MOTOR
INFORMATION SYSTEMS

IMPORTED CAR REPAIR MANUAL

20th Edition, Volume 2

First Printing

EDITORIAL DEVELOPMENT

Senior Editor
Warren Schildknecht, SAE

Quality Assurance Editor
Richard G. Glover, SAE

Assistant Special Projects Editor
Ron Lathrop

Technical Editors
Thomas H. Nash
Scott E. Mason, ASE
Richard H. Sparkes, ASE
Darren Costello
Duayn M. Verhelst, ASE
Michael A. Zimmerman, ASE
Gerald S. Athey
Jeff Finamore
Anthony W. Dutton
Uche-Uwa Ogu

John R. Lypen, SAE
Editorial Director

Marian A. Maasshoff, SAE
Executive Managing Editor

Authorized Distributor

For Information On MOTOR Products Call
1-800-4A-MOTOR (1-800-426-6867)

EDITORIAL PRODUCTION

Production Manager
Richard C. Grunz, ASE

Production Assistant
Julie Andrews
Catherine Starzyk

PRODUCT SUPPORT

Product Support Specialist
Donald J. Schall, ASE

BOOK PRODUCTION

Director of Technology
Robert Jaramillo

Production Manager
Catherine Cardon

Production Group
Michele L. Hawley
Frank Jannaro
Elizabeth Matteini
Elizabeth A. Summers
Susan J. Verhelst

MOTOR

**Published by Hearst Holdings, Inc.
A Unit of The Hearst Corporation**

5600 Crooks Road, Troy, MI 48098

Printed in the U.S.A.
Copyright © 1999 Hearst Business Publishing, Inc.
All rights reserved
ISBN 0-87851-991-2

VEHICLE IDENTIFICATION
INDEX

1st POSITION
COUNTRY OF ORIGIN
J = Japan
K = Korea
4 = U.S.A.
6 = Australia

2nd POSITION
MANUFACTURER
A = Mitsubishi
M = Mitsubishi
M = Hyundai (Precis)
P = Hyundai (Precis)

3rd POSITION
VEHICLE TYPE
H = Passenger Car
M = Passenger Car
3 = Passenger Car
4 = MPV
7 = Truck

4th POSITION - CARS
EXCEPT PRECIS
RESTRAINT SYSTEM
A = Driver & Pass Air Bag
B = Active Seat Belt (91-92)
B = Driver Air Bag (1993)
C = Passive Seat Belt
D = Active Seat Belt
E = Driver Air Bag
X = Driver Air Bag

PRECIS
DRIVE LINE TYPE
U = Right Hand Drive
V = Left Hand Drive

4th POSITION - TRUCKS/MPV
GVWR & BRAKE SYSTEM
HYDRAULIC
F = 4001 - 5000 lbs.
G = 5001 - 6000 lbs.
L = 4001 - 5000 lbs.
M = 5001 - 6000 lbs.

5th POSITION
EXCEPT PRECIS
VEHICLE LINE
A = Mirage
A = Galant (1999)
B = Expo LRV (FWD)
C = Diamante
C = Expo LRV (AWD)
D = 3000GT (FWD)
D = Expo (FWD)
D = Precis 3DR HB
E = 3000GT (AWD)
E = Expo (AWD)
F = Eclipse (FWD)
G = Eclipse (AWD)
H = Galant (FWD) 1993
J = Montero
J = Galant (1994-98)
K = Montero
K = Eclipse (FWD) (95-99)
L = Truck (RWD)
L = Eclipse (AWD)
L = Eclipse GSX (95-97)
M = Truck (4WD)
M = 3000GT (FWD)

5th POSITION (Cont'd)
N = 3000GT (AWD) VR4
P = Diamante
R = Galant (FWD)
R = Montero
S = Montero Sport (98-99)
S = Eclipse (FWD)
S = Truck (RWD)
T = Eclipse (AWD)
T = Truck (4WD)
T = Montero Sport
U = Mirage
V = Expo LRV (FWD)
V = 3000GT Conv. (FWD)
W = Expo LRV (AWD)
W = 3000GT Conv. (AWD)
X = Galant (AWD)
X = Eclipse Conv.
Y = Expo (FWD)
Z = Expo (AWD)
Y = Mirage
X = Eclipse Spyder

PRECIS
BODY TYPE
A = 5 Door Sedan
D = 3 Door Sedan
F = 4 Door Sedan

6th POSITION
EXCEPT PRECIS
SERIES
1 = Economy/Base
2 = Low
3 = Medium
4 = High
5 = Premium
5 = Sports
6 = Special
6 = Special
7 = Ultimate
8 = Sports
8 = Special

PRECIS
BODY STYLE & VERSION
1 = Standard
2 = Deluxe (GL)
3 = Super Deluxe (GLS)

7th POSITION - CARS
EXCEPT PRECIS
BODY STYLE
0 = 4 Door Wagon
1 = 2 Door Sedan
4 = 3 Door Hatchback
5 = 2 Door Convertible
6 = 4 Door Sedan
7 = 4 Door Hardtop (Pillared)
9 = 5 Door Wagon

PRECIS
RESTRAINT SYSTEM
1 = Active
1 = Passive (1994)
2 = Passive

7th POSITION - TRUCKS / MPV
BODY STYLE
1 = 5 Door Wagon
1 = Pickup - Short
2 = Pickup - Long

7th POSITION (Cont'd)
3 = 3 Door Metal Top
3 = Pickup - Extended Cab
4 = Pickup - Standard Cab
5 = Pickup - Extended Cab
9 = Pickup - Long Cab

8th POSITION
ENGINE CODE
A = 1.5L SOHC, MPI
A = 1.5L SOHC, MFI
B = 3.0L DOHC, MPI
B = 1.8L SOHC, MFI
C = 3.0L DOHC, Turbo
C = 1.8L SOHC, MFI
D = 1.8L SOHC, MPI
D = 2.0L SOHC, MFI
E = 2.6L
E = 2.0L DOHC, MFI
F = 2.0L DOHC, Turbo
G = 2.4L SOHC, MFI
H = 3.0L SOHC, MFI
J = 1468cc (Precis)
J = 3.0L DOHC, MFI
J = 1.5L MPI
K = 3.0L DOHC, Turbo
L = 2.4L DOHC, MFI
L = 3.0L SOHC, MFI
M = 3.5L
N = 2.5L SOHC, MPI
P = 3.0L SOHC, MFI
P = 3.5L SOHC, MFI
R = 2.0L DOHC, MPI
R = 3.5L SOHC, MFI
S = 3.0L SOHC, MPI
T = 1.8L SOHC, MPI
U = 2.0L DOHC, Turbo
V = 2.0L SOHC, MPI
W = 2.4L SOHC, MPI
Y = 1.6L SOHC, MFI
Y = 2.0L DOHC, MFI

9th POSITION
CHECK DIGIT

10th POSITION
MODEL YEAR
M = 1991
N = 1992
P = 1993
R = 1994
S = 1995
T = 1996
V = 1997
W = 1998
X = 1999

11th POSITION
ASSEMBLY PLANT
B = Bromont (Precis Only)
E = DSM (Diamond Star)
J = Nagoya-3
P = Nagoya
T = Tonsley Park
U = Mizushima
U = Ulsan (Precis only)
Y = Nagoya-1
Z = Okazaki

12th THRU 17th POSITION
PRODUCTION SEQUENCE
NUMBER

MT1139900284000X

Fig. 1 Mitsubishi

VEHICLE IDENTIFICATION

Fig. 2 Nissan Passenger Cars

1st Thru 3rd POSITION — MANUFACTURER
JN1 = Japan-Car
JN3 = Japan-Convertible
1N4 = USA-Car
3N1 = Mexico-Car

4th POSITION — ENGINE TYPE

ALTIMA
A = KA24DE, 2.4L-4Cyl.
B = KA24DE, 2.4L-4cyl.
D = KA24DE, 2.4L-4CYL.

MAXIMA
C = VG30DE, 3.0L-V6
E = VE30DE, 3.0L-V6
H = VG30i, 3.0L-V6

SENTRA/NX COUPE
A = GA16DE, 1.6L-4cyl.
E = GA16DE, 1.6L-4cyl.
R = SR20DE, 2.0L-4cyl.

STANZA
A = KA24DE, 2.4L-4cyl.
B = KA24DE, 2.4L-4cyl.
D = KA24DE, 2.4L-4cyl.
F = KA24E, 2.4L-4cyl.
H = KA24E, 2.4L-4cyl.
M = KA24DE, 2.4L-4cyl.
S = KA24E, 2.4L-4cyl.
F = KA24E, 2.4L-4cyl.

200SX
A = GA16DE, 1.6L-4cyl.
B = SR20DE, 2.0L-4cyl.

240SX
A = KA24DE, 2.4L-4cyl.
B = KA24DE, 2.4L-4cyl.
D = KA24DE, 2.4L-4cyl.
F = KA24E, 2.4L-4cyl.
H = KA24E, 2.4L-4cyl.
M = KA24DE, 2.4L-4cyl.
S = KA24E, 2.4L-4cyl.

300ZX
C = VG30DETT, 3.0L-V6 (twin turbo)
R = VG30DE, 3.0L-V6
T = VG33E, 3.3L-V6

5th & 6th POSITION — MODEL & SERIES
A2 = Maxima (A32)
B3 = Sentra / NX Coupe (B13)
B4 = Sentra / 200SX (B14)
J0 = Maxima (J30)
L0 = Altima (L30)
S3 = 240SX (S13)
S4 = 240SX (S14)
U2 = Stanza (U12)
U3 = Altima (U13)
Z2 = 300ZX (Z32)

7th POSITION — BODY TYPE CODE
1 = 4 Door Sedan
2 = 2 Door Sedan
2 = 2 Door Coupe (200SX)
4 = Coupe (240SX, Sentra/NX Coupe)
4 = 2 Seater (300ZX)
5 = 4 Door Sedan
6 = Coupe, T-Bar Roof (Sentra/NX Coupe)
6 = Fastback & Convertible (240SX)
6 = 2+2 Seater (300ZX)
7 = Convertible (1993-98)

8th POSITION — RESTRAINT SYSTEM
A = Passive 3 Point (Mechanical)
B = Passive 2 Point (Motorized)
B = Air Bag
C = Air Bag & Passive Belt
D = Driver & Pass Air Bag
D = Air Bags w/ 3-Point Belts
F = Air Bag & Passive Belt
H = Air Bag & Passive Belt
J = Passive 2 Point (Motorized) 4WD
P = Passive 2 Point (Motorized) 2WD
P = Automatic/Passive Seat Belts
S = Active Belt

9th POSITION — CHECK DIGIT

10th POSITION — MODEL YEAR
M = 1991
N = 1992
P = 1993
R = 1994
S = 1995
T = 1996
V = 1997
W = 1998
X = 1999

11th POSITION — ASSEMBLY PLANT
C = Smyrna, Tennessee
L = Aguascaliente, Mex.
M = Tochigi
T = Oppama
U = Zama
W = Kyushu
X = Nissha-Hiratsuka
4 = Aichi
5 = Murayama
9 = Fujijyu

12th Thru 17th POSITION — PRODUCTION SEQUENCE NUMBER

NS11399002009000X

Fig. 3 Nissan Light Duty Trucks

1st POSITION — NATION OF ORIGIN
J = Japan
1 = U.S.A.
4 = U.S.A.

2nd POSITION — MANUFACTURER
N = Nissan

3rd POSITION — VEHICLE TYPE
4 = MPV, U.S.A.
6 = Cargo, U.S.A.
6 = Commercial, Japan
6 = Truck, U.S.A.
8 = MPV, Japan

4th POSITION - EXC QUEST — ENGINE TYPE

PICK-UP
H = VG30E, 3.0L V6
S = KA24E, 2.4L 4cyl.
N = Z24i, 2.4L 4cyl.

PATHFINDER
A = VG33E
A = KA24DE, 2.4L 4cyl.
C = VG30DE, 3.0L V6
H = VG30i, 3.0L V6

FRONTIER
D = KA24DE
A = VG33E, 3.3L V6
R = VG30DE, 3.0L V6
T = VG33E, 3.3L V6

4th POSITION - QUEST
G.V.W.R. & BRAKE SYSTEM ASSIGNED BY CLASS

5th & 6th POSITION — MODEL & SERIES
D1 = Truck (D21)
D1 = Pathfinder (WD21)
D2 = Frontier (D22)
N1 = Quest MPV (V40)
N4 = Quest Cargo (V40)
R0 = Pathfinder (R50)

7th POSITION — BODY TYPE CODE
1 = Standard Wheelbase (Truck)
1 = MPV (Quest)
2 = Long Wheelbase (Truck)
4 = Cargo (Quest)
4 = 2 Door Pathfinder
5 = Cab & Chassis: Pathfinder
6 = King Cab (Truck)
6 = 2 Door Pathfinder
7 = 4 Door Pathfinder
8 = 4 Door Pathfinder

8th POSITION - EXC QUEST — MISCELLANEOUS INFORMATION
H = Heavy Duty
S = 2 Wheel Drive
T = 2 Wheel Drive
Y = 4 Wheel Drive

8th POSITION - QUEST — ENGINE TYPE
W = VG30E
I = VG30E
T = VG33E

9th POSITION — CHECK DIGIT

10th POSITION — MODEL YEAR
M = 1991
N = 1992
P = 1993
R = 1994
S = 1995
T = 1996
V = 1997
W = 1998
X = 1999

11th POSITION — ASSEMBLY PLANT
C = Smyrna, Tennessee
D = Avon Lake, Ohio
W = Kyushyu
X = Nissha-Hiratsuka

12th Thru 17th POSITION — PRODUCTION SEQUENCE NUMBER

NS11399002100000X

Fig. 4 Subaru

1st POSITION
NATION OF ORIGIN
J = Japan
4 = USA

2nd POSITION
MANUFACTURER
F = Fuji Heavy Industries LTD.
S = Subaru-Isuzu Automotive

3rd POSITION
VEHICLE TYPE
1 = Passenger Vehicle
2 = Multipurpose Vehicle (MPV)
3 = Passenger Vehicle
4 = Multipurpose Vehicle (MPV)
7 = Truck

4th POSITION
LINE TYPE
A = Fuji Subaru, L Line (82-89)
B = Loyal & XT Line (90-94)
B = Legacy Line (90-98)
C = SVX Line
G = Impreza Line
L = Justy Line
S = Forester Line

5th POSITION
BODY TYPE
A = Justy 3 Door
B = 4 Door Sedan (82-84)
C = Impreza & Legacy 4D
D = Justy 5 Door
D = Legacy Sedan
F = Hatchback (82-89)
F = Impreza Station Wagon
F = Forester
G = 3 Door Coupe
J = Legacy Station Wagon
J = Touring Wagon (1989)
K = Loyale Touring Wagon
K = Legacy Station Wagon
M = Station Wagon (82-84)
M = Impreza Coupe
N = Station Wagon (85-89)
N = Loyale Station Wagon
T = Brat (82-85)
U = Brat (86-87)
W = Hardtop (82-84)
X = XT & XT6
X = SVX

6th POSITION
ENGINE TYPE
1 = 1300cc
1 = 1800cc FWD
2 = 1600cc
2 = 1800cc

6th POSITION (cont'd)
ENGINE TYPE
2 = 2200cc AWD
2 = 1800cc AWD
2 = 1600cc 4WD
3 = 2200cc FWD
3 = 3300cc
4 = 1800cc
4 = 1800cc 4WD
5 = 1800cc AWD
6 = 2200cc & 2200cc 4WD
6 = 2500cc AWD
7 = 1800cc 4WD L Line & 1200cc J Line
8 = 3300cc AWD
8 = 2700cc L Line & 1200cc 4WD J Line
9 = 2700cc 4WD L Line (w/Air Susp.)

7th POSITION
MODEL INFORMATION
1 = Standard, Non Turbo RS, L
Impreza Base (95-98), Forester Base
2 = DL, RS, Legacy Base & Loyale
Impreza L & L+ M.T.
Legacy/Impreza Base (95-98)
LE SVX
3 = GL, RS Justy
Legacy L/L+/Outback
Impreza L / Outback (95-98)
L SVX, Forester L
4 = GL 10, XT6, Legacy LS.
Legacy L+ AT & LS
LS SVX
5 = GL 10 Turbo, GL F4WD 3D
Legacy LS & LS-L
LSL / LSI SVX
Impreza LS, LSI, LX
6 = RX Turbo, Loyale Turbo
Legacy LSI (95-98)
LSI SVX
Forester S
7 = GL Turbo
Loyale Turbo
Legacy LSI (95-98)
LSI SVX
Legacy GT (95-98)
Impreza RS
8 = Legacy Outback
Impreza Outback
Sport Utility Sedan
9 = Legacy Postal vehicle

8th POSITION
WEIGHT CLASS/RESTRAINT
PASSENGER CAR
1 = Active Restraint
2 = Passive Restraint
3 = Air Bag
5 = Active w/Dual Air Bags
TRUCK
A = Under 3000lb. GVW / Active
B = 3001 - 4000lb. GVW / Passive
C = Under 3000lb. GVW / Active
D = 3001 - 4000lb. GVW / Passive
MPV
A = Under 3000lb. GVW

8th POSITION (cont'd)
WEIGHT CLASS/RESTRAINT
MPV
B = 3001 - 4000lb. GVW
C = 4001 - 5000lb. GVW

9th POSITION
CHECK DIGIT

10th POSITION
MODEL YEAR
C = 1982
D = 1983
E = 1984
F = 1985
G = 1986
H = 1987
J = 1988
K = 1989
L = 1990
M = 1991
N = 1992
P = 1993
R = 1994
S = 1995
T = 1996
V = 1997
W = 1998
X = 1999

11th POSITION
ASSY PLANT/TRANSMISSION
GUNMA
A = Manual 4 Speed
B = Manual 5 Speed
C = Automatic 3 Speed, ECTV, 4EAT
D = Manual 5 Speed Dual Range
E = 4 Speed Dual Range
F = Automatic 3 Speed & ECTV (4WD)
G = Manual 5 Speed Full Time (4WD)
H = Elect Auto 4 Sp Full Time (4WD)
J = Dual Range-5MT Full Time (4WD)
LAFAYETTE
K = Electronic Automatic 4 Speed
1 = Manual 5 Speed
2 = Automatic 3 Speed, ECTV, 4EAT
3 = Automatic 3 Speed (4WD)
5 = Automatic 3 Speed & ECTV (4WD)
6 = Manual 5 Speed Full Time (4WD)
7 = Elect Auto 4 Sp Full Time (4WD)
9 = Electronic Automatic 4 Speed

12th THRU 17th POSITION
PRODUCTION SEQUENCE NUMBER

SB113990002000X

Fig. 5 Suzuki

1st POSITION
NATION OF ORIGIN
J = Japan
2 = Canada

2nd POSITION
MANUFACTURER
S = Suzuki

3rd POSITION
VEHICLE TYPE
2 = Passenger Car
3 = Multipurpose Vehicle (MPV)
4 = Truck W/2 Seats When Factory Delivers

4th POSITION
VEHICLE LINE
A = Swift
J = Esteem
J = Samurai
L = X-90
T = Sidekick
T = Vitara / Grand Vitara (1999)

5th POSITION - PASSENGER CARS
SERIES & RESTRAINT SYSTEM
A = 2 Door Hatchback, Active
A = 2WD, Active (1995)
B = 4 Door Hatchback, Active
B = 2WD, Active w/Air Bags (95-99)
C = 2 Door Hatchback, Passive
D = 4 Door Hatchback, Active
E = 4 Door Notchback, Passive
H = 4 Door Notchback, Active

5th POSITION - TRUCKS/MPV
SERIES
A = X-90, 2 Door (2WD)
A = Sidekick, 2 Door (4WD)
A = Vitara, 2 Door (4WD)
B = X-90, 2 Door (4WD)
C = Sidekick, 2 Door (2WD)
C = Samurai, (4WD)
C = Vitara, 2 Door (2WD)
D = Sidekick, 4 Door (4WD)
D = Vitara, 4 Door (4WD)
D = Samurai, (2WD)
E = Sidekick, 4 Door (2WD)
E = Vitara, 4 Door (2WD)

6th POSITION
ENGINE CODE
0 = 1.6L, 4 Cylinder
1 = 1.0L, 3 Cylinder (Swift)
1 = 1.6L, 4 Cylinder

6th POSITION (Cont'd)
0 = 1.6L, 4 Cylinder (Vitara)
2 = 1.3L, 4 Cylinder
2 = 1.8L, 4 Cylinder (Sidekick Sport)
3 = 1.3L, 4 Cylinder
3 = 1.6L, 4 Cylinder
4 = 1.0L, 3 Cylinder (Swift)
4 = 1.8L, 4 Cylinder
5 = 1.3L, 4 Cylinder
5 = 2.0L, 4 Cylinder (Vitara)
6 = 2.5L, 6 Cylinder (Vitara)

7th POSITION
DESIGN SEQUENCE
1 = Original Design
2 = Original Design
3 = Original Design
4 = Swift GTI
5 = Swift GA

8th POSITION
BODY TYPE
C = Canvas Top
H = 3 Door Hatchback
S = 4 Door Sedan
S = T-Bar Top
T = Truck
V = Hardtop
W = Wagon

9th POSITION
CHECK DIGIT

10th POSITION
MODEL YEAR
G = 1986
H = 1987
J = 1988
K = 1989
L = 1990
M = 1991
N = 1992
P = 1993
R = 1994
S = 1995
T = 1996
V = 1997
W = 1998
X = 1999

11th POSITION
ASSEMBLY PLANT
4 = Iwata
5 = Kosai
6 = CAMI

12th Thru 17th POSITION
PRODUCTION SEQUENCE NUMBER

SK113990008I000X

VEHICLE IDENTIFICATION

Fig. 6 Toyota Passenger Cars

1st POSITION
NATION OF ORIGIN
1 = USA
2 = Canada
4 = USA
J = Japan

2nd POSITION
MANUFACTURER
T = Toyota

3rd POSITION
VEHICLE TYPE
2 = Passenger Vehicle
3 = Multipurpose Passenger Vehicle
4 = Truck
5 = Incomplete Vehicle

4th POSITION
BODY / DRIVE TYPE
A = 2 Door Sedan 2WD
B = 4 Door Sedan 2WD
C = 2 Door Coupe 2WD
D = 3 Door Liftback 2WD
E = 4 Door Wagon 2WD
F = 2 Door Convertible 2WD

5th POSITION
ENGINE CODE
A = 4A-FE, 1.6L
B = 7A-FE, 1.8L
C = 5E-FE, 1.5L
D = 2JZ-GE, 3.0L
E = 2JZ-GTE, 3.0L Turbo
F = 1MZ-FE, 3.0L
G = 5S-FE, 2.2L
L = 2TZ-FE, 2.4L
R = 1ZZ-FE

6th POSITION
SERIES CODE
1 = 10, 111 SERIES
2 = 20, 110 SERIES
3 = 30, 130 SERIES
4 = 40, 140 SERIES

7th POSITION
RESTRAINT / GRADE
1 = Manual Belt
2 = Manual Belt w/ Air Bag
8 = Manual Belt w/Airbag & Side Airbag

8th POSITION
CARLINE
A = Supra
E = Avalon
F = Corolla
H = Pasco
K = Camry
L = Tercel
P = Solara
T = Tercel
T = Celica

9th POSITION
CHECK DIGIT

10th POSITION
MODEL YEAR
T = 1996
V = 1997
W = 1998
X = 1999

11th POSITION
ASSEMBLY PLANT

12th Thru 17th POSITION
PRODUCTION SEQUENCE NUMBER

TY113990434000X

Fig. 7 Toyota Light Duty Trucks

1st POSITION
NATION OF ORIGIN
1 = USA
2 = Canada
4 = USA
J = Japan

2nd POSITION
MANUFACTURER
T = Toyota

3rd POSITION
VEHICLE TYPE
3 = MPV
4 = Truck
5 = Incomplete Vehicle
6 = Bus

4th POSITION
BODY / DRIVE TYPE
G = 4 Door Wagon 2WD
H = 4 Door Wagon (ALL TRAC) 4WD
J = STD Cab 1/2 Ton 2WD
K = STD Cab 1/2 Ton 4WD
L = STD Cab 1 Ton 2WD
M = STD Cab 1 Ton 4WD
N = STD Cab, Short Wheel Base, 2WD
P = STD Cab, Short Wheel Base, 4WD
T = EXT Cab 1/2 Ton 2WD
U = EXT Cab 1/2 Ton 4WD
V = EXT Cab, Extra Long WB, 2WD
W = EXT Cab, Extra Long WB, 4WD

5th POSITION
ENGINE CODE
J = 1FZ-FE, 4.5L
K = 2TZ-FZE, 2.4L
L = 2TZ-FE, 2.4L
M = 3RZ-FE
N = 5VZ-FE, 3.4L
P = 3SFE, 2.0L
R = 1ZZ-FE

6th POSITION
SERIES CODE
1 = 10, 111 SERIES
2 = 20, 110 SERIES
3 = 30, 130 SERIES
4 = 40, 140 SERIES

7th POSITION
RESTRAINT SYSTEM / GRADE
1 = STD
2 = DLX
3 = LE
4 = SR 5
5 = VX
6 = SR 5 V6
7 = Limited

8th POSITION
CARLINE
C = Previa / Sienna
D = T100
J = Land Cruiser
M = Previa
N = Tacoma Pickup
R = 4 Runner
V = RAV 4

9th POSITION
CHECK DIGIT

10th POSITION
MODEL YEAR
T = 1996
V = 1997
W = 1998
X = 1999

11th POSITION
ASSEMBLY PLANT

12th Thru 17th POSITION
PRODUCTION SEQUENCE NUMBER

TY113990435000X

COMPUTER RELEARN PROCEDURES

INDEX

DESCRIPTION

A computer relearn procedure may be required on any vehicle equipped with body, engine or transmission control computers whenever battery power to the computer is interrupted. These computers gather and store information on vehicle operation. They use this information to provide maximum driveability and vehicle performance.

MITSUBISHI

ENGINE PERFORMANCE

If the battery has been disconnected or the ECM/PCM replaced, drive vehicle for approximately ten minutes to allow the ECM/PCM to relearn its operating values.

TCM RESETTING PROCEDURE

1. Disconnect negative battery cable before replacing transaxle or carrying out an overhaul.

2. After work has been completed, check Diagnostic Trouble Codes (DTC). If DTC No. 12 ("Battery power was disconnected since last power down " has been generated, this DTC must be cleared.
3. Select "Special function" on scan tool, then set scan tool to Quick Learn mode and carry out this operation from scan tool screen.
4. This procedure will cause the clutch volume index to be memorized by the TCM.

PINION FACTOR PROCEDURE

The TCM uses the rotation speed of the transaxle output shaft to calculate the vehicle speed and cumulative distance travelled. Because of this, it is necessary to input (or update) the tire size coefficient into the TCM memory after the TCM has been replaced or tire size has changed.
1. Connect scan tool to Data Link Connector (DLC).
2. Select the "Special function" on scan

tool and then set scan tool to Pinion Factor mode and carry out this operation from scan tool screen.
3. Then input (or update) tire size coefficient into TCM memory. Note new TCM's do not have tire size coefficient already input.

NISSAN

If a battery terminal is disconnected, the memory will return to the ECM value. The ECM will now start to self-control at its initial value. Engine operation can vary slightly when the terminal is disconnected. However, this is not an indication of a problem. Do not replace parts because of a slight variation.

SUBARU

If the battery has been disconnected or the ECM/PCM replaced, test drive the vehicle for approximately ten minutes for adaptation of new ECM/PCM.

AIR BAG SYSTEM PRECAUTIONS

INDEX

MITSUBISHI

DISARMING

1. Turn ignition to Lock position.
2. Disconnect and isolate battery ground cable.
3. **Wait at least 60 seconds after disconnection before performing repair procedures.** The Supplemental Restraint System (SRS) is designed to retain enough deployment voltage for a short time even after battery has been disconnected.

ARMING

1. Ensure no one is inside vehicle.
2. Connect battery ground cable and start engine.
3. Ensure SRS warning lamp lights for approximately seven seconds, and then goes off.
4. **If lamp operates as outlined,** SRS is functioning properly.
5. **If lamp does not operate as outlined,** an SRS condition is indicated.

NISSAN

DISARMING

1. Turn ignition switch to off position, then disconnect battery cables.
2. **On 1996 models,** wait a minimum of 10 minutes for air bag system to discharge.
3. **On 1997-99 models,** wait a minimum of three minutes for air bag system to discharge. The system will retain power after disconnection and it is possible for the air bag to deploy during this time.
4. **On 1996 models,** remove steering wheel lower lid, then disconnect air bag module electrical connector.

ARMING

1. **On 1996 models,** with battery cables disconnected, connect air bag module connector.
2. **On all models,** ensure no one is inside vehicle, then connect battery cables.
3. Turn ignition switch to On position and observe SRS warning lamp.
4. SRS lamp should light for approximately seven seconds, then go off. This indicates SRS is functioning properly.
5. If SRS warning lamp does not function

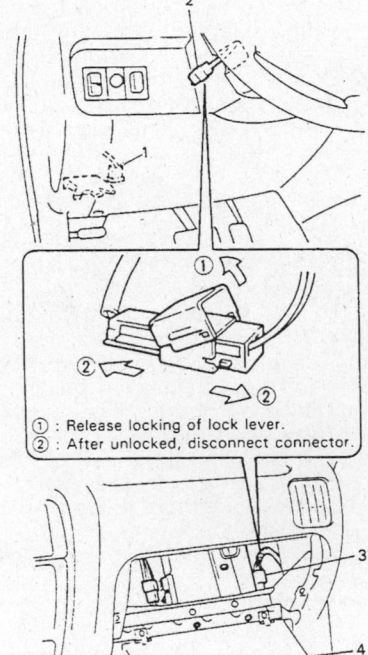

① : Release locking of lock lever.
② : After unlocked, disconnect connector.

1. Air bag fuse box
2. Yellow connector of driver air bag (inflator) module
3. Yellow connectors of passenger air bag (inflator) module
4. Glove box

SK8019400005000X

Fig. 1 Air bag system fuse & panel. Suzuki

as described, an SRS malfunction is indicated. Diagnose and repair as necessary.

SUBARU

DISARMING

1. Place ignition switch in off position.
2. Disconnect battery ground cable, then the positive cable.
3. **Wait 20 seconds before beginning repair procedures.**

ARMING

1. Ensure no one is inside vehicle.
2. With ignition switch in off position, connect battery positive cable, then the ground cable.
3. Wait at least 20 seconds, then turn ignition switch to On position and note air

bag warning lamp operation. Lamp should light for approximately eight seconds, then go off. If lamp remains illuminated or fails to light, an air bag system malfunction is indicated. Diagnose and repair as necessary.

SUZUKI

DISARMING

The Sensing and Diagnostic Module (SDM) provides reserve energy to the deployment loop and diagnostic monitoring of all system components. It can maintain sufficient deployment voltage for up to 10 seconds after the ignition has been turned Off, air bag fuse removed or battery disconnected.

1. Place front wheels in straight ahead position.
2. Turn ignition switch to Lock position and remove key, then disconnect battery ground cable.
3. Remove Air Bag-IG fuse from air bag fuse panel, **Fig. 1.** Air bag fuse box is located under lefthand side of instrument panel near junction/fuse panel.
4. Remove lefthand upper steering column cap, then unlock and disconnect driver's air bag module yellow connector.
5. Open glove compartment while pushing stopper from left and righthand sides, then remove compartment.
6. Disconnect passenger's air bag yellow connector.

ARMING

1. Turn ignition switch to Lock position and remove key.
2. Connect passenger's and driver's air bag yellow connectors. **Ensure connector lock levers lock securely.**
3. Install glove compartment and steering column upper lefthand cap, then install Air Bag-IG fuse.
4. Ensure no one is inside vehicle, then connect battery ground cable.
5. Turn ignition switch to On position and note air bag lamp operation.
6. If air bag lamp does not flash seven times, then go off, an SRS malfunction is indicated. Diagnose and repair as necessary.

TOYOTA

DISARMING

1. Note radio station settings before disconnecting battery, as all vehicle memory will be lost.
2. Turn ignition switch to Lock position, then disconnect battery ground cable.
3. **Wait at least 90 seconds after disconnection before proceeding with any service procedures.** Supplemental Restraint System (SRS) incorporates a back-up energy source that can maintain sufficient deployment voltage for up to 90 seconds after ignition switch has been placed in off position and battery disconnected.
4. **Never use an auxiliary power source during this procedure.**

ARMING

1. Ensure ignition switch is in Lock position and no one is inside vehicle.
2. Connect battery ground cable.
3. **Wait at least ten seconds before turning ignition switch from Lock position.**
4. Place ignition switch in Accessory or On position and ensure SRS lamp lights, then goes off after approximately six seconds.
5. If SRS warning lamp does not go off after six seconds, an SRS malfunction is stored in system memory. Diagnose and repair as necessary.
6. Reset radio stations and clock.

SERVICE REMINDER & WARNING LAMP RESET PROCEDURES

TABLE OF CONTENTS

Mitsubishi

INDEX

MALFUNCTION INDICATOR LAMP (MIL)

The MIL will illuminate to indicate an emission control item malfunction. When the malfunctioning system returns to its normal state, the MIL will go out.

Immediately after the ignition switch is placed in the On position, the MIL will light for five seconds to indicate proper operation.

MAINTENANCE REMINDER LAMP

MONTERO & TRUCK

An EGR warning lamp on the dash will illuminate at 50,000 miles to alert the driver to have the EGR system inspected and serviced.

Following inspection and maintenance, reset mileage sensor. Reset switch is located on the back of instrument panel either to the left of or below speedometer cable junction, **Fig. 1.** Slide switch to the opposite position to reset sensor lamp.

MAINTENANCE REQUIRED LAMP

VAN & WAGON

At 50,000, 80,000 and 100,000 miles the Maintenance Required lamp will be illuminated. **After performing the required service, reset switch located at rear of**

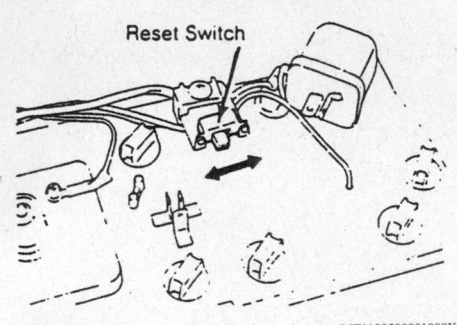

Fig. 1 EGR maintenance reminder lamp reset. 1985–86 Montero & Truck

MT1138500001000X

instrument cluster to turn lamp off, **Fig. 2.** At 120,000 miles, the bulb should be removed from the Maintenance Required lamp.

TRUCK

1988

At mileage of 50,000 and 100,000 the Maintenance Required lamp will be illuminated. **At 50,000 miles, after performing the required service, reset the switch located at front of instrument cluster to turn lamp off, Fig. 3.** At 100,000 miles, the bulb should be removed from the Maintenance Required lamp.

1989-96

At mileage of 50,000, 80,000 and 100,000 the Maintenance Required lamp will be illuminated. **At 50,000, 80,000 and 100,000 miles, after performing the required service, reset switch located at front of instrument cluster to turn lamp**

off, **Fig. 3.** At mileage above 120,000 miles, the bulb should be removed from the Maintenance Required lamp.

MONTERO

1988

At mileage of 50,000 and 100,000 the Maintenance Required lamp will be illuminated. **At 50,000 miles, after performing the required service, reset switch located at rear of instrument cluster to turn lamp off, Fig. 4.** At 100,000 miles, the bulb should be removed from the Maintenance Required lamp.

1989-96

At mileage of 50,000, 80,000 and 100,000 the Maintenance Required lamp will be illuminated. **After performing the required service, reset switch located at rear of instrument cluster to turn lamp off, Figs. 4 through 6.** At mileage above 120,000 miles on 1989 models, 150,000 miles on 1990-91 models or 100,000 miles on 1992–96 models, the bulb should be removed from the Maintenance Required lamp.

ANTI-LOCK BRAKE WARNING LAMP

The Anti-Lock warning lamp is used to warn of a system malfunction. It will be lit during engine start-up, but should go out when the self-diagnostic system determines that the system is functioning properly. If the lamp remains lit, a malfunction in the anti-lock brake system is indicated. Following diagnosis and repair of the system, the lamp may be turned off using a

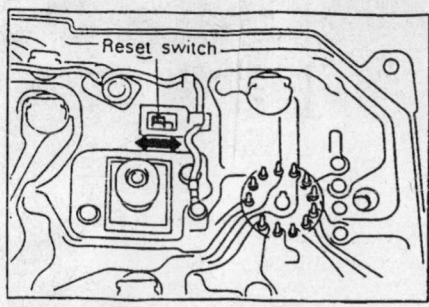

Fig. 2 Maintenance Required lamp reset. Van & Wagon

MT1138500002000X

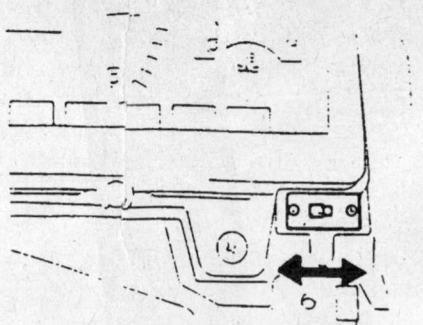

MT1139000003000X

Fig. 3 EGR/Maintenance Required lamp reset. Truck

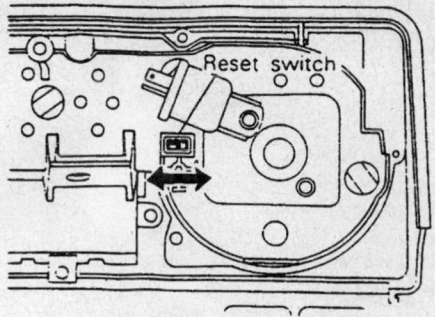

MT1138800004000X

Fig. 4 EGR/Maintenance Required lamp reset. 1988-91 Montero

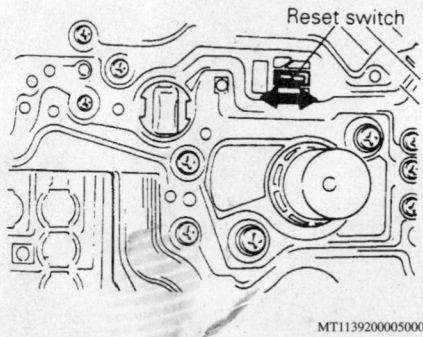

MT1139200005000X

Fig. 5 EGR/Maintenance Required lamp reset. 1992-93 Montero

Multi-Use Tester (MUT) diagnostic scan tool. Follow tool manufacturer's instructions.

AIR BAG WARNING LAMP

The diagnosis unit monitors the Supplemental Restraint System (SRS) and stores data concerning any faults detected in the system. When the ignition key is in the On or Start positions, the lamp should illuminate for approximately seven seconds, then turn off. This indicates the system is operating properly.

If the air bag warning lamp does not illuminate as described, stays on for longer than seven seconds or illuminates during vehicle operation, a system malfunction is indicated. **To reset the lamp, it is necessary to use a Multi-Use Tester (MUT) diagnostic scan tool. Follow tool manufacturer's instructions.**

CENTRAL WARNING DISPLAY

DIAMANTE

1999

Charge Warning Lamp

The warning lamp illuminates when the ignition key is in the On position and goes Off after engine is started. This indicator il-

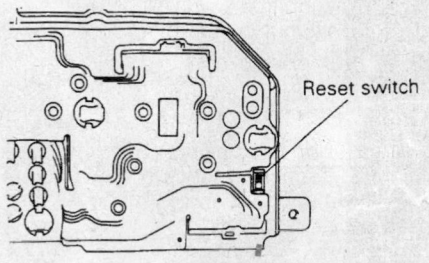

MT1139400006000X

Fig. 6 EGR/Maintenance Required lamp reset. 1994-96 Montero

luminates when the drive belt breaks or there is a malfunction in the charging system.

Oil Pressure Warning Lamp

The warning lamp illuminates when the ignition key is in the On position and goes Off after engine is started and oil pressure rises above specification.

Nissan

INDEX

AIR BAG WARNING LAMP

When the ignition key is placed in the On or Start positions, the air bag warning lamp will illuminate for approximately seven seconds, then turn off. This lamp cycle indicates the air bag system is functioning properly.

If the air bag warning lamp does not perform as described, the air bag system should be inspected and repaired as necessary.

ANTI-LOCK WARNING LAMP

This lamp will be illuminated when the ignition switch is placed in the On position as a bulb check. If the lamp remains illuminated or lights during vehicle operation, an anti-lock brake system malfunction is indicated. When the lamp is illuminated, place the ignition switch in the off position, then restart the engine. If the lamp still remains lit, the anti-lock brake system should be serviced. The basic brake system will remain functional, but without the assistance of anti-lock features. **After servicing the anti-lock brake system, the lamp will reset automatically when the ignition switch has been cycled to the off position and the vehicle has been driven at a speed exceeding 19 mph.**

AUTOMATIC TRANSMISSION OIL TEMPERATURE WARNING LAMP

This lamp will be illuminated wh__ __ the automatic transmission fluid tempera__ __ __re is __xcessive. **When the transmission fluid __ __ __rned to its normal temperature, __ __ill reset automatically.**

"__ __NGINE"

__ __ will be illumi-
__ __ is in the On
__. When the
__ __ go out. If
__ __ode has

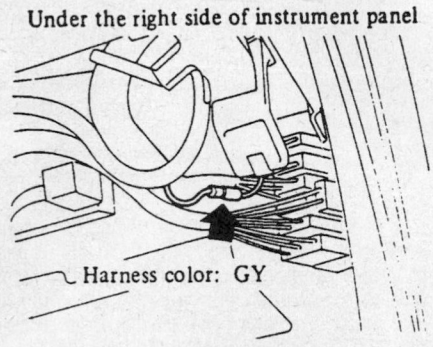

Under the right side of instrument panel

Harness color: GY

NS1138000001000X

Fig. 1 Oxygen sensor warning lamp electrical connector location. 1980-81 810

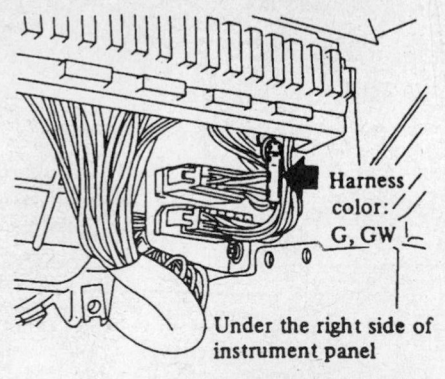

Harness color: G, GW

Under the right side of instrument panel

NS1138100003000X

Fig. 3 Oxygen sensor warning lamp electrical connector location. 1980-83 280ZX

been stored by the electronic control system. **After diagnosis and repair are complete, place the ignition switch in the off position, then clear stored diagnostic trouble codes by disconnecting battery ground cable momentarily.**

MALFUNCTION INDICATOR LAMP (MIL)

1993-99

The MIL will illuminate to indicate the presence of a system malfunction. The lamp will blink simultaneously with the ECM's red Light Emitting Diode (LED).

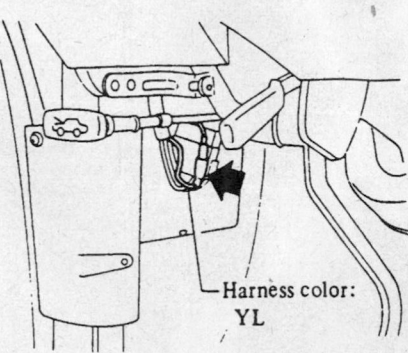

Harness color: YL

NS1138000002000X

Fig. 2 Oxygen sensor warning lamp electrical connector location. 1981-83 200SX

Following diagnosis and repair of all system malfunctions, reset the MIL by disconnecting battery ground cable momentarily. This will clear the ECM's memory.

COOLANT LEVEL WARNING LAMP

This lamp will be illuminated when the coolant level in the cooling system reservoir drops below the "MIN" level mark. **The lamp will reset when the coolant level is raised above the "MIN" mark.**

OXYGEN SENSOR

Refer to Figs. Figs. 1 through 26, when performing the following procedures.

After the vehicle has been operated for 30,000 or 50,000 miles, depending on model, the oxygen sensor warning lamp located on the instrument panel will light, indicating that the oxygen sensor should be inspected.

On 1980-85 models except 1985 Pickup, after the appropriate service has been performed, disconnect warning lamp electrical connector to prevent the lamp from lighting again.

On 1986-89 models except Pickup and Stanza Wagon, reset the warning lamp hold relay. After the third interval, at 90,000 miles, disconnect warning lamp electrical connector to prevent the light from lighting again.

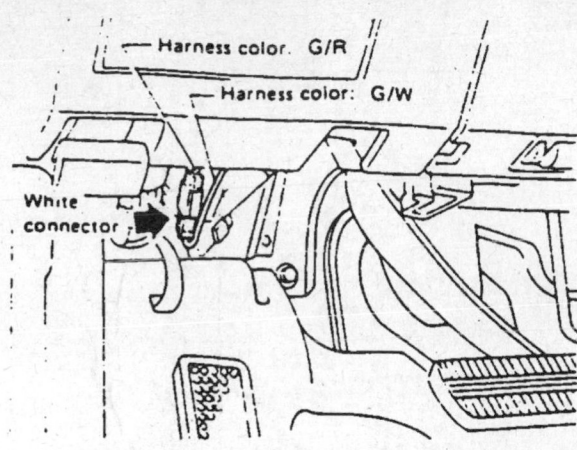

Fig. 4 Oxygen sensor warning lamp electrical connector location. 1982-83 Sentra & 1982-84 Pulsar

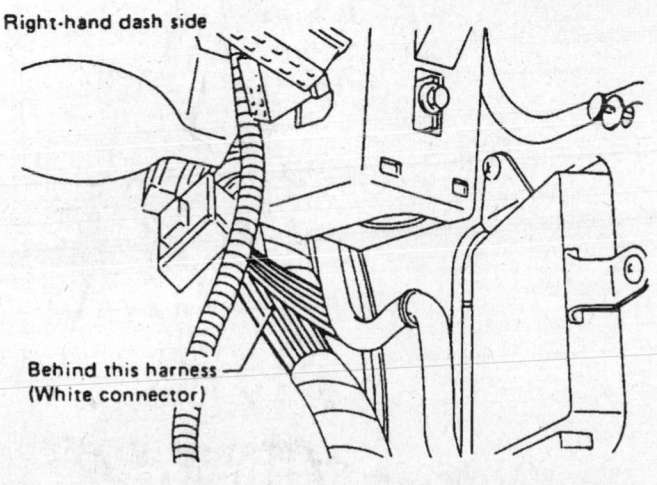

Fig. 6 Oxygen sensor warning lamp electrical connector location. 1984 200SX

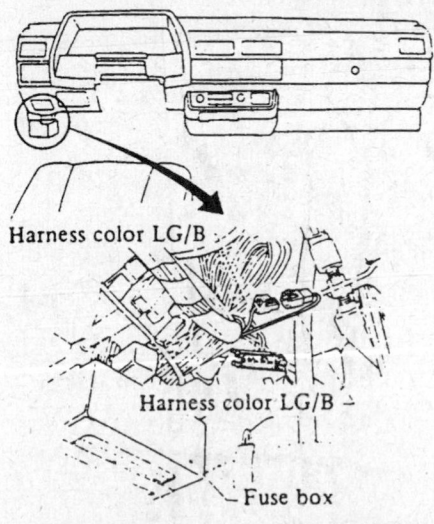

Fig. 8 Oxygen sensor warning lamp electrical connector location. 1984-86 Sentra & 1985-86 Pulsar

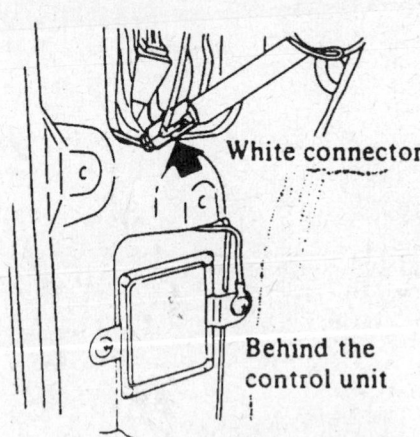

Fig. 9 Oxygen sensor warning lamp electrical connector location. 1984-86 Stanza except Wagon

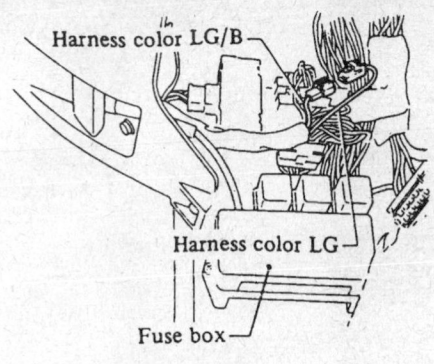

Fig. 5 Oxygen sensor warning lamp electrical connector location. 1983-87 Maxima

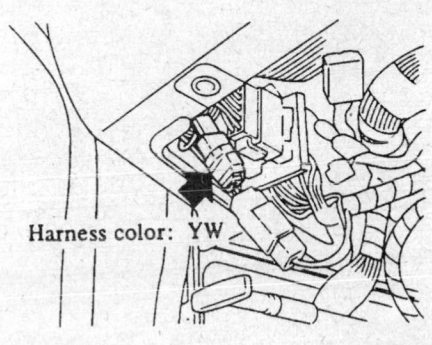

Fig. 7 Oxygen sensor warning lamp electrical connector location. 1985 California Pickup

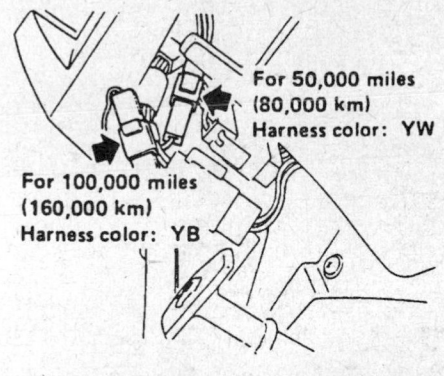

Fig. 10 Oxygen sensor warning lamp electrical connector location. 1985-86 Federal Pickup

On 1985 California Pickup, after the appropriate service has been performed, disconnect warning lamp electrical connector.

On 1985-86 Federal Pickup, disconnect the yellow wiring harness connector at 50,000 miles and the yellow/black wiring harness connector at 100,000 miles.

On 1986 California Pickup, depress hold relay reset button at 30,000 miles and, at 90,000 miles, disconnect yellow white electrical connector.

NS1138400011000X

Fig. 11 Oxygen sensor warning lamp electrical connector location. 1984-87 300ZX

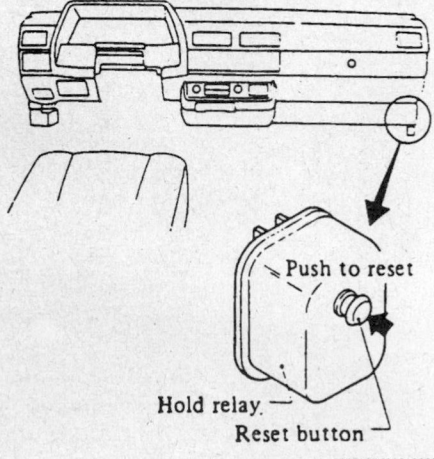

NS1138600013000X

Fig. 13 Oxygen sensor warning lamp hold relay location. 1986 Pulsar & 1986-89 Sentra

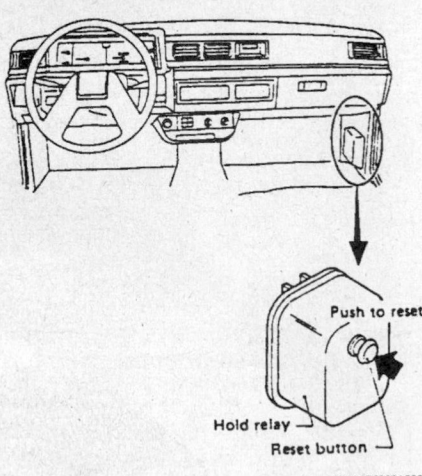

NS1138600015000X

Fig. 15 Oxygen sensor warning lamp hold relay location. 1986 Stanza except Wagon

On **1986-87 Stanza Wagon,** after appropriate service has been performed, remove warning lamp hold relay and use a suitable tool to reset. At 90,000 miles, disconnect warning lamp electrical connector.

On **1987 300ZX models with analog type instrument cluster,** after inspecting

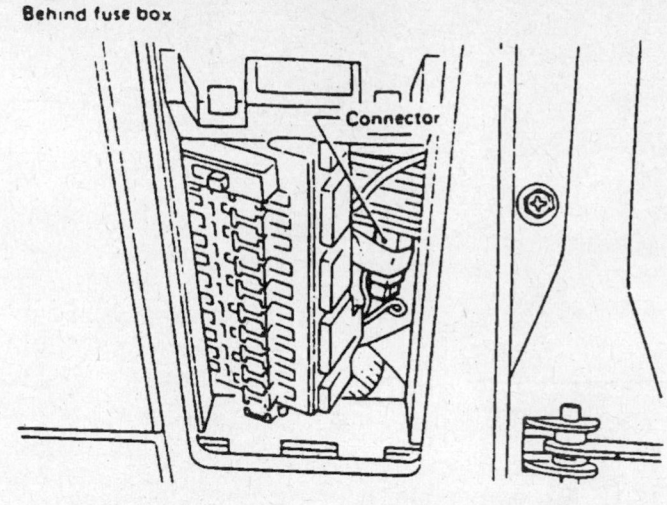

Behind fuse box

NS1138500012000X

Fig. 12 Oxygen sensor warning lamp electrical connector location. 1985-87 200SX

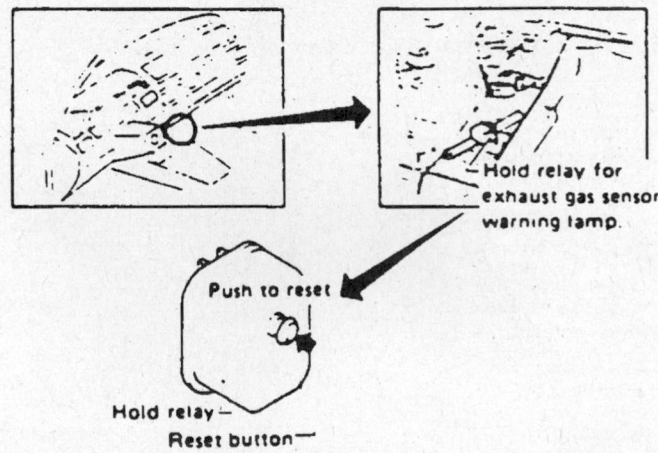

NS1138600014000X

Fig. 14 Oxygen sensor warning lamp hold relay location. 1986-87 200SX

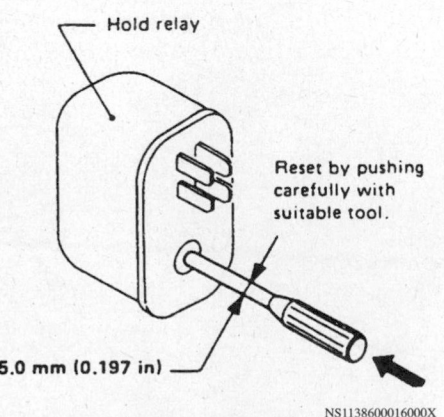

NS1138600016000X

Fig. 16 Oxygen sensor warning lamp hold relay location. 1986 Maxima

the oxygen sensor, disconnect the electrical connector for the mileage interval indicated in **Fig. 11,** to reset the oxygen sensor warning lamp.

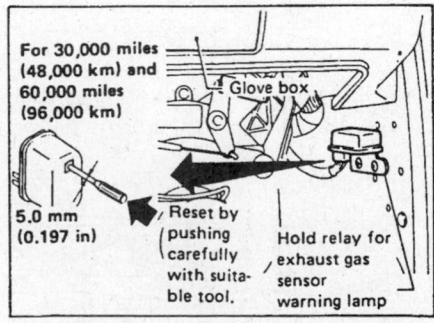

NS1138600017000X

Fig. 17 Oxygen sensor warning lamp hold relay. 1986 Stanza Wagon

On **1987 300ZX models with digital type instrument cluster,** after inspecting the oxygen sensor, depress and hold relay button to reset the oxygen sensor warning lamp at 30,000 and 60,000 mile intervals,

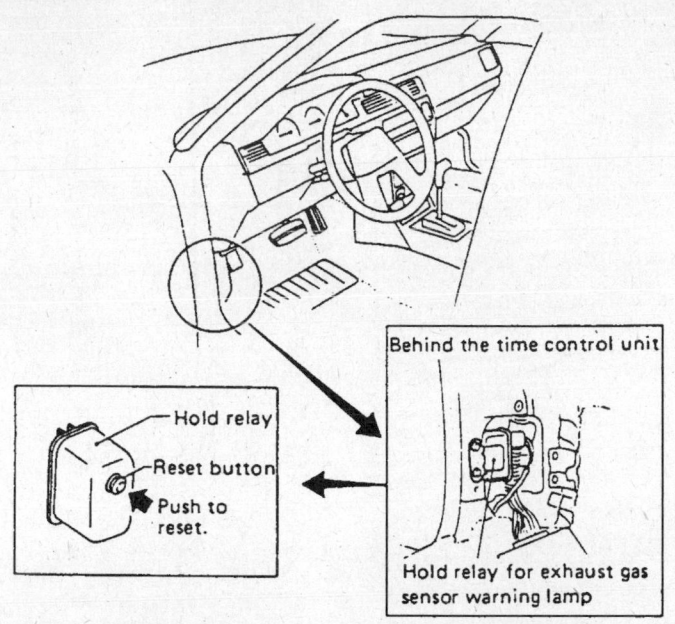

Fig. 18 Oxygen sensor warning lamp hold relay location. 1987 Maxima

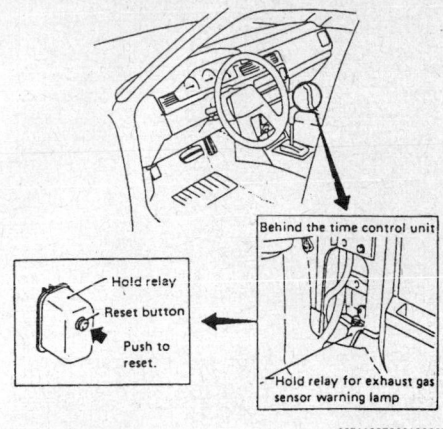

Fig. 19 Oxygen sensor warning lamp electrical connector & hold relay location. 1986 California Pickup

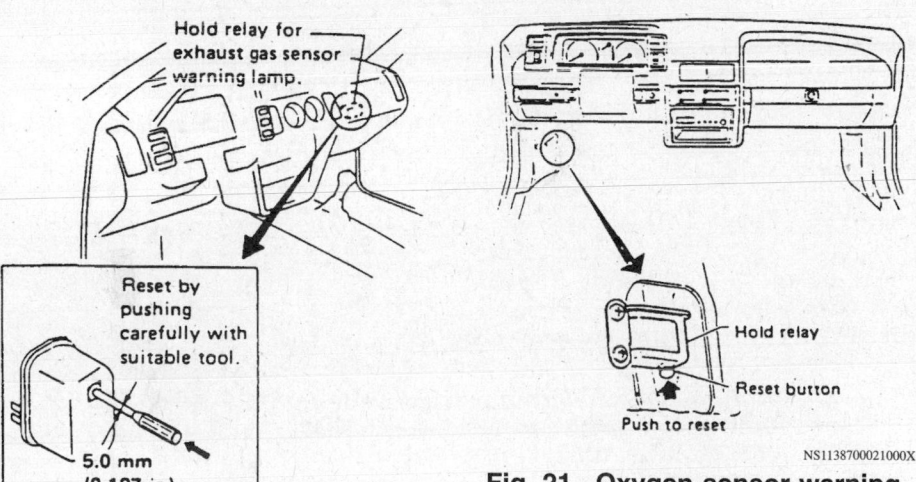

Fig. 20 Oxygen sensor warning lamp hold relay location. 1986 300ZX

Fig. 21 Oxygen sensor warning lamp hold relay location. 1987-89 Pulsar

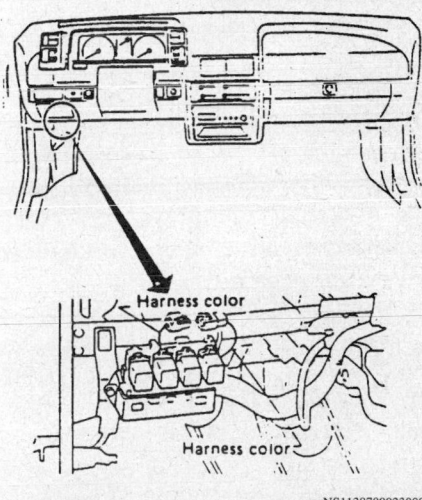

Fig. 23 Oxygen sensor warning lamp hold relay location. 1987 Stanza except Wagon

Fig. 26. At the 90,000 mile interval, disconnect the warning lamp electrical connector, **Fig. 11.**

WARNING DISPLAY
300ZX

This system monitors engine coolant level, washer fluid level and exterior lamp operation. When the ignition switch is placed in the On position, the "WASH" and "WATER" lamps should illuminate and, if systems are satisfactory, the "OK" lamp should also illuminate. Operation of the headlamps, stop lamps and tail lamps will not be checked until the system has been activated by depressing the brake pedal or placing the light switch in the On position. If a problem is detected in one of the monitored systems, the red warning display indicator lamp will be illuminated. Depressing the warning display check button will indicate which system is in need of attention.

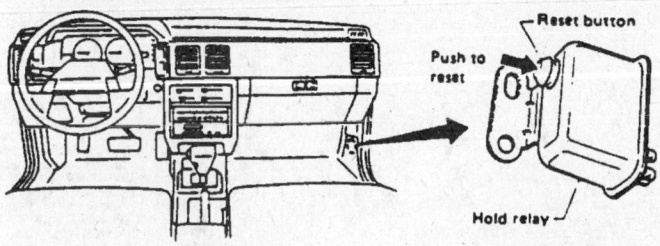

Fig. 22 Oxygen sensor warning lamp electrical connector location. 1987 Stanza except Wagon

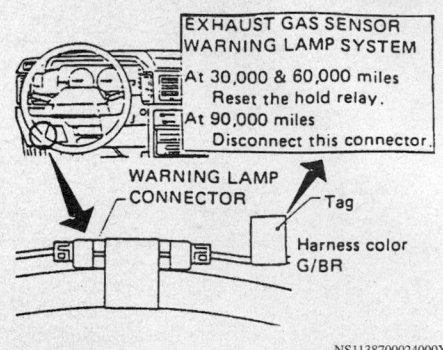

EXHAUST GAS SENSOR
WARNING LAMP SYSTEM

At 30,000 & 60,000 miles
Reset the hold relay.
At 90,000 miles
Disconnect this connector.

WARNING LAMP
CONNECTOR — Tag

Harness color
G/BR

NS1138700024000X

Fig. 24 Oxygen sensor warning lamp electrical connector location. 1987 Pulsar

After the indicated system has been serviced, the warning display will reset automatically.

TRACTION CONTROL/ SLIP INDICATOR LAMP

Drive wheel slippage is detected by the four wheel rotating signal. When wheel slip becomes excessive, the Traction Control System (TCS) operates causing the SLIP indicator lamp to illuminate. When the TCS off switch is used to cancel TCS function, the TCS OFF indicator lamp will illuminate. If a malfunction in the TCS system occurs, the SLIP indicator lamp and TCS OFF indicator lamp will light, shutting down the TCS operation. The indicator lamps will reset when the malfunction is corrected and vehicle is driven.

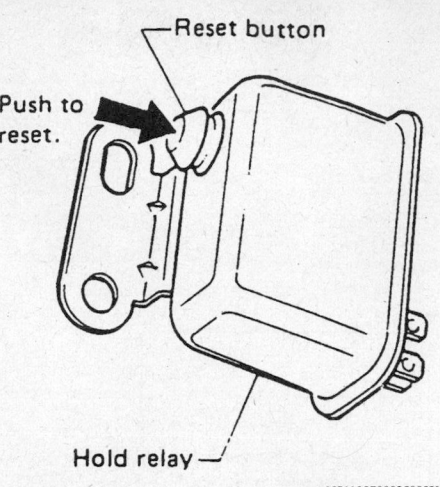

Reset button

Push to reset.

Hold relay —

NS1138700025000X

Fig. 25 Oxygen sensor warning lamp hold relay. 1987 Stanza Wagon

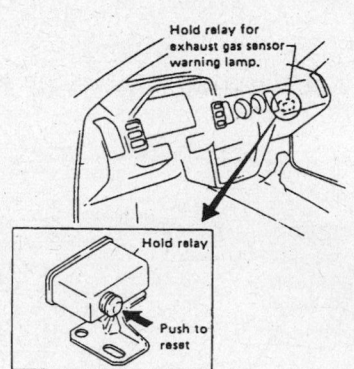

Hold relay for exhaust gas sensor warning lamp.

Hold relay

Push to reset

If sensor should be checked at 90,000 miles (144,000 km) of operation (After the third inspection), disconnect warning lamp harness connector.

NS1138700027000X

Fig. 27 Oxygen sensor warning lamp electrical connectors location. 1987 300ZX w/digital type instrument cluster

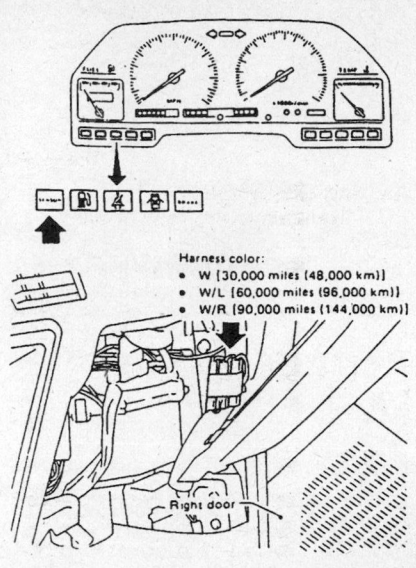

Harness color:
• W (30,000 miles (48,000 km))
• W/L (60,000 miles (96,000 km))
• W/R (90,000 miles (144,000 km))

Right door

NS1138700026000X

Fig. 26 Oxygen sensor warning lamp electrical connectors location. 1987 300ZX w/analog type instrument cluster

Subaru

INDEX

"CHECK ENGINE" LAMP

1985-86

The "Check Engine" lamp will illuminate when the ignition switch is in the On position. The lamp should go out shortly after the engine has been started. If it does not, the self-diagnostic system has detected a problem and stored a diagnostic trouble code. **After diagnosis and repair are complete, the self-diagnostic system memory will automatically be cleared of any stored diagnostic trouble codes.**

1987-99 EXCEPT 1990 LEGACY

The "Check Engine" lamp will be illuminated when the ignition switch is placed in the On position. When the engine is started, the lamp should go out. If it remains lit after engine start-up, the self-diagnostic system has detected a problem and stored a diagnostic trouble code. **After diagnosis and repair are complete, the self-diagnostic system memory can be cleared as follows:**

1. Start engine and run until normal operating temperature is reached.
2. Place ignition switch in off position, then connect test mode and read memory connectors.
3. Place ignition switch in On position without starting engine. "Check Engine" lamp should be illuminated.
4. Depress accelerator pedal completely, then return to half throttle and hold for two seconds.
5. Release accelerator pedal and start engine.
6. Drive vehicle at a speed above 5 mph for approximately one minute.
7. Allow engine to reach operating temperature at an engine speed above 1500 RPM. "Check Engine" lamp should blink.
8. Place ignition switch in off position, then disconnect test mode and read memory connectors.

1990 LEGACY

The "Check Engine" lamp will be illuminated when the ignition switch is placed in

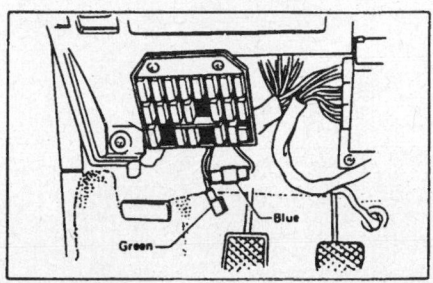

SB1139000001000X

Fig. 1   EGR maintenance lamp reset

the On position. When the engine is started, the lamp should go out. If it remains lit after engine start-up, the self-diagnostic system has detected a problem and stored a diagnostic trouble code. **After diagnosis and repair are complete, the self-diagnostic system memory can be cleared as follows:**

1. Start engine and allow to reach operating temperature.
2. Place ignition switch in off position, then connect test mode and read memory connectors.
3. Place ignition switch in On position without starting engine. "Check Engine" lamp should be illuminated.
4. Depress accelerator pedal completely, then return to half throttle and hold for two seconds.
5. Release accelerator pedal and start engine.
6. If "Check Engine" lamp remains lit, proceed as follows:
   a. Confirm diagnostic trouble code.
   b. Perform sequential checks of diagnostic trouble codes.
7. If lamp goes out, drive at a speed exceeding 7 mph for at least one minute.
8. **On models equipped with manual transaxle,** perform a fourth speed shift.
9. **On all models,** warm up engine by running above 2000 RPM, then observe "Check Engine" lamp.
10. If lamp does not blink, check again for diagnostic trouble codes, then repeat preceding step.
11. If lamp blinks, place ignition switch in off position.
12. Disconnect test and read mode connectors.

MALFUNCTION INDICATOR LAMP (MIL)

IMPREZA

The MIL will be illuminated when the ignition switch is placed in the On position, and should go out when the engine is started. If the MIL remains lit after engine start-up, the self-diagnostic system has detected a malfunction and has stored a diagnostic trouble code. **After diagnosis and repair are complete, the self-diagnostic system memory can be cleared of diagnostic trouble codes using a suitable scan tool. Follow tool manufacturer's instructions.**

AIR BAG WARNING LAMP

The air bag warning lamp, located inside the combination meter, will illuminate in the event of a poor connection or other air bag system malfunction. When the air bag system is functioning properly, the lamp should go out approximately eight seconds after the ignition switch is placed in the On position. The lamp can also be used to display stored diagnostic trouble codes.

Following system diagnosis and repair, clear air bag diagnostic trouble codes from memory using a suitable diagnostic scan tool. Follow tool manufacturer's instructions.

EGR MAINTENANCE REMINDER LAMP

The EGR maintenance reminder indicator lamp will be illuminated to indicate time for EGR maintenance. **After performing maintenance, reset reminder lamp. Remove instrument panel lower cover, then locate the three single pin electrical connectors located behind the fuse panel. Disconnect blue connector and connect it with the green connector, Fig. 1.**

Suzuki

INDEX

OXYGEN SENSOR MAINTENANCE REMINDER LAMP

1986-87 SAMURAI

A sensor lamp is located on the instrument panel to indicate proper operation of the oxygen sensor feedback circuit. Every 60,000 miles of vehicle operation, the lamp will begin to flash. **When the lamp begins to flash, the feedback circuit should be checked and the lamp reset using the following procedure:**

1. Ensure ignition switch is in the off position, then remove fuse panel cover and move cancel switch to On position, **Fig. 1.**
2. Turn ignition switch to On position and observe Sensor lamp. If lamp does not light (without flashing), inspect for defective bulb or open feed circuit and repair as necessary.
3. After lamp lights, start engine and allow to reach normal operating temperature.
4. Operate engine at 1500–2000 RPM while observing lamp.
5. If lamp flashed, system is operating properly. If lamp does not flash, a problem in the Computer Engine Control

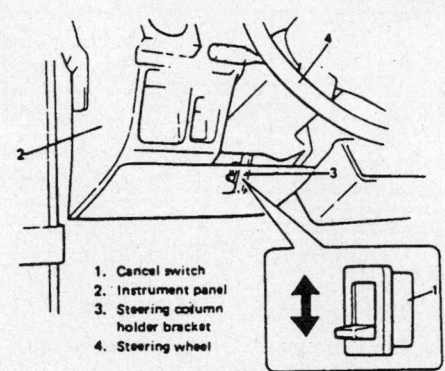

1. Cancel switch
2. Instrument panel
3. Steering column holder bracket
4. Steering wheel

SK1139000001000X

Fig. 1 Oxygen sensor indicator lamp cancel switch

System is indicated and diagnosis and system testing is required.

6. After proper system operation has been verified, place cancel switch in off position to reset automatic indicator system.

"CHECK ENGINE" LIGHT

1988-91 SAMURAI & SIDEKICK

The "Check Engine" light will flash or illu-

minate at 50,000, 80,000 and 100,000 miles to indicate emission maintenance is required. After performing the required maintenance the light may be reset by moving cancel switch to opposite position. Cancel switch is located under instrument panel to the left of the steering column.

MALFUNCTION INDICATOR LAMP

The Malfunction Indicator Lamp lights when the ignition switch is turned ON (but the engine not running) with the diagnosis switch terminal ungrounded regardless of the condition of the Electronic Fuel Injection system. This is only to check the malfunction indicator lamp bulb and its circuit. If there are no problems with the Electronic Fuel Injection system the malfunction indicator lamp turns off after the engine has started. Time to erase diagnostic trouble code memory thoroughly varies depending on ambient temperature as follows: over 32°F 60 seconds or longer, under 32°F select a place with higher temperature than 32°F.

Toyota

INDEX

ANTI-LOCK BRAKE SYSTEM WARNING LAMP

The anti-lock warning lamp is used to warn of a system malfunction. The lamp will be lit during engine start-up, but should go out when the self-diagnostic system verifies proper anti-lock operation. If the lamp remains lit, a malfunction in the anti-lock brake system is indicated. **After system diagnosis and repair are complete, the lamp can be reset using the following procedures.**

AVALON, CAMRY & SIENNA

1990-91

1. Place ignition switch in On position.
2. Disconnect check connector, **Fig. 1.**
3. Depress brake pedal completely at least eight times within three seconds, then ensure warning lamp diagnostic trouble code display indicates normal condition, **Fig. 2.**
4. Connect check connector.
5. Anti-lock warning lamp should not be illuminated. If it is, repeat reset procedure, ensure all requirements are met.

1992-99

1. Place ignition switch in On position.
2. **On Nippondenso systems** connect jumper tool No. 09843-18020, or equivalent, to terminals T_C and E1 of diagnostic connector link, **Figs. 3 and 4** and remove the short pin from DLC1 **Fig. 5.** Vehicle must be stopped at this time.
3. **On Bosch systems** connect jumper tool No. 09843-18020, or equivalent, to terminals T_C and E1 of diagnostic connector link, **Figs. 3 and 4.** Vehicle must be stopped at this time.
4. **On all systems** clear diagnostic trouble codes from ECU by fully depressing brake pedal at least eight times within three seconds.
5. Ensure warning lamp diagnostic trou-

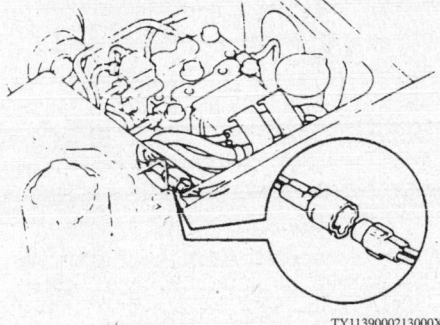

Fig. 1   Check connector location. 1990-91 Camry

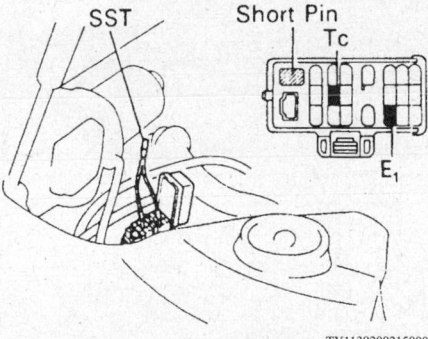

Fig. 3   Check connector location & terminal identification. 1992-96 Camry

ble code display indicates a normal condition, **Fig. 2.**
6. Remove check connectors, then ensure ABS warning lamp goes out.

CELICA & PASEO

1987-89

1. Place ignition switch in On position.
2. **On FWD models,** remove control relay bracket attaching bolt, **Fig. 6.**
3. **On all models,** disconnect check connector, **Figs. 6 and 7.**
4. Cycle brake pedal at least eight times within three seconds, then ensure

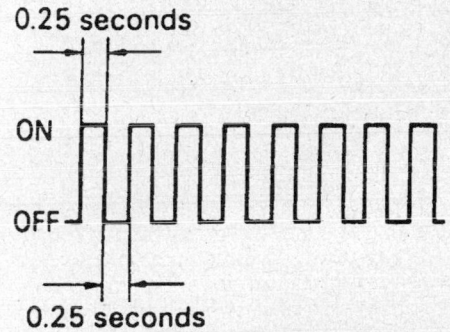

Fig. 2   Normal indication

warning lamp diagnostic trouble code display indicates a normal condition, **Fig. 2.**
5. Connect check connector.
6. Anti-lock warning lamp should not be illuminated.
7. **On FWD models,** install control relay attaching bolt.

1990-99

1. Place ignition switch in On position.
2. Connect jumper tool No. 09843-18020, or equivalent, to terminals T_C and E1 of diagnostic connector link, **Figs. 8 and 9.** Vehicle must be stopped at this time.
3. Clear ECU diagnostic trouble codes by fully depressing brake pedal at least eight times within three seconds.
4. Ensure warning lamp diagnostic trouble code display indicates a normal condition.
5. Remove jumper tool and ensure ABS warning lamp goes out.

CRESSIDA

1. Place ignition switch in On position.
2. Connect a suitable jumper wire between terminals T_C and E1 of diagnostic connector link, **Fig. 10.**
3. Fully depress brake pedal at lease eight times within three seconds, then ensure warning lamp diagnostic trouble code display indicates a normal

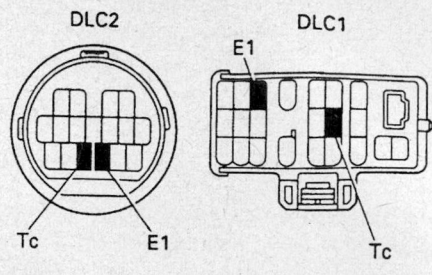

Fig. 4 Check connector terminal identification. Avalon, Sienna & 1997-98 Camry

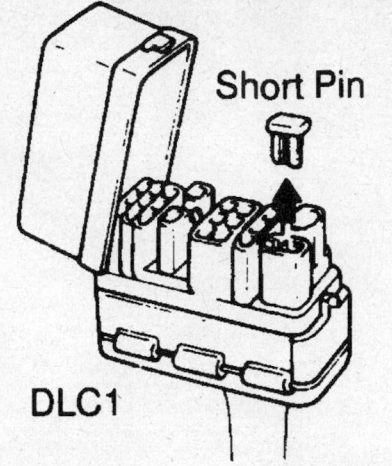

Fig. 5 Short pin location. Camry

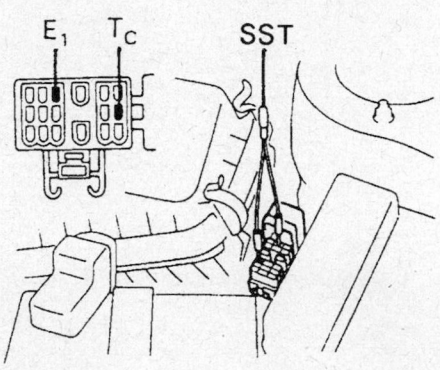

Fig. 8 Check connector location & terminal identification. 1990-93 Celica

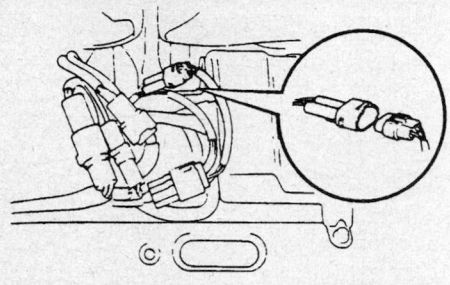

Fig. 7 Check connector location. 1987-89 Celica AWD

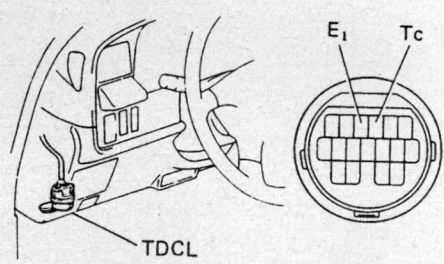

Fig. 10 Check connector location. Cressida

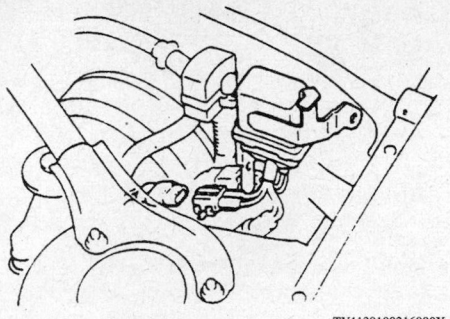

Fig. 6 Check connector location. 1987-89 Celica FWD

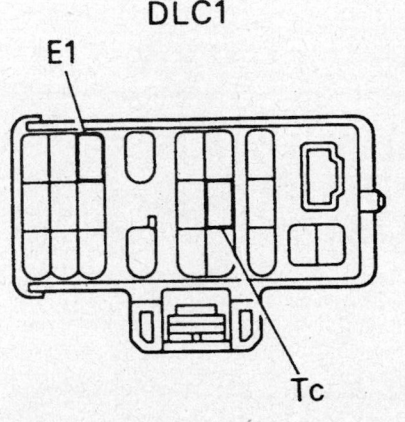

Fig. 9 Check connector terminal identification. RAV4 & 1994-98 Celica, Land Cruiser & Tacoma

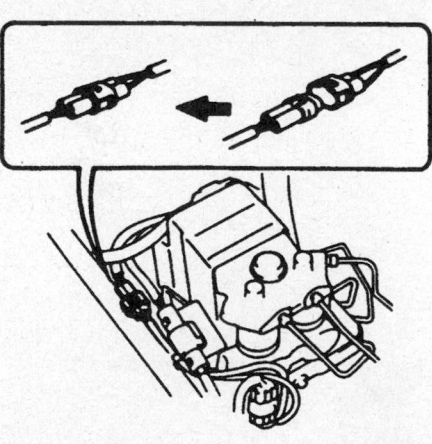

Fig. 11 Check connector location. 1988-92 Supra

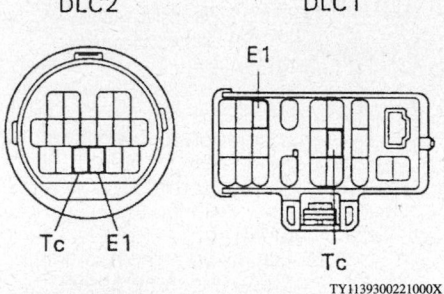

Fig. 12 Check connector terminal identification. 1993-98 Supra

condition, **Fig. 2.**
4. Disconnect jumper wire from diagnostic connector link.
5. Anti-lock warning lamp should not be illuminated.

LAND CRUISER & TACOMA

1. Place ignition switch in On position.
2. Connect jumper tool No. 09843-18020, or equivalent, to terminals T$_C$ and E1 of diagnostic connector link, **Fig. 9.** Vehicle must be stopped at this time.
3. Clear diagnostic trouble codes from ECU by fully depressing brake pedal at least eight times within three seconds.
4. Ensure warning lamp diagnostic trouble code display indicates a normal condition.
5. Remove jumper tool, then ensure ABS warning lamp goes out.

SUPRA
1988-92

1. Place ignition switch in On position.
2. Disconnect actuator check connector, **Fig. 11.**

3. Fully depress brake pedal at least eight times within three seconds, then ensure warning lamp diagnostic trouble code display indicates a normal condition, **Fig. 2.**
4. Connect actuator check connector.
5. Anti-lock warning lamp should not be illuminated. If it is, repeat reset procedure, ensure all requirements are met.

1993-98

1. Using a suitable jumper, connect DLC1 or DLC2 terminals T$_C$ and E1, **Fig. 12.** Remove short pin from DLC 1.
2. Fully depress brake pedal at least eight times within three seconds, then ensure warning lamp diagnostic trouble code display indicates a normal condition.
3. Remove jumper, then connect short pin to DLC1.

PICKUP & 4RUNNER

1. Place ignition switch in On position.
2. Disconnect service connector, **Fig. 13.** Ensure vehicle is not moving.

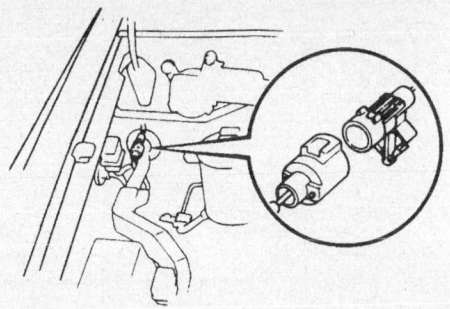

Fig. 13 Service connector location. Pickup & 4Runner

TY1139100222000X

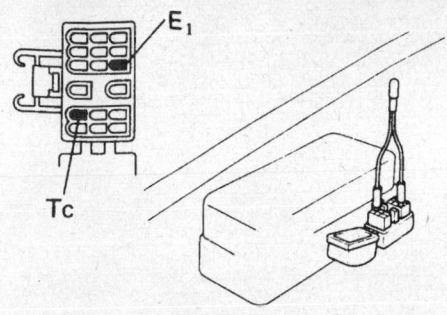

Fig. 14 Check connector location & terminal identification. Pickup

TY1139100223000X

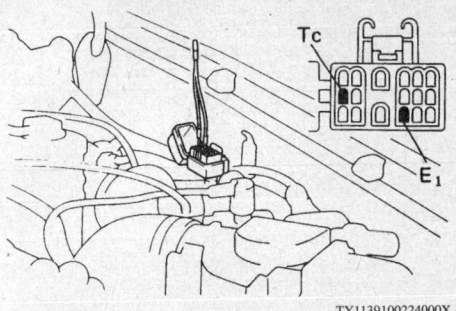

Fig. 15 Check connector location & terminal identification. 4Runner

TY1139100224000X

Fig. 16 Service connector location. Previa

TY1139100225000X

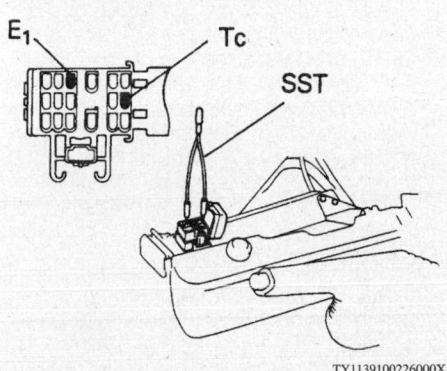

Fig. 17 Check connector location & terminal identification. Previa

TY1139100226000X

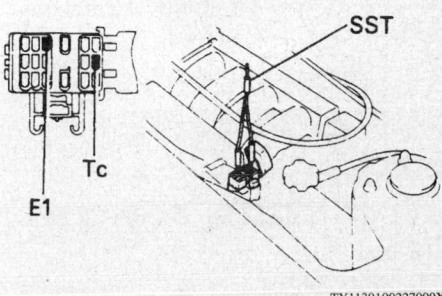

Fig. 18 Check connector location & terminal identification. MR2

TY1139100227000X

3. Connect a suitable jumper wire between terminals T_C and E_1 of check connector, **Figs. 14 and 15.**
4. Fully depress brake pedal at least eight times within three seconds, then ensure warning lamp diagnostic trouble code display indicates a normal condition, **Fig. 2.**
5. Connect service connector and remove jumper wire. Ensure warning lamp goes out.

RAV4

1. Using jumper tool No. 09843-18020, or equivalent, connect Data Link Connector (DLC1) terminals T_C and E1, **Fig. 9.**
2. Disconnect short pin from DLC1, then place ignition switch in On position.
3. **On AWD models,** fully depress brake pedal at least eight times within three seconds.
4. **On FWD models,** fully depress brake pedal at least eight times within five seconds.
5. **On all models,** ensure warning lamp diagnostic trouble code display indicates a normal condition.
6. Remove jumper tool and connect short pin to DLC1.

PREVIA

1. Place ignition switch in On position.
2. Disconnect service connector, **Fig. 16.**
3. Connect jumper wire tool No. 09843-18020, or equivalent, to check connector terminals T_C and E_1, **Fig. 17.** Ensure vehicle is not moving.
4. Clear ECU diagnostic trouble codes by fully depressing brake pedal at least eight times within three seconds.
5. Ensure warning lamp diagnostic trou-

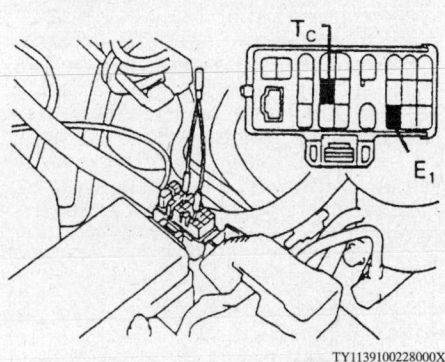

Fig. 19 Check connector location & terminal identification. T100

TY1139100228000X

ble code display indicates a normal condition, then connect service connector.
6. Remove jumper wire tool and ensure ABS warning lamp goes out.

MR2

1. Place ignition switch in On position.
2. Connect jumper wire tool No. 09843-18020, or equivalent, to check connector terminals T_C and E1, **Fig. 18.** Ensure vehicle is not moving.
3. Clear ECU diagnostic trouble codes by fully depressing brake pedal at least eight times within three seconds.
4. Ensure warning lamp diagnostic trouble code display indicates a normal condition, then remove jumper tool.
5. Ensure ABS warning lamp goes out.

T100

1. Place ignition switch in On position.

2. Connect jumper tool No. 09843-18020, or equivalent, to diagnostic connector link terminals T_C and E_1, **Fig. 19.** Ensure vehicle is not moving.
3. Clear ECU diagnostic trouble codes by fully depressing brake pedal at least eight times within three seconds.
4. Ensure warning lamp diagnostic trouble code display indicates a normal condition.
5. Remove jumper tool and ensure ABS warning lamp goes out.

AUTOMATIC TRANSMISSION OVERDRIVE LAMP

The "OD off" lamp will be illuminated when the ignition switch is in the On position and the Overdrive (OD) switch is in the off position. When the OD switch is placed in the On position, the "OD off" lamp should go out. If the lamp flashes when the switch is placed in the On position, a malfunction has been detected by the electronic control system. **After diagnosis and repair are complete, place the ignition switch in the off position, then clear ECU of diagnostic trouble codes as follows:**

1. **On Celica, MR2, Pickup, Previa, T100 and 4Runner models,** remove EFI fuse (15A) for at least ten seconds.
2. **On Cressida models,** remove EFI fuse (20A) for at least ten seconds.
3. **On Supra models,** remove DOME fuse for at least ten seconds.
4. **On all models,** it may be necessary to remove fuse for a longer period of time in cold weather conditions.

AUTOMATIC TRANSMISSION OIL TEMPERATURE WARNING LAMP

This lamp will be illuminated when automatic transmission or transfer case fluid temperature exceeds 302°F. If the lamp lights, allow vehicle to operate at idle speed until fluid temperature falls below 248°F; the lamp should go out. If it remains lit, the transmission or transfer case may require service. **When transmission or transfer case fluid has returned to its normal temperature, the lamp will reset automatically.**

MALFUNCTION INDICATOR LAMP (MIL)

CAMRY, CELICA, PASEO & SUPRA

The MIL will be illuminated when the ignition switch is in the On position with engine not running. When the engine is started, the MIL should go out. If it does not, the Electronic Control Unit (ECU) has detected a system malfunction and stored a diagnostic trouble code. **After diagnosis and repair are complete, place ignition switch in off position, then clear ECU diagnostic trouble codes as follows:**

1. **On 1985-86 Camry models,** remove ECU-B fuse for at least ten seconds.
2. **On 1985-86 Celica and Supra models,** remove STOP fuse for at least ten seconds.
3. **On 1987-89 models and 1990-95 models except Supra,** remove EFI fuse.
4. **On 1990-95 Supra models,** remove EFI (15A) fuse for at least 30 seconds.
5. **On 1996-99 models,** either remove EFI fuse, disconnect battery cable or use a suitable scan tool.
6. **On all models,** it may be necessary to remove fuse for a longer period of time during cold weather conditions.

It is also possible to clear ECU diagnostic trouble codes by disconnecting the battery ground cable, but this method will also erase clock, radio and radio alarm memory.

COROLLA & TERCEL

The MIL will be illuminated when the ignition switch is in the On position with engine not running. When the engine has been started, the MIL should go out. If it does not, the Electronic Control Unit (ECU) has detected a system malfunction and stored a diagnostic trouble code. **After diagnosis and repair are complete, place ignition switch in off position, then clear ECU diagnostic trouble codes as follows:**

1. **On all models except 1990-95 Tercel,** remove STOP (15A) fuse, **Fig. 20,** for at least ten seconds.
2. **On 1990-95 Tercel models,** remove EFI (15A) fuse for at least ten seconds.

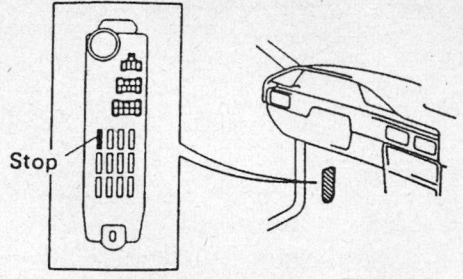

Fig. 20 STOP fuse location. Corolla & Tercel

TY1139100229000X

3. **On 1996-99 models,** either remove EFI fuse, disconnect battery cable or use a suitable scan tool.
4. **On all models,** it may be necessary to remove fuse for a longer period of time during cold weather conditions.

It is also possible to clear ECU diagnostic trouble codes by disconnecting the battery ground cable, but this method will also erase clock, radio and radio alarm memory.

CRESSIDA & VAN

The MIL will be illuminated when the ignition switch is in the On position with engine not running. When the engine has been started, the MIL should go out. If it remains lit, a diagnostic trouble code has been stored by the Electronic Control Unit (ECU). **After diagnosis and repair are complete, place ignition switch in off position, then clear diagnostic trouble codes from the ECU by removing the EFI (20A) fuse from the passenger compartment fuse panel for at least ten seconds. It may be necessary to remove the fuse for a longer period of time during cold weather conditions.** It is also possible to clear ECU diagnostic trouble codes by disconnecting the battery ground cable, but this method will also erase clock and radio memory.

LAND CRUISER, PICKUP, PREVIA, TACOMA, T100 & 4RUNNER

The MIL will be illuminated when the ignition switch is in the On position with engine not running. When the engine has been started, the lamp should go out. If it remains lit, a diagnostic trouble code has been stored by the Electronic Control Unit (ECU). **After diagnosis and repair are complete, place the ignition switch in the off position, then clear ECU diagnostic trouble codes as follows:**

1. **On models equipped with carbureted engine,** remove HAZ-HORN fuse from engine compartment relay panel.
2. **On models equipped with fuel injected engine,** remove EFI fuse from passenger compartment fuse panel.
3. **On all models,** the fuse must be removed for at least 30 seconds, possibly longer during cold weather conditions.

Diagnostic trouble codes can also be erased by disconnecting the battery ground

cable, but this method will also erase clock and radio memory.

RAV4

The MIL should light when the ignition switch is placed in the On position without starting the engine. When the engine is started, the lamp should go out. If it remains lit, a malfunction has been detected by the diagnostic system and has logged a diagnostic trouble code. If the malfunction does not occur again within three trips, the lamp will go out but a diagnostic trouble code will remain stored. **The lamp will reset automatically when diagnosis and repair are complete and diagnostic trouble codes have been cleared using one of the following procedures:**

1. Connect a suitable OBD II scan tool to instrument panel data link connector, then use tool to erase stored diagnostic trouble codes. Follow tool manufacturer's instructions.
2. Disconnect battery ground cable or EFI fuse. **Disconnecting ground cable will also erase clock and radio memory.**

MR2

The MIL will be illuminated when the ignition switch is in the On position with engine not running. When the engine has been started, the lamp should go out. If it remains lit, a diagnostic trouble code has been stored by the Electronic Control Unit (ECU). **After diagnosis and repair are complete, place ignition switch in off position, then remove the AM-2 fuse from the engine compartment relay panel on pre-1991 models or the EFI (15A) fuse on 1991–95 models.** The fuse must be removed for at least ten seconds, possibly longer during cold weather conditions. The lower the ambient temperature, the longer the fuse will have to be removed. Another method to erase stored diagnostic trouble codes is to disconnect the battery ground cable, but this method will also erase other memory, including clock and radio.

LOW COOLANT LEVEL LAMP

This lamp will be illuminated when the coolant level in the radiator drops below a pre-determined point. **To reset the lamp, bring the coolant to the proper level. Be sure to inspect the cooling system for leaks that may have precipitated the low coolant level condition.**

LOW OIL LEVEL WARNING LAMP

This lamp lights to indicate that the engine oil level is below a specified level. The lamp will be illuminated during engine start-up. If oil level is sufficient, the lamp will go out during engine operation. **The lamp will reset automatically when the oil level is corrected.**

OXYGEN SENSOR MAINTENANCE REMINDER LAMP

4 CYLINDER ENGINE

This lamp illuminates at 30,000 mile intervals. After performing the required service, reset lamp cancel switch. On Corolla models equipped with 3T-C engine and Celica and Corona models, the cancel switch is clipped to lefthand kick panel. On Corolla models equipped with 3A-C engine and Cressida and Tercel models, the cancel switch is located under instrument panel on the lower lefthand side. On 1980 Supra models, the cancel switch is located under the instrument panel to the left of the steering column. On 1981 Supra models, the cancel switch is clipped to the lefthand kick panel.

On 1980 models, use tool No. 09810-25010, or equivalent, to remove switch cover, then move switch lever to opposite position. On 1981 models, open the switch cover; then, using a screwdriver and working through the cover opening, move the switch lever to the opposite position.

TIMING BELT MAINTENANCE INDICATOR LAMP

PICKUP

Diesel Engine

After the timing belt has been replaced, the maintenance indicator lamp may be reset as follows:

1. Remove grommet from speedometer lens.
2. Insert a screwdriver into grommet hole and depress reset switch, **Fig. 21**.
3. Install grommet on speedometer lens.

AIR BAG SYSTEM WARNING LAMP

EXCEPT RAV4

The air bag system warning lamp is used

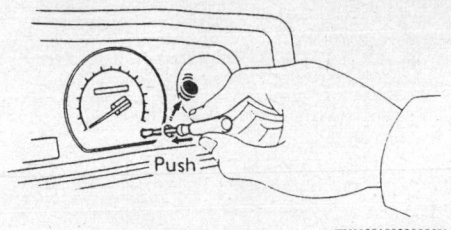

Fig. 21   Timing belt maintenance indicator lamp reset. Pickup w/diesel engine

to warn of a system malfunction. The lamp will light during engine start-up, but should go out when the self-diagnostic system determines that no malfunctions are present. If the lamp remains lit, a malfunction in the air bag system is indicated. **The air bag system must be diagnosed and repaired, then the following procedures can be used to reset the warning lamp.**

1. If Diagnostic Trouble Code 41 is not indicated, proceed as follows:
   a. Ensure ignition switch is in off position.
   b. Disconnect battery ground cable or remove ECU-B fuse for at least ten seconds.
   c. Connect battery ground cable or install ECU-B fuse. **Ensure ignition switch is in Lock position, or diagnostic system damage may occur.**
2. If Diagnostic Trouble Code 41 is indicated, proceed as follows:
   a. Connect service wires to check connector terminals T_C and AB.
   b. Place ignition switch in Accessory or On positions and wait approximately six seconds.
   c. Apply body ground to terminals T_C and AB alternately, twice in .5–1.5 second intervals beginning with terminal T_C, **Fig. 22**. When alternating ground applications, release one terminal from ground while applying it to other terminal.
   d. After a few seconds, the air bag lamp will blink in a 64 millisecond cycle, indicating cancellation is complete.

RAV4

The air bag or SRS warning lamp is intended to warn the driver of an air bag system malfunction. It is activated by the air bag sensor assembly. If the system is functioning properly, the lamp should light when the ignition switch is placed in the Accessory or On positions and should remain lit for approximately six seconds. If the lamp does not go out after this time or flashes, a malfunction has been detected and a diagnostic trouble code has been stored. **When diagnosis and repair are complete, placing the ignition switch in the off position will clear diagnostic trouble codes. This, in turn, will reset the warning lamp.**

ENGINE OIL REMINDER LAMP

PREVIA

At the specified engine oil change interval of 6,000 miles, an Oil Change reminder lamp on the instrument panel will be illuminated. After changing the engine oil and filter the lamp must be reset. To rest lamp, remove cover from instrument cluster, **Fig. 23,** then insert a small screwdriver or equivalent into plug opening to depress reset button.

TIRE PRESSURE WARNING LAMP

This warning lamp will illuminate when tire pressure falls below a specified psi. When the warning lamp illuminates, check the air pressure of the tire and adjust it to specified pressure. When the vehicle is driven more than 18 mph after the adjustment, the lamp will go Off.

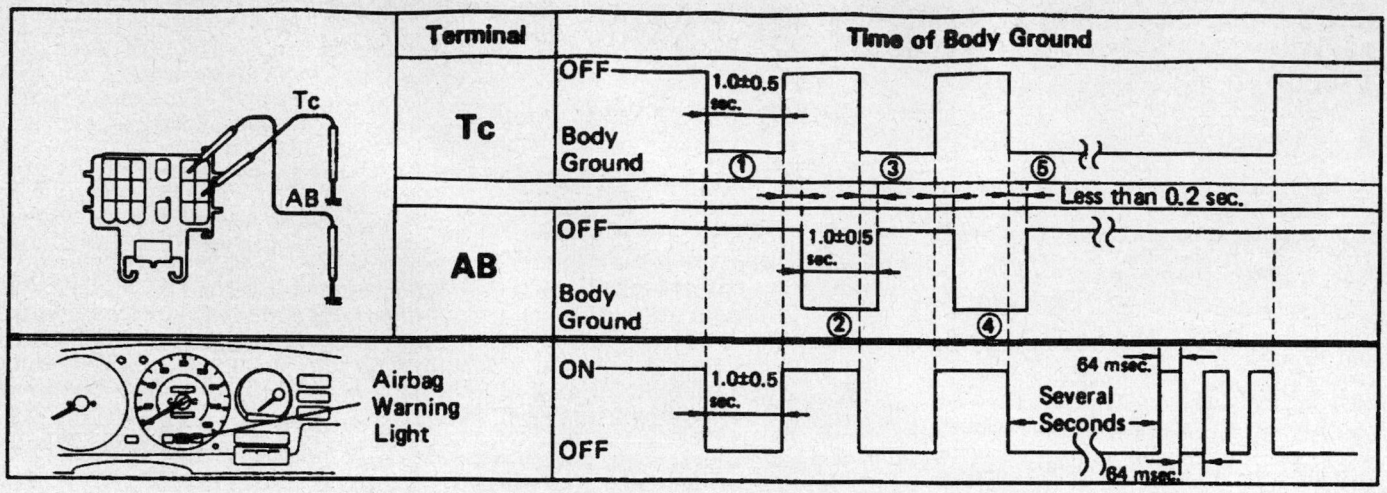

Fig. 22 Air bag warning lamp reset

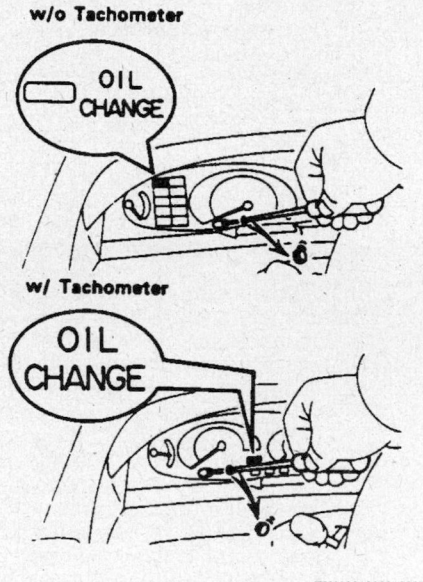

Fig. 23 Engine oil service reminder lamp reset. Previa

VEHICLE LIFT POINTS

TABLE OF CONTENTS

Mitsubishi

INDEX

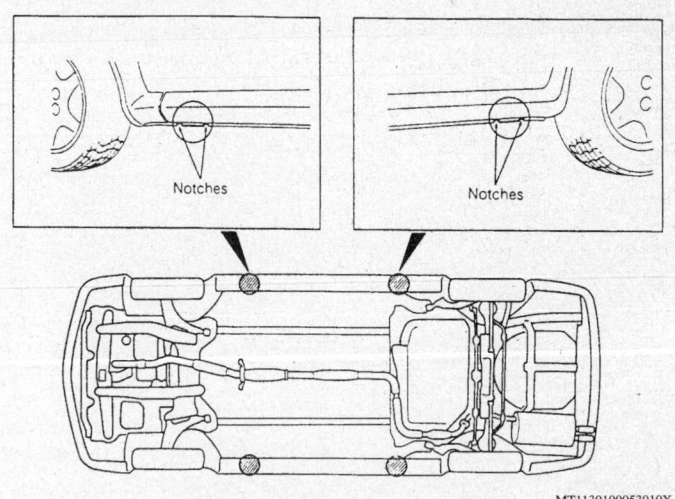

MT1139100053010X

Fig. 1 Diamante. Hoist

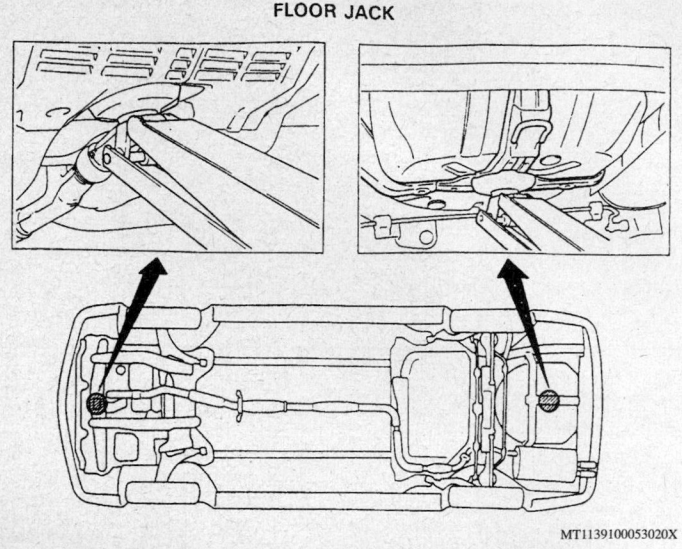

FLOOR JACK

MT1139100053020X

Fig. 2   1996 Diamante. Floor Jack

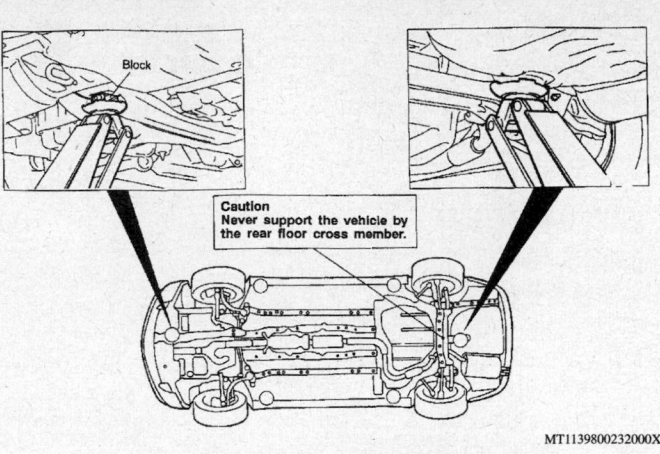

Block

Caution
Never support the vehicle by
the rear floor cross member.

MT1139800232000X

Fig. 3   1997-99 Diamante. Floor Jack

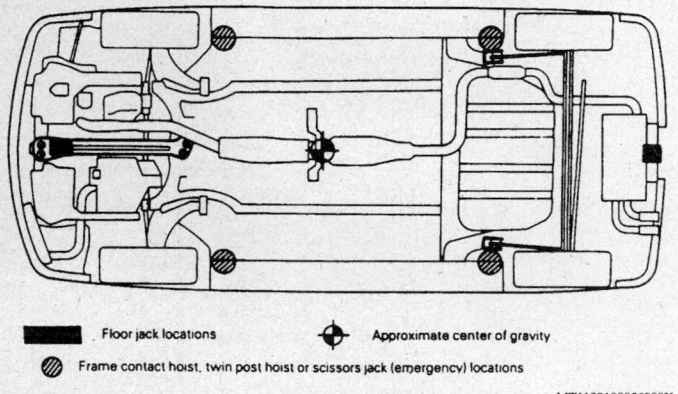

▬ Floor jack locations

⬥ Approximate center of gravity

▨ Frame contact hoist, twin post hoist or scissors jack (emergency) locations

MT1139100056000X

Fig. 4   Mirage. Floor Jack

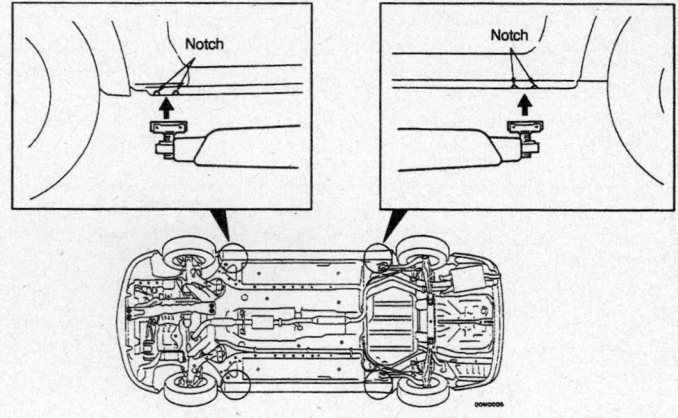

Notch

Notch

DOW0006

MT1139800234000X

Fig. 5   Mirage. Hoist

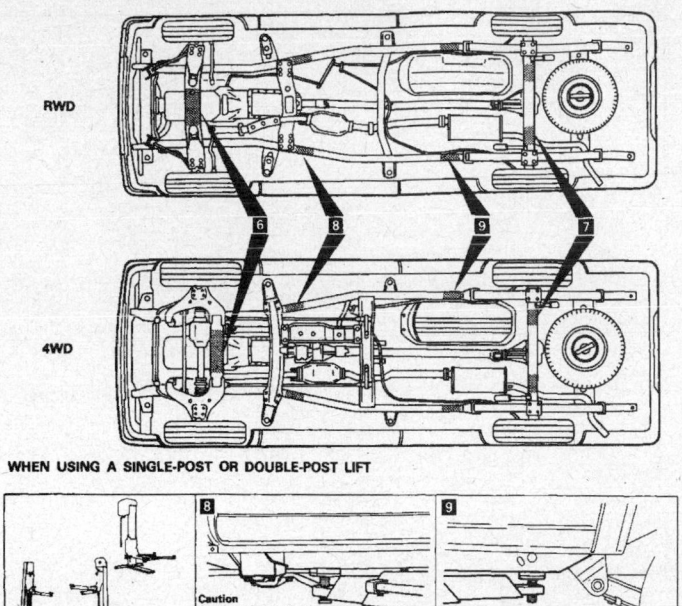

Fig. 6 Truck. Hoist

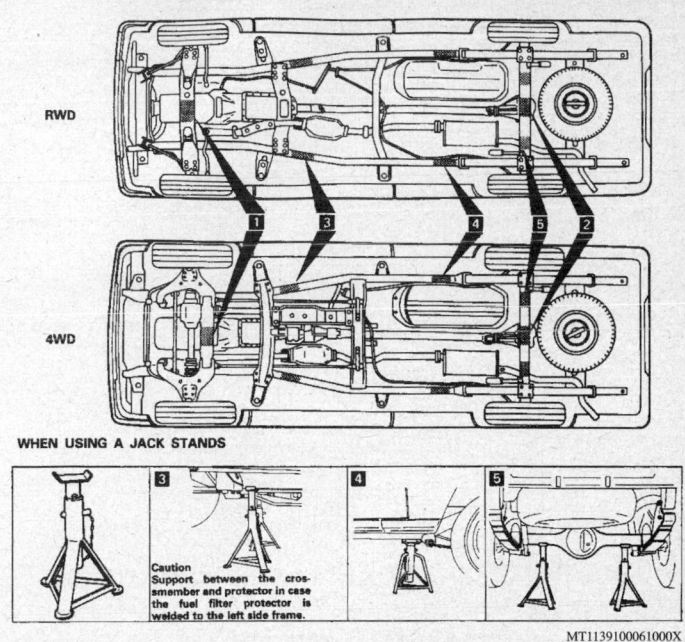

Fig. 7 Truck. Floor Jack

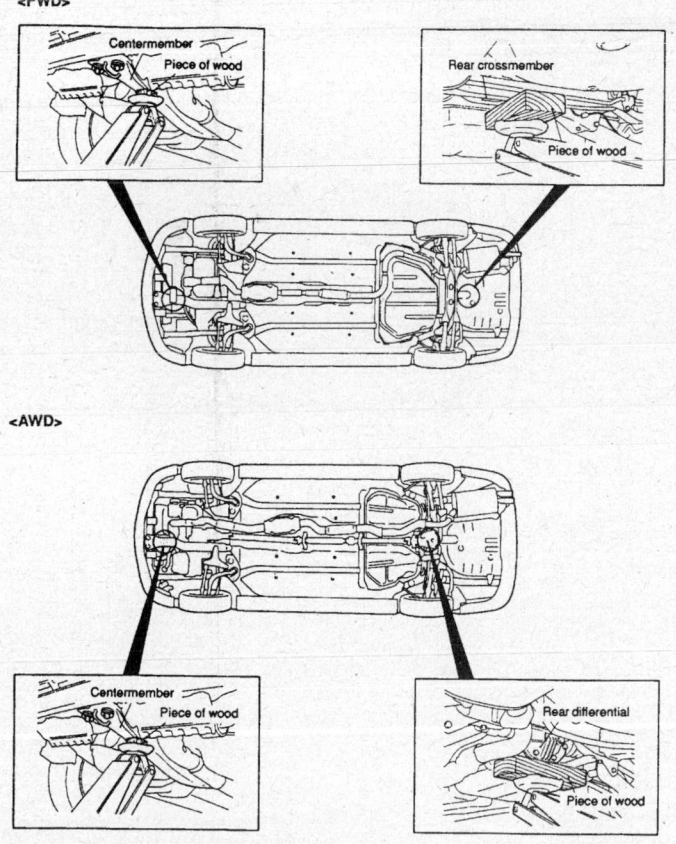

Fig. 8 Eclipse & Eclipse Spyder. Floor Jack

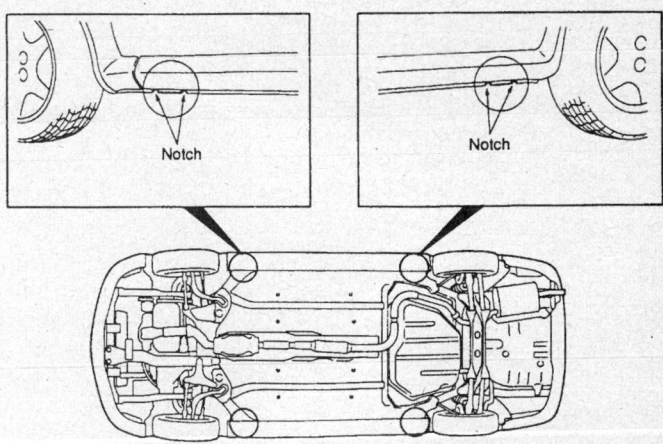

Fig. 9 Eclipse & Eclipse Spyder. Hoist

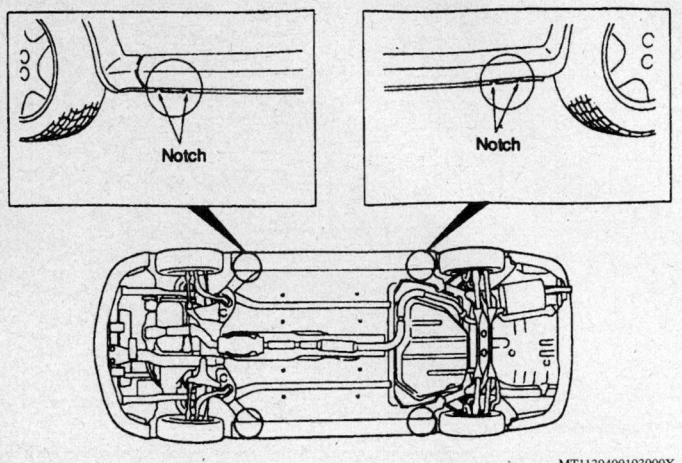

Fig. 10   Galant. Hoist

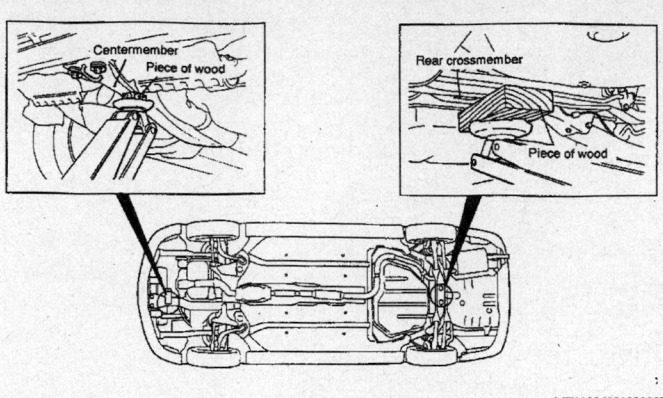

Fig. 11   Galant. Floor Jack

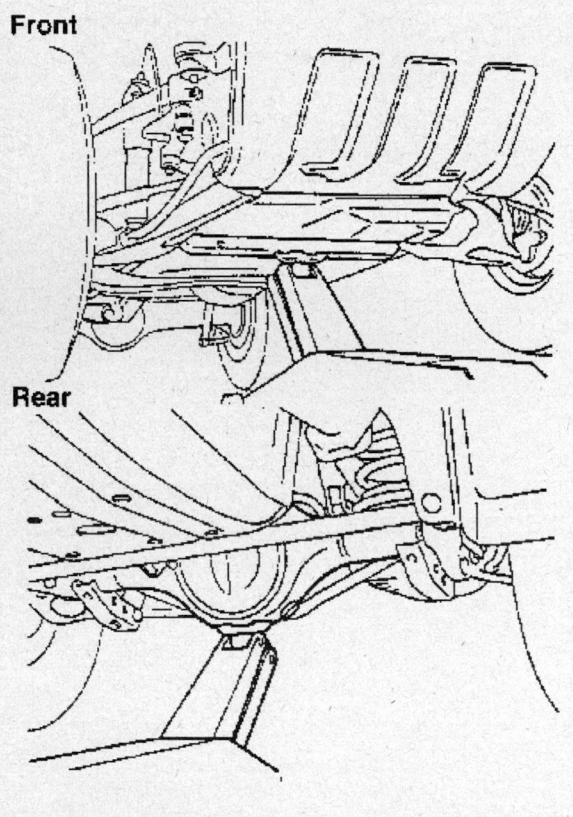

Fig. 12   Montero & Montero Sport. Floor Jack

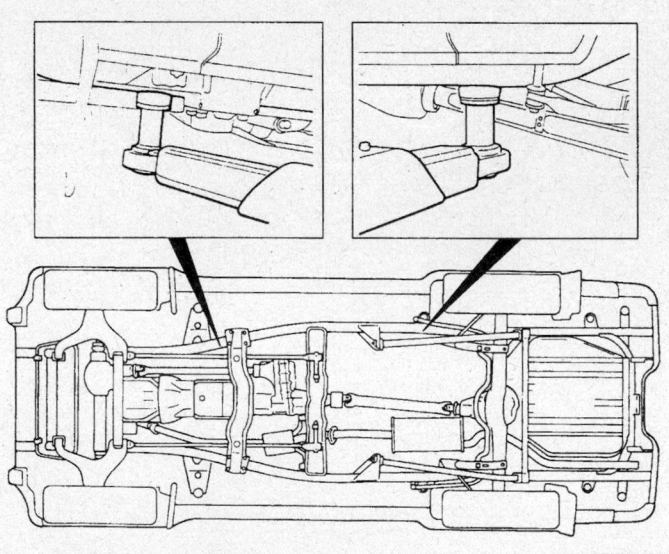

Fig. 13   Montero. Hoist

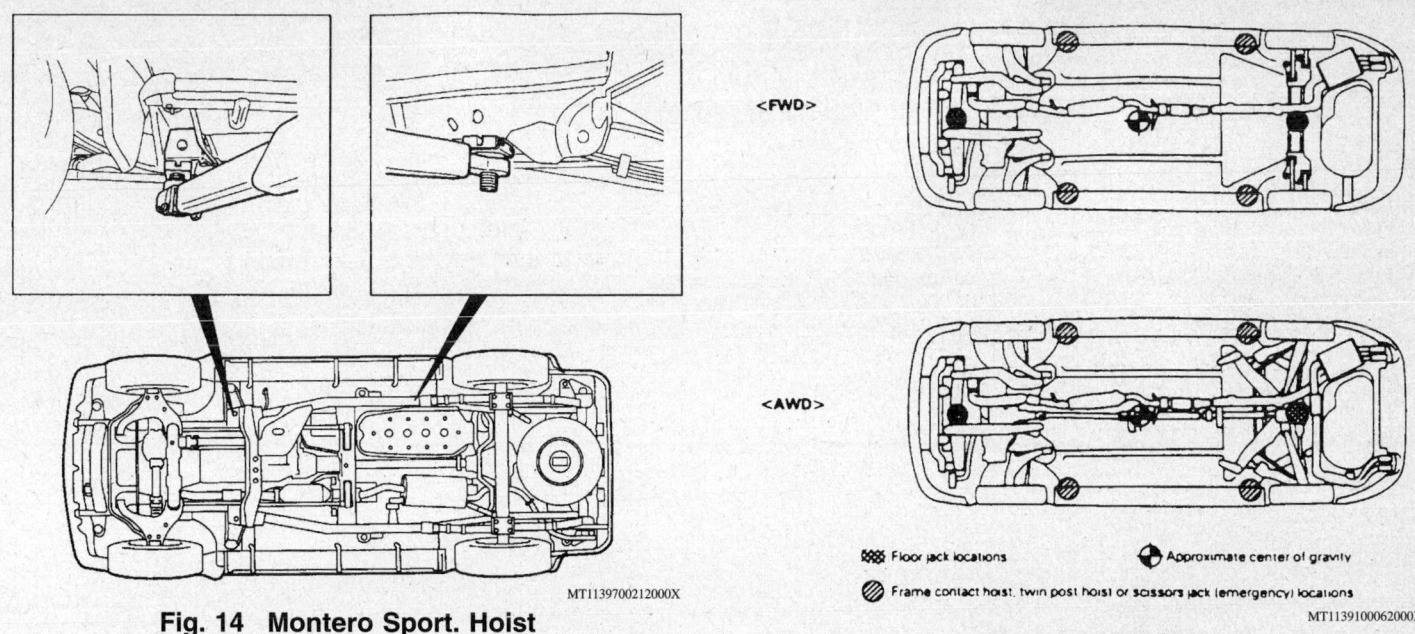

Fig. 14   Montero Sport. Hoist

MT1139700212000X

<FWD>

<AWD>

▨ Floor jack locations   ◆ Approximate center of gravity

◑ Frame contact hoist, twin post hoist or scissors jack (emergency) locations

MT1139100062000X

Fig. 15   3000GT

Nissan

INDEX

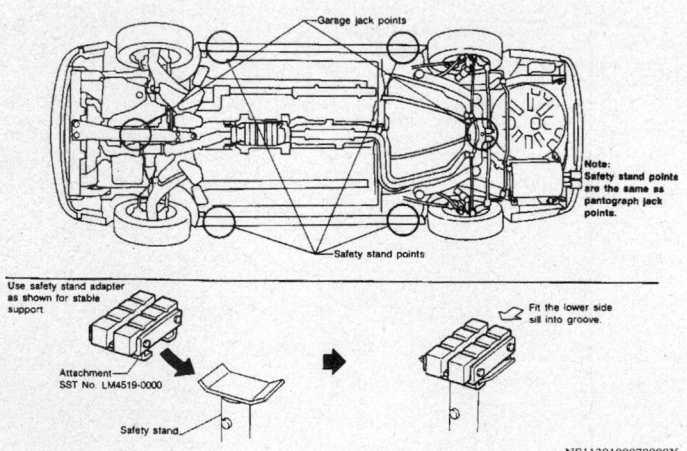

NS1139100078000X

Fig. 1 Altima. Floor Jack

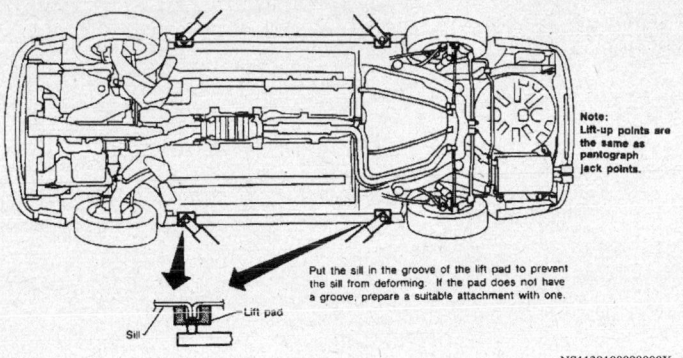

Note:
Lift-up points are the same as pantograph jack points.

Put the sill in the groove of the lift pad to prevent the sill from deforming. If the pad does not have a groove, prepare a suitable attachment with one.

Sill — Lift pad

NS1139100098000X

Fig. 2 Altima. Hoist

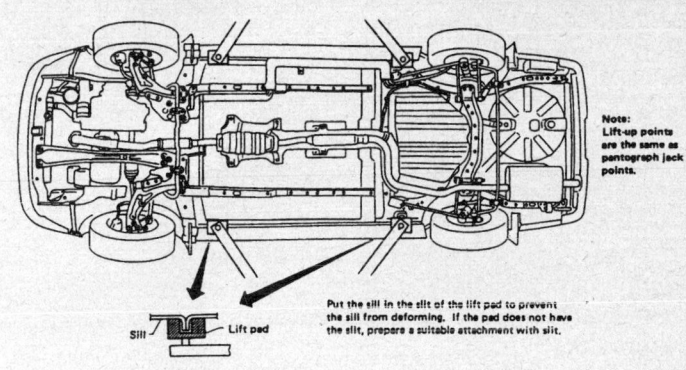

Note:
Lift-up points are the same as pantograph jack points.

Put the sill in the slit of the lift pad to prevent the sill from deforming. If the pad does not have the slit, prepare a suitable attachment with slit.

Sill — Lift pad

NS1139100067000X

Fig. 3 Maxima. Hoist

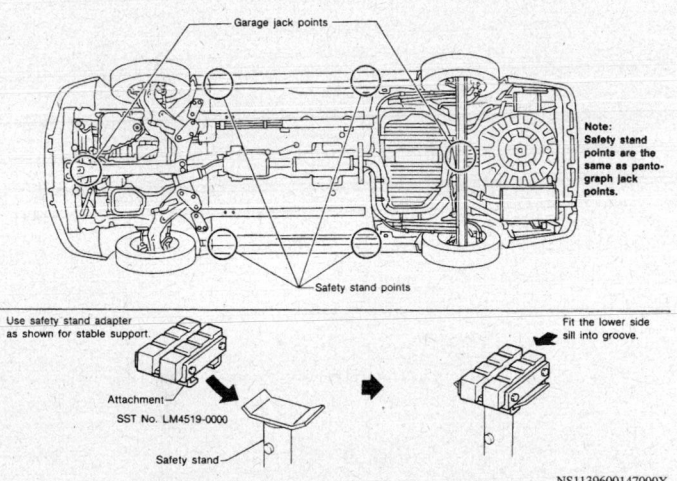

Garage jack points

Note:
Safety stand points are the same as pantograph jack points.

Safety stand points

Use safety stand adapter as shown for stable support.

Attachment
SST No. LM4519-0000

Safety stand

Fit the lower side sill into groove.

NS1139600147000X

Fig. 4 Maxima. Floor Jack

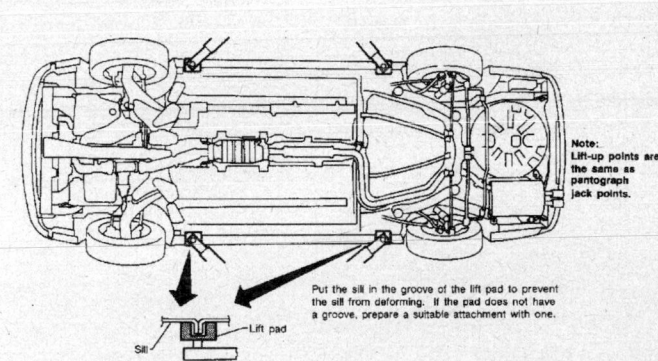

Note:
Lift-up points are the same as pantograph jack points.

Put the sill in the groove of the lift pad to prevent the sill from deforming. If the pad does not have a groove, prepare a suitable attachment with one.

Sill — Lift pad

NS1139800177000X

Fig. 5 Sentra & 200SX. Hoist

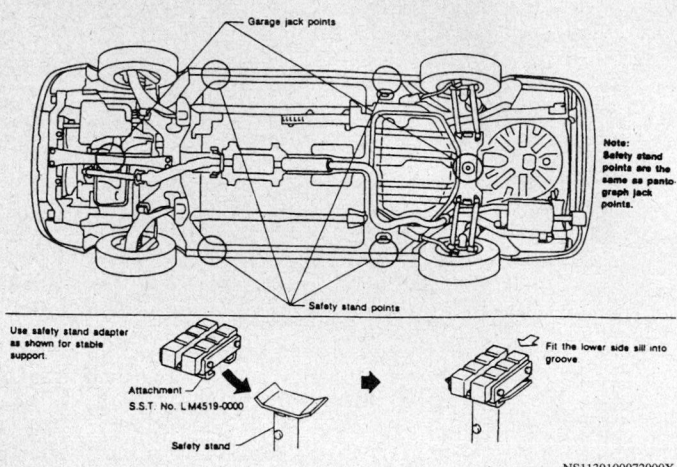

Fig. 6 Sentra & 200SX. Floor Jack

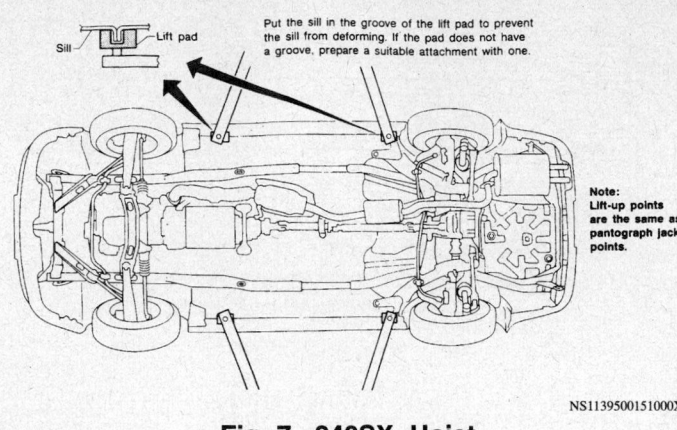

Fig. 7 240SX. Hoist

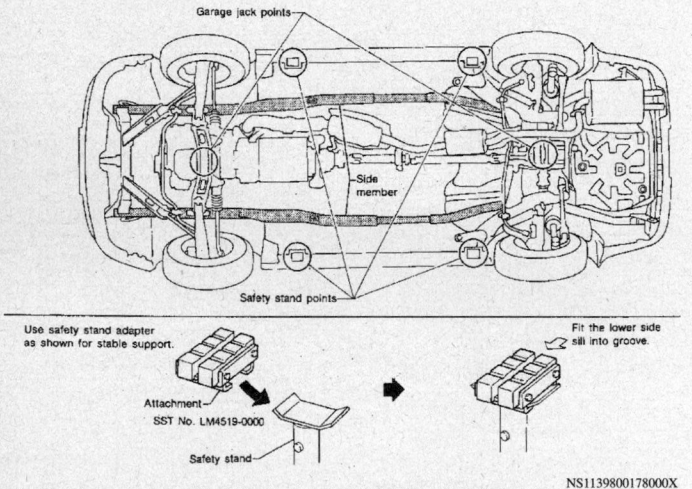

Fig. 8 240SX. Floor Jack

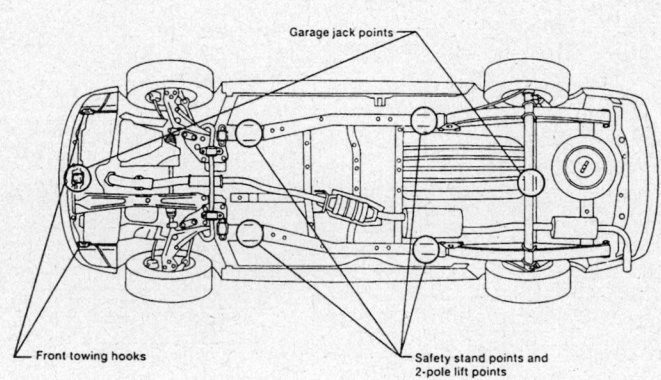

Fig. 9 Quest

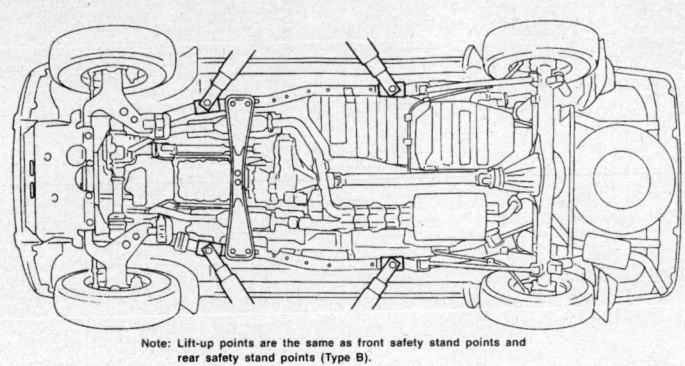

Note: Lift-up points are the same as front safety stand points and rear safety stand points (Type B).

NS1139600148000X

Fig. 10 Pathfinder. Hoist

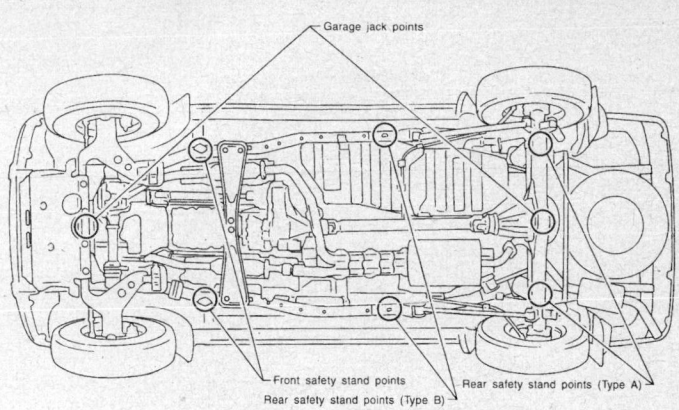

Garage jack points

Front safety stand points

Rear safety stand points (Type B)

Rear safety stand points (Type A)

Notes:
(1) Front and rear safety stand points (Type A) are the same as screw jack points.
(2) Rear safety stand points (Type B) are the same as rear 2-pole lift points.

NS1139600149000X

Fig. 11 Pathfinder. Floor Jack

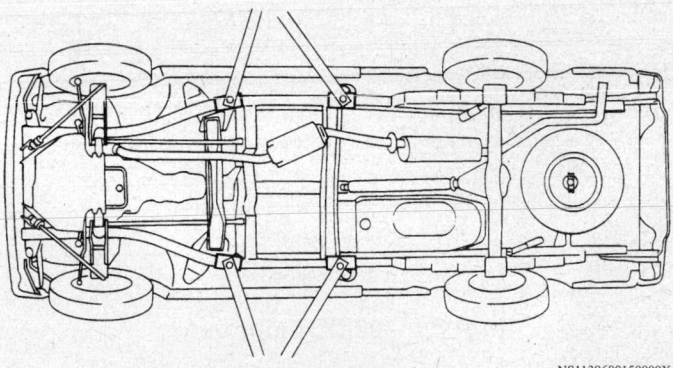

NS1139600150000X

Fig. 12 Frontier & Pickup. Hoist

2-WHEEL DRIVE
4-WHEEL DRIVE

NS1139100070000X

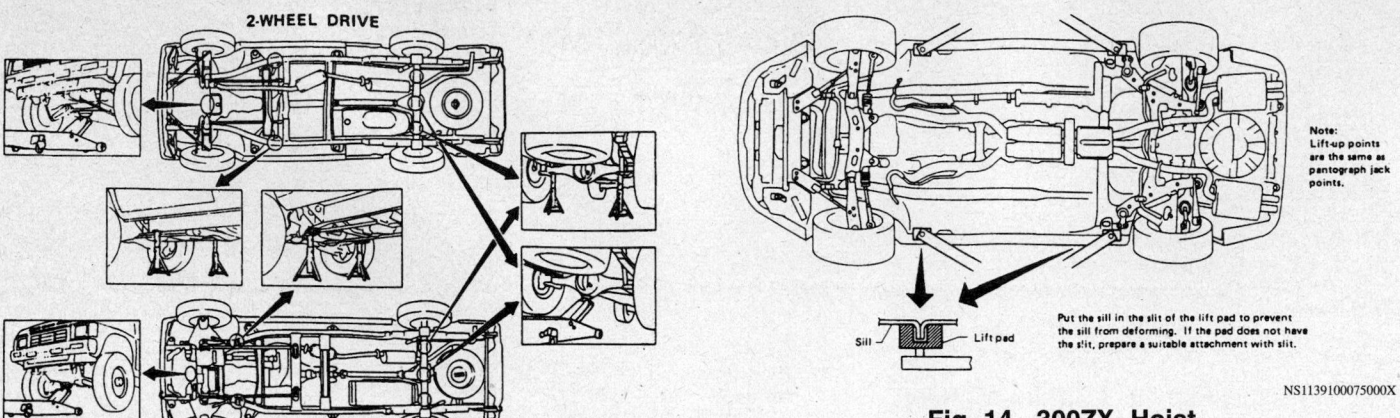

Fig. 13 Frontier & Pickup. Floor Jack

Note:
Lift-up points are the same as pantograph jack points.
Sill
Lift pad
Put the sill in the slit of the lift pad to prevent the sill from deforming. If the pad does not have the slit, prepare a suitable attachment with slit.

NS1139100075000X

Fig. 14 300ZX. Hoist

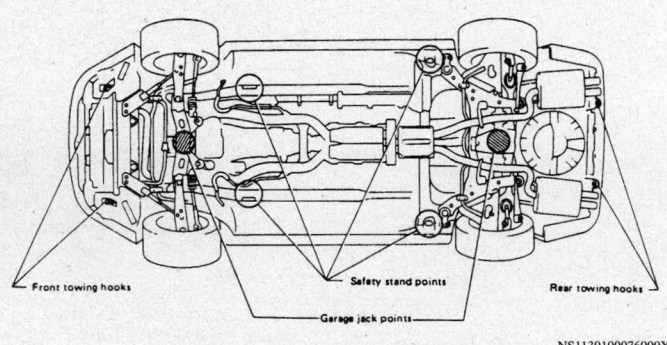

Front towing hooks
Safety stand points
Rear towing hooks
Garage jack points

NS1139100076000X

Fig. 15 300ZX. Floor Jack

Subaru

INDEX

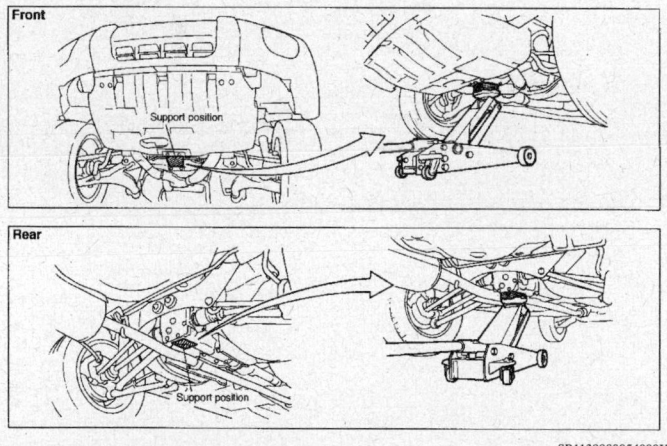

SB1139800054000X

Fig. 1   Forester. Floor Jack

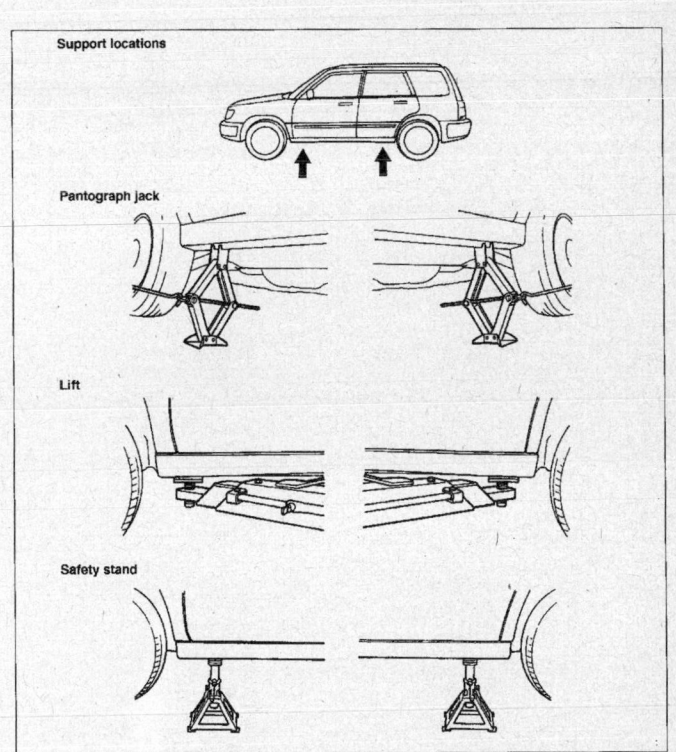

SB1139800055000X

Fig. 2   Forester. Hoist

VEHICLE LIFT POINTS

PANTOGRAPH JACK, SAFETY STAND AND LIFT

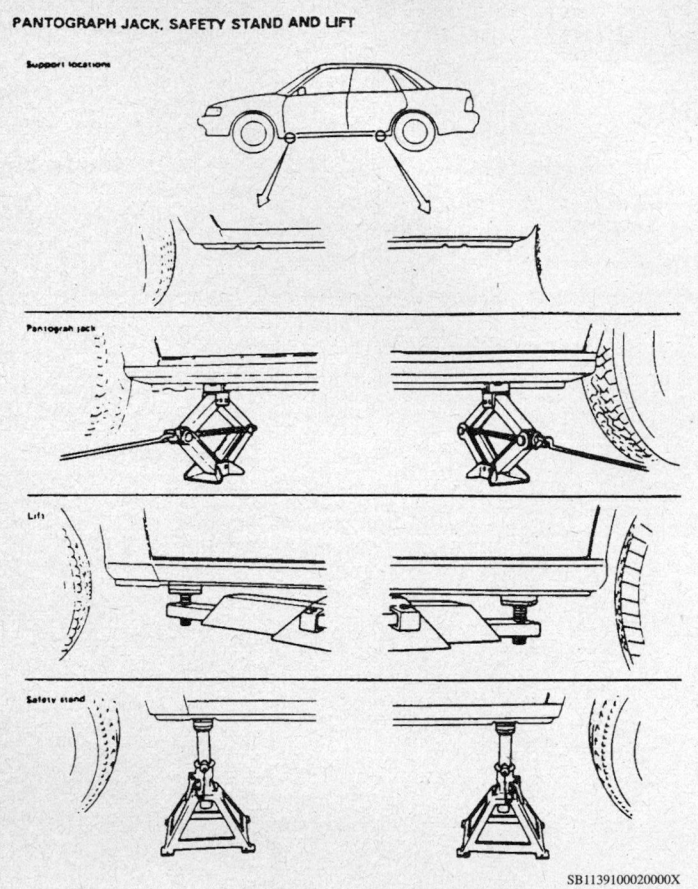

Support locations

Pantograph jack

Lift

Safety stand

SB1139100020000X

Fig. 3 Legacy

Support locations

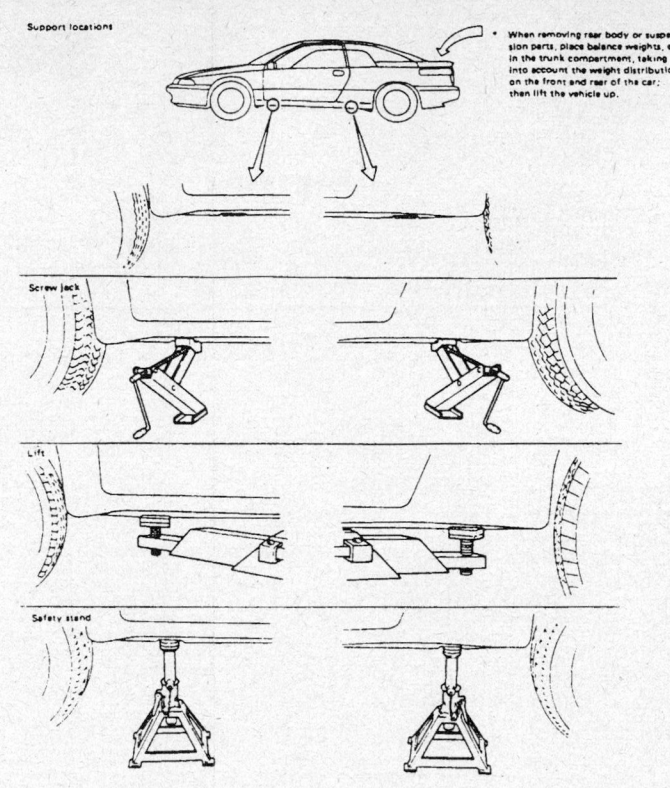

- When removing rear body or suspension parts, place balance weights, etc. in the trunk compartment, taking into account the weight distribution on the front and rear of the car; then lift the vehicle up.

Screw jack

Lift

Safety stand

SB1139100022000X

Fig. 4 SVX

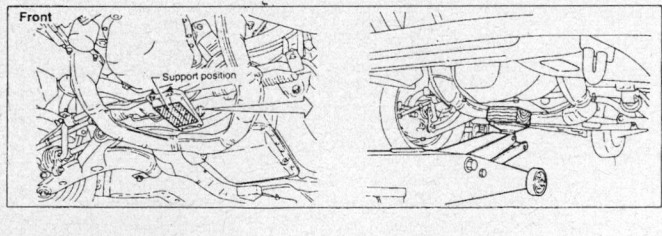

Front

Support position

Rear
FWD

Support position

AWD

Support position

SB1139100023000X

Fig. 5 Impreza. Floor Jack

Support locations

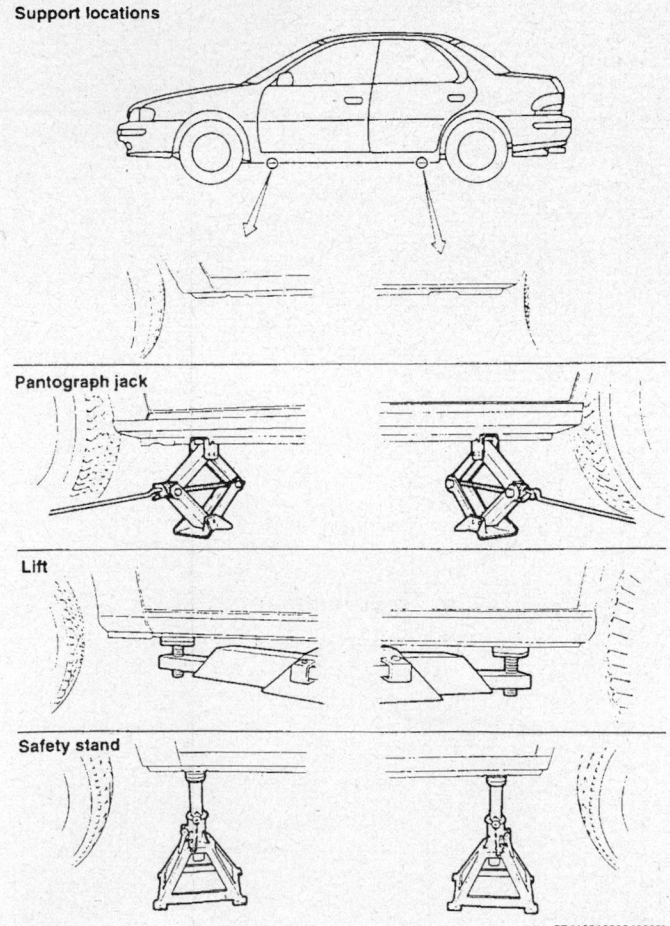

Pantograph jack

Lift

Safety stand

SB1139100024000X

Fig. 6 Impreza. Hoist

Suzuki

INDEX

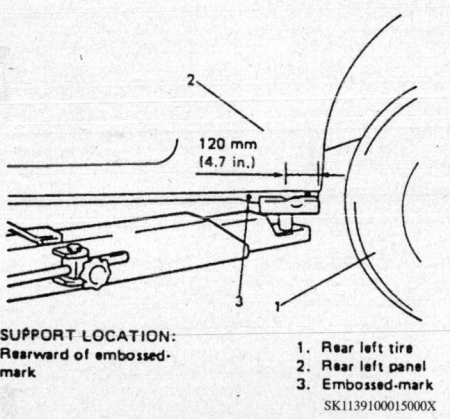

SUPPORT LOCATION:
Rearward of embossed-mark

1. Rear left tire
2. Rear left panel
3. Embossed-mark

SK1139100015000X

Fig. 1   Sidekick & X-90. Hoist (Front)

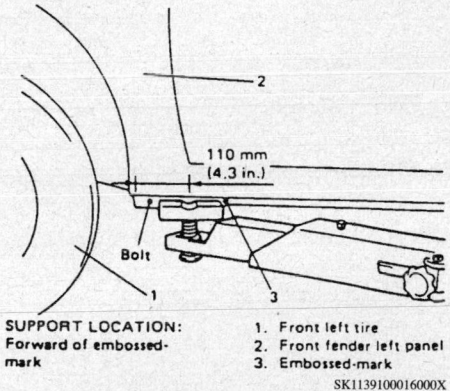

SUPPORT LOCATION:
Forward of embossed-mark

1. Front left tire
2. Front fender left panel
3. Embossed-mark

SK1139100016000X

Fig. 2   Sidekick & X-90. Hoist (Rear)

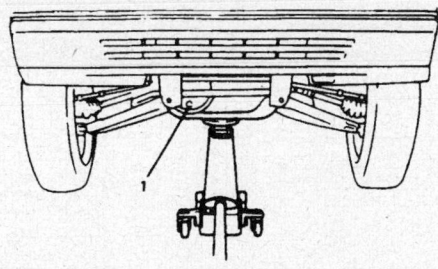

1. Front differential housing

SK1139100017000X

Fig. 3   Sidekick. Floor Jack (Front)

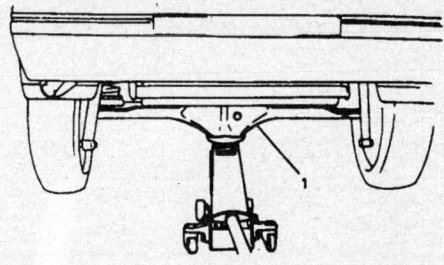

1. Rear axle

SK1139100018000X

Fig. 4   Sidekick. Floor Jack (Rear)

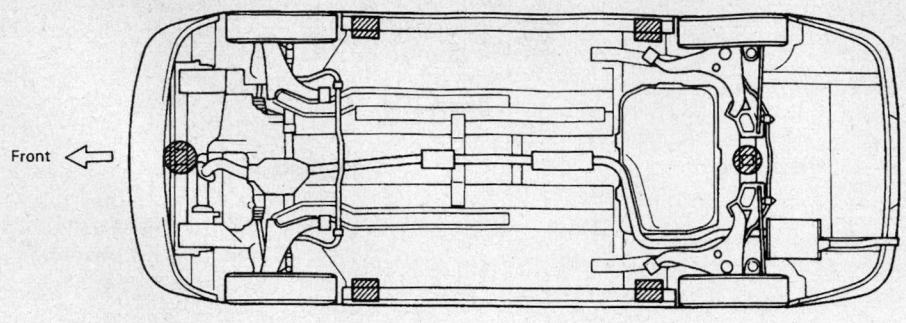

▨ : Support position for frame contact hoist and safety stand
◍ : Floor jack position

SK1139500053000X

Fig. 5   Esteem & Swift

When using frame contact hoist:

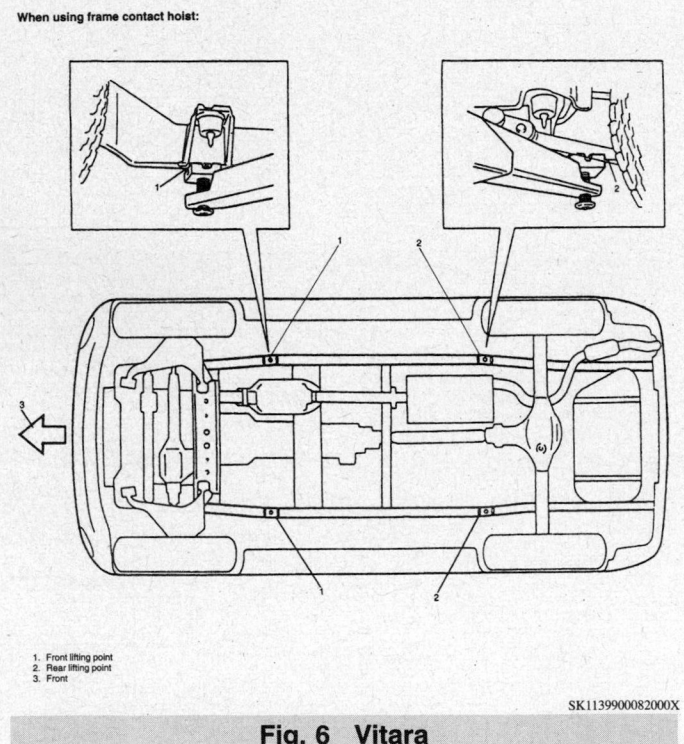

1. Front lifting point
2. Rear lifting point
3. Front

SK1139900082000X

Fig. 6   Vitara

Toyota

INDEX

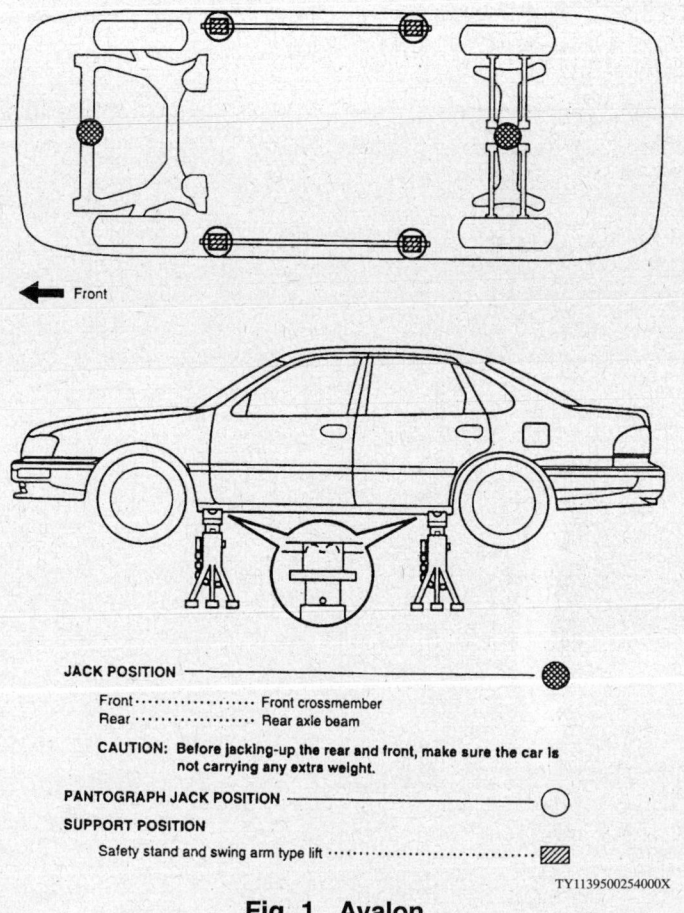

JACK POSITION ⬤

Front · · · · · · · · · · Front crossmember
Rear · · · · · · · · · · Rear axle beam

CAUTION: Before jacking-up the rear and front, make sure the car is not carrying any extra weight.

PANTOGRAPH JACK POSITION ◯

SUPPORT POSITION

Safety stand and swing arm type lift · · · · · · · · · · ▨

TY1139500254000X

Fig. 1 Avalon

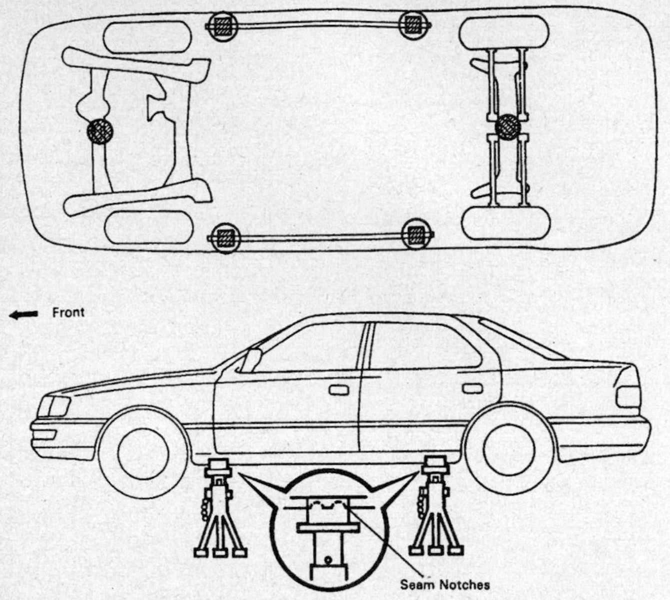

Front →

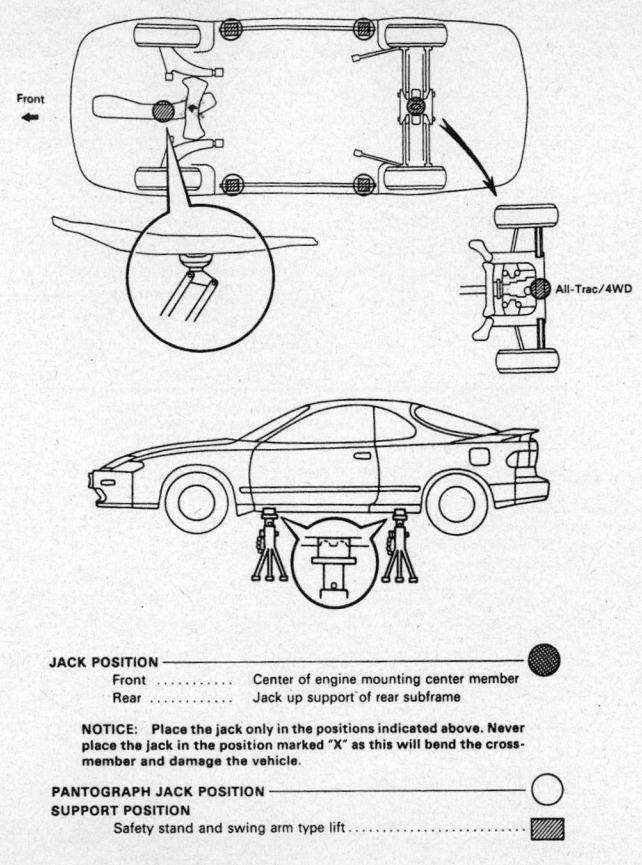

All-Trac/4WD

JACK POSITION ⬤

Front .... Front crossmember

Rear .... Rear axle beam

CAUTION: Before jacking-up the rear and front, make sure the car is not carrying any extra weight.

PANTOGRAPH JACK POSITION ○

SUPPORT POSITION

Safety stand and swing arm type lift .... ▨

TY1139600287000X

Seam Notches

← Front

Fig. 2 Camry & Camry Solara

JACK POSITION ⬤

Front .... Center of engine mounting center member

Rear .... Jack up support of rear subframe

NOTICE: Place the jack only in the positions indicated above. Never place the jack in the position marked "X" as this will bend the crossmember and damage the vehicle.

PANTOGRAPH JACK POSITION ○
SUPPORT POSITION

Safety stand and swing arm type lift .... ▨

TY1139100098000X

Fig. 3 Celica

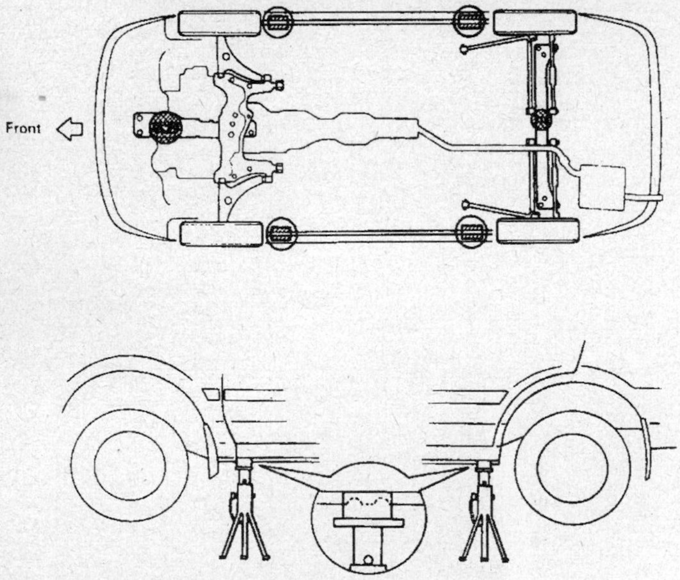

Front →

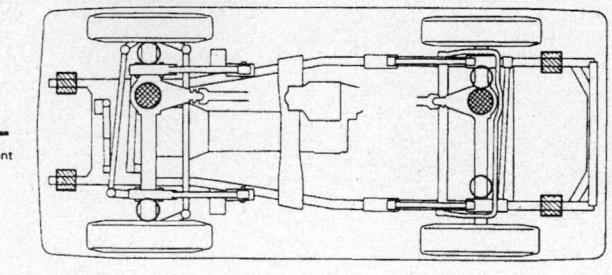

Front →

JACK POSITION ⬤

Front .... Front crossmember

Rear .... Rear axle beam

CAUTION: Before jacking-up the rear and front, make sure the car is not carrying any extra weight.

PANTOGRAPH JACK POSITION ○

SUPPORT POSITION

Safety stand and swing arm type lift .... ▨

TY1139100099000X

Fig. 4 Corolla

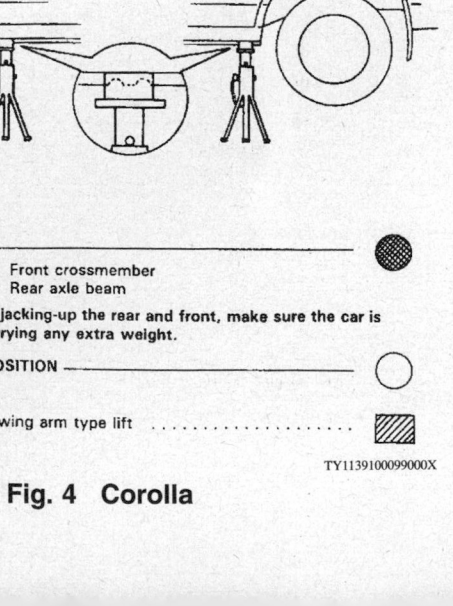

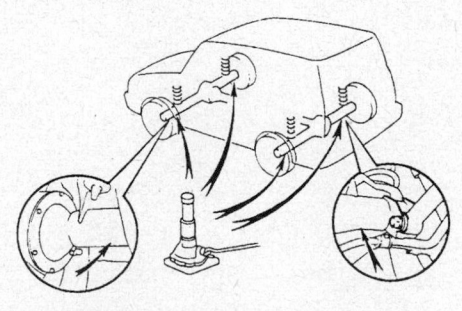

JACK POSITION ⬤

Front .... Under the front differential

Rear .... Under the rear differential

SCREW TYPE JACK POSITION ○

SUPPORT POSITION

Safety stand .... ▨

TY1139500255000X

Fig. 5 Land Cruiser

TOYOTA

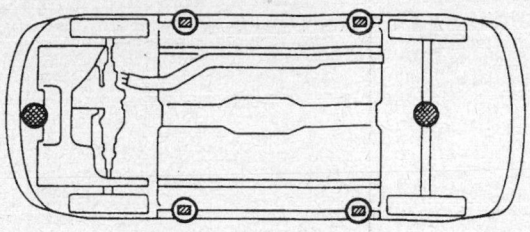

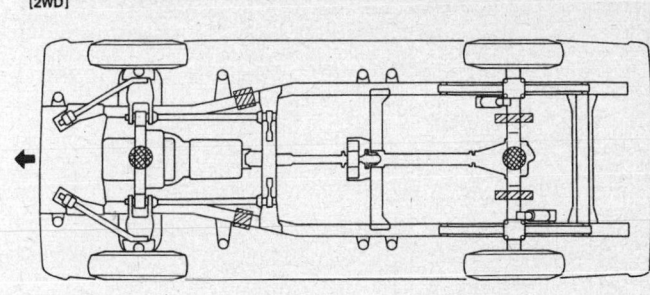

[2WD]

[4WD]

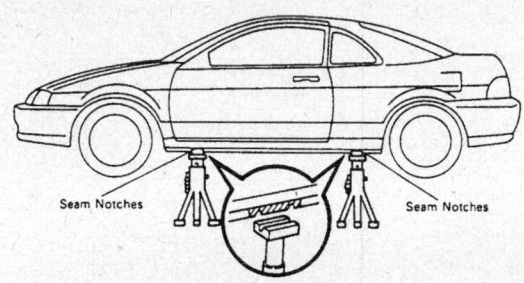

← Front

JACK POSITION ●
Front .... Front crossmember
Rear .... Rear axle beam
CAUTION: When jack-up the rear and front, make sure the car is not carrying any extra weight.

PANTOGRAPH JACK POSITION ○

SUPPORT POSITION
Safety stand and swing arm type lift .... ▨

TY1139100108000X

Fig. 6   Paseo

JACK POSITION .... ●
Front .... Center of crossmember
Rear .... Under the rear differential

SUPPORT POSITION
Safety stand .... ▨

TY1139100102000X

Fig. 7   T100

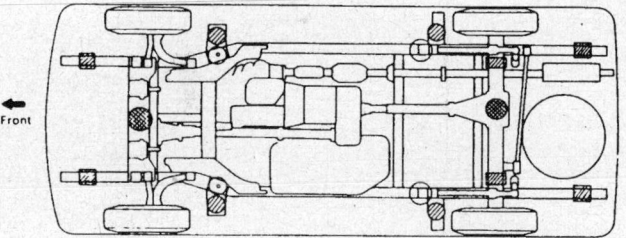

← Front

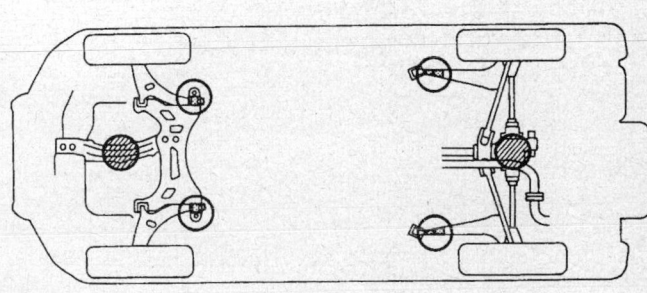

← Front

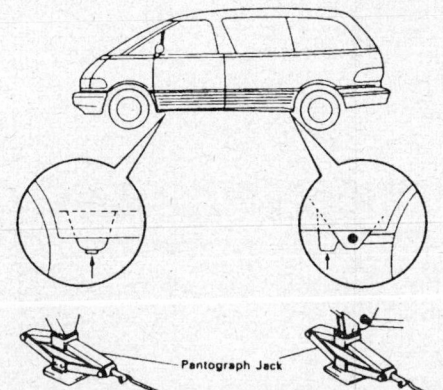

Pantograph Jack

JACK POSITION ●
Front .... Center of front suspension crossmember
Rear .... Center of rear axle housing

PANTOGRAPH JACK POSITION ○
SUPPORT POSITION
Safety stand .... ▨

SWING ARM TYPE LIFT POSITION ●

TY1139300106000X

Fig. 8   Previa

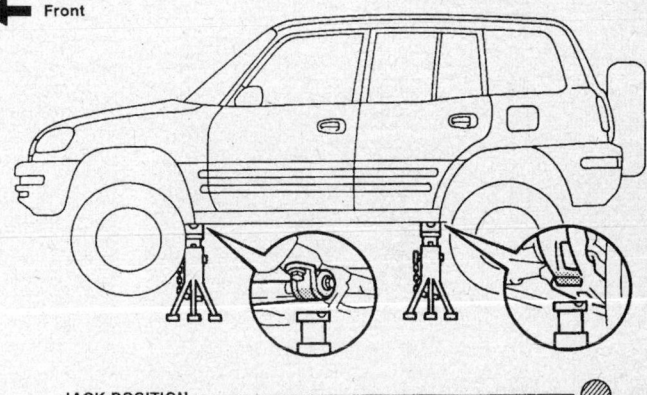

JACK POSITION ◐
Front ·············· Front crossmember
Rear ·············· Rear axle beam

CAUTION : Before jacking-up the rear and front, make sure the car is not carrying any extra weight.

PANTOGRAPH JACK POSITION ○

SUPPORT POSITION
Safety stand and swing arm type lift ············· ▨

TY1139600288000X

Fig. 9   RAV4. 1996-97

VEHICLE LIFT POINTS

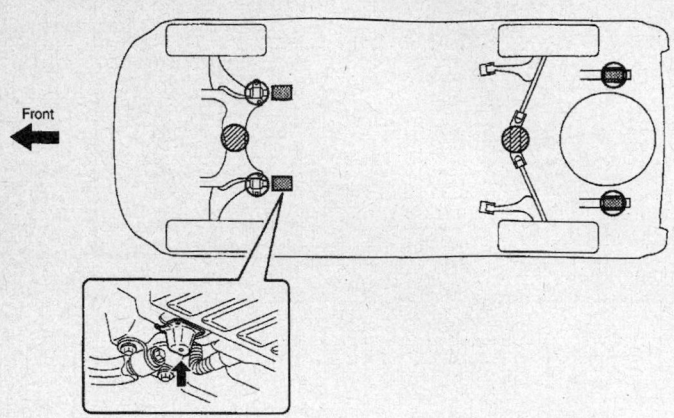

JACK POSITION ─────────────────── ●
  Front ─────── Front crossmember
  Rear ─────── Rear suspension member
  CAUTION : When jacking–up the rear and front, make sure the
              car is not carrying any extra weight.

SUPPORT POSITION
  Safety stand ───────────────── ▨

  Safety stand for removing the Traction Batteries ──────── ○

TY1139800342000X

Fig. 10   RAV4. 1998-99

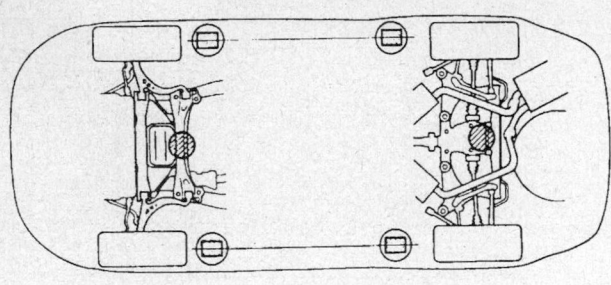

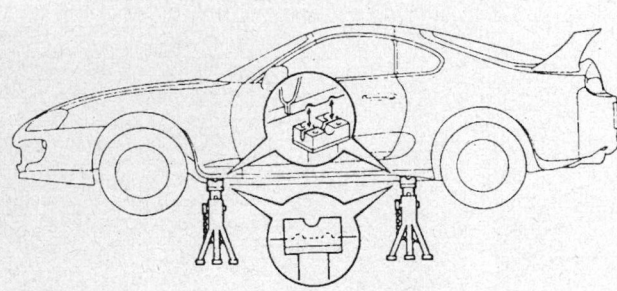

JACK POSITION ─────────────── ●
  Front .... Front crossmember
  Rear .... Rear axle beam
  CAUTION: Before jacking-up the rear and front, make sure the car is
             not carrying any extra weight.

PANTOGRAPH JACK POSITION ─────────── ○

SUPPORT POSITION
  Safety stand and swing arm type lift .... ▨

TY1139300104000X

Fig. 12   Supra

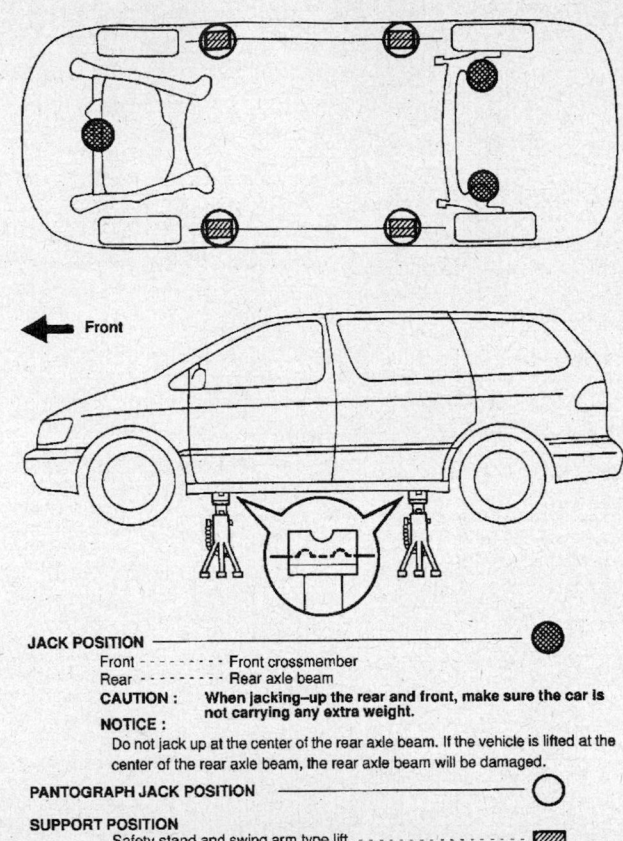

JACK POSITION ─────────────────── ●
  Front ─────── Front crossmember
  Rear ─────── Rear axle beam
  CAUTION :   When jacking–up the rear and front, make sure the car is
              not carrying any extra weight.
  NOTICE :
     Do not jack up at the center of the rear axle beam. If the vehicle is lifted at the
     center of the rear axle beam, the rear axle beam will be damaged.

PANTOGRAPH JACK POSITION ─────────── ○

SUPPORT POSITION
  Safety stand and swing arm type lift ─────────── ▨

TY1139800343000X

Fig. 11   Sienna

[2WD]

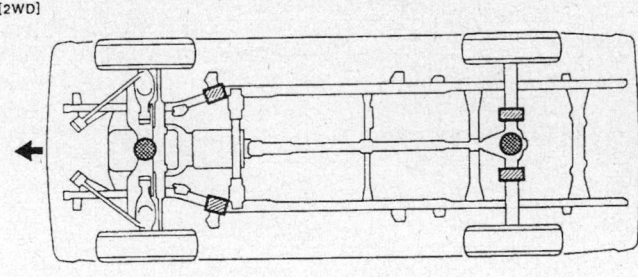

[4WD]

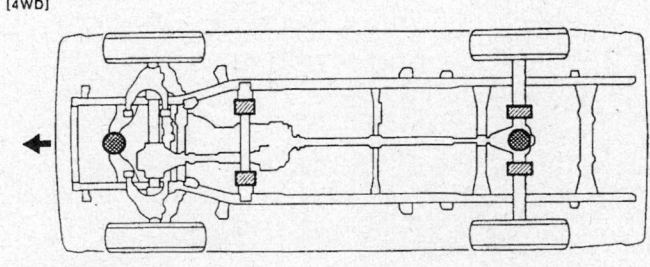

JACK POSITION . . . . ●
  Front . . . . Center of crossmember
  Rear . . . . Under the rear differential.

SUPPORT POSITION

  Safety stand . . . . ▨

TY1139500256000X

Fig. 13   Tacoma. 1996–98

TOYOTA

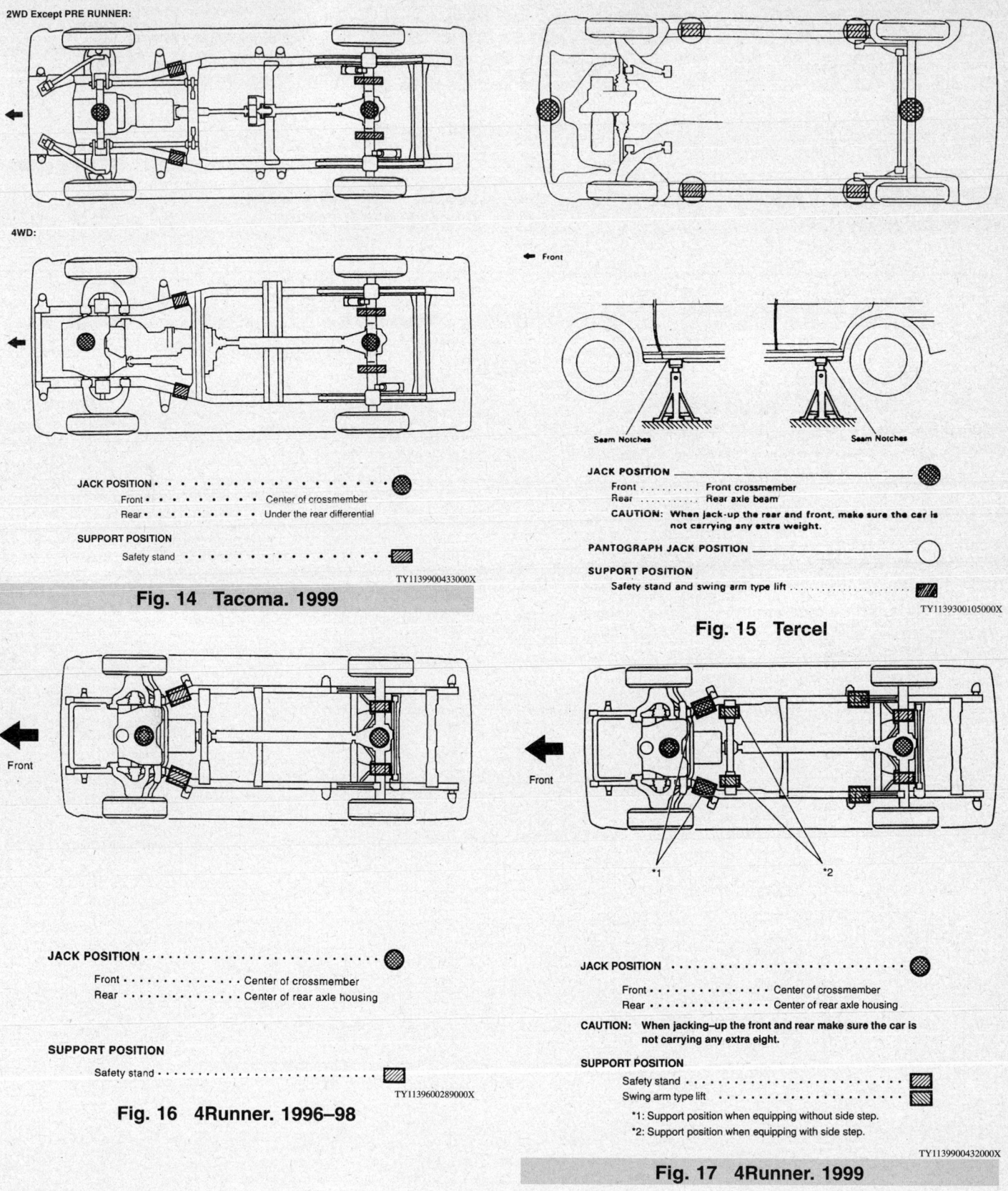

2WD Except PRE RUNNER:

4WD:

JACK POSITION • ⬤

Front • • • • • • • • • • • • • • Center of crossmember
Rear • • • • • • • • • • • • • • Under the rear differential

SUPPORT POSITION

Safety stand • ▨

TY1139900433000X

Fig. 14   Tacoma. 1999

← Front

Seam Notches   Seam Notches

JACK POSITION _____ ⬤

Front . . . . Front crossmember
Rear . . . . Rear axle beam
CAUTION: When jack-up the rear and front, make sure the car is
not carrying any extra weight.

PANTOGRAPH JACK POSITION _____ ◯

SUPPORT POSITION

Safety stand and swing arm type lift . . . . ▨

TY1139300105000X

Fig. 15   Tercel

Front

JACK POSITION • ⬤

Front • • • • • • • • • • • • • Center of crossmember
Rear • • • • • • • • • • • • • Center of rear axle housing

SUPPORT POSITION

Safety stand • ▨

TY1139600289000X

Fig. 16   4Runner. 1996–98

Front

*1   *2

JACK POSITION • ⬤

Front • • • • • • • • • • • • • Center of crossmember
Rear • • • • • • • • • • • • • Center of rear axle housing

CAUTION: When jacking–up the front and rear make sure the car is
not carrying any extra eight.

SUPPORT POSITION

Safety stand • ▨
Swing arm type lift • ▨

*1: Support position when equipping without side step.
*2: Support position when equipping with side step.

TY1139900432000X

Fig. 17   4Runner. 1999

ELECTRICAL SYMBOL & WIRE COLOR CODE IDENTIFICATION

TABLE OF CONTENTS

Electrical Symbol Identification

INDEX

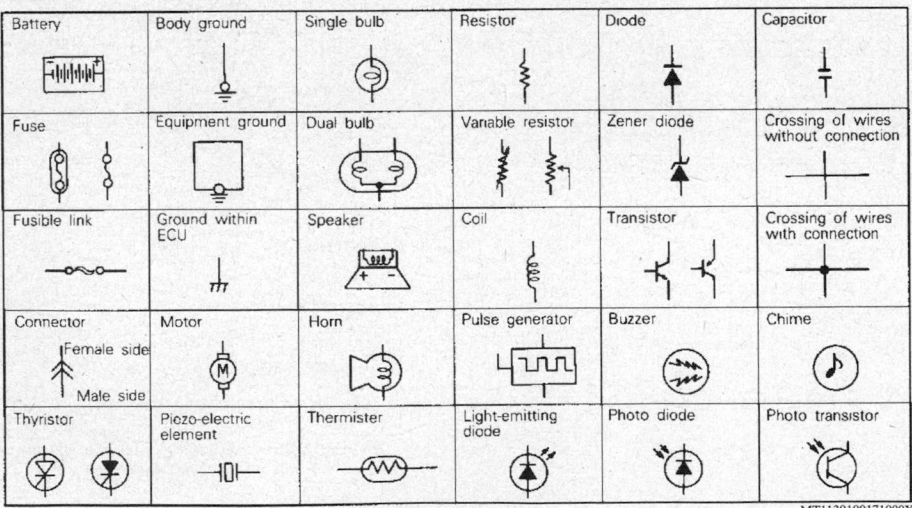

MT1139100171000X

Fig. 1 Mitsubishi

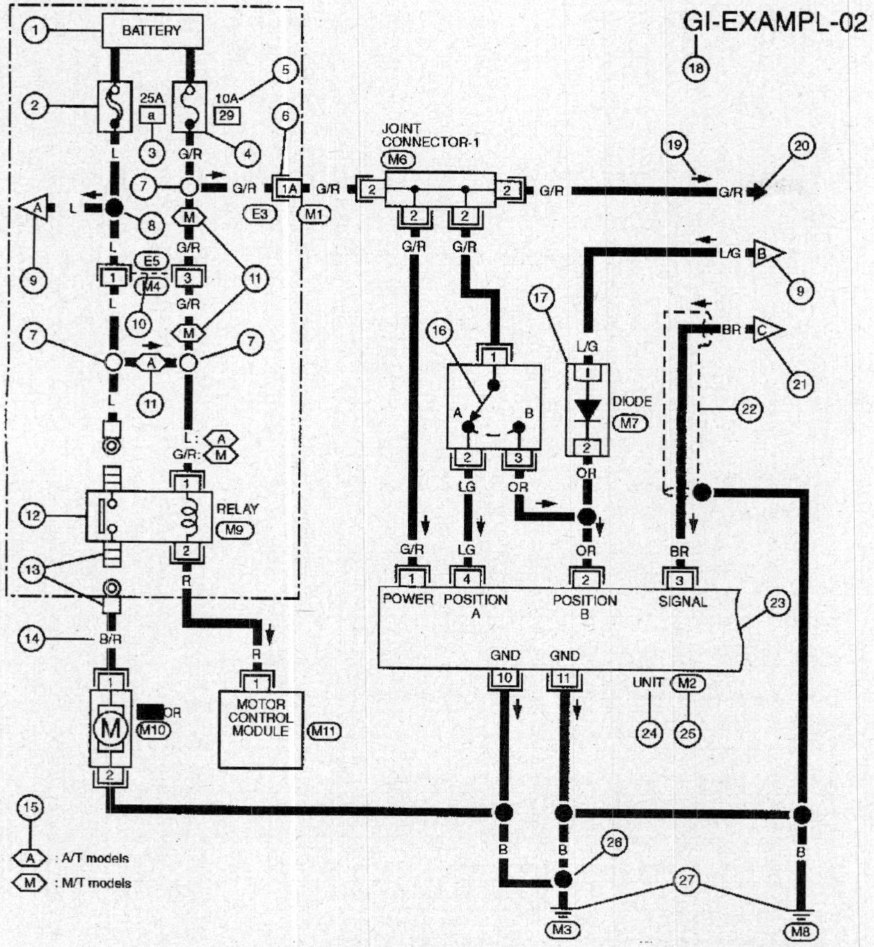

Number	Item	Description
①	Power condition	• This shows the condition when the system receives battery positive voltage (can be operated).
②	Fusible link	• The double line shows that this is a fusible link. • The open circle shows current flow in, and the shaded circle shows current flow out.
③	Fusible link/fuse location	• This shows the location of the fusible link or fuse in the fusible link or fuse box.
④	Fuse	• The single line shows that this is a fuse. • The open circle shows current flow in, and the shaded circle shows current flow out.
⑤	Current rating	• This shows the current rating of the fusible link or fuse.
⑥	Connectors	• This shows that connector (E3) is female and connector (M1) is male. • The G/R wire is located in the 1A terminal of both connectors. • Terminal number with an alphabet (1A, 5B, etc.) indicates that the connector is SMJ connector. Refer to GI-17.
⑦	Optional splice	• The open circle shows that the splice is optional depending on vehicle application.
⑧	Splice	• The shaded circle shows that the splice is always on the vehicle.
⑨	Page crossing	• This arrow shows that the circuit continues to an adjacent page. • The A will match with the A on the preceding or next page.
⑩	Common connector	• The dotted lines between terminals show that these terminals are part of the same connector.
⑪	Option abbreviation	• This shows that the circuit is optional depending on vehicle application.
⑫	Relay	• This shows an internal representation of the relay.
⑬	Connectors	• This shows that the connector is connected to the body or a terminal with bolt or nut.
⑭	Wire color	• This shows a code for the color of the wire. B = Black BR = Brown W = White OR = Orange R = Red P = Pink G = Green PU = Purple L = Blue GY = Gray Y = Yellow SB = Sky Blue LG = Light Green CH = Dark Brown DG = Dark Green When the wire color is striped, the base color is given first, followed by the stripe color as shown below: Example: L/W = Blue with White Stripe
⑮	Option description	• This shows a description of the option abbreviation used.
⑯	Switch	• This shows that continuity exists between terminals 1 and 2 when the switch is in the A position. Continuity exists between terminals 1 and 3 when the switch is in the B position.
⑰	Assembly parts	• Connector terminal in component shows that it is a harness incorporated assembly.
⑱	Cell code	• This identifies each page of the wiring diagram by section, system and wiring diagram page number.

NS11398001790020X

Fig. 2 Nissan (Part 2 of 3)

GI-EXAMPL-02

NS11398001790010X

Fig. 2 Nissan (Part 1 of 3)

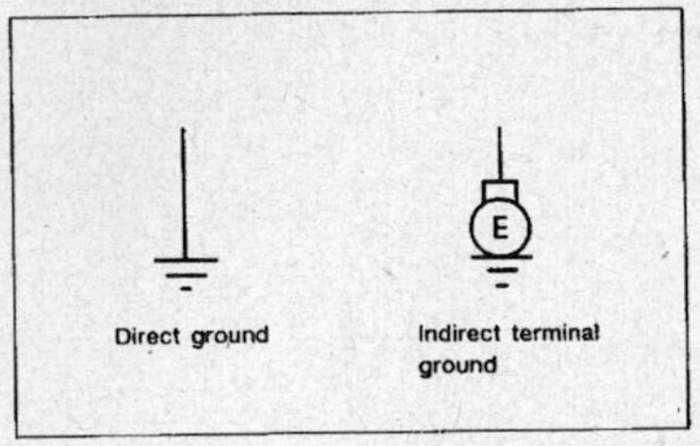

The ground points shown in the wiring diagram refer to the following:

- GB Body ground
- GE Engine ground
- GR Radio ground
- GD Rear defogger ground

All wiring harnesses are provided with a ground point which should be securely connected.

Direct ground · Indirect terminal ground

Relay type		Energizing circuit OFF	Energizing circuit ON
Normally-open type	4-pole	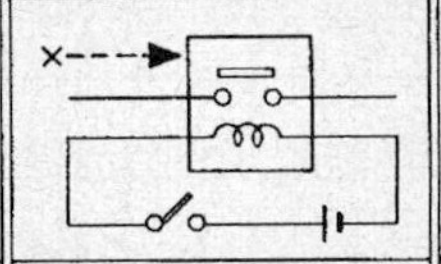	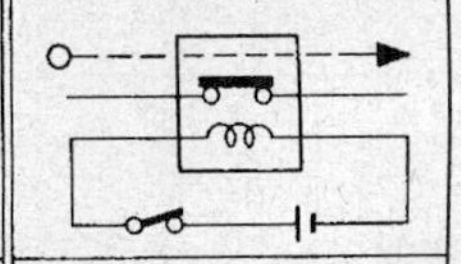
	6-pole	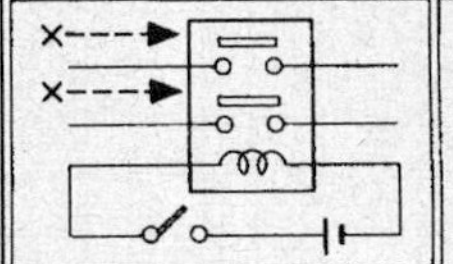	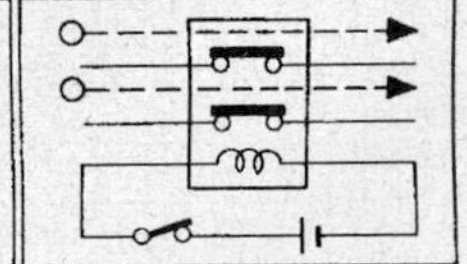
Normally-closed type	4-pole	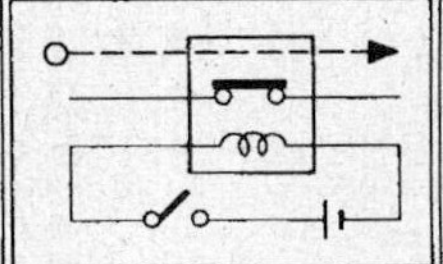	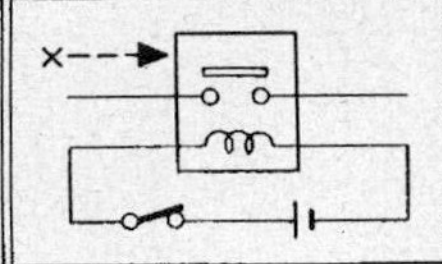
Mixed type	5-pole	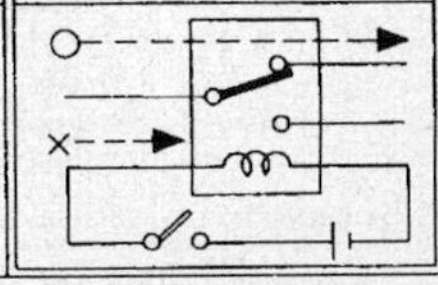	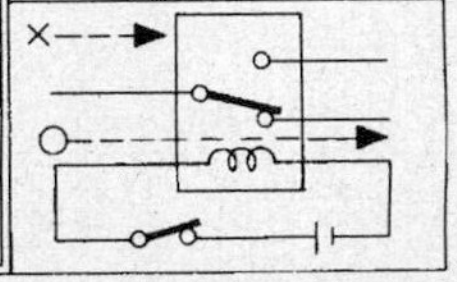

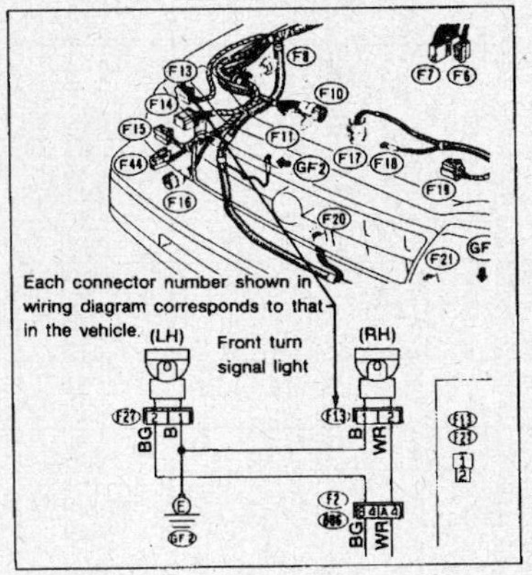

Number	Item	Description
19	Current flow arrow	• Arrow indicates electric current flow, especially where the direction of standard flow (vertically downward or horizontally from left to right) is difficult to follow. • A double arrow "◄►" shows that current can flow in either direction depending on circuit operation.
20	System branch	• This shows that the system branches to another system identified by cell code (section and system).
21	Page crossing	• This arrow shows that the circuit continues to another page identified by cell code. • The C will match with the C on another page within the system other than the next or preceding pages.
22	Shielded line	• The line enclosed by broken line circle shows shield wire.
23	Component box in wave line	• This shows that another part of the component is also shown on another page (indicated by wave line) within the system.
24	Component name	• This shows the name of a component.
25	Connector number	• This shows the connector number. • The letter shows which harness the connector is located in. Example: M: main harness. A coordinate grid is included for complex harnesses to aid in locating connectors.
26	Ground (GND)	• The line spliced and grounded under wire color shows that ground line is spliced at the grounded connector.
27	Ground (GND)	• This shows the ground connection.
28	Connector views	• This area shows the connector faces of the components in the wiring diagram on the page.
29	Common component	• Connectors enclosed in broken line show that these connectors belong to the same component.
30	Connector color	• This shows a code for the color of the connector. For code meaning, refer to wire color codes, Number 30 of this chart.
31	Fusible link and fuse box	• This shows the arrangement of fusible link(s) and fuse(s).
32	Reference area	• This shows that more information on the Super Multiple Junction (SMJ) and Joint Connectors (J/C) exists on the foldout page.

Fig. 2 Nissan (Part 3 of 3)

The first character of each connector number refers to the area or system of the vehicle, as indicated in table below.

Symbol	Wiring harness and Cord
F	Front wiring harness
B	Bulkhead wiring harness
E	Engine wiring harness
T	Transmission cord
D	Door cord LH & RH, Rear gate cord
I	Instrument panel wiring harness
R	Rear wiring harness, Rear defogger cord Room light cord, Fuel tank cord, Sunroof cord, Trunk lid cord
P	Floor wiring harness

Each connector number shown in wiring diagram corresponds to that in the vehicle.

Front turn signal light (RH) / (LH)

Fig. 3 Subaru

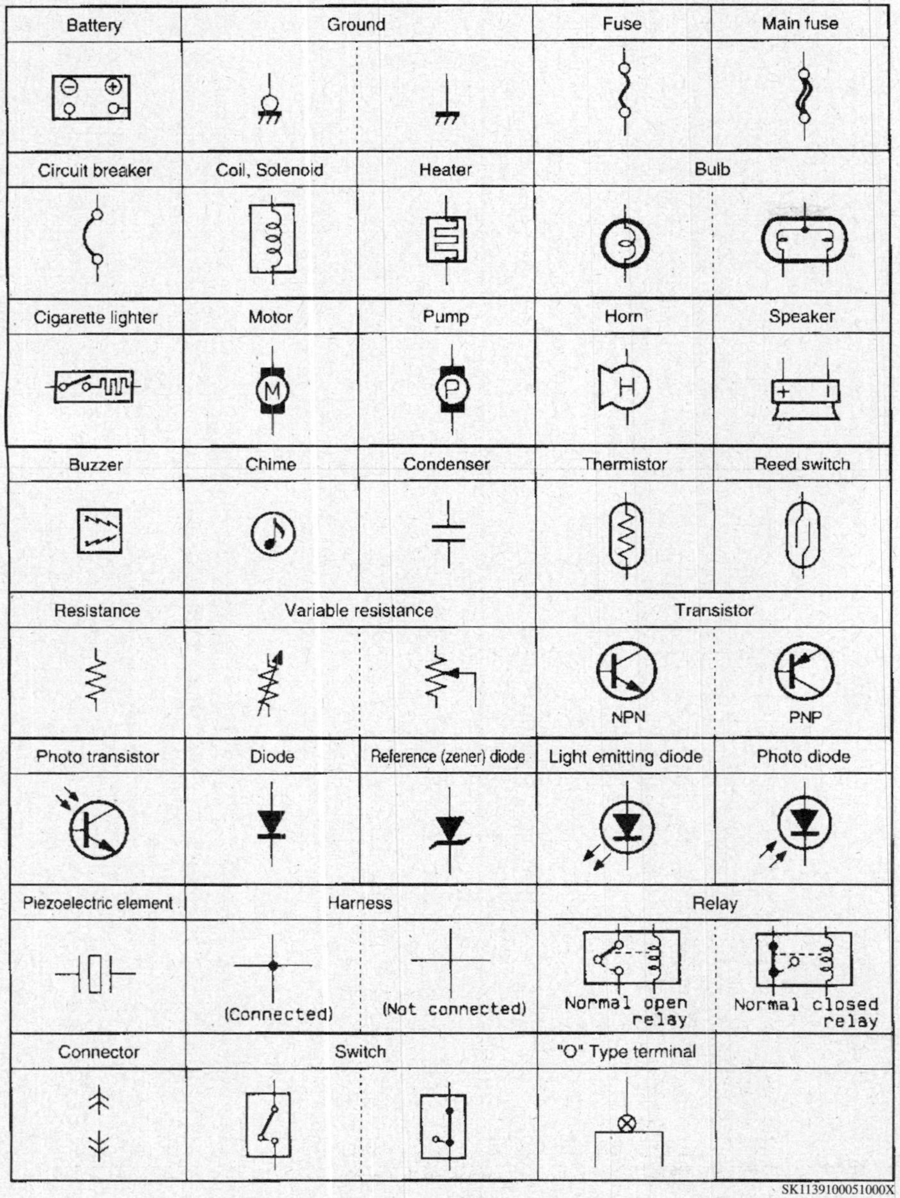

GROUND — The point at which wiring attaches to the Body, thereby providing a return path for an electrical circuit; without a ground, current cannot flow.

HEADLIGHTS
1. SINGLE FILAMENT — Current flow causes a headlight filament to heat up and emit light. A headlight may have either a single (1) filament or a double (2) filament.
2. DOUBLE FILAMENT

HORN — An electric device which sounds a loud audible signal.

IGNITION COIL — Converts low-voltage DC current into high-voltage ignition current for firing the spark plugs.

LIGHT — Current flow through a filament causes the filament to heat up and emit light.

LED (LIGHT EMITTING DIODE) — Upon current flow, these diodes emit light without producing the heat of a comparable light.

METER, ANALOG — Current flow activates a magnetic coil which causes a needle to move, thereby providing a relative display against a background calibration.

METER, DIGITAL — Current flow activates one or many LED's, LCD's, or fluorescent displays, which provide a relative or digital display.

MOTOR — A power unit which converts electrical energy into mechanical energy, especially rotary motion.

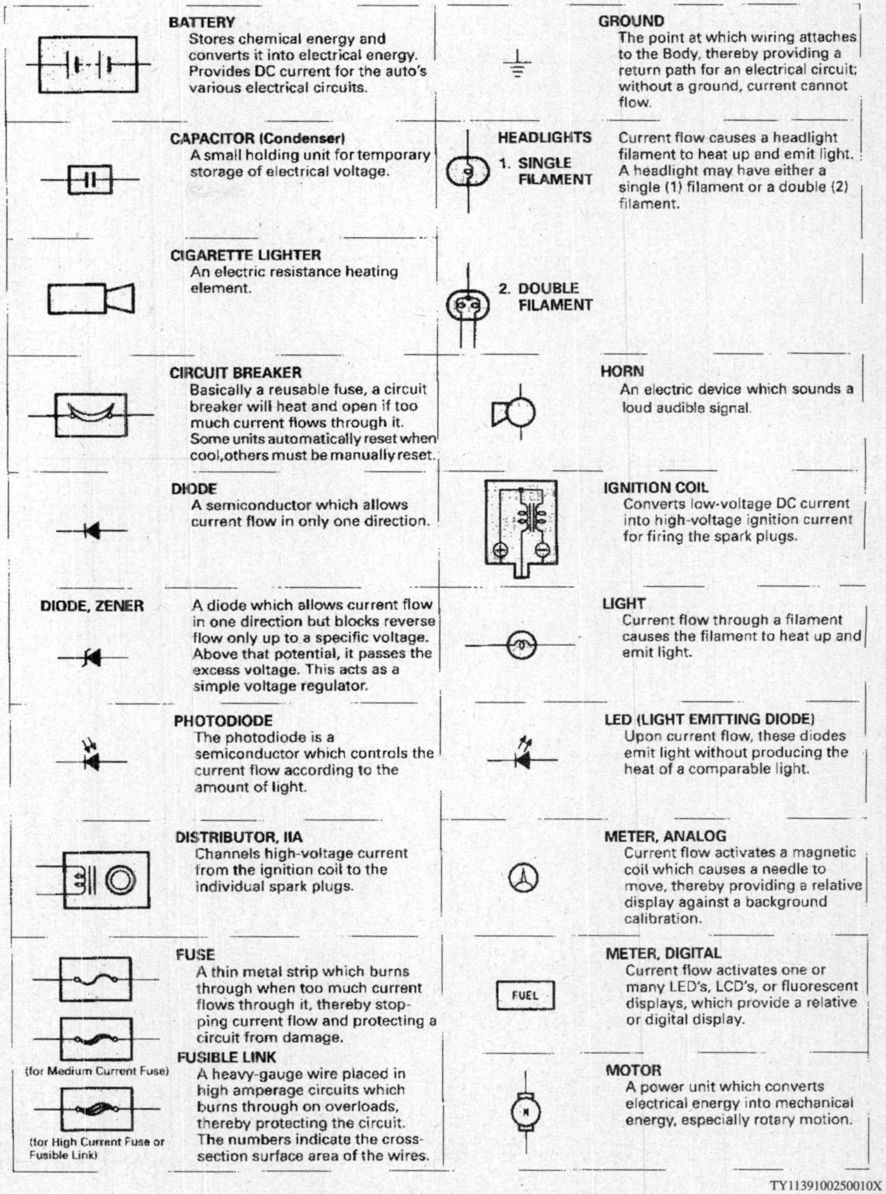

BATTERY — Stores chemical energy and converts it into electrical energy. Provides DC current for the auto's various electrical circuits.

CAPACITOR (Condenser) — A small holding unit for temporary storage of electrical voltage.

CIGARETTE LIGHTER — An electric resistance heating element.

CIRCUIT BREAKER — Basically a reusable fuse, a circuit breaker will heat and open if too much current flows through it. Some units automatically reset when cool, others must be manually reset.

DIODE — A semiconductor which allows current flow in only one direction.

DIODE, ZENER — A diode which allows current flow in one direction but blocks reverse flow only up to a specific voltage. Above that potential, it passes the excess voltage. This acts as a simple voltage regulator.

PHOTODIODE — The photodiode is a semiconductor which controls the current flow according to the amount of light.

DISTRIBUTOR, IIA — Channels high-voltage current from the ignition coil to the individual spark plugs.

FUSE — A thin metal strip which burns through when too much current flows through it, thereby stopping current flow and protecting a circuit from damage.

FUSIBLE LINK — A heavy-gauge wire placed in high amperage circuits which burns through on overloads, thereby protecting the circuit. The numbers indicate the cross-section surface area of the wires.
(for Medium Current Fuse or Fusible Link)
(for High Current Fuse or Fusible Link)

Fig. 5 Toyota (Part 1 of 2)

TY11391002500010X

SK11391010005100X

Battery	Ground	Coil, Solenoid	
Circuit breaker	Heater	Motor	Main fuse
Cigarette lighter			Fuse
	Bulb		
Buzzer	Chime	Condenser	Speaker
Resistance	Variable resistance		Horn
		Thermistor	Reed switch
Photo transistor	Diode	Reference (zener) diode	Transistor
			NPN / PNP
Piezoelectric element	Harness	Light emitting diode	Photo diode
Connector	Switch	(Connected) (Not connected)	Relay
		"O" Type terminal	Normal open relay / Normal closed relay

Fig. 4 Suzuki

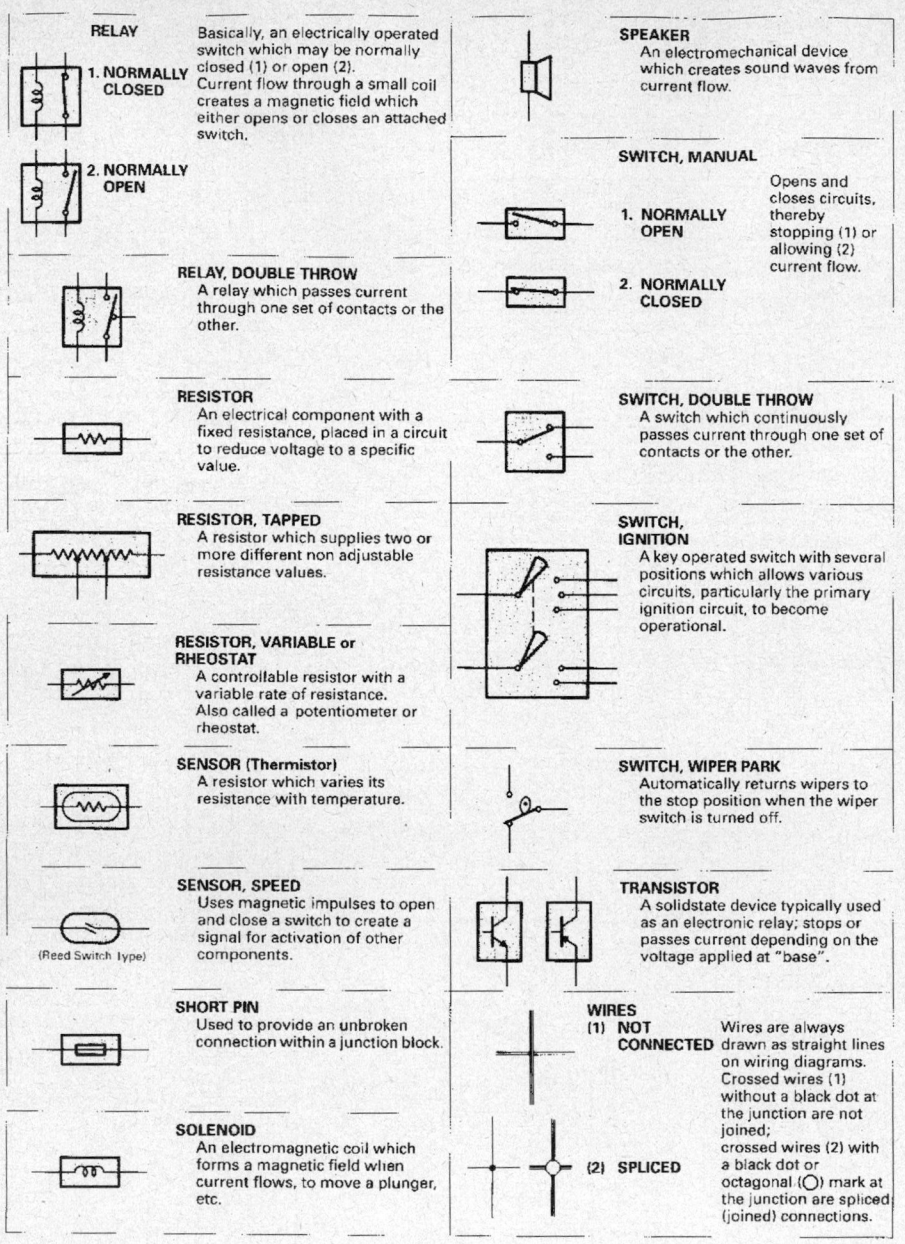

RELAY

1. NORMALLY CLOSED

2. NORMALLY OPEN

Basically, an electrically operated switch which may be normally closed (1) or open (2). Current flow through a small coil creates a magnetic field which either opens or closes an attached switch.

RELAY, DOUBLE THROW
A relay which passes current through one set of contacts or the other.

RESISTOR
An electrical component with a fixed resistance, placed in a circuit to reduce voltage to a specific value.

RESISTOR, TAPPED
A resistor which supplies two or more different non adjustable resistance values.

RESISTOR, VARIABLE or RHEOSTAT
A controllable resistor with a variable rate of resistance. Also called a potentiometer or rheostat.

SENSOR (Thermistor)
A resistor which varies its resistance with temperature.

SENSOR, SPEED
Uses magnetic impulses to open and close a switch to create a signal for activation of other components.

(Reed Switch Type)

SHORT PIN
Used to provide an unbroken connection within a junction block.

SOLENOID
An electromagnetic coil which forms a magnetic field when current flows, to move a plunger, etc.

SPEAKER
An electromechanical device which creates sound waves from current flow.

SWITCH, MANUAL

1. NORMALLY OPEN

2. NORMALLY CLOSED

Opens and closes circuits, thereby stopping (1) or allowing (2) current flow.

SWITCH, DOUBLE THROW
A switch which continuously passes current through one set of contacts or the other.

SWITCH, IGNITION
A key operated switch with several positions which allows various circuits, particularly the primary ignition circuit, to become operational.

SWITCH, WIPER PARK
Automatically returns wipers to the stop position when the wiper switch is turned off.

TRANSISTOR
A solidstate device typically used as an electronic relay; stops or passes current depending on the voltage applied at "base".

WIRES
(1) NOT CONNECTED

(2) SPLICED

Wires are always drawn as straight lines on wiring diagrams. Crossed wires (1) without a black dot at the junction are not joined; crossed wires (2) with a black dot or octagonal (○) mark at the junction are spliced (joined) connections.

TY1139100250020X

Fig. 5 Toyota (Part 2 of 2)

Wire Color Code Identification

Color	Manufacturer				
	Mitsubishi	**Nissan**	**Subaru**	**Suzuki**	**Toyota**
Black	B	B	B	B	B
Blue	L	L	L	Bl	L
Brown	BR	BR	Br	Br	BR
Dark Brown	—	CH	—	—	—
Dark Gray	DG	—	—	—	—
Gray	GR	GY	Gr	—	GR
Green	G	G	G	G	G
Light Blue	—	—	Lb	LBL	—
Light Green	LG	LG	Lg	Lg	LG
Orange	O	OR	Or	O	O
Pink	P	P	P	P	P
Purple	—	PU	—	—	—
Red	R	R	R	R	R
Sky Blue	SB	SB	—	—	SB
Violet	V	—	—	V	V
White	W	W	W	W	W
Yellow	Y	Y	Y	Y	Y

VEHICLE MAINTENANCE SCHEDULES

TABLE OF CONTENTS

Mitsubishi Diamante, Eclipse, Galant, Mirage & 3000GT

Recommended Service	Service Interval In Miles①																									
	3750	7500	11250	15000	18750	22500	26250	30000	33750	37500	41250	45000	48750	52500	56250	60000	63750	67500	71250	75000	78750	82500	86250	90000	93750	97500
BODY																										
Inspect Seat Belt Pretensioners & Supplemental Restraint System	colspan: 10 Years From Vehicle Build Date																									
BRAKES																										
Inspect Brake Pads		S	N	S		S		X		S		S		S		X		S		S		S		X		S
Inspect Brake Shoes, Wheel Cylinders & Parking Brake Operation			S					X				S				X		S				S		X		S
Inspect Brake Connections, Hoses & Lines, Except 1999 Galant	Every 12 Months																									
Inspect Brake Hoses, 1999 Galant			X					X				X				X		X				X		X		
CLUTCH & TRANSMISSION																										
Change Automatic Transmission Fluid & Filter, Except 1997–99 Diamante & Eclipse			S					S				S				S		S				S		S		
Change Automatic Transaxle Fluid & Filter, 1997–99 Diamante								S								S		S						S		
Change Automatic Transaxle External Filter, 1997–99 Eclipse			S					S				S				S		S				S		S		
Change Manual Transaxle & Transfer Case Lubricant			X					X				X				X		X				X		X		
DRIVE AXLE & DRIVESHAFT																										
Change Differential Lubricants & Driveshaft U-Joints			S					X				S				X		S				S		X		
Inspect CV & Driveshaft Boots For Damage Or Leakage			X					X				X				X		X				X		X		
ENGINE																										
Change Engine Coolant	Every 24 Months Or 30,000 Miles																									

Service Interval In Miles ①

Recommended Service	3750	7500	11250	15000	18750	22500	26250	30000	33750	37500	41250	45000	48750	52500	56250	60000	63750	67500	71250	75000	78750	82500	86250	90000	93750	97500
ENGINE																										
Change Engine Oil, Non-Turbo	Normal Service Every 12 Months Or 7,500 (Oil) Or 15,000 (Filter) Miles; Severe Service Every 3 Months Or 3,000 (Oil) Or 6,000 (Filter) Miles																									
Change Engine Oil, Turbo	Normal Service Every 6 Months Or 5,000 (Oil) Or 10,000 (Filter) Miles; Severe Service Every 3 Months Or 3,000 Miles																									
Inspect Coolant, Fuel & Vapor Hoses & Drive Belts, Exhaust System								X								X								X		
Inspect Cooling System & Protection Level				X				X				X				X				X				X		
Inspect Distributor Cap & Rotor & EVAP System																X										
Inspect Fuel System Connections, Lines, Tank & Filler Cap	Every 60 Months Or 50,000 Miles																									
Inspect & Adjust Engine Valve Clearance (Models w/Solid Valve Lifters)								X								X								X		
Replace Air Filter, 1996 Diamante								N								N								N		
Replace Air Filter, Eclipse, Galant, 3000GT & 1997-99 Diamante				S				X				S				X				S				X		
Replace Spark Plugs	Normal Service Platinum Tips Every 60,000 Miles, Regular Tips Every 30,000 Miles; Severe Service All Every 15,000 Miles																									
Replace Spark Plug Wires																X										
Replace Timing & Balancer Belts	Every 60,000 Miles Recommended																									
STEERING, SUSPENSION & TIRES																										
Inspect Ball Joint & Steering Linkage Grease Seals For Damage Or Leakage								X								X								X		
Inspect & Lubricate Rear Wheel Bearings	At Brake Inspections, Or Every 24 Months Or 30,000 Miles																									
Lubricate Ball Joint Grease Fittings				X				X				X				X				X				X		
Rotate Tires & Adjust Pressures		X		X		X		X		X		X		X		X		X		X		X		X		X

N — Normal Service
S — Severe Service
X — Normal Or Severe Service
① — After vehicles passes 99,000 mile mark return to beginning of mileage table & start cycle over again.

1996 Mitsubishi Montero, Montero Sport & Truck

Service Interval In Miles ①

Recommended Service	3600	7500	9000	12500	18000	21000	22500	27000	30000	33000	36000	37500	39000	42500	45000	48000	51000	54000	57000	60000	63000	67500	72000	81000	82500	84000	87000	90000	93000	99000
BODY																														
Inspect Seat Belt Pretensioners	colspan: 10 Years From Vehicle Build Date																													
Inspect Supplemental Restraint System	colspan: 10 Years From Vehicle Build Date																													
BRAKES																														
Inspect Brake Pads	S		S		N	S		S		S		S		N	S		S		N	S		S		S		N	S		S	
Inspect Brake Shoes, Wheel Cylinders & Parking Brake Operation			S			X		S		X		S			X		S			X		S		X		S		X		
Inspect Brake Connections, Hoses & Lines	Every 12 Months Or 15,000 Miles																													
CLUTCH & TRANSMISSION																														
Change Transmission & Transfer Case Fluid & Filter						X									X							X						X		
DRIVE AXLE & DRIVESHAFT																														
Change Differential Lubricants						S									S							S						X		
Inspect Driveshafts						X									X							X						X		
ENGINE																														
Change Engine Coolant	Every 24 Months Or 30,000 Miles																													
Change Engine Oil	Normal Service Every 7,500 Miles; Severe Service Every 3,000 Miles																													
Change Engine Oil Filter	Normal Service Every 15,000 Miles; Severe Service Every 6,000 Miles																													
Inspect Coolant, Fuel & Vapor Hoses, Montero, Montero Sport & Sport									X											X								X		
Inspect Cooling System Integrity & Protection Level	X			X		X			X	X				X	X			X		X		X	X			X		X		
Inspect Distributor Cap & Rotor & Distributor Spark Advance Systems									X											X						X		X		
Inspect Drive Belts & Exhaust System						X									X							X						X		
Inspect EVAP System For Leaks Or Clogging																				X								X		
Inspect Fuel System Connections, Lines, Tank & Filler Cap	Every 60 Months Or 50,000 Miles																													

VEHICLE MAINTENANCE SCHEDULES, 1996 MITSUBISHI MONTERO, MONTERO SPORT & TRUCK

Service Interval In Miles①

Recommended Service	3000	6000	7500	9000	12000	15000	18000	21000	24000	27000	30000	33000	36000	37500	39000	42000	45000	48000	51000	54000	57000	60000	63000	66000	67500	69000	72000	75000	78000	81000	84000	87000	90000	93000	96000	97500	99000
ENGINE																																					
Inspect & Adjust Engine Valve Clearance (Models w/Solid Valve Lifters)						X					X						X					X						X					X				
Replace Air Filter, Montero Sport & Truck						S					S						S					S						S					S				
Replace EVAP Canister, Van & Wagon w/FED Emissions											X											X															
Replace EVAP Canister, Montero									Every 100,000 Miles																												
Replace Spark Plugs									Normal Service Platinum Tips Every 60,000 Miles, Regular Tips Every 30,000 Miles; Severe Service All Every 15,000 Miles																												
Replace Spark Plug Wires																						X															
Replace Timing & Balancer Belts									Recommended Every 60,000 Miles																												
STEERING, SUSPENSION & TIRES																																					
Inspect Ball Joint & Steering Linkage Grease Seals For Damage Or Leakage											X											X											X				
Inspect & Lubricate Rear Wheel Bearings, Truck									Every 24 Months Or 30,000 Miles																												
Lubricate Ball Joint Grease Fittings						X					X						X					X						X					X				
Rotate Tires & Adjust Pressures			X			X			X		X			X			X			X		X			X			X			X		X			X	

N — Normal Service
S — Severe Service
X — Normal Or Severe Service
① — After vehicles passes 99,000 mile mark return to beginning of mileage table & start cycle over again.

1997-99 Mitsubishi Montero & Montero Sport

Recommended Service — Service Interval In Miles ①

(Mileage grid: 3,000-mile increments from 3,000 to 111,000 miles. S = Severe service, X = Normal/scheduled service; mileages below are in thousands of miles.)

BODY

Recommended Service	Schedule
Inspect Seat Belt Pretensioners & Supplemental Restraint System	10 Years From Vehicle Build Date

BRAKES

Recommended Service	Schedule
Inspect Brake Pads	S: 15, 30, 45, 60, 75, 90, 105
Inspect Brake Shoes, Wheel Cylinders & Parking Brake Operation	S: 15, 45, 75, 105; X: 30, 60, 90
Inspect Brake Connections, Hoses & Lines	Every 12 Months Or 15,000 Miles

CLUTCH & TRANSMISSION

Recommended Service	Schedule
Change Transmission Fluid & Filter & Transfer Case Lubricant, Except 1999	X: 30, 60, 90
Change Automatic Transmission Fluid, 1999 Montero Sport	X: 30, 60, 90
Check Automatic Transmission Fluid, 1999	X: 15, 45, 75, 105
Check Manual Transmission & Transfer Case Fluid, 1999	X: 30, 60, 90

DRIVE AXLE & DRIVESHAFT

Recommended Service	Schedule
Change Differential Lubricants	S: 15, 45, 75, 105; X: 30, 60, 90
Inspect CV & Driveshaft For Damage & Lubricate U-Joints	X: 15, 30, 45, 60, 75, 90, 105
Lubricate Ball Joint, 1999	X: 30, 60, 90

ENGINE

Recommended Service	Schedule
Change Engine Coolant	Every 24 Months Or 30,000 Miles
Change Engine Oil	Normal Service Every 7,500 Miles; Severe Service Every 3,000 Miles
Change Engine Oil Filter	Normal Service Every 15,000 Miles; Severe Service Every 6,000 Miles
Inspect Coolant, Fuel & Vapor Hoses & Drive Belts & EVAP & Exhaust	X: 30, 60, 90
Inspect Cooling System	X: 15, 30, 45, 60, 75, 90, 105
Inspect Distributor Cap & Rotor	X: 15, 45, 75, 105

VEHICLE MAINTENANCE SCHEDULES, 1997-99 MITSUBISHI MONTERO & MONTERO SPORT

Service Interval In Miles ①

Recommended Service	3000	6000	9000	12000	15000	18000	21000	24000	27000	30000	33000	36000	39000	42000	45000	48000	51000	54000	57000	60000	63000	66000	69000	72000	75000	78000	81000	84000	87000	90000	93000	96000	99000
ENGINE																																	
Inspect EVAP Control System, 1999																				X													
Inspect Fuel System & Filler Cap	Every 60 Months Or 50,000 Miles																																
Inspect & Adjust Engine Valve Clearance (Models w/Solid Valve Lifters)					X					X					X					X					X					X			
Replace Air Filter, Montero & Sport					S					X					S					X					S					X			
Replace Spark Plugs	Normal Service Platinum Tips Every 60,000 Miles, Regular Tips Every 30,000 Miles; Severe Service All Every 15,000 Miles																																
Replace Spark Plug Wires																				X													
Replace Timing & Balancer Belts	Recommended Every 60,000 Miles																																
STEERING, SUSPENSION & TIRES																																	
Inspect Ball Joint & Steering Linkage Grease Seals For Damage Or Leakage																				X													
Inspect & Lubricate Rear Wheel Bearings, Truck	Every 24 Months Or 30,000 Miles																																
Lubricate Ball Joint Grease Fittings					X					X					X					X					X					X			
Rotate Tires & Adjust Pressures		X		X		X		X		X		X		X		X		X		X		X		X		X		X		X		X	

N — Normal Service
S — Severe Service
X — Normal Or Severe Service
① — After vehicles passes 99,000 mile mark return to beginning of mileage table & start cycle over again.

1996-98 Nissan

Recommended Service & Service Interval (Months)

Service Interval In Miles

Recommended Service & Service Interval (Months)	3750	7500	11250	15000	18750	22500	26250	30000	33750	37500	41250	45000	48750	52500	56250	60000	63750	67500	71250	75000	78750	82500	86250	90000
BODY																								
Inspect Air Bag System									Every 10 Years															
BRAKES																								
Inspect Brake Lines & Cables (Every 12 Mos.)				X				X				X				X				X				X
Inspect Brake Pads, Shoes, Discs & Drums		S		X		S		X		S		X		S		X		S		X		S		X
CLUTCH & TRANSMISSION																								
Change Transmission & Transfer Fluid (Severe Service Every 24 Mos.)				S				S				S				S				S				S
Change Transmission Fluid (Every 12 Mos.)				X				X				X				X				X				X
Inspect Transfer Fluid, 4WD				N				N				N				N				N				N
Inspect Transfer Gear, 4WD		S		S		S		S		S		S		S		S		S		S		S		X
DRIVE AXLE & DRIVESHAFT																								
Change Differential Gear Oil (Standard Differential)				S				S				S				S				S				S
Change Differential Gear Oil (Limited Slip Differential)				X				X				X				X				X				X
Inspect Differential Gear Oil (Every 12 Mos.)				X				X				X				X				X				X
Inspect Driveshaft		S		X		S		X		S		X		S		X		S		X		S		X
Lubricate Driveshaft, ①		S		X		S		X		S		X		S		X		S		X		S		X
ENGINE																								
Change Engine Coolant								At 48 Months Or 60,000 Miles, Then Every 24 Months Or 30,000 Miles							X				X				X
Change Engine Oil, Except 300ZX (Turbo, Normal Service Every 6 Mos., Normal Service Every 6 Mos./Severe Service Every 3 Mos.)	S	X	S	X	S	X	S	X	S	X	S	X	S	X	S	X	S	X	S	X	S	X	S	X
Change Engine Oil, 300ZX Turbo						Normal Service, Every 6 Months Or 5,000 Miles/Severe Service, Every 3 Months Or 3,000 Miles																		
Change Engine Oil Filter, Except 300ZX Turbo	S	X	S	X	S	X	S	X	S	X	S	X	S	X	S	X	S	X	S	X	S	X	S	X
Change Engine Oil Filter, 1996 300ZX Turbo						Normal Service, Every 5,000 Miles/Severe Service, Every 3,000 Miles																		
Inspect Drive Belts, Except Frontier, Pathfinder & Truck						At 48 Months Or 60,000 Miles Then Every 12 Months Or 15,000 Miles																		
Inspect Drive Belts, Frontier, Pathfinder & Truck				X				X				X				X				X				X
Inspect Exhaust System (Normal Service Every 12 Mos./Severe Service Every 6 Mos.)		S		X		S		X		S		X		S		X		S		X		S		X
Inspect Fuel & EVAP Vapor Lines & Replace Air Filter (Every 24 Mos.)				X				X				X				X				X				X
Inspect Idle RPM, Sentra & 200SX 1.6L				X				X				X				X				X				X
Replace Air Induction Valve Filter, 2.4L KA24E				S				S				S				S				S				S
Replace Camshaft Timing Belt, 300ZX Turbo																X								
Replace Camshaft Timing Belt, Except 300ZX Turbo						Replace Every 105,000 Miles																		
Replace PCV Filter, 2.4L KA24E & Z24i																								X

Recommended Service & Service Interval (Months)

Service Interval In Miles

Service	3750	7500	11250	15000	18750	22500	26250	30000	33750	37500	41250	45000	48750	52500	56250	60000	63750	67500	71250	75000	78750	82500	86250	90000
ENGINE																								
Replace Spark Plugs, Platinum Tip Type																								X
Replace Spark Plugs, Conventional Type								X								X								X
STEERING, SUSPENSION & TIRES																								
Inspect Axle & Suspension Components (Normal Service Every 24 Mos./Severe Service Every 6 Mos.)		S		S		S		X		S		S		S		X		S		S		S		X
Inspect Front Suspension Ball Joints (Severe Service Every 6 Mos.)		S		S		S		S		S		S		S		S		S		S		S		S
Inspect Front Wheel Bearings, Frontier, Pathfinder & Truck				X				X				X				X				X				X
Inspect Steering Gear & Linkage (Normal Service Every 24 Mos./Severe Service Every 6 Mos.)		S		S		S		X		S		S		S		X		S		S		S		X
Inspect Steering Linkage Ball Joints (Severe Service Every 6 mos.)		S		S		S		S		S		S		S		S		S		S		S		S
Inspect Super HICAS Linkage, 300ZX Turbo		S		S		S		X		S		S		S		X		S		S		S		X
Repack Front Wheel Bearings, Frontier, Pathfinder & Truck 4WD②								X								X								X

N — Normal Service
S — Severe Service
X — Normal or Severe Service
Mos. — Months
① — Grease daily if immersed in water.
② — If operating frequently in water, repack bearings every 3 months or 3,750 miles.

1999 Nissan

Service Interval In Miles

Recommended Service & Service Interval (Months)	3750	7500	11250	15000	18750	22500	26250	30000	33750	37500	41250	45000	48750	52500	56250	60000	63750	67500	71250	75000	78750	82500	86250	90000
BODY																								
Inspect Air Bag System										Every 10 Years														
BRAKES																								
Inspect Brake Lines & Cables (Every 12 Mos.)				X				X				X				X				X				X
Inspect Brake Pads, Shoes, Discs & Drums		S		X		S		X		S		X		S		X		S		X		S		X
CLUTCH & TRANSMISSION																								
Inspect Automatic Transmission Fluid, Transfer Case Fluid & Manual Transmission Fluid ①								X								X								X
DRIVE AXLE & DRIVESHAFT																								
Inspect Differential Fluid (Less Limited Slip)①				X				X				X				X				X				X
Inspect Differential Fluid (With Limited Slip)①				X				X				X				X				X				X
Inspect Driveshaft Boots & Propeller Shaft, 4WD						X		X		X		X		X		X		X		X		X		X
Lubricate Propeller Shaft②						X		X		X		X		X		X		X		X		X		X
Replace Limited Slip Differential Fluid								X								X								X
ENGINE																								
Change Engine Coolant	At 60,000 Miles Or 48 Months, Then Every 30,000 Miles Or 24 Months Thereafter																							
Change Engine Oil & Filter	S	X	S	X	S	X	S	X	S	X	S	X	S	X	S	X	S	X	S	X	S	X	S	X
Inspect Drive Belts																X				X				X
Inspect EVAP Vapor & Fuel Lines																X								X
Inspect Exhaust System				X				X				X				X				X				X
Inspect Idle RPM, Sentra w/GA16DE Engine				X				X				X				X				X				X
Inspect Intake & Exhaust Valve Clearance, Altima, Maxima, Sentra & KA24DE Engine	Inspect Valve Clearance If Noise Increases																							
Replace Air Filter								X								X								X
Replace PCV Filter (KA24DE)								X								X								X
Replace Spark Plugs, Conventional								X								X								X
Replace Spark Plugs, Platinum Tip																								X
Replace Timing Belt	Every 105,000 Miles																							

Recommended Service & Service Interval (Months)

Recommended Service & Service Interval (Months)	Service Interval In Miles															
Months	3	7	11	15	18	22	26	30	33	37	41	45	48	52	56	60
Miles	3750	7500	11250	15000	18750	22500	26250	30000	33750	37500	41250	45000	48750	52500	56250	60000
STEERING, SUSPENSION & TIRES																
Inspect Steering Gear & Linkage, Axle & Suspension Parts	X			X		X		X		X		X		X		X
Inspect Front Wheel Bearing Grease, 2WD						X						X				
Inspect Front Wheel Bearing Grease, 4WD		X								X				X		
Replace Front Wheel Bearing Grease, 4WD③			X													

S — Severe Service
X — Normal Service
Mos. — Months

① — If towing a trailer, using a camper or a car stop carrier, or driving on rough or muddy roads, change fluid at every 30,000 miles or 24 months except for limited slip differential fluid. Change LSD fluid every 15,000 miles or 12 months.
② — Propeller shaft should be greased daily if it is immersed in water.
③ — If operating frequently in water, replace grease every 3750 miles or 3 months.

Subaru

Service interval headers below are given as **Service Interval In Miles** (in thousands). The leftmost label column is **Recommended Service & Service Interval (Months)**.

Legend: S, X, N = prescribed service actions at the indicated interval.

Recommended Service & Service Interval (Months)	7.5	15	22.5	30	37.5	45	52.5	60	67.5	75	82.5	90	97.5	105	112.5	120	127.5	135	142.5	150	157.5	165	172.5
BODY																							
Inspect Supplemental Restraint System								Every 10 Years															
BRAKES																							
Change Brake Fluid (Every 30 Mos.)																							
Inspect Brake Lines, Except 1999	S	X	S	X	S	X	S	X	S	X	S	X	S	X	S	X	S	X	S	X	S	X	S
Inspect Brake Line & Check Operation Of Parking & Service Brake System, 1999 All		X		X		X		X		X		X		X		X		X		X		X	
Inspect Brake System & Parking Brake Operation	S	X	S	X	S	X	S	X	S	X	S	X	S	X	S	X	S	X	S	X	S	X	S
Inspect Disc Brake Pads & Discs	S	X	S	X	S	X	S	X	S	X	S	X	S	X	S	X	S	X	S	X	S	X	S
Inspect Drum Brake Linings & Drums	S	X	S	X	S	X	S	X	S	X	S	X	S	X	S	X	S	X	S	X	S	X	S
Inspect Hill-Holder System Operation		X		X		X		X		X		X		X		X		X		X		X	
CLUTCH & TRANSMISSION																							
Change Automatic Transmission Fluid				S				S				S				S				S			
Change Manual Transmission Oil				S				S				S				S				S			
Inspect Automatic Transmission Fluid		N		N		N		N		N		N		N		N		N		N		N	
Inspect Clutch Operation	X		X		X		X		X		X		X		X		X		X		X		X
Inspect Manual Transmission Oil		N		N		N		N		N		N		N		N		N		N		N	
DRIVE AXLE & DRIVESHAFT																							
Change Front & Rear Differential Lubricant				S				S				S				S				S			
Inspect Front & Rear Axle Boots & Axle Shaft Joints	S	X	S	X	S	X	S	X	S	X	S	X	S	X	S	X	S	X	S	X	S	X	S
Inspect Front & Rear Differential Oil		N		N		N		N		N		N		N		N		N		N		N	
ENGINE																							
Change Engine Coolant (Every 30 Mos.)				X				X				X				X				X			
Change Engine Oil & Filter — First Interval 3 Months Or 3,000 Miles, Subsequent Intervals. Normal Service Every 12 Months Or 7,500 Miles/Severe Service Change More Often	X	X	X	X	X	X	X	X	X	X	X	X	X	X	X	X	X	X	X	X	X	X	X
Inspect Camshaft Timing Belt, Except 2.5L & 1996–98 2.2L CA														X									
Inspect Camshaft Timing Belt, 2.5L All & 1996–98 2.2L CA														X									
Inspect Camshaft Timing Belt, 1999 All														X									
Inspect Cooling System Hoses & Connections (Every 30 Mos.)	S	S	S	S	S	S	S	S	S	S	S	S	S	X	S	S	S	S	S	S	S	S	S
Inspect Drive Belts				X				X				X				X				X			
Inspect Fuel System Hoses & Connections				X				X				X				X				X			
Inspect Valve Clearance, 1.2L	X		X		X		X		X		X		X		X		X		X		X		X
Inspect Valve Clearance, 1.8L, 2.2L, 2.5L, 2.7L & 3.3L				X				X				X				X				X			

Recommended Service & Service Interval (Months)

Service Interval In Miles (×1,000)

Service	7.5	15	22.5	30	37.5	45	52.5	60	67.5	75	82.5	90	97.5	105	112.5	120	127.5	135	142.5	150	157.5	165	172.5
ENGINE																							
Inspect Valve Clearance, 1999 All														X									
Replace Air Filter (Every 30 Mos.)			X			X			X			X			X			X			X		
Replace Camshaft Timing Belt, 1.2L								X															
Replace Camshaft Timing Belt, 1.8L							X																
Replace Camshaft Timing Belt, 1996–98 2.2L FED								X															
Replace Camshaft Timing Belt, 1996–98 2.2L CA													X										
Replace Camshaft Timing Belt, 2.5L								X						X									
Replace Camshaft Timing Belt, 2.7L								X								X							
Replace Camshaft Timing Belt, 3.3L								X								X							
Replace Camshaft Timing Belt, 1999 All													X										
Replace Drive Belts, 1996-98 FED													X	X									
Replace Drive Belts, 1996-98 CA													X	X									
Replace Drive Belts, 1999 All													X										
Replace Fuel Filter, 1996–98 FED								X								X							
Replace Fuel Filter, 1996–98 CA											X					X							
Replace Spark Plugs, 1.2L, 1.8L, 2.2L & 2.7L				X				X								X							
Replace Spark Plugs, 2.5L & 3.3L								X								X							
STEERING & SUSPENSION																							
Inspect Front & Rear Wheel Bearing Lubricant												X											
Inspect Steering & Suspension	S	X	S	X	S	X	S	X	S	X	S	X	S	X	S	X	S	X	S	X	S	X	S
Lubricate Chassis	X	X	X	X	X	X	X	X	X	X	X	X	X	X	X	X	X	X	X	X	X	X	X

CA — California
FED — Federal
N — Normal Service
S — Severe Service
X — Normal or Severe Service
Mos. — Months

Suzuki Esteem & Swift

Recommended Service

Service Interval In Miles① (×1000)

Recommended Service	3/6	7.5	9	12	15	18	21	24	27	30	33	36	39	42	45	48	51	54	57	60	63	66	67.5	69	72	75	78	81	84	87	90	93	96	97.5	99
BODY																																			
Inspect Supplemental Restraint System	colspan: 10 Years From Vehicle Build Date																																		
Lubricate Door Hinges	At Every Engine Oil Change																																		
BRAKES																																			
Change Brake Fluid															X																				
Inspect Brake Fluid Level	At Every Engine Oil Change																																		
Inspect Brake Drums, Hoses, Lines, Pads, Rotors & Shoes		S			N					S					N					S						N					S				
Inspect Main Brake System Operation					X					X					X					X						X					X				
Inspect Parking Brake Operation	At Every Second Engine Oil Change																																		
CLUTCH & TRANSAXLE																																			
Change Automatic Transmission Fluid & Filter, Swift																	S																		
Change Manual Transaxle Lubricant, Swift		S			N					S					N					S						N									
Lubricate Transaxle Shift Control Lever & Shaft & Inspect Operation	At Every Engine Oil Change																																		
DRIVESHAFT																																			
Inspect CV Joint Boots		S			N					S					N					S						N					S				
ENGINE																																			
Change Engine Coolant															X																X				
Change Engine Oil & Filter, Except Swift GT	S	S	S	S	S	S	S	S	S	S	S	S	S	S	S	S	S	S	S	S	S	S	S	S	S	S	S	S	S	S	S	S	S	S	S

Service Interval In Miles①

Recommended Service	3000	6000	7500	9000	12000	15000	18000	21000	22500	24000	27000	30000	33000	36000	37500	39000	42000	45000	48000	51000	52500	54000	57000	60000	63000	66000	67500	69000	72000	75000	78000	81000	82500	84000	87000	90000	93000	96000	97500	99000
ENGINE																																								
Change Engine Oil & Filter, Swift GT	→ Normal Service Every 12 Months Or 5000 Miles; Severe Service Every 3 Months Or 3000 Miles																																							
Inspect Air Filter Element			S			S			S			S			S			S			S			S			S			S			S			S			S	
Inspect Distributor Cap & Rotor		S				S						S						S						S						S						S				
Inspect Drive Belts & Exhaust System												X												X												X				
Inspect Engine Valve Clearance, 1998 Swift												N												N												N				
Inspect Fuel System		S				S						X						S						X						S						X				
Inspect PCV Valve		S				S						S						S						S						S						S				
Inspect Spark Plug Wires		S				S						S						S						S						S						S				
Inspect Thermostatic Air Cleaner System & Replace Engine Air Filter												X												X												X				
Inspect Underhood Wiring Harness & Connections																								X																
Replace EVAP Canister Suction & Fuel Filter, 1998 Swift	→ Every 10 Years Or 120,000 Miles																																							
Replace Fuel Filter, Esteem & 1996–97 Swift	→ Normal Service Every 105 Months Or 105,000 Miles; Severe Service Every 60 Months Or 60,000 Miles																																							
Replace Spark Plugs												X												X												X				
Replace Spark Plug Wires																								X																
Replace Timing Belt②																																								

STEERING, SUSPENSION & TIRES

Service Interval In Miles①

Recommended Service	3000	6000	7500	9000	12000	15000	18000	21000	22500	24000	27000	30000	33000	36000	37500	39000	42000	45000	48000	51000	52500	54000	57000	60000	63000	66000	67500	69000	72000	75000	78000	81000	82500	84000	87000	90000	93000	96000	97500	99000
Inspect Steering & Suspension Systems	S	N	S	N	S	N	S	N	X	N	S	N	S	N	S	N	S	X	S	N	S	N	S	N	S	N	X	N	S	N	S	N	S	N	S	X	S	N	S	N
Rotate Tires & Adjust Pressure	S	N	S	N	S	N	S	N	X	N	S	N	S	N	S	N	S	X	S	N	S	N	S	N	S	N	X	N	S	N	S	N	S	N	S	X	S	N	S	N

N — Normal Service
S — Severe Service
X — Normal Or Severe Service

① — After vehicles passes 99,000 mile mark return to beginning of mileage table & start cycle over again.

② — Normal service on 1996–97 models except CA replace at 60,000 miles. Normal service on 1996–97 CA models & all 1998–99 models replace every 60,000 mile intervals. Normal service on 1996–97 models replace every 60 months or 60,000 miles. On all models operating in severe conditions replace every 60 months or 60,000 miles, then inspect at 90, 150 & 210 months or 90,000, 150,000 & 210,000 miles.

Suzuki Sidekick & X-90

Service Interval In Miles [1]

Recommended Service	3000	6000	9000	12000	15000	18000	21000	24000	27000	30000	33000	36000	39000	42000	45000	48000	51000	54000	57000	60000	63000	66000	69000	72000	75000	78000	81000	84000	87000	90000	93000	96000	99000
BODY																																	
Inspect Supplemental Restraint System	10 Years From Vehicle Build Date																																
Lubricate Door Hinges	At Every Engine Oil Change																																
BRAKES																																	
Change Brake Fluid					S					S					S					S					S					S			
Inspect Brake System					S					S					S					X					N					S			
Inspect Parking Brake	At Every Second Engine Oil Change																																
CLUTCH, TRANSMISSION & TRANSFER CASE																																	
Change Automatic Transmission Fluid & Filter, 3 Speed															S																		
Change Automatic Transmission Fluid & Filter, 4 Speed	Normal Service Every 100,000 Miles, Severe Service Every 15,000 Miles																																
Change Transmission & Transfer Case Lubricants					S					X					S					X					S					X			
Lubricate Transmission Shift Control Lever & Shaft & Inspect Operation	At Every Engine Oil Change																																
Replace Automatic Transmission Fluid Cooler Hoses															X															X			
DRIVE AXLE & DRIVESHAFT																																	
Change Differential Lubricant					S					X					S					X					S					X			
Inspect CV Joint Boots					S					N					S					N					S					N			
Inspect & Lubricate Driveshafts					S					X					S					X					S					X			
ENGINE																																	
Change Engine Coolant										X																				X			
Change Engine Oil & Filter & Inspect Air Filter Element	S	S	N	S	S	X	S	S	N	S	S	X	S	S	N	S	S	X	S	S	N	S	S	X	S	S	N	S	S	X	S	S	N
Inspect Catalytic Converter & Fuel Injector, Except Sport	Every 100,000 Miles																																
Inspect Coolant Level	At Every Engine Oil Change																																
Inspect Distributor Cap & Rotor					S															X										S			

Service Interval In Miles①

ENGINE

The following table lists the Recommended Service items and the mileage intervals at which each is marked (X = service, S = severe/supplemental service).

Recommended Service	Marked intervals (miles)
Inspect Emission System Hoses & Tubes	X: 60000
Inspect Valve Clearance & Fuel System & Idle Speed	S: 36000; X: 15000, 45000, 60000, 75000, 90000
Inspect Exhaust Heat Shields & System Integrity	S: 7500, 12000, 24000, 30000, 36000, 42000, 48000, 54000, 66000, 72000, 78000, 84000; X: 60000, 90000
Inspect Ignition Timing	X: 60000
Inspect Spark Plug Wires	S: 12000, 30000, 45000, 75000, 90000
Replace Air Filter Element & Inspect PCV Valve & Drive Belts	S: 15000, 45000, 75000; X: 30000, 60000, 90000
Replace Drive Belts	S: 30000, 60000; X: 60000
Replace EVAP Canister & Inspect ECM & Related Sensors	Every 100,000 Miles
Replace Spark Plug Wires, Exhaust System Hangers & Fuel Filler Cap	X: 60000
Replace O2 Sensor, Except Sport	Every 80,000 Miles
Replace PCV Valve & Inspect EGR System	Every 50,000 Miles
Replace Spark Plugs & Fuel Filter	X: 30000, 60000, 90000
Replace Timing Belt②	X: 60000

Service Interval In Miles①

Recommended Service	7500	15000	22500	30000	37500	45000	52500	60000	67500	75000	82500	90000	97500
STEERING, SUSPENSION & TIRES													
Inspect Power Steering Fluid Level	At Every Engine Oil Change												
Inspect Steering Wheel Freeplay, Gearbox Lubricant & Linkage	S	S	S	S	S	S	S	S	S	S	S	S	S
Inspect Free-Wheeling Hubs		X		X		X		X		X		X	
Inspect Wheel Bearings & Suspension & Rotate Tires & Adjust Pressure	S	N	S	N	S	N	S	N	S	N	S	N	S

N — Normal Service
S — Severe Service
X — Normal Or Severe Service
① — After vehicles passes 99,000 mile mark return to beginning of mileage table & start cycle over again.
② — Normal service on 1996–97 models except CA replace at 60,000 mile intervals. Normal service on 1996–97 CA models & all 1998 models replace every 60,000 miles & inspect at 90,000 miles. On 1997–99 models operating in severe conditions replace every 60 months or 60,000 miles, then inspect at 90, 150 & 210 months or 90,000, 150,000 & 210,000 miles.

Suzuki Vitara

Service Interval In Miles ①

Recommended Service	3000	6000	7500	9000	12000	15000	21000	22500	30000	33000	36000	37500	45000	48000	52500	54000	57000	60000	66000	67500	72000	75000	81000	82500	84000	90000	96000	99000
BRAKES																												
Inspect & Adjust Brake Pedal Stroke						X			X				X					X				X				X		
Inspect & Adjust Parking Brake Lever & Cable Lever Movement						X			X				X					X				X				X		
Inspect Brake Discs, Drums, Pads & Shoes			X			X		X	X			X	X		X			X		X		X		X		X		
Inspect Brake Fluid			X			X		X	X			X	X		X			X		X		X		X		X		
Inspect Brake Hoses & Pipes			X			X		X	X			X	X		X			X		X		X		X		X		
Replace Brake Fluid									X				X					X				X				X		
CLUTCH & TRANSAXLE																												
Change Automatic Transmission Fluid	At Every 100,000 Miles																											
Inspect Automatic Transmission Fluid Level			X		X	X		X	X			X	X		X			X		X		X		X		X		
Inspect Clutch Fluid Level			X			X		X	X			X	X		X			X		X		X		X		X		
Inspect Manual Transmission Fluid		X	X		X	X		X	X			X	X		X			X		X		X		X		X		
Inspect Transfer Case & Differential Fluids		X	X		X	X		X	X			X	X		X			X		X		X		X		X		
Replace Automatic Transmission Fluid Hose									X				X							X						X		
Replace Manual Transmission Fluid								X							X			X						X		X		
Replace Transfer Case & Differential Fluids								X					X					X						X		X		
DRIVESHAFT																												
Inspect Propeller Shafts			X			X		X	X			X	X		X			X		X		X		X		X		
ENGINE																												
Change Engine Coolant									X						X											X		
Change Engine Oil & Filter	S	S	X	S	S	X	S	X	X	S	S	X	X	S	X	S	S	X	S	X	S	X	S	X	S	X	S	S
Inspect Cooling System Hoses & Connections	S	S	X	S	S	X	S	X	X	S	S	X	X	S	X	S	S	X	S	X	S	X	S	X	S	X	S	S
Inspect Drive Belt								X																		X		

0-68

Service Interval In Miles ①

Recommended Service	3000	3600	7500	9000	12000	15000	18000	22500	24000	27000	30000	36000	37500	42000	45000	51000	54000	57000	60000	67500	69000	72000	75000	78000	81000	84000	87000	90000	97500
ENGINE																													
Inspect Emission Hoses & Tubes																			X										
Inspect Exhaust Pipes & Mounting		S	S			S		S			X		S		S			S	X	S			S					X	S
Inspect Fuel Lines & Connections											X								X									X	
Inspect Fuel Tank Cap											X		X						X									X	
Inspect Ignition Coil											X		X						X									X	
Inspect Three Way Catalytic Converter																			At 100,000 Miles										
Inspect Timing Belt, SOHC Engine																			X									X	
Inspect Valve Lash Clearance, SOHC Engine								X							X					X								X	
Inspect Wiring Harness & Connections, SOHC			S												X					X			S					X	
Replace Air Filter						S					X				S				X				S					X	
Replace Drive Belt											X								X									X	
Replace EVAP Canister																			At 100,000 Miles										
Replace Fuel Filter											X								X									X	
Replace Fuel Tank Cap											X								X									X	
Replace Ignition Wires, SOHC Engine																			At 100,000 Miles										
Replace PCV Valve											X									At 50,000 Miles & 100,000 Miles									
Replace Spark Plugs											X								X									X	
Replace Timing Belt, SOHC Engine																			At 100,000 Miles										
STEERING, SUSPENSION & TIRES																													
Inspect Power Steering	X		X		X	X		X			X		X		X		X		X	X			X		X			X	X
Inspect Steering System, Steering Wheel Movement & Steering Linkage	X		X		X	X		X			X		X		X		X		X	X			X		X			X	X
Inspect Suspension System	X		X		X						X		X		X				X	X			X					X	X
Inspect Wheel Bearings			X								X		X		X				X	X			X		X			X	X
Rotate Tires	X		X		X	X		X			X		X		X		X		X	X			X		X			X	X

S — Severe Service
X — Normal Service

Toyota Avalon, Camry, Celica, Corolla, Paseo, Supra & Tercel

Recommended Service

Service Interval In Miles ①

Recommended Service	5,000	7,500	10,000	15,000	20,000	22,500	25,000	30,000	35,000	37,500	40,000	45,000	50,000	52,500	55,000	60,000
BODY																
Inspect Body Fastener Security		S		S		S		S		S		S		S		S
Inspect Supplemental Restraint System	At 10 Years From Vehicle Build Date, Then Every 24 Months Thereafter															
BRAKES																
Inspect Main & Parking Brake Discs, Drums, Pads & Rotors, System Connections, Hoses & Lines	S	S	S	X	S	S	S	X	S	S	S	X	S	S	S	X
CLUTCH & TRANSMISSION																
Change Automatic Transmission Fluid & Filter				S				S				S				S
Change Manual Transmission Lubricant				S				S				S				S
Inspect Transmission For Leakage		X		X		X		X		X		X		X		X
DRIVE AXLE & DRIVESHAFT																
Change Differential Lubricant, Except Supra				S				S				S				S
Change Limited Slip Differential Lubricant, Supra				X				X				X				X
Inspect CV Joint Boots, Tighten Driveshaft Flange Bolts	S	S	S	X	S	S	S	X	S	S	S	X	S	S	S	X
Inspect CV Joints & Boots	S	S	S	X	S	S	S	X	S	S	S	X	S	S	S	X
ENGINE																
Change Engine Coolant	Every 24 Months Or 30,000 Miles															
Change Engine Oil & Filter ③	S	S	S	S	S	S	S	S	S	S	S	S	S	S	S	S
Inspect Drive Belts		X		X		X		X		X		X		X		X
Inspect Engine For Leakage		X		X		X		X		X		X		X		X
Inspect Engine Air Filter	S	S	S	S	S	S	S	S	S	S	S	S	S	S	S	S
Inspect EVAP Charcoal Canister								X								X
Inspect Exhaust Heat Shields & System Integrity				X				X				X				X
Inspect Fast Idle, Curb Idle Speed								X								X
Inspect Fuel & Vapor System Connections, Hoses, Lines & Tank Mounting Bands				X				X				X				X
Inspect Fuel Tank Cap Gasket								X								X
Inspect Supercharger Gear Oil Level								X								X
Isolate & Adjust Noisy Engine Valves								X								X
Replace Engine Air Filter				X				X				X				X
Replace Spark Plugs (Platinum Tip)								X								X

Service Interval In Miles①

Recommended Service	5000	7500	10000	15000	20000	25000	30000	35000	40000	45000	50000	55000	60000
ENGINE													
Replace Spark Plugs (Standard Tip)							X						X
Replace Timing Belt, 1996–97													X
Replace Timing Belt, 1998	Every 72 Months Or 90,000 Miles												
STEERING, SUSPENSION & TIRES													
Inspect Chassis Fastener Security	S		S		S		S		S		S		S
Inspect Steering Gear For Fluid Leakage			X		X		X		X		X		X
Inspect Steering Linkage & Ball Joints, Paseo & Tercel			S		S		S		S		S		S
Repack Rear Wheel Bearings, Paseo & Tercel			X		X		X		X		X		X
Rotate Tires	S	N	S	N	S	N	S	N	S	N	S	N	S

N — Normal Service
S — Severe Service
X — Normal Or Severe Service
ADD — Automatic Disconnecting Differential
① — After vehicle has passed 60,000 mile mark return to beginning of mileage table & start cycle over again.
② — Severe service models less turbocharger should be changed twice as often as shown; models w/turbocharger change every 2500 miles.
③ — Models w/turbocharger in severe service should be changed every 2500 miles.

Toyota 4Runner, Land Cruiser, Previa, RAV4, Sienna, Tacoma, Truck & T100

Service Interval In Miles①

Recommended Service	5,000	7,500	10,000	15,000	20,000	25,000	30,000	35,000	40,000	45,000	50,000	55,000	60,000
BODY													
Inspect Body Fastener Security②				S	S	S	S	S	S	S	S	S	S
Inspect Supplemental Restraint System	At 10 Years From Vehicle Build Date, Then Every 24 Months Thereafter												
BRAKES													
Inspect Main & Parking Brake Discs, Drums, Pads & Rotors, System Connections, Hoses & Lines④	S		S	X	S	S	X	S	S	X	S	S	X
CLUTCH & TRANSMISSION													
Change Automatic Transmission Fluid & Filter				S			S		S				X
Change Manual Transmission Lubricant							S						S
Change Transfer case Lubricant							S						S
Inspect Transmission For Leakage④			X			X				X			X
DRIVE AXLE & DRIVESHAFT													
Change Limited Slip Differential Lubricant, 1996–97 RAV4							X						X
Change Limited Slip Differential Lubricant, 1998 RAV4							X						X
Inspect CV Joint Boots, Tighten Driveshaft Flange Bolts, 1996–97 4WD	S	S	S	S	S	S	S	S	S	S	S	S	S
Inspect CV Joints & Driveshaft	S	X	S	X	S	X	S	X	S	X	S	X	X
Lubricate Driveshaft Bushing, 1996 4WD Models Except Previa, 1997–98 Land Cruiser, T100 4WD & Tacoma 4WD Less ADD				X			X			X			X
ENGINE													
Adjust Engine Valve 2R-E Engine							X						X
Change Engine Coolant,	Every 24 Months Or 30,000 Miles												
Change Engine Oil & Filter③	S	N	S	N	S	N	S	N	S	N	S	N	S
Inspect Drive Belts		X	X	X	X	X	N	X	X	X	X	X	X
Inspect Engine Air Filter④	S	S	S	S	S	S	S	S	S	S	S	S	S
Inspect Engine Idle Speed, Truck & 4Runner	X				X			X			X		
Inspect EVAP Charcoal Canister							X						X
Inspect Exhaust Heat Shields & System Integrity④		X		X		X				X			X
Inspect Fuel & Vapor System Connections, Hoses, Lines & Tank Mounting Bands							X						X
Inspect Fuel Tank Cap Gasket							X						X
Isolate & Adjust Noisy Engine Valves													X
Replace Engine Air Filter & Inspect Supercharger Gear Oil Level							X						X

Recommended Service — Service Interval In Miles[1]

Recommended Service	5000	7500	10000	15000	20000	22500	25000	30000	35000	37500	40000	45000	50000	52500	55000	60000
ENGINE																
Replace Spark Plugs (Platinum Tip)																X
Replace Spark Plugs (Standard Tip)								X								X
Replace Timing Belt, 1996-97																X
Replace Timing Belt, 1998	— Every 72 Months Or 90,000 Miles															
STEERING, SUSPENSION & TIRES																
Inspect Chassis Fastener Security[2]	S	S	S	S	S	S	S	S	S	S	S	S	S	S	S	S
Inspect Steering Gear For Fluid Leakage[4]				X				X				X				X
Inspect Steering Linkage & Ball Joints, Land Cruiser, Previa, RAV4, T100, Tacoma, Truck & 4Runner[4]	S	S	S	X	S	S	S	X	S	S	S	X	S	S	S	X
Lubricate Driveshaft, Steering & Suspension Grease Fittings, Land Cruiser, Previa, RAV4, T100, Tacoma, Truck & 4Runner[4]	S	S	S	X	S	S	S	X	S	S	S	X	S	S	S	X
Lubricate Steering Knuckle, 1996-97 Land Cruiser[4]	S	S	S	X	S	S	S	X	S	S	S	X	S	S	S	X
Repack Front Wheel Bearings, 1996 4Runner, T100 & Tacoma 4WD Less ADD				X				X				X				X
Rotate Tires	S	N	S	N	S	N	S	N	S	N	S	N	S	N	S	N

N — Normal Service
S — Severe Service
X — Normal Or Severe Service
ADD — Automatic Disconnecting Differential
[1] — After vehicle has passed 60,000 mile mark return to beginning of mileage table & start cycle over again.
[2] — Severe intervals apply to vehicles operating on muddy & rough roads. Pay particular attention to front & rear suspension mountings, leaf spring U-bolts, strut bar bracket-to-body bolts & seat installation bolts.
[3] — Models w/turbocharger in severe service should be changed every 2500 miles.
[4] — Perform these operations daily if vehicle travels off-road, through deep mud, sand or water.

GENERAL INFORMATION

Page No.

MITSUBISHI:
VEHICLE SERVICE:

GENERAL INFORMATION

Manual Information Locator, Inside Rear Cover

Specifications

GENERAL ENGINE SPECIFICATIONS

Year	Engine	Fuel System	Bore & Stroke	Compression Ratio	Maximum Net H.P. @ RPM	Maximum Torque, Ft. Lbs. @ RPM	Oil Pressure, Lbs.
1996	3.0L SOHC	MPI	3.587 X 2.992	10.0	175 @ 5500	185 @ 3000	11.4①
	3.0L DOHC	MPI	3.587 X 2.992	10.0	202 @ 6000	201 @ 3500	11.4①
1997–99	3.5L	MPI	3.65 X 3.37	9.0	210 @ 5000	231 @ 4000	11.4①

① — Minimum pressure @ curb idle speed.

TUNE UP SPECIFICATIONS

Year	Engine	Spark Plug Gap, Inch	Ignition Timing — Firing Order	Ignition Timing — Timing, °BTDC	Ignition Timing — Timing Mark Location	Idle Speed, RPM — Curb	Idle Speed, RPM — Fast	Fuel Pump Pressure, psi	Valve Lash — Intake	Valve Lash — Exhaust
1996	3.0L SOHC	.041	③	5④	Pulley	700N	①	47.6②	⑦	⑦
	3.0L DOHC	.041	③	5⑤	⑥	700N	①	47.6②	⑦	⑦
1997–99	3.5L	.041	⑧	5⑤	⑥	700N	①	47.0–50.0②	⑦	⑦

BTDC — Before Top Dead Center
N — Neutral
① — Controlled by idle speed control servo.
② — With fuel pressure regulator vacuum hose disconnected & plugged.
③ — Cylinder numbering from front of engine to rear: right bank, 1, 3, 5; left bank, 2, 4, 6. Firing order:

1–2–3–4–5–6. On SOHC engine, refer to **Fig. A.** On DOHC engine, refer to **Fig. B** for wire routing.
④ — With jumper wire connected between ignition timing adjustment connector & ground. Refer to **Fig. D.**
⑤ — Electronically controlled.
⑥ — Equipped w/crankshaft position sensor.

⑦ — Hydraulic valve lifters, no adjustment required.
⑧ — Cylinder numbering from front of engine to rear: right bank, 1, 3, 5; left bank, 2, 4, 6. Firing order: 1–2–3–4–5–6. Refer to **Fig. C** for wire routing.

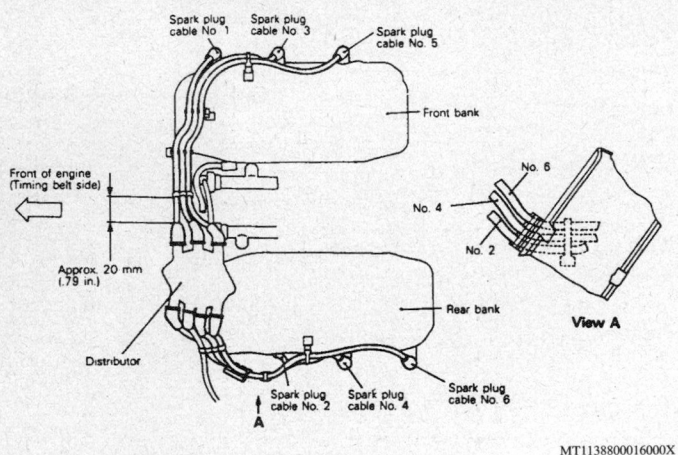

Fig. A

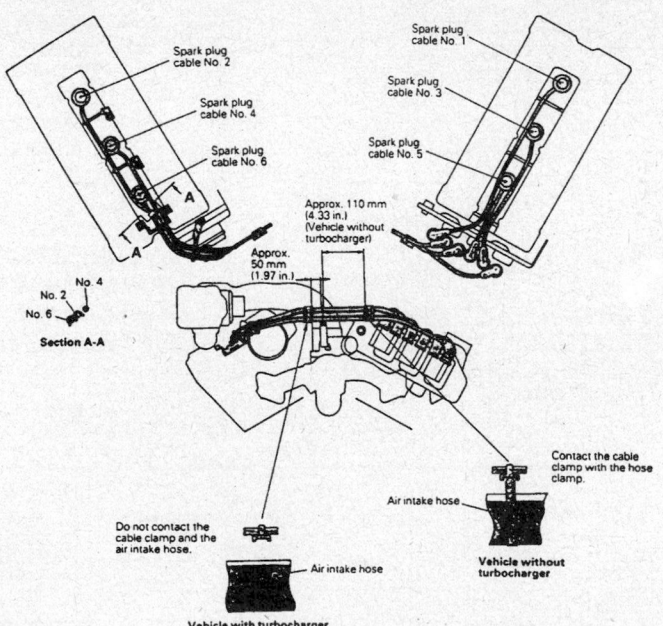

Fig. B

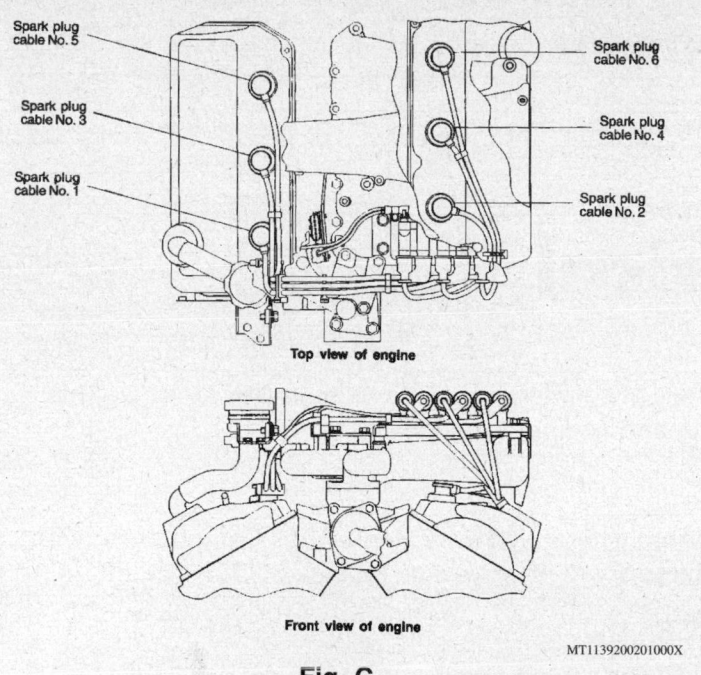

Top view of engine

Front view of engine

MT1139200201000X

Fig. C

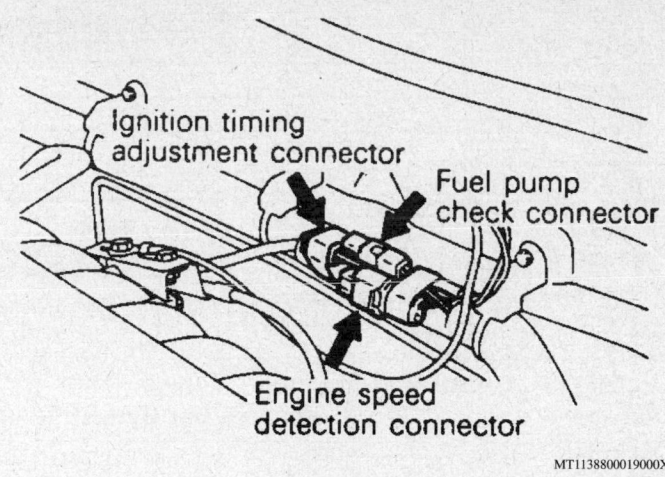

MT1138800019000X

Fig. D

FRONT WHEEL ALIGNMENT SPECIFICATIONS

Year	Caster Angle, Deg.		Camber Angle, Deg.		Toe, Inch①	Ball Joint Inspection③
	Limits	Desired	Limits	Desired		
1996	+2¼ to +3¼	+2¾	−½ to +½	0	−.12 to +.12	86.8–191.0②
1997–99	+2½ to +3½	+3	−½ to +½	0	−.12 to +.12	87.0–190.0②

① — Toe-in (+); toe-out (-).

② — Breakaway torque measurement using special service tool No. MB990326, or equivalent.

③ — Inch lbs.

REAR WHEEL ALIGNMENT SPECIFICATIONS

Year	Camber Angle, Deg.		Toe, Inch①	Ball Joint Inspection, Inch Lbs.
	Limits	Desired		
1996	−½ to +½	0	-.12 to + .12	17.36–79.11③
1997–99	④	②	.-012 to +.012	1.00–23.00③

① — Toe-in (+); toe-out (-).

② — 205/65R15 tires., -⅔. 215/60R16 tires, -⅚.

③ — Breakaway torque measurement using special service tool No. MB990326, or equivalent.

④ — 205/65R15 tires, -1⅙ to -⅙. 215/60R16 tires, -1⅓ to -⅓.

FLUID CAPACITIES & COOLING SYSTEM DATA

Year	Coolant Capacity, Qts.	Radiator Cap Relief Pressure, Lbs.	Thermo. Opening Temp., Deg. F	Fuel Tank, Gals.	Engine Oil Refill, Qts. ①	Trans. Fluid, Qts. ②
1996	8.5	13	180	19.0	4.7	7.9
1997	10.0	13	180	18.7	4.7	9.0
1998–99	10.0	13	180	18.7	4.7	9.0

① — Includes filter.

② — Approximate capacity; make final check w/dipstick.

MITSUBISHI DIAMANTE

LUBRICANT DATA

Year	Lubricant Type		
	Automatic Transaxle	Power Steering	Brake System
1996	Diamond ATF SP	Dexron II	DOT 3 or DOT 4
1997–99	Diamond ATF SPII	Dexron III	DOT 3 or DOT 4

Electrical

NOTE: On Air Bag Equipped Models, Refer To "Air Bag System Precautions" Located In Front Of This Manual For System Disarming and Arming Procedures.

NOTE: Refer To "Computer Relearn Procedures" Located In Front Of This Manual For Computer Relearn Procedures.

INDEX

PRECAUTIONS

AIR BAG SYSTEMS

Refer to "Air Bag System Precautions" in front of this manual for system disarming and arming procedures.

BATTERY GROUND CABLE

Prior to service, disconnect battery ground cable and isolate as required.

FUSE PANEL & FLASHER LOCATION

1996

The engine compartment fuse panel is located on the front righthand corner of the engine compartment, near the battery. The multi-purpose fuse block is located behind the lefthand side of the instrument panel, left of the steering column. The hazard and

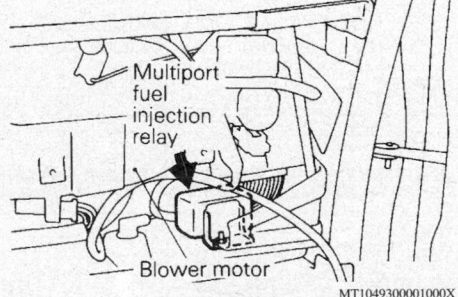

Fig. 1 Fuel pump relay location. 1996

turn signal flasher unit is mounted on the multi-purpose fuse block under the lefthand side of the instrument panel.

1997-99

The engine compartment fuse panel is located on the front lefthand side of the engine compartment. The multi-purpose fuse block is located behind the lefthand side of the instrument panel, left of the steering column. The hazard and turn signal flasher unit is mounted on the multi-purpose fuse block under the lefthand side of the instrument panel.

FUEL PUMP RELAY LOCATION

1996

The fuel pump relay, also known as the multi-port fuel injection relay, is located on the blower motor assembly housing, **Fig. 1.**

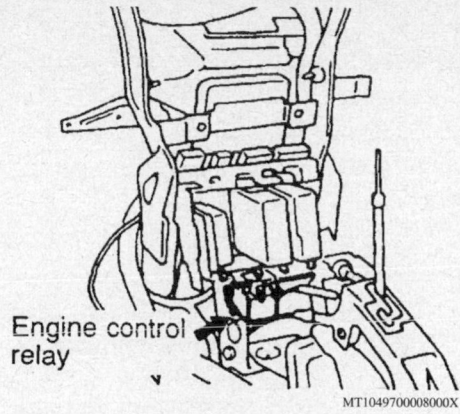

Fig. 2 Fuel pump relay location. 1997-99

1997-99

The fuel pump relay, also known as the engine control relay, is located under the front of the center console, **Fig. 2.**

RELAY CENTER LOCATION

1996

The main relay center is located on the front righthand side of the engine compartment, near the battery. An auxiliary relay cluster is located above the righthand front wheel housing.

1997-99

The relay center is located on the front lefthand side of the engine compartment.

STARTER

REPLACE

1996

1. Place gear selector lever in Neutral position.
2. Raise and support vehicle.
3. Drain transaxle oil and remove side undercover.
4. Remove air cleaner cover and air intake hose.
5. Remove electronically controlled suspension compressor assembly leaving hoses attached. Secure to body using suitable wire.
6. Disconnect transaxle control and speedometer cables.
7. Disconnect oil cooler lines.
8. Disconnect Park/Neutral position and kickdown servo switches.
9. Disconnect pulse generator and oil temperature sensor.
10. Raise transaxle to release pressure on transaxle mount bracket using suitable jack stand then disconnect transaxle mount.
11. Disconnect front height sensor rod.
12. Loosen tie rod end nut then disconnect tie rod from knuckle using steering linkage puller tool No. MB991113-01, or equivalent. **Ensure tie cord of tool is tied off correctly.**

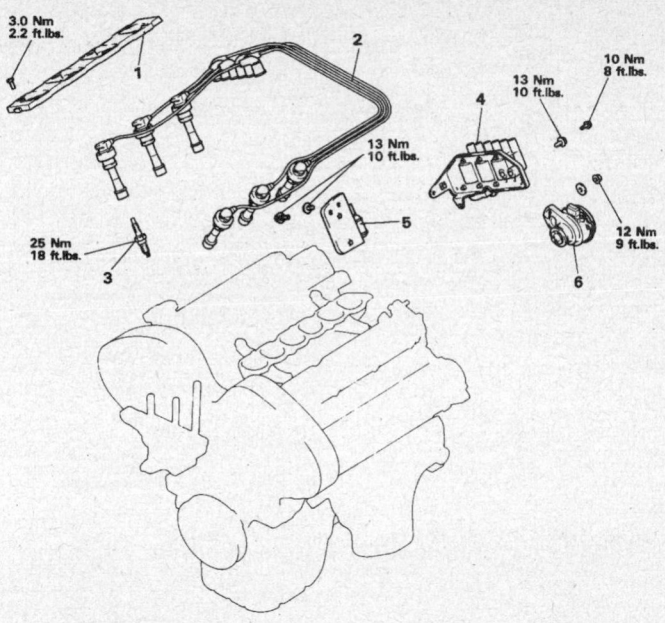

Fig. 3 Coil pack replacement. 3.0L engine

13. With transaxle properly supported, remove righthand crossmember.
14. Remove starter electrical connections, then starter assembly.
15. Reverse procedure to install.

1997-99

1. Remove air cleaner element and breather hose.
2. Remove volume air flow sensor and gasket.
3. Remove air cleaner cover and air intake hose assembly.
4. Remove air duct and air cleaner body.
5. Disconnect starter motor electrical connector.
6. Remove starter motor attaching bolts, then the starter motor.
7. Reverse procedure to install. **Torque** starter motor attaching bolts to 23 ft. lbs.

ALTERNATOR

REPLACE

1996

SOHC Engine

1. Remove intake air hose, then the alternator drive belt.
2. Remove roll stopper stay, then disconnect EGR temperature sensor connector.
3. Remove EGR pipe, then the air intake plenum stay.
4. Remove alternator mounting nut and bolt, then the alternator from the transaxle side through the bottom of the air intake plenum.
5. Reverse procedure to install.

DOHC Engine

1. Remove headlamp washer pump tank, then the condenser fan assembly.
2. Drain coolant into a suitable container.

3. Remove radiator upper hose, then the alternator drive belt.
4. Disconnect and remove alternator and alternator bracket assembly.
5. Remove alternator bracket, then the alternator.
6. Reverse procedure to install, set alternator in place prior to mounting alternator bracket.

1997-99

1. Remove alternator drive belt, then disconnect alternator harness connector.
2. Remove oil level dipstick.
3. Remove alternator adjustment bolt, then the through bolt and nut.
4. Remove alternator from mounting bracket.
5. Reverse procedure to install. **Torque** adjustment bolt to 16 ft. lbs. and through bolt nut to 33 ft. lbs.

DISTRIBUTOR

REPLACE

3.0L ENGINE

1. Disconnect coil and spark plug wires. **Mark position for installation reference.**
2. Rotate engine to position No. 1 cylinder at top dead center (TDC) on compression stroke.
3. Mark position of distributor rotor on distributor housing and distributor housing on intake manifold for correct installation.
4. Remove distributor mounting nut and distributor from engine.
5. Reverse procedure to install, aligning marks made during disassembly.

3.5L ENGINE

1. Remove engine cover.
2. Mark spark plug wires for installation reference.

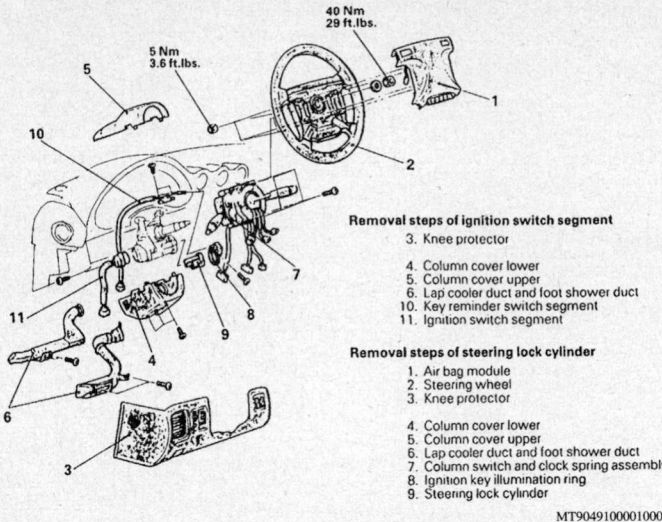

Removal steps of ignition switch segment

3. Knee protector
4. Column cover lower
5. Column cover upper
6. Lap cooler duct and foot shower duct
10. Key reminder switch segment
11. Ignition switch segment

Removal steps of steering lock cylinder

1. Air bag module
2. Steering wheel
3. Knee protector

4. Column cover lower
5. Column cover upper
6. Lap cooler duct and foot shower duct
7. Column switch and clock spring assembly
8. Ignition key illumination ring
9. Steering lock cylinder

MT9049100001000X

Fig. 4   Ignition switch & lock cylinder. 1996

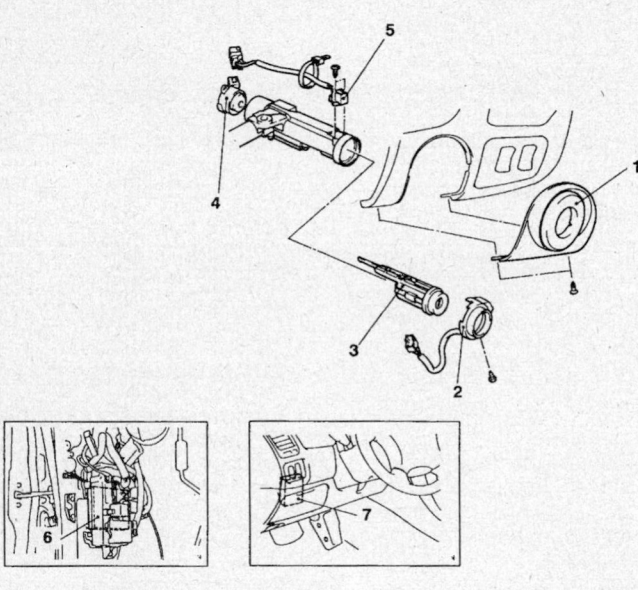

Steering lock cylinder and ignition switch removal steps

● Instrument lower cover (RH)

1. Key cylinder panel
2. Keyhole lighting ring

3. Steering lock cylinder
4. Ignition switch
5. Key reminder switch
6. ETACS-ECU
7. Instrument panel ECU

MT9129700010000X

Fig. 6   Ignition switch & lock cylinder. 1997–99

3. Disconnect spark plug wires from distributor.
4. Remove distributor retaining nut, then the distributor and distributor O-ring.
5. Reverse procedure to install. **Torque** distributor retaining nut to 17 ft. lbs.

COIL PACK
REPLACE
3.0L ENGINE

1. Remove center cover.
2. Remove spark plug wires.
3. Remove coil pack, refer to **Fig. 3** for replacement.
4. Refer to "Tune Up Specifications" for coil pack and spark plug wire routing.
5. Reverse procedure to install.

IGNITION LOCK
REPLACE
1996

1. Remove steering wheel as outlined under "Steering Wheel, Replace."
2. Remove upper and lower steering column covers, **Fig. 4.**
3. Remove knee protector.
4. Remove column switch as outlined under "Multi-Function Switch, Replace."
5. Remove ignition key illumination ring.
6. Insert ignition key into ignition lock cylinder and turn to ACC position.
7. Press lock cylinder lockpin down, **Fig. 5,** and remove lock cylinder.
8. Remove key reminder switch segment.

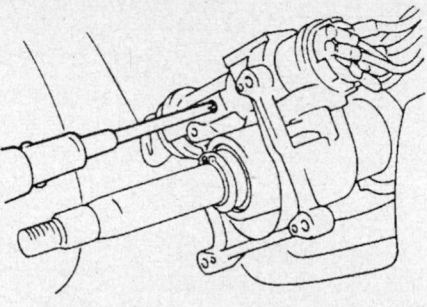

MT9129100003000X

Fig. 5   Ignition lock cylinder removal. 1996

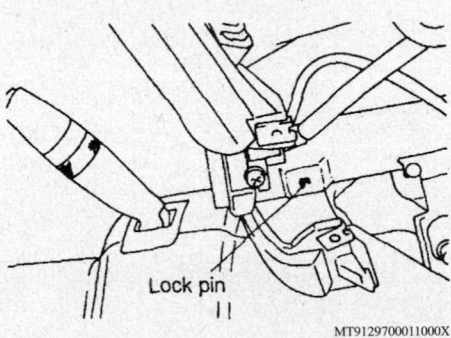

Lock pin

MT9129700011000X

Fig. 7   Ignition lock cylinder removal. 1997–99

9. Disconnect and remove ignition switch assembly.
10. Reverse procedure to install.

1997–99

1. Remove steering column upper and lower covers.
2. Remove hood lock and parking brake release handles from instrument panel lower cover.
3. Remove instrument panel lower cover.
4. Remove key cylinder panel from steering column, **Fig. 6.**
5. Remove keyhole lighting ring.
6. Insert key into steering lock cylinder and turn it to the ACC position.
7. Using a Phillips head screwdriver, push lockpin of steering lock cylinder inward, then pull steering lock cylinder out of column, **Fig. 7.**
8. Reverse procedure to install.

IGNITION SWITCH
REPLACE
1996

1. Remove knee protector from under steering column.
2. Remove upper and lower steering column covers, **Fig. 4.**
3. Disconnect ignition switch electrical connectors, then remove ignition switch from column.
4. Reverse procedure to install.

1997–99

1. Remove steering lock cylinder as outlined under "Ignition Lock, Replace."
2. Disconnect ignition switch electrical connectors.

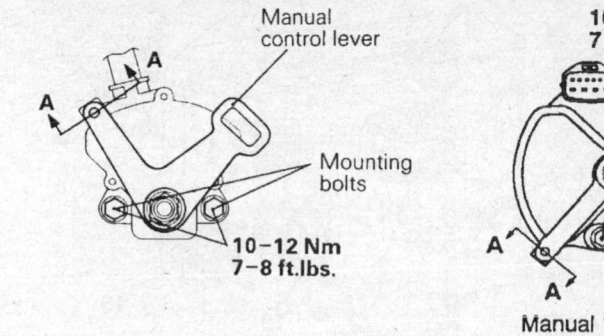

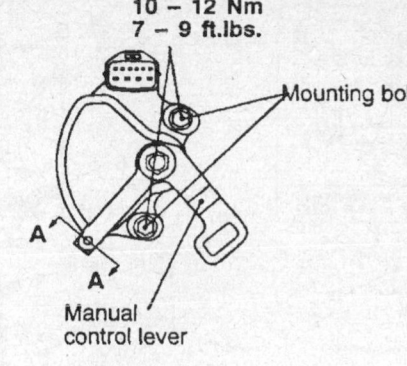

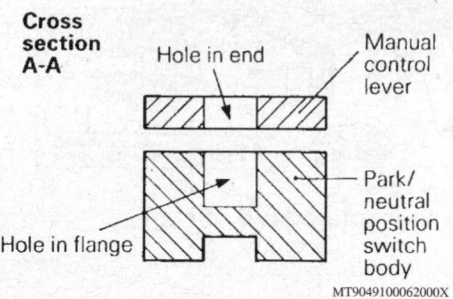

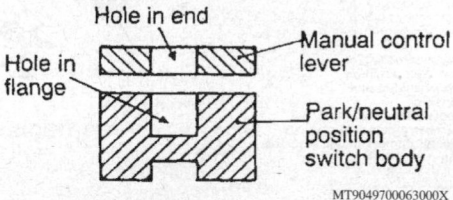

Fig. 8 Neutral safety switch alignment. 1996

MT9049100062000X

Fig. 9 Neutral safety switch alignment. 1997–99

MT9049700063000X

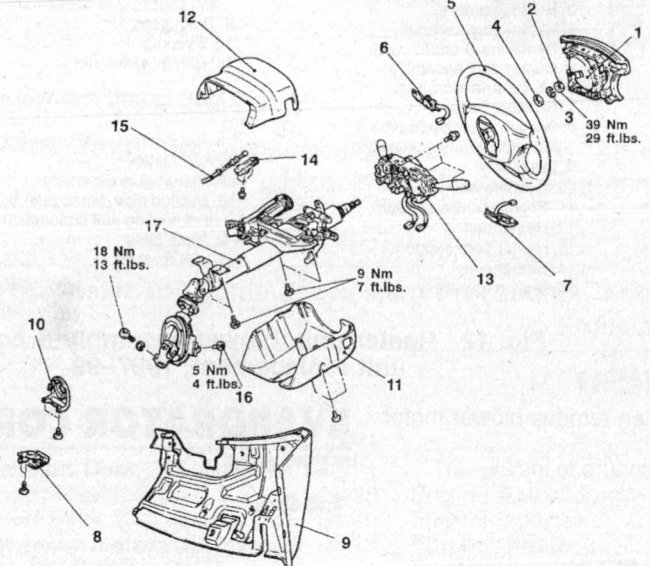

1. Air bag module
2. Steering wheel retaining nut
3. Spring washer
4. Flat washer
5. Steering wheel
6. Cruise control switch
7. Remote control switch
8. Lock release handle
9. Instrument panel lower cover
10. Key cylinder panel
11. Lower column cover
12. Upper column cover
13. Clock spring and column switch assembly
14. Cover
15. Key interlock cable (Shift lock)
16. Retainer mounting bolt
17. Steering column assembly

MT9049700064000X

Fig. 10 Steering column components. 1997–99

3. Remove ignition switch from steering column.
4. Reverse procedure to install.

NEUTRAL SAFETY SWITCH
REPLACE
1. Place selector lever in Neutral position.

2. Place manual control lever in Neutral position, then remove control lever retainer and lever.
3. Disconnect electrical harness, then remove switch retaining bolts and switch assembly.
4. Reverse procedure to install, then adjust as follows:
   a. With manual control lever in Neutral position, rotate switch body until hole in end of manual control lever

and hole in flange of park/neutral position switch are aligned, **Figs. 8 and 9.**
   b. Hold switch body in position, then **torque** retaining bolts to 7–9 ft. lbs.
   c. Lightly pull transaxle control cable and tighten adjusting nut.
   d. Ensure selector lever is in Neutral position.
   e. Check for proper operation.

MULTI-FUNCTION SWITCH
REPLACE
1996
1. Remove steering wheel as outlined under "Steering Wheel, Replace."
2. Remove knee protector, **Fig. 4.**
3. Remove upper and lower steering column covers.
4. Remove lap cooler and foot shower ducts.
5. Remove combination switch assembly.
6. Reverse procedure to install.

1997–99
1. Remove steering wheel as outlined under "Steering Wheel, Replace."
2. Remove cruise control and remote control switches, **Fig. 10.**
3. Remove lock release handle and instrument panel lower cover.
4. Remove key cylinder panel, then the upper and lower covers.
5. Remove clockspring and column switch assembly.
6. Reverse procedure to install.

STEERING WHEEL
REPLACE
1. Position front wheels in straight ahead position.
2. Remove air bag module as outlined in "Passive Restraint Systems."
3. Using suitable steering wheel puller, remove steering wheel.
4. Reverse procedure to install.

INSTRUMENT CLUSTER
REPLACE
1996
1. Remove cluster bezel.
2. Remove cluster retaining screws.
3. Disconnect speedometer cable at transaxle end.
4. Pull cluster rearward slightly and disconnect electrical connectors and speedometer cable.
5. Release speedometer adapter lock by turning adapter left or right.
6. Remove instrument cluster.
7. Reverse procedure to install.

1997–99
1. Remove cluster bezel attaching screws, then the bezel.
2. Remove combination meter attaching screws, then the meter.

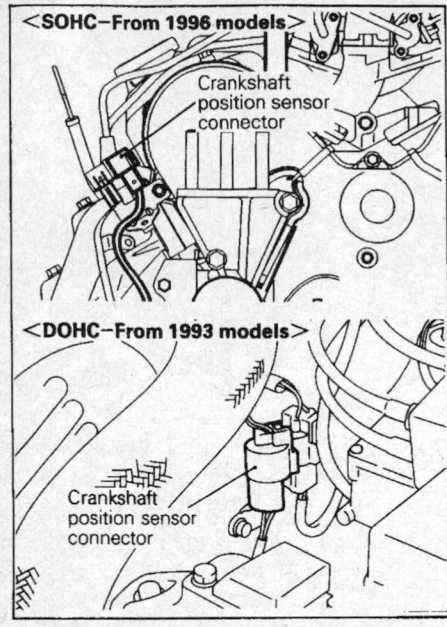

Fig. 1 Distributor & crankshaft position sensor connector locations

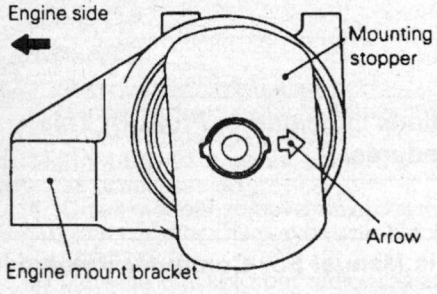

Fig. 3 Engine mounting stopper installation

FUEL SYSTEM PRESSURE RELIEF

1. Raise and support vehicle.
2. Disconnect fuel pump electrical connector.
3. Lower vehicle.
4. Start engine and allow to idle.
5. After engine has stopped, turn ignition switch to Off position, then disconnect battery ground cable.
6. After fuel system repairs are complete, reconnect fuel pump connector.

COMPRESSION PRESSURE

Ensure engine oil, starter motor and battery are in satisfactory condition. When checking compression, engine coolant should be at normal operating temperature, spark plugs should be removed and throttle valve should be wide open. Perform engine compression pressure test as follows:

1. Ensure lights, electric cooling fan and accessories are OFF.
2. Disconnect distributor or crankshaft position sensor, **Fig. 1**.

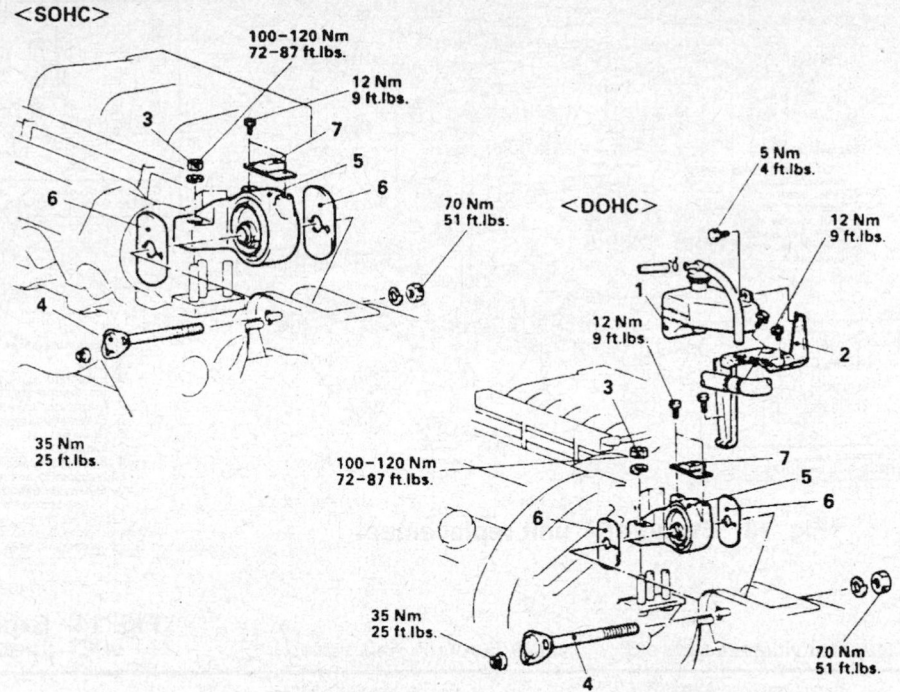

Fig. 2 Engine mount replacement

Removal steps
1. Reserve tank <Vehicles with ABS>
2. Reserve tank bracket <Vehicles with ABS>
3. Engine mount bracket mounting nuts
4. Engine mount bracket and body connection bolt
5. Engine mount bracket
6. Mounting stopper
7. Dynamic damper

3. Install compression gauge in spark plug holes.
4. With throttle valve fully open, crank engine at 250–400 RPM and record compression pressure.
5. **On models equipped with SOHC engine,** standard compression pressure is 196 psi.
6. **On models equipped with DOHC engine,** standard compression pressure is 185 psi.
7. **On SOHC engine,** limit compression pressure is 149 psi.
8. **On DOHC engine,** limit compression pressure is 139 psi.
9. **On all models,** difference between cylinders should not exceed 14 psi.
10. Connect distributor or crankshaft position sensor connector.
11. Install spark plugs and spark plug wires.
12. Erase diagnostic trouble code with scan tool or reconnect battery after ten seconds or more of disconnection. Code will set when crankshaft position sensor is disconnected.

ENGINE MOUNT
REPLACE
ENGINE

1. Using suitable floor jack, raise engine to release weight off mounts.

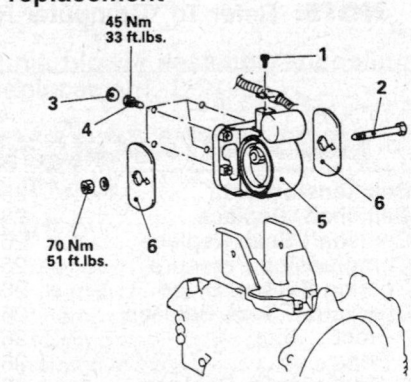

Removal steps
1. Engine harness attachment bolt
2. Transaxle mounting insulator attachment bolt
3. Cap
4. Transaxle mounting attachment bolt
5. Transaxle mounting bracket
6. Transaxle mounting stopper

Fig. 4 Transaxle mount replacement

2. Replace engine mounts in numbered sequence shown in **Fig. 2**, installing mounting stopper in direction shown, **Fig. 3**.

TRANSAXLE

1. Using suitable floor jack, raise transaxle to release weight off mounts.

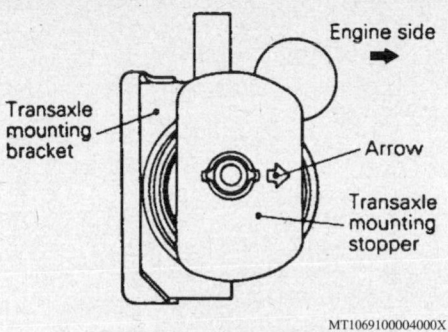

Fig. 5 Transaxle mounting stopper installation

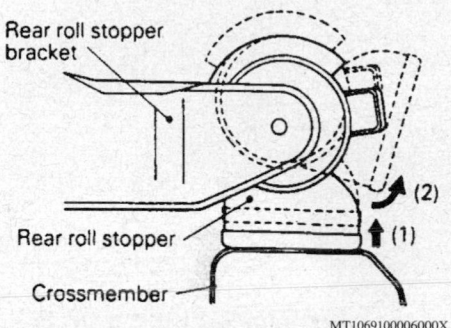

Fig. 7 Rotating roll stopper bracket

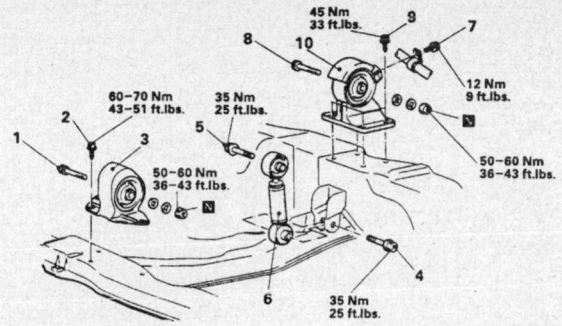

Removal steps for front roll stopper
1. Front roll stopper attachment bolt (engine side)
2. Front roll stopper attachment bolt (No.1 crossmember side)
3. Front roll stopper

Removal steps for engine damper
4. Engine damper lower attachment bolt
5. Engine damper upper attachment bolt
6. Engine damper

Removal steps for rear roll stopper
7. Hose installation bolt <Vehicles with 4WS>
8. Rear roll stopper attachment bolt (engine side)
9. Rear roll stopper attachment bolt (crossmember side)
10. Rear roll stopper

Fig. 6 Engine roll stopper & engine damper replacement

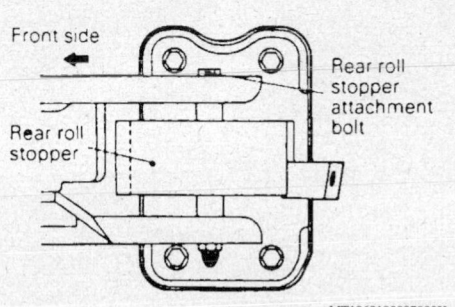

Fig. 8 Roll stopper bracket bolt installation

2. Replace transaxle mounts in numbered sequence shown in **Fig. 4**, installing mounting stopper in direction shown, **Fig. 5**.

ENGINE ROLL STOPPER & DAMPER

1. Using suitable floor jack raise transaxle to release weight off mounts.
2. Replace engine roll stopper and damper in numbered sequence shown in **Fig. 6**, turning roll stopper bracket in direction shown in **Fig. 7**.
3. Reverse procedure to install, installing rear roll stopper bracket and engine connection bolt as shown in **Fig. 8**.

ENGINE
REPLACE

1. Relieve fuel system pressure as outlined under "Precautions."
2. Mark and remove hood assembly.
3. Drain cooling system into a suitable container.
4. Remove front exhaust pipe.
5. Remove transaxle assembly as outlined under "Automatic Transaxle" section.
6. Remove radiator assembly.
7. Remove engine assembly from vehicle in numbered sequence shown in **Figs. 9 and 10**, noting the following:
   a. Remove power steering pump and air conditioner compressor and position aside, leaving hoses attached.
   b. Disconnect alternator wiring from engine compartment relay block.
   c. Support engine assembly using a suitable engine lifting device, then remove engine mounting bolts.
   d. After ensuring all hoses and electrical connections are disconnected, raise engine out of engine compartment.
8. Reverse procedure to install, installing engine mount bracket stopper as shown in **Fig. 3**.

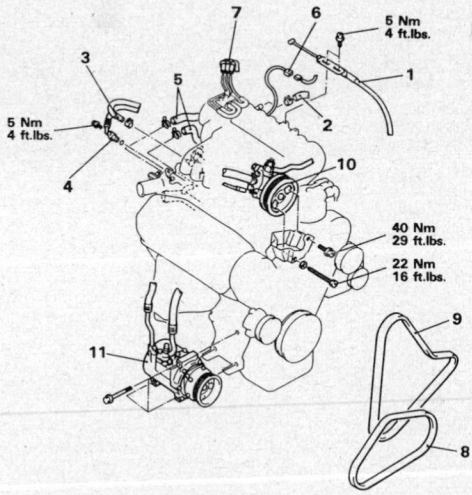

1. Accelerator cable connection
2. Brake booster vacuum hose connection
3. Fuel return hose connection
4. Fuel high pressure hose connection
5. Heater hose connection
6. EGR temperature sensor connector
7. Vacuum hose connector

● Adjustment Drive Belt Tension
8. Drive belt (air conditioning)
9. Drive belt (generator and power steering)
10. Power steering oil pump
11. Air conditioning compressor

Fig. 9 Engine assembly removal (Part 1 of 2). SOHC engine

12. ISC motor connector
12-1. Condenser connector
12-2. Ignition coil connector
13. TPS connector
14. Injector harness connector
15. Knock sensor connector
16. Air conditioning engine coolant
temperature switch connector

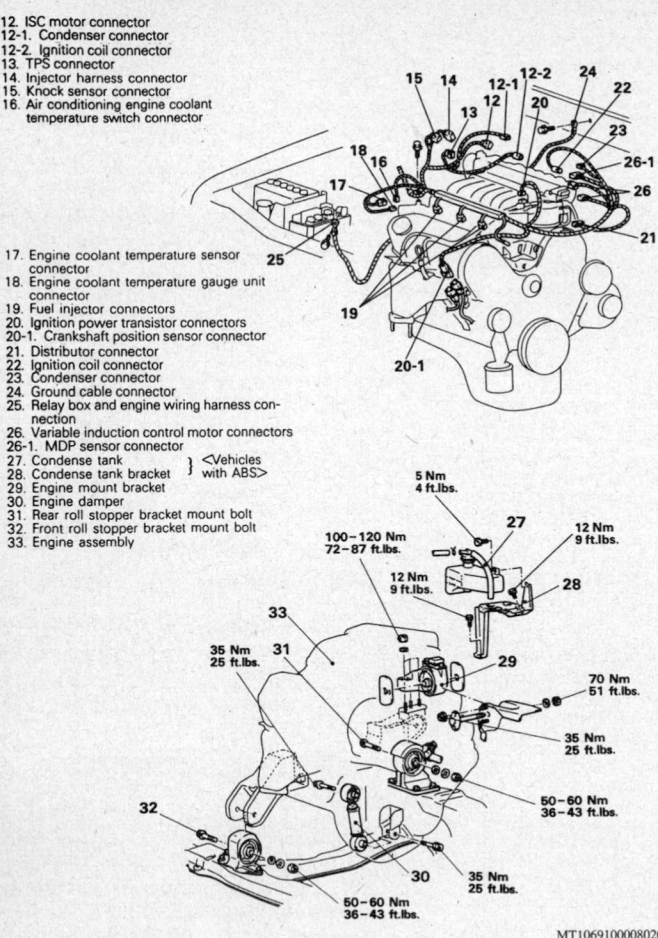

17. Engine coolant temperature sensor
connector
18. Engine coolant temperature gauge unit
connector
19. Fuel injector connectors
20. Ignition power transistor connectors
20-1. Crankshaft position sensor connector
21. Distributor connector
22. Ignition coil connector
23. Condenser connector
24. Ground cable connector
25. Relay box and engine wiring harness connection
26. Variable induction control motor connectors
26-1. MDP sensor connector
27. Condense tank   } <Vehicles
28. Condense tank bracket   with ABS>
29. Engine mount bracket
30. Engine damper
31. Rear roll stopper bracket mount bolt
32. Front roll stopper bracket mount bolt
33. Engine assembly

**Fig. 9   Engine assembly removal (Part 2 of 2).
SOHC engine**

INTAKE MANIFOLD
REPLACE

1. Release fuel system pressure as outlined under "Precautions."
2. Drain engine coolant, then remove
throttle body in numbered sequence
shown in **Fig. 11.**
3. Replace intake manifold plenum in
numbered sequence shown in **Fig. 12.**
4. Remove intake manifold in numbered
sequence shown in **Figs. 13 and 14.**
5. Reverse procedure to install, noting
the following:
  a. Refer to **Fig. 15** to identify intake
manifold front and rear banks.
  b. **Torque** intake manifold front bank
nuts to 4–6 ft. lbs.
  c. **Torque** intake manifold rear bank
nuts to 14–17 ft. lbs.
  d. **Torque** intake manifold front bank
nuts an additional 14–17 ft. lbs.
  e. **Torque** intake manifold rear bank
nuts an additional 14–17 ft. lbs.
  f. **Torque** intake manifold front bank
nuts an additional 14–17 ft. lbs.
  g. Install throttle body gasket as
shown in **Fig. 16.**

EXHAUST MANIFOLD
REPLACE

1. Release fuel system pressure as out-

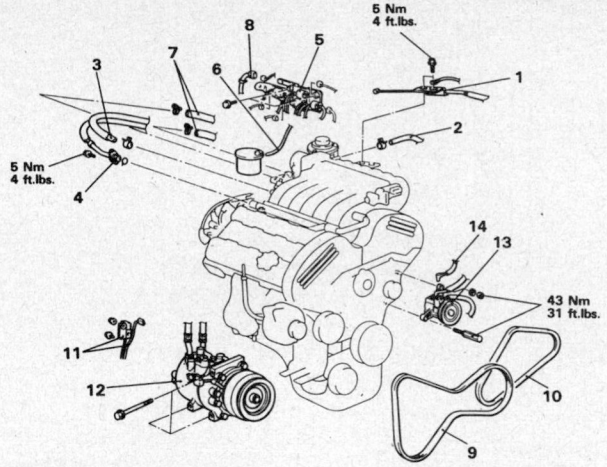

1. Accelerator cable connection
2. Brake booster vacuum hose connection
3. Fuel return hose connection
4. Fuel high pressure hose connection
5. Solenoid valve assembly
6. Vapor hose connection
7. Heater hose connection
8. EGR temperature sensor connector

9. Drive belt (Generator and air conditioning)
10. Drive belt (Power steering)
11. Generator harness connection
12. Air conditioning compressor
13. Power steering oil pump
14. Oil pressure switch connection
(Power steering)

MT1069100009010X

**Fig. 10   Engine assembly removal (Part 1 of 2).
DOHC engine**

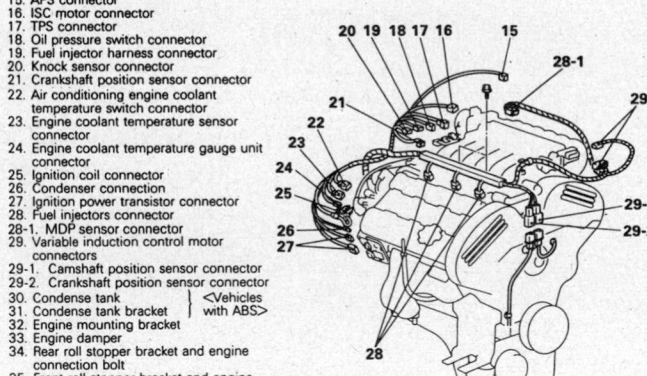

15. APS connector
16. ISC motor connector
17. TPS connector
18. Oil pressure switch connector
19. Fuel injector harness connector
20. Knock sensor connector
21. Crankshaft position sensor connector
22. Air conditioning engine coolant
temperature switch connector
23. Engine coolant temperature sensor
connector
24. Engine coolant temperature gauge unit
connector
25. Ignition coil connector
26. Condenser connection
27. Ignition power transistor connector
28. Fuel injectors connector
28-1. MDP sensor connector
29. Variable induction control motor
connectors
29-1. Camshaft position sensor connector
29-2. Crankshaft position sensor connector
30. Condense tank   } <Vehicles
31. Condense tank bracket   with ABS>
32. Engine mounting bracket
33. Engine damper
34. Rear roll stopper bracket and engine
connection bolt
35. Front roll stopper bracket and engine
connection bolt
36. Engine assembly

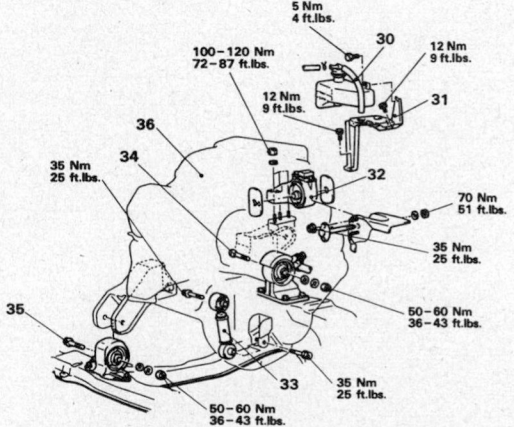

MT1069100009020X

**Fig. 10   Engine assembly removal (Part 2 of 2).
DOHC engine**

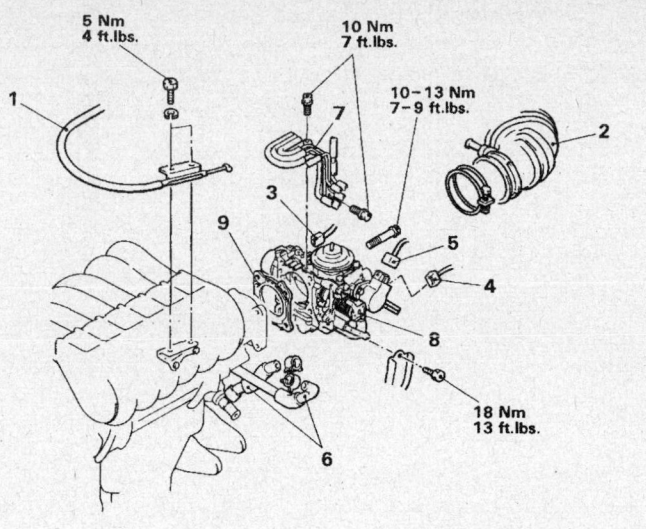

Removal steps

1. Accelerator cable connection
2. Air intake hose connection
3. TPS connector connection
4. ISC motor connector connection
5. APS connector connection
   <Vehicles with TCL>
6. Water hose connection
7. Vacuum pipe assembly
8. Throttle body
9. Gasket

MT1069300492000X

Fig. 11 Throttle body removal

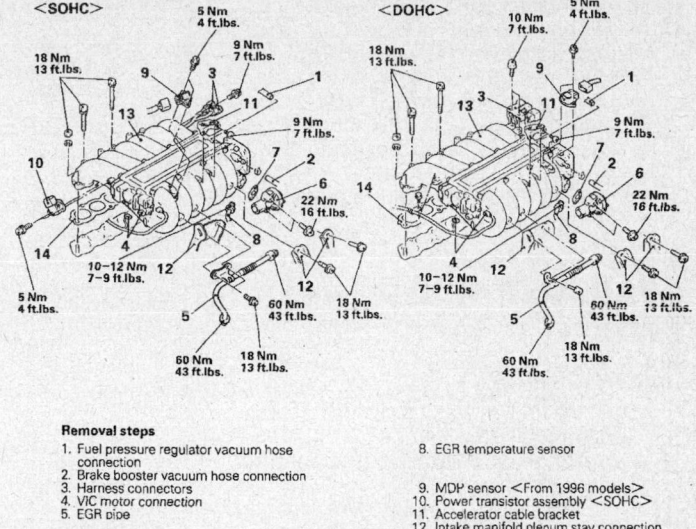

Removal steps

1. Fuel pressure regulator vacuum hose connection
2. Brake booster vacuum hose connection
3. Harness connectors
4. VIC motor connection
5. EGR pipe
6. EGR valve
7. EGR valve gasket
8. EGR temperature sensor
9. MDP sensor <From 1996 models>
10. Power transistor assembly <SOHC>
11. Accelerator cable bracket
12. Intake manifold plenum stay connection
13. Intake manifold plenum
14. Intake manifold plenum gasket

MT1069300493000X

Fig. 12 Intake manifold plenum removal

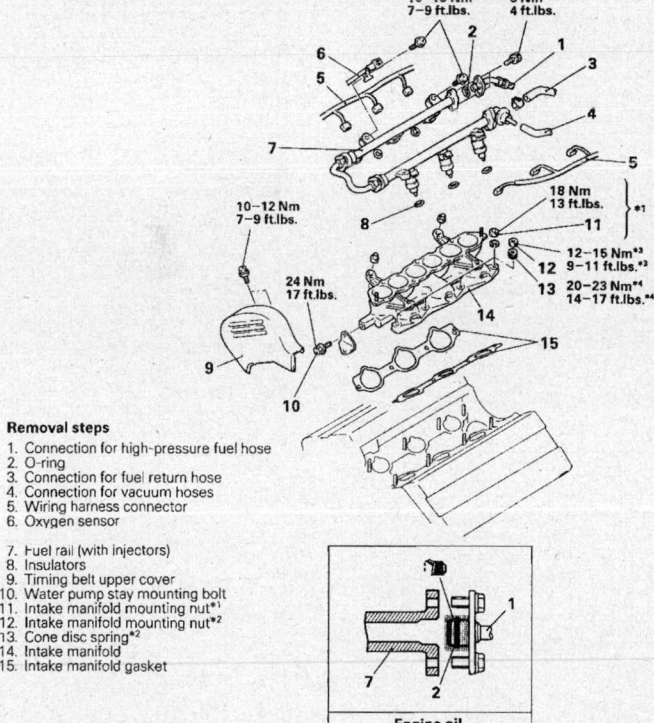

Removal steps

1. Connection for high-pressure fuel hose
2. O-ring
3. Connection for fuel return hose
4. Connection for vacuum hoses
5. Wiring harness connector
6. Oxygen sensor

7. Fuel rail (with injectors)
8. Insulators
9. Timing belt upper cover
10. Water pump stay mounting bolt
11. Intake manifold mounting nut*[1]
12. Intake manifold mounting nut*[2]
13. Cone disc spring*[2]
14. Intake manifold
15. Intake manifold gasket

MT1069300494000X

Fig. 13 Intake manifold replace. DOHC engine

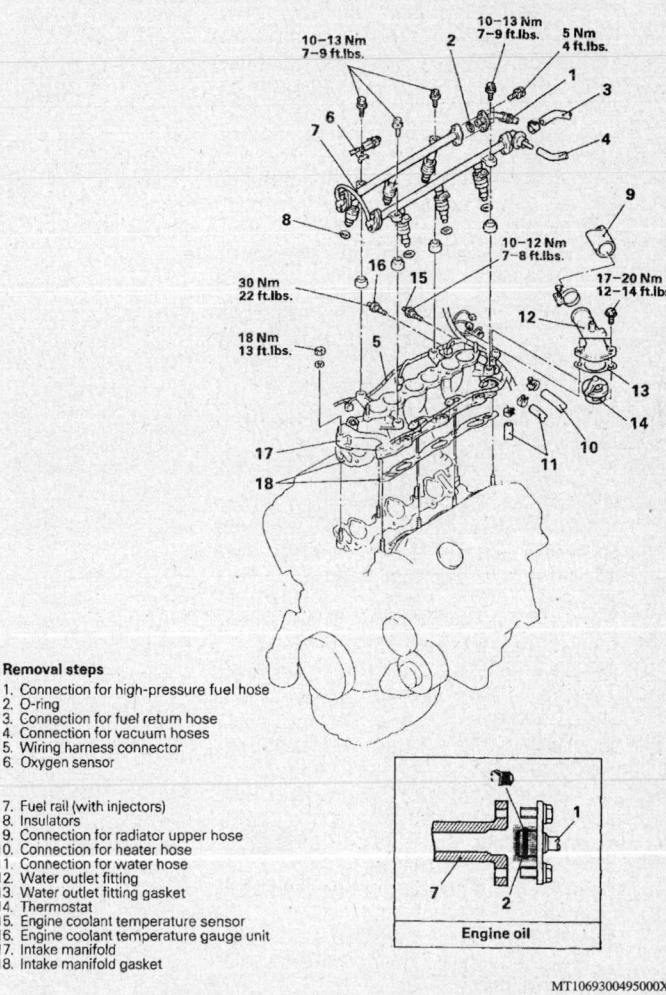

Removal steps

1. Connection for high-pressure fuel hose
2. O-ring
3. Connection for fuel return hose
4. Connection for vacuum hoses
5. Wiring harness connector
6. Oxygen sensor

7. Fuel rail (with injectors)
8. Insulators
9. Connection for radiator upper hose
10. Connection for heater hose
11. Connection for water hose
12. Water outlet fitting
13. Water outlet fitting gasket
14. Thermostat
15. Engine coolant temperature sensor
16. Engine coolant temperature gauge unit
17. Intake manifold
18. Intake manifold gasket

MT1069300495000X

Fig. 14 Intake manifold replace. SOHC engine

lined under "Precautions."

2. Replace exhaust manifold in numbered sequence shown in **Figs. 17 and 18,** noting the following:

a. **On models equipped with DOHC engine,** remove air conditioner compressor and position aside, leaving hoses attached.

b. **On all models,** disconnect front exhaust pipe.

CYLINDER HEAD

REPLACE

SOHC ENGINE

1. Relieve fuel system pressure as outlined under "Precautions."

2. Drain engine coolant into an approved container.

3. Remove exhaust manifold as outlined under "Exhaust Manifold, Replace."

4. Remove air plenum and intake manifold as outlined under "Air Plenum & Intake Manifold, Replace."

5. Remove timing belt as outlined under "Timing Belt, Replace."

6. Remove cylinder head in numbered sequence shown in **Fig. 19** using socket tool No. MD998051-01, or equivalent.

7. Reverse procedure to install, noting the following:

a. Lay cylinder head gasket on block with identification mark at front top, **Fig. 20.**

b. Install cylinder head bolt washers as shown in **Fig. 21.**

c. Using special socket tool and tightening sequence shown in **Fig. 21, torque** cylinder head bolts to 80 ft. lbs., in three steps.

DOHC ENGINE

1. Remove timing belt as outlined under "Timing Belt, Replace."

2. Remove camshafts as outlined under "Camshaft, Replace."

3. Remove exhaust manifolds as outlined under "Exhaust Manifold, Replace."

4. Drain engine coolant into an approved container.

5. Remove cylinder head in numbered sequence shown in **Fig. 22,** using cylinder head bolt wrench tool No. MD998051-01, or equivalent, to remove cylinder head bolts.

6. Using a suitable straightedge and feeler gauge, measure flatness of cylinder head and ensure head flatness is .0012 inch or less. If specification is exceeded, grind head no more than .008 inch.

7. Reverse numbered sequence shown in **Fig. 22** to install cylinder head, noting the following:

a. Lay cylinder head gasket on block with identification mark at front top, **Fig. 20.**

b. Using special socket tool and tightening sequence shown in **Fig. 23, torque** cylinder head bolts to 80 ft. lbs., in three steps.

c. Tighten valve cover bolts in se-

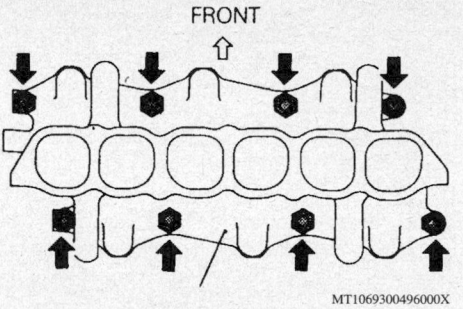

Fig. 15 Intake manifold bolt identification

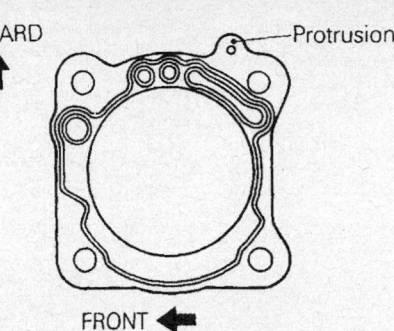

Fig. 16 Throttle body gasket installation

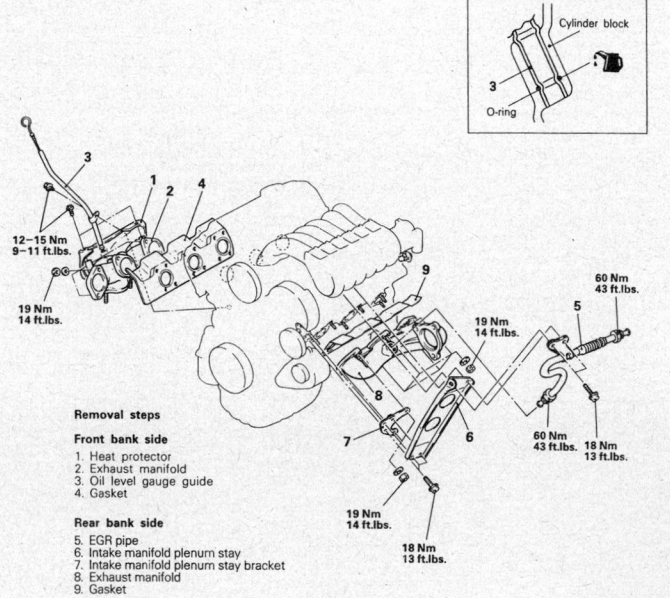

Removal steps

Front bank side
1. Heat protector
2. Exhaust manifold
3. Oil level gauge guide
4. Gasket

Rear bank side
5. EGR pipe
6. Intake manifold plenum stay
7. Intake manifold plenum stay bracket
8. Exhaust manifold
9. Gasket

Fig. 17 Exhaust manifold replacement. SOHC engine

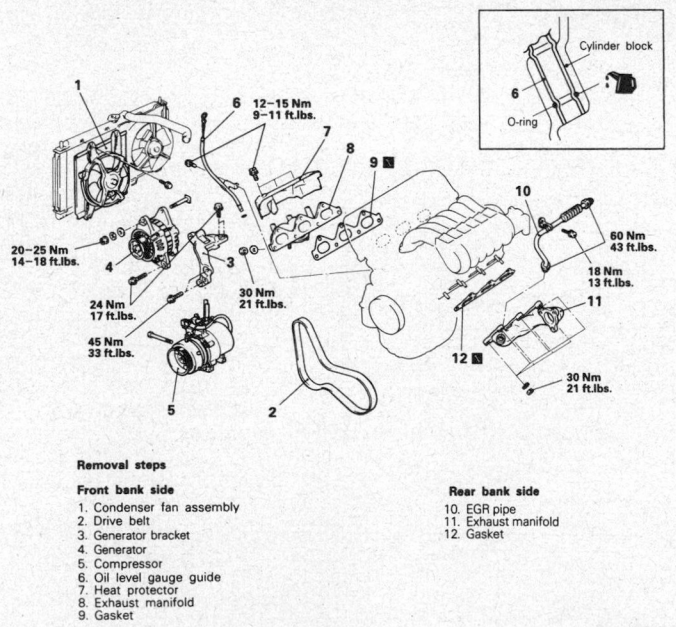

Removal steps

Front bank side
1. Condenser fan assembly
2. Drive belt
3. Generator bracket
4. Generator
5. Compressor
6. Oil level gauge guide
7. Heat protector
8. Exhaust manifold
9. Gasket

Rear bank side
10. EGR pipe
11. Exhaust manifold
12. Gasket

Fig. 18 Exhaust manifold replacement. DOHC engine

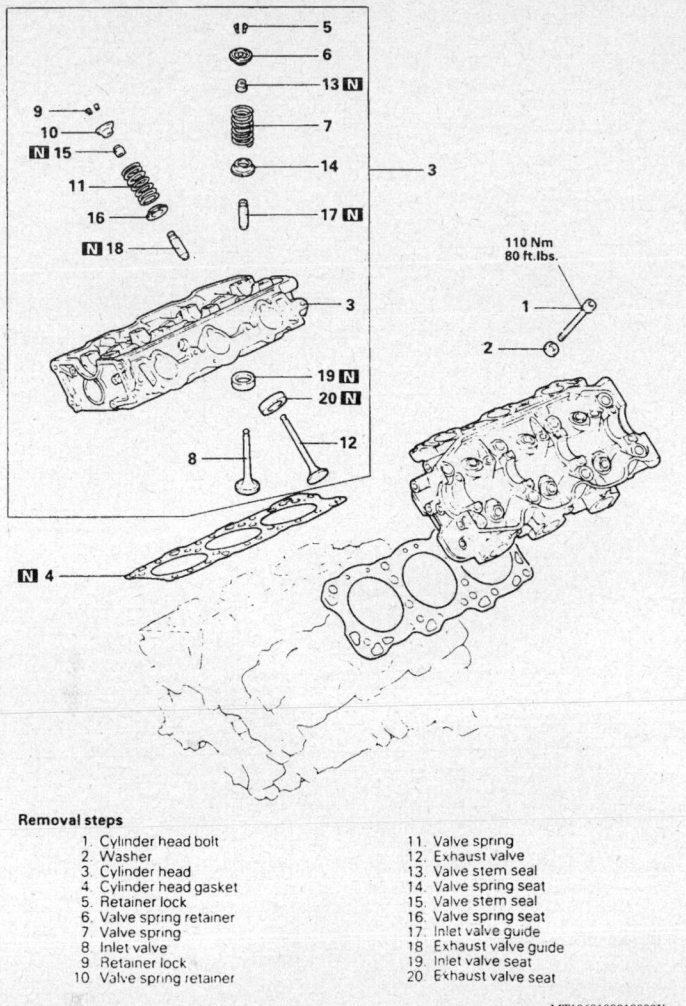

Removal steps

1. Cylinder head bolt
2. Washer
3. Cylinder head
4. Cylinder head gasket
5. Retainer lock
6. Valve spring retainer
7. Valve spring
8. Inlet valve
9. Retainer lock
10. Valve spring retainer
11. Valve spring
12. Exhaust valve
13. Valve stem seal
14. Valve spring seat
15. Valve stem seal
16. Valve spring seat
17. Inlet valve guide
18. Exhaust valve guide
19. Inlet valve seat
20. Exhaust valve seat

MT1069100010000X

Fig. 19 Cylinder head & valve replacement. SOHC engine

quence shown in **Fig. 24.** Install black colored bolts on engine front bank and green colored bolts on rear bank. Bolt No. 5 is longer than other bolts used.

VALVE ARRANGEMENT

Intake valves are on inside of cylinder head and exhaust valves are on outside of cylinder head.

VALVE CLEARANCE SPECIFICATIONS

Stem-To-Guide Clearance, Inch①

Intake	Exhaust
SOHC ENGINE	
.0012–.0024	.0020–.0035
DOHC ENGINE	
.0008–.0020	.0020–.0035

① — Not adjustable.

VALVE ADJUSTMENT

Automatic lash adjusters are used; therefore no adjustment is necessary.

ROCKER ARMS

SOHC ENGINE

1. Release fuel system pressure as outlined under "Precautions."
2. Remove timing belt as outlined under "Timing Belt, Replace."
3. Remove camshaft sprocket bolt using end yoke holder tool No. MB990767 and MD998719, or equivalents.
4. Attach lash adjuster retainer tool No. MD998443-01, or equivalent, before removing rocker assembly.
5. Remove camshaft and rocker arms in numbered sequence shown in **Fig. 25,** noting the following:
   a. Immerse lash adjuster in clean diesel fuel. Using small wire, move plunger up and down four to five times while pushing down lightly on check ball to bleed out air. Install lash adjuster into cylinder head.
   b. Apply sealant at four places shown in **Fig. 26.** Ensure sealant does not contact cam journal surface.
   c. Install rocker arms, shafts and bearing caps so mark on bearing cap faces same direction as arrow mark on cylinder head, **Fig. 27.**

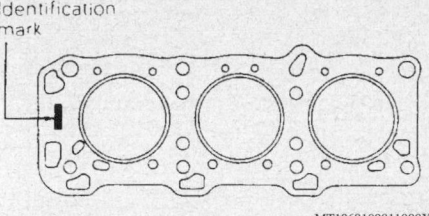

MT1069100011000X

Fig. 20 Cylinder head gasket identification mark

d. Install camshaft oil seal as outlined under "Camshaft Seal, Replace."
e. Install a .020 inch spacer onto circular packing driver tool No. MD998714-01, or equivalent, then install circular packing.

DOHC ENGINE

1. Release fuel system pressure as outlined under "Precautions."
2. Remove timing belt as outlined under "Timing Belt, Replace."
3. Remove camshaft oil seal as outlined under "Camshaft, Replace."
4. Replace rocker arm and camshaft in numbered sequence shown in **Fig. 28,** noting the following:
   a. Immerse lash adjuster in clean diesel fuel. Using small wire, move plunger up and down four to five times while pushing down lightly on check ball to bleed out air. Install lash adjuster into cylinder head.
   b. Turn crankshaft to bring No. 1 cylinder to TDC.
   c. Ensure rocker arm is installed correctly on valve lash adjuster and valve.
   d. Install camshaft noting identification mark stamped on hexagonal section. Camshaft marked with a V is intake side and camshaft marked with a D is exhaust side.
   e. Install camshafts with their dowel pins positioned as shown in **Fig. 29.**
   f. Install bearing caps noting identification mark and cap number. Bearing caps Nos. 2, 3 and 4 bear front mark. Install these caps with mark lined up with front mark on cylinder head. Caps marked with a " I" are for intake side and caps marked with an " E" are exhaust side.
   g. Tighten bearing cap bolts gradually in two or three steps and finally tighten to specification.
   h. Using circular packing installer tool No. MD998762, or equivalent, install circular packing.

TIMING BELT
REPLACE

With the timing belt removed, avoid turning the camshaft or crankshaft. If movement is required, exercise extreme caution to avoid valve damage caused by piston contact.

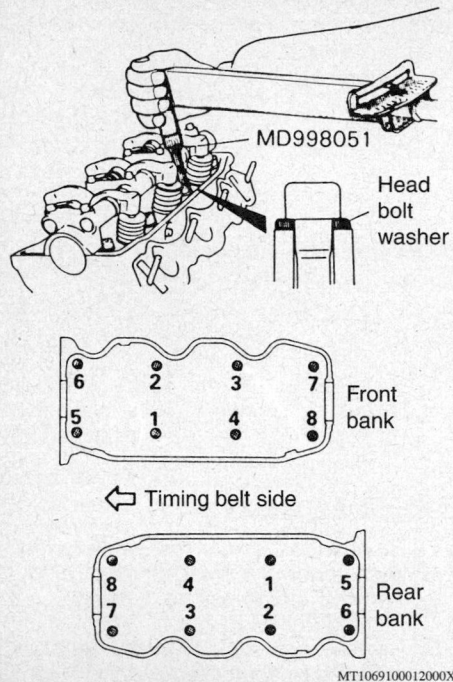

Head bolt washer

Front bank

← Timing belt side

Rear bank

MT1069100012000X

Fig. 21 Cylinder head bolt tightening sequence. SOHC engine

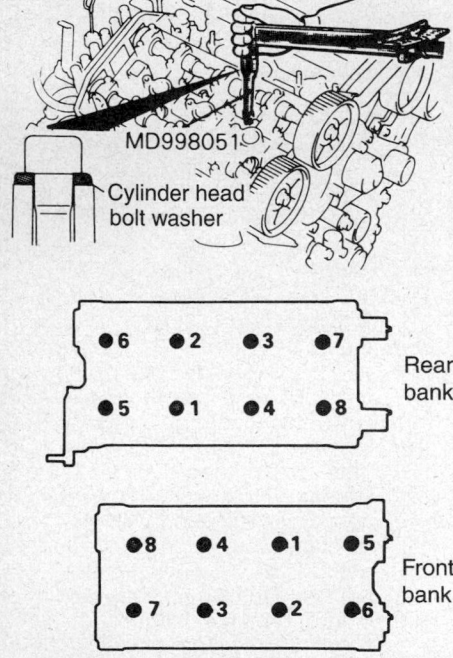

Cylinder head bolt washer

Rear bank

Front bank

MT1069800530000X

Fig. 23 Cylinder head bolt tightening sequence. DOHC engine

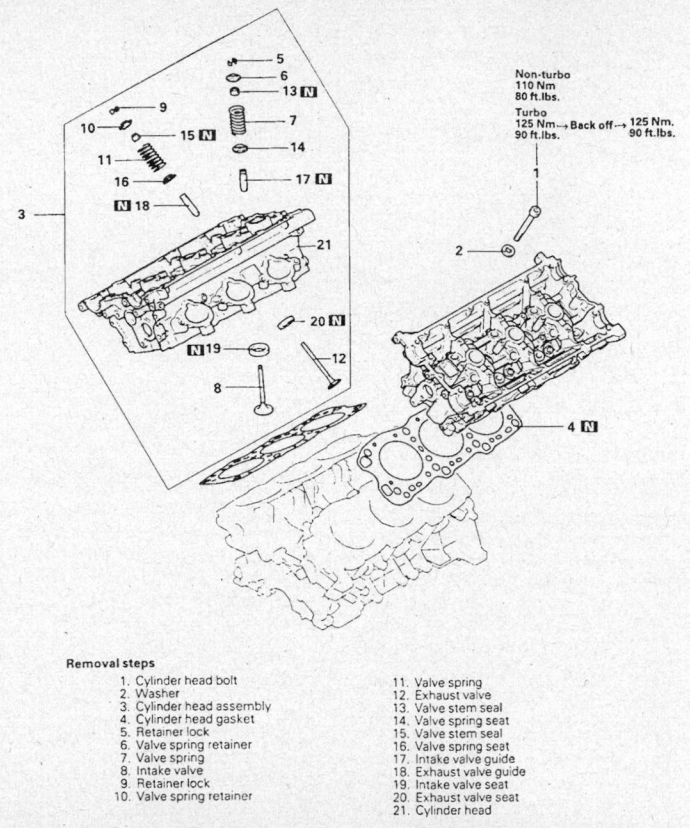

Removal steps

1. Cylinder head bolt
2. Washer
3. Cylinder head assembly
4. Cylinder head gasket
5. Retainer lock
6. Valve spring retainer
7. Valve spring
8. Intake valve
9. Retainer lock
10. Valve spring retainer
11. Valve spring
12. Exhaust valve
13. Valve stem seal
14. Valve spring seat
15. Valve stem seal
16. Valve spring seat
17. Intake valve guide
18. Exhaust valve guide
19. Intake valve seat
20. Exhaust valve seat
21. Cylinder head

MT1069100013000X

Fig. 22 Cylinder head & valve replacement. DOHC engine

Rear bank

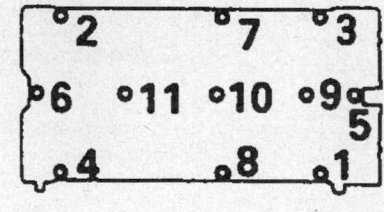

Front bank

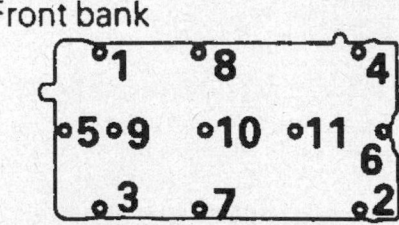

MT1069100014000X

Fig. 24 Valve cover bolt tightening sequence. DOHC engine

SOHC ENGINE

Removal

1. Release fuel system pressure as outlined under "Precautions."
2. Remove engine lower cover.
3. Raise and support engine, ensure weight is lifted off mounts.
4. Remove A/C and power steering/alternator drive belts.
5. Remove A/C tension pulley assembly and bracket.
6. Disconnect power steering switch connector, the remove power steering pump, suspend pump aside with wire, leave hoses attached.
7. Slightly raise engine and remove engine support bracket.
8. Raise engine slightly, then remove engine support bracket in reverse numbered sequence shown in **Fig. 30**, spraying lubricant on reamer bolt while slowly removing.
9. Using yoke holder tool No. MB990767 and crankshaft holder pins No. MD998719, or equivalents, remove crankshaft pulley.
10. Remove timing belt cover cap, upper front covers, lower cover and flange, **Fig. 31**.
11. Rotate engine to position No. 1 cylinder at TDC on compression stroke and align timing marks, **Figs. 32 and 33**.
12. Mark rotational direction of engine on timing belt.
13. Loosen timing belt tensioner bolt, then using a suitable screwdriver, turn tensioner counterclockwise to release belt tension, tighten tensioner bolt.
14. Remove timing belt.

Installation

1. Align timing marks, **Figs. 32 and 33**.
2. Keeping belt tight between each sprocket, install timing belt in the following order:
   a. Onto crankshaft sprocket.
   b. Over lefthand camshaft sprocket.
   c. Onto water pump pulley.
   d. Over righthand camshaft sprocket.
   e. Over tensioner pulley.
3. Install flange onto front end of crankshaft.

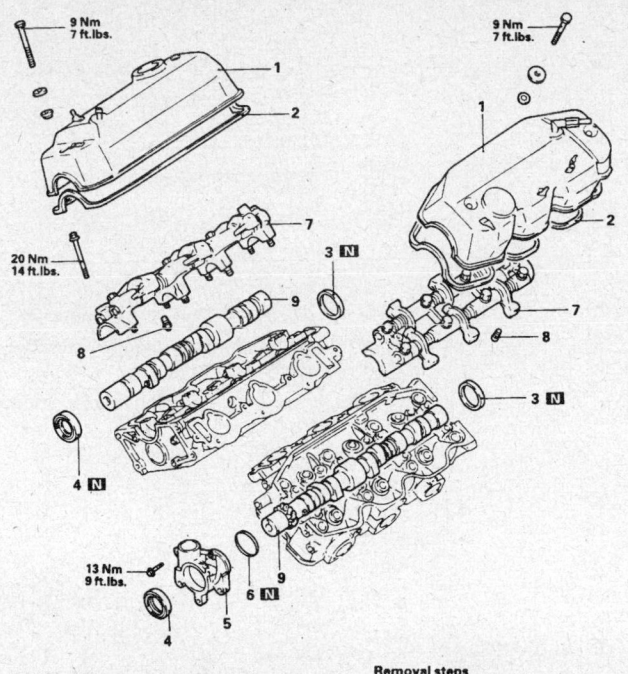

Fig. 26 Applying sealant to cylinder head. SOHC engine

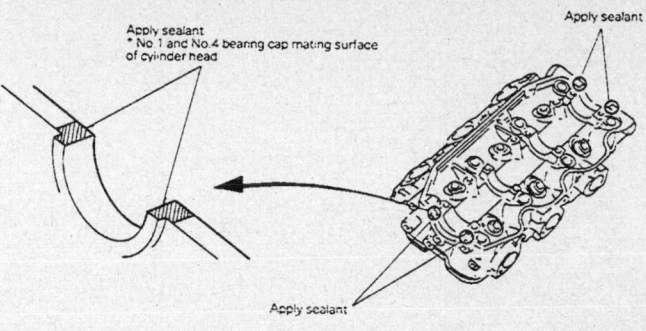

Removal steps
1. Rocker cover
2. Gasket
3. Circular packing
4. Camshaft oil seal
5. Distributor adaptor
6. O-ring
7. Rocker arms, shafts and bearing caps
8. Lash adjuster
9. Camshaft

MT1069100030000X

Fig. 25 Camshaft & rocker arm replacement. SOHC engine

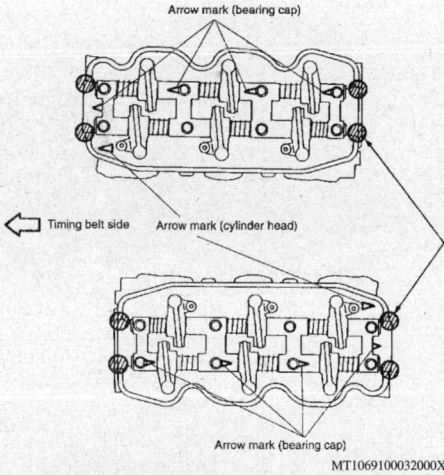

Arrow mark (bearing cap)

Timing belt side   Arrow mark (cylinder head)

Arrow mark (bearing cap)

MT1069100032000X

Fig. 27 Camshaft bearing caps installation. SOHC engine

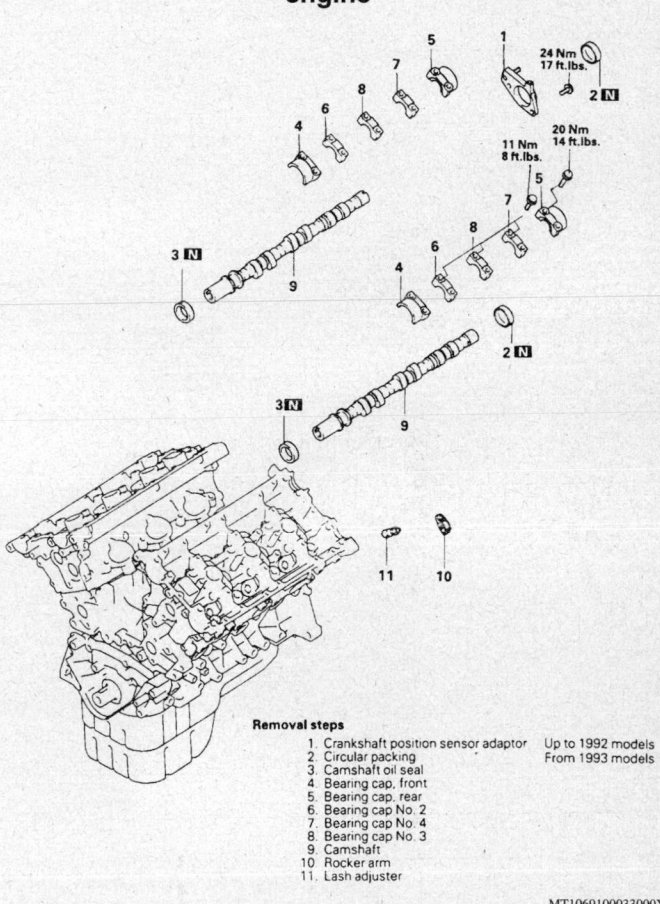

Removal steps
1. Crankshaft position sensor adaptor — Up to 1992 models
2. Circular packing — From 1993 models
3. Camshaft oil seal
4. Bearing cap, front
5. Bearing cap, rear
6. Bearing cap No. 2
7. Bearing cap No. 4
8. Bearing cap No. 3
9. Camshaft
10. Rocker arm
11. Lash adjuster

MT1069100033000X

Fig. 28 Camshaft & rocker arms replacement. DOHC engine

4. Install crankshaft wrench tool No. M998716-01, or equivalent, onto crankshaft.
5. Loosen tensioner lock bolt one or two turns and allow spring to tension timing belt.
6. Turn crankshaft two full turns clockwise. **Do not turn crankshaft counterclockwise as damage to valve components or pistons may occur.**
7. Align timing marks, **Figs. 32 and 33,** then tighten tensioner lock bolt to specification.
8. Measure timing belt tension using a suitable belt tension gauge. Belt tension should be 44.1–66.1 lbs.

9. Adjust timing belt as follows:
10. Install timing belt cover bolts as shown in **Fig. 34.**
11. Tighten crankshaft pulley using end yoke holder tools No. MD990767-01 and MD998719, or equivalents.
12. Install engine support bracket in numbered sequence shown in **Fig. 30.** Note bolt size when installing.
13. Install engine mount bracket stopper as shown in **Fig. 3.**

DOHC ENGINE
Removal

1. Release fuel system pressure as out-

lined under "Precautions."
2. Remove engine undercover.
3. Remove alternator as outlined under "Alternator, Replace" in "Electrical."
4. Raise and support engine ensuring weight is lifted off mounts.
5. Rotate engine to position No. 1 cylinder at top dead center on compression stroke to align (TDC) timing marks, **Fig. 35.**
6. Remove timing belt in numbered sequence shown in **Fig. 36,** noting the following:
   a. Secure camshaft pulley using end yoke holder tools No. MB990767-01 and MD998719, or equivalents, then remove crankshaft pulley bolt.
   b. Remove engine support bracket in

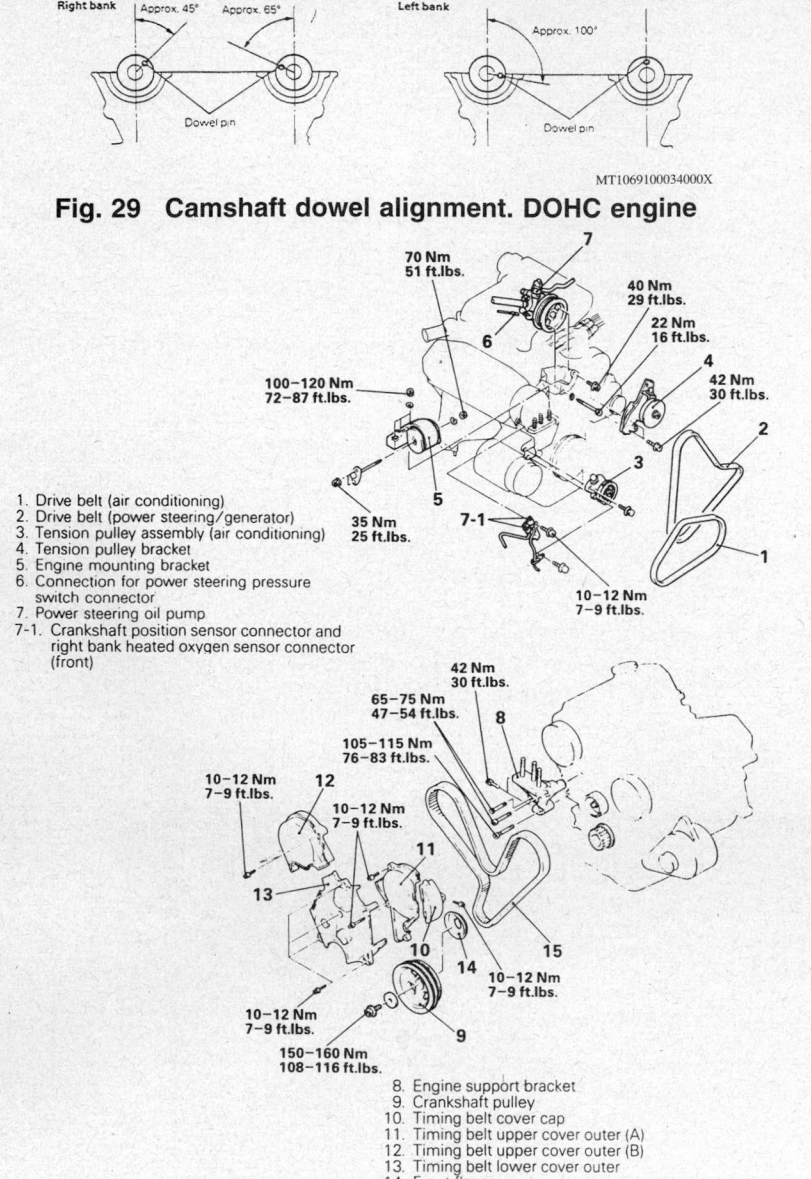

Fig. 29 Camshaft dowel alignment. DOHC engine

Fig. 31 Timing belt replacement. SOHC engine

1. Drive belt (air conditioning)
2. Drive belt (power steering/generator)
3. Tension pulley assembly (air conditioning)
4. Tension pulley bracket
5. Engine mounting bracket
6. Connection for power steering pressure switch connector
7. Power steering oil pump
7-1. Crankshaft position sensor connector and right bank heated oxygen sensor connector (front)

8. Engine support bracket
9. Crankshaft pulley
10. Timing belt cover cap
11. Timing belt upper cover outer (A)
12. Timing belt upper cover outer (B)
13. Timing belt lower cover outer
14. Front flange
• Adjustment of timing belt tension
15. Timing belt

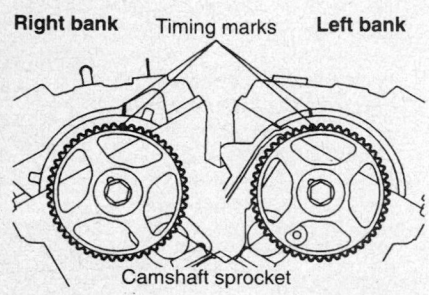

Right bank   Timing marks   Left bank

Camshaft sprocket

Fig. 33 Camshaft sprocket timing mark alignment. SOHC engine

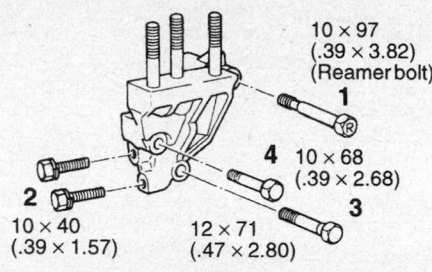

10 × 97 (.39 × 3.82) (Reamer bolt) **1**
10 × 68 (.39 × 2.68) **3**
10 × 40 (.39 × 1.57) **2**
12 × 71 (.47 × 2.80)
4

Thread diameter × length   mm (in.)

Fig. 30 Engine support bracket replacement

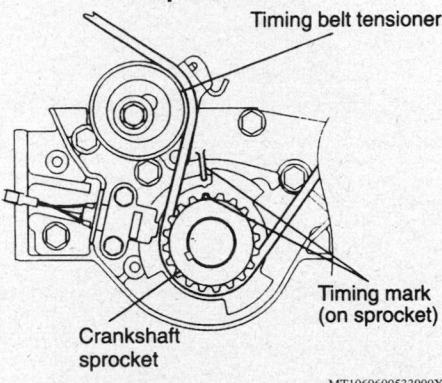

Timing belt tensioner

Timing mark (on sprocket)

Crankshaft sprocket

Fig. 32 Crankshaft sprocket timing mark alignment. SOHC engine

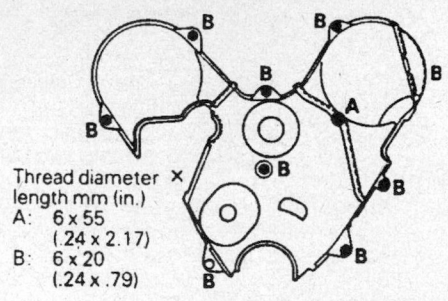

Thread diameter × length mm (in.)
A: 6 × 55 (.24 x 2.17)
B: 6 × 20 (.24 x .79)

Fig. 34 Timing belt cover bolt location. SOHC engine

reverse numbered sequence shown in **Fig. 30,** spraying lubricant on reamer bolt while slowly removing.

c. Mark rotational direction of engine on timing belt.
d. Loosen timing belt tensioner pulley center bolt, then remove timing belt.

Installation

Reverse numbered sequence shown in **Fig. 36** to install, noting the following:
1. Align timing marks, **Fig. 35.**
2. Install auto tensioner as follows:
   a. Clamp auto tensioner level and clamp in a soft jawed vise, **Fig. 37.**
   b. Close vise slowly until set hole in rod (A) is aligned with hole in cylinder (B).
   c. Insert a .055 inch diameter wire into set holes.
   d. Remove tensioner from vise and install onto engine.
3. With timing marks aligned, install timing belt as follows keeping belt tight between each sprocket:
   a. Shift timing mark on crankshaft sprocket by three teeth to lower position on No. 1 cylinder slightly from TDC position on compression stroke. **Turning camshaft sprocket with piston in No. 1 cylinder at TDC may cause valves to interfere with piston.**
   b. Ensure timing marks on camshaft sprockets for intake and exhaust valves are not within range A in **Fig. 38.** If timing mark is within range A, turn camshaft sprocket to move

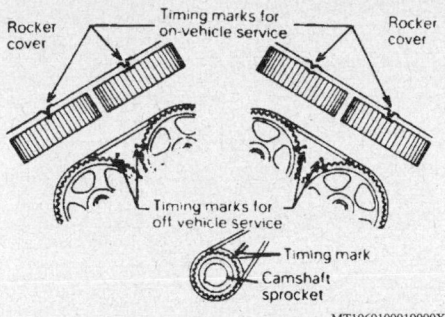

Fig. 35 Timing mark alignment. DOHC engine

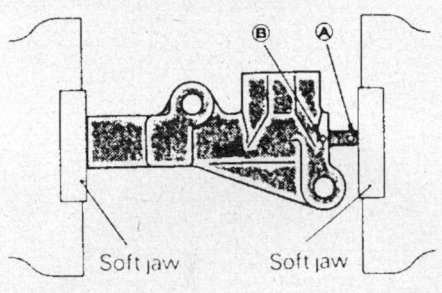

Fig. 37 Auto tensioner set holes. DOHC engine

timing mark to area closest to range A. **In range A, cam lobe on camshaft lifts valve through rocker arm and camshaft sprocket is apt to rotate by reaction force of valve spring. Use care not pinch finger between sprockets.**

c. Turn camshaft sprocket for either intake or exhaust valve to locate timing mark as shown in **Fig. 39**, then turn other camshaft to locate timing mark as shown. **If intake and exhaust valves of same cylinder lift at same time, interference with each other may result. Therefore, turn intake valve camshaft sprocket and exhaust valve camshaft alternately.**

d. Turn camshaft sprocket clockwise to align timing marks. If camshaft sprocket has been turned excessively, turn it counterclockwise to align timing marks.

e. Align timing mark of crankshaft sprocket. **Shift timing mark of crankshaft sprocket one tooth in counterclockwise direction to aid in belt installation.**

f. Using spring loaded binder clips, secure camshaft sprockets with suitable box end wrenches, then install timing belt in following order, ensuring not to allow belt to slack: (1) Front exhaust camshaft to (2) front intake camshaft to (3) water pump to (4) rear intake camshaft to (5) rear exhaust camshaft to (6) idler pulley to (7) crankshaft to (8) tensioner pulley, **Fig. 40.**

g. Turn tensioner pulley so that its pin holes are located above center bolt, then press tensioner pulley against

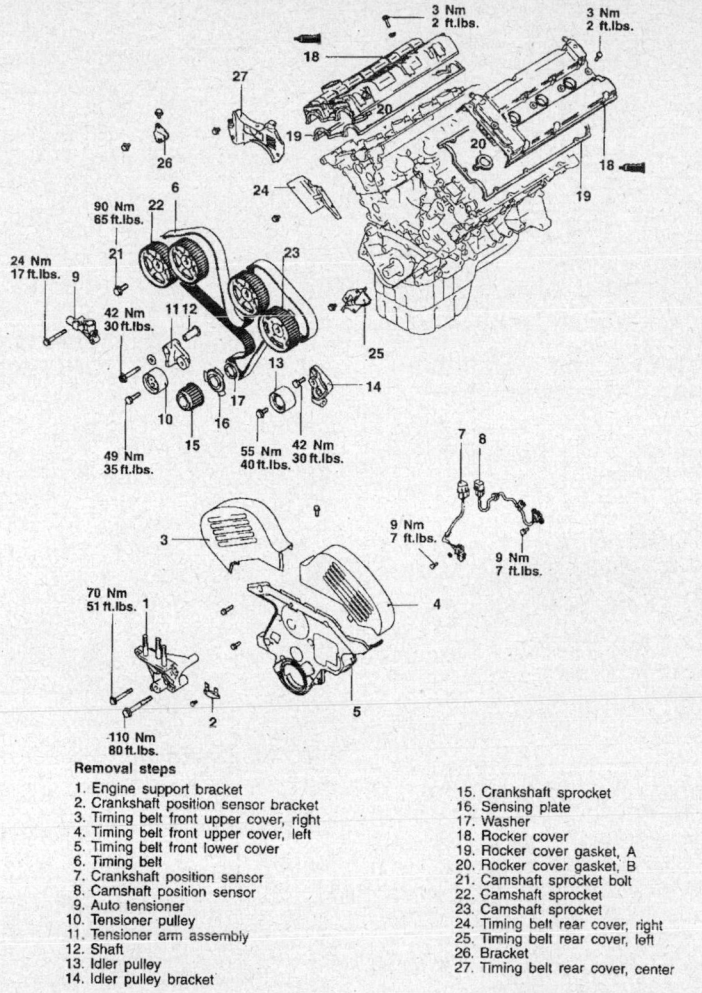

Removal steps
1. Engine support bracket
2. Crankshaft position sensor bracket
3. Timing belt front upper cover, right
4. Timing belt front upper cover, left
5. Timing belt front lower cover
6. Timing belt
7. Crankshaft position sensor
8. Camshaft position sensor
9. Auto tensioner
10. Tensioner pulley
11. Tensioner arm assembly
12. Shaft
13. Idler pulley
14. Idler pulley bracket
15. Crankshaft sprocket
16. Sensing plate
17. Washer
18. Rocker cover
19. Rocker cover gasket, A
20. Rocker cover gasket, B
21. Camshaft sprocket bolt
22. Camshaft sprocket
23. Camshaft sprocket
24. Timing belt rear cover, right
25. Timing belt rear cover, left
26. Bracket
27. Timing belt rear cover, center

Fig. 36 Timing belt replacement. DOHC engine

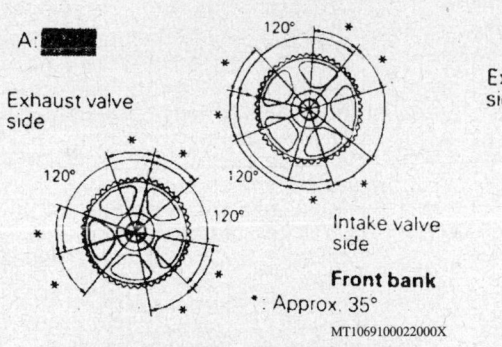

Fig. 38 Camshaft alignment positions. DOHC engine

timing belt and, at same time, temporarily tighten center bolt **Fig. 41.**

h. Ensure all timing marks are still aligned properly.

i. Remove paper clips.

4. Adjust timing belt as follows:
a. Rotate crankshaft ¼ turn counterclockwise, then rotate crankshaft clockwise until timing marks are aligned.

b. Loosen center bolt on tensioner pulley. Using tensioner pulley socket wrench tool No. MD998767, or

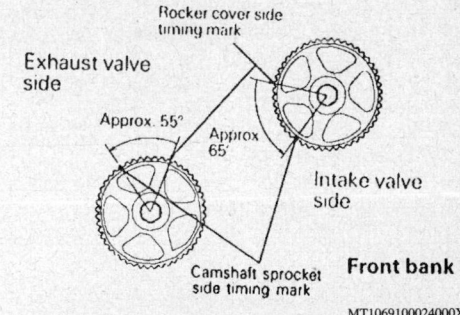

Fig. 39 Timing mark alignment. DOHC engine

equivalent, and torque wrench, apply 7 ft. lbs. tension to timing belt and, at same time, tighten tensioner center bolt.

c. Remove set pin from auto tensioner. At this time, ensure set pin can be easily removed.

d. Rotate crankshaft two turns clockwise and let stand for five minutes or more.

e. Again ensure set pin can be easily removed from, and installed to, auto tensioner. If set pin cannot be

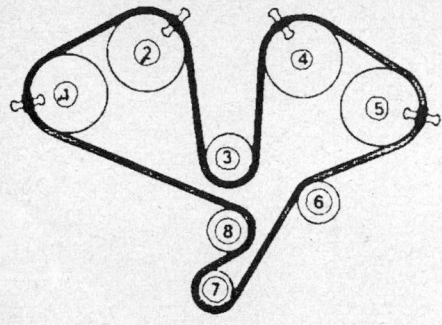

Fig. 40 Timing belt installation. DOHC engine

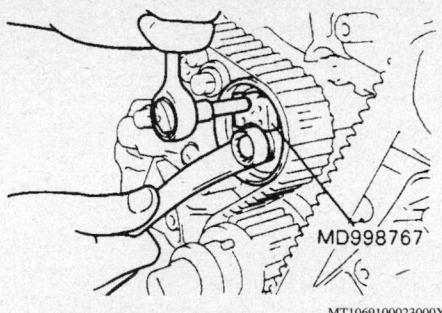

Fig. 41 Tensioner pulley adjustment. DOHC engine

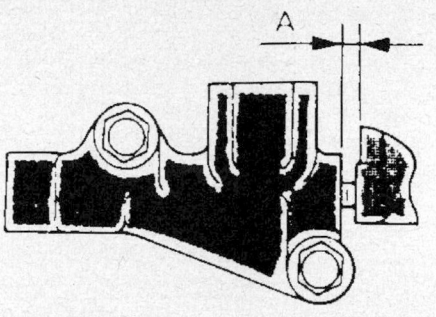

Fig. 42 Auto tensioner rod protrusion. DOHC engine

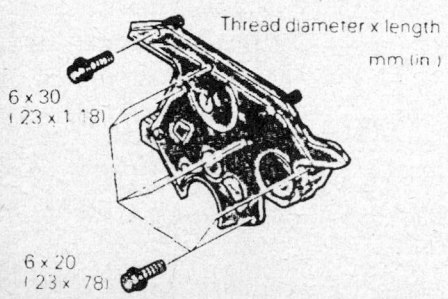

Fig. 43 Timing belt lower cover bolt location. DOHC engine

Fig. 44 Securing camshaft. DOHC engine

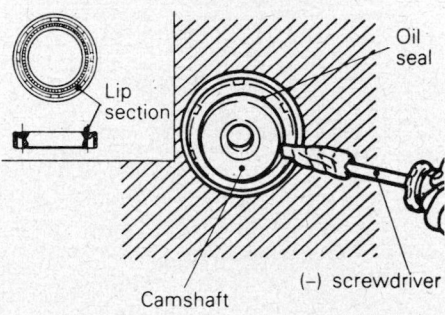

Fig. 45 Oil seal removal

easily inserted, auto tensioner is normal if its rod protrusion is within .149–.177 inch, **Fig. 42**. If protrusion is out of specification, repeat procedure.

   f. Ensure timing marks on all sprockets are aligned properly.

5. Install timing belt cover bolts as shown in **Fig. 43**.
6. Install engine support bracket in numbered sequence shown in **Fig. 30**. Note bolt size when installing.
7. Tighten crankshaft pulley using end yoke holder tools No. MD990767-01 and MD998719, or equivalents.
8. Install engine mount bracket stopper as shown in **Fig. 3**.

CAMSHAFT

REPLACE

Refer to "Rocker Arms, Replace" in this section for camshaft replacement procedures.

CAMSHAFT SEAL

REPLACE

1. Release fuel system pressure as outlined under "Precautions."
2. Remove timing belt as outlined under "Timing Belt, Replace."
3. **On models equipped with SOHC engine,** remove camshaft sprocket bolt using end yoke holder tool No. MB990767 and MD998719, or equivalents.
4. **On models equipped with DOHC engine,** remove rocker covers. Remove camshaft sprocket bolts by securing

camshaft with a suitable wrench as shown, **Fig. 44**.
5. **On all models,** cut out a portion in camshaft oil seal lip, **Fig. 45**.
6. Cover tip of a suitable screwdriver with a clean soft cloth and pry out seal at cut out portion of seal. **Use care not to damage camshaft or cylinder head.**
7. Lift camshaft from engine.
8. Reverse procedure to install, noting the following:
   a. Install oil seals using seal installation tool, No. MD998713-01, or equivalent, on SOHC engine or tool No. MD998761, or equivalent, on DOHC engine.
   b. **On models equipped with DOHC engine,** tighten rocker cover bolts in sequence shown in **Fig. 24**. Install black colored bolts on engine front bank and green colored bolts on rear bank. Bolt No. 5 is longer than other bolts used.

PISTON & ROD ASSEMBLY

1. Release fuel system pressure as outlined under "Precautions."
2. Drain engine coolant into an approved container.
3. Remove engine assembly as outlined under "Engine, Replace."
4. Remove timing belt as outlined under "Timing Belt, Replace."
5. Remove exhaust manifolds as outlined under "Exhaust Manifold, Replace."
6. Remove air plenum and intake manifold as outlined under " Intake Manifold, Replace."

7. Remove cylinder head as outlined under "Cylinder Head, Replace."
8. Remove engine oil pan.
9. Replace piston and connecting rod in numbered sequence shown in **Fig. 46**.
10. Reverse procedure to install.

CRANKSHAFT SEAL

REPLACE

FRONT

1. Release fuel system pressure as outlined under "Precautions."
2. Remove timing belt as outlined under "Timing Belt, Replace."
3. Remove crankshaft position sensor.
4. Remove crankshaft sprocket.
5. Remove crankshaft sensing blade and spacer key.
6. Cut out a portion in crankshaft oil seal lip, **Fig. 45**.
7. Cover tip of a suitable screwdriver with a clean soft cloth and pry out seal at cut out portion of seal. **Use care not to damage crankshaft or oil pump case.**
8. Reverse procedure to install, using seal installer tool No. MD998717, or equivalent, to install oil seal.

REAR

1. Release fuel system pressure as outlined under "Precautions."
2. Remove transaxle.
3. Secure crankshaft using end yoke holder tool No. MD998719, or equivalent, on SOHC engine or No. MD998754, or equivalent, on DOHC engine.
4. Remove adapter and driveplates.

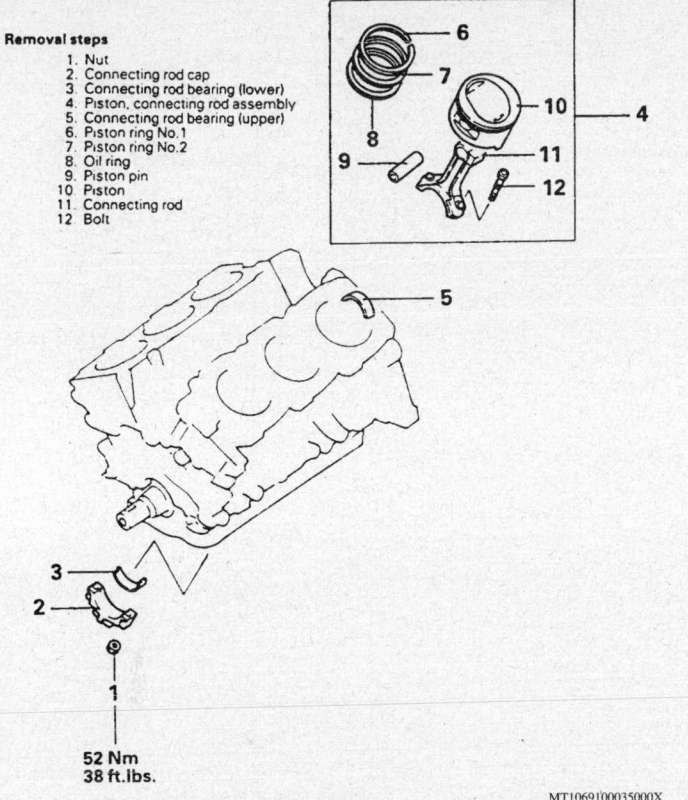

Removal steps
1. Nut
2. Connecting rod cap
3. Connecting rod bearing (lower)
4. Piston, connecting rod assembly
5. Connecting rod bearing (upper)
6. Piston ring No.1
7. Piston ring No.2
8. Oil ring
9. Piston pin
10. Piston
11. Connecting rod
12. Bolt

52 Nm
38 ft.lbs.

MT10691000035000X

Fig. 46   Piston & connecting rod replacement

23 Nm 17 ft.lbs.
24 Nm 17 ft.lbs.
75 Nm 55 ft.lbs.
13 Nm 10 ft.lbs.
24 Nm 17 ft.lbs.
55 Nm 40 ft.lbs.
75 Nm 55 ft.lbs.
10 Nm 8 ft.lbs.
19 Nm 14 ft.lbs.
10 Nm 8 ft.lbs.
14 Nm 11 ft.lbs.
19 Nm 14 ft.lbs.
45 Nm 33 ft.lbs.
40 Nm 29 ft.lbs.
6 Nm 5 ft.lbs.

Removal steps
1. Transmission stay, right
2. Transmission stay, left
3. Oil pressure switch
4. Oil pressure gauge unit
5. Oil filter
6. Oil cooler by-pass valve***
7. Oil filter bracket stay
8. Oil filter bracket
9. Oil filter bracket gasket
10. Drain plug
11. Drain plug gasket
12. Oil pan
13. Oil screen
14. Oil screen gasket
15. Plug
16. Relief spring
17. Relief plunger
18. Crankshaft oil seal
19. Oil pump case
20. Oil pump gasket
21. Oil pump cover
22. Oil pump outer rotor
23. Oil pump inner rotor

NOTE
* SOHC
** DOHC Non-turbo
*** DOHC Turbo

MT1099100001000X

Fig. 47   Oil pan & pump replacement. SOHC engine

5. Cut out a portion in camshaft oil seal lip, **Fig. 45.**
6. Cover tip of a suitable screwdriver with a clean soft cloth and pry out seal at cut out portion of seal. **Use care not to damage crankshaft.**
7. Reverse procedure to install, using seal installer tool No. MD998718-01, or equivalent, to install rear main oil seal.

OIL PAN
REPLACE

1. Release fuel system pressure as outlined under "Precautions."
2. Remove engine assembly as outlined under "Engine, Replace."
3. Remove timing belt as outlined under "Timing Belt, Replace."
4. Remove front exhaust pipe.
5. Drain engine oil into a suitable container.
6. Remove engine undercover.
7. Remove oil pan in numbered sequence shown in **Figs. 47 and 48.**
8. Reverse procedure to install, noting the following:
   a. Check oil pump components for cracks and wear.
   b. Install rotor on oil pump and ensure clearance is .0040–.0070 inch for body clearance and .0016–.0039 inch for side clearance, **Fig. 49.**
   c. Ensure oil cooler valve moves smoothly.
   d. Apply sealant to oil pan as shown in **Fig. 50.**
   e. Tighten oil pan bolts in sequence shown in **Fig. 51.**

OIL PUMP
REPLACE

Refer to "Oil Pan, Replace" for oil pump replacement procedure.

BELT TENSION DATA

Belt	Deflection @ 22 Lbs.	
	New, Inch	Used, Inch
SOHC ENGINE		
A/C	.256–.275	.275–.335
Alternator/ Power Steering	.157–.197	.236–.276
DOHC ENGINE		
A/C & Alternator	.138–.157	.157–.197
Power Steering	.300–.350	.410–.490

COOLING SYSTEM BLEED

These engines do not require a specified bleed procedure. After filling cooling system, run engine to operating temperature with radiator/pressure cap off. Air will then be automatically bled through cap opening.

THERMOSTAT
REPLACE

1. Relieve fuel system pressure as outlined under "Precautions."
2. Remove air intake hose.
3. **On models equipped with SOHC engine,** disconnect radiator upper hose.
4. **On models equipped with DOHC engine,** disconnect radiator lower hose.
5. **On all models,** remove water outlet housing.
6. Remove housing gasket and thermostat.
7. Reverse procedure to install. Position thermostat with jiggle valve lined up with mark on housing, **Fig. 52.**

WATER PUMP
REPLACE

1. Release fuel system pressure as outlined under "Precautions."
2. Remove timing belt as outlined under "Timing Belt, Replace."
3. Drain engine coolant into a suitable container.
4. Replace engine water pump in numbered sequence shown in **Figs. 53 and 54,** noting the following during installation:
   a. Coat inlet pipe O-ring with water to ease installation.
   b. **On models equipped with DOHC engine,** install water pump bolts as shown, **Fig. 55.**

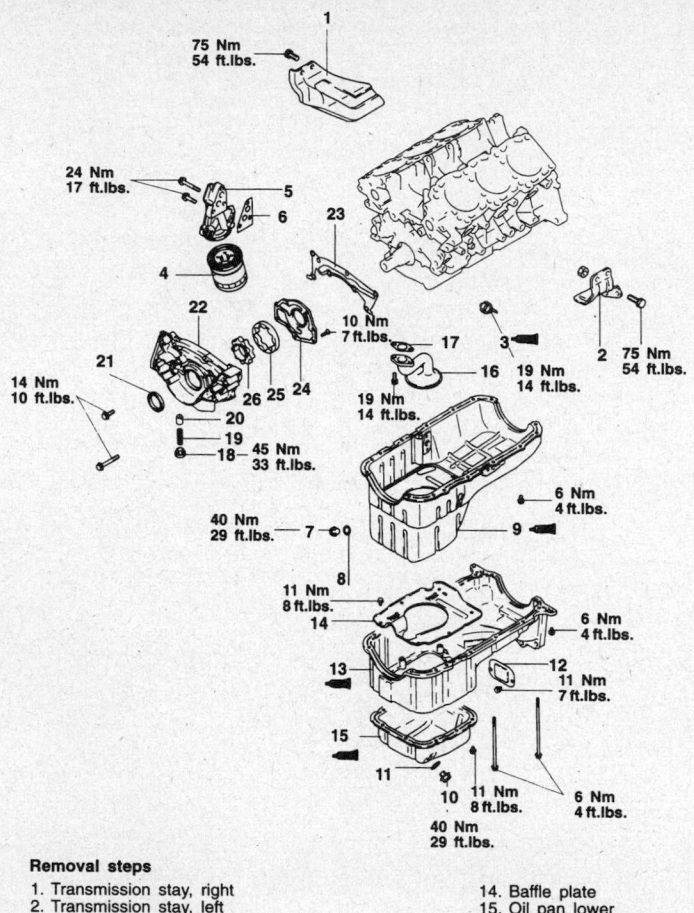

Removal steps
1. Transmission stay, right
2. Transmission stay, left
3. Oil pressure switch
4. Oil filter
5. Oil filter bracket
6. Oil filter bracket gasket
7. Drain plug
8. Drain plug gasket
9. Oil pan
10. Drain plug
11. Drain plug gasket
12. Cover
13. Oil pan upper
14. Baffle plate
15. Oil pan lower
16. Oil screen
17. Oil screen gasket
18. Plug
19. Relief spring
20. Relief plunger
21. Crankshaft oil seal
22. Oil pump case
23. Oil pump gasket
24. Oil pump cover
25. Oil pump outer rotor
26. Oil pump inner rotor

MT1069800532000X

Fig. 48   Oil pan & pump replacement. DOHC engine

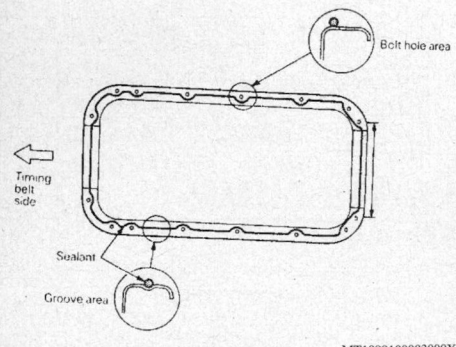

MT1099100003000X

Fig. 50   Applying sealant on oil pan

RADIATOR
REPLACE
1. Drain engine coolant, then remove drain plug and radiator cap.

2. Remove overflow hose and reserve tank, then the upper and lower radiator hoses.
3. Disconnect ATF cooler hoses from radiator, then plug and cover hoses and nipples.
4. Disconnect condenser and radiator fan motor connections, then remove upper insulator and radiator.
5. Remove condenser fan and radiator fan motor assembly.
6. Remove lower insulator and fan, then the resistor.
7. Remove fan motor, shroud, then the radiator.
8. Reverse procedure to install.

FUEL PUMP
REPLACE
1. Relieve fuel system pressure as outlined under "Precautions."

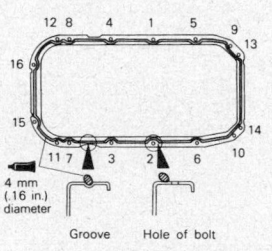

MT1099100002000X

Fig. 49   Oil pump clearance measurement

MT1099100004000X

Fig. 51   Oil pan tightening sequence

2. Drain fuel into an approved container.
3. Remove fuel pump in numbered sequence shown in **Fig. 56,** noting the following:
   a. Remove rear wheel steering cylinder attachment bolts and lower cylinder to provide working space.
   b. Remove center exhaust pipe and suspend to frame using wire.
4. Reverse procedure to install.

FUEL FILTER
REPLACE
1. Relieve fuel system pressure as outlined under "Precautions."
2. Drain fuel into an approved container.
3. Remove air intake hose.
4. Holding fuel filter with spanner, remove high pressure fuel hose and eye bolt. **Fuel pipe line has some residual pressure, cover with a rag to prevent spraying.**
5. Loosen flare nut to release connection with fuel main pipe, then remove fuel filter, **Fig. 57.**
6. Reverse procedure to install, **Fig. 58.**

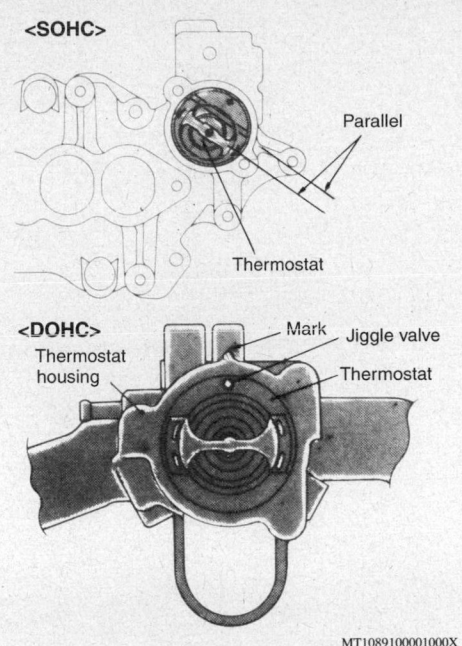

<SOHC>

Parallel

Thermostat

<DOHC>

Mark — Jiggle valve

Thermostat housing

Thermostat

MT1089100001000X

Fig. 52 Thermostat installation

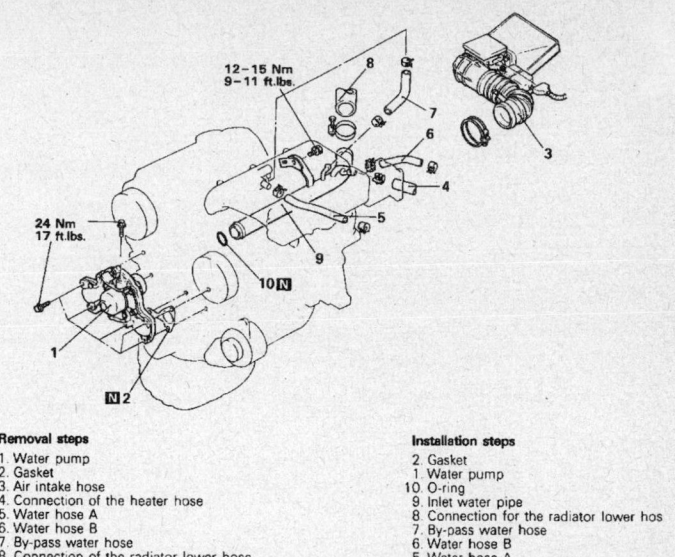

12–15 Nm
9–11 ft.lbs.

24 Nm
17 ft.lbs.

Removal steps

1. Water pump
2. Gasket
3. Air intake hose
4. Connection of the heater hose
5. Water hose A
6. Water hose B
7. By-pass water hose
8. Connection of the radiator lower hose
9. Inlet water pipe
10. O-ring

Installation steps

2. Gasket
1. Water pump
10. O-ring
9. Inlet water pipe
8. Connection for the radiator lower hos
7. By-pass water hose
6. Water hose B
5. Water hose A
4. Connection for the heater hose
3. Air intake hose

MT1089100002000X

Fig. 53 Water pump replacement. SOHC engine

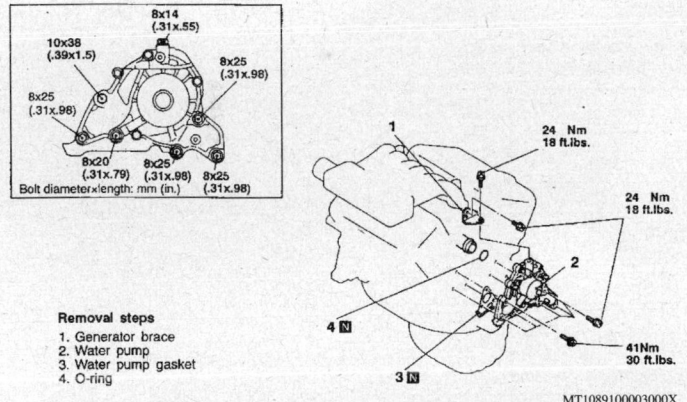

8x14
(.31x.55)

10x38
(.39x1.5)

8x25
(.31x.98)

8x25
(.31x.98)

8x20
(.31x.79)

8x25
(.31x.98)

8x25
(.31x.98)

Bolt diameter×length: mm (in.)

24 Nm
18 ft.lbs.

24 Nm
18 ft.lbs.

41Nm
30 ft.lbs.

Removal steps

1. Generator brace
2. Water pump
3. Water pump gasket
4. O-ring

MT1089100003000X

Fig. 54 Water pump replacement. DOHC engine

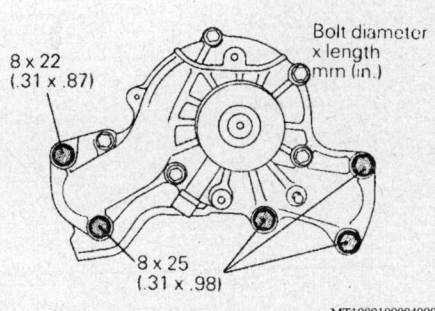

8 x 22
(.31 x .87)

Bolt diameter
x length
mm (in.)

8 x 25
(.31 x .98)

MT1089100004000X

Fig. 55 Water pump bolt locations. DOHC engine

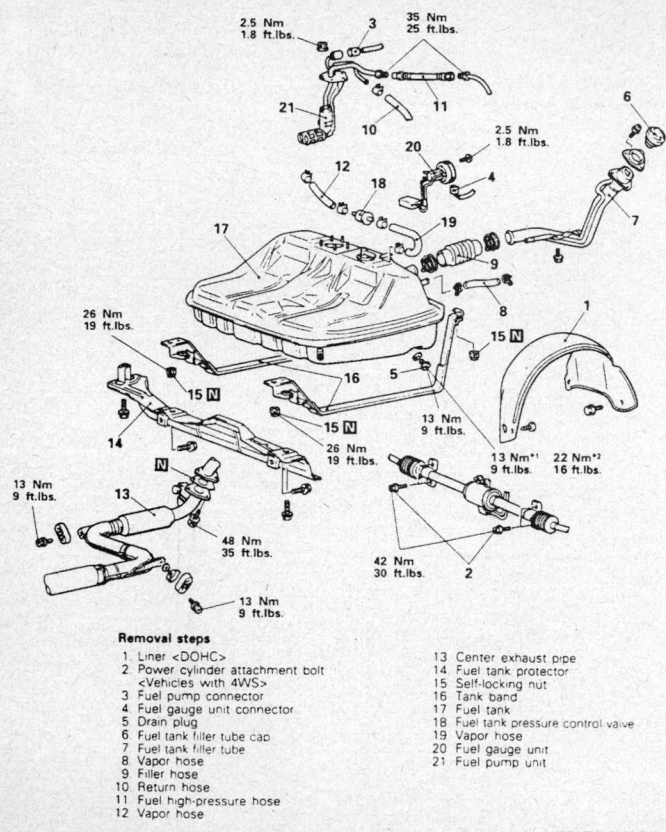

Removal steps
1. Liner <DOHC>
2. Power cylinder attachment bolt <Vehicles with 4WS>
3. Fuel pump connector
4. Fuel gauge unit connector
5. Drain plug
6. Fuel tank filler tube cap
7. Fuel tank filler tube
8. Vapor hose
9. Filler hose
10. Return hose
11. Fuel high-pressure hose
12. Vapor hose
13. Center exhaust pipe
14. Fuel tank protector
15. Self-locking nut
16. Tank band
17. Fuel tank
18. Fuel tank pressure control valve
19. Vapor hose
20. Fuel gauge unit
21. Fuel pump unit

MT1029100001000X

Fig. 56 Fuel tank & pump replacement

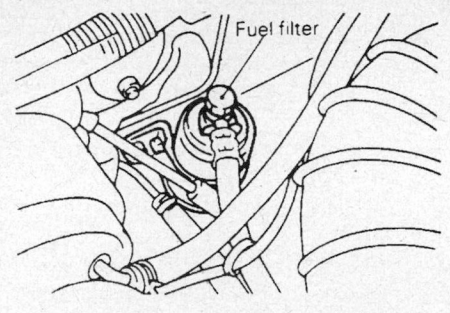

MT1029100002000X

Fig. 57 Fuel filter location

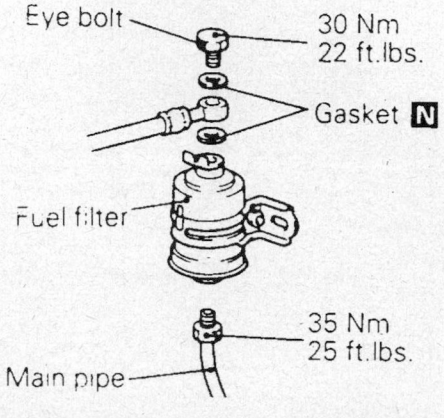

MT1029100003000X

Fig. 58 Fuel filter installation

TIGHTENING SPECIFICATIONS

Year	Component	Torque, Ft. Lbs.
1996	Air Intake Plenum Bolt & Nut	13
	Air Intake Plenum Stay Bolt	13
	Alternator	17
	Alternator Brace Bolt	10
	Alternator Bracket Bolt	17
	Alternator Bracket Side Bolt	84⑨
	Alternator Pivot Nut	17
	Auto Tensioner Bolt②	17
	Bearing Cap Bolts No. 2, 3, & 4①	57
	Bearing Cap Bolts No. 2, 3 & 4②	67
	Bearing Caps, Front & Rear Bolts①	57
	Bearing Caps, Front & Rear Bolts②	67
	Bellhousing Cover Bolt	24⑨
	Bracket Bolt	17
	Camshaft Sprocket Bolt	65
	Center Cover Bolt	84⑨
	Connecting Rod Cap Nut	38⑧
	Cooling Fan Bolt	96⑨
	Cooling Fan Bracket Bolt	30
	Crank Angle Sensor Adapter Bolt②	17
	Crank Angle Sensor Nut	108⑨
	Crankshaft Bearing Cap Bolt	⑦
	Crankshaft Bearing Cap Stay Bolt	35
	Crankshaft Pulley Bolt①	112
	Crankshaft Pulley Bolt②	134

Continued

TIGHTENING
SPECIFICATIONS—Continued

Year	Component	Torque, Ft. Lbs.
1996	Cylinder Head Bolts	④
	Detonation Sensor	17
	Distributor Adapter Bolts①	108⑨
	Distributor Nut	10
	Drive Belt Tensioner Nut①	36
	Driveplate Bolt	54
	EGR Pipe	13
	EGR Pipe Clamp Bolts	13
	EGR Pipe Flare Nuts	43
	EGR Valve Bolt	16
	Engine Coolant Temperature Gauge Unit	96⑨
	Engine Coolant Temperature Sensor	22
	Engine Support Bracket, 10mm Bolts①	43
	Engine Support Bracket, 12mm Bolts①	80
	Engine Support Bracket, 10mm Bolts②	51
	Engine Support Bracket, 12mm Bolts②	80
	Exhaust Manifold Heat Protector	10
	Exhaust Manifold Nut①	14
	Exhaust Manifold Nut②	33
	Exhaust Manifold Stay Bolt	44
	Exhaust Manifold Tightening Side Nut	108⑨
	Fan Pulley Bolt	96⑨
	Flywheel Bolt	54
	Fuel Pipe①	84⑨
	Fuel Pressure Regulator Bolt	84⑨
	Heat Pipe Bolt①	108⑨
	Idler Pulley Bolt①	36
	Idler Pulley Bolt②	40
	Idler Pulley Bracket Bolt②	30
	Ignition Coil Bolt①	24⑨
	Ignition Coil Bolt, 10mm Bolts②	84⑨
	Ignition Coil Bolt, 12mm Bolts②	108⑨
	Injector & Delivery Pipe Bolt	108⑨
	Intake Manifold	③
	Oil Filler①	84⑨
	Oil Filter Bracket Stay	⑤
	Oil Filter Bracket	⑥
	Oil Pan Bolt	48⑨
	Oil Pan Drain Plug	29
	Oil Pressure Switch①	84⑨
	Oil Pressure Switch②	14
	Oil Pump Cane Bolt	10
	Oil Pump Cover Bolt	84⑨
	Oil Screen Bolt	14
	Oil Seal Case Bolt	96⑨
	Oil Level Gauge Assembly Bolt	10
	Power Transistor Bolt①	43⑨
	Power Transistor Bolt②	16
	Rear Plate Bolt	96⑨
	Rocker Arms, Shaft & Bearing Cap Bolts①	14
	Rocker Cover Bolt①	84⑨
	Rocker Cover Bolt②	48⑨
	Roll Stopper Bracket, 10mm Bolts	30

Continued

TIGHTENING
SPECIFICATIONS—Continued

Year	Component	Torque, Ft. Lbs.
1996	Roll Stopper Bracket, 12mm Bolts	54
	Spark Plug	18
	Tensioner Arm Bolt②	30
	Tensioner Bracket Bolt①	30
	Tensioner Bracket Bolt②	17
	Tensioner Bracket Stay Bolt	17
	Tensioner Lock Bolt①	19
	Tensioner Pulley Nut②	35
	Tensioner Pulley Nut	36
	Thermo Switch	72⑨
	Thermostat Housing Bolt	14
	Throttle Body Bolt	96⑨
	Timing Belt Rear Cover Center Bolt②	17
	Transmission Stay	54
	Water Inlet Fitting Bolt	14
	Water Inlet Pipe Bolt	10
	Water Outlet Fitting Bolt	14
	Water Pump Bolt	17

① — SOHC engine.

② — DOHC engine.

③ — Refer to "Intake Manifold, Replace" for tightening procedure.

④ — Refer to "Cylinder Head, Replace" for tightening procedure.

⑤ — 8mm bolts, 9 ft. lbs.; 10mm bolts, 17 ft. lbs.

⑥ — Bolts marked "4"," 17 ft. lbs.; bolts marked "7," 10 ft. lbs.

⑦ — Bolts marked "9", 58 ft. lbs.; bolts marked "10," 69 ft. lbs.

⑧ — Tighten an additional 1/4 turn.

⑨ — Inch lbs.

3.5L Engine

NOTE: For Procedures Not Found In This Section, Refer To "3.5L Engine" In "Mitsubishi B-Series" Chassis Section.

NOTE: On Air Bag Equipped Models, Refer To "Air Bag System Precautions" Located In Front Of This Manual For System Disarming and Arming Procedures.

NOTE: Refer To "Computer Relearn Procedures" Located In Front Of This Manual For Computer Relearn Procedures.

INDEX

PRECAUTIONS

AIR BAG SYSTEMS

Refer to "Air Bag System Precautions" in front of this manual for system disarming and arming procedures.

BATTERY GROUND CABLE

Prior to service, disconnect battery ground cable and isolate as required.

FUEL SYSTEM PRESSURE RELIEF

1. Remove rear seat cushion.
2. Remove fuel pump floor cover plate, then disconnect fuel pump electrical connector.
3. Start and run engine until it stalls.
4. After engine has stopped, turn ignition switch to OFF position.
5. After fuel system repairs are complete, reconnect fuel pump connector.

COMPRESSION PRESSURE

Ensure engine oil, starter motor and battery are in satisfactory condition. When checking compression, engine coolant should be at normal operating temperature, spark plugs should be removed and throttle valve should be wide open.
1. Ensure lights, electric cooling fan and accessories are OFF.
2. Disconnect crankshaft position sensor electrical connector, **Fig. 1.**
3. Install compression gauge into spark plug holes.

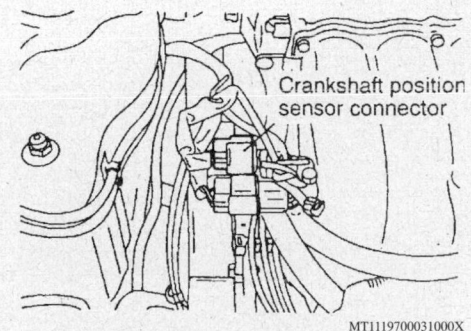

Crankshaft position sensor connector

MT1119700031000X

Fig. 1 Crankshaft position sensor connector location

4. With throttle valve fully open, crank engine at 250–400 RPM and record compression pressure.
5. Standard compression pressure is 171 psi.
6. Minimum compression pressure is 127 psi.
7. Difference between cylinders should not exceed 14 psi.

ENGINE MOUNT

REPLACE

ENGINE

1. Raise engine assembly until weight is removed from engine mount insulator, then support engine with a suitable lifting device.
2. Remove washer fluid tank.
3. Remove engine mount from vehicle in numbered sequence shown in **Fig. 2.**
4. Reverse procedure to install.

TRANSAXLE

1. Remove air cleaner assembly.
2. Remove battery and battery tray.
3. Remove front roll stopper as outlined under "Engine Roll Stoppers & Center Member."
4. Remove washer transmission and rear roll stopper coupling bolt.
5. Remove rear roll stopper bracket.
6. Using engine lifting tool Nos. MZ203827 and MB991453, or equivalents, raise and support engine.
7. Remove transaxle mount from vehicle in numbered sequence shown in **Fig. 3.**
8. Reverse procedure to install.

ENGINE ROLL STOPPERS & CENTER MEMBER

1. Remove engine roll stoppers and center member from vehicle in numbered sequence shown in **Fig. 4.**
2. Reverse procedure to install.

ENGINE

REPLACE

1. Relieve fuel system pressure as outlined under "Precautions."
2. Mark and remove hood assembly.
3. Drain cooling system and power steering fluid.
4. Remove radiator assembly.
5. Remove front exhaust pipe, washer fluid tank and engine cover.
6. Remove transaxle assembly.
7. Remove engine assembly from vehicle in numbered sequence shown in

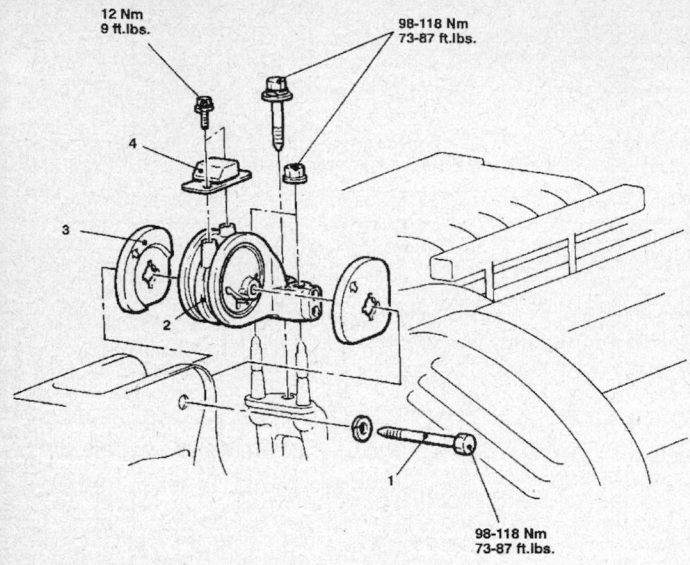

Removal steps

1. Mounting bolt for engine mount insulator
2. Engine mount bracket
3. Engine mount stopper
4. Dynamic damper

MT1069700498000X

Fig. 2 Engine mount replacement

Removal steps

1. Transaxle mount bracket
2. Transaxle mount stopper

MT1069700499000X

Fig. 3 Transaxle mount replacement

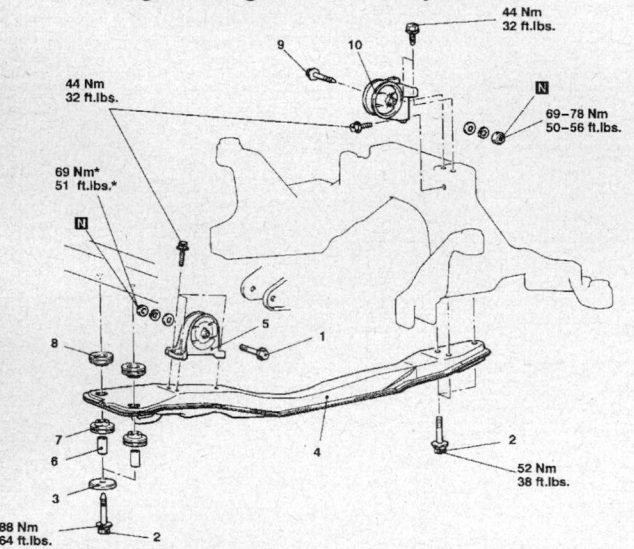

Front roll stopper & Center Member Removal steps

1. Coupling bolt for transaxle and front roll stopper
2. Mounting bolt for center member
3. Stopper
4. Center member
5. Front roll stopper
6. Collar
7. Bush (lower)
8. Bush (upper)

Rear roll stopper Removal steps

9. Coupling bolt between transaxle and rear roll stopper
10. Rear roll stopper

Caution

*: Indicates parts which should be temporarily tightened, and then fully tightened with the vehicle on the ground in the unladen condition.

MT1069700500000X

Fig. 4 Engine roll stoppers & center member replacement

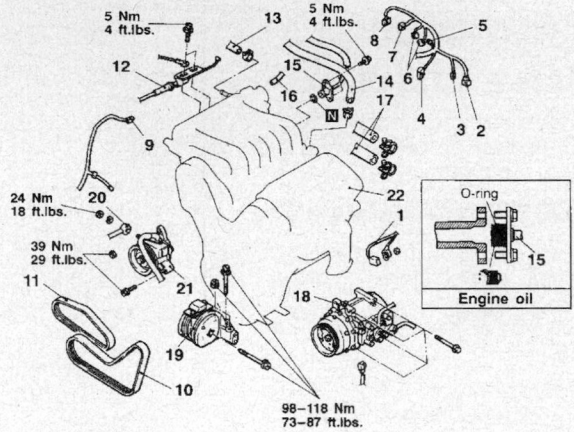

Removal Steps

1. Generator connector
2. Water temperature connector
3. Water temperature gauge connector
4. Injector harness connector
5. Condenser connector
6. Distributor connector
7. ISC servo connector
8. TPS connector
9. Crank angle sensor connector
10. Drive belt (for generator and A/C)
11. Drive belt (for power steering)
12. Connection of the accelerator cable
13. Connection of brake booster vacuum hose
14. Connection of fuel return hose
15. Connection of fuel high pressure hose
16. Connection of the purge hose
17. Connection of heater hose
18. A/C compressor
19. Engine mount
20. Pressure hose
21. Power steering oil pump
22. Engine assembly

MT1069700501000X

Fig. 5 Engine assembly removal

Fig. 5, noting the following:

a. Remove power steering pump and air conditioner compressor and position aside, leave hoses attached.

b. Support engine assembly using a suitable engine lifting device, then remove engine mounting bolts.

c. Ensure all hoses and electrical connections are disconnected, then raise engine out of engine compartment.

8. Reverse procedure to install.

BELT TENSION DATA

Belt	New, Inch	Used, Inch
1997		
Alternator & A/C	141–184	98–119
Power Steering	110–154	77–99
1998–99		
Alternator & A/C	174–218	120–142
Power Steering	135–179	93.8–116

COOLING SYSTEM BLEED

These engines do not require a specified bleed procedure. After filling cooling system, run engine to operating temperature with radiator/pressure cap off. Air will then be automatically bled through cap opening.

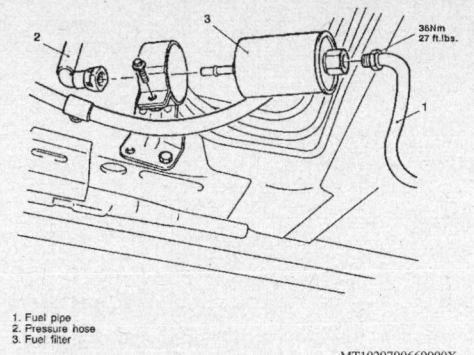

1. Fuel pipe
2. Pressure hose
3. Fuel filter

MT1029700669000X

Fig. 6   Fuel filter location

RADIATOR
REPLACE

Refer to "Radiator, Replace" in the "3.0L Engine" section for replacement procedure.

FUEL PUMP
REPLACE

1. Relieve fuel system pressure as out-lined under "Precautions."
2. Remove rear seat cushion, then the fuel gauge unit protector.
3. Disconnect fuel gauge unit and pump assembly electrical connector.
4. Remove fuel gauge unit and pump assembly from fuel tank.
5. Reverse procedure to install, noting the following:
   a. When installing fuel gauge unit, tilt float at end of unit towards the left. If unit is tilted towards the right it will touch the fuel tank reservoir.
   b. Align arrows on top of fuel tank with holes in the fuel gauge unit and pump assembly.

FUEL FILTER
REPLACE

1. Relieve fuel system pressure as outlined under "Precautions."
2. Remove fuel pump in numbered sequence shown in **Fig. 6.**
3. Reverse procedure to install.

TIGHTENING SPECIFICATIONS

Year	Component	Torque, Ft. Lbs.
1997–99	A/C & Alternator Belt Tensioner Pulley	36
	Alternator Bracket Bolt (M8)	36
	Alternator Bracket Bolt (M10)	17
	Alternator Pivot Nut	15
	Center Member Front Bolts	64
	Center Member Rear Bolts	38
	Crankshaft Pulley Bolt	134
	Engine Hood Hinge Bolts	108①
	Engine Mount Bolts	73-87
	Engine Mount Dynamic Damper	108①
	Front Roll Stopper Bracket Bolts	32
	Front Roll Stopper Through Bolt	51
	Fuel Pipe To Fuel Filter Flare Nut	27
	Hood Gas Spring Bolts	16
	Power Steering Pump Mounting Bolt	29
	Power Steering Pump Pressure Hose	18
	Rear Roll Stopper Bracket Bolts	32
	Rear Roll Stopper Through Bolt	50–56
	Transaxle Mount Bracket Bolt	60
	Transaxle Mount Through Bolt	58

① — Inch lbs.

Rear Axle & Suspension

NOTE: Refer To "Computer Relearn Procedures" Located In Front Of This Manual For Computer Relearn Procedures.

INDEX

PRECAUTIONS

BATTERY GROUND CABLE

Prior to service, disconnect battery ground cable and isolate as required.

HUB & BEARING
REPLACE

1. Raise and support vehicle, then remove rear tire and wheel assembly.
2. Remove rear axle hub in numbered sequence shown in **Figs. 1 and 2,** noting the following:
   a. When removing rear speed sensor, use care not to strike pole piece against teeth of rotor or other components.
   b. Remove brake caliper leaving brake hose attached, then support to frame using suitable wire. **Do not allow caliper to hang by hose.**
   c. Care must be taken not to scratch or damage teeth of speed sensor rotor. Rotor must never be dropped.
3. Reverse procedure to install, noting the following:
   a. **On 1996 models,** after tightening flange nut, crimp nut at concave portion of spindle.
   b. **On 1996 models,** install rear speed sensor and insert a .008–.028 inch feeler gauge between speed sensor pole piece and rotor's toothed surface and tighten.

REAR SUSPENSION
REPLACE
1996

1. Raise and support vehicle, then remove rear tire and wheel assembly.
2. **On sedan models,** remove trunk side trim panel.
3. **On all models,** support rear suspension using suitable jack stands.
4. Remove rear suspension in numbered sequence as shown in, **Fig. 3,** noting the following:
   a. Remove parking brake cable end.
   b. Prior to removing crossmember

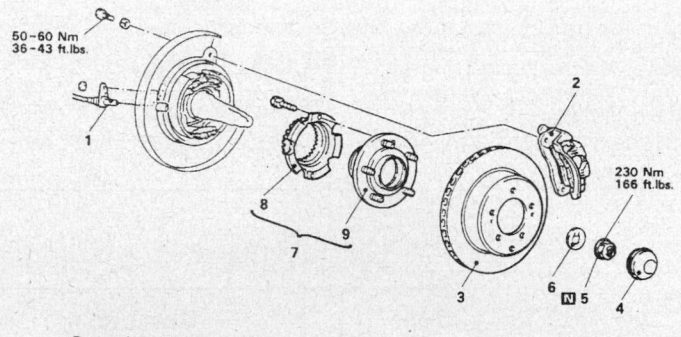

```
50-60 Nm
36-43 ft.lbs.
                                                    2

                                                    230 Nm
                                                    166 ft.lbs.

Removal steps
1  Rear speed sensor <Vehicles with ABS>
2  Caliper assembly
3  Brake disc
4  Hub cap
5  Flange nut
6  Tongued washer
7  Rear hub assembly
8  Rear rotor <Vehicles with ABS>
9  Rear hub unit bearing

Caution
The rear hub unit bearing should not
be dismantled.

MT3039100001000X
```

Fig. 1 Rear axle hub replacement. 1996

mounting nuts, support rear suspension using suitable jack stands.
   c. Remove crossmember mounting nuts and lower rear suspension out of vehicle.
5. Reverse procedure to install, noting the following on wagon models:
   a. Temporarily tighten lateral rod, upper control arms, shock absorbers and axle assembly attaching bolts.
   b. Install upper control arms ensuring attaching bolts are installed in proper direction, and tighten to specifications.
   c. Install rear springs with small end on top, ensuring step in pad aligns with end of spring.

1997–99

1. Remove rear seat assembly, then raise and support vehicle.
2. Remove center exhaust pipe.
3. Remove rear suspension in numbered sequence as shown in, **Fig. 4,** noting the following:
   a. Disconnect parking brake cable end from parking brake drum.
   b. Prior to removing crossmember

mounting nuts, support crossmember with a suitable jack.
4. Reverse procedure to install.

SHOCK ABSORBER
REPLACE
1996

1. Raise and support vehicle, then remove rear tire and wheel assembly.
2. Remove trunk side trim panel.
3. Remove shock absorber in numbered sequence shown in **Fig. 5.**
4. Reverse procedure to install.

1997–99

1. Remove rear seat, then the shock absorber upper flange nuts.
2. Raise and support vehicle, then remove shock absorber lower mounting bolt.
3. Remove shock absorber.
4. Reverse procedure to install

COIL SPRING
REPLACE

1. Remove shock absorber as outlined under "Shock Absorber, Replace."

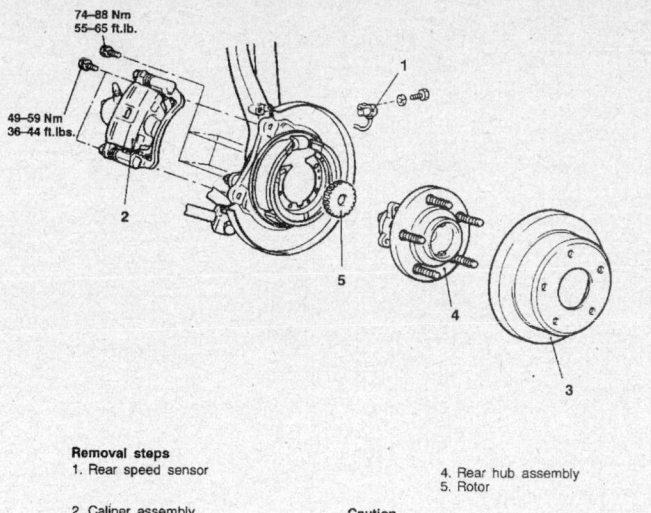

Removal steps

1. Rear speed sensor
2. Caliper assembly
3. Brake disc
4. Rear hub assembly
5. Rotor

Caution
The rear hub assembly should not be disassembled.

MT3039700073000X

Fig. 2   Rear axle hub replacement. 1997–99

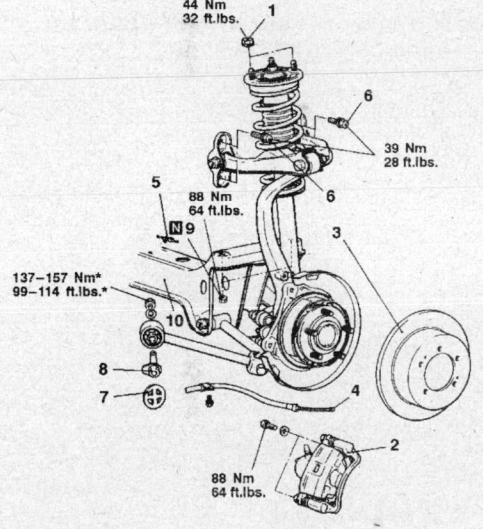

Removal steps

1. Shock absorber mounting nuts
2. Brake caliper assembly
3. Brake disc
4. Parking brake cable end
5. Rear speed sensor connector
6. Upper arm bracket mounting bolt
7. Grommet
8. Trailing arm mounting bolt
9. Crossmember mounting self-locking nuts
10. Rear suspension assembly

Caution
* Indicates parts which should be temporarily tightened, and then full tightened with the vehicles on the ground in the unladen condition.

MT2039700105000X

Fig. 4   Rear suspension assembly replacement. 1997–99

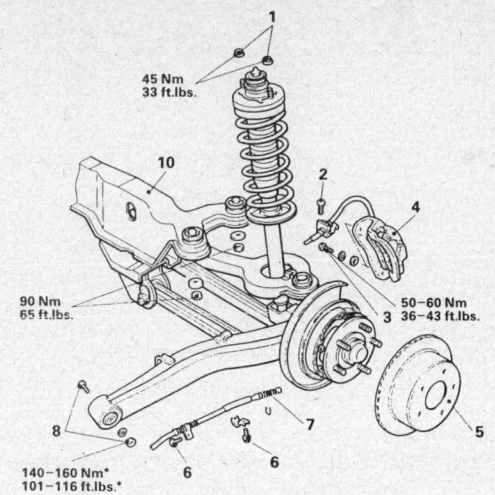

1. Shock absorber upper mounting nuts
2. Bolt
3. Brake caliper mounting bolts
4. Brake caliper assembly
5. Brake disc
6. Bolt
7. Parking brake cable end
8. Trailing arm mounting bolt and nut
9. Crossmember mounting nuts
10. Rear suspension assembly

Caution
*: Indicates parts which should be temporarily tightened, and then fully tightened with the vehicle on the ground in the unladen condition.

MT2039100001000X

Fig. 3   Rear suspension assembly replacement. 1996

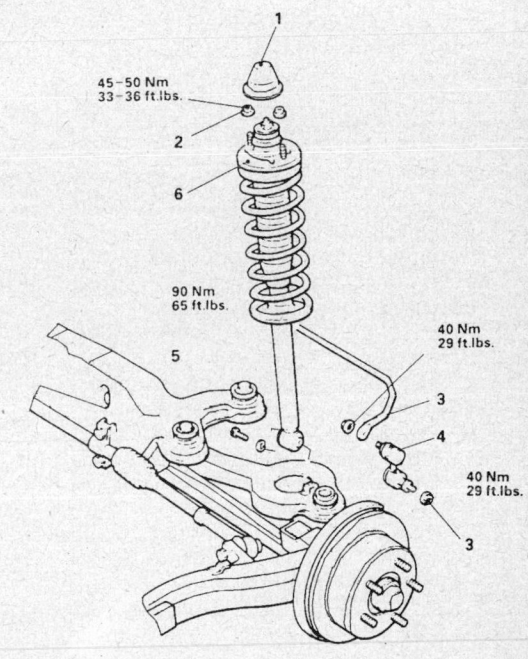

Removal steps

1. Cap
2. Shock absorber upper mounting nuts
3. Stabilizer link mounting nuts
4. Stabilizer link
5. Shock absorber mounting bolt
6. Shock absorber assembly

MT2039100004000X

Fig. 5   Shock absorber replacement. 1996

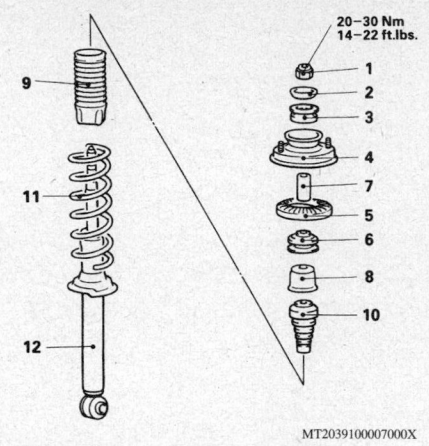

Disassembly steps
1. Piston rod tightening nut
2. Washer
3. Upper bushing (A)
4. Bracket assembly
5. Upper spring pad
6. Upper bushing (B)
7. Collar
8. Cup assembly
9. Dust cover
10. Bump rubber
11. Coil spring
12. Shock absorber

20–30 Nm
14–22 ft.lbs.

MT2039100007000X

Fig. 6 Exploded view of rear shock absorber assembly. 1996

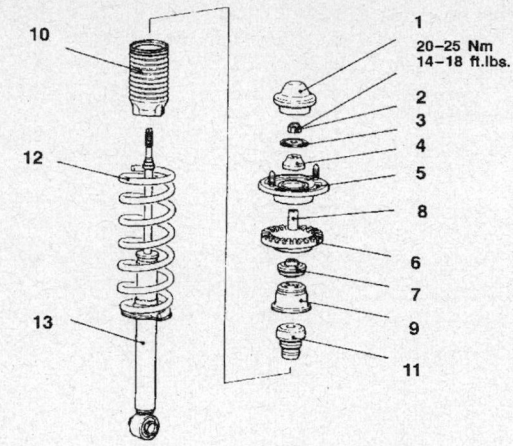

20–25 Nm
14–18 ft.lbs.

Disassembly steps
1. Cap
2. Self-locking nut
3. Washer
4. Upper bushing A
5. Bracket
6. Spring pad
7. Upper bushing B
8. Collar
9. Cup
10. Dust cover
11. Bump rubber
12. Coil spring
13. Shock absorber assembly

MT2039700106000X

Fig. 7 Exploded view of rear shock absorber assembly. 1997–99

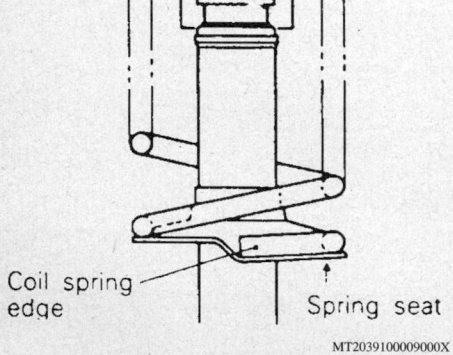

Coil spring edge

Spring seat

MT2039100009000X

Fig. 8 Coil spring installation

2. Compress coil spring using coil spring compression tools No. MB991237 and MB991239, or equivalent.
3. Separate coil spring from other shock absorber components in numbered sequence shown in **Figs. 6 and 7**.
4. Reverse procedure to install, noting the following:
   a. Align edge of coil spring as shown in **Fig. 8**.
   b. Position upper bracket as shown in **Figs. 9 and 10**, then tighten nuts and bolts to specifications.

CONTROL ARM

REPLACE

1996

1. Raise and support vehicle, then remove rear tire and wheel assembly.
2. Remove shock absorber as outlined under "Shock Absorber, Replace."
3. Remove assist link, lower and upper arm in numbered sequence shown in **Fig. 11**, noting the following:
   a. Remove ball joints using steering linkage puller tool No. MB991113, or equivalent.
   b. Loosen, but do not remove, cross-member mounting nuts to lower crossmember.
4. Reverse procedure to install.

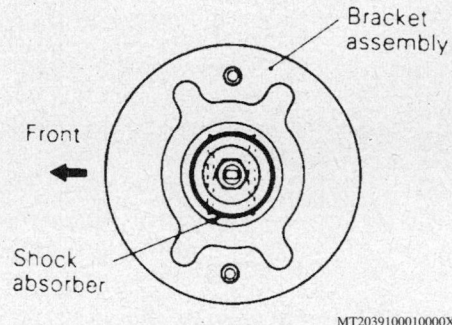

Bracket assembly

Front

Shock absorber

MT2039100010000X

Fig. 9 Upper bracket installation. 1996

1997-99

Upper

1. Raise and support vehicle, then remove wheel and tire assembly.
2. Remove upper control arm in numbered sequence shown in **Fig. 12**.
3. Reverse procedure to install.

Lower & Toe Control

1. Raise and support vehicle, then remove wheel and tire assembly.
2. Remove lower and toe control arms in numbered sequence shown in **Fig. 13**, noting the following:
   a. Before separating toe control arm ball joint from knuckle, tie cord of steering linkage puller tool No. MB991113, or equivalent, to nearby part, **Fig. 14**.
   b. Make mating marks on toe control arm and eccentric cam bolt, before removing cam bolt.
3. Reverse procedure to install.

Bracket

Front

Lower bushing inner pipe

MT2039700107000X

Fig. 10 Upper bracket installation. 1997–99

KNUCKLE

REPLACE

1997-99

1. Remove hub assembly as outlined under "Hub & Bearing, Replace."
2. Remove knuckle in numbered sequence shown in **Fig. 15**, noting the following:
   a. Before separating toe control arm ball joint from knuckle, tie cord of steering linkage puller tool No. MB991113, or equivalent, to nearby part, **Fig. 14**.
   b. Make mating marks on toe control arm and eccentric cam bolt, before removing cam bolt.
3. Reverse procedure to install.

TRAILING ARM

REPLACE

1. Raise and support vehicle, then remove rear tire and wheel assembly.
2. **On 1996 models**, remove trailing arm

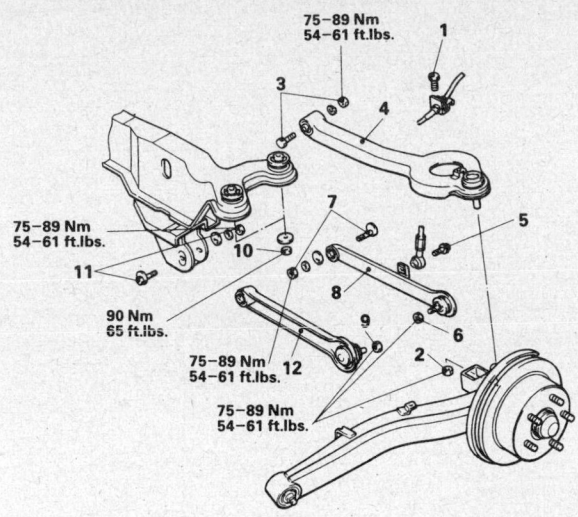

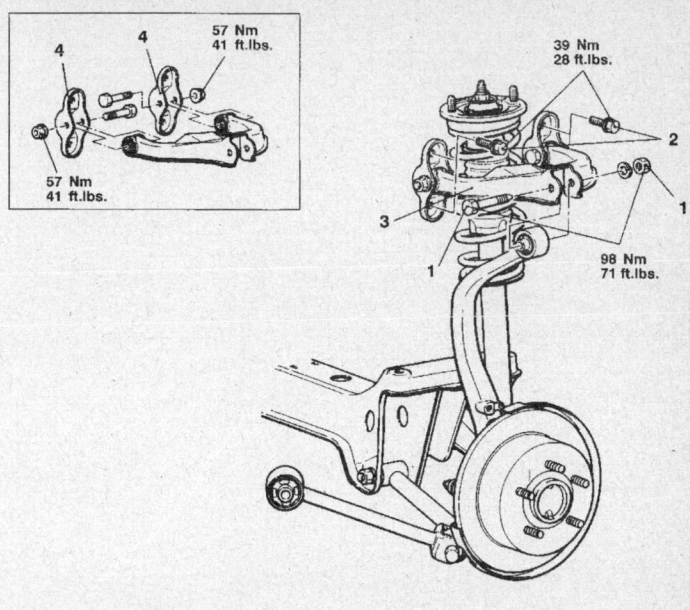

Upper arm removal steps
- Removal of shock absorber
1. Brake line clamp bolt
2. Self lock nut
3. Upper arm mounting bolt and nut
4. Upper arm

Lower arm removal steps
5. ECS height sensor rod
   <Vehicle equipped with ECS>
6. Self lock nut
7. Lower arm mounting bolt and nut
8. Lower arm

Assist link removal steps
9. Self lock nut
10. Crossmember mounting nuts
11. Assist link mounting bolt and nut
12. Assist link

MT2039100011000X

Fig. 11 Assist link, lower & upper arm replacement. 1996

Removal steps
1. Upper arm and knuckle connecting bolt and nut
2. Upper arm assembly mounting bolts
3. Upper arm assembly
4. Upper arm bracket

MT2039700108000X

Fig. 12 Upper arm assembly replacement. 1997–99

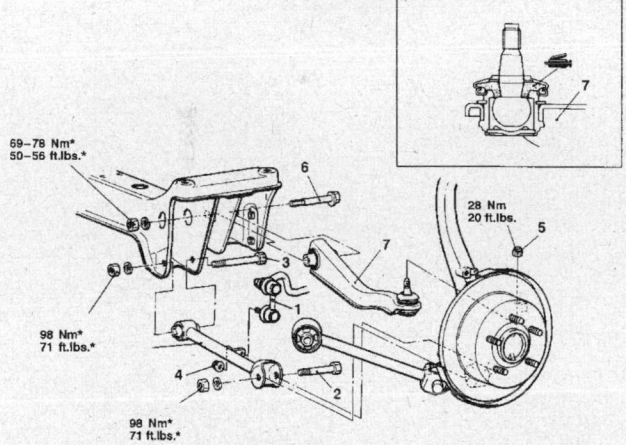

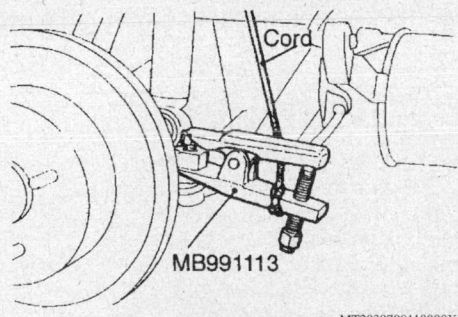

MB991113

MT2039700110000X

Fig. 14 Toe control arm ball joint removal. 1997–99

Lower arm assembly removal steps
1. Stabilizer link
2. Lower arm assembly and knuckle connection
3. Lower arm assembly mounting bolt
4. Lower arm assembly

Toe control arm assembly removal steps
5. Connection for toe control arm ball joint joint and knuckle
6. Toe control arm assembly mounting bolt
7. Toe control arm assembly

Caution
* Indicates parts which should be temporarily tightened, and then fully tightened with the vehicle on the ground in the unladen condition.

MT2039700109000X

Fig. 13 Lower & toe control arm replacement. 1997–99

in numbered sequence shown in **Fig. 16,** removing ball joints using steering linkage puller tool No. MB991113, or equivalent.
3. **On 1997–99 models,** remove trailing arm in numbered sequence shown in **Fig. 17.**
4. **On all models,** reverse procedure to install.

STABILIZER BAR
REPLACE

1. Raise and support vehicle, then remove rear tire and wheel assembly.
2. Remove stabilizer bar assembly in numbered sequence shown in **Figs. 18 and 19.**
3. Reverse procedure to install.

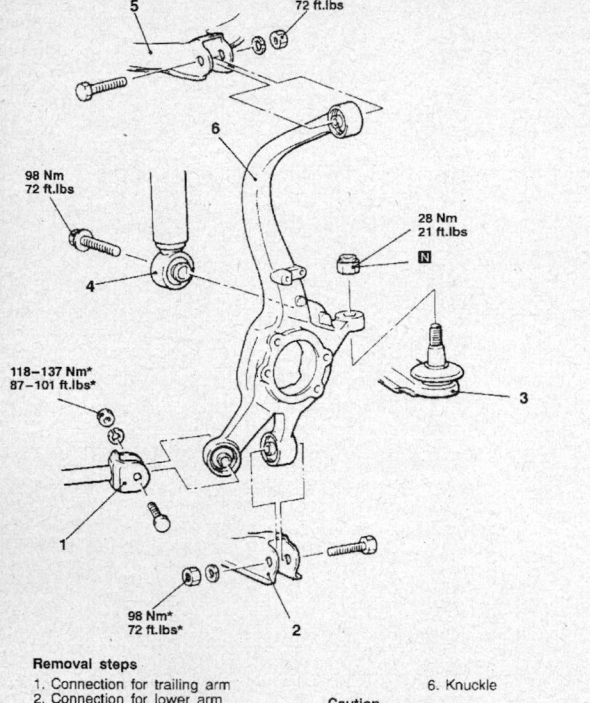

Removal steps
1. Connection for trailing arm
2. Connection for lower arm
3. Connection for toe control arm
4. Connection for shock absorber
5. Connection for upper arm

6. Knuckle

Caution
*: Indicates parts which should be temporarily tightened, and then fully tightened with the vehicle on the ground in the unladen condition.

MT2039700111000X

Fig. 15 Knuckle replacement. 1997–99

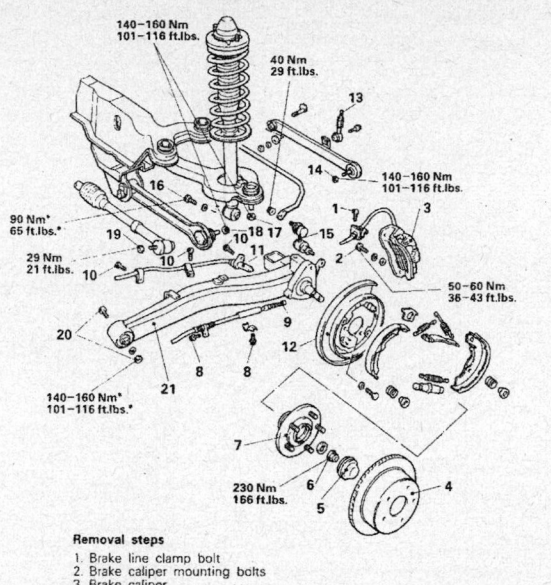

Removal steps
1. Brake line clamp bolt
2. Brake caliper mounting bolts
3. Brake caliper
4. Brake disk
5. Hub cap
6. Flange nut
7. Hub assembly
8. Bolt
9. Parking brake cable end
10. ABS speed sensor clamp bolts
11. ABS speed sensor
12. Backing plate
13. ECS height sensor rod
14. Self lock nut
15. Stabilizer link
16. Shock absorber mounting bolt
17. Self lock nut
18. Self lock nut
   <Vehicles not equipped with 4WS>
19. Power cylinder tie-rod connection nut <Vehicles equipped with 4WS>
20. Trailing arm mounting bolt and nut
21. Trailing arm

MT2039100013000X

Fig. 16 Trailing arm replacement. 1996

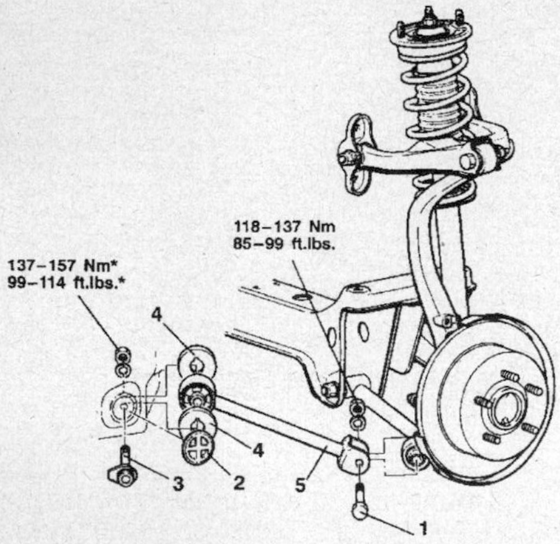

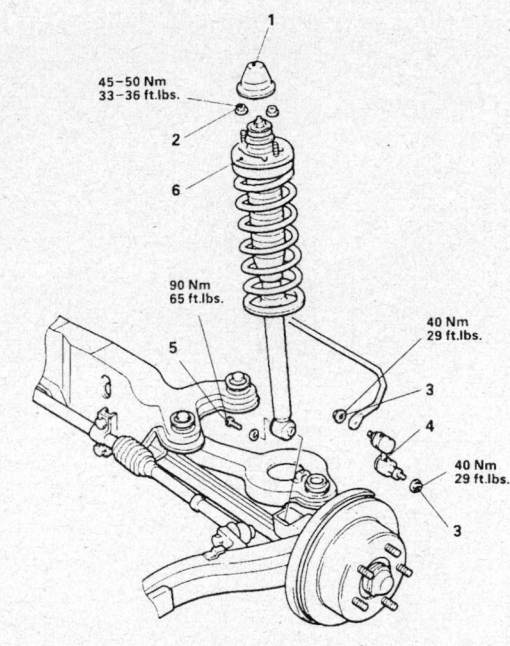

Removal steps
1. Connection for knuckle and trailing arm assembly
2. Grommet
3. Trailing arm assembly mounting bolt
4. Stopper
5. Trailing arm assembly

Caution
* Indicates parts which should be temporarily tightened, and then fully tightened with the vehicles on the ground in the unladen condition.

INSPECTION
• Check the bushings for wear and deterioration.
• Check the trailing arm for bends or damage.

MT2039700112000X

Fig. 17 Trailing arm replacement. 1997–99

Removal steps
1. Cap
2. Shock absorber upper mounting nuts
3. Stabilizer link mounting nuts
4. Stabilizer link
5. Shock absorber mounting bolt
6. Shock absorber assembly

MT2039100012000X

Fig. 18 Stabilizer bar assembly replacement. 1996

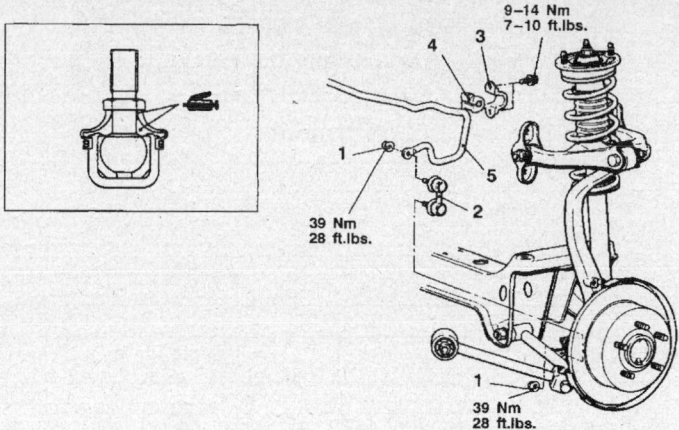

Disassembly steps
1. Stabilizer link mounting nuts
2. Stabilizer link
3. Stabilizer bar brackets
4. Bushing
5. Stabilizer

MT2039700113000X

**Fig. 19 Stabilizer bar assembly replacement.
1997–99**

TIGHTENING SPECIFICATIONS

Year	Component	Torque, Ft. Lbs.
1996	Air Tube Nuts	84①
	Axle Nut	166
	Backing Plate Bolts	40
	Caliper Mounting Bolt	36–43
	Hub Bearing Flange Nut	166
	Hub Nut	166
	Lateral Rod Mounting Bolt & Nut, Lower	110
	Lateral Rod Mounting Bolt & Nut, Upper	66
	Lower Arm & Assisting Arm Mounting Bolts	54–61
	Lower Control Arm Mounting Bolt & Nut	170
	Pipe Connections	11
	Piston Rod Nut	14–33
	Rear Suspension Assembly Mounting Nuts	65
	Shock Absorber Mounting Nuts, Sedan Lower	65
	Shock Absorber Mounting Nuts, Sedan Upper	33–36
	Shock Absorber Mounting Nuts, Wagon Lower	51
	Shock Absorber Mounting Nuts, Wagon Upper	33
	Stabilizer Link Bolts	29
	Trailing Arm Mounting Bolts & Nuts	101–116
	Upper Arm Mounting Bolts & Nuts	54–61
	Wheel Lug Nut	65–80
1997–99	Caliper Mounting Bolt	64
	Cross Member Mounting Self-Locking Nuts	64
	Shock Absorber Mounting Nut	32
	Stabilizer Link Bracket Bolts	7–10
	Stabilizer Link Mounting Nuts	28
	Toe Control Arm Ball Joint	20
	Toe Control Arm Mounting Bolt	50–56
	Trailing Arm Mounting Bolt	99–114

Continued

TIGHTENING SPECIFICATIONS—Continued

Year	Component	Torque, Ft. Lbs.
1997–99	Trailing Arm To Knuckle Bolt	85–99
	Upper Arm & Knuckle Connecting Bolt & Nut	71
	Upper Arm Bracket Bolt & Nut	41
	Upper Arm Bracket Mounting Bolts	28
	Wheel Lug Nut	65–80

① — Inch lbs.

Front Suspension & Steering

NOTE: On Air Bag Equipped Models, Refer To "Air Bag System Precautions" Located In Front Of This Manual For System Disarming & Arming Procedures.

NOTE: Refer To "Computer Relearn Procedures" Located In Front Of This Manual For Computer Relearn Procedures.

INDEX

PRECAUTIONS

AIR BAG SYSTEMS

Refer to "Air Bag System Precautions" in front of this manual for system disarming and arming procedures.

BATTERY GROUND CABLE

Prior to service, disconnect battery ground cable and isolate as required.

WHEEL BEARING

ADJUST

Bearing preload is preset to specified value by design and cannot be adjusted.

WHEEL HUB & STEERING KNUCKLE

REPLACE

1996

1. Replace hub, knuckle and bearing in numbered sequence shown in **Figs. 1 and 2,** noting the following:

a. Use care when handling pole piece at tip of speed sensor and toothed edge of rotor, if equipped.
b. Apply brake pressure, then remove driveshaft nut. **Do not apply vehicle weight to wheel bearing while loosening driveshaft nut.**
c. Disconnect ball joint and tie rod end using steering linkage puller tool No. MB990635-01, or equivalent. **Loosen but do not remove ball joint and tie rod end nuts until knuckle is ready to be removed.**
d. Using axle puller tool No. MB990241-01, or equivalent, press driveshaft from front hub.
e. Ensure driveshaft nut and washer are installed in direction shown in **Fig. 3.**
f. Temporarily install speed sensor to knuckle, if equipped, then insert a suitable thickness gauge between sensor pole piece and rotor toothed surface, **Fig. 4,** and tighten speed sensor at a position where clearance is .012–.035 inch. **If clearance cannot be obtained, check for improper installation of rotor.**

g. Remove hub, or hub and rotor, by attaching front hub remover/installer tool No. MB990998-01 and knuckle arm bridge tool No. MB991355, or equivalents to knuckle and hub. Secure knuckle in vise, then tighten nut of front hub remover/installer to remove hub, or hub and rotor from knuckle.
h. Remove wheel bearing inner race from front hub using side bearing puller tool No. MB990810-01, or equivalent. First, crush oil seal in two places to allow tabs of side bearing puller clearance to get under inner race.
i. Drive wheel bearing out using knuckle arm bridge tool No. MB991355, remover/installer disc tool No. MB990932-01 and handle tool No. MB990938-01, or equivalents.
j. Fill wheel bearing with multi-purpose grease and apply a thin coating to knuckle and bearing contact surfaces, then press in wheel bearing using rear suspension

bushing base tool No. MB990890-01 and rear suspension arbor tool No. MB990883-01, or equivalents.

k. Drive oil seal into knuckle using lower arm bushing arbor tool No. MB990947 and oil seal installer tool No. MB990955-01, or equivalents. Apply multi-purpose grease to lip of oil seal and surfaces of oil seal which contact front hub.

l. Use front hub remover/installer tool No. MB990998-01, or equivalent, to mount hub or hub and rotor onto knuckle. Tighten nut of hub remover/installer to specifications while rotating hub to seat bearing. Leave hub remover/installer in place while taking measurements described in Steps n and o.

m. Measure wheel bearing starting torque using hub remover/installer and a suitable inch pound torque wrench. Starting torque must be 16 inch lbs. or less and bearing must not feel rough when rotated.

n. Measure hub endplay using hub remover/installer and a suitable dial indicator. Endplay must be within .002 inch. If starting torque and endplay are not within limits specified, bearing, hub and/or knuckle may have been incorrectly installed. Repeat disassembly and assembly procedures.

o. Apply multi-purpose grease to lip and install driveshaft side oil seal into knuckle using rear suspension bushing base tool No. MB990890-01 and rear suspension arbor tool No. MB990883-01, or equivalents. Drive seal in until it contacts snap ring.

1997-99

1. Replace hub and knuckle in numbered sequence shown in **Fig. 5,** noting the following:
   a. Hold hub assembly with tool No. MB990767, or equivalent, when removing driveshaft nut.
   b. Before separating lower arm ball joint from knuckle, tie cord of steering linkage puller tool No. MB991113, or equivalent, to nearby part, **Fig. 6.**
2. Disassemble hub, knuckle and bearing assembly as shown in **Fig. 7,** noting the following:
   a. Secure assembly in a vise, then attach pressing tool Nos. MB990998 and MB991355, or equivalents, as shown in **Fig. 8.**
   b. Tighten nut of tool No. MB991355, or equivalent, to separate hub from knuckle assembly.
   c. Using puller tool No. MB990197, or equivalent, remove wheel bearing inner race from hub.
   d. Using a suitable press with a 2.4 inch (61 mm) adapter, remove wheel bearing from hub assembly.
3. Reverse procedure to assemble and install, noting the following:
   a. Fill wheel bearing with multi-purpose grease.
   b. Apply a thin coat of multi-purpose grease to knuckle and bearing contact surfaces.
   c. Apply multi-purpose grease to lip of oil seal and to surfaces of oil seal which contact front hub.
   d. Using front hub remover/installer tool No. MB990998, or equivalent, install hub assembly into knuckle. Rotate hub in order to seat bearing.
   e. **Torque** nut of front hub remover/installer tool to 145–188 ft. lbs., then measure hub rotation starting torque. Starting torque should be 16 inch lbs. or less. If starting torque exceeds specification, replace hub and bearing assembly.
   f. With hub and knuckle assembly mounted in a suitable vise, measure wheel bearing endplay. Endplay should not exceed .002 inch. If endplay exceeds specification, replace hub assembly
   g. Install driveshaft washer in direction shown in **Fig. 3.**

BALL JOINT

REPLACE

Refer to "Control Arm, Replace" for ball joint replacement procedure.

STRUT

REPLACE

1. Remove, install, disassemble and assemble strut assembly in numbered sequence shown in **Figs. 9 and 10,** noting the following:
   a. Hold spring upper seat using spring seat holder tool No. MB991176, or equivalent, then loosen but do not remove self-locking nut.
   b. Using spring compressor body and arm set tools No. MB991237 and MB991238, or equivalents, compress coil spring and remove self-locking nut.
   c. Line up holes in strut assembly spring lower seat with hole in spring upper seat. **This is more easily accomplished using a piece of pipe 10 mm x 300 mm.**
   d. Correctly align both ends of coil spring with grooves in spring seat.
   e. Apply multi-purpose grease to bearing portion of strut insulator. **Do not allow grease to adhere to insulator's rubber portion.**

CONTROL ARM

REPLACE

1. Replace lower control arm and ball joint in numbered sequence shown in **Fig. 11,** noting the following:
   a. Remove ball joint using ball joint remover tool No. MB991113, or equivalent. **Loosen but do not remove ball joint nut until lower control arm is ready to be removed.**
   b. Place lower arm bushing bracket so that its mounting surface tilts 5–7° with respect to bottom surface of lower arm, then install self-locking nut, **Fig. 12.**

STABILIZER BAR

REPLACE

1996

Replace stabilizer bar in numbered sequence shown in **Fig. 13.**

1997-99

1. Remove stabilizer bar in numbered sequence shown in **Fig. 14,** noting the following:

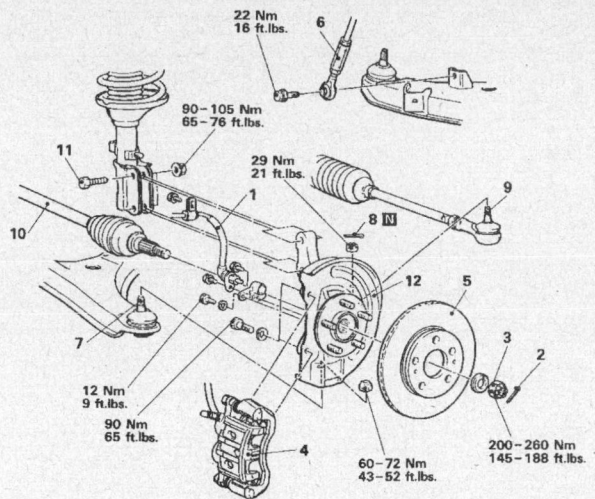

Removal steps
1. Front speed sensor <Vehicles with ABS>
2. Cotter pin
3. Drive shaft nut
4. Caliper assembly
5. Brake disc
6. Front height sensor <Vehicles with ACTIVE-ECS>
7. Connection for lower arm ball joint
8. Cotter pin
9. Connection for tie rod end
10. Drive shaft
11. Front strut mounting bolt
12. Hub and knuckle

MT2049100001000X

Fig. 1   Hub, knuckle & bearing replacement. 1996

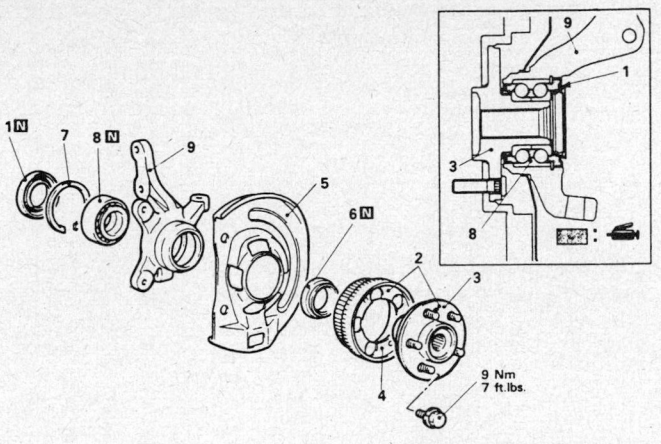

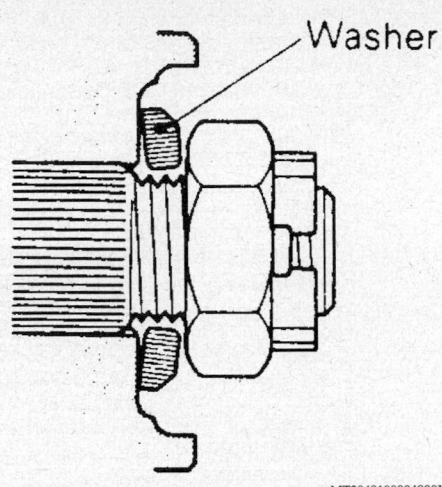

Disassembly steps

1. Oil seal (drive shaft side)
   ● Adjustment of wheel bearing starting torque
   ● Adjustment of hub end play
2. Hub and rotor <Vehicles with ABS>
3. Hub

4. Rotor <Vehicles with ABS>
5. Dust shield
6. Oil seal (hub side)
7. Snap ring
8. Wheel bearing
9. Knuckle

MT2049100002000X

Fig. 2   Hub, knuckle & bearing service. 1996

Fig. 3   Driveshaft nut & washer installation

MT2049100004000X

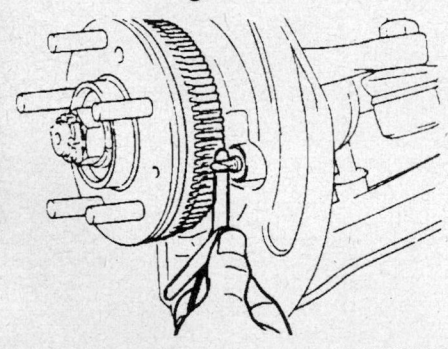

MT2049100005000X

Fig. 4   Speed sensor pole piece clearance check. 1996

a. Remove front exhaust pipe.
b. Remove lower control arm as outlined under "Control Arm, Replace."
2. Reverse procedure to install.

POWER STEERING GEAR

REPLACE

1996

1. Replace power steering gearbox in numbered sequence shown in **Fig. 15**, noting the following:
   a. Disconnect tie rod ends using steering linkage puller tool No. MB991113-01, or equivalent.
   b. Disconnect lines as necessary from control valve, remove control valve from gearbox, then secure to crossmember with wire.
   c. Move rack completely to right, remove gearbox from crossmember, then tilt gearbox downward and remove to left. **Pull out carefully and slowly to avoid damaging boots.**
   d. When installing mounting rubber, align projection of mounting rubber with indentation in crossmember.

1997-99

1. Replace power steering gearbox in

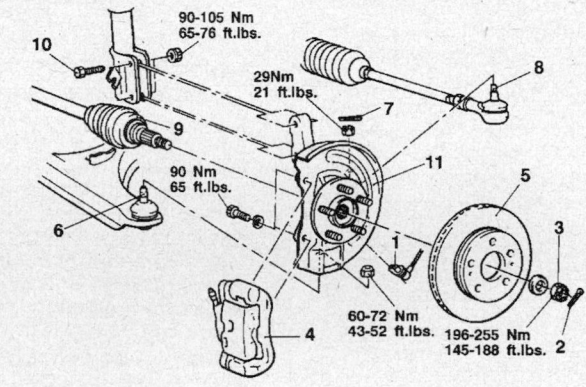

Removal steps

1. Front speed sensor
2. Cotter pin
3. Drive shaft nut
4. Caliper assembly
5. Brake disc
6. Connection for lower arm ball joint

7. Split pin
8. Connection for tie rod end
9. Drive shaft
10. Front strut mounting bolt
11. Hub and knuckle

MT2049700056000X

Fig. 5   Hub & knuckle replacement. 1997-99

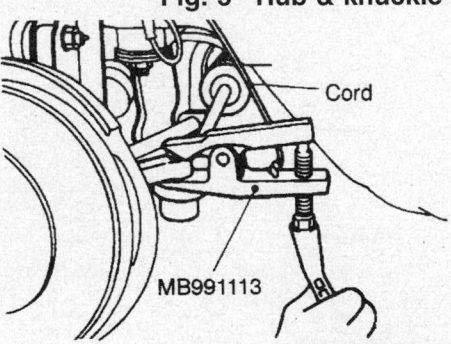

MT2029700044000X

Fig. 6   Lower control arm ball joint removal. 1997-99

numbered sequence shown in **Fig. 16**, noting the following:

a. Drain power steering fluid and support engine using suitable lifting device.
b. Remove center cross member and front exhaust pipe.
c. Before separating lower arm ball joint from knuckle, tie cord of steer-

ing linkage puller tool No. MB991113, or equivalent, to nearby part, **Fig. 6.**
2. Reverse procedure to install.

POWER STEERING PUMP

REPLACE

1996

1. Replace power steering pump in numbered sequence shown in **Figs. 17 and 18**, noting the following:
   a. **On SOHC engine,** raise connector of oil pressure hose upright and lift upward, then align concave portion of pump cover with fuel pipe and remove pump.
   b. **On all models,** connect pressure hose so that slit part contacts oil pumps guide bracket.

1997-99

Replace power steering pump in numbered sequence shown in **Fig. 19**.

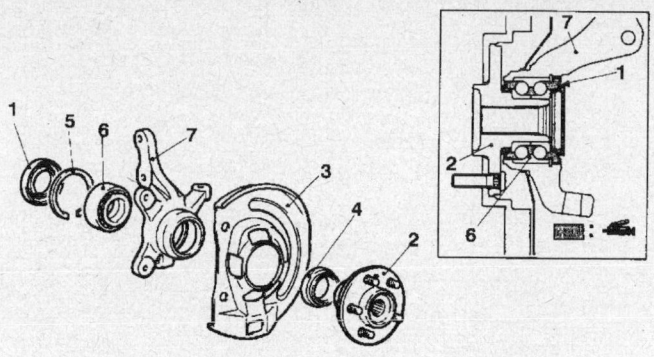

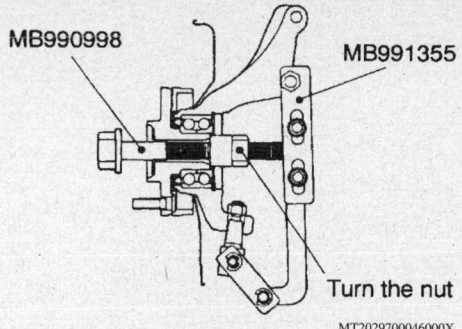

Fig. 8 Hub & knuckle separation.
1997–99

MT2029700046000X

Disassembly Procedure
1. Oil seal (Drive shaft side)
● Adjustment of the wheel bearing starting torque
● Adjustment of the hub end play
2. Hub

3. Dust shield
4. Oil seal
5. Snap ring
6. Wheel bearing
7. Knuckle

MT2029700045000X

Fig. 7 Hub, knuckle & bearing service. 1997–99

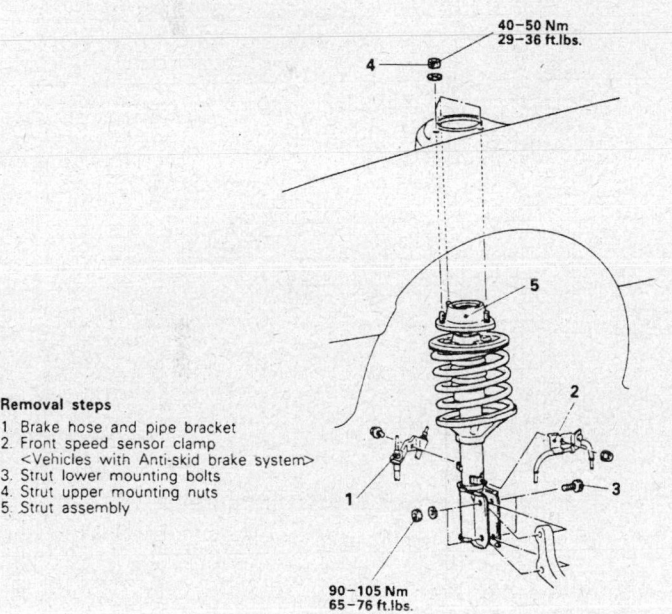

40–50 Nm
29–36 ft.lbs.

Removal steps
1. Brake hose and pipe bracket
2. Front speed sensor clamp
   <Vehicles with Anti-skid brake system>
3. Strut lower mounting bolts
4. Strut upper mounting nuts
5. Strut assembly

90–105 Nm
65–76 ft.lbs.

MT2029100004000X

Fig. 9 Strut assembly replacement

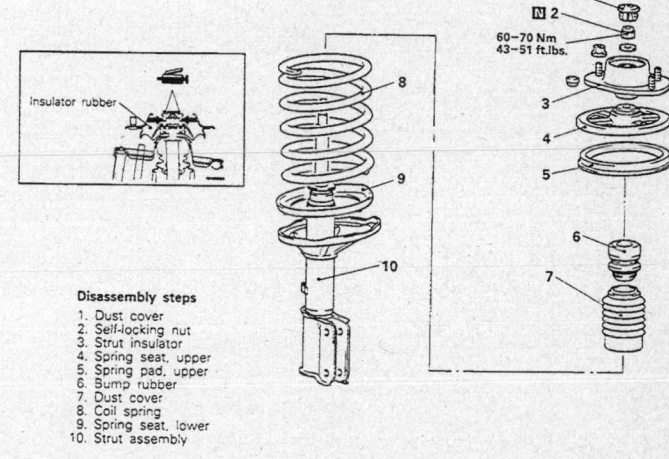

Disassembly steps
1. Dust cover
2. Self-locking nut
3. Strut insulator
4. Spring seat, upper
5. Spring pad, upper
6. Bump rubber
7. Dust cover
8. Coil spring
9. Spring seat, lower
10. Strut assembly

60–70 Nm
43–51 ft.lbs.

MT2029100005000X

Fig. 10 Strut assembly service

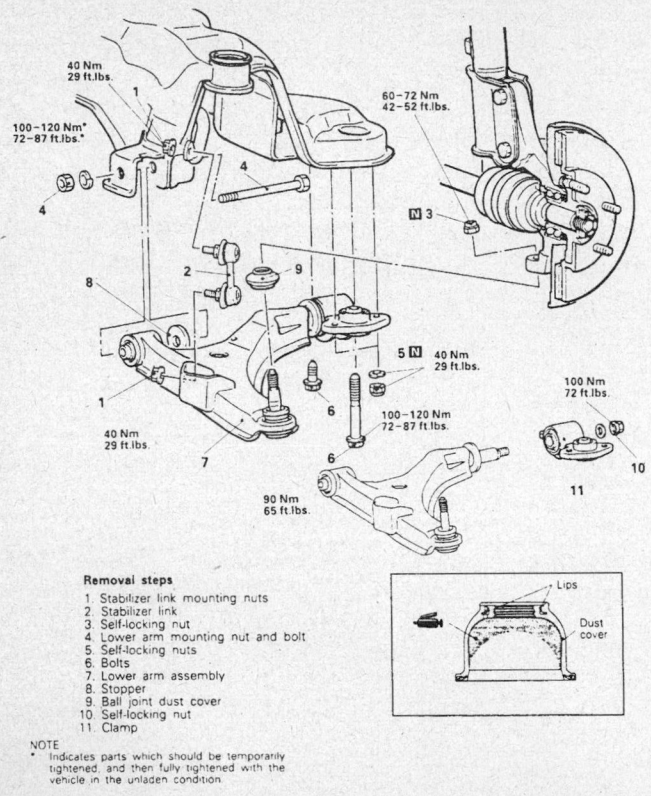

Removal steps

1. Stabilizer link mounting nuts
2. Stabilizer link
3. Self-locking nut
4. Lower arm mounting nut and bolt
5. Self-locking nuts
6. Bolts
7. Lower arm assembly
8. Stopper
9. Ball joint dust cover
10. Self-locking nut
11. Clamp

NOTE
* Indicates parts which should be temporarily tightened, and then fully tightened with the vehicle in the unladen condition.

MT2029100001000X

Fig. 11 Lower control arm & ball joint replacement

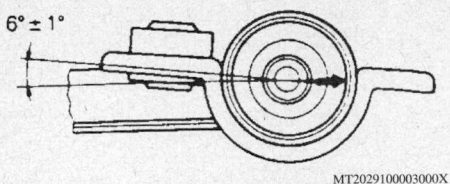

MT2029100003000X

Fig. 12 Lower arm clamp nut installation

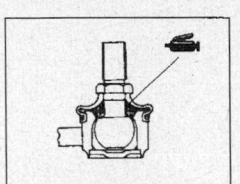

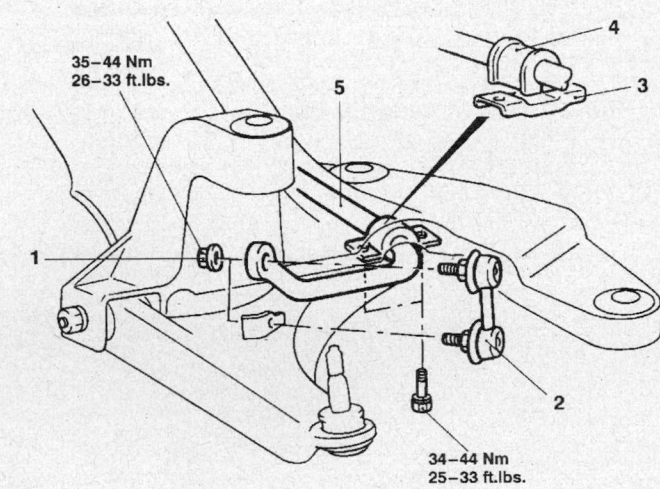

Removal steps

1. Stabilizer link mounting nut
2. Stabilizer link
3. Stabilizer bar bracket

4. Bushing
5. Stabilizer bar

MT2029700047000X

Fig. 14 Stabilizer bar replacement. 1997–99

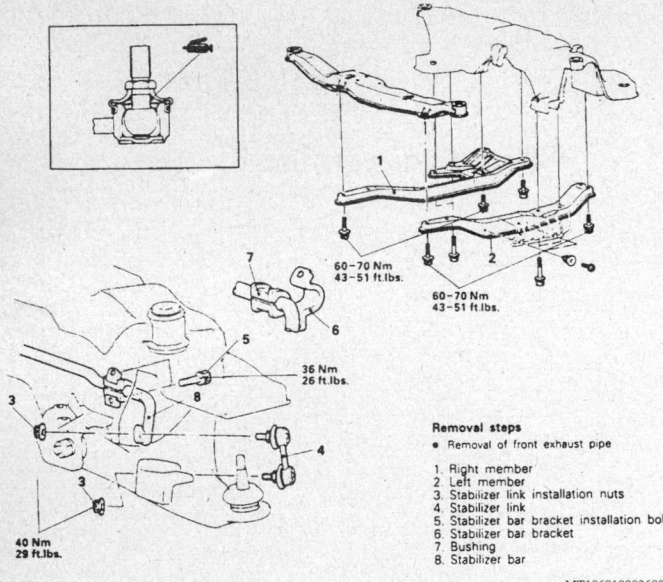

Removal steps

● Removal of front exhaust pipe

1. Right member
2. Left member
3. Stabilizer link installation nuts
4. Stabilizer link
5. Stabilizer bar bracket installation bolt
6. Stabilizer bar bracket
7. Bushing
8. Stabilizer bar

MT1069100036000X

Fig. 13 Stabilizer bar replacement. 1996

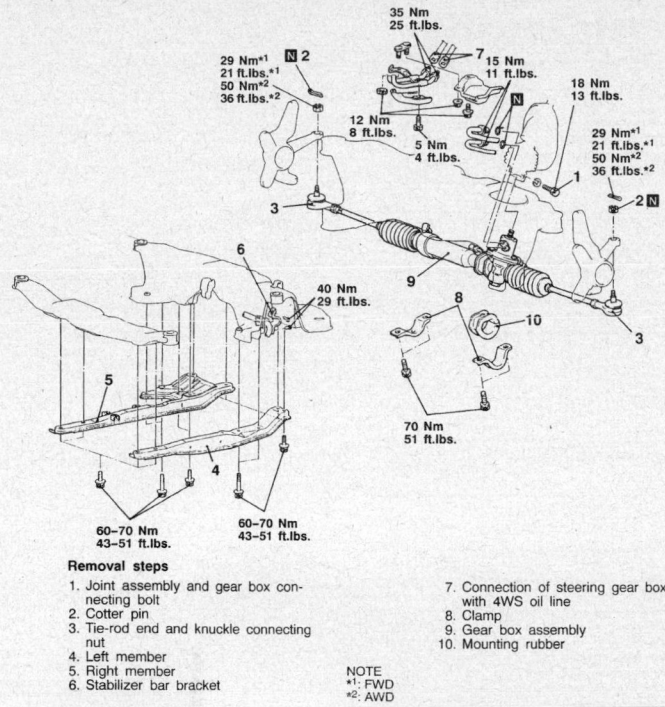

Removal steps

1. Joint assembly and gear box connecting bolt
2. Cotter pin
3. Tie-rod end and knuckle connecting nut
4. Left member
5. Right member
6. Stabilizer bar bracket

7. Connection of steering gear box with 4WS oil line
8. Clamp
9. Gear box assembly
10. Mounting rubber

NOTE
*1: FWD
*2: AWD

MT6039100001000X

Fig. 15   Power steering gearbox replacement. 1996

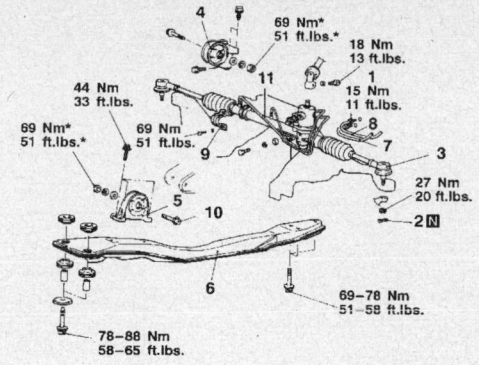

Removal steps

1. Joint assembly and gear box connecting bolt
2. Cotter pin
3. Connection for tie-rod end and knuckle
4. Rear roll stopper
5. Front roll stopper
6. Center member assembly
7. Pressure pipe
8. Return pipe

9. Clamp
10. Bolt
11. Gear box assembly

Caution
The fasteners marked * should be temporarily tightened before they are finally tightened once the total weight of the engine has been placed on the vehicle body.

MT6029700052000X

Fig. 16   Power steering gearbox replacement. 1997–99

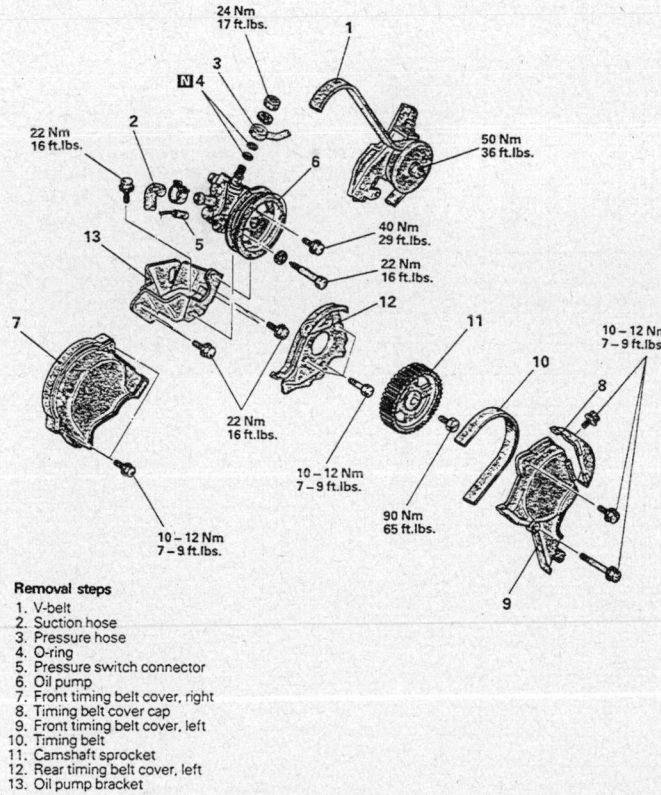

Removal steps

1. V-belt
2. Suction hose
3. Pressure hose
4. O-ring
5. Pressure switch connector
6. Oil pump
7. Front timing belt cover, right
8. Timing belt cover cap
9. Front timing belt cover, left
10. Timing belt
11. Camshaft sprocket
12. Rear timing belt cover, left
13. Oil pump bracket

MT1069100037000X

Fig. 17   Power steering pump replacement. 1996 SOHC engine

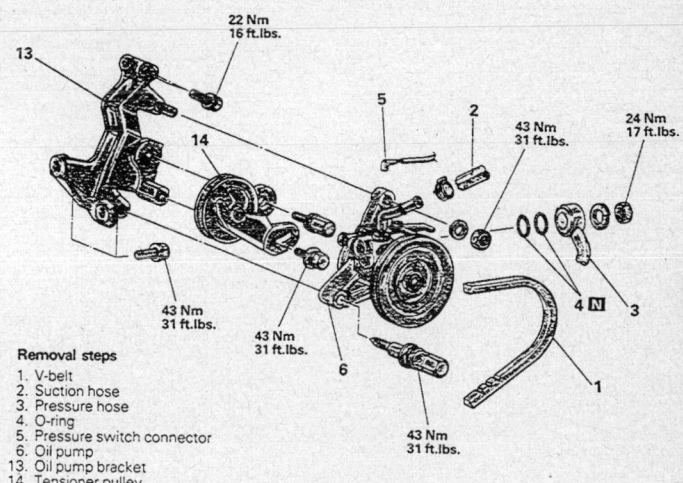

Removal steps

1. V-belt
2. Suction hose
3. Pressure hose
4. O-ring
5. Pressure switch connector
6. Oil pump
13. Oil pump bracket
14. Tensioner pulley

MT1069100038000X

Fig. 18   Power steering pump replacement. 1996 DOHC engine

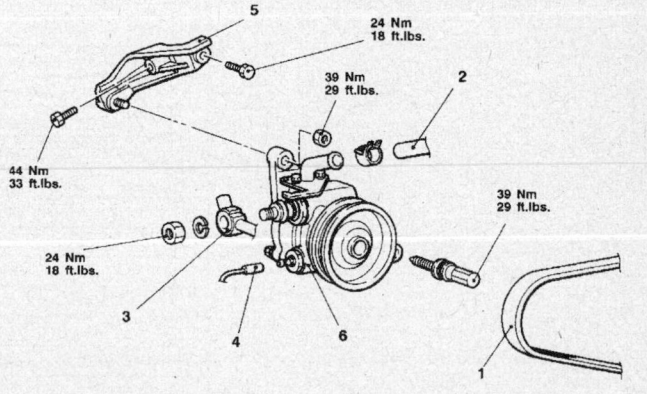

Removal steps

1. Drive-belt
2. Suction hose
3. Pressure hose

4. Pressure switch connector
5. Power steering pump bracket stay
6. Oil pump

MT6029700053000X

Fig. 19   Power steering pump replacement. 1997–99

TIGHTENING SPECIFICATIONS

Year	Component	Torque, Ft. Lbs.
1996	ABS Speed Sensor To Knuckle	108②
	Air Line To Strut Joint	84②
	Axle Nut	145–188
	Brake Caliper To Knuckle	65
	Camshaft Sprocket Bolt (SOHC Engine)	65
	Driveshaft Nut	145–188
	Front Height Sensor To Lower Arm	16
	Front Power Steering Pump Bracket Mounting Bolts (DOHC Engine)	16
	Front Power Steering Pump Mounting Bolts (DOHC Engine)	31
	Front Power Steering Pump Mounting Bolts (SOHC Engine)	16
	Front Power Steering Pump Pressure Hose To Pump	17
	Hub Nut	145–188
	Hub To ABS Rotor	84②
	Knuckle To Ball Joint	43–52
	Knuckle To Strut Assembly	65–76
	Knuckle To Tie Rod Assembly	21
	Lower Arm Clamp To Lower Arm	72
	Lower Arm To Crossmember Bolt	72–87
	Lower Arm To Crossmember Self Locking Nuts	29
	Lower Arm To Crossmember Through Bolt & Nut	72–87①
	Power Cylinder Control Valve To Mounting Plate	96②
	Power Cylinder Lines	11
	Power Steering Control Valve Mounting Plate To Valve Bracket	96②
	Power Steering Control Valve To Mounting Plate	96②
	Power Steering Gearbox Coupling Bolt	13
	Power Steering Gearbox To Crossmember	51
	Power Steering Lines	11
	Right & Left Member Bolts	43–51
	Stabilizer Bar Bracket	26
	Stabilizer Link Mounting Nut	29
	Strut Assembly Self Locking Nut	43–51
	Strut To Strut Tower	29–36
	Timing Cover Mounting Bolts (SOHC Engine)	84–108②
	Wheel Lug Nuts	65–79
1997–99	Brake Caliper Mounting Bolts	65
	Crossmember To Frame	58–65
	Driveshaft Nut	145–188
	Front Roll Stopper Through Bolt	51
	Front Roll Stopper To Crossmember	33
	Hub Nut	145–188
	Lower Control Arm Ball Joint Nut	43–52
	Lower Strut Mounting Bolts	65–76
	Power Steering Gear Pressure Hose Fitting	11
	Power Steering Gear Return Hose Fitting	11
	Power Steering Gear To Column Pinch Bolt	13
	Power Steering Pump Bracket	18

Continued

TIGHTENING
SPECIFICATIONS—Continued

Year	Component	Torque, Ft. Lbs.
1997–99	Power Steering Pump Pressure Hose Fitting	18
	Power Steering Pump To Bracket	29
	Rear Roll Stopper Through Bolt	51
	Tie Rod End To Knuckle	20
	Stabilizer Link Bracket Bolts	25–33
	Stabilizer Link Mounting Nut	26–33
	Strut Upper Attaching Nuts	29–36
	Wheel Lug Nut	65–80

① — Must be tightened while vehicle is unladen.
② — Inch lbs.

Wheel Alignment

INDEX

PRELIMINARY INSPECTION

1. Ensure tires are inflated to correct pressure, then check for uneven wear.
2. Check front wheel bearings, suspension arm and ball joints for damage. Replace components as necessary, to eliminate improper alignment due to faulty components.
3. Check steering gear for damage and adjust as necessary.
4. Check shocks for damage and replace as necessary.
5. Rock vehicle backward and forward and bounce it upward and downward to settle vehicle prior to alignment.
6. Ensure vehicle is unloaded and on a suitable alignment rack according to manufacturer's instructions. **When measuring equipment is attached directly to outer end of driveshaft and front wheels are on turntables, apply brake to prevent improper vehicle movement.**

FRONT WHEEL ALIGNMENT

CAMBER

Camber is preset during production and is not adjustable. If camber is out of specification, replace bent or damaged components.

CASTER

Caster has been preset during production and is not adjustable.

TOE-IN

1. Adjust toe-in by loosening clips and turning left and right tie rod turnbuckles equally in opposite directions, **Fig. 1.**
2. To increase toe-out, turn left turnbuckle toward front of vehicle and right turnbuckle toward rear of vehicle. To increase toe-in, turn turnbuckles in other direction.
3. Amount of toe-in adjustment is .24 inch for each half turn of left and right tie rods.

REAR WHEEL ALIGNMENT

CAMBER

1996

1. Turn lower arm mounting bolt to adjust rear camber, **Fig. 2.**
2. Loosen assist link mounting bolt prior to camber adjustment.
3. Difference between both wheels should not exceed ½.°

1997-99

Camber is preset during production and is not adjustable. If camber is out of specification, replace bent or damaged components.

TOE-IN

1996

Adjust rear toe-in by turning assist link mounting bolt an equal amount on both sides, **Fig. 3.**

1997-99

Rear toe adjustment is done by turning the toe control arm mounting bolt to the left or right by equal amounts, **Fig. 4.** One scale mark is equal to a change of .08 inch.

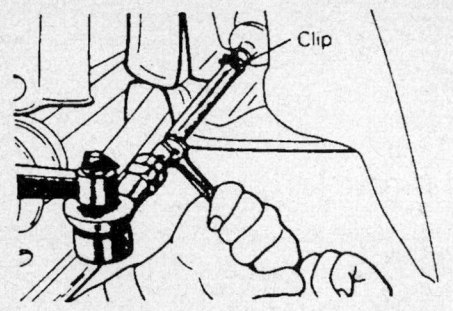

Fig. 1   Front toe-in adjustment.
1996

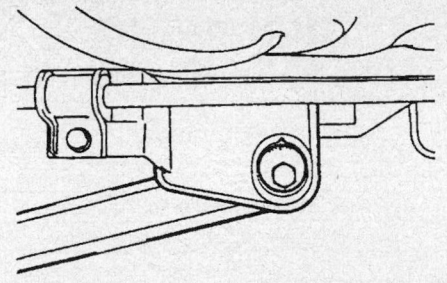

Fig. 2   Rear camber adjustment

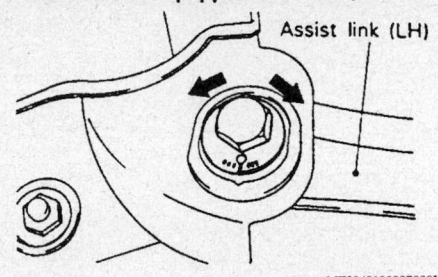

Fig. 3   Rear toe-in adjustment.
1996

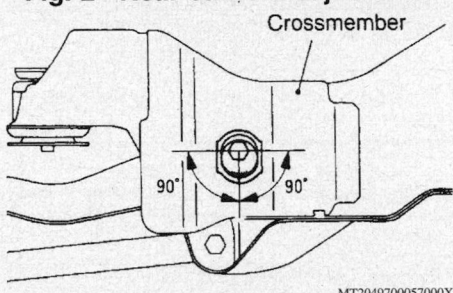

Fig. 4   Rear toe-in adjustment.
1997–99

MITSUBISHI ECLIPSE
INDEX OF SERVICE OPERATIONS

Specifications

GENERAL ENGINE SPECIFICATIONS

Year	Engine, Liter	Fuel System	Bore & Stroke	Compression Ratio	Maximum Net H.P. @ RPM	Maximum Torque, Ft. Lbs. @ RPM	Normal Oil Pressure, psi
1996–99	2.0L	Fuel Inj.	3.45 X 3.27	9.6	140 @ 6000	130 @ 4800	11.4②
	2.0L①	Fuel Inj.	3.35 X 3.46	8.5	④	⑤	11.4②
	2.4L	Fuel Inj.	3.41 X 3.94	③	141 @ 5500	148 @ 3000	11.4②

① — Turbocharged engine.
② — At idle speed w/oil temperature between 167–194°F.
③ — 1996–97, 9.5; 1998–99, 9.0 w/California emissions, 9.5 w/Federal emissions.

④ — 210 @ 6000 RPM w/manual transmission; 205 @ 6000 RPM w/automatic transmission.
⑤ — 214 @ 3000 RPM w/manual transmission; 220 @ 3000 RPM w/automatic transmission.

TUNE UP SPECIFICATIONS

Year	Engine Liter	Spark Plug Gap, Inch	Ignition Timing			Idle Speed, RPM				Fuel Pump Pressure, psi	Valve Lash
			Firing Order	Timing, °BTDC	Timing Mark Location	Curb②		Fast			
						Man. Trans.	Auto. Trans.	Man. Trans.	Auto. Trans.		
1996–99	2.0L	.050	1-3-4-2	12①	⑦	800	800N	④	④	47–50	③
	2.0L⑤	.030	1-3-4-2	5⑥	⑦	750	750N	④	④	33	③
	2.4L	.040	1-3-4-2	5⑥	⑦	750	750N	④	④	38	③

BTDC — Before Top Dead Center
N — Neutral
① — Electronically controlled.
② — When adjusting idle speed, set parking brake & chock drive wheels.

③ — Equipped w/hydraulic lash adjusters.
④ — Controlled by idle speed control servo.
⑤ — Turbocharged engine.

⑥ — With jumper wire connected between ignition timing adjustment connector & ground. Refer to **Fig. A.**
⑦ — Equipped w/crankshaft position sensor.

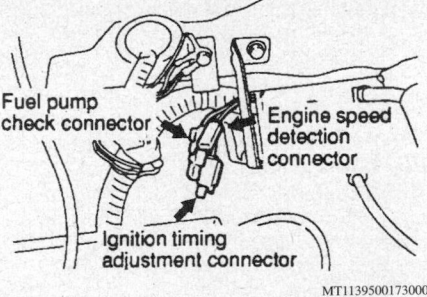

MT1139500173000X

Fig. A

FRONT WHEEL ALIGNMENT SPECIFICATIONS

Year	Model	Caster Angle, Deg.		Camber Angle, Deg.		Toe, Inch①	Ball Joint Wear
		Limits	Desired	Limits	Desired		
1996	Eclipse②	+2⅙ to +5⅚	+4⅓	-½ to +½	0	−.12 to +.12	④
	Eclipse③	+3⅙ to +6⅙	+4⅔	-7/12 to +5/12	-1/12	−.12 to +.12	④
1997–99	Eclipse②	+3⅙ to +6⅙	+4⅔	-7/12 to +5/12	-1/12	−.12 to +.12	④
	Eclipse③	+3⅙ to +6⅙	+4⅔	-⅚ to +⅙	-⅓	−.12 to +.12	④

① — Toe-in (+); toe-out (-).
② — 14 inch wheels.
③ — 16 inch wheels.
④ — Lateral lower arm ball joint breakaway torque, 9–30 ft. lbs.; stabilizer link ball joint breakaway torque, 4–13 inch lbs.

REAR WHEEL ALIGNMENT SPECIFICATIONS

Year	Model	Camber Angle, Deg.		Toe, Inch①
		Limits	Desired	
1996–99	Eclipse AWD③	-1⅚ to -⅚	-1⅓	0 to +.24
	Eclipse AWD④	-2⅙ to -1⅙	-1⅔	0 to +.24
	Eclipse FWD⑤	-1⅚ to -⅚	-1⅓	0 to +.24
	Eclipse FWD②	-2⅙ to -1⅙	-1⅔	0 to +.24

AWD — All Wheel Drive
FWD — Front Wheel Drive
① — Toe-in (+); toe-out (-).
② — 16 inch wheels.
③ — Manual transaxle.
④ — Automatic transaxle.
⑤ — 14 inch wheels.

FLUID CAPACITIES & COOLING SYSTEM DATA

Year	Engine	Coolant Capacity, Qts.	Radiator Cap Relief Pressure, Lbs.	Thermo. Opening Temp., °F	Fuel Tank, Gals.	Engine Oil Refill, Qts. ①	Transaxle Oil		Transfer Case Oil, Pts.	Rear Drive Axle Oil, Pts.
							Man. Trans. Pts.	Auto. Trans., Qts.②		
1996–99	2.0L Non-Turbo	7.4	14–18	195	16.9	4.5	4.2	9.1	—	—
	2.0L FWD Turbo	7.4	11–15	180	16.9	4.6	4.2	7.1	—	—
	2.0L AWD Turbo	7.4	11–15	180	16.9	4.6	4.6	7.1	1.06	1.8
	2.4L FWD	7.4	11–15	180	16.9	4.5	4.2	6.4	—	—
	2.4L AWD	7.4	11–15	180	16.9	4.5	—	6.4	1.06	1.8

AWD — All Wheel Drive
FWD — Front Wheel Drive
① — Includes filter.
② — Approximate; make final check w/dipstick.

LUBRICANT DATA

Year	Lubricant Type					
	Transmission		Transfer Case	Rear Axle	Power Steering	Brake System
	Manual	Automatic				
1996–99	①	②	75w/90 GL-4/5	GL-5	Dexron II/IIE/III	DOT 3 or 4

① — With non-turbocharged engine, Texaco MTX fluid FM or equivalent; with turbocharged engine, 75w/90 GL-4.
② — 1996, Dia ATF SP; 1997–99, Dia ATF SPII.

Electrical

NOTE: On Air Bag Equipped Models, Refer To "Air Bag System Precautions" Located In The Front Of This Manual For System Disarming & Arming Procedures.

NOTE: Refer To "Computer Relearn" Located In The Front Of This Manual For Computer Relearn Procedures.

INDEX

PRECAUTIONS

AIR BAG SYSTEMS

Refer to "Air Bag System Precautions" in the front of this manual for system disarming and arming procedures.

BATTERY GROUND CABLE

Prior to service, disconnect battery ground cable and isolate as required.

FUSE PANEL & FLASHER LOCATION

The multi-purpose fuse panel and dedicated fuse panel are located under the lefthand side of the instrument panel. On non-turbocharged models, the dedicated fuse panel/power distribution block is located on the front lefthand side of the engine compartment. On models equipped with 2.4L or turbocharged engines, the dedicated fuse panel/power distribution block is located on the righthand side of the engine compartment. The hazard and turn signal flasher is located behind the center of the instrument panel.

FUEL PUMP RELAY LOCATION

On non-turbocharged models, the fuel pump relay is located in the lefthand rear corner of the engine compartment.

On models equipped with 2.4L or turbocharged engines, the fuel pump relay is located behind the center of the instrument panel.

RELAY CENTER LOCATION

On non-turbocharged models, the main relay centers are located on the front lefthand side and rear lefthand side of the engine compartment.

On models equipped with 2.4L or turbocharged engines, the main relay centers are located on the righthand side of the engine compartment.

STARTER

REPLACE

1. Remove battery.
2. **On models equipped with turbocharged engine,** remove air hose.
3. **On models equipped with 2.4L engine,** remove air cleaner assembly and air intake hose.
4. **On all models,** remove starter terminal and connector.
5. Remove starter attaching bolts, then the starter.
6. Reverse procedure to install.

COIL PACK

REPLACE

1. **On models equipped 2.4L engine and turbocharged models,** remove center cover.
2. **On all models,** disconnect spark plug cables from ignition coil. **Label cables for installation reference.**
3. Remove coil pack mounting screws, then the coil pack.
4. Reverse procedure to install.

IGNITION LOCK

REPLACE

1. Remove steering wheel as outlined under "Steering Wheel, Replace."
2. Remove instrument panel lower cover.
3. Remove plug, then remove hood lock release handle, **Fig. 1.**
4. Remove upper and lower column covers.
5. Remove clock spring, column switch, then the ignition key illumination light.
6. Insert key in ignition lock cylinder and turn to ACC position.
7. Using a Phillips tip screwdriver, or equivalent, push lockpin of ignition lock cylinder inward, then pull ignition lock cylinder out, **Fig. 2.**
8. Remove key reminder switch segment and key hole illumination lamp, if equipped.
9. Remove ignition switch segment.
10. Reverse procedure to install. Apply a light coat of multi-purpose grease to areas shown, then ensure proper operation of key interlock system.

IGNITION SWITCH

REPLACE

Refer to "Ignition Lock, Replace," for ignition switch replacement procedures.

NEUTRAL SAFETY SWITCH

REPLACE

1. Place selector lever in Neutral position.
2. Place manual control lever in Neutral

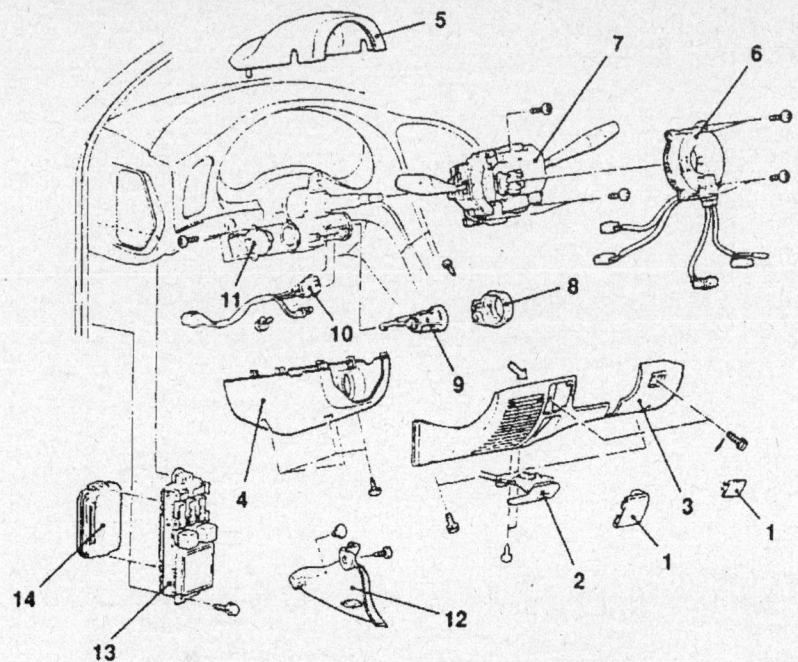

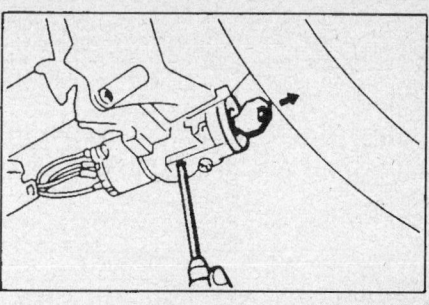

Fig. 2 Lock cylinder removal

1. Plug
2. Hood lock release handle
3. Instrument under cover
4. Column cover lower
5. Column cover upper
6. Clock spring
7. Column switch
8. Ignition key illumination ring or ring cover
9. Steering lock cylinder
10. Key reminder switch segment or key hole illumination light
11. Ignition switch segment
12. Cowl side trim (LH)
13. Junction block
14. ETACS-ECU

Fig. 1 Ignition switch replacement

position, then remove control lever retainer and lever.
3. Disconnect electrical harness, then remove switch retaining bolts and switch assembly.
4. Reverse procedure to install, then adjust as follows:
   a. With manual control lever in Neutral position, rotate switch body until wide end of control lever overlaps switch body flange.
   b. Hold switch body in position, then **torque** retaining bolts to 7–9 ft. lbs.

HEADLAMP SWITCH
REPLACE

Refer to "Combination Switch, Replace" for headlamp switch replacement procedure.

COMBINATION SWITCH
REPLACE

1. Remove air bag module as outlined under "Air Bag System."

2. Remove steering wheel as outlined under "Steering Wheel, Replace."
3. Remove column switch in numbered sequence, **Fig. 3.**
4. Reverse procedure to install.

DIMMER SWITCH
REPLACE

Refer to "Combination Switch, Replace" for dimmer switch replacement procedure.

STEERING WHEEL
REPLACE

1. Remove air bag mounting nut from back side, then disconnect electrical connector.
2. Remove horn pad attaching screws and pad.
3. Remove steering wheel attaching nut.
4. Scribe mating marks on steering shaft and steering wheel for installation reference.
5. Using a suitable steering wheel puller, remove steering wheel. **Do not ham-**

mer on steering wheel to remove. Damage to collapsible mechanism may occur.
6. Reverse procedure to install, noting the following:
   a. Align mating marks on steering shaft and steering wheel.
   b. **Torque** steering wheel attaching nut to 25–36 ft. lbs.

INSTRUMENT CLUSTER
REPLACE

1. Remove instrument cluster bezel.
2. Remove screws holding cluster to dash.
3. Gently pull cluster outward enough to remove connectors and clips from rear of cluster, allowing it to be removed.
4. Reverse procedure to install.

RADIO
REPLACE

1. Use plastic trim tool to pry lower part of radio panel out of console.
2. Remove floor console assembly.
3. Remove radio bracket.
4. Gently pull outward on radio assembly enough to remove connectors from rear of unit.
5. Reverse procedure to install.

WIPER MOTOR
REPLACE
FRONT

Remove front windshield wiper motor and transmission in numbered sequence, **Figs. 4 and 5,** noting the following:
1. Mark position of wiper arms before removal.
2. Reverse procedure to install.

REAR

Remove rear windshield wiper motor and transmission in numbered sequence, **Fig. 6,** noting the following:
1. Mark position of wiper arm before removal.
2. Reverse procedure to install.

WIPER SWITCH
REPLACE

Refer to "Combination Switch, Replace" procedure.

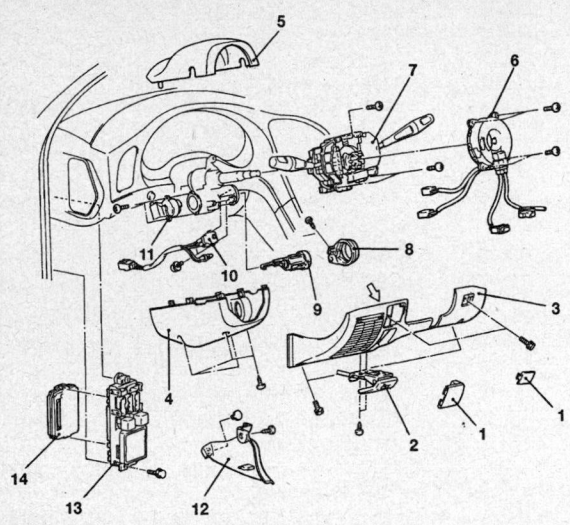

Steering lock cylinder removal steps

1. Plug
2. Hood lock release handle
3. Instrument under cover
4. Column cover lower
5. Column cover upper
6. Clock spring
7. Column switch
8. Ignition key illumination ring or ring cover
9. Steering lock cylinder

Key reminder switch segment or key hole illumination light removal steps

4. Column cover lower
5. Column cover upper
10. Key reminder switch segment or key hole illumination light

Ignition switch segment removal steps

4. Column cover lower
5. Column cover upper
11. Ignition switch segment

ETACS-ECU removal steps

12. Cowl side trim (L.H.)
13. Junction block
14. ETACS-ECU

CR9049500067000X

Fig. 3   Combination switch removal

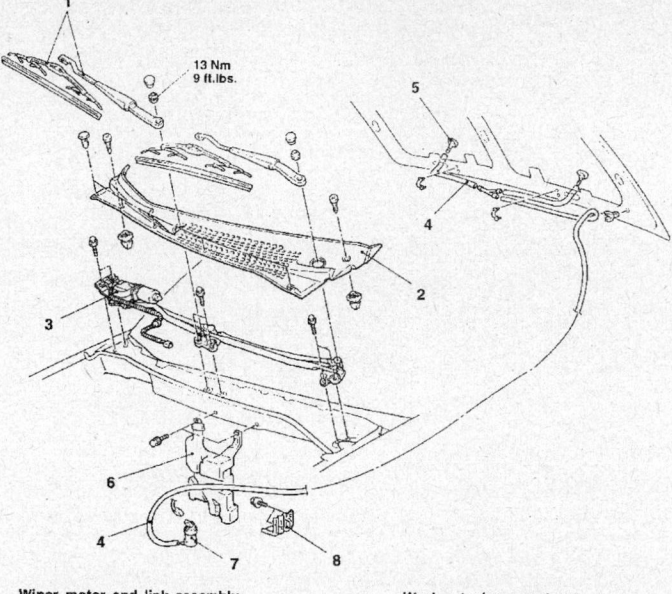

Wiper motor and link assembly removal steps

1. Wiper arm and blade assembly
2. Front deck garnish
3. Wiper motor and link assembly

Washer nozzle and washer hose removal steps

4. Washer hose connection
5. Washer nozzle

Washer tank removal steps

● Brake fluid reservoir tank mounting bolt
6. Washer tank
7. Washer motor
8. Washer tank bracket

MT9029800068000X

Fig. 4   Front wiper motor replacement. Non-turbocharged engine

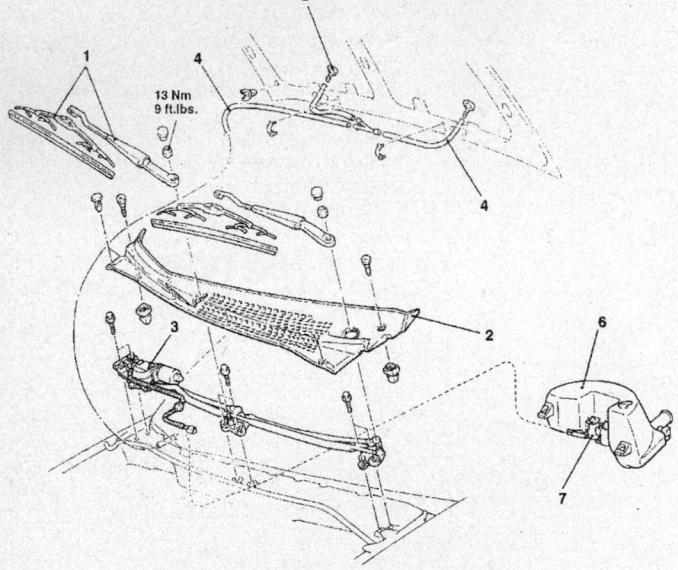

Wiper motor and link assembly removal steps

1. Wiper arm and blade assembly
2. Front deck garnish
3. Wiper motor and link assembly

Washer nozzle and washer hose removal steps

4. Washer hose connection
5. Washer nozzle

Washer tank removal steps

6. Washer tank
7. Washer motor

MT9029800069000X

Fig. 5   Front wiper motor replacement. Turbocharged engine

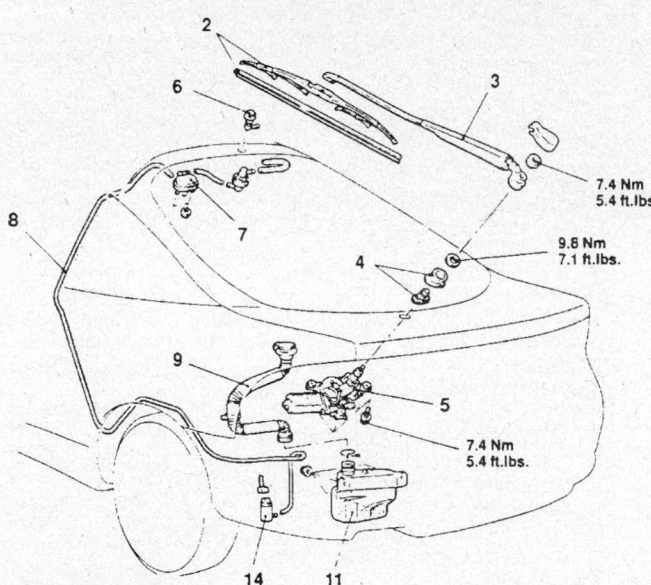

Rear wiper motor removal steps

2. Wiper blade
3. Wiper arm
4. Spacer assembly
● Liftgate lower trim

5. Rear wiper motor

Rear washer tank and hose removal steps

● Quarter upper trim (LH)
● Quarter lower trim (LH)

● Rear end trim
● Rear side trim
● Liftgate upper trim
6. Washer nozzle
7. Joint assembly
8. Tube assembly
9. Hose assembly
11. Rear washer tank
14. Rear washer motor

CR9029500133000X

Fig. 6   Rear wiper motor replacement

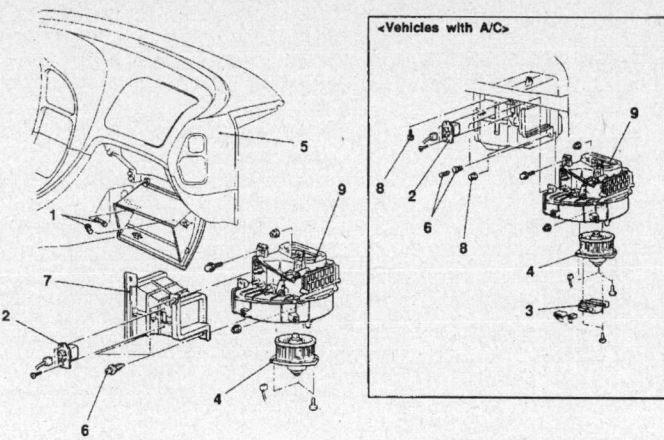

Resistor removal steps

1. Stopper
2. Resistor

Blower fan and motor removal steps

3. Automatic compressor ECM
   <Vehicles with A/C>
4. Blower fan and motor

Blower unit removal steps

5. Instrument panel

6. Clip
7. Joint duct <Vehicles without A/C>
8. Evaporator installation bolts and nut
   <Vehicles with A/C>
9. Blower unit assembly

CR7029500230000X

Fig. 7 Blower motor replacement

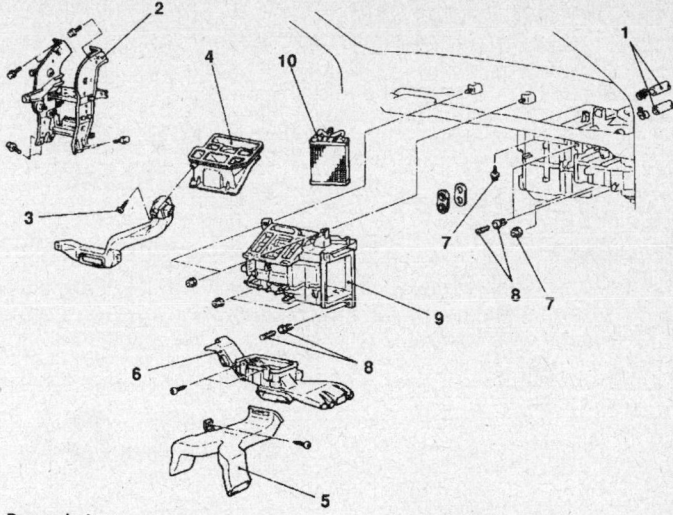

Removal steps

● Instrument panel

1. Heater hose connection
2. Center stay
3. Lap cooler duct installation screw
4. Center duct

5. Semi rear heater duct
6. Foot distribution duct
7. Evaporator installation bolt and nut
   <Vehicles with A/C>
8. Clip
9. Heater unit
10. Heater core

CR7029500231000X

Fig. 8 Exploded view of heater unit

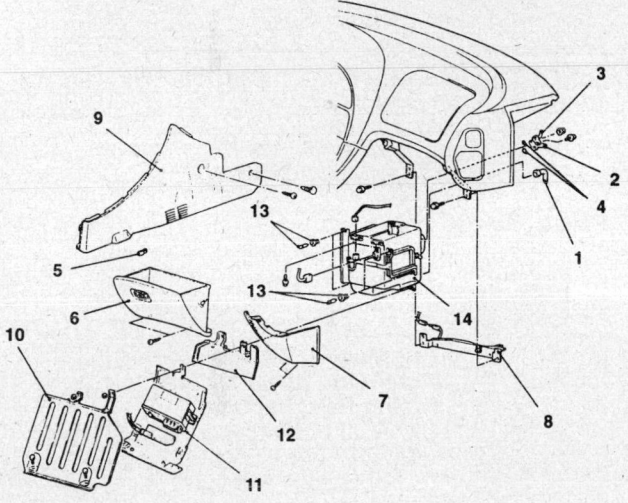

1. Drain hose
2. Suction pipe <2.0L Engine (Non-turbo)> or suction hose <2.0L Engine (Turbo)> and 2.4L Engine> connection
3. Liquid pipe connection
4. O-ring
5. Stopper
6. Glove box

7. Corner panel
8. Glove box under frame
9. Console side cover <R.H.>
10. Control unit cover
11. ABS-ECU bracket
12. Harness protector (Turbo)
13. Clip
14. Cooling unit

CR7029500232000X

Fig. 9 Evaporator replacement

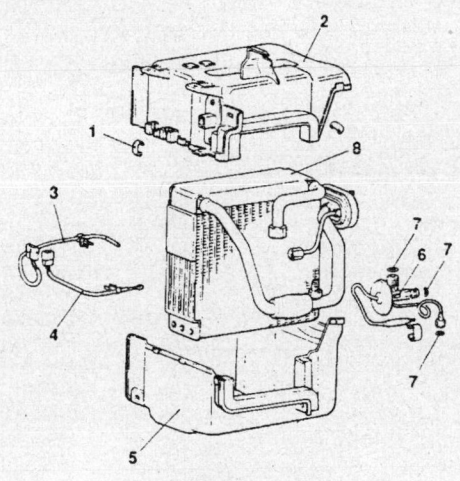

Disassembly steps

1. Clip
2. Evaporator case (upper)
3. Fin thermo sensor
4. Air inlet sensor
5. Evaporator case (lower)
6. Expansion valve
7. O-ring
8. Evaporator

CR7029500233000X

Fig. 10 Exploded view of evaporator unit

BLOWER MOTOR
REPLACE

Remove blower motor in numbered sequence, **Fig. 7,** noting the following:
1. Clean blower case before installation.
2. Reverse procedure to install.

HEATER CORE
REPLACE

Remove heater unit in numbered sequence, **Fig. 8,** noting the following:
1. Drain engine coolant.

2. Remove instrument panel as outlined in "Dash Panel Service."
3. Reverse procedure to install. Refill engine coolant.

EVAPORATOR CORE
REPLACE

Remove evaporator unit in numbered sequence, **Figs. 9 and 10,** noting the following:
1. Properly discharge refrigerant from A/C system as outlined in "Air Conditioning."

2. Plug refrigerant lines to prevent air from mixing when disconnecting them.
3. **On models equipped with non-turbocharged engine,** refill evaporator with 1.35 fl. oz. ND-OIL 8 compressor oil, or equivalent, before replacing evaporator.
4. **On models equipped with turbo-charged engine,** refill evaporator with 2.03 fl. oz. SUN PAG 56 compressor oil, or equivalent, before replacing evaporator.
5. **On all models,** reverse procedure to install, properly recharge A/C system as outlined in "Air Conditioning."

2.0L Engine

NOTE: On Air Bag Equipped Models, Refer To "Air Bag System Precautions" Located In The Front Of This Manual For System Disarming & Arming Procedures.

NOTE: Refer To "Computer Relearn" Located In The Front Of This Manual For Computer Relearn Procedures.

INDEX

PRECAUTIONS
AIR BAG SYSTEMS

Refer to "Air Bag System Precautions" in the front of this manual for system disarming and arming procedures.

BATTERY GROUND CABLE

Prior to service, disconnect battery ground cable and isolate as required.

FUEL SYSTEM PRESSURE RELIEF

1. Raise and support vehicle.
2. Disconnect fuel pump electrical connector. **Failure to relieve fuel system**

pressure prior to disconnecting fuel system components may cause fire or personal injury.
3. Lower vehicle.
4. Start and run engine until it stops. Allow engine to deplete fuel supply, then turn ignition off.
5. Disconnect battery ground cable.
6. Crank engine two or three times to release remaining fuel pressure.
7. After fuel system repairs are completed, reconnect fuel pump electrical connector.

COMPRESSION PRESSURE

1. Check engine oil level, then ensure battery and starter motor are in satisfactory condition.
2. Start and run engine until it reaches operating temperature.
3. Turn engine off and remove spark plugs.
4. Disconnect crankshaft position sensor connector. NOTE: Doing this will prevent engine control unit from carrying out ignition and fuel injection.
5. Cover spark plug hole with shop towel

Engine Liter	Compression Pressure, psi①	Minimum Pressure, psi	Max. Variation Between Cylinders, psi
2.0L②	170-225	100	25
2.0L③	178	133	14

① — At 250–400 psi. ② — Non-turbocharged engine. ③ — Turbocharged engine.

Fig. 1 Compression pressure data

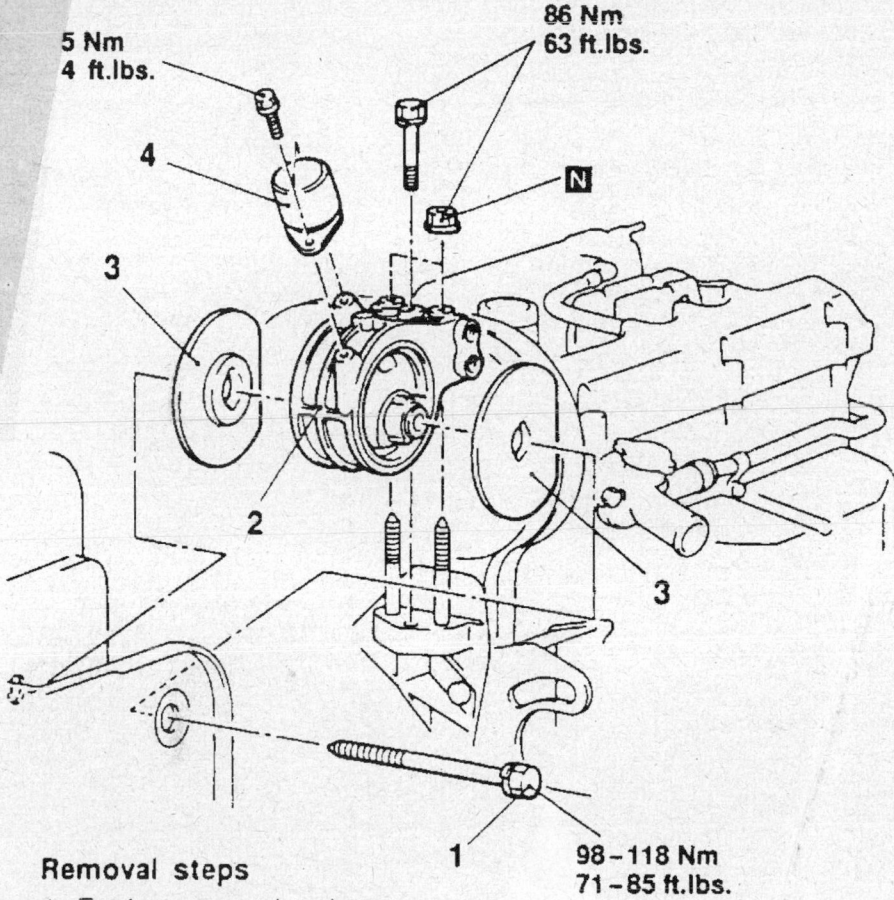

5 Nm
4 ft.lbs.

86 Nm
63 ft.lbs.

4

3

2

3

1

98 – 118 Nm
71 – 85 ft.lbs.

Removal steps

1. Engine mount insulator mounting bolt
2. Engine mount bracket
3. Engine mount stopper
4. Dynamic damper

CR1069500602000X

Fig. 2 Engine mount assembly

etc., and after engine has been cranked, check that no foreign material is adhering to shop towel.

  a. **Keep away from spark plug hole when cranking engine.**
  b. **If compression is measured with water, oil, fuel, etc., that has come from cracks inside cylinder, these materials will become heated and will gush out from spark plug hole, which is dangerous.**

6. Connect a suitable pressure gauge and crank engine at wide throttle valve wide open.
7. Repeat procedure at each cylinder, compare readings with specifications

shown in **Fig. 1.**

ENGINE MOUNT
REPLACE
EXCEPT ENGINE ROLL STOPPER

Remove engine mount in numbered sequence, **Fig. 2,** noting the following:

1. Slightly raise and support engine, removing weight of engine from mount.
2. Inspect insulators for damage or cracks and replace as necessary.
3. Check brackets and replace if deformed or damaged.

4. When installing mounting stoppers, ensure arrow on stopper faces center of engine, **Fig. 3.**
5. Reverse procedure to install.

ENGINE ROLL STOPPER

Remove engine roll stoppers in numbered sequence, **Fig. 4,** noting the following:

1. Slightly raise and support engine, removing weight of engine from mount.
2. Inspect insulators for damage or cracks and replace as necessary.
3. Inspect brackets and replace if deformed or damaged.
4. Inspect front roll stopper bracket assembly. If the dimension shown in **Fig. 5** is not 1.57–1.81 inches when the weight of the engine is on the body, replace the front roll stopper assembly.
5. When installing mounting stoppers, ensure arrow on stopper faces center of engine, **Fig. 3.**
6. Reverse procedure to install.

ENGINE
REPLACE

1. Release fuel system pressure as outlined under "Precautions."
2. Scribe reference marks between hood and hood hinges, then remove hood.
3. Drain cooling system as follows:
  a. Place temperature control lever in Hot position.
  b. Carefully remove radiator cap, then the radiator drain plug.
4. Remove transaxle assembly.
5. Remove radiator as outlined under "Radiator, Replace."
6. Remove engine components in numbered sequence as shown in **Figs. 6 and 7,** noting the following:
  a. Remove power steering pump from bracket with hoses attached, then secure pump aside with a piece of wire.
  b. Remove A/C compressor from bracket with hoses attached, then compressor pump aside with a piece of wire.
  c. Using a suitable engine hoist, slightly raise engine, then remove engine mount bracket.
  d. Ensure all cables, connectors and hoses are disconnected, then remove engine from engine compartment.
7. Reverse procedure to install.

INTAKE MANIFOLD
REPLACE
REMOVAL

Remove intake manifold in numbered sequence, **Figs. 8 and 9,** noting the following:

1. Drain coolant as follows:
  a. Place instrument panel temperature control lever in Hot position.
  b. Carefully remove radiator cap.
  c. Remove radiator drain plug.
2. Before disconnecting high pressure

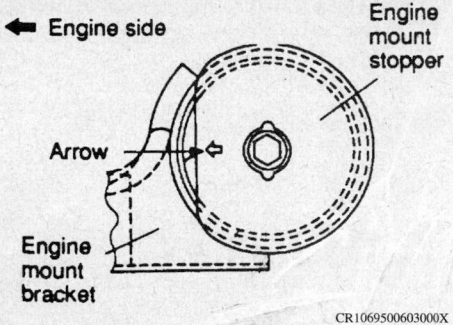

Fig. 3 Engine mount stopper installation

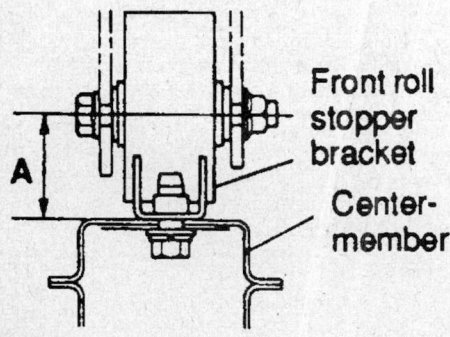

Fig. 5 Front roll stopper clearance

fuel line, release fuel pressure as outlined under "Precautions."
3. Remove delivery pipe, fuel injector and regulator as an assembly.

INSPECTION

Inspect intake manifold and air intake plenum (if equipped) as follows:
1. Check for damage, cracks or defects.
2. Ensure coolant and jet air passages are clear.
3. Check installation surfaces with a straightedge. Replace if deflection exceeds .012 inch.

INSTALLATION

Reverse removal procedure to install, noting the following:
1. Replace fuel injector O-rings.
2. Apply a light amount of new engine oil to fuel injector O-rings and high pressure fuel hose union.

EXHAUST MANIFOLD
REPLACE

Remove exhaust manifold in numbered sequence shown in **Figs. 10 and 11,** noting the following:
1. **On models equipped with turbocharged engine,** drain engine oil and coolant prior to removing exhaust manifold. To drain coolant, proceed as follows:
   a. Place instrument panel temperature control lever in Hot position.
   b. Carefully remove radiator cap.
   c. Remove radiator drain plug.
2. **On all models,** use oxygen sensor

socket No. MD998703, or equivalent, to remove oxygen sensor.
3. **On models equipped with turbocharged engine,** leave power steering hoses attached when disconnecting power steering pump. Position pump out of the way and secure with a piece of wire.
4. **On all models,** reverse procedure to install.
   a. **On models equipped with turbocharged engine,** apply machine oil to inner surface pipe flare prior to installing water pipe (18), **Fig. 11.**

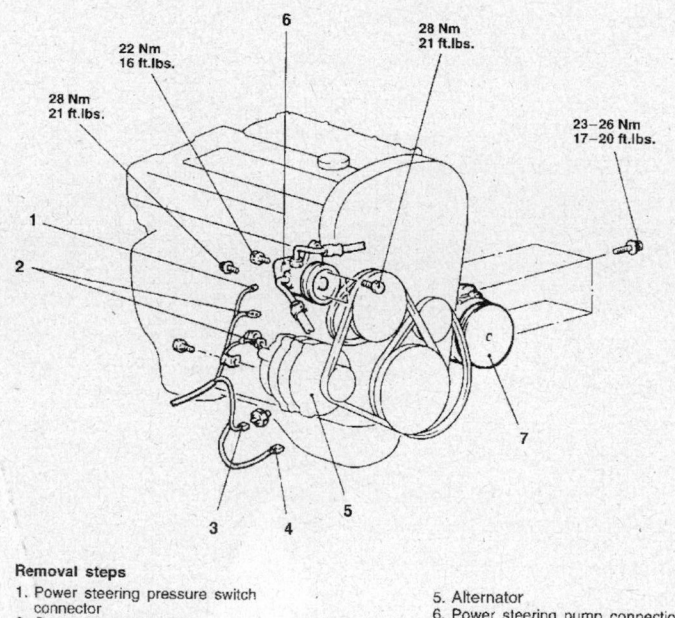

Removal steps
1. Power steering pressure switch connector
2. Generator connectors
3. Oil pressure switch connector
4. Oil pressure gauge unit connector
5. Alternator
6. Power steering pump connection
7. A/C compressor connection

Fig. 6 Engine replacement (Part 1 of 3). Turbocharged engine

CYLINDER HEAD
REPLACE

TURBOCHARGED ENGINE

1. Release fuel system pressure as outlined under "Precautions."
2. Remove cylinder head in numbered sequence as shown, **Fig. 12.**
3. Drain cooling system into an appropriate container.
4. Prior to removing upper radiator hose, mark hose clamp in relation to hose for installation reference.

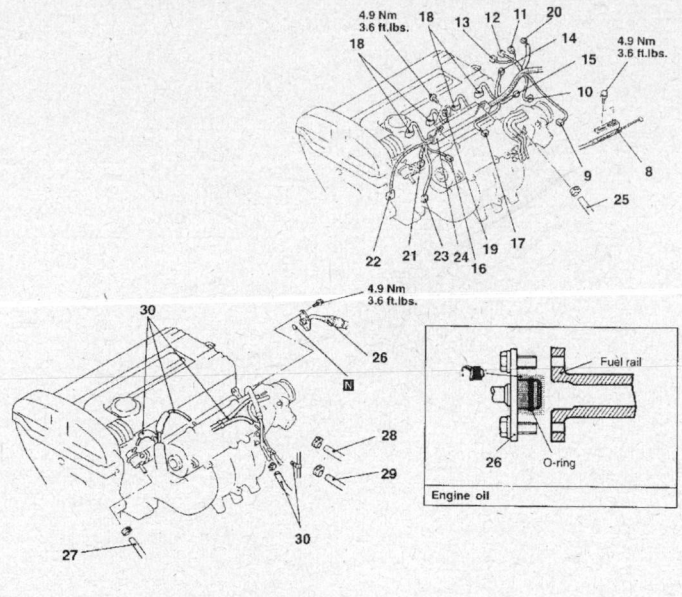

8. Accelerator cable connection
9. Idle air control motor connector
10. Knock sensor connector
11. Heated oxygen sensor connector
12. Engine coolant temperature gauge unit connector
13. Engine coolant temperature sensor connector
14. Ignition power transistor connector
15. Throttle position sensor connector
16. Capacitor connector
17. Manifold differential pressure sensor connector
18. Injector connectors
19. Ignition coil connector

20. Camshaft position sensor connector
21. Crankshaft position sensor connector
22. Air conditioning compressor connector
23. Evaporative emission purge solenoid valve connector
24. Control wiring harness
25. Brake booster vacuum hose connection
26. High-pressure fuel hose connection
27. Fuel return hose connection
28. Water hose A connection
29. Water hose B connection
30. Vacuum hoses connection

MT1069800535020X

Fig. 6   Engine replacement (Part 2 of 3). Turbocharged engine

31. Front exhaust pipe connection
32. Gasket
33. Engine mount bracket assembly
34. Engine assembly

MT1069800535030X

Fig. 6   Engine replacement (Part 3 of 3). Turbocharged engine

5. When disconnecting high pressure fuel hose, cover fuel pipe line with a shop towel. Some residual fuel pressure may be present.
6. Remove timing belt as outlined under "Timing Belt, Replace."
7. Using wrench tool No. MD998051, or equivalent, remove cylinder head attaching bolts in sequence as shown, **Fig. 13.** Loosen head bolts evenly, in two or three steps to prevent cylinder head warpage. When removing cylinder head use care not to disturb camshaft sprockets. After removing cylinder head, clean gasket surfaces on head and block.
8. Remove intake and exhaust manifolds.
9. Reverse procedure to install, noting the following:
   a. Tighten attaching nuts and bolts to specifications.
   b. Clean both cylinder head and cylinder block gasket surfaces, then install gasket with identification mark toward cylinder head, **Fig. 14.**
   c. When installing cylinder head bolts, the length below head of bolts should be within limit. If bolts are outside limit, replace bolts.
   d. Apply engine oil to bolt thread and washer.
   e. Using sequence shown in **Fig. 15, torque** cylinder head bolts in five steps: first step, all bolts to 58 ft. lbs.; second step, fully loosen all bolts; third step, all bolts to 15 ft. lbs.; fourth step, all bolts an additional 90°; fifth step, all bolts an additional 90.° **Ensure head bolt washers are correctly installed.**
   f. **Ensure tightening angle of 90° is obtained. If less than 90° is reached, head bolts will loosen.**
   g. Ensure camshaft and crankshaft timing marks are correctly aligned.
   h. When installing rocker cover, apply 3M sealant No. 8660, or equivalent, to semicircular packing.
   i. When installing high pressure fuel line, apply a small amount of gasoline to hose union. **Use caution not to damage O-ring.**
   j. Tighten fuel return hose fitting bolts to specifications.

NON-TURBOCHARGED ENGINE

1. Relieve fuel system pressure as outlined under "Precautions."
2. Drain engine coolant, then drain oil from crankcase.
3. Remove cylinder head as shown in **Fig. 16.**

4. Reverse procedure to install, noting the following:
   a. Prior to installation, inspect cylinder head bolts for stretching by placing a straightedge against bolt threads. If all threads do not contact straightedge, replace bolt.
   b. Clean bolt threads and lubricate with clean engine oil.
   c. Using sequence shown in **Fig. 17, torque** cylinder head bolts in four steps: first step, bolts 1 through 6 to 25 ft. lbs. and bolts 7 through 10 to 20 ft. lbs.; second step, bolts 1 through 6 to 50 ft. lbs. and bolts 7 through 10 to 20 ft. lbs.; third step, 1 through 6 to 50 ft. lbs. and bolts 7 through 10 to 20 ft. lbs.; fourth step, all bolts an additional 90.° **Do not use a torque wrench for final step.**
   d. When installing radiator hoses, align marks on clamps and respective hoses.

CRANKSHAFT
REPLACE
TURBOCHARGED ENGINE
Removal

1. Remove crankshaft in sequence as shown, **Figs.18 and 19.**

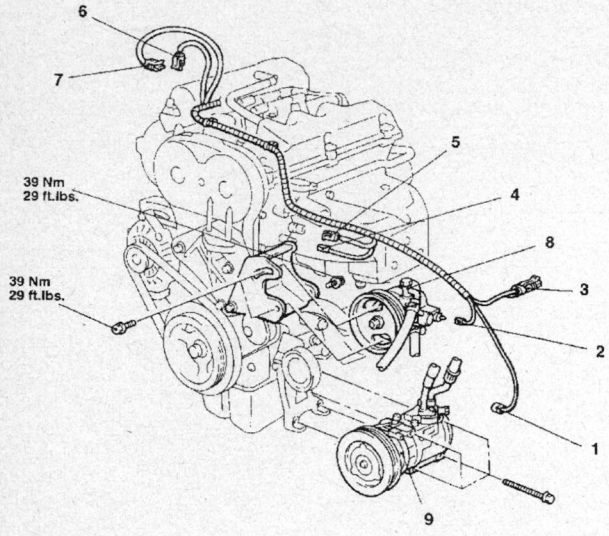

Removal steps

1. A/C compressor connector
2. Power steering pressure switch connector
3. Heated oxygen sensor connector
4. Engine coolant temperature gauge unit connector
5. Engine coolant temperature sensor connector
6. MAP sensor connector
7. Intake air temperature sensor connector
8. Power steering pump connection
9. A/C compressor connection

MT1069800536010X

Fig. 7   Engine replacement (Part 1 of 3). Non-turbocharged engine

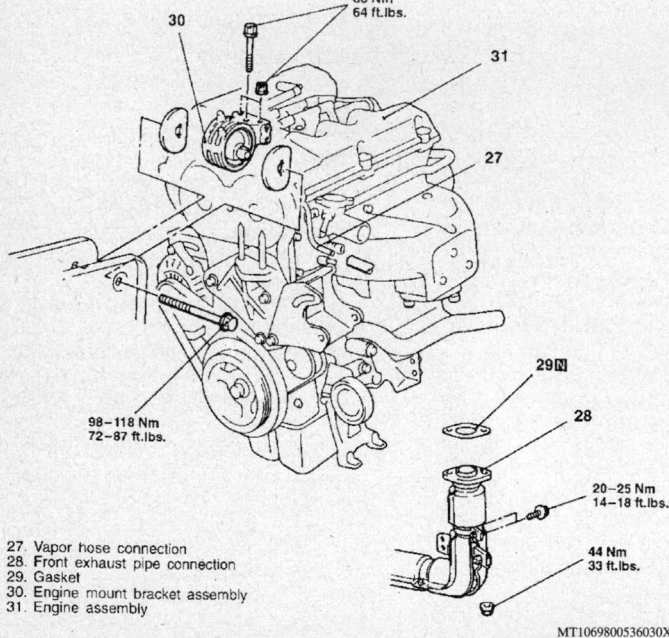

27. Vapor hose connection
28. Front exhaust pipe connection
29. Gasket
30. Engine mount bracket assembly
31. Engine assembly

MT1069800536030X

Fig. 7   Engine replacement (Part 3 of 3). Non-turbocharged engine

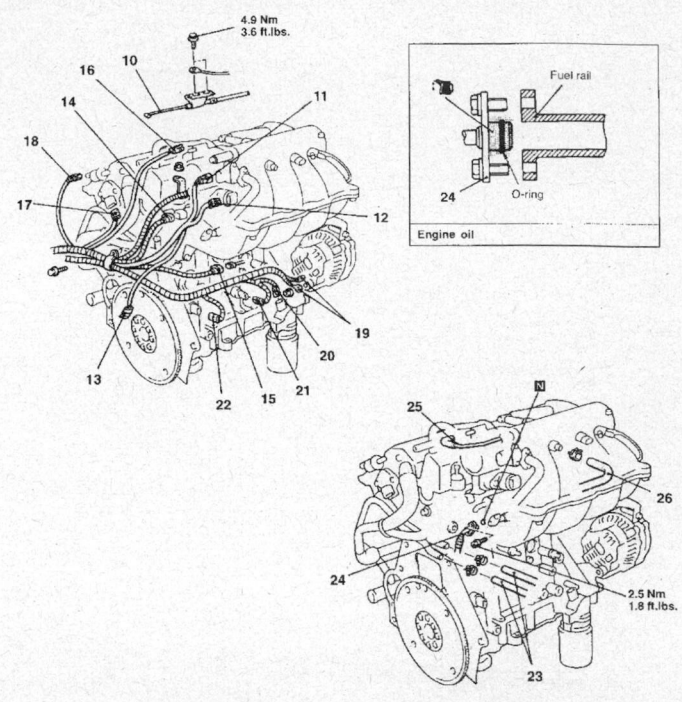

10. Accelerator cable connection
11. Throttle position sensor connector
12. Idle air control motor connector
13. Vehicle speed sensor connector <M/T>
14. Injector harness connector
15. Generator harness connector
16. Ignition coil connector
17. Camshaft position sensor connector
18. EGR solenoid valve connector
19. Generator connector
20. Crankshaft position sensor connector
21. Knock sensor connector
22. Oil pressure switch connector
23. Heater hose connection
24. High-pressure fuel hose connection
25. Purge air hose connection
26. Brake booster vacuum hose connection

MT1069800536020X

Fig. 7   Engine replacement (Part 2 of 3). Non-turbocharged engine

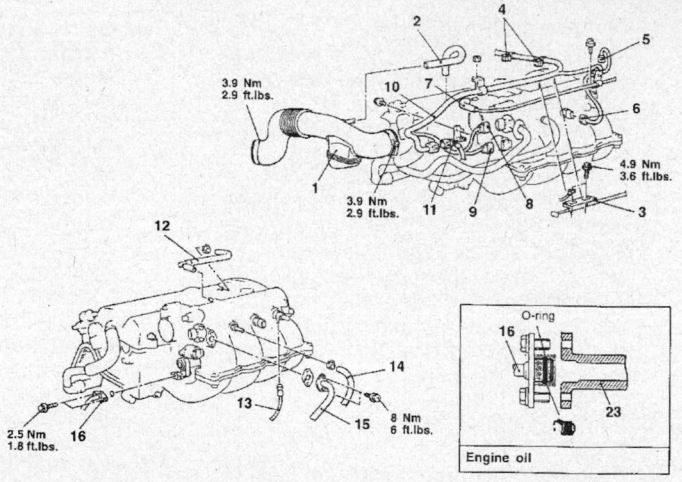

Removal steps

1. Air intake hose
2. Breather hose
3. Accelerator cable connection
4. Clip
5. MAP sensor connector
6. Charge temperature sensor connector
7. Vacuum hose connection
8. TPS connector
9. AIS motor connector
10. Control wiring harness
11. Generator wiring harness connection
12. PCV hose assembly
13. Vacuum hose connection
14. Brake booster vacuum hose connection
15. EGR pipe connection
16. High-pressure fuel hose connection

MT1059800047010X

Fig. 8   Intake manifold replacement (Part 1 of 2). Non-turbocharged engine

2.0L ENGINE

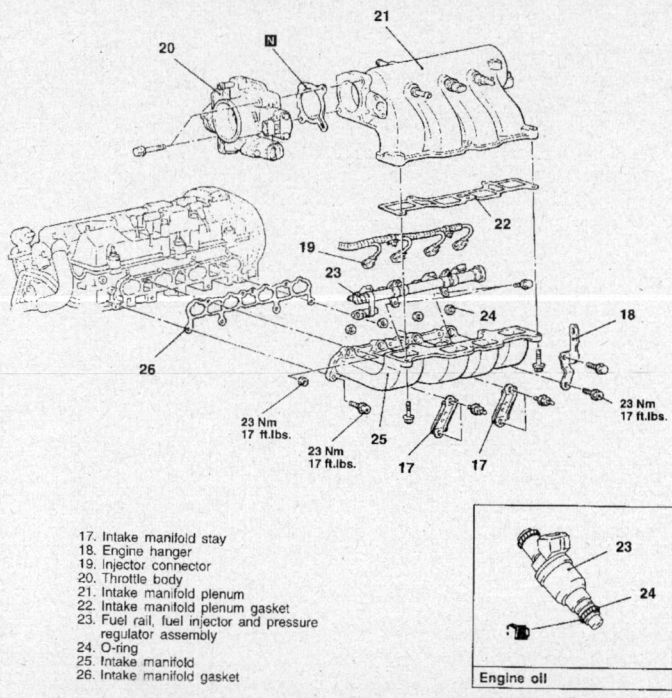

17. Intake manifold stay
18. Engine hanger
19. Injector connector
20. Throttle body
21. Intake manifold plenum
22. Intake manifold plenum gasket
23. Fuel rail, fuel injector and pressure regulator assembly
24. O-ring
25. Intake manifold
26. Intake manifold gasket

Engine oil

MT1059800047020X

Fig. 8   Intake manifold replacement (Part 2 of 2). Non-turbocharged engine

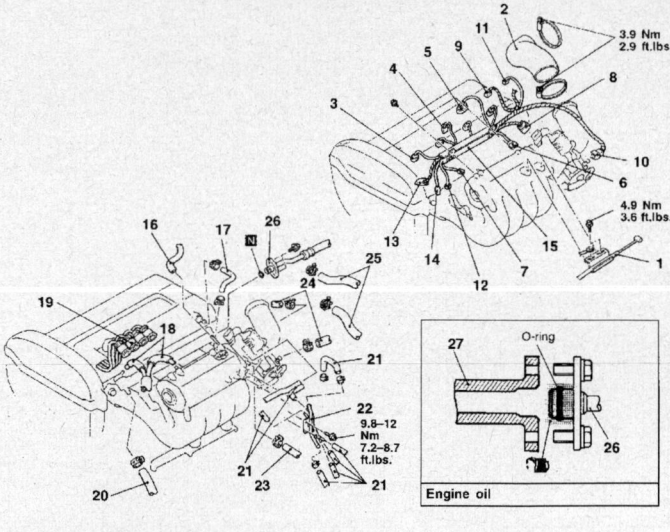

Removal steps

1. Accelerator cable connection
2. Air hose "C"
3. Injector connector
4. Ignition coil connector
5. Ignition power transistor connector
6. Manifold differential pressure sensor connector
7. Capacitor connector
8. TPS connector
9. Knock sensor connector
10. IAC motor connector
11. Camshaft position sensor connector
12. Evaporative emission purge solenoid valve connector
13. Crankshaft position sensor connector
14. Air conditioning compressor connector
15. Control wiring harness
16. Hose connection
17. PCV hose connection
18. Vacuum hose connection
19. Spark plug cable connection
20. Fuel return hose connection
21. Vacuum hose connection
22. Vacuum pipe
23. Brake booster vacuum hose connection
24. Heater hose connection
25. Heater hose connection
26. High-pressure fuel hose connection

MT1059800048010X

Fig. 9   Intake manifold replacement (Part 1 of 2). Turbocharged engine

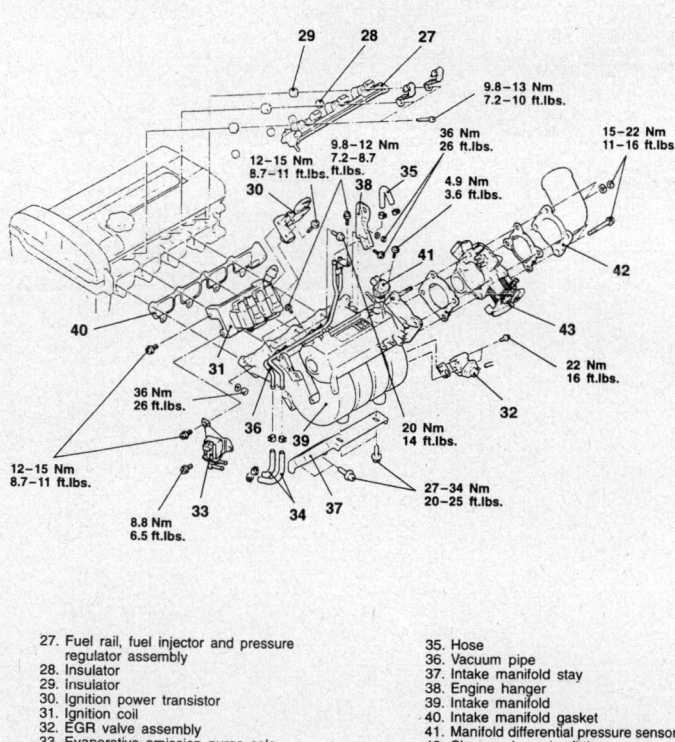

27. Fuel rail, fuel injector and pressure regulator assembly
28. Insulator
29. Insulator
30. Ignition power transistor
31. Ignition coil
32. EGR valve assembly
33. Evaporative emission purge solenoid valve assembly
34. Purge hoses
35. Hose
36. Vacuum pipe
37. Intake manifold stay
38. Engine hanger
39. Intake manifold
40. Intake manifold gasket
41. Manifold differential pressure sensor
42. Charge air cooler fitting
43. Throttle body

MT1059800048020X

Fig. 9   Intake manifold replacement (Part 2 of 2). Turbocharged engine

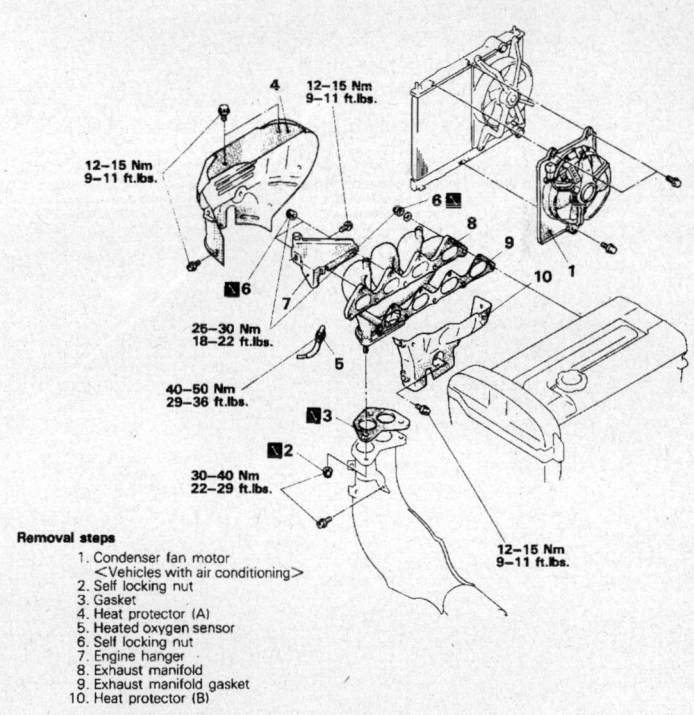

Removal steps

1. Condenser fan motor
   <Vehicles with air conditioning>
2. Self locking nut
3. Gasket
4. Heat protector (A)
5. Heated oxygen sensor
6. Self locking nut
7. Engine hanger
8. Exhaust manifold
9. Exhaust manifold gasket
10. Heat protector (B)

CR1079100007000X

Fig. 10   Exhaust manifold replacement. Non-turbocharged engine

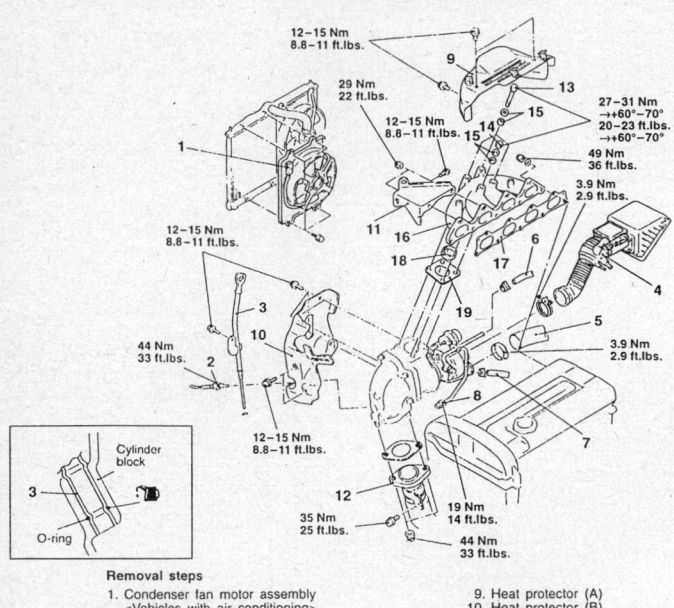

Removal steps
1. Condenser fan motor assembly <Vehicles with air conditioning>
2. Heated oxygen sensor <front>
3. Engine oil level gauge guide
4. Air cleaner and air intake hose assembly
5. Air hose (A) connection
6. Water hose connection
7. Water hose connection
8. Oil pipe (A) connection

9. Heat protector (A)
10. Heat protector (B)
11. Engine hanger
12. Front exhaust pipe connection
13. Flange bolts
14. Flange nut
15. Coned disc spring
16. Exhaust manifold
17. Exhaust manifold gasket
18. Ring
19. Gasket (A)

MT1079800023010X

Fig. 11 Exhaust manifold replacement (Part 1 of 2). Turbocharged engine

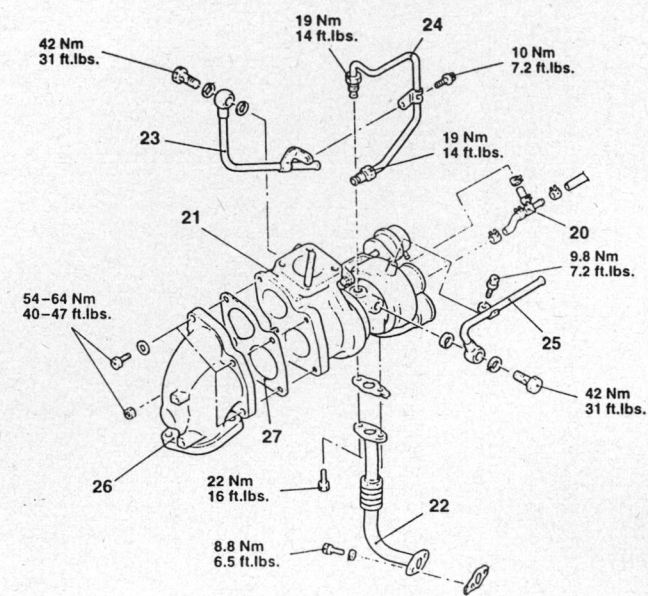

20. Vacuum hose assembly
21. Turbocharger assembly
22. Oil return pipe
23. Water pipe assembly (B)

24. Oil pipe assembly
25. Water pipe assembly (A)
26. Exhaust manifold fitting
27. Gasket

MT1079800023020X

Fig. 11 Exhaust manifold replacement (Part 2 of 2). Turbocharged engine

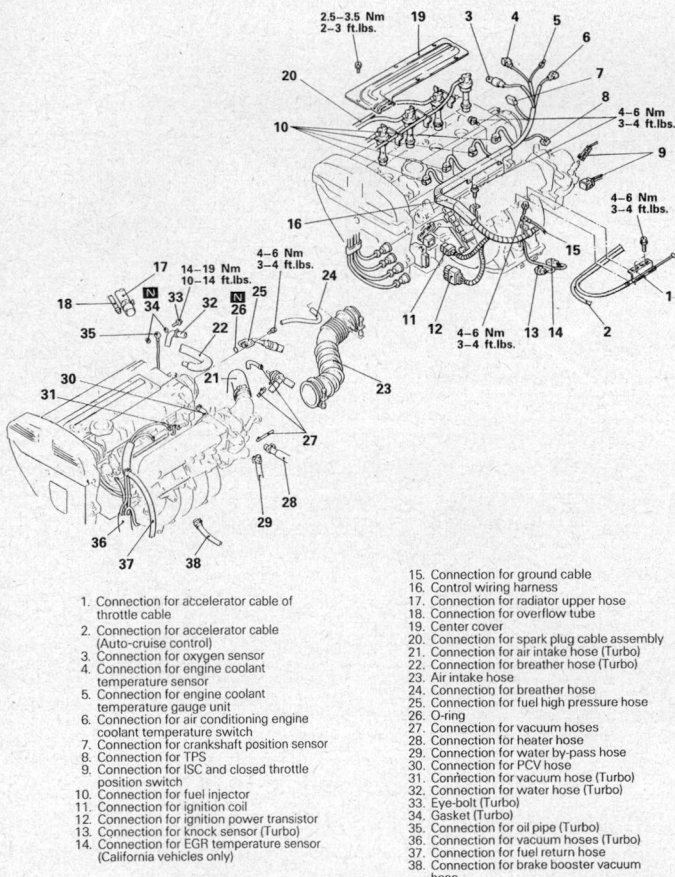

1. Connection for accelerator cable of throttle cable
2. Connection for accelerator cable (Auto-cruise control)
3. Connection for oxygen sensor
4. Connection for engine coolant temperature sensor
5. Connection for engine coolant temperature gauge unit
6. Connection for air conditioning engine coolant temperature switch
7. Connection for crankshaft position sensor
8. Connection for TPS
9. Connection for ISC and closed throttle position switch
10. Connection for fuel injector
11. Connection for ignition coil
12. Connection for ignition power transistor
13. Connection for knock sensor (Turbo)
14. Connection for EGR temperature sensor (California vehicles only)

15. Connection for ground cable
16. Control wiring harness
17. Connection for radiator upper hose
18. Connection for overflow tube
19. Center cover
20. Connection for spark plug cable assembly
21. Connection for air intake hose (Turbo)
22. Connection for breather hose (Turbo)
23. Air intake hose
24. Connection for breather hose
25. Connection for fuel high pressure hose
26. O-ring
27. Connection for vacuum hoses
28. Connection for heater hose
29. Connection for water by-pass hose
30. Connection for PCV hose
31. Connection for vacuum hose (Turbo)
32. Connection for water hose (Turbo)
33. Eye-bolt (Turbo)
34. Gasket (Turbo)
35. Connection for oil pipe (Turbo)
36. Connection for vacuum hoses (Turbo)
37. Connection for fuel return hose
38. Connection for brake booster vacuum hose

MT1069100084010X

Fig. 12 Cylinder head replacement (Part 1 of 2). Turbocharged engine

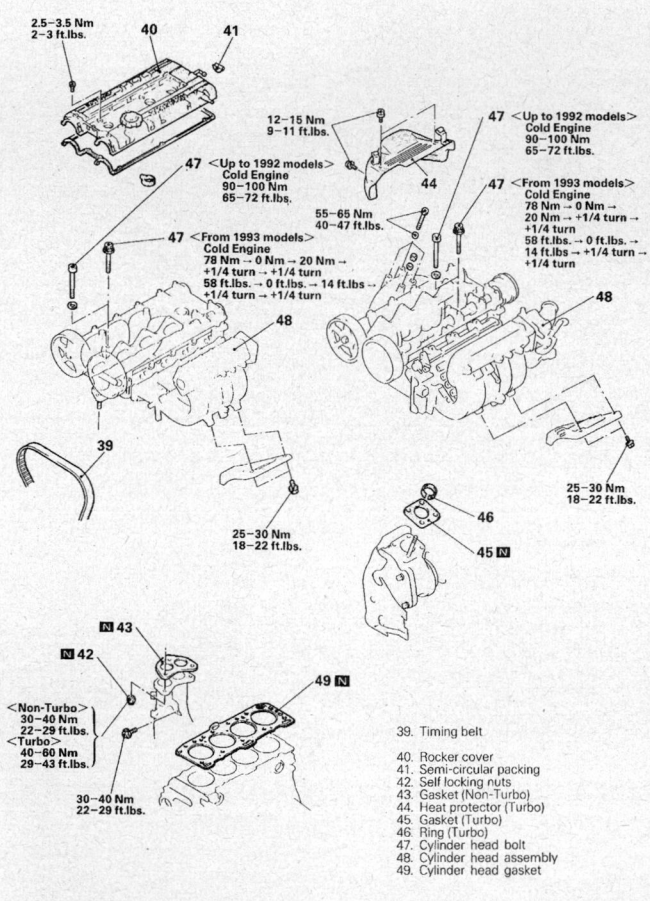

39. Timing belt
40. Rocker cover
41. Semi-circular packing
42. Self locking nuts
43. Gasket (Non-Turbo)
44. Heat protector (Turbo)
45. Gasket (Turbo)
46. Ring (Turbo)
47. Cylinder head bolt
48. Cylinder head assembly
49. Cylinder head gasket

MT1069100084020X

Fig. 12 Cylinder head replacement (Part 2 of 2). Turbocharged engine

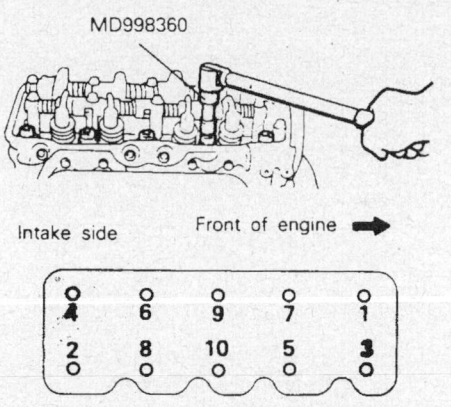

MD998360

Intake side   Front of engine ➡

| 4 | 6 | 9 | 7 | 1 |
| 2 | 8 | 10 | 5 | 3 |

Exhaust side

MT1069100081000X

Fig. 13   Cylinder head bolt loosening sequence. Turbocharged engine

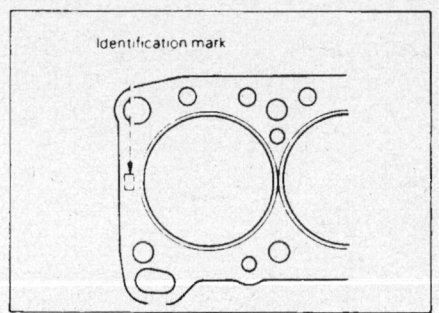

Identification mark

MT1069100082000X

Fig. 14   Cylinder head gasket identification mark. Turbocharged engine

Front of engine ➡

Intake side

| 7 | 5 | 2 | 4 | 10 |
| 9 | 3 | 1 | 6 | 8 |

Exhaust side

MT1069100083000X

Fig. 15   Cylinder head bolt tightening sequence. Turbocharged engine

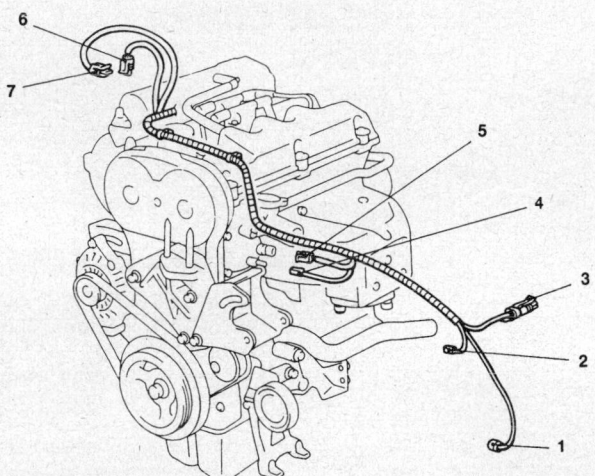

Removal steps
1. A/C compressor connector
2. Power steering pressure switch connector
3. Heated oxygen sensor connector
4. Engine coolant temperature gauge unit connector
5. Engine coolant temperature sensor connector
6. MAP sensor connector
7. Intake air temperature sensor connector

MT1069800537010X

Fig. 16   Cylinder head replacement (Part 1 of 3). Non-turbocharged engine

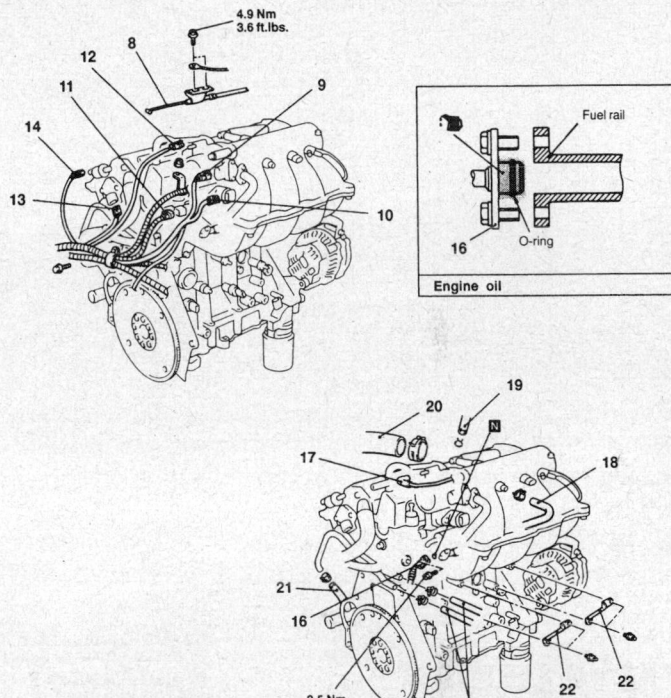

4.9 Nm
3.6 ft.lbs.

Fuel rail

O-ring

Engine oil

2.5 Nm
1.8 ft.lbs.

8. Accelerator cable connection
9. Throttle position sensor connector
10. Idle air control motor connector
11. Injector harness connector
12. Ignition coil connector
13. Camshaft position sensor connector
14. EGR solenoid valve connector
15. Heater hose connection
16. High-pressure fuel hose connection
17. Purge air hose connection
18. Brake booster vacuum hose connection
19. Overflow tube connection
20. Radiator upper hose connection
21. Water hose connection
22. Intake manifold stay

MT1069800537020X

Fig. 16   Cylinder head replacement (Part 2 of 3). Non-turbocharged engine

Installation

1. Reverse procedure shown in **Fig. 18**, noting the following:
   a. **Torque** bearing cap bedplate bolts to 18 ft. lbs. in sequence as shown, **Fig. 20**.
   b. Tighten bolts in sequence an additional 90–100.° **Do not exceed 100° of additional tightening.**

NON-TURBOCHARGED ENGINE

Removal

1. Remove crankshaft sprocket, oil pan, connecting rods and pistons.
2. Using tool No. MB995022, or equivalent, remove front crankshaft oil seal.

3. Gently pry out rear oil seal with screw driver.
4. Remove main bearing cap bedplate.
5. Remove lower bearings.
6. Remove crankshaft, then upper bearings.

Installation

Refer to **Fig. 21** when installing crankshaft.
1. Install crankshaft bearings on cylinder block.
2. Lubricate bearing surfaces, then install crankshaft.
3. Apply Loctite sealant No. 19614, or

equivalent to cylinder block as shown, **Fig. 22**.
4. Install bearing halves on bearing cap bedplate.
5. Install bearing cap bedplate on cylinder block.
6. Lightly lubricate bedplate bolts with engine oil, then install and finger tighten.
7. **Torque** bedplate bolts 1 through 10 in sequence to 55 ft. lbs.
8. **Torque** bedplate bolts A through K in sequence to 20 ft. lbs.

VALVE ARRANGEMENT

Intake valves are on the righthand side of

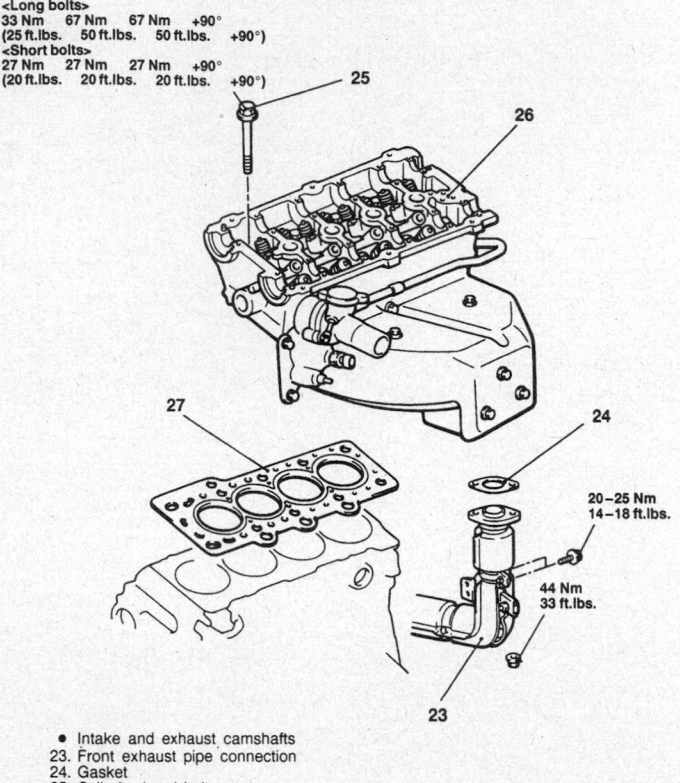

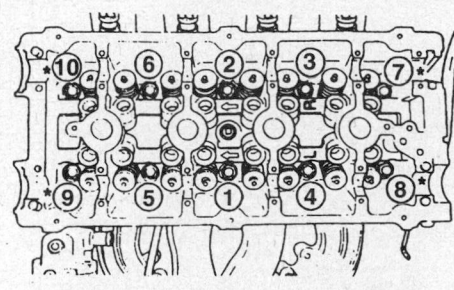

*Location of 110 mm (4.330 in.) short bolts.

CR1069500631000A

Fig. 17 Cylinder head bolt tightening sequence. Non-turbocharged engine

- Intake and exhaust camshafts
23. Front exhaust pipe connection
24. Gasket
25. Cylinder head bolt
26. Cylinder head
27. Cylinder head gasket

MT1069800537030X

Fig. 16 Cylinder head replacement (Part 3 of 3). Non-turbocharged engine

the engine and the exhaust valves are on the lefthand side of the engine.

again at low speed. Repeat this step to bleed air out of oil system.

VALVE LIFTERS

INSPECTION

Abnormal Noise

1. Operate engine to normal operating temperature.
2. While installed to cylinder head, press part of rocker arm that contacts lash adjuster.
3. If, when pressed, rocker arm is very hard to be depressed, adjuster is operating correctly.
4. If, when pressed, rocker arm is very easily depressed replace lash adjuster.
5. If there is a spongy feeling when pressed, air is mixed in with engine oil. The cause is insufficient amount of engine oil or damage to oil screen and/or gasket.
6. After finding and correcting cause, warm engine and drive at low speed for a short time. Then, after stopping engine and waiting a few minutes, drive

VALVE CLEARANCE SPECIFICATIONS

Engine, Liter	Clearance, Inch	
	Intake	Exhaust
1996–97		
2.0L ①	.0008–.0020	.0020–.0035
2.0L ②	.0019–.0026	.0029–.0037
1998		
2.0L ①	.0008–.0020	.0020–.0035
2.0L ②	.0009–.0037	.0020–.0037
1999		
2.0L ①	.0008–.0020	.0020–.0035
2.0L ②	.0009–.0025	.0020–.0037

① — Turbocharged engine.
② — Non-turbocharged engine.

VALVE ADJUSTMENT

These engines use hydraulic auto-lash adjusters. No adjustments are required.

ROCKER ARMS

REPLACE

Refer to "Camshaft, Replace" for rocker arm replacement procedure.

FRONT COVER

REPLACE

Refer to "Oil Pump, Replace" for front cover replacement procedure.

TIMING BELT

REPLACE

TURBOCHARGED ENGINE

With the timing belt removed, avoid turning the camshaft or crankshaft. If movement is required, exercise extreme caution to avoid valve damage caused by piston contact.

1. Remove undercover.
2. Remove clamp securing power steering pressure hose and air conditioner high pressure hose to body.
3. Using a wood block and a jack, place wood block under engine oil pan and raise engine only enough to relieve tension on top engine mount, then remove mount and bracket.
4. Remove the accessory drive belts. **Prior to removing water pump drive belt, loosen water pump pulley bolts.**
5. Remove tensioner pulley, bracket, crankshaft pulley and water pump pulley.
6. Remove timing belt upper, center and lower covers.
7. Rotate crankshaft clockwise to bring No. 1 cylinder to TDC of compression stroke. **Rotate crankshaft only in the clockwise direction. No. 1 cylinder is at TDC of compression stroke when timing marks on camshaft sprockets are aligned with upper surface of cylinder head and dowel pins on camshaft sprockets are facing up as shown, Fig. 23.** Crankshaft and oil pump sprockets must also be

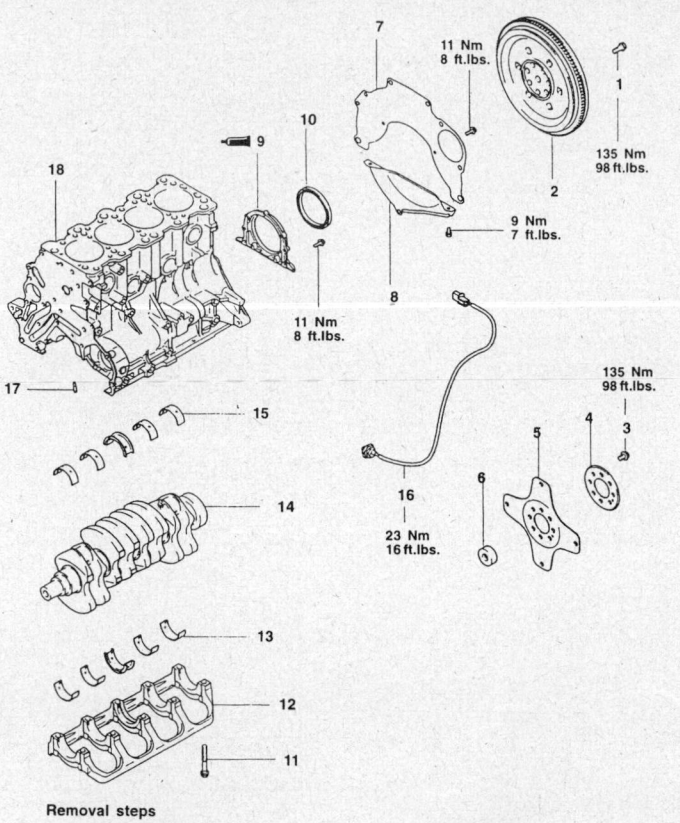

Lubricate all internal parts with engine oil during reassembly.

Removal steps

1. Flywheel bolt <M/T>
2. Flywheel <M/T>
3. Drive plate bolt
4. Adapter plate
5. Drive plate
6. Crankshaft bushing <A/T>
7. Rear plate
8. Bell housing cover
9. Oil seal case

10. Oil seal
11. Bearing cap bolt
12. Bearing cap
13. Crankshaft bearing (lower)
14. Crankshaft
15. Crankshaft bearing (upper)
16. Knock sensor
17. Oil jet
18. Cylinder block

MT1069800538000X

Fig. 18 Crankshaft replacement. 1996-97 turbocharged engine

Removal steps

1. Flywheel bolt <M/T>
2. Flywheel <M/T>
3. Drive plate bolt
4. Adapter plate
5. Drive plate
6. Crankshaft bushing <A/T>
7. Rear plate
8. Bell housing cover
9. Oil seal case
10. Oil seal

11. Bearing cap bolt
12. Bearing cap
13. Crankshaft bearing (lower)
14. Crankshaft
15. Thrust bearing
16. Crankshaft bearing (upper)
17. Knock sensor
18. Oil jet
19. Cylinder block

MT1069900555000X

Fig. 19 Crankshaft assembly. 1998-99 turbocharged engine

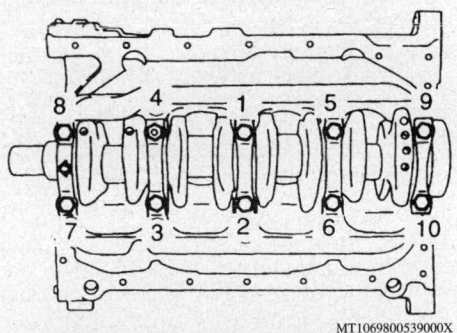

MT1069800539000X

Fig. 20 Main bearing cap bedplate tightening sequence. Turbocharged engine

MT1069800540000X

Fig. 21 Main bearing cap bedplate tightening sequence. Non-turbocharged engine

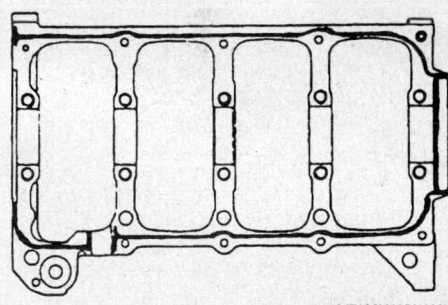

MT1069800541000X

Fig. 22 Sealant application. Non-turbocharged engine

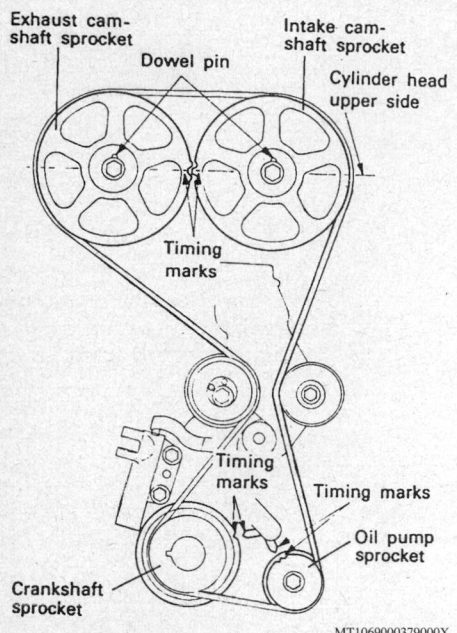

Fig. 23 Camshaft, crankshaft & oil pump sprocket timing marks. Turbocharged engine

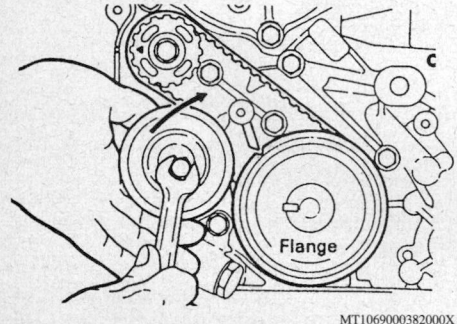

Fig. 26 Tensioning timing belt B. Turbocharged engine

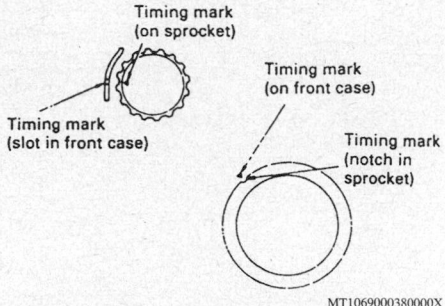

Fig. 24 Timing marks for timing belt B. Turbocharged engine

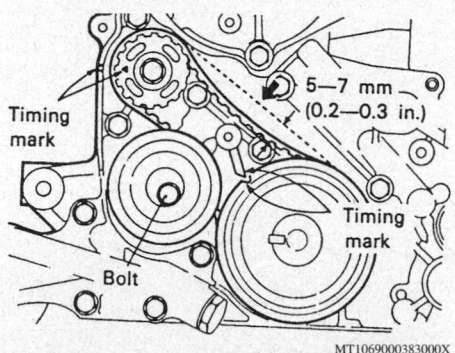

Fig. 27 Timing belt deflection. Turbocharged engine

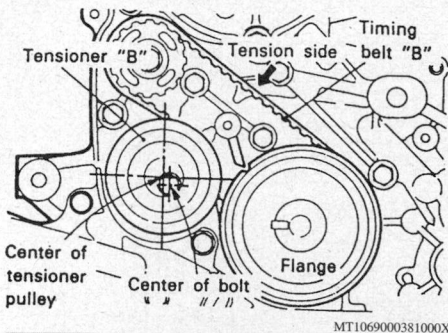

Fig. 25 Tensioner B pulley alignment location. Turbocharged engine

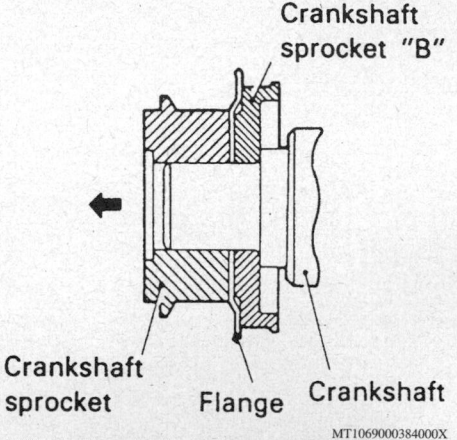

Fig. 28 Flange & crankshaft sprocket installation. Turbocharged engine

aligned with their respective timing marks. The crankshaft may need to be rotated up to six times before all timing marks are properly aligned due to the oil pump to balance shaft gear ratio.

8. Loosen center timing belt tensioner pulley bolt.
9. Move timing belt tensioner pulley toward water pump side, then remove timing belt.
10. Remove auto-tensioner. To check tensioner, position tensioner push rod against metal object (engine block, etc.), then apply a force of approximately 22–44 lbs. and measure push rod movement. Pushrod movement should be within .04 inch. If push rod movement is not within limits, replace auto-tensioner.
11. Remove tensioner pulley and arm, then idler pulley, if necessary.
12. Remove crankshaft sprocket bolt, special washer, sprocket, flange and crankshaft sensing blade.

13. Remove balance shaft timing belt tensioner, then timing belt.
14. Align timing marks of balance shaft sprocket and crankshaft sprocket "B," **Fig. 24**, then install timing belt "B" over both sprockets. When installing timing belt, ensure belt has no slack on tension side.
15. Adjust balance shaft timing belt tension as follows:
    a. Temporarily install balance shaft timing belt tensioner so center of tensioner pulley is left and above center of retaining bolt. Temporarily attach tensioner pulley so flange is toward front of engine, **Fig. 25**.
    b. Hold balance shaft timing belt tensioner up in direction shown by arrow in, **Fig. 26**, then place pressure on timing belt so tension side of belt is taut.
    c. Tighten balance shaft timing belt tensioner bolt to 11–16 ft. lbs. **When tightening bolt, do not allow tensioner pulley shaft to rotate.**
    d. To check belt tension, depress belt at point (A), **Fig. 27**. Belt deflection should be .20–.28 inch . If not, readjust belt tension.
16. Install crankshaft sprocket flange, sprocket and special washer. Tighten crankshaft sprocket bolt to 80–94 ft. lbs. **Ensure flange and sprocket are correctly installed as shown in Fig. 28.** Prior to installation, apply a light coat of engine oil to crankshaft sprock-

et bolt threads.
17. Install crankshaft sensing blade, if equipped.
18. If auto-tensioner rod is fully extended, proceed as follows:
    a. Position auto-tensioner level in soft jawed vise. If plug at bottom of tensioner protrudes, apply a plain washer to prevent plug from direct contact with vise.
    b. Slowly push tensioner rod in, using vise, until set hole (A) is aligned with hole (B) in tensioner cylinder, **Fig. 29**.
    c. Insert a .055 inch diameter wire into set holes, then remove auto-tensioner from vise.
19. Install auto-tensioner, then **torque** retaining bolt to 14–20 ft. lbs. **Leave wire installed in auto-tensioner.**
20. Install tensioner pulley onto tensioner arm, if removed.
21. Position hole in tensioner pulley shaft to left of center bolt, then tighten center bolt finger tight.
22. Rotate camshaft sprockets so that dowel pins are located on top, then align timing marks facing each other with top surface of cylinder head, **Fig.**

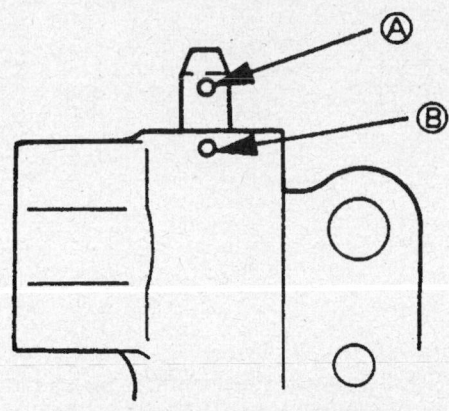

Fig. 29 Tensioner rod alignment. Turbocharged engine

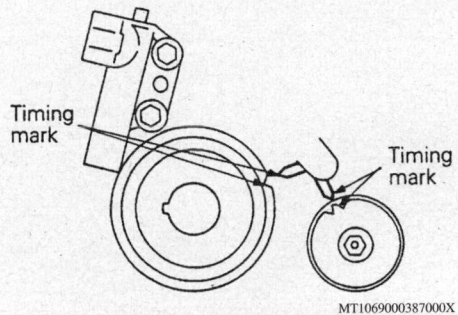

Fig. 32 Crankshaft & oil pump sprocket alignment. Turbocharged engine

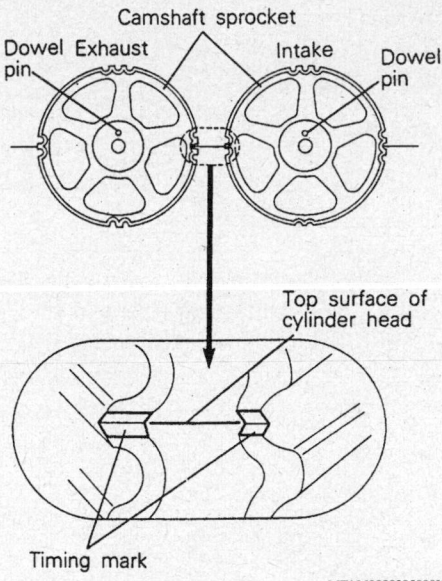

Fig. 30 Camshaft sprocket timing mark alignment. Turbocharged engine

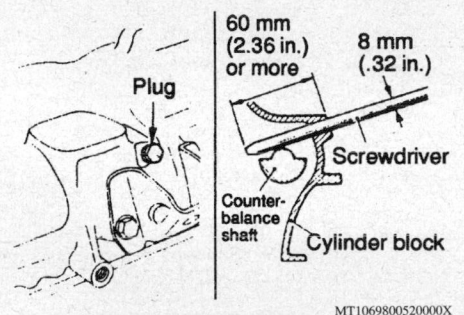

Fig. 33 Oil pump sprocket timing mark alignment inspection. Turbocharged engine

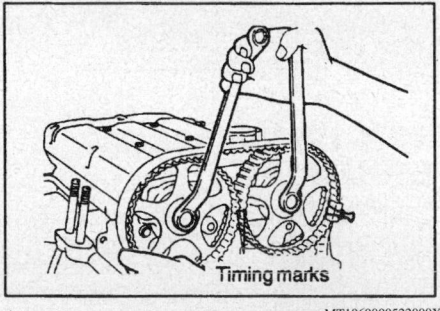

Fig. 35 Aligning camshaft timing marks. Turbocharged engine

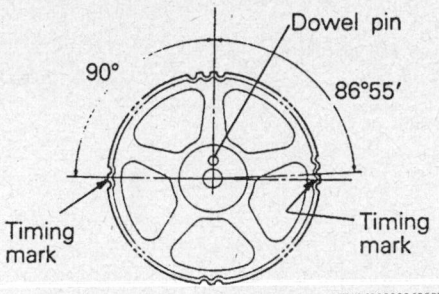

Fig. 31 Camshaft sprocket position. Turbocharged engine

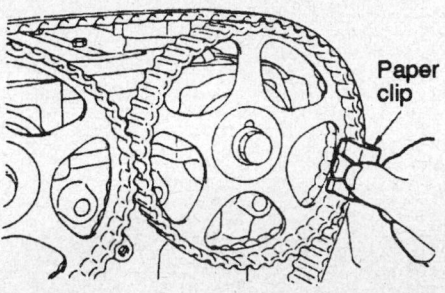

Fig. 34 Securing timing belt to camshaft sprocket. Turbocharged engine

30. The camshaft sprockets are interchangeable and have two sets of timing marks. When sprocket is mounted on the exhaust camshaft, use timing mark on right with dowel pin hole on top. For intake sprocket, use mark on left with dowel pin hole on top, **Fig. 31**

23. Align crankshaft sprocket and oil pump sprocket timing marks as shown, **Fig. 32.**
24. With oil pump sprocket timing marks aligned, remove plug from side of the engine and insert a screwdriver, with a shaft diameter of .31 inch, into hole, **Fig. 33.** If screwdriver can be inserted 2.36 inches or more, alignment is correct. If screwdriver can only be inserted .79–.98 inch, rotate oil pump sprocket one revolution and realign timing marks. Ensure screwdriver can be inserted 2.36 inches or more. This check is performed to ensure oil pump sprocket is properly positioned. Leave screwdriver inserted in hole until after timing belt has been installed.
25. Install timing belt over intake camshaft sprocket. Use a binder clip to hold timing belt to sprocket, **Fig. 34.**
26. Install timing belt over exhaust camshaft sprocket. Align sprocket timing marks using two box wrenches on sprocket bolts, **Fig. 35.** Use a binder clip to secure timing belt to sprocket.

27. Install timing belt to idler pulley, oil pump sprocket, crankshaft sprocket and tensioner pulley.
28. Remove binder clips.
29. Remove screwdriver securing oil pump sprocket in position, then install plug.

30. Set timing belt tensioner pulley so that holes are positioned at bottom, then press tensioner pulley against timing belt.
31. Install Mitsubishi setscrew tool No. MD998738, or equivalent, through left-hand engine support bracket.
32. Tighten the setscrew tool until it contacts tensioner arm, then tighten tool slightly more, **Fig. 36.**
33. Remove wire retaining auto-tensioner plunger, then remove setscrew tool.
34. Tighten timing belt tensioner pulley bolt.
35. Rotate crankshaft pulley 1/4 turn counterclockwise, then turn clockwise, aligning the crankshaft and camshaft timing marks.
36. Loosen tensioner pulley retaining bolt, then position Mitsubishi socket tool No. MD998767, or equivalent, and a suitable torque wrench to pulley, **Fig. 37.** Apply a torque of 2.6 ft. lbs., then tighten the retaining bolt while holding the pulley in position.
37. **Torque** timing belt tensioner pulley bolt to 35 ft. lbs.
38. Rotate engine clockwise two turns.
39. After approximately 15 minutes, measure auto-tensioner plunger protrusion from tensioner housing, **Fig. 38.** Plunger protrusion should be .15–.18 inch. If protrusion is not with in limits, adjust timing belt tension.
40. If clearance (A) can not be measured with engine in vehicle, proceed as follows:
   a. Screw in Mitsubishi setscrew tool

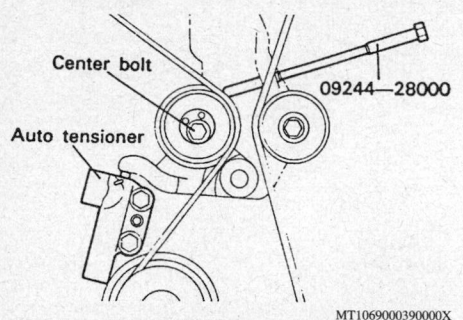

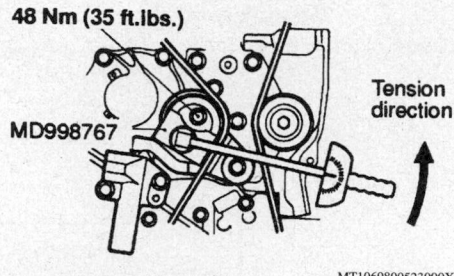

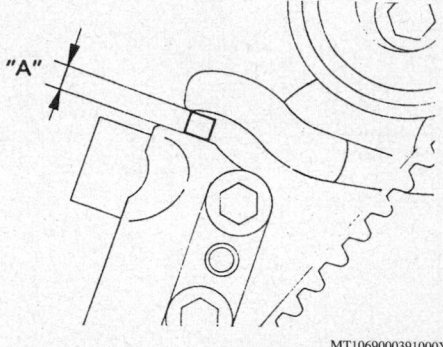

Fig. 36 Auto tensioner setscrew tool installation. Turbocharged engine

Fig. 37 Adjusting timing belt tension. Turbocharged engine

Fig. 38 Auto tensioner protrusion measurement. Turbocharged engine

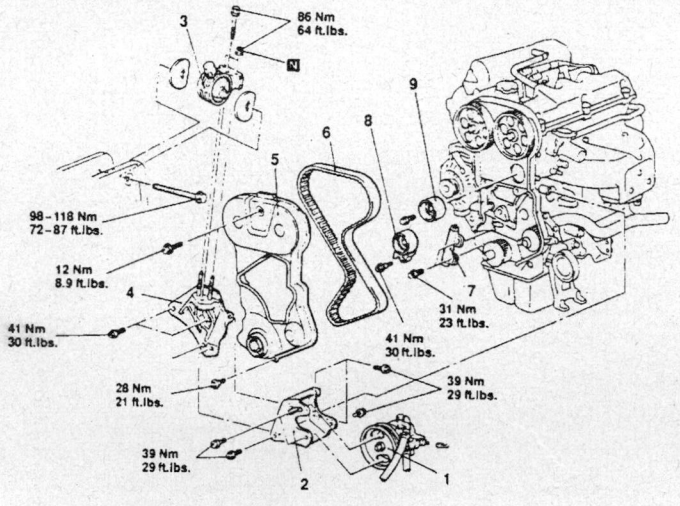

Removal steps
1. Power steering pump connection
2. Power steering pump bracket
3. Engine mount bracket assembly
4. Engine mount bracket
5. Front timing belt cover
6. Timing belt
7. Timing belt tensioner
8. Tensioner pulley
9. Idle pulley

Fig. 39 Timing belt assembly. Non-turbocharged engine

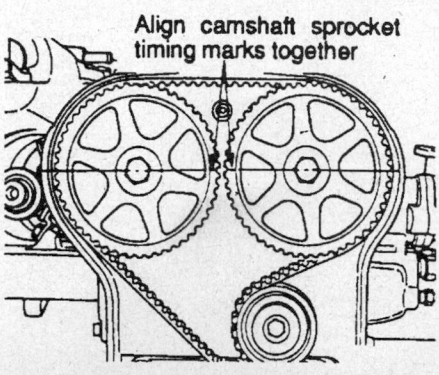

Fig. 40 Camshaft sprocket timing alignment. Non-turbocharged engine

No. MD998738, or equivalent, until end of tool makes contact with tensioner arm.
  b. Starting in this position, count number of turns of tool required to bring tensioner arm in contact with auto-tensioner body. Ensure contact is made within 2.5–3 turns, then remove tool.
  c. Install rubber plug into timing belt rear cover.
41. Reverse steps 1 through 9 to install remaining components, noting the following:
  a. When installing the rocker cover, apply 3M sealant No. 8660 or equivalent to semi-circular packing.

NON-TURBOCHARGED ENGINE

With the timing belt removed, avoid turning the camshaft or crankshaft. If movement is required, exercise extreme caution to avoid valve damage caused by piston contact.
1. Remove cooling system reserve tank, then the engine undercover.
2. Remove A/C compressor, power steering pump and alternator drive belts.
3. Remove crankshaft pulley.
4. Remove power steering pump from bracket, then with hoses attached, po-

sition out of the way.
5. Using a suitable jack and a block of wood, support engine under oil pan.
6. Remove engine mount bracket assembly, **Fig. 39**.
7. Remove timing belt front cover, then align camshaft and crankshaft sprocket timing marks, **Figs. 40 and 41**.
8. Loosen timing belt tensioner, then remove timing belt.
9. Remove timing belt tensioner and place in a soft jawed vice, **Fig. 42**.
10. Carefully compress tensioner plunger and insert a pin through tensioner body to hold plunger in place.
11. Ensure all timing marks are aligned, **Figs. 40 and 41**. If timing marks are not aligned properly, proceed as follows:
  a. Lower No. 1 piston from TDC by moving crankshaft sprocket 3 teeth before TDC. **No. 1 piston must be lowered to avoid valve contact.**
  b. Align camshaft sprocket timing marks.
  c. Align crankshaft sprocket with mark on oil pump housing.
12. Move crankshaft sprocket to ½ notch before TDC.

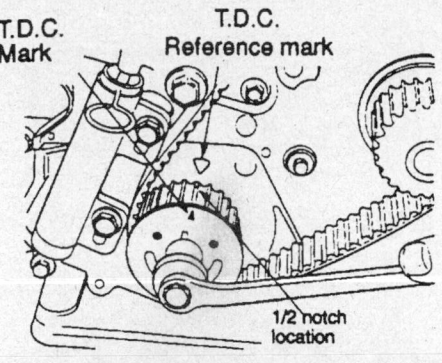

Fig. 41 Crankshaft sprocket alignment. Non-turbocharged engine

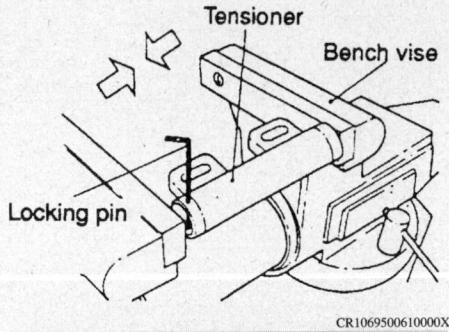

Fig. 42 Timing belt tensioner compression. Non-turbocharged engine

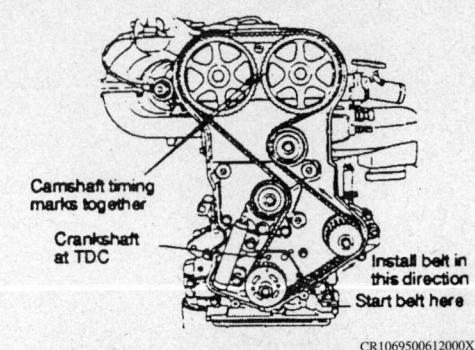

Fig. 43 Timing belt installation. Non-turbocharged engine

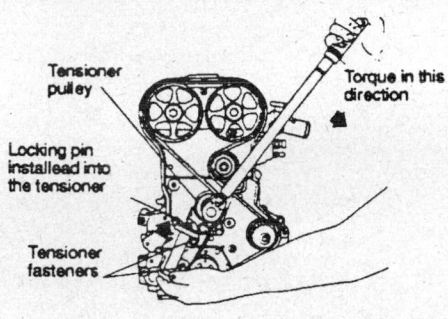

Fig. 44 Timing belt adjustment. Non-turbocharged engine

13. Install timing belt over crankshaft sprocket, water pump sprocket, idler pulley, camshaft sprockets and tensioner pulley, **Fig. 43.**
14. Align crankshaft sprocket with mark on oil pump housing.
15. Install tensioner. **Do not tighten attaching bolts.**
16. Using a suitable torque wrench, apply 21 ft. lbs. of torque to tensioner pulley, **Fig. 44.**
17. While applying torque to tensioner pulley, move tensioner up against pulley bracket and tighten attaching bolts to specifications.
18. Remove pin from tensioner body. Pretension is correct when pin can be removed and installed.
19. Rotate crankshaft two turns in normal direction of rotation and ensure timing marks are aligned. If timing marks are not aligned, timing belt must be removed and installed.
20. Install timing belt front cover, then the engine mount bracket assembly.
21. Remove jack and wooden block from under engine oil pan.
22. Install power steering pump to bracket.
23. Install crankshaft pulley, then the alternator drive belt.
24. Install A/C compressor and power steering pump drive belt.
25. Install engine undercover, then the cooling system reserve tank.

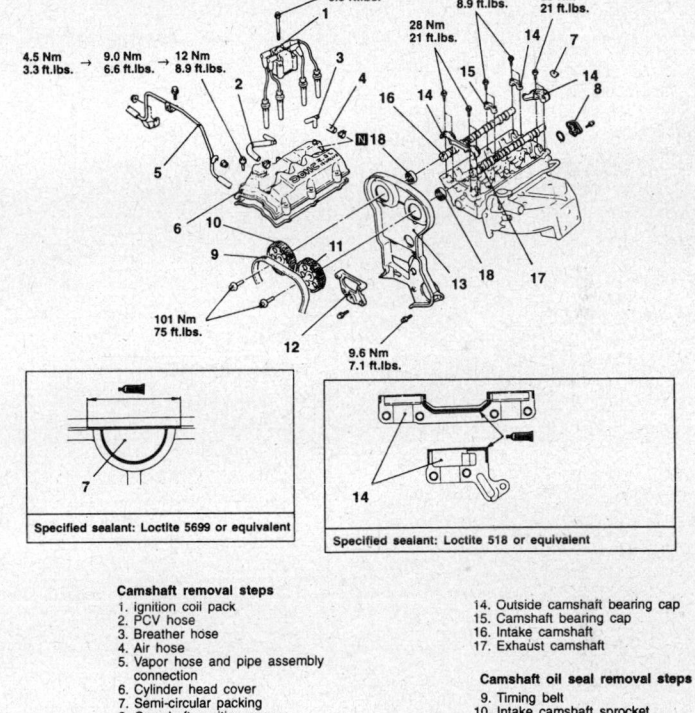

Fig. 45 Camshaft replacement. Non-turbocharged engine

CAMSHAFT

REPLACE

NON-TURBOCHARGED ENGINE

Removal

Remove camshaft in numbered sequence, **Fig. 45,** noting the following:
1. Release fuel system pressure as outlined under "Precautions."
2. Use camshaft sprocket holder and adapter tool Nos. MD990767 and MD998719, or equivalents, to ensure camshaft sprockets do not turn during removal.
3. Mark and identify intake camshaft and exhaust camshaft before removal as they are not interchangeable.
4. Remove camshaft endcaps, then loosen remaining camshaft bearing cap attaching bolts in sequence shown in **Fig. 46,** one camshaft at a time.
5. Remove camshaft oil seals using suitable screwdriver to pry seal out.

Installation
1. Install new camshaft oil seals using special oil seal seating tool Nos. MB991554 and MB998713, or equivalents, **Fig. 47.**
2. Install camshaft bearing cap attaching bolts in sequence shown in **Fig. 46,**

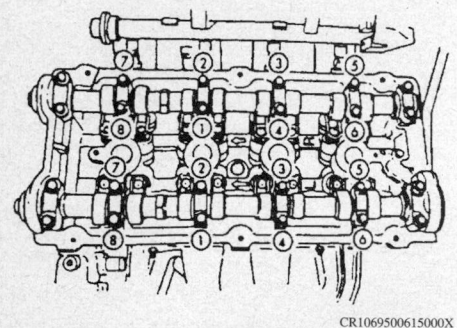

Fig. 46 Camshaft bearing caps. Non-turbocharged engine

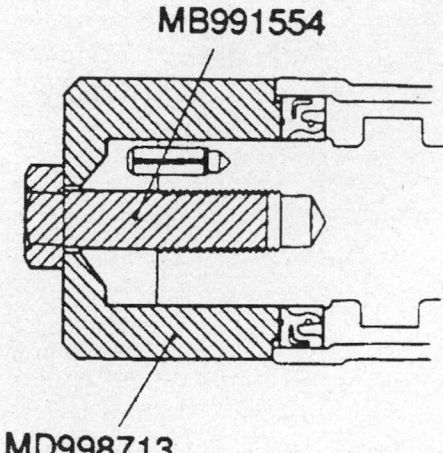

MB991554

MD998713

Fig. 47 Camshaft oil seal installation. Non-turbocharged engine

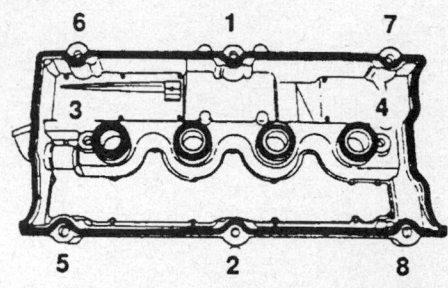

Fig. 48 Cylinder head cover installation. Non-turbocharged engine

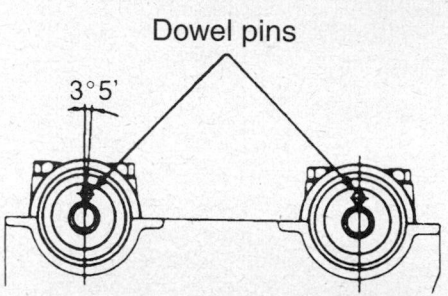

Dowel pins

3°5'

Exhaust side   Intake side

Fig. 50 Camshaft dowel pin alignment. Turbocharged engine

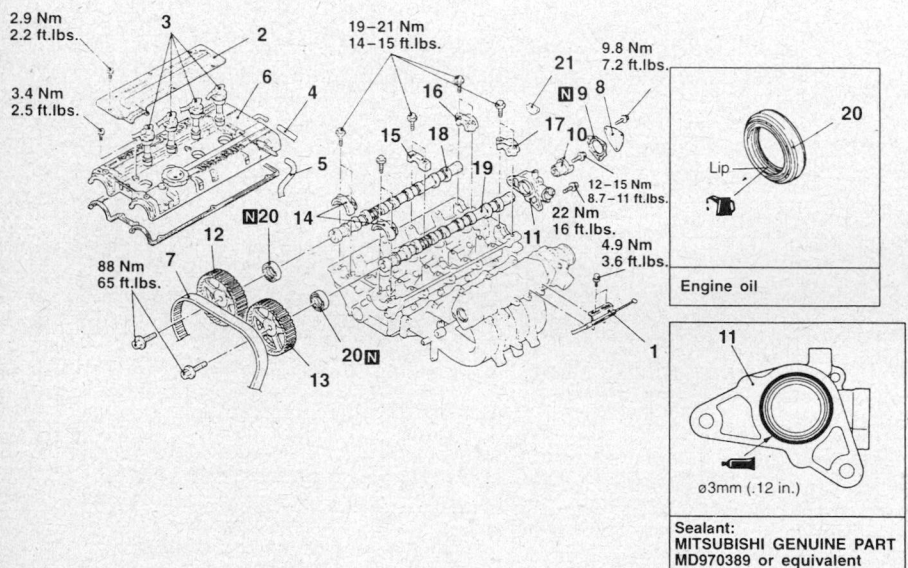

2.9 Nm 2.2 ft.lbs.
3.4 Nm 2.5 ft.lbs.
19–21 Nm 14–15 ft.lbs.
9.8 Nm 7.2 ft.lbs.
12–15 Nm 8.7–11 ft.lbs.
22 Nm 16 ft.lbs.
4.9 Nm 3.6 ft.lbs.
88 Nm 65 ft.lbs.

Lip
Engine oil

ø3mm (.12 in.)

Sealant: MITSUBISHI GENUINE PART MD970389 or equivalent

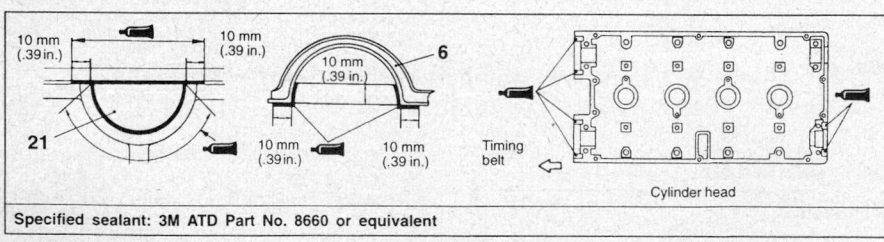

10 mm (.39 in.)
10 mm (.39 in.)
10 mm (.39 in.)
10 mm (.39 in.)
10 mm (.39 in.)

Timing belt

Cylinder head

Specified sealant: 3M ATD Part No. 8660 or equivalent

Removal steps
1. Accelerator cable connection
2. Center cover
3. Spark plug cable
4. Breather hose
5. PCV hose
6. Rocker cover
7. Timing belt
8. Cover
9. Gasket
10. Camshaft position sensing cylinder
11. Camshaft position sensor support
12. Exhaust camshaft sprocket
13. Intake camshaft sprocket
14. Front camshaft bearing cap
15. Camshaft bearing cap
16. Rear camshaft bearing cap (R.H.)
17. Rear camshaft bearing cap (L.H.)
18. Exhaust camshaft
19. Intake camshaft
20. Camshaft oil seal
21. Semi-circular packing

Installation steps
19. Intake camshaft
18. Exhaust camshaft
17. Rear camshaft bearing cap (R.H.)
16. Rear camshaft bearing cap (L.H.)
15. Camshaft bearing cap
14. Front camshaft bearing cap
20. Camshaft oil seal
13. Intake camshaft sprocket
12. Exhaust camshaft sprocket
11. Camshaft position sensor support
10. Camshaft position sensing cylinder
9. Gasket
8. Cover
7. Timing belt
6. Rocker cover
5. PCV hose
4. Breather hose
3. Spark plug cable
2. Center cover
1. Accelerator cable connection

Fig. 49 Camshaft replacement. Turbocharged engine

one camshaft at a time. Tighten to specifications.
3. Use camshaft sprocket holder and adapter tool Nos. MD990767 and MD998719, or equivalents, to ensure camshaft sprockets do not turn during installation.
4. Install cylinder head cover assembly to head and tighten in sequence shown in **Fig. 48. Torque** in three steps: first to 3.3 ft. lbs., then to 6.6 ft. lbs., finally to 9 ft. lbs.

TURBOCHARGED ENGINE

Removal

Refer to **Fig. 49** when removing camshafts, noting the following:
1. Using suitable wrench, hold camshaft at hexagonal portion when removing camshaft sprockets.
2. Loosen bearing caps in two or three steps.
3. If bearing cap is difficult to remove, lightly tap rear of camshaft with rubber mallet.
4. Tag and identify intake and exhaust camshafts as they are not interchangeable.

Installation

Refer to **Fig. 49** when installing camshafts, noting the following:
1. When installing a new camshaft, remove rocker arms, then install camshaft and bearing caps.
2. Ensure camshaft rotates freely.
3. Remove camshaft, then reinstall rocker arms.

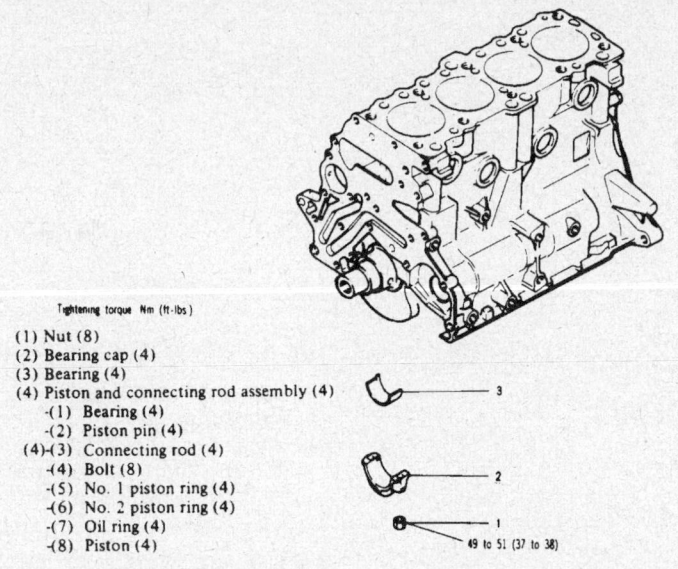

Tightening torque Nm (ft-lbs)

(1) Nut (8)
(2) Bearing cap (4)
(3) Bearing (4)
(4) Piston and connecting rod assembly (4)
  -(1) Bearing (4)
  -(2) Piston pin (4)
(4)-(3) Connecting rod (4)
  -(4) Bolt (8)
  -(5) No. 1 piston ring (4)
  -(6) No. 2 piston ring (4)
  -(7) Oil ring (4)
  -(8) Piston (4)

49 to 51 (37 to 38)

MT1069100087000X

Fig. 51 Piston & rod service

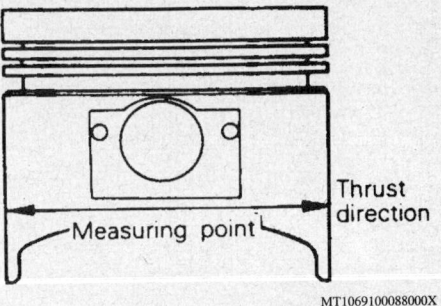

MT1069100088000X

Fig. 52 Piston measurements

4. Install camshaft, rotate so dowel pins are as shown in **Fig. 50,** and **torque** bearing caps to 14 ft. lbs. in two to three steps.

SILENT SHAFT

REPLACE

Refer to "Oil Pump, Replace" for silent shaft replacement procedure.

PISTON & ROD ASSEMBLY

Refer to **Fig. 51** when removing piston and rod assembly. Keep all components, such as connecting rod caps and bearings, in proper order for installation. Position each piston ring gap as far apart as possible and ensure each piston and rod are installed in the same cylinder bore as removed. Ensure connecting rod caps and bearings are placed on proper connecting rods, then tighten bolts to specification.

Pistons and rings are available in standard sizes and oversizes of .010, .020, .030 and .039 inch. Measure piston as shown, **Fig. 52.** Oversize pins are not available.

MAIN & ROD BEARINGS

Refer to "Crankshaft, Replace" for main bearing replacement.

OIL PAN

REPLACE

1. Remove oil pan mounting bolts, then tap oil pan remover tool between cylinder block and oil pan.
2. Remove oil pan by placing a brass bar at corner of oil pan remover tool, then tap with a hammer. **Do not use a screwdriver, chisel or similar tool when removing oil pan.**
3. Check oil pan and screen for damage, cracks or clogging and replace as necessary.
4. Using a wire brush, scrape clean all gasket surfaces of cylinder block and oil pan ensuring all loose material is removed.
5. Ensure gasket surfaces are free of oil and dirt, apply sealant, No. MD970389, or equivalent, around gasket surface of oil pan. Sealant should be applied in a continuous bead approximately .16 inch in diameter.
6. Assemble oil pan to cylinder block within 15 minutes after applying sealant. **After installing oil pan, wait at least 30 minutes before starting engine.**

OIL PUMP

REPLACE
REMOVAL

Refer to **Figs. 53 through 55,** when removing silent shaft, oil pump and front case, noting the following:
1. Position a suitable screwdriver between oil pan and cylinder block and slide along groove to remove.
2. Keep silent shaft in position by inserting a screwdriver through plug hole in left side of cylinder block, **Fig. 54.** Remove oil pump driven gear flange bolt.
3. If front case is sticking to cylinder, insert a suitable screwdriver into slot and pry up, **Fig. 55. Never attempt to pry at any other positions where flange**

is thinner. **Avoid impacting front of case for removal.**
4. Using removal tool No. MD998282-01, or equivalent, remove front and rear bearings from cylinder block.

INSPECTION

1. Ensure silent shaft oil holes are not clogged and journal is inspected for seizure, damage or contact with bearing. If so, replace bearing or front case assembly.
2. Measure silent shaft clearance. If clearance is excessive due to wear, replace silent shaft bearing, silent shaft or front case assembly. Clearance should be as follows:
   a. Right: front, .0008–.0024 inch; rear, .0020–.0036 inch.
   b. Left: front, .0008–.0021 inch; rear, .0020–.0036 inch.
3. Ensure oil pump side clearance of each gear is as follows:
   a. Drive gear: .0031–.0055 inch.
   b. Driven gear: .0024–.0047 inch.

INSTALLATION

1. Install silent shaft in cylinder block.
2. Install oil pump drive and driven gears in front case, ensure gear timing marks are aligned, **Fig. 56.**
3. Using small end of oil seal guide tool No. MD998375-01, or equivalent, install crankshaft front oil seal, **Fig. 57. If crankshaft front oil seal is already mounted to front case, use oil seal guide for protection of oil seal.**
4. Install front case.
5. Insert a screwdriver through plug hole in left side of cylinder block to keep shaft in position, then tighten bolt to specification.
6. Install oil filter bracket assembly and gasket, then tighten front case bolts and oil filter bracket bolts to specification.
7. Install plug cap.
8. Install oil screen and gasket, then clean gasket surfaces of cylinder block and oil pan.
9. Install oil pan gasket, if equipped, using a small amount of suitable gasket sealant. If no gasket is used, apply a .16 inch (4 mm) wide bead of suitable

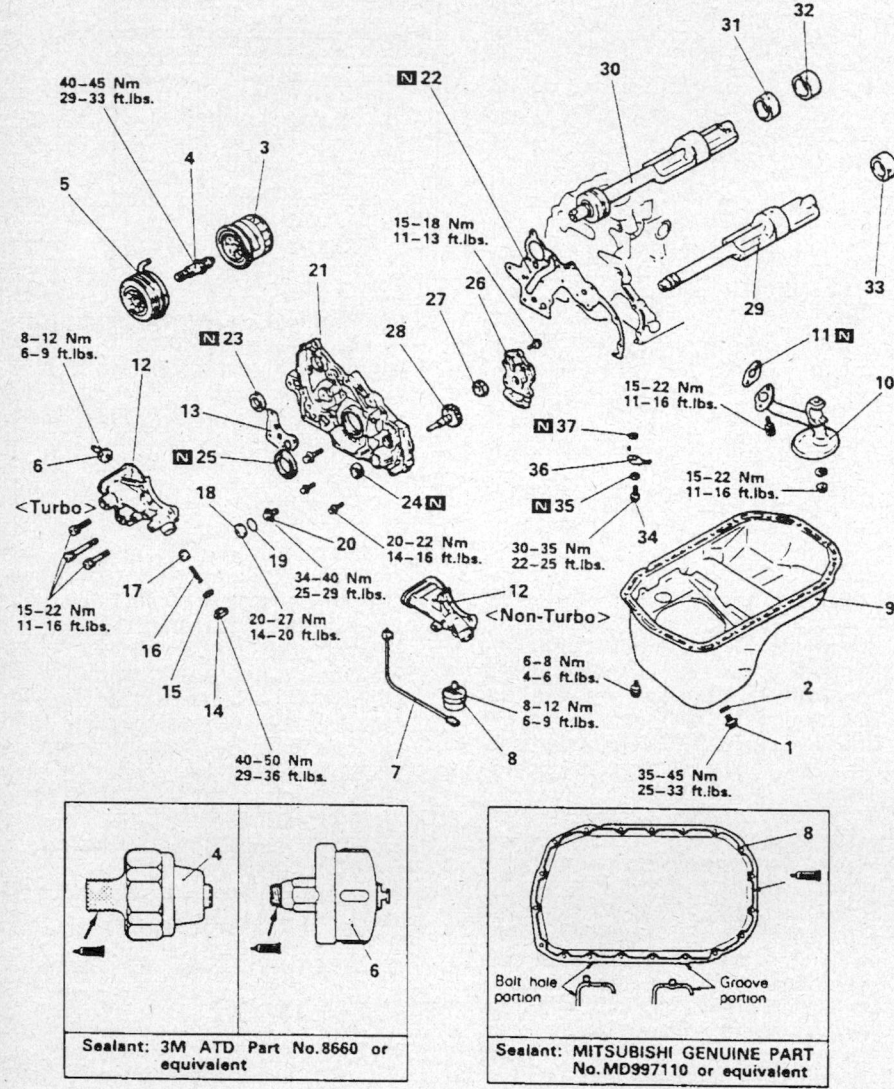

40–45 Nm / 29–33 ft.lbs.
15–18 Nm / 11–13 ft.lbs.
8–12 Nm / 6–9 ft.lbs.
15–22 Nm / 11–16 ft.lbs.
15–22 Nm / 11–16 ft.lbs.
20–22 Nm / 14–16 ft.lbs.
34–40 Nm / 25–29 ft.lbs.
20–27 Nm / 14–20 ft.lbs.
40–50 Nm / 29–36 ft.lbs.
6–8 Nm / 4–6 ft.lbs.
8–12 Nm / 6–9 ft.lbs.
30–35 Nm / 22–25 ft.lbs.
15–22 Nm / 11–16 ft.lbs.
35–45 Nm / 25–33 ft.lbs.

Sealant: 3M ATD Part No. 8660 or equivalent

Sealant: MITSUBISHI GENUINE PART No. MD997110 or equivalent

Disassembly steps

1. Drain plug
2. Gasket
3. Oil filter
4. Oil cooler bolt (Turbo)
5. Oil cooler (Turbo)
6. Oil pressure switch
7. Harness assembly
8. Oil pressure gauge unit
9. Oil pan
10. Oil screen
11. Gasket
12. Oil filter bracket
13. Gasket
14. Relief plug
15. Gasket
16. Relief spring
17. Relief plunger
18. Plug cap
19. O-ring
20. Driven gear bolt
21. Front case
22. Gasket
23. Oil seal
24. Silent shaft oil seal
25. Crankshaft front oil seal
26. Oil pump cover
27. Oil pump driven gear
28. Oil pump drive gear
29. Left silent shaft
30. Right silent shaft
31. Silent shaft front bearings
32. Right silent shaft rear bearing
33. Left silent shaft rear bearing
34. Check valve (Turbo)
35. Gasket (Turbo)
36. Oil jet (Turbo)
37. Gasket (Turbo)

MT1099100006000X

Fig. 53   Silent shaft, oil pump & front case components

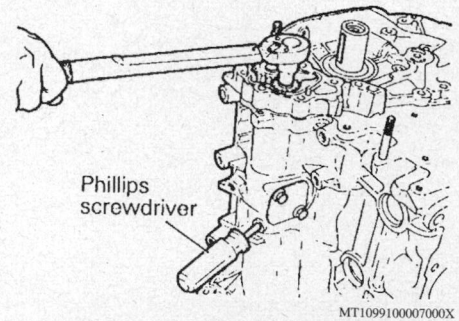

Phillips screwdriver

MT1099100007000X

Fig. 54   Flange bolt removal

sealant to entire circumference of oil pan flange.

10. Install oil pan and tighten bolts to specification. Note difference in bolt length as shown, **Fig. 58.**

BELT TENSION DATA

Year	Belt	New, Lbs.	Used, Lbs.
NON-TURBOCHARGED ENGINE			
1996–99	A/C	137–159	93–115
	Alt.	110–160	90–110
	Power Steering	137–159	93–115
TURBOCHARGED ENGINE			
1996–99	A/C	86–99	57–75
	Alt.	①	88–110
	Power Steering	110–154	77–99

① — 1996–98, 110–154; 1999, 132–17.6

COOLING SYSTEM BLEED

These engines do not require a specified bleed procedure. After filling cooling system, run engine to operating temperature with radiator/pressure cap off. Air will then be automatically bled through the cap opening.

THERMOSTAT
REPLACE

Remove thermostat in numbered sequence, **Fig. 59**, noting the following:

1. Drain coolant to below level of thermostat housing.
2. Mark and note the position of the hose clamps before removal.
3. Clean mating surfaces.
4. Reverse procedure to install, noting the following:
   a. Align hose clamps in position as marked.
   b. Ensure drain is closed, then refill

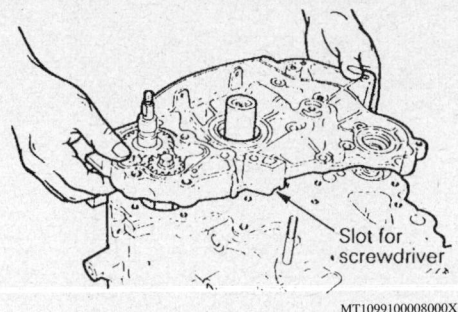

Fig. 55 Front case removal

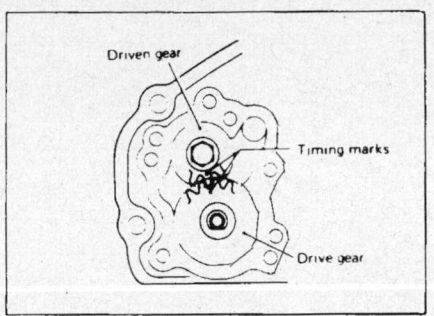

Fig. 56 Oil pump gear timing marks

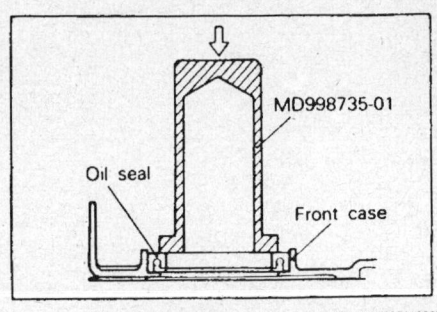

Fig. 57 Crankshaft front oil seal installation

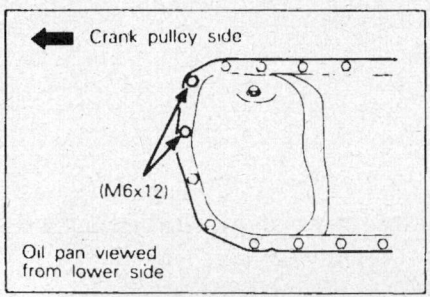

Fig. 58 Oil pan bolt location

coolant. Replace cap, then start engine until warm. Check for leaks, then recheck coolant and fill if necessary.

WATER PUMP

REPLACE

NON-TURBOCHARGED ENGINE

Remove water pump in numbered sequence, **Fig. 60,** noting the following:
1. Drain engine coolant as follows:
   a. Place instrument panel temperature control lever in Hot position.
   b. Carefully remove radiator cap.
   c. Remove radiator drain plug.
2. Remove timing belt rear cover as outlined under "Timing Belt, Replace."
3. Reverse procedure to install. Coat O-ring with water or coolant to ease installation.

TURBOCHARGED ENGINE

Remove water pump in numbered sequence, **Fig. 61,** noting the following:
1. Drain engine coolant as follows:
   a. Place instrument panel temperature control lever in Hot position.
   b. Carefully remove radiator cap.
   c. Remove radiator drain plug.
2. Remove timing belt rear cover as outlined under "Timing Belt, Replace."
3. Reverse procedure to install, noting the following:
   a. Coat O-ring with water or coolant to ease installation.
   b. Refer to bolt inset, **Fig. 61,** when installing water pump attaching bolts.

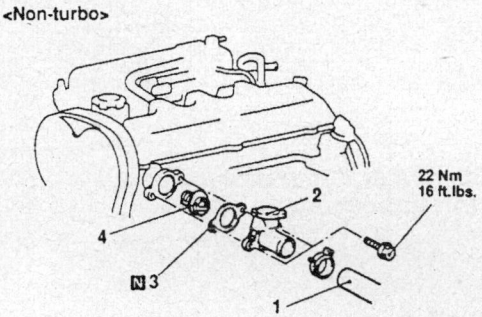

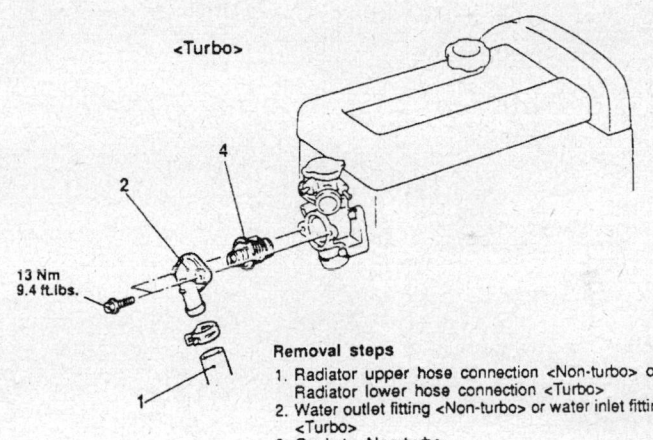

Removal steps
1. Radiator upper hose connection <Non-turbo> or Radiator lower hose connection <Turbo>
2. Water outlet fitting <Non-turbo> or water inlet fitting <Turbo>
3. Gasket <Non-turbo>
4. Thermostat

Fig. 59 Thermostat replacement

RADIATOR

REPLACE

Remove radiator in numbered sequence, **Figs. 62 and 63,** noting the following:
1. Drain engine coolant as follows:
   a. Place instrument panel temperature control lever in Hot position.
   b. Carefully remove radiator cap.
   c. Remove radiator drain plug.
2. Mark and note the position of the hose clamps before removal.
3. **On models equipped with turbocharged engine,** remove air cleaner bracket.
4. **On models equipped with automatic transaxle,** plug or cover nipples and hoses for cooling lines to ensure dust, dirt or other contaminants do not enter lines.
5. **On all models,** reverse procedure to install, noting the following:
   a. Align hose clamps in position as marked.
   b. **On models equipped with turbocharged engine,** install air cleaner bracket
   c. **On models equipped with automatic transaxle,** install cooling lines.
   d. **On all models,** ensure drain is closed, then refill coolant. Replace cap, start engine until warm. Check for leaks, then recheck coolant and fill if necessary.

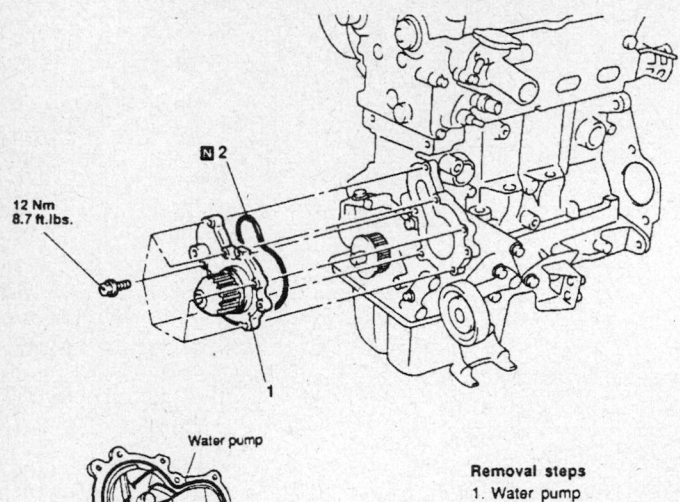

Removal steps
1. Water pump
2. O-ring

CR1089500146000X

Fig. 60 Water pump replacement. Non-turbocharged engine

Removal steps
1. Generator brace
2. Water pump
3. Water pump gasket
4. O-ring

CR1089500147000X

Fig. 61 Water pump replacement. Turbocharged engine

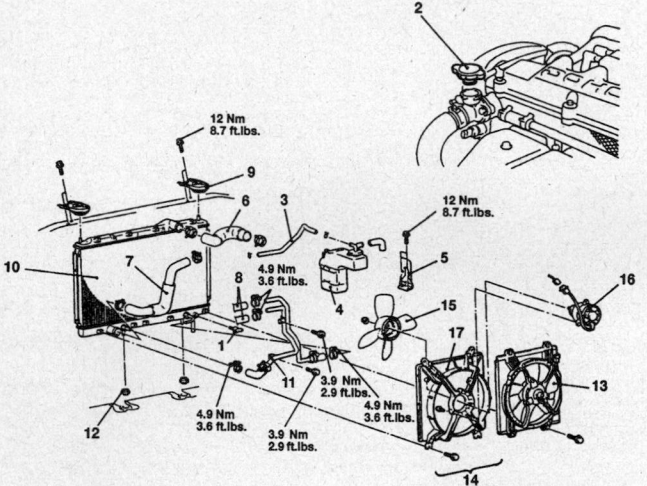

Radiator removal steps
1. Drain plug
2. Radiator cap
3. Overflow tube
4. Reserve tank
5. Reserve tank bracket
6. Radiator upper hose
7. Radiator lower hose
8. Transaxle fluid cooler hose connection <Vehicles with A/T>
9. Upper insulator
10. Radiator assembly
11. Transaxle fluid cooler hose and pipe assembly <Vehicles with A/T>
12. Lower insulator

13. Condenser fan motor assembly <Vehicles with A/C>
14. Radiator fan motor assembly
15. Fan
16. Radiator fan motor
17. Shroud

Radiator fan motor removal steps
11. Transaxle fluid cooler hose and pipe assembly <Vehicles with A/T>
14. Radiator fan motor assembly
15. Fan
16. Radiator fan motor
17. Shroud

CR1089500149000X

Fig. 62 Radiator replacement. Non-turbocharged engine

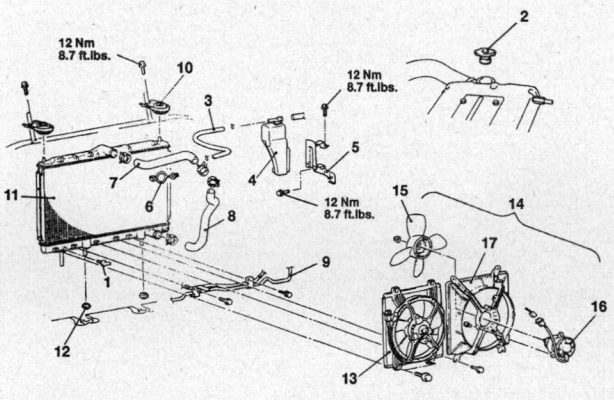

Radiator removal steps
1. Drain plug
2. Radiator cap
3. Overflow tube
4. Reserve tank
5. Reserve tank bracket
6. Clip
7. Radiator upper hose
8. Radiator lower hose
9. Transaxle fluid cooler hose and pipe assembly <Vehicles with A/T>
10. Upper insulator
11. Radiator assembly
12. Lower insulator
13. Condenser fan motor assembly <Vehicles with A/C>
14. Radiator fan motor assembly
15. Fan
16. Radiator fan motor
17. Shroud

Radiator fan motor removal steps
4. Reserve tank
9. Transaxle fluid cooler hose and pipe assembly <Vehicles with A/T>
14. Radiator fan motor assembly
15. Fan
16. Radiator fan motor
17. Shroud

CR1089500150000X

Fig. 63 Radiator replacement. Turbocharged engine

FUEL PUMP
REPLACE
FWD MODELS
Removal

Remove fuel pump in numbered sequence, **Fig. 64.**
1. Relieve fuel pressure as outlined under "Precautions."
2. Remove fuel from fuel tank into a suitable container.

3. When disconnecting high pressure fuel line, cover fuel line connection with rags to prevent spraying of fuel.
4. Remove rear seat cushion and floor plate for access to fuel pump.
5. Disconnect hoses and connectors to remove fuel pump

Installation

Reverse removal procedure to install, noting the following:
1. Align packing position projections with holes in fuel pump assembly.

2. Ensure fuel pump assembly and hoses are not leaking.
3. Before installing hole cover plate, apply suitable sealant to rear floor pan.

AWD MODELS
Removal

Relieve fuel pressure as outlined under "Precautions." and remove fuel pump in numbered sequence, **Fig. 65.**
1. Remove fuel from fuel tank into a suitable container.

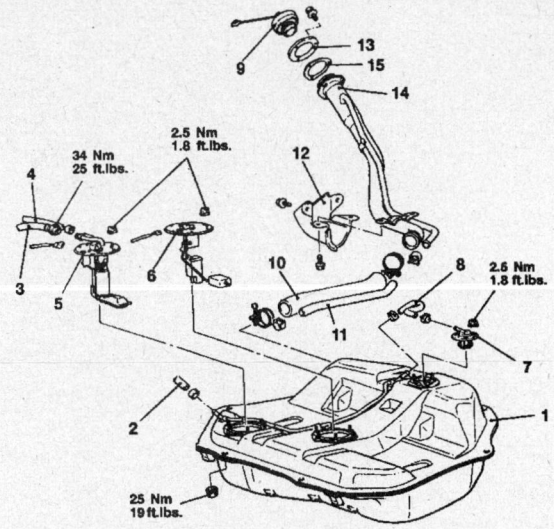

Removal steps
1. Fuel tank
2. Vapor hose
3. High-pressure fuel hose
4. Return hose
5. Fuel pump assembly
6. Fuel gauge unit
7. Fuel cut-off valve assembly
8. Vapor hose
9. Fuel tank filler tube cap
10. Filler hose
11. Vapor hose
12. Fuel tank filler tube protector
13. Reinforcement
14. Fuel tank filler tube assembly
15. Packing

NOTE
When replacing the fuel pump assembly or the fuel gauge unit only, it is possible to work from the service holes underneath the rear seat cushion without having to remove the fuel tank.

MT1029500670000X

Fig. 64 Fuel pump replacement. FWD models

2. When disconnecting high pressure fuel line, cover fuel line connection with rags to prevent spraying of fuel.
3. Remove rear seat cushion and floor plate for access to fuel pump.
4. Disconnect hoses and connectors to remove fuel pump

Installation

Reverse removal procedure to install, noting the following:
1. Ensure packing seal is not damaged or deformed.
2. Apply soapy water to fuel tank threads, then install fuel pump and cap.
3. Using special cap tightening tool No. MB991480, or equivalent. **Fig. 66.**
4. Ensure fuel pump assembly and hoses are not leaking.

FUEL FILTER
REPLACE

When replacing fuel filter, refer to **Fig. 67** for replacement procedure.
1. Relieve fuel pressure as outlined under "Precautions."
2. Remove battery and air intake hose to access fuel filter.
3. Reverse procedure to install.

TURBOCHARGER
REPLACE

1. Remove turbocharger components in order as shown, **Fig. 68.**

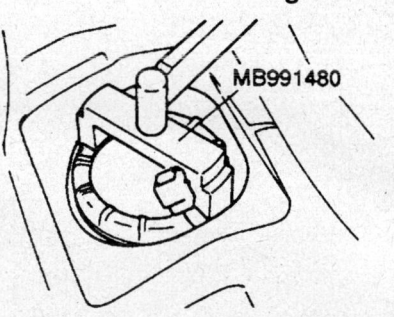

MB991480

CR1029503774000X

Fig. 66 Fuel pump cap installation. AWD models

2. Drain cooling system as follows:
   a. Place temperature control lever in Hot position.
   b. Carefully remove radiator cap.
   c. Remove radiator drain plug.
3. Drain engine oil into appropriate container.
4. Disconnect oxygen sensor electrical connector, then using oxygen sensor wrench tool No. MD998748, or equivalent, and an offset box-end wrench, remove oxygen sensor.
5. Remove power steering pump from

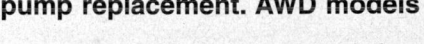

Removal Steps
1. Heated oxygen sensor connection
2. Center exhaust pipe
3. Protector
4. Band
5. Fuel tank
6. High-pressure fuel hose
7. Return hose
8. Suction hose
9. Pipe
10. Cap
11. Fuel gauge unit and pump assembly
12. Fuel gauge unit and pipe assembly
13. Tape
14. Vapor hose
15. Fuel cut-off valve assembly
16. Fuel tank filler tube cap
17. Filler hose
18. Vapor hose
19. Fuel tank filler tube protector
20. Reinforcement
21. Fuel tank filler tube assembly
22. Packing

MT1029500671000X

Fig. 65 Fuel pump replacement. AWD models

bracket with hoses attached, then secure pump aside with a piece of wire.
6. Remove turbocharger assembly with exhaust fitting, water pipes A and B and oil pipe attached.
7. **After disconnecting oil pipe, ensure foreign material does not enter oil passage hole of turbocharger.**
8. Reverse procedure to install, noting the following:
   a. Prior to installing turbocharger assembly, pour a small quantity of clean engine oil into oil supply pipe fitting hole in turbocharger.
   b. Clean alignment surfaces of turbocharger as shown, **Fig. 69. Use caution not to allow gasket or other foreign material to enter oil passage hole.**
   c. Use new gaskets, locknuts and O-rings.
   d. Install oxygen sensor using oxygen sensor wrench tool No. MD998748, or equivalent, and an offset box-end wrench, then connect oxygen sensor electrical connector.

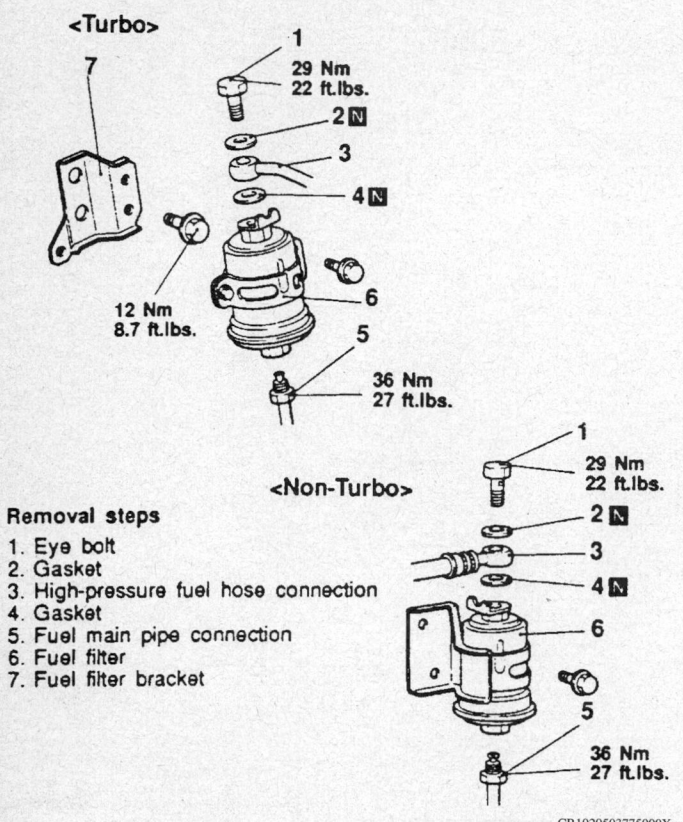

<Turbo>

1
29 Nm
22 ft.lbs.

2 N

3

4 N

6

12 Nm
8.7 ft.lbs.

5

36 Nm
27 ft.lbs.

<Non-Turbo>

1
29 Nm
22 ft.lbs.

2 N

3

4 N

6

5

36 Nm
27 ft.lbs.

Removal steps

1. Eye bolt
2. Gasket
3. High-pressure fuel hose connection
4. Gasket
5. Fuel main pipe connection
6. Fuel filter
7. Fuel filter bracket

CR1029503775000X

Fig. 67   Fuel filter replacement

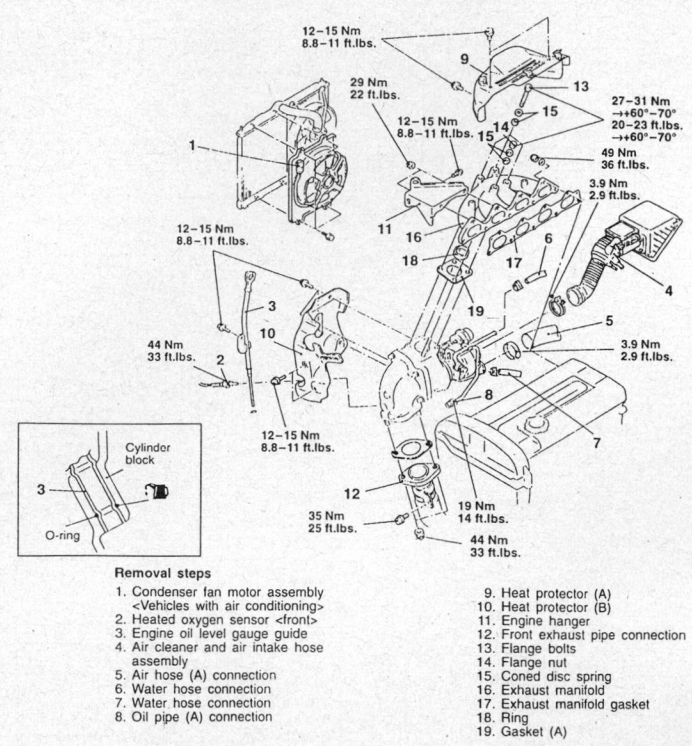

12–15 Nm
8.8–11 ft.lbs.

9

13

29 Nm
22 ft.lbs.

12–15 Nm
8.8–11 ft.lbs.

15   14   15

27–31 Nm
→+60°~70°
20–23 ft.lbs.
→+60°~70°

49 Nm
36 ft.lbs.

1

11   16

18

17

3.9 Nm
2.9 Nm

12–15 Nm
8.8–11 ft.lbs.

3

19

5

3.9 Nm
2.9 Nm

44 Nm
33 ft.lbs.

10

8

Cylinder block

3

O-ring

12–15 Nm
8.8–11 ft.lbs.

7

12

35 Nm
25 ft.lbs.

19 Nm
14 ft.lbs.

44 Nm
33 ft.lbs.

Removal steps

1. Condenser fan motor assembly
   <Vehicles with air conditioning>
2. Heated oxygen sensor <front>
3. Engine oil level gauge guide
4. Air cleaner and air intake hose assembly
5. Air hose (A) connection
6. Water hose connection
7. Water hose connection
8. Oil pipe (A) connection

9. Heat protector (A)
10. Heat protector (B)
11. Engine hanger
12. Front exhaust pipe connection
13. Flange bolts
14. Flange nut
15. Coned disc spring
16. Exhaust manifold
17. Exhaust manifold gasket
18. Ring
19. Gasket (A)

MT1079800023010X

Fig. 68   Turbocharger replacement (Part 1 of 2)

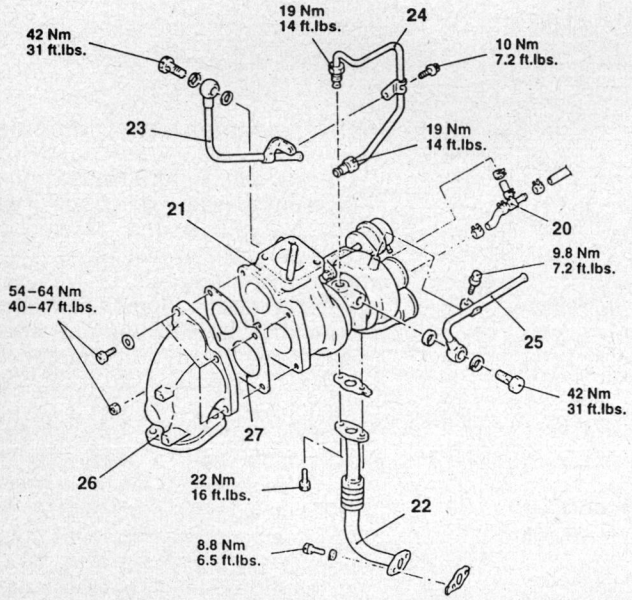

42 Nm
31 ft.lbs.

19 Nm
14 ft.lbs.

24

10 Nm
7.2 ft.lbs.

23

19 Nm
14 ft.lbs.

21

20

54–64 Nm
40–47 ft.lbs.

9.8 Nm
7.2 ft.lbs.

25

27

26

22 Nm
16 ft.lbs.

42 Nm
31 ft.lbs.

22

8.8 Nm
6.5 ft.lbs.

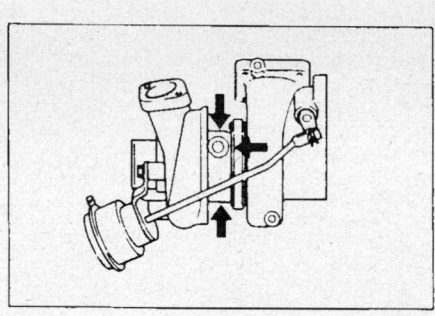

MT1059100007000X

Fig. 69   Turbocharger alignment surfaces

20. Vacuum hose assembly
21. Turbocharger assembly
22. Oil return pipe
23. Water pipe assembly (B)

24. Oil pipe assembly
25. Water pipe assembly (A)
26. Exhaust manifold fitting
27. Gasket

MT1079800023020X

Fig. 68   Turbocharger replacement (Part 2 of 2)

TIGHTENING SPECIFICATIONS

Year	Component	Torque, Ft. Lbs.
NON-TURBOCHARGED ENGINE		
1996–99	A/C Compressor Bracket	17–20
	Air Cleaner	72-84③
	Auto Tensioner	22
	Camshaft Bearing Cap Bolt	14
	Camshaft Sprocket	73
	Connecting Rod Bearing Caps	27②
	Crankshaft Bearing Caps (Inner)	55
	Crankshaft Bearing Caps (Outer)	20
	Crankshaft Pulley	48③
	Cylinder Head Bolt	①
	EGR Valve	16
	Engine Coolant Temperature Sensor	22
	Exhaust Manifold To Engine	17
	Exhaust Pipe Clamp Bolt	108③
	Exhaust Pipe To Hanger	108③
	Exhaust Pipe To Manifold	33
	Flywheel	98
	Fuel Gauge Unit (AWD)	36
	Fuel Gauge Unit (FWD)	22③
	Fuel Pump (Bolt)	22③
	Fuel Pump Cap	36
	Intake Manifold To Engine	17
	Oil Pan Drain Plug	25
	Oil Pump Cover	17
	Oil Screen	21
	Oxygen Sensor	22
	Throttle Body	11–16
	Timing Belt Front Cover, Bottom	21
	Timing Belt Front Cover, Top	108③
	Timing Belt Tensioner Pulley	20
	Water Pump	108③

Continued

2.0L ENGINE

TIGHTENING
SPECIFICATIONS—Continued

Year	Component	Torque, Ft. Lbs.
TURBOCHARGED ENGINE		
1996–99	Air Cleaner	72-84③
	Auto Tensioner	17
	Camshaft Bearing Cap Bolt	14
	Camshaft Sprocket	65
	Center Cover	26③
	Connecting Rod Bearing Caps	14.5④
	Crankshaft Bearing Cap	18④
	Crankshaft Pulley	18
	Crankshaft Sprocket	80–94
	Cylinder Head Bolt	①
	EGR Valve	16
	Electric Fuel Pump (Bolt)	22③
	Engine Coolant Temperature Sensor	22
	Engine Oil Cooler Mounting Bolt	29–33
	Exhaust Manifold To Engine	22
	Exhaust Manifold To Turbocharger	43
	Exhaust Pipe Clamp Bolt	108③
	Exhaust Pipe To Hanger	108③
	Exhaust Pipe To Manifold	33–36
	Flywheel	98
	Fuel Gauge Unit (AWD)	36
	Fuel Gauge Unit (FWD)	22③
	Heat Shield To Exhaust Manifold	9–11
	Intake Manifold To Engine	14
	Oil Filter Bracket	14
	Oil Pan	60③
	Oil Pan Drain Plug	29
	Oil Pressure Gauge Unit	40
	Oil Pressure Switch	84③
	Oil Pump Cover	12
	Oil Pump Driven Gear	84③
	Oil Return Pipe To Oil Pan	84③
	Oil Screen	14
	Oxygen Sensor	32
	Tensioner Pulley Bracket	17–20
	Throttle Body	14
	Timing Belt B Tensioner	14
	Timing Belt Front Cover	84–108③
	Timing Belt Tensioner Bolt	17–20
	Water Pump	9–11

① — Refer to "Cylinder Head, Replace."

② — Tighten an additional 90.°

③ — Inch lbs.

④ — Tighten an additional 90–100.°

2.4L Engine

NOTE: For Procedures Not Found In This Section, Refer To The "2.4L Engine" Section In The "Mitsubishi Galant" Chapter.

NOTE: On Air Bag Equipped Models, Refer To "Air Bag System Precautions" Located In The Front Of This Manual For System Disarming & Arming Procedures.

NOTE: Refer To "Computer Relearn" Located In The Front Of This Manual For Computer Relearn Procedures.

INDEX

PRECAUTIONS

AIR BAG SYSTEMS

Refer to "Air Bag System Precautions" in the front of this manual for system disarming and arming procedures.

BATTERY GROUND CABLE

Prior to service, disconnect battery ground cable and isolate as required.

ENGINE

REPLACE

1. Relieve fuel system pressure as outlined under "Precautions," then scribe and remove hood.
2. Drain engine coolant into a suitable container, then remove transaxle.
3. Remove radiator.
4. Remove engine assembly in numbered sequence shown in **Fig. 1,** noting the following:
   a. When removing power steering pump and A/C compressor, leave hoses attached and support aside.
   b. Ensure engine is supported when transaxle is removed. A block of wood placed between oil pan and a floor jack will suffice until a suitable engine lifting device can be installed.
5. Reverse procedure to install. Tighten all engine mounting bolts and nuts to specifications.

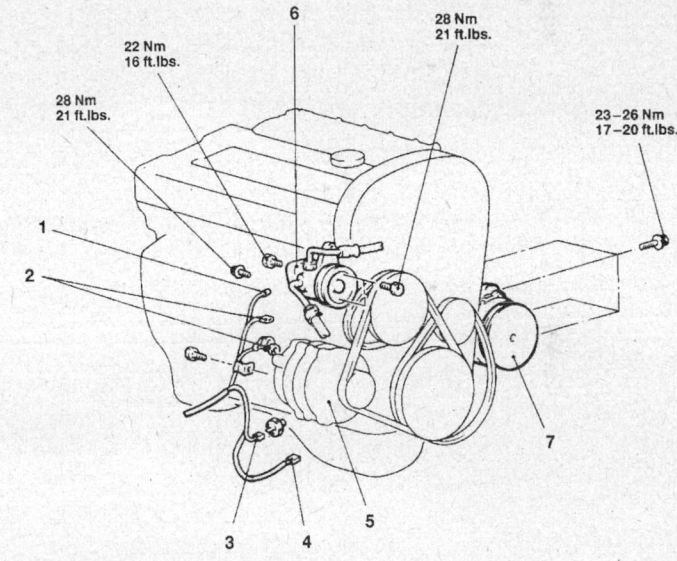

Removal steps
1. Power steering pressure switch connector
2. Generator connectors
3. Oil pressure switch connector
4. Oil pressure gauge unit connector
5. Generator
6. Power steering pump connection
7. A/C compressor connection

MT1069600342010X

Fig. 1 Engine replacement (Part 1 of 3)

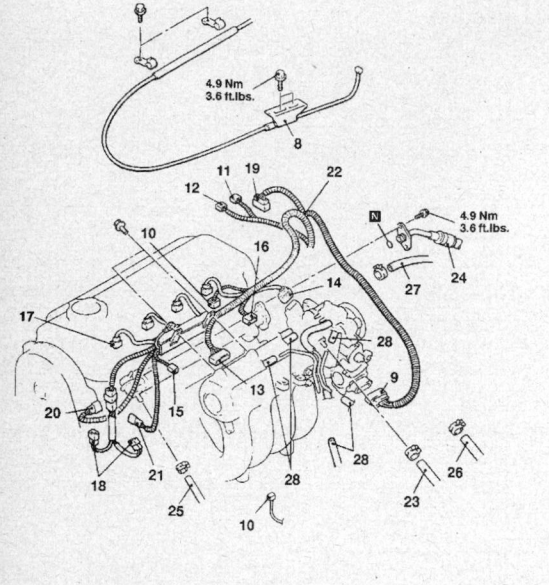

8. Accelerator cable connection
9. Idle air control motor connector
10. Heated oxygen sensor connector
11. Engine coolant temperature gauge unit connector
12. Engine coolant temperature sensor connector
13. Ignition power transistor connector
14. Throttle position sensor connector
15. Capacitor connector
16. Manifold differential pressure sensor connector
17. Injector connectors
18. Ignition coil connector

19. Camshaft position sensor connector
20. Crankshaft position sensor connector
21. Air conditioning compressor connector
22. Control wiring harness
23. Brake booster vacuum hose connection
24. High-pressure fuel hose connection
25. Fuel return hose connection
26. Water hose A connection
27. Water hose B connection
28. Vacuum hoses connection

MT1069600342020X

Fig. 1   Engine replacement (Part 2 of 3)

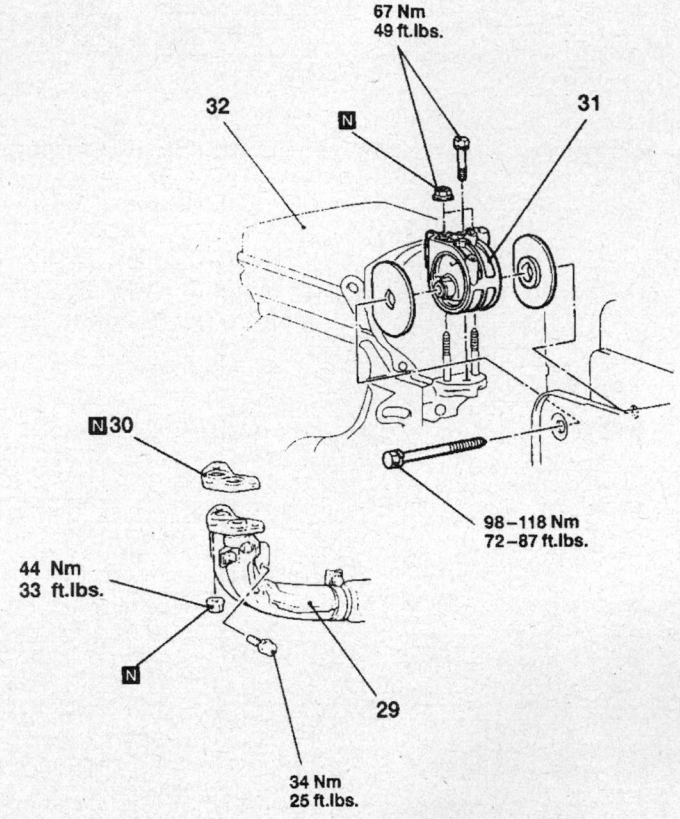

29. Front exhaust pipe connection
30. Gasket
31. Engine mount bracket assembly
32. Engine assembly

MT1069600342030X

Fig. 1   Engine replacement (Part 3 of 3)

TIGHTENING SPECIFICATIONS

Year	Component	Torque, Ft. Lbs.
1996–99	Accelerator Cable Bracket	43④
	Air Intake Hose Clamp	36④
	Alternator Adjustment Bolt	10
	Alternator Bracket Pivot Bolt	17
	Bellhousing Cover Bolts	84④
	Bellhousing Cover Bolts (Bolt & Flange, 1999)	18
	Bellhousing Cover Bolts (Bolt & Washer Assembled, 1999)	78④
	Camshaft Position Sensor Bolt	108④
	Center Member Attaching Bolts (Front)	64
	Center Member Attaching Bolts (Rear)	50–56
	Crankshaft Pulley Bolts	18
	Dynamic Damper Mounting Bolts	48④
	Engine Hanger To Exhaust Manifold Nuts	③
	Engine Mount Bracket Through Bolt	②
	Engine Mount Bracket To Engine Bolt & Nut	49
	Exhaust Manifold Mounting Nuts	20–22
	Front Exhaust Pipe Bracket Bolts	25
	Front Exhaust Pipe To Exhaust Manifold Nuts	33
	Front Roll Stopper Bracket Bolts	32
	Front Roll Stopper Bracket Through Bolt Nut	①
	Heat Protector	10
	High Pressure Fuel Hose Flange To Fuel Rail Bolts	43④
	Ignition Coil Assembly Mounting Bolt	84④
	Ignition Power Transistor Mounting Bolt	43④
	Oil Dipstick Tube Guide Bolt	43
	Power Steering Pump Mounting Bolt	21
	Power Steering Pump Pivot Bolt	16
	Power Steering Pump Pulley Bolts	21
	Rear Roll Stopper Bracket Bolts	32
	Rear Roll Stopper Bracket Through Bolt Nut	32
	Spark Plugs	18
	Timing Belt Auto Tensioner Bolt	17
	Timing Belt Auto Tensioner Pulley Center Bolt	35
	Timing Belt "B" Tensioner Pulley Center Bolt	14
	Timing Belt Front Cover Flange Bolts (M6)	96④
	Timing Belt Front Cover Washer Bolt (M6)	84④
	Timing Belt Front Cover Bolt (M8)	10
	Timing Belt Tensioner Pulley Bracket Bolt	17–19
	Transaxle Mount Bolt (6mm)	96④
	Transaxle Mount Bolt (8mm)	20
	Transaxle Mount Bolt (10mm)	36
	Transaxle Mount Bracket Bolt	51
	Water Inlet Pipe Bracket	10
	Water Pump Pulley Bolts	96④

① — 1996–98, 41 ft. lbs.; 1999, 63 ft. lbs.

② — 1996–98, 85 ft. lbs.; 1999, 60 ft. lbs.

③ — 1996–98, 18–21 ft. lbs.; 1999, 36 ft. lbs.

④ — Inch lbs.

Clutch & Manual Transaxle

INDEX

ADJUSTMENTS

CLUTCH PEDAL

1. Measure clutch pedal height "A" and clutch pedal clevis pin play "B," **Fig. 1.**
2. Clutch pedal height "A" should be 7.0–7.1 inches.
3. Clevis pin play "B" should be .04–.12 inch.
4. If either "A" or "B" are not within specification, adjust as follows:
   a. **On models less cruise control,** turn and adjust bolt ensure pedal height is correct, then secure by tightening locknut, **Fig. 2.**
   b. **On models equipped with cruise control,** disconnect clutch switch connector and turn the switch for standard clutch pedal height, then lock with the locknut.
   c. **On all models,** turn pushrod, **Fig. 3,** to adjust clutch pedal clevis pin play to proper value, then secure pushrod with locknut. **When adjusting clutch pedal clevis pin play, ensure pushrod is not pushed toward the master cylinder.**
5. Upon completing adjustments above, ensure clutch pedal freeplay (C) is .2–.5 inch.
6. Ensure distance (D) between clutch pedal pad and firewall, when clutch pedal is disengaged, **Fig. 4,** is 2.76 inches or more.
7. If clutch pedal freeplay (C) and distance (D) are not within specification, check for air in hydraulic system or a defective clutch or master cylinder assembly.

HYDRAULIC SYSTEM SERVICE

CLUTCH BOOSTER INSPECTION

1. Run engine for one minute or more, then turn engine off.
2. Step on clutch pedal several times with normal pressure.
3. If pedal depressed fully the first time but gradually becomes higher when depressed several times, the booster is operating correctly.
4. If pedal height remains unchanged, booster is faulty.
5. With engine off, step on clutch pedal

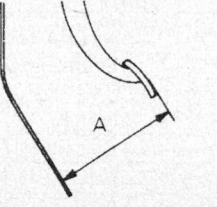
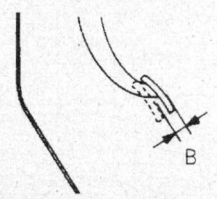

Fig. 1   Clutch pedal height & clevis pin play

MT5049100001000X

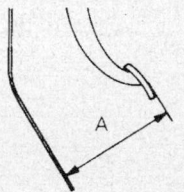
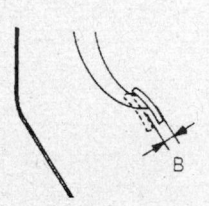

Fig. 3   Clutch pedal clevis pin play

MT5049100003000X

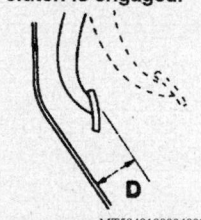

Fig. 4   Clutch pedal freeplay & distance to firewall

MT5049100004000X

several times with same foot pressure, then step on clutch pedal and start engine.
6. If pedal moves downward slightly, booster is in good condition. If there is no change in pedal height, booster is faulty.
7. With engine idling, step on clutch pedal and turn engine off.
8. If pedal height does not change, booster is operating correctly. If pedal height rises, booster is faulty.
9. If one or more of the above tests fail, ensure condition of valve and vacuum

Fig. 2   Locknut location

MT5049100002000X

hose and if necessary, replace booster.

CLUTCH CONTROL COMPONENTS, REPLACE

1. Remove air cleaner assembly.
2. Drain clutch system fluid into an appropriate container.
3. Remove clutch control components in numbered sequence as shown, **Fig. 5,** noting the following:
   a. Disconnect clutch hose from tube by securing nut on clutch hose, then loosen flare nut on clutch tube. Remove clip from clutch hose to remove clutch hose from bracket.
4. Adjust clearance between clutch booster pushrod and piston as outlined under "Clutch Booster Pushrod & Piston Clearance Adjust."

CLUTCH MASTER CYLINDER SERVICE

1. Remove piston stop ring, **Fig. 7.**
2. Remove piston assembly. **Do not damage master cylinder body or piston assembly. Do not disassemble piston assembly.**
3. Inspect inside cylinder body and piston for rust or scars and the piston cup for wear or deformation, replace as necessary.
4. Inspect clutch tube connection part for clogging.
5. Reverse procedure to assemble, tightening reservoir band.

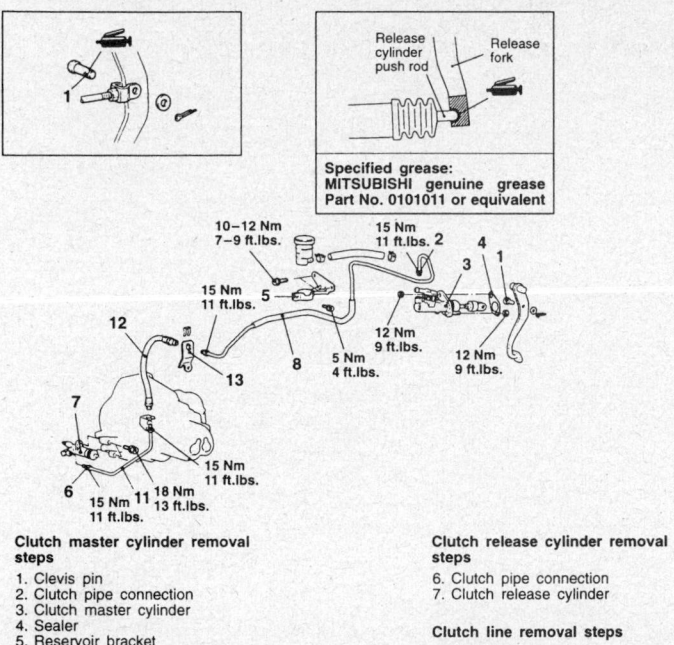

Clutch master cylinder removal steps

1. Clevis pin
2. Clutch pipe connection
3. Clutch master cylinder
4. Sealer
5. Reservoir bracket

Clutch release cylinder removal steps

6. Clutch pipe connection
7. Clutch release cylinder

Clutch line removal steps

8. Clutch pipe
11. Clutch pipe
12. Clutch hose
13. Clutch hose bracket

MT5049500054000X

Fig. 5 Clutch control component replacement. Non-turbocharged engine

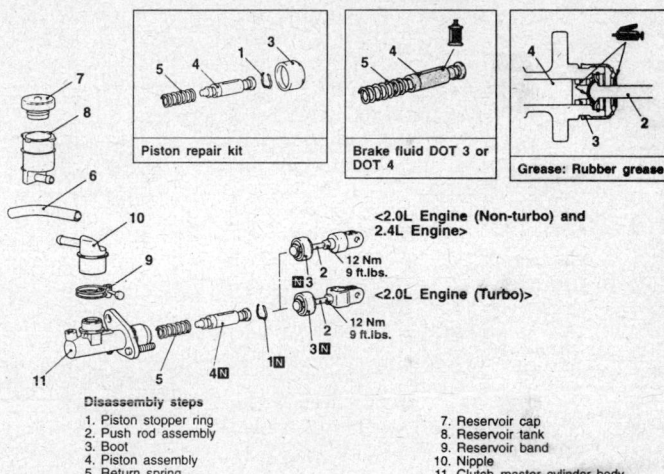

Clutch master cylinder removal steps

1. Clevis pin
2. Clutch pipe connection
3. Clutch master cylinder
4. Sealer
5. Reservoir bracket

Clutch release cylinder removal steps

6. Clutch release cylinder connection
7. Clutch release cylinder

Clutch line removal steps

8. Clutch pipe
9. Clutch pipe
10. Clutch fluid chamber
11. Clutch pipe
12. Clutch hose

MT5049500060000X

Fig. 6 Clutch control component replacement. Turbocharged engine

CLUTCH

REPLACE

1. Remove transaxle as outlined under "Transaxle, Replace."
2. Insert clutch disc guide tool No. MD998126, or equivalent, into center hole to prevent dropping of clutch disc, then diagonally loosen bolts that hold clutch cover assembly to remove clutch cover assembly. **Do not clean clutch disc or release bearing with cleaning solvent.**
3. Remove snap ring and clevis pin, then the release cylinder assembly, if equipped.
4. Remove return clip, then the release bearing.
5. Remove spring pins from clutch release fork and shaft using a suitable punch.
6. Install release shaft and packing, then the return spring and release fork.
7. Align lockpin holes of shift arm and control shaft, then drive in two new spring pins.
8. When installing spring pins, ensure spring pin slot direction is at right angles to center line of control shaft.
9. Remove grease from clutch facing by wiping with clean cloth.
10. Apply small amount of grease to clutch

disc spline and input shaft spline.
11. Using clutch installer tool No. MD998126, or equivalent, install clutch disc and clutch cover assembly to flywheel. When installing clutch disc, ensure surface with manufacturer's stamped mark is on pressure plate side.

SHIFT CABLE

REPLACE

Replace transaxle shift cables in num-

Disassembly steps

1. Piston stopper ring
2. Push rod assembly
3. Boot
4. Piston assembly
5. Return spring
6. Reservoir hose

7. Reservoir cap
8. Reservoir tank
9. Reservoir band
10. Nipple
11. Clutch master cylinder body

MT5049500062000X

Fig. 7 Clutch master cylinder

bered sequence shown in **Fig.8,** noting the following when installing:

1. Install shift lever assembly bushings with the side marked UP facing upward.
2. Install select cable as follows:
   a. Install select cable on the transaxle end.
   b. Place transaxle in Neutral position.
   c. Place gear selector in Neutral position.
   d. Adjust length of select cable then

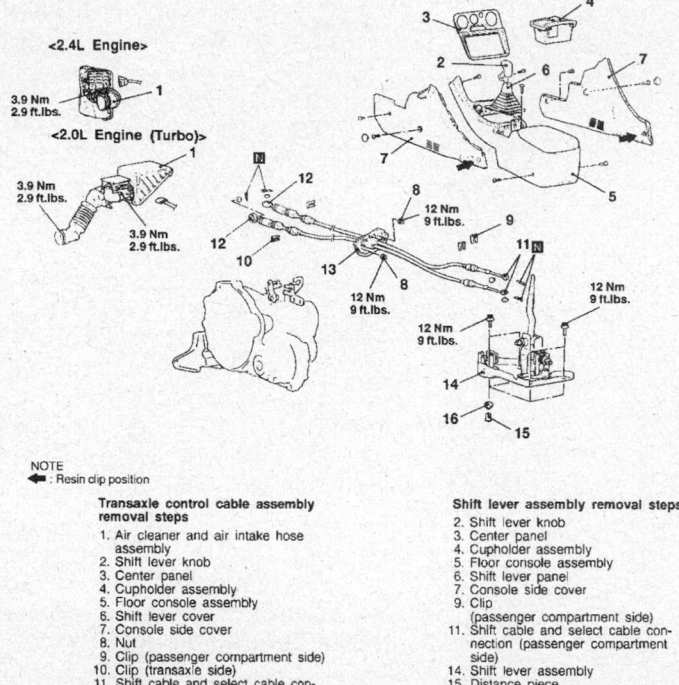

NOTE
◄ : Resin clip position

Transaxle control cable assembly removal steps

1. Air cleaner and air intake hose assembly
2. Shift lever knob
3. Center panel
4. Cupholder assembly
5. Floor console assembly
6. Shift lever cover
7. Console side cover
8. Nut
9. Clip (passenger compartment side)
10. Clip (transaxle side)
11. Shift cable and select cable connection (passenger compartment side)
12. Shift cable and select cable connection (transaxle side)
13. Shift cable and select cable assembly

Shift lever assembly removal steps

2. Shift lever knob
3. Center panel
4. Cupholder assembly
5. Floor console assembly
6. Shift lever panel
7. Console side cover
9. Clip (passenger compartment side)
11. Shift cable and select cable connection (passenger compartment side)
14. Shift lever assembly
15. Distance piece
16. Bushing

MT5039500128000X

Fig. 8 Shift cable replacement

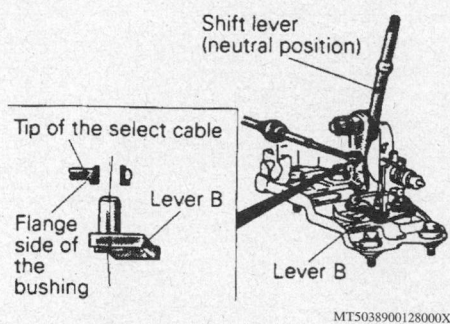

MT5038900128000X

Fig. 9 Select cable connection

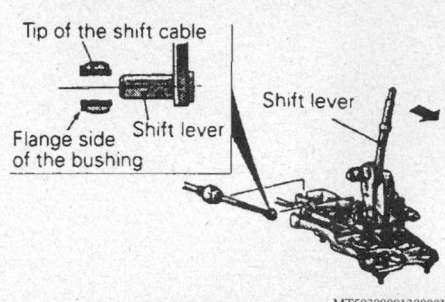

MT5038900130000X

Fig. 11 Shift cable connection

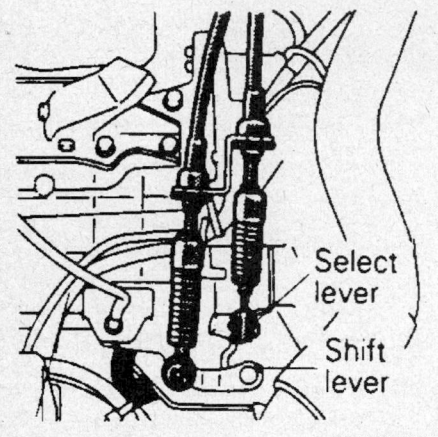

MT5038900129000X

Fig. 10 Transaxle control position

install cable onto gear selector assembly as shown, **Fig. 9.**
3. Install shift cable as follows:
   a. Install shift cable on the transaxle end.
   b. Keeping select lever on transaxle in the Neutral position, move shift lever on transaxle into 4th gear as shown, **Fig. 10.**
   c. Position gear selector lever into the 4th gear position, **Fig. 11,** and adjust length of shift cable and install cable onto the gear selector lever as shown.
4. Ensure transaxle controls function properly.

TRANSAXLE
REPLACE

1. Drain transaxle oil into a suitable container, then remove battery and engine undercover.
2. **On AWD models,** remove transfer assembly as outlined in "Transfer Cases."
3. **On all models,** remove transaxle in numbered sequences shown, **Figs. 12 and 13,** noting the following:
   a. When removing transaxle mounting bracket nuts, use a suitable garage jack to raise transaxle assembly slightly. **Do not allow transaxle to tilt.**
   b. Support engine using support tool No. MZ203827, or equivalent.
   c. Use separator tool No. MB991113, or equivalent, to free tie rod end, lateral lower arm and compression lower arm.
   d. Use a suitable pry bar to separate driveshaft from transaxle case.
   e. Insert plug tool No. MB991460, or equivalent, into transaxle case to prevent entry of foreign matter.
   f. Support driveshaft to prevent joints from flexing excessively.
   g. When removing clutch release cylinder, it is not necessary to disconnect hydraulic line; simply support cylinder aside.
4. Reverse procedure to install, noting the following:
   a. Do not allow serrated portion of driveshaft to damage oil seal.
   b. **On AWD models,** ensure driveshaft washer is installed with convex side facing outward, then use a torque wrench and holding tool No. MB990767, or equivalent.

TECHNICAL SERVICE BULLETINS
MANUAL TRANSAXLE GEAR OIL SPECIFICATION

Manual transaxles in these vehicles require API GL-4 gear oil. Use of other API gear oils, such as GL-5, may affect shift effort and result in internal transaxle damage due to chemical reactions with copper synchronizer rings. Mitsubishi Diamond Gear Lube No. A991ZC2X01 (SAE 75W–85W GL-4) or equivalent is recommended.

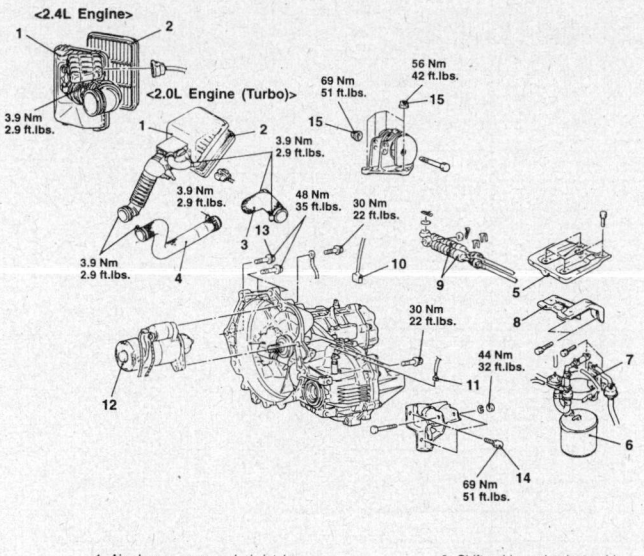

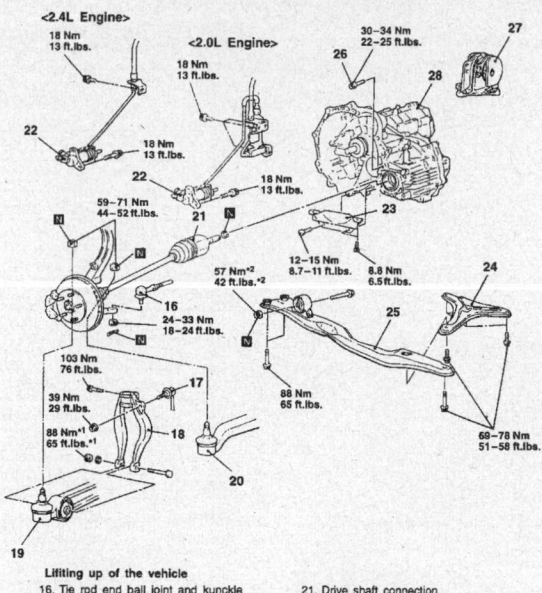

1. Air cleaner cover and air intake hose assembly
2. Air cleaner element
3. Air hose C <2.0L Engine (Turbo)>
4. Air hose A <2.0L Engine (Turbo)>
5. Battery tray
6. Evaporative emission canister <2.0L Engine (Turbo)>
7. Evaporative emission canister holder <2.0L Engine (Turbo)>
8. Battery tray stay

9. Shift cable and select cable connection
10. Backup light switch connector
11. Vehicle speed sensor connector
12. Starter motor
13. Transaxle assembly mounting bolts
14. Rear roll stopper bracket mounting bolts
15. Transaxle mounting bracket mounting nuts
• Supporting engine assembly

MT5039500130010X

Fig. 12 Transaxle replacement (Part 1 of 2). FWD models

Lifting up of the vehicle

16. Tie rod end ball joint and knuckle connection
17. Stabilizer link connection
18. Damper fork
19. Lateral lower arm ball joint and knuckle connection
20. Compression lower arm ball joint and knuckle connection

21. Drive shaft connection
22. Clutch release cylinder connection
23. Bell housing cover
24. Stay (R.H.)
25. Center member assembly
26. Transaxle assembly mounting bolt
27. Transaxle mounting
28. Transaxle assembly

MT5039500130020X

Fig. 12 Transaxle replacement (Part 2 of 2). FWD models

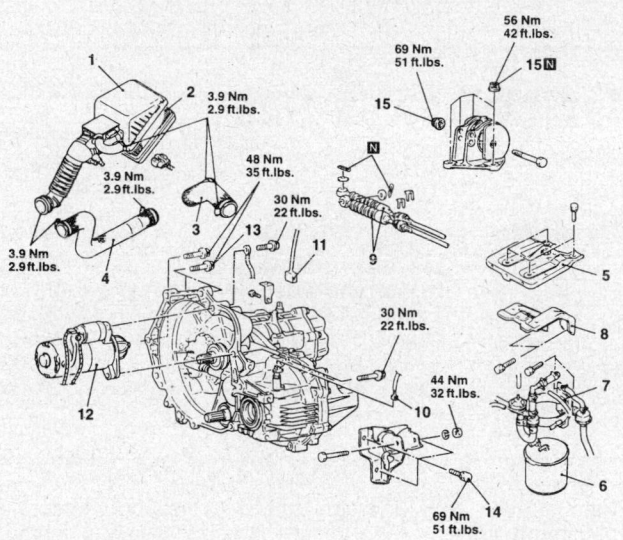

1. Air cleaner cover and air intake hose assembly
2. Air cleaner element
3. Air hose C
4. Air hose A
5. Battery tray
6. Evaporative emission canister
7. Evaporative emission canister holder
8. Battery tray stay

9. Shift cable and select cable connection
10. Backup light switch connector
11. Vehicle speed sensor connector
12. Starter motor
13. Transaxle assembly mounting bolts
14. Rear roll stopper bracket mounting bolts
15. Transaxle mounting bracket mounting nuts
• Supporting engine assembly

MT5039500131010X

Fig. 13 Transaxle replacement (Part 1 of 2). AWD models

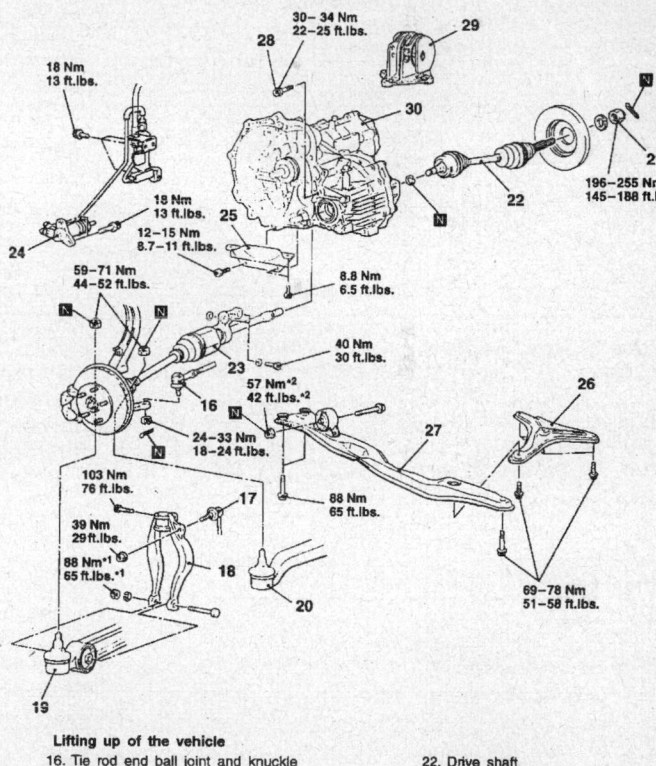

Lifting up of the vehicle

16. Tie rod end ball joint and knuckle connection
17. Stabilizer link connection
18. Damper fork
19. Lateral lower arm ball joint and knuckle connection
20. Compression lower arm ball joint and knuckle connection
21. Drive shaft nut

22. Drive shaft
23. Drive shaft with inner shaft connection
24. Clutch release cylinder connection
25. Bell housing cover
26. Stay (R.H.)
27. Center member assembly
28. Transaxle assembly mounting bolt
29. Transaxle mounting
30. Transaxle assembly

MT5039500131020X

Fig. 13 Transaxle replacement (Part 2 of 2). AWD models

TIGHTENING SPECIFICATIONS

Year	Component	Torque, Ft. Lbs.
1996–99	Back-Up Lamp Switch	24
	Bearing Retainer Bolt	14
	Clutch Cover Assembly	11–16
	Clutch Pedal Bracket	72-108①
	Clutch Pedal Support Bracket	72-108①
	Clutch Pedal To Support Bracket	14–18
	Clutch Release Cylinder	11–16
	Compression Lower Arm	44–52
	Flywheel Bolts	55
	Lower Arm Ball Joint To Knuckle	44–52
	Poppet Plug	27
	Rear Housing Cover Bolt	14
	Rear Roll Stopper Bracket	51
	Restrict Ball Assembly	24
	Shift And Select Cable To Transaxle	11–16
	Speedometer Sleeve Bolt	36①
	Starter Motor Mounting Bolt	20
	Stop Lamp Switch	24
	Tie Rod End To Knuckle	18–24
	Transaxle Case Tightening Bolt	29
	Transaxle Mounting Bolt	35
	Transfer Assembly Mounting Bolt	40–44
	Wheel Lug Nuts	65–80

① — Inch lbs.

Rear Axle & Suspension

INDEX

DIFFERENTIAL CARRIER

REPLACE

AWD MODELS

1. Drain differential fluid, then drain brake fluid into an appropriate container.
2. Remove differential carrier in numbered sequence as shown, **Fig. 1**, noting the following:
   a. Scribe marks on differential companion flange and flange yoke for installation reference, then separate differential carrier and propeller shaft. Suspend propeller shaft from vehicle body with wire, ensure there are no sharp bends in shaft assembly.
   b. Push lower part of knuckle to outside of vehicle, then separate driveshaft from differential carrier.

Suspend driveshaft from vehicle body with wire so as not to damage driveshaft joint.
   c. Removal differential carrier, then cover openings to prevent entry of foreign objects.
3. Reverse procedure to install.

PROPELLER SHAFT

REPLACE

1. Remove spacers, **Fig. 2**. Number of spacers differs on each vehicle. Note number of spacers and use for reference during installation.
2. Remove propeller shaft. Make mating marks on differential companion flange and flange yoke for reference during installation.
3. Insert piece of cloth or rag into boot opening, then remove propeller shaft

in a straight and level manner ensuring boot is not damaged through pinching.
4. **Do not lower rear end of vehicle as the oil will flow out of the transfer case and be cautious to avoid damage to the oil seal lip of the transfer case.**
5. **Use special tool provided as a cover to prevent the entry of foreign materials into the transfer case.**
6. Inspect sleeve yoke, center yoke, flange yoke and propeller shaft yokes for wear damage or cracks and replace as necessary.
7. Using a suitable dial indicator, measure propeller shaft runout. Runout for the front, center and rear propeller shafts should be .024 inch (.6 mm).
8. Set V-blocks as much as possible to the end of the shaft, then measure the deflection at the center of the shaft.

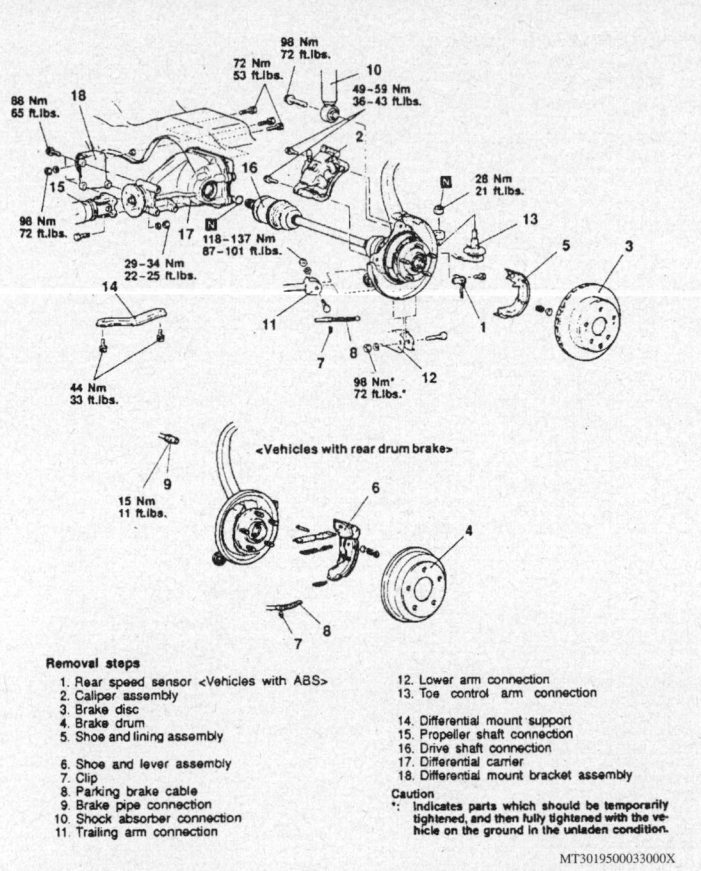

98 Nm
72 ft.lbs.

72 Nm
53 ft.lbs.

88 Nm
65 ft.lbs.

49-59 Nm
36-43 ft.lbs.

98 Nm
72 ft.lbs.

29-34 Nm
22-25 ft.lbs.

118-137 Nm
87-101 ft.lbs.

26 Nm
21 ft.lbs.

44 Nm
33 ft.lbs.

98 Nm*
72 ft.lbs.*

15 Nm
11 ft.lbs.

<Vehicles with rear drum brake>

Removal steps
1. Rear speed sensor <Vehicles with ABS>
2. Caliper assembly
3. Brake disc
4. Brake drum
5. Shoe and lining assembly

6. Shoe and lever assembly
7. Clip
8. Parking brake cable
9. Brake pipe connection
10. Shock absorber connection
11. Trailing arm connection

12. Lower arm connection
13. Toe control arm connection

14. Differential mount support
15. Propeller shaft connection
16. Drive shaft connection
17. Differential carrier
18. Differential mount bracket assembly

Caution
*: Indicates parts which should be temporarily tightened, and then fully tightened with the vehicle on the ground in the unladen condition.

MT3019500033000X

Fig. 1   Differential carrier replacement. AWD models

9. Inspect universal joints for smooth operation in all directions, then the center bearing for smooth movement and mounting rubber for damage or deterioration and replace as necessary.
10. Reverse procedure to install, noting the following:
   a. Install spacers and insulators as shown, **Fig. 3.**
   b. When installing center bearing, assemble the same spacers as removed from the bearing or new spacers of equal thickness.

HUB & BEARING

REPLACE

FWD MODELS

Replace rear axle hub assembly in numbered sequence as shown, **Fig. 4,** noting the following:
1. **Care must be used when handling the pole piece at tip of ABS speed sensor and toothed edge of rotor so as not to damage them or striking against other components.**
2. Remove caliper assembly and support to frame using suitable wire.
3. **Care must be taken not to scratch or scar ABS rotor's tooth surface and not to drop it. If rotor's toothed surface is chipped or is deformed, the ABS brake system might not operate accurately.**

AWD MODELS

1. Remove rear axle hub in numbered se-

quence as shown, **Fig. 5,** noting the following:
   a. **Care must be used when handling the pole piece at the tip of the ABS speed sensor and toothed edge of rotor ensuring not to damage them or strike against other components.**
   b. Remove caliper assembly and support to frame using suitable wire.
   c. Using end yoke holder tool No. MB990767-01, or equivalent, secure axle hub and remove companion flange self-locking nut.
   d. Using axle puller and slide hammer tools, No. MB990211-01 and MB990241-01, or equivalents, remove rear axle hub.
   e. Press off ABS rotor from axle hub.
   f. Press off outer bearing and dust shield from axle hub.
   g. Using seal remover tool No. MB990938-01 and MB990928-01, or equivalents, remove axle hub seal and inner bearing from axle housing.
2. Reverse procedure to install, noting the following:
   a. Install inner bearing using bearing installer tool Nos. MB990931-01 and MB990938-01, or equivalents.
   b. Install oil seal using oil seal installer tool No. MB990931-01, or equivalent. Apply multi-purpose grease to lip of oil seal.
   c. Install dust shields using ball joint dust cover installer tool No. MB990799-01, or equivalent.

Fig. 2   Propeller shaft removal

Gear oil:
API classification GL-4, SAE 75W-90 or 75W-85W

50-60 Nm
36-43 ft.lbs.

30 Nm
22 ft.lbs.

30 Nm
22 ft.lbs.

Removal steps
1. Self-locking nut
2. Insulator

3. Propeller shaft
4. Spacer

MT3039100002000X

   d. Install outer bearing after applying multi-purpose grease to bearing surfaces.
   e. Install ABS rotor with groove in surface pointing toward axle shaft flange.

WHEEL BEARING

ADJUST

FWD MODELS

1. Raise and support vehicle.
2. Remove caliper assembly and support to frame using suitable wire.
3. Turn hub several times to seat bearings.
4. Using a suitable spring scale, measure rotary starting torque.
5. Loosen or tighten hub nut to obtain a starting torque of 3.9 ft. lbs., or less. Replace rear hub bearing if necessary.

AWD MODELS

1. Raise and support vehicle.
2. Remove driveshaft from companion flange.
3. Remove caliper assembly and support to frame using suitable wire.
4. Turn hub several times to seat bearings.
5. Using a suitable spring scale, measure rotary starting torque.
6. If starting torque is not 9 inch lbs., or less, ensure torque of axle hub companion flange nut is correct. If flange torque is correct, replace axle hub bearing.

REAR SUSPENSION

REPLACE

1. Remove service lid trim from interior of vehicle, then raise and support vehicle.
2. Remove rear crossmember under cover panel, then remove center exhaust pipe.
3. **On AWD models,** remove propeller shaft assembly, **Fig. 6. Scribe marks on differential companion flange**

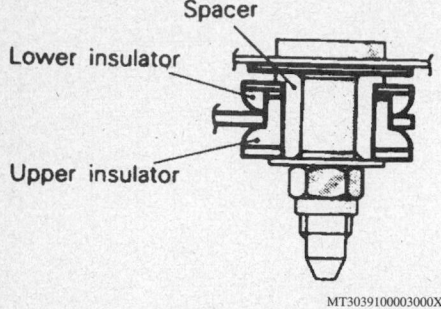

Fig. 3 Propeller shaft installation

and flange yoke for installation reference, then separate differential carrier and propeller shaft. Suspend propeller shaft from vehicle body with wire and ensure there are no sharp bends in shaft assembly.
4. **On all models,** remove brake caliper and brake assembly.
5. Remove parking brake cable.
6. **On models equipped with drum brakes,** remove brake hose connection.
7. **On all models,** remove upper arm bracket, then shock absorber cap and mounting nuts.
8. Remove speed sensor electrical connector, then the trailing arm grommet and mounting bolt.
9. **On AWD models,** support differential case with suitable jack stand, then remove crossmember mounting nuts.
10. **On FWD models,** support crossmember with suitable jack stand, then remove crossmember mounting nuts.
11. **On all models,** reverse procedure to install, noting the following:
    a. Bleed brake system as outlined under "Hydraulic Brake Systems."
    b. Inspect rear wheel alignment as outlined under " Wheel Alignment."

SHOCK ABSORBER
REPLACE

1. **On coupe models,** remove cover in luggage compartment to access shock absorber.
2. **On convertible models,** remove luggage compartment floor board, partition trim, rear end trim, then the luggage compartment side trim.
3. **On all models,** remove shock absorber assembly in numbered sequence as shown, **Fig. 7,** noting the following:
    a. Raise and support rear suspension before removing shock absorber.
    b. Remove shock absorber upper and lower mounting bolts, then the shock absorber assembly.
4. Reverse procedure to install, noting the following:
    a. Using a suitable coil spring, compress and insert coil spring on shock absorber.
    b. Align edge of coil spring to position as shown, **Fig. 8.**
    c. Fit dust cover over dust cup as shown, **Fig. 9.**

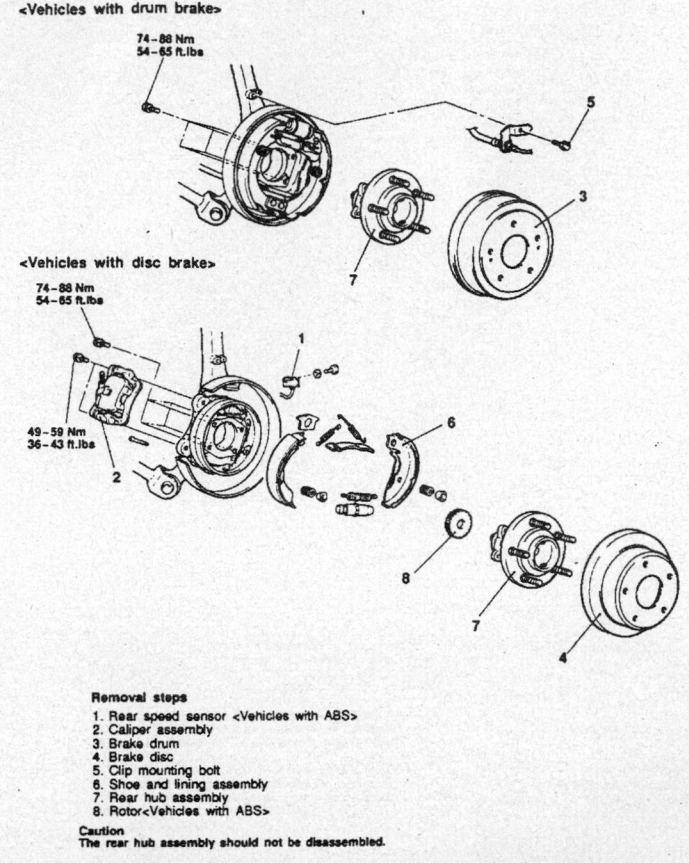

Fig. 4 Rear axle hub replacement. FWD models

Removal steps
1. Rear speed sensor <Vehicles with ABS>
2. Caliper assembly
3. Brake drum
4. Brake disc
5. Clip mounting bolt
6. Shoe and lining assembly
7. Rear hub assembly
8. Rotor<Vehicles with ABS>

Caution
The rear hub assembly should not be disassembled.

d. Position upper bracket as shown, then tighten piston nut to specifications.
e. Install coil spring, ensure lower edge fits into spring seat groove and upper edge fits into spring pad groove, then remove compression tool, **Fig. 10.**

SHOCK ABSORBER SERVICE

1. Disassemble shock absorber assembly in numbered sequence as shown, **Fig. 11,** noting the following:
    a. Before removing piston rod nut, compress coil spring using suitable coil spring compression tool.
    b. While holding piston rod, remove piston rod nut.

COIL SPRING
REPLACE

Remove and disassemble shock absorber assembly as outlined under "Shock Absorber, Replace."

CONTROL ARM
REPLACE
UPPER

1. Remove upper arm and connecting bolt, **Fig. 12.**
2. Remove upper arm assembly mounting bolts, then upper arm assembly.
3. Remove upper arm bracket.
4. Reverse procedure to install, noting the following:
    a. Install the upper arm bracket so that dimension "A" is 1.38–1.54 inches, **Fig. 13.**
    b. Install the upper arm bracket so that dimension "B" is 8.40 inches, **Fig. 14.**
    c. Install the upper arm bracket so that dimension "C" is 10.6 inches.

LOWER

1. Remove stabilizer link, **Fig. 15.**
2. Remove speed sensor clamp bolts, then the lower arm assembly and knuckle connecting bolt.
3. Remove lower arm assembly mounting bolt, then the lower arm assembly.
4. Loosen toe control arm joint and knuckle connection using steering linkage puller tool No. MB991113 or equivalent. **Tie cord from tool to vehicle,**

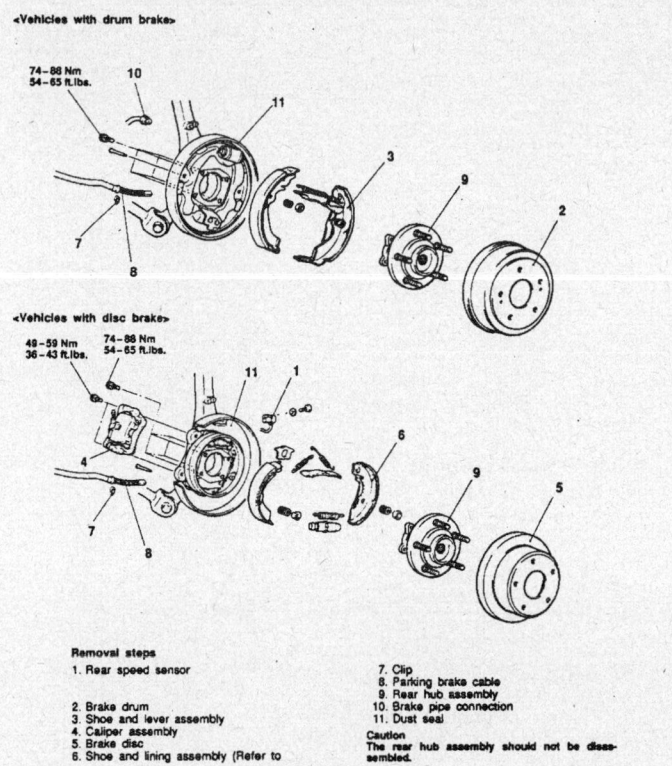

<Vehicles with drum brake>

74~88 Nm
54~65 ft.lbs.

<Vehicles with disc brake>

48~59 Nm
36~43 ft.lbs.

74~88 Nm
54~65 ft.lbs.

Removal steps

1. Rear speed sensor
2. Brake drum
3. Shoe and lever assembly
4. Caliper assembly
5. Brake disc
6. Shoe and lining assembly (Refer to

7. Clip
8. Parking brake cable
9. Rear hub assembly
10. Brake pipe connection
11. Dust seal

Caution
The rear hub assembly should not be disassembled.

MT2049500055000X

Fig. 5   Rear axle hub replacement. AWD models

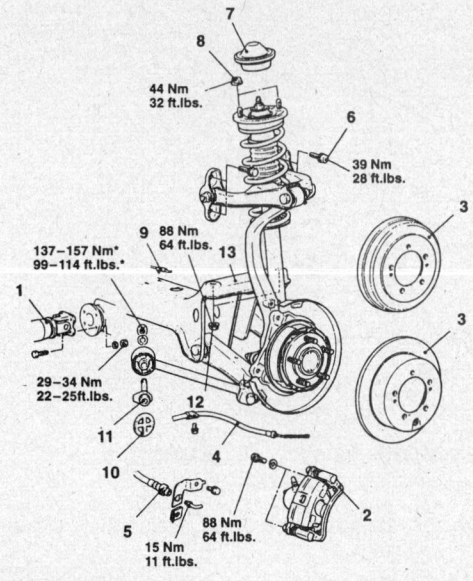

44 Nm
32 ft.lbs.

39 Nm
28 ft.lbs.

137~157 Nm*
99~114 ft.lbs.*

9 88 Nm
64 ft.lbs.

29~34 Nm
22~25 ft.lbs.

88 Nm
64 ft.lbs.

15 Nm
11 ft.lbs.

1. Propeller shaft connection <AWD>
2. Brake caliper assembly
   <Vehicles with disc brakes>
3. Brake disc <Vehicles with disc
   brakes> or brake drum <Vehicles
   with drum brakes>
4. Parking brake cable end
5. Brake hose connection
   <Vehicles with drum brakes>
6. Upper arm bracket mounting bolts

7. Cap
8. Shock absorber mounting nuts
9. Rear wheel-speed sensor connector
   <Vehicles with ABS>
10. Grommet
11. Trailing arm mounting bolt
12. Crossmember mounting self-locking
    nuts
13. Rear suspension assembly

Caution
* : indicates parts which should be temporarily tightened,
    and then fully tightened with the vehicles on the ground
    in the unladen condition.

MT2039500094000X

Fig. 6   Rear suspension replacement

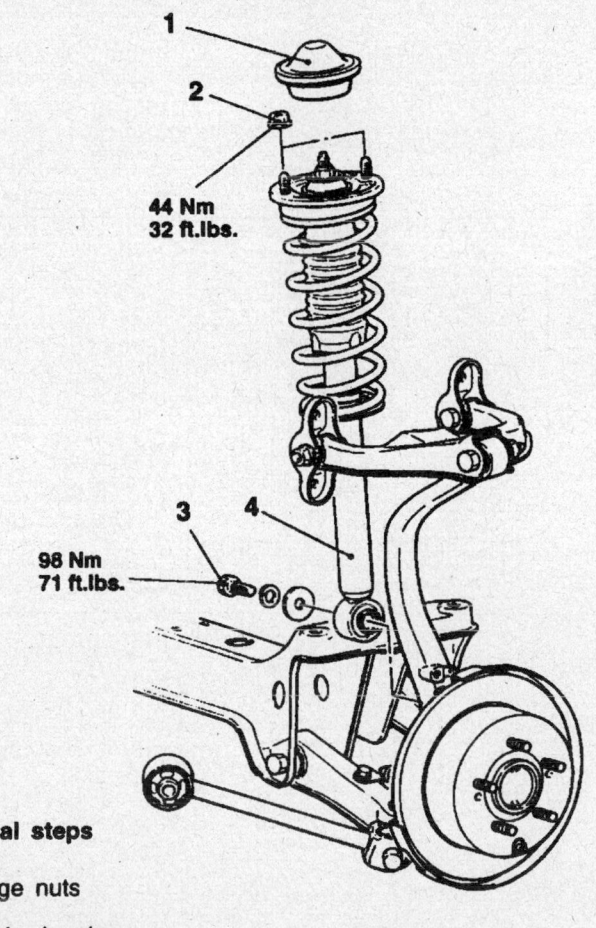

44 Nm
32 ft.lbs.

98 Nm
71 ft.lbs.

Removal steps

1. Cap
2. Flange nuts
3. Bolt
4. Shock absorber

MT2039500114000X

Fig. 7   Shock absorber replacement

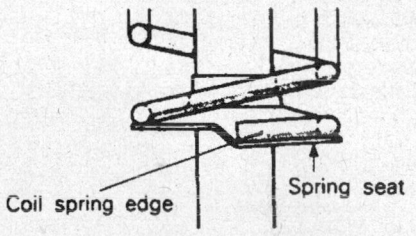

Coil spring edge   Spring seat

MT2039100018000X

Fig. 8   Coil spring installation

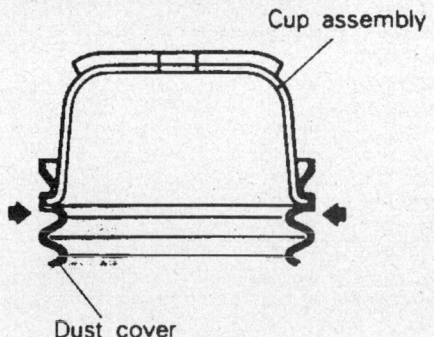

Cup assembly

Dust cover

MT2039100019000X

Fig. 9   Dust cover & cup installation

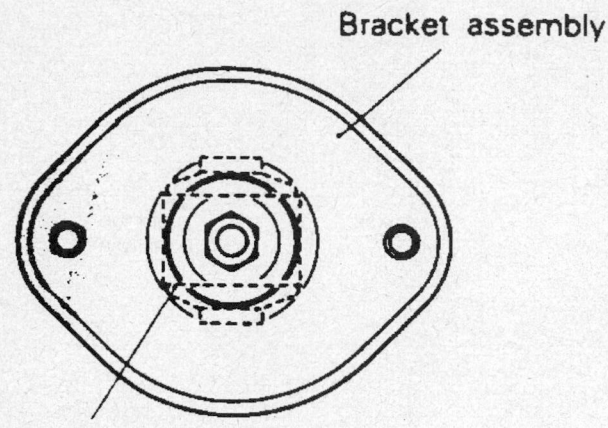

Bracket assembly

Shock absorber lower bushing

Fig. 10 Shock absorber upper bracket installation

MT2039100020000X

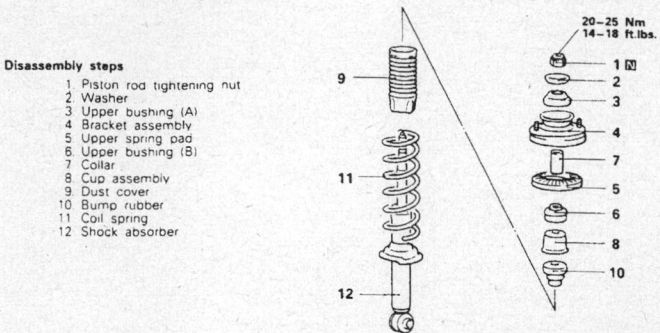

Disassembly steps
1. Piston rod tightening nut
2. Washer
3. Upper bushing (A)
4. Bracket assembly
5. Upper spring pad
6. Upper bushing (B)
7. Collar
8. Cup assembly
9. Dust cover
10. Bump rubber
11. Coil spring
12. Shock absorber

20–25 Nm
14–18 ft.lbs.

MT2039100016000X

Fig. 11 Shock absorber service

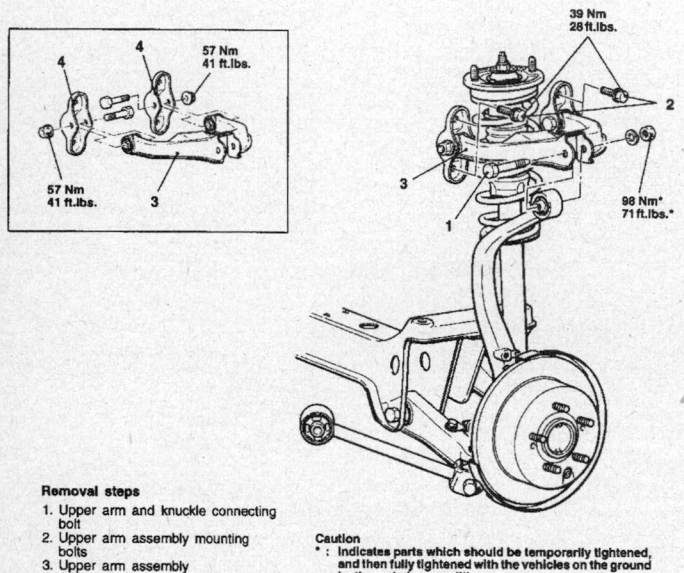

39 Nm
28 ft.lbs.

57 Nm
41 ft.lbs.

57 Nm
41 ft.lbs.

98 Nm*
71 ft.lbs.*

Removal steps
1. Upper arm and knuckle connecting bolt
2. Upper arm assembly mounting bolts
3. Upper arm assembly
4. Upper arm bracket

Caution
*: Indicates parts which should be temporarily tightened, and then fully tightened with the vehicles on the ground in the unladen condition.

MT2039500097000X

Fig. 12 Upper arm replacement

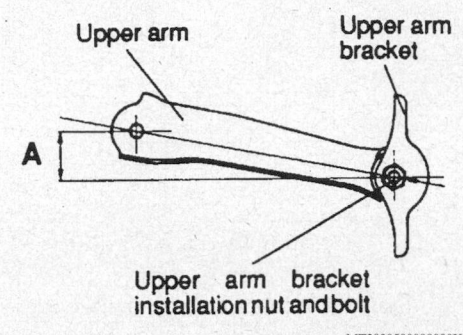

Upper arm

Upper arm bracket

A

Upper arm bracket installation nut and bolt

MT2039500098000X

Fig. 13 Upper arm bracket dimension A

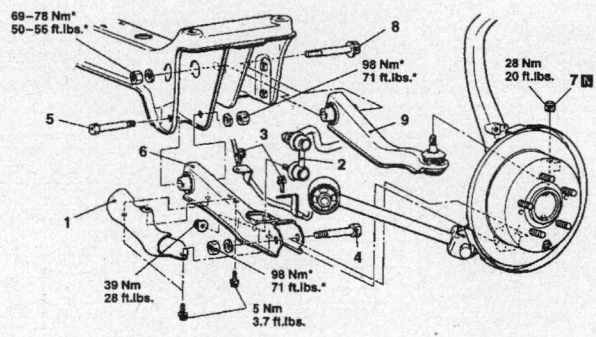

69–78 Nm*
50–56 ft.lbs.*

98 Nm*
71 ft.lbs.*

28 Nm
20 ft.lbs.

39 Nm
28 ft.lbs.

98 Nm*
71 ft.lbs.*

5 Nm
3.7 ft.lbs.

Lower arm assembly removal steps
1. Lower arm cover <Vehicles with aero parts>
2. Stabilizer link ball joint and lower arm connection
3. ABS wheel-speed sensor clamp bolts <Vehicles with ABS>
4. Lower arm assembly and knuckle connecting bolt
5. Lower arm assembly mounting bolt
6. Lower arm assembly

Toe control arm assembly removal steps
7. Toe control arm ball joint and knuckle connection
8. Toe control arm assembly mounting bolt
9. Toe control arm assembly

Caution
*: Indicates parts which should be temporarily tightened, and then fully tightened with the vehicles on the ground in the unladen condition.

MT2039500100000X

Fig. 15 Lower arm replacement

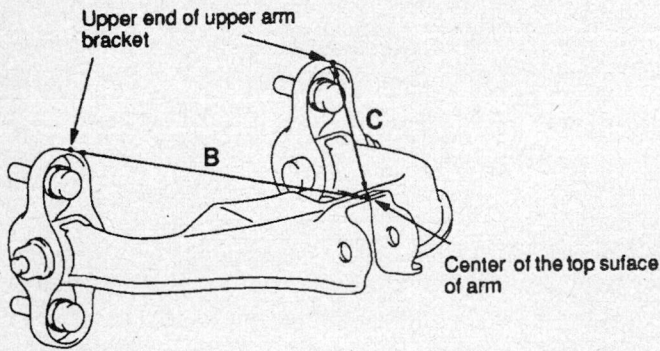

Upper end of upper arm bracket

C

B

Center of the top surface of arm

MT2039500099000X

Fig. 14 Upper arm bracket dimensions B & C

then loosen but do not remove nut, **Fig. 16.**

5. Scribe installation reference marks on toe control arm assembly mounting bolt, **Fig. 17,** then remove bolt and toe control arm assembly.
6. Reverse procedure to install.

TRAILING ARM
REPLACE

1. Remove knuckle and trailing arm assembly connecting bolt, **Fig. 18.**
2. Remove trailing arm assembly grommet, mounting bolt and stopper.
3. Remove trailing arm assembly.
4. Reverse procedure to install.

STABILIZER BAR
REPLACE

1. Remove lower arm cover.
2. Remove stabilizer link mounting nuts, then stabilizer link, **Fig. 19.**
3. Remove stabilizer bar brackets, bushing and stabilizer bar.
4. Inspect bushings for wear and deterioration, then inspect stabilizer bar for deterioration or damage.
5. Inspect stabilizer link ball joint dust cover for cracks. If dust cover is defective replace as follows:
   a. Remove clip ring and dust cover.
   b. Apply multi-purpose grease to the lip and inside of dust cover.
   c. Using vinyl tape, tape stabilizer link on protruding end, then install dust cover to stabilizer link.
   d. Secure dust cover by the clip ring.
6. Verify all bolts are straight and in good condition.
7. Reverse procedure to install.

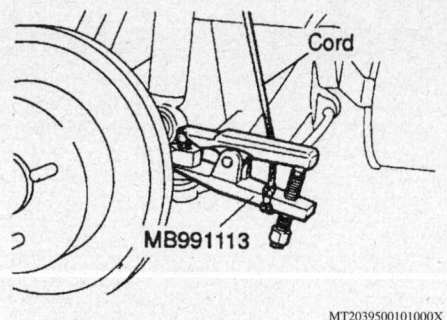

Fig. 16   Steering linkage puller installation

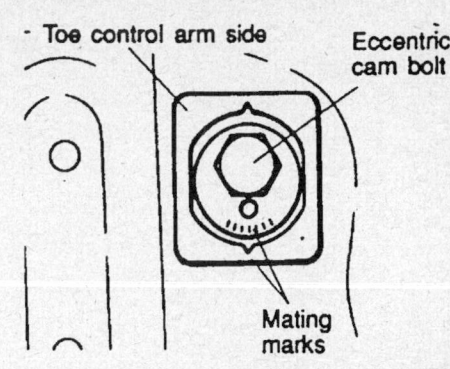

Fig. 17   Toe control arm assembly mounting bolt removal

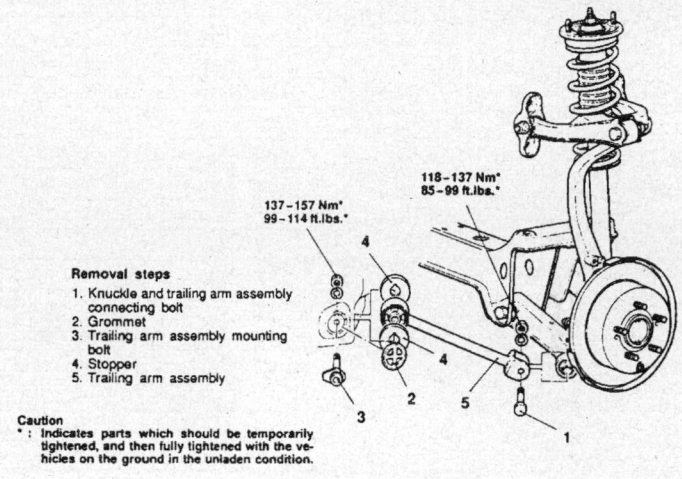

Fig. 18   Trailing arm replacement

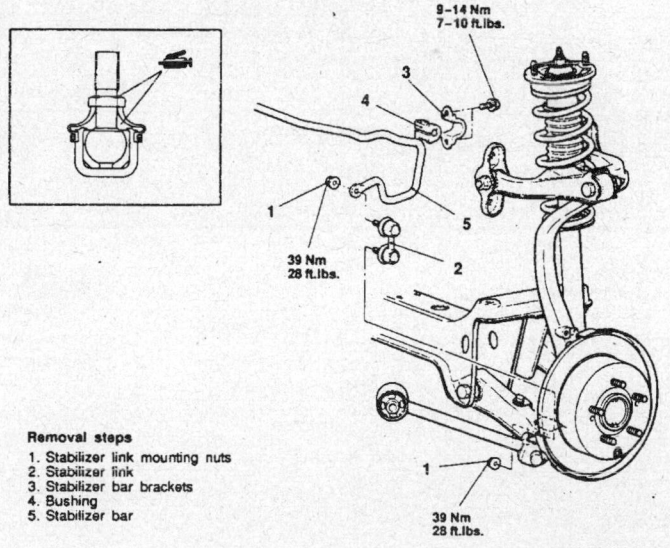

Fig. 19   Stabilizer replacement

TIGHTENING SPECIFICATIONS

For rear axle and suspension tightening specifications, refer to individual repair or replacement procedures and illustrations.

Year	Component	Torque, Ft. Lbs.
1996–99	Axle Nut	145–188
	Crossmember Self-Locking	64
	Differential Carrier To Differential Support Member	72
	Driveshaft Nut	188
	Hub Nut	145–188
	Lower Arm Assembly Mounting	71
	Lower Arm To Knuckle	71
	Piston Rod Nut	16
	Propeller Shaft To Differential	22–25
	Rear Brake Assembly Installation Bolt	64
	Shock Absorber Upper Mounting Nut	32
	Shock Absorber Lower Mounting Nut	71
	Stabilizer Bar Bracket	7–10
	Stabilizer Link Mounting	28
	Stabilizer Link To Stabilizer Bar	28
	Toe Control Arm Assembly Mounting	50–56
	Toe Control Arm Ball Joint to Knuckle	20
	Trailing Arm Mounting Bolt	99–114
	Trailing Arm To Knuckle	85–99
	Upper Arm Assembly	71
	Upper Arm Bracket	41
	Upper Arm Mounting	28
	Wheel Lug Nuts	65–80

Transfer Case

INDEX

PRECAUTIONS

BATTERY GROUND CABLE

Prior to service, disconnect battery ground cable and isolate as required.

TRANSFER CASE

REPLACE

1. Disconnect front exhaust pipe from engine.
2. Remove transfer case attaching bolts, then move transfer case to the left and lower front of transfer case.
3. Remove transfer case from propeller shaft, noting the following:
   a. Use caution not to damage transfer case oil seal lip.
   b. Suspend propeller shaft to prevent bending.
   c. Cover transfer case opening using plug tool No. MB991193, or equivalent, to prevent oil leakage and entry of foreign material.
4. Reverse procedure to install.

Front Suspension & Steering

NOTE: On Air Bag Equipped Models, Refer To "Air Bag System Precautions" Located In The Front Of This Manual For System Disarming & Arming Procedures.

NOTE: Refer To "Computer Relearn" Located In The Front Of This Manual For Computer Relearn Procedures.

INDEX

PRECAUTIONS

AIR BAG SYSTEMS

Refer to "Air Bag System Precautions" in the front of this manual for system disarming and arming procedures.

BATTERY GROUND CABLE

Prior to service, disconnect battery ground cable and isolate as required.

WHEEL BEARING

ADJUST

1. Inspect play of bearings while vehicle is jacked up and resting on floor jack.
2. Remove hub cap, then release parking brake.
3. Remove caliper assembly and brake disc, then measure bearing endplay.
4. Placing dial gauge against hub surface, move hub in axial direction and check for endplay.
5. Endplay should be .002 inch or less; if greater, the locknut should be tightened to specification and endplay measured again.
6. Replace rear hub bearing unit if an adjustment cannot be made to within limit.

WHEEL HUB & STEERING KNUCKLE

REPLACE
REMOVAL

Remove knuckle and hub assembly in numbered sequence, **Fig. 1**, noting the following:
1. Loosen driveshaft nut with vehicle on floor and brakes applied.

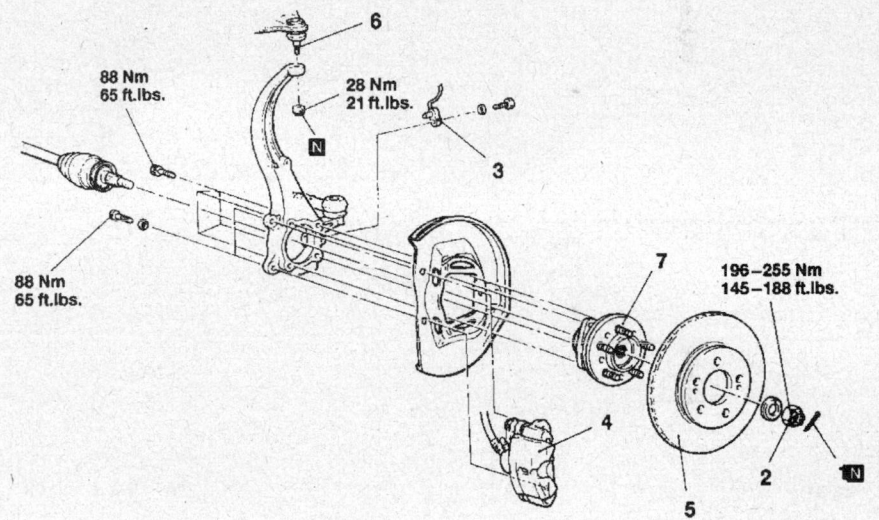

Removal steps
1. Cotter pin
2. Drive shaft nut
3. Front wheel speed sensor <Vehicles with ABS>
4. Caliper assembly
5. Brake disc
6. Upper arm ball joint and knuckle connection
7. Front hub assembly

Caution
The front hub assembly should not be disassembled.

CR3039500360000X

Fig. 1   Hub & knuckle replacement

2. Loosen, but do not remove, tie rod end nut.
3. Remove and suspend caliper assembly out of the way using a piece of wire.
4. Shift the knuckle to the outside in order to maintain the clearance between the front hub assembly mounting bolts and the driveshaft. **Do not damage the ball joint boot.**

INSTALLATION

Reverse removal procedure to install, noting the following:
1. Ensure to install driveshaft washer as

shown, **Fig. 2.**
2. After installing wheel, lower vehicle to ground, then final tighten driveshaft nut to specification.
3. Align holes, then install cotter pin.

HUB & BEARING SERVICE

The front hub assembly should not be disassembled. If required by damage or wear, it should be replaced.

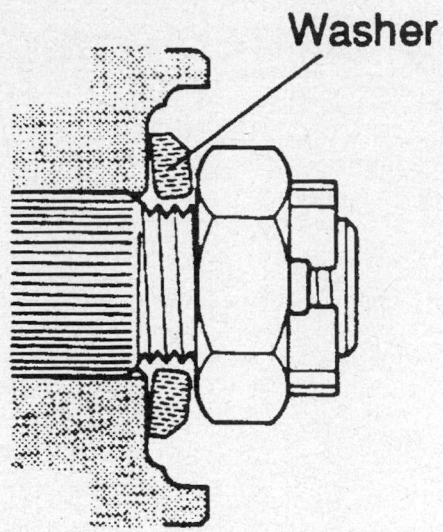

Fig. 2   Driveshaft washer installation

CR3039500362000X

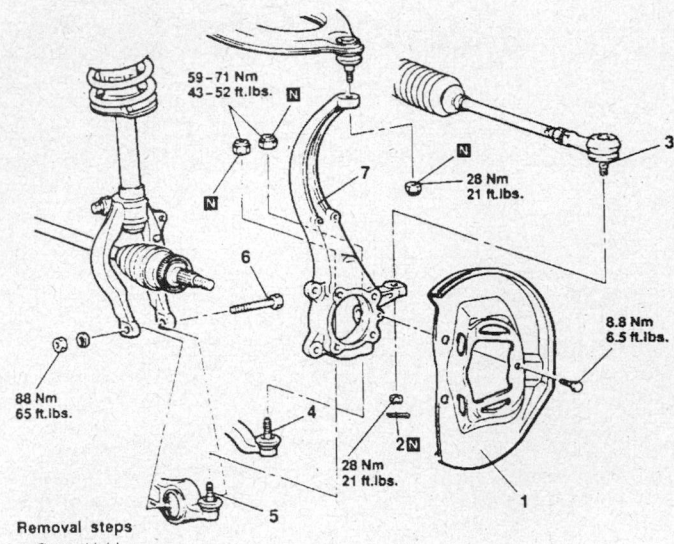

Removal steps
1. Dust shield
2. Cotter pin
3. Tie rod end connection
4. Compression lower arm connection
5. Lateral lower arm connection
6. Connection bolt of damper fork and lateral lower arm
7. Knuckle

CR3039500361000X

Fig. 3   Knuckle replacement

2. Shake ball joint several times, then install ball joint stud nut.
3. Using torque wrench tool No. MB990326, or equivalent, measure ball joint breakaway torque.
4. Ball joint breakaway torque should be 3–22 ft. lbs.
5. If breakaway torque exceeds specifications, replace ball joint.

BALL JOINT
REPLACE

Refer to "Control Arm, Replace" for ball joint replacement procedure.

STRUT
REPLACE
REMOVAL

Remove strut assembly in numbered sequence, **Fig. 4.**

INSTALLATION

Reverse removal procedure to install, noting the following:
1. Ensure spring is properly seated in upper and lower spring seat when installing.
2. Install strut upper bracket as shown in **Fig. 5,** then tighten strut rod nut to specifications.

STRUT SERVICE

Disassemble strut in numbered sequence, **Fig. 6,** noting the following:
1. Compress spring using spring compression tool Nos. MB991237 and MB991239, or equivalents, to ease in disassembly and assembly.

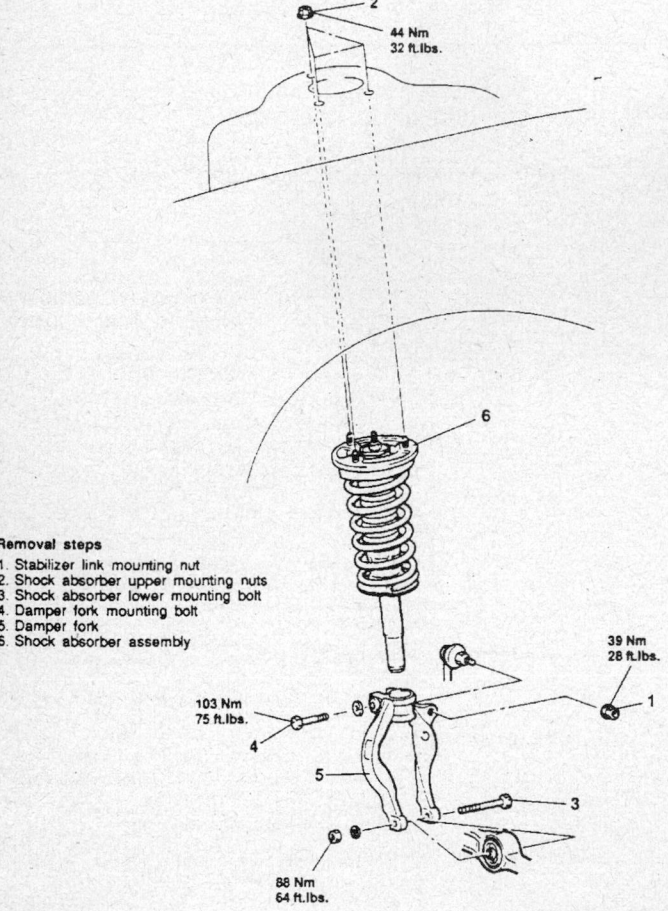

Removal steps
1. Stabilizer link mounting nut
2. Shock absorber upper mounting nuts
3. Shock absorber lower mounting bolt
4. Damper fork mounting bolt
5. Damper fork
6. Shock absorber assembly

CR2029500106000X

Fig. 4   Strut assembly removal

Disassemble knuckle assembly in numbered sequence, **Fig. 3,** noting the following:
1. Loosen, but do not remove, tie rod end nut.
2. Loosen, but do not remove, compression lower arm nut.
3. Loosen, but do not remove, lateral lower arm nut.

BALL JOINT INSPECTION

1. Disconnect ball joint from steering knuckle as outlined under "Ball Joint, Replace."

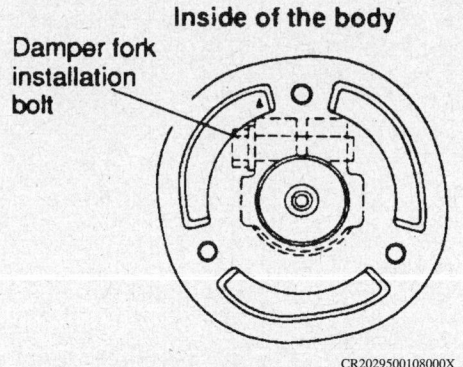

Damper fork installation bolt

Inside of the body

CR2029500108000X

Fig. 5   Upper bracket installation

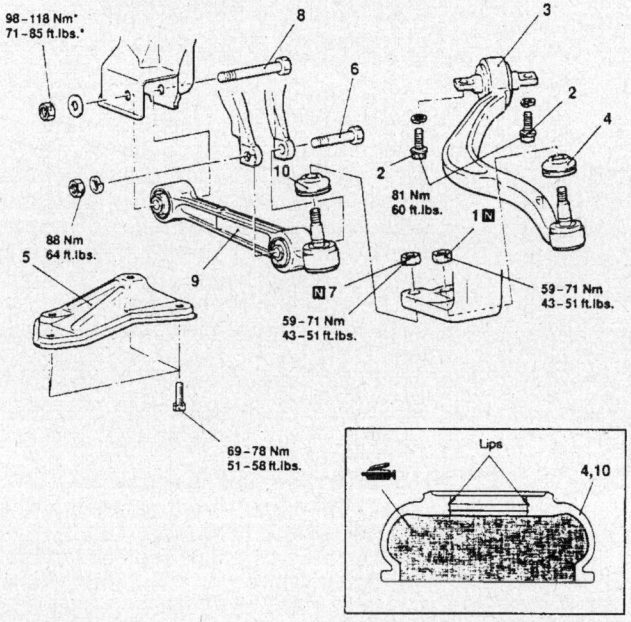

98–118 Nm*
71–85 ft.lbs.*

88 Nm
64 ft.lbs.

81 Nm
60 ft.lbs.

59–71 Nm
43–51 ft.lbs.

59–71 Nm
43–51 ft.lbs.

69–78 Nm
51–58 ft.lbs.

Lips

4,10

Compression lower arm assembly removal steps
1. Compression lower arm ball joint and knuckle connection
2. Compression lower arm mounting bolts
3. Compression lower arm assembly
4. Dust cover

Lateral lower arm assembly removal steps
5. Stay
6. Shock absorber lower mounting bolt
7. Lateral lower arm ball joint and knuckle connection
8. Lateral lower arm mounting bolt
9. Lateral lower arm assembly
10. Dust cover
Caution
*: Indicates parts which should be temporarily tightened, and then fully tightened with the vehicle on the ground in the unladen condition.

CR2029500109000X

Fig. 7   Compression & lateral lower arm replacement

CONTROL ARM
REPLACE
LOWER

Remove compression and lateral lower control arms in numbered sequence, **Fig. 7,** noting the following:
1. Loosen but do not remove compression lower arm ball joint.
2. Check compression lower arm ball joint breakaway torque. Torque should be 4–13 inch lbs. If reading exceeds specified amount, replace lower arm assembly.
3. Loosen but do not remove knuckle/lateral lower arm ball joint.
4. Check lateral lower arm ball joint breakaway torque. Torque should be

13 inch lbs. If reading exceeds specified amount, replace lower arm assembly.

STABILIZER BAR
REPLACE

Remove stabilizer bar in numbered sequence, **Fig. 8.** When installing the stabilizer bar ensure identification mark is at the left and dimension is as shown in **Fig. 9.**

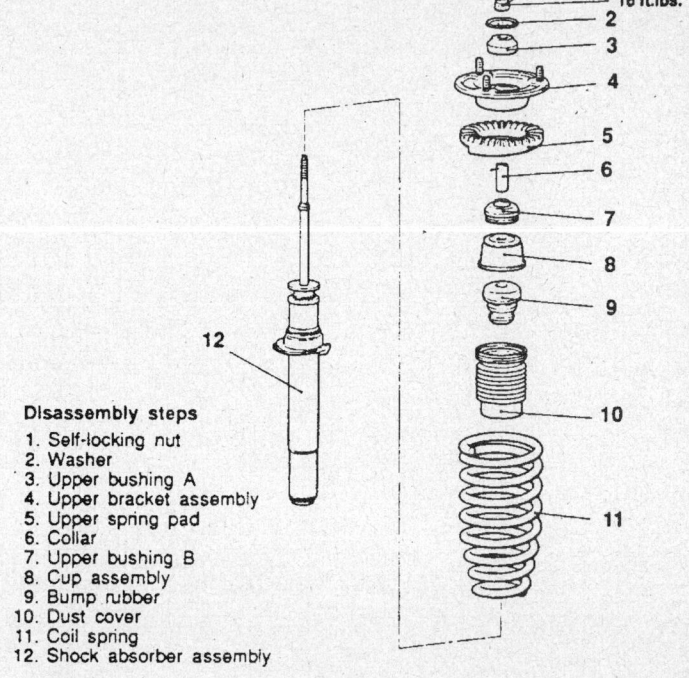

1N 25 Nm 16 ft.lbs.

Disassembly steps
1. Self-locking nut
2. Washer
3. Upper bushing A
4. Upper bracket assembly
5. Upper spring pad
6. Collar
7. Upper bushing B
8. Cup assembly
9. Bump rubber
10. Dust cover
11. Coil spring
12. Shock absorber assembly

CR2029500107000X

Fig. 6   Strut service

POWER STEERING GEAR
REPLACE

Remove rack and pinion in numbered sequence, **Figs. 10 and 11,** noting the following:
1. Turn rack completely to right, the disconnect gearbox from crossmember.
2. While tilting gearbox downward, remove from left side.
3. Reverse procedure to install.

POWER STEERING PUMP
REPLACE

Remove steering pump in numbered sequence, **Figs. 12 and 13** noting the following:
1. Remove reservoir cap and disconnect return hose to drain fluid.
2. Raise and support vehicle.
3. Cover alternator (located under oil pump) if any hoses are removed
4. Reverse procedure to install, ensuring to install oil pump in a position towards the front of the bracket, and adjust the belt tension using the air conditioning tension pulley. Bleed power steering system as outlined under "Power Steering System Bleed."

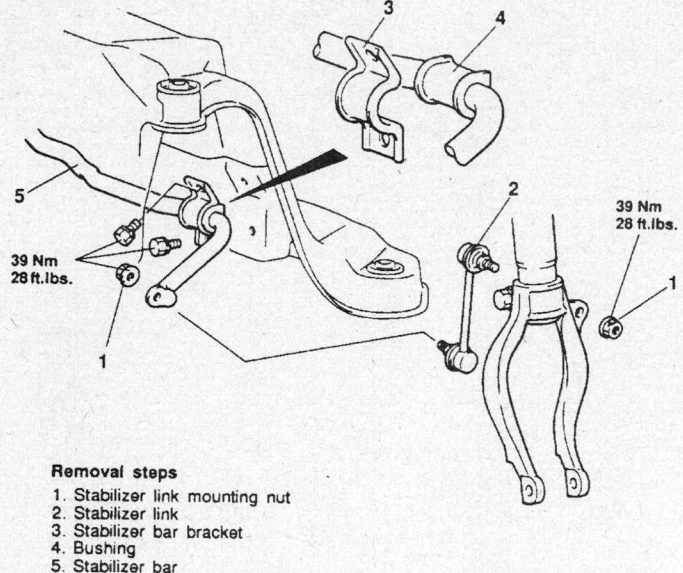

Removal steps
1. Stabilizer link mounting nut
2. Stabilizer link
3. Stabilizer bar bracket
4. Bushing
5. Stabilizer bar

CR2029500110000X

Fig. 8   Stabilizer bar replacement

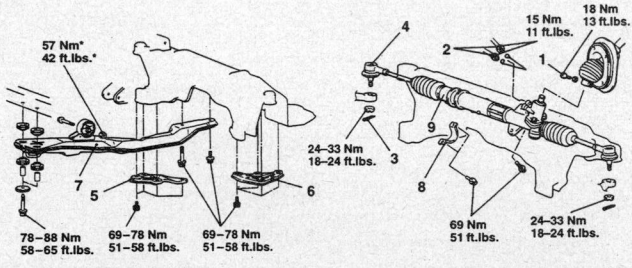

Removal steps
1. Joint assembly and gear box connecting bolt
2. Power steering pipe connection
3. Cotter pin
4. Tie rod end and knuckle connection
5. Stay (L.H.)
6. Stay (R.H.)
7. Center member assembly
8. Clamp
9. Gear box assembly

Caution
*: Indicates parts which should be initially tightened, and then fully tightened after placing the vehicle horizontally and loading the full weight of the engine on the vehicle body.

MT6029800061000X

Fig. 10   Power steering gear replacement. 2.0L non-turbocharged engine

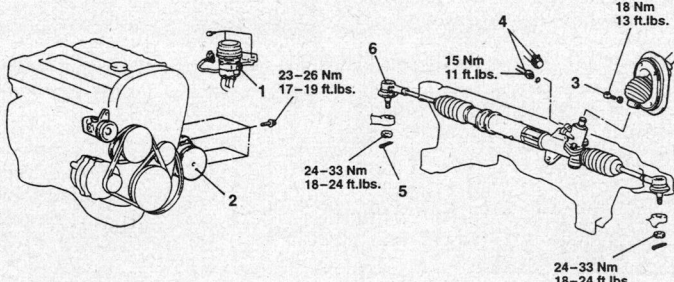

Removal steps
1. Brake fluid reservoir assembly
2. A/C compressor
3. Joint assembly and gear box connecting bolt
4. Power steering pipe connection
5. Cotter pin
6. Tie rod end and knuckle connection

MT6029800062000X

Fig. 11   Power steering gear replacement. 2.0L turbocharged & 2.4L engines

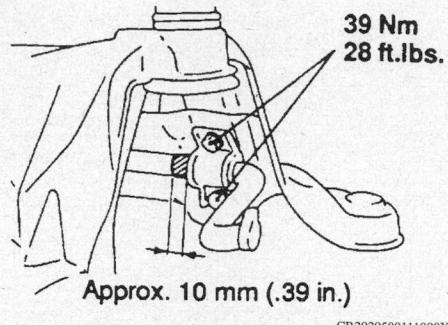

Approx. 10 mm (.39 in.)

CR2029500111000X

Fig. 9   Stabilizer bar bushing alignment

POWER STEERING SYSTEM BLEED

The hydraulic brake system must be bled if air has entered the system. This condition may be caused by low fluid level, a hydraulic fluid leak, the opening of a hydraulic line or replacement of a hydraulic system component. Symptoms include a loss of basic brake operation and/or a low or spongy brake pedal.

On models equipped with ABS, use a suitable filter when adding fluid to reservoir tank.

1. Ensure master cylinder reservoir is full. Add suitable brake fluid as needed, and securely reinstall the master cylinder cap.
2. Raise and support vehicle.
3. Position a drain pan under the wheel being bled.
4. Have an assistant depress the brake pedal with a slow even pressure and hold it. **Do not depress brake pedal fully to the end of the master cylinder stroke. This may cause damage to the master cylinder.**
5. Using a suitable wrench, open the bleeder valve one full turn. Watch for air bubbles in the fluid, and listen for air escaping from the system.
6. With the brake pedal still depressed, close the bleeder valve.
7. Have the assistant pump the brake pedal several times. **Do not depress brake pedal fully to the end of the master cylinder stroke, this may cause damage to the master cylinder.**
8. Repeat preceding bleed steps until all air is removed from the hydraulic system. **While bleeding the system, recheck brake fluid supply in the master cylinder often so as not to allow the master cylinder to run dry.**
9. Upon completion of hydraulic system bleeding, proceed as follows:
   a. Ensure the master cylinder reservoir is full. Add suitable brake fluid as needed, and securely reinstall the master cylinder cap.
   b. Lower the vehicle. Ensure brake pedal is firm and braking operation is satisfactory.

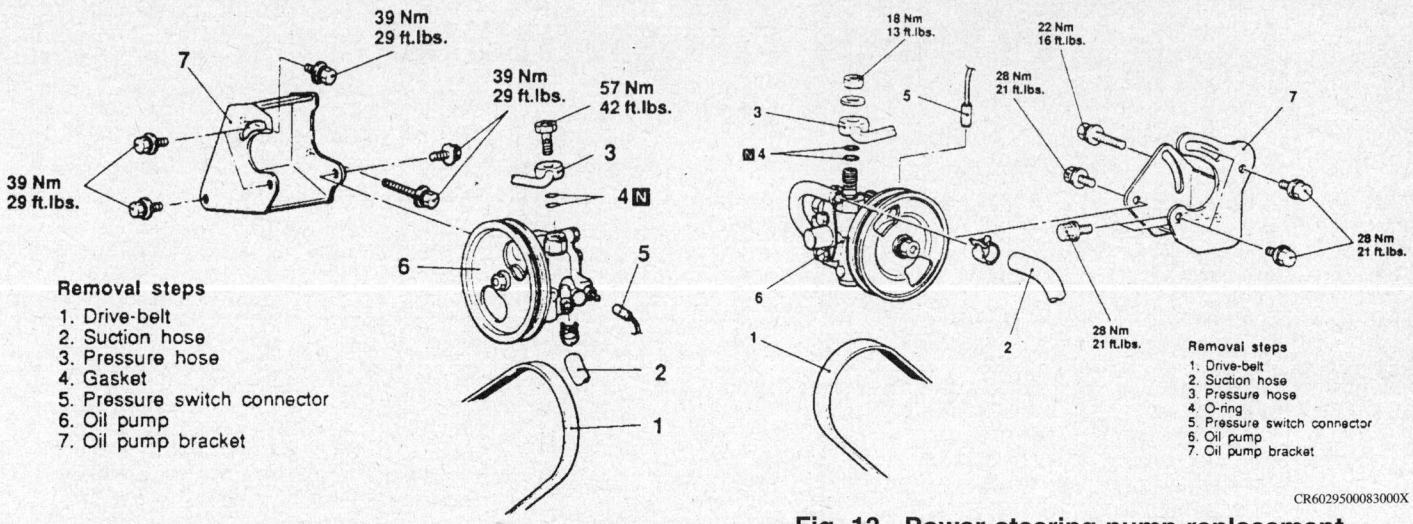

Fig. 12 Power steering pump replacement. Non-turbocharged engine

CR6029500082000X

Fig. 13 Power steering pump replacement. Turbocharged engine

CR6029500083000X

TIGHTENING SPECIFICATIONS

For rear axle and suspension tightening specifications, refer to individual repair or replacement procedure and illustrations.

Year	Component	Torque, Ft. Lbs.
1996–99	Axle Nut	145–188
	Caliper Assembly Mounting Bolt	36–43
	Compression Lower Arm	51–60
	Dampener Pivot	64
	Dampener To Strut Collar	75
	Driveshaft Nut	145–188
	Dust Shield	78②
	Hub Assembly To Knuckle	65
	Knuckle To Ball Joint	21
	Knuckle To Compression Lower Arm	43
	Knuckle Upper Mounting	21
	Lateral Lower Arm Ball Joint	60
	Lateral Lower Arm To Crossmember	71–85
	Power Steering Oil Pump To Bracket	21–29
	Stabilizer Bar Bracket	28
	Stabilizer Link To Dampener	28
	Stay To Crossmember	51–58
	Strut Lower Mounting	65
	Strut Top End Nut	16
	Strut Upper Mounting Nut	32
	Tie Rod End Ball Joint	21
	Upper Arm Pivot	41
	Upper Arm Shaft Assembly	62
	Upper Arm To Knuckle	20
	Wheel Lug Nuts	①

① — 1996–98, 88–108 ft. lbs.; 1999, 65–80 ft. lbs.
② — Inch lbs.

Wheel Alignment

INDEX

PRELIMINARY INSPECTION

1. Ensure tires are inflated to correct pressure, then check for uneven wear.
2. Check front wheel bearings, suspension arm and ball joints for damage and replace as necessary, to correct improper alignment due to faulty components.
3. Check steering gear and shocks for damage and replace as necessary.
4. Rock vehicle back and forth, then bounce it up and down to settle vehicle prior to alignment.
5. Ensure vehicle is unloaded and on a suitable alignment rack in accordance with manufacturer's instructions. **When measuring, equipment is attached directly to outer end of driveshaft and front wheels are on turntables. Apply brake to prevent vehicle movement.**

FRONT WHEEL ALIGNMENT

CAMBER

Camber is preset during production and is not adjustable. If camber is out of specification, replace bent or damaged components as necessary.

CASTER

Caster has been preset during production and is not adjustable.

TOE-IN

1. Adjust toe-in by loosening clips and

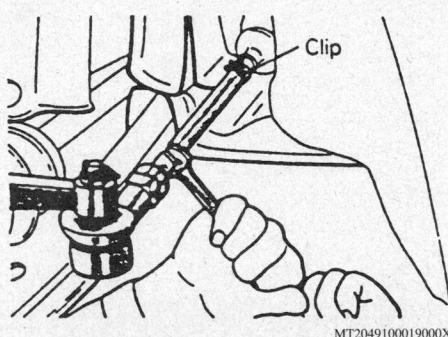

Fig. 1   Front toe-in adjustment

turning left and right tie rod turnbuckles equally in opposite directions. Refer to **Fig. 1.**
2. To increase toe-out, turn left turnbuckle toward front of vehicle and right turnbuckle toward rear of vehicle. To increase toe-in, turn turnbuckles in other direction.
3. Toe-in adjustment should be .24 inch for each half turn of left and right tie rods.

REAR WHEEL ALIGNMENT

CAMBER

FWD Models

Camber and toe-in have been preset during production and cannot be adjusted. If camber is out of specification, replace bent or damaged components as necessary.

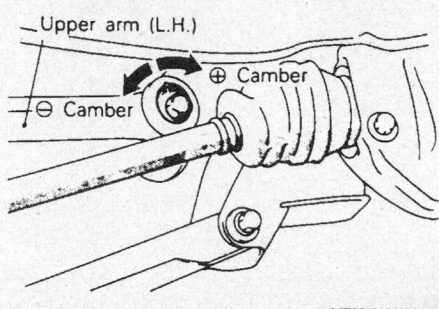

Fig. 2   Rear camber adjustment. AWD models

AWD Models

1. Measure camber with a camber/caster/kingpin gauge.
2. Adjust camber by moving mounting bolt located on crossmember side of upper arm. One graduation is equivalent to about ¼° in camber, **Fig. 2.**

TOE-IN

1. Adjust rear toe-in by moving mounting bolts located on crossmember side of the trailing arm.
2. Make adjustment by moving left and right bolts equally. One graduation changes toe by approximately .05 inch.

VEHICLE RIDE HEIGHT

There is no provision for adjustment of vehicle ride height on these vehicles. If ride height is not satisfactory, check for damaged or modified suspension components.

MITSUBISHI EXPO
INDEX OF SERVICE OPERATIONS

Specifications

GENERAL ENGINE SPECIFICATIONS

Year	Engine Liters	Fuel System	Bore & Stroke	Compression Ratio	Maximum Net H.P. @ RPM	Maximum Torque Ft. Lbs. @ RPM	Oil Pressure Ft. Lbs. @ idle
1996	1.8L	MFI	3.19 X 3.50	8.5	113 @ 6000	116 @ 4500	11.4
	2.4L	MFI	3.41 X 3.94	9.5	136 @ 5500	145 @ 4250	11.4

TUNE UP SPECIFICATIONS

Year	Engine	Spark Plug Gap, Inch	Ignition Timing			Idle Speed, RPM				Fuel Pump Pressure, psi	Valve Lash	
			Firing Order	Timing, °BTDC①	Timing Mark Location	Curb②		Fast			Intake	Exhaust
						Man. Trans.	Auto. Trans.	Man. Trans.	Auto. Trans.			
1996	1.8L	.041	1-3-4-2	5	③	700	700N	②	②	47–50	.008H	.012H
	2.4L	.041	1-3-4-2	5	③	750	750N	②	②	47–50	④	④

BTDC — Before Top Dead Center

① — With a jumper wire connected between ground & ignition timing adjustment connector. On 1.8L models, refer to **Fig. A**. On 2.4L models refer to **Fig. B**.

② — Controlled by idle speed control servo.

③ — Equipped w/crankshaft position sensor.

④ — Equipped w/hydraulic lifters no adjustment required.

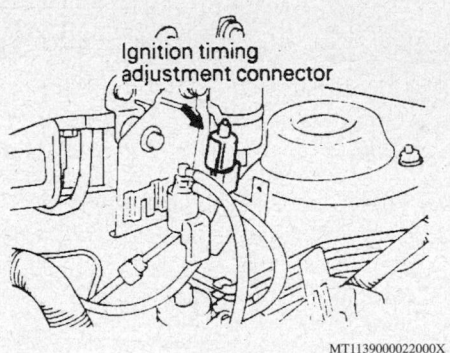

Ignition timing adjustment connector

MT1139000022000X

Fig. A

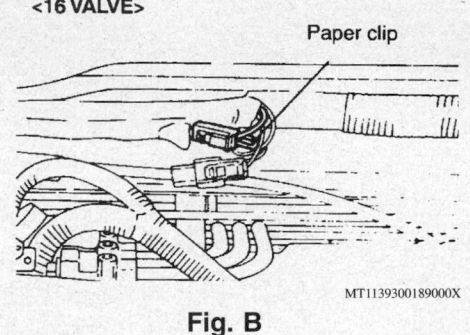

<16 VALVE>

Paper clip

MT1139300189000X

Fig. B

FRONT WHEEL ALIGNMENT SPECIFICATIONS

Year	Model	Caster Angle, Deg.		Camber Angle, Deg.		Toe, Inch①	Ball Joint Inspection Inch Lbs.
		Limits	Desired	Limits	Desired		
1996	FWD	+1½ to +2⅚	+2⅙	−⅙ to +⅚	+⅓	−.12 to +.12	17–78②
	AWD	+1⁵⁄₁₂ to +2¾	+2¹⁄₁₂	+⅙ to +1⅙	+⅔	−.12 to +.12	17–78②

AWD — All wheel drive

FWD — Front wheel drive

① — Toe-in (+); toe-out (-).

② — Breakaway torque measurement using tool No. MB990326, or equivalent.

REAR WHEEL ALIGNMENT SPECIFICATIONS

Year	Camber Angle, Deg.		Toe-In, Inch①
	Limits	Desired	
1996	−1 to 0	− ½	−0 to +.20

① — Toe-in (+); toe-out (-).

FLUID CAPACITIES & COOLING SYSTEM DATA

Year	Engine	Coolant Capacity, Qts.	Radiator Cap Relief Pressure, Lbs.	Thermo. Opening Temp., °F	Fuel Tank, Gals.	Engine Oil Refill, Qts. ①	Transaxle Oil		Transfer Case Oil, Pts.	Rear Drive Axle Oil, Pts.
							5 Speed, Pts.	Auto. Trans., Qts. ②		
1996	1.8L	6.3	13	180	③	4	3.8	6.4	—	—
	2.4L FWD	6.8	13	180	③	4.5	4.8	6.4	—	—
	2.4L AWD	6.8	13	180	③	4.5	4.8	6.9	1.2	1.48

AWD — All wheel drive
FWD — Front wheel drive
① — Includes filter.

② — Approximate, make final check w/dipstick.

③ — Expo, 15.9 gals.; Expo LRV, 14.5 gals.

LUBRICANT DATA

Year	Lubricant Type					
	Transaxle		Transfer Case	Rear Axle	Power Steering	Brake System
	Manual	Automatic				
1996	75W-90 GL-4/5	Dia ATF SP	75W-90 GL-4/5	GL-5	Dexron II/IIE/III	DOT 3 or 4

Electrical

NOTE: On Air Bag Equipped Models, Refer To "Air Bag System Precautions" Located In Front Of This Manual For System Disarming & Arming Procedures.

INDEX

PRECAUTIONS

AIR BAG SYSTEMS

Refer to "Air Bag System Precautions" in front of this manual for system disarming and arming procedures.

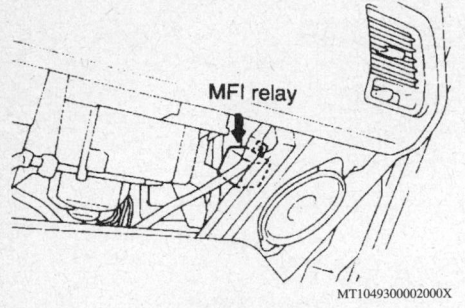

Fig. 1 Fuel pump relay location

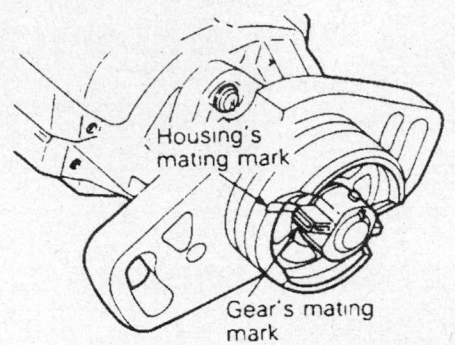

Fig. 2 Distributor housing mating marks

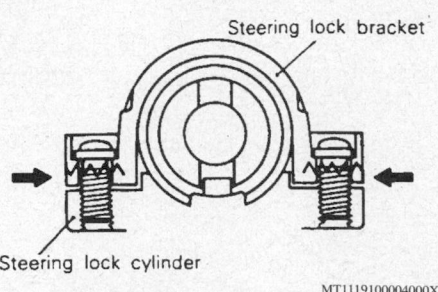

Fig. 3 Steering lock special bolts

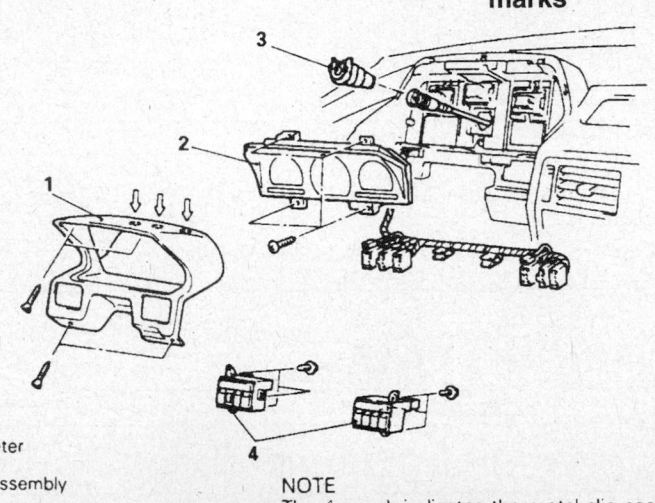

Removal steps
1. Meter hood
2. Combination meter
3. Adapter
4. Cluster switch assembly

NOTE
The ⇐ mark indicates the metal clip positions.

Fig. 4 Cluster switch removal

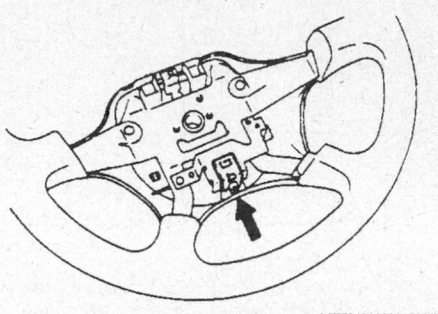

Fig. 5 Spring holder installation

BATTERY GROUND CABLE

Prior to service, disconnect battery ground cable and isolate as required.

FUSE PANEL & FLASHER LOCATION

Fuse panel is located under lefthand side of instrument panel, left of steering column. Hazard flasher unit is located above fuse panel.

FUEL PUMP RELAY LOCATION

The fuel pump relay, also known as multi-port fuel injection relay, is located under the righthand side of the instrument panel, **Fig. 1.**

RELAY CENTER LOCATION

Main relay centers are located on righthand side of engine compartment and behind lower lefthand side of instrument panel.

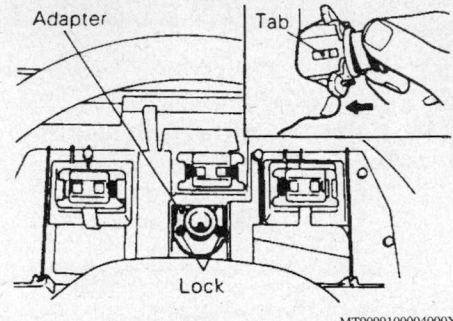

Fig. 6 Speedometer cable adapter lock

STARTER

REPLACE

1. Raise and support vehicle.
2. Disconnect starter electrical connections.
3. Remove starter bolts and starter.
4. Reverse procedure to install.

ALTERNATOR

REPLACE

1.8L ENGINE

1. Loosen alternator adjusting nut, push alternator toward engine and remove drive belt.

2. Disconnect alternator electrical connections.
3. Remove alternator brace assembly.
4. Remove alternator.
5. Reverse procedure to install.

2.4L ENGINE

1. Remove alternator harness connector lock bolt, then harness connector.
2. Remove alternator pivot bolt, then alternator.
3. Remove drive belt, water pump pulley bolt, then both water pump pulleys.
4. Remove alternator brace, then alternator.
5. Reverse procedure to install.

DISTRIBUTOR

REPLACE

1. Remove spark plug cables.
2. Disconnect distributor electrical connections.
3. Rotate engine to position piston for No. 1 cylinder at top dead center.
4. Remove distributor retainer bolt then distributor.
5. Reverse procedure to install, noting the following:
   a. Ensure piston for No. 1 cylinder is at top dead center.
   b. Align distributor housing and gear mating marks, **Fig. 2,** then install distributor on engine.

IGNITION LOCK

REPLACE

1. Disconnect hood lock release handle.
2. Remove instrument panel undercover.
3. Remove steering column lower cover.
4. Remove instrument cluster hood and upper column cover.
5. Remove steering wheel as outlined under "Steering Wheel, Replace."

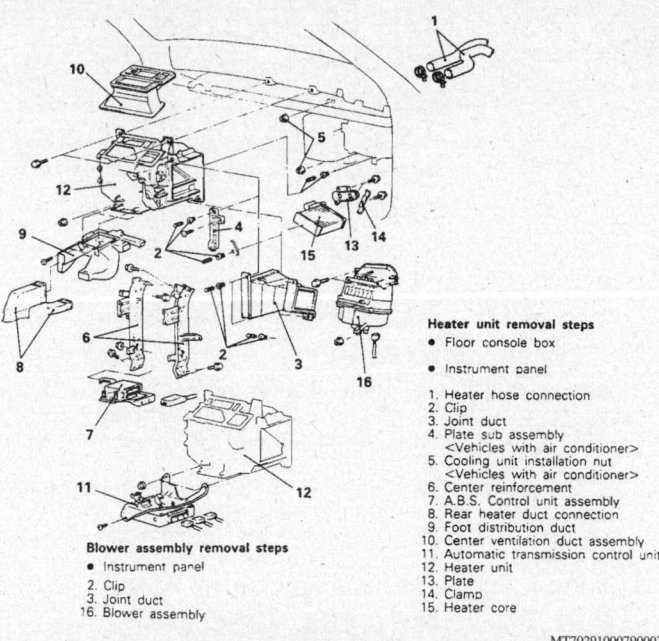

Heater unit removal steps
- Floor console box
- Instrument panel

1. Heater hose connection
2. Clip
3. Joint duct
4. Plate sub assembly
   <Vehicles with air conditioner>
5. Cooling unit installation nut
   <Vehicles with air conditioner>
6. Center reinforcement
7. A.B.S. Control unit assembly
8. Rear heater duct connection
9. Foot distribution duct
10. Center ventilation duct assembly
11. Automatic transmission control unit
12. Heater unit
13. Plate
14. Clamp
15. Heater core

MT7029100079000X

Blower assembly removal steps
- Instrument panel

2. Clip
3. Joint duct
16. Blower assembly

Fig. 7   Heater core & blower housing assembly replacement

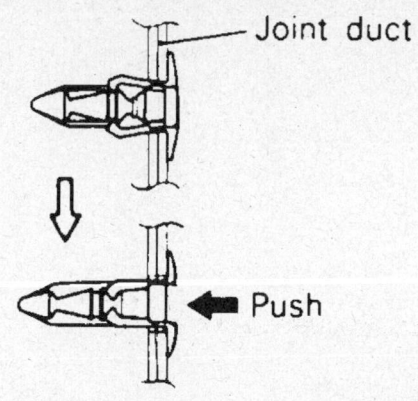

MT7029100080000X

Fig. 8   Retainer clip removal

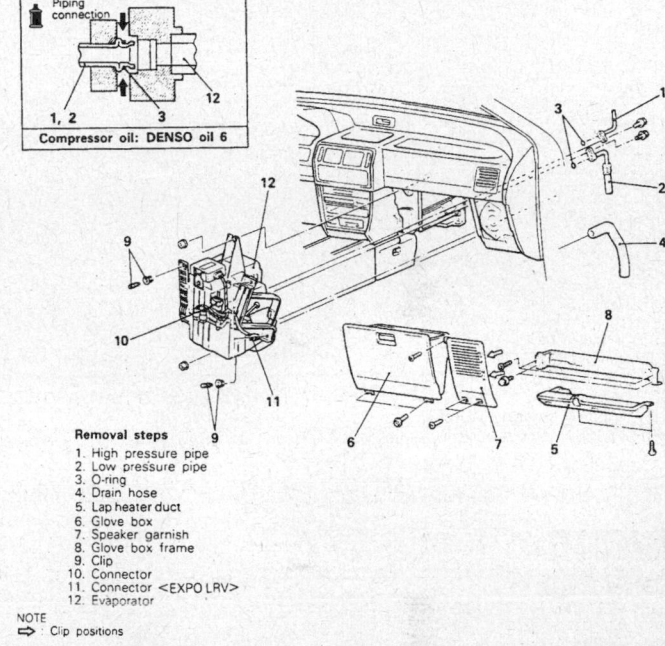

Compressor oil: DENSO oil 6

Removal steps
1. High pressure pipe
2. Low pressure pipe
3. O-ring
4. Drain hose
5. Lap heater duct
6. Glove box
7. Speaker garnish
8. Glove box frame
9. Clip
10. Connector
11. Connector <EXPO LRV>
12. Evaporator

NOTE
⇨ : Clip positions

MT7029100081000X

Fig. 9   Evaporator housing replacement

6. Using a hacksaw, cut special bolts used to secure steering lock, **Fig. 3.**
7. Reverse procedure to install, noting the following:
   a. Temporarily install steering lock bracket and steering lock on steering column.
   b. Ensure proper operation of steering lock.
   c. Tighten special bolts until heads twist off.

IGNITION SWITCH
REPLACE

1. Disconnect hood lock release handle.
2. Remove instrument panel undercover, then steering column lower cover.
3. Remove instrument cluster hood and upper column cover.
4. Insert ignition key into cylinder and turn to ACC position.
5. Using a small Phillips screwdriver, or equivalent, push lockpin of steering lock cylinder inward, then pull steering lock cylinder outward.
6. Disconnect key reminder switch.
7. Remove ignition switch segment.
8. Reverse procedure to install.

NEUTRAL SAFETY SWITCH
REPLACE

1. **On models with manual transmission,** disconnect switch electrical connections, then remove switch from transmission.
2. **On models with automatic transmission,** proceed as follows:
   a. Disconnect transmission gear selector cable from transmission.
   b. Disconnect position switch electrical connections.

c. Remove manual control lever, then switch.
3. **On all models,** reverse procedure to install.

COMBINATION SWITCH
REPLACE

1. Remove instrument cluster hood, **Fig. 4.**
2. Remove cluster switch retaining screws.
3. Pull cluster switch toward rear of vehicle and disconnect electrical connectors.
4. Remove switch from vehicle.
5. Reverse procedure to install.

STEERING WHEEL
REPLACE

1. Remove horn pad assembly.
2. Remove spring holder.
3. Remove steering wheel using a suitable steering wheel puller. **Do not**

hammer on steering column to remove it, doing so may damage collapsible mechanism.
4. Reverse procedure to install, noting the following:
   a. Install spring clip as shown in **Fig. 5.**
   b. Press downward on horn pad to install it on steering wheel.

INSTRUMENT CLUSTER
REPLACE

1. Remove instrument cluster hood, **Fig. 4.**
2. Remove instrument cluster retaining screws.
3. Pull instrument cluster rearward and remove adapter lock, **Fig. 6.**
4. Pull speedometer cable slightly into passenger compartment and remove rear side of adapter from cable.
5. After turning adapter so that notched section is aligned with tab on cable, remove adapter by sliding it backwards.

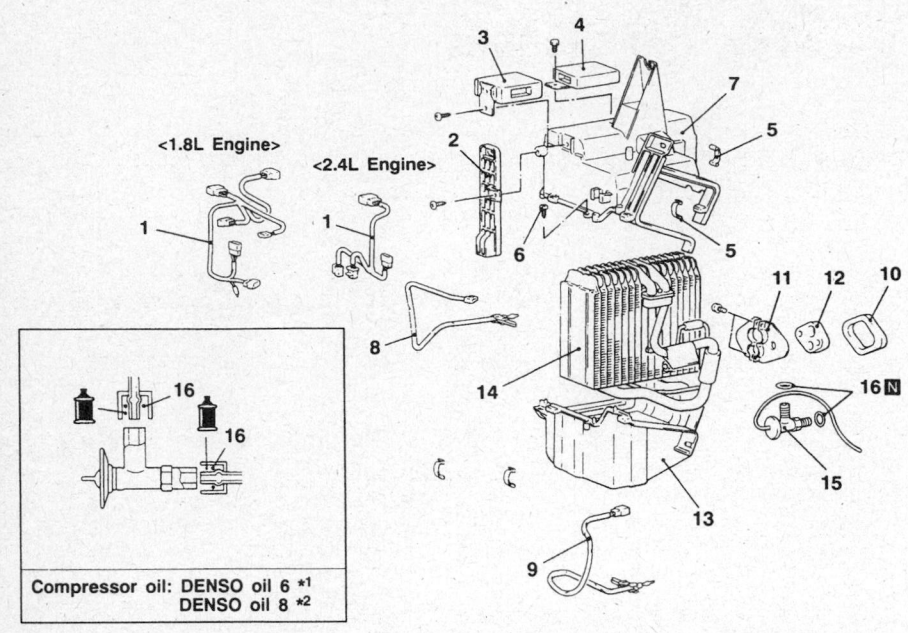

Compressor oil: DENSO oil 6 *1
DENSO oil 8 *2

Disassembly steps

1. Harness
2. Plate sub assembly
3. Auto compressor control unit
4. Belt lock controller <1.8L Engine>
5. Clip
6. Tapping screw
7. Evaporator case (upper)
8. Air inlet sensor
   <Up to 1993 models>
9. Air thermo sensor
10. Packing
11. Bracket
12. Grommet
13. Evaporator case (lower)
14. Evaporator assembly
15. Expansion valve
16. O-ring

NOTE
*1: Vehicles using R-12 refrigerant
*2: Vehicles using R-134a refrigerant

MT7029100082000X

Fig. 10 Evaporator housing service

6. Reverse procedure to install.

RADIO
REPLACE

1. Remove ashtray and center trim panel.
2. Remove radio bracket retaining bolts.
3. Pull radio assembly slightly into passengers compartment and disconnect electrical and antenna connections.
4. Remove radio from vehicle.
5. Reverse procedure to install.

WIPER MOTOR
REPLACE
FRONT

1. Remove wiper blades and arm assemblies.

2. Remove front deck garnish.
3. Loosen wiper motor assembly bolts, then remove wiper motor assembly.
4. Disconnect wiper linkage and motor electrical connections.
5. Remove wiper motor assembly.
6. Reverse procedure to install.

REAR

1. Remove wiper blades and arm assemblies.
2. Remove liftgate interior trim panel.
3. Disconnect wiper electrical connections, then remove wiper motor assembly.
4. Reverse procedure to install.

WIPER SWITCH
REPLACE
FRONT

Refer to "Column Switch, Replace" for windshield wiper switch replacement.

REAR

Refer to "Combination Switch, Replace" for rear window wiper switch replacement.

BLOWER MOTOR
REPLACE

1. Remove passengers lap heater duct.
2. Remove glove compartment.
3. Disconnect and remove blower resistor.
4. Remove speaker garnish and glove compartment frame.
5. Disconnect then remove blower motor assembly.
6. Reverse procedure to install.

HEATER CORE
REPLACE

1. Drain cooling system into a suitable container.
2. Remove floor console and instrument panel as outlined under "Dash Panel Service."
3. Remove blower motor housing assembly and heater core assembly in numbered sequence shown in **Fig. 7**, pushing in center of joint duct clip for removal, **Fig. 8**.
4. Reverse procedure to install.

EVAPORATOR CORE
REPLACE

1. Recover refrigerant from system as outlined under "Refrigerant Recovery."
2. Remove evaporator housing assembly in numbered sequence shown in **Fig. 9**, pushing in center of joint duct clip for removal, **Fig. 8**.
3. Disassemble evaporator housing assembly in numbered sequence shown in **Fig. 10**, noting the following:
   a. Remove housing clips using a suitable flat blade screwdriver.
   b. Loosen expansion valve flare nut using two wrenches.
4. Reverse procedure to install.

1.8L Engine

NOTE: On Air Bag Equipped Models, Refer To "Air Bag System Precautions" Located In Front Of This Manual For System Disarming & Arming Procedures.

NOTE: Prior To Performing Any Service Operations Listed In This Section, Consult The "Technical Service Bulletins " Section For Related Information.

INDEX

PRECAUTIONS

AIR BAG SYSTEMS

Refer to "Air Bag System Precautions" in front of this manual for system disarming and arming procedures.

BATTERY GROUND CABLE

Prior to service, disconnect battery ground cable and isolate as required.

FUEL SYSTEM PRESSURE RELIEF

1. Remove grommet below floor and disconnect fuel pump connector.
2. Start engine and allow engine to runout of fuel.
3. Crank engine two or three times to release remaining fuel pressure.
4. Place ignition switch to Off position.
5. After fuel system repairs are completed, connect fuel pump electrical connections.

COMPRESSION PRESSURE

Ensure engine oil, starter motor and battery are in satisfactory condition. When checking compression, engine coolant should be at normal operating temperature, spark plugs should be removed and throttle valve should be wide open. Correct compression pressures at engine cranking speed, should be 151 psi. Difference between cylinders should not exceed 14 psi.

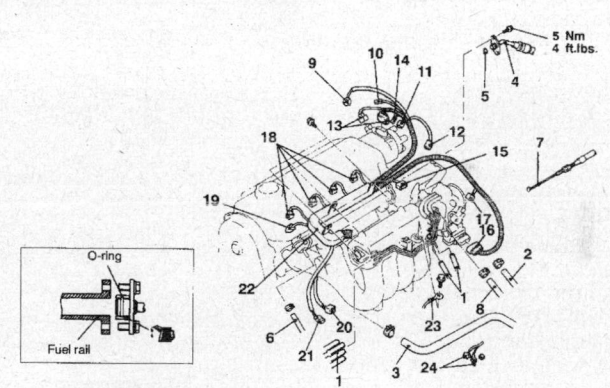

Removal steps
1. Vacuum hose connection
2. Heater hose connection (Thermostat housing to heater unit)
3. Heater hose connection (Heater unit to water inlet pipe)
4. High-pressure fuel hose connection
5. O-ring
6. Fuel return hose connection
7. Accelerator cable connection
8. Brake booster vacuum hose connection
9. Heated oxygen sensor connector <Vehicles for California>
10. Oil pressure switch connector
11. Engine coolant temperature gauge unit connector
12. Engine coolant temperature sensor connector
13. Distributor connector
14. Capacitor connector
15. MDP sensor connector
16. Idle air control motor connector
17. TPS connector
18. Injector connector
19. Crankshaft position sensor connector
20. Heated oxygen sensor connector
21. EGR temperature sensor connector <1995 models for Federal>
22. Control harness assembly
23. Ground wire
24. Generator harness connection

MT1069100102010X

Fig. 1 Engine replacement (Part 1 of 2)

ENGINE

REPLACE

1. Release fuel system pressure as outlined under "Precautions."
2. Mark hood hinge bolt location on hood, then remove hood.
3. Drain cooling system into an approved container.
4. Remove transaxle assembly as outlined under "Transaxle, Replace" in "Clutch & Manual Transaxle"section for models with manual transaxle or in

"Automatic Transaxle " unit repair section for models with automatic transaxle.

5. Remove radiator assembly.
6. Remove engine assembly in numbered sequence shown in **Fig. 1**, noting the following:
   a. Remove power steering pump with hoses attached, then support aside.
   b. Remove air conditioner compressor with hoses attached, then support aside.
   c. Support engine using a suitable jack stand.
   d. Remove engine hanger tool used when transaxle was removed.
   e. Support engine using a chain and suitable engine lifting device.
   f. Raise engine slightly to remove weight off mounts then remove engine mounts.
   g. Ensure all electrical and hose connections are disconnected then raise engine assembly out of vehicle.
   h. **Always insert a piece of wood between engine hanger assembly and front deck. Do not pinch hood weatherstrip between front deck and piece of wood.**
7. Reverse procedure to install, noting the following:
   a. Using a floor jack and a piece of wood, support engine on oil pan, then install engine mount bracket while adjusting position of engine.
   b. Remove engine lifting device allowing engine hanger tool to support engine until transaxle is installed.

INTAKE MANIFOLD
REPLACE

1. Release fuel system pressure as outlined under "Precautions."
2. Drain cooling system into an approved container.
3. Remove intake manifold in numbered sequence shown in **Fig. 2**, removing fuel delivery pipe leaving injectors and pressure regulator intact. **Do not drop injector when removing delivery pipe.**
4. Reverse procedure to install.

EXHAUST MANIFOLD
REPLACE

1. Replace exhaust manifold in numbered sequence shown in **Figs. 3 and 4.**
2. Reverse procedure to install.

CYLINDER HEAD
REPLACE
REMOVAL

1. Release fuel system pressure as outlined under "Precautions."
2. Drain cooling system into an approved container.
3. Remove cylinder head and gasket in

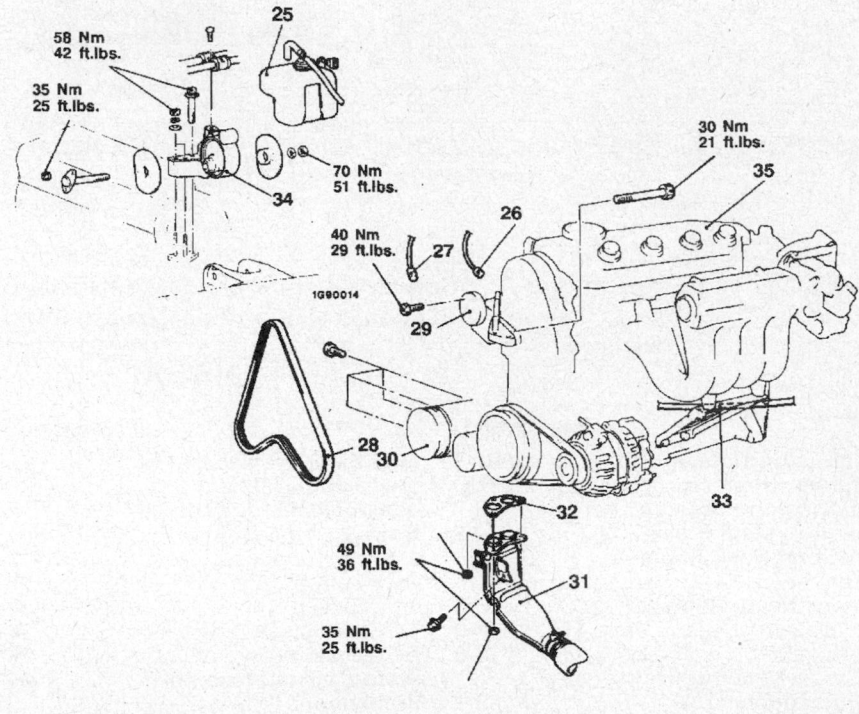

Removal steps
25. Condense tank
26. Power steering pressure switch connector
27. Air conditioning compressor connector
28. Drive belt
29. Power steering oil pump connection
30. Air conditioning compressor connection

31. Front exhaust pipe connection
32. Gasket
33. Starter and generator harness clamp
34. Engine mount bracket
35. Engine assembly

MT1069100102020X

Fig. 1 Engine replacement (Part 2 of 2)

numbered sequence shown in **Fig. 5**, noting the following:
a. Rotate engine so No. 1 cylinder is at top dead center on compression stroke and align camshaft timing mark, **Fig. 6.**
b. Tie camshaft sprocket and timing belt together so that position of camshaft sprocket will not move with respect to timing belt, **Fig. 7.**
c. Remove camshaft sprocket as outlined under "Timing Belt, Replace."
d. Loosen cylinder head bolts in two or three steps in numbered sequence shown in **Fig. 8. Use care not to damage plug guide, as plug guides cannot be replaced.**
4. Inspect cylinder head gasket surface for flatness by using a straightedge.

INSTALLATION

Reverse numbered sequence shown in **Fig. 5** to install, noting the following:
1. Clean cylinder gasket surface on both cylinder head and engine block.
2. Place cylinder head gasket on cylinder

block with identification mark facing upward on intake side, **Fig. 9.**
3. Measure cylinder head bolts and ensure bolts are less than 3.795 inches long.
4. Apply a small amount of oil to cylinder head bolt threads and to bolt washer. **Ensure cylinder head bolt is installed as shown in Fig. 10.**
5. Tighten cylinder head bolts in numbered sequence shown in **Fig. 11** in five steps as follows:
   a. **Torque** bolts to 54 ft. lbs.
   b. Completely loosen bolts.
   c. **Torque** bolts to 15 ft. lbs.
   d. Turn bolts 90° (1/4 turn).
   e. Turn bolts an additional 90° (1/4 turn).
6. Loosen water inlet pipe bolt, apply sealant to thermostat case, **Figs. 12 and 13.**
7. Apply a small amount of water to O-ring of water inlet pipe and press thermostat case assembly onto water inlet pipe.
8. Install thermostat case assembly

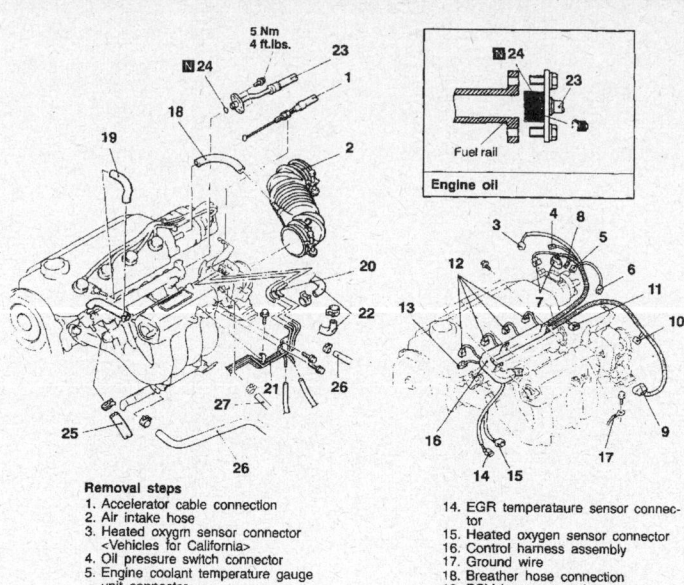

Removal steps
1. Accelerator cable connection
2. Air intake hose
3. Heated oxygn sensor connector <Vehicles for California>
4. Oil pressure switch connector
5. Engine coolant temperature gauge unit connector
6. Engine coolant temperature sensor connector
7. Distributor connector
8. Capacitor connector
9. IAC connector
10. TPS connector
11. MDP sensor connector

12. Injector connector
13. Crankshaft position sensor connector

14. EGR temperataure sensor connector
15. Heated oxygen sensor connector
16. Control harness assembly
17. Ground wire
18. Breather hose connection
19. PCV hose connection
20. Vacuum hose connection
21. Vacuum pipe
22. Water hose connection
23. High-pressure fuel hose connection
24. O-ring
25. Fuel return hose connection
26. Heater hose connection
27. Brake boster vacuum hose connection

MT1059100016010X

Fig. 2   Intake manifold replacement (Part 1 of 2)

28. Fuel rail, injector and pressure regulator assembly
29. Insulator
30. Insulator
31. Intake manifold stay
32. Intake manifold
33. Intake manifold gasket

34. Throttle body
35. EGR temperature sensor <1995 models for Federal>
36. EGR valve
37. MDP sensor

MT1059100016020X

Fig. 2   Intake manifold replacement (Part 2 of 2)

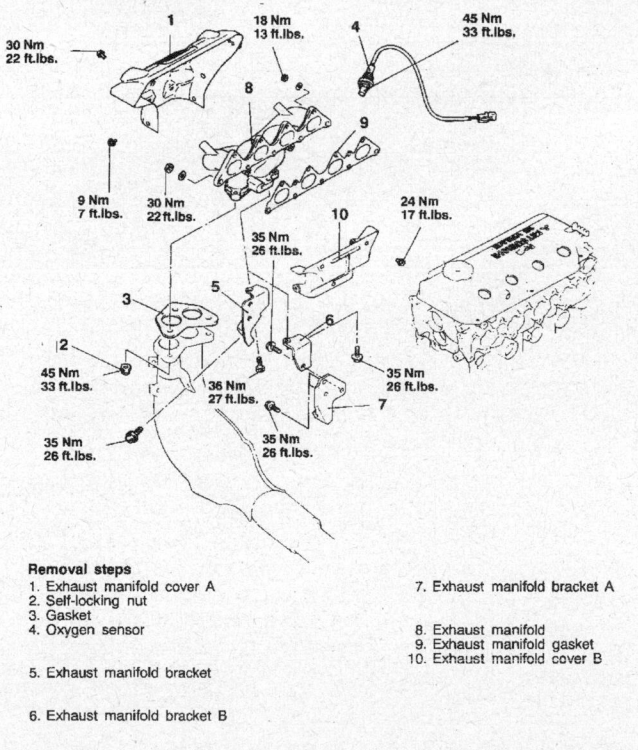

Removal steps
1. Exhaust manifold cover A
2. Self-locking nut
3. Gasket
4. Oxygen sensor

5. Exhaust manifold bracket

6. Exhaust manifold bracket B

7. Exhaust manifold bracket A

8. Exhaust manifold
9. Exhaust manifold gasket
10. Exhaust manifold cover B

MT1079100008000X

Fig. 3   Exhaust manifold replacement. Less California emissions

mounting bolt and tighten water inlet pipe bolt.
9. Install thermostat so jiggle valve is at top.

Removal steps
1. Heated oxygen sensor

2. Exhaust manifold bracket B
3. Exhaust manifold bracket A

4. Exhaust manifold cover A
5. Exhaust manifold
6. Exhaust manifold gasket

MT1079800024000X

Fig. 4   Exhaust manifold replacement. w/California emissions

cylinder head and exhaust valves are located on LH side of cylinder head.

VALVE ARRANGEMENT

Intake valves are located on RH side of

VALVE CLEARANCE SPECIFICATIONS

Valve stem to guide clearance with the engine hot is .008 for intake and .0012 inch for exhaust.

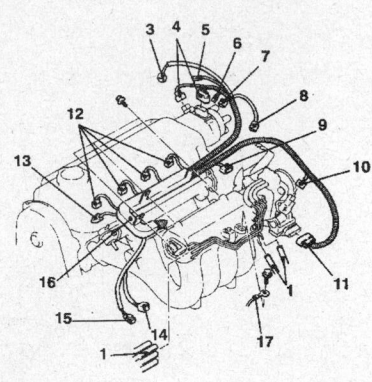

Removal steps

1. Vacuum hose connection
2. Air conditioning engine coolant temperature switch connector
3. Oxygen sensor or heated oxygen sensor connector
4. Distributor connector
5. Oil pressure switch connector
6. Capacitor connector
7. Engine coolant temperature gauge unit connector
8. Engine coolant temperature sensor connector
9. MDP sensor connector
10. TPS connector
11. Idle air control motor connector
12. Injector connector
13. Crankshaft position sensor connector
14. Heated oxygen sensor connector
15. EGR temperature sensor connector
16. Control harness assembly
17. Ground wire

MT1069800544010X

Fig. 5   Cylinder head replacement (Part 1 of 3)

VALVE ADJUSTMENT

1. Remove valve cover assembly as outlined under "Cylinder Head, Replace."
2. Position No. 1 cylinder at top dead center on compression stroke.
3. Adjust valve clearance at points shown in **Fig. 14** as follows:
   a. Loosen adjusting screw locknut.
   b. Using feeler gauge, adjust intake valve clearance to 0.008 inch and exhaust valve clearance to 0.012 inch by turning adjusting screw.
   c. While holding adjusting screw, tighten adjusting screw locknut.
4. Rotate engine crankshaft clockwise one complete turn to position No. 4 cylinder at top dead center on compression stroke.
5. Repeat Step 4 for points shown in **Fig. 15.**
6. Install valve cover.

ROCKER ARMS

REPLACE

Refer to "Camshaft, Replace" for rocker arm replacement procedure.

FRONT COVER

REPLACE

Refer to "Oil Pump, Replace" for front cover replacement procedure.

TIMING BELT

REPLACE

REMOVAL

With the timing belt removed, avoid turning the camshaft or crankshaft. If

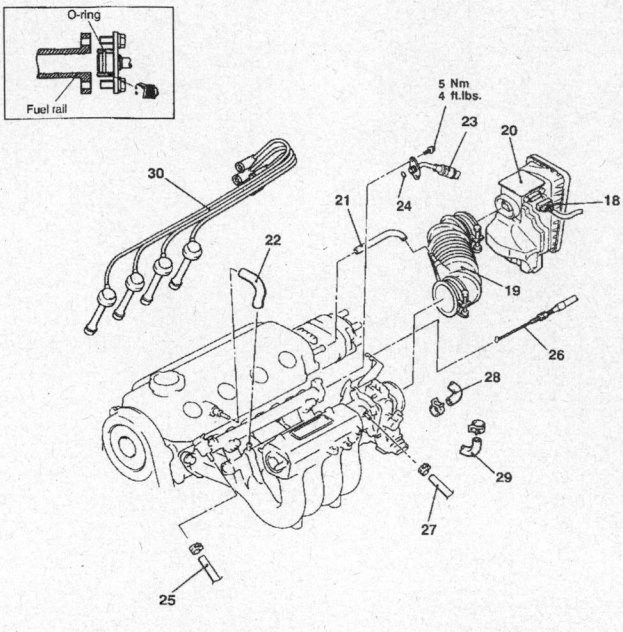

Removal steps

18. Volume air flow sensor connector
19. Air intake hose
20. Air cleaner case cover
21. Breather hose connection
22. PCV hose
23. High-pressure fuel hose connection
24. O-ring
25. Fuel return hose connection
26. Accelerator cable connection
27. Brake booster vacuum hose connection
28. Water hose connection (Thermostat case to throttle body)
29. Water hose connection (Throttle body to water inlet fitting)
30. Spark plug cable

MT1069800544020X

Fig. 5   Cylinder head replacement (Part 2 of 3)

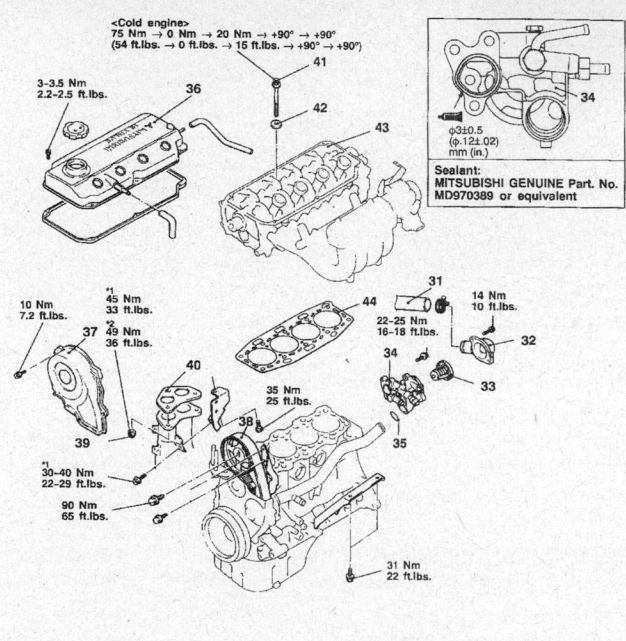

NOTE
*1: Except Vehicles for California
*2: Vehicles for California

Removal steps

31. Radiator lower hose connection
32. Water inlet fitting
33. Thermostat
34. Thermostat case assembly
35. O-ring
36. Rocker cover
37. Timing belt upper cover
38. Camshaft sprocket
39. Self-locking nuts
40. Gasket
41. Cylinder head bolt
42. Washer
43. Cylinder head assembly
44. Cylinder head gasket

MT1069800544030X

Fig. 5   Cylinder head replacement (Part 3 of 3)

1.8L ENGINE

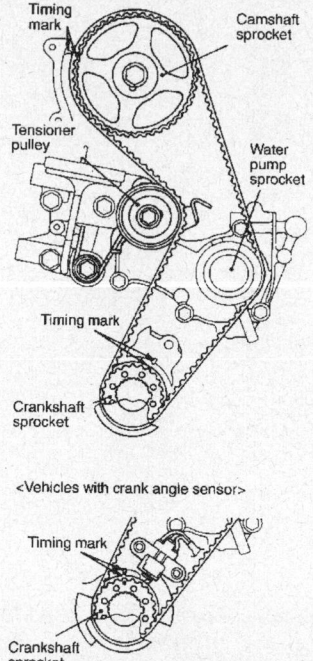

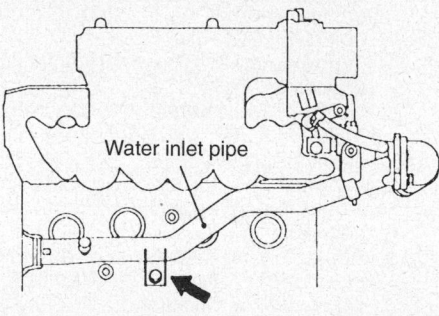

Fig. 6   Engine timing marks

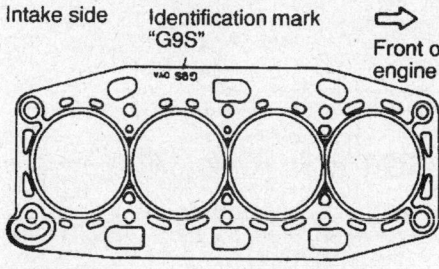

Fig. 9   Cylinder head gasket identification mark

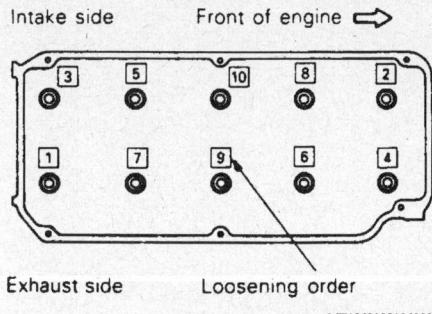

Fig. 7   Camshaft sprocket secured position

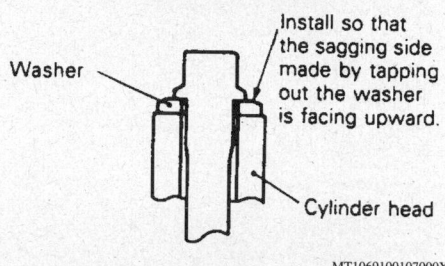

Fig. 10   Cylinder head bolt washer installation

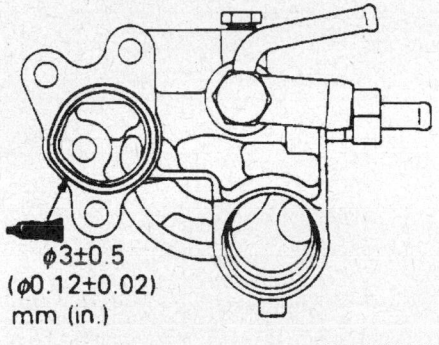

Fig. 13   Thermostat housing sealant location

Fig. 8   Cylinder head bolt loosening sequence

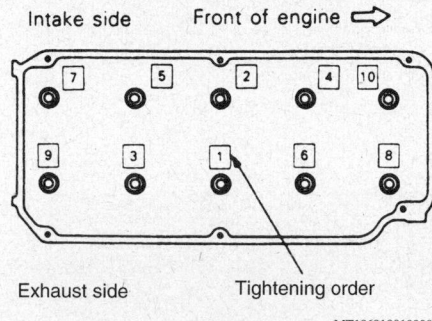

Fig. 11   Cylinder head bolt tightening sequence

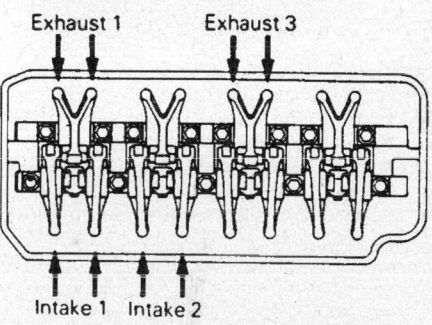

Fig. 14   Valve clearance adjustment w/No. 1 cylinder at TDC

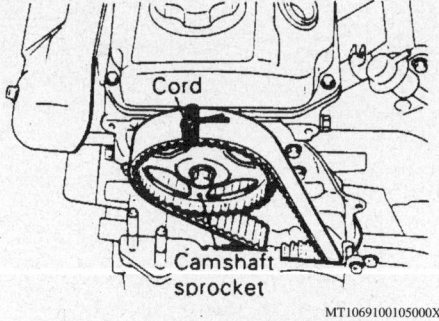

Fig. 12   Inlet water pipe mounting bolt location

movement is required, exercise extreme caution to avoid valve damage caused by piston contact. Never rotate the engine in a counterclockwise direction or damage to the engine will result.
1. Remove engine undercover.
2. Remove cooling system condenser tank.
3. Remove air conditioning and power steering line clamp, **Fig. 16.**

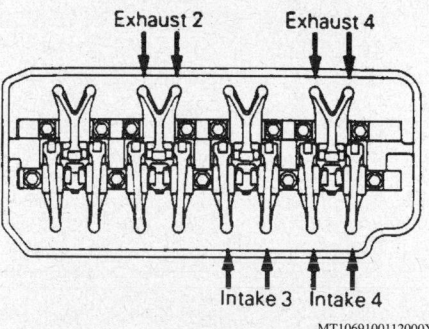

Fig. 15   Valve clearance adjustment w/No. 1 cylinder at BTDC

4. Raise and support vehicle.
5. Remove left front wheel, then the inner splash shield.
6. Remove power steering and air conditioning drive belt, then alternator drive belt.

7. Stop crankshaft pulley from turning using crankshaft pulley holder, then remove crankshaft bolt, washer and pulley.
8. Remove upper and lower timing belt covers, then flange.
9. If belt is to be reused, mark rotational direction for installation.
10. Turn crankshaft clockwise to align each timing mark and set No. 1 cylinder at compression top dead center (TDC), **Fig. 6.**
11. Loosen timing belt tensioner bolt, then press tensioner fully back clockwise using a screwdriver.
12. Temporarily tighten timing belt tensioner bolt and remove timing belt.
13. Loosen tensioner bolt and move tensioner as close to engine mount as possible with screwdriver, then tighten bolt.

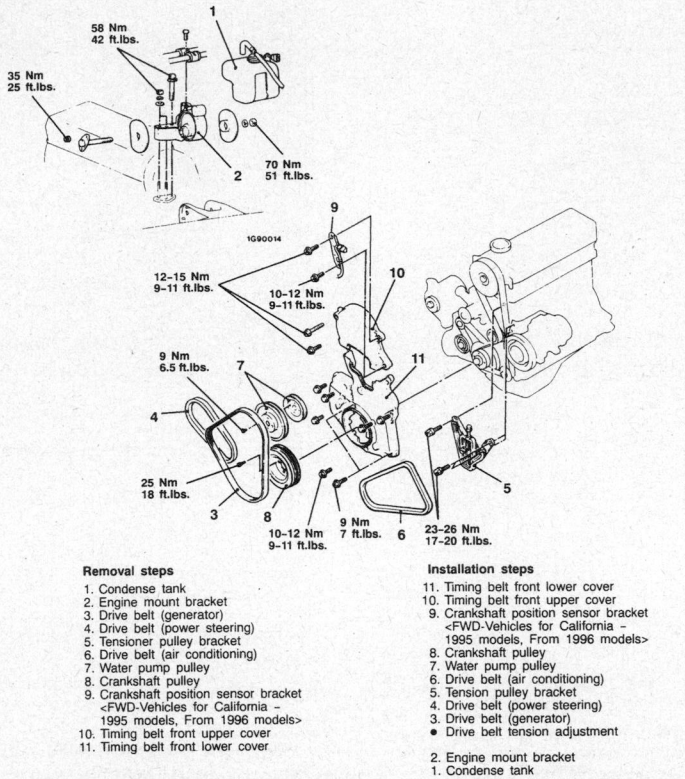

Fig. 16 Exploded view of timing belt

Removal steps
1. Condense tank
2. Engine mount bracket
3. Drive belt (generator)
4. Drive belt (power steering)
5. Tensioner pulley bracket
6. Drive belt (air conditioning)
7. Water pump pulley
8. Crankshaft pulley
9. Crankshaft position sensor bracket
   <FWD-Vehicles for California –
   1995 models, From 1996 models>
10. Timing belt front upper cover
11. Timing belt front lower cover

Installation steps
11. Timing belt front lower cover
10. Timing belt front upper cover
9. Crankshaft position sensor bracket
   <FWD-Vehicles for California –
   1995 models, From 1996 models>
8. Crankshaft pulley
7. Water pump pulley
6. Drive belt (air conditioning)
5. Tension pulley bracket
4. Drive belt (power steering)
3. Drive belt (generator)
● Drive belt tension adjustment

2. Engine mount bracket
1. Condense tank

MT1069100113000X

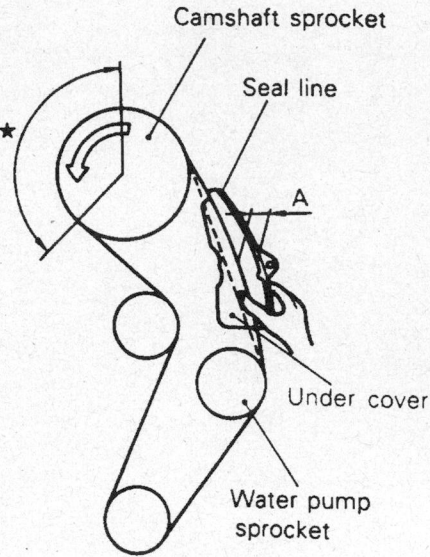

Fig. 17 Timing belt tension inspection

INSTALLATION

1. Ensure camshaft and crankshaft timing marks are aligned, **Fig. 6.**
2. Ensure tension side of belt is taut while installing timing belt over crankshaft, water pump and camshaft sprockets, then tensioner pulley.
3. Apply counterclockwise pressure (reverse of normal rotational direction) to camshaft sprocket and check that belt is fully tensioned, then ensure timing marks are properly aligned.
4. Loosen timing belt tensioner belt approximately ½ turn and allow tensioner spring to tension belt.
5. Rotate crankshaft clockwise two turns, then check timing marks.
6. Ensure timing belt is properly seated on sprockets, then tighten tensioner bolt to specifications.
7. Grasp timing belt with thumb and undercover with index finger and apply light pressure, Check clearance, **Fig. 17,** "A" between belt and undercover. Clearance should be approximately 1.18 inches.
8. Install crankshaft flange with flanged side out, **Fig. 18.**
9. Install timing belt upper and lower covers, then tighten bolts to specifications, **Fig. 19.** "A" bolts: 0.24 x 0.71 inch and "B" bolts: 0.24 x 1.18 inches.
10. Apply engine oil to bearing surface and thread section of crankshaft bolt, then install crankshaft bolt and tighten to specifications.
11. Install alternator drive belt, then air conditioning and power steering pump drive belt.

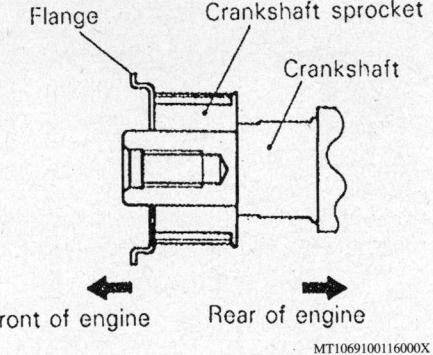

Fig. 18 Flange installation

12. Install left inner splash shield, then the wheel.
13. Lower vehicle.
14. Install clamp attaching air conditioning and power steering lines to engine mount.
15. Install cooling system condenser tank.
16. Install engine undercover.
17. Check and adjust ignition timing as necessary.

CAMSHAFT
REPLACE

1. Release fuel system pressure as outlined under "Precautions."
2. Rotate engine to position No. 1 cylinder at top dead center on compression stroke.
3. Remove camshaft, camshaft oil seal

rocker arms and shafts in numbered sequence shown in **Fig. 20,** noting the following:
a. Prevent camshaft from turning using end yoke holder, tool Nos. MB990767 and MD998719, or equivalent, and loosen camshaft sprocket bolt, then remove camshaft sprocket.
b. Do not disassemble rocker arm shafts unless component replacement is necessary.
4. Reverse procedure to install, noting the following:
a. If rocker arm shaft was disassembled, temporarily tighten rocker arm shaft bolt so all rocker arms on inlet side do not push valves. Install rocker arm shaft spring from above and position at right angle to plug guide, **Fig. 21.**
b. Tighten rocker arm shaft bolts to specification.
c. Using seal installation tool No. MD998713-01, or equivalent, install camshaft seal.
d. Install distributor as outlined under "Distributor, Replace" in "Electrical" section.
e. Adjust timing belt tension as outlined under "Timing Belt, Replace."
f. Adjust valve clearance as outlined under "Valve Adjustment."

PISTON & ROD ASSEMBLY

1. Release fuel system pressure as outlined under "Precautions."
2. Remove engine as outlined under "Engine, Replace."
3. Remove timing belt as outlined under "Timing Belt, Replace."
4. Remove water pump as outlined under "Water Pump, Replace."
5. Remove cylinder head as outlined under "Cylinder Head, Replace."

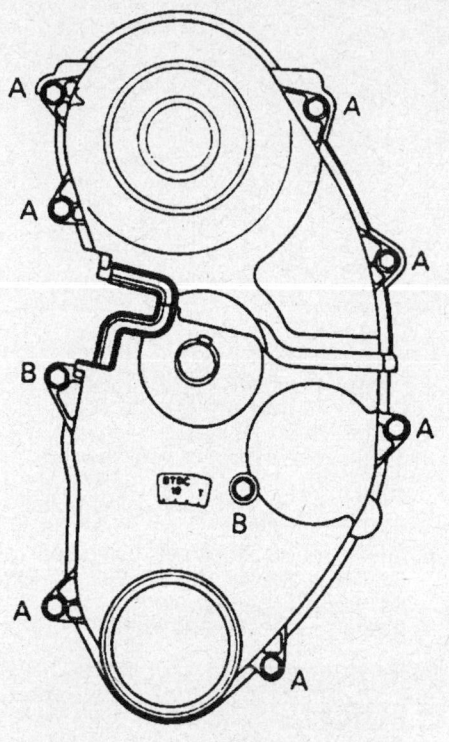

MT1069100117000X

Fig. 19 Timing belt cover bolt locations

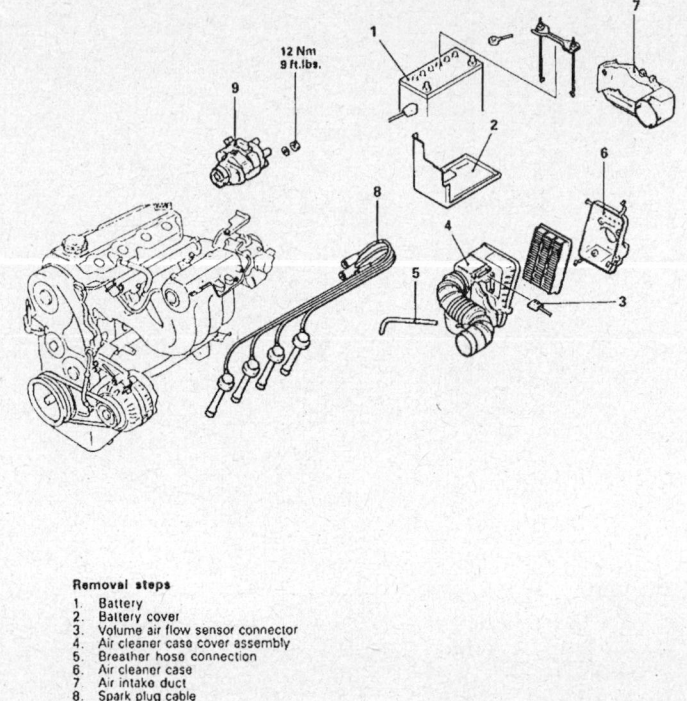

Removal steps

1. Battery
2. Battery cover
3. Volume air flow sensor connector
4. Air cleaner case cover assembly
5. Breather hose connection
6. Air cleaner case
7. Air intake duct
8. Spark plug cable
9. Distributor

MT1069100118010X

Fig. 20 Camshaft replacement (Part 1 of 2)

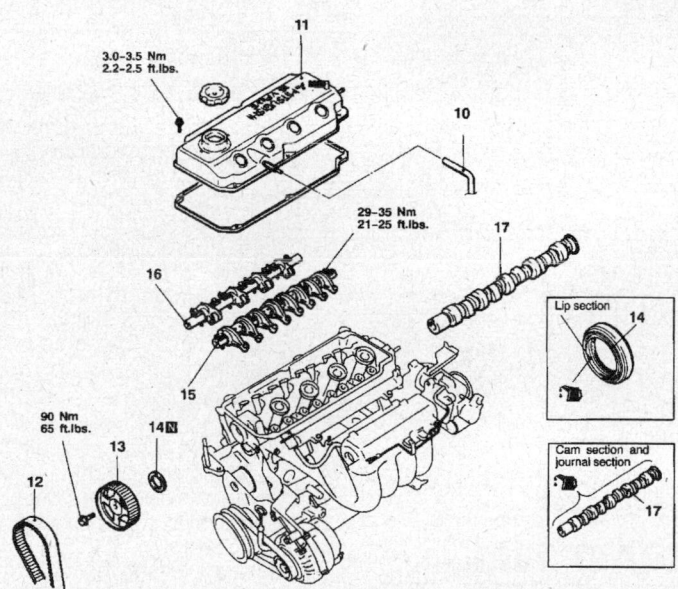

3.0–3.5 Nm
2.2–2.5 ft.lbs.

29–35 Nm
21–25 ft.lbs.

90 Nm
65 ft.lbs.

Lip section

Cam section and journal section

10. PCV hose connection
11. Rocker cover
12. Timing belt
13. Camshaft sprocket
14. Camshaft oil seal
15. Rocker arms and rocker arm shaft assembly (Intake side)
16. Rocker arms and rocker arm shaft assembly (Exhaust side)
17. Camshaft

MT1069100118020X

Fig. 20 Camshaft replacement (Part 2 of 2)

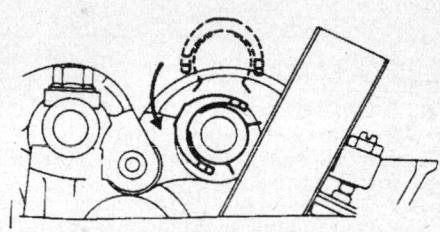

MT1069100120000X

Fig. 21 Rocker shaft spring installation

6. Remove oil pan as outlined under "Oil Pump, Replace."
7. Remove piston and connecting rod in numbered sequence shown in **Fig. 22**, marking large end of each connecting rod with cylinder number.
8. Reverse procedure to install, noting the following:
   a. Arrange piston ring oil gaps and piston as shown in **Fig. 23**.
   b. Use suitable thread protectors on connection rod studs prior to installation.
   c. Mate each connecting rod marking with appropriate cylinder.
   d. Install connecting rod bearing cap on connecting rod.
   e. Coat threads lightly with oil.
   f. Install both nuts finger tight.
   g. Alternately tighten each nut to specifications.

MAIN & ROD BEARINGS

When servicing crankshaft bearings refer to **Fig. 24**.

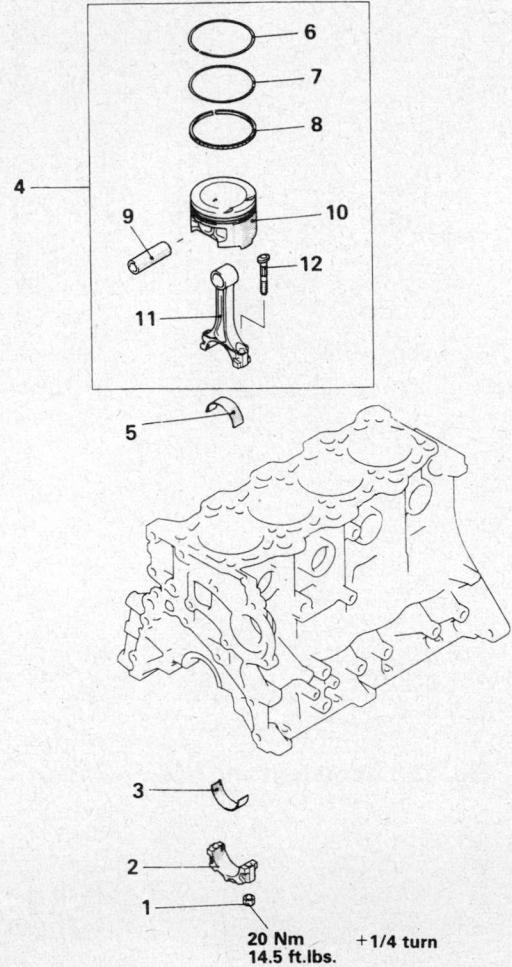

Disassembly steps
1. Nut
2. Connecting rod cap
3. Connecting rod bearing
4. Piston and connecting rod.
5. Connecting rod bearing
6. Piston ring No.1
7. Piston ring No.2
8. Oil ring
9. Piston pin
10. Piston
11. Connecting rod
12. Bolt

MT1069100121000X

Fig. 22 Exploded view of piston & connecting rod

1. Install bearing with oil groove on cylinder block side.
2. Install bearing with no oil groove on bearing cap side.
3. Install thrust bearing to No. 3 bearing (groove facing outside).
4. Install bearing caps so their arrows are positioned toward timing belt side.
5. Measure each bearing cap bolt and ensure bolt is less than 2.79 inches long.
6. Tighten bearing cap bolts to specification.
7. Ensure crankshaft turns freely and endplay is 0.0020–0.0098 inch.
8. Replace rear main oil seal as outlined under "Crankshaft Seal, Replace."

CRANKSHAFT SEAL

REPLACE

REAR

1. Remove transaxle assembly as outlined under "Transaxle, Replace" in "Clutch & Manual Transaxle" section for models with manual transaxle or in "Automatic Transaxle" unit repair section for models with automatic transaxle.
2. Remove flywheel or driveplate from rear of crankshaft.
3. Remove rear engine place and inspection cover.

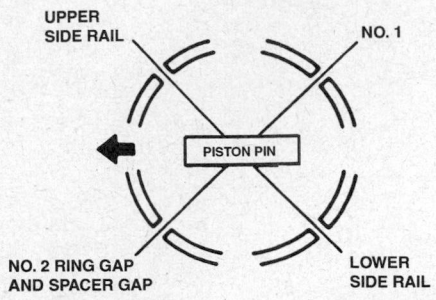

MT1069100122000X

Fig. 23 Piston pin & ring installation

4. Remove rear main oil seal case and oil seal.
5. Drive out old oil seal using suitable seal removal tool.
6. Install rear main oil seal using seal installer tool Nos. MB990938-01 and MD998776, or equivalent.
7. Reverse procedure to install.

OIL PAN

REPLACE

Refer to "Oil Pump, Replace" for oil pan replacement procedure.

OIL PUMP

REPLACE

REMOVAL

1. Release fuel system pressure as outlined under "Precautions."
2. Remove timing belt as outlined under "Timing Belt, Replace."
3. Remove water pump as outlined under "Water Pump, Replace."
4. Remove front case, oil pan and oil pump in numbered sequence shown in **Fig. 25**, marking alignment marks on outer and inner oil pump rotors for reassembly.

INSPECTION

1. Inspect oil pump rotor tip clearance and ensure a 0.0024–0.0071 inch clearance exists, **Fig. 26**.
2. Inspect oil pump rotor side clearance and ensure a 0.0016–0.0039 inch clearance exists, **Fig. 27**.
3. Inspect oil pump body clearance and ensure a 0.0039–0.0071 inch clearance exists, **Fig. 28**.

INSTALLATION

Reverse numbered sequence shown in **Fig. 25** to install, noting the following:
1. Apply engine oil to oil pump rotors.
2. Install oil pump rotors into pump body, aligning marks made during disassembly.
3. Apply sealant to oil pump case cover.
4. Install seal into oil pump case using seal installer tool No. MD998717-01, or equivalent.

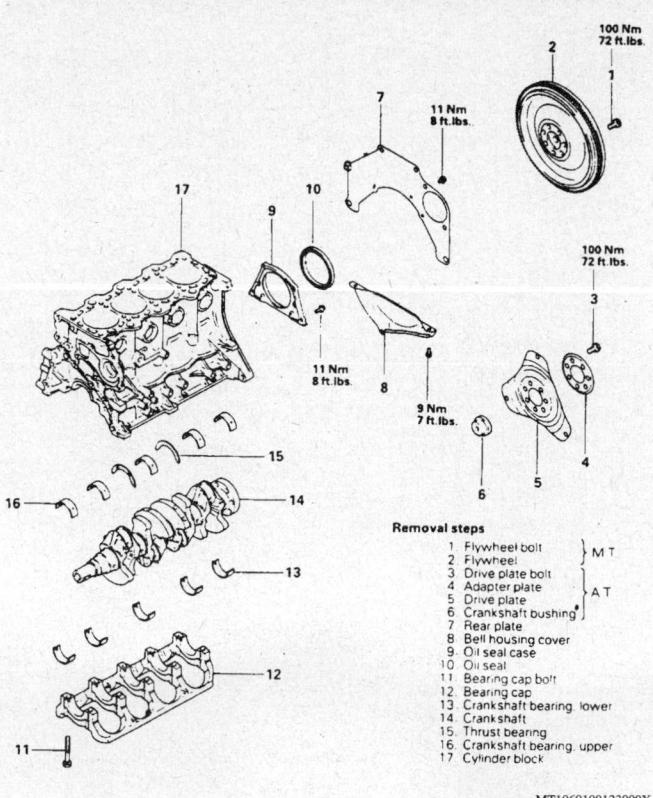

100 Nm 72 ft.lbs.
11 Nm 8 ft.lbs.
11 Nm 8 ft.lbs.
100 Nm 72 ft.lbs.
9 Nm 7 ft.lbs.
14 Nm 11 ft.lbs.

Removal steps

1. Flywheel bolt } M T
2. Flywheel
3. Drive plate bolt
4. Adapter plate } A T
5. Drive plate
6. Crankshaft bushing
7. Rear plate
8. Bell housing cover
9. Oil seal case
10. Oil seal
11. Bearing cap bolt
12. Bearing cap
13. Crankshaft bearing, lower
14. Crankshaft
15. Thrust bearing
16. Crankshaft bearing, upper
17. Cylinder block

MT1069100123000X

Fig. 24 Exploded view of crankshaft

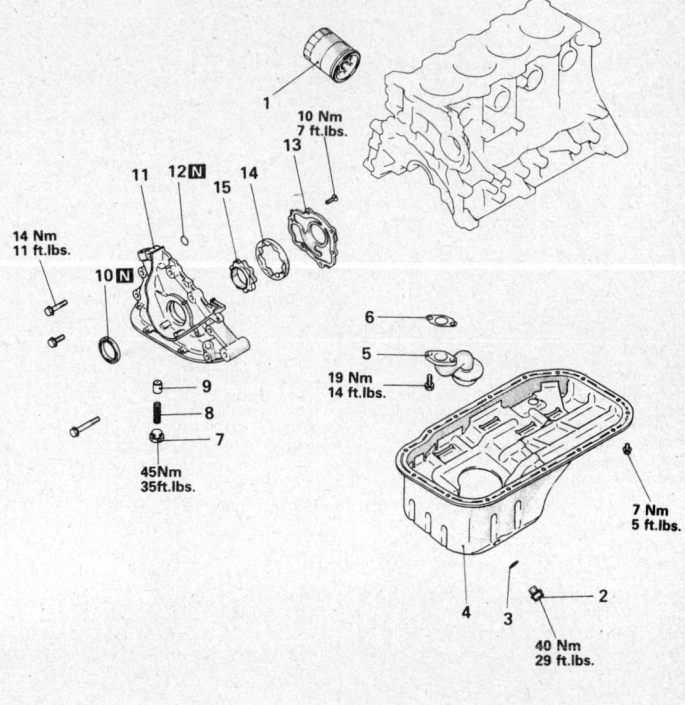

10 Nm 7 ft.lbs.
10 N
45Nm 35ft.lbs.
19 Nm 14 ft.lbs.
40 Nm 29 ft.lbs.
7 Nm 5 ft.lbs.

Removal steps

1. Oil filter
2. Drain plug
3. Drain plug gasket
4. Oil pan
5. Oil screen
6. Oil screen gasket
7. Relief plug
8. Relief spring
9. Relief plunger
10. Oil seal
11. Oil pump case
12. O-ring
13. Oil pump case cover
14. Outer rotor
15. Inner rotor

MT1099100039000X

Fig. 25 Exploded view of front case & oil pump

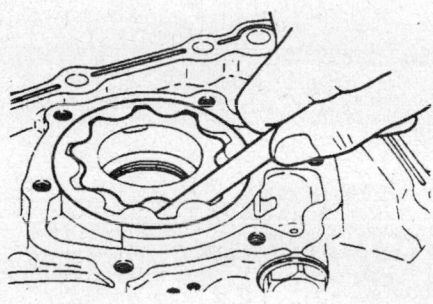

MT1099100040000X

Fig. 26 Rotor tip clearance inspection

5. Apply a 0.16 inch diameter bead of sealant to oil pan flange as shown, **Fig. 29.**

BELT TENSION DATA

Belt	Deflection At 22 Lbs.	
	New, Inches	Used, Inches①
Alt.	0.280–0.340	0.370
A/C	0.217–0.236	0.268–0.299
Power Steering	0.295–0.354	0.374–0.453

① — Belt used for 5 minutes or more.

COOLING SYSTEM BLEED

1. Remove air bleed bolt from on top of thermostat housing, **Fig. 30.**

2. Fill coolant system through air bleed bolt hole until full.
3. Install air bleed bolt.
4. Slowly pour coolant into radiator until radiator is full and fill reservoir tank to FULL line.
5. Install radiator cap, start engine and allow to idle.
6. After thermostat has opened, perform 3000 RPM racing three times.
7. Stop engine and allow to cool completely. **Failure to allow engine to fully cool may result in personal injury.**
8. Open radiator cap, if coolant level has dropped repeat Steps 4 through 8.
9. Replace radiator cap and check for coolant system leaks.

THERMOSTAT
REPLACE

1. Drain coolant into an approved container.
2. Disconnect upper radiator hose from thermostat housing.
3. Remove thermostat housing.
4. Install thermostat with jiggle valve at top, **Fig. 31.**

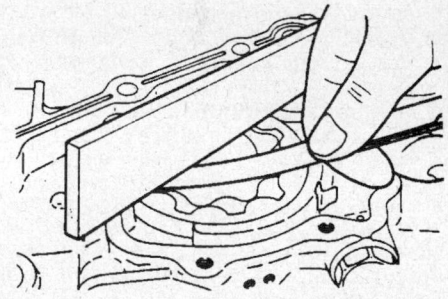

MT1099100041000X

Fig. 27 Rotor side clearance inspection

5. Reverse procedure to install, bleeding coolant system after installation is complete.

WATER PUMP
REPLACE

1. Remove timing belt as outlined under "Timing Belt, Replace."
2. Remove timing belt rear cover.
3. Remove water pump mounting bolts, then water pump, **Fig. 32.**

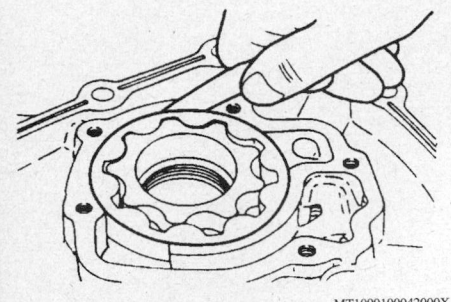

Fig. 28 Body clearance inspection

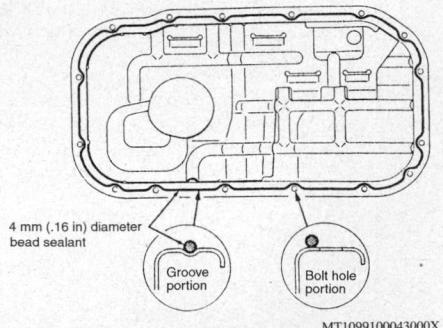

4 mm (.16 in) diameter bead sealant
Groove portion
Bolt hole portion

Fig. 29 Oil pan sealant location

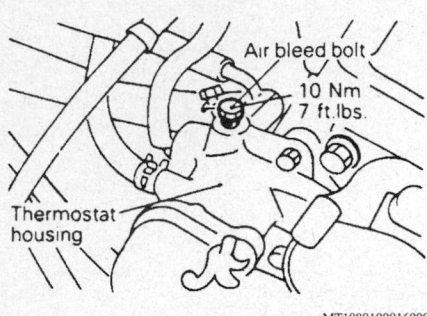

Air bleed bolt
10 Nm
7 ft.lbs.
Thermostat housing

Fig. 30 Cooling system air bleed bolt

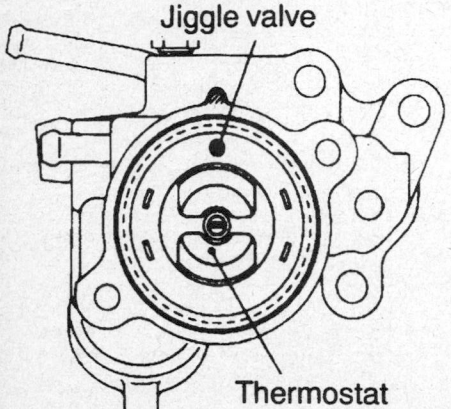

Jiggle valve

Thermostat

Fig. 31 Thermostat replacement

4. Reverse procedure to install, noting bolt length position shown in **Fig. 33.**

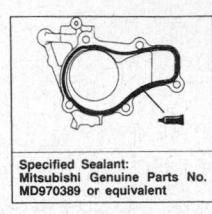

Specified Sealant: Mitsubishi Genuine Parts No. MD970389 or equivalent

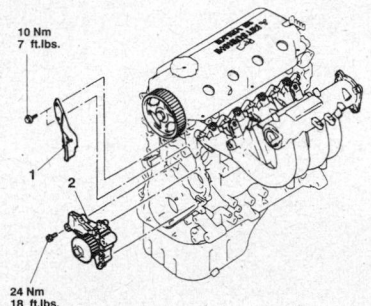

10 Nm
7 ft.lbs.

24 Nm
18 ft.lbs.

Removal steps
1. Timing belt rear cover
2. Water pump

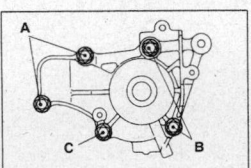

INSTALLATION SERVICE POINT

►A◄ **WATER PUMP INSTALLATION**

Water pump installation bolt size are different. Do not confuse them.

	Up to 1993 models	From 1994 models
A	8 × 20 (.31 × .79)	8 × 20 (.31 × .79)
B	8 × 35 (.31 × 1.38)	8 × 35 (.31 × 1.38)
C	8 × 35 (.31 × 1.38)	8 × 20 (.31 × .79)

Bolt diameter×length: mm (in.)

Fig. 32 Water pump replacement

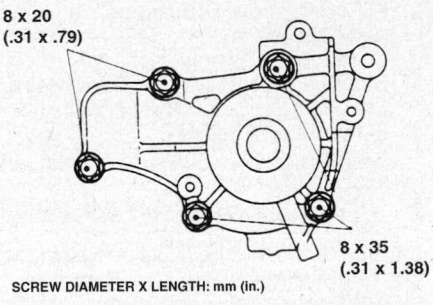

8 x 20
(.31 x .79)

8 x 35
(.31 x 1.38)

SCREW DIAMETER X LENGTH: mm (in.)

Fig. 33 Water pump bolt installation

RADIATOR
REPLACE

1. Drain engine coolant, then remove drain plug and radiator cap.
2. Remove overflow tube and reserve tank, then upper and lower radiator hoses.
3. **On models equipped with automatic transaxle,** remove ATF cooler hose, then plug hose and radiator nipple.
4. **On models equipped with air conditioning,** disconnect condenser fan connector.
5. **On all models,** disconnect radiator fan connector, then remove upper insulator and radiator assembly.
6. Remove resistor.
7. **On models equipped with air conditioning,** remove condenser fan motor assembly.
8. **On all models,** remove radiator fan motor assembly.
9. Remove lower insulator, fan, radiator fan motor and shroud.
10. Reverse procedure to install.

FUEL PUMP
REPLACE

This procedure has been revised by a Technical Service Bulletin.
1. Release fuel system pressure as outlined under "Precautions."
2. Remove fuel cap, then drain fuel tank into a suitable container.
3. Disconnect return, high pressure, vapor and filler hoses.
4. Disconnect fuel gauge unit and electric fuel pump electrical connections.
5. **On AWD models,** remove rear propeller shaft.
6. **On all models,** support fuel tank and remove fuel tank supports.
7. Lower fuel tank from vehicle.
8. Remove fuel pump from fuel tank.
9. Reverse procedure to install.

FUEL FILTER
REPLACE

This procedure has been revised by a Technical Service Bulletin.
1. Release fuel system pressure as outlined under "Precautions."
2. Remove air cleaner and intake hose.
3. Holding fuel filter with a spanner, remove eye bolt and high-pressure fuel hose. **As there will be some pressure remaining in fuel pipe line, cover it with a rag to prevent fuel from spraying out.**
4. Loosen flare nut then disconnect fuel main pipe connection.
5. Remove fuel filter, **Figs. 34 and 35.**
6. Reverse procedure to install.

TECHNICAL SERVICE BULLETINS
FUEL STARVATION

Fuel starvation can occur when in-tank fuel filter is clogged, typically by contaminated fuel.

To correct problem, proceed as follows:

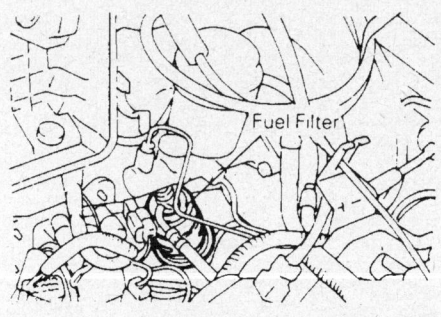

Fig. 34 Fuel filter location

1. Activate fuel pump with scan tool, then measure pump's supply voltage.
2. If voltage is less than 8 volts, inspect and repair fuel pump wiring harness.
3. If voltage is 8 volts or more, check system fuel pressure.
4. If system fuel pressure is within specifications, check system for other starvation problems. Specification is 38 psi at curb idle with fuel pressure regulator vacuum hose attached and 47–50 psi with hose disconnected.
5. If fuel system pressure is not within

specifications, remove fuel pump as described in "Fuel Pump, Replace" and check filter.
6. If filter is clean, replace fuel pump. If filter is clogged, proceed as follows:
   a. Carefully dislodge pump motor from bracket. On some models it may be necessary to remove lower bracket clamp to dislodge motor.
   b. Remove rubber pump vibration dampener, then retaining clip (or nut) and filter.
   c. Replace filter.
   d. **If filter is severely clogged, clean inside of fuel tank.**
7. Reverse procedure to install using new gasket.

IDLE VIBRATION

Some models (mostly equipped with automatic transaxles) may vibrate excessively at idle.

Radiator may be transmitting engine vibration through frame because mounting brackets are not centered on posts. To correct problem, proceed as follows:
1. Examine upper radiator mounting brackets. Brackets should be centered on post and radiator should move freely.

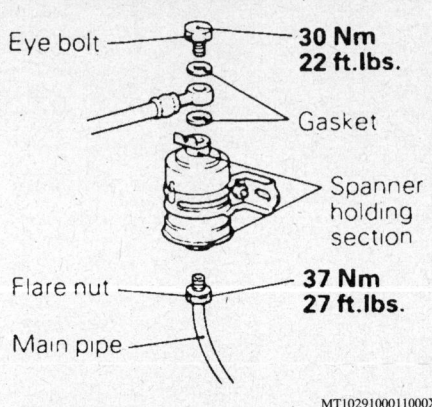

Fig. 35 Fuel filter installation

2. If brackets are not center, remove upper brackets and ensure bottom mounting posts are seating in lower brackets.
3. Center upper brackets over posts and tighten bolts to specifications.
4. Measure clearance between upper brackets and radiator top. Standard clearance is .0394 inch or more.

TIGHTENING SPECIFICATIONS

Year	Component	Torque, Ft. Lbs.
1996	Adjusting Screw Locknut	7
	Alternator Brace Bolt	17
	Alternator Brace Mounting Bolt	36
	Alternator Pivot Nut	33
	Bellhousing Cover Mounting Bolt	7
	Camshaft Sprocket Bolt	65
	Connecting Rod Cap Nut	②
	Crankshaft Bearing Cap Bolt	③
	Crankshaft Bolt	134
	Cylinder Head Bolt	①
	Distributor Mounting Nut	9
	Driveplate Bolt	72
	EGR Temperature Sensor (California)	8
	EGR Valve Mounting Bolt (California)	9
	Engine Coolant Temperature Gauge Unit	8
	Engine Coolant Temperature Sensor	22
	Engine Hanger Mounting Bolt	9
	Engine Support Bracket Left Mounting Bolt	36
	Exhaust Manifold Bracket Mounting Bolt	26
	Exhaust Manifold Cover "A" Mounting Bolt	22
	Exhaust Manifold Cover "B" Mounting Bolt	17
	Exhaust Manifold Mounting Nut	22
	Flywheel Bolt	72
	Fuel Delivery Pipe Mounting Bolt	9
	Fuel High Pressure Hose Union	25
	Fuel Pressure Regulator Bolt	7
	Fuel Pump Nut	1.8

Continued

TIGHTENING
SPECIFICATIONS—Continued

Year	Component	Torque, Ft. Lbs.
1996	Fuel Tank Drain Bolt	4
	Fuel Tank Mounting Nut	17
	Intake Manifold Mounting Bolt	14.5
	Intake Manifold Mounting Nut	14.5
	Intake Manifold Stay Mounting Bolt	22
	Oil Drain Plug	29
	Oil Level Gauge Guide Mounting Bolt	8
	Oil Pan Mounting Bolt	5
	Oil Pressure Switch	7
	Oil Pump Case Mounting Bolt	11
	Oil Screen	14
	Oil Seal Case Mounting Bolt	8
	Oxygen Sensor	33
	Rear Plate Mounting Bolt	8
	Relief Plug	35
	Rocker Arm Shaft Mounting Bolt	23
	Rocker Cover Mounting Bolt	2.4
	Spark Plug	18
	Thermostat Housing Mounting Bolt	18
	Throttle Body Mounting Bolt	14
	Throttle Position Sensor Bolt	1.4
	Timing Belt Cover Mounting Bolt	7
	Timing Belt Tensioner Bolt	18
	Timing Belt Tensioner Spring Bolt	33
	Water Outlet Fitting Mounting Bolt	14
	Water Pipe Mounting Bolt	10
	Water Pump Mounting Bolt	18

① — Refer to "Cylinder Head, Replace" for procedure.

② — 14.5 ft. lbs., then tighten an additional 90° (1/4 turn).

③ — 18 ft. lbs. then tighten an additional 90° (1/4 turn).

2.4L Engine

> **NOTE:** On Air Bag Equipped Models, Refer To "Air Bag System Precautions" Located In Front Of This Manual For System Disarming & Arming Procedures.

> **NOTE:** Prior To Performing Any Service Operations Listed In This Section, Consult The "Technical Service Bulletins" Section For Related Information.

INDEX

PRECAUTIONS

AIR BAG SYSTEMS

Refer to "Air Bag System Precautions" in front of this manual for system disarming and arming procedures.

BATTERY GROUND CABLE

Prior to service, disconnect battery ground cable and isolate as required.

FUEL SYSTEM PRESSURE RELIEF

1. Remove grommet below floor and disconnect fuel pump connector.
2. Start engine and allow engine to runout of fuel.
3. Crank engine two or three times to release remaining fuel pressure.
4. Place ignition switch to Off position.
5. After fuel system repairs are completed, connect fuel pump electrical connections.

COMPRESSION PRESSURE

Ensure engine oil, starter motor and battery are in satisfactory condition. When checking compression, engine coolant should be at normal operating temperature, spark plugs should be removed and throttle valve should be wide open. Correct com-

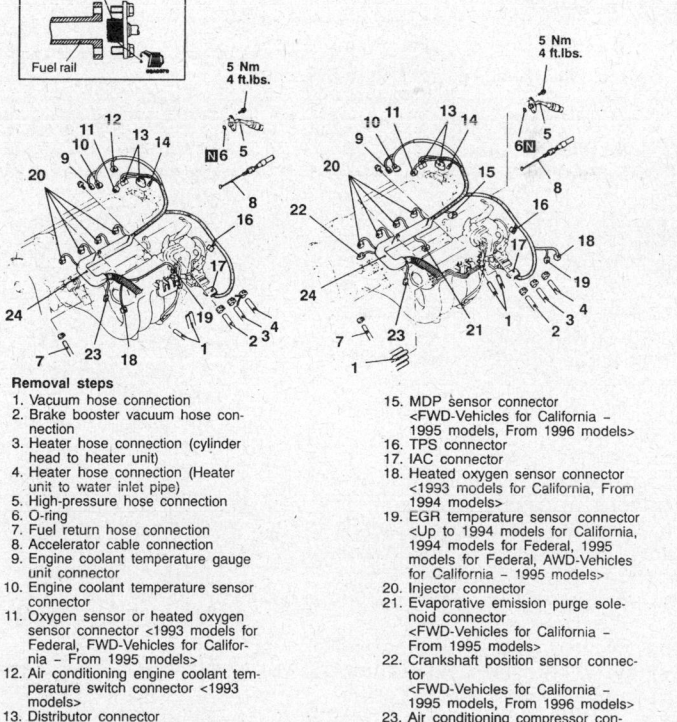

Removal steps
1. Vacuum hose connection
2. Brake booster vacuum hose connection
3. Heater hose connection (cylinder head to heater unit)
4. Heater hose connection (Heater unit to water inlet pipe)
5. High-pressure hose connection
6. O-ring
7. Fuel return hose connection
8. Accelerator cable connection
9. Engine coolant temperature gauge unit connector
10. Engine coolant temperature sensor connector
11. Oxygen sensor or heated oxygen sensor connector <1993 models for Federal, FWD-Vehicles for California – From 1995 models>
12. Air conditioning engine coolant temperature switch connector <1993 models>
13. Distributor connector
14. Capacitor connector

15. MDP sensor connector <FWD-Vehicles for California – 1995 models, From 1996 models>
16. TPS connector
17. IAC connector
18. Heated oxygen sensor connector <1993 models for California, From 1994 models>
19. EGR temperature sensor connector <Up to 1994 models for California, 1994 models for Federal, 1995 models for Federal, AWD-Vehicles for California – 1995 models>
20. Injector connector
21. Evaporative emission purge solenoid connector <FWD-Vehicles for California – From 1995 models>
22. Crankshaft position sensor connector <FWD-Vehicles for California – 1995 models, From 1996 models>
23. Air conditioning compressor connector
24. Control harness

MT1069100125010X

Fig. 1 Engine removal (Part 1 of 2)

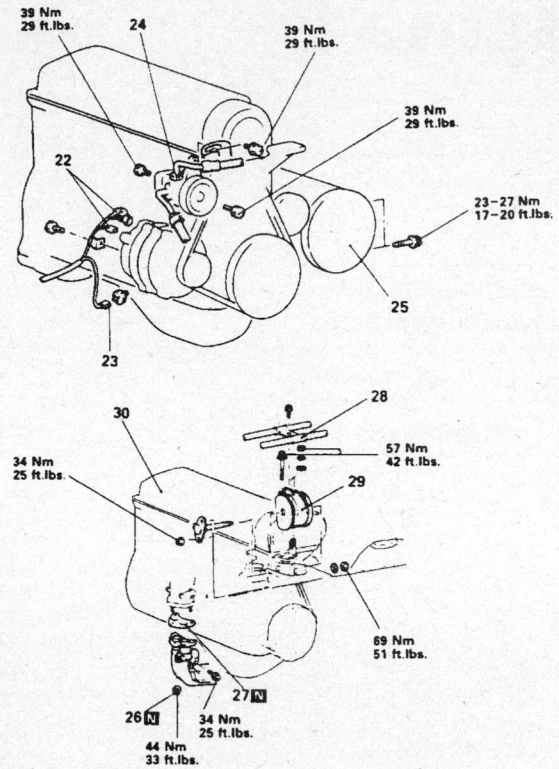

39 Nm
29 ft.lbs.

39 Nm
29 ft.lbs.

39 Nm
29 ft.lbs.

23–27 Nm
17–20 ft.lbs.

34 Nm
25 ft.lbs.

57 Nm
42 ft.lbs.

69 Nm
51 ft.lbs.

34 Nm
25 ft.lbs.

44 Nm
33 ft.lbs.

Removal steps

22 Connection for generator
23 Connection for oil pressure switch
● Drive belt tension adjustment

24 Power steering oil pump
25 Air conditioning compressor
26 Self-locking nuts
27 Gasket
28 Clamp of pressure hose (Power steering)
  and high pressure hose (Air conditioning)
29 Engine mount bracket
30 Engine assembly

MT1069100125020X

Fig. 1 Engine removal (Part 2 of 2)

Fuel rail

5 Nm
4 ft.lbs.

10 Nm
7 ft.lbs.

Engine oil

1. Air intake hose
2. Accelerator cable connection
3. Brake booster vacuum hose connection
4. Vacuum pipe and hose assembly connection
5. Water hose connection
6. High-pressure fuel hose connection
7. O-ring
8. PCV hose
9. Vacuum hose connection
10. Fuel return hose connection

MT1059300018010X

Fig. 2 Intake manifold removal (Part 1 of 2)

pression pressures at engine cranking speed is 139 psi minimum. Difference between cylinders should not exceed 14 psi.

ENGINE

REPLACE

1. Release fuel system pressure as outlined under "Precautions."
2. Mark hood hinge bolt location on hood, then remove hood.
3. Drain cooling system into a suitable container.
4. Remove radiator assembly.
5. Remove transaxle assembly as outlined under "Transaxle, Replace" in "Clutch & Manual Transaxle" section for models with manual transaxle or in "Automatic Transaxle" unit repair section for models with automatic transaxle.
6. Remove power steering pump and air conditioner compressor without disconnecting hoses, then support aside.
7. Remove engine assembly in numbered sequence shown in **Fig. 1**, noting the following:
   a. **On FWD models,** set engine hanger tool No. MB991191, or equivalent, on body to support engine assembly. **Always insert a piece**

of wood between engine hanger assembly and front deck, ensuring not to pinch hood weatherstrip.
   b. **On FWD models,** remove center member mounting bolt.
   c. **On AWD models,** when transaxle assembly is removed, center member assembly has also been removed.
   d. **On all models,** support engine using a floor jack and remove engine hanger assembly.
   e. Support engine using a chain and suitable engine lifting device.
   f. Raise engine slightly to remove weight off mounts then remove engine mounts.
   g. Ensure all electrical and hose connections are disconnected then raise engine assembly out of vehicle.
   h. **Always insert a piece of wood between engine hanger assembly and front deck. Also, do not pinch hood weatherstrip between front deck and piece of wood.**
8. Reverse procedure to install, noting the following:
   a. Using a floor jack and a piece of

wood, support engine on oil pan then install engine mount bracket while adjusting position of engine.
   b. Remove engine lifting device as allow engine hanger tool to support engine until transaxle is installed.

INTAKE MANIFOLD

REPLACE

1. Release fuel system pressure as outlined under "Precautions."
2. Drain cooling system into an approved container.
3. Remove intake manifold in numbered sequence shown in **Fig.2**, removing fuel delivery pipe but leaving injectors and pressure regulator intact. **Do not drop injector when removing delivery pipe.**
4. Reverse procedure to install.

EXHAUST MANIFOLD

REPLACE

1. Replace exhaust manifold in numbered sequence shown in **Fig. 3**.
2. Reverse procedure to install.

CYLINDER HEAD

REPLACE

This procedure has been revised by a technical service bulletin.

1. Release fuel system pressure as outlined under "Precautions."
2. Drain cooling system into an approved container.
3. Remove cylinder head and gasket in

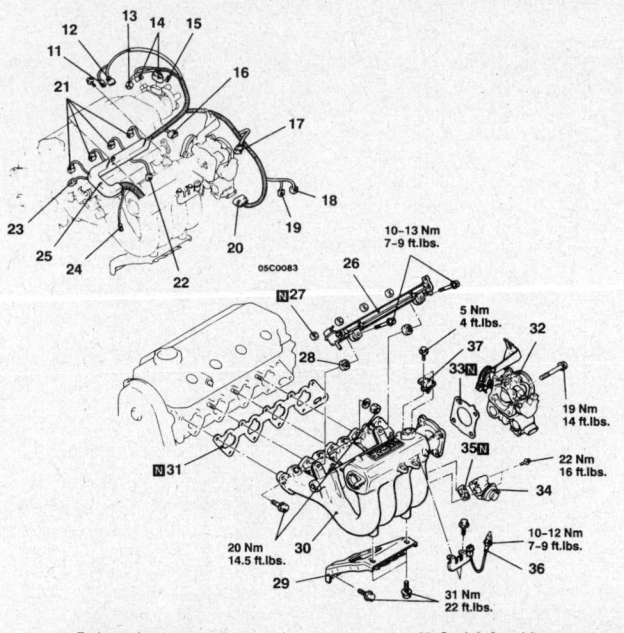

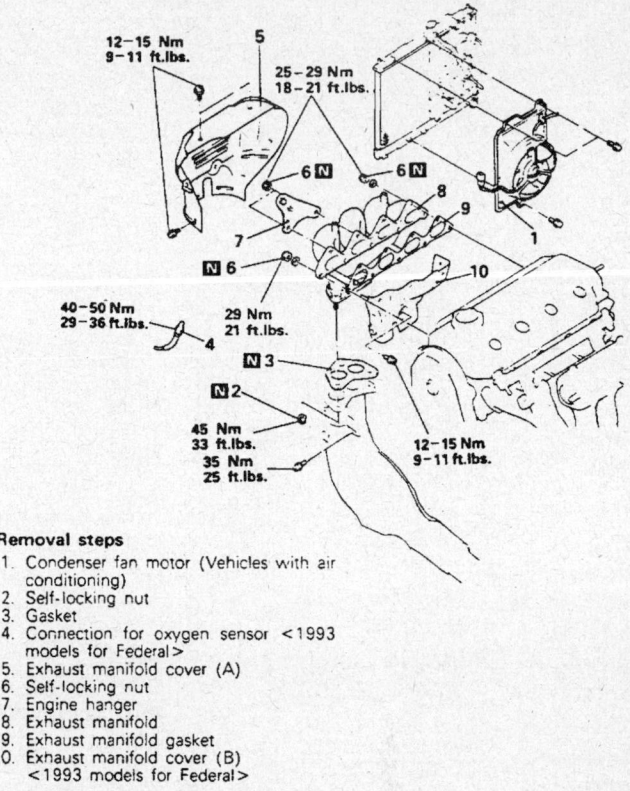

Removal steps

1. Condenser fan motor (Vehicles with air conditioning)
2. Self-locking nut
3. Gasket
4. Connection for oxygen sensor <1993 models for Federal>
5. Exhaust manifold cover (A)
6. Self-locking nut
7. Engine hanger
8. Exhaust manifold
9. Exhaust manifold gasket
10. Exhaust manifold cover (B) <1993 models for Federal>

MT1079300010000X

Fig. 3 Exhaust manifold removal

11. Engine coolant temperature gauge unit connector	23. Crankshaft posisiton sensor connector <FWD-vehicles for California – 1995 models, From 1996 models>
12. Engine coolant temperature sensor connector	24. Air conditioning compressor connector
13. Heated oxygen sensor connector <FWD-Vehicles for California>	25. Control harness
14. Distributor connector	26. Fuel rail, fuel injector and pressure regulator
15. Capacitor connector	27. Insulator
16. MDP sensor connector <FWD-vehicles for California – 1995 models, From 1996 models>	28. Insulator
17. TPS connector	29. Intake manifold stay
18. Heated oxygen sensor connector	30. Intake manifold
19. EGR temperature sensor connector <Except FWD-vehicles for California – 1995 models, From 1996 models>	31. Intake manifold gasket
20. IAC connector	32. Throttle body
21. Injector connector	33. Throttle body gasket
22. Solenoid valve connector <FWD-vehicles for California – 1995 models, From 1996 models>	34. EGR valve
	35. EGR gasket
	36. EGR temperature sensor <Except FWD-vehicles for California – 1995 models, From 1996 models>
	37. MDP sensor <FWD-vehicles for California – 1995 models, From 1996 models>

MT1059300018020X

Fig. 2 Intake manifold removal (Part 2 of 2)

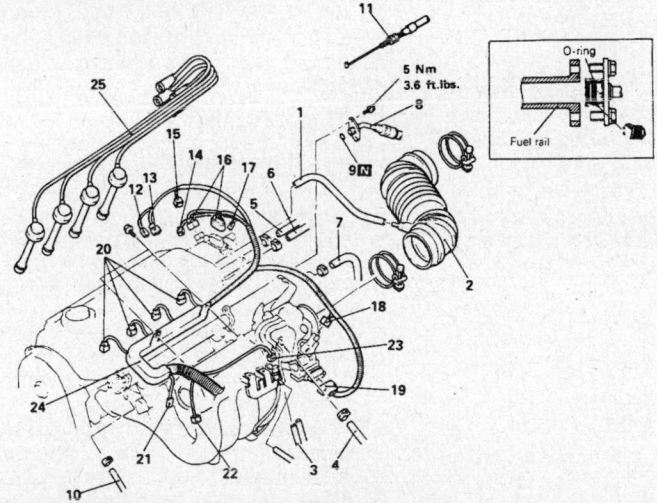

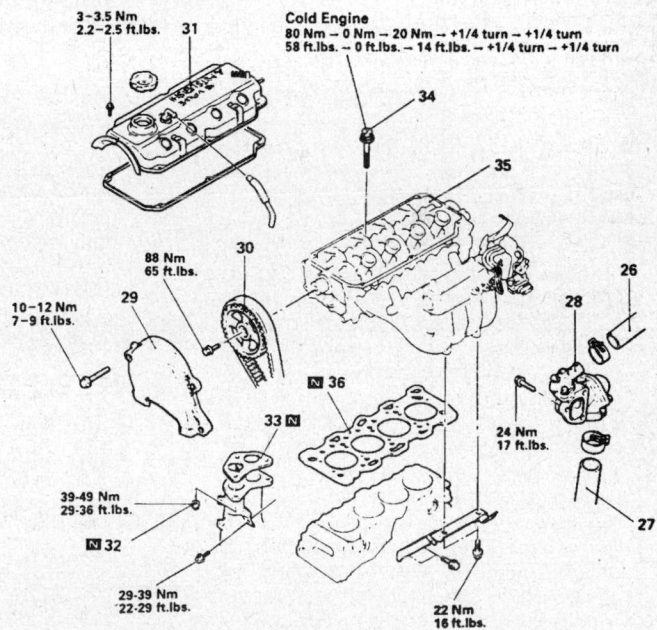

Removal steps

1. Breather hose
2. Air intake hose
3. Vacuum hose connection
4. Brake booster vacuum hose connection
5. Water hose connection (cylinder head → throttle body)
6. Heater hose connection (cylinder head → heater unit)
7. Water hose connection (throttle body → water inlet pipe)
8. Fuel high pressure hose connection
9. O-ring
10. Fuel return hose connection
11. Accelerator cable connection
12. Engine coolant temperature gauge unit connector
13. Engine coolant temperature sensor connector

14. Oxygen sensor connector <1993 models for Federal>
15. Air conditioning engine coolant temperature switch connector <1993 models>
16. Distributor connector
17. Condenser connector
18. TPS connector
19. IAC connector
20. Injector connector
21. Air conditioning compressor connector
22. Oxygen sensor connector <1993 models for California, From 1994 models>
23. EGR temperature sensor connector <1993 models for California, From 1994 models>
24. Control harness
25. Spark plug cable

26. Connection for radiator upper hose
27. Connection for radiator lower hose
28. Water inlet fitting, thermostat and thermostat case assembly
29. Timing belt upper cover
30. Camshaft sprocket
31. Rocker cover
32. Self-locking nuts
33. Gasket
34. Cylinder head bolt
35. Cylinder head assembly
36. Cylinder head gasket

MT1069100127020X

MT1069100127010X

Fig. 4 Cylinder head & gasket removal (Part 1 of 2)

Fig. 4 Cylinder head & gasket removal (Part 2 of 2)

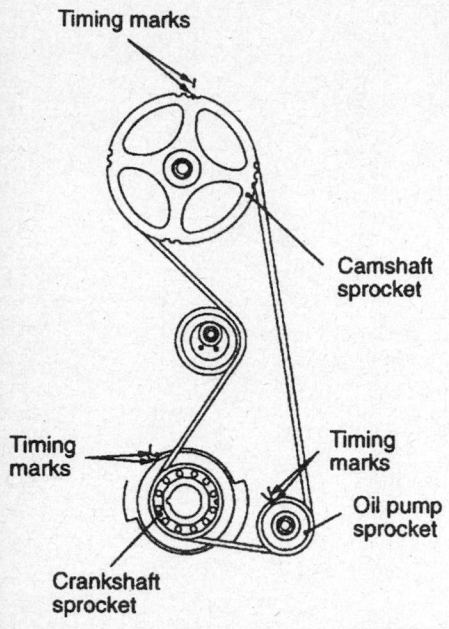

Fig. 5   Timing belt alignment marks

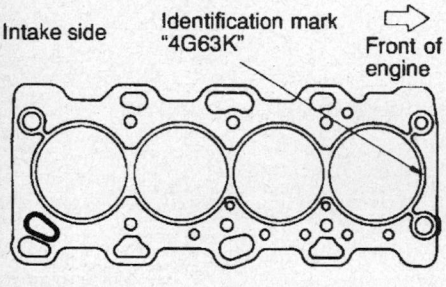

Fig. 8   Cylinder head gasket identification mark

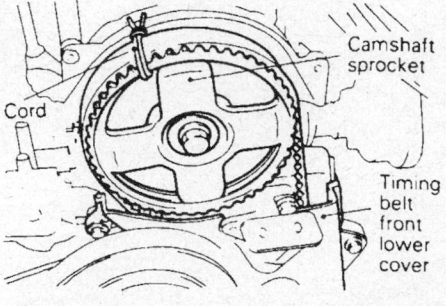

Fig. 6   Timing belt & camshaft sprocket

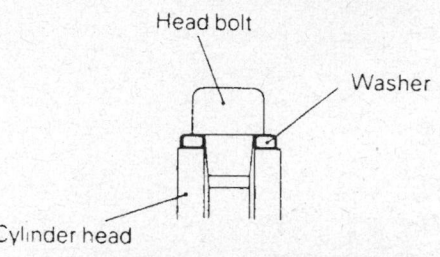

Fig. 9   Cylinder head bolt washer installation

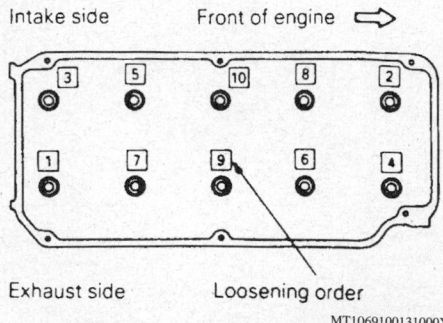

Fig. 7   Cylinder head bolt loosening sequence

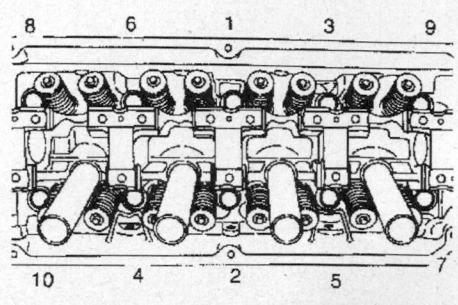

Fig. 10   Cylinder head bolt tightening sequence

numbered sequence shown in **Fig. 4**, noting the following:

a. Place a wooden block against engine oil pan and on a suitable floor jack, then raise engine to remove weight from engine mount.

b. Remove engine mount bracket.

c. Rotate engine so No. 1 cylinder is at top dead center on compression stroke and align camshaft timing mark, **Fig. 5**.

d. Tie camshaft sprocket and timing belt together so that position of camshaft sprocket will not move with respect to timing belt, **Fig. 6**.

e. Remove camshaft sprocket as outlined under "Timing Belt, Replace."

f. Loosen cylinder head bolts in two or three steps in numbered sequence shown in **Fig. 7**.

4. Inspect cylinder head gasket surface for flatness by using a straightedge.

5. Reverse procedure to install, noting the following:

a. Clean cylinder gasket surface on both cylinder head and engine block.

b. Place cylinder head gasket on cyl-

inder block with identification mark facing upward, **Fig. 8**. Cylinder **head gasket must be installed with identification mark properly positioned for oil passage hole alignment.**

c. Apply a small amount of oil to cylinder head bolt threads and to bolt washer. **Ensure cylinder head bolt is installed as shown in Fig. 9.**

d. **Torque** bolts to 58 ft. lbs., using sequence, **Fig. 10**. Completely loosen bolts and **torque** bolts to 14 ft. lbs. in sequence. Turn bolts 90° (¼ turn), then turn bolts an additional 90° (¼ turn).

VALVE ARRANGEMENT
FRONT TO REAR

I-E-E-I-I-E-E-I

VALVE CLEARANCE SPECIFICATIONS

Valve stem to guide clearance with engine cool is .0008–.0020 inch for intake valves and .0020–.0035 inch for exhaust valves.

VALVE ADJUSTMENT

These engines use hydraulic auto-lash adjusters. No adjustments are required.

ROCKER ARMS
REPLACE
REMOVAL

1. Release fuel system pressure as outlined under "Precautions."

2. Remove timing belt as outlined under "Timing Belt, Replace."

3. Replace camshaft, camshaft oil seal, rocker arms and rocker arm shafts in numbered sequence shown in **Fig. 11**, installing auto-lash adjuster holder tool No. MD998443, or equivalent, prior to removal of rocker arm and rocker shaft assembly, to ensure auto-lash adjuster is not allowed to fall.

INSTALLATION

1. Bleed auto-lash adjuster as follows:

a. Immerse lash adjuster in clean diesel fuel.

b. While lightly pushing down inner steel ball with a small wire, move plunger up and down several times to bleed air.

c. Remove small wire and press plunger. If plunger is hard to depress, lash adjuster is operating normal, proceed to Step e.

d. If plunger can be easily depressed, repeat Steps a through c. If plunger is still loose, replace lash adjuster.

e. **After bleeding hold adjuster upright to prevent diesel fuel from spilling out,** set lash adjuster on leak down tester, tool No. MD998440, or equivalent.

f. After plunger has depressed 0.008–0.020 inch, measure time taken for plunger to drop an additional 0.04 inch. If plunger drops 0.04 inch in 4–20 seconds, lash adjuster is operating correctly.

2. Reverse numbered sequence shown in **Fig. 11** to complete installation, noting the following:

a. Insert rocker arm shaft into front

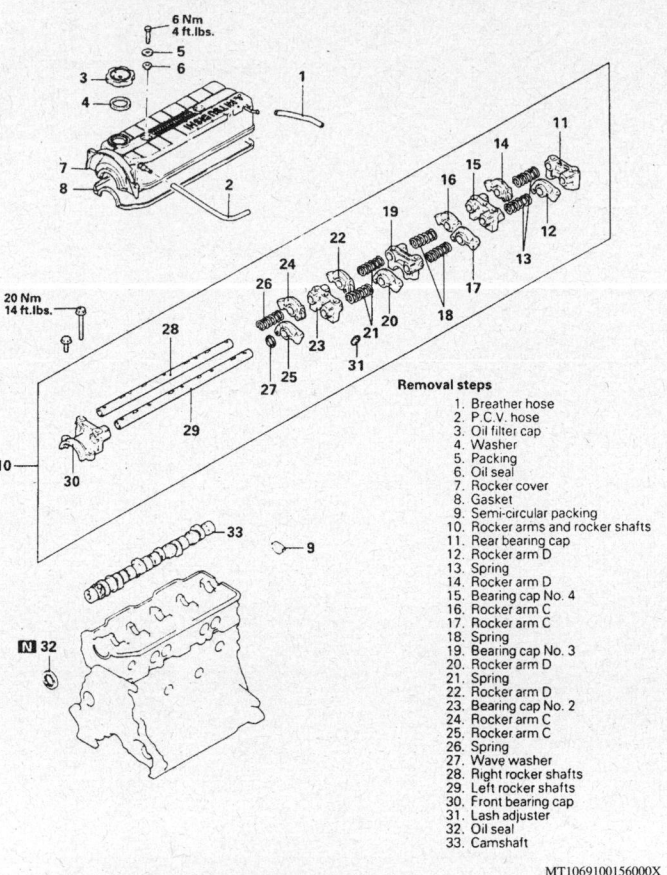

Removal steps

1. Breather hose
2. P.C.V. hose
3. Oil filter cap
4. Washer
5. Packing
6. Oil seal
7. Rocker cover
8. Gasket
9. Semi-circular packing
10. Rocker arms and rocker shafts
11. Rear bearing cap
12. Rocker arm D
13. Spring
14. Rocker arm D
15. Bearing cap No. 4
16. Rocker arm C
17. Rocker arm C
18. Spring
19. Bearing cap No. 3
20. Rocker arm D
21. Spring
22. Rocker arm D
23. Bearing cap No. 2
24. Rocker arm C
25. Rocker arm C
26. Spring
27. Wave washer
28. Right rocker shafts
29. Left rocker shafts
30. Front bearing cap
31. Lash adjuster
32. Oil seal
33. Camshaft

MT1069100156000X

Fig. 11 Exploded view of rocker arms & camshaft

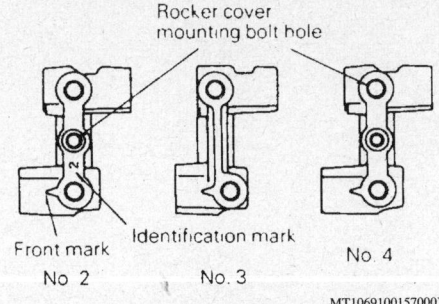

Fig. 12 Camshaft bearing caps identification

MT1069100157000X

bearing cap so notch on shaft faces up. Do not tighten at this time.

b. Install wave washer with raise side toward front bearing cap.

c. Install rocker arm marked "1-3" for cylinders 1 and 3 and rockers marked "2-4" for cylinders 2 and 4.

d. Identify bearing caps 2, 3 and 4 as shown in **Fig. 12**.

e. Install bearing caps with front marks pointing to camshaft sprocket side of engine.

f. Bleed auto-lash adjuster as outlined under Step 1, then insert adjuster into rocker arm securing with lash adjuster holder, tool No. MD998443-01, or equivalent.

g. Install camshaft oil seal using seal installation tool Nos. MD998306-01 and MD998307-01, or equivalent.

h. Apply sealant to outer circumference of circular packing then install on cylinder head.

FRONT COVER
REPLACE

Refer to "Oil Pump, Replace" for front cover replacement procedure.

TIMING BELT
REPLACE

With the timing belt removed, avoid turning the camshaft or crankshaft. If movement is required, exercise extreme

caution to avoid valve damage caused by piston contact. **Never rotate engine in a counterclockwise direction or damage to the engine will result.**

REMOVAL

1. Relieve fuel system pressure as described under "Precautions," then remove engine undercover.
2. Raise and support vehicle.
3. Remove left front wheel, then the inner splash shield.
4. Remove coolant reservoir tank, **Fig. 13**.
5. Support engine with suitable jack and wooden block under oil pan, and remove right hand engine mount.
6. Remove alternator and power steering pump drive belts, then tensioner pulley bracket.
7. Remove air conditioning drive belt, then water pump and crankshaft pulleys.

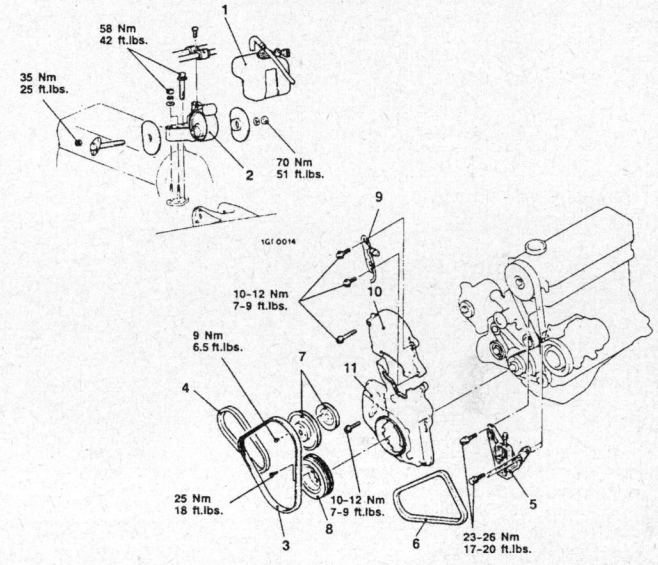

Installation steps

1. Condense tank
2. Engine mount bracket
3. Drive belt (generator)
4. Drive belt (power steering)
5. Tensioner pulley bracket
6. Drive belt (air conditioning)
7. Water pump pulley
8. Crankshaft pulley
9. Crankshaft position sensor bracket <FWD-Vehicles for California – 1995 models>
10. Timing belt front upper cover
11. Timing belt front lower cover

11. Timing belt front lower cover
10. Timing belt front upper cover
9. Crankshaft position sensor bracket <FWD-Vehicles for California – 1995 models>
8. Crankshaft pulley
7. Water pump pulley
6. Drive belt (air conditioning)
5. Tension pulley bracket
4. Drive belt (power steering)
3. Drive belt (generator)
• Drive belt tension adjustment
2. Engine mount bracket
1. Condense tank

MT1069100148000A

Fig. 13 Timing belt replacement

8. **On FWD California models,** remove crankshaft position sensor bracket.
9. **On all models,** remove upper and lower covers.
10. Rotate crankshaft clockwise and align timing marks, then remove auto tensioner, **Fig. 14**.
11. Mark directional rotation on timing belt and remove. **Keep timing belt, sprocket and tensioner free of oil and water; do not wash or lubricate these parts.**
12. Remove tensioner pulley and arm, then idler pulley, **Fig. 15**.
13. Remove camshaft sprocket.

INSTALLATION

1. Install crankshaft sprocket flange with raised side facing out, then install crankshaft sprocket and idle pulley.
2. Measure auto-tensioner plunger protrusion. Protrusion from housing

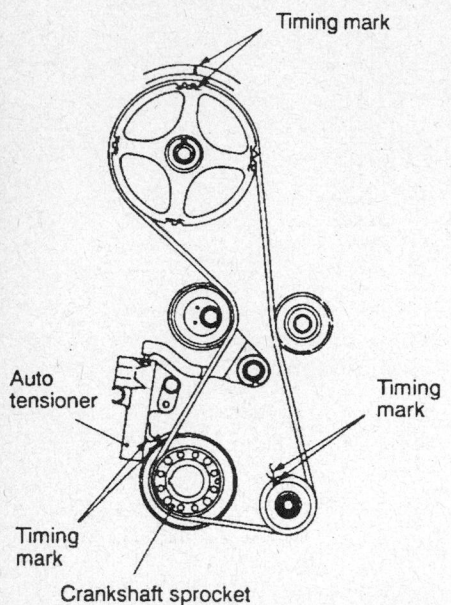

Fig. 14 Timing belt alignment

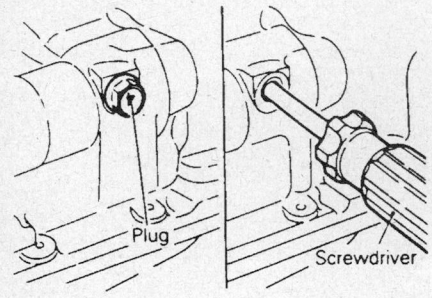

Fig. 16 Silent shaft blocking plug

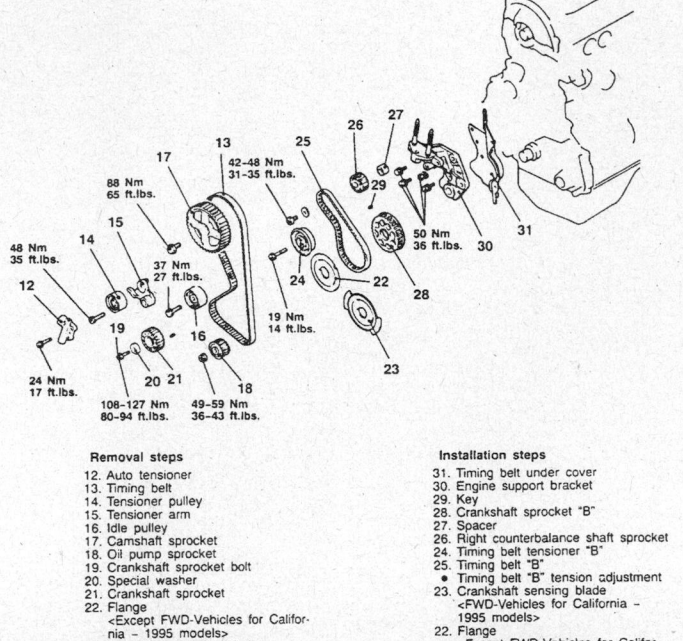

Removal steps
12. Auto tensioner
13. Timing belt
14. Tensioner pulley
15. Tensioner arm
16. Idle pulley
17. Camshaft sprocket
18. Oil pump sprocket
19. Crankshaft sprocket bolt
20. Special washer
21. Crankshaft sprocket
22. Flange
    <Except FWD-Vehicles for California – 1995 models>
23. Crankshaft sensing blade
    <FWD-Vehicles for California – 1995 models>
24. Timing belt tensioner "B"
25. Timing belt "B"
26. Right counterbalance shaft sprocket
27. Spacer
28. Crankshaft sprocket "B"
29. Key
30. Engine support bracket
31. Timing belt under cover

Installation steps
31. Timing belt under cover
30. Engine support bracket
29. Key
28. Crankshaft sprocket "B"
27. Spacer
26. Right counterbalance shaft sprocket
24. Timing belt tensioner "B"
25. Timing belt "B"
 • Timing belt "B" tension adjustment
23. Crankshaft sensing blade
    <FWD-Vehicles for California – 1995 models>
22. Flange
    <Except FWD-Vehicles for California – 1995 models>
21. Crankshaft sprocket
20. Special washer
19. Crankshaft sprocket bolt
18. Oil pump sprocket
17. Camshaft sprocket
16. Idle pulley
12. Auto tensioner
15. Tensioner arm
14. Tensioner pulley
13. Timing belt
 • Timing belt tension adjustment

Fig. 15 Timing & balance shaft replacement

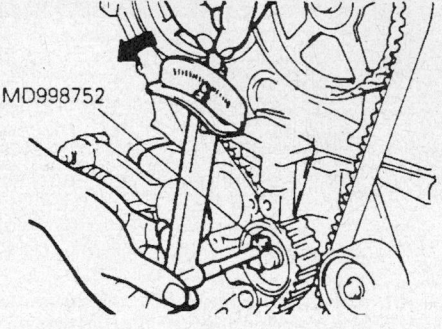

Fig. 17 Timing belt tensioner pulley & adjustment tools

should be .47 inch. If plunger is fully extended, proceed as follows:
 a. Keep auto-tensioner level and place in vice with soft jaws. If plug at bottom protrudes, keep it from touching vice with washer.
 b. Slowly compress plunger with vise pressure until hole in plunger aligns with housing hole.
 c. Hole plunger in place by inserting .055 inch pin or wire through aligned holes.
3. Remove auto-tensioner from vice and install. **Do not remove securing pin or wire.**
4. Install tensioner arm, then install tensioner pulley on arm.
5. Position tensioner pulley shaft pinhole to left of center bolt and finger-tighten bolt.
6. Ensure crankshaft and camshaft timing marks are aligned, **Fig. 14.**
7. With oil pump sprocket timing marks aligned, remove cylinder block plug and insert .31 inch diameter Phillips screwdriver through hole, **Fig. 16.** If screwdriver can be insert 2.4 inches or more, alignment is correct.
8. If screwdriver can only be inserted 0.8–1.0 inch, rotate oil pump sprocket one revolution and realign timing

marks. Ensure screwdriver can be inserted 2.4 inches or more.
9. Ensure oil pump sprocket is properly aligned and leave screwdriver in hole until after timing belt has been installed.
10. Install timing belt around crankshaft and oil pump sprockets, then idler pulley camshaft sprocket and tensioner pulley. **Hold belt so there is no slack on tension side and apply counterclockwise force on camshaft sprocket to aid tension. Ensure all timing marks remain aligned.**
11. Carefully position timing belt tensioner pulley against belt and tighten center bolt.
12. Rotate crankshaft pulley ¼ turn counterclockwise, then turn clockwise and align crankshaft and camshaft timing marks.
13. Loosen tensioner pulley retaining bolt, position special socket tools, **Fig. 17,** and **torque** to 2.6 ft. lbs., then tighten retaining bolt to specifications while holding pulley in position.
14. Install special set screw tool No. MD998738, or equivalent, through left hand engine support bracket, **Fig. 18.** Engine may need to be raised slightly to install set screw tool.
15. Tighten set screw tool until it contacts tensioner arm, then tighten tool slightly more.
16. Remove auto-tensioner retaining pin or wire, then remove set screw tool.
17. Rotate crankshaft clockwise two turns

and allow to sit for 15 minutes, then measure auto-tensioner plunger protrusion from housing dimension "A," **Fig. 19.** Distance should be .15–.18 inch. If not within specifications, adjust belt tension. Install rear cover rubber plug.
18. Install lower and upper covers, **Fig. 20,** and tighten to specifications.
19. **On FWD California models,** install crankshaft position sensor bracket.
20. **On all models,** install crankshaft and water pump pulleys, then tighten bolts to specifications.
21. Install air conditioning drive belt, then tension pulley bracket.
22. Install power steering pump and alternator drive belts, and adjust belt tensions.

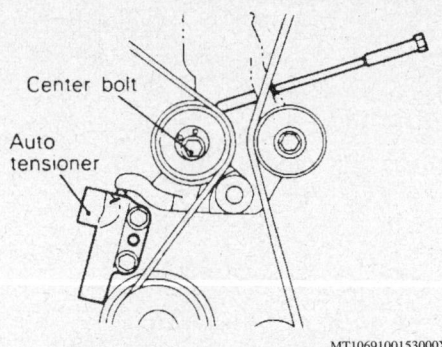

Fig. 18 Timing belt auto tensioner set screw

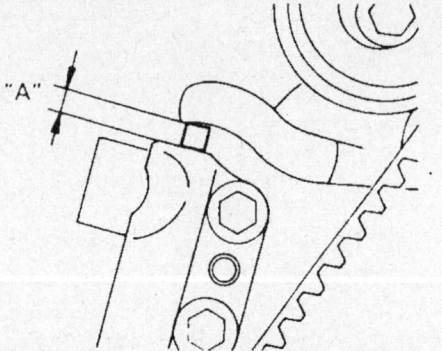

Fig. 19 Auto tensioner protrusion measurement

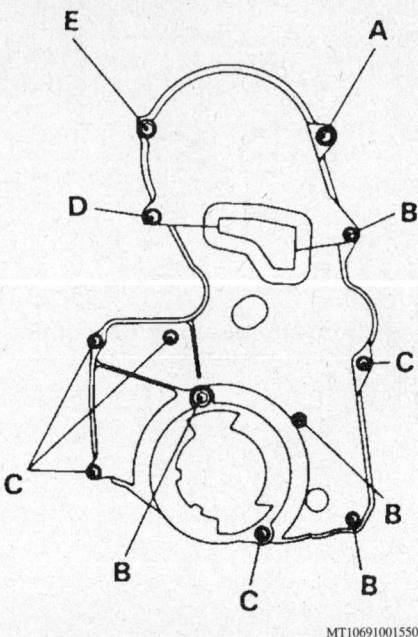

Fig. 20 Timing belt cover bolt locations (Part 1 of 2)

	1993 models	From 1994 models
A	6 × 20 (24 × .78) or 6 × 18 (24× 71)	8 × 28 (31 × 1.10)
B	6 × 22 (24 × 87) or 6 × 25 (24 × .98)	6 × 25 (24 × .98)
C	6 × 18 (24 × 71)	6 × 18 (24 × 71)
D	6 × 28 (24 × 1.10) or 6 × 25 (24 × .98)	8 × 35 (31 × 1.38)
E	6 × 50 (24 × 1.97)	8 × 50 (.31 × 1.97)

Bolt diameter × length   mm(in)

Fig. 20 Timing belt cover bolt locations (Part 2 of 2)

23. Install right hand engine mount and tighten bolts to specifications, then remove jack and wood block.
24. Install engine coolant reservoir and fill to proper lever, then install undercover.
25. Install left inner splash shield, then the wheel.
26. lower vehicle.
27. Check and adjust ignition timing.

CAMSHAFT
REPLACE

Refer to "Rocker Arms, Replace" for camshaft replacement procedure.

BALANCE SHAFT BELT
REPLACE
REMOVAL

1. Remove timing belt as described in "Timing Belt, Replace."
2. Remove cylinder block plug and insert .31 inch diameter Phillips screwdriver through hole to block left balance shaft, **Fig. 16,** then remove oil pump sprocket nut and sprocket.
3. Remove crankshaft sprocket bolt, washer and sprocket, then remove crankshaft flange, **Fig. 15.**
4. **On FWD California models,** remove crankshaft sensing blade.
5. **On all models,** remove balance shaft belt tensioner, then mark rotational direction on belt and remove. **Keep timing belt, sprocket and tensioner free of oil and water; do not wash or lubricate these parts.**
6. Remove right balance shaft sprocket and spacer, crankshaft sprocket and

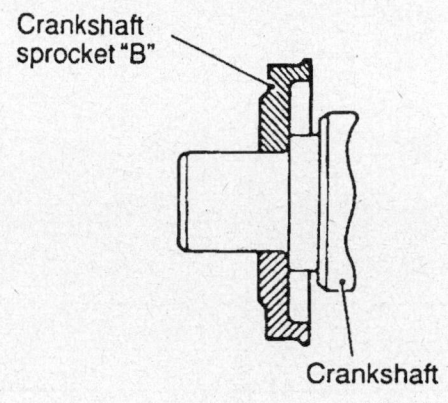

Fig. 21 Balance shaft sprocket installation

key, then engine support bracket and timing belt undercover.

INSTALLATION

1. Install timing belt undercover, then install engine support bracket, apply sealant to center bolt and tighten all bolts to specifications.
2. Install crankshaft sprocket, **Fig. 21.**
3. Apply thin coat of engine oil to outer inside diameter of space and install with chamfered end facing oil seal, **Fig. 22.**
4. Install right hand balance shaft sprocket.
5. Ensure balance shaft and crankshaft sprockets are properly aligned, **Fig. 23,** then fit balance shaft timing belt over crankshaft and balance shaft sprockets. **There should be no belt slack.**
6. Temporarily install tensioner with center of pulley to left and above installation bolt center, then temporarily install pulley with flange toward front of engine.
7. Hold tensioner up so that tension side of belt is taut and tighten tensioner bolt, then measure belt tension side deflection. Standard deflection is .20–.28 inch.
8. **On FWD California models,** install crankshaft sensing blade, **Fig. 24.**
9. **On all models,** install crankshaft flange, **Fig. 25.**
10. Install timing belt as described in "Tim-

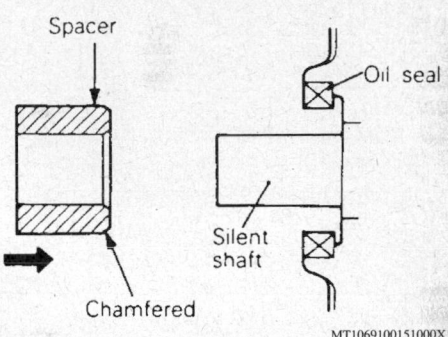

Fig. 22 Balance shaft sprocket spacer orientation

ing Belt, Replace."

SILENT SHAFT
REPLACE

Refer to "Oil Pump, Replace" for silent shaft replacement procedure.

PISTON & ROD ASSEMBLY
REPLACEMENT

1. Release fuel system pressure as outlined under "Precautions."
2. Remove engine as outlined under "Engine, Replace. "
3. Remove timing belt as outlined under "Timing Belt, Replace."
4. Remove water pump as outlined under "Water Pump, Replace."
5. Remove cylinder head as outlined under "Cylinder Head, Replace."
6. Remove oil pan as outlined under "Oil Pump, Replace. "
7. Remove piston and connecting rod in numbered sequence shown in **Fig. 26,**

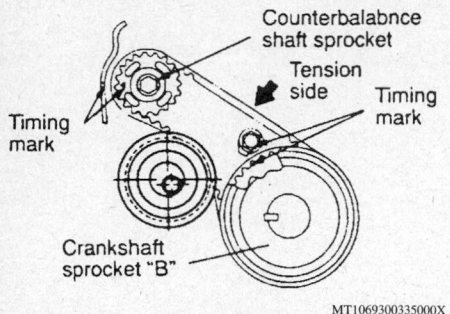

Fig. 23 Balance shaft belt timing marks

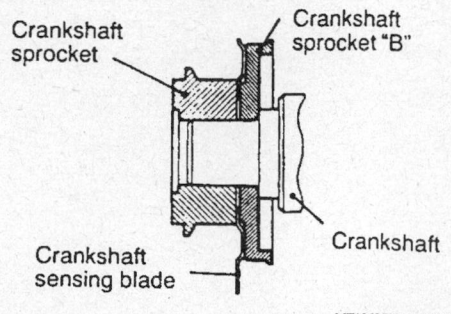

Fig. 24 Crankshaft sensing blade installation

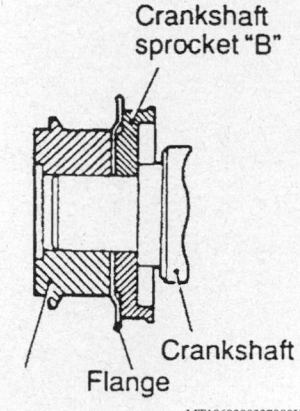

Fig. 25 Crankshaft flange installation

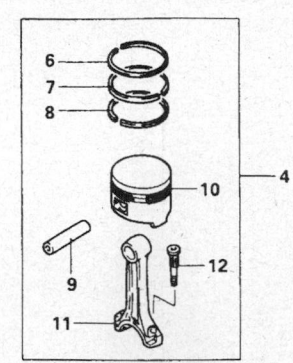

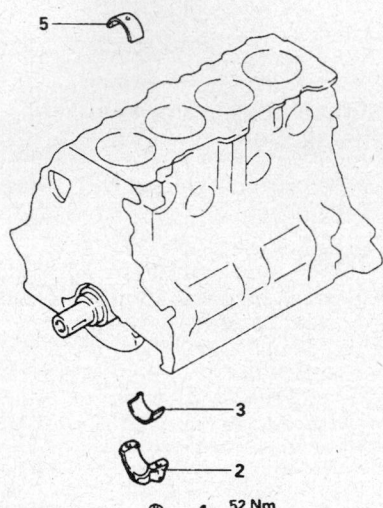

Removal steps
1. Nut
2. Connecting rod cap
3. Connecting rod bearing
4. Piston and connecting rod assembly
5. Connecting rod bearing
6. Piston ring No. 1
7. Piston ring No. 2
8. Oil ring
9. Piston pin
10. Piston
11. Connecting rod
12. Bolt

Fig. 26 Exploded view of piston & connecting rod

marking large end of each connecting rod with cylinder number.
8. Reverse procedure to install, noting the following:
   a. Arrange piston ring oil gaps and piston as shown in **Fig. 27.**
   b. Use suitable thread protectors on connecting rod studs prior to installation.
   c. Mate each connecting rod marking with appropriate cylinder.
   d. Install connecting rod bearing cap on connecting rod.
   e. Coat threads lightly with oil.
   f. Install both nuts finger tight.
   g. Alternately tighten each nut to specifications.

MAIN & ROD BEARINGS

When servicing crankshaft bearings refer to **Fig. 28.**

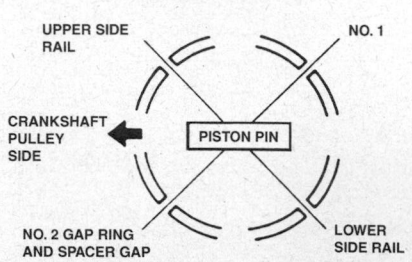

Fig. 27 Piston ring installation

1. Install bearing with oil groove on cylinder block side.
2. Install bearing with no oil groove on bearing cap side.
3. Install bearing caps so their arrows are positioned on timing belt side.
4. Tighten bearing cap bolts to specifications.
5. Ensure crankshaft turns freely and endplay is 0.0020–0.0071 inch.
6. Force oil separator into oil seal case so that oil hole in separator is directed downward.

OIL PAN
REPLACE

Refer to "Oil Pump, Replace" for oil pan replacement procedure.

OIL PUMP
REPLACE
REMOVAL

1. Release fuel system pressure as outlined under "Precautions."
2. Remove timing belt as outlined under "Timing Belt, Replace."
3. Remove balance shaft belt as described in "Balance Shaft Belt, Replace."
4. Remove components in numbered sequence shown in **Fig. 29,** noting the following:
   a. Remove oil pan by driving oil pan remover tool around pan.
   b. Remove plug on side of cylinder

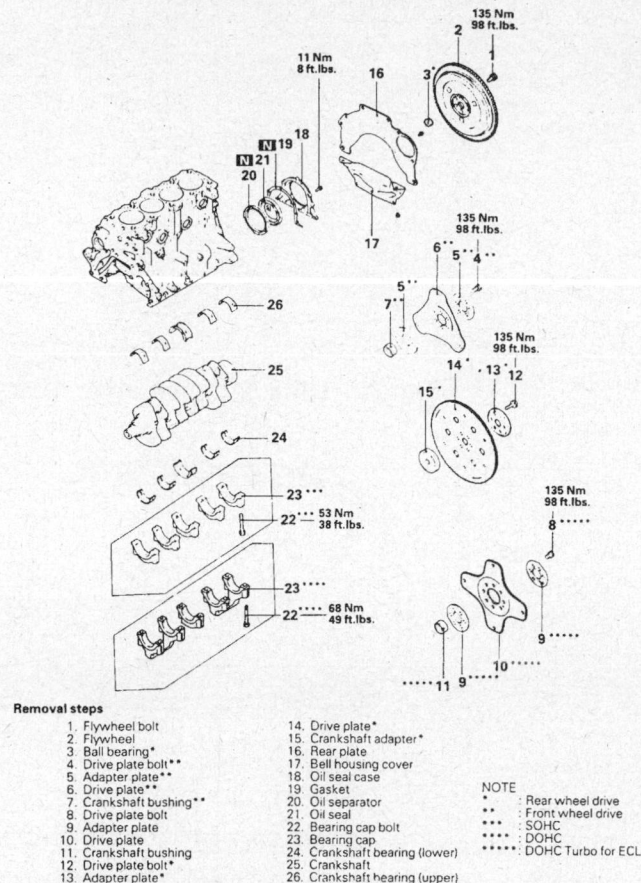

Removal steps

1. Flywheel bolt
2. Flywheel
3. Ball bearing*
4. Drive plate bolt**
5. Adapter plate**
6. Drive plate**
7. Crankshaft bushing**
8. Drive plate bolt
9. Adapter plate
10. Drive plate
11. Crankshaft bushing
12. Drive plate bolt*
13. Adapter plate*
14. Drive plate*
15. Crankshaft adapter*
16. Rear plate
17. Bell housing cover
18. Oil seal case
19. Gasket
20. Oil separator
21. Oil seal
22. Bearing cap bolt
23. Bearing cap
24. Crankshaft bearing (lower)
25. Crankshaft
26. Crankshaft bearing (upper)

NOTE
*   : Rear wheel drive
**   : Front wheel drive
***   : SOHC
**** : DOHC
***** : DOHC Turbo for ECLIPSE

MT1069100160000X

Fig. 28   Exploded view of crankshaft

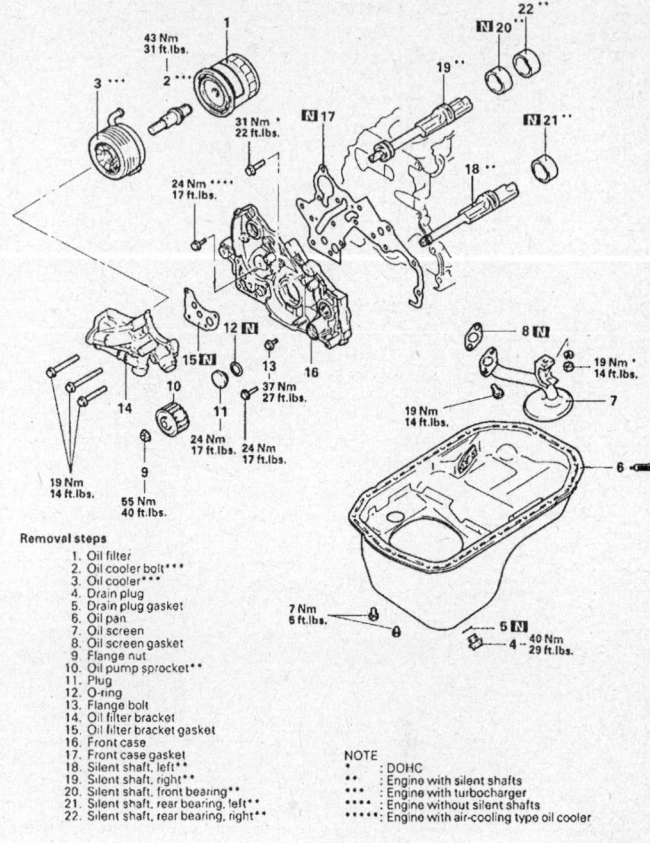

Removal steps

1. Oil filter
2. Oil cooler bolt***
3. Oil cooler***
4. Drain plug
5. Drain plug gasket
6. Oil pan
7. Oil screen
8. Oil screen gasket
9. Flange nut
10. Oil pump sprocket**
11. Plug
12. O-ring
13. Flange bolt
14. Oil filter bracket
15. Oil filter bracket gasket
16. Front case
17. Front case gasket
18. Silent shaft, left*
19. Silent shaft, right*
20. Silent shaft, front bearing**
21. Silent shaft, rear bearing, left**
22. Silent shaft, rear bearing, right**

NOTE
*   : DOHC
**   : Engine with silent shafts
***   : Engine with turbocharger
**** : Engine without silent shafts
***** : Engine with air-cooling type oil cooler

MT1099100044010X

Fig. 29   Oil pump, front case, silent shaft & oil pan replacement (Part 1 of 2)

block and insert a screwdriver into hole to prevent silent shaft from turning.
c. Loosen oil pump sprocket flange nut.
d. With silent shaft locked, remove flange bolt.

INSPECTION

1. Check gear contacting surface of front case and oil pump cover for step wear. If wear is evident, replace front case.
2. Check silent shaft journals for wear and damage. If excessive damage or wear is evident, check bearing. If necessary, replace silent shaft and/or bearing.
3. Inspect oil pump as follows:
   a. Assemble oil pump gear in front case and rotate gear to ensure smooth rotation with no looseness.
   b. Ensure no ridge wear exists on contact surface between front case and gear surface of oil pump cover.
   c. Ensure side clearance is 0.0031–0.0055 inch for drive gear and 0.0024–0.0047 inch for driven gear.

INSTALLATION

Reverse numbered sequence shown in **Fig. 29** to install, noting the following:
1. Install silent shaft and water pump seal using suitable seal installer tool.
2. Install crankshaft front seal using seal

installer, tool No. MD998375-01, or equivalent.
3. Apply engine oil amply to gears and line up alignment marks, **Fig. 30**.
4. Coat threads of oil pressure switch/gauge unit with 3M sealant, No. 8660, or equivalent.
5. Install front case as follows:
   a. Install crankshaft front oil seal guide, tool No. MD998285-01, or equivalent, on end of crankshaft and apply a small amount of oil to outside surface.
   b. Install front case assembly and temporarily tighten flange bolts.
   c. Mount oil filter bracket and tighten bolts to specifications, **Fig. 31. Bolt marked with asterisk 1 has a different tighten value.**
   d. Insert a screwdriver into silent shaft alignment hole on RH side of engine block.
   e. Secure oil pump driven gear onto left silent shaft by tightening flange bolt to specifications.
   f. Install new O-ring in groove of front case at plug position and install plug. Tighten to specifications.
   g. Lock silent shaft as outlined under Step d.
   h. Tighten flange bolt to specifications.
   i. Apply a 0.16 inch bead of sealant to oil pan as shown in **Fig. 32**.

j. Tighten oil pan bolts to specifications.

BELT TENSION DATA

Belt	Deflection @ 22 Lbs.	
	New, Inches	Used, Inches①
A/C	0.170–0.190	0.210–0.024
Alt.	0.300–0.350	0.400
Power Steering	0.180–0.220	0.240–0.280

① — Belt used for 5 minutes or more.

COOLING SYSTEM BLEED

These engines do not require a specified bleed procedure. After filling cooling system, run engine to operating temperature with radiator/pressure cap off. Air will then be automatically bled through cap opening.

THERMOSTAT

REPLACE

1. Drain coolant into suitable container.
2. Disconnect upper radiator, then remove thermostat housing attaching bolts.
3. Remove thermostat housing, then thermostat.

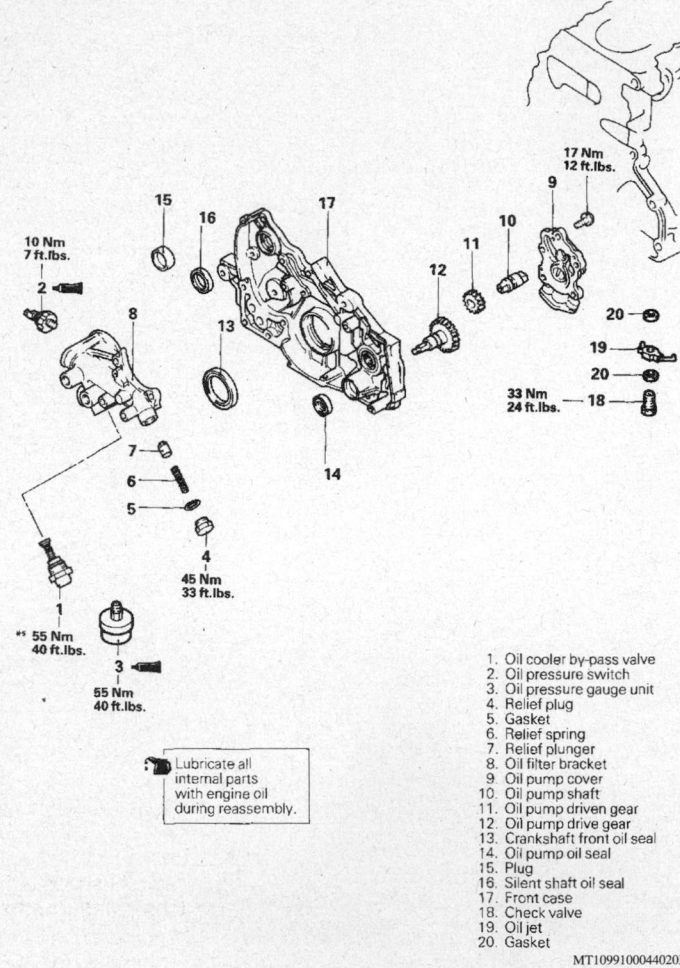

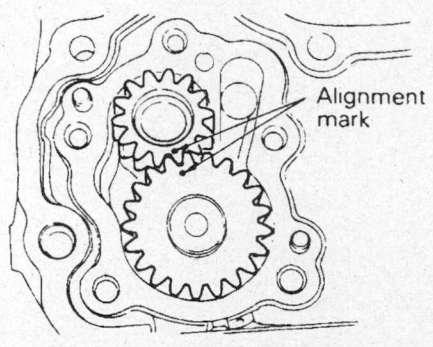

Fig. 30 Oil pump gear alignment marks

1. Oil cooler by-pass valve
2. Oil pressure switch
3. Oil pressure gauge unit
4. Relief plug
5. Gasket
6. Relief spring
7. Relief plunger
8. Oil filter bracket
9. Oil pump cover
10. Oil pump shaft
11. Oil pump driven gear
12. Oil pump drive gear
13. Crankshaft front oil seal
14. Oil pump oil seal
15. Plug
16. Silent shaft oil seal
17. Front case
18. Check valve
19. Oil jet
20. Gasket

Fig. 29 Oil pump, front case, silent shaft & oil pan replacement (Part 2 of 2)

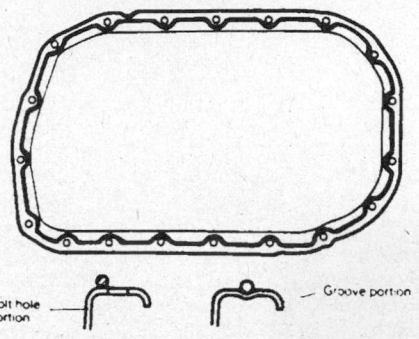

Fig. 32 Oil pan sealant location

7. Lower fuel tank from vehicle, then remove fuel pump from fuel tank.
8. Reverse procedure to install.

FUEL FILTER

REPLACE

This procedure has been revised by a technical service bulletin.
1. Release fuel system pressure as outlined under "Precautions."
2. Remove air cleaner and intake hose.
3. Holding fuel filter with a spanner, remove eye bolt and high-pressure fuel hose. **As there will be some pressure remaining in fuel pipe line, cover it with a rag to prevent fuel from spraying out.**
4. Loosen flare nut then disconnect fuel main pipe connection.
5. Remove fuel filter, **Figs. 35 and 36.**
6. Reverse procedure to install.

TECHNICAL SERVICE BULLETINS

FUEL STARVATION

Fuel starvation can occur when in-tank fuel filter is clogged, typically by contaminated fuel.

To correct problem, proceed as follows:
1. Activate fuel pump with scan tool, then measure pump's supply voltage.
2. If voltage is less than 8 volts, inspect and repair fuel pump wiring harness.
3. If voltage is 8 volts or more, check system fuel pressure.

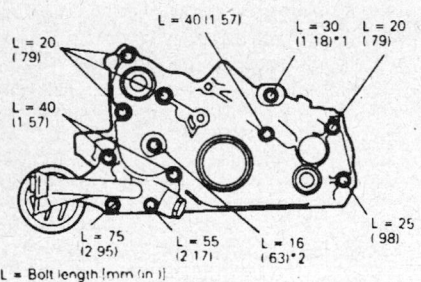

Fig. 31 Oil filter bracket bolt location

4. Reverse procedure to install, tightening attaching bolts to specifications.

WATER PUMP

REPLACE

1. Drain cooling system into an approved container.
2. Remove timing belts as outlined under "Timing Belt, Replace."
3. Remove alternator brace, **Fig. 33.**
4. Remove water pump built and water pump.
5. Remove water pump gasket and O-ring.

6. Reverse procedure to install, noting the following:
   a. Coat O-ring with water to ease installation.
   b. Install water pump bolts in correct location, **Fig. 34.**

RADIATOR

REPLACE

Service radiator as described in "1.8L engine."

FUEL PUMP

REPLACE

This procedure has been revised by a technical service bulletin.
1. Release fuel system pressure as outlined under "Precautions."
2. Remove fuel cap, then drain fuel tank into a suitable container.
3. Disconnect return, high pressure, vapor and filler hoses.
4. Disconnect fuel gauge unit and electric fuel pump electrical connections.
5. **On AWD models,** remove rear propeller shaft.
6. **On all models,** support fuel tank then remove fuel tank supports.

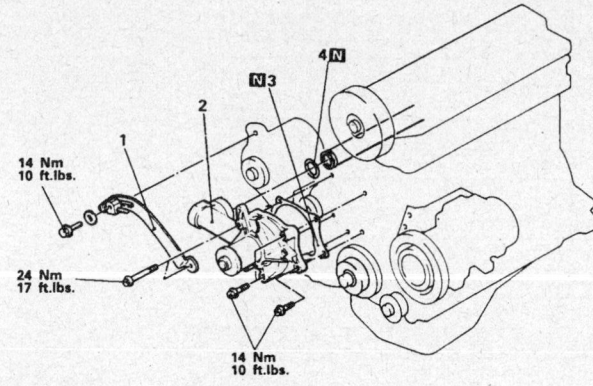

Removal steps
1. Alternator brace
2. Water pump
3. Water pump gasket
4. O-ring

MT1089100017000X

Fig. 33   Exploded view of water pump

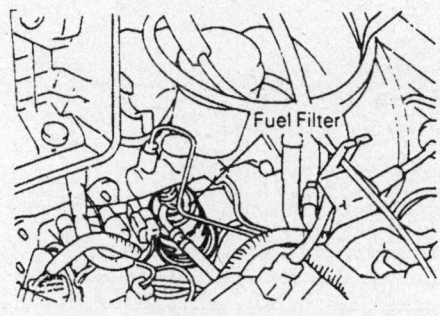

MT1029100012000X

Fig. 35   Fuel filter location

4. If system fuel pressure is within specifications, check system for other starvation problems. Specification is 38 psi at curb idle with fuel pressure regulator vacuum hose attached and 47–50 psi with hose disconnected.
5. If fuel system pressure is not within specifications, remove fuel pump as described in "Fuel Pump, Replace"

and check filter.
6. If filter is clean, replace fuel pump. If filter is clogged, proceed as follows:
   a. Carefully dislodge pump motor from bracket. On some models it may be necessary to remove lower bracket clamp to dislodge motor.
   b. Remove rubber pump vibration dampener, then retaining clip (or nut) and filter.
   c. Replace filter.
   d. **If filter is severely clogged, clean inside of fuel tank.**
7. Reverse procedure to install using new gasket.

IDLE VIBRATION

Some models (mostly equipped with automatic transaxles) may vibrate excessively at idle.

Radiator may be transmitting engine vibration through frame because mounting brackets are not centered on posts. To correct problem, proceed as follows:

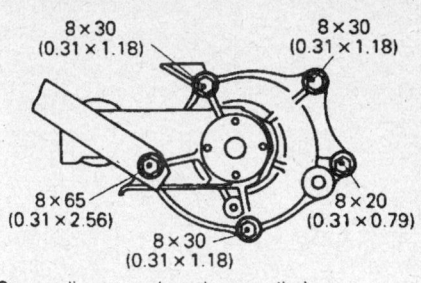

Screw diameter × length: mm (in.)

MT1089100018000X

Fig. 34   Water pump bolt location

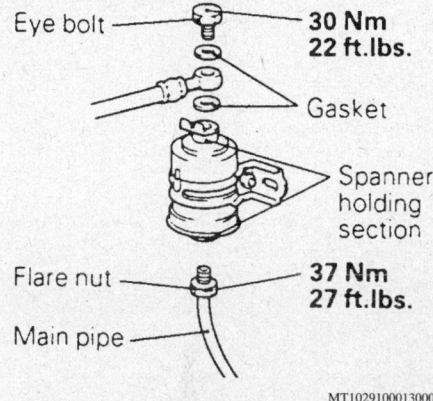

MT1029100013000X

Fig. 36   Fuel filter installation

1. Examine upper radiator mounting brackets. Brackets should be centered on post and radiator should move freely.
2. If brackets are not center, remove upper brackets and ensure bottom mounting posts are seating in lower brackets.
3. Center upper brackets over posts and tighten bolts to specifications.
4. Measure clearance between upper brackets and radiator top. Standard clearance is .0394 inch or more.

TIGHTENING SPECIFICATIONS

Year	Component	Torque, Ft. Lbs.
1996	Air Intake Plenum Bolt & Nut	13
	Air Intake Plenum Stay Bolt	13
	Air Outlet Fitting Bolt	14
	Alternator Brace Bolt	10
	Alternator Mounting Bolt	17
	Alternator Pivot Nut	17
	Camshaft Bearing Cap Bolt	⑤
	Camshaft Sprocket Bolt	65
	Connecting Rod Cap Nut	38
	Cooling Fan Bolt	8
	Crankshaft Bearing Cap Bolt	38
	Crankshaft Pulley Bolt	18
	Crankshaft Sprocket Bolt	87
	Cylinder Head Bolts	⑦
	Distributor Nut	8
	Driveplate Bolt	98
	EGR Valve Bolt	14
	Engine Coolant Temperature Gauge Unit	8
	Engine Coolant Temperature Sensor	22
	Engine Mount	⑧
	Engine Support Bracket Bolt	33
	Engine Support Bracket Bolt (Front)	43
	Engine Support Bracket Bolt (Left)	26
	Exhaust Fitting Bolt	43
	Exhaust Manifold Heat Protector Bolt	③
	Exhaust Manifold Nut	13
	Exhaust Pipe Support Bracket Bolt	26
	Flywheel Bolt	98
	Front Case Bolt	⑥
	Front Case Plug	17
	Fuel Pressure Regulator Bolt	7
	Idle Speed Control Servo Bolt	2.5
	Ignition Coil Bolt	10
	Intake Manifold Bolt & Nut	13
	Intake Manifold Stay Bolt	16
	Oil Cooler Bolt	31
	Oil Cooler By-Pass Valve	40
	Oil Delivery Body	8
	Oil Filter Bracket Bolt	14
	Oil Level Gauge Guise Bolt	②
	Oil Pan Bolt	5
	Oil Pan Drain Plug	29
	Oil Pressure Gauge Unit	40
	Oil Pressure Switch	7
	Oil Pump Check Valve	24
	Oil Pump Cover Bolt	12
	Oil Pump Sprocket Nut	40
	Oil Screen Bolt & Nut	14
	Oil Seal Case Bolt	8
	Power Transistor Bolt	10
	Relief Plug	33
	Rocker Cover Bolt	4
	Roll Stopper Bracket Bolt (Front)	47

Continued

2.4L ENGINE

TIGHTENING
SPECIFICATIONS—Continued

Year	Component	Torque, Ft. Lbs.
1996	Roll Stopper Bracket Bolt (Rear)	87
	Silent Shaft Flange Bolt (Left)	27
	Silent Shaft Sprocket Bolt (Right)	33
	Spark Plug	18
	Tensioner Bolt	35
	Tensioner "B" Bolt	14
	Tensioner Spacer	35
	Thermostat Case Nut	13
	Throttle Body Bolt	14
	Throttle Position Sensor Bolt	1.4
	Timing Belt Tensioner Pulley Center Bolt	35
	Timing Belt Upper Cover Bolts	8
	Water Inlet Pipe Bolt	10
	Water Outlet Fitting Bolt	14
	Water Pipe Bolt	④
	Water Pipe "A" & "B" Eye Bolt	31
	Water Pipe "A" Bolt	8
	Water Pipe "B" Flare Nut	33
	Water Pump Bolt	17
	Water Pump Pulley Bolt	①

① — Less cooling fan, 7 ft. lbs; w/cooling fan, 8 ft. lbs.

② — 8 mm bolts, 10 ft. lbs; 10 mm bolts, 43 ft. lbs.

③ — 6 mm bolts, 7 ft. lbs.; 8 mm bolts, 10 ft. lbs.; 10 mm bolts, 22 ft. lbs.

④ — 6 mm bolts, 8 ft. lbs.; 8 mm bolts, 10 ft. lbs.

⑤ — 8 mm x 25 mm bolts, 17 ft. lbs.; 8 mm x 65 mm bolts, 14 ft. lbs.

⑥ — 8 mm bolts, 17 ft. lbs.; 10 mm bolts, 22 ft. lbs.

⑦ — Refer to "Cylinder Head, Replace" for procedure.

⑧ — Mount bolt and nuts, 42 ft. lbs.; mount through bolt nut, 51 ft. lbs.; mount through bolt attaching nuts, 25 ft. lbs.

Clutch & Manual Transaxle

INDEX

ADJUSTMENTS

CLUTCH PEDAL

1. Measure clutch pedal height (A) and clutch pedal freeplay (B), **Fig. 1.**
2. Clutch pedal height should be 7.68–7.87 inches.
3. Clutch pedal clevis pin play should be 0.04–0.12 inch.
4. If clutch pedal height and freeplay are not within specifications, adjust as follows:
   a. **On models less cruise control,** turn adjusting bolt to adjust pedal to correct height.
   b. **On models with cruise control,** disconnect clutch switch, then turn clutch switch to adjust pedal to correct height.
   c. **On all models,** turn clutch master cylinder pushrod to adjust clutch pedal clevis pin play, **Fig. 2.**
   d. After completing adjustments, measure clutch pedal freeplay and clutch pedal floor clearance, **Fig. 3.** freeplay should be 0.24–0.51 inch and floor clearance should be 1.77 inches or more.
5. If clutch pedal freeplay and floor clearance is not within specifications, result is either air in hydraulic system or a faulty clutch master cylinder, clutch or interlock switch.

CLUTCH INTERLOCK SWITCH

1. Block front wheels, apply parking brake and place transaxle into 5th gear.
2. After adjusting clutch pedal, check clutch interlock as follows:
   a. Engine should not start even if ignition switch is turned to Start position with clutch pedal not depressed. If engine starts, check interlock switch and harness.
   b. Engine should start after clutch pedal has been fully depressed and ignition switch has been turned to Start position. If engine starts before clutch pedal is fully depressed, adjust clutch interlock.

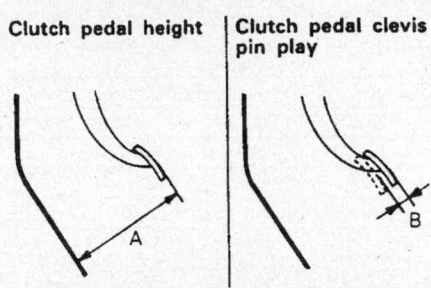

Fig. 1 Clutch pedal height & clevis pin freeplay

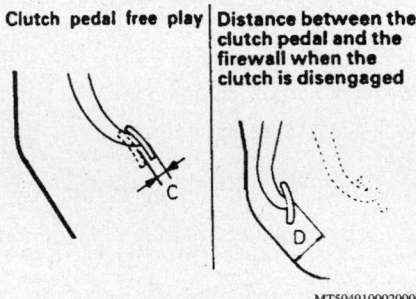

Fig. 3 Clutch pedal freeplay & floor clearance

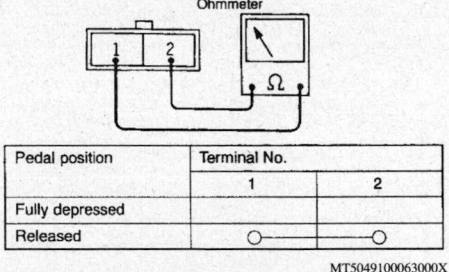

Fig. 5 Clutch interlock switch continuity test

Pedal position	Terminal No.	
	1	2
Fully depressed		
Released	○	○

3. Loosen clutch interlock switch locknut, depress clutch pedal six inches and adjust clearance to 0.14 inch, **Fig. 4.**
4. Connect ohmmeter to clutch interlock

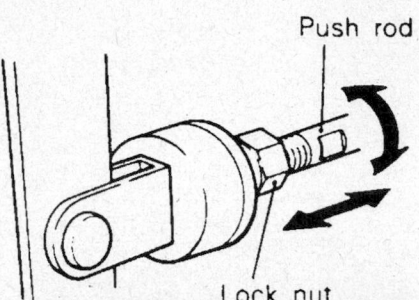

Fig. 2 Clevis pin adjustment

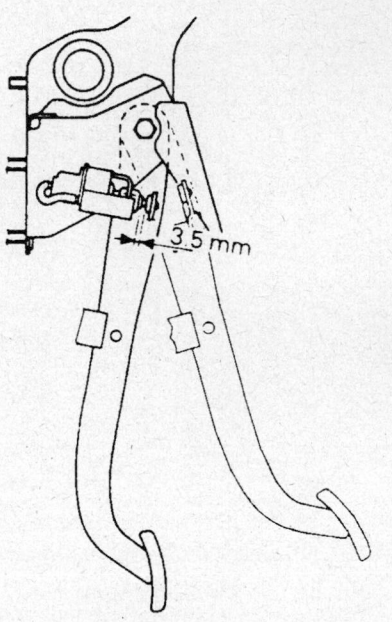

Fig. 4 Clutch interlock switch adjustment

switch terminals No. 1 and No. 2, **Fig. 5.**
5. With clutch pedal fully depressed no continuity should exist at terminals, **Fig. 5.**

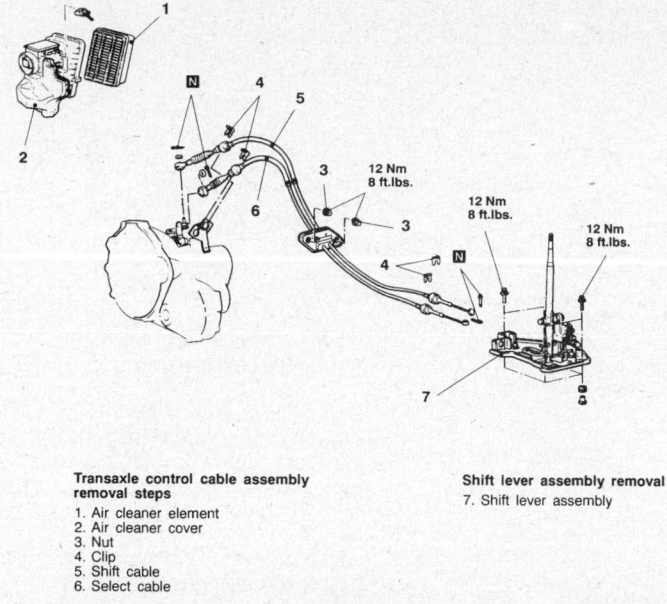

Transaxle control cable assembly removal steps
1. Air cleaner element
2. Air cleaner cover
3. Nut
4. Clip
5. Shift cable
6. Select cable

Shift lever assembly removal
7. Shift lever assembly

MT5049100022000X

Fig. 6   Exploded view of clutch control components

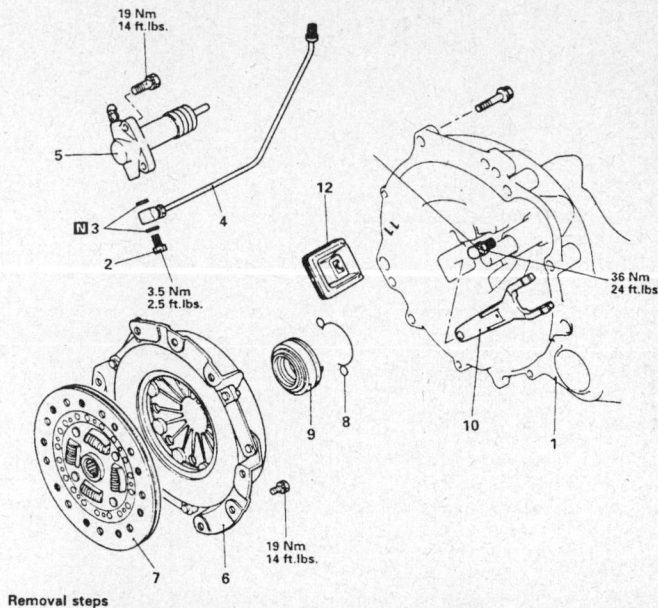

Removal steps
1. Transaxle assembly
2. Union bolt
3. Gasket
4. Clutch oil tube
5. Clutch release cylinder assembly
6. Clutch cover assembly
7. Clutch disc
8. Return clip
9. Clutch release bearing
10. Release fork
11. Fulcrum
12. Release fork boot

MT5049100023000X

Fig. 7   Exploded view of clutch assembly

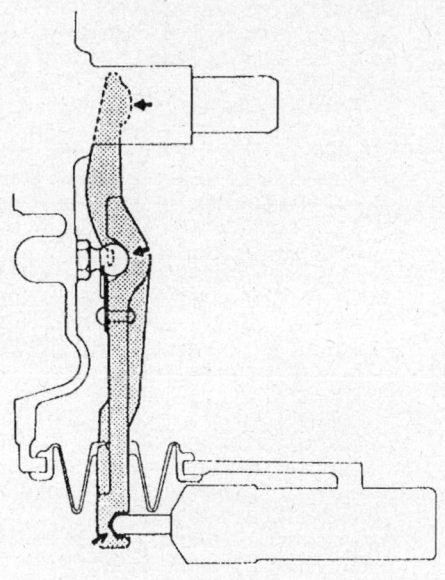

MT5049100024000X

Fig. 8   Release fork grease application

6. With clutch pedal released, continuity should exist between terminals No. 1 and No. 2, **Fig. 5.**

HYDRAULIC SYSTEM SERVICE

CLUTCH HYDRAULIC CONTROL COMPONENT, REPLACE

1. Drain clutch fluid from bleeder screw into a suitable container.
2. Remove clutch control components in numbered sequence shown in **Fig. 6.**
3. Reverse procedure to install, adjusting clutch pedal as outlined under "Adjustments."

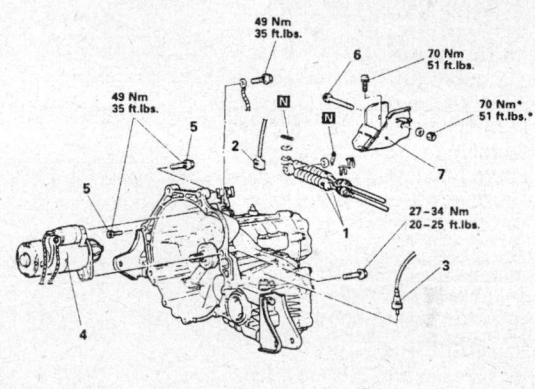

Removal steps
1. Control cable connection
2. Backup light switch connector
3. Speedometer cable connection
4. Starter motor
5. Transaxle assembly upper part coupling bolt
6. Transaxle mount bolt
7. Transaxle mount bracket

NOTE
For tightening locations indicated by the * symbol, first tighten temporarily, and then make the final tightening with the entire weight of the engine applied to the vehicle body.

MT5039100103010X

Fig. 9   Transaxle replacement (Part 1 of 2). FWD models

CLUTCH

REPLACE

1. Remove transaxle as outlined under "Manual Transaxle, Replace."
2. Remove clutch cover, disc and related components in numbered sequence shown in **Fig. 7.**
3. Reverse procedure to install, noting the following:
   a. Apply Mitsubishi grease part No. 0101011, or equivalent, on contact points of release fork shown in **Fig. 8.**
   b. Apply Mitsubishi grease part No. 0101011, or equivalent, to inside surface of release bearing.
   c. Apply Mitsubishi grease part No. 0101011, or equivalent, to clutch disc splines, then install clutch disc and cover using suitable alignment tool.

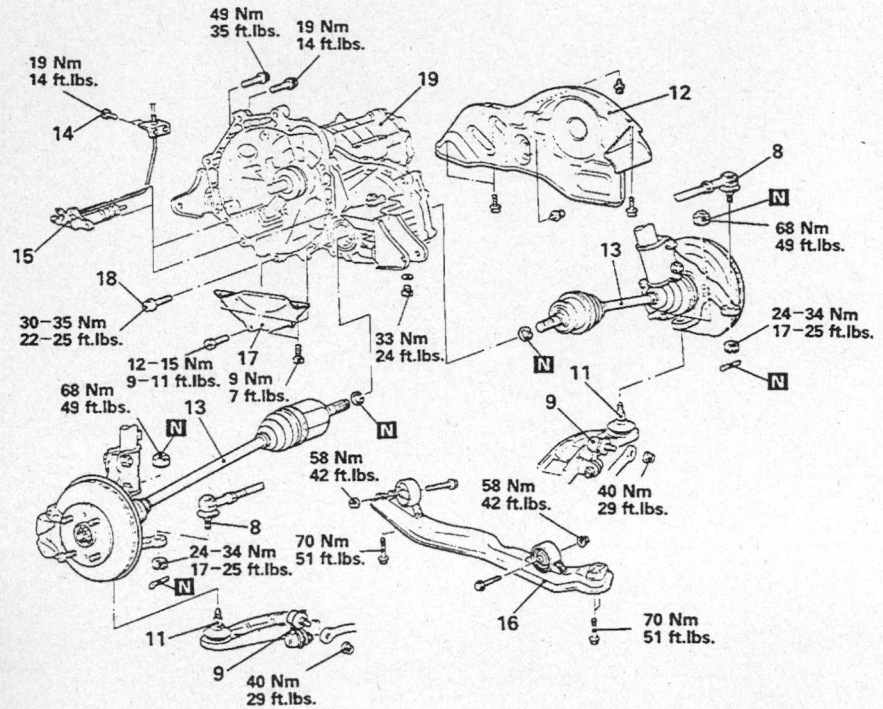

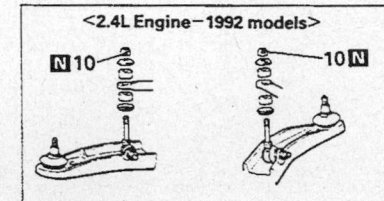

<2.4L Engine—1992 models>

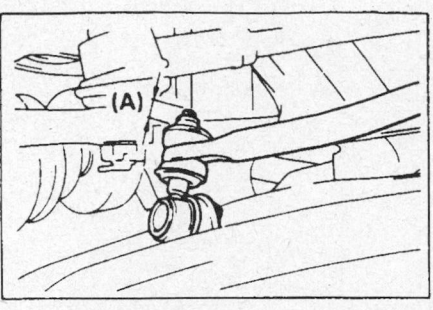

MT5039100104000X

Fig. 10 Stabilizer bar bolt protrusion

- Lift up of the vehicle
- 8 . Connection for tie rod end
- 9 . Connection for stabilizer bar <except 2.4L Engine—1992 models>
- 10. Self locking nut <2.4L Engine—1992 models>
- 11. Connection for lower arm ball joint
- 12. Under cover (RH)
- • Draining of the transaxle oil
- 13. Drive shaft connection
- 14. Clutch oil line bracket bolt
- 15. Connection for release cylinder
- 16. Center member <except 2.4L Engine—1992 models>
- 17. Bell housing cover
- 18. Transaxle assembly lower part coupling bolts
- 19. Transaxle assembly

MT5039100103020X

Fig. 9 Transaxle replacement (Part 2 of 2). FWD models

TRANSAXLE
REPLACE
FWD MODELS

1. Remove air cleaner assembly.
2. Remove transaxle in numbered sequence shown in **Fig. 9,** noting the following:
   - a. Remove starter motor assembly with cables attached, then support aside.
   - b. **On F5M22 transaxles,** support engine, using engine support hanger tool No. MB991191, or equivalent, to remove weight off transaxle mounting bolts.
   - c. **On F5M31 transaxles,** use a suitable floor jack to raise transaxle assembly until no weight is applied on transaxle mounting bolts.
   - d. **On all models,** remove transaxle mounting bolt.
   - e. Loosen tie rod end nut then disconnect tie rod end using steering linkage puller tool No. MB991113-01, or equivalent.
   - f. Loosen lower ball joint nut then disconnect ball joint using steering linkage puller tool No. MB991113-01, or equivalent.
   - g. Remove driveshafts as outlined in "Drive Axles"section.

   - h. Disconnect clutch hydraulic cylinder leaving hoses attached.
   - i. Support transaxle using a suitable jack stand, then move transaxle assembly to right and lower from vehicle.
3. Reverse procedure to install, ensuring stabilizer bar bolt protrusion is 0.3–0.4 inch, **Fig. 10.**

AWD MODELS

1. Remove air cleaner assembly.
2. Remove transaxle in numbered sequence shown in **Fig. 11,** noting the following:
   - a. Remove starter motor assembly with cables attached, then support aside.
   - b. Support engine, using engine support hanger tool No. MB991191, or equivalent, to remove weight off transaxle mounting bolts.
   - c. Remove transaxle mounting bolt.
   - d. Loosen tie rod end nut then disconnect tie rod end using steering linkage puller tool No. MB991113-01, or equivalent.
   - e. Loosen lower ball joint nut then disconnect ball joint using steering linkage puller tool No. MB991113-01, or equivalent.
   - f. Remove driveshafts as outlined in "Drive Axles"section.
   - g. Disconnect clutch hydraulic cylinder leaving hoses attached.
   - h. Remove propeller shaft.
   - i. Remove transfer case assembly and cover opening to prevent oil discharge or entry of foreign material.
   - j. Support transaxle using a suitable jack stand, then move transaxle assembly to right and lower from vehicle.
3. Reverse procedure to install, installing driveshafts as outlined in "Drive Axles" section.

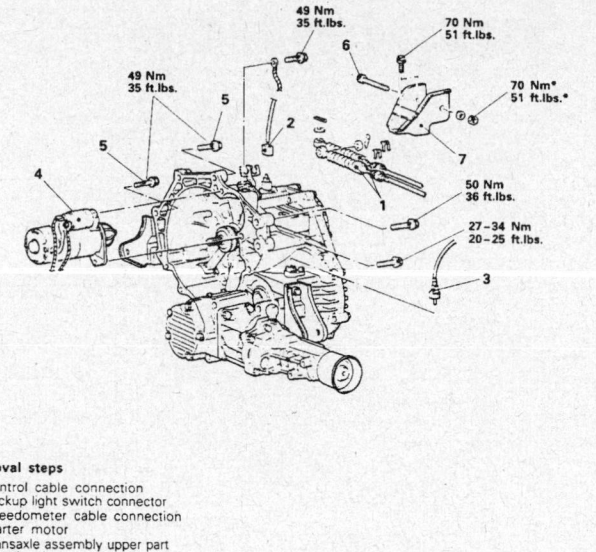

Removal steps
1. Control cable connection
2. Backup light switch connector
3. Speedometer cable connection
4. Starter motor
5. Transaxle assembly upper part coupling bolt
6. Transaxle mount bolt
7. Transaxle mount bracket

NOTE
For tightening locations indicated by the * symbol, first tighten temporarily, and then make the final tightening with the entire weight of the engine applied to the vehicle body.

MT5039100105010X

Fig. 11   Transaxle replacement (Part 1 of 2). AWD models

- ● Lifting up of the vehicle
- 8. Connection for tie rod end
- 9. Connection for stabilizer bar
- 10. Connection for lower arm ball joint
- ● Draining of the transaxle oil
- 11. Under cover (RH)
- 12. Drive shaft nut (RH)
- 13. Drive shaft (RH)
- 14. Connection for drive shaft and inner shaft
- 15. Clutch oil line bracket bolts
- 16. Connection for clutch release cylinder

17. Front exhaust pipe
18. Transfer assembly
19. Center member
20. Bell housing cover
21. Transaxle assembly lower part coupling bolts
22. Transaxle assembly

Transfer assembly removal steps
17. Front exhaust pipe
18. Transfer assembly

MT5039100105020X

Fig. 11   Transaxle replacement (Part 2 of 2). AWD models

TIGHTENING SPECIFICATIONS

For tightening specifications, refer to individual repair procedure or illustrations.

Year	Component	Torque, Ft. Lbs.
1996	Clutch Cover Bolts	14
	Clutch Hose Bracket Bolt	9
	Clutch Master Cylinder Nuts	9
	Clutch Oil Tube Union Bolt	2.5
	Clutch Release Cylinder Bolts	14
	Pipe Fitting Nuts	11
	Release Fork Bolt	24
	Reservoir Bracket Bolts	4
	Transaxle Coupling Bolts	①
	Transaxle Mount Bolts	51

① — Refer to "Transaxle, Replace" for procedure

Rear Axle & Suspension

INDEX

DIFFERENTIAL CARRIER

REPLACE

1. Raise and support vehicle.
2. Remove differential carrier and/or support member in numbered sequence shown in **Fig. 1,** noting the following:
   a. Remove nuts and bolts from driveshaft and companion flange then support driveshaft aside.
   b. Using slide hammer tool No. MB990211-01, or equivalent, remove companion shaft from differential carrier.
   c. Mark propeller shaft location for reference during assembly.
   d. Remove propeller shaft bolts, then support propeller shaft aside.
   e. Support differential carrier bolts using a suitable jack then remove differential carrier support bolts.
   f. Disconnect main muffler from center exhaust pipe. Support muffler with wire from frame.
3. Reverse procedure to install, noting the following:
   a. Install mount stopper as shown in **Fig. 2.**
   b. Install companion shaft into differential carrier using care not to damage oil seal.
   c. Identify RH and LH companion shafts prior to installation, **Fig. 3.**

SHOCK ABSORBER

REPLACE

1. Support lower arm using suitable jack.
2. Remove and disassemble shock absorber in numbered sequence shown in **Fig. 4.**
3. Reverse procedure to assemble and install.

COIL SPRING

REPLACE

1. Raise and support vehicle.
2. Remove rear stabilizer bar as outlined under "Stabilizer Bar, Replace."
3. Remove shock absorber as outlined under "Shock Absorber, Service."
4. Disconnect driveshaft from differential carrier and support aside.
5. Disconnect speed sensor clamp bolt.
6. Lower jack used to support lower arm and remove coil spring.
7. Remove spring seat.
8. Reverse procedure to install, ensuring coil spring seat properly into spring seat grooves.

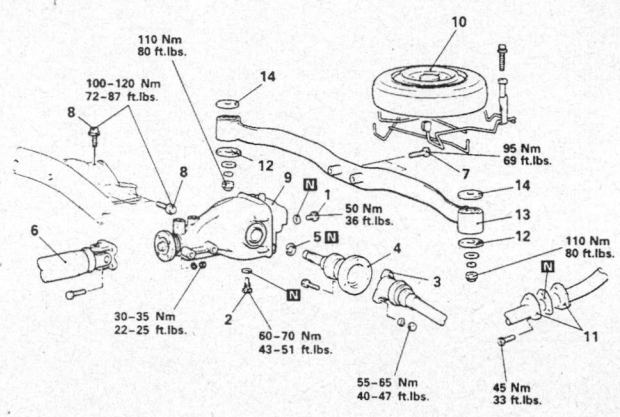

Fig. 1

110 Nm / 80 ft.lbs.	
100–120 Nm / 72–87 ft.lbs.	
95 Nm / 69 ft.lbs.	
50 Nm / 36 ft.lbs.	
30–35 Nm / 22–25 ft.lbs.	
60–70 Nm / 43–51 ft.lbs.	
55–65 Nm / 40–47 ft.lbs.	
45 Nm / 33 ft.lbs.	
110 Nm / 80 ft.lbs.	

Differential carrier removal steps

1. Filler plug
2. Drain plug
3. Drive shaft connection
4. Companion shaft
5. Circlip
6. Propeller shaft connection
7. Bolts
8. Bolts
9. Differential Carrier

Differential support member removal steps

7. Bolts
10. Spare tyre
11. Connection for main muffler and center exhaust pipe
12. Differential mount lower stopper
13. Differential support member
14. Differential mount upper stopper

Caution
If the thread section of the mounting bolts and nuts for the drive shaft and propeller shaft and the companion shaft have any oil or grease on them, there is a possibility that they may loosen, even if they are tightened to the specified torque, so the threads should always be cleaned before tightening.

MT3019100003000X

Fig. 1 Exploded view of differential carrier

Differential mount upper stopper

Differential mount lower stopper

MT3019100031000X

Fig. 2 Differential mount stoppers

CONTROL ARM

REPLACE

LOWER

1. Remove stabilizer bar as outlined under "Stabilizer Bar, Replace."
2. Remove shock absorber as outlined under "Shock Absorber, Service."
3. Remove coil spring as outlined under "Coil Spring, Replace."
4. Replace lower arm assembly in numbered sequence shown in **Figs. 5 and 6,** not removing AWD models rear hub assembly except when replacing bearing.

REAR CROSSMEMBER

REPLACE

1. Remove stabilizer bar as outlined under "Stabilizer Bar, Replace."
2. Remove shock absorber as outlined under "Shock Absorber, Service."
3. Make mating marks on lower arm shaft assembly and crossmember.
4. Remove coil spring as outlined under "Coil Spring, Replace."
5. **On AWD models,** mark then remove propeller shaft.
6. **On all models,** replace suspension crossmember in numbered sequence shown in **Figs. 7 and 8.**
7. Reverse procedure to install, ensuring coil spring is properly seated.

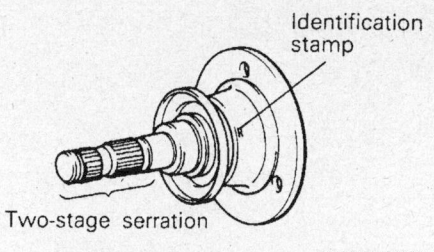

Fig. 3 Companion shaft identification mark

STABILIZER BAR

REPLACE

1. Raise and support vehicle.
2. Remove stabilizer bar link nut.
3. Remove stabilizer bar link bolt, spacer joint cups, rubber bushing and collar.
4. Support stabilizer bar and remove frame mount bracket bolts and bushings.
5. Remove stabilizer bar from vehicle.
6. Reverse procedure to install, noting the following:
   a. Position stabilizer bar by aligning painted section as shown, **Fig. 9.**
   b. Protrusion of stabilizer link bolt should be 0.98–1.06 inches, **Fig. 10.**

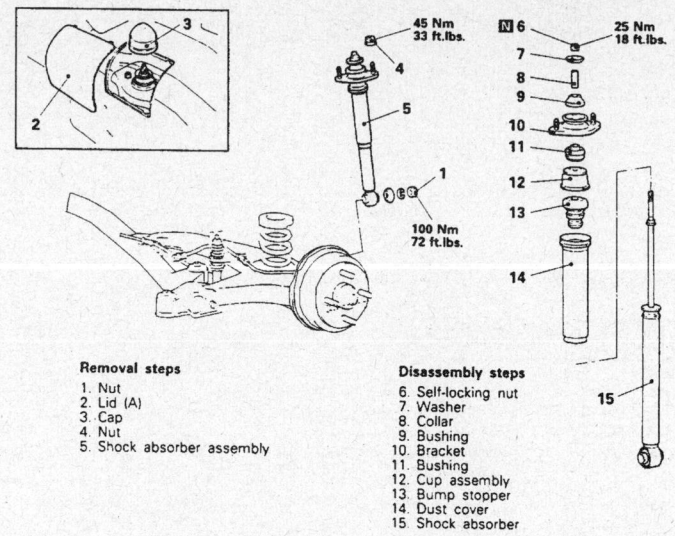

Removal steps
1. Nut
2. Lid (A)
3. Cap
4. Nut
5. Shock absorber assembly

Disassembly steps
6. Self-locking nut
7. Washer
8. Collar
9. Bushing
10. Bracket
11. Bushing
12. Cup assembly
13. Bump stopper
14. Dust cover
15. Shock absorber

Fig. 4 Exploded view of shock absorber

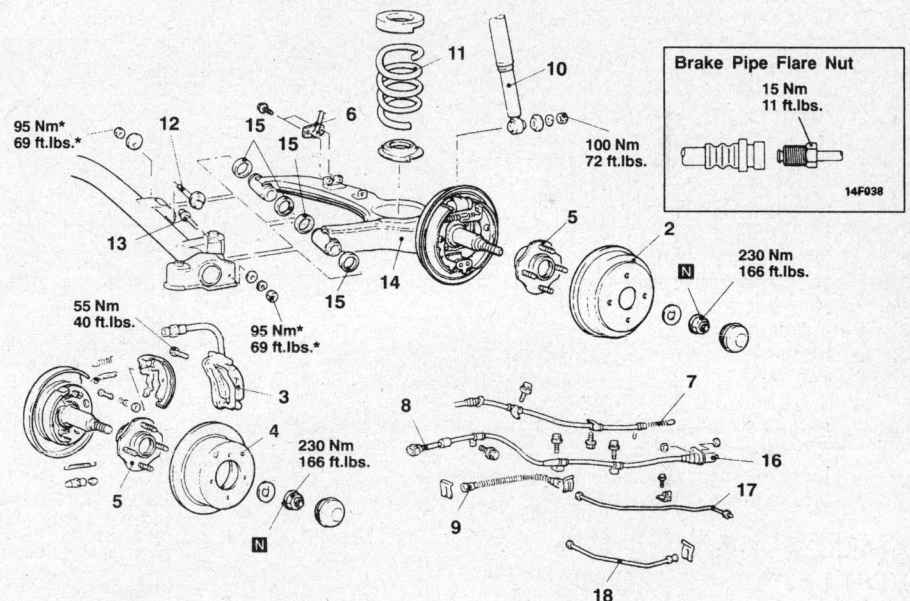

Brake Pipe Flare Nut
15 Nm
11 ft.lbs.

Removal steps
2. Brake drum
3. Caliper assembly <Vehicles with ABS>
4. Brake disk <Vehicles with ABS>
5. Hub assembly
6. Link bracket <EXPO>
7. Connection for parking brake cable and brake shoe
8. Rear sensor connector <Vehicles with ABS>
9. Brake hose
10. Shock absorber
11. Coil spring
12. Shaft assembly
13. Flange bolt

14. Lower arm assembly
15. Stopper
16. Rear speed sensor <Vehicles with ABS>
17. Brake pipe
18. Brake pipe <Vehicles with ABS>

Caution
(1) For vehicles with ABS, be careful not to damage the rotro teeth when removinb the jub assembly.
(2) For vehicles with ABS, when removing the speed sensor, be careful tht the end of the pole piece does not touch any other component.
(3) * Indicates parts which should be temporarily tightened, and then fully tightened with the vehicle on the ground in the unladen condition.

Fig. 5 Exploded view of lower arm. FWD models

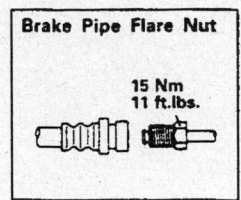

Brake Pipe Flare Nut

15 Nm
11 ft.lbs.

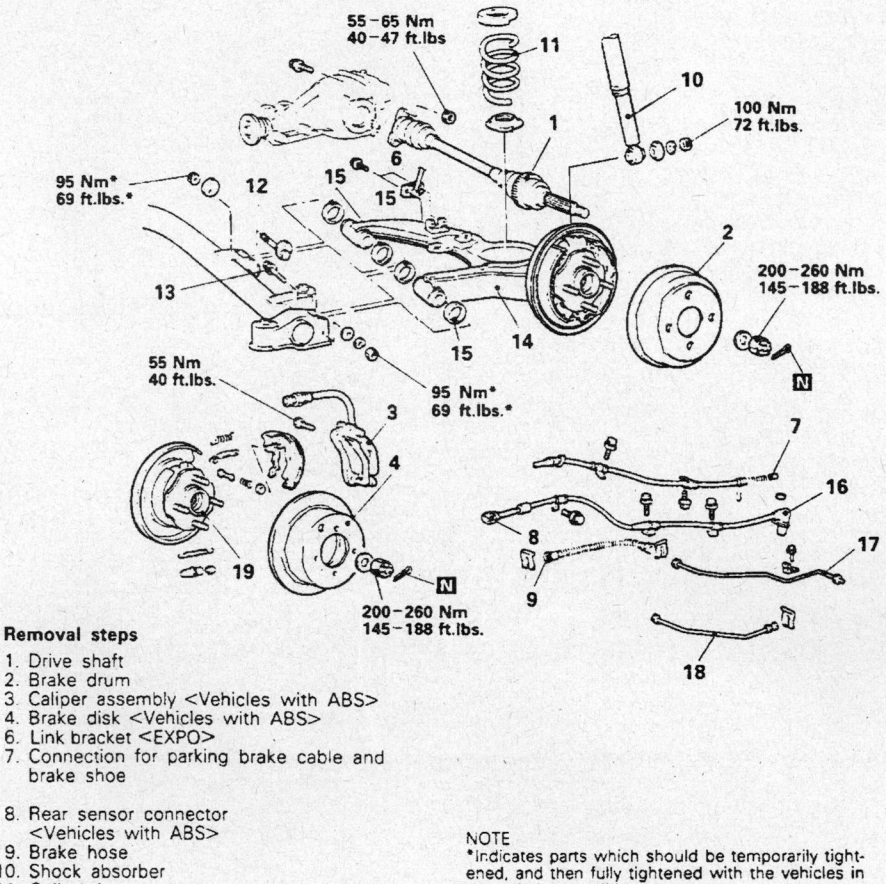

Removal steps

1. Drive shaft
2. Brake drum
3. Caliper assembly <Vehicles with ABS>
4. Brake disk <Vehicles with ABS>
6. Link bracket <EXPO>
7. Connection for parking brake cable and brake shoe

8. Rear sensor connector <Vehicles with ABS>
9. Brake hose
10. Shock absorber
11. Coil spring
12. Shaft assembly
13. Flange bolt
14. Lower arm assembly
15. Stopper
16. Rear speed sensor <Vehicles with ABS>
17. Brake pipe
18. Brake pipe <Vehicles with ABS>
19. Hub assembly

NOTE
*Indicates parts which should be temporarily tightened, and then fully tightened with the vehicles in the unladen condition.

Caution
(1) For vehicles with ABS, be careful not to damage the rotor teeth when removing the drive shaft.
(2) For vehicles with ABS, when removing the speed sensor, be careful that the end of the pole piece does not touch any other component.

MT2039100045000X

Fig. 6 Exploded view of lower arm. AWD models

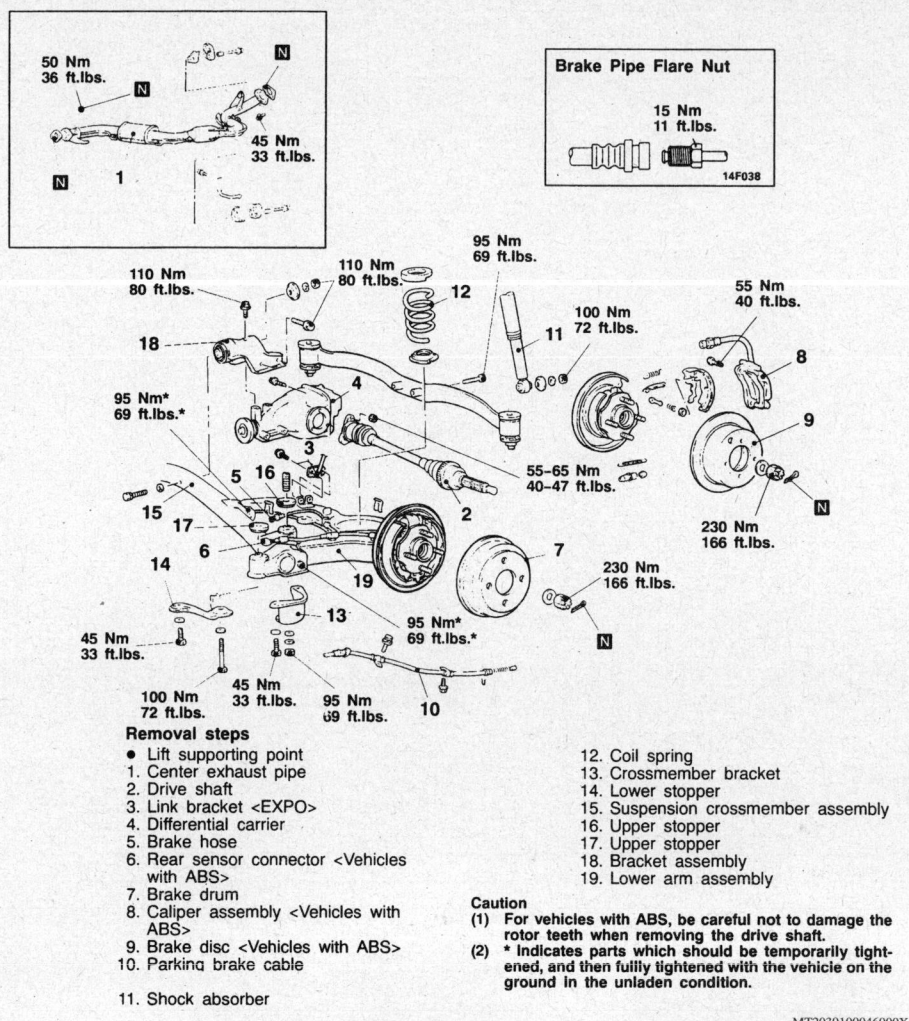

Fig. 7 Exploded view of suspension crossmember. FWD models

MT2039100046000X

Removal steps

- ● Lift supporting point
- 1. Center exhaust pipe
- 2. Drive shaft
- 3. Link bracket <EXPO>
- 4. Differential carrier
- 5. Brake hose
- 6. Rear sensor connector <Vehicles with ABS>
- 7. Brake drum
- 8. Caliper assembly <Vehicles with ABS>
- 9. Brake disc <Vehicles with ABS>
- 10. Parking brake cable
- 11. Shock absorber
- 12. Coil spring
- 13. Crossmember bracket
- 14. Lower stopper
- 15. Suspension crossmember assembly
- 16. Upper stopper
- 17. Upper stopper
- 18. Bracket assembly
- 19. Lower arm assembly

Caution
(1) For vehicles with ABS, be careful not to damage the rotor teeth when removing the drive shaft.
(2) * Indicates parts which should be temporarily tightened, and then fully tightened with the vehicle on the ground in the unladen condition.

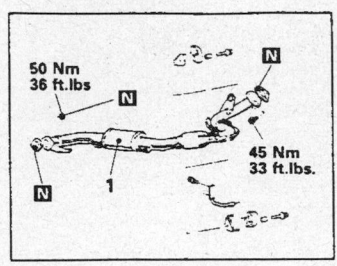

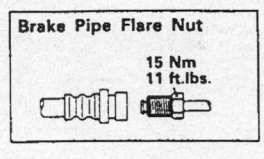

Brake Pipe Flare Nut

15 Nm
11 ft. lbs.

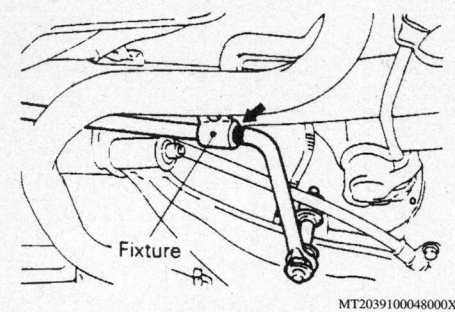

Fixture

MT2039100048000X

Fig. 9 Mounting stabilizer bar

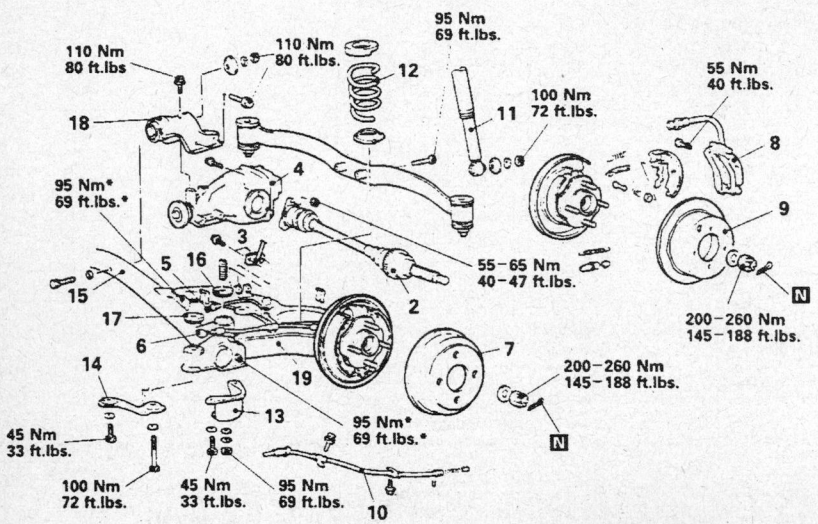

Removal steps

- Lift supporting point
1. Center exhaust pipe
2. Drive shaft
3. Link bracket <EXPO>
4. Differential carrier
5. Brake hose
6. Rear sensor connector.
   <Vehicles with ABS>
7. Brake drum
8. Caliper assembly <Vehicles with ABS>
9. Brake disk <Vehicles with ABS>
10. Parking brake cable

11. Shock absorber
12. Coil spring
13. Crossmember bracket
14. Lower stopper
15. Suspension crossmember assembly
16. Upper stopper
17. Upper stopper
18. Bracket assembly
19. Lower arm assembly

Caution
For vehicles with ABS, be careful not to damage the rotor teeth when removing the drive shaft.

NOTE
*Indicates parts which should be temporarily tightened, and then fully tightened with the vehicles in the unladen condition.

MT2039100047000X

Fig. 8 Exploded view of suspension crossmember. AWD models

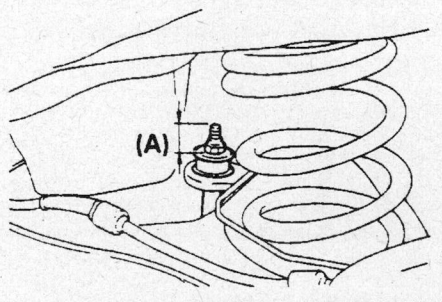

MT2039100049000X

**Fig. 10 Stabilizer bar bolt
protrusion**

TIGHTENING SPECIFICATIONS

For tightening specifications, refer to individual repair procedure or illustrations.

Year	Component	Torque, Ft. Lbs.
1996	Axle Nut, AWD	145–188
	Axle Nut, FWD	166
	Brake Caliper Mounting Bolts	40
	Crossmember Bracket Bolt	33
	Crossmember Bracket Nut	69
	Differential Carrier Mounting Bolts	①
	Driveshaft Connection Nuts	40–47
	Driveshaft Nut, AWD	145–188
	Driveshaft Nut, FWD	166
	Hub Nut, AWD	145–188
	Hub Nut, FWD	166
	Lower Arm Mounting Bolts	69
	Lower Stop Bolt, Front	33
	Lower Stop Bolt, Rear	72
	Shock Absorber Dust Cover Nut	18
	Shock Absorber Mounting Nuts, Lower	72
	Shock Absorber Mounting Nuts, Upper	33
	Wheel Bearing Nut, AWD	145–188
	Wheel Bearing Nut, FWD	166

① — Refer to "Differential Carrier, Replace" for procedure.

Front Suspension & Steering

NOTE: On Air Bag Equipped Models, Refer To "Air Bag System Precautions" Located In The Front Of This Manual For System Disarming & Arming Procedures.

INDEX

PRECAUTIONS

AIR BAG SYSTEMS

Refer to "Air Bag System Precautions" in the front of this manual for system disarming and arming procedures.

BATTERY GROUND CABLE

Prior to service, disconnect battery ground cable and isolate as required.

WHEEL HUB & STEERING KNUCKLE

REPLACE

Replace hub, knuckle and bearing in numbered sequence shown in **Figs. 1 and 2,** noting the following:

1. Remove caliper and suspend with wire, then remove driveshaft nut using end yoke holder, tool No. MB990767-01, or equivalent.
2. Disconnect ball joint and tie rod end using steering linkage puller, tool No. MB990635-01, or equivalent. **Loosen but do not remove ball joint and tie rod end nuts until knuckle is ready to be removed.**
3. Using a suitable axle shaft puller, press driveshaft from front hub.
4. Ensure driveshaft nut and washer are installed in direction shown in **Fig. 3.**
5. Temporarily install speed sensor to knuckle, if equipped, then insert a suitable thickness gauge between sensor pole piece and rotor toothed surface, **Fig. 4,** and tighten speed sensor at a position where clearance is 0.012–

0.035 inch. **If clearance cannot be obtained, check for improper installation of rotor.**
6. Remove hub by attaching front hub remover/installer, tool No. MB990998-01 and knuckle arm bridge tool No. MB991355, or equivalent, to knuckle and hub. Secure knuckle in vise, then tighten nut of front hub remover/installer to remove hub, or hub and rotor from knuckle.
7. Remove wheel bearing inner race from front hub using side bearing puller, tool No. MB990810-01, or equivalent. First, crush oil seal in two places to allow tabs of side bearing puller clearance to get under inner race.
8. Drive wheel bearing out using knuckle arm bridge, tool No. MB991355 remover/installer disc, tool No.

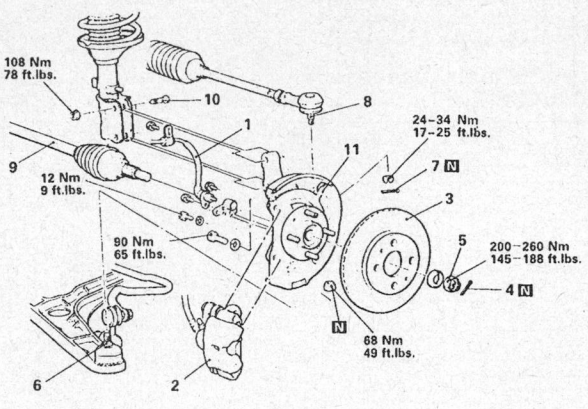

108 Nm
78 ft.lbs.

12 Nm
9 ft.lbs.

90 Nm
65 ft.lbs.

24–34 Nm
17–25 ft.lbs.

200–260 Nm
145–188 ft.lbs.

68 Nm
49 ft.lbs.

Removal steps
1. Front speed sensor
   <Vehicle with ABS>
2. Caliper assembly
3. Brake disc
4. Cotter pin
5. Drive shaft nut
6. Connection for lower arm ball joint
7. Cotter pin
8. Connection for tie rod end
9. Drive shaft
10. Front strut mounting bolt
11. Hub and knuckle

Caution
Be careful when handling the pole piece at the tip of the speed sensor and the toothed edge of the rotor so as not to damage them by striking against other parts.

MT2049100024000X

Fig. 1 Hub, knuckle & bearing replacement

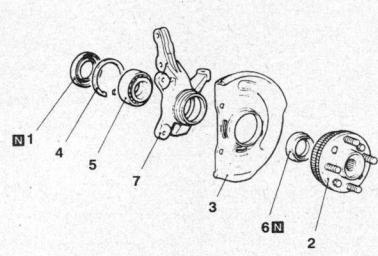
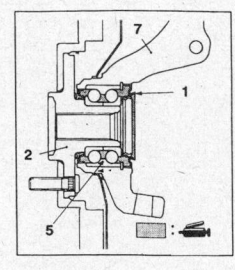

Disassembly steps
1. Inner oil seal
2. Hub
3. Dust cover
4. Snap ring
5. Wheel bearing
6. Outer oil seal
7. Knuckle

Reassembly steps
7. Knuckle
5. Wheel bearing
4. Snap ring
6. Outer oil seal
3. Dust cover
2. Hub
● Wheel bearing starting torque check
● Hub end play check
1. Inner oil seal

MT2049100025000X

Fig. 2 Servicing hub, knuckle & bearing

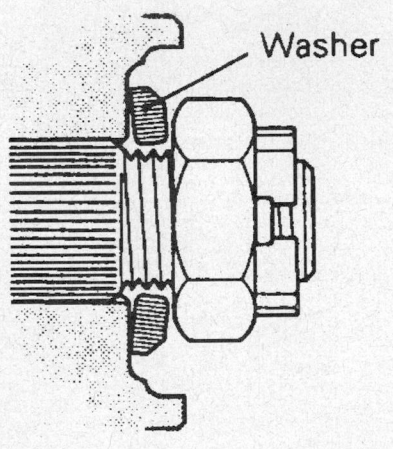

Washer

MT2049100026000X

Fig. 3 Driveshaft nut & washer installation

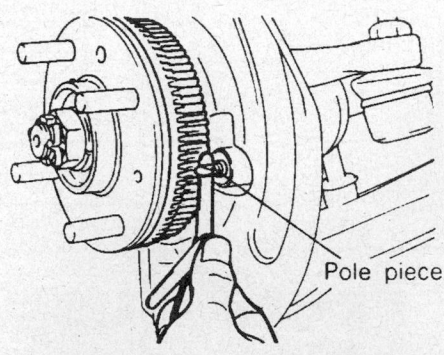

Pole piece

MT2049100027000X

Fig. 4 ABS speed sensor pole piece clearance check

MB990932-01 and handle, tool No. MB990938-01, or equivalent.

9. Fill wheel bearing with multi-purpose grease and apply a thin coating to knuckle and bearing contact surfaces, then press in wheel bearing using rear suspension bushing base, tool No. MB990890-01 and rear suspension arbor, tool No. MB990883-01, or equivalent.

10. Drive oil seal into knuckle using lower arm bushing arbor, tool No. MB990947-01 and rear suspension bushing base, tool No. MB990847-01, or equivalent. Apply multi-purpose grease to lip of oil seal and surfaces of oil seal which contact front hub.

11. Use front hub remover/installer, tool No. MB990998-01, or equivalent, to mount hub, or hub and rotor onto knuckle. **Torque** nut of hub remover/installer to 145–188 ft. lbs. while rotating hub to seat bearing. Leave hub remover/installer in place while taking measurements described in Steps 12 and 13.

12. Measure wheel bearing starting torque using hub remover/installer and a suitable inch pound torque wrench. Starting **torque** must be 16 inch lbs. or less and bearing must not feel rough when rotated.

13. Measure hub endplay using hub remover/installer and a suitable dial in-dicator, endplay must be within 0.002 inch. If starting torque and endplay are not within limits specified, bearing, hub and/or knuckle may have been incorrectly installed. Repeat disassembly and assembly procedures.

14. Apply multi-purpose grease to lip and install driveshaft side oil seal into knuckle using rear suspension bushing base, tool No. MB990890-01 and rear suspension arbor, tool No. MB990883-01, or equivalent. Drive seal in until it contacts snap ring.

BALL JOINT
REPLACE

Refer to "Control Arm, Replace" for ball joint replacement procedure.

STRUT
REPLACE

Remove, install, disassemble and assemble strut assembly in numbered sequence shown in **Figs. 5 and 6,** noting the following:
1. Secure lower arm assembly with wire, then disconnect strut assembly from knuckle.
2. Hold spring upper seat using spring

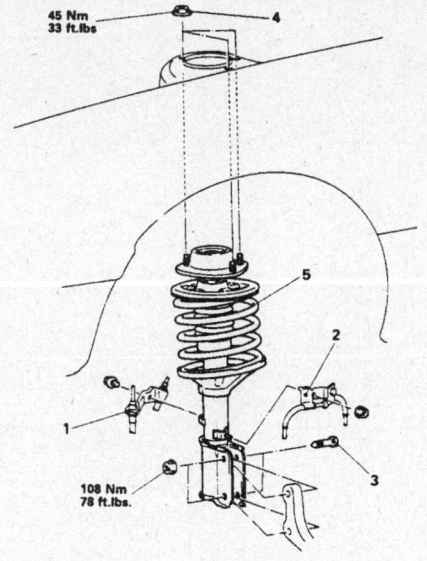

Removal steps
1. Brake pipe clamp
2. Front speed sensor clamp
   <Vehicles with ABS>
3. Bolts
4. Flange nut
5. Strut assembly

MT2029100020000X

Fig. 5   Strut assembly replacement

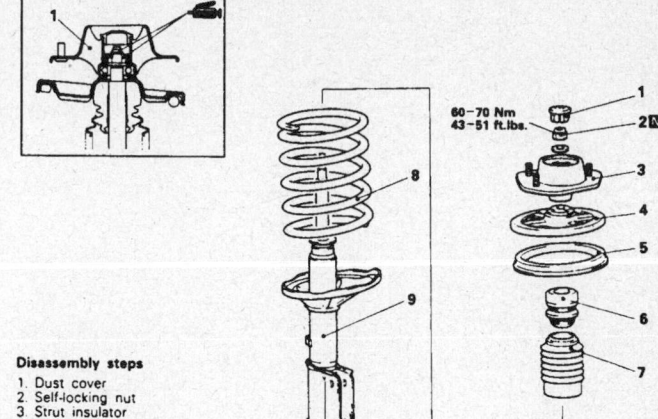

Disassembly steps
1. Dust cover
2. Self-locking nut
3. Strut insulator
4. Spring seat, upper
5. Spring pad, upper
6. Bump rubber
7. Dust cover
8. Coil spring
9. Strut assembly

MT2029100021000X

Fig. 6   Servicing strut assembly

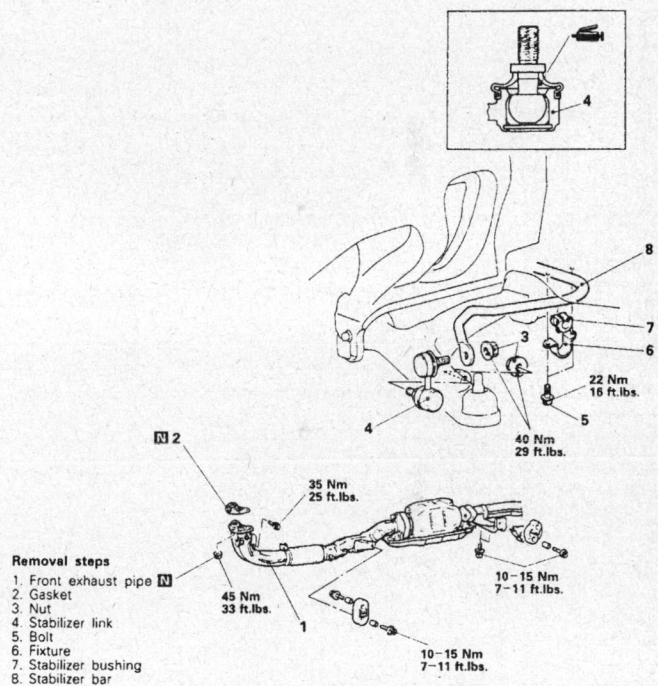

Removal steps
1. Front exhaust pipe
2. Gasket
3. Nut
4. Stabilizer link
5. Bolt
6. Fixture
7. Stabilizer bushing
8. Stabilizer bar

MT2029300022000X

Fig. 8   Stabilizer bar replacement

Removal steps
1. Stabilizer link
2. Self-locking nut
3. Bolt
4. Clamp
5. Lower arm

NOTE
* : Indicates parts which should be temporarily tightened, and then fully tightened with the vehicle in the unladen condition.

MT2029100019000X

Fig. 7   Lower control arm & ball joint replacement

seat holder MB991176, or equivalent, then loosen, but do not remove self-locking nut.
3. Using spring compressor body and arm set, tool Nos. MB991237 and MB991238 or their equivalents, compress coil spring and remove self-locking nut.

4. Line up holes in strut assembly spring lower seat with hole in spring upper seat. **This is more easily accomplished using a piece of pipe .394 x 11.82 inches.**
5. Correctly align both ends of coil spring with grooves in spring seat.
6. Apply multi-purpose grease to bearing

portion of strut insulator. **Do not allow grease to adhere to insulator's rubber portion.**

CONTROL ARM
REPLACE
LOWER

Replace lower control arm and ball joint in numbered sequence shown in **Fig. 7**.

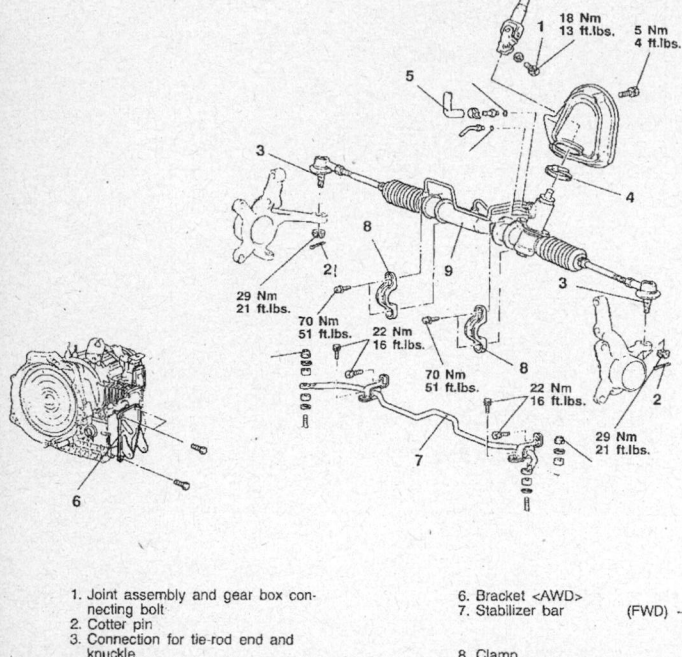

1. Joint assembly and gear box connecting bolt
2. Cotter pin
3. Connection for tie-rod end and knuckle
4. Band
5. Connection for return tube
6. Bracket <AWD>
7. Stabilizer bar   (FWD)
8. Clamp
9. Gear box assembly

MT6039100011000X

Fig. 9   Power steering gear replacement

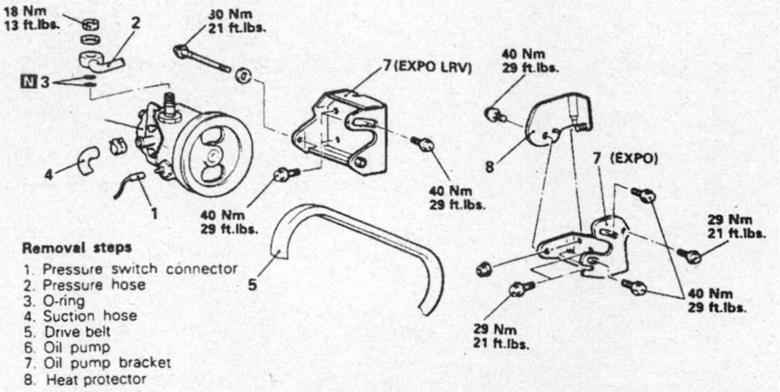

Disconnect knuckle from lower arm ball joint using steering linkage puller MB991113-01, or equivalent. **Loosen but do not remove ball joint nut until lower control arm is ready to be removed.**

STABILIZER BAR
REPLACE

This procedure has been revised by a technical service bulletin.

Replace stabilizer bar in numbered sequence shown in **Fig. 8 ,** noting the following:

1. **On LRV and AWD models,** remove propeller shaft, then disconnect front exhaust pipe and secure with wire. **Do not bend flexible joint of pipe excessively or damage to interior may result.**
2. **On all models,** when installing bar, align left edge of marking on stabilizer bar with edge of stabilizer bush, then tighten mounting bolt.
3. **On FWD models,** remove tie rod end using steering linkage puller, tool No. MB991113-01, or equivalent.

Removal steps
1. Pressure switch connector
2. Pressure hose
3. O-ring
4. Suction hose
5. Drive belt
6. Oil pump
7. Oil pump bracket
8. Heat protector

MT6039100012000X

Fig. 10   Power steering pump replacement

POWER STEERING GEAR
REPLACE

Replace power steering gearbox in numbered sequence shown in **Fig. 9.** Disconnect tie rod ends using steering linkage puller, tool No. MB991113-01, or equivalent.

POWER STEERING PUMP
REPLACE

Replace power steering pump in numbered sequence shown in **Fig. 10,** noting the following:

1. Before disconnecting pressure and suction hoses, place a rag over alternator to prevent fluid leaking into alternator.
2. When connecting pressure hose, install so that notched part contacts suction connector.

TIGHTENING SPECIFICATIONS

For tightening specifications, refer to individual repair or replacement procedures and illustrations.

Year	Component	Torque, Ft. Lbs.
1996	Axle Nut	145–188
	Driveshaft Nut	145–188
	Hub Nut	145–188
	Lower Arm Bracket Nuts	49
	Lower Arm Mounting Bolts	78
	Power Steering Pump Bracket Bolts	①
	Stabilizer Link Bracket Bolts	16
	Stabilizer Link Nuts	29
	Steering Gear Box Bracket Bolts	51
	Strut Flange Nuts	33
	Strut Pinch Bolts	78
	Strut Shaft Nut	43–51
	Wheel Bearing Nut	145–188

① — Refer to "Power Steering Pump, Replace" for procedure.

Wheel Alignment

INDEX

PRELIMINARY INSPECTION

1. Ensure tires are inflated to correct pressure, then check for uneven wear.
2. Check front wheel bearings, suspension arm and ball joints for damage and replace components as necessary to eliminate improper alignment.
3. Check steering gear for damage and adjust as necessary.
4. Check shocks for damage and replace as necessary.
5. Rock vehicle backward and forward and jounce it up and down to settle vehicle prior to alignment.
6. Ensure vehicle is unloaded and on a suitable alignment rack according manufacturer's instructions. **When measuring equipment is attached directly to outer end of driveshaft and front wheels are on turntables, apply brake to prevent vehicle movement.**

FRONT WHEEL ALIGNMENT

CAMBER

Camber is preset during production and is not adjustable. If camber is out of specification, replace bent or damaged components.

CASTER

Caster is preset during production and is not adjustable.

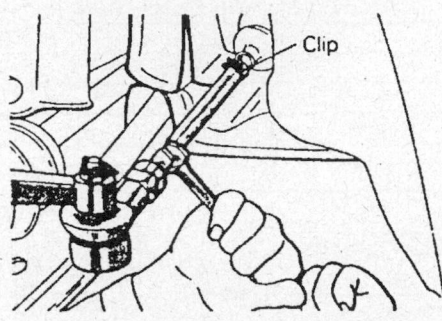

MT2049100028000X

Fig. 1   Front toe-in adjustment

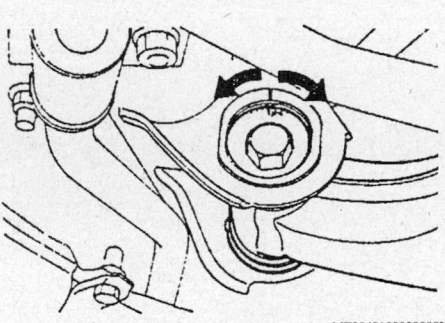

MT2049100029000X

Fig. 2   Rear toe-in adjustment

TOE-IN

1. Adjust toe-in by loosening clips and turning left and right tie rod turnbuckles equally in opposite directions. Refer to **Fig. 1.**

2. To increase toe-out, turn left turnbuckle toward front of vehicle and right turnbuckle toward rear of vehicle. To increase toe-in, turn turnbuckles in other direction.
3. Amount of toe-in adjustment is 0.24 inch for each half turn of left and right tie rods.

REAR WHEEL ALIGNMENT

CAMBER

Rear camber is preset to specifications and cannot be adjusted. If camber is out of specification, bent or damaged components must be replaced.

TOE-IN

1. Turn mounting bolts, located inside lower arms, equally to left and right sides. **Fig. 2.**
2. Toe adjustment changes approximately 0.08 inch for every scale gradation.

VEHICLE RIDE HEIGHT

There is no provision for adjustment of vehicle ride height on these vehicles. If ride height is not satisfactory, check for damaged or modified suspension components.

MITSUBISHI GALANT
INDEX OF SERVICE OPERATIONS

Specifications

GENERAL ENGINE SPECIFICATIONS

Year	Engine Liters	Fuel System	Bore & Stroke	Compression Ratio	Maximum Net H.P. @ RPM	Maximum Torque Ft. Lbs. @ RPM	Normal Oil Pressure, psi.
1996–97	2.4L ①	MFI	3.41 x 3.94	9.5	141 @ 5500	148 @ 3000	11.4③
	2.4L ②	MFI	3.41 x 3.94	9.5	138 @ 5500	148 @ 3000	11.4③
1998	2.4L	MFI	3.41 x 3.94	9.5	141 @ 5500	148 @ 3000	11.4③
1999	2.4L ①	MFI	3.41 x 3.94	9.5	145 @ 5500	155 @ 3000	11.4③
	2.4L ②	MFI	3.41 x 3.94	9.5	140 @ 5500	155 @ 3000	11.4③
	3.0L ①	MFI	3.56 x 2.99	9.0	195 @ 5500	205 @ 4500	11.6③
	3.0L ②	MFI	3.56 x 2.99	9.0	190 @ 5500	205 @ 4000	11.6③

MFI — Multi-Point Fuel Injection
① — Federal models.

② — California models.

③ — Minimum at idle speed w/oil temperature between 167–194° F.

TUNE UP SPECIFICATIONS

Year	Engine, Liter	Spark Plug Gap, Inch	Ignition Timing, Firing Order Fig.⑤	Ignition Timing, °BTDC⑥	Ignition Timing, Timing Mark Loc.	Idle Speed, RPM Curb② Man. Trans.	Idle Speed, RPM Curb② Auto. Trans.	Idle Speed, RPM Fast Man. Trans.	Idle Speed, RPM Fast Auto. Trans.	Fuel Pump Pressure, psi	Valve Lash Intake	Valve Lash Exhaust
1996–97	2.4L	.041	A	5	③	750	750N	④	④	47.6	①	①
1998	2.4L	.041	⑤	5	③	750	750N	④	④	47–50⑧	①	①
1999	2.4L	.041	⑤	5	③	750	750N	④	④	47–50⑧	①	①
	3.0L	.041	⑦	5	③	700	700N	④	④	47–50⑧	①	①

BTDC — Before Top Dead Center
N — Neutral
① — Hydraulic lifters, no adjustment required.
② — When adjusting idle speed, set parking brake & chock drive wheels.

③ — Equipped w/crankshaft position sensor.
④ — Controlled by idle speed control servo.
⑤ — Cylinder numbering from front of engine to rear, 1, 2, 3, 4. Firing order, 1–3–4–2.

⑥ — With jumper wire connected between ignition timing adjustment connector & ground. Refer to Fig. B.
⑦ — Firing order, 1–2–3–4–5–6.
⑧ — With vacuum hose disconnected from pressure regulator, engine at idle.

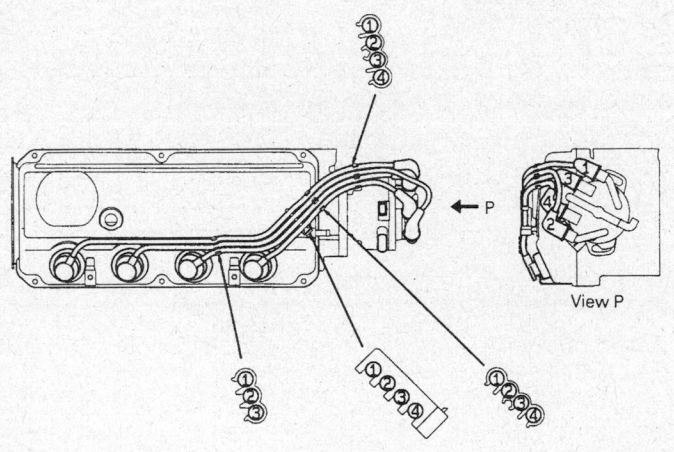

Fig. A

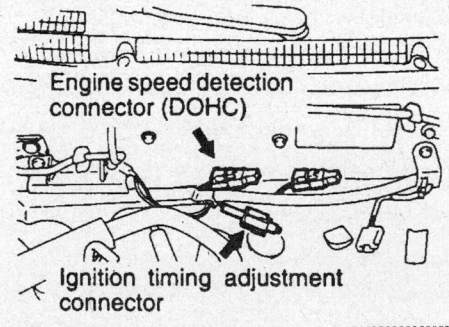

Engine speed detection connector (DOHC)

Ignition timing adjustment connector

MT1139000025000X

Fig. B

FRONT WHEEL ALIGNMENT SPECIFICATIONS

Year	Caster Angle, Deg.		Camber Angle, Deg.		Toe, Inch①	Ball Joint Inspection, Inch Lbs.	
	Limits	Desired	Limits	Desired		Upper	Lower
1996–98	+2⅝ to +5⅝	+4⅓	–½ to +½	0	–.12 to +.12	3–13②	4–22②
1999	+2½ to +3½	+3	–½ to +½	0	–.1 to +.1	—	22–54③

① — Toe-in (+); toe-out (-).

② — Breakaway measurement using special service tool No. MB990326, or equivalent.

③ — Breakaway measurement using tool No. MB991006, or equivalent.

REAR WHEEL ALIGNMENT SPECIFICATIONS

Year	Camber Angle, Deg.		Toe, Inch①	Ball Joint Inspection, Inch Lbs.	
	Limits	Desired		Upper	Lower
1996–99	–1⅝ to –⅝	–1⅓	0 to +.24	—	1–23②

① — Toe-in (+); toe-out (-).

② — Breakaway measurement using tool No. MB990326, or equivalent.

FLUID CAPACITIES & COOLING SYSTEM DATA

Year	Engine	Coolant Capacity, Qts.		Radiator Cap Relief Pressure, Lbs.	Thermo. Opening Temp., °F	Fuel Tank, Gals.	Engine Oil Refill, Qts.①	Transmission Oil	
		Less A/C	With A/C					5 Speed, Pts.	Auto. Trans., Qts.②
1996–97	2.4L	7.4	7.4	13	180	16.9	4.5	4.4	6.3
1998	2.4L	7.4	7.4	11–15	180	16.9	4.5	4.6	6.3
1999	2.4L	7.4	7.4	11–15	190	16.3	4.5	4.6	8.2
	3.0L	7.4	7.4	11–15	190	16.3	4.5	4.6	9.0

① — Includes filter.

② — Approximate, make final check w/dipstick.

LUBRICANT DATA

Year	Lubricant Type			
	Transmission		Power Steering	Brake System
	Manual	Automatic		
1996–97	75W-90 GL-4	Dia ATF SP	Dexron II/IIE/III	DOT 3 or 4
1998–99	75W-90, 75W-85W GL-4	Dia ATF SP II	Dexron II	DOT 3 or 4

Electrical

NOTE: On Air Bag Equipped Models, Refer To "Air Bag System Precautions" Located In The Front Of This Manual For System Disarming & Arming Procedures.

NOTE: Refer To "Computer Relearn Procedures" Located In The Front Of This Manual For Computer Relearn Procedures.

INDEX

PRECAUTIONS

AIR BAG SYSTEMS

Refer to "Air Bag System Precautions" in the front of this manual for system disarming and arming procedures.

BATTERY GROUND CABLE

Prior to service, disconnect battery ground cable and isolate as required.

FUSE PANEL & FLASHER LOCATION

The fuse panel is located behind the lefthand side of the instrument panel. The centralized junction box is mounted on the righthand wheelhouse in the engine compartment. The turn signal and hazard flasher is located behind the lower lefthand side of the instrument panel.

FUEL PUMP RELAY LOCATION

1996–98

The fuel pump relay (multi-point fuel injection MFI relay), is located on the lefthand side of the center console, **Fig. 1.**

1999

The fuel pump relay and MFI relay are located in the underhood relay fuse panel.

RELAY CENTER LOCATION

The main relay center is located on top of

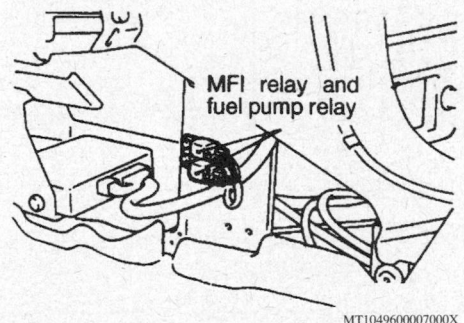

MT1049600007000X

Fig. 1 Fuel pump relay location. 1996–98

the righthand or lefthand wheelhouse in the engine compartment.

STARTER

REPLACE

1. Remove air cleaner assembly.
2. Disconnect starter cables.
3. Remove starter mounting bolts, then the starter.
4. Reverse procedure to install. **Torque** starter mounting bolts to 20–25 ft. lbs.

DISTRIBUTOR

REPLACE

1. Rotate crankshaft to No. 1 cylinder TDC, then remove spark plug cables.
2. Remove high tension cable from ignition coil.
3. Scribe alignment marks on distributor housing, then remove distributor.

4. Reverse procedure to install, noting the following:
   a. Ensure No. 1 cylinder is still at TDC.
   b. Align distributor housing and gear mating marks.
   c. Install distributor with housing and gear mating marks aligned as shown, **Fig. 2.**

IGNITION LOCK

REPLACE

1. Remove steering column shrouds.
2. Cut attaching bolts at steering lock bracket side using a suitable hacksaw, then remove bolts.
3. Remove ignition switch electrical connectors, then the lock assembly.
4. Reverse procedure to install, noting the following:
   a. Temporarily install ignition lock in alignment with column boss and check for proper switch operation.
   b. Steering lock bracket should be replaced when installing new ignition switch.
   c. Install special ignition lock attaching bolts and tighten until heads twist off.

IGNITION SWITCH

REPLACE

Remove ignition switch in numbered sequence, **Figs. 3 and 4.**

NEUTRAL SAFETY SWITCH

REPLACE

1. Disconnect all switch connections,

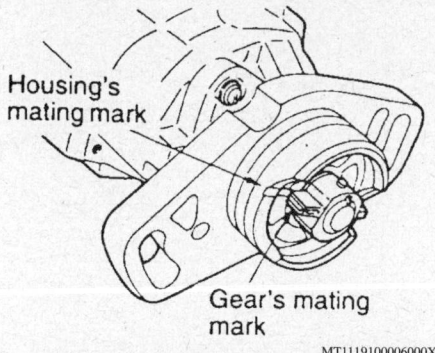

Fig. 2 Distributor gear alignment

then remove switch from transaxle.
2. Reverse procedure to install, then adjust switch as follows:
   a. Place selector lever and manual control lever in Neutral position.
   b. Rotate switch body, ensuring manual control lever hole and switch body hole are aligned, **Fig. 5.**
   c. **Torque** mounting bolts of the park/neutral position switch body to 7–9 ft. lbs. **Do not drop switch body.**
   d. Loosen nut as shown, **Fig. 6,** then lightly pull end of transaxle control cable in "F" direction by hand. **Torque** to 7–10 ft. lbs.
   e. With selector lever in Neutral position, ensure neutral start switch operates and functions on transaxle side in range which corresponds to each position of selector lever.

COMBINATION SWITCH
REPLACE

1. Refer to numbered sequence in **Fig. 3** when replacing combination switch.
2. Reverse procedure to install.

STEERING WHEEL
REPLACE

1. Disconnect negative battery cable.
2. **Wait at least 60 seconds after disconnecting battery cable before continuing with procedure.**
3. Remove air bag module mounting nut using a socket from back side of steering wheel.
4. When disconnecting the connector of the clock spring from air bag module, press air bag's lock toward outer side to spread it open.
5. Use a screwdriver to pry gently while removing connector.
6. Remove driver's air bag module.
7. Using a suitable steering wheel puller, remove steering wheel.
8. Reverse procedure to install, noting the following:
   a. Turn vehicles wheels straight ahead and align mating marks of the clockspring.
   b. Install steering wheel and **torque** nut to 30 ft. lbs.

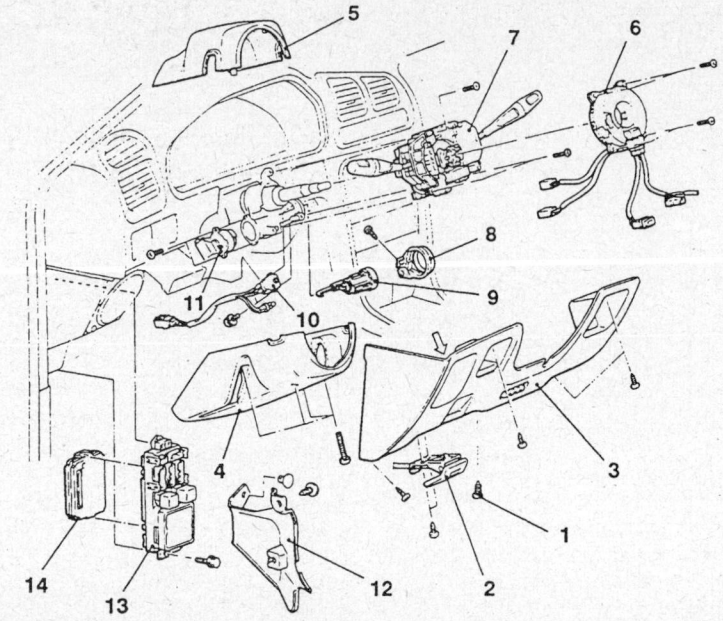

NOTE
The ⇐ mark indicates the sheet metal clip position.

● Steering wheel

1. Clip
2. Hood lock release handle
3. Instrument under cover
4. Column cover lower
5. Column cover upper
6. Clock spring
7. Column switch
8. Ignition key illumination ring or ring cover
9. Steering lock cylinder

Key reminder switch or key hole illumination light removal steps

4. Column cover lower
5. Column cover upper
10. Key reminder switch or key hole illumination light

Ignition switch removal steps

4. Column cover lower
5. Column cover upper
11. Ignition switch

BUZZER-ECU or ETACS-ECU removal steps

12. Cowl side trim (LH)
13. Junction block
14. BUZZER-ECU or ETACS-ECU

Fig. 3 Ignition switch & combination switch replacement. 1996–98

INSTRUMENT CLUSTER
REPLACE

To replace instrument cluster, refer to "Dash Panel Serivce."

RADIO
REPLACE

1. Pry off radio panel using a suitable tool.
2. Remove radio bracket attaching screws, then disconnect antenna and radio electrical connector.
3. Remove radio.
4. Reverse procedure to install.

WIPER MOTOR
REPLACE

1. Remove front deck and inlet garnish panels.
2. Remove linkage mounting bolts.
3. Remove wiper motor attaching bolts, then pull wiper motor slightly and disconnect motor and linkage assembly.
4. Remove wiper motor with linkage from

vehicle. If crank arm is to be removed, mark position of arm to wiper motor for assembly reference.
5. Reverse procedure to install.

WIPER SWITCH
REPLACE

Refer to "Column Switch, Replace" for wiper switch replacement procedure.

BLOWER MOTOR
REPLACE

1. Remove instrument panel lower cover.
2. **On models with A/C,** remove automatic compressor ECM.
3. **On all models,** remove blower motor attaching bolts, then the blower motor.
4. Reverse procedure to install.

HEATER CORE
REPLACE

Remove heater unit components in order as shown, **Fig. 7,** noting the following:

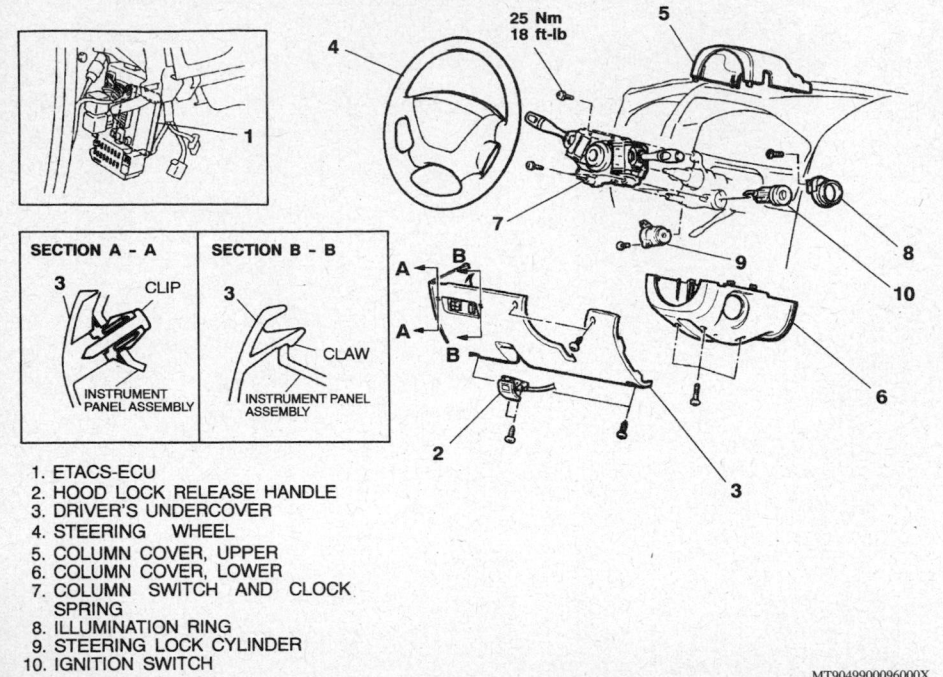

25 Nm
18 ft-lb

SECTION A - A | SECTION B - B

SECTION A - A
3   CLIP
INSTRUMENT PANEL ASSEMBLY

SECTION B - B
3
CLAW
INSTRUMENT PANEL ASSEMBLY

1. ETACS-ECU
2. HOOD LOCK RELEASE HANDLE
3. DRIVER'S UNDERCOVER
4. STEERING WHEEL
5. COLUMN COVER, UPPER
6. COLUMN COVER, LOWER
7. COLUMN SWITCH AND CLOCK SPRING
8. ILLUMINATION RING
9. STEERING LOCK CYLINDER
10. IGNITION SWITCH

MT9049900096000X

Fig. 4 Ignition switch & combination switch replacement. 1999

<SOHC>   <DOHC>

A   A Manual control lever

A   A

Manual control lever

Section A-A

Rod (ø5)   Manual control lever

Switch body

MT9099400007000X

Fig. 5 Neutral start switch measurement

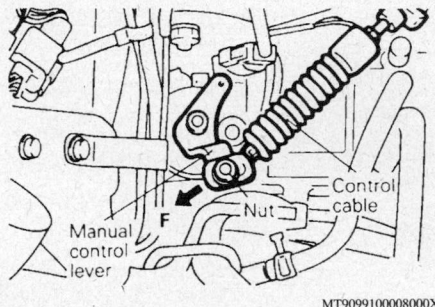

Manual control lever   Nut   Control cable

F

MT9099100008000X

Fig. 6 Manual control lever nut removal

1. Drain cooling system into suitable container.
2. Remove front seats and floor console **Figs. 8 and 9.**
3. Remove instrument panel as outlined under "Dash Panel Service."
4. **On models with A/C,** remove bolts and nuts attaching evaporator assembly to heater unit, then pull evaporator assembly out of heater unit.
5. **On all models,** remove heater unit from vehicle.
6. To prevent bolts from falling into blower assembly, set air selection damper to outside air induction position.
7. Remove heater core from heater unit.
8. Reverse procedure to install.

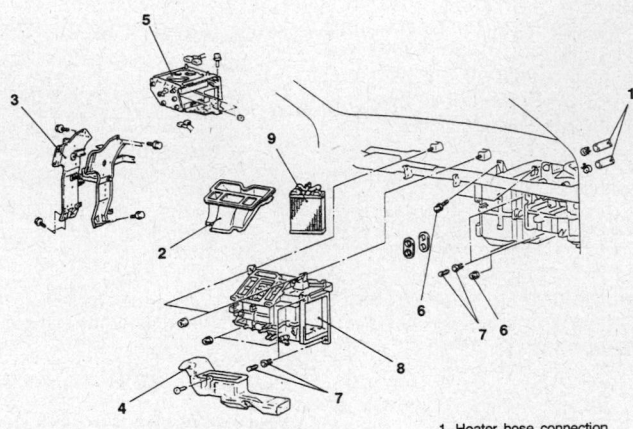

1. Heater hose connection
2. Center ventilation duct
3. Center reinforcement
4. Foot distribution duct
5. ECM bracket
6. Evaporator installation bolt and nut
7. Clip
8. Heater unit
9. Heater core

MT7029400084000X

Fig. 7 Exploded view of heater unit

EVAPORATOR CORE

REPLACE

1. Discharge refrigerant from system as outlined in "Air Conditioning" section.
2. Disconnect evaporator inlet pipe and suction hose. **Plug openings to prevent contamination.**
3. Remove components in numbered sequences, **Fig. 10.**
4. Reverse procedure to install, recharge A/C system with refrigerant as outlined in "Air Conditioning" section.

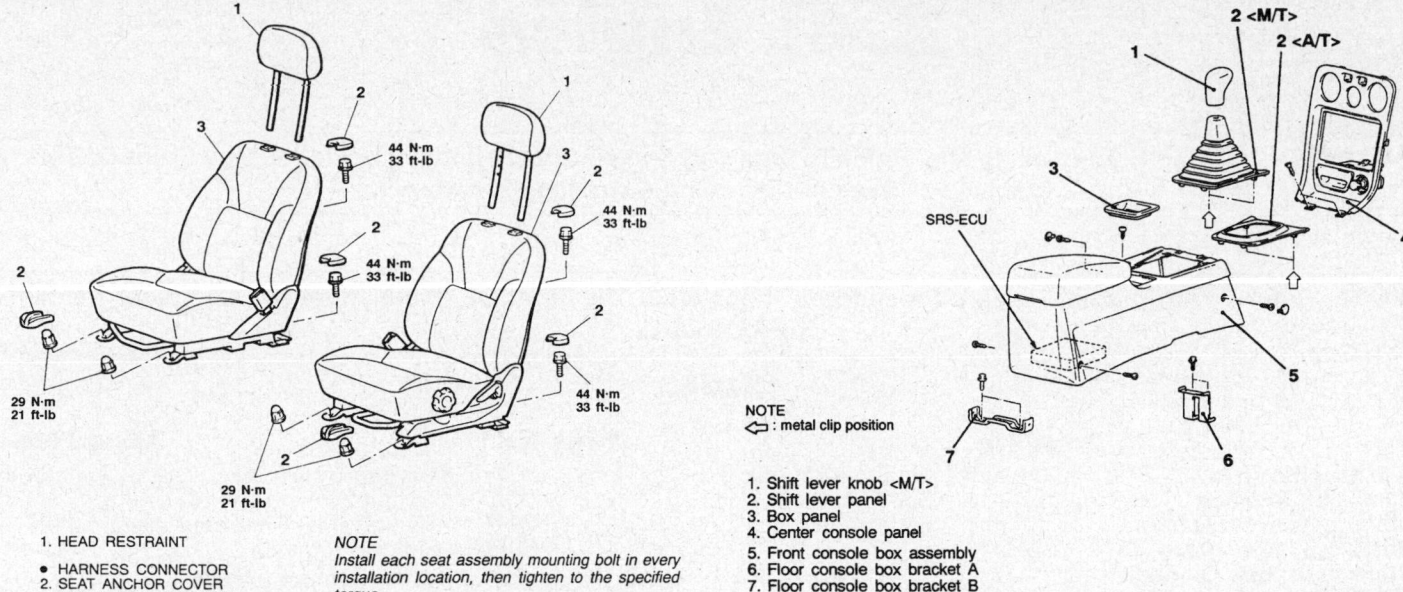

1. HEAD RESTRAINT
- HARNESS CONNECTOR
2. SEAT ANCHOR COVER
3. FRONT SEAT ASSEMBLY

NOTE
Install each seat assembly mounting bolt in every installation location, then tighten to the specified torque.

MT7029400086000X

Fig. 8 Front seat removal

NOTE
⟸ : metal clip position

1. Shift lever knob <M/T>
2. Shift lever panel
3. Box panel
4. Center console panel
5. Front console box assembly
6. Floor console box bracket A
7. Floor console box bracket B

MT7029400088000X

Fig. 9 Floor console removal

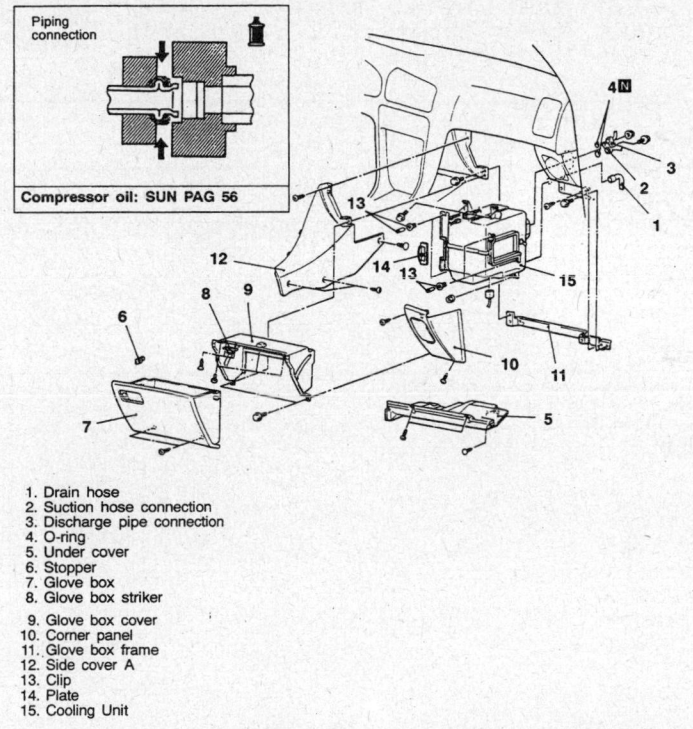

Compressor oil: SUN PAG 56

1. Drain hose
2. Suction hose connection
3. Discharge pipe connection
4. O-ring
5. Under cover
6. Stopper
7. Glove box
8. Glove box striker
9. Glove box cover
10. Corner panel
11. Glove box frame
12. Side cover A
13. Clip
14. Plate
15. Cooling Unit

MT7029400092000X

Fig. 10 Evaporator core replacement

2.4L Engine

NOTE: On Air Bag Equipped Models, Refer To "Air Bag System Precautions" Located In The Front Of This Manual For System Disarming & Arming Procedures.

NOTE: Refer To "Computer Relearn Procedures" Located In The Front Of This Manual For Computer Relearn Procedures.

INDEX

PRECAUTIONS

AIR BAG SYSTEMS

Refer to "Air Bag System Precautions" in the front of this manual for system disarming and arming procedures.

BATTERY GROUND CABLE

Prior to service, disconnect battery ground cable and isolate as required.

FUEL SYSTEM PRESSURE RELIEF

When service to any component necessitates working with the fuel system, fuel pressure in the system must be relieved. This is extremely important to reduce risk of personal injury, fire or explosion due to fuel spray and leakage. Relieve fuel system pressure as follows:

1. Remove rear seat cushion, then disconnect fuel pump wiring harness from floor wiring harness.
2. Start engine and allow all residual fuel in system to be consumed; when engine stalls, turn ignition switch to Off position.
3. Connect fuel pump wiring harness to floor wiring harness and install rear seat cushion, then continue with service.

COMPRESSION PRESSURES

Ensure engine oil, starter motor and battery are in satisfactory condition. When checking compression, engine coolant should be at normal operating temperature, spark plugs should be removed and throttle valve should be wide open. Minimum compression pressure at engine cranking speed is 145 psi. Difference between cylinders should not exceed 14 psi.

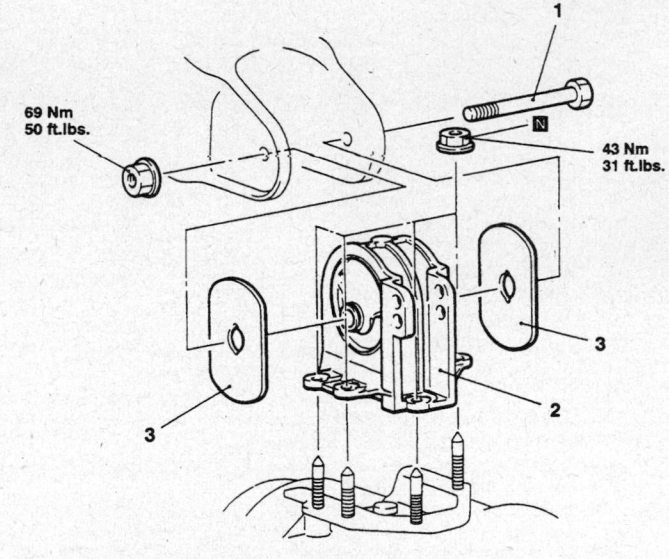

1. Transaxle mount insulator mounting bolt
2. Transaxle mount bracket
3. Transaxle mount stopper

MT1069100219000X

Fig. 1 Transaxle mount replacement

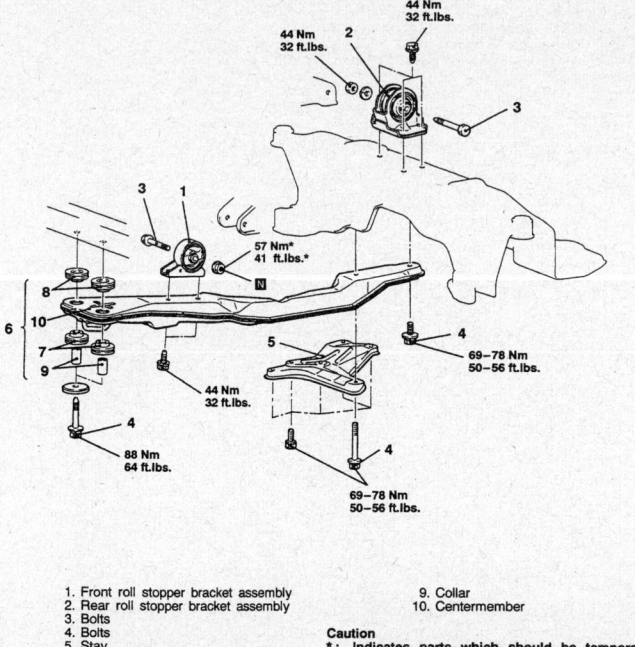

44 Nm
32 ft.lbs.
44 Nm
32 ft.lbs.
57 Nm*
41 ft.lbs.*
69–78 Nm
50–56 ft.lbs.
44 Nm
32 ft.lbs.
88 Nm
64 ft.lbs.
69–78 Nm
50–56 ft.lbs.
1. Front roll stopper bracket assembly
2. Rear roll stopper bracket assembly
3. Bolts
4. Bolts
5. Stay
6. Centermember assembly
7. Bushing (lower)
8. Bushing (upper)
9. Collar
10. Centermember
Caution
*: Indicates parts which should be temporarily tightened, and then fully tightened with the vehicle on the ground in the unladen condition.
MT1069100220000X

Fig. 2 Engine roll stopper & center member replacement

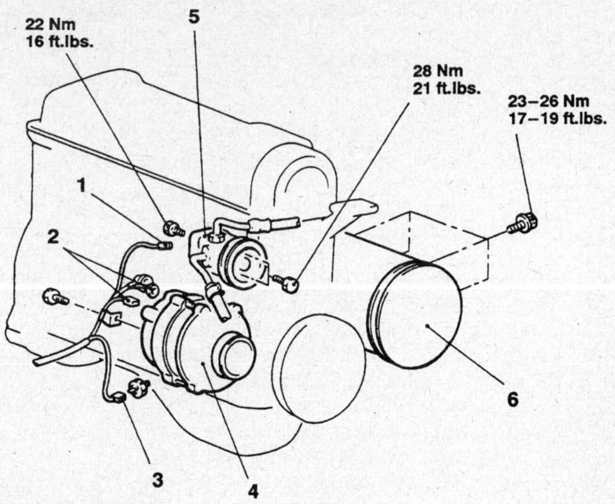

22 Nm
16 ft.lbs.
28 Nm
21 ft.lbs.
23–26 Nm
17–19 ft.lbs.
1. Power steering pressure switch connector
2. Generator harness
3. Oil pressure switch connector
4. Generator
5. Connection for power steering pump
6. Connection for A/C compressor
MT1069100221010X

Fig. 3 Engine replacement (Part 1 of 3). 1996–98

ENGINE MOUNT

REPLACE

ENGINE

Refer to "Engine, Replace" in this section for motor mount replacement information.

TRANSAXLE

1. Relieve fuel system pressure as outlined under " Precautions," then remove air cleaner assembly.
2. Using a suitable lifting device, raise engine and transaxle assembly slightly to alleviate pressure on transaxle mount.
3. Remove transaxle mount in numbered sequence, **Fig. 1.**
4. Reverse procedure to install. Tighten all bolts and nuts to specifications.

ROLL STOPPER & CENTER MEMBER

1. Relieve fuel system pressure as outlined under " Precautions."
2. Remove roll stopper and center member in numbered sequence, **Fig. 2.**
3. Reverse procedure to install. Tighten all bolts and nuts to specifications.

ENGINE

REPLACE

1996–98

1. Relieve fuel system pressure as outlined under " Precautions," then scribe and remove hood.
2. Drain engine coolant into a suitable container, then remove transaxle as outlined under "Transaxle, Replace" in "Clutch & Manual Transaxle" or " Automatic Transaxle" section.
3. Remove radiator as outlined under "Radiator, Replace, " then the engine lower cover.
4. Remove engine assembly in numbered sequence, **Fig. 3** noting the following:
   a. When removing power steering pump and A/C compressor, leave hoses attached and support aside.
   b. Ensure engine is supported when transaxle is removed. A block of wood placed between oil pan and a floor jack will suffice until a suitable engine lifting device can be installed.
5. Reverse procedure to install. Tighten all engine mounting bolts and nuts to specifications.

1999

1. Mark hood hinge to hood location for installation reference, then remove hood.
2. Relieve fuel system pressure as outlined under " Precautions."
3. Drain engine oil and coolant into suitable containers.
4. Remove air cleaner assembly.
5. Remove thermostat case assembly.
6. Remove radiator and reservoir.
7. Remove front exhaust pipe.
8. Remove engine assembly in numbered sequence, **Fig. 4.**
9. Reverse procedure to install, noting the following:
   a. **Torque** all mounting hardware to specification.
   b. Ensure engine mount stopper is installed in position with arrow pointing in direction shown, **Fig. 5.**
   c. Apply a small drop of clean engine oil to high pressure fuel rail fitting and install with a twisting motion using care not to damage O-ring seal.

INTAKE MANIFOLD

REPLACE

1. Relieve fuel system pressure as outlined under " Precautions," then drain engine coolant into a suitable container.
2. Remove intake manifold in numbered sequence shown, **Figs. 6 and 7** then inspect cylinder head mating surface for distortion using a straightedge and a feeler gauge. Distortion must be below .008 inch.
3. Reverse procedure to install. Tighten all bolts and nuts to specifications.

EXHAUST MANIFOLD

REPLACE

1. Relieve fuel system pressure as outlined under " Precautions."
2. Remove exhaust manifold in numbered sequence shown, **Figs. 8 and 9.**
3. Reverse procedure to install, tighten all bolts and nuts to specifications.

CYLINDER HEAD

REPLACE

1. Relieve fuel system pressure as outlined in "Precautions, " then drain engine coolant and oil into suitable containers.
2. Remove cylinder head and gasket in numbered sequence, **Fig. 10.** Loosen cylinder head bolts evenly, a little at a time, using head bolt tool No. MD991654, or equivalent.

3. Reverse procedure to install noting the following:
   a. Install new cylinder head gasket, **Fig. 11.**
   b. Measure shank length of each cylinder head bolt before installing, **Fig. 12.**
   c. Replace any bolt that measures more than 3.91 inches.
   d. Apply oil to threaded portion of bolts and washers.
   e. **Torque** bolts in sequence, **Fig. 13,** to 58 ft. lbs.
   f. Loosen bolts completely, then **torque** to 14.5 ft. lbs. in sequence.
   g. Make a paint mark across each bolt head and cylinder head.
   h. Turn each bolt in sequence, 90.°
   i. Tighten each bolt in sequence another 90° and ensure paint mark on bolt head and paint mark on cylinder head are aligned.

VALVE CLEARANCE SPECIFICATIONS

This engine uses hydraulic valve lash adjusters, no adjustments are required

VALVE ADJUSTMENT

This engine uses hydraulic valve lash adjusters, no adjustments are required. If an abnormal rattling noise is heard from the lash adjusters refer to "Hydraulic Lash Adjusters" for inspection and repair procedures.

HYDRAULIC LASH ADJUSTERS

Any air entering the high pressure chamber of the hydraulic lash adjuster can cause the adjuster to make a rattling noise. Use the following procedure to check and replace adjuster.

1. Check engine oil for any of the following conditions:
   a. If oil level is low, air will be sucked in from the oil strainer and will mix in the oil passage.
   b. If oil level is excessive, oil will be stirred by the crankshaft, causing a large amount of air mix in the oil.
   c. If oil is deteriorated, it will not easily separate from air and amount of air mixed in oil will increase.
2. If engine oil exhibits any of the above conditions, add or change engine oil as necessary.
3. Start engine and gently accelerate several times. If rattling noise stops, air is bled from high pressure chamber and adjuster is operating normally. If rattling noise does not stop, check lash adjusters as follows:
   a. Stop engine and remove rocker arm cover.
   b. Set No. 1 piston to top dead center of compression stroke.
   c. Push rocker arm as indicated in **Fig. 14.**
   d. Slowly rotate crankshaft 360° and push rocker arms indicated in **Fig. 15.**

e. If rocker arm can be pushed easily, lash adjuster either has air in high pressure chamber or it is faulty and should be replaced.
4. To determine if the lash adjuster is faulty, proceed as follows:
   a. Remove rocker arms as outlined under "Rocker Arms, Replace."
   b. Immerse lash adjuster in clean diesel fuel.
   c. Using a small wire, lightly push down inner steel ball four or five times, **Fig. 16.**
   d. Remove small wire and press plunger. If plunger is hard to press in, adjuster is normal. If plunger is easy to push in, lash adjuster is faulty and must be replaced. **After air bleeding is complete, hold lash adjuster upright to prevent inside diesel fuel from spilling.**
   e. Air must be bled from new hydraulic lash adjusters prior to installation.

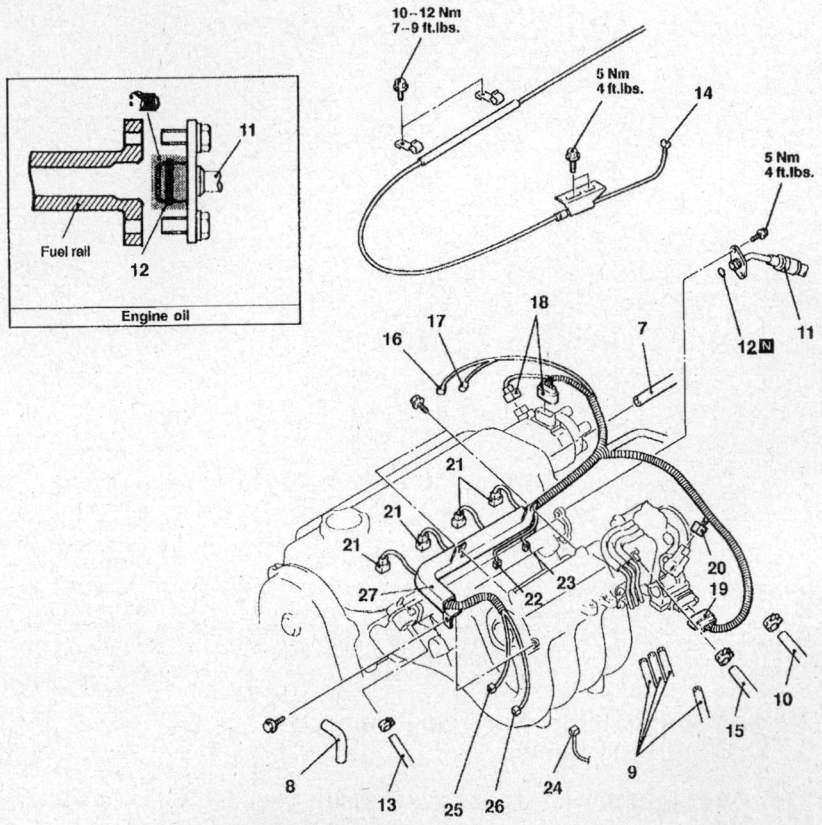

Fig. 3   Engine replacement (Part 2 of 3). 1996–98

7. Breather hose connection
8. PCV hose
9. Vacuum hose connection
10. Water hose connection
11. Fuel high-pressure hose connection
12. O-ring
13. Fuel return hose connection
14. Accelerator cable connection
15. Brake booster vacuum hose connection
16. Engine coolant temperature gauge unit connector
17. Engine coolant temperature sensor connector
18. Distributor connector
19. Idle speed control motor connector
20. Throttle position sensor connector
21. Injector connectors
22. Control wiring harness and heated oxygen sensor wiring harness connection
23. EGR temperature sensor connector
24. Heated oxygen sensor connector
25. Condenser connector
26. Refrigerant temperature switch connector
27. Control harness

MT1069100221020X

ROCKER ARMS
REPLACE

Refer to "Camshaft, Replace" for rocker arm replacement procedure.

TIMING BELT
REPLACE

With the timing belt removed, avoid turning the camshaft or crankshaft. If movement is required, exercise extreme caution to avoid valve damage caused by piston contact. Never rotate the engine in a counterclockwise direction or possible engine damage will result.

1. Relieve fuel system pressure as outlined under " Precautions," then remove engine lower cover.
2. Timing belt upper and lower cover bolts are of varying length. Note location of each bolt on removal for installation reference.

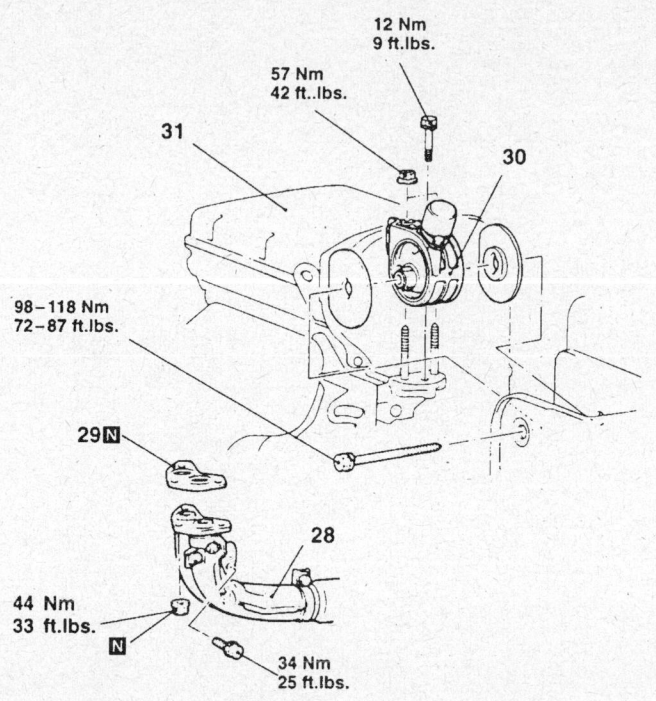

28. Front exhaust pipe connection
29. Gasket
30. Engine mount bracket
31. Engine assembly

MT1069100221030X

Fig. 3   Engine replacement (Part 3 of 3). 1996–98

Fig. 4   Engine replacement (Part 1 of 2). 1999

1. ACCELERATOR CABLE CONNECTION
2. PURGE HOSE CONNECTION
3. BRAKE BOOSTER VACUUM HOSE CONNECTION
4. VACUUM HOSE CONNECTION <VEHICLES WITH AUTO-CRUISE CONTROL SYSTEM>
5. IGNITION COIL CONNECTOR
6. INJECTOR CONNECTOR
7. IBNITION FAILURE SENSOR CONNECTOR
8. MANIFOLD DIFFERENTIAL PRESSURE SENSOR CONNECTOR
9. THROTTLE POSITION SENSOR CONNECTOR
10. IDLE AIR CONTROL MOTOR CONNECTOR
11. EVAPORATIVE EMISSION PURGE SOLENOID VALVE CONNECTOR
12. EGR SOLENOID VALVE CONNECTOR
13. HIGH-PRESSURE FUEL HOSE CONNECTION
14. FUEL RETURN HOSE CONNECTION
15. PRESSURE TUBE CONNECTION

MT1069900567010X

3. Remove timing belt in numbered sequence shown, **Figs. 17 and 18**, noting the following:
   a. When removing belt, turn crankshaft in direction of normal rotation to align timing marks, then loosen tensioner pulley center bolt and move pulley toward water pump.
   b. If timing belt is to be reused, mark direction of rotation for installation reference.
4. Remove timing belt "B" in numbered sequence shown, **Fig. 19**, noting the following:
   a. When removing crankshaft sprocket, secure flywheel or driveplate with holding tool No. MD998781, or equivalent, then use sprocket removal tool No. MD998778, or equivalent, to separate sprocket from shaft.
   b. If timing belt "B" is to be reused, mark direction of normal rotation on belt for installation reference.
5. Reverse procedure to install, noting the following:
   a. When installing timing belt "B," ensure crankshaft sprocket "B" timing mark and silent shaft sprocket timing mark are aligned, **Fig. 20**, then fit timing belt "B" over crankshaft sprocket "B" and silent shaft

sprocket. There should be no slack in belt.
   b. To adjust timing belt "B" tension, temporarily secure tensioner such that center of pulley is offset from installation bolt as shown, **Fig. 21**, then attach tensioner pulley with

flange toward front of engine. Hold tensioner up in direction of arrow, **Fig. 22**, then exert pressure on belt until tension side is taut. Tighten bolt to secure tensioner in place. **Do not allow tensioner pulley shaft to rotate with bolt.**

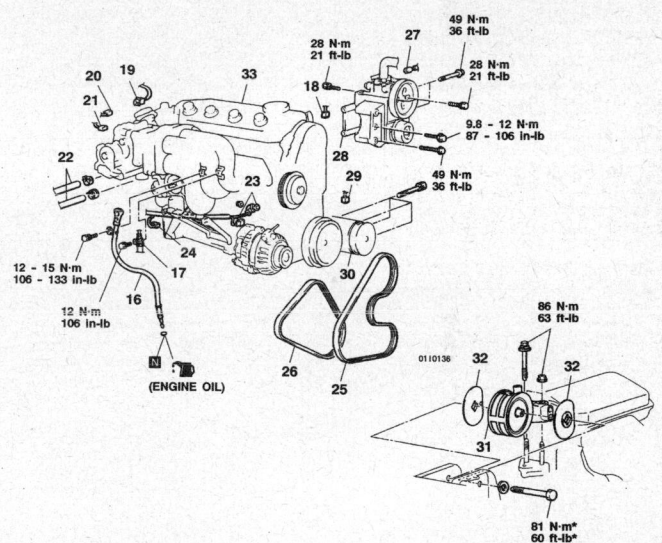

16. OIL DIPSTICK AND DIPSTICK GUIDE
17. PRESSURE HOSE CONNECTION
18. CRANKSHAFT POSITION SENSOR CONNECTOR
19. HEATED OXYGEN SENSOR CONNECTOR <VEHICLES FOR CALIFORNIA>
20. CAMSHAFT POSITION SENSOR CONNECTOR
21. ENGINE COOLANT TEMPERATURE SENSOR CONNECTOR
22. HEATER HOSE CONNECTION
23. GENERATOR CONNECTOR
24. OIL PRESSURE SWITCH CONNECTOR
25. DRIVE BELT (POWER STEERING OIL PUMP AND A/C COMPRESSOR)
26. DRIVE BELT (GENERATOR)
27. POWER STEERING PRESSURE SWITCH CONNECTOR
28. POWER STEERING OIL PUMP AND BRACKET ASSEMBLY
29. A/C COMPRESSOR ASSEMBLY CONNECTOR
30. A/C COMPRESSOR
• TRANSAXLE ASSEMBLY
30. A/C COMPRESSOR
31. ENGINE MOUNT BRACKET
32. ENGINE MOUNT STOPPER
33. ENGINE ASSEMBLY

MT1069900567020X

Fig. 4   Engine replacement (Part 2 of 2). 1999

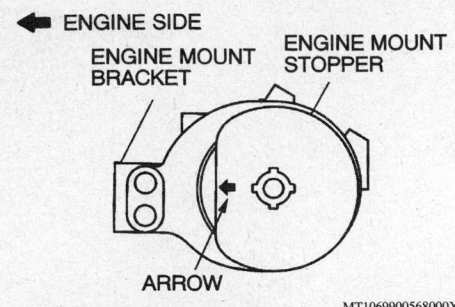

Fig. 5 Engine mount stopper installation. 1999 2.4L engine

MT1069900568000X

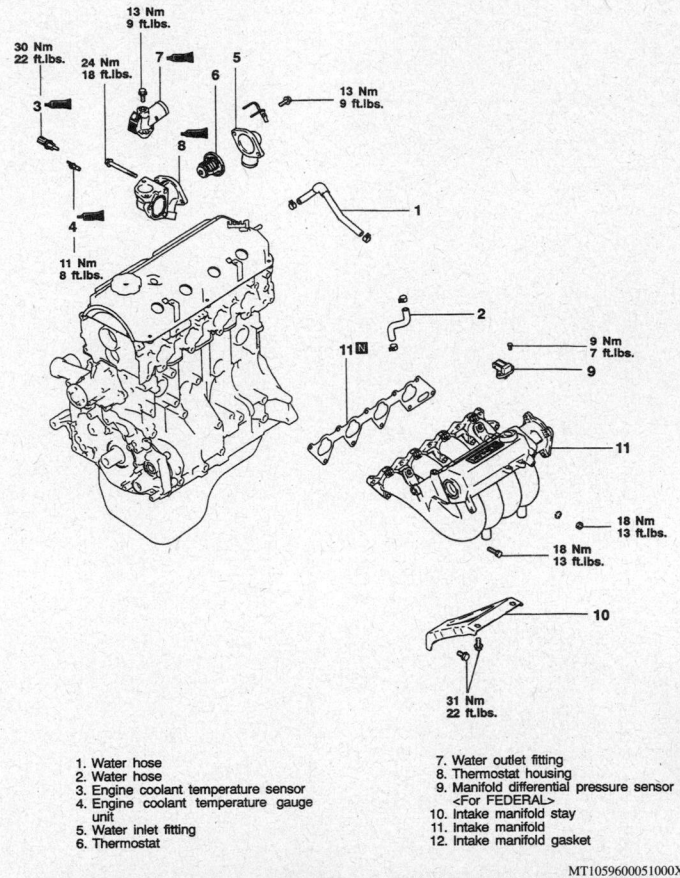

1. Water hose
2. Water hose
3. Engine coolant temperature sensor
4. Engine coolant temperature gauge unit
5. Water inlet fitting
6. Thermostat
7. Water outlet fitting
8. Thermostat housing
9. Manifold differential pressure sensor <For FEDERAL>
10. Intake manifold stay
11. Intake manifold
12. Intake manifold gasket

MT1059600051000X

Fig. 6 Intake manifold replacement. 1996–98

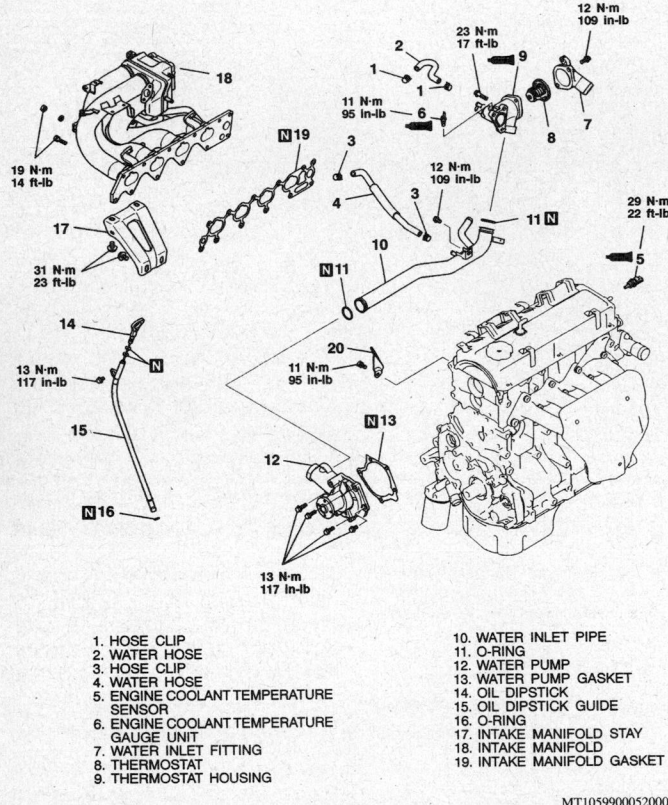

1. HOSE CLIP
2. WATER HOSE
3. HOSE CLIP
4. WATER HOSE
5. ENGINE COOLANT TEMPERATURE SENSOR
6. ENGINE COOLANT TEMPERATURE GAUGE UNIT
7. WATER INLET FITTING
8. THERMOSTAT
9. THERMOSTAT HOUSING
10. WATER INLET PIPE
11. O-RING
12. WATER PUMP
13. WATER PUMP GASKET
14. OIL DIPSTICK
15. OIL DIPSTICK GUIDE
16. O-RING
17. INTAKE MANIFOLD STAY
18. INTAKE MANIFOLD
19. INTAKE MANIFOLD GASKET

MT1059900052000X

Fig. 7 Intake manifold replacement. 1999

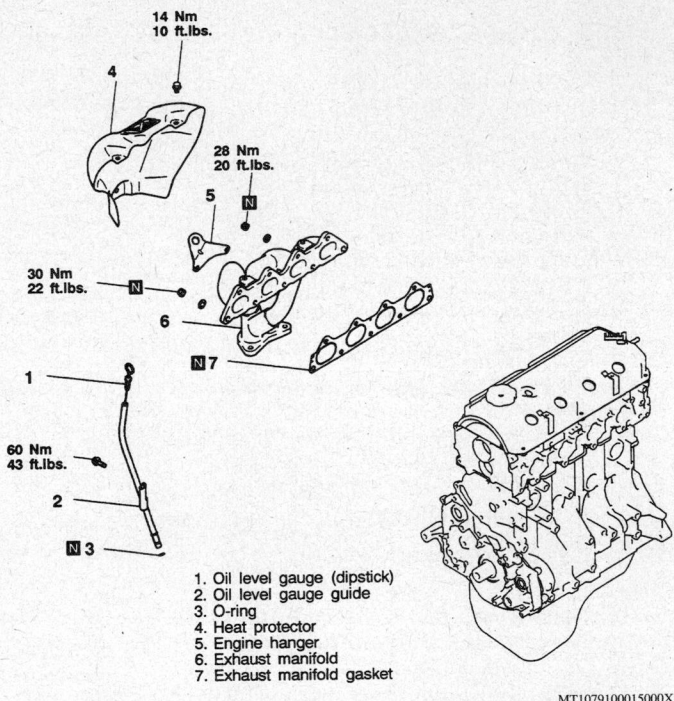

1. Oil level gauge (dipstick)
2. Oil level gauge guide
3. O-ring
4. Heat protector
5. Engine hanger
6. Exhaust manifold
7. Exhaust manifold gasket

MT1079100015000X

Fig. 8 Exhaust manifold replacement. 1996–98

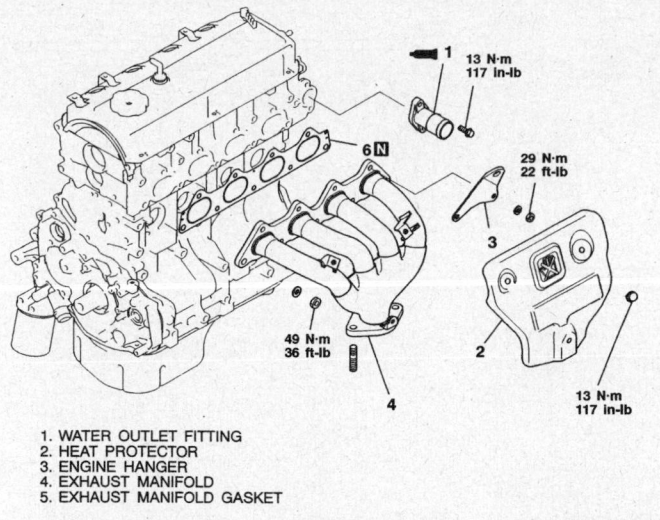

Fig. 9   Exhaust manifold replacement. 1999

1. WATER OUTLET FITTING
2. HEAT PROTECTOR
3. ENGINE HANGER
4. EXHAUST MANIFOLD
5. EXHAUST MANIFOLD GASKET

MT1079900026000X

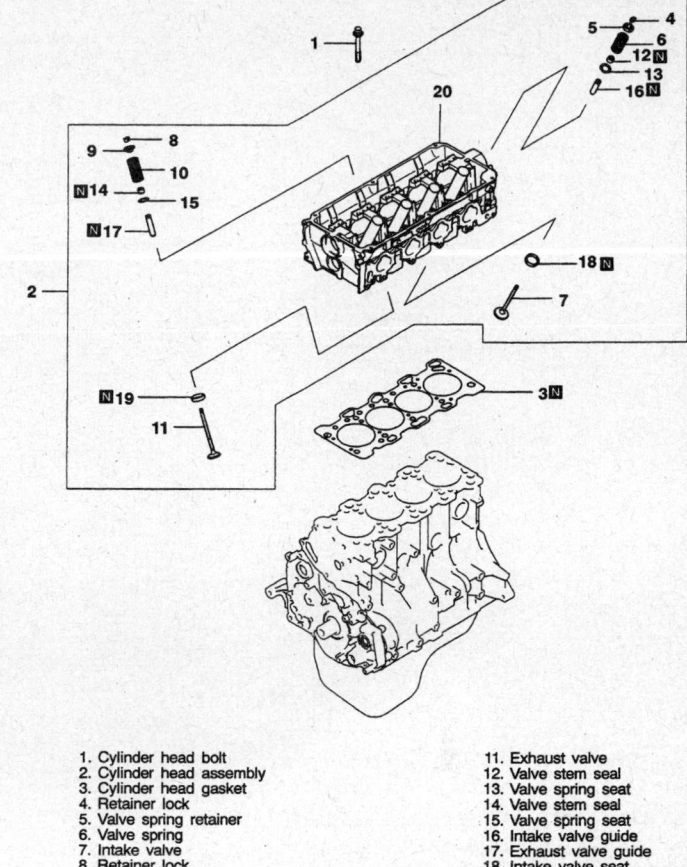

1. Cylinder head bolt
2. Cylinder head assembly
3. Cylinder head gasket
4. Retainer lock
5. Valve spring retainer
6. Valve spring
7. Intake valve
8. Retainer lock
9. Valve spring retainer
10. Valve spring
11. Exhaust valve
12. Valve stem seal
13. Valve spring seat
14. Valve stem seal
15. Valve spring seat
16. Intake valve guide
17. Exhaust valve guide
18. Intake valve seat
19. Exhaust valve seat
20. Cylinder head

MT1069600569000X

Fig. 10   Cylinder head replacement

c. Inspect timing belt "B" tension by pressing on belt at point A, **Fig. 21.** If deflection is not .20–.28 inch, adjust tension.
d. When installing timing belt "B," ensure flange is installed, **Fig. 23,**
e. Before installing timing belt auto tensioner, use a vise to compress pushrod gently into cylinder until pin holes in cylinder and pushrod align, then insert set pin.
f. When installing timing belt, align timing marks on camshaft, crankshaft and oil pump sprockets, then remove plug from cylinder block and insert suitable Phillips head screwdriver at least 2.36 inches into block, **Fig. 24,** to hold silent shaft in place. If screwdriver travels only .8–1 inch before contacting silent shaft, rotate sprocket once and realign timing mark, then insert screwdriver fully.
g. Position timing belt first over crankshaft sprocket, then over oil pump sprocket and, finally, over camshaft sprocket. There should be no slack in belt.
h. When preparing timing belt tensioner for belt tension adjustment, position tensioner pulley with pin holes at bottom, then press pulley against timing belt and tighten bolt only enough to secure pulley. Thread special tool through left engine support bracket as shown, **Fig. 25,** to exert pressure on tensioner pulley, then remove set pin and tighten center bolt to specifications. Remove tool.
i. To adjust timing belt tension, rotate crankshaft ¼ turn counterclockwise, then rotate clockwise until timing marks align. Loosen tensioner pulley bolt, then use tension adjustment tool No. MD998767, or equivalent, and a torque wrench to tighten bolt to specifications while applying 2.6 ft. lbs. of tension to belt. Finally, rotate crankshaft

through two full clockwise revolutions, realign timing marks and measure auto tensioner protrusion, **Fig. 26** (dimension " A") after leaving engine undisturbed for 15 minutes. If protrusion is not .150–.177 inch, repeat tension adjustment procedure.
j. Install timing covers, ensure bolts are reinstalled in their proper location.

CAMSHAFT
REPLACE

1. Relieve fuel system pressure as outlined under " Precautions," then remove battery and timing belt upper cover.
2. Remove camshaft and oil seal in numbered sequence shown, **Figs. 27 and 28,** noting the following:
   a. Use special tools to remove camshaft sprocket as shown, **Fig. 29.**
   b. Before removing rocker arm and shaft assembly, install valve lash adjuster holder tools No. MD998443, or equivalent, to prevent adjusters from falling out.
3. Reverse procedure to install, noting the following:
   a. When installing rocker arm and

shaft assembly, temporarily tighten rocker shaft with bolt to prevent arms on intake side from pushing valves. Ensure rocker shaft springs are at right angles to plug guides.
   b. Ensure rocker shaft notches are positioned as shown, **Fig. 30.**
   c. Use seal installation tool No. MD998713, or equivalent, to install camshaft oil seal. Apply clean engine oil to oil seal lip prior to installation.
   d. When installing distributor, rotate crankshaft until No. 1 cylinder reaches camshaft position on compression stroke, then align mating marks on distributor housing and coupling key. Ensure distributor mounting stud bolt is aligned with slot in distributor flange.
   e. Tighten all bolts and nuts to specifications; inspect and adjust ignition timing as necessary.

CRANKSHAFT SEAL
REPLACE

1. Relieve fuel system pressure as outlined under " Precautions," then remove timing belt "B" as outlined under "Timing Belt, Replace."

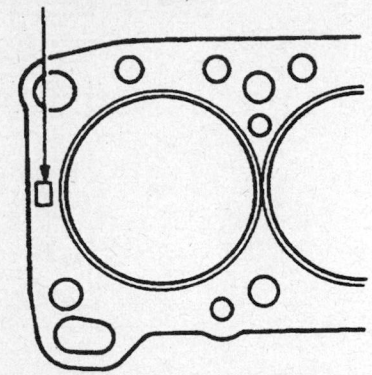

Identification mark

Fig. 11 Cylinder head gasket orientation

MT1069600570000X

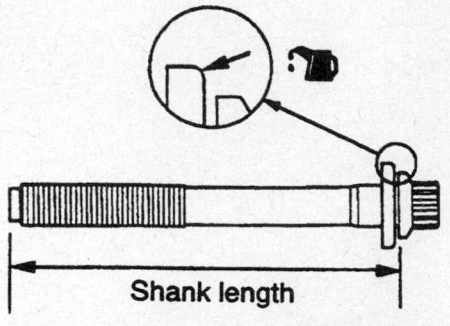

Shank length

MT1069600571000X

Fig. 12 Cylinder head bolt shank measurement

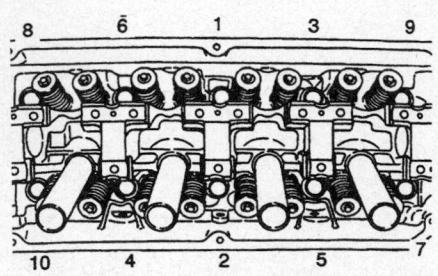

MT1069600572000X

Fig. 13 Cylinder head bolt tightening sequence

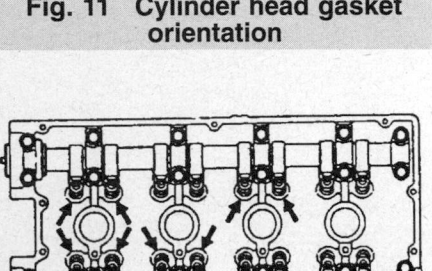

MT1069400327000X

Fig. 14 Hydraulic lash adjuster inspection

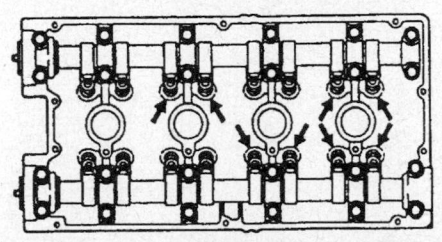

MT1069400328000X

Fig. 15 Hydraulic lash adjuster inspection

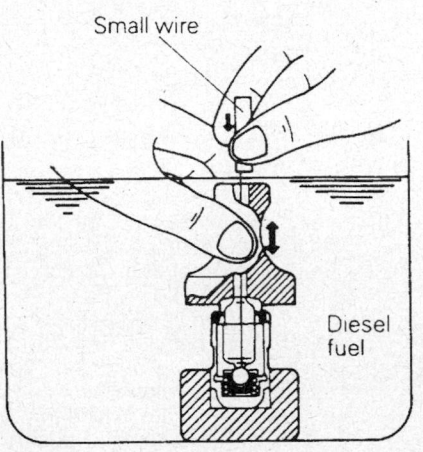

Small wire

Diesel fuel

MT1069400329000X

Fig. 16 Bleeding hydraulic lash adjuster

2. Remove crankshaft seal with a suitable removal tool.
3. Reverse procedure to install. Apply clean engine oil to outer edge of seal lip before installation.

CRANKSHAFT REAR OIL SEAL

REPLACE

1. Relieve fuel system pressure as outlined under "Precautions," then remove transaxle.
2. **On models with manual transaxle,** remove clutch cover and disc as as outlined in "Clutch & Manual Transaxle" section.
3. **On all models,** remove oil pan as outlined under "Oil Pan, Replace."
4. Remove crankshaft rear oil seal in numbered sequence shown, **Fig. 31.**
5. Reverse procedure to install, noting the following:
   a. Apply clean engine oil to outer edge of seal lip.
   b. Use a suitable soft-faced hammer and seal installation tools No. MB990938 and MD998776, or equivalents, to install crankshaft rear oil seal.
   c. Tighten all bolts and nuts to specifications.

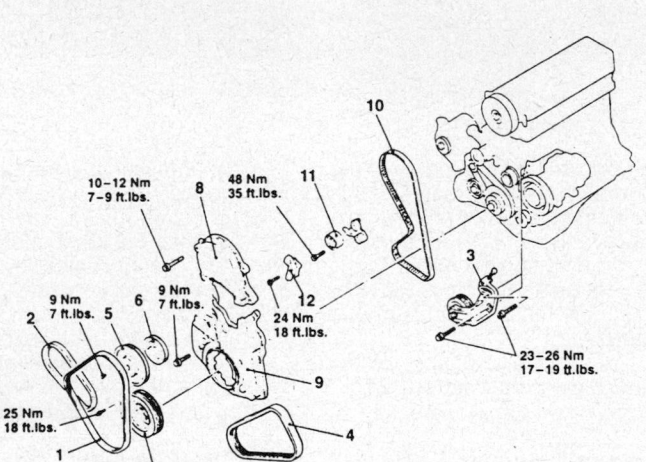

- Drive Belt Tension Adjustment

1. Drive belt (Generator)
2. Drive belt (Power steering)
3. Tensioner pulley bracket
4. Drive belt (A/C)
5. Water pump pulley
6. Power steering pulley
7. Crankshaft pulley
8. Timing belt front upper cover
9. Timing belt front lower cover

- Timing belt tension adjustment
10. Timing belt
11. Tension pulley
12. Auto tensioner

10-12 Nm 7-9 ft.lbs.
48 Nm 35 ft.lbs.
9 Nm 7 ft.lbs.
9 Nm 7 ft.lbs.
24 Nm 18 ft.lbs.
25 Nm 18 ft.lbs.
23-26 Nm 17-19 ft.lbs.

MT1069100232000X

Fig. 17 Timing belt replacement. 1996-98

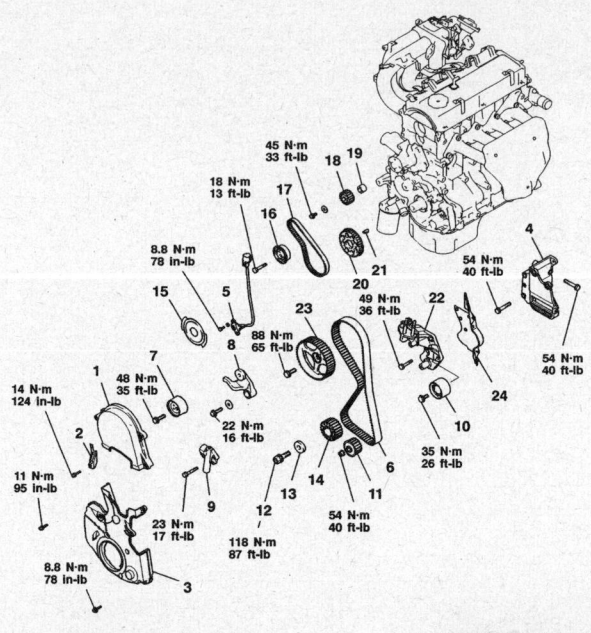

45 N·m
33 ft-lb
18 N·m
13 ft-lb
8.8 N·m
78 in-lb
88 N·m
65 ft-lb
49 N·m
36 ft-lb
54 N·m
40 ft-lb
48 N·m
35 ft-lb
22 N·m
16 ft-lb
14 N·m
124 in-lb
11 N·m
95 in-lb
23 N·m
17 ft-lb
118 N·m
87 ft-lb
35 N·m
26 ft-lb
54 N·m
40 ft-lb
54 N·m
40 ft-lb
8.8 N·m
78 in-lb

1. TIMING BELT FRONT UPPER
   COVER
2. CONNECTOR BRACKET
3. TIMING BELT FRONT LOWER
   COVER
4. POWER STEERING PUMP
   BRACKET
5. CRANKSHAFT POSITION SENSOR
6. TIMING BELT
7. TENSIONER PULLEY
8. TENSIONER ARM
9. AUTO-TENSIONER
10. IDLER PULLEY

11. OIL PUMP SPROCKET
12. CRANKSHAFT BOLT
13. CRANKSHAFT PULLEY WASHER
14. CRANKSHAFT SPROCKET
15. CRANKSHAFT SENSING BLADE
16. TENSIONER "B"
17. TIMING BELT "B"
18. COUNTERBALANCE SHAFT
    SPROCKET
19. SPACER
20. CRANKSHAFT SPROCKET "B"
21. KEY
22. ENGINE SUPPORT BRACKET
23. CAMSHAFT SPROCKET

MT1069900573000X

Fig. 18   Timing belt & timing belt "B" replacement. 1999

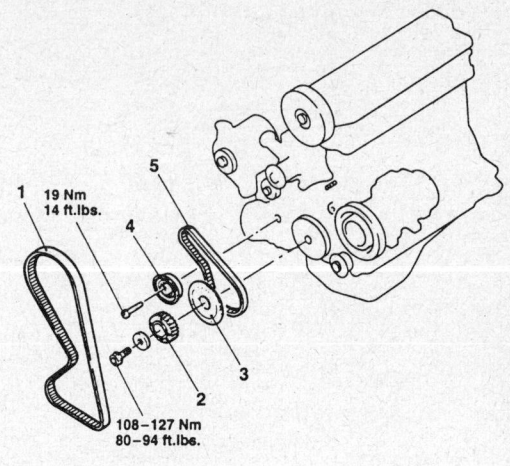

1   19 Nm
    14 ft.lbs.
108–127 Nm
80–94 ft.lbs.

1. Timing belt
2. Crankshaft sprocket
3. Flange
4. Timing belt B tensioner
5. Timing belt B

MT1069100233000X

Fig. 19   Timing belt "B" replacement. 1996–98

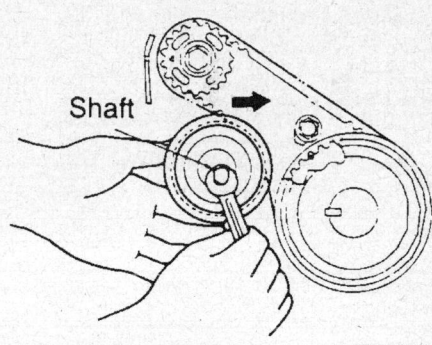

Shaft

MT1069100236000X

Fig. 22   Timing belt "B" tension adjustment

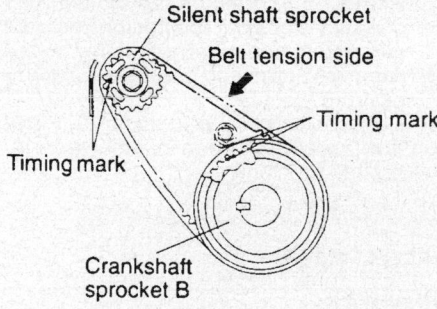

Silent shaft sprocket
Belt tension side
Timing mark
Timing mark
Crankshaft sprocket B

MT1069100234000X

Fig. 20   Timing belt "B" mark alignment

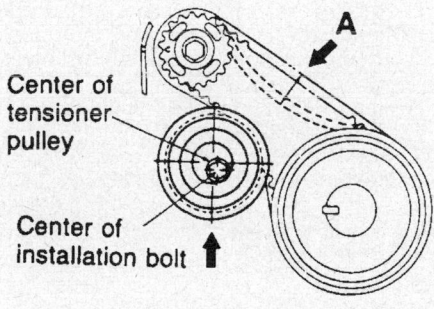

A

Center of
tensioner
pulley

Center of
installation bolt

MT1069100235000X

Fig. 21   Timing belt "B" tensioner orientation & tension inspection point

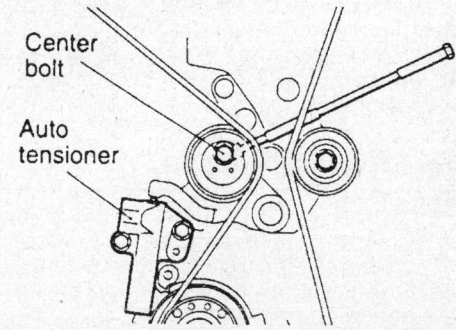

Center
bolt

Auto
tensioner

MT1069100239000X

Fig. 25   Tool installation & release of auto tensioner

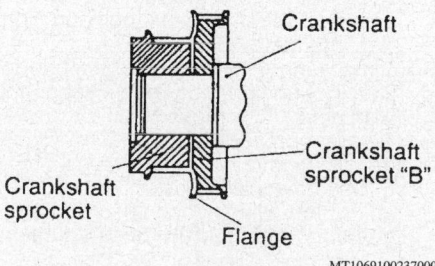

Crankshaft
Crankshaft
sprocket "B"
Crankshaft
sprocket
Flange

MT1069100237000X

Fig. 23   Timing belt "B" flange position

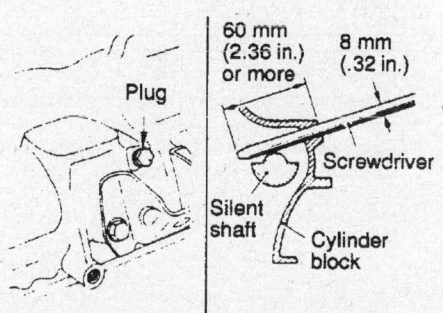

Plug

60 mm
(2.36 in.)
or more

8 mm
(.32 in.)

Screwdriver

Silent
shaft

Cylinder
block

MT1069100238000X

Fig. 24   Screwdriver installation in silent shaft access plug

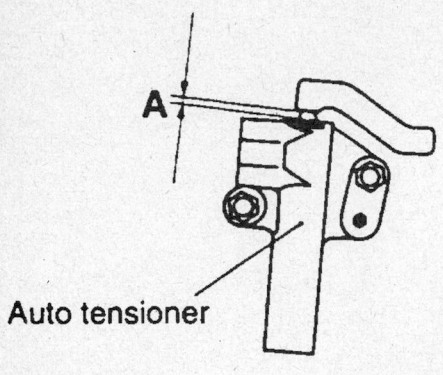

Fig. 26 Auto tensioner protrusion

OIL PAN

REPLACE

1. Relieve fuel system pressure as outlined under " Precautions," then drain engine oil into a suitable container.
2. Remove dipstick tube and front exhaust pipe.
3. Remove oil pan and screen in numbered sequence shown, **Fig. 32.**
4. Reverse procedure to install.

BELT TENSION DATA

Belt	Deflection, Inch	
	New	Used
A/C	.22–.24	.26–.30
Alternator	.30–.35	.39
Power Steering	.18–.22	.24–.28

COOLING SYSTEM BLEED

This engine does not require a specified bleed procedure. After filling cooling system, start engine and remove radiator cap. Air will then be automatically bled through cap opening.

THERMOSTAT

REPLACE

1. Drain engine coolant into a suitable container, then disconnect lower radiator hose. **Mark hose position for installation reference.**
2. Remove water outlet fitting, then the thermostat.
3. Reverse procedure to install, noting the following:
   a. Ensure thermostat is installed with jiggle valve facing straight up and is aligned with mark on thermostat case.

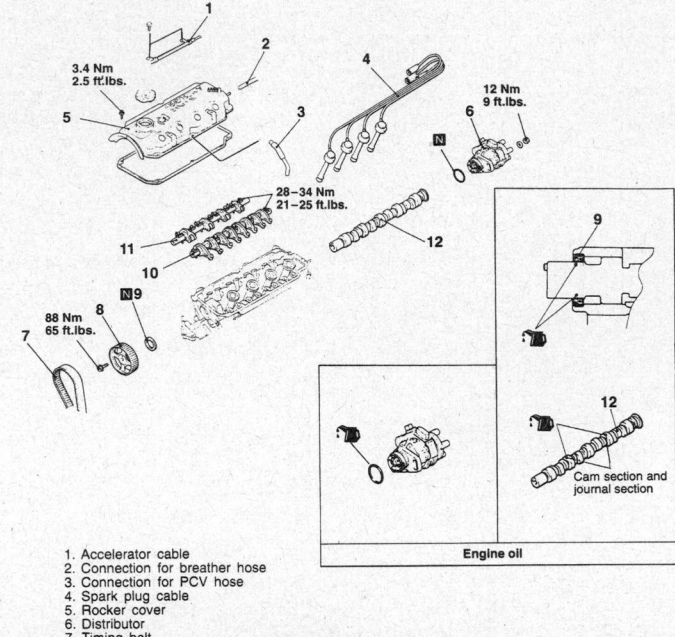

1. Accelerator cable
2. Connection for breather hose
3. Connection for PCV hose
4. Spark plug cable
5. Rocker cover
6. Distributor
7. Timing belt
8. Camshaft sprocket
9. Camshaft oil seal
10. Rocker arm and shaft assembly (Intake side)
11. Rocker arm and shaft assembly (Exhaust side)
12. Camshaft

Fig. 27 Camshaft replacement. 1996–98

   b. Tighten water outlet fitting bolts to specifications.

WATER PUMP

REPLACE

1. Relieve fuel system pressure as outlined under " Precautions," then drain engine coolant into a suitable container.
2. Remove timing belt as outlined under "Timing Belt, Replace."
3. Remove water pump.
4. Reverse procedure to install.

RADIATOR

REPLACE

1. Remove radiator drain plug and drain coolant.
2. Remove radiator cap, then the overflow tube.
3. Remove upper and lower coolant hoses from radiator.
4. **On models with automatic transaxle,** disconnect fluid cooler lines from radiator.
5. **On all models,** remove upper insulators, then the radiator assembly.
6. Remove condenser and radiator fan motor assemblies from radiator.
7. Remove shroud from radiator.
8. Reverse procedure to install.

FUEL PUMP

REPLACE

1. Relieve fuel system pressure as outlined under " Precautions," then remove rear seat cushion.
2. Remove fuel tank protector, then disconnect electrical connector from fuel gauge unit and pump assembly.
3. Remove pump and gauge unit assembly from fuel tank.
4. Reverse procedure to install. Tilt float to lefthand side when inserting assembly into fuel tank.

FUEL FILTER

REPLACE

1. Relieve fuel system pressure as outlined under " Precautions," then remove air intake hose, **Fig. 33.**
2. Using a spanner wrench, hold fuel filter in place and remove eye bolt and high pressure hose.
3. With spanner wrench still attached to filter, loosen flare nut, then disconnect main pipe and remove filter.
4. Reverse procedure to install, noting the following:
   a. Use a new filter gasket.
   b. Tighten all fittings to specifications.
   c. Inspect filter and fuel lines for leaks.

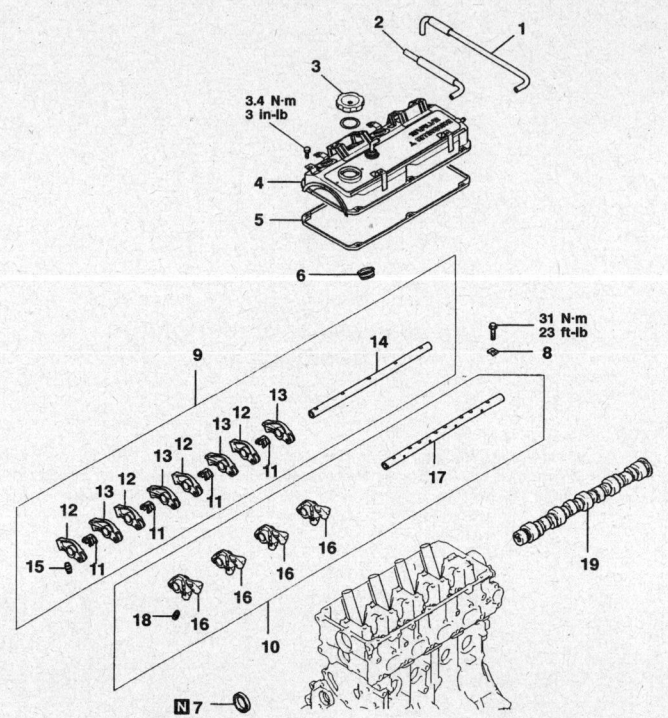

1. BREATHER HOSE
2. PCV HOSE
3. OIL FILLER CAP
4. ROCKER COVER
5. ROCKER COVER GASKET
6. OIL SEAL
7. OIL SEAL
8. ROCKER SHAFT CAP
9. ROCKER ARMS AND ROCKER ARM SHAFT
10. ROCKER ARMS AND ROCKER ARM SHAFT

11. ROCKER SHAFT SPRING
12. ROCKER ARM "B"
13. ROCKER ARM "A"
14. ROCKER ARM SHAFT (INTAKE SIDE)
15. LASH ADJUSTER
16. ROCKER ARM "C"
17. ROCKER ARM SHAFT (EXHAUST SIDE)
18. LASH ADJUSTER
19. CAMSHAFT

MT1069900574000X

Fig. 28   Camshaft replacement. 1999

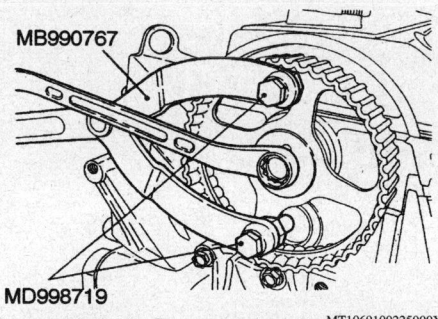

MB990767

MD998719

MT1069100225000X

Fig. 29   Camshaft sprocket removal

NOTCH

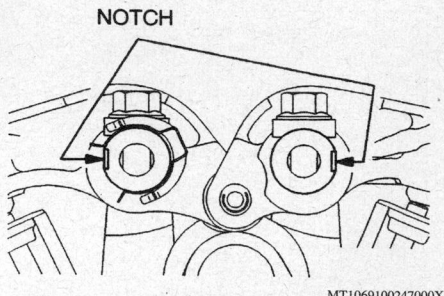

MT1069100247000X

Fig. 30 Rocker shaft notch positions

⚠ **CAUTION**

On the flexible wheel equipped engines, do not remove any of the bolts "A" of the flywheel shown in the illustration. The balance of the flexible flywheel is adjusted in an assembled condition. Removing the bolt, therefore, can cause the flexible flywheel to be out of balance, giving damage to the flywheel.

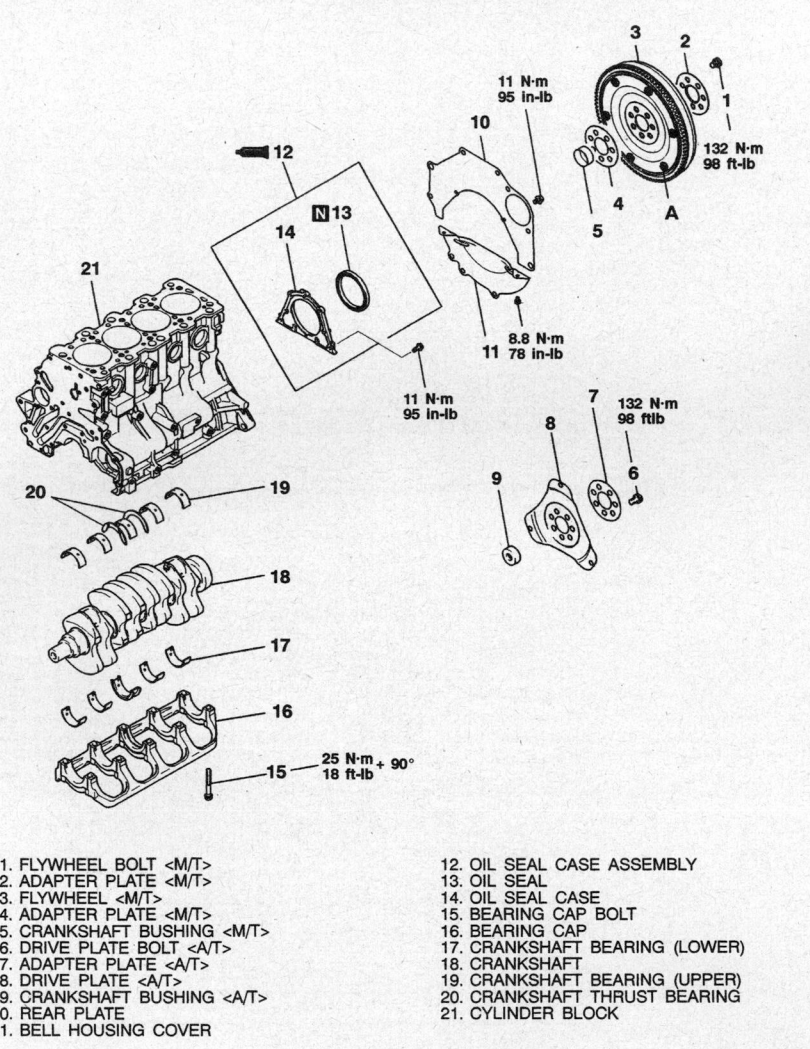

1. FLYWHEEL BOLT <M/T>
2. ADAPTER PLATE <M/T>
3. FLYWHEEL <M/T>
4. ADAPTER PLATE <M/T>
5. CRANKSHAFT BUSHING <M/T>
6. DRIVE PLATE BOLT <A/T>
7. ADAPTER PLATE <A/T>
8. DRIVE PLATE <A/T>
9. CRANKSHAFT BUSHING <A/T>
10. REAR PLATE
11. BELL HOUSING COVER
12. OIL SEAL CASE ASSEMBLY
13. OIL SEAL
14. OIL SEAL CASE
15. BEARING CAP BOLT
16. BEARING CAP
17. CRANKSHAFT BEARING (LOWER)
18. CRANKSHAFT
19. CRANKSHAFT BEARING (UPPER)
20. CRANKSHAFT THRUST BEARING
21. CYLINDER BLOCK

MT1069100251000X

Fig. 31 Crankshaft rear oil seal replacement

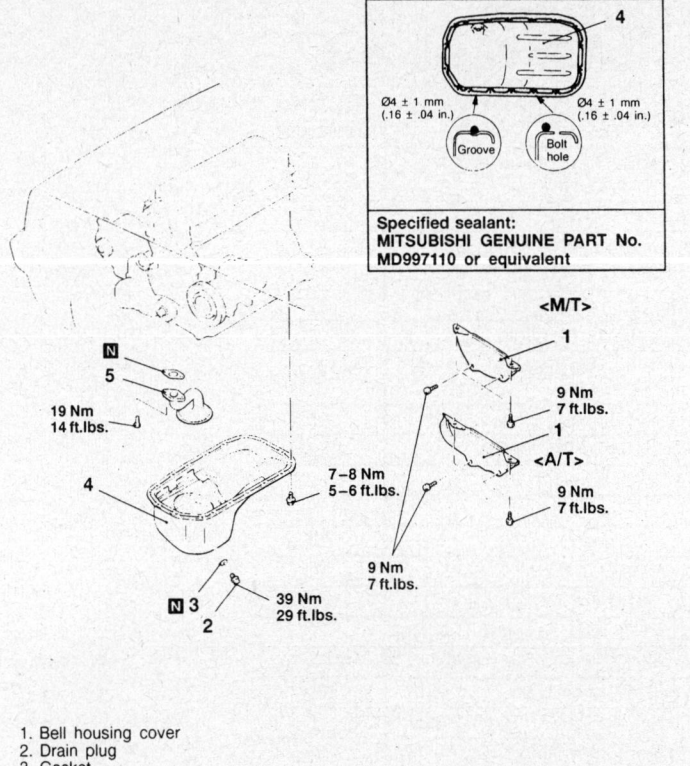

1. Bell housing cover
2. Drain plug
3. Gasket
4. Oil pan
5. Oil screen

Fig. 32 Oil pan & screen replacement

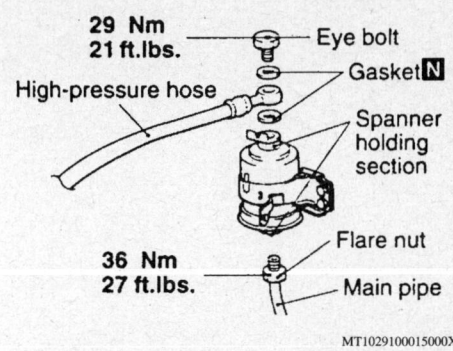

Fig. 33 Fuel filter replacement

TIGHTENING SPECIFICATIONS

Year	Component	Torque, Ft. Lbs.
1996–99	Air Intake Hose Clamp	36 ②
	Alternator Adjustment Bolt	9–11
	Alternator Bracket Pivot Bolt	18
	Bellhousing Cover Bolts	84②
	Camshaft Sprocket Bolt	65
	Center Member Attaching Bolts (Front)	64
	Center Member Attaching Bolts (Rear)	50–56
	Crankshaft Pulley Bolts	18
	Crankshaft Sprocket Bolts	80–94
	Cylinder Head Bolts	①
	Distributor Mounting Nut	108②
	Driveplate To Output Flange Bolts	94–101
	Dynamic Damper Mounting Bolts	48②
	EGR Valve Mounting Bolts	16
	Engine Hanger To Exhaust Manifold Nuts	18–21
	Engine Hanger To Intake Manifold Bolt	15
	Engine Hanger To Intake Manifold Nut	26
	Engine Mount Bracket Through Bolt	85
	Engine Mount Bracket To Engine Bolt & Nut	41
	Exhaust Manifold Cover Bolts	9–11
	Exhaust Manifold Mounting Nuts	18–21
	Flywheel To Output Flange Bolts	94–101
	Front Exhaust Pipe Bracket Bolts	25

Continued

TIGHTENING
SPECIFICATIONS—Continued

Year	Component	Torque, Ft. Lbs.
1996–99	Front Exhaust Pipe To Exhaust Manifold Nuts	32
	Front Roll Stopper Bracket Bolts	32
	Front Roll Stopper Bracket Through Bolt Nut	41
	Fuel Filter Eye Bolt	21
	Fuel Filter Main Pipe Flare Nut	27
	Fuel Rail To Intake Manifold Bolts	7–10
	High Pressure Fuel Hose Flange To Fuel Rail Bolts	48②
	Intake Manifold Mounting Bolts & Nuts	15
	Intake Manifold Stay Bolts	19–24
	Oil Drain Plug	29
	Oil Pan Bolts	60-72②
	Oil Screen Bolts	14
	Power Steering Pump Pulley Bolts	21
	Rear Roll Stopper Bracket Bolts	32
	Rear Roll Stopper Bracket Through Bolt Nut	32
	Rocker Arm & Shaft Mounting Bolts	21–25
	Rocker Cover Bolts	36②
	Thermostat Case To Engine Block Bolts	18
	Throttle Body Mounting Bolts	14
	Timing Belt Auto Tensioner Bolt	18
	Timing Belt Auto Tensioner Pulley Center Bolt	35
	Timing Belt "B" Tensioner Pulley Center Bolt	14
	Timing Belt Lower Cover Bolts	①
	Timing Belt Tensioner Pulley Bracket Bolts	17–19
	Timing Belt Upper Cover Bolts	①
	Transaxle Mount Bracket Nuts	31
	Transaxle Mount Bracket Through Bolt	50
	Vacuum Pipe Bracket To Intake Manifold Bolts	84②
	Water Outlet Fitting	10
	Water Pump Bolts	9–11

① — Refer to "Cylinder Head, Replace" for procedure.

② — Inch lbs.

3.0L Engine

29-21

NOTE: For Procedures Not Listed In This Section, Refer To The Engine Section Of The "Mitsubishi Pickups" Chapter.

NOTE: On Air Bag Equipped Models, Refer To "Air Bag System Precautions" Located In The Front Of This Manual For System Disarming & Arming Procedures.

NOTE: Refer To "Computer Relearn Procedures" Located In The Front Of This Manual For Computer Relearn Procedures.

INDEX

PRECAUTIONS

AIR BAG SYSTEMS

Refer to "Air Bag System Precautions" in the front of this manual for system disarming and arming procedures.

BATTERY GROUND CABLE

Prior to service, disconnect battery ground cable and isolate as required.

FUEL SYSTEM PRESSURE RELIEF

When service to any component necessitates working with the fuel system, fuel pressure in the system must be relieved. This is extremely important to reduce risk of personal injury, fire or explosion due to fuel spray and leakage. Relieve fuel system pressure as follows:

1. Remove rear seat cushion, then disconnect fuel pump wiring harness from floor wiring harness.
2. Start engine and allow all residual fuel in system to be consumed; when engine stalls, turn ignition switch to Off position.
3. Connect fuel pump wiring harness to floor wiring harness and install rear seat cushion, then continue with service.

COMPRESSION PRESSURES

1. Ensure engine oil is at proper level and that starter and battery are functioning properly.
2. Warm vehicle to normal operating temperature.
3. Turn lights and accessories Off.

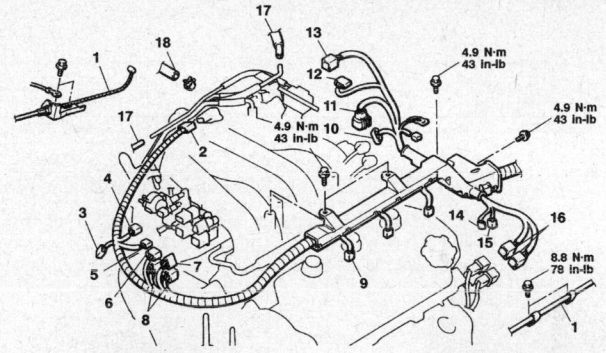

REMOVAL STEPS
1. ACCELERATOR CABLE CONNECTION
2. MANIFOLD DIFFERENTIAL PRESSURE SENSOR CONNECTOR
3. CONTROL WIRING HARNESS AND POWER STEERING WIRING HARNESS COMBINATION CONNECTOR
4. EGR SOLENOID VALVE CONNECTOR
5. EVAPORATIVE EMISSION PURGE SOLENOID VALVE CONNECTOR
6. KNOCK SENSOR CONNECTOR
7. CRANKSHAFT POSITION SENSOR CONNECTOR
8. RIGHT BANK HEATED OXYGEN SENSOR CONNECTOR <VEHICLES FOR CALIFORNIA>
9. INJECTOR CONNECTOR
10. DISTRIBUTOR CONNECTOR
11. CONTROL WIRING HARNESS AND INJECTOR WIRING HARNESS COMBINATION CONNECTOR
12. THROTTLE POSITION SENSOR CONNECTOR
13. IDLE AIR CONTROL MOTOR CONNECTOR
14. ENGINE COOLANT TEMPERATURE GAUGE UNIT CONNECTOR
15. ENGINE COOLANT TEMPERATURE SENSOR CONNECTOR
16. LEFT BANK HEATED OXYGEN SENSOR CONNECTOR <VEHICLES FOR CALIFORNIA>
17. VACUUM HOSE CONNECTION
18. BRAKE BOOSTER VACUUM HOSE CONNECTION

MT1069900575010X

Fig. 1 Engine replacement (Part 1 of 2)

4. Set gear selector to Park.
5. Remove spark plug cables and spark plugs.
6. Disconnect crankshaft position sensor to prevent ECU from activating ignition and fuel injection systems.
7. Install a suitable compression gauge into spark plug mounting hole.
8. Crank engine with throttle valve fully open and measure compression.
9. Compression should be between 83–119 psi at normal engine cranking speed. Difference between cylinders should be less than 14 psi.

ENGINE MOUNT

REPLACE

1. Support engine with a suitable jack.
2. Hold engine assembly with a chain block or suitable support device.
3. Place a suitable jack beneath engine

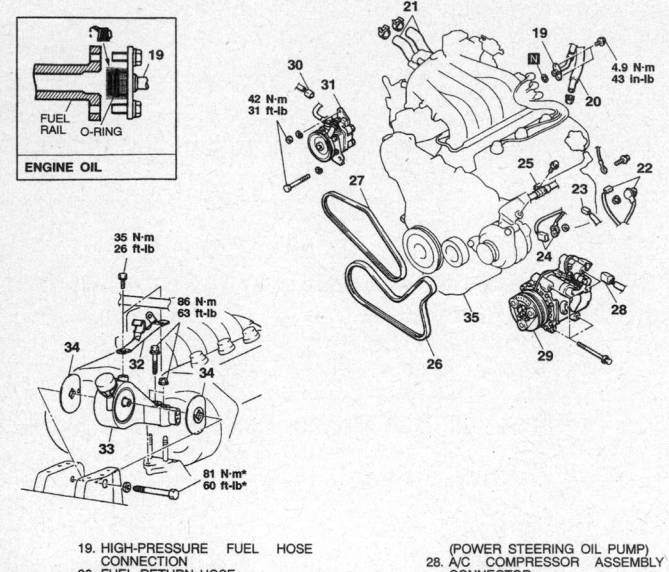

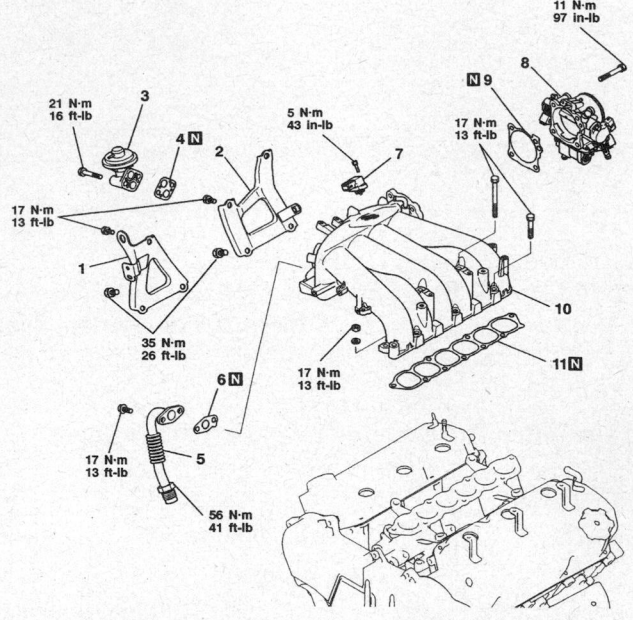

19. HIGH-PRESSURE FUEL HOSE CONNECTION
20. FUEL RETURN HOSE CONNECTION
21. HEATER HOSE CONNECTION
22. STARTER CONNECTOR
23. OIL PRESSURE SWITCH CONNECTOR
24. GENERATOR CONNECTOR
25. SUCTION HOSE CONNECTION
26. DRIVE BELT (GENERATOR AND A/C COMPRESSOR)
27. DRIVE BELT

(POWER STEERING OIL PUMP)
28. A/C COMPRESSOR ASSEMBLY CONNECTOR
29. A/C COMPRESSOR
30. POWER STEERING PRESSURE SWITCH CONNECTOR
31. POWER STEERING OIL PUMP
32. ENGINE MOUNT STAY
● TRANSAXLE ASSEMBLY (REFER TO GROUP 23A, TRANSAXLE ASSEMBLY.)
33. ENGINE MOUNT BRACKET
34. ENGINE MOUNT STOPPER
35. ENGINE ASSEMBLY

MT1069900575020X

Fig. 1 Engine replacement (Part 2 of 2)

1. INTAKE MANIFOLD PLENUM STAY, FRONT
2. INTAKE MANIFOLD PLENUM STAY, REAR
3. EGR VALVE
4. EGR VALVE GASKET
5. EGR PIPE

6. EGR PIPE GASKET
7. MANIFOLD DIFFERENTIAL PRESSURE SENSOR
8. THROTTLE BODY
9. THROTTLE BODY GASKET
10. INTAKE MANIFOLD PLENUM

MT1069900576000X

Fig. 2 Intake manifold plenum replacement

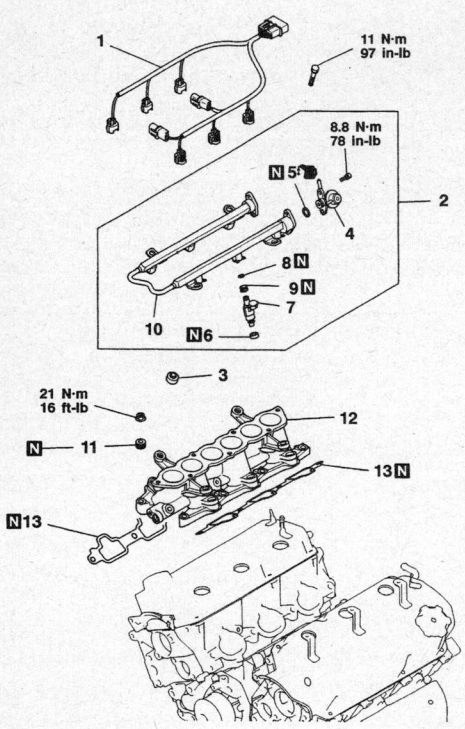

1. INJECTOR HARNESS
2. INJECTOR AND FUEL RAIL
3. INSULATOR
4. FUEL PRESSURE REGULATOR
5. O-RING
6. INSULATOR
7. INJRCTOR

8. O-RING
9. GROMMET
10. FUEL RAIL
11. CONED DISC SPRING
12. INTAKE MANIFOLD
13. INTAKE MANIFOLD GASKET

MT1069900577000X

Fig. 3 Intake manifold replacement

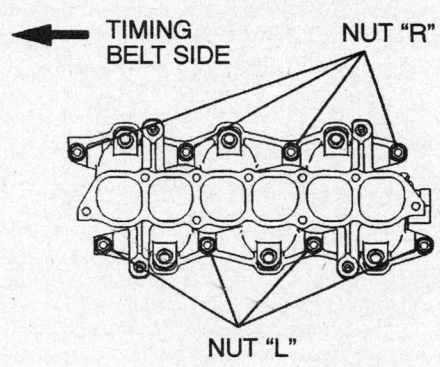

TIMING BELT SIDE ←   NUT "R"

NUT "L"

MT1069900578000X

Fig. 4 Intake manifold tightening sequence

oil pan using a block of wood to prevent damage to pan.
4. Jack up engine so that weight of engine is no longer being supported by engine mount.
5. Remove engine mount/bracket assembly from engine.
6. Reverse procedure to install.

ENGINE

REPLACE

1. Mark hood hinge to hood location for assembly reference, then remove hood.
2. Relieve fuel system pressure as outlined under "Precautions."

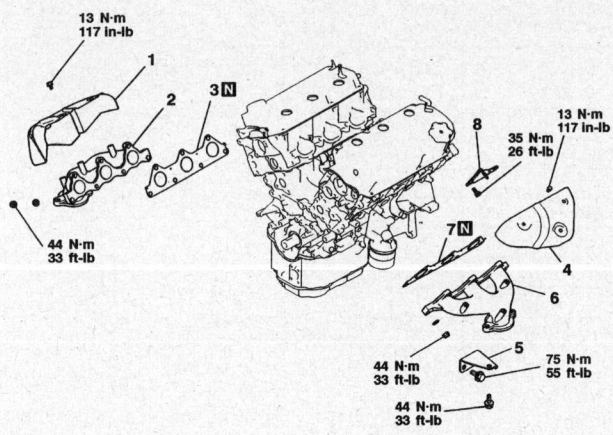

1. HEAT PROTECTOR, RIGHT
2. EXHAUST MANIFOLD, RIGHT
3. EXHAUST MANIFOLD GASKET
4. HEAT PROTECTOR, LEFT
5. EXHAUST MANIFOLD STAY
6. EXHAUST MANIFOLD, LEFT
7. EXHAUST MANIFOLD GASKET
8. ENGINE HANGER

MT1069900579000X

Fig. 5 Exhaust manifold replacement. Federal engine

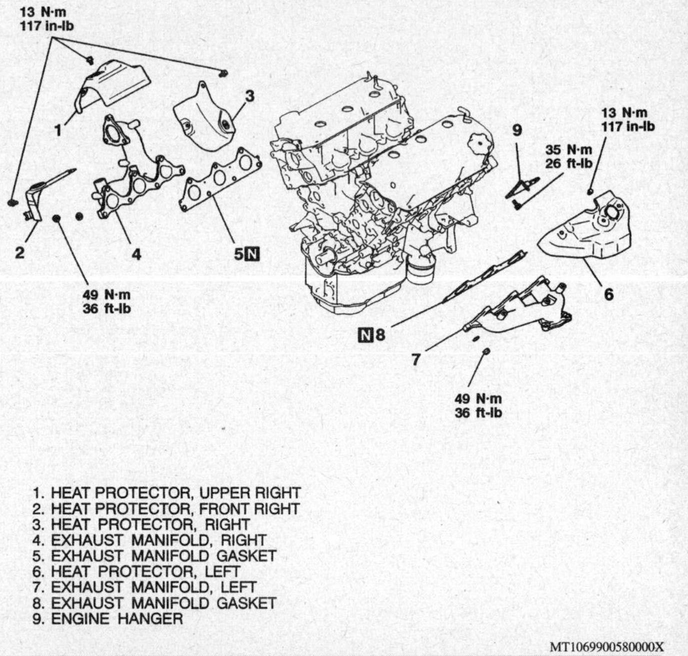

1. HEAT PROTECTOR, UPPER RIGHT
2. HEAT PROTECTOR, FRONT RIGHT
3. HEAT PROTECTOR, RIGHT
4. EXHAUST MANIFOLD, RIGHT
5. EXHAUST MANIFOLD GASKET
6. HEAT PROTECTOR, LEFT
7. EXHAUST MANIFOLD, LEFT
8. EXHAUST MANIFOLD GASKET
9. ENGINE HANGER

MT1069900580000X

Fig. 6 Exhaust manifold replacement. California engine

3. Drain engine coolant and oil into suitable containers.
4. Remove air cleaner assembly.
5. Remove radiator and reservoir assembly.
6. Remove front exhaust pipe.
7. Remove engine assembly in numbered sequence, **Fig. 1**.
8. Reverse procedure to install, tighten all engine mounting bolts and nuts to specifications.

INTAKE MANIFOLD
REPLACE

1. Relieve fuel system pressure as outlined under " Precautions."
2. Remove intake manifold plenum in numbered sequence, **Fig. 2**, then remove intake manifold in numbered sequence, **Fig. 3**.
3. Reverse procedure to install, noting the following:

a. Refer to **Fig. 4** when installing intake manifold.
b. **Torque** nuts "R" to 56 inch lbs.
c. **Torque** nuts "L" to 16 ft. lbs.
d. **Torque** nuts "R" to 16 ft. lbs.
e. **Torque** nuts "L" to 16 ft. lbs.
f. **Torque** nuts "R" to 16 ft. lbs.

EXHAUST MANIFOLD
REPLACE

Remove exhaust manifolds in numbered sequence, **Figs. 5 and 6**. Reverse numerical sequence to install, tighten all nuts and bolts to specification.

TIGHTENING SPECIFICATIONS

Year	Component	Torque, Ft. Lbs.
1999	Alternator Bolt (M8)	15
	Alternator Bracket Bolt	36
	Alternator Nut	32
	Drive Belt Tensioner Pulley Nut	36
	Engine Hanger	26
	Exhaust Gas Recirculation Pipe Bolt	13
	Exhaust Gas Recirculation Pipe Flare Nut	41
	Exhaust Manifold Nuts	33
	Exhaust Manifold Stay Bolt (M10)	33
	Exhaust Manifold Stay Bolt (M12)	55
	Fuel Pressure Regulator Bolt	78①
	Fuel Rail Bolt	97①
	Heat Protector Bolt	117①
	Intake Manifold Nut	16
	Intake Manifold Plenum Bolt & Nut	13
	Intake Manifold Plenum Stay Bolt (M8)	13
	Intake Manifold Plenum Stay Bolt (M10)	26
	Manifold Differential Pressure Sensor	43①
	Throttle Body Bolt	97①

① — Inch lbs.

Clutch & Manual Transaxle

INDEX

ADJUSTMENTS

CLUTCH PEDAL

1996-98

1. Turn up carpeting underneath clutch pedal and measure clutch pedal height, **Fig. 1.**
2. Standard value of measurement "A" is 7.0–7.1 inches.
3. If pedal height is not as specified, loosen locknut and adjust pedal height using adjusting bolt, clutch pedal position switch or push rod.
4. Measure clutch pedal clevis pin free play.
5. Standard value of measurement "B" is .04–.12 inch.
6. If clutch pedal clevis pin play is not as specified, adjust with push rod.
7. Do not push in master cylinder push rod at this time.
8. After completing adjustments, confirm that clutch pedal free play "C," **Fig. 2,** is .24–.51 inch and that distance between firewall and clutch pedal, "D," **Fig. 2,** is 1.97 inch or more with clutch disengaged.

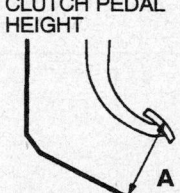
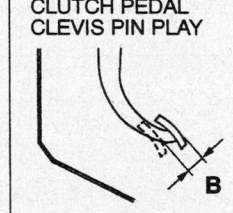

MT5049800082000X

Fig. 1 Clutch pedal height & clevis pin free play measurements A & B

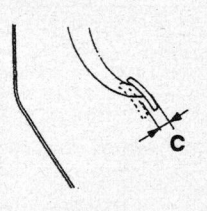
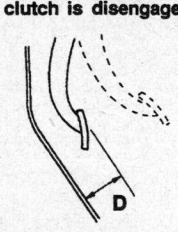

MT5049800083000X

Fig. 2 Clutch pedal free play measurements C & D

9. If clutch pedal free play and distance between firewall and clutch pedal are not as specified, inspect for air in hydraulic system or faulty clutch master cylinder or clutch.

1999

1. Turn back carpet under clutch pedal.
2. Measure clutch pedal height "A," **Fig. 1,** and clutch pedal clevis pin play "B," **Fig. 1.**
3. Standard value for "A" is 6.44–6.56

inches, standard value for "B" is .04–.12 inch.
4. If height of clutch pedal is not as specified, loosen locking nut and adjust pedal height to specified value using adjusting bolt or pushrod.
5. After adjustments, confirm that clutch pedal free play, " C," **Fig. 2,** is .2–.5 inch.

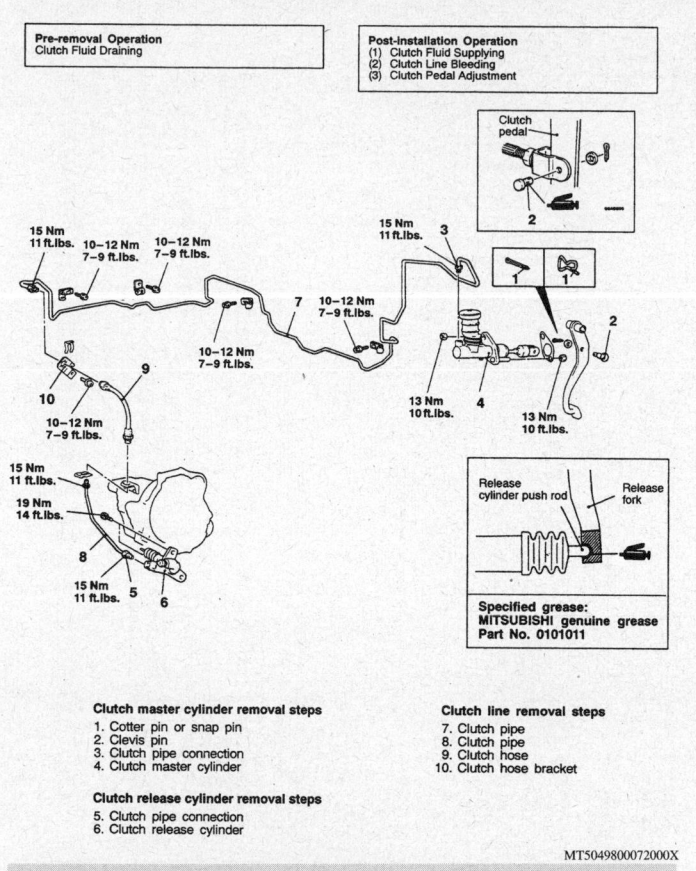

Fig. 3 Exploded view of clutch control system. 1996–98

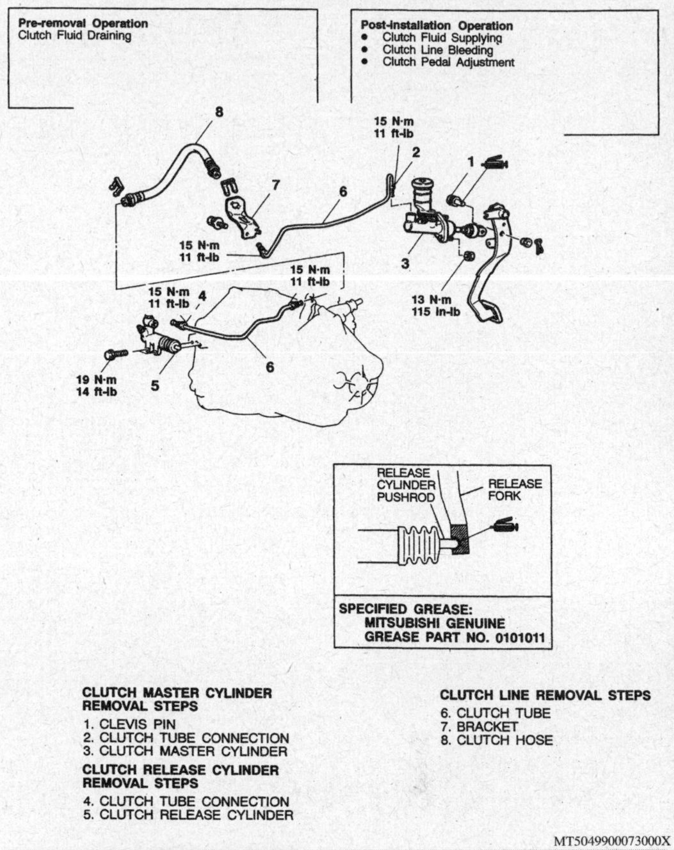

Fig. 4 Exploded view of clutch control system. 1999

6. Confirm that distance between clutch pedal and firewall, " D," **Fig. 2,** is 2.4 inches or more when clutch is disengaged.
7. If measured free play and distance are not as specified, inspect for air in clutch hydraulic system or for a faulty clutch master cylinder or clutch assembly.

HYDRAULIC SYSTEM SERVICE

CLUTCH MASTER & RELEASE CYLINDER, REPLACE

Refer to **Figs.3 and 4,** when replacing the clutch master and release cylinder.

CLUTCH

REPLACE

1. Remove transaxle as outlined under "Transaxle, Replace."

2. Insert clutch disc guide tool No. MD998126, or equivalent, into center hole to prevent dropping of clutch disc, then diagonally loosen bolts that hold clutch cover assembly to remove clutch cover assembly. **Do not clean clutch disc or release bearing with cleaning solvent.**
3. Remove snap ring, clevis pin and release cylinder assembly.
4. Remove return clip, then the release bearing.
5. Remove spring pins from clutch release fork and shaft using a suitable punch.
6. Install release shaft and packings, then the return spring and release fork.
7. Align lockpin holes of shift arm and control shaft, then using pin installer tool No. MD998245, or equivalent, drive in two new spring pins.
8. When installing spring pins ensure spring pin slot direction is at right angles to center line of control shaft.

9. Remove grease from clutch facing by wiping with clean cloth.
10. Apply small amount of grease to clutch disc spline and input shaft spline.
11. Using tool No. MD998126, or equivalent, install clutch disc and clutch cover assembly to flywheel. When installing clutch disc, make certain that surface with manufacturer's stamped mark is on pressure plate side.

TRANSAXLE

REPLACE

Remove transaxle in numbered sequence, **Figs. 5 and 6.** Install in reverse order of removal.

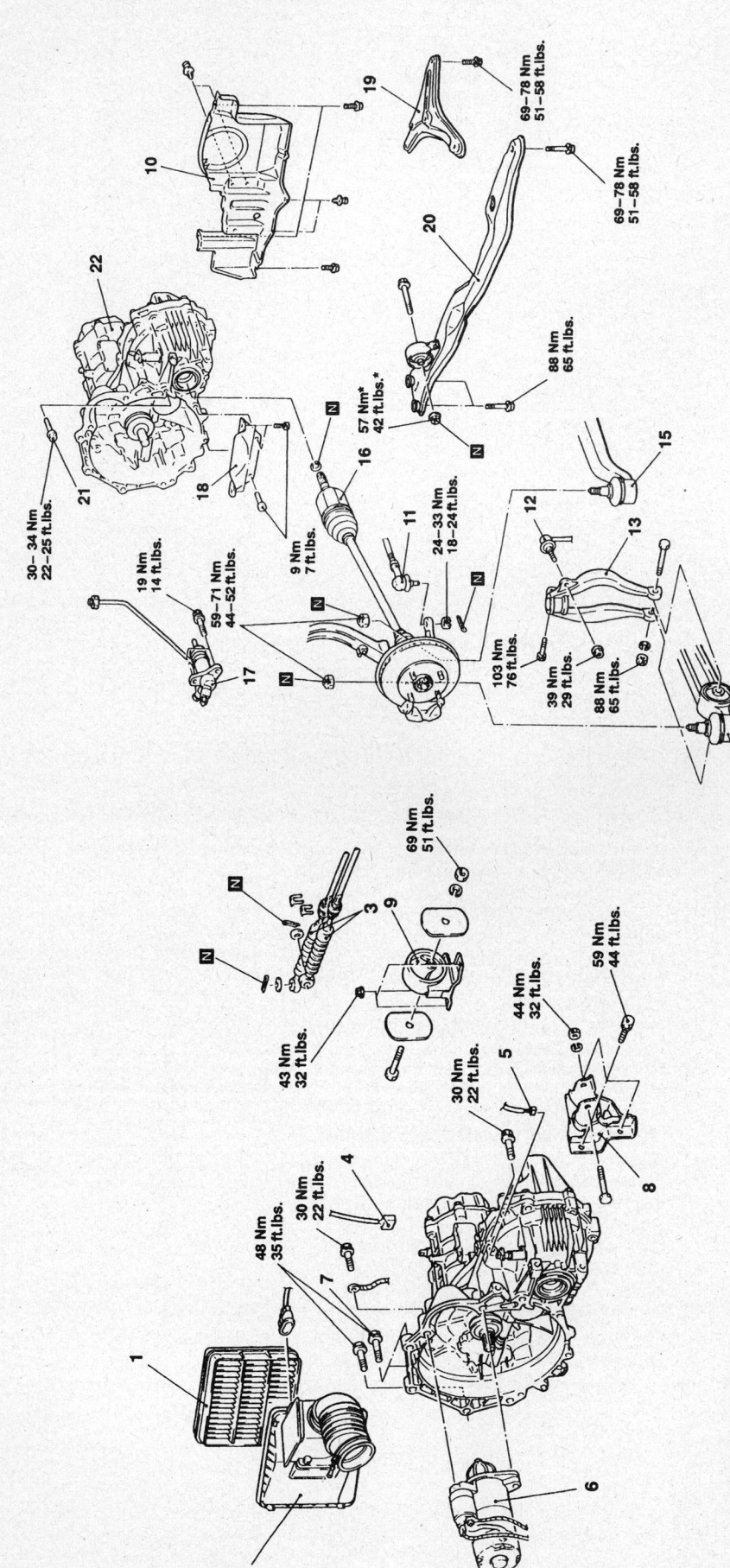

Fig. 5 Transaxle replacement (Part 2 of 2). 1996–98

69–78 Nm
51–58 ft.lbs.

69–78 Nm
51–58 ft.lbs.

88 Nm
65 ft.lbs.

57 Nm*
42 ft.lbs.*

24–33 Nm
18–24 ft.lbs.

9 Nm
7 ft.lbs.

30–34 Nm
22–25 ft.lbs.

19 Nm
14 ft.lbs.

59–71 Nm
44–52 ft.lbs.

103 Nm
76 ft.lbs.

39 Nm
29 ft.lbs.

88 Nm
65 ft.lbs.

Lifting up of the vehicle

10. Under cover (R.H.)
11. Connection for tie rod end
12. Connection for stabilizer link
13. Damper fork
14. Connection for lateral lower arm
15. Connection for compression lower arm
16. Connection for drive shaft
17. Connection for clutch release cylinder

18. Bell housing cover
19. Stay (R.H.)
20. Center member assembly
21. Transaxle assembly lower part coupling bolt
22. Transaxle assembly

Caution
*: Indicates parts which should be temporarily tightened, and then fully tightened with the vehicle on the ground in the unladen condition.

Removal steps

1. Air cleaner element
2. Air cleaner cover and hose assembly
3. Connection for shift cable and select cable
4. Backup light switch connector
5. Speedometer connector
6. Starter motor
7. Transaxle assembly upper part coupling bolts
8. Rear roll stopper bracket
9. Transaxle mounting
• Supporting engine assembly

69 Nm
51 ft.lbs.

43 Nm
32 ft.lbs.

44 Nm
32 ft.lbs.

59 Nm
44 ft.lbs.

30 Nm
22 ft.lbs.

30 Nm
22 ft.lbs.

48 Nm
35 ft.lbs.

Fig. 5 Transaxle replacement (Part 1 of 2). 1996–98

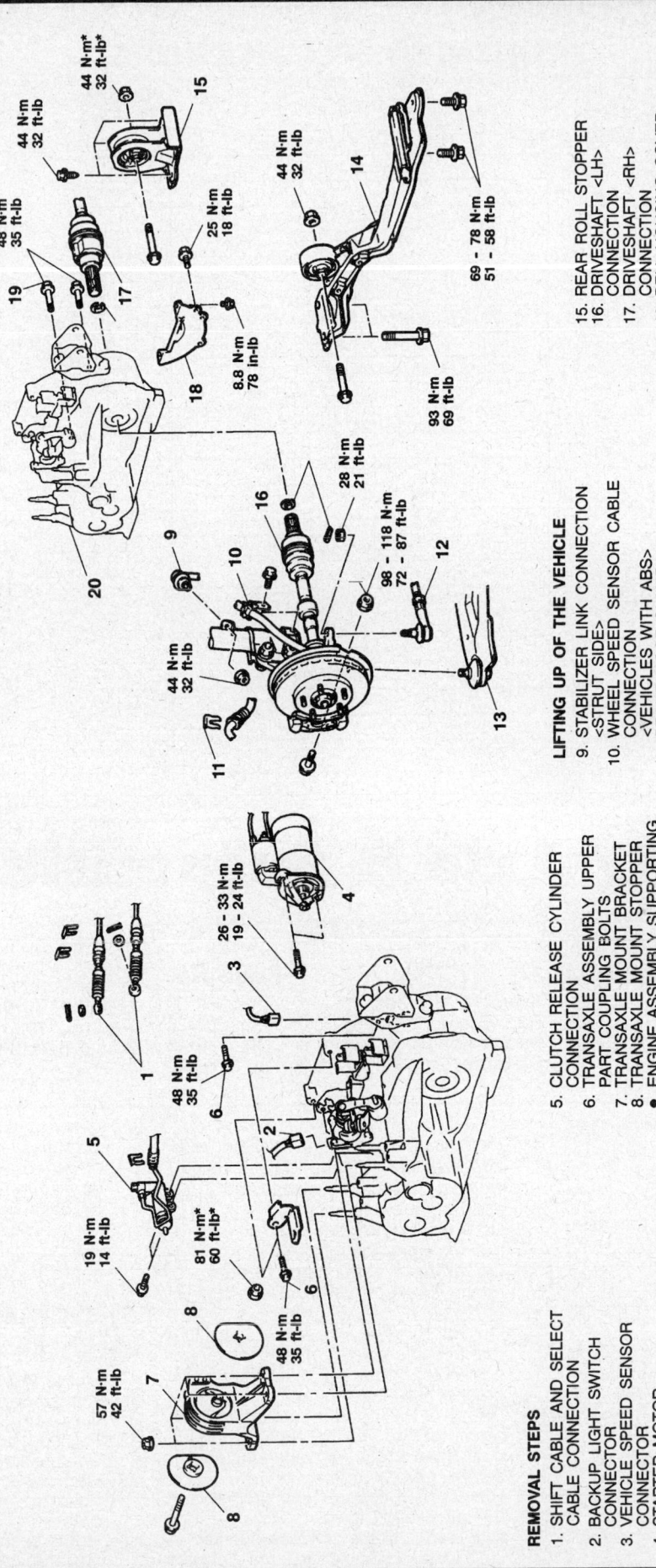

**44 N·m*
32 ft-lb***

**44 N·m
32 ft-lb**

**48 N·m
35 ft-lb**

**25 N·m
18 ft-lb**

**44 N·m
32 ft-lb**

**8.8 N·m
78 in-lb**

**69 - 78 N·m
51 - 58 ft-lb**

**93 N·m
69 ft-lb**

**28 N·m
21 ft-lb**

**98 - 118 N·m
72 - 87 ft-lb**

**44 N·m
32 ft-lb**

MT503990015102OX

Fig. 6 Transaxle replacement (Part 2 of 2). 1999

LIFTING UP OF THE VEHICLE

9. STABILIZER LINK CONNECTION
   <STRUT SIDE>
10. WHEEL SPEED SENSOR CABLE
    CONNECTION
    <VEHICLES WITH ABS>
11. BRAKE HOSE CLAMP
12. TIE ROD END CONNECTION
13. LOWER ARM CONNECTION
14. CENTERMEMBER ASSEMBLY

15. REAR ROLL STOPPER
16. DRIVESHAFT <LH>
17. DRIVESHAFT <RH>
    CONNECTION
18. BELL HOUSING COVER
19. TRANSAXLE ASSEMBLY LOWER
    PART COUPLING BOLTS
20. TRANSAXLE ASSEMBLY

**26 - 33 N·m
19 - 24 ft-lb**

**48 N·m
35 ft-lb**

**19 N·m
14 ft-lb**

**81 N·m*
60 ft-lb***

**48 N·m
35 ft-lb**

**57 N·m
42 ft-lb**

MT503990015101OX

Fig. 6 Transaxle replacement (Part 1 of 2). 1999

REMOVAL STEPS

1. SHIFT CABLE AND SELECT
   CABLE CONNECTION
2. BACKUP LIGHT SWITCH
   CONNECTOR
3. VEHICLE SPEED SENSOR
   CONNECTOR
4. STARTER MOTOR

5. CLUTCH RELEASE CYLINDER
   CONNECTION
6. TRANSAXLE ASSEMBLY UPPER
   PART COUPLING BOLTS
7. TRANSAXLE MOUNT BRACKET
8. TRANSAXLE MOUNT STOPPER
• ENGINE ASSEMBLY SUPPORTING

TIGHTENING SPECIFICATIONS

Year	Component	Torque, Ft. Lbs.
1996–99	Bellhousing Cover Bolts	84-108②
	Brake Booster Nut	8–12
	Clutch Cover Assembly	11–15
	Clutch Line Tube Flare Nut	11
	Clutch Master Cylinder To Firewall	7–11
	Clutch Pedal Bracket	72-108②
	Clutch Pedal Support Bracket	72-108②
	Clutch Pedal Support Bracket To Firewall	7–11
	Clutch Release Cylinder	11–15
	Clutch Release Cylinder To Union Bolt	14–18
	Clutch Release Fork Fulcrum	24
	Clutch Tube Bracket	72-108②
	Driveshaft Nut	144–188
	Flywheel Attaching Bolt	98
	Lower Arm Ball Joint To Knuckle	43–52
	Pedal Rod To Clutch Pedal Support Bracket	12–19
	Tie Rod End To Knuckle	17–25
	Transaxle Case To Transaxle	40-43
	Transaxle Mount Bracket To Body	29–36
	Transaxle Mount Bracket To Transaxle	43–58
	Transaxle Mounting Bolts	①
	Transaxle Oil Drain Plug	22–25
	Transaxle Oil Filler Plug	22–25
	Transaxle Stay To Engine	47–61

① — 12mm bolts, 32–39 ft. lbs.; 10mm bolts, 22–25 ft. lbs.;
8mm bolts, 7–9 ft. lbs.
② — Inch lbs.

Rear Axle & Suspension

INDEX

HUB & BEARING SERVICE

Refer to **Fig. 1,** when replacing rear axle hub.

WHEEL BEARING

ADJUST

Using a suitable spring scale, ensure rear hub rotary sliding resistance is no more than 3.9 lbs. on 1996–98 models and 13 ft. lbs on 1999 models, with caliper or drum removed.

REAR SUSPENSION

REPLACE

Refer to **Figs. 2 and 3** for rear suspension replacement.

1. Remove rear seat, then raise and support rear of vehicle and remove rear wheels, center exhaust pipe and shock absorber mounting nuts.
2. **On models with disc brakes,** remove brake caliper and rotor.
3. **On models with drum brakes,** remove brake drum and disconnect brake hose.
4. **On all models,** disconnect parking brake cable and rear speed sensor connector, then remove upper arm bracket mounting bolt.
5. Remove trailing arm mounting bolt, grommet and crossmember mounting nuts, then lower rear suspension assembly from vehicle.
6. Reverse procedure to install, noting the following:
   a. Bleed brake system as outlined in "Hydraulic Brake Systems" section.
   b. Adjust parking brake and inspect wheel alignment as necessary.
   c. Tighten all rear suspension assembly nuts and bolts to specifications in **Figs. 2 and 3.**

SHOCK ABSORBER

REPLACE

Refer to **Fig. 4,** when replacing the rear shock absorber.
1. Raise and support vehicle.
2. Position jack under torsion axle and arm assembly.
3. Remove shock absorber cap, shock absorber upper, then lower attaching nuts.
4. Remove shock absorber from vehicle.
5. Reverse procedure to install.

⚠ CAUTION
The rear hub unit bearing should not be dismantled.

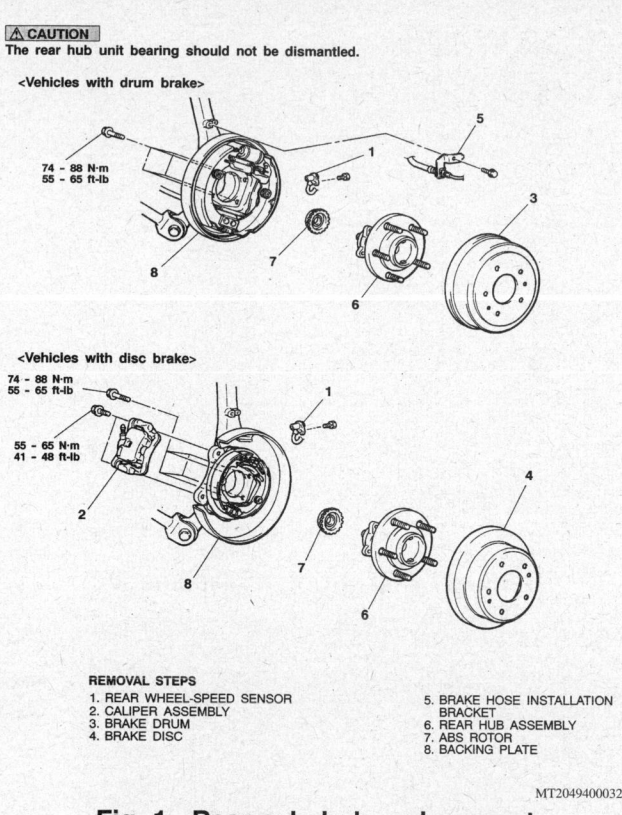

REMOVAL STEPS
1. REAR WHEEL-SPEED SENSOR
2. CALIPER ASSEMBLY
3. BRAKE DRUM
4. BRAKE DISC
5. BRAKE HOSE INSTALLATION BRACKET
6. REAR HUB ASSEMBLY
7. ABS ROTOR
8. BACKING PLATE

MT2049400032000X

Fig. 1   Rear axle hub replacement

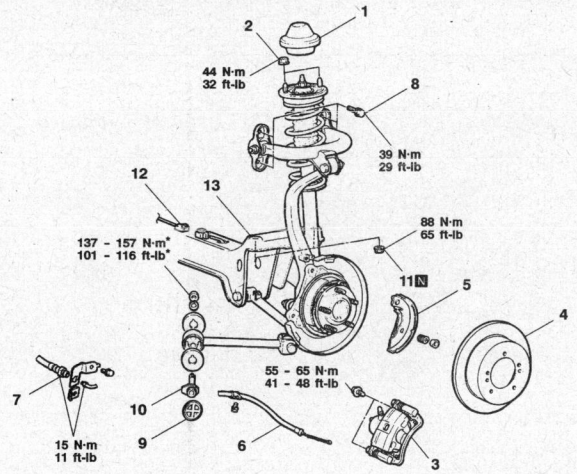

1. CAP
2. SHOCK ABSORBER MOUNTING NUTS
3. BRAKE CALIPER ASSEMBLY
4. BRAKE DISC OR BRAKE DRUM
5. SHOE AND LINING ASSEMBLY
6. PARKING BRAKE CABLE CONNECTION
7. BRAKE HOSE CONNECTION <VEHICLES WITH DRUM BRAKE>
8. UPPER ARM MOUNTING BOLTS
9. GROMMET
10. TRAILING ARM MOUNTING BOLT
11. CROSSMEMBER MOUNTING NUTS
12. REAR WHEEL SPEED SENSOR CONNECTOR CONNECTION <VEHICLES WITH ABS>
13. REAR SUSPENSION ASSEMBLY

MT2039900116000X

Fig. 3   Rear suspension replacement. 1999

COIL SPRING
REPLACE

1. Remove shock absorber assembly. Refer to procedure outlined under "Shock Absorber, Replace."
2. Disassemble shock absorber compo-

nents in order as shown, **Fig. 5.**
3. Reverse procedure to install.

Removal steps
1. Shock absorber mounting nuts
2. Brake drum
3. Parking brake cable end
4. Brake hose connection
5. Rear speed sensor connector <Vehicles with ABS>
6. Upper arm bracket mounting bolt
7. Grommet
8. Trailing arm mounting bolt
9. Crossmember mounting self-locking nuts
10. Rear suspension assembly

Caution
* Indicates parts which should be temporarily tightened, and then full tightened with the vehicles on the ground in the unladen condition.

MT2039600115000X

Fig. 2   Rear suspension replacement. 1996–98

CONTROL ARM
REPLACE
LOWER

1. Remove lower control arm and toe control arm assemblies in numbered sequence shown, **Figs. 6 and 7.**
2. Reverse procedure to install, noting the following:
   a. Tighten all bolts and nuts to specifications, **Fig. 6.**
   b. Inspect and adjust rear wheel alignment as necessary.

KNUCKLE
REPLACE

Refer to **Fig. 8** when replacing rear suspension knuckle.

TRAILING ARM
REPLACE

1. Remove trailing arm assembly in numbered sequence shown, **Fig. 9.**
2. Reverse procedure to install, noting the following:
   a. Tighten all bolts and nuts to specifications, **Fig. 9.**
   b. Inspect and adjust rear wheel alignment as necessary.

STABILIZER BAR
REPLACE

1. Remove stabilizer bar in numbered sequence, **Figs. 10 and 11.**
2. Reverse procedure to install, tighten bolts and nuts to specifications.

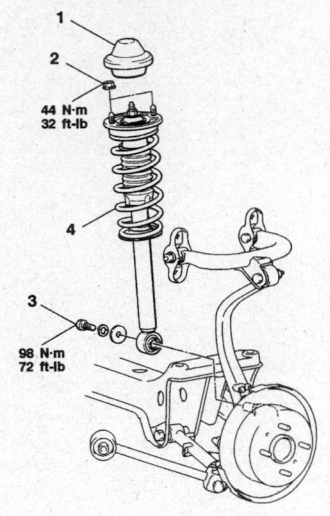

1. CAP
2. SHOCK ABSORBER MOUNTING NUTS
3. BOLT
4. SHOCK ABSORBER ASSEMBLY

MT2039900117000X

Fig. 4 Rear shock absorber replacement

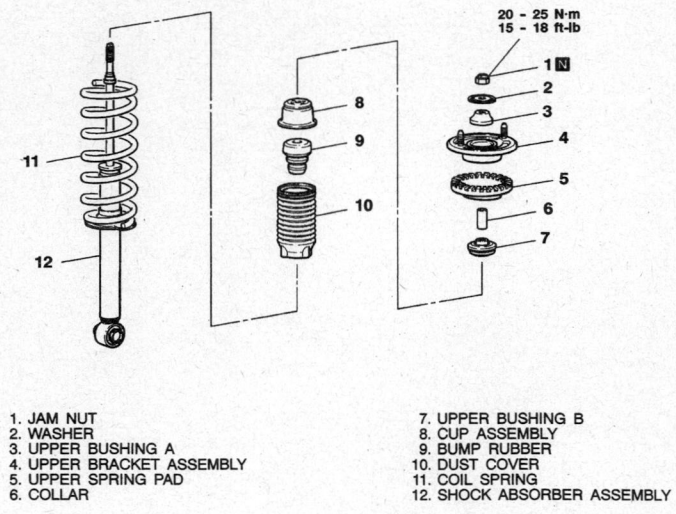

1. JAM NUT	7. UPPER BUSHING B
2. WASHER	8. CUP ASSEMBLY
3. UPPER BUSHING A	9. BUMP RUBBER
4. UPPER BRACKET ASSEMBLY	10. DUST COVER
5. UPPER SPRING PAD	11. COIL SPRING
6. COLLAR	12. SHOCK ABSORBER ASSEMBLY

MT2039100055000X

Fig. 5 Coil spring replacement

Lower arm assembly removal steps

1. Stabilizer link
2. ABS speed sensor clamp bolts <Vehicles with ABS>
3. Lower arm assembly and knuckle connection
4. Lower arm assembly mounting bolt
5. Lower arm assembly

Toe control arm assembly removal steps

6. Connection for toe control arm ball joint joint and knuckle
7. Toe control arm assembly mounting bolt
8. Toe control arm assembly

Caution
* Indicates parts which should be temporarily tightened, and then fully tightened with the vehicle in the unladen condition.

MT2039400070000X

Fig. 6 Lower control arm & toe control arm replacement. 1996–98

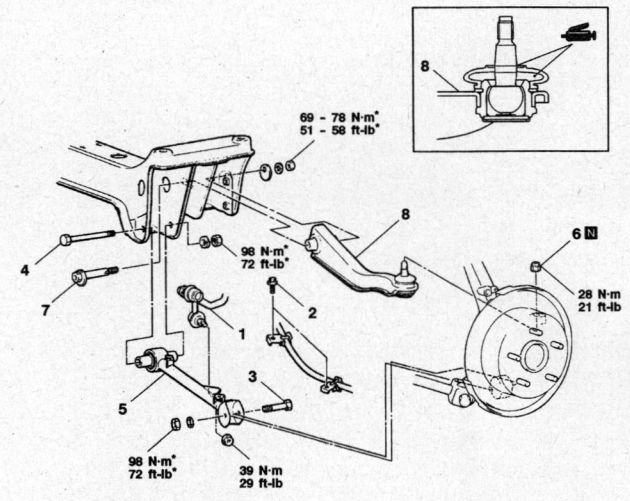

LOWER ARM ASSEMBLY

1. STABILIZER LINK CONNECTION
2. WHEEL SPEED SENSOR MOUNTING BOLTS
3. LOWER ARM ASSEMBLY AND KNUCKLE CONNECTING BOLT
4. LOWER ARM ASSEMBLY MOUNTING BOLT
5. LOWER ARM ASSEMBLY

TOE CONTROL ARM ASSEMBLY

6. TOE CONTROL ARM AND KNUCKLE CONNECTION
7. TOE CONTROL ARM ASSEMBLY MOUNTING BOLT
8. TOE CONTROL ARM ASSEMBLY

MT2039900118000X

Fig. 7 Lower control arm & toe control arm replacement. 1999

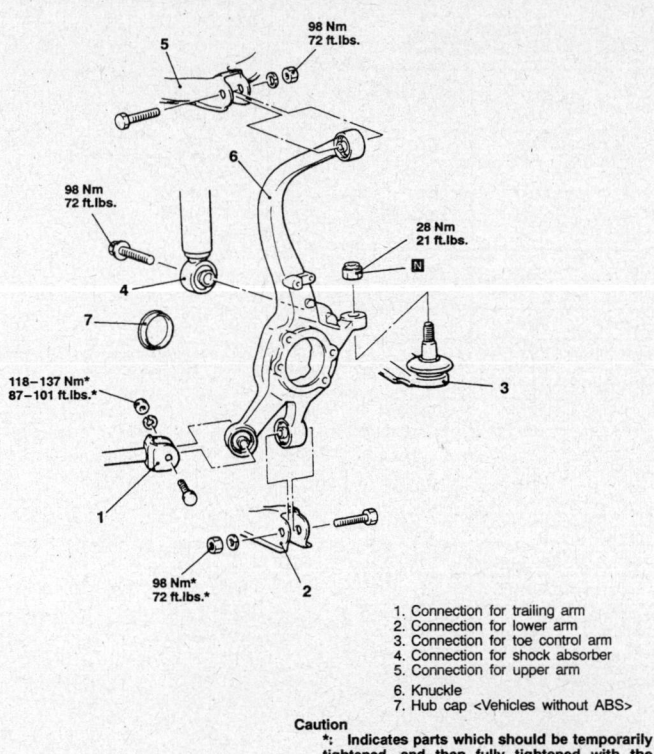

1. Connection for trailing arm
2. Connection for lower arm
3. Connection for toe control arm
4. Connection for shock absorber
5. Connection for upper arm
6. Knuckle
7. Hub cap <Vehicles without ABS>

Caution
*: Indicates parts which should be temporarily
    tightened, and then fully tightened with the
    vehicle on the ground in the unladen condition.

MT2039400071000X

Fig. 8   Rear suspension knuckle replacement

1. Connection for knuckle and trailing
   arm assembly
2. Grommet
3. Trailing arm assembly mounting
   bolt
4. Stopper
5. Trailing arm assembly

Caution
* Indicates parts which should be temporarily
tightened, and then fully tightened with the
vehicles in the unladen condition.

MT2039400066000X

Fig. 9   Trailing arm replacement

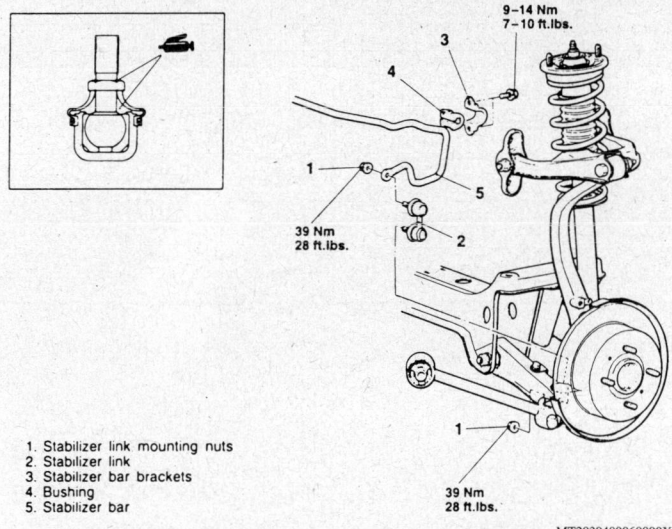

1. Stabilizer link mounting nuts
2. Stabilizer link
3. Stabilizer bar brackets
4. Bushing
5. Stabilizer bar

MT2039400060000X

**Fig. 10   Stabilizer bar assembly replacement.
1996–98**

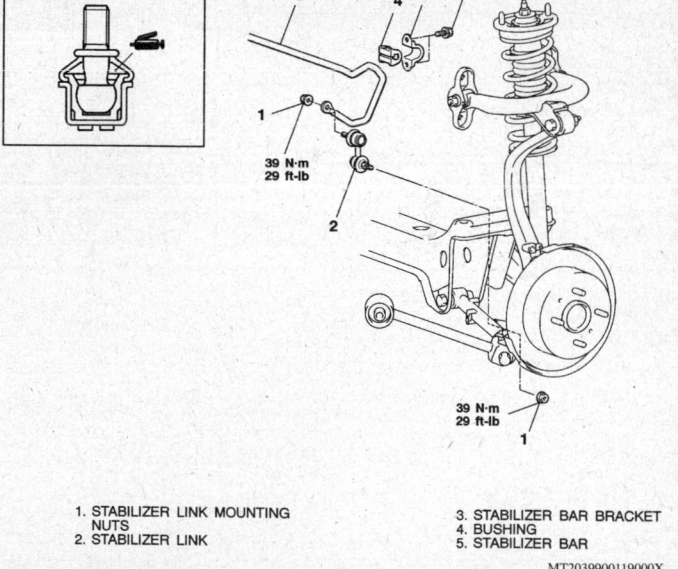

1. STABILIZER LINK MOUNTING
   NUTS
2. STABILIZER LINK
3. STABILIZER BAR BRACKET
4. BUSHING
5. STABILIZER BAR

MT2039900119000X

Fig. 11   Stabilizer bar assembly replacement. 1999

TIGHTENING SPECIFICATIONS

Year	Component	Torque, Ft. Lbs
1996–98	Brake Backing Plate Assembly Bolts	54–65
	Brake Hose To Brake Tube Fitting	11
	Caliper Bolts	36–43
	Crossmember Nuts	64
	Knuckle To Upper Arm Through Bolt Nut	72
	Lower Arm Assembly Mounting Bolt & Nut	71
	Lower Arm Assembly To Knuckle Bolt & Nut	71
	Shock Absorber Lower Mounting Bolt	72
	Shock Absorber Upper Mounting Nuts	32
	Stabilizer Bar Bracket Bolts	7–10
	Stabilizer Link Mounting Nuts	28
	Toe Control Arm Assembly Mounting Bolt & Nut	50–56
	Toe Control Arm Ball Joint Nut	20
	Trailing Arm Front Through Bolt Nut	99–114
	Trailing Arm To Knuckle Through Bolt Nut	85–99
	Upper Arm Bracket Bolts	28
	Wheel Lug Nuts	65–80
1999	Brake Caliper Assembly Bolt	41–48
	Brake Hose	11
	Crossmember To Body Nut	65
	Lower Arm Assembly Nut	72
	Shock Absorber Assembly To Knuckle Bolt	72
	Shock Absorber Jam Nut	15–18
	Stabilizer Bar Bracket Bolt	32
	Stabilizer Link Nut	29
	Toe Control Arm To Crossmember Nut	51–58
	Toe Control Arm Assembly To Knuckle Jam Nut	21
	Trailing Arm To Body Nut	101–116
	Trailing Arm To Knuckle Nut	87–101
	Upper Arm Assembly To Body Bolt	29
	Upper Arm Assembly To Knuckle Nut	72
	Upper Arm To Upper Arm Bracket Nut	42

Front Suspension & Steering

NOTE: On Air Bag Equipped Models, Refer To "Air Bag System Precautions" Located In The Front Of This Manual For System Disarming & Arming Procedures.

NOTE: Refer To "Computer Relearn Procedures" Located In The Front Of This Manual For Computer Relearn Procedures.

INDEX

PRECAUTIONS

BATTERY GROUND CABLE

Prior to service, disconnect battery ground cable and isolate as required.

AIR BAG SYSTEMS

Refer to "Air Bag System Precautions" in the front of this manual for system disarming and arming procedures.

WHEEL BEARING

ADJUST

Bearing preload is preset to specified value by design and cannot be adjusted.

WHEEL HUB & STEERING KNUCKLE

REPLACE

1. Raise and support vehicle, then remove front wheels.
2. Remove hub assembly in numbered sequence shown, **Figs. 1 and 2.** Do not disconnect brake hose from caliper; support assembly aside, but do not allow caliper to hang by brake hose.
3. Remove knuckle in numbered sequence shown, **Figs. 3 and 4.** Use ball joint remover tool No. MB991113, or equivalent, to remove ball joints.
4. Reverse procedure to install.

BALL JOINT

REPLACE

Refer to "Control Arm, Replace" for ball joint replacement procedure.

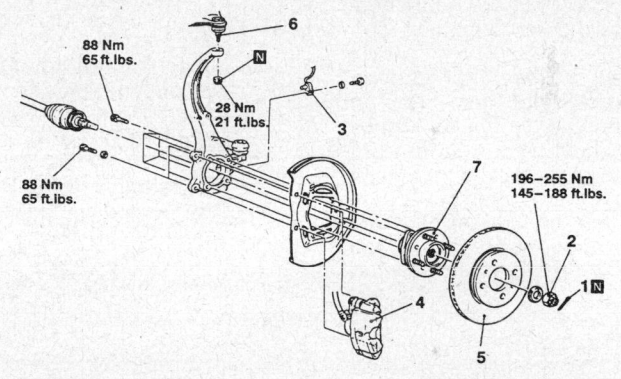

1. Cotter pin
2. Drive shaft nut
3. Front speed sensor <Vehicles with ABS>
4. Caliper assembly
5. Brake disc
6. Connection for upper arm
7. Front hub assembly

Caution
The front hub assembly should not be disassembled.

MT2049400034000X

Fig. 1 Hub assembly replacement. 1996–98

SHOCK ABSORBER

REPLACE

1. Raise and support vehicle, then remove front wheel.
2. Remove shock absorber in numbered sequence shown, **Figs. 5 and 6.**
3. Reverse procedure to install.

CONTROL ARM

REPLACE

LOWER

1. Raise and support vehicle, then remove front wheels.
2. Remove compression lower arm and/or lateral lower arm in numbered sequence shown, **Figs. 7 and 8.** Use ball joint remover tool No. MB991113, or equivalent, when disconnecting compression lower arm ball joint and knuckle.

3. Reverse procedure to install.

UPPER

1. Raise and support front of vehicle.
2. Remove upper arm assembly in numbered sequence shown, **Fig. 9.**
3. Reverse procedure to install. Inspect and adjust wheel alignment as necessary.

STABILIZER BAR

REPLACE

When replacing stabilizer bar refer to **Figs. 10 and 11** for replacement procedures.

POWER STEERING GEAR

REPLACE

1996-98

1. Drain power steering fluid as follows:

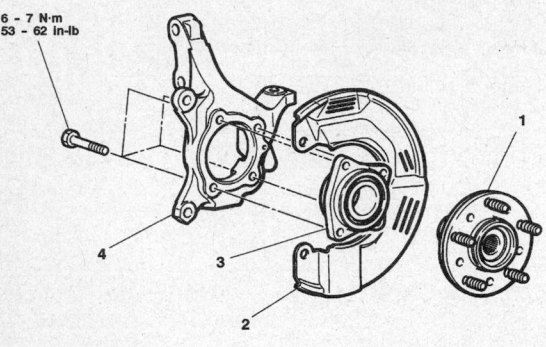

DISASSEMBLY STEPS
1. HUB
2. DUST COVER
3. WHEEL BEARING
4. KNUCKLE

ASSEMBLY STEPS
4. KNUCKLE
3. WHEEL BEARING
2. DUST COVER
1. HUB
● WHEEL BEARING BREAKAWAY TORQUE CHECK
● HUB END PLAY CHECK

MT2029900049000X

Fig. 2 Hub assembly replacement. 1999

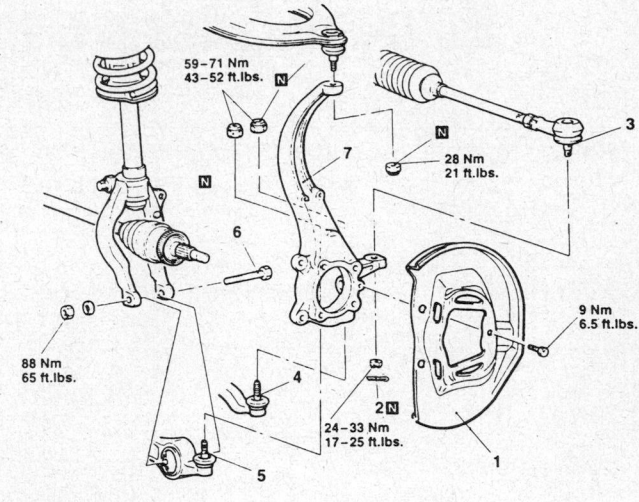

Removal steps
1. Dust shield
2. Cotter pin
3. Connection for tie rod end
4. Connection for compression lower arm
5. Connection for lateral lower arm
6. Connection bolt of damper fork and lateral lower arm
7. Knuckle

MT2049400035000X

Fig. 3 Knuckle replacement. 1996–98

a. Raise and support front of vehicle, then disconnect power steering fluid return hose.
b. Connect a vinyl hose to return hose and drain fluid into a suitable container.
c. Disconnect coil wire to prevent engine from starting, then crank engine intermittently while turning steering wheel back and forth between stops to purge remaining fluid from power steering circuit.
2. Remove stabilizer bar as outlined under "Stabilizer Bar, Replace," then remove power steering gear in numbered sequence shown, **Fig. 12**, noting the following:
a. Use ball joint remover tool No. MB991113, or equivalent, when removing tie rod ends.
b. In order to gain enough clearance to remove power steering gear from vehicle, it may be necessary to remove bolt from engine rear roll stopper bracket and lower rear of engine slightly.
3. Reverse procedure to install. Fill power steering fluid reservoir and bleed air from system as follows:
a. Raise and support vehicle, then rotate oil pump pulley several times by hand and turn steering wheel back and forth between stops through 5 or 6 cycles.
b. Disconnect coil wire to prevent engine from starting, then crank engine intermittently while turning steering wheel back and forth between stops. **Ensure reservoir is kept full during bleeding pro-**

cess. Do not attempt to bleed system with engine running.
c. After turning steering wheel from stop to stop 5 or 6 times, connect coil wire and start engine.
d. Turn steering wheel from stop to stop until no bubbles appear in reservoir. Ensure fluid is not milky and fluid level does not diminish greatly when steering wheel is turned.

1999

1. Drain power steering fluid into suitable container.
2. Remove center cross member, front exhaust pipe and stabilizer bar.
3. Remove power steering gear box in numbered sequence, **Fig. 13.**
4. Reverse procedure to install, **torque all nuts and bolts to specifications.**

POWER STEERING PUMP
REPLACE

1. Drain power steering fluid as follows:
a. Raise and support front of vehicle, then disconnect power steering fluid return hose.
b. Connect a vinyl hose to return hose and drain fluid into a suitable container.
c. Disconnect coil wire to prevent en-

gine from starting, then crank engine intermittently while turning steering wheel back and forth between stops to purge remaining fluid from power steering circuit.
2. Remove power steering pump in numbered sequence shown, **Figs. 14 and 15.**
3. Reverse procedure to install. Adjust pump drive belt tension as necessary.
4. Bleed air from power steering fluid as follows:
a. Raise and support vehicle, then rotate oil pump pulley several times by hand and turn steering wheel back and forth between stops through 5 or 6 cycles.
b. Disconnect coil wire to prevent engine from starting, then crank engine intermittently while turning steering wheel back and forth between stops. **Ensure reservoir is kept full during bleeding process. Do not attempt to bleed system with engine running.**
c. After turning steering wheel from stop to stop 5 or 6 times, connect coil wire and start engine.
d. Turn steering wheel from stop to stop until no bubbles appear in reservoir. Ensure fluid is not milky and fluid level does not diminish greatly when steering wheel is turned.

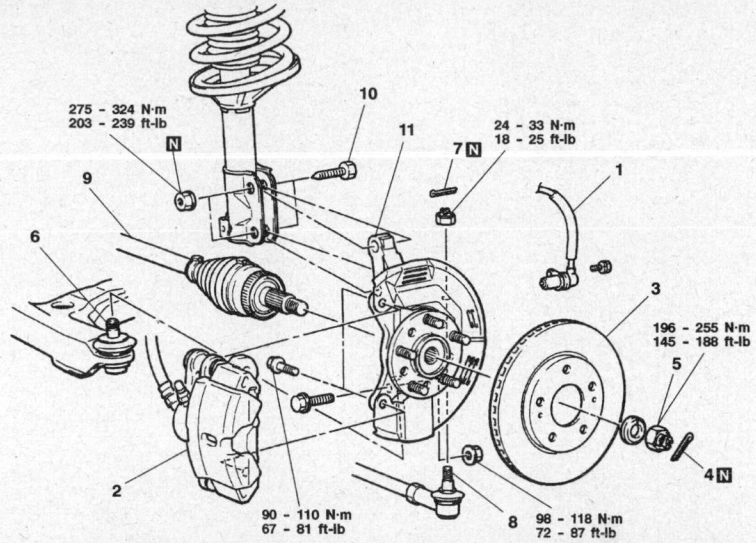

275 – 324 N·m
203 – 239 ft-lb

24 – 33 N·m
18 – 25 ft-lb

196 – 255 N·m
145 – 188 ft-lb

90 – 110 N·m
67 – 81 ft-lb

98 – 118 N·m
72 – 87 ft-lb

1. FRONT SPEED SENSOR
   <VEHICLES WITH ABS>
2. CALIPER ASSEMBLY
3. BRAKE DISC
4. COTTER PIN
5. DRIVESHAFT NUT
6. LOWER ARM BALL JOINT
   CONNECTION
7. COTTER PIN
8. TIE ROD END CONNECTION
9. DRIVESHAFT
10. FRONT STRUT MOUNTING BOLT
    AND NUT
11. HUB AND KNUCKLE

MT2029900048000X

Fig. 4   Knuckle replacement. 1999

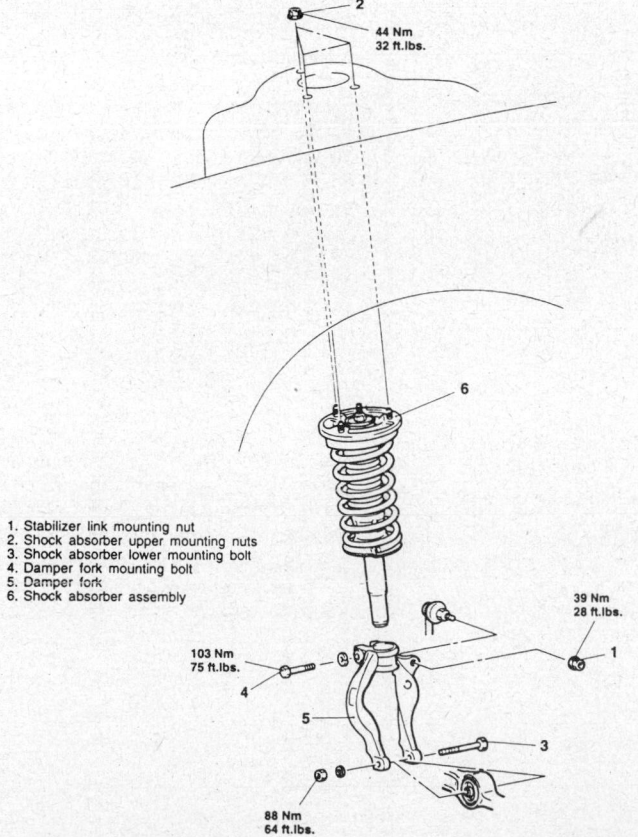

44 Nm
32 ft.lbs.

39 Nm
28 ft.lbs.

103 Nm
75 ft.lbs.

88 Nm
64 ft.lbs.

1. Stabilizer link mounting nut
2. Shock absorber upper mounting nuts
3. Shock absorber lower mounting bolt
4. Damper fork mounting bolt
5. Damper fork
6. Shock absorber assembly

MT2029400027000X

Fig. 5   Shock absorber replacement. 1996–98

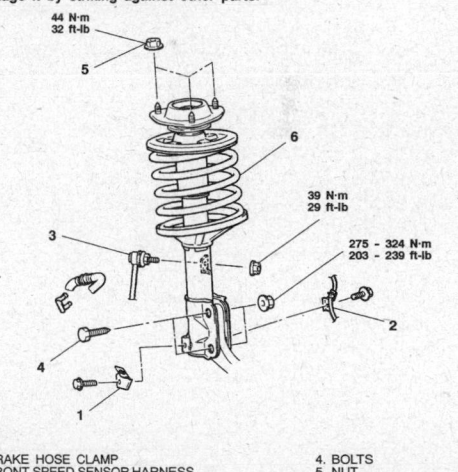

44 N·m
32 ft-lb

39 N·m
29 ft-lb

275 – 324 N·m
203 – 239 ft-lb

1. BRAKE HOSE CLAMP
2. FRONT SPEED SENSOR HARNESS
   CLAMP <VEHICLES WITH ABS>
3. STABILIZER LINK
4. BOLTS
5. NUT
6. STRUT ASSEMBLY

MT2029900050000X

Fig. 6   Shock absorber replacement. 1999

FRONT SUSPENSION & STEERING

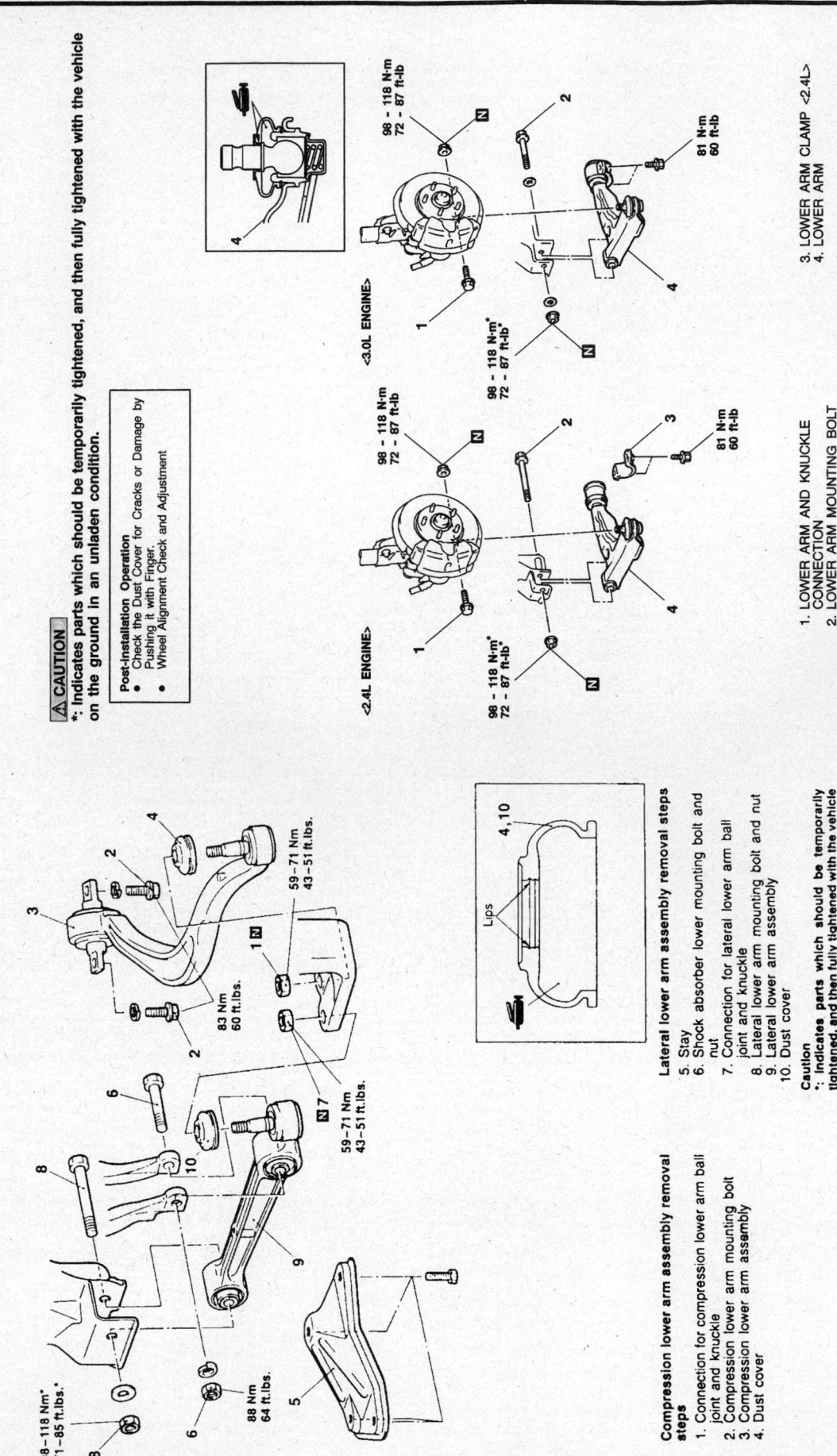

⚠ CAUTION

*: Indicates parts which should be temporarily tightened, and then fully tightened with the vehicle on the ground in an unladen condition.

Post-installation Operation
- Check the Dust Cover for Cracks or Damage by Pushing it with Finger.
- Wheel Alignment Check and Adjustment

<3.0L ENGINE>

98 – 118 N·m
72 – 87 ft-lb

81 N·m
60 ft-lb

98 – 118 N·m*
72 – 87 ft-lb*

<2.4L ENGINE>

98 – 118 N·m
72 – 87 ft-lb

81 N·m
60 ft-lb

98 – 118 N·m*
72 – 87 ft-lb*

3. LOWER ARM CLAMP <2.4L>
4. LOWER ARM

1. LOWER ARM AND KNUCKLE CONNECTION
2. LOWER ARM MOUNTING BOLT

Fig. 8 Lower control arm replacement. 1999

MT20299005100X

Compression lower arm assembly removal steps

1. Connection for compression lower arm ball joint and knuckle
2. Compression lower arm mounting bolt
3. Compression lower arm assembly
4. Dust cover

Lateral lower arm assembly removal steps

5. Stay
6. Shock absorber lower mounting bolt and nut
7. Connection for lateral lower arm ball joint and knuckle
8. Lateral lower arm mounting bolt and nut
9. Lateral lower arm assembly
10. Dust cover

Caution
*: Indicates parts which should be temporarily tightened, and then fully tightened with the vehicle in the unladen condition.

59 – 71 Nm
43–51 ft.lbs.

83 Nm
60 ft.lbs.

59 – 71 Nm
43–51 ft.lbs.

98 – 118 Nm*
71–85 ft.lbs.*

88 Nm
64 ft.lbs.

Lips

4, 10

MT20294000250X0X

MT20294000025000X

Fig. 7 Lower control arm replacement. 1996–98

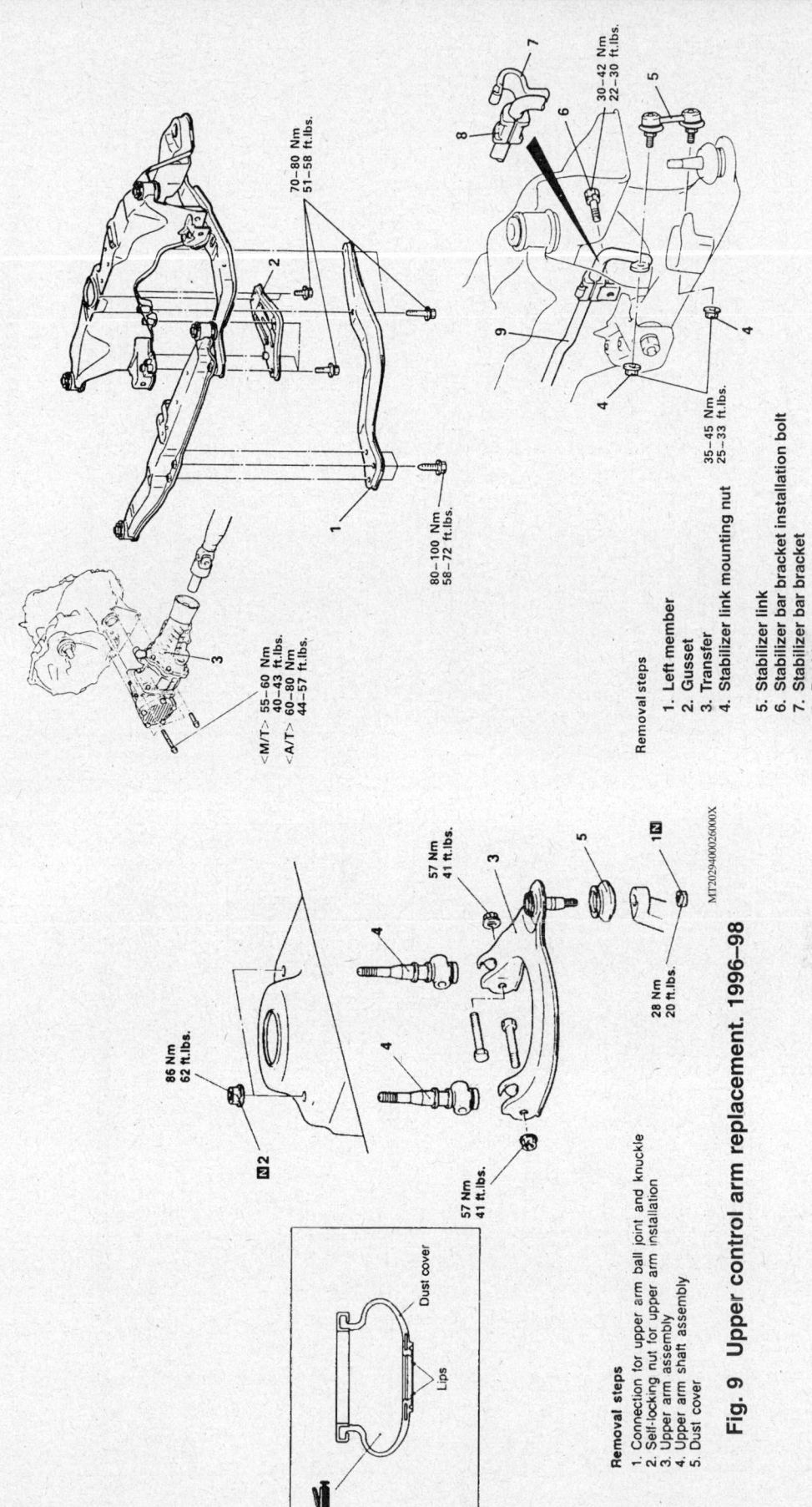

MT2029400029000X

70–80 Nm
51–58 ft.lbs.

30–42 Nm
22–30 ft.lbs.

80–100 Nm
58–72 ft.lbs.

<M/T> 55–60 Nm
40–43 ft.lbs.
<A/T> 60–80 Nm
44–57 ft.lbs.

35–45 Nm
25–33 ft.lbs.

Removal steps
1. Left member
2. Gusset
3. Transfer
4. Stabilizer link mounting nut
5. Stabilizer link
6. Stabilizer bar bracket installation bolt
7. Stabilizer bar bracket
8. Bushing
9. Stabilizer bar

Fig. 10 Stabilizer bar replacement. 1996–98

57 Nm
41 ft.lbs.

28 Nm
20 ft.lbs.

86 Nm
62 ft.lbs.

57 Nm
41 ft.lbs.

MT2029400026000X

Dust cover

Lips

Removal steps
1. Connection for upper arm ball joint and knuckle
2. Self-locking nut for upper arm installation
3. Upper arm assembly
4. Upper arm shaft assembly
5. Dust cover

Fig. 9 Upper control arm replacement. 1996–98

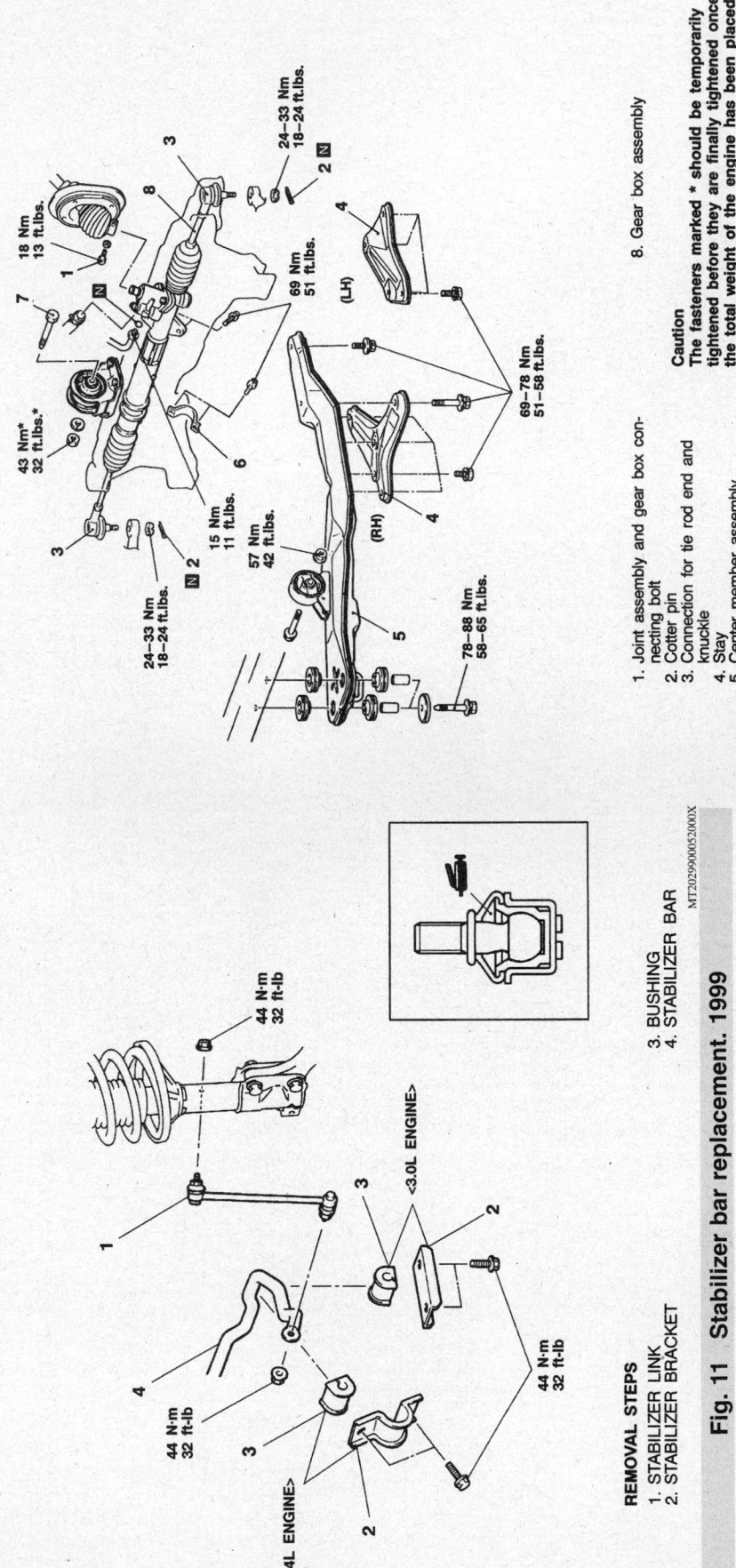

1. Joint assembly and gear box connecting bolt
2. Cotter pin
3. Connection for tie rod end and
   knuckle
4. Stay
5. Center member assembly
6. Clamp
7. Bolt
8. Gear box assembly

Caution
The fasteners marked * should be temporarily
tightened before they are finally tightened once
the total weight of the engine has been placed
on the vehicle body.

Fig. 12 Power steering gear replacement

REMOVAL STEPS

1. STABILIZER LINK
2. STABILIZER BRACKET
3. BUSHING
4. STABILIZER BAR

Fig. 11 Stabilizer bar replacement. 1999

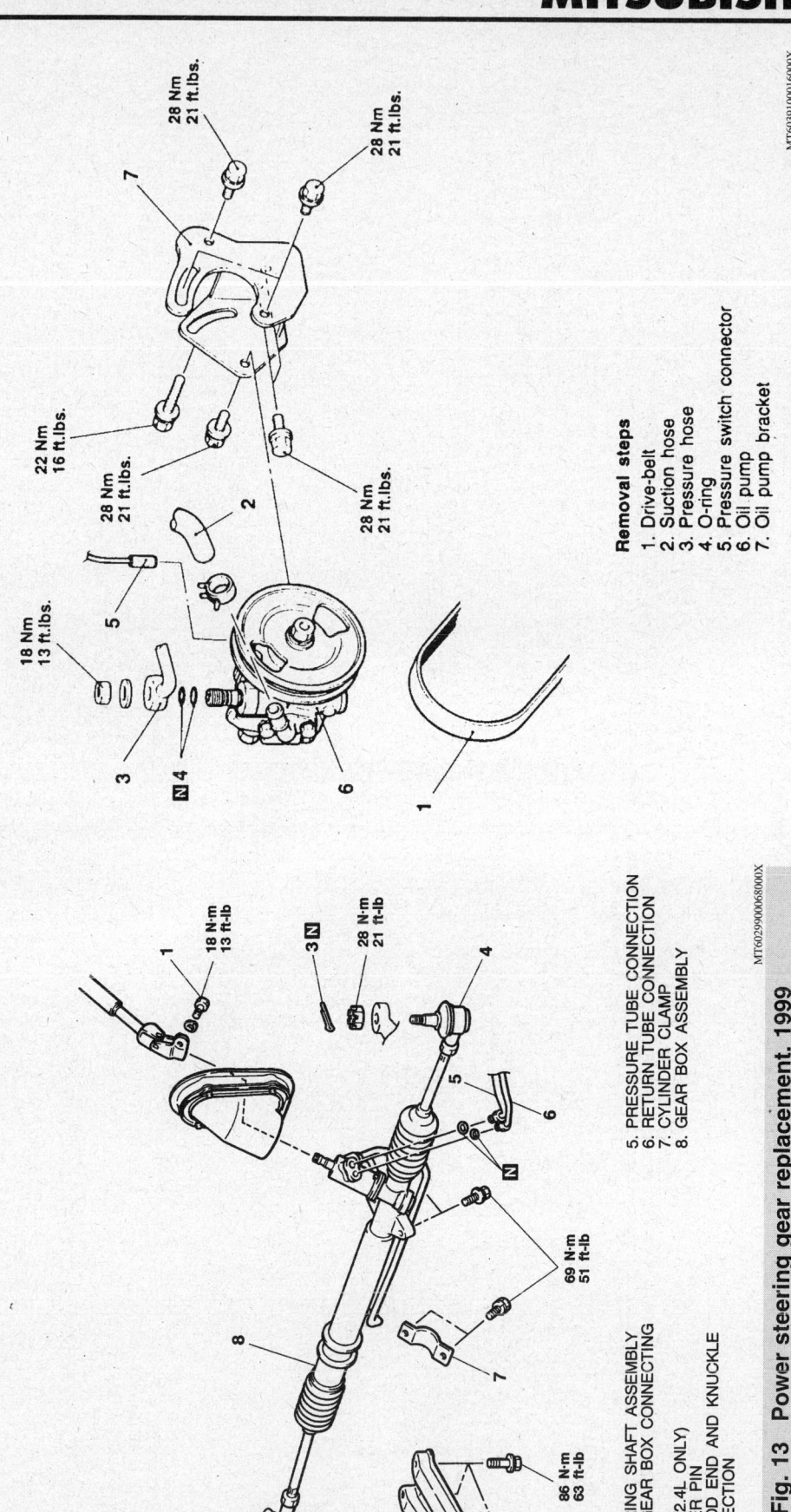

MT6039100016000X

Removal steps

1. Drive-belt
2. Suction hose
3. Pressure hose
4. O-ring
5. Pressure switch connector
6. Oil pump
7. Oil pump bracket

28 Nm
21 ft.lbs.

28 Nm
21 ft.lbs.

22 Nm
16 ft.lbs.

28 Nm
21 ft.lbs.

28 Nm
21 ft.lbs.

18 Nm
13 ft.lb.

Fig. 14 Power steering pump replacement. 1996–98

MT6029900068000X

1. STEERING SHAFT ASSEMBLY
   AND GEAR BOX CONNECTING
   BOLT
2. STAY (2.4L ONLY)
3. COTTER PIN
4. TIE ROD END AND KNUCKLE
   CONNECTION

5. PRESSURE TUBE CONNECTION
6. RETURN TUBE CONNECTION
7. CYLINDER CLAMP
8. GEAR BOX ASSEMBLY

18 N·m
13 ft-lb

28 N·m
21 ft-lb

69 N·m
51 ft-lb

86 N·m
63 ft-lb

Fig. 13 Power steering gear replacement. 1999

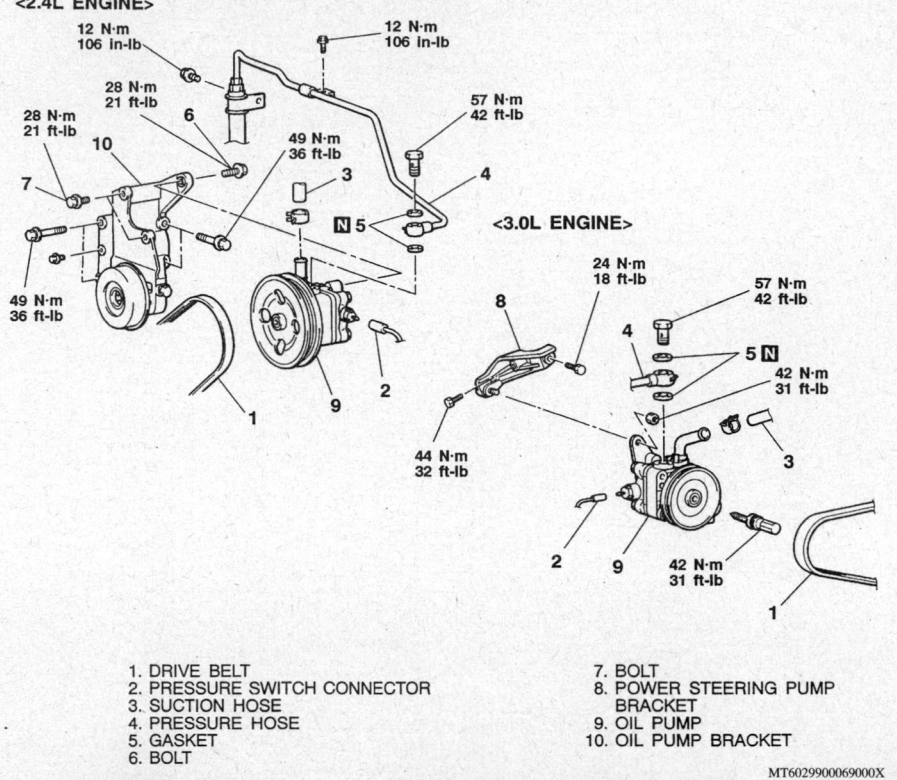

<2.4L ENGINE>

12 N·m
106 in-lb

12 N·m
106 in-lb

28 N·m
21 ft-lb

57 N·m
42 ft-lb

28 N·m
21 ft-lb

49 N·m
36 ft-lb

<3.0L ENGINE>

49 N·m
36 ft-lb

24 N·m
18 ft-lb

57 N·m
42 ft-lb

42 N·m
31 ft-lb

44 N·m
32 ft-lb

42 N·m
31 ft-lb

1. DRIVE BELT
2. PRESSURE SWITCH CONNECTOR
3. SUCTION HOSE
4. PRESSURE HOSE
5. GASKET
6. BOLT
7. BOLT
8. POWER STEERING PUMP
   BRACKET
9. OIL PUMP
10. OIL PUMP BRACKET

MT6029900069000X

Fig. 15 Power steering pump replacement. 1999

TIGHTENING SPECIFICATIONS

Year	Component	Torque, Ft. Lbs
1996–98	Brake Dust Shield Mounting Bolts	7
	Caliper Mounting Bolts	65
	Compression Lower Arm Ball Joint Nut	43–51
	Compression Lower Arm Mounting Bolts	60
	Damper Fork Mounting Bolt	75
	Driveshaft Nut	145–188
	Hub Mounting Bolts	65
	Knuckle To Upper Arm Nut	21
	Lateral Lower Arm Ball Joint Nut	43–51
	Lateral Lower Arm Mounting Bolt Nut	71–85
	Lateral Lower Arm To Damper Fork Through Bolt Nut	65
	Power Steering Gear & Joint Connecting Bolt	13
	Power Steering Gear Fluid Fitting	11
	Power Steering Pump Adjustment Bolt	16
	Power Steering Pump Bracket Mounting Bolts	21
	Power Steering Pump Pressure Hose Nut	13
	Shock Absorber Lower Mounting Nut	64
	Shock Absorber Upper Mounting Nuts	32
	Stabilizer Bar Bracket Bolts	28
	Stabilizer Link Mounting Nut	28
	Tie Rod End Nut	17–25
	Upper Arm Pivot Shaft Mounting Bolts	62
	Upper Arm To Pivot Shaft Bolts	41
	Wheel Lug Nuts	65–80
1999	Brake Assembly Mounting Bolt	66–81
	Brake Disc Bleeder Screw	71①
	Brake Tube Flare Nut	11
	Lower Arm Clamp Bolt	60
	Lower Arm To Crossmember Bolt	60
	Lower Arm To Crossmember Nut	72–87
	Lower Arm To Knuckle	72–87
	Power Steering Front/Rear Bracket Bolt (3.0L)	12
	Power Steering Gear Box Stay Bolt	63
	Power Steering Hose Flare Nut	25
	Power Steering Oil Pump Bolt/Nut (3.0L)	31
	Power Steering Pressure Switch	15
	Power Steering Pump Bracket Bolt (M8 2.4L)	21
	Power Steering Pump Bracket Bolt (M10 2.4L)	36
	Power Steering Pump Bracket Bolt (M8 3.0L)	18
	Power Steering Pump Bracket Bolt (M10 3.0L)	32
	Power Steering Pump Eye Bolt	42
	Power Steering Suction Pipe Bolt	30–35
	Pressure Hose Bolt (2.4L)	106①
	Stabilizer Bracket Bolt	32
	Stabilizer Link Nut	29
	Strut Assembly Jam Nut	44–51
	Strut Assembly To Body Nut	32
	Strut Assembly To Knuckle	203–239
	Tie Rod End Jam Nut	36–40
	Tie Rod End To Knuckle Nut	21

① — Inch Lbs.

Wheel Alignment

INDEX

PRELIMINARY INSPECTION

1. Ensure tires are inflated to correct pressure, then check for uneven wear.
2. Check front wheel bearings, suspension arm and ball joints for damage and replace components as necessary.
3. Check steering gear for damage and adjust as necessary.
4. Check shocks for damage and replace as necessary.
5. Rock vehicle backward and forward and bounce it upward and downward to settle vehicle prior to alignment.
6. Ensure vehicle is unloaded and on a suitable alignment rack according manufacturers' instructions. **When measuring equipment is attached directly to outer end of driveshaft and front wheels are on turntables, apply brake to prevent improper vehicle movement.**

FRONT WHEEL ALIGNMENT

CAMBER

Camber on these vehicles is preset to specifications and cannot be adjusted. If camber is out of specification, bent or damaged components must be replaced.

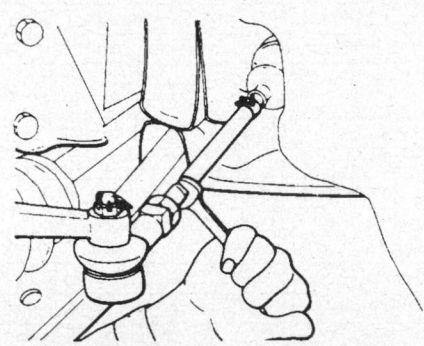

MT2049100036000X

Fig. 1   Front toe-in adjustment

CASTER

Caster is preset to specifications and cannot be adjusted. If caster is out of specification, bent or damaged components must be replaced.

TOE-IN

1. Adjust toe-in by undoing clips and turning left and right tie rod turnbuckles by same amount in opposite directions, **Fig. 1.**
2. To increase toe-out, turn left turnbuckle toward front of vehicle and right turnbuckle toward rear of vehicle. To increase toe-in, turn turnbuckles in other direction. Toe-in is adjusted .24 inch for each half turn of left and right tie rods.
3. After adjusting toe-in, check that steering wheel turning angle is within specification.

REAR WHEEL ALIGNMENT

CAMBER

Camber and toe-in are preset to specifications and cannot be adjusted. If camber is out of specification, bent or damaged components must be replaced.

TOE-IN

Rear toe-in is preset to specifications and cannot adjusted. If rear toe-in is out of specification, bent or damaged components must be replaced.

VEHICLE RIDE HEIGHT

There is no provision for adjustment of vehicle ride height. If ride height is not satisfactory, inspect suspension for damaged or modified components.

Specifications

GENERAL ENGINE SPECIFICATIONS

Year	Engine Liters	Fuel System	Bore & Stroke	Compression Ratio	Maximum Net H.P. @ RPM	Maximum Torque Ft. Lbs. @ RPM	Oil Pressure, psi
1996–99	1.5L	Fuel Inj.	2.97 X 3.23	9.2②	92 @ 6000	93 @ 3000	11.4①
	1.8L	Fuel Inj.	3.19 X 3.50	9.5	113 @ 6000③	116 @ 4500	11.4①

① — Minimum pressure at idle speed.
② — 1997–99: 9.0
③ — 1997–99: 111 H.P. @ 5500 RPM w/CA emissions.

TUNE UP SPECIFICATIONS

Year & Engine	Spark Plug Gap, Inch	Ignition Timing			Idle Speed, RPM②		Fuel Pressure psi	Valve Lash, Inch			
		Firing Order①	Timing ° BTDC	Timing Mark Location	Curb	Fast		Cold		Hot	
								Intake	Exhaust	Intake	Exhaust
1996											
1.5L	.041	①	5⑥	④	750	③	48	.004	.007	.008	.010
1.8L	.041	①	5⑥	④	700	③	50	.004	.008	.008	.012
1997–99											
1.5L	.041	①	5	④	750	③	48	.004⑦	.007	.008	.020
1.8L	.041	⑤	5	④	700	③	50	.004⑦	.008	.008	.012

BTDC — Before Top Dead Center
N — Neutral
① — Cylinder numbering from front of engine to rear, 1, 2, 3, 4. Firing order, 1–3–4–2.
② — When adjusting idle speed, set parking brake & chock drive wheels.
③ — Controlled by idle speed control servo.
④ — Equipped w/crankshaft position sensor.
⑤ — Equipped w/camshaft position sensor. Ignition coil (A) fires spark plug Nos. 1 & 4; ignition coil (B) fires spark plug Nos. 2 & 3.
⑥ — With jumper wire connected between ignition timing adjustment connector & ground. Refer to **Fig. C.**
⑦ — 1998–99: Equipped w/automatic lash adjusters.

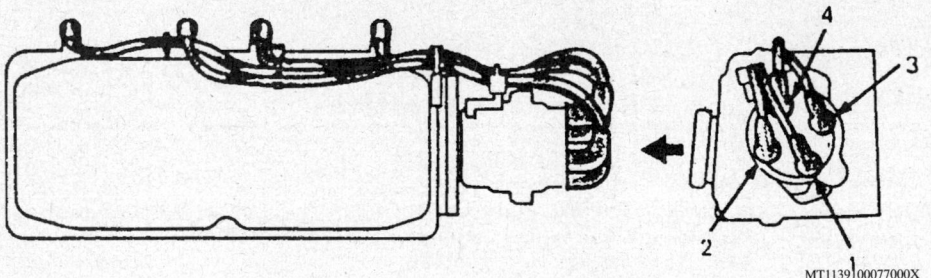

Fig. A

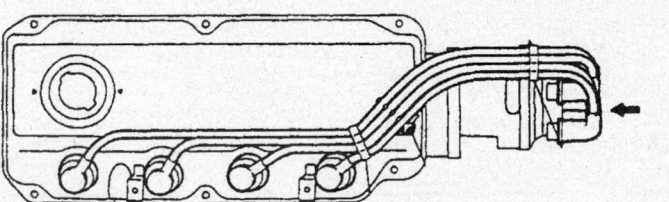
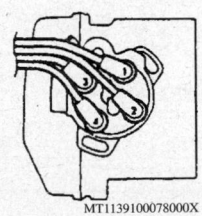

Fig. B

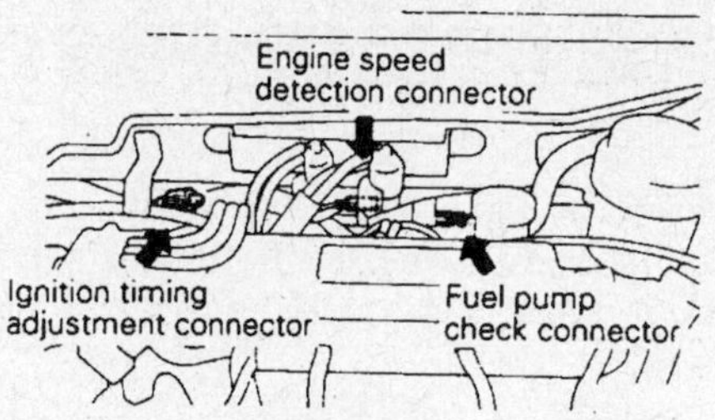

Fig. C Ignition timing adjustment connector

FRONT WHEEL ALIGNMENT SPECIFICATIONS

Year	Caster Angle, Deg.		Camber Angle, Deg.		Toe, Inch①	Ball Joint Wear
	Limits	Desired	Limits	Desired		
1996	—	+2¼	-½ to +½	0	-.12 to +.12	②
1997–99	+2⅓ to +3⅓	+2⅚	-½ to +½	0	-.12 to +.12	②

① — Toe-in (+); toe-out (-).

② — Lower arm ball joint break away torque, 9–56 inch lbs.

REAR WHEEL ALIGNMENT SPECIFICATIONS

Year	Camber Angle, Deg.		Toe, Inch①	Thrust Angle
	Limits	Desired		
1996	-1⅙ to -⅙	-⅔	+.04 to +.20	—
1997–99	-1⅙ to -⅙	-⅔	+.04 to +.20	-.15 to +.15

① — Toe-in (+); toe-out (-).

FLUID CAPACITIES & COOLING SYSTEM DATA

Year	Engine	Coolant Capacity, Qts.	Radiator Cap Relief Pressure, Lbs.	Thermo. Opening Temp. °F	Fuel Tank, Gals.	Engine Oil Refill, Qts. ①	Transmission Oil	
							Manual, Pts.	Auto. Trans., Qts. ②
1996	1.5L	5.3	13.0	190	13.2	3.5	3.8	6.3
	1.8L	6.3	13.0	180	13.2	4.0	3.8	6.3
1997–99	1.5L	5.3	9.2	180	13.2	3.5	⑤③	8.2
	1.8L	6.3	9.2	180	13.2	4.0	⑥④	8.2

① — Includes filter.

② — Approximate; make final check w/dipstick.

③ — 1998–99: 2.2 pts.

④ — 1998–99: 2.3 pts.

⑤ — 1997: 4.4 pts.

⑥ — 1997: 4.6 pts.

LUBRICANT DATA

Year	Lubricant Type			
	Transmission		Power Steering	Brake System
	Manual	Automatic		
1996–99	75W-90 GL-4/5	Diamond ATF SP II	Dexron II/IIE/III	DOT 3 or 4

Electrical

NOTE: On Air Bag Equipped Models, Refer To "Air Bag System Precautions" Located In The Front Of This Manual For System Disarming & Arming Procedures.

INDEX

PRECAUTIONS

AIR BAG SYSTEMS

Refer to "Air Bag System Precautions" in front of this manual for system disarming and arming procedures.

BATTERY GROUND CABLE

Prior to service, disconnect battery ground cable and isolate as required.

FUSE PANEL & FLASHER LOCATION

The multi-purpose fuse panel is located behind the lefthand side of the instrument panel, left of the steering column. The turn signal and hazard flasher is mounted on the multi-purpose fuse panel.

FUEL PUMP RELAY LOCATION

The multi-port fuel injection relay is located behind the center of the instrument panel.

RELAY CENTER LOCATION

The main relay centers are located behind the lefthand side of instrument panel and on the right and left sides of the engine compartment.

STARTER
REPLACE

1. Remove air cleaner assembly and intake manifold stay.
2. Remove starter cover.
3. Disconnect starter cables.
4. Remove starter mounting bolts, then starter assembly.
5. Reverse procedure to install, noting the following:
   a. **On 1996 models, torque** starter mounting bolts to 22 ft. lbs.
   b. **On 1997–99 models, torque** starter mounting bolts to 36 ft. lbs.

ALTERNATOR
REPLACE

1. Remove all drive belts.
2. **On models equipped with 1.5L engine,** remove water pump pulley.
3. **On all models,** disconnect alternator electrical connectors.
4. Remove alternator mounting bracket attaching bolts, then the bracket.
5. Remove alternator from vehicle.
6. Reverse procedure to install. Adjust drive belt tension as outlined under "Belt Tension Data" in the appropriate engine section.

DISTRIBUTOR
REPLACE
1.5L ENGINE

1. Remove distributor cap.
2. Rotate crankshaft until distributor rotor lines up with No. 1 spark plug wire on distributor cap.

3. Align notch on crankshaft with mark on timing indicator.
4. Remove distributor hold-down, then the distributor.
5. Reverse procedure to install, noting following:
   a. Align mark on distributor housing with mark on drive gear, then install distributor.
   b. With distributor installed, align mark on flange with center of mounting stud, then tighten distributor hold-down bolt.

1.8L ENGINE

1. Remove spark plug cables.
2. Remove distributor cap.
3. Rotate crankshaft until distributor rotor lines up with No. 1 spark plug wire on distributor cap.
4. Align notch on crankshaft with mark on timing indicator.
5. Remove distributor hold-down, then distributor.
6. Reverse procedure to install, noting the following:
   a. Align mark on distributor housing with mark on drive gear, then install distributor.
   b. With distributor installed, align mark on flange with center of mounting stud, then tighten distributor hold-down.

COIL PACK
REPLACE
1.8L ENGINE

1. Disconnect spark plug leads from coil.
2. Remove ignition coil pack attaching bolts.
3. Remove coil pack.

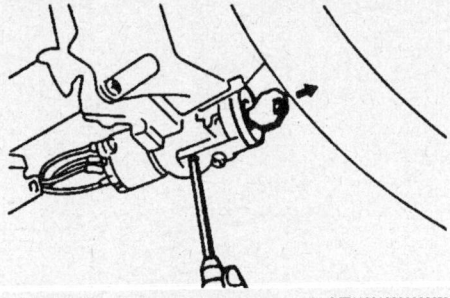

Fig. 1   Lock cylinder removal

4. Reverse procedure to install.

IGNITION LOCK
REPLACE

1. Remove knee protector and steering column shrouds.
2. Insert key into cylinder lock and turn to ACC position.
3. Push lockpin inward, **Fig. 1,** then remove cylinder lock.
4. Reverse procedure to install.

IGNITION SWITCH
REPLACE

Remove components in order as outlined in **Figs. 2 and 3,** noting the following:
1. Remove steering lock cylinder as follows:
   a. Insert key in lock cylinder and turn to ACC position.
   b. Using a small screwdriver, push lock cylinder lockpin in, **Fig. 1,** then remove lock cylinder.
2. Reverse procedure to install, noting following:
   a. With ignition switch Off or with key removed and brake pedal depressed, ensure shift lever cannot be moved from Park position.

NEUTRAL SAFETY SWITCH
REPLACE

1. Place selector lever in Neutral position.
2. Place manual control lever in Neutral position, then remove control lever retainer and lever.
3. Disconnect electrical harness, then remove switch retaining bolts and switch assembly.
4. Reverse procedure to install, noting following:
   a. With manual control lever in Neutral position, rotate switch body until wide end of manual control lever aligns with switch body flange.
   b. Hold switch body in position, then **torque** retaining bolts to 7–9 ft. lbs.

MULTI-FUNCTION SWITCH
REPLACE

1. Remove steering wheel as outlined under "Steering Wheel, Replace."

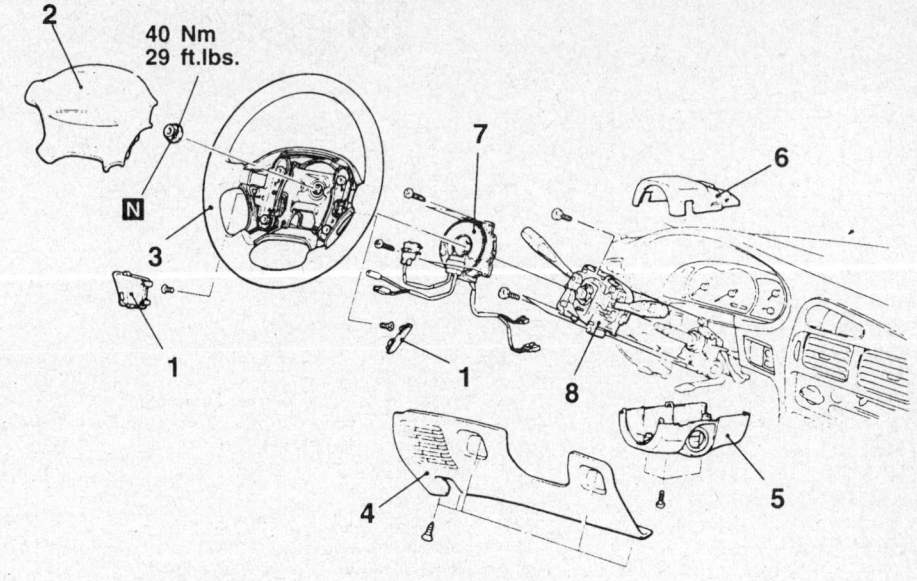

Removal steps <1993 models>

3. Steering wheel
4. Knee protector
5. Column cover lower
6. Column cover upper
8. Column switch

Removal steps

1. Cover
2. Air bag module
3. Steering wheel
4. Knee protector
5. Column cover lower
6. Column cover upper
7. Clock spring
8. Column switch

Fig. 2   Ignition switch replacement. 1996

2. **On models equipped with tilt steering,** set tilt position of steering shaft to lowest position.
3. **On all models,** remove air bag clockspring.
4. Disconnect column switch electrical connectors, then remove cable band.
5. Remove column switch attaching screws, then the column switch from steering shaft.
6. Reverse procedure to install.

STEERING WHEEL
REPLACE

1. Carefully remove air bag module from steering wheel.
2. Remove steering wheel attaching nut.
3. Scribe mating marks on steering shaft and steering wheel for installation reference.
4. Using a suitable steering wheel puller, remove steering wheel. **Do not hammer on steering wheel to remove. Damage to collapsible mechanism may occur.**
5. Reverse procedure to install, noting following:
   a. Align mating marks on steering shaft and steering wheel.

b. **Torque** steering wheel attaching nut 25–33 ft. lbs.

INSTRUMENT CLUSTER
REPLACE

1. Remove instrument cluster bezel attaching screws, then the bezel from the instrument panel.
2. Remove instrument cluster attaching screws, then pull cluster rearward.
3. Pull speedometer cable slightly into passenger compartment, then remove cable adapter lock.
4. Remove instrument cluster from instrument panel.
5. Reverse procedure to install.

RADIO
REPLACE
1996

On some models, the radio fuse is located on the rear of the radio. If the radio fuse needs to be replaced, it will be necessary to remove the radio.
1. Pry off center panel using a suitable tool, then remove panel from instrument panel.

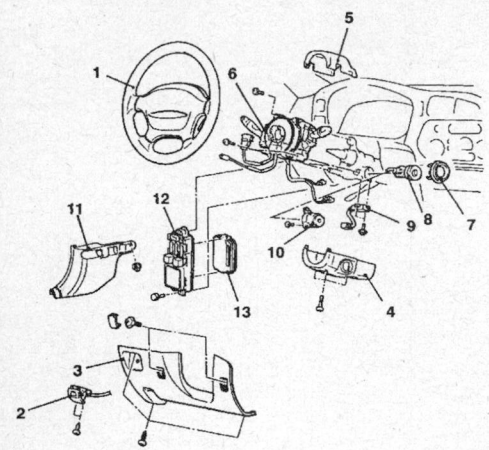

13 Nm
9 ft.lbs.

5 Nm
4 ft.lbs.

9 Nm
7 ft.lbs.

Steering lock cylinder removal steps

1. Steering wheel
2. Hood lock release handle
3. Instrument under cover
4. Column cover, lower
5. Column cover, upper
6. Clock spring and column switch assembly
7. Ring cover
8. Steering lock cylinder

Key reminder switch removal steps

4. Column cover, lower
5. Column cover, upper
9. Key reminder switch

Ignition switch removal steps

4. Column cover, lower
5. Column cover, upper
10. Ignition switch

BUZZER-ECU or ETACS-ECU removal steps

11. Cowl side trim (LH)
12. Junction block
13. BUZZER-ECU or ETACS-ECU

MT9049700065000X

Fig. 3   Ignition switch replacement. 1997–99

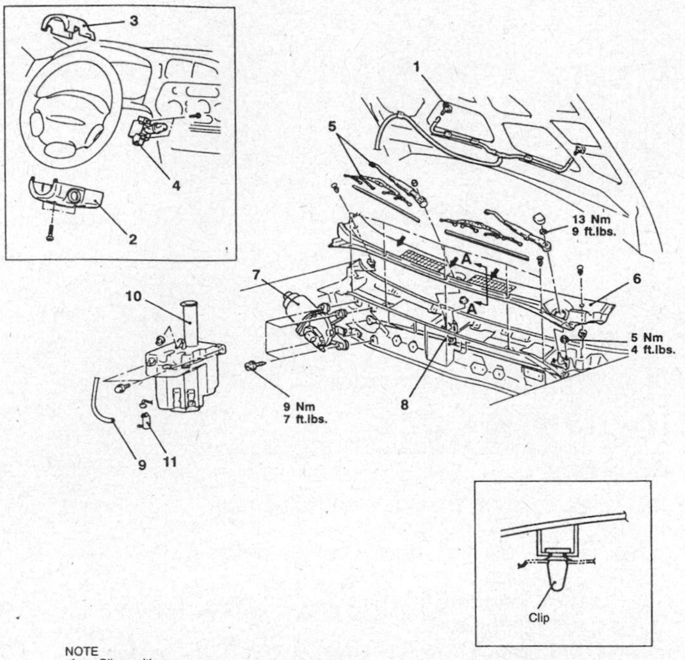

NOTE
◀ : Clip position

1. Washer nozzle assembly

Wiper and washer switch removal steps

2. Column cover, lower
3. Column cover, upper
4. Wiper and washer switch

Wiper motor and linkage removal steps

5. Wiper arm and blade assembly
6. Front deck garnish
7. Wiper motor
8. Linkage

Clip

Washer tank removal steps

● Draining of washer fluid
● Front bumper
9. Washer hose
10. Washer tank
11. Washer motor

MT9029700067000X

Fig. 4   Wiper & washer assembly replacement. 1997–99

2. Remove radio bracket attaching screws, then the radio bracket.
3. Pull radio outward enough to gain access to rear of radio.
4. Disconnect antenna lead wire and electrical connector, then remove radio.
5. Reverse procedure to install.

1997–99

1. Remove audio panel attaching screws, then the audio panel.
2. Remove radio mounting bracket attaching screws, then the brackets.
3. Remove radio from instrument panel.
4. Reverse procedure to install.

WIPER MOTOR

REPLACE

1996

1. Remove pivot shaft attaching nuts, then push pivot shaft inward.
2. Remove wiper motor attaching bolts, then pull wiper motor slightly and disconnect motor and linkage assembly.
3. Remove wiper motor with linkage from vehicle. **Mark position of crank arm to wiper motor, if necessary to remove.**
4. Reverse procedure to install.

1997–99

Replace wiper motor, linkage and washer tank in order as shown in **Fig. 4.** Reverse procedure to install.

WIPER SWITCH

REPLACE

Replace wiper switch in order as shown in **Fig. 4.**

BLOWER MOTOR

REPLACE

1996

Replace blower motor as shown in **Fig. 5.**

1997–99

1. Replace blower motor as shown in **Fig. 6,** noting the following,
   a. Drain cooling system into appropriate container.
   b. Remove air cleaner cover and air intake hose.
   c. Remove instrument panel.

HEATER CORE

REPLACE

1996

Remove heater unit components in order as shown in, **Fig. 7,** noting the following:

1. Drain cooling system into appropriate container.
2. Remove front seats and floor console, **Figs. 8 and 9,** then instrument panel as outlined under "Instrument Cluster, Replace."
3. **On models equipped with A/C,** remove bolts and nuts attaching evaporator assembly to heater unit.
4. **On all models,** pull evaporator assembly outward, then remove heater unit.
5. Remove heater core fastening clips.
6. Remove heater core from heater unit. **Use caution not to damage heater core fins or pad part of heater core.**
7. Reverse procedure to install.

1997–99

1. Drain engine coolant and discharge A/C refrigerant into a suitable recovery device.
2. Remove air cleaner and air intake hose.
3. Remove instrument panel as outlined in "Dash Panel Service."
4. Remove joint duct assembly, then evaporator case as outlined under "Evaporator Core, Replace."
5. Remove heater core in numbered sequence shown in **Fig. 10.**
6. Reverse procedure to install.

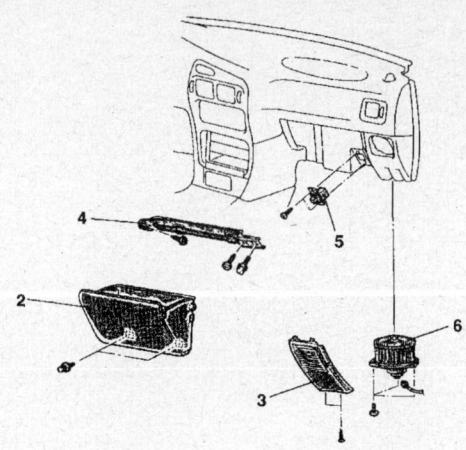

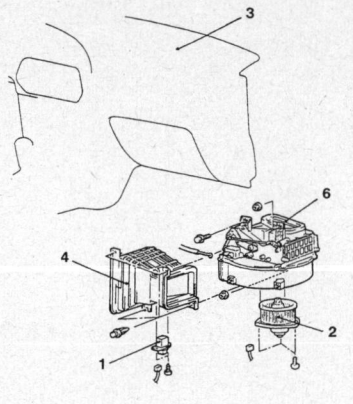

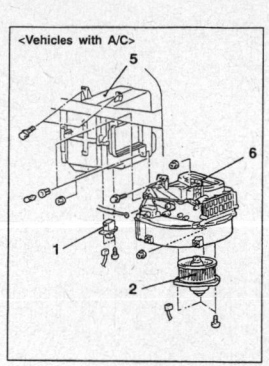

Resistor removal steps

2. Glove box
3. Corner panel
4. Glove box frame
5. Resistor

Blower motor assembly removal

6. Blower motor assembly

MT7029700407000X

Fig. 5   Blower motor replacement. 1996

1. Resistor
2. Blower fan and motor

Blower unit removal steps

3. Instrument panel
4. Joint duct <Vehicles without A/C>
5. Evaporator <Vehicles with A/C>
6. Blower unit assembly

MT7029900423000X

Fig. 6   Replace blower motor. 1997-99

EVAPORATOR CORE
REPLACE
1996

1. Discharge A/C refrigerant into a suitable recovery device, then remove evaporator core in numbered sequence shown, **Fig. 11.**
2. Reverse procedure to install.

1997-99

1. Discharge A/C refrigerant into a suitable recovery device, then remove evaporator case in numbered sequence shown, **Fig. 12.**
2. Remove evaporator core in numbered sequence shown, **Fig. 13.**
3. Reverse procedure to install.

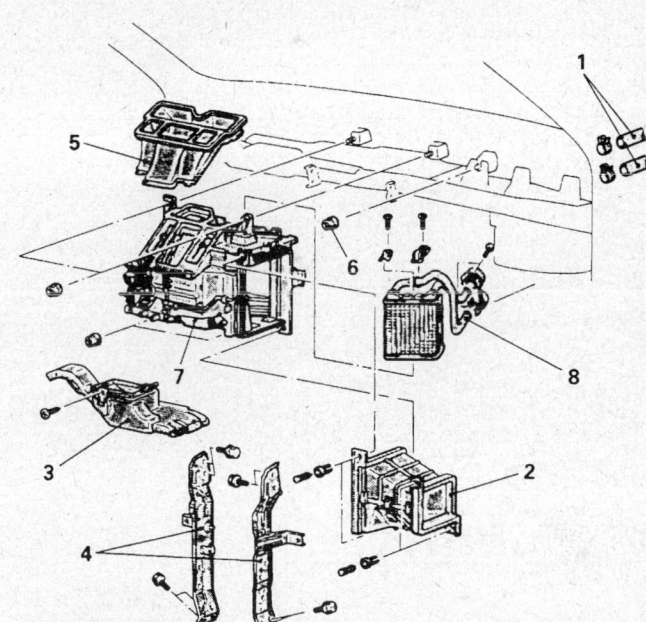

Removal steps

1. Heater hose connection
2. Joint duct
   <Vehicles without air conditioning>
3. Foot duct
4. Center reinforcement
5. Center ventilation duct
6. Evapolator installation nut
   <Vehicles with air conditioning>
7. Heater unit
8. Heater core

MT7029400094000X

Fig. 7   Heater unit & core replacement. 1996

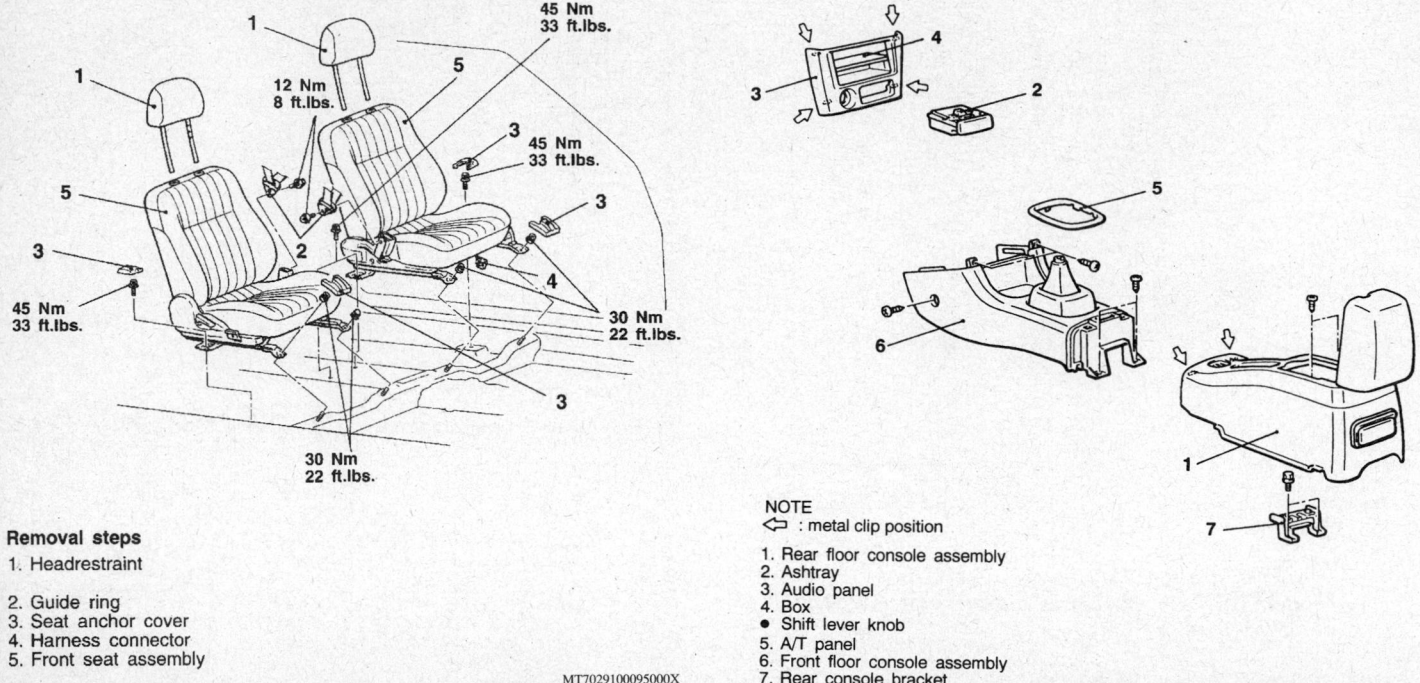

Removal steps

1. Headrestraint

2. Guide ring
3. Seat anchor cover
4. Harness connector
5. Front seat assembly

MT7029100095000X

Fig. 8   Front seat removal. 1996

NOTE
⇦ : metal clip position

1. Rear floor console assembly
2. Ashtray
3. Audio panel
4. Box
● Shift lever knob
5. A/T panel
6. Front floor console assembly
7. Rear console bracket

MT7029400098000X

Fig. 9   Floor console removal. 1996

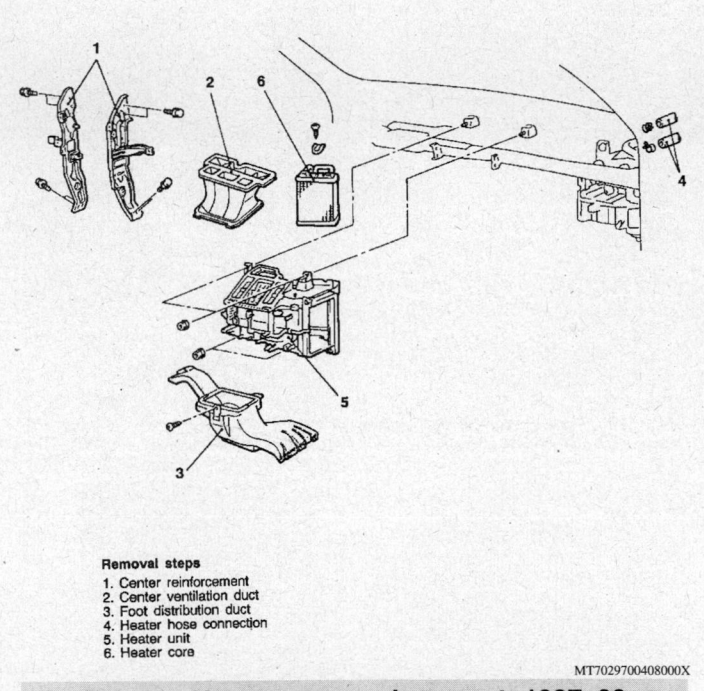

Removal steps
1. Center reinforcement
2. Center ventilation duct
3. Foot distribution duct
4. Heater hose connection
5. Heater unit
6. Heater core

MT7029700408000X

Fig. 10   Heater core replacement. 1997–99

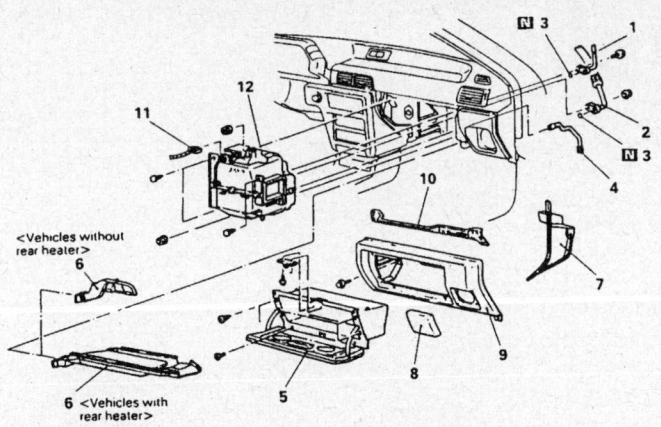

1. Liquid pipe connection
2. Suction hose connection
3. O-rings
4. Drain hose
5. Glove box
6. Lap heater duct <vehicles without rear heater> or shower duct <vehicles with rear heater>
7. Cowl side trim
8. Speaker cover
9. Knee protector, R.H.
10. Glove box frame
11. Connection of the connector (12P) for auto compressor control unit
12. Evaporator

MT7029100102000X

Fig. 11 Evaporator core replacement. 1996

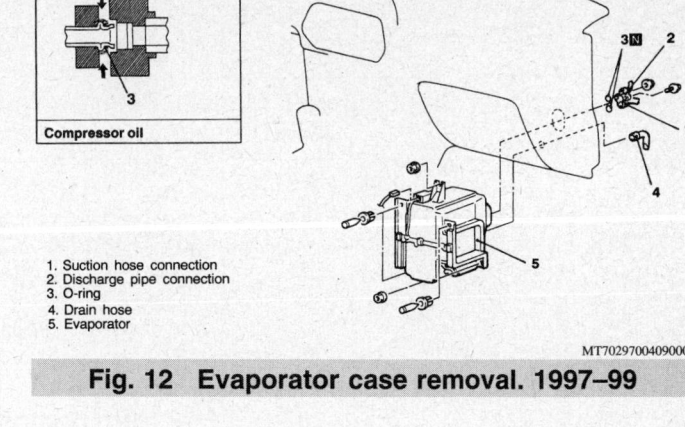

1. Suction hose connection
2. Discharge pipe connection
3. O-ring
4. Drain hose
5. Evaporator

MT7029700409000X

Fig. 12 Evaporator case removal. 1997–99

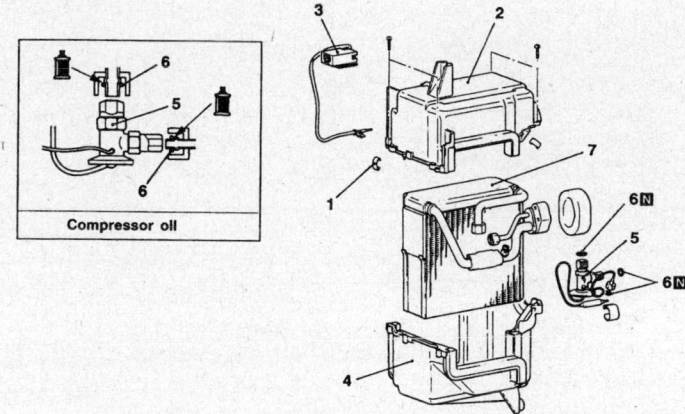

Disassembly steps

1. Clip
2. Evaporator cover (upper)
3. Thermostat (Automatic compressor-ECU)
4. Evaporator cover (lower)
5. Expansion valve
6. O-ring
7. Evaporator

MT7029700410000X

Fig. 13 Evaporator core replacement. 1997–99

MITSUBISHI MIRAGE

1.5L Engine

NOTE: On Air Bag Equipped Models, Refer To "Air Bag System Precautions" Located In Front Of This Manual For System Disarming & Arming Procedures.

NOTE: Prior To Performing Any Service Operations Listed In This Section, Consult The "Technical Service Bulletins" For Related Information.

INDEX

PRECAUTIONS

AIR BAG SYSTEMS

Refer to "Air Bag System Precautions" in front of this manual for system disarming and arming procedures.

FUEL SYSTEM PRESSURE RELIEF

1. Disconnect fuel pump harness connector at rear side of fuel tank. **Cover fuel pipe line with rag after relieving pressure as residual pressure may still remain.**
2. Start engine and let idle until engine stops by itself, then turn ignition switch to Off. **Failure to relieve fuel system pressure prior to disconnecting fuel system components may cause fire or personal injury.**
3. Disconnect battery ground cable.
4. Connect fuel pump harness connector.
5. After repairs have been completed, connect positive battery terminal to fuel pump drive terminal and negative terminal to chassis. Ensure fuel pump operates at this time.

BATTERY GROUND CABLE

Prior to service, disconnect battery ground cable and isolate as required.

COMPRESSION PRESSURE

Standard compression pressure is 192 psi. Minimum compression pressure is 137 psi. Maximum difference between cylinders is 14 psi, 1996–98.

Standard compression pressure is 188 psi. Minimum compression pressure is 133 psi. Maximum difference between cylinders is 14 psi, 1999.

ENGINE MOUNT

REPLACE

1. Raise and support engine to reduce weight upon mounts.
2. Remove power steering pressure hose and A/C high pressure hose.
3. Remove engine mount bracket and body connection bolt.
4. Remove engine mount bracket and mounting stopper.
5. Reverse procedure to install.

ENGINE

REPLACE

1. Relieve fuel system pressure as outlined under "Precautions," then scribe and remove hood.
2. Drain engine coolant into a suitable container, then remove transaxle as outlined in "Clutch & Manual Transaxle" or in "Automatic Transmission/Transaxle" section.
3. Remove radiator assembly.
4. Remove front exhaust pipe.
5. Remove engine assembly in numbered sequence outlined in **Figs. 1 and 2.** Support A/C compressor and power steering pump aside with hoses attached.

6. Reverse procedure to install. Tighten all bolts to specifications.

INTAKE MANIFOLD

REPLACE

When replacing intake manifold, remove and install manifold in numbered sequence as shown, **Figs. 3 and 4.**

EXHAUST MANIFOLD

REPLACE

When replacing exhaust manifold, remove and install manifold in numbered sequence as outlined in **Fig. 5.**

CYLINDER HEAD

REPLACE

1. Reduce fuel system pressure as outlined under "Precautions."
2. Drain engine coolant and oil into suitable containers.
3. Remove air intake hose.
4. Remove thermostat case assembly.
5. Remove cylinder head and gasket in numbered sequence shown, **Fig. 6,** noting following:
   a. After timing belt upper cover is removed, rotate crankshaft in direction of normal rotation until timing marks align.
   b. Remove camshaft sprocket using sprocket remover . MB990767 and MD998719, or equivalents.

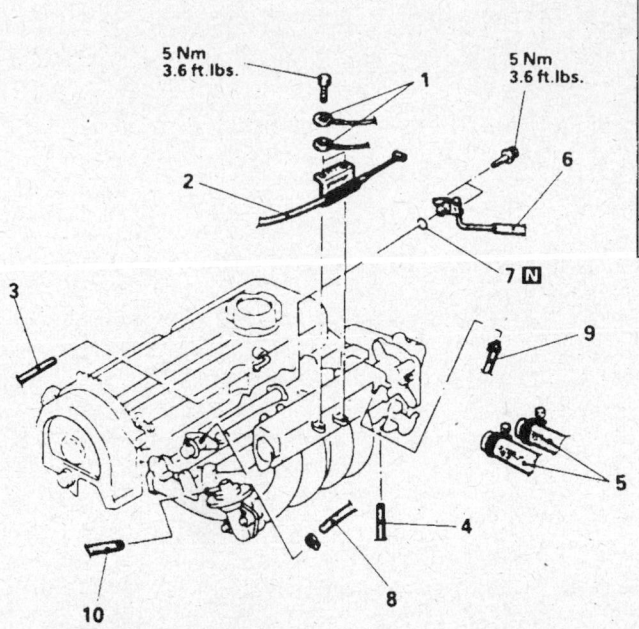

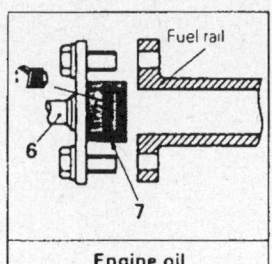

Fig. 1 Engine replacement. (Part 1 of 2) 1996

MT1069300252010X

Removal steps
1. Ground cable connection
2. Accelerator cable connection
3. Breather hose connection
4. Vacuum hose connection
5. Heater hose connection
6. High-pressure hose connection
7. O-ring
8. Return hose connection
9. Brake booster vacuum hose connection
10. Vacuum hose connection

c. Remove cylinder head bolts in sequence shown, **Fig. 7,** in two or three steps.
6. Reverse procedure to install, noting the following:
   a. Install new head gasket on block with "ICG" identification mark facing up.
   b. Tighten cylinder head bolts in order outlined in the following steps, first tighten to 36 ft. lbs., second fully loosen in reverse order, thirdly tighten to 14 ft. lbs., next tighten additional 90° of a turn and finally tighten additional 90° of a turn in order outlined in **Fig. 8.**

VALVE CLEARANCE SPECIFICATIONS

Refer to "Tune Up Specifications" for valve clearance.

VALVE ADJUSTMENT

1996–97

1. With engine at operating temperature, remove rocker arm cover.
2. Disconnect high tension lead from ignition coil.

3. While observing rocker arms on No. 4 cylinder, rotate crankshaft clockwise until exhaust valve is closing and intake valve is slightly open. Ensure timing mark on crankshaft pulley is aligned with "T" mark on lower timing cover case and No. 1 cylinder is at top dead center (TDC) compression stroke. Check and adjust valve clearance for both intake and exhaust valves of No. 1 cylinder, intake valve of No. 2 cylinder and exhaust valve of No. 3 cylinder. If valve clearance is not as specified, adjust valves as follows:
   a. Loosen rocker arm locknut.
   b. Turn adjusting screw while measuring clearance with a feeler gauge, **Fig. 9,** until screw contacts feeler gauge.
   c. Hold adjusting screw in place and tighten locknut to specifications.
4. Rotate crankshaft clockwise 360 degrees then check and adjust valve clearance for exhaust valve of No. 2 cylinder, intake valve of No. 3 cylinder and intake and exhaust valves of No. 4 cylinder.
5. After completing adjustment, install rocker arm cover and connect ignition coil high tension lead.
6. Tighten rocker arm cover bolts to specifications.

1998–99

These engines use hydraulic auto-lash adjusters. No adjustments are required.

ROCKER ARMS

REPLACE

Refer to "Camshaft, Replace" for rocker arm and shaft replacement procedure.

VALVE GUIDES

1. Press old valve guide from cylinder head toward lower surface using a suitable pushrod and press.
2. Ream each valve guide bore in cylinder head to outer diameter of replacement valve guide, **Fig. 10.** Never use a valve guide of same size as removed guide.
3. **On 1996 models,** press fit new valve guide into top of cylinder head until a protrusion of .579–.602 inch is obtained.
4. **On 1997–99 models,** press fit new valve guide in to top of cylinder head until a protrusion of .670 inch is obtained.
5. **On 1996–97 models,** note that valve guides for intake and exhaust are of different lengths. Intake guides are 1.791 inches long; exhaust guides are 1.988 inches long.
6. **On 1998–99 models,** intake guides are 1.732 inches long; exhaust guides are 1.949 inches long.
7. **On all models,** after installation of new valve guides, insert valve and ensure it slides freely, then check for proper clearance. If clearance is not correct, ream valve guide until proper clearance is obtained. Refer to " Valve Specifications" for stem to guide clearance.

TIMING BELT

REPLACE

REMOVAL

1. Disconnect breather and secondary air hoses, then remove air cleaner assembly, air intake duct and heated air duct.
2. Disconnect accelerator cable and oxygen sensor lead, and remove spark plug wires.
3. Remove accessory drive belts.
4. Support engine as needed, then remove left engine mount bracket.
5. Remove power steering pump and water pump pulleys.
6. Remove upper and lower timing belt covers.
7. Remove damper pulley, crankshaft pulley.
8. Rotate crankshaft in normal direction of rotation until timing marks are aligned, **Fig. 11,** loosen belt tensioner bolts and move timing belt tensioner fully toward water pump, then tighten bolts to hold tensioner. **Crankshaft should always be turned only clockwise.**
9. Loosen timing belt tensioner bolts.

10. Loosen camshaft sprocket bolt using camshaft sprocket MD998715, or equivalent.

11. Move timing belt tensioner to water pump side and temporarily tighten adjusting bolt.

12. Remove timing belt. If timing belt is to be reused, place an arrow mark indicating turning direction (direction of engine rotation) to ensure proper installation.

13. Inspect belt and replace if any of following conditions are noted:
    a. Hardened back surface rubber. With back surface glossy, nonelastic and so hard that no mark is produced when fingernail is forced into surface.
    b. Cracked back surface rubber or separated canvas.
    c. Cracks at tooth bottom or side of belt.

INSTALLATION

1. Install timing belt tensioner as follows:
   a. Tighten camshaft sprocket bolt to specification.
   b. Mount tensioner, spring and spacer, then temporarily tighten pivot bolt.
   c. Temporarily tighten adjusting bolt, then install bottom end of spring into front case.
   d. Secure tensioner to position nearest water pump.

2. Ensure timing marks are aligned, **Fig. 11.**

3. Install timing belt over crankshaft sprocket, then the camshaft sprocket, keeping tension side of belt tight as belt is installed. If used belt is installed, ensure belt is installed in original direction.

4. Apply counterclockwise force to camshaft sprocket to tighten tension side of belt. Ensure timing marks remain aligned.

5. **On 1996 models,** install crankshaft pulley to prevent belt from slipping off sprocket.

6. **On 1997–99 models,** adjust belt tension as follows:
   a. Loosen tensioner bolts to allow tensioner to bear against belt, then tighten adjusting bolt and pivot bolt. **Tighten adjusting bolt first to prevent tensioner from rotating away from belt.**
   b. Rotate crankshaft clockwise one full revolution, then realign crankshaft sprocket timing mark with pointer. **Crankshaft must be rotated smoothly, in clockwise direction. Do not apply any force other than spring force of tensioner to timing belt.**
   c. Loosen tensioner pivot and adjusting bolts, then tighten adjuster bolt and pivot bolt. **Tighten adjusting bolt first to prevent tensioner from rotating away from belt.**
   d. Check belt tension by holding belt, **Fig. 12,** and applying thumb pressure to tension side of belt. Tension is correct when tooth of belt covers

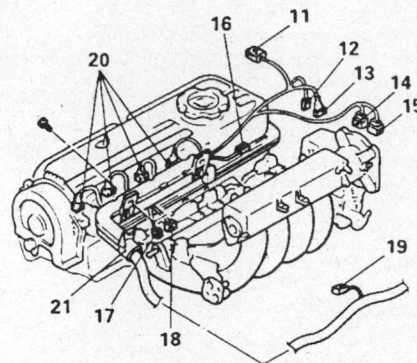

16. Throttle position sensor connector
17. Intake air temperature sensor

11. Oxygen sensor connector
12. Ignition coil connector
13. CKP sensor and CMP sensor connector
14. Engine coolant temperature sensor connector
15. Engine coolant temperature gauge unit connector
16. Throttle position sensor connector
17. Intake air temperature sensor
18. EGR temperature sensor
19. Idle air control motor
20. Injector connector
21. Control harness

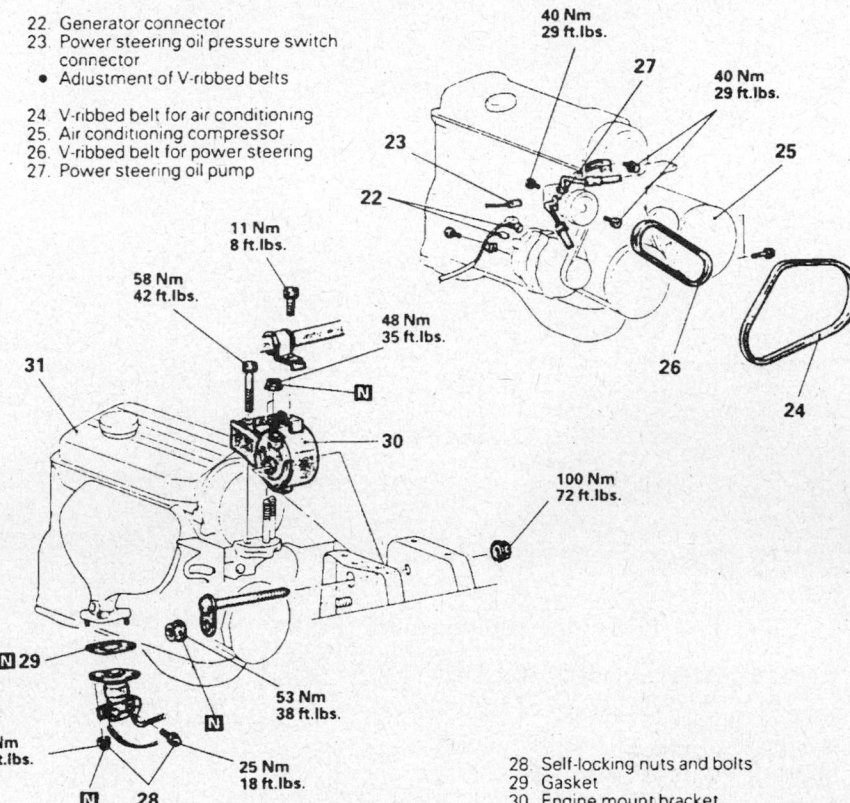

22. Generator connector
23. Power steering oil pressure switch connector
• Adjustment of V-ribbed belts

24. V-ribbed belt for air conditioning
25. Air conditioning compressor
26. V-ribbed belt for power steering
27. Power steering oil pump

28. Self-locking nuts and bolts
29. Gasket
30. Engine mount bracket
31. Engine assembly

MT1069300252020X

Fig. 1   Engine replacement. (Part 2 of 2) 1996

approximately ¼ width of tensioner adjuster bolt.
   e. Rotate crankshaft clockwise, one full revolution and ensure timing marks line up.

7. **On all models,** reverse procedure to install. Adjust valve clearances as required.

CAMSHAFT

REPLACE

REMOVAL

Remove camshaft in numbered sequence, **Fig. 13,** noting the following:

1. Release fuel system pressure as outlined under "Precautions."
2. Use camshaft sprocket holder and adapter . MD998719 and MB990767, or equivalents, to ensure camshaft sprockets do not turn during removal.
3. **On 1996 models,** check and adjust valve clearance as required.
4. **On 1997–99 models,** attach lash adjuster MD998443, or equivalent, before removing rocker assembly.
5. **On all models,** mark and identify rocker arms and rocker shafts before removal, as they are not interchangeable.
6. Remove camshaft oil seals using suitable screw driver to pry seal out.

INSTALLATION

Reverse procedures to install noting the following:

1. Install oil seals using seal installation

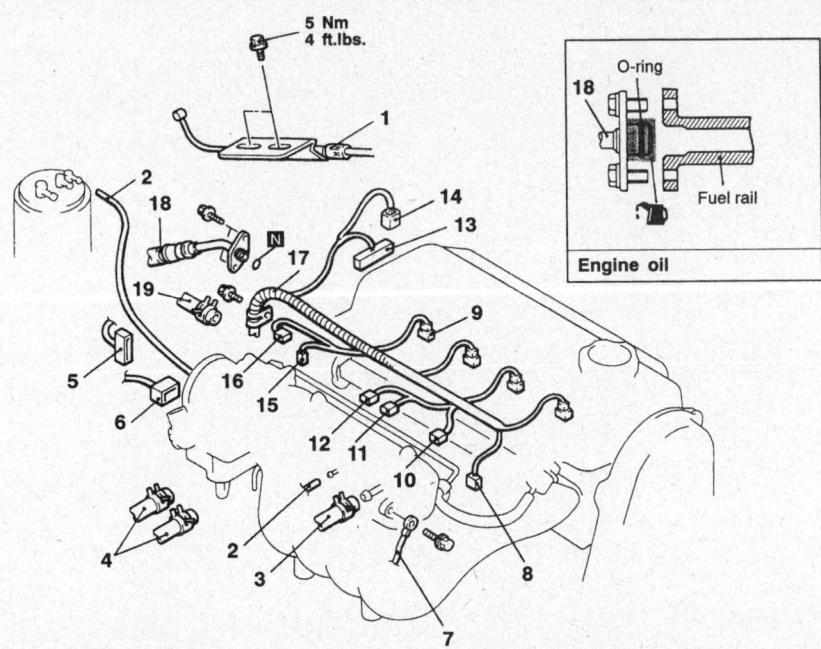

**5 Nm
4 ft.lbs.**

Engine oil

Removal steps
1. Accelerator cable connection
2. Vacuum hose connection
3. Brake booster vacuum hose connection
4. Heater hose connection
5. Throttle position sensor connector
6. Idle speed control connector
7. Ground cable connection
8. Heated oxygen sensor connector
9. Injector connector
10. Intake air temperature sensor connector
11. Evaporative emission purge solenoid connector

12. EGR solenoid connector
13. Distributor connector
14. Heated oxygen sensor connector <Vehicles for California>
15. Engine coolant temperature gauge unit connector
16. Engine coolant temperature sensor connector
17. Control wiring harness
18. High-pressure fuel hose connection
19. Fuel return hose connection

MT1069900556010X

Fig. 2   Engine replacement. (Part 1 of 2) 1997–99

MD998713, or equivalent.
2. Install rocker arm shafts with notched side toward timing belt.
3. Install camshaft sprocket and timing belt, and ensure timing marks are aligned, **Fig. 11.** Tighten camshaft sprocket bolt to specification.
4. Install rocker arms with identification marks positioned as shown, **Fig. 14.**
5. Position large chamfer end of rocker shaft toward timing belt side of engine.
6. **On 1996 models,** temporarily set valve clearances to cold engine clearance specifications.
7. **On 1997–99 models,** fit lash adjuster onto rocker arm without allowing diesel fuel to spill out, keeping special MD998443 attached.
8. **On all models,** install gasket in rocker cover groove, then temporarily install rocker cover.
9. Start and operate engine at idle speed until normal operating temperature is reached and adjust valve clearances as required.

PISTON & ROD ASSEMBLY

Piston and rod are assembled with indented arrow on piston and embossed numeral on rod facing toward front of engine, **Fig. 15.**

PISTONS, PINS & RINGS

Pistons and rings are available in standard size and oversizes of .010, .020, .030 and .039 inch. Oversize pins are not available.

MAIN & ROD BEARINGS

Main and rod bearings are available in undersizes of .010, .020 and .030 inch.
Main bearing caps are installed with arrows facing front of engine.

CRANKSHAFT REAR OIL SEAL
REPLACE

1. Remove transmission, clutch assembly and flywheel or flex plate, as equipped.
2. Remove rear oil seal case and separate: oil seal, case and separator, if equipped, **Fig. 16.**
3. Drive in oil seal from inside of case, **Fig. 17,** noting the following:
   a. Ensure oil seal plate fits properly in inner contact surface of seal case, if equipped.
   b. **On 1996 models,** use seal installer MD998011, or equivalent.
   c. **On 1997–99 models,** use seal install MD998718, or equivalent.
4. Install separator with oil hole facing bottom of case, if equipped.
5. Apply engine oil to oil seal lips.
6. Install oil seal case in cylinder block.

OIL PAN
REPLACE

On some models, it may be necessary to remove engine from vehicle to gain access to oil pan.
1. Raise and support vehicle, remove engine splash pan, if equipped, then drain crankcase into appropriate container.
2. Remove oil pressure sender unit, if necessary.
3. Remove oil pan bolts, then the oil pan using gasket cutter MD998727, or equivalent, to break seal of oil pan gasket.
4. Remove oil pump pickup, if necessary.
5. Reverse procedure to install, noting following:
   a. Tighten oil pump pickup bolts to specifications.
   b. Tighten oil pan bolts to specifications.

OIL PUMP
REPLACE

To remove oil pump pickup, refer to "Oil Pan, Replace."
1. Remove timing belt as outlined under "Timing Belt, Replace."
2. Remove oil pan and oil screen, then the front case.
3. Remove oil pump cover, then the inner and outer gears from front case. Mark outer gear surface facing timing case so it can be installed in same direction.
4. Remove relief valve plug, spring and valve.
5. Reverse procedure to install, noting following:
   a. Lubricate oil pump internal components with engine oil before installing.
   b. Tighten oil pump cover attaching bolts to specification.
   c. After installing oil pump cover,

check to ensure oil pump gears rotate smoothly. Tighten relief valve plug to specification.

d. When installing front case attaching bolts, refer to **Fig. 18,** and note that bolts installed in location "A" are 1.18 inches in length, bolts installed in location "B" are .79 inches in length and bolts installed in location "C" are 2.36 inches in length **on 1996 models only.**

e. **On all models,** when installing oil seal, lubricate seal lips with engine oil, then position seal on crankshaft and tap into front case using seal installer MD998304, or equivalent.

f. Before installing oil pan, apply sealer at four front case and rear oil seal case to cylinder block mating surfaces.

g. Tighten front timing case attaching bolts and oil pan attaching bolts to specification.

BELT TENSION DATA

Belt	Tension lbs.	
	New	Used ①
A/C	143–187	99–121
Alternator	88–132	99–121
Power Steering	143–187	99–121

① — Used five minutes or more.

COOLING SYSTEM BLEED

These engines do not require a specified bleed procedure. After filling cooling system, run engine to operating temperature with radiator/pressure cap off. Air will then be automatically bled through cap opening.

THERMOSTAT
REPLACE

1. Drain engine coolant into suitable container.
2. Remove upper radiator hose from thermostat housing.
3. Remove thermostat housing attaching bolts, then the housing.
4. Remove thermostat, then the thermostat gasket.
5. Reverse procedure to install. Tighten bolts to specifications.

WATER PUMP
REPLACE

1. Drain cooling system.
2. **On models equipped with power steering,** remove power steering pump and bracket leaving hoses connected, and secure pump aside.
3. **On all models,** remove timing belt as outlined under "Timing Belt, Replace."
4. Remove alternator brace and disconnect hoses from water pump.
5. Remove water pump bolts, noting length and position for installation reference, then the water pump, gasket and O-ring.

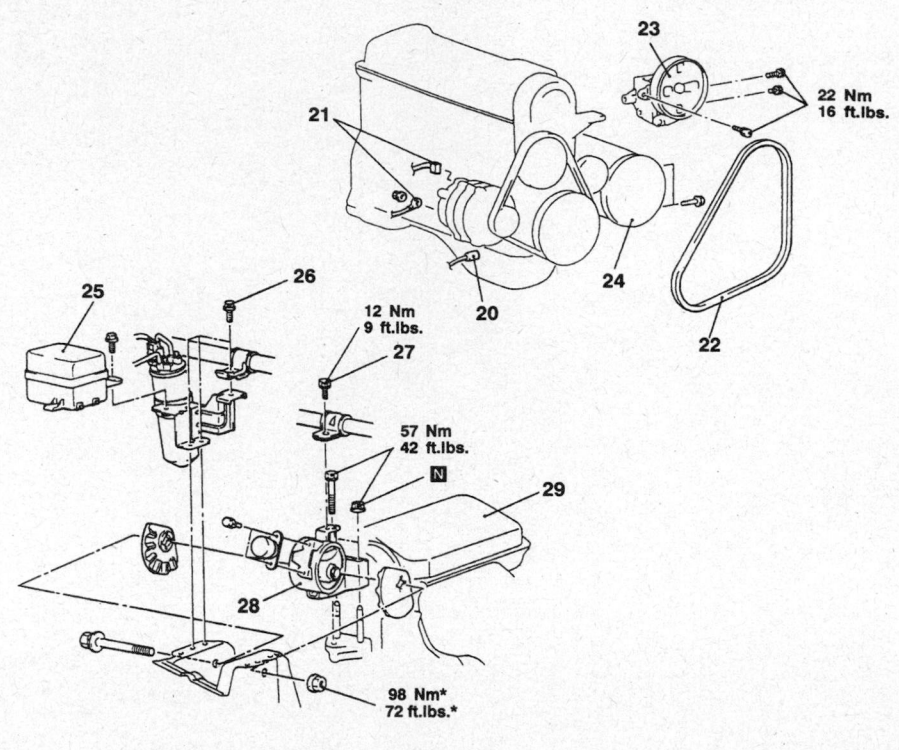

20. Oil pressure switch connector
21. Generator connector
22. Drive belt (Power steering and A/C)
23. Power steering oil pump and bracket assembly
24. Air conditioning compressor
● Transaxle assembly
25. Air conditioning relay box
26. Air conditioning receiver bracket mounting bolts
27. Power steering hose mounting bolt
28. Engine mount bracket
29. Engine assembly

Caution
Mounting locations marked by * should be provisionally tightened, and then fully tightened when the body is supporting the full weight of the engine.

MT1069900556020X

Fig. 2   Engine replacement. (Part 2 of 2) 1997–99

6. Reverse procedure to install, noting following:
a. **On 1996 models, torque** 28 mm pump bolts to 10 ft. lbs. and 65 mm pump bolt to 17 ft. lbs.
b. **On 1997–99 models, torque** 14 mm, 25 mm and 30 mm bolts to 11 ft. lbs.
c. **On all models,** refer to **Figs. 19 and 20** for bolt length and position.
d. **Torque** 50 mm bolt to 17 ft. lbs.

RADIATOR
REPLACE

1. Drain engine coolant, then remove overflow and reserve tank.
2. Remove upper and lower radiator hoses.
3. **On models equipped with automatic transaxle,** remove ATC cooler hose, then plug hose and nipple.
4. **On all models,** remove radiator fan motor connector, then the upper insulator.

5. Remove radiator and fan motor assembly, then the engine coolant temperature switch connector.
6. Remove radiator fan motor assembly and engine coolant temperature switch, then the lower insulator.
7. Reverse procedure to install.

FUEL PUMP
REPLACE

The following procedure has been revised by a Technical Service Bulletin.
1. Relieve fuel system pressure as outlined under "Precautions."
2. Remove fuel tank cap, raise and support rear of vehicle and drain fuel into suitable container.
3. Disconnect filler hose from tank, support tank with suitable jack and remove nuts securing tank straps.
4. Lower fuel tank, then mark and disconnect fuel hoses, vapor hoses and electrical connectors.

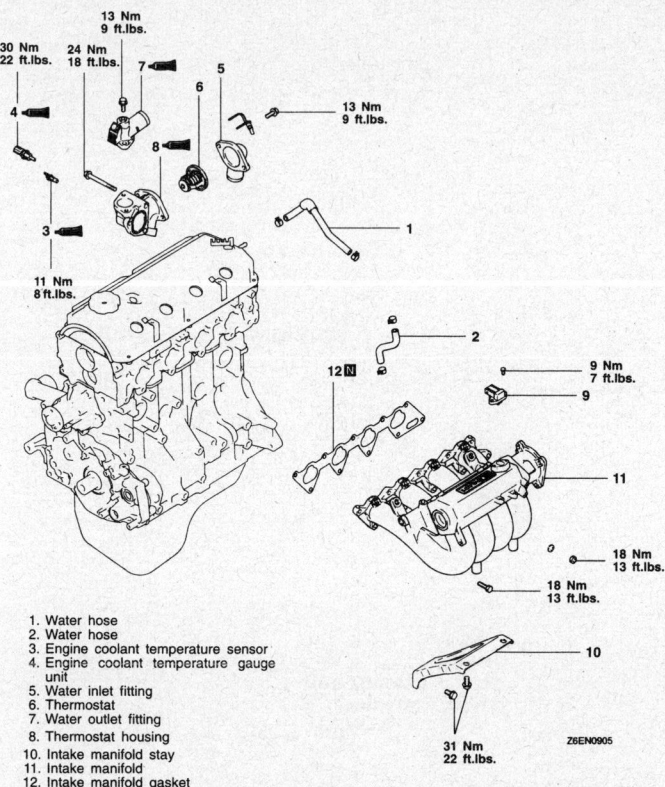

1. Water hose
2. Water hose
3. Engine coolant temperature sensor
4. Engine coolant temperature gauge unit
5. Water inlet fitting
6. Thermostat
7. Water outlet fitting
8. Thermostat housing
10. Intake manifold stay
11. Intake manifold
12. Intake manifold gasket

MT1059300026000X

Fig. 3   Intake manifold replacement. 1996

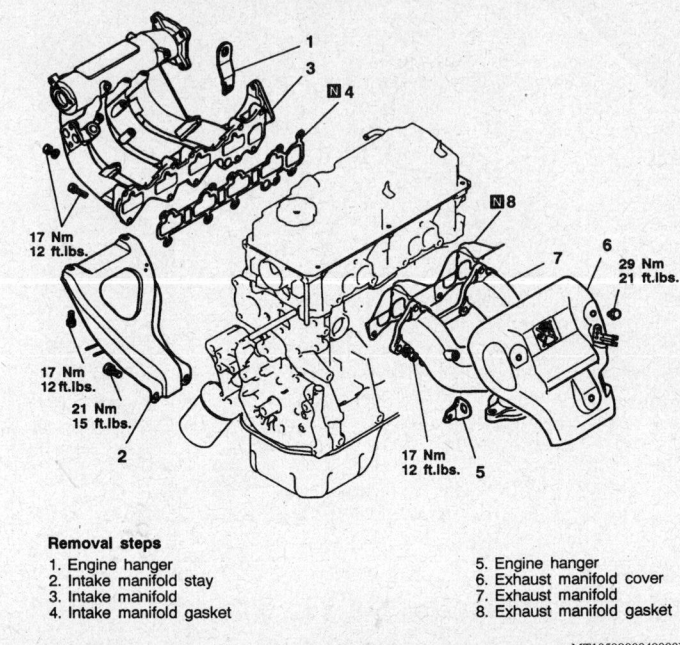

Removal steps

1. Engine hanger
2. Intake manifold stay
3. Intake manifold
4. Intake manifold gasket
5. Engine hanger
6. Exhaust manifold cover
7. Exhaust manifold
8. Exhaust manifold gasket

MT1059900049000X

Fig. 4   Intake & exhaust manifold replacement. 1997-99

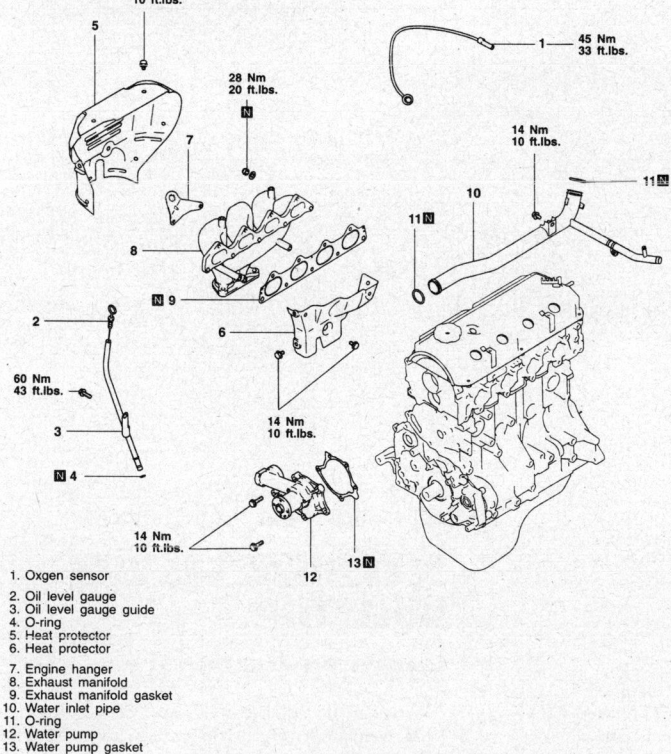

1. Oxgen sensor
2. Oil level gauge
3. Oil level gauge guide
4. O-ring
5. Heat protector
6. Heat protector
7. Engine hanger
8. Exhaust manifold
9. Exhaust manifold gasket
10. Water inlet pipe
11. O-ring
12. Water pump
13. Water pump gasket

MT1079100016000X

Fig. 5   Exhaust manifold replacement. 1996

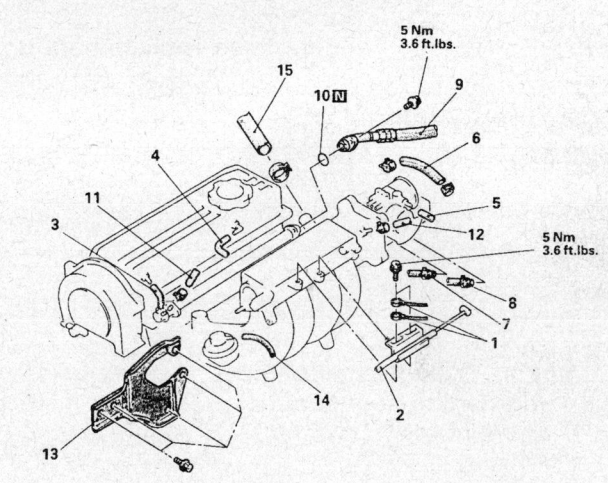

Removal steps

1. Ground cable connection
2. Accelerator cable connection
3. PCV hose connection
4. Breather hose connection
5. Vacuum hose connection
6. Water hose connection
   (Throttle body → thermostat housing)
7. Water hose connection
   (Throttle body → water inlet pipe)
8. Water hose connection
   (Heater unit → thermostat housing)
9. Fuel high-pressure hose connection
10. O-ring
11. Return hose connection
12. Brake booster vacuum hose connection
13. Engine mounting stay
14. Vacuum hose
15. Radiator upper hose

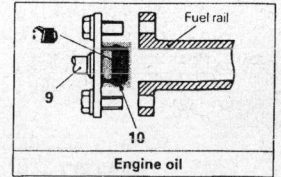

MT1069300256010X

Fig. 6   Cylinder head replacement (Part 1 of 2)

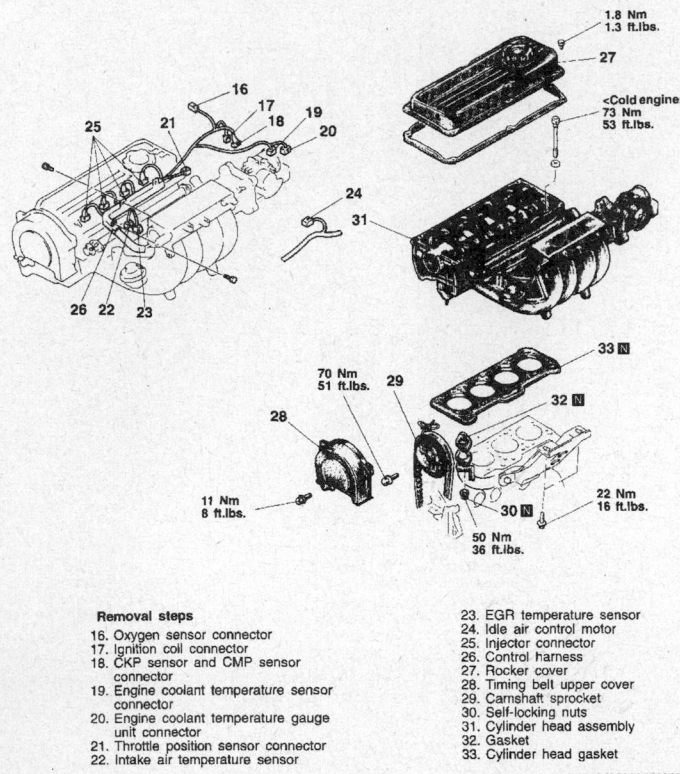

1.8 Nm
1.3 ft.lbs.
— 27

<Cold engine>
73 Nm
53 ft.lbs.

24
31

70 Nm
51 ft.lbs. 29
28

33 Ⓝ
32 Ⓝ

11 Nm
8 ft.lbs.
30 Ⓝ

22 Nm
16 ft.lbs.

50 Nm
36 ft.lbs.

Removal steps
16. Oxygen sensor connector
17. Ignition coil connector
18. CKP sensor and CMP sensor connector
19. Engine coolant temperature sensor connector
20. Engine coolant temperature gauge unit connector
21. Throttle position sensor connector
22. Intake air temperature sensor

23. EGR temperature sensor
24. Idle air control motor
25. Injector connector
26. Control harness
27. Rocker cover
28. Timing belt upper cover
29. Camshaft sprocket
30. Self-locking nuts
31. Cylinder head assembly
32. Gasket
33. Cylinder head gasket

MT1069300256020X

Fig. 6 Cylinder head replacement (Part 2 of 2)

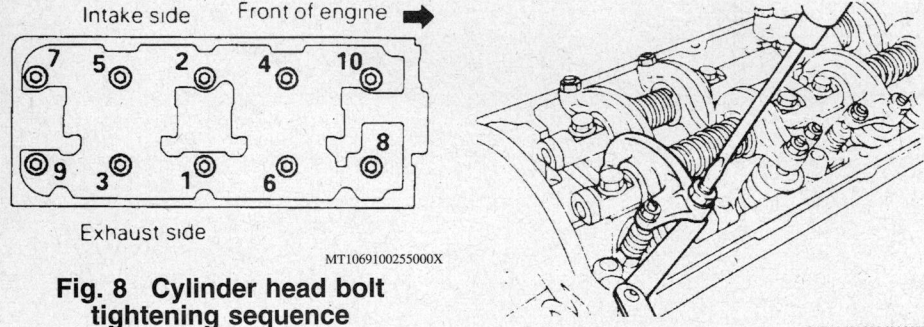

MT1069100255000X

Fig. 8 Cylinder head bolt tightening sequence

MT1069100260000X

Fig. 9 Valve clearance adjustment

Size mm (in.)	Size mark	Cylinder head hole size mm (in.)
0.05 (.002) O.S.	5	12.050 – 12.068 (.4744 – .4751)
0.25 (.010) O.S.	25	12.250 – 12.268 (.4823 – .4830)
0.50 (.020) O.S.	50	12.500 – 12.518 (.4921 – .4928)

MT1069100266000X

Fig. 10 Valve guide & guide bore oversizes

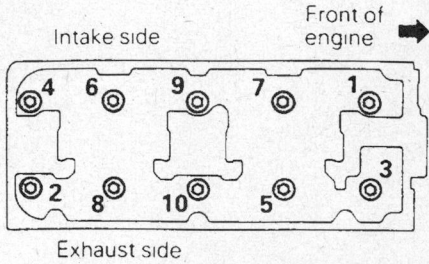

MT1069100254000X

Fig. 7 Cylinder head bolt loosening sequence

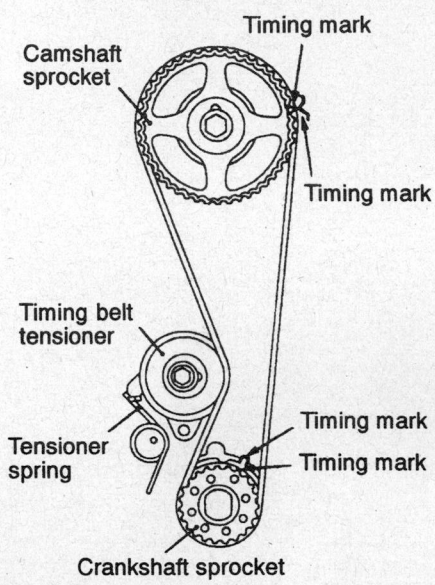

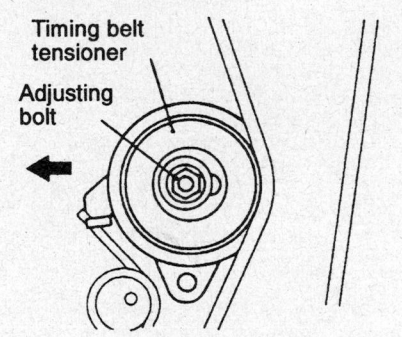

MT1069900559000X

Fig. 11 Camshaft & crankshaft sprocket timing marks

5. Remove nuts securing fuel pump assembly, then the fuel pump and gasket.
6. Reverse procedure to install.

FUEL FILTER
REPLACE
1. Release fuel system pressure as outlined under "Precautions."

2. Remove air cleaner and air intake hose.
3. Hold fuel filter with spanner and remove eye bolt, **Fig. 21.** Cover fuel pipe line with rag to prevent remaining fuel from spraying out.
4. Hold fuel filter with spanner and loosen flare nut, then disconnect fuel main pipe connection.

TECHNICAL SERVICE BULLETINS

FUEL STARVATION

Fuel starvation can occur when the in-tank fuel filter is clogged, typically by contaminated fuel.

Use the following procedure to correct this problem.
1. Activate fuel pump with scan tool, then

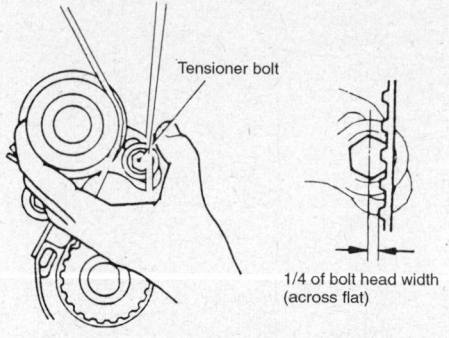

Fig. 12 Timing belt tension inspection

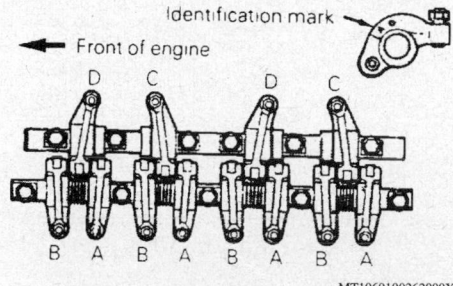

Fig. 14 Rocker arm & shaft installation

measure pump supply voltage.

2. If voltage is less than eight volts, inspect and repair fuel pump wiring harness.
3. If voltage is eight or more volts, check system fuel pressure.
4. Fuel system pressure should be 38 psi at curb idle with fuel pressure regulator vacuum hose attached and 47–50 psi with hose disconnected.
5. If system pressure is within specifications, check system for other starvation problems.
6. If fuel system pressure is not within specifications, remove fuel pump as outlined in "Fuel Pump, Replace" and check filter.
7. If filter is clean, replace fuel pump. If filter is clogged, replace filter as outlined in "Fuel Filter, Replace."
8. **If filter is severely clogged, clean inside of fuel tank.**

IDLE VIBRATION

Some of these models may vibrate excessively at idle.

This condition could be caused by an incorrectly mounted radiator. If the radiator mounting brackets are not centered on their posts, the radiator will transmit engine vibration through the frame. Use the following procedure to correct problem.

1. Examine upper radiator mounting brackets. Brackets should be centered on post

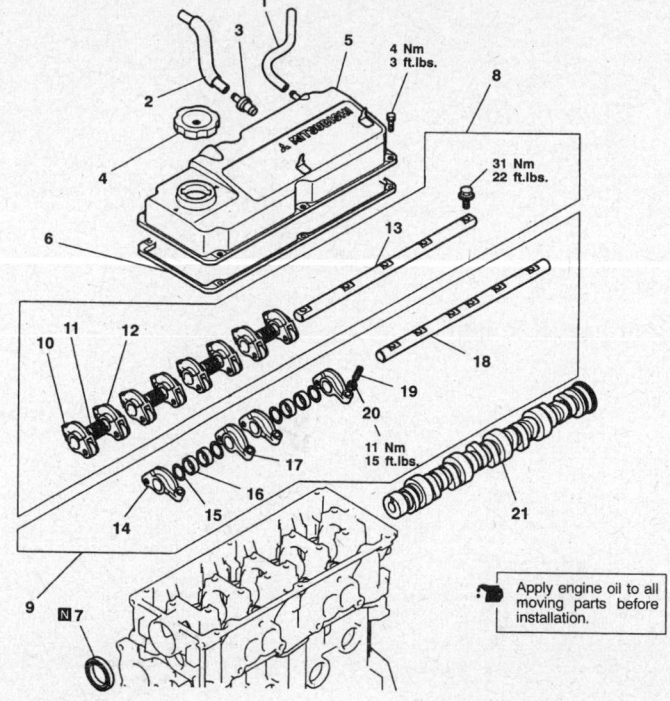

Removal steps
1. Breather hose
2. PCV hose
3. PCV valve
4. Oil filler cap
5. Rocker cover
6. Rocker cover gasket
7. Camshaft oil seal
8. Rocker arm and shaft assembly (intake)
9. Rocker arm and shaft assembly (exhaust)

10. Rocker arm A
11. Rocker arm spring
12. Rocker arm B
13. Rocker arm shaft
14. Rocker arm C
15. Wave washer
16. Spacer
17. Rocker arm D
18. Rocker arm shaft
19. Adjusting screw
20. Nut
21. Camshaft

Fig. 13 Camshaft removal

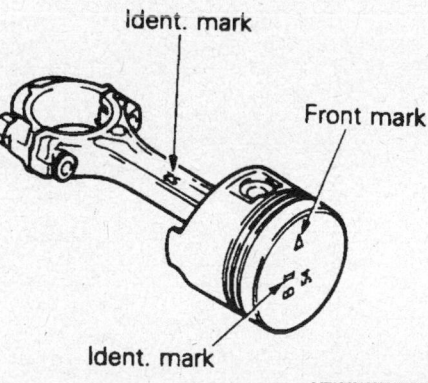

Fig. 15 Piston & rod assembly

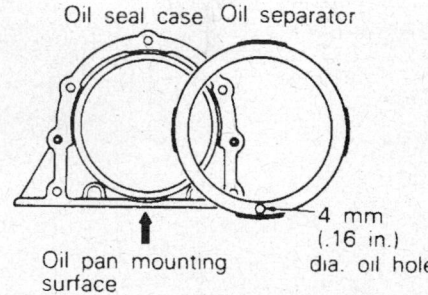

Fig. 16 Disassembled view of oil seal case & separator

2. If brackets are not centered, remove upper brackets. Ensure bottom mounting posts are in lower brackets.
3. Center upper brackets over posts and

tighten bolts to specifications.
4. Measure clearance between upper brackets and radiator top. Standard clearance is .0394 inch or more.

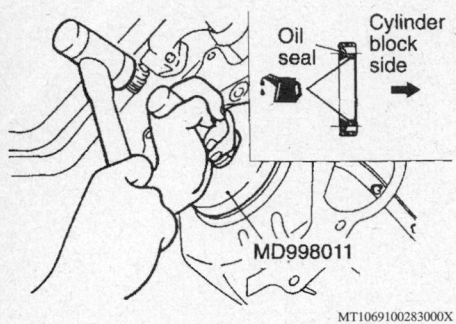

Fig. 17 Rear seal installation

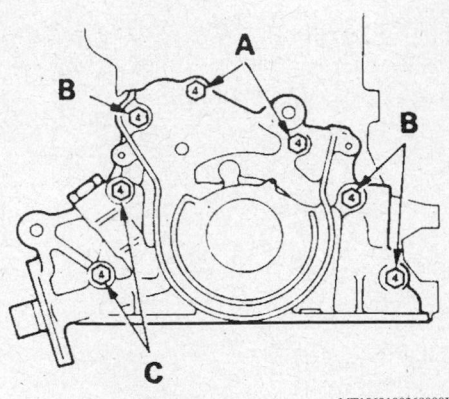

Fig. 18 Front case cover bolt locations

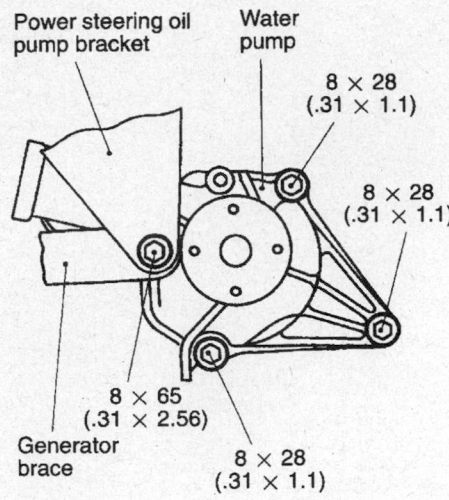

Screw diameter × length: mm (in.)

Fig. 19 Water pump bolt lengths & locations. 1996

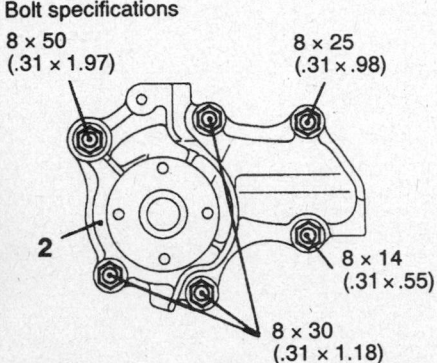

Fig. 20 Water pump bolt lengths & locations. 1997-99

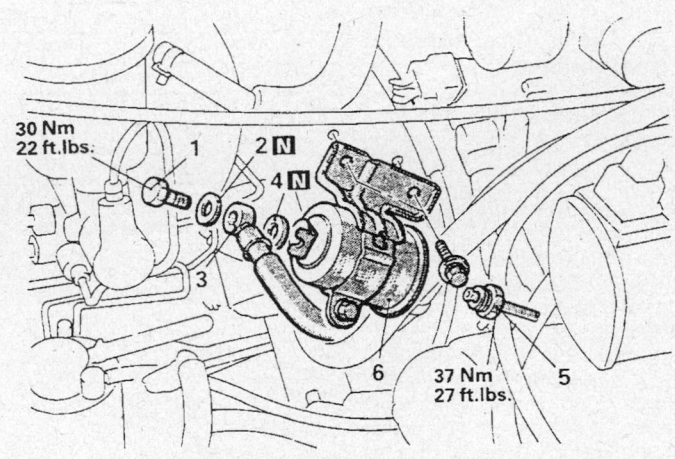

Removal steps
1. Eye bolt
2. Gasket
3. High-pressure fuel hose connection
4. Gasket
5. Fuel main pipe connection
6. Fuel filter

Fig. 21 Fuel filter replacement

TIGHTENING SPECIFICATIONS

Year	Component	Torque/ Ft. Lbs.
1996–99	A/C Compressor To Bracket	17–20
	Accelerator Cable Adjusting Bolt	36–48④
	Ball Joint Attaching Nut	43–52
	Camshaft Bolts	22
	Camshaft Sprocket Bolt	47–54
	Connecting Rod Cap	①
	Control Wiring Harness Protector To Air Intake Plenum	36–48④
	Crankshaft Bearing Caps	36–39
	Crankshaft Pulley To Crankshaft Sprocket	9–11
	Crankshaft Sprocket Bolt	51–72
	Cylinder Head Bolts	②
	Distributor Mounting Nut	84–108④
	Driveplate	94–101
	Engine Ground Cable Bolt	20–24
	Engine Mount Bracket Nut And Bolt	36–47
	Engine Mount Insulator Nut (Large)	65–80
	Engine Mount Insulator Nut (Small)	33–43
	Engine To Transaxle (8 mm)	84–96④
	Engine To Transaxle (10 mm)	22–25
	Engine To Transaxle (12 mm)	31–40
	Exhaust Manifold Bolts/Nuts	21
	Flywheel	94–101
	Front Case Bolt	7–11
	Front Engine Support Bracket Bolt	36–51
	Front Exhaust Pipe Clamp Bolt	25
	Front Exhaust Pipe Support Bracket Bolt	22–30
	Front Exhaust Pipe To Exhaust Manifold	36
	Front Roll Stopper Bracket Bolt	40–54
	Front Roll Stopper Insulator Nut	33–43
	Fuel High Pressure Hose To Delivery Pipe	36–48④
	Intake Manifold Bolts/Nuts	11–14
	Intake Manifold Stay	13–18
	Left Engine Support Bracket Bolt	22–30
	Main Bearing Cap	36–40
	Oil Filter	96–108④
	Oil Pan Bolts	48–72④
	Oil Pan Drain Plug	25–33
	Oil Pressure Switch	11–16
	Oil Pump Cover Bolt	72–84④
	Oil Screen	13
	Power Steering Oil Pump Brace Bolt	29
	Power Steering Oil Pump To Bracket	33–40
	Rear Plate Bolt	72–84④
	Rear Roll Stopper Bracket Bolt	80–94
	Rear Roll Stopper Insulator Nut	33–43
	Relief Valve Plug	29–36
	Rocker Arm Shaft Bolt	14–20
	Rocker Cover Bolt	14–20④
	Roll Rod Bracket To Body Bolt	51–65
	Roll Rod To Engine Bolt	40–47
	Surge Tank To Intake Manifold Bolts And Nuts	11–14
	Thermostat Housing Attaching Bolts	108④
	Tie Rod Attaching Nut	11–25
	Timing Belt Lower Cover	84–108④
	Timing Belt Tensioner	14–20

Continued

TIGHTENING SPECIFICATIONS—Continued

Year	Component	Torque/ Ft. Lbs.
1996–99	Timing Belt Upper Cover	84–108④
	Transaxle Mounting Bolts	43–58
	Transaxle To Engine Mounting Bolts	②
	Valve Adjusting Screw Nut	9–13
	Water Pump Bolts	③
	Water Pump Pulley Bolt	72–84④

① — Tighten in four steps: torque to 14.5 ft. lbs.; then back off; torque again to 14.5 ft. lbs.; then tighten an additional ¼ turn.
② — Refer to "Cylinder Head, Replace" for tightening sequence.
③ — Refer to "Water Pump, Replace" for procedure.
④ — Inch lbs.

1.8L Engine

NOTE: On Air Bag Equipped Models, Refer To "Air Bag System Precautions" Located In The Front Of This Manual For System Disarming & Arming Procedures.

INDEX

PRECAUTIONS

AIR BAG SYSTEMS

Refer to "Air Bag System Precautions" in front of this manual for system disarming and arming procedures.

FUEL SYSTEM PRESSURE RELIEF

1. Disconnect fuel pump harness connector at fuel tank rear side. **Cover fuel pipe line with rag after relieving pressure as residual pressure may still remain.**
2. Start engine and let idle until engine stops, then turn ignition switch to Off. **Failure to relieve fuel system pressure prior to disconnecting fuel system components may cause fire or personal injury.**
3. Disconnect battery ground cable.
4. Connect fuel pump harness connector.
5. After repairs have been completed, connect positive battery terminal to fuel pump drive terminal and negative terminal to chassis. Ensure fuel pump operates at this time.

BATTERY GROUND CABLE

Prior to service, disconnect battery ground cable and isolate as required.

COMPRESSION PRESSURE

Standard compression pressure is 199 psi. Minimum compression pressure is 151 psi. Difference between cylinders should not exceed 14 psi.

ENGINE MOUNT

REPLACE

1. Raise and support engine to reduce weight upon mounts.
2. Remove power steering pressure hose from mounting bracket.
3. Remove engine mount bracket and connecting bolt.
4. Reverse procedure to install.

ENGINE

REPLACE

1. Release fuel system pressure as outlined under "Precautions."

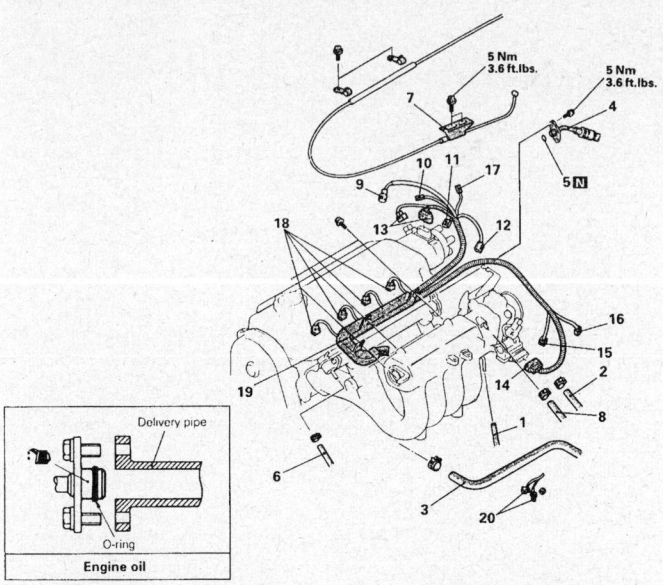

Removal steps
1. Vacuum hose connection
2. Heater hose connection (Thermostat housing → heater unit)
3. Heater hose connection (Heater unit → Water inlet pipe)
4. Fuel high pressure hose connection
5. O-ring
6. Fuel return hose connection
7. Accelerator cable connection
8. Brake booster vacuum hose connection
9. Oxygen sensor connector
10. Oil pressure switch connector
11. Engine temperature gauge unit connector
12. Engine coolant temperature sensor connector
13. Distributor connector
14. Idle air control motor connector
15. Heated oxygen sensor connector (front) <Vehicles for California>
16. EGR temperature sensor connector <Vehicles for California>
17. Throttle position sensor connector
18. Injector connector
19. Control harness assembly
20. Generator harness connection

MT1069100284010X

Fig. 1 Engine replacement (Part 1 of 2) 1996

2. Remove engine hood.
3. Drain engine coolant into appropriate container.
4. Remove transaxle assembly.
5. Remove radiator assembly.
6. Remove power steering oil pump from bracket with hose attached, tie with a cord and place aside.
7. Remove engine assembly in numbered sequence as outlined in **Figs. 1 and 2**, noting the following:
   a. **On models equipped with A/C,** disconnect A/C compressor connector and remove compressor from compressor bracket with hose attached.
   b. **On all models,** connect engine assembly to engine hoist.
   c. Place piece of wood between oil pan and jack, then after raising engine until no weight is on engine mount brackets, remove engine mount brackets.
   d. After checking that all cables, hoses and harness connections are disconnected from engine, slowly remove engine assembly upward from engine compartment.
8. Reverse procedure to install, noting following:
   a. Ensure cables, harnesses and hose connections are clear of engine assembly.
   b. Install engine mount brackets using engine support MZ203827, or equivalent, to support engine assembly while installing transaxle.

Removal steps
21. Power steering oil pressure switch connector
22. Air conditioning compressor connector
23. V-ribbed belt
24. Power steering oil pump connection
25. Air conditioning compressor connection
26. Front exhaust pipe connection
27. Gasket
28. Starter and generator harness clamp
29. Engine mount bracket
30. Engine assembly

MT1069100284020X

Fig. 1 Engine replacement (Part 2 of 2) 1996

INTAKE MANIFOLD
REPLACE
1996

1. Release fuel system pressure as outlined under " Precautions."
2. Drain cooling system into an approved container.
3. Remove intake manifold in numbered sequence shown in **Fig. 3**, removing fuel delivery pipe leaving injectors and pressure regulator intact. **Do not drop injector when removing delivery pipe.**
4. Reverse procedure to install.

1997-99

1. Release fuel system pressure as outlined under " Precautions."
2. Drain cooling system into an approved container.
3. Remove intake manifold in numbered sequence outlined in **Fig. 4.**
4. Reverse procedure to install.

EXHAUST MANIFOLD
REPLACE
1996

1. Replace exhaust manifold in numbered sequence shown in **Figs. 5 and 6.**
2. Reverse procedure to install.

1997-99

1. Replace exhaust manifold in numbered sequence outlined in **Fig. 4.**
2. Reverse procedure to install.

CYLINDER HEAD
REPLACE
REMOVAL

1. Release fuel system pressure as outlined under " Precautions."
2. Drain cooling system into an approved container.
3. Remove cylinder head and gasket in

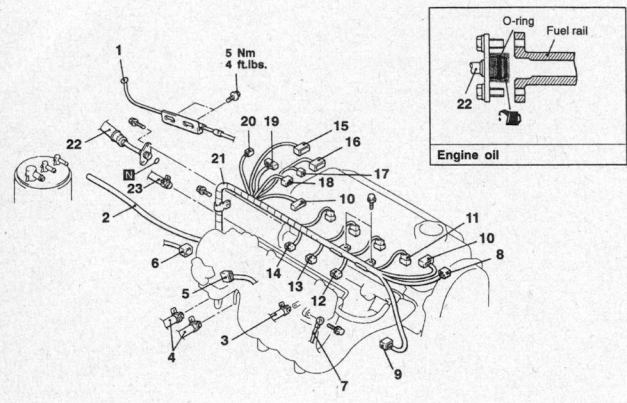

Removal steps
1. Accelerator cable connection
2. Vacuum hose connection
3. Brake booster vacuum hose connection
4. Heater hose connection
5. Throttle position sensor connector
6. Idle speed control connector
7. Ground cable connection
8. Crank angle sensor connector
9. Heated oxygen sensor connector
10. Ignition coil connector
11. Injector connector
12. Evaporative emission purge solenoid
13. EGR solenoid connector
14. Manifold differential pressure sensor connector
15. Heated oxygen sensor connector <Vehicle for California>
16. Ignition failure sensor connector
17. Engine coolant temperature gauge unit connector
18. Engine coolant temperature sensor connector
19. Camshaft position sensor connector
20. Noise condensor connector
21. Control wiring harness
22. High-pressure fuel hose connection
23. Fuel return hose connection

MT1069900561010X

Fig. 2 Engine replacement (Part 1 of 2) 1997-99

24. Oil pressure switch connector
25. Generator connector
26. Drive belt (Power steering and A/C)
27. Power steering pump bracket stay
28. Power steering oil pump and bracket assembly
29. Air conditioning compressor
● Transaxle assembly
30. Air conditioning relay box
31. Air conditioning receiver bracket mounting bolts
32. Power steering hose mounting bolt
33. Engine mount bracket
34. Engine mount assembly

Caution
Mounting locations marked by * should be provisionally tightened, and then fully tightened when the body is supporting the full weight of the engine.

MT1069900561020X

Fig. 2 Engine replacement (Part 2 of 2) 1997-99

numbered sequence, **Figs. 7 and 8,** noting the following:

a. Rotate engine so No. 1 cylinder is at top dead center on compression stroke and align camshaft timing mark, **Fig. 9.**
b. Tie camshaft sprocket and timing belt together so that position of camshaft sprocket will not move with respect to timing belt, **Fig. 10.**
c. Remove camshaft sprocket as outlined under "Timing Belt, Replace."
d. Loosen cylinder head bolts in two or three steps in numbered sequence outlined in **Figs. 11 and 12. Use care not to damage plug guide, as plug guides cannot be replaced.**
4. Inspect cylinder head gasket surface for flatness by using a straightedge.

INSTALLATION

Reverse numbered sequence outlined in **Figs. 7 and 8** to install, noting the following:
1. Clean cylinder gasket surface on both cylinder head and engine block.
2. Place cylinder head gasket on cylinder block with identification mark facing upward on intake side, **Fig. 13.**
3. Measure cylinder head bolts and ensure bolts are less than 3.795 inches long.
4. Apply a small amount of oil to cylinder head bolt threads and to bolt washer. **Ensure cylinder head bolt is installed as shown in Fig. 14.**
5. Tighten cylinder head bolts in numbered sequence shown in **Figs.15 and 16** in five steps as follows:
   a. **Torque** bolts to 54 ft. lbs.
   b. Completely loosen bolts.
   c. **Torque** bolts to 15 ft. lbs.
   d. Turn bolts 90° (¼ turn).

e. Turn bolts an additional 90° (¼ turn).
6. Loosen water inlet pipe bolt, apply sealant to thermostat case, **Figs. 17 and 18.**
7. Apply a small amount of water to O-ring of water inlet pipe and press thermostat case assembly onto water inlet pipe.
8. Install thermostat case assembly mounting bolt and tighten water inlet pipe bolt.
9. Install thermostat so jiggle valve is at top.

VALVE ARRANGEMENT

Intake valve are located on RH side of cylinder head and exhaust valves are located on LH side of cylinder head.

VALVE CLEARANCE SPECIFICATIONS

On 1996 models, valve stem guide clearance with engine hot is .008 for intake and .0010 inch for exhaust. On 1997–99 models, valve stem clearance with engine hot is .008 for intake and .0020 for exhaust.

VALVE ADJUSTMENT
1996-97

1. Remove valve cover assembly as outlined under "Cylinder Head, Replace."

2. Position No. 1 cylinder at top dead center on compression stroke.
3. Adjust valve clearance at points shown in **Fig. 19** as follows:
   a. Loosen adjusting screw locknut.
   b. Using feeler gauge, adjust intake valve clearance to 0.008 inch and exhaust valve clearance to 0.012 inch by turning adjusting screw.
   c. While holding adjusting screw, tighten adjusting screw locknut.
4. Rotate engine crankshaft clockwise one complete turn to position No. 4 cylinder at top dead center on compression stroke.
5. Repeat Step 4 for points shown in **Fig. 20.**
6. Install valve cover.

1998-99

Equipped with hydraulic lash adjusters. No adjustment is required.

ROCKER ARMS
REPLACE

Refer to "Camshaft, Replace" for rocker arm replacement procedure.

FRONT COVER
REPLACE

Refer to "Oil Pump, Replace" for front cover replacement procedure.

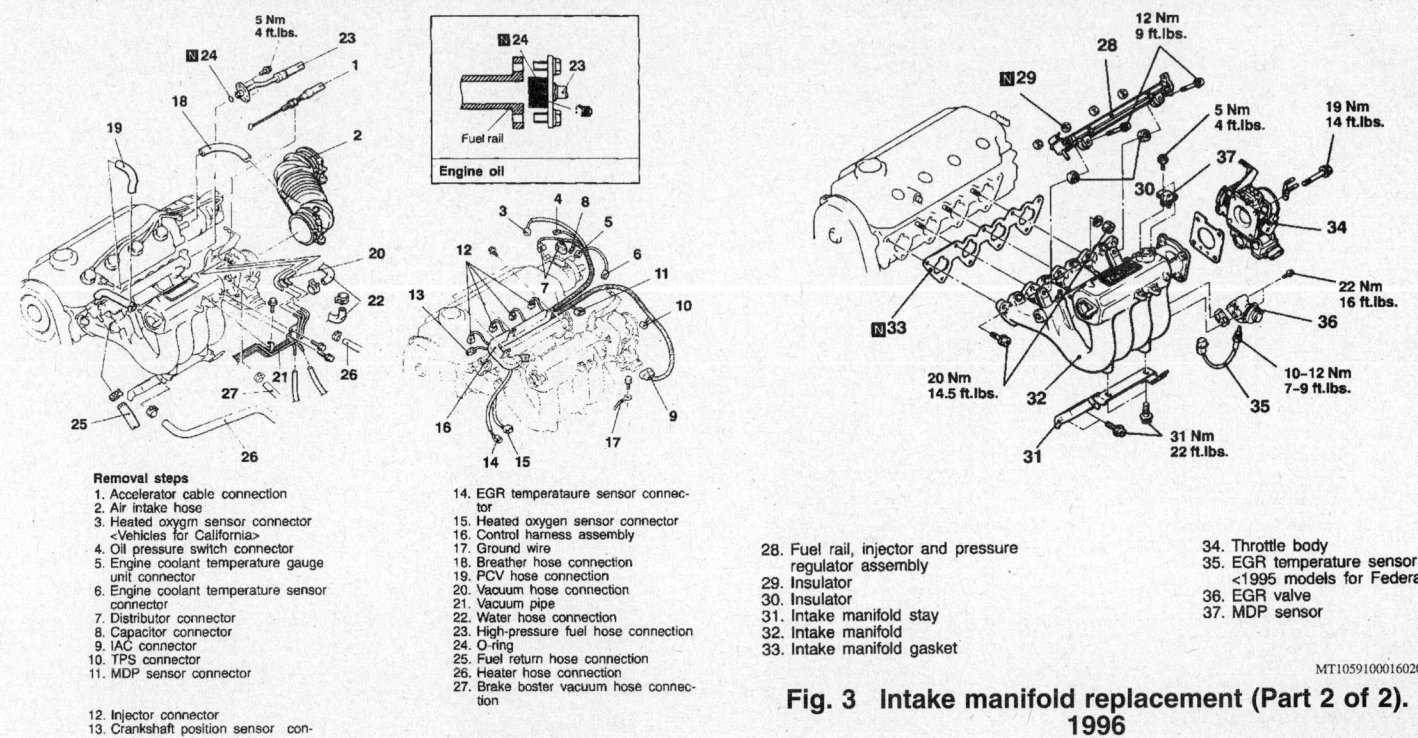

Removal steps
1. Accelerator cable connection
2. Air intake hose
3. Heated oxygen sensor connector <Vehicles for California>
4. Oil pressure switch connector
5. Engine coolant temperature gauge unit connector
6. Engine coolant temperature sensor connector
7. Distributor connector
8. Capacitor connector
9. IAC connector
10. TPS connector
11. MDP sensor connector

12. Injector connector
13. Crankshaft position sensor connector

14. EGR temperataure sensor connector
15. Heated oxygen sensor connector
16. Control harness assembly
17. Ground wire
18. Breather hose connection
19. PCV hose connection
20. Vacuum hose connection
21. Vacuum pipe
22. Water hose connection
23. High-pressure fuel hose connection
24. O-ring
25. Fuel return hose connection
26. Heater hose connection
27. Brake boster vacuum hose connection

28. Fuel rail, injector and pressure regulator assembly
29. Insulator
30. Insulator
31. Intake manifold stay
32. Intake manifold
33. Intake manifold gasket

34. Throttle body
35. EGR temperature sensor <1995 models for Federal>
36. EGR valve
37. MDP sensor

MT1059100016020X

Fig. 3 Intake manifold replacement (Part 2 of 2). 1996

MT1059100016010X

Fig. 3 Intake manifold replacement (Part 1 of 2). 1996

TIMING BELT

REPLACE
REMOVAL

1. Remove engine undercover.
2. Remove timing belt in numbered sequence outlined in **Figs. 21 and 22,** noting the following:
   a. Remove air conditioning and power steering line clamp.
   b. Remove power steering and air conditioning drive belt, then the alternator drive belt.
   c. Stop crankshaft pulley from turning using crankshaft pulley holder, then remove crankshaft bolt, washer and pulley.
   d. Remove upper and lower timing belt covers, then the flange.
   e. If belt is to be reused, mark rotational direction for installation.
   f. Turn crankshaft clockwise to align each timing mark and set No. 1 cylinder at top dead center (TDC) of compression stroke, **Fig. 23.**
   g. Loosen timing belt tensioner bolt, then press tensioner fully back clockwise using a screwdriver.
   h. Temporarily tighten timing belt tensioner bolt and remove timing belt.
   i. Loosen tensioner bolt and move tensioner as close to engine mount as possible with screwdriver, then tighten bolt.

INSTALLATION

Reverse numbered sequence outlined in **Figs. 21 and 22,** noting the following:
1. Ensure camshaft and crankshaft timing marks are aligned, **Fig. 23.**

2. Ensure tension side of belt is taut while installing timing belt over crankshaft, water pump and camshaft sprockets, then the tensioner pulley.
3. Apply counterclockwise pressure (reverse of normal rotational direction) to camshaft sprocket and check that belt is fully tensioned. Ensure timing marks are properly aligned.
4. Loosen timing belt tensioner belt approximately ½ turn and allow tensioner spring to tension belt.
5. Rotate crankshaft clockwise two turns, then check timing marks.
6. Ensure timing belt is properly seated on sprockets, then tighten tensioner bolt to specifications.
7. Tighten timing belt tensioner locking bolt to specified torque.
8. Check and adjust ignition timing as necessary.

CAMSHAFT

REPLACE

1. Release fuel system pressure as outlined under "Precautions."
2. Remove air cleaner assembly.
3. Remove timing belt as outlined under "Timing Belt, Replace."
4. Rotate engine to position No. 1 cylinder at top dead center on compression stroke.
5. **On 1998–99 models,** set lash adjuster tool No. MD998443, or equivalent, to prevent lash adjuster from coming free.
6. **On all models,** remove camshaft, camshaft oil seal rocker arms and

shafts in numbered sequence shown in **Figs. 24 and 25,** noting the following:
   a. Prevent camshaft from turning using end yoke holder, tool Nos. MB990767 and MD998719, or equivalent, and loosen camshaft sprocket bolt, then remove camshaft sprocket.
   b. Do not disassemble rocker arm shafts unless component replacement is necessary.
7. Reverse procedure to install, noting the following:
   a. **On 1996–97 models,** if rocker arm shaft was disassembled, temporarily tighten rocker arm shaft bolt so all rocker arms on inlet side do not push valves. Install rocker arm shaft spring from above and position at right angle to plug guide, **Fig. 26.**
   b. **On 1998–99 models,** fit lash adjuster onto rocker arm without allowing diesel fuel to spill out. Fit special tool No. MD998443, or equivalent, to prevent lash adjuster from coming free.
   c. **On all models,** install rocker arm shafts, place end with notched side toward timing belt side.
   d. Move rocker arms until they touch rocker arm shaft mounting bosses on cylinder head.
   e. Tighten rocker arm shaft bolts to specification.
   f. Using seal installation MD998713-01, or equivalent, install camshaft seal.

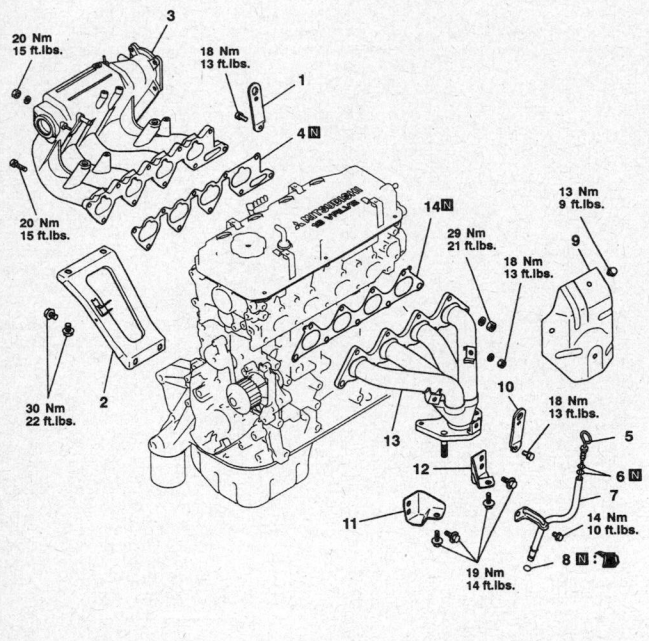

Removal steps

1. Engine hanger
2. Intake manifold stay
3. Intake manifold
4. Intake manifold gasket
5. Oil dipstick
6. O-ring
7. Oil dipstick guide
8. O-ring
9. Exhaust manifold cover
10. Engine hanger
11. Exhaust manifold bracket A
12. Exhaust manifold bracket B
13. Exhaust manifold
14. Exhaust manifold gasket

MT1059900050000X

Fig. 4 Intake & exhaust manifold replacement. 1997–99

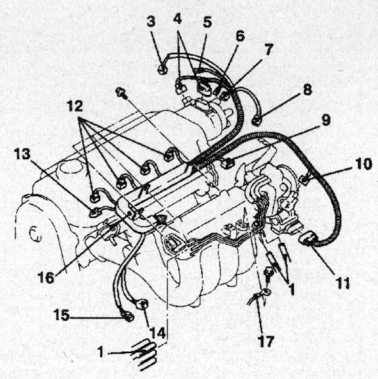

Removal steps

1. Exhaust manifold cover A
2. Self-locking nut
3. Gasket
4. Oxygen sensor

5. Exhaust manifold bracket

6. Exhaust manifold bracket B

7. Exhaust manifold bracket A

8. Exhaust manifold
9. Exhaust manifold gasket
10. Exhaust manifold cover B

MT1079100008000X

Fig. 5 Exhaust manifold replacement. w/Federal emissions

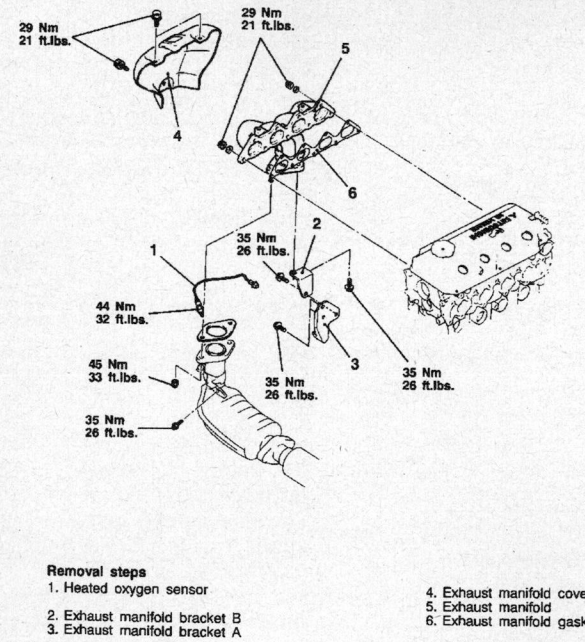

Removal steps

1. Heated oxygen sensor

2. Exhaust manifold bracket B
3. Exhaust manifold bracket A

4. Exhaust manifold cover A
5. Exhaust manifold
6. Exhaust manifold gasket

MT1079800024000X

Fig. 6 Exhaust manifold replacement. 1996 w/California emissions

Removal steps

1. Vacuum hose connection
2. Air conditioning engine coolant temperature switch connector
3. Oxygen sensor or heated oxygen sensor connector

4. Distributor connector
5. Oil pressure switch connector
6. Capacitor connector
7. Engine coolant temperature gauge unit connector
8. Engine coolant temperature sensor connector
9. MDP sensor connector

10. TPS connector
11. Idle air control motor connector
12. Injector connector
13. Crankshaft position sensor connector
14. Heated oxygen sensor connector
15. EGR temperature sensor connector
16. Control harness assembly
17. Ground wire

MT1069800544010X

Fig. 7 Cylinder head replacement (Part 1 of 3) 1996

PISTON & ROD ASSEMBLY

1. Release fuel system pressure as outlined under " Precautions."
2. Remove engine as outlined under "Engine, Replace."
3. Remove timing belt as outlined under

" Timing Belt, Replace."
4. Remove water pump as outlined under
"Water Pump, Replace."
5. Remove cylinder head as outlined
under "Cylinder Head, Replace."

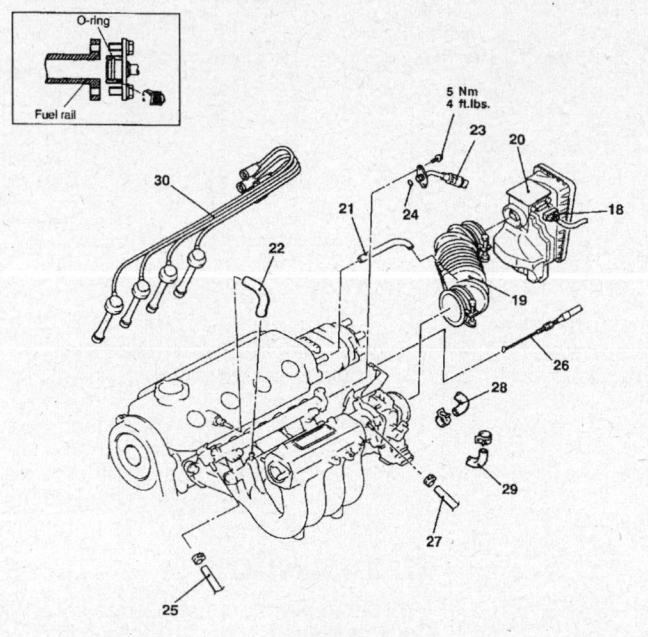

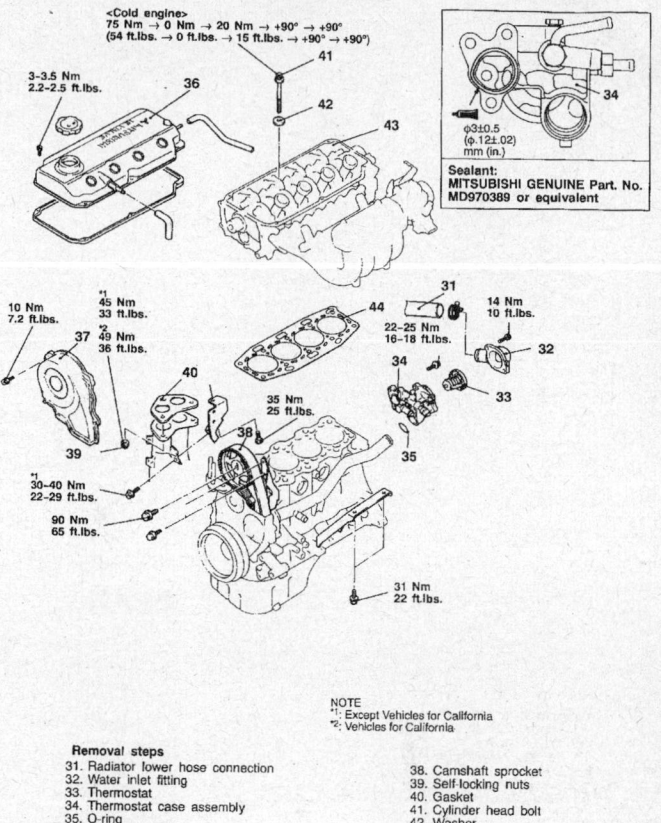

Removal steps

18. Volume air flow sensor connector	26. Accelerator cable connection
19. Air intake hose	27. Brake booster vacuum hose connection
20. Air cleaner case cover	28. Water hose connection
21. Breather hose connection	(Thermostat case to throttle body)
22. PCV hose	29. Water hose connection
23. High-pressure fuel hose connection	(Throttle body to water inlet fitting)
24. O-ring	30. Spark plug cable
25. Fuel return hose connection	

MT1069800544020X

Fig. 7 Cylinder head replacement (Part 2 of 3) 1996

NOTE
*1: Except Vehicles for California
*2: Vehicles for California

Removal steps

31. Radiator lower hose connection	38. Camshaft sprocket
32. Water inlet fitting	39. Self-locking nuts
33. Thermostat	40. Gasket
34. Thermostat case assembly	41. Cylinder head bolt
35. O-ring	42. Washer
36. Rocker cover	43. Cylinder head assembly
37. Timing belt upper cover	44. Cylinder head gasket

MT1069800544030X

Fig. 7 Cylinder head replacement (Part 3 of 3) 1996

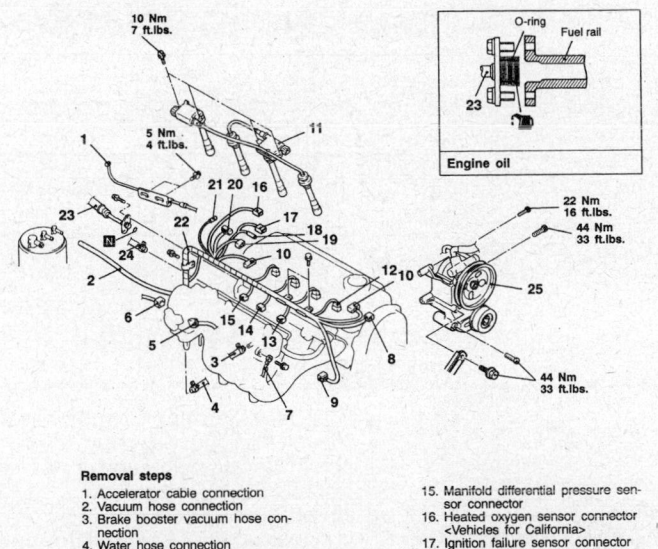

Removal steps

1. Accelerator cable connection	15. Manifold differential pressure sensor connector
2. Vacuum hose connection	16. Heated oxygen sensor connector
3. Brake booster vacuum hose connection	<Vehicles for California>
4. Water hose connection	17. Ignition failure sensor connector
5. Throttle position sensor connector	18. Engine coolant temperature gauge unit connector
6. Idle speed control connector	19. Engine coolant temperature sensor connector
7. Ground cable connection	20. Camshaft position sensor connector
8. Crankshaft position sensor connector	21. Noise condenser connector
9. Heated oxygen sensor connector	22. Control wiring harness
10. Ignition coil connector	23. High-pressure fuel hose connection
11. Ignition coil assembly	24. Fuel return hose connection
12. Injector connector	25. Power steering oil pump and bracket assembly
13. Evaporative emission purge solenoid connector	
14. EGR solenoid valve connector	

MT1069900562010X

**Fig. 8 Cylinder head replacement (Part 1 of 2)
1997-99**

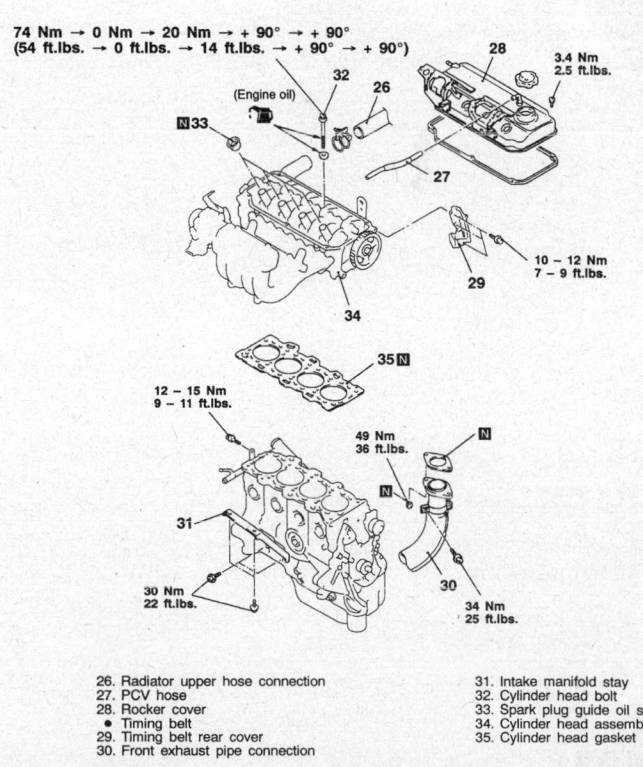

Removal steps

26. Radiator upper hose connection	31. Intake manifold stay
27. PCV hose	32. Cylinder head bolt
28. Rocker cover	33. Spark plug guide oil seal
• Timing belt	34. Cylinder head assembly
29. Timing belt rear cover	35. Cylinder head gasket
30. Front exhaust pipe connection	

MT1069900562020X

**Fig. 8 Cylinder head replacement (Part 2 of 2)
1997-99**

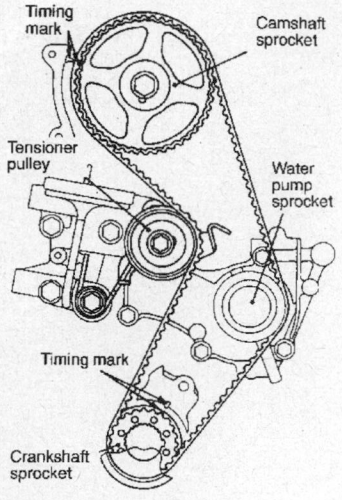

<Vehicles with crank angle sensor>

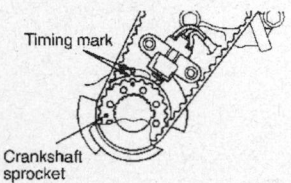

MT1069100104000X

Fig. 9   Engine timing marks

6. Remove oil pan as outlined under "Oil Pump, Replace."
7. Remove piston and connecting rod in numbered sequence shown in **Fig. 27,** marking large end of each connecting rod with cylinder number.
8. Reverse procedure to install, noting the following:
   a. Arrange piston ring oil gaps and piston as outlined in **Fig. 28.**
   b. Use suitable thread protectors on connection rod studs prior to installation.
   c. Mate each connecting rod marking with appropriate cylinder.
   d. Install connecting rod bearing cap on connecting rod.
   e. Coat threads lightly with oil.
   f. Install both nuts finger tight.
   g. Alternately tighten each nut to specifications.

MAIN & ROD BEARINGS

Refer to "Crankshaft, Replace" for main bearing replacement.

CRANKSHAFT SEAL
REPLACE
FRONT

1. Release fuel system pressure as outlined under " Precautions."
2. Remove timing belt as outlined under " Timing Belt, Replace."
3. **On 1998–99 models,** remove crankshaft position sensor.

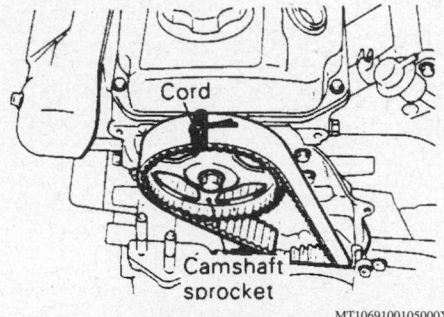

MT1069100105000X

Fig. 10   Camshaft sprocket secured position

4. **On all models,** remove crankshaft sprocket.
5. Remove crankshaft sensing blade, spacer and front oil seal.
6. Reverse procedure to install, using seal installer 998717, or equivalent, to install oil seal.

REAR

1. Remove transaxle assembly as outlined under "Transaxle, Replace" in "Clutch & Manual Transaxle" section for models with manual transaxle or in "Automatic Transaxle" unit repair section for models with automatic transaxle.
2. Remove flywheel or driveplate from rear of crankshaft.
3. Remove rear engine place and inspection cover.
4. Remove rear main oil seal case and oil seal.
5. Drive out old oil seal using suitable seal removal tool.
6. Reverse procedure to install, Note: install rear main oil seal using seal installer tool Nos. MB990938-01 and MD998776, or equivalents.

OIL PAN
REPLACE

Refer to "Oil Pump, Replace" for oil pan replacement procedure.

OIL PUMP
REPLACE
REMOVAL

1. Release fuel system pressure as outlined under " Precautions."
2. Remove timing belt as outlined under "Timing Belt, Replace."
3. Remove water pump as outlined under "Water Pump, Replace."
4. Remove front case, oil pan and oil pump in numbered sequence shown in **Fig. 29,** marking alignment marks on outer and inner oil pump rotors for reassembly.

INSPECTION

1. Inspect oil pump rotor tip clearance and ensure a .0024–.0071 inch clearance exists, **Fig. 30.**
2. Inspect oil pump rotor side clearance

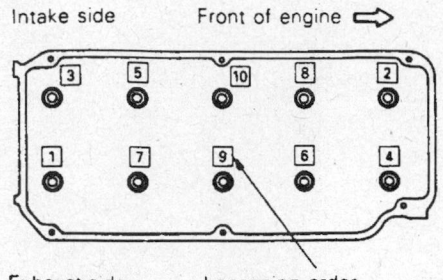

MT1069100106000X

Fig. 11   Cylinder head bolt loosening sequence. 1996

and ensure a .0016–.0039 inch clearance exists, **Fig. 31.**
3. Inspect oil pump body clearance and ensure a .0039–.0071 inch clearance exists, **Fig. 32.**

INSTALLATION

Reverse numbered sequence shown in **Fig. 29** to install, noting the following:
1. Apply engine oil to oil pump rotors.
2. Install oil pump rotors into pump body, aligning marks made during disassembly.
3. Apply sealant to oil pump case cover.
4. Install seal into oil pump case using seal installer MD998717-01, or equivalent.
5. Apply a 0.16 inch diameter bead of sealant to oil pan flange as shown, **Fig. 33.**

BELT TENSION DATA

Belt	Tension lbs.	
	New	Used①
Alt.	110–154	77–99
Power Steering & A/C	143–187	99–121

① — Belt used for 5 minutes or more.

COOLING SYSTEM BLEED

1. Remove air bleed bolt from on top of thermostat housing, **Fig. 34.**
2. Fill coolant system through air bleed bolt hole until full.
3. Install air bleed bolt.
4. Slowly pour coolant into radiator until radiator is full and fill reservoir tank to FULL line.
5. Install radiator cap, start engine and allow to idle.
6. After thermostat has opened, perform 3000 RPM racing three times.
7. Stop engine and allow to cool completely. **Failure to allow engine to fully cool may result in personal injury.**
8. Open radiator cap, if coolant level has dropped repeat Steps 4 through 8.
9. Replace radiator cap and check for coolant system leaks.

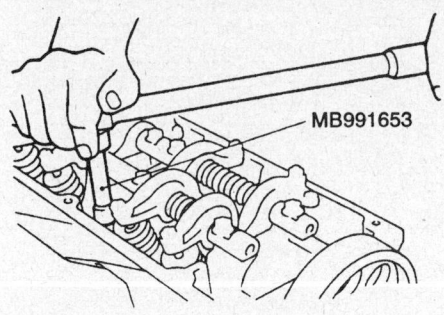

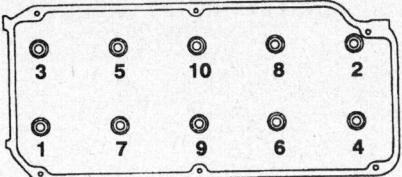

Intake side ⇦ **Front of engine**

Exhaust side

MT1069900563000X

Fig. 12 Cylinder head bolt loosening sequence. 1997-99

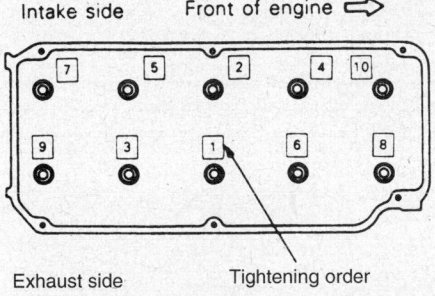

Intake side   Front of engine ⇨

Exhaust side   Tightening order

MT1069100108000X

Fig. 15 Cylinder head bolt tightening sequence. 1996

THERMOSTAT
REPLACE

1. Drain coolant into an approved container.
2. **On 1996 models,** disconnect upper radiator hose from thermostat housing.
3. **On 1997–99 models,** disconnect lower radiator hose from thermostat housing.
4. **On all models,** remove thermostat housing.
5. Install thermostat with jiggle valve at top, **Fig. 35.**
6. Reverse procedure to install, bleeding coolant system after installation is complete.

WATER PUMP
REPLACE

1. Drain engine coolant into suitable container.
2. Remove timing belt as outlined under "Timing Belt, Replace."

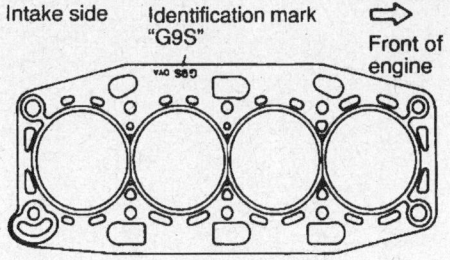

Intake side   Identification mark "G9S"   ⇨ Front of engine

Exhaust side

MT1069300338000X

Fig. 13 Cylinder head gasket identification mark

3. Remove timing belt rear cover.
4. Remove water pump mounting bolts, then water pump, **Fig. 36.**
5. Reverse procedure to install, noting bolt length position shown in **Fig. 37.**

FUEL PUMP
REPLACE

This procedure has been revised by a Technical Service Bulletin.
1. Release fuel system pressure as outlined under "Precautions."
2. Remove fuel cap, then drain fuel tank into a suitable container.
3. Disconnect return, high pressure, vapor and filler hoses.
4. Disconnect fuel gauge unit and electric fuel pump electrical connections.
5. **On 1996 models,** disconnect rear ABS speed sensor connector.
6. **On 1997–99 models,** remove the rear seat cushion.
7. **On all models,** support fuel tank and remove fuel tank supports.
8. Lower fuel tank from vehicle.
9. Remove fuel pump from fuel tank.
10. Reverse procedure to install.

FUEL FILTER
REPLACE

This procedure has been revised by a Technical Service Bulletin.
1. Release fuel system pressure as outlined under "Precautions."
2. Remove air cleaner and intake hose.
3. Holding fuel filter with a spanner, remove eye bolt and high-pressure fuel hose. **As there will be some pressure remaining in fuel pipe line, cover it with a rag to prevent fuel from spraying out.**
4. Loosen flare nut then disconnect fuel main pipe connection.
5. Remove fuel filter, **Figs. 38 and 39.**
6. Reverse procedure to install.

RADIATOR
REPLACE

1. Drain engine coolant, then remove drain plug and radiator cap.
2. Remove overflow tube and reserve tank, then upper and lower radiator hoses.
3. **On models equipped with automat-**

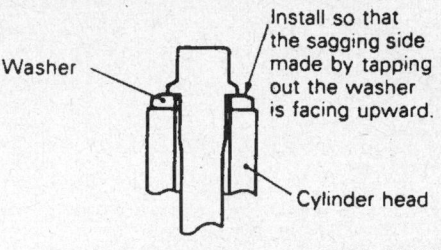

Washer   Install so that the sagging side made by tapping out the washer is facing upward.

Cylinder head

MT1069100107000X

Fig. 14 Cylinder head bolt washer installation

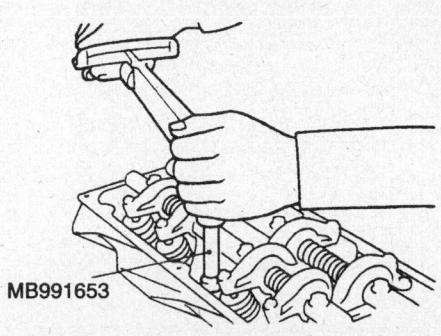

MB991653

Intake side   ⇦ Front of engine

Exhaust side

MT1069900564000X

Fig. 16 Cylinder head bolt tightening sequence. 1997-99

ic transaxle, remove ATF cooler hose, then plug hose and radiator nipple.
4. **On models equipped with air conditioning,** disconnect condenser fan connector.
5. **On all models,** disconnect radiator fan connector, then remove upper insulator and radiator assembly.
6. Remove resistor.
7. **On models equipped with air conditioning,** remove condenser fan motor assembly.
8. **On all models,** remove radiator fan motor assembly.
9. Remove lower insulator, fan, radiator fan motor and shroud.
10. Reverse procedure to install.

TECHNICAL SERVICE BULLETINS

FUEL STARVATION

Fuel starvation can occur when in-tank fuel filter is clogged, typically by contaminated fuel.

To correct problem, proceed as follows:
1. Activate fuel pump with scan tool, then measure pump's supply voltage.

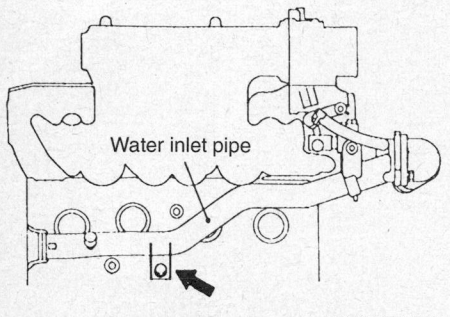

Fig. 17 Inlet water pipe mounting bolt location

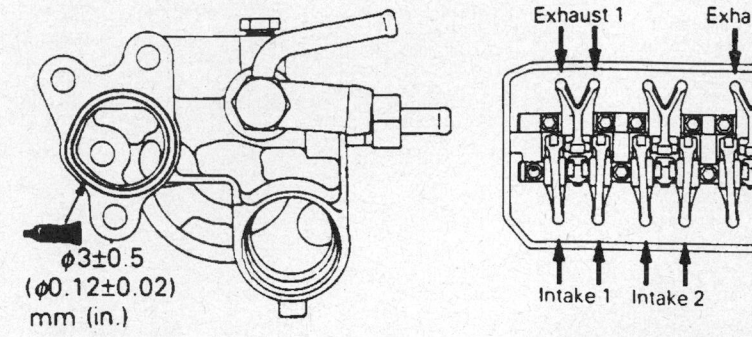

Fig. 18 Thermostat housing sealant location

Fig. 19 Valve clearance adjustment w/No. 1 cylinder at TDC. 1996–97

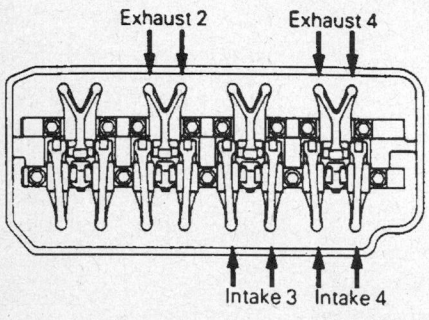

Fig. 20 Valve clearance adjustment w/No. 1 cylinder at BTDC

2. If voltage is less than 8 volts, inspect and repair fuel pump wiring harness.
3. If voltage is 8 volts or more, check system fuel pressure.
4. If system fuel pressure is within specifications, check system for other starvation problems. Specification is 38 psi at curb idle with fuel pressure regulator vacuum hose attached and 47–50 psi with hose disconnected.
5. If fuel system pressure is not within specifications, remove fuel pump as described in "Fuel Pump, Replace" and check filter.
6. If filter is clean, replace fuel pump. If filter is clogged, proceed as follows:
   a. Carefully dislodge pump motor from bracket. On some models it may be necessary to remove lower bracket clamp to dislodge motor.
   b. Remove rubber pump vibration dampener, then retaining clip (or nut) and filter.
   c. Replace filter.
   d. **If filter is severely clogged, clean inside of fuel tank.**
7. Reverse procedure to install using new gasket.

IDLE VIBRATION

Some models (mostly equipped with automatic transaxles) may vibrate excessively at idle.

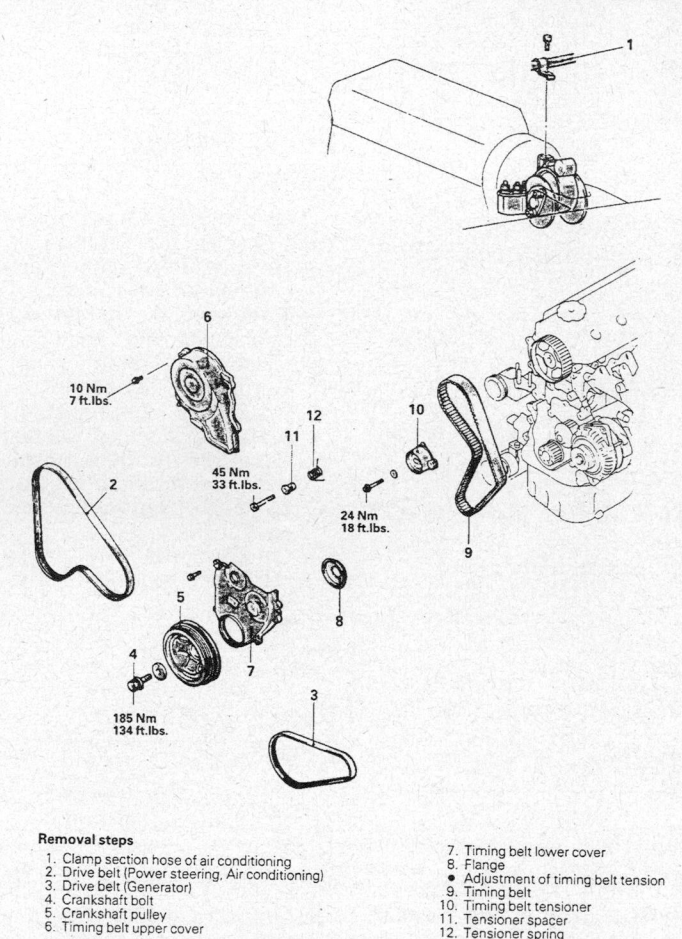

Removal steps
1. Clamp section hose of air conditioning
2. Drive belt (Power steering, Air conditioning)
3. Drive belt (Generator)
4. Crankshaft bolt
5. Crankshaft pulley
6. Timing belt upper cover
7. Timing belt lower cover
8. Flange
● Adjustment of timing belt tension
9. Timing belt
10. Timing belt tensioner
11. Tensioner spacer
12. Tensioner spring

Fig. 21 Timing belt replacement. 1996

Radiator may be transmitting engine vibration through frame because mounting brackets are not centered on posts. To correct problem, proceed as follows:
1. Examine upper radiator mounting brackets. Brackets should be centered on post and radiator should move freely.
2. If brackets are not center, remove upper brackets and ensure bottom mounting posts are seating in lower brackets.
3. Center upper brackets over posts and tighten bolts to specifications.
4. Measure clearance between upper brackets and radiator top. Standard clearance is .0394 inch or more.

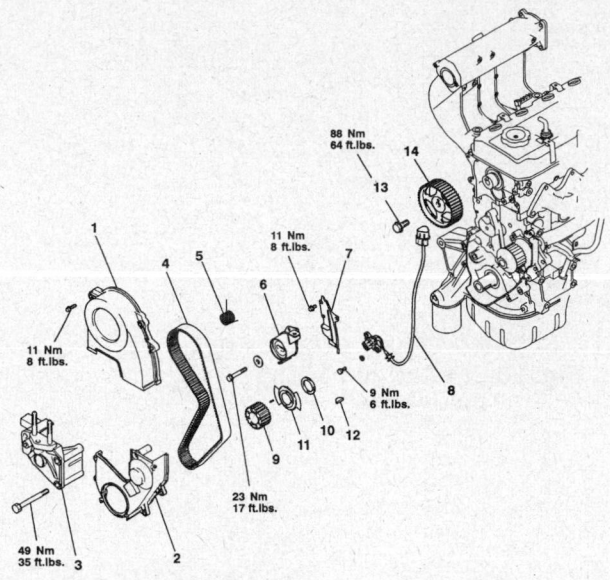

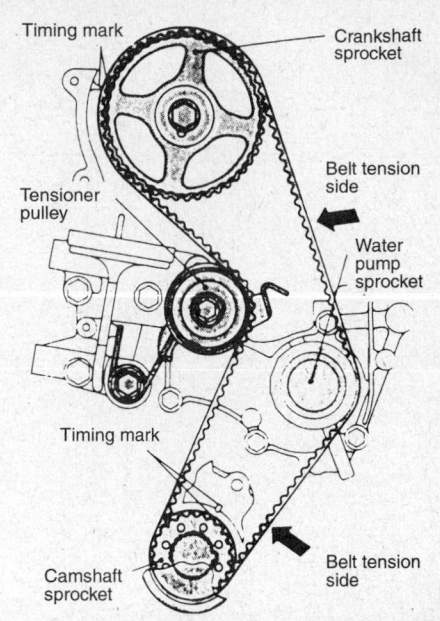

MT1069100287000X

Fig. 23 Timing belt alignment

Removal steps

1. Timing belt front upper cover
2. Timing belt front lower cover
3. Engine support bracket, right
4. Timing belt
5. Tensioner spring
6. Timing belt tensioner
7. Timing belt rear cover
8. Crankshaft angle sensor
9. Crankshaft sprocket
10. Crankshaft spacer
11. Crankshaft sensing plate
12. Crankshaft key
13. Camshaft sprocket bolt
14. Camshaft sprocket

MT1069900565000X

Fig. 22 Timing belt replacement. 1997-99

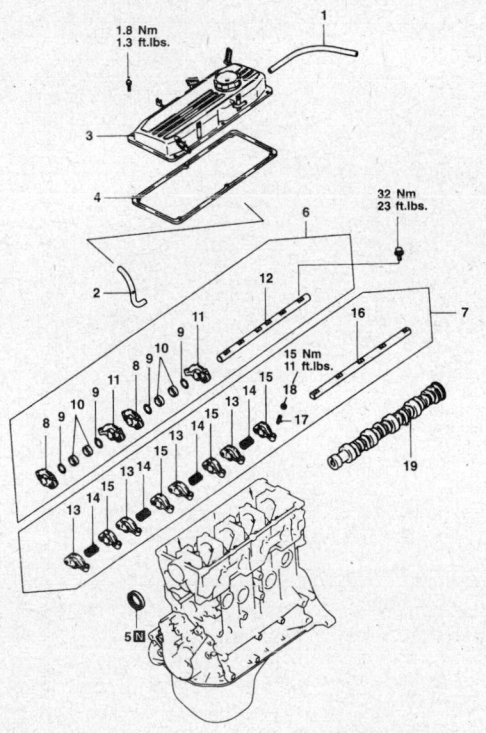

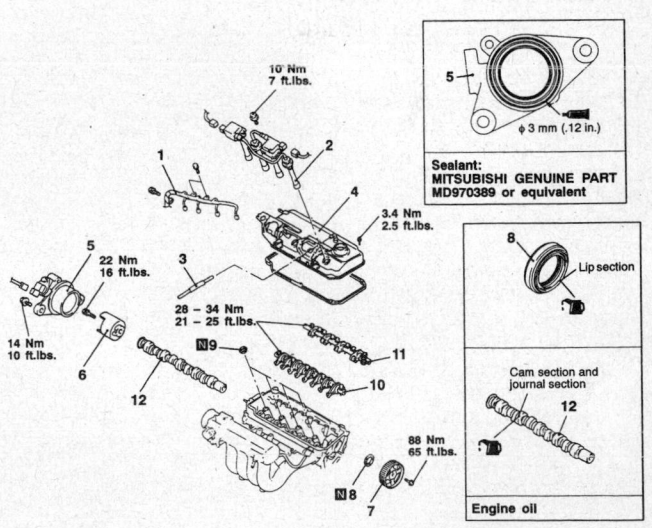

Removal steps

1. Breather hose
2. PCV hose
3. Rocker cover
4. Rocker cover gasket
   Valve clearance preadjustment
5. Oil seal
6. Rocker arms and rocker arm shaft
7. Rocker arms and rocker arm shaft
8. Rocker arm D
9. Wave washer
10. Spacer
11. Rocker arm C
12. Rocker arm shaft (exhaust side)
13. Rocker arm B
14. Rocker arm spring
15. Rocker arm A
16. Rocker arm shaft (intake side)
17. Adjusting screw
18. Nut
19. Camshaft

MT1069100118000X

Fig. 24 Camshaft replacement. 1996

Removal steps

1. Control harness connection
2. Spark plug cable
3. PCV hose connection
4. Rocker cover
   ● Valve clearance adjustment
5. Camshaft position sensor support
6. Camshaft position sensing cylinder
7. Camshaft sprocket
8. Camshaft oil seal
9. Spark plug guide oil seal
10. Rocker arm and shaft assembly (intake side)
11. Rocker arm and shaft assembly (exhaust side)
12. Camshaft

MT1069900566000X

Fig. 25 Camshaft replacement. 1997-99

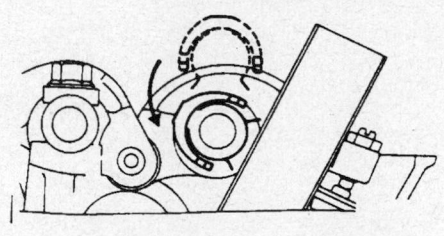

Fig. 26 Rocker shaft spring installation. 1996–97

MT1069100120000X

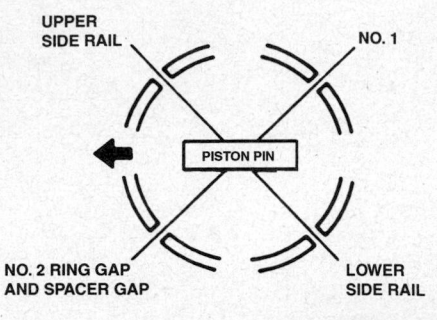

Fig. 28 Piston pin & ring installation

MT1069100122000X

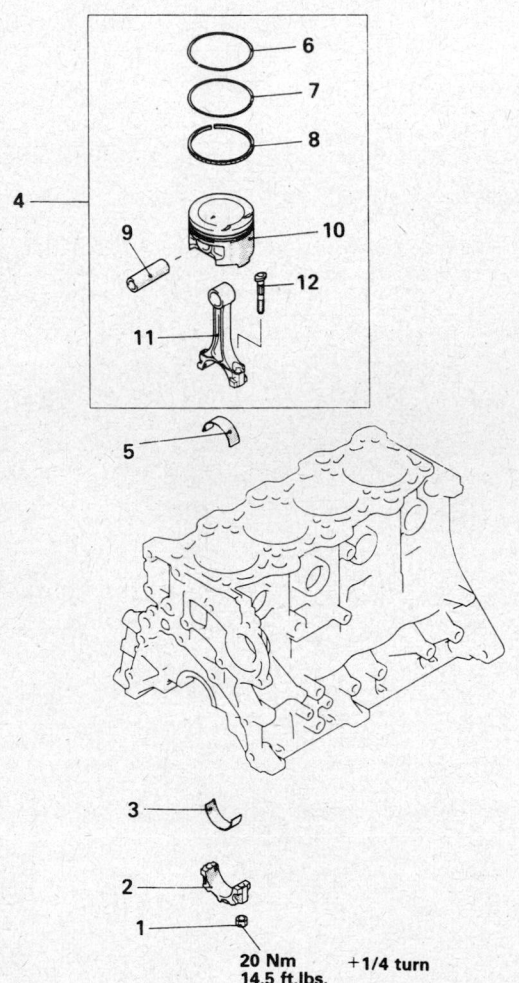

Fig. 27 Exploded view of piston & connecting rod

MT1069100121000X

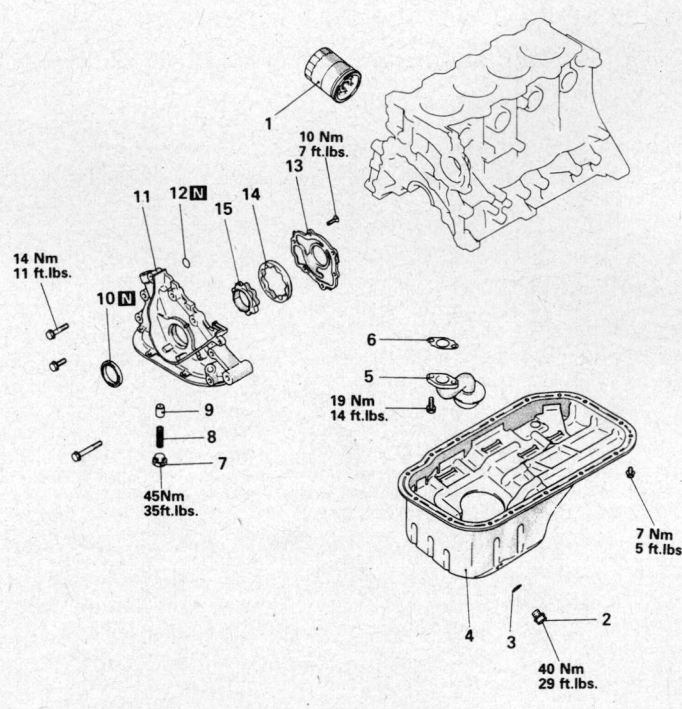

Fig. 29 Exploded view of front case & oil pump

MT1099100039000X

Disassembly steps

1. Nut
2. Connecting rod cap
3. Connecting rod bearing
4. Piston and connecting rod.
5. Connecting rod bearing
6. Piston ring No.1
7. Piston ring No.2
8. Oil ring
9. Piston pin
10. Piston
11. Connecting rod
12. Bolt

Removal steps

1. Oil filter
2. Drain plug
3. Drain plug gasket
4. Oil pan
5. Oil screen
6. Oil screen gasket
7. Relief plug
8. Relief spring
9. Relief plunger
10. Oil seal
11. Oil pump case
12. O-ring
13. Oil pump case cover
14. Outer rotor
15. Inner rotor

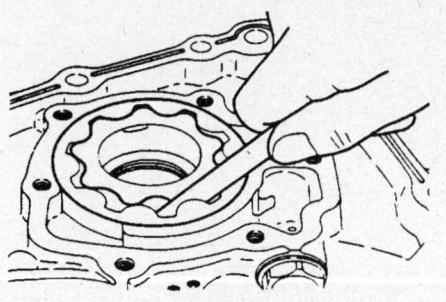

MT1099100040000X

Fig. 30 Rotor tip clearance inspection

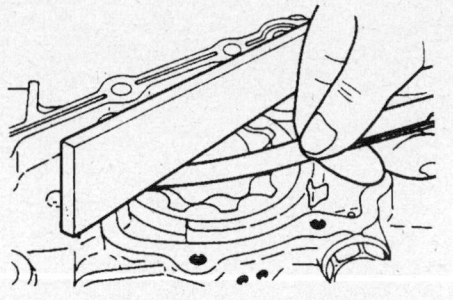

MT1099100041000X

Fig. 31 Rotor side clearance inspection

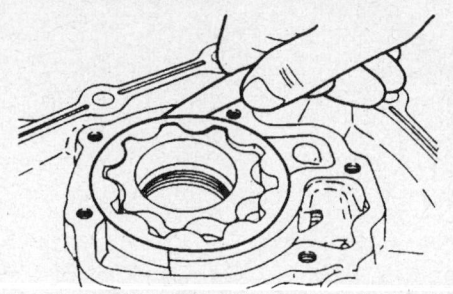

MT1099100042000X

Fig. 32 Body clearance inspection

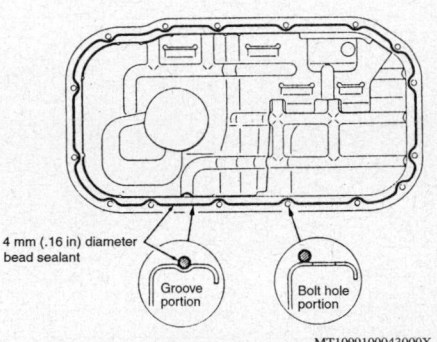

MT1099100043000X

Fig. 33 Oil pan sealant location

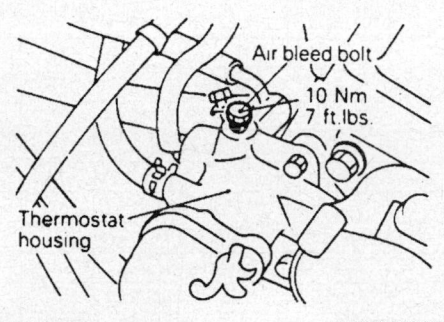

MT1089100016000X

Fig. 34 Cooling system air bleed bolt

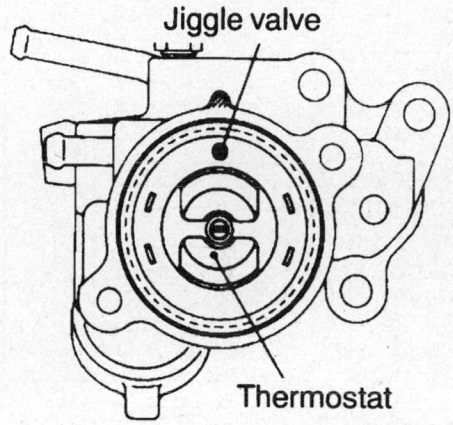

MT1069300341000X

Fig. 35 Thermostat replacement

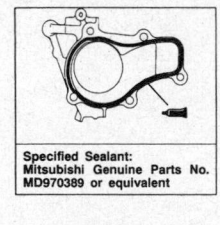

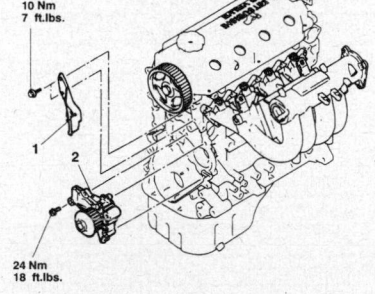

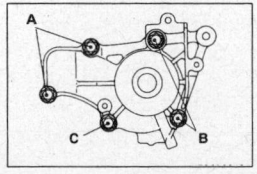

INSTALLATION SERVICE POINT

▶A◀ WATER PUMP INSTALLATION

Water pump installation bolt size are different. Do not confuse them.

	Up to 1993 models	From 1994 models
A	8 × 20 (.31 × .79)	8 × 20 (.31 × .79)
B	8 × 35 (.31 × 1.38)	8 × 35 (.31 × 1.38)
C	8 × 35 (.31 × 1.38)	8 × 20 (.31 × .79)

Bolt diameter×length: mm (in.)

MT1089100014000X

Fig. 36 Water pump replacement

Specified Sealant: Mitsubishi Genuine Parts No. MD970389 or equivalent

10 Nm 7 ft.lbs.

24 Nm 18 ft.lbs.

Removal steps
▶A◀ 1. Timing belt rear cover
2. Water pump

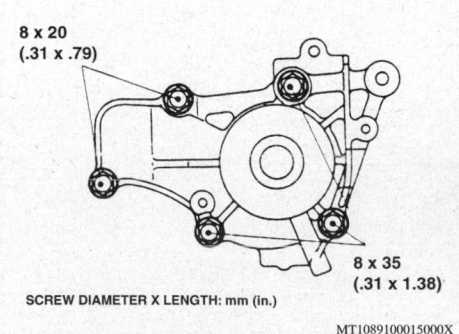

8 x 20 (.31 x .79)

8 x 35 (.31 x 1.38)

SCREW DIAMETER X LENGTH: mm (in.)

MT1089100015000X

Fig. 37 Water pump bolt installation

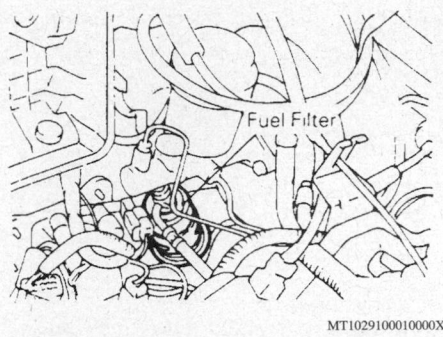

Fig. 38 Fuel filter location

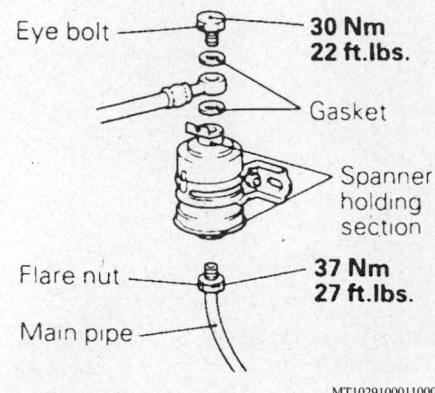

Fig. 39 Fuel filter installation

TIGHTENING SPECIFICATIONS

Year	Component	Torque, Ft. Lbs.
1996–99	Adjusting Screw Locknut	84④
	Alternator Brace Bolt	17
	Alternator Brace Mounting Bolt	36
	Alternator Pivot Nut	33
	Bellhousing Cover Mounting Bolt	84④
	Camshaft Sprocket Bolt	65
	Connecting Rod Cap Nut	②
	Crankshaft Bearing Cap Bolt	③
	Crankshaft Bolt	134
	Cylinder Head Bolt	①
	Distributor Mounting Nut	108④
	Driveplate Bolt	72
	EGR Temperature Sensor (California)	96⑤
	EGR Valve Mounting Bolt (California)	108④
	Engine Coolant Temperature Gauge Unit	96④
	Engine Coolant Temperature Sensor	22
	Engine Hanger Mounting Bolt	108④
	Engine Support Bracket Left Mounting Bolt	36
	Exhaust Manifold Bracket Mounting Bolt	26
	Exhaust Manifold Cover "A" Mounting Bolt	22
	Exhaust Manifold Cover "B" Mounting Bolt	17
	Exhaust Manifold Mounting Nut	22
	Flywheel Bolt	72
	Fuel Delivery Pipe Mounting Bolt	108④
	Fuel High Pressure Hose Union	25
	Fuel Pressure Regulator Bolt	84④
	Fuel Pump Nut	20④
	Fuel Tank Drain Bolt	48④
	Fuel Tank Mounting Nut	17
	Intake Manifold Mounting Bolt	14.5
	Intake Manifold Mounting Nut	14.5
	Intake Manifold Stay Mounting Bolt	22
	Oil Drain Plug	29
	Oil Level Gauge Guide Mounting Bolt	96④
	Oil Pan Mounting Bolt	60④
	Oil Pressure Switch	84④
	Oil Pump Case Mounting Bolt	11
	Oil Screen	14
	Oil Seal Case Mounting Bolt	96④

Continued

1.8L ENGINE

TIGHTENING
SPECIFICATIONS—Continued

Year	Component	Torque, Ft. Lbs.
1996–99	Oxygen Sensor	33
	Rear Plate Mounting Bolt	96④
	Relief Plug	35
	Rocker Arm Shaft Mounting Bolt	23
	Rocker Cover Mounting Bolt	35④
	Spark Plug	18
	Thermostat Housing Mounting Bolt	18
	Throttle Body Mounting Bolt	14
	Throttle Position Sensor Bolt	15④
	Timing Belt Cover Mounting Bolt	84④
	Timing Belt Tensioner Bolt	18
	Timing Belt Tensioner Spring Bolt	33
	Water Outlet Fitting Mounting Bolt	14
	Water Pipe Mounting Bolt	10
	Water Pump Mounting Bolt	18

① — Refer to "Cylinder Head, Replace" for procedure.
② — 14.5 ft. lbs., then tighten an additional 90° (1/4 turn).
③ — 18 ft. lbs. then tighten an additional 90° (1/4 turn).
④ — Inch lbs.

Clutch & Manual Transaxle

INDEX

ADJUSTMENTS

CLUTCH PEDAL

Cable Operated

1. Measure distance between upper surface of floor board and top of clutch pedal.
2. Pedal height should be 6.2–6.4 inches.
3. If clutch pedal height is not as specified in step 1, check pedal stopper of pedal support member for deterioration and replace as necessary.
4. Measure clutch pedal freeplay "B," **Fig. 1.** Freeplay should be .8–1.2 inches.
5. If freeplay is not as specified in step 5, turn outer cable adjusting nut at bulkhead in engine compartment and adjust clutch cable freeplay "C" to .20–.25 inch, **Fig. 2.**
6. After adjusting pedal freeplay, depress clutch pedal several times, then with pedal fully depressed check clutch pedal to floor board clearance.
7. Clearance should be 3.1 inches or more.
8. If clutch pedal clearance is not as specified in step 5 or if clutch pedal stroke is not as specified in step 6,

clutch assembly is defective. Repair clutch assembly as required.

Hydraulic Operated

1. Measure clutch pedal height (A) and clutch pedal clevis pin play (B), **Fig. 3.**
2. Clutch pedal height (A) should be 6.4–6.5 inches.
3. Clevis pin play (B) should be .04–.12 inch.
4. If either (A) or (B) are not within correct range, adjust as follows:
   a. Turn and adjustment bolt so pedal height is correct, then secure by tightening locknut, **Fig. 4.**
   b. Disconnect clutch switch connector and turn switch for standard clutch pedal height, then secure with locknut.
   c. Turn pushrod, **Fig. 5,** to adjust clutch pedal clevis pin play to proper value, then secure pushrod with locknut. **When adjusting clutch pedal clevis pin play, ensure pushrod is not pushed toward master cylinder.**
   d. Check that interlock switch outlined in **Fig. 6,** is depressed full stroke at 5.6 inch. If necessary,
5. After completing adjustments, ensure

clutch pedal freeplay (C) is .2–.5 inch. In addition, confirm that distance (D) between clutch pedal pad and firewall when clutch pedal is disengaged, **Fig. 7,** is 2.8 inches or more.
6. If clutch pedal freeplay (C) and distance (D) are not within correct range, check for air in hydraulic system, defective clutch or master cylinder assembly.

HYDRAULIC SYSTEM SERVICE

CLUTCH SYSTEM BLEED

1. Loosen bleeder screw at release cylinder.
2. Push pedal down slowly, when pedal is at bottom of pedal stroke tighten bleeder screw.
3. Repeat procedure until all air is expelled from system.
4. **Depress clutch pedal again after it returns to top of stroke.**

CLUTCH RELEASE CYLINDER, REPLACE

1. Disconnect hydraulic clutch line, **Fig. 8.**

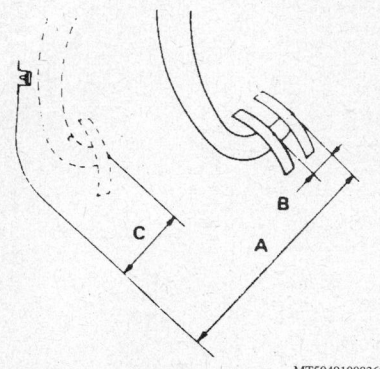

Fig. 1 Clutch pedal height, freeplay & floorboard clearance measurement

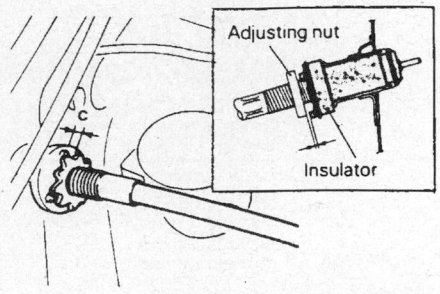

Fig. 2 Clutch pedal freeplay adjustment

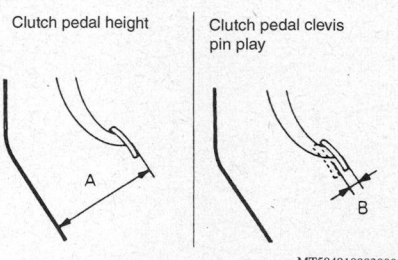

Fig. 3 Clutch pedal height & clevis pin play

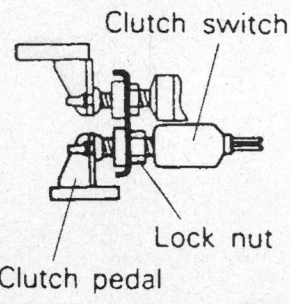

Fig. 4 Locknut location

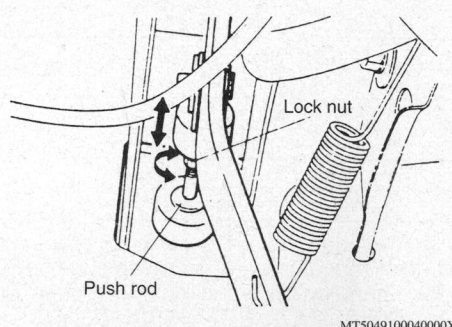

Fig. 5 Clutch pedal clevis pin play adjustment

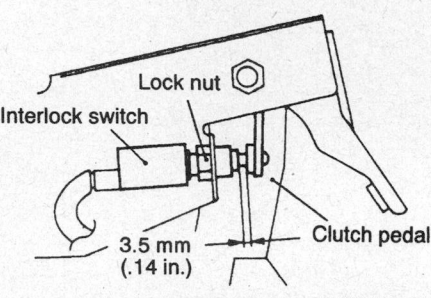

Fig. 6 Interlock switch check & adjustment

2. Remove clevis pin and snap ring.
3. Remove release cylinder attaching bolts, then the release cylinder.
4. Reverse procedure to install, noting following:
   a. Coat clevis pin with Molywhite TA No. 2 grease, or equivalent, when installing.

CLUTCH
REPLACE

1. Remove transaxle as outlined under "Transaxle, Replace" in the "Clutch & Manual Transaxle" section.
2. Insert clutch disc guide MD998126, or equivalent, into center hole to prevent dropping of clutch disc, then diagonally loosen bolts that hold clutch cover assembly to remove clutch cover assembly. **Do not clean clutch disc or release bearing with cleaning solvent.**
3. Remove snap ring, clevis pin and release cylinder assembly, if equipped.
4. Remove return clip, then the release bearing.
5. Remove spring pins from clutch release fork and shaft using a suitable punch.
6. Install release shaft and packings, then the return spring and release fork.
7. Align lockpin holes of shift arm and control shaft and, using MD998245, or equivalent, drive in two new spring pins.
8. When installing spring pins ensure spring pin slot direction is at right angles to center line of control shaft.

9. Remove grease from clutch facing by wiping with clean cloth.
10. Apply small amount of grease to clutch disc spline and input shaft spline.
11. Using MD998126, or equivalent, install clutch disc and clutch cover assembly to flywheel. When installing clutch disc, make certain that surface with manufacturer's stamped mark is on pressure plate side.

TRANSAXLE
REPLACE

1. Drain transaxle fluid and clutch fluid into appropriate containers.
2. Remove undercover.
3. Remove air cleaner assembly.
4. Remove battery and battery tray.
5. Disconnect clutch cable or tube, as equipped, from transaxle case.
6. Disconnect shift and select cables from transaxle case.
7. Disconnect back-up light switch electrical connector, speedometer cable and ground cable from transaxle case.
8. Disconnect starter motor wiring harness, then remove starter motor attaching bolts and starter motor.
9. Disconnect stabilizer bar from lower control arm.
10. Remove transaxle mount bracket.
11. Remove front driveshafts as follows:
    a. Loosen ball joint stud nut, then break ball joint loose from steering knuckle using a suitable tool.
    b. Loosen tie rod end stud nut, then disconnect tie rod end from steering knuckle using a suitable tool.
    c. **On models equipped with drive-**

shaft center bearing, remove bearing snap ring. Lightly tap tripod joint outer race to remove driveshaft from transaxle, then remove center bearing. **Do not insert pry bar between transaxle case and driveshaft or remove driveshaft from Birfield joint side.**
    d. **On models less driveshaft center bearing,** insert suitable pry bar between transaxle case and driveshaft, then pry driveshaft from transaxle. **Do not pull on driveshaft or insert pry bar deep enough to damage oil seal.**
    e. **On all models,** secure driveshaft to body.
12. Remove bellhousing cover attaching bolts and cover.
13. Support transaxle assembly with a suitable jack.
14. Remove transaxle mounting strut, then the mounting bracket bolt caps, bolts and brackets.
15. Carefully lower transaxle assembly from vehicle.
16. Reverse procedure to install, noting following:
    a. Tighten tie rod end stud nut, ball joint stud nut and transaxle mounting bracket to transaxle attaching bolts to specification.
    b. Tighten transaxle mounting bracket to body attaching bolts, bellhousing cover attaching bolts and starter motor attaching bolts to specification.
    c. Tighten filler and drain plugs, transaxle to engine attaching bolts, transaxle mounting strut to transaxle attaching bolts, and transaxle mounting strut to bracket attaching bolts to specification.

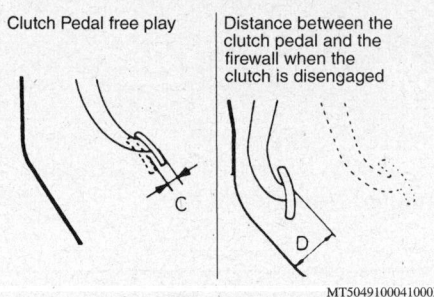

Fig. 7 Clutch pedal freeplay & distance to firewall when engaged

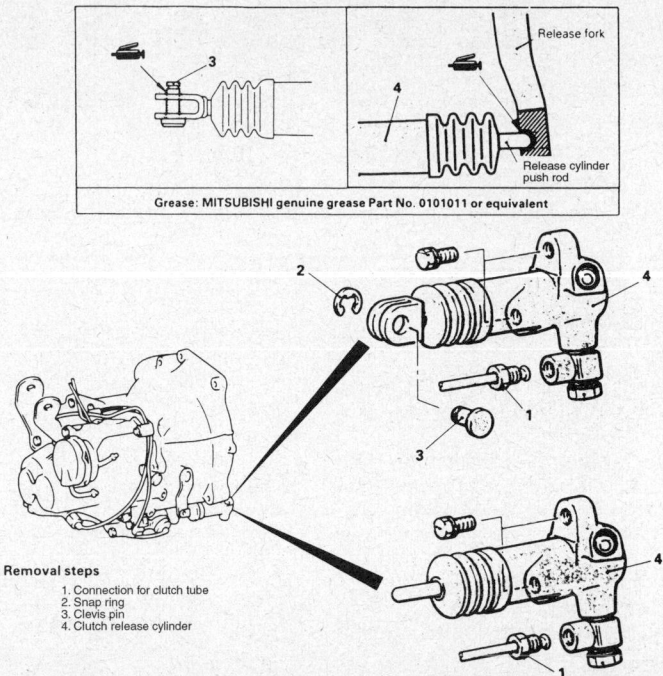

Fig. 8 Clutch release cylinder replacement

TIGHTENING SPECIFICATIONS

Year	Component	Torque/ Ft. Lbs.
1996–99	Ball Joint Stud Nut	43–52
	Back-Up Light Switch	22–25
	Bellhousing Cover Bolts	33
	Clutch Master Cylinder To Firewall	7–11
	Clutch Release Cylinder	11–16
	Clutch To Flywheel	11–15
	Drain Plug	22–25
	Filler Plug	22–25
	Flywheel	94–101
	Lower Arm Ball Joint	43–52
	Reservoir Band	48–60①
	Starter Motor	20–25
	Tie Rod End Nut	11–25
	Transaxle Mounting Bracket To Body	65–80
	Transaxle Mounting Bracket To Transaxle	43–58
	Transaxle Mounting Bolts (.31 Inch Diameter Bolts)	84–108①
	Transaxle Mounting Bolts (.39 Inch Diameter Bolts)	22–25
	Transaxle Mounting Bolts (.47 Inch Diameter Bolts)	32–39
	Transaxle Mounting Stud To Bracket	33–43
	Transaxle Mounting Stud To Transaxle	43–51
	Wheel Lug Nut	65–80

① — Inch lbs.

Rear Axle & Suspension

INDEX

HUB & BEARING
REPLACE

1. Raise and support vehicle, then remove rear wheel and rear speed sensor.
2. Disconnect parking brake cable, then remove caliper bolts and support caliper aside without disconnecting hydraulic tube.
3. Remove brake disc or drum, hub nut cap and flange nut, then slide hub assembly and rotor off axle.
4. Reverse procedure to install, noting following:
   a. Do not disassemble rear hub unit.
   b. Do not allow rotor teeth to be damaged in any way; ABS malfunction will result.
   c. **On 1996 models,** adjust clearance between pole piece and rotor teeth .012–.035 inch.,
   d. **On 1997–99 models,** adjust clearance between pole piece and rotor teeth .004–.079 inch.

STRUT
REPLACE

1. Remove quarter trim lid and strut upper flange self-locking nuts.
2. Remove two bolts to disconnect lower arm and trailing arm from lower end of strut assembly, then the strut.
3. Reverse procedure to install. Tighten bolts and nuts to specifications.

CONTROL ARM
REPLACE

1. Remove control arms in numbered sequence, **Fig. 1.** Scribe mating marks on toe-in or camber adjustment bolts prior to removing control link and lower arm.
2. Reverse procedure to install. Inspect and adjust wheel alignment as necessary.

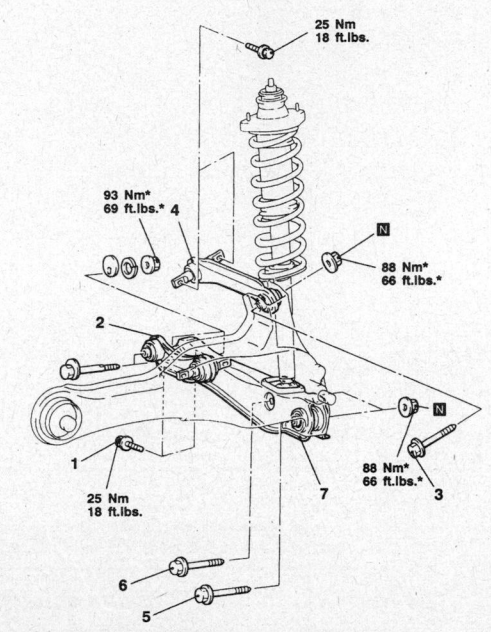

Control link removal steps
1. Control link and trailing arm connection
2. Control link

Upper link removal steps
3. Upper link and trailing arm connection
4. Upper link

Lower arm removal steps
1. Control link and trailing arm connection
5. Lower arm and trailing arm connection
6. Strut assembly and lower arm connection
7. Lower arm

Caution
* Indicates parts which should be temporarily tightened, and then fully tightened with the vehicle on the ground in the unladen condition.

MT2039300082000X

Fig. 1   Control arm replacement

TRAILING ARM
REPLACE

1. Remove rear brake assembly, then the hub as outlined under " Hub & Bearing, Replace."
2. Remove trailing arm in numbered sequence shown, **Fig. 2.** When removing speed sensor, do not allow pole piece to contact rotor teeth or other parts.
3. Reverse procedure to install, noting following:
   a. When installing rear speed sensor, adjust clearance between pole piece and rotor toothed surface to .012–.035 inch.
   b. Bleed brake system as necessary.

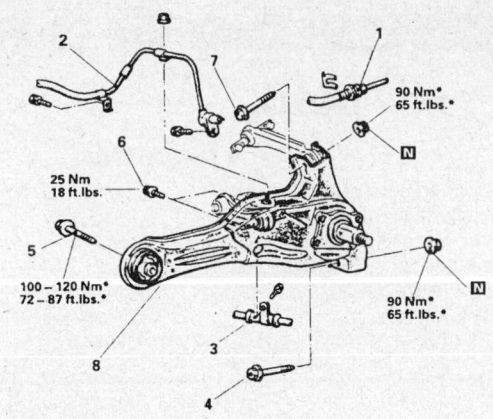

Removal steps
1. Brake hose
2. Rear speed sensor <Vehicles with ABS>
3. Parking brake cable
4. Lower arm and trailing arm connection
5. Trailing arm and body connection
6. Control link and trailing arm connection
7. Upper link and trailing arm connection
8. Trailing arm

NOTE
* Indicates parts which should be temporarily tightened, and then fully tightened with the vehicles in the unladen condition.

MT2039300083000X

Fig. 2   Trailing arm replacement

TIGHTENING SPECIFICATIONS

Year	Component	Torque/ Ft. Lbs.
1996–99	Axle Nut	130
	Control Link Mounting Bolts	18
	Control Link Nuts	51
	Flange Nut	130
	Hub Nut	130
	Lower Arm To Strut Bolt	65
	Lower Arm To Trailing Arm Bolt	65
	Rotor To Hub Bolts	108②
	Strut Cap Nut	18
	Strut Upper Flange Nuts	①
	Trailing Arm Front Mount Bolt	72–87
	Upper Link Mounting Bolts	18
	Upper Link To Trailing Arm Nut	65
	Wheel Lug Nut	65–80

① — 1996; 20 ft. lbs. 1997–99; 33 ft. lbs.

② — Inch lbs.

Front Suspension & Steering

INDEX

WHEEL HUB & STEERING KNUCKLE
REPLACE

When replacing drive hub and knuckle assembly, refer to **Fig. 1.**
1. Raise and support vehicle, then remove front wheels.
2. Remove cotter pin, wheel bearing nut and washer.
3. Disconnect brake caliper assembly and support using suitable wire.
4. Disconnect lower control arm ball joint from knuckle using a suitable tool.
5. Disconnect tie rod end from knuckle using a suitable tool.
6. Remove driveshaft from hub, then the circlip.
7. Remove hub and knuckle as an assembly from strut assembly.
8. Reverse procedure to install.

HUB SERVICE

1. Attach tool Nos. MB990998-01 and MB991056, or equivalents, to knuckle and hub, then secure knuckle in vise.
2. Remove hub from knuckle by tightening nut of tool.
3. Remove dust cover, then the hub and disc assembly attaching bolts and nuts.
4. Remove brake disc, then the inner oil seal.
5. Remove inner bearing inner race, then the outer bearing inner race using suitable tools.
6. Remove outer oil seal, then the outer and inner bearing outer race using a suitable punch. **If either outer or inner race needs replacement, they should be replaced as a set.**
7. Install outer and inner bearing outer race using a suitable tool.
8. Pack outer and inner bearing inner race with suitable grease, then install bearings.
9. Drive outer oil seal into knuckle using a suitable tool until it is flush with knuckle end surface.
10. Apply suitable grease to lip and side lip of oil seal.
11. Install brake disc, then the hub and disc assembly attaching bolts and nuts. Tighten nuts to specification.
12. Install dust cover, then the inner bearing into knuckle.

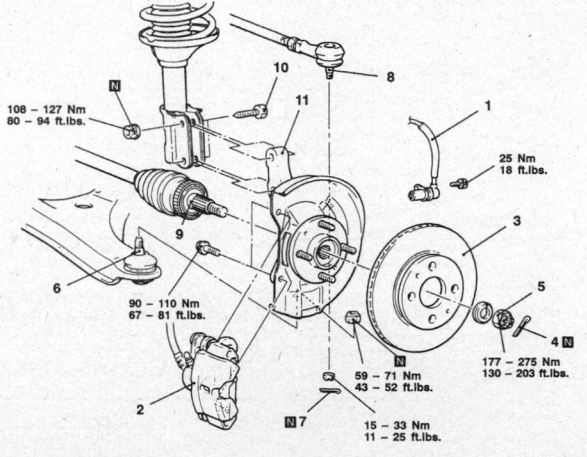

Removal steps
1. Front speed sensor <Vehicles with ABS>
2. Caliper assembly
3. Brake disc
4. Cotter pin
5. Drive shaft nut
⬥ Lower arm and stabilizer bar connection
6. Lower arm ball joint connection
7. Cotter pin
8. Tie rod end connection
9. Drive shaft
10. Front strut mounting bolt and nut
11. Hub and knuckle

Caution
1. For vehicles with ABS, be careful when handling the pole piece at the tip of the speed sensor so as not to damage it by striking against other parts.
2. For vehicles with ABS, be careful not to damage the rotors installed to the R.J. outer race during removal and installation of the drive shaft.

MT2049300039000X

Fig. 1   Axle hub replacement

13. Rotate hub to seat bearing, then check hub turning torque. Turning torque should be 11.3 inch lbs. or less.
14. Mount knuckle in vise, then check hub endplay using a suitable dial gauge. Endplay should be .008 inch.
15. If turning torque and hub endplay are not as specified, hub and/or knuckle may have been installed incorrectly. Repeat service procedures.
16. Install inner oil seal using suitable tool until it projects from knuckle to a height of .10 inch, then apply grease to lip of seal.

BALL JOINT INSPECTION

1. Disconnect ball joint from steering knuckle as outlined under "Ball Joint, Replace."
2. Shake ball joint several times, then install ball joint stud nut.
3. Using torque wrench MB990326, or equivalent, measure ball joint breakaway torque.

4. Ball joint breakaway torque should be 9–56 inch lbs.
5. If breakaway torque exceeds specifications, replace ball joint.

BALL JOINT
REPLACE
LOWER

Refer to "Control Arm, Replace" for ball joint replacement procedure.

STRUT
REPLACE

1. Remove brake hose bracket attaching bolt, then the brake hose bracket.
2. Disconnect strut assembly from knuckle arm, **Fig. 2.**
3. Remove dust cover from strut assembly.
4. Hold piston rod with a suitable hex wrench, then remove strut assembly attaching nut using MB991036, or equivalent.

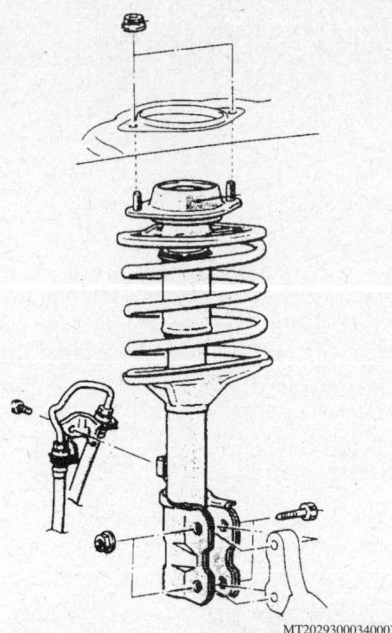

Fig. 2 Strut replacement

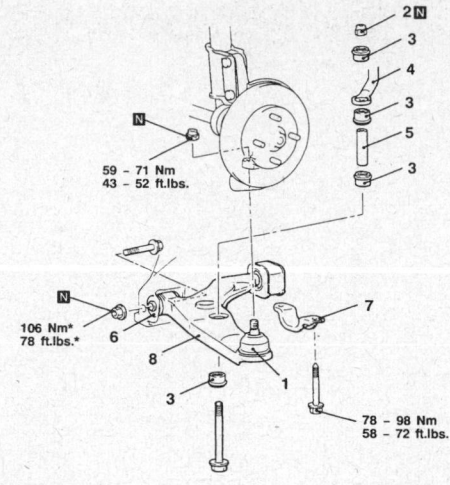

Removal steps
1. Lower arm ball joint connection
2. Self-locking nut
3. Stabilizer rubber
4. Stabilizer bar
5. Collar
6. Lower arm front bushing connection
7. Support bracket
8. Lower arm assembly

Caution
*: Indicates parts which should be temporarily tightened, and then fully tightened with the vehicle on the ground in the unladen condition.

MT2029300033000X

Fig. 3 Lower control arm replacement

5. Remove stopper and stopper rubber insulator, then the strut assembly.
6. Reverse procedure to install. Tighten all bolts and nuts to specifications.

STRUT SERVICE
DISASSEMBLE
1. Remove rubber insulator.
2. Compress coil spring using spring compressor body MB991237 and arm set MB991238, or equivalents.
3. Hold piston rod with suitable Hex wrench, then remove piston rod attaching nut using MB991036, or equivalent.
4. Remove support, spring seat, coil spring and rubber bumper from strut.
5. Remove bearing from support using a suitable brass rod.

INSPECTION
Check all strut assembly components for wear or damage and replace as necessary.

ASSEMBLE
Coil springs have color marks to indicate coil spring identification and load classification. This identification mark indicates applicable vehicle model equipped with that particular coil spring. When replacing coil spring, be sure to use spring having appropriate identification mark.
1. With support facing black retainer side of bearing, press bearing into support using suitable tool.
2. Compress spring using compressor MB990987, or equivalent, then install spring into strut.
3. Extend piston rod as far as possible, then install rubber bumper.
4. Install spring upper seat onto piston rod.
5. Install support on piston rod, then tighten nut to specification using suitable tool.

6. Align both ends of coil spring with grooves in spring seat, then slowly loosen spring compressor. Ensure spring seat does not become twisted.
7. Install rubber insulator on strut assembly.

CONTROL ARM
REPLACE
LOWER
1. Raise and support vehicle, then remove front wheel.
2. Remove lower arm in sequence, **Fig. 3.**
3. Reverse procedure to install, noting following:
   a. Tighten stabilizer bar mounting bolt self-locking nut until .87 inch of bolt protrudes above nut.
   b. Tighten all bolts and nuts to specifications.

STABILIZER BAR
REPLACE
1. Raise and support vehicle.
2. Remove undercover attaching bolt, then the undercover.
3. Remove stabilizer bar to lower control arm attaching bolt and nut.
4. Remove joint cup, bushing and collar.
5. Remove fixture attaching bolts, then the upper and lower fixtures from stabilizer bar.
6. Remove stabilizer bar from vehicle.
7. Reverse procedure to install, noting following:
   a. Tighten fixture attaching bolts to specification.
   b. When installing ends of stabilizer bar to control arm, tighten self locking attaching nut so distance from

base of nut to end of bolt is .83–.91 inch.

POWER STEERING GEAR
REPLACE
When replacing power steering gearbox, refer to **Fig. 4.**
1. Raise and support vehicle, then remove front wheels.
2. Disconnect return hose and drain power steering fluid into appropriate container.
3. Remove shaft assembly and gearbox attaching bolt.
4. Remove tie rod end ball joint from knuckle, using a suitable tool.
5. Remove power steering feed hose, then the dust cover band.
6. Remove gear housing clamp attaching bolts, then the gear housing clamps.
7. Remove gear housing mounting rubber, then the steering gear assembly.
8. Reverse procedure to install.

MANUAL STEERING GEAR
REPLACE
When removing manual steering gearbox, refer to **Fig. 5.**
1. Raise and support from of vehicle, then remove wheel and tire assembly.
2. Remove shaft assembly and gearbox attaching bolt.
3. Remove tie rod end ball joint from knuckle, using a suitable tool.
4. Remove dust cover band.
5. Remove gear housing clamp attaching bolts, then the gear housing clamps.
6. Remove gear housing mounting rubber, then the steering gear assembly.
7. Reverse procedure to install.

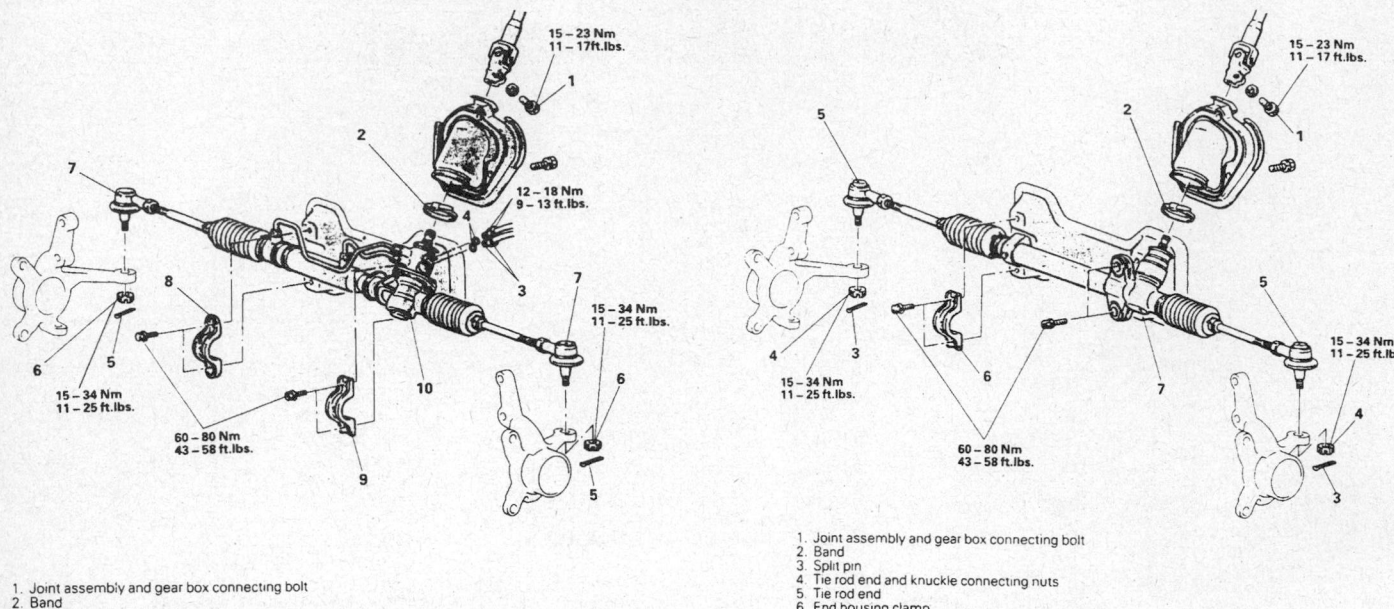

Fig. 4 **Power steering gear replacement**

1. Joint assembly and gear box connecting bolt
2. Band
3. Pressure tube and return tube
4. O-ring
5. Cotter pin
6. Tie rod end and knuckle connecting nut
7. Tie rod end
8. Gear housing clamp
9. Cylinder clamp
10. Gear box assembly

MT6039100022000X

1. Joint assembly and gear box connecting bolt
2. Band
3. Split pin
4. Tie rod end and knuckle connecting nuts
5. Tie rod end
6. End housing clamp
7. Gear box assembly

MT6039100021000X

Fig. 5 **Manual steering gear replacement**

TIGHTENING SPECIFICATIONS

Year	Component	Torque/Ft. Lbs.
1996–99	Axle Nut	130–203
	Caliper To Knuckle	90–110
	Center Member Rear Mounting Bolt	43–58
	Driveshaft Nut	144–188
	Gearbox To Body	51
	Hub Nut	130–203
	Joint To Gearbox	11–17
	Knuckle To Strut Assembly	80–94
	Lower Arm Ball Joint	43–52
	Lower Arm Front Mounting Nut	69–87
	Lower Arm Rear Mounting Bolt	43–58
	Pressure Tube To Gearbox	9–13
	Rack Support Cover Locking Nut	36–51
	Rear Roll Stopper Mounting Nut	33–43
	Return Tube To Gearbox	9–13
	Stabilizer Bar Mounting Bolt	12–19
	Stabilizer Link Mounting Nut	40–51
	Strut Assembly To Knuckle	80–94
	Strut Top End Nut	43–51
	Strut Upper Mounting Nut	25–36
	Tie Rod End Ball Joint	11–25
	Tie Rod End Locknut	25–36
	Tie Rod End To Knuckle	11–25
	Tie Rod To Rack	58–72
	Wheel Lug Nut	65–80

Wheel Alignment

INDEX

PRELIMINARY INSPECTION

1. Ensure tires are inflated to correct pressure, then check for uneven wear.
2. Check front wheel bearings, suspension arm and ball joints for damage and replace as necessary, to eliminate improper alignment due to faulty components.
3. Check steering gear for damage and replace as necessary.
4. Check shocks for damage and replace as necessary.
5. Rock vehicle back and forth and bounce upward and downward to settle vehicle prior to alignment.
6. Ensure vehicle is unloaded and on a suitable alignment rack according to manufacturers' instructions. **When measuring equipment is attached directly to outer end of driveshaft and front wheels are on turntables, apply brake to prevent improper vehicle movement.**

FRONT WHEEL ALIGNMENT

CAMBER

Camber refers to the angle at which a wheel leans in or out, **Fig. 1**. Positive camber is when wheel leans outward and negative camber is when wheel leans inward.

Camber on these vehicles is preset to specification and cannot be adjusted. If camber is out of specification, bent or damaged components must be replaced.

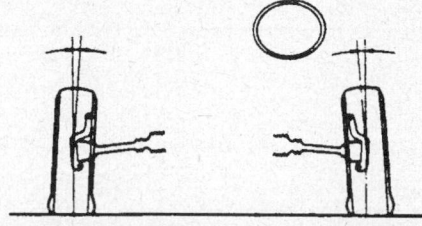

MT2049100040000X

Fig. 1   Camber adjustment

CASTER

Caster angle refers the to angle at which wheel center deviates from vertical when viewed from side, **Fig. 2**. Caster is preset to specification and cannot be adjusted. If caster is out of specification, bent or damaged components must be replaced.

TOE

As viewed from above, wheels must be set so distances A and B, **Fig. 3**, measured at wheel rims and at axle height, are different at a given value. If distance A is smaller than distance B, setting is known as toe-in. If distance A is greater than distance B, setting is known as toe-out. toe setting is given in inches and refers to difference between A and B. If distances A and B are same, toe setting is 0.

1. Adjust toe-in by undoing clips and turning left and right tie rod turnbuckles by same amount in opposite directions.
2. To increase toe-out, turn left turnbuckle toward front of vehicle and right turnbuckle toward rear of vehicle. To increase toe-in, turn turnbuckles in opposite direction.
3. Toe-in is adjusted .48 inch for each half turn of left and right tie rods.
4. After adjusting toe-in, check that steering wheel turning angle is within specification.

REAR WHEEL ALIGNMENT

CAMBER

Camber and toe-in are preset to specification and cannot be adjusted. If camber is out of specification, bent or damaged components must be replaced.

TOE

As viewed from above, wheels must be set so distances A and B, **Fig. 3**, measured at wheel rims and at axle height, are different at a given value. If distance A is smaller than distance B, setting is known as toe-in. If distance A is greater than distance B, setting is known as toe-out. Toe setting is given in inches and refers to difference between A and B. If distances A and B are same, toe setting is 0.

Rear toe-in is preset to specification and cannot be adjusted. If rear toe-in is out of specification, bent or damaged components must be replaced.

VEHICLE RIDE HEIGHT

There is no provision for adjustment of vehicle ride height. If ride height is not satisfactory, inspect suspension components for damage or modification.

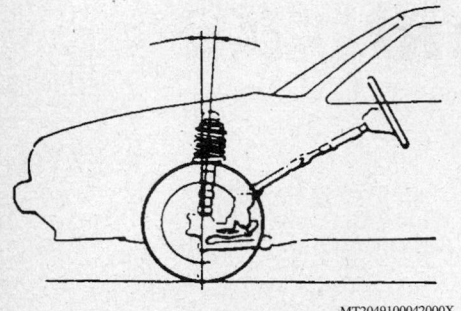

Fig. 2 Caster adjustment

MT2049100042000X

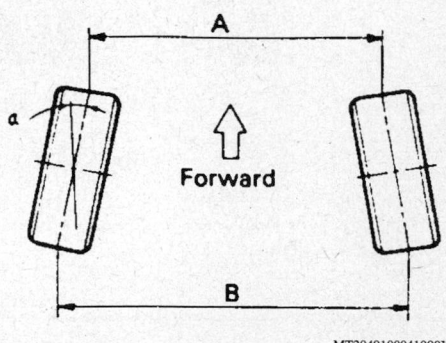

MT2049100041000X

Fig. 3 Toe adjustment

MITSUBISHI LIGHT TRUCKS

INDEX OF SERVICE OPERATIONS

Specifications

GENERAL ENGINE SPECIFICATIONS

Year	Engine Liters	Fuel System	Bore & Stroke	Compression Ratio	Maximum Net HP @ RPM	Maximum Torque Ft. Lbs. @ RPM	Oil Pressure, psi①
1996	2.4L	Fuel Inj.	3.41 X 3.94	8.5	116 @ 5000	136 @ 3500	11.4
	3.0L	Fuel Inj.	3.59 X 2.99	9.0	177 @ 5500	188 @ 4500	11.4
	3.5L	Fuel Inj.	3.66 X 3.38	9.5	215 @ 5000	228 @ 3000	11.4
1997–98	2.4L	Fuel Inj.	3.41 X 3.94	9.5	132 @ 5500	148 @ 2750	11.4
	3.0L	Fuel Inj.	3.59 X 2.99	9.0	173 @ 5250	188 @ 4000	11.4
	3.5L	Fuel Inj.	3.66 X 3.38	9.0	200 @ 5000	228 @ 3500	11.4
1999	2.4L	Fuel Inj.	3.41 X 3.94	9.0	132 @ 5500	148 @ 2750	11.4
	3.0L	Fuel Inj.	3.59 X 2.99	9.0	173 @ 5250	188 @ 4000	11.4
	3.5L	Fuel inj.	3.66 X 3.38	9.0	200 @ 5000	228 @ 3500	11.4

① — Minimum pressure @ curb idle.

TUNE UP SPECIFICATIONS

Year & Engine	Spark Plug Gap, Inch	Firing Order, Fig.	Ignition Timing Timing BTDC	Ignition Timing Timing Mark Location	Curb Idle Speed② Man. Trans.	Curb Idle Speed② Auto. Trans.	Fast Idle Speed Man. Trans.	Fast Idle Speed Auto. Trans.	Fuel Pressure psi	Valve Lash
1996										
2.4L	.041	A	5①	⑦	750	750N	④	④	47-50	⑤
3.0L	.041	⑥	5③	⑦	700	700N	④	④	47-50	⑤
3.5L	.041	F⑥	5①	⑦	700	700N	④	④	47-50	⑤
1997–99										
2.4L	.041	A	5①	⑦	700	700	④	④	47-50	⑤
3.0L	.041	⑥	5③	⑦	700	700	④	④	47-50	⑤
3.5L	.041	F⑥	5①	⑦	700	700	④	④	47-50	⑤

BTDC — Before Top Dead Center

N — Neutral

① — With jumper wire connected between ignition timing adjustment connector and ground. Refer to Figs.C through E.

② — When adjusting idle speed, set parking brake & chock drive wheels.

③ — Electronically controlled.

④ — Controlled by idle speed control servo.

⑤ — Equipped with hydraulic valve lash adjusters.

⑥ — Cylinder numbering from front of engine to rear: right bank, 1, 3, 5; left bank, 2, 4, 6. Firing order: 1–2–3–4–5–6.

⑦ — Equipped w/crankshaft position sensor.

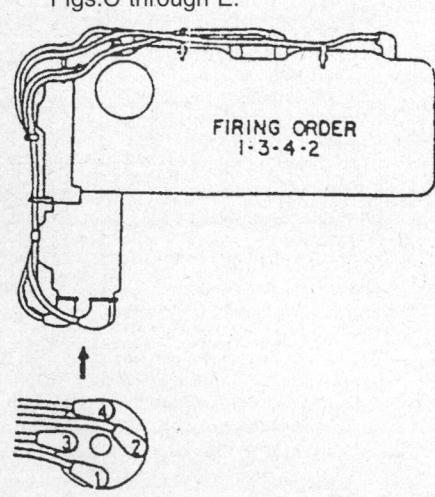

FIRING ORDER 1-3-4-2

MT1139100084000X

Fig. A

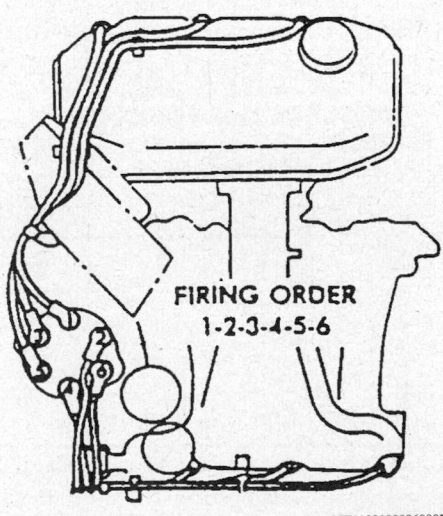

FIRING ORDER 1-2-3-4-5-6

MT1139100086000X

Fig. B

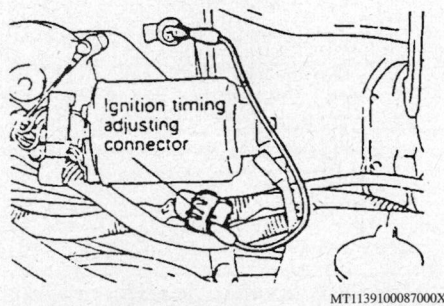

Ignition timing adjusting connector

MT1139100087000X

Fig. C   Ignition timing adjustment connector. Montero & Montero Sport w/3.0L engine

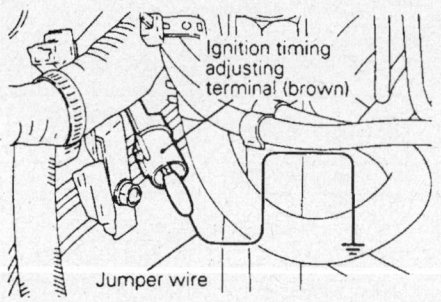

Fig. D Ignition timing adjustment connector. Montero w/3.5L engine

MT1138800030000X

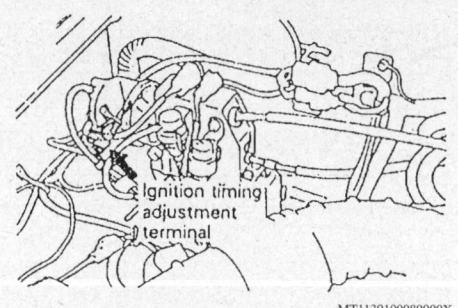

MT1139100089000X

Fig. E Ignition timing adjustment connector. Pickup & Montero Sport w/2.4L engine

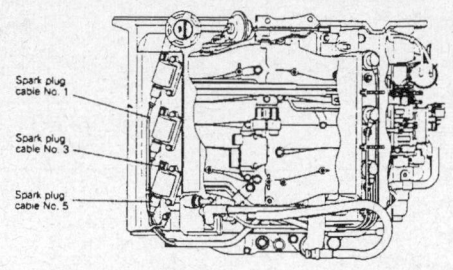

MT1139400174000X

Fig. F

FRONT WHEEL ALIGNMENT SPECIFICATIONS

Year	Model	Caster Angle, Deg.		Camber Angle, Deg.		Toe, Inch①	Kingpin Inclination, Deg.	Ball Joint Wear
		Limits	Desired	Limits	Desired			
1996–99	Montero	+2 to +4	+3	+1/6 to +1 1/6	+2/3	0 to +.28	14¹³/₁₅	②
	Montero Sport	+1²/₃ to +3²/₃	+2²/₃	+1/6 to +1¹/₆	+2/3	0 to +.28	—	②
	Pickup	+1¹/₂ to +3¹/₂	+2¹/₂	+1/6 to +1¹/₆	+2/3	+.08 to +.35	—	③

① — Toe-in (+); toe-out (-).

② — Upper ball joint starting torque, 7–30 inch lbs.; stabilizer link ball joint starting torque, 15–27 inch lbs.; lower ball joint end play, .012 maximum.

③ — Upper ball joint starting torque, 7–30 inch lbs.; lower ball joint end play, .020 maximum.

REAR WHEEL ALIGNMENT SPECIFICATIONS

Year	Model	Camber Angle, Deg.		Toe, Inch①
		Limits	Desired	
1996–99	Montero & Montero Sport	—	0	0
	Pickup	—	0	0

① — Toe-in (+); toe-out (-).

FLUID CAPACITIES & COOLING SYSTEM DATA

Model & Engine	Coolant Capacity, Qts.		Radiator Cap Relief Pressure, Lbs.	Thermo. Opening Temp., °F	Fuel Tank, Gals.	Engine Oil Refill, Qts.①	Transmission Oil		Transfer Case Oil, Pts.	Drive Axle Oil, Pts.	
	Less A/C	With A/C					5 Speed, Pts.	Auto. Trans., Qts.②		Front	Rear
Montero 3.0L	10.0	10.0	13	190	24.3	5.2	5.2	9.0	③	2.6	5.4
Montero 3.5L	10.0	10.0	13	180	24.3	5.2	5.2	9.0	③	2.6	5.4
Montero Sport 2.4L	⑤	⑤	13	190	19.5	4.5	4.8	10.4	③	2.6	3.2
Montero Sport 3.0L	⑥	⑥	13	190	19.5	5.2	4.8	10.4	③	2.6	5.5
Pickup 2.4L	6.3	6.4	13	190	④	4.0	4.8	7.7	—	—	3.2

① — Includes filter, unless otherwise noted.

② — Approximate; make final check with dipstick.

③ — V4AW2 & V5MT1, 4.8 pts.; V4AW3, 5.2 pts.

④ — Standard body, 13.7 gals.; long body & extended cab, 18.2 gals.

⑤ — With rear heat, 9.5 qts. Less rear heat 8.5 qts.

⑥ — With rear heat, 10.6 qts. Less rear heat, 9.5 qts.

LUBRICANT DATA

| Year | Lubricant Type | | | | | |
| | Transmission | | Transfer Case | Rear Axle | Power Steering | Brake System |
	Manual	Automatic				
1996–99	75W-90 GL-4	Dia ATF SP	75W-90 GL-4	GL-5①	Dexron II/IIE/III	DOT 3 or 4

① — With limited slip differential, use
Mitsubishi part No. 8149630EX, or
equivalent.

Electrical

NOTE: Refer To "Computer Relearn Procedures" Located In The Front Of This Manual For Computer Relearn Procedures.

NOTE: On Air Bag Equipped Models, Refer To "Air Bag System Precautions" Located In The Front Of This Manual For System Disarming & Arming Procedures.

INDEX

PRECAUTIONS
AIR BAG SYSTEMS

Refer to "Air Bag System Precautions" in the front of this manual for system disarming and arming procedures.

BATTERY GROUND CABLE

Prior to service, disconnect battery ground cable and isolate as required.

FUSE PANEL & FLASHER LOCATION

On Montero, the fuse panel is located on side of left end of instrument panel. There is an A/C fuse located on evaporator and a headlight fuse located in front left corner of engine compartment. Flashers are located on the left kick panel.

On Montero Sport models, the fuse panel is located under the dash panel on the left side. The flasher is located next to the fuse panel.

On Pickup, the fuse panel is located on the instrument panel to the left of steering wheel. Flashers are located under the left corner of instrument panel.

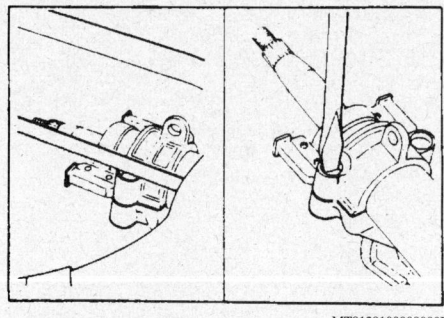

Fig. 1 Ignition lock removal

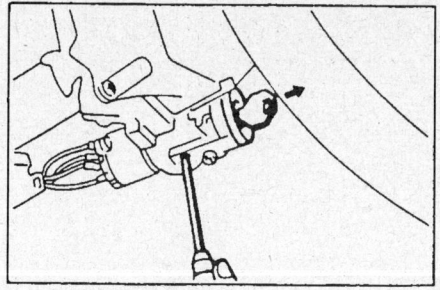

Fig. 2 Lock cylinder removal

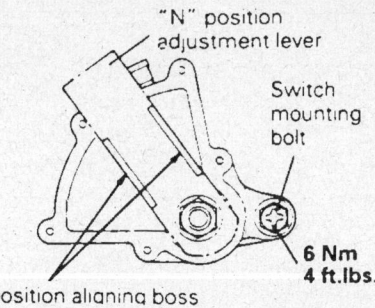

Fig. 3 Positioning selector lever. 1996 Montero

FUEL PUMP RELAY LOCATION

MONTERO & MONTERO SPORT

The multi-port fuel injection (MFI) relay is located behind the righthand side of the instrument panel, right of the glove compartment.

PICKUP

The multi-port fuel injection (MFI) relay is located below the righthand side of the instrument panel, behind the right kick panel.

RELAY CENTER LOCATION

On Montero and Montero Sport, the main relay centers are located on the upper lefthand side of the engine compartment and behind the lefthand side of the instrument panel.

On Pickup, the main relay center is located behind the lower lefthand corner of the instrument panel.

STARTER

REPLACE

1. **On Montero models,** drain transmission fluid, then remove transmission fluid cooler lines.
2. **On Montero Sport models,** remove the following:
   a. Under cover.
   b. Front differential actuator assembly.
   c. Right front engine mount heat shield.
3. **On all models,** remove starter cover, then disconnect starter cables.
4. Remove starter mounting bolts, then the starter.
5. Reverse procedure to install, noting the following:
   a. Before mounting starter, clean mating surfaces of starter and engine.
   b. Install starter and **torque** mounting bolts to 20–25 ft. lbs.

DISTRIBUTOR

REPLACE

1. Remove distributor cap with spark plug wires attached.

2. Turn engine No. 1 cylinder to top dead center (TDC).
3. Disconnect distributor electrical connections.
4. Remove distributor retaining nut, then the distributor.
5. Reverse procedure to install, noting the following:
   a. Ensure engine No. 1 cylinder is at TDC.
   b. Align distributor housing and gear mating marks.
   c. Install distributor into engine while aligning groove cut of the distributor installation flange with center of retaining stud.

COIL PACK

REPLACE

2.4L ENGINE

The ignition coil is located on top of the engine, near the base of the distributor and is mounted with two screw.

3.0L ENGINE

The power transistor and ignition coil located on the top lefthand front of the engine and are mounted with a screws.

3.5L ENGINE

The ignition power transistor is located on top of intake manifold and is mounted with a screw. The secondary ignition coils are located on top of spark plugs on lefthand side of engine and may be replaced by hand.

IGNITION LOCK

REPLACE

PICKUP

1. Remove steering column shrouds.
2. Cut groove in attaching bolt head using a suitable hacksaw, then remove bolts, **Fig. 1.**
3. Remove ignition switch electrical connectors, then the lock assembly.
4. Reverse procedure to install, noting the following:
   a. Temporarily install ignition lock in alignment with column boss and check for proper switch operation.
   b. Steering lock bracket should be replaced when installing new ignition switch.

c. Install special ignition lock attaching bolts and tighten until heads twist off.

MONTERO & MONTERO SPORT

Refer to "Ignition Switch, Replace" in this section for ignition lock procedure.

IGNITION SWITCH

REPLACE

1. Remove knee protector, if necessary.
2. Remove column shrouds, then the switch electrical connectors.
3. Remove switch attaching screws, then remove lock cylinder from switch as follows:
   a. Insert key in lock cylinder and turn to ACC position.
   b. Using a small screwdriver, push lock cylinder lockpin in, **Fig. 2,** then remove lock cylinder.
4. Reverse procedure to install.

NEUTRAL SAFETY SWITCH

REPLACE

PICKUP

1. Disconnect switch electrical connector, then remove switch from transmission case. Allow fluid to drain into a suitable container.
2. Move selector lever to Park and Neutral positions. Ensure switch operating lever fingers are centered in switch opening in transmission case.
3. Install switch using a new seal and **torque** to 25 ft. lbs.
4. Using a suitable ohmmeter, ensure continuity is present between center pin of switch and transmission case. **Continuity should exist only when transmission is in Park or Neutral.**
5. Add transmission fluid as required to fill transmission to proper level.

MONTERO & MONTERO SPORT

1996 Montero

1. Remove neutral start switch attaching screws.

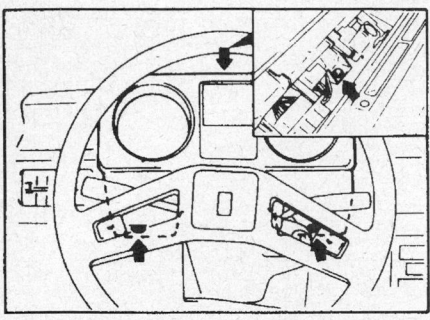

Fig. 4 Instrument cluster mounting screw locations. 1996 Montero

Fig. 5 Instrument cluster electrical connectors. 1996 Montero

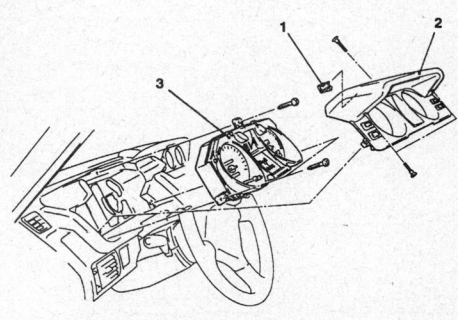

Combination meter removal steps
1. Meter hood plug
2. Meter bezel
3. Combination meter

MT9099700027000X

Fig. 6 Instrument cluster removal. 1997–99 Montero

2. Disconnect switch electrical connector, then remove switch from vehicle.
3. Reverse procedure to install, then adjust as follows:
   a. Move selector lever to Neutral position.
   b. Loosen adjusting nut of control cable.
   c. Loosen park/neutral position switch mounting bolt.
   d. Turn park/neutral position switch so bosses on switch align with neutral position adjustment lever, **Fig. 3**.
   e. **Torque** switch mounting bolt to 4 ft. lbs.
   f. Gently pull end of transmission control cable toward front of vehicle and **torque** adjusting nut to 17 ft. lbs.
   g. Ensure selector lever is in Neutral position, then check each position of selector lever for proper operation.

1997–99 Montero & Montero Sport

1. Remove neutral start switch attaching screws.
2. Disconnect switch electrical connector, then remove switch from vehicle.
3. Reverse procedure to install, then adjust as follows:
   a. Move selector lever to Neutral position.
   b. Loosen adjusting nut of control cable.
   c. Gently pull end of transmission control cable toward front of vehicle and **torque** adjusting nut to 17 ft. lbs.
   d. Ensure selector lever is in Neutral position, then check each position of selector lever for proper operation.

STEERING WHEEL

REPLACE

1. Remove air bag module.
2. Remove horn pad attaching screw(s) and horn pad.
3. Remove steering wheel attaching nut.
4. Scribe mating marks on steering shaft and steering wheel for installation reference.
5. Using a suitable steering wheel puller,

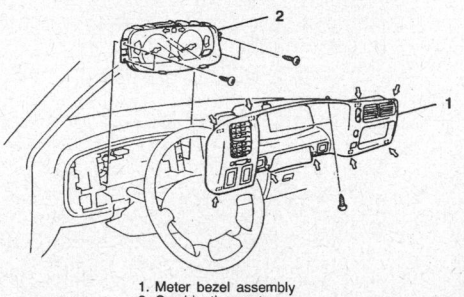

1. Meter bezel assembly
2. Combination meter

MT9099700028000X

Fig. 7 Instrument cluster removal. 1997–99 Montero Sport

remove steering wheel. **Do not hammer on steering wheel to remove. Damage to the collapsible mechanism may occur.**
6. Reverse procedure to install, noting the following:
   a. Align mating marks on steering shaft and steering wheel.
   b. **Torque** steering wheel attaching nut to 29 ft. lbs.

INSTRUMENT CLUSTER

REPLACE

1996 MONTERO

1. Remove instrument cluster upper trim cover.
2. Remove attaching screws from bottom of instrument cluster, then the attaching bolt from upper part of cluster, **Fig. 4.**
3. Disconnect speedometer cable and all electrical connectors from rear of cluster, **Fig. 5,** then remove cluster.
4. Reverse procedure to install.

1997–99 MONTERO & MONTERO SPORT

Refer to **Figs. 6 and 7,** for instrument cluster removal.

PICKUP

1. Remove hazard warning switch and hole cover using a suitable trim tool.
2. Remove four instrument cluster bezel attaching screws, then remove bezel.

3. Remove four instrument cluster attaching screws.
4. Disconnect speedometer cable and all wire connectors from rear of cluster, then remove cluster from instrument panel.
5. Reverse procedure to install.

MULTI-FUNCTION SWITCH

REPLACE

1996

1. **On Montero models,** remove dash panel lower cover.
2. **On all models,** remove steering wheel as outlined under "Steering Wheel, Replace."
3. **On models equipped with tilt steering,** set the tilt position of the steering shaft to the lowest position.
4. **On all models,** remove column upper and lower covers.
5. Disconnect multi-function switch electrical connectors, then remove the cable band.
6. Remove multi-function switch attaching screws, then the multi-function switch from steering shaft.
7. Reverse procedure to install.

1997–99

Montero

1. Remove upper and lower column covers.
2. Remove multi-function switch retaining screws, then remove multi-function switch.
3. Reverse procedure to install.

Montero Sport

1. Position front wheels straight ahead, then remove ignition key.
2. Remove air bag module, then remove steering wheel.
3. Remove upper and lower column covers, then remove clock spring assembly.
4. Remove multi-function switch retaining screws, then remove multi-function switch.

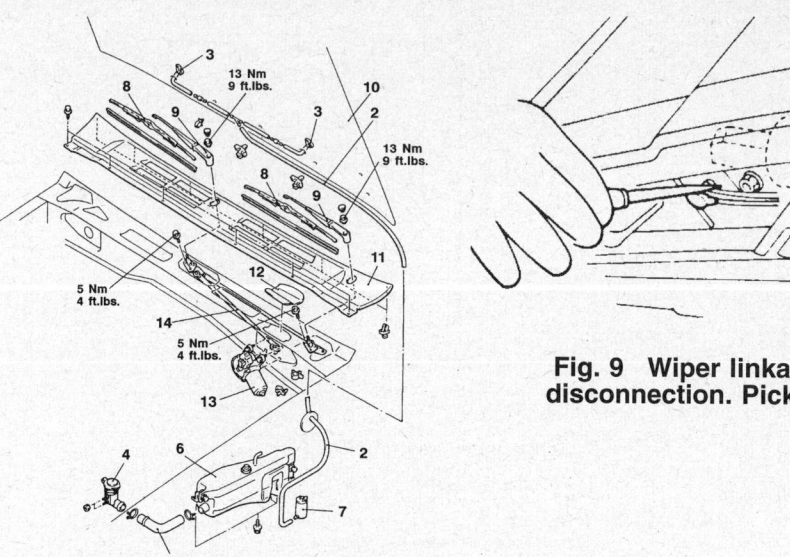

5 Nm
4 ft.lbs.

5 Nm
4 ft.lbs.

13 Nm
9 ft.lbs.

13 Nm
9 ft.lbs.

Linkage removal steps
Washer tank removal steps

MT9029900071000X

Fig. 8 Wiper linkage disconnection. Montero & Montero Sport

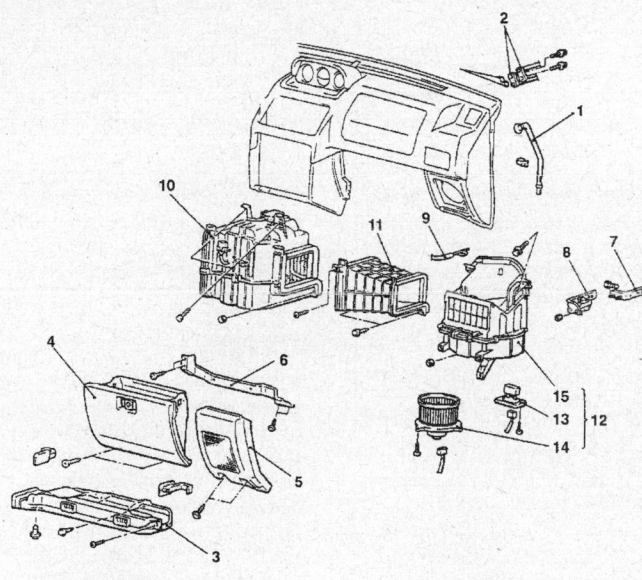

Removal steps
- Recover Refrigerant as Required.
1. Drain hose
   <Vehicles with air conditioning>
2. Liquid pipe and suction hose connection <Vehicles with air conditioning>
3. Foot shower duct (R.H.)
4. Glove box
5. Corner cover
6. Lower frame
7. Engine control relay assembly
8. Bracket
9. Air selection control wire connection
10. Evaporator
    <Vehicles with air conditioning>

11. Duct joint
    <Vehicles without air conditioning>
12. Blower assembly
13. Resistor
14. Blower motor assembly
15. Blower case assembly

Blower motor assembly removal steps
3. Foot shower duct (R.H.)
14. Blower motor assembly

Resistor removal steps
3. Foot shower duct (R.H.)
13. Resistor

MT7029800411000X

Fig. 11 Blower motor replacement. Montero

MT9029100003000X

Fig. 9 Wiper linkage disconnection. Pickup

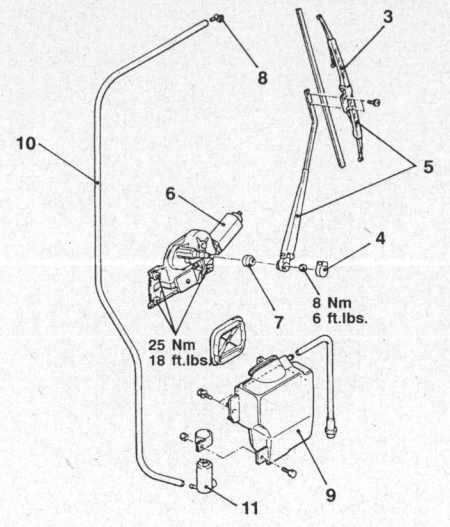

8 Nm
6 ft.lbs.

25 Nm
18 ft.lbs.

MT9029900072000X

Fig. 10 Rear wiper motor installation

5. Reverse procedure to install.

RADIO
REPLACE

On some models, the radio fuse is located on the rear of the radio. If radio fuse is to be replaced, it is necessary to remove the radio.

MONTERO & MONTERO SPORT

1. Remove radio trim panel using suitable trim stick.
2. Remove radio bracket attaching screws, then the radio with cassette player or CD player, if equipped.
3. Disconnect antenna lead and electrical connectors from rear of radio.
4. Remove radio from instrument panel.
5. Reverse procedure to install.

PICKUP

1. Remove heater control lever knob.
2. Pry off center panel using a suitable tool, then remove panel from instrument panel.
3. Remove radio bracket attaching screws, then the radio bracket.
4. Pull radio outward enough to gain access to rear of radio.
5. Disconnect antenna lead wire and electrical connector, then remove radio.
6. Reverse procedure to install.

WIPER MOTOR
REPLACE
FRONT
Montero & Montero Sport

1. Remove wiper arms, front deck garnish, then the arm shaft locknut and push shaft inward as outlined in **Fig. 8.**

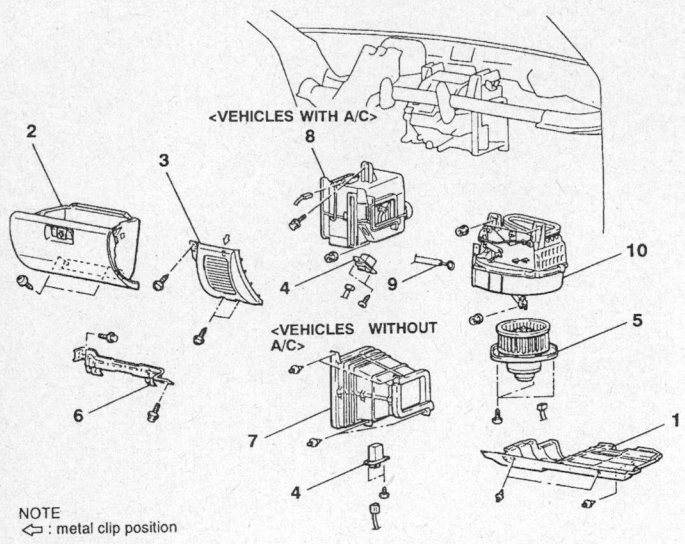

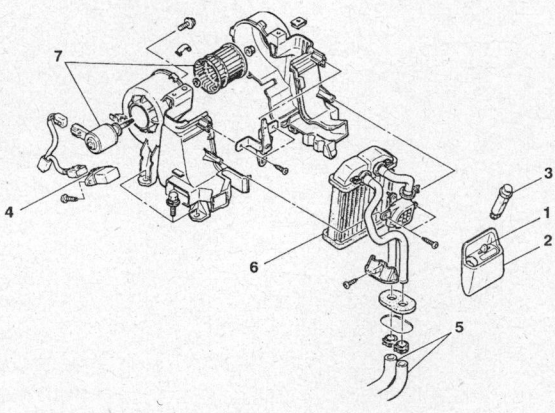

NOTE
◁ : metal clip position

RESISTOR, BLOWER FAN AND MOTOR REMOVAL STEPS
1. UNDER COVER
2. GLOVE BOX ASSEMBLY
3. CORNER COVER
4. RESISTOR
5. BLOWER FAN AND MOTOR

BLOWER CASE REMOVAL STEPS
● INSTRUMENT PANEL
6. GLOVE BOX FRAME
7. JOINT DUCT <VEHICLES WITHOUT A/C>
8. EVAPORATOR <VEHICLES WITH A/C>
9. INSIDE/OUTSIDE AIR CHANGEOVER DAMPER CABLE CONNECTION
10. BLOWER CASE ASSEMBLY

MT7029700367000X

REAR HEATER UNIT SWITCH REMOVAL STEPS
1. KNOB
2. REAR HEATER CONTROL PANEL ASSEMBLY
3. REAR HEATER SWITCH

FAN MOTOR ASSEMBLY REMOVAL STEPS
▶ REAR FLOOR CONSOLE

4. RESISTOR
● DRAINING AND SUPPLYING OF COOLANT
5. REAR HEATER HOSE CONNECTION
6. REAR HEATER CORE ASSEMBLY
7. FAN MOTOR ASSEMBLY

MT7029700387000X

Fig. 12   Front blower motor replacement. Montero Sport

Fig. 13   Rear blower motor & heater core replacement. Montero Sport

2. Remove bolts securing motor bracket to body, disconnect linkage, then remove wiper motor assembly. **Scribe marks on linkage for installation reference.**
3. Reverse procedure to install.

Pickup

1. Remove wiper arms and blades.
2. Insert a trim stick into front deck garnish and pry off.
3. Using a suitable screwdriver, disconnect wiper linkage, **Fig. 9,** then remove wiper motor.
4. Reverse procedure to install.

REAR

1. Remove spare wheel from rear door.
2. Raise wiper arm pivot cover, then remove pivot shaft locking nut.
3. Remove wiper arm and shield cap, **Fig. 10.**
4. Remove nut and collar.
5. Remove hatch trim.
6. Remove rear wiper motor bracket mounting nuts, then remove rear wiper motor assembly from hatch.
7. Reverse procedure to install.

WIPER SWITCH

REPLACE

FRONT

Refer to "Multi-Function Switch, Replace" procedure.

REAR

1996

1. Pry switch from instrument cluster using suitable tool.
2. Disconnect switch electrical connector, then remove switch.
3. Reverse procedure to install.

1997-99

Refer to "Multi-Function Switch, Replace" procedure.

BLOWER MOTOR

REPLACE

MONTERO

Refer to **Fig. 11,** for blower motor replacement.

MONTERO SPORT

Front

Refer to **Fig. 12,** for front blower motor replacement.

Rear

Refer to **Fig. 13,** for rear blower motor and rear heater core replacement.

PICKUP

1. Remove glove compartment stopper, then the glove compartment and frame.
2. Disconnect air selection control wire from blower assembly.

3. Remove duct, then disconnect blower motor electrical connector.
4. Remove bolts attaching blower assembly to heater housing.
5. Remove blower fan from blower motor.
6. Reverse procedure to install, noting the following:
   a. Place air selection lever in Outside Air position.
   b. Press air selection damper against stopper, then connect air selection control wire inner cable to end of air selection damper lever.
   c. Secure outer cable with clip.

HEATER CORE

REPLACE

MONTERO

1. Place temperature control lever in Hot position, then drain cooling system into appropriate container.
2. Disconnect heater hoses from heater core, then plug heater core fittings to prevent coolant spillage.
3. Remove instrument panel as outlined under "Dash Panel Service" in the "Unit Repair" section.
4. Proceed as follows:
   a. Remove foot shower ducts and lap cooler duct, **Fig. 14.**
   b. **On models equipped with A/C,** remove evaporator unit attaching nuts, then the heater unit.
   c. **On models less A/C,** remove joint duct.
   d. **On all models,** remove center duct, then the center reinforcement.
   e. Remove heater unit, then the heater core.
5. Reverse procedure to install.

MONTERO SPORT

Front

1. Drain coolant into a suitable container,

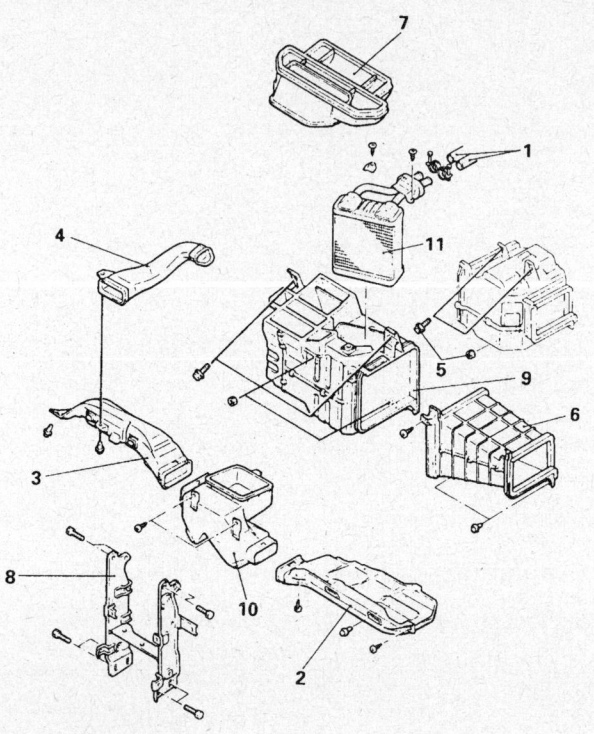

1. Connection for water hoses
2. Foot shower duct (RH)
3. Foot shower duct (LH)
4. Lap cooler duct A
5. Evaporator mounting bolt and nut <Vehicles with A/C>
6. Joint duct <Vehicles without A/C>
7. Center duct assembly
8. Center reinforcement
9. Heater unit
10. Foot distribution duct
11. Heater core

MT7029100108000X

Fig. 14 Heater unit replacement. Montero

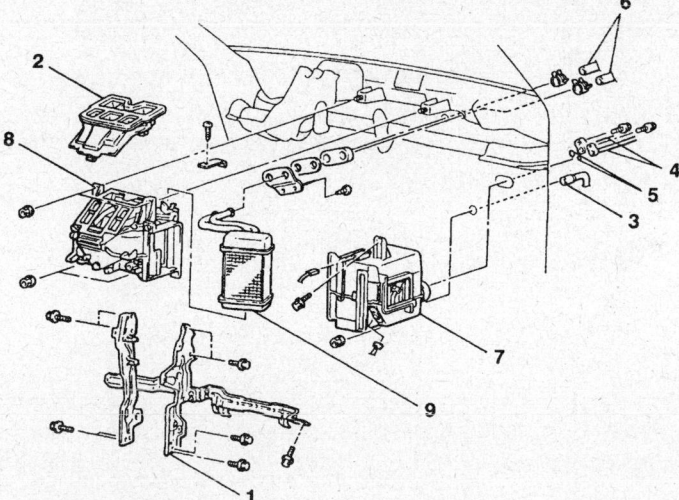

REMOVAL STEPS

1. CENTER REINFORCEMENT
2. CENTER VENTILATION DUCT
3. DRAIN HOSE <VEHICLES WITH A/C>
4. SUCTION PIPE OR HOSE AND DISCHARGE PIPE CONNECTION <VEHICLES WITH A/C>
5. O-RING
6. HEATER HOSE CONNECTION
7. EVAPORATOR <VEHICLES WITH A/C>
8. HEATER UNIT
9. HEATER CORE

MT7029700390000X

Fig. 16 Heater unit removal. Montero Sport

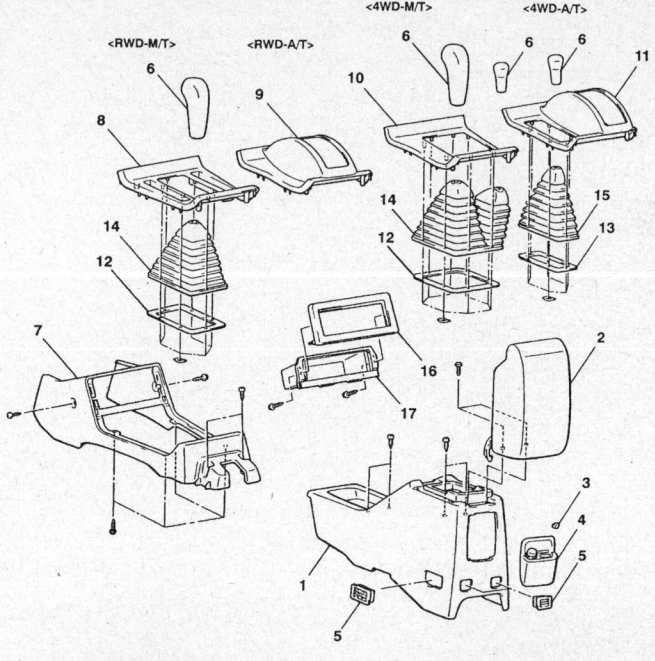

REMOVAL STEPS

1. REAR FLOOR CONSOLE ASSEMBLY
2. CONSOLE LID ASSEMBLY
3. KNOB
4. REAR HEATER CONTROL PANEL ASSEMBLY
5. FOOT GRILL
6. SHIFT LEVER KNOB
7. FRONT FLOOR CONSOLE ASSEMBLY
8. CONSOLE PANEL A <RWD-M/T>
9. CONSOLE PANEL B <RWD-A/T>
10. CONSOLE PANEL C <4WD-M/T>
11. CONSOLE PANEL D <4WD-A/T>
12. SHIFT LEVER BOOT REINFORCEMENT <M/T>
13. TRANSFER LEVER BOOT REINFORCEMENT <4WD-A/T>
14. SHIFT LEVER BOOT <M/T>
15. TRANSFER LEVER BOOT <4WD-A/T>
16. CONSOLE PANEL
17. BOX

MT7029700388000X

Fig. 15 Floor console removal. Montero Sport

then remove floor console in sequence, **Fig. 15.**

2. Remove instrument panel as outlined under "Dash Panel Service" in the "Unit Repair" section.
3. Remove heater unit in sequence, **Fig. 16.**
4. Reverse procedure to install.

Rear

Refer to "Blower Motor, Replace" for rear heater core replacement.

PICKUP

1. Place temperature control lever in extreme right position.
2. Loosen radiator drain plug and drain cooling system into appropriate container.
3. Remove air filter, then remove hose clamps and disconnect heater hoses from heater core.
4. Remove dash panel as outlined under "Dash Panel Service" in the "Unit Repair" section.
5. Remove heater duct, then the center ventilator duct.
6. Remove defroster duct, then the center reinforcement.
7. Remove heater unit and grommet.
8. Separate heater core from heater unit.
9. Remove hose cover, joint hose clamp,

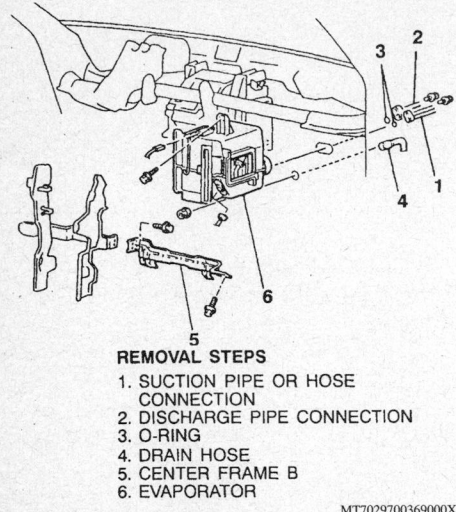

REMOVAL STEPS
1. SUCTION PIPE OR HOSE CONNECTION
2. DISCHARGE PIPE CONNECTION
3. O-RING
4. DRAIN HOSE
5. CENTER FRAME B
6. EVAPORATOR

MT7029700369000X

Fig. 17 Evaporator replacement. Montero Sport

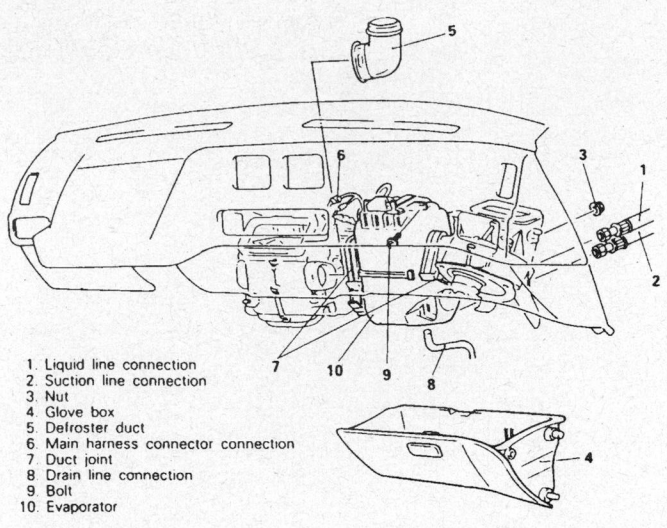

1. Liquid line connection
2. Suction line connection
3. Nut
4. Glove box
5. Defroster duct
6. Main harness connector connection
7. Duct joint
8. Drain line connection
9. Bolt
10. Evaporator

MT7029100109000X

Fig. 18 Evaporator core replacement. Pickup

joint hose and support plate from end of heater core.
10. Reverse procedure to install.

EVAPORATOR CORE

REPLACE

MONTERO

1. Recover refrigerant as outlined under "Air Conditioning," then disconnect evaporator inlet pipe and suction hose. Plug openings to prevent contamination.
2. Remove drain hose.
3. Remove glove compartment stopper, then the glove compartment.
4. Remove speaker grille.

5. Remove lower frame and foot shower duct.
6. Disconnect air conditioner wiring harness.
7. Remove evaporator unit.
8. Remove air conditioner control unit.
9. Remove evaporator case halves retaining screws and clips.
10. Separate case halves, then remove air thermo sensor, air inlet sensor and expansion valve.
11. Remove high/low pressure extension pipe.
12. Remove evaporator assembly.
13. Reverse procedure to install.

MONTERO SPORT

1. Recover refrigerant as outlined under

"Air Conditioning."
2. Remove under cover and glove box.
3. Remove evaporator in sequence, **Fig. 17**.
4. Reverse procedure to install.

PICKUP

1. Recover refrigerant as outlined under "Air Conditioning," then disconnect evaporator inlet pipe and suction hose. Plug openings to prevent contamination.
2. Remove nut, glove compartment and defroster duct, **Fig. 18**.
3. Disconnect main harness connector, duct joint and drain hose.
4. Remove bolt, then the evaporator.
5. Reverse procedure to install.

2.4L Engine

NOTE: Refer To "Computer Relearn Procedures" Located In The Front Of This Manual For Computer Relearn Procedures.

NOTE: On Air Bag Equipped Models, Refer To "Air Bag System Precautions" Located In The Front Of This Manual For System Disarming & Arming Procedures.

NOTE: For Procedures Not Found In This Section, Refer To The Engine Section Of The "Mitsubishi Expo" Chapter.

INDEX

PRECAUTIONS

AIR BAG SYSTEMS

Refer to "Air Bag System Precautions" in the front of this manual for system disarming and arming procedures.

FUEL SYSTEM PRESSURE RELIEF

1. Disconnect fuel pump harness connector at the fuel tank rear side. **Cover fuel pipe line with rag after relieving pressure as certain pressure may still remain.**
2. Start engine and let idle until engine stops by itself, then turn ignition switch to Off. **Failure to relieve fuel system pressure prior to disconnecting fuel system components may cause fire or personal injury.**
3. Connect fuel pump harness connector.
4. After repairs have been completed, connect positive battery terminal to fuel pump drive terminal and the negative terminal to the chassis. Ensure fuel pump operates at this time.

BATTERY GROUND CABLE

Prior to service, disconnect battery ground cable and isolate as required.

COMPRESSION PRESSURE

Compression pressure should be a minimum 127 psi on 1996 engines and 145 psi on 1997–99 engines with a maximum difference of 14 psi between cylinders.

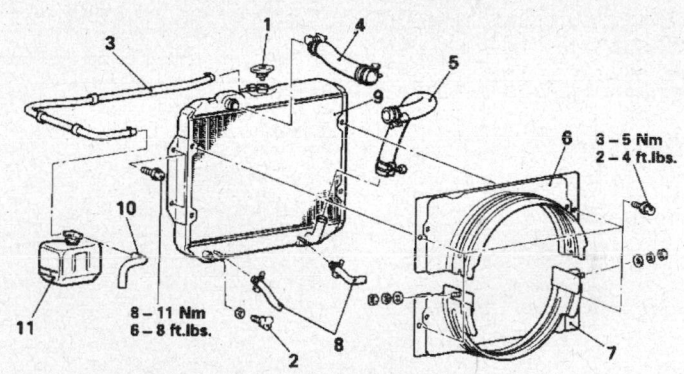

Removal steps
1. Radiator cap
2. Drain plug
3. Overflow hose
4. Radiator upper hose
5. Radiator lower hose
6. Radiator upper shroud
7. Radiator lower shroud
8. Automatic transmission oil cooler hose connection <A/T>
9. Radiator
10. Overflow tube
11. Reserve tank

MTI069100291000X

Fig. 1   Radiator assembly. Pickup

ENGINE

REPLACE

1. Relieve fuel system pressure as outlined under "Precautions."
2. Scribe reference marks between hood and hood hinges, then remove hood.
3. Drain cooling system into an appropriate container as follows:
   a. Place temperature control lever in Hot position.
   b. Carefully remove radiator cap.
   c. Remove radiator drain plug.
4. Remove transmission assembly.
5. Remove radiator components in order as shown, **Figs. 1 and 2,** noting the following:
   a. Prior to removing radiator hoses, mark hose clamps in relation to hoses for installation reference.
   b. After disconnecting transmission cooler lines on models equipped with automatic transmission, plug or cover ends of lines to prevent entry of dirt or foreign material.
6. Remove engine components in order as shown, **Figs. 3 and 4,** noting the following:
   a. Remove A/C compressor from bracket with hoses attached, then support compressor pump aside

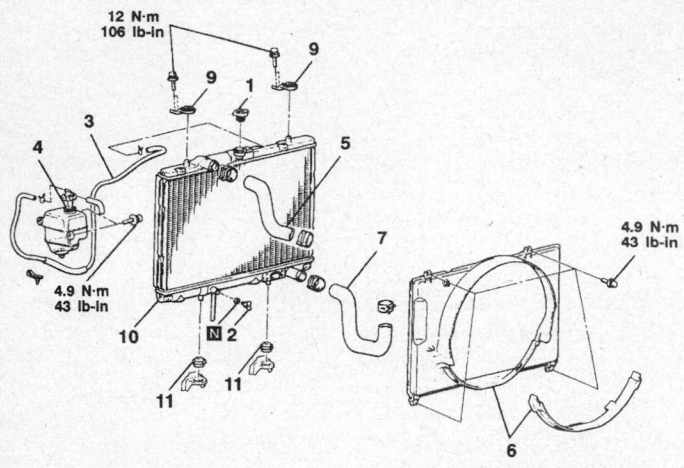

1. RADIATOR CAP
2. DRAIN PLUG
3. RUBBER HOSE CONNECTION
4. RESERVE TANK ASSEMBLY
5. RADIATOR UPPER HOSE
6. SHROUD ASSEMBLY
7. RADIATOR LOWER HOSE
9. RADIATOR SUPPORT
10. RADIATOR
11. LOWER INSULATOR

MT1069700488000X

Fig. 2 Radiator assembly. Montero Sport

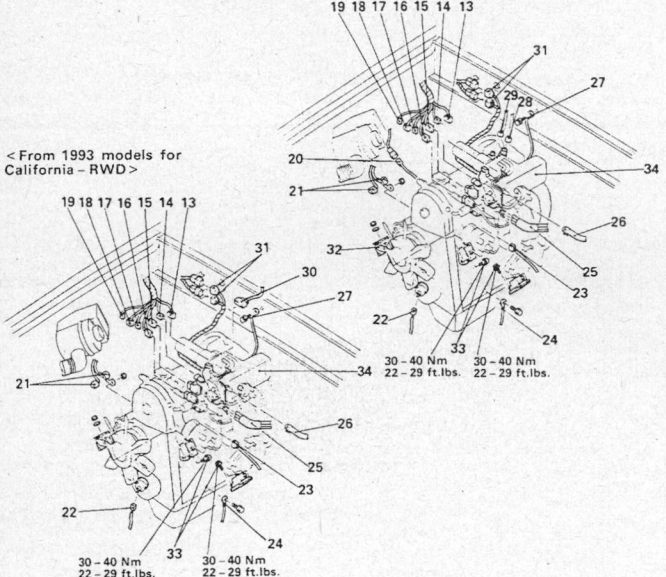

< From 1993 models for California – RWD >

Removal steps

13. Throttle position sensor connector
14. Ignition coil connector
15. Power transistor connector
16. EGR temperature sensor connector
17. Engine coolant temperature gauge unit connector
18. Engine coolant temperature sensor connector
19. Thermal switch connector <A/T>
20. Oxygen sensor connector
21. Generator connector
22. Oil pressure gauge unit connector
23. Air conditioning engine coolant temperature switch connector <A/C>
24. Ground cable connection
25. Emission control vacuum hose connection
26. Brake booster vacuum hose connection
27. Ground cable connection
28. Idle speed control motor connector
29. Idle speed control motor position sensor connector
30. Idle air control motor connector
31. Control wiring harness connector
32. Heat protector
33. Engine mounting bolt
34. Engine assembly

MT1069100292020X

Fig. 3 Engine assembly (Part 2 of 2). Pickup

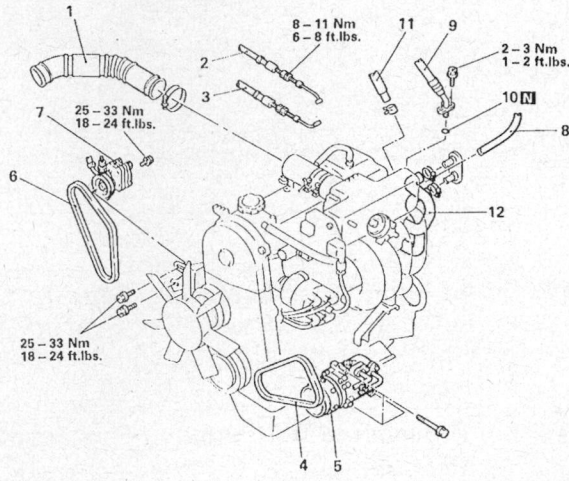

Removal Steps

1. Air cleaner duct
2. Accelerator cable connection
3. Throttle control cable connection

<A/T>
4. Air conditioning compressor drive belt

5. Compressor

6. Power steering oil pump drive belt
7. Power steering oil pump
8. Cruise control vacuum hose connection <Vehicles with cruise control>
9. High pressure fuel hose connection
10. O-ring
11. Fuel return hose connection
12. Water hose connection

MT1069100292010X

Fig. 3 Engine assembly (Part 1 of 2). Pickup

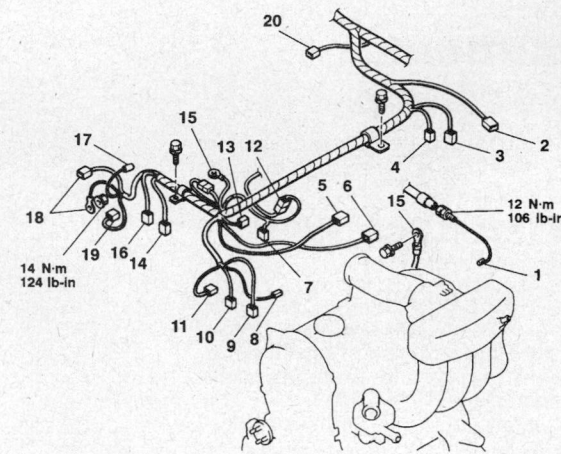

1. ACCELERATOR CABLE CONNECTION
2. MANIFOLD DIFFERENTIAL PRESSURE SENSOR CONNECTOR <FEDERAL>
3. THROTTLE POSITION SENSOR CONNECTOR
4. IDLE AIR CONTROL MOTOR CONNECTOR
5. EGR SOLENOID CONNECTOR <FEDERAL>
6. EVAPORATIVE EMISSION PURGE SOLENOID
7. CAPACITOR
8. MAGNETIC CLUTCH AND REFRIGERANT TEMPERATURE SWITCH CONNECTOR
9. IGNITION POWER TRANSISTOR CONNECTOR
10. IGNITION COIL CONNECTOR
11. ENGINE COOLANT TEMPERATURE SENSOR CONNECTOR
12. FRONT WIRING HARNESS AND INJECTION WIRING HARNESS COMBINATION
13. CRANKSHAFT POSITION SENSOR
14. DISTRIBUTOR SIGNAL GENERATOR
15. GROUND CABLE
16. HEATED OXYGEN SENSOR CONNECTOR <CALIFORNIA>
17. POWER STEERING PRESSURE SWITCH CONNECTOR
18. GENERATOR CONNECTOR
19. OIL PRESSURE SWITCH CONNECTOR
20. ENGINE COOLANT TEMPERATURE GAUGE UNIT CONNECTOR

MT1069700489010X

Fig. 4 Engine assembly (Part 1 of 2). Montero Sport

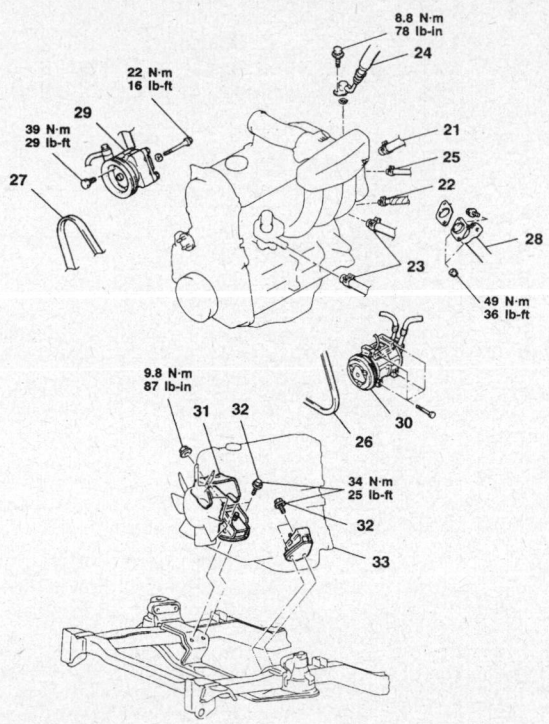

21. BRAKE BOOSTER VACUUM HOSE CONNECTION
22. VACUUM HOSE CONNECTION
23. HEATER HOSE CONNECTION
24. HIGH-PRESSURE FUEL HOSE CONNECTION
25. FUEL RETURN HOSE CONNECTION
26. DRIVE BELT (FOR A/C)
27. DRIVE BELT (FOR POWER STEERING)
28. FRONT EXHAUST PIPE CONNECTION
29. POWER STEERING OIL PUMP ASSEMBLY
30. A/C COMPRESSOR ASSEMBLY
31. HEAT PROTECTOR
32. ENGINE SUPPORT FRONT INSULATOR ATTACHING BOLT
33. ENGINE ASSEMBLY

MT1069700489020X

Fig. 4 Engine assembly (Part 2 of 2). Montero Sport

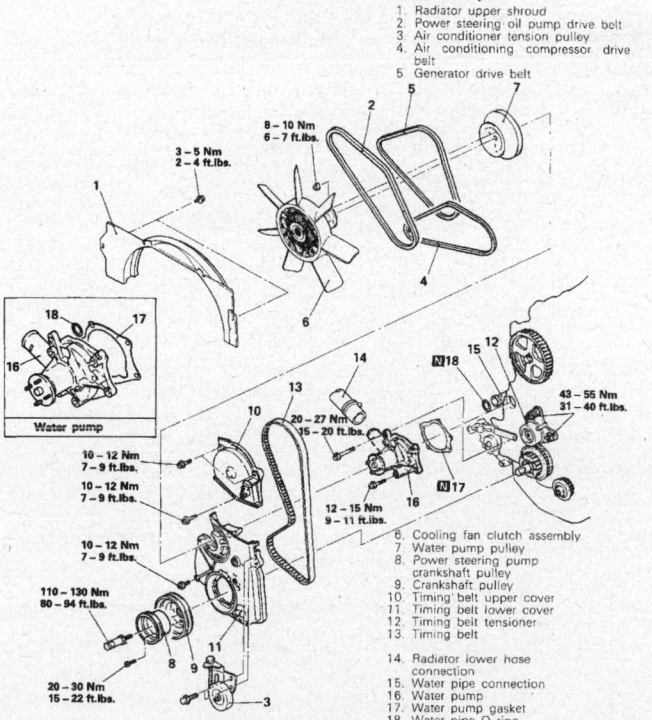

Removal steps
1. Radiator upper shroud
2. Power steering oil pump drive belt
3. Air conditioner tension pulley
4. Air conditioning compressor drive belt
5. Generator drive belt

6. Cooling fan clutch assembly
7. Water pump pulley
8. Power steering pump crankshaft pulley
9. Crankshaft pulley
10. Timing belt upper cover
11. Timing belt lower cover
12. Timing belt tensioner
13. Timing belt
14. Radiator lower hose connection
15. Water pipe connection
16. Water pump
17. Water pump gasket
18. Water pipe O-ring

MT1089500087000X

Fig. 6 Water pump assembly

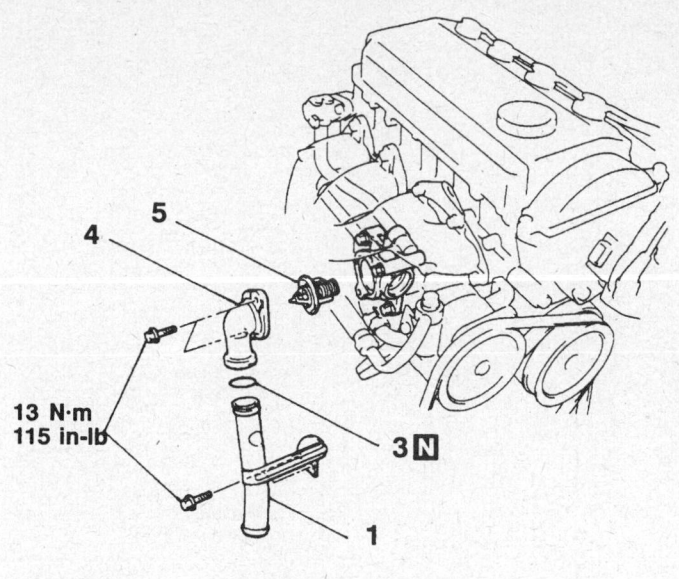

1. RADIATOR LOWER PIPE ASSEMBLY
3. O-RING
4. WATER INLET FITTING
5. THERMOSTAT

MT1089900132000X

Fig. 5 Thermostat removal

with a piece of wire.
b. Remove power steering pump from bracket with hoses attached, then secure pump aside with a piece of wire.
c. When disconnecting high pressure fuel hose, cover fuel pipe line with a shop towel. **Some residual fuel pressure may be present.**
d. Ensure all cables, connectors and hoses are disconnected, then remove engine from engine compartment.
7. Reverse procedure to install.

BELT TENSION DATA

Component	Deflection, Inch①
PICKUP	
Water Pump	0.27–0.39
Power Steering Pump	0.23–0.35
A/C Compressor	0.33–0.39
MONTERO SPORT	
A/C Compressor	0.24–0.26
Alternator	0.28–0.35
Power Steering	0.22–0.30

① — With 22 lbs. of force is applied.

COOLING SYSTEM BLEED

These engines do not require a specified

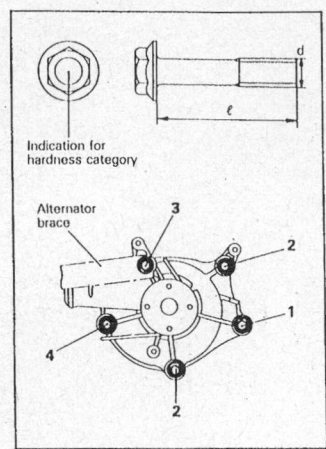

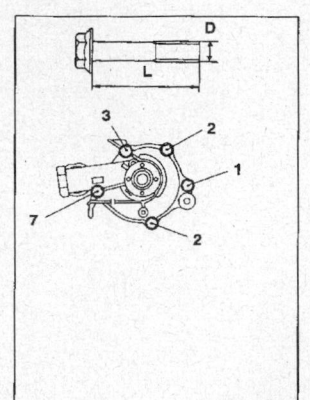

No.	Hardness category (Head mark)	d × ℓ mm (in.)	Torque Nm (ft.lbs.)
1	4T	8×20 (.31×.79)	12 – 15 (9 – 11)
2	4T	8×30 (.31×1.18)	12 – 15 (9 – 11)
3	7T	8×65 (.31×2.26)	20 – 27 (15 – 20)
4	4T	8×40 (.31×1.57)	12 – 15 (9 – 11)

MT1069100293000X

Fig. 7 Water pump attaching bolts. 1996

No.	HARDNESS CATEGORY (HEAD MARK)	BOLT DIAMETER × LENGTH mm (in)
1	4T	8 × 14 (0.3 × 0.6)
2		8 × 22 (0.3 × 0.9)
3		8 × 28 (0.3 × 1.1)
7		

MT1069800545000X

Fig. 8 Water pump attaching bolts. 1997-99

bleed procedure. After filling cooling system, run engine to operating temperature with radiator/pressure cap off. Air will then be automatically bled through cap opening.

THERMOSTAT
REPLACE

1. Drain cooling system into a appropriate container.
2. Remove thermostat as outlined in **Fig. 5.**
3. Reverse procedure to install, then ensure thermostat flange is correctly seated in the thermostat housing socket.

WATER PUMP
REPLACE

Remove water pump components in order as shown, **Fig.6,** noting the following:
1. Drain cooling system into appropriate container as follows:
   a. Place temperature control lever in Hot position.
   b. Carefully remove radiator cap.
   c. Remove radiator drain plug.
2. Prior to removing water pump drive belt, loosen water pump attaching bolts.
3. Remove timing belt covers and timing belts as outlined under " Timing Belt, Replace."
4. Reverse procedure to install, noting the following:
   a. Coat outer diameter of O-ring with water to ease installation.
   b. Refer to bolt chart, **Figs. 7 and 8,** when installing water pump attaching bolts.
   c. Install timing belts and timing belt covers.

FUEL PUMP
REPLACE
MONTERO SPORT

Refer to **Fig. 9,** for fuel pump replacement procedures.

PICKUP

1. Release fuel system pressure as outlined under " Precautions."
2. Drain fuel tank into a appropriate container.
3. Lower fuel tank using suitable jack.
4. Disconnect all electrical and hose connections.
5. Remove fuel pump/sending unit retaining nuts.
6. Remove fuel pump from fuel tank.
7. Reverse procedure to install, noting the following:
   a. Install check valve as shown, **Fig. 10.**
   b. Install overfill limiter valve with arrow pointing toward engine side fuel hose.
   c. Do not allow the main hose to become twisted when tightening.

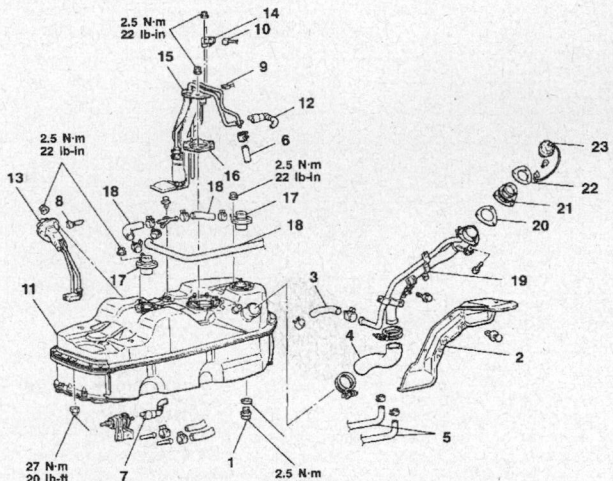

1. DRAIN PLUG
2. FUEL TANK FILTER TUBE PROTECTOR

FUEL TANK REMOVAL STEPS
3. LEVELING HOSE
4. FILLER HOSE
5. VAPOR HOSE CONNECTION (FUEL TANK FILLER TUBE SIDE)
6. RETURN HOSE CONNECTION (FUEL TANK SIDE)
7. HIGH-PRESSURE FUEL HOSE CONNECTION (FUEL LINE SIDE)
8. FUEL GAUGE UNIT CONNECTOR
9. FUEL PUMP CONNECTOR
10. FUEL TANK DIFFERENTIAL PRESSURE SENSOR CONNECTOR
11. FUEL TANK
12. HIGH-PRESSURE FUEL HOSE
13. FUEL GAUGE UNIT
14. FUEL TANK DIFFERENTIAL PRESSURE SENSOR
15. FUEL PUMP ASSEMBLY
16. PACKING
17. FUEL CUT-OFF VALVE
18. VAPOR HOSE

FUEL TANK FILLER TUBE REMOVAL STEPS
2. FUEL TANK FILLER TUBE PROTECTOR
3. LEVELING HOSE
4. FILLER HOSE
5. VAPOR HOSE CONNECTION (FUEL TANK FILLER TUBE SIDE)
19. FUEL TANK FILLER TUBE
20. PACKING
21. FUEL TANK FILLER TUBE EXTENSION
22. PACKING
23. FUEL TANK FILLER TUBE CAP

MT1029801308000X

Fig. 9 Fuel pump replacement. Montero Sport

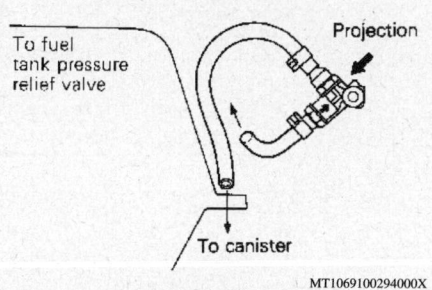

Fig. 10 Check valve installation. Pickup

FUEL FILTER
REPLACE

1. Release fuel system pressure as outlined under " Precautions."

2. Drain fuel tank into a appropriate container.
3. **On Montero Sport models,** press retainer in on high pressure line to release quick connect fitting.
4. **On Pickup models,** hold fuel filter with a wrench and remove eye bolt retaining fuel high pressure hose with an eye wrench, **Fig. 11.**
5. **On all models,** inspect hose and pipes for cracks, damage or clogging and replace as necessary.
6. Inspect evaporative emission canister for clogging and replace as necessary.
7. Inspect check valve and fuel filter for clogging or damage and replace as necessary.
8. Remove protector of fuel filter, then disconnect fuel filter mounting bolt.
9. Remove fuel filter and high pressure

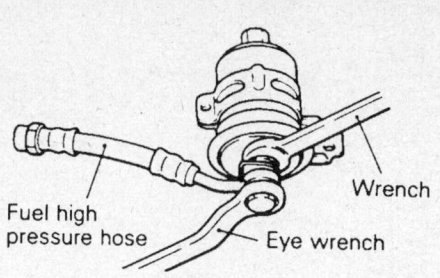

Fig. 11 Fuel filter replacement. Pickup

hose assembly.

TIGHTENING SPECIFICATIONS

Year	Component	Torque/ Ft. Lbs.
1996–99	Accelerator Cable Nut	72–96③
	Air Cleaner Bolt	14–22
	Air Intake Pipe	84–108③
	Camshaft Bearing Cap Bolts	②
	Camshaft Sprocket Bolt	58–72
	Clutch Hose To Tube	9–12
	Connecting Rod Cap Nuts	37–38
	Cooling Fan	84–108③
	Crankshaft Pulley Bolt	15–21
	Crankshaft Rear Oil Seal Case Bolts	84–108③
	Crankshaft Sprocket Bolt	80–94
	Cylinder Head Bolts	①
	Driveplate/Flywheel Bolt	94–101
	Engine Mount Bracket Bolt/Nut	36–47
	Engine Mounting Crossmember To Body	65–80
	Engine Mounting Crossmember To Strut Bar	65–90
	Engine Mount Insulator Nut (Large)	43–58
	Engine Mount Insulator Nut (Small)	22–29
	Engine Support Front Insulator To Engine	22–24
	Exhaust Pipe Support Bracket Bolt	22–30
	Front Case Bolts	15–19
	Front Engine Support Bracket Bolt	29-36
	Front Exhaust Pipe Clamp Bolt	14–22
	Front Exhaust Pipe To Exhaust Manifold	22–29
	Front Exhaust Pipe To Under Catalytic Converter	36–50
	Front Roll Stopper Bracket Bolt	29–36
	Front Roll Stopper Bracket Nut	36–47
	High Pressure Fuel Hose	12-24③
	Intake Manifold Stay Bolt	13–18
	Jet Valve	13–15
	Left Engine Support Bracket	29–36
	Lower Arm Ball Joint To Knuckle	43–52
	Main Bearing Cap Bolts	37–39
	Oil Filter Bracket Bolts	11–15

TIGHTENING
SPECIFICATIONS—Continued

Year	Component	Torque/ Ft. Lbs.
1996–99	Oil Pan Bolts	48–72 ③
	Oil Pan Drain Plug	26–32
	Oil Pressure Gauge Unit	72–96 ③
	Oil Pressure Switch	72–96 ③
	Oil Pump Cover Bolts	11–13
	Oil Pump Driven Gear Bolt	25–28
	Oil Pump Sprocket Bolt/Nut	36–43
	Oil Screen Bolts	11–15
	Power Steering Oil Pump Bracket	18–24
	Power Steering Oil Pump Lower Bolt	14–20
	Power Steering Oil Pump Upper Bolt	18–24
	Power Steering Pressure Hose To Oil Pump	29–36
	Propeller Shaft	36–43
	Radiator Upper Shroud	24–48 ③
	Rear Engine Insulator To Rear Engine Mounting Bracket	51–69
	Rear Roll Stopper Bracket Bolt	80–94
	Rear Roll Stopper Insulator Bolt	29–36
	Rear Roll Stopper Insulator Nut	22–29
	Relief Valve Plug	29–36
	Right Engine Support Bracket	29–36
	Right Silent Shaft Sprocket Bolt	25–28
	Rocker Arm Adjusting Nuts	72–84 ③
	Rocker Arm Shaft Bolts	14–15
	Rocker Cover Bolts	48–60 ③
	Silent Shaft Sprocket Bolt	31–35
	Strut Bar To Lower Arm	61–80
	Tensioner "B" Bolt	11–15
	Tensioner Spacer	32–39
	Tie Rod End To Knuckle	17–25
	Timing Belt Lower Cover Bolts	84–108 ③
	Timing Belt Tensioner Bolt	30–40
	Timing Belt Upper Cover Bolts	84–108 ③
	Transaxle Mount Bracket Bolt	29–36
	Transaxle Mount Insulator Nut	43–58
	Water Pump Pulley Bolt	72–84

① — Torque to 58 ft. lbs., completely loosen, torque to 15 ft. lbs. Tighten 90°, then an additional 90°.

② — 8 X 25 bolts, 15–19 ft. lbs.; 8 X 65 bolts, 14–15 ft. lbs.

③ — Inch lbs.

NOTE: Refer To "Computer Relearn Procedures" Located In The Front Of This Manual For Computer Relearn Procedures.

NOTE: On Air Bag Equipped Models, Refer To "Air Bag System Precautions" Located In The Front Of This Manual For System Disarming & Arming Procedures.

NOTE: For Procedures Not Found In This Section, Refer To The Engine Section of The "Mitsubishi 3000GT" Chapter.

INDEX

PRECAUTIONS

AIR BAG SYSTEMS

Refer to "Air Bag System Precautions" in the front of this manual for system disarming and arming procedures.

FUEL SYSTEM PRESSURE RELIEF

1. Remove carpet from cargo compartment, then remove bolts from floor cover.
2. Disconnect fuel pump electrical connection.
3. Start engine and let idle until all residual fuel is consumed, then turn ignition switch to Off position. **Failure to relieve fuel system pressure prior to disconnecting fuel system components may cause fire or personal injury.**
4. Connect fuel pump electrical connection.
5. Install cargo compartment floor cover and bolts then install carpet. **Torque** bolts to 9 ft. lbs.
6. After repairs have been completed, connect battery cable and ensure fuel pump operates properly.

BATTERY GROUND CABLE

Prior to service, disconnect battery ground cable and isolate as required.

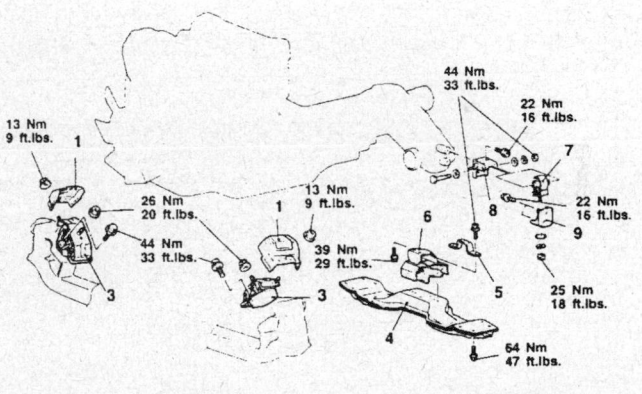

Removal steps of front engine mount

- Removal of Engine Assembly

1. Heat protector
2. Front insulator stopper
3. Engine support front insulator

Removal steps of rear engine mount

4. No. 2 crossmember
5. Stopper
6. Engine support rear insulator

Removal steps of transfer roll stopper

7. Transfer support insulator
8. Transfer mounting bracket
9. Transfer support bracket

MT1069500320000X

Fig. 1 Engine mount replacement. Montero w/manual transmission

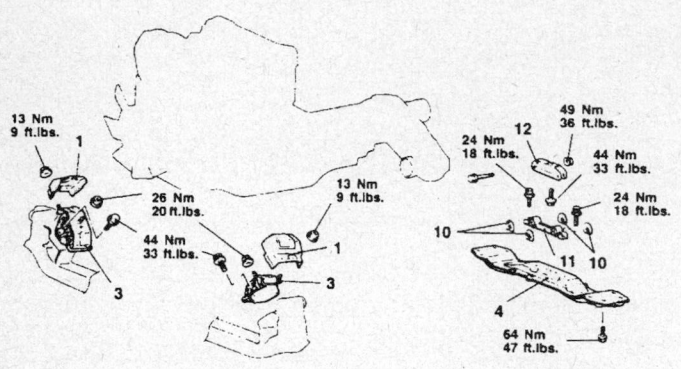

Removal steps of front engine mount

- Removal of Engine Assembly

1. Heat protector
3. Engine support front insulator

Removal steps of rear engine mount

4. No. 2 crossmember
10. Stopper
11. Engine support rear insulator
12. Engine support rear bracket

MT1069500321000X

Fig. 2 Engine mount replacement. Montero w/automatic transmission

REMOVAL STEPS
1. HEAT PROTECTOR
2. FRONT INSULATOR STOPPER
3. FRONT ENGINE SUPPORT INSULATOR

Caution
*: Indicates parts which should be initially tightened, and then fully tightened after placing the vehicle horizontally and loading the full weight of the engine on the vehicle body.

MT1069800546000X

Fig. 3 Engine mount replacement. Montero Sport

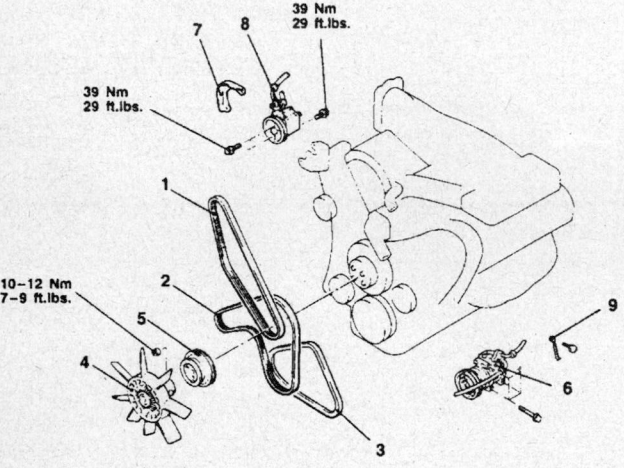

Removal Steps
1. Power steering drive belt
2. Generator drive belt
3. A/C drive belt
4. Cooling fan
5. Water pump pulley
6. A/C compressor
7. Cover
8. Power steering pump
9. Ground cable connection

MT1069500322010X

Fig. 4 Engine replacement (Part 1 of 2). Montero & Montero Sport

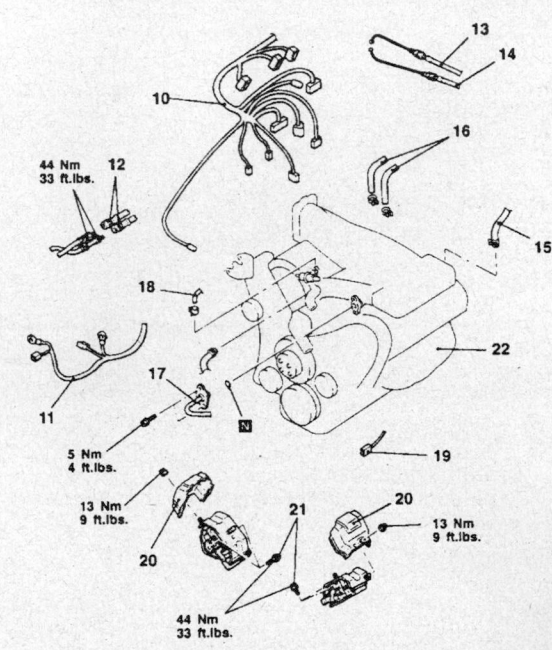

10. Engine control harness connection
11. Generator and starter harness connection
12. Engine oil cooler hose connection
13. Accelerator cable connection
14. Throttle cable connection
15. Brake booster vacuum hose connection
16. Heater hose connection
17. Fuel hose connection
18. Fuel return hose connection
19. Oil pressure switch harness connection
20. Heat protectors
21. Engine mounting bolt
22. Engine assembly

MT1069500322020X

Fig. 4 Engine replacement (Part 2 of 2). Montero & Montero Sport

COMPRESSION PRESSURE

Compression pressure should be a minimum 127 psi with a maximum difference of 14 psi between cylinders.

ENGINE MOUNT
REPLACE

1. Raise and support vehicle, then remove snow protection lower cover, undercover, skid plate, transfer case protector and cross shaft protector as required.

2. Lower vehicle, then remove engine mounts in numbered sequence shown, **Figs. 1 through 3.**
3. Reverse procedure to install. Tighten all bolts and nuts to specifications, **Figs. 1 through 3.**

ENGINE
REPLACE

Refer to **Figs. 4 and 5,** when replacing engine.
1. Relieve fuel system pressure as outlined under " Precautions."

2. Scribe hood hinge locations and remove hood.
3. Drain engine coolant, engine oil, transfer case fluid and transmission oil into appropriate containers.
4. **On models equipped with manual transmission,** drain clutch hydraulic fluid into appropriate containers.
5. **On models equipped with A/C,** discharge refrigerant into appropriate container.
6. **On all models,** raise and support vehicle, then remove snow protection undercover, skid plate, transfer case protector and cross shaft protector.

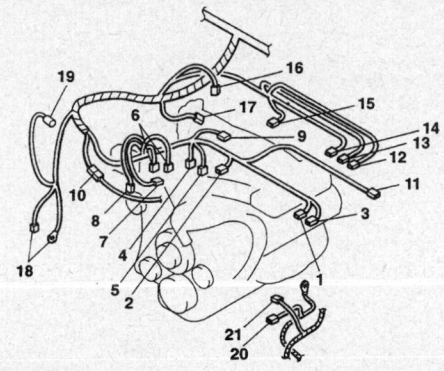

REMOVAL STEPS
1. IGNITION COIL 1 CONNECTOR
2. IGNITION COIL 2 CONNECTOR
3. IGNITION COIL 3 CONNECTOR
4. CAMSHAFT POSITION SENSOR CONNECTOR
5. CRANKSHAFT POSITION SENSOR CONNECTOR
6. IGNITION POWER TRANSISTOR CONNECTOR
7. CAPACITOR CONNECTOR
8. ENGINE COOLANT TEMPERATURE SENSOR CONNECTOR
9. ENGINE COOLANT TEMPERATURE GAUGE UNIT CONNECTOR
10. FRONT WIRING HARNESS AND INJECTION WIRING HARNESS COMBINATION CONNECTOR
11. MANIFOLD DIFFERENTIAL PRESSURE SENSOR <FEDERAL>
12. EGR SOLENOID CONNECTOR <FEDERAL>
13. EVAPORATIVE EMISSION PURGE SOLENOID CONNECTOR
14. LEFT BANK HEATED OXYGEN SENSOR CONNECTOR (FRONT) <CALIFORNIA>
15. RIGHT BANK HEATED OXYGEN SENSOR CONNECTOR (FRONT) <CALIFORNIA>
16. THROTTLE POSITION SENSOR CONNECTOR
17. IDLE AIR CONTROL MOTOR CONNECTOR
18. GENERATOR CONNECTOR
19. POWER STEERING PRESSURE SWITCH CONNECTOR
20. MAGNETIC CLUTCH AND REFRIGERANT TEMPERATURE SWITCH CONNECTOR
21. OIL PRESSURE SWITCH CONNECTOR

MT1069800547010X

Fig. 5 Engine replacement (Part 1 of 2). Montero Sport

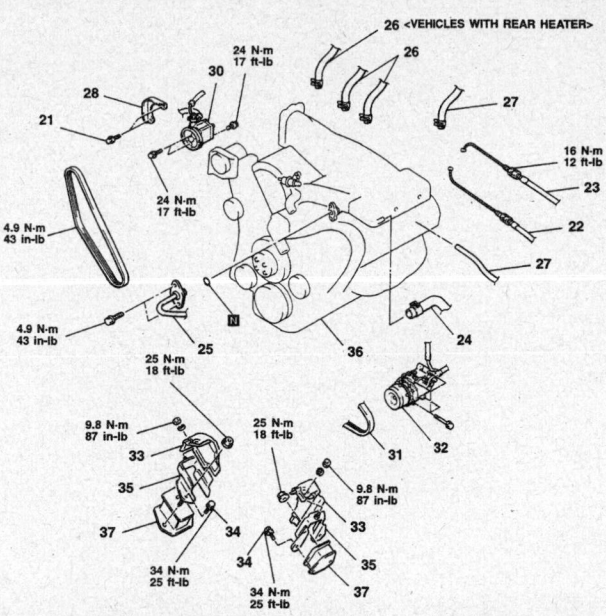

22. ACCELERATOR CABLE CONNECTION
23. THROTTLE CABLE CONNECTION
24. FUEL RETURN HOSE CONNECTION
25. HIGH-PRESSURE FUEL HOSE CONNECTION
26. HEATER HOSE CONNECTION
27. VACUUM HOSE CONNECTION
28. POWER STEERING DRIVE BELT COVER
29. DRIVE BELT (FOR POWER STEERING)
30. POWER STEERING OIL PUMP ASSEMBLY
31. DRIVE BELT (FOR A/C)
32. A/C COMPRESSOR ASSEMBLY
33. HEAT PROTECTOR
34. ENGINE SUPPORT FRONT INSULATOR ATTACHING BOLT
35. ENGINE SUPPORT FRONT INSULATOR STOPPER
36. ENGINE ASSEMBLY
37. ENGINE SUPPORT FRONT INSULATOR

MT1069800547020X

Fig. 5 Engine replacement (Part 2 of 2). Montero Sport

14. Remove A/C compressor and position aside. **Leave compressor lines connected.**
15. Disconnect oil cooler hoses from engine.
16. Remove power steering pump, if equipped and position aside. **Leave pressure and return hoses connected.**
17. Disconnect fuel high pressure hose. **Cover fuel pipe line with a rag as fuel pressure may remain.**
18. Disconnect fuel return hose.
19. Disconnect vacuum hose.
20. Disconnect water hoses from engine.
21. Disconnect electrical wiring and electrical sensors.
22. Remove ignition coil and power transistor assembly.
23. Disconnect purge hose and brake booster hose.
24. Disconnect accelerator cable, bracket, and cruise control cable, if equipped.
25. Remove heat protector, then the engine mounting bolts.
26. Connect suitable engine lifting equipment, ensure all cables, hoses and harness connectors are positioned aside, then remove engine assembly.
27. Reverse procedure to install.

INTAKE MANIFOLD
REPLACE

1. Relieve fuel system pressure as outlined under "Precautions," then drain

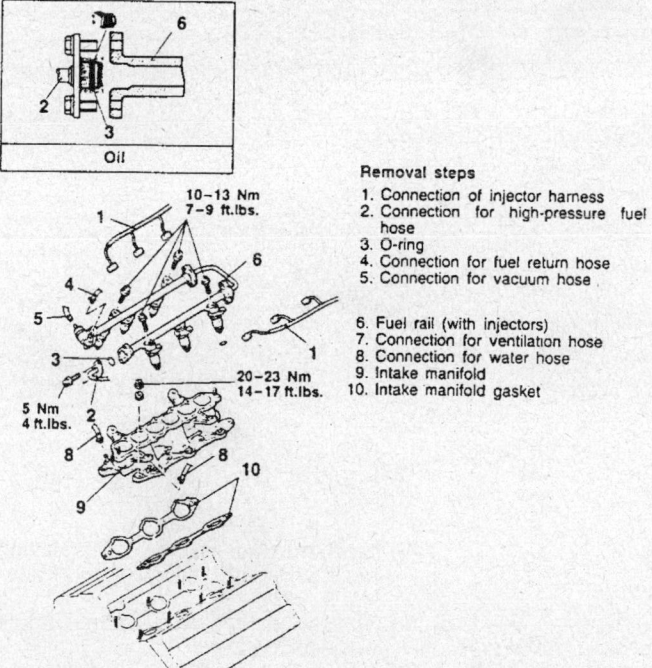

Removal steps
1. Connection of injector harness
2. Connection for high-pressure fuel hose
3. O-ring
4. Connection for fuel return hose
5. Connection for vacuum hose
6. Fuel rail (with injectors)
7. Connection for ventilation hose
8. Connection for water hose
9. Intake manifold
10. Intake manifold gasket

MT1059500043000X

Fig. 6 Intake manifold replacement

7. Remove transmission and transfer case assembly. Refer to "Transmission, Replace" in appropriate transmission section.
8. Disconnect radiator upper and lower hoses and overflow tube, then remove fan shroud.
9. **On models equipped with automatic transmission,** remove oil cooler hose and tube assemblies.
10. **On all models,** remove radiator and bushings.
11. Disconnect front exhaust pipe from engine.
12. Remove air cleaner duct.
13. Remove engine drive belts.

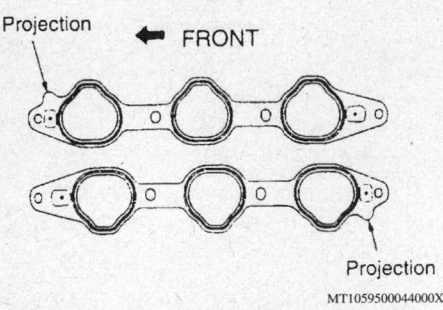

Fig. 7 Intake manifold gasket installation

MT1059500044000X

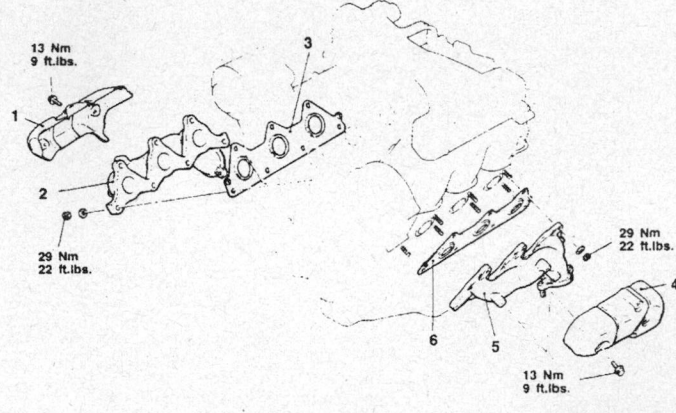

Removal steps (Right)
- Air duct and air cleaner cover
1. Heat protector (R.H.)
2. Exhaust manifold (R.H.)
3. Gasket

Removal steps (Left)
- Battery and battery tray
4. Heat protector (L.H.)
5. Exhaust manifold (L.H.)
6. Gasket

MT1079500020000X

Fig. 8 Exhaust manifold replacement

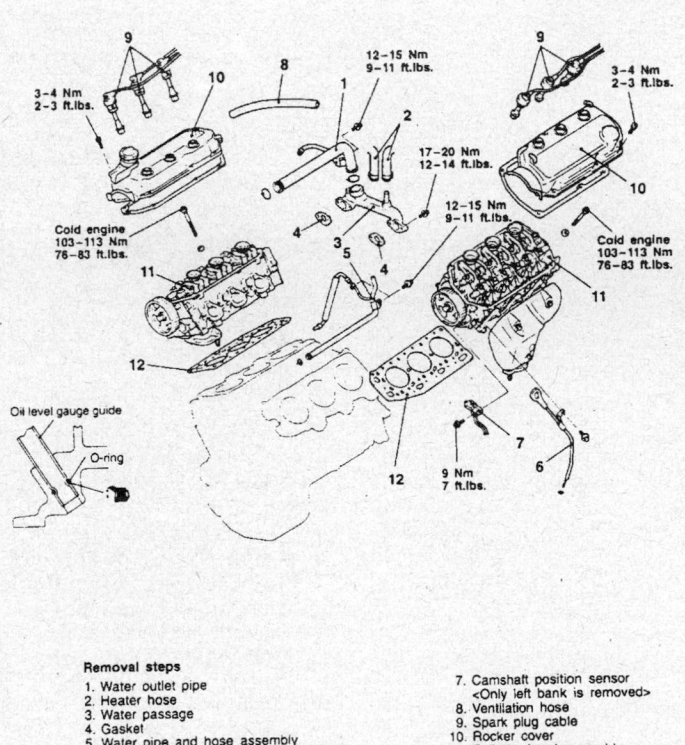

Removal steps
1. Water outlet pipe
2. Heater hose
3. Water passage
4. Gasket
5. Water pipe and hose assembly
6. Oil level gage guide
   <Only left bank is removed>
7. Camshaft position sensor
   <Only left bank is removed>
8. Ventilation hose
9. Spark plug cable
10. Rocker cover
11. Cylinder head assembly
12. Cylinder head gasket

MT1069500329000X

Fig. 9 Cylinder head replacement

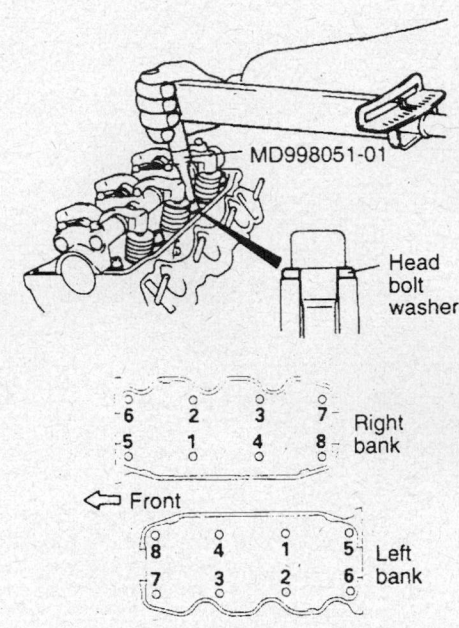

MT1069500330000X

Fig. 10 Cylinder head bolt sequence

engine coolant into a suitable container.

2. Remove intake manifold plenum, then the manifold in numbered sequence as shown, **Fig. 6.**

3. Reverse procedure to install, noting the following:
   a. Install intake manifold gaskets as shown, **Fig. 7.**
   b. When installing intake manifold mounting nuts, first **torque** right bank nuts to 5 ft. lbs., then the left bank nuts to 14–17 ft. lbs. Finally, **torque** right bank nuts to 14–17 ft. lbs.

EXHAUST MANIFOLD
REPLACE

1. Relieve fuel system pressure as outlined under " Precautions."
2. **On Federal models,** remove front exhaust pipe.
3. **On California models,** remove warm up three way catalytic converter.

4. **On all models,** remove exhaust manifold in numbered sequence as shown, **Fig. 8.**
5. Reverse procedure to install. Tighten to specifications.

CYLINDER HEAD
REPLACE

Refer to **Fig. 9,** when replacing the cylinder head noting the following:
1. Drain engine coolant into suitable container, then remove timing belt & intake manifold.
2. Remove cylinder head bolts in three steps in sequence shown in **Fig. 10,** using head bolt replacement tool No. MD998051-01, or equivalent.

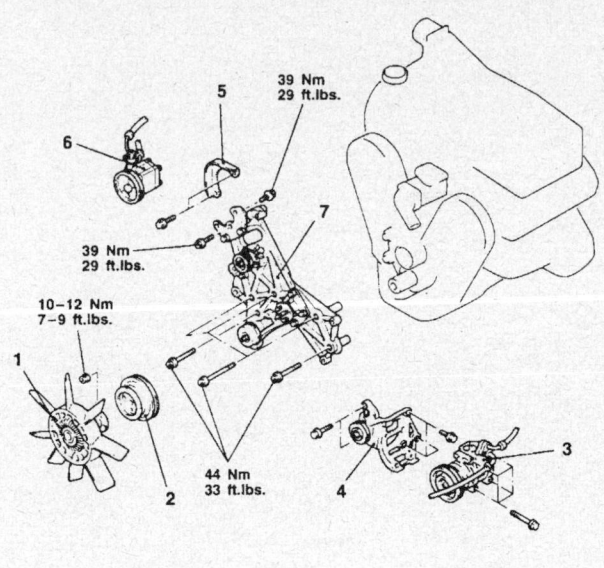

Removal steps
1. Cooling fan clutch assembly
2. Water pump pulley
3. Compressor <A/C>
4. Compressor bracket <A/C>
5. Cover
6. Power steering oil pump
7. Accessory mount

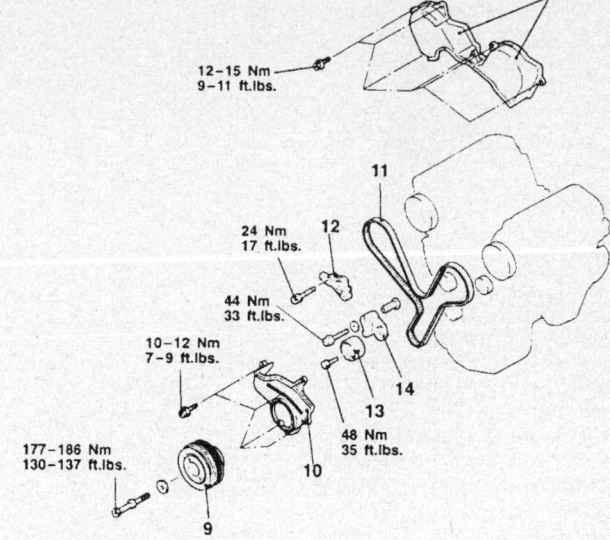

8. Timing belt upper cover
9. Crankshaft pulley
10. Timing belt lower cover
11. Timing belt
12. Auto tensioner
13. Tension pulley
14. Tension arm assembly

MT1069500325020X

Fig. 11   Timing belt replacement (Part 2 of 2)

3. Reverse procedure to install, noting the following:
   a. When installing cylinder head gasket, degrease gasket mounting surface, then lay gasket on cylinder block with ID mark at front top.
   b. **Torque** cylinder head bolts to 76–83 ft. lbs., in three steps in sequence shown in **Fig. 10,** using head bolt replacement tool No. MD998051-01, or equivalent.
   c. Rinse mounting location of water pipe O-ring and water pipe with water then install. **Do not apply oil or grease to O-ring. Insert water pipe until its end bottoms.**
   d. Bend tabs of water passage gasket onto water passage, then install. Ensure gasket does not slip.

VALVE ADJUSTMENT

This engine uses automatic valve lash adjusters. No valve adjustment is required.

TIMING BELT
REPLACE

With timing belt removed, avoid turning the camshaft or crankshaft. If movement is required, exercise extreme caution to avoid valve damage caused by piston contact,
1. Drain engine coolant into suitable container.
2. Remove timing belt in numbered sequence as shown, **Fig. 11,** noting the following:
   a. When removing A/C compressor

and power steering pump, leave hoses attached and support aside.
   b. Use pulley remover tool No. MB990767-01, or equivalent, to remove crankshaft pulley.
   c. Loosen timing belt tensioner bolt, then rotate tensioner counterclockwise.
   d. Remove timing belt. **Ensure direction of normal rotation is marked on belt if it is to be reused.**

Fig. 12   Timing marks alignment

MT1069500326000X

3. Reverse procedure to install, noting the following:
   a. If auto tensioner rod is fully extended, gently push rod into cylinder by clamping tensioner assembly in a soft jawed vise until set hole in rod aligns with hole in cylinder wall, then insert a stiff wire through set hole to keep rod in place.
   b. Align timing marks of camshaft sprockets and crankshaft sprocket to bring No. 1 cylinder to TDC as shown in **Fig. 12.**
   c. Route timing belt over crankshaft sprocket, idler pulley and LH side camshaft sprocket, then route timing belt over water pump pulley, RH side camshaft sprocket and timing belt tensioner. **RH side camshaft sprocket turns easily due to spring force applied and may cause personal injury if fingers are caught.**
   d. Turn RH side camshaft sprocket counterclockwise until tension side of timing belt is firmly stretched, then ensure all timing marks are aligned.
   e. Use tool No. MD998767, or equivalent, to push the tension pulley into timing belt, then temporarily tighten tensioner bolt.
   f. Using tool No. MD998769, or equivalent, rotate crankshaft ¼ turn clockwise, then turn crankshaft again until timing marks are aligned.
   g. Loosen tensioner bolt and apply 3.3 ft. lbs. of **torque** to timing belt, then tighten tensioner bolt.
   h. Remove setting wire from auto tensioner, then rotate crankshaft two turns and ensure timing marks are aligned.

i. Wait five minutes and measure auto tensioner push rod protrusion. If protrusion is not 0.15–0.20 inch, repeat steps "f" through "i."

CRANKSHAFT SEAL
REPLACE
FRONT

1. Remove timing belt as outlined under "Timing Belt, Replace," then remove crankshaft sprocket, position sensor, sensing blade and spacer.
2. Remove key from keyway, then separate oil seal from case as follows:
   a. Cut out a small portion of crankshaft oil seal lip.
   b. Cover tip of a suitable screwdriver with a cloth, then insert into seal cutout and pry away from oil pump case.
3. Reverse procedure to install. Drive seal in until flush with surface of oil pump case using seal installation tool No. MD998717, or equivalent.

REAR

1. Remove transmission assembly, then the outer adapter plate and driveplate.
2. Remove driveplate to output flange adapter, then remove oil seal from engine as follows:
   a. Cut out a small portion of crankshaft oil seal lip.
   b. Cover tip of a suitable screwdriver with a cloth, then insert into seal cutout and pry away from engine.
3. Reverse procedure to install. Drive seal in using seal installation tool No. MD998718-01, or equivalent.

OIL PAN
REPLACE

Refer to "Oil Pan, Replace" in the 3.5L engine section.

BELT TENSION DATA

Component	Deflection, Inch①	
	New	Used ②
MONTERO		
Alternator③	.22–.33	.31–.35
Power Steering Pump	.37–.45	.45–.53
MONTERO SPORT		
Alternator ④	.22–.29	.31–.35
Power Steering Pump	.44–.52	.56–.64
PICKUP		
A/C Compressor	—	.33–.39
Power Steering Pump	—	.23–.35
Water Pump	.26–.32	.32–.39

① — With 22 lbs. of force applied.
② — Used 5 minutes or more.
③ — Measured between water pump pulley & alternator.
④ — Measure between alternator pulley & cooling fan pulley.

Fig. 13 Water pump replacement

Removal steps <3.0L – 12VALVE engine>

1. Radiator hose
2. Water hose
3. Water inlet fitting
4. Water inlet fitting gasket
11. Tensioner bracket stay
15. Water pump
16. Water pump gasket
17. O-ring

Removal steps <3.0L-24VALVE engines>

• Thermostat
1. Radiator hose
2. Water hose
5. Water outlet fitting bracket
6. Water outlet fitting
7. O-ring
8. Gasket
9. Thermostat case
10. Gasket
12. Water pump bracket
15. Water pump
16. Water pump gasket
17. O-ring

COOLING SYSTEM BLEED

This engine does not require a specified bleed procedure. After filling cooling system, run engine to operating temperature with radiator/pressure cap off. Air will then be automatically bled through cap opening.

THERMOSTAT
REPLACE

1. Drain cooling system into appropriate container.
2. Disconnect radiator hose from thermostat housing.
3. Remove thermostat housing retaining bolts, then thermostat housing and thermostat.
4. Reverse procedure to install.

WATER PUMP
REPLACE

Remove water pump in numbered sequence as shown in **Fig. 13,** noting the following:
1. Drain cooling system into appropriate container.
2. Relieve fuel system pressure as outlined under " Precautions."
3. Reverse procedure to install, noting the following:
   a. Coat O-ring with water to ease installation.
   b. Tighten water pump attaching bolts to specifications.

RADIATOR
REPLACE

1. Drain engine coolant into suitable container, then remove engine under cover.
2. Remove air cleaner case.
3. Remove transmission oil cooler hose.
4. Remove radiator upper hose and radiator shroud, over flow hose and reserve tank.
5. Remove radiator lower hose, then radiator.
6. Reverse procedure to install.

FUEL PUMP
REPLACE
MONTERO & MONTERO SPORT

1. Remove drain plug from fuel tank and drain fuel into suitable container, then remove cargo compartment carpet.
2. Release fuel system pressure as outlined under " Precautions."
3. Remove floor cover, then packing.
4. Disconnect fuel pump electrical connection.
5. Disconnect high pressure fuel hose at body side main pipe connection, then at pump side connection.
6. Disconnect fuel return hose connection.

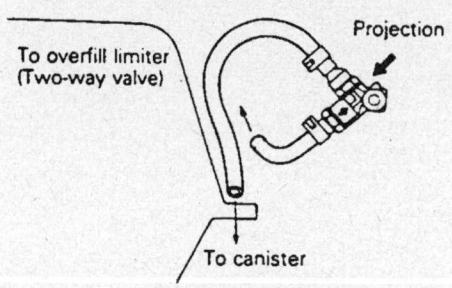

Fig. 14 Check valve installation. Pickup

7. Remove fuel pump assembly.
8. Reverse procedure to install.

PICKUP

1. Release fuel system pressure as outlined under " Precautions."
2. Drain fuel tank into a suitable container.
3. Lower fuel tank using suitable jack.
4. Disconnect all electrical and hose connections.

5. Remove fuel pump/sending unit retaining nuts.
6. Remove fuel pump from fuel tank.
7. Reverse procedure to install, noting the following:
   a. Install check valve as shown, **Fig. 14.**
   b. Install overfill limiter valve with arrow pointing toward engine side fuel hose.
   c. Do not allow the main hose to become twisted when tightening.

FUEL FILTER
REPLACE

1. Release fuel system pressure as outlined under " Precautions."
2. Drain fuel tank into a suitable container.
3. **On Montero & Pickup models,** hold fuel filter with a wrench and remove eye bolt retaining fuel high pressure hose with an eye wrench, **Fig. 15.**
4. **On Montero Sport models,** press retainer in on high pressure fuel line quick connect fitting to release.
5. **On all models,** inspect hose and pipes

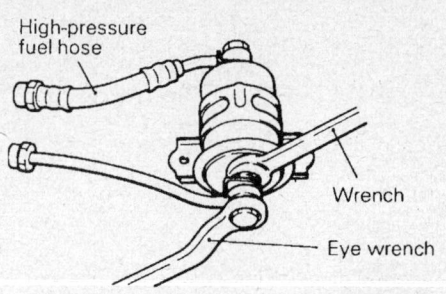

Fig. 15 Fuel filter replacement

for cracks, damage or clogging and replace as necessary.
6. Inspect evaporative emission canister for clogging and replace as necessary.
7. Inspect check valve and fuel filter for clogging or damage and replace as necessary.
8. Remove protector of fuel filter, then disconnect fuel filter mounting bolt.
9. Remove fuel filter and high pressure hose assembly.
10. Reverse procedure to install.

TIGHTENING SPECIFICATIONS

Year	Component	Torque/Ft. Lbs.
1996–99	Accelerator Cable	36–48⑪
	Air Cleaner Body Installation Bolt	72–84⑪
	Air Intake Plenum Stay	11–14
	Air Intake Plenum To Intake Manifold Bolt	9–10
	Air Intake Plenum To Intake Manifold Nut	90–114⑪
	Alternator Brace Bolt	8–11
	Alternator Bracket Bolt	15–21
	Alternator Stay Bolt	15–21
	Alternator Stay To Alternator Bracket	14–21
	Alternator Stay To Exhaust Manifold	11–16
	Alternator Support Nut	14–18
	Alternator Tension Pulley Bracket To Engine	24–36
	Alternator Tension Pulley	29–43
	Bearing Cap Bolt	55–61
	Bellhousing Cover To Engine	72–84⑪
	Bellhousing Cover To Transmission	22–30
	Bracket To Exhaust Manifold	11–14
	Camshaft Bearing Cap Bolt	⑩
	Camshaft Sprocket Bolt	58–72
	Clutch Control Cable Bracket To Transmission	11–16
	Clutch Hose Bracket To Transmission	11–16
	Clutch Release Cylinder To Transmission	11–16
	Connecting Rod Cap Nut	37–38
	Cooling Fan Bracket	③
	Cooling Fan To Cooling Fan Bracket	84–108⑪
	Crankshaft Pulley	108–116
	Cylinder Head Bolt	①
	Distributor Adapter To Engine	9–10
	Distributor Adapter Bolt	9–11
	Driveshaft Nut	145–188
	EGR Pipe	11–14

TIGHTENING
SPECIFICATIONS—Continued

Year	Component	Torque/ Ft. Lbs.
1996–99	Engine Damper To Crossmember	29–36
	Engine Damper To Engine	22–28
	Engine Hanger To Exhaust Manifold	11–16
	Engine Mount Bracket Nut	44–57
	Engine Mount Insulator Nut (Large)	44–57
	Engine Mount Insulator Nut (Small)	22–28
	Engine Mount Insulator	22–29
	Engine Mounting Rear Insulator To Engine⑤	13–18
	Engine Mounting Rear Insulator To Engine Support Rear Bracket⑥	11–18
	Engine Oil Feed Hose Assembly To Engine Oil Cooler	22–25
	Engine Oil Return Hose Assembly To Engine Oil Cooler	22–25
	Engine Support Bracket (Left)	15–21
	Engine Support Bracket (Right)	②
	Engine Support Bracket	⑨
	Engine Support Rear Bracket To Engine⑥	13–18
	Engine To Engine Mounting Front Insulator	9–15
	Engine To Transmission Stay (Right)	⑦
	Exhaust Manifold To Engine	11–16
	Flywheel/Driveplate Bolt	53–55
	Front Exhaust Pipe To Exhaust Manifold	22–28
	Front Insulator Stopper To Frame	22–29
	Front Roll Stopper Bracket To Center member	29–36
	Front Roll Stopper Insulator Nut	37–47
	Front Suspension Crossmember To Differential	58–72
	Front Suspension Crossmember To Frame	72–87
	Fuel High Pressure Hose To Delivery Pipe	18–25
	Fuel Hose Clamp To Rear Cylinder Head	9–10
	Heat Protector	48–84⑪
	Heat Protector To Engine Mount Insulator	72–108⑪
	Heat Protector To Exhaust Manifold	9–11
	High Pressure Fuel Hose	④
	Ignition Coil Assembly Bolt	14–22
	Intake Manifold To Engine	11–14
	Lower Arm Ball Joint To Knuckle	44–52
	No. 2 Crossmember To Frame	40–54
	Oil Cooler Hose	29–32
	Oil Filter Bracket Bolt	9–11
	Oil Level Gauge Guide To Engine	14–21
	Oil Pan Bolt	48–72⑪
	Oil Pan Drain Plug	26–32
	Oil Pressure Switch	72–108⑪
	Oil Pump Bracket	25–33
	Oil Pump Case Bolt	9–10
	Oil Pump Cover Screw	72–108⑪
	Oil Pump Mounting Bracket	25–33
	Oil Relief Valve Plug	29–36
	Oil Screen Bolt	11–15
	Plate To Frame	13–18
	Plate To Transfer Mounting Insulator	13–18

Continued

3.0L ENGINE

TIGHTENING
SPECIFICATIONS—Continued

Year	Component	Torque/Ft. Lbs.
1996–99	Power Steering Oil Pump	25–33
	Power Steering Oil Pump Bracket To Front Cylinder Head	13–18
	Power Steering Oil Pump To Bracket	13–18
	Power Steering Pressure Hose To Oil Pump	29–36
	Radiator Shroud To Radiator	24–60⑪
	Radiator Upper Shroud To Radiator Lower Shroud	72–96⑪
	Rear Engine Support Member To Frame⑥	84–108⑪
	Rear Engine Support Member To No. 2 Crossmember⑥	13–18
	Rear Plate Bolt	72–84⑪
	Rear Roll Stopper Bracket To Crossmember	29–36
	Rear Roll Stopper Insulator Nut	22–29
	Rocker Arm And Shaft Assembly	14–15
	Rocker Cover Bolt	72–84⑪
	Roll Stopper Bracket (A)	24–36
	Roll Stopper Bracket (B)	⑧
	Starter Bolt	20–25
	Support Plate To No. 2 Crossmember⑤	13–18
	Tension Adjusting Bolt	14–20
	Tension Pulley Bracket	24–36
	Tie Rod End To Knuckle	18–24
	Timing Belt Cover Bolt	84–108⑪
	Timing Belt Tensioner Bolt	16–21
	Transfer Mounting Bracket To Transfer	22–29
	Transmission Mount Bracket To Body	29–36
	Transmission Mount Bracket To Transaxle	44–57
	Transmission Mount Insulator Nut	44–57
	Transmission Mounting Plate	90–102⑪
	Transmission Stay To Engine	47–61
	Transmission Stay To Transmission Assembly	22–30
	Water Inlet Pipe To Front Cylinder Head	9–10
	Water Pump Bolts	14–20

① — Torque to 76–83 ft. lbs. in three steps.
② — 10 X 22 mm (.39 X .87 inch) bolts, 24–36 ft. lbs.; 12 X 22 mm (.47 X .87 inch) & 12 X 32 mm (.47 X 1.26 inch) bolts, 47–61 ft. lbs.
③ — Except 12 X 100 mm (.47 X 3.93 inches) bolts, 24–36 ft. lbs.; 12 X 100 mm (.47 X 3.93 inches) bolts, 47–61 ft. lbs.
④ — Montero, 7–9 ft. lbs.; Pickup, 12–24 inch lbs.
⑤ — Models w/manual transmission.
⑥ — Models w/automatic transmission.
⑦ — 10 X 30 mm (.39 X 1.18 inches) bolts, 24–36 ft. lbs.; 12 X 35 mm (.47 X 1.37 inches) & 12 X 50 mm (.47 X 1.96 inches) bolts, 47–61 ft. lbs.
⑧ — 10 X 25 mm (.39 X .98 inch) bolts, 24–36 ft. lbs.; 12 X 30 mm (.47 X 1.18 inches) bolts, 47–61 ft. lbs.
⑨ — 10 X 53 mm (.39 X 2.09 inches) bolts, 47–54 ft. lbs.; 12 X 56 mm (.47 X 2.20 inches) bolts, 76–83 ft. lbs.; 10 X 450 mm (.39 X 1.57 inches) bolts, 26–36 ft. lbs.
⑩ — Bearing cap bolts No. 2, 3 & 4, 8 ft. lbs. Bearing caps front & rear, 14 ft. lbs.
⑪ — Inch lbs.

3.5L Engine

NOTE: Refer To "Computer Relearn Procedures" Located In The Front Of This Manual For Computer Relearn Procedures.

NOTE: On Air Bag Equipped Models, Refer To "Air Bag System Precautions" Located In The Front Of This Manual For System Disarming & Arming Procedures.

INDEX

PRECAUTIONS

AIR BAG SYSTEMS

Refer to "Air Bag System Precautions" in the front of this manual for system disarming and arming procedures.

FUEL SYSTEM PRESSURE RELIEF

1. Remove carpet from cargo compartment, then remove bolts from floor cover.
2. Disconnect fuel pump electrical connection.
3. Start engine and let idle until all residual fuel is consumed, then turn ignition switch to Off position. **Failure to relieve fuel system pressure prior to disconnecting fuel system components may cause fire or personal injury.**
4. Connect fuel pump electrical connection.
5. Install cargo compartment floor cover and bolts then install carpet. **Torque** bolts to 9 ft. lbs.
6. After repairs have been completed, connect battery cable and ensure fuel pump operates properly.

BATTERY GROUND CABLE

Prior to service, disconnect battery ground cable and isolate as required.

COMPRESSION PRESSURE

Compression pressure should be a minimum 127 psi with a maximum difference of 14 psi between cylinders.

ENGINE MOUNT

REPLACE

Refer to **Fig. 1,** when replacing engine mounts.

ENGINE

REPLACE

1. Scribe and remove hood, then remove battery, tray and cruise control intermediate link.
2. Relieve fuel system pressure as outlined under "Precautions," then remove radiator assembly, skid plate, lower cover and front exhaust pipe.
3. Remove transmission and transfer assembly.
4. Remove engine assembly from vehicle in numbered sequence shown, **Figs. 2 through 4,** noting the following:
   a. When removing power steering pump and A/C compressor, leave hoses attached and support aside.
   b. When disconnecting oil cooler hose, use a spanner wrench, or equivalent.
5. Reverse procedure to install.

INTAKE MANIFOLD

REPLACE

1. Relieve fuel system pressure as outlined under " Precautions," then drain engine coolant into a suitable container.
2. Remove intake manifold plenum, then the manifold in numbered sequence as shown, **Figs. 5 and 6.**
3. Reverse procedure to install, noting the following:

a. Install intake manifold gaskets as shown, **Figs. 7 and 8.**
b. When installing intake manifold mounting nuts, first **torque** right-bank nuts to 2.2–3.6 ft. lbs., then the left bank nuts to 9–11 ft. lbs. Finally, **torque** right bank nuts to 9–11 ft. lbs.

EXHAUST MANIFOLD

REPLACE

1. Relieve fuel system pressure as outlined under "Precautions," then remove engine lower cover.
2. Remove exhaust manifold in numbered sequence as shown, **Figs. 9 and 10.**
3. Reverse procedure to install. Tighten all bolts and nuts to specifications.

CYLINDER HEAD

REPLACE

Refer to **Figs. 11 and 12,** when replacing the cylinder head noting the following:
1. Release fuel system pressure as outlined under " Precautions."
2. Drain engine coolant into suitable container, then remove timing belt, intake manifold and exhaust manifolds.
3. Using sequence shown in **Fig. 13,** remove cylinder head bolts in three steps.
4. Reverse procedure to install, noting the following:
   a. When installing cylinder head gasket, degrease gasket mounting surface, then lay gasket on cylinder block with ID mark at front top.
   b. Using sequence shown in **Fig. 13,** **torque** cylinder head bolts in two or three steps to 76–83 ft. lbs.
   c. Rinse mounting location of water

pipe O-ring and water pipe with water then install. **Do not apply oil or grease to O-ring. Insert water pipe until its end bottoms.**
d. Bend tabs of water passage gasket onto water passage, then install. Ensure gasket does not slip.
e. Install thermostat with jiggle valve straight up.

VALVE ADJUSTMENT

This engine is equipped with automatic valve lash adjusters, no adjustments are required.

TIMING BELT

REPLACE

With timing belt removed, avoid turning the camshaft or crankshaft. If movement is required, exercise extreme caution to avoid valve damage caused by piston contact.
1. Release fuel system pressure as outlined under " Precautions."
2. Remove radiator assembly, alternator, battery, tray, skid plate and engine lower cover.
3. Remove timing belt in numbered sequence as shown, **Figs. 14 and 15,** noting the following:
   a. When removing A/C compressor and power steering pump, leave hoses attached and support aside.
   b. Use pulley remover tool No. MB990767-01, or equivalent, to remove crankshaft pulley.
   c. When removing timing belt, align timing marks as shown, **Figs. 16 and 17,** ensure direction of normal rotation is marked on belt if it is to be reused.
4. Reverse procedure to install, noting the following:
   a. If auto tensioner rod is fully extended, gently push rod into cylinder by clamping tensioner assembly in a soft jawed vise until set hole in rod aligns with hole in cylinder wall, then insert a stiff wire through set hole to keep rod in place.
   b. When installing timing belt, install crankshaft pulley and turn crankshaft sprocket timing mark forward three teeth to move No. 1 piston slightly past top dead center. **Prevent piston from contacting valves during this procedure.**
   c. Align left camshaft sprocket with timing mark, then align right camshaft sprocket with timing mark and prevent rotation using suitable wrenches.
   d. When camshaft sprockets are aligned with timing marks, clamp timing belt over each sprocket using suitable binder clips, then slip belt over water pump pulley and idler pulley.
   e. After aligning crankshaft sprocket timing marks, rotate crankshaft counterclockwise slightly, then place timing belt over crankshaft sprocket and tensioner pulley.

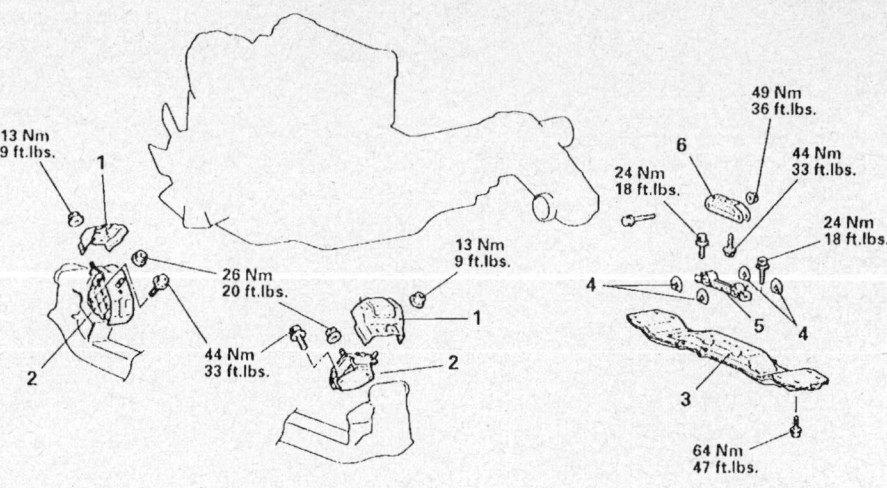

Removal steps of front engine mount
• Removal of Engine Assembly

1. Heat protector
2. Engine support front insulator

Removal steps of rear engine mount
3. No. 2 crossmember
4. Stopper
5. Engine support rear insulator
6. Engine support rear bracket

MT1069100314000X

Fig. 1 Engine mount replacement

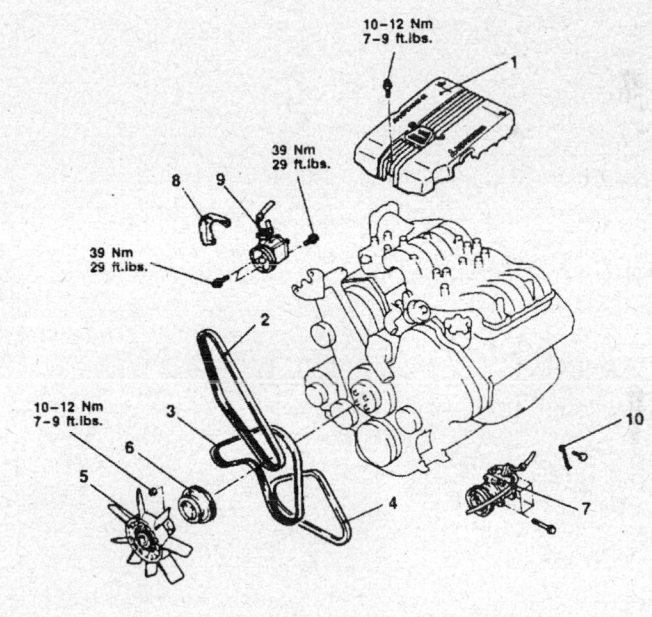

Removal Steps
1. Intake manifold plenum cover
2. Power steering drive belt
3. Generator drive belt
4. A/C drive belt
5. Cooling fan
6. Water pump pulley
7. A/C compressor
8. Cover
9. Power steering pump
10. Ground cable connection

MT1069100315010A

Fig. 2 Engine replacement (Part 1 of 2). 1996

f. Position tensioner pulley pin hole at top, then press tensioner pulley onto timing belt and tighten set bolt until snug. Align crankshaft sprocket timing marks and ensure all timing marks are aligned, then remove binder clips from timing belt.
g. To adjust timing belt tension, rotate crankshaft ¼ turn counterclockwise and then back to position where timing marks align, then loosen tensioner pulley center bolt. Using tensioner tool No. MD998767, or equivalent, and a torque wrench, apply a **torque** of 7 ft. lbs. to timing belt while tightening pulley center bolt to specifications. Remove auto tensioner set pin and measure rod protrusion. If protrusion is not .150–.196 inch, repeat adjustment procedure.

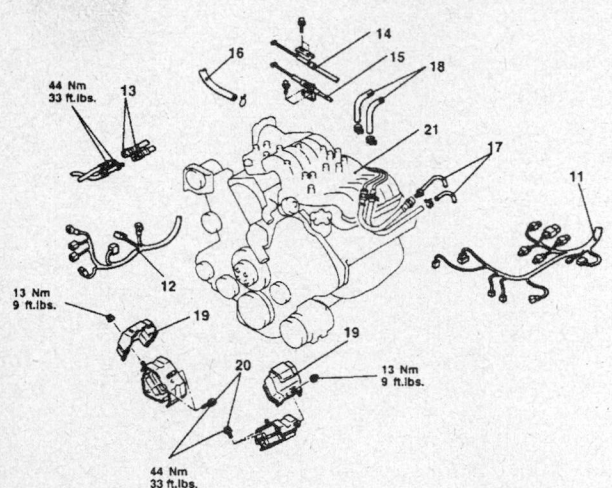

11. Engine control harness connection
12. Generator and starter harness connection
13. Engine oil cooler hose connection
14. Accelerator cable connection
15. Throttle cable connection
16. Brake booster vacuum hose connection
17. Fuel hose connection
18. Heater hose connection
19. Heat protectors
20. Engine mounting bolt
21. Engine assembly

MT1069100315020A

Fig. 2 Engine replacement (Part 2 of 2). 1996

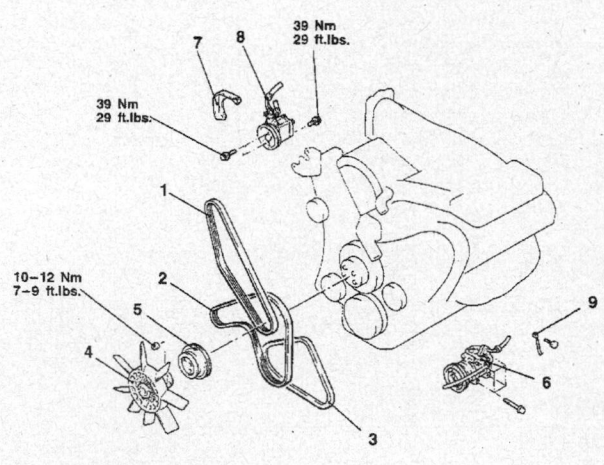

Removal Steps
1. Power steering drive belt
2. Generator drive belt
3. A/C drive belt
4. Cooling fan
5. Water pump pulley
6. A/C compressor
7. Cover
8. Power steering pump
9. Ground cable connection

MT1069800548010X

Fig. 3 Engine replacement (Part 1 of 2). 1997–99 Montero & 1997–98 Montero Sport

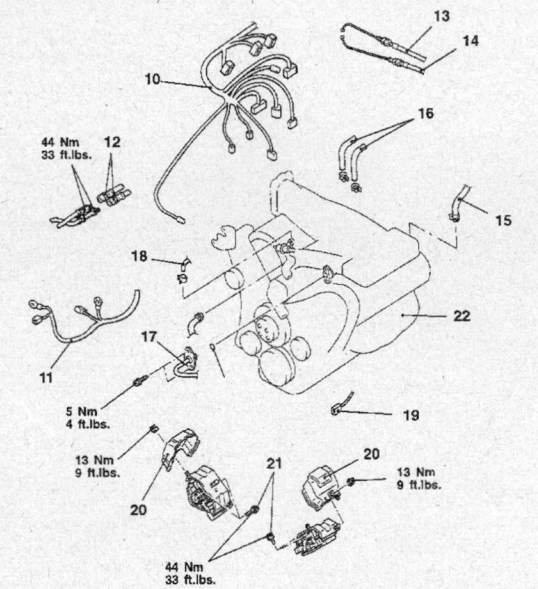

10. Engine control harness connection
11. Generator and starter harness connection
12. Engine oil cooler hose connection
13. Accelerator cable connection
14. Throttle cable connection
15. Brake booster vacuum hose connection
16. Heater hose connection
17. Fuel hose connection
18. Fuel return hose connection
19. Oil pressure switch harness connection
20. Heat protectors
21. Engine mounting bolt
22. Engine assembly

MT1069800548020X

Fig. 3 Engine replacement (Part 2 of 2). 1997–99 Montero & 1997-98 Montero Sport

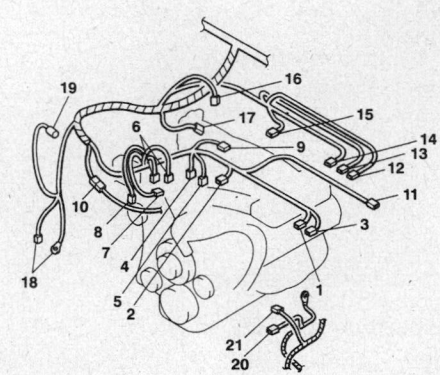

1. IGNITION COIL 1 CONNECTOR
2. IGNITION COIL 2 CONNECTOR
3. IGNITION COIL 3 CONNECTOR
4. CAMSHAFT POSITION SENSOR CONNECTOR
5. CRANKSHAFT POSITION SENSOR CONNECTOR
6. IGNITION POWER TRANSISTOR CONNECTOR
7. CAPACITOR CONNECTOR
8. ENGINE COOLANT TEMPERATURE SENSOR CONNECTOR
9. ENGINE COOLANT TEMPERATURE GAUGE UNIT CONNECTOR
10. FRONT WIRING HARNESS AND INJECTION WIRING HARNESS COMBINATION CONNECTOR
11. MANIFOLD DIFFERENTIAL PRESSURE SENSOR
12. EGR SOLENOID CONNECTOR
13. EVAPORATIVE EMISSION PURGE SOLENOID CONNECTOR
14. LEFT BANK HEATED OXYGEN SENSOR CONNECTOR (FRONT) <CALIFORNIA>
15. RIGHT BANK HEATED OXYGEN SENSOR CONNECTOR (FRONT) <CALIFORNIA>
16. THROTTLE POSITION SENSOR CONNECTOR
17. IDLE AIR CONTROL MOTOR CONNECTOR
18. GENERATOR CONNECTOR
19. POWER STEERING PRESSURE SWITCH CONNECTOR
20. MAGNETIC CLUTCH AND REFRIGERANT TEMPERATURE SWITCH CONNECTOR
21. OIL PRESSURE SWITCH CONNECTOR

MT1069900268010X

Fig. 4 Engine replacement (Part 1 of 2). 1999 Montero Sport

CRANKSHAFT SEAL

REPLACE

FRONT

1. Remove timing belt as outlined under "Timing Belt, Replace," then remove crankshaft sprocket, position sensor, sensing blade and spacer.
2. Remove key from keyway, then separate oil seal from case as follows:
   a. Cut out a small portion of crankshaft oil seal lip.
   b. Cover tip of a suitable screwdriver with a cloth, then insert into seal cutout and pry away from oil pump case.
3. Drive seal in until flush with surface of oil pump case using seal installation tool No. MD998717, or equivalent.

REAR

1. Remove transmission assembly, then the outer adapter plate and driveplate.
2. Remove driveplate to output flange adapter, then remove oil seal from engine as follows:
   a. Cut out a small portion of crankshaft oil seal lip.

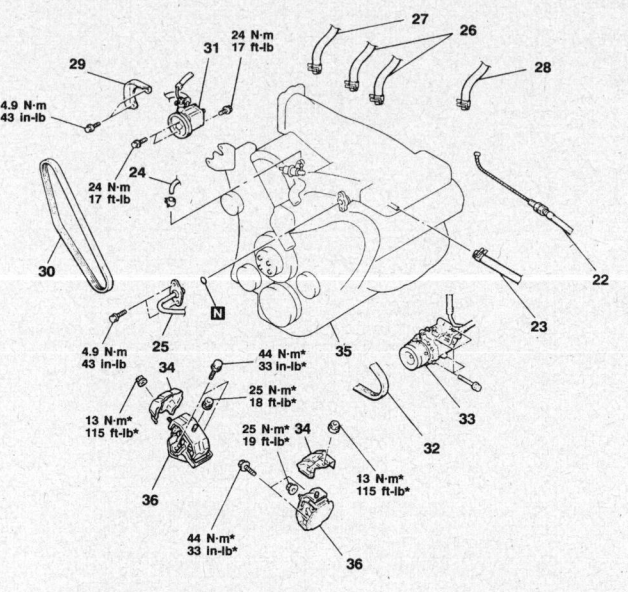

22. THROTTLE CABLE CONNECTION
23. VACUUM HOSE CONNECTION
24. FUEL RETURN HOSE CONNECTION
25. HIGH-PRESSURE FUEL HOSE CONNECTION
26. HEATER HOSE CONNECTION
27. HEATER HOSE CONNECTION <VEHICLES WITH REAR HEATER>
28. VACUUM HOSE CONNECTION
29. POWER STEERING DRIVE BELT COVER
30. DRIVE BELT (FOR POWER STEERING)
31. POWER STEERING PUMP ASSEMBLY
32. DRIVE BELT (FOR A/C)
33. A/C COMPRESSOR ASSEMBLY
34. HEAT PROTECTOR
35. ENGINE ASSEMBLY
36. ENGINE SUPPORT FRONT INSULATOR

MT1069900268020X

Fig. 4   Engine replacement (Part 2 of 2). 1999 Montero Sport

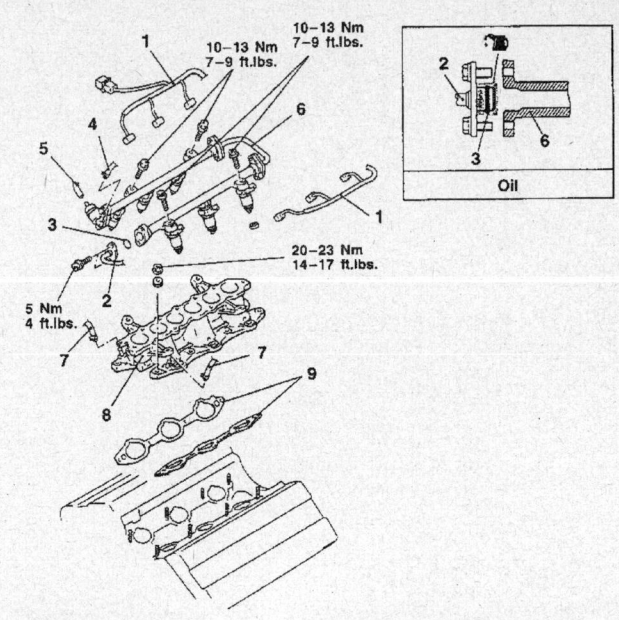

Removal steps

1. Injector harness connection
2. High-pressure fuel hose connection
3. O-ring
4. Fuel return hose connection
5. Vacuum hose connection
6. Fuel rail (with injectors)
7. Water hose connection
8. Intake manifold
9. Intake manifold gasket

MT1059100028000X

Fig. 5   Intake manifold replacement. DOHC engine

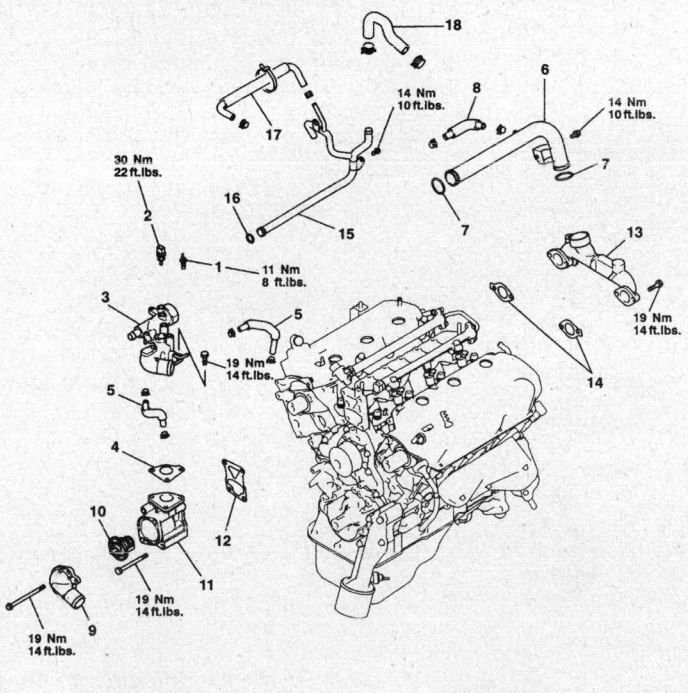

1. Engine coolant temperature gauge unit
2. Engine coolant temperature sensor
3. Water outlet fitting
4. Water outlet fitting gasket
5. Water hose
6. Water outlet pipe
7. O-ring
8. Water hose
9. Water inlet fitting
10. Thermostat
11. Thermostat case
12. Thermostat case gasket
13. Water passage
14. Gasket
15. Water pipe
16. O-ring
17. Water hose
18. Water hose

MT1059700045010X

Fig. 6   Intake manifold replacement (Part 1 of 2). SOHC engine

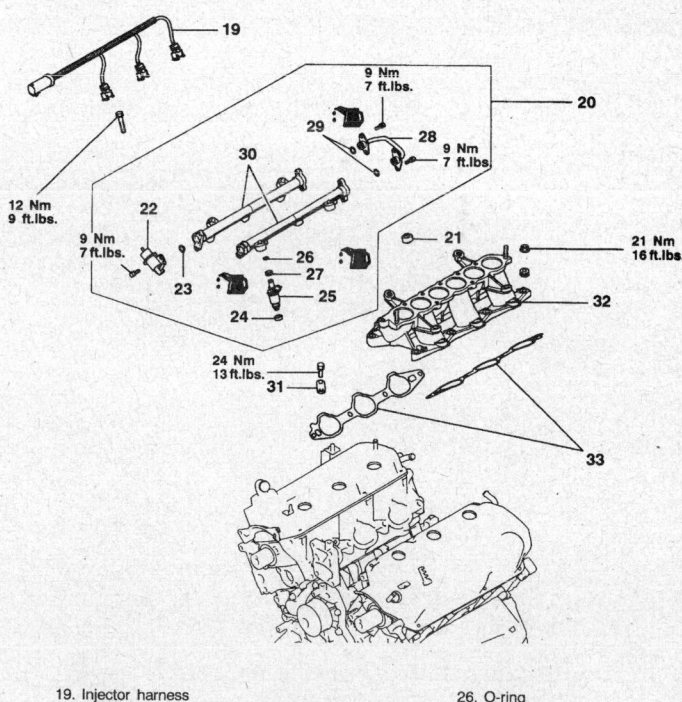

19. Injector harness
20. Injector and fuel rail
21. Insulator
22. Fuel pressure regulator
23. O-ring
24. Insulator
25. Injector
26. O-ring
27. Grommet
28. Fuel pipe
29. O-ring
30. Fuel rail
31. Bracket
32. Intake manifold
33. Intake manifold gasket

MT1059700045020X

Fig. 6   Intake manifold replacement (Part 2 of 2). SOHC engine

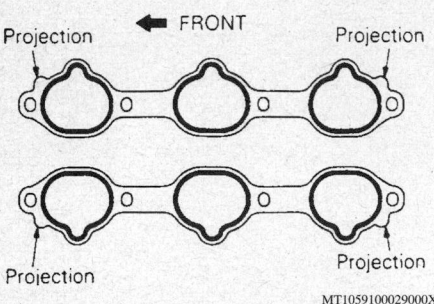

Fig. 7 Intake manifold gasket orientation. DOHC engine

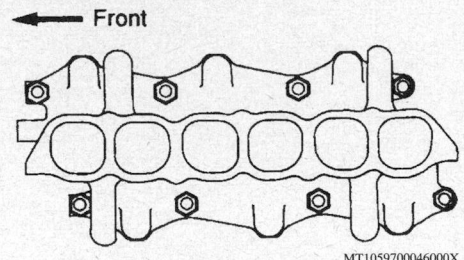

Fig. 8 Intake manifold gasket orientation. SOHC engine

Removal steps of exhaust manifold (Right)
- Air duct and air creaner cover
1. EGR pipe
2. Gasket
3. Heat protector (R.H.)
4. Exhaust manifold (R.H.)
5. Gasket

Removal steps of exhaust manifold (Left)
- Battery and battery tray
6. Heat protector (L.H.)
7. Exhaust manifold (L.H.)
8. Gasket

Fig. 9 Exhaust manifold replacement. DOHC engine

b. Cover tip of a suitable screwdriver with a cloth, then insert into seal cutout and pry away from engine.
3. Reverse procedure to install. Drive seal in using seal installation tool No. MD998718-01, or equivalent.

OIL PAN
REPLACE
LOWER

1. Remove skid plate, lower cover and front exhaust pipe, then drain engine oil into a suitable container.
2. Separate oil pan from engine, noting the following:
   a. It may be necessary to free pan by placing a wooden block against it and tapping with a hammer.
   b. **Do not attempt to remove pan using oil pan remover tool No. MD998727, or equivalent; damage to aluminum components may result.**
3. Reverse procedure to install, noting the following:
   a. Ensure oil pan mating surfaces are clean, then apply Mitsubishi sealant No. MD970389, or equivalent, in a continuous bead as shown, **Fig. 18.**

b. Install oil pan on engine block within 30 minutes of sealant application.
c. Tighten oil pan mounting bolts to specifications in sequence shown, **Fig. 18.**

UPPER

1. Remove lower oil pan as outlined in this section, then remove front differential carrier.
2. Remove upper oil pan in sequence as shown, **Fig. 19.**
3. Reverse procedure to install, noting the following:
   a. Clean upper oil pan mating surfaces, then apply Mitsubishi sealant No. MD970389, or equivalent, in a continuous bead as shown, **Fig. 20.**
   b. Install upper oil pan on cylinder block within 30 minutes of sealant application.
   c. Tighten upper oil pan mounting

bolts to specifications in sequence shown, **Fig. 20.**

BELT TENSION DATA

Component	Inch Deflection①	
	New Belt	Used Belt②
Alternator	.22–.30③	.31–.35③
Power Steering Pump	.43–.51	.55–.63
A/C Compressor	.20–.24	.26–.30

① — With 22 lbs. of force applied.
② — Used 5 minutes or more.
③ — Measured between water pump pulley & alternator.

COOLING SYSTEM BLEED

This engine does not require a specified bleed procedure. After filling cooling system, run engine to operating temperature with radiator/pressure cap off. Air will then be automatically bled through cap opening.

THERMOSTAT
REPLACE

1. Drain engine coolant into a suitable container, then disconnect lower radiator hose and remove water inlet fitting.
2. Remove thermostat from engine.
3. Reverse procedure to install, noting the following:
   a. Install thermostat with jiggle valve facing straight up.
   b. Tighten water inlet fitting mounting bolts to specifications.

WATER PUMP
REPLACE

1. Drain engine coolant into a suitable container, then remove timing belt as outlined under "Timing Belt, Replace."
2. Remove thermostat as outlined under "Thermostat, Replace," then remove water pump in numbered sequence as shown, **Fig. 21.**
3. Reverse procedure to install, noting the following:
   a. When installing O-ring, rinse mounting location with water. **Do not apply oil or grease to O-ring.**
   b. Tighten all bolts and nuts to specifications.

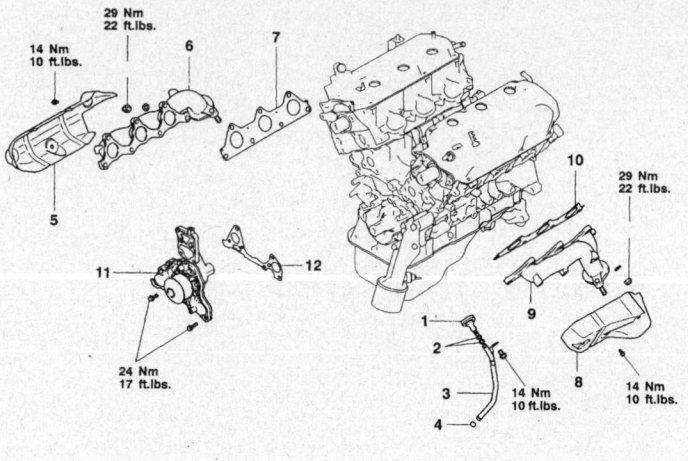

1. Oil level gauge
2. O-ring
3. Oil level gauge guide
4. O-ring
5. Heat protector, right
6. Exhaust manifold, right
7. Exhaust manifold gasket
8. Heat protector, left
9. Exhaust manifold, left
10. Exhaust manifold gasket
11. Water pump
12. Water pump gasket

MT1079700021000X

Fig. 10   Exhaust manifold replacement. SOHC engine

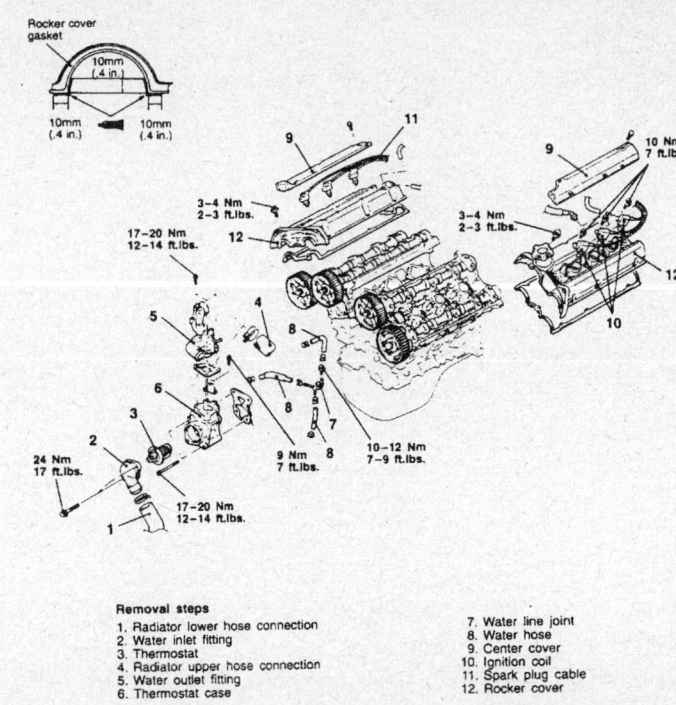

Removal steps

1. Radiator lower hose connection	7. Water line joint
2. Water inlet fitting	8. Water hose
3. Thermostat	9. Center cover
4. Radiator upper hose connection	10. Ignition coil
5. Water outlet fitting	11. Spark plug cable
6. Thermostat case	12. Rocker cover

MT1069500331010X

Fig. 11   Cylinder head replacement (Part 1 of 2). DOHC engine

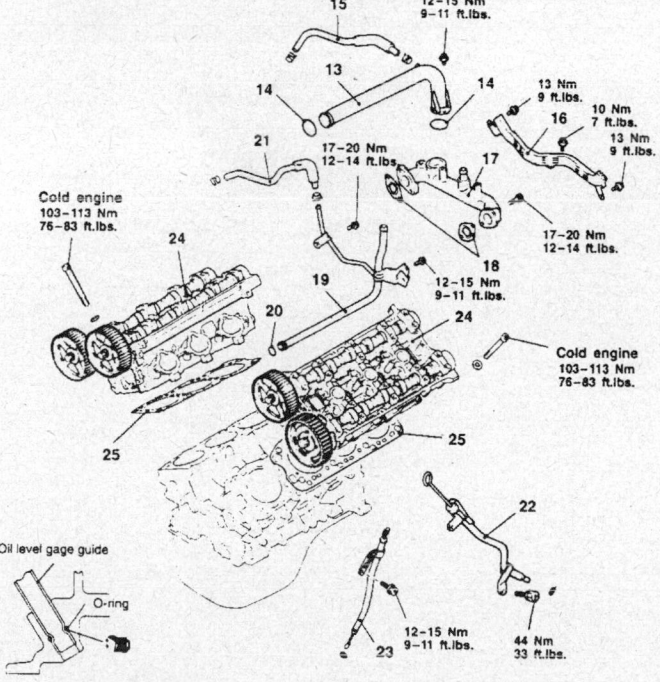

13. Water outlet pipe
14. O-ring
15. Water hose
16. Spark plug cable support
17. Water passage
18. Gasket
19. Water pipe assembly
20. O-ring
21. Water hose
22. Oil filler pipe
23. Oil level gage guide
24. Cylinder head assembly
25. Cylinder head gasket

MT1069500331020X

Fig. 11   Cylinder head replacement (Part 2 of 2). DOHC engine

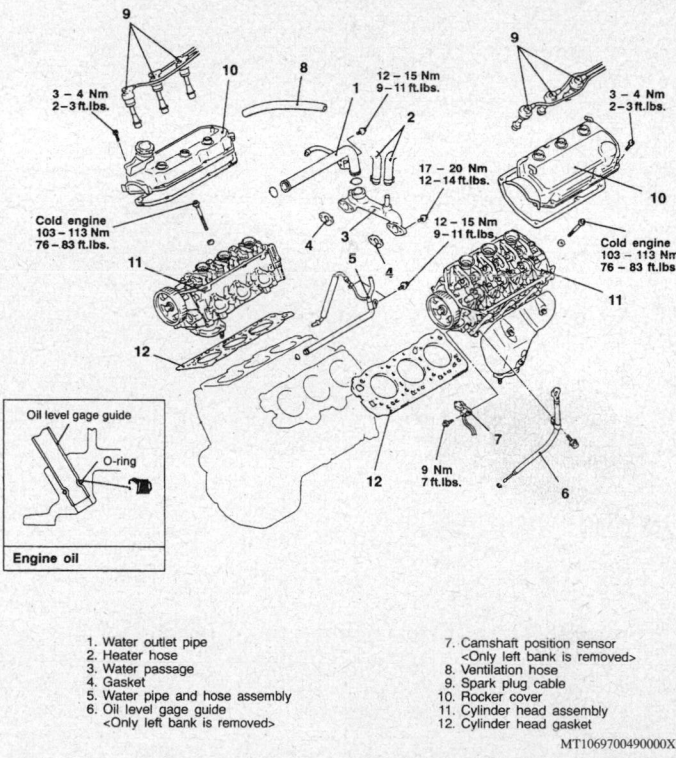

1. Water outlet pipe
2. Heater hose
3. Water passage
4. Gasket
5. Water pipe and hose assembly
6. Oil level gage guide
    <Only left bank is removed>
7. Camshaft position sensor
    <Only left bank is removed>
8. Ventilation hose
9. Spark plug cable
10. Rocker cover
11. Cylinder head assembly
12. Cylinder head gasket

MT1069700490000X

Fig. 12   Cylinder head replacement. SOHC engine

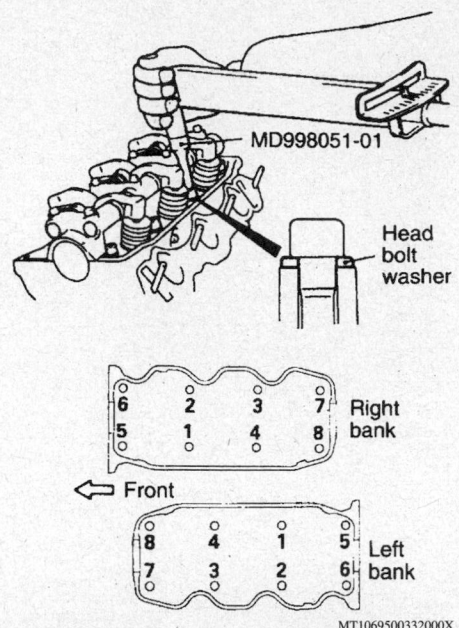

Fig. 13 Cylinder head bolt loosening & tightening sequence

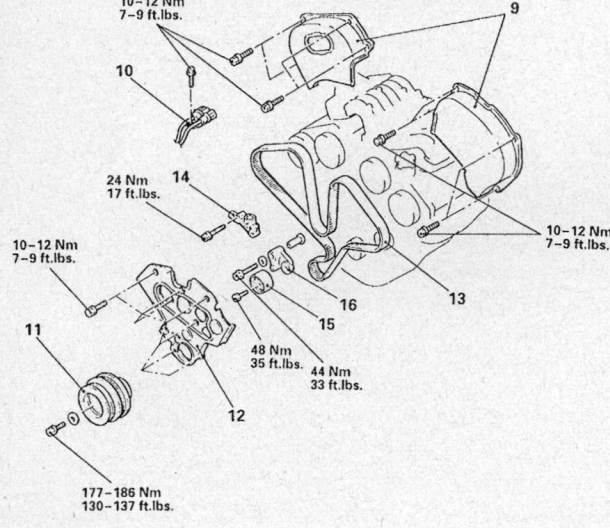

9. Timing belt upper cover
10. Crankshaft position sensor connector
11. Crankshaft pulley
12. Timing belt lower cover
• Adjustment of timing belt tension
13. Timing belt
14. Auto tensioner
15. Tension pulley
16. Tension arm assembly

MT1069100316020X

Fig. 14 Timing belt replacement (Part 2 of 2). DOHC engine

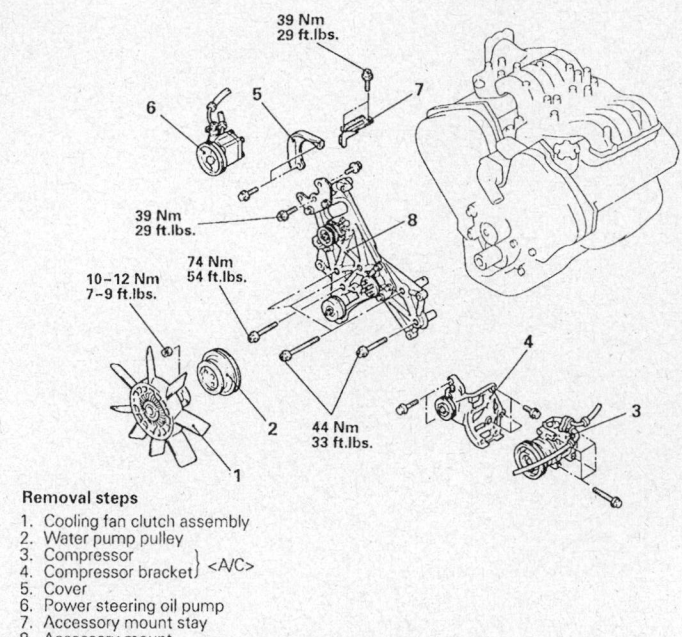

Removal steps
1. Cooling fan clutch assembly
2. Water pump pulley
3. Compressor
4. Compressor bracket } <A/C>
5. Cover
6. Power steering oil pump
7. Accessory mount stay
8. Accessory mount

MT1069100316010X

Fig. 14 Timing belt replacement (Part 1 of 2). DOHC engine

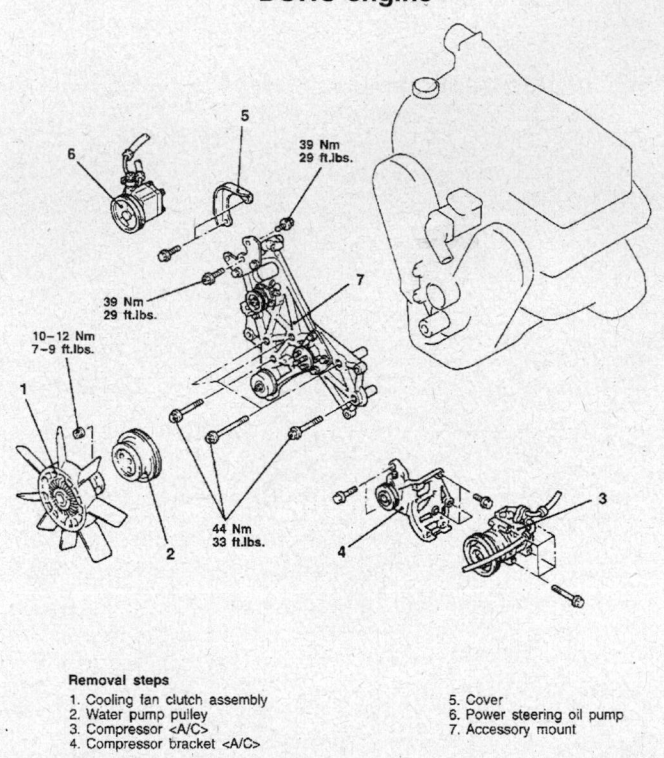

Removal steps
1. Cooling fan clutch assembly
2. Water pump pulley
3. Compressor <A/C>
4. Compressor bracket <A/C>
5. Cover
6. Power steering oil pump
7. Accessory mount

MT1069800549010X

Fig. 15 Timing belt replacement (Part 1 of 2). SOHC engine

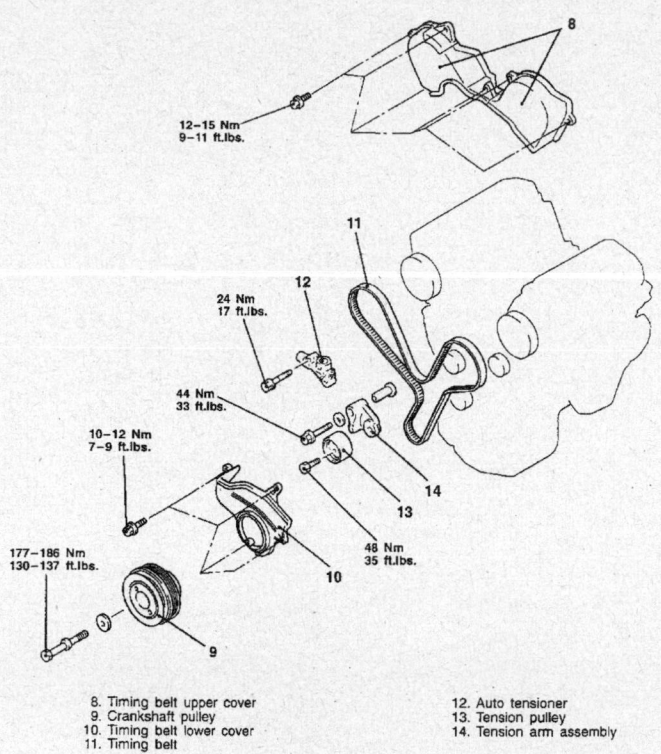

12–15 Nm
9–11 ft.lbs.

24 Nm
17 ft.lbs.

44 Nm
33 ft.lbs.

10–12 Nm
7–9 ft.lbs.

177–186 Nm
130–137 ft.lbs.

48 Nm
35 ft.lbs.

8. Timing belt upper cover
9. Crankshaft pulley
10. Timing belt lower cover
11. Timing belt

12. Auto tensioner
13. Tension pulley
14. Tension arm assembly

MT1069800549020X

Fig. 15 Timing belt replacement (Part 2 of 2). SOHC engine

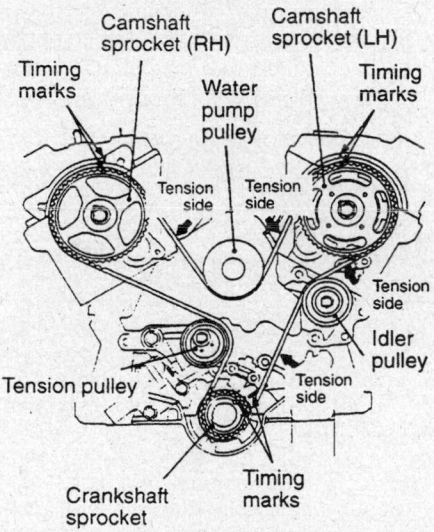

Camshaft sprocket (RH)

Camshaft sprocket (LH)

Timing marks

Water pump pulley

Timing marks

Tension side

Tension side

Tension side

Tension side

Idler pulley

Tension pulley

Tension side

Crankshaft sprocket

Timing marks

MT1069700492000X

Fig. 17 Timing mark alignment. SOHC engine

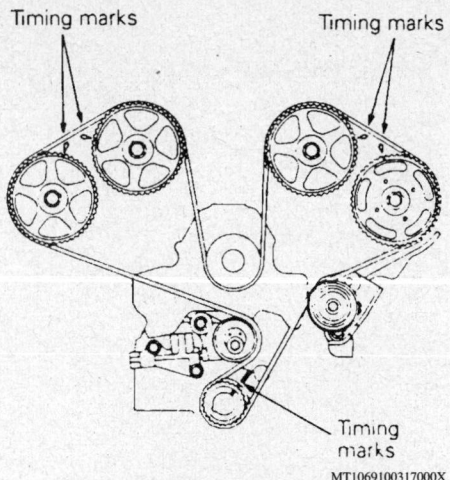

Timing marks

Timing marks

Timing marks

MT1069100317000X

Fig. 16 Timing mark alignment. DOHC engine

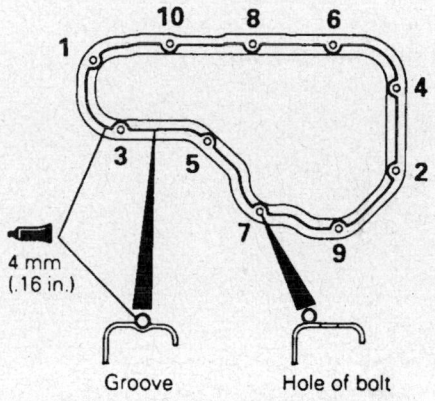

1 3 5 7 9 10 8 6 4 2

4 mm (.16 in.)

Groove

Hole of bolt

MT1099100053000X

Fig. 18 Lower oil pan sealant application & bolt tightening sequence

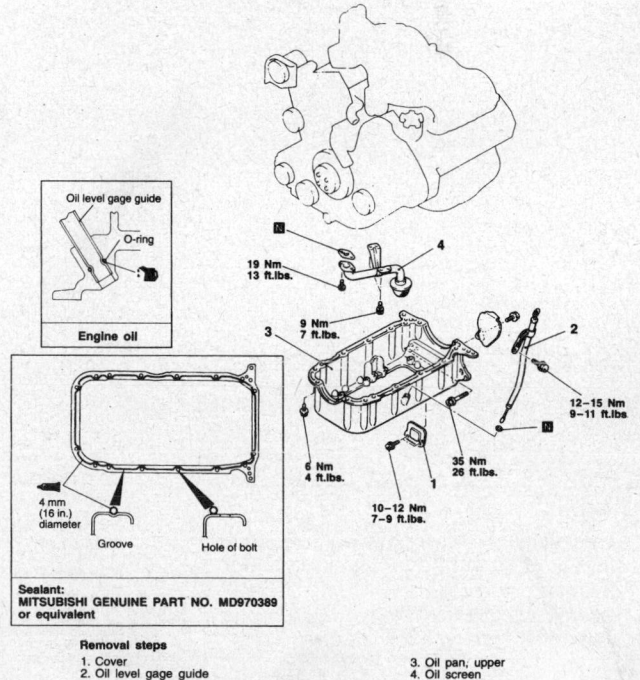

Oil level gage guide
O-ring
Engine oil

19 Nm
13 ft.lbs.

9 Nm
7 ft.lbs.

12–15 Nm
9–11 ft.lbs.

35 Nm
26 ft.lbs.

6 Nm
4 ft.lbs.

10–12 Nm
7–9 ft.lbs.

4 mm (16 in.) diameter

Groove

Hole of bolt

Sealant:
MITSUBISHI GENUINE PART NO. MD970389 or equivalent

Removal steps
1. Cover
2. Oil level gage guide

3. Oil pan, upper
4. Oil screen

MT1099100054000X

Fig. 19 Upper oil pan replacement

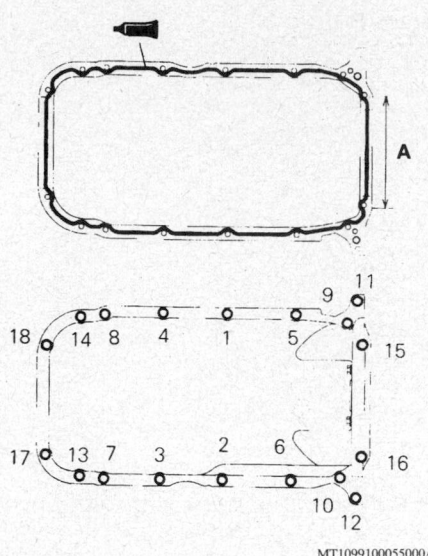

Fig. 20 Upper oil pan sealant application & bolt tightening sequence

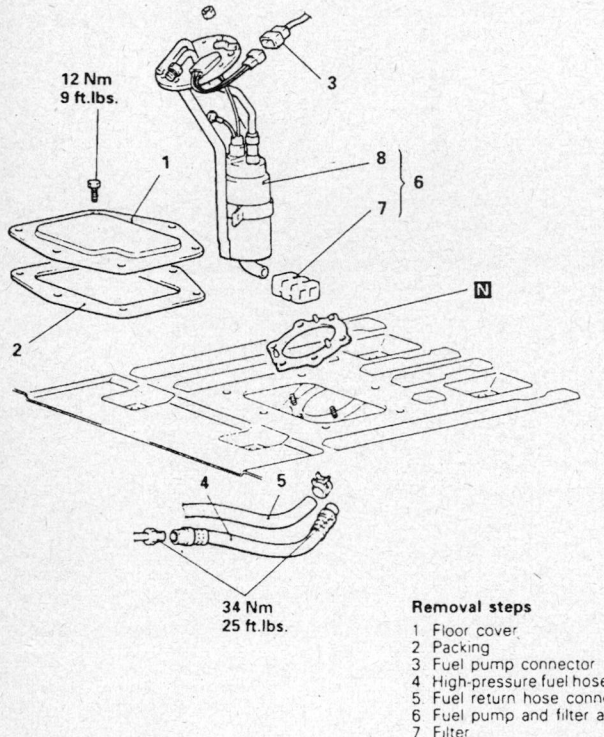

Removal steps
1. Floor cover
2. Packing
3. Fuel pump connector
4. High-pressure fuel hose
5. Fuel return hose connection
6. Fuel pump and filter assembly
7. Filter
8. Fuel pump assembly

MT1029100019000X

Fig. 22 Fuel pump replacement

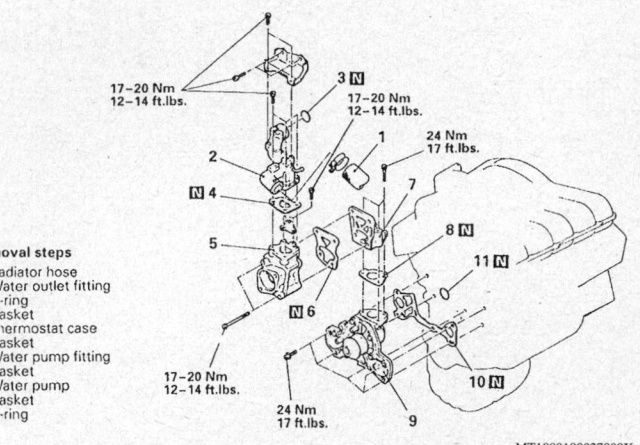

Removal steps
1. Radiator hose
2. Water outlet fitting
3. O-ring
4. Gasket
5. Thermostat case
6. Gasket
7. Water pump fitting
8. Gasket
9. Water pump
10. Gasket
11. O-ring

MT1089100027000X

Fig. 21 Water pump replacement

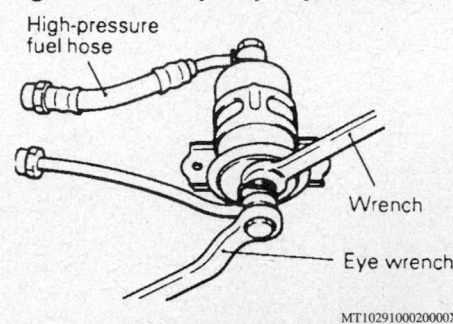

MT1029100020000X

Fig. 23 Fuel filter replacement

lined under "Precautions," then drain fuel tank into a suitable container. Remove rear carpet, then remove fuel pump in numbered sequence shown, **Fig. 22.**

2. Reverse procedure to install. Tighten all bolts and fittings to specifications.

FUEL FILTER
REPLACE

1. Release fuel system pressure as outlined under "Precautions."
2. Drain fuel tank into a suitable container.
3. Hold fuel filter with a wrench and remove eye bolt retaining fuel high pressure hose with an eye wrench, **Fig. 23.**
4. Inspect hose and pipes for cracks, damage or clogging and replace as necessary.
5. Inspect evaporative emission canister for clogging and replace as necessary.
6. Inspect check valve and fuel filter for clogging or damage and replace as necessary.
7. Remove protector of fuel filter, then disconnect fuel filter mounting bolt.
8. Remove fuel filter and high pressure hose assembly.
9. Reverse procedure to install.

RADIATOR
REPLACE

1. Drain engine coolant into suitable container, then remove engine under cover.
2. Remove air cleaner case, then remove transmission oil cooler hose.
3. Remove radiator upper hose and radiator shroud, over flow hose and reserve tank.
4. Remove radiator lower hose, then radiator.
5. Reverse procedure to install.

FUEL PUMP
REPLACE

1. Relieve fuel system pressure as out-

TIGHTENING SPECIFICATIONS

Year	Component	Torque/Ft. Lbs.
1996–99	Camshaft Sprocket Bolt	65
	Cooling Fan To Water Pump Pulley Bolts	84–108②
	Crankshaft Position Sensor Bracket Bolt	84②
	Crankshaft Pulley Bolt	130–137
	Cylinder Head Bolts	①
	Dipstick Tube Bracket Bolt	9–11
	EGR Pipe Flange Bolts	13
	Engine Mount Bolts	33
	Engine Mount Heat Protector Nuts	108②
	Engine Mount Nuts	20
	Engine Oil Cooler Hose Fittings	33
	Engine Oil Cooler Hose To Cooler Eye Bolts	22–25
	Engine Oil Cooler Hose To Engine Eye Bolts	29–33
	Engine Oil Drain Plug	29
	Engine Rear Support Insulator To Crossmember Bolts	18
	Engine Support Rear Bracket Nut	36
	Engine Support Rear Bracket To Engine Bolt	33
	Exhaust Manifold Heat Protector Bolts	9–11
	Exhaust Manifold Mounting Nuts	22
	Fuel Gauge Sending Unit Mounting Nuts	24②
	Fuel Pump Floor Access Cover Bolts	108②
	Fuel Pump Mounting Nuts	24②
	Fuel Rail Mounting Bolts	84–108②
	Fuel Tank Drain Plug	14
	Fuel Tank Support Nuts	18–22
	High Pressure Fuel Hose Fittings	25
	High Pressure Fuel Hose To Fuel Rail Flange Bolts	12–24②
	Ignition Coil Wire Bracket Bolts	84②
	Intake Manifold Mounting Nuts	9–11
	Intake Manifold Plenum Cover Bolt	84–108②
	Lower Oil Pan Bolts	84–108②
	Oil Screen Bracket Bolts	84②
	Oil Screen Flange Bolts	13
	Power Steering Pump Bolts	29
	Rear Crossmember Mounting Bolts	47
	Rocker Cover Bolts	24–36②
	Thermostat Case To Water Pump Fitting Bolts	12–14
	Timing Belt Auto Tensioner Bolt	17
	Timing Belt Lower Cover Bolts	84–108②
	Timing Belt Tension Arm Bolts	33
	Timing Belt Tensioner Pulley Center Bolt	35
	Timing Belt Upper Cover Bolts	84–108②
	Upper Oil Pan Bolts	48②
	Upper Oil Pan To Transmission Bolts	26
	Water Outlet Fitting To Thermostat Case Bolts	12–14
	Water Pump Mounting Bolts	17

① — Refer to "Cylinder Head, Replace" for tightening procedure.

② — Inch lbs.

Clutch & Manual Transmission

NOTE: Refer To "Computer Relearn Procedures" Located In The Front Of This Manual For Computer Relearn Procedures.

NOTE: On Air Bag Equipped Models, Refer To "Air Bag System Precautions" Located In The Front Of This Manual For System Disarming & Arming Procedures.

INDEX

PRECAUTIONS

AIR BAG SYSTEMS

Refer to "Air Bag System Precautions" in the front of this manual for system disarming and arming procedures.

BATTERY GROUND CABLE

Prior to service, disconnect battery ground cable and isolate as required.

ADJUSTMENTS

CLUTCH PEDAL

Cable Operated

1. Measure clutch pedal height as shown, **Fig. 1.** Clutch pedal height should be 6.5–6.7 inches. If clutch pedal height is not as specified, rotate pedal stopper until specified dimension is obtained.
2. Measure clutch pedal freeplay by lightly depressing on clutch pedal until light resistance is felt. Clutch pedal freeplay should be .8–1.4 inches. If clutch pedal freeplay is not as specified, pull clutch cable lightly at toe board, then rotate adjusting nut until adjusting nut to insulator clearance, **Fig. 2,** is .12–.16 inch.
3. Check clutch pedal height and freeplay after making adjustments.
4. Measure distance between face of clutch pedal and floor board, with clutch pedal depressed. Distance should be 2.4 inches or more.

Hydraulically Operated

1. Measure clutch pedal height (A) and clutch pedal freeplay (B), **Fig. 3.** Clutch pedal height should be as follows:
   a. **On Pickup models,** 6.5–6.7 inches.
   b. **On Montero models,** 7.3–7.5 inches.

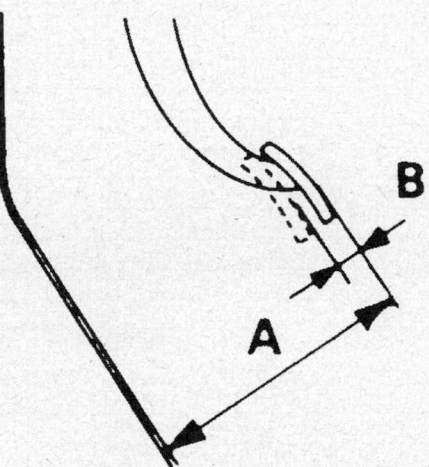

MT5049100043000X

Fig. 1 Clutch pedal height adjustment. Pickup

c. **On Montero Sport models,** 6.9–7.1 inches.
2. Clutch pedal freeplay should be as follows:
   a. **On Montero models,** .04–.12 inch.
   b. **On Montero Sport models,** .24–.51 inch.
   c. **On Pickup models,** .8–1.4 inches.
3. If clutch pedal height and freeplay are not within specification, adjust as follows:
   a. Back off pedal stopper bolt until it does not contact pedal arm, **Fig. 4.**
   b. Loosen pushrod locknut, then adjust pedal height to specified value by turning the pushrod, **Fig. 4.**
   c. Turn pedal stopper bolt until it comes into contact with pedal arm, then tighten the locknut.
4. After above adjustment is completed, depress clutch pedal and check the clutch pedal to floorboard clearance (C), **Fig. 3.** Pedal to floorboard clearance should be 2.4 inches or more on

Pickup or 1.4 inches or more on Montero.
5. If clutch pedal to floorboard clearance is less than specified value, check for air in hydraulic system or defective clutch assembly.

HYDRAULIC SYSTEM SERVICE

CLUTCH SLAVE CYLINDER, REPLACE

Replace clutch slave cylinder in sequence as shown, **Figs. 5 through 7.**

CLUTCH

REPLACE

PICKUP

1. Remove transmission and transfer case assembly, if applicable, as outlined under "Transmission, Replace."
2. Insert suitable tool into center hole to prevent dropping clutch disc, then diagonally loosen bolts holding clutch cover assembly and remove assembly.
3. Remove clutch disc and tool.
4. Remove two return clips on transmission side, then the release bearing.
5. Remove shift arm spring pin and control lever shaft assembly with 3/16 inch punch, then remove clutch shift arm, two felt packing and two return springs.
6. Apply grease to inside surface of bushing and oil seal lips and apply engine oil to two felt packing.
7. Insert clutch control lever and shaft assembly into transmission case from left, then install clutch shift arm, two felt packing, and two return springs onto shaft.
8. Align lockpin holes on shift arm and

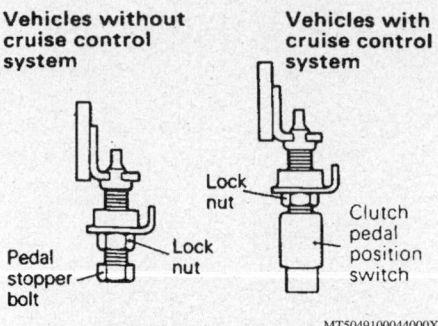

Fig. 2 Clutch pedal freeplay adjustment. Pickup

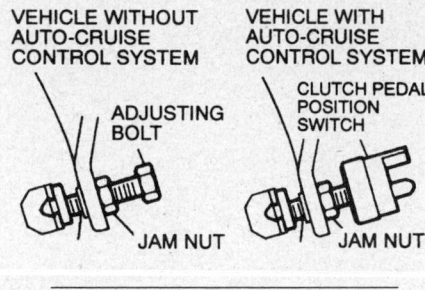

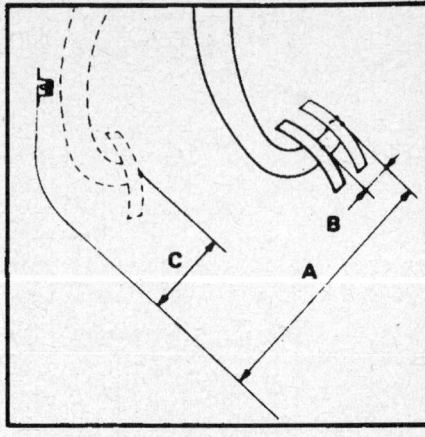

Fig. 4 Clutch pedal height & freeplay adjustment

control shaft, then drive in two spring pins. Ensure spring pin slot direction is at right angles to control shaft.

9. Apply ample amount of rubber grease to outer surface of piston and piston cup and insert them in release cylinder, then install pushrod and rubber boot.
10. Install release cylinder assembly to transmission case.
11. Fill groove of bearing inside diameter with grease.
12. Install release bearing to transmission front bearing retainer, then install return clips.
13. Rub grease in clutch disc spline and transmission main gear spline.
14. Using suitable tool, install clutch disc and clutch cover assembly on flywheel. When installing clutch disc, make certain that surface with manufacturer's stamped mark is on pressure plate side.
15. Install transmission.

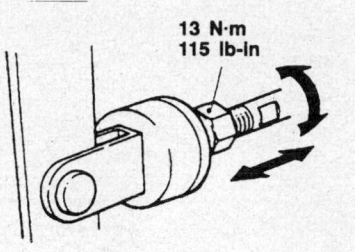

Fig. 3 Clutch pedal height, freeplay & floorboard clearance

MONTERO & MONTERO SPORT

1. Remove transmission and transfer case assembly as outlined under "Transmission, Replace."
2. Insert tool No. MB998127, or equivalent, in center hole to prevent dropping of clutch disc.
3. Diagonally loosen bolts that hold clutch cover assembly and remove assembly.
4. Slide release fork in direction of arrow, **Fig. 8,** to disengage fulcrum from clip.
5. Pack release fork fulcrum hole and release cylinder pushrod hole with grease.
6. Pack grease in groove on release bearing inside diameter.
7. Clean clutch facing and pressure plate with clean cloth.
8. Lightly grease clutch disc spline and main drive gear spline of transmission.
9. Using tool No. MB998127, or equivalent, install clutch disc and clutch cover assembly on flywheel. When installing clutch disc, make certain that surface with manufacturer's stamped mark is on pressure plate side.

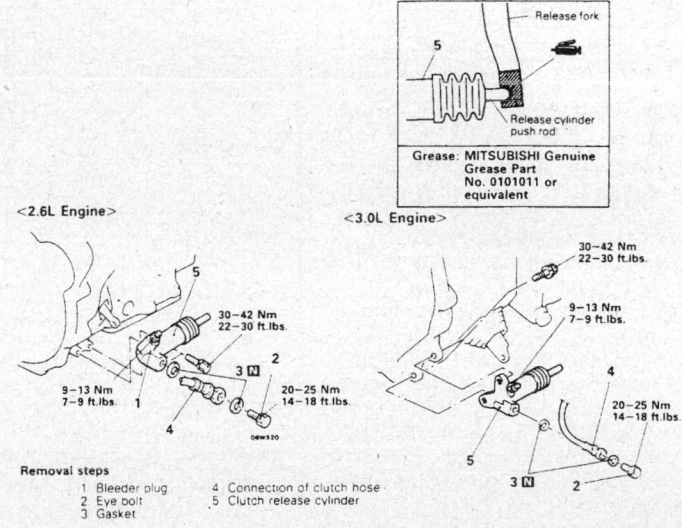

Fig. 5 Clutch slave cylinder replacement. Montero

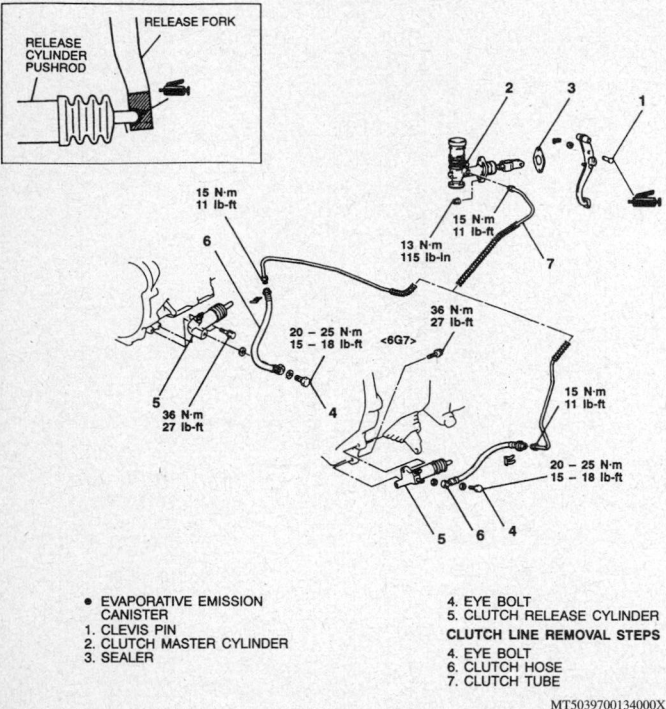

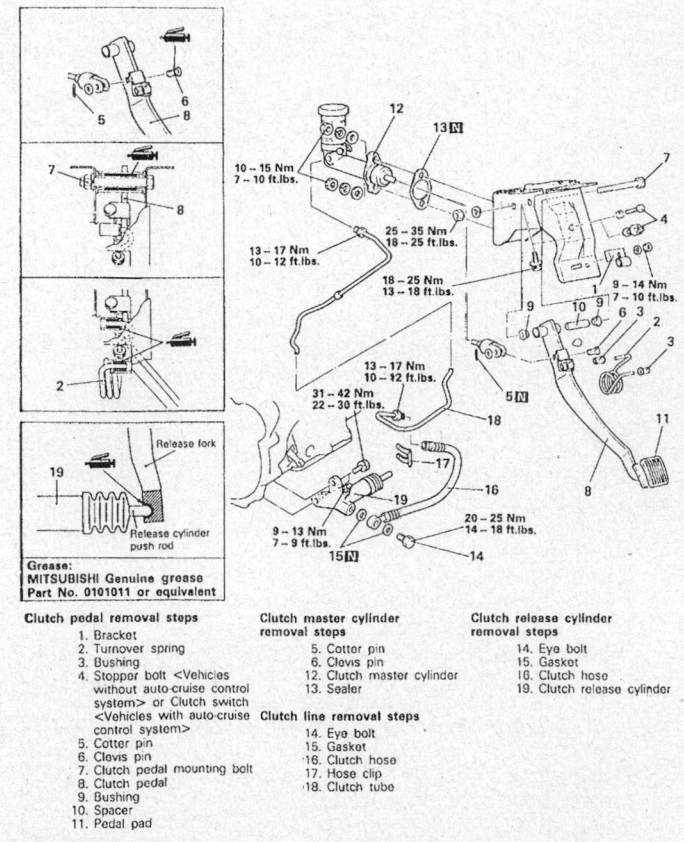

- EVAPORATIVE EMISSION CANISTER
1. CLEVIS PIN
2. CLUTCH MASTER CYLINDER
3. SEALER

4. EYE BOLT
5. CLUTCH RELEASE CYLINDER

CLUTCH LINE REMOVAL STEPS
4. EYE BOLT
6. CLUTCH HOSE
7. CLUTCH TUBE

MT5039700134000X

Fig. 6 Clutch slave cylinder replacement. Montero Sport

Clutch pedal removal steps
1. Bracket
2. Turnover spring
3. Bushing
4. Stopper bolt <Vehicles without auto-cruise control system> or Clutch switch <Vehicles with auto-cruise control system>
5. Cotter pin
6. Clevis pin
7. Clutch pedal mounting bolt
8. Clutch pedal
9. Bushing
10. Spacer
11. Pedal pad

Clutch master cylinder removal steps
5. Cotter pin
6. Clevis pin
12. Clutch master cylinder
13. Sealer

Clutch line removal steps
14. Eye bolt
15. Gasket
16. Clutch hose
17. Hose clip
18. Clutch tube

Clutch release cylinder removal steps
14. Eye bolt
15. Gasket
16. Clutch hose
19. Clutch release cylinder

Grease:
MITSUBISHI Genuine grease
Part No. 0101011 or equivalent

MT5049100048000X

Fig. 7 Clutch slave cylinder replacement. Pickup

TRANSMISSION

REPLACE

PICKUP

1. Remove mounting bolts from stopper plate, then the control lever assembly with the stopper plate.
2. Remove the front exhaust pipe assembly.
3. Drain transmission into a suitable container.
4. Mark then remove the propeller shaft assembly.
5. Disconnect back-up light and speedometer cable from transmission, **Fig. 9.**
6. Remove exhaust pipe bracket.
7. Remove bellhousing inspection cover.
8. Disconnect clutch release cable.
9. Support transmission with a suitable jack.
10. Remove rear engine support insulator and transmission mounting nuts and separate from the transmission.
11. Remove No. 2 crossmember mounting bolts then the crossmember.
12. Remove transmission from vehicle by moving reward then lowing.
13. Reverse procedure to install.

MONTERO & MONTERO SPORT

1. Remove transmission and transfer case levers.
2. Remove transfer case protector.
3. Disconnect and remove front exhaust pipe.
4. Drain transmission and transfer case fluid into a suitable container.

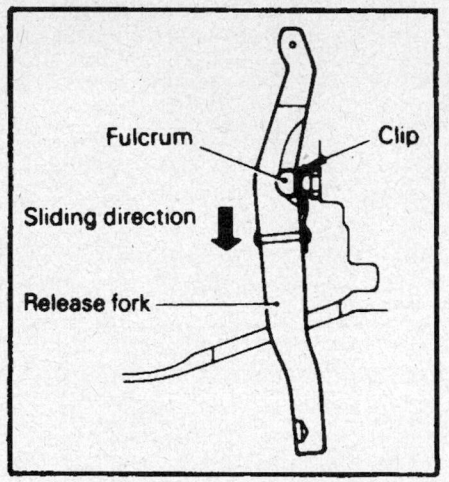

MT5049100049000X

Fig. 8 Release fork disengagement. Montero & Montero Sport

5. Mark then remove front and rear propeller shafts.
6. Replace transmission and transfer case assembly in numbered sequence shown in **Figs. 10 and 11,** noting the following:
   a. Remove clutch master cylinder actuator and suspend from body with hoses attached.
   b. Support transmission with a suit-

able transmission jack prior to removing transfer case roll stopper.
   c. Remove transmission and transfer case assembly by slowly pulling it toward the rear of the vehicle then tilt the front of the assembly downward and slowly lower assembly out of the vehicle.
7. Install control housing as follows:
   a. Remove adhesive sticking control housing bolts and bolt holes, **Fig. 12.**
   b. Apply 3M Stud Locking adhesive No. 4170, or equivalent, to bolts at section marked with a circled A.
   c. **On Montero models,** bolts labeled A are .3 inch in diameter and 1.6 inches long.
   d. **On Montero models,** bolts labeled B are reamer bolts .3 inch in diameter and 1.6 inches long.
   e. **On Montero models,** bolts labeled C are .3 inch in diameter and 1 inches long.
   f. **On Montero Sport models,** bolts labeled A are .3 inch in diameter and .7 inch long.
   g. **On Montero Sport models,** bolts labeled B are reamer bolts .3 inch in diameter and .8 inch long.
   h. **On Montero Sport models,** bolts labeled C are .3 inch in diameter and .9 inch long.

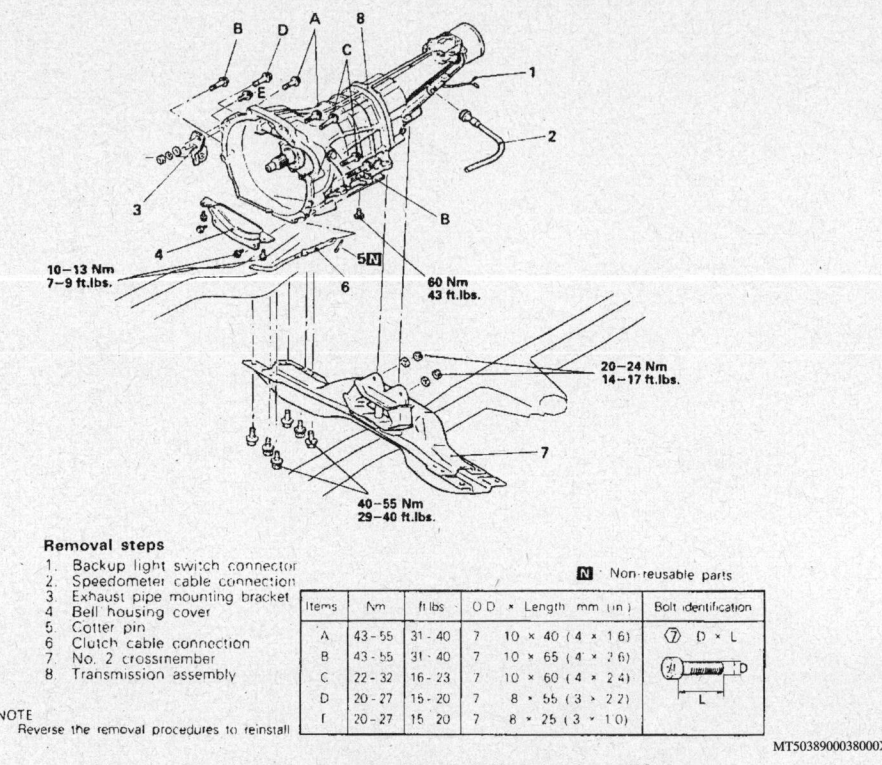

Removal steps
1. Backup light switch connector
2. Speedometer cable connection
3. Exhaust pipe mounting bracket
4. Bell housing cover
5. Cotter pin
6. Clutch cable connection
7. No. 2 crossmember
8. Transmission assembly

N Non-reusable parts

NOTE
Reverse the removal procedures to reinstall.

Items	Nm	ft lbs	O.D. × Length mm (in)	Bolt identification
A	43 – 55	31 - 40	7	10 × 40 (4 × 1.6)	⑦ D × L
B	43 – 55	31 - 40	7	10 × 65 (4 × 2.6)	
C	22 - 32	16 - 23	7	10 × 60 (4 × 2.4)	
D	20 - 27	15 - 20	7	8 × 55 (3 × 2.2)	
E	20 - 27	15 - 20	7	8 × 25 (3 × 1.0)	

MT5038900038000X

Fig. 9 Transmission replacement. Pickup

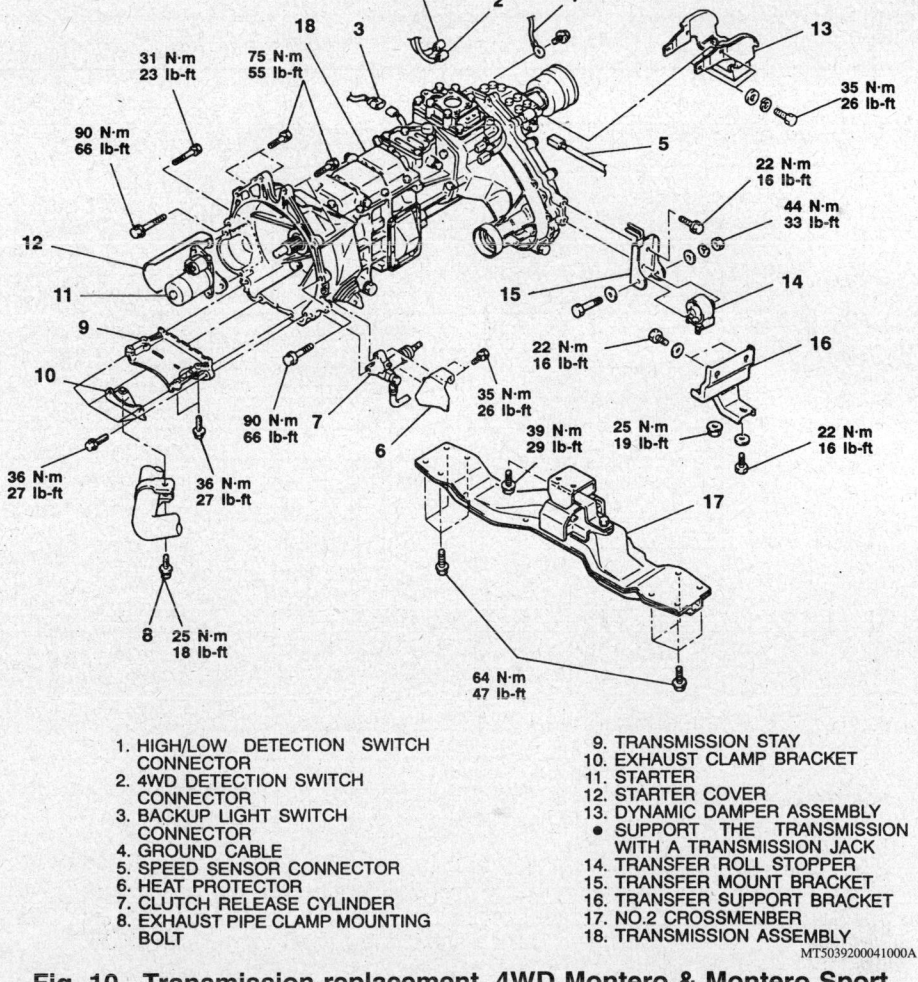

1. HIGH/LOW DETECTION SWITCH CONNECTOR
2. 4WD DETECTION SWITCH CONNECTOR
3. BACKUP LIGHT SWITCH CONNECTOR
4. GROUND CABLE
5. SPEED SENSOR CONNECTOR
6. HEAT PROTECTOR
7. CLUTCH RELEASE CYLINDER
8. EXHAUST PIPE CLAMP MOUNTING BOLT
9. TRANSMISSION STAY
10. EXHAUST CLAMP BRACKET
11. STARTER
12. STARTER COVER
13. DYNAMIC DAMPER ASSEMBLY
● SUPPORT THE TRANSMISSION WITH A TRANSMISSION JACK
14. TRANSFER ROLL STOPPER
15. TRANSFER MOUNT BRACKET
16. TRANSFER SUPPORT BRACKET
17. NO.2 CROSSMEMBER
18. TRANSMISSION ASSEMBLY

MT5039200041000A

Fig. 10 Transmission replacement. 4WD Montero & Montero Sport

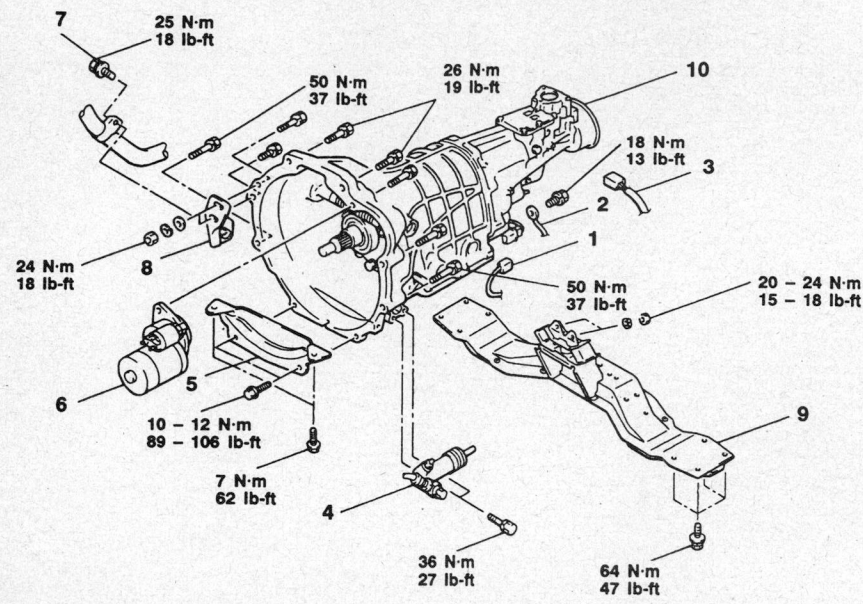

1. BACKUP LIGHT SWITCH CONNECTOR
2. GROUND CABLE CONNECTION
3. SPEED SENSOR CONNECTION
4. CLUTCH RELEASE CYLINDER
5. BELL HOUSING COVER
6. STARTER MOTOR
7. EXHAUST PIPE CLAMP MOUNTING BOLT
8. EXHAUST PIPE CLAMP MOUNTING BRACKET
● SUPPORT THE TRANSMISSION WITH A TRANSMISSION JACK
9. NO.2 CROSSMENBER ASSEMBLY
10. TRANSMISSION ASSEMBLY

MT5039700135000X

Fig. 11 Transmission replacement. 2WD Montero Sport

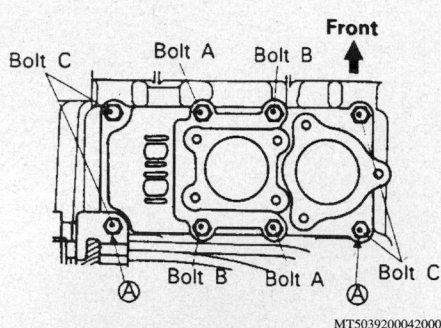

MT5039200042000X

Fig. 12 Control housing installation. Montero & Montero Sport

TIGHTENING SPECIFICATIONS

Year	Component	Torque/ Ft. Lbs.
1996–99	Adapter Cover Bolts	17 ③
	Adapter Part Poppet Spring Installation Screw Plug④	35
	Adapter Part Side Poppet Spring Installation Screw Plug④	22–30
	Back Light Switch	22–30
	Bellhousing Attaching Bolts	84–108⑧
	Bleeder Plug	84–108⑧
	Brake Pedal To Pedal Support③	18–25
	Chain Cover Bolt	22–30
	Clutch Cover Assembly To Flywheel	11–15
	Clutch Flare Nut	10–12
	Clutch Housing Mounting Bolts	86
	Clutch Master Cylinder To Firewall①	60–84⑧
	Clutch Master Cylinder To Firewall③	7–10
	Clutch Pedal Bracket①	13–18
	Clutch Pedal To Pedal Bracket①	18–25
	Clutch Release Cylinder Mounting Bolt①	22–29
	Control Housing Bolt	11–15
	Control Housing To Cover	84–108⑧
	Engine Mounting Rear Insulator To No. 2 Crossmember	13–18
	Engine Mounting Rear Insulator To Transmission	13–18

Continued

TIGHTENING
SPECIFICATIONS—Continued

Year	Component	Torque/ Ft. Lbs.
1996–99	Exhaust Pipe Mounting Bracket Mounting Bolts	15–20
	Extension Housing & Transmission Case Connection Bolt	11–15
	Eye Bolt	14–18
	Flywheel Bolt	54
	Front Exhaust Pipe Mounting Bolt	15–22
	Fulcrum	22–30
	Neutral Return Plunger Plug	35
	No. 2 Crossmember To Frame⑦	40–54
	No. 2 Crossmember Mounting Bolts⑥	29–36
	Oil Drain Plug⑤	43
	Oil Filler & Drain Plug④	17
	Oil Filler Drain Plug①	40–61
	Oil Filler Plug⑤	22—25
	Pedal Support Member Mounting Bolt③	72–108⑧
	Plugs	15
	Power Take-Off Cover Bolts	14
	Pulse Generator Bolt	7–9
	Pulse Rotor Bolt	11–15
	Release Cylinder To Transmission Case	22–30
	Rear Engine Support Insulator To Transmission⑥	14—17
	Reservoir Band	48–60⑧
	Seal Plug	22–30
	Select Plunger Plug	22–25
	Shift Knob⑥	46–63⑧
	Side Cover Bolt	60–84⑧
	Slotted Nut	15–43
	Speedometer Sleeve Clamp Bolt⑥	84–108⑧
	Starter Motor Mounting Bolt②	20–25
	Starting Motor Mounting Bolts⑥	16–23
	Stopper Bracket Assembly Attaching Bolt	11–15
	Stopper Plate To Control Housing⑥	60–109⑧
	Transmission Case & Clutch Housing	86
	Transmission Case & Lower Case	17
	Transmission Case PTO Cover	14
	Transmission To Engine (A)⑦	47–61
	Transmission To Engine (B)⑦	58–72
	Transmission To Engine⑤	32–39
	Transmission To Exhaust Pipe Mounting Bracket	15–20
	Transmission To Transmission Stay	22–30
	Undercover Attaching Bolt	60–84⑧

① — Montero & Montero Sport.
② — Models except Pickup.
③ — Pickup.
④ — Montero & Montero Sport 4WD.
⑤ — 2WD models.
⑥ — Pickup.
⑦ — 4WD models.
⑧ — Inch lbs.

Rear Axle & Suspension

INDEX

REAR AXLE

REPLACE

MONTERO & MONTERO SPORT

1. Raise and support vehicle.
2. Support rear axle using suitable jack stands.
3. Remove rear axle assembly in numbered sequence as shown, **Figs. 1 and 2,** noting the following:
   a. Make alignment marks on flange yoke of rear propeller shaft and flange of differential.
   b. After supporting axle assembly by floor jack, remove lower arm assembly.
   c. Remove rear axle assembly toward the rear of the vehicle. **Use care not to allow axle to fall.**
4. Reverse procedure to install, noting the following:
   a. **On Montero models,** install lateral rod bolt from the axle housing side.
   b. Install lower arm washers as shown **Fig. 3.**
   c. After installing stabilizer bar bracket, ensure amount of projection of stabilizer bar bolt is .59–.67 inch.
5. **On all models,** align propeller shaft mating marks made during disassembly.

REAR AXLE SHAFT

REPLACE

REMOVAL

1. Raise and support rear of vehicle, then remove rear wheel and brake drum and disconnect brake hose from wheel cylinder.
2. Disconnect bearing case from axle housing end, **Figs. 4 through 7.**
3. Remove brake backing plate, if equipped, bearing case, and axle shaft as an assembly, using slide hammer and adapter tool No. MB990211-01 and axle puller tool No. MB990241-01, or equivalents, to remove axle shaft if necessary.
4. Remove O-ring and wheel bearing preload shims.
5. Using slide hammer and adapter tool No. MB990211-01 and seal removal tool No. MB990212, or equivalents, remove oil seal.

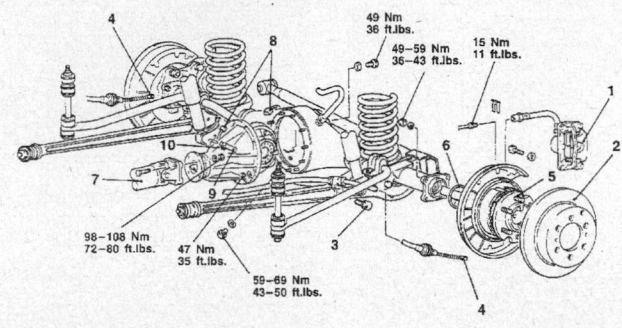

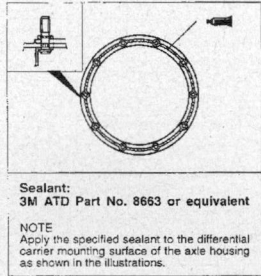

Fig. 1 Axle assembly replacement. Montero

Removal steps
1. Rear brake assembly
2. Brake disc
3. Parking brake cable attaching bolt
4. Parking brake cable end
5. Rear axle shaft assembly
6. O-ring
7. Rear propeller shaft
8. Rear differential lock position harness connector
9. Hose <Vehicles with rear differential lock>
10. Differential carrier

Sealant:
3M ATD Part No. 8663 or equivalent

NOTE
Apply the specified sealant to the differential carrier mounting surface of the axle housing as shown in the illustrations.

MT3039100008000X

6. **On Pickup models,** proceed as follows:
   a. Remove wheel bearing by first removing lock washer, then using locknut spanner wrench tool No. MB990785-01, or equivalent, remove the locknut.
   b. Remove washers, then reinsert locknut on axle shaft approximately three turns.
7. **On Montero and Montero Sport models,** proceed as follows:
   a. Remove one backing plate retaining bolt.
   b. Push bearing case down to expose bearing retainer.
   c. Apply protective tape on bearing case.
   d. Secure axle shaft assembly then, using suitable grinder, shave off a point of the bearing retainer until thickness is about .08 inch, **Fig. 8. Use care not to damage bearing case or axle shaft.**
   e. Using a suitable chisel, cut retainer ring and remove retainer.

8. **On all models,** install rear axle bearing case removal tool No. MB991560, or equivalent, as shown, **Fig. 9.**
9. Remove wheel bearing by turning nuts evenly.
10. Using hammer and drift punch, remove bearing outer race from bearing case.
11. Check all components for wear or damage and check axle shaft for runout.

INSTALLATION

1. After applying specified grease to outer surface of wheel bearing outer race and lip of new oil seal, drive them into bearing case using handle tool No. MB990938-01 and bearing and oil seal installer tool No. MB990937-01, or equivalents.
2. Slide bearing case and wheel bearing over axle shaft, lubricate wheel bearing rollers, then install wheel bearing inner race with axle bearing remover/installer tool No. MB990799, or equivalent.

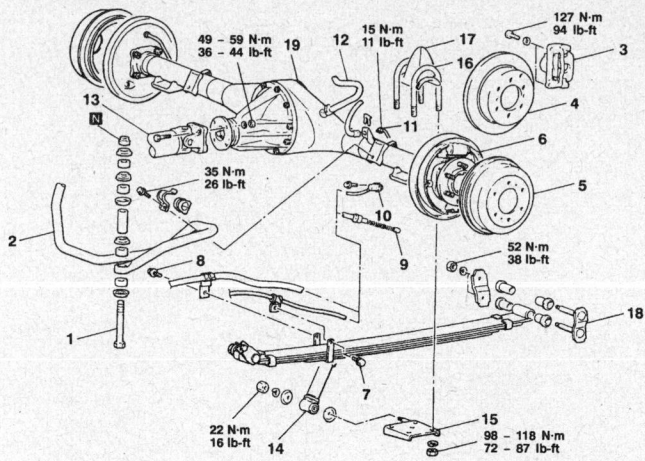

Fig. 2 Axle assembly replacement. Montero Sport

1. STABILIZER BAR MOUNTING BOLT
2. STABILIZER BAR
3. CALIPER ASSEMBLY <VEHICLES WITH DISC BRAKES>
4. BRAKE DISC <VEHICLES WITH DISC BRAKES>
5. BRAKE DRUM <VEHICLES WITH DRUM BRAKES>
6. SHOE AND LIMING ASSEMBLY (REFER TO GROUP 35A, REAR DRUM BRAKE OR REFER TO GROUP 36, PARKING BRAKE DRUM. >
7. PARKING BRAKE CABLE ATTACHING BOLT
8. SPEED SENSOR ATTACHING BOLT <VEHICLES WITH ABS>
9. PARKING BRAKE CABLE CONNECTION
10. SPEED SENSOR CONNECTION <VEHICLES WITH ABS>
11. BRAKE TUBE
12. BREATHER HOSE
13. PROPELLER SHAFT
14. SHOCK ABSORBER
15. U-BOLT SEAT
16. U-BOLT
17. BUMP STOPPER
18. SHACKLE ASSEMBLY
19. AXLE ASSEMBLY

MT2039700104000X

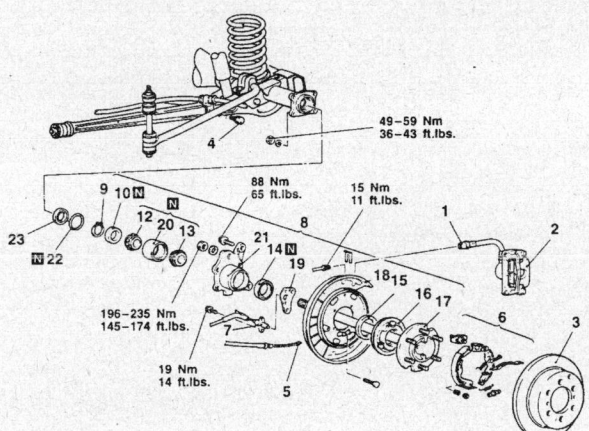

Fig. 4 Exploded view of axle shaft. Montero

Removal steps
1. Connection for brake pipe
2. Rear brake assembly
3. Brake disc
4. Parking brake cable attaching bolt
5. Parking cable end
6. Parking brake assembly
7. Speed sensor <Vehicles with ABS>
8. Axle shaft assembly
9. Snap ring
10. Retainer
11. Axle shaft sub assembly (Parts from step 13 to step 17)
12. Bearing inner race (inner)
13. Bearing inner race (outer)
14. Oil seal
15. Dust cover <Vehicles without ABS>
16. Rotor assembly <Vehicles with ABS>
17. Axle shaft
18. Backing plate
19. Speed sensor bracket <Vehicles with ABS>
20. Bearing outer race
21. Bearing case
22. O-ring
23. Oil seal

Installation steps
23. Oil seal
22. O-ring
21. Bearing case
20. Bearing outer race
19. Sped sensor bracket <Vehicles with ABS>
18. Backing plate
17. Axle shaft
16. Rotor assembly <Vehicles with ABS>
15. Dust cover <Vehicles with ABS>
13. Bearing inner race (outer)
14. Oil seal
12. Bearing inner race (inner)
10. Retainer
9. Snap ring
8. Axle shaft assembly
7. Speed sensor <Vehicles with ABS>

6. Parking brake assembly

5. Parking cable end
3. Brake disc
2. Rear brake assembly
1. Connection for brake pipe

MT3039100006000X

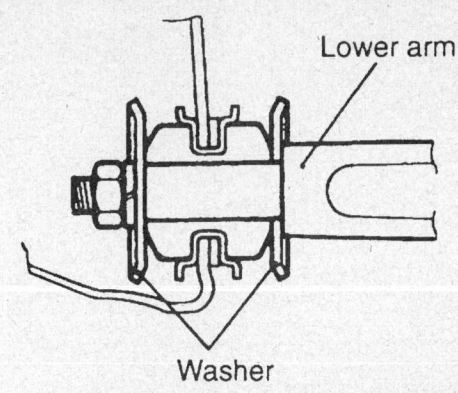

MT3039500056000X

Fig. 3 Lower arm washer installation. Montero

3. **On Pickup models,** proceed as follows:
   a. Install washer, lock washer and locknut, tighten locknut to specifications with locknut spanner wrench tool No. MB990785-01, or equivalent.
   b. Bend tab on lock washer into groove on locknut, tightening nut as necessary to align tab and groove.

4. **On all models,** install bearing retainer as follows:
   a. Press on bearing retainer while confirming that 11,023 lbs. of pressure or more is needed to start the bearing retainer on the axle shaft and 17,637 lbs. of pressure or more is used for the final pressure input.
   b. Install retainer snap ring, and measure clearance (A) as shown **Fig. 10,** is less than .0065 inch.

5. Lubricate lip of new oil seal, then using oil seal installer tool No. MB990930-01 and handle tool No. MB990938, or equivalents, drive oil seal into axle housing.

6. Adjust axial play of rear axle shaft as follows:
   a. Remove any old sealant and rust from mating surfaces of bearing case and axle housing.
   b. Insert a .04 inch shim and O-ring into left side of axle housing and apply semi-drying sealer to mating surface of bearing case.
   c. Insert left side axle shaft assembly into left side of axle housing, then tighten bearing case to specifications.
   d. Insert right side axle shaft assembly into right side axle housing without using shim or O-ring, then **torque** bearing case to 4 ft. lbs. Measure gap between bearing case and axle housing.
   e. Loosen nut and separate right side axle shaft assembly from axle housing.
   f. Using a shim with thickness equal to that of measured gap and a shim with thickness of .0020–.0079 inch, insert shims and O-ring into axle housing, then apply semi-drying sealant to mating surface of bearing case.

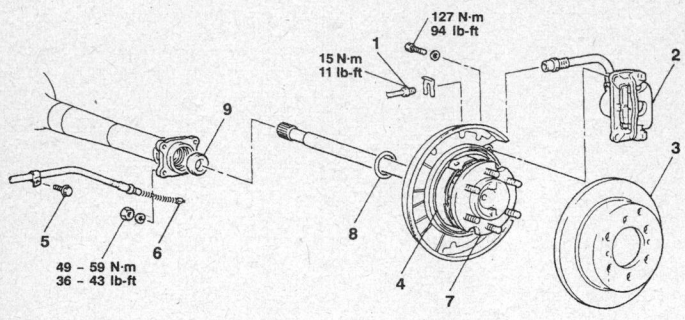

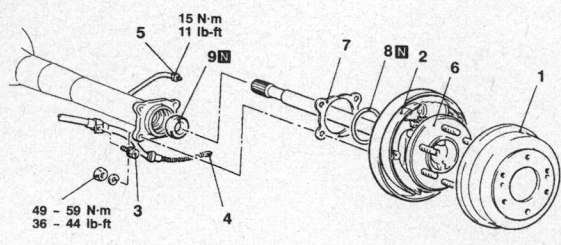

1. BRAKE TUBE
2. CALIPER ASSEMBLY
3. BRAKE DISC
4. PARKING BRAKE SHOE

5. PARKING BRAKE CABLE AND
   SPEED SENSOR <VEHICLES WITH
   ABS> ATTACHING BOLT
6. PARKING BRAKE CABLE
7. AXLE SHAFT ASSEMBLY
8. O-RING
9. OIL SEAL

MT3039700070000X

Fig. 5 Exploded view of axle shaft. Montero Sport w/disc brakes

1. BRAKE DRUM
2. SHOE AND LINING ASSEMBLY

3. PARKING BRAKE CABLE, SPEED
   SENSOR CABLE <VEHICLES WITH
   ABS> ATTACHMENT BOLT
4. PARKING BRAKE CABLE
   CONNECTION

5. BRAKE TUBE
● AXLE SHAFT END PLAY
  ADJUSTMENT <VEHICLES
  WITHOUT ABS>
6. AXLE SHAFT ASSEMBLY
7. SHIM <VEHICLES WITHOUT ABS>
8. O-RING
9. OIL SEAL

MT3039700071000X

Fig. 6 Exploded view of axle shaft. Montero Sport w/drum brakes

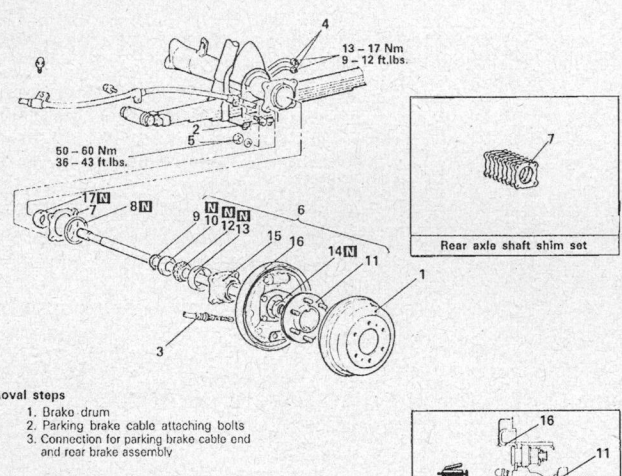

Rear axle shaft shim set

Removal steps
1. Brake drum
2. Parking brake cable attaching bolts
3. Connection for parking brake cable end
   and rear brake assembly

4. Brake tube connection
5. Nut
   Adjustment of rear axle shaft end play
6. Rear axle shaft assembly
   (with parking brake cable)
7. Shim
8. O-ring
9. Snap ring
10. Retainer ring
11. Rear axle shaft
12. Bearing inner race
13. Bearing outer race
14. Oil seal

15. Bearing case
16. Backing plate
17. Oil seal

MT3039100007000X

Fig. 7 Exploded view of axle shaft. Pickup

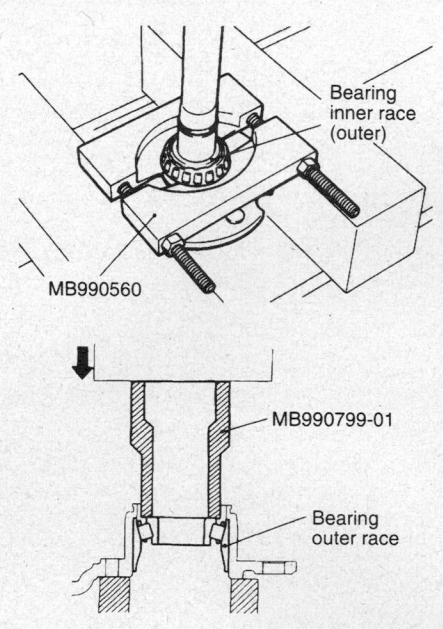

Fig. 9 Wheel bearing removal

11. Connect brake line to wheel cylinder, then install rear brake drum and wheel.

DIFFERENTIAL CARRIER
REPLACE

1. Drain gear oil into appropriate container.
2. Remove parking brake cable adjusting nuts, then disconnect parking brake cables.
3. Raise and support vehicle, then remove wheel and tire assembly.
4. Remove brake drum, then the axle shaft assembly as previously described.
5. Disconnect rear propeller shaft from differential assembly.
6. Remove differential carrier.
7. Reverse procedure to install.

g. Insert right side axle shaft assembly into right side axle housing, then tighten bearing case to specifications.
h. Using dial indicator, check that axial play of axle shaft is .002–.008 inch. If not, adjust shim thickness.
7. Lubricate bearing case and axle housing end.
8. Attach brake assembly, with wheel cylinder, to axle housing.
9. Insert O-ring between axle housing end and bearing case, then apply semi-drying sealant to bearing case.
10. Tighten bearing case to specifications.

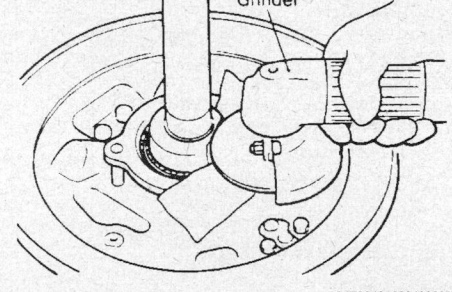

MT2049100043000X

Fig. 8 Bearing retainer removal

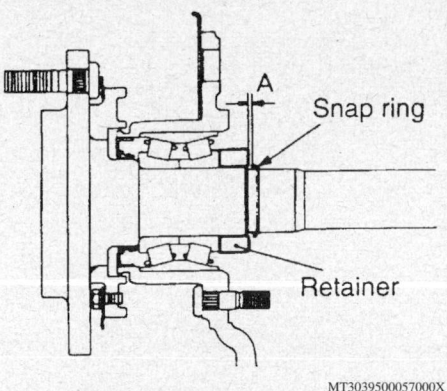

Fig. 10 Axle bearing retainer snap ring clearance

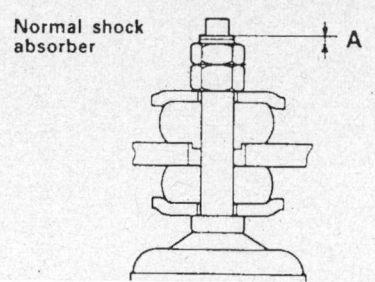

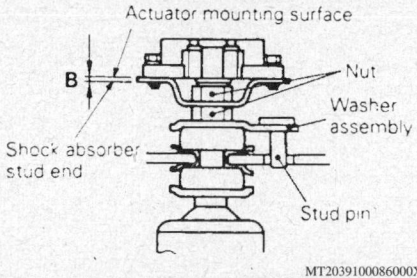

Fig. 11 Variable shock absorber actuator installation

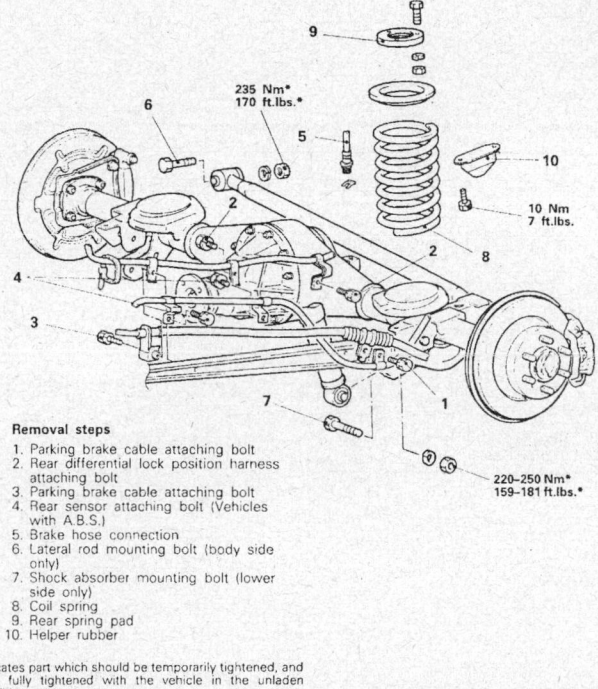

Removal steps
1. Parking brake cable attaching bolt
2. Rear differential lock position harness attaching bolt
3. Parking brake cable attaching bolt
4. Rear sensor attaching bolt (Vehicles with A.B.S.)
5. Brake hose connection
6. Lateral rod mounting bolt (body side only)
7. Shock absorber mounting bolt (lower side only)
8. Coil spring
9. Rear spring pad
10. Helper rubber

NOTE
*: Indicates part which should be temporarily tightened, and then fully tightened with the vehicle in the unladen condition.

Fig. 12 Coil spring replacement

SHOCK ABSORBER
REPLACE

1. Raise rear of vehicle, then position jackstands under frame side sills.
2. Disconnect variable shock absorbers actuator, if equipped.
3. Remove wheel and tire assembly, then disconnect shock absorbers at upper and lower mountings, then remove from vehicle.

4. Reverse procedure to install, noting the following:
   a. Tighten shock absorber attaching nuts to specification.
   b. **On models equipped with variable shock absorbers,** tighten nuts so dimension "A" is .04–.08 inch and dimension "B" is .06–.10 inch, **Fig. 11.**

COIL SPRING
REPLACE

1. Raise and support vehicle.
2. Support rear axle using suitable jack stand.
3. Remove coil spring in numbered sequence as shown **Fig. 12,** while slowly lowering jack supporting axle housing to remove coil spring.
4. Reverse procedure to install.

LEAF SPRING
REPLACE

1. Loosen rear wheel lug nuts, then jack up rear of vehicle with jack placed under differential.
2. Remove rear wheels and support vehicle on axle stands placed forward of rear spring front bracket, with jack still applying slight upward pressure on axle assembly, **Fig. 13.**
3. Make mating marks on rear propeller shaft flange yoke and companion flange of differential case to facilitate installation, then remove propeller shaft.
4. Remove adjusting nuts, then disconnect parking brake cables.
5. Loosen joint between brake hose and brake line and pull out stops to disconnect brake hose.
6. Disconnect rear cable of parking brake at balancer.
7. **On 4WD models,** disconnect breather hose.
8. **On all models,** disconnect shock absorbers at lower end.
9. Remove spring U-bolts, then the spring seats.
10. Remove spring shackle pin nuts, then the shackle plate. **Ensure not to drop axle housing from jack.**
11. Remove axle housing by slowly lowering jack.
12. Reverse procedure to install, noting the following:
    a. Align match marks when installing propeller shaft.
    b. Install spring support so distance between hole on load sensing proportioning valve lever and spring support hole is 6.77–6.93 inches.
    c. Bleed rear brake system.

CONTROL ARM
REPLACE
LOWER

1. Raise and support vehicle.
2. Support rear axle using suitable jack stand.
3. Replace lower arm in numbered sequence as shown **Fig. 14,** installing lower arm front bushing as shown **Fig. 15.**

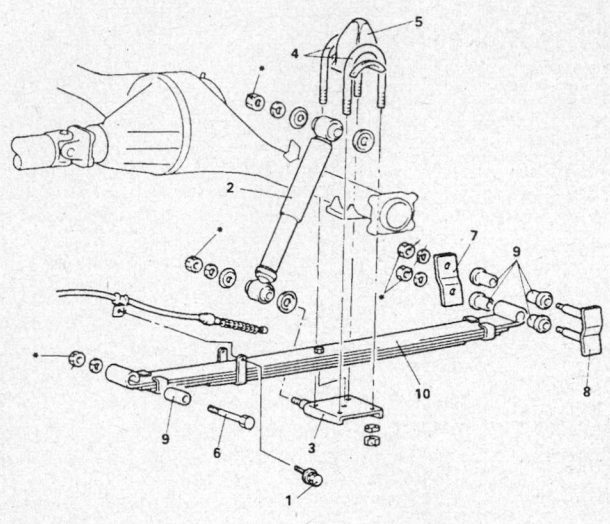

Removal steps

1. Parking brake cable attaching bolt
2. Shock absorber
3. U-bolt seat
4. U-bolts
5. Bump stopper
6. Bolt

7. Shackle plate
8. Shackle assembly
9. Rubber bushing
10. Rear spring

NOTE
* Tighten when the vehicle is unloaded.

MT2039100087000X

Fig. 13   Leaf spring replacement

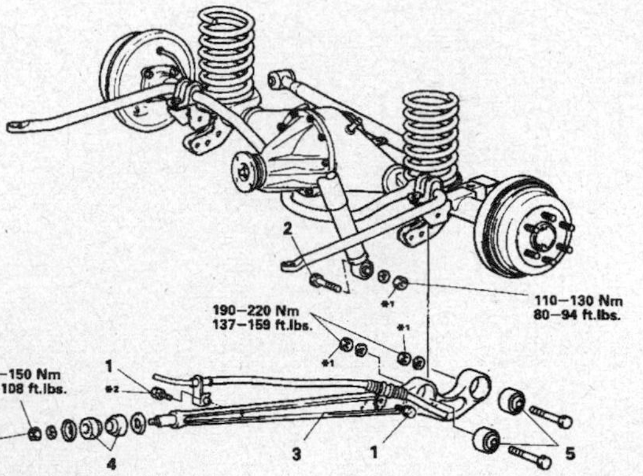

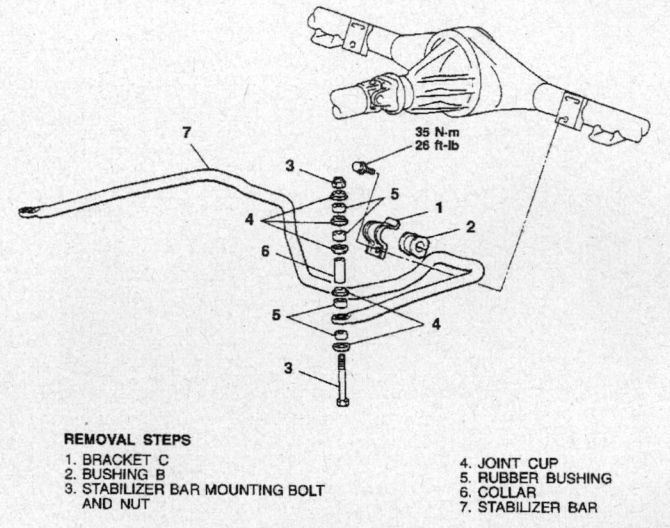

Removal steps

1. Parking brake cable attaching bolt
2. Shock absorber mounting bolts (Lower side)
3. Lower arm
4. Lower arm front bushing
5. Lower arm rear bushing

190—220 Nm
137—159 ft.lbs.

110—130 Nm
80—94 ft.lbs.

130—150 Nm
94—108 ft.lbs.

NOTE
(1) *¹ : Tighten when the vehicle is unloaded.
(2) The part with *² is available only for the 4-door models.

MT2039100089000X

Fig. 14   Lower arm replacement

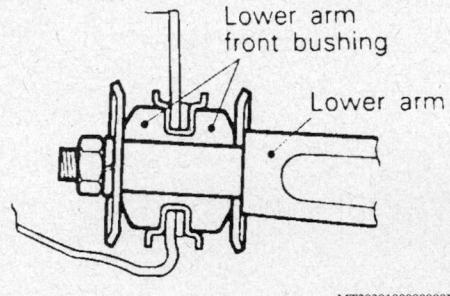

Lower arm front bushing

Lower arm

MT2039100090000X

Fig. 15   Lower arm bushing installation

STABILIZER BAR

REPLACE

1. Raise and support vehicle.
2. Remove rear stabilizer bar in numbered sequence as shown **Fig. 16.**
3. Reverse procedure to install.

LATERAL ROD

REPLACE

1. Raise and support vehicle.
2. Disconnect shock absorber lower mounting bolt.

REMOVAL STEPS

1. BRACKET C
2. BUSHING B
3. STABILIZER BAR MOUNTING BOLT AND NUT

4. JOINT CUP
5. RUBBER BUSHING
6. COLLAR
7. STABILIZER BAR

35 N·m
26 ft-lb

MT2039100091000X

Fig. 16   Stabilizer bar replacement

3. Disconnect left brake cable attaching bolt.
4. Remove rear differential lock position harness attaching bolt.
5. Disconnect rear anti-lock brake sensor (ABS) sensor attaching bolt.
6. Disconnect lower arm, then remove arm from vehicle.
7. Reverse procedure to install.

TIGHTENING SPECIFICATIONS

Year	Component	Torque/ Ft. Lbs.
1996–99	Axle Bumper To Body	72–108 ⑤
	Bearing Case To Axle Housing	36–43
	Brake Line Flare Nut	9–12
	Differential Carrier To Axle Housing	④
	Differential Drain Plug	36–51
	Differential Filler Plug	29–43
	Front Pin Assembly Mounting Bolt	10–14
	Front Pin Assembly Mounting Nut	33–43
	Lateral Rod Mounting Bolt	72–87
	Lateral Rod Mounting Nut	80–94
	Leaf Spring Front Mounting Bolt	87–116
	Lower Control Arm To Axle Housing	137–159
	Lower Control Arm To Body	94–108
	Pinion Yoke Nut	159
	Propeller Shaft	36–43
	Rear Axle Bearing Locknut	130–159
	Shackle Assembly Mounting Nut	33–43
	Shock Absorber Mounting Nut	②
	Stabilizer Bar To Axle Housing	22–29
	U-Bolt Mounting Nut	①
	Wheel Lug Nuts	③

① — Montero & Montero Sport, 61–80 ft. lbs.; Pickup, 72–87 ft. lbs.

② — Montero & Montero Sport: upper, 11 ft. lbs.; lower, 65–76 ft. lbs.; Pickup: upper, 9–13 ft. lbs.; lower, 7–10 ft. lbs.

③ — Montero & Montero Sport, 72–87 ft. lbs.; Pickup, 87–101 ft. lbs.

④ — Montero & Montero Sport w/3.0L, 29–40 ft. lbs.; Pickup, 18–22 ft. lbs.

⑤ — Inch lbs.

Transfer Case

INDEX

TRANSFER CASE

REPLACE

The transmission and transfer case are removed as an assembly. Refer to removal procedure as outlined under "Transmission, Replace."

FLUID CHANGE

1. Raise and support vehicle, then drain transfer case fluid. Refer to **Fig. 1,** for drain plug location.

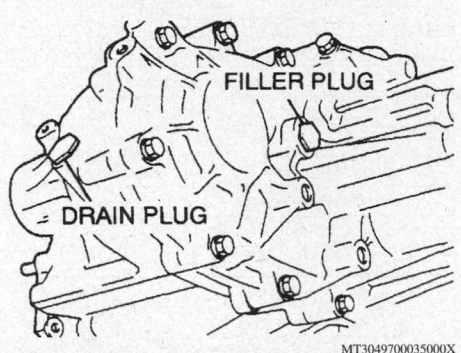

FILLER PLUG

DRAIN PLUG

MT3049700035000X

Fig. 1 Drain & fill plug locations

2. After fluid has drained, tighten drain plug to specifications.
3. Refer to **Fig. 1,** for fill plug location, then fill with specified fluid to bottom of fill plug opening.
4. Tighten filler plug to specifications.
5. Lower vehicle, then test drive and ensure proper operation of transfer case.

TIGHTENING SPECIFICATIONS

Year	Component	Torque/ Ft. Lbs.
1996–99	Adapter To Transfer Case Mounting Bolts & Nuts	22–30
	Extension Housing & Transmission Case Connection Bolt	11–15
	Oil Filler & Drain Plug①	22–25
	Rear Cover Bolt②	60–84③
	Transfer Adapter & Transmission Case Coupling Bolt	11–15
	Transfer Case Adapter To Transmission Case Mounting Bolts	30
	Transfer Mounting Bracket To Pipe	25–40
	Transfer Mounting Bracket To Transmission	13–18
	Transfer Mounting Bracket Mounting Bolts	13–18
	Transmission Case & Transfer Adapter	30
	4WD Indicator Light Switch	22

① — Transfer case.

② — Montero & Montero Sport transfer case assembly.

③ — Inch lbs.

Front Suspension & Steering

INDEX

HUB SERVICE

MONTERO & MONTERO SPORT

Removal

1. Remove wheel and tire assembly, then the brake caliper assembly with brake hose connected. **Suspend caliper assembly from frame using a wire hook to prevent damage to brake hose.**
2. Remove automatic freewheeling hub cover. When cover cannot be loosened by hand, protect cover with shop towel to prevent damage, then loosen cover using a suitable oil filter wrench.
3. Remove O-ring from hub cover, then the snap ring and spacer.
4. Remove automatic freewheeling hub using tool No. MD998360, or equivalent, **Figs. 1 and 2.**
5. Remove lock washer, then the hub locknut using tool No. MB990954, or equivalent, **Fig. 3.**
6. Pull front hub with brake disc from knuckle, using care not to drop outer wheel bearing inner race.
7. Remove grease from inside front hub, then using a suitable drift, drive bearing races from hub.
8. Place alignment marks on brake disc and hub, then separate hub and disc as necessary.
9. Inspect all components for wear and damage. Measure spindle bearing seating area diameter, **Fig. 4.** Diameter should be 1.7805–1.7812 inches.

Disassemble

1. Remove cover, then the O-ring.
2. Remove housing, then depress brake "B" and remove C-ring.
3. Remove brakes "B" and "A," then the brake spring.
4. Remove housing snap ring, then using tool No. MB990811-01, or equivalent, depress drive gear and remove retainer and C-ring.
5. Using tool No. MB990811-01, or equivalent, and a suitable press, remove drive gear, slide gear and return spring.
6. Remove retainer "B," then the retainer bearing.
7. Remove drive gear snap ring and discard.

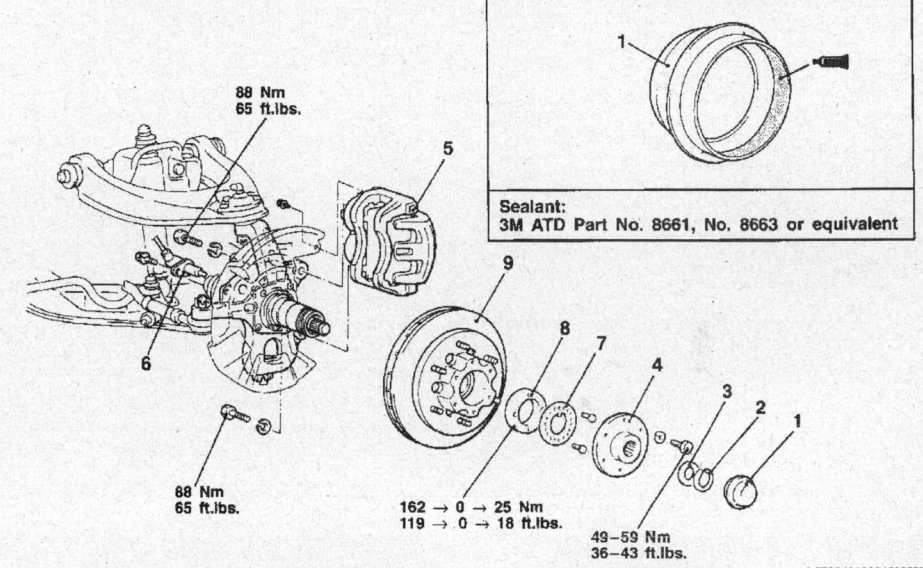

Fig. 1 Exploded view of front axle hub. 1996

88 Nm
65 ft.lbs.

88 Nm
65 ft.lbs.

162 → 0 → 25 Nm
119 → 0 → 18 ft.lbs.

49–59 Nm
36–43 ft.lbs.

Sealant:
3M ATD Part No. 8661, No. 8663 or equivalent

MT2049100045000X

8. Remove retainer "A," then the drive gear.
9. Depress cam, then remove slide gear C-ring.
10. Remove cam, then the spring holder, shift spring and slide gear.

Assemble

Reverse disassemble procedure to assemble, noting the following:
1. Apply suitable grease to mounting surfaces of all components.
2. Pack groove in brake "B," groove around outside of retainer and both sides of bearing with suitable grease.
3. Install return spring with smaller coil diameter side toward spring seat.

Installation

1. Apply grease to wheel bearing outer races, then using a suitable drift, drive outer races into front hub.
2. Pack inner and outer bearings with suitable grease. Apply grease to oil seal lip.
3. Evenly coat inner wall of front hub with grease.
4. Position inner bearing and oil seal on hub, then install oil seal using tool No. MB990985, or equivalent.
5. If removed, install brake disc on front hub, **Fig. 1,** tightening attaching bolts alternately and evenly to 36–44 ft. lbs. After assembling, check brake disc runout. Brake disc runout should not exceed .006 inch.
6. Carefully install front hub on steering knuckle spindle.
7. Install outer bearing on spindle, then install and **torque** spindle nut to 94–145 ft. lbs. Loosen spindle nut and re-tighten to 18 ft. lbs., then back-off and install lock washer. **If hole in lock washer is not aligned with hole in spindle nut, then nut may be loosened up to an additional 20° to obtain proper alignment.**
8. Measure force required to rotate front hub, using a suitable spring scale, **Fig. 5.** The force required to rotate front hub assembly should be between .9–4.1 lbs. If not within specification, readjust bearings as outlined in step 7.
9. Apply grease to inner surface of freewheeling hub body assembly.
10. Apply semi-dry sealant to front hub surface to which the freewheeling hub body assembly is attached.
11. Install freewheeling hub body assembly on front hub, then tighten attaching bolts to specification.
12. Install freewheeling hub cover and tighten to specification.

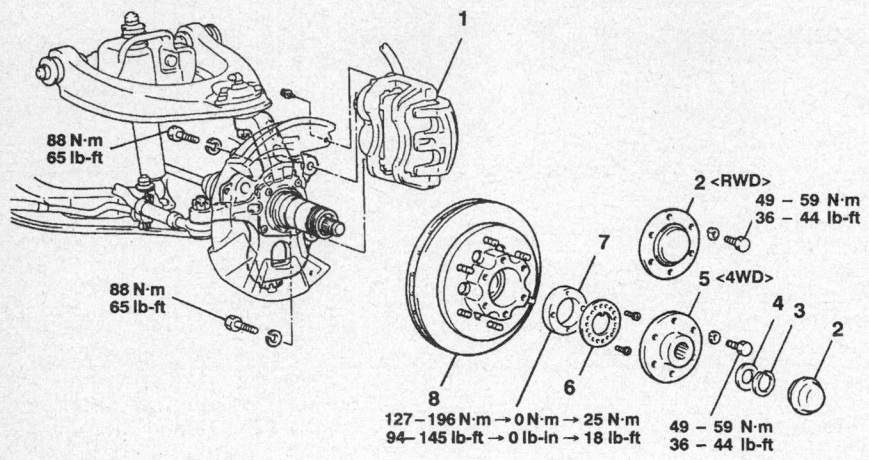

1. CALIPER ASSEMBLY
2. HUB CAP
● DRIVE SHAFT END PLAY
ADJUSTMENT <4WD>
3. SNAP RING
4. SHIM
5. DRIVE FLANGE

● HUB ROTARY SLIDING
RESISTANCE AND WHEEL
BEARING AXIAL MOVEMENT
ADJUSTMENT <4WD>
6. SPRING WASHER
7. JAM NUT
8. FRONT HUB ASSEMBLY

Fig. 2 Exploded view of front axle hub. 1997–99

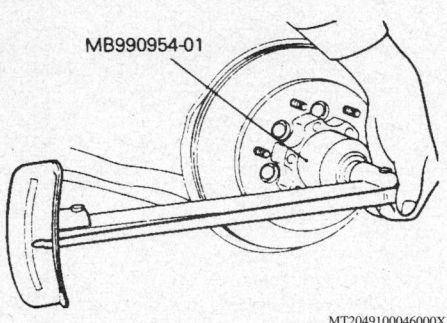

Fig. 3 Spindle nut removal

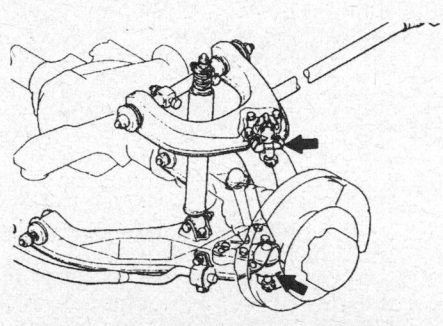

**Fig. 6 Lower ball joint dust
cover inspection**

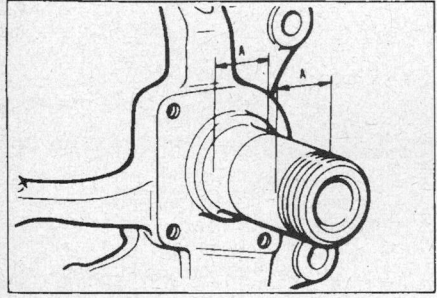

Fig. 4 Spindle inspection

13. Install brake caliper assembly.

BALL JOINT INSPECTION

LOWER

1. These components are permanently lubricated. They do not require periodic lubrication. Damaged seals and boots should be replaced to prevent leakage or contamination to grease.
2. Inspect dust cover and boots for proper sealing, leakage and damage. Replace if defective, **Fig. 6.**

UPPER

1. Using suitable socket and torque wrench, measure breakaway torque of ball joint.
2. Torque reading should be 7–30 inch lbs. if measurement exceeds this limit, replace ball joint.
3. If measurement is lower than limit, ball joint may still be used.

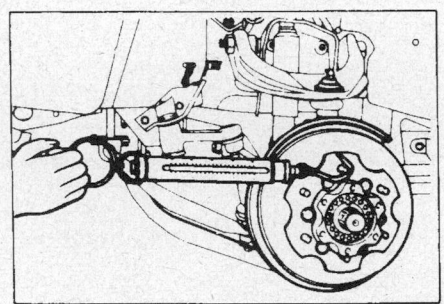

**Fig. 5 Front hub assembly
bearing adjustment**

4. Rotate ball joint and ensure smooth rotation without excessive play.

TORSION BAR

REPLACE

1. Remove torsion bar locknut.
2. Measure distance "A" from end of anchor bolt to outer edge of nut, then remove torsion bar adjusting nut. If torsion bar is to be reused, when reinstalling nut ensure distance " A" equals the value found prior to removal of nut.
3. Remove seat-holding nut, anchor bolt and nuts.
4. Remove torsion bar assembly.
5. Move the dust covers of the front and rear anchor arms and make mating marks on the anchor arms and the torsion bar. Remove the anchor arms from the torsion bar.
6. Reverse procedure to install, noting the following:
   a. When installing torsion bar, note that the marked end of the bar is to

be installed toward the rear of the vehicle.
b. Apply suitable grease to the torsion bar serrations and dust covers.
c. If torsion bar is to be reused, reinstall anchor arms, ensuring they line up with mating marks.
d. Apply suitable grease to threaded part of anchor bolt.
e. **On Pickup models,** when using a new torsion bar, perform the following prior to installing torsion bar adjusting nut. Offset the torsion bar's and rear anchor arm's phase so value of projection "B," **Fig. 7,** of the anchor bolt (from the rear anchor arm) is 1.42 inches. As a temporary adjustment of vehicle height, tighten torsion bar adjusting nut until amount of projection of anchor bolt is 2.48 inches.
f. **On all models,** tighten torsion bar adjusting nut until amount of projection of anchor bolt is 3.15 inches.

STABILIZER BAR

REPLACE

MONTERO, MONTERO SPORT & 4WD PICKUP

1. Remove stabilizer bar from lower arm and stabilizer link assembly.
2. Inspect stabilizer bar, bushings, and stabilizer link assembly and replace as necessary.
3. Install stabilizer bar, noting the following:
   a. When installing stabilizer link assembly to No. 1 crossmember, tighten self locking nut, ensuring

distance from base of nut to top of stud is .24–.31 inch.

b. When installing ends of stabilizer bar to lower arms, tighten self-locking nuts, ensuring distance from base of nut to end of bolt is .24–.31 inch.

c. Tighten stabilizer bracket attaching nuts to specification.

2WD PICKUP

1. Disconnect strut bar at lower control arm.
2. Disconnect strut bar at strut bar bracket and slide bar out.
3. Disconnect stabilizer bar at stabilizer bracket and at stabilizer links and remove bar.
4. Inspect stabilizer bar, strut bar and bushings, then replace as necessary.
5. Reverse procedure to install, noting the following:
   a. LH strut bar is marked with an "L."
   b. Strut bar bushings for front side and rear side are different. Bushing with convex surface is installed on front side.
   c. When installing strut bar to strut bar bracket, distance between face of innermost nut and end of strut bar should be 2.9 inches. Tighten top end nut to specification after vehicle is lowered to ground. Check caster adjustment and correct as necessary, then adjust distance between nut face and bar end as necessary.
   d. When installing stabilizer bar to links, tighten first nut, ensuring distance between top of nut and end of bolt is .87–.94 inch
   e. Tighten stabilizer bracket attaching bolts to specification.

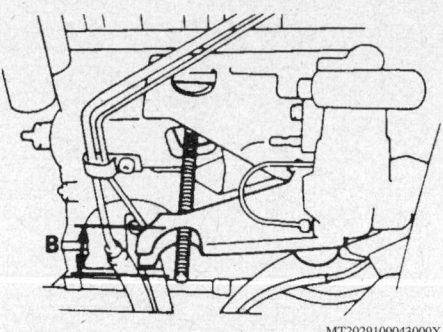

MT2029100043000X

Fig. 7 Anchor bolt installation measurement

STRUT BAR
REPLACE
2WD PICKUP

Refer to "Stabilizer Bar, Replace" for strut bar replacement procedure.

POWER STEERING GEAR
REPLACE
MONTERO & MONTERO SPORT

1. Remove clamp bolt that connects steering shaft to steering gear mainshaft.
2. Using tool Nos. MB990716 and MB990717, or equivalents, disconnect pressure and return hoses from steering gear.
3. Using tool No. MB990635, or equivalent, disconnect pitman arm from relay rod.

4. Remove steering gear.
5. Using tool No. MB990915, or equivalent, remove pitman arm from steering gear.
6. Reverse procedure to install.

PICKUP

1. Disconnect steering shaft from input worm shaft.
2. Using tool No. MB990635, or equivalent, disconnect tie rod and pitman arm from relay rod.
3. Remove air cleaner, then disconnect pressure and return hoses from steering gear and remove undercover.
4. Loosen steering gear mounting bolts.
5. **On models equipped with automatic transmission,** remove throttle linkage and throttle linkage splash shield.
6. **On models equipped with manual transmission,** remove starter.
7. **On all models,** remove steering gear from below vehicle.
8. Using tool No. MB990809, or equivalent, remove pitman arm.
9. Reverse procedure to install.

MANUAL STEERING GEAR
REPLACE
PICKUP

1. Remove clamp bolt connecting steering shaft and steering gear.
2. Using tool No. MB990635, or equivalent, disconnect tie rod and pitman arm from relay rod.
3. Remove steering gear downward from body frame.
4. Using tool No. MB990809, or equivalent, remove pitman arm from cross shaft.
5. Reverse procedure to install.

TIGHTENING SPECIFICATIONS

Year	Component	Torque/Ft. Lbs.
1996–99	Anchor Arm	69–87
	Anchor Arm Locknut	29–36
	Automatic Free Wheeling Hub Cover	13–25
	Axle Nut	144–188
	Bearing Cap	40–47
	Bracket To Differential Carrier	58–80
	Brake Tube Flare Nut	9–12
	Brake Tube To Front Brake	9–12
	Bump Stop To Lower Arm	14–22
	Center Bearing Bracket To Engine Strut Assembly	26–33
	Center Member Rear Mounting Bolt	43–58
	Companion Flange To Drive Pinion	116–159
	Differential Case To Drive Gear	58–65
	Differential Cover To Differential Carrier	11–16
	Differential Mounting Brackets To Frame	58–80
	Disc Cover To Strut Assembly	72–108④
	Drain Plug	43–51
	Driveshaft Nut	144–188
	Engine Mount Bracket To Crossmember	22–29
	Filler Plug	29–43
	Freewheeling Hub Body Or Front Hub Assembly	36–43
	Freewheeling Hub Cover	7–10④
	Front Anchor Arm To Upper Arm	51–69
	Front Hub To Brake Disc	36–43
	Front Propeller Shaft To Differential Carrier	36–43
	Front Shock Absorber To Crossmember	9–13
	Front Shock Absorber To Lower Arm②	11–16
	Front Suspension Crossmember Mounting Bolts	72–87
	Housing Tube To Differential Carrier	58–72
	Hub Nut	144–188
	Knuckle Arm To Ball Joint	43–52
	Knuckle Arm To McPherson Strut Assembly	58–72
	Knuckle Spindle To Slotted Nut	⑦
	Knuckle To Front Brake Assembly	58–72
	Knuckle To Front Brake Tube	36–43
	Knuckle To Tie Rod Assembly	33
	Left Differential Mounting Bracket To Differential Carrier	58–72
	Lower Arm Ball Joint	43–52
	Lower Arm Bushing	90–112
	Lower Arm Mounting Shaft Mounting Nut	69–87
	Lower Arm Rear Mounting Bolt	43–58
	Lower Arm Shaft①	101–116
	Lower Arm Shaft Bolt	58–69
	Lower Arm Shaft Flange	72–96④
	Lower Arm To Ball Joint⑥	39–54
	Lower Arm To Ball Joint⑤	22–30
	Lower Arm To Suspension Crossmember	80–94
	Lower Ball Joint to Knuckle	87–130
	Pinion Yoke Nut	⑧
	Rear Roll Stopper Mounting Nut	33–43
	Rebound Stop To Rebound Stop Bracket	14–22

Continued

TIGHTENING
SPECIFICATIONS—Continued

Year	Component	Torque/ Ft. Lbs.
1996–99	Rebound Stop To Upper Arm	72–108④
	Right Differential Mounting Bracket To Housing Tube	58–72
	Right Driveshaft To Inner Shaft	36–43
	Shock Absorber Ring Nut	101–108
	Spring Seat To Strut Assembly	29–36
	Stabilizer Bar Bracket	72–108④
	Stabilizer Bar Mounting Bolt	12–19
	Stabilizer Bar To Lower Arm	7–14
	Stabilizer Link Mounting Nut	40–51
	Strut Assembly To Brake Assembly	58–72
	Strut Bar Bracket To Frame	25–33
	Strut Bar Locknut①	54–61
	Strut Bar To Lower Arm	43–51
	Strut Bar To Strut Bar Bracket Mounting Nut	54–61
	Strut Insulator To Body	18–25
	Strut Mounting Self Locking Nut	29–36
	Suspension Crossmember Mounting Bolts To Frame	36–48④
	Suspension Crossmember To Body	87–116
	Suspension Crossmember To Steering Gearbox	51–65
	Tie Rod And Turnbuckle Locking Nut	36–40
	Tie Rod End Ball Joint	11–25
	Tie Rod End To Knuckle Arm	25–33
	Torsion Bar Adjusting Nut To Torsion Bar Locknut	29–36
	Transfer Assembly	40–43
	Undercover To Frame	84–108④
	Under Skid Plate To side Frame	13–18
	Upper Arm Shaft To Crossmember	72–87
	Upper Ball Joint To Knuckle	43–65
	Wheel Lug Nuts	③

① — Must be tightened while vehicle is unladen.

② — Montero & Montero Sport.

③ — Montero & Montero Sport, 72–87 ft. lbs.; Pickup, 87–101 ft. lbs.

④ — Inch lbs.

⑤ — 2WD.

⑥ — 4WD.

⑦ — Three steps, first to 22 ft. lbs., back off to 0 ft. lbs., then finally to 8 ft. lbs.

⑧ — Montero: w/auto transmission, 137 ft. lbs. w/manual transmission, 159 ft. lbs. Montero Sport & Pickup: 159 ft. lbs.

Wheel Alignment

INDEX

PRELIMINARY INSPECTION

1. Ensure tires are inflated to correct pressure, then check for uneven wear.
2. Inspect front wheel bearings, suspension arm and ball joints for damage and replace as necessary.
3. Inspect steering gear for damage and adjust as necessary.
4. Inspect shocks for damage and replace as necessary.
5. Rock vehicle backward and forward and bounce it upward and downward to settle vehicle prior to alignment.
6. Ensure vehicle is unloaded and on a suitable alignment rack according to manufacturers' instructions. **When measuring equipment is attached directly to outer end of driveshaft and front wheels are on turntables, apply brake to prevent improper vehicle movement.**

FRONT WHEEL ALIGNMENT

CAMBER

Montero, Montero Sport & 4WD Pickup

Adjust camber by adjusting number of shims between upper arm shaft and arm post of side frame. A .039 inch adjustment of shim thickness provides approximately 13 minutes adjustment of camber, **Fig. 1**.

2WD Pickup

1. Hold upper arm shaft to crossmember bolt and remove nut from engine compartment side.
2. Adjust number of shims between upper arm shaft and crossmember. A total of approximately .16 inch of shim thickness is standard camber. A .039 inch adjustment of shim thickness provides approximately 13 minutes adjustment of camber.

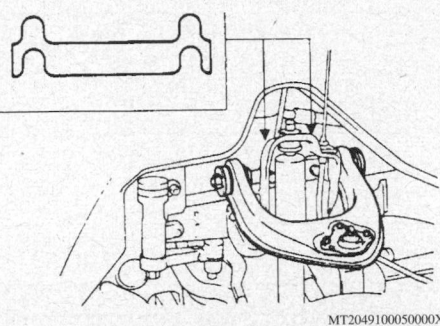

Fig. 1   Front camber adjustment. Montero, Montero Sport & 4WD Pickup

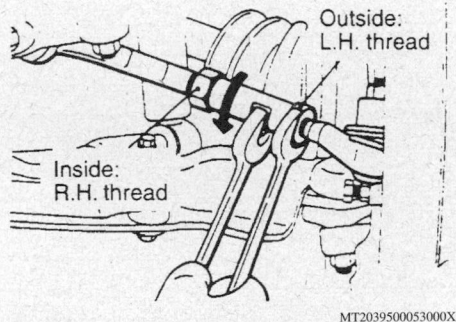

Fig. 2   Front toe-in adjustment. Montero, Montero Sport & 4WD Pickup

CASTER

Adjustment of caster on these vehicles is made by turning the eccentrics on upper arm shaft. A half turn of upper arm shaft will cause .049 inch fore or aft movement of upper arm shaft, resulting in 3 ¾° caster adjustment.

TOE-IN

Montero, Montero Sport & 4WD Pickup

1. Adjust toe-in by turning left and right tie rod turnbuckles equal amounts in opposite directions, **Fig. 2**.
2. Toe-in on left wheel is reduced by turning tie rod toward front of vehicle or increased by turning tie rod toward rear of vehicle. Toe-in on right wheel is reduced by turning tie rod toward rear of vehicle or increased by turning tie rod toward front of vehicle. A half turn of turnbuckles changes toe-in approximately .3 inch.

2WD Pickup

1. Adjust toe-in by turning left tie rod turnbuckle. Toe-in is increased by turning tie rod toward front of vehicle or decreased by turning tie rod toward rear of vehicle. One complete turn of turnbuckle changes toe-in adjustment by approximately .3 inch
2. After adjusting toe-in, check difference in length of left and right tie rods. If difference is greater than .2 inch, remove right tie rod and adjust length until difference is reduced to .2 inch or less. "L" stamped on outer surface of tie rod indicates LH thread.

REAR WHEEL ALIGNMENT

CAMBER

Rear camber is preset to specification and cannot be adjusted. If camber is out of specification, bent or damaged components must be replaced.

TOE-IN

Rear toe-in is preset to specification and cannot be adjusted. If rear toe-in is out of specification, bent or damaged components must be replaced.

VEHICLE RIDE HEIGHT

There is no provision for adjustment of vehicle ride height on these models. If ride height is not satisfactory, inspect suspension components for damage or modification.

MITSUBISHI 3000GT
INDEX OF SERVICE OPERATIONS

Specifications

GENERAL ENGINE SPECIFICATIONS

Year	Engine, Liter	Fuel System	Bore & Stroke	Compression Ratio	Maximum Net H.P. @ RPM	Maximum Torque, Ft. Lbs. @ RPM	Normal Oil Pressure, psi
1996–97	3.0L	MFI	3.59 X 2.99	10.0	218 @ 6000	205 @ 4500	11.4②
1996–99	3.0L①	MFI	3.59 X 2.99	8.0	320 @ 6000	315 @ 2500	11.4②
1998–99	3.0L	MFI	3.59 X 2.99	8.9:1	161 @ 5500	185 @ 4000	11.4②

MFI — Multi-Port Fuel Injection.
① — Turbocharged engine.

② — At idle speed w/oil temperature between 167–194°F.

TUNE UP SPECIFICATIONS

Year	Engine Liter	Spark Plug Gap, Inch	Ignition Timing			Idle Speed, RPM				Fuel Pump Pressure, psi	Valve Lash
			Firing Order	Timing, °BTDC	Timing Mark Location	Curb②		Fast			
						Man. Trans.	Auto. Trans.	Man. Trans.	Auto. Trans.		
1996-99	3.0L	.041	1-2-3-4-5-6	5①	⑥	700	700N	④	④	38	③
	3.0L⑤	.041	1-2-3-4-5-6	5①	⑥	700	700N	④	④	34	③

BTDC — Before Top Dead Center
N — Neutral
① — Electronically controlled.
② — When adjusting idle speed, set parking brake & chock drive wheels.

③ — Equipped w/hydraulic lash adjusters.
④ — Controlled by idle speed control servo.

⑤ — Turbocharged engine.
⑥ — Equipped w/crankshaft position sensor.

FRONT WHEEL ALIGNMENT SPECIFICATIONS

Year	Caster Angle, Deg.		Camber Angle, Deg.		Toe, Inch①	Ball Joint Wear
	Limits	Desired	Limits	Desired		
1996–99	+3⁵/₁₂ to +4⁵/₁₂	+3¹¹/₁₂	–½ to +½	0	–.12 to +.12	②

AWD — All Wheel Drive
FWD — Front Wheel Drive
① — Toe-in (+); toe-out (-).

② — Lateral lower arm ball joint breakaway torque, 86–191 inch lbs.; stabilizer link ball joint breakaway torque, 15–28 inch lbs.

REAR WHEEL ALIGNMENT SPECIFICATIONS

Year	Model	Camber Angle, Deg.		Toe, Inch①
		Limits	Desired	
1996–99	FWD	–½ to +½	0	-.08 to +.10
	AWD	–⅓ to +⅔	⅙	-.08 to +.10

AWD — All Wheel Drive   FWD — Front Wheel Drive   ① — Toe-in (+); toe-out (-).

FLUID CAPACITIES & COOLING SYSTEM DATA

Year	Model & Engine	Coolant Capacity, Qts.	Radiator Cap Relief Pressure, Lbs.	Thermo. Opening Temp., °F	Fuel Tank, Gals.	Engine Oil Refill, Qts. ①	Transaxle Oil		Transfer Case Oil, Pts.	Rear Drive Axle Oil, Pts.
							Man. Trans, Pts.	Auto. Trans., Qts.②		
1996–99	3.0L Non-Turbo	8.5	13	③	19.8	4.5	4.8	7.9	—	—
	3.0L Turbo	8.5	13	170	19.8	4.9	5.0	7.9	1.60	2.3

AWD — All Wheel Drive
FWD — Front Wheel Drive
① — Includes filter.

② — Approximate; make final check w/dipstick.

③ — On 1996 models; 170°F; on 1997–99 models 180°F.

LUBRICANT DATA

Year	Lubricant Type					
	Transmission		Transfer Case	Rear Axle	Power Steering	Brake System
	Manual	Automatic				
1996–99	75w/90 GL-4	Dia ATF SP	75w/90 GL-4	GL-5	Dexron II/IIE/III	DOT 3 or 4

Electrical

NOTE: On Air Bag Equipped Models, Refer To "Air Bag System Precautions" Located In The Front Of This Manual For System Disarming & Arming Procedures.

INDEX

PRECAUTIONS

AIR BAG SYSTEMS

Refer to "Air Bag System Precautions" in the front of this manual for system disarming and arming procedures.

BATTERY GROUND CABLE

Prior to service, disconnect battery ground cable and isolate as required.

FUSE PANEL & FLASHER LOCATION

The fuse panel is located under the left-hand side of the instrument panel. There are fuses located in the relay box on the right and left sides of the engine compartment. The turn signal and hazard flasher unit is located under the lefthand side of the instrument panel, near the lower kick panel.

FUEL PUMP RELAY LOCATION

The fuel pump relay is located on the righthand side of the engine compartment, near the relay box.

RELAY CENTER LOCATION

The main relay centers are located on the righthand side and lefthand rear corner of the engine compartment.

STARTER

REPLACE

MANUAL TRANSAXLE

FWD Models

1. Raise and support vehicle.

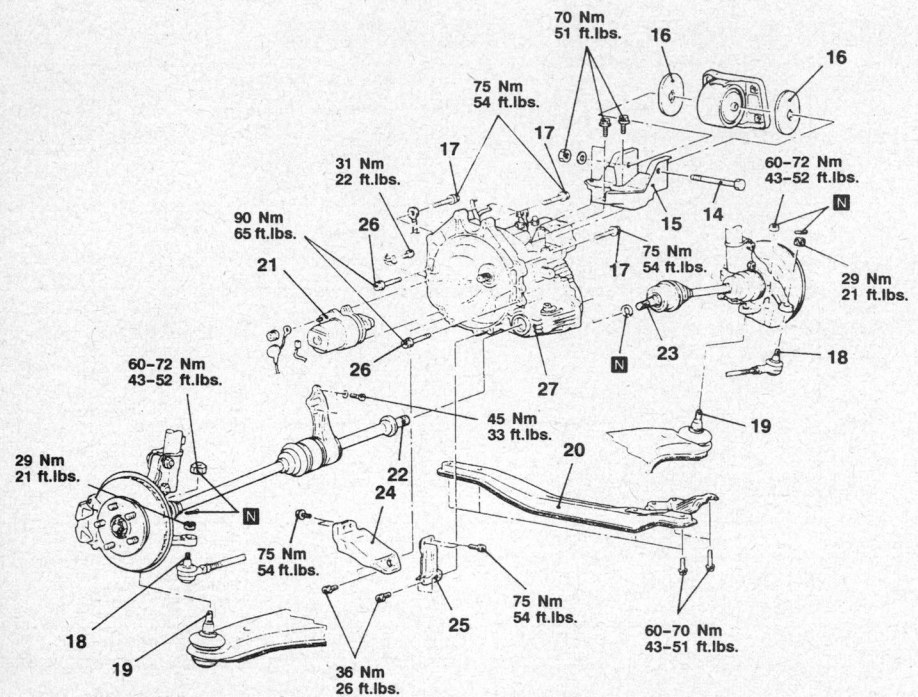

14. Transaxle mount connection
15. Transaxle mount bracket
16. Mounting stopper
17. Transaxle assembly upper part coupling bolt
18. Tie rod end connection
19. Lower arm ball joint connection
20. Right member
21. Starter
22. Drive shaft (Left side), Inner shaft assembly
23. Drive shaft (Right side)
24. Transaxle stay (Front bank side)
25. Transaxle stay (Rear bank side)
26. Transaxle assembly lower part coupling bolt
27. Transaxle assembly

MT1129100002000X

Fig. 1 Starter replacement. FWD w/manual transaxle

2. Drain transmission fluid into appropriate container.
3. Remove engine lower cover.
4. Remove battery and battery tray, then the washer tank.
5. Remove air cleaner cover and air intake hose.
6. Remove clutch release cylinder and oil line bracket without disconnecting oil coupling, then secure to body using suitable wire.
7. Disconnect transaxle control and speedometer cables.
8. Raise transaxle with suitable jack to release pressure on transaxle mount bracket, then disconnect transaxle mount.
9. Remove transaxle mounting stopper, **Fig. 1.**
10. Loosen tie rod end nut then disconnect tie rod from knuckle using steering linkage puller tool No. MB991113-01, or equivalent. **Ensure tie cord of tool is tied off correctly.**
11. Repeat step 10 on lower ball joint.
12. With transaxle properly supported, remove righthand crossmember.
13. Remove starter electrical connections, then the starter assembly.
14. Reverse procedure to install, noting the following:
    a. Install mounting stopper as shown, **Fig. 2.**
    b. **Torque** starter bolts to 65 ft. lbs.
    c. **Torque** righthand crossmember bolts to 43–51 ft. lbs.
    d. **Torque** lower ball joint nut to 43–52 ft. lbs. and tie rod end nut to 22 ft. lbs.
    e. **Torque** transaxle mount bracket bolts to 51 ft. lbs.
    f. **Torque** clutch tube bracket bolts to 13 ft. lbs.

AWD Models

1. Raise and support vehicle.
2. Drain transaxle oil into appropriate container and remove engine lower cover.
3. Disconnect front exhaust pipe and support from frame.
4. Remove rear propeller shaft and support aside. **Suspend propeller shaft so it is not sharply bent.**
5. Remove transfer assembly mounting bolts, then the transfer assembly.
6. Remove air cleaner hoses, air cleaner, air intake hose and vacuum pipe.
7. Remove battery and battery tray, then the washer tank.
8. Disconnect transaxle control cable.
9. Remove clutch release cylinder and oil line bracket without disconnecting oil coupling, then secure to body using suitable wire.
10. Raise transaxle to release pressure on transaxle mount bracket using suitable jack stand then disconnect transaxle mount.

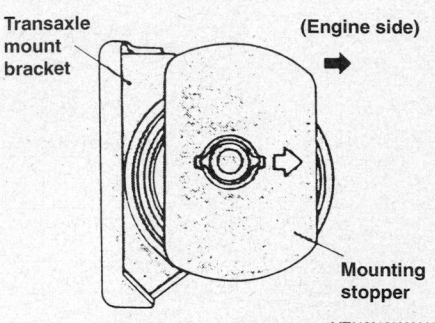

MT1129100003000X

Fig. 2 Mounting stopper installation. FWD

11. Remove transaxle mounting stopper, **Fig. 3.**
12. Loosen tie rod end nut, then disconnect tie rod from knuckle using steering linkage puller tool No. MB991113-01, or equivalent. **Ensure tie cord of tool is tied off correctly.**
13. Repeat step 12 on lower ball joint.
14. With transaxle properly supported, remove righthand crossmember.
15. Remove starter electrical connections, then the starter assembly.
16. Reverse procedure to install, noting the following:
    a. Install mounting stopper as shown, **Fig. 2.**
    b. **Torque** starter bolts to 65 ft. lbs.
    c. **Torque** righthand crossmember bolts to 43–51 ft. lbs.
    d. **Torque** lower ball joint nut to 43–52 ft. lbs. and tie rod end nut to 36 ft. lbs.
    e. **Torque** transaxle mount bracket bolts to 51 ft. lbs.
    f. **Torque** clutch tube bracket bolts to 13 ft. lbs.
    g. **Torque** transfer assembly mounting bolts to 61–65 ft. lbs.

AUTOMATIC TRANSAXLE

1. Place gear selector lever into Neutral position.
2. Raise and support vehicle.
3. Drain transaxle oil into appropriate container and remove front and side lower covers.
4. Remove battery and battery tray, then the washer tank.
5. Remove air cleaner cover and air intake hose.
6. Disconnect transaxle control and speedometer cables.
7. Disconnect oil cooler lines.
8. Disconnect Park/Neutral position and kickdown servo switches.
9. Disconnect pulse generator and oil temperature sensor.
10. Raise transaxle to release pressure on transaxle mount bracket using suitable jack stand, then disconnect transaxle mount.
11. Loosen tie rod end nut then disconnect tie rod from knuckle using steering linkage puller tool No. MB991113-01, or equivalent. **Ensure tie cord of tool is tied off correctly.**
12. Repeat step 11 on lower ball joint.

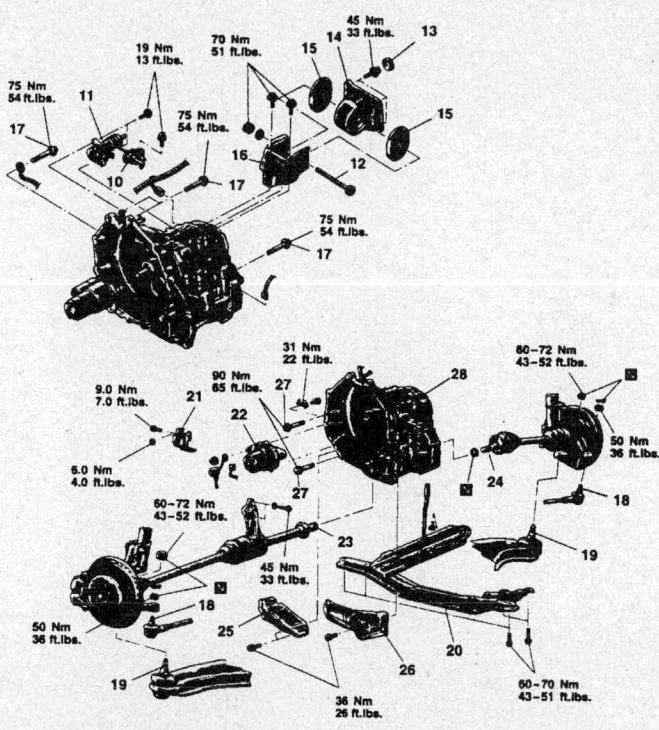

10. Clutch tube bracket connection
11. Clutch release cylinder connection
12. Transaxle mount connection
13. Plug
14. Transaxle mount bracket (Body side)
15. Mounting stopper
16. Transaxle mount bracket (Transaxle side)
17. Transaxle assembly lower part coupling bolt
18. Tie rod end connection
19. Lower arm ball joint connection
20. Right member

21. Starter cover
22. Starter
23. Drive shaft (Left side). Inner shaft assembly
24. Drive shaft (Right side)
25. Transaxle stay connection (Front bank side)
26. Transaxle stay connection (Rear bank side)
27. Transaxle assembly lower part coupling bolt
28. Transaxle assembly

MT1129500034000X

Fig. 3   Starter replacement. AWD w/manual transaxle

13. With transaxle properly supported, remove righthand crossmember, **Fig. 4.**
14. Remove starter electrical connections, then the starter assembly.
15. Reverse procedure to install, noting the following:
    a. **Torque** starter bolts to 22 ft. lbs.
    b. **Torque** righthand crossmember bolts to 43–51 ft. lbs.
    c. **Torque** lower ball joint nut to 43–52 ft. lbs. and tie rod end nut to 22 ft. lbs.
    d. **Torque** transaxle mount bracket bolts to 51 ft. lbs.

COIL PACK
REPLACE

1. Disconnect spark plug cables from ignition coil. **Label cables for installation reference.**
2. Remove coil pack mounting screws, then the coil pack.
3. Reverse procedure to install.

IGNITION LOCK
REPLACE

1. Remove ignition switch or lock cylinder in numbered sequence as shown, **Fig. 5**, noting the following:

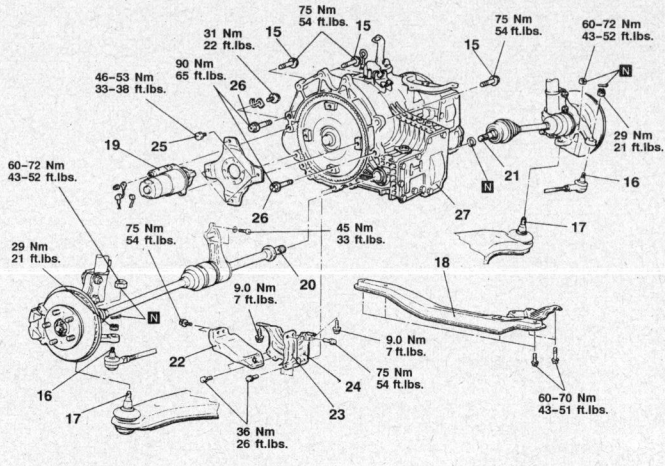

15. Transaxle assembly upper part coupling bolt
16. Tie rod end connection
17. Lower arm ball joint connection
18. Right member
19. Starter
20. Drive shaft (left side), Inner shaft assembly

21. Drive shaft (right side)
22. Transaxle stay (front bank side)
23. Transaxle stay (rear bank side)
24. Bell housing cover
25. Special bolts
26. Transaxle assembly lower part coupling bolt
27. Transaxle assembly

MT1129100005000X

Fig. 4   Starter replacement w/automatic transaxle

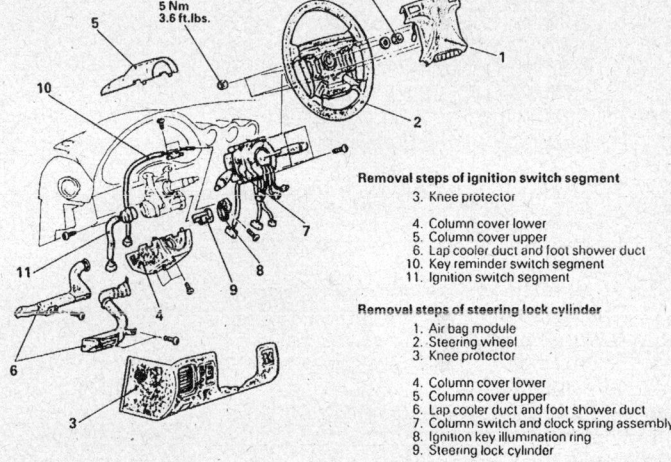

Removal steps of ignition switch segment

3. Knee protector

4. Column cover lower
5. Column cover upper
6. Lap cooler duct and foot shower duct
10. Key reminder switch segment
11. Ignition switch segment

Removal steps of steering lock cylinder

1. Air bag module
2. Steering wheel
3. Knee protector

4. Column cover lower
5. Column cover upper
6. Lap cooler duct and foot shower duct
7. Column switch and clock spring assembly
8. Ignition key illumination ring
9. Steering lock cylinder

MT9049100001000X

Fig. 5   Ignition switch replacement

a. Remove steering wheel as outlined under "Steering Wheel, Replace."
b. To remove clockspring connector from air bag module, force lock outward and pry it with a suitable screwdriver as shown, **Fig. 6.** Ensure no excessive force is applied when connector is removed. **The removed air bag module should be stored in a clean, dry, flat place with pad cover facing up.**
c. Remove upper and lower steering column cover screws and covers, ensuring not to break cover grippers, **Fig. 7.**
d. Insert ignition key into ignition lock cylinder and turn to Acc position.
e. Press down lockpin using a suitable Phillips head screwdriver to remove lock cylinder, **Fig. 8.**

2. Reverse numbered sequence as shown, **Fig. 5** to assemble, noting the following:
   a. Line up "Neutral" mark of clockspring with mating mark to center clockspring. **If clockspring is not centered, problems such as intermediate failure of steering wheel to turn or broken ribbon cable in clockspring could occur. As a result, they might hinder proper operation of SRS, resulting in serious injury.**

IGNITION SWITCH
REPLACE

Refer to "Ignition Lock, Replace" for ignition switch replacement procedures.

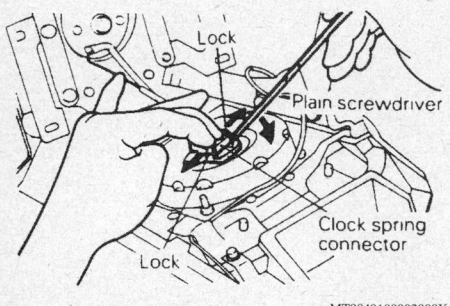

Fig. 6   Air bag clockspring connector removal

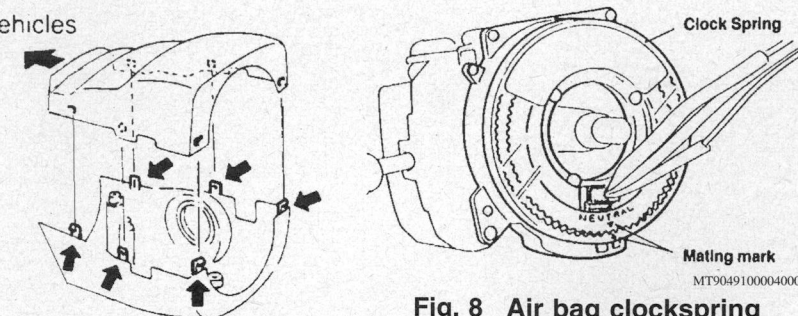

Front of vehicles

Fig. 7   Upper & lower column cover removal

Fig. 8   Air bag clockspring alignment

NEUTRAL SAFETY SWITCH

REPLACE

1. Place selector lever in Neutral position.
2. Place manual control lever in Neutral position, then remove control lever retainer and lever.
3. Disconnect electrical harness, then remove switch retaining bolts and switch assembly.
4. Reverse procedure to install, then adjust as follows:
   a. With manual control lever in Neutral position, rotate switch body until wide end of control lever overlaps switch body flange.
   b. Hold switch body in position, then **torque** retaining bolts to 7–9 ft. lbs.

HEADLAMP SWITCH

REPLACE

Refer to "Combination Switch, Replace" for headlamp switch replacement procedure.

COMBINATION SWITCH

REPLACE

1. Remove steering wheel as outlined under "Steering Wheel, Replace."
2. Remove knee protector as follows:
   a. Remove hood lock handle.
   b. Remove rheostat and switch garnish.
   c. Remove knee protector screws and knee protector, **Fig. 9.**
3. Remove upper and lower steering column cover screws, then remove covers ensuring not to break cover grippers, **Fig. 7.**
4. Remove lap cooler and foot shower duct.
5. Remove right and left column switches.
6. Reverse procedure to install.

DIMMER SWITCH

REPLACE

Refer to "Combination Switch, Replace" for dimmer switch replacement procedure.

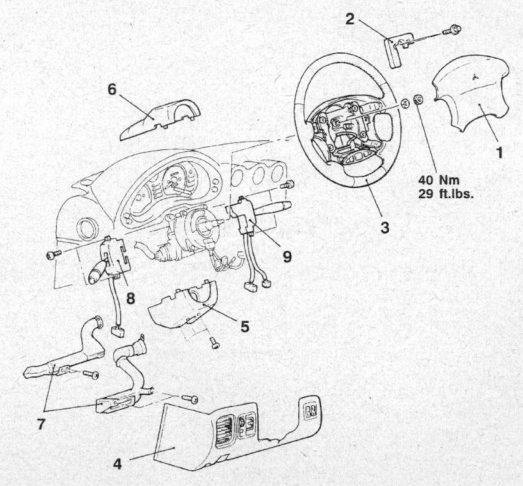

Removal steps

1. Air bag module (Refer to GROUP 52B.)
2. Weight
3. Steering wheel
4. Knee protector (Refer to GROUP 52A – Instrument Panel.)
5. Column cover, lower
6. Column cover, upper
7. Lap cooler duct and foot shower duct
8. Column switch, left (For lighting switch, dimmer/passing switch and turn signal switch)
9. Column switch, right (For wiper and washer switch)

Fig. 9   Column switch replacement

STEERING WHEEL

REPLACE

1. Remove air bag module mounting nut using a socket wrench from back side. **Wait at least one minute after disconnecting battery ground cable before doing any further work on vehicle.** SRS system is designed to retain enough voltage to deploy air bag for a short time even after battery has been disconnected.
2. To remove clockspring connector from air bag module, force lock outward and pry it with a suitable screwdriver as shown, **Fig. 6.** Ensure no undue force is applied when connector is removed. **The removed air bag module should be stored in a clean, dry, flat place with pad cover facing up.**
3. Remove steering wheel using suitable puller.
4. Reverse procedure to install, noting the following:
   a. Line up the "Neutral" mark of clockspring with the mating mark to cen-

ter clockspring, **Fig. 8.** If clockspring is not centered, problems such as intermediate failure of the steering wheel to turn or broken ribbon cable in clockspring could occur. As a result, they might hinder proper operation of SRS, resulting in serious injury.

INSTRUMENT CLUSTER

REPLACE

COMBINATION METERS

1. Remove knee protector as follows:
   a. Remove hood lock handle.
   b. Remove rheostat and switch garnish.
   c. Remove knee protector screws and knee protector.
2. Remove upper and lower steering column cover screws then remove covers ensuring not to break cover grippers, **Fig. 7.**
3. Remove meter bezel, **Fig. 10.**

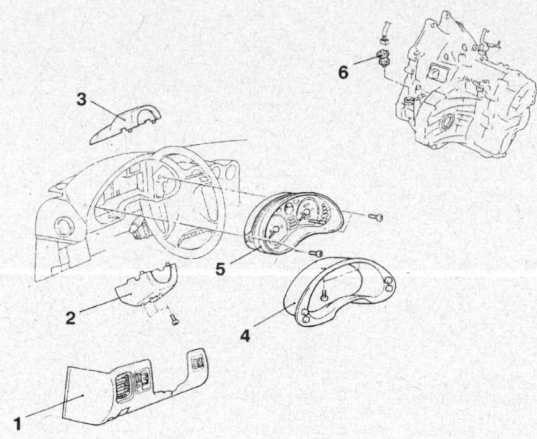

Removal steps

1. Knee protector

2. Column cover, lower

3. Column cover, upper
4. Meter bezel
5. Combination meter
6. Vehicles speed sensor

MT9099100003000X

Fig. 10 Combination meter replacement

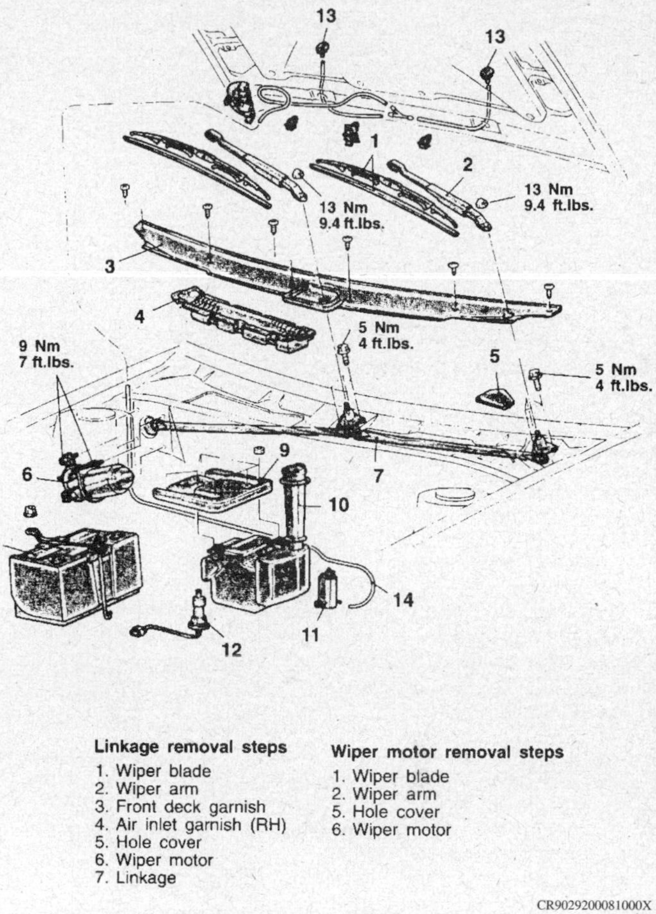

4. Remove combination meter attaching screws.
5. **On models with mechanical speedometer,** disconnect speedometer cable at transaxle end of cable.
6. **On all models,** pull combination meter slightly toward vehicle interior, release wiring harness and speedometer adapter (if equipped) by turning to left or right.
7. Reverse procedure to install.

COMBINATION GAUGES

1. Remove instrument panel as outlined under "Instrument Panel, Replace" in "Dash Panel Service."
2. Remove air distribution duct.
3. Disconnect combination gauge electrical connections.
4. Remove combination gauge attaching screws, then the combination gauges.
5. Reverse procedure to install.

RADIO
REPLACE

1. Pry off radio panel using a suitable tool, then remove panel from floor console.
2. Remove radio bracket attaching screws, then disconnect antenna and radio electrical connector.
3. Remove radio from floor console.
4. Reverse procedure to install.

WIPER MOTOR
REPLACE
FRONT

1. Remove wiper arm attaching bolt, then remove wiper arm.
2. Unsnap hole cover assembly, **Fig. 11.**
3. Disconnect wiper motor electrical connector.

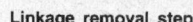

Linkage removal steps

1. Wiper blade
2. Wiper arm
3. Front deck garnish
4. Air inlet garnish (RH)
5. Hole cover
6. Wiper motor
7. Linkage

Wiper motor removal steps

1. Wiper blade
2. Wiper arm
5. Hole cover
6. Wiper motor

CR9029200081000X

Fig. 11 Front wiper motor replacement

4. Remove wiper motor attaching bolts, then remove wiper motor.
5. Reverse procedure to install. **Torque** wiper motor attaching bolts to 7 ft. lbs. and wiper arm nuts to 9.4 ft. lbs.

REAR

1. Remove wiper arm and wiper blade, **Fig. 12.**
2. Remove wiper arm spacer, then the hatch trim.
3. Remove rear wiper motor bracket mounting nuts, then remove rear wiper motor assembly from hatch.
4. Reverse procedure to install.

WIPER SWITCH
REPLACE

Refer to "Combination Switch, Replace" procedure.

BLOWER MOTOR
REPLACE

1. Drain engine coolant into suitable container.
2. Remove instrument panel as outlined under Instrument Panel, Replace.
3. Remove instrument panel lower cover.
4. Remove blower motor attaching bolts, then the blower motor, **Fig. 13.**

5. Reverse procedure to install.

HEATER CORE
REPLACE

1. Drain coolant into a suitable container and disconnect heater hoses.
2. Remove center console and instrument panel as outlined under "Instrument Panel, Replace" in "Dash Panel Service."
3. Remove center reinforcement, **Fig. 14.**
4. Remove lower cover, foot shower, distribution and lap cooler ducts.
5. **On models with A/C,** remove evaporator assembly as outlined under "Evaporator Core, Replace."
6. **On all models,** remove center duct.
7. To prevent bolts from falling into blower assembly, set air selection damper to outside air induction position.
8. Remove heater unit assembly.
9. Remove plate from heater unit.
10. Remove heater core from heater unit. **Use caution not to damage heater core fins or pad part of heater core.**
11. Reverse procedure to install.

EVAPORATOR CORE
REPLACE

1. Discharge refrigerant into an approved

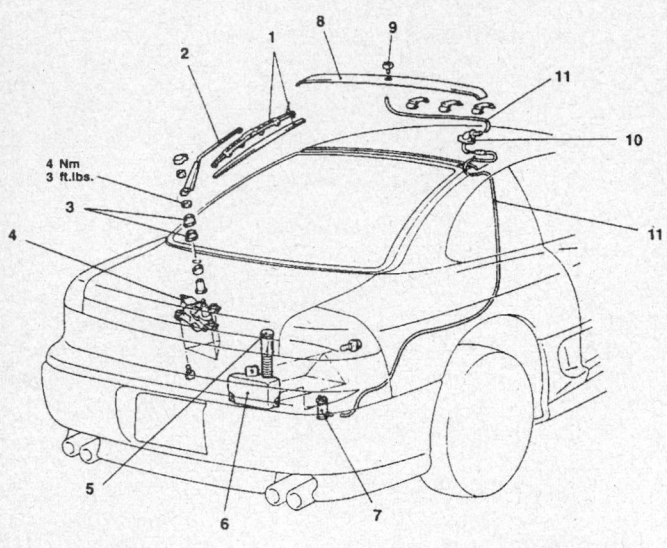

Wiper motor removal steps

1. Wiper blade
2. Wiper arm
3. Spacer
• Liftgate lower trim

4. Wiper motor

Washer tank removal steps

• Rear end trim

5. Cap
6. Washer tank
7. Washer motor

Washer tube removal steps

• Front pillar trim (RH)
• Quarter trim (RH)
• Quarter upper trim (RH)
• Rear roof rail trim
• Rear side trim (RH)

8. Liftgate upper moulding
9. Washer nozzle
10. Tube and grommet assembly
11. Washer tube

MT9029500051000X

Fig. 12   Rear wiper motor replacement

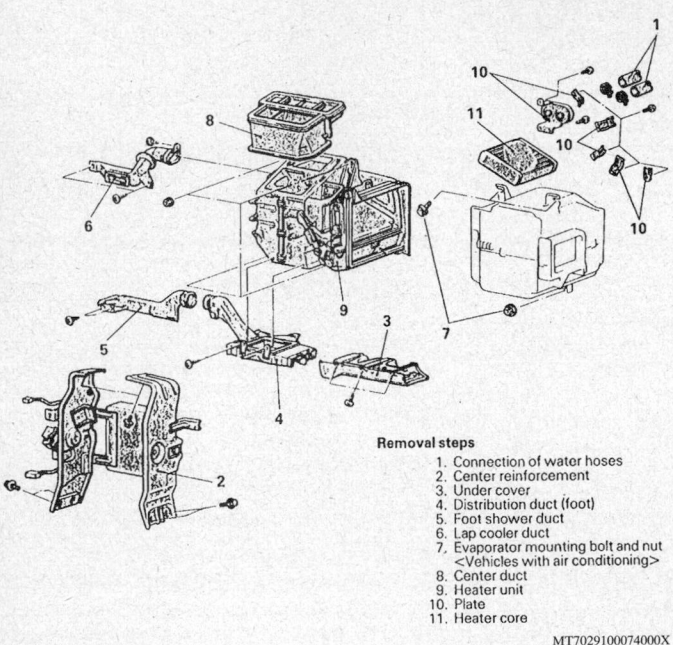

Removal steps

1. Connection of water hoses
2. Center reinforcement
3. Under cover
4. Distribution duct (foot)
5. Foot shower duct
6. Lap cooler duct
7. Evaporator mounting bolt and nut
   <Vehicles with air conditioning>
8. Center duct
9. Heater unit
10. Plate
11. Heater core

MT7029100074000X

Fig. 14   Exploded view of heater unit

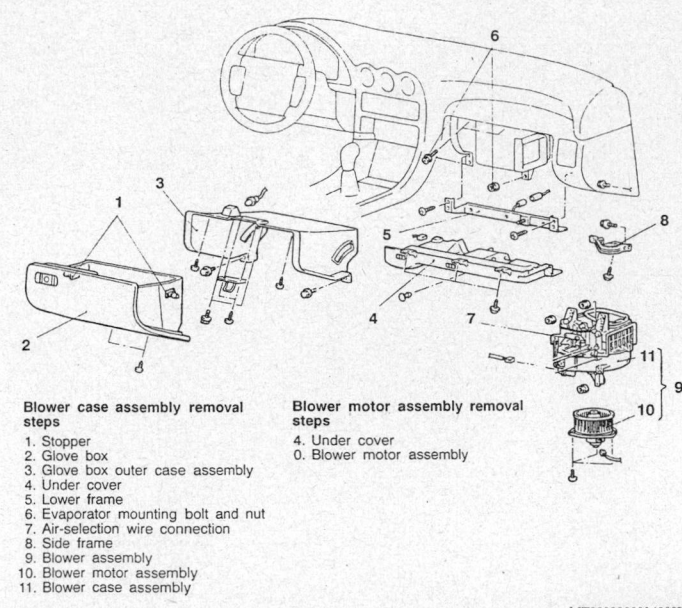

Blower case assembly removal steps

1. Stopper
2. Glove box
3. Glove box outer case assembly
4. Under cover
5. Lower frame
6. Evaporator mounting bolt and nut
7. Air-selection wire connection
8. Side frame
9. Blower assembly
10. Blower motor assembly
11. Blower case assembly

Blower motor assembly removal steps

4. Under cover
0. Blower motor assembly

MT9099900034000X

Fig. 13   Blower motor removal

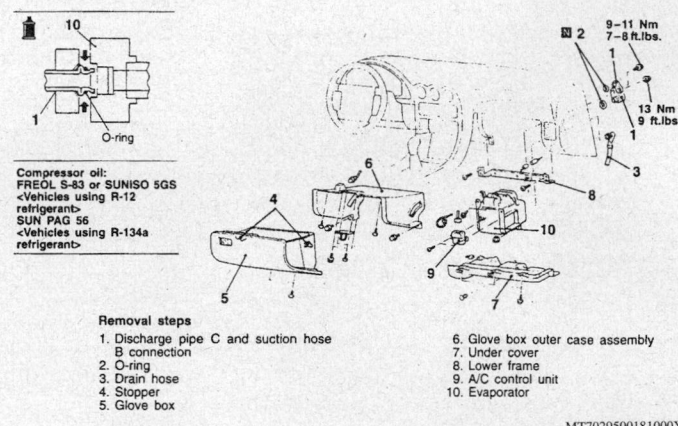

Compressor oil:
FREOL S-83 or SUNISO 5GS
<Vehicles using R-12 refrigerant>
SUN PAG 56
<Vehicles using R-134a refrigerant>

Removal steps

1. Discharge pipe C and suction hose B connection
2. O-ring
3. Drain hose
4. Stopper
5. Glove box

6. Glove box outer case assembly
7. Under cover
8. Lower frame
9. A/C control unit
10. Evaporator

MT7029500181000X

Fig. 15   Evaporator core replacement

recovery device as outlined in "Air Conditioning."
2. Disconnect suction hose and liquid pipe from evaporator.
3. Remove glove compartment stoppers, then the glove compartment, **Fig. 15.**
4. Remove lower frame, then the right-hand foot shower duct, if applicable.
5. Disconnect body wiring harness and A/C wiring harness connectors.
6. Remove A/C control unit.
7. Remove drain hose, then the evaporator.
8. Remove evaporator core from case as shown, **Fig. 16.**
9. Reverse procedure to install.

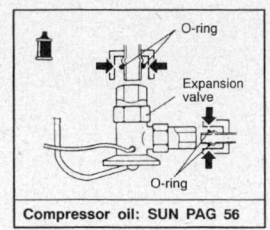

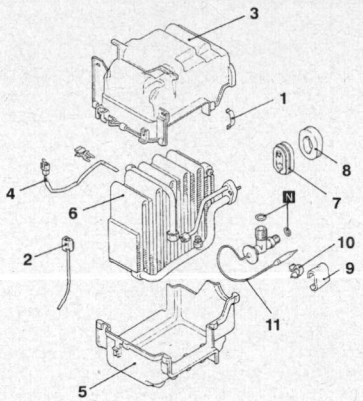

Disassembly steps

1. Clips
2. Auto compressor controller \<DOHC>
3. Evaporater case (upper)
4. Air thermo sensor
5. Evaporator case (lower)

6. Evaporator assembly
7. Grommet
8. Insulator
9. Rubber insulator
10. Clip
11. Expansion valve

MT7029500182000X

Fig. 16   Exploded view of evaporator unit

3.0L Engine

NOTE: On Air Bag Equipped Models, Refer To "Air Bag System Precautions" Located In The Front Of This Manual For System Disarming & Arming Procedures.

NOTE: Prior To Performing Any Service Operations Listed In This Section, Consult The "Technical Service Bulletins" Section For Related Information.

INDEX

PRECAUTIONS

AIR BAG SYSTEMS

Refer to "Air Bag System Precautions" in the front of this manual for system disarming and arming procedures.

BATTERY GROUND CABLE

Prior to service, disconnect battery ground cable and isolate as required.

Engine	Standard, psi @ RPM	Minimum, psi @ RPM	Maximum Variation Between Cylinders, psi
DOHC①	185 @ 250-400	139 @ 250-400	14
DOHC②	156 @ 250-400	115 @ 250-400	14
SOHC	171 @ 250-400	127 @ 250-400	14

① — Non-turbocharged. ② — Turbocharged.

Fig. 1   Compression pressure data

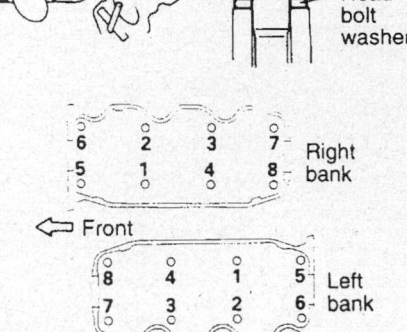

Head bolt washer

Fig. 2   Engine mount replacement

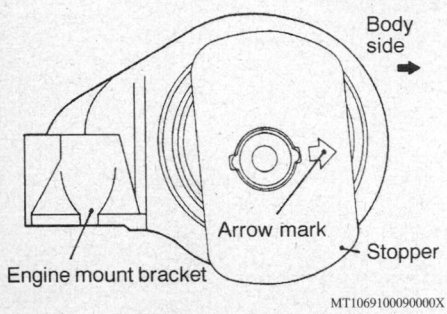

Fig. 3   Engine mounting stopper installation

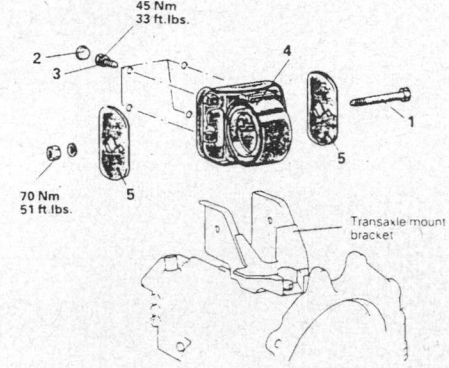

45 Nm 33 ft.lbs.

70 Nm 51 ft.lbs.

Removal steps
1. Transaxle mount bracket and transaxle connection bolt
2. Cap
3. Transaxle mount bracket installation bolt
4. Transaxle mount bracket
5. Mounting stopper

Fig. 4   Transaxle mount replacement

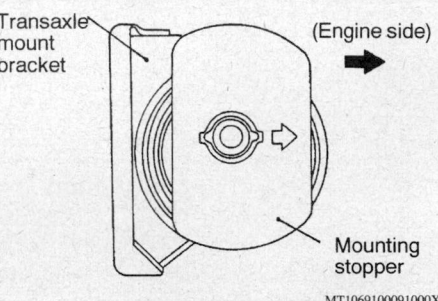

Fig. 5   Transaxle mounting stopper installation

FUEL SYSTEM PRESSURE RELIEF

Before any fuel system service can be performed, the fuel pressure in the fuel system must be released to prevent personal injury or damage to the vehicle.

1. Remove fuel gauge cover in luggage compartment.
2. Disconnect fuel pump harness connector.
3. Start engine and allow to idle.
4. When engine stops idling, turn ignition switch to Off position.
5. After fuel system repairs are complete, connect fuel pump harness connector.
6. Apply body sealant No. 8509, or equivalent, to fuel gauge cover, then install cover.

COMPRESSION PRESSURE

Refer to **Fig. 1** for compression pressure data.

ENGINE MOUNT
REPLACE
ENGINE

1. Raise and support engine to remove weight off mounts using suitable engine jack.
2. Replace engine mounts in numbered sequence as shown, **Fig. 2**, moving cruise control actuator out of the way.
3. Ensure arrow mark on mounting stopper is pointing away from engine when installing engine mounting bracket, **Fig. 3**.

TRANSAXLE

1. Using suitable transmission jack, raise and support transaxle to remove weight off mounts.
2. Remove air cleaner assembly.
3. Replace transaxle mounts in numbered sequence as shown, **Fig. 4**.
4. Ensure arrow mark on mounting stopper is pointing toward engine when attaching transaxle mounting bracket, **Fig. 5**.

ENGINE ROLL STOPPER

1. **On turbocharged models,** remove condenser, then condenser cooling fan assembly and left catalytic converter.
2. **On all models,** replace engine front and rear roll stopper brackets in numbered sequence as shown, **Fig. 6**. Slightly raise rear roll stopper bracket, then twist rear roll stopper bracket up and lift upward to remove, **Fig. 7**.
3. When installing rear roll stopper bracket, install bracket and bracket to engine bolt as shown, **Fig. 8**.

ENGINE
REPLACE

1. Release fuel system pressure as outlined under "Precautions."

2. Remove cruise control pump and link assembly as outlined in "Speed Control Systems."
3. Mark and remove hood assembly.
4. **On turbocharged models,** remove air hose and air pipe assembly.
5. **On all models,** remove front exhaust pipe assembly.
6. Remove transaxle assembly.
7. Remove radiator assembly.
8. Remove engine assembly in numbered sequence as shown, **Figs. 9 and 10,** noting the following:
   a. Disconnect air conditioner compressor and power steering oil pump leaving hoses connected.
   b. Using suitable engine lifting device, raise and support engine to remove weight off mounts, then remove engine mount bracket as outlined under "Engine Mount, Replace."
   c. Ensure cables, hoses and wire harness connectors are removed, raise engine assembly upward out of engine compartment.
9. Reverse procedure to install, **Fig. 10,** noting the following:
   a. Ensure all cables hoses and wire harness connectors are in correct position before completing engine installation.
   b. Ensure arrow mark on stopper is in

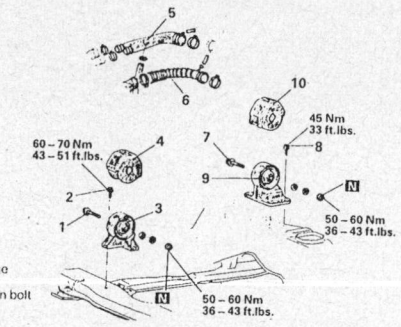

Front stopper bracket removal steps
1. Front roll stopper bracket and engine connection bolt
2. Front roll stopper bracket installation bolt
3. Front roll stopper bracket
4. Heat protector <Turbo>

Rear roll stopper bracket removal steps
5. Air hose A <Turbo>
6. Air intake hose C <Turbo>
7. Rear roll stopper bracket and engine connection bolt
8. Rear roll stopper bracket installation bolt
9. Rear roll stopper bracket
10. Heat protector <Turbo>

MT1069100093000X

Fig. 6 Engine roll stopper replacement

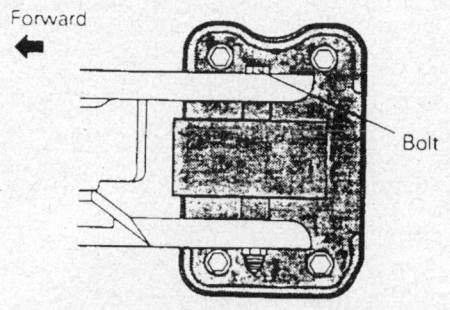

Fig. 8 Rear roll stopper installation

direction shown, **Fig. 3,** when attaching engine mounting bracket.

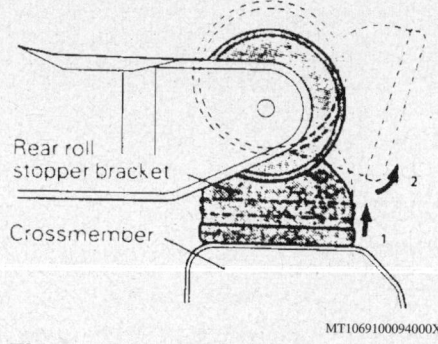

MT1069100094000X

Fig. 7 Rear roll stopper removal

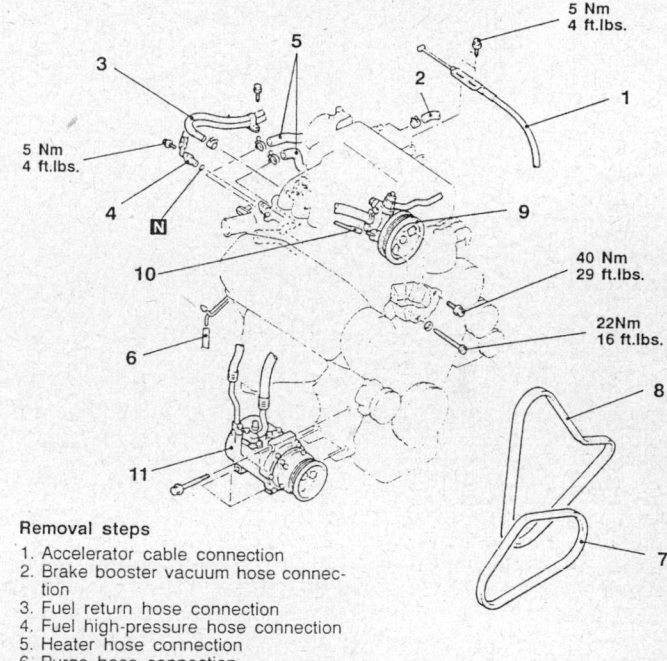

Removal steps
1. Accelerator cable connection
2. Brake booster vacuum hose connection
3. Fuel return hose connection
4. Fuel high-pressure hose connection
5. Heater hose connection
6. Purge hose connection
7. Drive belt (air conditioning)
8. Drive belt (generator and power steering)
9. Power steering oil pump
10. Power steering pressure switch connector
11. Air conditioning compressor

MT1069900550010X

Fig. 9 Engine replacement (Part 1 of 2). SOHC engine

INTAKE MANIFOLD
REPLACE
AIR INTAKE PLENUM

1. Release fuel system pressure as outlined under "Precautions."
2. Replace air intake plenum in numbered sequence shown, **Figs. 11 and 12,** leaving hoses attached to throttle body when removing plenum.
3. When installing throttle body, ensure gasket protrusion is toward top.

AIR INTAKE MANIFOLD

1. Release fuel system pressure as outlined under "Precautions."
2. Drain engine coolant into an appropriate container.
3. Remove air intake plenum as outlined previously.
4. Replace intake manifold in numbered sequence shown, **Fig. 13.**
5. Install gaskets with protrusions in position shown, **Fig. 14.**
6. **On turbocharged models,** tighten intake manifold mounting nuts using the following procedure:
   a. **Torque** nuts in front bank to 2.2–3.6 ft. lbs.
   b. **Torque** nuts in rear bank to 9–11 ft. lbs.

c. **Torque** nuts in front bank to 9–11 ft. lbs.
d. Repeat steps b and c one more time.
7. **On all models,** apply lubricant sparingly to intake manifold mounting nuts.

EXHAUST MANIFOLD
REPLACE

1. **On turbocharged models,** remove turbocharger assembly as outlined under "Turbocharger, Replace."
2. **On non-turbocharged models,** remove front exhaust pipe and condenser fan motor assembly.
3. **On all models,** replace exhaust manifold in numbered sequence as shown, **Figs. 15 and 16.**

4. **On turbocharged models,** install rear exhaust manifold nuts in the following order:
   a. **Torque** nuts marked A to 22 ft. lbs., **Fig. 17.**
   b. **Torque** nuts marked B to 34–38 ft. lbs.
   c. Back off nuts marked B until a **torque** of 7 ft. lbs. is reached.
   d. **Torque** nuts marked B to 21–22 ft. lbs., **Fig. 17.**
   e. Install cone disc spring with grooved side facing up, then the nut, cone disc spring and washer in direction shown.
5. **On turbocharged models,** with the exhaust manifold stay resting on exhaust manifold, fit it along manifold over studs.
6. **On turbocharged models,** install

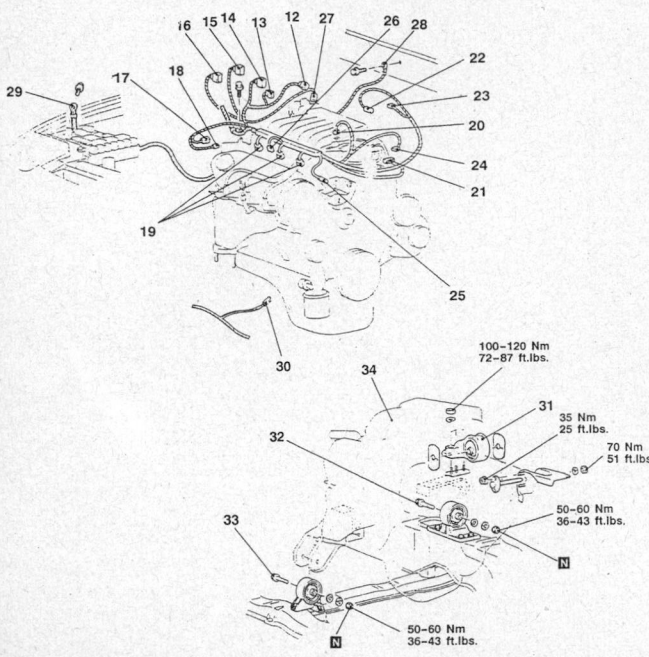

100–120 Nm
72–87 ft.lbs.

35 Nm
25 ft.lbs.

70 Nm
51 ft.lbs.

50–60 Nm
36–43 ft.lbs.

50–60 Nm
36–43 ft.lbs.

12. Idle air control motor connection
13. TPS connection
14. Injector harness connection
15. EGR solenoid valve connector
16. Evaporative emission purge solenoid valve connector
17. Engine coolant temperature sensor connection
18. Engine coolant temperature gauge unit connection
19. Fuel injectors connection
20. Ignition power transistor connection
21. Camshaft position sensor connector
22. Ignition coil connection
23. Condenser connection

24. Right bank heated oxygen sensor (front) connector
25. Crankshaft position sensor connector
26. Left bank heated oxygen sensor (front) connector
27. Manifold differential pressure sensor connector
28. Ground cable connection
29. Relay box and engine control harness connection
30. Oil pressure gauge unit connection
31. Engine mount bracket
32. Rear roll stopper bracket mount bolt
33. Front roll stopper bracket mount bolt
34. Engine assembly

MT1069900550020X

Fig. 9 Engine replacement (Part 2 of 2). SOHC engine

front exhaust manifold nuts in the following order:
a. **Torque** nuts marked C to 22 ft. lbs., **Fig. 18.**
b. Temporarily install turbocharger assembly.
c. **Torque** nut marked D to 22 ft. lbs.
d. **Torque** nuts marked E and F to 34–38 ft. lbs.
e. Back off nuts marked E and F until a **torque** of 7 ft. lbs. is reached.
f. **Torque** nuts marked E and F to 21–22 ft. lbs.
g. Install cone disc spring with grooved side facing up, then the nut, cone disc spring and washer in direction shown.

CYLINDER HEAD
REPLACE

1. Remove timing belt as outlined under "Timing Belt, Replace."
2. Remove camshafts as outlined under "Camshaft, Replace."
3. Remove exhaust manifolds as outlined under "Exhaust Manifold, Replace."
4. Remove cylinder head and valves in numbered sequence as shown, **Fig. 19,** noting the following:

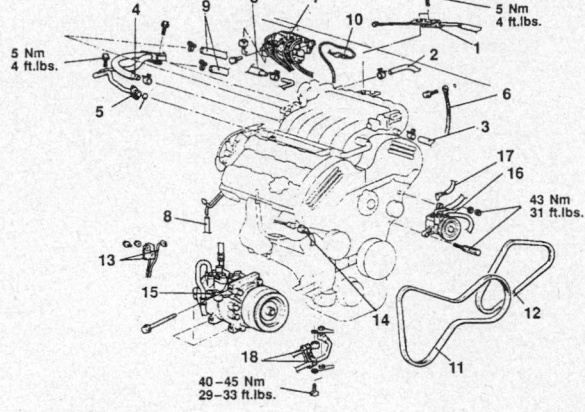

5 Nm
4 ft.lbs.

5 Nm
4 ft.lbs.

43 Nm
31 ft.lbs.

40–45 Nm
29–33 ft.lbs.

Removal steps

1. Accelerator cable connection
2. Brake booster vacuum hose connection
3. Booster vacuum hose connection <Turbo>
4. Fuel return hose connection
5. Fuel high pressure hose connection
6. Ground cable connection
7. Solenoid valve assembly
8. Vapor hose connection
9. Heater hose connection
10. EGR temperature sensor connector <Vehicles for California>

11. Drive belt (Generator and air conditioning)
12. Drive belt (Power steering)
13. Generator harness connection
14. Heated oxygen sensor connector <Turbo>
15. Air conditioning compressor
16. Power steering oil pump
17. Oil pressure switch connector (Power steering)
18. Oil cooler pipes connection <Turbo>

MT1069500332010X

Fig. 10 Engine replacement (Part 1 of 2). DOHC engine

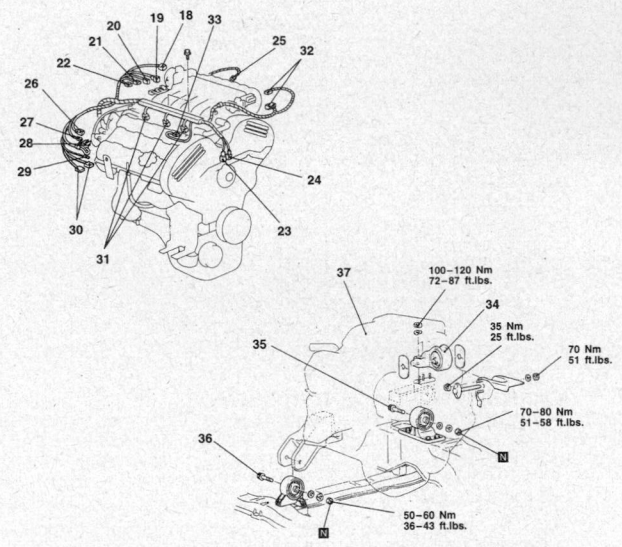

100–120 Nm
72–87 ft.lbs.

35 Nm
25 ft.lbs.

70 Nm
51 ft.lbs.

70–80 Nm
51–58 ft.lbs.

50–60 Nm
36–43 ft.lbs.

18. Idle air control motor connector
19. TPS connector
20. Oil pressure harness connector
21. Fuel injector harness connector
22. Knock sensor connector
23. Crankshaft position sensor connector
24. Camshaft position sensor connector
25. Manifold differential pressure sensor connector
26. Engine coolant temperature sensor connector
27. Engine coolant temperature gauge unit connector
28. Capacitor connector

29. Ignition coil connector
30. Power transistor connector
31. Fuel injector connector
32. Variable induction motor connector <Non-Turbo>
33. Left bank heated oxygen sensor (front) connector
34. Engine mounting bracket
35. Rear roll stopper bracket and engine connection bolt
36. Front roll stopper bracket and engine connection bolt
37. Engine assembly

MT1069500332020X

Fig. 10 Engine replacement (Part 2 of 2). DOHC engine

a. Using cylinder head bolt wrench tool No. MD998051-01, or equivalent, remove cylinder head bolts.
b. Using suitable valve spring com-

pressor tool, remove valve spring retaining locks.
5. Using a suitable straightedge and feeler gauge, measure flatness of cylinder

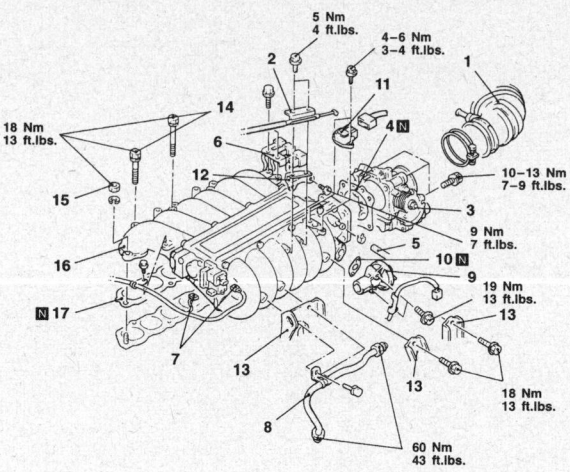

Removal steps

1. Air intake hose connection
2. Accelerator cable connection
3. Throttle body assembly
4. Throttle body gasket
5. Brake booster vacuum hose connection
6. Harness connectors
7. VIC motor connection
8. EGR pipe
9. EGR valve
10. EGR valve gasket
11. Manifold differential pressure sensor
12. Accelerator cable bracket
13. Intake manifold plenum stay connection
14. Intake manifold plenum installation bolts
15. Intake manifold plenum installation nuts
16. Intake manifold plenum
17. Intake manifold plenum gasket

MT1069100097000X

Fig. 11 Air intake plenum replacement. Non-turbocharged engine

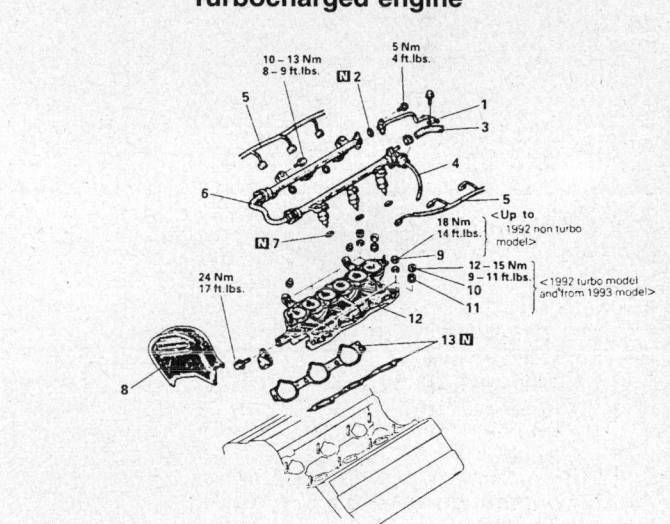

1. Air hose A connection
2. Accelerator cable connection
3. Throttle body assembly
4. Throttle body gasket
5. Air pipe A
6. Vacuum hose connection
7. Brake booster vacuum hose connection
8. Harness connector
9. Clutch booster vacuum hose connection
10. Manifold differential pressure sensor
11. EGR valve
12. EGR valve gasket
13. EGR pipe installation bolts
14. EGR pipe gasket
15. Intake manifold plenum stay connection
16. Intake manifold plenum installation bolts
17. Intake manifold plenum installation nuts
18. Intake manifold plenum
19. Intake manifold plenum gasket

MT1069100098000X

Fig. 12 Air intake plenum replacement. Turbocharged engine

head. Measurement should be .0012 inch or less for DOHC engines and .0020 or less for SOHC engines. If specification is greater, machine head no more than .008 inch.

6. Reverse procedure to install, **Fig. 19**, noting the following:

   a. Install spring seat, then the valve stem oil seal using valve stem oil seal installer tool No. MD998763, or equivalent. **incorrect installation of seal without using oil seal installer tool will result in poor sealing and cause oil leakage down valve guide. Never reuse oil seals.**

   b. Valve springs should be installed with enamel coated side toward valve spring retainer.

   c. Using suitable valve spring compression tool, install valve spring retainers.

   d. Ensure correct head gasket is used on engine. Cylinder head gaskets marked with a 72S2 are for SOHC engines and gaskets marked with a 72D4 are for DOHC engines.

   e. Apply a light coat of clean engine oil to cylinder head bolts and ensure bolt threads in block are clean.

   f. **Ensure cylinder head bolt washers are installed with chamfer side facing upward.**

   g. **On 1996 models,** tighten cylinder head bolts in sequence, **Fig. 20.**

   h. **On 1996 models less turbo, torque** to 80 ft. lbs. using 3 even steps.

   i. **On 1996 models equipped with turbo,** tighten as follows: first step,

   torque to 91 ft. lbs. using 3 even steps; second step, loosen all bolts; third step, **torque** to 91 ft. lbs. using 3 even steps.

   j. **On 1997–99 models,** tighten cylinder head bolts in sequence, **Fig. 20.**

   k. **On 1997–99 SOHC models, torque** to 76–83 ft. lbs. using 3 even steps.

Fig. 13 Intake manifold replacement

Removal steps

1. Connection for high-pressure fuel hose
2. O-ring
3. Connection for fuel return hose
4. Connection for vacuum hoses
5. Connection for injector connector
6. Fuel rail (with injectors)
7. Insulators
8. Timing belt upper cover
9. Intake manifold mounting nut <1992 non turbo model>
10. Intake manifold mounting nut <1992 turbo model and from 1993 model>
11. Cone disc spring <1992 turbo model and from 1993 model>
12. Intake manifold
13. Intake manifold gasket

MT1059100008000X

   l. **On 1997–99 DOHC models less turbo, torque** to 76–83 ft. lbs. using 3 even steps.

   m. **On 1997–99 DOHC models equipped with turbo,** tighten in 3 steps as follows: First step, **torque** to 87–94 ft. lbs. using 3 even steps; second step, loosen all bolts; third step, **torque** to 87–94 ft. lbs. using 3 even steps.

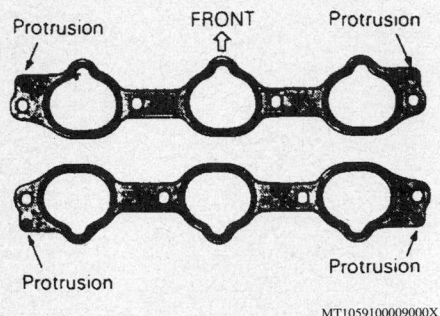

Fig. 14 Intake manifold gasket installation

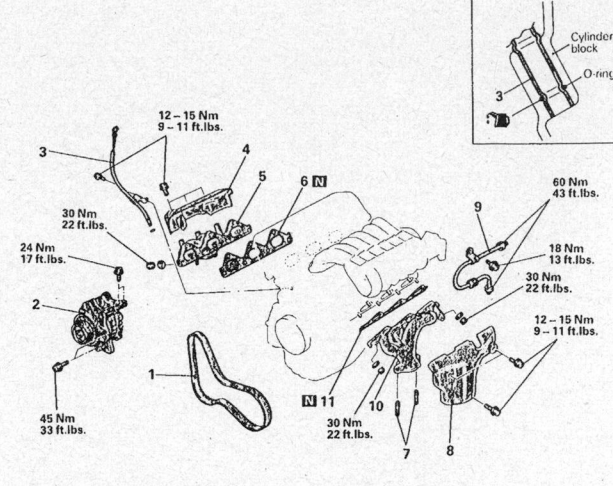

Removal steps of exhaust manifold (front)
1. Drive belt

2. Generator assembly
3. Oil level gauge guide
4. Heat protector
5. Exhaust manifold (front)
6. Gasket

Removal steps of exhaust manifold (rear)
7. Stud
8. Heat protector
9. EGR pipe <Vehicles for California>
10. Exhaust manifold (rear)
11. Gasket

Fig. 15 Exhaust manifold replacement. Non-turbocharged engine

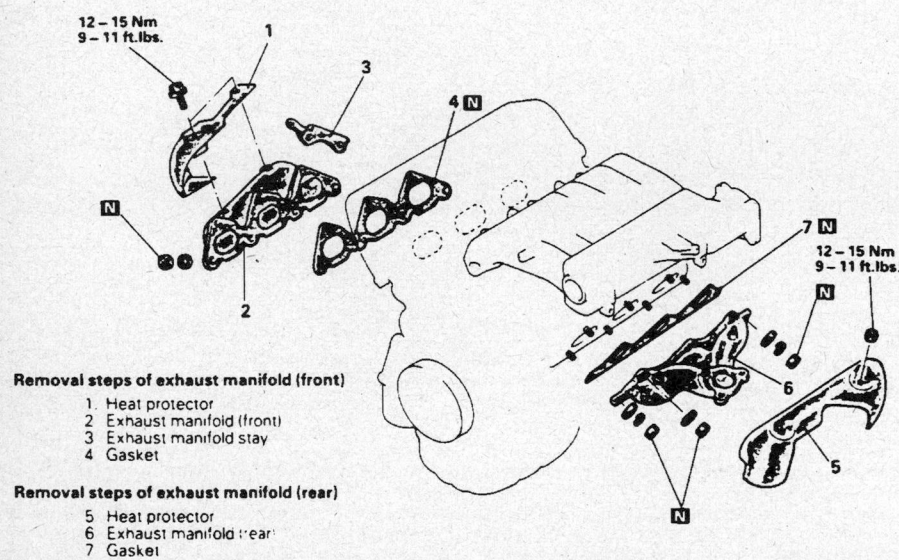

Removal steps of exhaust manifold (front)
1. Heat protector
2. Exhaust manifold (front)
3. Exhaust manifold stay
4. Gasket

Removal steps of exhaust manifold (rear)
5. Heat protector
6. Exhaust manifold (rear)
7. Gasket

Fig. 16 Exhaust manifold replacement. Turbocharged engine

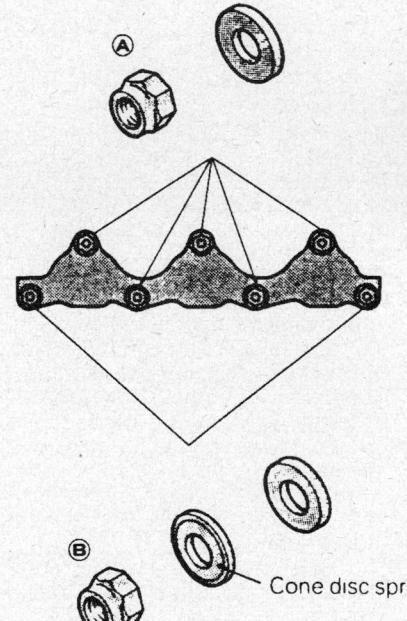

Fig. 17 Rear exhaust manifold nut installation. Turbocharged engine

VALVE COVER

REPLACE

1. Remove timing belt as outlined under "Timing Belt, Replace."
2. Remove intake manifold as outlined under "Intake Manifold, Replace."
3. Replace camshaft oil seals in numbered sequence as shown, **Fig. 21,** noting the following:
   a. Using a suitable wrench on hexagonal part of camshaft, loosen camshaft sprocket bolt.
   b. Cut out a portion in camshaft oil seal lip, **Fig. 22.**

c. Cover tip of a suitable screwdriver with a clean soft cloth and pry out seal at cut out portion of seal. **Use care not to damage camshaft or cylinder head.**

4. Reverse procedure to install, **Fig. 21,** noting the following:
   a. Apply small amount of engine oil to seal lip.
   b. Using camshaft oil seal installer tool No. MD998761, or equivalent, insert oil seal.
   c. Using a suitable wrench on hexagonal part of camshaft, tighten camshaft sprocket pulley bolt to

specifications.
   d. Tighten valve cover bolts in order as shown, **Fig. 23.** No. 5 bolt (.79 inch) in rear bank differs from other bolts in length. Remaining bolts in rear bank are .39 inch long. Bolts are color coded for installation, front bank bolts are black and rear bank bolts are green. When rocker

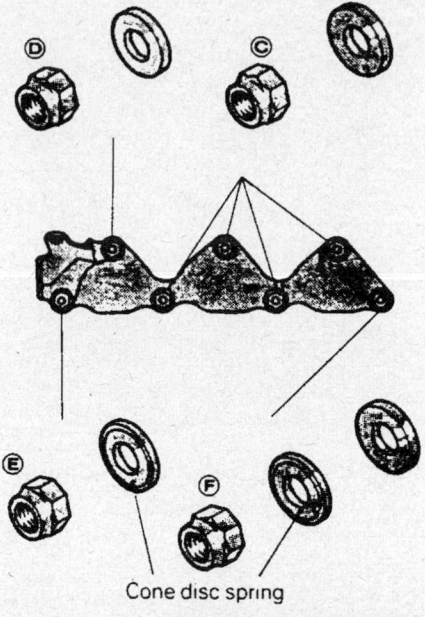

MT1079100007000X

Fig. 18 Front exhaust manifold nut installation. Turbocharged engine

Cone disc spring

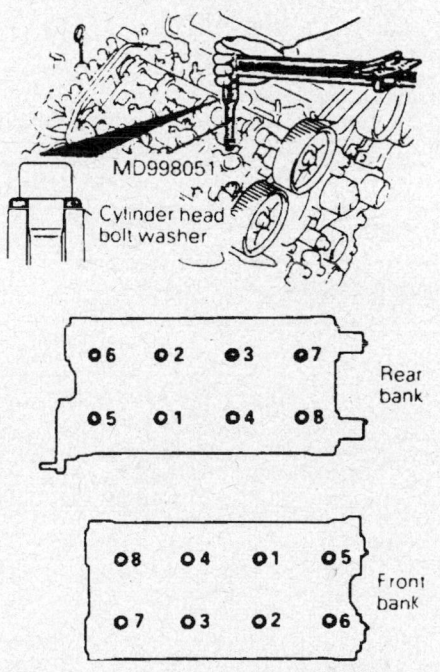

MD998051

Cylinder head bolt washer

Rear bank

Front bank

MT1099100033000X

Fig. 20 Cylinder head tightening sequence

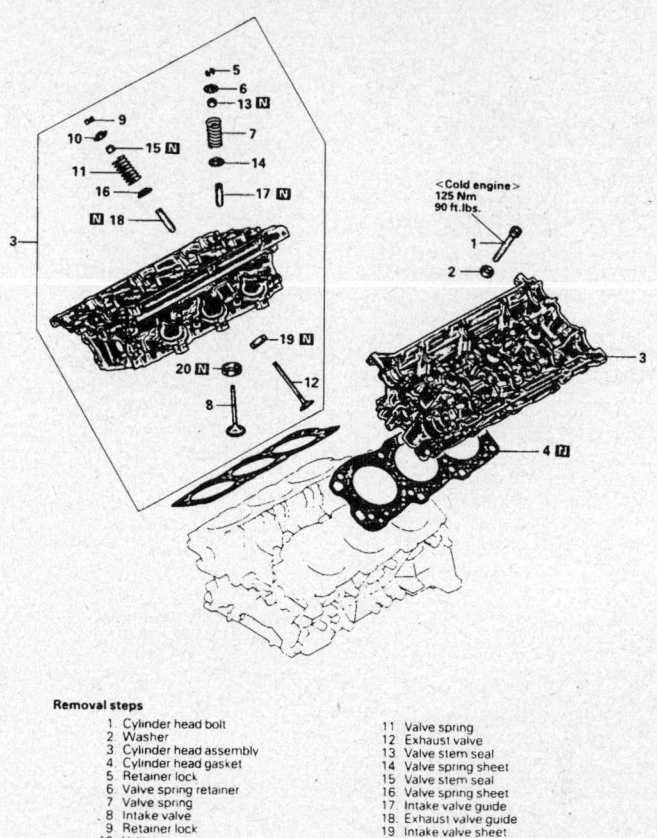

<Cold engine>
125 Nm
90 ft.lbs.

Removal steps

1. Cylinder head bolt
2. Washer
3. Cylinder head assembly
4. Cylinder head gasket
5. Retainer lock
6. Valve spring retainer
7. Valve spring
8. Intake valve
9. Retainer lock
10. Valve spring retainer
11. Valve spring
12. Exhaust valve
13. Valve stem seal
14. Valve spring sheet
15. Valve stem seal
16. Valve spring sheet
17. Intake valve guide
18. Exhaust valve guide
19. Intake valve sheet
20. Exhaust valve sheet

MT1099100032000X

Fig. 19 Cylinder head & valve replacement

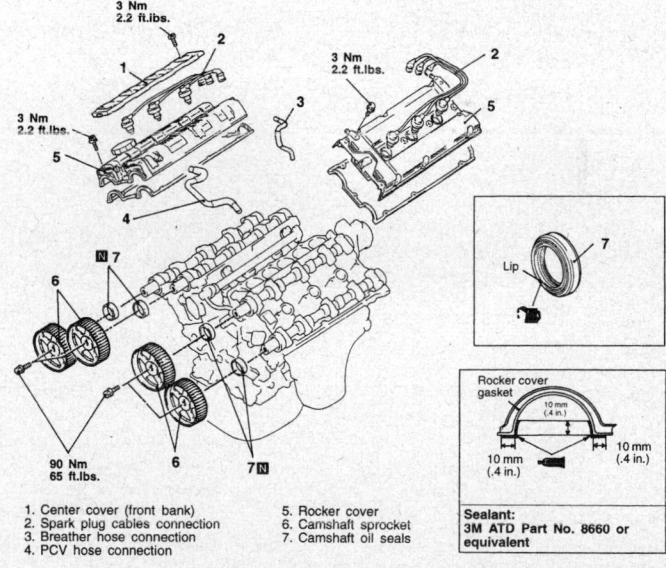

3 Nm
2.2 ft.lbs.

3 Nm
2.2 ft.lbs.

3 Nm
2.2 ft.lbs.

90 Nm
65 ft.lbs.

Lip

Rocker cover gasket

10 mm
(.4 in.)

10 mm
(.4 in.)

10 mm
(.4 in.)

Sealant:
3M ATD Part No. 8660 or equivalent

1. Center cover (front bank)
2. Spark plug cables connection
3. Breather hose connection
4. PCV hose connection
5. Rocker cover
6. Camshaft sprocket
7. Camshaft oil seals

MT1099100026000X

Fig. 21 Camshaft oil seal replacement

cover gasket has been replaced, tighten bolts in this order to specification.

VALVE CLEARANCE SPECIFICATIONS

Year	Valve Clearance, Inch	
	Intake	Exhaust
1997–99 SOHC	.0012–.0024	.0020–.0035
1996–99 DOHC	.0008–.0020	.0020–.0035

VALVE ADJUSTMENT

Because automatic lash adjusters are used, no adjustment is necessary.

TIMING BELT

REPLACE

SOHC ENGINE

Removal

The timing belt should be replaced every 60,000 miles.
1. Release fuel system pressure as outlined under "Precautions."
2. Remove engine undercover.
3. Remove air conditioning, power steering and alternator drive belts.
4. Remove air conditioning tension pulley and bracket.
5. Raise and support engine ensuring weight is lifted off mounts.
6. Remove engine mounting bracket.
7. Remove power steering pump with hoses attached and place aside.
8. Remove engine support bracket mounting bolts in reverse order of numbered sequence shown in **Fig. 24**, spraying lubricant on the reamer bolt while removing slowly.
9. Secure camshaft pulley end using yoke holder tool Nos. MB990767 and MB998719, or equivalents, when removing crankshaft pulley.
10. Remove timing belt cover cap.
11. Remove timing belt upper and lower cover outers, then remove front flange.
12. Rotate engine to position No. 1 cylinder at TDC on compression stroke to align timing marks, **Fig. 25**
13. Loosen timing belt tensioner bolt, then turn tensioner counterclockwise to release tension from belt and tighten in released position.
14. Remove timing belt.

Installation

1. Align camshaft and crankshaft sprockets timing marks **Fig. 25**.
2. Install timing belt as follows:
   a. Install timing belt on crankshaft sprocket.
   b. Route timing belt over lefthand camshaft sprocket.
   c. Route timing belt onto water pump sprocket.
   d. Route timing belt over righthand

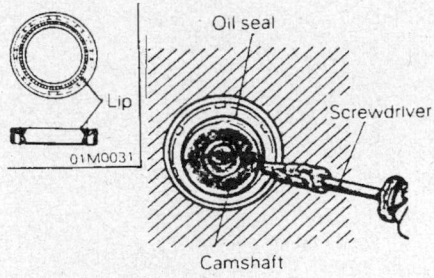

Fig. 22   Oil seal removal

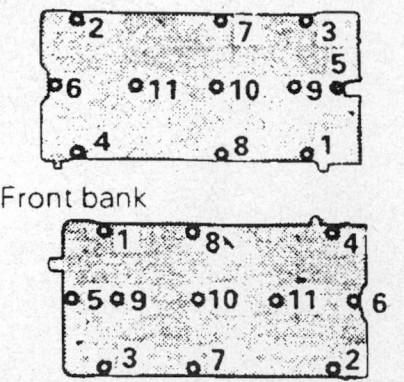

Rear bank

Front bank

Fig. 23   Valve cover tightening sequence

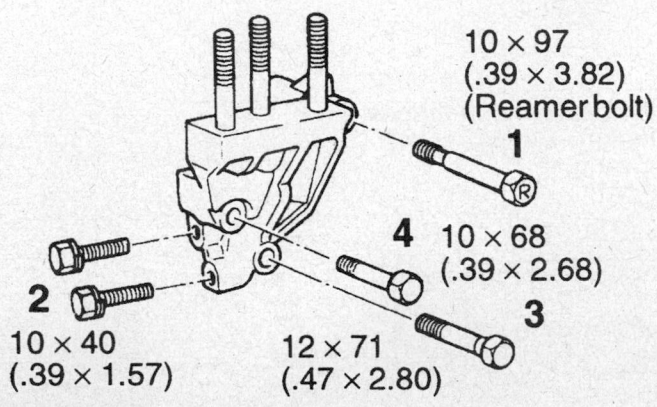

10 × 97
(.39 × 3.82)
(Reamer bolt)   **1**

10 × 68
(.39 × 2.68)   **4**

10 × 40
(.39 × 1.57)   **2**

12 × 71
(.47 × 2.80)   **3**

Thread diameter × length   mm (in.)

Fig. 24   Engine support bracket replacement. SOHC engine

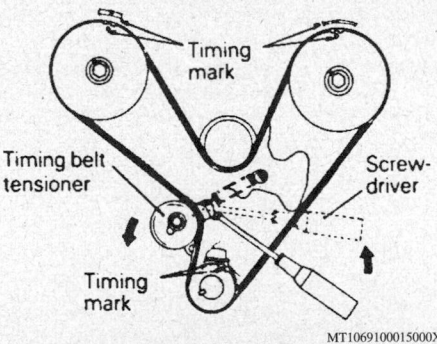

Fig. 25   Timing mark alignment. SOHC engine

camshaft sprocket.
   e. Route timing belt over tensioner pulley.
3. Adjust timing belt as follows:
   a. Install crankshaft flange.
   b. Loosen tensioner retainer bolt and allow tensioner spring tension to tighten timing belt.
   c. Turn crankshaft two turns clockwise with crankshaft tool No. MD998716, or equivalent.
   d. Align timing marks. **Do not turn crankshaft counterclockwise as damage to valve components or pistons may occur.**
   e. Tighten tension retainer bolts.
   f. Measure timing belt tension using a suitable belt tension gauge. Belt tension should be 44.1–66.1 lbs.
4. Install timing belt cover bolts as shown in **Fig. 26**.
5. Tighten crankshaft pulley using end yoke holder tool Nos. MB990767 and MD998719, or equivalents.
6. Install engine support bracket in numbered sequence shown in **Fig. 24**. **Note bolt size when installing.**
7. Install power steering oil pump and tighten mounting bolt.
8. Install power steering oil pump pressure switch connector.
9. Install tension pulley bracket and tighten mounting bolts.
10. Install air conditioning tension pulley assembly.
11. Install undercovers.

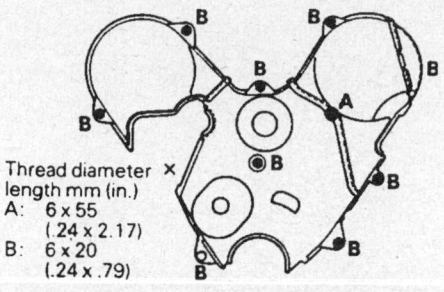

Thread diameter ×
length mm (in.)
A: 6 × 55
(.24 × 2.17)
B: 6 × 20
(.24 × .79)

MT1069100018000X

Fig. 26 Timing belt cover bolt location. SOHC engine

DOHC ENGINE

The timing belt should be replaced every 60,000 miles.

1. **On models less active aero system,** remove lefthand lower cover.
2. **On models with active aero system,** remove front lower cover in numbered sequence as shown, **Fig. 27.** Install air dam link assembly in the operative condition for ease of front lower cover panel.
3. **On all models,** remove cruise control pump and link assembly as outlined in "Speed Control Systems."
4. Remove alternator assembly.
5. Using suitable engine lifting device, raise and support engine to remove weight off engine mounts.
6. Remove timing belt in numbered sequence as shown, **Fig. 28,** noting the following:
   a. Using crankshaft pulley holder and end yoke holder tools, No. MD998754 and MB990767-01, or equivalents, remove crankshaft pulley.
   b. Remove engine support bracket in numbered sequence as shown, **Fig. 29.** While spraying lubricant, slowly remove reamer bolt.
   c. Remove timing belt as outlined in steps d through f.
   d. Align timing marks, **Fig. 30.**
   e. Mark rotational direction on back side of timing.
   f. Loosen center bolt on tensioner pulley, then remove timing belt. **Coolant or oil on timing belt shortens belt life drastically, removed timing belt, sprocket and tensioner must be free from oil and coolant.**
7. Install auto tensioner as follows:
   a. Secure auto tensioner in a soft jaw vise in a level position, **Fig. 31.**
   b. Push in rod slowly with vise until set hole (A) is aligned with pin hole (B).
   c. Insert a .055 inch thick wire into set and pin holes.
   d. Remove auto tensioner from vise and install on engine.
8. Align timing marks on camshaft or crankshaft sprocket.
9. Install crankshaft pulley. Shift timing mark on crankshaft sprocket by three teeth to lower the position on the No. 1 cylinder slightly from the TDC position

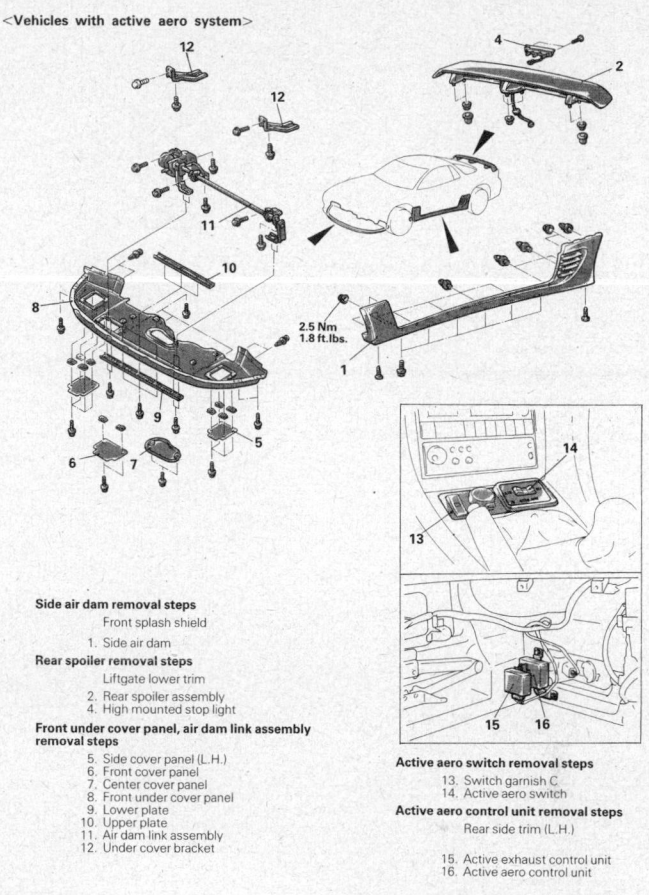

<Vehicles with active aero system>

2.5 Nm
1.8 ft.lbs.

Side air dam removal steps
   Front splash shield
1. Side air dam
Rear spoiler removal steps
   Liftgate lower trim
2. Rear spoiler assembly
4. High mounted stop light
Front under cover panel, air dam link assembly removal steps
5. Side cover panel (L.H.)
6. Front cover panel
7. Center cover panel
8. Front under cover panel
9. Lower plate
10. Upper plate
11. Air dam link assembly
12. Under cover bracket

Active aero switch removal steps
13. Switch garnish C
14. Active aero switch
Active aero control unit removal steps
   Rear side trim (L.H.)
15. Active exhaust control unit
16. Active aero control unit

MT1099100015000X

Fig. 27 Active aero system component removal. DOHC engine

on compression stroke. **Turning camshaft sprocket with piston in No. 1 cylinder at TDC may cause valves to interfere with piston.**

10. Ensure timing marks on camshaft sprockets for intake and exhaust valves are not within range A in **Fig. 32.** If timing mark is within range A, turn camshaft sprocket to move timing mark to area closest to range A. **In range A, cam lobe on camshaft lifts valve through rocker arm and camshaft sprocket is apt to rotate by reaction force of valve spring. Use care not to have finger pinched between sprockets.**

11. Turn camshaft sprocket for either intake or exhaust valve to locate timing mark as shown, **Fig. 33,** then turn other camshaft to locate timing mark as shown. **If intake and exhaust valves of same cylinder lift at the same time, interference with each other may result. Therefore, turn intake valve camshaft sprocket and exhaust valve camshaft alternately.**

12. Turn camshaft sprocket clockwise to align timing marks. If camshaft sprocket has been turned excessively, turn it counterclockwise to align timing marks.

13. Align timing mark of crankshaft sprocket. **Shift timing mark of crankshaft sprocket one tooth in counterclock-**

wise direction to aid in belt installation.

14. Using spring loaded paper clips, secure camshaft sprockets with suitable box end wrenches, then install timing belt in the following order: (1) Front exhaust camshaft to (2) front intake camshaft to (3) water pump to (4) rear intake camshaft to (5) rear exhaust camshaft to (6) idler pulley to (7) crankshaft to (8) tensioner pulley, **Fig. 34.** Do not allow belt to slacken.

15. Turn tensioner pulley, ensure pin holes are located above center bolt, then press tensioner pulley against timing belt and, at the same time, temporarily tighten center bolt, **Fig. 35.**

16. Ensure all timing marks are still aligned properly.

17. Remove loaded paper clips.

18. Adjust timing belt as follows:
   a. Rotate crankshaft ¼ turning counterclockwise, then rotate clockwise until timing marks are aligned.
   b. Loosen center bolt on tensioner pulley. Using tensioner pulley socket wrench tool No. MD998767, or equivalent, and torque wrench, apply a torque of 7 ft. lbs. to timing belt and tighten tensioner center bolt simultaneously.
   c. Remove set pin from auto tensioner, ensure set pin cam be easily removed.

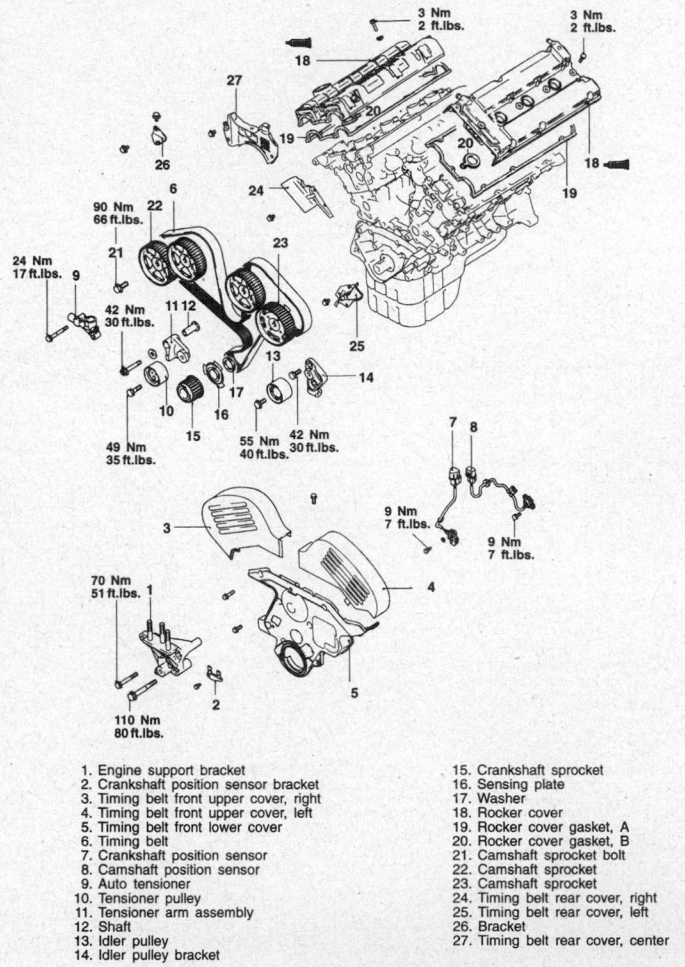

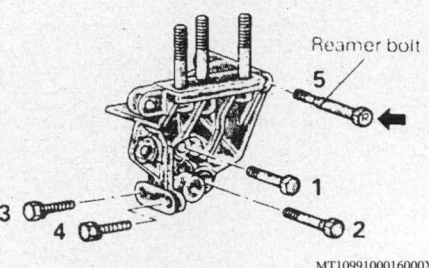

Fig. 29 Engine support bracket removal. DOHC engine

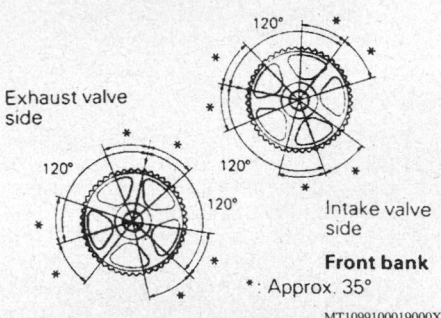

Fig. 32 Intake & exhaust camshaft alignment. DOHC engine

1. Engine support bracket
2. Crankshaft position sensor bracket
3. Timing belt front upper cover, right
4. Timing belt front upper cover, left
5. Timing belt front lower cover
6. Timing belt
7. Crankshaft position sensor
8. Camshaft position sensor
9. Auto tensioner
10. Tensioner pulley
11. Tensioner arm assembly
12. Shaft
13. Idler pulley
14. Idler pulley bracket
15. Crankshaft sprocket
16. Sensing plate
17. Washer
18. Rocker cover
19. Rocker cover gasket, A
20. Rocker cover gasket, B
21. Camshaft sprocket bolt
22. Camshaft sprocket
23. Camshaft sprocket
24. Timing belt rear cover, right
25. Timing belt rear cover, left
26. Bracket
27. Timing belt rear cover, center

Fig. 28 Timing belt replacement. DOHC engine

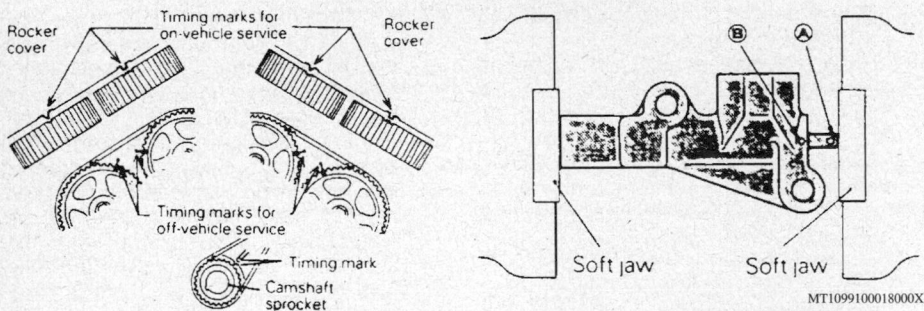

Fig. 30 Timing mark alignment. DOHC engine

d. Rotate crankshaft two turns clockwise and let stand for five minutes or more.
e. Ensure set pin can be easily removed from, and installed to, the auto tensioner. If set pin cannot be easily inserted, the auto tensioner is normal if its rod protrusion is within .149–.177 inch, **Fig. 36.** If protrusion is out of specification, repeat procedure.
f. Ensure timing marks on all sprockets are aligned properly.

19. Reverse procedure to install as shown, **Fig. 28,** noting the following:

Fig. 31 Timing belt auto tensioner adjustment. DOHC engine

a. Install lower timing cover bolts as shown, **Fig. 37.**
b. Install engine support bracket bolts as shown, **Fig. 38.** While installing reamer bolt, tighten slowly while spraying lubricant on reamer area.
c. Install crankshaft pulley using removal tools.

CAMSHAFT
REPLACE

1. Remove valve covers as outlined under "Valve Cover, Replace."
2. Replace rocker arm and camshaft in

numbered sequence as shown, **Figs. 39 and 40,** noting the following:
a. Immerse lash adjuster in clean diesel fuel. Using small wire, move plunger up and down four to five times while pushing down lightly on the check ball to bleed out air. Install lash adjuster into cylinder head.
b. Turn crankshaft to bring No. 1 cylinder to TDC.
c. Ensure rocker arm is installed correctly on valve lash adjuster and valve.
d. Install camshaft noting identification mark stamped on hexagonal section. Camshaft marked with a V is the intake side and camshaft marked with a C is exhaust side.
e. Install camshafts with their dowel pins positioned as shown, **Fig. 41.**
f. Install bearing caps noting identification mark and cap number. Bearing caps Nos. 2, 3 and 4 bear the front mark. Install these caps with mark lined up with front mark on cylinder head. Caps marked with an I are for intake side and caps marked with an E are exhaust side, **Fig. 42.**
g. Tighten bearing cap bolts gradually in two or three steps, then tighten to specifications.
h. Using semicircular packing installer tool No. MD998762, or equivalent, install semicircular packing.

PISTON & ROD ASSEMBLY

1. Drain engine coolant into an approved container.
2. Remove engine assembly as outlined under" Engine, Replace."

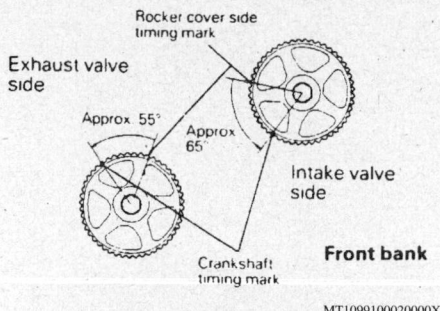

Fig. 33 Intake & exhaust camshaft sprocket alignment. DOHC engine

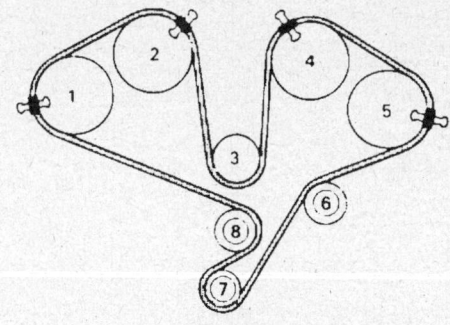

MT1099100021000X

Fig. 34 Timing belt installation. DOHC engine

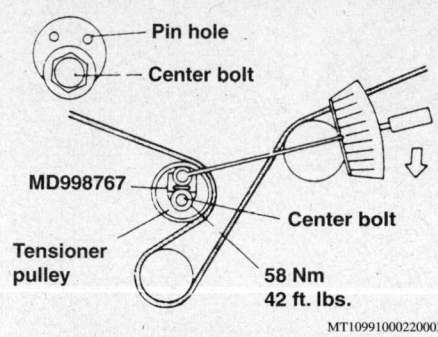

MT1099100022000X

Fig. 35 Timing belt tension adjustment. DOHC engine

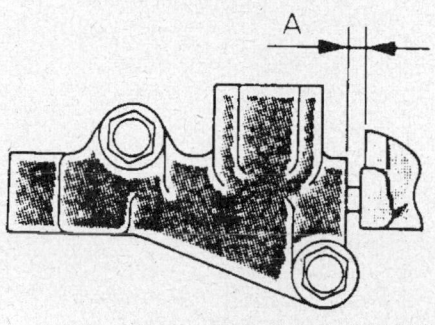

MT1099100023000X

Fig. 36 Auto adjuster rod protrusion. DOHC engine

3. Remove timing belt as outlined under "Timing Belt, Replace."
4. Remove exhaust manifolds as outlined under "Exhaust Manifold, Replace."
5. Remove air plenum and intake manifold as outlined under "Intake Manifold, Replace."
6. Remove cylinder head as outlined under "Cylinder Head, Replace."
7. Remove engine oil pan.
8. Replace piston and connecting rod in numbered sequence shown in **Fig. 43**, noting the following:

   a. Using piston ring expander, fit No. 2 and then No. 1 piston ring into position.
   b. The ring end is marked with identification. **SOHC No. 1 ring 1R, No. 2 ring 2R; DOHC No. 1 ring T, No. 2 ring T2.**
   c. Pistons for SOHC engine include those for right bank and left bank identified by an R for right bank and L for left bank.

When installing piston and rod assemblies, ensure front marks are pointed toward front of engine (timing belt side), **Fig. 43**.

OIL PAN
REPLACE

1. Drain engine oil into an appropriate container.
2. **On models with active aero system,** remove front lower cover in numbered sequence as shown, **Fig. 27,** then install air dam link assembly in operative

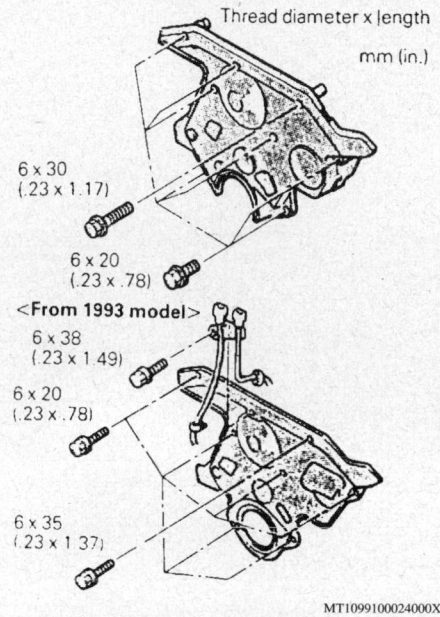

MT1099100024000X

Fig. 37 Lower timing belt cover installation. DOHC engine

condition for ease of front lower cover panel installation.
3. **On all models,** remove engine lower cover.
4. Remove front exhaust pipe.
5. Remove transfer assembly.
6. Replace oil pan and screen in numbered sequence as shown, **Fig. 44.**
7. Reverse procedure to install, noting the following:

   a. Apply a .16 inch diameter bead of sealant around oil pan flange.
   b. Tighten oil pan bolts in sequence as shown, **Fig. 45.**

OIL PUMP
REPLACE

1. Remove engine assembly as outlined under "Engine, Replace."
2. Remove timing belt as outlined under "Timing Belt, Replace."
3. Remove oil pan and pump assembly in numbered sequence as shown, **Fig. 46.**
4. Reverse procedure to install, **Fig. 46,** noting the following:

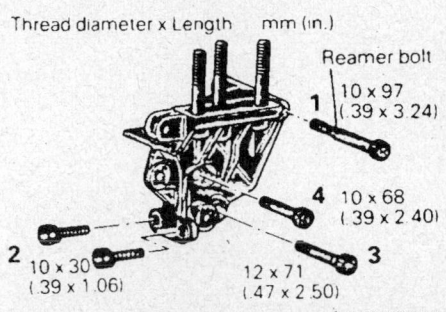

MT1099100025000X

Fig. 38 Engine support bracket installation. DOHC engine

a. Install front oil seal using oil seal installer tool No. MD998717, or equivalent.
b. Apply a .16 inch diameter bead of sealant around oil pan flange.
c. Tighten oil pan bolts in sequence as shown, **Fig. 45.**

OIL PUMP SERVICE

1. Inspect oil pump by assembling rotor on oil pump. Ensure a .0039–.0071 inch body and .0016–.0037 inch side clearance, **Fig. 47.**
2. **On turbocharged models,** ensure oil cooler bypass valve moves smoothly and dimension marked L is 1.358 inches long under normal temperature and humidity and 1.57 inches long after being dipped into oil with a temperature of 212°F.

OIL COOLER
REPLACE

1. Drain engine oil into an appropriate container.
2. Remove front splash shield, then the oil cooler engine oil feed hose.
3. Remove oil cooler engine oil return hose, then the oil cooler engine oil return tube.
4. Remove engine oil cooler.
5. Reverse procedure to install.

BELT TENSION DATA

Adjust belts by applying 22 lbs. of force to belt midway between pulleys as shown, **Fig. 48,** ensure deflection is as specified in **Fig. 49.**

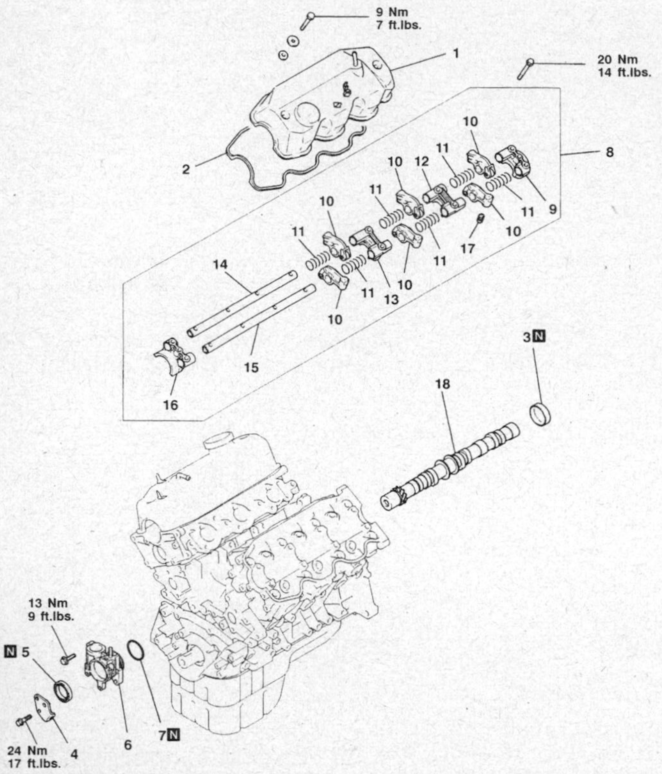

Fig. 39 diagram labels:

9 Nm
7 ft.lbs.

20 Nm
14 ft.lbs.

13 Nm
9 ft.lbs.

24 Nm
17 ft.lbs.

Removal steps
1. Rocker cover
2. Gasket
3. Circular packing
4. Intake manifold plenum stay bracket "A"
5. Camshaft oil seal
6. Distributor adaptor
7. O-ring
8. Rocker arm and rocker arm shaft
9. Bearing cap No. 4
10. Rocker arm
11. Spring
12. Bearing cap No. 3
13. Bearing cap No. 2
14. Rocker arm shaft "B"
15. Rocker arm shaft "A"
16. Bearing cap No. 1
17. Lash adjuster
18. Camshaft

MT1069900552000X

Fig. 39   Rocker arm & camshaft replacement. SOHC engine

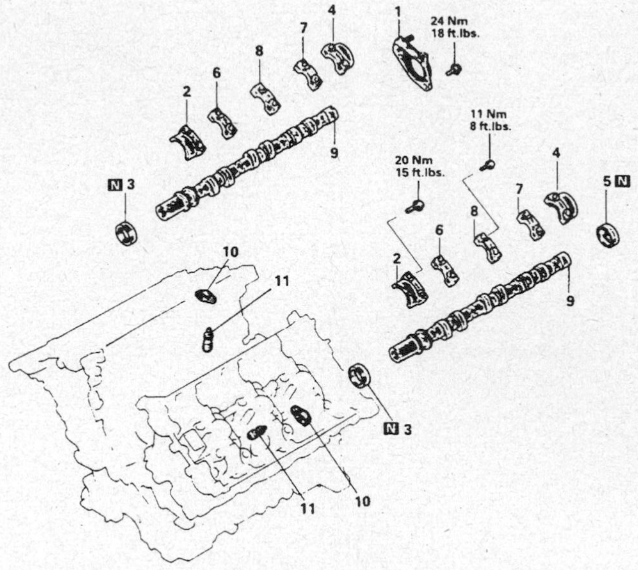

Fig. 40 diagram labels:

24 Nm
18 ft.lbs.

11 Nm
8 ft.lbs.

20 Nm
15 ft.lbs.

Removal steps
1. Crank angle sensor adaptor
2. Bearing cap front
3. Oil seal
4. Bearing cap rear
5. Circular packing
6. Bearing cap No. 2
7. Bearing cap No. 4
8. Bearing cap No. 3
9. Camshaft
10. Rocker arm
11. Lash adjuster

Installation steps
11. Lash adjuster
10. Rocker arm
9. Camshaft
8. Bearing cap No. 3
7. Bearing cap No. 4
6. Bearing cap No. 2
4. Bearing cap rear
2. Bearing cap front
5. Circular packing
3. Oil seal
1. Crank angle sensor adaptor

MT1099100029000X

Fig. 40   Rocker arm & camshaft replacement. DOHC engine

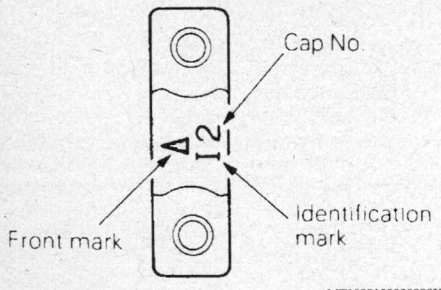

Cap No.
Front mark
Identification mark

MT1099100030000X

Fig. 41   Camshaft installation

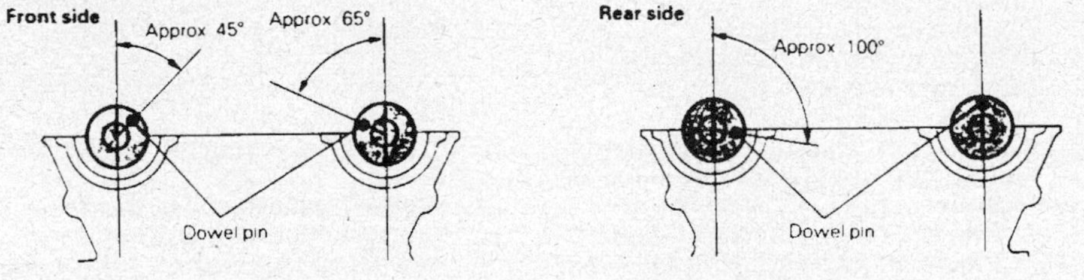

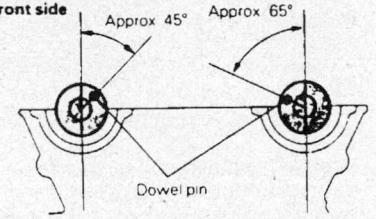

Front side — Approx 45° — Approx 65° — Dowel pin

Rear side — Approx 100° — Dowel pin

MT1099100031000X

Fig. 42   Camshaft bearing cap identification

COOLING SYSTEM BLEED

These engines do not require a specified bleed procedure. After filling cooling system, run engine to operating temperature with radiator/pressure cap off. Air will then be automatically bled through the cap opening.

THERMOSTAT
REPLACE

1. Drain coolant into an appropriate container.

2. Remove thermostat in numbered sequence as shown, **Fig. 50.**
3. Reverse procedure to install, noting the following:
   a. Install thermostat to the intake manifold, **Fig. 51.**
   b. Align air intake hose "A" notches with marks on air intake hoses "B and C." Insert hoses into air intake hose "A" until bottomed out, **Fig. 52.**

WATER PUMP
REPLACE

1. Drain engine coolant into an appropriate container.

2. Remove power transistor and ignition coil assembly.
3. Remove timing belt as outlined under "Timing Belt, Replace."
4. Remove water pump.
5. Reverse procedure to install, **Figs. 53 and 54,** noting the following:
   a. Install water pump bolts in correct location as shown, **Fig. 55.**
   b. Replace inlet water pipe O-ring at both ends and apply water to O-ring to help installation. **Do not allow engine oil or other contaminates to adhere to O-ring.**

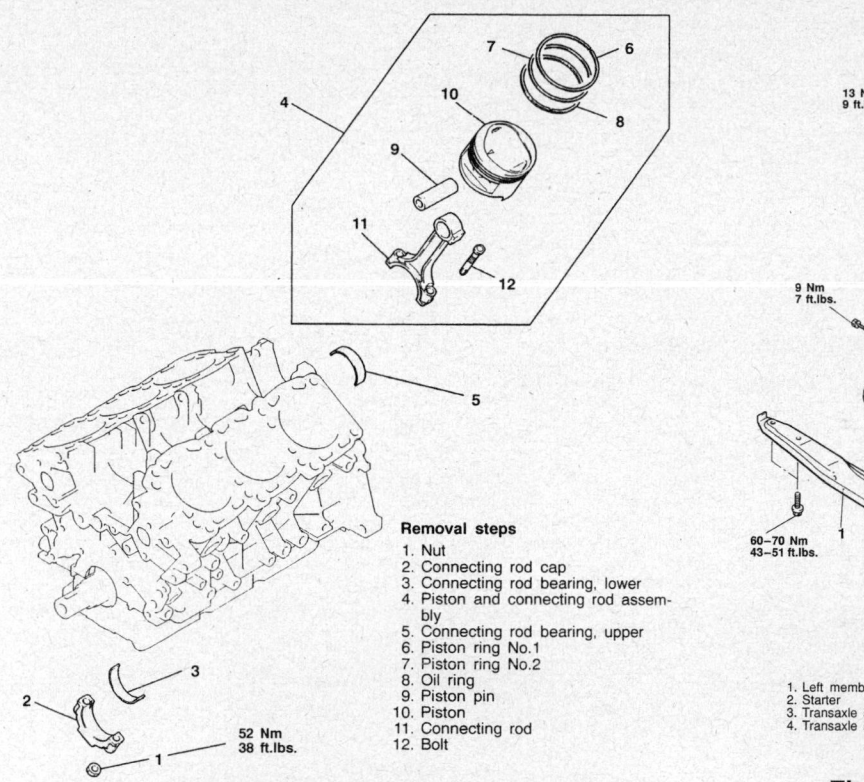

Removal steps

1. Nut
2. Connecting rod cap
3. Connecting rod bearing, lower
4. Piston and connecting rod assembly
5. Connecting rod bearing, upper
6. Piston ring No.1
7. Piston ring No.2
8. Oil ring
9. Piston pin
10. Piston
11. Connecting rod
12. Bolt

52 Nm
38 ft.lbs.

MT1069900553000X

Fig. 43 Piston & connecting rod replacement

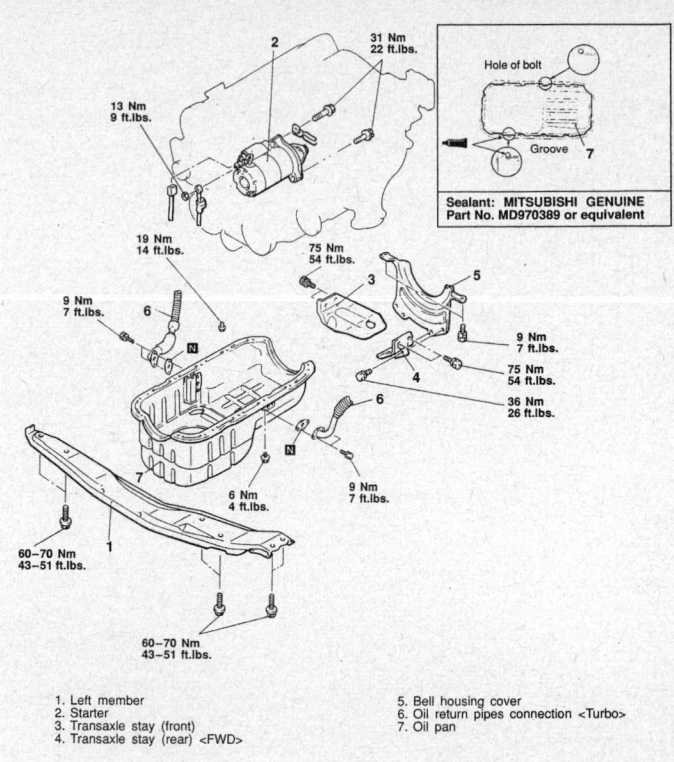

Sealant: MITSUBISHI GENUINE Part No. MD970389 or equivalent

1. Left member
2. Starter
3. Transaxle stay (front)
4. Transaxle stay (rear) <FWD>
5. Bell housing cover
6. Oil return pipes connection <Turbo>
7. Oil pan

MT1099100035000X

Fig. 44 Oil pan & screen replacement

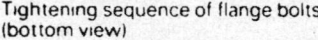

Tightening sequence of flange bolts (bottom view)

Front of engine (Timing belt side)

MT1099100036000X

Fig. 45 Oil pan tightening sequence

RADIATOR

REPLACE

Refer to **Fig. 56,** when replacing radiator.

FUEL PUMP

REPLACE

1. Drain fuel from fuel tank into an appropriate container.
2. Release fuel system pressure as outlined under "Precautions."
3. Remove fuel pump in numbered sequence as shown, **Fig. 57,** noting the following:
   a. Cover body side high pressure fuel hose connection with a shop towel to prevent splash of fuel that could be caused by residual pressure in fuel line.

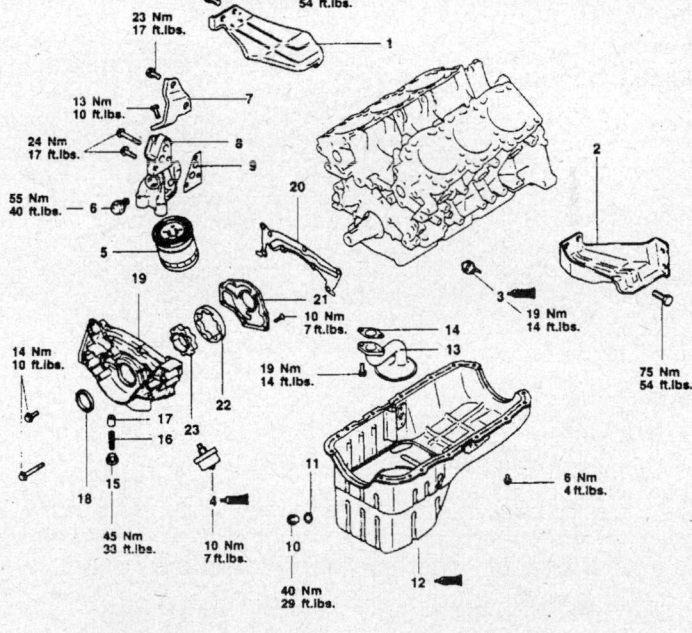

Removal steps

1. Transmission stay, right
2. Transmission stay, left
3. Oil pressure switch
4. Oil pressure gauge unit
5. Oil filter
6. Oil cooler by-pass valve <Turbo>
7. Oil filter bracket stay <Turbo>
8. Oil filter bracket
9. Oil filter bracket gasket
10. Drain plug
11. Drain plug gasket
12. Oil pan
13. Oil screen
14. Oil screen gasket
15. Plug
16. Relief spring
17. Relief plunger
18. Crankshaft oil seal
19. Oil pump case
20. Oil pump gasket
21. Oil pump cover
22. Oil pump outer rotor
23. Oil pump inner rotor

MT1099500060000X

Fig. 46 Oil pan & pump replacement

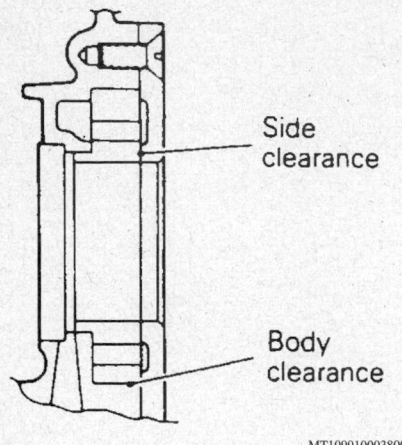

Fig. 47 Oil pump inspection

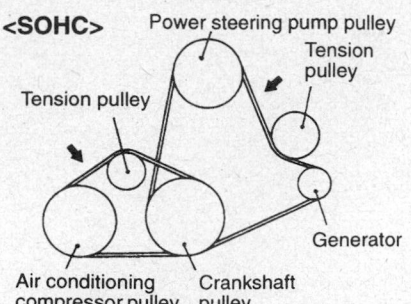

<SOHC>

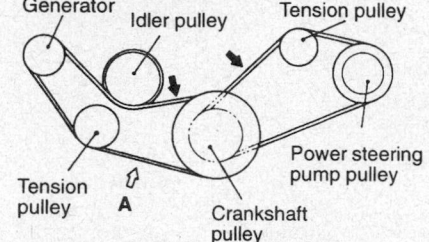

<DOHC without air conditioning>

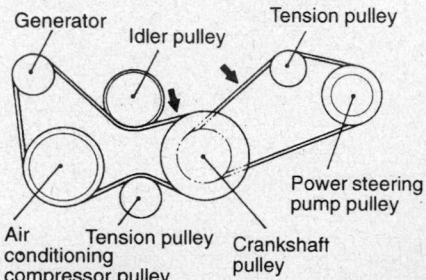

<DOHC with air conditioning>

Fig. 48 Drive belt adjustment

<Vehicle without air conditioning>

Items		Specification
For generator	Tension N (lbs.)	350–600 (77–132)
	Deflection mm (in.) <Reference value>	4.0–5.5 (.16–.22)
For P/S pump	Tension N (lbs.)	250–500 (55–110)
	Deflection mm (in.) <Reference value>	9.5–13.5 (.37–.53)

<Vehicle with air conditioning>

Items		Specification
For generator and A/C compressor	Tension N (lbs.)	350–600 (77–132)
	Deflection mm (in.) <Reference value>	4.0–5.5 (.16–.22)
For P/S pump	Tension N (lbs.)	250–500 (55–110)
	Deflection mm (in.) <Reference value>	9.5–13.5 (.37–.53)

MT1069100100000X

Fig. 49 Drive belt tension data

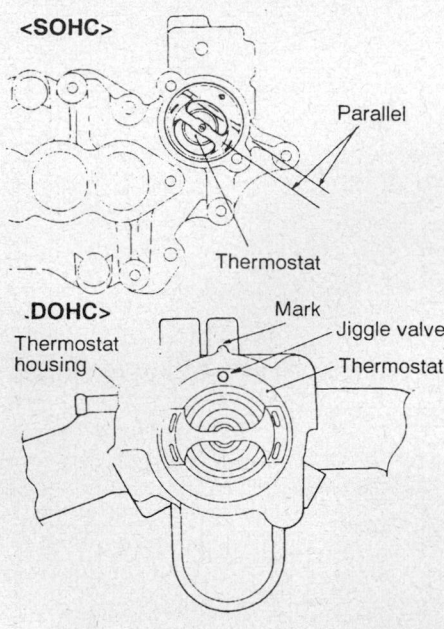

MT1089900130000X

Fig. 51 Thermostat installation

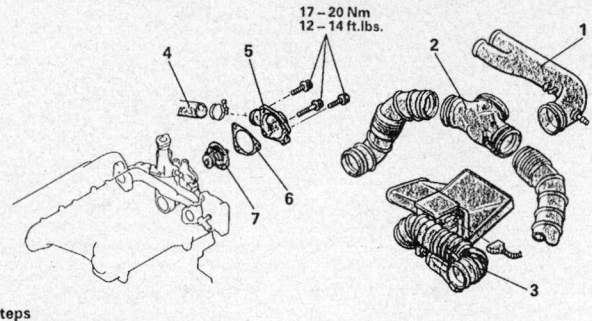

Removal steps
1. Air hose A <Turbo>
2. Air intake hose A <Turbo>
3. Air intake hose <Non-Turbo>
4. Connection of radiator lower hose
5. Water inlet fitting
6. Gasket
7. Thermostat

MT1089100009000X

Fig. 50 Thermostat replacement

b. Hold pump side nut while disconnecting pump side of high pressure fuel hose.
4. Reverse procedure to install, noting the following:
   a. Align three projections of packing with holes in fuel pump and gauge assembly.
   b. Install overfill limiter valve as shown, **Fig. 58.**
   c. Apply body sealant to fuel gauge cover.
5. Reverse procedure to install.

FUEL FILTER
REPLACE

1. Drain fuel from fuel tank into an appropriate container.
2. Release fuel system pressure as outlined under "Precautions."
3. Remove eye bolt while holding fuel filter nut securely **Fig. 59. Cover hose connection with rags to prevent splash of fuel that could be caused by some residual pressure in the** fuel pipe line.
4. Remove fuel main pipe connection.
5. Remove mounting bolt.
6. Reverse procedure to install, noting the following:
   a. Insert main pipe at connector part of the high pressure fuel pipe, **Fig. 60,** then manually screw in main pipe flare nut.
   b. Holding fuel filter nut, tighten flare nut and eye bolt to specifications.
   c. Install filter to bracket.

TURBOCHARGER
REPLACE

1. Remove radiator assembly.
2. Remove right transaxle stay.
3. Remove front exhaust pipe.
4. Remove front and rear turbocharger assembly in numbered sequence as shown, **Figs. 61 and 62,** noting the following:
   a. Disconnect oxygen sensor connector, then remove oxygen sensor using oxygen sensor wrench tool No. MD998770, or equivalent.

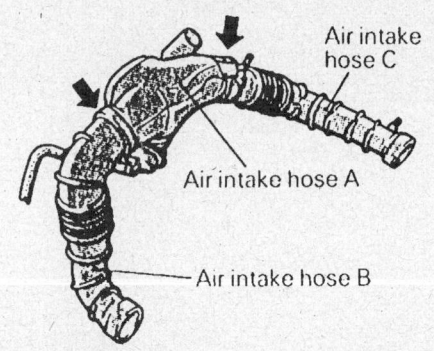

Fig. 52 Air intake hose "A" installation

MT1089100011000X

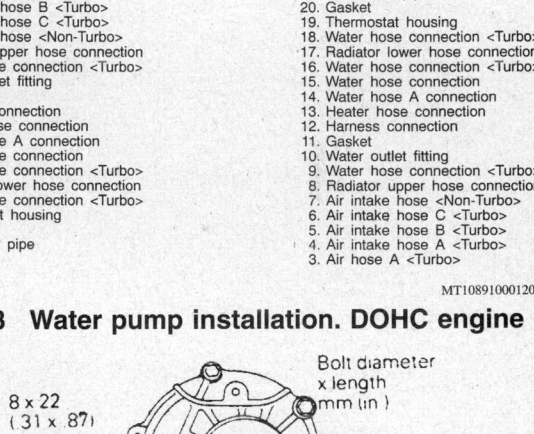

Fig. 53 Water pump installation. DOHC engine

MT1089100012000X

Removal steps
1. Water pump
2. Gasket
3. Air hose A <Turbo>
4. Air intake hose A <Turbo>
5. Air intake hose B <Turbo>
6. Air intake hose C <Turbo>
7. Air intake hose <Non-Turbo>
8. Radiator upper hose connection
9. Water hose connection <Turbo>
10. Water outlet fitting
11. Gasket
12. Harness connection
13. Heater hose connection
14. Water hose A connection
15. Water hose connection
16. Water hose connection <Turbo>
17. Radiator lower hose connection
18. Water hose connection <Turbo>
19. Thermostat housing
20. Gasket
21. Inlet water pipe
22. O-ring

Installation steps
2. Gasket
1. Water pump
22. O-ring
21. Inlet water pipe
20. Gasket
19. Thermostat housing
18. Water hose connection <Turbo>
17. Radiator lower hose connection
16. Water hose connection <Turbo>
15. Water hose connection
14. Water hose A connection
13. Heater hose connection
12. Harness connection
11. Gasket
10. Water outlet fitting
9. Water hose connection <Turbo>
8. Radiator upper hose connection
7. Air intake hose <Non-Turbo>
6. Air intake hose C <Turbo>
5. Air intake hose B <Turbo>
4. Air intake hose A <Turbo>
3. Air hose A <Turbo>

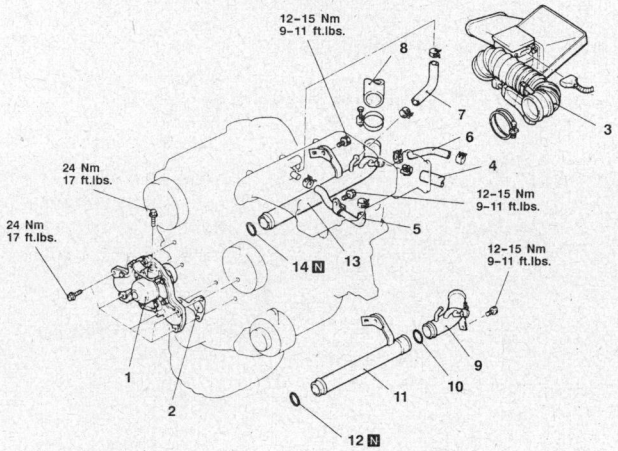

Removal steps
1. Water pump
2. Gasket
3. Air intake hose
4. Heater hose connection
5. Water hose A
6. Water hose B
7. By-pass water hose
8. Radiator lower hose connection
9. Inlet water pipe B
   <Vehicles with manual transaxle>
10. O-ring
   <Vehicles with manual transaxle>
11. Inlet water pipe A
   <Vehicles with manual transaxle>
12. O-ring
   <Vehicles with manual transaxle>
13. Inlet water pipe A
   <Vehicles with automatic transaxle>
14. O-ring
   <Vehicles with automatic transaxle>

Installation steps
1. Water pump
2. Gasket
14. O-ring
   <Vehicles with automatic transaxle>
13. Inlet water pipe A
   <Vehicles with automatic transaxle>
12. O-ring
   <Vehicles with manual transaxle>
11. Inlet water pipe A
   <Vehicles with manual transaxle>
10. O-ring
   <Vehicles with manual transaxle>
9. Inlet water pipe B
   <Vehicles with manual transaxle>
8. Radiator lower hose connection
7. By-pass water hose
6. Water hose B
5. Water hose A
4. Heater hose connection
3. Air intake hose

MT1089900128000X

Fig. 54 Water pump installation. SOHC engine

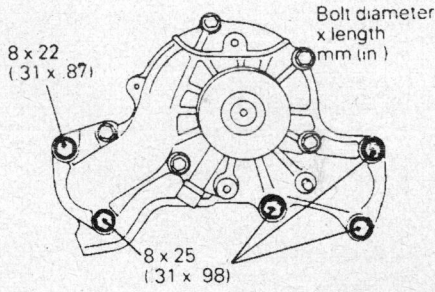

Bolt diameter
x length
mm (in.)

8 x 22
(31 x .87)

8 x 25
(31 x .98)

MT1089100013000X

Fig. 55 Water pump replacement

b. Disconnect A/C compressor connectors, leaving hoses connected.
5. Reverse numbered sequence as shown, **Figs. 61 and 62.**
6. Install front turbocharger, noting the following:
   a. Clean alignment surfaces as shown, **Fig. 63,** then apply clean engine oil through oil pipe hole.
   b. Install oxygen sensor using oxygen sensor tool.
   c. Align marks indicated by arrows and insert securely into stepped portion of pipe or until seated, **Figs. 64 through 68.**

TECHNICAL SERVICE BULLETINS

VALVE NOISE AT START-UP

1996 DOHC Engine

It is normal to hear valve noise during the first two minutes after engine start-up. The noise is caused by air in the high pressure chamber inside the automatic valve lash adjusters. Replacing valve lash adjusters will probably not eliminate valve noise. The following procedures will bleed air out of the adjusters and to confirm that the adjusters do not require replacement.

1. Verify engine oil level and quality, correct as necessary.
2. Start engine, if valve noise continues for longer than two minutes after start-up, proceed as follows:
   a. Warm engine to normal operating temperature. Gradually increase idle speed to 3000 RPM, then back down to normal idle speed. Repeat this process several times (maximum of ten times).
   b. Remove oil cap on rocker cover and verify noise is coming from valve lash adjusters.

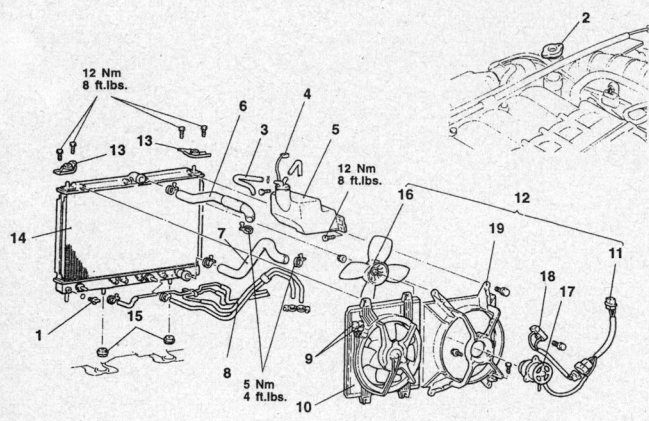

Radiator removal steps
1. Drain plug
2. Cap
3. Overflow tube
4. Water level sensor connector
5. Reserve tank
6. Radiator upper hose
7. Radiator lower hose
8. Automatic transaxle oil cooler hoses <Vehicles with A/T>
9. Condenser fan motor connector <Vehicles with air conditioning>
10. Condenser fan motor assembly <Vehicles with air conditioning>
11. Radiator fan motor connector
12. Radiator fan motor assembly
13. Upper insulator
14. Radiator assembly
15. Lower insulator

16. Fan
17. Radiator fan motor
18. Resistor
19. Shroud

Radiator fan motor assembly removal steps
1. Drain plug
2. Cap
6. Radiator upper hose
9. Condenser fan motor connector <Vehicles with air conditioning>
10. Condenser fan motor assembly <Vehicles with air conditioning>
11. Radiator fan motor connector
12. Radiator fan motor assembly
16. Fan
17. Radiator fan motor
18. Resistor
19. Shroud

MT1089500079000X

Fig. 56   Radiator replacement

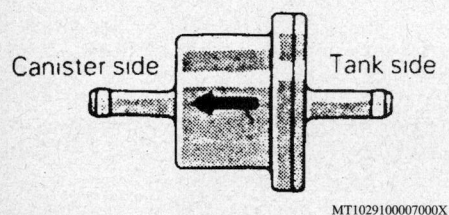

MT1029100007000X

Fig. 58   Overfill limiter valve installation

c. Remove rocker cover.
d. Verify camshaft lobe is on flat side.
e. Using finger pressure, push down on rocker arm over the head of each valve lash adjuster.
f. If the head of adjuster sinks when pressure is applied, adjuster must be replaced.
g. If the head of adjuster stays firm when pressure is applied, adjuster is operating normally.

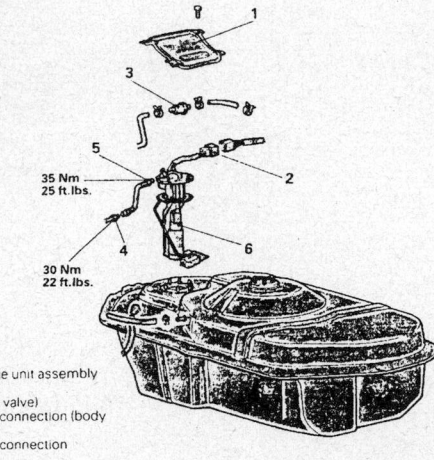

Removal steps
1. Fuel gauge cover
2. Fuel pump and fuel gauge unit assembly connector
3. Overfill limiter (Two-way valve)
4. High pressure fuel hose connection (body side)
5. High pressure fuel hose connection (fuel pump side)
6. Fuel pump and fuel gauge unit assembly

MT1029100006000X

Fig. 57   Fuel pump replacement

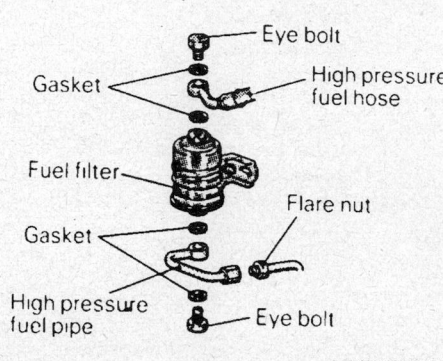

MT1029100009000X

Fig. 60   Fuel filter installation

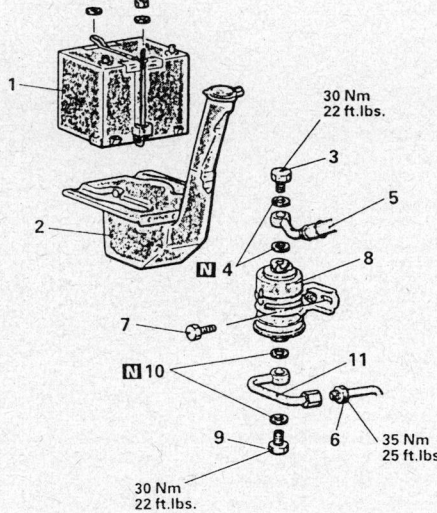

REMOVAL STEPS
1. Battery
2. Battery tray with washer tank assembly
3. Eye bolt
4. Gasket
5. High pressure fuel hose
6. Connection of fuel main pipe
7. Mounting bolt
8. Fuel filter
9. Eye bolt
10. Gasket
11. High pressure fuel pipe

MT1029100008000X

Fig. 59   Fuel filter removal

3.0L ENGINE

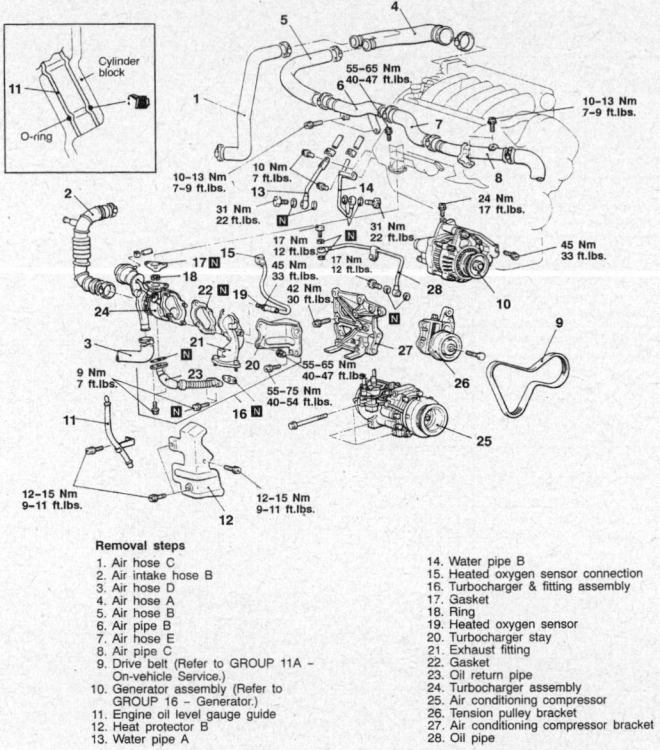

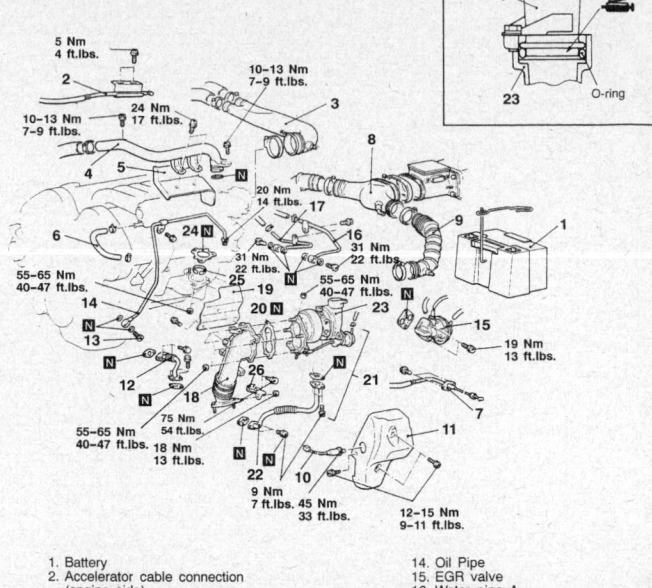

Removal steps

1. Air hose C
2. Air intake hose B
3. Air hose D
4. Air hose A
5. Air hose B
6. Air pipe B
7. Air hose E
8. Air pipe C
9. Drive belt (Refer to GROUP 11A – On-vehicle Service.)
10. Generator assembly (Refer to GROUP 16 – Generator.)
11. Engine oil level gauge guide
12. Heat protector B
13. Water pipe A
14. Water pipe B
15. Heated oxygen sensor connection
16. Turbocharger & fitting assembly
17. Gasket
18. Ring
19. Heated oxygen sensor
20. Turbocharger stay
21. Exhaust fitting
22. Gasket
23. Oil return pipe
24. Turbocharger assembly
25. Air conditioning compressor
26. Tension pulley bracket
27. Air conditioning compressor bracket
28. Oil pipe

MT1059100040000X

Fig. 61 Front turbocharger replacement

1. Battery
2. Accelerator cable connection (engine side)
3. Air hose A
4. Air pipe A
5. Heat protector F
6. Clutch booster vacuum hose
7. Accelerator cable connection (pedal side)
8. Air intake hose A
9. Air intake hose C
10. Heated oxygen sensor
11. Heat protector D
12. EGR pipe
13. Eye bolt
14. Oil Pipe
15. EGR valve
16. Water pipe A
17. Water pipe B
18. Exhaust fitting
19. Heat protector E
20. Gasket
21. Turbocharger & return pipe assembly
22. Oil return pipe
23. Turbocharger assembly
24. Gasket
25. Ring
26. Exhaust fitting stay

MT1059100041000X

Fig. 62 Rear turbocharger replacement

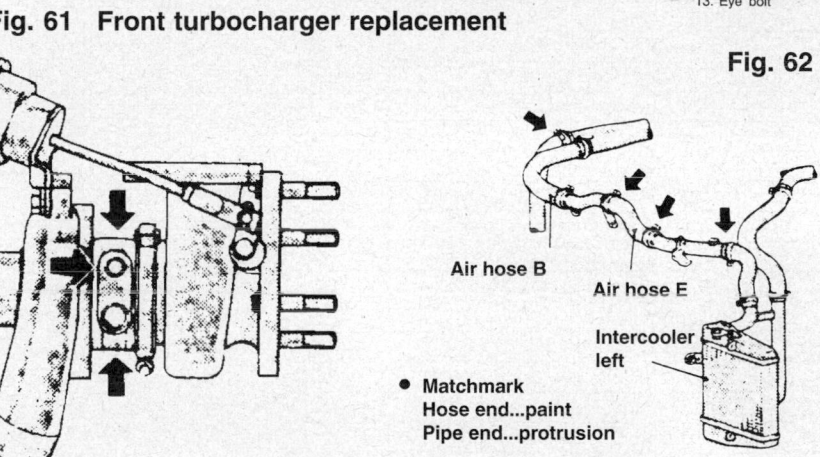

Fig. 63 Service points of turbocharger replacement

MT1059100010000X

Fig. 64 Air hose "E & B" installation. Front turbocharger

MT1059100011000X

Fig. 65 Air hose "D & C" installation. Front turbocharger

MT1059100012000X

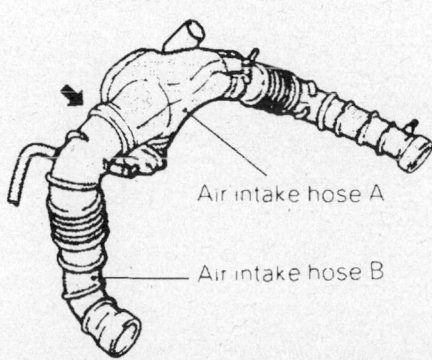

Fig. 66 Air intake hose "B" installation. Front turbocharger

MT1059100013000X

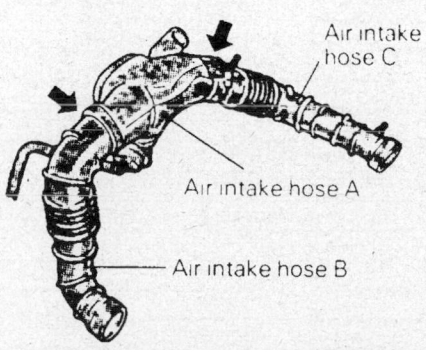

Fig. 67 Air intake hose "A & C" installation. Rear turbocharger

MT1059100014000X

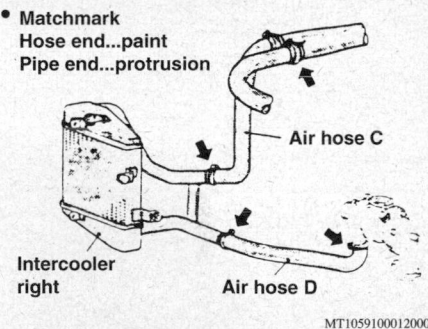

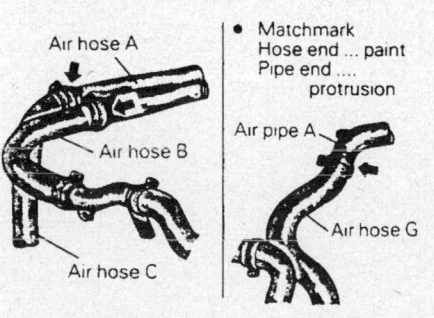

Fig. 68 Air pipe & hose "A" installation. Rear turbocharger

MT1059100015000X

TIGHTENING SPECIFICATIONS

Year	Component	Torque/ Ft. Lbs.
1996-99	Air Intake Plenum Bolt & Nut	13
	Air Intake Plenum Stay Bolt	13
	Alternator	17
	Alternator Brace Bolt	10
	Alternator Bracket Bolt	17
	Alternator Bracket Side Bolt	7
	Alternator Pivot Nut	17
	Auto Tensioner Bolt	17
	Bearing Caps Bolts No. 2, 3 & 4 (SOHC)	14
	Bearing Caps Bolts No. 2, 3 & 4 (DOHC)	8
	Bearing Caps, Front & Rear	14
	Bellhousing Cover Bolt	7
	Bracket Bolts	17
	Camshaft Sprocket Bolt	66
	Center Cover Bolt	2
	Connecting Rod Cap Nut	38
	Cooling Fan Bolt	8
	Cooling Fan Bracket Bolt	30
	Crank Angle Sensor Adapter Bolt (DOHC)	17
	Crank Angle Sensor Nut	9
	Crankshaft Bearing Cap Bolt (DOHC)	67
	Crankshaft Bearing Cap Bolt (SOHC)	59
	Crankshaft Bearing Cap Bolt (Turbo)	54
	Crankshaft Pulley Bolt	136
	Cylinder Head Bolts	①
	Detonation Sensor	17
	EGR Pipe	13
	EGR Valve	16
	Engine Coolant Temperature Gauge Unit	8
	Engine Coolant Temperature Sensor	22
	Engine Support Bracket	②
	Exhaust Manifold Heat Protector	10
	Exhaust Manifold Nut (DOHC)	33
	Exhaust Manifold Nut (SOHC)	14
	Exhaust Manifold Nut (Turbo)	22
	Exhaust Manifold Stay Bolt	44
	Exhaust Manifold Tightening Side Nut	9
	Fan Pulley Bolt	8
	Flywheel Bolt	54
	Fuel Filter Eye Bolts	22
	Fuel Filter Flare Nuts	25
	Fuel Pressure Regulator Bolt	7
	Idler Pulley Bolt	40
	Idler Pulley Bracket Bolt	30
	Ignition Coil Bolt	③
	Injector & Fuel Rail Bolt	9
	Intake Manifold Front Side Nut	17
	Intake Manifold Nut (DOHC)	16
	Intake Manifold Nut (SOHC)	13
	Oil Filter Bracket Stay	④
	Oil Filter Bracket	⑤
	Oil Level Gauge Assembly Bolt	10
	Oil Pan Bolt	4
	Oil Pan Drain Plug	29
	Oil Pressure Switch	14

Continued

3.0L ENGINE

TIGHTENING
SPECIFICATIONS—Continued

32-27

Year	Component	Torque/Ft. Lbs.
1996-99	Oil Pump Case Bolt	10
	Oil Pump Cover Bolt	10
	Oil Screen Bolt	14
	Oil Seal Case Bolt	8
	Power Transistor Bolt (SOHC)	4
	Power Transistor Bolt (DOHC)	9
	Rear Plate Bolt	8
	Rocker Cover Bolt (SOHC)	7
	Rocker Cover Bolt (DOHC)	2
	Roll Stopper Bracket	⑥
	Spark Plug	18
	Tensioner Arm Bolt	30
	Tensioner Bracket Bolt (SOHC)	30
	Tensioner Bracket Bolt (DOHC)	14
	Tensioner Bracket Stay Bolt	17
	Tensioner Pulley Nut	35
	Thermo Switch	6
	Thermostat Housing Bolt	14
	Throttle Body Bolt	8
	Timing Belt Rear Cover Center Bolt	17
	Transmission Stay	54
	Water Inlet Fitting Bolt	14
	Water Inlet Pipe Bolt	10
	Water Outlet Fitting Pipe Bolt	14
	Water Pump Bolt	17

① — Refer to "Cylinder Head, Replace."

② — 10 mm bolts, 51 ft. lbs.; 12 mm bolts, 80 ft. lbs.

③ — 10 mm bolts, 7 ft. lbs.; 12 mm bolts, 9 ft. lbs.

④ — 8 mm bolts, 9 ft. lbs.; 10 mm bolts, 17 ft. lbs.

⑤ — Bolts marked No. 4, 17 ft. lbs. ; bolts marked No. 7, 10 ft. lbs.

⑥ — 10 mm bolts, 36–43 ft. lbs.; 12 mm bolts, 51–58 ft. lbs.

Clutch & Manual Transaxle

INDEX

ADJUSTMENTS

CLUTCH PEDAL

1. Measure clutch pedal height as shown, **Fig. 1.**
2. **On FWD models,** clutch pedal height should be 6.97–7.17 inches.
3. **On AWD models,** clutch pedal height should be 7.20–7.40 inches.
4. If clutch pedal height is not as specified, adjust as follows:
   a. **On models less cruise control,** turn and adjust bolt to obtain correct pedal height.
   b. **On models with cruise control,** disconnect clutch switch and turn switch to obtain correct pedal height.
5. Measure clutch pedal stroke, **Fig. 2.** If pedal stroke is not 6.29 inches or more, turn pushrod to obtain correct stroke.
6. Release pedal gradually from its full stroke position to measure amount of return made by pedal until interlock switch makes as operating sound, **Fig. 3.**
7. If amount of pedal return is not .394–.591 inch, adjust by loosening locknut and turning interlock switch.
8. **On AWD models,** measure pedal play by depressing pedal two or three times to eliminate booster negative pressure with engine off, then push pedal with finger to measure play, **Fig. 4.**
9. **On all models,** measure clearance at point where clutch disengages, **Fig. 5.** On AWD models, engine must be idling.
10. Bleed hydraulic system or check master cylinder, release cylinder and hoses if clutch pedal play and clearance are not as follows:
    a. **On FWD models,** total play should be .24–.51 inch.
    b. **On AWD models,** total play should be .49–.79 inch.
    c. **On all models,** clearance from floorboard to clutch pedal pad with pedal depressed should be 2.2 inches or more.

CLUTCH BOOSTER PUSHROD & PISTON CLEARANCE

AWD

1. Measure dimension (B) between mas-

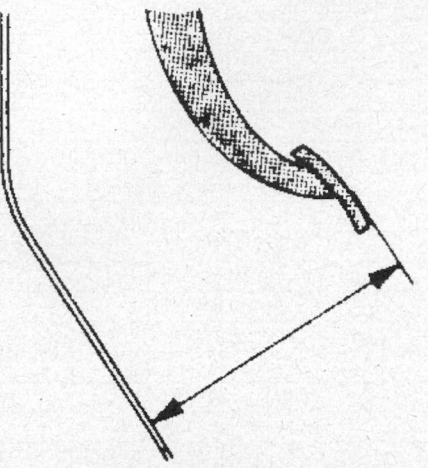

Fig. 1 Clutch pedal height inspection

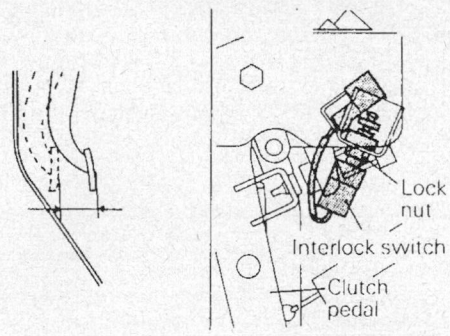

Fig. 3 Clutch pedal interlock operation inspection

ter cylinder and face and piston, **Fig. 6.** Measure with square placed on master cylinder end face then subtract thickness of square equaling (B).
2. Obtain dimension (C) between clutch booster mounting surface and master cylinder end face, **Fig. 7.**
3. Measure dimension (D) between master cylinder mounting surface on clutch booster and the pushrod end, **Fig. 8.** Measure with square placed on clutch booster, then subtract thickness of square equaling (D).
4. Using measured values obtained in steps 1 through 3, obtain clearance for dimension (A), **Fig. 9,** between clutch

Fig. 2 Clutch pedal stroke inspection

booster pushrod and piston using following formula: $(A(A = B - C - D))$.
5. If clearance is not within .0082–.0181 inch, adjust by changing pushrod length by turning adjustable end of pushrod. **When clutch booster negative pressure of 9.7 psi is applied, the clearance (A) becomes .0039–.0118 inch.**

HYDRAULIC SYSTEM SERVICE

CLUTCH BOOSTER INSPECTION

1. Run engine for one minute or more, then turn engine off.
2. Step on clutch pedal several times with normal pressure.
3. If pedal depressed fully the first time but gradually becomes higher when depressed several times, the booster is operating correctly.
4. If pedal height remains unchanged, booster is faulty.
5. With engine off, step on clutch pedal several times with same foot pressure, then step on clutch pedal and start engine.
6. If pedal moves downward slightly, booster is in good condition. If there is no change in pedal height, booster is faulty.
7. With engine idling, step on clutch pedal and turn engine off.
8. If pedal height does not change, booster is operating correctly. If pedal height rises, booster is faulty.
9. If one or more of the above tests fail, ensure condition of valve and vacuum hose and if required, replace booster.

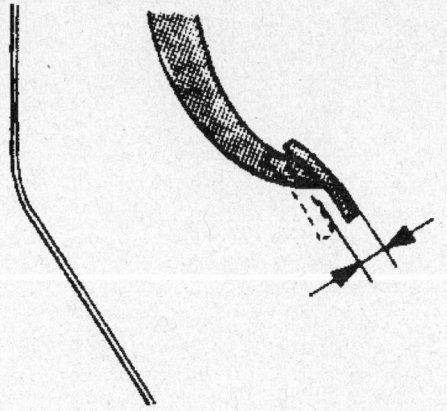

Fig. 4 Clutch pedal freeplay check. AWD

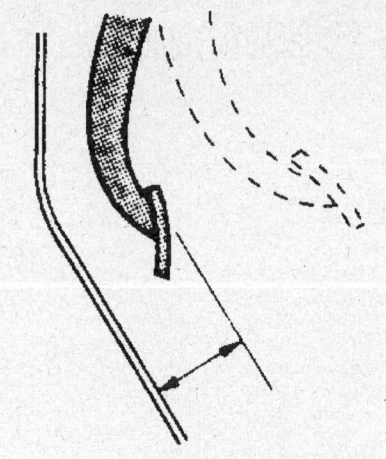

Fig. 5 Clutch disengagement check

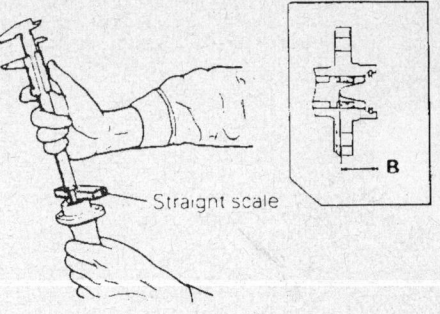

Fig. 6 Pushrod clearance measurement (B). AWD

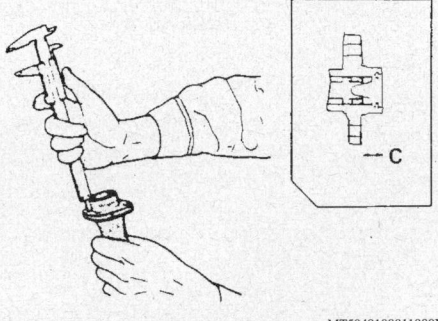

Fig. 7 Pushrod clearance measurement (C). AWD

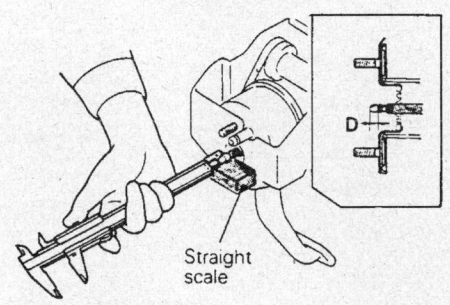

Fig. 8 Pushrod clearance measurement (D). AWD

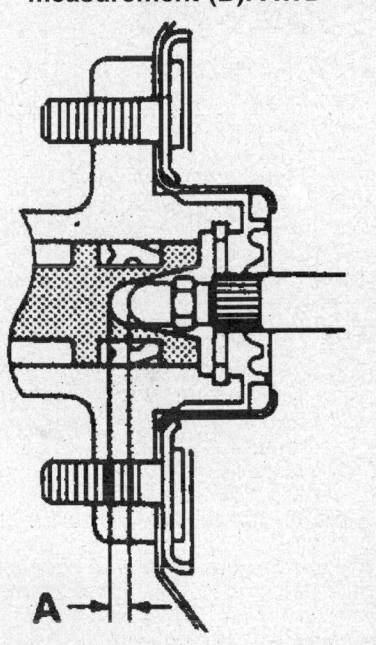

Fig. 9 Pushrod clearance measurement (A). AWD

CLUTCH CONTROL COMPONENTS, REPLACE

1. Remove air cleaner assembly.
2. Drain clutch system fluid into an appropriate container.
3. Remove clutch control components in numbered sequence as shown, **Fig. 10**, noting the following:
   a. Disconnect clutch hose from tube by securing nut on clutch hose, then loosen flare nut on clutch tube. Remove clip from clutch hose to remove clutch hose from bracket.
   b. **On AWD models,** use a flat type box wrench to remove clutch release cylinder bolts.
4. **On AWD models,** reverse procedure to install. Temporarily tighten flare nut by hand, then tighten to specifications and ensure clutch hose does not become twisted.
5. **On all models,** adjust clearance between clutch booster pushrod and piston as outlined under "Clutch Booster Pushrod & Piston Clearance Adjust."

CLUTCH MASTER CYLINDER SERVICE

1. Remove piston stop ring (FWD) or the snap ring (AWD) while depressing the piston, **Fig. 11**.
2. Remove piston assembly. **Do not damage master cylinder body or piston assembly. Do not disassemble piston assembly.**

3. Inspect inside cylinder body and piston for rust or scars and the piston cup for wear or deformation, replace as necessary.
4. Inspect clutch tube connection part for clogging.
5. Reverse procedure to assemble, tightening reservoir band.

CLUTCH
REPLACE

1. Remove transaxle as outlined under "Transaxle, Replace."
2. Insert clutch disc guide tool No. MD998126, or equivalent, into center hole to prevent dropping of clutch disc, then diagonally loosen bolts that hold clutch cover assembly to remove clutch cover assembly. **Do not clean clutch disc or release bearing with cleaning solvent.**
3. Remove snap ring and clevis pin, then the release cylinder assembly, if equipped.
4. Remove return clip, then the release bearing.
5. Remove spring pins from clutch release fork and shaft using a suitable punch.
6. Install release shaft and packing, then the return spring and release fork.
7. Align lockpin holes of shift arm and control shaft, then drive in two new spring pins.
8. When installing spring pins, ensure

spring pin slot direction is at right angles to center line of control shaft.
9. Remove grease from clutch facing by wiping with clean cloth.
10. Apply small amount of grease to clutch disc spline and input shaft spline.
11. Using clutch installer tool No. MD998126, or equivalent, install clutch disc and clutch cover assembly to flywheel. When installing clutch disc, ensure surface with manufacturer's stamped mark is on pressure plate side.

SHIFT CABLE
REPLACE

Replace transaxle shift cables in numbered sequences shown in **Fig. 12,** noting the following when installing:
1. Install shift lever assembly bushings with the side marked UP facing upward.
2. Install select cable as follows:
   a. Install select cable on the transaxle end.
   b. Place transaxle in Neutral position.

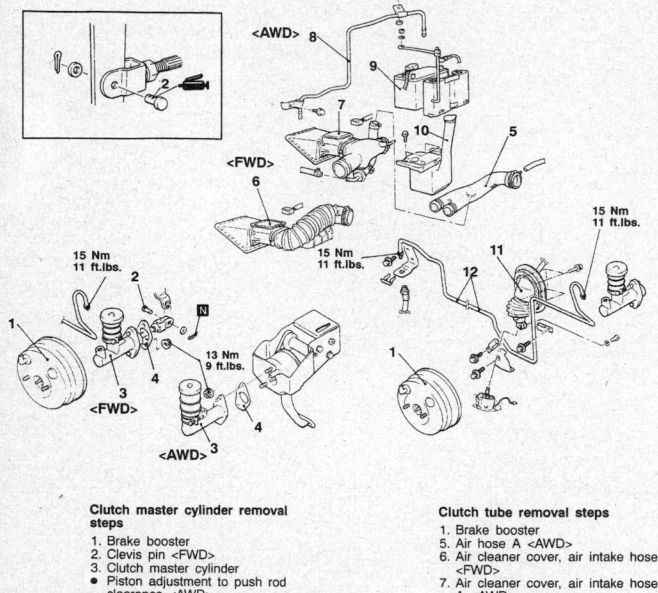

Clutch master cylinder removal steps

1. Brake booster
2. Clevis pin <FWD>
3. Clutch master cylinder
   • Piston adjustment to push rod clearance <AWD>
4. Sealer

Clutch tube removal steps

1. Brake booster
5. Air hose A <AWD>
6. Air cleaner cover, air intake hose <FWD>
7. Air cleaner cover, air intake hose A <AWD>
8. Vacuum pipe <AWD>
9. Battery
10. Battery seat, washer tank
11. Steering column assembly
12. Clutch tube

MT5049100015010X

Fig. 10 Clutch control component replacement (Part 1 of 2)

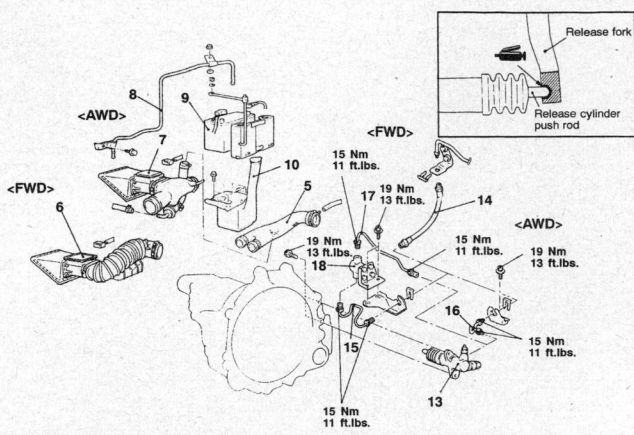

Clutch release cylinder removal steps

5. Air hose A <AWD>
6. Air cleaner cover, air intake hose <FWD>
7. Air cleaner cover, air intake hose A <AWD>
8. Vacuum pipe <AWD>
9. Battery
10. Battery seat, washer tank
13. Clutch release cylinder

Clutch hose removal steps

5. Air hose A <AWD>
6. Air cleaner cover, air intake hose <FWD>
7. Air cleaner cover, air intake hose A <AWD>

8. Vacuum pipe <AWD>
9. Battery
10. Battery seat, washer tank
14. Clutch hose

Clutch tube A, tube B, tube C, damper removal steps

5. Air hose A <AWD>
6. Air cleaner, air intake hose <FWD>
7. Air cleaner cover, air intake hose A <AWD>
8. Vacuum pipe <AWD>
9. Battery
10. Battery seat, washer tank
15. Clutch tube A <AWD>
16. Clutch tube B <AWD>
17. Clutch tube C <AWD>
18. Clutch damper <FWD>

MT5049100015020X

Fig. 10 Clutch control component replacement (Part 2 of 2)

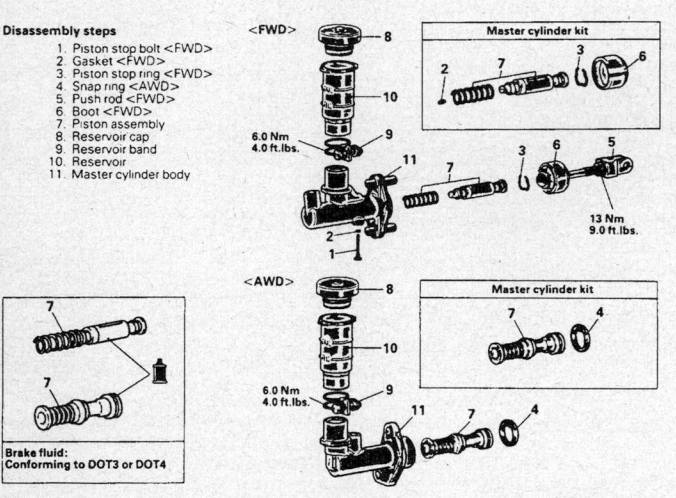

Disassembly steps

1. Piston stop bolt <FWD>
2. Gasket <FWD>
3. Piston stop ring <FWD>
4. Snap ring <AWD>
5. Push rod <FWD>
6. Boot <FWD>
7. Piston assembly
8. Reservoir cap
9. Reservoir band
10. Reservoir
11. Master cylinder body

Brake fluid: Conforming to DOT3 or DOT4

Fig. 11 Clutch master cylinder

c. Place gear selector in Neutral position.
d. Adjust length of select cable then install cable onto gear selector assembly as shown, **Fig. 13.**
3. Install shift cable as follows:
   a. Install shift cable on the transaxle end.
   b. Keeping select lever on transaxle in the Neutral position, move shift lever on transaxle into 4th gear as shown, **Fig. 14.**
   c. Position gear selector lever into the 4th gear position, **Fig. 15,** and adjust length of shift cable and install cable onto the gear selector lever as shown.
4. Ensure transaxle controls function properly.

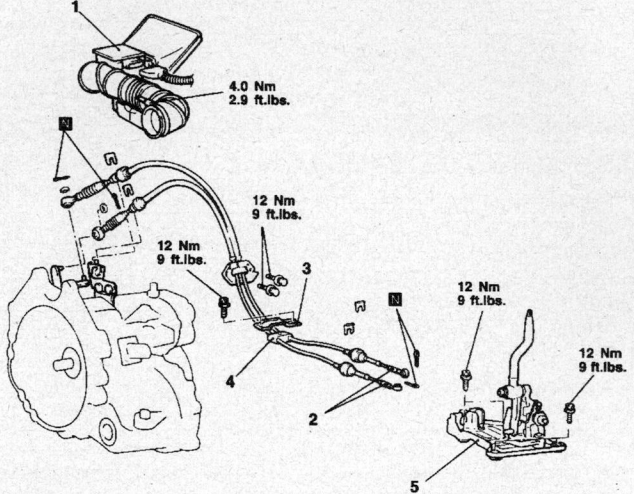

Transaxle control cable assembly removal steps

1. Air cleaner, Air intake hose
2. Transaxle control cable assembly connection (Shift lever assembly side)
3. Retainer
4. Transaxle control cable assembly

Shift lever assembly removal steps

1. Air cleaner, Air intake hose
2. Transaxle control cable assembly connection (Shift lever assembly side)
5. Shift lever assembly

MT5038900125000X

Fig. 12 Shift cable replacement

TRANSAXLE
REPLACE

1. Drain transaxle fluid into an appropriate container.
2. **On models with an active aero system,** remove active front venturi skirt in numbered sequence as shown, **Fig. 16.**
3. **On AWD models,** remove transfer assembly as outlined under "Transfer

Case, Replace."
4. **On all models,** remove front exhaust pipe.
5. Remove front lower cover.
6. Remove transaxle in numbered sequence as shown, **Figs. 17 and 18,** noting the following:
   a. Remove clutch release cylinder and clutch oil line bracket bolts, then secure to body using suitable wire without disconnecting oil line coupling.

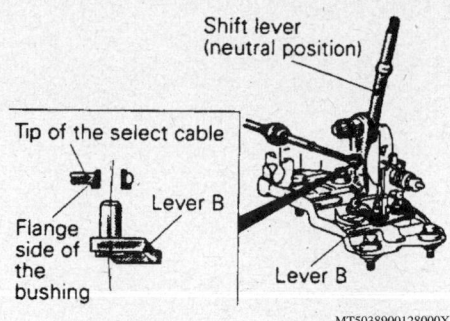

Fig. 13 Select cable connection

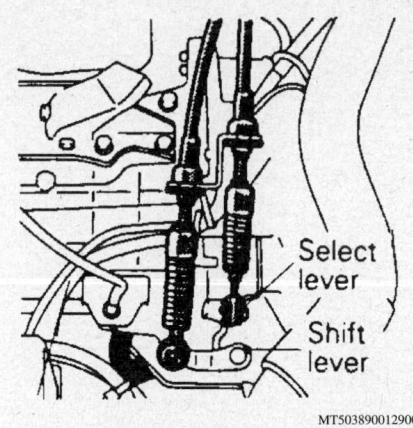

Fig. 14 Transaxle control position

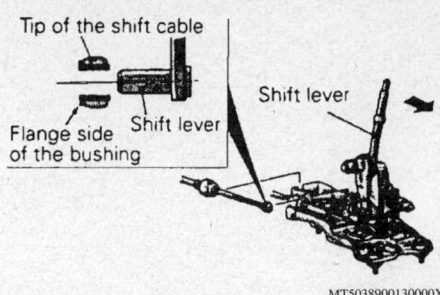

Fig. 15 Shift cable connection

b. Raise transaxle assembly using suitable transmission stand to release weight off mounts, then remove transaxle mount insulator bolt.

c. Loosen, but do not remove, tie rod ends using ball joint puller tool No. MB991113-01, or equivalent.

d. Loosen, but do not remove, lower arm ball joint using ball joint tool.

e. Remove lefthand driveshaft bearing bracket bolts, then insert pry bar between bearing bracket and cylinder block, **Fig. 19.**

f. Remove lefthand driveshaft and inner shaft assembly from transaxle. **Remove driveshaft and inner shaft as an assembly together with hub, knuckle and other parts.**

g. Suspend removed lefthand driveshaft and inner shaft assembly with suitable wire to prevent shaft from sharply bending or turning at each joint.

h. To remove righthand driveshaft from transaxle assembly, apply pry bar to protrusion, **Fig. 20.** Remove driveshaft as an assembly together with hub, knuckle and other parts.

i. Suspend removed lefthand driveshaft assembly with suitable wire to prevent shaft from sharply bending or turning at each joint.

j. Support transaxle assembly with a suitable transaxle stand, then remove transaxle assembly lower part coupling and lower transaxle assembly.

7. Reverse procedure to install, **Fig. 21.**

TECHNICAL SERVICE BULLETINS

MANUAL TRANSAXLE GEAR OIL SPECIFICATION

Manual transaxles in these vehicles require API GL-4 gear oil. Use of other API gear oils, such as GL-5, may affect shift effort and result in internal transaxle damage due to chemical reactions with copper synchronizer rings. Mitsubishi Diamond Gear Lube No. A991ZC2X01 (SAE 75W-85W GL-4) or equivalent is recommended.

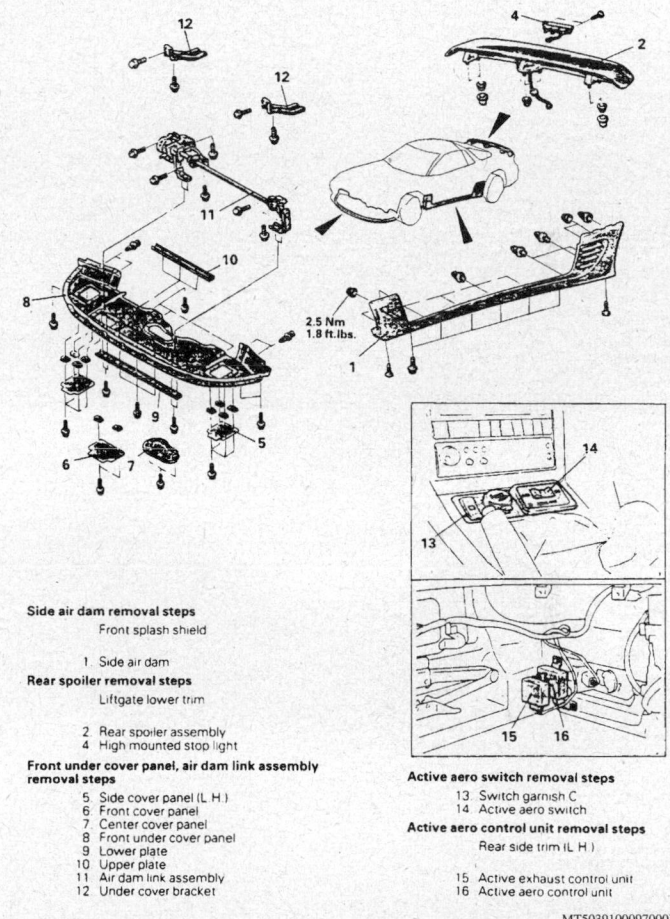

Side air dam removal steps
  Front splash shield
  1. Side air dam
Rear spoiler removal steps
  Liftgate lower trim
  2. Rear spoiler assembly
  4. High mounted stop light
Front under cover panel, air dam link assembly removal steps
  5. Side cover panel (L.H.)
  6. Front cover panel
  7. Center cover panel
  8. Front under cover panel
  9. Lower plate
  10. Upper plate
  11. Air dam link assembly
  12. Under cover bracket

Active aero switch removal steps
  13. Switch garnish C
  14. Active aero switch
Active aero control unit removal steps
  Rear side trim (L.H.)
  15. Active exhaust control unit
  16. Active aero control unit

Fig. 16 Active aero component replacement

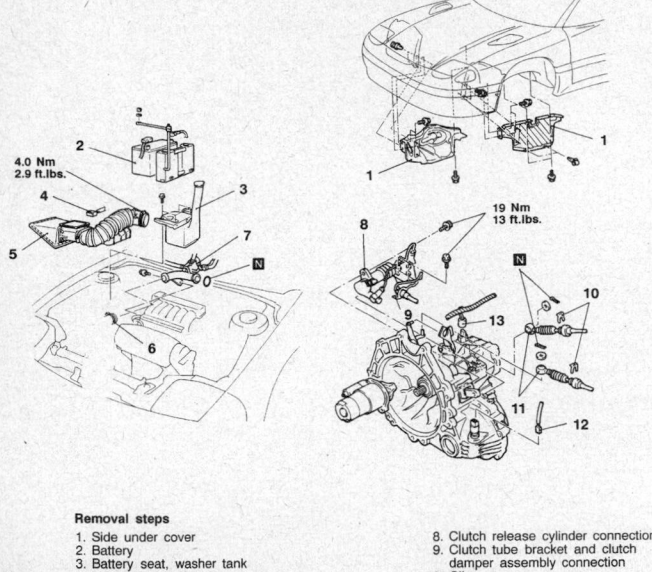

Removal steps

1. Side under cover
2. Battery
3. Battery seat, washer tank
4. Volume air flow sensor connector
5. Air cleaner cover, air intake hose
6. Radiator lower hose connection <SOHC>
7. Water inlet pipe B connection <SOHC>
8. Clutch release cylinder connection
9. Clutch tube bracket and clutch damper assembly connection
10. Clip
11. Transaxle control cable connection
12. Speedometer connector connection
13. Back-up light switch connector

MT5039100098010X

Fig. 17 Transaxle assembly replacement (Part 1 of 2). FWD

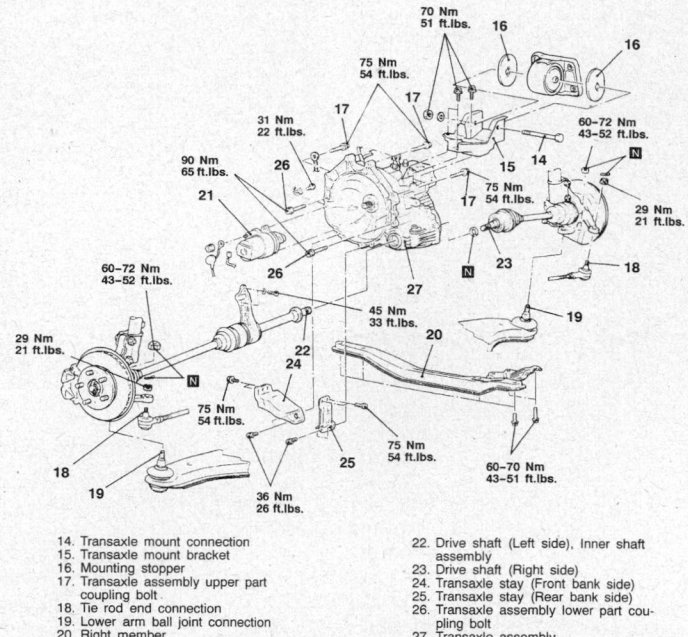

14. Transaxle mount connection
15. Transaxle mount bracket
16. Mounting stopper
17. Transaxle assembly upper part coupling bolt
18. Tie rod end connection
19. Lower arm ball joint connection
20. Right member
21. Starter
22. Drive shaft (Left side), Inner shaft assembly
23. Drive shaft (Right side)
24. Transaxle stay (Front bank side)
25. Transaxle stay (Rear bank side)
26. Transaxle assembly lower part coupling bolt
27. Transaxle assembly

MT5039100098020X

Fig. 17 Transaxle assembly replacement (Part 2 of 2). FWD

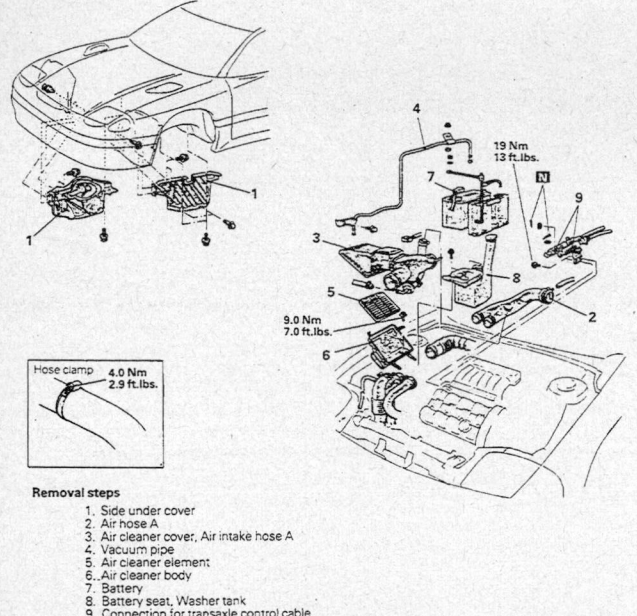

Hose clamp   4.0 Nm 2.9 ft.lbs.

Removal steps

1. Side under cover
2. Air hose A
3. Air cleaner cover, Air intake hose A
4. Vacuum pipe
5. Air cleaner element
6. Air cleaner body
7. Battery
8. Battery seat, Washer tank
9. Connection for transaxle control cable

MT5039100099010X

Fig. 18 Transaxle assembly replacement (Part 1 of 2). AWD

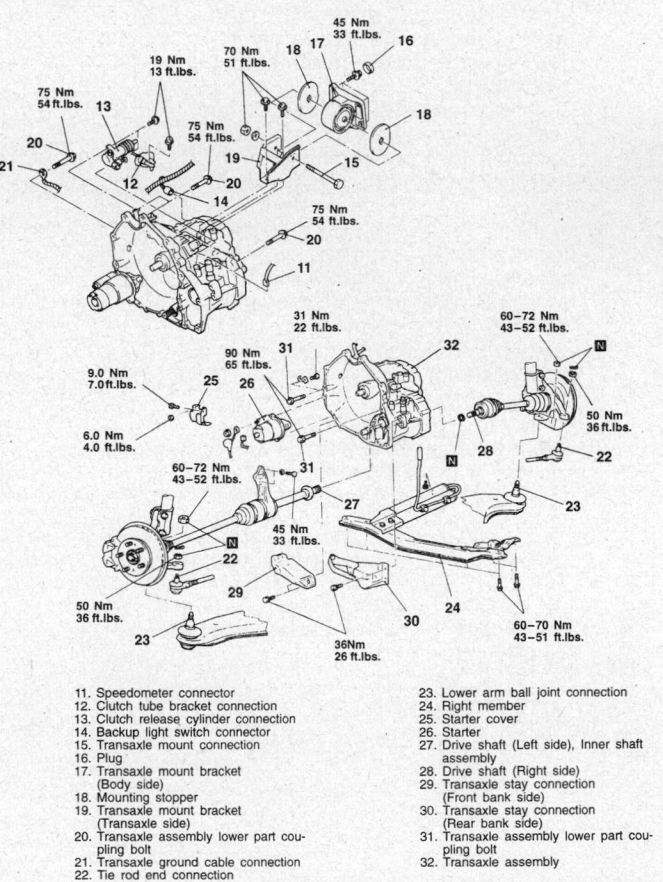

11. Speedometer connector
12. Clutch tube bracket connection
13. Clutch release cylinder connection
14. Backup light switch connector
15. Transaxle mount connection
16. Plug
17. Transaxle mount bracket (Body side)
18. Mounting stopper
19. Transaxle mount bracket (Transaxle side)
20. Transaxle assembly lower part coupling bolt
21. Transaxle ground cable connection
22. Tie rod end connection
23. Lower arm ball joint connection
24. Right member
25. Starter cover
26. Starter
27. Drive shaft (Left side), Inner shaft assembly
28. Drive shaft (Right side)
29. Transaxle stay connection (Front bank side)
30. Transaxle stay connection (Rear bank side)
31. Transaxle assembly lower part coupling bolt
32. Transaxle assembly

MT5039100099020X

Fig. 18 Transaxle assembly replacement (Part 2 of 2). AWD

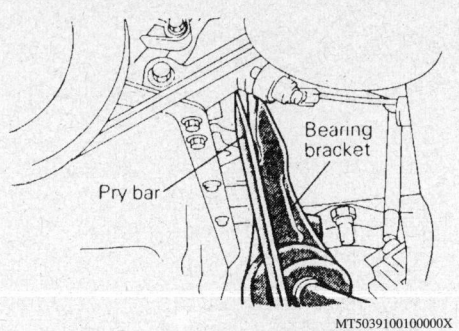
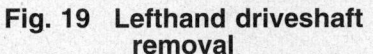

MT5039100100000X

Fig. 19 Lefthand driveshaft removal

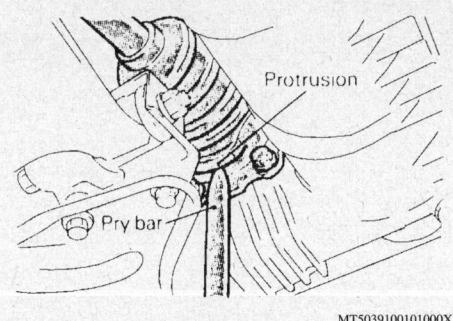

MT5039100101000X

Fig. 20 Righthand driveshaft removal

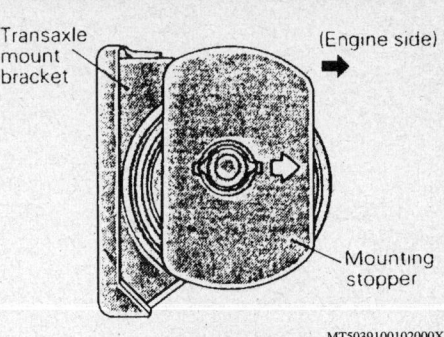

MT5039100102000X

Fig. 21 Mounting stopper installation

TIGHTENING SPECIFICATIONS

Year	Component	Torque/ Ft. Lbs.
1996–99	Back-Up Lamp Switch	24
	Brake Pedal Shaft	22
	Clutch Cover Bolt	14
	Clutch Master Cylinder Bolt	9
	Clutch Pedal Bolt	22
	Clutch Release Cylinder	14
	Clutch Tube Bolt	11
	Clutch Vacuum Line Bolt	11–13
	Flywheel Bolt	54
	RH Member Bolt	43–51
	Starter Cover Bolt	7
	Stop Lamp Switch	10
	Tie Rod End	22
	Transaxle Coupling Bolt	54
	Transaxle Mount	51
	Transaxle Stay	26
	Transfer Case To Transaxle	64
	Wheel Lug Nuts	87–101

Rear Axle & Suspension

INDEX

DIFFERENTIAL CARRIER
REPLACE

1. Drain differential fluid into an appropriate container.
2. Remove center exhaust pipe.
3. Remove driveshaft as outlined under "Driveshaft, Replace" in "All Wheel Drive."
4. Remove propeller shaft.
5. Remove differential carrier in numbered sequence as shown, **Fig. 1.**
6. Hold bottom of differential carrier and remove rear wheel oil pump through mounting hole, then the differential carrier.
7. Reverse procedure to install.

PROPELLER SHAFT
REPLACE

1. Remove spacers, **Fig. 2.** Number of spacers differs on each vehicle. Note number of spacers and use for reference during installation.
2. Remove propeller shaft. Make mating marks on differential companion flange and flange yoke for reference during installation.
3. Insert piece of cloth or rag into boot opening, then remove propeller shaft in a straight and level manner ensuring boot is not damaged through pinching.
4. **Do not lower rear end of vehicle as the oil will flow out of the transfer case and be cautious to avoid damage to the oil seal lip of the transfer case.**
5. **Use plug tool No. MB991193, or equivalent, provided as a cover to prevent entry of foreign materials into transfer case.**
6. Inspect sleeve yoke, center yoke, flange yoke and propeller shaft yokes for wear damage or cracks and replace as necessary.
7. Using a suitable dial indicator, measure propeller shaft runout. Runout for the front, center and rear propeller shafts should be .024 inch (.6 mm).
8. Set V-blocks as much as possible to the end of the shaft, then measure the deflection at the center of the shaft.
9. Inspect universal joints for smooth operation in all directions, then the center bearing for smooth movement and

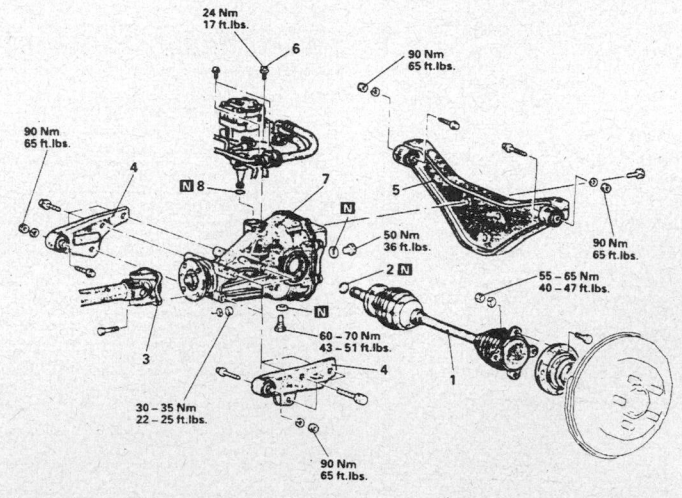

Removal steps
1. Drive shaft
2. Circlip
3. Propeller shaft connection
4. Differential support assembly
5. Differential support member assembly
6. Rear wheel oil pump installation bolt
7. Differential carrier
8. O-ring

MT3019100002000X

Fig. 1 Differential carrier replacement. AWD

mounting rubber for damage or deterioration and replace as necessary.
10. Reverse procedure to install, noting the following:
  a. Install spacers and insulators as shown, **Fig. 3.**
  b. When installing center bearing, assemble the same spacers as removed from the bearing or new spacers of equal thickness.

HUB & BEARING
REPLACE
FWD MODELS

This procedure has been revised by Technical Service Bulletin.
Replace rear axle hub assembly in numbered sequence as shown, **Fig. 4,** noting the following:
1. **Care must be used when handling the pole piece at tip of ABS speed sensor and toothed edge of rotor so**

as not to damage them or striking against other components.
2. Remove caliper assembly and support to frame using suitable wire.
3. **Care must be taken not to scratch or scar ABS rotor's tooth surface and not to drop it. If rotor's toothed surface is chipped or is deformed, the ABS brake system might not operate accurately.**
4. If wheel bearing inner race remains on spindle when rear hub bearings or assembly are removed, replace rear hub bearing with a new part. If rear hub is installed with inner race on spindle, the oil seal lip will reverse causing bearing looseness and lubricant leakage.

AWD MODELS

1. Remove rear axle hub in numbered sequence as shown, **Fig. 5,** noting the following:
  a. **Care must be used when handling the pole piece at the tip of the ABS speed sensor and**

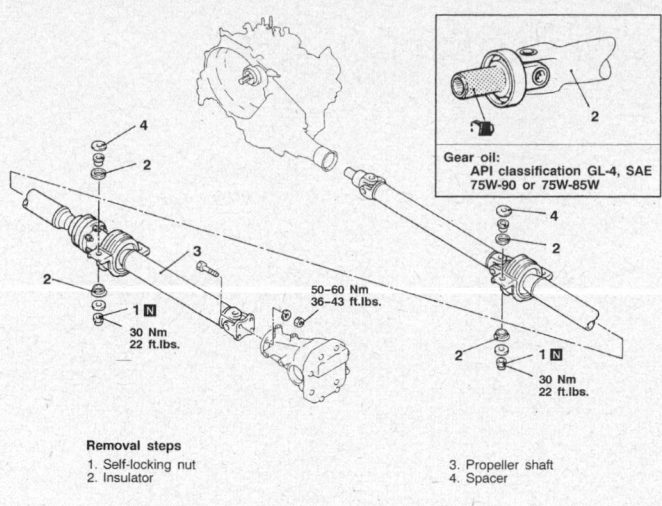

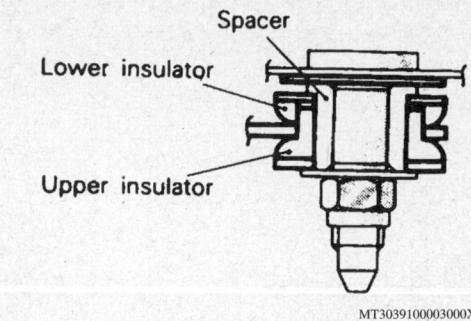

Fig. 3 Propeller shaft installation

Removal steps
1. Self-locking nut
2. Insulator
3. Propeller shaft
4. Spacer

Fig. 2   Propeller shaft removal

toothed edge of rotor ensuring not to damage them or strike against other components.
b. Remove caliper assembly and support to frame using suitable wire.
c. Using end yoke holder tool No. MB990767-01, or equivalent, secure axle hub and remove companion flange self-locking nut.
d. Using axle puller and slide hammer tool Nos. MB990211-01 and MB990241-01, or equivalents, remove rear axle hub.
e. Using rear rotor ABS tool No. MB990560, or equivalent, press off ABS rotor from axle hub.
f. Press off outer bearing and dust shield from axle hub.
g. Using seal remover tool Nos. MB990938-01 and MB990928-01, or equivalents, remove axle hub seal and inner bearing from axle housing.
2. Reverse procedure to install, noting the following:
a. Install inner bearing using bearing installer tool Nos. MB990931-01 and MB990938-01, or equivalents.
b. Install oil seal using oil seal installer tool No. MB990931-01, or equivalent. Apply multi-purpose grease to lip of oil seal.
c. Install dust shields using ball joint dust cover installer tool No. MB990799-01, or equivalent.
d. Install outer bearing after applying multi-purpose grease to bearing surfaces.
e. Install ABS rotor with groove in surface pointing toward axle shaft flange.

WHEEL BEARING
ADJUST
FWD MODELS

1. Raise and support vehicle.
2. Remove caliper assembly and support to frame using suitable wire.
3. Turn hub several times to seat bearings.

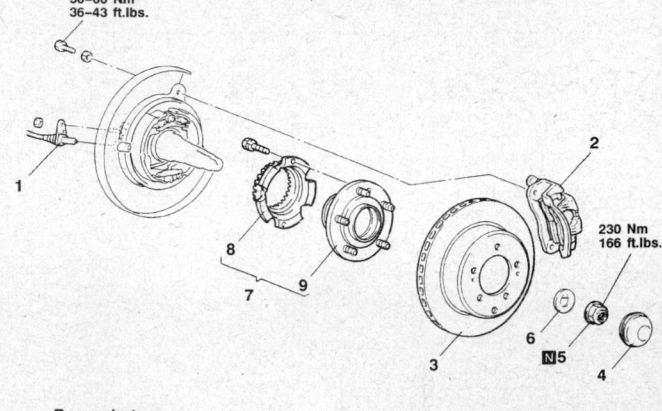

Removal steps
1. Rear speed sensor <Vehicles with ABS>
2. Caliper assembly
3. Brake disc
4. Hub cap
5. Wheel bearing nut
6. Tongued washer
7. Rear hub assembly
8. Rear ABS rotor <Vehicles with ABS>
9. Rear hub unit bearing

Caution
Rear hub unit bearing cannot be disassembled.

Fig. 4   Rear axle hub replacement. FWD

4. Using a suitable spring scale, measure rotary starting torque.
5. Loosen or tighten hub nut to obtain a starting torque of 16 inch lbs. or less. Replace rear hub bearing if necessary.

AWD MODELS

1. Raise and support vehicle.
2. Remove driveshaft from companion flange.
3. Remove caliper assembly and support to frame using suitable wire.
4. Turn hub several times to seat bearings.
5. Using a suitable spring scale, measure rotary starting torque.
6. If starting torque is not 7 inch lbs. or less, ensure torque of axle hub companion flange nut is correct. If flange torque is correct, replace axle hub bearing.

REAR SUSPENSION
REPLACE
FWD MODELS

1. Raise and support vehicle, then remove rear wheels.
2. Remove shock absorber trim cover from inside luggage compartment.
3. Remove exhaust muffler assembly.
4. Remove rear suspension assembly in numbered sequence as shown, **Fig. 6,**

supporting crossmember with transmission jack, then remove crossmember mounting nut and rear suspension assembly.
5. Reverse procedure to install, noting the following:
a. Install exhaust muffler.
b. Verify rear wheel alignment.
c. Verify parking brake operation.
d. Install shock absorber trim cover in luggage compartment.

AWD MODELS

1. Remove shock absorber cover from luggage compartment.
2. Remove center exhaust pipe and main muffler.
3. Remove rear suspension in numbered sequence as shown, **Fig. 7,** noting the following:
a. Before removing crossmember bracket, support differential case with a suitable transmission jack.
b. Remove crossmember mounting nuts and bolts.
c. Lower rear suspension using two assistants to help support suspension on transmission stand. **Rear suspension is very heavy and damage or personal injury could occur if rear suspension is not supported correctly.**
4. Reverse procedure to install, noting the following:
a. Bleed power steering system as

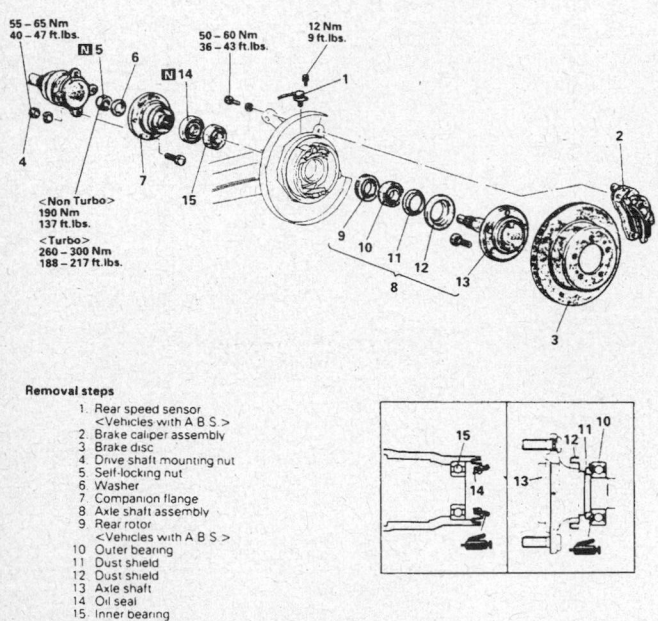

Removal steps

1. Rear speed sensor
   <Vehicles with A B S.>
2. Brake caliper assembly
3. Brake disc
4. Drive shaft mounting nut
5. Self-locking nut
6. Washer
7. Companion flange
8. Axle shaft assembly
9. Rear rotor
   <Vehicles with A B S>
10. Outer bearing
11. Dust shield
12. Dust shield
13. Axle shaft
14. Oil seal
15. Inner bearing

MT2049100014000X

Fig. 5   Rear axle hub replacement. AWD

outlined under "Bleeding System" in "Power Steering Service."
b. Verify rear wheel alignment and operation of parking brake.

SHOCK ABSORBER
REPLACE

1. Remove cover in luggage compartment to access shock absorber.
2. Remove shock absorber assembly in numbered sequence as shown, **Fig. 8,** noting the following:
   a. Raise and support rear suspension before removing shock absorber.
   b. Remove shock absorber upper and lower mounting bolts, then the shock absorber assembly.
3. Reverse procedure to install, noting the following:
   a. Using a suitable coil spring, compress and insert coil spring on shock absorber.
   b. Align edge of coil spring to position as shown, **Fig. 9.**
   c. Fit dust cover over dust cup as shown, **Fig. 10.**
   d. Position upper bracket as shown, then tighten piston nut to specifications.
   e. Install coil spring, ensure lower edge fits into spring seat groove and upper edge fits into spring pad groove, then remove compression tool, **Fig. 11.**

SHOCK ABSORBER SERVICE

1. Disassemble shock absorber assembly in numbered sequence as shown, **Fig. 12,** noting the following:
   a. Before removing piston rod nut,

compress coil spring using suitable coil spring compression tool.
b. While holding piston rod, remove

piston rod nut.

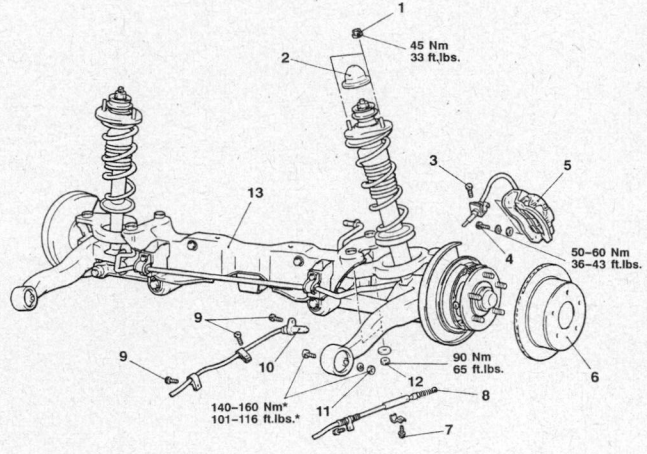

Removal steps

1. Shock absorber mounting nuts (upper)
2. Cap
3. Brake tube clamp bolt
4. Brake caliper mounting bolt
5. Brake caliper assembly
6. Brake disc
7. Parking brake cable clamp bolt
8. Parking brake cable end (Refer to GROUP 36.)
9. Rear speed sensor clamp bolt <ABS>
10. ABS speed sensor <ABS>
11. Trailing arm mounting bolt and nut
12. Crossmember mounting nut
13. Rear suspension assembly

Caution
*: Indicates parts which should be temporarily tightened, and then fully tightened with the vehicle on the ground in an unladen condition.

MT2039100024000X

Fig. 6   Rear suspension assembly replacement. FWD

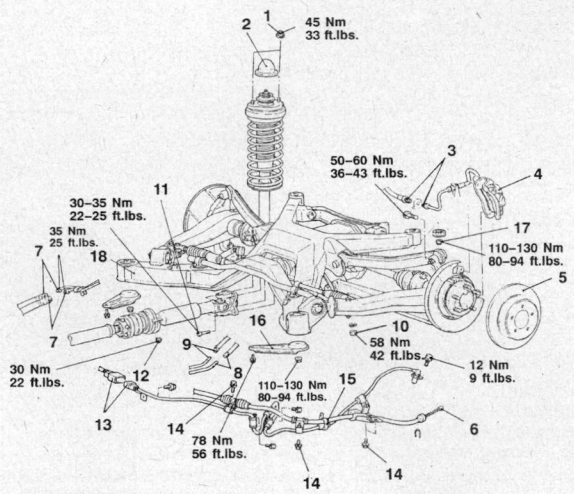

Removal steps

1. Shock absorber mounting nuts (upper)*
2. Cap*
3. Brake tube to brake hose connection* (Refer to GROUP 35A – Brake Line.)
4. Brake caliper*
5. Brake disc*
6. Parking brake cable end* (Refer to GROUP 36 – Parking Brake.)
7. Pressure tube assembly to pipe assembly connection <4WS>
8. Feed pipe assembly to suction hose connection <4WS>
9. Return pipe assembly to rubber hose connection <4WS>
10. Power cylinder tie rod coupling nut <4WS>* or assist link coupling nut <except 4WS>*
11. Differential carrier to propeller shaft coupling bolt
12. Center bearing mounting nut
13. Harness connector <ABS>*
14. Parking brake cable and ABS sensor fixing bolt <ABS>*
15. Cable band*
16. Crossmember bracket*
17. Crossmember mounting nut (on differential side)*
18. Rear suspension assembly

NOTE
Parts marked with * are symmetrical.

MT2039100025000X

Fig. 7   Rear suspension assembly replacement. AWD

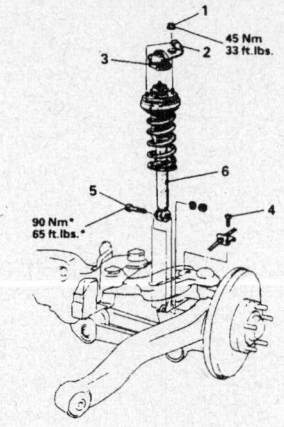

Removal steps
1. Shock absorber upper mounting nut
2. ECS connector (ECS)
3. Cap
4. Brake line clamp bolt
5. Shock absorber lower mounting bolt
6. Shock absorber

NOTE
indicates parts which should be temporarily tightened, and then fully tightened with the vehicle in the unladen condition

MT2039100015000X

Fig. 8 Shock absorber assembly replacement

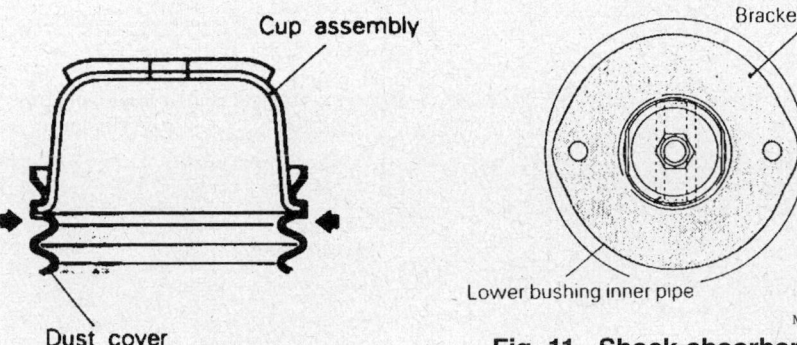

Cup assembly

Dust cover

MT2039100019000X

Fig. 10 Dust cover & cup installation

Bracket assembly

Lower bushing inner pipe

MT2039100021000X

Fig. 11 Shock absorber upper bracket installation

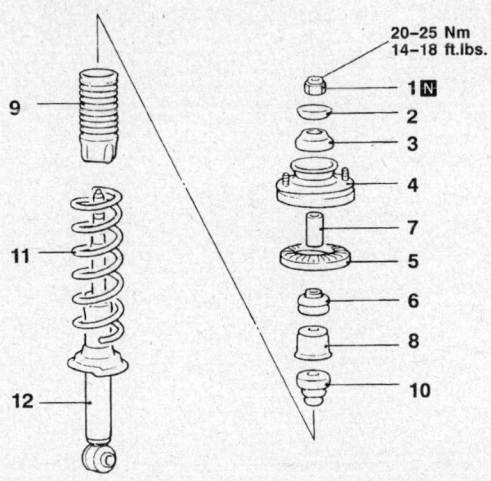

Disassembly steps
1. Piston rod tightening nut
2. Washer
3. Upper bushing (A)
4. Bracket assembly
5. Upper spring pad
6. Upper bushing (B)
7. Collar
8. Cup assembly
9. Dust cover
10. Bump rubber
11. Coil spring
12. Shock absorber

MT2039100017000X

Fig. 12 Shock absorber disassembly

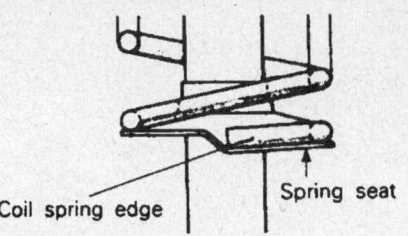

Coil spring edge — Spring seat

MT2039100018000X

Fig. 9 Coil spring installation

COIL SPRING
REPLACE

Remove and disassemble shock absorber assembly as outlined under "Shock Absorber, Replace."

CONTROL ARM
REPLACE
FWD MODELS

1. Remove shock absorber assembly as outlined under " Shock Absorber, Replace."
2. Remove upper and lower control arms and assist link in numbered sequence as shown, **Fig. 13**, noting the following:
   a. Using ball joint remover tool No. MB991113-01, or equivalent, remove ball joints from the knuckle. **Loosen but do not remove ball joint nut.**

AWD MODELS

Remove upper and lower control arms in numbered sequence as shown, **Fig. 14**, then using ball joint remover tool No. MB991113-01, or equivalent, disconnect upper and lower arm ball joint from knuckle. **Loosen, but do not remove ball joint nut.**

TRAILING ARM
REPLACE
FWD MODELS

1. Remove trailing arm in numbered sequence as shown, **Fig. 15**, noting the following:
   a. Using ball joint remover tool No. MB991113-01, or equivalent, remove knuckle from lower arm, upper arm and assist link.
   b. **Do not remove nut from ball joint. Suspend special tool with a rope to prevent it from dropping.**
2. Reverse procedure to install, noting the following:
   a. Install stabilizer link as describer under "Stabilizer Bar, Replace."
   b. Verify wheel alignment and operation of parking brake.

AWD MODELS

1. Remove trailing arm in numbered sequence as shown, **Fig. 16**, noting the following:
   a. Using end yoke holder tool No.

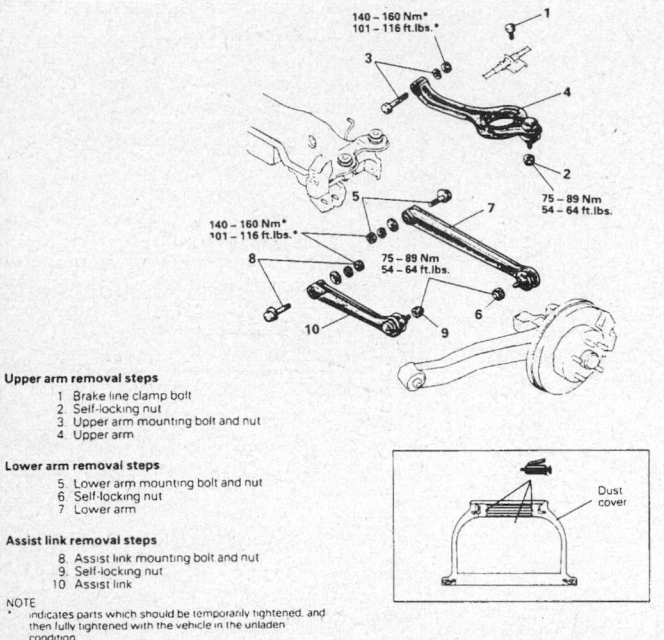

Upper arm removal steps
1. Brake line clamp bolt
2. Self-locking nut
3. Upper arm mounting bolt and nut
4. Upper arm

Lower arm removal steps
5. Lower arm mounting bolt and nut
6. Self-locking nut
7. Lower arm

Assist link removal steps
8. Assist link mounting bolt and nut
9. Self-locking nut
10. Assist link

NOTE
*: Indicates parts which should be temporarily tightened, and then fully tightened with the vehicle in the unladen condition

MT2039100042000X

Fig. 13 Upper & lower control arm & assist link replacement. FWD

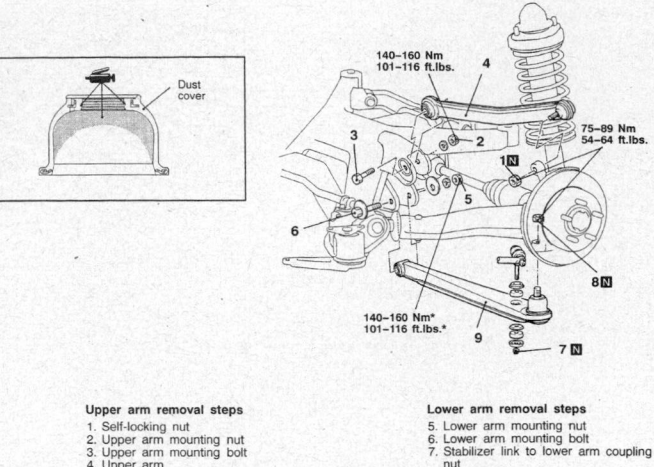

Upper arm removal steps
1. Self-locking nut
2. Upper arm mounting nut
3. Upper arm mounting bolt
4. Upper arm

Lower arm removal steps
5. Lower arm mounting nut
6. Lower arm mounting bolt
7. Stabilizer link to lower arm coupling nut
8. Self-locking nut
9. Lower arm

Caution
*: Indicates parts which should be temporarily tightened, and then fully tightened with the vehicle on the ground in an unladen condition.

MT2039100041000X

Fig. 14 Upper & lower control arm replacement. AWD

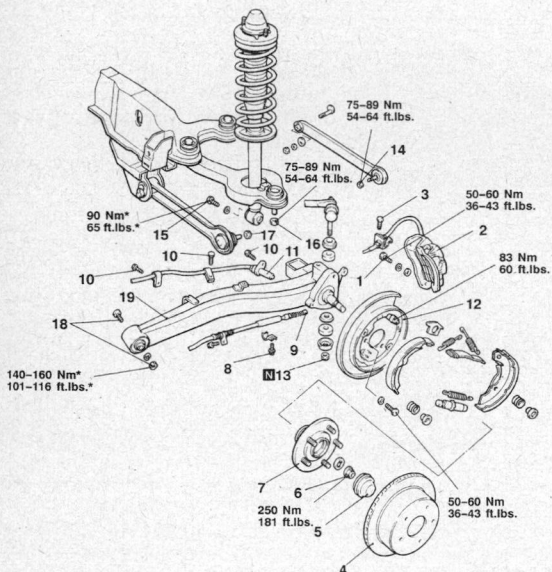

Removal steps

1. Brake caliper mounting bolt	13. Stabilizer link mounting nut
2. Brake caliper	14. Self-locking nut
3. Brake tube clamp bolt	15. Shock absorber mounting bolt (upper)
4. Rear brake disc	16. Self-locking nut
5. Hub cap	17. Self-locking nut
6. Wheel bearing nut	18. Trailing arm mounting bolt and nut
7. Rear hub assembly	19. Trailing arm assembly
8. Parking brake cable clamp bolt	
9. Parking brake cable end (Refer to GROUP 36 – Parking Brake.)	
10. Rear speed sensor clamp bolt <ABS>	
11. ABS speed sensor <ABS>	
12. Backing plate	

Caution
*: Indicates parts which should be temporarily tightened, and then fully tightened with the vehicle on the ground in an unladen condition.

MT2039100035000X

Fig. 15 Trailing arm replacement. FWD

MB990767-01, or equivalent, secure rear axle shaft then remove self-locking nut.
b. Using axle puller and slide hammer tool Nos. MB990211-01 and MB990241-01, or equivalents, remove rear axle hub.

c. Using ball joint remover tool No. MB991113-01, or equivalent, loosen and disconnect ball joint from knuckle. **Loosen, but do not remove ball joint nut.**
2. Replace connecting rod as follows:
   a. Remove trailing arm bushing.

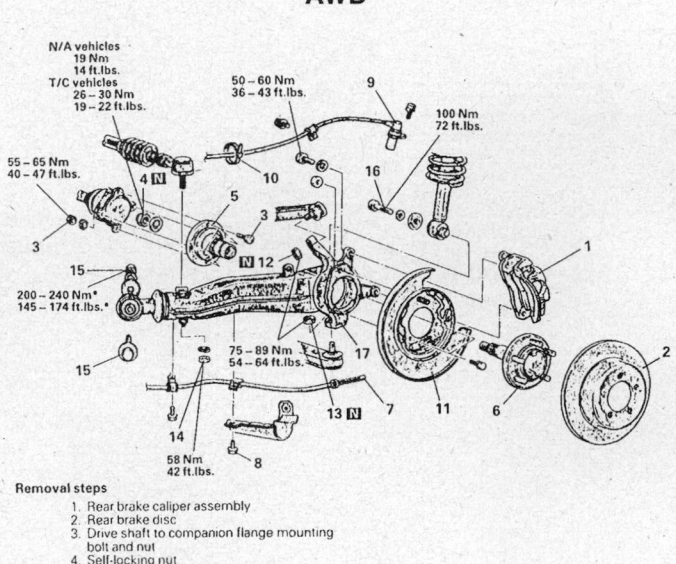

N/A vehicles
19 Nm
14 ft.lbs.
T/C vehicles
26 – 30 Nm
19 – 22 ft.lbs.

Removal steps
1. Rear brake caliper assembly
2. Rear brake disc
3. Drive shaft to companion flange mounting bolt and nut
4. Self-locking nut
5. Companion flange
6. Rear axle shaft
7. Parking brake cable end
8. Parking brake cable clamp bolt
9. Rear speed sensor (ABS)
10. Rear speed sensor cable and parking brake cable bands (ABS)
11. Dust shield
12. Self-locking nut (upper arm)
13. Self-locking nut (lower arm)
14. Tie rod end mounting nut
15. Trailing arm mounting bolt and nut
16. Rear shock absorber mounting bolt
17. Trailing arm

NOTE
For tightening points marked with *, first temporarily tighten and then ground the vehicle to torque to specification where the vehicle is empty

MT2039100037000X

Fig. 16 Trailing arm replacement. AWD

b. Remove connecting rod nut and bolt.
c. Install rod remover and installer tool No. MB9911254, or equivalent, as shown in **Fig. 17.**
d. Apply lubricant to sliding points (A). Install bolt (B) in trailing arm.
e. Using a suitable wrench, turn screw (C) to remove connecting rod.
f. Installation of special tool should be performed with screw shaft and

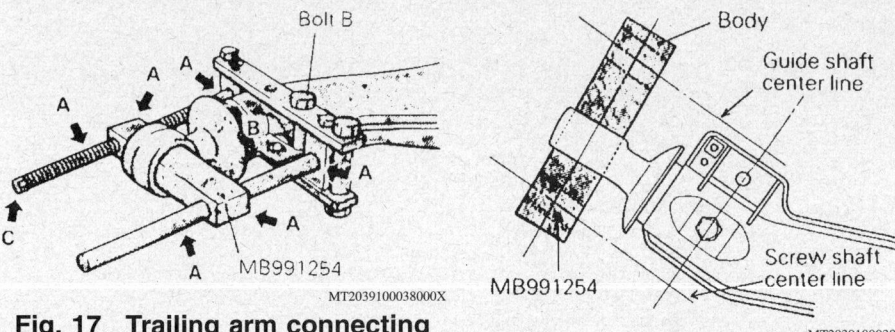

Fig. 17 Trailing arm connecting rod replacement. AWD

Fig. 18 Trailing arm connecting rod installation. AWD

guide shaft center lines oriented as shown, **Fig. 18.**

  g. Apply soapy water to rubber portion of connecting rod, then reverse procedure to install connecting rod.

3. Reverse procedure to install.

STABILIZER BAR
REPLACE
AWD MODELS

1. Remove rear suspension in numbered sequence as shown, **Fig. 19,** noting the following:
   a. Support rear suspension with a suitable transmission jack.
   b. Remove crossmember bracket nut and bracket.
   c. Lower transmission jack to obtain a gap between rear suspension and body.
   d. Remove stabilizer bar.
2. Check stabilizer link ball joint stud starting torque as follows:
   a. Move stabilizer link ball joint stud from side to side several times.
   b. Install two nuts on ball joint and measure ball joint starting torque, **Fig. 20.**
   c. If starting torque is not 15–28 lbs., replace stabilizer link.
3. Reverse procedure to install, noting the following:
   a. Hold stabilizer link with wrench and tighten locknut so that protrusion is .197–.276 inch, **Fig. 21.**

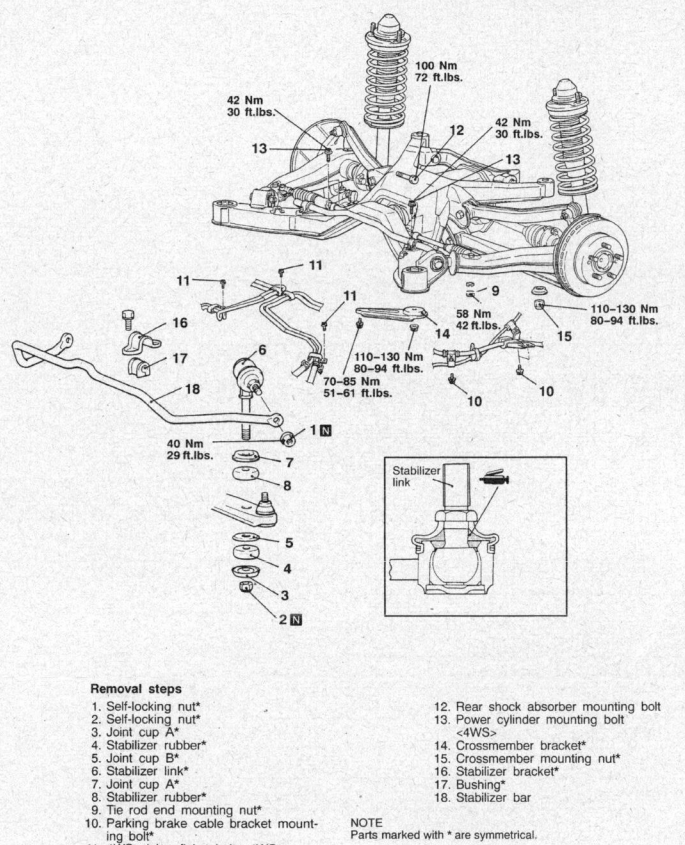

Removal steps

1. Self-locking nut*
2. Self-locking nut*
3. Joint cup A*
4. Stabilizer rubber*
5. Joint cup B*
6. Stabilizer link*
7. Joint cup A*
8. Stabilizer rubber*
9. Tie rod end mounting nut*
10. Parking brake cable bracket mounting bolt*
11. 4WS piping fixing bolt <4WS>
12. Rear shock absorber mounting bolt
13. Power cylinder mounting bolt <4WS>
14. Crossmember bracket*
15. Crossmember mounting nut*
16. Stabilizer bracket*
17. Bushing*
18. Stabilizer bar

NOTE
Parts marked with * are symmetrical.

Fig. 19 Stabilizer bar replacement. AWD

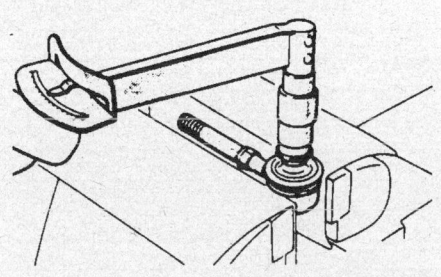

Fig. 20 Stabilizer link ball joint starting torque inspection. AWD

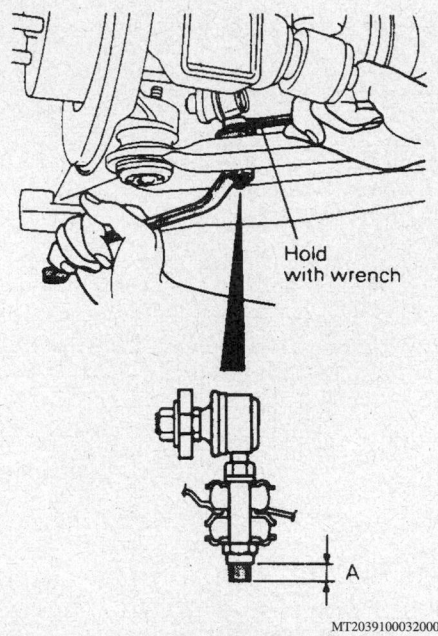

MT2039100032000X

**Fig. 21 Stabilizer link installation.
AWD**

TIGHTENING SPECIFICATIONS

For rear axle and suspension tightening specifications,
refer to individual repair or replacement procedures
and illustrations.

Year	Component	Torque/ Ft. Lbs.
AWD MODELS		
1996–99	ABS Cable Attaching Bolt	9
	ABS Rear Speed Sensor Bolt	9
	Brake Caliper Bolt	65
	Center Bearing Nut	33
	Crossmember Bracket Bolt	43–51
	Crossmember Bracket Nut	72–87
	Crossmember Nut (Differential Side)	72–87
	Differential Carrier To Propeller Shaft Coupling	30–35
	Driveshaft To Companion Flange	40–47
	Lower Control Arm Inner Nut & Bolt	101–116①
	Lower Control Arm Self-Locking Nut	72
	Power Cylinder Bolt (4WS)	30
	Pressure Tube Assembly To Pump (4WS)	30
	Self-Locking Nut	②
	Shock Absorber Lower Mount	72
	Shock Absorber Piston Rod Nut	14–18
	Shock Absorber Upper Mount	33
	Tie Rod End	42
	Trailing Arm	145–174①
	Upper Control Arm Inner Nut & Bolt	101–116①
	Upper Control Arm Self-Locking Nut	54–64
	Wheel Lug Nuts	87–101

Continued

TIGHTENING SPECIFICATIONS—Continued

For rear axle and suspension tightening specifications,
refer to individual repair or replacement procedures
and illustrations.

Year	Component	Torque/ Ft. Lbs.
FWD MODELS		
1996–99	Assist Arm Self-Locking Nut	54–64
	Brake Caliper	65
	Crossmember Nut	65
	Lower Control Arm Self-Locking Nut	43–52
	Shock Absorber Lower Mount	65①
	Shock Absorber Piston Rod Nut	14–18
	Shock Absorber Upper Mount	33
	Stabilizer Bar Bolt	29
	Stabilizer Bar Self-Locking Nut	29
	Trailing Arm Nut & Bolt	101–116①
	Upper Control Arm Self-Locking Nut	54–64
	Wheel Bearing Nut	145–188
	Wheel Lug Nuts	87–101

① — Tighten temporarily, then tighten to specifications once vehicle is unladen.
② — Non-turbo, 137 ft. lbs.; turbo, 188–217 ft. lbs.

Transfer Case

INDEX

PRECAUTIONS

AIR BAG SYSTEMS

Refer to "Air Bag System Precautions" in the front of this manual for system disarming and arming procedures.

BATTERY GROUND CABLE

Prior to service, disconnect battery ground cable and isolate as required.

TRANSFER CASE

REPLACE

1. Disconnect front exhaust pipe from engine.
2. Remove transfer case attaching bolts, then move transfer case to the left and lower front of transfer case.
3. Remove transfer case from propeller shaft, noting the following:

a. Use caution not to damage transfer case oil seal lip.
b. Suspend propeller shaft to prevent bending.
c. Cover transfer case opening using plug tool No. MB991193, or equivalent, to prevent oil leakage and entry of foreign material.
4. Reverse procedure to install.

Front Suspension & Steering

NOTE: On Air Bag Equipped Models, Refer To "Air Bag System Precautions" Located In The Front Of This Manual For System Disarming & Arming Procedures.

INDEX

PRECAUTIONS

AIR BAG SYSTEMS

Refer to "Air Bag System Precautions" in the front of this manual for system disarming and arming procedures.

BATTERY GROUND CABLE

Prior to service, disconnect battery ground cable and isolate as required.

WHEEL BEARING

ADJUST

Bearing preload is pre-set to the specified value by design and therefore cannot be adjusted.

WHEEL HUB & STEERING KNUCKLE

REPLACE

1. Raise and support vehicle.
2. Remove hub and knuckle in numbered sequence as shown, **Fig. 1,** noting the following:
   a. Remove front speed sensor bracket to knuckle mounting bolt, then the speed sensor. **Use care when handling the pole piece at the tip of the speed sensor and toothed surface of the ABS rotor so as not to strike or damage them.**
   b. Loosen driveshaft nut while vehicle is on floor with brakes applied. **Do not apply full vehicle load on wheel bearing when loosening.**
   c. Remove caliper assembly mount bolts and suspend from frame using suitable wire without disconnecting the brake hose.
   d. Disconnect lower ball joint using ball joint remover tool No. MB990635-01, or equivalent. **Loosen, but do not remove ball joint nut.**
   e. Disconnect tie rod end using ball

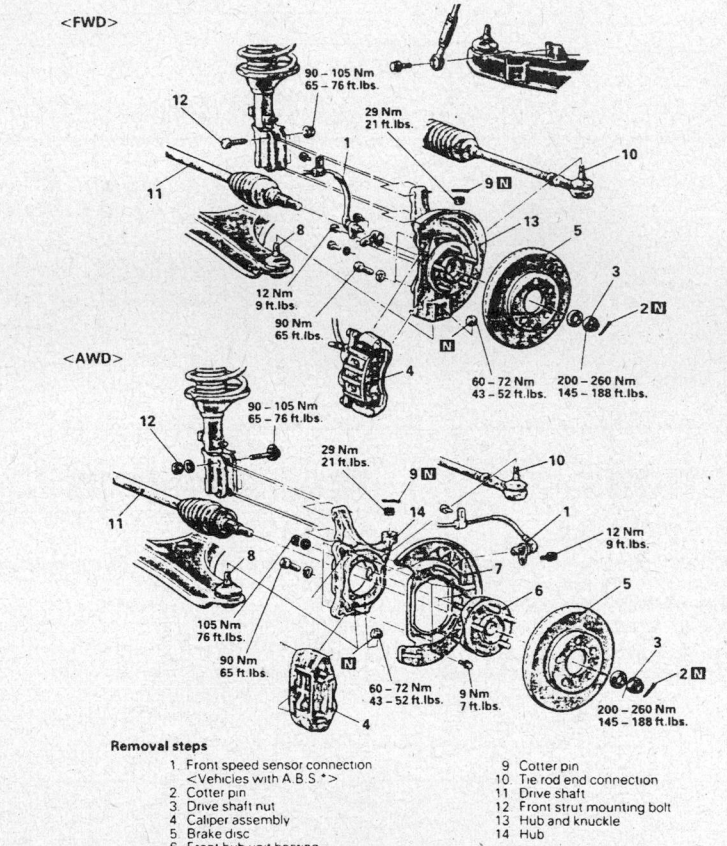

Fig. 1 Hub & knuckle removal

Removal steps

1. Front speed sensor connection <Vehicles with A.B.S.*>
2. Cotter pin
3. Drive shaft nut
4. Caliper assembly
5. Brake disc
6. Front hub unit bearing
7. Dust shield
8. Lower arm ball joint connection
9. Cotter pin
10. Tie rod end connection
11. Drive shaft
12. Front strut mounting bolt
13. Hub and knuckle
14. Hub

NOTE
* Anti-lock braking system

MT2049100015000X

joint remover tool. **Loosen, but do not remove tie rod end locknut.**
f. Remove driveshaft using axle puller tool No. MB990241-01, or equivalent.
g. Use care not to damage ABS rotor installed to the outer driveshaft outer race when removing hub.
3. Measure front hub unit bearing rotation

starting torque as follows:
a. Install front hub remover and installer tool No. MB990998-01, or equivalent, on the front hub unit bearing, **Fig. 2.**
b. While holding tool bolt, tighten to specification.
c. Turn hub to seat bearing in grease.
d. Measure rotation starting torque

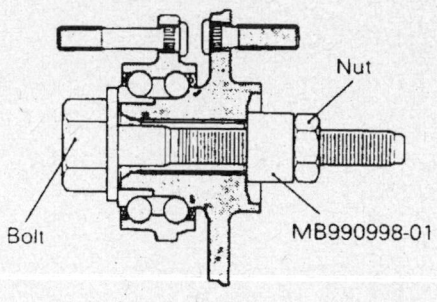

Fig. 2 Bearing installer tool installation

MT2049100016000X

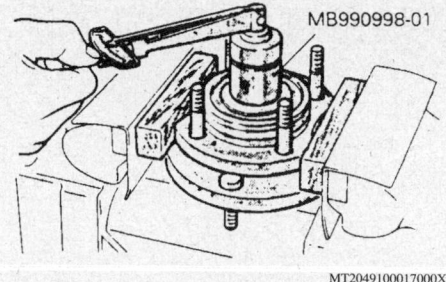

Fig. 3 Hub torque measurement

MT2049100017000X

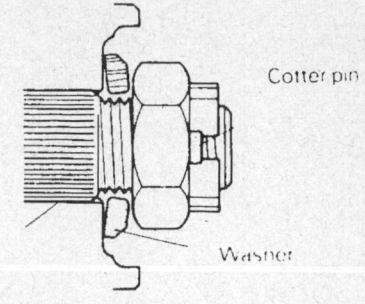

MT2049100018000X

Fig. 4 Driveshaft nut installation

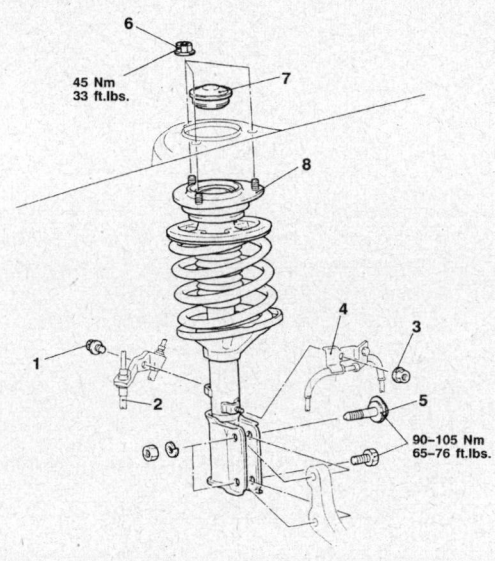

45 Nm
33 ft.lbs.

90–105 Nm
65–76 ft.lbs.

Removal steps

1. Brake hose tube clamp mounting bolt
2. Brake hose tube clamp
3. Front speed sensor clamp mounting nut <ABS>
4. Front speed sensor clamp <ABS>
5. Strut lower mounting bolt
6. Strut upper mounting bolt
7. Dust cover
8. Strut assembly

MT2029100011000X

Fig. 5 Strut assembly replacement

and ensure it is 16 inch lbs. or less, **Fig. 3.**

4. Reverse procedure to install, noting the following:
   a. Ensure washer and wheel bearing nut are installed as shown, **Fig. 4.**
   b. After installing wheel, lower vehicle and tighten nut to specifications.
   c. If position of cotter key holes does not line up, tighten to specification.
   d. Install cotter key.

BALL JOINT INSPECTION

1. Disconnect ball joint from steering knuckle as outlined under "Ball Joint, Replace."
2. Shake ball joint several times, then install ball joint stud nut.
3. Using torque wrench tool No. MB990326, or equivalent, measure ball joint breakaway torque.
4. Ball joint breakaway torque should be 7–16 ft. lbs.

5. If breakaway torque exceeds specifications, replace ball joint.

BALL JOINT
REPLACE

Refer to "Control Arm, Replace" for ball joint replacement procedure.

STRUT
REPLACE

1. Replace strut assembly in numbered sequence as shown, **Fig. 5.**
2. Reverse procedure to assemble and install, noting the following:
   a. Assemble spring upper seat on piston rod of strut aligning notch in rod with notch in seat.
   b. Install coil spring while aligning four holes in upper seat with four holes in lower seat using a .3 inch diameter by 11.8 inch long rod, **Fig. 6.**
   c. With coil spring still compressed, secure upper seat and finger-tighten the self-locking nut.

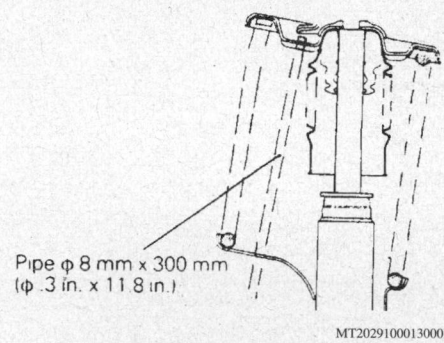

Pipe φ 8 mm x 300 mm
(φ .3 in. x 11.8 in.)

MT2029100013000X

Fig. 6 Spring upper seat installation

   d. Align both ends of the coil spring with grooves in spring seat, then slowly loosen compression tool.
   e. Using seat holder tool No. MB991176 or equivalent, tighten to specification.

STRUT SERVICE

1. Disassemble strut assembly in numbered sequence as shown, **Fig. 7**, noting the following:
   a. Secure upper seat using spring seat holder tool No. MB991176, or equivalent, then loosen strut self-locking nut. **Loosen, but do not remove self-locking nut until the next step is performed.**
   b. Compress coil spring using a suitable coil spring compression tool, then remove self-locking nut.

CONTROL ARM
REPLACE
LOWER

1. Replace lower control arm and ball joint in numbered sequence as shown, **Fig. 8,** noting the following:
   a. Remove ball joint using ball joint remover tool No. MB991113-01, or equivalent. **Loosen, but do not remove ball joint nut until lower control arm is ready to be removed.**
   b. Position lower arm bushing bracket with mounting surface tilting 5°–7° with respect to bottom surface of lower arm, then install self-locking nut, **Fig. 9.**

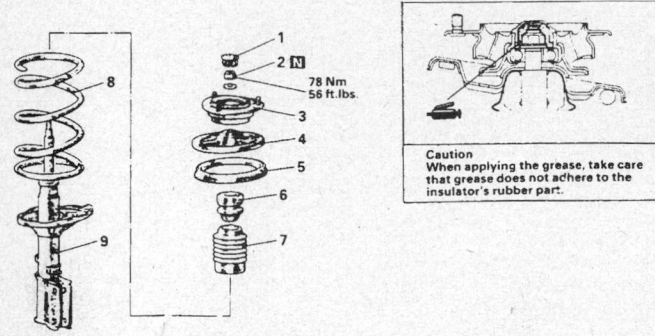

Disassembly steps
1. Dust shield
2. Self-locking nut
3. Strut insulator assembly
4. Spring upper seat assembly
5. Upper spring pad
6. Bump rubber
7. Dust shield
8. Front coil spring
9. Strut assembly

MT2029100012000X

Fig. 7 Strut assembly removal

MT2029100010000X

Fig. 9 Lower arm clamp nut installation

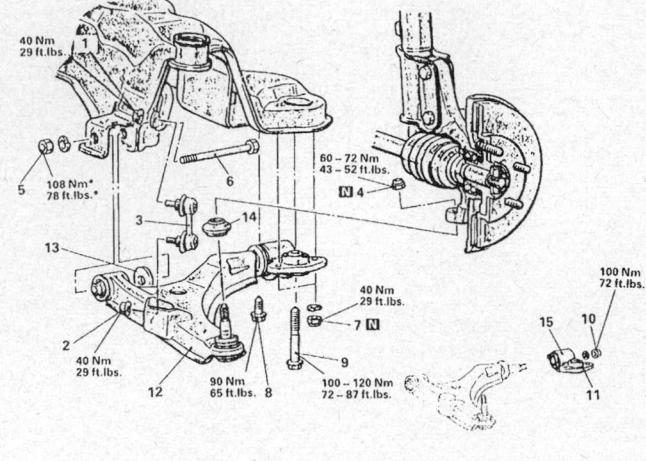

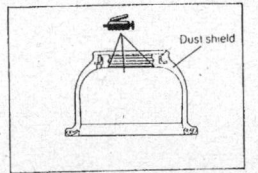

Removal steps
1. Stabilizer link mounting nut (stabilizer bar side)
2. Stabilizer link mounting nut (lower arm side)
3. Stabilizer link
4. Self-locking nut connecting lower arm ball joint to knuckle
5. Lower arm mounting nut
6. Lower arm mounting bolt
7. Clamp mounting self-locking nut
8. Clamp mounting bolt (small)
9. Clamp mounting bolt (large)
10. Lower arm clamp mounting self-locking nut
11. Lower arm mounting clamp
12. Lower arm
13. Stopper
14. Dust shield
15. Rod bushing

NOTE
For tightening points marked with *, first temporarily tighten them, then ground the vehicle and torque to specification where the vehicle is empty.

MT2029100009000X

Fig. 8 Lower control arm & ball joint replacement

STABILIZER BAR
REPLACE

1. Remove front exhaust pipe, then the front lower cover.
2. Remove right and left members in numbered sequence as shown, **Fig. 10.**
3. Replace stabilizer bar in numbered sequence shown, **Fig. 11.**
4. Reverse procedure to install, noting the following:
   a. Align left stabilizer bar bushing with marking on bar and temporarily tighten stabilizer bar bracket, **Fig. 12.**
   b. Mount stabilizer bar right bracket and temporarily tighten.
   c. Temporarily install both ends of the stabilizer bar on the links, then tighten stabilizer bar mounting brackets bolts.
   d. Bleed power steering system and align front suspension. Refer to "Power Steering System Bleed."

POWER STEERING GEAR
REPLACE

1. Drain power steering system fluid into an appropriate container.
2. Remove front exhaust pipe, then the transfer assembly.
3. Remove power steering gear in numbered sequence as shown, **Fig. 13,** noting the following:
   a. Disconnect tie rod end using ball

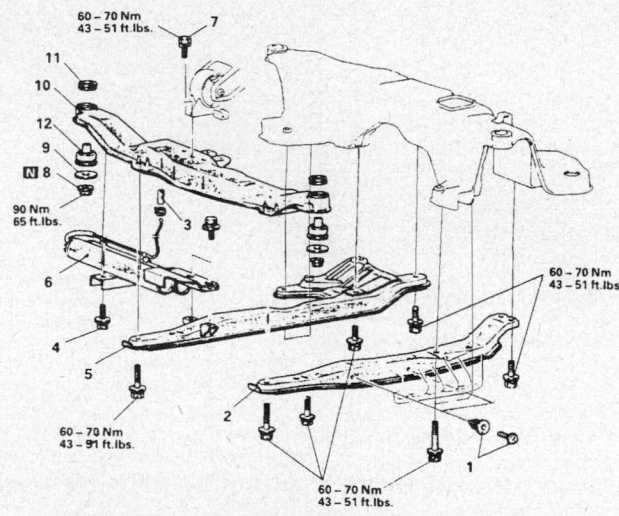

Removal steps of No. 1 crossmember, left member, right member
1. Cover installation screw
2. Left member
3. Connection of clutch vacuum hose <Turbo>
4. Vacuum tank installation bolt <Turbo>
5. Right member
6. Vacuum tank <Turbo>
7. Front roll stopper installation bolt
8. No. 1 crossmember installation nut
9. Lower plate
10. No. 1 crossmember
11. Stopper (B)
12. Bushing (B)

MT2029100016000X

Fig. 10 Right & left member replacement

joint remover tool No. MB991113-01, or equivalent.
b. When removing steering gear,

move gear completely to right and then remove gear from crossmember.

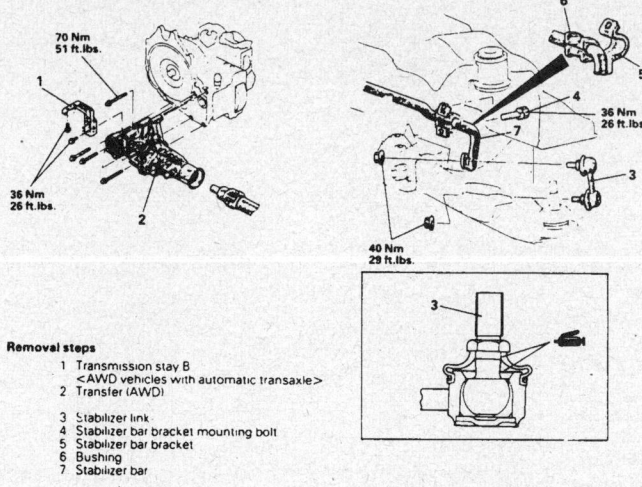

Removal steps

1 Transmission stay B
  <AWD vehicles with automatic transaxle>
2 Transfer (AWD)

3 Stabilizer link
4 Stabilizer bar bracket mounting bolt
5 Stabilizer bar bracket
6 Bushing
7 Stabilizer bar

MT2029100017000X

Fig. 11 Stabilizer bar replacement

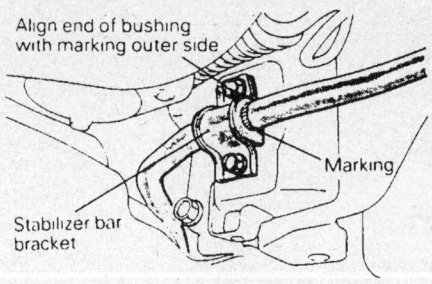

MT2029100018000X

Fig. 12 Stabilizer bar bracket position

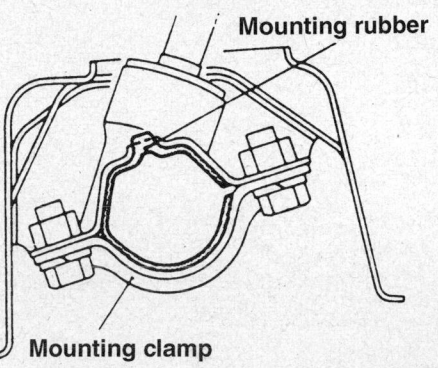

MT6039100002000X

Fig. 14 Rubber mount installation

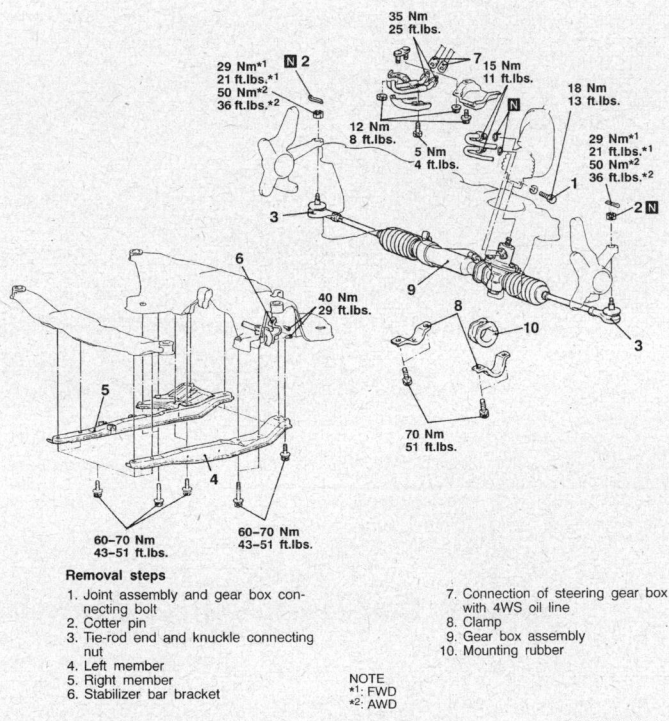

Removal steps

1. Joint assembly and gear box connecting bolt
2. Cotter pin
3. Tie-rod end and knuckle connecting nut
4. Left member
5. Right member
6. Stabilizer bar bracket

7. Connection of steering gear box with 4WS oil line
8. Clamp
9. Gear box assembly
10. Mounting rubber

NOTE
*1: FWD
*2: AWD

MT6039100001000X

Fig. 13 Power steering gear replacement

c. Tilt steering gear downward and re-move from left side.
4. Ensure total pinion torque while rotating pinion gear at a rate of one rotation every four to six seconds is 5–11 inch lbs.
5. Reverse procedure to install, noting the following:
   a. Keep projection of mounting rubber as shown, **Fig. 14.**
   b. Bleed power steering system as outlined under "Power Steering System Bleed."

POWER STEERING PUMP
REPLACE
FRONT

1. Drain power steering fluid into an appropriate container.
2. Replace power steering pump in numbered sequence as shown, **Figs. 15 and 16,** noting the following:
   a. Connect pressure hose ensuring

slit part contacts the oil pump guide bracket, **Fig. 17.**
   b. Bleed power steering system as outlined under "Power Steering System Bleed."

REAR

1. Drain power steering fluid into an appropriate container.
2. Remove main muffler assembly.
3. Remove rear power steering pump in numbered sequence as shown, **Fig. 18,** noting the following:
   a. Support differential case using a suitable transmission jack, then re-move crossmember bracket and crossmember mounting nuts on differential side.
   b. Slightly lower crossmember assembly.
4. Reverse procedure to install, noting the following:
   a. Bleed power steering system as outlined under "Power Steering System Bleed."
   b. Bleed the four wheel steering (4WS) system as outlined under " Bleeding System" in "Power Steering Service."

REAR POWER CYLINDER
REPLACE

1. Raise and support vehicle.

<SOHC>

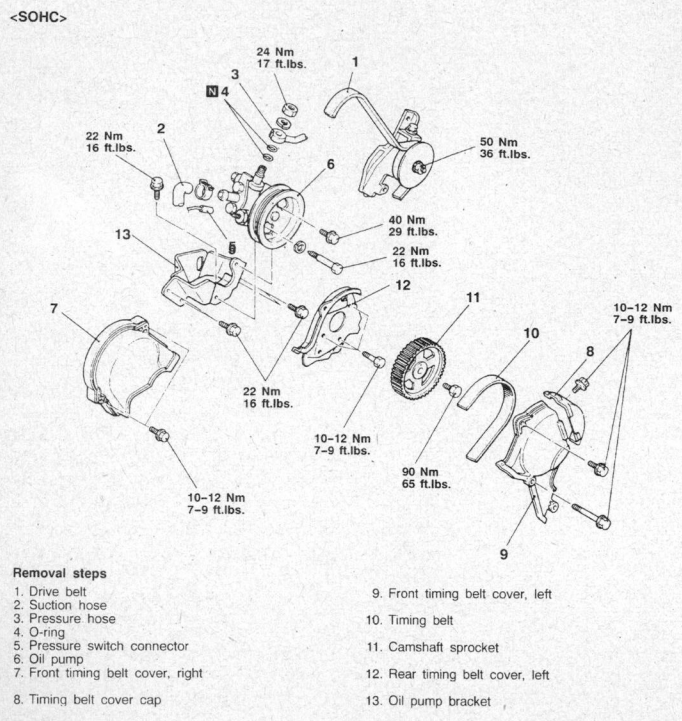

Removal steps

1. Drive belt
2. Suction hose
3. Pressure hose
4. O-ring
5. Pressure switch connector
6. Oil pump
7. Front timing belt cover, right
8. Timing belt cover cap
9. Front timing belt cover, left
10. Timing belt
11. Camshaft sprocket
12. Rear timing belt cover, left
13. Oil pump bracket

MT6029900067000X

Fig. 15 Front power steering pump replacement. SOHC engine

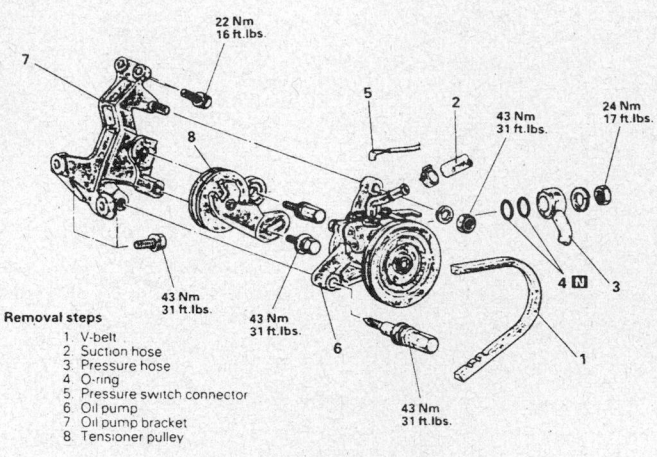

Removal steps

1. V-belt
2. Suction hose
3. Pressure hose
4. O-ring
5. Pressure switch connector
6. Oil pump
7. Oil pump bracket
8. Tensioner pulley

MT6039100004000X

Fig. 16 Front power steering pump replacement. DOHC engine

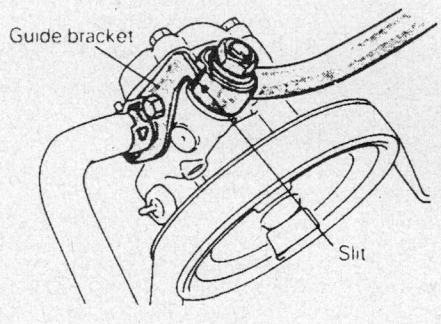

MT6039100005000X

Fig. 17 Pressure hose installation

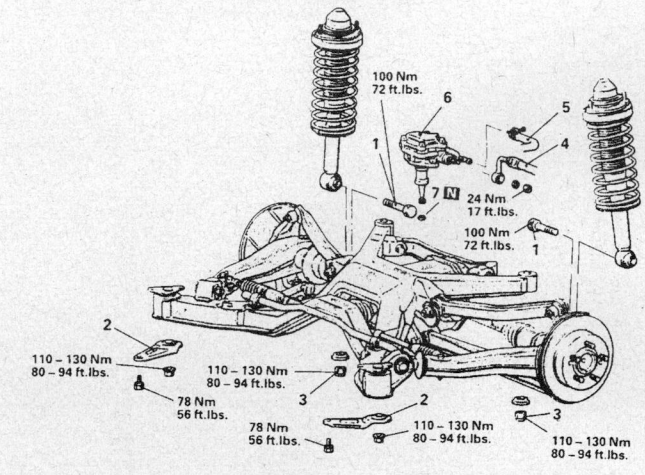

Removal steps

1. Rear shock absorber lower mounting bolt
2. Crossmember bracket
3. Crossmember mounting nut (on differential side)
4. Pressure hose
5. Suction hose
6. Rear-wheel oil pump
7. O-ring

NOTE
Do not disassemble the rear-wheel oil pump

MT6039100006000X

Fig. 18 Rear power steering pump replacement

2. Clean steering system piping using suitable steam cleaner or equivalent.
3. Drain steering system fluid into an appropriate container.
4. Remove main muffler assembly.
5. Remove rear power cylinder in numbered sequence as shown, **Fig. 19**, noting the following:
   a. Before removing crossmember self-locking nut, support differential case with a suitable transmission jack, then remove self-locking nut.
   b. Secure power cylinder on tie rod side with a suitable spanner wrench and remove power cylinder mounting nut.
6. Inspect tie rod swing torque as follows:
   a. Swing tie rod ten times, hard.
   b. Point tie rod end down, then attach a suitable spring scale as shown and measure swing torque, **Fig. 20**.
   c. If swing torque is more than 26 inch lbs., replace tie rod.
   d. If swing torque is less than 4 inch

lbs., the ball joint may be reused as long as it operates smoothly and is not loose.
7. Inspect power cylinder slide resistance as follows:
   a. Place piston in neutral position.
   b. Wrap wire around tie rod end, then measure slide resistance using a suitable spring scale, **Fig. 21**.
   c. If slide resistance is more than 15 lbs., replace power cylinder.
   d. If resistance is less than 15 lbs., the power cylinder may be reused as long as it slides smoothly and is not loose.
8. Reverse procedure to install, noting the following:
   a. Secure power cylinder to crossmember.
   b. Move power cylinder piston rod over its full stroke to determine its Neutral position.
   c. Align tie rod ends and installation holes at trailing arm.

d. When tie rod ends and installation holes on the trailing arm do not meet, loosen tie rod end securing nut, then adjust length. **The dust cover fastener clip should be removed for this step.**
e. The difference between lengths of left and right tie rods should be less than .039 inch. **The threads of the tie rod ends may be used as a guide for this step.**
f. Bleed power steering system as outlined under "Power Steering System Bleed."

REAR POWER CYLINDER CONTROL VALVE
REPLACE

1. Raise and support vehicle.
2. Clean steering system piping using suitable steam cleaner or equivalent.

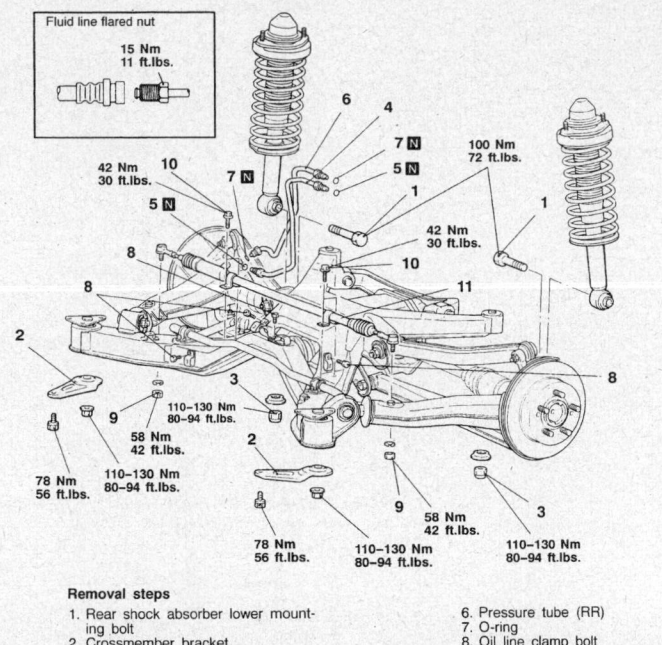

Fluid line flared nut
15 Nm
11 ft.lbs.

42 Nm
30 ft.lbs.

100 Nm
72 ft.lbs.

42 Nm
30 ft.lbs.

78 Nm
56 ft.lbs.

110–130 Nm
80–94 ft.lbs.

58 Nm
42 ft.lbs.

110–130 Nm
80–94 ft.lbs.

78 Nm
56 ft.lbs.

58 Nm
42 ft.lbs.

110–130 Nm
80–94 ft.lbs.

110–130 Nm
80–94 ft.lbs.

Removal steps

1. Rear shock absorber lower mounting bolt
2. Crossmember bracket
3. Crossmember mounting nut
   (on differential side)
4. Pressure tube (RL)
5. O-ring

6. Pressure tube (RR)
7. O-ring
8. Oil line clamp bolt
9. Tie rod end nut
10. Power cylinder installation bolt
11. Power cylinder

MT6039100007000X

**Fig. 19 Rear power cylinder (steering gear)
replacement**

3. Drain steering system fluid into an appropriate container.
4. Remove the rear suspension assembly as outlined under " Rear Suspension, Replace" in "Rear Axle &
   Suspension."
5. Replace control valve and related
   components in numbered sequence
   as shown, **Fig. 22.**
6. Raise and support vehicle.
7. Clean steering system piping using
   suitable steam cleaner or equivalent.
8. Drain steering system fluid into an appropriate container.
9. Remove the rear suspension assembly as outlined under " Rear Suspension, Replace" in "Rear Axle &
   Suspension."
10. Replace control valve and related
    components in numbered sequence
    as shown, **Fig. 22.**
11. Bleed power steering system as out-
    lined under "Power Steering System
    Bleed."

POWER STEERING SYSTEM BLEED

2WS SYSTEM

The hydraulic brake system must be
bled if air has entered the system. This condition may be caused by low fluid level, a
hydraulic fluid leak, the opening of a hydraulic line or replacement of a hydraulic
system component. Symptoms include a
loss of basic brake operation and/or a low
or spongy brake pedal.

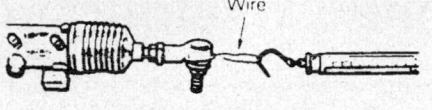

Wire

MT6039100009000X

**Fig. 21 Power cylinder slide
resistance inspection**

On models equipped with ABS, use a
suitable filter when adding fluid to reservoir
tank.

1. Ensure master cylinder reservoir is full.
   Add suitable brake fluid as needed,
   and securely reinstall the master cylinder cap.
2. Raise and support vehicle.
3. Position a drain pan under the wheel
   being bled.
4. Have an assistant depress the brake
   pedal with a slow even pressure and
   hold it. **Do not depress brake pedal
   fully to the end of the master cylinder stroke. This may cause damage
   to the master cylinder.**
5. Using a suitable wrench, open the
   bleeder valve one full turn. Watch for
   air bubbles in the fluid, and listen for air
   escaping from the system.
6. With the brake pedal still depressed,
   close the bleeder valve.
7. Have the assistant pump the brake
   pedal several times. **Do not depress
   brake pedal fully to the end of the
   master cylinder stroke, this may
   cause damage to the master cylinder.**

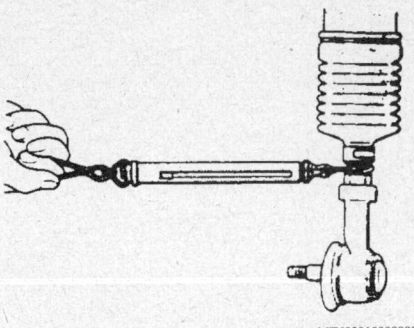

MT6039100008000X

**Fig. 20 Tie rod swing torque
inspection**

8. Repeat preceding bleed steps until all
   air is removed from the hydraulic system. **While bleeding the system, recheck brake fluid supply in the
   master cylinder often so as not to
   allow the master cylinder to run dry.**
9. Upon completion of hydraulic system
   bleeding, proceed as follows:
   a. Ensure the master cylinder reser-
      voir is full. Add suitable brake fluid
      as needed, and securely reinstall
      the master cylinder cap.
   b. Lower the vehicle. Ensure brake
      pedal is firm and braking operation
      is satisfactory.

4WS SYSTEM

1. Bleed air from power steering system
   as previously outlined.
2. Raise and support vehicle just off
   ground.
3. Start engine and allow to idle.
4. Loosen bleeder screw on left side of
   control valve and install air bleeder set
   tool No. MB991230, or equivalent, on
   bleeder screw, **Fig. 23.**
5. Turn steering wheel to left stop, then
   immediately return it to center position.
   Air will be discharged with fluid. **Ensure reservoir is kept filled.**
6. Repeat preceding step two or three
   times until all air is bled from system.
7. Repeat preceding bleed steps using
   right side bleeder screw.
8. Turn ignition switch to Off position.
9. Install air bleeder tool on rear power
   cylinder, **Fig. 24.**
10. Start engine, place transaxle in Drive
    position and raise indicated vehicle
    speed to 43–50 mph to circulate fluid.
    **Ensure vehicle is properly support-
    ed and secured for this step. Use ex-
    treme caution when working
    around moving wheels.**
11. Reduce indicated vehicle speed to 19–
    25 mph, turn steering wheel from stop
    to stop. Air will be bleed into reservoir
    at this time. When steering wheel is at
    each stop air will circulate inside spe-
    cial hose.
12. Repeat preceding step several times
    until no more air is seen in reservoir.

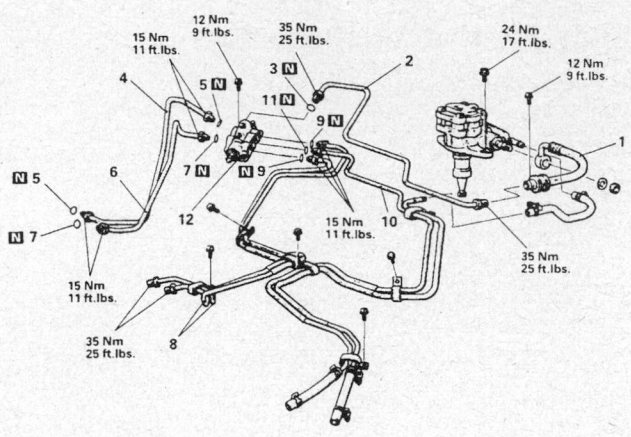

Removal steps

1. Pressure hose
2. Pressure tube
3. O-ring
4. Pressure tube (RR)
5. O-ring
6. Pressure tube (RL)
7. O-ring
8. Pressure tube (FL, FR)
9. O-ring
10. Return pipe
11. O-ring
12. Control valve

MT6039100010000X

Fig. 22   Rear power cylinder control valve replacement

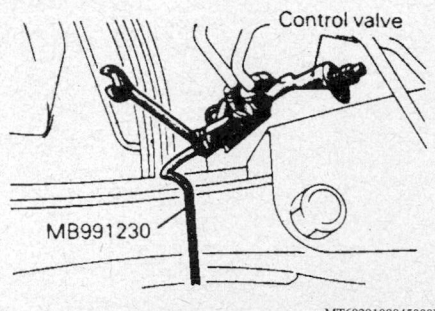

MT6029100045000X

Fig. 23   4WS system bleed

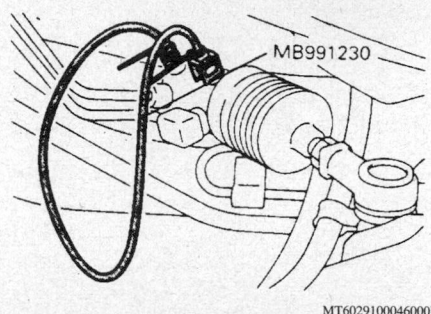

MT6029100046000X

Fig. 24   Rear power cylinder bleed

TIGHTENING SPECIFICATIONS

For rear axle and suspension tightening specifications, refer to individual repair or replacement procedure and illustrations.

Year	Component	Torque/Ft. Lbs.
1996–99	Air Bag Module	4
	Axle Shaft Nut	145–188
	Crossmember Attaching Bolt	43–51
	Crossmember Attaching Nut	58–72
	Crossmember Lower Plate Self-Locking Nut	65
	Dust Plate Bolt (AWD)	7
	Driveshaft Nut	145–188
	Front Brake Caliper	65
	Front Roll Stopper Bolt	43–51
	Front Speed Sensor Attaching Bolt	9
	Front Strut Lower Mount Bolt	65–76
	Front Strut Piston Rod Nut	56
	Hub Nut	145–188
	Inner Shaft Bracket Bolt	33
	Lower Ball Joint Nut	43–52
	Lower Ball Joint To Steering Knuckle Nut	43–52
	Lower Control Arm Clamp Long Bolt	72–87
	Lower Control Arm Clamp Mounting Nut	72
	Lower Control Arm Clamp Nut	29
	Lower Control Arm Clamp Short Bolt	65①
	Lower Control Arm Nut	72–87①
	Power Steering Gearbox Line Fittings (4WS)	25
	Power Steering Line Fitting	11
	Power Steering Line Inner Bracket (4WS)	4

Continued

TIGHTENING SPECIFICATIONS—Continued

For rear axle and suspension tightening specifications,
refer to individual repair or replacement procedure
and illustrations.

Year	Component	Torque/Ft. Lbs.
1996–99	Power Steering Line Outer Bracket (4WS)	8
	Power Steering Pump Bracket Lower Bolt	31
	Power Steering Pump Bracket Upper Bolt	16
	Power Steering Pump Plug	18–22
	Power Steering Pump Pressure Hose Nut	17
	Power Steering Pump Tensioner Pulley	31
	Power Steering Pump To Bracket	31
	Power Steering Rack Bracket Attaching Bolts	51
	Power Steering Rack To Steering Column Linkage	13
	Stabilizer Bar Bracket Bolt	26
	Stabilizer Link Nut	29
	Steering Column Shaft Joint	13
	Steering Column Support	8
	Steering Wheel	29
	Tie Rod End Attaching Nut	21–36
	Tie Rod End Locking Nut	36–40
	Wheel Lug Nuts	87–101

① — Tighten temporarily, tighten to specifications when vehicle is unladen.

Wheel Alignment

INDEX

PRELIMINARY INSPECTION

1. Ensure tires are inflated to correct pressure, then check for uneven wear.
2. Check front wheel bearings, suspension arm and ball joints for damage and replace as necessary, to correct improper alignment due to faulty components.
3. Check steering gear and shocks for damage and replace as necessary.
4. Rock vehicle back and forth, then bounce it up and down to settle vehicle prior to alignment.
5. Ensure vehicle is unloaded and on a suitable alignment rack in accordance with manufacturer's instructions. **When measuring, equipment is attached directly to outer end of driveshaft and front wheels are on turntables. Apply brake to prevent vehicle movement.**

FRONT WHEEL ALIGNMENT

CAMBER

1. Install wheel alignment gauge attachment tool No. MB991004, or equivalent. Tighten to front driveshaft nut specification.
2. To adjust, turn upper bolt on strut lower mount. One graduation is equivalent to about 1/3° camber.

CASTER

Caster has been preset during production and is not adjustable.

TOE-IN

1. Adjust toe-in by loosening clips and turning left and right tie rod turnbuckles equally in opposite directions. Refer to **Fig. 1.**
2. To increase toe-out, turn left turnbuckle toward front of vehicle and right turnbuckle toward rear of vehicle. To increase toe-in, turn turnbuckles in other direction.
3. Toe-in adjustment should be .24 inch for each half turn of left and right tie rods.

REAR WHEEL ALIGNMENT

CAMBER

FWD Models

1. Make adjustment with crossmember side assist link mounting bolt loosened.
2. Adjust camber by turning lower arm mounting bolt (crossmember side). One graduation is equivalent to about 1/4° in camber.
3. If camber is adjusted, ensure toe-in is also adjusted.

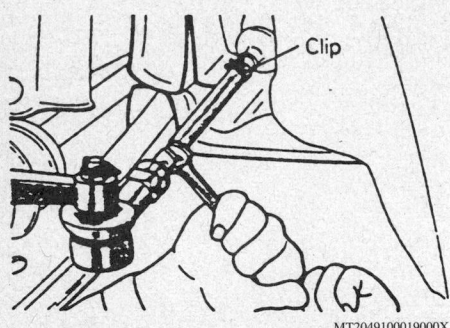

Fig. 1   Front toe-in adjustment

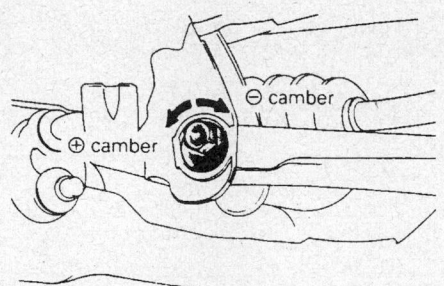

Fig. 2   Rear camber adjustment.
AWD

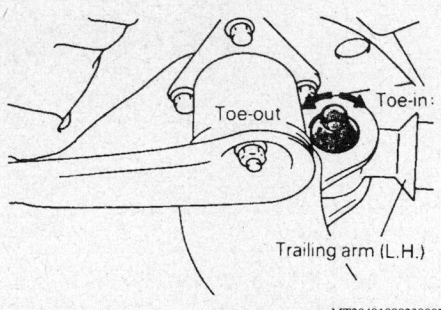

Fig. 3   Rear toe-in adjustment.
AWD

AWD Models

1. Measure camber with a camber/caster/kingpin gauge.
2. Adjust camber by moving mounting bolt located on crossmember side of lower arm. One graduation is equivalent to about 1/5° in camber, **Fig. 2.**

TOE-IN

FWD Models

Adjust rear toe-in by turning the crossmember side assist link mounting bolts on both sides the same amount. One graduation changes toe by approximately .19 inch.

AWD Models

1. Adjust rear toe-in by moving mounting bolts located on crossmember side of the trailing arm.

2. Make adjustment by moving left and right bolts equally. One graduation changes toe by approximately .08 inch, **Fig. 3.**

VEHICLE RIDE HEIGHT

There is no provision for adjustment of vehicle ride height on these vehicles. If ride height is not satisfactory, check for damaged or modified suspension components.

MITSUBISHI UNIT REPAIR

TABLE OF CONTENTS

Air Conditioning

NOTE: On Air Bag Equipped Models, Refer To "Air Bag System Precautions" Located In The Front Of This Manual For System Disarming & Arming Procedures.

NOTE: Prior To Performing Any Service Operations Listed In This Section, Consult The "Technical Service Bulletins" Section For Related Information.

INDEX

PRECAUTIONS

AIR BAG SYSTEMS

Refer to "Air Bag System Precautions" in the front of this manual for system disarming and arming procedures.

BATTERY GROUND CABLE

Prior to service, disconnect battery ground cable and isolate as required.

REFRIGERANT

R-134a is a hydrofluorocarbon refriger-

Garage ambient temperature °C (°F)	21 (70)	26.7 (80)	32.2 (90)	37.8 (100)
Discharge air temperature °C (°F)	0.0–3.0 (32.0–37.4)	0.0–3.0 (32.0–37.4)	0.0–4.0 (32.0–39.2)	0.0–4.0 (32.0–39.2)
Compressor high pressure kPa (psi)	650–700 (92.5–99.6)	740–790 105.3–113.4	980–1020 139.4–145.1	1650–1200 163.6–130.7
Compressor low pressure kPa (psi)	130–140 (18.5–27.5)	130–190 18.5–27.5	130–190 (18.5–27.5)	130–190 (18.5–27.5)

MT7029100183000X

Fig. 1 A/C performance chart. 1996–97 Diamante

ant designed to protect the earth's ozone layer. **However, use of an approved R-134a recovery device is required when it is necessary to discharge the** A/C system for any reason. While this transparent, colorless refrigerant is not flammable or explosive, it is dangerous because its rapid evaporation rate causes it to

Garage ambient temperature °C (°F)	21 (70)	26.7 (80)	32.2 (90)	37.8 (100)
Discharge air temperature °C (°F)	0.0–3.0 (32.0–37.4)	0.0–3.0 (32.0–37.4)	0.0–4.0 (32.0–39.2)	0.0–4.0 (32.0–39.2)
Compressor high pressure kPa (psi)	650–700 (92.5–99.6)	740–790 (105.3–113.4)	980–1020 (139.4–145.1)	1650–1200 (163.6–130.7)
Compressor low pressure kPa (psi)	130–140 (18.5–27.5)	130–190 (18.5–27.5)	130–190 (18.5–27.5)	130–190 (18.5–27.5)

MT7029900418000X

Fig. 2   A/C performance chart. 1998–99 Diamante

Garage ambient temperature °C (°F)	20 (68)	25 (77)	35 (95)	40 (104)
Discharge air temperature °C (°F)	2.5–5.0 (37–41)	3.0–6.0 (37–43)	3.5–7.5 (38–46)	4.0–8.0 (39–46)
Compressor high pressure kPa (psi)	700–900 (101.6–130.6)	740–1,100 (107.4–159.6)	750–1,350 (108.8–195.4)	960–1,570 (139.3–227.8)
Compressor low pressure kPa (psi)	140 (20.3)	140–210 (20.3–30.5)	140–220 (20.3–31.9)	150–230 (21.8–33.4)

MT7029500184000X

Fig. 3   A/C performance chart. Eclipse

Garage ambient temperature °C (°F)	21 (70)	26.7 (80)	32.2 (90)	37.8 (100)	43.3 (110)
Discharge air temperature °C (°F)	2.8–4.4 (37–40)	3.3–5.0 (38–41)	3.9–5.6 (39–42)	4.4–7.2 (40–45)	4.4–7.8 (40–46)
Compressor discharge pressure kPa (psi)	758–1,310 (110–190)	896–1,517 (130–220)	1,103–1,793 (160–260)	1,310–1,999 (190–290)	1,517–2,206 (220–320)
Evaporator suction pressure kPa (psi)	131–165 (19–24)	138–179 (20–26)	145–186 (21–27)	152–193 (22–28)	159–200 (23–29)

MT7029100113000X

Fig. 4   A/C performance chart. Pickup

Garage ambient temperature °C (°F)	20 (68)	25 (77)	35 (95)	40 (104)
Discharge air temperature °C (°F)	2.5–4.5 (37–40)	2.5–4.5 (33–40)	4.0–6.5 (39–44)	6.5–9.0 (44–48)
Compressor high pressure kPa (psi)	765–960 (111.0–139.3)	765–960 (111.0–139.3)	1,325–1,420 (192.2–206.0)	1,570–1,765 (227.8–256.1)
Compressor low pressure kPa (psi)	40–135 (5.8–19.6)	40–135 (5.8–19.6)	80–175 (11.6–25.4)	155–255 (22.5–37.0)

MT7029600187000X

Fig. 5   A/C performance chart. Galant

Garage ambient temperature °C (°F)	21 (70)	26.7 (80)	32.2 (90)	37.8 (100)	43.3 (110)
Discharge air temperature °C (°F)	2.5–5.0 (36.5–41.0)	3.0–5.5 (37.4–41.9)	3.0–6.0 (37.4–42.8)	3.5–7.5 (38.3–45.5)	3.5–8.0 (38.3–46.4)
Compressor discharge pressure kPa (psi)	650–890 (92.5–126.6)	740–1,040 (105.3–147.9)	750–1,130 (106.7–160.7)	920–1,320 (135.1–187.7)	1,150–1,410 (163.6–200.5)
Compressor suction pressure kPa (psi)	140–210 (19.9–29.9)	140–210 (19.9–29.9)	140–210 (19.9–29.9)	150–220 (21.3–31.3)	150–220 (21.3–31.3)

MT7029300115000X

Fig. 6   A/C performance chart. 1996 Mirage

Garage ambient temperature °C (°F)	20 (68)	25 (77)	35 (95)	40 (104)
Discharge air temperature °C (°F)	2.5–4.5 (37–40)	2.5–4.5 (33–40)	4.0–6.5 (39–44)	6.5–9.0 (44–48)
Compressor high pressure kPa (psi)	765–960 (111.0–139.3)	765–960 (111.0–139.3)	1,325–1,420 (192.2–206.0)	1,570–1,765 (227.8–256.1)
Compressor low pressure kPa (psi)	40–135 (5.8–19.6)	40–135 (5.8–19.6)	80–175 (11.6–25.4)	155–255 (22.5–37.0)

MT7029900419000X

Fig. 7   A/C performance chart. 1997–99 Mirage

Garage ambient temperature °C (°F)	21 (70)	26.7 (80)	32.2 (90)	37.8 (100)	43.3 (110)
Discharge air temperature °C (°F)	3.0–6.0 (37.4–42.8)	3.0–7.0 (37.4–44.4)	3.5–7.5 (38.3–45.5)	4.0–8.0 (39.2–46.4)	4.5–8.5 (40.1–47.3)
Compressor discharge pressure kPa (psi)	961–1,402 (139–203)	1,029–1,471 (149–213)	1,108–1,549 (161–225)	1,245–1,745 (181–253)	1,304–1,902 (189–276)
Compressor suction pressure kPa (psi)	98–216 (14–31)	98–226 (14–33)	108–235 (16–34)	137–265 (20–38)	157–275 (23–40)

MT7029600188000X

Fig. 8   A/C performance chart. Montero

GARAGE AMBIENT TEMPERATURE °C (°F)	20 (68)	25 (77)	35 (95)	40 (104)
DISCHARGE AIR TEMPERATURE °C (°F)	6.5–11.0 (44.0–52.0)	6.5–10.5 (44.0–51.0)	6.5–10.5 (44.0–51.0)	7.0–11.0 (45.0–52.0)
COMPRESSOR HIGH PRESSURE kPa (psi)	1,088 (158)	1,401 (203)	1,666 (242)	1,842 (267)
COMPRESSOR LOW PRESSURE kPa (psi)	147 (21)	157 (23)	157 (23)	157 (23)

MT7029700332000X

Fig. 9   A/C performance chart. 1996–98 Montero Sport

GARAGE AMBIENT TEMPERATURE °C (°F)	20 (68)	25 (77)	35 (95)	40 (104)
Discharge air temperature °C (°F)	4.9–6.5 (40.1–43.7)	5.0–7.0 (41.0–44.6)	7.2–9.2 (45.0–48.6)	8.5–10.5 (47.3–50.9)
Compressor high pressure kPa (psi)	830–1,130 (120–164)	1,000–1,300 (145–189)	1,200–1,500 (174–218)	1,550–1,850 (225–268)
Compressor low pressure kPa (psi)	95–195 (14–28)	105–209 (15–30)	125–229 (18–33)	145–245 (21–36)

MT7029900420000X

Fig. 10   A/C performance chart. 1999 Montero Sport

Garage ambient temperature °C (°F)	21 (70)	26.7 (80)	32.2 (90)	37.8 (100)	43.3 (110)
Discharge air temperature °C (°F)	0.0–3.0 (32.0–37.4)	1.0–4.0 (33.8–39.2)	1.0–4.0 (33.8–39.2)	1.0–4.0 (33.8–39.2)	2.0–5.0 (35.6–41.0)
Compressor discharge pressure kPa (psi)	690–740 (98.1–105.3)	780–830 (110.9–118.1)	870–920 (123.7–130.9)	1,080–1,130 (153.6–160.7)	1,210–1,260 (172.1–179.2)
Compressor suction pressure kPa (psi)	130–190 (18.5–27.5)	130–190 (18.5–27.5)	130–190 (18.5–27.5)	130–190 (18.5–27.5)	130–190 (18.5–27.5)

MT7029100117000X

Fig. 11   A/C performance chart. 3000GT

freeze anything it contacts. **For this reason, it is extremely important to wear protective goggles and clothing to prevent refrigerant from contacting skin and eyes.**

If R-134a refrigerant does enter the eyes, it is best to rinse them with a few drops of sterile mineral oil and plenty of cold water. Contact a physician even if irritation ceases.

Do not expose R-134a refrigerant to temperatures above 104°F as pressure may increase beyond system or container capacity. It is also important to keep R-134a containers upright while charging the A/C system to prevent the liquid portion of the refrigerant from entering the system.

Do not allow R-134a refrigerant to come into contact with finished or bright metal surfaces. The metal will tarnish and, if exposed to moisture, corrode.

TROUBLESHOOTING

SIGHT GLASS REFRIGERANT LEVEL

1. Clean refrigerant level sight glass, then start engine.
2. Push A/C button to operate compressor, place blower switch to high position and move temperature lever to the extreme left.
3. Allow system to operate for several minutes, then check sight glass as follows:
   a. If sight glass is clear, magnetic clutch is engaged, compressor discharge line is warm and compressor inlet line is cool, the system has a full charge.
   b. If sight glass is clear, magnetic clutch is engaged and there is no difference in temperature between compressor inlet and discharge lines, the system has lost some refrigerant.
   c. If sight glass is clear and magnetic clutch is disengaged, clutch is defective or system is out of refrigerant.
   d. If foam or bubbles are present in sight glass, system could be low on refrigerant. **Occasional foam or bubbles are normal when temperature is above 110°F or below 70°F.**
4. Allow engine to run at 1500 RPM, then block airflow through condenser to increase compressor discharge pressure to 206–220 psi. If foam or bubbles are still present in sight glass, system is low on refrigerant. **The refrigerant system should not be low on charge unless there is a leak. Repair leak as required, then repeat test.**

AIR CONDITIONING

Model	Compressor Type	Oil Charge (Fl. Oz.) When Changing Component				
		Compressor	Condenser	Evaporator	Lines	Receiver Drier
Diamante	MSC105	③	.50	2.00	.30	.30
Eclipse①	MSC105CVS	③	.50	2.00	.30	.30
Eclipse②	10PA17C	③	1.40	1.40	.30	.30
Galant	MSC105CVS	③	.50	2.00	.30	.30
Mirage	FX105V	③	.50	2.00	.30	.30
Montero	10PA15	③	1.40	1.40	.30	.30
Montero Sport	10PA15	③	.70	2.40	.30	.30
Pickup	MSC90C	③	.50	2.00	.30	.30
3000GT	MSC105	③	.50	2.00	.30	.30

① — 2.0L turbocharged engine & 2.4L engine.
② — 2.0L non-turbocharged engine.
③ — To determine correct oil charge, measure amount of oil drained from old compressor, then adjust new compressor oil charge to match.

Fig. 12 Oil charge specifications chart

PERFORMANCE TEST

Before performing this test a visual inspection of system should be made to ensure system is operating efficiently and correctly. Move vehicle out of direct sunlight.
1. Connect suitable tachometer and manifold gauge set, then start engine.
2. Press A/C button, then reset the control buttons to the maximum cooling position in manual mode as follows:
   a. Place mode selection button in face position.
   b. Place temperature control button in maximum cooling position.
   c. Place air selection button in recirculation position.
   d. Place blower switch in high speed position.
3. Run engine at 1000 RPM with A/C clutch engaged.
4. Engine should be warmed up with doors and windows closed.
5. Insert suitable thermometer in left center A/C outlet and operated engine for approximately 20 minutes.
6. Note discharge air temperature and refer to A/C performance temperature chart, **Figs. 1 through 11.** If clutch cycles, take reading before clutch disengages.

LEAK TEST

Testing the refrigerant system for leaks is one of the most important phases of troubleshooting. One or more of the methods outlined will prove useful in detecting leaks or checking connections if service is performed. Before beginning any leak test, attach a manifold gauge set and note pressure. If little or no pressure is indicated, a partial charge must be supplied. Inspect all connections, compressor head gasket, oil filler plug and compressor shaft seal for leaks.

R-12 leak detectors will not detect R-134a leaks. For R-134a systems, an electronic type leak detector is recommended.

ELECTRONIC LEAK DETECTORS

The following procedure has been revised by a Technical Service Bulletin.

There are a number of electronic leak detectors available to perform leak tests. It is necessary to obtain a detector conforming to SAE J1627 requirements. Refer to the operating instructions for the unit being used and follow these general procedures:
1. To ensure accuracy of test results, perform test only when ambient temperature is at least 60°F and compressor drive belt tension is correct.
2. Ensure system pressure is at least 50 psi before beginning test. If necessary, add refrigerant until proper pressure is reached. In most cases, this will require no more than four ounces of refrigerant.
3. If area to be tested is excessively dirty, clean it with a dry shop towel and compressed air prior to testing. **Do not use cleaning agents; a false detector reading may result.**
4. Move detector probe one to two inches per second in areas of suspected leaks, approximately ¼ inch from surface. **Do not allow probe tip to touch any surfaces or to become contaminated by dirt or moisture.**
5. Position probe below test points, as refrigerant gas is heavier than air.
6. Inspect service access gauge port valve fittings, particularly when valve caps are missing, as dirt accumulations can destroy sealing area of valve core when manifold gauge set is attached. Replace missing valve caps after cleaning valve core area. **Valve caps should only be finger tightened. Using pliers to tighten valve caps may distort sealing surface of valve.**
7. Thoroughly inspect bulkhead evaporator fittings, as O-rings in these fittings are a common source of leakage.
8. Leak test A/C evaporator as follows:
   a. Run A/C on highest setting for 15 seconds, then turn system off and wait for refrigerant to accumulate in evaporator case. Refer to leak detector instructions for accumulation time.
   b. After accumulation time has elapsed, insert leak detector probe into evaporator drain tube (if no condensation is present). Probe may also be inserted through a heater vent close to evaporator case.
   c. Listen for leak detector alarm. If alarm sounds, a leak exists at evaporator.
9. Check for leaks in manifold gauge set and hoses, as well as in remainder of system.

FLAME TYPE (HALIDE) LEAK DETECTORS

When using flame type detectors, avoid inhaling fumes produced by burning refrigerant. Do not use this type of detector where concentrations of combustible gases, dusts or vapors may exist.
1. Adjust detector flame as low as possible to obtain maximum sensitivity. Ensure copper element is cherry red and is not burned away. Flame will be almost colorless.
2. Slowly move detector along areas of suspected leaks. A slight leak will cause flame to change to a bright yellow or green color; a significant leak will be indicated by a brilliant blue flame. Position detector below areas being tested, as refrigerant gas is heavier than air. **Dust in pickup hose may cause a change in flame color. If this is not remedied, a false diagnosis may result. Store leak detector in a clean place and ensure hose is free of dust before leak testing.**
3. Check for leaks in manifold gauge set and hoses, as well as in remainder of system.
4. Use a suitable small fan to ventilate areas where leak detector indicates refrigerant constantly. These areas are contaminated with refrigerant and must be ventilated before leak can be pinpointed.

FLUID LEAK DETECTORS

Apply leak detector solution around joints to be tested. A cluster of bubbles will form immediately if there is a leak. A white foam that forms after a short while will indicate an extremely small leak. In some confined areas, such as sections of the evaporator and condenser, electronic leak detectors will be more useful.

DISCHARGING SYSTEM

R-134a systems require the use of special service equipment designed specifically to be compatible with them. R-12 service equipment cannot be used on R-134a systems. Recovery and recycling stations must also be compatible with the type of refrigerant in use; a station will be contaminated if it is used in conjunction with an incompatible refrigerant.

Refrigerant recovery and recycling stations allow the retention and reuse of refrigerant after contaminants and moisture have been removed. When using such a station, follow the manufacturer's operating instructions, noting the following:

1. **Use extreme caution and observe all safety and service precautions related to the use of refrigerants.**
2. Connect refrigerant recycling station hose(s) to vehicle A/C service port(s) and recovery station inlet fitting. Use hoses equipped with shutoff devices or check valves located within 12 inches of hose ends to minimize introduction of air into recycling station and to minimize amount of refrigerant released when hose ends are disconnected.
3. Turn recycling station on to begin recovery process. Allow station to pump refrigerant from A/C system until station pressure gauge indicates vacuum.
4. After vehicle A/C system has been evacuated, close station inlet valve, if equipped.
5. Turn station off. Some stations may be shut off automatically by a low pressure switch.
6. Allow vehicle A/C system to remain closed for approximately two minutes. Observe vacuum level indicated on gauge. If pressure does not rise, disconnect recycling station hose(s).
7. If system pressure rises, repeat recovery steps until vacuum level remains stable for two minutes.

8. Service A/C system as necessary, then evacuate and recharge A/C system.

SYSTEM EVACUATION
VACUUM PUMP

Vacuum pumps suitable for removing air and moisture from A/C systems are commercially available. The system pump down specification used as a reference point is 28–29½ inches Hg vacuum. However, this reading can be attained at or near sea level only. For each 1000 feet of altitude at which this operation is performed, the reading will be one inch of vacuum higher. For example, at an elevation of 5000 feet, only 23–24½ inches Hg vacuum can be obtained. **The system refrigerant must be completely recovered before it can be evacuated. Damage to the vacuum pump will result if pressurized refrigerant is allowed to enter.**

1. Connect vacuum pump to gauge manifold. With gauges connected to system, remove vacuum hose connector cap and connect gauge manifold center hose to vacuum pump connector. Place high and low side compressor service valve, if used, in middle position and open high and low side gauge manifold hand valves.
2. Operate vacuum pump for at least 30 minutes to remove air and moisture. Observe compound gauge to ensure system pumps down into vacuum. System should reach 28–29½ inches Hg vacuum within five minutes. If system does not pump down, inspect all connections and leak test if necessary.
3. Close gauge manifold hand valves and shut off vacuum pump.
4. Evaluate system's ability to hold vacuum pressure. Observe compound gauge and ensure needle does not rise at a rate exceeding one inch Hg vacuum every four or five minutes. If gauge rises at too rapid a rate, supply partial charge and leak test, then recover refrigerant as described under "Discharging System."
5. If system holds vacuum, charge with refrigerant.

CHARGING STATION

A vacuum pump is built into the charging station and is designed to withstand repeat-

ed and prolonged use without damage. Complete moisture removal from the system is possible only with a vacuum pump constructed for that purpose.

The system refrigerant must be completely recovered before it can be evacuated. Damage to the vacuum pump will result if pressurized refrigerant is allowed to enter.

1. Connect hose to vacuum pump if system refrigerant was recovered through charging station.
2. Open charging station low side gauge hand valve.
3. Connect station to 110V current.
4. Activate vacuum pump according to station manufacturer's instructions.
5. Evacuate system with vacuum pump until low pressure gauge reads at least 28 inches Hg vacuum. Continue evacuating system for an additional 15 minutes for routine system service or 20–30 minutes if any components have been replaced.
6. Close low side gauge hand valve, then turn off vacuum pump.
7. Evaluate system's ability to hold vacuum. Observe low side gauge and ensure needle does not rise at a rate exceeding one inch Hg vacuum every four to five minutes. If low side gauge indication rises at too rapid a rate, supply a partial charge and leak test, then evacuate system again.
8. If system holds vacuum, charge with refrigerant.

CHARGING SYSTEM

Use instructions provided with charging station. Follow these procedures to prevent charging station from being exposed accidentally to the vehicle's high-side system pressure:

1. Do not connect high pressure line to A/C system.
2. Always keep high pressure valve closed on charging station.
3. Perform all evacuation and charging through receiver/drier low-side pressure service fitting.

OIL CHARGE

When replacing an A/C component, refer to the oil charge specifications chart, **Fig. 12,** for oil charge specifications.

A/C SPECIFICATIONS

Model	Refrigerant (R134a) Capacity, Lbs.	Compressor Oil Viscosity	Total System Oil Capacity, Oz.	Compressor Oil Level, Inches	Compressor Clutch Air Gap, Inch
1996					
Diamante	1.63–1.74	①	5.70–6.40	②	.010–.020
Eclipse⑤	1.54–1.63	①	5.70–6.40	②	.016–.026
Eclipse⑥	1.54–1.63	④	2.70–4.10	②	.014–.026
Galant	1.44–1.52	①	5.10–5.75	②	.016–.025
Mirage	1.62–1.88	①	4.40–5.10	②	.016–.026

Continued

A/C SPECIFICATIONS—Continued

Model	Refrigerant (R134a) Capacity, Lbs.	Compressor Oil Viscosity	Total System Oil Capacity, Oz.	Compressor Oil Level, Inches	Compressor Clutch Air Gap, Inch
1996					
Montero	1.31–1.44	④	2.70	②	.014–.026
Pickup	1.63–1.75	①	4.10–4.80	②	.014–.030
3000GT	1.63–1.75	①	5.40–7.00	②	.010–.020
1997–98					
Diamante	1.44–1.52	①	5.10–5.70	②	.016–.025
Eclipse⑤	1.54–1.63	①	5.70–6.40	②	.012–.020
Eclipse⑥	1.54–1.63	④	2.70–4.10	②	.014–.026
Galant	1.44–1.52	①	4.10	②	.016–.026
Mirage	1.23–1.31	①	4.10	②	.016–.026
Montero	1.31–1.44	④	4.10	②	.014–.026
Montero Sport	1.44–1.50	①	5.70	②	③
3000GT	1.63	①	8.60–10.0	②	.010–.020
1999					
Diamante	1.31–1.41	①	4.90–5.60	②	.012–.020
Eclipse⑤	1.54–1.63	①	5.70–6.40	②	.012–.020
Eclipse⑥	1.54–1.63	④	2.70–4.10	②	.014–.025
Galant	1.48–1.56	①	4.10	②	⑦
Mirage	1.23–1.31	①	4.10	②	.012–.020
Montero	1.31–1.44	④	4.10	②	.014–.025
Montero Sport	1.44–1.50	①	5.70	②	.010–.020
3000GT	1.63–1.75	①	8.60–10.0	②	.012–.020

① — SUN PAG 56, or equivalent.
② — Oil level inches cannot be checked.
③ — 1997; .016–.024. 1998; .010–.020.
④ — DENSO Oil 8, or equivalent.
⑤ — 2.0L turbocharged & 2.4L engine.
⑥ — 2.0L non-turbocharged engine.
⑦ — 2.4L engine; .012–.020. 3.0L engine; .016–.024.

BELT TENSION

Model	Engine	A/C Compressor Belt Deflection, Inch
1996		
Diamante	3.0L	.16–.22
Eclipse	2.0L Non-Turbo	.39–.43
	2.0L Turbo & 2.4L	.26–.30
Galant	2.4L	.26–.32
Mirage	1.5L	.24–.28
	1.8L	.27–.30
Montero	3.0L	.26–.29
	3.5L	.26–.30
Pickup & Montero Sport	2.4L & 3.0L	.33–.39
3000GT	3.0L	.16–.22
1997		
Diamante	3.5L	.16–.22
Eclipse	2.0L Non-Turbo	.39–.43
	2.0L Turbo & 2.4L	.26–.30
Galant	2.4L	.26–.32
Mirage	1.5L	.24–.28
	1.8L	.27–.30
Montero	3.5L	.26–.30
Montero Sport	2.4L	.24–.26
	3.0L	.22–.26

Continued

BELT TENSION—Continued

Model	Engine	A/C Compressor Belt Deflection, Inch
1997		
3000GT	3.0L	.295–.374
1998		
Diamante	3.5L	.31–.38
Eclipse	2.0L Non-Turbo	.39–.43
	2.0L Turbo & 2.4L	.26–.30
Galant	2.4L	.26–.32
Mirage	1.5L & 1.8L	.18–.24
Montero	3.5L	.26–.30
Montero Sport	2.4L	.24–.26
	3.0L	.22–.26
3000GT	3.0L	.295–.374
1999		
Diamante	3.5L	.31–.38
Eclipse	2.0L Non-Turbo	.39–.43
	2.0L Turbo & 2.4L	.26–.30
Galant	2.4L	.46–.60
Mirage	1.5L & 1.8L	.18–.24
Montero	3.5L	.26–.30
Montero Sport	2.4L	.24–.26
	3.0L	.22–.26
3000GT	3.0L	.295–.374

TECHNICAL SERVICE BULLETINS

AIR CONDITIONING ODOR

An A/C odor may be created when condensation forms in and around the A/C evaporator. The condensation eventually mixes with airborne pollutants to form growths of bacteria and/or fungi. This produces an unpleasant or musty odor when the blower is turned on.

To remove this odor and prevent new bacteria growth, Mitsubishi Air Conditioner Treatment should be applied. This treatment kills bacteria and fungi growths inside the A/C system and leaves a protective film that guards against new growth for at least one year.

The A/C treatment is applied to the evaporator core through the fresh air inlet. This is done using compressed air, an air gun and the product's applicator nozzle. Use treatment from case part No. A993ZC1X01 and nozzle/adapter kit part No. A993ZC1X02.

Cooling Fans

TABLE OF CONTENTS

Electric Cooling Fans

INDEX

PRECAUTIONS

AIR BAG SYSTEMS

Refer to "Air Bag System Precautions" in the front of this manual for system disarming and arming procedures.

BATTERY GROUND CABLE

Prior to service, disconnect battery ground cable and isolate as required.

TROUBLESHOOTING

FAN MOTOR DOES NOT OPERATE WHEN COOLANT TEMPERATURE IS HIGH

1. Burned out fusible link.
2. Poor electrical connection or break in harness.
3. Faulty relay.
4. Faulty engine coolant temperature sensor.
5. Faulty motor.

FAN MOTOR OPERATES WHEN COOLANT TEMPERATURE IS LOW

1. Faulty engine coolant temperature sensor.
2. Short circuit to body in harness.
3. Faulty relay.

COMPONENT DIAGNOSIS & TESTING

DIAMANTE

ENGINE COOLANT TEMPERATURE SENSOR

1. Drain cooling system, then remove coolant temperature sensor from engine.
2. Submerge sensor end of coolant temperature sensor as shown in **Fig. 1.**
3. Connect ohmmeter across coolant temperature sensor terminals.
4. The resistance should be as follows:
   a. 2.1–2.7 kohms at 68°F.
   b. .9–1.3 kohms at 104°F.
   c. .26–.36 kohms at 176°F.

FAN RELAY

1996

1. With radiator fan relay disconnected,

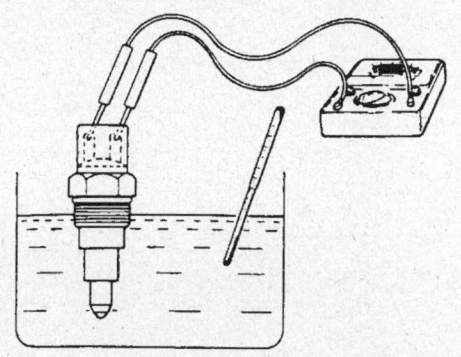

Fig. 1   Coolant temperature sensor inspection

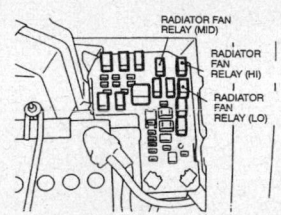

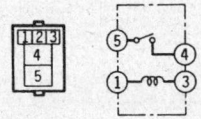

BATTERY VOLTAGE	TERMINAL No.			
	1	3	4	5
Not supplied	○—○			
Supplied	⊕—	—○	○—	—○

MT1089900119000X

Fig. 3   Radiator fan relay inspection. 1997–99 Diamante

use suitable ohmmeter to inspect for continuity between terminals 2 and 4, **Fig. 2,** continuity should exist. inspect for continuity between terminals 1 and 3; continuity should not exist.
2. Apply battery positive voltage to terminal 2 and battery negative to terminal 4, then inspect for continuity between terminals 1 and 3; continuity should exist.

1997–99

Refer to **Fig. 3** when testing the Low, Mid or High radiator fan relays.

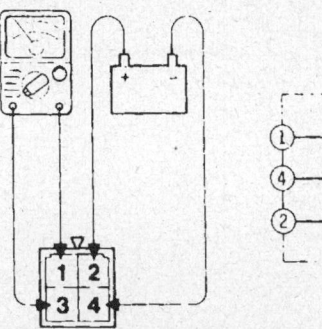
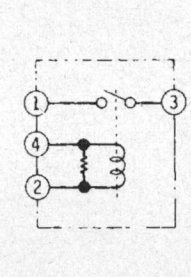

MT1089300091000X

Fig. 2   Radiator fan relay testing. Diamante

RADIATOR FAN MOTOR

1996

1. Disconnect fan motor connection.
2. Connect battery to terminals as shown in **Fig. 4.** Motor should operate smoothly.

1997–99

Refer to **Fig. 5** when testing radiator fan motor.

CONDENSER FAN MOTOR

1996

1. Apply battery voltage terminal 3 and battery negative to terminal 4 as shown in **Fig. 6,** motor should turn.
2. To inspect resistor, measure resistance between terminals 1 and 2, resistance should be .29 ohms.

1997–99

1. Apply battery voltage to terminal 1 and ground terminal 2, **Fig. 7.** Motor should run at low speed.
2. Apply battery voltage to terminal 3 and ground terminal 4, **Fig. 7.** Motor should run at high speed.
3. Replace condenser fan motor if low or high speed tests fail.

ECLIPSE

ENGINE COOLANT TEMPERATURE SENSOR

1. Drain cooling system, then remove coolant temperature sensor from engine.

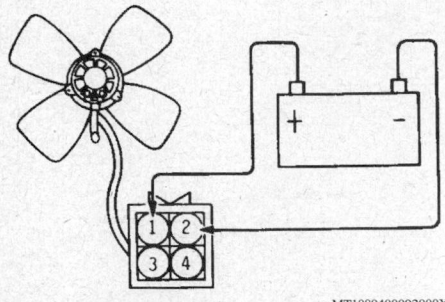

Fig. 4   Radiator fan motor testing. Eclipse & 1996 Diamante

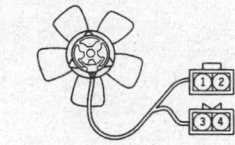

TERMINALS CONNECTED TO THE BATTERY				RADIATOR FAN MOTOR ROTATION
1	2	3	4	
		⊕	⊖	Low
	⊖	⊕	⊖	Medium
⊕	⊖	⊕	⊖	High

Fig. 5   Radiator fan motor inspection. 1997–99 Diamante

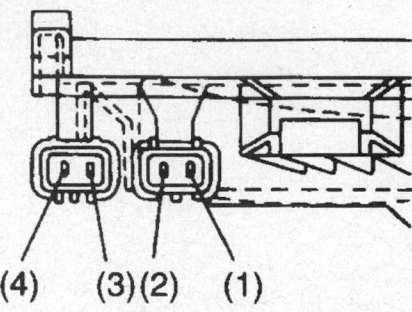

Fig. 6   Condenser fan motor testing. 1996 Diamante

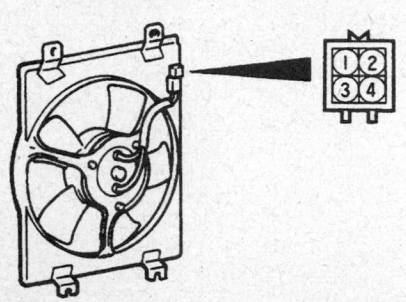

Fig. 7   Condenser fan terminal identification. 1997–99 Diamante

<2.0L Engine (Non-turbo)>

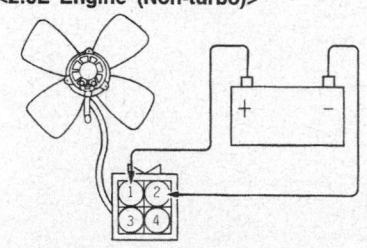

<Except 2.0L Engine (Non-turbo)>

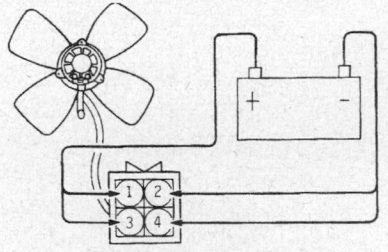

Fig. 8   Radiator fan motor inspection. Eclipse

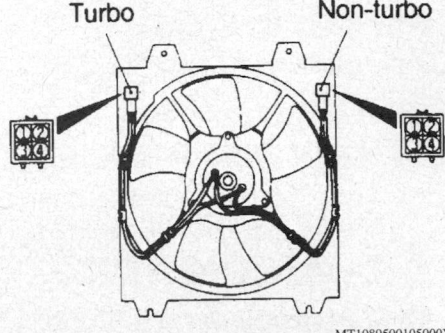

Fig. 9   Condenser fan motor testing. Eclipse

2. Submerge sensor end of coolant temperature sensor as shown in **Fig. 1.**
3. Connect ohmmeter across sensor terminals.
4. Resistance should be as follows:
   a. 5.1–6.3 kohms at 32°F.
   b. 2.1–2.7 kohms at 68°F.
   c. .9–1.3 kohms at 104°F.
   d. .26–.36 kohms at 176°F.

FAN RELAY

1. With radiator fan relay disconnected, use suitable ohmmeter to inspect for continuity between terminals 1 and 3; continuity should exist. Inspect for continuity between terminals 4 and 5; continuity should not exist.
2. Apply battery positive voltage to terminal 1 and battery negative to terminal 3, then inspect for continuity between terminals 4 and 5; continuity should exist.

RADIATOR FAN MOTOR

1. Disconnect fan motor connection.
2. Connect battery to terminals as shown, **Fig. 8.** Motor should operate smoothly.

CONDENSER FAN MOTOR

1. Apply battery positive voltage to terminal 1 of the and battery negative to terminal 4, motor should operate smoothly. Apply battery positive voltage to terminal 3 and battery negative to terminal 2, **Fig. 9,** motor should operate faster.

GALANT & MIRAGE

ENGINE COOLANT TEMPERATURE SENSOR

1. Drain cooling system, then remove Engine Coolant Temperature Sensor from intake manifold.
2. Submerge sensor end of Engine Coolant Temperature Sensor as shown, **Fig. 1,** in warm water.
3. Connect ohmmeter across terminals.
4. Resistance should be as follows:
   a. 2.1–2.7 kohms at 68°F.
   b. .9–1.3 kohms at 104°F.
   c. .26–.36 kohms at 176°F.

RADIATOR FAN RELAY

Mirage & 1996-98 Galant

1. With radiator fan relay disconnected, use suitable ohmmeter to inspect for continuity between terminals 1 and 3, **Fig. 10.** Continuity should exist. Inspect terminals 4 and 5, continuity

should not exist.
2. Apply battery positive voltage to terminal 1 and battery negative to terminal 3, then inspect for continuity between terminals 4 and 5, continuity should exist.
3. If relay does not perform as outlined above, replace.

1999 Galant

1. With radiator fan relay disconnected, use suitable ohmmeter to inspect for continuity between terminals 1 and 3, **Fig. 11.** Continuity should exist. Inspect terminals 2 and 5, continuity should not exist.
2. Apply battery positive voltage to terminal 3 and battery negative to terminal 1, then inspect for continuity between terminals 2 and 5, continuity should exist.
3. If relay does not perform as outlined above, replace.

RADIATOR FAN MOTOR

1. Disconnect fan motor connection.
2. Connect battery to terminals as shown in **Figs. 12 and 13.** Motor should operate smoothly.

FAN CONTROL MODULE

1999 Galant

1. Remove condenser fan motor electrical connector.
2. Start engine and allow to idle.

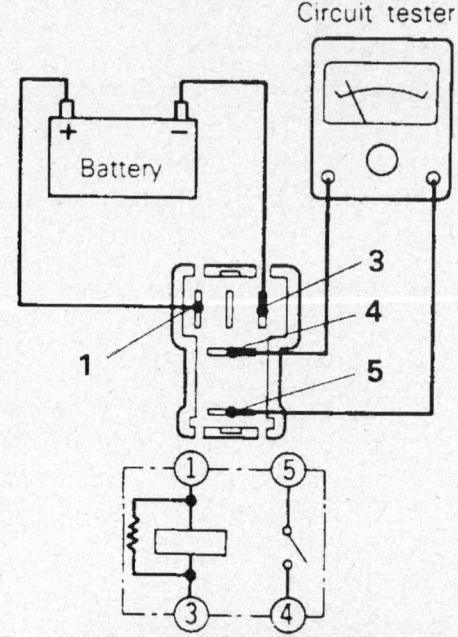

Fig. 10 Radiator fan relay testing. Mirage & 1996–98 Galant

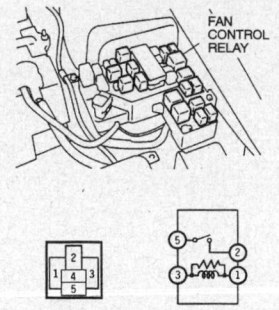

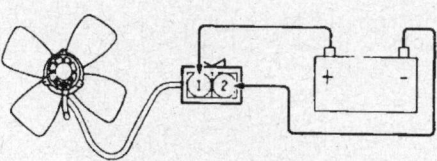

BATTERY VOLTAGE	TERMINAL NO.			
	1	2	3	5
When current is not supplied	○——		——○	
When current is supplied	○——		⊕	○

Fig. 11 Radiator fan relay testing. 1999 Galant

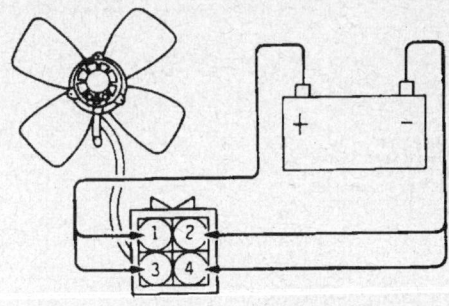

Fig. 12 Radiator fan motor testing. Galant

Fig. 13 Radiator fan motor testing. Mirage

3. Turn A/C switch on and maintain engine coolant temperature of 176° or less.
4. Measure voltage between fan control module side connector terminals.
5. Voltage should change as follows:
   a. 0 volt.
   b. **On models equipped with 2.4L engine,** 5.6–10.8 volts.
   c. **On models equipped with 3.0L engine,** 4.2–9.4 volts.
   d. **On all models,** 9.4–14.6 volts.
6. If voltage does not cycle as indicated, replace radiator fan motor and fan control module assembly.

CONDENSER FAN MOTOR

1. Disconnect fan motor connection.
2. Apply battery positive voltage to terminal 1 of the gray connector and battery negative to terminal 2, motor should operate smoothly.
3. Apply battery positive voltage to terminal 1 of the black connector and battery negative to terminal 2, motor should operate faster.

MONTERO, MONTERO SPORT & PICKUP

ENGINE COOLANT TEMPERATURE SENSOR

1. Drain cooling system, then remove coolant temperature sensor from engine.
2. Submerge sensor end of coolant temperature sensor as shown in **Fig. 1**.
3. Connect ohmmeter across sensor terminals.
4. **On Montero models,** resistance should be as follows:
   a. 2.4 kohms at 68°F.
   b. 1.1 kohms at 104°F.
   c. .3 kohms at 176°F.
5. **On Montero Sport models,** resis-

tance should be as follows:
   a. 2.1–2.7 kohms at 68°F.
   b. .26–.36 kohms at 176°F.
6. **On Pickup models,** resistance should be as follows:
   a. 2.20–2.60 kohms at 68°F.
   b. 258–330 ohms at 176°F.

CONDENSER FAN MOTOR

1. Disconnect condenser fan electrical connection.
2. **On Montero & pickup models,** apply battery voltage to terminal 2 and battery negative to terminal 1. Motor should turn smoothly.
3. **On Montero Sport models,** apply battery voltage to terminal 1 and battery negative to terminal 2. Motor should turn smoothly.

3000GT

ENGINE COOLANT TEMPERATURE SENSOR

1. Drain cooling system, then remove coolant temperature sensor from engine.
2. Submerge sensor end of coolant temperature sensor as shown in **Fig. 1**.
3. Connect ohmmeter across sensor terminals.
4. Resistance should be as follows:
   a. 2.4 kohms at 68°F.
   b. 1.1 kohms at 104°F.
   c. .3 kohms at 176°F.

FAN RELAY

1996

1. With radiator fan relay disconnected, use suitable ohmmeter to inspect for continuity between terminals 1 and 3; continuity should exist. Inspect for continuity between terminals 4 and 5; continuity should not exist.
2. Apply battery positive voltage to terminal 1 and battery negative to terminal 3, then inspect for continuity between terminals 4 and 5; continuity should exist.

1997-99

1. With radiator fan relay disconnected, use suitable ohmmeter to inspect for continuity between terminals 2 and 4; continuity should exist. Inspect for continuity between terminals 1 and 3; continuity should not exist.
2. Apply battery positive voltage to terminal 2 and battery negative to terminal 4, then inspect for continuity between terminals 1 and 3; continuity should exist.

RADIATOR FAN MOTOR

1. Disconnect fan motor connection.
2. Connect battery to terminals as shown in **Fig. 14.** Motor should operate smoothly.

CONDENSER FAN MOTOR

1996-98

1. Apply battery voltage terminal 3 and battery negative to terminal 4 as shown in **Fig. 15,** motor should turn. Apply battery voltage to terminal 1 and battery negative to terminal 2; motor should turn.

1999

1. Apply battery voltage terminal 2 and battery negative to terminal 3 as shown in **Fig. 16,** motor should operate. Apply battery voltage to terminal 1 and battery negative to terminal 3; motor should operate faster.

COMPONENT REPLACEMENT

Refer to **Figs. 17 through 28** for component replacement.

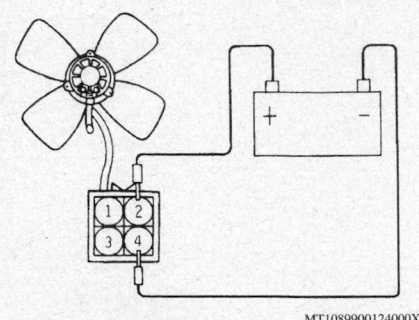

MT1089900124000X

Fig. 14 Radiator fan motor inspection. 3000GT

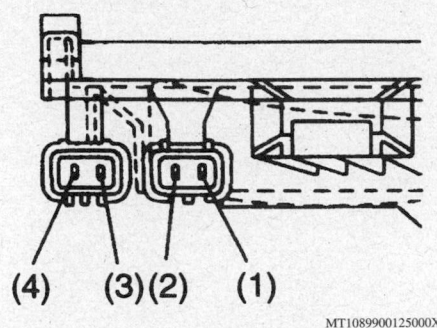

(4) (3)(2) (1)

MT1089900125000X

Fig. 15 Condenser fan motor testing. 1996–98 3000GT

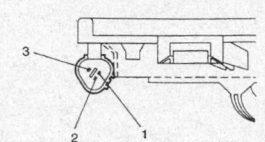

Terminal No.			Condenser fan
1	2	3	
	⊕	⊖	Low speed
⊕		⊖	High speed

MT1089900126000X

Fig. 16 Condenser fan motor testing. 1999 3000GT

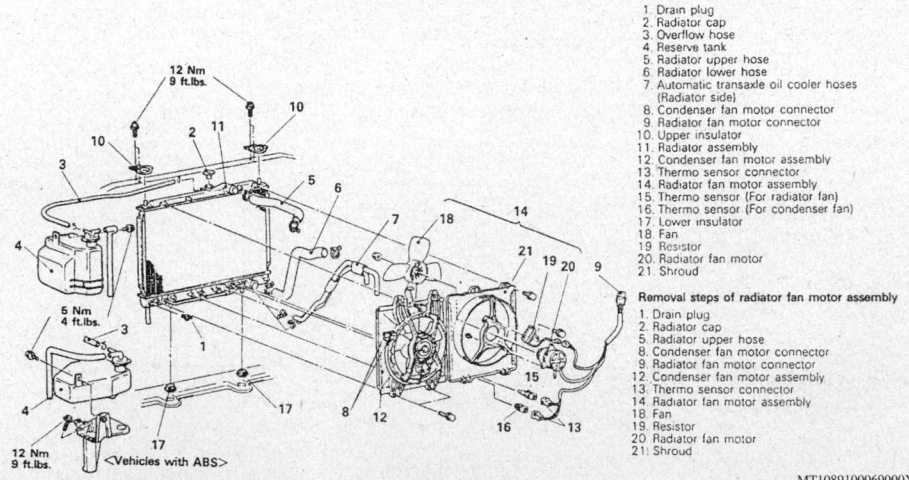

Removal steps of radiator
1. Drain plug
2. Radiator cap
3. Overflow hose
4. Reserve tank
5. Radiator upper hose
6. Radiator lower hose
7. Automatic transaxle oil cooler hoses (Radiator side)
8. Condenser fan motor connector
9. Radiator fan motor connector
10. Upper insulator
11. Radiator assembly
12. Condenser fan motor assembly
13. Thermo sensor connector
14. Radiator fan motor assembly
15. Thermo sensor (For radiator fan)
16. Thermo sensor (For condenser fan)
17. Lower insulator
18. Fan
19. Resistor
20. Radiator fan motor
21. Shroud

Removal steps of radiator fan motor assembly
1. Drain plug
2. Radiator cap
5. Radiator upper hose
8. Condenser fan motor connector
9. Radiator fan motor connector
12. Condenser fan motor assembly
13. Thermo sensor connector
14. Radiator fan motor assembly
18. Fan
19. Resistor
20. Radiator fan motor
21. Shroud

MT1089100069000X

Fig. 17 Component replacement. 1996 Diamante

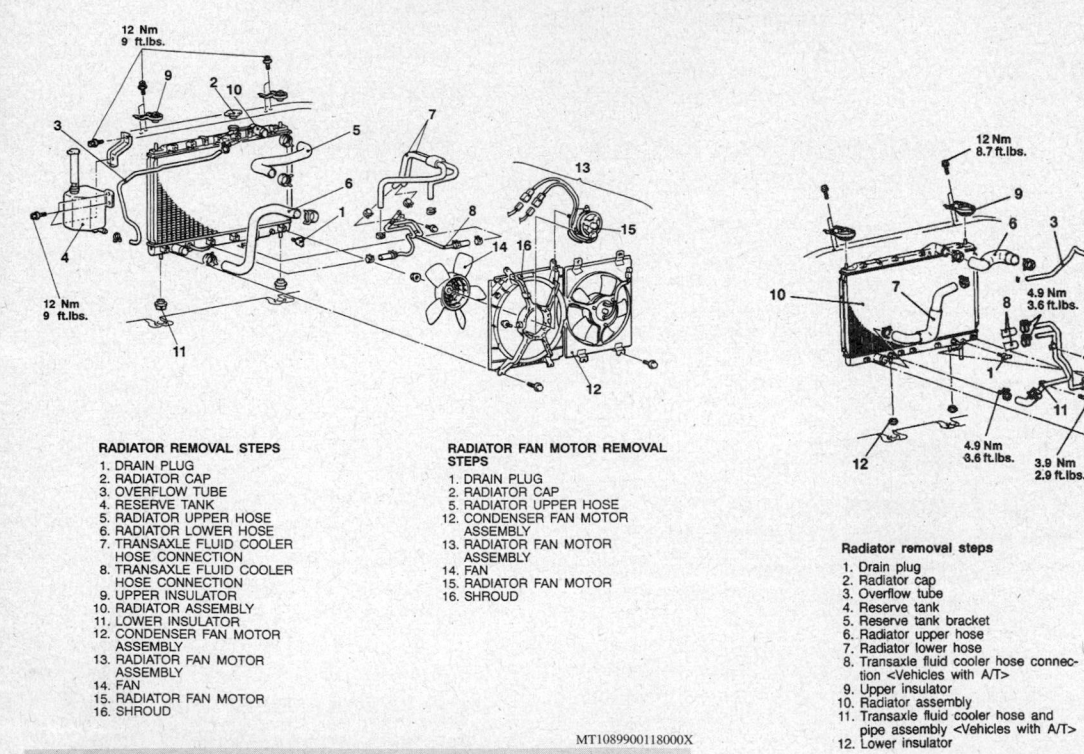

RADIATOR REMOVAL STEPS
1. DRAIN PLUG
2. RADIATOR CAP
3. OVERFLOW TUBE
4. RESERVE TANK
5. RADIATOR UPPER HOSE
6. RADIATOR LOWER HOSE
7. TRANSAXLE FLUID COOLER HOSE CONNECTION
8. TRANSAXLE FLUID COOLER HOSE CONNECTION
9. UPPER INSULATOR
10. RADIATOR ASSEMBLY
11. LOWER INSULATOR
12. CONDENSER FAN MOTOR ASSEMBLY
13. RADIATOR FAN MOTOR ASSEMBLY
14. FAN
15. RADIATOR FAN MOTOR
16. SHROUD

RADIATOR FAN MOTOR REMOVAL STEPS
1. DRAIN PLUG
2. RADIATOR CAP
5. RADIATOR UPPER HOSE
12. CONDENSER FAN MOTOR ASSEMBLY
13. RADIATOR FAN MOTOR ASSEMBLY
14. FAN
15. RADIATOR FAN MOTOR
16. SHROUD

MT1089900118000X

Fig. 18 Component replacement. 1997–99 Diamante

Radiator removal steps
1. Drain plug
2. Radiator cap
3. Overflow tube
4. Reserve tank
5. Reserve tank bracket
6. Radiator upper hose
7. Radiator lower hose
8. Transaxle fluid cooler hose connection <Vehicles with A/T>
9. Upper insulator
10. Radiator assembly
11. Transaxle fluid cooler hose and pipe assembly <Vehicles with A/T>
12. Lower insulator
13. Condenser fan motor assembly <Vehicles with A/C>
14. Radiator fan motor assembly
15. Fan
16. Radiator fan motor
17. Shroud

Radiator fan motor removal steps
11. Transaxle fluid cooler hose and pipe assembly <Vehicles with A/T>
14. Radiator fan motor assembly
15. Fan
16. Radiator fan motor
17. Shroud

MT1089500109000X

Fig. 19 Component replacement. Eclipse w/2.0L non-turbo engine

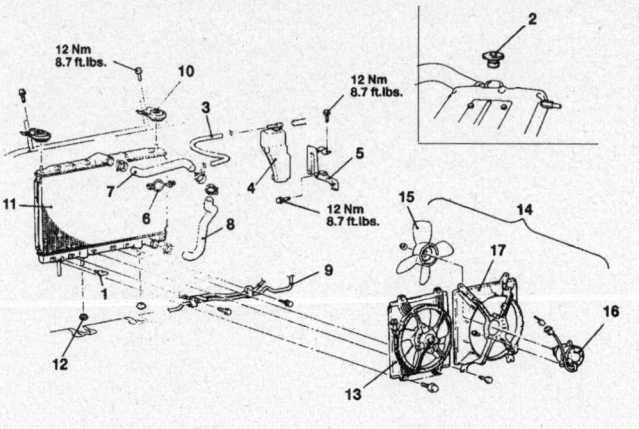

Radiator removal steps
1. Drain plug
2. Radiator cap
3. Overflow tube
4. Reserve tank
5. Reserve tank bracket
6. Clip
7. Radiator upper hose
8. Radiator lower hose
9. Transaxle fluid cooler hose and pipe assembly <Vehicles with A/T>
10. Upper insulator
11. Radiator assembly
12. Lower insulator
13. Condenser fan motor assembly <Vehicles with A/C>
14. Radiator fan motor assembly
15. Fan
16. Radiator fan motor
17. Shroud

Radiator fan motor removal steps
4. Reserve tank
9. Transaxle fluid cooler hose and pipe assembly <Vehicles with A/T>
14. Radiator fan motor assembly
15. Fan
16. Radiator fan motor
17. Shroud

MT1089500110000X

Fig. 20 Component replacement. Eclipse w/2.0L turbo engine

Radiator removal steps
1. Drain plug
2. Radiator cap
3. Overflow tube
4. Reserve tank
5. Reserve tank bracket
6. Radiator upper hose
7. Radiator lower hose
8. Transaxle fluid cooler hose and pipe assembly <Vehicles with A/T>
9. Upper insulator
10. Radiator assembly
11. Lower insulator
12. Condenser fan motor assembly <Vehicles with A/C>
13. Radiator fan motor assembly
14. Fan
15. Radiator fan motor
16. Shroud

Radiator fan motor removal steps
4. Reserve tank
8. Transaxle fluid cooler hose and pipe assembly <Vehicle with A/T>
13. Radiator fan motor assembly
14. Fan
15. Radiator fan motor
16. Shroud

MT1089600111000X

Fig. 21 Component replacement. Eclipse w/2.4L engine

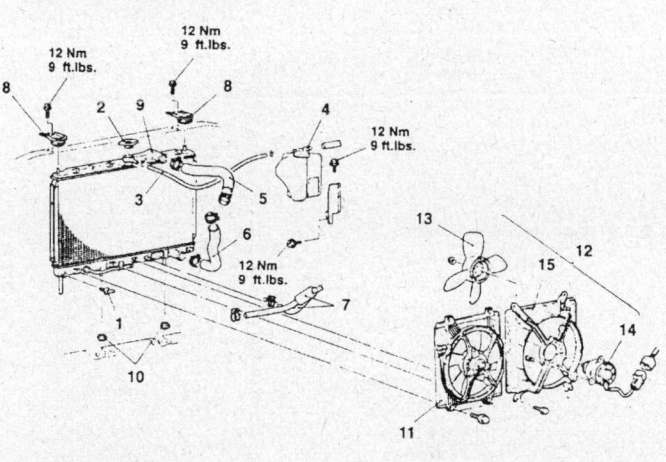

Radiator removal steps
1. Drain plug
2. Radiator cap
3. Overflow tube
4. Reserve tank
5. Radiator upper hose
6. Radiator lower hose
7. Transaxle fluid cooler hose connection <Vehicles with A/T>
8. Upper insulator
9. Radiator assembly
10. Lower insulator
11. Condenser fan motor assembly <Vehicles with A/C>
12. Radiator fan motor assembly
13. Fan
14. Radiator fan motor
15. Shroud

Radiator fan motor removal steps
1. Drain plug
2. Radiator cap
5. Radiator upper hose
11. Condenser fan motor assembly <Vehicles with A/C>
12. Radiator fan motor assembly
13. Fan
14. Radiator fan motor
15. Shroud

MT1089400073000X

Fig. 22 Component replacement. 1996–98 Galant

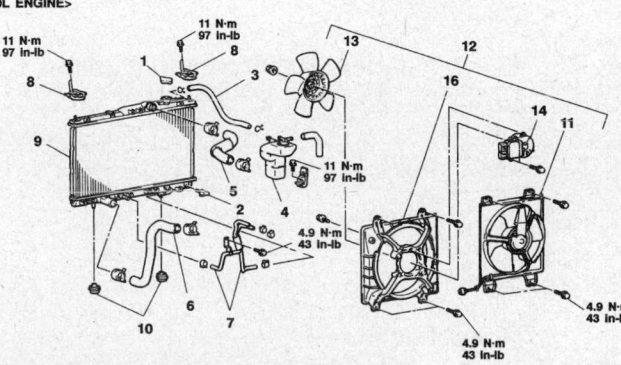

MT1089900127010X

Fig. 23 Component replacement (Part 1 of 2). 1999 Galant

RADIATOR REMOVAL STEPS
1. RADIATOR CAP
2. DRAIN PLUG
3. RUBBER HOSE CONNECTION
4. RESERVE TANK ASSEMBLY
5. RADIATOR UPPER HOSE
6. RADIATOR LOWER HOSE
7. A/T OIL COOLER HOSE CONNECTION <A/T>
8. RADIATOR SUPPORT
9. RADIATOR
10. LOWER INSULATOR
11. CONDENSER FAN MOTOR ASSEMBLY <3.0L ENGINE>
12. RADIATOR FAN MOTOR ASSEMBLY
13. FAN
14. RADIATOR FAN MOTOR
15. PACKING <2.4L ENGINE>
16. SHROUD

RADIATOR FAN MOTOR ASSEMBLY REMOVAL STEPS
1. RADIATOR CAP
2. DRAIN PLUG
5. RADIATOR UPPER HOSE
11. CONDENSER FAN MOTOR ASSEMBLY <3.0L ENGINE>
12. RADIATOR FAN MOTOR ASSEMBLY
13. FAN
14. RADIATOR FAN MOTOR
15. PACKING <2.4L ENGINE>
16. SHROUD

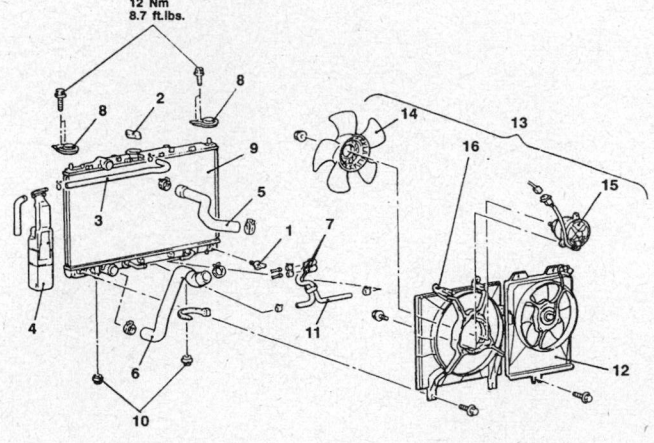

Fig. 23   Component replacement (Part 2 of 2). 1999 Galant

Radiator removal steps
1. Drain plug
2. Radiator cap
3. Overflow hose
4. Reserve tank
5. Radiator upper hose
6. Radiator lower hose
7. A/T oil cooler hose connection
8. Upper insulator
9. Radiator assembly
10. Lower insulator
11. A/T oil cooler hose assembly
12. Condenser fan motor assembly <Vehicle with A/C>
13. Radiator fan motor assembly

Radiator fan motor removal steps
1. Drain plug
2. Radiator cap
3. Overflow hose
5. Radiator upper hose
12. Condenser fan motor assembly <Vehicles with A/C>
14. Fan
15. Radiator fan motor
16. Shroud

Fig. 24   Component replacement. Mirage

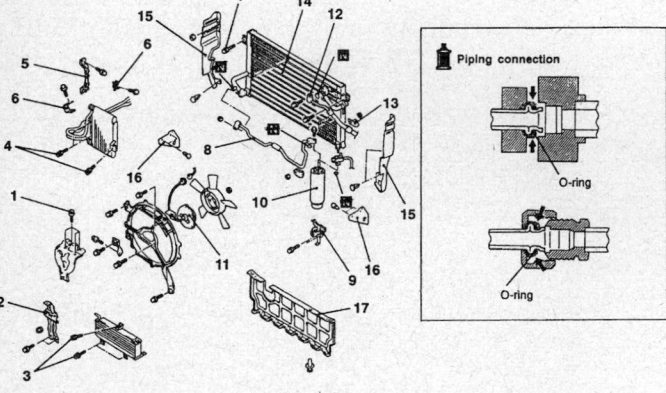

Removal steps
1. Hood latch bracket assembly mounting bolt
2. Hood latch stay
3. Transmission oil cooler mounting bolt <A/T>
4. Engine oil cooler mounting bolt
5. Engine oil cooler bracket
6. Bracket
7. Condenser mounting bolt
8. High pressure pipe A
9. Receiver bracket
10. Receiver
11. Condenser fan motor
12. High pressure hose connection
13. High pressure hose bracket
14. Condenser
15. Headlight side seal
16. Frame side seal
17. Under seal

Fig. 25   Component replacement. Montero & Montero Sport

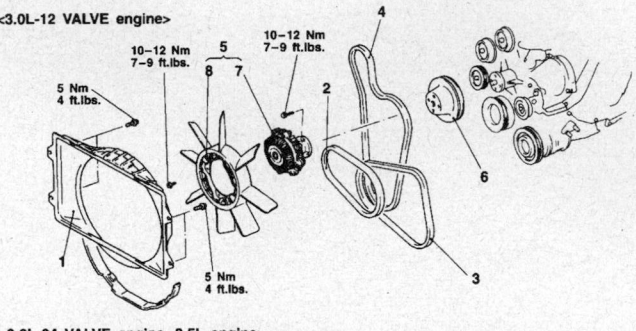

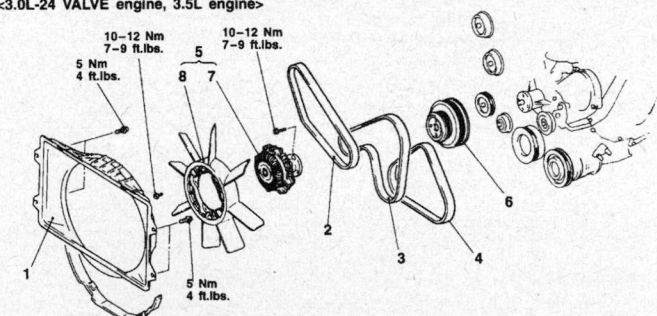

Removal steps <3.0L-12 VALVE engine>
1. Shroud
2. Drive belt (Power steering)
3. Drive belt (Air conditioning)
4. Drive belt (Generator)
5. Cooling fan and fan clutch assembly
6. Pulley
7. Fan clutch
8. Cooling fan

Removal steps <3.0L-24 VALVE engine, 3.5L engine>
1. Shroud
2. Drive belt (Power steering)
3. Drive belt (Generator)
4. Drive belt (Air conditioning)
5. Cooling fan and fan clutch assembly
6. Pulley
7. Fan clutch
8. Cooling fan

Fig. 26   Cooling fan replacement. Montero & Montero Sport

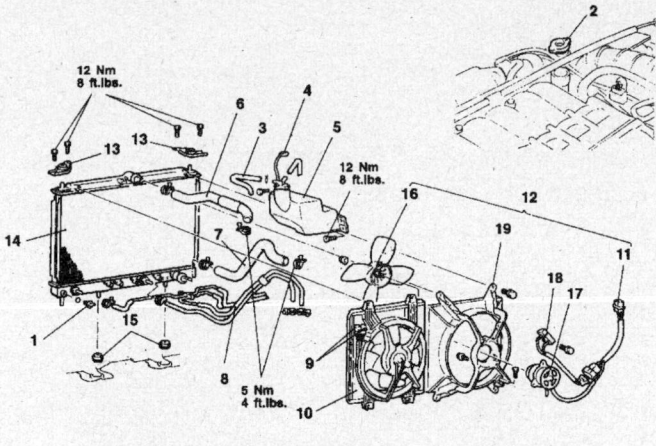

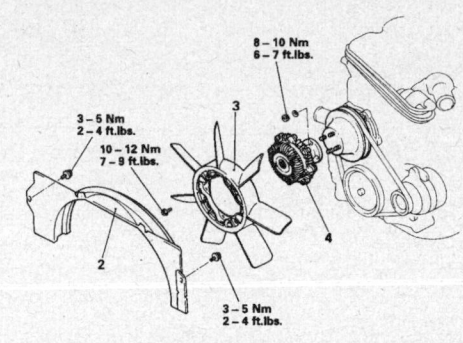

2.4L Engine

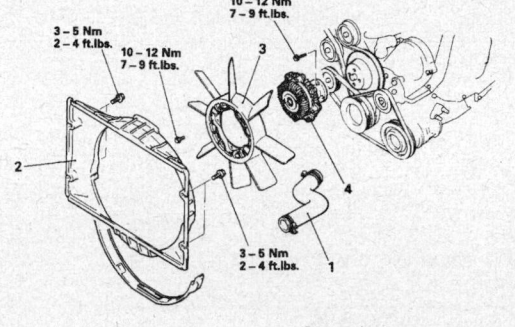

3.0L Engine

Radiator removal steps
1. Drain plug
2. Cap
3. Overflow tube
4. Water level sensor connector
5. Reserve tank
6. Radiator upper hose
7. Radiator lower hose
8. Automatic transaxle oil cooler hoses <Vehicles with A/T>
9. Condenser fan motor connector <Vehicles with air conditioning>
10. Condenser fan motor assembly <Vehicles with air conditioning>
11. Radiator fan motor connector
12. Radiator fan motor assembly
13. Upper insulator
14. Radiator assembly
15. Lower insulator

16. Fan
17. Radiator fan motor
18. Resistor
19. Shroud

Radiator fan motor assembly removal steps
1. Drain plug
2. Cap
6. Radiator upper hose
9. Condenser fan motor connector <Vehicles with air conditioning>
10. Condenser fan motor assembly <Vehicles with air conditioning>
11. Radiator fan motor connector
12. Radiator fan motor assembly
16. Fan
17. Radiator fan motor
18. Resistor
19. Shroud

MT1089100077000X

Fig. 27 Component replacement. 3000GT

Removal steps
1. Radiator upper hose
2. Radiator upper shroud <2.4L Engine>
   Radiator shroud <3.0L Engine>
3. Cooling fan
4. Fan clutch

MT1089300116000X

Fig. 28 Cooling fan replacement. Pickup

Viscous Clutch Cooling Fans

INDEX

PRECAUTIONS

AIR BAG SYSTEMS

Refer to "Air Bag System Precautions" in the front of this manual for system disarming and arming procedures.

BATTERY GROUND CABLE

Prior to service, disconnect battery ground cable and isolate as required.

COMPONENT SERVICE

INSPECTION

Cooling Fan

1. Inspect fan blades for cracks or other signs of damage.
2. Inspect fan hub and bolt hole areas for cracks or other signs of damage.

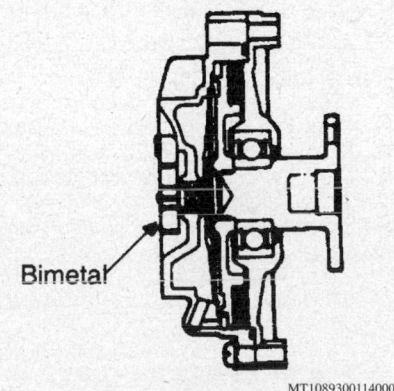

Bimetal

MT1089300114000X

Fig. 1 Fan clutch

3. Replace cooling fan if any portion appears to be cracked or otherwise damaged.

Fan Clutch

1. Inspect fan clutch for fluid leaks at case joints and seals. **Fluid loss will result in decreased fan rotation and engine overheating.**
2. Rotate fan by hand. If moderate resistance is noted, fan clutch operation is satisfactory; if little or no resistance is felt, fan clutch should be replaced.
3. Inspect bi-metal strip, **Fig. 1,** for signs of damage.

COMPONENT REPLACEMENT

Refer to "Electric Cooling Fans" section when replacing the cooling fan or any related components.

Dash Gauges

NOTE: On Air Bag Equipped Models, Refer To "Air Bag System Precautions" Located In The Front Of This Manual For System Disarming & Arming Procedures.

NOTE: Refer To The "Dash Panel Service" Section For Dash Panel Removal Procedures.

NOTE: Refer To The "Electronic Instrumentation" Section In MOTOR'S "Imported Engine Performance & Driveability Manual" For Information Related To Electronic Instrumentation.

INDEX

PRECAUTIONS

AIR BAG SYSTEMS

Refer to "Air Bag System Precautions" in the front of this manual for system disarming and arming procedures.

BATTERY GROUND CABLE

Prior to service, disconnect battery ground cable and isolate as required.

GAUGES

DESCRIPTION

FUEL

When the ignition key is placed in the On position, power is supplied to the fuel gauge. When the fuel tank is full, the fuel gauge unit's resistance is very low and current flow is high, causing the indicator to reside in the Full or "F" range. A low fuel level generates high resistance at the unit and reduces current flow to the gauge, causing the indicator to move toward the Empty or "E" range.

COOLANT TEMPERATURE

When the ignition key is placed in the On position, power is supplied to the coolant temperature gauge. When the coolant temperature is high, the temperature gauge unit's resistance is very low and current flow is high, causing the indicator to reside in the Hot or "H" range. A low coolant temperature generates high resistance at the unit and reduces current flow to the gauge, causing the indicator to move toward the Cool or "C" range.

OIL PRESSURE

When the ignition key is placed in the On position, power is supplied to the oil pressure gauge. When the oil pressure is high, the gauge's internal contacts remain closed for a longer period of time. This allows more current to flow and causes the gauge needle to swing toward the high pressure side. When the pressure is low, the gauge contacts open in a short period of time to reduce current flow in the circuit and cause the needle to swing toward the low pressure side.

DIAGNOSIS & TESTING

FUEL GAUGE

Except Pickup

Refer to **Figs. 1 through 8** for fuel gauge diagnosis.

Pickup

1. Disconnect electrical connector from fuel gauge unit in fuel tank.
2. Ground harness side connector through a 12 volt 3.4 watt test lamp.
3. Turn ignition switch to On position.
4. Test light should light and gauge needle should move.
5. If test light lights and needle does not move, replace fuel gauge.
6. If light does not light and needle does not move, check for a blown fuse or a broken wire.

COOLANT TEMPERATURE

Refer to **Fig. 9** for coolant temperature gauge diagnosis.

OIL PRESSURE

Refer to **Fig. 10** for oil pressure gauge diagnosis.

METERS

DESCRIPTION

Voltmeter

When the ignition key is placed in the On position, power is supplied to the voltmeter. The meter should indicate approximately 12 volts until the engine is started and the charging system begins to operate. If the charging system is functioning properly, the meter should indicate 12–16 volts while the engine is running.

DIAGNOSIS & TESTING

Voltmeter

Refer to **Fig. 11** for voltmeter diagnosis and testing procedures.

WARNING LAMPS

DESCRIPTION

Oil Pressure

The oil pressure warning lamp illuminates when the ignition key is placed in the On position, but will go out after the engine has started unless a problem exists in the oil circulation system. The lamp will also light during driving if oil fails to circulate properly or if pressure drops.

Brake

The brake warning lamp illuminates when the ignition key is placed in the On position, but will go out after the engine has started. However, if the parking brake is applied or if the brake fluid level is low, the lamp will remain lit.

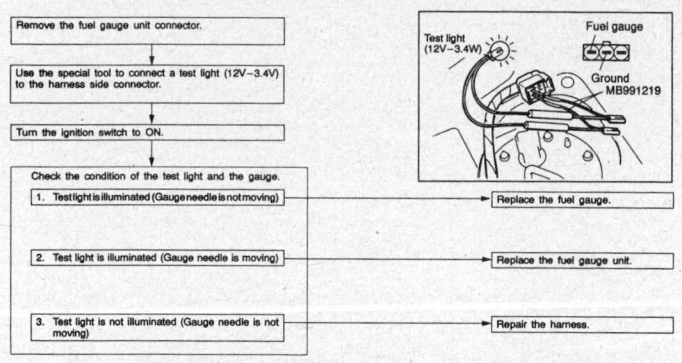

Fig. 1   Fuel gauge diagnosis. 1996 Diamante & 1996–98 Galant

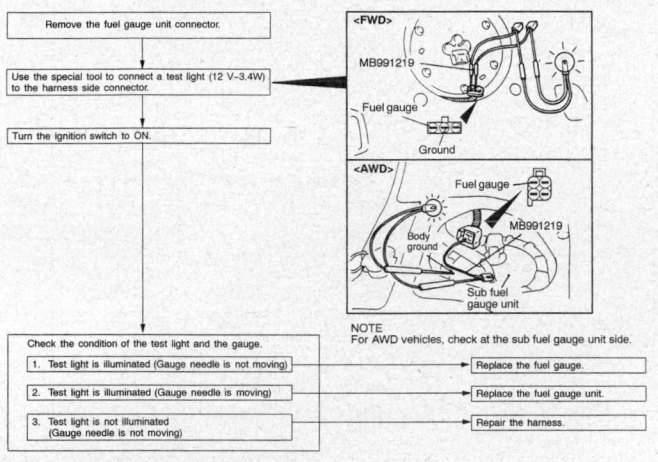

Fig. 3   Fuel gauge diagnosis. Eclipse

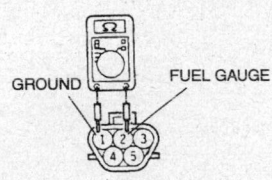

1. Check that resistance value between the fuel gauge terminal and ground terminal is at the standard value when the fuel gauge unit float is between point F (highest) and point E (lowest).

   Standard value:
   Point F: 3 – 5 Ω
   Point E: 110 – 112 Ω

2. Check that resistance value changes smoothly when the float moves slowly between point F (highest) and point E (lowest).

3. If all checks are correct, go to fuel gauge unit float height check. If any check is not correct, replace the fuel gauge unit.

MT9099900032000X

Fig. 4   Fuel gauge diagnosis. 1999 Galant

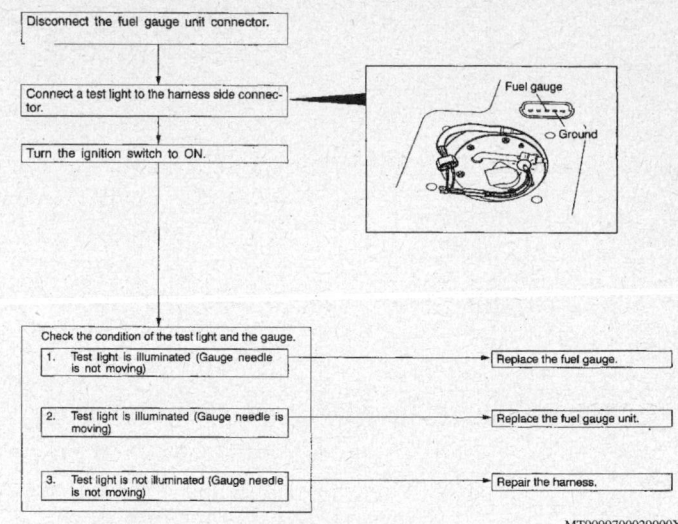

Fig. 2   Fuel gauge diagnosis. 1997–99 Diamante

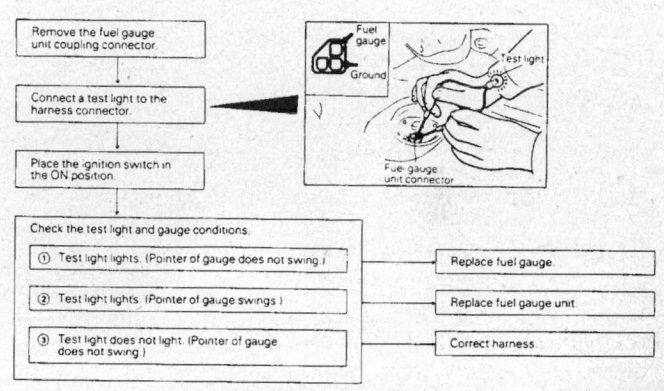

MT9099100018000X

Fig. 5   Fuel gauge diagnosis. Montero & 1996 Mirage

SPEEDOMETER

INSPECTION

A speedometer test drum and related equipment are required for completion of the following procedure.

1. Ensure tire pressures are correct, then position vehicle on speedometer test drum.

2. **On models equipped with Traction Control (TCL),** place TCL switch in Off position.

3. **On all models,** set parking brake, then secure vehicle as required by speedometer test equipment. **Failure to do so may allow vehicle to move unexpectedly during testing.**

4. Simulate a range of vehicle speeds, noting the following:

   a. **Do not operate clutch suddenly or change indicated speed rapidly during testing.**

   b. When standard indication reaches 20 mph, allowable indication range is 19–22 mph; at 40 mph, allowable range is 38–44 mph; at 60 mph, allowable range is 57–66 mph; at 80 mph, allowable range is 76–88 mph; at 100 mph, allowable range is 94–110 mph.

Low Fuel

The low fuel lamp illuminates when the fuel level in the tank falls below a specific level.

Seat Belt

The seat belt warning lamp illuminates for six seconds after the ignition key has been placed in the On position, regardless of whether the drivers seat belt has been fastened.

Four Wheel Steering Oil Level

The four wheel steering oil level warning lamp illuminates when the power steering oil level in the reservoir tank is low.

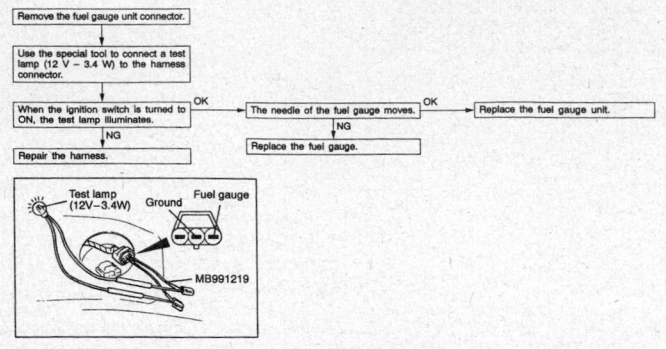

Fig. 6   Fuel gauge diagnosis. 1997–99 Mirage

MT9099900030000X

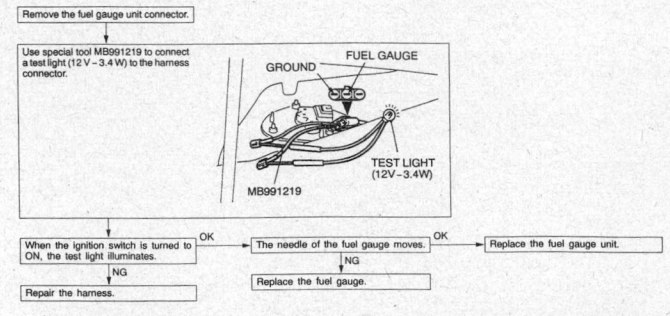

Fig. 7   Fuel gauge diagnosis. Montero Sport

MT9099900031000X

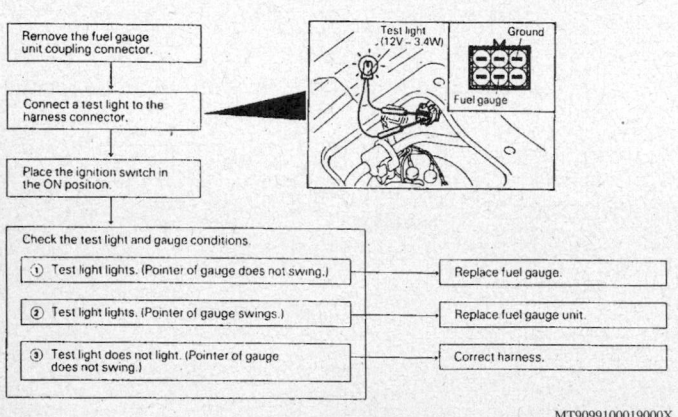

Fig. 8   Fuel gauge diagnosis. 3000GT

MT9099100019000X

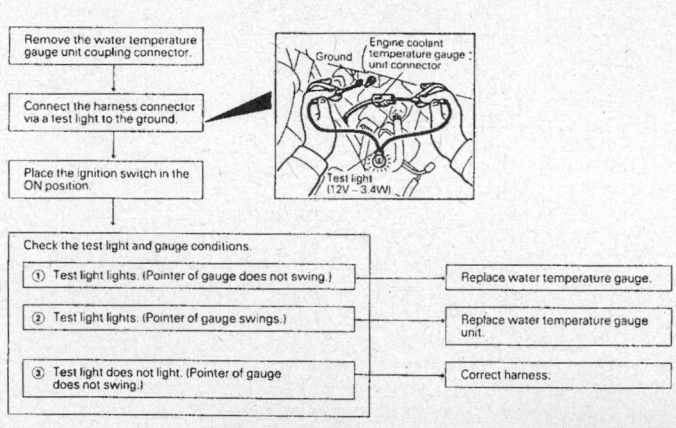

Fig. 9   Coolant temperature gauge diagnosis

MT9099100022000X

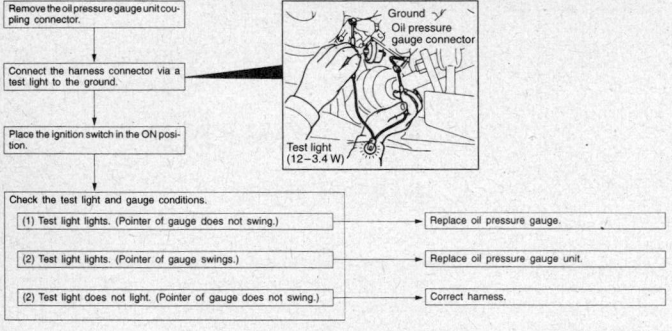

Fig. 10   Oil pressure gauge diagnosis

MT9099100023000X

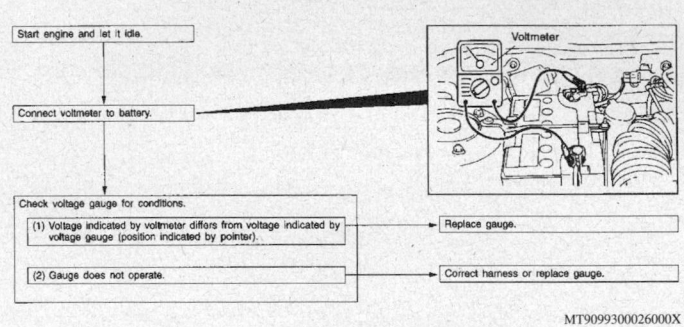

Fig. 11   Voltmeter diagnosis

MT9099300026000X

Starter Motors

INDEX

GENERAL INFORMATION

The starting system includes the battery, starter motor, magnet switch, ignition switch, Park/Neutral Position (PNP) switch (on models equipped with an automatic transmission), starter or PNP switch relays, connecting wires and battery cables.

When the ignition switch is turned to the Start position, current flows to energize the solenoid windings of the starter motor. As a result, the solenoid plunger and clutch shift lever (on reduction drive units) operate to cause the clutch pinion to engage with the flywheel ring gear, **Figs. 1 through 3.** At the same time, the magnet switch contacts close to energize the starter motor windings.

The overrunning running clutch pinion gear prevents damage that could be caused by overrunning the starter armature when the engine is started. When the engine is started, the ignition switch must be turned back to the On position to prevent damage to the starter motor or ring gear.

DESCRIPTION

MANUAL TRANSMISSION/TRANSAXLE

The interlock or clutch switch contact is switched Off when the clutch pedal is depressed, when the ignition switch is turned to the Start position, electricity flows to the starter or inhibitor relay and the starter motor. The contact of the starter is switched On and the starter motor is activated.

If the ignition switch is turned to the Start position without depressing the clutch pedal, electricity flows to the starter or inhibitor relay (coil), the interlock switch (contacts) and to ground. This results in that the contacts of the starter relay are switched Off and the power to the starter motor is interrupted.

AUTOMATIC TRANSMISSION/TRANSAXLE

when the ignition switch is turned to the Start position while the gear selector is in "P" or "N" position, the contact (magnetic switch) of the starter is switched On and the starter motor is activated.

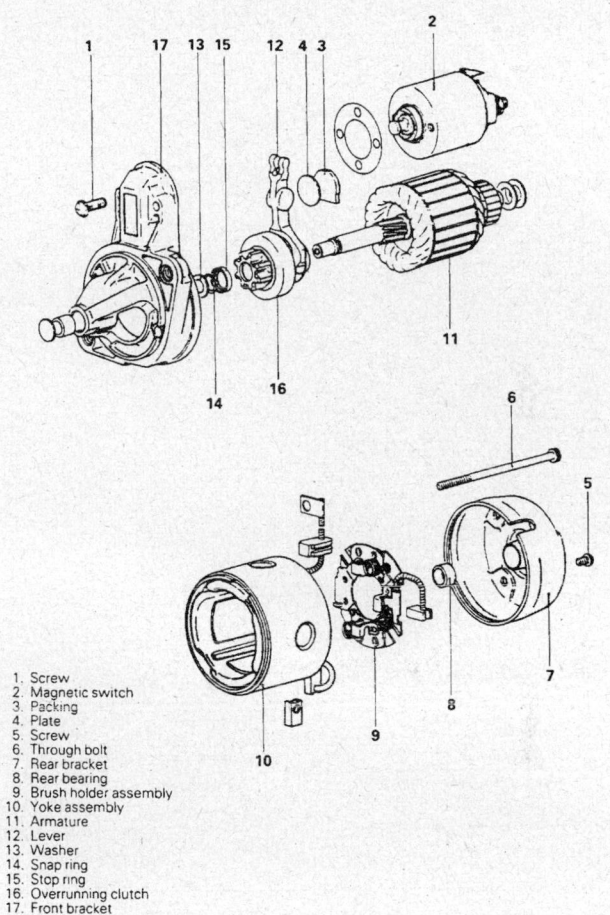

1. Screw
2. Magnetic switch
3. Packing
4. Plate
5. Screw
6. Through bolt
7. Rear bracket
8. Rear bearing
9. Brush holder assembly
10. Yoke assembly
11. Armature
12. Lever
13. Washer
14. Snap ring
15. Stop ring
16. Overrunning clutch
17. Front bracket

MT1129100006000X

Fig. 1 Exploded view of direct drive starter

TROUBLESHOOTING

Refer to **Fig. 4** when troubleshooting the starting system.

DIAGNOSIS & TESTING

PINION GAP INSPECTION

1. Disconnect field coil wire from "M" terminal of magnetic switch, **Fig. 5.**
2. Connect a 12 volt battery between "S" and "M" terminals. **This test must be performed in less than 10 seconds to prevent coil from burning out.**
3. Measure pinion gap with a suitable feeler gauge, **Fig. 6.**
4. If pinion gap is not as specified under "Starter Specifications," adjust by adding or removing gaskets between magnetic switch and front bracket.

MAGNETIC SWITCH PULL-IN TEST

1. Disconnect field coil wire from "M" terminal of magnetic switch, **Fig. 5.**
2. Connect a 12 volt battery between "S" and "M" terminals. **This test must be performed in less than 10 seconds to prevent coil from burning out.**
3. If pinion moves out, then pull-in coil is

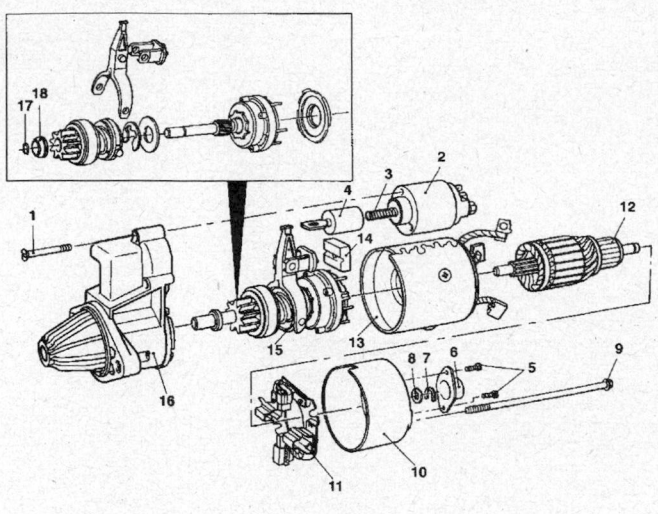

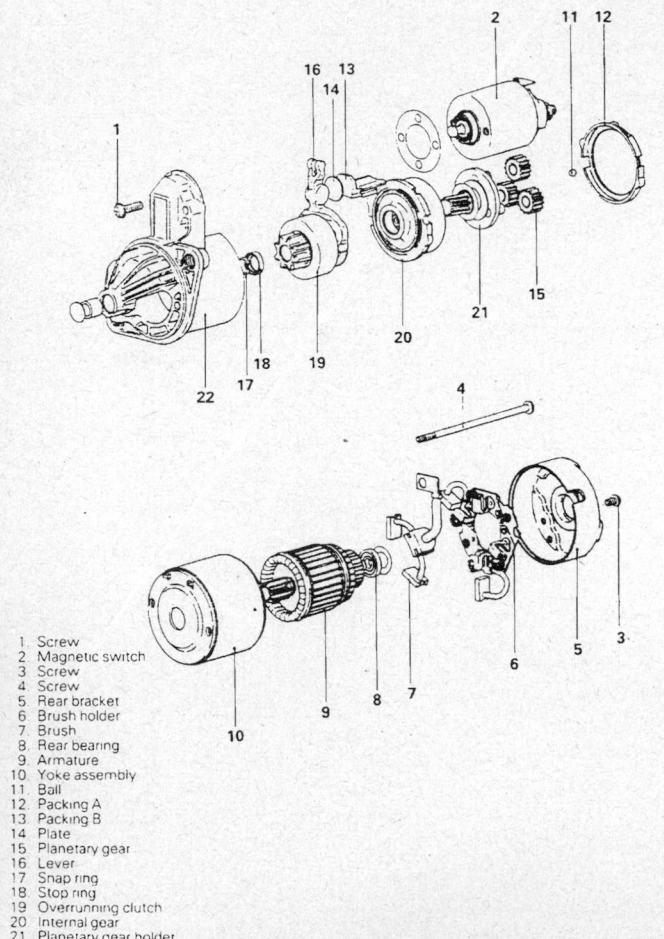

1. Screw
2. Magnetic switch
3. Screw
4. Screw
5. Rear bracket
6. Brush holder
7. Brush
8. Rear bearing
9. Armature
10. Yoke assembly
11. Ball
12. Packing A
13. Packing B
14. Plate
15. Planetary gear
16. Lever
17. Snap ring
18. Stop ring
19. Overrunning clutch
20. Internal gear
21. Planetary gear holder
22. Front bracket

MT1129100007000X

**Fig. 2 Exploded view of reduction drive starter.
Except 1997–99 Diamante**

Disassembly steps

1. Screw
2. Magnetic switch
3. Spring
4. Solenoid barrel
5. End cover screws
6. End cover
7. C clip
8. Flat washer
9. Through bolts
10. Rear housing

11. Brush holder
12. Armature assembly
13. Yoke assembly
14. Rubber seal
15. Overrunning clutch, drive pinion assembly and gear set
16. Front housing
17. Stop ring
18. Snap ring

MT1129700040000X

**Fig. 3 Exploded view of reduction drive starter.
1997–99 Diamante**

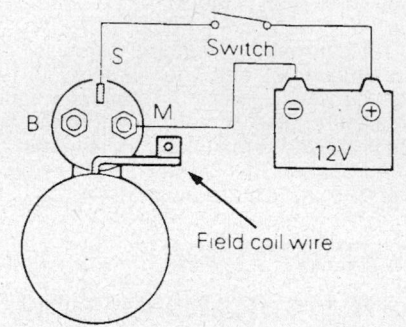

MT1129100010000X

Fig. 5 Magnetic switch inspection

Probable condition	Probable cause	Remedy
Engine will not crank.	Battery charge low	Charge or replace battery.
	Battery cables loose, corroded or worn	Repair or replace cables.
	Inhibitor switch faulty (Vehicle with automatic transaxle only)	Adjust or replace switch.
	Fusible link blown	Replace fusible link.
	Starter motor faulty	Repair starter motor.
	Ignition switch faulty	Replace ignition switch.
Engine cranks slowly	Battery charge low	Charge or replace battery.
	Battery cables loose, corroded or worn	Repair or replace cables.
	Starter motor faulty	Repair starter motor.
Starter keeps running.	Starter motor faulty	Repair starter motor.
	Ignition switch faulty	Replace ignition switch.
Starter spins but engine will not crank.	Short in wiring	Repair wiring.
	Pinion gear teeth broken or starter motor faulty	Repair starter motor.
	Ring gear teeth broken	Replace flywheel ring gear or torque converter.

MT1129100009000X

Fig. 4 Starting system troubleshooting chart

operating correctly. If pinion does not move out, replace magnetic switch.

MAGNETIC SWITCH HOLD-IN TEST

1. Disconnect field coil wire from "M" terminal of magnetic switch, **Fig. 5.**

2. Connect a 12 volt battery between "S" terminal and body ground, **Fig. 7.** This test must be performed in less than ten seconds to prevent coil from burning out.

3. If pinion remains out, magnetic switch is operating correctly. If pinion moves

in, hold-in circuit is open and the magnetic switch must be replaced.

FREE RUNNING TEST

1. Place starter in a suitable soft jawed vise.

2. Connect a fully charged 12 volt battery, ammeter and voltmeter to starter motor as shown in **Fig. 8** using a suitable 0–100 amperage ammeter, voltmeter and carbon pile rheostat.

3. Rotate carbon pile rheostat to full resistance position.

4. Adjust rheostat until battery voltage shown on the voltmeter matches free running test voltage listed under "Starter Specifications."

5. Confirm that the maximum amperage is as indicated under "Starter Specifications" chart in this section, ensure starter motor turns smoothly and freely.

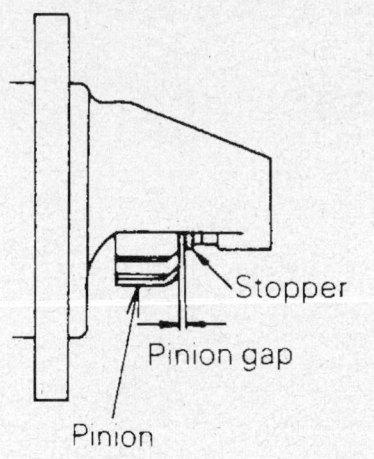

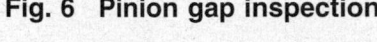

Fig. 6   Pinion gap inspection

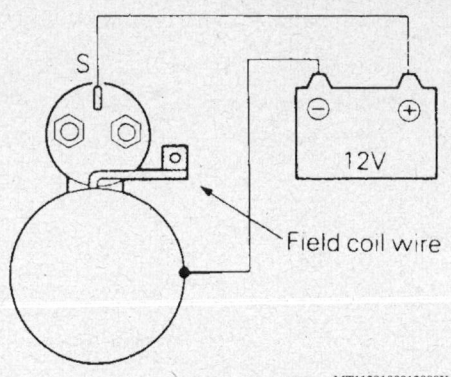

Fig. 7   Magnetic switch hold-in function inspection

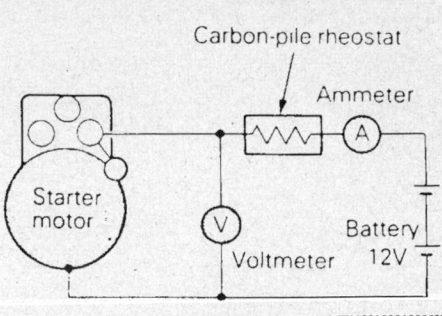

Fig. 8   Free running test connections

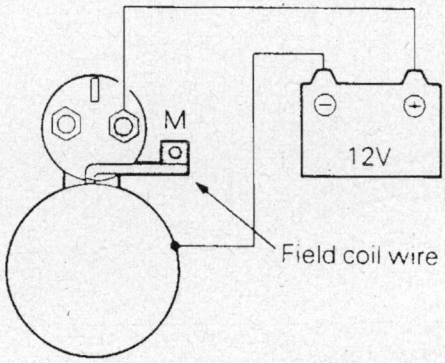

Fig. 9   Magnetic switch return function inspection

MAGNETIC SWITCH RETURN TEST

1. Disconnect field coil wire from "M" terminal of magnetic switch, **Fig. 9.**
2. Connect a 12 volt battery between "M" terminal and body ground. **This test must be performed in less than ten seconds to prevent coil from burning out.**
3. Pull pinion out and release. If pinion quickly returns to its original position, magnetic switch is operating correctly. If pinion does not return, replace magnetic switch.

STARTER & THEFT ALARM STARTER RELAY INSPECTION

For relay testing, refer to **Figs. 10 through 16.**

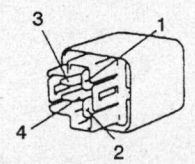

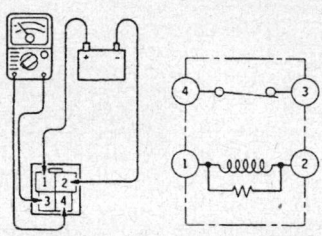

	TERMINAL No.			
	1	2	3	4
Battery voltage				
Not supplied	○———○			
Supplied	⊕———⊝		○———○	

Fig. 10   Starter relay test. Diamante

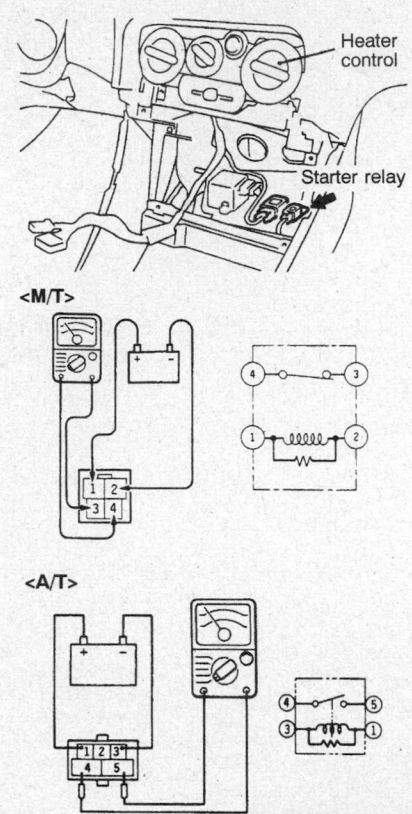

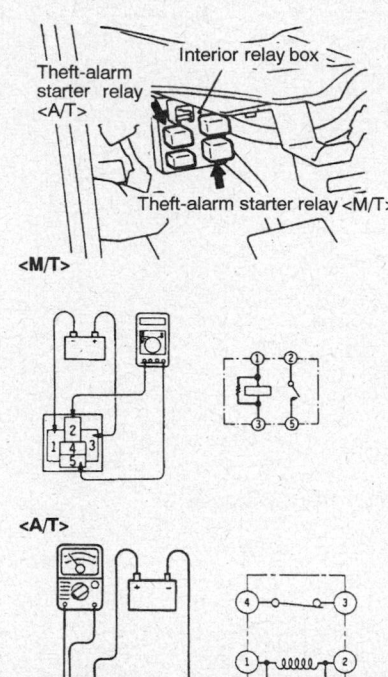

<M/T>

Battery voltage	Terminal No.			
	1	2	3	4
Power is not supplied	○—	—○	○—	—○
Power is supplied	⊕—	—⊖		

<A/T>

Battery voltage	Terminal No.				
	1	2	3	4	5
Power is not supplied	○—	—○			
Power is supplied	⊕—	—⊖	○—	—○	

MT1129900043000X

Fig. 11 Starter relay test. Eclipse

<M/T>

Battery voltage	Terminal No.			
	1	2	3	5
Power is not supplied	○—	—○		
Power is supplied	⊖—	—⊕	○—	—○

<A/T>

Battery voltage	Terminal No.			
	1	2	3	4
Power is not supplied	○—	—○	○—	—○
Power is supplied	⊕—	—⊖		

MT1129900044000X

Fig. 12 Theft alarm starter relay test. Eclipse

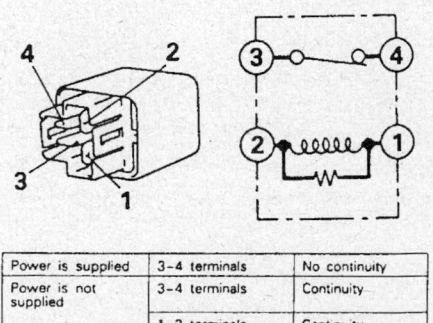

Power is supplied	3–4 terminals	No continuity
Power is not supplied	3–4 terminals	Continuity
	1–2 terminals	Continuity

MT1129200017000X

**Fig. 13 Starter relay test. Montero
& Pickup**

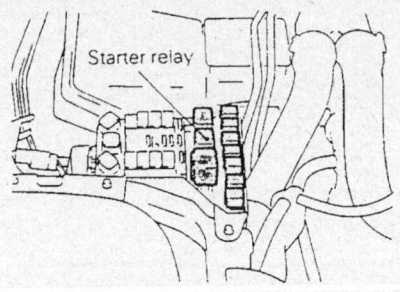

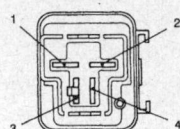

1. Set an ohmmeter check that there is continuity when the (+) terminal of the tester is connected to terminal 4 of the starter relay and the (−) terminal is connected to terminal 2.
2. Next, check that there is no continuity continuity when the (+) terminal is connected to terminal 2 and the (−) terminal is connected to terminal 4.
3. If the continuity checks in step 1 and 2 show a defect, replace the starter relay.

MT1129700041000X

Fig. 15   Starter relay test. 1997–99 Mirage

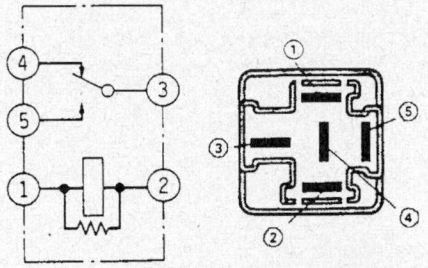

Power is supplied	3-4 terminals	No continuity
	3-5 terminals	Continuity
Power is not supplied	3-4 terminals	Continuity
	3-5 terminals	No continuity
	1-2 terminals	Continuity

MT1129100015000X

Fig. 14   Starter relay test. 3000GT & 1996 Mirage

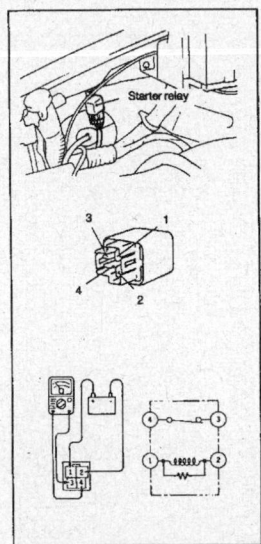

Battery voltage	Terminal No.			
Battery voltage	1	2	3	4
Not supplied	○—○		○	○
Supplied	⊕—⊖		○—○	

MT1129400039000X

Fig. 16   Starter relay test. 1996–98 Galant

STARTER SPECIFICATIONS

Model	Drive Type	Output, kW	Pinion Gap, Inch	Commutator		Free Speed Test		
				Runout, Inch	Diameter, Inch	Terminal Voltage	Max. Current, Amps	Min. RPM
Diamante	Reduction	1.20	.020–.079	.0020	①	11.0	90	3000
Eclipse & Eclipse Spyder	Direct⑤	.95	—	—	—	11.0	—	—
	Reduction⑥	1.40	.020–.079	.0020	1.158	11.0	90	3000
Galant	Reduction	1.20	.020–.079	.0020	1.158	11.0	90	3000
Mirage	Direct③	.70	.020–.079	.0020	1.260	11.5	60	6000
	Direct②	.90	.020–.079	.0020	1.260	11.5	60	6000
	Reduction④	1.20	.020–.079	.0020	1.158	11.0	90	2800
Montero & Montero Sport	Reduction	1.20	.020–.079	.0020	1.157	11.0	90	3000
Pickup	Direct⑧	.90	.020–.079	.0020	1.260	11.5	60	6600
	Reduction⑦	1.20	.020–.079	.0020	1.157	11.0	90	3000
3000GT	Reduction	1.20	.020–.079	.0020	1.158	11.0	90	3000

① — 1996: 1.158. 1997–99: 1.27.
② — 1.5L engine w/automatic transaxle & 1.8L engine w/manual transaxle.
③ — 1.5L engine w/manual transaxle.
④ — 1.8L engine w/automatic transaxle.
⑤ — 2.0L non-turbocharged engine.
⑥ — 2.0L turbocharged engine & 2.4L engine.
⑦ — 2.4L engine w/automatic transmission & 3.0L engine.
⑧ — 2.4L engine w/manual transmission.

Alternators

INDEX

GENERAL INFORMATION

When the ignition switch is turned to the On position and before the engine starts, current flows through the charging indicator light then to the alternator and ground, causing the charging light to illuminate.

Once the engine starts, battery voltage is applied to the alternator "S" or "R" terminal. The battery voltage imposed on this terminal is monitored by the IC voltage regulator, and according to the voltage detected the IC voltage regulator regulates the alternator field coil current, thus controlling the alternator current.

Once the alternator starts alternator starts generating current, a slightly higher voltage than battery voltage is applied to terminal "L." This prevents current from flowing to the charging indicator light and the light goes off.

At alternator terminal "B," a load current proportional to the battery voltage is produced and is sent to any load. The alternator relay provides charge to the battery even when the charging indicator light bulb is burnt out.

TROUBLESHOOTING

1. If charging indicator light does not illuminate when Ignition switch is turned to On position (before engine starts), check charge indicator lamp bulb.
2. If charging indicator light fails to go off once engine starts, check drive belt tension and IC voltage regulator.
3. If battery is discharged or overcharged, check IC voltage regulator.
4. If charging warning light illuminates dimly, check diode inside combination meter for a short.

DIAGNOSIS & TESTING

IN-VEHICLE TESTS

ALTERNATOR OUTPUT WIRE VOLTAGE DROP TEST

This test judges whether or not the wiring between alternator "B" terminal and battery positive terminal is sound by voltage drop method.
1. Refer to **Fig. 1** when preparing the charging system as follows:
   a. Turn ignition switch to Off position.
   b. disconnect battery ground cable.
   c. Disconnect alternator output lead from alternator terminal "B."
   d. Connect a 0–100 DC ammeter in series to terminal "B" and the dis-

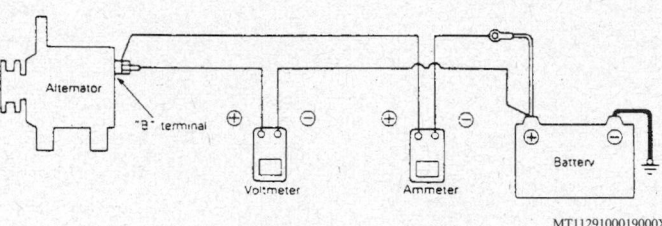

MT1129100019000X

Fig. 1   Voltage drop test

connected output lead. Connect positive lead of meter to terminal "B" and negative lead to disconnected output wire.
   e. Connect positive lead of a digital voltmeter to alternator terminal "B" and negative lead to battery positive terminal.
   f. Connect battery ground cable.
2. Start engine.
3. Turn headlights and small lights On or Off and adjust engine speed so that ammeter reads 20 amps and read value on voltmeter under this condition.
4. If voltmeter indicates maximum value of .2 volts, system is operating correctly.
5. If voltmeter indicates a value that is larger than the standard value, poor wiring is suspected between terminal "B" and battery positive terminal.
6. After completion of test, set engine speed at idle, turn Off lights and ignition switch.
7. Disconnect battery ground.
8. Disconnect ammeter and voltmeter then reconnect alternator output wire and connect battery ground cable.

OUTPUT CURRENT TEST

This test judges whether or not the alternator gives an output current that is equivalent to the normal output.
1. Ensure battery condition is in sound state and that the tension of the alternator drive belt is correct as outlined under "Drive Belt Tension" in the appropriate engine section.
2. Refer to **Fig. 2** when preparing the charging system as follows:
   a. Turn ignition switch to Off position.
   b. Disconnect battery ground cable.
   c. Disconnect alternator output wire from terminal "B."
   d. Connect a 0–100 DC ammeter positive lead to terminal "B" and the negative lead to the disconnected output wire. **Tighten all connections using suitable bolt and nut as a heavy current will flow. Do**

not relay on clips.
   e. Connect a 0–20 voltmeter positive lead to alternator terminal "B" and negative lead to a sound ground.
   f. Connect an engine tachometer then the battery ground cable.
3. Ensure voltmeter reads same voltage as battery.
4. Turn headlights On and start engine.
5. Set headlight on high beam and heater blower switch on high, quickly increase engine speed to 2500 RPM and read maximum output current indicated on ammeter.
6. Calculate output limit value. Limit value is equal to 70% of output rating listed under "Alternator Specifications" in this section.
7. Ammeter reading must be higher than limit value. If reading is lower and output wire is satisfactory, replace alternator.
8. Normal output current value is shown in nameplate attached to alternator. The output current value changed with electrical load and temperature. therefore the normal output current may not be obtained if the vehicle electrical load, at time of test, is small. In such a case, discharge battery by leaving headlights on or by using another vehicle's lights to increase load.
9. After completion of test, set engine speed at idle and turn off lights and ignition switch.
10. Disconnect battery ground cable.
11. Disconnect ammeter and voltmeter then reconnect alternator output wire and connect battery ground cable.

REGULATED VOLTAGE TEST

The purpose of this test is to check that the electronic voltage regulator controls the voltage correctly.
1. Prepare charging system, **Fig. 3,** as follows:
   a. Ensure battery condition is good and alternator drive belt tension is correct. Refer to "Belt Tension Data" in appropriate engine section.

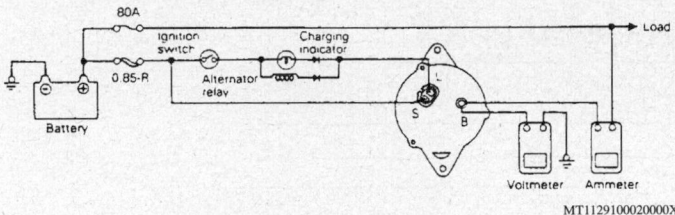

Fig. 2   Output current test

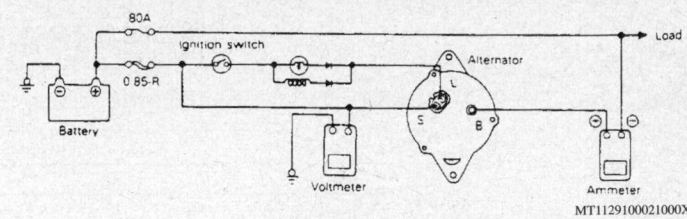

Fig. 3   Regulated voltage test

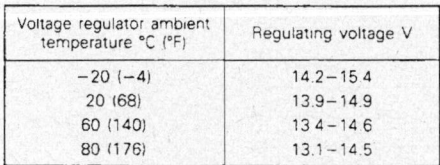

Voltage regulator ambient temperature °C (°F)	Regulating voltage V
−20 (−4)	14.2–15.4
20 (68)	13.9–14.9
60 (140)	13.4–14.6
80 (176)	13.1–14.5

MT1129100022000X

Fig. 4   Regulated voltage table

  b. Turn ignition switch to Off position.
  c. Disconnect battery ground cable.
  d. Connect the positive lead of a digital voltmeter to terminal "S" of the alternator and the negative lead to a sound ground or battery ground terminal.
  e. Disconnect alternator output wire from terminal "B."
  f. Connect the positive lead of a 0–100 ammeter to terminal "B" and the negative lead to the disconnected output wire.
  g. Connect an engine tachometer and then the battery ground cable.
2. Turn ignition switch to On position. If voltmeter reads zero volts, there is an open circuit in wire between alternator terminal "S" and battery positive terminal.
3. Start engine. Keep all electrical components Off.
4. run engine at 2500 RPM and read voltmeter when output current drops to 10 amps or less.
5. If voltmeter reading agrees with the value shown in **Fig. 4**, the voltage regulator is functioning correctly. If reading is other than standard value, replace the voltage regulator.
6. After completion of test, set engine speed at idle, turn Off ignition switch.
7. Disconnect battery ground.
8. Disconnect ammeter and voltmeter then reconnect alternator output wire and connect battery ground cable.

BENCH TESTS

ROTOR

1. Check rotor for continuity. Ensure

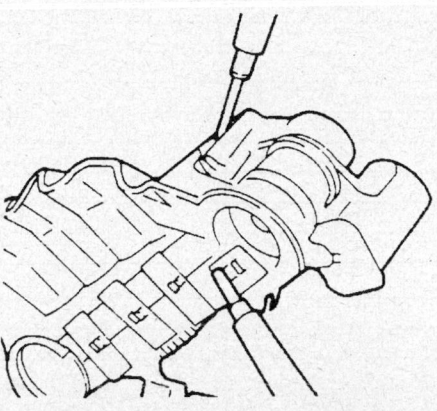

MT1129100023000X

Fig. 5   Positive rectifier test

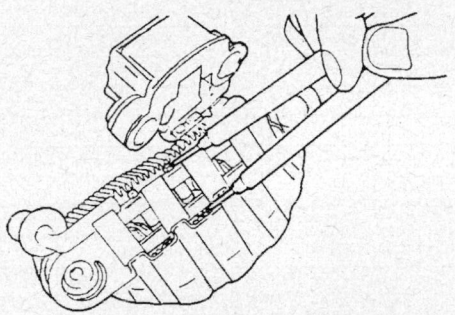

MT1129100025000X

Fig. 7   Diode trio test

there is continuity between slip rings.
2. If resistance is not 3–5 ohms, a short exists in rotor. If no continuity exists or if there is a short, replace rotor assembly.
3. Ensure there is no continuity between slip ring and core. If continuity exists,

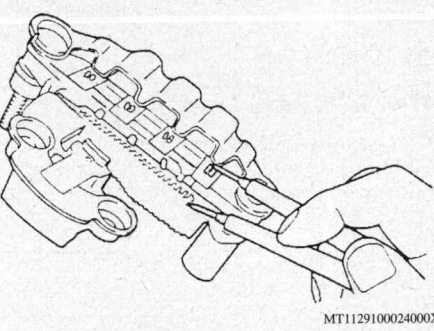

MT1129100024000X

Fig. 6   Negative rectifier test

replace rotor assembly.

STATOR

1. Ensure continuity exists between coil leads. Replace stator if no continuity exists.
2. Ensure there is no continuity between coil and core. Replace stator is continuity exists.

RECTIFIERS

Positive Rectifier Test

Ensure continuity exists in only one direction between positive rectifier and stator coil lead, **Fig. 5**. If continuity exists in both directions, diode is shorted and rectifier must be replaced.

Negative Rectifier Test

Ensure continuity exists in only one direction between negative rectifier and stator coil lead, **Fig. 6**. If continuity exists in both directions, diode is shorted and rectifier must be replaced.

Diode Trio Test

Ensure continuity exists in only one direction between both ends of each diode, **Fig. 7**. If continuity exists in both directions, diode is faulty and heat sink assembly must be replaced.

ALTERNATOR SPECIFICATIONS

Model	Engine, Liter	Identification Number	Output Rating, Amps①⑤
1996			
Diamante	3.0L	—	90
Eclipse	2.0L⑦	A002T81292	90
	2.0L⑧	A002T81292	90
	2.4L	A002T81292	90
Galant	2.4L	A2TA0891	90
Mirage	1.5L	—	70
	1.8L	—	75
Montero	3.0L⑨	—	75
	3.0L⑥	—	90
	3.5L	—	90
Pickup	2.4L	—	40
	3.0L	—	65
3000GT	3.0L	—	95
1997–99			
Diamante	3.5L	—	110
Eclipse & Eclipse Spyder	2.0L③⑦	A2TA0891	75
	2.0L④⑦	A2TA0892	75
	2.0L③⑧	A2TA0891	75
	2.0L④⑧	A2TA0892	75
	2.4L③	A2TA0891	75
	2.4L④	A2T82791	90
Galant	2.4L	A2TA82791	90
Mirage	1.5L	A2TA5191	80
	1.8L	②	80
Montero	3.5L	—	85
Montero Sport	2.4L	—	85
	3.0L	—	85
3000GT	3.0L SOHC	—	90
	3.0L DOHC	—	110

① — At 12 volts.

② — 1997–98: A2TA4991. 1999: A2TA5391.

③ — Manual transaxle.

④ — Automatic transaxle.

⑤ — Internal voltage regulator.

⑥ — 24 valve engine.

⑦ — Non-turbocharged engine.

⑧ — Turbocharged engine.

⑨ — 12 valve engine.

Speed Control Systems

NOTE: On Air Bag Equipped Models, Refer To "Air Bag System Precautions" Located In The Front Of This Manual For System Disarming & Arming Procedures.

INDEX

PRECAUTIONS

AIR BAG SYSTEMS

Refer to "Air Bag System Precautions" in the front of this manual for system disarming and arming procedures.

BATTERY GROUND CABLE

Prior to service, disconnect battery ground cable and isolate as required.

TROUBLESHOOTING

Refer to **Figs. 1 through 5** when troubleshooting the speed control system.

ADJUSTMENTS

SPEED CONTROL CABLE

MIRAGE

1. Turn all accessories off, warm up engine until specified idle speed is reached, then turn engine off.
2. Remove air cleaner, then depress accelerator pedal completely, ensure throttle valve operates smoothly from full close to full open.
3. Remove actuator cover.
4. **On models equipped with automatic transaxle or SOHC engine,** turn ignition switch to On position for 15 seconds, ensure throttle lever returns.
5. **On all models,** check the inner cable (throttle valve side) for too much or too little slack. Cable deflection should measure .04–.08 inch. If not within specified limits, adjust as follows:
   a. Loosen the adjustment bolts at the air intake plenum side and free inner cable, **Fig. 6.** Adjust cable to specified limits. **Excessive cable deflection will cause vehicle speed to drop; excessive cable tension will cause idle speed to increase.**
   b. After adjustment of the cable, en-

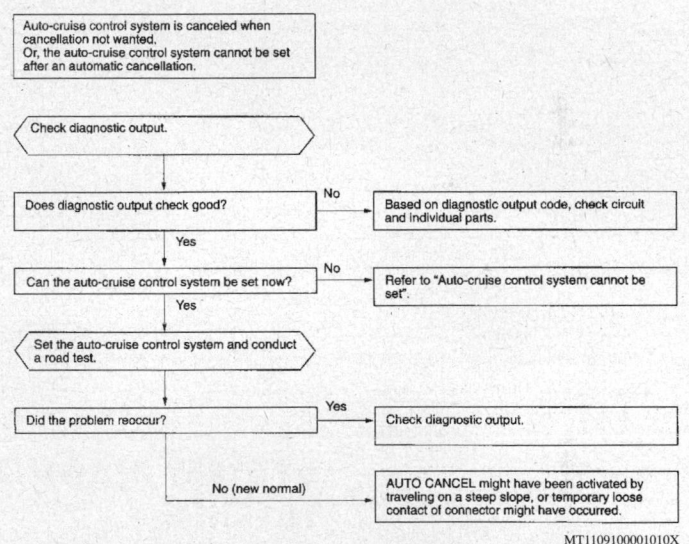

Fig. 1 Troubleshooting (Part 1 of 4). Mirage

sure throttle lever contacts idle position switch.
6. Adjust cable (accelerator pedal side) as follows:
   a. Loosen cable locknut.
   b. Adjust inner cable deflection to 0–.04 inch on models with manual transaxle or .08–.12 inch on models with automatic transaxle, then tighten adjusting bolt, **Fig. 7,** or locknut. **Use caution not to decrease play in cable B (throttle valve side). Use caution not to decrease play in cable B (throttle valve side).**
   c. Ensure throttle lever travels distance shown in **Fig. 8.**
   d. Ensure throttle valve fully opens and closes when operating accelerator pedal.
   e. Install air cleaner.

ECLIPSE

2.0L Non-Turbocharged Engine

Hold link (C), **Fig. 9,** where it contacts link (B), then secure the speed control cable in position.

PICKUP

1. Turn all accessories off, warm up engine until specified idling speed is reached, then turn engine off.
2. Remove air cleaner, then depress the accelerator pedal down, ensure throttle valve operates smoothly from full close to full open.
3. Remove actuator cover.
4. Loosen locknuts of the cables and let inner cables sag.
5. Contact lever P to stopper, then turn adjusting nut to lengthen outer cable,

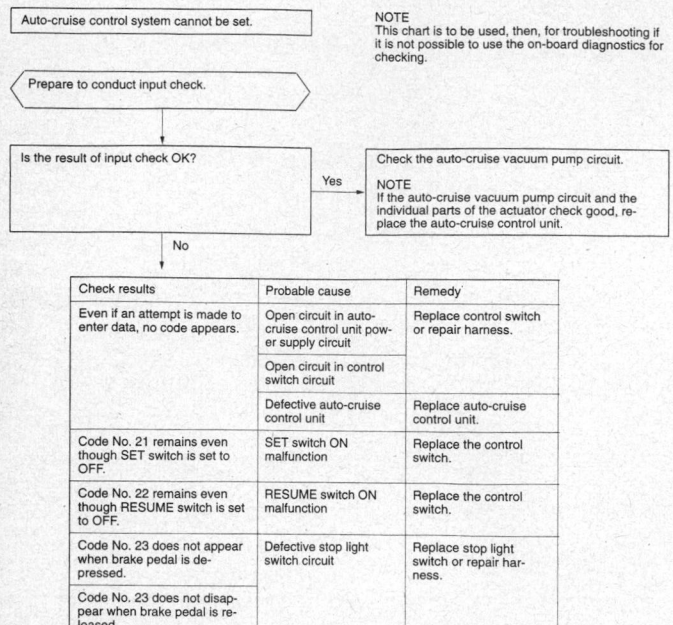

NOTE
This chart is to be used, then, for troubleshooting if it is not possible to use the on-board diagnostics for checking.

Auto-cruise control system cannot be set.

Prepare to conduct input check.

Is the result of input check OK? — Yes → Check the auto-cruise vacuum pump circuit.
NOTE
If the auto-cruise vacuum pump circuit and the individual parts of the actuator check good, replace the auto-cruise control unit.

No ↓

Check results	Probable cause	Remedy
Even if an attempt is made to enter data, no code appears.	Open circuit in auto-cruise control unit power supply circuit	Replace control switch or repair harness.
	Open circuit in control switch circuit	
	Defective auto-cruise control unit	Replace auto-cruise control unit.
Code No. 21 remains even though SET switch is set to OFF.	SET switch ON malfunction	Replace the control switch.
Code No. 22 remains even though RESUME switch is set to OFF.	RESUME switch ON malfunction	Replace the control switch.
Code No. 23 does not appear when brake pedal is depressed.	Defective stop light switch circuit	Replace stop light switch or repair harness.
Code No. 23 does not disappear when brake pedal is released.		
Code No. 26 does not disappear when clutch pedal is released. <M/T>	Defective clutch switch circuit	Replace clutch switch or repair harness.
Code No. 26 does not disappear when SELECT lever is placed in a position other than "N" and "P". <A/T>	Defective Park/Neutral position switch circuit	Replace Park/Neutral position switch or repair harness.
Code No. 25 does not appear when vehicle is traveling at less than 40 km/h (25 mph).	Defective vehicle speed sensor circuit	Check or repair vehicle speed sensor circuit.
Code No. 25 does not disappear or code No. 24 does not appear when vehicle speed is increased to more than approximately 40 km/h (25 mph).		

MT1109100001020X

Fig. 1 Troubleshooting (Part 2 of 4). Mirage

Trouble symptom	Probable cause	Remedy
• The set vehicle speed varies greatly upward or downward. • "Hunting" (repeated alternating acceleration and deceleration) occurs after setting is made.	Malfunction of the vehicle speed sensor circuit	Repair the vehicle speed sensor system, or replace the part.
	Malfunction of the speedometer cable or speedometer drive gear	
	Auto-cruise vacuum pump circuit poor contact	Repair the auto-cruise vacuum pump system, or replace the part.
	Malfunction of the auto-cruise vacuum pump	
	Malfunction of the auto-cruise control unit	Replace the auto-cruise control unit.
The auto-cruise control system is not canceled when the brake pedal is depressed.	Brake switch (for auto-cruise control) malfunction (short-circuit)	Repair the harness or replace the stop light switch.
	Auto-cruise vacuum pump drive circuit short-circuit	Repair the harness or replace the auto-cruise vacuum pump.
	Malfunction of the auto-cruise control unit	Replace the auto-cruise control unit.
The auto-cruise control system is not canceled when the clutch pedal is depressed. <M/T> (It is canceled, however, when the brake pedal is depressed.)	Damaged or disconnected wiring of clutch switch input circuit	Repair the harness, or repair or replace the clutch switch.
	Clutch switch improper installation (won't switch ON)	
	Malfunction of the auto-cruise control unit	Replace the auto-cruise control unit.
The auto-cruise control system is not canceled when the shift lever is moved to the "N" position. <A/T> (It is canceled, however, when the brake pedal is depressed.)	Damaged or disconnected wiring of Park/Neutral position switch input circuit	Repair the harness, or repair or replace the Park/Neutral position switch.
	Improper adjustment of Park/Neutral position switch	
	Malfunction of the auto-cruise control unit	Replace the auto-cruise control unit.

MT1109100001030X

Fig. 1 Troubleshooting (Part 3 of 4). Mirage

until just before the lever P begins to operate, **Fig. 10**.
6. Turn back adjusting nut ½ turn, then tighten locking nut. Deflection of cable A should be between 0–.04 inch.
7. Turn adjusting nut of cable B at carburetor or throttle body for a distance of 0–.08 inch between levers C and P, **Fig. 11**.

AUTO CRUISE CONTROL CABLE

DIAMANTE, MONTERO & MONTERO SPORT

1. Inspect cables for sharp bends and straighten as necessary.
2. Fully depress accelerator pedal to ensure throttle lever moves smoothly from closed to open position.
3. Determine point at which intermediate link (A), **Figs. 12 and 13**, contacts link (B), then unscrew adjusting nut (A) approximately one full turn in this position.
4. Ensure inner cable play is .04–.08 inch, then secure cable with locknut.

GALANT, 3000GT & ECLIPSE w/2.0L TURBOCHARGED & 2.4L ENGINES

1. Determine position at which intermediate link (C), **Fig. 14**, touches link (B). At this contact point, loosen adjusting nut approximately one turn.

2. Ensure inner cable play is .04–.08 inch, then secure cable with locknut.

SYSTEM DIAGNOSIS & TESTING

Auto Cruise Control Signal Circuit Inspection

Refer to **Figs. 15 through 17** for test procedure.

Accessing Diagnostic Trouble Codes

Using suitable scan tool, connect cable to Data Link Connector (DLC). follow scan tool manufacturer's instructions for obtaining trouble codes, then refer to "Diagnostic Trouble Code Interpretation."

Diagnostic Trouble Code Interpretation

Refer to **Figs. 18 through 23** for diagnostic trouble code interpretation.

Wiring Diagrams

Refer to **Figs. 24 through 33** for wiring diagrams.

Diagnostic Tests

Refer to **Figs. 34 through 150** for diagnostic tests and inspection procedures.

Clearing Diagnostic Trouble Codes

Refer to scan tool manufacturer's instructions when clearing trouble codes.

COMPONENT DIAGNOSIS & TESTING

Stop Lamp/Brake Switch

1. Disconnect electrical connector from switch.
2. Check for continuity between terminals of switch, **Figs. 151 and 152**.

Clutch Switch

1. Disconnect electrical connector from switch.
2. Check for continuity between terminals when clutch pedal is depressed.

Trouble symptom	Probable cause	Remedy
Cannot accelerate or resume speed by using the RESUME switch.	Open or short circuit in RESUME switch circuit in control switch	Replace the control switch.
	Auto-cruise vacuum pump circuit poor contact	Repair the harness or replace the auto-cruise vacuum pump and actuator.
	Malfunction of the auto-cruise vacuum pump and actuator (including air leaks from negative pressure passage)	
	Malfunction of the auto-cruise control unit.	Replace the auto-cruise control unit.
Auto-cruise control system can be set while traveling at a vehicle speed of less than 40 km/h (25 mph), or there is no automatic cancellation at that speed	Malfunction of the vehicle speed sensor circuit	Repair the vehicle speed sensor system, or replace the part.
	Malfunction of the speedometer cable or the speedometer drive gear	
	Malfunction of the auto-cruise control unit.	Replace the auto-cruise control unit.
The auto-cruise control switch indicator light does not illuminate. (But auto-cruise control system is normal.)	Damaged or disconnected bulb of auto-cruise control switch indicator	Repair the harness or replace the control switch.
	Harness damaged or disconnected	
Malfunction of control function by ON/OFF switching of 4 A/T accelerator switch (Non-operation of damper clutch, 2nd gear hold, etc.)	Malfunction of circuit related to accelerator switch OFF function	Repair the harness or replace the part.
	Malfunction of the auto-cruise control unit.	
Overdrive is not canceled during fixed speed driving. <A/T>	Malfunction of circuit related to overdrive cancellation, or malfunction of auto-cruise control unit	Repair the harness or replace the part.
No shift to overdrive during manual driving. <A/T>		
The auto-cruise control indicator light does not illuminate. (But auto-cruise control system is normal.)	Damaged or disconnected bulb of indicator light	Repair the harness or replace the bulb.
	Harness damaged or disconnected	

MT1109100001040X

Fig. 1 Troubleshooting (Part 4 of 4). Mirage

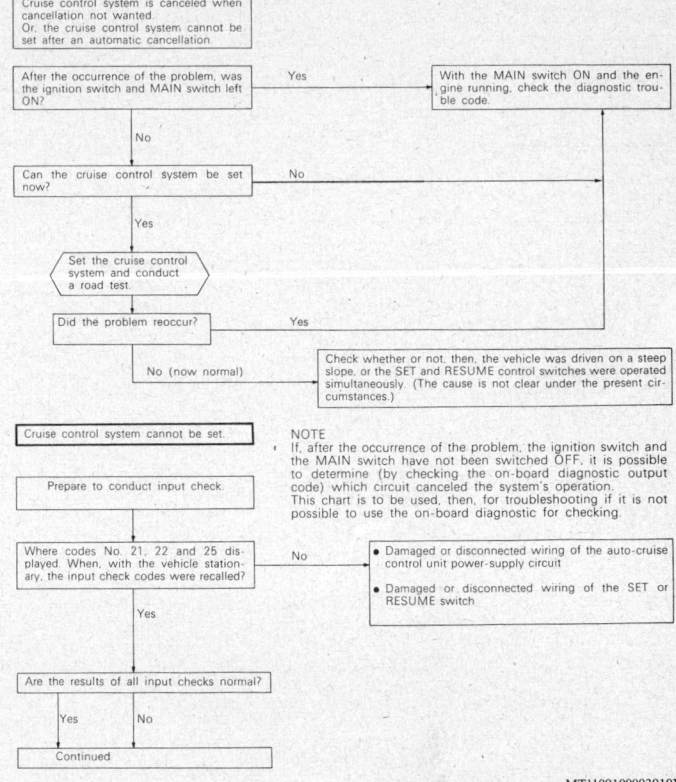

MT1109100003010X

Fig. 2 Troubleshooting (Part 1 of 3). Pickup

Park/Neutral Position (PNP) Switch

1. Disconnect electrical connector from switch.
2. Place selector lever in the N, then P ranges to check switch. Check continuity between terminals as shown in **Figs. 153 and 154.**

Speed Control Actuator

ELECTRICAL TYPE
CONTINUITY INSPECTION
Except Pickup

1. Disconnect electrical connector.
2. Measure clutch coil resistance between terminals 1 and 2, **Fig. 155.** Standard value is 20 ohms.

Pickup

1. Disconnect electrical connector.
2. Measure resistance value of clutch coil, between terminals 1 and 2, **Fig. 155.** Standard value is 45–65 ohms.
3. Measure resistance value of clutch coil, between terminals 1 and 3, **Fig. 155.** Standard value is 25–35 ohms.
4. Measure resistance value of clutch coil, between terminals 1 and 4, **Fig. 155.** Standard value is 18–28 ohms.

ACTUATOR OPERATION INSPECTION

Except Pickup

1. Connect terminal 1 of actuator through ammeter to battery positive terminal, **Fig. 156.**
2. Connect terminal 2 to battery negative terminal.
3. Solenoid should emit an audible click and ammeter should measure .5–.7 amps. If not, proceed as follows:
   a. If no solenoid noise is heard and ammeter reads 0 amps, check for damaged or disconnected clutch coil wiring.
   b. If no solenoid sound is heard, but ammeter reads infinite, check for clutch coil short circuit.

Pickup

1. Disconnect actuator, then connect battery voltage and an ammeter, **Fig. 157.**
2. Apply 16 inches vacuum to actuator. Ensure actuator operation is as specified in **Fig. 158.**
3. Disconnect wire from terminal 2 and ensure actuator is as specified in **Fig. 159.**
4. Disconnect wire on terminal 2 then from terminal 3 one at a time and ensure actuator is as specified in **Fig. 160.**

MOTOR PULL DIRECTION & LIMIT SWITCH OPERATION INSPECTION

Except Pickup

1. Connect ammeters to actuator side connector, **Fig. 161.**
2. Current should be cut off when selector is turned in Pull (fully open) direction for full stroke. Ammeter A1 should read .5–.7 amps. Ammeter A2 should read less than .5 amps, when current is on.
3. If selector moves in Pull direction, ammeter reads .5–.7 amps, but ammeter A2 reads 1 amp or more, check the following:
   a. Improper gear backlash, burning between shaft and metal, or insufficient thrust clearance.
4. If selector does not move, ammeter A1 reads .5–.7 amps and ammeter A2 reads 1 amp or more, check the following:
   a. Burned shaft or motor, or foreign material caught between gears.
5. If selector does not move, ammeter A1 reads .3–.7 amps and ammeter A2 reads .0 amps, check the following:
   a. Damaged or disconnected internal lead wire or motor wiring, poor contact of limit switch, or open diode.
6. With selector stroke in the intermediate level, disconnect connection to terminal 1, then cut the current flow to the clutch coil.
7. If selector does not return to original position, even if current is cut to the clutch coil, check for clutch plate remaining engaged with clutch.

Continued from the preceding page.

Yes | No

Check results	Probable cause	Remedy	Check chart No.
Code No. 21 remains even though SET switch is set to OFF.	SET switch ON malfunction	Replace the control switch.	No. 2
	SET switch input line short-circuit	Repair the harness.	
Code No. 22 remains even though RESUME switch is set to OFF.	RESUME switch ON malfunction	Replace the control switch.	No. 3
	RESUME switch input line short-circuit	Repair the harness.	
Code No. 23 remains even though CANCEL switch is set to OFF.	Malfunction of the CANCEL circuit (ON malfunction)	Check or repair each CANCEL circuit.	No. 6, 7
Code No. 25 does not disappear, and code No. 24 does not appear, even though vehicle speed reaches approximately 40 km/h (25 mph) or higher.	Malfunction of the vehicle-speed sensor circuit (damaged or disconnected wiring, or short-circuit)	Check or repair the vehicle speed sensor circuit.	No. 4

Check the actuator circuit?

NOTE
If the results of the check of the actuator circuit and of the actuator itself reveal no abnormal condition, replace the cruise control unit.

Symptom	Probable cause	Remedy
• The set vehicle speed varies greatly upward or downward. "Hunching" (repeated alternating acceleration and deceleration) occurs after setting is made.	Malfunction of the vehicle speed sensor circuit	Repair the vehicle-speed sensor system, or replace the part.
	Malfunction of the speedometer cable or speedometer drive gear	
	Malfunction of the vacuum circuit	Repair vacuum system, or replace the part.
	Actuator circuit poor contact	Repair the actuator system, or replace the part.
	Malfunction of the actuator	
	Malfunction of the Cruise control unit	Replace the cruise control unit.
The cruise control system is not canceled when the brake pedal is depressed.	Damaged or disconnected wiring of the stop light switch input circuit; brake switch (for cruise control) malfunction (short-circuit)	Repair the harness or replace the stop light switch.
	Actuator drive circuit short-circuit	Repair the harness or replace the actuator.
	Malfunction of the cruise control unit	Replace the cruise control unit.

MT1109100003020X

Fig. 2   Troubleshooting (Part 2 of 3). Pickup

Symptom	Probable cause	Remedy
The auto-cruise control system is not canceled when the clutch pedal is depressed. (It is canceled, however, when the brake pedal is depressed.)	Damaged or disconnected wiring of clutch switch input circuit	Repair the harness, or repair or replace the clutch switch.
	Clutch switch improper installation (won't switch ON)	
	Malfunction of the auto-cruise control unit	Replace the auto-cruise control unit.
Cannot decelerate by using the SET switch	Temporary damaged or disconnected wiring of SET switch input circuit	Repair the harness or replace the SET switch.
	Actuator circuit poor contact	Repair the harness or replace the actuator.
	Malfunction of the actuator	
	Malfunction of the auto-cruise control unit	Replace the auto-cruise control unit.
Cannot accelerate or resume speed by using the RESUME switch	Damaged or disconnected wiring, or short-circuit, of RESUME switch input circuit	Repair the harness or replace the RESUME switch.
	Actuator circuit poor contact	Repair the harness or replace the actuator.
	Malfunction of the actuator	
	Malfunction of the auto-cruise control unit	Replace the auto-cruise control unit.
Auto-cruise control system can be set while traveling at a vehicle speed of less than 40 km/h (25 mph), or there is no automatic cancelation at that speed	Malfunction of the vehicle speed sensor circuit	Repair the vehicle speed sensor system, or replace the part
	Malfunction of the speedometer cable or the speedometer drive gear	
	Malfunction of the auto-cruise control unit	Replace the auto-cruise control unit.

MT1109100003030X

Fig. 2   Troubleshooting (Part 3 of 3). Pickup

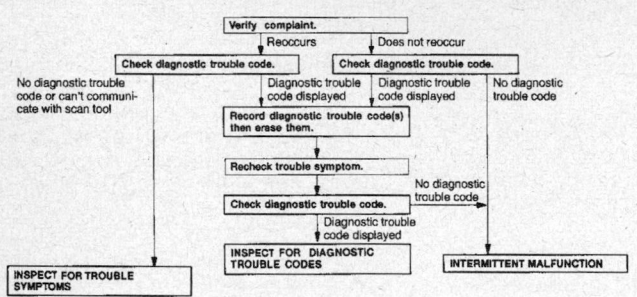

NOTE
Before carrying out trouble diagnosis, check all the following items.
1. Is the vacuum hose correctly installed and undamaged?
2. Are the auto-cruise, accelerator, and throttle cables routed correctly?
3. Do the link assembly and cables move smoothly?
4. Is the play of each cable within its standard value?

MT1109400043000X

Fig. 3   Troubleshooting. Galant, Eclipse, Montero & Montero Sport

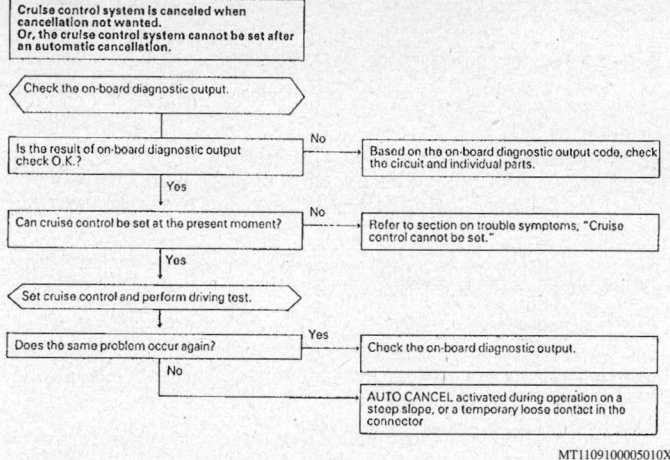

MT1109100005010X

Fig. 4   Troubleshooting (Part 1 of 4). 3000GT

MOTOR RELEASE DIRECTION & LIMIT SWITCH OPERATION INSPECTION

Except Pickup

1. Connect ammeters to actuator side connector, **Fig. 162.**
2. Turn selector in the Release (fully closed), direction. Current should be cut off, ammeter A1 should read .5–.7 amps, ammeter A2 should read less than .5 amps when current is on.
3. If the selector moves in the Release direction, ammeter reads .5–.7 amps,

but ammeter A2 reads 1 amp or more, check the following:
a. Improper gear backlash, burning between shaft and metal, or insufficient thrust clearance.
4. If selector does not move, ammeter A1 reads .5–.7 amps, but ammeter A2 reads 1 amp or more, check the following:
a. Burned shaft or motor, or foreign material caught between gears.
5. If selector does not move, ammeter A1 reads .30007 amps and ammeter A2 reads .0 amps, check the following:

a. Damaged or disconnected internal lead wire or motor wiring, poor limit switch contact, or open diode.

VACUUM TYPE

1. Remove actuator.
2. Apply vacuum to actuator and ensure holder moves more than 1.38 inches. In addition, ensure there is no change in position of holder when vacuum is maintained.
3. Install actuator and inspect and adjust cruise control cable.

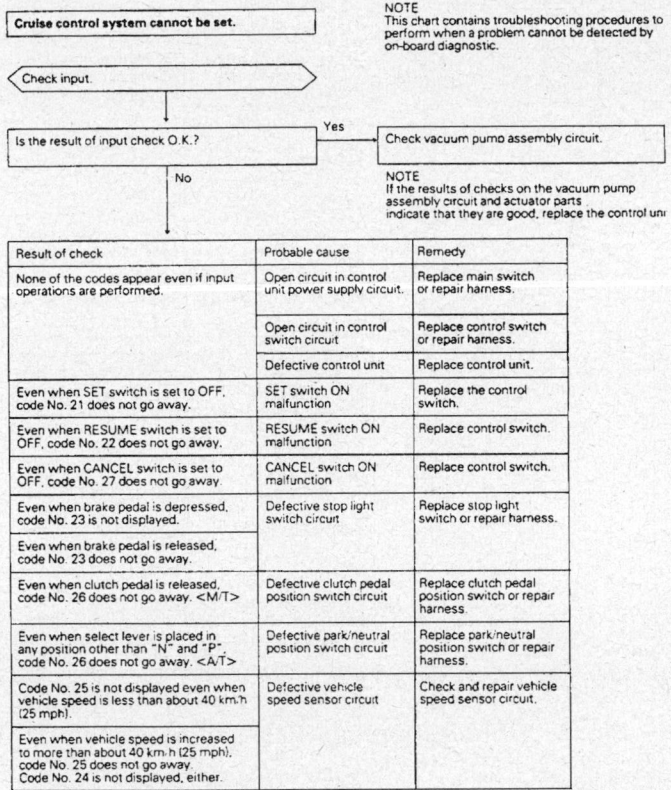

Fig. 4 Troubleshooting (Part 2 of 4). 3000GT

MT1109100005020X

Result of check	Probable cause	Remedy
None of the codes appear even if input operations are performed.	Open circuit in control unit power supply circuit	Replace main switch or repair harness.
	Open circuit in control switch circuit	Replace control switch or repair harness.
	Defective control unit	Replace control unit.
Even when SET switch is set to OFF, code No. 21 does not go away.	SET switch ON malfunction	Replace the control switch.
Even when RESUME switch is set to OFF, code No. 22 does not go away.	RESUME switch ON malfunction	Replace control switch.
Even when CANCEL switch is set to OFF, code No. 27 does not go away.	CANCEL switch ON malfunction	Replace control switch.
Even when brake pedal is depressed, code No. 23 is not displayed.	Defective stop light switch circuit	Replace stop light switch or repair harness.
Even when brake pedal is released, code No. 23 does not go away.		
Even when clutch pedal is released, code No. 26 does not go away. <M/T>	Defective clutch pedal position switch circuit	Replace clutch pedal position switch or repair harness.
Even when select lever is placed in any position other than "N" and "P", code No. 26 does not go away. <A/T>	Defective park/neutral position switch circuit	Replace park/neutral position switch or repair harness.
Code No. 25 is not displayed even when vehicle speed is less than about 40 km/h (25 mph).	Defective vehicle speed sensor circuit	Check and repair vehicle speed sensor circuit.
Even when vehicle speed is increased to more than about 40 km/h (25 mph), code No. 25 does not go away. Code No. 24 is not displayed, either.		

Flowchart:
- Cruise control system cannot be set.
- NOTE: This chart contains troubleshooting procedures to perform when a problem cannot be detected by on-board diagnostic.
- Check input.
- Is the result of input check O.K.? → Yes → Check vacuum pump assembly circuit.
  - NOTE: If the results of checks on the vacuum pump assembly circuit and actuator parts indicate that they are good, replace the control unit.
- No ↓

Trouble symptom	Probable cause	Remedy
• The set vehicle speed varies greatly upward or downward. • "Hunting" (repeated alternating acceleration and deceleration) occurs after setting is made.	Malfunction of the vehicle speed sensor circuit	Repair the vehicle speed sensor system, or replace the part.
	Malfunction of the speedometer cable or speedometer drive gear <Up to 1993 models (Non turbo)>	
	Vacuum pump assembly circuit poor contact	Repair the actuator system, or replace the part.
	Malfunction of the vacuum pump assembly (including air leaks from negative pressure passage)	
	Malfunction of the ECU	Replace the ECU.
The cruise control system is not canceled when the brake pedal is depressed.	Brake switch (for cruise control) malfunction (short-circuit)	Repair the harness or replace the stop light switch.
	Vacuum pump assembly drive circuit short-circuit	Repair the harness or replace the vacuum pump assembly.
	Malfunction of the ECU	Replace the ECU.
The cruise control system is not canceled when the clutch pedal is depressed. <M/T> (It is canceled, however, when the brake pedal is depressed.)	Damaged or disconnected wiring of clutch switch input circuit	Repair the harness, or repair or replace the clutch switch.
	Clutch switch improper installation (won't switch ON)	
	Malfunction of the ECU	Replace the ECU.
The cruise control system is not canceled when the shift lever is moved to the "N" position. - <A/T> (It is canceled, however, when the brake pedal is depressed.)	Damaged or disconnected wiring of park/neutral position switch input circuit	Repair the harness, or repair or replace the park/neutral position switch.
	Improper adjustment of park/neutral position switch	
	Malfunction of the ECU	Replace the ECU.
Cannot decelerate by using the SET switch.	Temporary damaged or disconnected wiring of control switch input circuit	Repair the harness or replace the control switch.
	Vacuum pump assembly circuit poor contact	Repair the harness or replace the vacuum pump assembly.
	Malfunction of the vacuum pump assembly	
	Malfunction of the ECU	Replace the ECU.

NOTE
ECU: Electronic control unit

MT1109100005030A

Fig. 4 Troubleshooting (Part 3 of 4). 3000GT

Trouble symptom	Probable cause	Check chart No.	Remedy
• The set vehicle speed varies greatly upward or downward. • "Hunching" (repeated alternating acceleration and deceleration) occurs after setting is made.	Malfunction of the vehicle speed sensor circuit	No. 4	Repair the vehicle speed sensor system, or replace the part.
	Malfunction of the speedometer cable or speedometer drive gear		
	Vacuum pump assembly circuit poor contact	No. 5	Repair the actuator system, or replace the part.
	Malfunction of the vacuum pump assembly (including air leaks from negative pressure passage)		
	Malfunction of the ECU	–	Replace the ECU.
The cruise control system does not cancel when the brake pedal is depressed.	Brake switch (for cruise control) malfunction (short-circuit)	No. 6	Repair the harness or replace the stop light switch.
	Vacuum pump assembly drive circuit short-circuit	No. 5	Repair the harness or replace the vacuum pump assembly.
	Malfunction of the ECU	–	Replace the ECU.
The cruise control system does not cancel when the clutch pedal is depressed. <M/T> (It cancels, however, when the brake pedal is depressed.)	Damaged or disconnected wiring of clutch pedal position switch input circuit	If the input check code No. 26 indicates a malfunction. No. 7	Repair the harness, or repair or replace the clutch pedal position switch.
	Clutch pedal position switch improper installation (won't switch ON)		
	Malfunction of the ECU	–	Replace the ECU.
The cruise control system does not cancel when the shift lever is moved to the "N" position. <A/T> (It cancels, however, when the brake pedal is depressed.)	Damaged or disconnected wiring or park/neutral position switch input circuit	If the input check code No. 26 indicates a malfunction. No. 8	Repair the harness, or repair or replace the park/neutral position switch.
	Improper adjustment of park/neutral position switch		
	Malfunction of the ECU	–	Replace the ECU.
Cannot decelerate by using the SET switch.	Temporary damaged or disconnected wiring of control switch input circuit	No. 2	Repair the harness or replace the control switch.
	Vacuum pump assembly circuit poor contact	No. 5	Repair the harness or replace the vacuum pump assembly.
	Malfunction of the vacuum pump assembly		
	Malfunction of the ECU	–	Replace the ECU.

MT1109100005040X

Fig. 4 Troubleshooting (Part 4 of 4). 3000GT

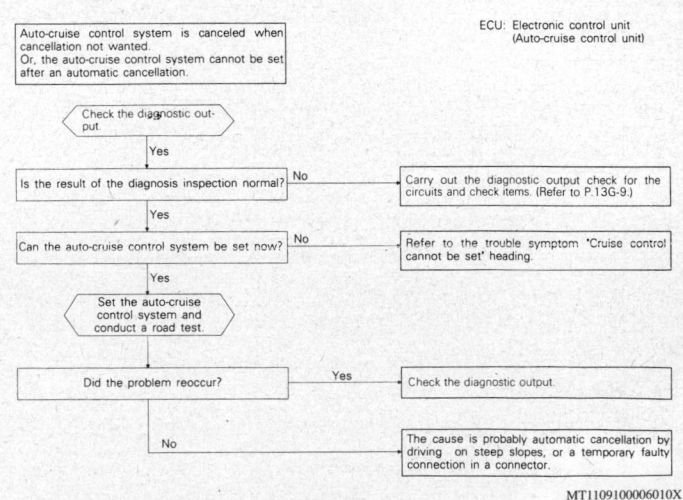

ECU: Electronic control unit (Auto-cruise control unit)

Flowchart:
- Auto-cruise control system is canceled when cancellation not wanted. Or, the auto-cruise control system cannot be set after an automatic cancellation.
- Check the diagnostic output.
- Is the result of the diagnosis inspection normal? → No → Carry out the diagnostic output check for the circuits and check items. (Refer to P.13G-9.)
  - Yes ↓
- Can the auto-cruise control system be set now? → No → Refer to the trouble symptom "Cruise control cannot be set" heading.
  - Yes ↓
- Set the auto-cruise control system and conduct a road test.
- Did the problem reoccur? → Yes → Check the diagnostic output.
  - No ↓
- The cause is probably automatic cancellation by driving on steep slopes, or a temporary faulty connection in a connector.

MT1109100006010X

Fig. 5 Troubleshooting (Part 1 of 5). Diamante

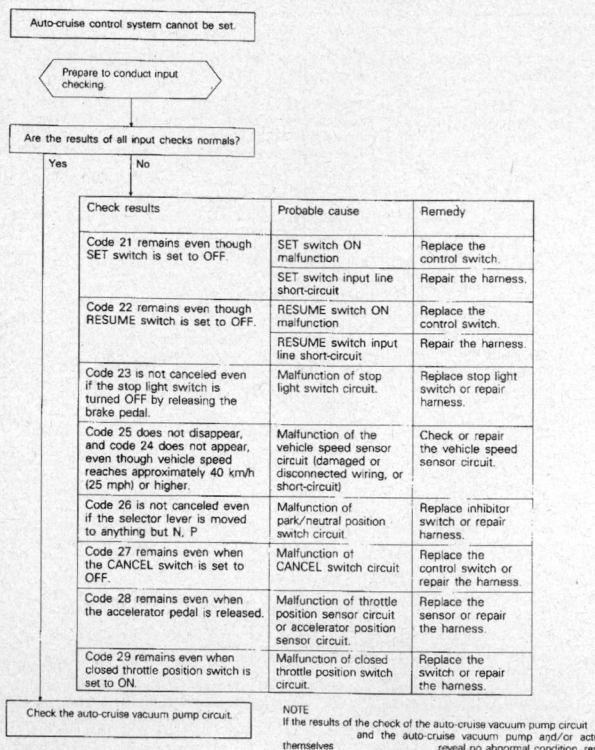

Check results	Probable cause	Remedy
Code 21 remains even though SET switch is set to OFF.	SET switch ON malfunction	Replace the control switch.
	SET switch input line short-circuit	Repair the harness.
Code 22 remains even though RESUME switch is set to OFF.	RESUME switch ON malfunction	Replace the control switch.
	RESUME switch input line short-circuit	Repair the harness.
Code 23 is not canceled even if the stop light switch is turned OFF by releasing the brake pedal.	Malfunction of stop light switch circuit.	Replace stop light switch or repair harness.
Code 25 does not disappear, and code 24 does not appear, even though vehicle speed reaches approximately 40 km/h (25 mph) or higher.	Malfunction of the vehicle speed sensor circuit (damaged or disconnected wiring, or short-circuit).	Check or repair the vehicle speed sensor circuit.
Code 26 is not canceled even if the selector lever is moved to anything but N, P.	Malfunction of park/neutral position switch circuit.	Replace inhibitor switch or repair harness.
Code 27 remains even when the CANCEL switch is set to OFF.	Malfunction of CANCEL switch circuit.	Replace the control switch or repair the harness.
Code 28 remains even when the accelerator pedal is released.	Malfunction of throttle position sensor circuit or accelerator position sensor circuit.	Replace the sensor or repair the harness.
Code 29 remains even when closed throttle position switch is set to ON.	Malfunction of closed throttle position switch circuit.	Replace the switch or repair the harness.

NOTE
If the results of the check of the auto-cruise vacuum pump circuit and the auto-cruise vacuum pump and/or actuator themselves reveal no abnormal condition, replace the electronic control unit (ECU).

MT1109100006020X

Fig. 5 Troubleshooting (Part 2 of 5). Diamante

Trouble symptom	Probable cause	Remedy
• The set vehicle speed varies gratly upward or downward. • "Hunching" (repeated alternating acceleration and deceleration) occurs after setting is made.	Malfunction of the vehicle speed sensor circuit	Repair the vehicle speed sensor system, or replace the part.
	Malfunction of the speedometer cable or speedometer drive gear	
	Auto-cruise vacuum pump circuit poor contact	Repair auto-cruise vacuum pump assembly or replace the part.
	Malfunction of the ECU	Replace the ECU.
The auto-cruise control system is not canceled when the brake pedal is depressed.	Damaged or disconnected wiring of the stop light switch input circuit brake switch (for auto-cruise control) malfunction (short-circuit)	Repair the harness or replace the stop light switch.
	Auto-cruise vacuum pump drive circuit short-circuit	Repair the harness or replace the auto-cruise vacuum pump.
	Malfunction of the ECU	Replace the ECU

NOTE
ECU: Electronic control unit

MT1109100006030X

Fig. 5 Troubleshooting (Part 3 of 5). Diamante

Trouble symptom	Probable cause	Remedy
The auto-cruise control system is not canceled when the selector lever is moved to the "N" position. (Vehicles with an automatic transaxle) (It is canceled, however, when the brake pedal is depressed.)	Damaged or disconnected wiring of park/neutral position switch input circuit	Repair the harness, or repair or replace the park/neutral position switch
	Improper adjustment of park/neutral position switch	
	Malfunction of the ECU	Replace the ECU.
Cannot decelerate by using the SET switch	Temporary damaged or disconnected wiring of SET switch input circuit	Repair the harness or replace the auto-cruise control switch.
	Auto-cruise vacuum pump circuit poor contact	Repair the harness or replace the auto-cruise vacuum pump.
	Malfunction of the vacuum pump assembly (including air leaks from negative pressure passage)	
	Malfunction of the ECU	Replace the ECU.
Cannot accelerate or resume speed by using the RESUME switch.	Damaged or disconnected wiring, or short-circuit, of RESUME switch input circuit	Repair the harness or replace the auto-cruise control switch.
	Auto-cruise vacuum pump circuit poor contact	Repair the harness or replace the auto-cruise vacuum pump.
	Malfunction of the vacuum pump assembly (including air leaks from negative pressure passage)	
	Malfunction of the ECU	Replace the ECU.
Cruise control does not cancel even when the CANCEL switch is set to ON. (However, it is cancelled when the brake pedal is depressed.)	Broken wire in the CANCEL switch circuit inside the control switch	Repair the harness or replace the auto-cruise control switch.
	Malfunction of the ECU	Replace the ECU.

MT1109100006040X

Fig. 5 Troubleshooting (Part 4 of 5). Diamante

Trouble symptom	Probable cause	Remedy
Auto-cruise control system can be set while traveling at a vehicle speed of less than 40 km/h (25 mph), or there is no automatic cancellation at that speed	Malfunction of the vehicle-speed sensor circuit	Repaire the vehicle-speed sensor system, or replace the part.
	Malfunction of the speedometer cable or the speedometer drive gear	
	Malfunction of the ECU	Replace the ECU.
The indicator lamp of the main switch does not illuminate. (But auto-cruise control system is normal.)	Damaged or disconnected bulb of indicator lamp Malfunction of the main switch	Repair the harness or replace the main switch.
	Harness damaged or disconnected	
Malfunction of control function by ON/OFF switching of ELC 4 A/T accelerator switch (Non-operation of damper clutch, 2nd gear hold, etc.)	Malfunction of circuit related to accelerator switch OFF function	Repair the harness or replace the part.
	Malfunction of the ECU	Replace the ECU
Overdrive is not canceled during fixed speed driving	Malfunction of circuit related to overdrive cancelation, or malfunction of ECU	Repair the harness or replace the part.
No shift to overdrive during manual driving		

MT1109100006050X

Fig. 5 Troubleshooting (Part 5 of 5). Diamante

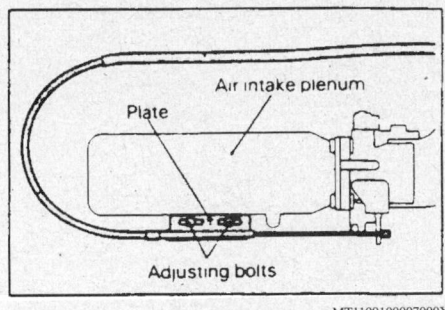

Fig. 6 Speed control inner cable adjustment (throttle valve side). Mirage

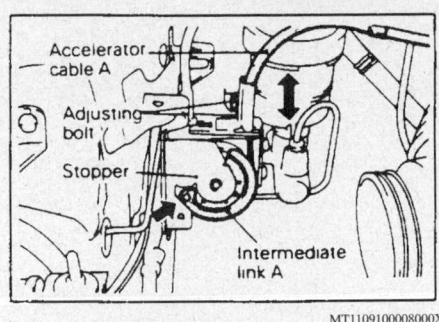

Fig. 7 Speed control inner cable adjustment (accelerator pedal side). Mirage

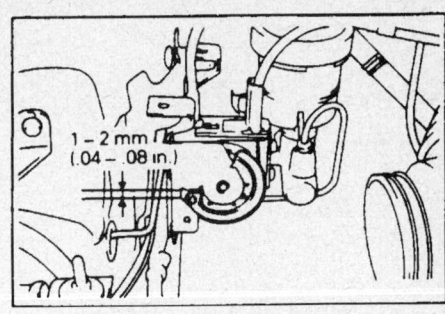

Fig. 8 Throttle lever measurement. Mirage

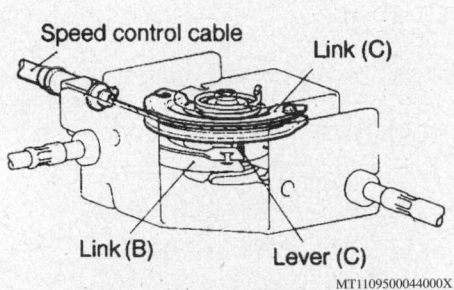

Fig. 9 Speed control cable adjustment. Eclipse w/2.0L non-turbocharged engine

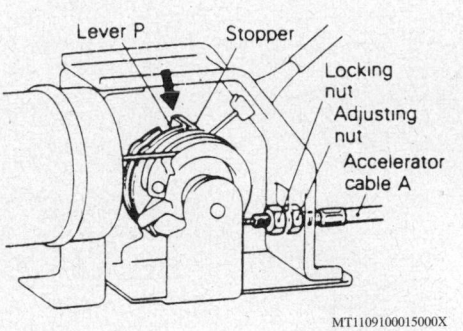

Fig. 10 Speed control outer cable freeplay adjustment. Pickup

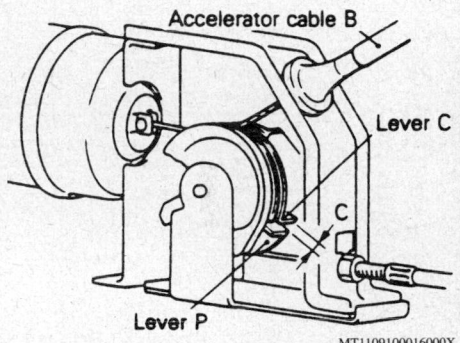

Fig. 11 Speed control cable B freeplay adjustment. Pickup

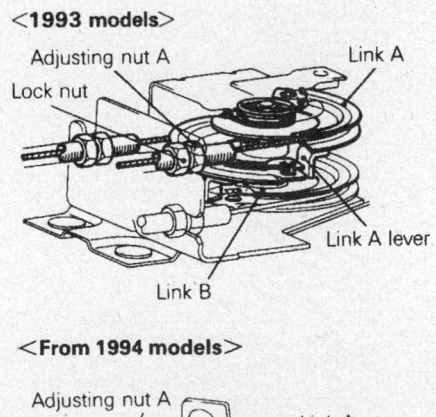

Fig. 12 Auto cruise control cable adjustment. Diamante

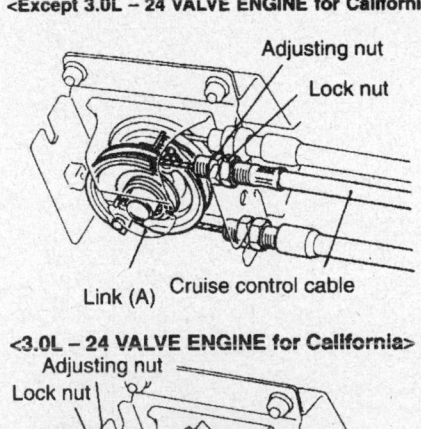
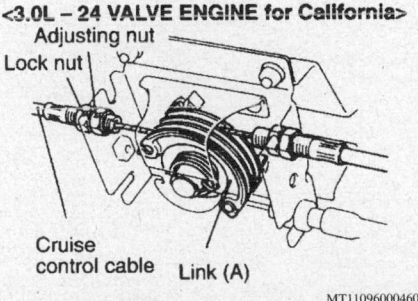

Fig. 13 Auto cruise control cable adjustment. Montero & Montero Sport

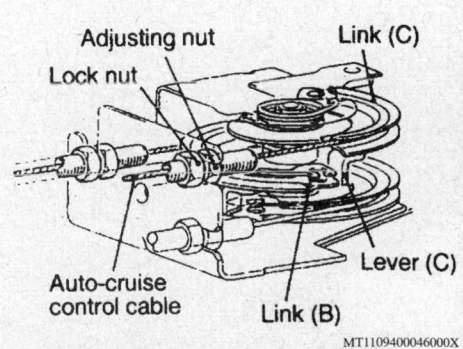

Fig. 14 Auto cruise control cable adjustment. Galant, 3000GT & Eclipse w/2.0L turbocharged & 2.4L Engine

Left table (Fig. 15, Part 1 of 2):

Terminal No.	Check item	Check conditions		Normal condition
1	Clutch pedal position switch input <M/T>	When pedal is not depressed	When clutch pedal position switch is OFF	Battery positive voltage
		When pedal is depressed	When clutch pedal position switch is ON	0V
	Park/neutral position switch input <A/T>	When selector lever is in a position other than N range	When park/neutral position switch is OFF	Battery positive voltage
		When selector lever is in N range	When park/neutral position switch is ON	0V
2	ECU power supply	When ignition switch is ON		Battery positive voltage
3	Power supply for OD signal control <A/T>	When ignition switch is ON		Battery positive voltage
4	Closed throttle position switch output	When accelerator pedal is depressed	When closed throttle position switch is OFF	4.5–5.5V
		When accelerator pedal is not depressed	When closed throttle position switch is ON	0V
5	Throttle position sensor input	When accelerator pedal is fully depressed		4.0–5.5V
		When accelerator pedal is released		0.5–0.7V
6	Ground	At all times		Continuity
8	Ground	At all times		Continuity
10	OD control output <A/T>	When OD switch is ON		Battery positive voltage
		When OD switch is OFF		0V
11	OD switch input <A/T>	When OD switch is ON		Battery positive voltage
		When OD switch is OFF		0V
12 13	Auto-cruise vacuum pump release valve and control valve input	When driving at constant speed using the SET switch	Release valve closed	0V
			Control valve closed	0V
12 13		When accelerating with the RESUME switch while driving at constant speed	Release valve closed	0V
			Release valve closed	0V
12 13		When decelerating with the SET switch while driving at constant speed	Release valve closed	0V
			Control valve open	Battery positive voltage
12		When canceling constant-speed driving with the CANCEL switch	Release valve open	Battery positive voltage
13			Control valve open	Battery positive voltage

MT1109500151010X

Fig. 15 Auto cruise control signal circuit inspection (Part 1 of 2). Eclipse, 3000GT & Montero

Right table (Fig. 15, Part 2 of 2):

Terminal No.	Check item	Check conditions		Normal condition
14	Ground	At all times		Continuity
15	Stop light switch input	When brake pedal is depressed	When stop light switch is ON	Battery positive voltage
		When brake pedal is not depressed	When stop light switch is OFF	0V
16	ECU backup power supply	At all times		Battery positive voltage
18	Auto-cruise control switch input	When SET switch is pressed	When SET switch is ON	3V
		When SET switch is not pressed	When SET switch is OFF	0V
		When RESUME switch is pressed	When RESUME switch is ON	6V
		When RESUME switch is not pressed	When RESUME switch is OFF	0V
		When CANCEL switch is pressed	When CANCEL switch is ON	Battery positive voltage
		When CANCEL switch is not pressed	When CANCEL switch is OFF	0V
19	Vehicle speed sensor input	When vehicle is moved forwards and backwards, sensor turns ON and OFF repeatedly.	When sensor is ON	0V
			When sensor is OFF	4.5 V or more
20	ACC power supply	When ignition switch is in ACC position		Battery positive voltage
23	Indicator input (inside combination meter)	When driving at constant speed	When indicator is illuminated	0V
		When constant-speed driving is cancelled	When indicator is switched off	Battery positive voltage
24	Diagnosis control input	When ignition switch is ON		4V or more
25	Surge absorption circuit terminal	When auto-cruise main switch is ON		Battery positive voltage
26	Auto-cruise vacuum pump motor input	When driving at constant speed using the SET switch	Motor stopped	Battery positive voltage
		When accelerating with the RESUME switch while driving at constant speed	Motor running	0V
		When decelerating with the SET switch while driving at constant speed	Motor stopped	Battery positive voltage
		When cancelling constant-speed driving with the CANCEL switch	Motor stopped	Battery positive voltage

MT1109500151020X

Fig. 15 Auto cruise control signal circuit inspection (Part 2 of 2). Eclipse, 3000GT & Montero

Bottom left table (Fig. 16, Part 1 of 3):

TERMINAL NO.	CHECK ITEM	CHECKING REQUIREMENTS		NORMAL CONDITION
1	THROTTLE POSITION SENSOR INPUT	WHEN ACCELERATOR PEDAL IS FULLY DEPRESSED		4.6–5.5 V
		WHEN ACCELERATOR PEDAL IS RELEASED		0.3–1.0 V
2	CLOSED THROTTLE POSITION SWITCH OUTPUT	WHEN ACCELERATOR PEDAL IS DEPRESSED	WHEN CLOSED THROTTLE POSITION SWITCH IS OFF	4.5–5.5 V
		WHEN ACCELERATOR PEDAL IS NOT DEPRESSED	WHEN CLOSED THROTTLE POSITION SWITCH IS ON	0 V
3	"ACC" POWER SUPPLY	WHEN IGNITION SWITCH IS IN "ACC" POSITION		BATTERY POSITIVE VOLTAGE
4	STOPLIGHT SWITCH INPUT	WHEN BRAKE PEDAL IS DEPRESSED	WHEN STOPLIGHT SWITCH IS ON	BATTERY POSITIVE VOLTAGE
		WHEN BRAKE PEDAL IS NOT DEPRESSED	WHEN STOPLIGHT SWITCH IS OFF	0 V
5	DIAGNOSIS CONTROL INPUT	WHEN IGNITION SWITCH IS "ON"		4 V OR MORE
6	ECU BACKUP POWER SUPPLY	ALWAYS		BATTERY POSITIVE VOLTAGE
7 8	AUTO-CRUISE VACUUM PUMP RELEASE VALVE AND CONTROL VALVE INPUT	WHEN DECELERATING WITH THE "SET" SWITCH WHILE DRIVING AT CONSTANT SPEED	CONTROL VALVE OPEN	BATTERY POSITIVE VOLTAGE
			RELEASE VALVE CLOSED	0 V
7 8		WHEN CANCELLING AUTO-CRUISE CONTROL BY THE "CANCEL" SWITCH	CONTROL VALVE OPEN	BATTERY POSITIVE VOLTAGE
			RELEASE VALVE OPEN	BATTERY POSITIVE VOLTAGE
9	GROUND	ALWAYS		CONTINUITY

MT1109700155010X

Fig. 16 Auto cruise control signal circuit inspection (Part 1 of 3). Mirage & Montero Sport

Bottom right table (Fig. 16, Part 2 of 3):

TERMINAL NO.	CHECK ITEM	CHECKING REQUIREMENTS		NORMAL CONDITION
10	A/T CONTROL OUTPUT	OD SWITCH ON		BATTERY POSITIVE VOLTAGE
		OD SWITCH OFF		0 V
11	VEHICLE SPEED SENSOR INPUT	WHEN THE VEHICLE MOVES FORWARD AND REVERSES, THE VEHICLE SPEED SENSOR TURNS ON AND OFF REPEATEDLY	WHEN THE SENSOR IS ON	0 V
			WHEN THE SENSOR IS OFF	4.5 V OR MORE
12	AUTO-CRUISE CONTROL SWITCH INPUT	WHEN THE AUTO-CRUISE CONTROL SWITCH HAS NOT BEEN OPERATED	WHEN ALL SWITCHES ARE "OFF"	0 V
		WHEN THE AUTO-CRUISE CONTROL SWITCH IS PUSHED DOWN	WHEN "SET" SWITCH IS "ON"	3 V
		WHEN THE AUTO-CRUISE CONTROL SWITCH IS PUSHED UP	WHEN "RESUME" SWITCH IS "ON"	6 V
		WHEN THE AUTO-CRUISE CONTROL SWITCH IS PULLED FORWARD	WHEN "CANCEL" SWITCH IS "ON"	BATTERY POSITIVE VOLTAGE
13	GROUND	ALWAYS		CONTINUITY
14	CLUTCH PEDAL POSITION SWITCH INPUT <M/T>	WHEN PEDAL IS NOT DEPRESSED	WHEN THE CLUTCH PEDAL POSITION SWITCH IS "OFF"	4.5 V OR MORE
		WHEN THE CLUTCH PEDAL IS DEPRESSED	WHEN THE CLUTCH PEDAL POSITION SWITCH IS "ON"	0 V
	PARK/NEUTRAL POSITION SWITCH INPUT <A/T>	WHEN THE SELECTOR LEVER IS IN A POSITION OTHER THAN "N" OR "P" RANGE	WHEN THE PARK/NEUTRAL POSITION SWITCH IS "OFF"	BATTERY POSITIVE VOLTAGE
		WHEN THE SELECTOR LEVER IS IN "N" OR "P" RANGE	WHEN THE PARK/NEUTRAL POSITION SWITCH IS "ON"	0 V

MT1109700155020X

Fig. 16 Auto cruise control signal circuit inspection (Part 2 of 3). Mirage & Montero Sport

SPEED CONTROL SYSTEMS

TERMINAL NO.	CHECK ITEM	CHECKING REQUIREMENTS		NORMAL CONDITION
15	PUMP POWER SUPPLY	IGNITION SWITCH "ON" MAIN SWITCH "ON" STOPLIGHT SWITCH: "ON"		BATTERY POSITIVE VOLTAGE
16	ECU POWER SUPPLY	IGNITION SWITCH: "ON" MAIN SWITCH "ON"		BATTERY POSITIVE VOLTAGE
17	INDICATOR INPUT (INSIDE COMBINATION METER)	WHEN DRIVING AT CONSTANT SPEED	WHEN INDICATOR IS ILLUMINATED	0 V
		WHEN CONSTANT-SPEED DRIVING IS CANCELLED	WHEN INDICATOR IS SWITCHED OFF	BATTERY POSITIVE VOLTAGE
18	AUTO-CRUISE VACUUM PUMP MOTOR INPUT	WHEN DRIVING AT CONSTANT SPEED USING THE "SET" SWITCH	MOTOR STOPPED/ RUNNING	BATTERY POSITIVE VOLTAGE/0 V
		WHEN ACCELERATING WITH THE "RESUME" SWITCH WHILE DRIVING AT CONSTANT SPEED	MOTOR STOPPED/ RUNNING	BATTERY POSITIVE VOLTAGE/0 V
		WHEN DECELERATING WITH "SET" SWITCH WHILE DRIVING AT CONSTANT SPEED	MOTOR STOPPED	BATTERY POSITIVE VOLTAGE
		WHEN CANCELLING CONSTANT SPEED DRIVING WITH THE "CANCEL" SWITCH	MOTOR STOPPED	BATTERY POSITIVE VOLTAGE

MT1109700155030X

Fig. 16 Auto cruise control signal circuit inspection (Part 3 of 3). Mirage & Montero Sport

Terminal No.	Check item	Check conditions		Normal condition
1	Clutch pedal position switch input <M/T>	When pedal is not depressed	When clutch pedal position switch is OFF	Battery positive voltage
		When pedal is depressed	When clutch pedal position switch is ON	0V
	Park/neutral position switch input <A/T>	When select lever is in a position other than N range	When park/neutral position switch is OFF	5V
		When select lever is in N range	When park/neutral position switch is ON	0V
2	ECU power supply	When ignition switch is ON		Battery positive voltage
3	Power supply for OD signal control <A/T>	–		Battery positive voltage
4	Closed throttle position switch output	When accelerator pedal is depressed	When idle switch is OFF	4.5–5.5V
		When accelerator pedal is not depressed	When idle switch is ON	0V
5	Throttle position sensor input	When accelerator pedal is fully depressed		4.0–5.5V
		When accelerator pedal is released		0.5–0.7V
6	Ground	–		Continuity
8	Ground	–		Continuity
10	OD control output <A/T>	When OD switch is ON		Battery positive voltage
		When OD switch is OFF		0V
11	OD switch input <A/T>	When OD switch is ON		Battery positive voltage
		When OD switch is OFF		0V
12 13	Auto-cruise vacuum pump release valve and control valve input	When driving at constant speed using the SET switch	Release valve closed	0V
			Control valve closed	0V
12 13		When accelerating with the RESUME switch while driving at constant speed	Release valve closed	0V
			Control valve closed	0V
12 13		When decelerating with the SET switch while driving at constant speed	Release valve closed	0V
			Control valve open	Battery positive voltage
12 13		When cancelling constant-speed driving with the CANCEL switch	Release valve open	Battery positive voltage
			Control valve open	Battery positive voltage
14	Ground	–		Continuity

MT1109400152010X

Fig. 17 Auto cruise control signal circuit inspection (Part 1 of 2). Galant

Terminal No.	Check item	Check conditions		Normal condition
15	Stop light switch input	When brake pedal is depressed	When stop light switch is ON	Battery positive voltage
		When brake pedal is not depressed	When stop light switch is OFF	0V
16	ECU backup power supply	–		Battery positive voltage
18	Auto-cruise control switch input	When SET switch is pressed	When SET switch is ON	3V
		When SET switch is not pressed	When SET switch is OFF	0V
		When RESUME switch is pressed	When RESUME switch is ON	6V
		When RESUME switch is not pressed	When RESUME switch is OFF	0V
		When CANCEL switch is pressed	When CANCEL switch is ON	Battery positive voltage
		When CANCEL switch is not pressed	When CANCEL switch is OFF	0V
19	Vehicle speed sensor input	When vehicle is moved forwards and backwards, sensor turns ON and OFF repeatedly.	When sensor is ON	0V
			When sensor is OFF	4.5 V or more
20	ACC power supply	When ignition switch is in ACC position		Battery positive voltage
23	Indicator input (inside combination meter)	When driving at constant speed	When indicator is illuminated	0V
		When constant-speed driving is cancelled	When indicator is switched off	Battery positive voltage
24	Diagnosis control input	When ignition switch is ON		4V or more
26	Auto-cruise vacuum pump motor input	When driving at constant speed using the SET switch	Motor stopped	Battery positive voltage
		When accelerating with the RESUME switch while driving at constant speed	Motor running	0V
		When decelerating with the SET switch while driving at constant speed	Motor stopped	Battery positive voltage
		When cancelling constant-speed driving with the CANCEL switch	Motor stopped	Battery positive voltage

MT1109400152020X

Fig. 17 Auto cruise control signal circuit inspection (Part 2 of 2). Galant

CODE NO.	ON-BOARD DIAGNOSTIC ITEMS
11	Electric vacuum pump drive system
12	Vehicle speed sensor system
14	Electric vacuum pump power supply system
15	Auto-cruise control switch
16	Auto-cruise control-ECU
17	Throttle position sensor/accelerator pedal position sensor system

MT1109900161000X

Fig. 18 Diagnostic Trouble Code Inspection Chart. Diamante

Code No.				On-board diagnostic items
Scan tool mode	General scan tool mode	*MIL		
35	P0500	15		Vehicle speed signal system
86	–	34		Auto-cruise control switch
87	–	34		Auto-cruise control switch
15		34		Speed control servo solenoid valve system
02	P0605	53		Powertrain control module (PCM)
82	–	77		Auto-cruise control relay system

NOTE
*MIL: Check engine/Malfunction indicator lamp

MT1109900180000X

Fig. 19 Diagnostic Trouble Code Inspection Chart. Eclipse w/2.0L Non-Turbocharged Engine

Code No.	On-board diagnostic items
11	Auto-cruise vacuum pump drive system
12	Vehicle speed signal system
14	Auto-cruise vacuum pump power supply system
15	Auto-cruise control switch
16	Auto-cruise control-ECU
17	Throttle position sensor system

MT1109900198000X

Fig. 20 Diagnostic Trouble Code Inspection Chart. Eclipse w/2.0L Turbocharged & 2.4L Engines

Code No.	On-board diagnostic items
11	Auto-cruise vacuum pump drive system
12	Vehicle speed sensor system
14	Auto-cruise vacuum pump power supply system
15	Auto-cruise control switch
16	Auto-cruise control-ECU
17	Throttle position sensor system

MT1109900221000X

Fig. 21 Diagnostic Trouble Code Inspection Chart. Galant & Mirage

Code No.	On-board diagnostic items
11	Auto-cruise vacuum pump drive system
12	Vehicle speed signal system
14	Auto-cruise vacuum pump power supply system
15	Auto-cruise control switch
16	Auto-cruise control-ECU
17	Throttle position sensor system

MT1109900241000X

Fig. 22 Diagnostic Trouble Code Inspection Chart. Montero & Montero Sport

Code No.	On-board diagnostic items
11	Auto-cruise vacuum pump drive system
12	Vehicle speed signal system
15	Auto-cruise control switch
16	Auto-cruise control-ECU
17	Throttle position sensor system

MT1109900263000X

Fig. 23 Diagnostic Trouble Code Inspection Chart. 3000GT

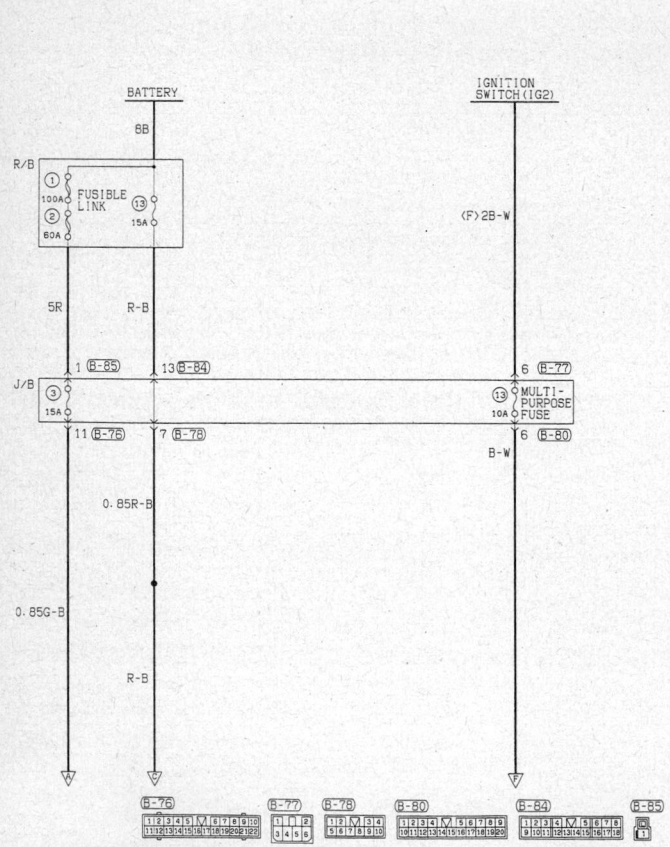

MT1109900284010X

Fig. 24 Wiring diagram (Part 1 of 6). Diamante

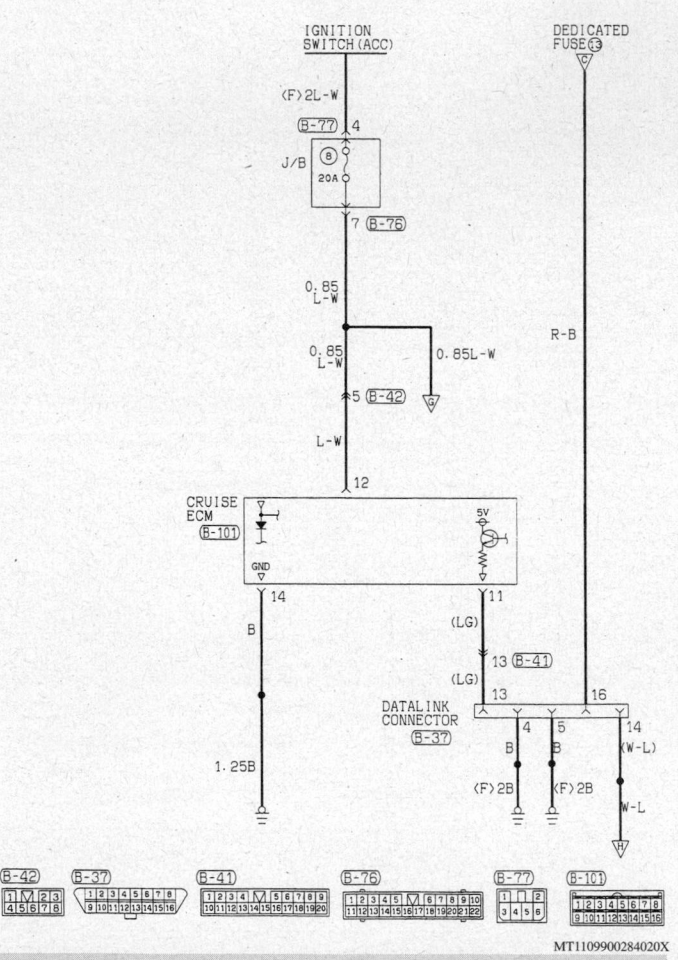

MT1109900284020X

Fig. 24 Wiring diagram (Part 2 of 6). Diamante

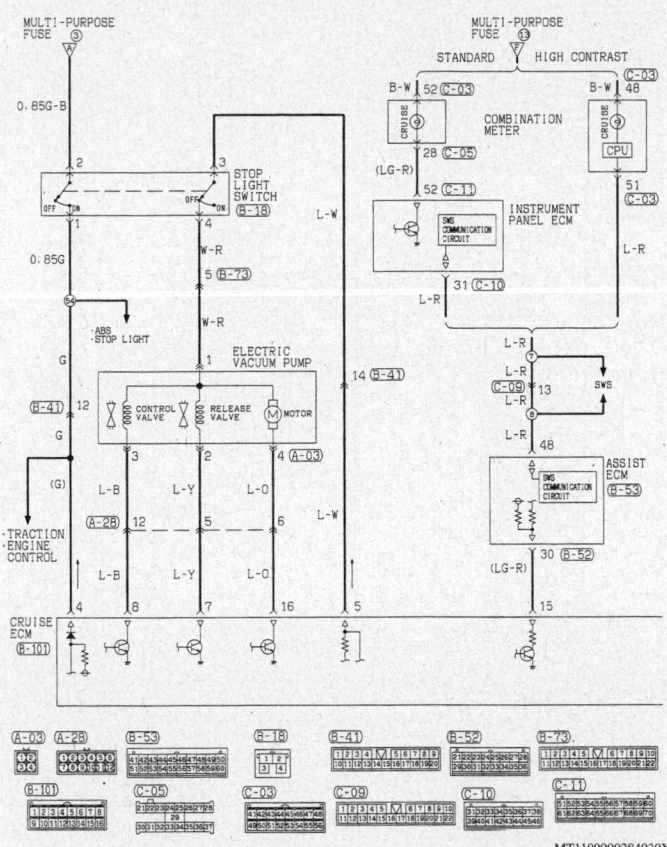

Fig. 24   Wiring diagram (Part 3 of 6). Diamante

MT1109900284030X

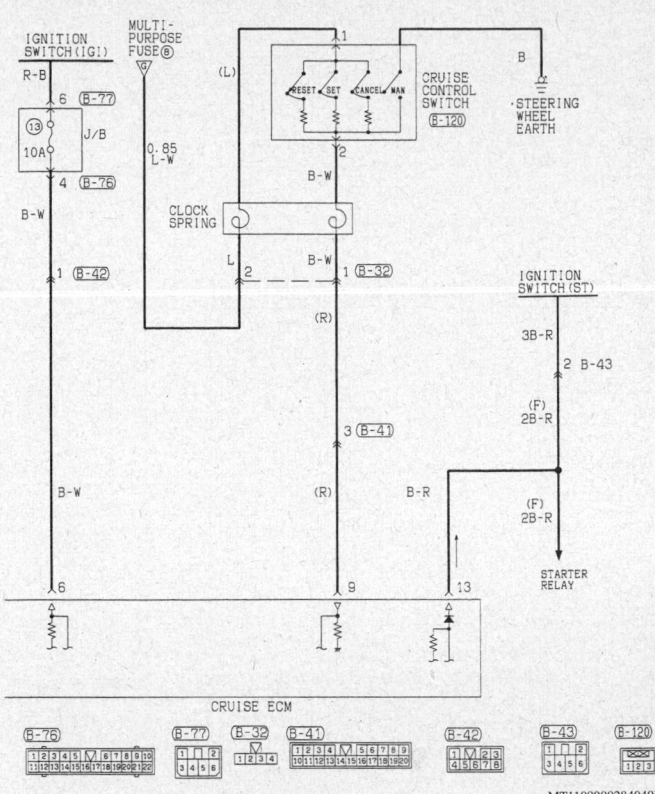

Fig. 24   Wiring diagram (Part 4 of 6). Diamante

MT1109900284040X

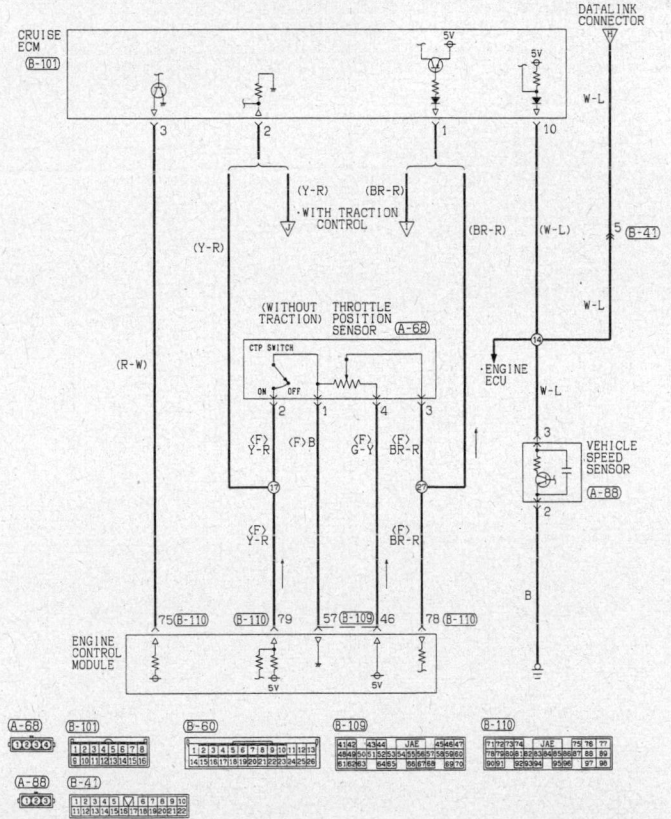

Fig. 24   Wiring diagram (Part 5 of 6). Diamante

MT1109900284050X

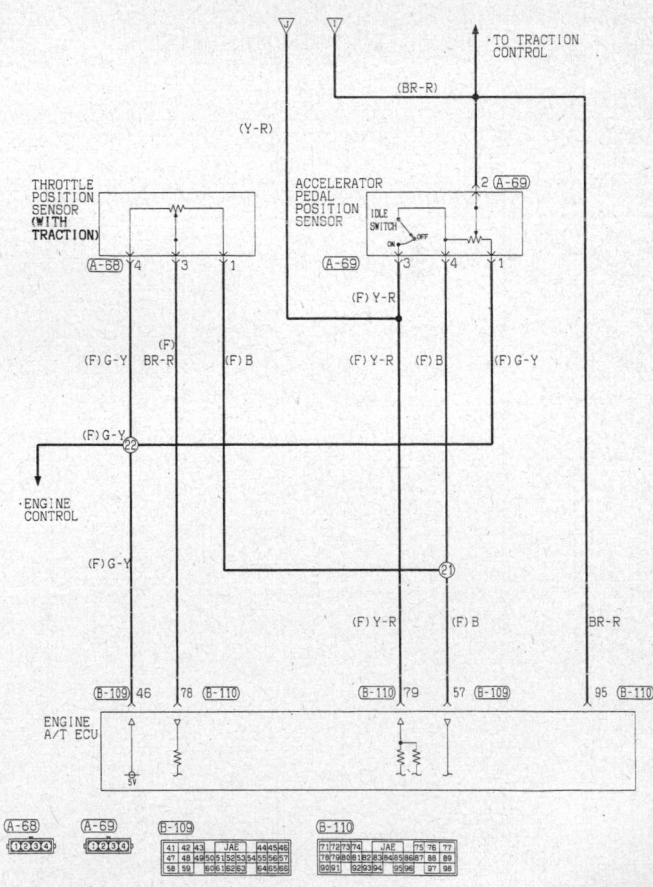

Fig. 24   Wiring diagram (Part 6 of 6). Diamante

MT1109900284060X

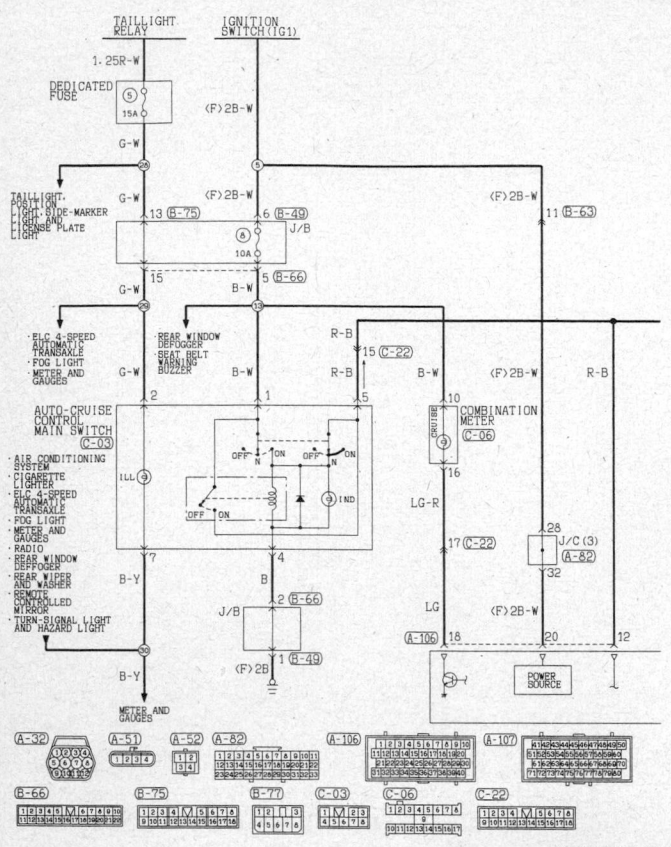

Fig. 25 Wiring diagram (Part 1 of 6). Eclipse w/2.0L non-turbocharged engine

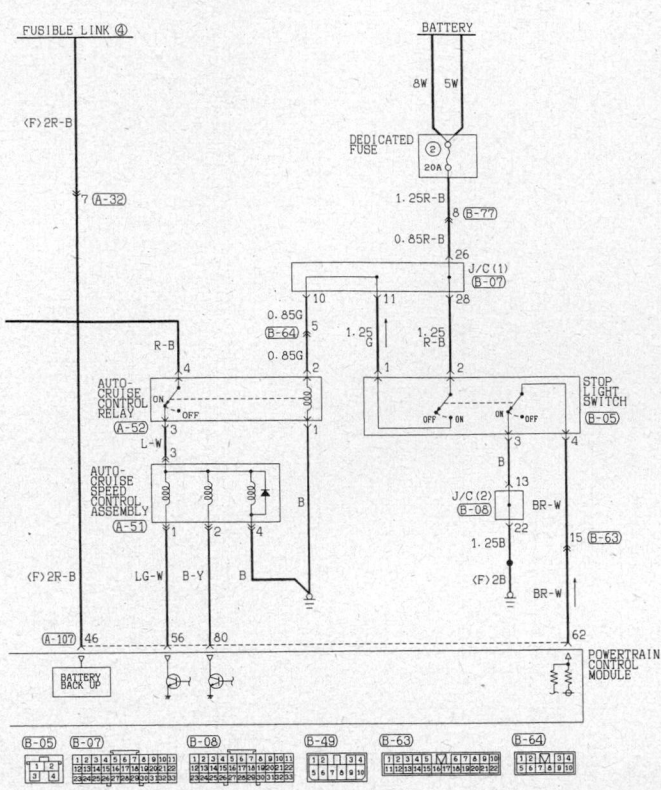

Fig. 25 Wiring diagram (Part 2 of 6). Eclipse w/2.0L non-turbocharged engine

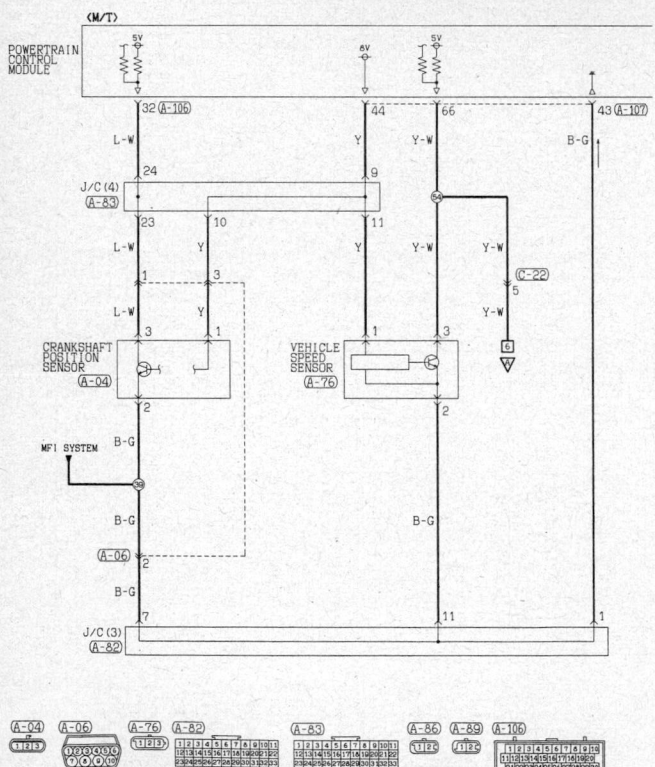

Fig. 25 Wiring diagram (Part 3 of 6). Eclipse w/2.0L non-turbocharged engine

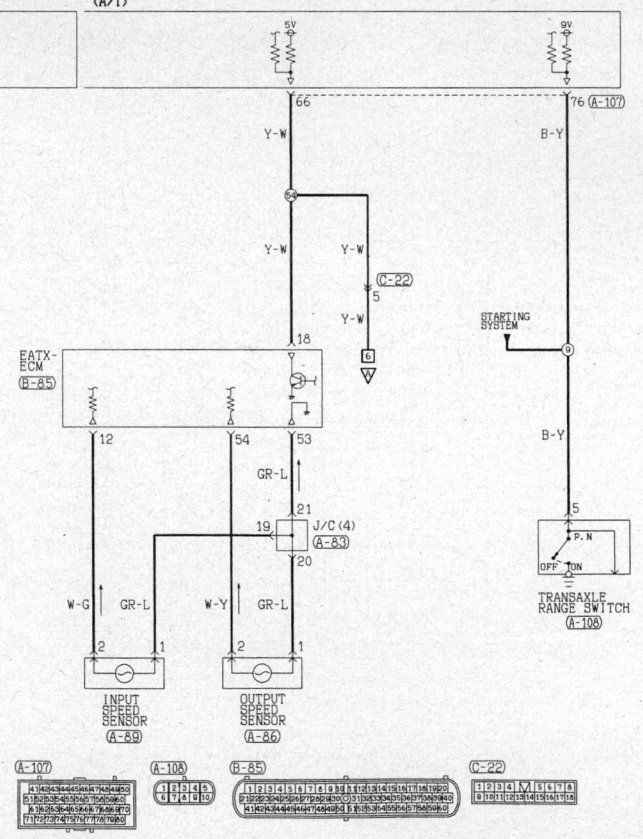

Fig. 25 Wiring diagram (Part 4 of 6). Eclipse w/2.0L non-turbocharged engine

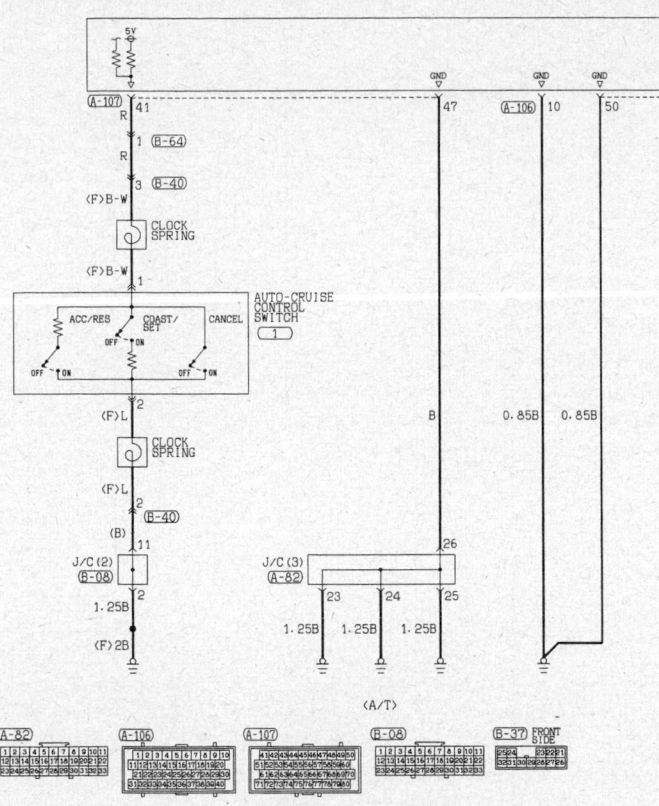

Fig. 25 Wiring diagram (Part 5 of 6). Eclipse w/2.0L non-turbocharged engine

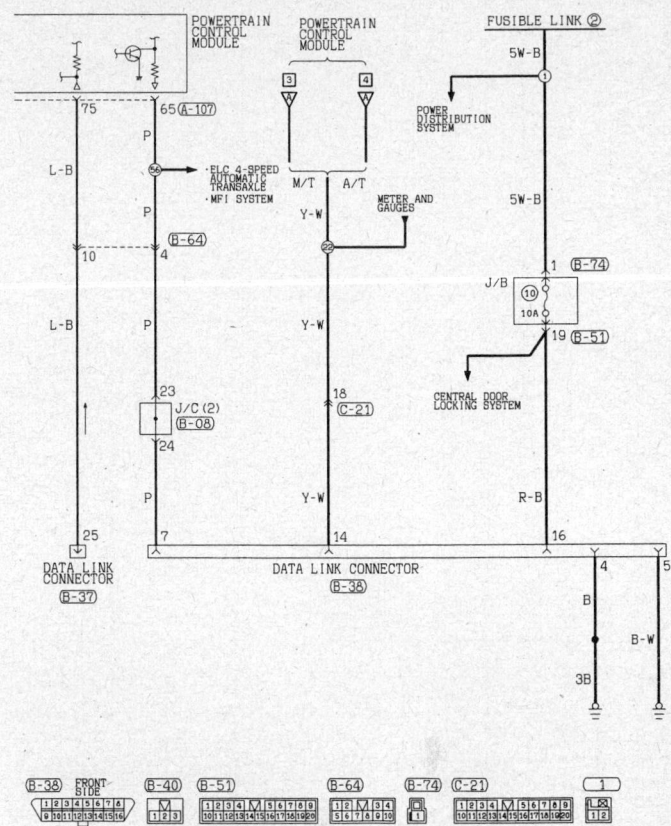

Fig. 25 Wiring diagram (Part 6 of 6). Eclipse w/2.0L non-turbocharged engine

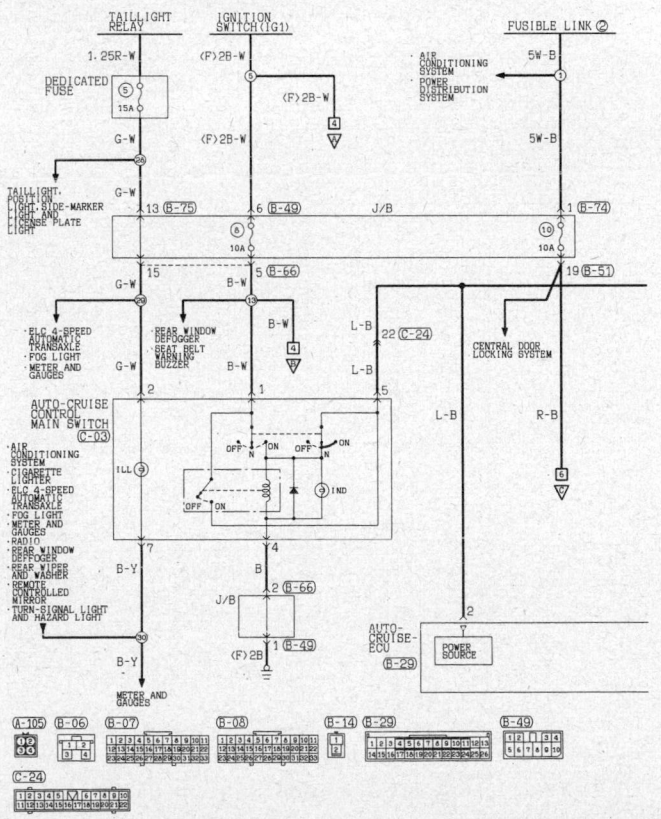

Fig. 26 Wiring diagram (Part 1 of 6). Eclipse w/2.0L turbocharged & 2.4L engines

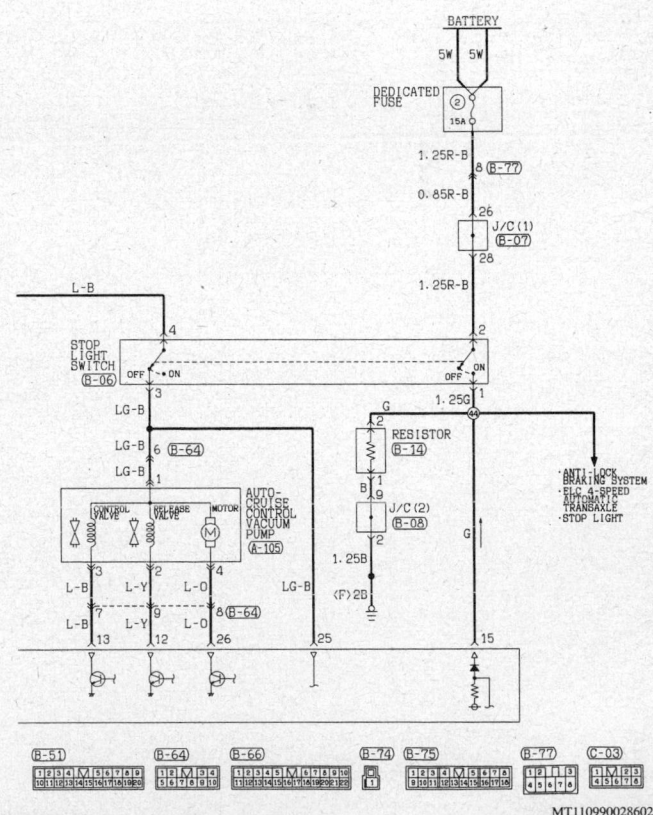

Fig. 26 Wiring diagram (Part 2 of 6). Eclipse w/2.0L turbocharged & 2.4L engines

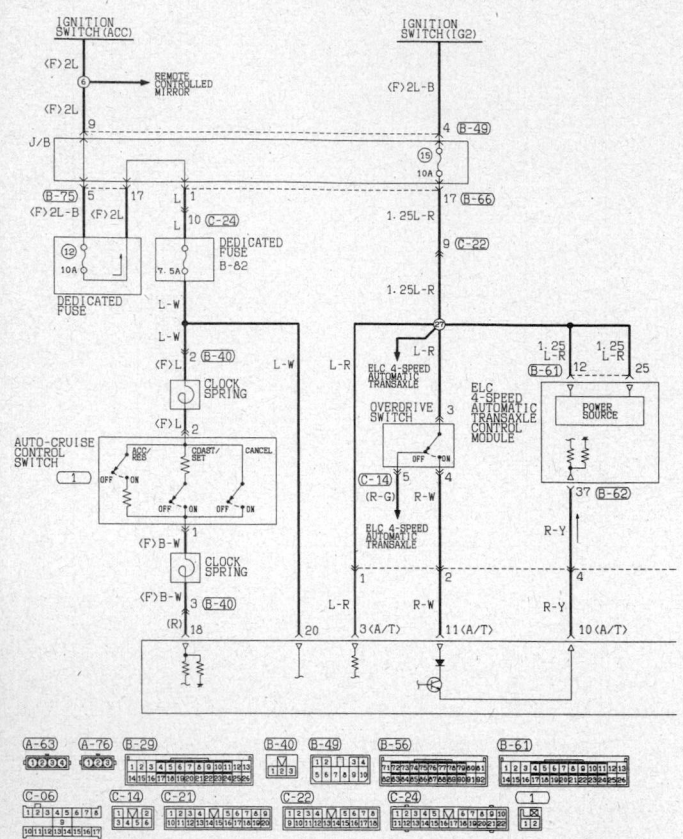

Fig. 26 Wiring diagram (Part 3 of 6). Eclipse w/2.0L turbocharged & 2.4L engines

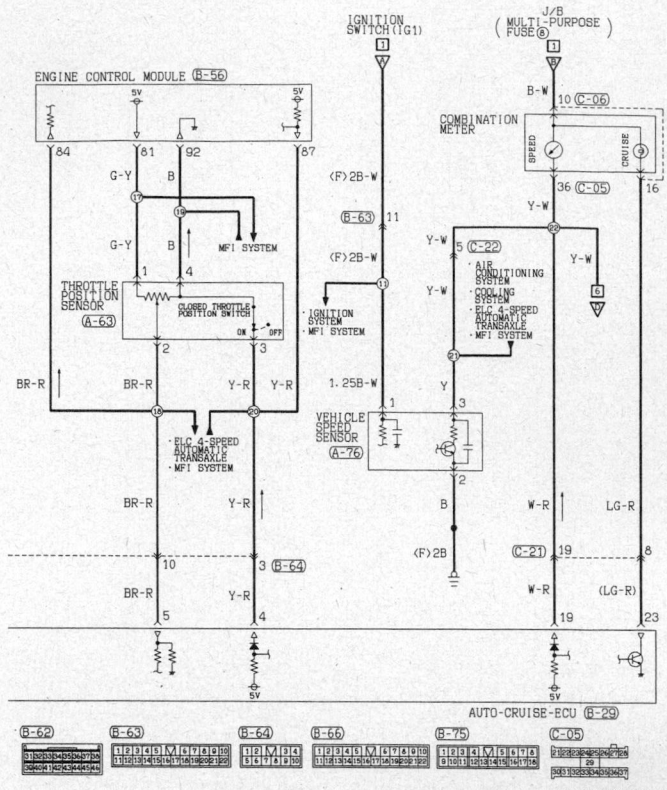

Fig. 26 Wiring diagram (Part 4 of 6). Eclipse w/2.0L turbocharged & 2.4L engines

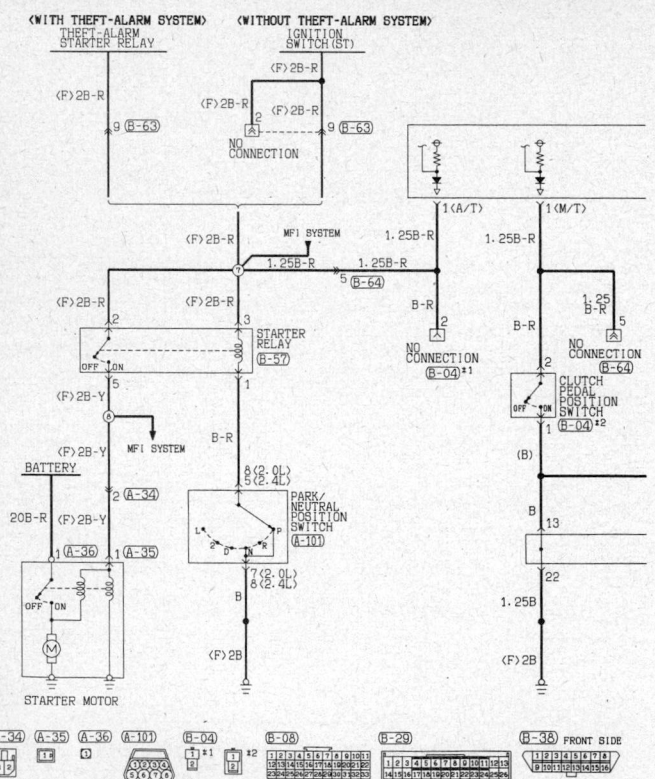

Fig. 26 Wiring diagram (Part 5 of 6). Eclipse w/2.0L turbocharged & 2.4L engines

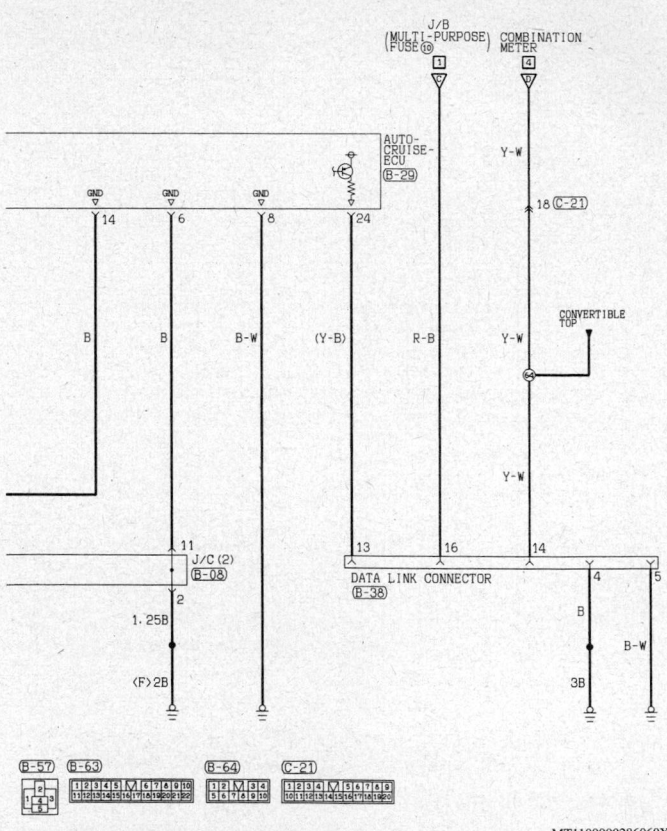

Fig. 26 Wiring diagram (Part 6 of 6). Eclipse w/2.0L turbocharged & 2.4L engines

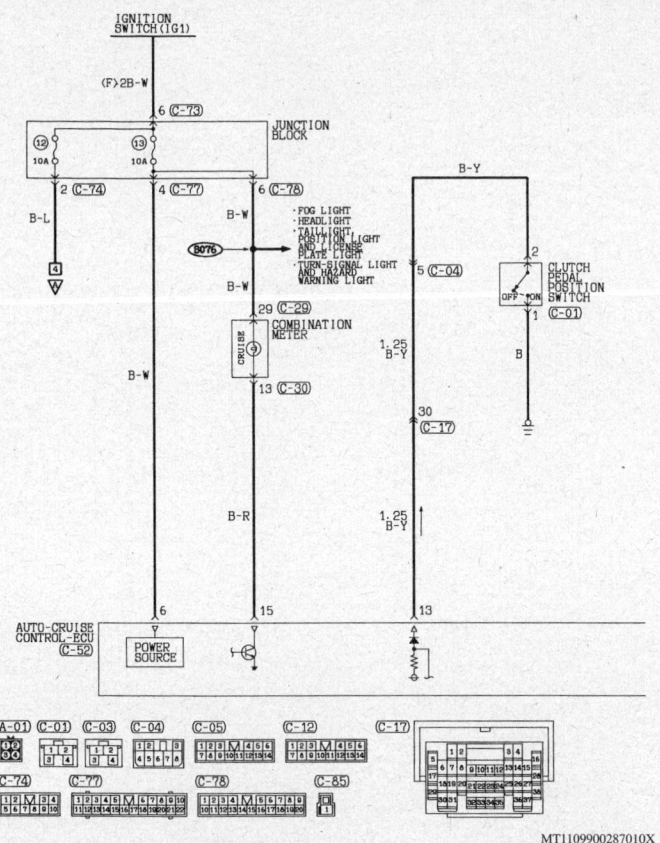

Fig. 27 Wiring diagram (Part 1 of 4). Galant w/manual transaxle

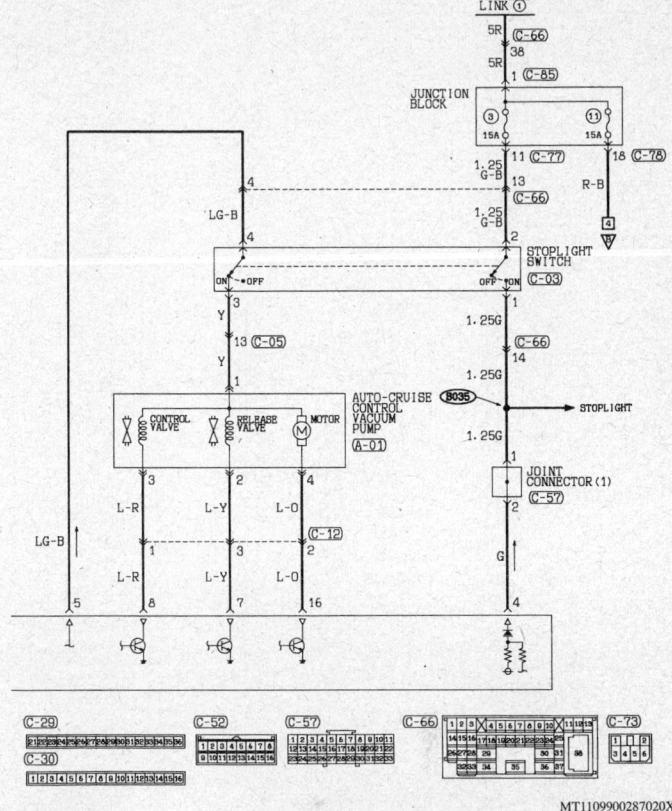

Fig. 27 Wiring diagram (Part 2 of 4). Galant w/manual transaxle

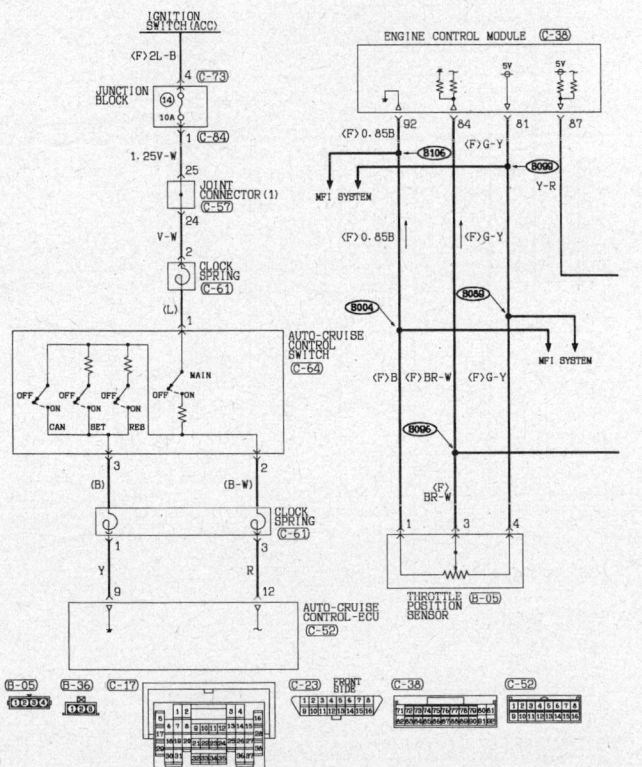

Fig. 27 Wiring diagram (Part 3 of 4). Galant w/manual transaxle

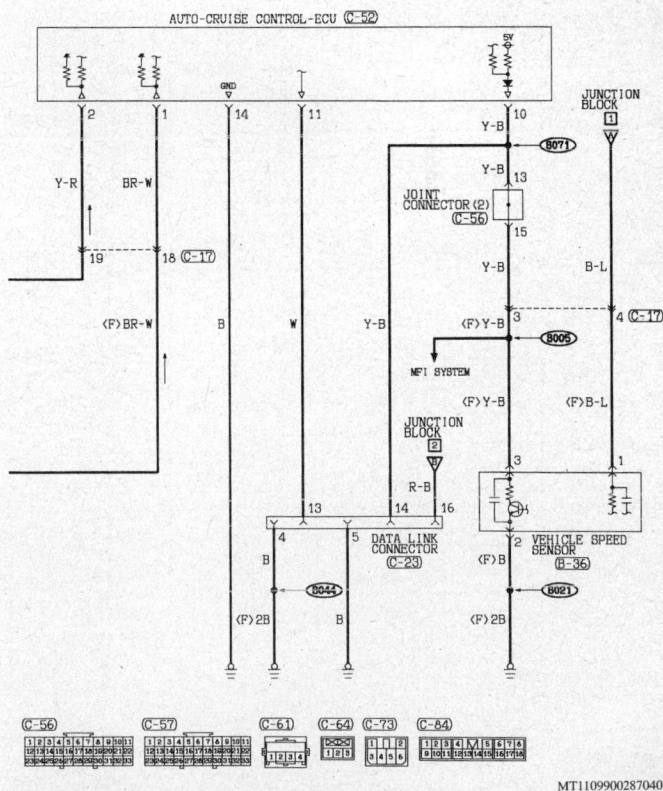

Fig. 27 Wiring diagram (Part 4 of 4). Galant /manual transaxle

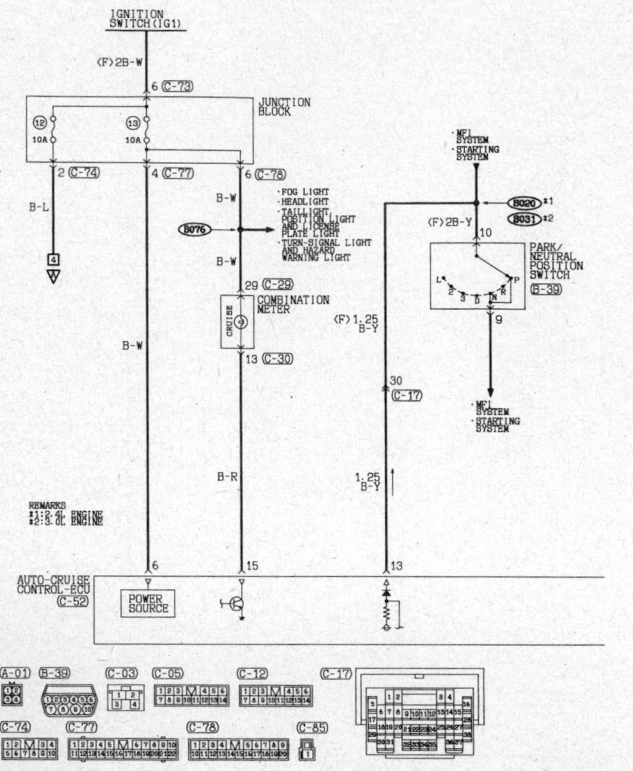

Fig. 28   Wiring diagram (Part 1 of 4). Galant w/automatic transaxle

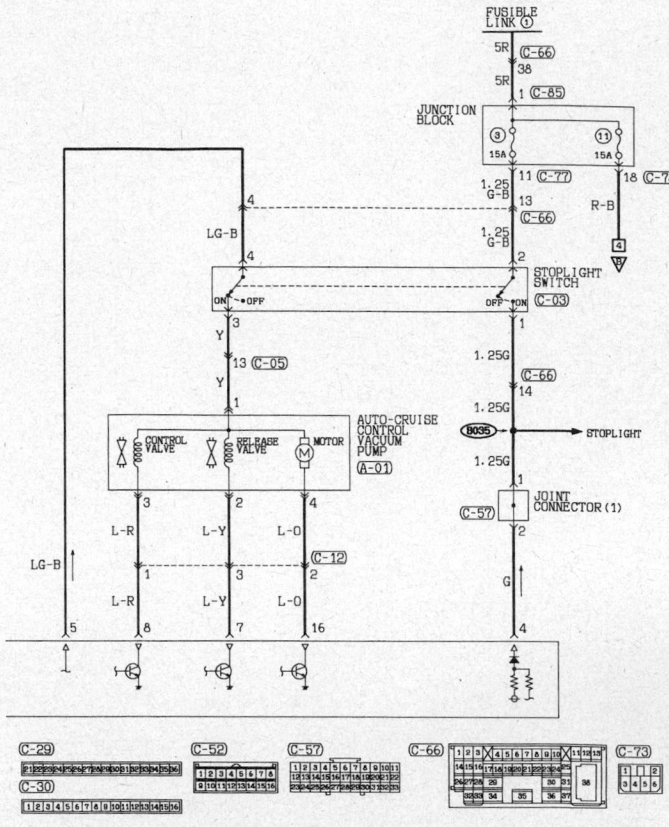

Fig. 28   Wiring diagram (Part 2 of 4). Galant w/automatic transaxle

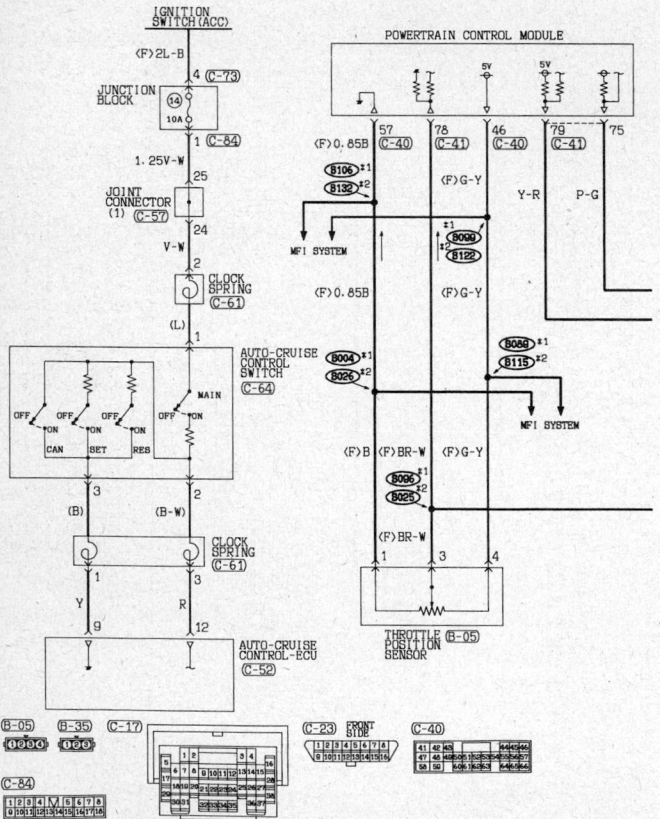

Fig. 28   Wiring diagram (Part 3 of 4). Galant w/automatic transaxle

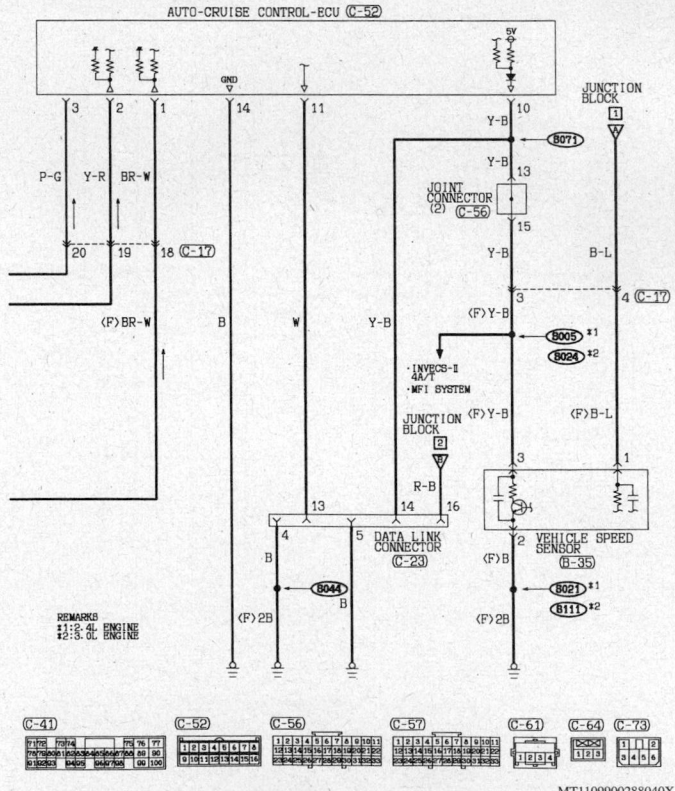

Fig. 28   Wiring diagram (Part 4 of 4). Galant w/automatic transaxle

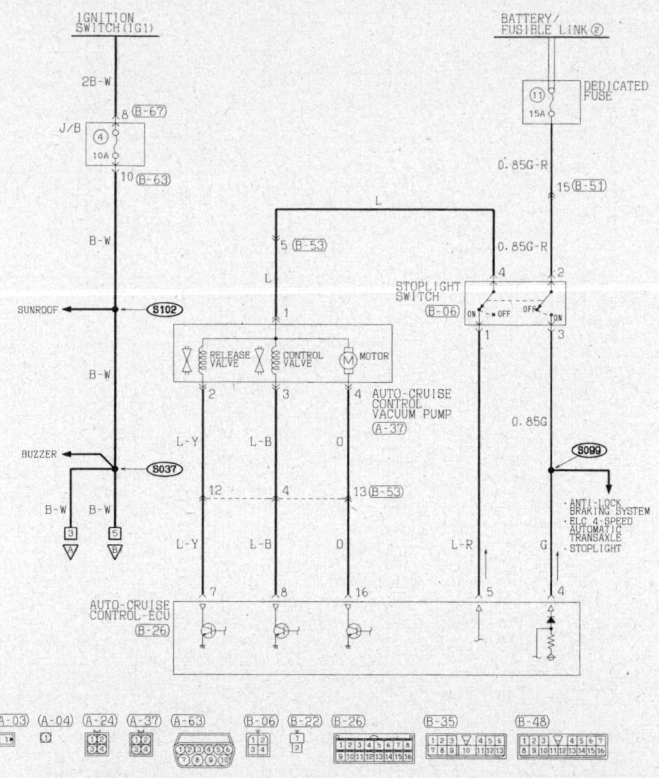

Fig. 29 Wiring diagram (Part 1 of 5). Mirage

MT1109900289010X

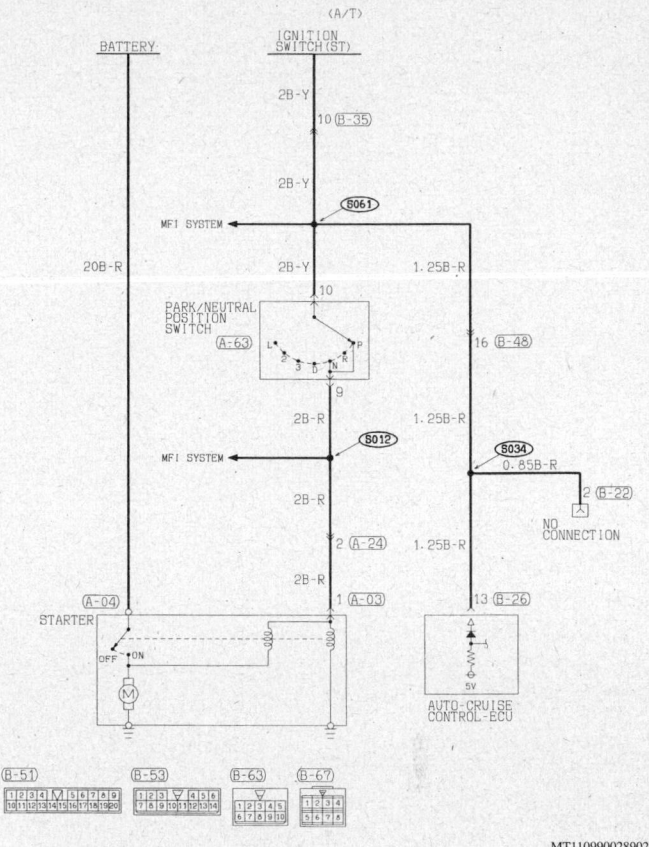

Fig. 29 Wiring diagram (Part 2 of 5). Mirage

MT1109900289020X

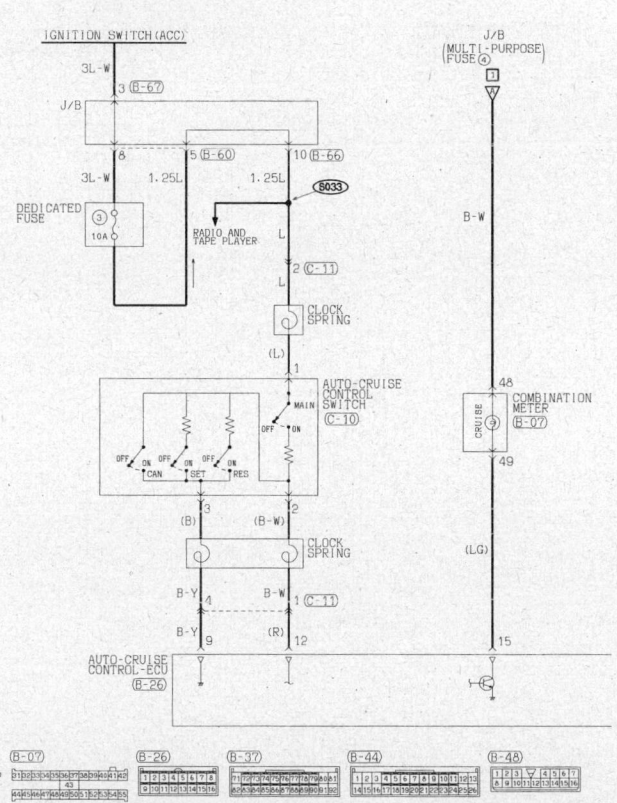

Fig. 29 Wiring diagram (Part 3 of 5). Mirage

MT1109900289030X

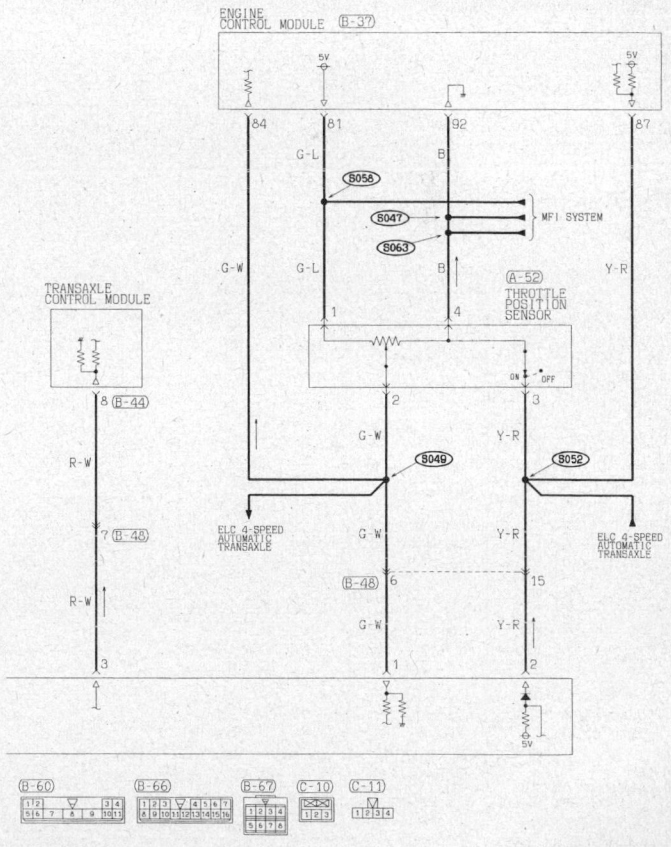

Fig. 29 Wiring diagram (Part 4 of 5). Mirage

MT1109900289040X

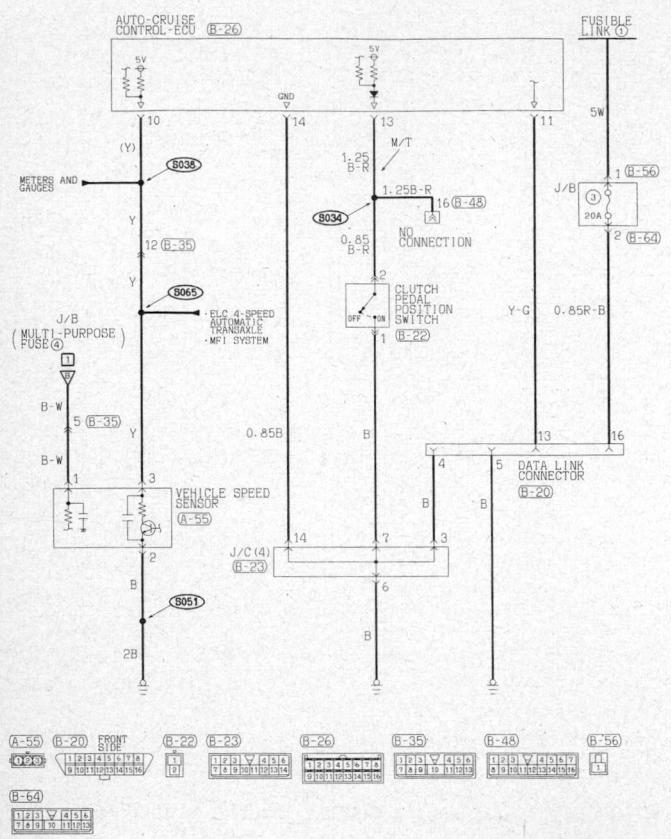

Fig. 29 Wiring diagram (Part 5 of 5). Mirage

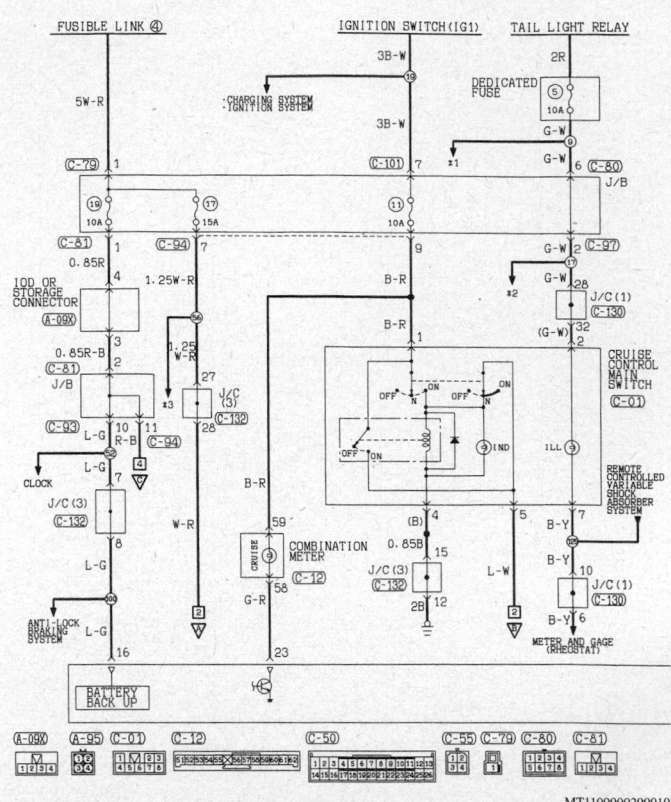

Fig. 30 Wiring diagram (Part 1 of 4). Montero

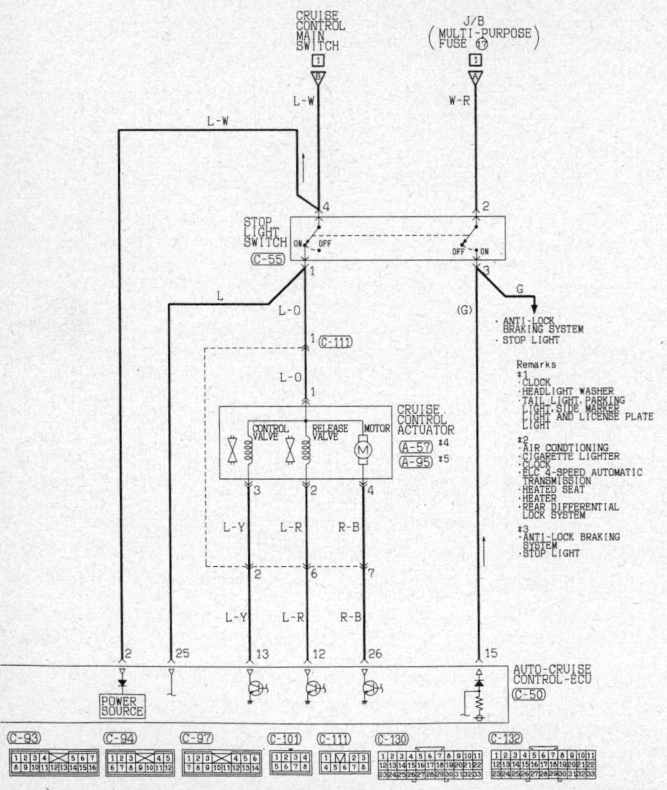

Fig. 30 Wiring diagram (Part 2 of 4). Montero

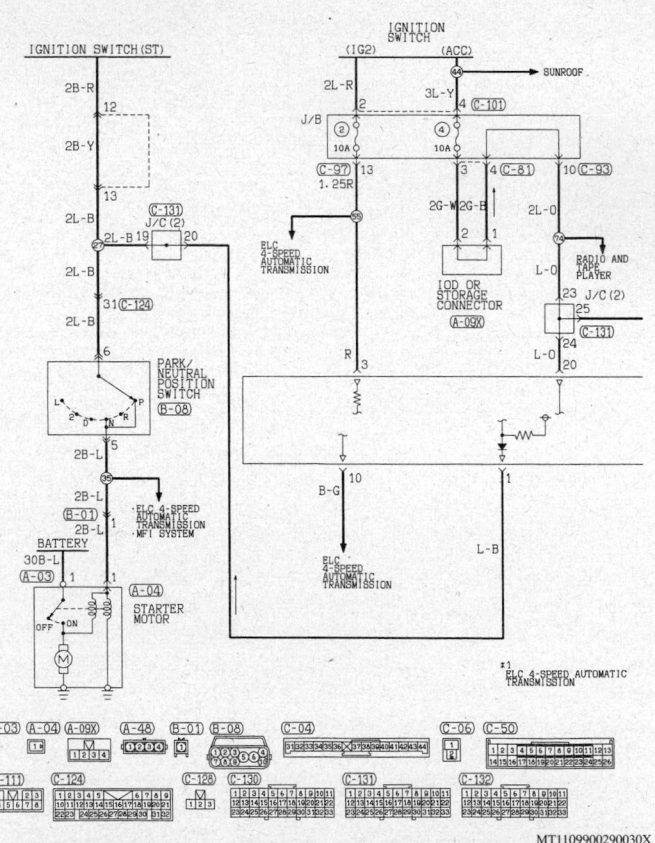

Fig. 30 Wiring diagram (Part 3 of 4). Montero

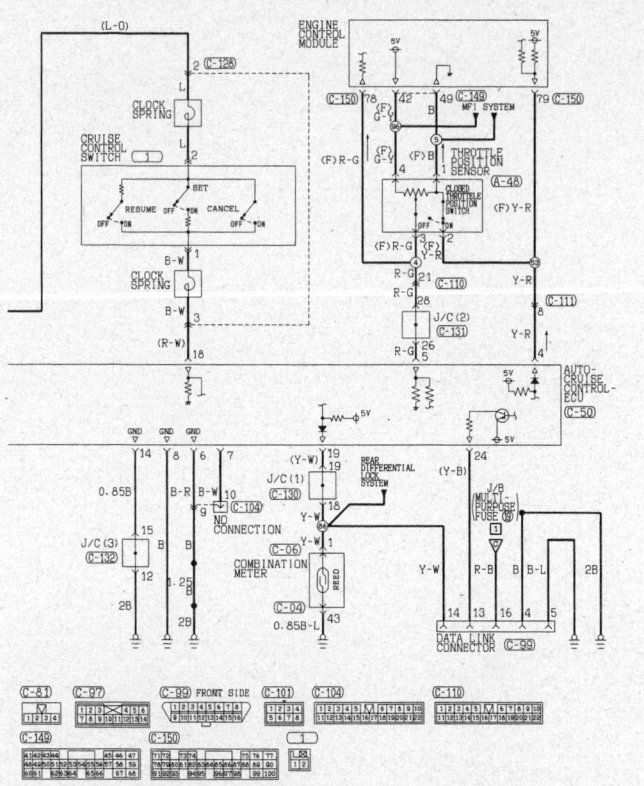

Fig. 30 Wiring diagram (Part 4 of 4). Montero

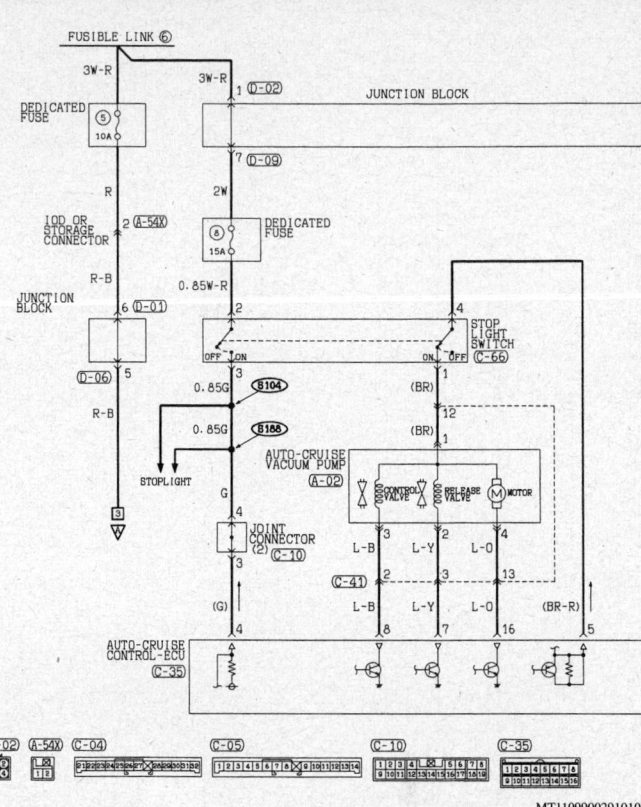

Fig. 31 Wiring diagram (Part 1 of 7). Montero Sport

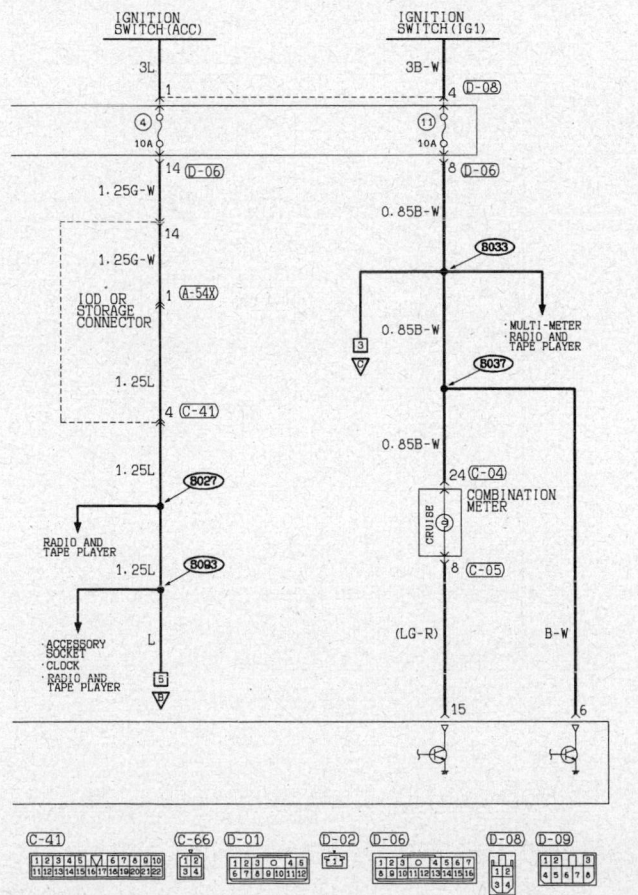

Fig. 31 Wiring diagram (Part 2 of 7). Montero Sport

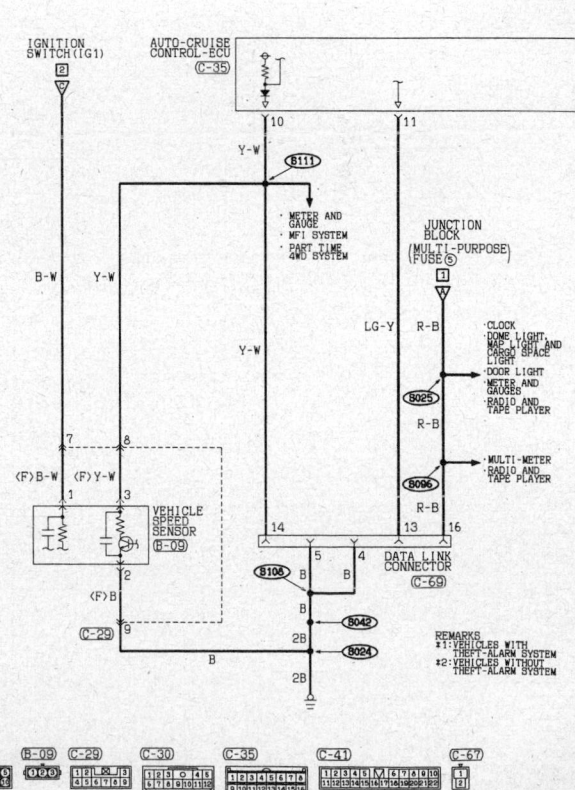

Fig. 31 Wiring diagram (Part 3 of 7). Montero Sport

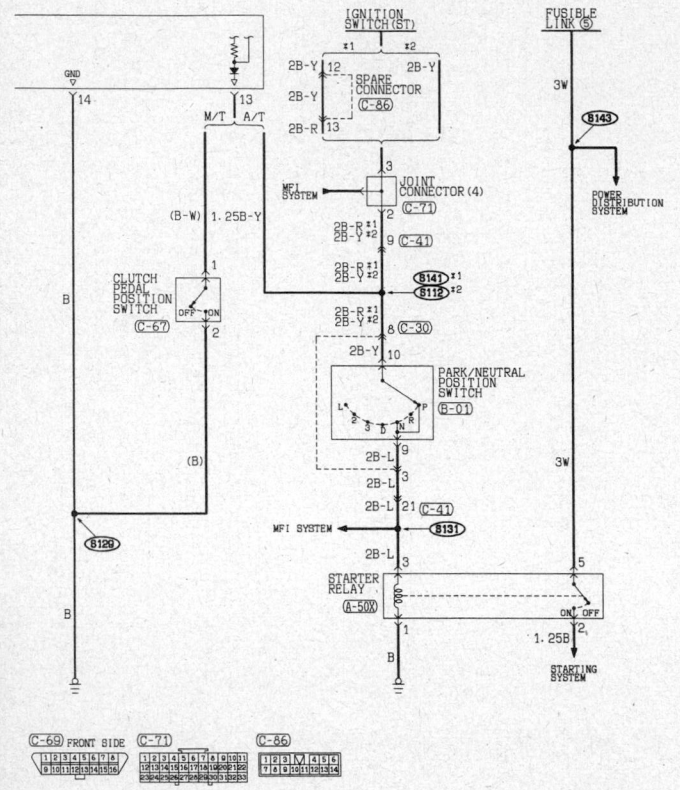

Fig. 31 Wiring diagram (Part 4 of 7). Montero Sport

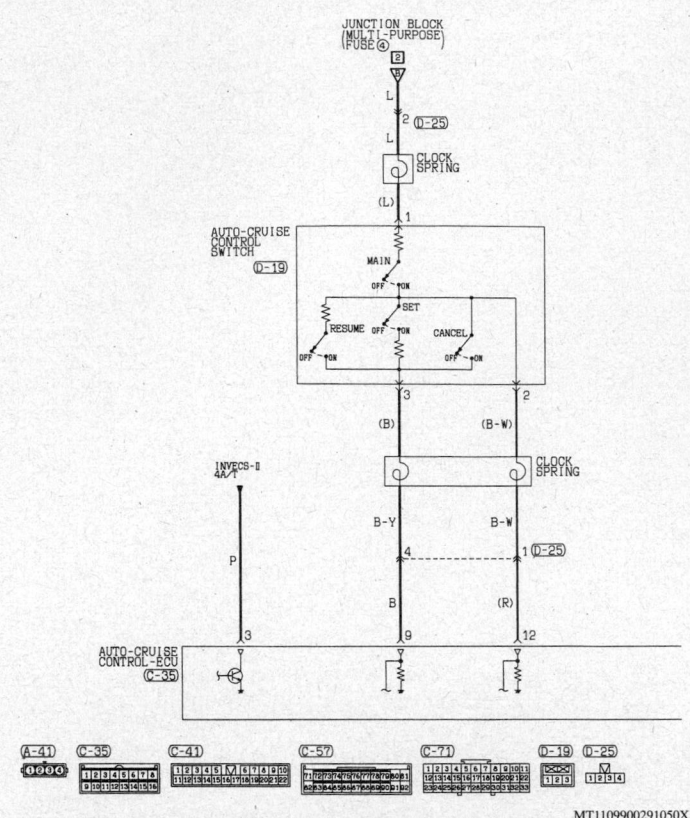

Fig. 31 Wiring diagram (Part 5 of 7). Montero Sport

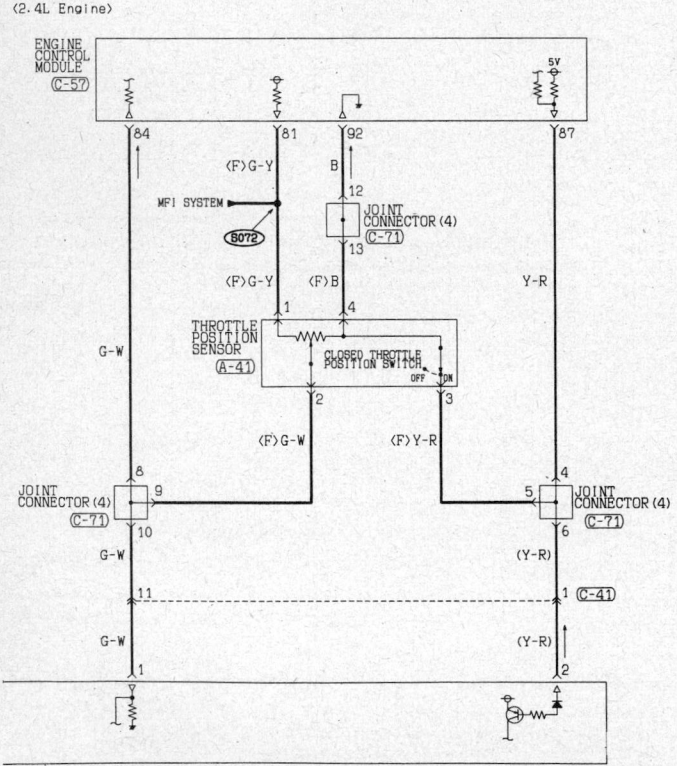

Fig. 31 Wiring diagram (Part 6 of 7). Montero Sport

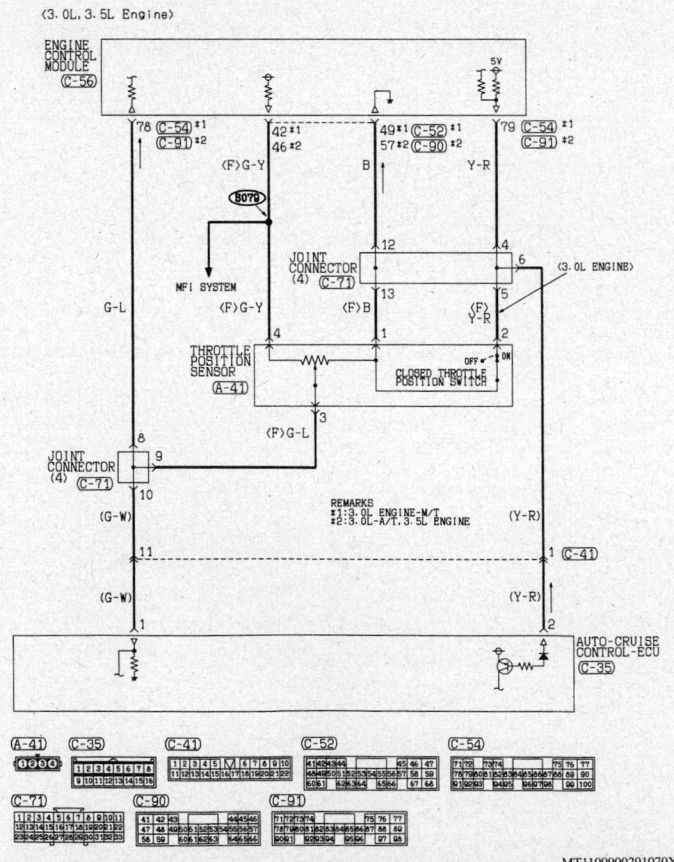

Fig. 31 Wiring diagram (Part 7 of 7). Montero Sport

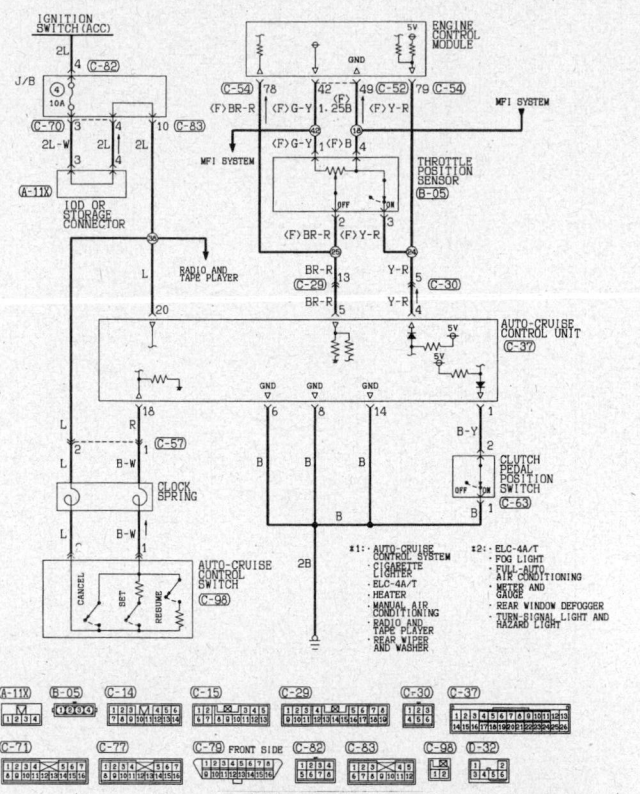

Fig. 32 Wiring diagram (Part 1 of 3). 3000GT w/manual transaxle

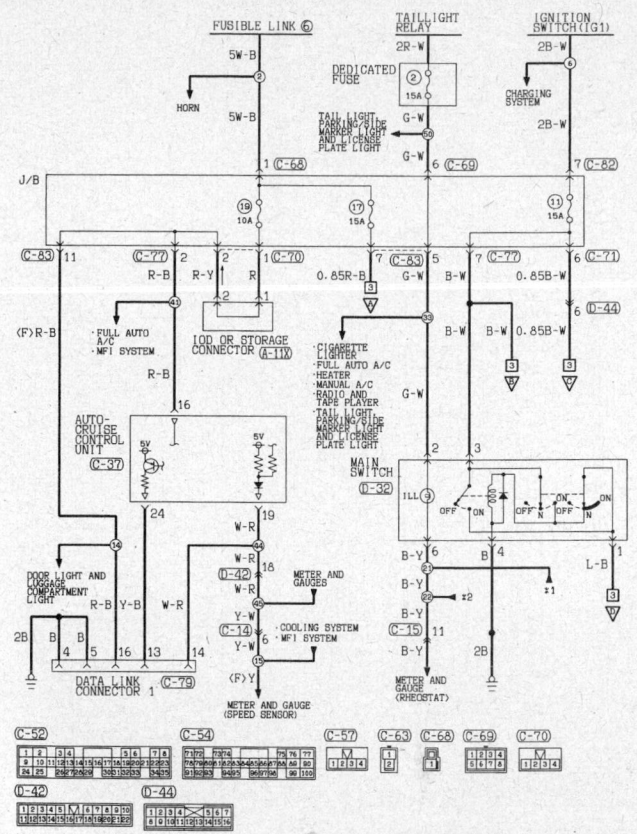

Fig. 32 Wiring diagram (Part 2 of 3). 3000GT w/manual transaxle

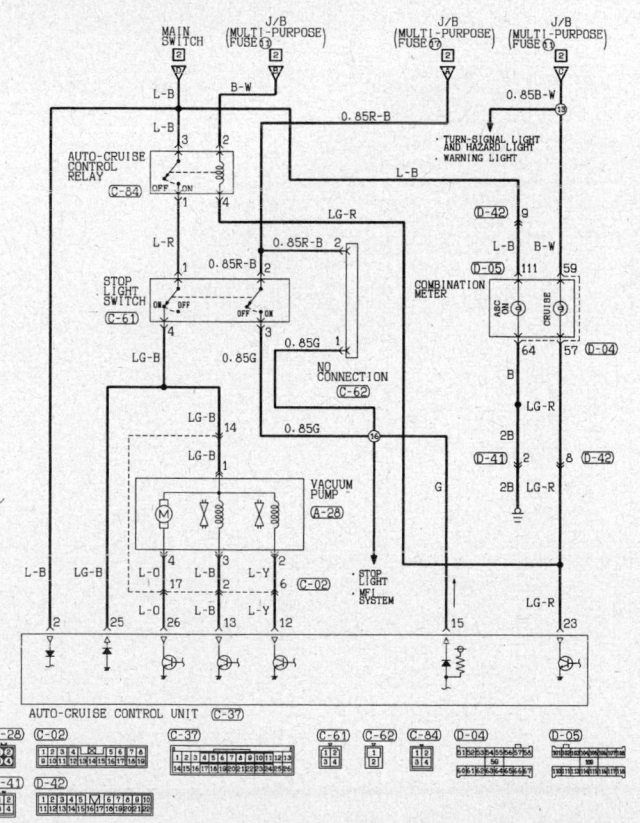

Fig. 32 Wiring diagram (Part 3 of 3). 3000GT w/manual transaxle

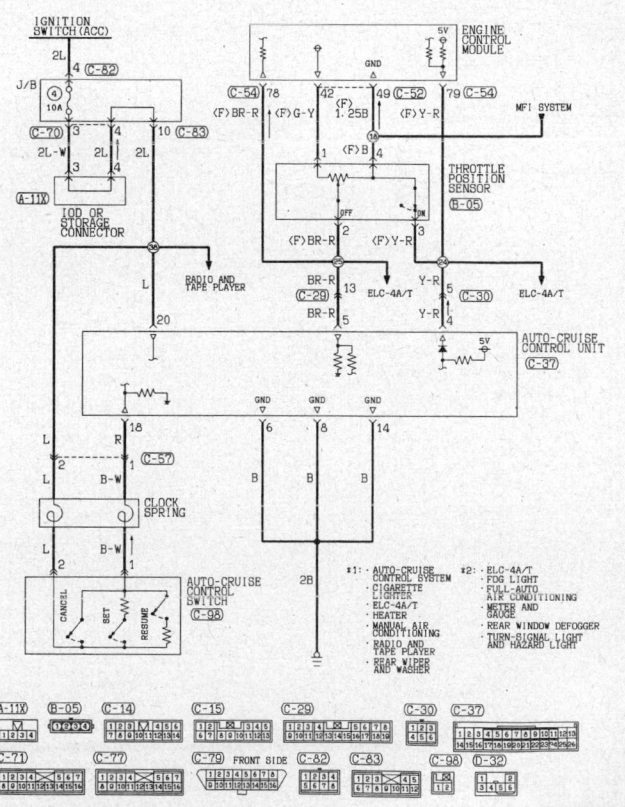

Fig. 33 Wiring diagram (Part 1 of 4). 3000GT w/automatic transaxle

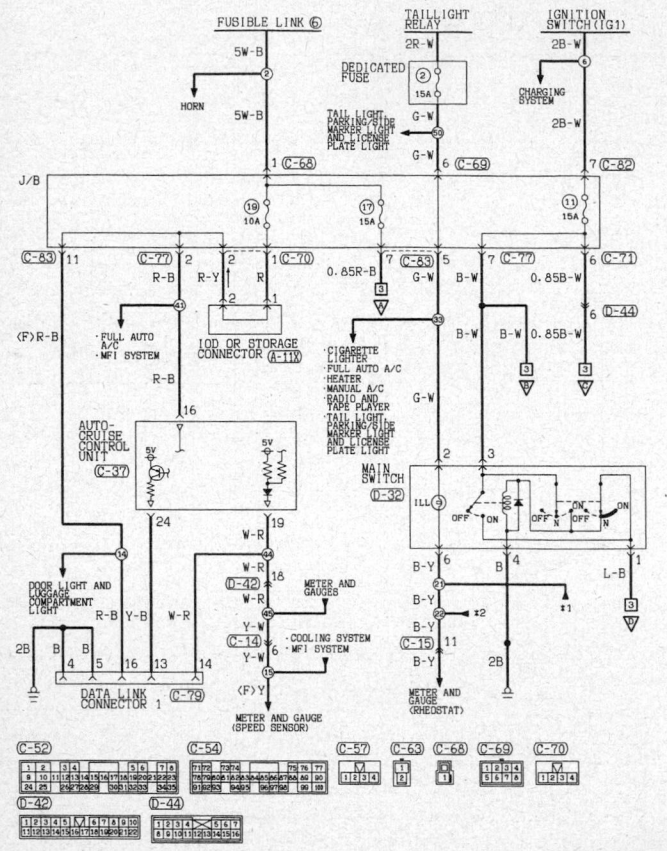

Fig. 33   Wiring diagram (Part 2 of 4). 3000GT w/automatic transaxle

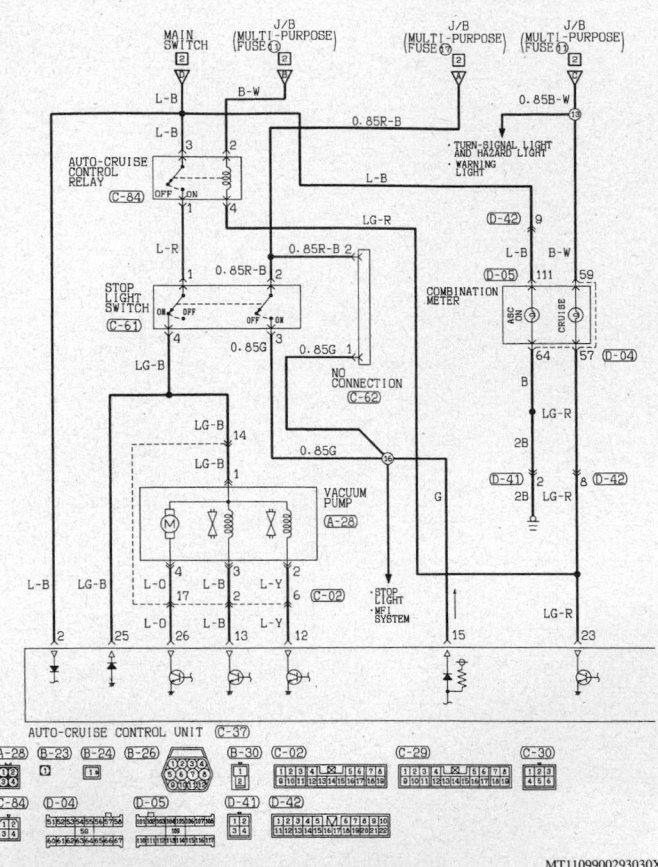

Fig. 33   Wiring diagram (Part 3 of 4). 3000GT w/automatic transaxle

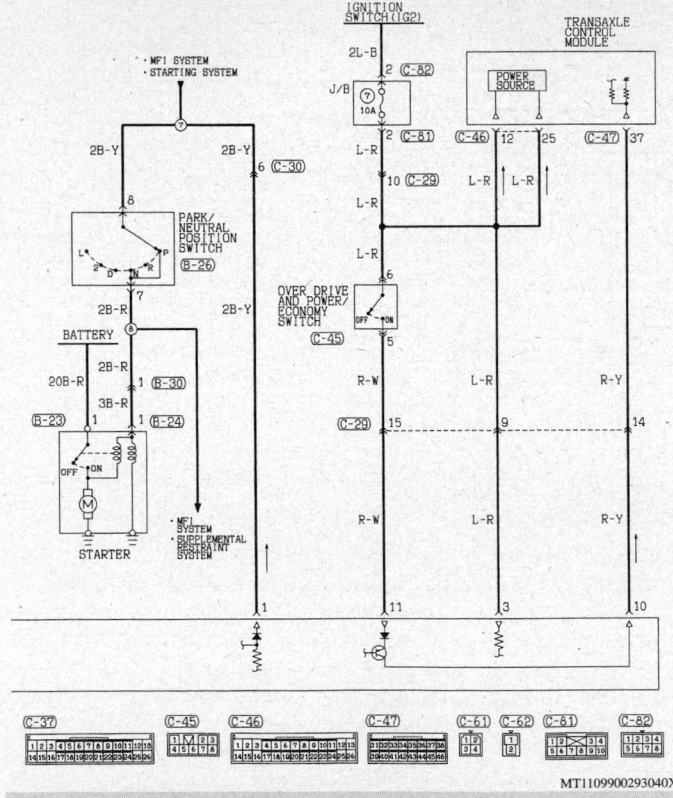

Fig. 33   Wiring diagram (Part 4 of 4). 3000GT w/automatic transaxle

DIAGNOSTIC CHART INDEX

Code/ Inspection Procedure	Description	Page No.	Fig. No.
DIAMANTE			
Code 11	Electric Vacuum Pump Drive System	33-50	34
Code 12	Vehicle Speed Signal System	33-50	35
Code 14	Electric Vacuum Pump Power Supply System	33-51	36
Code 15	Auto Cruise Control Switch	33-51	37
Code 16	Auto Cruise Control ECU	33-51	38
Code 17	TPS/APPS System	33-51	39
—	Inspection Procedure Chart	33-51	40
Inspection Procedure 1	Communication w/Scan Tool Not Possible	33-51	41
Inspection Procedure 2	Communication w/Scan Tool Not Possible	33-51	42
Inspection Procedure 3	Input Switch Inspection w/Scan Tool Not Possible	33-52	43
Inspection Procedure 4	Auto Cruise Does Not Cancel	33-52	44
Inspection Procedure 5	Auto Cruise Does Not Cancel	33-52	45
Inspection Procedure 6	Auto Cruise Does Not Cancel	33-52	46
Inspection Procedure 7	Auto Cruise Cannot Be Set	33-52	47
Inspection Procedure 8	Hunting Occurs At Set Speed	33-52	48
Inspection Procedure 9	Auto Cruise Indicator Does Not Illuminate	33-52	49
Inspection Procedure 10	Stop Lamp Switch Circuit Inspection	33-53	50
Inspection Procedure 11	PNP Switch Inspection	33-53	51
ECLIPSE w/2.0L NON-TURBOCHARGED ENGINE			
Code 02	PCM	33-53	56
Code 15	Speed Control Servo Solenoid	33-53	55
Code 35	Vehicle Speed Signal System	33-53	52
Code 82	Auto Cruise Control Relay System	33-53	57
Code 86	Auto Cruise Control Switch	33-53	53
Code 87	Auto Cruise Control Switch	33-53	54
—	Inspection Procedure Chart	33-53	58
Inspection Procedure 1	Communication w/Scan Tool Not Possible	33-53	59
Inspection Procedure 2	Auto Cruise Does Not Cancel When Engine Speed Increases	33-54	60
Inspection Procedure 3	Auto Cruise Does Not Cancel	33-54	61
Inspection Procedure 4	Auto Cruise Does Not Cancel	33-54	62
Inspection Procedure 5	Auto Cruise Does Not Cancel	33-54	63
Inspection Procedure 6	Auto Cruise Cannot Be Set	33-54	64
Inspection Procedure 7	Hunting Occurs At Set Speed	33-54	65
Inspection Procedure 8	Auto Cruise Lamp Does Not Illuminate	33-54	66
Inspection Procedure 9	Auto Cruise Lamp Does Not Illuminate	33-54	67
Inspection Procedure 10	Auto Cruise Lamp Does Not Illuminate	33-54	68

Continued

DIAGNOSTIC CHART INDEX—Continued

Code/ Inspection Procedure	Description	Page No.	Fig. No.
ECLIPSE w/2.0L TURBOCHARGED & 2.4L ENGINES			
Code 11	Auto Cruise Vacuum Pump Drive System	33-55	69
Code 12	Vehicle Speed Signal System	33-55	70
Code 14	Auto Cruise Vacuum Pump Power Supply System	33-55	71
Code 15	Auto Cruise Control Switch	33-55	72
Code 16	Auto Cruise Control ECU	33-55	73
Code 17	TPS System	33-55	74
—	Inspection Procedure Chart	33-56	75
Inspection Procedure 1	Communication w/Scan Tool Not Possible	33-56	76
Inspection Procedure 2	Communication w/Scan Tool Not Possible	33-56	77
Inspection Procedure 3	Input Switch Inspection w/Scan Tool Not Possible	33-56	78
Inspection Procedure 4	Auto Cruise Does Not Cancel	33-56	79
Inspection Procedure 5	Auto Cruise Does Not Cancel	33-57	80
Inspection Procedure 6	Auto Cruise Does Not Cancel	33-57	81
Inspection Procedure 7	Auto Cruise Does Not Cancel	33-57	82
Inspection Procedure 8	Auto Cruise Cannot Be Set	33-57	83
Inspection Procedure 9	Auto Cruise Cannot Be Set	33-57	84
Inspection Procedure 10	Hunting Occurs At Set Speed	33-57	85
Inspection Procedure 11	Auto Cruise Lamp Does Not Illuminate	33-57	86
Inspection Procedure 12	Auto Cruise Lamp Does Not Illuminate	33-58	87
Inspection Procedure 13	Auto Cruise Lamp Does Not Illuminate	33-58	88
Inspection Procedure 14	Stop Lamp Switch Inspection	33-58	89
Inspection Procedure 15	CPS or PNP Switch Inspection	33-58	90
GALANT & MIRAGE			
Code 11	Auto Vacuum Pump Drive System	33-58	91
Code 12	Vehicle Speed Signal System	33-58	92
Code 14	Auto Cruise Vacuum Pump Power Supply	33-58	93
Code 15	Auto Cruise Control Switch	33-58	94
Code 16	Auto Cruise Control ECU	33-58	95
Code 17	TPS System	33-59	96
—	Inspection Procedure Chart	33-59	97
Inspection Procedure 1	Communication w/Scan Tool Not Possible	33-59	98
Inspection Procedure 2	Communication w/Scan Tool Not Possible	33-59	99
Inspection Procedure 3	Input Switch Inspection w/Scan Tool Not Possible	33-59	100
Inspection Procedure 4	Auto Cruise Will Not Cancel	33-59	101
Inspection Procedure 5	Auto Cruise Will Not Cancel	33-60	102
Inspection Procedure 6	Auto Cruise Will Not Cancel	33-60	103

Continued

DIAGNOSTIC CHART INDEX—Continued

Code/ Inspection Procedure	Description	Page No.	Fig. No.
GALANT & MIRAGE			
Inspection Procedure 7	Auto Cruise Will Not Cancel	33-60	104
Inspection Procedure 9	Auto Cruise Cannot Be Set	33-60	105
Inspection Procedure 10	Hunting Occurs At Set Speed	33-60	106
Inspection Procedure 11	Auto Cruise Lamp Does Not Illuminate	33-60	107
Inspection Procedure 12	Stop Lamp Switch Inspection	33-60	108
Inspection Procedure 13	CPS Or PNP Switch Inspection	33-60	109
MONTERO & MONTERO SPORT			
Code 11	Auto Cruise Vacuum Pump	33-61	110
Code 12	Vehicle Speed Signal System	33-61	111
Code 14	Auto Cruise Vacuum Pump Power Supply	33-61	112
Code 15	Auto Cruise ECU	33-61	113
Code 16	Auto Cruise ECU	33-61	114
Code 17	TPS System	33-61	115
—	Inspection Procedure Chart	33-61	116
Inspection Procedure 1	Communication w/Scan Tool Not Possible	33-61	117
Inspection Procedure 2	Communication w/Scan Tool Not Possible	33-62	118
Inspection Procedure 3	Input Switch Inspection w/Scan Tool Not Possible	33-62	119
Inspection Procedure 4	Auto Cruise Does Not Cancel	33-62	120
Inspection Procedure 5	Auto Cruise Does Not Cancel	33-62	121
Inspection Procedure 6	Auto Cruise Does Not Cancel	33-62	122
Inspection Procedure 7	Auto Cruise Cannot Set	33-62	123
Inspection Procedure 8	Auto Cruise Cannot Set	33-63	124
Inspection Procedure 9	Hunting Occurs At Set Speed	33-63	125
Inspection Procedure 10	Auto Cruise Lamp Does Not Illuminate	33-63	126
Inspection Procedure 11	Auto Cruise Lamp Does Not Illuminate	33-63	127
Inspection Procedure 12	Auto Cruise Lamp Does Not Illuminate	33-63	128
Inspection Procedure 13	Stop Lamp Switch Inspection	33-63	129
Inspection Procedure 14	PNP Switch Inspection	33-63	130
3000GT			
Code 11	Auto Cruise Vacuum Pump Drive System	33-63	131
Code 12	Vehicle Speed Signal System	33-64	132
Code 15	Auto Cruise Control ECU	33-64	133
Code 16	Auto Cruise Control ECU	33-64	134
Code 17	TPS System	33-64	135
—	Inspection Procedure Chart	33-64	136
Inspection Procedure 1	Communication w/Scan Tool Not Possible	33-64	137

Continued

DIAGNOSTIC CHART INDEX—Continued

Code/ Inspection Procedure	Description	Page No.	Fig. No.
3000GT			
Inspection Procedure 2	Communication w/Scan Tool Not Possible	33-64	138
Inspection Procedure 3	Communication w/Scan Tool Not Possible	33-65	139
Inspection Procedure 4	Auto Cruise Does Not Cancel	33-65	140
Inspection Procedure 5	Auto Cruise Does Not Cancel	33-65	141
Inspection Procedure 6	Auto Cruise Does Not Cancel	33-65	142
Inspection Procedure 7	Auto Cruise Does Not Cancel	33-65	143
Inspection Procedure 8	Auto Cruise Cannot Be Set	33-65	144
Inspection Procedure 9	Hunting Occurs At Set Speed	33-65	145
Inspection Procedure 10	Auto Cruise Lamp Does Not Illuminate	33-65	146
Inspection Procedure 11	Auto Cruise Lamp Does Not Illuminate	33-66	147
Inspection Procedure 12	Auto Cruise Lamp Does Not Illuminate	33-66	148
Inspection Procedure 13	Stop Lamp Switch	33-66	149
Inspection Procedure 14	CPS Or PNP Switch	33-66	150

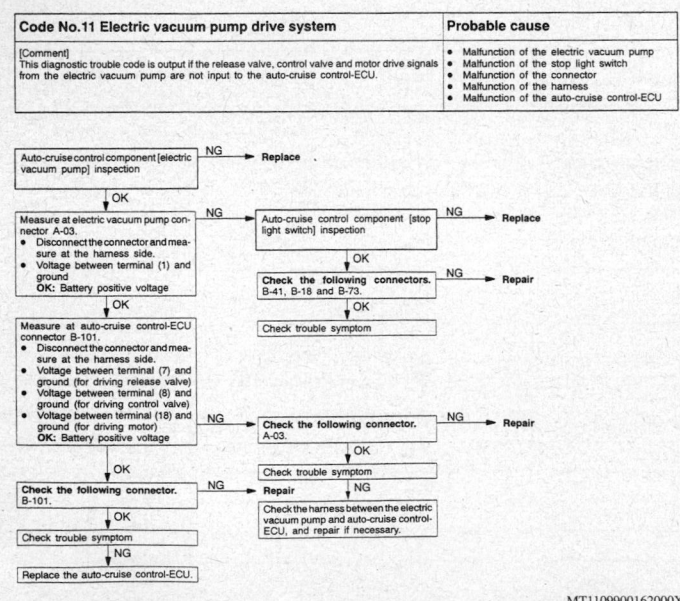

MT1109900162000X

Fig. 34   Code 11: Electric Vacuum Pump Drive System. Diamante

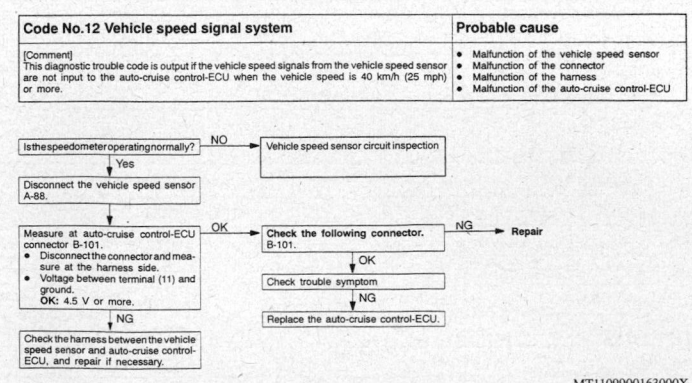

MT1109900163000X

Fig. 35   Code 12: Vehicle Speed Signal System. Diamante

Code No.14 Electric vacuum pump power supply system	Probable cause
This diagnostic trouble code is output if the electric vacuum pump release valve, control valve and motor driving signals are not input into the cruise control ECU.	• Stop lamp switch fault • Connector fault • Harness fault • Cruise control ECU fault

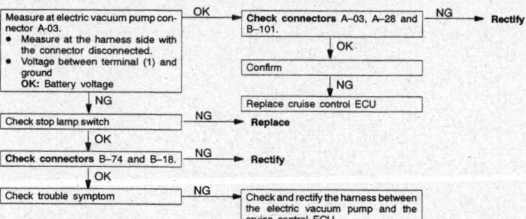

MT1109900164000X

Fig. 36 Code 14: Electric Vacuum Pump Power Supply System. Diamante

Code No.16 Auto-cruise control-ECU	Probable cause
[Comment] This diagnostic trouble code is output if there is an abnormality in the CANCEL hold circuit or the microprocessor monitor circuit in the auto-cruise control-ECU.	• Malfunction of the auto-cruise control-ECU

Replace the auto-cruise control-ECU.

MT1109900166000X

Fig. 38 Code 16: Auto Cruise Control ECU. Diamante

TROUBLE SYMPTOM		INSPECTION PROCEDURE No.
Communication with scan tool is not possible.	Communication with all systems is not possible.	1
	Communication with auto-cruise control-ECU only is not possible.	2
Input switch inspection using the scan tool is not possible. (However, diagnosis inspection is possible.)		3
Auto-cruise control is not cancelled.	Even if brake pedal is depressed	4
	Even if select lever is set to N range	5
	Even if CANCEL switch is set to ON	6
Auto-cruise control cannot be set.		7
Hunting (repeated acceleration and deceleration) occurs at the set vehicle speed.		8
Auto-cruise control indicator light inside combination meter does not illuminate. (However, auto-cruise control is normal.)		9

MT1109900168000X

Fig. 40 Inspection Procedure Chart. Diamante

Code No.15 Auto-cruise control switch	Probable cause
[Comment] This diagnostic trouble code is output if the cruise control RESUME switch, SET switch or CANCEL switch remains ON.	• Malfunction of the auto-cruise control switch

MT1109900165000X

Fig. 37 Code 15: Auto Cruise Control Switch. Diamante

Code No.17 Throttle position sensor/accelerator pedal position sensor system	Probable cause
[Comment] This diagnostic trouble code is output if a voltage of 1.5 V or more when the closed throttle position switch is ON or 0.2 V or less when the closed throttle position switch is OFF is output for a continuous period of 4 seconds or more.	• Malfunction of the throttle position sensor/ accelerator pedal position sensor • Malfunction of the connector • Malfunction of the harness • Malfunction of the auto-cruise control-ECU

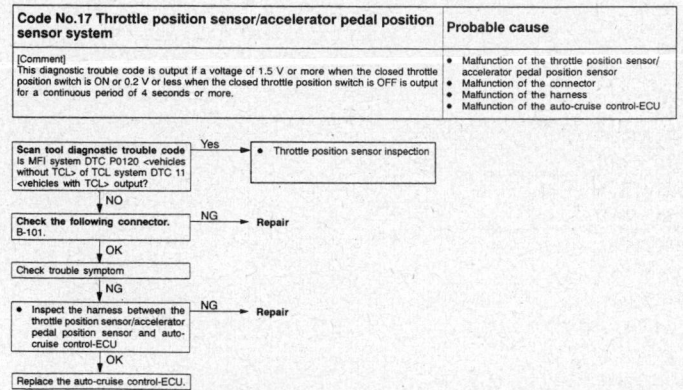

MT1109900167000X

Fig. 39 Code 17: TPS/APPS System. Diamante

Communication with scan tool is not possible. (Communication with all systems is not possible.)	Probable cause
[Comment] The reason is probably a defect in the power supply system (including ground) for the diagnosis line.	• Malfunction of the connector • Malfunction of the harness

MT1109900169000X

Fig. 41 Inspection Procedure 1: Communication w/Scan Tool Not Possible. Diamante

Communication with scan tool is not possible. (Communication with auto-cruise control-ECU only is not possible.)	Probable cause
[Comment] The cause is probably a malfunction of auto-cruise control ECU power supply main switch circuit or a malfunction of auto-cruise control-ECU ground circuit.	• Malfunction of the connector • Malfunction of the harness • Malfunction of the auto-cruise control-ECU

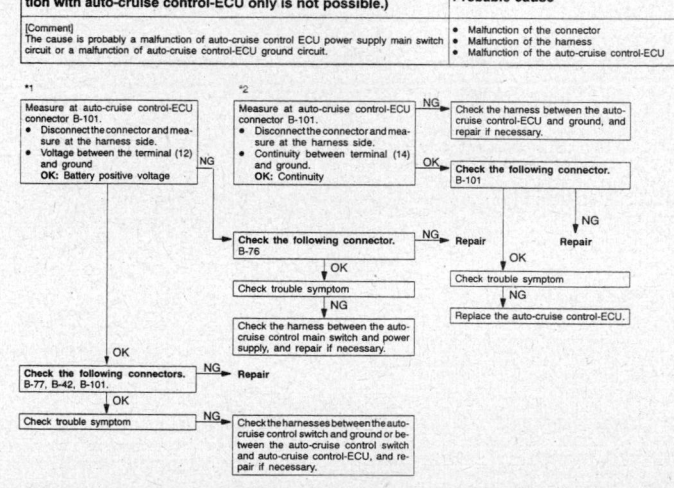

NOTE: *1 indicates malfunction of the auto-cruise control-ECU power supply circuit.

NOTE: *2 indicates malfunction of the auto-cruise control-ECU ground circuit.

MT1109900170000X

Fig. 42 Inspection Procedure 2: Communication w/Scan Tool Not Possible. Diamante

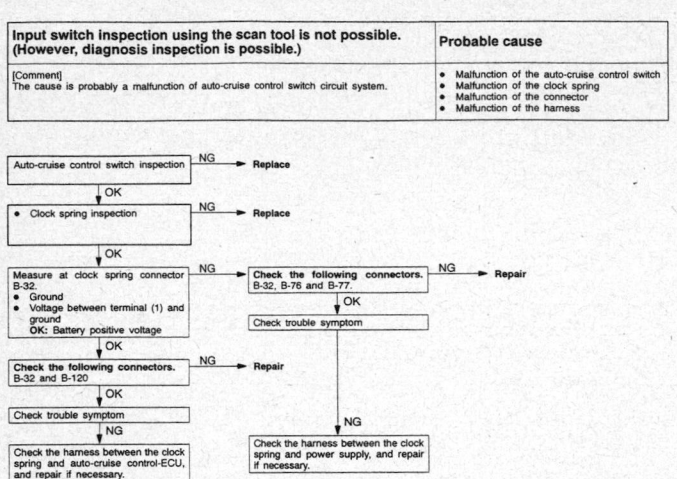

Fig. 43 Inspection Procedure 3: Input Switch Inspection w/Scan Tool Not Possible. Diamante

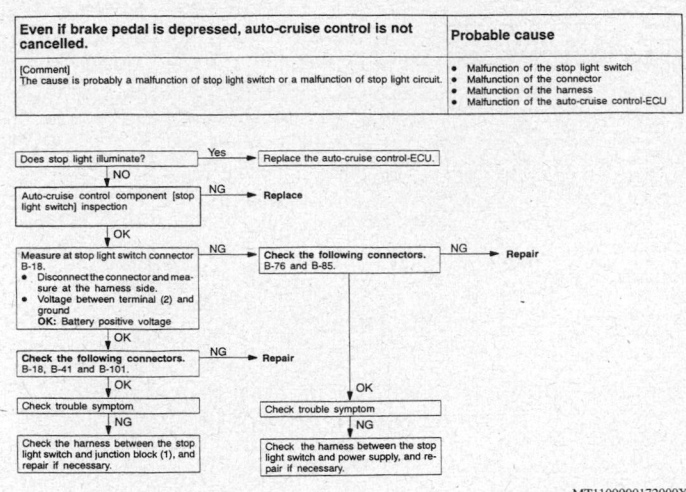

Fig. 44 Inspection Procedure 4: Auto Cruise Does Not Cancel. Diamante

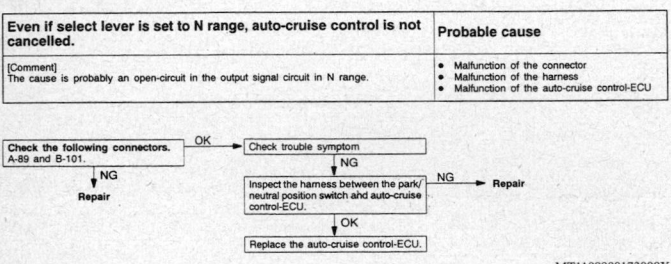

Fig. 45 Inspection Procedure 5: Auto Cruise Does Not Cancel. Diamante

Even if auto-cruise control CANCEL switch is set to ON, auto-cruise control is not cancelled.	Probable cause
[Comment] The cause is probably an open-circuit in the circuit inside the CANCEL switch.	• Malfunction of the auto-cruise control-ECU

Replace the auto-cruise control switch.

MT1109900174000X

Fig. 46 Inspection Procedure 6: Auto Cruise Does Not Cancel. Diamante

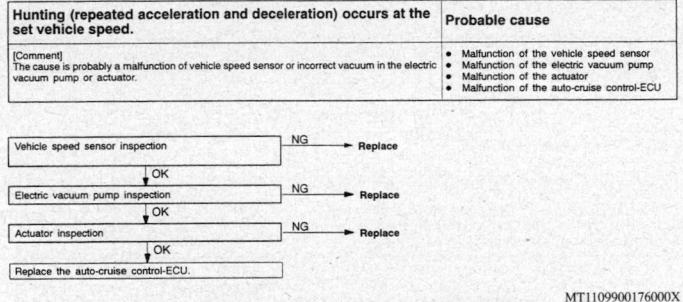

Fig. 48 Inspection Procedure 8: Hunting Occurs At Set Speed. Diamante

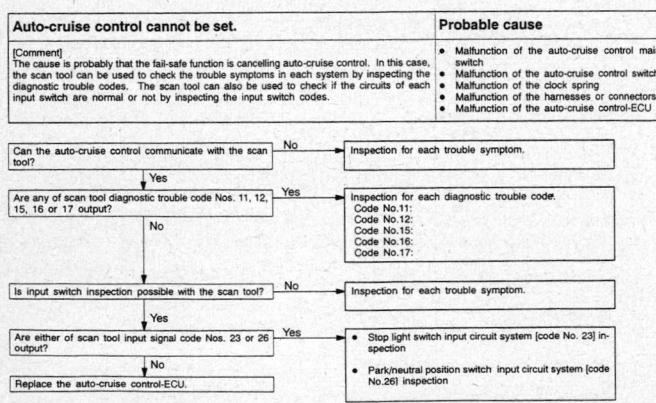

Fig. 47 Inspection Procedure 7: Auto Cruise Cannot Be Set. Diamante

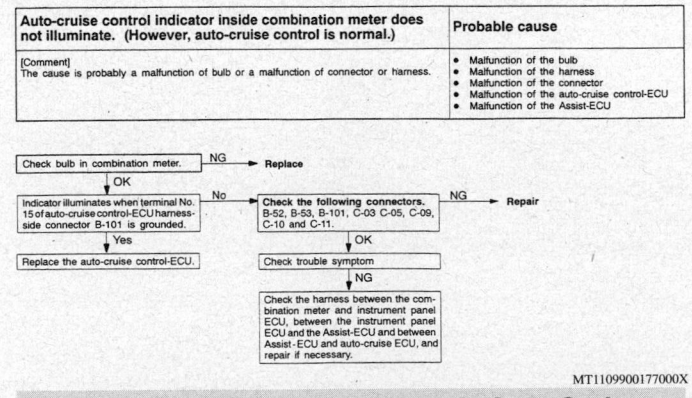

Fig. 49 Inspection Procedure 9: Auto Cruise Indicator Does Not Illuminate. Diamante

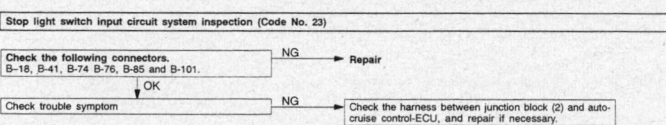

Stop light switch input circuit system inspection (Code No. 23)

Check the following connectors.
B-18, B-41, B-74 B-76, B-85 and B-101. → NG → Repair

↓ OK

Check trouble symptom → NG → Check the harness between junction block (2) and auto-cruise control-ECU, and repair if necessary.

MT1109900178000X

Fig. 50 Inspection Procedure 10: Stop Lamp Switch Circuit Inspection. Diamante

Code No.	Scan tool	35	Vehicle speed signal system	Probable cause
	General scan tool	P0500		
	MIL	15		

[Comment]
No distance sensor signal detected during load conditions.

- Malfunction of the vehicle speed sensor <M/T>.
- Malfunction of the input speed sensor or output speed sensor <A/T>.
- Malfunction of the connector.
- Malfunction of the harness.
- Malfunction of the PCM.

Vehicle speed sensor circuit system check [Vehicle speed sensor <M/T>. input speed sensor or output speed sensor <A/T>]

MT1109900181000X

Fig. 52 Code 35: Vehicle Speed Signal System. Eclipse w/2.0L Non-Turbocharged Engine

Code No.	Scan tool	87	Auto-cruise control switch	Probable cause
	General scan tool	–		
	MIL	34		

[Comment]
Speed control switch input below minimum acceptable voltage.

- Malfunction of the auto-cruise control switch.

Replace the auto-cruise control switch.

MT1109900183000X

Fig. 54 Code 87: Auto Cruise Control Switch. Eclipse w/2.0L Non-Turbocharged Engine

Code No.	Scan tool	02	Powertrain control module (PCM)	Probable cause
	General scan tool	P0605		
	MIL	53		

[Comment]
Internal powertrain control module fault is detected.

- Malfunction of the PCM.

Replace the powertrain control module.

MT1109900185000X

Fig. 56 Code 02: PCM. Eclipse w/2.0L Non-Turbocharged Engine

Code No.	Scan tool	82	Auto-cruise control relay system	Probable cause
	General scan tool	–		
	MIL	77		

[Comment]
An open or shorted condition is detected in the speed control servo power relay control circuit.

- Malfunction of the speed control servo.
- Malfunction of the auto-cruise control relay.
- Malfunction of the connector.
- Malfunction of the harness.
- Malfunction of the PCM.

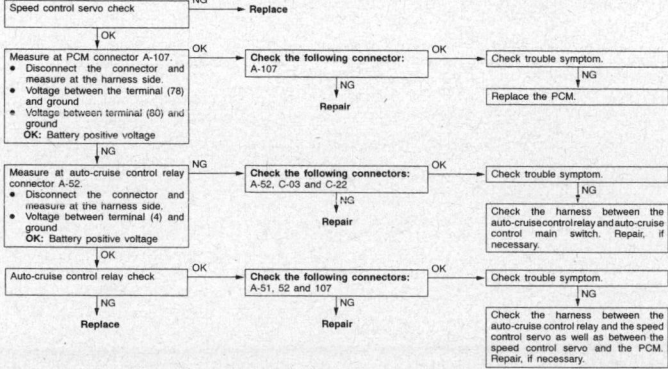

MT1109900186000X

Fig. 57 Code 82: Auto Cruise Control Relay System. Eclipse w/2.0L Non-Turbocharged Engine

Park/neutral position switch input circuit system inspection (Code No. 26)

Check the harness between auto-cruise control-ECU and power supply.

MT1109900179000X

Fig. 51 Inspection Procedure 11: PNP Switch Inspection. Diamante

Code No.	Scan tool	86	Auto-cruise control switch	Probable cause
	General scan tool	–		
	MIL	34		

[Comment]
Speed control switch input above maximum acceptable voltage.

- Malfunction of the auto-cruise control switch.

Replace the auto-cruise control switch.

MT1109900182000X

Fig. 53 Code 86: Auto Cruise Control Switch. Eclipse w/2.0L Non-Turbocharged Engine

Code No.	Scan tool	15	Speed control servo solenoid system	Probable cause
	General scan tool	–		
	MIL	34		

[Comment]
An open or shorted condition is detected in either the speed control vacuum or vent solenoid control circuits.

- Malfunction of the speed control servo.
- Malfunction of the connector.
- Malfunction of the harness.
- Malfunction of the PCM.

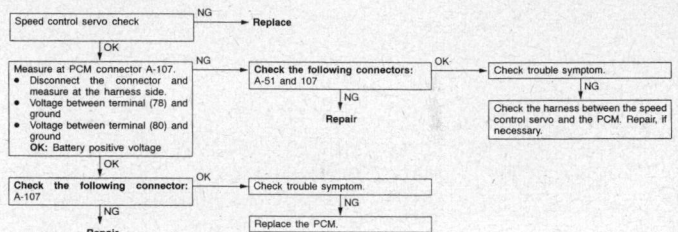

MT1109900184000X

Fig. 55 Code 15: Speed Control Servo Solenoid. Eclipse w/2.0L Non-Turbocharged Engine

Trouble symptom		Inspection procedure No.
Communication with scan tool is not possible.		1
Auto-cruise control does not cancel.	When engine speed rises suddenly	2
	When brake pedal is depressed	3
	When selector lever is set to N range <A/T>	4
	When CANCEL switch is set to ON	5
Auto-cruise control cannot be set.		6
Hunting (repeated acceleration and deceleration) occurs at the set vehicle speed.		7
When the auto-cruise control main switch is ON, the switch indicator on the instrument panel does not illuminate. (However, auto-cruise control is normal.)		8
Auto-cruise control main switch illumination light does not illuminate.		9
Auto-cruise control indicator light inside combination meter does not illuminate. (However, auto-cruise control is normal.)		10

MT1109900187000X

Fig. 58 Inspection Procedure Chart. Eclipse w/2.0L Non-Turbocharged Engine

Communication with scan tool is not possible.		Probable cause
[Comment] A defect in the power supply system (including ground) for the diagnostic line may be present.		- Malfunction of the connector. - Malfunction of the harness.

MT1109900188000X

Fig. 59 Inspection Procedure 1: Communication w/Scan Tool Not Possible. Eclipse w/2.0L Non-Turbocharged Engine

When engine speed rises suddenly, auto-cruise control does not cancel.	Probable cause
[Comment] A malfunction of powertrain control module may exist.	• Malfunction of the PCM.

Replace the powertrain control module.

MT1109900189000X

Fig. 60 Inspection Procedure 2: Auto Cruise Does Not Cancel When Engine Speed Increases. Eclipse w/2.0L Non-Turbocharged Engine

When selector lever is set to N range, auto-cruise control does not cancel. <A/T>	Probable cause
[Comment] An open-circuit in the output signal circuit in N range may be present.	• Malfunction of the connector. • Malfunction of the harness. • Malfunction of the PCM.

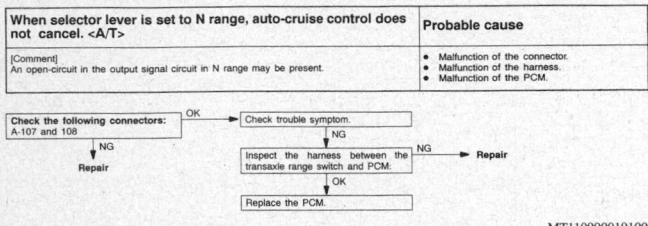

Fig. 62 Inspection Procedure 4: Auto Cruise Does Not Cancel. Eclipse w/2.0L Non-Turbocharged Engine

Auto-cruise control cannot be set.	Probable cause
[Comment] A malfunction of the auto-cruise control switch circuit may exist.	• Malfunction of the auto-cruise control switch. • Malfunction of the clock spring. • Malfunction of the connector. • Malfunction of the harness.

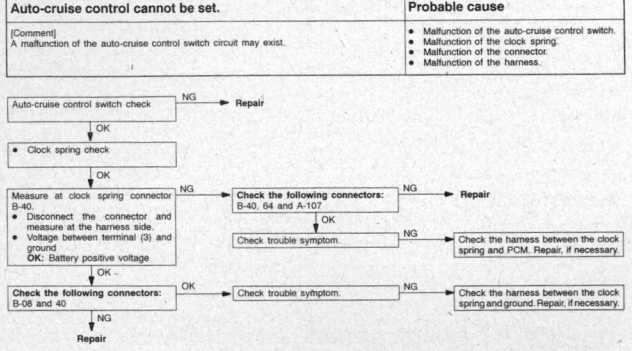

Fig. 64 Inspection Procedure 6: Auto Cruise Cannot Be Set. Eclipse w/2.0L Non-Turbocharged Engine

When the auto-cruise control main switch is ON, the switch indicator on the instrument panel does not illuminate. (However, auto-cruise control is normal.)	Probable cause
[Comment] Blown bulb in auto-cruise control main switch.	• Malfunction of the auto-cruise control main switch.

Replace the auto-cruise control main switch.

MT1109900195000X

Fig. 66 Inspection Procedure 8: Auto Cruise Lamp Does Not Illuminate. Eclipse w/2.0L Non-Turbocharged Engine

Auto-cruise control main switch illumination light does not illuminate.	Probable cause
[Comment] A malfunction of the auto-cruise control main switch, harness, or connector may exist.	• Malfunction of the auto-cruise control main switch. • Malfunction of the connector. • Malfunction of the harness.

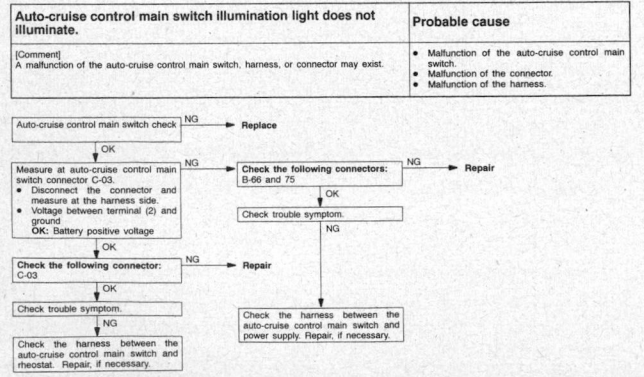

MT1109900196000X

Fig. 67 Inspection Procedure 9: Auto Cruise Lamp Does Not Illuminate. Eclipse w/2.0L Non-Turbocharged Engine

When brake pedal is depressed, auto-cruise control does not cancel.	Probable cause
[Comment] A malfunction of the stop light switch or stop light circuit may exist.	• Malfunction of the stop light switch. • Malfunction of the connector. • Malfunction of the harness. • Malfunction of the PCM.

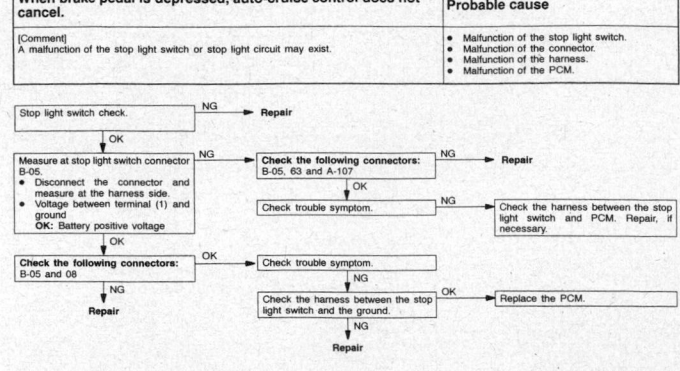

MT1109900190000X

Fig. 61 Inspection Procedure 3: Auto Cruise Does Not Cancel. Eclipse w/2.0L Non-Turbocharged Engine

When auto-cruise control CANCEL switch is set to ON, auto-cruise control does not cancel.	Probable cause
[Comment] An open-circuit inside the CANCEL switch may be present.	• Malfunction of the auto-cruise control switch.

Replace the auto-cruise control switch.

MT1109900192000X

Fig. 63 Inspection Procedure 5: Auto Cruise Does Not Cancel. Eclipse w/2.0L Non-Turbocharged Engine

Hunting (repeated acceleration and deceleration) occurs at the set vehicle speed.	Probable cause
[Comment] A malfunction of a speed sensor, the speed control servo, or the vacuum supply may be present.	• Malfunction of the vehicle speed sensor <M/T>. • Malfunction of the input speed sensor or output speed sensor <A/T>. • Malfunction of the speed control servo. • Malfunction of the vacuum supply. • Malfunction of the PCM.

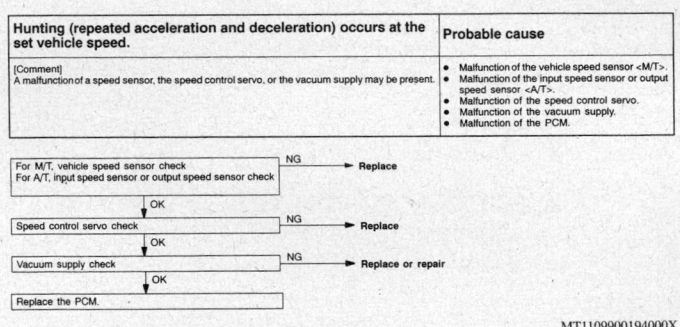

MT1109900194000X

Fig. 65 Inspection Procedure 7: Hunting Occurs At Set Speed. Eclipse w/2.0L Non-Turbocharged Engine

Auto-cruise control indicator inside combination meter does not illuminate. (However, auto-cruise control is normal.)	Probable cause
[Comment] A malfunction of the bulb, connector, or harness may be present.	• Malfunction of the bulb. • Malfunction of the harness. • Malfunction of the connector. • Malfunction of the PCM.

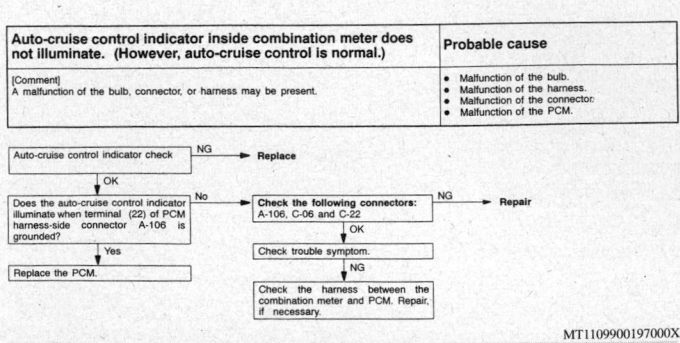

MT1109900197000X

Fig. 68 Inspection Procedure 10: Auto Cruise Lamp Does Not Illuminate. Eclipse w/2.0L Non-Turbocharged Engine

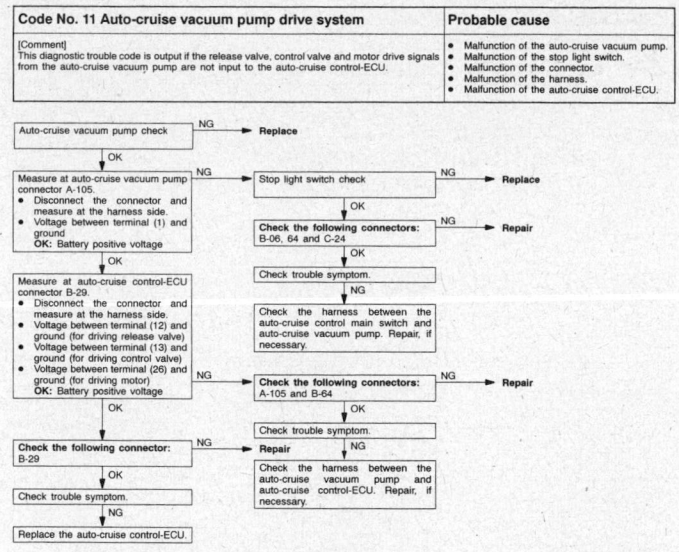

Fig. 69   Code 11: Auto Cruise Vacuum Pump Drive System. Eclipse w/2.0L Turbocharged & 2.4L Engines

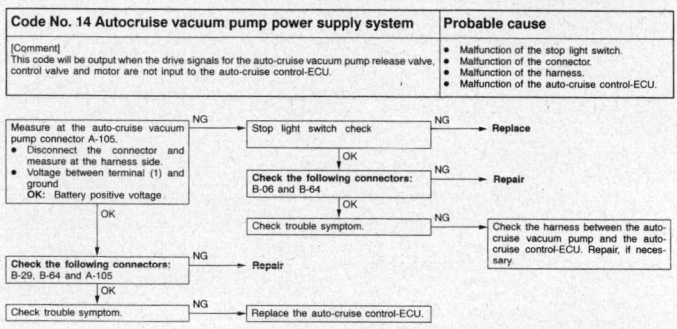

Fig. 71   Code 14: Auto Cruise Vacuum Pump Power Supply System. Eclipse w/2.0L Turbocharged & 2.4L Engines

Code No. 16 Auto-cruise control-ECU	Probable cause
[Comment] This diagnostic trouble code is output if there is an abnormality in the CANCEL hold circuit or the microprocessor monitor circuit in the auto-cruise control-ECU.	• Malfunction of the auto-cruise control-ECU.

Replace the auto-cruise control-ECU.

MT1109900203000X

Fig. 73   Code 16: Auto Cruise Control ECU. Eclipse w/2.0L Turbocharged & 2.4L Engines

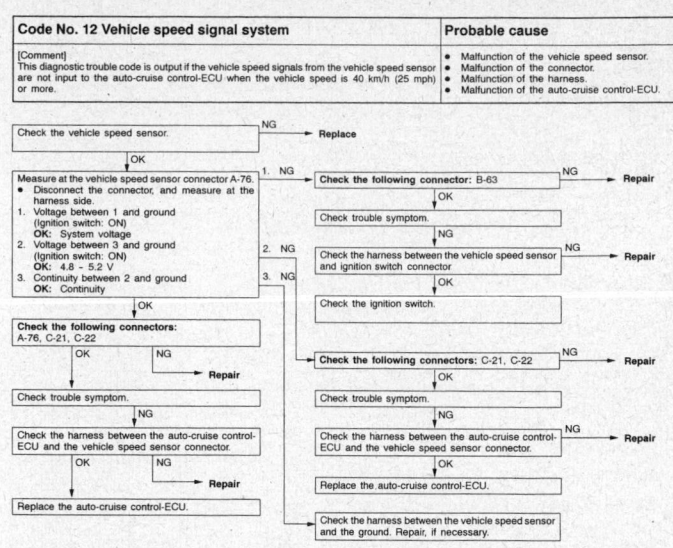

Fig. 70   Code 12: Vehicle Speed Signal System. Eclipse w/2.0L Turbocharged & 2.4L Engines

Code No. 15 Auto-cruise control switch	Probable cause
[Comment] This diagnostic trouble code is output if the RESUME switch or SET switch remains ON.	• Malfunction of the auto-cruise control switch.

Replace the auto-cruise control switch.

MT1109900202000X

Fig. 72   Code 15: Auto Cruise Control Switch. Eclipse w/2.0L Turbocharged & 2.4L Engines

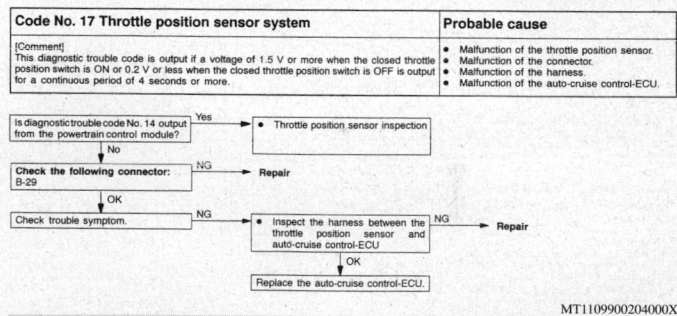

Fig. 74   Code 17: TPS System. Eclipse w/2.0L Turbocharged & 2.4L Engines

Trouble symptom		Inspection procedure No.
Communication with scan tool is not possible.	Communication with all systems is not possible.	1
	Communication with auto-cruise control-ECU only is not possible.	2
Input switch inspection using the scan tool is not possible. (However, diagnostic inspection is possible.)		3
Auto-cruise control does not cancel.	When brake pedal is depressed	4
	When clutch pedal is depressed <M/T>	5
	When select lever is set to N range <A/T>	6
	When CANCEL switch is set to ON	7
The diagnosis result displayed on the scan tool is normal even though auto-cruise control cannot be set.		8
Auto-cruise control cannot be set.		9
Hunting (repeated acceleration and deceleration) occurs at the set vehicle speed.		10
When the auto-cruise control main switch is ON, the switch indicator on the instrument panel does not illuminate. (However, auto-cruise control is normal.)		11
Auto-cruise control main switch illumination light does not illuminate.		12
Auto-cruise control indicator light inside combination meter does not illuminate. (However, auto-cruise control is normal.)		13

MT1109900205000X

Fig. 75   Inspection Procedure Chart. Eclipse w/2.0L Turbocharged & 2.4L Engines

Communication with scan tool is not possible. (Communication with auto-cruise control-ECU only is not possible.)	Probable cause
[Comment] A malfunction of auto-cruise control main switch circuit or a malfunction of auto-cruise control-ECU ground circuit may be present.	• Malfunction of the auto-cruise control main switch. • Malfunction of the connector. • Malfunction of the harness. • Malfunction of the auto-cruise control-ECU.

1. Auto-cruise control main switch circuit malfunction

2. Auto-cruise control-ECU ground circuit malfunction

MT1109900207000X

Fig. 77   Inspection Procedure 2: Communication w/Scan Tool Not Possible. Eclipse w/2.0L Turbocharged & 2.4L Engines

Communication with scan tool is not possible. (Communication with all systems is not possible.)	Probable cause
[Comment] A defect in the power supply system (including ground) for the diagnostic line may be present.	• Malfunction of the connector. • Malfunction of the harness.

MT1109900206000X

Fig. 76   Inspection Procedure 1: Communication w/Scan Tool Not Possible. Eclipse w/2.0L Turbocharged & 2.4L Engines

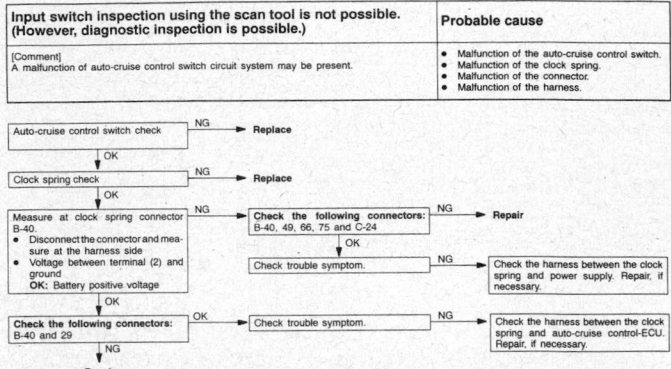

Input switch inspection using the scan tool is not possible. (However, diagnostic inspection is possible.)	Probable cause
[Comment] A malfunction of auto-cruise control switch circuit system may be present.	• Malfunction of the auto-cruise control switch. • Malfunction of the clock spring. • Malfunction of the connector. • Malfunction of the harness.

MT1109900208000X

Fig. 78   Inspection Procedure 3: Input Switch Inspection w/Scan Tool Not Possible. Eclipse w/2.0L Turbocharged & 2.4L Engines

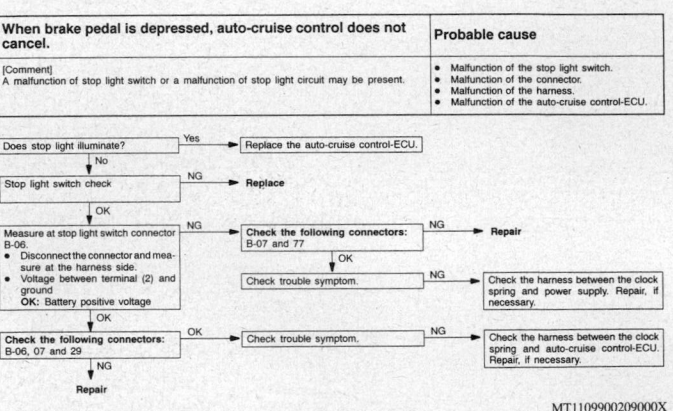

When brake pedal is depressed, auto-cruise control does not cancel.	Probable cause
[Comment] A malfunction of stop light switch or a malfunction of stop light circuit may be present.	• Malfunction of the stop light switch. • Malfunction of the connector. • Malfunction of the harness. • Malfunction of the auto-cruise control-ECU.

MT1109900209000X

Fig. 79   Inspection Procedure 4: Auto Cruise Does Not Cancel. Eclipse w/2.0L Turbocharged & 2.4L Engines

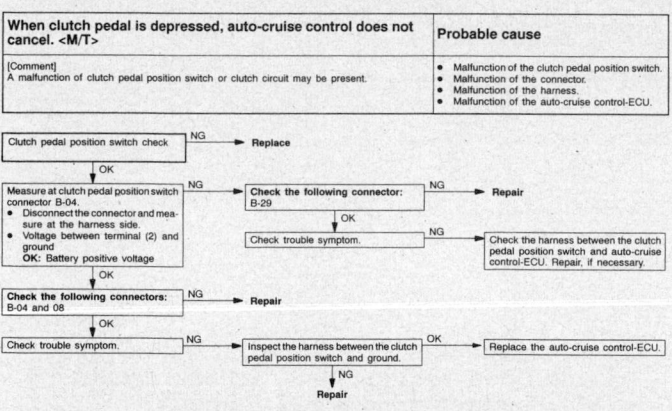

Fig. 80 Inspection Procedure 5: Auto Cruise Does Not Cancel. Eclipse w/2.0L Turbocharged & 2.4L Engines

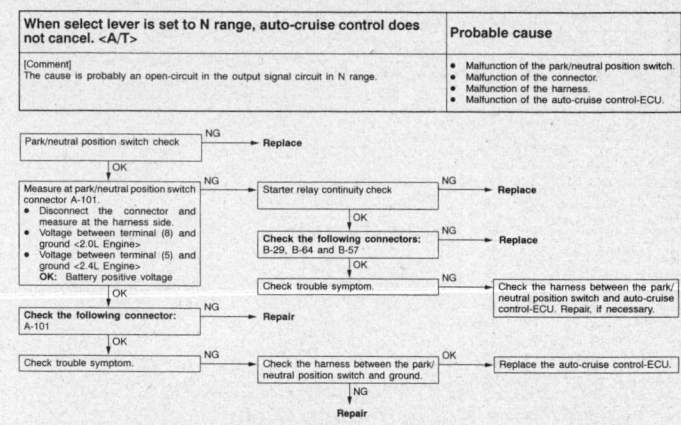

Fig. 81 Inspection Procedure 6: Auto Cruise Does Not Cancel. Eclipse w/2.0L Turbocharged & 2.4L Engines

When auto-cruise control CANCEL switch is set to ON, auto-cruise control does not cancel.	Probable cause
[Comment] An open-circuit in the circuit inside the CANCEL switch may be present.	• Malfunction of the auto-cruise control switch.

Replace the auto-cruise control switch.

MT1109900212000X

Fig. 82 Inspection Procedure 7: Auto Cruise Does Not Cancel. Eclipse w/2.0L Turbocharged & 2.4L Engines

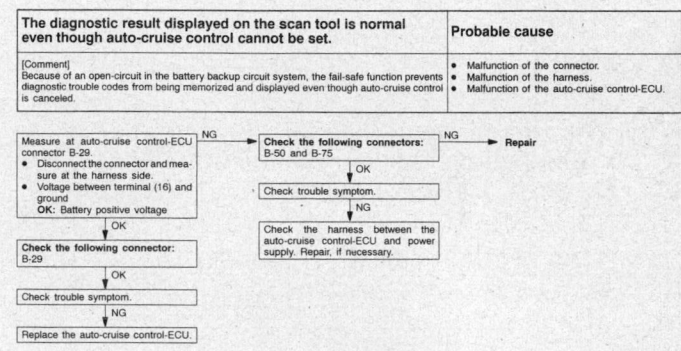

Fig. 83 Inspection Procedure 8: Auto Cruise Cannot Be Set. Eclipse w/2.0L Turbocharged & 2.4L Engines

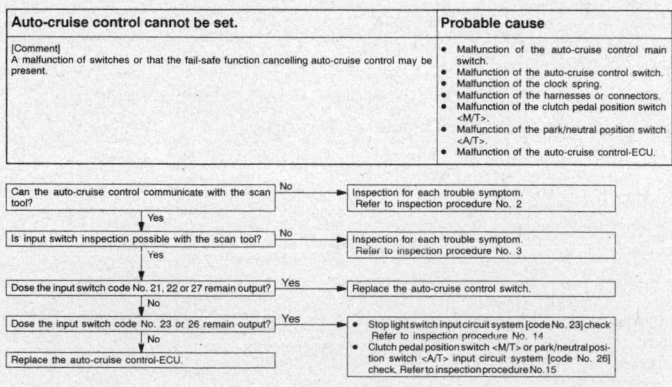

Fig. 84 Inspection Procedure 9: Auto Cruise Cannot Be Set. Eclipse w/2.0L Turbocharged & 2.4L Engines

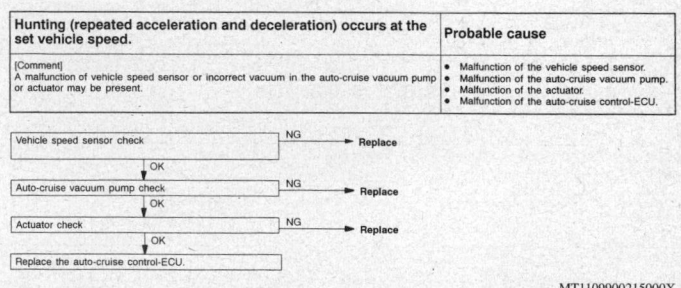

Fig. 85 Inspection Procedure 10: Hunting Occurs At Set Speed. Eclipse w/2.0L Turbocharged & 2.4L Engines

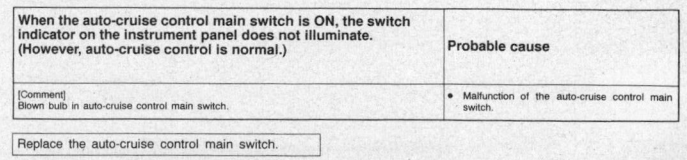

Fig. 86 Inspection Procedure 11: Auto Cruise Lamp Does Not Illuminate. Eclipse w/2.0L Turbocharged & 2.4L Engines

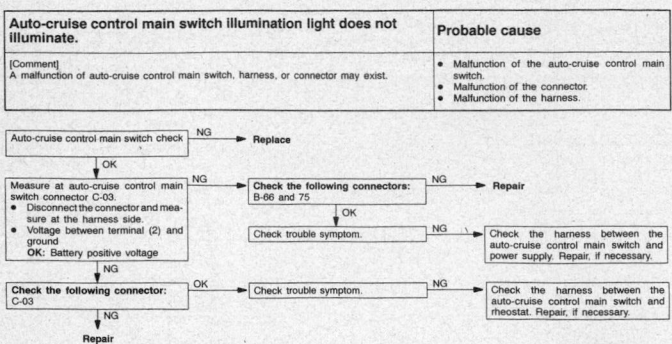

Auto-cruise control main switch illumination light does not illuminate.	Probable cause
[Comment] A malfunction of the auto-cruise control main switch, harness, or connector may exist.	• Malfunction of the auto-cruise control main switch. • Malfunction of the connector. • Malfunction of the harness.

MT1109900217000X

Fig. 87 Inspection Procedure 12: Auto Cruise Lamp Does Not Illuminate. Eclipse w/2.0L Turbocharged & 2.4L Engines

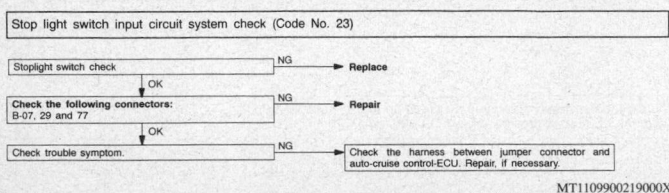

MT1109900219000X

Fig. 89 Inspection Procedure 14: Stop Lamp Switch Inspection. Eclipse w/2.0L Turbocharged & 2.4L Engines

Code No. 11 Auto-cruise vacuum pump drive system	Probable cause
This diagnostic trouble code is output if the release valve, control valve or motor drive signals from the auto-cruise vacuum pump are not input to the auto-cruise control-ECU.	• Malfunction of the auto-cruise vacuum pump • Malfunction of the connector • Malfunction of the harness • Malfunction of the auto-cruise control-ECU

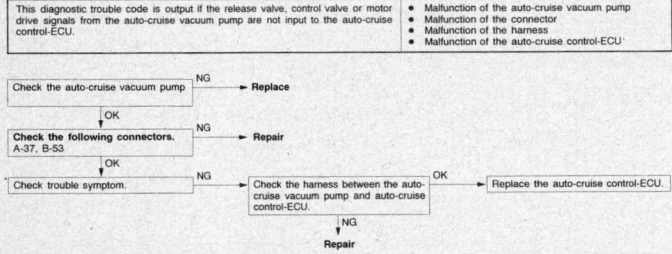

MT1109900222000X

Fig. 91 Code 11: Auto Vacuum Pump Drive System. Galant & Mirage

Code No. 14 Auto-cruise vacuum pump power supply system	Probable cause
This diagnostic trouble code is output when none of the drive signals from the release valve, control valve and motor of the auto-cruise vacuum pump are input to the auto-cruise control-ECU.	• Malfunction of the stop light switch • Malfunction of the connector • Malfunction of the harness • Malfunction of the auto-cruise control-ECU • Malfunction of the auto-cruise vacuum pump

MT1109900224000X

Fig. 93 Code 14: Auto Cruise Vacuum Pump Power Supply. Galant & Mirage

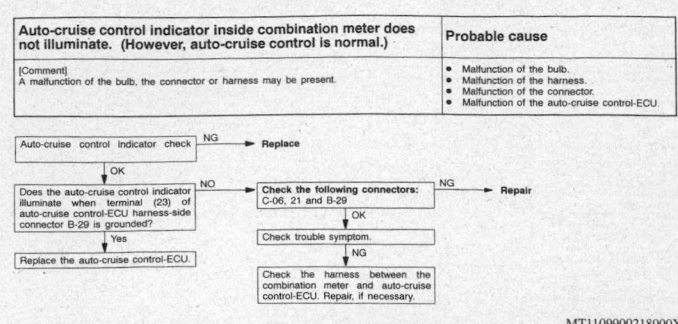

Auto-cruise control indicator inside combination meter does not illuminate. (However, auto-cruise control is normal.)	Probable cause
[Comment] A malfunction of the bulb, the connector or harness may be present.	• Malfunction of the bulb. • Malfunction of the harness. • Malfunction of the connector. • Malfunction of the auto-cruise control-ECU.

MT1109900218000X

Fig. 88 Inspection Procedure 13: Auto Cruise Lamp Does Not Illuminate. Eclipse w/2.0L Turbocharged & 2.4L Engines

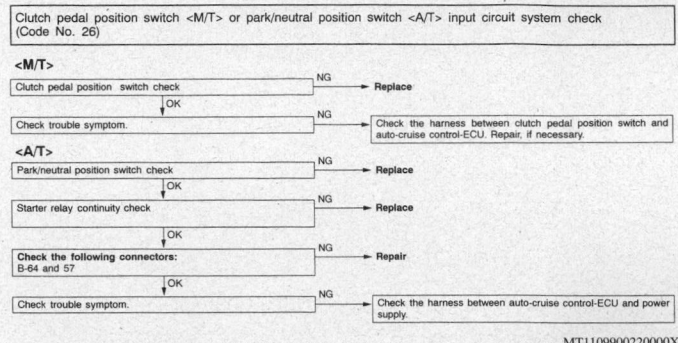

MT1109900220000X

Fig. 90 Inspection Procedure 15: CPS or PNP Switch Inspection. Eclipse w/2.0L Turbocharged & 2.4L Engines

Code No. 12 Vehicle speed signal system	Probable cause
This diagnostic trouble code is output if the vehicle speed signals from the vehicle speed sensor are not input to the auto-cruise control-ECU when the vehicle speed is 40 km/h or more.	• Malfunction of the vehicle speed sensor • Malfunction of the connector • Malfunction of the harness • Malfunction of the auto-cruise control-ECU

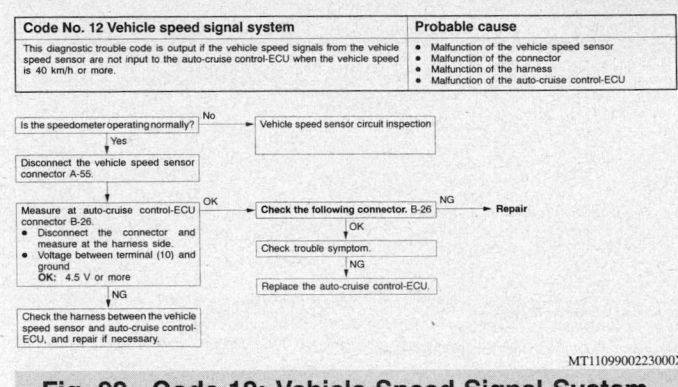

MT1109900223000X

Fig. 92 Code 12: Vehicle Speed Signal System. Galant & Mirage

Code No. 15 Auto-cruise control switch	Probable cause
This diagnostic trouble code is output if the cruise control RESUME switch, SET switch or CANCEL switch remains ON.	• Malfunction of the auto-cruise control switch

Replace the auto-cruise control switch.

MT1109900225000X

Fig. 94 Code 15: Auto Cruise Control Switch. Galant & Mirage

Code No. 16 Auto-cruise control ECU	Probable cause
This diagnostic trouble code is output if there is an abnormality in the CANCEL hold circuit or the microprocessor monitor circuit in the auto-cruise control-ECU.	• Malfunction of the auto-cruise control-ECU

Replace the auto-cruise control-ECU.

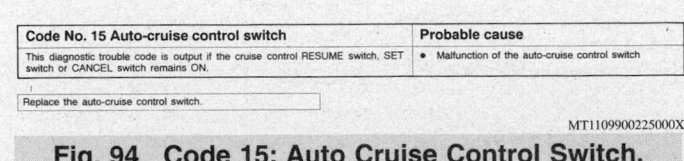

MT1109900226000X

Fig. 95 Code 16: Auto Cruise Control ECU. Galant & Mirage

Code No.17 Throttle position sensor system

This diagnostic trouble code is output if a voltage of 1.5 V or more (when the closed throttle position switch is ON) or 0.2 V or less (when the closed throttle position switch is OFF) is output for a continuous period of 4 seconds or more.

Probable cause
- Malfunction of the throttle position sensor
- Malfunction of the connector
- Malfunction of the harness
- Malfunction of the auto-cruise control-ECU

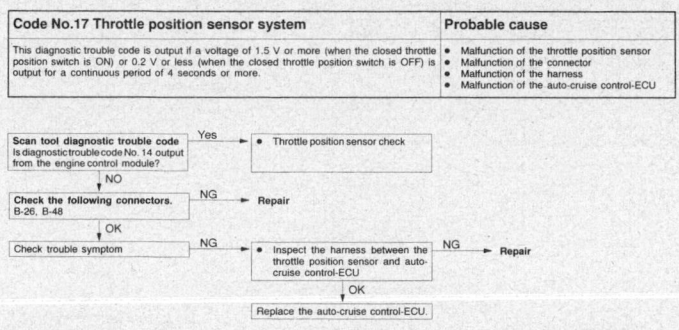

MT1109900227000X

Fig. 96   Code 17: TPS System. Galant & Mirage

Trouble symptom		Inspection procedure No.
Communication with scan tool is not possible.	Communication with all systems is not possible.	1
	Communication with auto-cruise control-ECU only is not possible.	2
Input switch inspection using the scan tool is not possible. (However, diagnosis inspection is possible.)		3
Auto-cruise control is not cancelled.	Even if brake pedal is depressed	4
	Even if clutch pedal is depressed <M/T>	5
	Even if select lever is set to N range <A/T>	6
	Even if CANCEL switch is set to ON	7
Auto-cruise control cannot be set.		9
Hunting (repeated acceleration and deceleration) occurs at the set vehicle speed.		10
Auto-cruise control indicator light inside combination meter does not illuminate. (However, auto-cruise control is normal.)		11

MT1109900228000X

Fig. 97   Inspection Procedure Chart. Galant & Mirage

Communication with scan tool is not possible. (Communication with all systems, is not possible.)

The reason is probably a defect in the power supply system (including ground) for the diagnosis line.

Probable cause
- Malfunction of the connector
- Malfunction of the harness

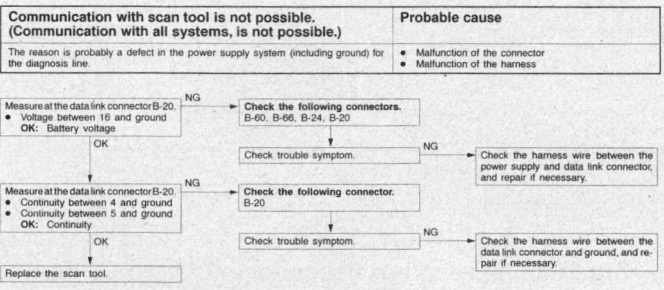

MT1109900229000X

Fig. 98   Inspection Procedure 1: Communication w/Scan Tool Not Possible. Galant & Mirage

Communication with scan tool is not possible (Communication with auto-cruise control-ECU only is not possible.)

The cause is probably a malfunction of the auto-cruise control switch circuit or a malfunction of the auto-cruise control-ECU ground circuit.

Probable cause
- Malfunction of the auto-cruise control switch
- Malfunction of the connector
- Malfunction of the harness
- Malfunction of the auto-cruise control-ECU

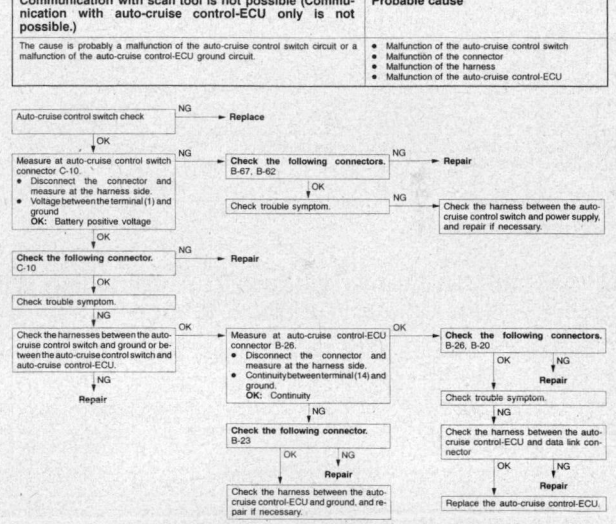

MT1109900230000X

Fig. 99   Inspection Procedure 2: Communication w/Scan Tool Not Possible. Galant & Mirage

Input switch inspection using the scan tool is not possible. (However, diagnosis inspection is possible.)

The cause is probably a malfunction of auto-cruise control switch circuit system.

Probable cause
- Malfunction of the auto-cruise control switch
- Malfunction of the clock spring
- Malfunction of the connector
- Malfunction of the harness

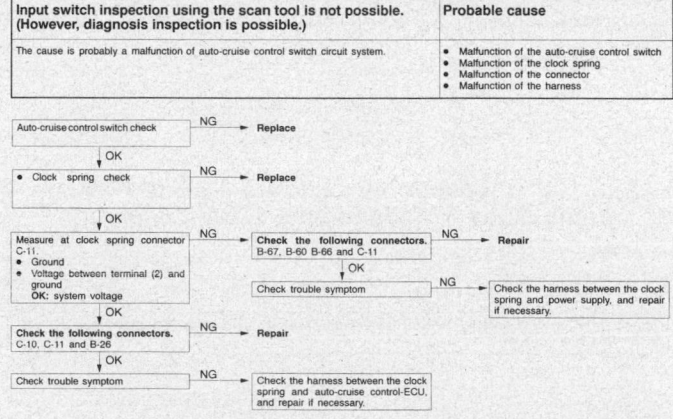

MT1109900231000X

Fig. 100   Inspection Procedure 3: Input Switch Inspection w/Scan Tool Not Possible. Galant & Mirage

Even if brake pedal is depressed, auto-cruise control is not cancelled.

The cause is probably a malfunction of stop light switch or a malfunction of stop light circuit.

Probable cause
- Malfunction of the stop light switch
- Malfunction of the connector
- Malfunction of the harness
- Malfunction of the auto-cruise control-ECU

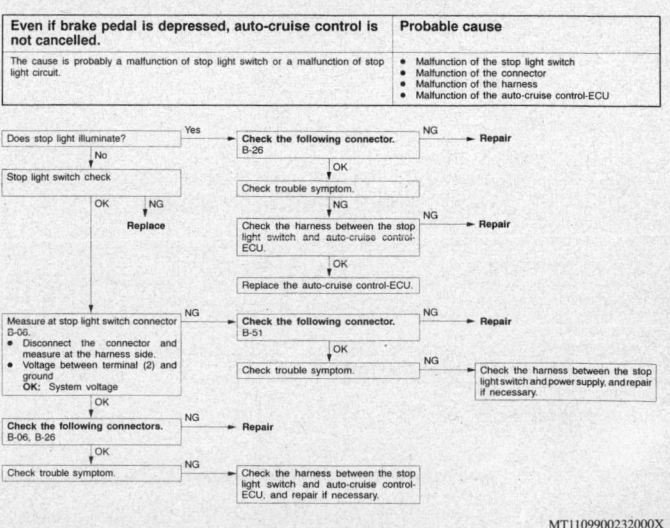

MT1109900232000X

Fig. 101   Inspection Procedure 4: Auto Cruise Will Not Cancel. Galant & Mirage

Even if clutch pedal is depressed, auto-cruise control is not cancelled. <M/T>	Probable cause
The cause is probably a malfunction of clutch pedal position switch or clutch circuit.	• Malfunction of the clutch pedal position switch • Malfunction of the connector • Malfunction of the harness • Malfunction of the auto-cruise control-ECU

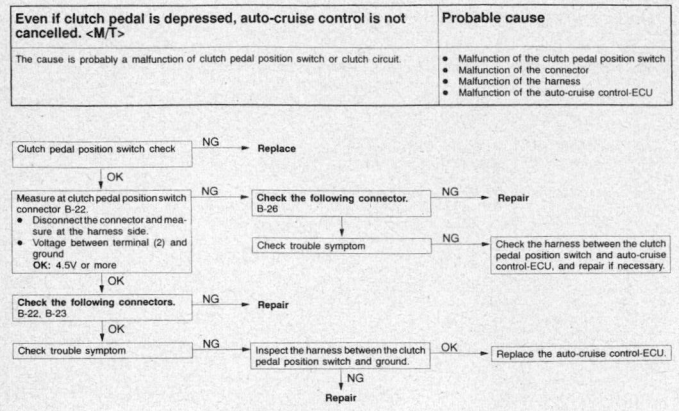

Fig. 102 Inspection Procedure 5: Auto Cruise Will Not Cancel. Galant & Mirage

Even if auto-cruise control CANCEL switch is set to ON, auto-cruise control is not cancelled.	Probable cause
The cause is probably an open-circuit in the circuit inside the CANCEL switch.	• Malfunction of the auto-cruise control switch

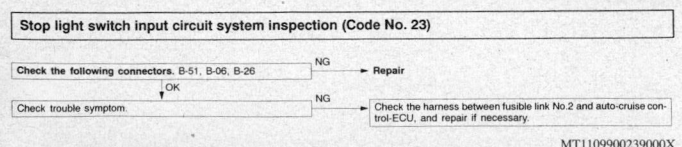

Replace the auto-cruise control switch.

Fig. 104 Inspection Procedure 7: Auto Cruise Will Not Cancel. Galant & Mirage

Hunting (repeated acceleration and deceleration) occurs at the set vehicle speed.	Probable cause
The cause is probably a malfunction of vehicle speed sensor or incorrect vacuum in the motor-driven vacuum pump or actuator.	• Malfunction of the vehicle speed sensor • Malfunction of the motor-driven vacuum pump • Malfunction of the actuator • Malfunction of the auto-cruise control-ECU

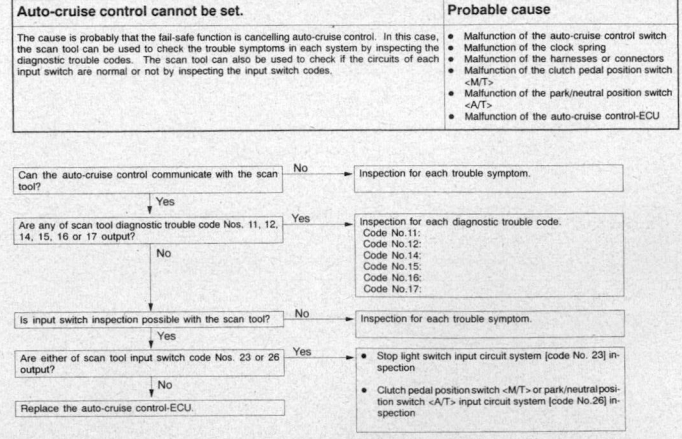

MT1109900237000X

Fig. 106 Inspection Procedure 10: Hunting Occurs At Set Speed. Galant & Mirage

Stop light switch input circuit system inspection (Code No. 23)

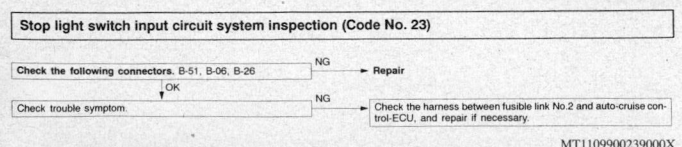

MT1109900239000X

Fig. 108 Inspection Procedure 12: Stop Lamp Switch Inspection. Galant & Mirage

Even if select lever is set to N range, auto-cruise control is not cancelled. <A/T>	Probable cause
The cause is probably an open-circuit in the output signal circuit in N range.	• Malfunction of the park/neutral position switch • Malfunction of the connector • Malfunction of the harness • Malfunction of the auto-cruise control-ECU

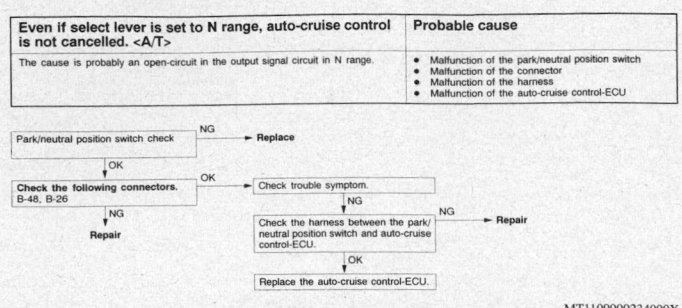

MT1109900234000X

Fig. 103 Inspection Procedure 6: Auto Cruise Will Not Cancel. Galant & Mirage

Auto-cruise control cannot be set.	Probable cause
The cause is probably that the fail-safe function is cancelling auto-cruise control. In this case, the scan tool can be used to check the trouble symptoms in each system by inspecting the diagnostic trouble codes. The scan tool can also be used to check if the circuits of each input switch are normal or not by inspecting the input switch codes.	• Malfunction of the auto-cruise control switch • Malfunction of the clock spring • Malfunction of the harnesses or connectors • Malfunction of the clutch pedal position switch <M/T> • Malfunction of the park/neutral position switch <A/T> • Malfunction of the auto-cruise control-ECU

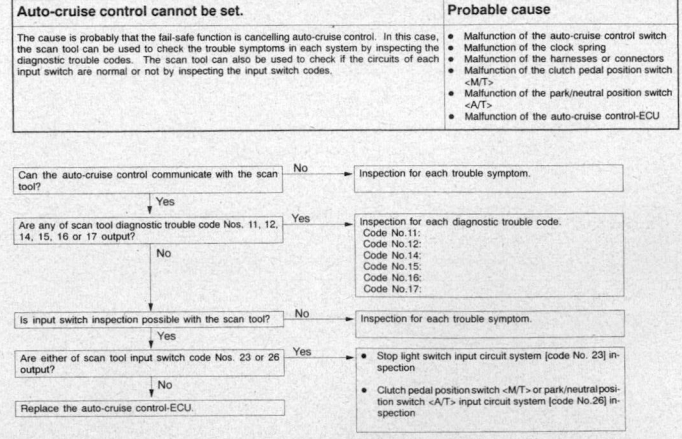

MT1109900236000X

Fig. 105 Inspection Procedure 9: Auto Cruise Cannot Be Set. Galant & Mirage

Auto-cruise control indicator lamp inside combination meter does not illuminate. (However, auto-cruise control is normal.)	Probable cause
The cause is probably a malfunction of the valve or a malfunction of the connector or harness.	• Malfunction of the valve • Malfunction of the harness • Malfunction of the connector • Malfunction of the auto-cruise control-ECU

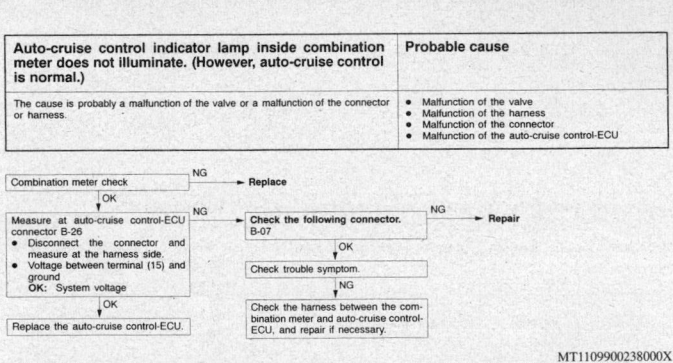

MT1109900238000X

Fig. 107 Inspection Procedure 11: Auto Cruise Lamp Does Not illuminate. Galant & Mirage

Clutch pedal position switch <M/T> or park/neutral position switch <A/T> input circuit system inspection (Code No. 26)

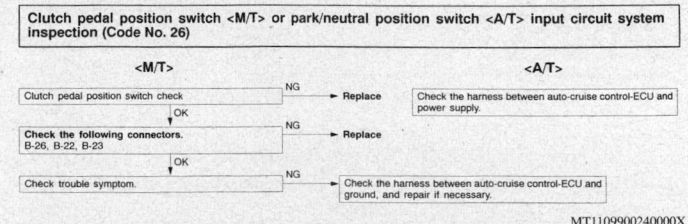

MT1109900240000X

Fig. 109 Inspection Procedure 13: CPS Or PNP Switch Inspection. Galant & Mirage

Code No.11 Auto-cruise vacuum pump drive system	Probable cause
[Comment] This diagnostic trouble code is output if the release valve, control valve and motor drive signals from the auto-cruise vacuum pump are not input to the auto-cruise control-ECU.	• Malfunction of the auto-cruise vacuum pump • Malfunction of the stop light switch • Malfunction of the connector • Malfunction of the harness • Malfunction of the auto-cruise control-ECU

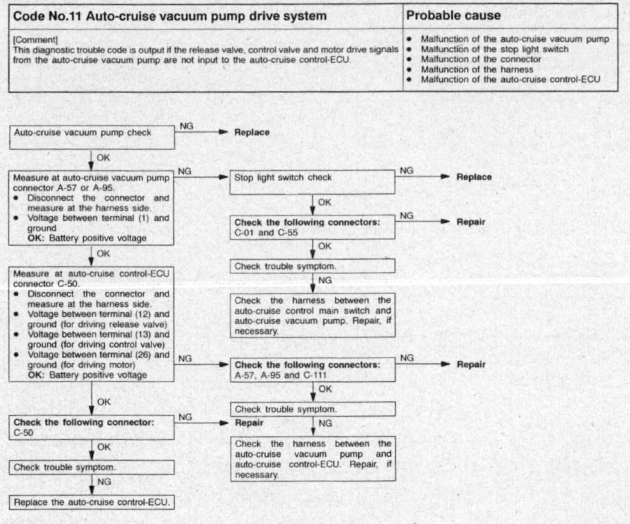

Fig. 110   Code 11: Auto Cruise Vacuum Pump. Montero & Montero Sport

Code No.14 Autocruise vacuum pump power supply system	Probable cause
[Comment] This code will be output when the drive signals for the auto-cruise vacuum pump release valve, control valve and motor are not input to the auto-cruise control-ECU.	• Malfunction of the stop light switch • Malfunction of the connector • Malfunction of the harness • Malfunction of the auto-cruise control-ECU

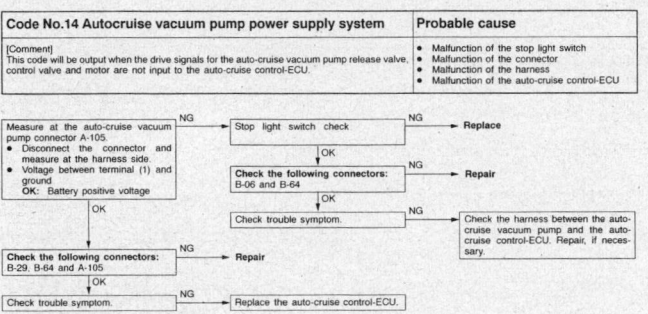

Fig. 112   Code 14: Auto Cruise Vacuum Pump Power Supply. Montero & Montero Sport

Code No.16 Auto-cruise control-ECU	Probable cause
[Comment] This diagnostic trouble code is output if there is an abnormality in the CANCEL hold circuit or the microprocessor monitor circuit in the auto-cruise control-ECU.	• Malfunction of the auto-cruise control-ECU

Replace the auto-cruise control-ECU.

MT1109900246000X

Fig. 114   Code 16: Auto Cruise ECU. Montero & Montero Sport

Trouble symptom		Inspection procedure No.
Communication with scan tool is not possible.	Communication with all systems is not possible.	1
	Communication with auto-cruise control-ECU only is not possible.	2
Input switch inspection using the scan tool is not possible. (However, diagnostic inspection is possible.)		3
Auto-cruise control does not cancel.	When brake pedal is depressed	4
	When select lever is set to N range	5
	When CANCEL switch is set to ON	6
The diagnosis result displayed on the scan tool is normal even though auto-cruise control cannot be set.		7
Auto-cruise control cannot be set.		8
Hunting (repeated acceleration and deceleration) occurs at the set vehicle speed.		9
When the auto-cruise control main switch is ON, the switch indicator on the instrument panel does not illuminate. (However, auto-cruise control is normal.)		10
Auto-cruise control main switch illumination light does not illuminate.		11
Auto-cruise control indicator light inside combination meter does not illuminate. (However, auto-cruise control is normal.)		12

MT1109900248000X

Fig. 116   Inspection Procedure Chart. Montero & Montero Sport

Code No.12 Vehicle speed signal system	Probable cause
[Comment] This diagnostic trouble code is output if the vehicle speed signals from the vehicle speed sensor are not input to the auto-cruise control-ECU when the vehicle speed is 40 km/h (25 mph) or more.	• Malfunction of the vehicle speed sensor • Malfunction of the connector • Malfunction of the harness • Malfunction of the auto-cruise control-ECU

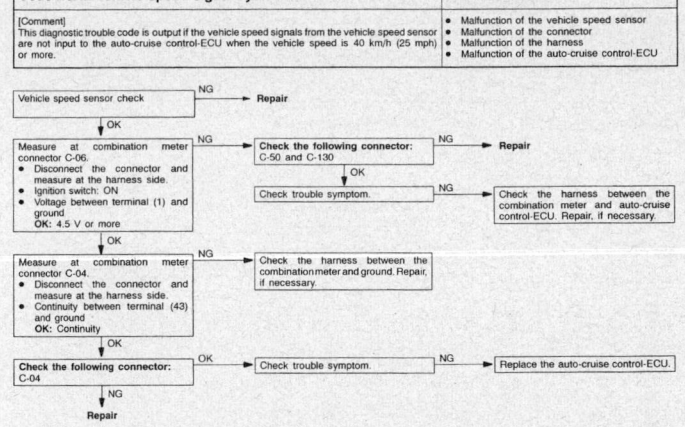

MT1109900243000X

Fig. 111   Code 12: Vehicle Speed Signal System. Montero & Montero Sport

Code No.15 Auto-cruise control-ECU	Probable cause
[Comment] This diagnostic trouble code is output if the RESUME switch or SET switch remains ON.	• Malfunction of the auto-cruise control switch

Replace the auto-cruise control switch.

MT1109900245000X

Fig. 113   Code 15: Auto Cruise ECU. Montero & Montero Sport

Code No.17 Throttle position sensor system	Probable cause
[Comment] This diagnostic trouble code is output if a voltage of 1.5 V or more (when the closed throttle position switch is ON) or 0.2 V or less (when the closed throttle position switch is OFF) is output for a continuous period of 4 seconds or more.	• Malfunction of the throttle position sensor • Malfunction of the connector • Malfunction of the harness • Malfunction of the auto-cruise control-ECU

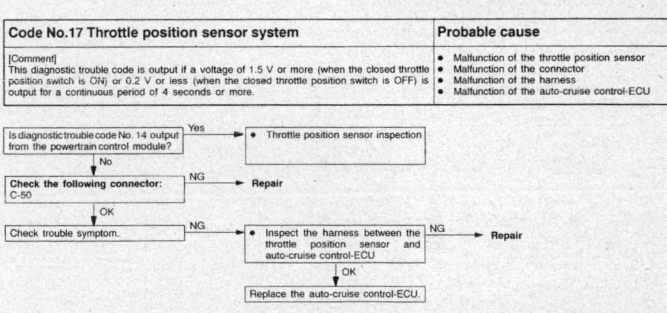

MT1109900247000X

Fig. 115   Code 17: TPS System. Montero & Montero Sport

Communication with scan tool is not possible. (Communication with all systems is not possible.)	Probable cause
[Comment] A defect in the power supply system (including ground) for the diagnostic line may be present.	• Malfunction of the connector • Malfunction of the harness

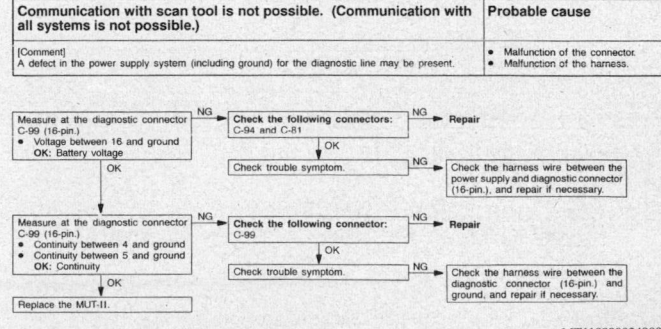

MT1109900249000X

Fig. 117   Inspection Procedure 1: Communication w/Scan Tool Not Possible. Montero & Montero Sport

Communication with scan tool is not possible. (Communication with auto-cruise control-ECU only is not possible.)	Probable cause
[Comment] A malfunction of the auto-cruise control main switch circuit or a malfunction of the auto-cruise control-ECU ground circuit may be present.	• Malfunction of the auto-cruise control main switch. • Malfunction of the connector. • Malfunction of the harness. • Malfunction of the auto-cruise control-ECU.

1. Auto-cruise control main switch circuit malfunction

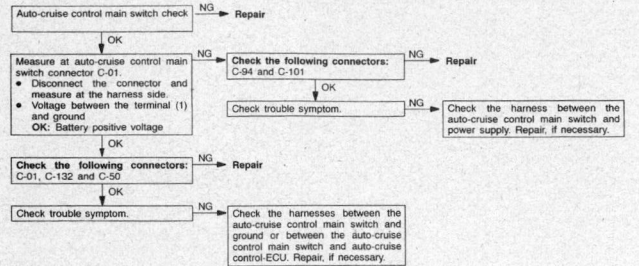

2. Auto-cruise control-ECU ground circuit malfunction

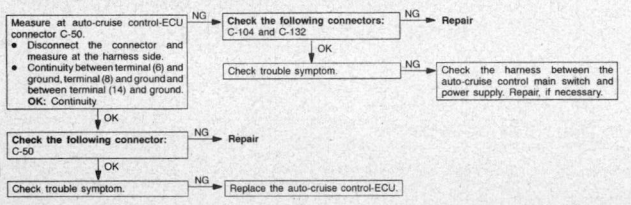

MT1109900250000X

Fig. 118   Inspection Procedure 2: Communication w/Scan Tool Not Possible. Montero & Montero Sport

When brake pedal is depressed, auto-cruise control does not cancel.	Probable cause
[Comment] A malfunction of stop light switch or a malfunction of stop light circuit may be present.	• Malfunction of the stop light switch. • Malfunction of the connector. • Malfunction of the harness. • Malfunction of the auto-cruise control-ECU.

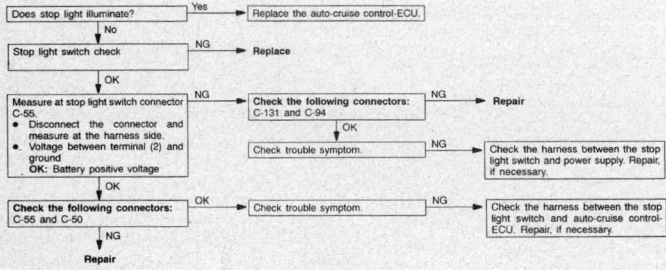

MT1109900252000X

Fig. 120   Inspection Procedure 4: Auto Cruise Does Not Cancel. Montero & Montero Sport

When auto-cruise control CANCEL switch is set to ON, auto-cruise control does not cancel.	Probable cause
[Comment] An open-circuit in the circuit inside the CANCEL switch may be present.	• Malfunction of the auto-cruise control switch.

Replace the auto-cruise control switch.

MT1109900254000X

Fig. 122   Inspection Procedure 6: Auto Cruise Does Not Cancel. Montero & Montero Sport

Input switch inspection using the scan tool is not possible. (However, diagnostic inspection is possible.)	Probable cause
[Comment] A malfunction of auto-cruise control switch circuit system may be present.	• Malfunction of the auto-cruise control switch. • Malfunction of the clock spring. • Malfunction of the connector. • Malfunction of the harness.

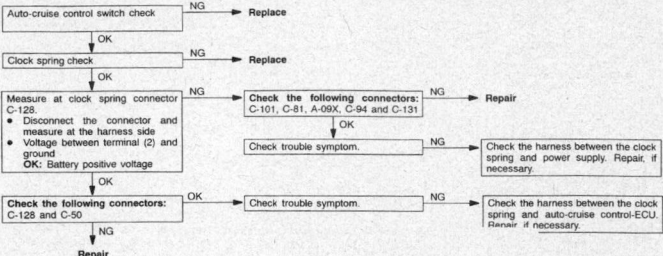

MT1109900251000X

Fig. 119   Inspection Procedure 3: Input Switch Inspection w/Scan Tool Not Possible. Montero & Montero Sport

When select lever is set to N range, auto-cruise control does not cancel.	Probable cause
[Comment] The cause is probably an open-circuit in the output signal circuit in N range.	• Malfunction of the park/neutral position switch. • Malfunction of the connector. • Malfunction of the harness. • Malfunction of the auto-cruise control-ECU.

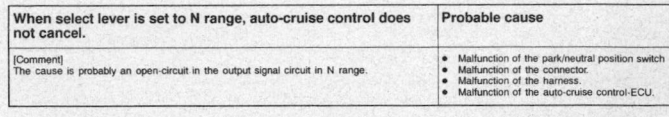
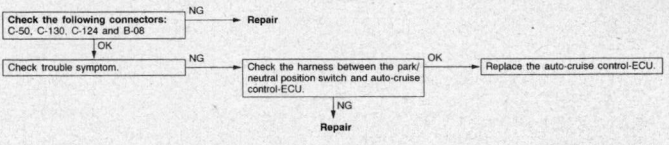

MT1109900253000X

Fig. 121   Inspection Procedure 5: Auto Cruise Does Not Cancel. Montero & Montero Sport

The diagnostic result displayed on the scan tool is normal even though auto-cruise control cannot be set.	Probable cause
[Comment] Because of an open-circuit in the battery backup circuit system, the fail-safe function prevents diagnostic trouble codes from being memorized and displayed even though auto-cruise control is canceled.	• Malfunction of the connector. • Malfunction of the harness. • Malfunction of the auto-cruise control-ECU.

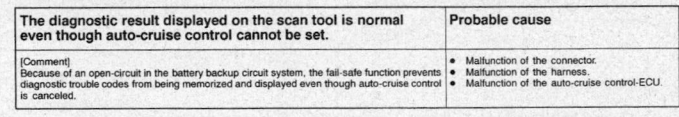
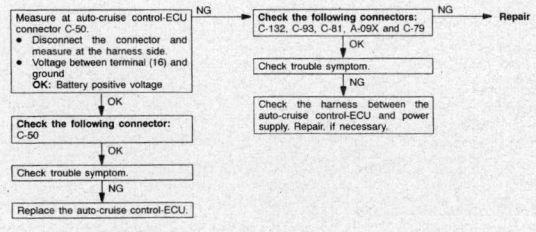

MT1109900255000X

Fig. 123   Inspection Procedure 7: Auto Cruise Cannot Set. Montero & Montero Sport

Auto-cruise control cannot be set.	Probable cause
[Comment] A malfunction of switches or that the fail-safe function cancelling auto-cruise control may be present.	• Malfunction of the auto-cruise control main switch. • Malfunction of the auto-cruise control switch. • Malfunction of the clock spring. • Malfunction of the harnesses or connectors. • Malfunction of the park/neutral position switch. • Malfunction of the auto-cruise control-ECU.

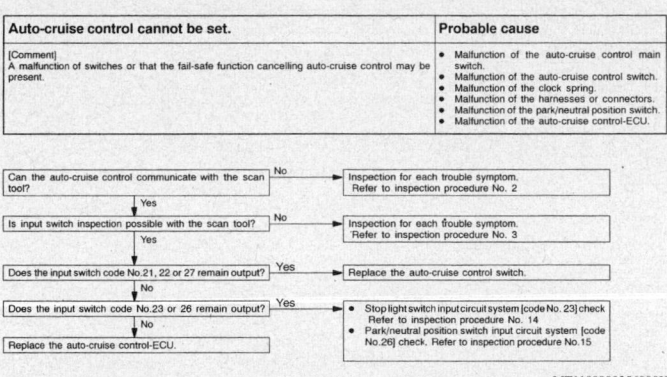

MT1109900256000X

Fig. 124 Inspection Procedure 8: Auto Cruise Cannot Set. Montero & Montero Sport

When the auto-cruise control main switch is ON, the switch indicator on the instrument panel does not illuminate. (However, auto-cruise control is normal.)	Probable cause
[Comment] Blown bulb in auto-cruise control main switch.	• Malfunction of the auto-cruise control main switch.

Replace the auto-cruise control main switch.

MT1109900258000X

Fig. 126 Inspection Procedure 10: Auto Cruise Lamp Does Not illuminate. Montero & Montero Sport

Auto-cruise control indicator inside combination meter does not illuminate. (However, auto-cruise control is normal.)	Probable cause
[Comment] A malfunction of the bulb, the connector or harness may be present.	• Malfunction of the bulb. • Malfunction of the harness. • Malfunction of the connector. • Malfunction of the auto-cruise control-ECU.

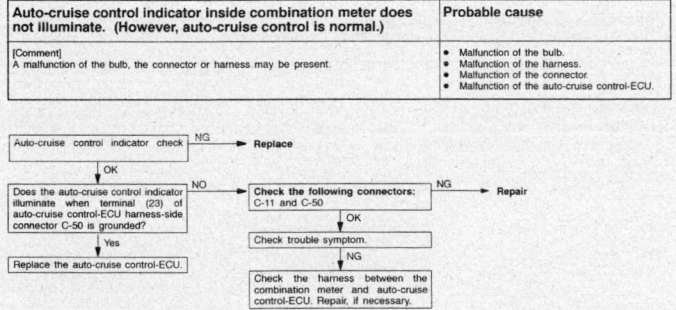

MT1109900260000X

Fig. 128 Inspection Procedure 12: Auto Cruise Lamp Does Not illuminate. Montero & Montero Sport

Park/neutral position switch input circuit system check (Code No. 26)

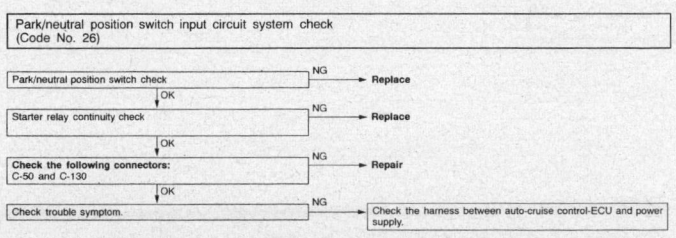

MT1109900262000X

Fig. 130 Inspection Procedure 14: PNP Switch Inspection. Montero & Montero Sport

Hunting (repeated acceleration and deceleration) occurs at the set vehicle speed.	Probable cause
[Comment] A malfunction of vehicle speed sensor or incorrect vacuum in the auto-cruise vacuum pump or actuator may be present.	• Malfunction of the vehicle speed sensor. • Malfunction of the auto-cruise vacuum pump. • Malfunction of the actuator. • Malfunction of the auto-cruise control-ECU.

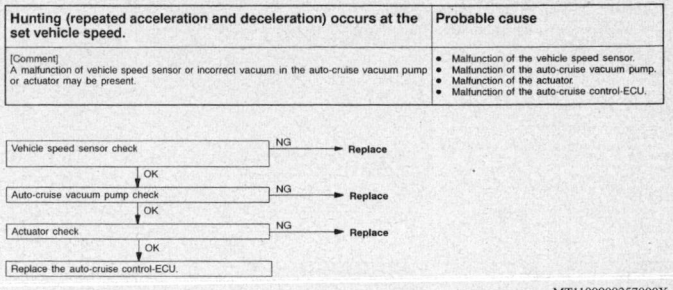

MT1109900257000X

Fig. 125 Inspection Procedure 9: Hunting Occurs At Set Speed. Montero & Montero Sport

Auto-cruise control main switch illumination light does not illuminate.	Probable cause
[Comment] A malfunction of auto-cruise control main switch, harness, or connector may exist.	• Malfunction of the auto-cruise control main switch. • Malfunction of the connector. • Malfunction of the harness.

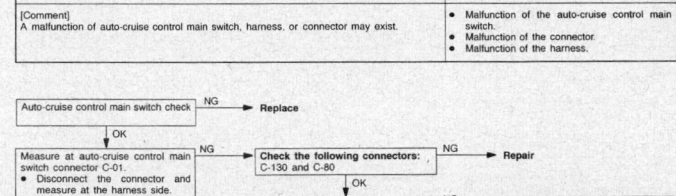

MT1109900259000X

Fig. 127 Inspection Procedure 11: Auto Cruise Lamp Does Not illuminate. Montero & Montero Sport

Stop light switch input circuit system check (Code No. 23)

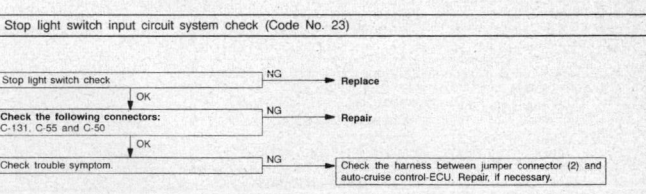

MT1109900261000X

Fig. 129 Inspection Procedure 13: Stop Lamp Switch Inspection. Montero & Montero Sport

Code No. 11 Auto-cruise vacuum pump drive system	Probable cause
This diagnostic trouble code is output if the release valve, control valve and motor drive signals from the auto-cruise vacuum pump are not input to the auto-cruise control-ECU.	• Malfunction of the auto-cruise vacuum pump • Malfunction of the stop light switch • Malfunction of the connector • Malfunction of the harness • Malfunction of the auto-cruise control-ECU

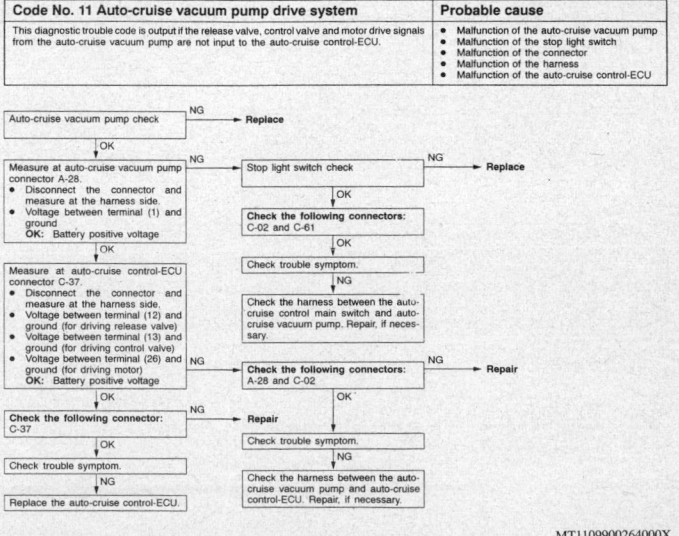

MT1109900264000X

Fig. 131 Code 11: Auto Cruise Vacuum Pump Drive System. 3000GT

Code No. 12 Vehicle speed signal system	Probable cause
This diagnostic trouble code is output if the vehicle speed signals from the vehicle speed sensor are not input to the auto-cruise control-ECU when the vehicle speed is 40 km/h (25 mph) or more.	• Malfunction of the vehicle speed sensor • Malfunction of the connector • Malfunction of the harness • Malfunction of the auto-cruise control-ECU

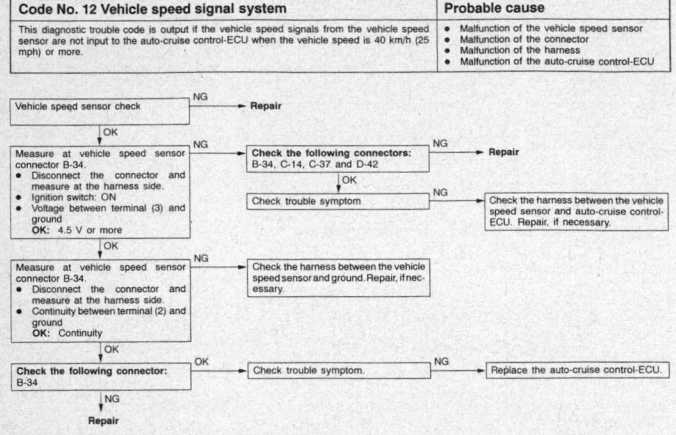

MT1109900265000X

Fig. 132   Code 12: Vehicle Speed Signal System. 3000GT

Code No. 16 Auto-cruise control-ECU	Probable cause
[Comment] This diagnostic trouble code is output if there is an abnormality in the CANCEL hold circuit or the microprocessor monitor circuit in the auto-cruise control-ECU.	• Malfunction of the auto-cruise control-ECU

Replace the auto-cruise control-ECU.

MT1109900267000X

Fig. 134   Code 16: Auto Cruise Control ECU. 3000GT

Code No. 15 Auto-cruise control-ECU	Probable cause
[Comment] This diagnostic trouble code is output if the RESUME switch or SET switch remains ON.	• Malfunction of the auto-cruise control switch

Replace the auto-cruise control switch.

MT1109900266000X

Fig. 133   Code 15: Auto Cruise Control ECU. 3000GT

Code No. 17 Throttle position sensor system	Probable cause
[Comment] This diagnostic trouble code is output if a voltage of 1.5 V or more when the closed throttle position switch is ON or 0.2 V or less when the closed throttle position switch is OFF is output for a continuous period of 4 seconds or more.	• Malfunction of the throttle position sensor • Malfunction of the connector • Malfunction of the harness • Malfunction of the auto-cruise control-ECU

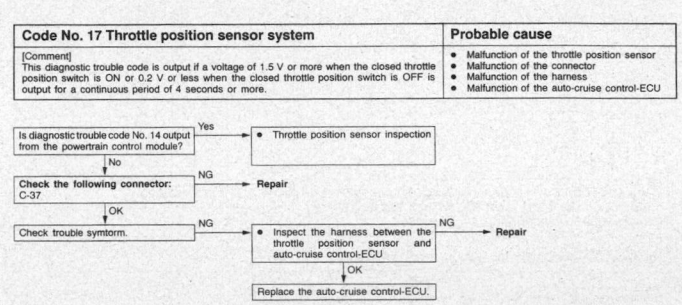

MT1109900268000X

Fig. 135   Code 17: TPS System. 3000GT

Trouble symptom		Inspection procedure No.
Communication with scan tool is not possible.	Communication with all systems is not possible.	1
	Communication with auto-cruise control-ECU only is not possible.	2
Input switch inspection using the scan tool is not possible. (However, diagnostic inspection is possible.)		3
Auto-cruise control does not cancel.	When brake pedal is depressed	4
	When clutch pedal is depressed <M/T>	5
	When select lever is set to N range <A/T>	6
	When CANCEL switch is set to ON	7
Auto-cruise control cannot be set.		8
Hunting (repeated acceleration and deceleration) occurs at the set vehicle speed.		9
When the auto-cruise control main switch is ON, the switch indicator on the instrument panel does not illuminate. (However, auto-cruise control is normal.)		10
Auto-cruise control main switch illumination light does not illuminate.		11
Auto-cruise control indicator light inside combination meter does not illuminate. (However, auto-cruise control is normal.)		12

MT1109900269000X

Fig. 136   Inspection Procedure Chart. 3000GT

Communication with scan tool is not possible. (Communication with all systems is not possible.)	Probable cause
A defect in the power supply system (including ground) for the diagnostic line may be present.	• Malfunction of the connector. • Malfunction of the harness.

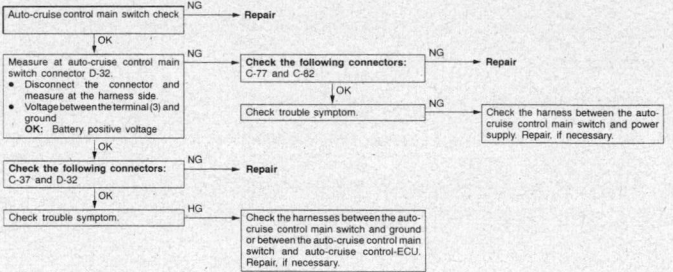

MT1109900270000X

Fig. 137   Inspection Procedure 1: Communication w/Scan Tool Not Possible. 3000GT

Communication with scan tool is not possible. (Communication with auto-cruise control-ECU is only not possible.)	Probable cause
A malfunction of Auto-cruise control main switch circuit or a malfunction of auto-cruise control-ECU ground circuit may be present.	• Malfunction of the auto-cruise control main switch. • Malfunction of the connector. • Malfunction of the harness. • Malfunction of the auto-cruise control-ECU.

1. **Auto-cruise control main switch circuit or a malfunction**

2. **Auto-cruise control-ECU ground circuit malfunction**

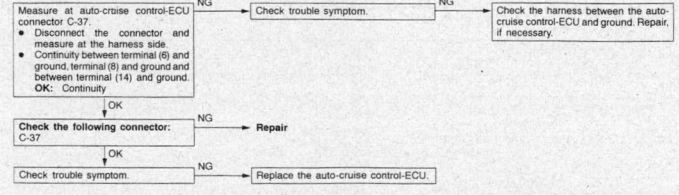

MT1109900271000X

Fig. 138   Inspection Procedure 2: Communication w/Scan Tool Not Possible. 3000GT

Input switch inspection using the scan tool is not possible. (However, diagnostic inspection is possible.)	Probable cause
A malfunction of auto-cruise control switch circuit system may be present.	• Malfunction of the auto-cruise control switch. • Malfunction of the clock spring. • Malfunction of the connector. • Malfunction of the harness.

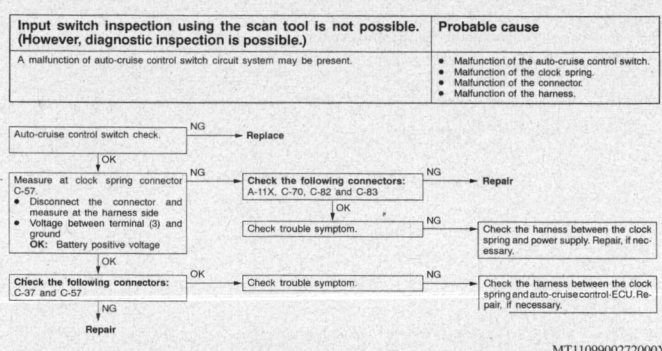

Fig. 139   Inspection Procedure 3: Communication w/Scan Tool Not Possible. 3000GT

When brake pedal is depressed, auto-cruise control does not cancel.	Probable cause
A malfunction of stop light switch or a malfunction of stop light circuit may be present.	• Malfunction of the stop light switch. • Malfunction of the connector. • Malfunction of the harness. • Malfunction of the auto-cruise control-ECU.

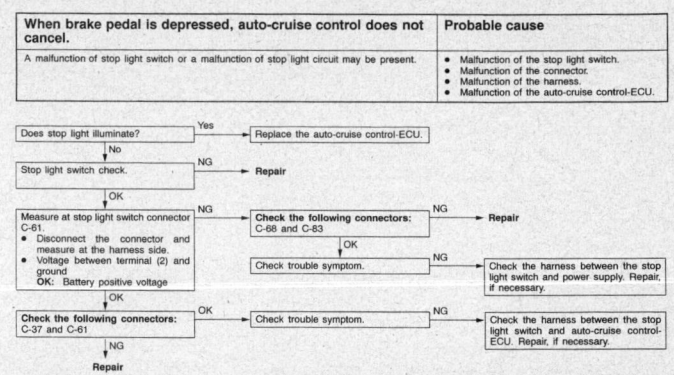

Fig. 140   Inspection Procedure 4: Auto Cruise Does Not Cancel. 3000GT

When clutch pedal is depressed, auto-cruise control does not cancel. <M/T>	Probable cause
A malfunction of the clutch pedal position switch or clutch circuit may be present.	• Malfunction of the clutch pedal position switch. • Malfunction of the connector. • Malfunction of the harness. • Malfunction of the auto-cruise control-ECU.

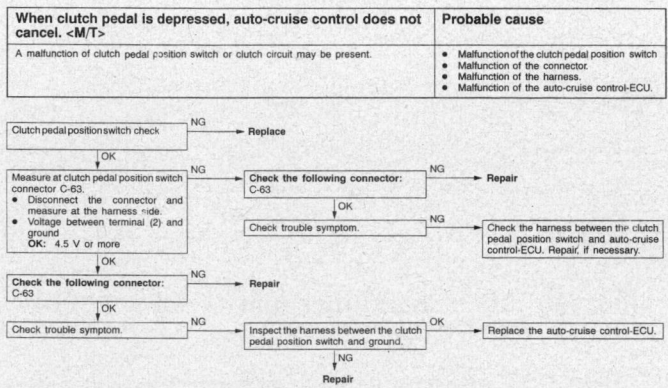

Fig. 141   Inspection Procedure 5: Auto Cruise Does Not Cancel. 3000GT

When select lever is set to N range, auto-cruise control does not cancel. <A/T>	Probable cause
The cause is probably an open-circuit in the output signal circuit in N range.	• Malfunction of the park/neutral position switch. • Malfunction of the connector. • Malfunction of the harness. • Malfunction of the auto-cruise control-ECU.

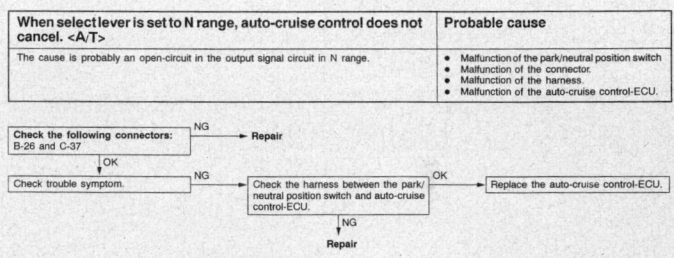

Fig. 142   Inspection Procedure 6: Auto Cruise Does Not Cancel. 3000GT

When auto-cruise control CANCEL switch is set to ON, auto-cruise control does not cancel.	Probable cause
An open-circuit in the circuit inside the CANCEL switch may be present.	• Malfunction of the auto-cruise control switch.

Replace the auto-cruise control switch.

Fig. 143   Inspection Procedure 7: Auto Cruise Does Not Cancel. 3000GT

Auto-cruise control cannot be set.	Probable cause
A malfunction of switches or that the fail-safe function cancelling auto-cruise control may be present.	• Malfunction of the auto-cruise control main switch. • Malfunction of the auto-cruise control switch. • Malfunction of the clock spring. • Malfunction of the harnesses or connectors. • Malfunction of the clutch pedal position switch <M/T>. • Malfunction of the park/neutral position switch <A/T>. • Malfunction of the auto-cruise control-ECU.

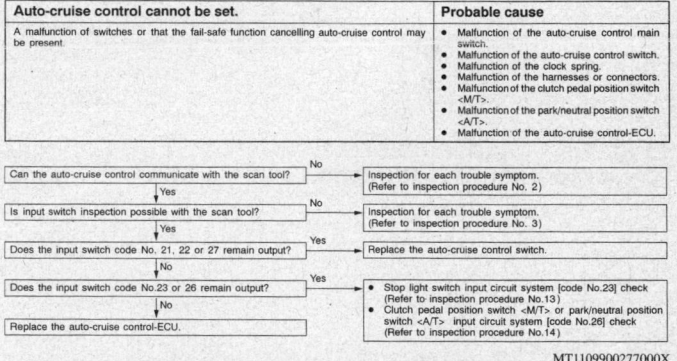

Fig. 144   Inspection Procedure 8: Auto Cruise Cannot Be Set. 3000GT

Hunting (repeated acceleration and deceleration) occurs at the set vehicle speed.	Probable cause
A malfunction of vehicle speed sensor or incorrect vacuum in the auto-cruise vacuum pump or actuator may be present.	• Malfunction of the vehicle speed sensor. • Malfunction of the auto-cruise vacuum pump. • Malfunction of the actuator. • Malfunction of the auto-cruise control-ECU.

Fig. 145   Inspection Procedure 9: Hunting Occurs At Set Speed. 3000GT

When the auto-cruise control main switch is ON, the switch indicator on the instrument panel does not illuminate. (However, auto-cruise control is normal.)	Probable cause
Blown bulb in auto-cruise control main switch.	• Malfunction of the auto-cruise control main switch.

Replace the auto-cruise control main switch.

Fig. 146   Inspection Procedure 10: Auto Cruise Lamp Does Not Illuminate. 3000GT

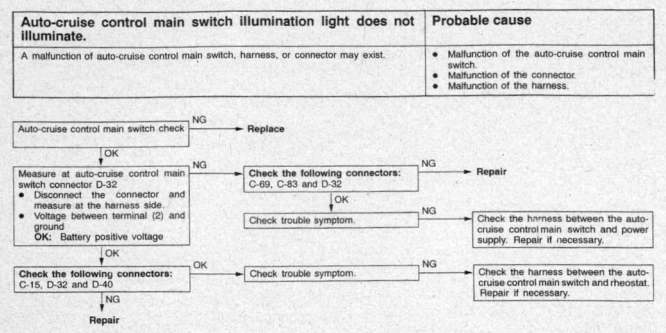

Auto-cruise control main switch illumination light does not illuminate.	Probable cause
A malfunction of auto-cruise control main switch, harness, or connector may exist.	• Malfunction of the auto-cruise control main switch. • Malfunction of the connector. • Malfunction of the harness.

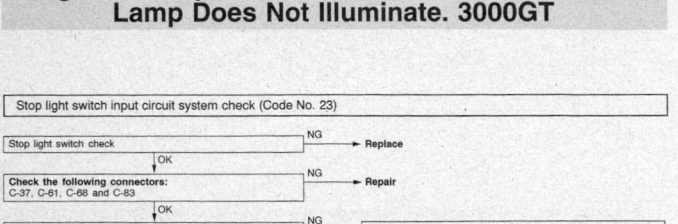

MT1109900280000X

Fig. 147 Inspection Procedure 11: Auto Cruise Lamp Does Not Illuminate. 3000GT

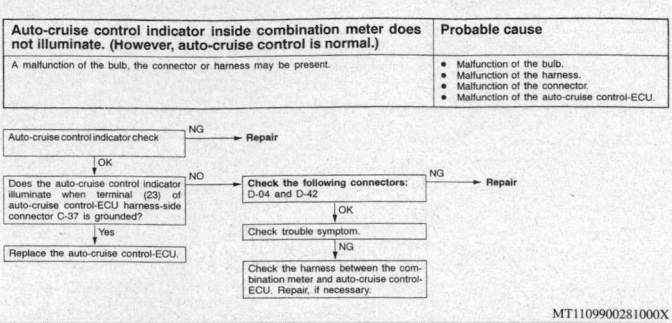

Auto-cruise control indicator inside combination meter does not illuminate. (However, auto-cruise control is normal.)	Probable cause
A malfunction of the bulb, the connector or harness may be present.	• Malfunction of the bulb. • Malfunction of the harness. • Malfunction of the connector. • Malfunction of the auto-cruise control-ECU.

MT1109900281000X

Fig. 148 Inspection Procedure 12: Auto Cruise Lamp Does Not Illuminate. 3000GT

Stop light switch input circuit system check (Code No. 23)

Stop light switch check	→ NG → Replace
Check the following connectors: C-37, C-61, C-68 and C-83	→ NG → Repair
Check trouble symptom.	→ NG → Check the harness between junction block and auto-cruise control-ECU. Repair, if necessary.

MT1109900282000X

Fig. 149 Inspection Procedure 13: Stop Lamp Switch. 3000GT

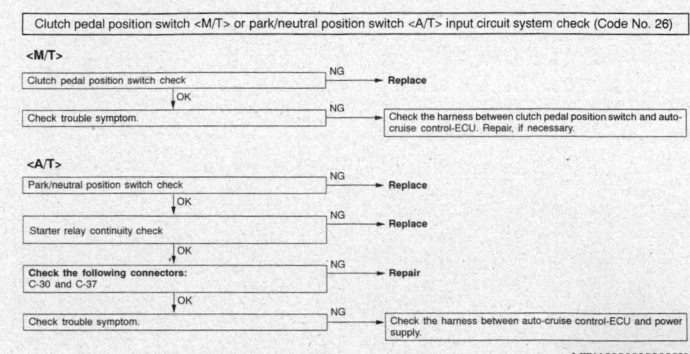

Clutch pedal position switch <M/T> or park/neutral position switch <A/T> input circuit system check (Code No. 26)

MT1109900283000X

Fig. 150 Inspection Procedure 14: CPS Or PNP Switch. 3000GT

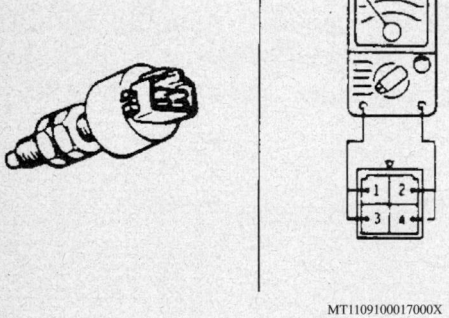

MT1109100017000X

Fig. 151 Stop lamp/brake switch terminal identification

○─○ :Continuity

Switch Terminal / Measurement conditions	Brake switch		Stop light switch	
	1	4	2	3
When brake pedal depressed.			○─○	○─○
When brake pedal not depressed.	○─○	○─○		

MT1109100018000X

Fig. 152 Stop lamp/brake switch continuity chart

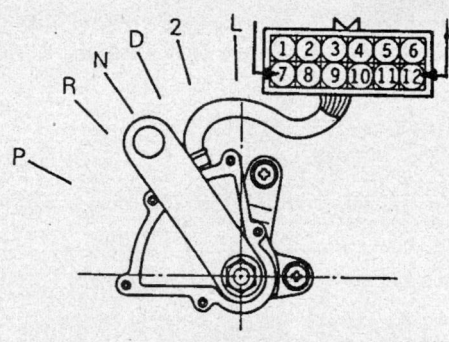

MT1109200019000X

Fig. 153 PNP switch N & P position inspection. Montero & Montero Sport

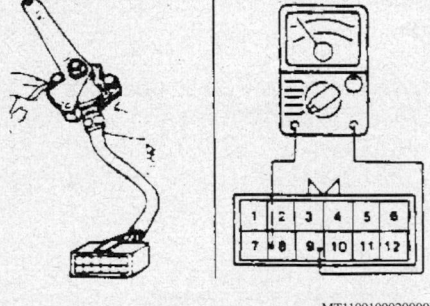

MT1109100020000X

Fig. 154 PNP switch N & P position inspection. Diamante, Eclipse, Galant, Mirage, Pickup & 3000GT

MT1109100021000X

Fig. 155 Actuator inspection

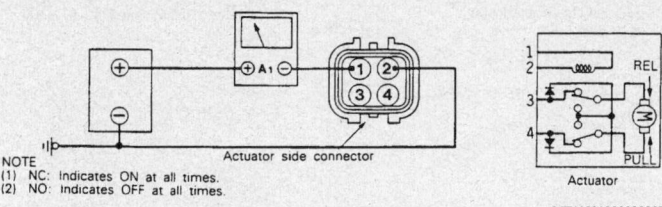

NOTE
(1) NC: Indicates ON at all times.
(2) NO: Indicates OFF at all times.

MT1109100022000X

Fig. 156 Actuator circuit inspection. Except Pickup

Judgement		Probable cause
Normal	Abnormal	
Holder moves in PULL direction • Gage indicates negative pressure • Ammeter indicates 1.5A or less	Holder does not move in PULL direction • Ammeter: 0A	Open circuit in lead wire Open circuit in valve solenoid coil
	Holder does not move in PULL direction • Ammeter: 0.7 – 1.5A • No gauge indication	Faulty solenoid valve in actuator (foreign matter caught inside)
	Holder does not move in PULL direction • Ammeter: 0.5 – 0.6A • Gauge gives indication	Open circuit in VAC side solenoid or valve remaining closed
	Holder once moves in PULL direction but soon moves back • Ammeter: 0.4 – 0.5A	Open circuit in VENT1 or VENT2 solenoid

MT1109100024000X

Fig. 158 Actuator operation inspection (VAC, VENT1, VENT2 solenoids on). Pickup

Judgement		Probable cause
Normal	Abnormal	
Holder keeps its position • Gauge negative pressure reading constant • Ammeter: 0.5 – 0.6A	Holder returns to initial position • Gauge reading constant • Ammeter: 0.5 – 0.6A	Leaks from VENT1 or VENT2 valve seal (foreign matter caught in valve.)
	Holder returns to initial position • Gauge reading: 0 mmHg. (0 in. Hg.) • Ammeter: 0.5 – 0.6A	VAC valve and VENT valves both sealing poorly

MT1109100025000X

Fig. 159 Actuator operation inspection (VAC solenoids off). Pickup

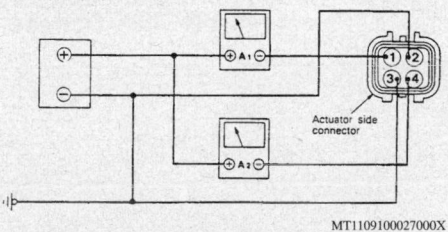

MT1109100027000X

Fig. 161 Motor pull direction & limit switch operation. Except Pickup

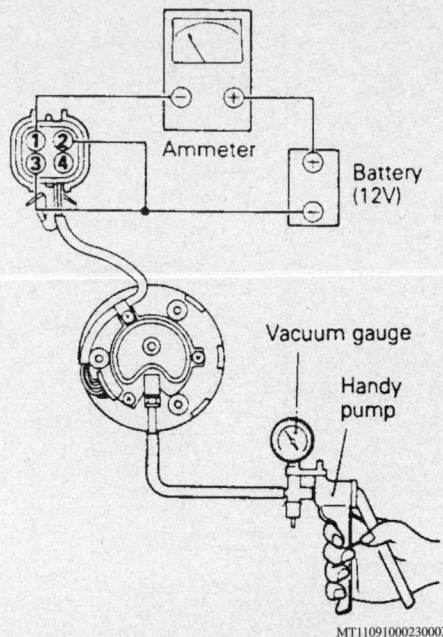

MT1109100023000X

Fig. 157 Actuator operation inspection. Pickup

Judgement		Probable cause
Normal	Abnormal	
Holder returns to initial position • Gauge negative pressure reading remains as (2) • Ammeter: 0.2 – 0.4A	Holder does not return to initial position • Gauge negative pressure reading remaining as (2)	• VENT valve binding • Atmosphere section filter completely loaded

MT1109100026000X

Fig. 160 Actuator operation inspection (VAC or VENT1, VENT2 solenoids off). Pickup

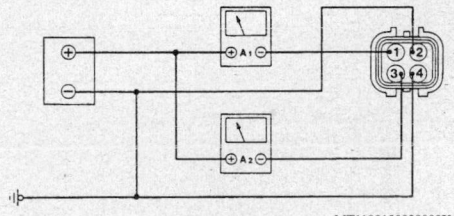

MT1109100028000X

Fig. 162 Motor release direction & limit switch operation. Except Pickup

COMPONENT REPLACEMENT

Refer to numbered sequences shown in **Figs. 163 through 172** for component replacement.

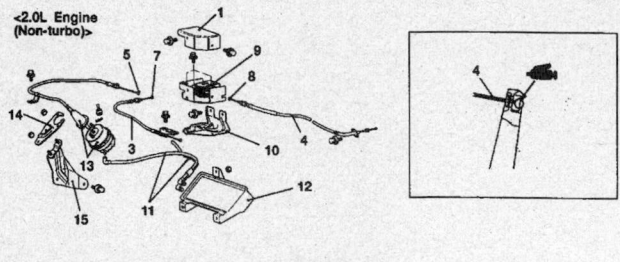

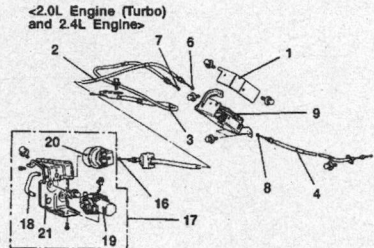

Auto-cruise control cable, throttle cable and accelerator cable removal steps
1. Link protector
 • Auto-cruise control cable adjustment
2. Auto-cruise control cable <2.0L Engine (Turbo) and 2.4L Engine>
3. Throttle cable
4. Accelerator cable

Link assembly removal steps
1. Link protector
 • Auto-cruise control cable adjustment
5. Speed control assembly connection <2.0L Engine (Non-turbo)>
6. Auto-cruise control cable connection <2.0L Engine (Turbo) and 2.4L Engine>
7. Throttle cable connection
8. Accelerator cable connection
9. Link assembly

10. Link bracket <2.0L Engine (Non-turbo)>

Reservoir assembly and speed control assembly removal steps <2.0L Engine (Non-turbo)>
11. Vacuum hose connection
12. Reservoir assembly
13. Speed control assembly
14. Actuator upper bracket
15. Actuator lower bracket

Vacuum pump and actuator removal steps <2.0L Engine (Turbo) and 2.4L Engine>
16. Auto-cruise control cable connection
17. Auto-cruise vacuum pump and actuator assembly
18. Vacuum hose
19. Auto-cruise vacuum pump
20. Actuator
21. Actuator bracket

MT1109500154010X

Fig. 163   Speed control component replacement (Part 1 of 3). Eclipse

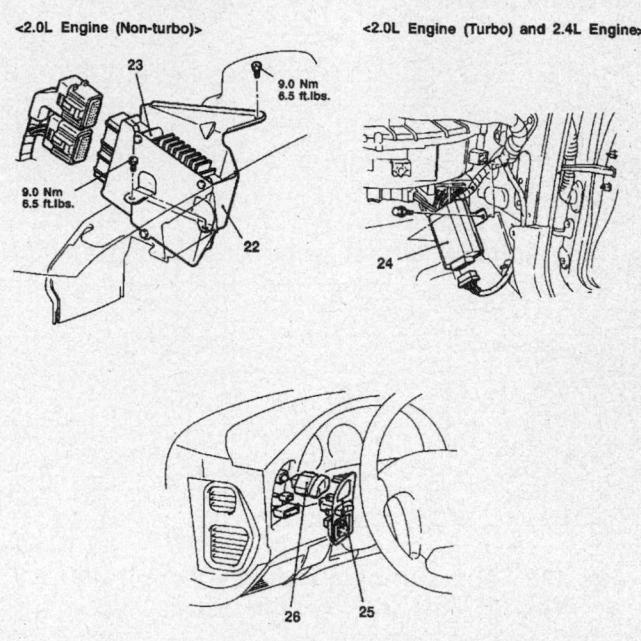

Powertrain control module removal steps <2.0L Engine (Non-turbo)>
 • Air cleaner
22. Powertrain control module bracket
23. Powertrain control module

Auto-cruise control – ECU removal steps <2.0L Engine (Turbo) and 2.4L Engine>
 • Cowl side trim
24. Auto-cruise control-ECU

Auto-cruise control main switch removal steps
25. Instrument panel switch
26. Auto-cruise control main switch

MT1109500154020X

Fig. 163   Speed control component replacement (Part 2 of 3). Eclipse

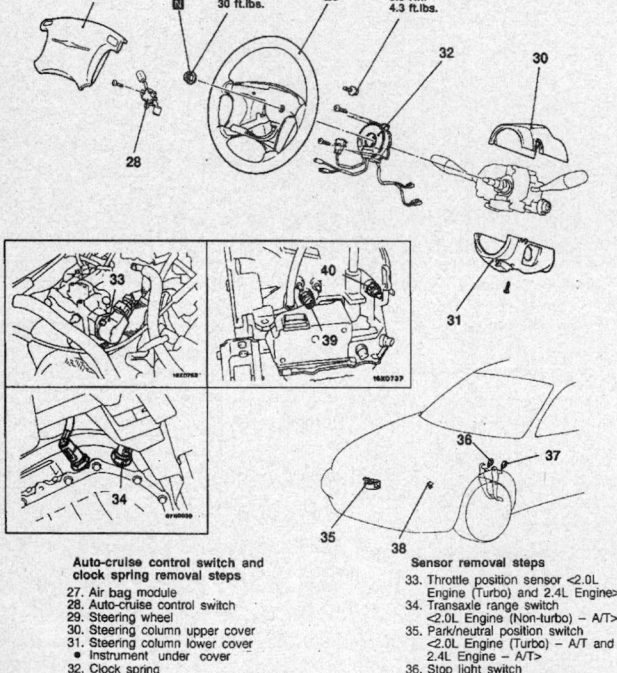

Auto-cruise control switch and clock spring removal steps
27. Air bag module
28. Auto-cruise control switch
29. Steering wheel
30. Steering column upper cover
31. Steering column lower cover
32. Clock spring

Sensor removal steps
33. Throttle position sensor <2.0L Engine (Turbo) and 2.4L Engine>
34. Transaxle range switch <2.0L Engine (Non-turbo) – A/T>
35. Park/neutral position switch <2.0L Engine (Turbo) – A/T and 2.4L Engine – A/T>
36. Stop light switch
37. Clutch pedal position switch <2.0L Engine (Turbo) – M/T and 2.4L Engine – M/T>
38. Vehicle speed sensor <Except 2.0L Engine (Non-turbo) – A/T>
39. Input speed sensor <2.0L Engine (Non-turbo) – A/T>
40. Output speed sensor <2.0L Engine (Non-turbo) – A/T>

MT1109500154030X

Fig. 163   Speed control component replacement (Part 3 of 3). Eclipse

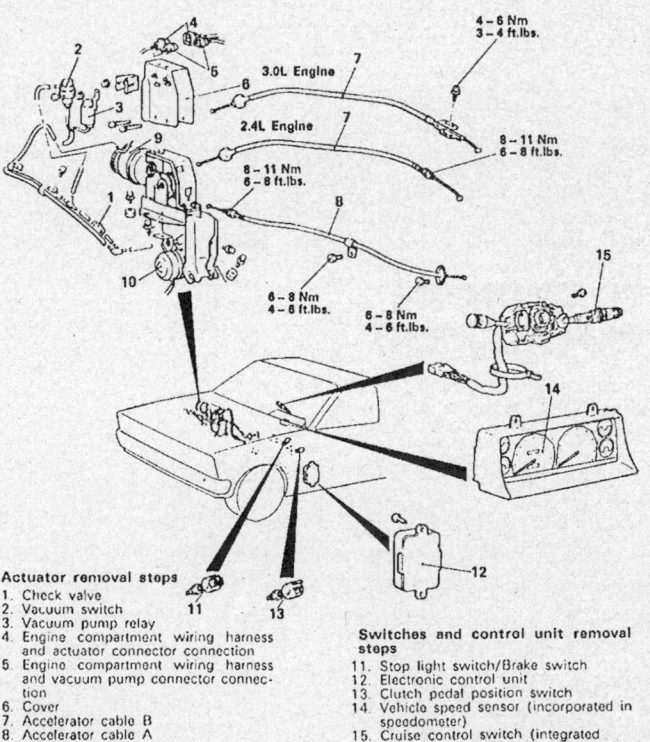

Actuator removal steps
1. Check valve
2. Vacuum switch
3. Vacuum pump relay
4. Engine compartment wiring harness and actuator connector connection
5. Engine compartment wiring harness and vacuum pump connector connection
6. Cover
7. Accelerator cable B
8. Accelerator cable A
9. Actuator assembly
10. Vacuum pump

Switches and control unit removal steps
11. Stop light switch/Brake switch
12. Electronic control unit
13. Clutch pedal position switch
14. Vehicle speed sensor (incorporated in speedometer)
15. Cruise control switch (integrated into column switch)

MT1109100033000X

Fig. 164   Speed control component replacement. Pickup

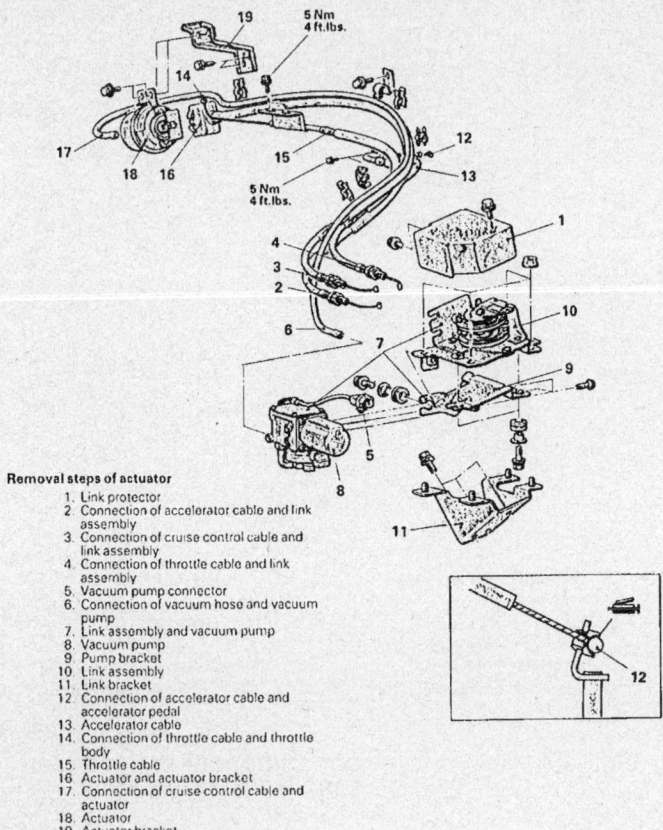

Removal steps of actuator
1. Link protector
2. Connection of accelerator cable and link assembly
3. Connection of cruise control cable and link assembly
4. Connection of throttle cable and link assembly
5. Vacuum pump connector
6. Connection of vacuum hose and vacuum pump
7. Link assembly and vacuum pump
8. Vacuum pump
9. Pump bracket
10. Link assembly
11. Link bracket
12. Connection of accelerator cable and accelerator pedal
13. Accelerator cable
14. Connection of throttle cable and throttle body
15. Throttle cable
16. Actuator and actuator bracket
17. Connection of cruise control cable and actuator
18. Actuator
19. Actuator bracket

MT1109100034010X

Fig. 165 Speed control component replacement (Part 1 of 2). 3000GT

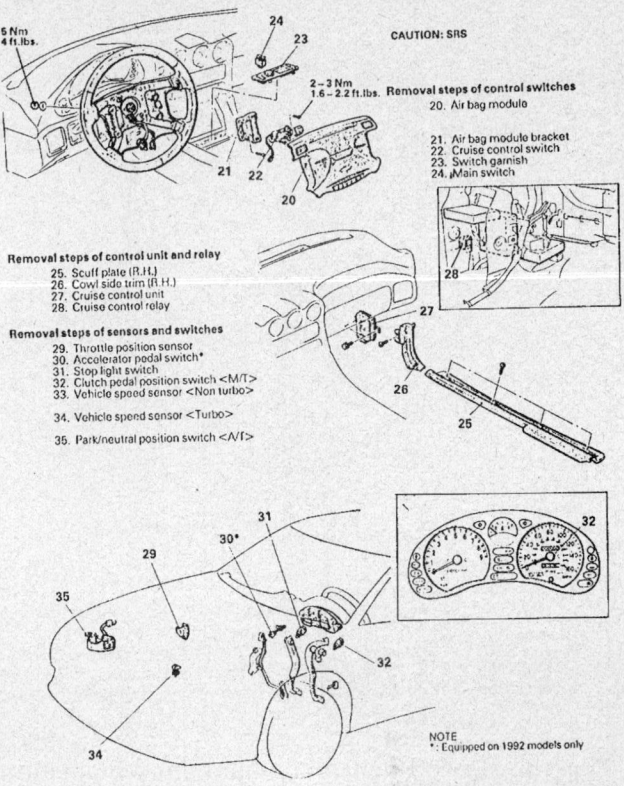

CAUTION: SRS

Removal steps of control switches
20. Air bag module
21. Air bag module bracket
22. Cruise control switch
23. Switch garnish
24. Main switch

Removal steps of control unit and relay
25. Scuff plate (R.H.)
26. Cowl side trim (R.H.)
27. Cruise control unit
28. Cruise control relay

Removal steps of sensors and switches
29. Throttle position sensor
30. Accelerator pedal switch*
31. Stop light switch
32. Clutch pedal position switch <M/T>
33. Vehicle speed sensor <Non turbo>
34. Vehicle speed sensor <Turbo>
35. Park/neutral position switch <A/t>

NOTE
*: Equipped on 1992 models only

MT1109100034020X

Fig. 165 Speed control component replacement (Part 2 of 2). 3000GT

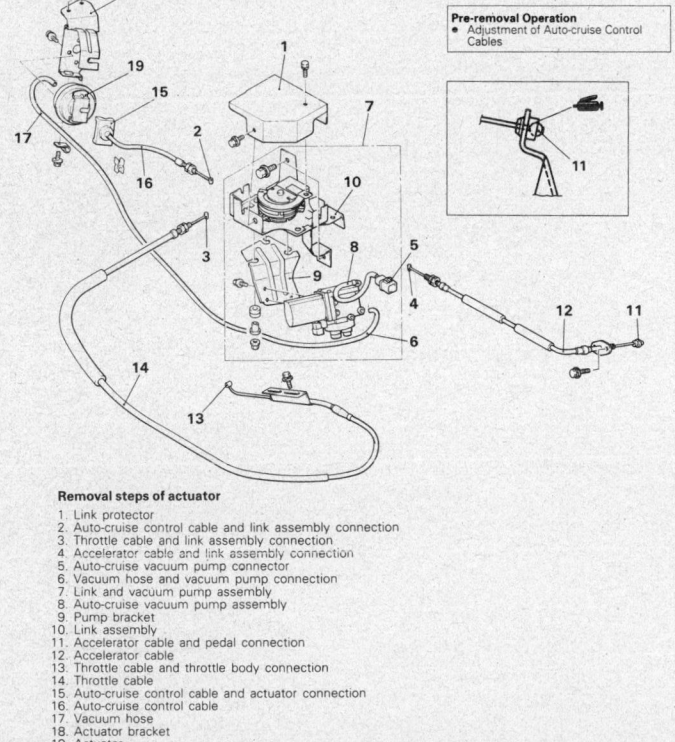

Pre-removal Operation
• Adjustment of Auto-cruise Control Cables

Removal steps of actuator
1. Link protector
2. Auto-cruise control cable and link assembly connection
3. Throttle cable and link assembly connection
4. Accelerator cable and link assembly connection
5. Auto-cruise vacuum pump connector
6. Vacuum hose and vacuum pump connection
7. Link and vacuum pump assembly
8. Auto-cruise vacuum pump assembly
9. Pump bracket
10. Link assembly
11. Accelerator cable and pedal connection
12. Accelerator cable
13. Throttle cable and throttle body connection
14. Throttle cable
15. Auto-cruise control cable and actuator connection
16. Auto-cruise control cable
17. Vacuum hose
18. Actuator bracket
19. Actuator

MT1109100036010X

Fig. 166 Speed control component replacement (Part 1 of 2). 1996 Diamante

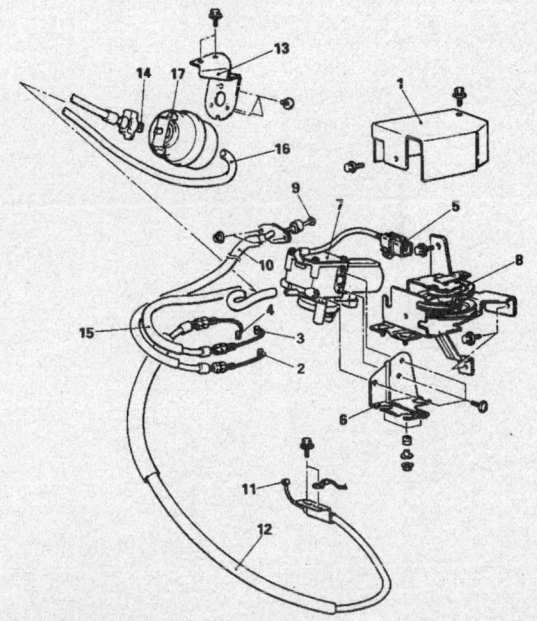

Removal stemps of actuator
1. Link protector
2. Accelerator cable and link assembly connection
3. Auto-cruise control cable and link assembly connection
4. Throttle cable and link assembly connection
5. Auto-cruise vacuum pump connector
6. Pump bracket
7. Auto-cruise vacuum pump assembly
8. Link assembly
9. Accelerator cable and pedal connection
10. Accelerator cable
11. Throttle cable and throttle body connection
12. Throttle cable
13. Actuator bracket
14. Auto-cruise control cable and actuator connection
15. Auto-cruise control cable
16. Vacuum hose
17. Actuator

MT1109100036020X

Fig. 166 Speed control component replacement (Part 2 of 2). 1996 Diamante

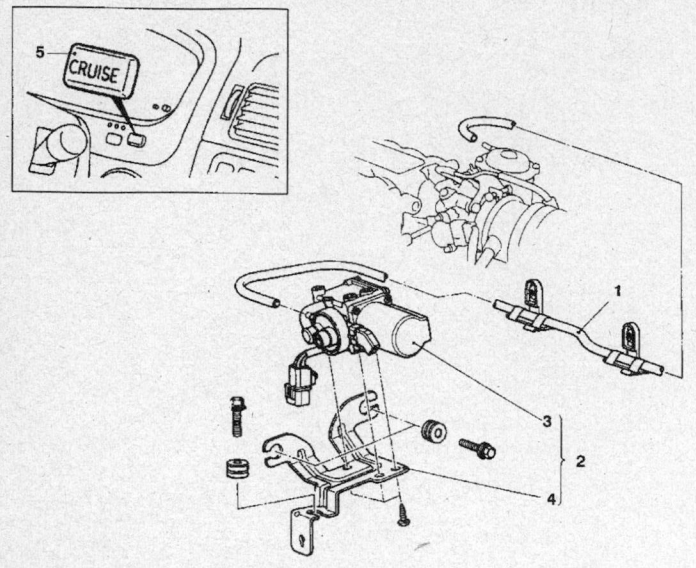

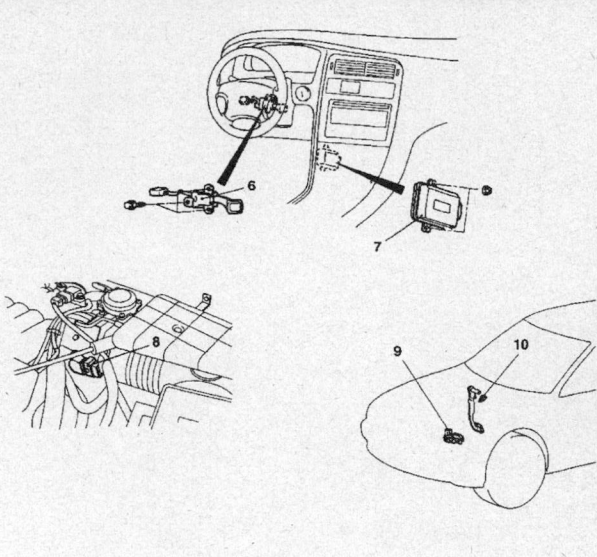

Vacuum pump removal steps
1. Vacuum hose
2. Electric vacuum pump and bracket assembly
3. Electric vacuum pump

Main switch removal steps
4. Bracket
5. Main switch

MT1109700156010X

Fig. 167 Speed control component replacement (Part 1 of 2). 1997–99 Diamante

Control switch removal steps
- Airbag module
6. Control switch

Control unit removal steps
- Floor console box assembly
- Center air outlet assembly

- Ash tray
- Air conditioner control unit and radio/tape player
7. Cruise control ECU

Sensor removal steps
8. Throttle position sensor
9. Inhibitor switch
10. Stop lamp switch

MT1109700156020X

Fig. 167 Speed control component replacement (Part 2 of 2). 1997–99 Diamante

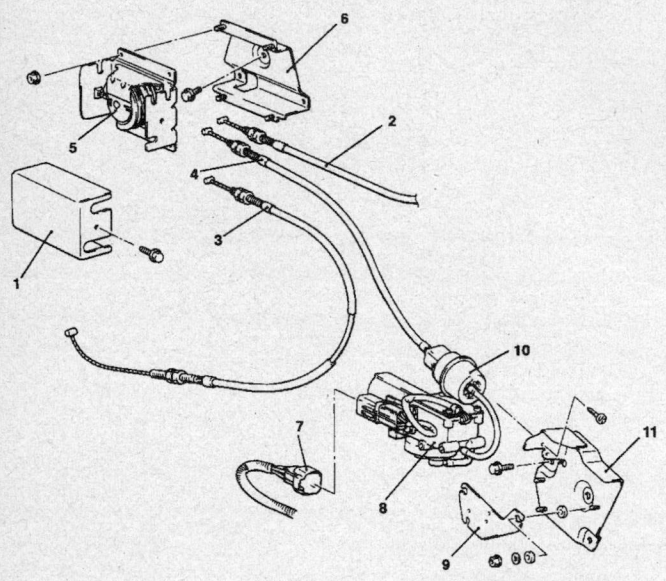

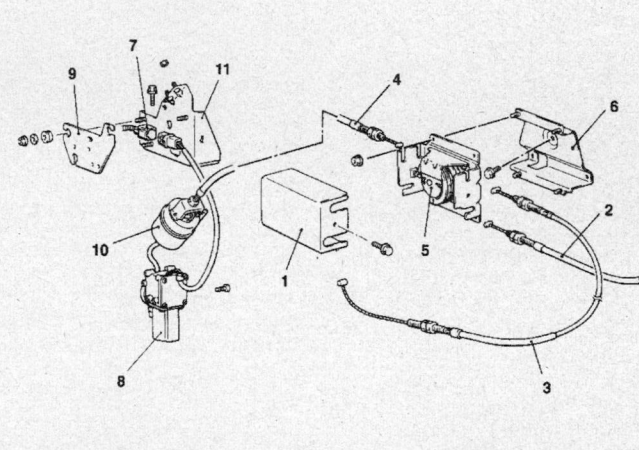

Intermediate link removal steps
1. Link protector
2. Accelerator cable and link connection
3. Throttle cable and link connection
4. Cruise control cable and link connection
5. Intermediate link
6. Link bracket

Actuator removal steps
4. Cruise control cable and link connection
7. Wiring connector
8. Vacuum pump
9. Pump bracket
10. Actuator
11. Actuator bracket

MT1109200037010X

Fig. 168 Speed control component replacement (Part 1 of 2). Montero except 1996 w/3.0L 24 valve engine & California emissions

Intermediate link removal steps
1. Link protector
2. Accelerator cable and link connection
3. Throttle cable and link connection
4. Cruise control cable and link connection
5. Intermediate link
6. Link bracket

Actuator removal steps
4. Cruise control cable and link connection
7. Wiring connector
8. Vacuum pump
9. Pump bracket
10. Actuator
11. Actuator bracket

MT110920003701AX

Fig. 168 Speed control component replacement (Part 1 of 2). 1996 Montero w/3.0L 24 valve engine & California emissions

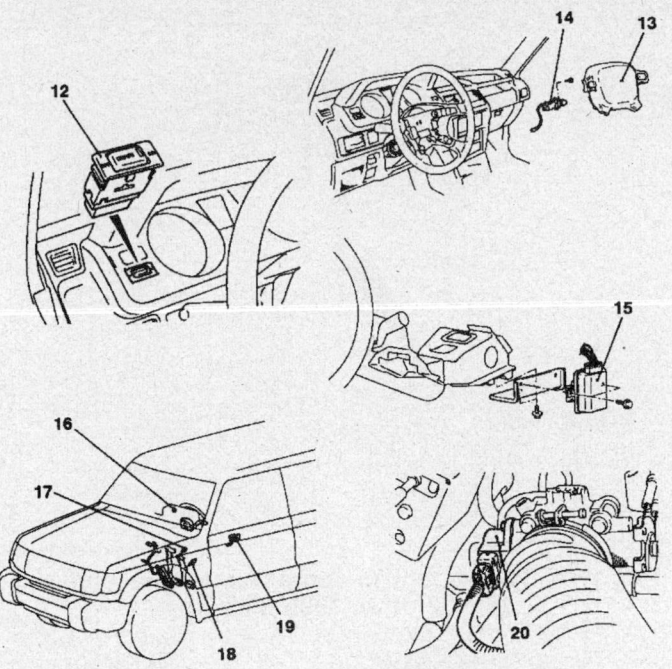

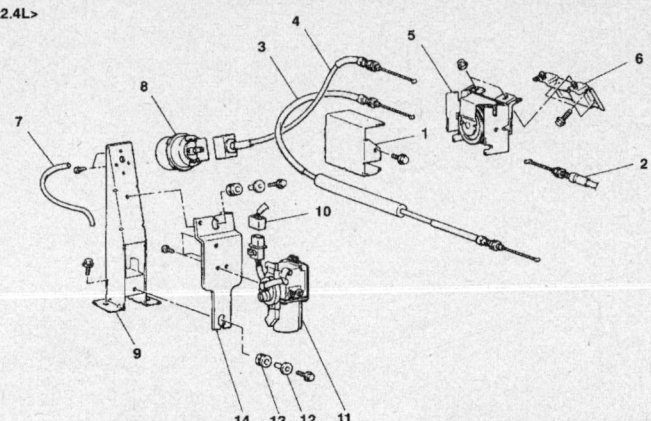

Removal steps of switches
12. Main switch
13. Air bag module
14. Control switch

Removal steps of control unit
● Instrument panel
15. Control unit

Removal steps of sensors
16. Vehicle speed sensor (reed switch)
17. Stop light switch
18. Clutch pedal position switch <M/T>
19. Park/Neutral position switch <A/T>
20. TPS (Throttle position sensor)

MT1109200037020X

Fig. 168 Speed control component replacement (Part 2 of 2). Montero

LINK ASSEMBLY REMOVAL STEPS
1. LINK PROTECTOR
2. ACCELERATOR CABLE (LINK ASSEMBLY SIDE)
3. THROTTLE CABLE (LINK ASSEMBLY SIDE)
4. CRUISE CONTROL CABLE (LINK ASSEMBLY SIDE)
5. LINK ASSEMBLY
6. LINK BRACKET

ACTUATOR REMOVAL STEPS
4. CRUISE CONTROL CABLE (ACTUATOR SIDE)
7. VACUUM HOSE
8. ACTUATOR
9. ACTUATOR BRACKET

VACUUM PUMP REMOVAL STEPS
7. VACUUM HOSE
10. WIRING CONNECTOR
11. VACUUM PUMP
12. DISTANCE PIECE
13. RUBBER MOUNT
14. PUMP BRACKET

MT1109700158010X

Fig. 169 Speed control component replacement (Part 1 of 2). Montero Sport w/2.4L engine

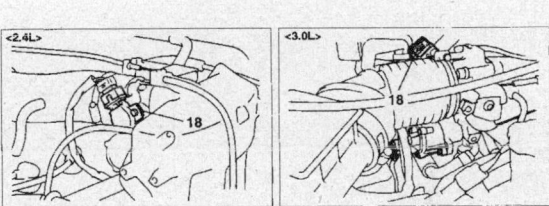

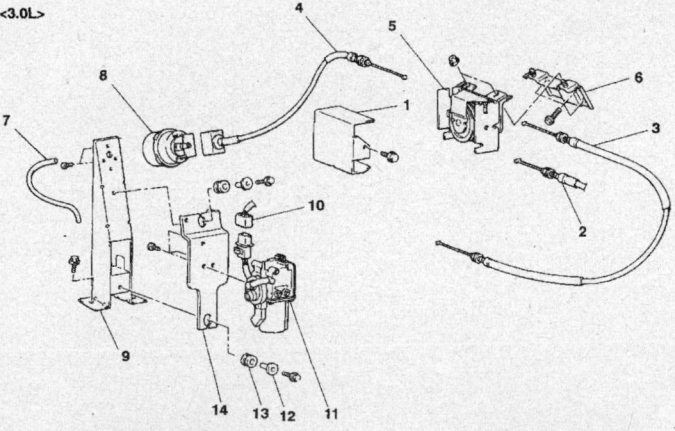

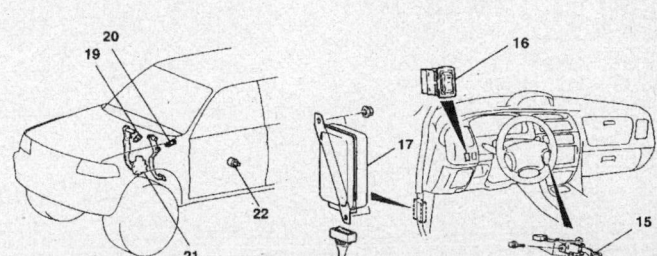

LINK ASSEMBLY REMOVAL STEPS
1. LINK PROTECTOR
2. ACCELERATOR CABLE (LINK ASSEMBLY SIDE)
3. THROTTLE CABLE (LINK ASSEMBLY SIDE)
4. CRUISE CONTROL CABLE (LINK ASSEMBLY SIDE)
5. LINK ASSEMBLY
6. LINK BRACKET

ACTUATOR REMOVAL STEPS
4. CRUISE CONTROL CABLE (ACTUATOR SIDE)
7. VACUUM HOSE
8. ACTUATOR
9. ACTUATOR BRACKET

VACUUM PUMP REMOVAL STEPS
7. VACUUM HOSE
10. WIRING CONNECTOR
11. VACUUM PUMP
12. DISTANCE PIECE
13. RUBBER MOUNT
14. PUMP BRACKET

MT110970015801AX

Fig. 169 Speed control component replacement (Part 1 of 2). Montero Sport w/3.0L engine

CONTROL SWITCH REMOVAL STEPS
● AIR BAG MODULE

15. CONTROL SWITCH

MAIN SWITCH REMOVAL STEPS
● METER BEZEL ASSEMBLY

16. MAIN SWITCH

CONTROL UNIT REMOVAL STEPS
● COWL SIDE TRIM

17. CONTROL-ECU

SENSOR REMOVAL STEPS
18. THROTTLE POSITION SENSOR
19. STOPLIGHT SWITCH
20. CLUTCH PEDAL POSITION SWITCH
21. PARK/NEUTRAL POSITION SWITCH <A/T>
22. VEHICLE SPEED SENSOR

MT1109700158020X

Fig. 169 Speed control component replacement (Part 2 of 2). Montero Sport

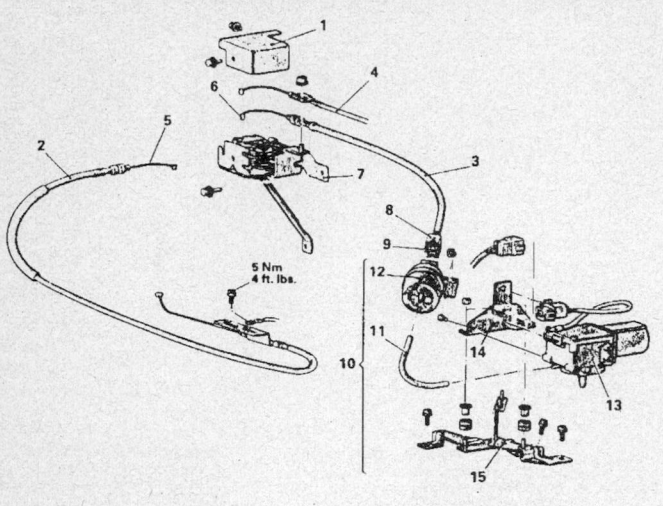

Throttle cable and auto-cruise control cable removal steps

1. Link protector
2. Throttle cable
3. Auto-cruise control cable

Link assembly removal steps

1. Link protector
4. Accelerator cable connection
5. Throttle cable connection
6. Auto-cruise control cable connection
7. Link assembly

Actuator removal steps

8. Cover
9. Auto-cruise control cable connection
10. Actuator and pump assembly (Part No. 11–15)
11. Vacuum hose
12. Actuator
13. Vacuum pump
14. Pump bracket
15. Actuator and pump bracket

MT1109300039010X

Fig. 170 Speed control component replacement (Part 1 of 3). 1996 Mirage

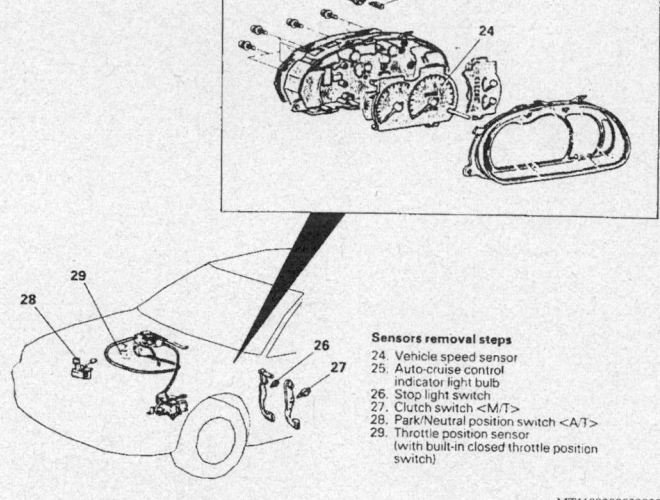

Sensors removal steps

24. Vehicle speed sensor
25. Auto-cruise control indicator light bulb
26. Stop light switch
27. Clutch switch <M/T>
28. Park/Neutral position switch <A/T>
29. Throttle position sensor (with built-in closed throttle position switch)

MT1109300039020X

Fig. 170 Speed control component replacement (Part 2 of 3). 1996 Mirage

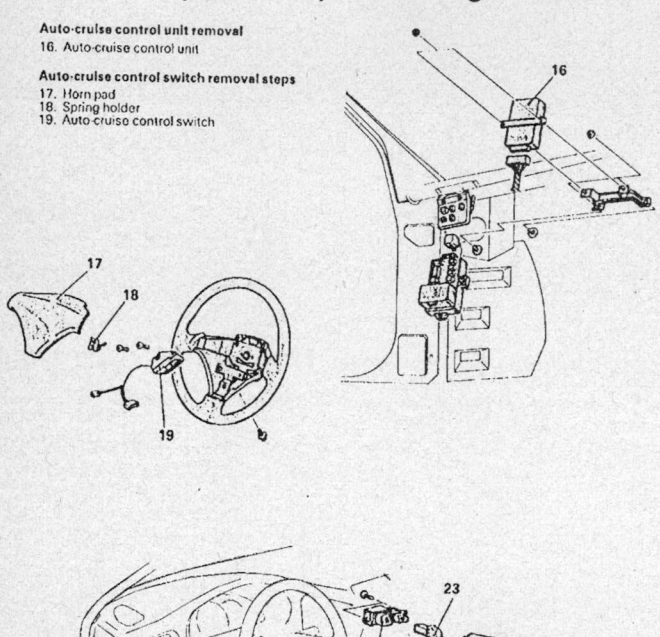

Auto-cruise control unit removal

16. Auto-cruise control unit

Auto-cruise control switch removal steps

17. Horn pad
18. Spring holder
19. Auto-cruise control switch

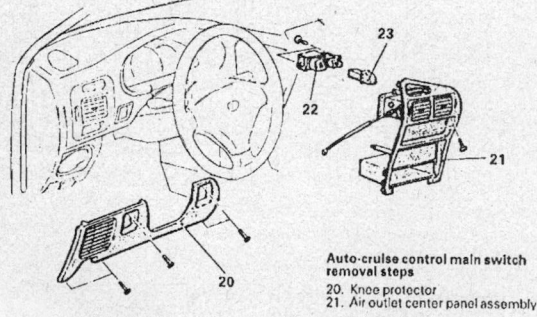

Auto-cruise control main switch removal steps

20. Knee protector
21. Air outlet center panel assembly
22. Switch holder
23. Auto-cruise control main switch

MT1109300039030X

Fig. 170 Speed control component replacement (Part 3 of 3). 1996 Mirage

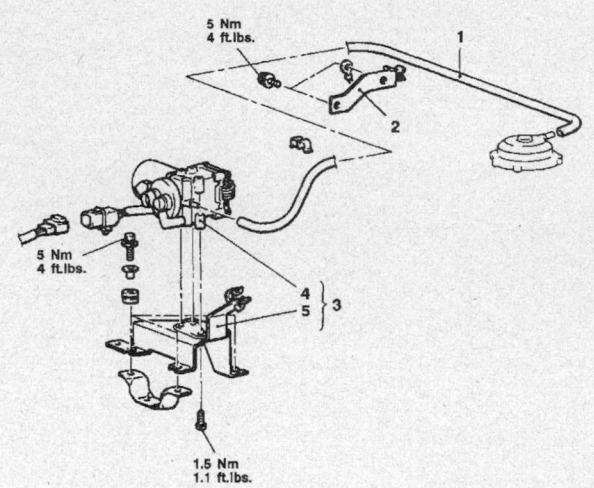

5 Nm
4 ft.lbs.

5 Nm
4 ft.lbs.

1.5 Nm
1.1 ft.lbs.

Auto-cruise vacuum pump removal steps

1. Vacuum hose
2. Bracket
3. Auto-cruise vacuum pump and bracket assembly
4. Auto-cruise vacuum pump assembly
5. Pump bracket

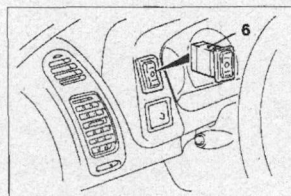

Main switch removal

6. Main switch

MT1109700157010X

Fig. 171 Speed control component replacement (Part 1 of 2). 1997–99 Mirage

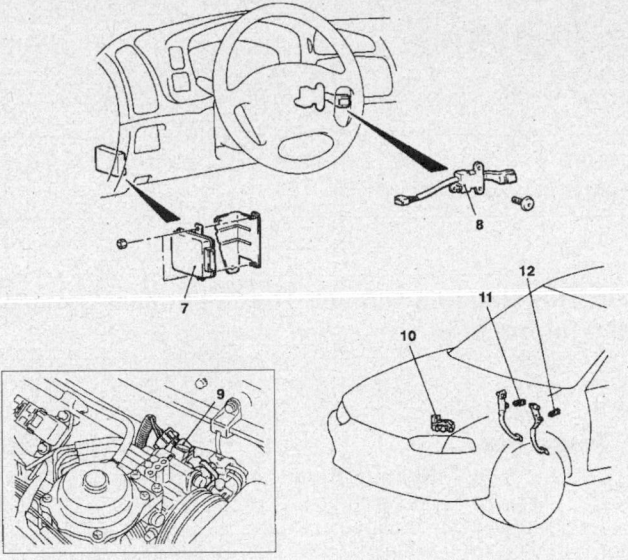

Control unit removal
- 7. Auto-cruise control-ECU
     Control switch removal

Control switch removal
- Air bag module
8. Control switch

Sensor removal
- 9. Throttle position sensor
- 10. Park/neutral position switch <A/T>
- 11. Stop light switch
- 12. Clutch pedal position switch <M/T>

MT1109700157020X

**Fig. 171   Speed control component replacement
(Part 2 of 2). 1997–99 Mirage**

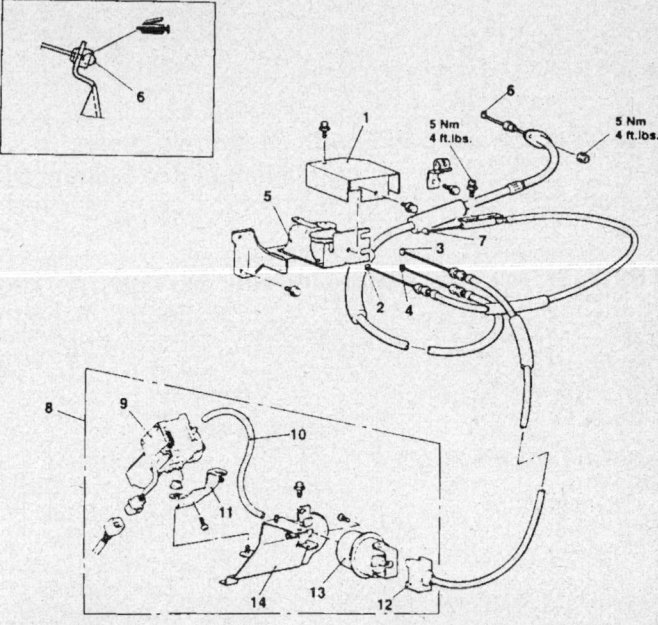

Link assembly removal steps
1. Link protector
2. Throttle cable connection
3. Auto-cruise control cable connection
4. Accelerator cable connection
5. Link assembly
6. Accelerator cable connection
7. Throttle cable connection

Actuator removal steps
8. Auto-cruise actuator assembly
9. Auto-cruise vacuum pump assembly
10. Vacuum hose
11. Pump bracket
12. Auto-cruise control cable connection
13. Actuator
14. Actuator bracket

MT1109400042010X

**Fig. 172   Speed control component replacement
(Part 1 of 3). Galant**

Main switch removal steps
15. Instrument panel switch
16. Main switch

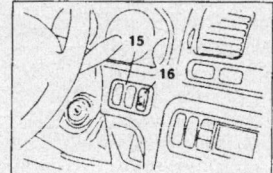

CAUTION: SRS
Before removal of air bag module
and clock spring, refer to
Precautions

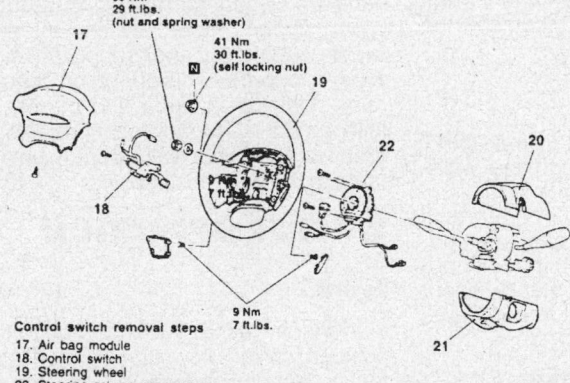

Control switch removal steps
17. Air bag module
18. Control switch
19. Steering wheel
20. Steering column upper cover
21. Steering column lower cover
- Instrument under cover

22. Clock spring

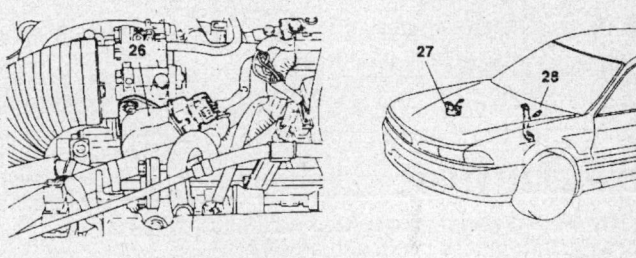

Sensor removal steps
26. Throttle position sensor
27. Park/neutral position switch
28. Stop light switch

MT1109400042030X

**Fig. 172   Speed control component replacement
(Part 3 of 3). Galant**

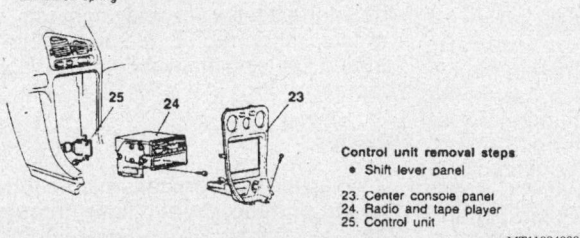

Control unit removal steps
- Shift lever panel

23. Center console panel
24. Radio and tape player
25. Control unit

MT1109400042020X

**Fig. 172   Speed control component replacement
(Part 2 of 3). Galant**

Wiper Systems

NOTE: On Air Bag Equipped Models, Refer To "Air Bag System Precautions" Located In The Front Of This Manual For System Disarming & Arming Procedures.

NOTE: Prior To Performing Any Service Operations Listed In This Section, Consult The "Technical Service Bulletins" Section For Related Information.

INDEX

PRECAUTIONS
AIR BAG SYSTEMS

Refer to "Air Bag System Precautions" in the front of this manual for system disarming and arming procedures.

BATTERY GROUND CABLE

Prior to service, disconnect battery ground cable and isolate as required.

DESCRIPTION

Two wiper systems are utilized on these vehicles: a manual system and an ETACS controlled system. The manual system is controlled by a dash or column mounted switch. On all models with the ETACS system except the 3000GT, the system utilizes a vehicle speed response type intermittent wiper system, mist wiper action and washer interlock. The 3000GT uses an electronically controlled intermittent wiper system.

WIPER OPERATION
Front

When the wiper switch is at the "LO" position and ignition switch is in On position, current flows through the wiper motor low speed brush, wiper switch and ground. The wipers then operate at low speed. When the wiper switch is at the "HI" position and ignition switch is in On position, current flows through the wiper motor high speed brush, wiper switch and ground. The wipers then operate at high speed.

Rear

With the rear wiper switch in the On position, current flows through the wiper switch, rear wiper motor and ground causing the rear wiper to operate.

WIPER AUTOMATIC STOP
Front

When the wiper switch is turned to the "OFF" position, current flows through the wiper motor low speed brush, wiper switch, intermittent control relay, wiper motor cam contacts and ground. This allows the wiper motor to continue operating until the blades return to the park (auto stop) position. When the blades reach the park position, the wiper motor contacts open and current flow to ground is interrupted, causing the wipers to stop.

Rear

With the wiper switch set to the "OFF" position, current flows through the wiper motor cam contacts, wiper switch, and ground causing the wiper to operate until the wiper returns to the park (auto stop) position. When the blades reach the park position, the wiper motor contacts open, which interrupts the current flow and causes the wiper motor to stop.

WIPER INTERMITTENT OPERATION
Front

With the ignition switch turned to the On position and the wiper switch set to the "INT" position, current flows through the intermittent relay, wiper switch and ground, causing the intermittent relay contacts to open and close repeatedly. When the contacts are closed, current flows through the low speed brush, wiper switch, intermittent wiper control relay and ground, causing the wiper to operate. The operation of the wiper opens the relay contacts and causes current to flow through the wiper motor cam contacts and ground. The wipers will operate until they return to the park position.

Rear

With the ignition switch turned to the On position and the wiper switch set to the "INT" position, current flows through the intermittent relay, wiper switch and ground, causing the intermittent relay contacts to open and close repeatedly. When the contacts are closed, current flows through the wiper motor, wiper switch, intermittent wiper control relay and ground, causing the wiper to operate. This operation causes the relay contacts to open and current flows through the wiper motor cam contacts and ground. The wiper will operate until it returns to the park position.

WASHER OPERATION
Front

With the washer switch turned to the On position, current flows through the intermittent wiper relay and ground, causing the intermittent wiper relay internal contacts to close. Once closed, current flows through the intermittent wiper relay contacts, wiper switch, wiper motor, washer motor and ground, causing the washers and wipers to operate.

Rear

When the rear washer switch is turned to the On position, current flows through the rear washer switch, washer motor and ground, causing the washer to operate.

Problem	Probable cause(s)	Checking procedure	Remedy
The wipers don't operate when the wiper switch is set to the "INT" position. (The wipers do operate, however, when the wiper switch is set to the "1" (low speed) position.)	Damage or disconnection of the wiring of the wiper switch ("INT") input circuit.	If a malfunction is discovered as a result of the checking of the input, conduct check of the individual part and circuit.	Repair the wiring harness, or replace the column switch.
	Damage or disconnection of the wiring of the wiper switch ("INT").		
	Damage or disconnection of the wiring of the ignition switch input circuit.	If a malfunction is discovered as a result of the checking of the input, conduct check of the individual part and circuit.	Repair the wiring harness.
	Damage or disconnection of the wiring of the wiper relay activation circuit.	Conduct check of the individual part and circuit.	Repair the wiring harness, or replace the column switch.
	Malfunction of the wiper relay.		
	Malfunction of the electronic control unit.	–	Replace the electronic control unit.
The wipers don't stop when the wiper switch is OFF. (This problem occurs at the low speed of the wipers.) NOTE If the wipers continue operating (without stopping) at the "2" position (high speed) of the wiper switch, there is a short-circuit in the circuit at the wiper motor high-speed side.	Short-circuit in the wiper switch ("INT") input circuit.	If a malfunction is discovered as a result of the checking of the input, conduct check of the individual part and circuit.	Repair the wiring harness, or replace the column switch.
	Short-circuit in the wiper switch ("INT").		
	Short-circuit in the wiper relay activation circuit.	Conduct check of the individual part and circuit.	Repair the wiring harness.
	Malfunction of the electronic control unit.	–	Replace the electronic control unit.
When the wiper switch is set to the "INT" position, the wipers operate continuously at low speed, not intermittent operation. (The wipers stop, however, when the wiper switch is set to "OFF".)	Short-circuit in the wiper switch ("INT") input circuit.	If a malfunction is discovered as a result of the checking of the input conduct check of the individual part and circuit.	Repair the wiring harness, or replace the column switch.
	Short-circuit in the wiper switch ("INT").		
	Malfunction of the electronic control unit.		Replace the electronic control unit.
The intermittent time does not change when the intermittent variable volume switch setting is changed.	Damage or disconnection of the wiring of the intermittent variable volume switch input circuit.	If a malfunction is discovered as a result of the checking of the input conduct check of the individual part and circuit.	Repair the wiring harness, or replace the column switch.
	Damage or disconnection of the wiring of the intermittent variable volume switch.		
	Malfunction of the electronic control unit.		Replace the electronic control unit.

MT9029100005010X

Fig. 1   Wiper system troubleshooting chart (Part 1 of 2). 3000GT

Problem	Probable cause(s)	Checking procedure	Remedy
The wipers do not function when the washer switch is switched ON for 0.6 second or longer. (With the wiper switch at the "INT" position, intermittent operation of the wipers is normal, and the washer function is normal.)	Damage or disconnection of the wiring of the washer switch input circuit.	If a malfunction is discovered as a result of the checking of the input conduct check of the individual part and circuit.	Repair the wiring harness, or replace the column switch.
	Damage or disconnection of the wiring of the washer switch.		
	Malfunction of the electronic control unit.	–	Replace the electronic control unit.
The wipers do not function when the washer switch is switched ON for less than 0.6 second. (The wipers and washer do function, however, when the washer switch is switched ON for 0.6 second or longer.)	Malfunction of the electronic control unit.		Replace the electronic control unit.

NOTE
"ECU" (electronic control unit) indicates the ETACS unit.

MT9029100005020X

Fig. 1   Wiper system troubleshooting chart (Part 2 of 2). 3000GT

WIPER DOES NOT OPERATE IN INTERMITTENT MODE

Check intermittent wiper relay terminal voltage.

WIPER FAILS TO STOP

Check wiper motor.

SYSTEM DIAGNOSIS & TESTING

GALANT

INTERMITTENT WIPER SYSTEM

1. **On 1996 models,** select intermittent wiper operation while measuring voltage at steering column switch terminal 7, **Fig. 2.** Voltage should alternate between zero and battery voltage.
2. **On 1997–99 models,** select intermittent wiper operation while measuring voltage at steering column switch terminal 8, **Fig. 3.** Voltage should alternate between zero and battery voltage.
3. **On all models,** if voltage remains at zero, inspect intermittent wiper relay or switch. Replace as necessary.
4. If voltage indication remains at battery voltage, inspect intermittent wiper relay. Replace as necessary.

ECLIPSE

INTERMITTENT WIPER SYSTEM

Refer to "Galant" in this section for intermittent wiper system inspection procedure.

3000GT

Connect a multi-use tester or voltmeter between the ETACS terminal and ground as shown in **Fig. 4.** The buzzer of the tester should sound or the needle of the voltmeter should move when each switch or sensor is activated. If the buzzer does not sound or the voltmeter does not move there is a problem in that switch or switch input circuit.

CIRCUIT TESTS

Power Supply & Ground

1. Ensure terminal voltage is zero volts at ECU connector 14, with ignition switch in "OFF" position and battery voltage is present in "ACC" position, **Fig. 5.**

TROUBLESHOOTING

FRONT WIPER SYSTEM

LESS ETACS SYSTEM

Wipers Do Not Operate

1. Ensure fuse is not blown.
2. Ensure proper ground connection.

Wipers Do Not Operate At High Or Low Speed

Check wiper switch.

Wipers Do Not Operate In Intermittent Mode

Check intermittent wiper relay terminal voltage.

Wipers Fail To Stop

Check wiper motor.

Interval Period Will Not Adjust

1. Check interval adjustment switch.
2. Check intermittent wiper relay.

Washer Does Not Work

1. If wiper still operates when attempting to activate washer, check washer motor.
2. If wiper does not operate when attempting to activate washer, check washer switch.

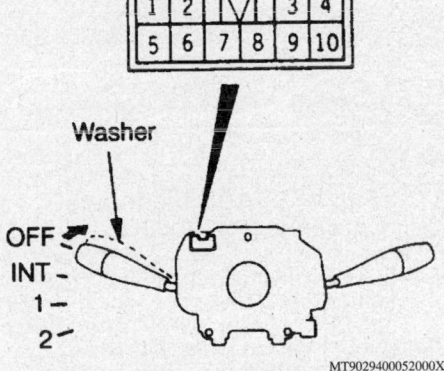

Fig. 2   Wiper & washer switch terminal identification. 1996 Galant & Eclipse

MT9029400052000X

Wipers Do Not Operate In Coordination w/Washer

Check intermittent wiper relay.

WITH ETACS SYSTEM

Refer to **Fig. 1** when troubleshooting the ETACS wiper system.

REAR WIPER SYSTEM

WIPER DOES NOT OPERATE

1. Check fuse.
2. Check for ground connection.

MT9029700062000X

Fig. 3 Wiper & washer switch terminal identification. 1997–99 Galant & Eclipse

A/INT Switch Input Circuit

1. Ensure terminal voltage is 5 volts at ECU connector 9 without anti-theft system or connector 11 with anti-theft system, with wiper switch in "OFF" position and zero volts in "INT" position.
2. Ensure no continuity exists between ECU connector terminal 9 without anti-theft system or connector 11 with anti-theft system and ground, with wiper switch in "OFF" position.
3. Ensure continuity exists between ECU connector terminal 9 without anti-theft system or connector 11 with anti-theft system and ground, with wiper switch in "INT" position, **Fig. 5**.

Intermittent Variable Volume Switch Input Circuit

1. Ensure terminal voltage is 0–2.5 volts at ECU connector terminal 13 without anti-theft system or connector 15 with anti-theft system.
2. Ensure continuity between intermittent variable volume switch connector terminal 13 without anti-theft system or connector 15 with anti-theft system and ground. Resistance should be 0–1000 ohms, and should change with movement of the intermittent variable volume, **Fig. 5**.

Wiper Relay Activation Circuit

1. Ensure terminal voltage is zero volts at ECU connector terminal 4 without anti-theft system or connector 6 with anti-theft system, with wiper and ignition switch Off.
2. Ensure battery voltage is present at ECU connector terminal 4 without anti-theft system or connector 6 with anti-theft system with wiper switch "OFF" and ignition switch in "ACC" position, **Fig. 5**.

Washer Switch Input Circuit

1. Ensure terminal voltage is zero volts at ECU connector terminal 58 without anti-theft system or connector 60 with anti-theft system, with washer switch Off and ignition switch in "ACC" position.
2. Ensure battery voltage is present at

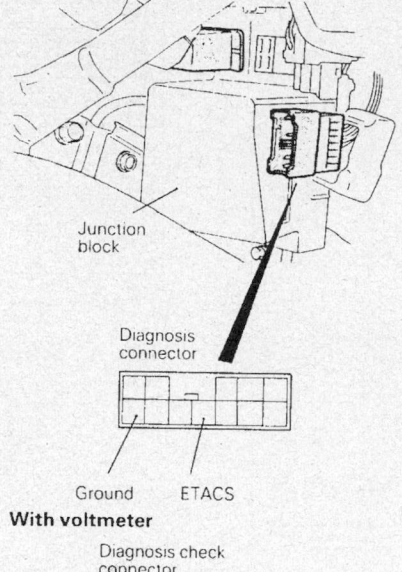

With voltmeter

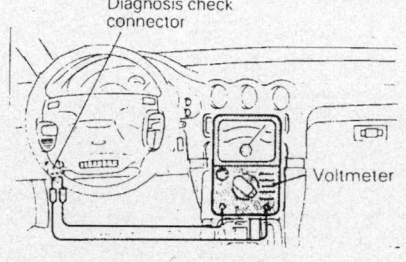

With multi-use tester

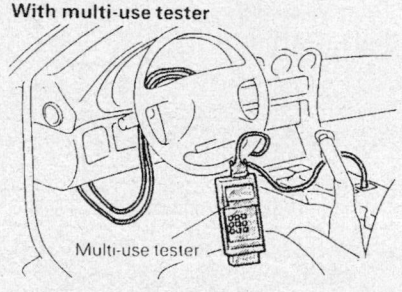

MT9029100009000X

Fig. 4 ETACS diagnosis connector. 3000GT

ECU connector terminal 58 without anti-theft system or connector 60 with anti-theft system with washer switch On and ignition switch is the "ACC" position, **Fig. 5**.

DIAMANTE

Connect a multi-use tester or voltmeter between the ETACS terminal and ground as shown in **Fig. 6**. The buzzer of the tester should sound or the needle of the voltmeter should move the switch is activated. If the buzzer does not sound or the voltmeter does not move there is a problem in that switch or switch input circuit.

COMPONENT DIAGNOSIS & TESTING
PICKUP

Wiper Motor

Refer to **Fig. 7** for connector terminal identification.

ETACS unit (ECU)

*1: Vehicles without theft-alarm system
*2: Vehicles with theft-alarm system

MT9029100010000X

Fig. 5 ETACS control unit terminal identification. 3000GT

1. To check low speed operation, connect battery positive to terminal 3 and battery negative to terminal 1. Motor should operate at low speed.
2. To check high speed operation, connect battery positive to terminal 3 and battery negative to terminal 2. Motor should operate at high speed.
3. To check auto stop function operation, proceed as follows:
   a. Connect battery positive to terminal 3 and battery negative to terminal 1, then run wipers at low speed. When terminal 3 is disconnected, motor should stop.
   b. Connect terminals 1 and 4, then connect B+ to terminal 3 and battery ground to wiper motor bracket. Wiper motor should start to run, then stop.

MONTERO & MONTERO SPORT

Front Wiper Motor

1. Connect battery positive to wiper motor as shown in **Fig. 8** and check operation of motor at high and low speeds.
2. With motor running at low speed, disconnect battery to stop motor.
3. Reconnect battery as shown in **Fig. 9**, then ensure motor starts to run at low speed and stops at automatic stop position.

Wiper & Washer Switch

Disconnect column switch connector and ensure continuity exists between terminals as shown in **Figs. 10 and 11**.

Intermittent Wiper Relay

1. With column switch connected, turn ignition switch to ACC position.
2. **On models without variable intermittent controls,** wipers should cycle at approximately 3–6 second intervals.
3. **On models with variable intermittent controls,** wipers should cycle approximately every three seconds on "fast" or 12 seconds on "slow."

Washer Motor

1. Ensure washer reservoir is full.

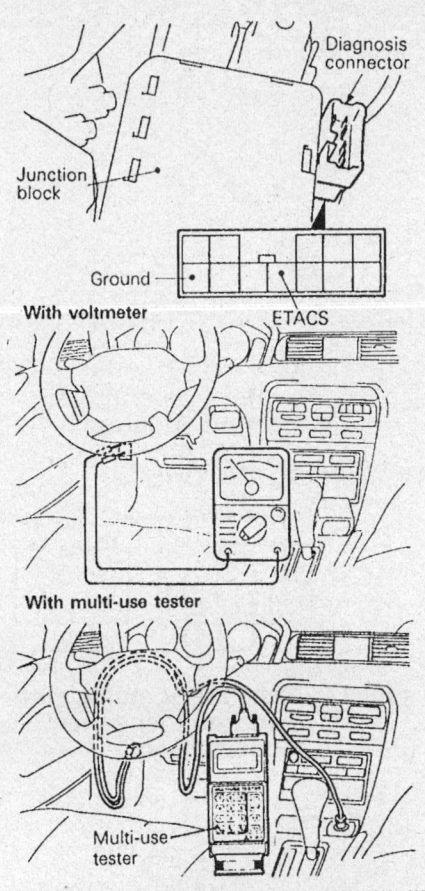

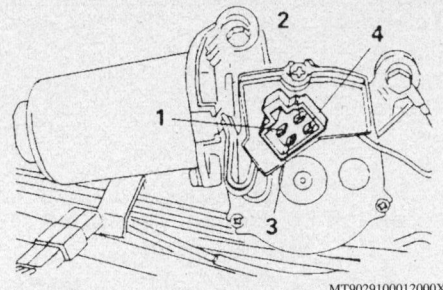

Fig. 7 Wiper motor connector identification. Pickup

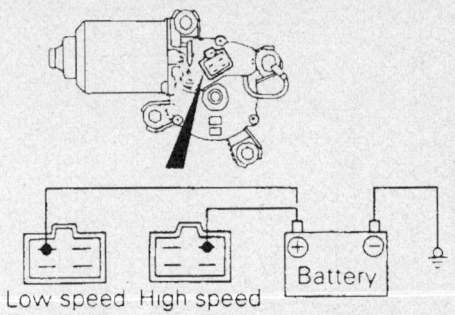

Fig. 8 Wiper motor high & low speed operation inspection. Montero & Montero Sport

Switch position		Terminal				
		6	7	8	9	10
	OFF		O	O		
Wiper switch	1 (LO)			O	—	O
	2 (HI)				O	O
Washer switch	ON	O				

Fig. 11 Front wiper & washer switch inspection. Montero & Montero Sport

2. Connect battery to wiper motor as shown in **Fig. 19.** Ensure motor works at high speed.
3. Operate wiper at low speed and disconnect lead from battery.
4. Connect battery as shown in **Fig. 20.** Ensure motor starts on low speed, then stops at automatic stop position.

Wiper & Washer Switch

1. Remove steering column undercover.
2. Disconnect column switch connector and check continuity at terminals as shown in **Figs. 21 and 22.**
3. If results are not as specified, replace switch.

Intermittent Wiper Relay

1. With column switch connector connected, place ignition switch in Accessory position.
2. Set wiper switch to intermittent function and note operation time. When set to fastest speed, wipers should cycle at three second intervals; at slowest speed, wipers should cycle at approximately 12 second intervals.
3. If results are not as specified, replace relay.

Washer Motor

1. Fill washer tank with water, then disconnect motor connector.
2. Apply battery voltage to motor terminals, **Fig. 23.**
3. If a strong spray of water is emitted from ducts, motor operation is satisfactory; if not, replace motor.

ECLIPSE

Front Wiper Motor

Do not remove motor and link assembly for inspection purposes.

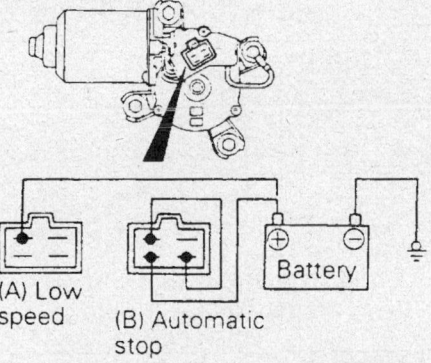

Fig. 6 ETACS diagnostic connector. Diamante

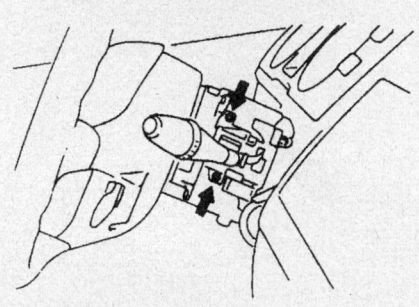

Fig. 9 Front wiper motor auto stop operation inspection. Montero & Montero Sport

2. With battery connected as shown in **Fig. 12,** washer motor should operate properly.

Rear Wiper & Washer Switch

Operate switch and check continuity between terminals as shown in **Figs. 10 and 13.**

Rear Wiper Motor

1. Disconnect wiper motor connector.
2. **On Montero models,** connect battery positive to terminal 3 as shown in Fig.

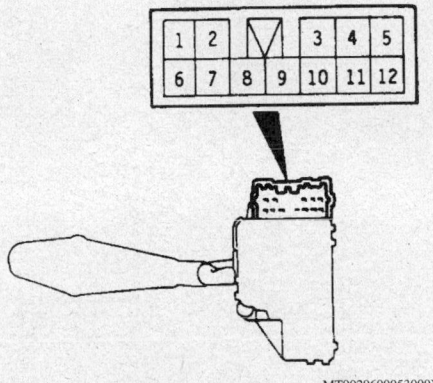

Fig. 10 Wiper & washer switch terminal identification. Montero & Montero Sport

14. Motor should operate.
3. **On Montero Sport models,** connect battery positive to terminal 2 as shown in **Fig. 15.** Motor should operate.
4. **On all models,** with wiper motor running, disconnect battery ground to stop motor.
5. Reconnect battery as shown in **Figs. 16 and 17.** Motor should start to run, then stop in auto stop position.

Rear Washer Motor

1. Ensure washer reservoir is full.
2. With battery connected as shown in **Fig. 12,** washer should operate properly.

GALANT

Wiper Motor

1. Connect battery to wiper motor as shown in **Fig. 18.** Ensure motor works at low speed.

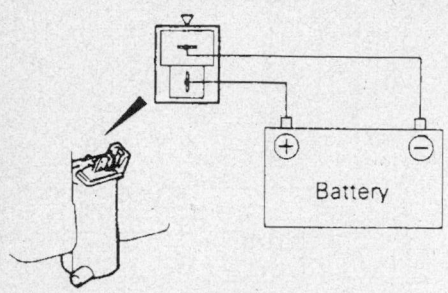

Fig. 12 Washer motor inspection. Diamante, Montero & Montero Sport

OPERATION CHECK

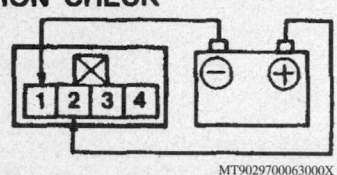

Fig. 15 Rear wiper motor inspection. Montero Sport

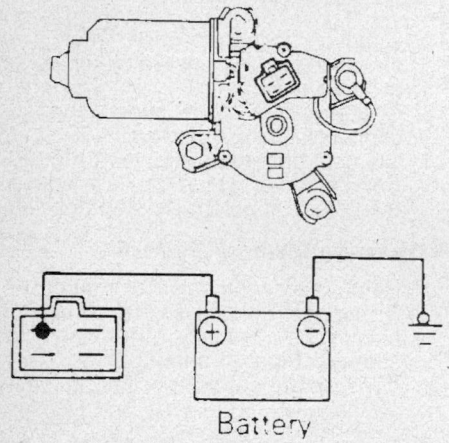

Fig. 18 Low speed wiper motor operation. Galant & Mirage

Switch position		Terminal No.				
		5	6	7	8	9
Wiper switch	OFF		○—	—○		
	1 (LO)			○—	—○	—○
	2 (HI)				○—	—○
Washer switch	ON	○—				—○

MT9029400056000X

Fig. 21 Wiper & washer switch continuity chart. 1996 Galant & Mirage

1. Connect battery to wiper motor terminals, **Fig. 24,** for low and high speed operation. Ensure motor operates at each speed when battery voltage is applied.
2. To inspect stop position operation, proceed as follows:
   a. Run wiper motor at low speed, then remove battery voltage supply and stop motor.

Switch position		Terminal			
		2	3	4	10
Wiper switch	OFF				
	INT		○—		—○
	ON			○—	—○
Washer switch	ON	○—			—○

MT9029600055000X

Fig. 13 Rear wiper & washer switch inspection. Montero & Montero Sport

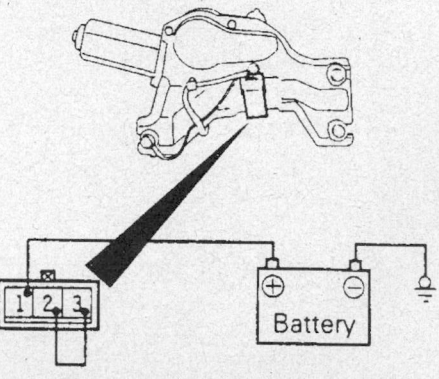

Fig. 16 Rear wiper motor auto stop operation inspection. Montero

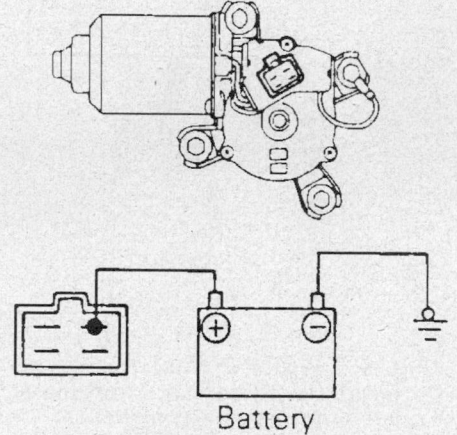

MT9029100024000X

Fig. 19 High speed wiper motor operation. Galant & Mirage

b. Reconnect battery, **Fig. 24,** ensure motor runs at low speed until it reaches its automatic stop position.

Front Wiper & Washer Switch

Refer to "Galant" in this section for switch inspection procedure.

Rear Wiper Motor

Do not remove the wiper motor for testing purposes.
1. Connect battery as shown in **Fig. 25** and ensure proper low and high speed operation.
2. Connect jumper and battery as shown in **Fig. 25.** Ensure motor starts to run, then stops in automatic stop position.

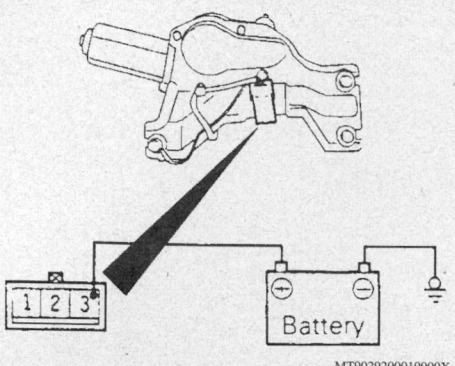

MT9029200019000X

Fig. 14 Rear wiper motor inspection. Montero

STOP POSITION CHECK

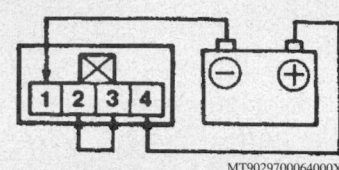

MT9029700064000X

Fig. 17 Rear wiper motor auto stop operation inspection. Montero Sport

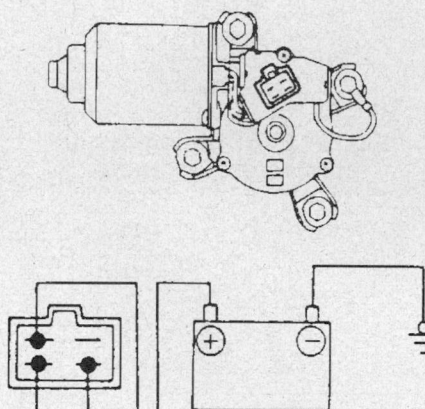

MT9029100025000X

Fig. 20 Wiper motor stop position. Galant & Mirage

Switch position		Terminal No.				
		6	7	8	9	10
Wiper switch	OFF		○—	—○		
	INT		○—	—○		
	1 (LO)			○—	—○	—○
	2 (HI)				○—	—○
Washer switch	ON	○—				—○

MT9029700065000X

Fig. 22 Wiper & washer switch continuity chart. 1997–99 Galant & Mirage

Rear Wiper & Washer Switch

Disconnect switch, then ensure continuity exists between terminals as shown in **Figs. 26 through 27.**

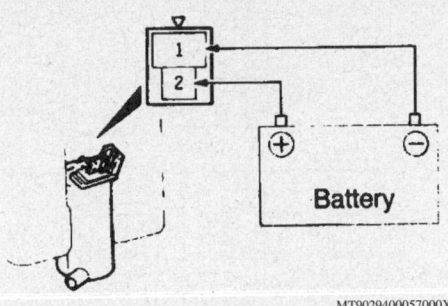

Fig. 23 Washer motor inspection. Galant, Mirage & Eclipse

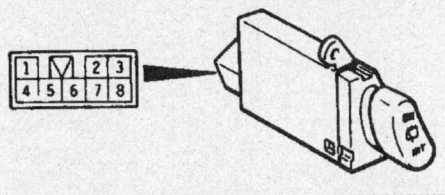

Fig. 26 Rear wiper & washer switch terminal identification. Eclipse

Washer Motor

Refer to "Galant" in this section for washer motor inspection procedure.

MIRAGE

Front Wiper Motor

1. Connect battery to wiper motor as shown in **Fig. 18.** Ensure motor works at low speed.
2. Connect battery to wiper motor as shown in **Fig. 19.** Ensure motor works at high speed.
3. Operate wipers at low speed and disconnect lead from battery.
4. Connect battery as shown in **Fig. 20.** Ensure motor starts on low speed, then stops at automatic stop position.

Front Wiper & Washer Switch

Refer to "Galant" in this section for switch inspection procedure.

Rear Wiper Motor

1. Connect battery as shown in **Fig. 28** and ensure rear wiper motor operates properly.
2. Connect jumper and battery as shown in **Fig. 29.** Ensure motor starts to run, then stops in automatic stop position.

Rear Wiper & Washer Switch

Operate switch and check for continuity between terminal as shown in **Fig. 30.** If results are not as specified, replace switch.

DIAMANTE

Wiper Motor

1. To check low and high speed operation of wiper motor, connect battery as shown in **Fig. 31.**

Inspection while operating

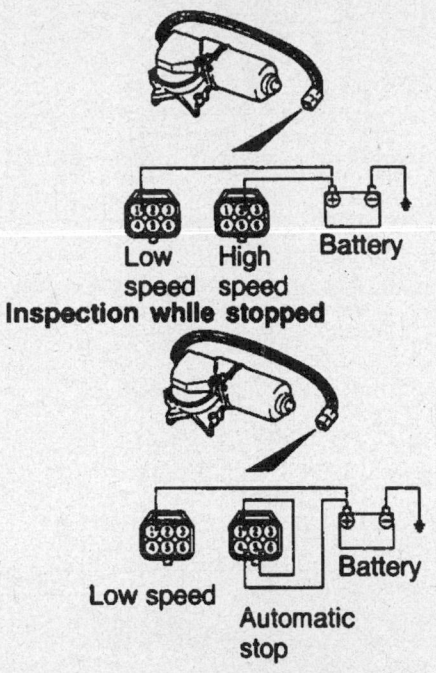

Inspection while stopped

Fig. 24 Front wiper motor inspection. Eclipse

Switch position		Terminal No.						
		3	7	5	6	8	1	4
Wiper switch	OFF			○	○			
	INT	○	○	○				ILL
	LO			○	○	○		
Washer switch	OFF							
	ON	○				○		

Fig. 27 Rear wiper & washer switch inspection. Eclipse

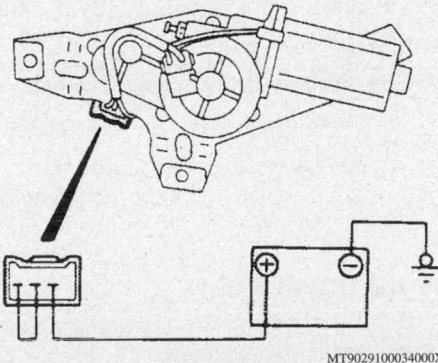

Fig. 29 Rear wiper automatic stop operation inspection. Mirage

2. To check wiper automatic stop position, run motor at low speed and disconnect battery, then connect jumper wire and battery as shown in **Fig. 32.** Motor should run at low speed, then stop in auto stop position.

Inspection while operating

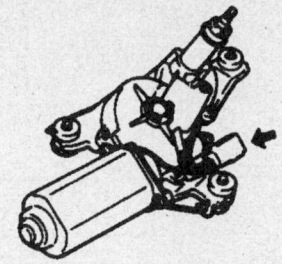

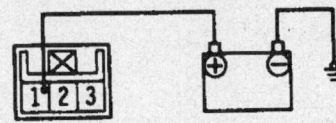

Inspection while stopped

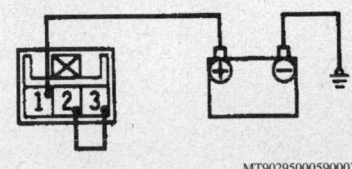

Fig. 25 Rear wiper operation inspection. Eclipse

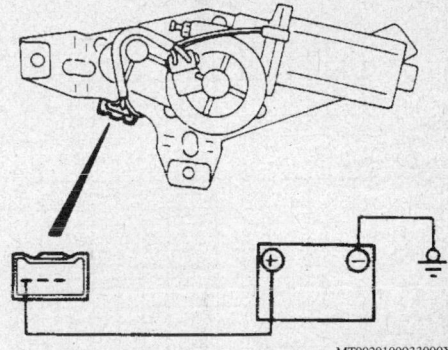

Fig. 28 Rear wiper low speed operation inspection. Mirage

Wiper & Washer Switch

1. Disconnect column switch connector.
2. Operate switch and ensure continuity exists between terminals as shown in **Figs. 33 and 34.**
3. If results are not as specified, replace switch.

Wiper Relay

1. Turn column switch to Off or AUTO position. Ensure continuity exists between terminals 3 and 10 and between terminals 1 and 12. Ensure no continuity exists between terminal 3 and 12, **Fig. 35.**
2. Connect B+ to terminal 12 and battery negative to terminal 1, then ensure battery voltage is present at terminal 3.

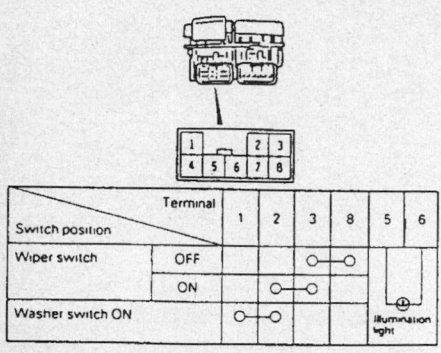

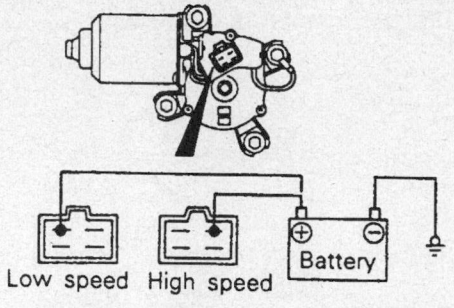

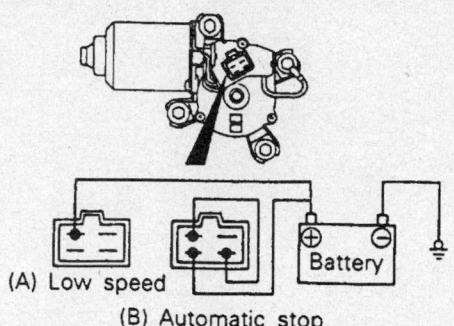

Switch position \ Terminal		1	2	3	8	5	6
Wiper switch	OFF			○—○			
	ON		○—○				
Washer switch ON		○—○					Illumination light

NOTE
○—○ indicates that there is continuity between the terminals.

MT9029100035000X

Fig. 30 Rear wiper & washer switch continuity chart. Mirage

Low speed High speed Battery

MT9029100036000X

Fig. 31 Wiper motor high & low speed operation inspection. Diamante

(A) Low speed Battery

(B) Automatic stop

MT9029100037000X

Fig. 32 Wiper motor in auto stop operation inspection. Diamante

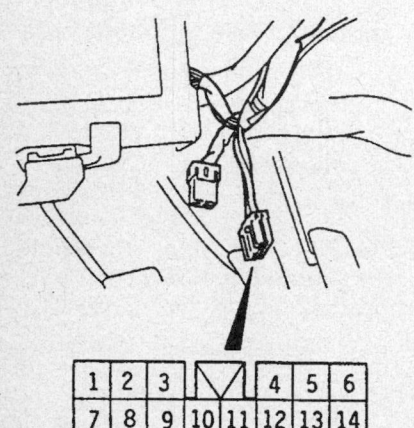

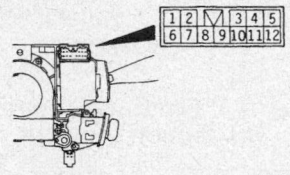

Switch position		Terminal Numbers						
		3	7	8	9	10	11	6
Wiper switch	OFF							
	INT		○—	——	——	—○		
	LO			○—	—○		
	HI				○—○		
Intermittent variable speed switch		○—	——	——	—○		
Washer switch ON						○—○	

MT9029700066000X

Fig. 34 Wiper & washer switch inspection. 1997–99 Diamante

Switch position \ Terminal		3	4	7	8	9	10	11	12
Wiper switch	OFF	○—	——	——	——	—○			
	AUTO			○—	—○			
	1 (LO)	○—	—○					
	2 (HI)					○—○		
Variable intermittent wiper control switch			○—	—○				
Washer switch	ON						○—○

NOTE
○—○ indicates that there is continuity between the terminals.

MT9029100038000X

Fig. 33 Wiper & washer switch inspection. 1996 Diamante

Washer Motor

1. Ensure washer reservoir is full.
2. With battery connected as shown in **Fig. 12,** washer motor should operate properly.

Washer Fluid Level Sensor

1. Remove washer fluid level sensor from washer tank.
2. Connect circuit tester to connector of washer fluid lever sensor.
3. When float is raised, no continuity should exist. When float is lowered, continuity should exist.

3000GT

Front Wiper Motor

1. To ensure proper low and high speed operation of wiper motor, connect battery as shown in **Fig. 36.**
2. To check motor automatic stop position, run motor at low speed, then disconnect battery and connect jumper wire and battery as shown in **Fig. 36.**

Front Wiper & Washer Switch

1. Remove knee protector and column cover.
2. Disconnect switch connector.
3. Operate switch and ensure continuity between terminals as shown in **Fig. 37.**

Front Wiper Relay

Refer to **Fig. 38** for terminal identification when checking wiper relay.
1. Ensure continuity exists between terminals 5 and 11, and 6 and 10. Ensure no continuity exists between terminal 6 and 11.
2. Connect battery positive to terminal 5 and battery negative to terminal 11, ensure battery voltage is at terminal 6.

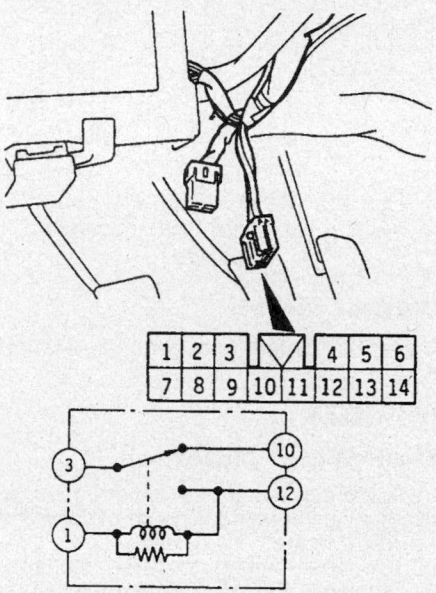

MT9029100039000X

Fig. 35 Wiper relay inspection. Diamante

Rear Wiper Motor

1. Connect battery as shown in **Fig. 39** ensure proper motor operation.
2. Connect jumper and battery as shown in **Fig. 39,** ensure motor starts to run, then stops in automatic stop position.

Rear Wiper & Washer Switch

1. Remove switch from knee pad protector.
2. Operate switch and check continuity between terminal as shown in **Fig. 40.**
3. If results are not as specified, replace switch.

Rear Intermittent Wiper Relay

With wipers operating, connect voltmeter to terminal 2 as shown in **Fig. 41.** With wipers stationary, no voltage should exist; with wipers in motion, battery voltage should exist.

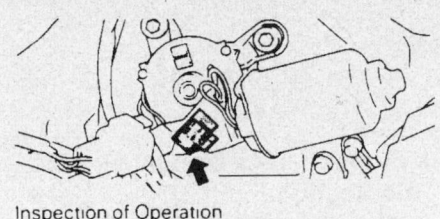

Inspection of Operation

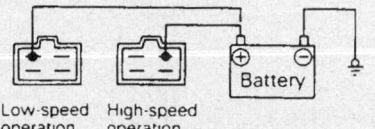

Low-speed operation   High-speed operation

Inspection of Stop Position

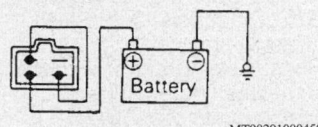

MT9029100045000X

Fig. 36 Front wiper motor connector identification. 3000GT

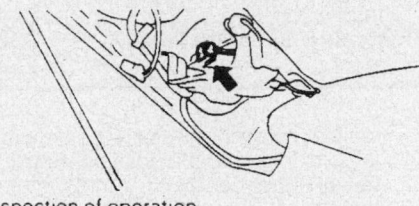

Inspection of operation

Inspection of stop position

MT9029100048000X

Fig. 39 Rear wiper motor connector identification. 3000GT

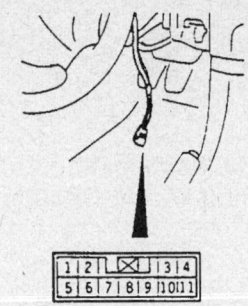

Switch position	Terminal No	3	4	5	6	7	8	9	10
Wiper switch	OFF				○		○		○
	INT	○	○		○		○	○	
	LO			○—○			○		
	HI			○		○			
Variable intermittent wiper control switch			○				○		
Washer switch					○—○		○		

NOTE
○—○ denotes that there is continuity between the terminals

MT9029100046000X

Fig. 37 Wiper & washer switch continuity chart. 3000GT

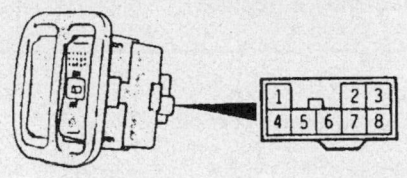

Switch position	Terminal	2	4	5	6	7	8	1	3
Wiper switch	OFF	○—○							
	INT	○—○		○—○					
	ON			○—○				ILL	
Washer switch	OFF								
	ON	○—	—○	—○					

NOTE
○—○ denotes that there is continuity between the terminals.

MT9029100049000X

Fig. 40 Rear wiper & washer continuity chart. 3000GT

Connector B

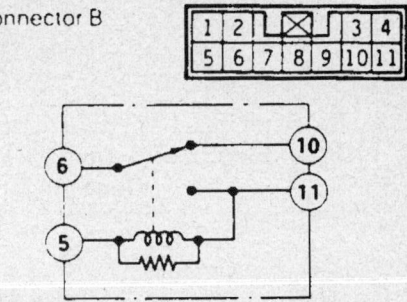

MT9029100047000X

Fig. 38 Wiper relay connector identification. 3000GT

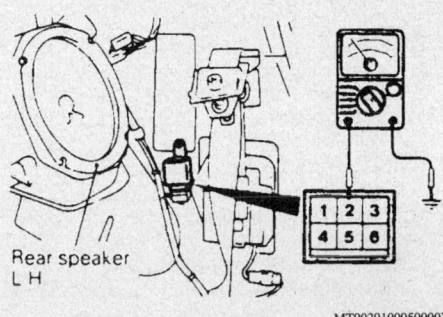

Rear speaker L H

MT9029100050000X

Fig. 41 Intermittent relay connector identification. 3000GT

Air Bag System

NOTE: Electrical Symbol & Wire Color Code Identification Located In The Front Of This Manual May Be Used As An Aid When Using Wiring Circuits Found In This Section.

INDEX

AIR BAG SYSTEM DISARMING & ARMING

Disarming

AIR BAG SYSTEM

1. Turn ignition to Lock position.
2. Disconnect and isolate battery ground cable.
3. **Wait at least 60 seconds after disconnection before performing repair procedures.** The Supplemental Restraint System (SRS) is designed to retain enough deployment voltage for a short time even after battery has been disconnected.

SEAT BELT PRETENSIONERS

Diamante

The seat belt pretensioner safety lock lever must be in the locked position whenever the pretensioner unit is not fitted to the vehicle.

1. Disarm air bag system as outlined under "Air Bag System Disarming & Arming."
2. Remove the front scuff plate, then the rear scuff plate.
3. Remove lower portion of the center pillar lower trim panel.
4. Remove upper portion of the center pillar lower trim panel.
5. Remove seat belt sash guide.
6. Remove upper center pillar trim panel.
7. Move the pretensioner safety lock lever to the locked position, **Fig. 1.**

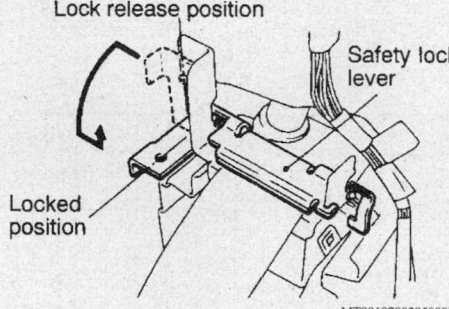

Fig. 1   Seat belt pretensioner safety lock lever locked & lock release positions. Diamante

MT8019700295000X

Arming

AIR BAG SYSTEM

1. Ensure no one is inside vehicle.
2. Connect battery ground cable and start engine.
3. Ensure SRS warning lamp lights for approximately seven seconds, and then goes off.
4. **If lamp operates as outlined,** SRS is functioning properly.
5. **If lamp does not operate as outlined,** an SRS condition is indicated. Refer to "Diagnosis & Testing. "

SEAT BELT PRETENSIONERS

Diamante

The seat belt pretensioner safety lock lever must be in the locked position whenever the pretensioner unit is not fitted to the vehicle.

1. With seat belt pretensioner properly in-

stalled, move pretensioner safety lock lever to lock release position, **Fig. 1.**
2. Install upper center pillar trim panel.
3. Install seat belt sash guide.
4. Install upper portion of the center pillar lower trim.
5. Install lower portion of center pillar lower trim panel.
6. Install rear scuff plate, then the front scuff plate.
7. Arm air bag system as outlined under "Air Bag System Disarming & Arming."

DESCRIPTION & OPERATION

MONTERO & MONTERO SPORT

The SRS consists of lefthand and righthand front impact sensors, driver's and front passenger's air bag modules, and the SRS diagnosis unit with a safing impact sensor.

The air bags will deploy when the safing sensor and either or both impact sensors simultaneously activate while the ignition is turned On. This is designed to occur in frontal or near frontal impacts of moderate to severe force.

DIAMANTE, ECLIPSE, GALANT, MIRAGE & 3000GT

The SRS consists of driver's and front passenger's air bag modules, and the SRS diagnosis unit with safing impact and analog G-sensors. The 1999 Galant also incorporates side air bag modules into the seat back portions of the front seats. A side impact sensor is used to activate these air bag modules.

SDU Terminal No.	Harness Connector (No. of Terminals, Color)	Destination of Harness	Corrective Action
1	2 pins, red	Clock spring	Replace clock spring.
2			
3	No connection		
4			
5	2 pins, green	Body wiring harness → Air bag module (passenger's side)	Correct or replace body wiring harness
6			
7		Body wiring harness	
8			
9		Body wiring harness → Diagnosis check pin	Correct or replace control wiring, instrument panel wiring harness or body wiring harness.
10		Body wiring harness → Control wiring harness → Ignition switch (ST)	
11		Body wiring harness → Multi-purpose fuse No. 11	
12		Body wiring harness → Multi-purpose fuse No. 18	
13		Body wiring harness → Instrument panel wiring harness → SRS warning light	
14	14 pins, red		
15		Body wiring harness → Front wiring harness → Front impact sensor (R.H.) – positive (+) terminal	Replace the sensor cable*
16		Body wiring harness → Front wiring harness → Front impact sensor (L.H.) – positive (+) terminal	
17		Body wiring harness → Front wiring harness → Front impact sensor (L.H.) – negative (–) terminal	
18		Body wiring harness → Front wiring harness → Front impact sensor (R.H.) – negative (–) terminal	
19		Body wiring harness → Junction block → Body wiring harness → Ground	Correct or replace body wiring harness.
20			

NOTE
(1) The sensor cable marked with * is available as service part.
(2) The sensor cable used as a replacement part is routed along the body wiring harness.

MT8019400084000X

Fig. 2   SRS wire service chart. 1996 Diamante, Galant & 3000GT

SRS-ECU TERMINAL NO.	DESTINATION OF HARNESS	CORRECTIVE ACTION
1, 2	–	–
3	Body wiring harness → Ground	Correct or replace the body wiring harness.
4	Body wiring harness → Instrument panel wiring → SRS warning light	Correct or replace each wiring harness.
5, 6	Body wiring harness → Air bag module (Front passenger's side)	Correct or replace the body wiring harness.
7, 8	Body wiring harness → Clock spring → Air bag module (Driver's side)	Correct or replace each wiring harness. Replace the clock spring.
9	Body wiring harness → Junction block (fuse No.5)	Correct or replace the body wiring harness.
10, 11	–	–
12	Body wiring harness → Junction block (fuse No.13)	Correct or replace the body wiring harness.
13 to 15	–	–
16	Body wiring harness → Data link connector	Correct or replace the body wiring harness.
17 to 20	–	–
21, 22	Body wiring harness → Side air bag module (LH)	Correct or replace the body wiring harness.
23, 24	Body wiring harness → Side air bag module (RH)	Correct or replace the body wiring harness.
25 to 33	–	–
34, 35, 36	Body wiring harness → Floor wiring harness → Side impact sensor (LH)	Correct or replace each wiring harness.
37 to 39	–	–
40, 41, 42	Body wiring harness → Floor wiring harness → Side impact sensor (RH)	Correct or replace each wiring harness.

MT8019900328000X

Fig. 4   SRS wire service chart. 1999 Galant w/side air bag

Air bags will deploy when the analog G-sensor and safing G-sensor activate while the ignition is turned On. This is designed to occur in frontal or near frontal impacts of moderate to severe force.

On Diamante models, the seat belt pretensioner, which is deployed manually, is built into the front seat belt retractors. The seat belt pretension activates to retract the seat belt and remove looseness in the event of a collision in which deceleration exceeds a specified value. The pretensioner consist of G-sensor, needle, activating agent and gas generating agent.

SRS-ECU terminal No.	Destination of harness	Corrective action
1 to 4	–	–
5	Body wiring harness → Clockspring → Air bag module (Driver's side)	Correct or replace each wiring harness. Replace clockspring.
6		
7	Body wiring harness → Air bag module (Front passenger's side)	Correct or replace each wiring harness.
8		
9,10	–	–
11	Body wiring harness → Date link connector	Correct or replace each wiring harness.
12	–	–
13	Body wiring harness → Junction block	Correct or replace each wiring harness.
14	Body wiring harness → Junction block	
15	Body wiring harness → SRS warning light	
16 to 19	–	–
20	Body wiring harness → Ground	Correct or replace body wiring harness.
21		

MT8019700221000X

Fig. 3   SRS wire service chart. 1997–99 Diamante, Eclipse, Galant less side air bag, Mirage & 3000GT

PRECAUTIONS

It is necessary to disarm the Supplemental Restraint System (SRS) prior to servicing any systems or components that may cause an air bag to deploy unexpectedly. Failure to do so may result in serious injury and vehicle damage. Refer to "Air Bag System Disarming & Arming" in this section for procedures.

1. Do not use any electrical test equipment on or near SRS components, except those specified in procedures.
2. **Never use analog ohmmeters or other powered test instruments on air bag units.**
3. **Do not disconnect any SRS components, fuses or connectors until battery ground cable has been disconnected for at least 60 seconds** to avoid storing false diagnostic trouble codes in the SRS Electronic Control Unit (ECU).
4. Always replace clockspring when replacing a deployed air bag module.
5. **Never attempt to repair following components:**
   a. Front impact sensors.
   b. SRS Diagnosis Unit (SDU).
   c. Clockspring.
   d. Air bag module.
   e. If any of these components are diagnosed as faulty, they should be replaced as outlined under "Component Service."
6. Do not attempt to repair SRS wiring harness connectors. Replace harness if any connectors are diagnosed as faulty. If wires are diagnosed as faulty, replace or repair harness according to tables shown in **Figs. 2 through 9**.
7. After disconnecting battery cable, wait 60 seconds or more before beginning repair procedures.
8. SRS components should not be subjected to heat over 200°F. Remove front impact sensors, SRS diagnosis unit, air bag module and clockspring before drying or baking vehicle after painting.

SRS-ECU Terminal No.	Harness Connector (No. of Terminals, Color)	Destination of Harness	Corrective Action
1 to 4	21 pins, yellows	–	–
5		Body wiring harness → Clock spring → Air bag module (Driver's side)	Correct or replace body wiring harness. Replace clock spring
6			
7		Body wiring harness → Air bag module (Front passenger's side)	Correct or replace body wiring harness
8			
9, 10		–	–
11		Body wiring harness → Data link connector	Correct or replace body wiring harness
12		–	–
13		Body wiring harness → Junction block (fuse No.3)	Correct or replace body wiring harness
14		Body wiring harness → Junction block (fuse No.8)	
15		Body wiring harness → Instrument panel wiring harness → SRS warning light	
16 to 19		–	–
20		Body wiring harness → Ground	Correct or replace body wiring harness
21			

MT8019600176000X

Fig. 5   SRS wire service chart. 1996 Eclipse

SDU Terminal No.	Harness Connector (No. of Terminals, Color)	Destination of Harness	Corrective Action
1	2 pins, red	Dash wiring harness → Clock spring	Correct or replace each wiring harness Replace clock spring
2			
3 and 4	Unused terminals	–	–
5	2 pins, green	Dash wiring harness → Front passenger's air bag module	Correct or replace each wiring harness
6			
11 and 12	14 pins, red	–	–
13	14 pins, red	Dash wiring harness → Diagnosis connector	Correct or replace each wiring harness
14		Dash wiring harness → Control wiring harness → Dash wiring harness → Ignition switch (ST)	
15		Dash wiring harness → Junction block (fuse No. 18)	
16		Dash wiring harness → Junction block (fuse No. 12)	
17		Dash wiring harness → Instrument panel wiring harness → SRS warning light	
18			
20		Dash wiring harness → Front wiring harness → Front impact sensor (LH)	Correct or replace with sensor cable*
21			
19		Dash wiring harness → Front wiring harness → Front impact sensor (RH)	
22			
23		Dash wiring harness → Ground	Correct or replace dash wiring harness
24			

NOTE
(1) The sensor cable marked with* is available as service part.
(2) The sensor cable used as a replacement part is routed along the front wiring harness and front wiring harness.

MT8019600174000X

Fig. 7   SRS wire service chart. 1996 Montero

9. Do not paint air bag to correct cosmetic flaws. Replacement is necessary to correct such flaws.
10. Inspect SRS warning lamp operation to ensure system is functioning properly when service is complete.

SCHEDULED MAINTENANCE

SRS WARNING LAMP INSPECTION

When the ignition switch is turned to the On position or the engine is started, the SRS warning lamp will light for about seven seconds, then go Off. If the lamp operates as specified, the system is functioning properly. If the lamp stays lit more than seven seconds or lights when driving, a system malfunction or condition is indicated. Refer to "Diagnosis and Testing."

Harness Connector (No. of Terminals, Color)	SRS-ECU Terminal No.	Destination of Harness	Corrective Action
21 pins	1 to 4	–	–
	5 to 6	Body wiring harness → Clock spring → Air bag module (Driver's side)	Replace clock spring. Correct or replace body wiring harness
	7 to 8	Body wiring harness → Air bag module (Front passenger's side)	Correct or replace body wiring harness
	9 to 10	–	–
	11	Body wiring harness → Data link connector	Correct or replace body wiring harness
	12	–	–
	13	Body wiring harness → Junction block (fuse No. 7)	Correct or replace body wiring harness
	14	Body wiring harness → Junction block (fuse No. 2)	
	15	Body wiring harness → SRS warning light	
	16 to 19	–	–
	20	Body wiring harness → Junction block → Body wiring harness → Ground	Correct or replace body wiring harness
	21		

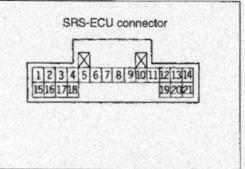
SRS-ECU connector
| 1 | 2 | 3 | 4 | ☒ | 5 | 6 | 7 | 8 | ☒ | 9 | 10 | 11 | 12 | 13 | 14 |
| 15 | 16 | 17 | 18 | | | | | | | | | 19 | 20 | 21 | |

MT8019600181000X

Fig. 6   SRS wire service chart. 1996 Mirage

SRS-ECU terminal No.	Harness Connector (No. of terminals, Color)	Destination of Harness	Corrective Action
1 to 4	21 pins, yellow	–	–
5	21 pins, yellow	Dash wiring harness → Clockspring → Air bag module (Driver's side)	Correct or replace dash wiring harness. Replace clockspring.
6	21 pins, yellow		
7	21 pins, yellow	Dash wiring harness → Air bag module (Front passenger's side)	Correct or replace dash wiring harness.
8	21 pins, yellow		
9,10	21 pins, yellow	–	–
11	21 pins, yellow	Dash wiring harness → Data link connector	Correct or replace dash wiring harness.
12,18	21 pins, yellow	Dash wiring harness → Front wiring harness → Front impact sensor (L.H.)	Correct or replace sensor cable.*
13	21 pins, yellow	Dash wiring harness → Junction block (fuse No.18)	Correct or replace dash wiring harness.
14	21 pins, yellow	Dash wiring harness → Junction block (fuse No.12)	
15	21 pins, yellow	Dash wiring harness → Instrument panel wiring harness → SRS warning light	
16	21 pins, yellow	–	–
17,19	21 pins, yellow	Dash wiring harness → Front wiring harness → Front impact sensor (R.H.)	Correct or replace sensor cable.*
20	21 pins, yellow	Dash wiring harness → Ground	Correct or replace dash wiring harness.
21	21 pins, yellow		

NOTE
(1) The sensor cable marked with* is available as service part.
(2) The sensor cable used as a replacement part is routed along the dash wiring harness and front wiring harness.

MT8019700222000X

Fig. 8   SRS wire service chart. 1997–99 Montero

FRONT IMPACT SENSOR INSPECTION

1. Remove righthand and lefthand front splash shields or extensions.
2. Ensure arrow mark on sensor is facing front of vehicle.
3. Inspect sensor frame mounting location condition and ensure it is free from deformities or rust. **SRS may not activate properly if an impact sensor is not installed properly.**
4. Inspect sensor for dents, cracks, deformities or rust.
5. Inspect sensor harnesses for binds, connectors for damage and terminals for deformities.

SIDE IMPACT SENSOR INSPECTION

1. Inspect sensor and bracket for dents, cracks or deformation.
2. Inspect connector for damage and terminals for deformation.
3. Ensure there is no bending or corrosion in center pillar. **SRS may not activate properly if an impact sensor is not installed properly.**

SRS DIAGNOSIS UNIT (SDU) INSPECTION

1. Inspect case and brackets for dents, cracks, deformities, or rust. **SRS may**

SRS-ECU TERMINAL NO.	DESTINATION OF HARNESS	CORRECTIVE ACTION
1 TO 4	–	–
5	BODY WIRING HARNESS → CLOCKSPRING → AIR BAG MODULE (DRIVER'S SIDE)	CORRECT OR REPLACE EACH WIRING HARNESS. REPLACE THE CLOCKSPRING.
6		
7	BODY WIRING HARNESS → AIR BAG MODULE (FRONT PASSENGER'S SIDE)	CORRECT OR REPLACE EACH WIRING HARNESS.
8		
9,10		
11	BODY WIRING HARNESS → DATE LINK CONNECTOR	CORRECT OR REPLACE EACH WIRING HARNESS.
12,17	BODY WIRING HARNESS → FRONT WIRING HARNESS → FRONT IMPACT SENSOR (LH)	SENSOR CABLE* INSTALLATION PROCEDURES
13	BODY WIRING HARNESS → JUNCTION BLOCK (FUSE NO.11)	CORRECT OR REPLACE EACH WIRING HARNESS.
14	BODY WIRING HARNESS → JUNCTION BLOCK (FUSE NO.10)	
15	BODY WIRING HARNESS → SRS WARNING LIGHT	
16		
18,19	BODY WIRING HARNESS → FRONT WIRING HARNESS → FRONT IMPACT SENSOR (RH)	SENSOR CABLE* INSTALLATION PROCEDURES
20	BODY WIRING HARNESS → GROUND	CORRECT OR REPLACE THE BODY WIRING HARNESS.
21		

NOTE*: The sensor cable is available as service part.

MT8019700223000X

Fig. 9   SRS wire service chart. Montero Sport

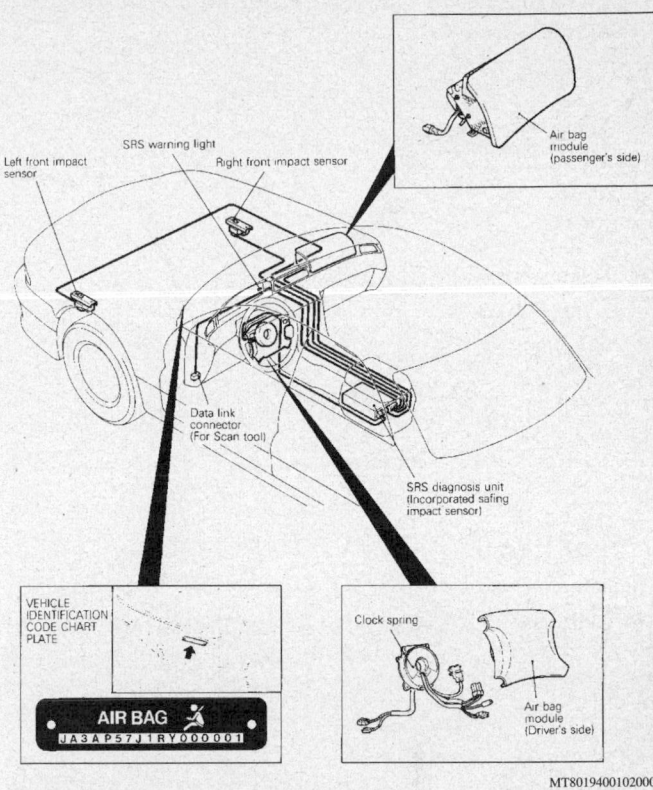

MT8019400102000X

Fig. 10   SRS component locations. 1996 Diamante

not activate properly if SDU is improperly installed.
2. Inspect SDU connectors for damaged or deformed terminals.
3. Inspect lock lever for damage or rust.

AIR BAG MODULE INSPECTION

Driver

1. Remove module as described under "Component Service."
2. Inspect pad cover for dents, cracks or deformities.
3. Inspect hooks and connector for deformities and binding harness.
4. Inspect air bag inflator case for damage.
5. Install air bag module to steering wheel to inspect fit and alignment.

Passenger

1. Remove module as described under "Component Service."
2. Inspect cover for dents, cracks and deformities.
3. Inspect connector for deformed terminal and binding harness.
4. Inspect inflator case for damage.

Side

1. Inspect deployment for dents, cracks and deformities.
2. Inspect connector for damage, terminals for deformation and harness for binds.

CLOCKSPRING INSPECTION

1. Remove clockspring as described under "Component Service."
2. Inspect connectors, protective tube and terminals for damage and deformities.
3. Visually inspect case and gears for damage.

STEERING WHEEL, COLUMN & INTERMEDIATE JOINT INSPECTION

1. Inspect wiring harness, connectors

and terminals for damage and deformities.
2. Install air bag module to inspect fit and alignment.
3. Inspect steering wheel for noise, binding, difficult operation or excessive freeplay.

WIRING HARNESS & BODY INSPECTION

1. Inspect harness connectors for damaged or deformed terminals.
2. Inspect harness for any crimps or binding.
3. Inspect harness wiring for any fraying or damage.
4. Replace harness or connectors if they show any signs of damage.

SEAT BELT PRETENSIONERS INSPECTION

Diamante

Inspect seat belt pretensioners for dents, cracks, deformation and rust. If dents, cracks, deformation or rust is present, replace the seat belt pretensioner. Refer to "Component Service" for procedure.

COMPONENT LOCATIONS

Refer to **Figs. 10 through 18** for SRS component locations.

DIAGNOSIS & TESTING

Refer to MOTOR's Air Bag Manual for complete air bag system diagnosis and testing information.

COLLISION INSPECTION

On vehicles which have experienced an air bag system deployment, certain air bag components must be replaced. To determine which components require replacement, refer to MOTOR's Air Bag Manual.

SRS DIAGNOSIS UNIT MEMORY INSPECTION

Perform the following steps to inspect and service the SRS after a collision, whether or not an air bag has been deployed:
1. Connect scan tool to diagnostic check connector.
2. Read all displayed DTCs. **If battery power supply has been disconnected or disrupted by collision, scan tool cannot communicate with SRS diagnosis unit. Inspect, and if necessary, repair body wiring harness before proceeding further.**
3. Read service data, then erase DTCs.
4. Read and record all DTCs displayed after 45 seconds. Refer to "Diagnosis and Testing" for DTC diagnosis.

REPAIR PROCEDURE

Air Bag(s) Deployed In Collision

1. Inspect clockspring for any visible damage such as dents, cracks or deformation, and replace as necessary.
2. Inspect wiring harness built into steering wheel and connectors for damage

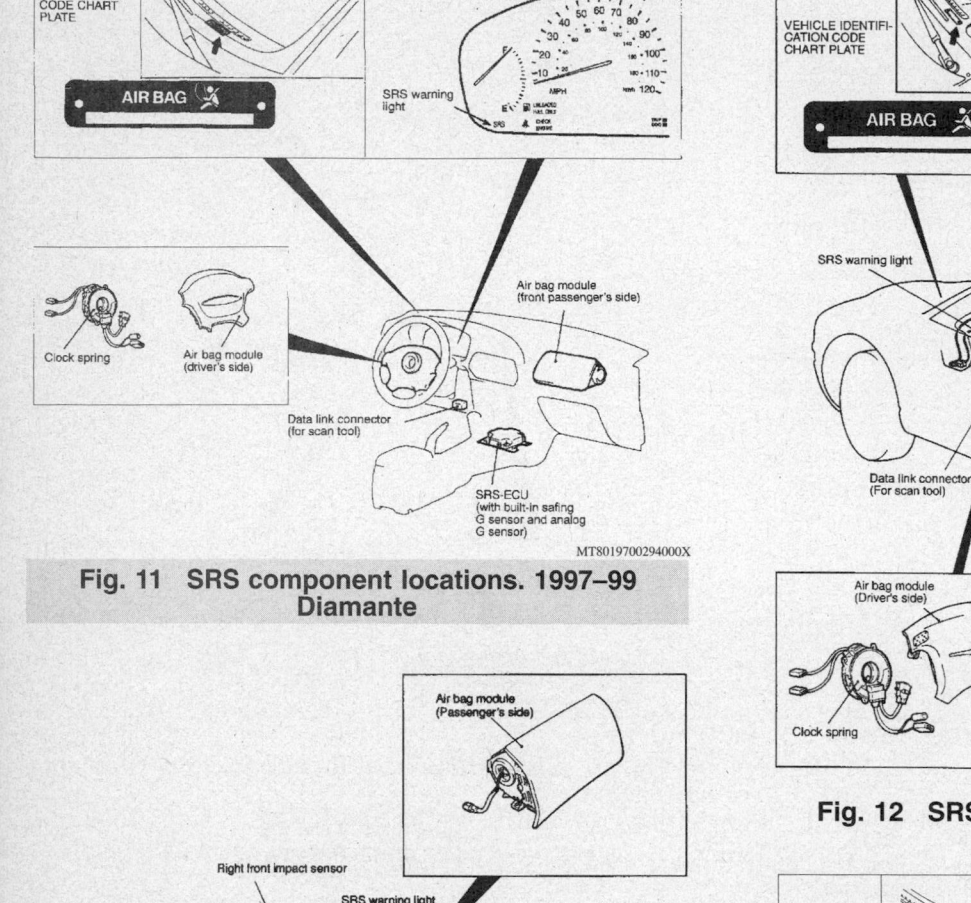

Fig. 11   SRS component locations. 1997–99 Diamante

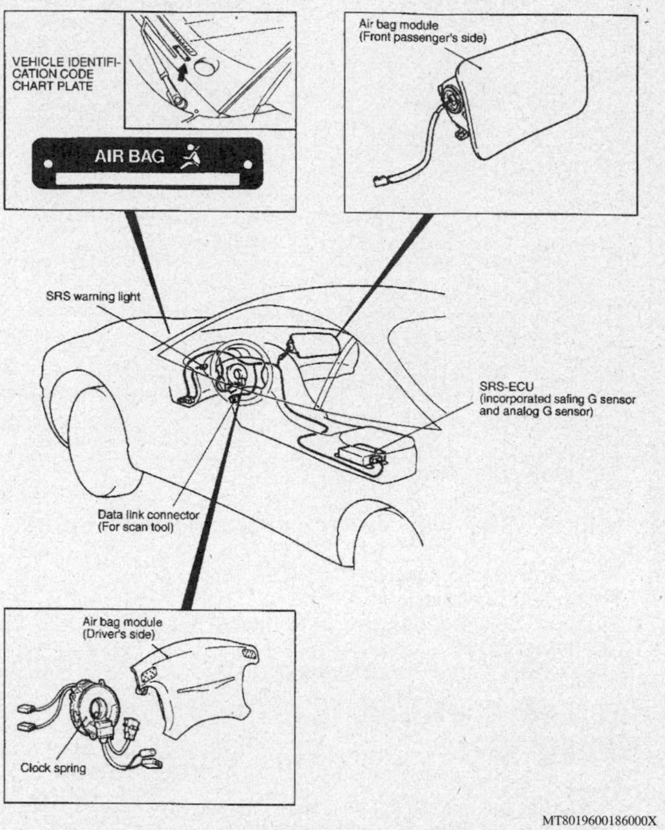

MT8019700294000X

Fig. 12   SRS component locations. Eclipse

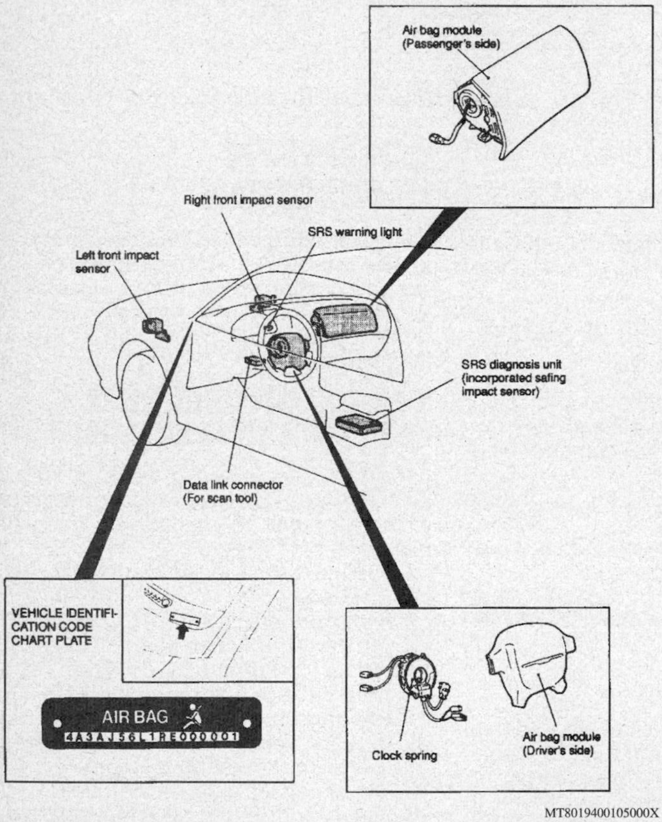

MT8019600186000X

Fig. 13   SRS component locations. 1996–98 Galant

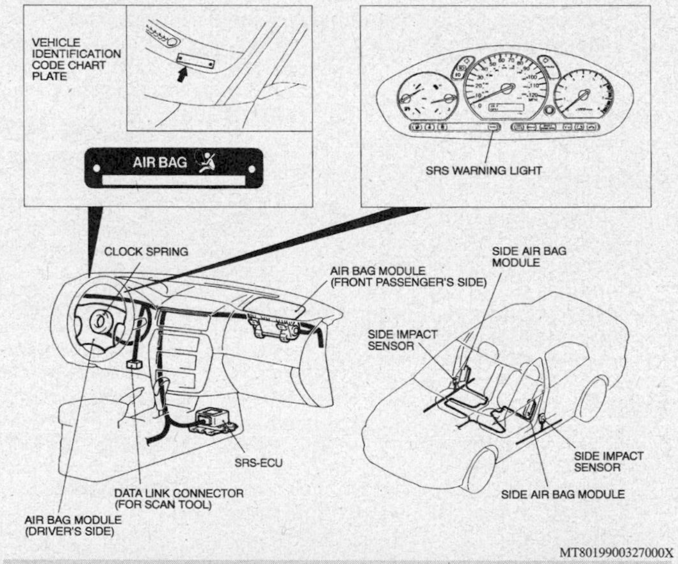

MT8019400105000X

Fig. 14   SRS component locations. 1999 Galant

MT8019900327000X

and terminals for deformities.
3. Inspect steering wheel, column and intermediate joint for noise, binding, difficult operation and excessive freeplay.
4. Inspect harness for binding, connectors for damage and poor connections, and terminals for deformities.

Seat Belt Pretensioner Deployed In Collision

Deployed seat belt pretensioners must be replaced, refer to "Component Service."

Air Bag(s) Did Not Deploy

Inspect SRS components as described under "Scheduled Maintenance" for visible damage such as dents, cracks or deformities and replace as necessary.

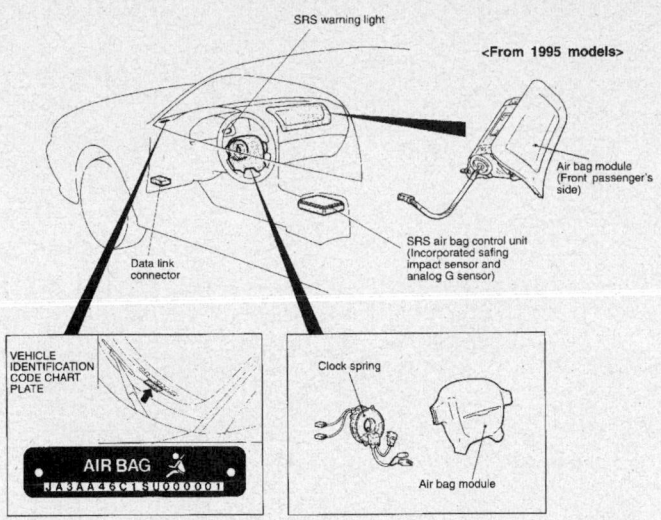

Fig. 15 SRS component locations. Mirage

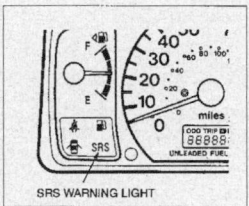

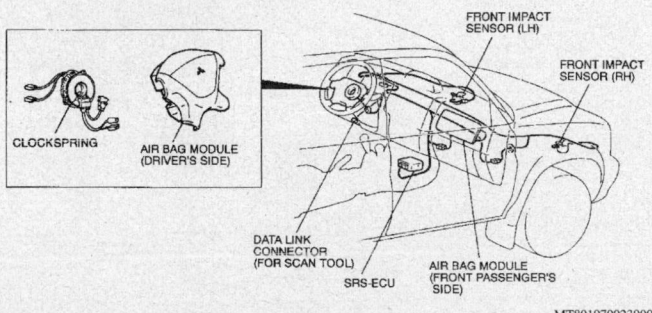

Fig. 17 SRS component locations. Montero Sport

COMPONENT SERVICE

AIR BAG MODULE REPLACEMENT

DRIVER

1. Set front wheels in straight ahead position, then remove ignition key.
2. Remove air bag module mounting nut from rear side of steering wheel, **Figs. 19 through 27.**
3. Spread air bag connector lock by pressing toward outer side with screwdriver, then disconnect clockspring connector.
4. Remove air bag module.
5. Remove clockspring.
6. Reverse procedure to install. **Ensure clockspring mating marks are properly aligned.**

PASSENGER

1. Remove glove compartment.
2. **On Montero and Montero Sport**

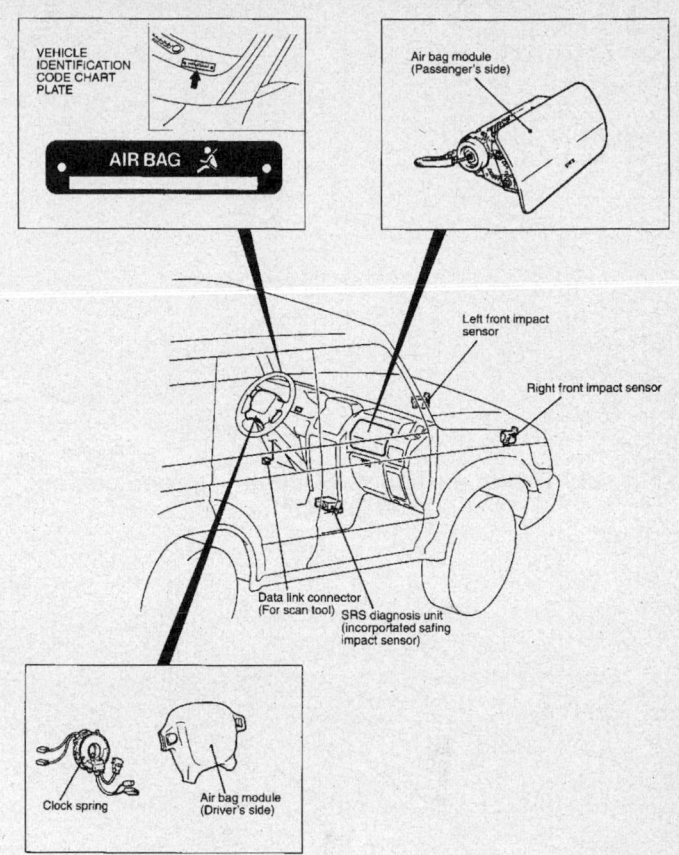

Fig. 16 SRS component locations. Montero

Name	Symbol	Name	Symbol
Data link connector <From 1994 models>	D	Front impact sensor	A
Data link connector <Up to 1993 models>	C	SRS diagnosis unit	B

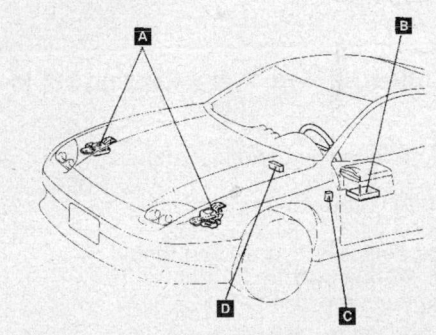

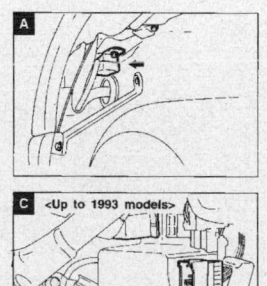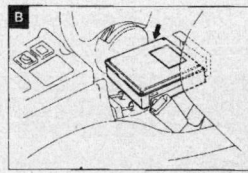

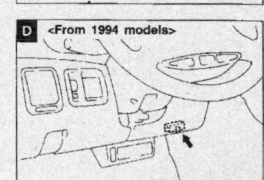

Fig. 18 SRS component locations. 3000GT

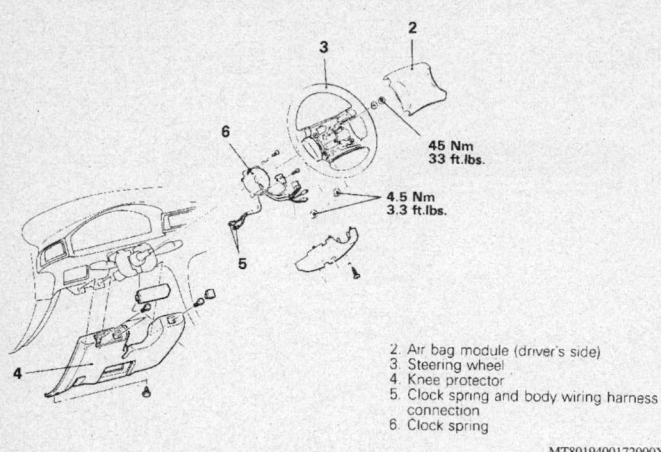

Fig. 19   Driver air bag & clockspring replacement.
1996 Diamante

2. Air bag module (driver's side)
3. Steering wheel
4. Knee protector
5. Clock spring and body wiring harness connection
6. Clock spring

MT8019400172000X

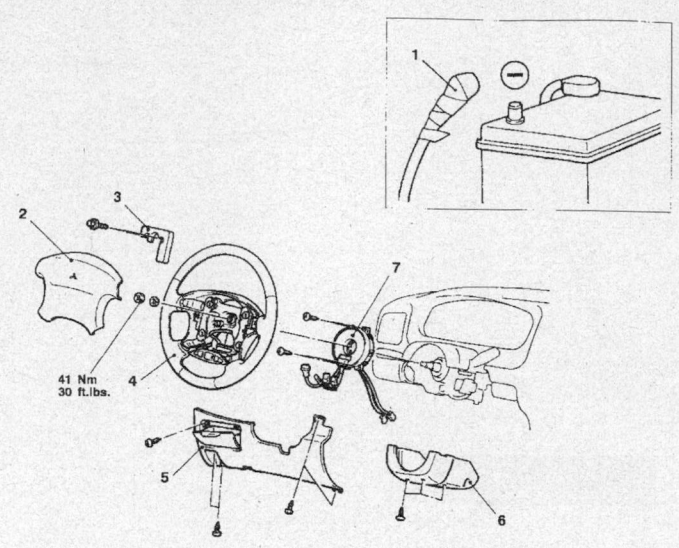

1. Negative (−) battery cable connection
2. Air bag module
3. Weight
4. Steering wheel
5. Instrument lower panel
6. Column cover lower
7. Clock spring

MT8019700299000X

Fig. 20   Driver air bag & clockspring replacement.
1997–99 Diamante

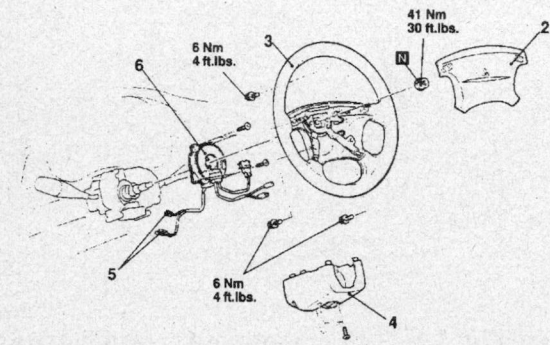

2. Air bag module
3. Steering wheel
4. Column cover lower
5. Clock spring and body wiring harness connection
6. Clock spring

MT8019400148000X

Fig. 21   Driver air bag & clockspring replacement.
Eclipse

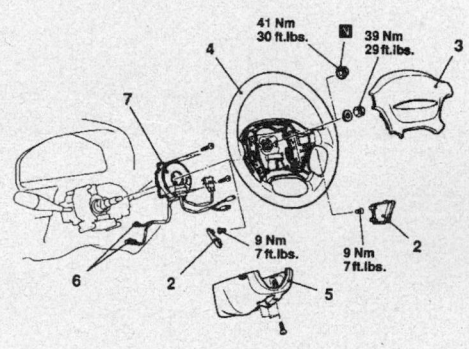

2. Steering wheel lower cover
3. Air bag module (Driver's side)
4. Steering wheel
5. Column cover lower
6. Clock spring and body wiring harness connection
7. Clock spring

MT8019400150000X

Fig. 22   Driver air bag & clockspring replacement.
1996–98 Galant

models, remove righthand foot shower duct.

3. **On 3000GT models,** remove cross pipe cover.

4. **On all models,** remove air bag module, **Figs. 28 through 36.**

5. Reverse procedure to install.

CLOCK SPRING, REPLACE

Refer to **Figs. 19 through 27** when replacing clock spring.

DIAMANTE, ECLIPSE, GALANT, MIRAGE, MONTERO & MONTERO SPORT

1. Set steering wheel in the straight ahead position, then remove ignition key.

2. Remove driver's air bag module as outlined under "Air Bag Module, Replace."

3. **On Montero models,** remove cap from lower portion of steering wheel.

4. **On Diamante models,** remove steering wheel weight retaining screw, then the weight.

5. **On all models,** remove steering wheel

to steering shaft retaining nut.

6. Use steering wheel puller to remove steering wheel. **Do not hammer on wheel.**

7. **On Diamante models,** remove instrument panel lefthand lower panel attaching screws, then the panel.

8. **On all models,** remove lower steering column cover.

9. Disconnect clock spring electrical connectors.

10. Remove clock spring retaining screws, then the clock spring.

11. Prior to installation of the air bag mod-

ule, a pre-installation inspection procedure must be performed. Refer to "Pre-Installation Inspection."

12. Reverse procedure to install, noting the following:

a. Ensure front wheels are in straight-ahead position.

b. **If clock spring mating marks, Fig. 37,** are not properly aligned, steering wheel may not turn completely, or flat cable in clock spring may be severed.

c. **On Eclipse models,** turn clock spring fully clockwise, then turn

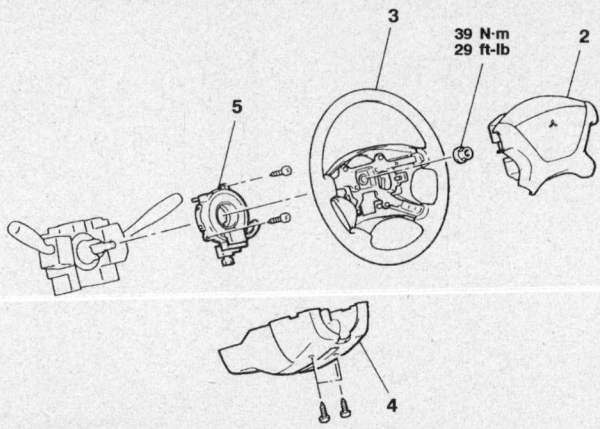

AIR BAG MODULE REMOVAL STEPS
- POST-INSTALLATION INSPECTION
1. NEGATIVE (–) BATTERY CABLE CONNECTION
2. AIR BAG MODULE
- PRE-INSTALLATION INSPECTION

CLOCK SPRING REMOVAL STEPS
- POST-INSTALLATION INSPECTION
1. NEGATIVE (–) BATTERY CABLE CONNECTION
2. AIR BAG MODULE
3. STEERING WHEEL
4. COLUMN COVER LOWER
5. CLOCK SPRING
- PRE-INSTALLATION INSPECTION

MT8019900329000X

Fig. 23 Driver air bag & clockspring replacement. 1999 Galant

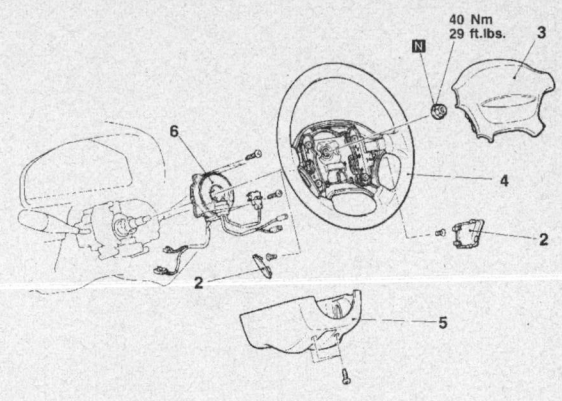

2. Cover
3. Air bag module
4. Steering wheel
5. Lower column cover
6. Clock spring

MT8019400151000X

Fig. 24 Driver air bag & clockspring replacement. Mirage

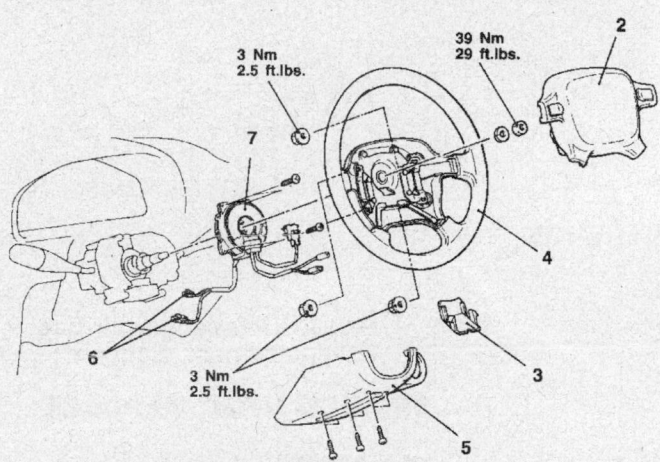

Clock spring removal steps
- Post-installation inspection

2. Air bag module (Driver's side)
3. Cap
4. Steering wheel
5. Column cover lower
6. Clock spring and body wiring harness connection
7. Clock spring

MT8019200215000X

Fig. 25 Driver air bag & clockspring replacement. Montero

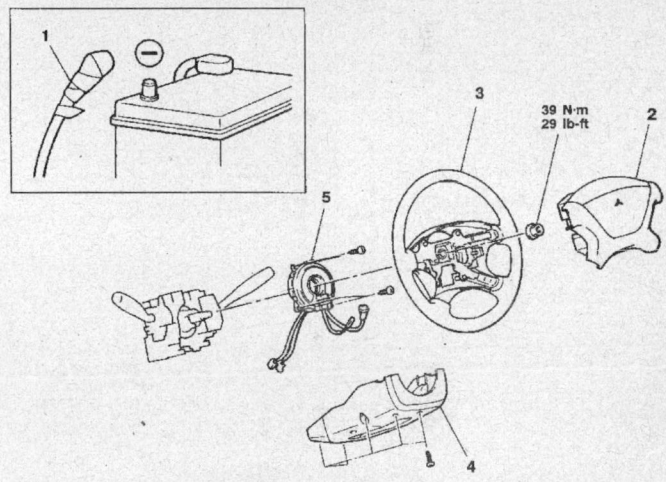

1. NEGATIVE (–) BATTERY CABLE CONNECTION
2. AIR BAG MODULE
3. STEERING WHEEL
4. COLUMN COVER LOWER
5. CLOCK SPRING

MT8019700274000X

Fig. 26 Driver air bag & clock spring replacement. Montero Sport

back approximately 3 1/8 turns to align mating marks.

d. **On Galant and Montero models,** turn clock spring fully clockwise, then turn back approximately 3 1/3 turns to align mating marks.

e. **On Diamante, Mirage and Montero Sport models,** turn clock spring fully clockwise, then turn back approximately 3 4/5 turns to align mating marks.

f. **On all models,** after securing steering wheel, turn from lock to lock to verify normal operation.

g. Arm SRS as outlined under "Air Bag System Disarming & Arming."

h. Perform post installation inspection. Refer to "Post Installation Inspection" for procedure.

3000GT

1. Set steering wheel in the straight-ahead position, then remove ignition key.

2. Remove driver's air bag module as outlined under "Air Bag Module, Replace."

3. Remove weight retaining bolt from steering wheel, then the weight

4. Remove steering wheel to steering shaft retaining nut.

5. Use steering wheel puller to remove steering wheel. **Do not hammer on wheel.**

6. Remove knee protector from lefthand side of instrument panel.

7. Remove lower steering column cover.

8. Remove the floor console.

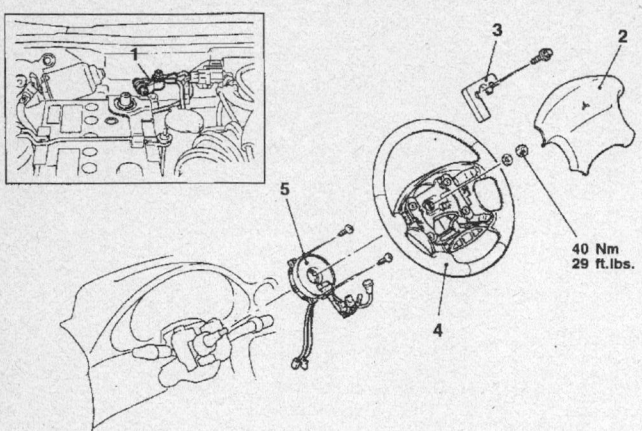

1. Negative (–) battery cable connection
2. Air bag module (Driver's side)
3. Weight
4. Steering wheel
● Knee protector
● Column cover
● Floor console
5. Clock spring

MT8019700275000X

Fig. 27   Driver air bag & clock spring replacement. 3000GT

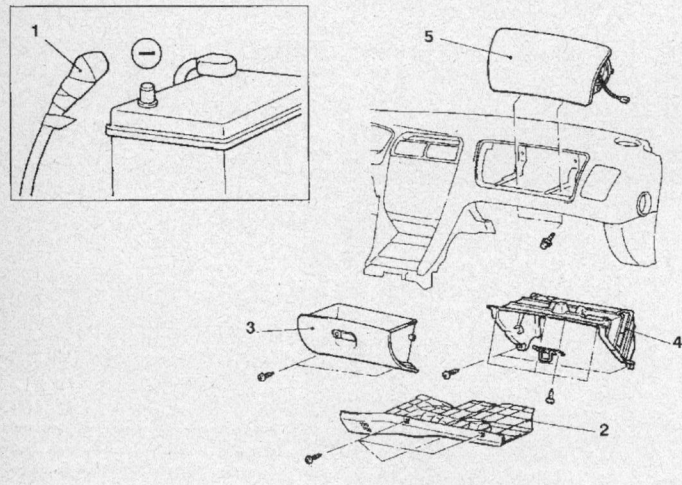

1. Negative (–) battery cable connection
2. Undercover

3. Glove box assembly
4. Glove box case
5. Air bag module

MT8019700300000X

Fig. 29   Passenger's air bag replacement. 1997–99 Diamante

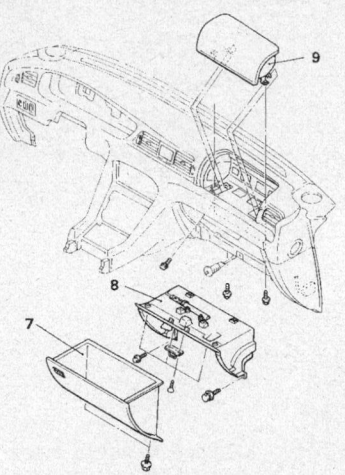

7. Glove box
8. Glove box outer case
9. Air bag module (passenger's side)

MT8019400153000X

Fig. 28   Passenger air bag replacement. 1996 Diamante

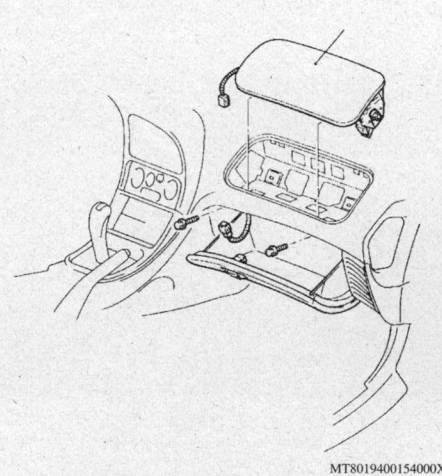

MT8019400154000X

Fig. 30   Passenger air bag replacement. Eclipse

SRS-ECU UNIT, REPLACE

DIAMANTE

1. Disarm SRS as outlined under "Air Bag System Disarming & Arming."
2. Remove foot rest, **Fig. 38.**
3. Remove left and right center console side covers.
4. Remove left and right floor carpet reinforcements.
5. Remove harness protector.
6. Disconnect electrical connectors from engine ECU, automatic transaxle ECU and automatic transaxle control relay.
7. Remove attaching nuts, then the engine ECU, automatic transaxle ECU and automatic transaxle control relay.
8. Disconnect SRS-ECU electrical connector.
9. Remove SRS-ECU to mounting bracket retaining bolts, then the SRS-ECU.
10. Reverse procedure to install, noting the following:
    a. Ensure SRS-ECU is properly installed. Improper installation may affect SRS operation.
    b. Tighten SRS-ECU mounting bolts

9. Disconnect clock spring electrical connectors.
10. Remove clock spring retaining screws, then the clock spring.
11. Prior to installation of the air bag module a pre-installation inspection procedure must be performed. Refer to "Pre-Installation Inspection."
12. Reverse procedure to install, noting the following:
    a. Ensure front wheels are in straight-ahead position.
    b. **If clock spring mating marks, Fig. 37,** are not properly aligned,

steering wheel may not turn completely, or flat cable in clock spring may be severed. Turn clock spring fully clockwise, then turn back approximately 3 ⁴/₅ turns to align mating marks.
    c. After securing steering wheel, turn from lock to lock to verify normal operation.
    d. Arm SRS as outlined under "Air Bag System Disarming & Arming."
    e. Perform post installation inspection. Refer to "Post Installation Inspection" for procedure.

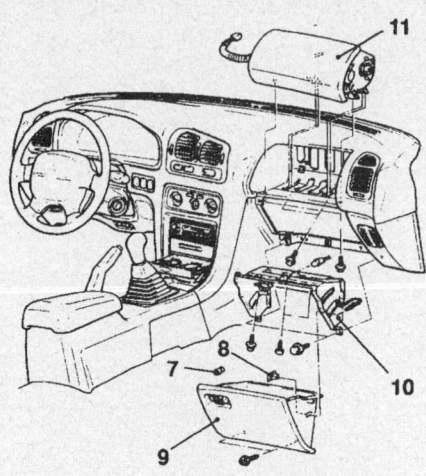

8. Catcher
9. Glove box
10. Glove box cover
11. Air bag module

MT8019400156000X

Fig. 31 Passenger air bag replacement. 1996–98 Galant

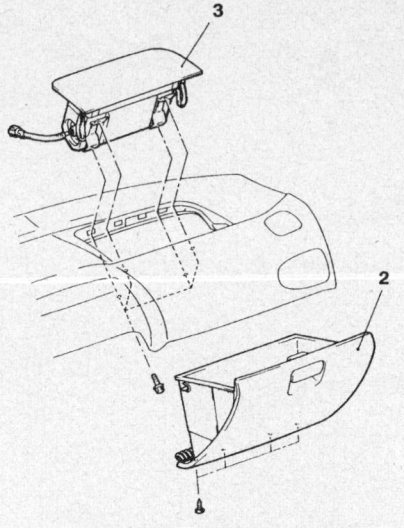

AIR BAG MODULE REMOVAL STEPS

- POST-INSTALLATION INSPECTION
1. NEGATIVE (–) BATTERY CABLE CONNECTION
2. GLOVE BOX ASSEMBLY
3. AIR BAG MODULE
- PRE-INSTALLATION INSPECTION

MT8019900330000X

Fig. 32 Passenger air bag replacement. 1999 Galant

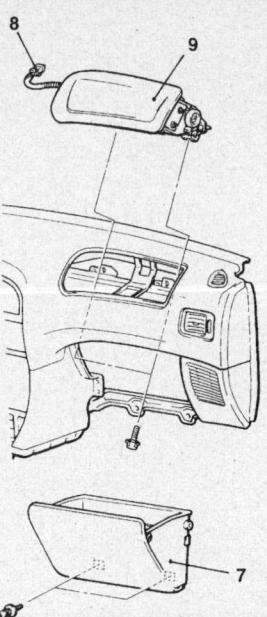

7. Glove box
8. Air bag module and body wiring harness connection
9. Air bag module

MT8019400157000X

Fig. 33 Passenger air bag replacement. Mirage

to specifications.
c. Arm SRS as outlined under "Air Bag System Disarming & Arming."
d. Perform post installation inspection. Refer to "Post Installation Inspection" for procedure.

ECLIPSE

1. Disarm SRS as outlined under "Air Bag System Disarming & Arming."
2. Open center floor console door and remove inner box, **Fig. 39.**
3. Disconnect SRS-ECU electrical connector.
4. Remove SRS-ECU to mounting bracket retaining nuts, then the SRS-ECU.
5. **On models with manual transaxle,** remove shift lever knob.
6. **On all models,** remove ashtray from center console.
7. Remove trim panel from front of center console.
8. Remove center floor console retaining screws, then the center console.
9. Remove SRS-ECU mounting bracket mounting bolts, then the bracket.
10. Reverse procedure to install, noting the following:
    a. Ensure SRS-ECU is properly installed. Improper installation may affect SRS operation.
    b. Tighten SRS-ECU mounting bolts to specifications.
    c. Arm SRS as outlined under "Air Bag System Disarming & Arming."
    d. Perform post installation inspection. Refer to "Post Installation Inspection" for procedure.

GALANT

1. Disarm SRS as outlined under "Air Bag System Disarming & Arming."
2. Open center floor console door and remove inner box, **Figs. 40 and 41.**
3. **On models with manual transaxle,**

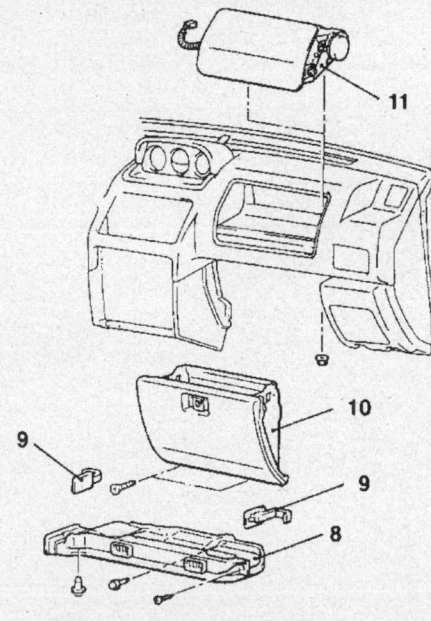

8. Foot shower duct (R.H.)
9. Stopper
10. Glove box
11. Air bag module (Passenger's side)

MT8019600216000X

Fig. 34 Passenger air bag replacement. Montero

remove shift lever knob.
4. **On all models,** remove shift lever panel.
5. Remove coin tray from center console.

MIRAGE

6. Remove trim panel from front of center console.
7. Remove center floor console retaining screws, then the center console.
8. Disconnect SRS-ECU electrical connector.
9. Remove SRS-ECU to mounting bracket retaining nuts, then the SRS-ECU.
10. Remove SRS-ECU mounting bracket mounting bolts, then the bracket.
11. Reverse procedure to install, noting the following:
    a. Ensure SRS-ECU is properly installed. Improper installation may affect SRS operation.
    b. Tighten SRS-ECU mounting bolts to specifications.
    c. Arm SRS as outlined under "Air Bag System Disarming & Arming."
    d. Perform post installation inspection. Refer to "Post Installation Inspection" for procedure.

MIRAGE

1. Disarm SRS as outlined under "Air Bag System Disarming & Arming."
2. Open rear center floor console door and remove inner box.
3. Remove rear center floor control mounting screws, then the console.
4. Remove ashtray.
5. Remove radio trim panel, then the storage box.
6. **On models with manual transaxle,** remove shift lever knob.
7. **On all models,** remove shift lever panel.

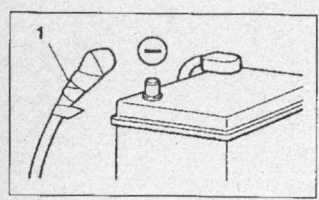

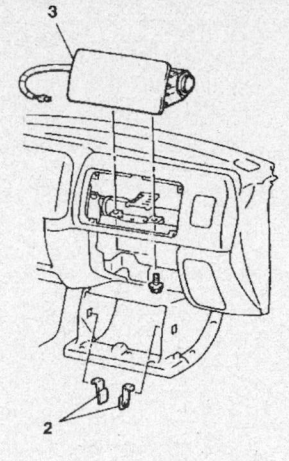

1. NEGATIVE (−) BATTERY CABLE
   CONNECTION

2. STOPPER
3. AIR BAG MODULE

MT8019700281000X

Fig. 35 Passenger's air bag replacement. Montero Sport

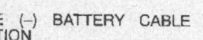

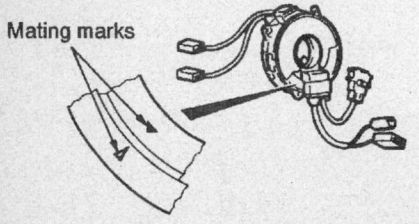

Mating marks

12. Glove box assembly
13. Cross pipe cover
14. Air bag module (passenger's side)

MT8019400158000X

Fig. 36 Passenger air bag replacement. 3000GT

MT8019700283000X

Fig. 37 Clock spring mating mark alignment

8. Remove front center floor console retaining screws, then the center console.
9. Disconnect Anti-Lock Brake System Electronic Control Unit (ABS-ECU) electrical connector, if equipped.
10. Remove ABS-ECU mounting bolts, then the ABS-ECU, if equipped.
11. Disconnect SRS-ECU electrical connector.
12. Remove SRS-ECU to mounting bracket retaining nuts, then the SRS-ECU, **Fig. 42.**
13. Reverse procedure to install, noting the following:
    a. Ensure SRS-ECU is properly installed. Improper installation may affect SRS operation.
    b. Tighten SRS-ECU mounting bolts to specifications.
    c. Arm SRS as outlined under "Air Bag System Disarming & Arming."
    d. Perform post installation inspection. Refer to "Post Installation Inspection" for procedure.

MONTERO

1. Disarm SRS as outlined under "Air Bag System Disarming & Arming."
2. Remove switch panel from rear center floor console.

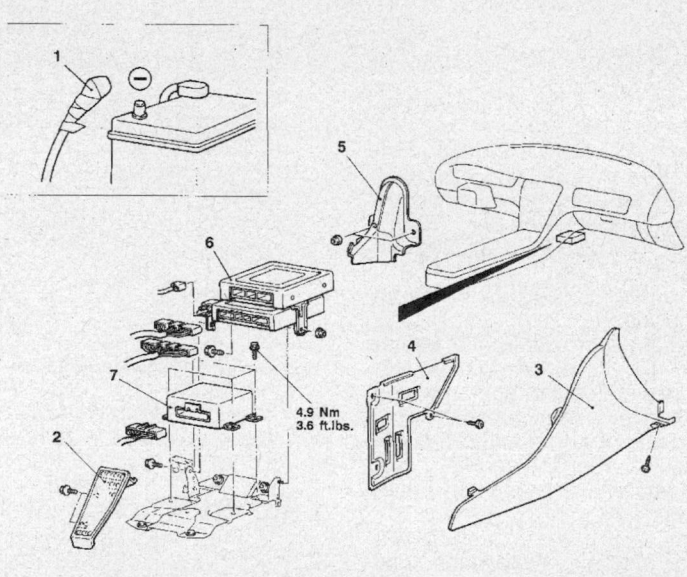

1. Negative (−) battery cable connection
2. Footrest
3. Console side cover (LH and RH)
4. Floor carpet reinforcement (LH and RH)
5. Harness protector
6. Engine ECU, A/T-ECU and A/T control relay
7. SRS-ECU

4.9 Nm
3.6 ft.lbs.

MT8019700301000X

Fig. 38 SRS-ECU replacement. Diamante

3. Remove suspension control switch or cover from rear center floor console.
4. Remove rear center floor console mounting screws, then the rear center console, **Fig. 43.**
5. **On models with manual transaxle,** remove shift lever knob.
6. **On all models,** remove transfer shift lever knob.
7. Disconnect front center floor console electrical connectors.

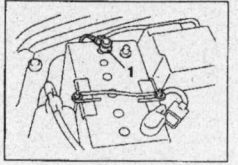
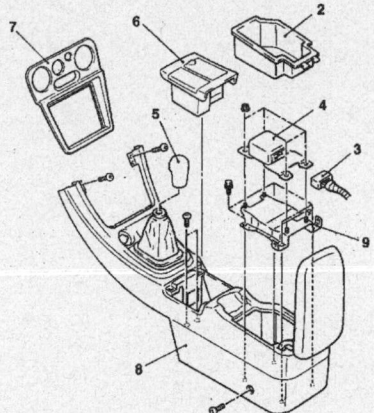

1. Negative (–) battery cable connection
2. Inner box
3. SRS-ECU and harness connector connection

4. SRS-ECU
5. Shift lever knob <M/T>
6. Ashtray
7. Center console panel
8. Floor console assembly
9. Bracket

MT8019700284000X

Fig. 39 SRS-ECU replacement. Eclipse

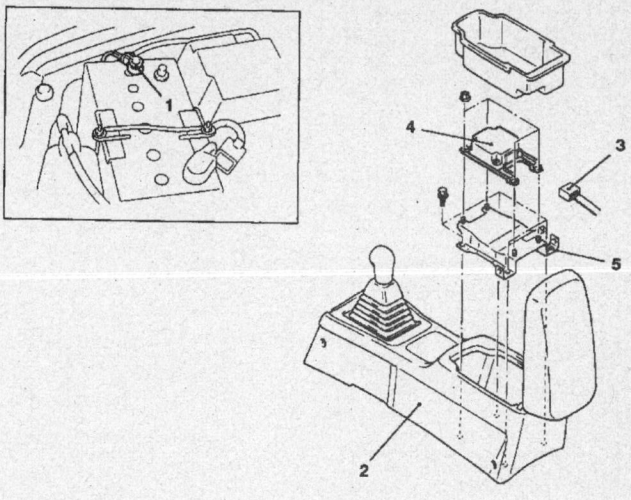

1. Connection for the negative (–) battery cable
2. Floor console assembly

3. SRS-ECU and harness connector connection
4. SRS-ECU
5. Bracket

MT8019700285000X

Fig. 40 SRS-ECU replacement. 1996–98 Galant

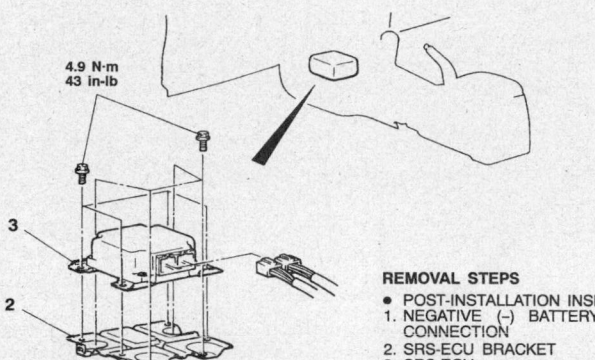

4.9 N·m
43 in-lb

REMOVAL STEPS
● POST-INSTALLATION INSPECTION
1. NEGATIVE (–) BATTERY CABLE CONNECTION
2. SRS-ECU BRACKET
3. SRS-ECU

MT8019900331000X

Fig. 41 SRS-ECU replacement. 1999 Galant

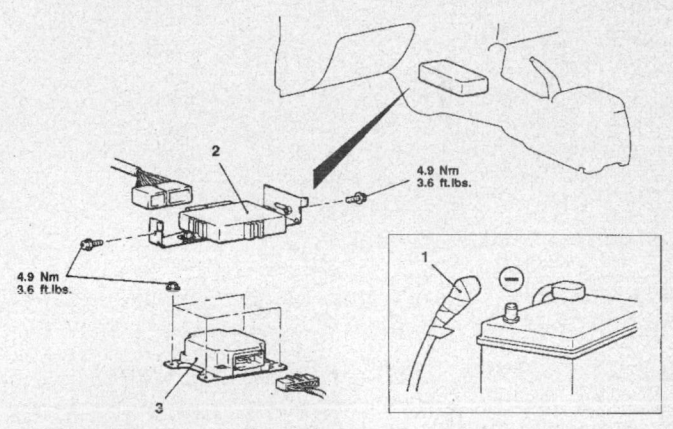

4.9 N·m
3.6 ft.lbs.

4.9 N·m
3.6 ft.lbs.

1. Negative (–) battery cable connection
2. ABS-ECU <Vehicles with ABS>
3. SRS-ECU

MT8019700287000X

Fig. 42 SRS-ECU replacement. Mirage

8. Remove front center floor console retaining screws, then the center console.
9. Disconnect SRS-ECU electrical connector.
10. Remove SRS-ECU to mounting bracket retaining nuts, then the SRS-ECU.
11. Reverse procedure to install, noting the following:
   a. Ensure SRS-ECU is properly installed. Improper installation may affect SRS operation.
   b. Tighten SRS-ECU mounting bolts to specifications.
   c. Arm SRS as outlined under "Air Bag System Disarming & Arming."
   d. Perform post installation inspection. Refer to "Post installation Inspection" for procedure.

MONTERO SPORT

1. Disarm SRS as outlined under "Air Bag System Disarming & Arming."
2. Remove rear center floor console mounting screws, then disconnect electrical connectors and remove the rear center console.
3. **On models with manual transaxle,** remove shift lever knob.

4. **On all models,** remove transfer shift lever knob.
5. Disconnect front center floor console electrical connectors.
6. Remove front center floor console retaining screws, then the center console.
7. Disconnect SRS-ECU electrical connector.
8. Remove SRS-ECU to mounting bracket retaining bolts, then the SRS-ECU, **Fig. 44.**
9. Reverse procedure to install, noting the following:
   a. Ensure SRS-ECU is properly installed. Improper installation may affect SRS operation.
   b. Tighten SRS-ECU mounting bolts to specifications.
   c. Arm SRS as outlined under "Air Bag System Disarming & Arming."
   d. Perform post installation inspection. Refer to "Post Installation Inspection" for procedure.

3000GT

1. Disarm SRS as outlined under "Air Bag System Disarming & Arming."
2. Remove cup holder from rear center floor console, **Fig. 45.**
3. Remove retaining screw cover plug from rear center floor console.
4. Remove rear center floor console retaining screws, then the console.
5. Disconnect SRS-ECU electrical connector.
6. Remove SRS-ECU to mounting bracket retaining bolts, then the SRS-ECU.
7. Reverse procedure to install, noting the following:
   a. Ensure SRS-ECU is properly installed. Improper installation may affect SRS operation.
   b. Tighten SRS-ECU mounting bolts to specifications.
   c. Arm SRS as outlined under "Air Bag System Disarming & Arming."

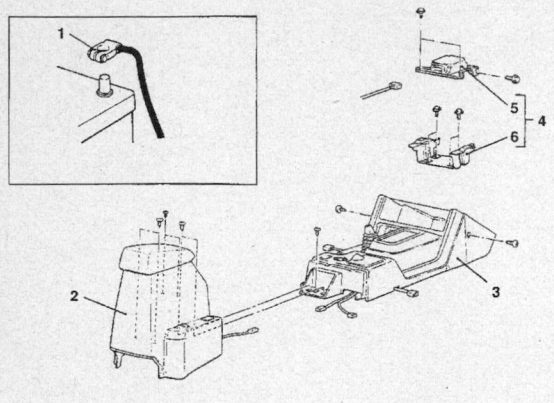

1. Negative (–) battery cable connection
2. Rear console assembly
3. Front console assembly
4. SRS air bag control unit assembly
5. SRS air bag control unit (SRS-ECU)
6. Bracket

MT8019800326000X

Fig. 43   SRS-ECU replacement. Montero

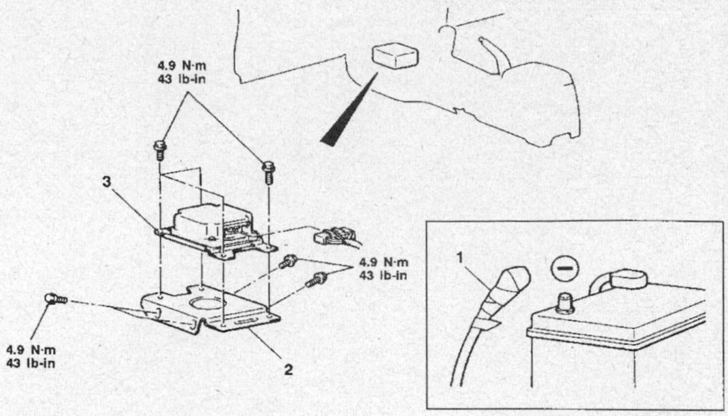

1. NEGATIVE (–) BATTERY CABLE CONNECTION
2. SRS-ECU BRACKET
3. SRS-ECU

MT8019700289000X

Fig. 44   SRS-ECU replacement. Montero Sport

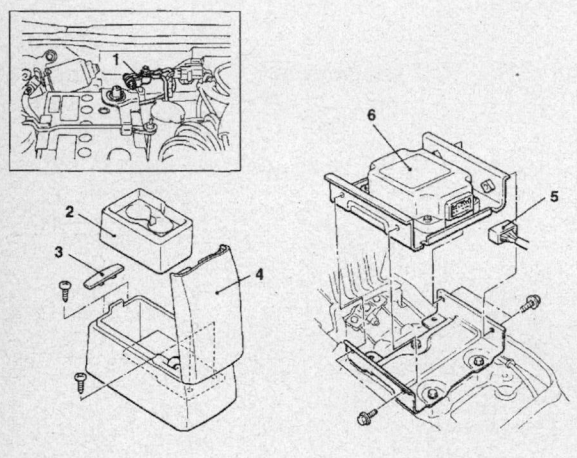

1. Negative (–) battery cable connection
2. Cup holder
3. Console plug
4. Rear console assembly
5. SRS-ECU and harness connector connection
6. SRS-ECU

MT8019700290000X

Fig. 45   SRS-ECU replacement. 3000GT

d. Perform post installation inspection. Refer to "Post Installation Inspection" for procedure.

FRONT IMPACT SENSOR REPLACEMENT

1. Remove shield, **Figs. 46 through 50.**
2. Remove front impact sensor.
3. Reverse procedure to install, noting following:
   a. Install sensor with arrow facing front of vehicle.
   b. Bend wiring harness slightly to remove slack, and clip securely.

SIDE IMPACT SENSOR

Refer to **Fig. 51** for side impact sensor replacement.

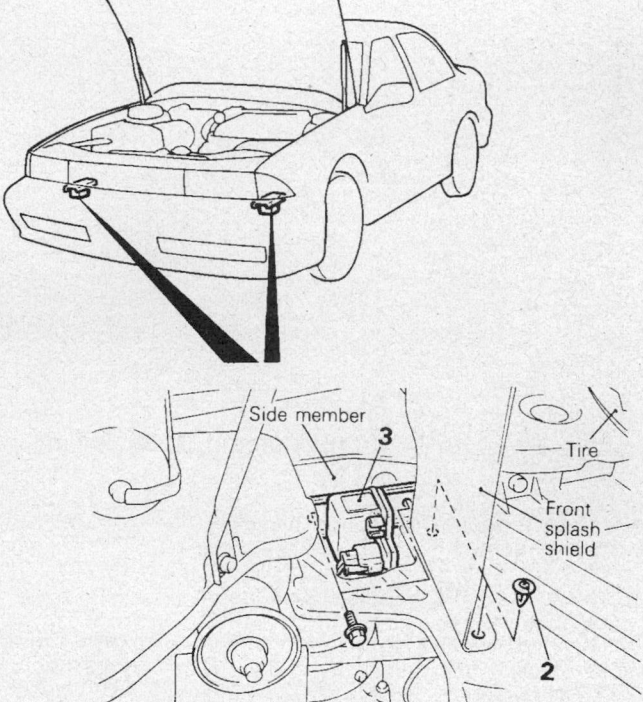

2. Front splash shield attaching clips
3. Front impact sensor

MT8019400166000X

Fig. 46   Front sensor replacement. Diamante

SEAT BELT PRETENSIONER, REPLACE

DIAMANTE

The seat belt pretensioner safety lock lever must be in the locked position whenever the pretensioner unit is not fitted to the vehicle.

1. Disarm air bag system as outlined under "Air Bag System Disarming & Arming."

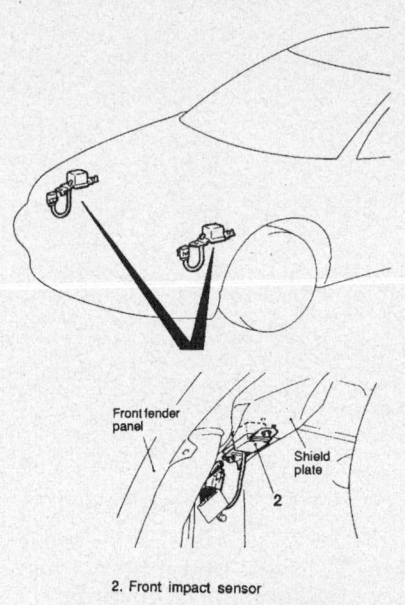

2. Front impact sensor

MT8019400167000X

Fig. 47 Front sensor replacement. Eclipse

2. Front impact sensor

MT8019400168000X

Fig. 48 Front sensor replacement. Galant

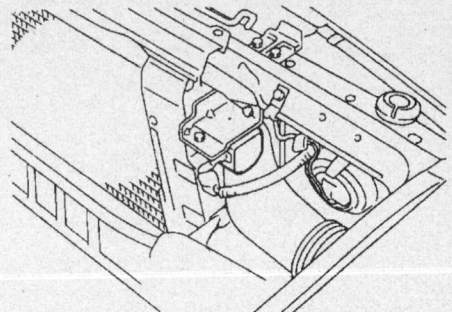

MT8019200218000X

Fig. 49 Front sensor replacement. Montero & Montero Sport

2. Remove the front scuff plate, then the rear scuff plate.
3. Remove lower portion of the center pillar lower trim panel.
4. Remove upper portion of the center pillar lower trim panel by carefully disengaging trim clips.
5. Remove seat belt sash guide.
6. Remove upper center pillar trim panel.
7. Move the pretensioner safety lock lever to the locked position, **Fig. 1.**
8. Remove the seat belt guide to center pillar retaining screw, **Fig. 52.**
9. Remove seat belt shoulder anchor to center pillar bolt.
10. Remove seat belt pretensioner to center pillar attaching bolts.
11. Reverse procedure to install, noting the following:
    a. Tighten seat belt pretensioner to center pillar attaching bolts to specifications.
    b. After the seat belt pretensioner has been fitted to the vehicle, refer to "Air Bag System Disarming & Arming."

POST INSTALLATION INSPECTION

1. After repairs are complete, connect battery ground cable.
2. Turn ignition On and observe SRS warning lamp.
3. If lamp is lit for approximately seven seconds, then goes off and remains off for at least 45 seconds, SRS is functioning properly.
4. If lamp does not perform as described, refer to "Diagnosis & Testing."

AIR BAG MODULE DISPOSAL PROCEDURES

Before scrapping a vehicle equipped with air bag(s), or prior to disposing of an air

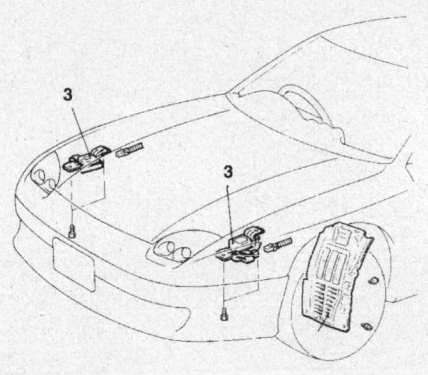

3. Front impact sensor

MT8019400169000X

Fig. 50 Front sensor replacement. 3000GT

bag module, the module must be deployed. If vehicle is to be scrapped, deploy air bag(s) inside vehicle. If vehicle is to continue in service, air bags must be removed and deployed outside vehicle.

UNDEPLOYED AIR BAG MODULE DISPOSAL

Deployment Inside Vehicle

1. Move vehicle to an isolated area.
2. Disconnect and remove battery from vehicle. **Wait at least 60 seconds after disconnection before performing any further steps. SRS is designed to retain enough deployment voltage for a short time even after battery has been disconnected.**
3. Remove lower steering column cover.
4. Disconnect clock spring red 2-pin connector from body wiring connector.
5. Remove glove compartment and outer

case, then disconnect passenger's air bag module red 2-pin connector from body wiring harness.
6. Connect two 20 ft. long wires to the two leads of SRS air bag adapter harness "A" No. MB686560, or equivalent. Cover connections with tape. **Other ends of two wires should be connected to each other to prevent unwanted deployment.**
7. Connect adapter harness "A" to clock spring connector.
8. Connect harness "A" to passenger red 2-pin connector and pass deployment wires out of vehicle.
9. Cover vehicle.
10. From as far away as possible, in a shielded position, disconnect the two wires from each other. **Read the following cautions before proceeding:**
    a. **Ensure no people, animals, equipment or objects are in or near vehicle before deploying air bag in this manner. Wear safety glasses and protective gloves.**
    b. Connect the two wires to a fully charged 12 volt battery. Deployment should occur.
    c. **Inflator will be quite hot immediately after deployment. Wait 30 minutes to allow air bag to cool.**
    d. **Do not inhale gas from air bag.**
    e. **Dispose of air bag as outlined under "Deployed Air Bag Module Disposal."**
    f. If air bag module fails to deploy, contact Mitsubishi Motor Corporation.

Deployment Outside Vehicle

1. Disconnect and remove battery from vehicle. **Wait at least 60 seconds**

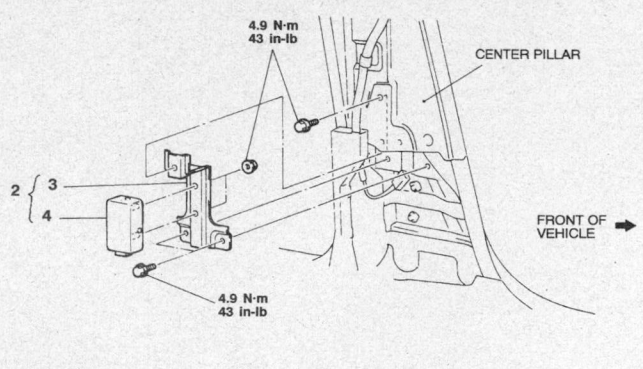

REMOVAL STEPS
- POST-INSTALLATION INSPECTION
- CENTER PILLAR LOWER TRIM
- SEAT BELT
1. NEGATIVE (–) BATTERY CABLE CONNECTION
2. SIDE IMPACT SENSOR AND BRACKET

3. BRACKET
4. SIDE IMPACT SENSOR
- PRE-INSTALLATION INSPECTION

NOTE
The illustration above shows the side impact sensor (LH). The position of the side impact sensor (RH) is symmetrical to this.

MT8019900332000X

Fig. 51 Side impact sensor replacement. 1999 Galant

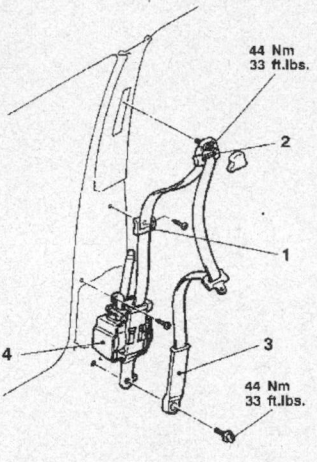

1. Seat belt guide
2. Shoulder anchor
3. Anchor plate
4. Pretensioner seatbelt

MT8019700296000X

Fig. 52 Seat belt pretensioner replacement. Diamante

after disconnection before performing any further steps. SRS is designed to retain enough deployment voltage for a short time even after battery has been disconnected.

2. Remove air bag module as outlined under "Air Bag Module, Replace."
3. Connect two 20 ft. long wires to the two leads of SRS air bag adapter harness "B" No. MB628919 (driver) or harness "A" No. MB686560 (passenger), or equivalents, and cover connections with tape. **The other ends of two wires should be connected to each other to prevent unwanted deployment.**
4. Place air bag module with pad cover facing upward in a flat, spacious area at least 20 feet away from any people, animals, equipment or other objects.
5. Connect adapter harness "B" to air bag module connector.
6. Install four nuts and bolts on rear side of driver's air bag module, then tie with thick wire.
7. Pass adapter harness "B" under a discarded tire and wheel assembly, then connect to air bag module.
8. Insert air bag module onto wheel and tire assembly, then secure with wires attached to bolt holes. Ensure module is facing upward, **Fig. 53. Leave some space below wheel for deployment wires.**
9. Place three tires without rims on top of tire and wheel assembly with air bag module attached. Secure all tires with rope at four locations.
   a. **Do not perform deployment outside if a strong wind is blowing. Even in a slight breeze, the air bag should be deployed downwind from battery.**
   b. **Ensure no people, animals, equipment or objects are nearby.** Module will jump upward about five to 10 feet into the air.

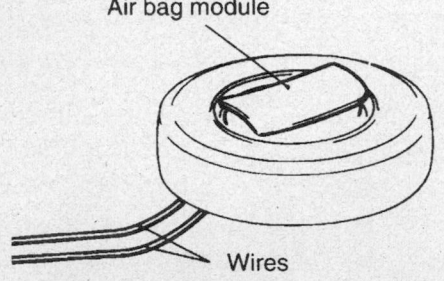

Air bag module

Wires

MT8019400170000X

Fig. 53 Positioning air bag module to tire & wheel assembly

10. From as far away as possible, in a shielded position, disconnect two connected wires from each other and connect them to a fully charged 12 volt battery, **Fig. 54.**
11. **Inflator will be quite hot immediately after deployment. Wait 30 minutes to allow air bag to cool.**
12. **Do not inhale gas from air bag.**
13. **Dispose of air bag as outlined under "Deployed Air Bag Module Disposal."**
14. If air bag module fails to deploy, contact Mitsubishi Motor Corporation.

DEPLOYED AIR BAG MODULE DISPOSAL

After deployment, the air bag module should be placed in a sealed plastic bag and disposed of in same manner as any other scrap parts, except that the following points should be carefully noted during disposal:

1. **Inflator will be quite hot immediately after deployment. Wait 30 minutes to allow air bag to cool.**
2. Do not put water or oil on air bag after deployment.
3. There may be material adhered to

module that could irritate eyes and/or skin. Wear gloves and safety glasses when handling a deployed air bag. **If material comes in contact with eyes and/or skin, rinse affected area immediately with a large amount of clear water. Seek medical attention if any irritation develops.**
4. Place deployed air bag in a hermetically sealed container and discard it.

SEAT BELT PRETENSIONER DISPOSAL

Before scrapping a vehicle equipped with seat belt pretensioners, or prior to disposing of a seat belt pretensioner, the pretensioner must be deployed. Seat belt pretensioner must be removed and deployed outside vehicle.

UNDEPLOYED SEAT BELT PRETENSIONER DISPOSAL

Deployment Outside Vehicle

1. Remove seat belt pretensioner as outlined under "Seat Belt Pretensioner, Replace. **The seat belt pretensioner safety lock lever must be in the locked position whenever the pretensioner unit is not fitted to the vehicle."**
2. Using a piece of rope at least 20 ft. in length, attach rope to pretensioner fitted seat belt as shown in **Fig. 55.**
3. Position pretensioner fitted seat belt on a concrete or other suitable floor surface, then place the pretensioner safety lock lever in the lock release position, **Fig. 1.** Use care in handling the pretensioner fitted seat belt when the safety lock lever is in the lock release position. Any shock may cause the pretensioner to deploy.
4. Position four tires without wheels around the pretensioner fitted seat belt. Place another tire with wheel over the four tires. Pass rope attached to

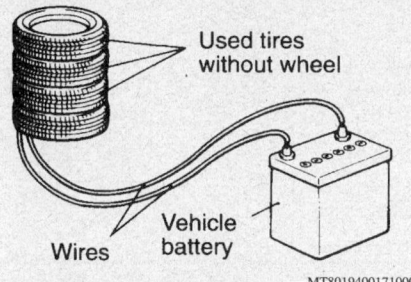

Fig. 54 Air bag module deployment

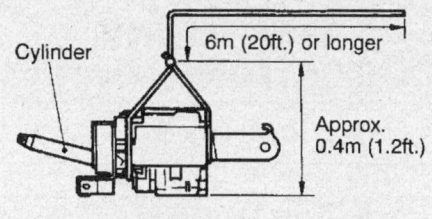

Fig. 55 Attaching rope to seat belt pretensioner for pretensioner disposal. Diamante

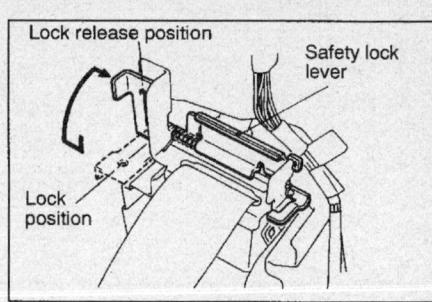

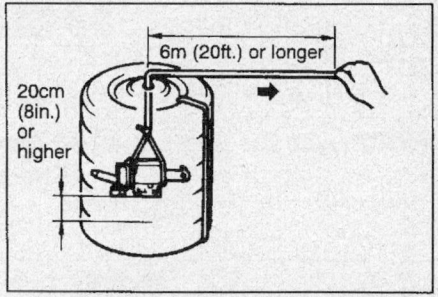

Fig. 56 Positioning seat belt pretensioner deployment. Diamante

pretensioner fitted seat belt through center hole of wheel. Secure all tires together with rope.

5. From a distance of at least 20 ft. from the pretensioner fitted seat belt, raise the seat belt pretensioner at least eight inches off floor, **Fig. 56.**
6. Ensure no one is within 20 ft. of the seat belt pretensioner.
7. Release the rope, allowing the pretensioner to drop to the concrete floor. The seat belt tensioner should deploy. If the seat belt pretensioner fails to deploy, contact Mitsubishi Motor Corporation.

DEPLOYED SEAT BELT PRETENSIONER DISPOSAL

After deployment, the seat belt pretensioner should be placed in a sealed plastic bag and disposed of in same manner as any other scrap parts, except that the following points should be carefully noted during disposal:

1. **Inflator will be quite hot immediately after deployment. Wait 30 minutes to allow air bag to cool.**
2. Do not put water or oil on air bag after deployment.
3. There may be material adhered to module that could irritate eyes and/or skin. Wear gloves and safety glasses when handling a deployed air bag. **If material comes in contact with eyes and/or skin, rinse affected area immediately with a large amount of clear water. Seek medical attention if any irritation develops.**
4. Place deployed air bag in a hermetically sealed container and discard it.

TIGHTENING SPECIFICATIONS

Year	Component	Torque, Ft. Lbs.
DIAMANTE		
1996–99	Seat Belt Shoulder Anchor Bolt	33
	Seat Pretensioner Anchor Bolt	33
	SRS-ECU Screws	3.6
	Steering Wheel Nut	30
ECLIPSE		
1996–99	Driver's Air Bag Module Screws	4
	Steering Wheel Nut	30
GALANT		
1996–99	Driver's Air Bag Module Screws	7
	Steering Wheel	30
MIRAGE		
1996–99	Driver's Air Bag Module Screws	4
	SRS-ECU Bolts & Nuts	3.6
	Steering Wheel Nut	30
MONTERO		
1996–99	Driver's Air Bag Module Screws	6.6
	Steering Wheel	29
MONTERO SPORT		
1997–99	Driver's Air Bag Module Screws	78①
	Front Impact Sensor Bolts	43①
	SRS-ECU Bolts & Nuts	43①
	Steering Wheel	29

Continued

TIGHTENING
SPECIFICATIONS—Continued

Year	Component	Torque, Ft. Lbs.
3000GT		
1996–99	Steering Wheel Nut	29

① — Inch lbs.

Dash Panel Service

NOTE: On Air Bag Equipped Models, Refer To "Air Bag System Precautions" Located In The Front Of This Manual For System Disarming & Arming Procedures.

NOTE: Refer To "Dash Gauges" Section For Related Information.

INDEX

PRECAUTIONS

AIR BAG SYSTEMS

Refer to "Air Bag System Precautions" in the front of this manual for system disarming and arming procedures.

BATTERY GROUND CABLE

Prior to service, disconnect battery ground cable and isolate as required.

DASH PANEL

REPLACE

DIAMANTE

1. Disconnect battery ground cable.
2. Remove ashtray from floor console, floor console attaching screws, then console assembly.
3. Remove plug, knee protector and support bracket, then column cover, **Figs. 1 and 2.**
4. Remove glove compartment striker, glove compartment, then glove compartment outer case.
5. Remove undercover attaching screw, audio panel, then radio and tape player.
6. Remove heater control panel assembly, cup holder, then speakers.
7. Remove meter bezel, combination meter.
8. Disconnect speedometer cable at transmission, remove lock of speedometer cable adapter from instrument panel, **Fig. 3.**

9. Pull cable slightly toward vehicle interior, then remove speedometer cable adapter.
10. Remove steering column attaching bolts, then disconnect harness connector.
11. Remove glove compartment light switch, then instrument panel assembly.
12. Reverse procedure to install.

ECLIPSE

1. Remove steering wheel as outlined in "Electrical" section of "Eclipse" chassis section.
2. Remove center console assembly as follows:
   a. Remove center console panel, **Fig. 4.**
   b. Remove ashtray and cup holder assembly.
   c. **On models with manual transaxle,** remove shift knob.
   d. **On all models,** remove center console assembly.
3. Remove combination meter bezel, then the combination meter, **Fig. 5.**
4. Remove radio and tape player.
5. Remove console side cover and sunglasses holder.
6. Remove glove box and passenger air bag assembly.
7. Remove hood lock release handle, then the lefthand side instrument under cover.
8. Remove center outlet assembly by pushing lever pin to disconnect air outlet changeover damper cable, **Fig. 6.**

9. Remove heater control assembly.
10. Remove instrument panel switch and righthand instrument under cover.
11. Remove speakers from top of instrument panel.
12. Remove instrument panel from vehicle.
13. Reverse procedure to install, noting the following:
    a. Set temperature control knob on heater control assembly to "MAX HOT" position.
    b. Set air mix damper lever at top of heater unit to "MAX HOT" position, then install cable to lever pin, **Fig. 7.**
    c. Push outer cable in direction of arrow as shown in **Fig. 7,** ensure there is no looseness in cable, then secure it with clip.
    d. Set knob for air outlet changeover on heater control assembly to the "DEF" position.
    e. Set air outlet changeover damper lever of heater unit to the "DEF" position, then install cable to lever pin, **Fig. 6.**

GALANT

1. Remove dash panel in numbered sequence shown, **Figs. 8 and 9.**
2. Reverse procedure to install, noting the following:
   a. Connect cool air bypass damper lever cable by turning lever on air outlet fully upward, then positioning lever on heater unit fully downward

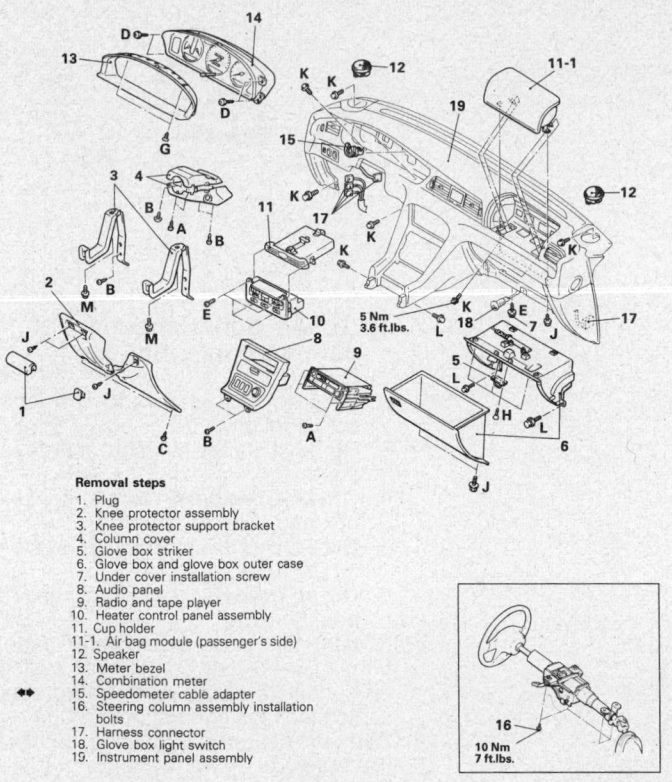

Removal steps
1. Plug
2. Knee protector assembly
3. Knee protector support bracket
4. Column cover
5. Glove box striker
6. Glove box and glove box outer case
7. Under cover installation screw
8. Audio panel
9. Radio and tape player
10. Heater control panel assembly
11. Cup holder
11-1. Air bag module (passenger's side)
12. Speaker
13. Meter bezel
14. Combination meter
15. Speedometer cable adapter
16. Steering column assembly installation bolts
17. Harness connector
18. Glove box light switch
19. Instrument panel assembly

MT9149100017000X

Fig. 1   Exploded view of instrument panel. 1996 Diamante

NOTE
(1) ⇦ : metal clip position
(2) ⬅ : plastic clip position

REMOVAL STEPS
1. COLUMN COVER
2. HOOD LOCK RELEASE HANDLE
3. PARKING BRAKE RELEASE HANDLE
4. INSTRUMENT PANEL LOWER COVER ASSEMBLY (LH)
5. KEY CYLINDER PANEL
6. INSTRUMENT PANEL ECU
7. METER BEZEL
8. COMBINATION METER
9. CENTER AIR OUTLET ASSEMBLY
10. ASHTRAY
11. AIR CONTROL PANEL ASSEMBLY & AUDIO UNIT
12. UNDERCOVER ASSEMBLY
13. GLOVEBOX ASSEMBLY
14. GLOVEBOX OUTER CASE
15. PASSENGER SIDE AIRBAG MODULE
16. CONSOLE SIDE COVER ASSEMBLY
17. FLOOR CARPET REAR REINFORCEMENT
18. HARNESS CONNECTOR
19. PLUG
20. STEERING COLUMN MOUNTING BOLT
21. INSTRUMENT PANEL

MT9149900034000X

Fig. 2   Exploded view of instrument panel. 1997–99 Diamante

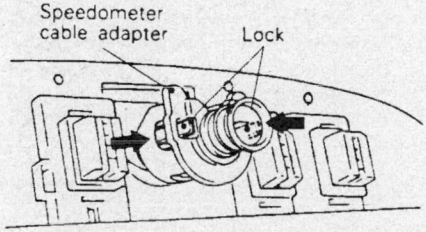

MT9149100018000X

Fig. 3   Speedometer cable adapter removal. Diamante

and fitting cable over connection point.

MIRAGE

1. Remove dash panel in numbered sequence as shown, **Figs. 10 and 11** noting the following:
   a. Remove cool air bypass lever cable of the air outlet center panel assembly at the heater unit side.
   b. Remove the air outlet center panel assembly mounting screws, then the air outlet center panel assembly.
   c. Remove the adapter lock from the instrument panel then pull speedometer cable slightly into the passenger compartment and remove the adapter.
2. Reverse procedure to install, noting the following:
   a. Install air outlet center panel assembly to instrument panel.
   b. Turn cool air bypass lever of air out-

let center panel assembly fully upward.
   c. Turn cool air bypass damper lever at the heater unit side fully downward and install the cool air bypass lever cable.

MONTERO & MONTERO SPORT

1. Remove floor console as follows:
   a. Remove switch panel, suspension control switch and rear console harness connector, **Figs. 12 through 14.**
   b. Remove side panel (A), then the rear console assembly.
   c. **On models with manual trans-**

Removal steps
1. Center console panel
2. Ashtray and cupholder assembly
3. Ashtray
4. Cup holder
5. Shift lever knob <M/T>
6. Floor console assembly
7. Ashtray illumination light bracket

NOTE
⇦ : Metal clip position

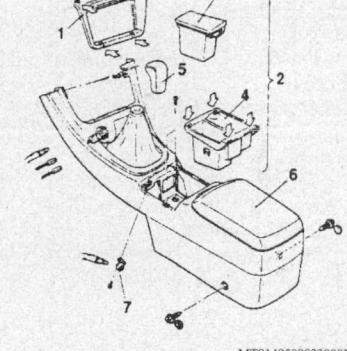

MT9149500023000X

Fig. 4   Exploded view of center console assembly. Eclipse

mission, remove shift knob.
   d. **On all models,** remove transfer shift lever, then floor console harness connector.
   e. Remove front console assembly. On models with automatic transmissions, set selector lever to "L" position when removing console assembly.
2. Remove hood lock release and fuel filler door lock release handle, then instrument under and corner covers, **Figs. 15 through 17.**
3. Remove glove compartment stopper, then the glove compartment assembly.
4. Remove center panel, heater control assembly, then radio.
5. Remove meter hood, meter bezel,

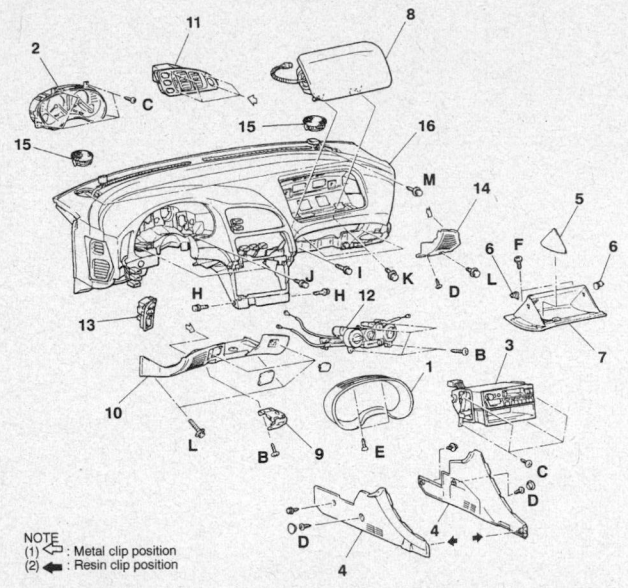

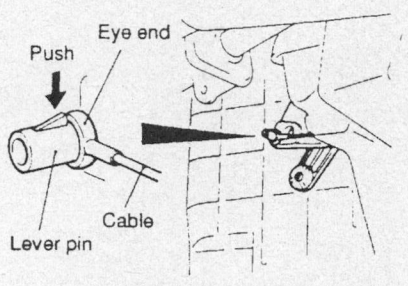

Fig. 6 Air outlet changeover damper cable. Eclipse

a. Remove shift knob and floor console, **Fig. 21.**
b. Remove panel (A) and shift lever boots.
c. **On 4WD models,** remove console box and console cover.
d. **On 4WD models,** remove console mounting bracket.
e. **On all models,** remove accessory box.
14. Disconnect side instrument panel, front harness, air conditioner switch, air conditioner unit, radio and ground cable electrical connectors.
15. Remove instrument panel assembly.
16. Reverse procedure to install.

3000GT

1. Remove console assembly as follows:
   a. Remove cup holder and console plug, **Fig. 22.**
   b. Remove rear console assembly.
   c. Remove radio panel and radio.
   d. Remove switch trim panel C and console side cover.
   e. Remove front console trim panel.
   f. **On models with manual transaxle,** remove shift lever knob.
   g. **On all models,** remove front console assembly.
2. Remove hood release handle and rheostat, **Fig. 23.**
3. Remove switch trim panel B and knee protector assembly.
4. Remove steering column cover.
5. Remove glove compartment striker, glove compartment and cross pipe cover.
6. Using a flat tip screwdriver, remove center air outlet assembly.
7. Remove heater control assembly retaining screws.
8. Remove meter bezel.
9. Remove combination meter.
10. **On models with mechanical type speedometer,** proceed as follows:
    a. Disconnect speedometer at transaxle, then remove adapter locks from instrument panel.
    b. Slightly pull speedometer cable toward passenger compartment and remove adapter.
11. **On all models,** remove speaker or instrument panel top covers.
12. Disconnect instrument panel harness connector.
13. Remove steering column retaining bolts.
14. Remove instrument panel assembly.
15. Reverse procedure to install.

NOTE
(1) ◁▷ : Metal clip position
(2) ◀▶ : Resin clip position

Removal steps
1. Meter bezel
2. Combination meter
3. Radio and tape player, and box
4. Console side cover
5. Sunglasses holder
6. Stopper
7. Glove box
8. Passenger's side air bag module assembly
9. Hood lock release handle
10. Instrument under cover L.H.
11. Center air outlet assembly
12. Heater control assembly
13. Instrument panel switch
14. Instrument under cover R.H.
15. Front speaker
16. Instrument panel assembly

MT9149500024000X

Fig. 5 Exploded view of instrument panel. Eclipse

then combination meter.
6. Disconnect speedometer cable at transmission, remove lock of speedometer cable adapter from instrument panel. **Fig. 18.**
7. Pull cable slightly toward vehicle interior, then remove speedometer cable adapter.
8. Remove column cover, clock if equipped, side defroster garnish, then door mirror control switch.
9. Remove front speakers, rheostat, rear wiper and washer switch, then door lock switch.
10. Remove ventilation control wire, then harness connector.
11. Remove steering column attaching bolts, then panel assembly.
12. Reverse procedure to install noting the following:
    a. When installing ventilation wire, set cool air bypass dial to closed position, **Fig. 19.**
    b. Close cool air bypass lever at heater unit side.
    c. Install wire and secure with clip.

PICKUP

1. Remove hazard warning flasher switch, **Fig. 20.**
2. Remove meter hood hole cover.
3. Tilt steering column down, then remove meter hood retaining screws.
4. Remove meter hood and meter assembly retaining screws.
5. Pull meter assembly outward, then disconnect speedometer cable and meter

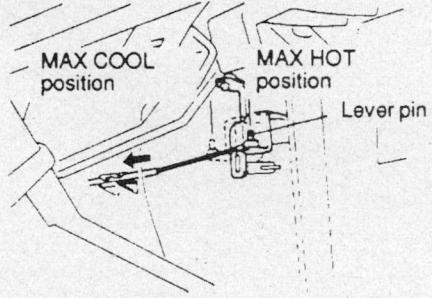

MT9149500026000X

Fig. 7 Heater control unit installation. Eclipse

assembly electrical connectors.
6. Remove fuse box cover and fuse box assembly.
7. Remove glove compartment stopper, then the glove compartment.
8. Remove defrost duct, then disconnect air, mode and temperature selection control wires.
9. Remove speaker bezel.
10. Remove accessory box, or clock, if equipped.
11. Remove instrument panel top hole covers.
12. Remove center cover retaining screws, center reinforcement and center cover.
13. Remove console retaining screws from center reinforcement, floor console bracket and floor console assembly as follows:

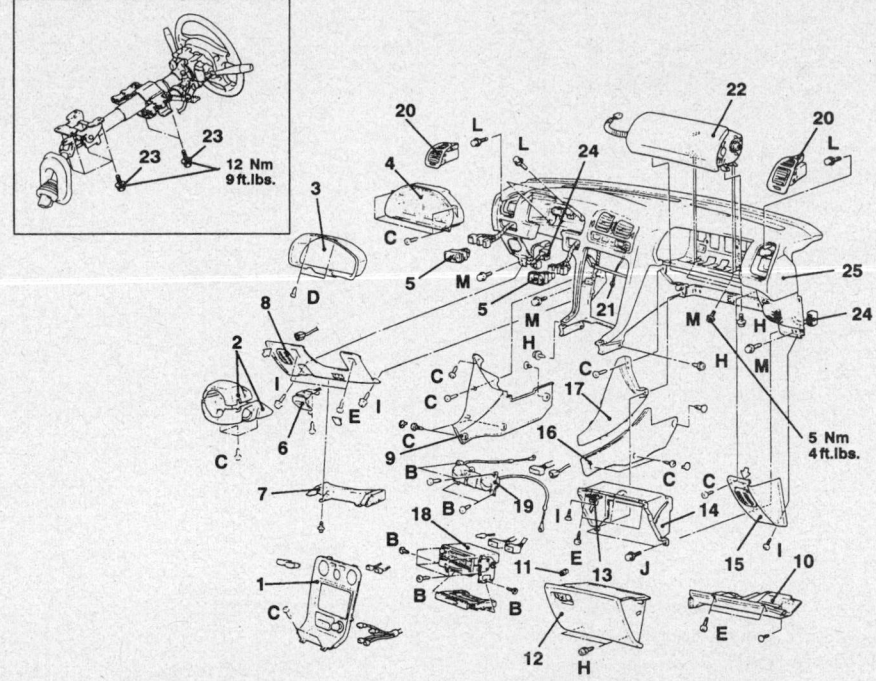

Removal steps

1. Center console panel	16. Side cover lower A
2. Column cover	17. Side cover upper A
3. Meter bezel	18. Radio and tape player, box, and
4. Combination meter	cup holder
5. Instrument panel switch	19. Heater control assembly
6. Hood lock release handle	20. Side air outlet assembly
7. Shower foot duct	21. Cool air bypass damper lever
8. Instrument under cover	cable connection
9. Side cover B	22. Passenger-side air bag module
10. Under cover	assembly
11. Stopper	23. Steering column assembly
12. Glove box	installation bolts
13. Glove box striker	24. Harness connector
14. Glove box cover	25. Instrument panel assembly
15. Corner panel	

MT9149400012000X

Fig. 8   Instrument panel replacement. 1996–98 Galant

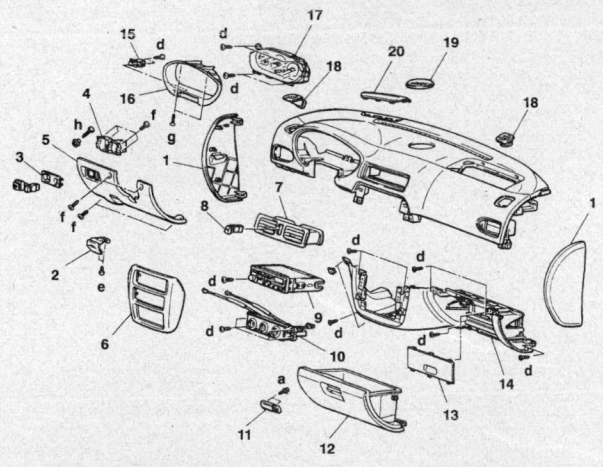

REMOVAL STEPS

1. INSTRUMENT PANEL SIDE COVER
2. HOOD LOCK RELEASE HANDLE
3. SWITCH PANEL ASSEMBLY
4. CONNECTOR HOLDER
5. FRONT DRIVER'S SIDE UNDER
   COVER
6. CENTER PANEL ASSEMBLY
• FOOT DISTRIBUTION DUCT
7. CENTER AIR OUTLET ASSEMBLY
8. HAZARD WARNING LIGHT SWITCH
9. RADIO AND TAPE PLAYER
10. HEATER CONTROL ASSEMBLY

11. GLOVE BOX STRIKER
12. GLOVE BOX
13. FRONT PASSENGER'S UNDER
    COVER PLUG
14. FRONT PASSENGER'S SIDE
    UNDER COVER
15. RHEOSTAT
16. METER BEZEL
17. COMBINATION METER
18. SIDE DEFROSTER GRILLE
19. SPEAKER GRILLE
• FRONT PILLAR TRIM
20. INSTRUMENT PANEL UPPER PLUG

(Continued on next removal step)

MT9149900033010X

**Fig. 9   Instrument panel replacement (Part 1 of 2).
1999 Galant**

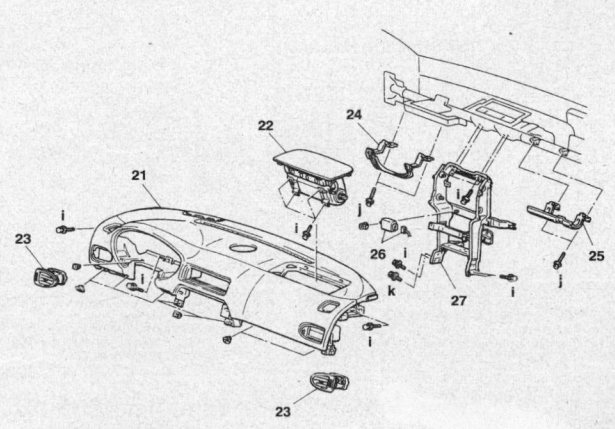

REMOVAL STEPS

21. INSTRUMENT PANEL ASSEMBLY	25. KNEE ABSORBER (PASSENGER'S
22. AIR BAG MODULE (PASSENGER'S	SIDE)
SIDE)	26. AUTO-CRUISE CONTROL-ECU
23. SIDE AIR OUTLET ASSEMBLY	27. INSTRUMENT PANEL CENTER
24. KNEE ABSORBER (DRIVER'S SIDE)	REINFORCEMENT

MT9149900033020X

**Fig. 9   Instrument panel replacement (Part 2 of 2).
1999 Galant**

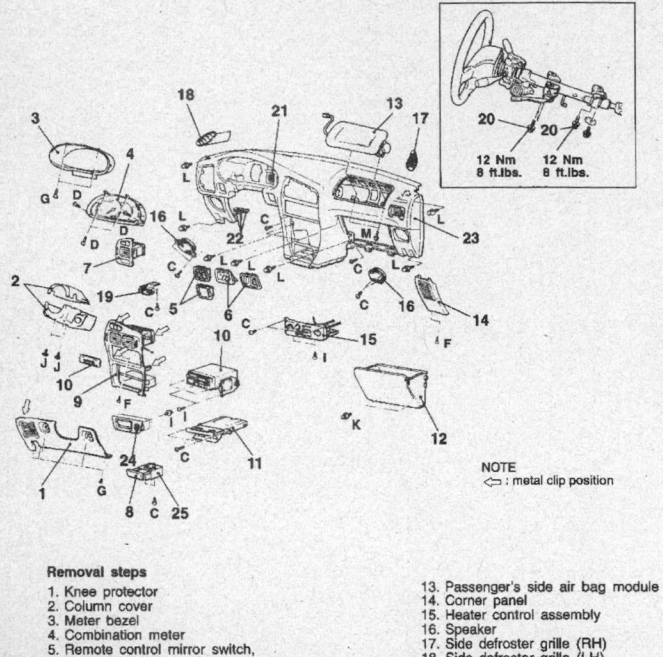

Removal steps

1. Knee protector
2. Column cover
3. Meter bezel
4. Combination meter
5. Remote control mirror switch, rheostat or plug
6. Coin box or rear wiper washer switch
7. Air outlet panel assembly
8. Ashtray
9. Air outlet center panel assembly
10. Radio and tape player or radio plug
11. Cup holder
12. Glove box
13. Passenger's side air bag module
14. Corner panel
15. Heater control assembly
16. Speaker
17. Side defroster grille (RH)
18. Side defroster grille (LH)
19. Hood lock release handle
20. Steering column assembly installation bolts
21. Adapter
22. Harness connector
23. Instrument panel assembly
24. Ashtray panel
25. Ashtray bracket

MT9149300002000X

Fig. 10   Exploded view of instrument panel. 1996 Mirage

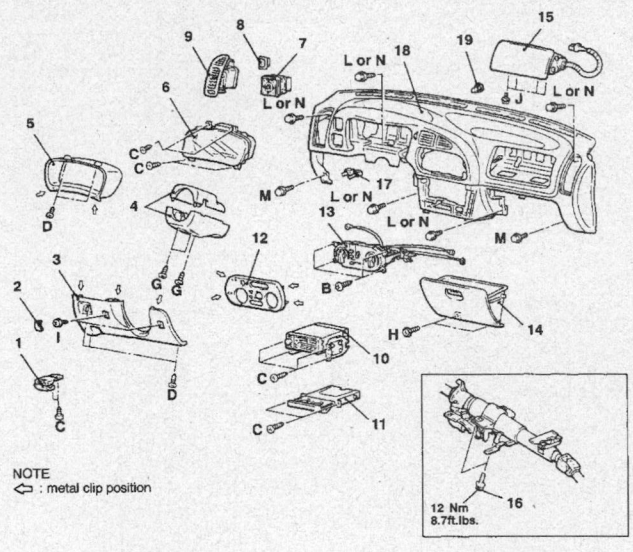

Removal steps

● Rheostat

1. Hood lock release handle
2. Knee protector plug
3. Knee protector assembly
4. Column cover
5. Meter bezel
6. Combination meter
7. Door mirror control switch or plug
8. Auto-cruise control main switch, fog light switch or plug
9. Side air outlet assembly
10. Radio and tape player
11. Cup holder
12. Heater control panel
13. Heater control assembly
14. Glove box
15. Front passenger's air bag module assembly
16. Steering column assembly installation bolt
17. Harness connector
18. Instrument panel assembly
19. Grommet

MT9149700027000X

Fig. 11   Exploded view of instrument panel. 1997–99 Mirage

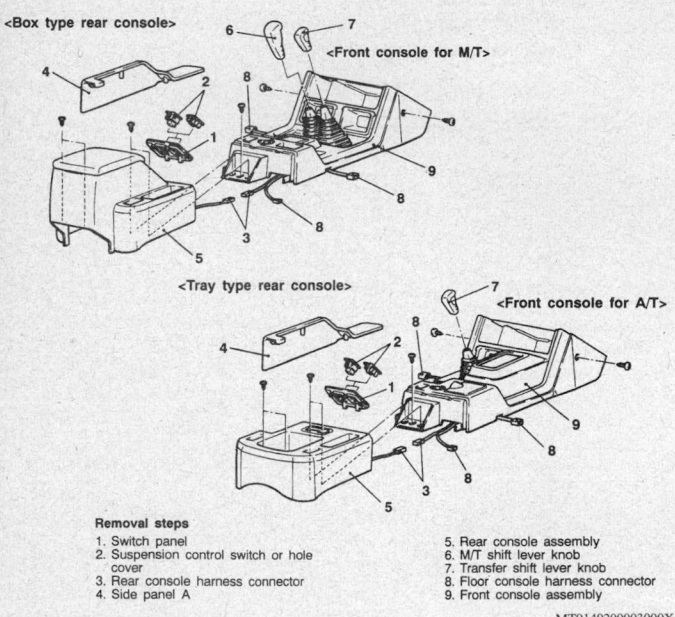

Removal steps

1. Switch panel
2. Suspension control switch or hole cover
3. Rear console harness connector
4. Side panel A
5. Rear console assembly
6. M/T shift lever knob
7. Transfer shift lever knob
8. Floor console harness connector
9. Front console assembly

MT9149200003000X

Fig. 12   Exploded view of floor console. 1996–97 Montero

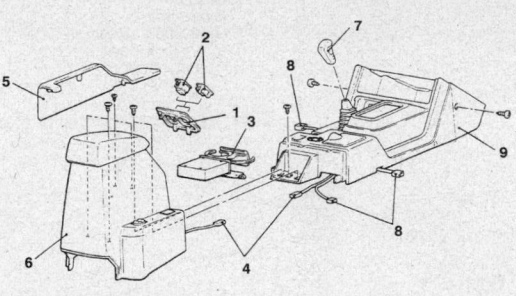

Removal steps

1. Switch panel
2. Suspension control switch or hole cover
3. Cup holder assembly
4. Rear console harness connector
5. Side panel A
6. Rear console assembly
7. Transfer shift lever knob
8. Floor console harness connector
9. Front console assembly

MT9149900031000X

Fig. 13   Exploded view of floor console. 1998–99 Montero

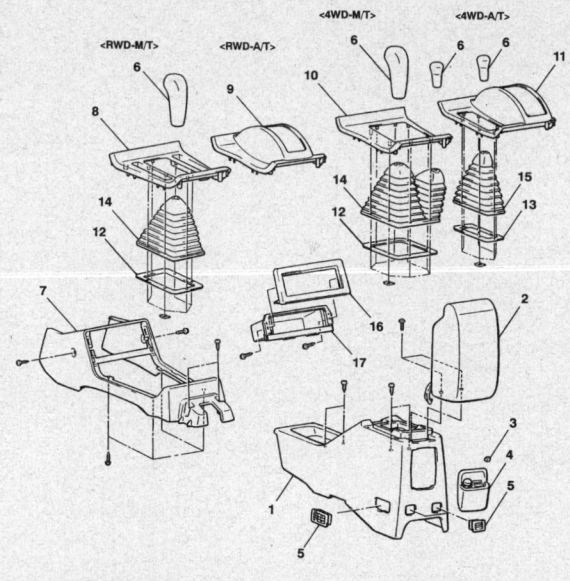

1. REAR FLOOR CONSOLE ASSEMBLY
2. CONSOLE LID ASSEMBLY
3. KNOB
4. REAR HEATER CONTROL PANEL ASSEMBLY
5. FOOT GRILL
6. SHIFT LEVER KNOB
7. FRONT FLOOR CONSOLE ASSEMBLY
8. CONSOLE PANEL A <RWD-M/T>
9. CONSOLE PANEL B <RWD-A/T>

10. CONSOLE PANEL C <4WD-M/T>
11. CONSOLE PANEL D <4WD-A/T>
12. SHIFT LEVER BOOT REINFORCEMENT <M/T>
13. TRANSFER LEVER BOOT REINFORCEMENT <4WD-A/T>
14. SHIFT LEVER BOOT <M/T>
15. TRANSFER LEVER BOOT <4WD-A/T>
16. CONSOLE PANEL
17. BOX

MT9149900032000X

Fig. 14   Exploded view of floor console. Montero Sport

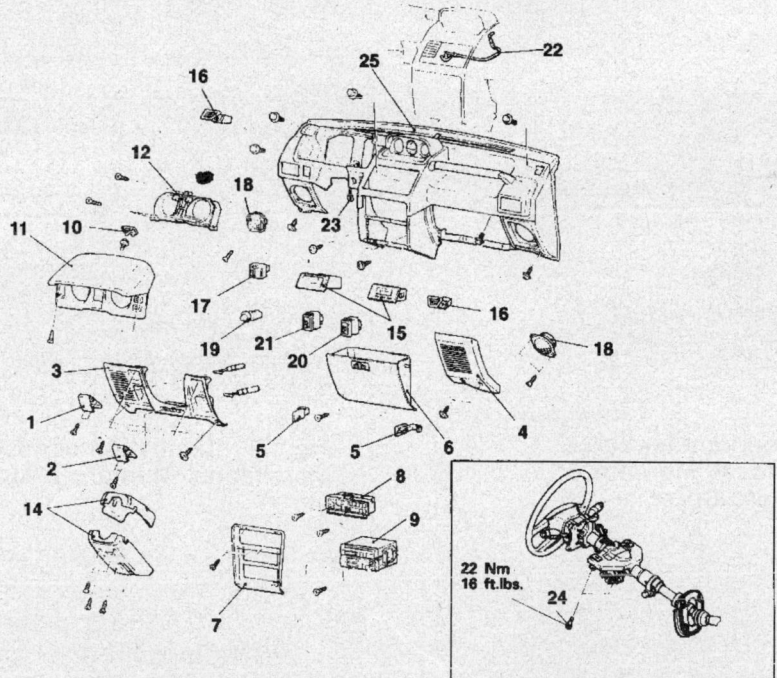

22 Nm
16 ft.lbs.

Removal steps

1. Hood lock release handle
2. Fuel filler door lock release handle
3. Instrument under cover
4. Instrument corner cover
5. Glove box stopper
6. Grove box assembly
7. Center panel A
8. Heater control assembly
9. Radio and tape player
10. Meter hood plug
11. Meter bezel assembly
12. Combination meter

14. Column cover
15. Clock or clock plug
16. Side defroster garnish
17. Door mirror control switch
18. Front speaker
19. Rheostat
20. Rear wiper and washer switch
21. Door lock switch
22. Ventilation control wire
23. Harness connector
24. Steering column installation bolts
25. Instrument panel assembly

MT9149200004000X

Fig. 15   Exploded view of instrument panel. 1996 Montero

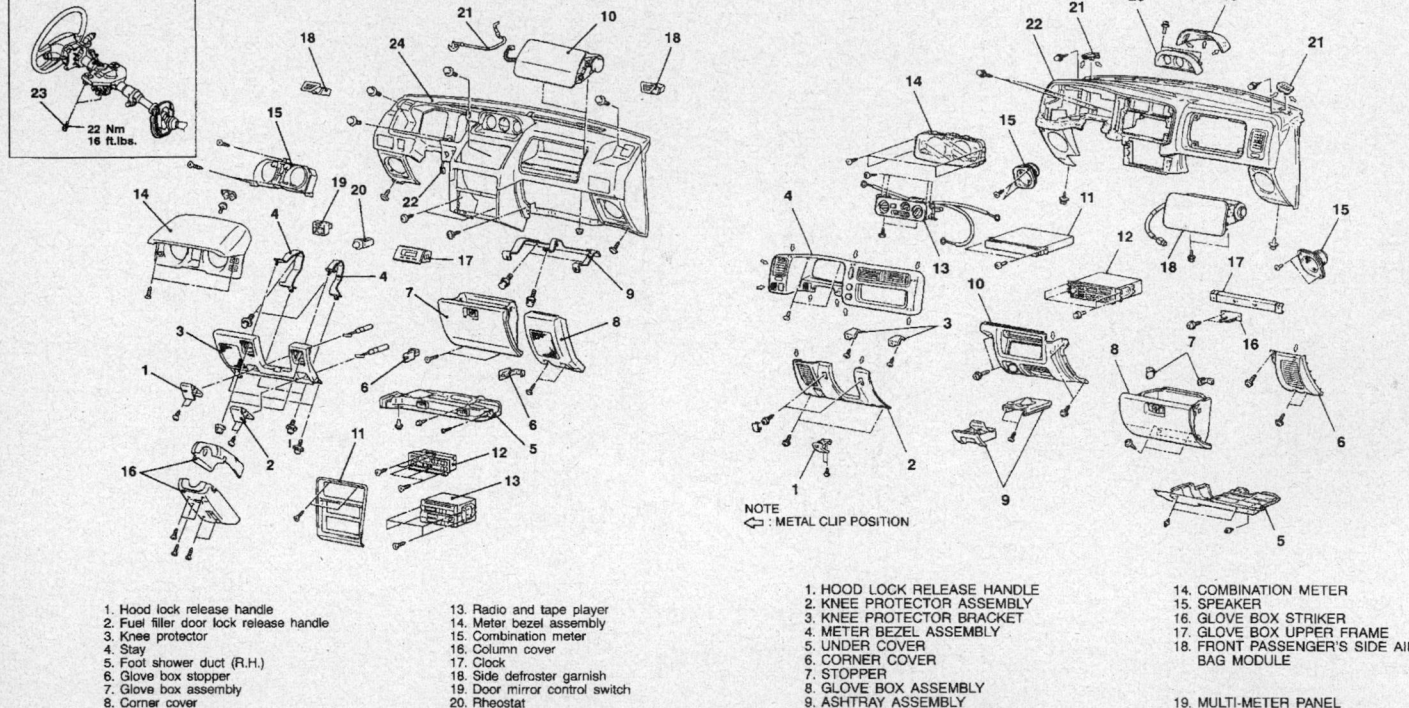

1. Hood lock release handle
2. Fuel filler door lock release handle
3. Knee protector
4. Stay
5. Foot shower duct (R.H.)
6. Glove box stopper
7. Glove box assembly
8. Corner cover
9. Stay
10. Passenger-side air bag module assembly
11. Center panel
12. Heater control assembly
13. Radio and tape player
14. Meter bezel assembly
15. Combination meter
16. Column cover
17. Clock
18. Side defroster garnish
19. Door mirror control switch
20. Rheostat
21. Ventilation control wire
22. Harness connector
23. Steering column installation bolts
24. Instrument panel assembly

MT9149700028000X

Fig. 16   Exploded view of instrument panel. 1997–99 Montero

1. HOOD LOCK RELEASE HANDLE
2. KNEE PROTECTOR ASSEMBLY
3. KNEE PROTECTOR BRACKET
4. METER BEZEL ASSEMBLY
5. UNDER COVER
6. CORNER COVER
7. STOPPER
8. GLOVE BOX ASSEMBLY
9. ASHTRAY ASSEMBLY
10. CENTER UNDER COVER ASSEMBLY
11. CUP HOLDER ASSEMBLY
12. RADIO AND TAPE PLAYER
13. HEATER CONTROL ASSEMBLY
14. COMBINATION METER
15. SPEAKER
16. GLOVE BOX STRIKER
17. GLOVE BOX UPPER FRAME
18. FRONT PASSENGER'S SIDE AIR BAG MODULE

19. MULTI-METER PANEL
20. MULTI-METER ASSEMBLY
21. SIDE DEFROSTER GRILL
22. INSTRUMENT PANEL ASSEMBLY

MT9149700029000X

Fig. 17   Exploded view of instrument panel. Montero Sport

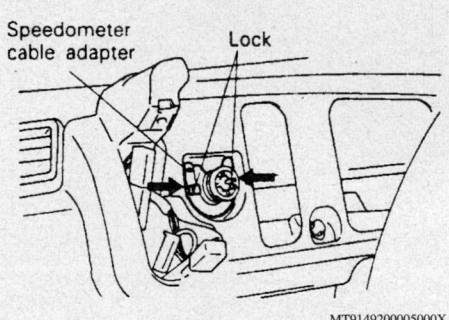

MT9149200005000X

Fig. 18   Speedometer cable adapter removal. Montero & Montero Sport

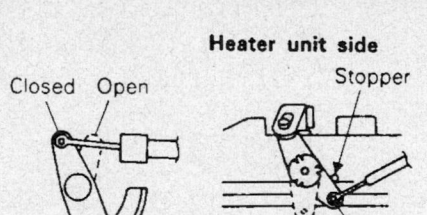

MT9149200006000X

Fig. 19   Ventilation control wire installation. Montero & Montero Sport

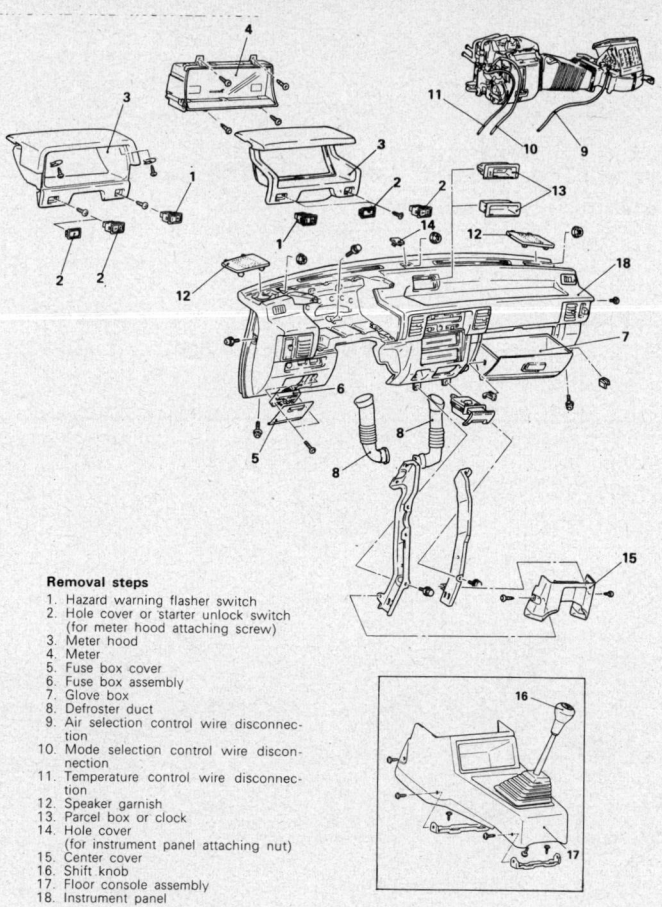

Removal steps
1. Hazard warning flasher switch
2. Hole cover or starter unlock switch (for meter hood attaching screw)
3. Meter hood
4. Meter
5. Fuse box cover
6. Fuse box assembly
7. Glove box
8. Defroster duct
9. Air selection control wire disconnection
10. Mode selection control wire disconnection
11. Temperature control wire disconnection
12. Speaker garnish
13. Parcel box or clock
14. Hole cover (for instrument panel attaching nut)
15. Center cover
16. Shift knob
17. Floor console assembly
18. Instrument panel

MT9149100008000X

Fig. 20 Exploded view of instrument panel. Pickup

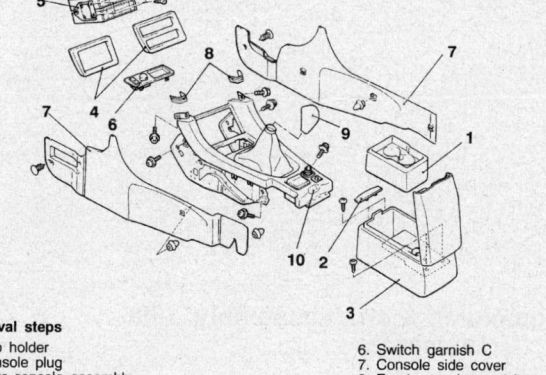

Removal steps
1. Cup holder
2. Console plug
3. Rear console assembly
4. Radio panel
5. Radio
6. Switch garnish C
7. Console side cover
8. Front console garnish
9. Manual transaxle shift lever knob
10. Front console assembly

MT9149100015000X

Fig. 22 Exploded view of console assembly. 3000GT

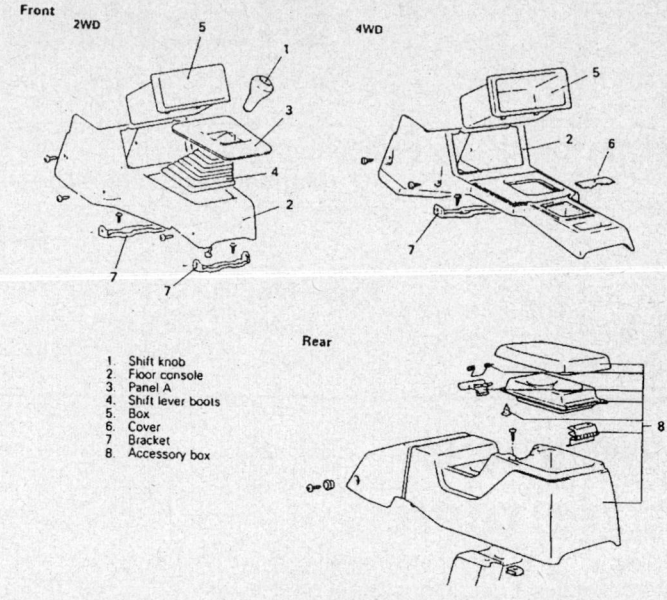

1. Shift knob
2. Floor console
3. Panel A
4. Shift lever boots
5. Box
6. Cover
7. Bracket
8. Accessory box

MT9149100009000X

Fig. 21 Exploded view of console assembly. Pickup

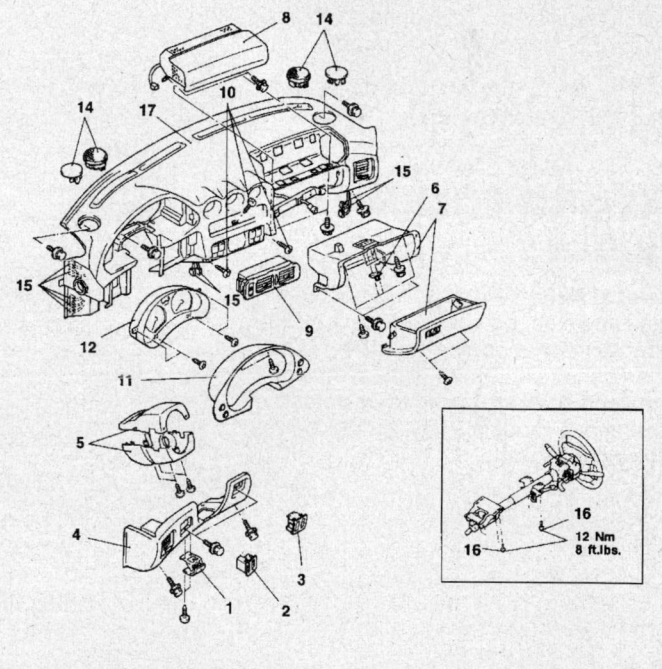

1. Hood lock release handle
2. Rheostat
3. Switch garnish B
4. Knee protector assembly
5. Column cover
6. Glove box striker
7. Glove box and cross pipe cover
8. Passenger seat air bag module
9. Center air outlet assembly
10. Heater control assembly installation screws
11. Meter bezel
12. Combination meter
14. Speaker or plug
15. Harness connector
16. Steering shaft mounting bolts
17. Instrument panel assembly

MT9149700030000X

Fig. 23 Exploded view of instrument panel. 3000GT

Steering Columns

NOTE: On Air Bag Equipped Models, Refer To "Air Bag System Precautions" Located In The Front Of This Manual For System Disarming & Arming Procedures.

INDEX

PRECAUTIONS

AIR BAG SYSTEMS

Refer to "Air Bag System Precautions" in the front of this manual for system disarming and arming procedures.

BATTERY GROUND CABLE

Prior to service, disconnect battery ground cable and isolate as required.

STEERING COLUMN SERVICE

Refer to **Figs. 1 through 11** for steering column and steering shaft service. On Galant and Mirage models, the steering column and shaft cannot be disassembled. If column and shaft are found to be defective on the above models, they should be replaced as an assembly.

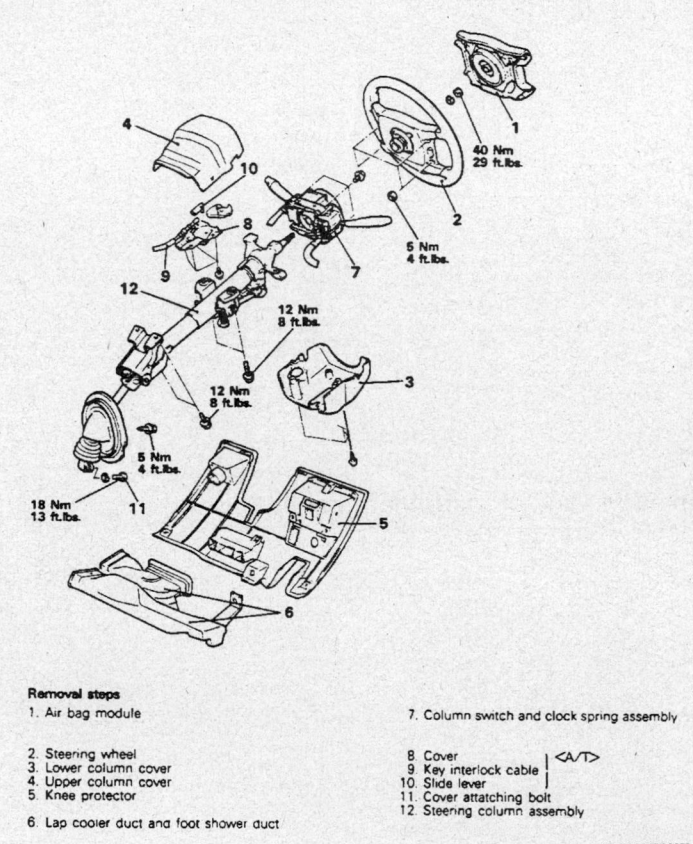

Removal steps

1. Air bag module
2. Steering wheel
3. Lower column cover
4. Upper column cover
5. Knee protector
6. Lap cooler duct and foot shower duct
7. Column switch and clock spring assembly
8. Cover   \<A/T\>
9. Key interlock cable
10. Slide lever
11. Cover attaching bolt
12. Steering column assembly

MT6049100002000X

Fig. 1   Steering column & shaft assembly. 1996 Diamante

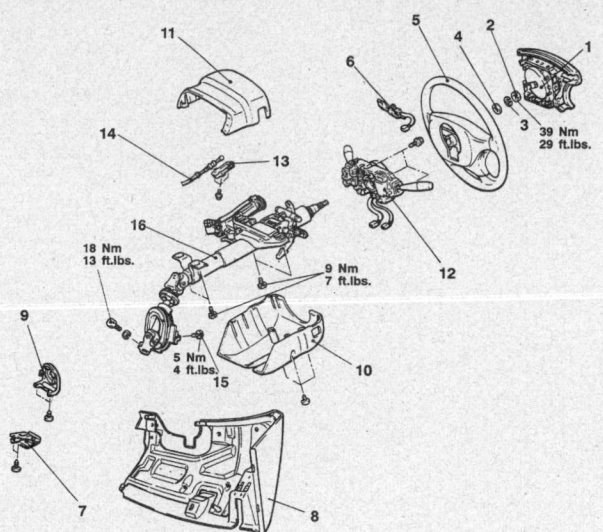

REMOVAL STEPS

1. AIR BAG MODULE
2. STEERING WHEEL RETAINING NUT
3. SPRING WASHER
4. FLAT WASHER
5. STEERING WHEEL
6. CRUISE CONTROL SWITCH
7. LOCK RELEASE HANDLE
8. INSTRUMENT PANEL LOWER COVER
9. KEY CYLINDER PANEL
10. LOWER COLUMN COVER
11. UPPER COLUMN COVER
12. CLOCK SPRING AND COLUMN SWITCH ASSEMBLY (REFER TO GROUP 52B)
13. COVER
14. KEY INTERLOCK CABLE (SHIFT LOCK)
15. RETAINER MOUNTING BOLT
16. STEERING COLUMN ASSEMBLY

MT6049900021000X

Fig. 2   Steering column & shaft assembly. 1997–99 Diamante

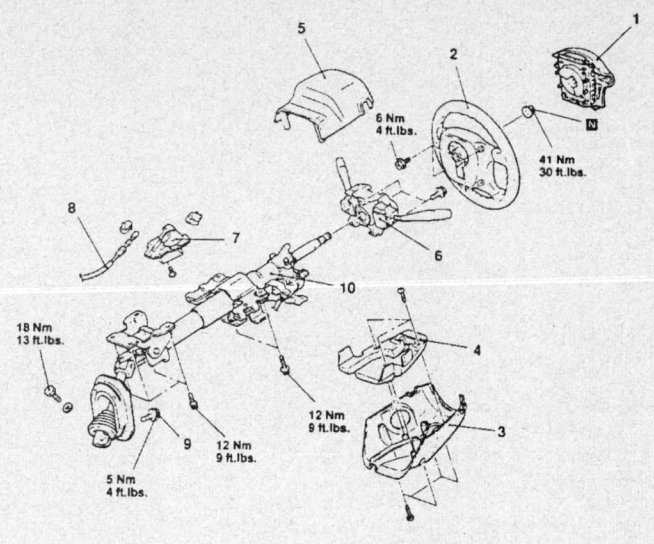

Removal steps

1. Air bag module
2. Steering wheel
3. Lower column cover
4. Column pad
5. Upper column cover
6. Clock spring and column switch assembly
7. Cover
8. Key interlock cable
9. Retainer attachment bolt
10. Steering column assembly

MT6049500018000X

Fig. 3   Steering column & shaft assembly. Eclipse

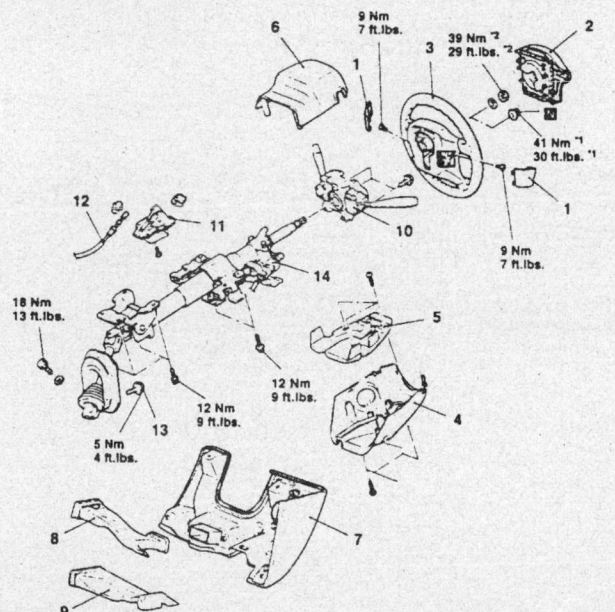

Removal steps

1. Steering wheel lower cover
2. Air bag module
3. Steering wheel
4. Lower column cover
5. Column pad
6. Upper column cover
7. Instrument under cover
8. Lap cooler duct
9. Foot shower duct
10. Clock spring and column switch assembly
11. Cover   <A/T>
12. Key interlock cable
13. Retainer attachment bolt
14. Steering column assembly

NOTE
*1: Case of self locking nut
*2: Case of nut and spring washer

MT6049400010000X

Fig. 4   Steering column & shaft assembly. 1996–98 Galant

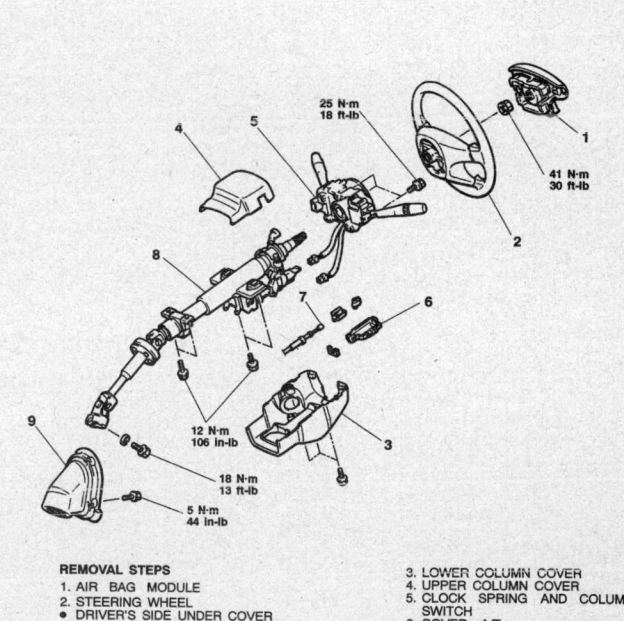

REMOVAL STEPS

1. AIR BAG MODULE
2. STEERING WHEEL
• DRIVER'S SIDE UNDER COVER
3. LOWER COLUMN COVER
4. UPPER COLUMN COVER
5. CLOCK SPRING AND COLUMN SWITCH
6. COVER <A/T>
7. KEY INTERLOCK CABLE <A/T>
8. STEERING SHAFT ASSEMBLY
9. STEERING COVER ASSEMBLY

Required Special Tool:
MB990803: Steering Wheel Puller

MT6049900022000X

Fig. 5   Steering column & shaft assembly. 1999 Galant

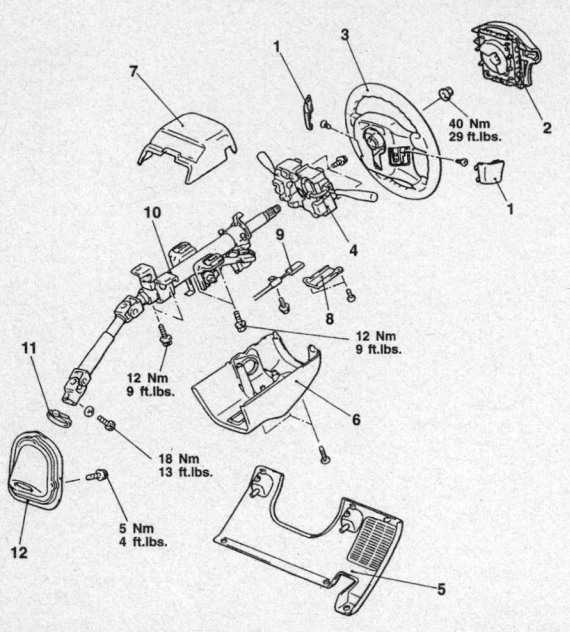

Removal steps
1. Cover
2. Air bag module
3. Steering wheel
4. Column switch assembly
5. Knee protector
6. Lower column cover
7. Upper column cover
8. Cover <A/T>
9. Connection for key interlock cable <A/T>
10. Steering column assembly
11. Band
12. Steering cover

MT6049400013000X

Fig. 6   Steering column & shaft assembly. 1996 Mirage

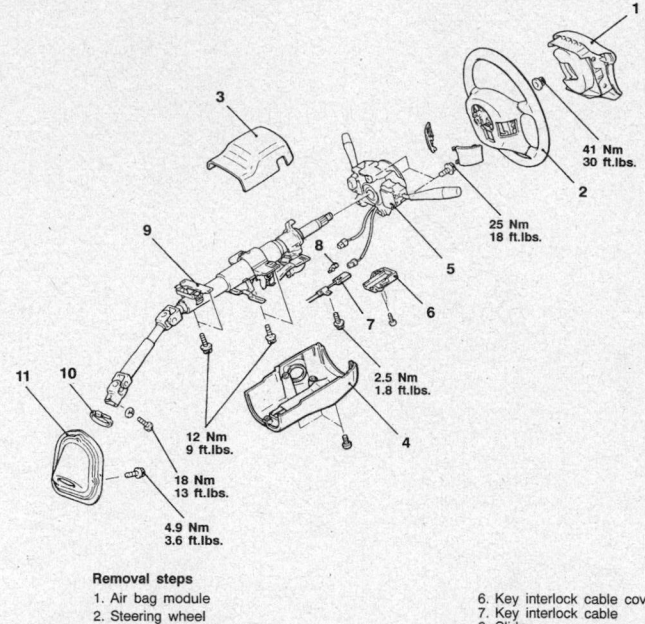

Removal steps
1. Air bag module
2. Steering wheel
3. Upper column cover
4. Lower column cover
5. Clock spring and column switch
6. Key interlock cable cover
7. Key interlock cable
8. Slider
9. Steering shaft assembly
10. Band
11. Steering cover assembly

MT6049900023000X

Fig. 7   Steering column & shaft assembly. 1997–99 Mirage

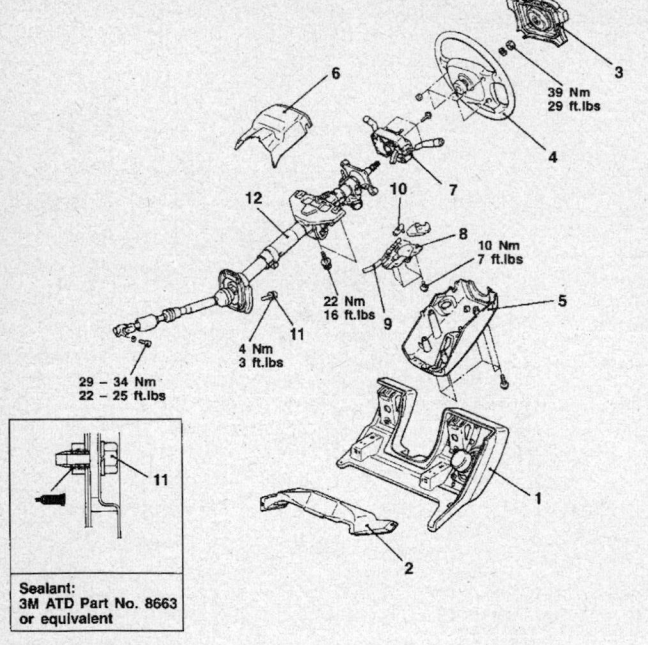

Sealant:
3M ATD Part No. 8663
or equivalent

Removal steps
1. Knee protector
2. Foot shower duct
3. Air bag module
4. Steering wheel
5. Lower column cover
6. Upper column cover
7. Column switch
8. Cover <A/T>
9. Key interlock cable <A/T>
10. Slide lever <A/T>
11. Cover attaching bolt
12. Steering column and shaft assembly

MT6049200014000A

Fig. 8   Steering column & shaft assembly. Montero

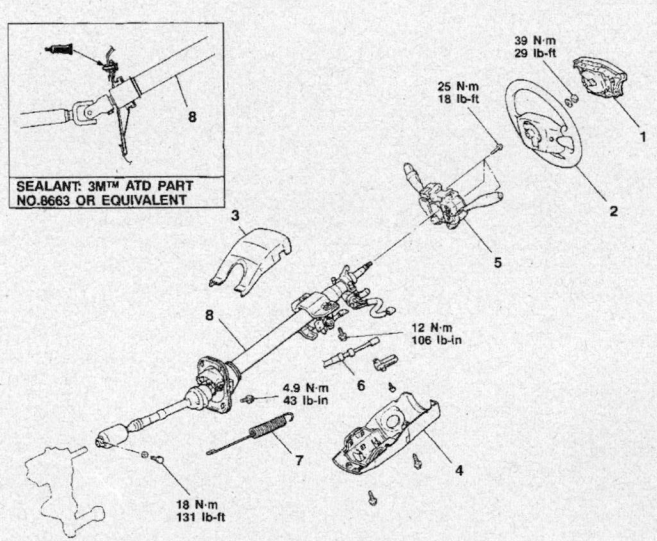

SEALANT: 3M™ ATD PART NO. 8663 OR EQUIVALENT

1. AIR BAG MODULE
2. STEERING WHEEL
   • KNEE PROTECTOR ASSEMBLY
3. UPPER COLUMN COVER ASSEMBLY
4. LOWER COLUMN COVER ASSEMBLY
5. CLOCK SPRING AND COLUMN SWITCH
6. KEY INTERLOCK CABLE <A/T>
7. BRAKE PEDAL RETURN SPRING
8. STEERING COLUMN ASSEMBLY

MT6049700020000X

Fig. 9   Steering column & shaft assembly. Montero Sport

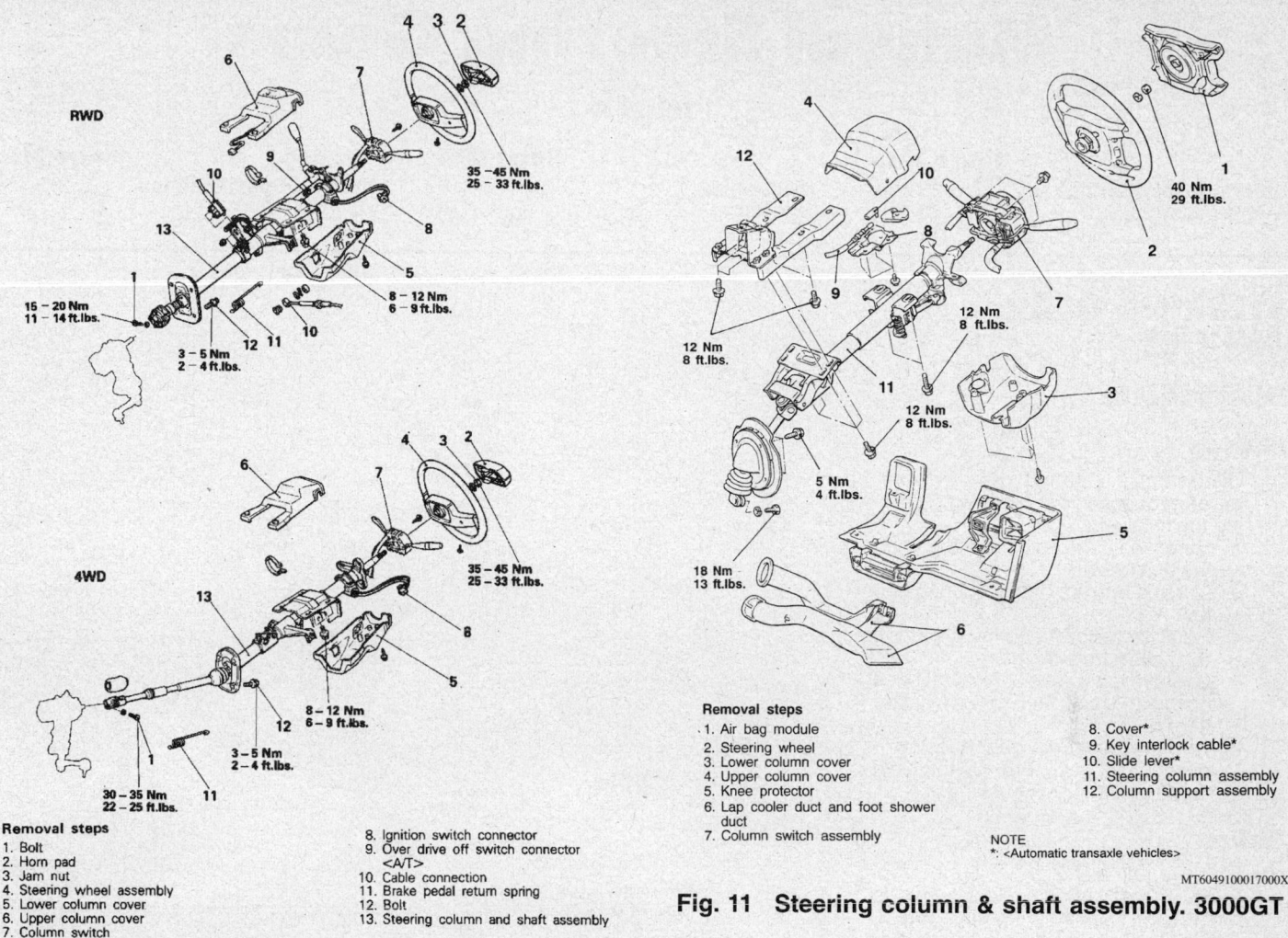

RWD

35 – 45 Nm
25 – 33 ft.lbs.

8 – 12 Nm
6 – 9 ft.lbs.

15 – 20 Nm
11 – 14 ft.lbs.

3 – 5 Nm
2 – 4 ft.lbs.

4WD

35 – 45 Nm
25 – 33 ft.lbs.

8 – 12 Nm
6 – 9 ft.lbs.

3 – 5 Nm
2 – 4 ft.lbs.

30 – 35 Nm
22 – 25 ft.lbs.

Removal steps

1. Bolt
2. Horn pad
3. Jam nut
4. Steering wheel assembly
5. Lower column cover
6. Upper column cover
7. Column switch

8. Ignition switch connector
9. Over drive off switch connector <A/T>
10. Cable connection
11. Brake pedal return spring
12. Bolt
13. Steering column and shaft assembly

MT6049100015000X

Fig. 10   Steering column & shaft assembly. Pickup

40 Nm
29 ft.lbs.

12 Nm
8 ft.lbs.

12 Nm
8 ft.lbs.

12 Nm
8 ft.lbs.

5 Nm
4 ft.lbs.

18 Nm
13 ft.lbs.

Removal steps

1. Air bag module
2. Steering wheel
3. Lower column cover
4. Upper column cover
5. Knee protector
6. Lap cooler duct and foot shower duct
7. Column switch assembly

8. Cover*
9. Key interlock cable*
10. Slide lever*
11. Steering column assembly
12. Column support assembly

NOTE
*: <Automatic transaxle vehicles>

MT6049100017000X

Fig. 11   Steering column & shaft assembly. 3000GT

Manual Steering Gears

INDEX

STEERING GEAR SERVICE

DISASSEMBLE

Mirage

1. Disassemble steering gear in numbered sequence as shown, **Fig. 1**, noting the following:
   a. Remove tie rod end snap ring, then the dust cover.
   b. Cut and remove band securing bellow.
   c. Remove bellow securing clip, then the bellow from tie rod.
   d. Unstake tab washer which attaches tie rod and rack, then remove tie rod from rack.
   e. Remove rack from gear housing in direction shown, **Fig. 2,** to avoid damaging gearbox bushing.

Pickup

1. Remove jam nut; then, using tool No. MB990809-01, or equivalent, separate pitman arm from steering gear, **Fig. 3.** Drain lubricant.
2. Remove dust cover attaching bolts, then the dust cover.
3. Remove breather plug.
4. Remove adjusting cover locknut, then the attaching bolts with washers.
5. Remove side cover, then the packing.
6. Remove cross shaft, then the adjusting cover cap.
7. Remove adjusting cover locknut, then the adjusting cover.
8. Remove end cover retaining bolts, then the end cover.
9. Remove adjusting shims and retain to facilitate assembly.
10. Remove bearing (16), then the mainshaft assembly.
11. Remove second bearing (18), then the oil seal (19).
12. Separate oil seal (20) from gearbox housing.

INSPECTION

Mirage

1. Check rack support for uneven wear.
2. Check rack support spring for deterioration.
3. Check cushion rubber for cracking.
4. Check rack and pinion for worn or damaged tooth surfaces.
5. Check ball bearings and needle roller bearings for uneven rotation.
6. Check ball joint dust cover for cracks.

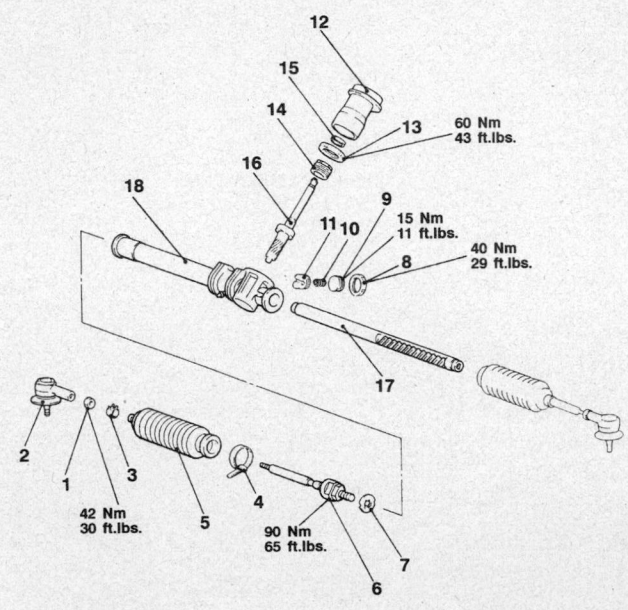

Disassembly steps

1. Tie-rod end lock nut	10. Rack support spring
2. Tie-rod end	11. Rack support
3. Bellows clip	12. Joint cover
4. Bellows band	13. Locking nut
5. Bellows	14. Top cover
6. Tie-rod	15. Oil seal
7. Tab washer	16. Pinion
● Total pinion torque adjustment	17. Rack
8. Locking nut	18. Gear housing
9. Rack support cover	

MT6039100023000X

Fig. 1   Exploded view of manual steering gear. Mirage

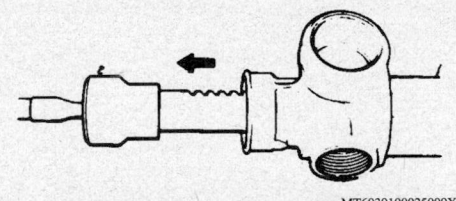

MT6039100025000X

Fig. 2   Rack removal from gear housing. Mirage

Pickup

1. Check ball nut for smooth rotation and endplay.
2. Check bearing for seizure and discoloration, then for a rough rolling surface.
3. Check oil seal for cracks and damage.
4. Check mainshaft and cross shaft tooth surfaces for wear and damage.
5. Check pitman arm for wear and damage.

ASSEMBLE

Mirage

1. Reverse disassembly procedure in **Fig. 1** to assemble, noting the following:
   a. Apply a coat of grease to surface of rack support that contacts the rack, then install rack support to the rack.
   b. Fill inner side of rack support spring with grease, then install rack support spring to rack housing.
   c. Install rubber cushion to rack support cover.
   d. Apply 3M ATD No. 8663 or equivalent sealant to threaded part of rack support cover, then install rack support cover to rack housing.
2. Adjust total pinion and tighten as follows:
   a. Position rack at its center then **torque** rack support cover to 11 ft. lbs.

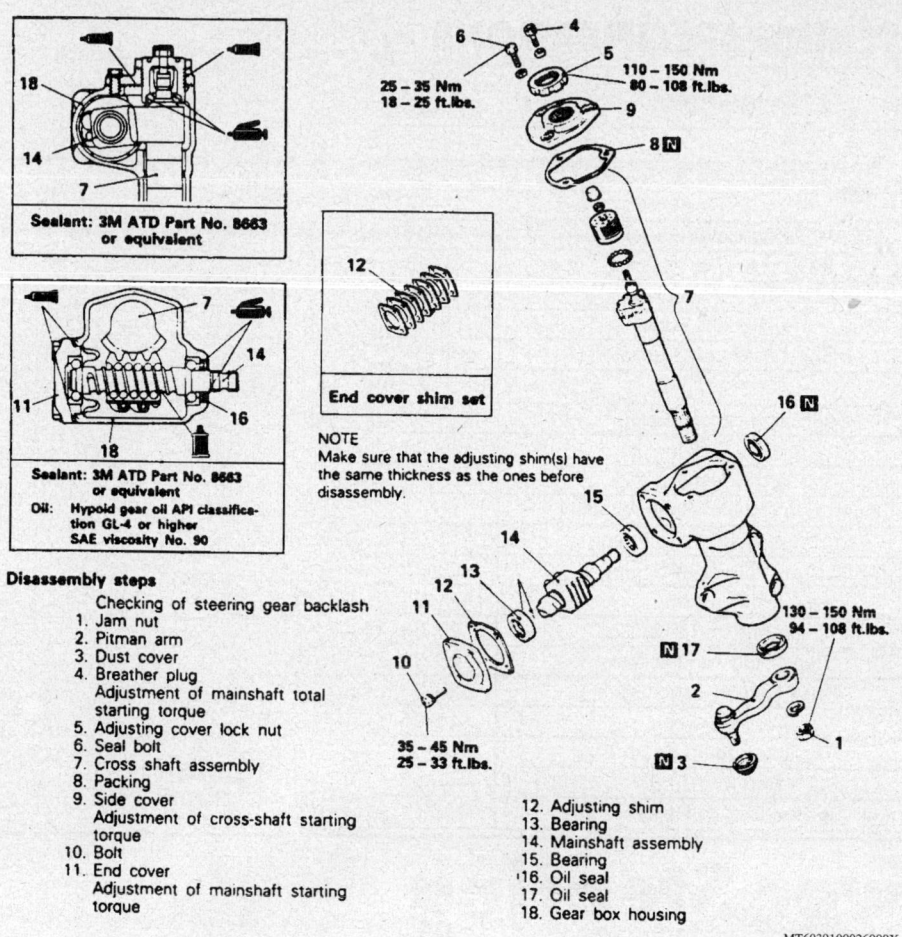

Sealant: 3M ATD Part No. 8663 or equivalent

Sealant: 3M ATD Part No. 8663 or equivalent
Oil: Hypoid gear oil API classification GL-4 or higher SAE viscosity No. 90

25 – 35 Nm
18 – 25 ft.lbs.

110 – 150 Nm
80 – 108 ft.lbs.

End cover shim set

NOTE
Make sure that the adjusting shim(s) have the same thickness as the ones before disassembly.

35 – 45 Nm
25 – 33 ft.lbs.

130 – 150 Nm
94 – 108 ft.lbs.

Disassembly steps

Checking of steering gear backlash
1. Jam nut
2. Pitman arm
3. Dust cover
4. Breather plug
   Adjustment of mainshaft total starting torque
5. Adjusting cover lock nut
6. Seal bolt
7. Cross shaft assembly
8. Packing
9. Side cover
   Adjustment of cross-shaft starting torque
10. Bolt
11. End cover
    Adjustment of mainshaft starting torque

12. Adjusting shim
13. Bearing
14. Mainshaft assembly
15. Bearing
16. Oil seal
17. Oil seal
18. Gear box housing

Fig. 3 Exploded view of manual steering gear. Pickup

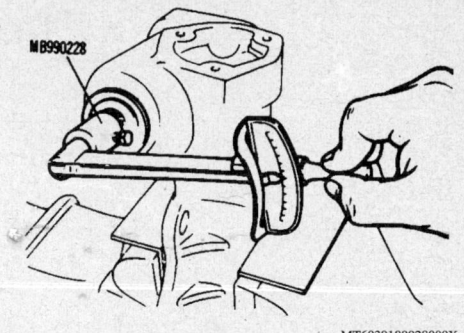

Fig. 4 Mainshaft preload measurement. Pickup

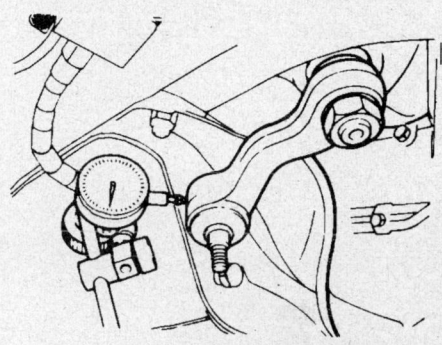

Fig. 5 Steering gear backlash measurement. Pickup

b. From neutral position, rotate pinion shaft clockwise one complete turn within 4–6 seconds using socket tool No. MB991006-01, or equivalent.

c. Loosen rack support cover 30–60° and adjust pinion **torque** to 5–11 inch lbs. from 0–90° and to 2–9 inch lbs. from 90° to rack stop.

d. If specified value cannot be reached, check rack support cover and components.

e. After adjustment, tighten support cover locknut.

Pickup

1. Adjust position of gear housing as to allow level installation of mainshaft. Press oil seals into housing using tool No. MB990925, or equivalent, then apply lubricant.

2. Apply lubricant to tooth and sliding surfaces of mainshaft and bearings, then install them into gear housing.

3. Install bearing (16).

4. Apply sealant to adjusting shims of same thickness as removed during disassembly, then install adjusting shims and end cover into gear housing and tighten attaching bolts. Measure mainshaft starting torque using tool No. MB990228-01, or equivalent, **Fig.**

4. Starting **torque** should be 3–5 inch lbs. If measured torque is not as specified, remove shims and add shims to reduce starting torque or remove shims to increase starting torque. Tighten attaching bolts to specifications.

5. Install adjusting cover, then apply sealant to base of threads on adjusting bolt. Temporarily tighten locknut with chamfered end facing downward. Place center portion of cross shaft in a vise, then measure starting torque. Starting **torque** should be 3.4–6.9 inch lbs. If measured torque is not as specified, adjust by rotating adjusting bolt as necessary.

6. Install cross shaft assembly into gear housing with mainshaft ball nut at center of gear housing, in a straight ahead position.

7. After adjustment, retain adjusting cover using tool No. MB990914, or equivalent, then **torque** locknut to 18–25 ft.lbs.

8. Apply sealant to component threads, except breather plug mounting hole. Apply grease to annular bearing of cross shaft, then temporarily screw in adjusting cover using tool No. MB990914, or equivalent.

9. Install adjusting cover locknut using

tool Nos. MB991149 and MB990914, or equivalents.

10. Adjust mainshaft total starting torque as follows:
    a. Rotate cross shaft approximately 36° to ensure proper fit between teeth, then with mainshaft in Neutral position (straight ahead), measure combined starting torque of mainshaft using tool No. MB990228-01, or equivalent.
    b. Starting **torque** should be 7.7–8.6 inch lbs.
    c. If starting torque is not as specified, rotate adjusting cover in or out as necessary.

11. Install adjusting cover locknut, then **torque** to 80–108 ft. lbs.

12. Install breather plug, then the dust cover.

13. Install pitman arm and align mating marks. Install jam nut and **torque** to 94–108 ft. lbs.

14. Adjust steering gear backlash with mainshaft, cross shaft and pitman arm in neutral position as follows:
    a. Inject a small amount of gear oil through the breather plug hole to lubricate bearings and shaft gear teeth.
    b. Move pitman arm 3–5 times in each direction to ensure is properly meshed with gear teeth.
    c. Using a dial indicator, **Fig. 5**, measure steering gear backlash at the pitman arm. If reading exceeds .02 inch, replace mainshaft.

TIGHTENING SPECIFICATIONS

Year	Component	Torque, Ft. Lbs.
MIRAGE		
1996–99	Gearbox To Body	43–58
	Joint To Gearbox	11–17
	Rack Support Cover Locking Nut	36–51
	Tie Rod End To Knuckle	11–25
	Tie Rod End Locknut	25–36
	Tie Rod To Rack	58–72
	Top Cover Locking Nut	36–51
PICKUP		
1996	Adjusting Cover Locknut	80–108
	End Cover	25–33
	Gearbox Installation	25–40
	Gearbox To Column Shaft Assembly	11–14
	Idler Arm Support To Frame	25–29
	Idler Arm To Idler Arm Support	29–43
	Pitman Arm	94–108
	Pitman Arm To Relay Rod	25–33
	Relay Rod To Idler Arm	25–33
	Relay Rod To Pitman Arm	25–33
	Side Cover	18–25
	Tie Rod End To Knuckle	25–33
	Tie Rod End To Pipe	47–58
	Tie Rod End To Relay Rod	33

Power Steering

NOTE: On Air Bag Equipped Models, Refer To "Air Bag System Precautions" Located In The Front Of This Manual For System Disarming & Arming Procedures.

NOTE: For Procedures Not Found In This Section, Refer To The "Four Wheel Steering" Section.

INDEX

POWER STEERING PRESSURE SPECIFICATIONS

Year	Model	Pump Pressure, psi		Retention Pressure, psi
		Gauge Valve Closed①	Gauge Valve Open①	
1996	Diamante	1067–1166	114–142	1067–1166
	Eclipse	1209–1309	114–142	1209–1309
	Galant	1209–1309	114–142	1209–1309
	Mirage	1351–1451	114–142	1351–1451
	Montero	②	114–142	②
	Pickup	1067–1166	114–142	1067–1166
	3000GT	1067–1166	114–142	1067–1166
1997	Diamante	1676	114–142	1676
	Eclipse & Eclipse Spyder	1209–1309	114–142	1209–1309
	Galant	1209–1309	114–142	1209–1309
	Mirage	1422	28–71	1422
	Montero	1205–1305	114–142	1205–1305
	Montero Sport	1204–1305	116–145	1204–1305
	3000GT	1067–1166	114–142	1067–1166
1998	Diamante	1676	114–142	1676
	Eclipse & Eclipse Spyder	1209–1309	114–142	1209–1309
	Galant	1209–1309	114–142	1209–1309
	Mirage	1422	28–71	1422
	Montero	1205–1305	114–142	1205–1305
	Montero Sport	1204–1305	116–145	1204–1305
	3000GT	1067–1166	114–142	1067–1166
1999	Diamante	1676	114–142	1676
	Eclipse & Eclipse Spyder	1209–1309	114–142	1209–1309
	Galant	1276	116–145	1276
	Mirage	1422	28–71	1422
	Montero	1205–1305	114–142	1205–1305
	Montero Sport	1204–1305	114–142	1204–1305
	3000GT	1067–1166	114–142	1067–1166

① — With special tool installed; refer to text.

② — 3.0L 12-valve engine, 1067–1166 psi; 3.0L 24-valve & 3.5L engines, 1205–1305 psi.

PRECAUTIONS

AIR BAG SYSTEMS

Refer to "Air Bag System Precautions" in the front of this manual for system disarming and arming procedures.

BATTERY GROUND CABLE

Prior to service, disconnect battery ground cable and isolate as required.

MAINTENANCE

FLUID CHANGE

1. Raise and support vehicle.
2. Disconnect return hose.
3. Connect a vinyl hose to return hose to drain oil into a suitable container.
4. Disconnect ignition coil high tension cable.
5. Rotate engine using starter motor and turn steering wheel from stop to stop to drain fluid from system. **Do not crank engine longer than ten seconds at a time.**
6. Connect return hose, fill reservoir with fluid and bleed air from system as outlined under "Power Steering System Service."

TROUBLESHOOTING

Refer to **Figs. 1 through 2** for troubleshooting procedures.

DIAGNOSIS & TESTING

OIL PUMP PRESSURE TESTS

EXCEPT PICKUP

The following procedures require the use of oil pressure gauge assembly tool No. MB990662, or equivalent. All models except 1996 Eclipse with 2.0L nonturbocharged engine require power steering oil pressure gauge pump side adapter tool No. MB990993-01 and power steering oil pressure gauge hose side adapter tool No. MB990994-01, or equivalents; 1996 Eclipse models equipped with 2.0L nonturbocharged engine require power steering oil pressure gauge pump side adapter tool No. MB991548 and power steering oil pressure gauge hose side adapter tool No. MB991549, or equivalents.

Oil Pump Relief Pressure Inspection

1. Disconnect pressure hose from oil pump, then connect special tools as shown, **Fig. 3.**
2. Bleed air from system as outlined under "Power Steering System Service," then turn steering wheel from stop to stop until fluid temperature in reservoir is 122–140°F.
3. Start engine and run at 900–1100 RPM.
4. Fully close shutoff valve and ensure oil pump relief pressure is as specified in "Power Steering Pressure Specifications" chart. **Do not leave shutoff valve closed for more than ten seconds, as damage or injury may occur.**
5. If pressure is not within specified range, service oil pump as outlined under "Power Steering System Service."

Symptom	Probable cause	Remedy
Excessive play of steering wheel	Loose rack support cover	Retighten
	Loose steering gear mounting bolts	Retighten
	Loose or worn stud of tie-rod end	Retighten or replace as necessary
Steering wheel operation is hard (Improper power assist)	Drive belt slippage	Check
	Damaged drive belt	Replace
	Low fluid level	Refill
	Air in the fluid	Bleed
	Twisted or damaged hoses	Correct the routing or replace
	Improper oil pump pressure	Repair or replace oil pump
	Sticky flow control valve	Replace
	Excessive internal oil pump leakage	Replace damaged parts
	Excessive oil leaks from rack & pinion in gear box	Replace damaged parts
	Bent or damaged gear box or valve body seal ring	Replace ·

MT6029100002010X

Fig. 1   Troubleshooting chart (Part 1 of 2). Mirage

Symptom	Probable cause	Remedy
Excessive play of steering wheel	Excessive play in steering gear box	Repair
	Loose steering gear mounting bolts	Retighten
	Loose or worn stud of tie rod end	Retighten or replace as necessary
Steering wheel operation is hard (insufficient power assist)	Loose belt	Adjust the belt tension
	Damaged belt	Replace the belt
	Low fluid level	Refill with fluid
	Air in fluid line	Bleed the system
	Twisted or damage hoses	Correct the hose routing or replace the hoses
	Fluid leakage	Repair or replace
	Malfunction of gear box	Check and replace the gear box if necessary
	Malfunction of oil pump	Check the oil pump pressure and re-pair oil pump
Rattling noise	Loose installation of oil pump or gear box	Retighten the oil pump or gear box
	Loose oil pump pulley nut	Retighten the oil pump pulley nut
	Interference around column or between pressure hose and other parts	Correct or replace the pressure hose and the parts around the column
	Abnormal noise inside of gear box and oil pump	Replace the gear box or oil pump

MT6029100003010X

Fig. 2   Troubleshooting chart (Part 1 of 2). Montero, Montero Sport & Pickup

6. Remove special tools and bleed system as outlined under "System Service."

No Load Pressure Inspection

1. Disconnect pressure hose from oil pump then connect special tools as shown, **Fig. 3.**
2. Bleed air from system as outlined under "Power Steering System Service," then turn steering wheel from stop to stop until fluid temperature in reservoir is 122–140°F.
3. Start engine and run at 900–1100 RPM.
4. Check hydraulic pressure and ensure it is as specified in the "Power Steering Pressure Specifications" chart.
5. If pressure is not within specification, probable causes include a clogged pressure line or faulty steering gearbox. Check and repair as necessary.
6. Remove special tools and bleed system as outlined under "Power Steering System Service."

Steering Gear Retention Hydraulic Pressure Inspection

1. Disconnect pressure hose from oil pump then connect special tools as shown, **Fig. 3.**

2. Bleed air from system as outlined under "Power Steering System Service," then turn steering wheel from stop to stop until fluid temperature in reservoir is 122–140°F.
3. Start engine and run at 900–1100 RPM.
4. Fully close, then fully open shutoff valve.
5. Turn steering wheel from stop to stop,

Symptom	Probable cause	Remedy
Steering wheel does not return properly	Excessive turning resistance of tie-rod ball joint	Replace
	Excessively tightened rack support cover	Adjust
	Rough turning of inner tie-rod and/or ball joint	Replace
	Worn steering shaft joint and/or body grommet	Correct or replace
	Bent rack	Replace
	Damaged pinion bearing	Replace
	Twisted or damaged hoses	Reroute or replace
	Damaged flow control valve	Replace
	Damaged oil pump input shaft bearing	Replace
Noise	Hissing Noise in Steering Gear — There is some noise in all power steering systems. One of the most common is a hissing sound when the steering wheel is turned and the car is not moving. This noise will be most evident when turning the wheel while the brakes are applied. There is no relationship between this noise and steering performance. Do not replace the valve unless the "hissing" noise is extremely objectionable. A replacement valve will also have a slight noise, and is not always a cure for the condition.	
Rattling or chucking noise in rack & pinion	Pressure hose touching other parts of vehicle	Reroute
	Loose gear box mounting bolts	Retighten
	Loose tie-rod end ball joint	Retighten
	Worn tie-rod end ball joint	Replace
Groaning noise in oil pump	Low fluid level	Refill
	Air in the fluid	Bleed
	Loose pump mounting bolts	Retighten

MT6029100002020X

Fig. 1   Troubleshooting chart (Part 2 of 2). Mirage

Symptom	Probable cause	Remedy
Shrill noise	Air sucked into oil pump	Check the oil level and hose clips, bleed the system or replace the oil pump
	Oil pump seizure	Replace the oil pump
Squealing noise	Loose belt	Adjust the belt deflection
	Oil pump seizure	Replace the oil pump
Hissing noise	Air sucked into oil pump	Check the oil level and hose clips, bleed the system
	Damage to the olive of the gear box port section	Replace the gear box
	Malfunction of return hose	Replace the hose
Whistling noise	Malfunction of gear box port section	Replace the gear box
Droning noise	Loose mounting bolt on oil pump or oil pump bracket	Retighten the pump bracket or pump mounting bolt
	Poor condition of oil pump body*	Replace the oil pump
Squeaking noise	Malfunction of steering stopper contact	Check and adjust the steering stopper
	Interference of wheel with vehicle body	Adjust the steering angle
	Malfunction of gear box	Replace the gear box
Vibration**	Air suction	Bleed the system
	Malfunction of gear box	Replace the gear box
Oil leakage from hose connection	Improperly tightened flare nut Incorrectly inserted hose Improperly clamped hose	Check, and repair or replace
Oil leakage from hose assembly	Damaged or clogged hose Hose connector malfunction	Replace
Oil leakage from reservoir	Improperly welded pipe	Weld the pipes or replace
	Overflow	Bleed the system or adjust the oil level
Oil leakage from oil pump	Malfunction oil pump housing	Replace the oil pump
	Malfunction of O-ring and/or oil seal	Replace the O-ring and oil seal
Oil leakage from gear box	Malfunction of gear box housing (including leakage from air hole)	Replace the gear box
	Malfunction of O-ring and/or oil seal	Replace the O-ring and oil seal

NOTE
* A slight "beat noise" is produced by the oil pump; this is not a malfunction. (This noise occurs particularly when a stationary steering effort is made.)
** A slight vibration may be felt when the stationary steering effort is made due to the condition of the road surface. To check whether the vibration actually exists or not, test-drive the vehicle on a dry concrete or asphalt surface. Moreover, a very slight amount of vibration is not a malfunction.

MT6029100003020X

Fig. 2   Troubleshooting chart (Part 2 of 2). Montero, Montero Sport & Pickup

then ensure retention pressure is as specified in "Power Steering Pressure Specifications " chart.
6. If pressure is not as specified, service steering gearbox and repeat steps for establishing correct retention pressure.
7. Remove special tools and bleed system.

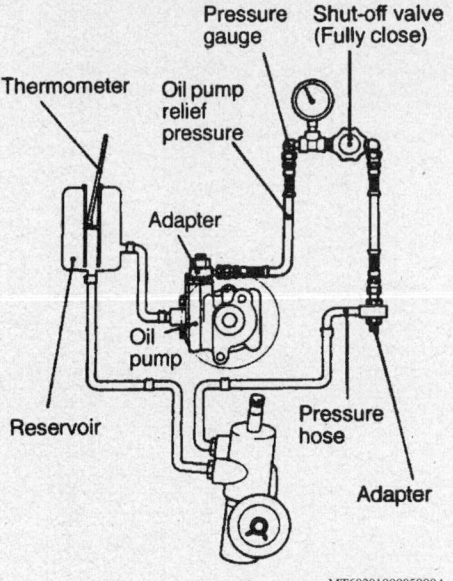

Fig. 3 Pressure gauge installation. Except Pickup

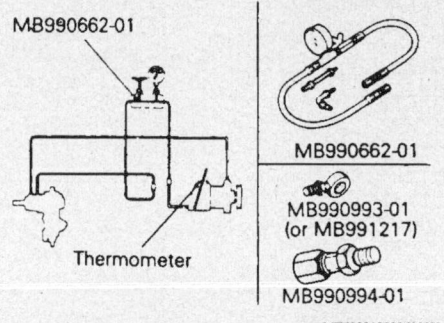

Fig. 4 Pressure gauge installation. Pickup

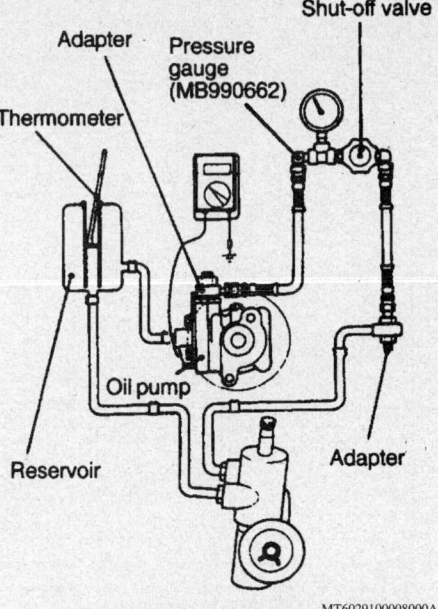

Fig. 5 Pressure gauge & ohmmeter installation

PICKUP

1. Disconnect pressure hose from pump and install special tools as shown, **Fig. 4.**
2. Bleed power steering system as outlined under "Power Steering System Service."
3. Start engine and raise engine temperature to 131°F.
4. Raise engine idle to 1000 RPM.
5. Close shutoff valve completely and read pressure. Pressure should read as specified in "Power Steering Pressure Specifications " chart. **Do not keep valve closed for more than ten seconds.**
6. If pressure is not within specification, replace pump.
7. Open shutoff valve completely and read pressure. Pressure should read as specified in "Power Steering Pressure Specifications" chart.
8. If pressure is not within specification, check for clogged hoses.
9. With the shutoff valve open, turn steering wheel from stop to stop and measure maximum oil pressure.
10. If pressure is not as specified in "Power Steering Pressure Specifications" chart, replace power steering gearbox.

OIL PRESSURE SWITCH TEST

The following procedures require the use of oil pressure gauge assembly tool No. MB990662, or equivalent. All models except 1996 Eclipse with 2.0L non-turbocharged engine require power steering oil pressure gauge pump side adapter tool No. MB990993-01 and power steering oil pressure gauge hose side adapter tool No. MB990994-01, or equivalents; 1996 Eclipse models equipped with 2.0L non-turbocharged engine require power steering oil pressure gauge pump side adapter tool No. MB991548 and power steering oil

pressure gauge hose side adapter tool No. MB991549, or equivalents.

1. Disconnect pressure hose from oil pump, then connect special tools as shown, **Fig. 5.**
2. Bleed air from system as outlined under "Power Steering System Service," then turn steering wheel from stop to stop until fluid temperature in reservoir is 122–140°F.
3. Start engine and allow to idle.
4. Disconnect connector of pressure switch and place an ohmmeter in position.
5. Gradually close shutoff valve and increase hydraulic pressure, then record switch activation pressure.
6. Pressure should be 213–284 psi when switch activates.
7. Gradually open shutoff valve and decrease hydraulic pressure and record pressure when switch deactivates.
8. Pressure should be 100–171 psi when switch deactivates.
9. Replace switch if not as specified.
10. Remove special tools and bleed system as outlined under "Power Steering System Service."

ELECTRONIC POWER STEERING (EPS) SYSTEM DIAGNOSIS

GALANT

Refer to **Fig. 6** for EPS system diagnostic procedures and **Fig. 7** for symptom charts.

DIAMANTE

Refer to **Fig. 8** for EPS system diagnostic procedures and **Fig. 9** for symptom charts.

ELECTRONIC POWER STEERING (EPS) SYSTEM COMPONENT TESTING

DIAMANTE & GALANT

EPS Solenoid Continuity Inspection

Check for continuity between solenoid valve terminals with the connector disconnected.

EPS Solenoid Current Inspection

1. If dummy speed oscillator tool No. MB991139, or equivalent, is to be used, proceed as follows:
   a. Set speed selection switch to zero mph.
   b. Turn cruise control main switch to off, then start engine and allow to idle.
   c. Set vehicle speed to 6–12 mph and ensure monitor light is flashing.
   d. If light remains illuminated and does not flash, move vehicle forward 1.0–1.3 feet.
2. If multi-use tester tool No. MB991341, or equivalent, is used, proceed as follows:
   a. Connect multi-use tester to self diagnostic connector and cigarette lighter.
   b. Input simulated vehicle speed, using vehicle speed signal function.
   c. If simulated vehicle speed cannot be input, a message will be displayed on testers display to move vehicle forward 1.0–1.31 feet.
3. Disconnect EPS solenoid valve wiring harness connector and connect a voltmeter between the two connectors as shown, **Fig. 10. Do not ground the solenoid terminal.**
4. Ensure solenoid current is .9–1.1 amps with vehicle at 0 mph, **Figs. 11 and 12.**
5. If current does not decrease as simulated speed increases, check EPS control.
6. **On models equipped with four speed automatic transaxle,** there will be a three speed hold caused by the fail safe function when multi-use tester is used. Therefore, disconnect the battery ground cable for ten seconds.

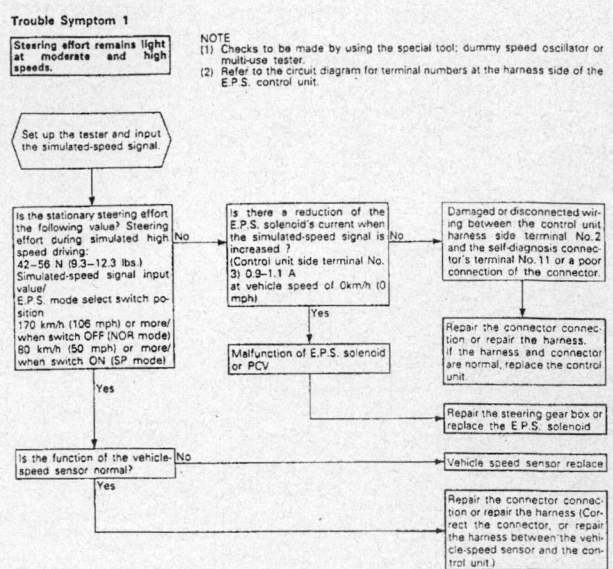

Symptom	Malfunction system	Check items
1. Steering effort remains light at moderate and high speeds	Control unit	Steering effort (full turn simulated by tester)
		E.P.S. solenoid current relative to vehicle speed change
	Steering gear box	E.P.S. solenoid activation
		P.C.V. activation
	Vehicle speed sensor	Vehicle speed sensor operation
2. Required steering effort is always great	Steering gear box	E.P.S. solenoid valve continuity
		E.P.S. solenoid activation
		P.C.V. activation
	Wiring harness or fuse	Fuse blown or not
		E.P.S. solenoid harness
	Control unit	*Fail-safe system activation
		Each harness continuity, and control unit power supply circuit
		Control unit activation
3. No change of the steering effort characteristic when the E.P.S. mode-select switch is used	E.P.S. mode-select switch	Continuity of E.P.S. mode-select switch
	Control unit	Each harness continuity, and control unit power supply circuit
		Control unit activation

NOTE
(1) For checking procedures for each problem, refer to the flow-chart type of troubleshooting guide
(2) To release the fail-safe system where indicated by the * symbol, set the ignition switch to the "ACC" or "LOCK" position, and then start the engine once again.
(3) P.C.V. = Pressure control valve

MT6029100009000X

Fig. 6   EPS diagnosis. Galant

Trouble Symptom 1

Steering effort remains light at moderate and high speeds.

NOTE
(1) Checks to be made by using the special tool: dummy speed oscillator or multi-use tester.
(2) Refer to the circuit diagram for terminal numbers at the harness side of the E.P.S. control unit.

MT6029100010010X

Fig. 7   EPS symptom charts (Part 1 of 3). Galant

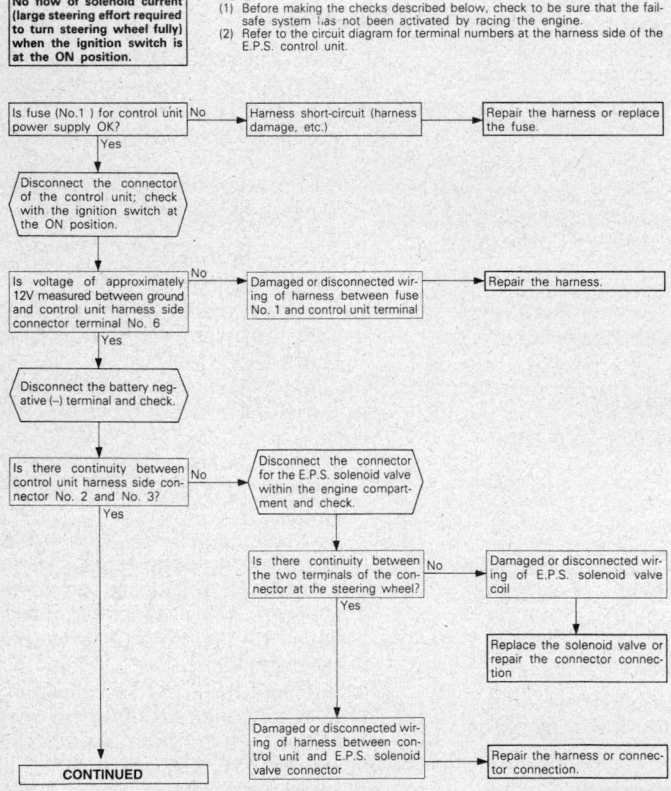

NOTE
(1) Before making the checks described below, check to be sure that the fail-safe system has not been activated by racing the engine.
(2) Refer to the circuit diagram for terminal numbers at the harness side of the E.P.S. control unit.

MT6029100010020X

Fig. 7   EPS symptom charts (Part 2 of 3). Galant

Never drive vehicle with the tester connected.

Mode Selector Switch Test

Refer to **Fig. 13** for a continuity test of the EPS mode selector switch.

POWER STEERING SYSTEM SERVICE

POWER STEERING SYSTEM BLEED

DIAMANTE, ECLIPSE, GALANT, MIRAGE & 3000GT

1. Raise and support vehicle.
2. Manually turn oil pump several complete turns.
3. Turn steering wheel from stop to stop.
4. Disconnect ignition coil high tension cable.
5. Rotate engine using starter motor and turn steering wheel from stop to stop for 15–20 seconds, refilling fluid in reservoir as necessary. **Only bleed system while cranking engine. Never bleed system with engine running.**
6. Connect ignition coil cable, then start engine and allow to idle.
7. Turn steering wheel from stop to stop until no air bubbles appear in fluid in reservoir.
8. Confirm fluid is not milky and fluid level does not change significantly when steering wheel is turned from stop to stop.
9. Ensure fluid level does not change by more than .2 inch when engine is turned off.
10. If fluid level change is more than specified, all air has not been bled from system. Leave steering system

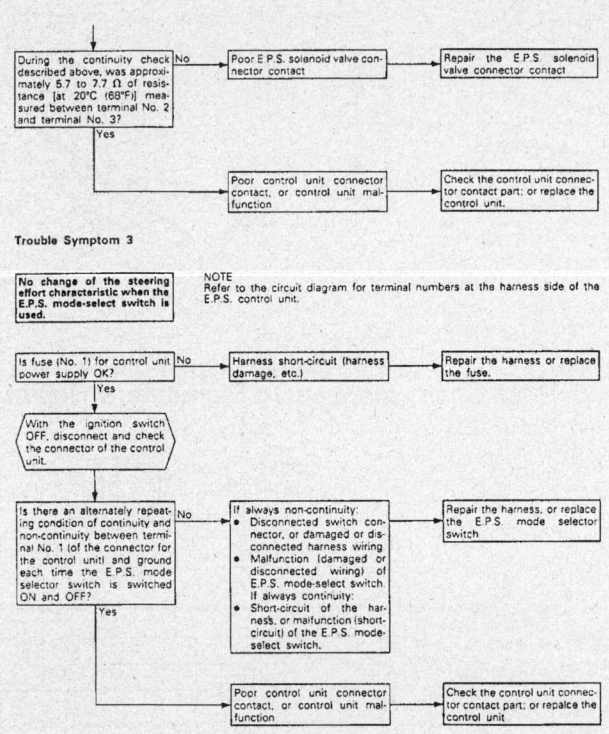

Trouble Symptom 3

Fig. 7   EPS symptom charts (Part 3 of 3). Galant

MT6029100010030X

Trouble symptom	Trouble area	Inspection item
Steering wheel movement is heavy. (When ignition key is turned to ON, no current flows through the solenoid.)	Steering gear and linkage	Solenoid valve continuity
		Solenoid or PCV operation is faulty.
	Harness or fuse	Blown fuse
		Remove the control unit connector and check the continuity in the solenoid harness (between terminals No. 2 and No. 3).
	Control unit	Turn the ignition key momentarily to ACC or LOCK and check if the fail-safe function is operating.
		Check for continuity in each harness and for abnormalities in the control unit power circuit.
While driving at medium or high speed, steering remains light.	Control unit	Use a tester to check the stationary steering effort.
		Check the solenoid current in relation to changes in vehicle speed.
	Steering gear and linkage	Solenoid or PCV operation.

NOTE
P.C.V. = Proportioning control valve

MT6029100011000X

Fig. 8   EPS diagnosis. Diamante

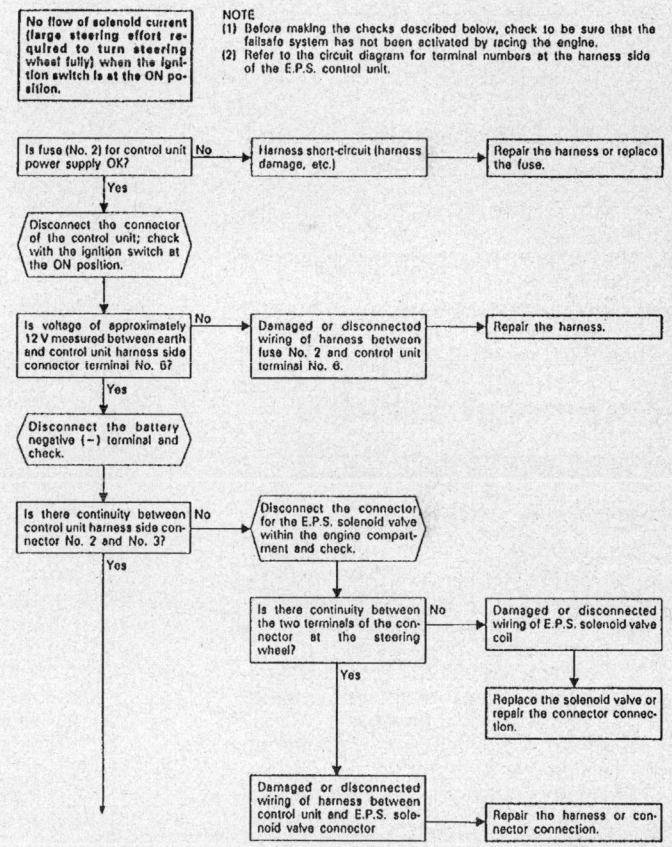

Fig. 9   EPS symptom charts (Part 2 of 3). Diamante

MT6029100012020X

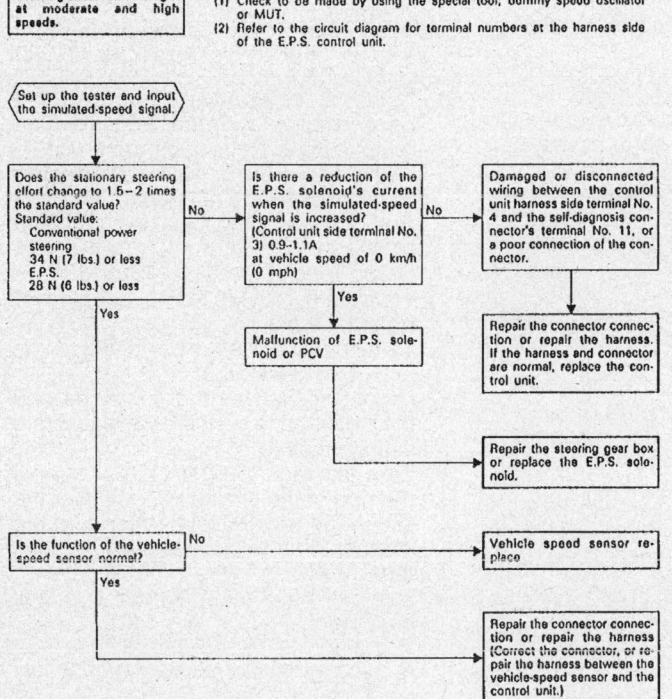

Fig. 9   EPS symptom charts (Part 1 of 3). Diamante

MT6029100012010X

undisturbed for several minutes, then repeat bleed procedure.

MONTERO, MONTERO SPORT & PICKUP

1. Fill power steering reservoir, then raise and support front of vehicle so that front wheels clear floor.
2. Remove ignition coil high tension cable.
3. Rotate engine using starter motor and turn steering wheel from stop to stop for 15–20 seconds refilling fluid in reservoir as necessary. **Only bleed system while cranking engine. Never bleed system with engine running.**
4. Lower front of vehicle.
5. Connect one end of a vinyl hose to the breather plug on the gearbox and place the other end into a suitable container.
6. Start engine and allow to idle.
7. Keeping reservoir full, loosen breather plug and turn steering wheel from stop

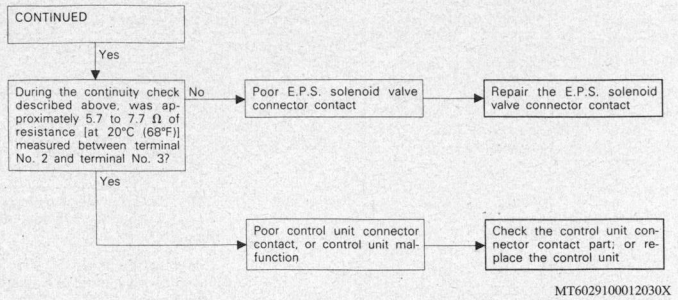

Fig. 9 EPS symptom charts (Part 3 of 3). Diamante

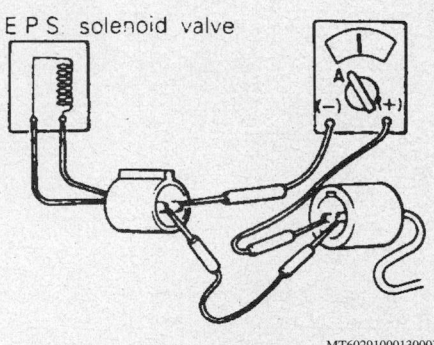

Fig. 10 EPS solenoid current inspection. Diamante & Galant

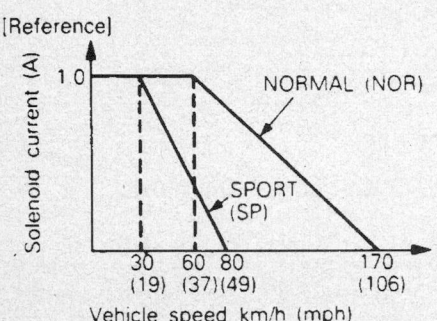

Fig. 11 EPS solenoid operating current. Galant

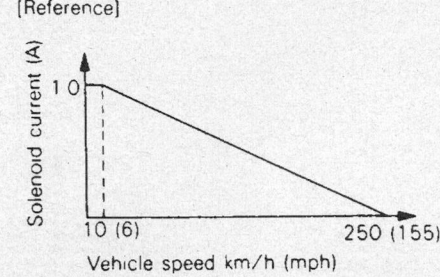

Fig. 12 EPS solenoid operating current. Diamante

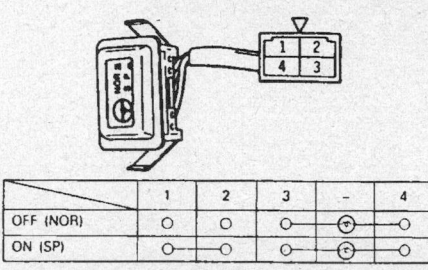

	1	2	3	–	4
OFF (NOR)	O	O	O─(+)		─O
ON (SP)	O──O		O─(+)		─O

NOTE
o─o indicates that there is continuity between the terminals.

Fig. 13 EPS mode switch test. Diamante & Galant

to stop until no air can be seen in vinyl hose.

8. After completion, tighten breather plug and check fluid.

9. When turning steering wheel from stop to stop, ensure fluid level does not change by more than .2 inch.

Component Service

POWER STEERING GEAR

Diamante & Galant

1. Disassemble power steering gear in numbered sequence shown in **Figs. 14 through 20,** noting the following:
   a. Tie rod and rack retaining tab must be unstaked with a chisel.
   b. Tool No. MB991204, or equivalent, may be used to remove rack support cover from gearbox.
   c. When removing pinion, gently tap with a plastic hammer.
   d. When removing oil seal from rack bushing, do not damage oil seal press fitting surface.
   e. Remove ball bearing from gear housing using a brass bar.
   f. Remove needle roller bearing from rack housing using special tool No. MB991120, or equivalent.
   g. When removing back-up washer and oil seal from gear housing, do not damage inner surface of gear housing rack cylinder.

2. Inspect rack tooth surfaces for damage or wear, then check oil seal contact surfaces for uneven wear.

3. Inspect rack for bends.

4. Check pinion gear tooth surfaces for damage or wear, then check for worn or defective seals.

5. Check bearing for roughness, abnormal noise and excessive play during operation.

6. Check needle roller bearings for roller slip-off.

7. Check rack housing cylinder inner surface for damage.

8. Check mounting rubber for cracks or damage. Replace as required.

9. Reverse numbered sequence shown in **Figs. 14 through 20** to assemble, noting the following:
   a. When installing back-up washer and oil seal, coat seal with Dexron II ATF, then press back-up and oil seal into rack housing to specified position.
   b. When installing needle roller bearing, apply even pressure to prevent housing damage.
   c. Apply coating of multipurpose grease to rack tooth face.
   d. When installing rack assembly, cover rack serrations with tool No. MB991213, or equivalent, then match oil seal center with rack to prevent retainer spring from slipping and slowly insert rack from power cylinder side.
   e. When installing rack bushing and stopper, wrap rack end with vinyl tape and apply a coating of Dexron II ATF.
   f. Install seal rings using tool No. MB991317, or equivalent.
   g. When installing end plug, secure threaded portion at two points using a punch.
   h. Adjust total pinion **torque** to 5–11 inch lbs.
   i. When installing tie rod, fold tab washer end into tie rod notch.
   j. Pack dust cover interior with multipurpose grease.

Eclipse

Disassemble power steering gear in numbered sequence shown in **Fig. 21,** noting the following:

1. Using a screwdriver, remove dust cover from tie rod end. Loosen, then remove boot retaining band.

2. Using a chisel, unstake tab washer which fixes tie rod and rack.

3. Remove end plug caulking and end plug.

4. Using special tool No. MB991204, or equivalent, remove rack support cover from gearbox.

5. Using a plastic hammer, gently tap the pinion to remove it.

6. Using a socket, remove the oil seal and the ball bearing from the valve housing simultaneously.

7. Turn the rack stopper clockwise until the end of the circlip comes out of the slot in the rack housing, then turn the stopper counterclockwise to remove the circlip.

8. Remove rack, rack stopper and rack bushing.

9. Partially bend oil seal and remove from rack bushing. Do not damage oil seal press fitting surface.

10. Using a brass bar, remove the ball bearing from the gear housing.

11. Using special tool No. MB991120, or equivalent, remove the needle roller bearing from the rack housing.

12. Remove the back-up washer and oil seal from the gear housing, using caution to avoid damaging inner surface of rack cylinder.

13. Inspect the rack tooth surfaces for

damage or wear, then the oil seal contact surfaces for uneven wear.

14. Inspect the rack for bends.
15. Check the pinion gear tooth surfaces for damage or wear, then check for worn or defective seal.
16. Check bearing for roughness or abnormal noise during operation, check the bearing for play.
17. Check the needle roller for bearings for roller slip-off.
18. Check the cylinder inner surface of the rack housing for damage.
19. Check mounting rubber for cracks or damage. Replace as required.
20. Reverse numbered sequence shown in **Fig. 21,** to assemble steering gear, noting the following.
    a. When installing back-up washer and oil seal, coat seal with Dexron II ATF and press washer and seal into rack housing to specified position.
    b. It will be necessary to use installer tool No. MB991199, guide tool No. MB991099 and bar tool No. MB991197, or equivalents, to install back-up washer and oil seal.
    c. When installing needle roller bearing, press evenly as valve housing is aluminum.
    d. It will be necessary to use installer tool Nos. MB990938 and MB991202, or equivalents, to install needle roller and ball bearings.
    e. When installing oil seal and O-ring, press fit oil seal until it reaches rack bush end.
    f. Apply coating of multipurpose grease to rack tooth face.
    g. When installing rack assembly, cover rack serrations with tool No. MB991213, or equivalent, then match oil seal center with rack to prevent retainer spring from slipping and slowly insert rack from power cylinder side.
    h. When installing rack bushing and stopper, wrap rack end with vinyl tape and apply a coating of Dexron II ATF.
    i. Install seal rings using tool No. MB991317, or equivalent.
    j. When installing end plug, secure threaded portion at two points using a punch.
    k. Adjust total pinion **torque** to 6–12 inch lbs.
    l. When installing tie rod, fold tab washer end into tie rod notch.
    m. Pack dust cover interior with multipurpose grease.

Mirage & 3000GT

1. Disassemble steering gear in numbered sequence shown in **Figs. 22 and 23,** noting the following:
   a. Unstake tie rod end tab washer.
   b. Using socket tool No. MB990607, or equivalent, remove rack support cover.
   c. Using a plastic hammer, lightly tap on pinion shaft to remove.
   d. Turn rack stopper clockwise until end of circlip is visible.
   e. Turn rack stopper counterclockwise to remove circlip, **Fig. 24.**

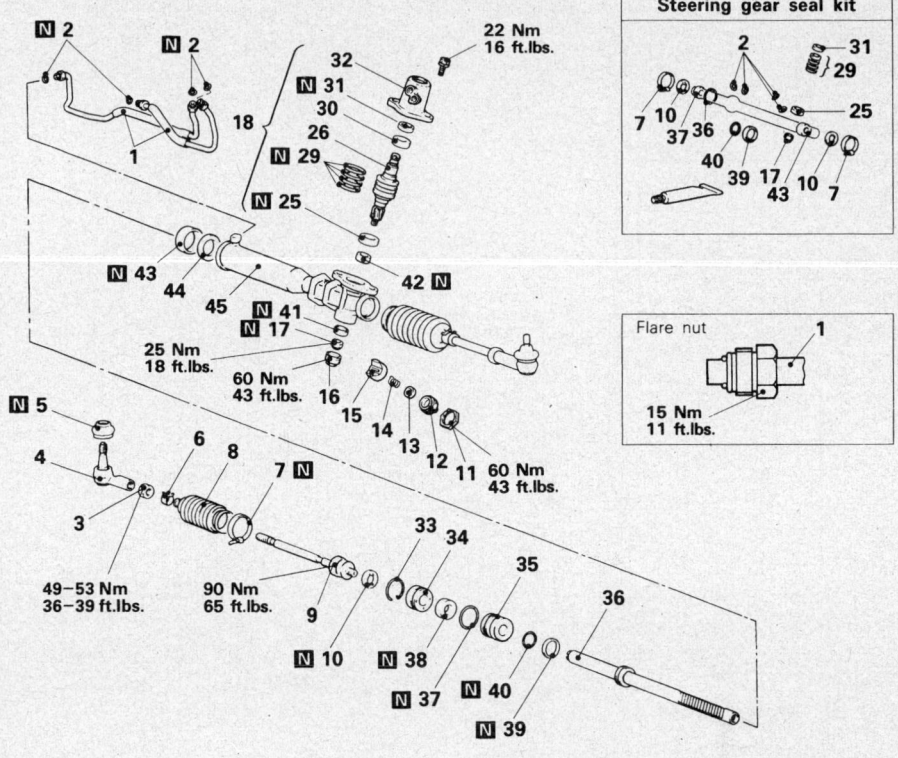

Disassembly steps

1. Feed tube
2. O-ring
3. Tie rod end locking nut
4. Tie rod end
5. Dust cover
6. Bellows clip
7. Bellows band
8. Bellows
9. Tie rod
10. Tab washer
    Adjustment of total pinion torque
11. Locking nut
12. Rack support cover
13. Cushion rubber
14. Rack support spring
15. Rack support
16. End plug
17. Self-locking nut
18. Valve housing assembly

25. Oil seal
26. Pinion and valve assembly
29. Seal ring
30. Ball bearing
31. Oil seal
32. Valve housing
33. Circlip
34. Rack stopper
35. Rack bushing
36. Rack
37. O-ring
38. Oil seal
39. Seal ring
40. O-ring
41. Ball bearing
42. Needle roller bearing
43. Oil seal
44. Back-up washer
45. Rack housing

MT6029100017000X

Fig. 14 Exploded view of power steering gear. 1996 Diamante w/conventional steering gear

f. Remove rack slowly, **Fig. 25.**
g. Remove oil seal using suitable oil seal remover tool.
h. Remove ball bearing using brass bar tool No. MB990939, or equivalent.
i. Remove needle roller bearing using bearing tool No. MB991120, or equivalent.
j. Remove oil seal from housing using a piece of pipe.

2. Reverse numbered sequence shown in **Figs. 22 and 23** to assemble, noting the following:
   a. Using rack installer tool No. MB991212, or equivalent, press back-up washer and oil seal into rack housing.
   b. Install needle roller bearing using bearing installation tool No.

MB991120, or equivalent.
c. Apply a coat of multipurpose grease to rack teeth face. **Do not close vent hose in rack with grease.**
d. Cover rack serrations with special rack installer tool, apply Dexron II ATF fluid to tool.
e. Align oil seal center with rack to prevent retainer spring from slipping and slowly insert rack from power cylinder side.
f. Wrap vinyl tape around end of rack, and install rack bushing and stopper.
g. Insert circlip to rack stopper through cylinder hole. Turn rack stopper clockwise and insert circlip firmly, **Fig. 26.**

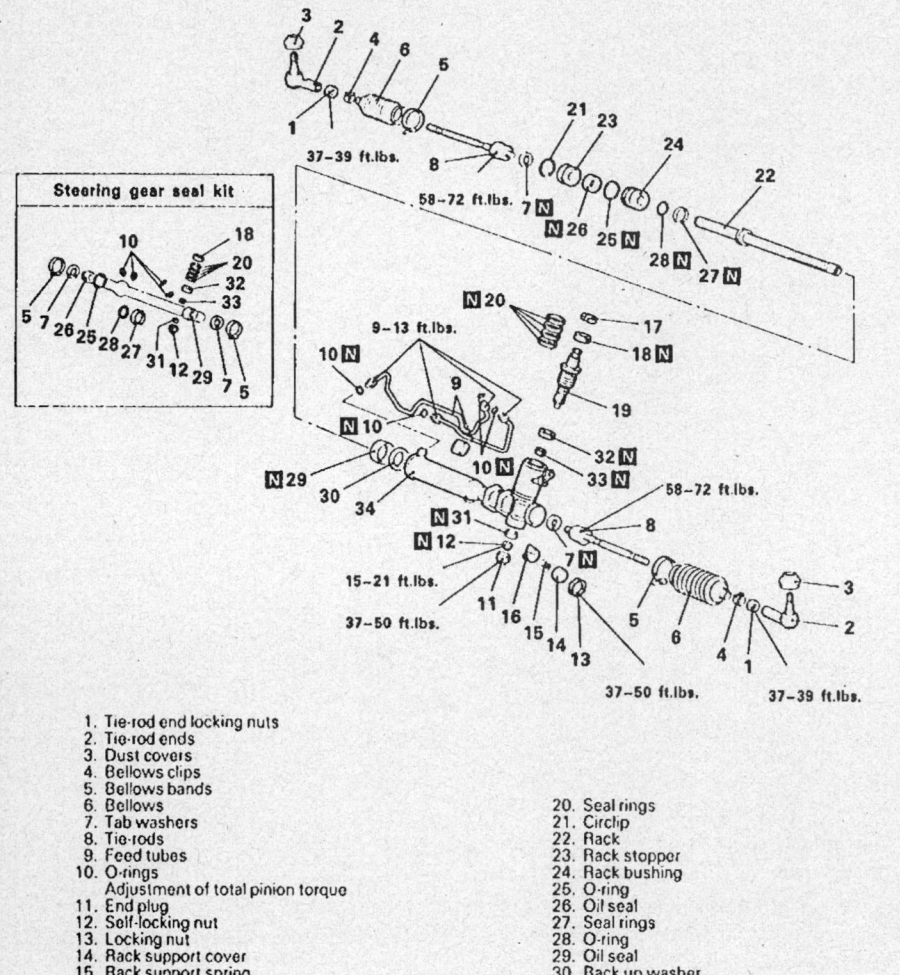

Steering gear seal kit

1. Tie-rod end locking nuts
2. Tie-rod ends
3. Dust covers
4. Bellows clips
5. Bellows bands
6. Bellows
7. Tab washers
8. Tie-rods
9. Feed tubes
10. O-rings
    Adjustment of total pinion torque
11. End plug
12. Self-locking nut
13. Locking nut
14. Rack support cover
15. Rack support spring
16. Rack support
17. Snap ring
18. Oil seal
19. Pinion and valve assembly

20. Seal rings
21. Circlip
22. Rack
23. Rack stopper
24. Rack bushing
25. O-ring
26. Oil seal
27. Seal rings
28. O-ring
29. Oil seal
30. Back up washer
31. Ball bearing
32. Oil seal
33. Needle roller bearing
34. Rack housing

MT6029100022000X

Fig. 15 Exploded view of power steering gear. 1996 Diamante w/electronic steering gear

h. Apply multipurpose grease to pinion gear and housing, wrap tape around serrated part.

i. Use seal ring installer tool No. MB991317, or equivalent, to install seal ring, then install pinion and valve assembly into valve housing.

j. Install valve housing seal using suitable seal installation tool and allow seal upper surface to project outward .040 inch, **Fig. 27.**

k. Apply 3M ATD sealant part No. 8663, or equivalent, to end plug threads, then install end plug securing in place using a suitable punch.

l. To adjust total pinion torque, center rack, then use torque wrench socket tool No. MB990607, or equivalent, to **torque** rack support cover to 11 ft. lbs. Then, from neutral position, rotate pinion shaft clockwise one turn within four to six seconds. Loosen rack support cover 30–60° and adjust **torque** to 5–11 inch lbs., then lock rack support cover with locknut.

Montero, Montero Sport & Pickup

1. Disassemble power steering gear in numbered sequence shown in **Figs. 28 and 29,** noting the following:
   a. Remove pitman arm using removal tool No. MB990809-01, or equivalent.
   b. Position mainshaft and cross shaft in straight ahead position, then tap bottom of cross shaft lightly with a plastic hammer to remove the cross shaft and side cover.
   c. **Do not remove packing unless fluid is leaking from threads of adjusting bolt.**
   d. **On Pickup models,** remove valve housing locknut using housing nut wrench tool No. MB990852-01, or equivalent, then remove rack piston from mainshaft by turning it clockwise. **Use care not to lose 26 balls inside rack piston.** Remove top cover and mainshaft from valve housing by using spanner wrench tool No. MB990201-01, or equiva-

lent, then install top cover on valve housing and remove top cover bearing and seal using suitable bearing removal tool.

   e. **On Montero and Montero Sport models,** remove rack piston from mainshaft by turning it counterclockwise. **Use care not to lose 26 balls inside rack piston.** Remove locknut using spanner wrench tool No. MB991367, or equivalent, and guide mainshaft out while pressing bearing race so balls do not drop out, then remove valve housing oil seal and bearing using a suitable bearing removal tool.

2. **On all models,** reverse numbered sequence shown in **Figs. 28 and 29** to assemble power steering gear, noting the following:
   a. Apply grease to bearing surface of side cover needle bearing and install the 33 rollers.
   b. Apply grease to bottom of side cover, then position new O-ring on the cover.
   c. Install adjusting bolt and plate into slot on top of cross shaft. Install plate with chamfered side toward cross shaft mating surface.
   d. Adjust cross shaft endplay to 0–.002 inch, using spacers as necessary.
   e. Install side cover onto cross shaft, tighten with adjusting bolt, then tighten locknut temporarily.
   f. Apply thin coat of grease to gear housing U-packing and oil seal, then press them into housing using tool Nos. MB990938 and MB990926, or equivalents.
   g. Apply thin coat of grease to lip of valve housing oil seal, then press it into housing.
   h. Press ball bearing into top cover, then install thrust plate, needle roller bearing and second thrust plate into cover. **Install the thinner of the two thrust plates on top cover side.**
   i. Install, then temporarily tighten top cover.
   j. Using tool No. MB990853, or equivalent, and a spring scale, **torque** top cover to 14–19 lbs., then loosen cover completely. Rotate input worm shaft and check for smooth operation.
   k. Measure starting torque using tool No. MB990228, or equivalent, while turning input worm shaft and note the value.
   l. Tighten top cover until starting **torque** of input worm shaft is 1.8–2.7 inch lbs., more than value measured in preceding step.
   m. Install valve housing nut, then **torque** to 131–166 ft. lbs.
   n. Measure starting torque again while turning input worm shaft. Preload should measure 2–6 inch lbs. If not, loosen valve housing nut and repeat steps for establishing correct preload.
   o. Secure gear housing in a vise, then

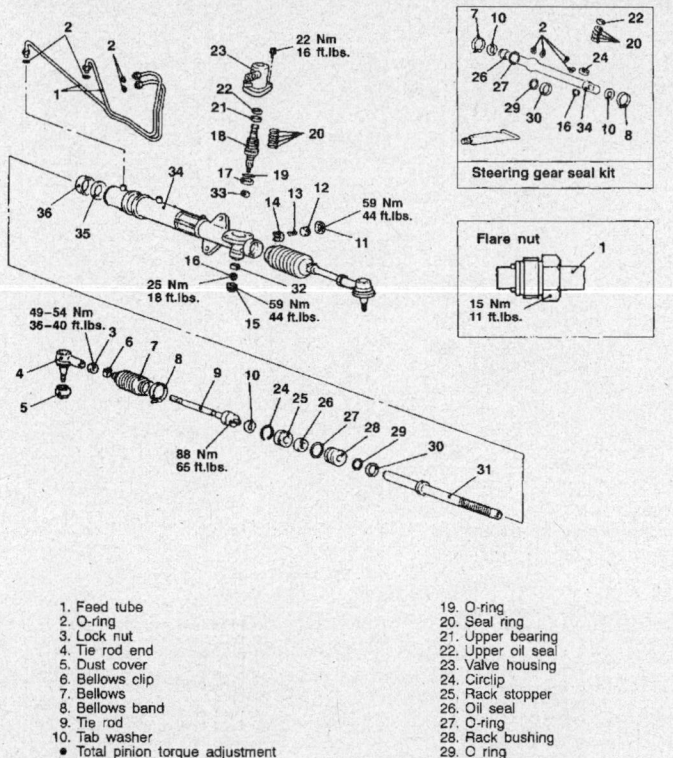

1. Feed tube
2. O-ring
3. Lock nut
4. Tie rod end
5. Dust cover
6. Bellows clip
7. Bellows
8. Bellows band
9. Tie rod
10. Tab washer
● Total pinion torque adjustment
11. Lock nut
12. Rack support cover
13. Rack support spring
14. Rack support
15. End plug
16. Lock nut
17. Lower oil seal
18. Pinion and valve assembly
19. O-ring
20. Seal ring
21. Upper bearing
22. Upper oil seal
23. Valve housing
24. Circlip
25. Rack stopper
26. Oil seal
27. O-ring
28. Rack bushing
29. O ring
30. Seal ring
31. Rack
32. Lower bearing
33. Needle roller bearing
34. Rack housing
35. Back-up washer
36. Oil seal

MT6029700054000X

Fig. 16 Exploded view of power steering gear. 1997–98 Diamante

install screw unit.

p. Install valve housing attaching bolts, then **torque** to 33–39 ft. lbs. Rotate input worm shaft to move rack piston to the Neutral position.

q. Install cross shaft with side cover to gear housing. **Torque** attaching bolts to 33–39 ft. lbs. When installing cross shaft assembly, apply a thin coat of Dexron II to rack piston teeth and shaft and multi-purpose grease to lip of oil seal. **Do not rotate side cover when installing.** Wrap cross shaft serration of with vinyl tape, then install it carefully to avoid damaging seal.

3. Measure total starting torque of input worm shaft, in the Neutral position, and adjust to 4–8 inch lbs. Ensure screw unit operates smoothly throughout its entire range.

4. Connect cross shaft to pitman arm. Ensure slit on tip of shaft is aligned with mark on pitman arm and tighten to specifications.

POWER STEERING PUMP

Diamante & Galant

1. Disassemble power steering pump in numbered sequence shown in **Figs. 30 through 34,** using a plastic hammer to remove pulley by lightly tapping rotor side of pulley shaft.

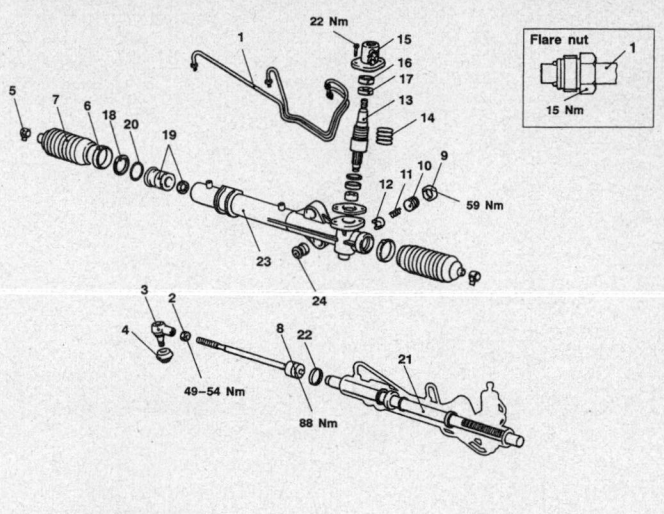

DISASSEMBLY STEPS
1. FEED TUBE
2. LOCK NUT
3. TIE ROD END
4. DUST COVER
5. CLIP
6. BAND
7. BELLOWS
● TOTAL PINION ROTATION TORQUE ADJUSTMENT
8. TIE ROD
9. LOCK NUT
10. RACK SUPPORT COVER
11. SPRING
12. RACK SUPPORT
13. PINION AND VALVE ASSEMBLY
14. SEAL RING
15. VALVE HOUSING
16. UPPER OIL SEAL
17. UPPER BEARING
18. CIRCLIP
19. RACK BUSH ASSEMBLY
20. O-RING
21. RACK ASSEMBLY
22. OIL SEAL
23. RACK HOUSING
24. RACK HOUSING MOUNT BUSH

MT6029900063000X

Fig. 17 Exploded view of power steering gear. 1999 Diamante

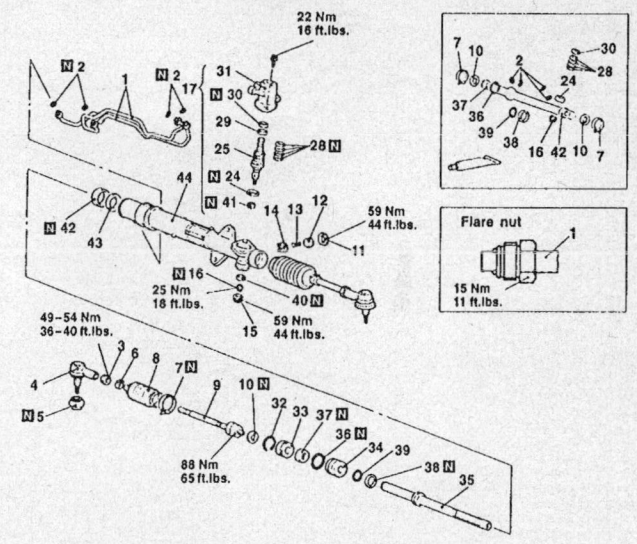

Disassembly steps
1. Feed tube
2. O-ring
3. Tie rod end locking nut
4. Tie rod end
5. Dust cover
6. Bellows clip
7. Bellows band
8. Bellows
9. Tie rod
10. Tab washer
● Total pinion torque adjustment
11. Locking nut
12. Rack support cover
13. Rack support spring
14. Rack support
15. End plug
16. Self-locking nut
17. Valve housing assembly
24. Oil seal
25. Pinion and valve assembly
26. Seal ring
27. O-ring
28. Seal ring
29. Ball bearing
30. Oil seal
31. Valve housing
32. Circlip
33. Rack stopper
34. Rack bushing
35. Rack
36. O-ring
37. Oil seal
38. Seal ring
39. O-ring
40. Ball bearing
41. Needle roller bearing
42. Oil seal
43. Back-up washer
44. Rack housing

MT6029400018000X

Fig. 18 Exploded view of power steering gear. 1996–98 Galant w/conventional steering gear

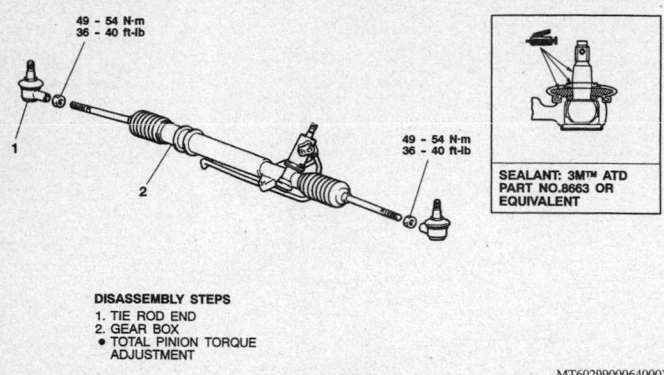

Fig. 19 Exploded view of power steering gear. 1999 Galant

DISASSEMBLY STEPS
1. TIE ROD END
2. GEAR BOX
● TOTAL PINION TORQUE ADJUSTMENT

SEALANT: 3M™ ATD PART NO.8663 OR EQUIVALENT

MT6029900064000X

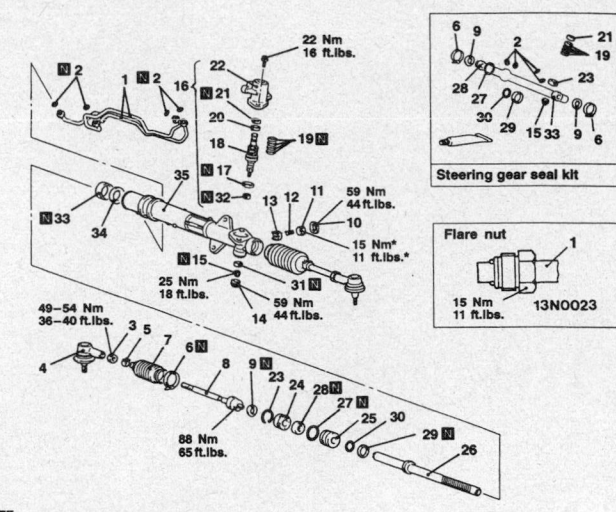

NOTE
*: Return the rack support cover 30° – 60°.

Disassembly steps

1. Feed tube
2. O-ring
3. Tie rod end locking nut
4. Tie rod end
5. Bellows clip
6. Bellows band
7. Bellows
8. Tie rod
9. Tab washer
● Total pinion torque adjustment
10. Locking nut
11. Rack support cover
12. Rack support spring
13. Rack support
14. End plug
15. Self-locking nut
16. Valve housing assembly
17. Oil seal
18. Pinion and valve assembly
19. Seal ring
20. Ball bearing
21. Oil seal
22. Valve housing
23. Circlip
24. Rack stopper
25. Rack bushing
26. Rack
27. O-ring
28. Oil seal
29. Seal ring
30. O-ring
31. Ball bearing
32. Needle roller bearing
33. Oil seal
34. Back-up washer
35. Rack housing

MT6029400020000X

Fig. 20 Exploded view of power steering gear. Galant w/electronic steering gear

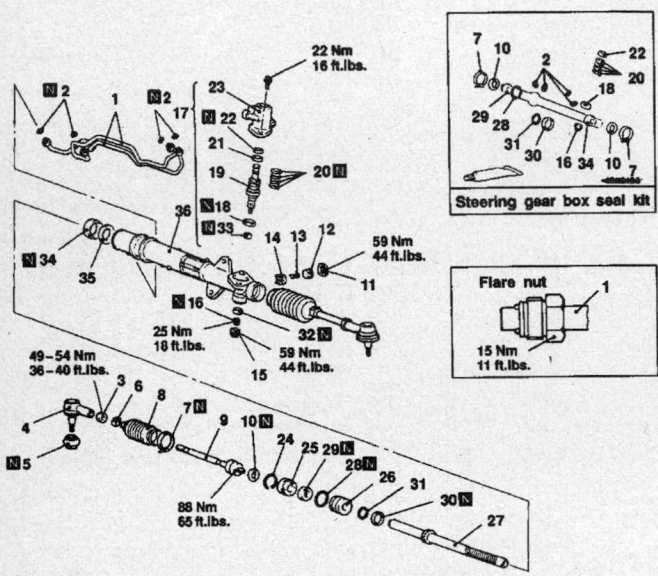

Steering gear box seal kit

Flare nut
15 Nm
11 ft.lbs.

MT6029500050000X

Disassembly steps

1. Feed tube
2. O-ring
3. Tie rod end locking nut
4. Tie rod end
5. Dust cover
6. Bellows clip
7. Bellows band
8. Bellows
9. Tie rod
10. Tab washer
● Total pinion torque adjustment
11. Locking nut
12. Rack support cover
13. Rack support spring
14. Rack support
15. End plug
16. Self-locking nut
17. Valve housing assembly
18. Oil seal
19. Pinion and valve assembly
20. Seal ring
21. Ball bearing
22. Oil seal
23. Valve housing
24. Circlip
25. Rack stopper
26. Rack bushing
27. Rack
28. O-ring
29. Oil seal
30. Seal ring
31. O-ring
32. Ball bearing
33. Needle roller bearing
34. Oil seal
35. Back-up washer
36. Rack housing

Fig. 21 Exploded view of power steering gear. Eclipse

2. Inspect flow control spring for wear.
3. Inspect shaft for signs of wear and bending.
4. Check groove of rotor vane for "stepped" wear.
5. Check contact surface of cam ring and vanes for " stepped" wear.
6. Check for broken vanes.
7. Install vane in rotor then measure gap between vane and rotor groove. Gap should not exceed .0024 inch.

8. Place a dial indicator at end of pulley shaft, **Fig. 35.**
9. Move pulley assembly up and down and measure freeplay. Freeplay should not exceed .004 inch.
10. Reverse numbered sequence shown in **Figs. 30 and 31** to assemble power steering pump, noting the following:
   a. Install spring in oil pump body with larger diameter end at terminal assembly side.

b. Apply Dexron II ATF fluid to O-rings, flow control valve, cam vanes & cam ring.
c. Align dowel pin of pump body with dowel pin hole of side plate to install side plate.
d. Install rotor to pulley assembly with rotor punch mark at pump cover side.
e. Install rotor snap ring and ensure snap ring is properly countersunk.
f. Align dowel pin cutouts in side plate with dowel pin holes of cam ring then install cam ring with punch mark toward pump body side.
g. Install vanes on rotor as shown in **Fig. 36.**

Eclipse w/2.0L Turbocharged & 2.4L Engines, Mirage & 3000GT

1. Disassemble power steering pump in numbered sequence shown in **Figs. 37 through 40.**
2. Measure gap between vane and rotor. Gap limit is .0024 inch.
3. Using a dial gauge at the end of the pump shaft, move pulley up and down and ensure movement is less than .004 inch.
4. Reverse numbered sequence in **Figs. 37 through 40.** to assemble, noting the following:
   a. Install piston rod spring into pump

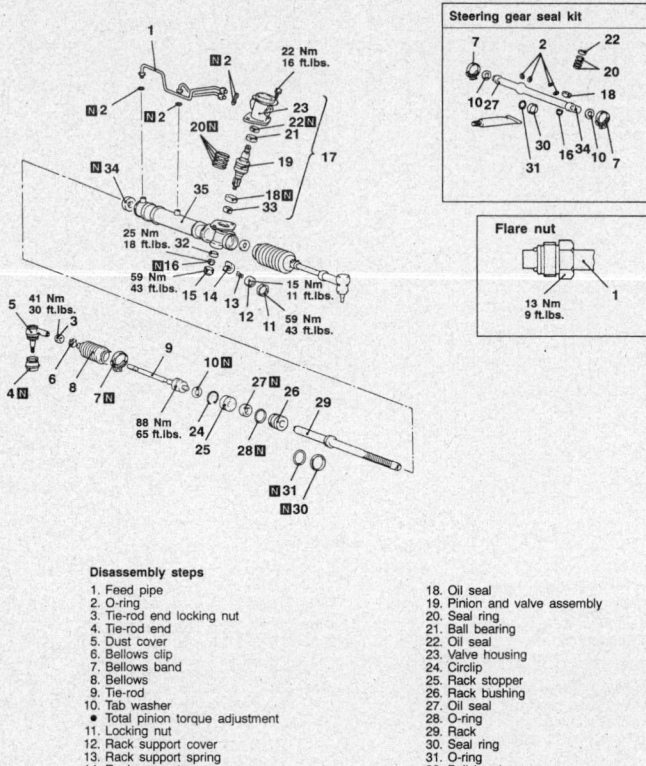

Disassembly steps

1. Feed pipe
2. O-ring
3. Tie-rod end locking nut
4. Tie-rod end
5. Dust cover
6. Bellows clip
7. Bellows band
8. Bellows
9. Tie-rod
10. Tab washer
    • Total pinion torque adjustment
11. Locking nut
12. Rack support cover
13. Rack support spring
14. Rack support
15. End plug
16. Self-locking nut
17. Valve housing assembly
18. Oil seal
19. Pinion and valve assembly
20. Seal ring
21. Ball bearing
22. Oil seal
23. Valve housing
24. Circlip
25. Rack stopper
26. Rack bushing
27. Oil seal
28. O-ring
29. Rack
30. Seal ring
31. O-ring
32. Ball bearing
33. Needle roller bearing
34. Oil seal
35. Rack housing

MT6029100024000X

Fig. 22   Exploded view of power steering gear. Mirage

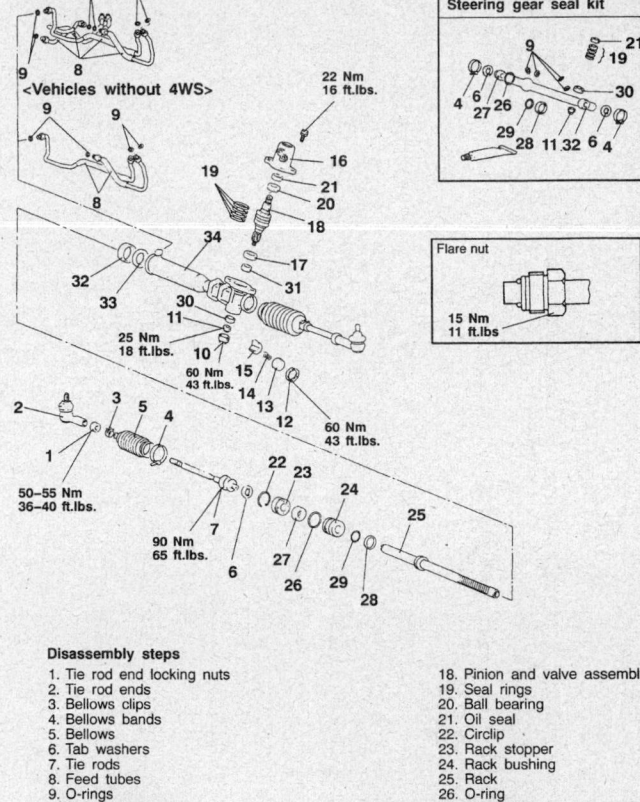

Disassembly steps

1. Tie rod end locking nuts
2. Tie rod ends
3. Bellows clips
4. Bellows bands
5. Bellows
6. Tab washers
7. Tie rods
8. Feed tubes
9. O-rings
   • Total pinion torque adjustment
10. End plug
11. Self-locking nut
12. Locking nut
13. Rack support cover
14. Rack support spring
15. Rack support
16. Valve housing
17. Oil seal
18. Pinion and valve assembly
19. Seal rings
20. Ball bearing
21. Oil seal
22. Circlip
23. Rack stopper
24. Rack bushing
25. Rack
26. O-ring
27. Oil seal
28. Seal rings
29. O-ring
30. Ball bearing
31. Needle roller bearing
32. Oil seal
33. Back-up washer
34. Rack housing

MT6029100025000X

Fig. 23   Exploded view of power steering gear. 3000GT

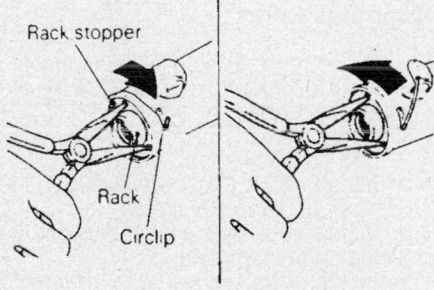

MT6029100026000X

Fig. 24   Circlip removal. Mirage & 3000GT

body with larger diameter end at terminal assembly side.

b. Apply Dexron II ATF to O-rings, flow control valve, rotor vanes and cam ring prior to installation.

c. Drive pulley shaft oil seal into pump body using suitable seal installation tool.

d. Align dowel pin of pump body with dowel pin hole of side plate to install side plate.

e. Install rotor onto pulley assembly so that rotor punch mark is at pump cover side.

f. Ensure rotor snap is properly installed.

g. Align dowel pin of pump body with dowel holes of cam ring, then install so that cam ring's punch mark is at pump body side.

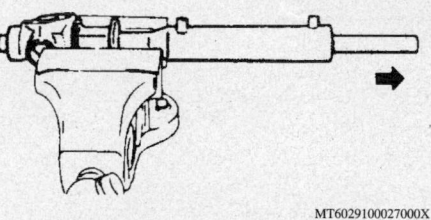

MT6029100027000X

Fig. 25   Rack removal. Mirage & 3000GT

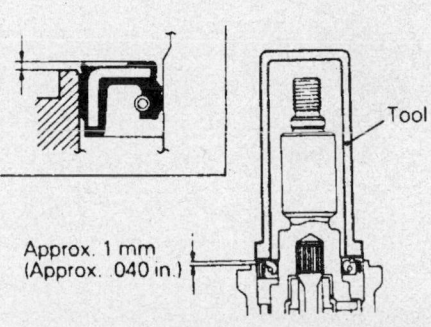

MT6029100029000X

Fig. 27   Oil seal installation. Mirage & 3000GT

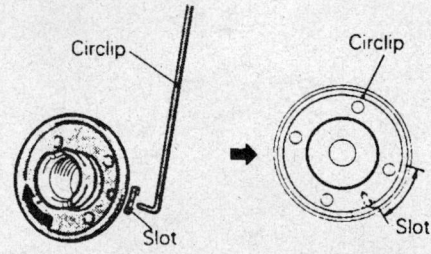

MT6029100028000X

Fig. 26   Circlip installation. Mirage & 3000GT

h. Install vanes in rotor as shown, **Figs. 37 through 40.**

i. Align pump cover dowel pins and install pump cover.

Eclipse w/2.0L Non-Turbocharged Engine

1. Disassemble power steering pump in numbered sequence shown, **Fig. 41.** Secure pulley with tool No. MB990767, or equivalent, when removing mounting nuts.

2. Reverse numbered sequence to reassemble, noting the following:

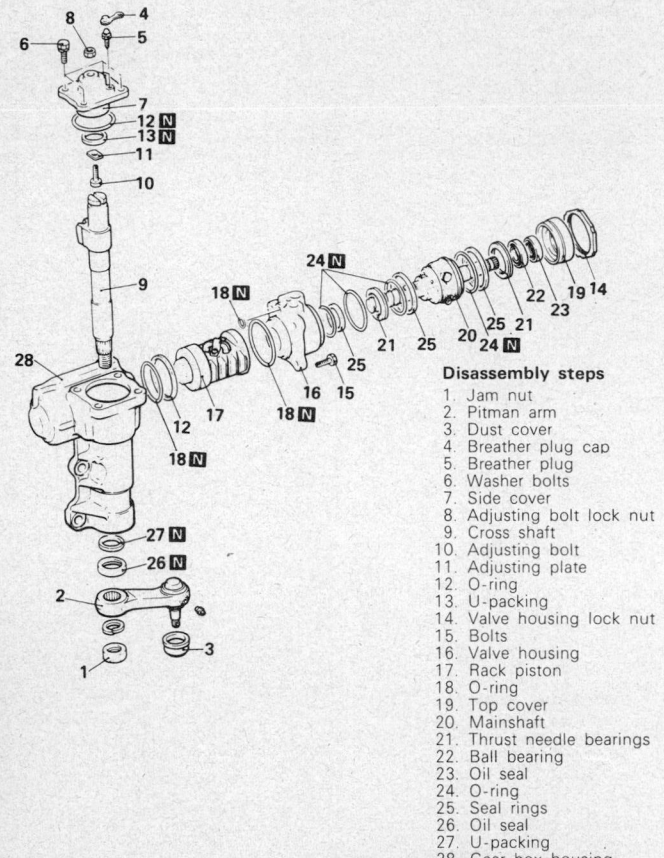

Disassembly steps

1. Jam nut
2. Pitman arm
3. Dust cover
4. Breather plug cap
5. Breather plug
6. Washer bolts
7. Side cover
8. Adjusting bolt lock nut
9. Cross shaft
10. Adjusting bolt
11. Adjusting plate
12. O-ring
13. U-packing
14. Valve housing lock nut
15. Bolts
16. Valve housing
17. Rack piston
18. O-ring
19. Top cover
20. Mainshaft
21. Thrust needle bearings
22. Ball bearing
23. Oil seal
24. O-ring
25. Seal rings
26. Oil seal
27. U-packing
28. Gear box housing

MT6029100030000X

**Fig. 28 Exploded view of power steering gear.
Pickup**

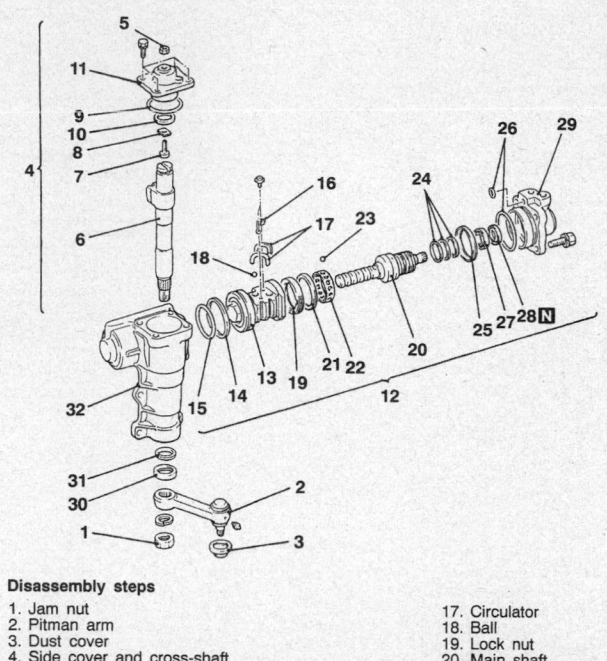

Disassembly steps

1. Jam nut
2. Pitman arm
3. Dust cover
4. Side cover and cross-shaft assembly
5. Adjusting bolt lock nut
6. Cross-shaft
7. Adjusting bolt
8. Adjusting plate
9. O-ring
10. Y-packing
11. Side cover
12. Main shaft and valve assembly
13. Rack piston
14. Seal ring
15. O-ring
16. Circulator holder
17. Circulator
18. Ball
19. Lock nut
20. Main shaft
21. Bearing race
22. Cage
23. Ball
24. Seal ring
25. Bearing race
26. O-ring
27. Bearing
28. Oil seal
29. Valve housing
30. Oil seal
31. Y-packing
32. Gear box housing

MT6029100031000X

**Fig. 29 Exploded view of steering gear. Montero &
Montero Sport**

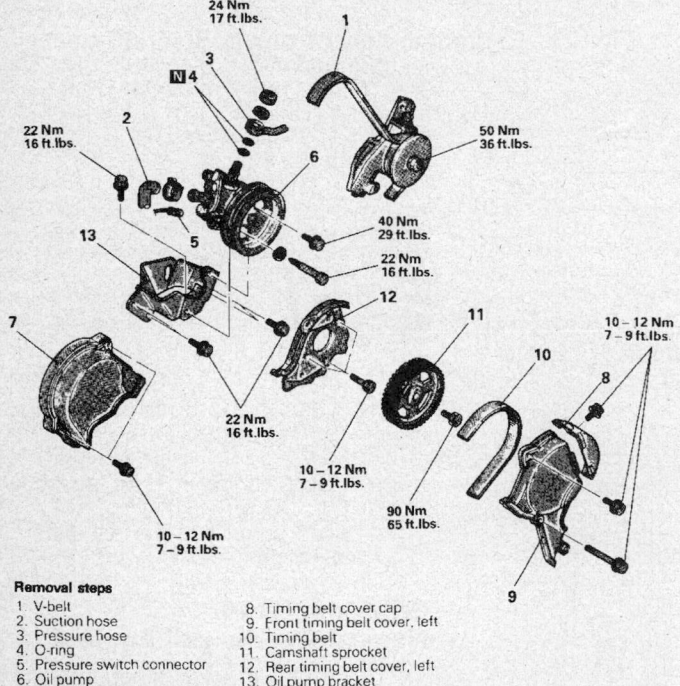

Removal steps

1. V-belt
2. Suction hose
3. Pressure hose
4. O-ring
5. Pressure switch connector
6. Oil pump
7. Front timing belt cover, right
8. Timing belt cover cap
9. Front timing belt cover, left
10. Timing belt
11. Camshaft sprocket
12. Rear timing belt cover, left
13. Oil pump bracket

MT6029100035000X

**Fig. 30 Exploded view of power steering pump.
1996 Galant & Diamante w/SOHC engine**

a. Install oil seal using installation tool Nos. MB990938 and MB991203, or equivalents.
b. Apply Dexron II ATF to all O-rings prior to installation.
c. Install rotor on shaft with punch mark at pump cover side.
d. Install cam ring with punch mark facing pump cover.
e. Install rotor vanes with rounded edges facing cam ring.
f. Secure pulley with tool No. MB990767 and spacer tool No. MD998719, or equivalents, when installing pulley locknut.
3. Inspect flow control valve for clogging, shaft for damage or excessive wear, rotor and vane groove for "stepped" wear and vanes for damage.
4. Measure clearance between shaft and oil pump body using a suitable micrometer and caliper gauge as follows:
a. Measure inside diameter of oil pump body bore, then measure outside diameter of shaft.
b. Subtract shaft diameter from oil pump body bore diameter to obtain clearance measurement. Clearance should not exceed .0276 inch.

Montero & Montero Sport

1. Disassemble power steering pump in numbered sequence shown in **Fig. 42**.
2. Reverse numbered sequence shown

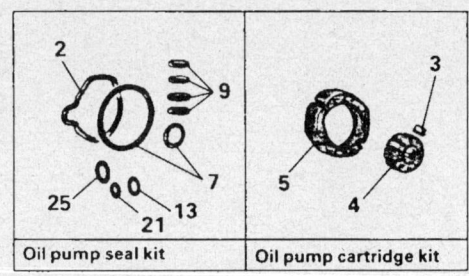

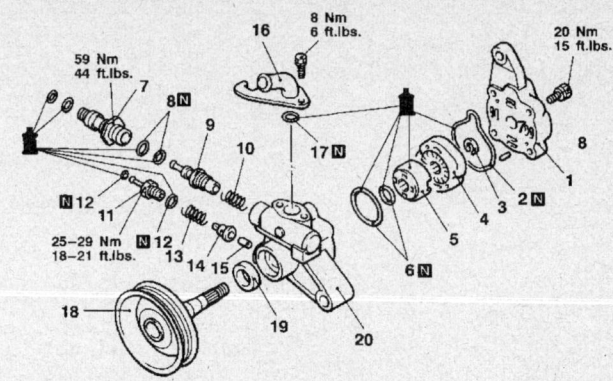

<DOHC Engine>

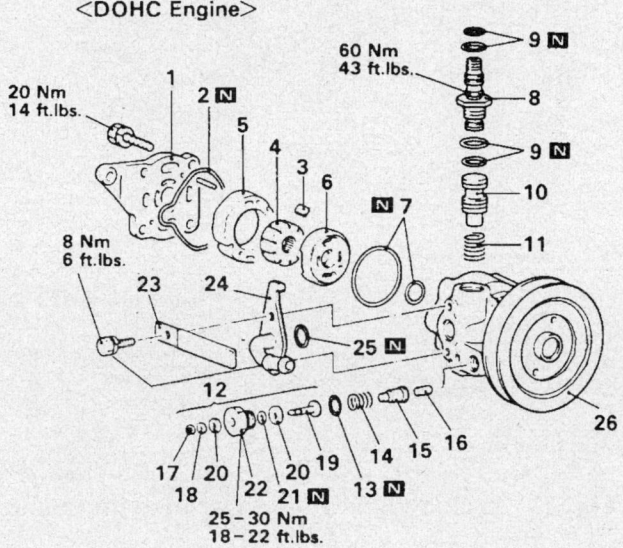

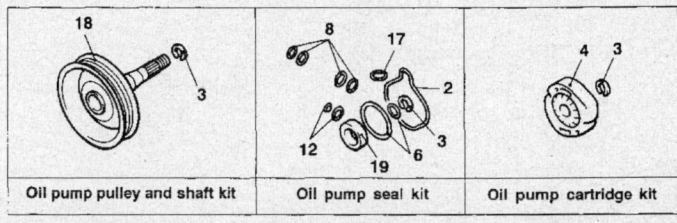

| Oil pump pulley and shaft kit | Oil pump seal kit | Oil pump cartridge kit |

1. Pump cover
2. O-ring
3. Snap ring
4. Oil pump cartridge
5. Side plate
6. O-ring
7. Connector
8. O-ring
9. Flow control valve
10. Flow control spring
11. Terminal assembly
12. O-ring
13. Plunger spring
14. Plunger
15. Piston rod
16. Suction connector
17. O-ring
18. Pulley and shaft
19. Shaft oil seal
20. Oil pump

MT6029700056000X

Fig. 32 Exploded view of power steering pump. 1997–99 Diamante

Disassembly steps

1. Pump cover
2. O-ring
3. Vanes
4. Rotor
5. Cam ring
6. Side plate
7. O-ring
8. Connector
9. O-ring
10. Flow control valve
11. Flow control spring
12. Terminal assembly
13. O-ring
14. Spring
15. Plunger
16. Piston rod
17. Snap ring
18. Terminal
19. Washer
20. Insulator
21. O-ring
22. Plug
23. Clip
24. Suction connector
25. O-ring
26. Oil pump body and Pulley assembly

Caution
Do not disassemble the flow control valve.

MT6029400036000X

Fig. 31 Exploded view of power steering pump. 1996 Diamante w/DOHC engine

in **Fig. 42** to assemble, noting the following:

a. Install flow control valve spring with larger diameter end at terminal side.
b. Line up dowel pin hole with dowel pin in bump body when installing side plate.

c. Install rotor with punch mark at pump cover side.
d. Ensure rotor snap ring is properly installed.
e. Install cam ring with the punch mark facing the side plate.
f. Install vanes as shown in **Fig. 36.**

Pickup

1. Disassemble power steering pump in numbered sequence shown in **Fig. 43.**
2. Reverse numbered sequence shown in **Fig. 43** to assemble, noting the following:
   a. If flow control valve is to be replaced, match identification mark on housing with mark on valve.
   b. Install flow control spring, flow control valve and connector to pump body.
   c. Install rotor with the countersunk portion toward pump cover side.
   d. Ensure rotor snap ring is installed correctly.
   e. Install vanes in rotor as shown in **Fig. 36.**
   f. Align dowel pin with dowel pin holes when installing cam ring with punch mark at pump body side.

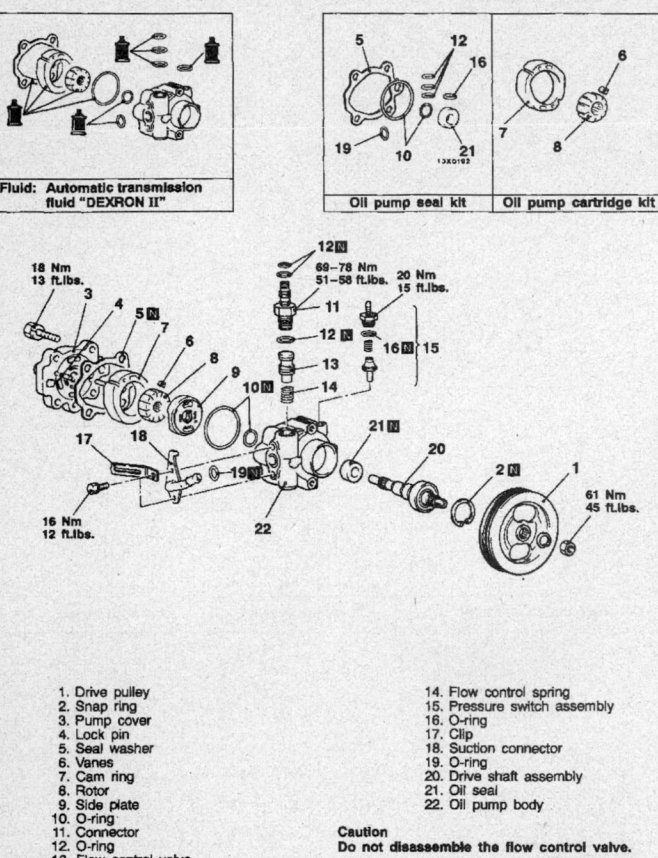

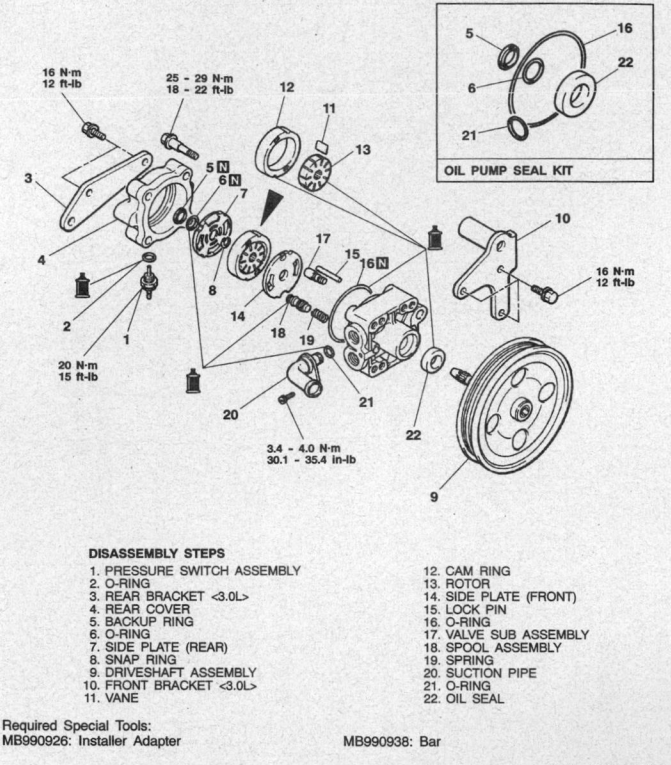

Fluid: Automatic transmission fluid "DEXRON II"

Oil pump seal kit | Oil pump cartridge kit

OIL PUMP SEAL KIT

18 Nm
13 ft.lbs.

69–78 Nm
51–58 ft.lbs.

20 Nm
15 ft.lbs.

16 Nm
12 ft.lbs.

61 Nm
45 ft.lbs.

1. Drive pulley
2. Snap ring
3. Pump cover
4. Lock pin
5. Seal washer
6. Vanes
7. Cam ring
8. Rotor
9. Side plate
10. O-ring
11. Connector
12. O-ring
13. Flow control valve

14. Flow control spring
15. Pressure switch assembly
16. O-ring
17. Clip
18. Suction connector
19. O-ring
20. Drive shaft assembly
21. Oil seal
22. Oil pump body

Caution
Do not disassemble the flow control valve.

MT6029700057000X

Fig. 33 Exploded view of power steering pump. 1997–98 Galant

16 N·m
12 ft-lb

25 – 29 N·m
18 – 22 ft-lb

16 N·m
12 ft-lb

20 N·m
15 ft-lb

3.4 – 4.0 N·m
30.1 – 35.4 in-lb

DISASSEMBLY STEPS

1. PRESSURE SWITCH ASSEMBLY
2. O-RING
3. REAR BRACKET <3.0L>
4. REAR COVER
5. BACKUP RING
6. O-RING
7. SIDE PLATE (REAR)
8. SNAP RING
9. DRIVESHAFT ASSEMBLY
10. FRONT BRACKET <3.0L>
11. VANE

12. CAM RING
13. ROTOR
14. SIDE PLATE (FRONT)
15. LOCK PIN
16. O-RING
17. VALVE SUB ASSEMBLY
18. SPOOL ASSEMBLY
19. SPRING
20. SUCTION PIPE
21. O-RING
22. OIL SEAL

Required Special Tools:
MB990926: Installer Adapter   MB990938: Bar

MT6029900065000X

Fig. 34 Exploded view of power steering pump. 1999 Galant

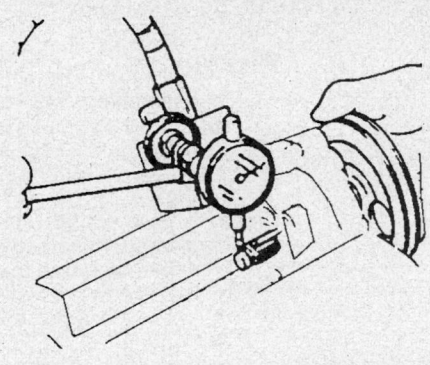

MT6029100037000X

Fig. 35 Pump backlash measurement. Diamante & Galant

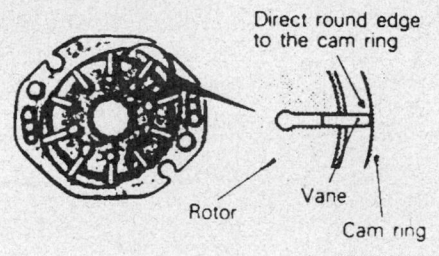

Direct round edge to the cam ring

Rotor

Vane

Cam ring

MT6029100038000X

Fig. 36 Rotor vane orientation

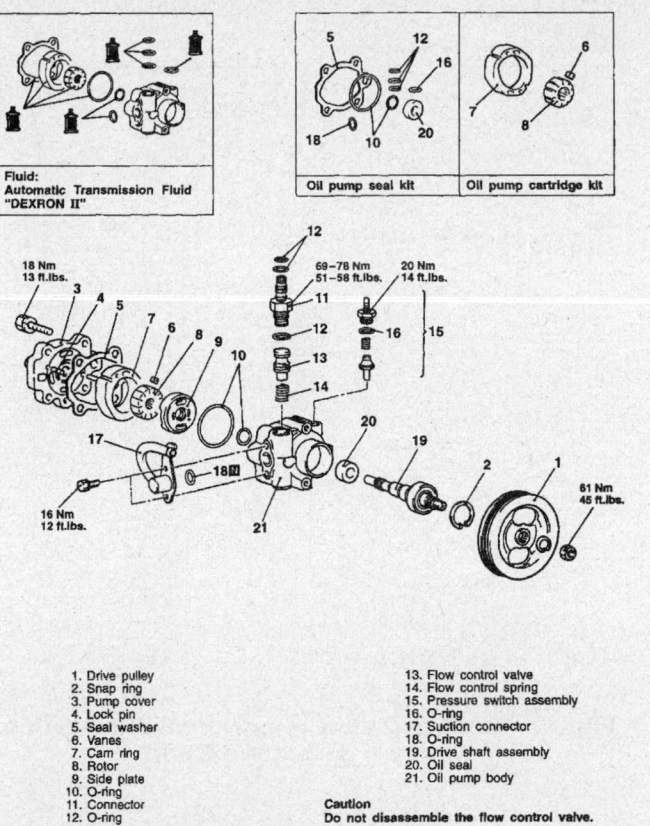

1. Drive pulley
2. Snap ring
3. Pump cover
4. Lock pin
5. Seal washer
6. Vanes
7. Cam ring
8. Rotor
9. Side plate
10. O-ring
11. Connector
12. O-ring
13. Flow control valve
14. Flow control spring
15. Pressure switch assembly
16. O-ring
17. Suction connector
18. O-ring
19. Drive shaft assembly
20. Oil seal
21. Oil pump body

Caution
Do not disassemble the flow control valve.

MT6029700058000X

Fig. 37 Exploded view of power steering pump. Eclipse w/2.0L turbocharged & 2.4L engines

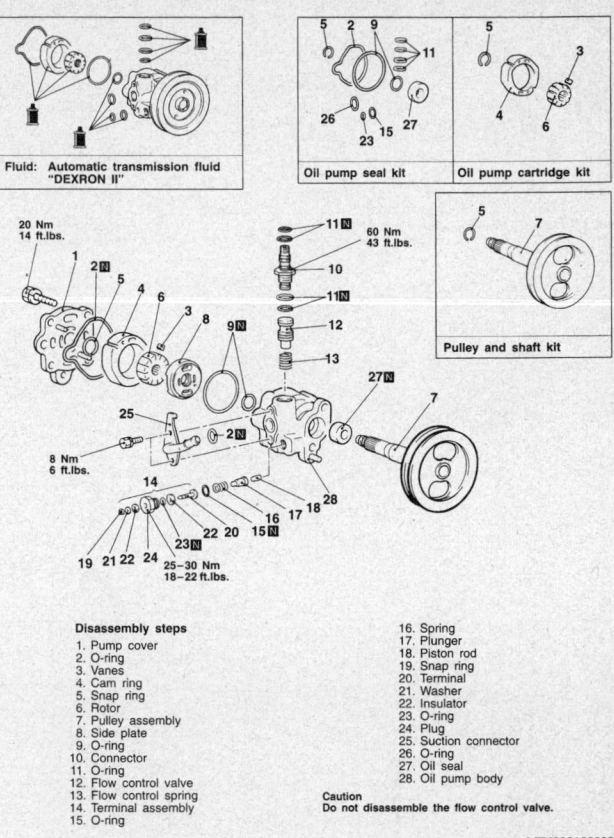

Disassembly steps
1. Pump cover
2. O-ring
3. Vanes
4. Cam ring
5. Snap ring
6. Rotor
7. Pulley assembly
8. Side plate
9. O-ring
10. Connector
11. O-ring
12. Flow control valve
13. Flow control spring
14. Terminal assembly
15. O-ring
16. Spring
17. Plunger
18. Piston rod
19. Snap ring
20. Terminal
21. Washer
22. Insulator
23. O-ring
24. Plug
25. Suction connector
26. O-ring
27. Oil seal
28. Oil pump body

Caution
Do not disassemble the flow control valve.

MT6029100039000X

Fig. 38 Exploded view of steering pump. 1996 Mirage

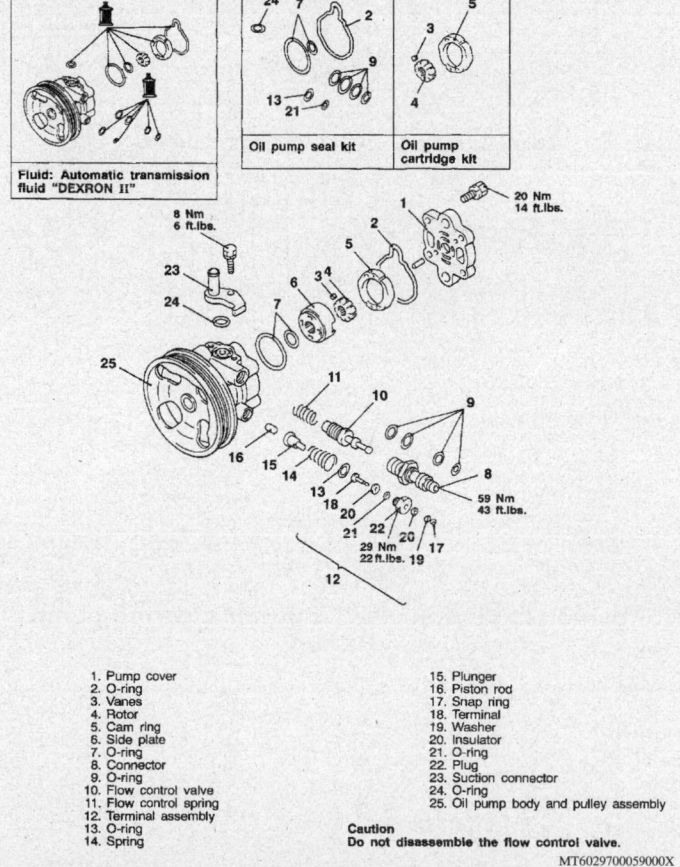

1. Pump cover
2. O-ring
3. Vanes
4. Rotor
5. Cam ring
6. Side plate
7. O-ring
8. Connector
9. O-ring
10. Flow control valve
11. Flow control spring
12. Terminal assembly
13. O-ring
14. Spring
15. Plunger
16. Piston rod
17. Snap ring
18. Terminal
19. Washer
20. Insulator
21. O-ring
22. Plug
23. Suction connector
24. O-ring
25. Oil pump body and pulley assembly

Caution
Do not disassemble the flow control valve.

MT6029700059000X

Fig. 39 Exploded view of power steering pump. 1997–99 Mirage

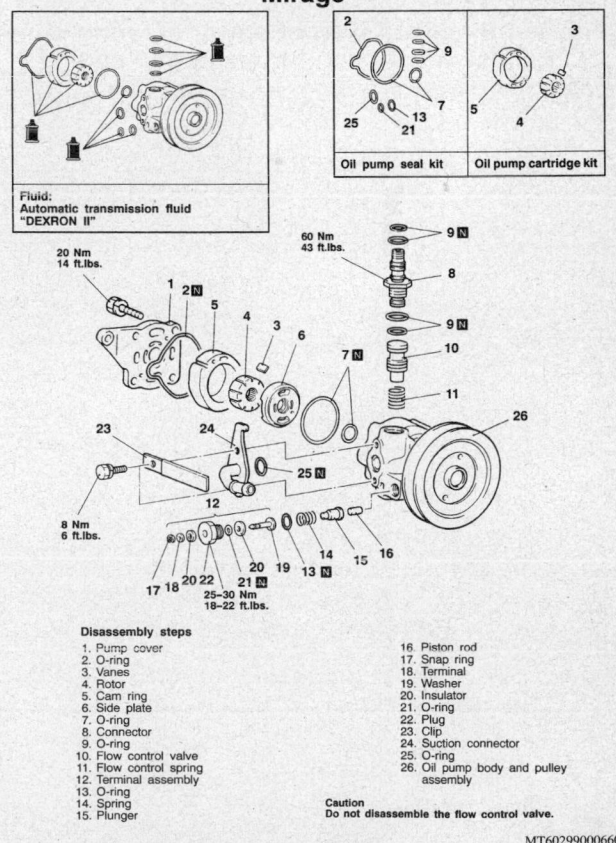

Disassembly steps
1. Pump cover
2. O-ring
3. Vanes
4. Rotor
5. Cam ring
6. Side plate
7. O-ring
8. Connector
9. O-ring
10. Flow control valve
11. Flow control spring
12. Terminal assembly
13. O-ring
14. Spring
15. Plunger
16. Piston rod
17. Snap ring
18. Terminal
19. Washer
20. Insulator
21. O-ring
22. Plug
23. Clip
24. Suction connector
25. O-ring
26. Oil pump body and pulley assembly

Caution
Do not disassemble the flow control valve.

MT6029900066000X

Fig. 40 Exploded view of power steering pump. 3000GT

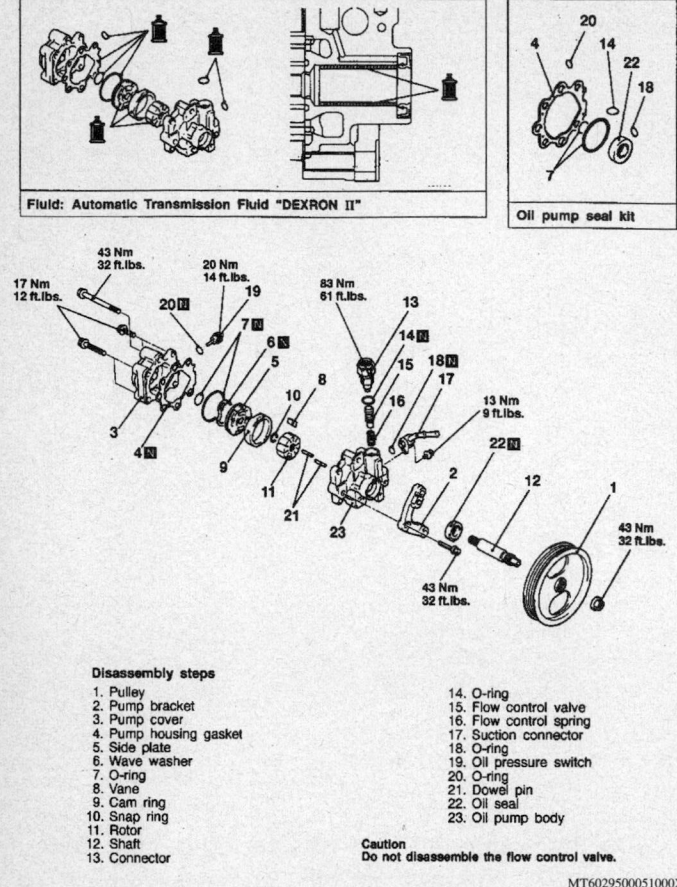

Disassembly steps
1. Pulley
2. Pump bracket
3. Pump cover
4. Pump housing gasket
5. Side plate
6. Wave washer
7. O-ring
8. Vane
9. Cam ring
10. Snap ring
11. Rotor
12. Shaft
13. Connector
14. O-ring
15. Flow control valve
16. Flow control spring
17. Suction connector
18. O-ring
19. Oil pressure switch
20. O-ring
21. Dowel pin
22. Oil seal
23. Oil pump body

Caution
Do not disassemble the flow control valve.

MT6029500051000X

**Fig. 41 Exploded view of power steering pump.
Eclipse w/2.0L non-turbocharged engine**

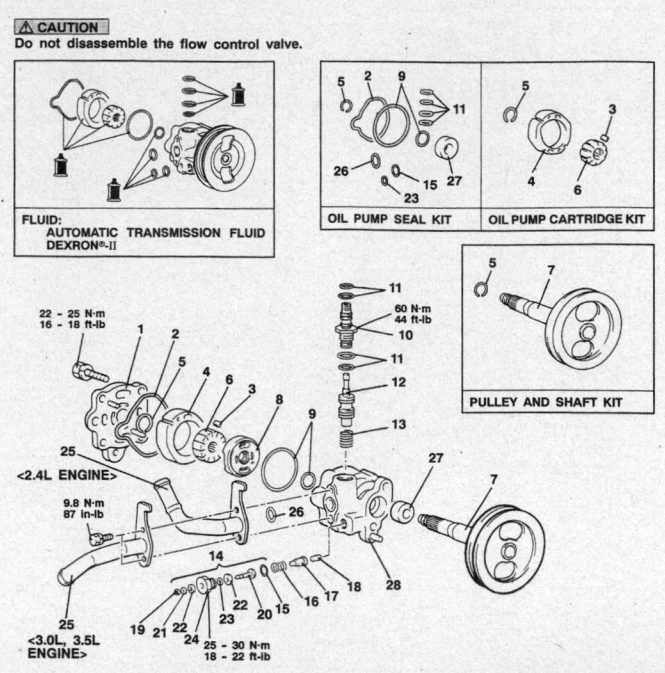

MT6029100040000X

**Fig. 42 Exploded view of power steering pump.
Montero & Montero Sport**

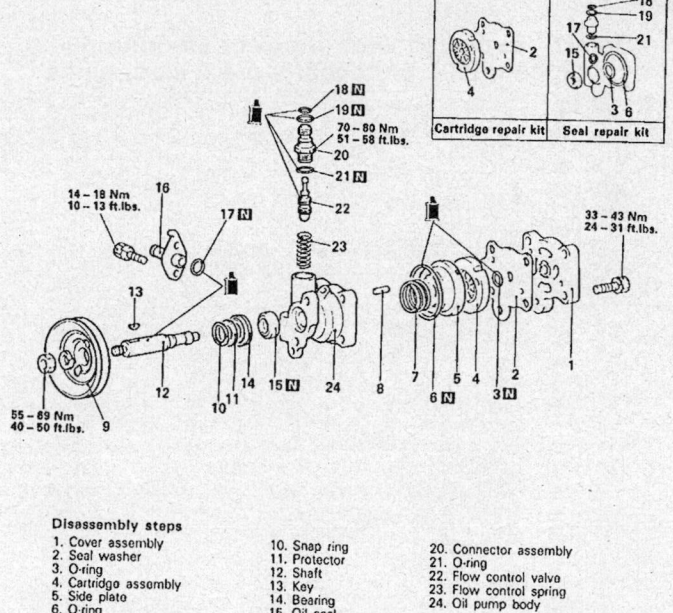

Disassembly steps
1. Cover assembly
2. Seal washer
3. O-ring
4. Cartridge assembly
5. Side plate
6. O-ring
7. Side plate spring
8. Dowel pin
9. Pulley
10. Snap ring
11. Protector
12. Shaft
13. Key
14. Bearing
15. Oil seal
16. Suction connector
17. O-ring
18. O-ring
19. O-ring
20. Connector assembly
21. O-ring
22. Flow control valve
23. Flow control spring
24. Oil pump body

: Automatic transmission fluid "DEXRON II"

MT6029100041000X

**Fig. 43 Exploded view of power steering pump.
Pickup**

TIGHTENING SPECIFICATIONS

Year	Component	Torque, Ft. Lbs.
DIAMANTE		
1996–99	Control Valve Bolts	8
	Crossmember Mounting Bolts	43–51
	Flow Connector Fitting To Power Steering Pump Body	43
	Hose Bracket Bolts	7
	Joint Assembly Clamp Bolt	13
	Oil Reservoir Mounting Bracket Mounting Bolts	8
	Oil Reservoir To Mounting Bracket Bolts	8
	PCV Assembly	13
	Pinion & Valve Nut	18
	Power Steering Gearbox Mounting Clamp Bolts	51
	Power Steering Pump Bracket Bolts	16
	Power Steering Pump Rear Cover Bolts	14
	Power Steering Pump Terminal Fitting	18–22
	Pressure Hose To Power Steering Pump Fitting	17
	Pressure Tube To Pressure Hose Fitting	25
	Rack Support Nut	43
	Stabilizer Bar Bracket Bolts	29
	Steering Shaft End Plug	43
	Steering Shaft Flange To Gearbox Bolts	16
	Suction Connector To Power Steering Pump Bolts	6
	Tie Rod End Jam Nuts	36–39
	Tie Rod End To Knuckle Nuts	21
	Tie Rod To Rack Housing	65

Continued

TIGHTENING
SPECIFICATIONS—Continued

Year	Component	Torque, Ft. Lbs.
ECLIPSE & ECLIPSE SPYDER		
1996–99	Center Member To Crossmember	58–65
	Center Member To Support	51–58
	Cooler Tube Bracket	34①
	End Plug	44
	End Plug Self-Locking Nut	18
	Feed Tube Flare Nut	11
	Gearbox Retaining Clamps	51
	Oil Pump Adjusting Bolt③	29
	Oil Pump Adjusting Bolt④	16
	Oil Pump Bracket To Engine③	29
	Oil Pump Bracket To Engine④	21
	Oil Pump Cover④	13
	Oil Pump Cover, Long Bolts③	32
	Oil Pump Cover, Short Bolts③	12
	Oil Pump Flow Control Valve Connector③	61
	Oil Pump Flow Control Valve Connector④	51–58
	Oil Pump Pulley③	32
	Oil Pump Pulley④	45
	Pinion & Valve Assembly	16
	Pipe Connections To Gearbox	11
	Power Steering Hose Brackets	8
	Power Steering Oil Pressure Switch	14
	Pressure Hose To Oil Pump③	42
	Pressure Hose To Oil Pump④	13
	Rack Support Cover Locknut	44
	Steering Shaft Joint To Gearbox	13
	Suction Connector To Oil Pump③	9
	Suction Connector To Oil Pump④	12
	Tie Rod End Jam Nut	36–40
	Tie Rod End To Knuckle	18–24

TIGHTENING
SPECIFICATIONS—Continued

Year	Component	Torque, Ft. Lbs.
GALANT		
1996–99	Center Member To Crossmember	58–65
	Center Member To Support	51–58
	End Plug	44
	End Plug Self-Locking Nut	18
	Feed Tube Flare Nut	11
	Flow Control Valve Connector	51–58
	Gearbox Retaining Clamps	51
	Oil Pump Adjusting Bolt	16
	Oil Pump Bracket To Engine	21
	Oil Pump Cover	13
	Oil Pump Pivots	21
	Oil Pump Pressure Hose	13
	Oil Pump Pulley	45
	Pinion & Valve Assembly	16
	Pipe Connections To Gearbox	11
	Pipe Connections To Hoses	25
	Power Steering Hose Brackets	9
	Power Steering Oil Pressure Switch	15
	Rack Support Locknut	44
	Steering Shaft Joint To Gearbox	13
	Suction Connector To Oil Pump	12
	Tie Rod End Jam Nut	36–40
	Tie Rod End To Knuckle	18–24
	Tie Rod To Rack	65
MIRAGE		
1996–99	End Plug	43
	End Plug Self-Locking Nut	18
	Feed Tube Flare Nut	9
	Flow Control Valve Connector	43
	Gearbox Retaining Clamps	51
	Oil Pump Adjusting Bolt	29
	Oil Pump Bracket To Engine⑤	16
	Oil Pump Bracket To Engine②	29
	Oil Pump Cover	14
	Oil Pump Pivot	17
	Oil Pump To Oil Pump Bracket	29
	Oil Reservoir	48①
	Power Steering Hose Brackets	9
	Pressure Pipe To Gearbox	11
	Pressure Pipe To Oil Pump	13
	Rack Support Cover Locking Nut	43
	Return Pipe To Gearbox	11
	Steering Shaft Grommet	48①
	Steering Shaft Joint To Gearbox	13
	Suction Connector To Oil Pump	6
	Terminal Assembly To Oil Pump	18–22
	Tie Rod End Jam Nut	30
	Tie Rod End To Knuckle	11–25
	Tie Rod To Rack	65
	Valve Housing	16

Continued

TIGHTENING
SPECIFICATIONS—Continued

Year	Component	Torque, Ft. Lbs.
MONTERO & MONTERO SPORT		
1996–99	Flow Connector Fitting To Power Steering Pump Body	43
	Hose Bracket Bolts	9
	Idler Arm Support Mounting Nuts	40–47
	Idler Arm To Support Nut	101
	Joint Assembly Clamp Bolt	22–25
	Oil Reservoir Mounting Nuts	9
	Outer Tie Rod End To Inner Tie Rod End Jam Nuts	53
	Pitman Arm To Power Steering Gearbox Nut	108–123
	Power Steering Gearbox Adjusting Bolt Locknut	27
	Power Steering Gearbox Mounting Nuts	40–47
	Power Steering Gearbox Side Cover Bolts	36
	Power Steering Pump Bracket Mounting Bolts	29
	Power Steering Pump Rear Cover Bolts	14
	Power Steering Pump Terminal Plug	18–22
	Pressure Hose Fitting At Gearbox	11
	Pressure Hose Fitting At Pump	14
	Pressure Pipe To Pressure Hose Fitting	25
	Relay Rod To Idler Arm Ball Joint Nut	33
	Relay Rod To Inner Tie Rod End Ball Joint Nut	33
	Relay Rod To Pitman Arm Nut	33
	Return Hose Fitting	11
	Suction Connector To Power Steering Pump Body Bolts	6

Continued

TIGHTENING
SPECIFICATIONS—Continued

Year	Component	Torque, Ft. Lbs.
PICKUP		
1996	Breather Pipe To Engine	6–9
	Breather Plug	24–48①
	Column Shaft Assembly To Steering Gearbox (2WD)	11–14
	Column Tube Clamp Bolt	36–48①
	Dash Panel Cover	24–48①
	Idler Arm Support To Frame	25–29
	Idler Arm To Idler Arm Support	29–43
	Joint Assembly To Steering Gearbox (4WD)	22–25
	Locknut Less Special Tool	130–166
	Locknut w/Special Tool	98–127
	Oil Pump Body To Oil Pump Bracket (2WD)	18–24
	Oil Pump Body To Oil Pump Bracket (4WD)	25–33
	Oil Pump Bracket (RH Front, 2WD)	12–19
	Oil Pump Bracket (RH Front, 4WD)	18–24
	Oil Pump Bracket (RH Rear)	12–19
	Oil Pump Bracket To Engine (Front)	18–24
	Oil Pump Connector Assembly	51–58
	Oil Pump Cover (2WD) ③	13–16
	Oil Pump Reservoir Assembly	7–10
	Oil Pump Suction Connector (2WD) ③	48–84①
	Oil Pump To Pressure Hose	12–19
	Pitman Arm	94–108
	Pitman Arm To Relay Rod	33
	Power Gearbox	40–47
	Power Steering Adjusting Bolt Locknut	22–33
	Power Steering Gearbox Side Cover	22–33
	Power Steering Gearbox To Pressure Hose	9–13
	Power Steering Gearbox To Return Hose	9–13
	Power Steering Valve Housing	33–40
	Pressure Hose Clip	7–10
	Pressure Hose Gearbox Side	9–14
	Pressure Hose To Oil Pump Side	12–19
	Pressure Tube Flare Nut (2WD)	9–14
	Relay Arm To Idler Arm	33
	Relay Rod To Pitman Arm	33
	Return Hose Clip	7–10
	Return Hose Or Tube	9–14
	Socket Assembly To Yoke (2WD)	14–18
	Steering Wheel Locknut	25–33
	Tie Rod End To Knuckle	33
	Tie Rod End To Pipe (2WD)	36–40
	Tie Rod End To Pipe (4WD)	47–58
	Tie Rod End To Relay Rod	33
	Tilt Bracket Bolts	6–9
	Tube Clip (4WD)	7–10
	Tube Stay	7–10

Continued

TIGHTENING
SPECIFICATIONS—Continued

Year	Component	Torque, Ft. Lbs.
3000GT		
1996–99	Cooler Tube Clamps	48①
	Gearbox Assembly Clamps	51
	Joint Assembly & Gearbox Connecting Bolt	13
	LH Member Installation Bolts	43–51
	Oil Pump Bracket Lower Bolt	31
	Oil Pump Bracket Upper Bolt	16
	Oil Pump To Bracket Lower Bolt	31
	Oil Pump To Bracket Upper Nut	31
	Oil Reservoir Mounting Bolts	8
	Pressure Hose To Oil Pump	17
	Pressure Tube To Pressure Hose Connector	25
	Return Hose To Cooler Tube Clamps	8
	RH Member Installation Bolts	43–51
	Stabilizer Bar Bracket	29
	Steering Column Support Assembly	8
	Steering Column To Joint Assembly	13
	Steering Gearbox Clamp	51
	Steering Wheel Locknut	29
	Tie Rod End & Knuckle Connecting Nut	36
	Tubing Clamp	48①
	Tubing Connectors To Gearbox	11
	Tubing Hold-Down Clamp	8

① — Inch lbs.

② — 1.8L engine.

③ — 2.0L non-turbocharged engine.

④ — 2.0L turbocharged engine & 2.4L engine.

⑤ — 1.5L engine.

Four Wheel Steering

NOTE: On Air Bag Equipped Models, Refer To " Air Bag System Precautions" Located In The Front Of This Manual For System Disarming & Arming Procedures.

NOTE: For Procedures Not Found In This Section, Refer To The "Power Steering" Section.

INDEX

STEERING PRESSURE SPECIFICATIONS

Model	Disp., Qts. @ mph	Relief Set Pressure, psi
Diamante	1.06 @ 31	569
3000GT	1.06 @ 31	569

PRECAUTIONS

AIR BAG SYSTEMS

Refer to "Air Bag System Precautions" in the front of this manual for system disarming and arming procedures.

BATTERY GROUND CABLE

Prior to service, disconnect battery ground cable and isolate as required.

DESCRIPTION

The Four Wheel Steering (4WS) system is designed to improve handling under a variety of conditions by adding steering control to the vehicle's rear wheels. A conventional steering gear is utilized to control front wheel steering; the addition of a vane type rear oil pump and hydraulic double action power cylinder allows full four wheel steering control. The power cylinder acts as a rear wheel steering gear.

TROUBLESHOOTING

Refer to **Fig. 1** when troubleshooting the Four Wheel Steering (4WS) system.

DIAGNOSIS & TESTING

FUNCTIONAL INSPECTION

1. Raise and support vehicle.

2. Start engine, place transaxle in Drive

3. Quickly turn steering wheel from stop

Malfunction symptom	Malfunctioning system	Inspection item
4WS does not operate	Power cylinder	Tie rod swing torque
		Power cylinder slide resistance
	Rear oil pump	Flow volume check
	Control valve	
Poor steering feeling Feeling of friction in steering Poor steering return	Steering gears and linkage	Rack cracks or deformation
Steering wheel efforts excessive	Control valve	Oil leakage from control valve joint
	Power cylinder	Oil leakage from piston rod
	Oil line	Pressure hose breakage
	Oil reservoir	Oil reservoir deformation or oil leakage
Rear wheels cannot be steered Poor rear wheels return Hydraulic pressure for rear wheel is constantly high	Control valve	Stuck control valve spool
	Power cylinder	Stuck power cylinder
	Rear oil pump	Relief valve remains open
Long rear wheel steering delay Poor steering response Poor steering return	Power cylinder	Excessive power cylinder friction
		Looseness in power cylinder tie rod ball joint
		Ball joint dust cover cracks
Poor rear wheel steering response Poor rear wheel steering range	Control valve	Oil leakage from control valve spool
	Power cylinder	Oil leakage from power cylinder
	Rear oil pump	Extreme oil pump internal wear
Poor steerability (extreme tire wear)	Power cylinder	Tie rod length improperly adjusted after toe-in adjustment

MT6029100042000X

Fig. 1   4WS system troubleshooting chart

range and raise indicated vehicle speed to 50 mph. **Ensure vehicle is properly supported and secured for this step. Use extreme caution when working around moving wheels.**

to stop, ensure rear wheels steer in same direction as front wheels.

REAR OIL PUMP DISCHARGE FLOW VOLUME INSPECTION

1. Disconnect pressure hose from rear oil

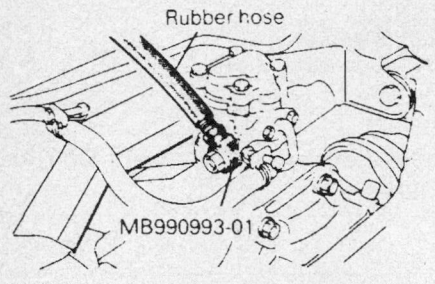

Fig. 2 Adapter tool connection

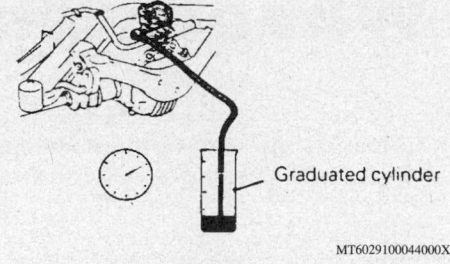

Fig. 3 Flow volume measurement

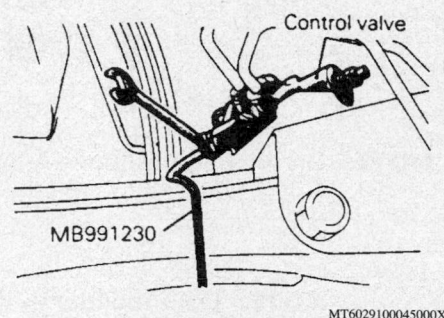

Fig. 4 4WS system bleed

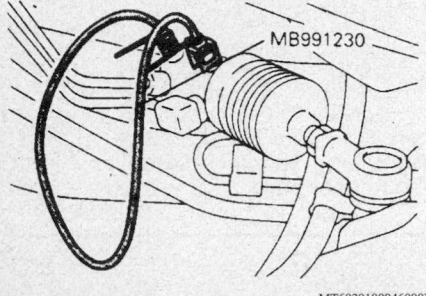

Fig. 5 Rear power cylinder bleed

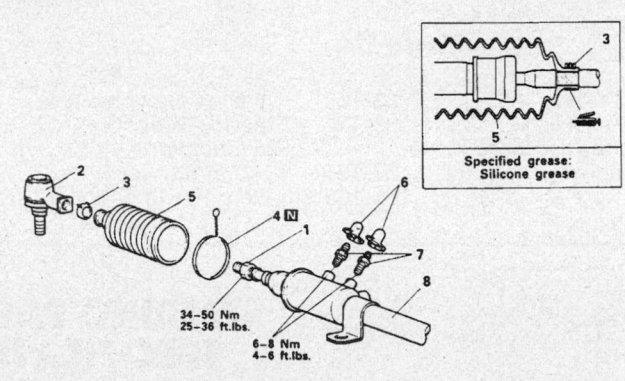

Disassembly steps
1. Nut
2. Tie rod end assembly
3. Clip
4. Wire
5. Dust cover
6. Bleeder caps
7. Bleeder screws
8. Cylinder assembly

Fig. 6 Rear power cylinder service

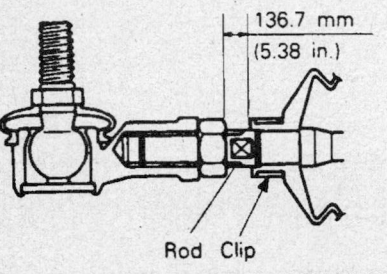

Fig. 7 Tie rod installation. Diamante

pump and install power steering oil pressure gauge adapter tool No. MB990993-01, or equivalent, **Fig. 2.**
2. Connect a suitable rubber hose to tool and place other end into a two quart graduated container.
3. Raise and support vehicle.
4. Start engine and place transaxle in Drive position, then slowly raise indicated vehicle speed to 31 mph and hold, measuring discharge flow volume for 30 seconds, **Fig. 3. Ensure vehicle is properly supported and secured for this step. Use extreme caution when working around moving wheels.**
5. If the discharge flow volume is not as specified in " Power Steering Pressure Specifications" chart, rear oil pump should be replaced.

SYSTEM SERVICE

4WS SYSTEM BLEED

1. Bleed air from power steering system as outlined in the " Power Steering" section.

2. Raise and support vehicle just off ground.
3. Start engine and allow to idle.
4. Loosen bleeder screw on left side of control valve and install air bleeder set tool No. MB991230, or equivalent, on bleeder screw, **Fig. 4.**
5. Turn steering wheel to left stop, then immediately return it to center position. Air will be discharged with fluid. **Ensure reservoir is kept filled.**
6. Repeat preceding step two or three times until all air is bled from system.
7. Repeat preceding bleed steps using right side bleeder screw.
8. Turn ignition switch to Off position.
9. Install air bleeder tool on rear power cylinder, **Fig. 5.**
10. Start engine, place transaxle in Drive position and raise indicated vehicle speed to 43–50 mph to circulate fluid. **Ensure vehicle is properly supported and secured for this step. Use extreme caution when working around moving wheels.**
11. Reduce indicated vehicle speed to 19–25 mph, turn steering wheel from stop to stop. Air will be bleed into reservoir at this time. When steering wheel is at each stop air will circulate inside special hose.
12. Repeat preceding step several times until no more air is seen in reservoir.

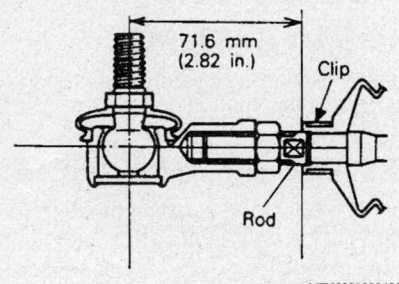

Fig. 8 Tie rod installation. 3000GT

REAR POWER CYLINDER (STEERING GEAR) SERVICE

Service rear power cylinder (steering gear) in numbered sequence shown in **Fig. 6**, positioning tie rod end as shown in **Figs. 7 and 8.**

REAR POWER STEERING PUMP SERVICE

The rear power steering pump is not serviceable and must be replaced if inoperative.

TIGHTENING SPECIFICATIONS

Year	Component	Torque, Ft. Lbs.
DIAMANTE		
1996–99	Bleeder Screw	7
	Control Valve Mounting Bolt	8
	Fluid Line Flare Nuts	11
	Front Pressure Tubes To Control Valve	11
	Pipe Assembly To Pressure Tube Connectors	25
	Power Cylinder Bolt	30
	Pressure Hose To Pressure Tube Connector	11
	Pressure Tube To Control Valve	11
	Rear Oil Pump	17
	Rear Pipe Assembly Hold-Down Brackets	9
	Rear RH Pressure Tube To Control Valve	11
	Tie Rod End Nuts	30
3000GT		
1996–99	Bleeder Screw	7
	Control Valve Mounting Bolt	9
	Fluid Line Flare Nuts	11
	Front Pressure Tubes To Control Valve	11
	Pipe Assembly To Pressure Tube Connectors	25
	Power Cylinder Bolt	30
	Power Cylinder Boot Bolt	30
	Power Cylinder To Joint Nut	30
	Pressure Hose To Pressure Tube Connector	25
	Pressure Tube To Control Valve	25
	Rear Pipe Assembly Hold Down Brackets	9
	Rear RH Pressure Tube To Control Valve	11
	Tie Rod End Nuts	42

Disc Brakes

TABLE OF CONTENTS

Mirage

INDEX

APPLICATION CHART

Year	Model	Caliper No.
FRONT		
1996	2 Door 1.5L	MR31S
	2 Door 1.8L	MR34V
	4 Door	MR34V
REAR		
1996	All	AD30P

BRAKE SYSTEM BLEED

The hydraulic brake system must be bled if air has entered the system. This could be caused by an open in the system, or replacement of a hydraulic system component. Symptoms include loss of brake operation, and a low or spongy brake pedal.

On models with ABS, use a suitable filter when adding fluid to reservoir tank.

1. Ensure master cylinder reservoir is full. Add suitable brake fluid as needed, and securely reinstall the master cylinder cap.
2. Raise and support vehicle.
3. Position a drain pan under the wheel being bled.
4. Have an assistant depress the brake pedal with a slow even pressure and hold it. **Do not press brake pedal to the end of the master cylinder stroke. This may cause damage to the master cylinder.**
5. Using a suitable wrench, open the bleeder valve one full turn. Watch for air bubbles in the fluid, and listen for air escaping from the system.
6. With the brake pedal still depressed, close the bleeder valve.
7. Have the assistant pump the brake pedal several times. **Pressing brake pedal to the end of the master cylinder stroke, this may cause damage to the master cylinder.**
8. Repeat preceding bleed steps until all air is removed from the hydraulic system. **While bleeding the system, re-check brake fluid supply in the master cylinder often. Do not allow the master cylinder to run dry.**
9. After system bleed, proceed as follows:
   a. Ensure the master cylinder reservoir is full. Add suitable brake fluid as needed.
   b. Lower the vehicle and ensure brake pedal is firm and braking operation is satisfactory.

BRAKE PAD SERVICE
REPLACEMENT
Front

1. Raise and support vehicle then remove wheel.
2. Remove guide/slide pins, **Figs. 1 through 5.**
3. Lift caliper assembly and support to frame suing suitable wire. **Guide pin is** coated with special grease. Be careful not to remove grease and ensure no dirt adheres to pin.
4. Remove inner & outer shims, anti-squeak shims and pad assembly.
5. Measure hub torque with pad removed to measure brake drag after pad installation, **Fig. 6.**
6. Securely attach pad clip to caliper support.
7. Press piston into cylinder. **Ensure piston boot does not become caught during installation.**
8. Lower caliper body and install lower guide pin, tightening to specification.
9. Check brake drag as follows:
   a. Start engine and hold brake pedal down for five seconds.
   b. Stop engine.
   c. Turn brake disc forward ten times.
   d. Check brake drag. If the difference between brake drag and hub torque measured in this procedure exceeds 4.4 lbs., disassemble piston and clean. Check piston and caliper for corrosion or worn parts.

Rear

1. Raise and support vehicle and remove wheel.

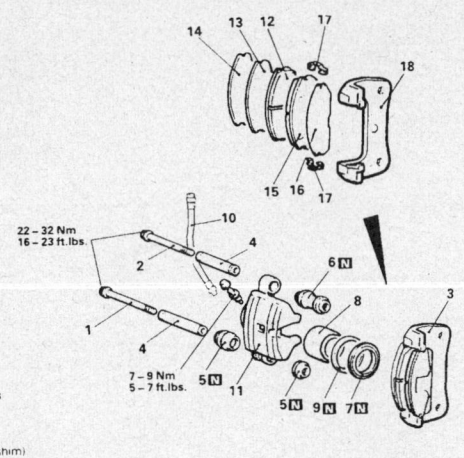

MT4079100001000X

Fig. 1   Exploded view of MR31S front disc brake assembly. 1996

Caliper disassembly steps
1 Sleeve bolt A
2 Sleeve bolt B
3 Caliper support
   (pad, retainer, shim)
4 Sleeve
5 Sleeve boot
6 Bushing
7 Dust boot
8 Piston
9 Piston seal
10 Brake hose
11 Caliper body

Pad assembly disassembly steps
1 Sleeve bolt A
2 Sleeve bolt B
3 Caliper support
   (pad, retainer, shim)
12 Pad assembly
13 Anti-squeak shim (inner)
14 Inner shim
15 Pad assembly
16 Anti-squeak shim (outer)
17 Pad retainer
18 Caliper support

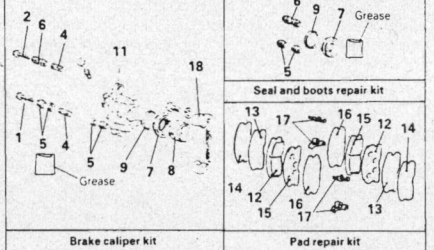

2. Loosen parking brake cable from inside vehicle then disconnect parking brake cable end on rear brake assembly.
3. Remove lower lockpin, **Fig. 7.**
4. Lift caliper assembly and secure to frame using suitable wire.
5. Remove outer shim and pad assembly.
6. Remove pad clips "C" and "B."
7. Measure hub torque with pad removed to be able to measure brake drag torque after installation, **Fig. 6.**
8. Attach pad clip to caliper support.
9. Clean piston surface then use rear disc brake piston driver tool No. MB990652, or equivalent, to thread piston into cylinder. **Ensure the stopper grove of piston correctly fits to projection on pads rear surface.**
10. Install pads and shims onto caliper assembly.
11. Lower caliper assembly and install lockpin. **Ensure piston boot does not become caught when lowering the caliper into place.**
12. Check brake drag torque as follows:
    a. Start engine and hold brake pedal down for five seconds.
    b. Stop engine and turn disc rotor forward ten times.
    c. If difference between brake drag torque and hub torque exceeds 4.4 lbs., disassemble piston and clean piston. Check for corrosion, wear or damaged on brake caliper components.

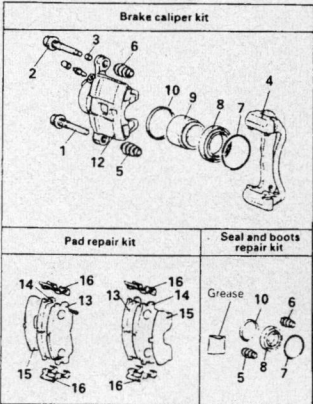

MT4079100002000X

Fig. 2   Exploded view of MR34V front disc brake assembly. 1996

Caliper assembly disassembly steps
1 Guide pin
2 Lock pin
3 Bushing
4 Caliper support (pad, clip, shim)
5 Guide pin boot
6 Lock pin boot
7 Boot ring
8 Piston boot
9 Piston
10 Piston seal
11 Brake hose
12 Caliper body

Pad assembly disassembly steps
1 Lock pin
2 Guide pin
3 Bushing
4 Caliper support
   (pad, clip, shim)
13 Pad and wear indicator assembly
14 Pad assembly
15 Outer shim
16 Clip

CALIPER SERVICE

REPLACEMENT

Front

1. Raise and support vehicle, then remove wheel.
2. Disconnect and cap brake hose.
3. Remove sleeve bolts, sleeves, boot pins and bushings, then the caliper body from torque member.
4. Reverse procedure to install, noting the following:
   a. Replace bushing and pin boot.
   b. Tighten sleeve bolts to specifications.
   c. Bleed brake system as outlined in "Brake System Bleed."

Rear

1. Raise and support vehicle, then remove wheel.
2. Disconnect and cap brake hose.
3. Disconnect parking brake cable.
4. Remove upper and lower guide pin then the caliper assembly.
5. Reverse procedure to install, noting the following:
   a. Replace bushing and pin boot.
   b. Tighten sleeve bolts to specifications.
   c. Bleed brake system as outlined in "Brake System Bleed."

OVERHAUL & INSPECTION

Front

1. Place rag in front of piston, then remove piston and dust boot by applying compressed air through brake hose fitting hole. **Keep fingers clear of front of piston.**
2. Remove piston seal. Use caution not to scratch the cylinder walls.
3. Check cylinder and piston for wear, damage and/or corrosion. Repair or replace as required.
4. Check caliper body and sleeve for wear. Replace as required.
5. Apply suitable brake fluid to the cylinder walls.
6. Apply an even coat of suitable grease to the new piston seal, then install seal in cylinder.
7. Install piston into cylinder. Use caution not to twist piston seal.
8. Apply suitable grease to dust boot, then install boot on piston and cylinder.

Rear

1. Remove caliper.
2. Disassemble caliper in numbered sequence, **Fig. 7,** noting the following:
   a. Use rear disc brake piston driver tool No. MB990652, or equivalent, to remove piston from caliper assembly.

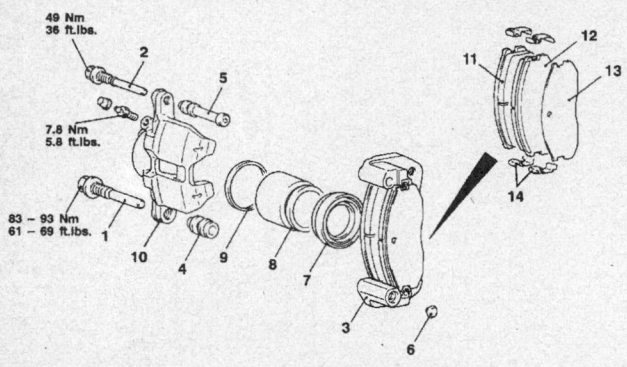

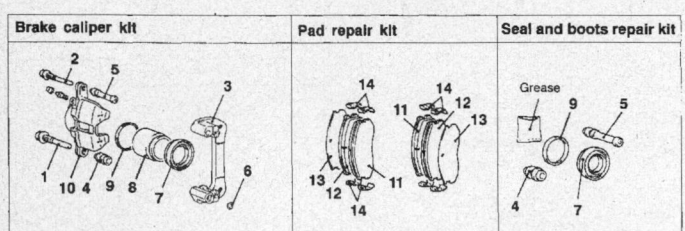

Fig. 3   Exploded view of front disc brake assembly. 1997–98

MT4079700037000X

Caliper assembly disassembly steps
1. Slide pin (M14)
2. Slide pin (M10)
3. Torque member (pad, pad liner, shim)
4. Boot
5. Bush
6. Plug
7. Piston boot
8. Piston
9. Piston seal
10. Caliper body

Pad assembly disassembly steps
1. Slide pin (M14)
2. Slide pin (M10)
3. Torque member (pad, pad liner, shim)
11. Pad and wear indicator assembly <L.H.> or pad assembly <R.H.>
12. Pad assembly
13. Outer shim (coated with rubber)
14. Pad liner

Fig. 4   Exploded view of front disc brake assembly. 1999 w/13 inch wheels

MT4079900040000X

Caliper assembly disassembly steps
1. Slide pin (M14)
2. Slide pin (M10)
3. Torque member, pad, pad clip, shim assembly
4. Torque member
5. Boot
6. Bush
7. Plug
8. Piston boot
9. Piston
10. Piston seal
11. Caliper body

Pad assembly disassembly steps
1. Slide pin (M14)
2. Slide pin (M10)
3. Torque member, pad, pad liner, shim assembly
12. Pad and wear indicator assembly <L.H.> or pad assembly <R.H.>
13. Pad assembly
14. Outer shim (coated with rubber)
15. Pad clip

b. Remove piston seal with fingers. **Do not use a screwdriver or other tool to prevent damage to cylinder inner surface.**

c. Use a .75 inch diameter steel pipe to press the spring case into the caliper body, then remove snap ring from caliper body using suitable snap ring pliers, **Fig. 8.**

3. Reverse numbered sequence, **Fig. 7** when assembling caliper, noting the following:

a. Use a .75 inch diameter steel pipe to press the spring case into the caliper body, then install snap ring into caliper body using suitable snap ring pliers. **Attach snap ring to caliper body with opening facing the bleeder.**

b. Push piston into caliper using piston driver tool and align groove, **Fig. 9.**

c. When installing brake pads, pins in pad must be placed in grooves in piston.

ROTOR
REPLACE
FRONT

1. Raise and support vehicle, then remove wheel.

2. Remove caliper as described under "Caliper Service" and secure aside. **Do not allow caliper to hang from brake hose.**

3. Remove rotor from hub.

4. Reverse procedure to install.

REAR

1. Raise and support vehicle, then remove rear wheels.

2. Loosen parking brake adjusting nut.

3. Remove parking brake cable retaining clip and spring, then disconnect parking brake cable.

4. Remove caliper bolts, then lift off caliper and secure aside.

5. Remove rotor retaining screw, then the rotor.

6. Reverse procedure to install, noting the following:

a. Tighten fasteners to specifications.

b. Adjust parking brake as outlined under "Adjustments."

ADJUSTMENTS
PARKING BRAKE

1. Pull parking brake lever with a force of approximately 45 lbs. and count number of clicks. Lever stroke should be 5–7 clicks.

2. If parking brake lever stroke is not within specifications, proceed as follows:

a. Remove center console, then loosen adjusting nut on end of cable rod to free parking brake cable.

b. With engine idling, depress brake pedal several times and confirm that the pedal stroke stops changing. **If pedal stroke stops changing, it indicates that automatic adjusting mechanism is functioning properly to adjust clearance between pads and disc to correct value.**

c. Ensure parking lever on caliper side is in contact with the stopper.

d. Turn adjusting nut to adjust parking brake lever stroke to specified range. **If number of brake lever notches engaged are less than specified value, cable has been pulled excessively and failure of the automatic adjuster mechanism may result.**

e. After adjusting lever stroke, raise and support rear of vehicle. With parking brake lever released, turn rear wheels to ensure rear brakes are not dragging.

f. Ensure parking brake lever on caliper side is in contact with the stopper.

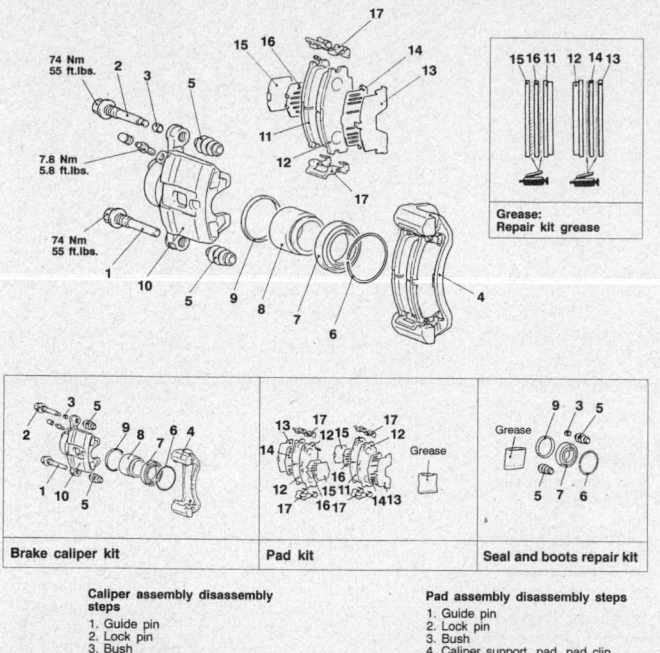

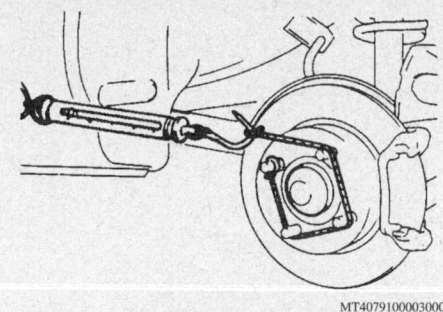

Fig. 6 Hub & brake drag torque measurement

Caliper assembly disassembly steps
1. Guide pin
2. Lock pin
3. Bush
4. Caliper support, pad, pad clip, shim assembly
5. Boot
6. Boot ring
7. Piston boot
8. Piston
9. Piston seal
10. Caliper body

Pad assembly disassembly steps
1. Guide pin
2. Lock pin
3. Bush
4. Caliper support, pad, pad clip, shim assembly
11. Pad and wear indicator assembly <L.H.> or pad assembly <R.H.>
12. Pad assembly
13. Outer shim
14. Outer shim
15. Inner shim
16. Inner shim
17. Pad clip

MT4079900041000X

Fig. 5 Exploded view of front disc brake assembly. 1999 w/14 inch wheels

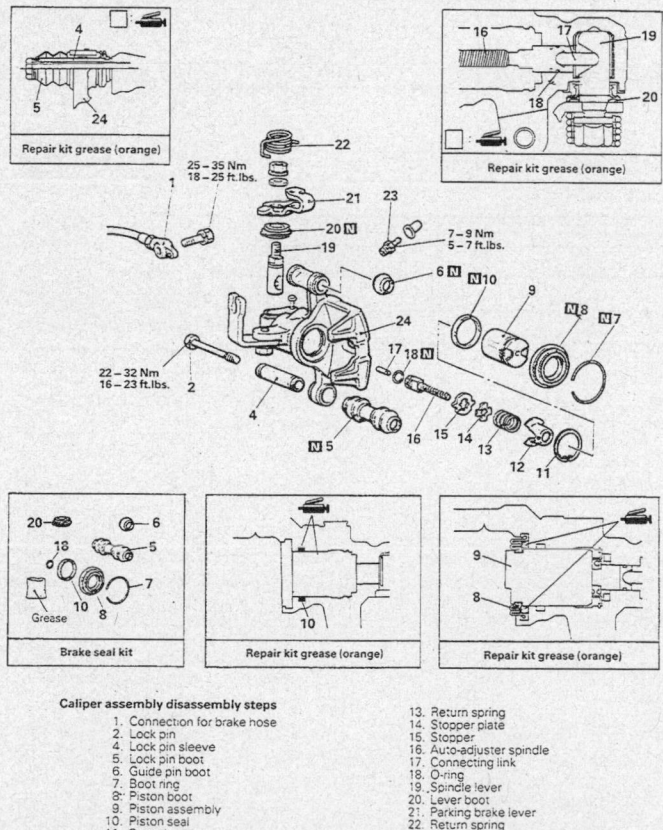

MT4079100004010X

Fig. 7 Exploded view of rear disc brake assembly (Part 1 of 2)

Caliper assembly disassembly steps
1. Connection for brake hose
2. Lock pin
4. Lock pin sleeve
5. Lock pin boot
6. Guide pin boot
7. Boot ring
8. Piston boot
9. Piston assembly
10. Piston seal
11. Snap ring
12. Spring case
13. Return spring
14. Stopper plate
15. Stopper
16. Auto-adjuster spindle
17. Connecting link
18. O-ring
19. Spindle lever
20. Lever boot
21. Parking brake lever
22. Return spring
23. Bleeder screw
24. Caliper body

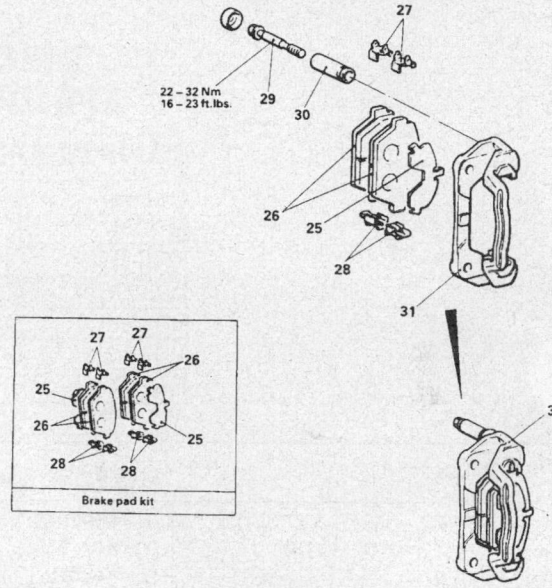

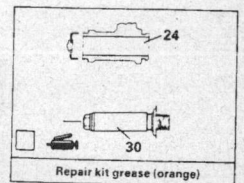

Pad assembly disassembly steps
2. Lock pin
3. Support mounting (pad, shim, clip)
25. Outer shim
26. Pad assembly
27. Pad clip C
28. Pad clip B
29. Guide pin
30. Guide pin sleeve
31. Support mounting

MT4079100004020X

Fig. 7 Exploded view of rear disc brake assembly (Part 2 of 2)

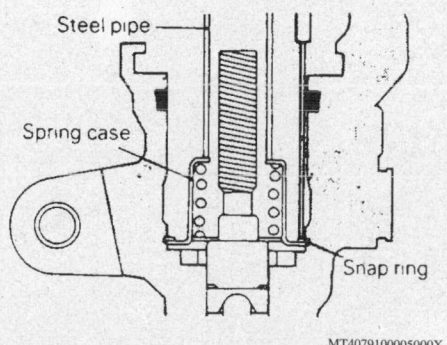

MT4079100005000X

Fig. 8 Spring case removal

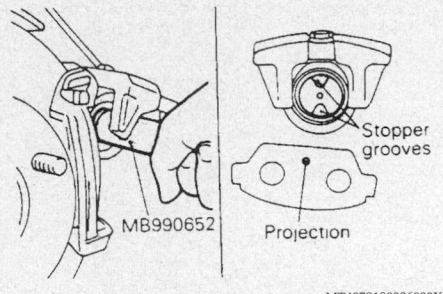

Fig. 9 Caliper piston installation

DISC BRAKE SPECIFICATIONS

CALIPER SPECIFICATIONS

Caliper Model	Caliper Bore Diameter, Inch
FRONT	
MR31S	2.0100
MR34V	2.1250
1997–99	2.1300
REAR	
All	1.1875

ROTOR SPECIFICATIONS

Rotor Type	Nominal Thickness, Inch	Minimum Refinish Thickness, Inch	Lateral Runout (T.I.R.), Inch
1996–98 FRONT			
Solid Rotor	.510	.450	.003
Ventilated Rotor	.710	.650	.003
1999 FRONT			
13 Inch Wheel	.710	.650	.003
14 Inch Wheel	.940	.880	.003
REAR			
All	.370	.330	.003

TIGHTENING SPECIFICATIONS

Year	Component	Torque, Ft. Lbs.
1996–99	Bleeder Screw	5–7
	Caliper Brake Line Hollow Bolt	22
	Caliper Mounting Bolt	65
	Flared Brake Line Nuts	9–12
	Front Brake Assembly Mounting Bolt	58–72
	Guide Pin (M-R31S Type)	61–69
	Guide Pin (M-R34V Type)	27–36
	Guide Pin (M-R46V Type)	46–62
	Guide Pin (1997–99 M10 Pin)	36
	Guide Pin (1997–99 M14 Pin)	61–69
	Lockpin (M-R31S & M-R34V Type)	27–36
	Lockpin (M-R46V)	46–62
	Wheel Bearing Nut	108–145
	Wheel Lug Nut	87–101

Eclipse & Galant

INDEX

APPLICATION CHART

Year	Model	Caliper No.
FRONT		
1996–99	Eclipse FWD	MR46V
	Eclipse AWD	MR56W
	Galant	MR46V
REAR		
1996–99	Eclipse	MR45S

BRAKE SYSTEM BLEED

The hydraulic brake system must be bled if air has entered the system. This condition may be caused by low fluid level, a hydraulic fluid leak, the opening of a hydraulic line or replacement of a hydraulic system component. Symptoms include a loss of basic brake operation and/or a low or spongy brake pedal.

On models equipped with ABS, use a suitable filter when adding fluid to reservoir tank.

1. Ensure master cylinder reservoir is full. Add suitable brake fluid as needed, and securely reinstall the master cylinder cap.
2. Raise and support vehicle.
3. Position a drain pan under the wheel being bled.
4. Have an assistant depress the brake pedal with a slow even pressure and hold it. **Do not depress brake pedal fully to the end of the master cylinder stroke. This may cause damage to the master cylinder.**
5. Using a suitable wrench, open the bleeder valve one full turn. Watch for air bubbles in the fluid, and listen for air escaping from the system.
6. With the brake pedal still depressed, close the bleeder valve.
7. Have the assistant pump the brake pedal several times. **Do not depress brake pedal fully to the end of the master cylinder stroke, this may cause damage to the master cylinder.**
8. Repeat preceding bleed steps until all air is removed from the hydraulic system. **While bleeding the system, recheck brake fluid supply in the**
master cylinder often so as not to allow the master cylinder to run dry.
9. Upon completion of hydraulic system bleeding, proceed as follows:
   a. Ensure the master cylinder reservoir is full. Add suitable brake fluid as needed, and securely reinstall the master cylinder cap.
   b. Lower the vehicle. Ensure brake pedal is firm and braking operation is satisfactory.

BRAKE PAD SERVICE

REPLACEMENT

Front

1. Raise and support vehicle, then remove wheel.
2. Remove lower lockpin, **Figs. 1 and 2,**

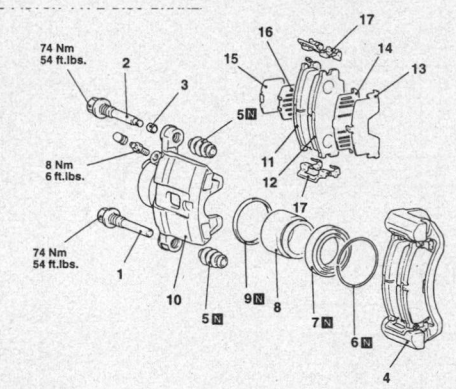

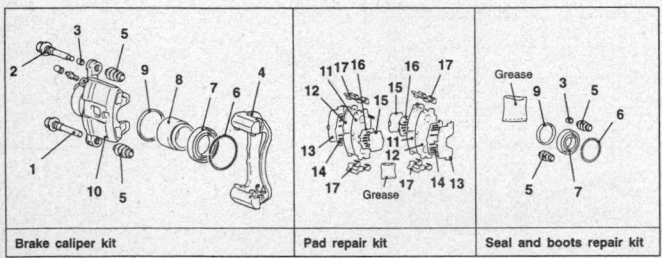

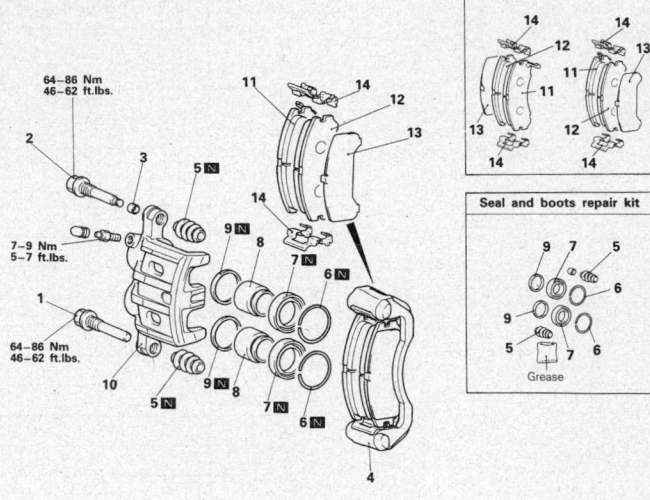

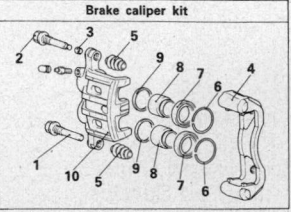

Pad repair kit

Seal and boots repair kit

Brake caliper kit

Caliper assembly disassembly steps

1. Guide pin
2. Lock pin
3. Bush
4. Caliper support (Pad, clip, shim)
5. Boot
6. Boot ring
7. Piston boot
8. Piston
9. Piston seal
10. Caliper body

Pad assembly disassembly steps

1. Guide pin
2. Lock pin
3. Bush
4. Caliper support (Pad, clip, shim)
11. Pad and wear indicator assembly
12. Pad assembly
13. Outer shim
14. Clip

MT4079100008000A

Brake caliper kit

Caliper assembly disassembly steps

1. Guide pin
2. Lock pin
3. Bushing
4. Caliper support (pad, clip, shim)
5. Boot
6. Boot ring
7. Piston boot
8. Piston
9. Piston seal
10. Caliper body

Pad assembly disassembly steps

1. Guide pin
2. Lock pin
3. Bushing
4. Caliper support (pad, clip, shim)
11. Pad and wear indicator assembly
12. Pad assembly
13. Outer shim (stainless)
14. Outer shim (coated with rubber)
15. Inner shim (stainless)
16. Inner shim (coated with rubber)
17. Clip

MT4079100007000A

Fig. 1   Exploded view of MR46V disc brake assembly

Fig. 2   Exploded view of MR56W disc brake assembly

and lift caliper body upward, then support caliper with wire. **Lockpin is coated with special grease. Use caution not to remove grease and ensure no dirt adheres to pin.**

3. Remove inner shim(s), anti-squeak shim and pad assemblies from support mounting.
4. Remove pad clips.
5. Measure hub torque with pad removed to aid in measuring brake drag torque after pad installation, **Fig. 3.**
6. Install pad clips, pad assemblies, inner shim(s) and anti-squeak shim onto the support mounting.
7. Apply a coating of suitable grease to the pad and anti-squeak shim contact surface and to the anti-squeak shim and inner shim contact surface. **Ensure grease does not come in contact with brake pad assemble.**
8. Lower caliper body into position, then install lower lockpin tightening to specification.
9. Check brake drag torque as follows:
   a. Start engine and hold brake pedal down for five seconds.
   b. Stop engine and turn brake rotor forward ten turns.
   c. Check brake drag using suitable tool.
   d. If the difference between brake drag torque and hub torque ex-

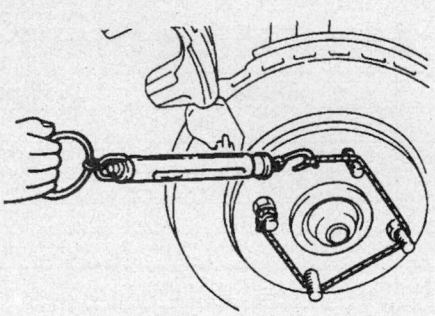

MT4079100009000X

Fig. 3   Hub & brake drag torque measurement

ceeds 3 ft. lbs., disassemble caliper assembly, clean and check for corrosion, worn or damaged parts.
10. Install wheel.

Rear

1. Raise and support vehicle, then remove wheel.
2. Remove parking brake cable.
3. Remove lower lockpin, **Fig. 4,** and lift caliper body upward, then support caliper with wire. **Lockpin is coated with special grease. Use caution not to remove grease and ensure no dirt adheres to pin.**

4. Remove outer shim and pad assembly from caliper support.
5. Remove pad clips.
6. Measure hub torque with pad removed to aid in measuring brake drag torque after pad installation, **Fig. 3.**
7. Press piston into cylinder using a suitable tool. Ensure stopper grooves in rear of piston are in the vertical position.
8. Install pad clips, then the pad and shim as an assembly onto the caliper support. Pins on back side of brake pad must be placed in grooves of piston.
9. Lower caliper body into position, then install lower lockpin tightening to specification.
10. With engine running, forcefully depress brake pedal five to six times and ensure the stroke of the parking brake lever is .078 inch or less, **Fig. 5.**
11. Check brake drag torque as follows:
    a. Start engine and hold brake pedal down for five seconds.
    b. Stop engine and turn brake rotor forward ten turns.
    c. Check brake drag using suitable tool.
    d. If the difference between brake drag torque and hub torque exceeds 3 ft. lbs., disassemble caliper

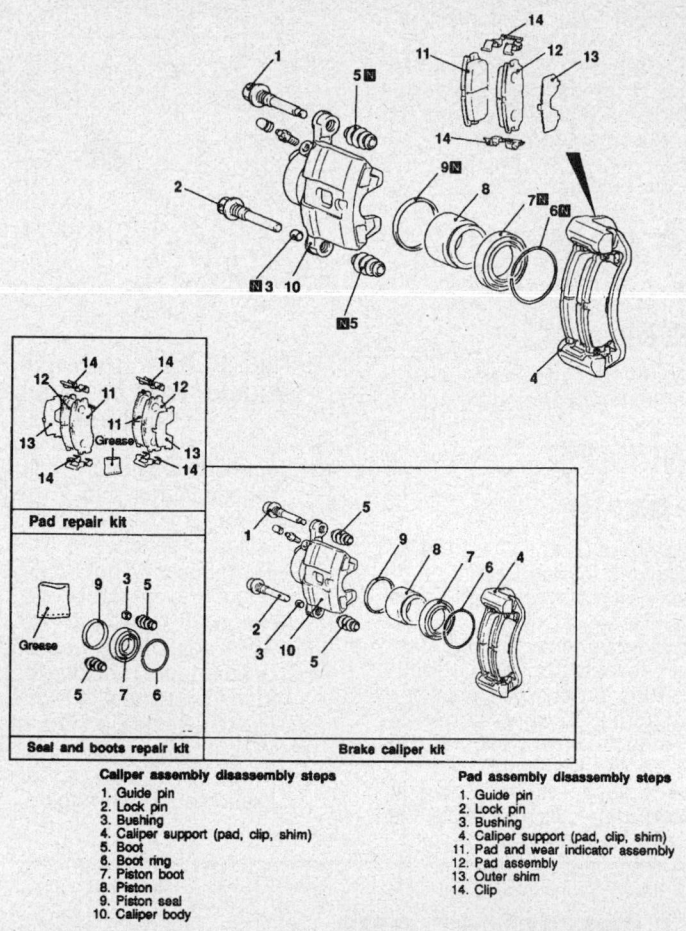

Fig. 4 Exploded view of MR45S disc brake assembly

Caliper assembly disassembly steps
1. Guide pin
2. Lock pin
3. Bushing
4. Caliper support (pad, clip, shim)
5. Boot
6. Boot ring
7. Piston boot
8. Piston
9. Piston seal
10. Caliper body

Pad assembly disassembly steps
1. Guide pin
2. Lock pin
3. Bushing
4. Caliper support (pad, clip, shim)
11. Pad and wear indicator assembly
12. Pad assembly
13. Outer shim
14. Clip

MT4079100011000A

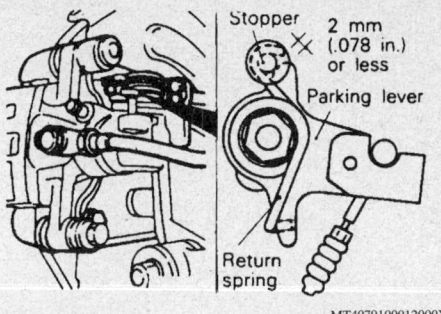

Fig. 5 Parking brake adjustment

MT4079100012000X

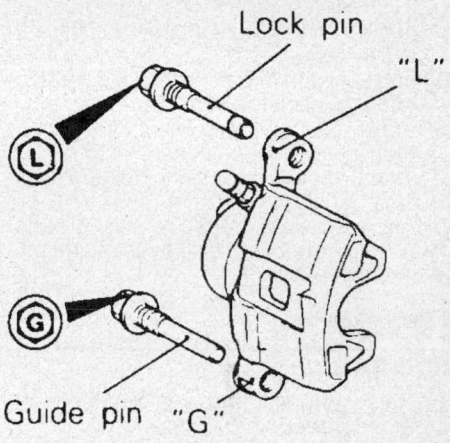

Fig. 6 Caliper bolt location. MR46V caliper

MT4079100013000X

assembly, clean and check for corroded, worn or damaged parts.
12. Install wheel.

CALIPER SERVICE
REPLACEMENT
Front

1. Raise and support vehicle, then remove wheel.
2. Disengage strut brake hose clips, then disconnect brake hose.
3. Remove lockpins, then the caliper assembly.
4. Reverse procedure to install, noting the following:
   a. Replace pin boots.
   b. **On models equipped with MR46V calipers,** install guide and lockpin so identification mark on pin matches mark on caliper body, **Fig. 6.**
   c. **On all models,** bleed brake system as outlined under "Brake System Bleed."

Rear

1. Raise and support vehicle, then remove rear wheel.
2. Disconnect parking brake cable from caliper assembly.

3. Disconnect brake hoses and brake tubes.
4. Remove lockpins from caliper assembly, noting position for installation reference.
5. Remove caliper assembly to adapter attaching bolts.
6. Remove caliper assembly.
7. Reverse procedure to install, noting the following:
   a. Install lockpins into original position using marks on pin head and marks on caliper body.
   b. Tighten bolts to specifications.
   c. Bleed brake system as outlined under "Brake System Bleed."

OVERHAUL & INSPECTION
Front

1. Remove boot ring.
2. Place rag in front of piston, then remove piston and dust boot by applying compressed air through brake hose fitting hole. Keep fingers clear of front of piston.
3. Remove piston seal. Use caution not to scratch the cylinder walls.
4. Remove sleeve and boot from caliper body.
5. Check cylinder and piston for wear, damage and/or corrosion. Repair or replace as required.

6. Check caliper body and sleeve for wear. Replace as required.
7. Apply suitable brake fluid to the cylinder walls.
8. Apply an even coat of suitable grease to the new piston seal, then install seal in cylinder.
9. Install piston into cylinder. Use caution not to twist piston seal.
10. Apply suitable grease to dust boot, then install boot on piston.
11. Attach piston boot onto cylinder with the boot ring.
12. Apply suitable grease to sliding parts of caliper body and sleeves, guide pin and lockpin boot.

Rear

1. Remove boot ring.
2. Place rag in front of piston, then remove piston and dust boot by applying compressed air through brake hose fitting hole. Keep fingers clear of front of piston.
3. Remove piston seal. Use caution not to scratch the cylinder walls.
4. Remove sleeve and boot from caliper body.
5. Check cylinder and piston for wear, damage and/or corrosion. Repair or replace as required.
6. Check caliper body and sleeve for wear. Replace as required.
7. Apply suitable brake fluid to the cylinder walls.
8. Apply an even coat of suitable grease

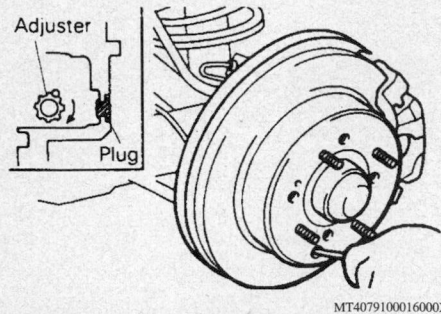

Fig. 7 Parking brake adjuster rotation

MT4079100016000X

to the new piston seal, then install seal in cylinder.
9. Install piston into cylinder. Use caution not to twist piston seal.
10. Apply suitable grease to dust boot, then install boot on piston.
11. Attach piston boot onto cylinder with the boot ring.
12. Apply suitable grease to sliding parts of caliper body and sleeves, guide pin and lockpin boot.

ROTOR
REPLACE

1. Raise and support vehicle, then remove wheel.

2. Separate caliper from adapter as described under "Brake Pad Service." It is not necessary to disconnect brake hose from caliper; suspend caliper aside with suitable wire to prevent brake hose damage.
3. Remove rotor assembly from hub.
4. Reverse procedure to install.

PARKING BRAKE SERVICE
ADJUSTMENT

Refer to "Adjustments" in this section for parking brake adjustment procedures.

ADJUSTMENTS
PARKING BRAKE

1. Pull parking brake lever with a force of approximately 45 lbs. and count number of clicks. Lever stroke should be as follows:
2. Lever should move three to five clicks.
3. If parking brake lever stroke is not within specifications, proceed as follows:
   a. Remove center console, then loosen adjusting nut on end of cable rod to free parking brake cable.
   b. Remove adjustment hole plug in disc rotor, then use a suitable flat

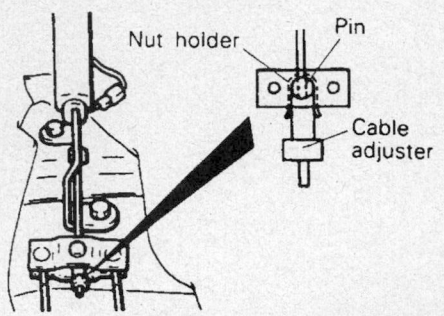

Fig. 8 Parking brake cable adjuster freeplay inspection. Eclipse

MT4079100017000X

screwdriver to turn adjuster in direction shown, **Fig. 7.**
c. Return adjuster five notches in opposite direction.
d. Turn adjusting nut to adjust parking brake lever stroke to specified range.
e. After adjustment has been made, ensure there is no play between adjusting nut and pin, **Fig. 8.**
f. Raise and support rear of vehicle.
g. With parking brake lever released, turn rear wheel to ensure rear brakes are not dragging.

DISC BRAKE SPECIFICATIONS
CALIPER SPECIFICATIONS

Model	Caliper Bore Diameter, Inch
FRONT	
Eclipse Non-Turbo	2.3750
Eclipse FWD Turbo	2.3750
Eclipse AWD Turbo①	1.6875
Galant	2.3750
REAR	
Eclipse FWD	1.3750
Eclipse AWD	1.3750

① — Two piston caliper.

ROTOR SPECIFICATIONS

Year	Model	Nominal Thickness, Inch	Minimum Refinish Thickness, Inch	Lateral Runout (T.I.R.), Inch
FRONT				
1996–99	All	.940	.880	.0031
REAR				
1996–99	Eclipse	.390	.330	.0031

TIGHTENING SPECIFICATIONS

Year	Component	Torque, Ft. Lbs.
ECLIPSE		
1996–99	Bleeder Screw	6
	Brake Hose To Front Caliper	11
	Brake Hose To Rear Caliper	11
	Caliper Body To Caliper Support	54
	Front Caliper To Backing Plate	65
	Rear Caliper To Backing Plate	36–43
	Rear Hub To Knuckle	54–65
	Wheel Lug Nuts	87–101
GALANT		
1996–99	Bleeder Screw	6
	Brake Hose To Caliper	22
	Caliper Body To Caliper Support	54
	Front Caliper To Backing Plate	65
	Rear Caliper To Backing Plate	36–43
	Rear Hub To Knuckle	54–65
	Wheel Lug Nuts	87–101

Diamante & 3000GT

INDEX

BRAKE SYSTEM BLEED

The hydraulic brake system must be bled if air has entered the system. Air may enter due to low fluid level, a hydraulic fluid leak, the opening of a hydraulic line or replacement of a hydraulic system component. Symptoms include loss of brake operation and/or a low or spongy brake pedal.

On models equipped with ABS, use a suitable filter when adding fluid to reservoir tank.

1. Ensure master cylinder reservoir is full. Add suitable brake fluid as needed, and securely reinstall the master cylinder cap.
2. Raise and support vehicle.
3. Position a drain pan under the wheel being bled.
4. Have an assistant depress the brake pedal with a slow even pressure and hold it. **Do not depress brake pedal fully to the end of the master cylinder stroke. This may cause damage to the master cylinder.**
5. Using a suitable wrench, open the bleeder valve one full turn. Watch for air bubbles in the fluid, and listen for air escaping from the system.
6. With the brake pedal still depressed, close the bleeder valve.

7. Have the assistant pump the brake pedal several times. **Do not depress brake pedal fully to the end of the master cylinder stroke, this may cause damage to the master cylinder.**
8. Repeat steps 4 through 7 until all air is removed from the hydraulic system. **While bleeding the system, recheck brake fluid supply in the master cylinder often so as not to allow the master cylinder to run dry.**
9. Upon completion of hydraulic system bleeding, proceed as follows:
   a. Ensure the master cylinder reservoir is full. Add suitable brake fluid as needed, and securely reinstall the master cylinder cap.
   b. Lower the vehicle. Ensure brake pedal is firm and braking operation is satisfactory.

BRAKE PAD SERVICE

REPLACEMENT

FRONT

FWD Models

1. Raise and support vehicle, then remove wheel.

2. Remove lower guide pin and pivot caliper assembly up and support using suitable wire.
3. Remove brake pads, pad clips and outer shim, **Fig. 1.**
4. Measure rotating torque of hub with brake pads removed using a suitable spring scale, **Fig. 2.**
5. Clean piston surface and push into caliper using suitable tool. **Ensure piston boot does not become wedged.**
6. Install pad clips and pads onto caliper.
7. Lower caliper assembly and install lower guide pin.
8. Check brake drag as follows:
   a. Start engine and hold brake pedal down for five seconds.
   b. Stop engine and turn brake rotor forward ten turns.
   c. Check brake drag using suitable tool.
   d. If the difference between brake drag torque and hub torque exceeds 3 ft. lbs., disassemble caliper assembly, clean and check for corrosion, worn or damaged parts.

3000GT AWD

1. Raise and support vehicle and remove wheel.
2. Remove pad pin clip and while holding

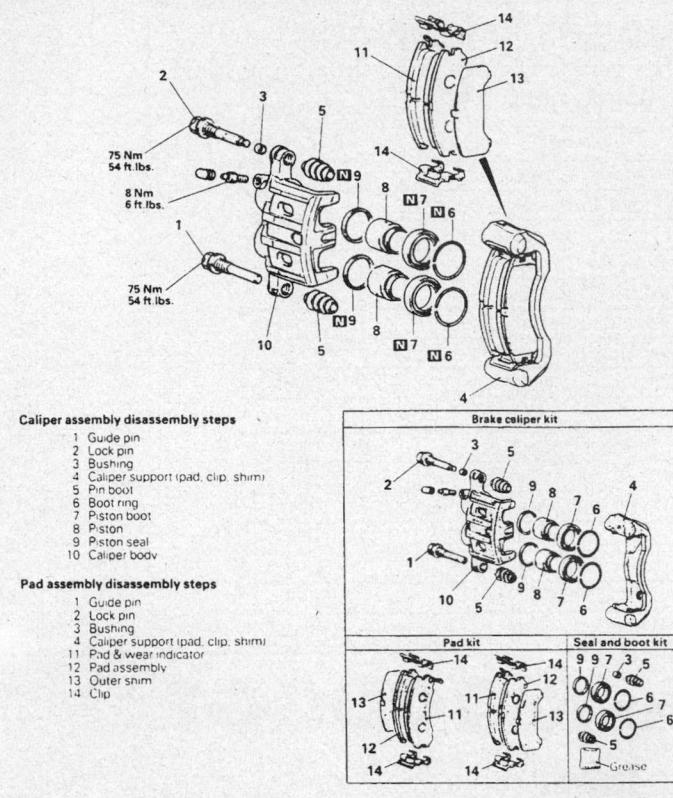

Caliper assembly disassembly steps
1. Guide pin
2. Lock pin
3. Bushing
4. Caliper support (pad, clip, shim)
5. Pin boot
6. Boot ring
7. Piston boot
8. Piston
9. Piston seal
10. Caliper body

Pad assembly disassembly steps
1. Guide pin
2. Lock pin
3. Bushing
4. Caliper support (pad, clip, shim)
11. Pad & wear indicator
12. Pad assembly
13. Outer shim
14. Clip

Fig. 1 Exploded view of front disc brake caliper. FWD models

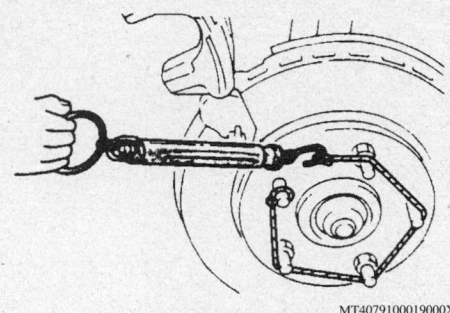

Fig. 2 Hub & brake drag torque measurement

cross spring with hand, remove pad pins, **Fig. 3.**
3. Using a suitable screwdriver, remove pads and shims.
4. Measure rotating torque of hub with brake pads removed using a suitable spring scale, **Fig. 2.**
5. Clean piston surface and push into caliper using suitable tool. **Ensure piston boot does not become wedged.**
6. Apply repair kit grease to both sides of inner shims. **Ensure grease does not come in contact with frictional surface of brake pads, grease should never squeeze out from around shim.**
7. Check brake drag as follows:
   a. Start engine and hold brake pedal down for five seconds.
   b. Stop engine and turn brake rotor forward ten turns.
   c. Check brake drag using suitable tool.
   d. If the difference between brake drag torque and hub torque exceeds 3 ft. lbs., disassemble caliper assembly, clean and check for corrosion, worn or damaged parts.

REAR
1. Loosen parking brake cable from interior end of cable and disconnect parking brake cable from rear brake caliper assembly.
2. Remove lower lockpin. Lift caliper assembly and support with suitable wire. **Do not smear grease on lockpin and ensure it is free of dirt.**

3. Remove outer shim, pad assembly, pad clip and inner shims, **Figs. 4 through 6.**
4. Measure rotating torque of hub with brake pads removed using a suitable spring scale, **Fig. 2.** On models with Viscous Coupling Unit (VCU) equipped Limited Slip Differential (LSD), disengage the driveshaft and companion flange.
5. Clean piston surface and push into caliper using suitable tool. **Ensure piston boot does not become wedged.**
6. Attach pad clip and pads to caliper support.
7. Check brake drag as follows:
   a. Start engine and hold brake pedal down for five seconds.
   b. Stop engine and turn brake rotor forward ten turns.
   c. Check brake drag using suitable tool.
   d. If the difference between brake drag torque and hub torque exceeds 3 ft. lbs., disassemble caliper assembly, clean and check for corrosion, worn or damaged parts.

CALIPER SERVICE
REPLACEMENT
1. Disconnect and plug brake hose.
2. Remove upper and lower caliper mounting bolts.
3. Remove caliper assembly; then, if necessary, separate from brake pads as outlined under "Brake Pad Service."

4. Reverse procedure to install, noting the following:
   a. Measure brake drag torque as outlined under "Brake Pad Service."
   b. Tighten brake hose fitting to specifications.
   c. Bleed brake system as outlined under "Brake System Bleed."

INSPECTION
Front
1. Raise and support vehicle and remove wheel.
2. Remove brake caliper.
3. Disassemble caliper assembly in numbered sequence shown in **Figs. 1 and 3,** noting the following:
   a. Remove pistons by placing a hammer handle in caliper to keep pistons even then send compressed air to break hose opening. **Use care not to pinch fingers when removing pistons. Send compressed air gradually. If one piston is removed, the others will not be able to be removed.**
   b. Remove piston seal with finger.
   c. Clean piston surface and inner cylinder with alcohol or specified brake fluid.
4. Reverse numbered sequence in **Figs. 1 and 3** to assemble caliper. On FWD models, match guide and lockpins identification marks with marks on caliper body when installing.

Rear
1. Raise and support vehicle and remove wheel.
2. Remove brake caliper.
3. Disassemble caliper assembly in numbered sequence shown in **Figs. 4 through 6,** noting the following:
   a. Protect caliper body with shop towel. Blow compressed air through brake hose opening to remove piston boot and piston.
   b. Remove piston seal using finger.
   c. Clean piston and inner cylinder using alcohol or brake fluid.
4. Reverse numbered sequence in **Figs. 4 through 6** to assemble caliper. On AWD models, match guide and lockpins identification marks with marks on caliper body when installing.

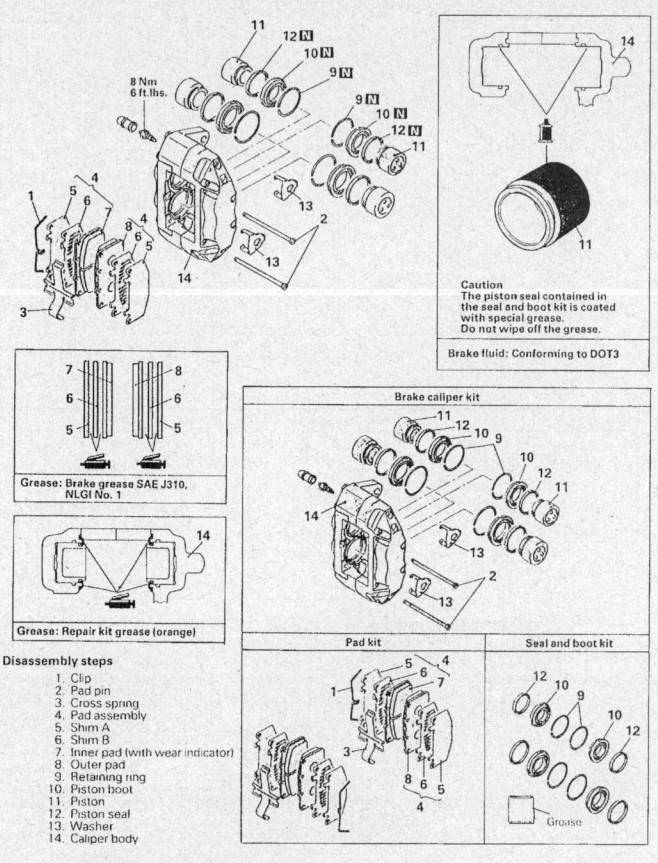

MT4079100020000X

Fig. 3   Exploded view of front disc brake caliper. 3000GT AWD

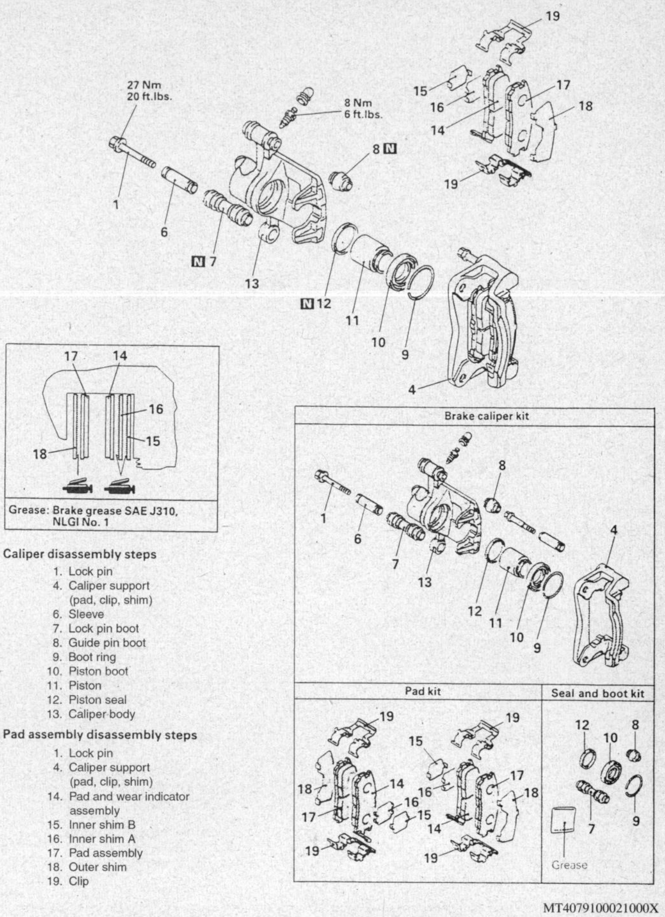

MT4079100021000X

Fig. 4   Exploded view of rear disc brake caliper. 3000GT FWD & 1996 Diamante

PARKING BRAKE SERVICE

OVERHAUL

1. Raise and support vehicle, then remove rear wheels.
2. Remove rear disc caliper from adapter as outlined under " Brake Pad Service."
3. Disassemble parking brakes in numbered sequence shown in **Figs. 7 through 9,** noting the following:
   a. **When removing speed sensor from knuckle, use care not to hit pole piece at its tip against the rotor teeth or other parts.**
   b. Using axle shaft holding tool No. MB990767-01, or equivalent, secure axle shaft and remove companion flange self locking nut.
   c. Using axle shaft puller tool Nos. MB990211-01 and MB990241-01, or equivalents, remove axle shaft from trailing arm.
4. Reverse numbered sequence shown in **Figs. 7 through 9** to assemble parking brakes, noting the following:
   a. Install shoe on anchor spring, **Fig. 10. Each shoe to anchor spring has a unique spring load and**

spring marked "a" is painted for identification. Figure shown is for left wheel.
   b. Install adjuster facing left adjusting bolt to vehicle front and right adjusting bolt to vehicle rear.
   c. Secure axle shaft using special tool and install companion flange self locking nut.
   d. **On FWD models,** after tightening flange nut to specifications, align with spindle's indentation and crimp, **Fig. 11.**
   e. **On all models,** insert a .008–.028 inch feeler gauge between speed sensor pole piece and rotor teeth and tighten speed sensor in position where gap is within this range over entire circumference.

ADJUSTMENTS
PARKING BRAKE

1. Pull parking brake lever with a force of approximately 45 lbs. and count number of clicks. Lever stroke should be three to five clicks.
2. If parking brake lever stroke is not within specifications, proceed as follows:
   a. Remove cup holder and plug then

loosen the adjusting nut on parking brake cable end so cable becomes free.
   b. With engine idling, depress brake pedal several times and confirm that the pedal stroke stops changing. **If pedal stroke stops changing, it indicates that automatic adjusting mechanism is functioning properly to adjust clearance between pads and disc to correct value.**
   c. Disconnect driveshaft and companion flange.
   d. Remove rotor adjusting hole plug and turn adjuster in direction shown in **Fig. 12,** until brake is slightly applied.
   e. Turn adjuster five notches in opposite direction to obtain the .0075 inch shoe to drum clearance.
   f. Turn parking brake cable adjusting nut to obtain a lever stroke of three to five clicks.
   g. After adjustment, ensure there is no play between the adjuster nut and pin.
   h. After adjustments have been made, ensure parking brake operates properly.

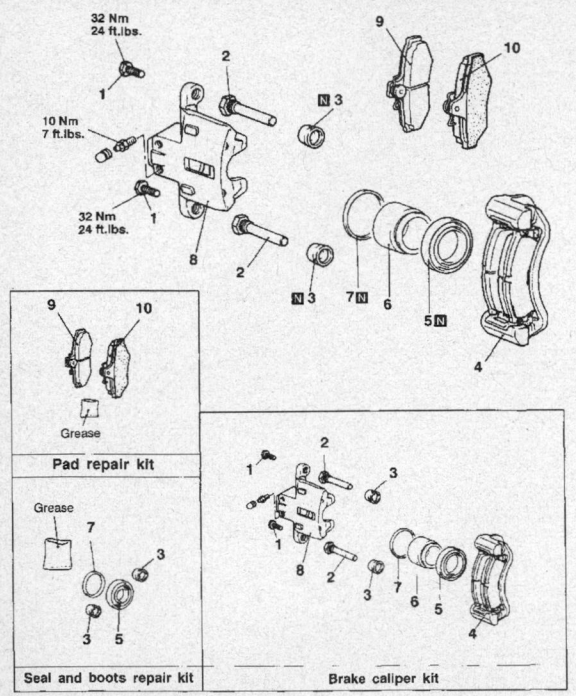

Caliper assembly disassembly steps
1. Guide pin locking bolts
2. Guide pin
3. Boot
4. Caliper support (pads)
5. Piston boot
6. Piston
7. Piston seal

8. Caliper body

Pad assembly disassembly steps
1. Locking bolts
2. Guide pin
3. Boot
4. Caliper support (pads)
9. Pad and wear indicator assembly
10. Pad assembly

MT4079700038000X

**Fig. 5   Exploded view of rear disc brake caliper.
1997–99 Diamante**

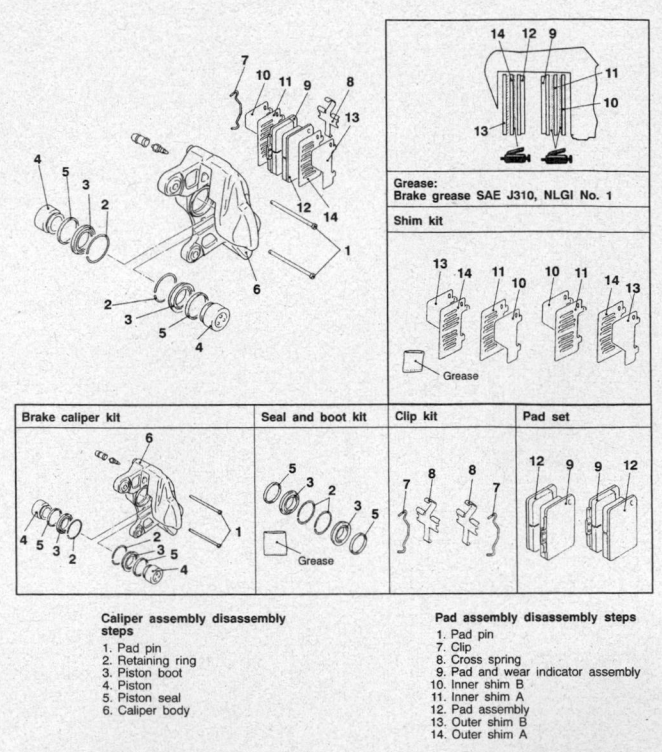

Grease:
Brake grease SAE J310, NLGI No. 1

Caliper assembly disassembly steps
1. Pad pin
2. Retaining ring
3. Piston boot
4. Piston
5. Piston seal
6. Caliper body

Pad assembly disassembly steps
1. Pad pin
7. Clip
8. Cross spring
9. Pad and wear indicator assembly
10. Inner shim B
11. Inner shim A
12. Pad assembly
13. Outer shim B
14. Outer shim A

MT4079900042000X

**Fig. 6   Exploded view of rear disc brake caliper.
3000GT AWD**

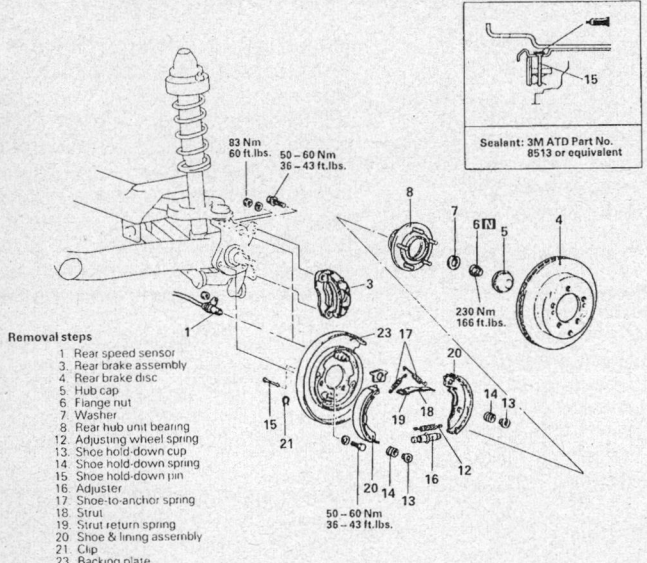

Sealant: 3M ATD Part No. 8513 or equivalent

Removal steps
1. Rear speed sensor
3. Rear brake assembly
4. Rear brake disc
5. Hub cap
6. Flange nut
7. Washer
8. Rear hub unit bearing
12. Adjusting wheel spring
13. Shoe hold-down cup
14. Shoe hold-down spring
15. Shoe hold-down pin
16. Adjuster
17. Shoe-to-anchor spring
18. Strut
19. Strut return spring
20. Shoe & lining assembly
21. Clip
23. Backing plate

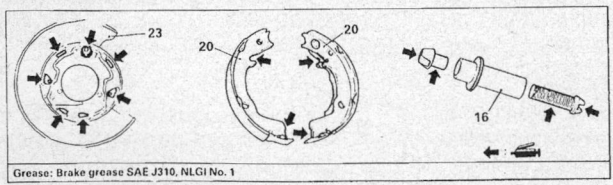

Grease: Brake grease SAE J310, NLGI No. 1

MT4079100024000X

**Fig. 7   Exploded view of parking brake assembly.
3000GT FWD & 1996 Diamante**

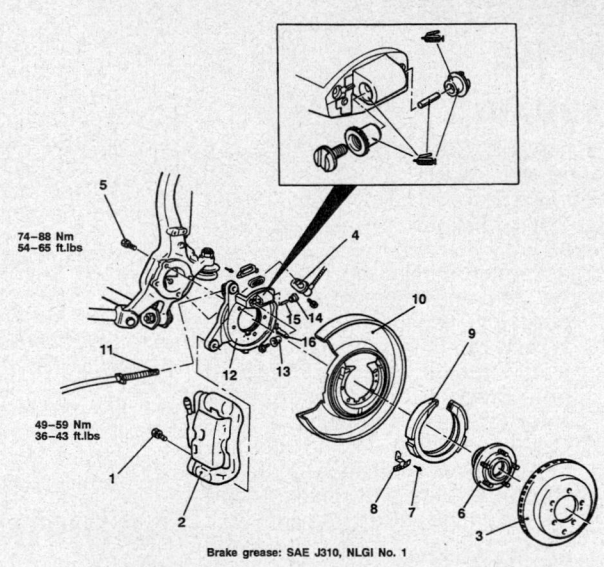

Brake grease: SAE J310, NLGI No. 1

REMOVAL STEPS
1. CALIPER ATTACHING BOLTS
2. CALIPER
3. DISC
4. SPEED SENSOR
5. HUB RETAINING BOLTS
6. HUB
7. SHOE HOLD DOWN SPRING SCREW
8. SHOE HOLD DOWN SPRING
9. SHOE
10. SPLASH SHIELD
11. PARKING BRAKE CABLE TO LEVER CONNECTION
12. BACKING PLATE
13. ADJUSTER STAR WHEEL
14. TAPPET
15. PUSHROD
16. LEVER

MT4079900043000X

**Fig. 8   Exploded view of parking brake assembly.
1997–99 Diamante**

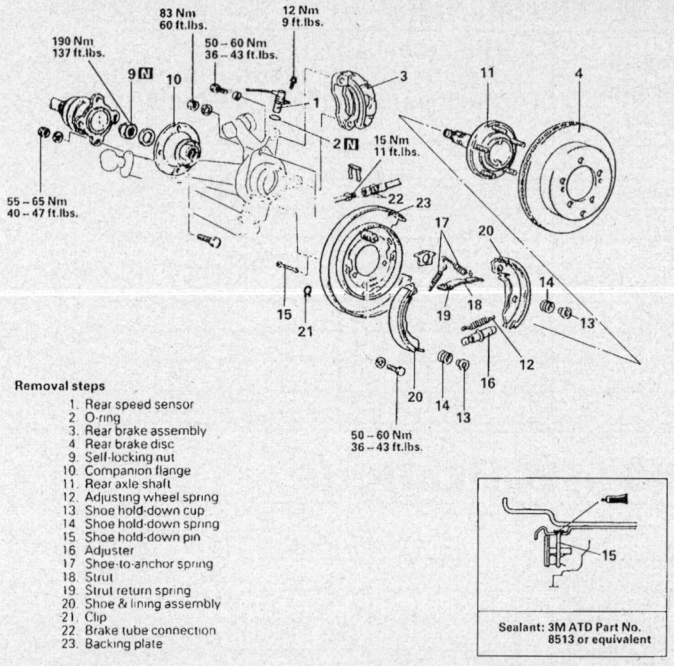

Removal steps

1. Rear speed sensor
2. O-ring
3. Rear brake assembly
4. Rear brake disc
9. Self-locking nut
10. Companion flange
11. Rear axle shaft
12. Adjusting wheel spring
13. Shoe hold-down cup
14. Shoe hold-down spring
15. Shoe hold-down pin
16. Adjuster
17. Shoe-to-anchor spring
18. Strut
19. Strut return spring
20. Shoe & lining assembly
21. Clip
22. Brake tube connection
23. Backing plate

Sealant: 3M ATD Part No. 8513 or equivalent

MT4079100025000X

Fig. 9 Exploded view of parking brake assembly. 3000GT AWD

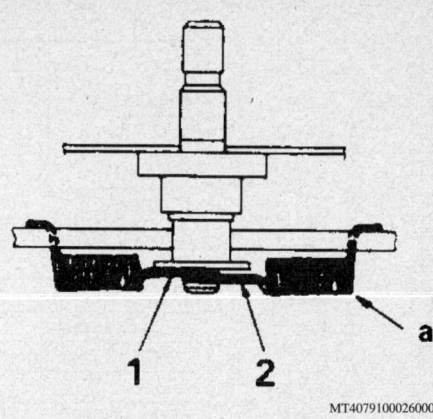

MT4079100026000X

Fig. 10 Shoe installation

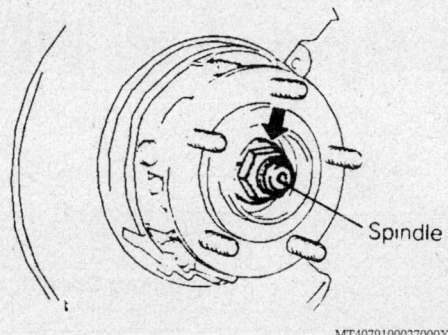

MT4079100027000X

Fig. 11 Flange nut installation. FWD models

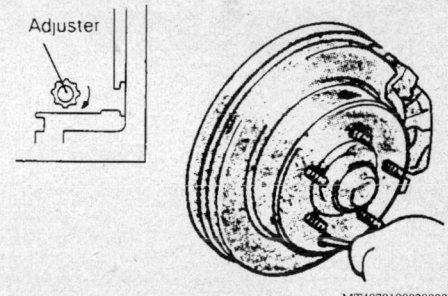

MT4079100028000X

Fig. 12 Parking brake adjustment

DISC BRAKE SPECIFICATIONS

CALIPER SPECIFICATIONS

Model	Caliper Bore Dia., Inch
FRONT	
Diamante	1.6875①
3000GT AWD	②
3000GT FWD	1.6825①
REAR	
1996 Diamante	1.3750
1997–99 Diamante	1.5000
3000GT AWD	1.5000
3000GT FWD	1.3750

① — Two piston caliper.
② — Four piston caliper, two at 1.5938 inches and two at 1.6875 inches.

ROTOR SPECIFICATIONS

Model	Nominal Thickness, Inch	Minimum Refinish Thickness, Inch	Lateral Runout (T.I.R.), Inch
FRONT			
Diamante	.940	.880	.0028
3000GT AWD	1.180	1.120	.0040
3000GT FWD	.940	.880	.0040
REAR			
1996 Diamante	.710	.650	.0031
1997–99 Diamante Sedan	.410	.330	.0020
3000GT AWD	.790	.720	.0031
3000GT FWD	.710	.650	.0031

TIGHTENING SPECIFICATIONS

Year	Component	Torque, Ft. Lbs.
1996–99	Bleeder Screws	6
	Brake Rotor	36–43
	Caliper Lockpin	54
	Caliper Mounting Bolts	65
	Flared Brake Line Nuts	11
	Wheel Lug Nuts	87–101

Montero, Montero Sport & Pickup

INDEX

BRAKE SYSTEM BLEED

The hydraulic brake system must be bled if air has entered the system. Air may enter due to low fluid level, a hydraulic fluid leak, opening of a hydraulic line or replacement of a hydraulic system component. Symptoms include loss of brake operation and/or a low or spongy brake pedal.

On models with ABS, use a suitable filter when adding fluid to reservoir tank.

1. Ensure master cylinder reservoir is full. Add suitable brake fluid as needed, and securely reinstall the master cylinder cap.
2. Raise and support vehicle.
3. Position a drain pan under the wheel being bled.
4. Have an assistant depress the brake pedal with a slow even pressure and hold it. **Do not depress brake pedal fully to the end of the master cylinder stroke. This may cause damage to the master cylinder.**
5. Using a suitable wrench, open the bleeder valve one full turn. Watch for air bubbles in the fluid, and listen for air escaping from the system.
6. With the brake pedal still depressed, close the bleeder valve.
7. Have the assistant pump the brake pedal several times. **Do not depress brake pedal fully to the end of the master cylinder stroke, as this may cause damage to the master cylinder.**
8. Repeat preceding bleed steps until all air is removed from the hydraulic system. **While bleeding the system, recheck brake fluid supply in the master cylinder often so as not to allow the master cylinder to run dry.**
9. Upon completion of hydraulic system bleeding, proceed as follows:
   a. Ensure the master cylinder reservoir is full. Add suitable brake fluid as needed, and securely reinstall the master cylinder cap.
   b. Lower the vehicle. Ensure brake pedal is firm and braking operation is proper.

BRAKE PAD SERVICE

REPLACEMENT

1. Raise and support vehicle, then remove front wheel.
2. Remove lockpin bolt, **Figs. 1 through 4.**
3. Lift up caliper body, using the guide pin bolt as a fulcrum. Use wire to suspend the caliper.
4. Remove inner and outer shims, pad assemblies, and pad clips from caliper support.
5. Measure hub torque using a suitable spring scale to determine brake drag torque after pan installation, **Fig. 5.**
6. Inspect all components, replacing as necessary.
7. Clean exposed part of piston, then compress piston.
8. Reverse procedure to install, ensure pad clips, shims, and pads are properly installed.
9. Measure brake drag torque as follows:

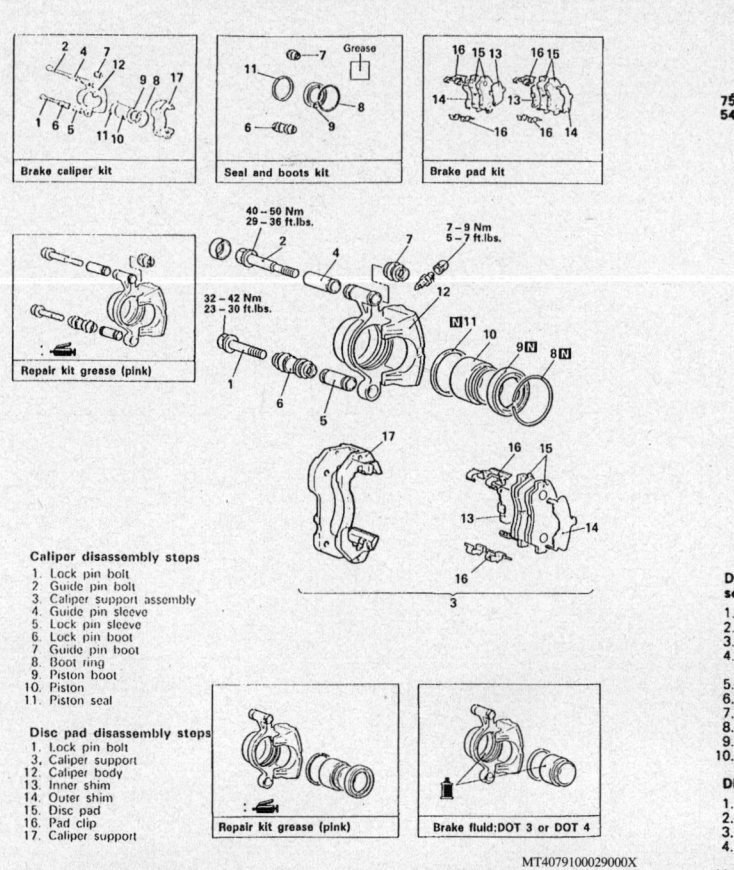

Fig. 1 Exploded view of disc brake assembly. Pickup

Caliper disassembly steps
1. Lock pin bolt
2. Guide pin bolt
3. Caliper support assembly
4. Guide pin sleeve
5. Lock pin sleeve
6. Lock pin boot
7. Guide pin boot
8. Boot ring
9. Piston boot
10. Piston
11. Piston seal

Disc pad disassembly steps
1. Lock pin bolt
3. Caliper support
12. Caliper body
13. Inner shim
14. Outer shim
15. Disc pad
16. Pad clip
17. Caliper support

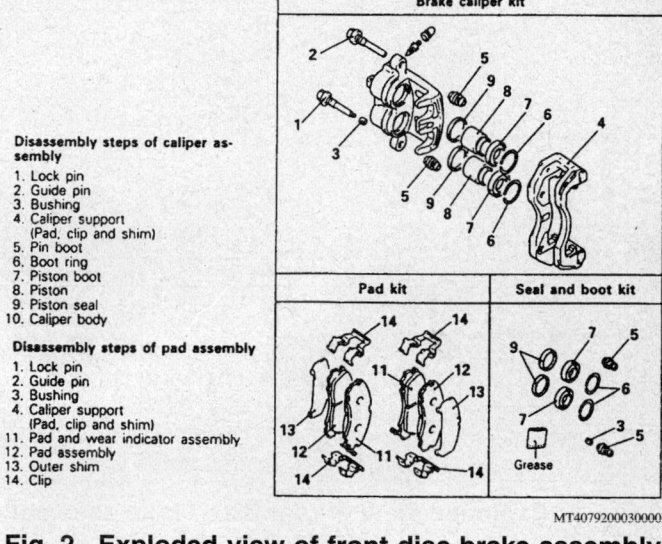

Fig. 2 Exploded view of front disc brake assembly. Montero & Montero Sport

Disassembly steps of caliper assembly
1. Lock pin
2. Guide pin
3. Bushing
4. Caliper support (Pad, clip and shim)
5. Pin boot
6. Boot ring
7. Piston boot
8. Piston
9. Piston seal
10. Caliper body

Disassembly steps of pad assembly
1. Lock pin
2. Guide pin
3. Bushing
4. Caliper support (Pad, clip and shim)
11. Pad and wear indicator assembly
12. Pad assembly
13. Outer shim
14. Clip

a. Start engine and hold brake pedal down for five seconds.
b. Stop engine and turn brake rotor forward ten turns.
c. Check brake drag using suitable tool.
d. **On Pickup models,** it will be necessary to disassemble caliper assembly, clean and check for corrosion, worn or damaged parts if difference between brake drag torque and hub torque exceeds 3 ft. lbs.
e. **On Montero and Montero Sport models,** it will be necessary to disassemble caliper assembly, clean and check for corrosion, worn or damaged parts if difference between front brake drag torque and hub torque exceeds 4 ft. lbs. or difference between rear brake drag torque and hub torque exceeds 13 ft. lbs.
10. **On all models,** install wheel.

CALIPER SERVICE

REPLACEMENT

1. Raise and support vehicle, then remove front wheel.
2. Disconnect brake hose.
3. Remove caliper from vehicle.
4. Reverse procedure to install, noting the following:

a. Tighten brake hose to specifications.
b. Bleed brake system as outlined under "Brake System Bleed."

OVERHAUL & INSPECTION

PICKUP

1. Remove dust boot.
2. Cover inner side of caliper with rag, then slowly inject compressed air through brake hose fitting to push out piston.
3. Remove piston seal, being careful not to damage cylinder.
4. Clean all metal parts and piston seal with brake fluid and clean dust boot with alcohol.
5. Check components for wear or damage, replacing as necessary. Use new piston seal, dust boot, and boot ring.
6. Apply rubber grease supplied with repair kit to piston seal, fit seal into cylinder groove, and install piston by hand, being careful not to twist seal.
7. Apply grease supplied with repair kit to dust boot attaching groove in caliper, then install dust boot.
8. Install brake pad.
9. Apply specified grease to the outer surface of guide pin and lockpin sleeves and the caliper body contact-

ing surfaces of lockpin and guide pin boots, then install lockpin and guide pin.

MONTERO & MONTERO SPORT

Front

1. Remove caliper from as outlined in this section.
2. Disassemble caliper in numbered sequence shown in **Fig. 2,** noting the following:
   a. Using compressed air, remove pistons from caliper. **When removing pistons, use the handle of a plastic hammer to adjust height of pistons to ensure both pistons protrude evenly and to protect them from damage.**
   b. Remove piston seals using finger tip only.
3. Reverse numbered sequence shown in **Fig. 2** to assemble, installing guide and lockpins so that each head mark of pin matches mark located on caliper body.

Rear

Refer to **Fig. 3** and "Pickup" under "Caliper Service" for service procedures.

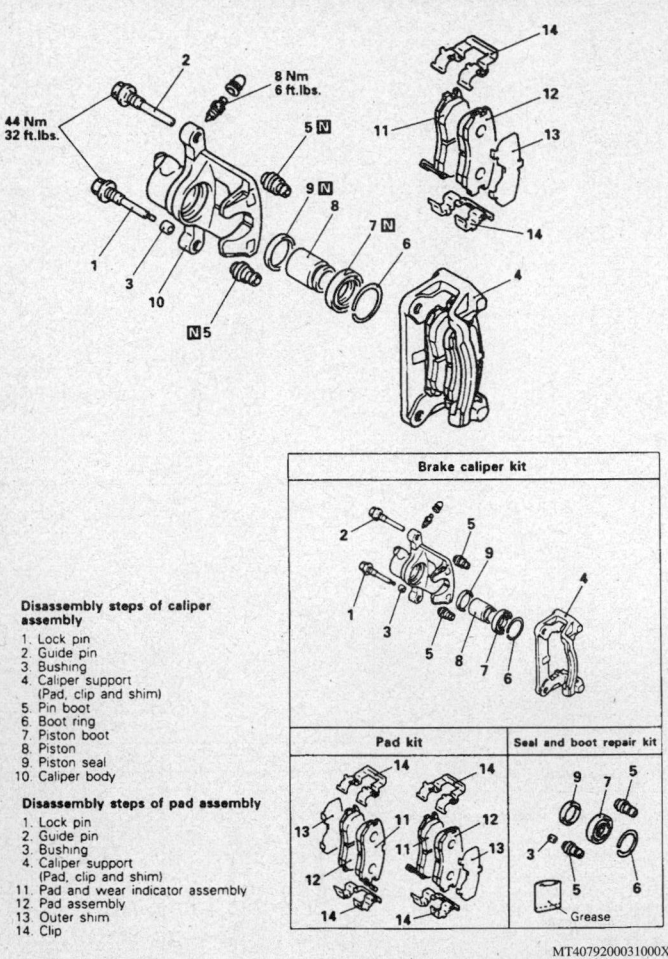

Disassembly steps of caliper assembly
1. Lock pin
2. Guide pin
3. Bushing
4. Caliper support (Pad, clip and shim)
5. Pin boot
6. Boot ring
7. Piston boot
8. Piston
9. Piston seal
10. Caliper body

Disassembly steps of pad assembly
1. Lock pin
2. Guide pin
3. Bushing
4. Caliper support (Pad, clip and shim)
11. Pad and wear indicator assembly
12. Pad assembly
13. Outer shim
14. Clip

MT4079200031000X

Fig. 3 Exploded view of rear disc brake assembly. Montero

CALIPER ASSEMBLY DISASSEMBLY STEPS
1. CLIP
2. PAD PIN
3. SPRING
4. INNER SHIM
5. PAD AND WEAR INDICATOR ASSEMBLY
6. PAD ASSEMBLY
7. OUTER SHIM
8. RETAINING RING
9. PISTON BOOT
10. PISTON
11. PISTON SEAL
12. SLEEVE BOLT
13. BUSHING
14. SLEEVE
15. PIN BOOT
16. INNER CALIPER
17. TORQUE PLATE
18. BLEEDER SCREW

PAD ASSEMBLY DISASSEMBLY STEPS
1. CLIP
2. PAD PIN
3. SPRING
4. INNER SHIM
5. PAD AND WEAR INDICATOR ASSEMBLY
6. PAD ASSEMBLY
7. OUTER SHIM

MT4079700039000X

Fig. 4 Exploded view of rear disc brake assembly. Montero Sport

ROTOR
REPLACE
2WD MODELS

1. Disconnect battery ground cable.
2. Raise and support vehicle.
3. Remove front brake assembly and suspend assembly with wire.
4. Remove hub cap, then the cotter pin.
5. Remove slotted nut and washer, then the outer bearing.
6. Remove front hub and rotor assembly.
7. Reverse procedure to install, noting the following:
   a. Tighten slotted wheel bearing nut to specifications.
   b. Loosen slotted nut completely.
   c. **Retorque** slotted nut to 6 ft. lbs.

4WD MODELS

1. Place free wheeling hub in "Free" position.
2. Rotate hub cover counterclockwise and remove.
3. Remove snap ring from end of driveshaft.
4. Remove adjusting shims (if equipped).
5. Remove automatic free wheeling hub

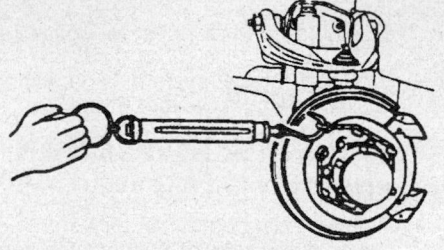

MT4079100032000X

Fig. 5 Hub & brake drag torque measurement

bolts then the hub.
6. Remove locknut lock washer.
7. Remove disc brake assembly as outlined under "Caliper Service."
8. Remove locknut using socket wrench tool No. MB990954-01, or equivalent, then the front hub and disc assembly.
9. Reverse procedure to install, noting the following:
   a. Adjust wheel bearing preload by using socket wrench tool to **torque** the locknut to 94–145 ft. lbs. Completely loosen locknut, then **torque** locknut to 18 ft. lbs. and loosen 30–40.°

b. Align key of brake marked "B" on free wheeling hub and keyway of knuckle spindle and loosely install free wheeling hub assembly.
c. Ensure wheel hub and free wheeling hub are brought into contact when free wheeling hub is forced lightly against the wheel hub. If not, turn hub until contact is made.
d. Use a suitable spring scale to measure front hub turning resistance. Ensure difference of turning resistance between automatic free wheeling hub and wheel hub (without free wheeling hub installed) is 3.1 lbs. If resistance exceeds limit, disassemble and reassemble free wheeling hub.
e. Rotate driveshaft forward and backward and set driveshaft to position where endplay is maximum. Set dial indicator on rotor with pointer on driveshaft then move driveshaft in axial direction and measure endplay.
f. If endplay is not .008–.020 inch, adjust by adding or removing shims.

DISC BRAKE SPECIFICATIONS

CALIPER SPECIFICATIONS

Model	Caliper Bore Diameter, Inch
FRONT	
Montero & Montero Sport	1.6875①
Pickup	2.2500
REAR	
Montero	1.6875
Montero Sport	1.7000

① — Two piston caliper.

ROTOR SPECIFICATIONS

Model	Nominal Thickness, Inch	Minimum Refinish Thickness, Inch	Lateral Runout (T.I.R.), Inch
FRONT			
Montero & Montero Sport	.940	.882	.004
Pickup	—	.803	.006
REAR			
Montero	.710	.646	.003
Montero Sport	.700	.650	.003

TIGHTENING SPECIFICATIONS

Year	Component	Torque, Ft. Lbs.
MONTERO & MONTERO SPORT		
1996–99	Bleeder Screw	5–7
	Brake Booster To Pedal Support	6–9
	Brake Line Flare Nut	9–12
	Brake Pedal Shaft	18–25
	Caliper Attaching Bolts (Front)	65
	Caliper Attaching Bolts (Rear)	65
	Guide Pin Bolt	29–36
	Lockpin Bolt	23–30
	Master Cylinder To Booster	6–9
	Master Cylinder To Brake Line Connector	18–25
	Mounting Support To Knuckle	58–72
	Pedal Support Member Attaching Bolt	13–18
	Piston Stopper	1–2
	Reservoir Stopper Bolt	1–2
	Speed Sensor Bolt	14
	Wheel Bearing Nut	①
	Wheel Lug Nuts	87–101

Continued

TIGHTENING SPECIFICATIONS—Continued

Year	Component	Torque, Ft. Lbs.
PICKUP		
1996	Bleeder Screw	5–7
	Brake Line Flare Nut	9–12
	Caliper Support Mounting Bolt	58–72
	Guide Pin Bolt	29–36
	Lockpin Bolt	23–30
	Master Cylinder To Brake Booster	6–9
	Master Cylinder To Brake Line Connector	18–25
	Piston Stopper	1–2
	Wheel Bearing Nut	①
	Wheel Lug Nuts	87–101

① — On 2WD models, torque to 22 ft. lbs., then loosen and torque back to 6 ft. lbs.; on 4WD models, torque to 94–145 ft. lbs., then loosen and torque back to 18 ft. lbs.

Drum Brakes

INDEX

BRAKE SERVICE

For drum brake service procedures, refer to **Figs. 1 through 4.**

ADJUSTMENTS

SERVICE BRAKES

Rear brakes should be adjusted after rear brake service or before adjusting parking brake. These brakes have self-adjusting shoe mechanisms that maintain correct brake lining to drum clearances at all times. The automatic self-adjusting mechanism operates whenever the parking brake lever is applied on all models except the Duo-Servo type. These contain a self-adjusting mechanism which operates when the brakes are applied as the vehicle is moving rearward.

PARKING BRAKE

Montero & Montero Sport

1. Pull parking brake lever with force of approximately 45 lbs., noting the following:
   a. Lever stroke should be four to six notches.
2. If lever stroke is not as indicated, pull parking brake lever repeatedly to adjust shoe clearance, then adjust parking brake lever stroke by turning cable adjusting nut.
3. Raise and support rear of vehicle and, with parking brake lever released, turn rear wheels to ensure rear brakes are not dragging.

Eclipse & Galant

1. Pull parking brake lever with a force of approximately 45 lbs. and count number of clicks. Lever stroke should be five to seven clicks.
2. If parking brake lever stroke is not within specifications, proceed as follows:
   a. Remove center console, then loosen adjusting nut to end of cable rod to free parking brake cable.
   b. With engine idling, depress brake pedal several times and confirm that the pedal stroke stops changing. **If pedal stroke stops changing, it indicates that automatic adjusting mechanism is functioning properly to adjust clearance between drum and shoe assembly to correct value.**
   c. Turn adjusting nut to adjust parking brake lever stroke to specified range. **If number of brake lever notches engaged is less than specified value, cable has been pulled excessively and failure of the automatic adjuster mechanism may result.**
   d. After adjusting lever stroke, raise and support rear of vehicle. With parking brake lever released, turn rear wheels to ensure rear brakes are not dragging.

Mirage

1. Pull parking brake lever with a force of approximately 45 lbs. and count number of clicks. Lever stroke should be five to seven clicks.
2. If parking brake lever stroke is not within specifications, proceed as follows:
   a. Remove center console, then with parking brake lever released, loosen cable adjuster locknut.
   b. After slacking off parking brake cable locknut, tighten cable adjuster locknut to take up slack in cable. **Excessive pulling of cable may result in failure of the automatic adjuster mechanism.**
   c. Pull parking brake lever repeatedly while depressing brake pedal until no more clicks are heard from the automatic adjuster mechanism.
   d. Adjust parking brake lever to the specified stroke, then secure with locknut.
   e. After adjusting lever stroke, raise and support rear of vehicle. With parking brake lever released, turn rear wheels to ensure rear brakes are not dragging.

Pickup

1. Adjust rear brake shoe clearance.
2. **On 2WD models,** adjust turnbuckle so that lever stroke is 16–17 notches with pulling force of 66 lbs.
3. **On 4WD models,** turn adjusting nut to

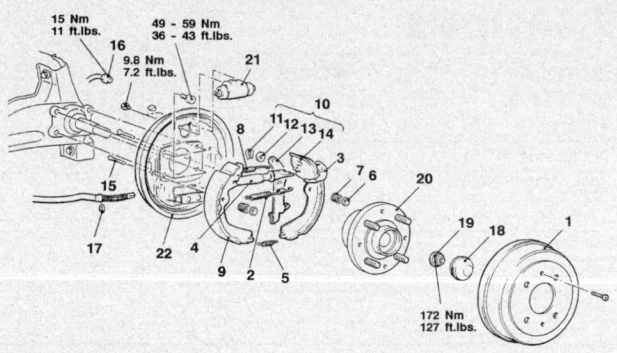

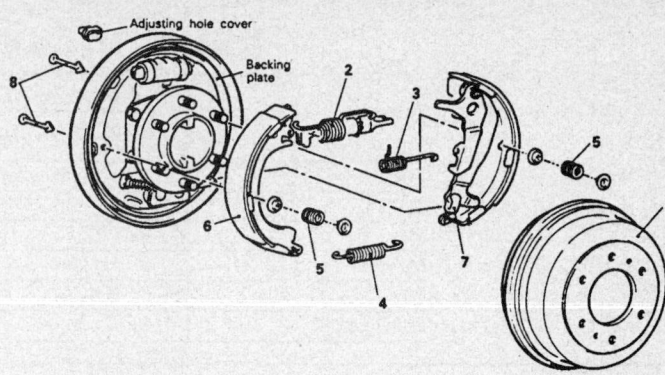

Rear drum brake removal steps
1. Brake drum
2. Shoe-to-lever spring
3. Adjuster lever
4. Auto adjuster assembly
5. Retainer spring
6. Shoe hold-down cup
7. Shoe hold-down spring
8. Shoe-to-shoe spring
9. Shoe and lining assembly
10. Shoe, lining and lever assembly
11. Retainer
12. Wave washer
13. Parking lever
14. Shoe and lining assembly
15. Shoe hold-down pin
16. Brake pipe connection
17. Snap ring
18. Hub cap

19. Flange nut
20. Rear hub assembly
21. Wheel cylinder
22. Backing plate

Wheel cylinder removal steps
1. Brake drum
2. Shoe-to-lever spring
8. Shoe-to-shoe spring
16. Brake pipe connection
21. Wheel cylinder

Caution
When removing the rear hub assembly, the wheel bearing inner race may be left at the spindle side. In this case, always replace the rear hub assembly, otherwise the hub will damage the oil seal, causing oil leaks or excessive play.

MT4089700009000X

Fig. 1 Exploded view of drum brake assembly. Mirage

1. Brake drum
2. Shoe return spring with brake shoe adjuster
3. Adjusting spring
4. Shoe retainer spring
5. Shoe hold-down spring
6. Shoe and lining assembly
7. Shoe and lever assembly
8. Shoe hold-down pin

MT4089100004000X

Fig. 2 Exploded view of drum brake assembly. Pickup

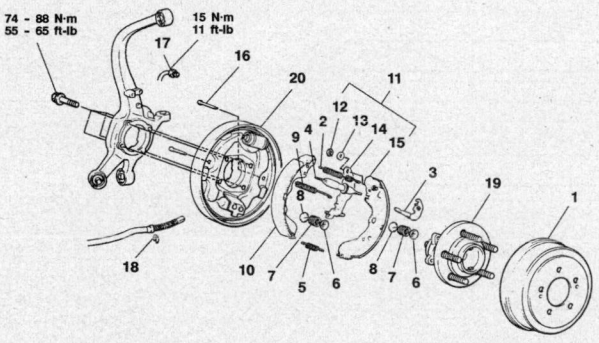

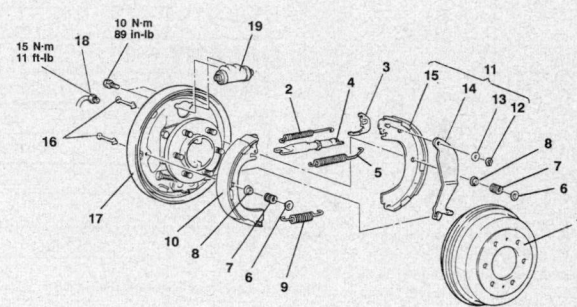

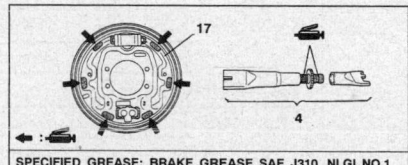 SPECIFIED GREASE: BRAKE GREASE SAE J310, NLGI NO.1

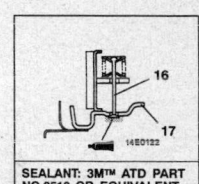 SEALANT: 3M™ ATD PART NO.8513 OR EQUIVALENT

REAR DRUM BRAKE REMOVAL STEPS
1. BRAKE DRUM
2. SHOE-TO-LEVER SPRING
3. ADJUSTER LEVER
4. AUTO ADJUSTER ASSEMBLY
5. RETAINER SPRING
6. SHOE HOLD-DOWN CUP
7. SHOE HOLD-DOWN SPRING
8. SHOE HOLD-DOWN CUP
9. SHOE-TO-SHOE SPRING
10. SHOE AND LINING ASSEMBLY
11. SHOE AND LEVER ASSEMBLY
12. RETAINER
13. WAVE WASHER
14. PARKING LEVER
15. SHOE AND LINING ASSEMBLY
16. SHOE HOLD-DOWN PIN
17. BACKING PLATE (REFER TO GROUP 27, REAR AXLE SHAFT.)

WHEEL CYLINDER REMOVAL STEPS
1. BRAKE DRUM
18. BRAKE TUBE CONNECTION
19. WHEEL CYLINDER

MT4089700008000X

Fig. 4 Exploded view of drum brake assembly. Montero Sport

5. **On 2WD models,** ensure balancer is almost parallel with center line of vehicle.
6. **On 4WD models,** ensure joint and equalizer are at right angles to each other.
7. **On all models,** if after above adjustments, stroke is not 16–17 notches, rear brake automatic adjusters are malfunctioning. Correct as necessary.

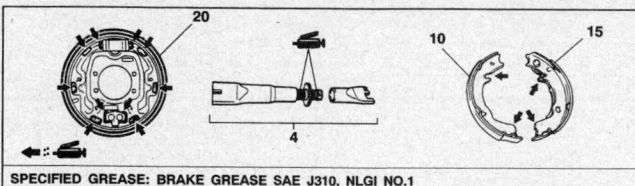
SPECIFIED GREASE: BRAKE GREASE SAE J310, NLGI NO.1

REAR DRUM BRAKE REMOVAL STEPS
1. BRAKE DRUM
2. SHOE-TO-LEVER SPRING
3. ADJUSTER LEVER
4. AUTO ADJUSTER ASSEMBLY
5. RETAINER SPRING
6. SHOE HOLD-DOWN CUP
7. SHOE HOLD-DOWN SPRING
8. SHOE HOLD-DOWN CUP
9. SHOE-TO-SHOE SPRING
10. SHOE AND LINING ASSEMBLY
11. SHOE AND LEVER ASSEMBLY
12. RETAINER
13. WAVE WASHER
14. PARKING LEVER
15. SHOE AND LINING ASSEMBLY
16. SHOE HOLD-DOWN PIN
17. BRAKE TUBE CONNECTION
18. SNAP RING
19. REAR HUB ASSEMBLY
20. BACKING PLATE

MT4089400007000X

Fig. 3 Exploded view of drum brake assembly. Eclipse & Galant

obtain lever stroke as described in preceding step.

4. **On all models,** ensure rear parking brake cable is not taut.

DRUM BRAKE SPECIFICATIONS

Model	Brake Drum Inside Dia., Inch	Maximum Refinish Dia., Inch	Rear Wheel Cylinder Bore, Inch
Eclipse	8.00	8.10	.813
Galant	9.00	9.10	.750
Mirage	7.10	7.20	.750
Montero Sport	10.10	10.71	.900
Pickup 2WD	10.00	10.08	.930
Pickup 4WD	10.00	10.08	.870

TIGHTENING SPECIFICATIONS

Year	Component	Torque, Ft. Lbs.
ECLIPSE		
1996–99	Backing Plate To Knuckle	60
	Bleeder Screw	6
	Flared Brake Line Nuts	11
	Wheel Cylinder Bolt	7
GALANT		
1996–99	Backing Plate To Knuckle	60
	Bleeder Screw	6
	Flared Brake Line Nuts	11
	Wheel Cylinder Bolt	7
MIRAGE		
1996–99	Backing Plate & Rear Axle Beam	36–43
	Bleeder Screw	5–7
	Flared Brake Line Nuts	9–12
	Rear Drum Brake Wheel Cylinder & Backing Plate	6–9
	Wheel Bearing Nut	108–145
MONTERO SPORT		
1996–99	Bleeder Screw	5–7
	Brake Line Flare Nut	9–12
	Wheel Cylinder To Backing Plate	13–15
PICKUP		
1996	Bleeder Screw	5–7
	Brake Line Flare Nut	9–12
	Wheel Cylinder To Backing Plate	13–15

Hydraulic Brake Systems

NOTE: On Air Bag Equipped Models, Refer To "Air Bag System Precautions" Located In The Front Of This Manual For System Disarming & Arming Procedures.

INDEX

PRECAUTIONS

AIR BAG SYSTEMS

Refer to "Air Bag System Precautions" in the front of this manual for system disarming and arming procedures.

BATTERY GROUND CABLE

Prior to service, disconnect battery ground cable and isolate as required.

DIAGNOSIS & TESTING

PROPORTIONING VALVE

Except Pickup

1. Connect two pressure gauges to proportioning valve, one to the output side and one to the input side, **Fig. 1.**
2. Bleed system after connecting gauges.
3. Depress brake pedal and ensure measured values are within specifications shown in "Hydraulic Brake System Specifications" chart at end of this section.

Pickup

1. Check load proportioning valve spring length with vehicle on flat ground.
2. Press load sensor lever and measure distance between spring ends, **Fig. 2.**
3. Distance should be between 6.93–7.05 inches.
4. Connect two pressure gauges to proportioning valve, one to the output side and one to the input side, **Fig. 3.**
5. Bleed system after connecting gauges, then remove load sensor spring.
6. Depress brake pedal and ensure measured values are within specifications as shown in "Hydraulic Brake System Specifications" chart at the end of this section.
7. Install load sensor spring, then supply load to rear of vehicle so that distance between load sensing proportioning valve lever and hole for support come to midpoint of standard value range with lever slightly pressed in, **Fig. 2.**

8. **On 4WD models with heavy duty suspension,** output pressure should be 299–583 psi at an input pressure of 1991 psi.
9. **On 2WD models with heavy duty suspension,** output pressure should be 512–683 psi at an input pressure of 1991 psi.
10. **On all models,** after checking load sensing proportioning valve, adjust spring length as necessary.

ADJUSTMENTS

BRAKE BOOSTER PUSHROD

1. Remove master cylinder as outlined under "Component Replacement," then proceed as follows:
   a. Measure distance between master cylinder end face and piston, **Fig. 4.** Position a square (straight scale) against edge of master cylinder, then measure and subtract thickness of the square to determine dimension B.
   b. Find dimension C by measuring distance between brake booster mounting surface and the end face, **Fig. 5.**
   c. Measure distance between master cylinder mounting surface and the pushrod end, **Fig. 6.** Find dimension D by subtracting the square's thickness from the measurement taken.
   d. Find brake booster to primary piston clearance dimension A, **Fig. 7,** using the formula $A = B - C - D$. Refer to **Fig. 8** for proper clearance specifications.
   e. If dimension A is not as specified, adjust brake booster pushrod as shown, **Fig. 9.**

COMPONENT REPLACEMENT

MASTER CYLINDER

Except Diamante & Eclipse

1. Disconnect brake fluid sensor electri-

cal connector from master cylinder reservoir.
2. Position a drain pan under master cylinder.
3. **On models with separately mounted reservoir,** disconnect reservoir hoses from the master cylinder.
4. **On all models,** disconnect brake lines from the master cylinder. Plug all lines and fittings.
5. Remove master cylinder to brake booster attaching nuts.
6. Pull master cylinder outward and away from brake booster.
7. Reverse procedure to install, noting the following:
   a. Prior to master cylinder installation, adjust brake booster pushrod as described under "Adjustments" in this section.
   b. Bleed master cylinder and hydraulic system as described under "Brake System Bleed" in this section.

Diamante

1. Position a drain pan under master cylinder.
2. Remove brake line connectors, then brake lines.
3. Remove proportioning valve.
4. Remove ABS connector assembly.
5. Remove master cylinder attaching bolts, then the master cylinder.
6. Reverse procedure to install, noting the following:
   a. Prior to master cylinder installation, adjust brake booster pushrod as described under "Adjustments."
   b. Bleed hydraulic system as described under "Brake System Bleed."

Eclipse

1. Drain brake fluid from reservoir.
2. **On models equipped with manual transaxle,** remove clutch fluid reservoir bracket.
3. **On models equipped with 2.0L non-turbocharged engine,** remove battery, relay assembly mounting bolts and washer tank mounting bolts.

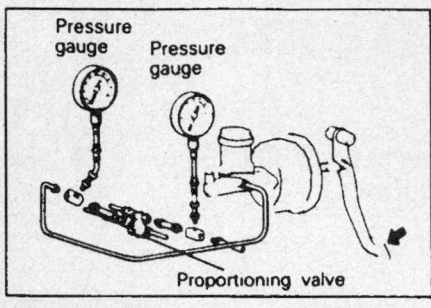

Fig. 1 Proportioning valve pressure gauge test connection. Except Pickup

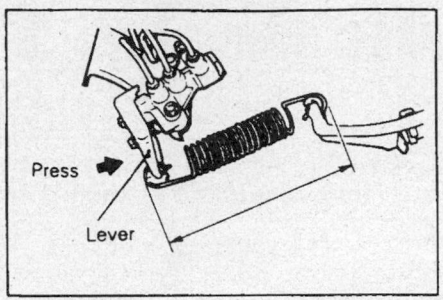

Fig. 2 Load sensing proportioning valve spring. Pickup

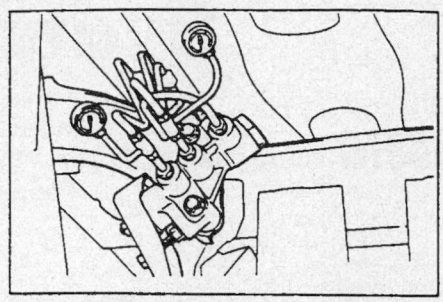

Fig. 3 Load sensing proportioning valve. Pickup

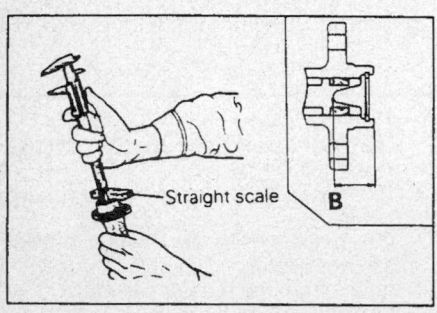

Fig. 4 Distance B measurement between master cylinder end face & piston

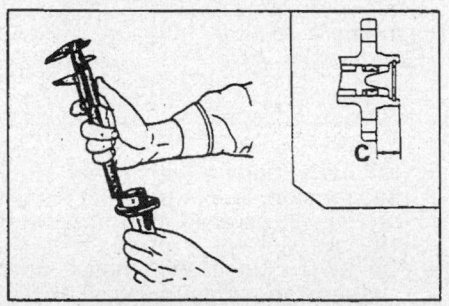

Fig. 5 Distance C measurement between brake booster mounting on master cylinder & end face

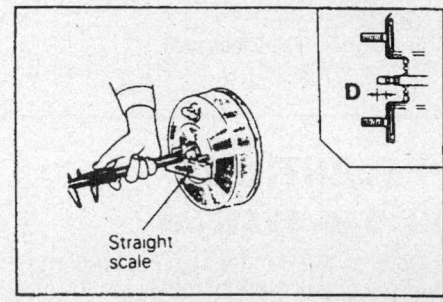

Fig. 6 Distance D measurement between master cylinder mounting surface & pushrod end

4. **On models equipped with 2.0L turbocharged engine and 2.4L engine,** proceed as follows:
   a. Remove center member assembly mounting bolts, engine mount bracket, A/C compressor mounting bolts, then the A/C high pressure hose clamp mounting bolts.
   b. Remove power steering pressure hose, pipe and return pipe clamp mounting bolts.
5. **On all models,** remove brake fluid reservoir from mounting bracket, then disconnect brake tubes at master cylinder.
6. Remove bolts securing master cylinder to power booster, then remove cylinder from vehicle.
7. Reverse procedure to install, noting the following:
   a. Adjust brake booster pushrod clearance as outlined under "Adjustments."
   b. Bleed master cylinder and brake system as outlined under "Brake System Bleed."

WHEEL CYLINDER

Removal

1. Remove wheel, drum and brake shoes.
2. Loosen brake line fitting at wheel cylinder. Do not pull metal line away from cylinder.
3. Remove screw holding cylinder to backing plate.
4. Separate wheel cylinder from brake line and backing plate by pulling cylin-

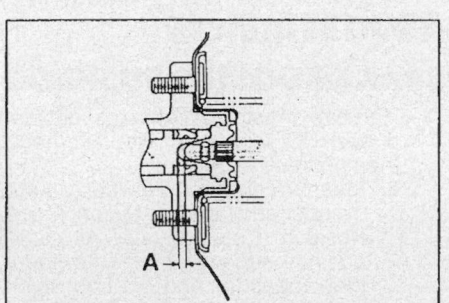

Fig. 7 Brake booster to primary piston clearance dimension A

der outward and away from backing plate.

Installation

1. Wipe end of hydraulic line to remove any foreign matter.
2. Position wheel cylinder to backing plate. Install brake line to cylinder and start connecting fitting.
3. Secure wheel cylinder to backing plate, then complete tightening of brake line fitting.
4. Install brake shoes, drum and wheel.
5. Bleed system as outlined under "Brake System Bleed."

COMPONENT SERVICE

MASTER CYLINDER

SERVICE

1. Disassemble master cylinder in numbered sequence shown, **Figs. 10**

through 12. Note the position of all parts as they are removed for proper installation.
2. **On models equipped with attached reservoir master cylinder,** remove reservoir screw and cap, brake fluid sensor, float, then the reservoir, **Figs. 10 and 11.**
3. **On models equipped with separately mounted reservoir,** remove nipple, **Fig. 12.**
4. **On models equipped with separately mounted reservoir,** use a wooden stick or dowel to depress primary piston into cylinder bore.
5. **On all models,** with pushrod depressed, remove piston stopper bolt, then the piston stopper ring.
6. Release pushrod, then remove piston assemblies. If secondary piston assembly is stuck in the bore, apply a light amount of compressed air to the secondary outlet port until piston assembly works free.
7. Reverse procedure to assemble, noting the following:
   a. **On models equipped with separate reservoir,** when replacing nipples, ensure primary and secondary nipples are installed properly, **Fig. 13.**
   b. **On all models,** use all parts contained in repair kit.
   c. Coat all components with clean brake fluid.

CLEANING & INSPECTION

Examine reservoirs for foreign matter and check all passages for restrictions. If there is any indication of contamination or

Model	Year	Booster Size, Inches	Pushrod Clearance, Inch
Diamante	1996	—	.0260–.0330
	1997–99	—	.0200–.0120
Eclipse & Eclipse Spyder	1996–99	—	.0260–.0340
Galant	1996	7 & 8③	.0160–.0240
		9④	.0240–.0310
	1997–99	—	.0240–.0310①
		—	.0160–.0240②
Mirage	1996	7	.0160–.0240
		8	.0180–.0260
	1997–99	—	.0256–.0335
Montero	1996–99	—	.0260–.0350
Montero Sport	1997–99	—	.0280–.0430
Pickup	1996	—	.0040–.0200
3000GT	1996–99	7 & 8	.0220–.0300
		9	.0260–.0330

① — Single booster assembly.
② — Dual booster assembly.
③ — SOHC engine w/ABS.
④ — SOHC engine less ABS.

Fig. 8 Brake booster rod adjustment specifications

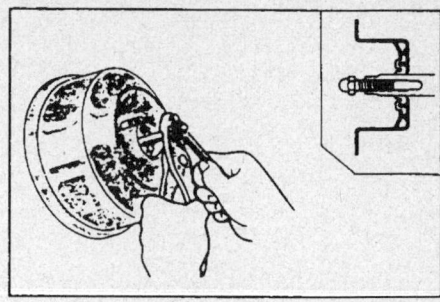

MT4099100011000X

Fig. 9 Brake booster pushrod adjustment

evidence of corrosion, service the hydraulic system as needed, then flush the entire system as outlined under "Brake System Bleed."

When disassembled, wash all parts in denatured alcohol or clean brake fluid. Use an air hose to blow out all passages, orifices and valve holes. Air dry and place parts on clean paper or lint-free cloth.

1. Check components for wear, damage, or corrosion. Replace as needed.
2. Check master cylinder bore for scoring, rust or pitting. Replace as necessary.

WHEEL CYLINDER

OVERHAUL

Note position of all parts as they are removed for proper installation, **Fig. 14.**

Disassemble

1. Remove boots, piston, cups and spring from wheel cylinder.
2. Wipe cylinder walls with denatured alcohol or clean brake fluid.
3. Examine cylinder bore. A scored bore may be honed, unless bore diameter will be increased by more than .005 inch. Replace as necessary.
4. Check pistons for wear or damage. Replace as necessary.

Assemble

1. Before assembling, wash hands with soap and water so as not to contaminate rubber parts.
2. Use all parts contained in repair kit. Lubricate cylinder walls and rubber parts with clean brake fluid.
3. Carefully install spring, cups, pistons and boots in housing.

BRAKE SYSTEM BLEED

MASTER CYLINDER

1. If master cylinder has been replaced or overhauled and reservoir is empty, proceed as follows:
   a. Fill reservoir with clean brake fluid, then disconnect brake lines at master cylinder.
   b. Depress pedal slowly and hold pedal in depressed position.
   c. Place fingers over outlet port, then release brake pedal.
   d. Repeat above steps several times. Refill reservoir suitable brake fluid.

HYDRAULIC SYSTEM

The hydraulic brake system must be bled if air has entered the system. This condition may be precipitated by low fluid level,

a hydraulic fluid leak, the opening of a hydraulic line or replacement of a hydraulic system component. Symptoms include a loss of brake operation and/or a low or spongy brake pedal.

1. Ensure master cylinder reservoir is full. Add suitable brake fluid as needed, and securely reinstall the master cylinder cap.
2. Raise and support vehicle.
3. Position a drain pan under the wheel being bled.
4. Have an assistant depress the brake pedal with a slow even pressure and hold it. **Do not depress brake pedal fully to the end of the master cylinder stroke. This may cause damage to the master cylinder.**
5. Using a suitable wrench, open the bleeder valve one full turn. Watch for air bubbles in the fluid, and listen for air escaping from the system.
6. With the brake pedal still depressed, close the bleeder valve.
7. Have the assistant pump the brake pedal several times. **Do not depress brake pedal fully to the end of the master cylinder stroke, this may cause damage to the master cylinder.**
8. Repeat preceding bleed steps until all air is removed from the hydraulic system. **While bleeding the system, recheck brake fluid supply in the master cylinder often so as not to allow the master cylinder to run dry.**
9. Upon completion of hydraulic system bleeding, proceed as follows:
   a. Ensure the master cylinder reservoir is full. Add suitable brake fluid as needed, and securely reinstall the master cylinder cap.
   b. Lower the vehicle. Ensure brake pedal is firm and braking operation is proper.

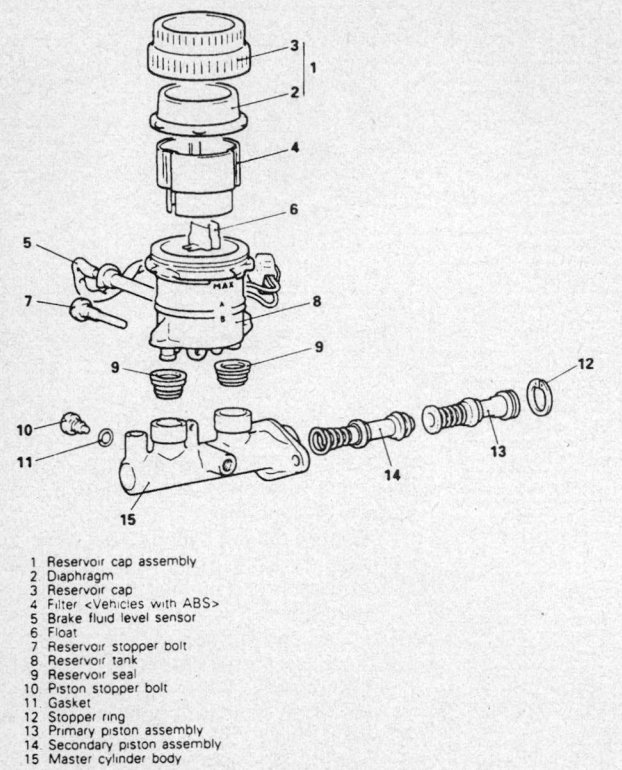

1. Reservoir cap assembly
2. Diaphragm
3. Reservoir cap
4. Filter <Vehicles with ABS>
5. Brake fluid level sensor
6. Float
7. Reservoir stopper bolt
8. Reservoir tank
9. Reservoir seal
10. Piston stopper bolt
11. Gasket
12. Stopper ring
13. Primary piston assembly
14. Secondary piston assembly
15. Master cylinder body

MT4099100002000X

Fig. 10 Exploded view of attached reservoir master cylinder. Except 1997–99 Diamante

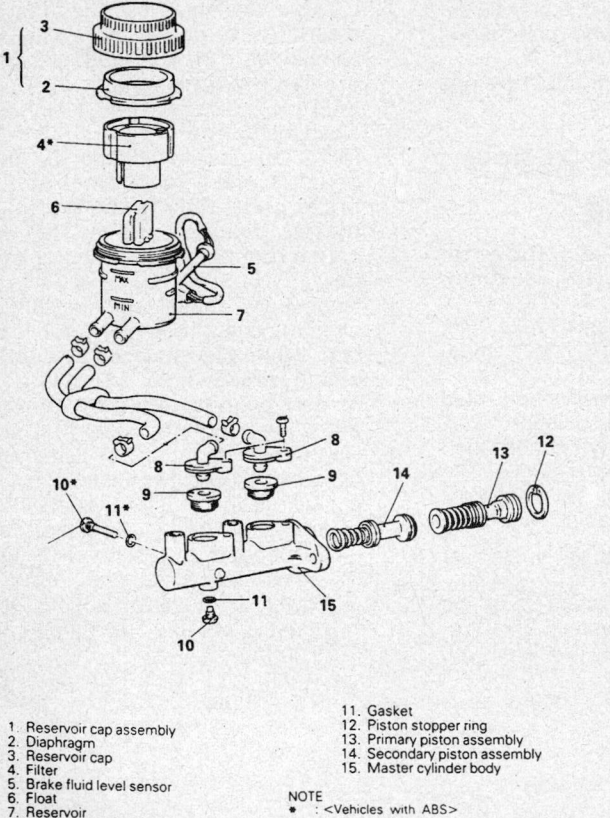

1. Reservoir cap assembly
2. Diaphragm
3. Reservoir cap
4. Filter
5. Brake fluid level sensor
6. Float
7. Reservoir
8. Nipple
9. Reservoir seal
10. Piston stopper bolt
11. Gasket
12. Piston stopper ring
13. Primary piston assembly
14. Secondary piston assembly
15. Master cylinder body

NOTE
* : <Vehicles with ABS>

MT4099100004000X

Fig. 12 Exploded view of separate reservoir master cylinder

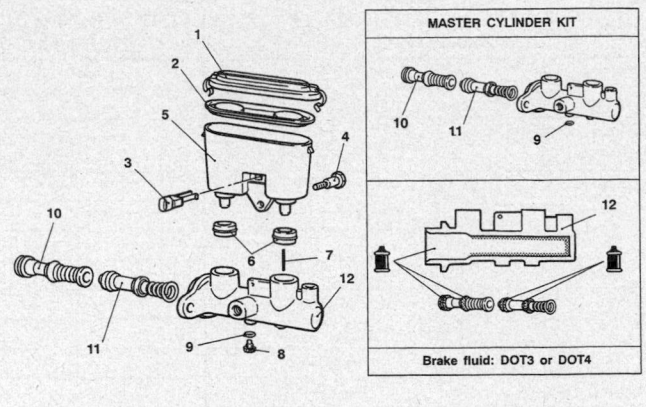

DISASSEMBLY STEPS
1. RESERVOIR CAP ASSEMBLY
2. DIAPHRAGM
3. BRAKE FLUID LEVEL SENSOR
4. RESERVOIR BOLT
5. RESERVOIR
6. RESERVOIR SEALS
7. PISTON STOPPER PIN (ABS VEHICLES)

8. PISTON STOPPER BOLT (NON ABS VEHICLES)
9. GASKET (NON ABS VEHICLES)
10. PRIMARY PISTON ASSEMBLY
11. SECONDARY PISTON ASSEMBLY
12. MASTER CYLINDER BODY

MT4099900016000X

Fig. 11 Exploded view of attached reservoir master cylinder. 1997–99 Diamante

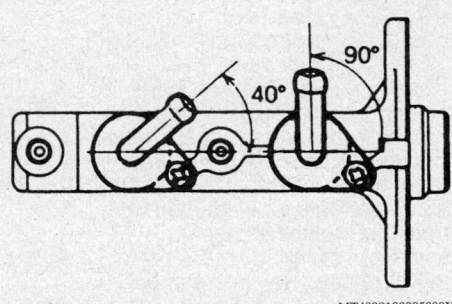

MT4099100005000X

Fig. 13 Brake fluid nipple orientation

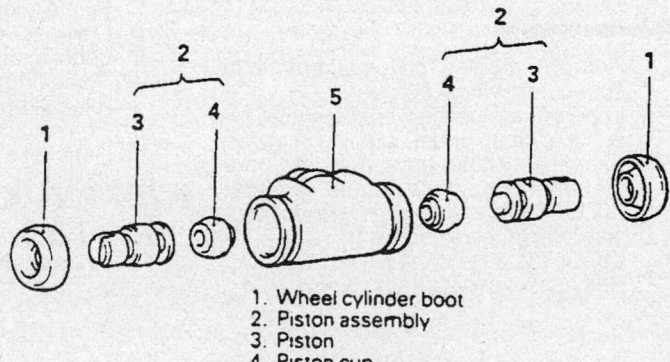

1. Wheel cylinder boot
2. Piston assembly
3. Piston
4. Piston cup
5. Wheel cylinder body

MT4099100006000X

Fig. 14 Exploded view of wheel cylinder

HYDRAULIC BRAKE SYSTEM SPECIFICATIONS

| Model | Proportioning Valve | | |
| | Input Pressure, psi | Output Pressure, psi | |
		@ Input Pressure Shown	Max. Difference Between LH & RH Brake Lines
1996			
Diamante	1138	676–747	57
Eclipse②	925	462–533	57
Eclipse①	996	569–640	57
Galant	996	604	57
Mirage②	996	604	57
Mirage①	1067	676	57
Montero	1422	873–1001	—
	2560	1129–1314	—
Pickup	1991	370–540	—
3000GT	1138	744–815	57
1997			
Diamante	—	483–544	57
Eclipse②	925	462–533	57
Eclipse①	996	569–640	57
Galant	—	617	57
Mirage⑤	—	566–680	59.6
Mirage⑥	—	619–733	59.6
Montero③	2560	1129–1314	—
Montero④	2560	1863–2147	—
Montero Sport	640	398–455	—
3000GT	906	651–723	—
1998			
Diamante	—	249–391	57
Eclipse②	925	462–533	57
Eclipse①	996	569–640	57
Galant	—	617	57
Mirage⑤	—	566–680	59.6
Mirage⑥	—	619–733	59.6
Montero③	2560	1129–1314	—
Montero④	2560	1863–2147	—
Montero Sport	640	398–455	—
3000GT	906	651–723	—
1999			
Diamante	—	249–391	57
Eclipse②	925	462–533	57
Eclipse①	996	569–640	57
Galant	—	619–732	57
Mirage⑤	—	566–680	59.6
Mirage⑥	—	619–733	59.6
Montero③	2560	1129–1314	—
Montero④	2560	1863–2147	—
Montero Sport	640	398–455	—
3000GT	906	651–723	—

① — With ABS.
② — Less ABS.
③ — With load sensing spring @ 8.9 inches
④ — With load sensing spring @ 10.1 inches.
⑤ — 2 door models
⑥ — 4 door models

TIGHTENING SPECIFICATIONS

Year	Component	Torque, Ft. Lbs.
DIAMANTE		
1996–99	Bleeder Screw	6
	Brake Booster To Pedal Support Bracket	10
	Brake Pedal Support Bolt	22
	Brake Pedal Support Bracket	7
	Flared Line Fittings	11
	Master Cylinder To Brake Booster	7
	Piston Stopper Bolt	24①
	Vacuum Hose Fitting	11–13
ECLIPSE		
1996–99	Bleeder Screw	5–7
	Brake Booster Nuts	8–12
	Brake Hose Bracket Bolts	12–19
	Flared Brake Line Nuts	9–12
	Master Cylinder To Brake Booster	6–9
	Nipple Screw	12–24①
	Pedal Rod To Clutch Pedal Bracket	12–19
	Pedal Rod To Pedal Support Bracket	12–19
	Pedal Support Bracket Bolts	6–9
	Pedal Support Nut	7–11
	Piston Stopper Bolt	12–24①
	Vacuum Hose Fitting	11–13
	Wheel Cylinder	7
GALANT		
1996–99	Bleeder Screw	6
	Brake Booster	10
	Brake Hose Bracket	12–19
	Brake Pedal Shaft	23
	Flared Brake Line Nuts	11
	Hydraulic Unit	12–19
	Master Cylinder To Brake Booster	7
	Parking Brake Lever	29–40
	Pedal Support Bracket Installation Nut	7
	Vacuum Hose Fitting	11–13
	Wheel Cylinder Bolt	7
MIRAGE		
1996–99	Bleeder Screw	5–7
	Brake Booster & Pedal Support Member (Right Side)	8–12
	Flared Brake Line Nuts	9–12
	Master Cylinder	6–9
	Pedal Support Member	12–15
	Piston Stopper Bolt	12–24①
	Reservoir	12–24①
	Sleeve Bolt	16–23
	Vacuum Hose Fitting	11–13
MONTERO & MONTERO SPORT		
1996–99	Bleeder Screw	5–7
	Brake Booster To Pedal Support	6–9
	Brake Line Flare Nut	9–12
	Brake Pedal Shaft	18–25
	Master Cylinder To Brake Booster	6–9
	Master Cylinder To Brake Line Connector	18–25
	Pedal Support Member	13–18
	Piston Stopper	12–24①
	Reservoir Stopper Bolt	12–24①

Continued

TIGHTENING SPECIFICATIONS—Continued

Year	Component	Torque, Ft. Lbs.
PICKUP		
1996	Bleeder Screw	5–7
	Brake Booster To Pedal Support Member	6–9
	Brake Line Flare Nut	9–12
	Brake Pedal Shaft	18–25
	Master Cylinder To Brake Booster	6–9
	Master Cylinder To Brake Line Connector	18–25
	Piston Stopper	12–24①
	Reservoir Stopper Belt	12–24①
	Vacuum Hose Fitting	11–13
3000GT		
1996–99	Bleeder Screw	6
	Brake Booster	10
	Brake Pedal Support Bolt	22
	Brake Pedal Support Bracket	9
	Flared Brake Line Fittings	11
	Master Cylinder To Brake Booster	7
	Vacuum Hose Fitting	11–13

① — Inch lbs.

Power Brake Units

INDEX

DESCRIPTION

The power brake unit is a vacuum assist diaphragm assembly which multiplies the force exerted on the master cylinder piston in order to increase the hydraulic pressure delivered to the wheel calipers. This effectively decreases the effort necessary to attain sufficient stopping performance.

Vacuum assist units are powered by the opposition of engine vacuum to atmospheric pressure. A piston, cylinder and flexible diaphragm utilize this energy to provide brake assistance. The diaphragm is balanced with engine vacuum until the brake pedal is depressed, allowing atmospheric pressure to unbalance the unit and apply force to the brake system.

The basic brake system will operate even if the power unit fails, although more effort is required at the pedal to achieve the same amount of braking performance attainable with a functional power assist unit.

TROUBLESHOOTING

1. Run engine for two minutes, then turn engine off. Depress brake pedal slowly several times.
2. Pedal should go down farther the first

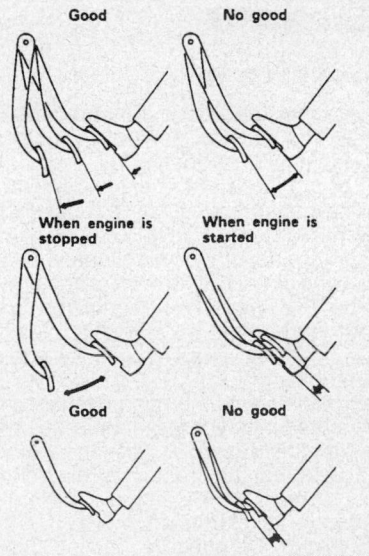

MT4039100001000X

Fig. 1 Brake booster functional inspection

Good / No good

When engine is stopped

When engine is started

Good / No good

time and rise gradually the second and third time, **Fig. 1.** If pedal height remains the same booster is faulty.

3. With engine off, depress brake pedal several times, **Fig. 1.** There should be no change in pedal stroke.
4. With brake pedal depressed, start engine. Pedal should go down slightly, if no change in pedal, booster is faulty.
5. With engine running and brake pedal depressed, stop engine.
6. If after 30 seconds there is no change in pedal movement, the booster is in good condition, **Fig. 1.** If pedal rises booster is faulty.

POWER BRAKE UNIT SERVICE

REPLACEMENT

1. Remove master cylinder as outlined in "Hydraulic Brake Systems" section.
2. Disconnect vacuum hose from power brake booster.
3. Remove pin connecting power brake rod with pedal.
4. Remove booster attaching nuts and remove booster.
5. Reverse procedure to install.

SERVICE

These units cannot be overhauled and must be replaced in the event of a malfunction.

PUSHROD ADJUSTMENT

Refer to "Adjustments" in "Hydraulic Brake Systems" section, for pushrod adjustment procedures.

Anti-Lock Brakes

NOTE: On Air Bag Equipped Models, Refer To "Air Bag System Precautions" Located In The Front Of This Manual For System Disarming & Arming Procedures.

NOTE: Wire Color Code Identification & Electrical Symbol Identification Located In The Front Of This Manual May Be Used As An Aid When Using Wiring Circuits Found In This Section.

INDEX

PRECAUTIONS

AIR BAG SYSTEMS

Refer to "Air Bag System Precautions" in the front of this manual for system disarming and arming procedures.

BATTERY GROUND CABLE

Prior to service, disconnect battery ground cable and isolate as required.

DESCRIPTION

The Anti-Lock Braking System (ABS) prevents wheels from locking up when braking, regardless of the surface conditions. This allows the vehicle to stop in a shorter distance and allows the driver to maintain directional control of the vehicle during heavy braking.

During normal braking conditions, the ABS operates like a conventional diagonally split hydraulic power assist system. During heavy braking, however, each wheel's braking pressure is modulated according to its speed. To maintain stability, both rear wheels receive the same signal.

TROUBLESHOOTING

GENERAL FAULT DIAGNOSIS

Except Pickup

Problems related to the Anti-Lock Brake System (ABS) can generally be classified as electrical or hydraulic.

For problems in the electrical system, a self-diagnostic function is built into the Electronic Control Unit (ECU), allowing the ABS warning lamp to illuminate as a warning to the driver in the event of an abnormality. In this instance, inspections can be performed with a voltmeter, Multi-Use Tester (MUT), oscilloscope or the ABS warning lamp.

Problems with the hydraulic system can be located in the same manner as ordinary brakes. It is, however, necessary to determine whether the problem is related to ordinary brake components or to the components related to the ABS.

Refer to "Diagnosis & Testing" for diagnostic test procedures.

Pickup

Refer to **Figs. 1 and 2** for troubleshooting procedures.

TRANSIENT FAULT DIAGNOSIS

In electronic control systems, momentary problems can occur in electronic circuits and input and output signals, and this can result in temporary trouble symptoms or a diagnostic trouble code being recorded by means of ECU on-board diagnostics. If the cause of the problem is continuous, the location of the abnormality can be discovered by checking according to the diagnosis chart classified by trouble symptoms. However, the symptoms of some transient problems may return to normal by themselves, so there is a possibility that the cause of the problem will be unclear.

The causes of problems in vehicles with temporary malfunctions include vibration, heat and excessive electrical resistance. By performing an inspection according to the following simulation method, the trouble symptom can be recreated.

1. If main cause is possibly vibration, perform the following:
   a. Gently shake connector up, down, right and left.
   b. Gently shake wiring harness up, down, right and left.
   c. Gently rock each sensor by hand.
   d. Gently shake other moving parts.

Condition of warning light	Main causes
Warning light will not come on even when ignition switch is "ON" with engine stop.	• Warning light bulb has run out. • Warning light drive circuit has been broken. • Control unit power circuit has been broken.
Warning light keeps on lighting	• Warning light drive circuit has been short-circuited. • Fail safe is working as a result of self-check.

MT4029100001000X

Fig. 1 Troubleshooting chart: Warning light. Pickup

Malfunction mode	Malfunction cause	Remedy
There is no input of signal in the control unit.	Harness between sensors is broken.	Check harness.
	Sensor is out of order.	Check sensor.
The sensor outputs abnormal signal to the control unit.	Sensor is not properly installed.	Check installation.
	Specified tire and wheel are not installed.	Check tire and wheel.
	Sensor is out of order.	Check sensor.

MT4029100002000X

Fig. 2 Troubleshooting chart: Malfunction mode. Pickup

2. If any wires or connections break during inspection, replace with new ones.
3. The vehicle speed sensors are particularly subject to intermittently poor contacts due to movement of suspension while driving, so it is desirable that a driving test be conducted while monitoring sensor signals.
4. If main cause is probably heat, use a hair dryer to heat suspected component. **Do not heat component above 176°F.**
5. If main cause is probably excessive electrical resistance, turn all electrical switches, including headlights and rear defogger, to On positions.

DIAGNOSIS & TESTING

Accessing Diagnostic Trouble Codes

If using a scan tool, turn the ignition switch to the Off position and connect a suitable diagnostic scan tool to the Data Link Connector (DLC). The DLC is located under the lefthand side of the instrument panel.

If an analog voltmeter is to be used to access diagnostic trouble codes, use special harness tool, **Fig. 3,** to connect it between the DLC diagnostic output and ground terminals. Specific diagnostic trouble codes are indicated by sweeps of the voltmeter needle as follows:

1. Following an initial pause of approximately three seconds, needle will begin to indicate "tens" digit of diagnostic trouble code. This digit will be represented by 1.5 second sweeps.
2. A two second pause will follow "tens" digit indication, then "ones" digit will be indicated by sweeps of approximately .5 seconds each. These will be separated from one another by .5 second pauses.

After obtaining any diagnostic trouble codes, proceed to "Diagnostic Trouble Code Interpretation" for diagnostic trouble code identification and diagnosis.

Diagnostic Trouble Code Interpretation

Refer to the "Diagnostic Chart Index" for diagnostic trouble code interpretation.

Wiring Diagrams

Refer to **Figs. 4 through 21** for ABS wiring diagrams.

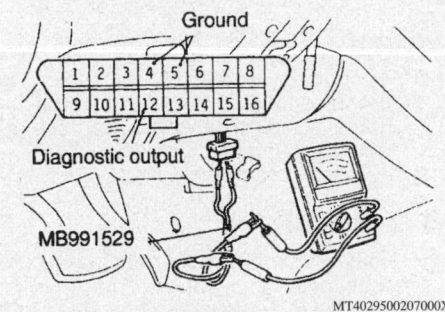

MT4029500207000X

Fig. 3 Voltmeter diagnostic trouble code retrieval

Diagnostic Tests

DIAMANTE

1996

Refer to **Figs. 22 through 39** for diagnostic flowcharts corresponding to specific diagnostic trouble codes.

1997-98

Refer to **Figs. 40 through 53** for diagnostic flowcharts corresponding to specific diagnostic trouble codes.

1999

Refer to **Figs. 54 through 69** for diagnostic flowcharts corresponding to specific diagnostic trouble codes.

ECLIPSE

1996-97

AWD Models

Refer to **Figs. 70 through 76** for diagnostic flowcharts corresponding to specific diagnostic trouble codes.

FWD Models

Refer to **Figs. 77 through 84** for diagnostic flowcharts corresponding to specific diagnostic trouble codes.

1998-99

AWD Models

Refer to **Figs. 85 through 99** for diagnostic flowcharts corresponding to specific diagnostic trouble codes.

FWD Models

Refer to **Figs. 100 through 113** for diagnostic flowcharts corresponding to specific diagnostic trouble codes.

GALANT

1996-98

Refer to **Figs. 114 through 134** for diag-

nostic flowcharts corresponding to specific diagnostic trouble codes.

1999

Refer to **Figs. 135 through 138** for diagnostic flowcharts corresponding to specific diagnostic trouble codes.

MIRAGE

1996

Refer to **Figs. 139 through 158** for diagnostic flowcharts corresponding to specific diagnostic trouble codes.

1997-99

Refer to **Figs. 159 through 172** for diagnostic flowcharts corresponding to specific diagnostic trouble codes.

MONTERO

1996-97

Refer to **Figs. 173 through 185** for diagnostic flowcharts corresponding to specific diagnostic trouble codes.

1998-99

Refer to **Figs. 186 through 207** for diagnostic flowcharts corresponding to specific diagnostic trouble codes.

MONTERO SPORT

Refer to **Figs. 208 through 215** for diagnostic flowcharts corresponding to specific diagnostic trouble codes.

PICKUP

Refer to **Fig. 216** to interpret diagnostic trouble code output.

3000GT

1996-97

Refer to **Figs. 217 through 230** for diagnostic flowcharts corresponding to specific diagnostic trouble codes.

1998-99

Refer to **Figs. 231 through 245** for diagnostic flowcharts corresponding to specific diagnostic trouble codes.

Clearing Diagnostic Trouble Codes

To clear diagnostic trouble codes, use the Multi-Use Tester (MUT) and follow manufacturer's instructions for erasure.

SYSTEM SERVICE

Brake System Bleed

1. Bleed brake master cylinder as follows:
   a. Fill master cylinder reservoir with DOT 3 or DOT 4 brake fluid, then depress brake pedal fully and plug master cylinder outlet fitting.
   b. With fitting opening plugged, release brake pedal. Perform this operation several times to fill master cylinder with brake fluid and purge all air.
2. Start engine and bleed air from hydraulic lines. Refer to **Figs. 246 through 248** for hydraulic line bleed sequence. **Ensure master cylinder reservoir is kept full during bleed procedure.**
3. Ensure brake pedal feels firm when applied. Check and fill master cylinder reservoir as necessary.

Component Replacement

BRAKE FLUID PRESSURE SWITCH

AWD Models

1. Disconnect pressure switch electrical connector.
2. Remove brake line connection.
3. Remove pressure switch from side of hydraulic unit.
4. Reverse procedure to install.

ELECTRONIC CONTROL UNIT & POWER RELAY

1. Remove ECU electrical connector mounting screws, then the ECU.
2. Remove ABS power relay, located under lefthand side of instrument panel.
3. Reverse procedure to install.

FRONT SPEED SENSOR

Except Pickup

1. Remove front toothed rotor.
2. Remove front speed sensor connector.
3. Remove front speed sensor and bracket.
4. Temporarily install sensor into knuckle.
5. Secure clip so white-painted portion is non twisted.
6. Insert a feeler gauge between speed sensor pole piece and rotor toothed surface.
7. Tighten front speed sensor bracket and toothed rotor attaching bolts.
8. **On 3000GT and 1996 Mirage models,** ensure a gap of .012–.035 inch exists between pole piece and rotor. If this gap cannot be reached, rotor may be improperly installed.
9. **On 1997–99 Mirage models,** ensure a gap of .004–.079 inch exists between pole piece and rotor. If this gap cannot be reached, rotor may be improperly

installed.
10. **On Montero and Montero Sport models,** ensure a gap of .008–.039 inch exists between pole piece and rotor. If this gap cannot be reached, rotor may be improperly installed.
11. **On Diamante, Galant and Eclipse models,** ensure a gap of 1.11–1.12 inches exists between sensor installation surface and rotor toothed surface.

Pickup

1. Disconnect electrical connector to speed sensor.
2. Remove speed sensor to rear axle attaching bolt, then the speed sensor.
3. Reverse procedure to install.

G-SENSOR

1. Disconnect G-sensor electrical connections.
2. Remove G-sensor bracket and G-sensor.
3. Reverse procedure to install.

HYDRAULIC UNIT

The hydraulic unit must never be disassembled, subjected to impact or turned upside down. Do not loosen bolts.

Galant

1. Drain brake fluid from reservoir and remove air intake hose.
2. Remove hydraulic unit in numbered sequence, **Figs. 249 and 250. Exercise caution during removal; unit is heavy and must be handled carefully.**
3. Reverse procedure to install, noting the following:
   a. Ensure brake lines are connected to proper ports, **Figs. 251 and 252.**
   b. Bleed brake system as outlined under "Brake System Bleed" in this section.

Eclipse

1. Drain brake fluid from reservoir, then remove lefthand splash shield and headlamp.
2. **On models equipped with 2.0L non-turbocharged engine,** remove air cleaner assembly, Engine Control Module (ECM), relay box bracket and power steering oil reservoir mounting bolts.
3. **On models equipped with 2.0L turbocharged engine and 2.4L engine,** remove power steering pressure and return pipe clamp mounting bolts.
4. **On all models,** remove hydraulic unit from vehicle in numbered sequence, **Fig. 253. Exercise caution when removing unit; it is heavy and must be handled carefully.**
5. Reverse procedure to install, noting the following:
   a. Ensure brake pipes are connected to proper ports, **Fig. 254.**
   b. Bleed brake system as outlined under "Brake System Bleed" in this section.

Mirage

Remove hydraulic unit in numbered sequence as shown in **Fig. 255,** keeping brake pipes in order when installing, **Fig. 256.** Brake system must be bled as described under "Brake System Bleed" in this section.

Montero & Montero Sport

Remove the hydraulic relay and unit in numbered sequence shown in **Figs. 257 and 258.** Brake system must be bled as described under "Brake System Bleed" in this section.

Diamante

1. Remove the hydraulic relay unit in numbered sequence as shown in **Figs. 259 and 260** pushing the unit rearward so that it does not come in contact with the piping on the A/C receiver.
2. Reverse numbered sequence to install. Brake system must be bled as outlined under "Brake System Bleed" in this section.

3000GT

1. Remove splash shield, then disconnect and remove relay box.
2. Remove hydraulic unit in numbered sequence shown in **Fig. 261,** noting the following:
   a. When removing brake tubes, pull up relay box with harness attached and insert a suitable wrench under relay box.
   b. Remove hydraulic unit along with bracket from wheelhouse.
3. Reverse procedure to install, noting the following:
   a. Ensure ground cable is properly attached.
   b. Bleed brake system as outlined under "Brake System Bleed" in this section.

MODULATOR

Pickup

1. Disconnect brake tubes.
2. Remove filter spacer, air filter and washer.
3. Disconnect vacuum hose.
4. Remove modulator to bracket attaching screws, then the modulator.
5. Reverse procedure to install.

REAR SPEED SENSOR

Except Pickup

1. Remove rear toothed rotor.
2. Remove rear speed sensor connector.
3. Remove rear speed sensor.
4. Temporarily install speed sensor in backing plate.
5. Secure clip so white-painted portion is non twisted.
6. Insert a feeler gauge between speed sensor pole piece and rotor toothed surface.
7. Tighten rear toothed rotor attaching bolts.
8. **On all models except Montero, 3000GT and Eclipse** ensure a gap of

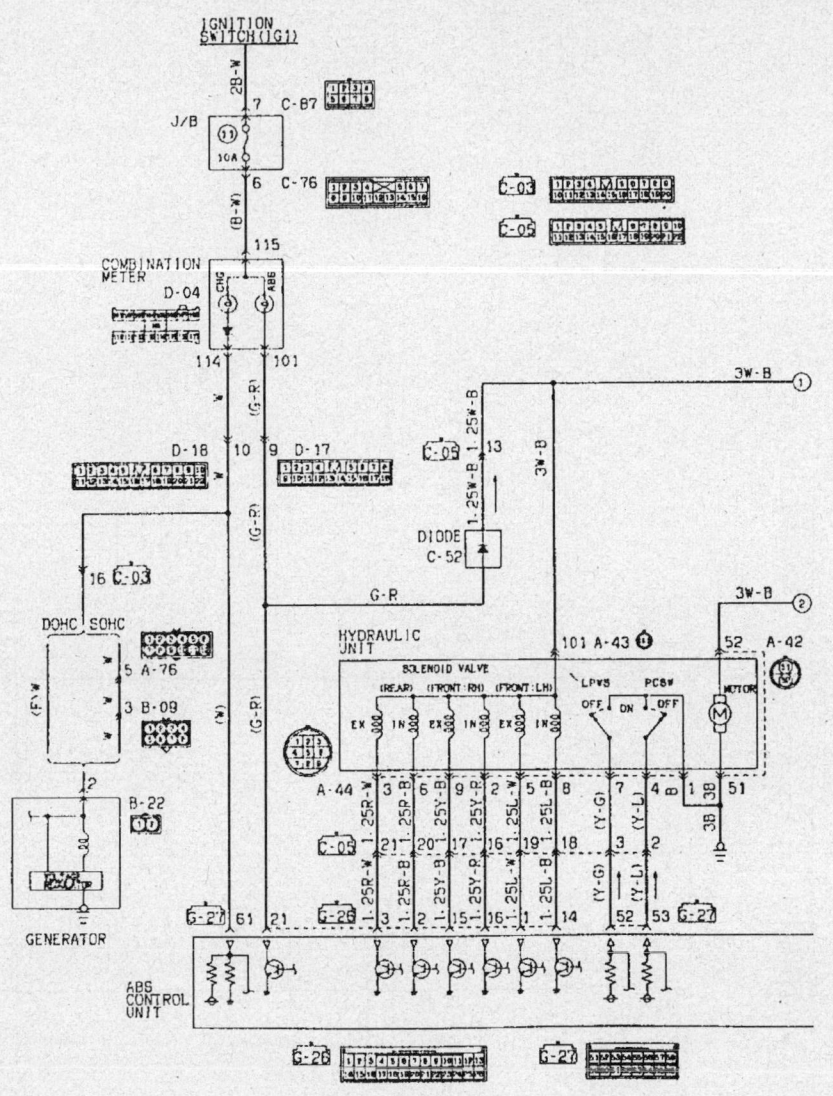

Fig. 4   ABS wiring diagram (Part 1 of 4). 1996 Diamante

.012–.035 inch exists between pole piece and rotor.

9. **On 3000GT models,** ensure a gap of .008–.028 inch exists between pole piece and rotor.

10. **On Galant and Eclipse models,** ensure a gap of 1.11–1.12 inches exists between sensor mounting surface and rotor.

11. **On all models,** slowly spin rotor one full revolution to ensure sensor pole piece does not come in contact with rotor.

Pickup

1. Disconnect electrical connector to speed sensor.

2. Remove speed sensor to rear axle attaching bolt, then the speed sensor.

3. Reverse procedure to install.

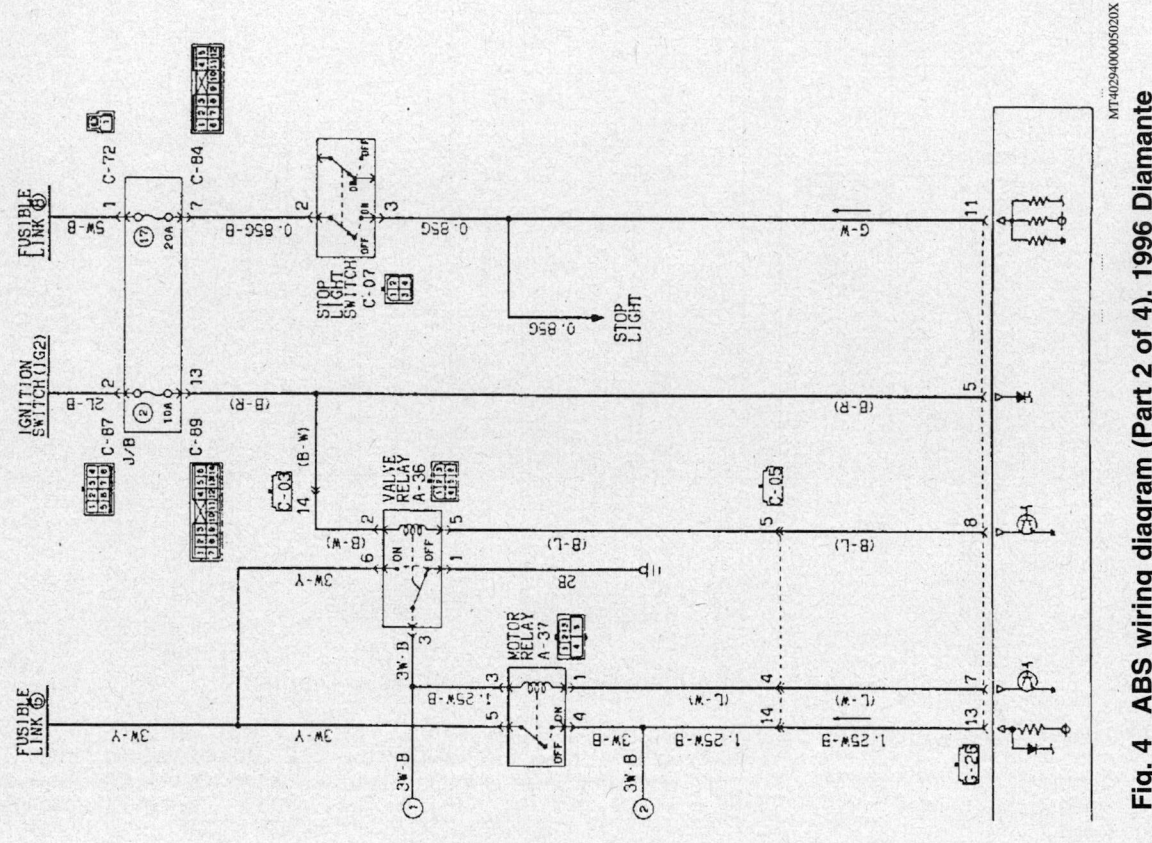

Fig. 4 ABS wiring diagram (Part 2 of 4). 1996 Diamante

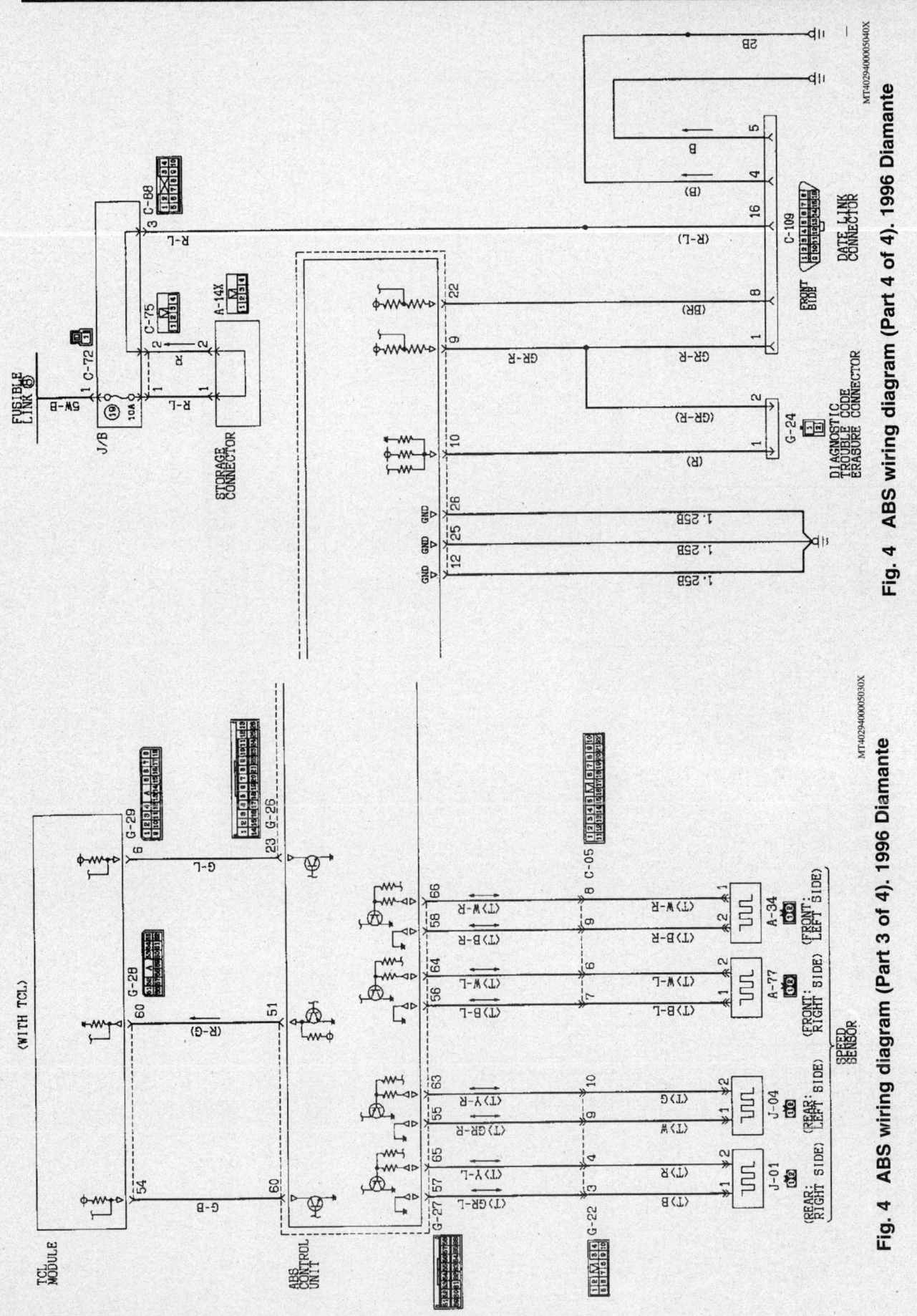

Fig. 4   ABS wiring diagram (Part 4 of 4). 1996 Diamante

Fig. 4   ABS wiring diagram (Part 3 of 4). 1996 Diamante

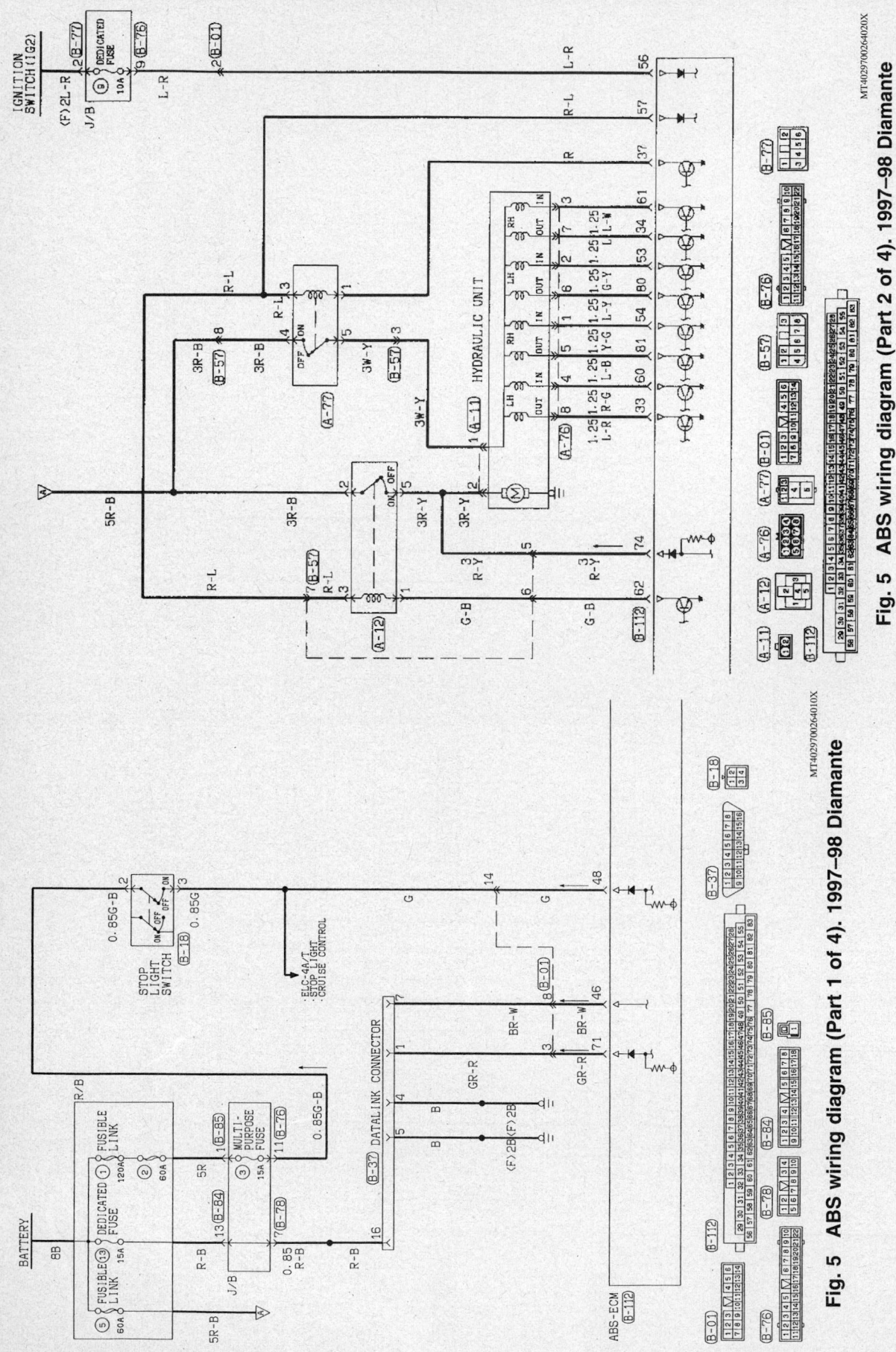

Fig. 5 ABS wiring diagram (Part 2 of 4). 1997-98 Diamante

Fig. 5 ABS wiring diagram (Part 1 of 4). 1997-98 Diamante

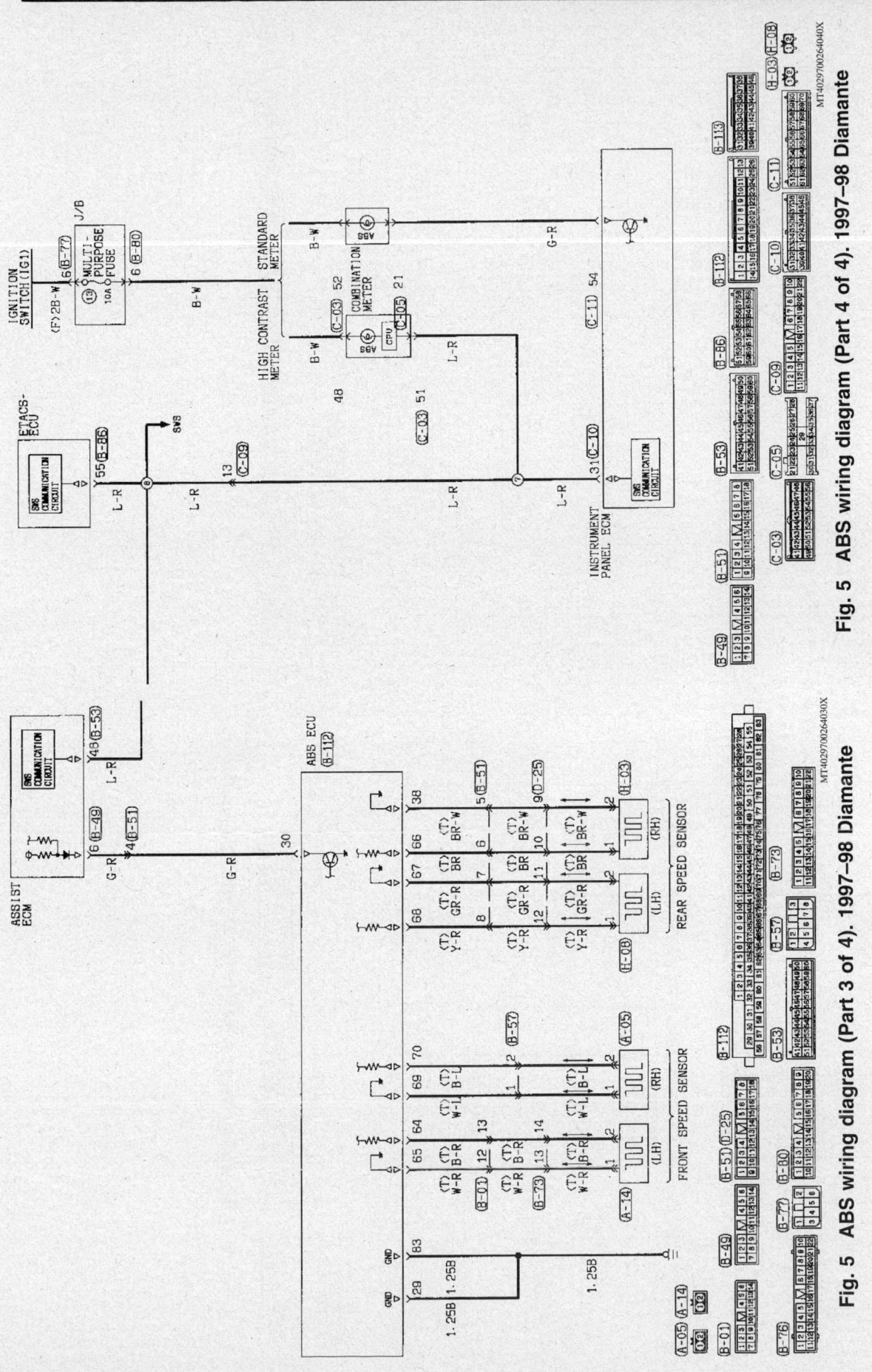

Fig. 5 ABS wiring diagram (Part 4 of 4). 1997–98 Diamante

Fig. 5 ABS wiring diagram (Part 3 of 4). 1997–98 Diamante

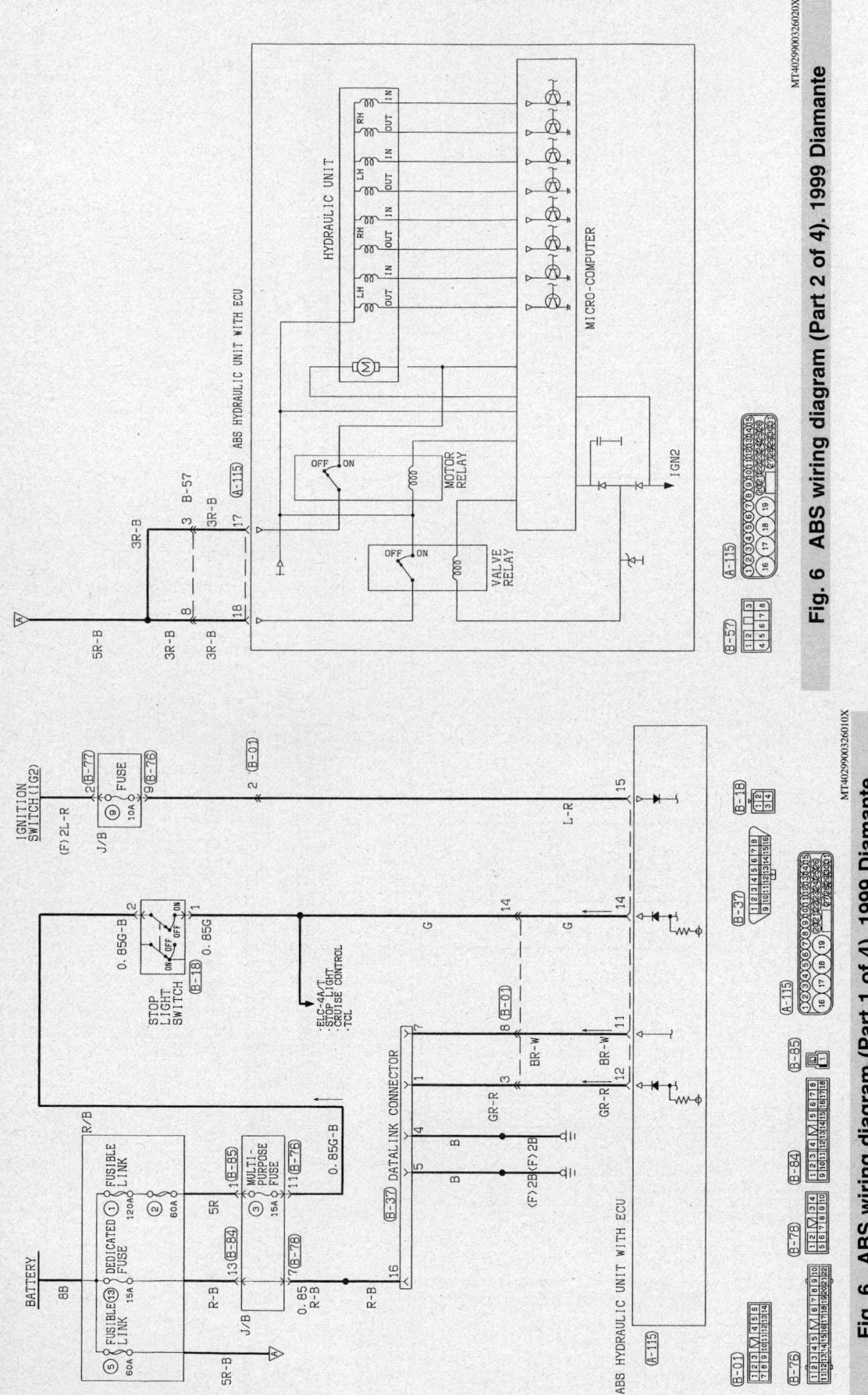

Fig. 6 ABS wiring diagram (Part 2 of 4). 1999 Diamante

Fig. 6 ABS wiring diagram (Part 1 of 4). 1999 Diamante

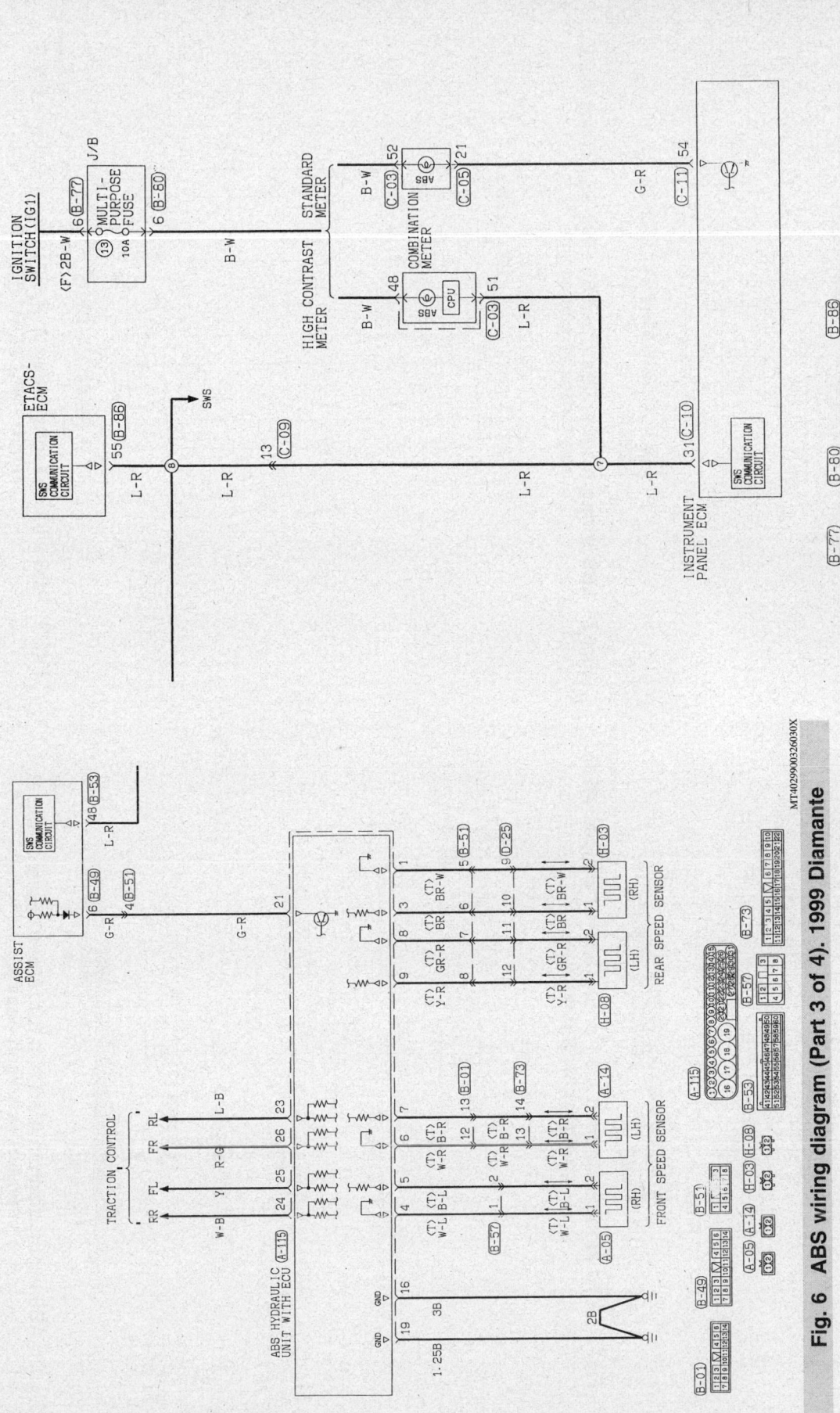

Fig. 6 ABS wiring diagram (Part 4 of 4). 1999 Diamante

Fig. 6 ABS wiring diagram (Part 3 of 4). 1999 Diamante

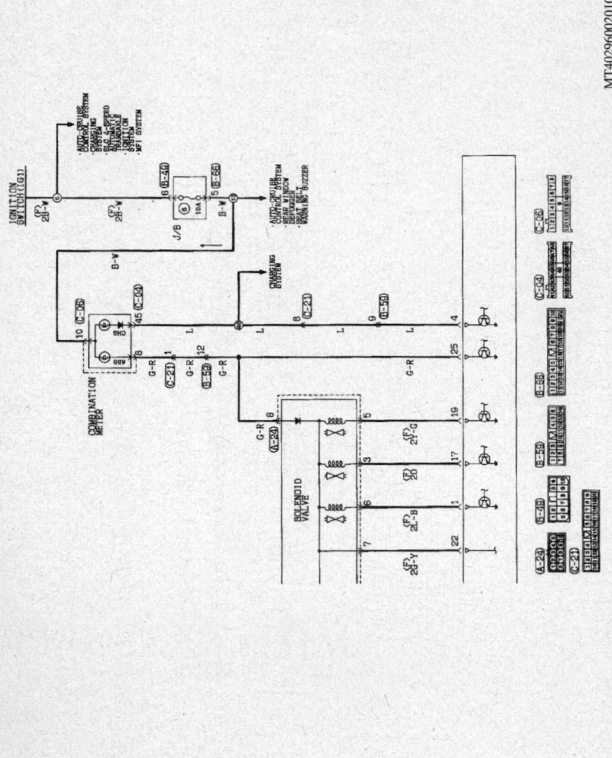

Fig. 7 ABS wiring diagram (Part 1 of 5). 1996–97 Eclipse w/2.0L non-turbocharged engine

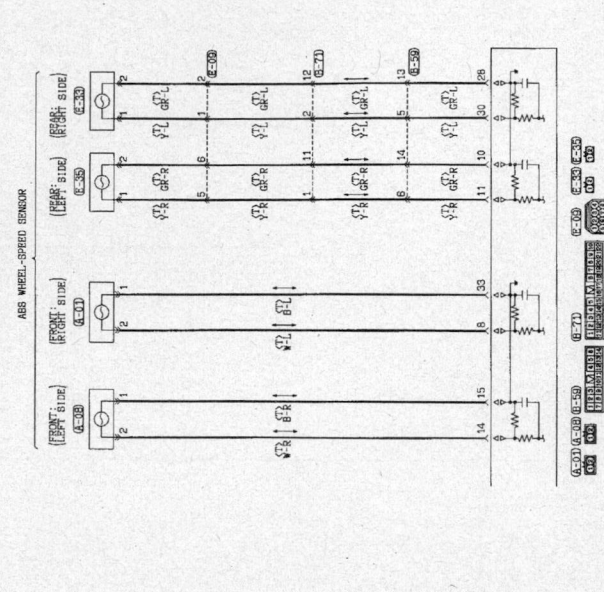

Fig. 7 ABS wiring diagram (Part 2 of 5). 1996–97 Eclipse w/2.0L non-turbocharged engine

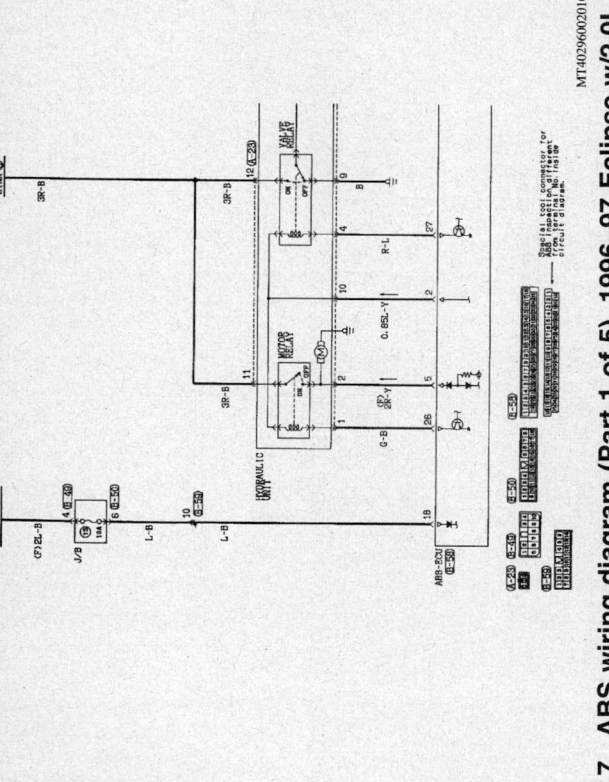

Fig. 7 ABS wiring diagram (Part 3 of 5). 1996–97 Eclipse w/2.0L non-turbocharged engine

Fig. 7 ABS wiring diagram (Part 4 of 5). 1996–97 Eclipse w/2.0L non-turbocharged engine

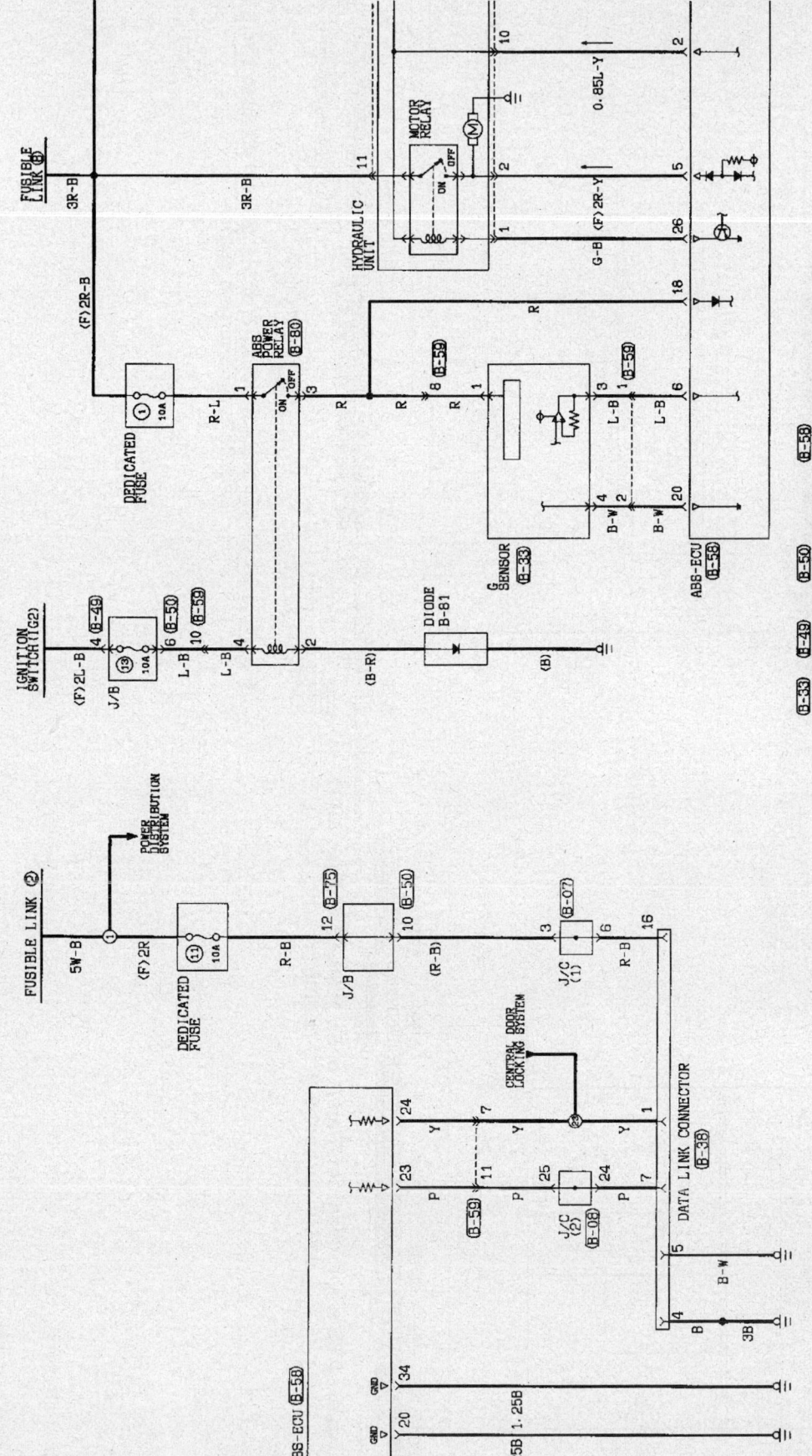

MT40296002020010X

Fig. 8 ABS wiring diagram (Part 1 of 5). 1996-97 Eclipse AWD w/2.0L turbocharged engine

MT40296002010050X

Fig. 7 ABS wiring diagram (Part 5 of 5). 1996-97 Eclipse w/2.0L non-turbocharged engine

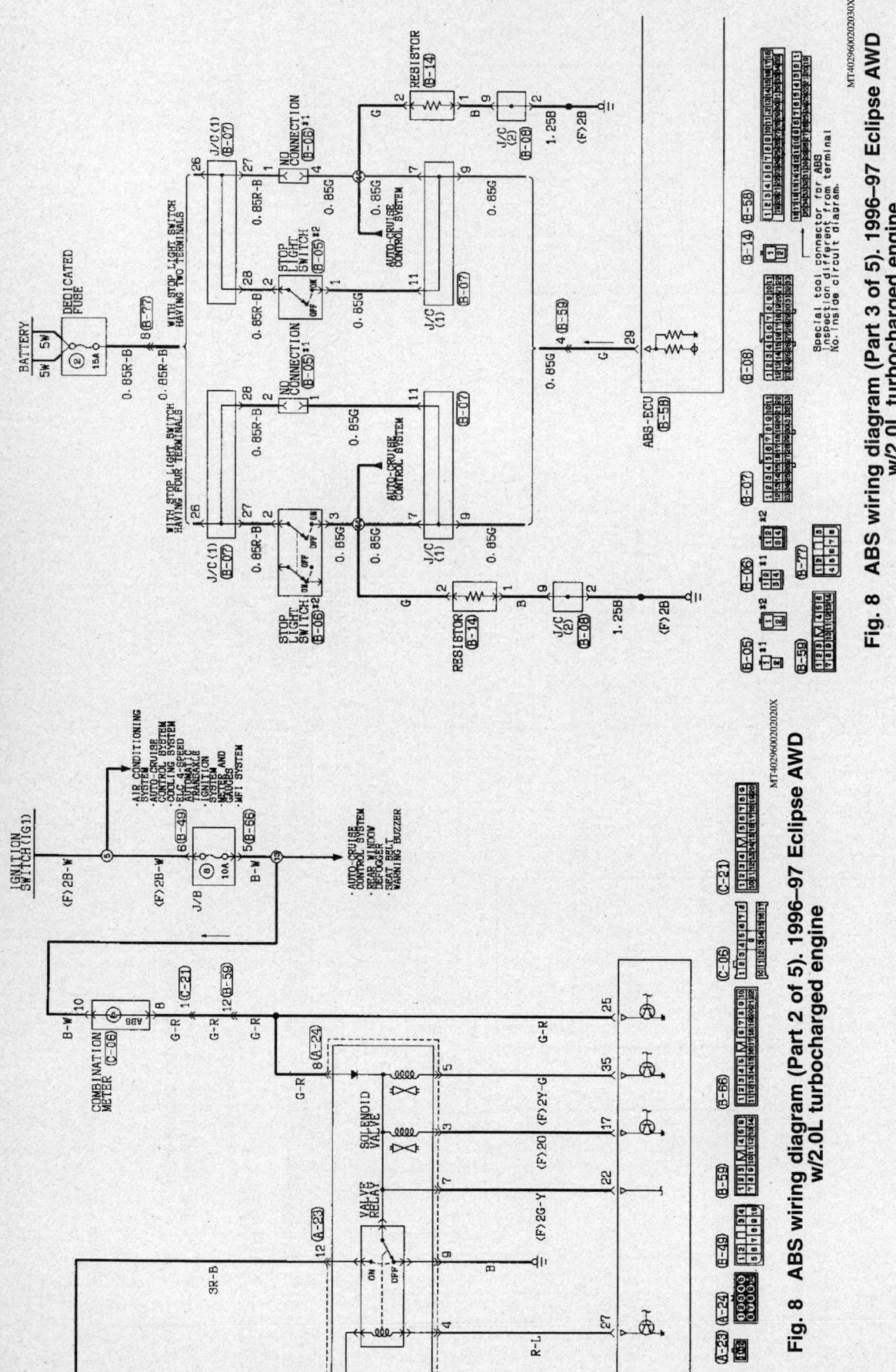

Fig. 8 ABS wiring diagram (Part 3 of 5). 1996-97 Eclipse AWD w/2.0L turbocharged engine

Fig. 8 ABS wiring diagram (Part 2 of 5). 1996-97 Eclipse AWD w/2.0L turbocharged engine

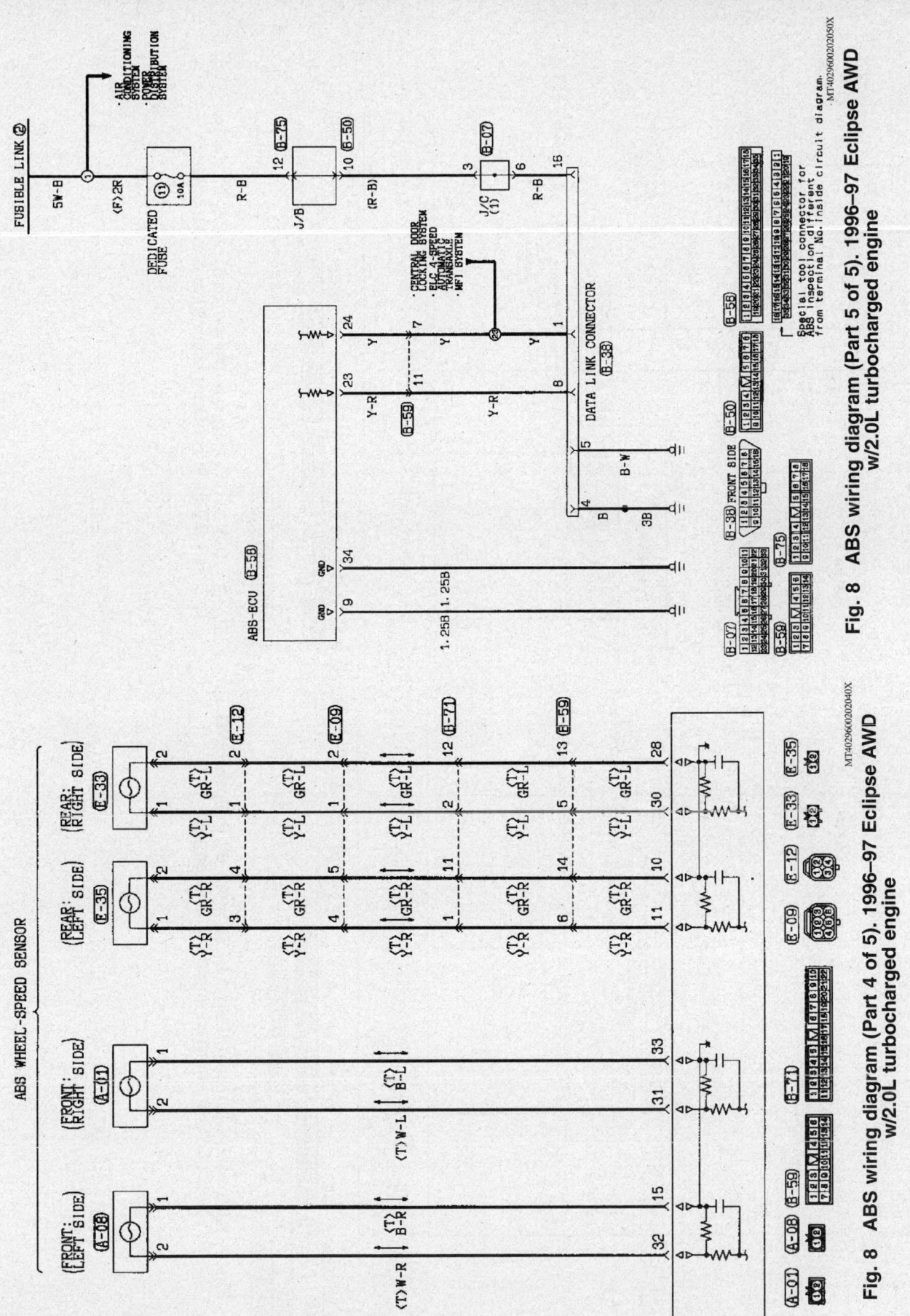

Fig. 8   ABS wiring diagram (Part 5 of 5). 1996-97 Eclipse AWD
w/2.0L turbocharged engine

Fig. 8   ABS wiring diagram (Part 4 of 5). 1996-97 Eclipse AWD
w/2.0L turbocharged engine

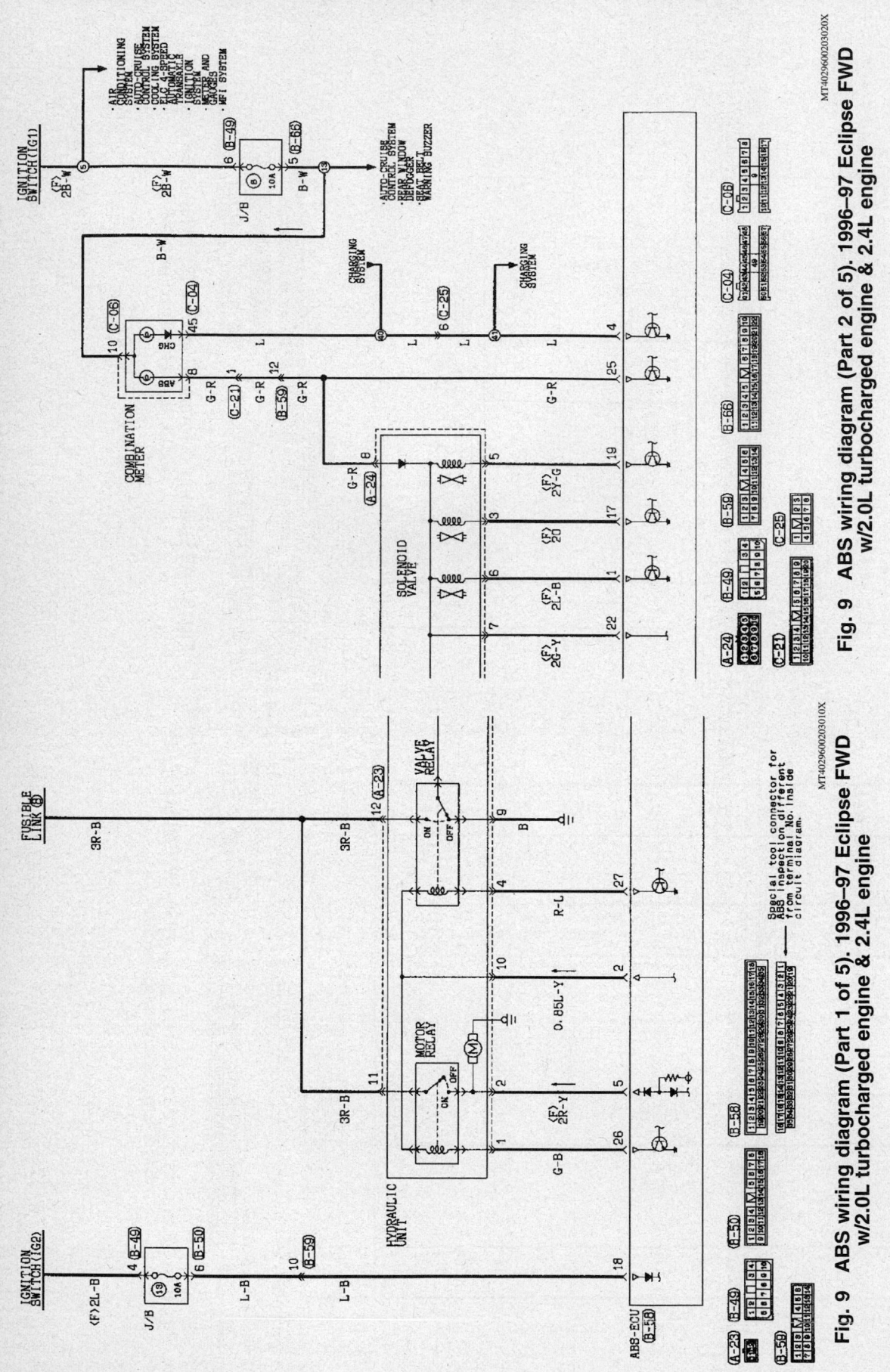

Fig. 9   ABS wiring diagram (Part 2 of 5). 1996–97 Eclipse FWD w/2.0L turbocharged engine & 2.4L engine

Fig. 9   ABS wiring diagram (Part 1 of 5). 1996–97 Eclipse FWD w/2.0L turbocharged engine & 2.4L engine

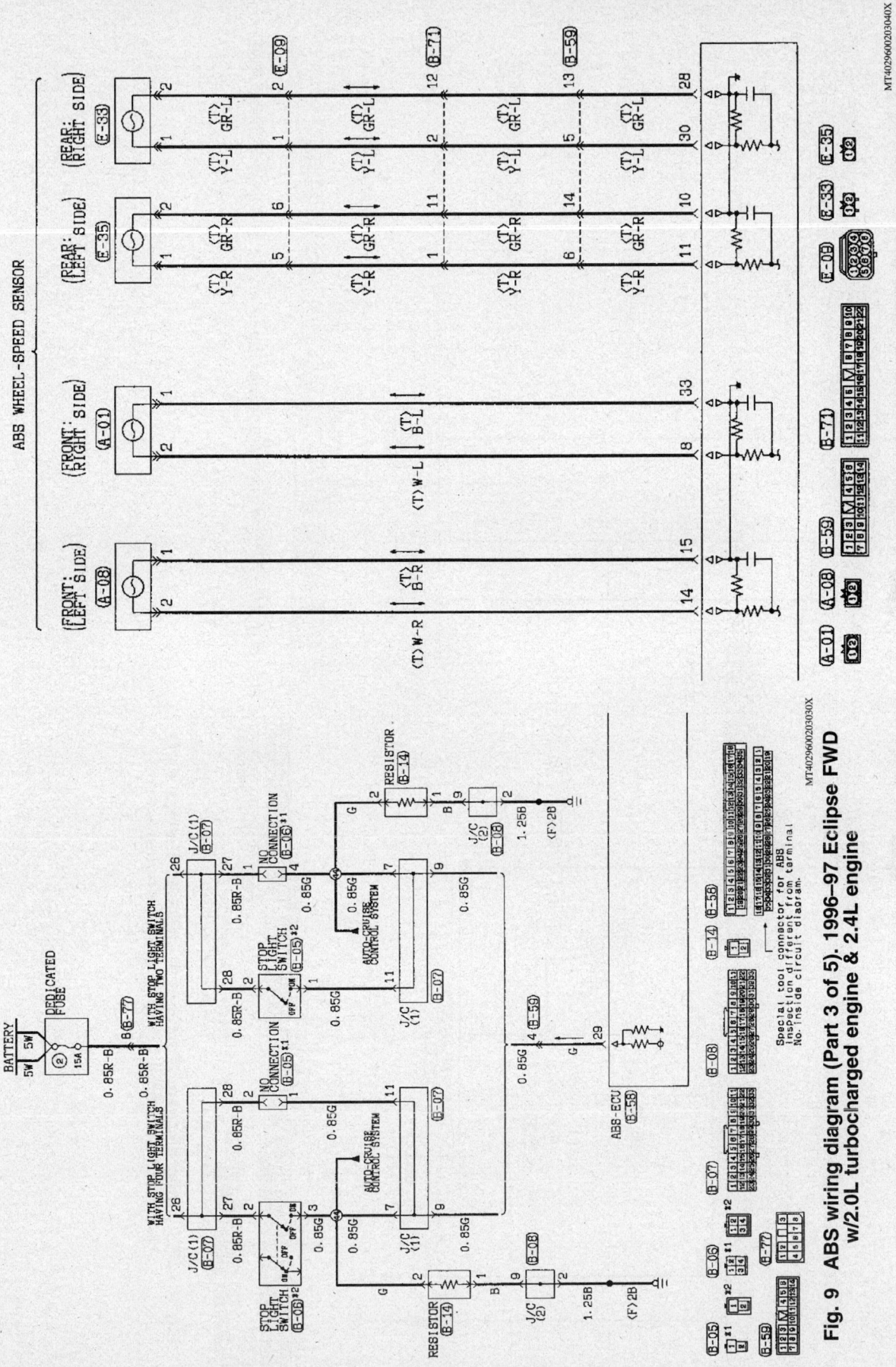

MT402960020304OX

Fig. 9 ABS wiring diagram (Part 4 of 5). 1996-97 Eclipse FWD w/2.0L turbocharged engine & 2.4L engine

MT402960020303OX

Fig. 9 ABS wiring diagram (Part 3 of 5). 1996-97 Eclipse FWD w/2.0L turbocharged engine & 2.4L engine

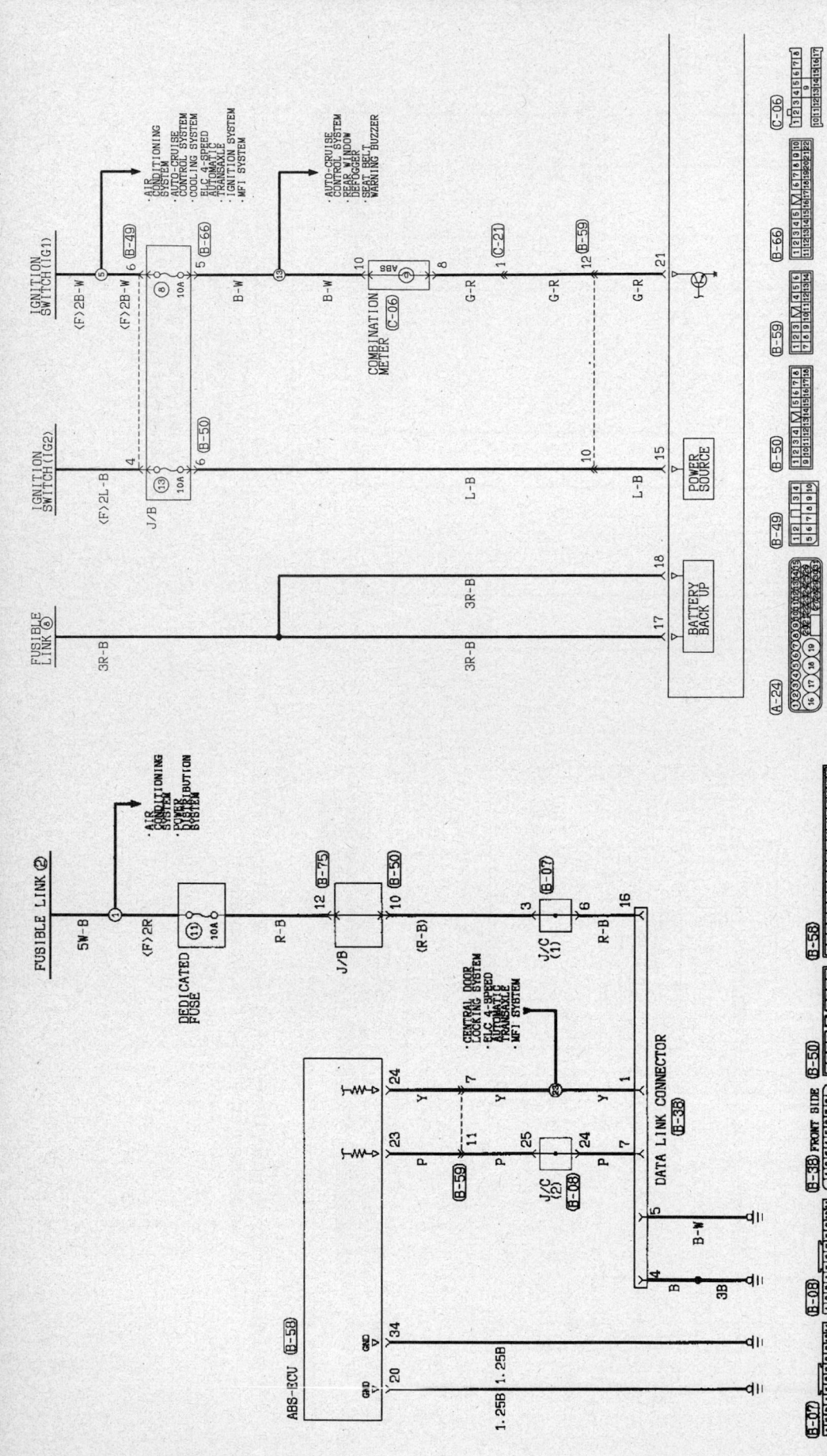

Fig. 10 ABS wiring diagram (Part 1 of 5). 1998-99 Eclipse AWD

Fig. 9 ABS wiring diagram (Part 5 of 5). 1996-97 Eclipse FWD w/2.0L turbocharged engine & 2.4L engine

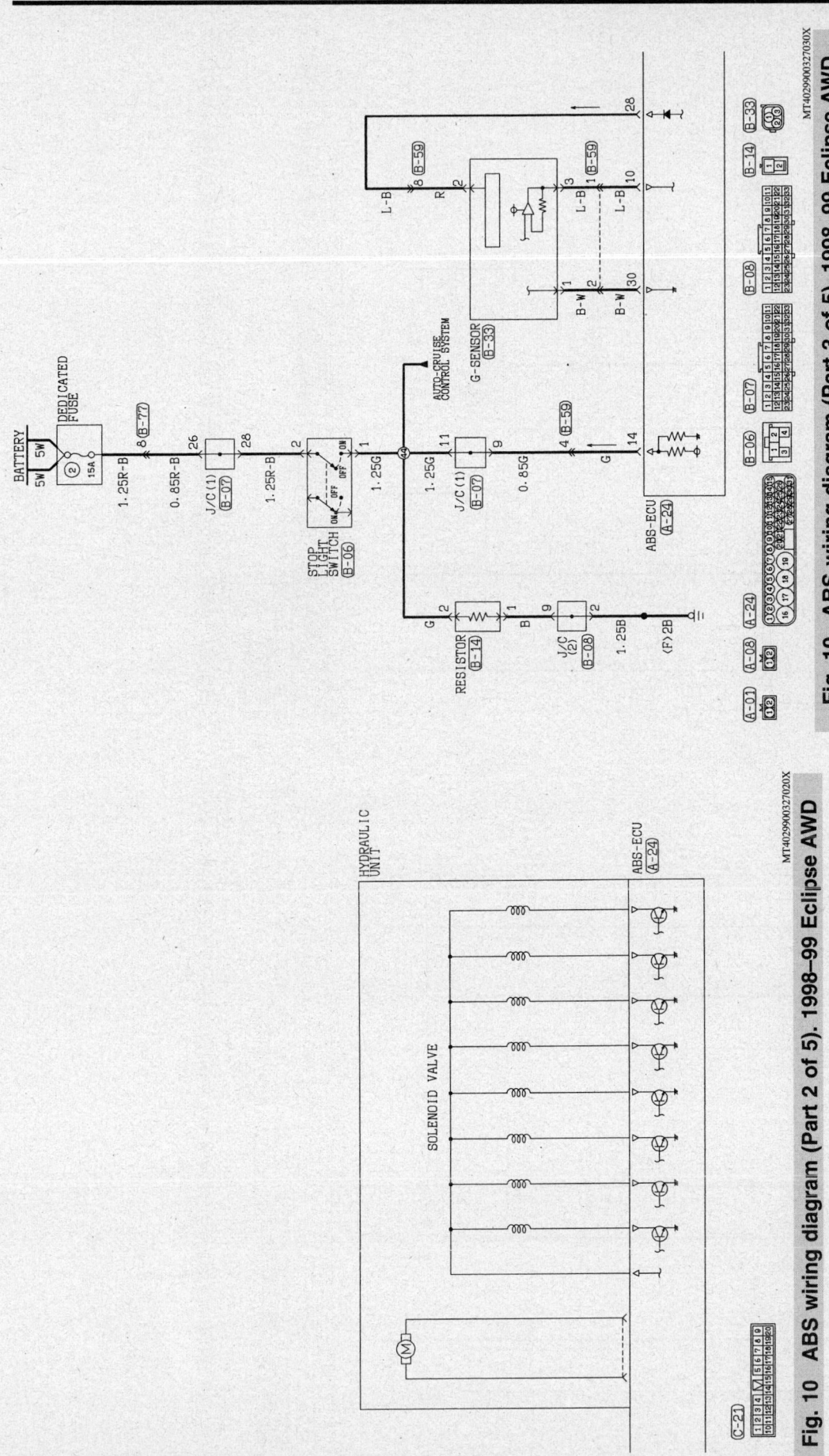

MT402990032703QX

Fig. 10   ABS wiring diagram (Part 3 of 5). 1998–99 Eclipse AWD

MT402990032702QX

Fig. 10   ABS wiring diagram (Part 2 of 5). 1998–99 Eclipse AWD

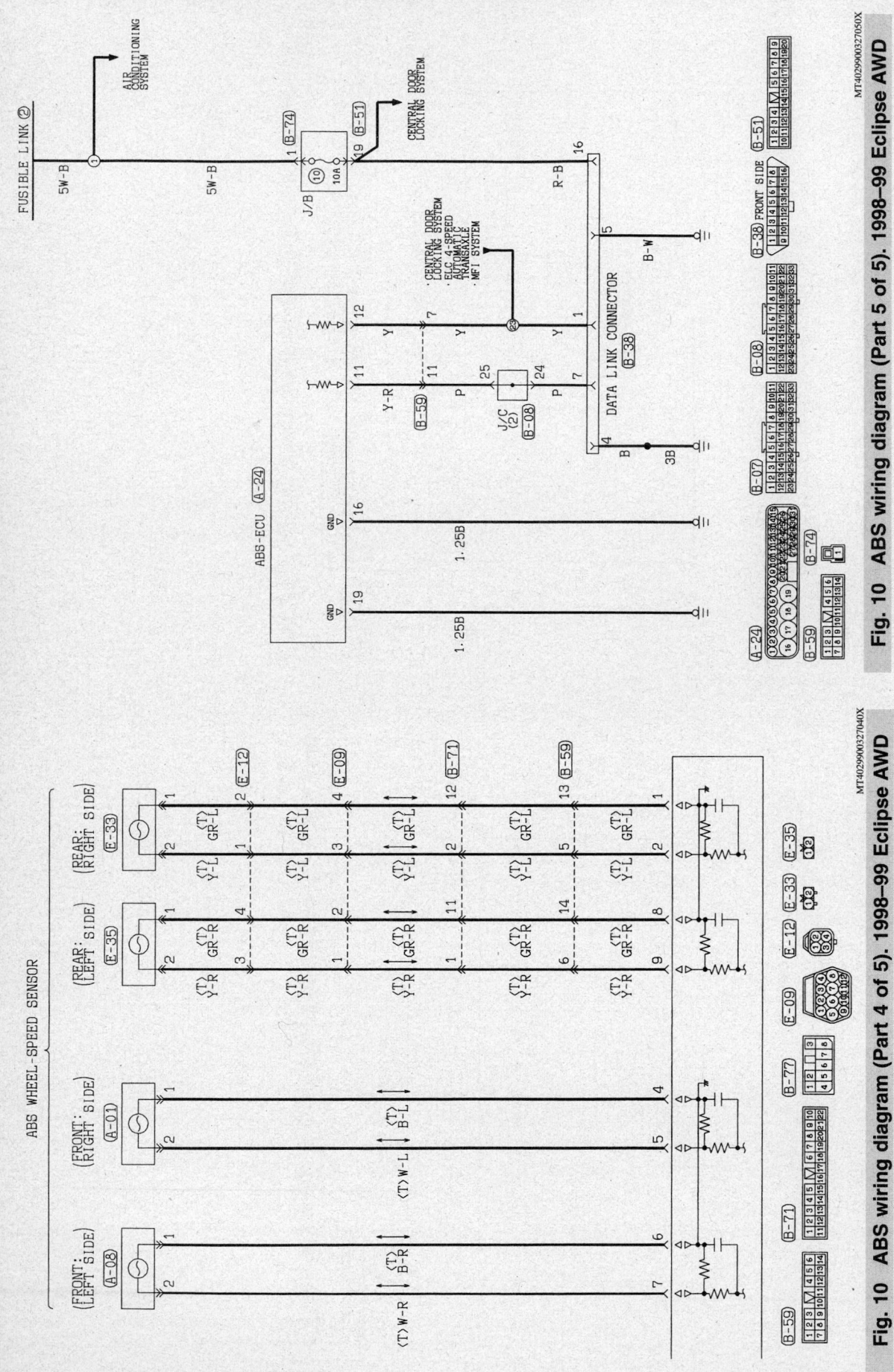

Fig. 10 ABS wiring diagram (Part 5 of 5). 1998–99 Eclipse AWD

Fig. 10 ABS wiring diagram (Part 4 of 5). 1998–99 Eclipse AWD

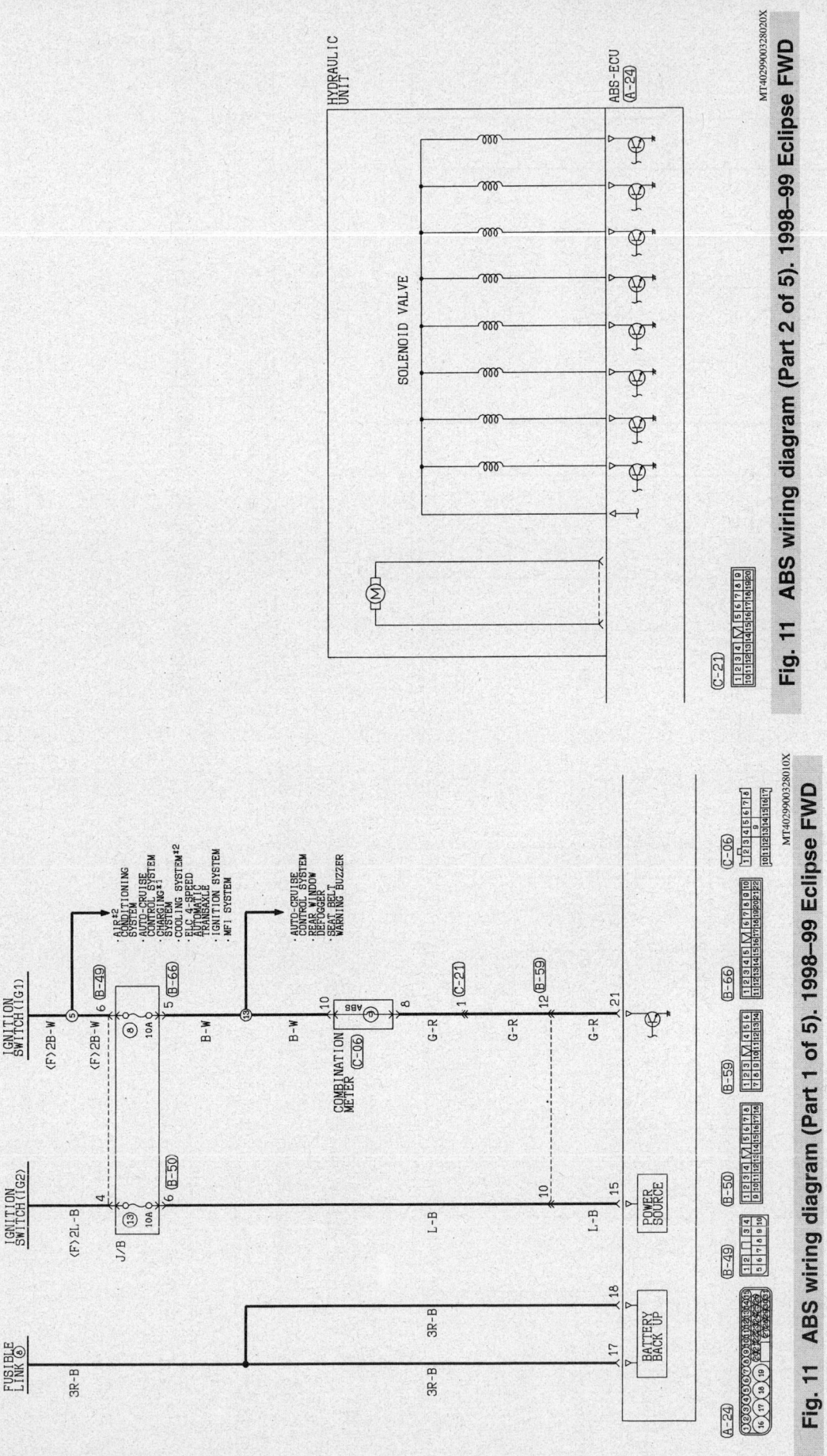

Fig. 11 ABS wiring diagram (Part 2 of 5). 1998–99 Eclipse FWD

Fig. 11 ABS wiring diagram (Part 1 of 5). 1998–99 Eclipse FWD

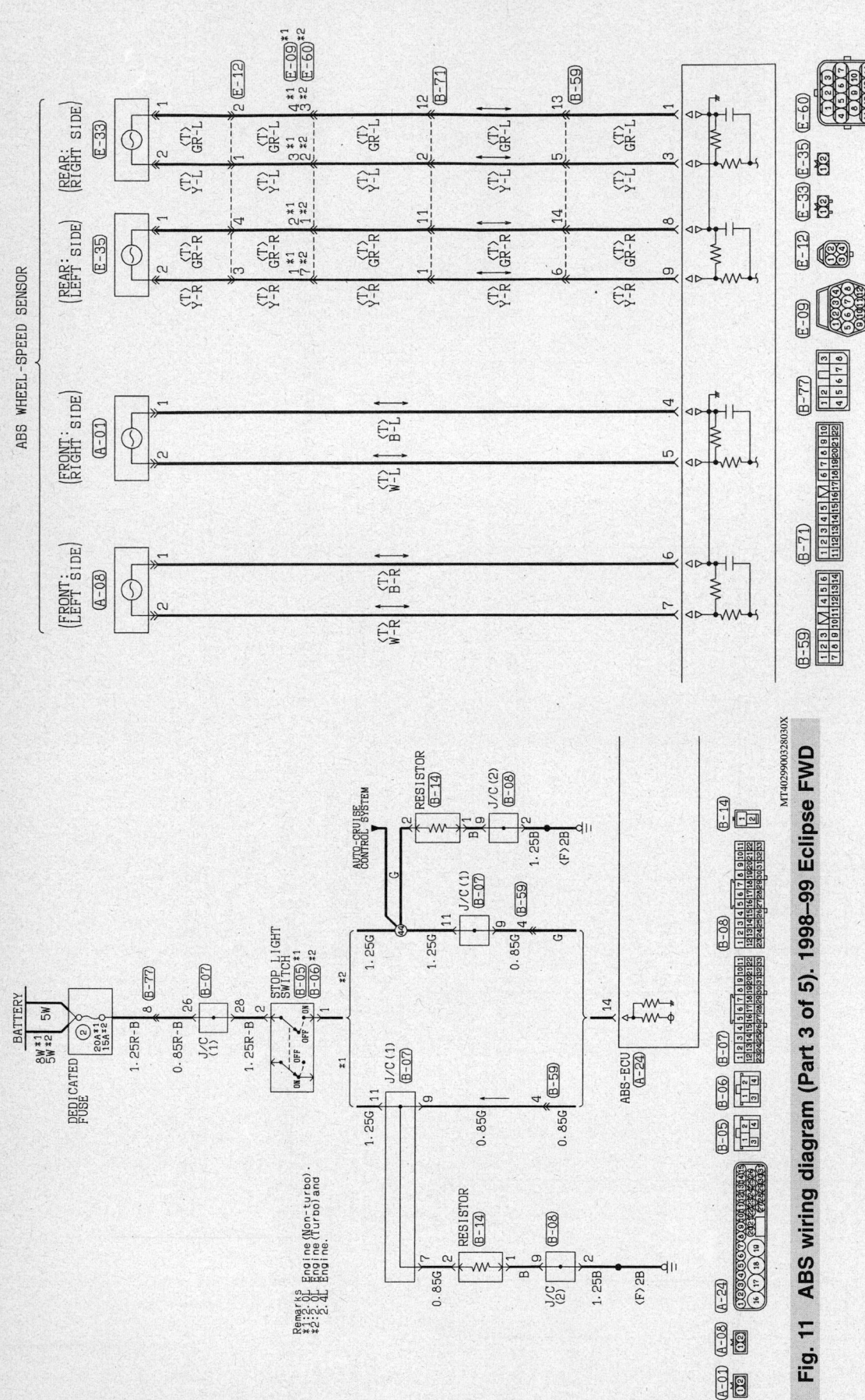

Fig. 11 ABS wiring diagram (Part 4 of 5). 1998–99 Eclipse FWD

Fig. 11 ABS wiring diagram (Part 3 of 5). 1998–99 Eclipse FWD

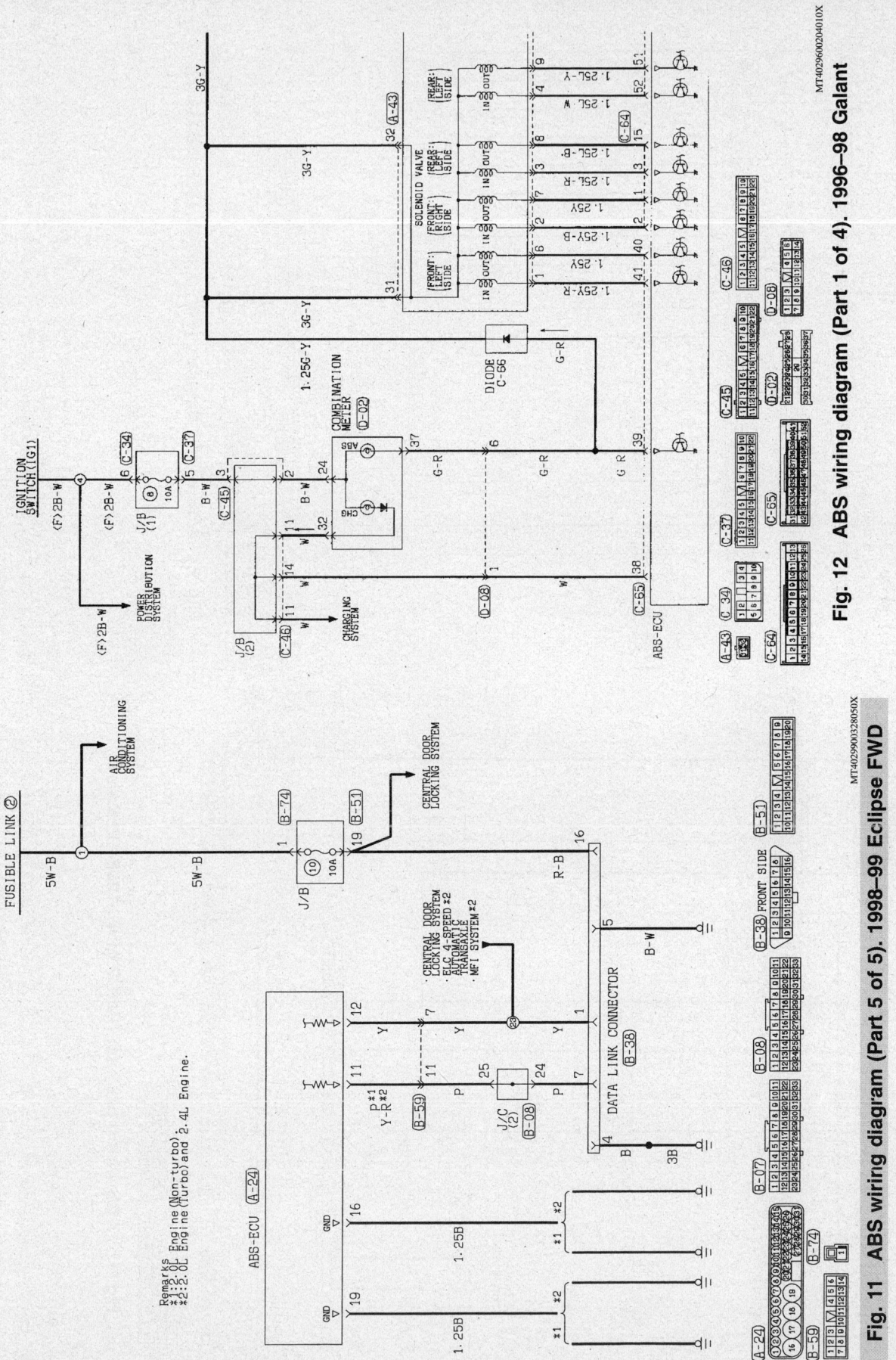

Fig. 12 ABS wiring diagram (Part 1 of 4). 1996–98 Galant

Fig. 11 ABS wiring diagram (Part 5 of 5). 1998–99 Eclipse FWD

Remarks: Engine (Non-turbo).
*1: 2.0L Engine (Non-turbo).
*2: 2.0L Engine (Turbo) and 2.4L Engine.

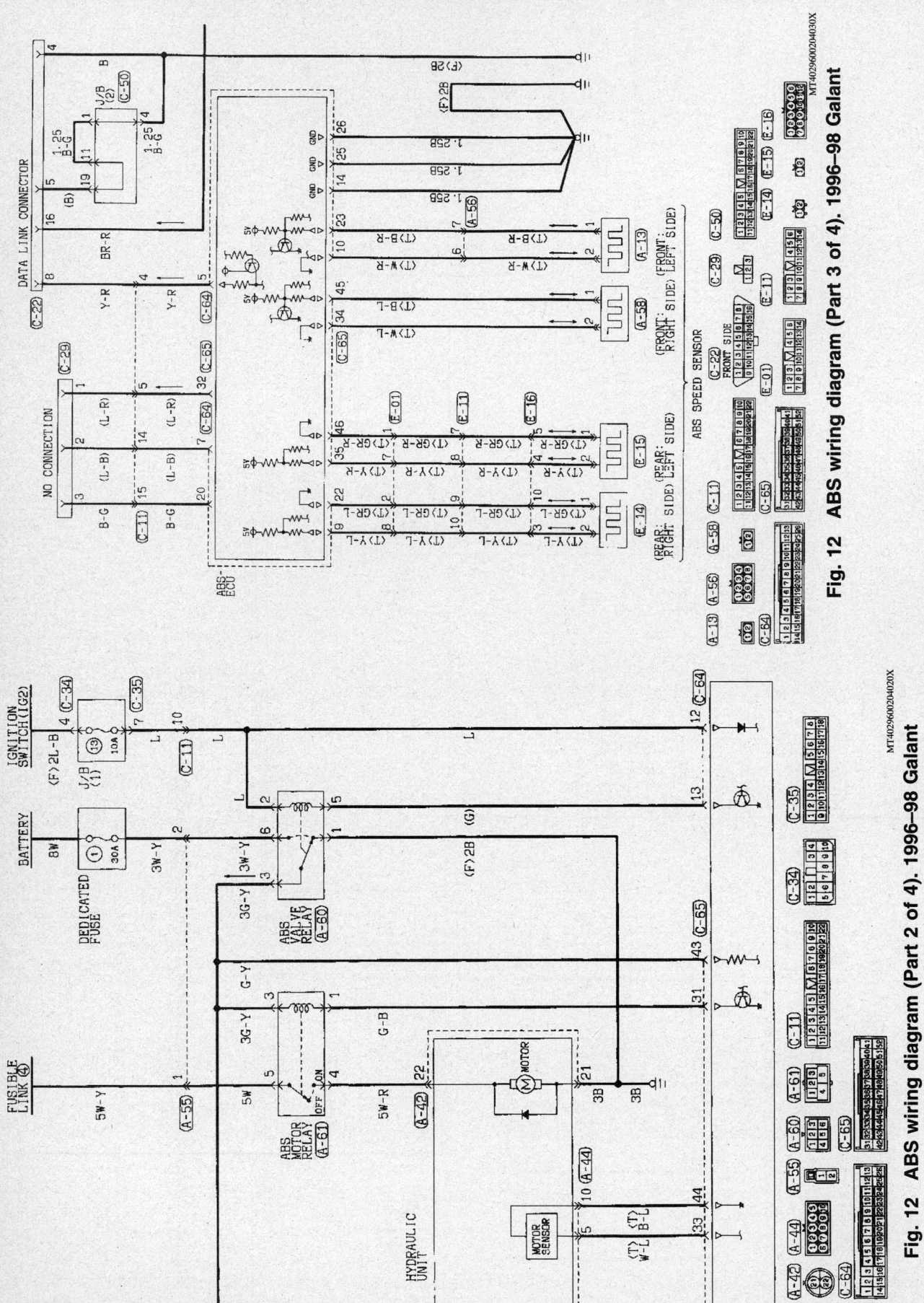

Fig. 12 ABS wiring diagram (Part 3 of 4). 1996–98 Galant

Fig. 12 ABS wiring diagram (Part 2 of 4). 1996–98 Galant

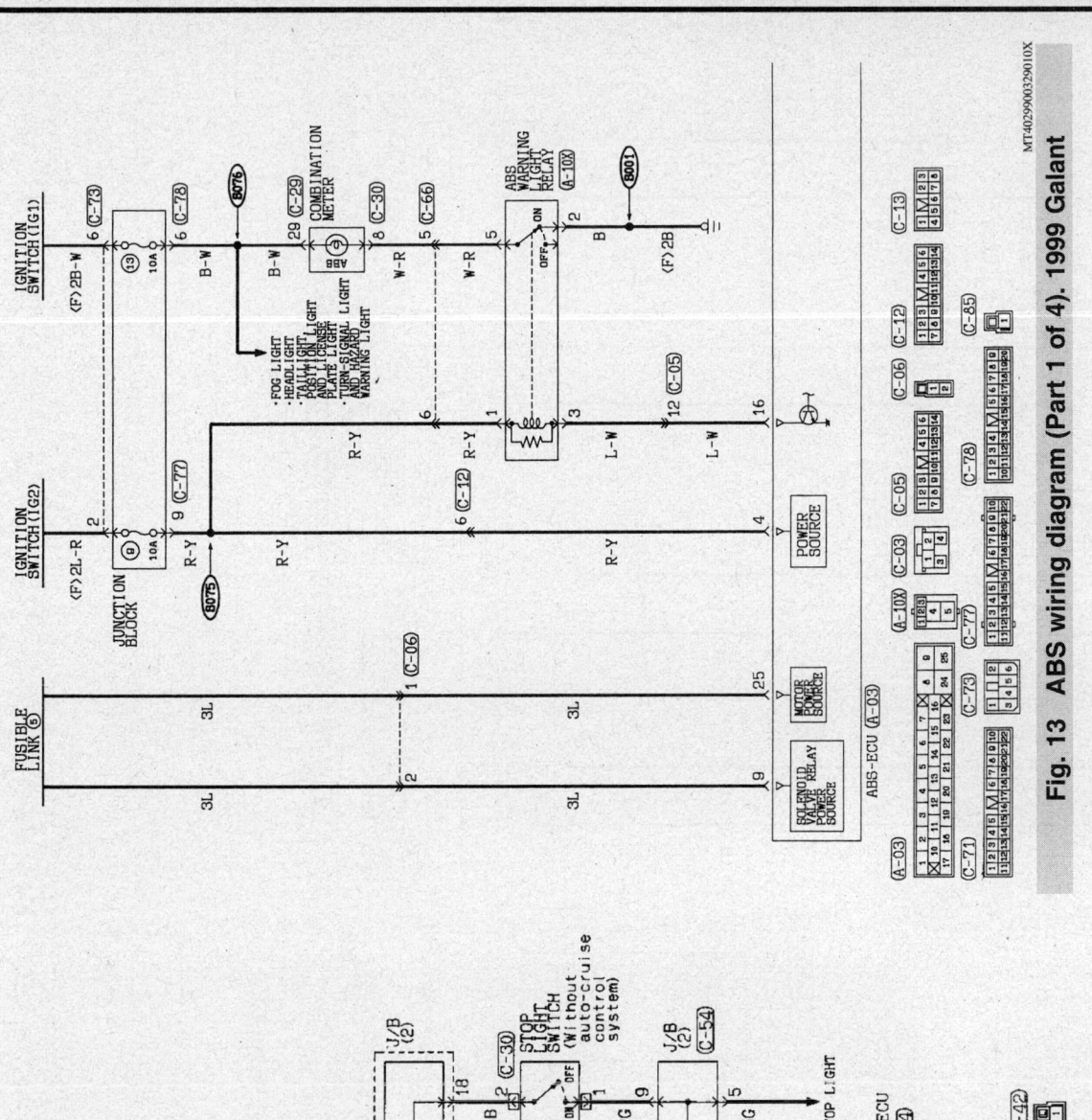

Fig. 13 ABS wiring diagram (Part 1 of 4). 1999 Galant

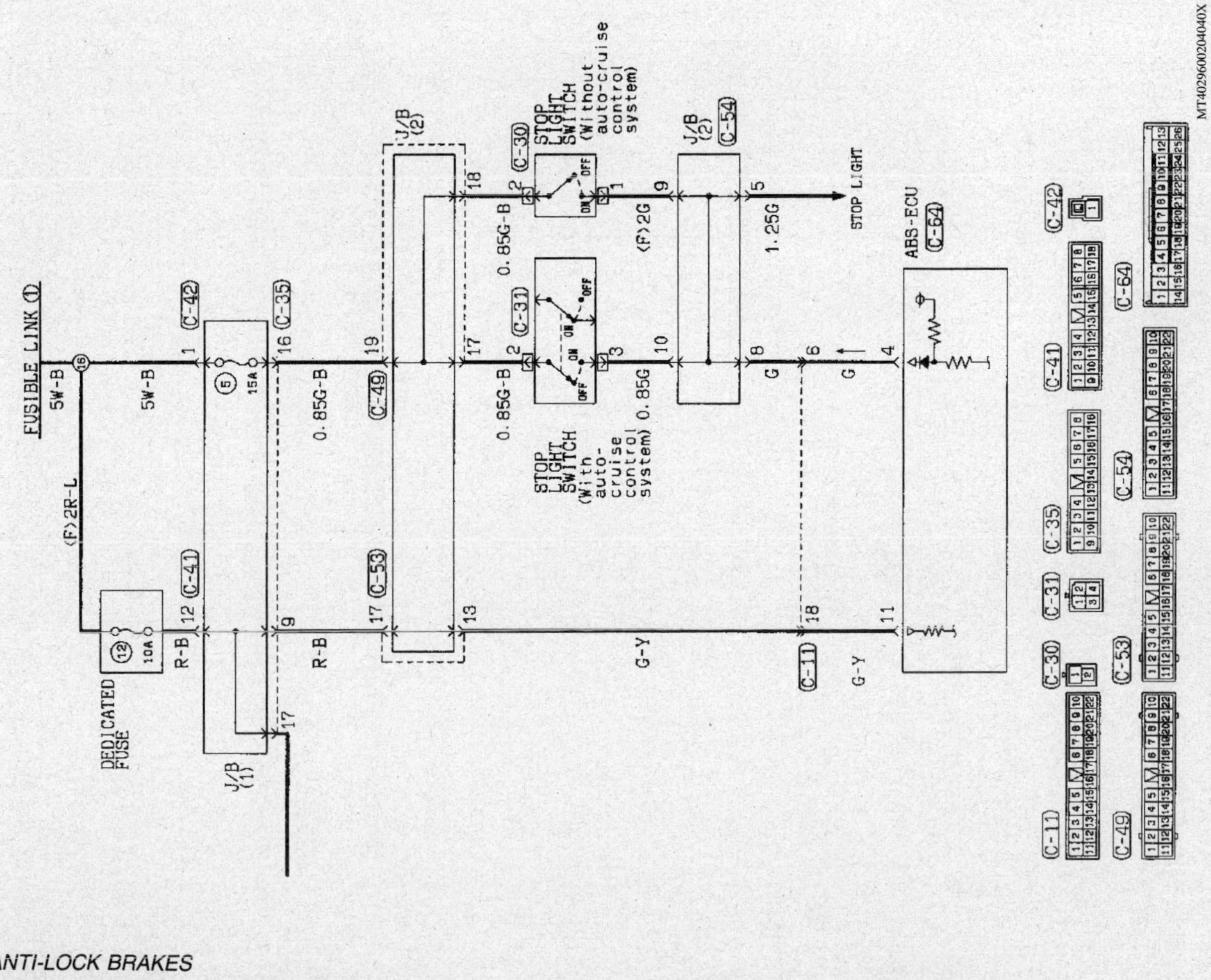

Fig. 12 ABS wiring diagram (Part 4 of 4). 1996–98 Galant

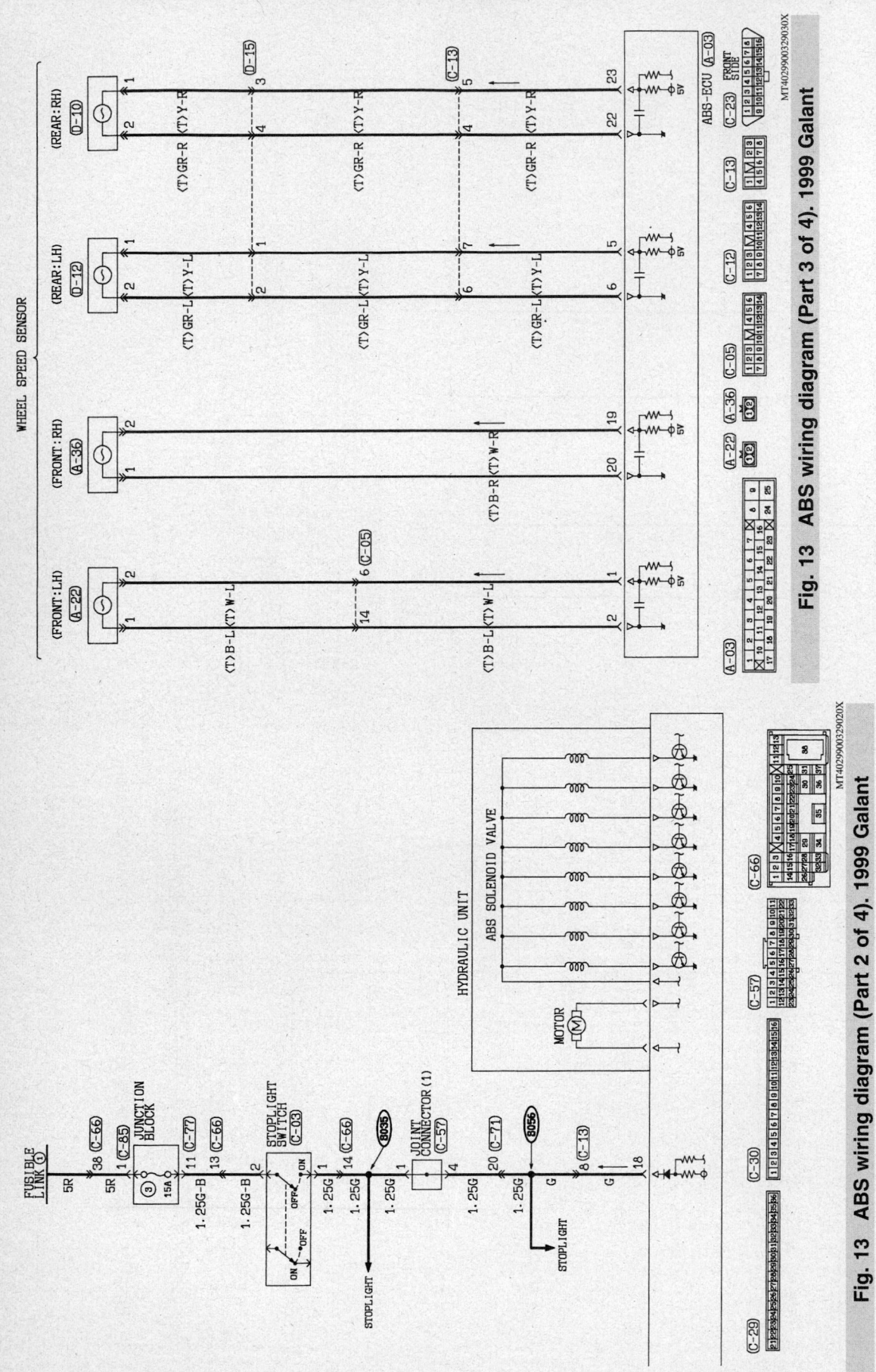

Fig. 13 ABS wiring diagram (Part 3 of 4). 1999 Galant

Fig. 13 ABS wiring diagram (Part 2 of 4). 1999 Galant

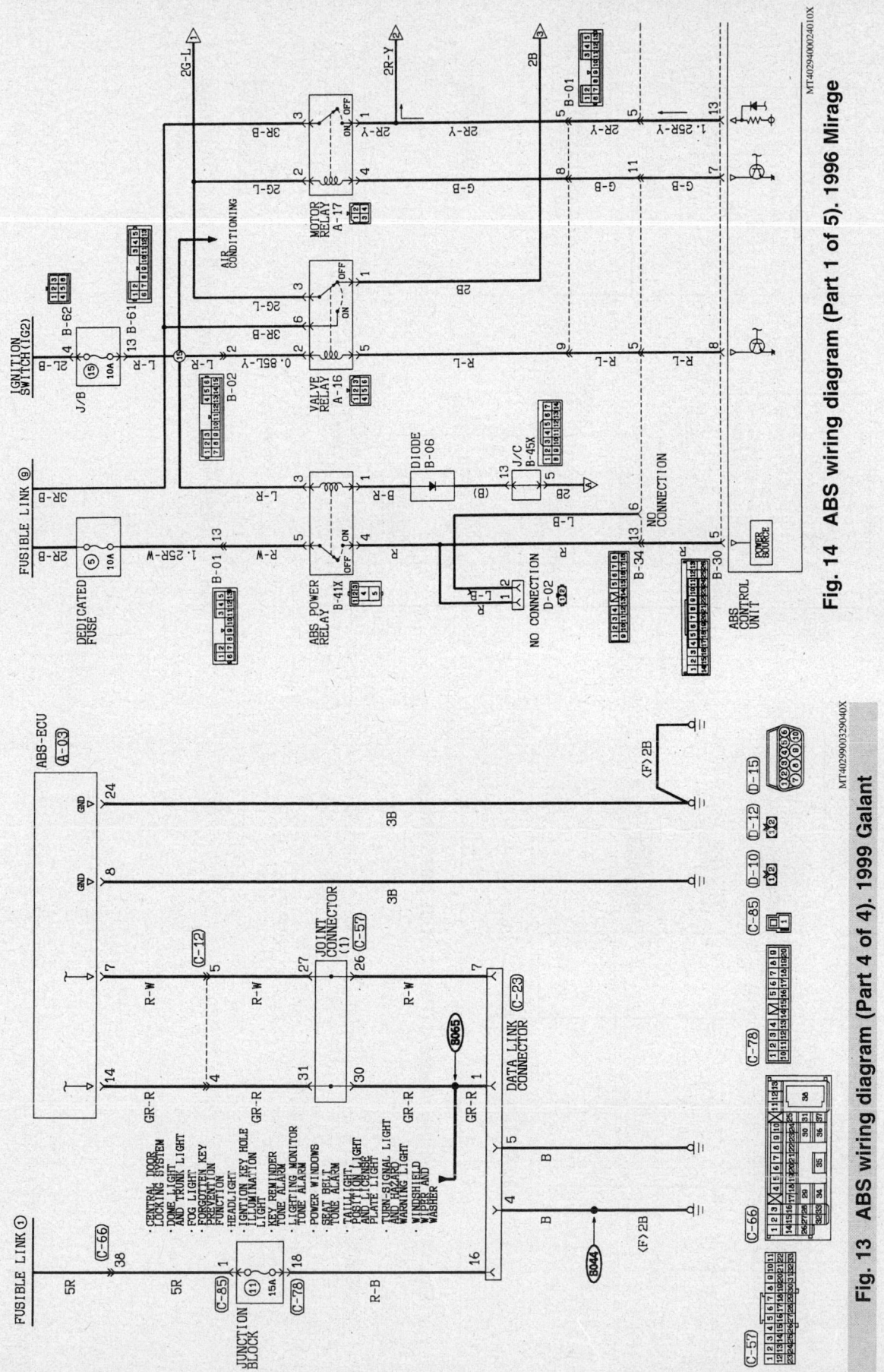

Fig. 14 ABS wiring diagram (Part 1 of 5). 1996 Mirage

Fig. 13 ABS wiring diagram (Part 4 of 4). 1999 Galant

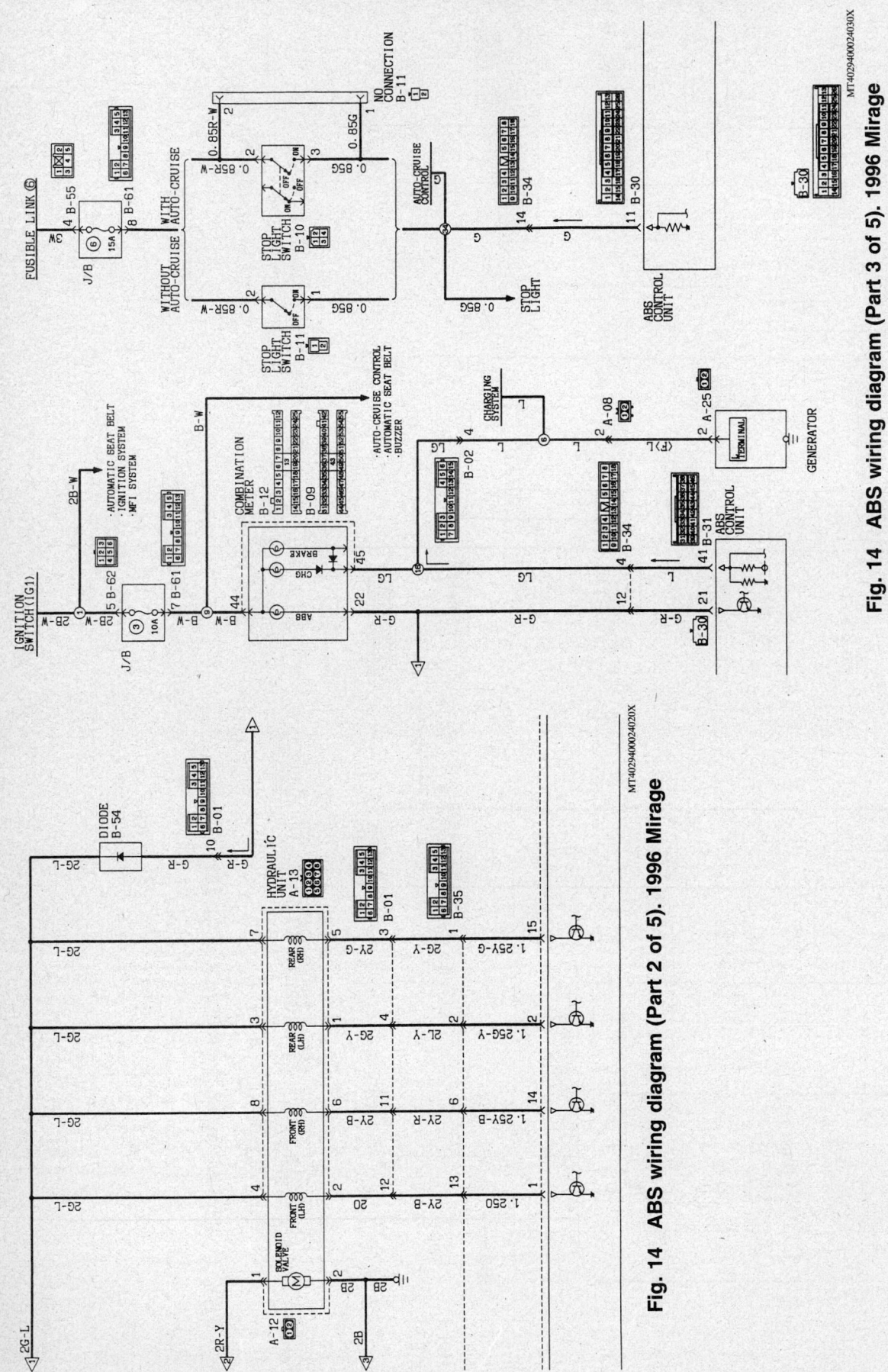

Fig. 14 ABS wiring diagram (Part 3 of 5). 1996 Mirage

Fig. 14 ABS wiring diagram (Part 2 of 5). 1996 Mirage

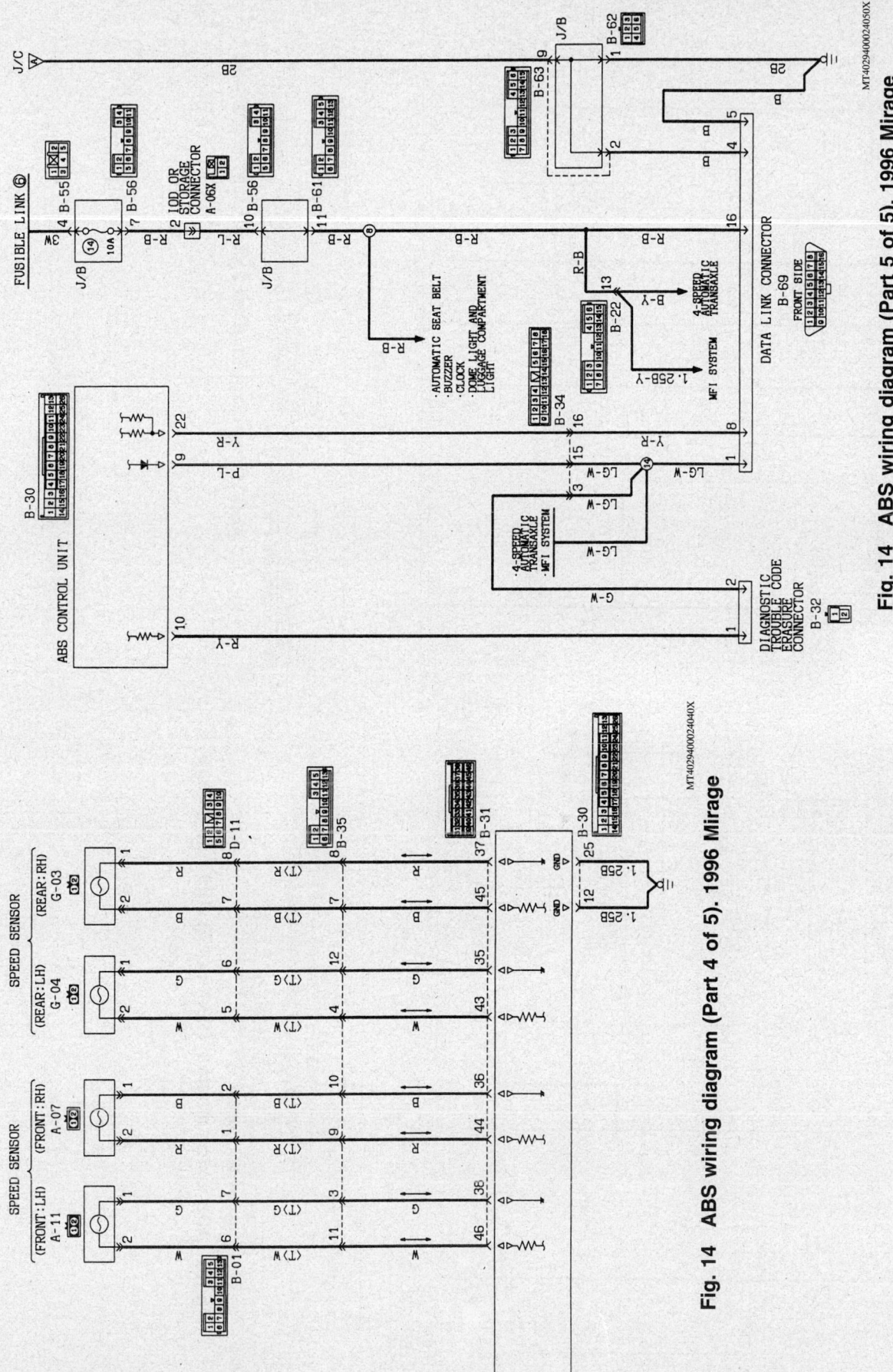

Fig. 14 ABS wiring diagram (Part 5 of 5). 1996 Mirage

Fig. 14 ABS wiring diagram (Part 4 of 5). 1996 Mirage

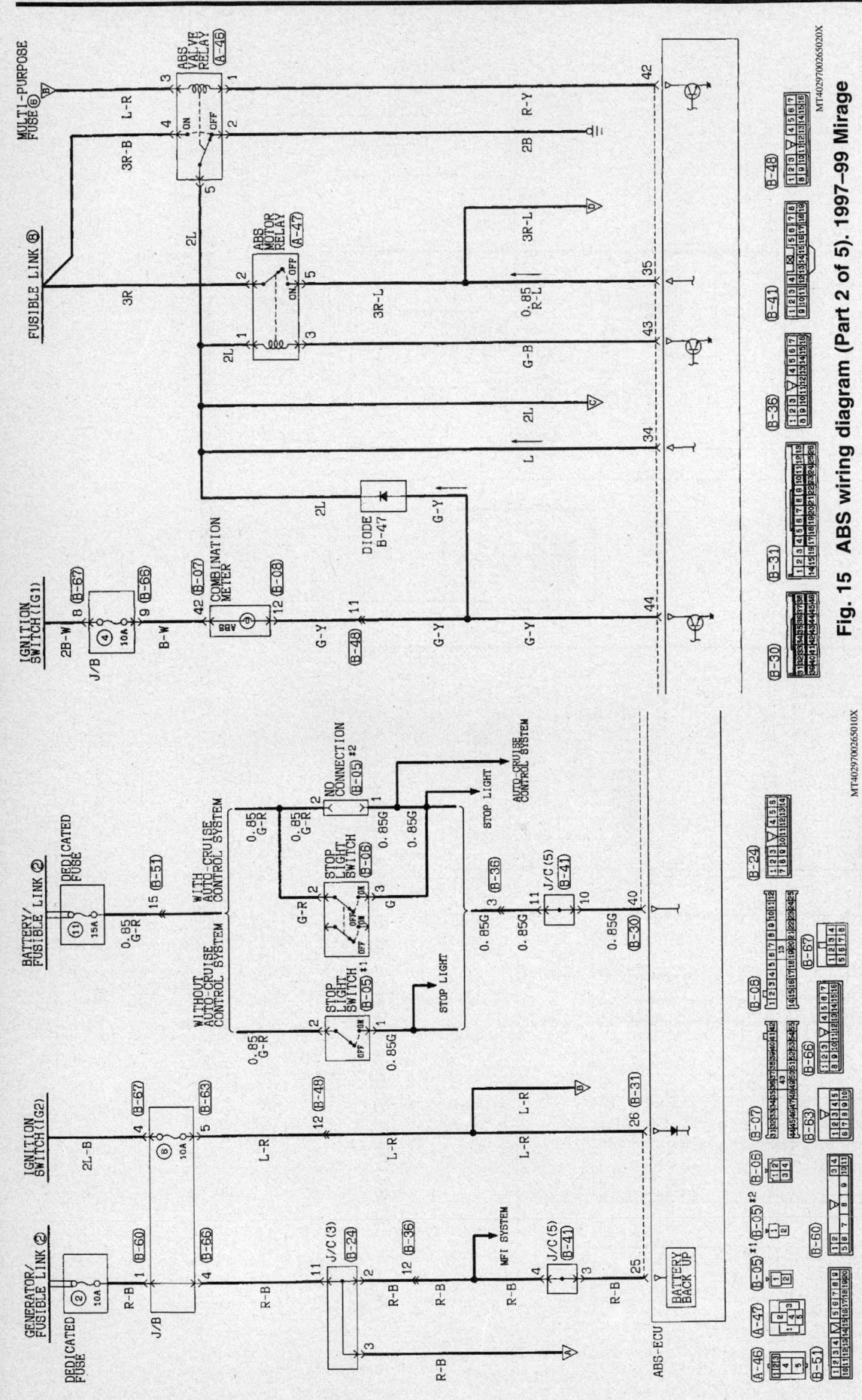

Fig. 15 ABS wiring diagram (Part 2 of 5). 1997–99 Mirage

Fig. 15 ABS wiring diagram (Part 1 of 5). 1997–99 Mirage

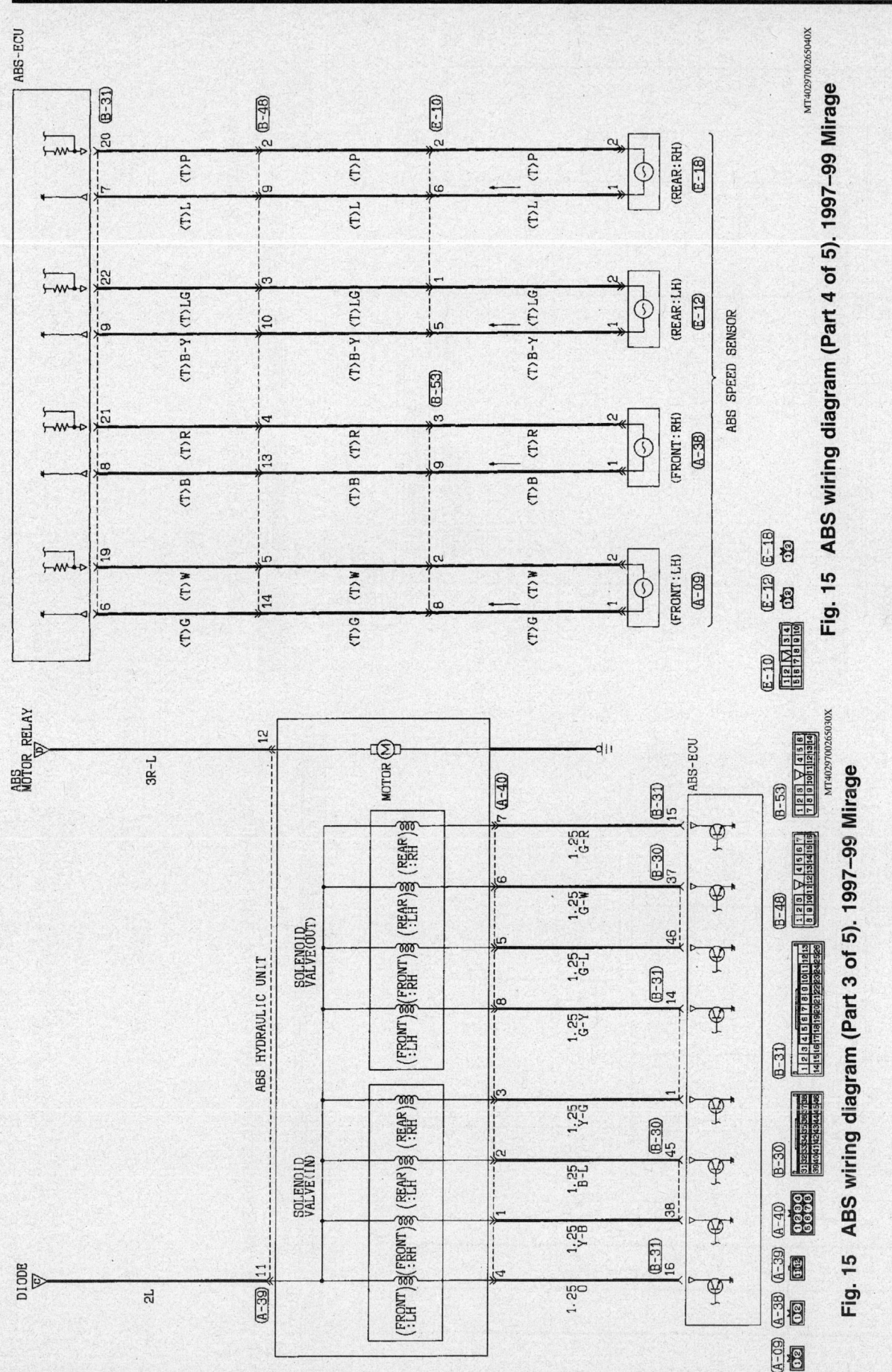

Fig. 15 ABS wiring diagram (Part 4 of 5). 1997–99 Mirage

Fig. 15 ABS wiring diagram (Part 3 of 5). 1997–99 Mirage

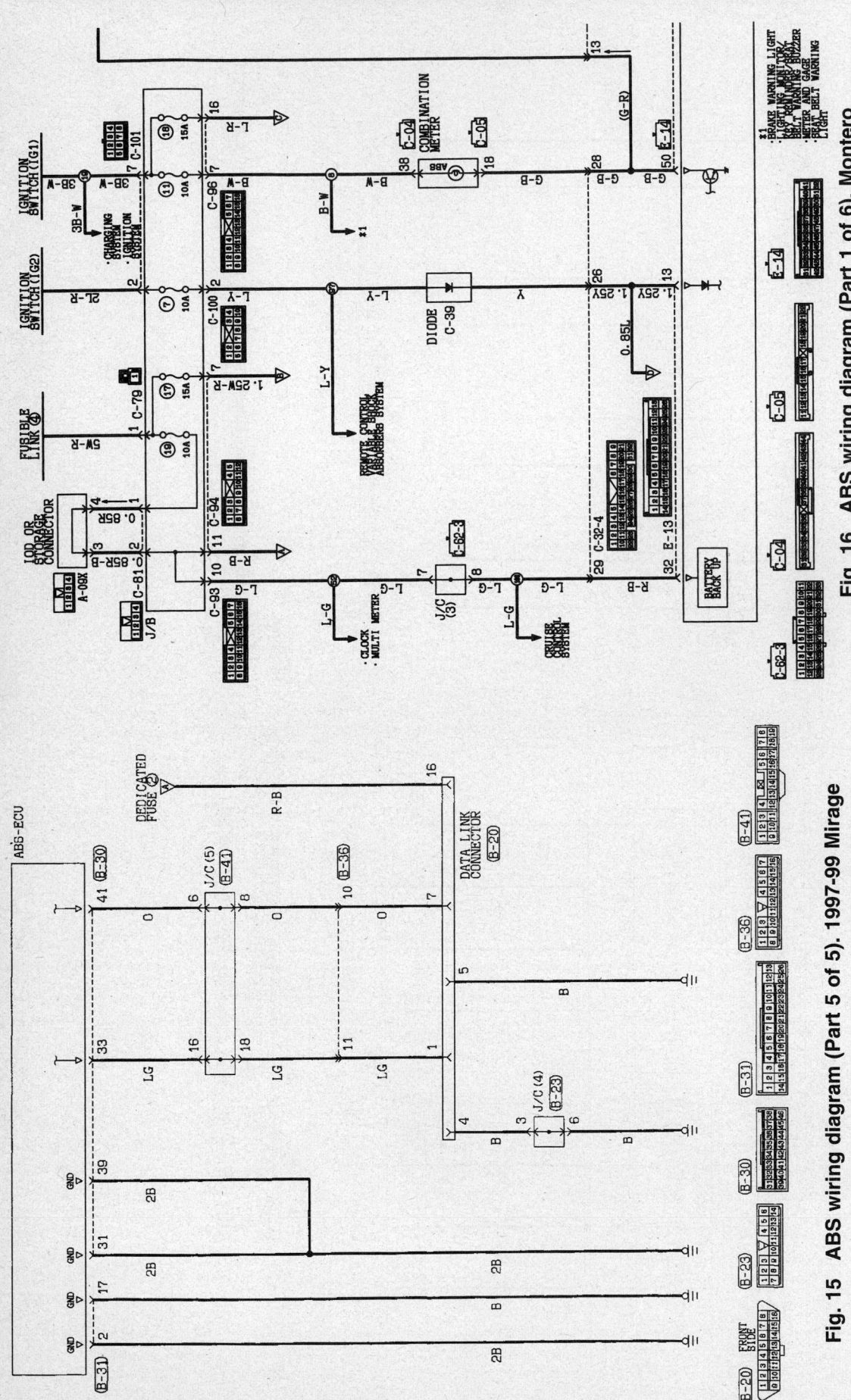

Fig. 16 ABS wiring diagram (Part 1 of 6). Montero

Fig. 15 ABS wiring diagram (Part 5 of 5). 1997-99 Mirage

ANTI-LOCK BRAKES

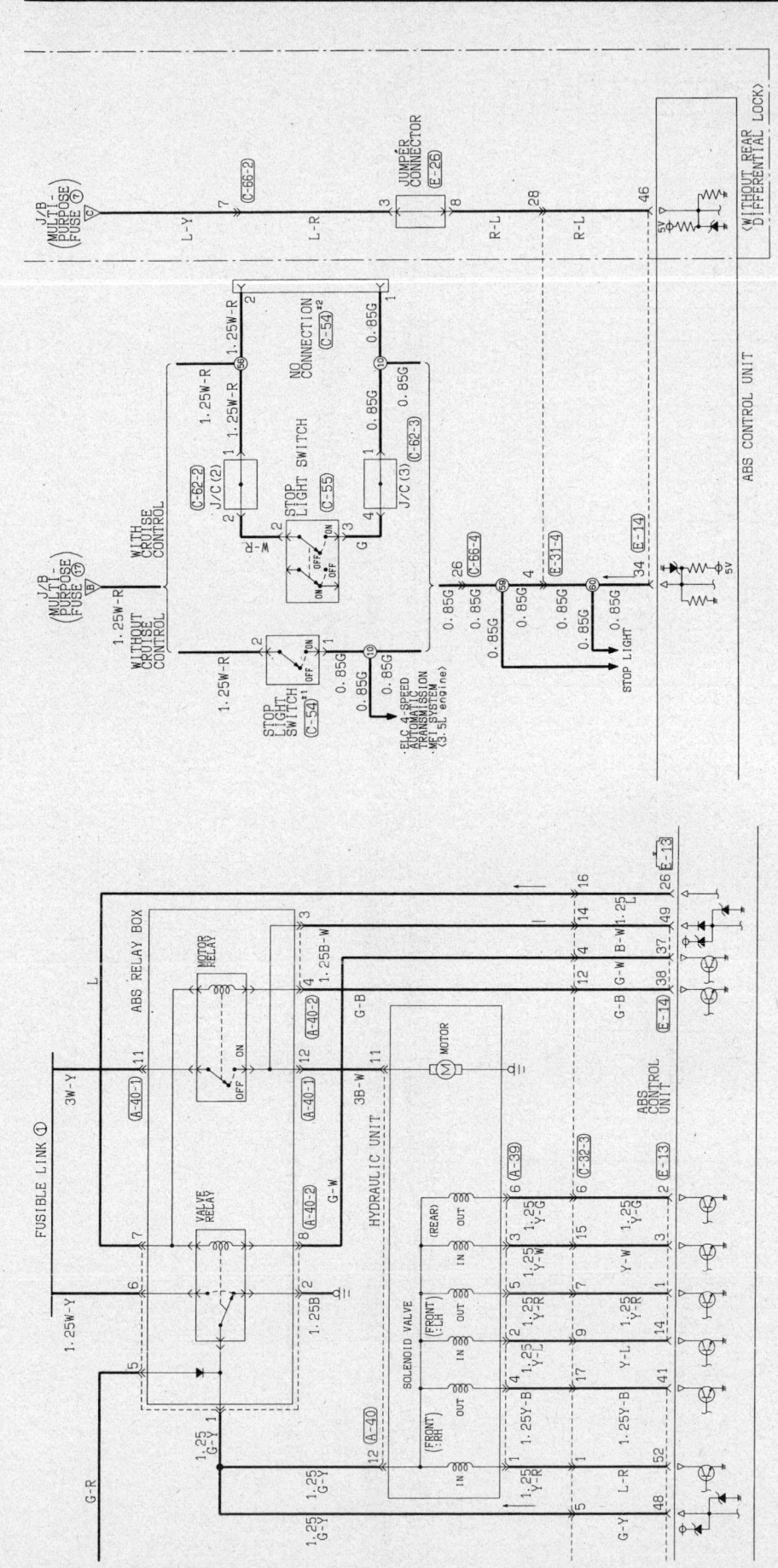

Fig. 16 ABS wiring diagram (Part 3 of 6). Montero

Fig. 16 ABS wiring diagram (Part 2 of 6). Montero

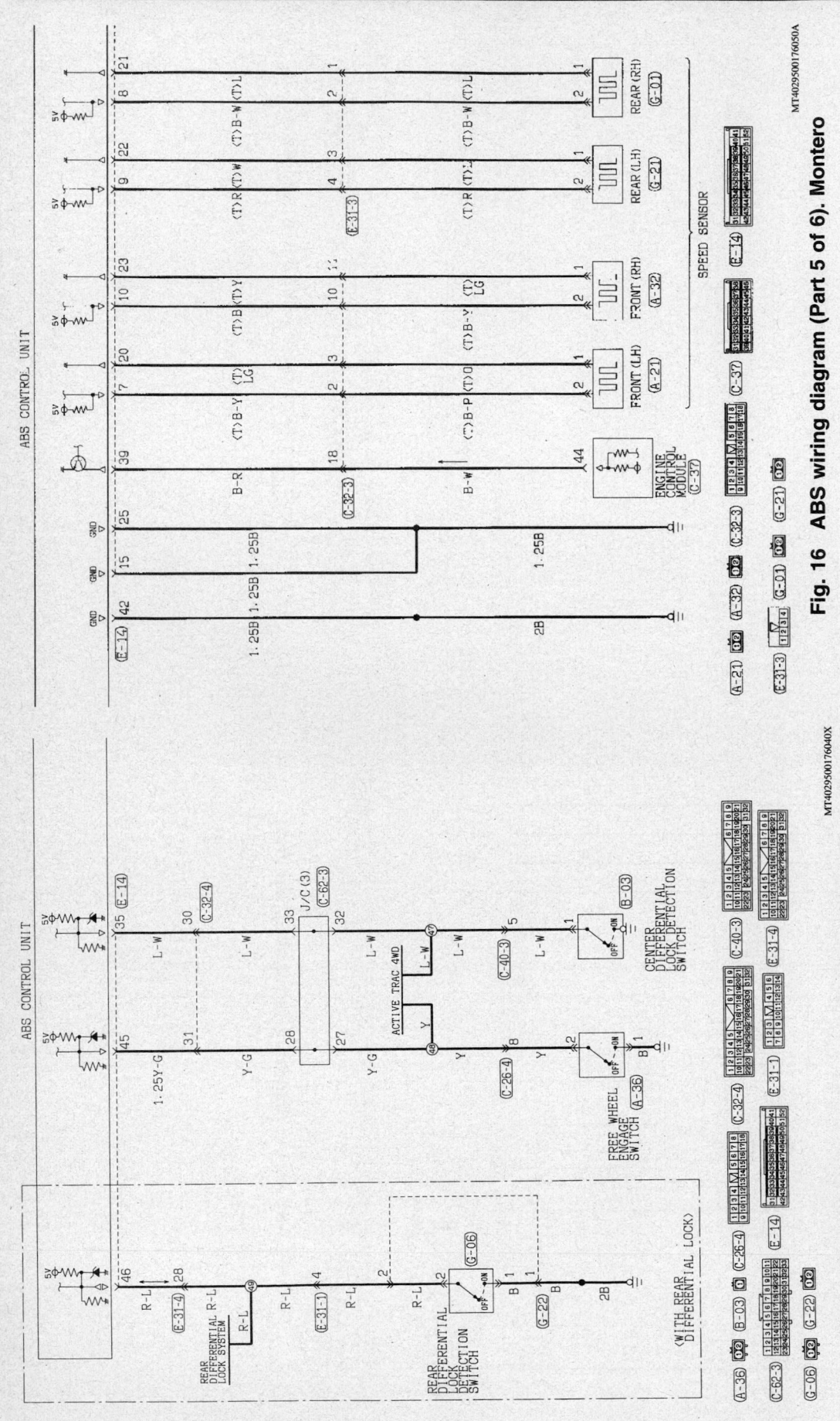

Fig. 16 ABS wiring diagram (Part 5 of 6). Montero

Fig. 16 ABS wiring diagram (Part 4 of 6). Montero

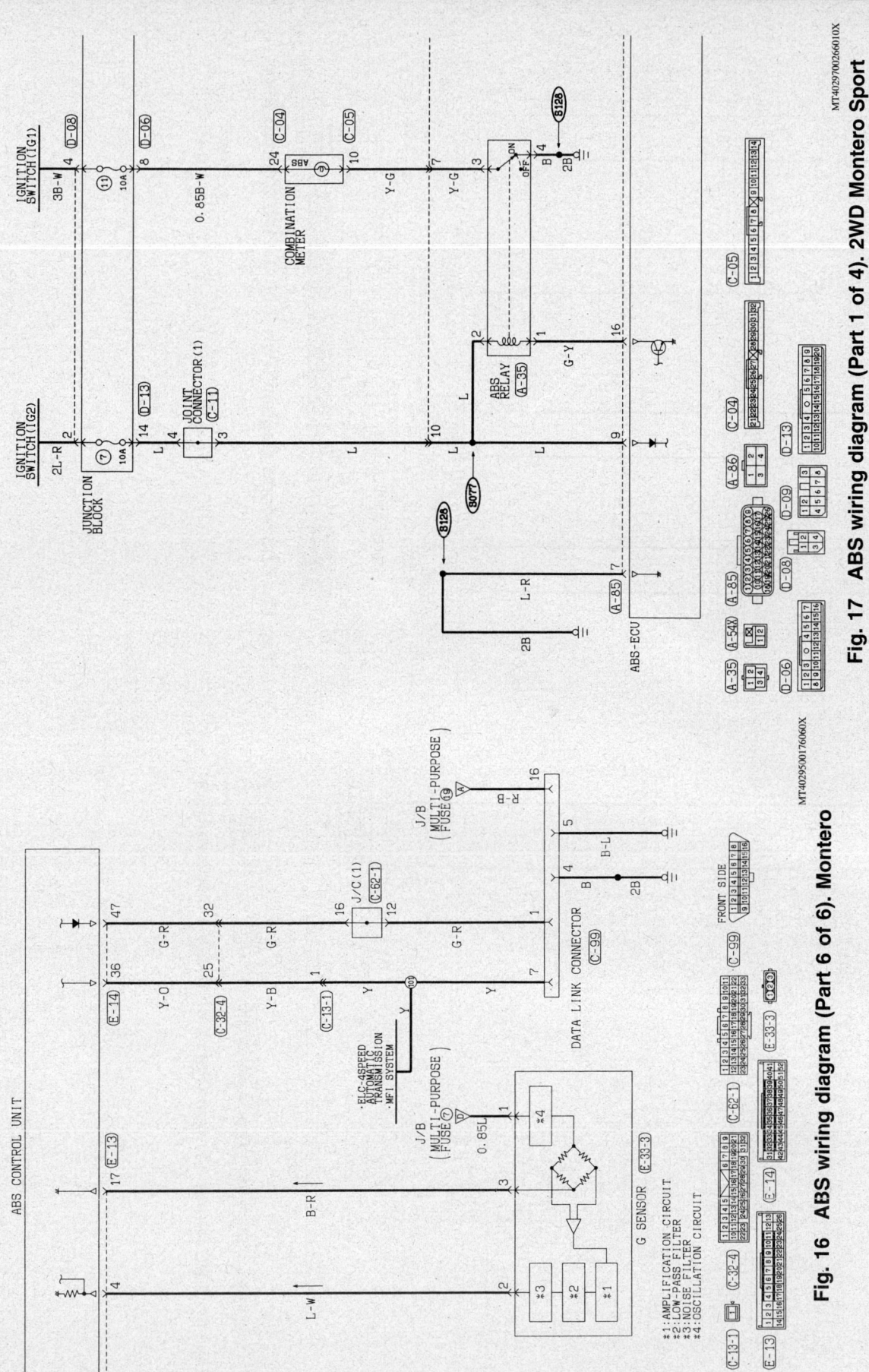

Fig. 17 ABS wiring diagram (Part 1 of 4). 2WD Montero Sport

Fig. 16 ABS wiring diagram (Part 6 of 6). Montero

*1: AMPLIFICATION CIRCUIT
*2: LOW-PASS FILTER
*3: NOISE FILTER
*4: OSCILLATION CIRCUIT

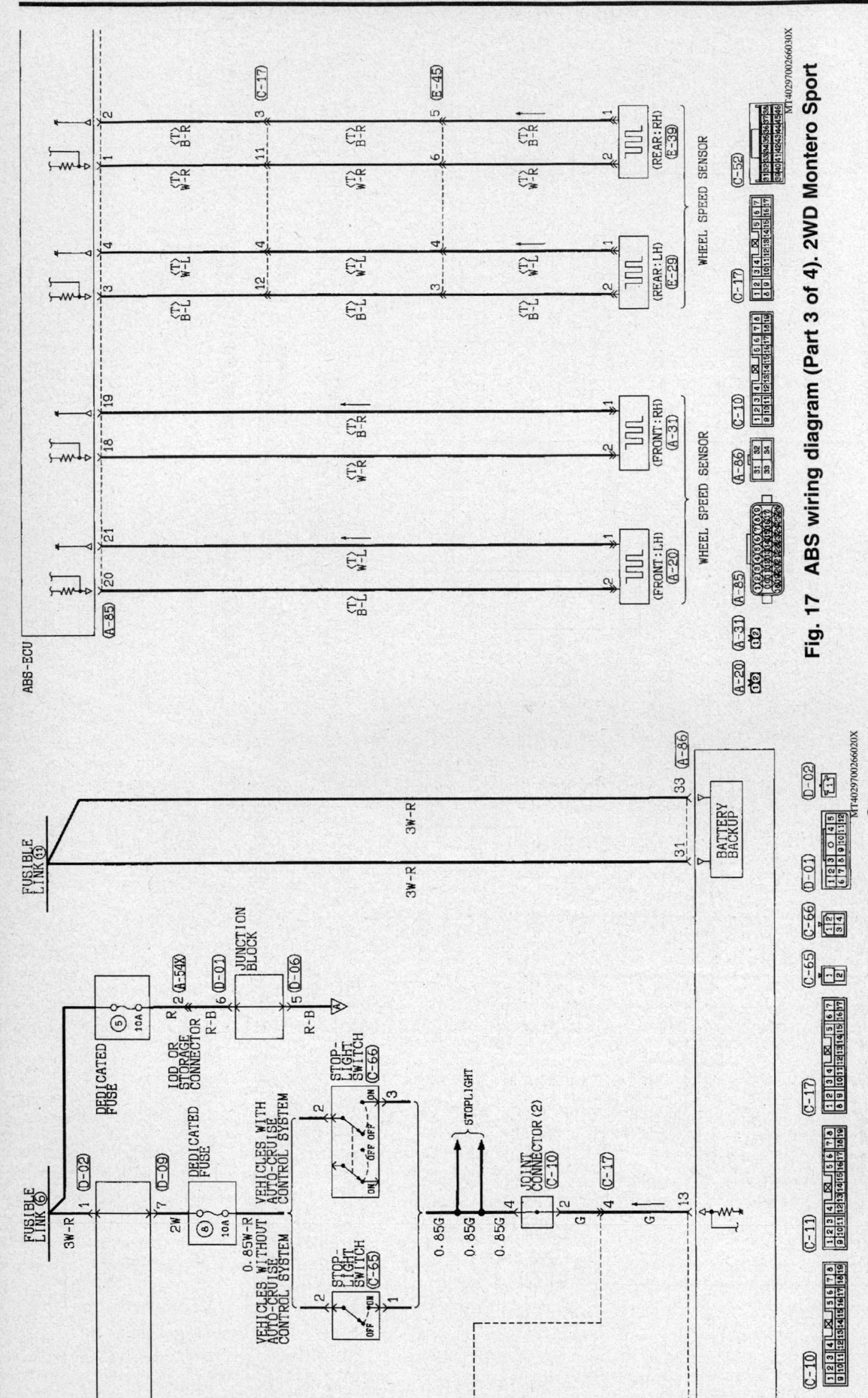

Fig. 17 ABS wiring diagram (Part 3 of 4). 2WD Montero Sport

Fig. 17 ABS wiring diagram (Part 2 of 4). 2WD Montero Sport

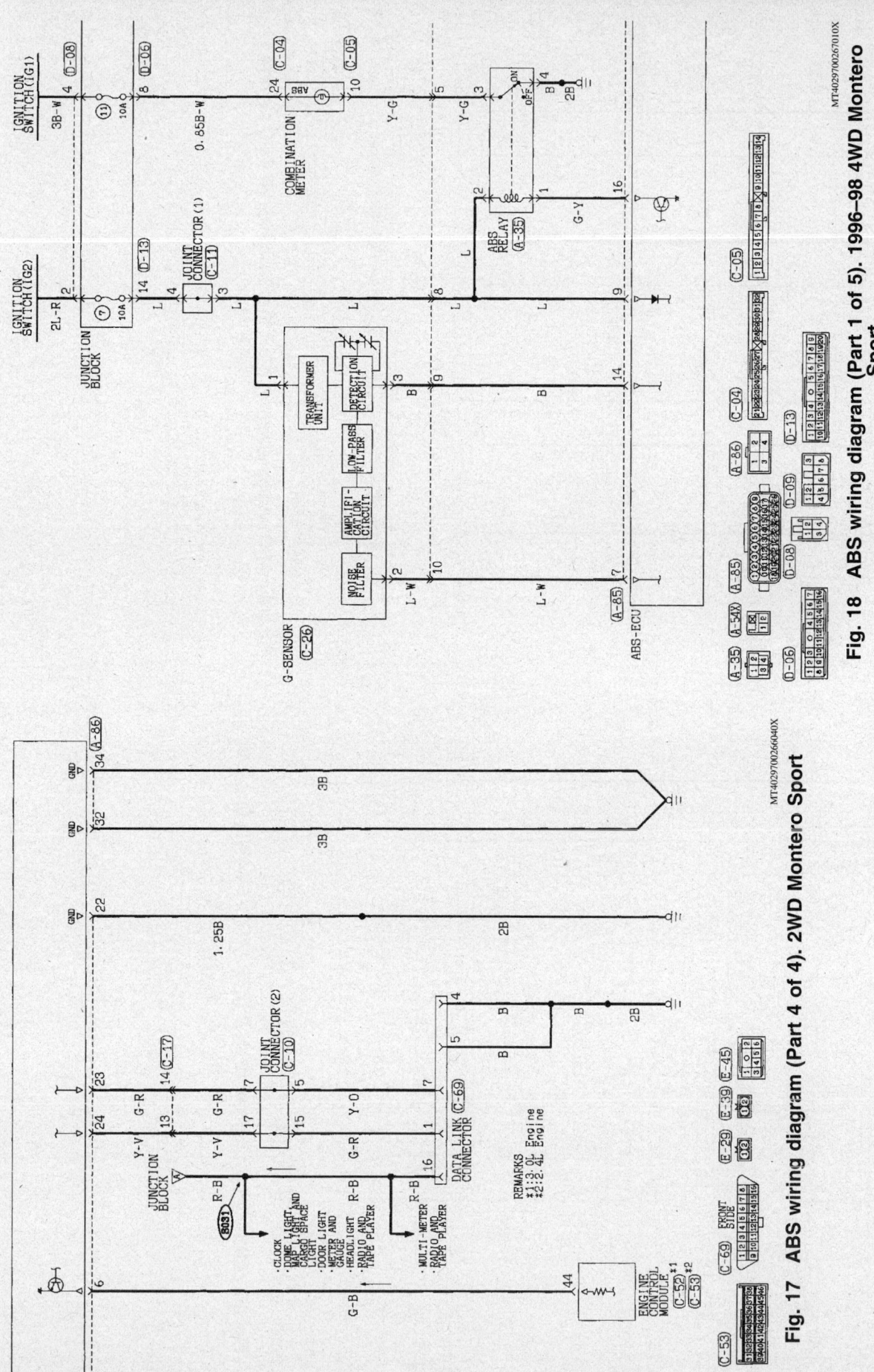

Fig. 18 ABS wiring diagram (Part 1 of 5). 1996–98 4WD Montero Sport

Fig. 17 ABS wiring diagram (Part 4 of 4). 2WD Montero Sport

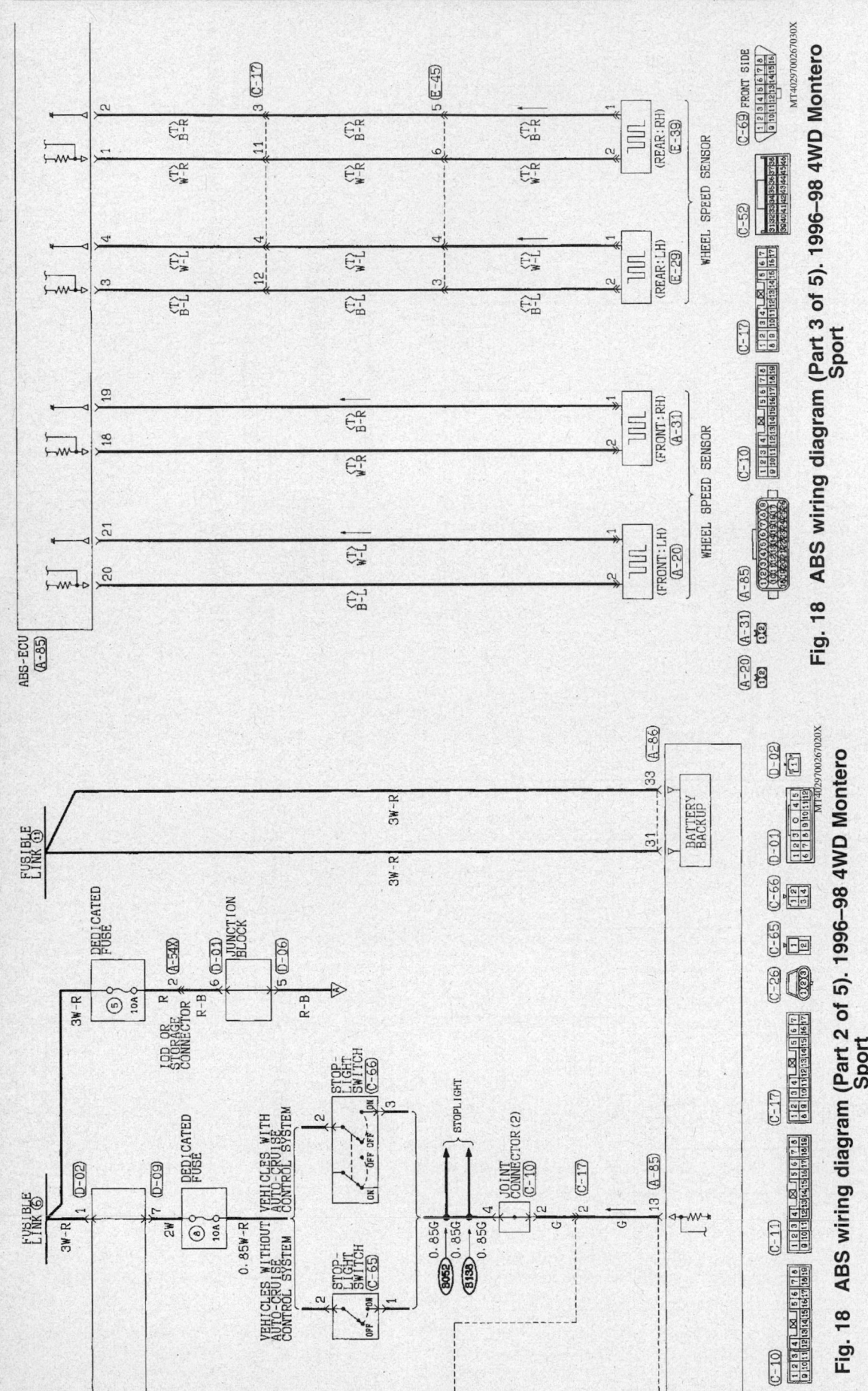

Fig. 18 ABS wiring diagram (Part 3 of 5). 1996-98 4WD Montero Sport

Fig. 18 ABS wiring diagram (Part 2 of 5). 1996-98 4WD Montero Sport

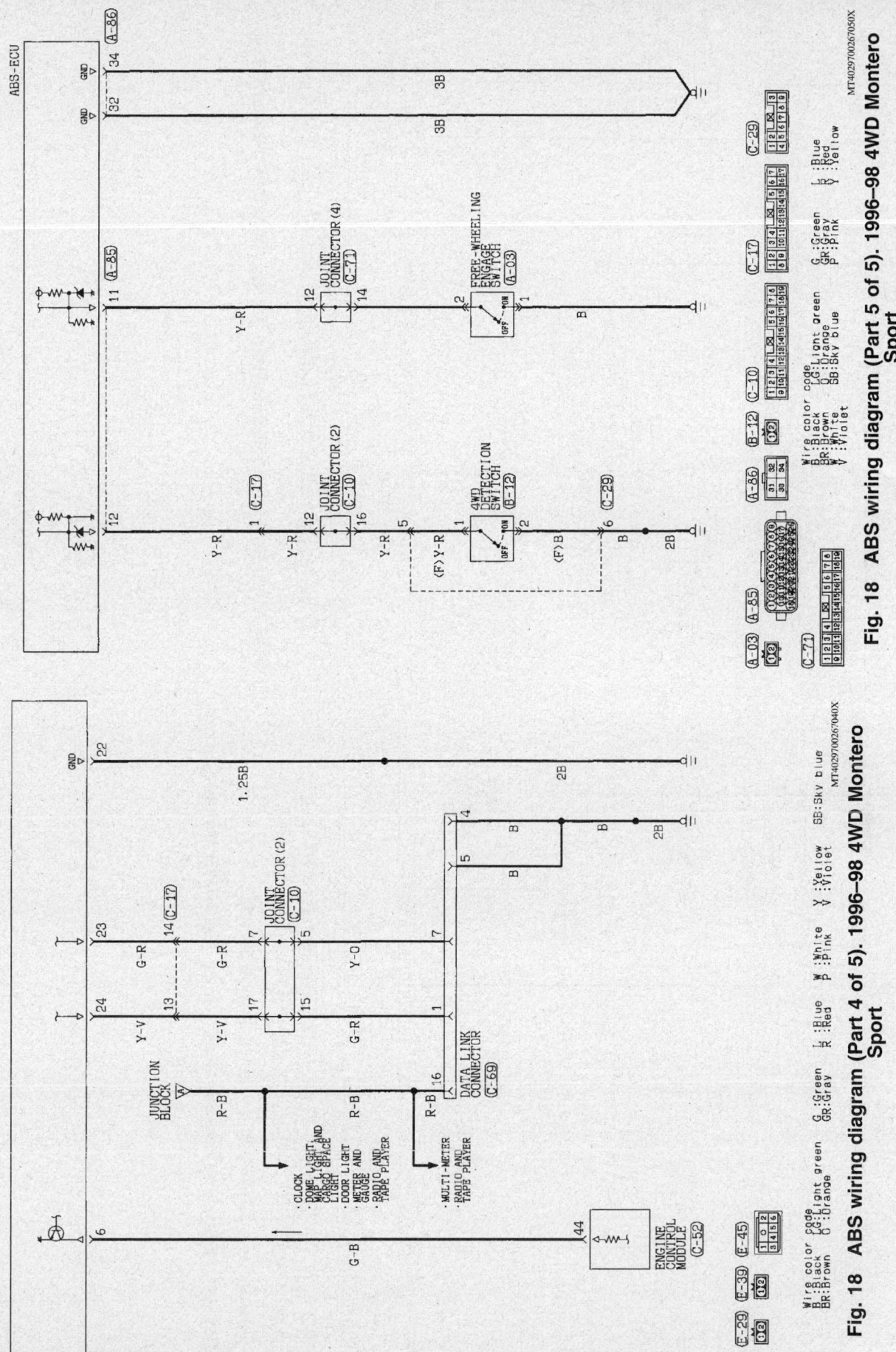

Fig. 18 ABS wiring diagram (Part 5 of 5). 1996–98 4WD Montero Sport

Fig. 18 ABS wiring diagram (Part 4 of 5). 1996–98 4WD Montero Sport

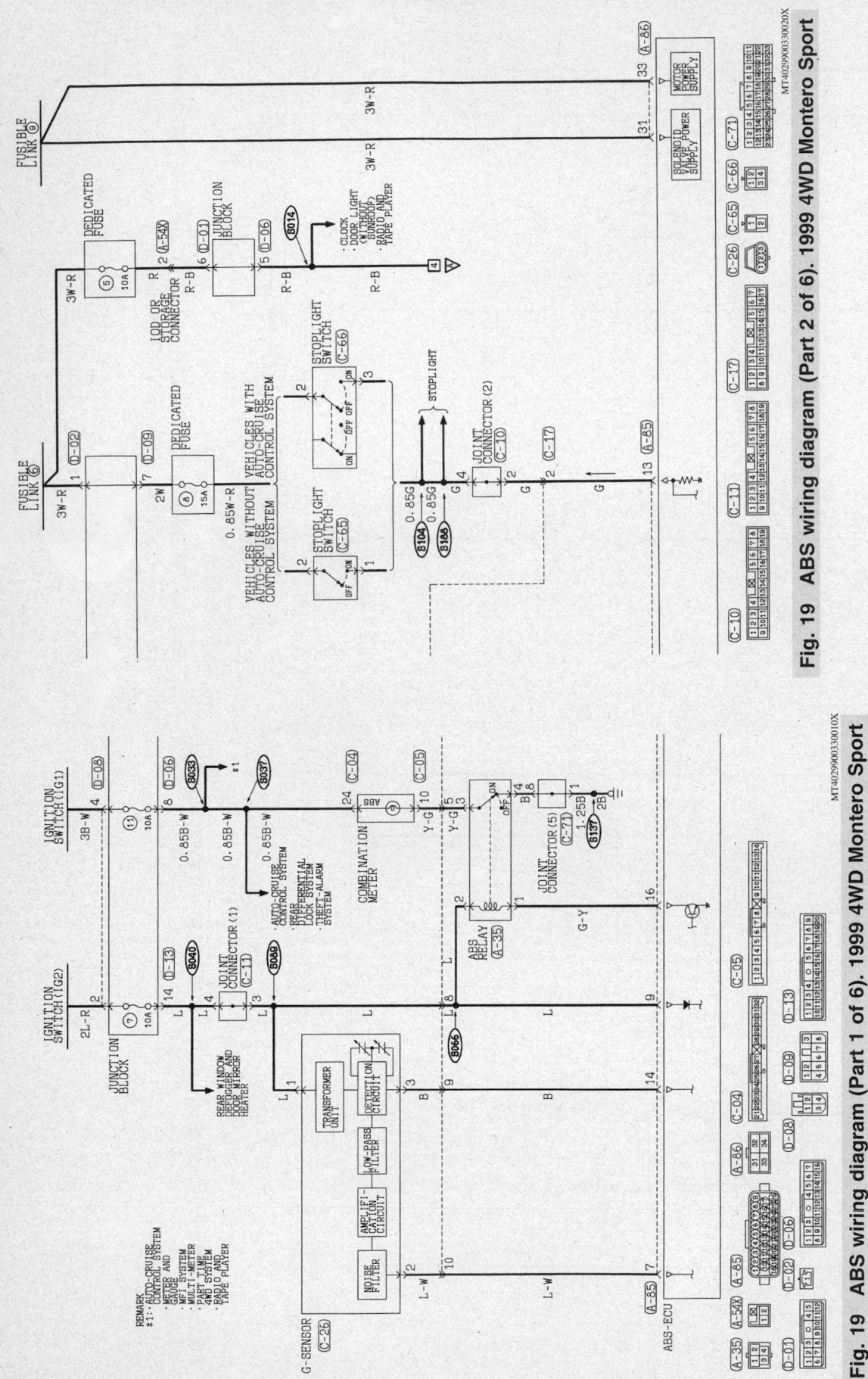

Fig. 19 ABS wiring diagram (Part 2 of 6). 1999 4WD Montero Sport

Fig. 19 ABS wiring diagram (Part 1 of 6). 1999 4WD Montero Sport

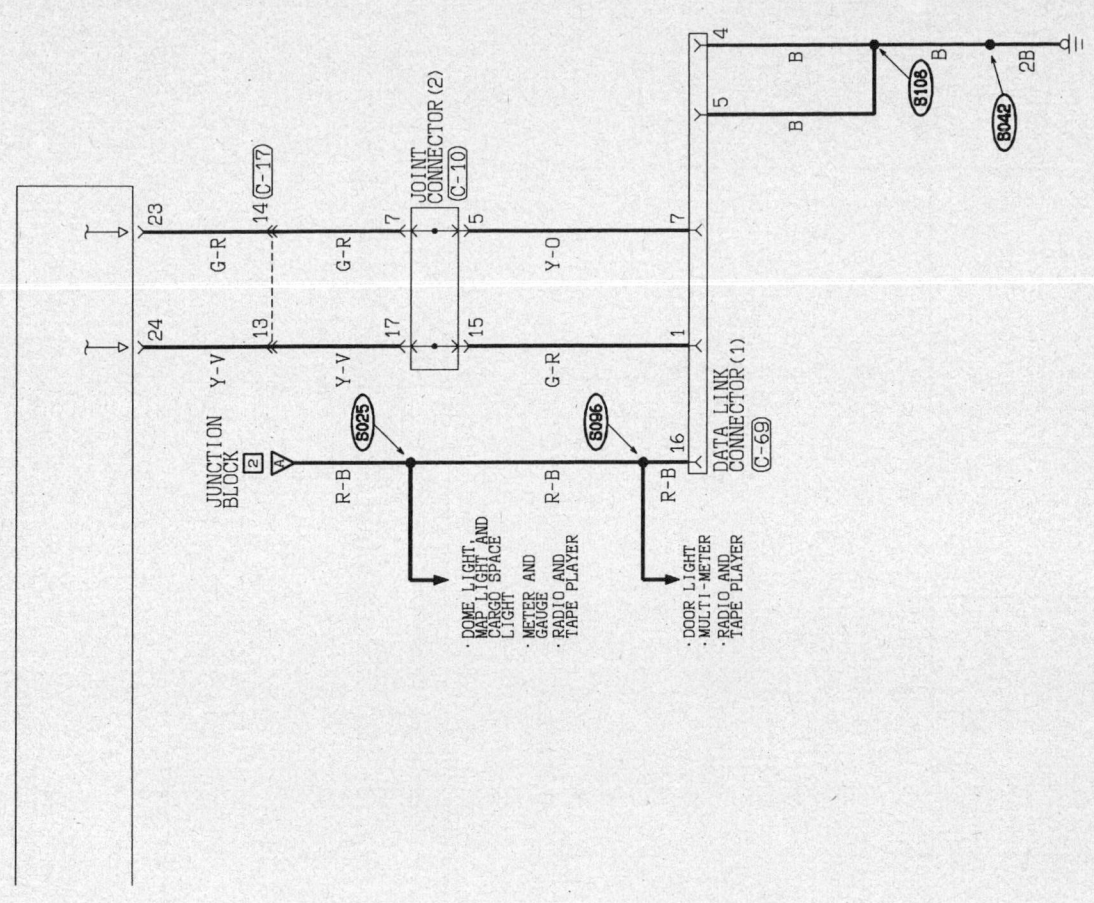

Fig. 19 ABS wiring diagram (Part 4 of 6). 1999 4WD Montero Sport

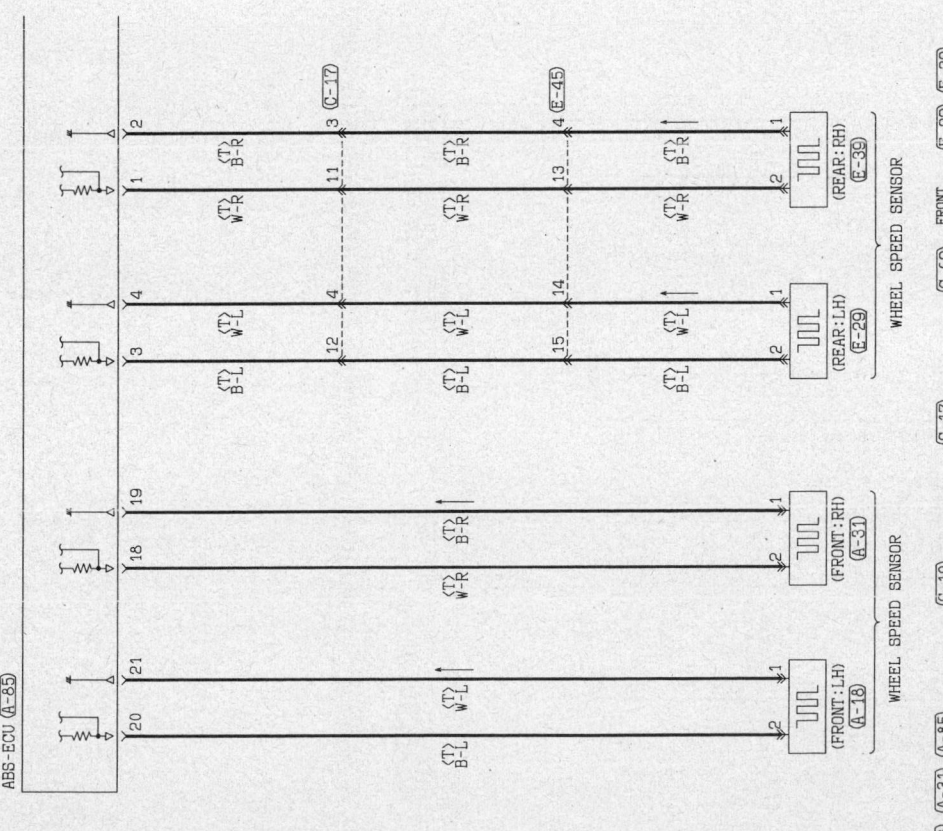

Fig. 19 ABS wiring diagram (Part 3 of 6). 1999 4WD Montero Sport

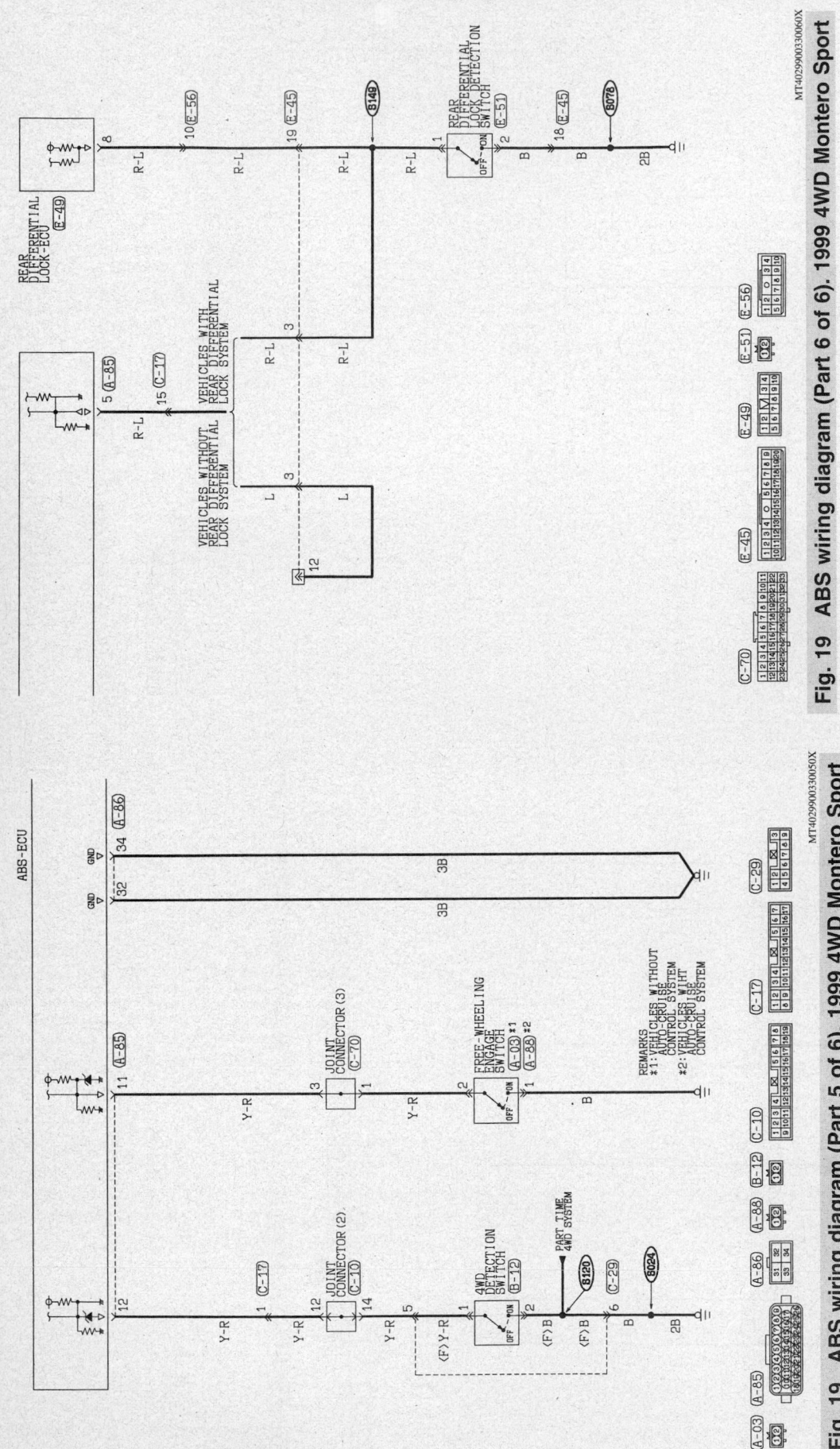

Fig. 19 ABS wiring diagram (Part 6 of 6). 1999 4WD Montero Sport

Fig. 19 ABS wiring diagram (Part 5 of 6). 1999 4WD Montero Sport

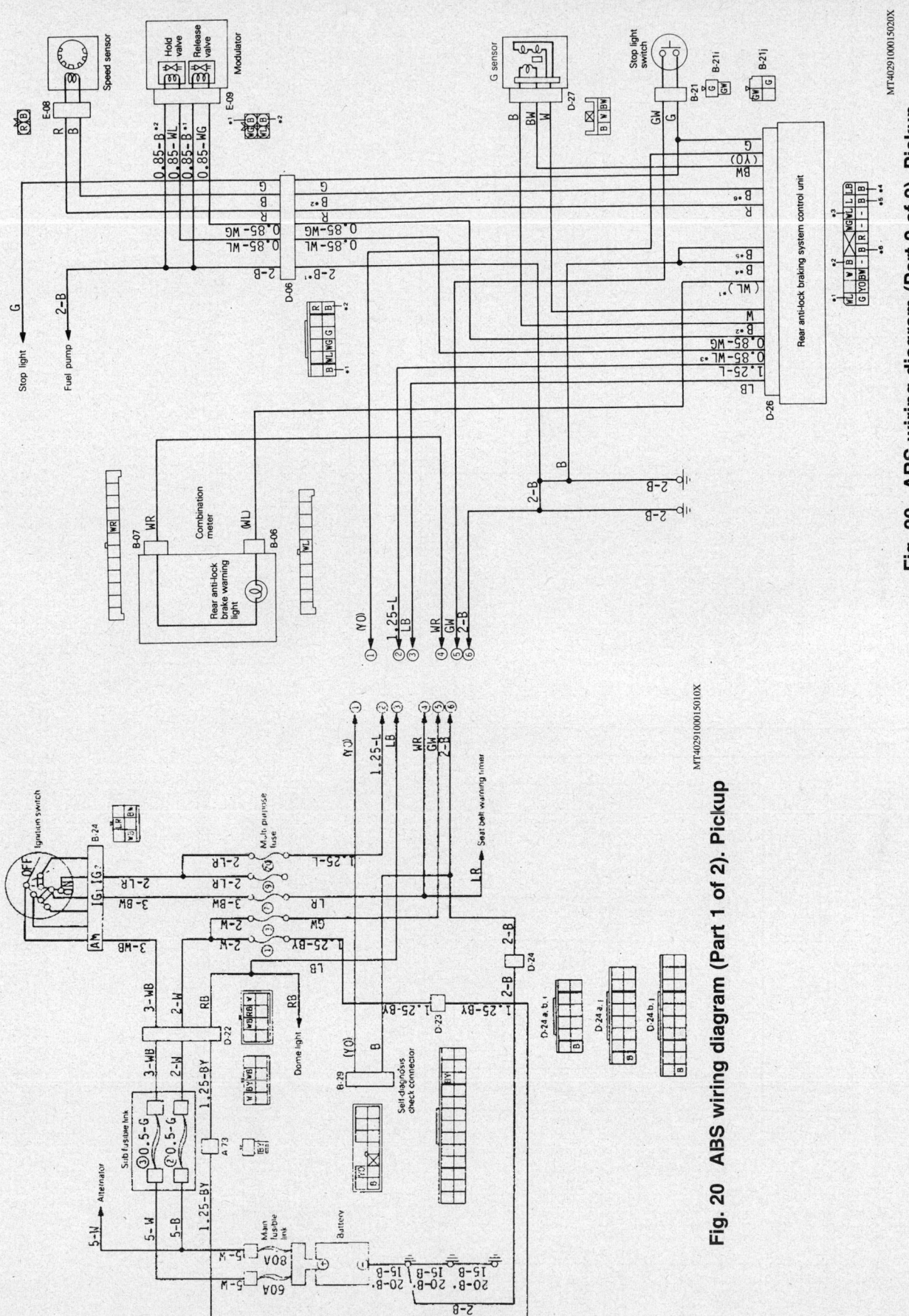

Fig. 20 ABS wiring diagram (Part 2 of 2). Pickup

Fig. 20 ABS wiring diagram (Part 1 of 2). Pickup

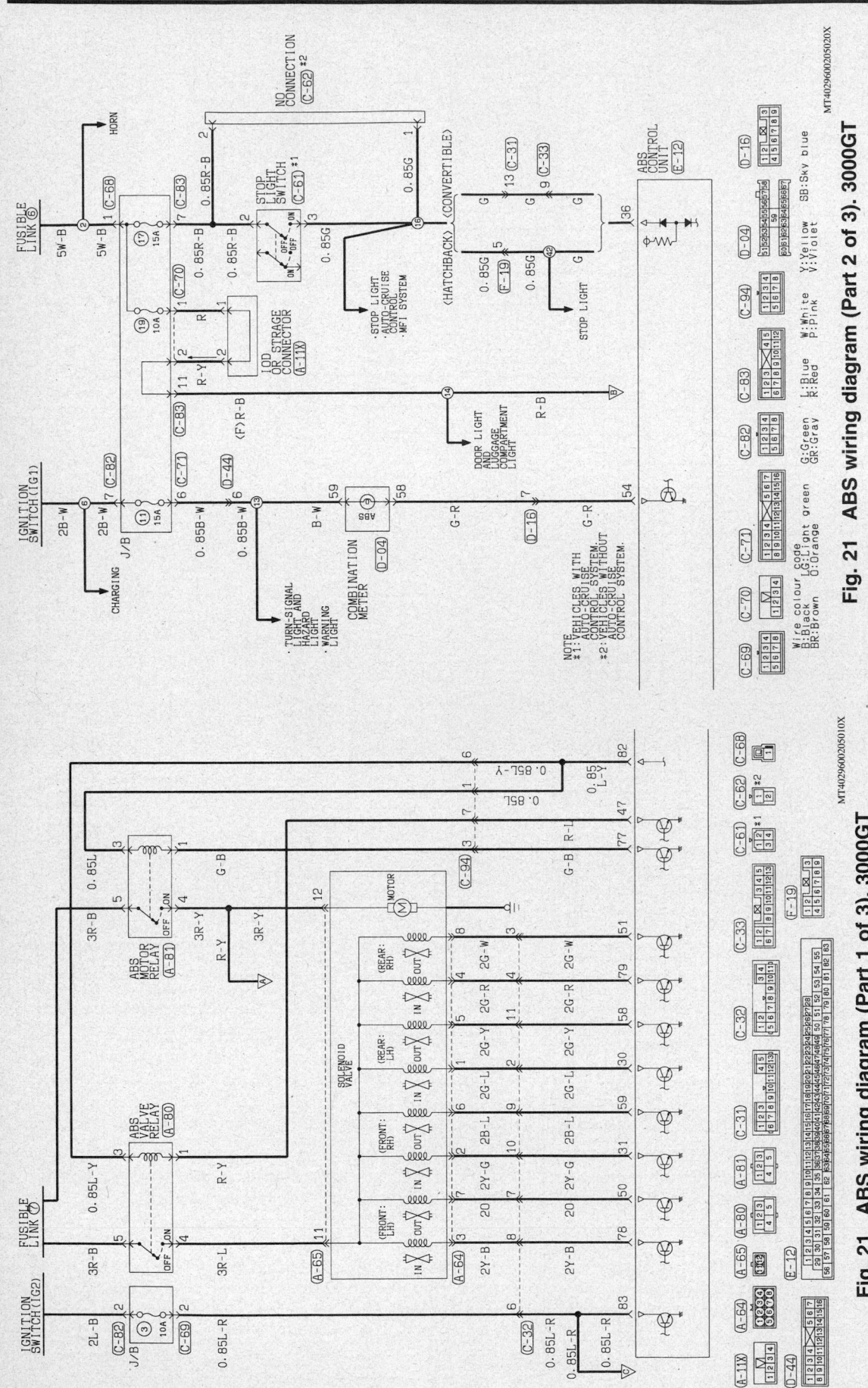

Fig. 21   ABS wiring diagram (Part 2 of 3). 3000GT

Fig. 21   ABS wiring diagram (Part 1 of 3). 3000GT

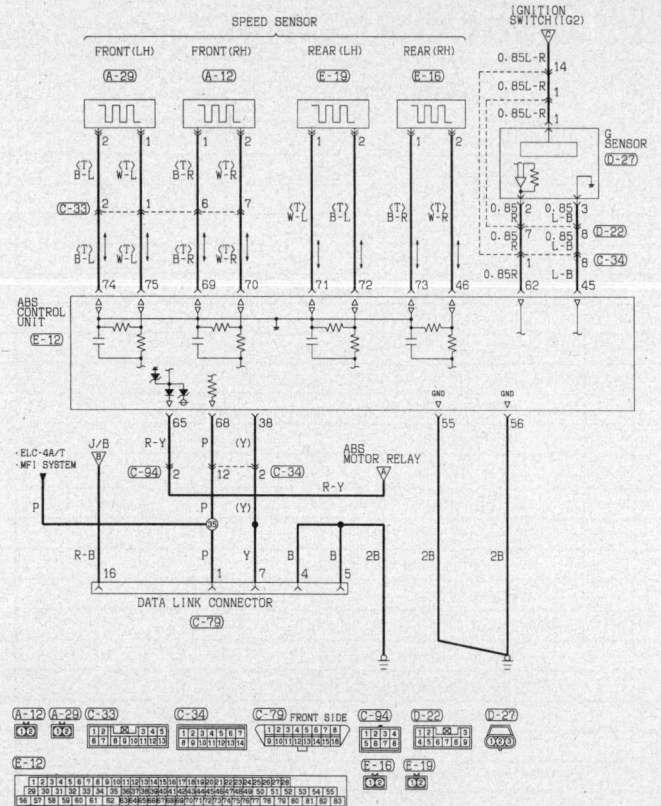

Fig. 21 ABS wiring diagram (Part 3 of 3). 3000GT

DIAGNOSTIC CHART INDEX

Code/Procedure	Description	Page No.	Fig. No.
1996 DIAMANTE			
—	Diagnostic Procedure Chart	33-218	22
Flowchart A	ABS Light Does Not Illuminate w/Key ON	33-219	23
Flowchart B	ABS Light Remains Illuminated w/Engine Running	33-220	24
Flowchart C	ABS Light Blinks Twice When Key Is Turned ON, Then Does Not Illuminate	33-220	25
Flowchart D	ABS Light Switches Off When Key Is Turned To START	33-220	26
Flowchart E	ABS Light Remains Illuminated w/Engine Running	33-221	27
Flowchart F	Abnormal ABS Operation	33-221	28
Code 11	Wheel Speed Sensors	33-221	29
Code 12	Wheel Speed Sensors	33-221	29
Code 13	Wheel Speed Sensors	33-221	29
Code 14	Wheel Speed Sensors	33-221	29
Code 15	Speed Sensor Circuit	33-222	30
Code 16	Power Supply Voltage	33-222	31
Code 21	Wheel Speed Sensors	33-221	29
Code 22	Wheel Speed Sensors	33-221	29
Code 23	Wheel Speed Sensors	33-221	29
Code 24	Wheel Speed Sensors	33-221	29
Code 25	Wheel Speed Sensors	33-221	29
Code 31	Wheel Speed Sensors	33-221	29
Code 32	Wheel Speed Sensors	33-221	29
Code 35	Generator Output Voltage	33-223	32
Code 37	Power Source Pressure For Hydraulic Unit Low	33-223	33
Code 41	Solenoid Valve Drive Circuit	33-223	34

ANTI-LOCK BRAKES

Continued

DIAGNOSTIC CHART INDEX—Continued

Code/ Procedure	Description	Page No.	Fig. No.
1996 DIAMANTE			
Code 42	Solenoid Valve Drive Circuit	33-223	34
Code 43	Solenoid Valve Drive Circuit	33-223	34
Code 44	Solenoid Valve Drive Circuit	33-223	34
Code 45	Solenoid Valve Drive Circuit	33-223	34
Code 46	Solenoid Valve Drive Circuit.	33-223	34
Code 51	Valve Relay Drive Circuit.	33-223	35
Code 52	Valve Relay Off & Motor Monitor Low	33-223	36
Code 53	Valve Relay Off & Motor Monitor Low	33-223	36
Code 54	Motor Relay	33-224	37
Code 61	Hydraulic Unit	33-224	38
1997–98 DIAMANTE			
Code 11	Wheel Speed Sensors	33-225	40
Code 12	Wheel Speed Sensors	33-225	40
Code 13	Wheel Speed Sensors	33-225	40
Code 14	Wheel Speed Sensors	33-225	40
Code 15	Wheel Speed Sensor Circuit	33-225	41
Code 16	Power Supply System	33-225	42
Code 21	Wheel Speed Sensor Circuit	33-225	43
Code 22	Wheel Speed Sensor Circuit	33-225	43
Code 23	Wheel Speed Sensor Circuit	33-225	43
Code 24	Wheel Speed Sensor Circuit	33-225	43
Code 38	Stop Light Switch System	33-226	44
Code 41	Solenoid Valve	33-226	45
Code 42	Solenoid Valve	33-226	45
Code 43	Solenoid Valve	33-226	45
Code 44	Solenoid Valve	33-226	45
Code 45	Solenoid Valve	33-226	46
Code 46	Solenoid Valve	33-226	46
Code 47	Solenoid Valve	33-226	46
Code 48	Solenoid Valve	33-226	46
Code 51	Valve Relay	33-226	47
Code 53	Motor Relay	33-226	48
Inspection Procedure 1	Communication w/Scan Tool Not Possible.	33-226	49
Inspection Procedure 2	Communication w/Scan Tool Not Possible	33-227	50
Inspection Procedure 3	ABS Warning Lamp Does Not Illuminate w/Key ON	33-227	51
Inspection Procedure 4	ABS Warning Lamp Remains Illuminated w/Engine Running	33-227	52
Inspection Procedure 5	Abnormal Brake Operation	33-227	53
1999 DIAMANTE			
—	Diagnostic Trouble Code Inspection Chart	33-228	54
Code 11	Wheel Speed Sensor Open Circuit	33-228	55
Code 12	Wheel Speed Sensor Open Circuit	33-228	55
Code 13	Wheel Speed Sensor Open Circuit	33-228	55
Code 14	Wheel Speed Sensor Open Circuit	33-228	55
Code 15	Wheel Speed Sensor Abnormal Output	33-228	56
Code 16	Power Supply System	33-228	57
Code 21	Wheel Speed Sensor Short Circuit	33-228	58
Code 22	Wheel Speed Sensor Short Circuit	33-228	58
Code 23	Wheel Speed Sensor Short Circuit	33-228	58
Code 24	Wheel Speed Sensor Short Circuit	33-228	58
Code 38	Stop Lamp Switch System	33-228	59
Code 41	Solenoid Inlet Valve	33-228	60

Continued

DIAGNOSTIC CHART INDEX—Continued

Code/ Procedure	Description	Page No.	Fig. No.
1999 DIAMANTE			
Code 42	Solenoid Inlet Valve	33-228	60
Code 43	Solenoid Inlet Valve	33-228	60
Code 44	Solenoid Inlet Valve	33-228	60
Code 45	Solenoid Outlet Valve	33-229	61
Code 46	Solenoid Outlet Valve	33-229	61
Code 47	Solenoid Outlet Valve	33-229	61
Code 48	Solenoid Outlet Valve	33-229	61
Code 51	Valve Relay	33-229	62
Code 53	Motor Relay	33-229	63
—	Inspection Procedure Chart	33-229	64
Inspection Procedure 1	Communication w/Scan Tool Not Possible.	33-229	65
Inspection Procedure 2	Communication w/Scan Tool Not Possible	33-229	66
Inspection Procedure 3	ABS Warning Lamp Does Not Illuminate w/Key ON	33-229	67
Inspection Procedure 4	ABS Warning Lamp Remains Illuminated w/Engine Running	33-230	68
Inspection Procedure 5	Abnormal Brake Operation	33-230	69
1996–97 ECLIPSE AWD			
Code 11	Wheel Speed Sensor Open Circuit	33-230	70
Code 12	Wheel Speed Sensor Open Circuit	33-230	70
Code 13	Wheel Speed Sensor Open Circuit	33-230	70
Code 14	Wheel Speed Sensor Open Circuit	33-230	70
Code 15	Wheel Speed Sensor System	33-230	71
Code 21	G-Sensor System	33-230	72
Code 22	Stop Light Switch System	33-230	73
Code 41	Solenoid Valve System	33-231	74
Code 42	Solenoid Valve System	33-231	74
Code 43	Solenoid Valve System	33-231	74
Code 51	Valve Relay System	33-231	75
Code 52	Motor Relay, Motor System	33-231	76
1996–97 ECLIPSE FWD			
Code 11	Wheel Speed Sensor Open Circuit	33-231	77
Code 12	Wheel Speed Sensor Open Circuit	33-231	77
Code 13	Wheel Speed Sensor Open Circuit	33-231	77
Code 14	Wheel Speed Sensor Open Circuit	33-231	77
Code 15	Wheel Speed Sensor System	33-232	78
Code 16	Power Supply System	33-232	79
Code 21	Wheel Speed Sensor Excessive Gap Or Short Circuit	33-232	80
Code 22	Wheel Speed Sensor Excessive Gap Or Short Circuit	33-232	80
Code 23	Wheel Speed Sensor Excessive Gap Or Short Circuit	33-232	80
Code 24	Wheel Speed Sensor Excessive Gap Or Short Circuit	33-232	80
Code 38	Stop Light Switch System	33-232	81
Code 41	Solenoid Valve System	33-232	82
Code 42	Solenoid Valve System	33-232	82
Code 43	Solenoid Valve System	33-232	82
Code 51	Valve Relay System	33-232	83
Code 53	Motor Relay, Motor System	33-233	84
1998–99 ECLIPSE AWD			
—	Diagnostic Trouble Code Inspection Chart	33-233	85
Code 11	Wheel Speed Sensor System	33-233	86
Code 12	Wheel Speed Sensor System	33-233	86
Code 13	Wheel Speed Sensor System	33-233	86
Code 14	Wheel Speed Sensor System	33-233	86

Continued

DIAGNOSTIC CHART INDEX—Continued

Code/ Procedure	Description	Page No.	Fig. No.
1998–99 ECLIPSE AWD			
Code 15	Wheel Speed Sensor System	33-233	87
Code 16	Power Supply System	33-233	88
Code 21	Wheel Speed Sensor Excessive Gap	33-234	89
Code 22	Wheel Speed Sensor Excessive Gap	33-234	89
Code 23	Wheel Speed Sensor Excessive Gap	33-234	89
Code 24	Wheel Speed Sensor Excessive Gap	33-234	89
Code 26	G-Sensor System	33-234	90
Code 38	Stop Light Switch System	33-234	91
Code 51	Valve power Supply	33-234	92
Code 53	Pump Motor	33-234	93
—	Inspection Procedure Chart	33-234	94
Inspection Procedure 1	Communication w/Scan Tool Not Possible	33-234	95
Inspection Procedure 2	Communication w/Scan Tool Not Possible	33-235	96
Inspection Procedure 3	ABS Warning Lamp Does Not Illuminate w/Key ON	33-235	97
Inspection Procedure 4	ABS Warning Lamp Remains Illuminated w/Engine Running	33-235	98
Inspection Procedure 5	Abnormal Brake Operation	33-235	99
1998–99 ECLIPSE FWD			
—	Diagnostic Trouble Code Inspection Chart	33-236	100
Code 11	Wheel Speed Sensor Open Circuit	33-236	101
Code 12	Wheel Speed Sensor Open Circuit	33-236	101
Code 13	Wheel Speed Sensor Open Circuit	33-236	101
Code 14	Wheel Speed Sensor Open Circuit	33-236	101
Code 15	Wheel Speed Sensor System	33-236	102
Code 16	Power Supply System	33-236	103
Code 21	Wheel Speed Sensor Excessive Gap Or Short Circuit	33-236	104
Code 22	Wheel Speed Sensor Excessive Gap Or Short Circuit	33-236	104
Code 23	Wheel Speed Sensor Excessive Gap Or Short Circuit	33-236	104
Code 24	Wheel Speed Sensor Excessive Gap Or Short Circuit	33-236	104
Code 38	Stop Lamp Switch System	33-237	105
Code 51	Valve Power Supply	33-237	106
Code 53	Pump Motor	33-237	107
—	Inspection Procedure Chart	33-237	108
Inspection Procedure 1	Communication w/Scan Tool Not Possible	33-237	109
Inspection Procedure 2	Communication w/Scan Tool Not Possible	33-237	110
Inspection Procedure 3	ABS Warning Lamp Does Not Illuminate w/Key ON	33-238	111
Inspection Procedure 4	ABS Warning Lamp Remains Illuminated w/Engine Running	33-238	112
Inspection Procedure 5	Abnormal Brake Operation	33-238	113
1996–98 GALANT			
—	Diagnostic Trouble Code Inspection Chart	33-238	114
Code 11	Wheel Speed Sensor Circuit Open	33-238	115
Code 12	Wheel Speed Sensor Circuit Open	33-238	115
Code 13	Wheel Speed Sensor Circuit Open	33-238	115
Code 14	Wheel Speed Sensor Circuit Open	33-238	115
Code 16	Power Supply System	33-239	116
Code 21	Wheel Speed Sensor Short Circuit	33-239	117
Code 22	Wheel Speed Sensor Short Circuit	33-239	117
Code 23	Wheel Speed Sensor Short Circuit	33-239	117

Continued

DIAGNOSTIC CHART INDEX—Continued

Code/ Procedure	Description	Page No.	Fig. No.
1996–98 GALANT			
Code 24	Wheel Speed Sensor Short Circuit	33-239	117
Code 25	Wheel Speed Sensor Excessive Gap	33-239	118
Code 26	Wheel Speed Sensor Excessive Gap	33-239	118
Code 27	Wheel Speed Sensor Excessive Gap	33-239	118
Code 28	Wheel Speed Sensor Excessive Gap	33-239	118
Code 33	Stop Lamp Switch System	33-239	119
Code 35	Wheel Speed Sensor Pulse Processing	33-239	120
Code 36	Wheel Speed Sensor Pulse Processing	33-239	120
Code 37	Wheel Speed Sensor Pulse Processing	33-239	120
Code 38	Wheel Speed Sensor Pulse Processing	33-239	120
Code 41	Solenoid Valve	33-239	121
Code 42	Solenoid Valve	33-239	121
Code 43	Solenoid Valve	33-239	121
Code 44	Solenoid Valve	33-239	121
Code 45	Solenoid Valve	33-239	121
Code 46	Solenoid Valve	33-239	121
Code 47	Solenoid Valve	33-239	121
Code 48	Solenoid Valve	33-239	121
Code 51	Valve Relay ON Not Possible	33-240	122
Code 52	Valve Relay OFF Not Possible	33-240	123
Code 53	Motor Relay ON Not Possible	33-240	124
Code 54	Motor Relay OFF Not Possible	33-240	125
—	Inspection Procedure Chart	33-240	126
Inspection Procedure 1	Communication w/Scan Tool Not Possible	33-240	127
Inspection Procedure 2	Communication w/Scan Tool Not Possible	33-241	128
Inspection Procedure 3	ABS Warning Lamp Does Not Illuminate w/Key ON	33-241	129
Inspection Procedure 4	ABS Warning Lamp Remains Illuminated w/Engine Running	33-241	130
Inspection Procedure 5	ABS Warning Lamp Turns Off 1 Second After Key Is ON	33-241	131
Inspection Procedure 6	ABS Warning Lamp Flashes w/Key ON	33-241	132
Inspection Procedure 7	ABS Warning Lamp Turns Off w/Key In START Position	33-241	133
Inspection Procedure 8	Abnormal Brake Operation	33-242	134
1999 GALANT			
—	Diagnostic Trouble Code Inspection Chart	33-242	135
Code 11	Wheel Speed Sensor Open Or Short Circuit	33-242	136
Code 12	Wheel Speed Sensor Open Or Short Circuit	33-242	136
Code 13	Wheel Speed Sensor Open Or Short Circuit	33-242	136
Code 14	Wheel Speed Sensor Open Or Short Circuit	33-242	136
Code 38	Stop Lamp Switch	33-243	137
Code 41	Solenoid Valve or Hydraulic Unit Malfunction	33-243	138
Code 51	Solenoid Valve or Hydraulic Unit Malfunction	33-243	138
Code 53	Solenoid Valve or Hydraulic Unit Malfunction	33-243	138
1996 MIRAGE			
Code 11	Speed Sensors (Open Circuit)	33-244	139
Code 12	Speed Sensors (Open Circuit)	33-244	139
Code 13	Speed Sensors (Open Circuit)	33-244	139
Code 14	Speed Sensors (Open Circuit)	33-244	139
Code 15	Speed Sensors (Open Circuit)	33-244	139
Code 21	Speed Sensors (Short Circuit)	33-244	140

Continued

DIAGNOSTIC CHART INDEX—Continued

Code/ Procedure	Description	Page No.	Fig. No.
1996 MIRAGE			
Code 22	Speed Sensors (Short Circuit)	33-244	140
Code 23	Speed Sensors (Short Circuit)	33-244	140
Code 24	Speed Sensors (Short Circuit)	33-244	140
Code 25	Open Circuit In Both Rear Wheel Speed Sensors	33-244	141
Code 31	Front Wheel Speed Sensor Rotors	33-244	142
Code 32	Front Wheel Speed Sensor Rotors	33-244	142
Code 16	Drop Of Battery Voltage & Drop Of Generator Output Voltage	33-245	143
Code 35	Drop Of Battery Voltage & Drop Of Generator Output Voltage	33-245	143
Code 41	Solenoid Valves	33-245	144
Code 42	Solenoid Valves	33-245	144
Code 43	Solenoid Valves	33-245	144
Code 44	Solenoid Valves	33-245	144
Code 51	Valve Relay No. 1	33-245	145
Code 52	Valve Relay No. 2	33-245	146
Code 53	Motor Relay No. 1	33-246	147
Code 54	Motor Relay No. 2	33-246	148
Code 55	Motor Sticking	33-246	149
Code 62	Hydraulic Unit	33-246	150
—	Trouble Symptom Chart	33-247	151
Inspection Procedure 1	—	33-247	152
Inspection Procedures 2 & 3	—	33-247	153
Inspection Procedure 4 & 5	—	33-247	154
Inspection Procedure 6	—	33-248	155
Inspection Procedure 7	—	33-248	156
Inspection Procedure 9	—	33-248	157
Inspection Procedure 10	—	33-248	158
1997–99 MIRAGE			
Code 11	Wheel Speed Sensor	33-249	159
Code 12	Wheel Speed Sensor	33-249	159
Code 13	Wheel Speed Sensor	33-249	159
Code 14	Wheel Speed Sensor	33-249	159
Code 21	Wheel Speed Sensor	33-249	159
Code 22	Wheel Speed Sensor	33-249	159
Code 23	Wheel Speed Sensor	33-249	159
Code 24	Wheel Speed Sensor	33-249	159
Code 15	Wheel Speed Sensor	33-249	160
Code 16	Power Supply System	33-249	161
Code 33	Stop Light Switch System	33-249	162
Code 41	Solenoid Valve	33-249	163
Code 42	Solenoid Valve	33-249	163
Code 43	Solenoid Valve	33-249	163
Code 44	Solenoid Valve	33-249	163
Code 51	Valve Relay	33-250	164
Code 53	Motor Relay	33-250	165
1996–97 MONTERO			
Code 11	Wheel Speed Sensor Open Circuit	33-251	173
Code 12	Wheel Speed Sensor Open Circuit	33-251	173
Code 13	Wheel Speed Sensor Open Circuit	33-251	173
Code 14	Wheel Speed Sensor Open Circuit	33-251	173

Continued

DIAGNOSTIC CHART INDEX—Continued

Continued

DIAGNOSTIC CHART INDEX—Continued

Code/Procedure	Description	Page No.	Fig. No.
MONTERO SPORT			
Code 11	Wheel Speed Sensor	33-259	208
Code 12	Wheel Speed Sensor	33-259	208
Code 13	Wheel Speed Sensor	33-259	208
Code 14	Wheel Speed Sensor	33-259	208
Code 21	Wheel Speed Sensor	33-259	208
Code 22	Wheel Speed Sensor	33-259	208
Code 23	Wheel Speed Sensor	33-259	208
Code 24	Wheel Speed Sensor	33-252	208
Code 15	Wheel Speed Sensor	33-252	209
Code 16	Power Supply System	33-260	210
Code 25	4WD Detection Switch	33-260	211
Code 26	Freewheel Engage Switch	33-261	212
Code 32	G-Sensor System	33-261	213
Code 33	Stoplight Switch System	33-262	214
Code 41	Hydraulic Unit Relay, Valve Or Malfunction	33-262	215
Code 42	Hydraulic Unit Relay, Valve Or Malfunction	33-262	215
Code 43	Hydraulic Unit Relay, Valve Or Malfunction	33-262	215
Code 51	Hydraulic Unit Relay, Valve Or Malfunction	33-262	215
Code 53	Hydraulic Unit Relay, Valve Or Malfunction	33-262	215
PICKUP			
—	Diagnostic Trouble Codes	33-263	216
1996 3000GT			
Code 11	Wheel Speed Sensor System Open Circuit	33-263	217
Code 12	Wheel Speed Sensor System Open Circuit	33-263	217
Code 13	Wheel Speed Sensor System Open Circuit	33-263	217
Code 14	Wheel Speed Sensor System Open Circuit	33-263	217
Code 15	Wheel Speed Sensor System Output Signal Abnormal	33-263	220
Code 16	ABS ECU Power Supply System Voltage Abnormally Low Or High	33-264	221
Code 21	Wheel Speed Sensor System Shorted	33-264	222
Code 22	Wheel Speed Sensor System Shorted	33-264	222
Code 23	Wheel Speed Sensor System Shorted	33-264	222
Code 24	Wheel Speed Sensor System Shorted	33-264	222
Code 26	G-Sensor System Open, Shorted Or Signal Abnormal	33-264	225
Code 38	Stop Light Switch System Open Circuit Or ON Trouble	33-264	226
Code 41	Solenoid Valve Systems	33-265	228
Code 42	Solenoid Valve Systems	33-265	228
Code 43	Solenoid Valve Systems	33-265	228
Code 44	Solenoid Valve Systems	33-265	228
Code 45	Solenoid Valve Systems	33-265	228
Code 46	Solenoid Valve Systems	33-265	228
Code 47	Solenoid Valve Systems	33-265	228
Code 48	Solenoid Valve Systems	33-265	228
Code 51	ABS Valve Relay System	33-265	229
Code 53	HU Pump Motor Or ABS Motor Relay System.	33-265	230
1997 3000GT AWD			
Code 11	Wheel Speed Sensor System Open Circuit	33-263	218
Code 12	Wheel Speed Sensor System Open Circuit	33-263	218
Code 13	Wheel Speed Sensor System Open Circuit	33-263	218
Code 14	Wheel Speed Sensor System Open Circuit	33-263	218
Code 15	Wheel Speed Sensor System Output Signal Abnormal	33-263	220
Code 16	ABS ECU Power Supply System Voltage Abnormally Low Or High	33-264	221
Code 21	Wheel Speed Sensor System Shorted	33-264	223
Code 22	Wheel Speed Sensor System Shorted	33-264	223
Code 23	Wheel Speed Sensor System Shorted	33-264	223
Code 24	Wheel Speed Sensor System Shorted	33-264	223

Continued

DIAGNOSTIC CHART INDEX—Continued

Code/Procedure	Description	Page No.	Fig. No.
1997 3000GT AWD			
Code 38	Stop Light Switch System Open Circuit Or ON Trouble	33-265	227
Code 41	Solenoid Valve Systems	33-265	228
Code 42	Solenoid Valve Systems	33-265	228
Code 43	Solenoid Valve Systems	33-265	228
Code 44	Solenoid Valve Systems	33-265	228
Code 45	Solenoid Valve Systems	33-265	228
Code 46	Solenoid Valve Systems	33-265	228
Code 47	Solenoid Valve Systems	33-265	228
Code 48	Solenoid Valve Systems	33-265	228
Code 51	ABS Valve Relay System	33-265	229
Code 53	HU Pump Motor Or ABS Motor Relay System	33-265	230
1997 3000GT FWD			
Code 11	Wheel Speed Sensor System Open Circuit	33-263	219
Code 12	Wheel Speed Sensor System Open Circuit	33-263	219
Code 13	Wheel Speed Sensor System Open Circuit	33-263	219
Code 14	Wheel Speed Sensor System Open Circuit	33-263	219
Code 15	Wheel Speed Sensor System Output Signal Abnormal	33-263	220
Code 16	ABS ECU Power Supply System Voltage Abnormally Low Or High	33-264	221
Code 21	Wheel Speed Sensor System Shorted	33-264	224
Code 22	Wheel Speed Sensor System Shorted	33-264	224
Code 23	Wheel Speed Sensor System Shorted	33-264	224
Code 24	Wheel Speed Sensor System Shorted	33-264	224
Code 38	Stop Light Switch System Open Circuit Or ON Trouble	33-265	227
Code 41	Solenoid Valve Systems	33-265	228
Code 42	Solenoid Valve Systems	33-265	228
Code 43	Solenoid Valve Systems	33-265	228
Code 44	Solenoid Valve Systems	33-265	228
Code 45	Solenoid Valve Systems	33-265	228
Code 46	Solenoid Valve Systems	33-265	228
Code 47	Solenoid Valve Systems	33-265	228
Code 48	Solenoid Valve Systems	33-265	228
Code 51	ABS Valve Relay System	33-265	229
Code 53	HU Pump Motor Or ABS Motor Relay System	33-265	230
1998–99 3000GT			
—	Diagnostic Trouble Code Inspection Chart	33-266	231
Code 11	Wheel Speed Sensor Open Circuit	33-266	232
Code 12	Wheel Speed Sensor Open Circuit	33-266	232
Code 13	Wheel Speed Sensor Open Circuit	33-266	232
Code 14	Wheel Speed Sensor Open Circuit	33-266	232
Code 15	Wheel Speed Sensor Output Signal Abnormal	33-266	233
Code 16	ABS-ECU Voltage Low Or High	33-266	234
Code 21	Wheel Speed Sensor Shorted	33-266	235
Code 22	Wheel Speed Sensor Shorted	33-266	235
Code 23	Wheel Speed Sensor Shorted	33-266	235
Code 24	Wheel Speed Sensor Shorted	33-266	235
Code 38	Stop Lamp Switch System	33-267	236
Code 41	Solenoid Valve	33-267	237
Code 42	Solenoid Valve	33-267	237
Code 43	Solenoid Valve	33-267	237
Code 44	Solenoid Valve	33-267	237
Code 45	Solenoid Valve	33-267	237
Code 46	Solenoid Valve	33-267	237
Code 47	Solenoid Valve	33-267	237
Code 48	Solenoid Valve	33-267	237
Code 51	ABS Valve Relay System	33-267	238

Continued

DIAGNOSTIC CHART INDEX—Continued

Code/ Procedure	Description	Page No.	Fig. No.
1998–99 3000GT			
Code 53	HU Pump Or ABS Motor Relay System	33-267	239
—	Inspection Procedure Chart	33-267	240
Inspection Procedure 1	Communication w/Scan Tool Not Possible	33-268	241
Inspection Procedure 2	Communication Between Scan Tool & ABS-ECU Not Possible	33-268	242
Inspection Procedure 3	ABS Warning Lamp Does Not Illuminate w/Key ON	33-268	243
Inspection Procedure 4	ABS Warning Lamp Remains Illuminated w/Key ON	33-268	244
Inspection Procedure 5	Brake Operation Abnormal	33-268	245

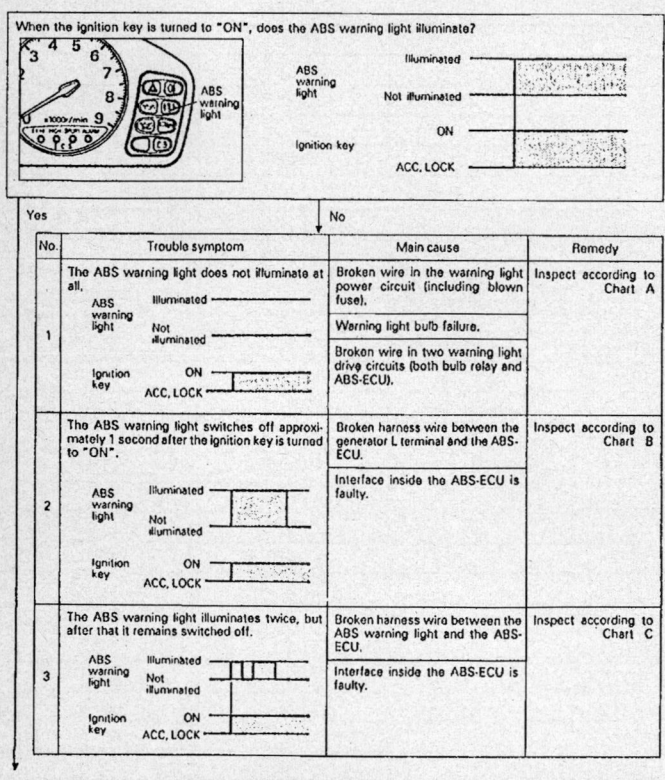

MT4029100094010X

Fig. 22 Diagnostic procedure chart (Part 1 of 4).
1996 Diamante

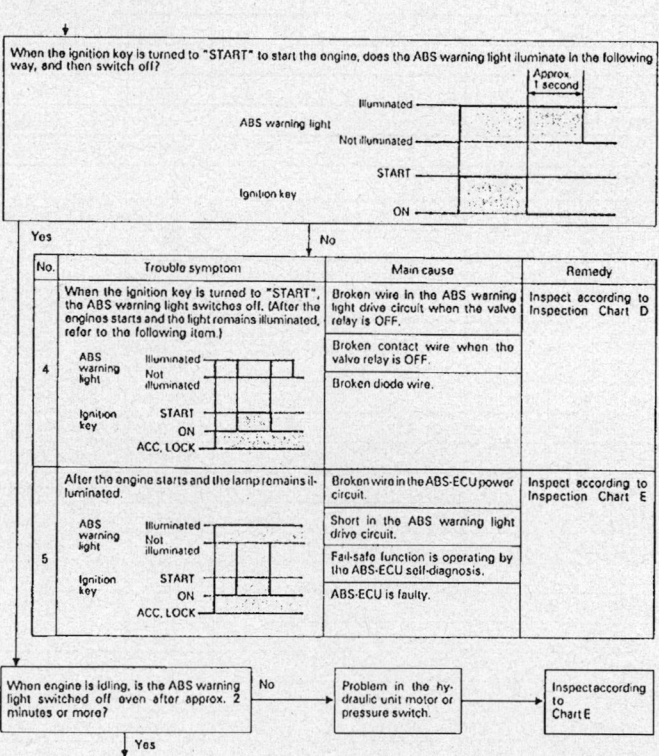

MT4029100094020X

Fig. 22 Diagnostic procedure chart (Part 2 of 4).
1996 Diamante

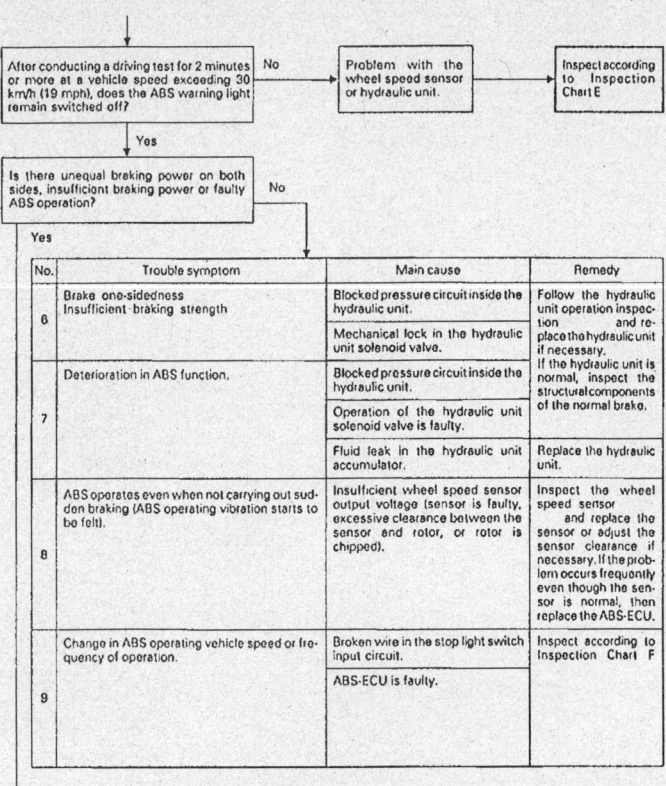

Fig. 22   Diagnostic procedure chart (Part 3 of 4).
1996 Diamante

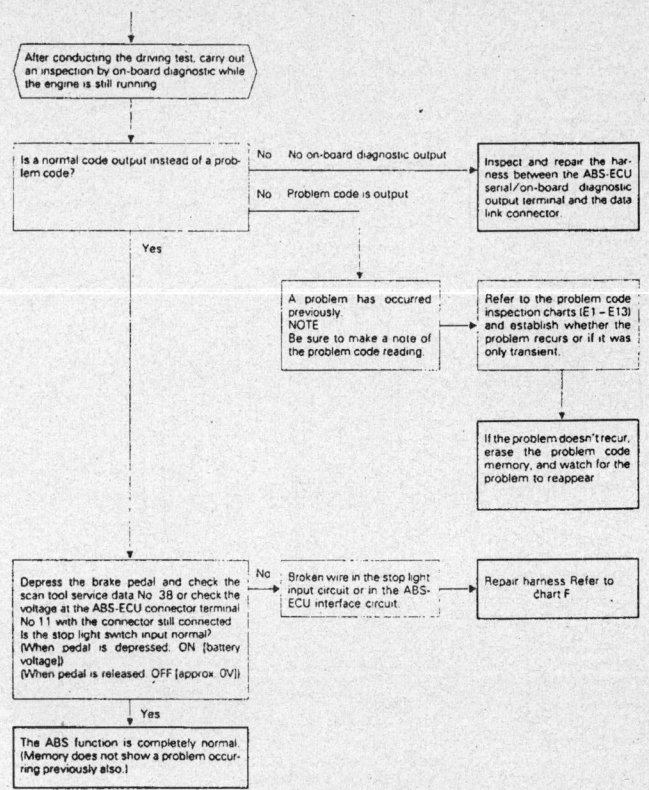

Fig. 22   Diagnostic procedure chart (Part 4 of 4).
1996 Diamante

A	When ignition key is turned to "ON", ABS warning light does not illuminate

Comment: When power is supplied to the ABS-ECU, the valve relay changes from OFF to ON·OFF·ON by the initial check, and thus even if there is a problem with the light illumination circuit that is driven by the ABS-ECU, the light will illuminate twice when the valve relay is OFF. Accordingly, there is a strong possibility that the problem is in the light bulb or in the power supply to the light.

Hint: When other warning lights also do not illuminate, the cause is probably a blown fuse.

MT4029100095010X

Fig. 23   Diagnostic Flowchart A: ABS Light Does
Not Illuminate w/Key On. (Part 1 of 3). 1996
Diamante

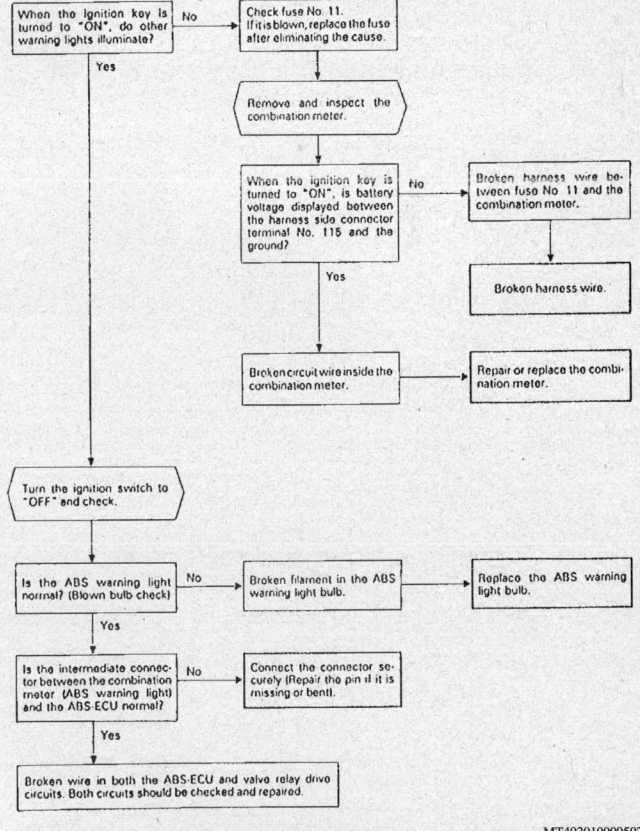

Fig. 23   Diagnostic Flowchart A: ABS Light Does
Not Illuminate w/Key On. (Part 2 of 3). 1996
Diamante

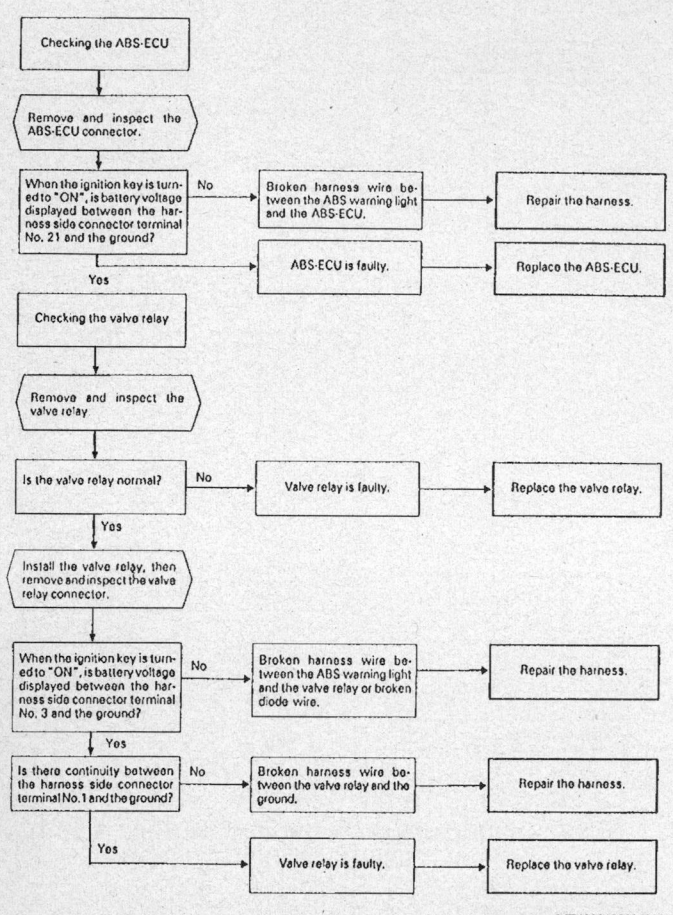

Fig. 23   Diagnostic Flowchart A: ABS Light Does Not Illuminate w/Key On. (Part 3 of 3). 1996 Diamante

MT4029100095030X

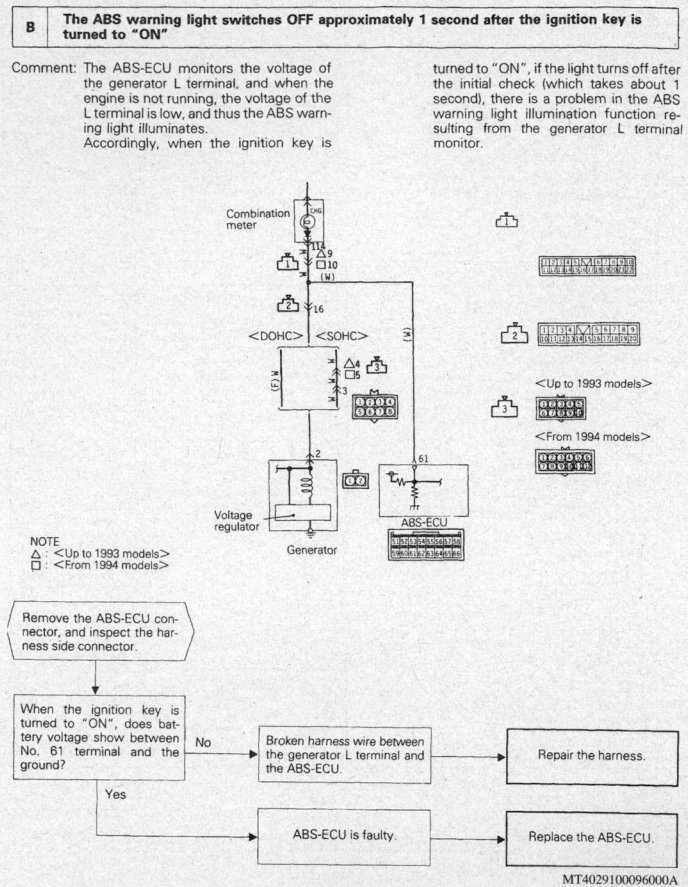

B   The ABS warning light switches OFF approximately 1 second after the ignition key is turned to "ON"

Comment: The ABS-ECU monitors the voltage of the generator L terminal, and when the engine is not running, the voltage of the L terminal is low, and thus the ABS warning light illuminates. Accordingly, when the ignition key is turned to "ON", if the light turns off after the initial check (which takes about 1 second), there is a problem in the ABS warning light illumination function resulting from the generator L terminal monitor.

MT4029100096000A

Fig. 24   Diagnostic Flowchart B: ABS Light Remains Illuminated w/Engine Running. 1996 Diamante

C   The ABS warning light illuminates twice after the ignition key is turned to "ON", but after that it remains switched off

Comment: The ABS-ECU causes the ABS warning light to illuminate during the initial check. The valve relay changes from OFF to OFF→ON by the initial check, and if there is a broken wire in the light drive circuit from the ABS-ECU, the light will illuminate when the valve relay is OFF. Accordingly, if the ignition key is "ON", and the light illuminates twice and then switches off, there is a problem in the ABS-ECU drive circuit.

MT4029100097000X

Fig. 25   Diagnostic Flowchart C: ABS Light Blinks Twice When Key Is Turned On, Then Does Not Illuminate. 1996 Diamante

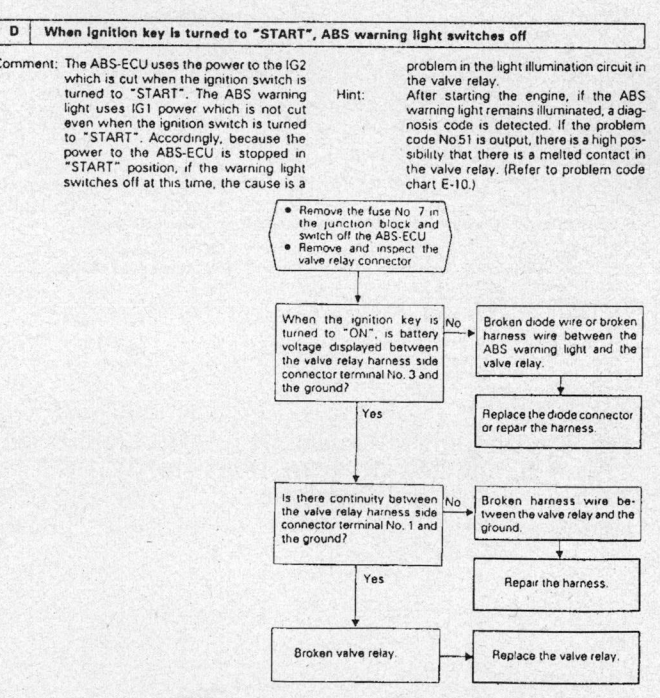

D   When ignition key is turned to "START", ABS warning light switches off

Comment: The ABS-ECU uses the power to the IG2 which is cut when the ignition switch is turned to "START". The ABS warning light uses IG1 power which is not cut even when the ignition switch is turned to "START". Accordingly, because the power to the ABS-ECU is stopped in "START" position, if the warning light switches off at this time, the cause is a problem in the light illumination circuit in the valve relay.

Hint: After starting the engine, if the ABS warning light remains illuminated, a diagnosis code is detected. If the problem code No.51 is output, there is a high possibility that there is a melted contact in the valve relay. (Refer to problem code chart E-10.)

MT4029100098000X

Fig. 26   Diagnostic Flowchart D: ABS Light Switches Off When Key Is Turned To Start. 1996 Diamante

ANTI-LOCK BRAKES

E	Even after the engine is stated, the ABS warning light remains illuminated

Comment: This symptom occurs when the ABS-ECU is not functioning due to a broken wire, etc., in the ABS-ECU power circuit, when the fail-safe function is operating to isolate the system, or when there is a isolate the system, or when there is a short in the warning light drive circuit.

Hint: Check the on-board diagnostic output and if there is no output voltage, or the scan tool and the ABS-ECU cannot communicate, then there is a high possibility that power is not being supplied to the ABS-ECU.

Caution
If a problem code is output, there is a high possibility that the fail-safe function is operating. In this case, to check if there is a current problem, the memory should be temporarily erased, and the engine should be restarted.

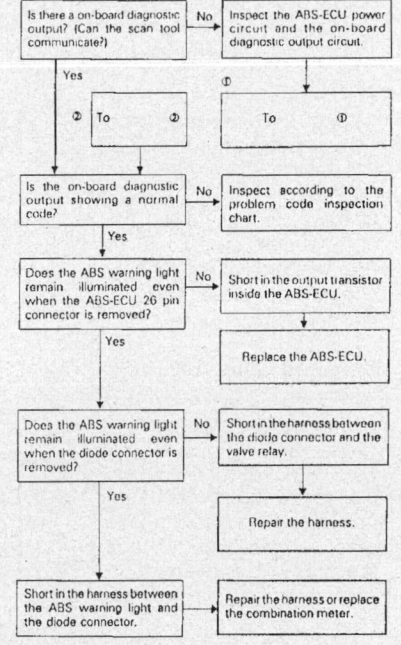

Fig. 27 Diagnostic Flowchart E: ABS Light Remains Illuminated w/Engine Running (Part 1 of 2). 1996 Diamante

MT4029100099010X

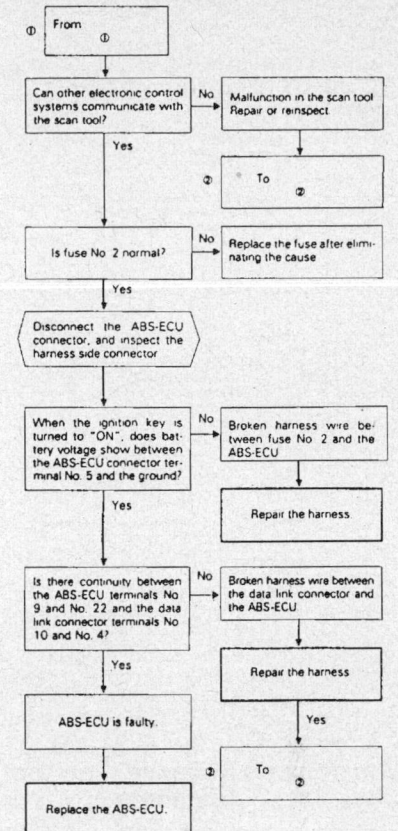

MT4029100099020X

Fig. 27 Diagnostic Flowchart E: ABS Light Remains Illuminated w/Engine Running (Part 2 of 2). 1996 Diamante

F	Change in ABS operating vehicle speed or frequency of operation

Comment: If the stop light switch ON signal is not input even once after the engine is started, the ABS control commences when the vehicle speed reaches 15 km/h (9 mph) or above. (Control is possible if the signal is input even once and the vehicle speed is approximately 6 km/h (4 mph) or above.) This symptom indicates a broken wire in the stop light switch.

Hint: When the stop light is illuminating normally, if the scan tool service data shows No. 39 even if the brake pedal is depressed, then there is a broken harness wire in the stop light switch input circuit, or the ABS-ECU interface circuit is faulty.

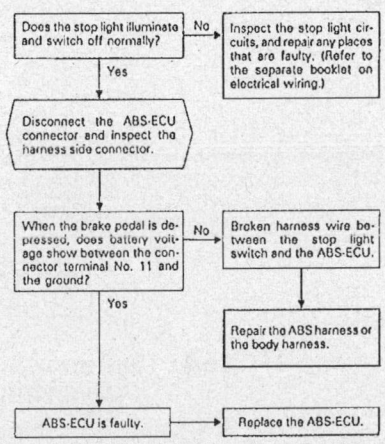

MT4029100100000X

Fig. 28 Diagnostic Flowchart F: Abnormal ABS Operation. 1996 Diamante

E-2	When diagnostic trouble codes No. 11, No. 12, No. 13 or No. 14 are displayed

Comment: These codes are displayed when the sensor with the broken wire can be distinguished, and sensor output drops due to a faulty sensor or a bent rotor, etc., and anti-lock control is continuously operating.

Hint: If there is currently a broken wire in the sensor circuit, when the engine is restarted, the display switches to diagnostic trouble code No. 15. If the same code is displayed even after restarting the engine, the problem is not a broken circuit wire, but something such as an excessive sensor gap.

Remedy: Inspect according to "Wheel Speed Sensor Inspection Flow Chart " while referring to the above.

E-3	When diagnostic trouble codes No. 21, No. 22, No. 23 or No. 24 are displayed

Comment: These problem codes are displayed when a broken wire cannot be verified, but when the vehicle speed reaches 10 km/h (6 mph) or more, no pulses are input.

Hint: The cause is likely to be either a short between the sensor harnesses, a short in the sensor + wire with the body, or an excessive sensor gap.

Remedy: Inspect according to "Wheel Speed Sensor Inspection Flow Chart " while referring to the above.

E-4	When diagnostic trouble code No. 25 is displayed

Comment: A problem in both rear wheel sensors is diagnosed when the signal from either of the front wheel speed sensors is diagnosed as normal, and the wheel speed of both rear wheels is 0 km/h (0 mph) for a continuous 20 second period, even if the wheel speed of the front wheels is 11 km/h (7 mph) or more.

Hint: This code is displayed when there is a short in the sensor harnesses of both rear wheels, or if there is low output from both rear wheel sensors.

Remedy: Inspect according to "Wheel Speed Sensor Inspection Flow Chart " while referring to the above.

NOTE
If the vehicle is raised up, or if the wheels are stuck and only the front wheels are moving, after approximately 20 seconds the ABS warning light will illuminate, and the system will be isolated.
Thus, this code can be output even when the system is normal, so it is only output during a current problem, and is not kept in memory from a previous problem. Accordingly, before turning the ignition switch to OFF, the problem code should be read and written down.

E-5	When diagnostic trouble code No. 31 or No. 32 is displayed

Comment: These codes are displayed when a chipped rotor tooth or a jammed rotor (one tooth) is detected.
Also, they show that there is a request of brake fluid pressure control with the stop light switch OFF from when the vehicle is stationary until the vehicle speed exceeds approximately 15 km/h (9 mph). If the vehicle repeats start and stop and the condition above is detected five times, the ABS warning light will illuminate.

Hint: There is a strong chance that the wheel speed sensor output is low due to a bent rotor tooth or excessive sensor gap. Low sensor output could also be caused by a rare short in the sensor coil.

Remedy: Inspect according to "Wheel Speed Sensor Inspection Flow Chart " while referring to the above.

MT4029100104010X

Fig. 29 Codes 11, 12, 13, 14, 21, 22, 23, 24, 25, 31 & 32: Wheel Speed Sensors (Part 1 of 3). 1996 Diamante

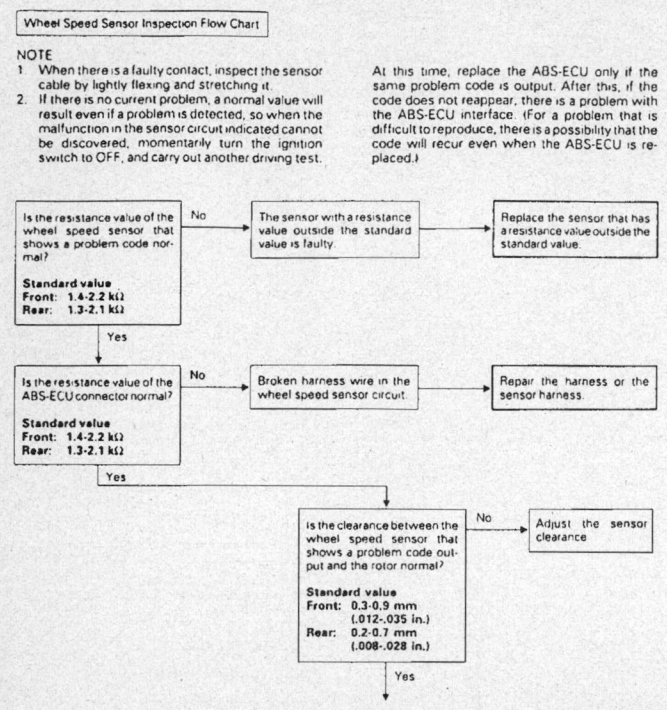

Wheel Speed Sensor Inspection Flow Chart

NOTE
1. When there is a faulty contact, inspect the sensor cable by lightly flexing and stretching it.
2. If there is no current problem, a normal value will result even if a problem is detected, so when the malfunction in the sensor circuit indicated cannot be discovered, momentarily turn the ignition switch to OFF, and carry out another driving test.

At this time, replace the ABS-ECU only if the same problem code is output. After this, if the code does not reappear, there is a problem with the ABS-ECU interface. (For a problem that is difficult to reproduce, there is a possibility that the code will recur even when the ABS-ECU is replaced.)

Fig. 29 Codes 11, 12, 13, 14, 21, 22, 23, 24, 25, 31 & 32: Wheel Speed Sensors (Part 2 of 3). 1996 Diamante

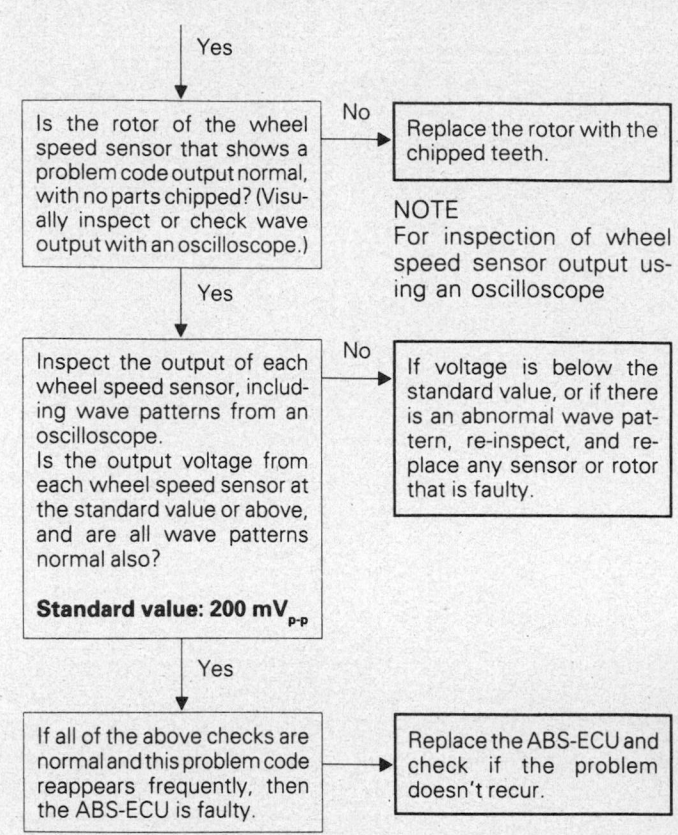

Fig. 29 Codes 11, 12, 13, 14, 21, 22, 23, 24, 25, 31 & 32: Wheel Speed Sensors (Part 3 of 3). 1996 Diamante

E-1 When diagnostic trouble code No. 15 is displayed

Comment: There is a broken + wire or – wire in one or more of the four wheel speed sensors detected by a broken wire inspection by the ABS-ECU hardware circuit. In this instance, inspect all of the wheel speed sensors, as it cannot be determined which single wheel is abnormal.

Hint: When using the scan tool, up to 4 codes are displayed.
When this code (No. 15) appears, and a problem code for a specific wheel (nos. 11–14) is also displayed, it is likely that there is a broken wire in the wheel speed sensor indicated by these codes.

NOTE
1. When there is a faulty contact, inspect the sensor cable by lightly flexing and stretching it.
2. If there is no current problem, a normal value will result even if a problem is detected, so when the malfunction in the sensor circuit indicated cannot be discovered, momentarily turn the ignition switch to OFF, and carry out another driving test. At this time, replace the ABS-ECU only if the same problem code is output. After this, if the code does not reappear, there is a problem with the ABS-ECU interface. (For a problem that is difficult to reproduce, there is a possibility that the code will recur even when the ABS-ECU is replaced.)

Fig. 30 Code 15: Speed Sensor Circuit (Part 1 of 2). 1996 Diamante

E-6 When diagnostic trouble code No. 16 is displayed

Comment: This indicates that the ABS-ECU power voltage is lower than the standard value. If the voltage returns to standard voltage or above, this problem code will not be output.

Caution
If the battery voltage drops during inspection, this code will be output as a current problem, and correct diagnosis of the problem cannot be made. Before carrying out the following inspection, check the battery level, and refill it if necessary.

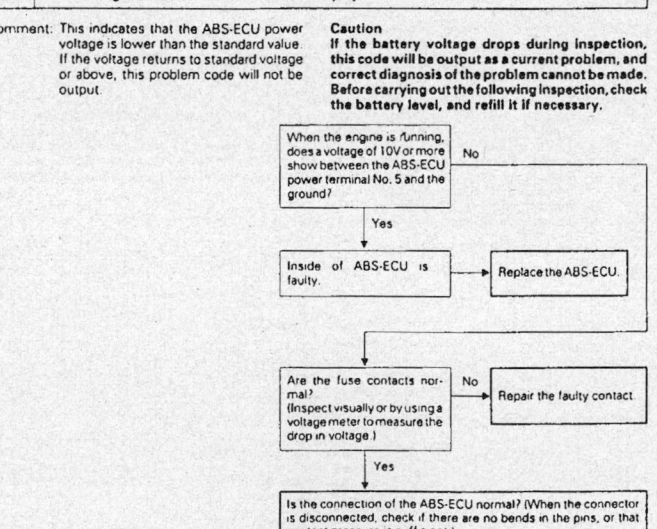

Fig. 31 Code 16: Power Supply Voltage. 1996 Diamante

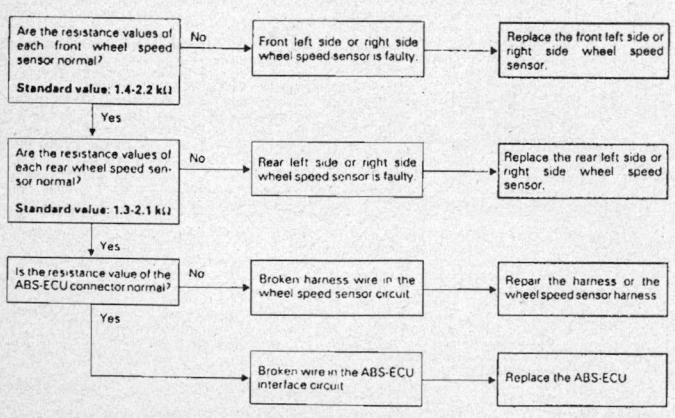

Fig. 30 Code 15: Speed Sensor Circuit (Part 2 of 2). 1996 Diamante

E-7	When diagnostic trouble code No. 35 is displayed

Comment: This indicates that the output voltage of the generator L terminal is low when the ignition key is turned to "ON" and the engine is stopped, or when the engine is running.
If the voltage returns to standard voltage or above, this problem code will not be output.

Hint: When the output voltage of the generator L terminal is low, the charge warning light will illuminate. This code also ap-

pears when there is a short in the generator L terminal monitor circuit, but not if there is a broken wire in that circuit.
If the scan tool service data displays No. 35, this problem code is output.

NOTE
If the engine is stopped, this code will be output, even if the situation is normal, so the following inspection should only be carried out if the code is output while the engine is running.

```
┌─────────────────────────┐
│ Remove the ABS-ECU con-  │
│ nector, and inspect the  │
│ harness side connector.  │
└─────────────────────────┘
             │
             ▼
┌─────────────────────────┐   No   ┌─────────────────────────┐
│ When the ignition key is in │──────▶│ Generator is faulty, or there │
│ the "ON" position, does a   │       │ is a short in the harness     │
│ voltage of 7V or more show  │       │ between the ABS-ECU and       │
│ between terminal No. 61 and │       │ the generator.                │
│ the ground?                 │       └─────────────────────────┘
└─────────────────────────┘                     │
             │ Yes                               ▼
             │                    ┌─────────────────────────┐
             │                    │ Repair the harness or replace │
             │                    │ the generator.                │
             │                    └─────────────────────────┘
             ▼
┌─────────────────────────┐        ┌─────────────────────┐
│ Inside of ABS-ECU is faulty │──────▶│ Replace the ABS-ECU. │
└─────────────────────────┘        └─────────────────────┘
```

MT4029100106000X

Fig. 32 Code 35: Generator Output Voltage. 1996 Diamante

E-9	When diagnostic trouble codes No. 41, No. 42, No. 43, No. 44, No. 45 or No. 46 are displayed

Comment: The ABS-ECU normally monitors the solenoid valve drive circuit. If there is no current flowing to the solenoid when the solenoid is ON, or the current continues to flow to the solenoid even when

the solenoid is OFF, the ABS-ECU diagnoses a broken wire or short in the solenoid coil or a broken wire or short in the harness, and this problem code is output.

```
┌─────────────────────────┐
│ Remove the hydraulic unit 9 │
│ pin connector and the 1 pin │
│ connector, and inspect the  │
│ hydraulic unit side connec- │
│ tor.                        │
└─────────────────────────┘
             │
             ▼
┌─────────────────────────┐   No   ┌─────────────────────┐
│ Is the resistance value of the │──────▶│ Replace the          │
│ solenoid valve that shows a    │       │ hydraulic unit       │
│ problem code within the        │       └─────────────────────┘
│ standard range?                │
│ Standard value: 2.8–3.4 kΩ     │
└─────────────────────────┘
             │ Yes
             ▼
┌─────────────────────────┐
│ Connect the hydraulic unit 9 │
│ pin connector and the 1 pin  │
│ connector, and remove and    │
│ inspect the ABS-ECU con-     │
│ nector.                      │
└─────────────────────────┘
             │
             ▼
┌─────────────────────────┐   No   ┌─────────────────────────┐
│ If the resistance value of the │──────▶│ Broken harness wire or   │
│ solenoid valve that shows a    │       │ short in the solenoid    │
│ problem code is measured       │       │ valve that has a re-     │
│ between the ABS-ECU connector  │       │ sistance value outside of │
│ and the hydraulic unit 1 pin   │       │ the standard value range. │
│ connector (No. 101) terminal,  │       └─────────────────────────┘
│ is the value within the stan-  │
│ dard range?                    │
│ Standard value: 2.8–3.4 kΩ     │
└─────────────────────────┘
             │ Yes                          │
             │                              ▼
             │                    ┌─────────────────────┐
             │                    │ Repair the harness.  │
             │                    └─────────────────────┘
             ▼
┌─────────────────────────┐        ┌─────────────────────┐
│ Broken harness wire or short │──────▶│ Replace the ABS-ECU. │
│ in the ABS-ECU interface.    │       └─────────────────────┘
└─────────────────────────┘
```

MT4029100108000X

Fig. 34 Codes 41, 42, 43, 44, 45 & 46: Solenoid Valve Drive Circuit. 1996 Diamante

E-8	When diagnostic trouble code No. 37 is displayed

Comment: This indicates that the power source pressure for the hydraulic unit is low. If the pressure returns to standard value or above, this problem code will not be output.

Remedy: While the engine is idling, wait for the pressure to return (motor and pump drive). If the problem continues after approximately 35 seconds or more have passed, the problem code will change over to No. 61 (inspect according to Inspection chart D-12).

Hint: This problem code will be output even if there is a broken wire in the LPWS input harness. (ON problem [short] is not detected.)
LPWS: Low pressure warning switch

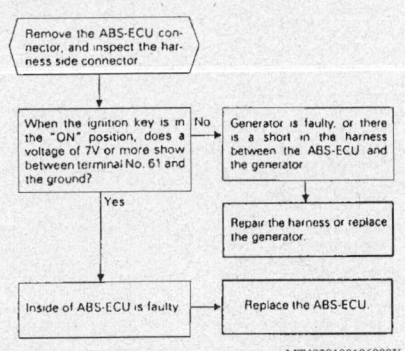

LPWS ON — ABS warning light is not illuminated
LPWS OFF — ABS warning light is illuminated

A   B

Point A 12.5 ± 1.0 MPa (1,778 ± 142 psi)
Point B 16.0 MPa (2,276 psi or less)

MT4029100107000X

Fig. 33 Code 37: Power Source Pressure For Hydraulic Unit Low. 1996 Diamante

E-10	When diagnostic trouble code No. 51 is displayed

Comment: During the initial check when the ignition switch is turned to "ON", if power is being supplied to the solenoid when the valve relay is OFF, the ABS-ECU diagno-

ses a melted relay contact or a short in the valve relay drive circuit, and the problem code No. 51 is output.

```
┌─────────────────────────┐   No   ┌─────────────────────┐
│ Is the valve relay normal?  │──────▶│ Valve relay is faulty. │
└─────────────────────────┘        └─────────────────────┘
             │ Yes                           │
             ▼                               ▼
┌─────────────────────────┐        ┌─────────────────────┐
│ Remove and inspect the     │        │ Replace the valve relay. │
│ ABS-ECU 26 pin connector.  │        └─────────────────────┘
└─────────────────────────┘
             │
             ▼
┌─────────────────────────┐   No   ┌─────────────────────────┐
│ Is the resistance value be-  │──────▶│ Short in the harness between │
│ tween the ABS-ECU harness    │       │ the ABS-ECU and the valve    │
│ side connector terminal No.  │       │ relay (coil).                │
│ 8 and the ground ∞Ω?         │       └─────────────────────────┘
└─────────────────────────┘                     │
             │ Yes                               ▼
             │                    ┌─────────────────────┐
             │                    │ Repair the harness.  │
             │                    └─────────────────────┘
             ▼
┌─────────────────────┐        ┌─────────────────────┐
│ ABS-ECU is faulty.   │──────▶│ Replace the ABS-ECU. │
└─────────────────────┘        └─────────────────────┘
```

MT4029100109000X

Fig. 35 Code 51: Valve Relay Drive Circuit. 1996 Diamante

E-11	When diagnostic trouble code No. 52 or No. 53 is displayed

Comment: During the initial check when the ignition switch is turned to "ON", if power is not being supplied to the solenoid when the valve relay is ON, the ABS-ECU diagnoses an OFF problem in the valve relay (not turned ON), and outputs the problem code No. 52. Also, when the motor pump receives a signal to turn ON and voltage at the motor monitor is LOW, the ABS-ECU outputs the problem code No. 53.

Hint: Because the same circuit is used as the power supply circuit for the valve relay and the motor relay, inspection of the circuit between the ABS fusible link (6)

and the valve relay is necessary for both code Nos. 52 and 53.
However, if the ABS system stops functioning after the sound of the motor is heard, or if it stops functioning when the motor relay is force-driven by the scan tool actuator test (No. 08), the power supply and the valve relay system can be considered normal.

Caution
As there is a problem that the accumulator pressure could become higher than necessary, resulting in a bad effect on the system, it is best not to carry out actuator test No. 8 if possible.

MT4029100110010X

Fig. 36 Codes 52 & 53: Valve Relay Off & Motor Monitor Low (Part 1 of 3). 1996 Diamante

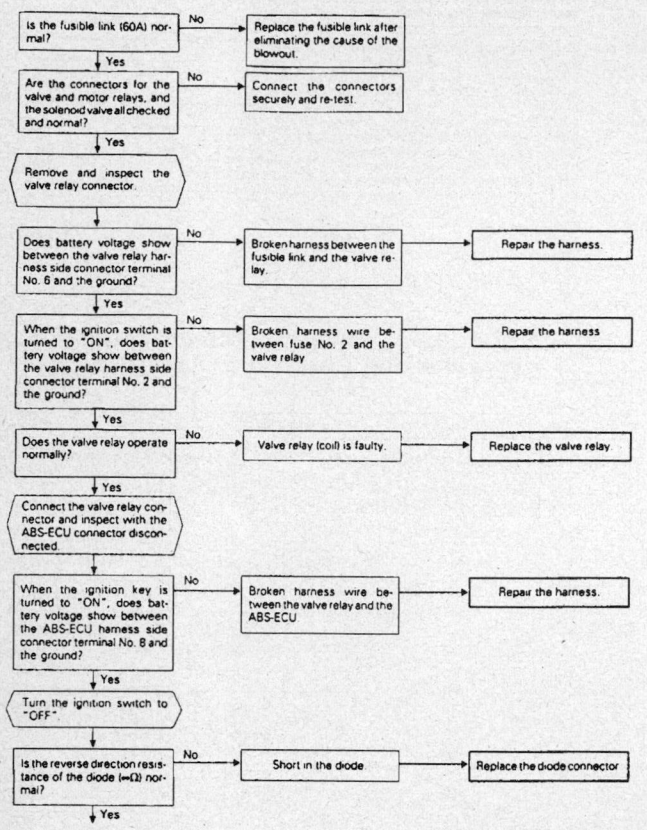

Fig. 36   Codes 52 & 53: Valve Relay Off & Motor Monitor Low (Part 2 of 3). 1996 Diamante

MT4029100110020X

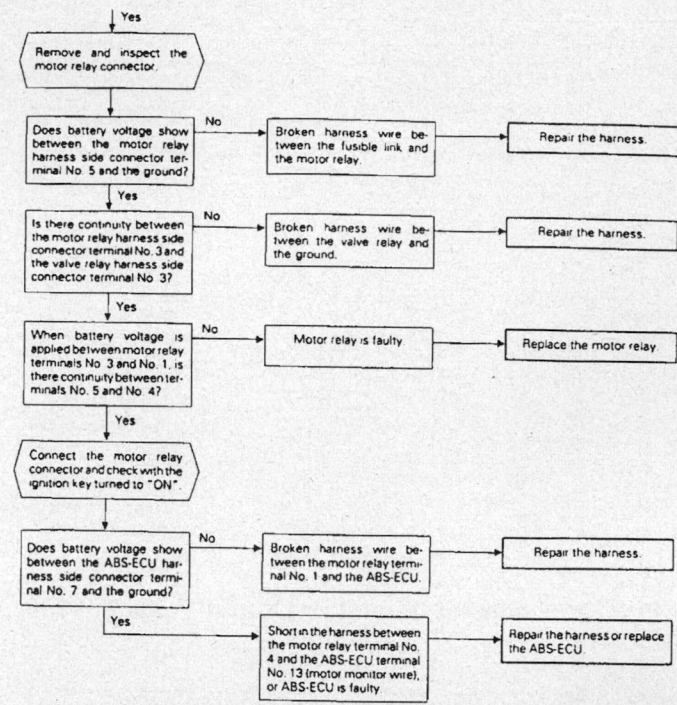

Fig. 36   Codes 52 & 53: Valve Relay Off & Motor Monitor Low (Part 3 of 3). 1996 Diamante

MT4029100110030X

E-12 | When diagnostic trouble code No. 54 is displayed

Comment: When the pump motor receives a signal to turn OFF and the motor monitor is ON, if a melted contact, etc. is diagnosed in the motor relay, the ABS-ECU outputs the problem code No. 54.

Hint: Because the motor monitor wire is pulled up into the ABS-ECU by the IG power, this problem code is output if there is a broken wire in the harness, even if the motor relay and the motor are normal.

Caution
If there is a melted contact in the motor relay, the motor will keep turning, even if the ignition witch is turned to OFF. In such a case, immediately remove the fusible link (60A) or disconnect the hydraulic unit 2 pin connector. Excessive running of the motor will cause a reduction in the efficiency of the hydraulic unit solenoid valve.

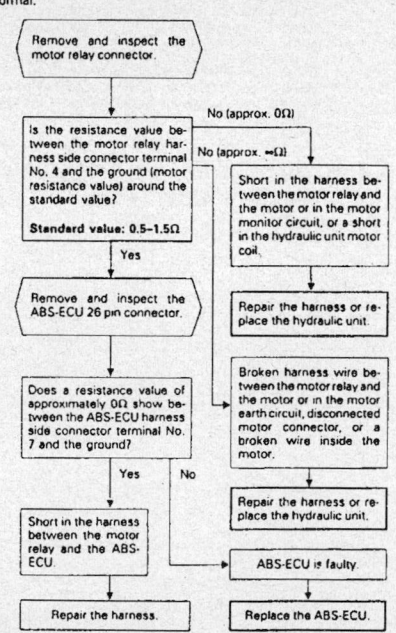

MT4029100111000X

Fig. 37   Code 54: Motor Relay. 1996 Diamante

E-13 | When diagnostic trouble code No. 61 is displayed

Comment: The ABS-ECU outputs this problem code No. 61 in the following cases if there is a fault inside the hydraulic unit.

(1) Even when the pump motor operates for 34 seconds due to demand of the pressure control switch, and then alternately switches OFF for 8.5 seconds and ON for 8.5 seconds, repeating this intermittent operation 4 times (total approx. 1 minute 40 seconds), the accumulator does not recover pressure equal to the pressure control switch standard amount or higher.

(2) When the low pressure warning switch outputs OFF (low pressure) for approximately 35 seconds after the engine is started.

(3) When low pressure warning switch ON (high pressure) is detected after the engine is started, and then the low pressure warning switch outputs OFF (low pressure) for 10 seconds or longer.

(4) When the pressure control switch is ON (high pressure side) and the low pressure warning switch is OFF (low pressure side).

Hint: After starting the engine, if the ABS warning light illuminates after the motor has been operating intermittently as in (1) above, it is clear that this problem code is output under the conditions in (1) due to faulty pump pressure accumulation.

After starting the engine, if the scan tool service data displays No. 37 (ON [high pressure side]), it is clear that this problem code is output under the conditions in (1)

REMEDY FOR FAULTY PUMP PRESSURE ACCUMULATION

1. Operation to expel N₂ (nitrogen) gas
For a vehicle that hasn't been used for a long period, the high pressure N₂ (nitrogen) gas that is stored inside the hydraulic unit accumulator passes through the rubber diaphragm and collects around the hydraulic unit pump, and this prevents oil pressure from building up even if the hydraulic unit pump is turning, so the following procedure should be carried out to expel the N₂ (nitrogen) that has collected around the pump.

(1) When Using The Scan Tool
With the brake pedal depressed, carry out scan tool actuator tests No. 04 – 06 in the following way (The collected gas is leaked into the reservoir by means of the forced actuation of the solenoid valve.)

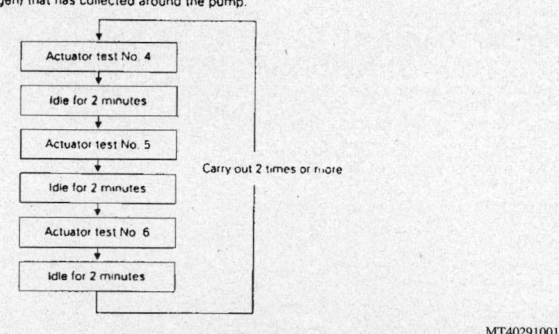

MT4029100112010X

Fig. 38   Code 61: Hydraulic Unit (Part 1 of 2). 1996 Diamante

(2) When Not Using The Scan Tool
Start the engine, leave it idling for 2 minutes, and then stop the engine.
Repeat this 10 times or more.
(The collected gas is leaked into the reservoir in the same way as when using the scan tool, by the repeated short-term operation of the solenoid valve during the initial check.)

INSPECTION OF PRESSURE SWITCHES (WHEN THE MOTOR DOES NOT OPERATE AFTER THE ENGINE HAS BEEN TURNED ON)

2. After carrying out the above, if it is normal (No abnormality is detected in the above cases (1) to (3)], carry out a normal bleeding of the brake lines.
3. After carrying out the above, if the motor operates intermittently and this problem code is output, the motor or pump operation is faulty, so replace the hydraulic unit.

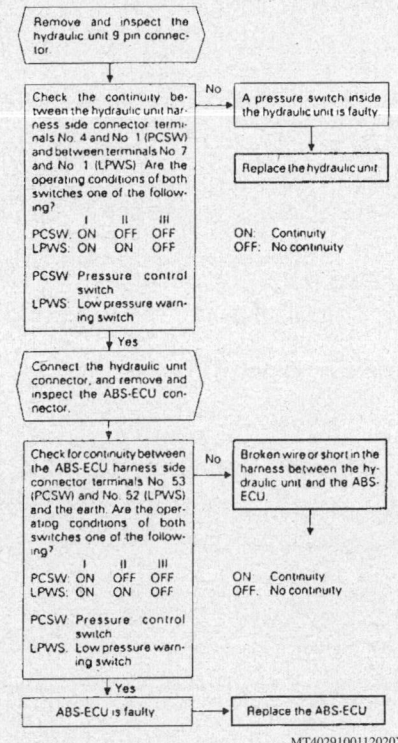

Fig. 38   Code 61: Hydraulic Unit (Part 2 of 2). 1996 Diamante

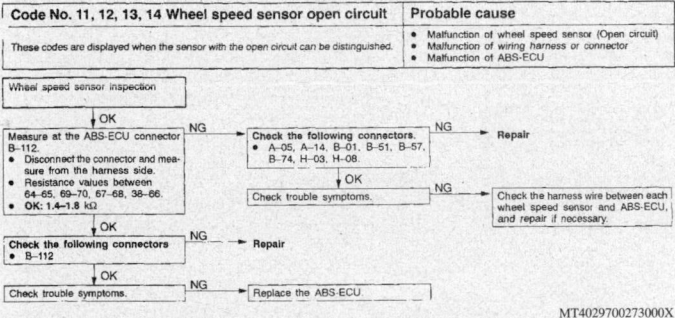

Fig. 40   Codes 11, 12, 13 & 14: Wheel Speed Sensors. 1997–98 Diamante

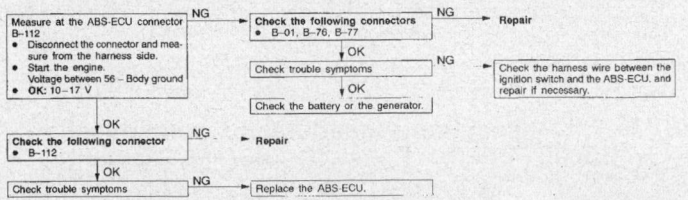

Fig. 42   Code 16: Power Supply System. 1997–98 Diamante

E-14	When diagnostic trouble code No. 62 is displayed

Comment: Diagnostic trouble code No. 62 is a problem code that is output when the ABS is unable to operate for a long period of time. However, it is possible that the problem could be caused not only by a faulty hydraulic unit, but also by a malfunctioning wheel speed sensor.

Caution
The problem code No. 62 is detected in the following cases, even if the ABS system is normal.
• If the parking brake is not fully released, or if the brakes are dragging while driving on snow or ice.
• When driving with left and right tyres of different sizes (difference in tyre diameter or uneven wear).
• When driving for a long period of time on roads with low friction coefficients, such as ice-covered roads.

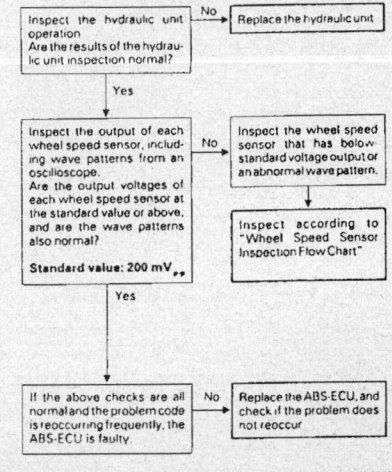

Fig. 39   Code 62: Hydraulic Unit Or Wheel Speed Sensor. 1996 Diamante

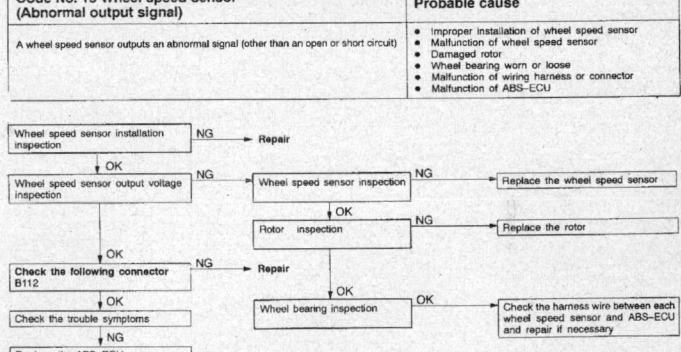

Fig. 41   Code 15: Wheel Speed Sensor Circuit. 1997–98 Diamante

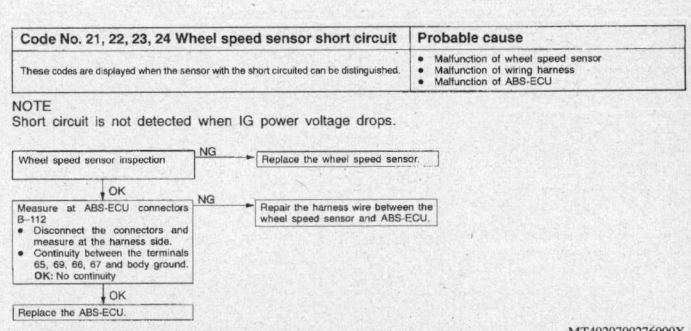

Fig. 43   Codes 21, 22, 23 & 24: Wheel Speed Sensor Circuit. 1997–98 Diamante

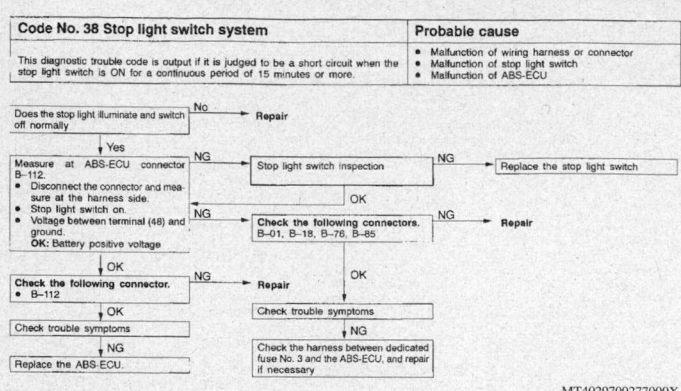

Fig. 44   Code 38: Stop Light Switch System. 1997–98 Diamante

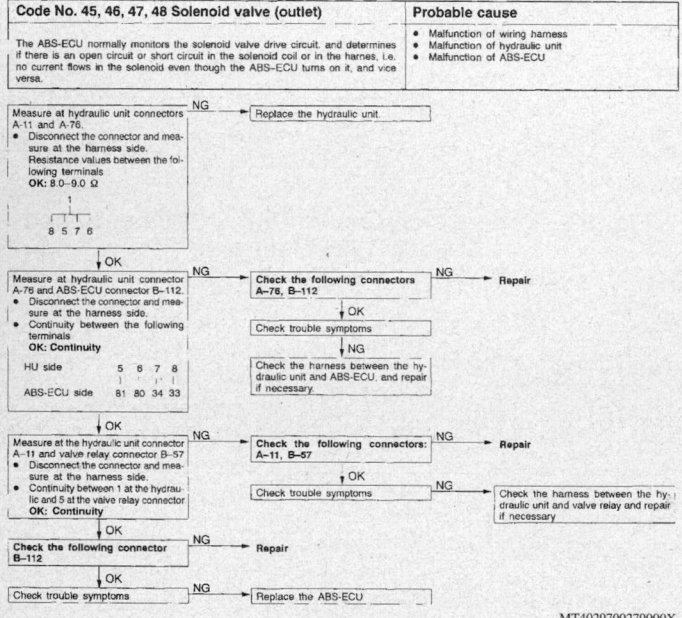

Fig. 46   Codes 45, 46, 47 & 48: Solenoid Valve. 1997–98 Diamante

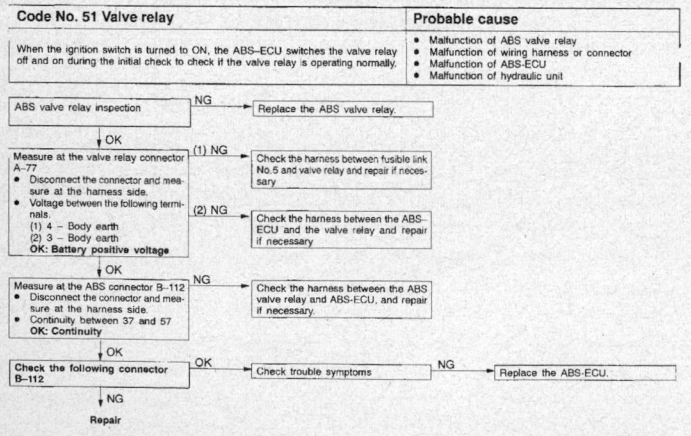

Fig. 47   Code 51: Valve Relay. 1997–98 Diamante

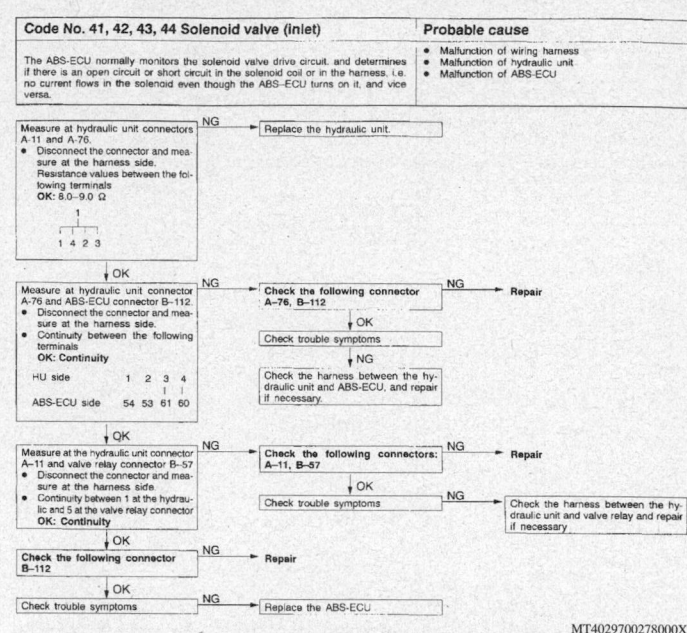

Fig. 45   Codes 41, 42, 43 & 44: Solenoid Valve. 1997–98 Diamante

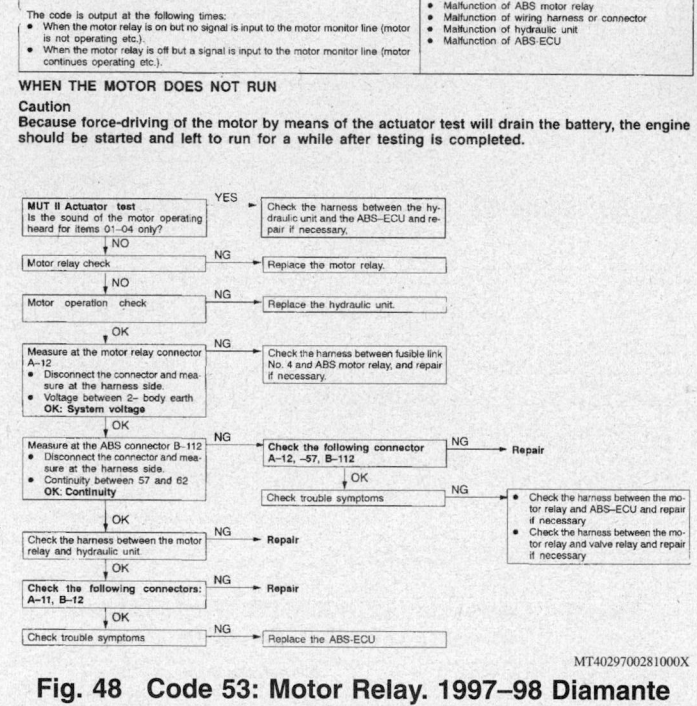

Fig. 48   Code 53: Motor Relay. 1997–98 Diamante

Communication with scan tool is not possible. (Communication with all systems is not possible.)	Probable cause
The reason is probably a defect in the power supply system (including ground) for the diagnostic line.	• Malfunction of connector • Malfunction of harness

MT4029700309000X

Fig. 49   Inspection Procedure 1: Communication w/Scan Tool Not Possible. 1997–98 Diamante

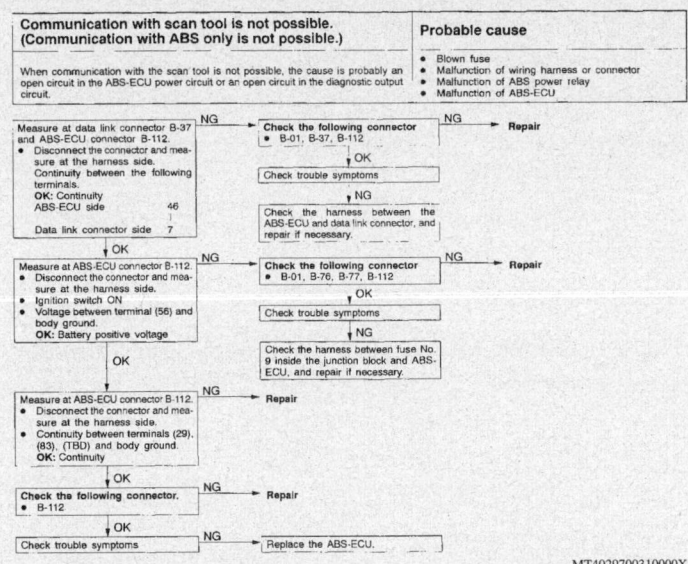

Fig. 50 Inspection Procedure 2: Communication w/ABS Not Possible. 1997–98 Diamante

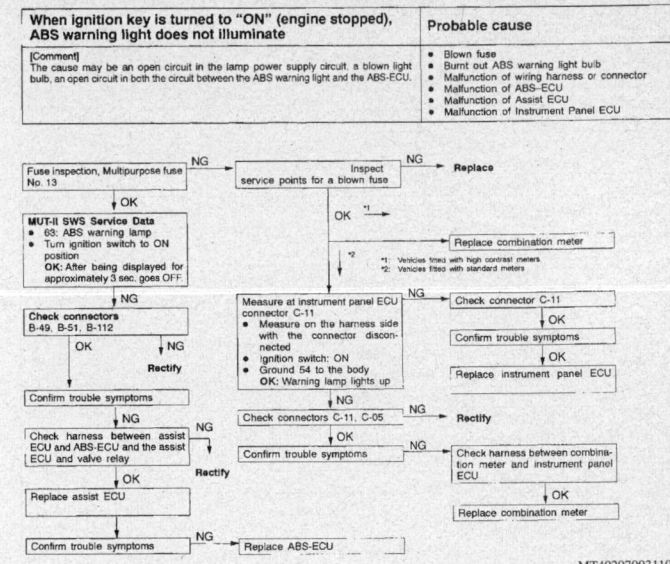

Fig. 51 Inspection procedure 3: ABS light does not illuminate w/key on. 1997–98 Diamante

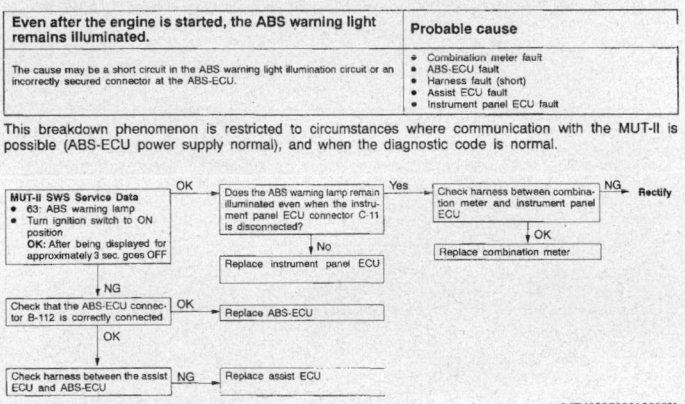

Fig. 52 Inspection Procedure 4: ABS Light Remains Illuminated w/Engine Running. 1997–98 Diamante

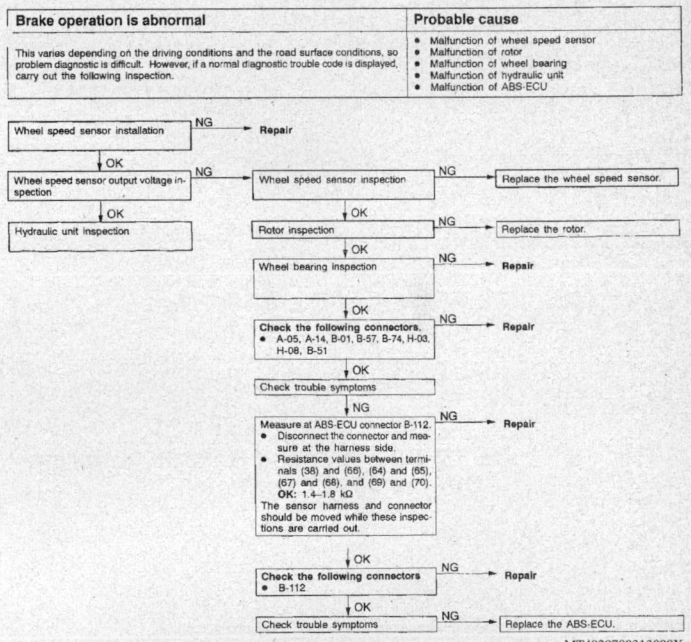

Fig. 53 Inspection Procedure 5: Brake Operation Abnormal. 1997–98 Diamante

DIAGNOSTIC TROUBLE CODE NO.	INSPECTION ITEM		DETECTION CONDITIONS
11	Front right wheel speed sensor		
12	Front left wheel speed sensor	Open circuit	B, C
13	Rear right wheel speed sensor		
14	Rear left wheel speed sensor		
15	Wheel speed sensor output signal abnormal		A, B
16	Power supply system		A, B, C
21	Front right wheel speed sensor		
22	Front left wheel speed sensor	Short circuit	B, C
23	Rear right wheel speed sensor		
24	Rear left wheel speed sensor		
38	Stop light switch system		B, C
41	Front right solenoid valve (inlet)		
42	Front left solenoid valve (inlet)		B, C
43	Rear right solenoid valve (inlet)		
44	Rear left solenoid valve (inlet)		
45	Front right solenoid valve (outlet)		
46	Front left solenoid valve (outlet)		B, C
47	Rear right solenoid valve (outlet)		
48	Rear left solenoid valve (outlet)		
51	Valve relay		A, B, C
53	Motor relay		B
63	ABS–ECU		A, B, C

Detection conditions

A: During system check immediately after starting
B: While ABS control is not operating while driving
C: While ABS control is operating

MT4029900419000X

Fig. 54 Diagnostic Trouble Code Inspection Chart. 1999 Diamante

---

Code No. 15 Wheel speed sensor (Abnormal output signal)	Probable cause
[Comment] A wheel speed sensor outputs an abnormal signal (other than an open or short circuit)	• Improper installation of wheel speed sensor • Malfunction of wheel speed sensor • Damaged rotor • Wheel bearing worn or loose • Malfunction of wiring harness or connector • Malfunction of ABS-ECU

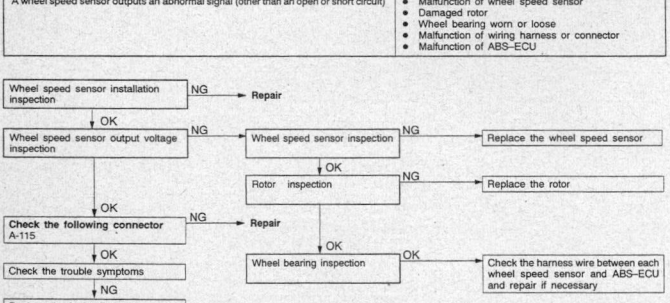

MT4029900421000X

Fig. 56 Code 15: Wheel Speed Sensor Abnormal Output. 1999 Diamante

---

Code No. 21, 22, 23, 24 Wheel speed sensor short circuit	Probable cause
[Comment] These codes are displayed when the sensor with the short circuit can be distinguished.	• Malfunction of wheel speed sensor • Malfunction of wiring harness • Malfunction of ABS-ECU

NOTE
Short circuit is not detected when IG power voltage drops.

MT4029900423000X

Fig. 58 Codes 21, 22, 23 & 24: Wheel Speed Sensor Short Circuit. 1999 Diamante

---

Code No. 11, 12, 13, 14 Wheel speed sensor open circuit	Probable cause
[Comment] These codes are displayed when the sensor with the open circuit can be distinguished.	• Malfunction of wheel speed sensor (Open circuit) • Malfunction of wiring harness or connector • Malfunction of ABS-ECU

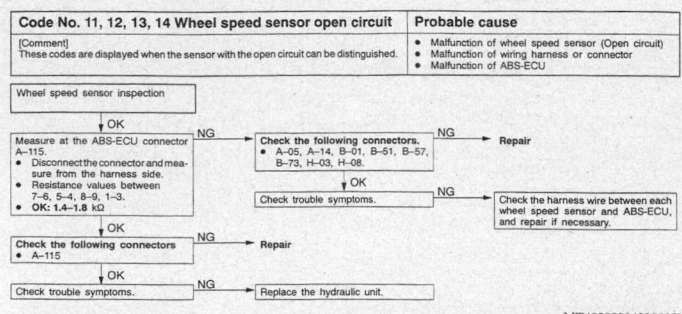

MT4029900420000X

Fig. 55 Codes 11, 12, 13 & 14: Wheel Speed Sensor Open Circuit. 1999 Diamante

---

Code No. 16 Power supply system	Probable cause
[Comment] This diagnostic trouble code is output when the ABS-ECU power voltage is outside the standard value. Furthermore, if the voltage returns to normal, this diagnostic trouble code will not be output.	• Malfunction of wiring harness or connector. • Malfunction of battery or alternator • Malfunction of ABS-ECU

Caution
If the battery voltage drops during inspection, this code will be output as a current problem, and correct diagnostic of the problem cannot be made.
Before carrying out the following inspection, check the battery condition, and recharge it if necessary.

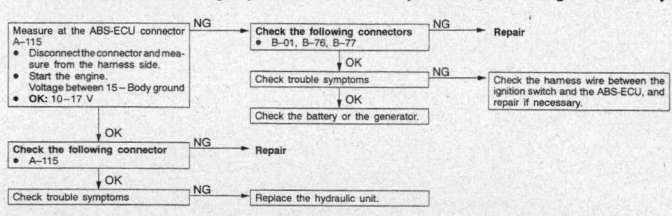

MT4029900422000X

Fig. 57 Code 16: Power Supply System. 1999 Diamante

Code No. 38 Stop light switch system	Probable cause
[Comment] This diagnostic trouble code is output if it is judged to be a short circuit when the stop light switch is ON for a continuous period of 15 minutes or more.	• Malfunction of wiring harness or connector • Malfunction of stop light switch • Malfunction of ABS-ECU

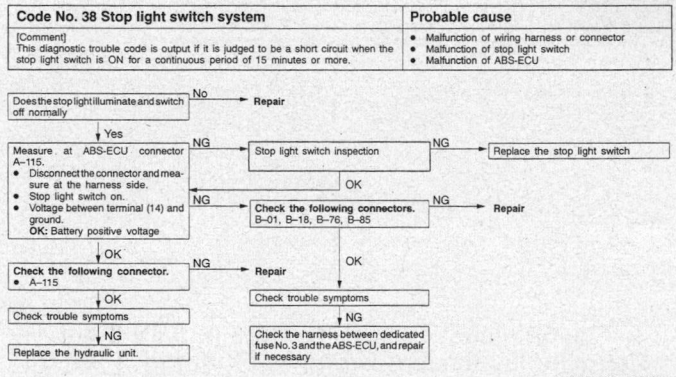

MT4029900424000X

Fig. 59 Code 38: Stop Lamp Switch System. 1999 Diamante

Code No. 41, 42, 43, 44 Solenoid valve (inlet)	Probable cause
[Comment] The ABS-ECU normally monitors the solenoid valve drive circuit. and determines if there is an open circuit or short circuit in the solenoid coil, i.e. no current flows in the solenoid even though the ABS-ECU turns it on, and vice versa.	• Malfunction of wiring harness • Malfunction of hydraulic unit • Malfunction of ABS-ECU
Refer to Troubleshooting procedure for DTC No. 16	

MT4029900425000X

Fig. 60 Codes 41, 42, 43 & 44: Solenoid Inlet Valve. 1999 Diamante

Code No. 45, 46, 47, 48 Solenoid valve (outlet)	Probable cause
[Comment] The ABS-ECU normally monitors the solenoid valve drive circuit, and determines if there is an open circuit or short circuit in the solenoid coil or in the harness, i.e. no current flows in the solenoid even though the ABS-ECU turns it on, and vice versa.	• Malfunction of wiring harness • Malfunction of hydraulic unit • Malfunction of ABS-ECU
Refer to Troubleshooting procedure for DTC No. 16	

MT4029900426000X

Fig. 61 Codes 45, 46, 47 & 48: Solenoid Outlet Valve. 1999 Diamante

Code No. 51 Valve relay	Probable cause
[Comment] When the ignition switch is turned to ON, the ABS-ECU switches the valve relay off and on during the initial check to check if the valve relay is operating normally.	• Malfunction of ABS valve relay • Malfunction of wiring harness or connector • Malfunction of ABS-ECU • Malfunction of hydraulic unit
Refer to Troubleshooting procedure for DTC No. 16	

MT4029900427000X

Fig. 62   Code 51: Valve Relay. 1999 Diamante

Code No. 53 Motor relay, motor	Probable cause
[Comment] The code is output at the following times: • When the motor relay is on but no signal is input to the motor monitor line (motor is not operating etc.). • When the motor relay is off but a signal is input to the motor monitor line (motor continues operating etc.).	• Malfunction of ABS motor relay • Malfunction of wiring harness or connector • Malfunction of hydraulic unit • Malfunction of ABS-ECU
Refer to Troubleshooting procedure for DTC No. 16	

MT4029900428000X

Fig. 63   Code 53: Motor Relay. 1999 Diamante

TROUBLE SYMPTOM		INSPECTION PROCEDURE NO.
Communication with scan tool is not possible.	Communication with all systems is not possible.	1
	Communication with ABS only is not possible.	2
When the ignition key is turned to "ON" (engine stopped), the ABS warning light does not illuminate.		3
After the engine starts, the light remains illuminated.		4
Faulty ABS operation	Unequal braking power on both sides	5
	Insufficient braking power	
	ABS operates under normal braking conditions	
	ABS operates before vehicle stops under normal braking conditions	
	Large brake pedal vibration when ABS operates	
	Large brake pedal vibration (Caution 2.)	–

MT4029900429000X

Fig. 64   Inspection Procedure Chart. 1999 Diamante

Communication with scan tool is not possible. (Communication with all systems is not possible.)	Probable cause
[Comment] The reason is probably a defect in the power supply system (including ground) for the diagnostic line.	• Malfunction of connector • Malfunction of harness

MT4029900430000X

Fig. 65   Inspection Procedure 1: Communication w/Scan Tool Not Possible. 1999 Diamante

Communication with scan tool is not possible. (Communication with ABS only is not possible.)	Probable cause
[Comment] When communication with the scan tool is not possible, the cause is probably an open circuit in the ABS-ECU power circuit or an open circuit in the diagnostic output circuit.	• Blown fuse • Malfunction of wiring harness or connector • Malfunction of ABS power relay • Malfunction of ABS-ECU

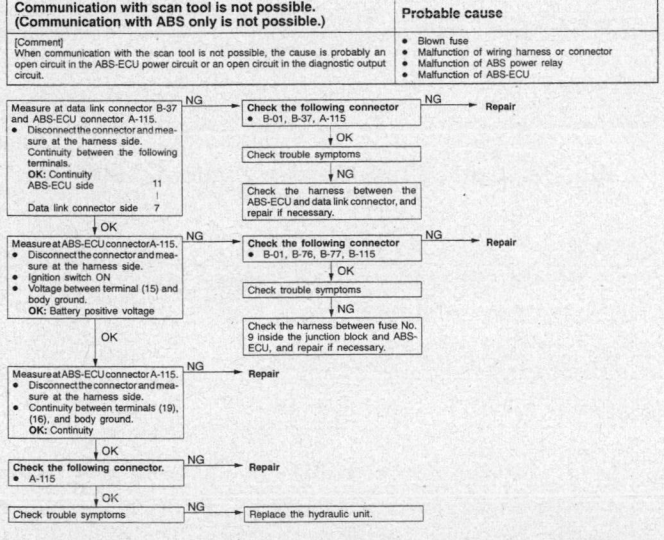

MT4029900431000X

Fig. 66   Inspection Procedure 2: Communication w/Scan Tool Not Possible. 1999 Diamante

When ignition key is turned to "ON" (engine stopped), ABS warning light does not illuminate	Probable cause
[Comment] The cause may be an open circuit in the lamp power supply circuit, a blown light bulb, an open circuit in both the circuit between the ABS warning light and the ABS-ECU and the Assist-ECU or between the Assist-ECU and the warning light.	• Blown fuse • Burnt out ABS warning light bulb • Malfunction of wiring harness or connector • Malfunction of ABS-ECU • Malfunction of Assist-ECU • Malfunction of Instrument Panel ECU

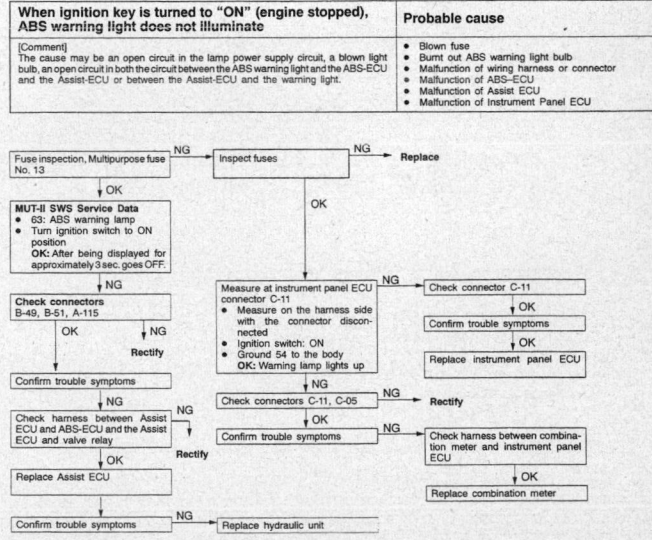

MT4029900432000X

Fig. 67   Inspection Procedure 3: ABS Warning Lamp Does Not Illuminate w/Key ON. 1999 Diamante

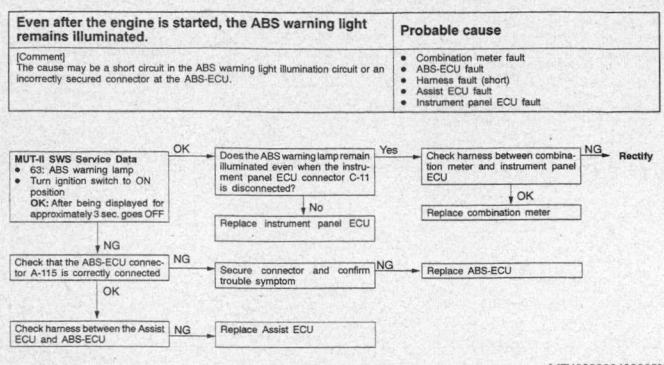

Fig. 68 Inspection Procedure 4: ABS Warning Lamp Remains Illuminated w/Engine Running. 1999 Diamante

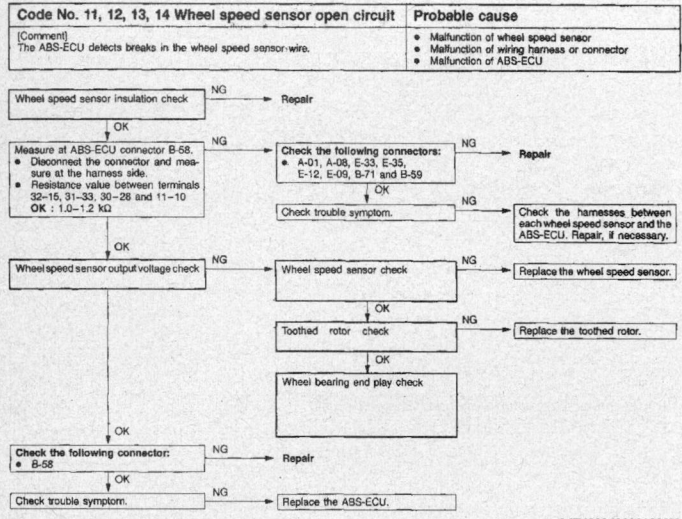

Fig. 70 Codes 11, 12, 13 & 14: Wheel Speed Sensor Open Circuit. 1996–97 Eclipse AWD

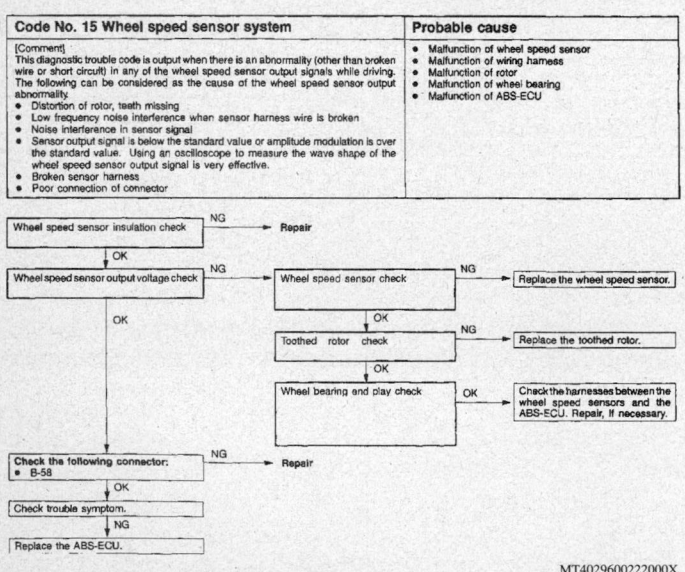

Fig. 71 Code 15: Wheel Speed Sensor System. 1996–97 Eclipse AWD

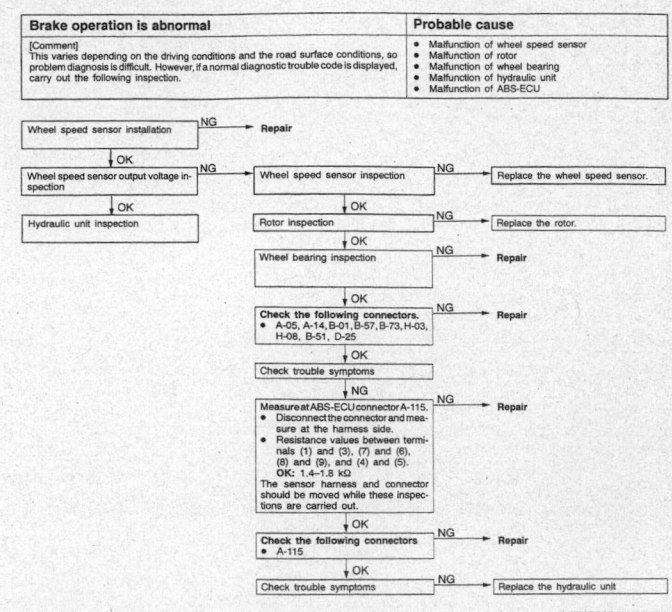

Fig. 69 Inspection Procedure 5: Abnormal Brake Operation. 1999 Diamante

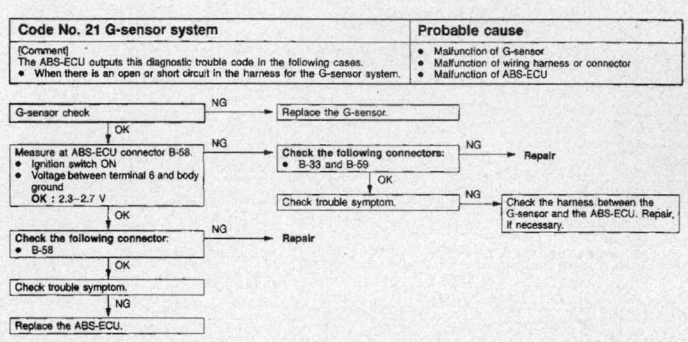

Fig. 72 Code 21: G-Sensor System. 1996–97 Eclipse AWD

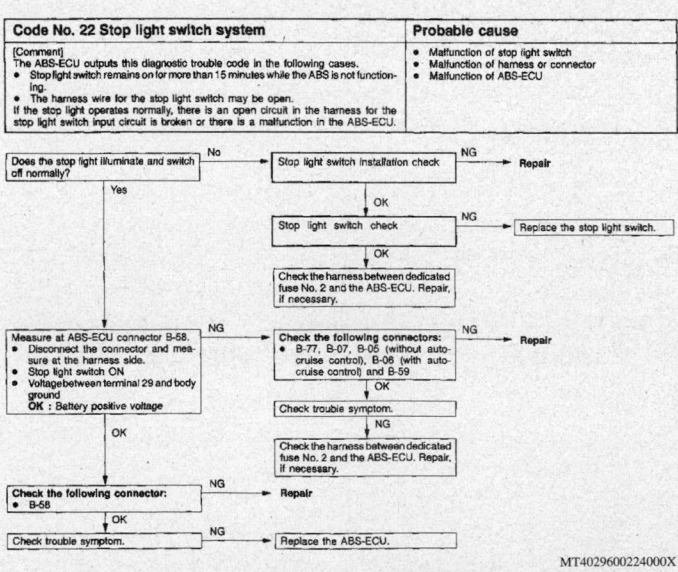

Fig. 73 Code 22: Stop Light Switch System. 1996–97 Eclipse AWD

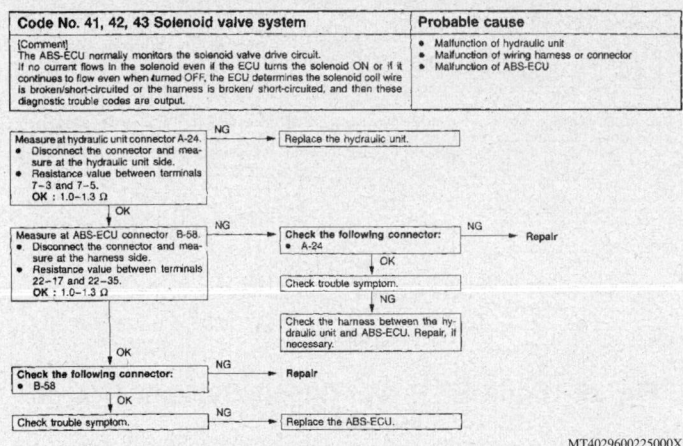

Code No. 41, 42, 43 Solenoid valve system	Probable cause
[Comment] The ABS-ECU normally monitors the solenoid valve drive circuit. If no current flows in the solenoid even if the ECU turns the solenoid ON or if it continues to flow even when turned OFF, the ECU determines the solenoid coil wire is broken/short-circuited or the harness is broken/short-circuited, and then these diagnostic trouble codes are output.	• Malfunction of hydraulic unit • Malfunction of wiring harness or connector • Malfunction of ABS-ECU

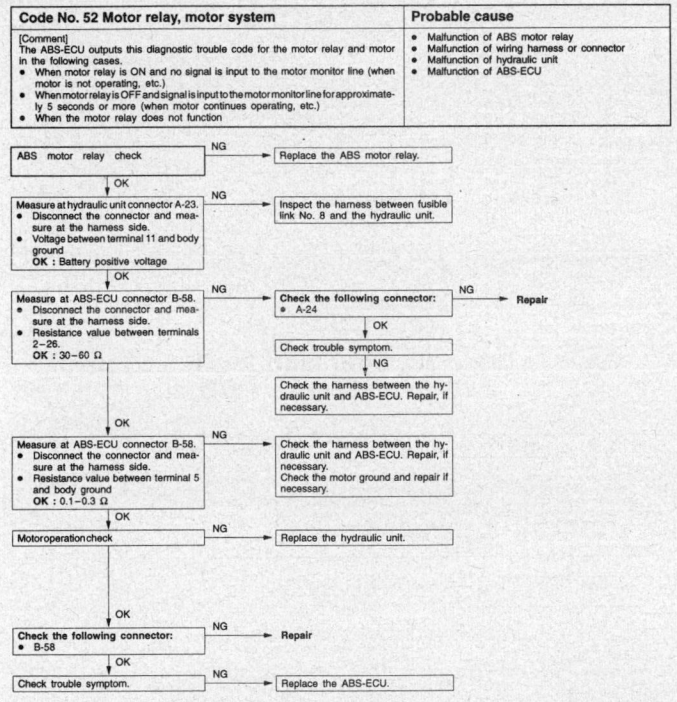

Fig. 74 Codes 41, 42 & 43: Solenoid Valve System. 1996–97 Eclipse AWD

Code No. 51 Valve relay system	Probable cause
[Comment] When the ignition switch is turned ON, the ABS-ECU switches the valve relay OFF and ON for an initial check, compares the voltage of the signal to the valve relay and valve power monitor line voltage to check whether the valve relay operation is normal. In addition, normally it monitors whether or not there is power in the valve power monitor line since the valve relay is normally ON. If the supply of power to the valve power monitor line is interrupted, this diagnostic trouble code will be output.	• Malfunction of ABS valve relay • Malfunction of wiring harness or connector • Malfunction of hydraulic unit • Malfunction of ABS-ECU

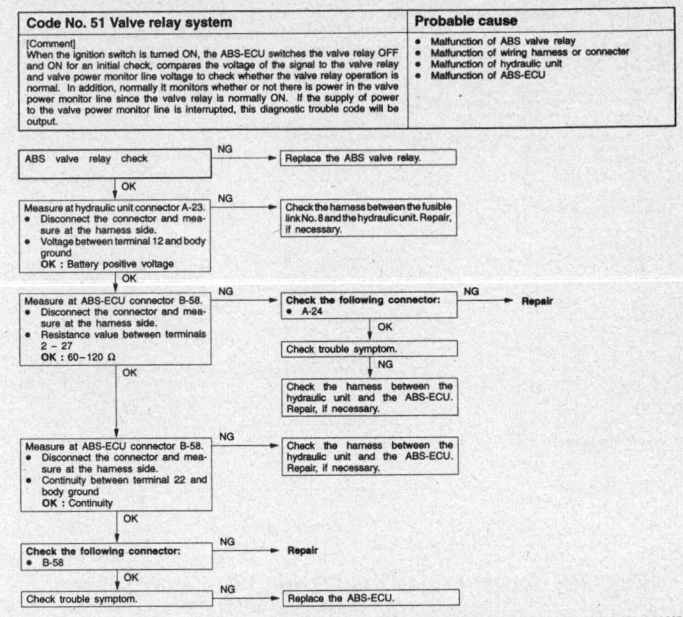

Fig. 75 Code 51: Valve Relay System. 1996–97 Eclipse AWD

Code No. 52 Motor relay, motor system	Probable cause
[Comment] The ABS-ECU outputs this diagnostic trouble code for the motor relay and motor in the following cases. • When motor relay is ON and no signal is input to the motor monitor line (when motor is not operating, etc.) • When motor relay is OFF and signal is input to the motor monitor line for approximately 5 seconds or more (when motor continues operating, etc.) • When the motor relay does not function	• Malfunction of ABS motor relay • Malfunction of wiring harness or connector • Malfunction of hydraulic unit • Malfunction of ABS-ECU

Fig. 76 Code 52: Motor Relay, Motor System. 1996–97 Eclipse AWD

Code No. 11, 12, 13, 14 Wheel speed sensor open circuit	Probable cause
[Comment] The ABS-ECU detects breaks in the wheel speed sensor wire.	• Malfunction of wheel speed sensor • Malfunction of wiring harness or connector • Malfunction of ABS-ECU

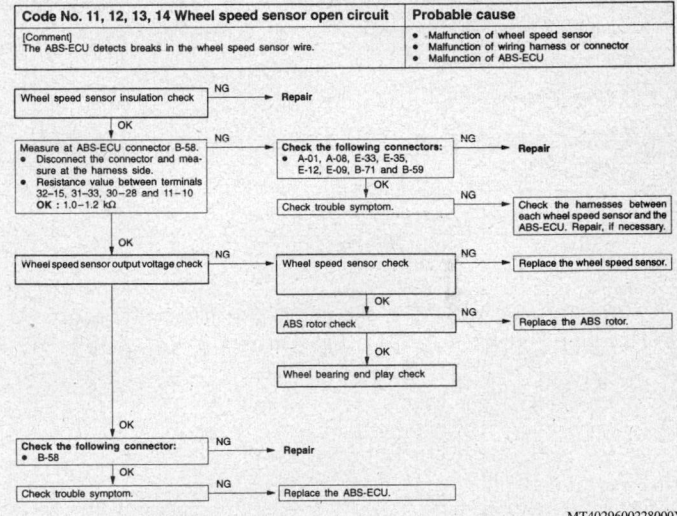

Fig. 77 Codes 11, 12, 13 & 14: Wheel Speed Sensor Open Circuit. 1996–97 Eclipse FWD

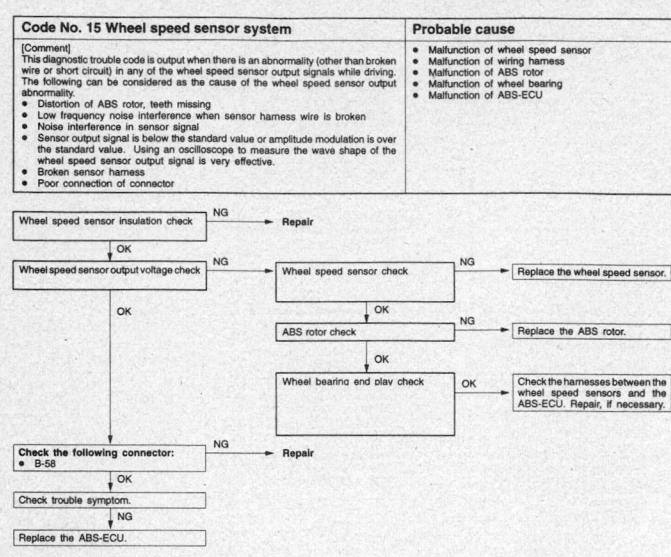

Code No. 15 Wheel speed sensor system	Probable cause
[Comment] This diagnostic trouble code is output when there is an abnormality (other than broken wire or short circuit) in any of the wheel speed sensor output signals while driving. The following can be considered as the cause of the wheel speed sensor output abnormality. • Distortion of ABS rotor, teeth missing • Low frequency noise interference when sensor harness wire is broken • Noise interference in sensor signal • Sensor output signal is below the standard value or amplitude modulation is over the standard value. Using an oscilloscope to measure the wave shape of the wheel speed sensor output signal is very effective. • Broken sensor harness • Poor connection of connector	• Malfunction of wheel speed sensor • Malfunction of wiring harness • Malfunction of ABS rotor • Malfunction of wheel bearing • Malfunction of ABS-ECU

Fig. 78   Code 15: Wheel Speed Sensor System. 1996–97 Eclipse FWD

Code No. 21, 22, 23, 24 Wheel speed sensor excessive gap or short circuit	Probable cause
[Comment] These diagnostic trouble codes are output when the detection speed of the wheel speed sensors is below the standard value.	• Improper installation of wheel speed sensor • Malfunction of wheel speed sensor (intermittent open circuit or short circuit) • Malfunction of rotor (chipped tooth or rotor not installed) • Noise interference in wheel speed sensor • Malfunction of ABS-ECU

NOTE
1. Momentary interruptions within approximately 100 ms are not detected.
2. To inspect the twisted pair wires in the wheel speed sensor, check if there is any damage to the cables, and flex the cables to check for any open circuits.

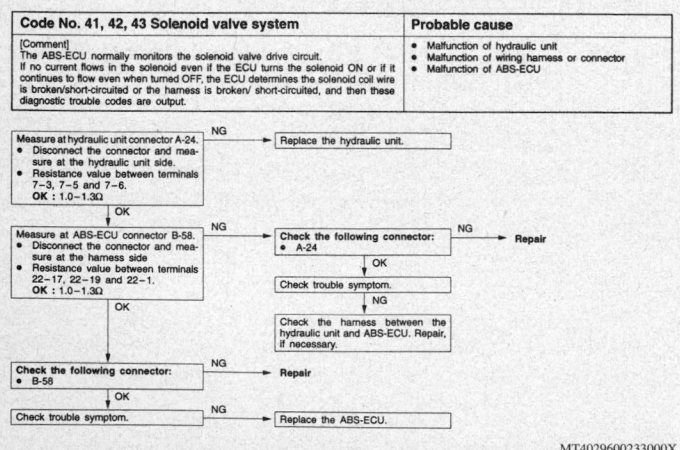

Fig. 80   Codes 21, 22, 23 & 24: Wheel Speed Sensor Excessive Gap Or Short Circuit. 1996–97 Eclipse FWD

Code No. 41, 42, 43 Solenoid valve system	Probable cause
[Comment] The ABS-ECU normally monitors the solenoid valve drive circuit. If no current flows in the solenoid even if the ECU turns the solenoid ON or it it continues to flow even when turned OFF, the ECU determines the solenoid coil wire is broken/short-circuited or the harness is broken/ short-circuited, and then these diagnostic trouble codes are output.	• Malfunction of hydraulic unit • Malfunction of wiring harness or connector • Malfunction of ABS-ECU

Fig. 82   Codes 41, 42 & 43: Solenoid Valve System. 1996–97 Eclipse FWD

Code No. 16 Power supply system	Probable cause
[Comment] This diagnostic trouble code is output when the ABS-ECU power voltage is outside the standard value. Furthermore, if the voltage returns to normal, this diagnostic trouble code will not be output.	• Malfunction of wiring harness or connector • Malfunction of battery or generator • Malfunction of ABS-ECU

Caution
If the battery voltage drops during check, this code will be output as a current problem, and correct diagnostic of the problem cannot be made.
Before carrying out the following check, check the battery condition, and recharge it if necessary.

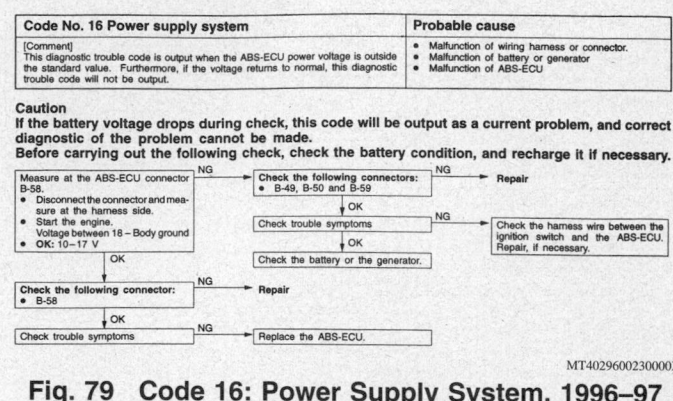

Fig. 79   Code 16: Power Supply System. 1996–97 Eclipse FWD

Code No. 38 Stop light switch system	Probable cause
[Comment] The ABS-ECU outputs this diagnostic trouble code in the following cases. • Stop light switch remains on for more than 15 minutes while the ABS is not functioning. • The harness wire for the stop light switch may be open-circuited. If the stop light operates normally, there is an open circuit in the harness for the stop light switch input circuit or there is a malfunction in the ABS-ECU.	• Malfunction of stop light switch • Malfunction of harness or connector • Malfunction of ABS-ECU

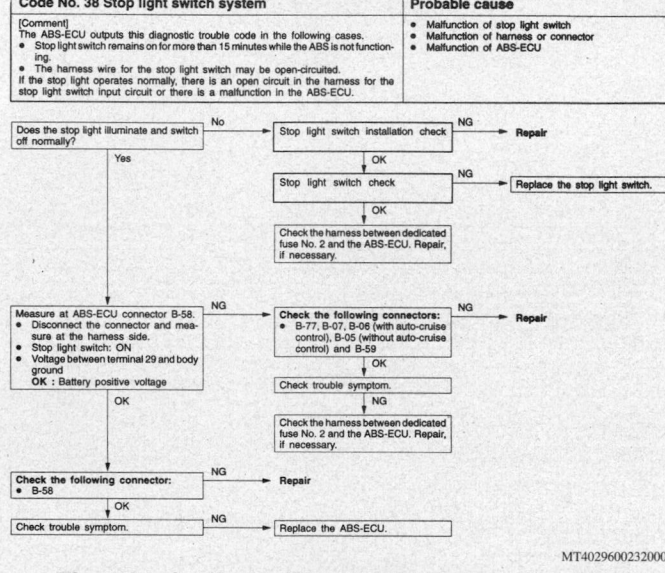

Fig. 81   Code 38: Stop Light Switch System. 1996–97 Eclipse FWD

Code No. 51 Valve relay system	Probable cause
[Comment] When the ignition switch is turned ON, the ABS-ECU switches the valve relay OFF and ON for an initial check, compares the voltage of the signal to the valve relay and valve power monitor line to check whether the valve relay operation is normal. In addition, normally it monitors whether or not there is power in the valve power monitor line since the valve relay is normally ON. If the supply of power to the valve power monitor line is interrupted, this diagnostic trouble code will be output.	• Malfunction of ABS valve relay • Malfunction of wiring harness or connecter • Malfunction of hydraulic unit • Malfunction of ABS-ECU

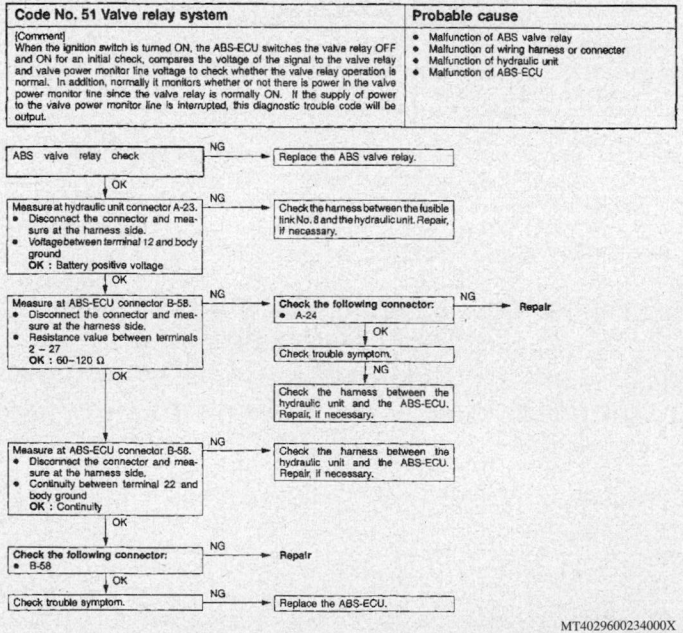

Fig. 83   Code 51: Valve Relay System. 1996–97 Eclipse FWD

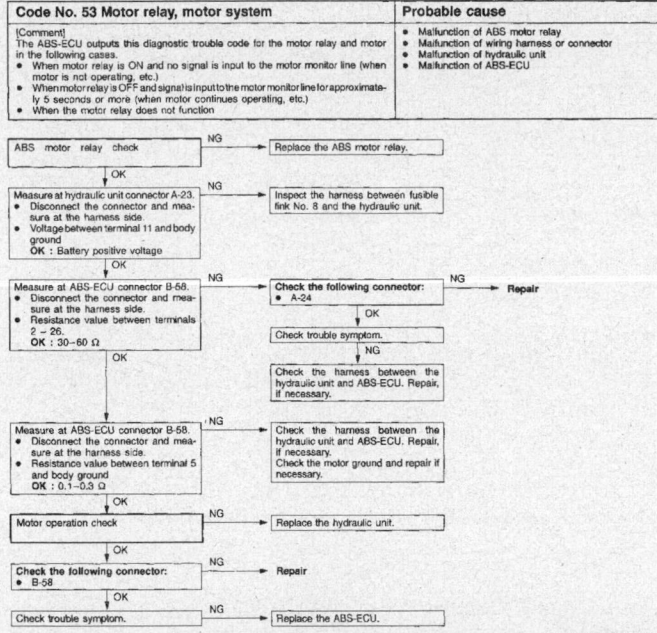

Fig. 84 Code 53: Motor Relay, Motor System. 1996–97 Eclipse FWD

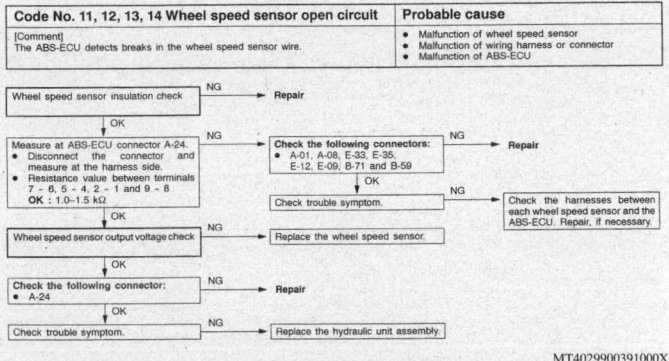

Fig. 86 Codes 11, 12, 13 & 14: Wheel Speed Sensor System. 1998–99 Eclipse AWD

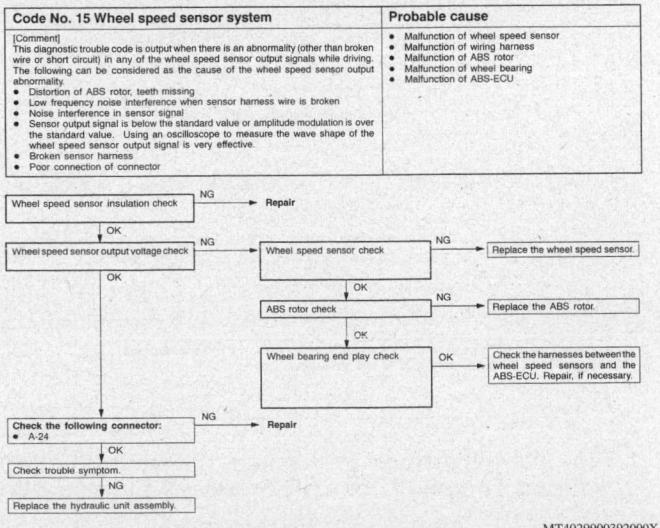

Fig. 87 Code 15: Wheel Speed Sensor System. 1998–99 Eclipse AWD

Diagnosis code No.	Inspection item	Diagnosis content
11	Front right wheel speed sensor	Open circuit
12	Front left wheel speed sensor	
13	Rear right wheel speed sensor	
14	Rear left wheel speed sensor	
15	Wheel speed sensor	Abnormal output signal
16	Power supply system	
21	Front right wheel speed sensor	Short circuit
22	Front left wheel speed sensor	
23	Rear right wheel speed sensor	
24	Rear left wheel speed sensor	
26	G sensor	
38	Stop light switch system	
41	Front right inlet solenoid valve	
42	Front left inlet solenoid valve	
43	Rear right inlet solenoid valve	
44	Rear left inlet solenoid valve	
45	Front right outlet solenoid valve	
46	Front left outlet solenoid valve	
47	Rear right outlet solenoid valve	
48	Rear left outlet solenoid valve	
51	Valve power supply	
53	Pump motor	
63	ABS-ECU	

Fig. 85 Diagnostic Trouble Code Inspection Chart. 1998–99 Eclipse AWD

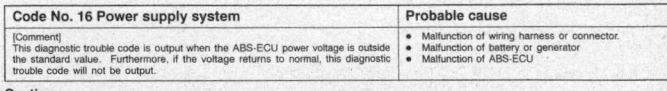
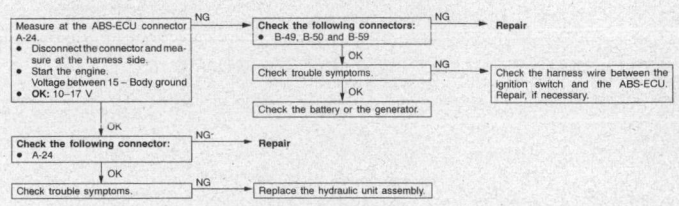

Fig. 88 Code 16: Power Supply System. 1998–99 Eclipse AWD

Code No. 21, 22, 23, 24 Wheel speed sensor excessive gap or short circuit	Probable cause
[Comment] These diagnostic trouble codes are output when the detection speed of the wheel speed sensors is below the standard value.	• Improper installation of wheel speed sensor • Malfunction of wheel speed sensor (intermittent open circuit or short circuit) • Malfunction of ABS rotor (chipped tooth or rotor not installed) • Noise interference in wheel speed sensor • Malfunction of ABS-ECU

NOTE
1. Momentary interruptions within approximately 100 ms are not detected.
2. To inspect the twisted pair wires in the wheel speed sensor, check if there is any damage to the cables, and flex the cables to check for any open circuits.

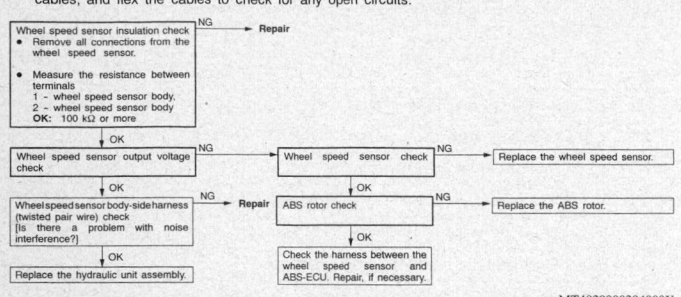

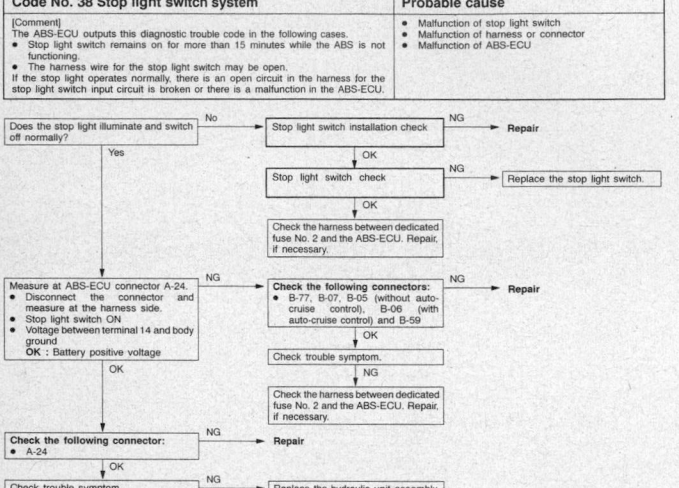

Fig. 89   Codes 21, 22, 23 & 24: Wheel Speed Sensor Excessive Gap. 1998–99 Eclipse AWD

Code No. 38 Stop light switch system	Probable cause
[Comment] The ABS-ECU outputs this diagnostic trouble code in the following cases. • Stop light switch remains on for more than 15 minutes while the ABS is not functioning. • The harness wire for the stop light switch may be open. If the stop light switch operates normally, there is an open circuit in the harness for the stop light switch input circuit is broken or there is a malfunction in the ABS-ECU.	• Malfunction of stop light switch • Malfunction of harness or connector • Malfunction of ABS-ECU

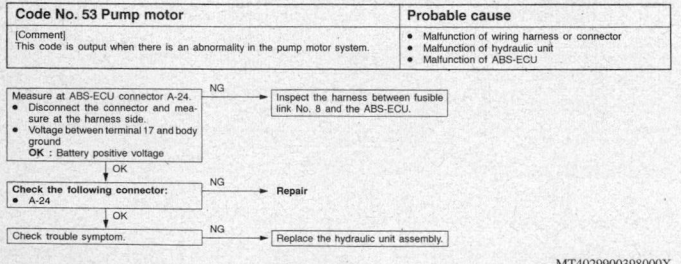

Fig. 91   Code 38: Stop Light Switch System. 1998–99 Eclipse AWD

Code No. 53 Pump motor	Probable cause
[Comment] This code is output when there is an abnormality in the pump motor system.	• Malfunction of wiring harness or connector • Malfunction of hydraulic unit • Malfunction of ABS-ECU

Fig. 93   Code 53: Pump Motor. 1998–99 Eclipse AWD

Code No. 26 G-sensor system	Probable cause
[Comment] The ABS-ECU outputs this diagnostic trouble code in the following cases. • When there is an open or short circuit in the harness for the G-sensor system.	• Malfunction of G-sensor • Malfunction of wiring harness or connector • Malfunction of ABS-ECU

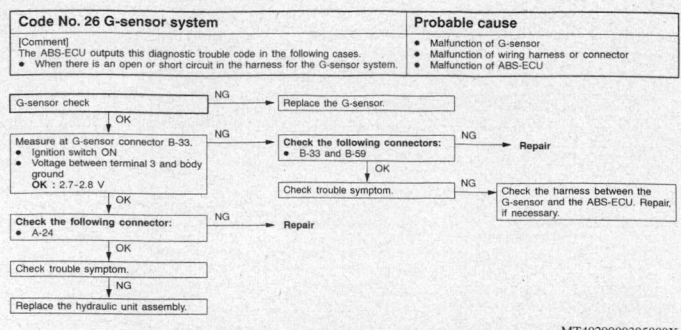

Fig. 90   Code 26: G-Sensor System. 1998–99 Eclipse AWD

Code No. 51 Valve power supply	Probable cause
[Comment] This code is output when there is an abnormality in the solenoid valve power supply system.	• Malfunction of wiring harness or connecter • Malfunction of ABS-ECU • Blown fuse

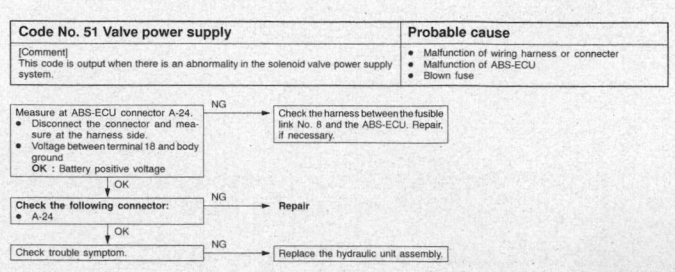

Fig. 92   Code 51: Valve Power Supply. 1998–99 Eclipse AWD

Trouble symptom		Inspection procedure No.
Communication with scan tool is not possible.	Communication with all systems is not possible.	1
	Communication with ABS only is not possible.	2
When the ignition key is turned to "ON" (engine stopped), the ABS warning light does not illuminate.		3
After the engine starts, the ABS warning light remains illuminated.		4
Faulty ABS operation	Unequal braking power on both sides	5
	Insufficient braking power	
	ABS operates under normal braking conditions	
	ABS operates before vehicle stops under normal braking conditions	
	Large brake pedal vibration (Caution 2.)	–

Fig. 94   Inspection Procedure Chart. 1998–99 Eclipse AWD

Communication with scan tool is not possible. (Communication with all systems is not possible.)	Probable cause
[Comment] The reason is probably a defect in the power supply system (including ground) for the diagnostic line.	• Malfunction of connector • Malfunction of harness • Improper scan tool <MUT-II> ROM pack

Fig. 95   Inspection Procedure 1: Communication w/Scan Tool Not Possible. 1998–99 Eclipse AWD

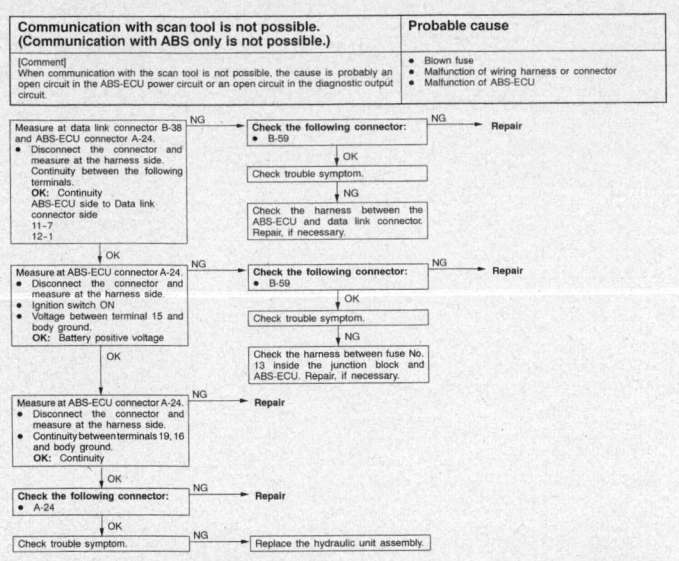

Fig. 96 Inspection Procedure 2: Communication w/Scan Tool Not Possible. 1998–99 Eclipse AWD

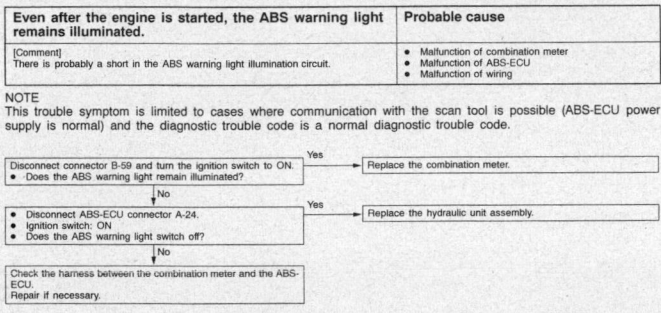

Fig. 98 Inspection Procedure 4: ABS Warning Lamp Remains Illuminated w/Engine Running. 1998–99 Eclipse AWD

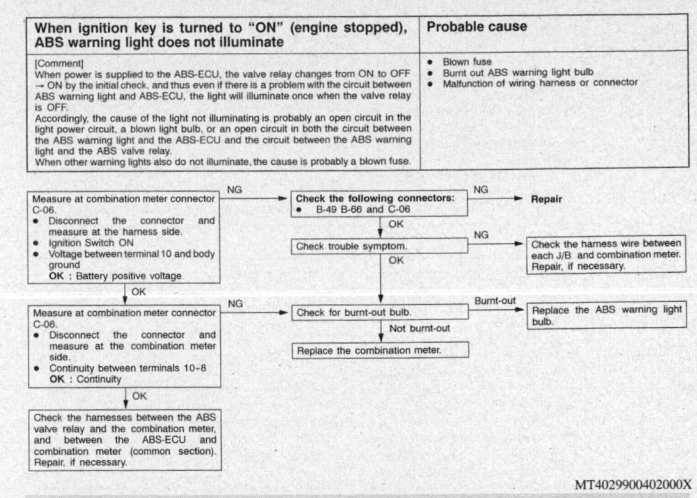

Fig. 97 Inspection Procedure 3: ABS Warning Lamp Does Not Illuminate w/Key ON. 1998–99 Eclipse AWD

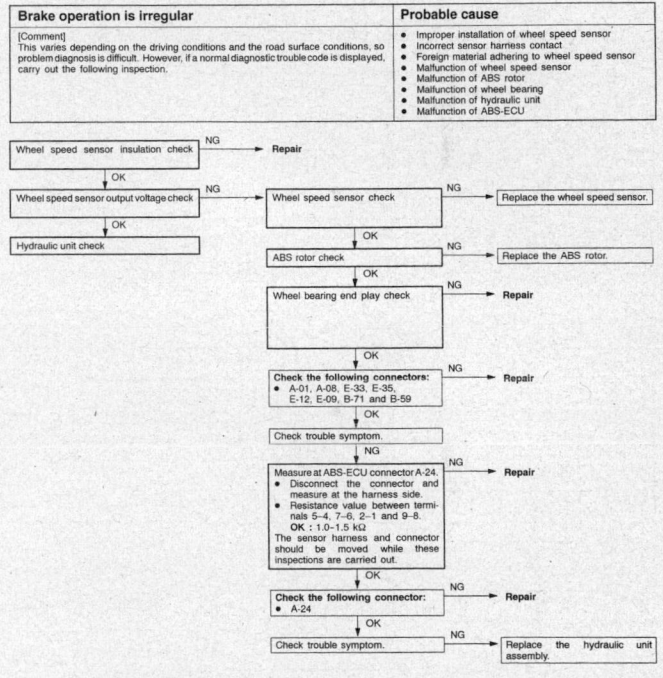

Fig. 99 Inspection Procedure 5: Abnormal Brake Operation. 1998–99 Eclipse AWD

Diagnosis code No.	Inspection item	Diagnosis content
11	Front right wheel speed sensor	Open circuit
12	Front left wheel speed sensor	
13	Rear right wheel speed sensor	
14	Rear left wheel speed sensor	
15	Wheel speed sensor	Abnormal output signal
16	Power supply system	
21	Front right wheel speed sensor	Short circuit
22	Front left wheel speed sensor	
23	Rear right wheel speed sensor	
24	Rear left wheel speed sensor	
38	Stop light switch system	
41	Front right inlet solenoid valve	
42	Front left inlet solenoid valve	
43	Rear right inlet solenoid valve	
44	Rear left inlet solenoid valve	
45	Front right outlet solenoid valve	
46	Front left outlet solenoid valve	
47	Rear right outlet solenoid valve	
48	Rear left outlet solenoid valve	
51	Valve power supply	
53	Pump motor	
63	ABS-ECU	

MT4029900405000X

Fig. 100   Diagnostic Trouble Code Inspection Chart. 1998–99 Eclipse FWD

Code No. 15 Wheel speed sensor system

	Probable cause
[Comment] This diagnostic trouble code is output when there is a malfunction (other than broken wire or short circuit) in any of the wheel speed sensor output signals while driving. The following can be considered as the cause of the wheel speed sensor output malfunction. • Distortion of rotor, teeth missing • Low frequency noise interference when sensor harness wire is broken • Noise interference in sensor signal • Sensor output signal is below the standard value or amplitude modulation is over the standard value. Using an oscilloscope to measure the wave shape of the wheel speed sensor output signal is very effective. • Broken sensor harness • Poor connection of connector	• Malfunction of wheel speed sensor • Malfunction of wiring harness • Malfunction of ABS rotor • Malfunction of wheel bearing • Malfunction of ABS-ECU

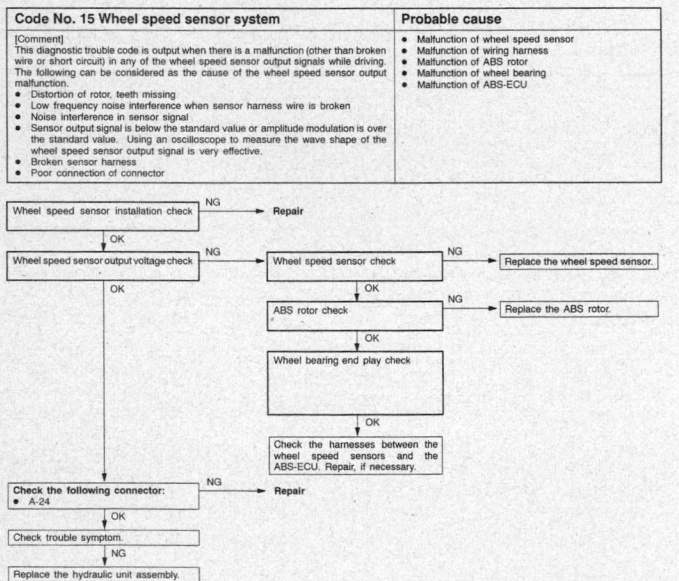

MT4029900407000X

Fig. 102   Code 15: Wheel Speed Sensor System. 1998–99 Eclipse FWD

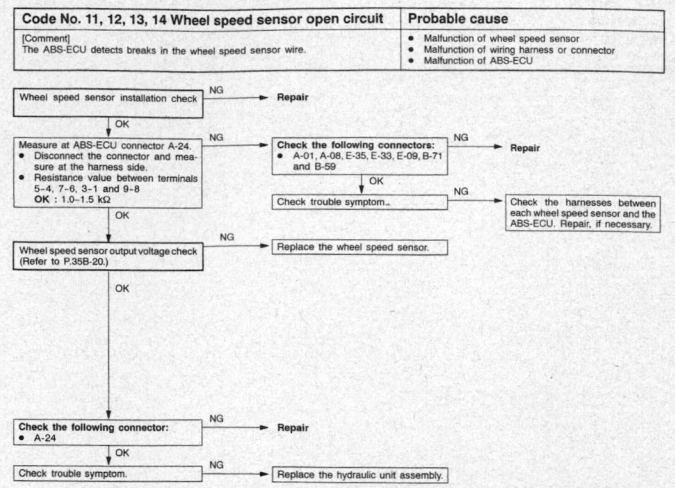

Code No. 11, 12, 13, 14 Wheel speed sensor open circuit

	Probable cause
[Comment] The ABS-ECU detects breaks in the wheel speed sensor wire.	• Malfunction of wheel speed sensor • Malfunction of wiring harness or connector • Malfunction of ABS-ECU

MT4029900406000X

Fig. 101   Codes 11, 12, 13 & 14: Wheel Speed Sensor Open Circuit. 1998–99 Eclipse FWD

Code No. 16 Power supply system

	Probable cause
[Comment] This diagnostic trouble code is output when the ABS-ECU power voltage is outside the standard value. Furthermore, if the voltage returns to normal, this diagnostic trouble code will not be output.	• Malfunction of wiring harness or connector. • Malfunction of battery or generator. • Malfunction of ABS-ECU

Caution
If the battery voltage drops during check, this code will be output as a current problem, and correct diagnostic of the problem cannot be made.
Before carrying out the following check, check the battery condition, and recharge it if necessary.

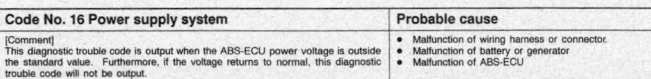
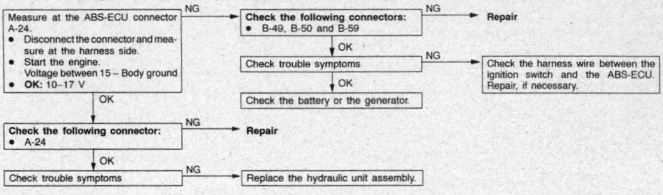

MT4029900408000X

Fig. 103   Code 16: Power Supply System. 1998–99 Eclipse FWD

Code No. 21, 22, 23, 24 Wheel speed sensor excessive gap or short circuit

	Probable cause
[Comment] These diagnostic trouble codes are output when the detection speed of the wheel speed sensors is below the standard value.	• Improper installation of wheel speed sensor • Malfunction of wheel speed sensor (intermittent open circuit or short circuit) • Malfunction of ABS rotor (chipped tooth or rotor not installed) • Noise interference in wheel speed sensor • Malfunction of ABS-ECU

NOTE
1. Momentary interruptions within approximately 100 ms are not detected.
2. To inspect the twisted pair wires in the wheel speed sensor, check if there is any damage to the cables, and flex the cables to check for any open circuits.

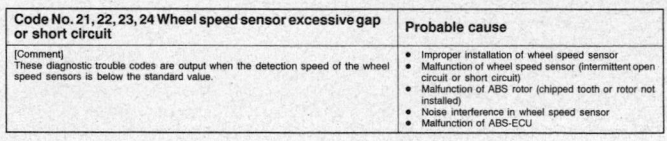
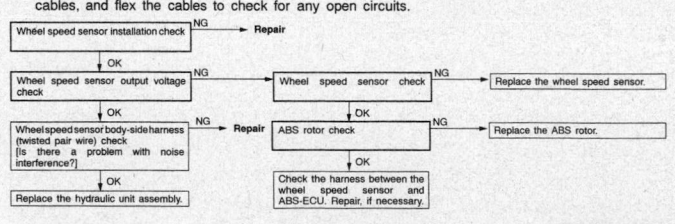

MT4029900409000X

Fig. 104   Codes 21, 22, 23 & 24: Wheel Speed Sensor Excessive Gap Or Short Circuit. 1998–99 Eclipse FWD

Code No. 38 Stop light switch system	Probable cause
[Comment] The ABS-ECU outputs this diagnostic trouble code in the following cases. • Stop light switch remains on for more than 15 minutes while the ABS is not functioning. • The harness wire for the stop light switch may be open-circuited. If the stop light operates normally, there is an open circuit in the harness for the stop light switch input circuit or there is a malfunction in the ABS-ECU.	• Malfunction of stop light switch • Malfunction of harness or connector • Malfunction of ABS-ECU

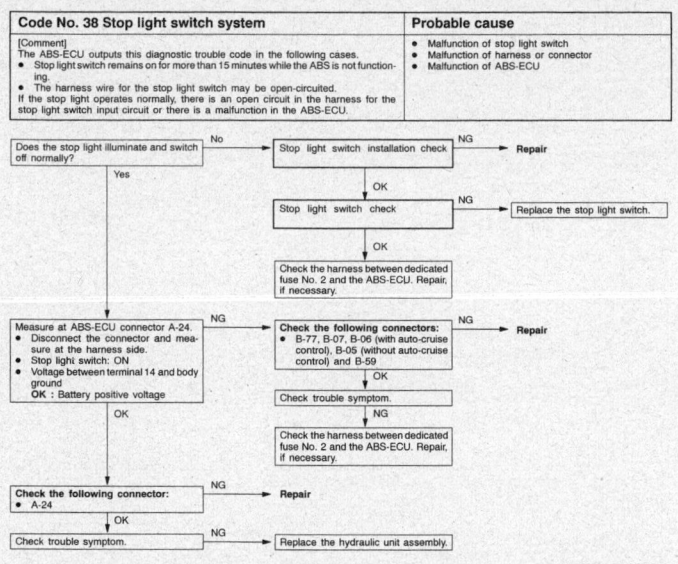

Fig. 105   Code 38: Stop Lamp Switch System. 1998–99 Eclipse FWD

Code No. 53 Pump motor	Probable cause
[Comment] This code is output when there is an abnormality in the pump motor system.	• Malfunction of wiring harness or connector • Malfunction of hydraulic unit • Malfunction of ABS-ECU

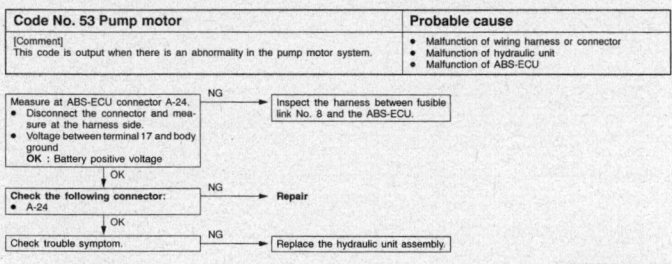

MT4029900412000X

Fig. 107   Code 53: Pump Motor. 1998–99 Eclipse FWD

Communication with scan tool is not possible. (Communication with all systems is not possible.)	Probable cause
[Comment] The reason is probably a defect in the power supply system (including ground) for the diagnostic line.	• Malfunction of connector • Malfunction of harness • Improper scan tool <MUT-II> ROM pack

MT4029900414000X

Fig. 109   Inspection Procedure 1: Communication w/Scan Tool Not Possible. 1998–99 Eclipse FWD

Code No. 51 Valve power supply	Probable cause
[Comment] This code is output when there is an abnormality in the solenoid valve power supply system.	• Malfunction of wiring harness or connector • Malfunction of ABS-ECU • Blown fuse

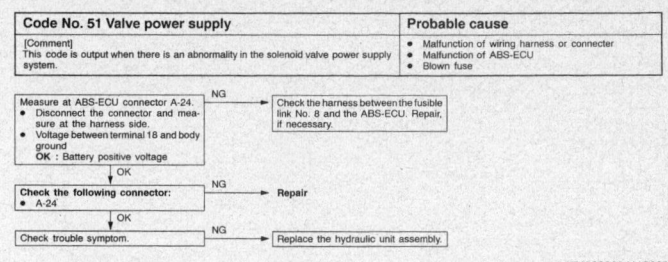

MT4029900411000X

Fig. 106   Code 51: Valve Power Supply. 1998–99 Eclipse FWD

Trouble symptom		Inspection procedure No.
Communication with scan tool is not possible.	Communication with all systems is not possible.	1
	Communication with ABS only is not possible.	2
When the ignition key is turned to "ON" (engine stopped), the ABS warning light does not illuminate.		3
After the engine starts, the ABS warning light remains illuminated.		4
Faulty ABS operation	Unequal braking power on both sides	5
	Insufficient braking power	
	ABS operates under normal braking conditions	
	ABS operates before vehicle stops under normal braking conditions	
	Large brake pedal vibration (Caution 2.)	–

MT4029900413000X

Fig. 108   Inspection Procedure Chart. 1998–99 Eclipse FWD

Communication with scan tool is not possible. (Communication with ABS only is not possible.)	Probable cause
[Comment] When communication with the scan tool is not possible, the cause is probably an open circuit in the ABS-ECU power circuit or an open circuit in the diagnostic output circuit.	• Blown fuse • Malfunction of wiring harness or connector • Malfunction of ABS-ECU

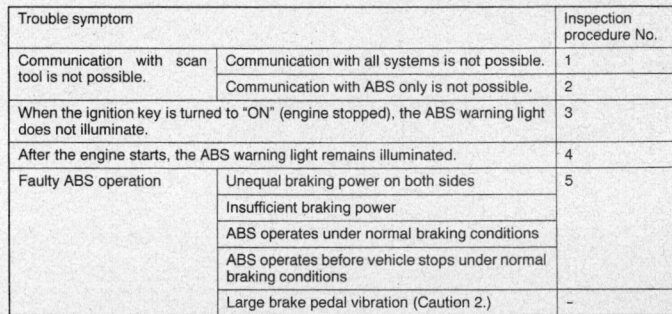

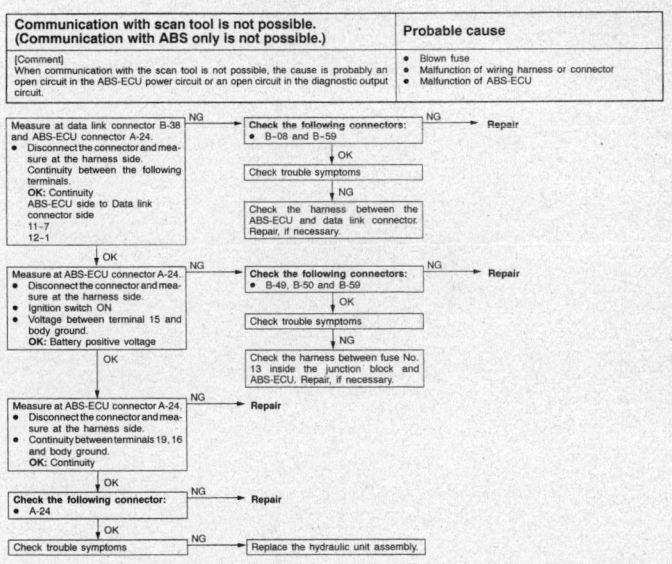

MT4029900415000X

Fig. 110   Inspection Procedure 2: Communication w/Scan Tool Not Possible. 1998–99 Eclipse FWD

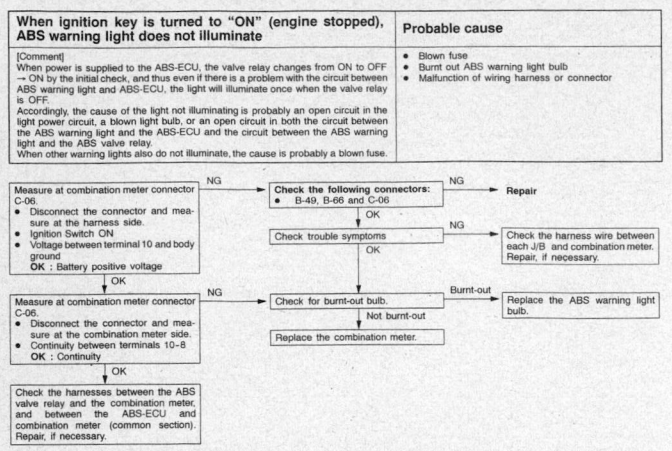

When ignition key is turned to "ON" (engine stopped), ABS warning light does not illuminate | **Probable cause**

[Comment]
When power is supplied to the ABS-ECU, the valve relay changes from ON to OFF → ON by the initial check, and thus even if there is a problem with the circuit between ABS warning light and ABS-ECU, the light will illuminate once when the valve relay is OFF.
Accordingly, the cause of the light not illuminating is probably an open circuit in the light power circuit, a blown light bulb, or an open circuit in both the circuit between the ABS warning light and the ABS-ECU and the circuit between the ABS warning light and the ABS valve relay.
When other warning lights also do not illuminate, the cause is probably a blown fuse.

Probable cause:
- Blown fuse
- Burnt out ABS warning light bulb
- Malfunction of wiring harness or connector

Fig. 111   Inspection Procedure 3: ABS Warning Lamp Does Not Illuminate w/Key ON. 1998–99 Eclipse FWD

MT4029900416000X

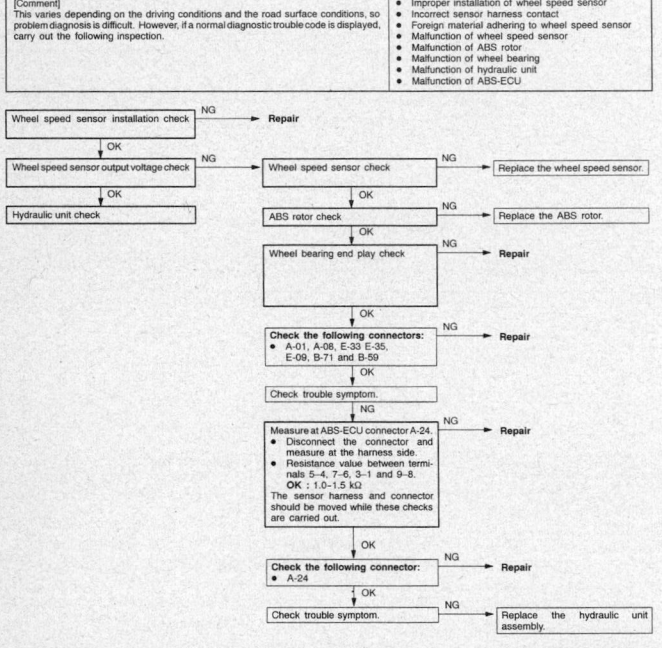

Brake operation is irregular | **Probable cause**

[Comment]
This varies depending on the driving conditions and the road surface conditions, so problem diagnosis is difficult. However, if a normal diagnostic trouble code is displayed, carry out the following inspection.

Probable cause:
- Improper installation of wheel speed sensor
- Incorrect sensor harness contact
- Foreign material adhering to wheel speed sensor
- Malfunction of wheel speed sensor
- Malfunction of ABS rotor
- Malfunction of wheel bearing
- Malfunction of hydraulic unit
- Malfunction of ABS-ECU

MT4029900418000X

Fig. 113   Inspection Procedure 5: Abnormal Brake Operation. 1998–99 Eclipse FWD

Even after the engine is started, the ABS warning light remains illuminated. | **Probable cause**

[Comment]
There is probably a short in the ABS warning light illumination circuit.

Probable cause:
- Malfunction of combination meter
- Malfunction of ABS-ECU
- Malfunction of wiring

NOTE
This trouble symptom is limited to cases where communication with the scan tool is possible (ABS-ECU power supply is normal) and the diagnostic trouble code is a normal diagnostic trouble code.

- Disconnect connector B-59 and turn the ignition switch to ON.
- Does the ABS warning light remain illuminated? — Yes → Replace the combination meter.
  - No
- Disconnect ABS-ECU connector A-24.
- Ignition switch: ON
- Does the ABS warning light switch off? — Yes → Replace the hydraulic unit assembly.
  - No

Check the harness between the combination meter and the ABS-ECU.
Repair if necessary.

MT4029900417000X

Fig. 112   Inspection Procedure 4: ABS Warning Lamp Remains Illuminated w/Engine Running. 1998–99 Eclipse FWD

Diagnostic trouble code no.	Inspection item		Detection conditions
11	Front right wheel speed sensor	Open circuit	B, C
12	Front left wheel speed sensor		
13	Rear right wheel speed sensor		
14	Rear left wheel speed sensor		
16	Power supply system		A, B, C
21	Front right wheel speed sensor	Short circuit	B, C
22	Front left wheel speed sensor		
23	Rear right wheel speed sensor		
24	Rear left wheel speed sensor		
25	Front right wheel speed sensor	Excessive gap	B, C
26	Front left wheel speed sensor		
27	Rear right wheel speed sensor		
28	Rear left wheel speed sensor		
33	Stop light switch system		B, C
35	Front right wheel speed sensor	Pulse processing [wheel speed input corresponding to a vehicle speed of 300 km/h (186 mph) or more]	B, C
36	Front left wheel speed sensor		
37	Rear right wheel speed sensor		
38	Rear left wheel speed sensor		
41	Front right solenoid valve (inside)		B, C
42	Front left solenoid valve (inside)		
43	Rear right solenoid valve (inside)		
44	Rear left solenoid valve (inside)		
45	Front right solenoid valve (outside)		
46	Front left solenoid valve (outside)		
47	Rear right solenoid valve (outside)		
48	Rear left solenoid valve (outside)		
51	Valve relay	ON impossible	A, B, C
52	Valve relay	OFF impossible	A
53	Motor relay	ON impossible	B
54	Motor relay	OFF impossible	B, C

Detection conditions
A: During system check immediately after starting
B: While ABS control is not operating while driving
C: While ABS control is operating

MT4029900369000X

Fig. 114   Diagnostic Trouble Code Inspection Chart. 1996–98 Galant

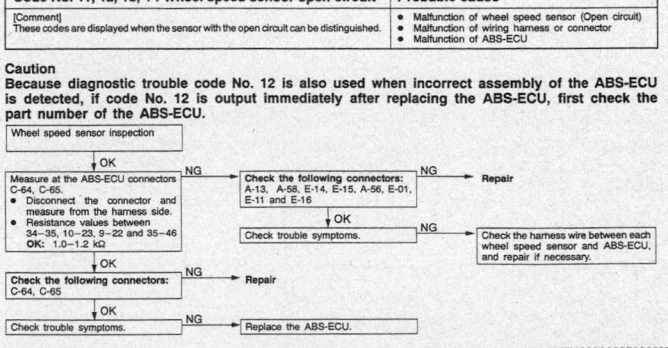

Code No. 11, 12, 13, 14 Wheel speed sensor open circuit | **Probable cause**

[Comment]
These codes are displayed when the sensor with the open circuit can be distinguished.

Probable cause:
- Malfunction of wheel speed sensor (Open circuit)
- Malfunction of wiring harness or connector
- Malfunction of ABS-ECU

Caution
Because diagnostic trouble code No. 12 is also used when incorrect assembly of the ABS-ECU is detected, if code No. 12 is output immediately after replacing the ABS-ECU, first check the part number of the ABS-ECU.

MT4029900370000X

Fig. 115   Codes 11, 12, 13 & 14: Wheel Speed Sensor Circuit Open. 1996–98 Galant

Code No. 16 Power supply system	Probable cause
[Comment] This diagnostic trouble code is output when the ABS-ECU power voltage is outside the standard value. Furthermore, if the voltage returns to normal, this diagnostic trouble code will not be output.	• Malfunction of wiring harness or connector. • Malfunction of battery or alternator • Malfunction of ABS-ECU

Caution
If the battery voltage drops during inspection, this code will be output as a current problem, and correct diagnostic of the problem cannot be made.
Before carrying out the following inspection, check the battery condition, and recharge it if necessary.

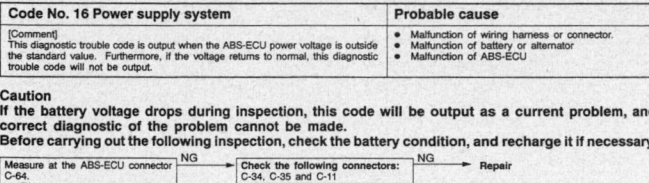

Fig. 116 Code 16: Power Supply System. 1996–98 Galant

Code No. 25, 26, 27, 28 Wheel speed sensor excessive gap	Probable cause
[Comment] These diagnostic trouble codes are output when the detection speed of the wheel speed sensors is below the standard value.	• Improper installation of wheel speed sensor • Malfunction of wheel speed sensor (intermittent open circuit or short circuit) • Malfunction of ABS rotor (chipped tooth or ABS rotor not installed) • Noise interference in wheel speed sensor • Malfunction of ABS-ECU

NOTE
1. Momentary interruptions within approximately 100 ms are not detected.
2. To inspect the twisted pair wires in the wheel speed sensor, check if there is any damage to the cables, and flex the cables to check for any open circuits.

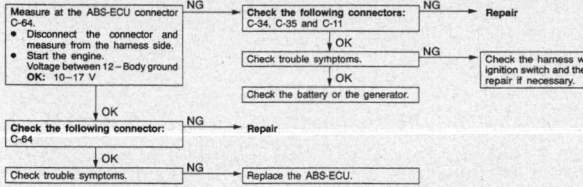

Fig. 118 Code 25, 26, 27 & 28: Wheel Speed Sensor Excessive Gap. 1996–98 Galant

Code No. 35, 36, 37, 38 Wheel speed sensor pulse processing	Probable cause
[Comment] These diagnostic trouble codes are output if a sensor pulse corresponding to a vehicle speed of 300 km/h (186 mph) or more is input to the wheel speed signal circuit due to ignition noise or excessive axle vibration.	• Malfunction of wiring harness • Malfunction of wheel speed sensor • Malfunction of ABS rotor • Malfunction of wheel bearing • Noise interference in wheel speed signal • Malfunction of ABS-ECU

NOTE
To inspect the twisted pair wires in the wheel speed sensors, check if there is any damage to the cables, and flex the cables to check for any open circuits.

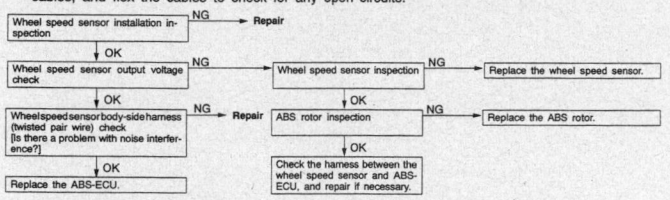

Fig. 120 Codes 35, 36, 37 & 38: Wheel Speed Sensor Pulse Processing. 1996–98 Galant

Code No. 21, 22, 23, 24 Wheel speed sensor short circuit	Probable cause
[Comment] These codes are displayed when the sensor with the short circuited can be distinguished.	• Malfunction of wheel speed sensor (short at (+) side or layer short) • Malfunction of wiring harness • Malfunction of ABS-ECU

NOTE
Short circuit is not detected when IG power voltage drops.

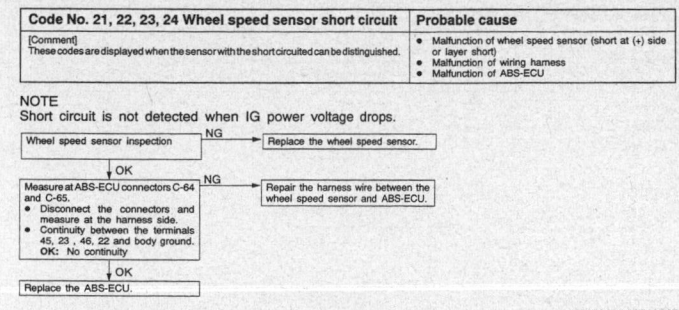

Fig. 117 Codes 21, 22, 23 & 24: Wheel Speed Sensor Short Circuit. 1996–98 Galant

Code No. 33 Stop light switch system	Probable cause
[Comment] This diagnostic trouble code is output if it is judged to be an open circuit when the stop light switch is ON for a continuous period of 15 minutes or more, or if it is judged to be a short circuit when the pedal stroke sensor output voltage is above the specified value and the switch is OFF for a constant period of time.	• Malfunction of wiring harness or connector • Malfunction of pedal stroke sensor (ON or OFF malfunction of stop light switch) • Malfunction of ABS-ECU

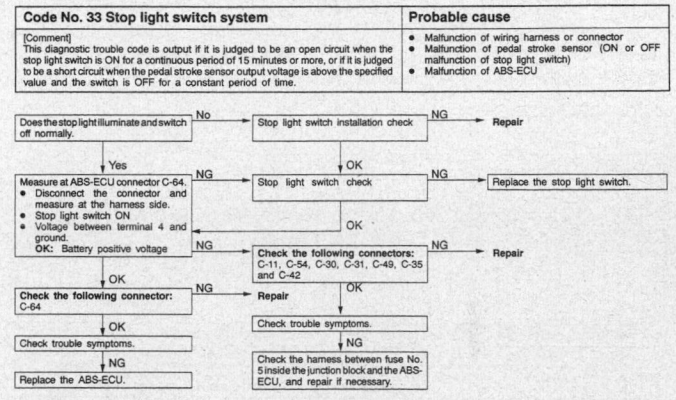

Fig. 119 Code 33: Stop Lamp Switch System. 1996–98 Galant

Code No. 41, 42, 43, 44, 45, 46, 47, 48 Solenoid valve	Probable cause
[Comment] The ABS-ECU normally monitors the solenoid valve drive circuit. If there is no current flowing to the solenoid even when the solenoid is ON, or the current continues to flow to the solenoid even when the solenoid is OFF, the ABS-ECU diagnostic a open circuit or short in the solenoid coil or a open circuit or short in the harness, and this diagnostic trouble code is output.	• Malfunction of wiring harness • Malfunction of hydraulic unit • Malfunction of ABS-ECU

Caution
• A valve malfunction is not detected when IG power voltage drops (less than 9 V).
• If power is not being supplied to the solenoid valve because connector A-43 is disconnected, all diagnostic trouble codes except code Nos. 41 and 46 will be output.

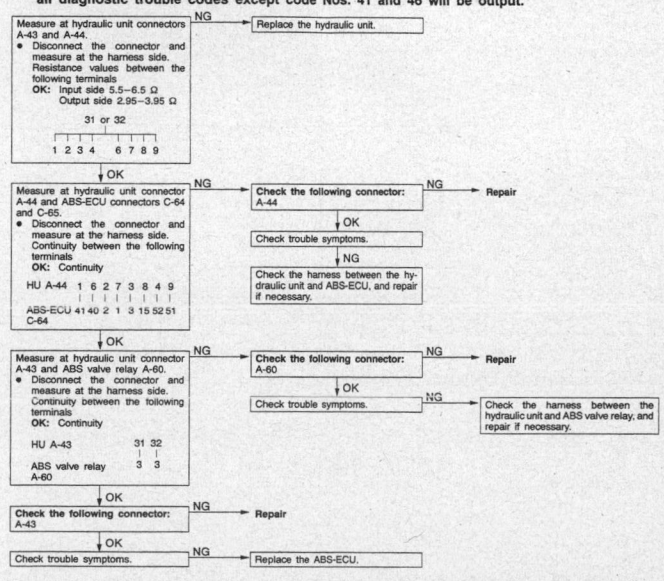

Fig. 121 Codes 41, 42, 43, 44, 45, 46, 47 & 48: Solenoid Valve 1996–98 Galant

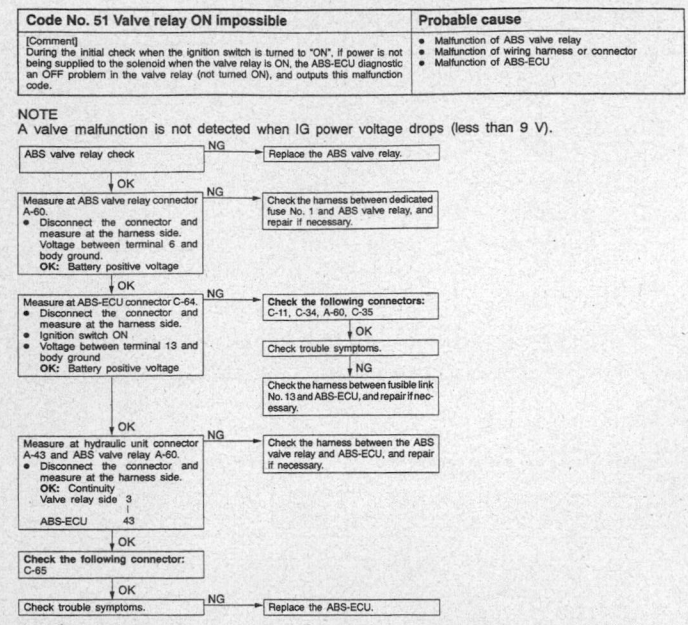

Code No. 51 Valve relay ON impossible	Probable cause
[Comment] During the initial check when the ignition switch is turned to "ON", if power is not being supplied to the solenoid when the valve relay is ON, the ABS-ECU diagnostic an OFF problem in the valve relay (not turned ON), and outputs this malfunction code.	• Malfunction of ABS valve relay • Malfunction of wiring harness or connector • Malfunction of ABS-ECU

NOTE
A valve malfunction is not detected when IG power voltage drops (less than 9 V).

MT4029900377000X

Fig. 122   Code 51: Valve Relay On Not Possible. 1996–98 Galant

Code No. 53 Motor relay, motor ON impossible	Probable cause
[Comment] This diagnostic trouble code is output if a motor relay ON instruction has been given but the motor revolution sensor signal has not risen above 150 Hz.	• Malfunction of ABS motor relay • Malfunction of wiring harness or connector • Malfunction of hydraulic unit • Malfunction of ABS-ECU

Caution
Because force-driving of the motor by means of the actuator test will drain the battery, the engine should be started and left to run for a while after testing is completed.

MT4029900379000X

Fig. 124   Code 53: Motor Relay On Not Possible. 1996–98 Galant

Code No. 52 Valve relay OFF impossible	Probable cause
[Comment] During the initial check when the ignition switch is turned to "ON", if power is being supplied to the solenoid when the valve relay is OFF, the ABS-ECU diagnostic a melted relay contact or a short in the valve relay drive circuit, and this diagnostic trouble code is output.	• Malfunction of ABS valve relay • Malfunction of wiring harness (Short circuited) • Malfunction of ABS-ECU

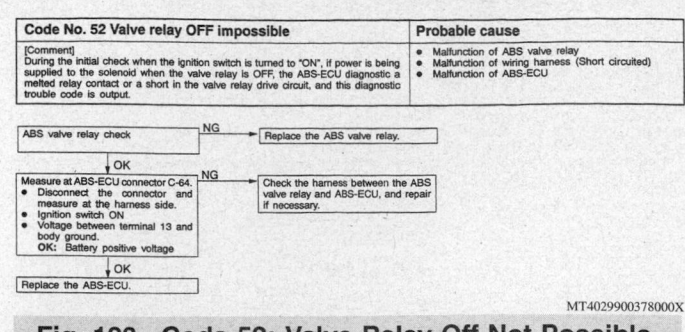

MT4029900378000X

Fig. 123   Code 52: Valve Relay Off Not Possible. 1996–98 Galant

Code No. 54 Motor relay, motor OFF impossible	Probable cause
[Comment] This diagnostic trouble code is output if a signal of 150 Hz or above is input to the ABS-ECU from the motor revolution sensor even though the motor relay is OFF.	• Malfunction of wiring harness or connector • Malfunction of hydraulic unit • Malfunction of ABS motor relay • Noise interference in motor rotating sensor circuit • Malfunction of ABS-ECU

Caution
If there is a melted contact in the motor relay, the motor will keep turning, even if the ignition switch is turned to OFF. In such a case, immediately remove the fusible link No. 4 or disconnect the hydraulic unit connector. Excessive running of the motor will cause the battery to discharge.

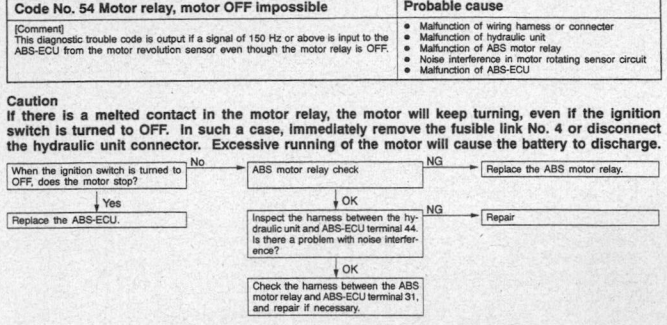

MT4029900380000X

Fig. 125   Code 54: Motor Relay OFF Not Possible. 1996–98 Galant

Trouble symptom		Inspection procedure No.
Communication with scan tool is not possible.	Communication with all systems is not possible.	1
	Communication with ABS only is not possible.	2
When the ignition key is turned to "ON" (engine stopped), the ABS warning light does not illuminate.		3
After the engine starts, the light remains illuminated.		4
The ABS warning light switches off approximately 1 second after the ignition key is turned to "ON". (Engine not running)		5
After the ignition key is turned to "ON", the ABS warning light flashes.		6
When the ignition key is turned to "START", the ABS warning light switches off.		7
Faulty ABS operation	Unequal braking power on both sides	8
	Insufficient braking power	
	ABS operates under normal braking conditions	
	ABS operates before vehicle stops under normal braking conditions	
	Large brake pedal vibration when ABS operates	
	Large brake pedal vibration (Caution 2.)	–

MT4029900381000X

Fig. 126   Inspection Procedure Chart. 1996–98 Galant

Communication with scan tool is not possible. (Communication with all systems is not possible.)	Probable cause
[Comment] The reason is probably a defect in the power supply system (including ground) for the diagnostic line.	• Malfunction of connector • Malfunction of harness

MT4029900382000X

Fig. 127   Inspection Procedure 1: Communication w/Scan Tool Not Possible. 1996–98 Galant

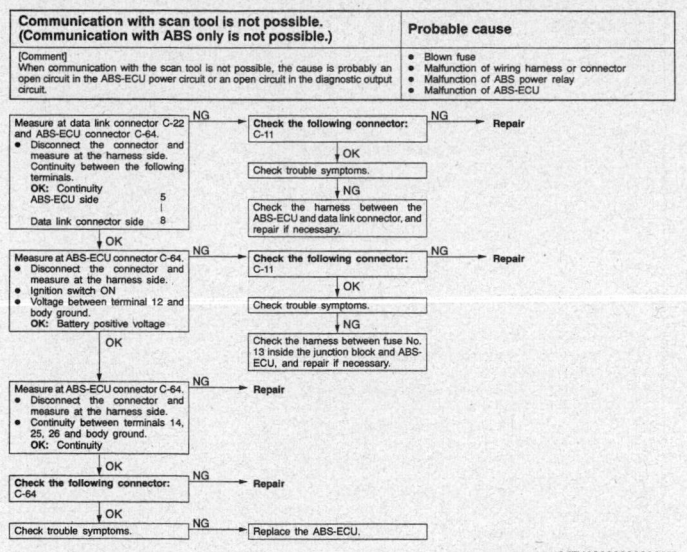

MT4029900383000X

Fig. 128 Inspection Procedure 2: Communication w/Scan Tool Not Possible. 1996–98 Galant

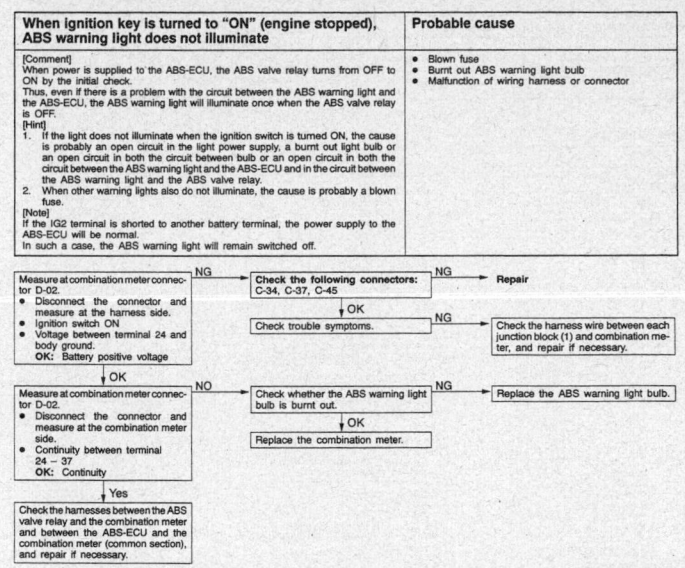

MT4029900384000X

Fig. 129 Inspection Procedure 3: ABS Warning Lamp Does Not Illuminate w/Key On. 1996–98 Galant

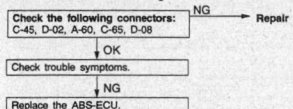

Even after the engine is started, the ABS warning light remains illuminated.	Probable cause
[Comment] There is probably a short in the ABS warning light illumination circuit. In addition, if the charge light is illuminated at the same time, the cause is likely to be the warning light illumination circuit between the generator and the ABS-ECU.	• Malfunction of combination meter • Malfunction of ABS valve relay • Malfunction of ABS-ECU • Malfunction of wiring harness

NOTE
This trouble symptom is limited to cases where communication with the scan tool is possible (ABS-ECU power supply is normal) and no diagnostic trouble code is displayed.

MT4029900385000X

Fig. 130 Inspection Procedure 4: ABS Warning Lamp Remains Illuminated w/Engine Running. 1996–98 Galant

The ABS warning light flashes when the ignition switch is turned to "ON"	Probable cause
[Hint] The cause is probably an open circuit (defective contact) in the ABS warning light circuit.	• Malfunction of connector

NOTE
If the ABS warning light is flashing, the reason may be that the diagnostic display mode using the warning light is active. [Diagnostic display mode using the warning light can be cancelled by turning the ignition switch to OFF or driving the car forward until the vehicle speed reaches 10 km/h (6 mph)].

MT4029900387000X

Fig. 132 Inspection Procedure 6: ABS Warning Lamp Flashes w/Key On. 1996–98 Galant

The ABS warning light switches OFF approximately 1.0 second after the ignition key is turned to "ON". (Engine not running)	Probable cause
[Comment] The ABS-ECU monitors the voltage of the generator L terminal, and when the engine is not running, the voltage of the L terminal is low, and thus the ABS warning light illuminates. [Hint] Accordingly, when the ignition key is turned to "ON", if the light turns off after the initial check (which takes about 1.0 second), there is a problem in the ABS warning light illumination function resulting from the generator L terminal monitor.	• Malfunction of wiring harness or connector • Malfunction of generator • Malfunction of ABS-ECU

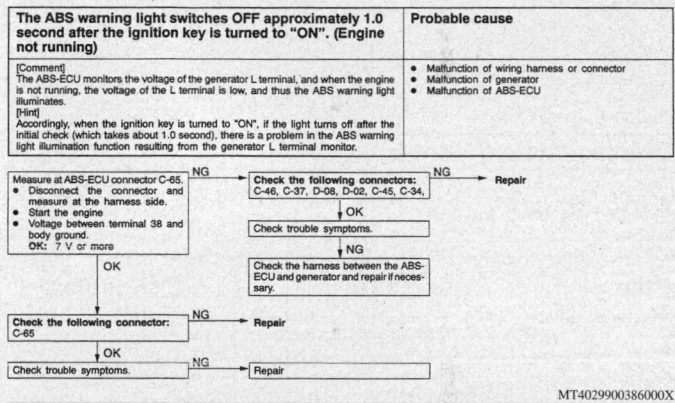

MT4029900386000X

Fig. 131 Inspection Procedure 5: ABS Warning Lamp Turns Off 1 Second After Key Is On. 1996–98 Galant

When ignition key is turned to "START", ABS warning light switches off	Probable cause
[Comment] The ABS-ECU uses the power to the IG2 which is cut when the ignition switch is turned to "START". The ABS warning light uses IG1 power which is not cut even when the ignition switch is turned to "START". [Hint] Accordingly, because the power to the ABS-ECU is stopped in "START" position, if the warning light switches off at this time, the cause is a problem in the light illumination circuit in the valve relay.	• Malfunction of wiring harness or connector • Malfunction of ABS valve relay • Malfunction of ignition switch

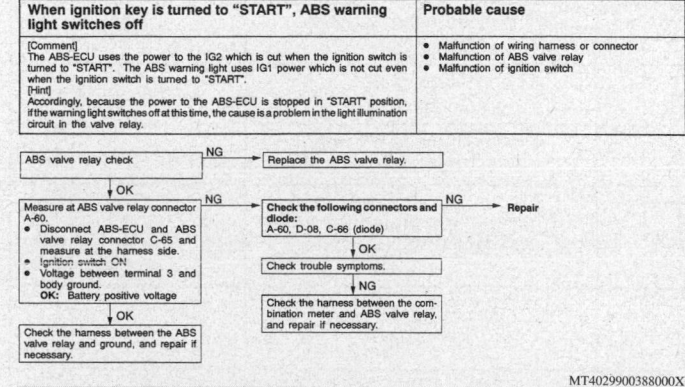

MT4029900388000X

Fig. 133 Inspection Procedure 7: ABS Warning Lamp Turns Off w/Key In Start Position. 1996–98 Galant

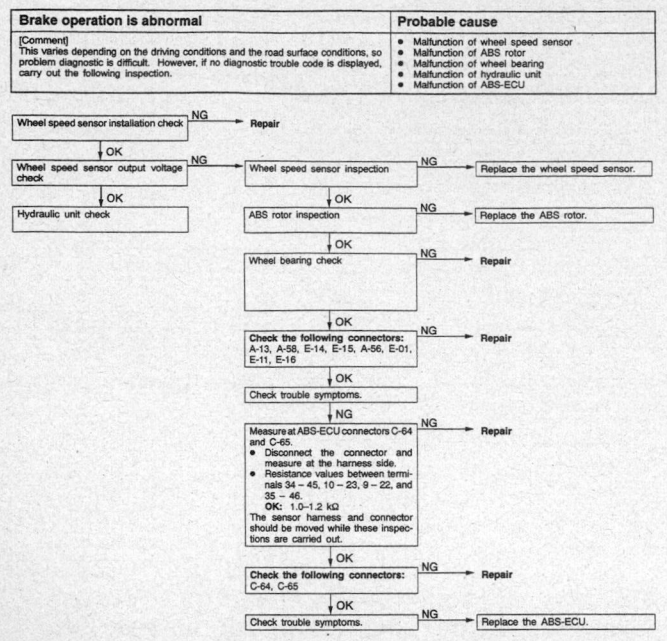

Brake operation is abnormal	Probable cause
[Comment] This varies depending on the driving conditions and the road surface conditions, so problem diagnostic is difficult. However, if no diagnostic trouble code is displayed, carry out the following inspection.	• Malfunction of wheel speed sensor • Malfunction of ABS rotor • Malfunction of wheel bearing • Malfunction of hydraulic unit • Malfunction of ABS-ECU

MT4029900389000X

Fig. 134   Inspection Procedure 8: Abnormal Brake Operation. 1996–98 Galant

DIAGNOSTIC TROUBLE CODE NO.	INSPECTION ITEM	DIAGNOSTIC CONTENT
11	Front right wheel speed sensor	Open circuit or short circuit
12	Front left wheel speed sensor	
13	Rear right wheel speed sensor	
14	Rear left wheel speed sensor	
16	Power supply system	ABS-ECU power supply voltage below or above the standard value. Not displayed if the voltage recovers.
21	Front right wheel speed sensor	
22	Front left wheel speed sensor	
23	Rear right wheel speed sensor	
24	Rear left wheel speed sensor	
38	Stoplight switch system	
41	Solenoid valve inside hydraulic unit	Open circuit or short circuit
42	ABS-ECU	
51	Hydraulic unit solenoid valve relay open or short circuit	
53	Malfunction of hydraulic unit	
63	ABS-ECU	

MT4029900435000X

Fig. 135   Diagnostic Trouble Code Inspection Chart. 1999 Galant

Codes 11, 12, 13 & 14

Wheel Speed Sensor

Cause

Faulty Wheel Speed Sensor, Wiring Harness, Connector Or Hydraulic Assembly

Step	Inspection	Connector	Value	Outcome	Go To Step	Repair
1	Check Wheel Speed Sensor Installation	—	—	OK	2	—
				NG	—	Install Sensor Correctly
2	Check Speed Sensor Circuit At ABS-ECU	A-03, Terminals 1 & 2	1.0–1.5 Kohms	OK	2a	—
				NG	3	—
2a	Check Speed Sensor Circuit At ABS-ECU	A-03, Terminals 19 & 20	1.0–1.5 Kohms	OK	2b	—
				NG	4	—
2b	Check Speed Sensor Circuit At ABS-ECU	A-03, Terminals 5 & 6 or 22 & 23	1.0–1.5 Kohms	OK	6	—
				NG	5	—
3	Check Harness Between Connectors	A-03 & A-22	—	OK	7	—
				NG	9	Repair As Required
4	Check Harness Between Connectors	A-03 & A-36	—	OK	7	—
				NG	9	Repair As Required
5	Check Harness Between Connectors	A-03, D-10 & D-12	—	OK	7	—
				NG	9	Repair As Required
6	Check Wheel Speed Sensor Output Voltage	—	70mv w/Voltmeter, 200 mv w/Oscilloscope	OK	9	Replace Hydraulic Assembly
				NG	7	
7	Check Wheel Speed Sensor Or ABS Rotor	—	Internal Resistance, 1.0–1.5 kohm	OK	—	Test Complete
				NG	—	Repair/Replace As Required
8	Check Wheel Bearing	—	—	OK	—	—
				NG	9	Replace Wheel Speed Sensor
9	Check System Components & Wiring	—	—	OK	—	Test Complete
				NG	—	Repair As Required

Fig. 136   Codes 11, 12, 13 & 14: Wheel Speed Sensor Open Or Short Circuit. 1999 Galant

ANTI-LOCK BRAKES

Code 38				Cause		
Stop Lamp Switch System				**Faulty Switch, Wiring Or Hydraulic Assembly**		
Step	Inspection	Connector	Value	Outcome	Go To Step	Repair
1	Check Switch Operation	—	—	OK	3	—
				NG	2	
2	Check Switch Installation	—	—	OK	4	
				NG	7	Repair/Replace As Required
3	Check Switch Circuit	A-03, Terminals 13 & Ground	Approx. 12v	OK	7	Replace Hydraulic Assembly
				NG	5	
4	Check Switch When Released	—	Continuity	OK	6	—
				NG	7	Replace Switch
5	Check Harness Between Connectors	A-03 & C-66	—	OK	8	—
				NG	7	Repair/Replace As Required
6	Check Wire Between Fuseable Link No. 1 & Switch Connector	C-03	—	OK	7	—
				NG	7	Repair/Replace As Required
7	Check System Components	—	—	OK	—	Test Complete
				NG	—	Repair/Replace As Required

Fig. 137   Code 38: Stop Lamp Switch. 1999 Galant

Codes 41, 51 & 53				Cause		
Solenoid Valve Or Hydraulic Unit Malfunction				**Faulty Wiring Or Hydraulic Assembly**		
Step	Inspection	Connector	Value	Outcome	Go To Step	Repair
1	Check Solenoid Valve Or Motor Power Supply Circuit	A-03, Terminal 9 & Ground Or 25 & Ground	Approx. 12	OK	3	Replace Hydraulic Assembly
				NG	2	—
2	Check Harness Between Fuseable Link No. 5 & connector	A-03	—	OK	3	—
				NG	3	Repair/Replace As Required
3	Check Components	—	—	OK	—	Test Complete
				NG	—	Repair/Replace As Required

Fig. 138   Codes 41, 51 & 53: Solenoid Valve or Hydraulic Unit Malfunction. 1999 Galant

INSPECTION PROCEDURE FOR DIAGNOSTIC TROUBLE CODES

Code No. 15 Open circuit in sensor	Probable cause
[Comment] There is a broken + wire or − wire in one or more of the four wheel speed sensors detected by a open circuit inspection by the ABS-ECU hardware circuit. In this case, if a driving test is carried out at 10 km/h (6.2 mph) or more, the diagnostic trouble code (No. 11−14) for the abnormal wheel will be displayed. Also, if the diagnostic trouble code for the abnormal wheel is not displayed, the problem is transient. [Hint] When using the scan tool, previous diagnostic trouble codes are displayed. When this code (No. 15) appears, and a diagnostic trouble code for a specific wheel (nos. 11−14) is also displayed, it is likely that there is a open circuit in the wheel speed sensor indicated by these codes.	Open circuit in wheel speed sensor

Code Nos. 11, 12, 13, 14 Open circuit in wheel speed sensor	Probable cause
[Comment] These codes are displayed when the sensor with the open circuit can be distinguished.	Open circuit in wheel speed sensor
	Broken wiring harness, disconnected connector
	Malfunction of ABS-ECU

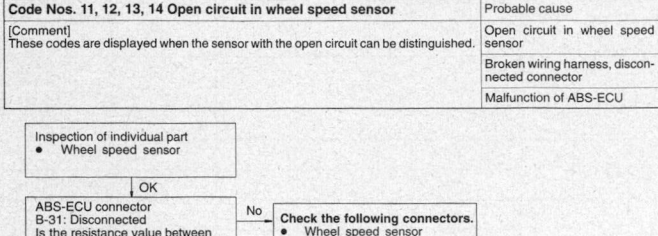

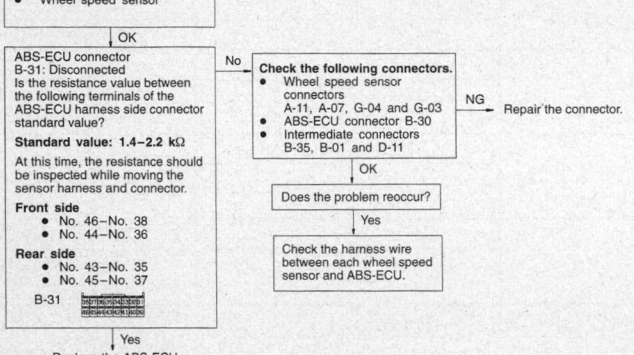

MT4029100124000X

Fig. 139   Codes 11, 12, 13, 14 & 15: Speed Sensors (Open Circuit). 1996 Mirage

Code No. 25 Open or short circuit in both rear wheel speed sensors	Probable cause
[Comment] A problem in both rear wheel sensors is diagnosed when the signal from either of the front wheel speed sensors is diagnosed as normal, and the wheel speed of both rear wheels is 0 km/h (0 mph) for a continuous 20 second period, even if the wheel speed of the front wheels is 11 km/h (7 mph) or more. [Hint] This code is displayed when there is a short in the sensor harnesses of both rear wheels, or if there is low output from both rear wheel sensors. NOTE If the vehicle is raised up, or if the wheels are stuck and only the front wheels are moving, after approximately 20 seconds the ABS warning light will illuminate, and the system will be isolated. Thus, this code can be output even when the system is normal, so it is only output during a current problem, and is not kept in memory from a previous problem. Accordingly, before turning the ignition switch to OFF, the diagnostic trouble code should be read and written down.	Improper installation of rear wheel speed sensor
	Malfunction of rear wheel speed sensor
	Malfunction of rotor
	Malfunction of wheel bearing
	Shortcircuited harness wire
	Malfunction of ABS-ECU

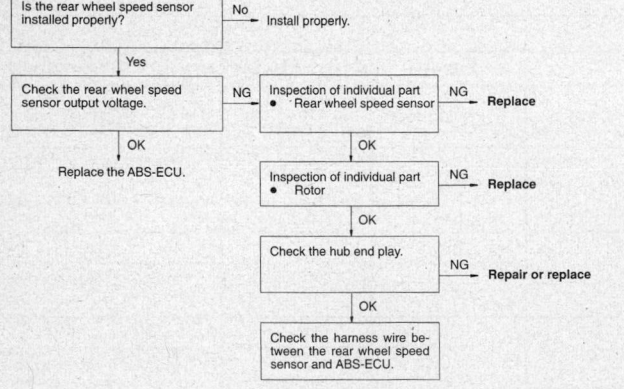

MT4029100126000X

Fig. 141   Code 25: Open Circuit In Both Rear Wheel Speed Sensors. 1996 Mirage

Code Nos. 21, 22, 23, 24 Short circuited wheel speed sensor	Probable cause
[Comment] These diagnostic trouble codes are displayed when a open circuit cannot be verified, but when the vehicle speed reaches 10 km/h (6 mph) or more, no pulses are input. [Hint] The cause is likely to be either a short between the sensor harnesses, a short in the sensor + wire with the body, or an excessive sensor gap.	Improper installation of wheel speed sensor
	Malfunction of wheel speed sensor
	Malfunction of rotor
	Malfunction of wheel bearing
	Shortcircuited harness wire
	Malfunction of ABS-ECU

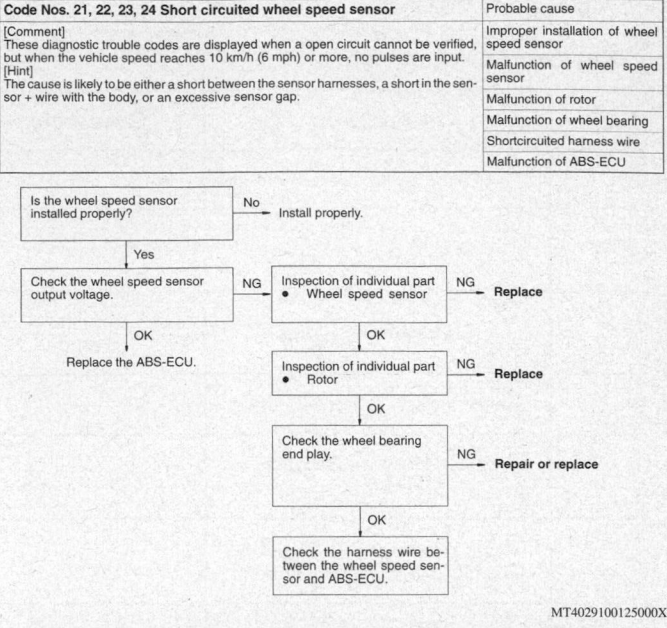

MT4029100125000X

Fig. 140   Codes 21, 22, 23 & 24: Speed Sensors (Short Circuit). 1996 Mirage

Code Nos. 31, 32, Incorrect number of rotor teeth	Probable cause
[Comment] These codes are displayed when a chipped rotor tooth or a jammed rotor (one tooth) is detected, or if sensor output is low due to a defective sensor and warped rotor and continuous anti-lock braking occurs. Also, they show that there is a request of brake fluid pressure control with the stop light switch OFF from when the vehicle is stationary until the vehicle speed exceeds approximately 15 km/h (9.3 mph). If the vehicle repeats start and stop and the condition above is detected five times, the ABS warning light will illuminate. [Hint] There is a strong chance that the wheel speed sensor output is low due to a bent rotor tooth or excessive sensor gap. Low sensor output could also be caused by a rare short in the sensor coil.	Improper installation of wheel speed sensor
	Malfunction of wheel speed sensor
	Malfunction of rotor
	Malfunction of wheel bearing
	Shortcircuited harness wire
	Malfunction of ABS-ECU

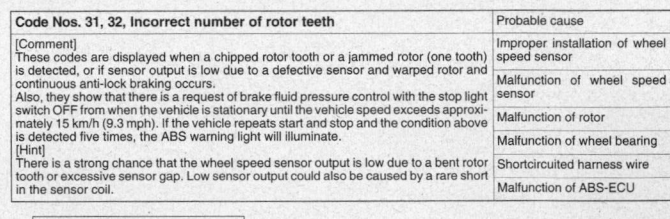

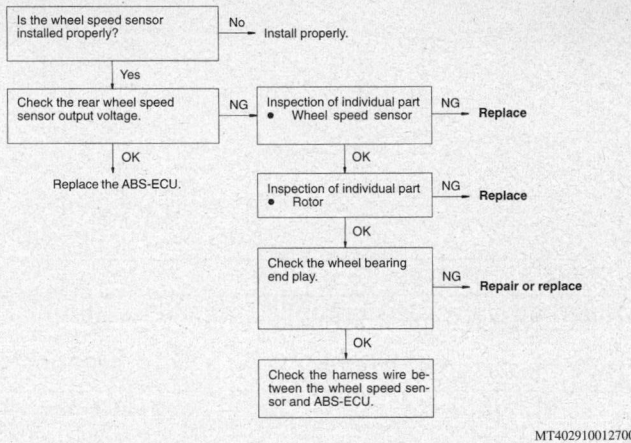

MT4029100127000X

Fig. 142   Codes 31 & 32: Front Wheel Speed Sensor Rotors. 1996 Mirage

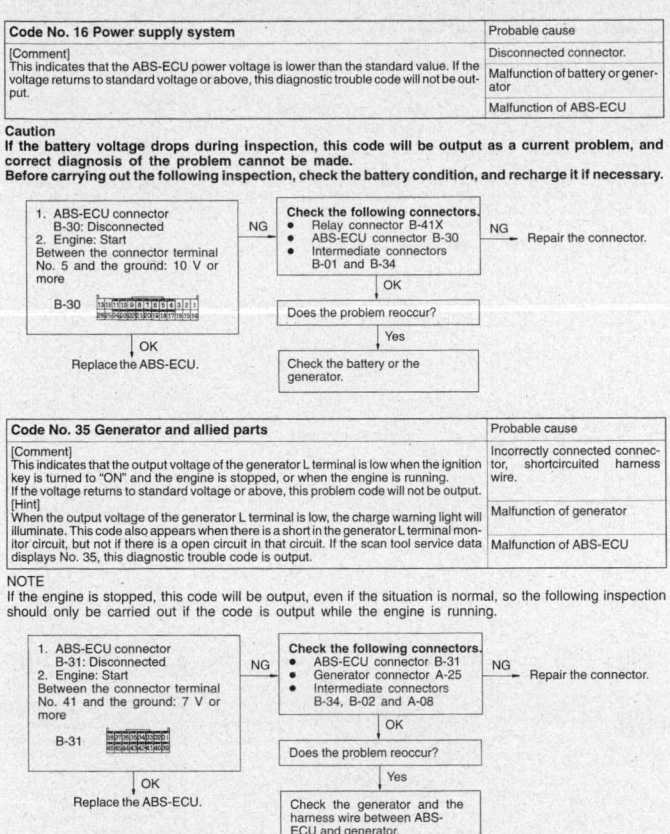

Code No. 16 Power supply system	Probable cause
[Comment] This indicates that the ABS-ECU power voltage is lower than the standard value. If the voltage returns to standard voltage or above, this diagnostic trouble code will not be output.	Disconnected connector.
	Malfunction of battery or generator
	Malfunction of ABS-ECU

Caution
If the battery voltage drops during inspection, this code will be output as a current problem, and correct diagnosis of the problem cannot be made.
Before carrying out the following inspection, check the battery condition, and recharge it if necessary.

Code No. 35 Generator and allied parts	Probable cause
[Comment] This indicates that the output voltage of the generator L terminal is low when the ignition key is turned to "ON" and the engine is stopped, or when the engine is running. If the voltage returns to standard voltage or above, this problem code will not be output. [Hint] When the output voltage of the generator L terminal is low, the charge warning light will illuminate. This code also appears when there is a short in the generator L terminal monitor circuit, but not if there is a open circuit in that circuit. If the scan tool service data displays No. 35, this diagnostic trouble code is output.	Incorrectly connected connector, shortcircuited harness wire.
	Malfunction of generator
	Malfunction of ABS-ECU

NOTE
If the engine is stopped, this code will be output, even if the situation is normal, so the following inspection should only be carried out if the code is output while the engine is running.

MT4029100128000X

Fig. 143   Codes 16 & 35: Drop Of Battery Voltage & Drop Of Generator Output Voltage. 1996 Mirage

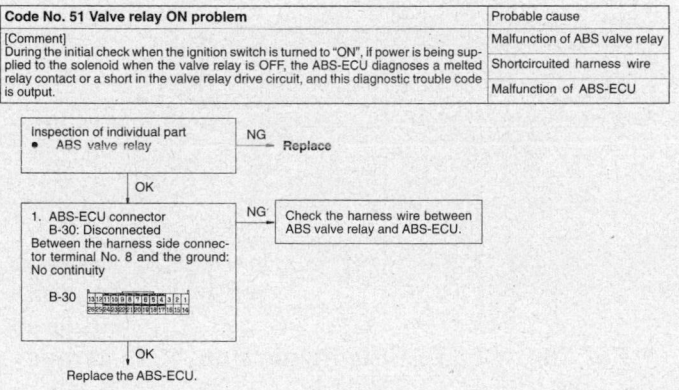

Code No. 51 Valve relay ON problem	Probable cause
[Comment] During the initial check when the ignition switch is turned to "ON", if power is being supplied to the solenoid when the valve relay is OFF, the ABS-ECU diagnoses a melted relay contact or a short in the valve relay drive circuit, and this diagnostic trouble code is output.	Malfunction of ABS valve relay
	Shortcircuited harness wire
	Malfunction of ABS-ECU

MT4029100130000X

Fig. 145   Code 51: Valve Relay No. 1. 1996 Mirage

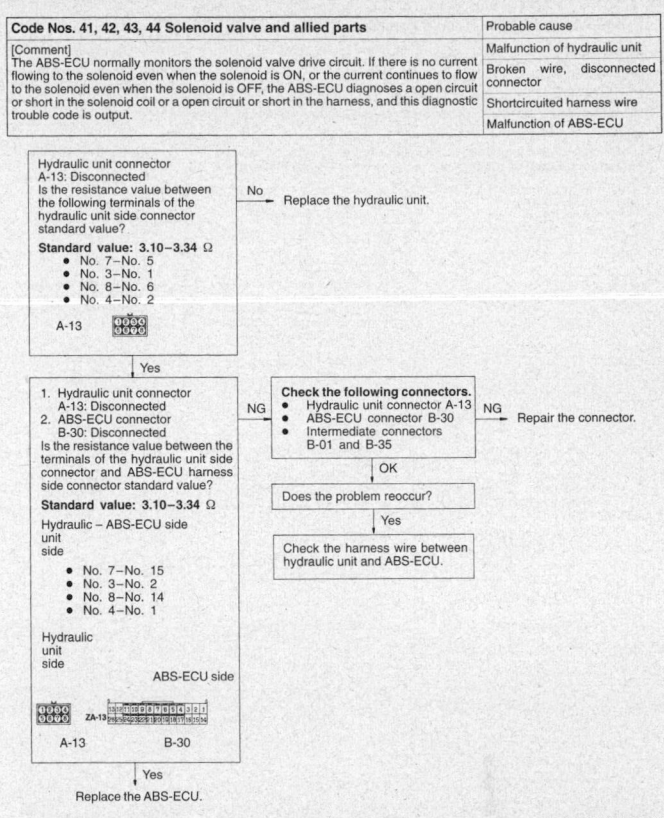

Code Nos. 41, 42, 43, 44 Solenoid valve and allied parts	Probable cause
[Comment] The ABS-ECU normally monitors the solenoid valve drive circuit. If there is no current flowing to the solenoid even when the solenoid is ON, or the current continues to flow to the solenoid even when the solenoid is OFF, the ABS-ECU diagnoses a open circuit or short in the solenoid coil or a open circuit or short in the harness, and this diagnostic trouble code is output.	Malfunction of hydraulic unit
	Broken wire, disconnected connector
	Shortcircuited harness wire
	Malfunction of ABS-ECU

MT4029100129000X

Fig. 144   Codes 41, 42, 43 & 44: Solenoid Valves. 1996 Mirage

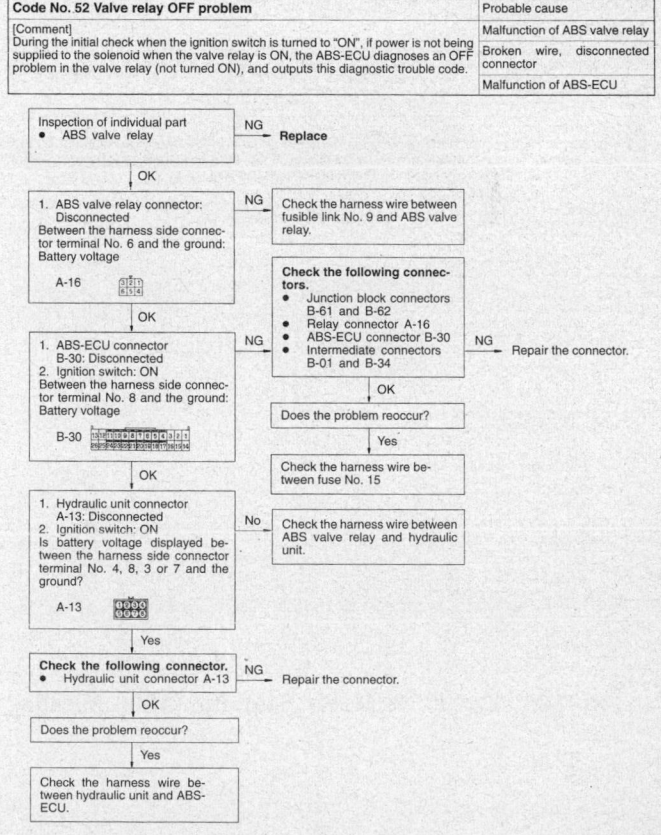

Code No. 52 Valve relay OFF problem	Probable cause
[Comment] During the initial check when the ignition switch is turned to "ON", if power is not being supplied to the solenoid when the valve relay is ON, the ABS-ECU diagnoses an OFF problem in the valve relay (not turned ON), and outputs this diagnostic trouble code.	Malfunction of ABS valve relay
	Broken wire, disconnected connector
	Malfunction of ABS-ECU

MT4029100131000X

Fig. 146   Code 52: Valve Relay No. 2. 1996 Mirage

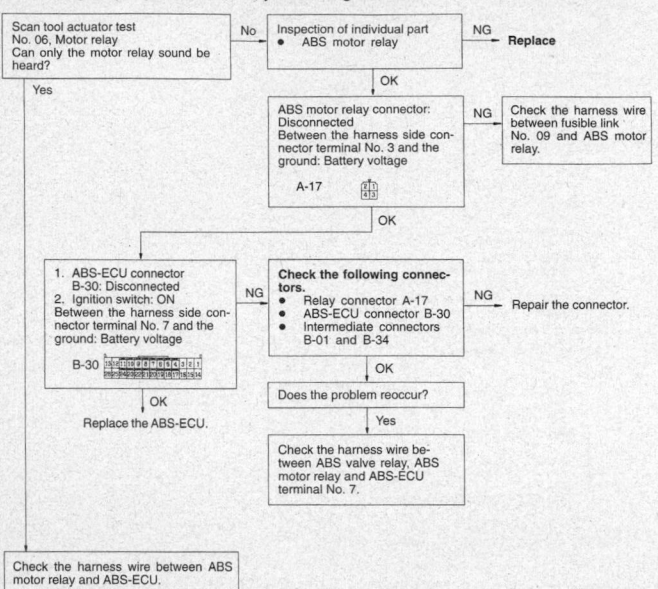

Code No. 53 Motor relay, motor OFF problem	Probable cause
[Comment] When the motor pump receives a signal to turn ON and voltage at the motor monitor is LOW, the ABS-ECU outputs this diagnostic trouble code. [Hint] If the sound of the motor relay operation can be heard when the No. 6 motor relay is driven by a scan tool actuator test, there is probably a short in the motor monitor wire.	Malfunction of ABS motor relay
	Defective harness wire, disconnected connector
	Malfunction of ABS-ECU

Caution
In the case of actuator test No. 06, the engine should be started left running for a while after the test is completed to prevent the battery from being drained.

MT4029100132000X

Fig. 147 Code 53: Motor Relay No. 1. 1996 Mirage

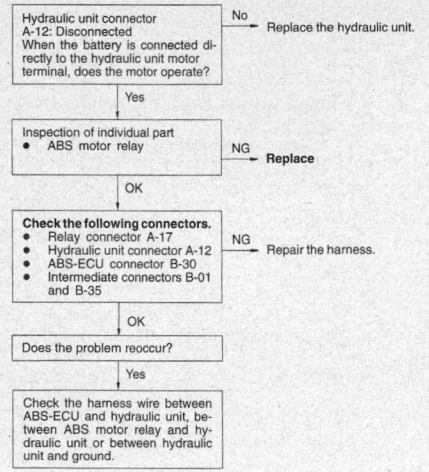

Code No. 55 Motor and allied parts	Probable cause
[Comment] The ABS-ECU drives the motor after the initial check, and if the motor is diagnosed as not running normally, the motor is driven again when the vehicle speed is 10 km/h (6.2 mph). If the motor operation is diagnosed as not normal at this time also, this diagnostic trouble code is output. [Hint] It is possible for this diagnostic trouble code to be output when there is an abnormality in the motor relay or motor harnesses. If the noise from the motor is not heard after starting the engine without depressing the brake pedal, the rotating shaft of the motor is probably stuck. When the No. 06 motor relay is driven by a scan tool actuator test and the motor doesn't operate, the same judgement is possible.	Malfunction of hydraulic unit
	Bad contact of connector
	Defective harness wire

Caution
If the battery is depleted or if the generator L terminal voltage is low, the motor will not be driven, so when carrying out the motor drive check, check to be sure that these things are normal. Carry out the motor drive check while the vehicle is stationary.

MT4029100134000X

Fig. 149 Code 55: Motor Sticking. 1996 Mirage

Code No. 54 Motor relay, motor ON problem	Probable cause
[Comment] When the pump motor receives a signal to turn OFF and the motor monitor is ON, if a melted contact, etc. is diagnosed in the motor relay, the ABS-ECU outputs this diagnostic trouble code. [Hint] Because the motor monitor wire is pulled up into the ABS-ECU by the IG power, this diagnostic trouble code is output if there is a open circuit in the harness, even if the motor relay and the motor are normal.	Malfunction of ABS motor relay
	Malfunction of hydraulic unit
	Broken wire, disconnected connector
	Malfunction of ABS-ECU

Caution
If there is a melted contact in the motor relay, the motor will keep turning, even if the ignition switch is turned to OFF. In such a case, immediately remove the fusible link (60 A) or disconnect the hydraulic unit A-12 connector. Excessive running of the motor will cause the battery to discharge.

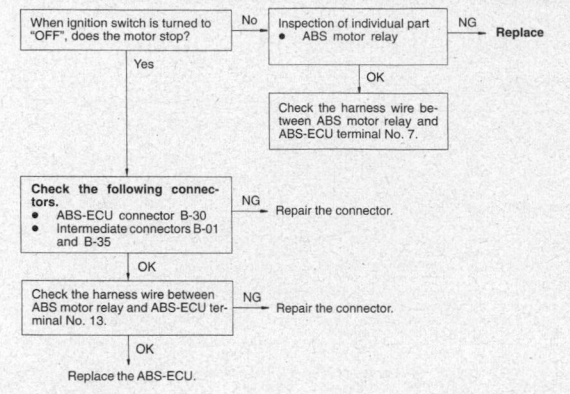

MT4029100133000X

Fig. 148 Code 54: Motor Relay No. 2. 1996 Mirage

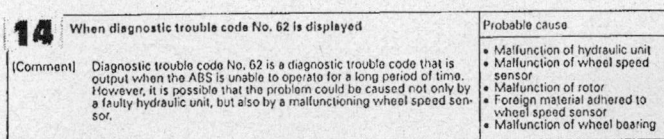

14 When diagnostic trouble code No. 62 is displayed	Probable cause
[Comment] Diagnostic trouble code No. 62 is a diagnostic trouble code that is output when the ABS is unable to operate for a long period of time. However, it is possible that the problem could be caused not only by a faulty hydraulic unit, but also by a malfunctioning wheel speed sensor.	Malfunction of hydraulic unit
	Malfunction of wheel speed sensor
	Malfunction of rotor
	Foreign material adhered to wheel speed sensor
	Malfunction of wheel bearing

Caution
The diagnostic trouble code No. 62 is detected in the following cases, even if the ABS system is normal. To be sure, the user should be questioned to check if the appropriate driving is not being carried out.

• If the parking brake is not fully released, of if the brakes are dragging while driving on snow or ice.
• When driving with left and right tires of different sizes (difference in tire diameter or uneven wear).
• When driving for a long period of time on roads with low friction coefficients, such as ice-covered roads.

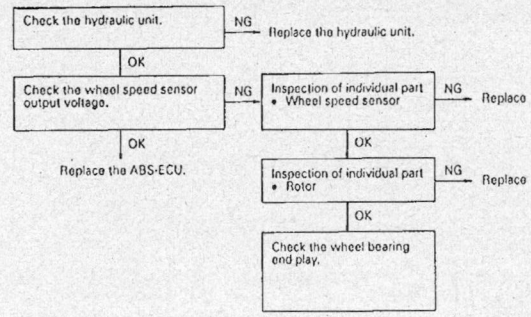

MT4029100135000X

Fig. 150 Code 62: Hydraulic Unit. 1996 Mirage

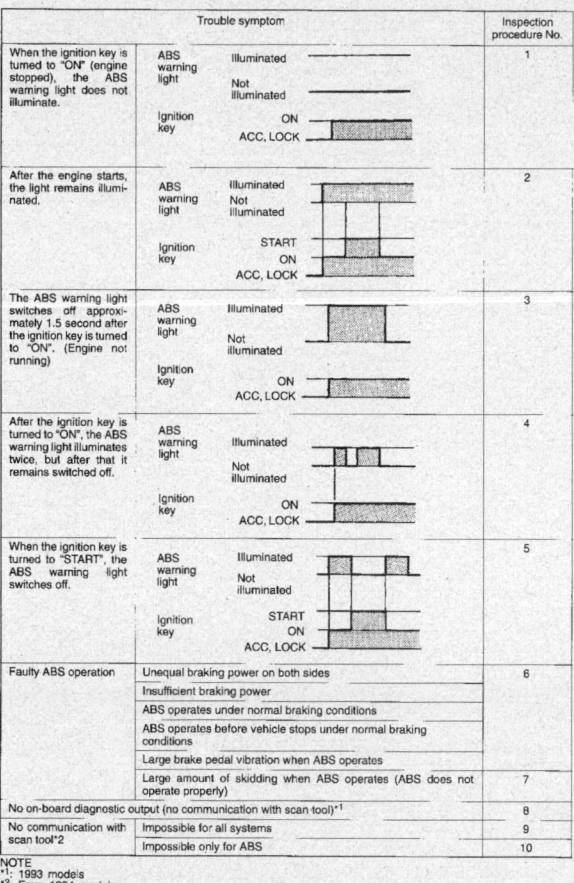

Fig. 151 Trouble symptom inspection chart. Mirage

MT4029100114000A

INSPECTION PROCEDURE 1

When ignition key is turned to "ON" (engine stopped), ABS warning light does not illuminate	Probable cause
[Comment] When power is supplied to the ABS-ECU, the valve relay changes from OFF to ON→OFF→ON by the initial check, and thus even if there is a problem with the circuit between ABS warning light and ABS-ECU, the light will illuminate twice when the valve relay is OFF. Accordingly, the cause of the light not illuminating is probably an open circuit in the light power circuit, a blown bulb, or an open circuit in both the circuit between the ABS warning light and the ABS-ECU and the circuit between the ABS warning light and the ABS valve relay. [Hint] When other warning lights also do not illuminate, the cause is probably a blown fuse.	Blown fuse
	Burnt out ABS warning light bulb
	Broken wire, disconnected connector

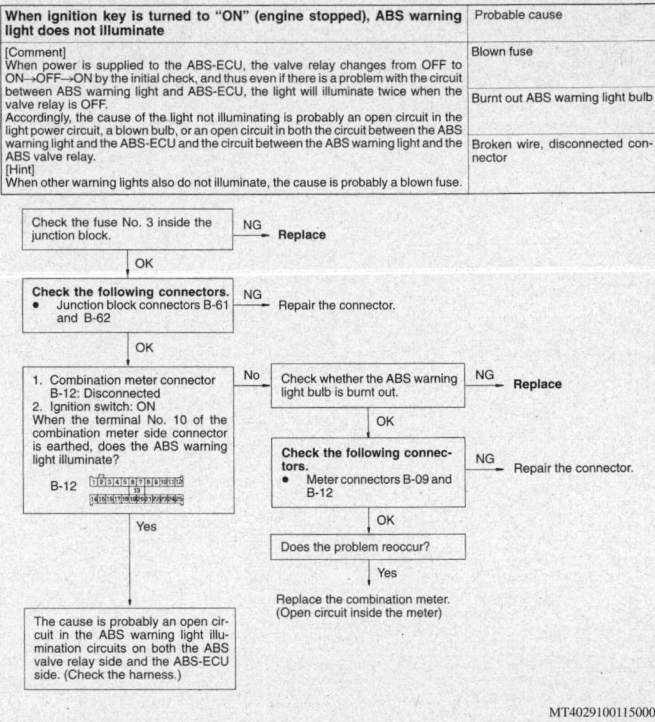

Fig. 152 Inspection chart 1. 1996 Mirage

MT4029100115000X

INSPECTION PROCEDURE 2

Even after the engine is started, the ABS warning light remains illuminated	Probable cause
[Comment] There is probably a short in the ABS warning light illumination circuit.	Malfunction of combination meter
	Malfunction of ABS-ECU
	Shortcircuited harness wire

NOTE
This trouble symptom is limited to cases where communication with the scan tool is possible (ABS-ECU power supply is normal) and the diagnostic trouble code is a normal diagnostic trouble code.

INSPECTION PROCEDURE 3

The ABS warning light switches OFF approximately 1.5 second after the ignition key is turned to "ON"	Probable cause
[Comment] The ABS-ECU monitors the voltage of the generator L terminal, and when the engine is not running, the voltage of the L terminal is low, and thus the ABS warning light illuminates. Accordingly, when the ignition key is turned to "ON", if the light turns off after the initial check (which takes about 1.5 second), there is a problem in the ABS warning light illumination function resulting from the generator L terminal monitor.	Broken wire, disconnected connector
	Malfunction of ABS-ECU

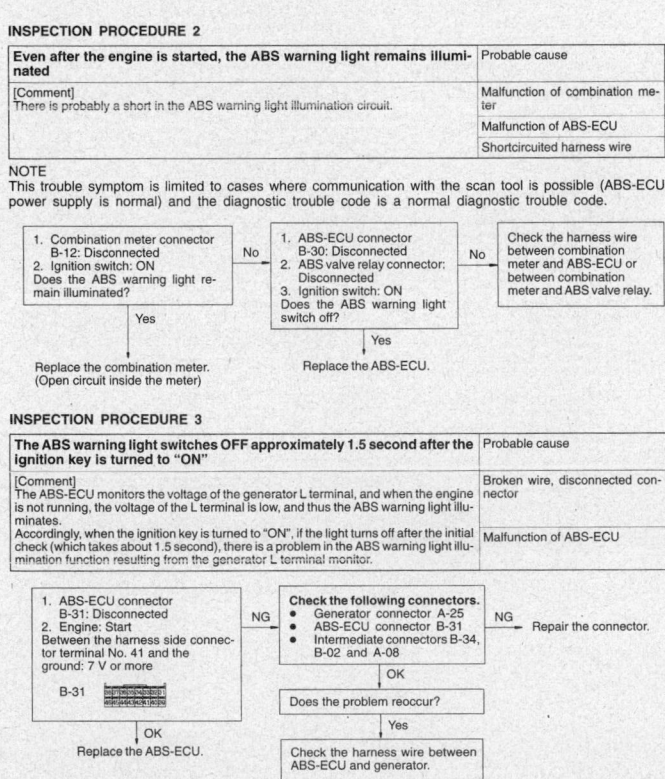

Fig. 153 Inspection charts 2 & 3. 1996 Mirage

MT4029100116000X

INSPECTION PROCEDURE 4

The ABS warning light illuminates twice after the ignition key is turned to "ON", but after that it remains switched off	Probable cause
[Comment] The ABS-ECU causes the ABS warning light to illuminate during the initial check. The valve relay changes from OFF to ON→OFF→ON by the initial check, and if there is a open circuit in the light drive circuit from the ABS-ECU, the light will illuminate when the valve relay is OFF. Accordingly, if the ignition key is "ON", and the light illuminates twice and then switches off, there is a problem in the ABS-ECU drive circuit.	Broken wire, disconnected connector
	Malfunction of ABS-ECU

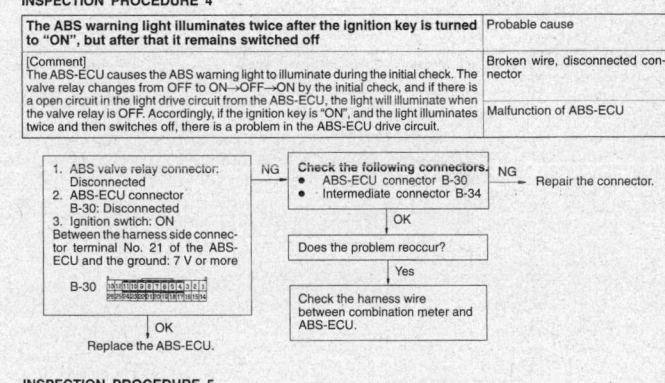

INSPECTION PROCEDURE 5

When ignition key is turned to "START", ABS warning light switches off	Probable cause
[Comment] The ABS-ECU uses the power to the IG2 which is cut when the ignition switch is turned to "START". The ABS warning light uses IG1 power which is not cut even when the ignition switch is turned to "START". Accordingly, because the power to the ABS-ECU is stopped in "START" position, if the warning light switches off at this time, the cause is a problem in the light illumination circuit in the valve relay.	Malfunction of ABS valve relay
	Broken wire, disconnected connector

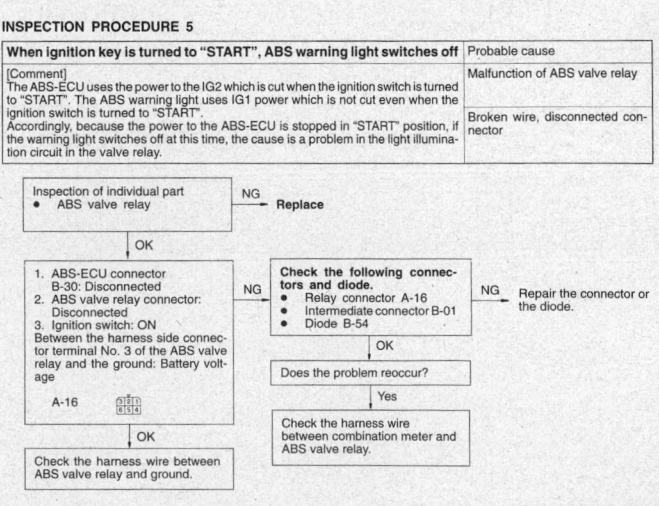

MT4029100117000X

Fig. 154 Inspection chart 4 & 5. 1996 Mirage

INSPECTION PROCEDURE 6

Brake operation is abnormal	Probable cause
[Comment] This varies depending on the driving conditions and the road surface conditions, so problem diagnosis is difficult. However, if a normal diagnostic trouble code is displayed, carry out the following inspection.	Improper installation of wheel speed sensor
	Bad contact of wheel speed sensor harness connector
	Malfunction of wheel speed sensor
	Malfunction of rotor
	Foreign material adhered to wheel speed sensor
	Malfunction of wheel bearing
	Malfunction of hydraulic unit
	Malfunction of ABS-ECU

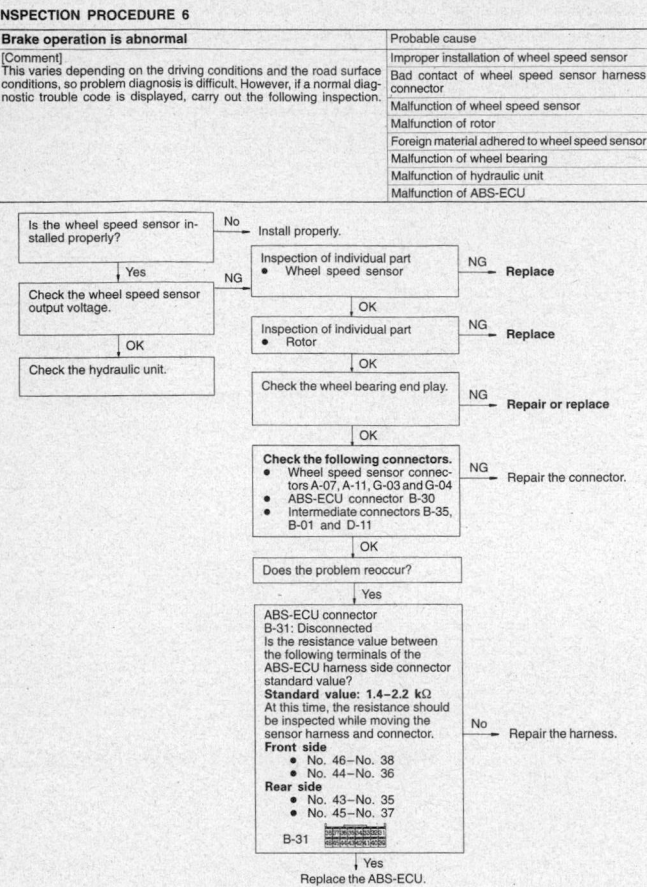

Fig. 155   Inspection chart 6. 1996 Mirage

MT4029100118000X

No communication with scan tool (impossible for all systems) <From 1994 models>	Probable cause
[Hint] Faulty power supply for diagnostic line (incl. grounding) is suspected.	Defective harness or connector

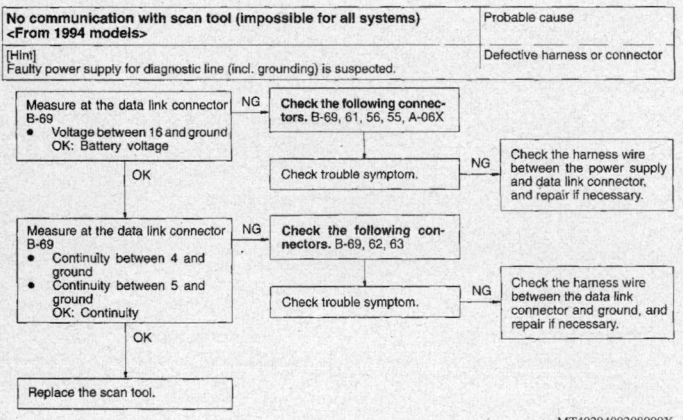

Fig. 157   Inspection chart 9. 1996 Mirage

MT4029400208000X

INSPECTION PROCEDURE 7

ABS function does not easily operate	Probable cause
[Comment] If the stop light switch ON signal is not input to the ABS-ECU even once after the engine has been started, the ABS control starting vehicle speed becomes 15 km/h (9.3 mph) or more. [If the signal is input even once, control is possible at a vehicle speed of 6 km/h (3.7 mph) or more.] This symptom occurs when there is an open circuit in the stop light switch. [Hint] When the illumination and switching off of the stop light switch is normal and scan tool service data No. 36 displays "OFF" even though the brake pedal is depressed, there is an open circuit in the stop light switch input circuit, or the ABS-ECU interface circuit is defective.	Blown fuse
	Malfunction of stop light switch
	Malfunction of hydraulic unit
	Broken wire, disconnected connector
	Malfunction of ABS-ECU

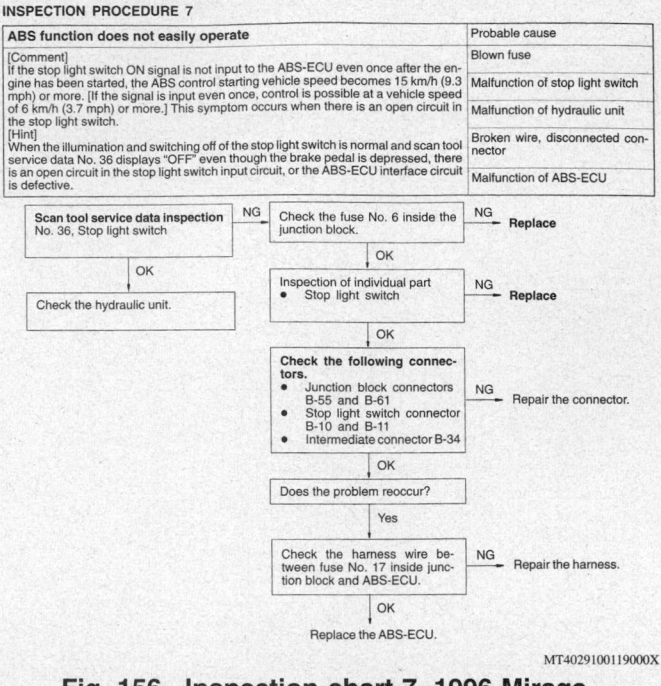

Fig. 156   Inspection chart 7. 1996 Mirage

MT4029100119000X

No communication with scan tool (impossible only for ABS) <From 1994 models>	Probable cause
[Hint] Open circuit in ABS diagnostic output circuit or power supply circuit (incl. ground circuit) is suspected.	Blown fuse
	Malfunction of ABS power relay
	Broken wire, disconnected connector
	Malfunction of ABS-ECU

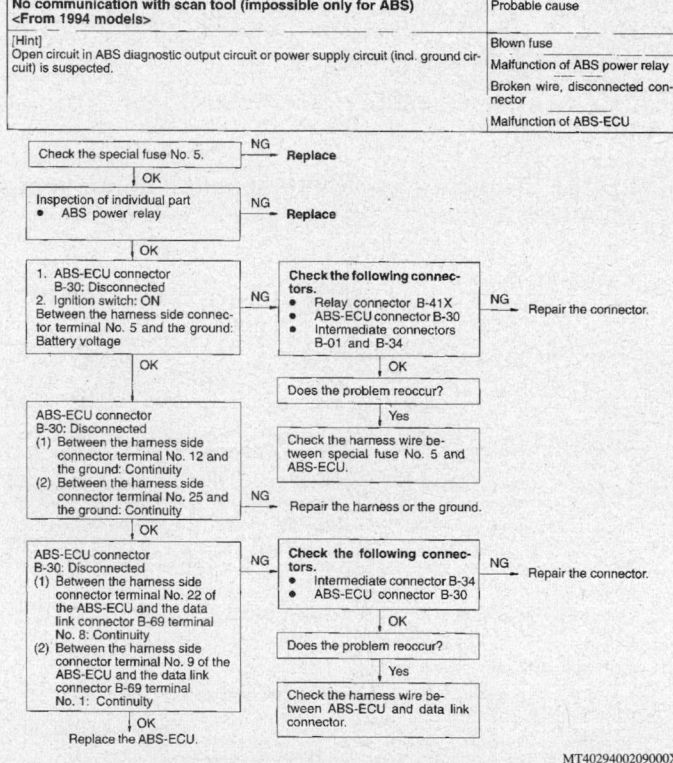

Fig. 158   Inspection chart 10. 1996 Mirage

MT4029400209000X

Code Nos. 11, 12, 13, 14 Wheel speed sensor open circuit or short circuit	Probable cause
Code Nos. 21, 22, 23, 24 Wheel speed sensor	
Code Nos.11, 12, 13, 14 are output when the ABS-ECU detects an open circuit or short circuit in at least one of the four wheel-speed sensors.	• Malfunction of wheel speed sensor • Malfunction of wiring harness or connector • Malfunction of ABS-ECU
Code Nos.21, 22, 23, 24 are output under the following cases: • When an open circuit cannot be found, but more than one wheel-speed sensor does not output any signal during driving at 8 km/h (5 mph) or higher. • When a chipped or plugged-up rotor tooth, etc. is detected during driving at 40 km/h (25 mph) or more.	• Malfunction of wheel-speed sensor • Malfunction of rotor • Malfunction of wheel bearing • Malfunction of wiring harness or connector • Malfunction of ABS-ECU

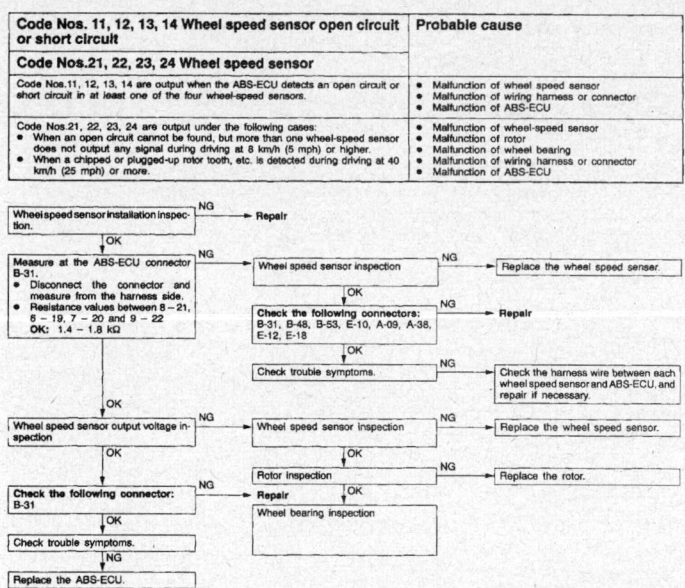

Fig. 159   Codes 11, 12, 13, 14, 21, 22, 23 & 24: Wheel Speed Sensor. 1997–99 Mirage

Code No. 16 Power supply system	Probable cause
The voltage of the ABS-ECU power supply or the voltage of the valve relay power supply drops lower or rises higher than the specified value. If the voltage returns to the specified value, this code is no longer output.	• Malfunction of wiring harness or connector. • Malfunction of ABS-ECU

Caution
If battery voltage drops or rises during inspection, this code will be output as well. If the voltage returns to standard value, this code is no longer output.
Before carrying out the following inspection, check the battery level, and refill it if necessary.

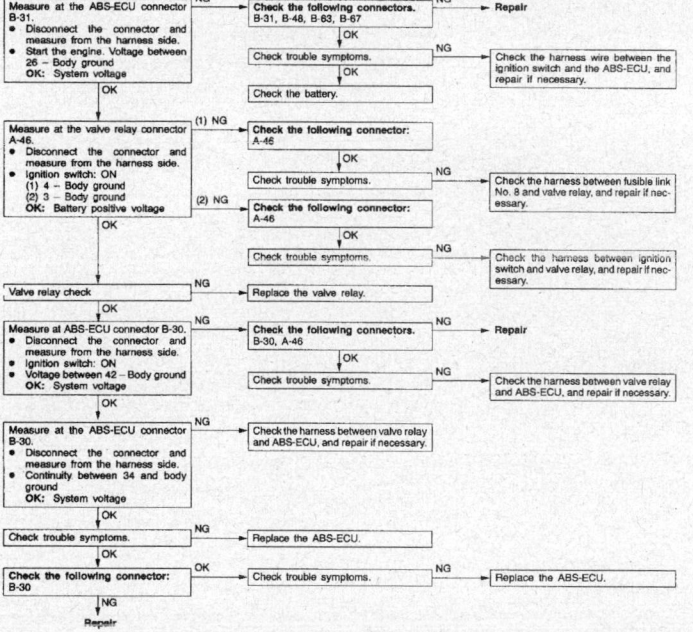

Fig. 161   Code 16: Power Supply System. 1997–99 Mirage

Code No. 15 Wheel speed sensor (Abnormal output signal)	Probable cause
A wheel speed sensor outputs an abnormal signal (other than an open or short-circuit).	• Improper installation of wheel speed sensor • Malfunction of wheel speed sensor • Malfunction of rotor • Malfunction of wheel bearing • Malfunction of wiring harness or connector • Malfunction of ABS-ECU

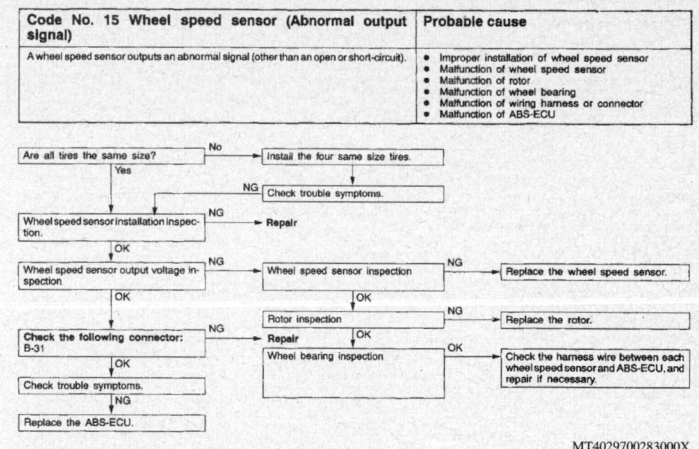

Fig. 160   Code 15: Wheel Speed Sensor. 1997–99 Mirage

Code No. 33 Stop light switch system	Probable cause
This code is output when the stop light switch is not be turned off (when the stop light switch stays on for 15 minutes or more although the ABS is not operating).	• Malfunction of stop light switch • Malfunction of harness or connector • Malfunction of ABS-ECU

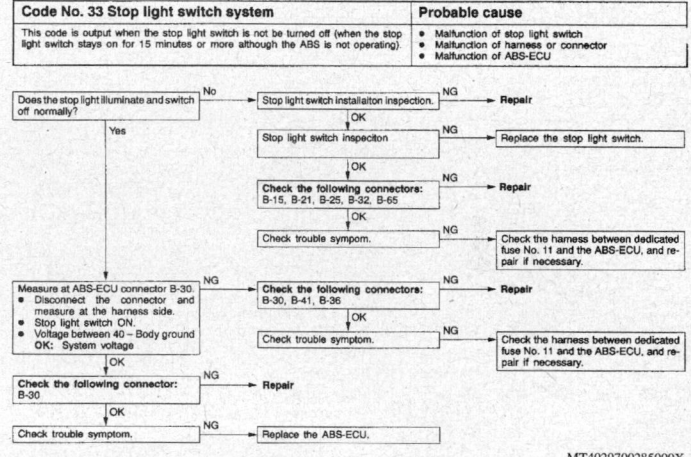

Fig. 162   Code 33: Stop Light Switch System. 1997–99 Mirage

Code Nos.41, 42, 43, 44 Solenoid valve	Probable cause
The ABS-ECU always monitors the solenoid valve drive circuit. It determines that there is an open or short-circuit in the solenoid coil or in a harness: • When no current flows in the solenoid even though the ABS-ECU turns on it, and vice versa.	• Malfunction of wiring harness • Malfunction of hydraulic unit • Malfunction of ABS-ECU

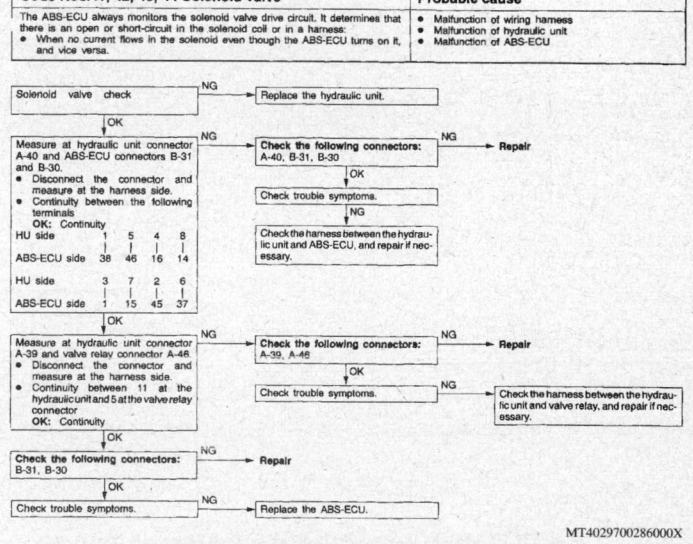

Fig. 163   Codes 41, 42, 43 & 44: Solenoid Valve. 1997–99 Mirage

Code No.51 Valve relay	Probable cause
When the ignition switch is turned to ON, the ABS-ECU switches the valve relay off and on during the initial check. In that way, the ABS-ECU compares the signals sent to the valve relay with the voltage in the valve relay monitor line. That is how to check if the valve relay is operating normally. The ABS-ECU always checks if current flows in the valve relay monitor line, too. It determines that there is an open circuit when no current flows. If no current flows in the valve relay monitor line, this diagnostic trouble code is output.	• Malfunction of valve relay • Malfunction of wiring harness or connector • Malfunction of ABS-ECU • Malfunction of hydraulic unit

NOTE
Whenever reading the diagnostic trouble codes using the ABS warning light (refer to P.35B-7), this diagnostic trouble code will be output. That is not a malfunction but because the valve relay connector is disconnected. After repairing all other malfunctions, connect the valve relay connector again to check the valve relay. Then check that the ABS warning light does not illuminate. If it illuminates, the valve relay may be defective. So carry out the following procedure.

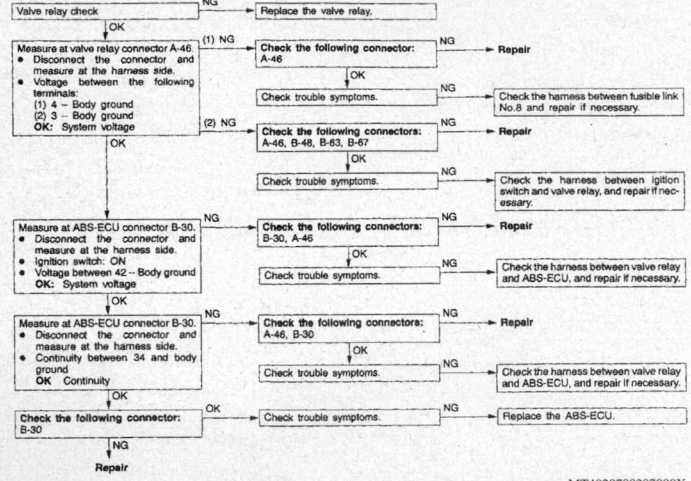

Fig. 164   Code 51: Valve Relay. 1997–99 Mirage

MT4029700287000X

Communication with scan tool is not possible. (Communication with all systems is not possible.)	Probable cause
The reason is probably defect in the power supply system (including ground) for the diagnostic line.	• Malfunction of wiring harness or connector

MT4029700314000X

Fig. 166   Inspection Procedure 1: Communication w/Scan Tool Not Possible. 1997–99 Mirage

Communication with scan tool is not possible. (Communication with ABS only is not possible.)	Probable cause
When communication with the scan tool is not possible, the cause is probably an open circuit in the ABS-ECU power circuit or an open circuit in the diagnostic output circuit.	• Blown fuse • Malfunction of wiring harness or connector • Malfunction of ABS-ECU

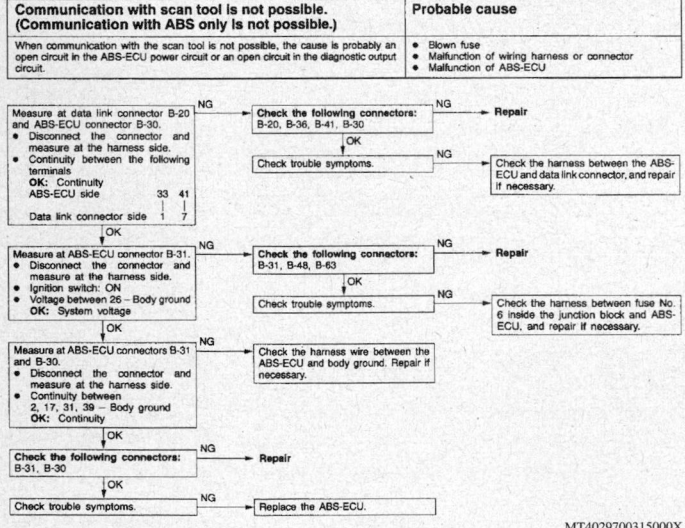

Fig. 167   Inspection Procedure 2: Communication w/ABS Not Possible. 1997–99 Mirage

MT4029700315000X

Code No.53 Motor relay, motor	Probable cause
This code is output at the following times: • When the motor relay is on but no signal is input to the motor monitor line (motor is not operating, etc.) • When the motor relay is off but a signal is input to the motor monitor line (motor continues operating, etc.) • When the motor relay does not operate	• Malfunction of motor relay • Malfunction of wiring harness or connector • Malfunction of hydraulic unit • Malfunction of ABS-ECU

\<When the motor does not run\>

Caution
The engine should be started and left to run for a while after testing is completed, because force-driving of the motor by means of the actuator test will drain the battery.

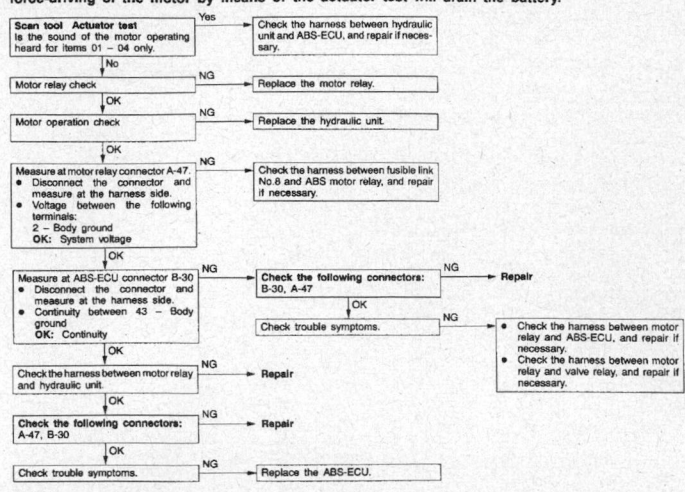

Caution
If there is a melted contact in the motor relay, the motor will keep running, even if the ignition switch is turned off. In this case, immediately remove the fusible link No.8, or disconnect the hydraulic unit connector A-39 or motor relay connector A-47. Excessive running of the motor will waste the battery.

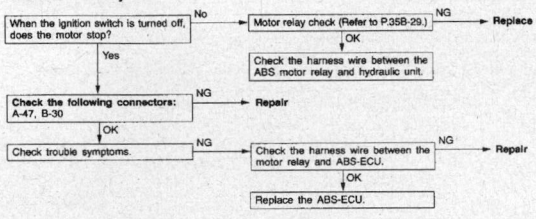

MT4029700288000X

Fig. 165   Code 53: Motor Relay. 1997–99 Mirage

When ignition key is turned to "ON" (engine stopped), ABS warning light does not illuminate.	Probable cause
The cause may be: an open circuit in the light power supply circuit, a blown light bulb, an open circuit in both the circuit between the ABS warning light and the ABS-ECU.	• Blown fuse • Burnt out ABS warning light bulb • Malfunction of wiring harness or connector

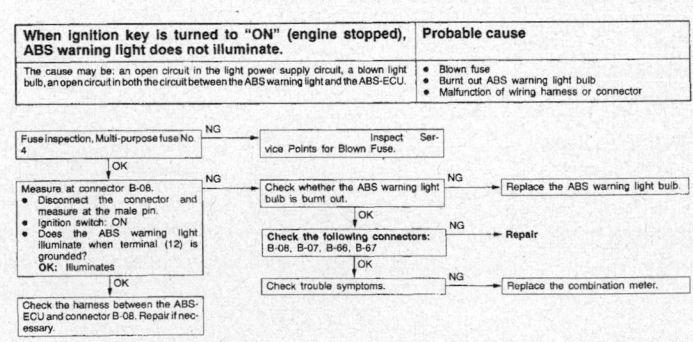

MT4029700316000X

Fig. 168   Inspection Procedure 3: ABS Light Does Not Illuminate w/Key In On Position. 1997–99 Mirage

Even after the engine is started, the ABS warning light remains illuminated.	Probable cause
The cause is probably a short-circuit in the ABS warning light illumination circuit.	• Malfunction of combination meter • Malfunction of ABS-ECU • Malfunction of wiring harness

NOTE
This trouble symptom is limited to cases where communication with the scan tool is possible (ABS-ECU power supply is normal) and the diagnostic trouble code is a normal diagnostic trouble code.

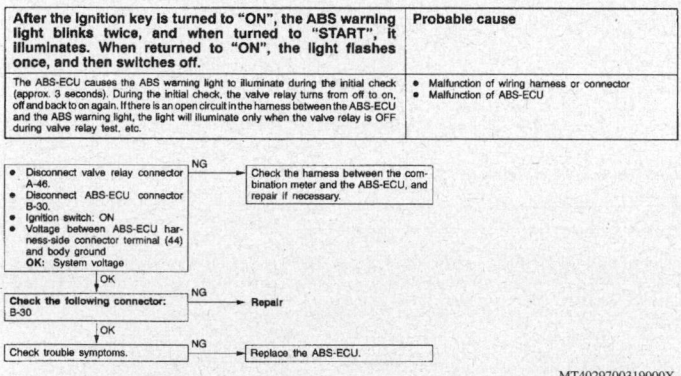

Fig. 169 Inspection Procedure 4: ABS Light Remains Illuminated w/Engine Running. 1997–99 Mirage

After the ignition key is turned to "ON", the ABS warning light blinks twice, and when turned to "START", it illuminates. When returned to "ON", the light flashes once, and then switches off.	Probable cause
The ABS-ECU causes the ABS warning light to illuminate during the initial check (approx. 3 seconds). During the initial check, the valve relay turns from off to on, off and back to on again. If there is an open circuit in the harness between the ABS-ECU and the ABS warning light, the light will illuminate only when the valve relay is OFF during valve relay test, etc.	• Malfunction of wiring harness or connector • Malfunction of ABS-ECU

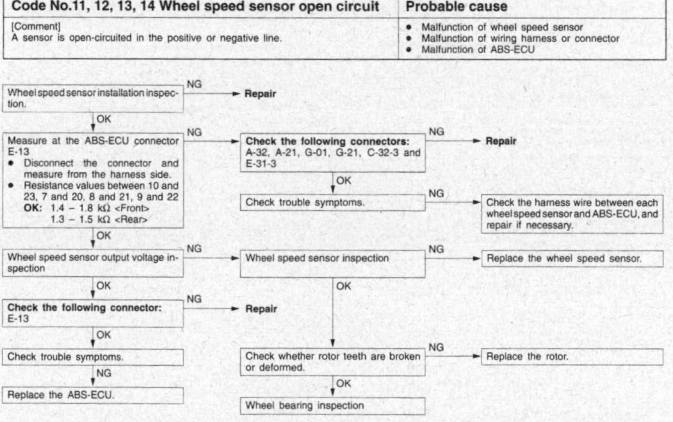

Fig. 171 inspection Procedure 6: ABS Light Blinks Twice When Key Is In On Position, Remains Illuminated In START Position, Then Blinks Once & Shuts Off When Key Is Returned To ON Position. 1997–99 Mirage

Code No.11, 12, 13, 14 Wheel speed sensor open circuit	Probable cause
[Comment] A sensor is open-circuited in the positive or negative line.	• Malfunction of wheel speed sensor • Malfunction of wiring harness or connector • Malfunction of ABS-ECU

Fig. 173 Codes 11, 12, 13 & 14: Wheel Speed Sensor Open Circuit. 1996–97 Montero

When the ignition key is turned to "START", the ABS warning light does not illuminate.	Probable cause
Current does not flow in the ABS warning light when the ignition switch is turned to "START". Current flows in the ABS warning light even when the ignition switch is turned to "START". Therefore, the valve relay, which current is supplied through the ABS-ECU, turns off when the ignition switch is at "START". However, the warning light circuit of the valve relay must turn on in turn. So the cause must be a defective circuit on valve relay side.	• Malfunction of wiring harness or connector • Malfunction of ABS-ECU

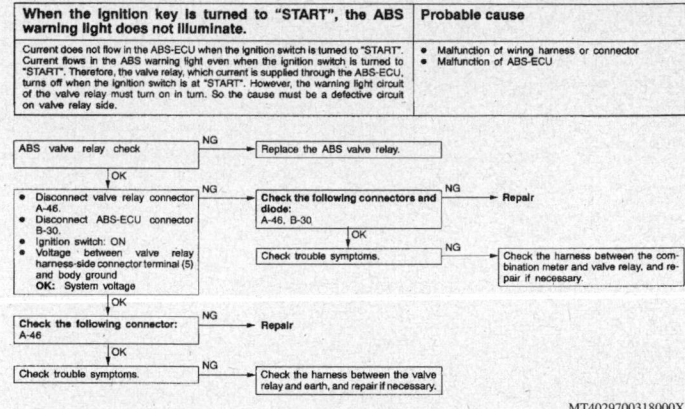

Fig. 170 Inspection Procedure 5: ABS Light Does Not Illuminate w/Key In Start Position. 1997–99 Mirage

Brake operation is abnormal.	Probable cause
This varies depending on the driving conditions and the road surface conditions, so problem diagnostic trouble is difficult. However, if a normal diagnostic trouble code is displayed, carry out the following inspection.	• Improper installation of wheel speed sensor • Incorrect sensor harness contact • Foreign material adhering to wheel speed sensor • Malfunction of wheel speed sensor • Malfunction of rotor • Malfunction of wheel bearing • Malfunction of hydraulic unit • Malfunction of ABS-ECU

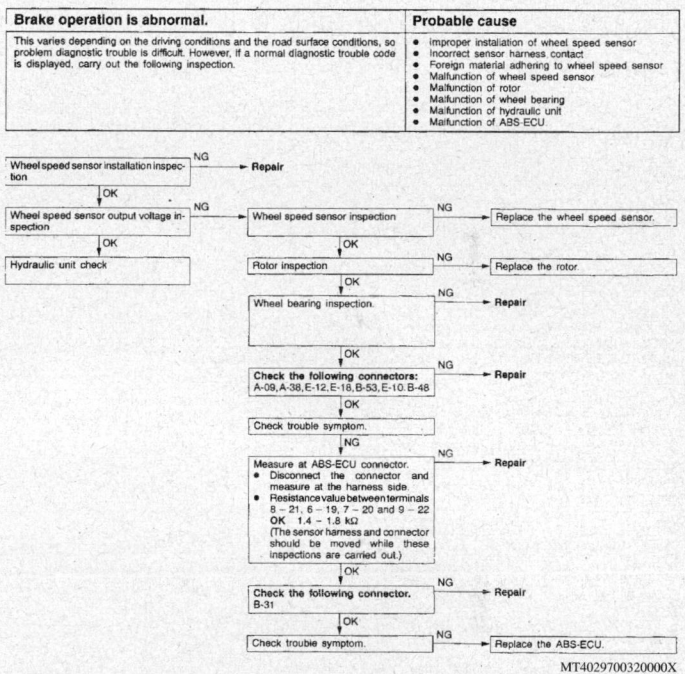

Fig. 172 Inspection Procedure 7: Brake Operation Abnormal. 1997–99 Mirage

Code No.15 Wheel speed sensor (Defective output signal)	Probable cause
[Comment] A malfunction (other than an open or short-circuit) is detected in the output signal from a wheel speed sensor while driving.	• Improper installation of wheel speed sensor • Malfunction of wheel speed sensor • Malfunction of rotor • Malfunction of wheel bearing • Malfunction of wiring harness or connector • Malfunction of ABS-ECU

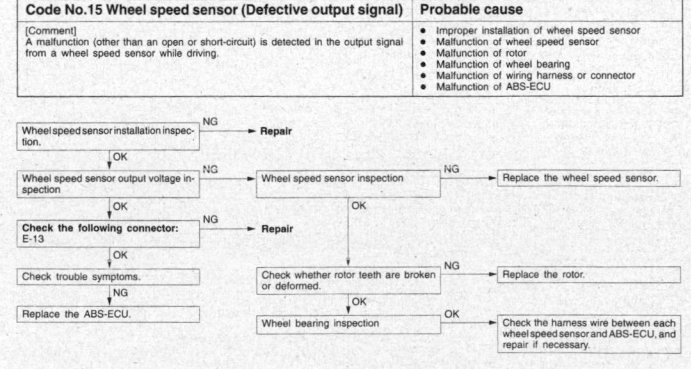

Fig. 174 Code 15: Wheel Speed Sensor Defective Output Signal. 1996–97 Montero

Code No.16 Power supply system	Probable cause
[Comment] The ABS-ECU power supply voltage or the solenoid valve power supply voltage is less than the specified value. If the voltage returns to the specified value, this code is no longer output.	• Malfunction of wiring harness or connector. • Malfunction of ABS-ECU.

Caution
If the battery voltage drops or rises during inspection, this code will be output as a current problem, and correct diagnosis of the problem cannot be made.
Before carrying out the following inspection, check the battery level, and refill it if necessary.

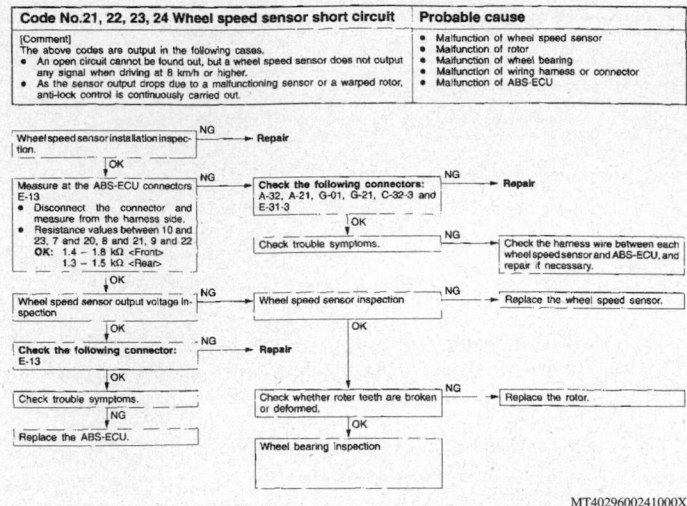

MT4029600240000X

Fig. 175   Code 16: Power Supply System. 1996–97 Montero

Code No.21, 22, 23, 24 Wheel speed sensor short circuit	Probable cause
[Comment] The above codes are output in the following cases. • An open circuit cannot be found out, but a wheel speed sensor does not output any signal when driving at 8 km/h or higher. • As the sensor output drops due to a malfunctioning sensor or a warped rotor, anti-lock control is continuously carried out.	• Malfunction of wheel speed sensor • Malfunction of rotor • Malfunction of wheel bearing • Malfunction of wiring harness or connector • Malfunction of ABS-ECU

MT4029600241000X

Fig. 176   Codes 21, 22, 23 & 24: Wheel Speed Sensor Short Circuit. 1996–97 Montero

Code No.25 Free wheel engage switch	Probable cause
[Comment] There is an open circuit in the free-wheeling engage switch system.	• Malfunction of wiring harness or connector • Malfunction of 4WD indicator ECU • Malfunction of ABS-ECU

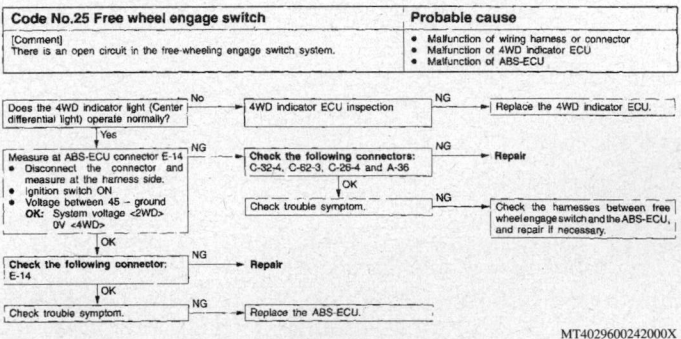

MT4029600242000X

Fig. 177   Code 25: Free Wheel Engage Switch. 1996–97 Montero

Code No.26 Centre differential lock detection switch	Probable cause
[Comment] The above codes are output in the following cases. • There is an open circuit in the center differential lock detection switch system. • The free wheel engage switch remains off and the center differential lock detection switch remains on at a vehicle speed of 15 km/h or more for 5 seconds or more.	• Malfunction of wiring harness or connector • Malfunction of free wheel engage switch • Malfunction of 4WD indicator ECU • Malfunction of center differential lock detection switch • Malfunction of ABS-ECU

Trouble symptom	Main cause	Remedy
Even when the transfer shift lever is in the "4H" position, the 4WD front wheel indicator light does not illuminate.	Broken harness wire between the 4WD indicator ECU and the free-wheel engage switch, or broken earth wire from the free-wheel engage switch.	Repair the harness
	Free wheel engage switch is defective	Replace the switch
Even when the transfer shift lever is in the "4H" position, the 4WD center differential light does not illuminate.	Broken harness wire between the 4WD indicator ECU and the center differential lock switch	Repair the harness
	Broken wire in the 4WD indicator ECU circuit	4WD indicator ECU inspection
4WD indicator center differential light illuminates regardless of the position of the transfer shift lever.	Short in the harness wire in the center differential lock detection switch circuit	Repair the harness
	Center differential lock detection switch is defective	Replace the switch
	Short inside the ABS-ECU circuit	Replace the ABS-ECU
	Short inside the the 4WD indicator ECU circuit	4WD indicator ECU inspection
No indicator is illuminated	Power circuit in the 4WD indicator ECU circuit	Repair the harness
	4WD indicator ECU is defective	4WD indicator ECU inspection

NOTE
When checking a short in the ABS-ECU circuit, remove the ABS-ECU connector and check if the 4WD indicator returns to normal. If it returns to normal, the ABS-ECU is defective. Furthermore, if the ABS-ECU is normal, then the 4WD indicator ECU will be defective.

MT4029600243000X

Fig. 178   Code 26: Center Differential Lock Detection Switch. 1996–97 Montero

Code No.27 Rear differential lock detection switch <Vehicles with rear differential lock>	Probable cause
[Comment] There is an open circuit in the rear differential lock detection switch system.	• Malfunction of wiring harness or connector • Malfunction of rear differential lock ECU • Malfunction of ABS-ECU

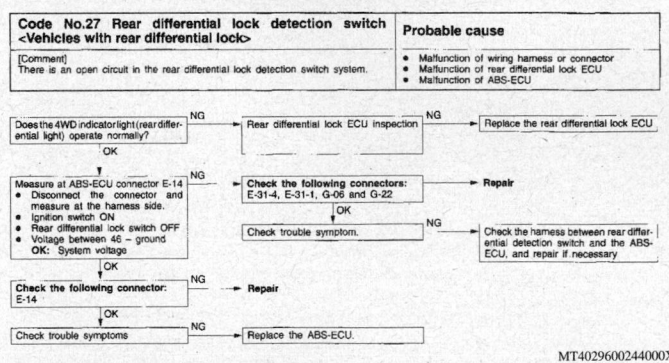

MT4029600244000X

Fig. 179   Code 27: Rear Differential Lock Detection Switch. 1996–97 Montero w/rear differential lock

Code No.27 Rear differential lock detection switch <Vehicles without rear differential lock>	Probable cause
[Comment] For vehicles without rear differential lock, battery positive voltage is applied to the ABS-ECU terminal no. 46. This diagnostic trouble code is output when this line is interrupted.	• Malfunction of wiring harness or connector • Malfunction of ABS-ECU

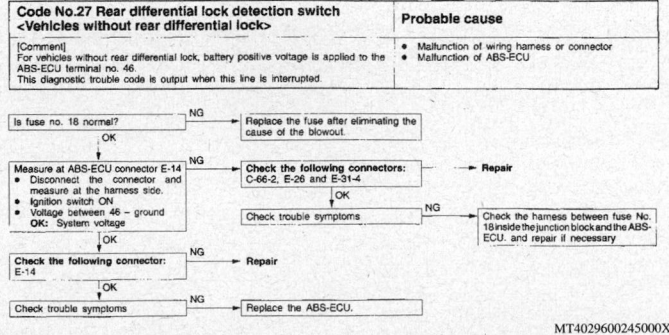

MT4029600245000X

Fig. 180   Code 27: Rear Differential Lock Detection Switch. 1996–97 Montero less rear differential lock

Code No.32 G-sensor system

Probable cause
- Malfunction of G-sensor
- Malfunction of wiring harness or connector
- Malfunction of ABS-ECU

[Comment]
The above codes are output in the following case.
- The G sensor output is less than 0.5 V or more than 4.5 V.
- There is an open or short circuit in the G sensor system.

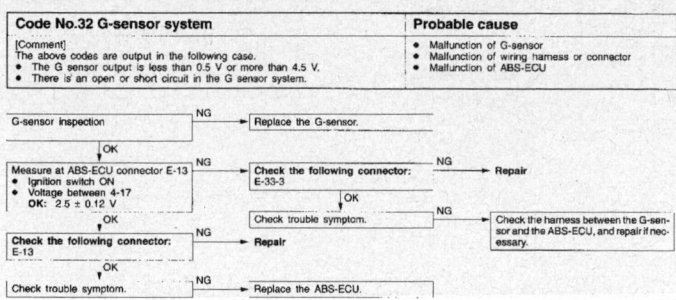

Fig. 181 Code 32: G-Sensor System. 1996–97 Montero

Code No.41, 42, 43 solenoid valve

Probable cause
- Malfunction of wiring harness
- Malfunction of hydraulic unit
- Malfunction of ABS-ECU

[Comment]
The ABS-ECU always monitors the solenoid drive circuit and judge that there is an open or short circuit in the solenoid coils in the following cases.
No current is being supplied to a solenoid even though that solenoid is on.
Current continues to be supplied to a solenoid even though that solenoid is off.

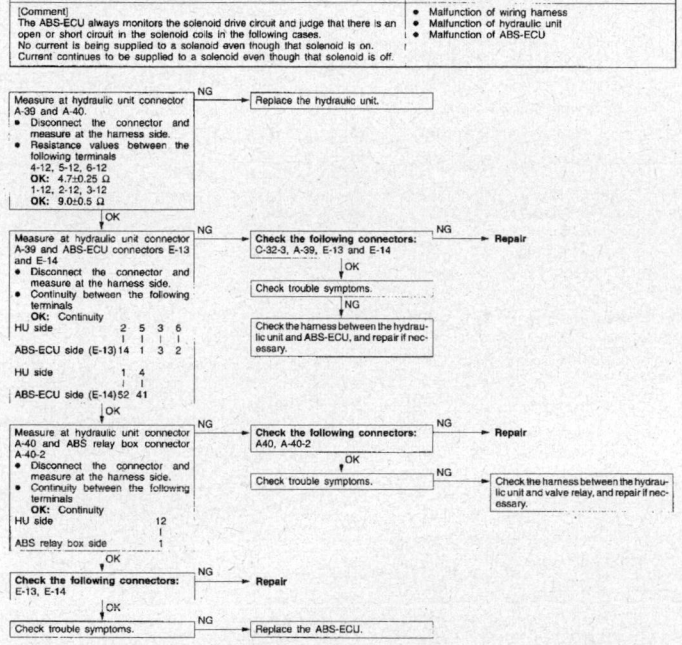

Fig. 183 Codes 41, 42 & 43: Solenoid Valve. 1996–97 Montero

Code No.33 Stop light switch system

Probable cause
- Malfunction of stop light switch
- Malfunction of harness or connector
- Malfunction of ABS-ECU

[Comment]
The above codes are output in the following cases.
- The stop light switch can not be turned off. (the stop light switch stays on for 15 minutes or more even though the ABS is not operating)
- There is an open circuit in the stop light switch system.

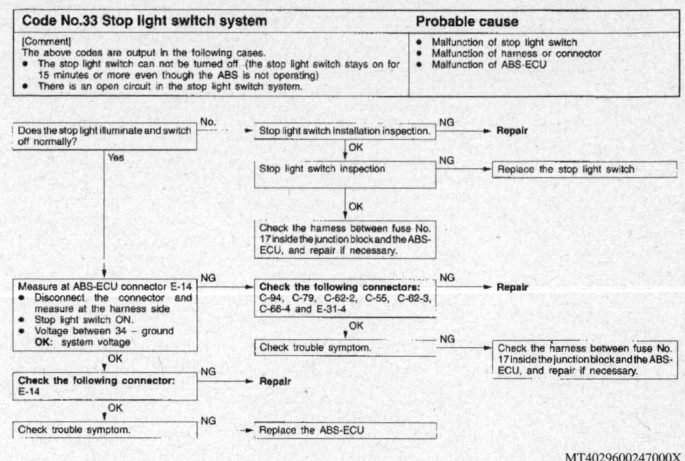

Fig. 182 Code 33: Stop Light Switch System. 1996–97 Montero

Code No.51 Valve relay

Probable cause
- Malfunction of valve relay
- Malfunction of wiring harness or connector
- Malfunction of ABS-ECU
- Malfunction of hydraulic unit

[Comment]
When the ignition switch is turned to ON, the ABS-ECU switches the valve relay off and on to check it as the initial check. The valve relay is normally on. So, if power is not being supplied to the relay, the ABS-ECU will judge that the valve relay is defective.

NOTE
Whenever reading the diagnostic trouble codes using the ABS warning light, this diagnostic trouble code will be output. That is because the valve relay has been removed. Repair all locations indicated by other diagnostic trouble codes, and then connect the valve relay connector. When the ABS warning light still indicates No.51 even after that, a malfunction in the valve relay system may be present. So, the following checks should then be carried out.

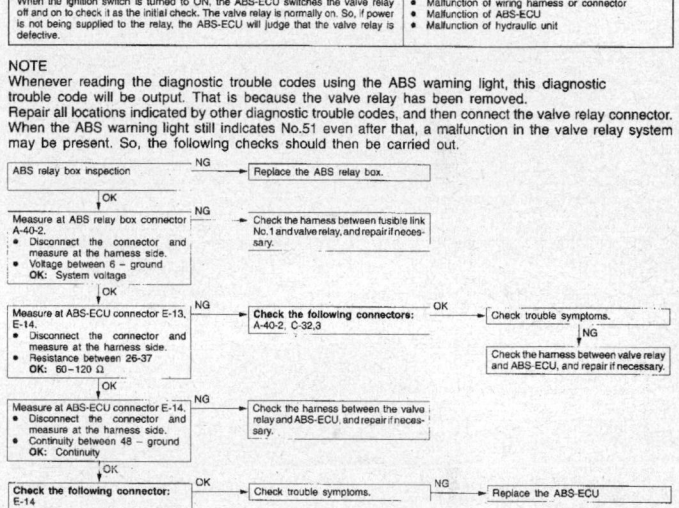

Fig. 184 Code 51: Valve Relay. 1996–97 Montero

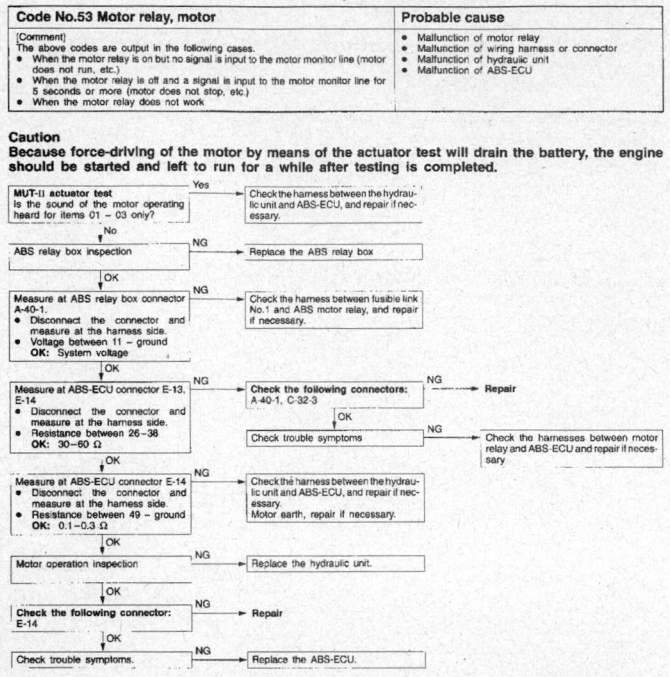

Code No.53 Motor relay, motor	Probable cause
[Comment] The above codes are output in the following cases. • When the motor relay is on but no signal is input to the motor monitor line (motor does not run, etc.) • When the motor relay is off and a signal is input to the motor monitor line for 5 seconds or more (motor does not stop, etc.) • When the motor relay does not work	• Malfunction of motor relay • Malfunction of wiring harness or connector • Malfunction of hydraulic unit • Malfunction of ABS-ECU

Caution
Because force-driving of the motor by means of the actuator test will drain the battery, the engine should be started and left to run for a while after testing is completed.

MT4029600250000X

Fig. 185   Code 53: Motor Relay & Motor Operation. 1996–97 Montero

Diagnosis code no.	Inspection item
27	Rear differential lock detection switch <Vehicles with rear differential lock>
	Rear differential lock detection switch <Vehicles without rear differential lock>
32	G-sensor system
33	Stop light switch system
41	Front right solenoid valve
42	Front left solenoid valve
43	Rear solenoid valve
51	Valve relay
53	Motor relay, motor
63	Replace the ABS-ECU
64	Replace the ABS-ECU

MT4029900347020X

Fig. 186   Diagnostic Trouble Code Inspection Chart (Part 2 of 2). 1998–99 Montero

Diagnosis code no.	Inspection item	Diagnosis content
11	Front right wheel speed sensor	Open or short circuit
12	Front left wheel speed sensor	
13	Rear right wheel speed sensor	
14	Rear left wheel speed sensor	
15	Wheel speed sensor	Abnormal output signal
16	Power supply system	
21	Front right wheel speed sensor	Defective sensor
22	Front left wheel speed sensor	
23	Rear right wheel speed sensor	
24	Rear left wheel speed sensor	
25	Free wheel engage switch	
26	Center differential lock detection switch	

MT4029900347010X

Fig. 186   Diagnostic Trouble Code Inspection Chart (Part 1 of 2). 1998–99 Montero

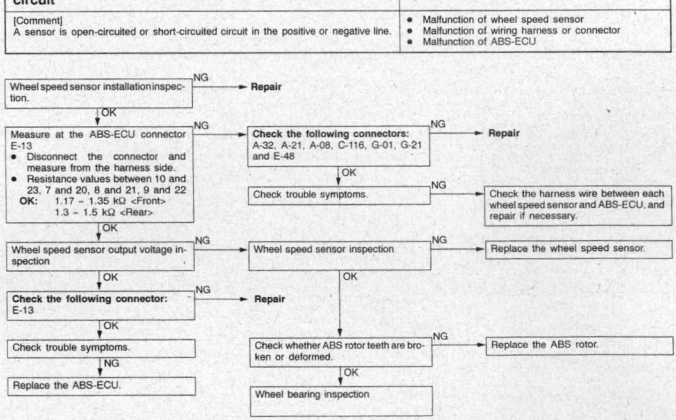

Code No.11, 12, 13, 14 Wheel speed sensor open or short circuit	Probable cause
[Comment] A sensor is open-circuited or short-circuited circuit in the positive or negative line.	• Malfunction of wheel speed sensor • Malfunction of wiring harness or connector • Malfunction of ABS-ECU

MT4029900348000X

Fig. 187   Codes 11, 12, 13 & 14: Wheel Speed Sensor Open Or Short Circuit. 1998–99 Montero

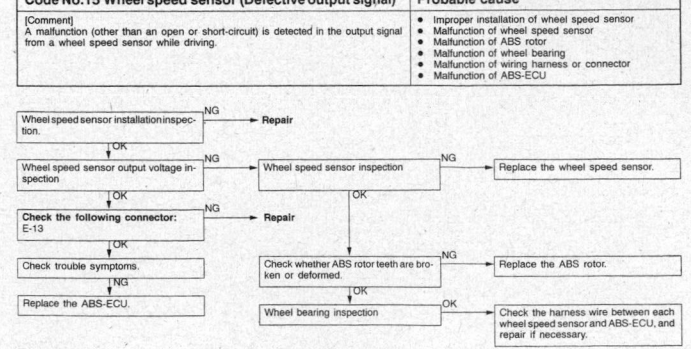

Code No.15 Wheel speed sensor (Defective output signal)	Probable cause
[Comment] A malfunction (other than an open or short-circuit) is detected in the output signal from a wheel speed sensor while driving.	• Improper installation of wheel speed sensor • Malfunction of wheel speed sensor • Malfunction of ABS rotor • Malfunction of wheel bearing • Malfunction of wiring harness or connector • Malfunction of ABS-ECU

MT4029900349000X

Fig. 188   Code 15: Wheel Speed Sensor. 1998–99 Montero

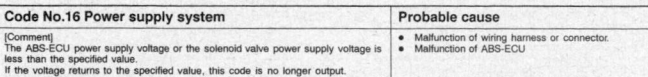

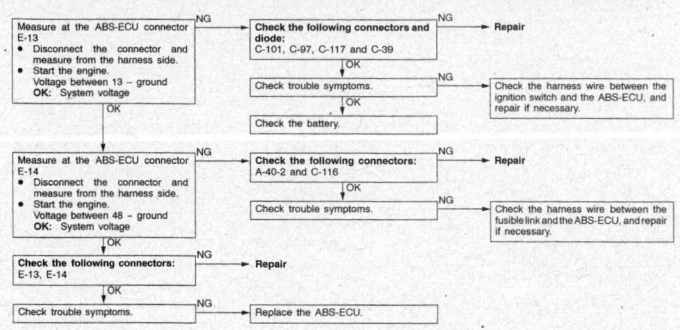

Fig. 189   Code 16: Power Supply System. 1998–99 Montero

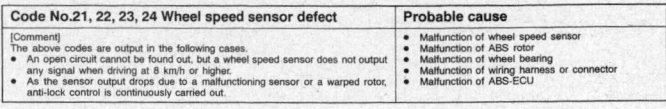

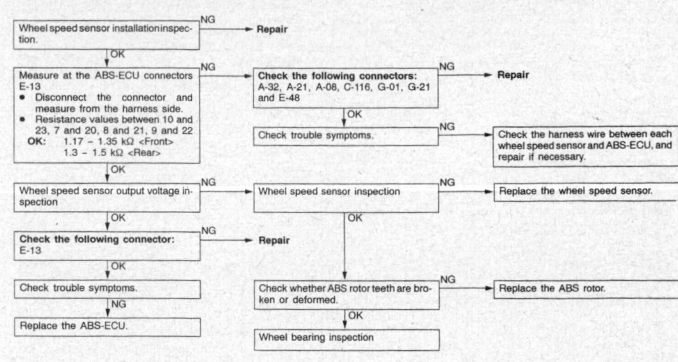

Fig. 190   Codes 21, 22, 23, & 24: Wheel Speed Sensor Malfunction. 1998–99 Montero

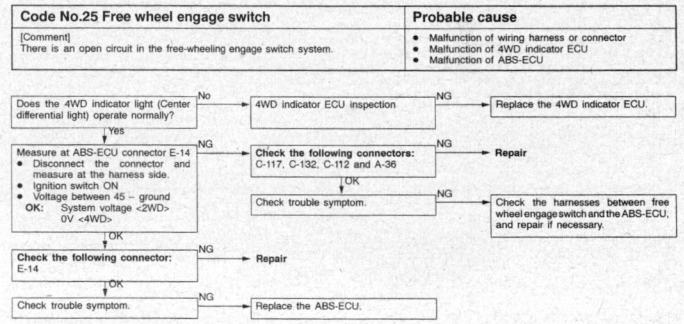

Fig. 191   Code 25: Free Wheel Engage Switch. 1998–99 Montero

Trouble symptom	Main cause	Remedy
Even when the transfer shift lever is in the "4H" position, the 4WD front wheel indicator light does not illuminate.	Broken harness wire between the 4WD indicator ECU and the free-wheel engage switch, or broken earth wire from the free-wheel engage switch.	Repair the harness
	Free wheel engage switch is defective	Replace the switch
Even when the transfer shift lever is in the "4H" position, the 4WD center differential light does not illuminate.	Broken harness wire between the 4WD indicator ECU and the center differential lock switch	Repair the harness
	Broken wire in the 4WD indicator ECU circuit	4WD indicator ECU inspection
4WD indicator center differential light illuminates regardless of the position of the transfer shift lever	Short in the harness wire in the center differential lock detection switch circuit	Repair the harness
	Center differential lock detection switch is defective	Replace the switch
	Short inside the ABS-ECU circuit	Replace the ABS-ECU
	Short inside the the 4WD indicator ECU circuit	4WD indicator ECU inspection
No indicator is illuminated	Power circuit in the 4WD indicator ECU circuit	Repair the harness
	4WD indicator ECU is defective	4WD indicator ECU inspection

NOTE
When checking a short in the ABS-ECU circuit, remove the ABS-ECU connector and check if the 4WD indicator returns to normal. If it returns to normal, the ABS-ECU is defective. Furthermore, if the ABS-ECU is normal, then the 4WD indicator ECU will be defective.

Fig. 192   Code 26: Center Differential Lock Detection Switch. 1998–99 Montero

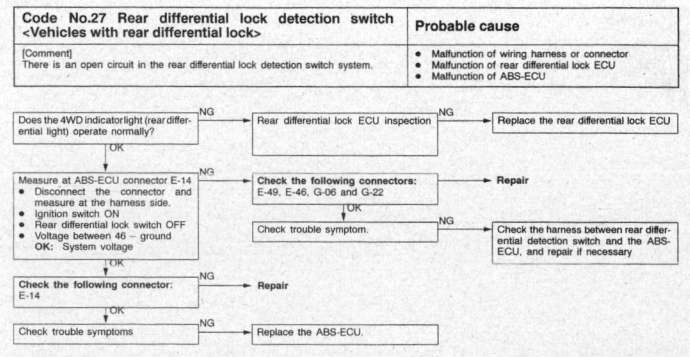

Fig. 193   Code 27: Rear Differential Lock Detection Switch. 1998–99 Montero w/Rear Differential Lock

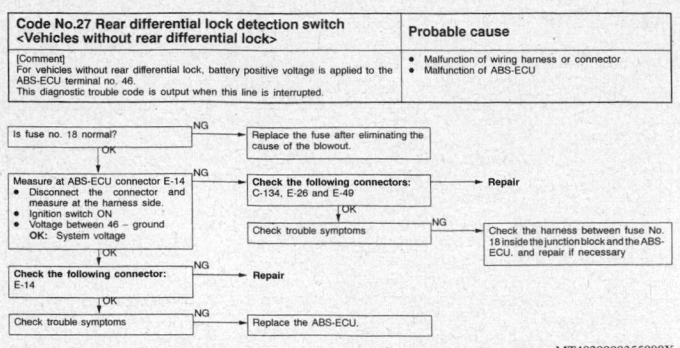

Fig. 194 Code 27: Rear Differential Lock Detection Switch. 1998–99 Montero Less Rear Differential Lock

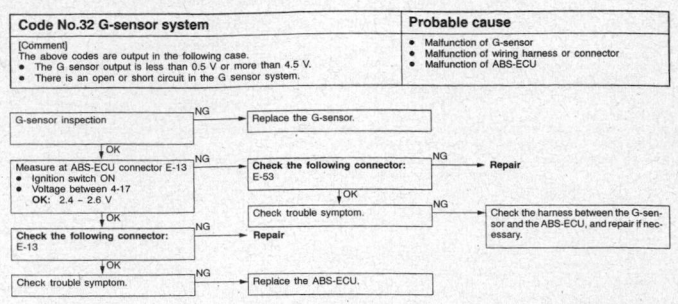

Fig. 195 Code 32: G Sensor System. 1998–99 Montero

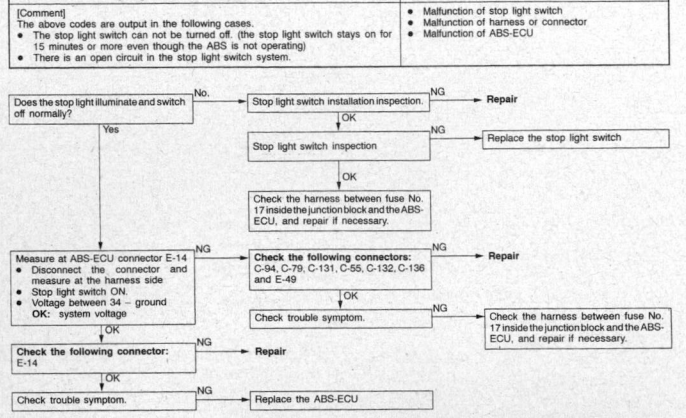

Fig. 196 Code 33: Stop Lamp Switch System. 1998–99 Montero

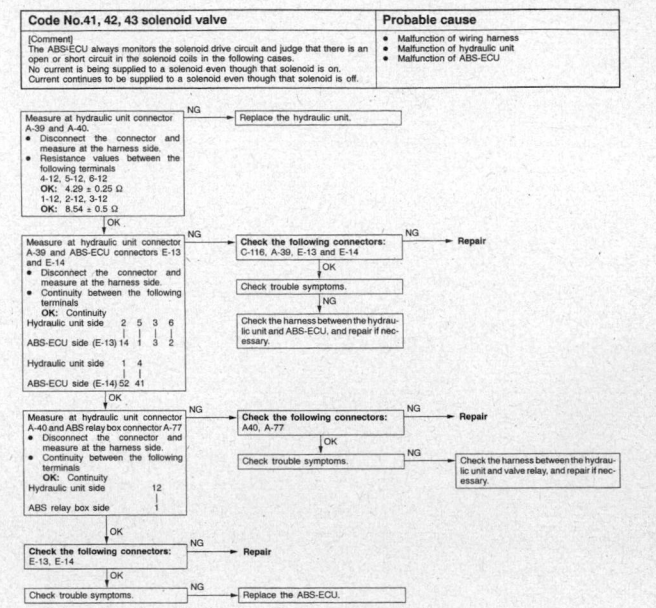

Fig. 197 Codes 41, 42 & 43: Solenoid Valve. 1998–99 Montero

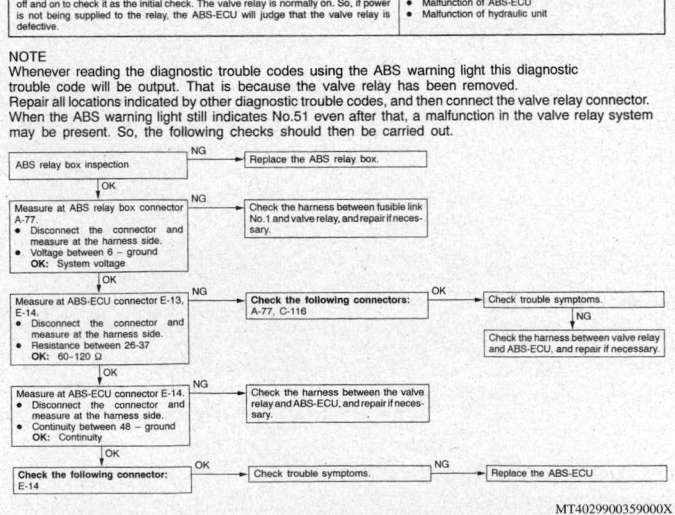

Fig. 198 Code 51: Valve Relay. 1998–99 Montero

Code No.53 Motor relay, motor	Probable cause
[Comment] The above codes are output in the following cases. • When the motor relay is on but no signal is input to the motor monitor line (motor does not run, etc.) • When the motor relay is off and a signal is input to the motor monitor line for 5 seconds or more (motor does not stop, etc.) • When the motor relay does not work	• Malfunction of motor relay • Malfunction of wiring harness or connector • Malfunction of hydraulic unit • Malfunction of ABS-ECU

Caution
The engine should be started and left to run for a while after testing is completed because force-driving of the motor by means of the actuator test will drain the battery.

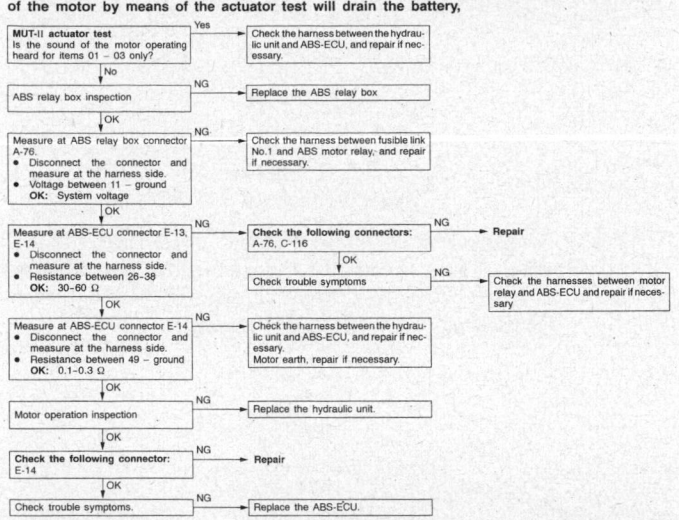

MT4029900360000X

Fig. 199   Code 53: Motor Relay. 1998–99 Montero

Communication with MUT-II is not possible. (Communication with all system is not possible.)	Probable cause
[Comment] The reason is probably a defect in the power supply system (including earth) for the diagnosis line.	• Malfunction of connector • Malfunction of harness

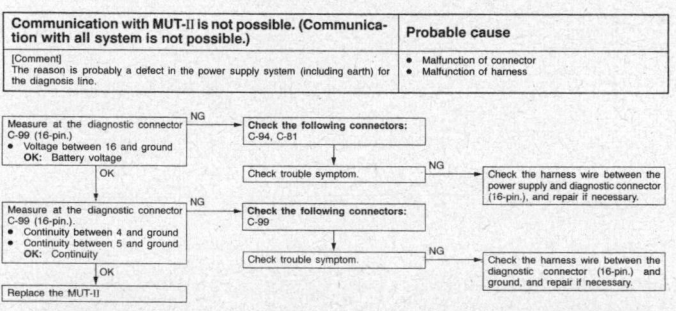

MT4029900362000X

Fig. 201   Inspection Procedure 1: Communication w/Scan Tool Not Possible. 1998–99 Montero

When ignition key is turned to "ON" (engine stopped), ABS warning light does not illuminate	Probable cause
[Comment] When power is supplied to the ABS-ECU, the valve relay turns from off to on, off and back to on again as an initial check. Because of this, the ABS warning light will illuminate twice when the valve relay is off even if there is a problem with the circuit between the ABS warning light and the ABS-ECU. Accordingly, if the light does not illuminate, the cause is probably one of the following items. An open circuit in the light power supply circuit A blown light bulb An open circuit in both the circuit between the ABS warning light and the ABS-ECU and in the circuit between the ABS warning light and the valve relay	• Blown fuse • Burnt out ABS warning light bulb • Malfunction of wiring harness or connector

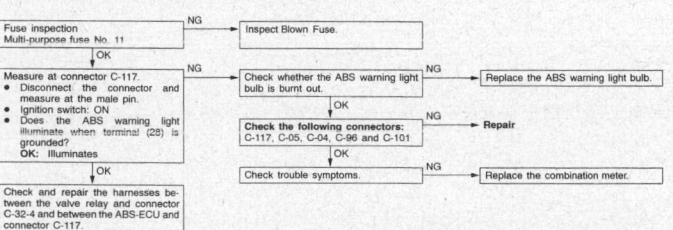

MT4029900364000X

Fig. 203   Inspection Procedure 3: ABS Warning Lamp Does Not Illuminate w/Key On. 1998–99 Montero

Trouble symptom		Inspection procedure No.
Communication with MUT-II is not possible.	Communication with all systems is not possible.	1
	Communication with ABS only is not possible.	2
When the ignition key is turned to "ON" (engine stopped), the ABS warning light does not illuminate.		3
After the engine starts, the light remains illuminated.		4
When the ignition key is turned to "START", the ABS warning light does not illuminate.		5
After the ignition key is turned to "ON", the ABS warning light blinks twice, and when turned to "START", it illuminates. When returned to "ON", the light flashes once, and then switches off.		6
Faulty ABS operation	Unequal braking power on both sides	7
	Insufficient braking power	7
	ABS operates under normal braking conditions	7
	ABS operates before vehicle stops under normal braking conditions	7
	Large brake pedal vibration (Caution 2.)	–

MT4029900361000X

Fig. 200   Inspection Procedure Chart. 1998–99 Montero

Communication with MUT-II is not possible. (Communication with ABS only is not possible.)	Probable cause
[Comment] When communication with the MUT-II is not possible, the cause is probably an open circuit in the ABS-ECU power circuit or an open circuit in the diagnosis output circuit.	• Blown fuse • Malfunction of wiring harness or connecter • Malfunction of ABS-ECU

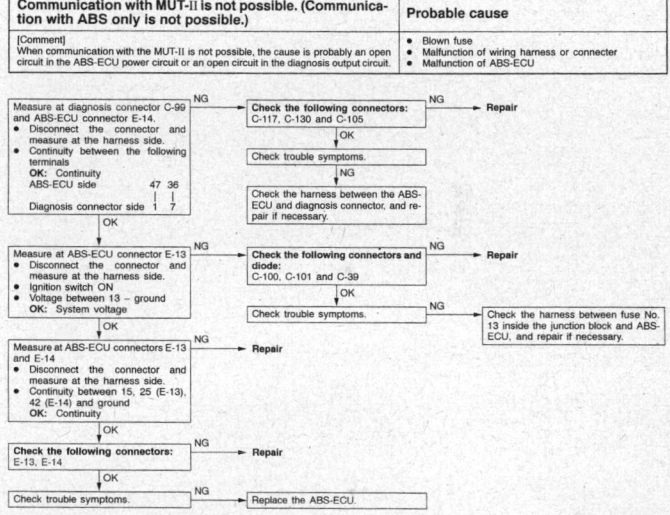

MT4029900363000X

Fig. 202   Inspection Procedure 2: Communication w/Scan Tool Not Possible. 1998–99 Montero

Even after the engine is started, the ABS warning light remains illuminated.	Probable cause
[Comment] A short-circuit in the ABS warning light illumination circuit may be present.	• Malfunction of combination meter • Malfunction of ABS-ECU • Malfunction of wiring harness

NOTE
This trouble symptom is limited to cases where communication with the MUT-II is possible (ABS-ECU power supply is normal) and the diagnosis code is a normal diagnosis code.

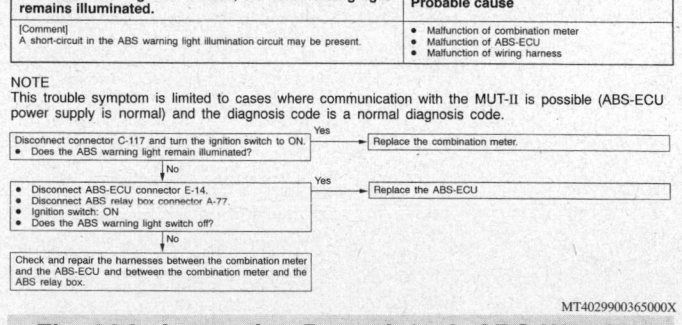

MT4029900365000X

Fig. 204   Inspection Procedure 4: ABS Warning Lamp Remains Illuminated w/Engine Running. 1998–99 Montero

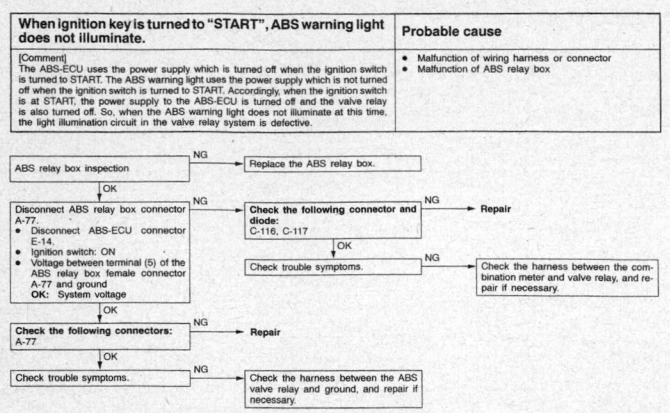

When ignition key is turned to "START", ABS warning light does not illuminate.	Probable cause
[Comment] The ABS-ECU uses the power supply which is turned off when the ignition switch is turned to START. The ABS warning light uses the power supply which is not turned off when the ignition switch is turned to START. Accordingly, when the ignition switch is at START, the power supply to the ABS-ECU is turned off and the valve relay is also turned off. So, when the ABS warning light does not illuminate at this time, the light illumination circuit in the valve relay system is defective.	• Malfunction of wiring harness or connector • Malfunction of ABS relay box

MT4029900366000X

Fig. 205   Inspection Procedure 5: ABS Warning Lamp Does Not Illuminate w/key In Start Position. 1998–99 Montero

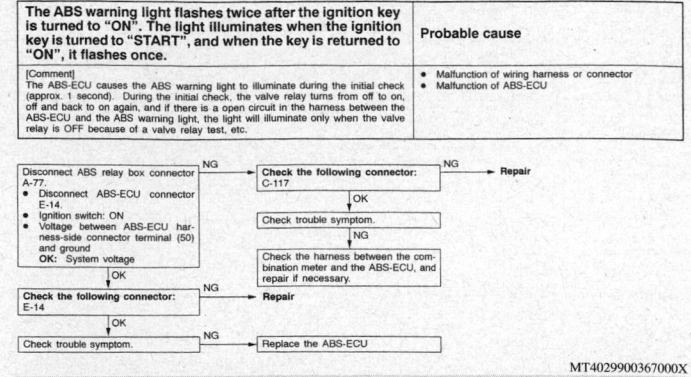

The ABS warning light flashes twice after the ignition key is turned to "ON". The light illuminates when the ignition key is turned to "START", and when the key is returned to "ON", it flashes once.	Probable cause
[Comment] The ABS-ECU causes the ABS warning light to illuminate during the initial check (approx. 1 second). During the initial check, the valve relay turns from off to on, off and back to on again, and if there is an open circuit in the harness between the ABS-ECU and the ABS warning light, the light will illuminate only when the valve relay is OFF because of a valve relay test, etc.	• Malfunction of wiring harness or connector • Malfunction of ABS-ECU

MT4029900367000X

Fig. 206   Inspection Procedure 6: ABS Warning Lamp Flashes Twice w/Key On, Remains Illuminated During Start, Then Flashes Once When Key Is Returned To ON. 1998–99 Montero

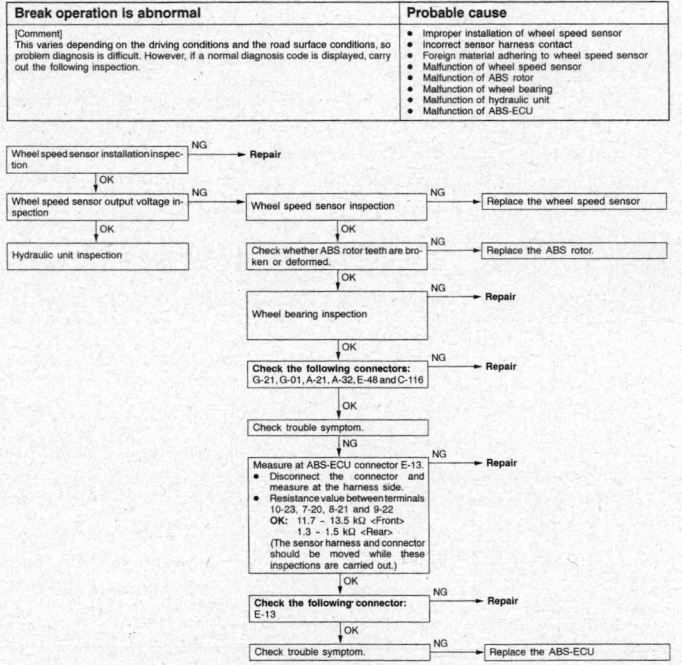

Break operation is abnormal	Probable cause
[Comment] This varies depending on the driving conditions and the road surface conditions, so problem diagnosis is difficult. However, if a normal diagnosis code is displayed, carry out the following inspection.	• Improper installation of wheel speed sensor • Incorrect sensor harness contact • Foreign material adhering to wheel speed sensor • Malfunction of wheel speed sensor • Malfunction of ABS rotor • Malfunction of wheel bearing • Malfunction of hydraulic unit • Malfunction of ABS-ECU

MT4029900368000X

Fig. 207   Inspection Procedure 7: Abnormal Brake Operation. 1998–99 Montero

Codes 11, 12, 13, 14, 21, 22, 23 & 24				Cause		
Wheel Speed Sensor (Open Or Short Circuit)				**Faulty Speed Sensor. Loose Or Broken Wiring. Faulty Hydraulic Assembly.**		
Step	Inspection	Connector	Value	Outcome	Go To Step	Repair
1	Check Sensor Installation	—	—	OK	2	—
				NG	—	Repair/Replace Sensor
2	Check Sensor Circuit at ABS-ECU, Terminals 1 & 2, 3 & 4, 18 & 19, 20 & 21	A-85	1.3–1.5 K ohms	OK	4	—
				NG	3	—
3	Check For Harness Damage	A-20, A-31, E-29, E-39 & A-85	—	OK	5	—
				NG	—	Repair/Replace Wiring or Harness
4	Sensor Output Voltage	—	70Mv	OK	7	—
				NG	6	—
5	Check Wiring Between Sensor Connectors & ABS-ECU	Sensor Connectors A-20, A-31, E-29 & E-39	—	—	—	Repair/Replace Wiring Harness or Connectors as Required.
		ABS-ECU Connector A-85	—	—	—	
6	Check Sensor Internal Resistance	—	1.3–1.5 K ohms	OK	8	—
				NG	—	Repair/Replace Sensor
	Check Sensor Insulation Resistance	—	100 K ohms	OK	8	—
				NG	—	Repair/Replace Sensor
7	Check Connector for Damage	A-85	—	OK	—	Replace Hydraulic Assembly
				NG	—	Repair/Replace as Required
8	Check Tone Wheel	—	—	OK	9	—
				NG	—	Replace Tone Wheel
9	Check Wheel Bearing	—	—	—	—	Replace as Required

Fig. 208   Codes 11, 12, 13, 14 21, 22, 23 & 24: Wheel Speed Sensor. Montero Sport

Code 15				Cause		
Wheel Speed Sensor (Abnormal Output Signal)				**Faulty Sensor, Tone Wheel, Bearing Or Wiring**		
Step	Inspection	Connector	Value	Outcome	Go To Step	Repair
1	Check Sensor Installation	—	—	OK	2	—
				NG	—	Repair/Replace As Required
2	Check Sensor Output	—	70Mv	OK	4	—
				NG	3	—
3	Check Resistance Of Sensors	—	Internal 1.3–15. K ohms	OK	5	—
				NG	—	Repair/Replace As Required
			Insulation 100 K ohms	OK	5	—
				NG	—	Repair/Replace As Required
4	Check Harness	A-85	—	OK	5	—
				NG	—	Repair/Replace As Required
5	Check Toothed ABS Rotor	—	—	OK	6	—
				NG	—	Repair/Replace As Required
6	Check Wheel Bearing	—	—	OK	—	Test Complete
				NG	—	Repair/Replace As Required

Fig. 209   Code 15: Wheel Speed Sensor. Montero Sport

Code 16				Cause		
Power Supply System				**Wiring Or Hydraulic Assembly Fault**		
Step	Inspection	Connector	Value	Outcome	Go To Step	Repair
1	Check Power Supply At ABS-ECU	A-85	Approx. 12v	OK	3	—
				NG	2	—
2	Check Harness For Damage	A-85 & D-08	—	OK	4	—
				NG	—	Repair/Replace As Required
3	Check Harness For Damage	A-85	—	OK	—	Replace Hydraulic Unit
				NG	—	Repair/Replace As Required
4	Check Wires Between Ignition Switch & ABS-ECU	D-08 & A-85	—	OK	—	Test Complete
				NG	—	Repair/Replace As Required

Fig. 210   Code 16: Power Supply System. Montero Sport

Code 25				Cause		
4WD Detection Switch				**Malfunction Of Switch, Hydraulic Assembly Or Indicator ECU**		
Step	Inspection	Connector	Value	Outcome	Go To Step	Repair
1	Does 4WD Indicator Illuminate Properly?	—	—	YES	2	—
				NO	—	Repair /Replace Indicator-ECU
2	Check Switch At ABS-ECU Terminals 12 & Ground	A-85	Approx. 12v	OK	3	—
				NG	4	—
3	Check Harness For Damage	A-85	—	OK	—	Replace Hydraulic Assembly
				NG	—	Repair/Replace As required
4	Check Harness For Damage	A-85 & B-12	—	OK	5	—
				NG	—	Repair/Replace As required
5	Check Harness Wires Between Switch & ABS-ECU	B-12 & A-85	—	OK	—	Test Complete
				NG	—	Repair/Replace As required

Fig. 211   Code 25: 4WD Detection Switch. Montero Sport 4WD

Code 26				Cause		
Freewheel Engage Switch				**Malfunction Of Switch, Hydraulic Assembly Or Indicator ECU**		
Step	Inspection	Connector	Value	Outcome	Go To Step	Repair
1	Does 4WD Indicator Illuminate Properly?	—	—	YES	2	—
				NO	3	—
2	Check Switch At ABS-ECU Terminals 11 & Ground	A-85	Approx. 12v	OK	4	—
				NG	5	—
3	Check Operation Of 4WD Indicator With ABS-ECU Disconnected			OK	—	Replace ABS-ECU
				NG	—	Continue Test
3a	Does Not Illuminate In 4H Position	—	—	—	—	Repair Wire Or Ground Between Indicator-ECU & Switch
						Replace Switch
3b	Lights Regardless Of Transfer Case Position	—	—	—	—	Repair Short In 4WD Detection Switch Circuit
3c	Check The Following In Order: 4WD Detection Switch, ABS-ECU, 4WD Indicator-ECU	—	—	NG	—	Repair Damaged Wiring, Harness Or Suspect Component
4	Check Harness For Damage	A-03 & A-85	—	OK	6	—
				NG	—	Repair/Replace As required
5	Check Harness For Damage	A-85		OK	—	Test Complete
				NG	—	Replace Hydraulic Assembly

Fig. 212   Code 26: Freewheel Engage Switch. 4WD Montero Sport

Code 32				Cause		
G-Sensor System				**Malfunction Of Sensor Or Hydraulic Assembly**		
Step	Inspection	Connector	Value	Outcome	Go To Step	Repair
1	Check Sensor Using Tool No. MB991348 Or Equivalent	Terminals 2 & 3	2.4–2.6v	OK	1b	—
				NG	—	Replace Sensor
1b	Check Sensor With Arrow Facing Down		3.4–3.6v	OK	2	—
				NG	—	Replace Sensor
2	Check Sensor circuit At ABS-ECU	A-85 Terminals 7 & 14	2.4–2.6v	OK	3	—
				NG	4	—
3	Check Harness For Damage	A-85	—	OK	—	Replace Hydraulic Assembly
				NG	—	Repair/Replace As Required
4	Check Harness For Damage	A-85 & C-26	—	OK	5	—
				NG	—	Repair/Replace As Required
5	Check Harness Between Sensor & ABS-ECU	C-26 & A-85	—	OK	—	Test Complete
				NG	—	Repair/Replace As Required

Fig. 213   Code 32: G-Sensor System. Montero Sport 4WD

Code 33				Cause		
Stoplight Switch System				Faulty Switch, Wiring Or Hydraulic Assembly		
Step	Inspection	Connector	Value	Outcome	Go To Step	Repair
1	Check Switch Operation	—	—	OK	3	—
				NG	2	—
2	Check Switch Installation	—	—	OK	4	—
				NG	—	Repair/Replace As Required
3	Check Switch Circuit	A-85, Terminals 13 & Ground	Approx. 12v	OK	6	—
				NG	5	—
4	Check Switch When Released	—	Continuity	OK	7	—
				NG	—	Replace Switch
5	Check Connectors for Damage	A-85, C-10 & C17	—	OK	8	—
				NG	—	Repair/Replace As Required
6	Check Connector For Damage	A-85	—	OK	—	Replace Hydraulic Assembly
				NG	—	Repair/Replace As Required
7	Check Connectors For Damage	A-85, C-65 & C-66	—	OK	9	—
				NG	—	Repair/Replace As Required
8	Check Wires Between Switch & ABS-ECU	C-65, C-66 & A-85	—	OK	—	Test Complete
				NG	—	Repair/Replace As Required
9	Check Wires Between Fuse 8 & ABS-ECU	A-85	—	OK	—	Test Complete
				NG	—	Repair/Replace As Required

Fig. 214   Code 33: Stoplight Switch System. Montero Sport

Codes 41, 42, 43, 51 & 53				Cause		
Solenoid Valve Inside Hydraulic Unit, HU Valve Relay Open Or Short Or HU Malfunction.				Damaged Wiring Harness & Connector. Faulty Hydraulic Assembly.		
Step	Inspection	Connector	Value	Outcome	Go To Step	Repair
1	Power Supply Circuit @ ABS-ECU	A-86	12 volts	Yes	3	—
				No	2	—
2	Inspect Harness Connector For Damage	A-86	—	OK	4	
				NG	—	Repair Or Replace As Required
3	Inspect Harness Connector For Damage	A-86	—	OK		Replace Hydraulic Unit
				NG	—	Repair Or Replace As Required
4	Inspect Harness Wire Between Fuseable Link 9 And ABS-ECU.	A-86	—	OK	—	—
				NG	—	Repair Or Replace As Required. Confirm No Fault Codes Are Present

Fig. 215   Codes 41, 42, 43, 51 & 53: Hydraulic Unit Relay, Valve Or Malfunction. Montero Sport

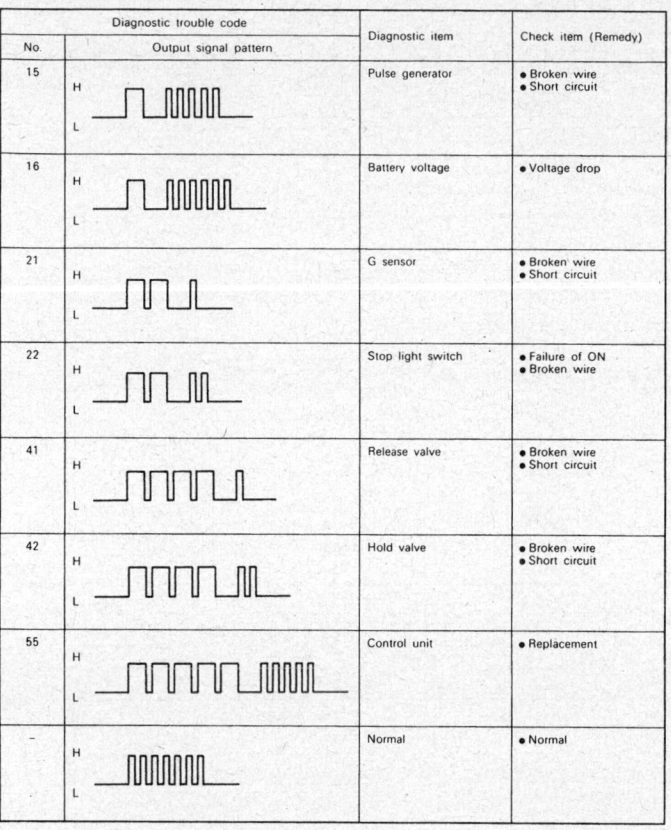

Diagnostic trouble code		Diagnostic item	Check item (Remedy)
No.	Output signal pattern		
15	H / L	Pulse generator	• Broken wire • Short circuit
16	H / L	Battery voltage	• Voltage drop
21	H / L	G sensor	• Broken wire • Short circuit
22	H / L	Stop light switch	• Failure of ON • Broken wire
41	H / L	Release valve	• Broken wire • Short circuit
42	H / L	Hold valve	• Broken wire • Short circuit
55	H / L	Control unit	• Replacement
–	H / L	Normal	• Normal

MT4029100158000X

Fig. 216   Diagnostic Trouble Codes. Pickup

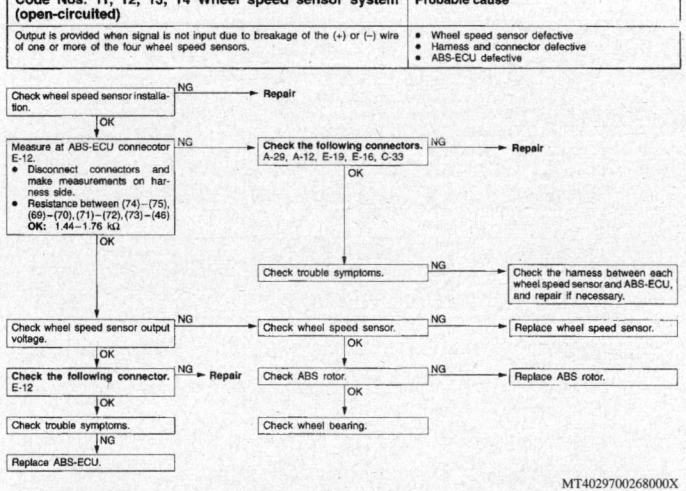

MT4029700268000X

Fig. 218   Codes 11, 12, 13 & 14: Wheel Speed Sensor System Open Circuit. 1997 3000GT AWD

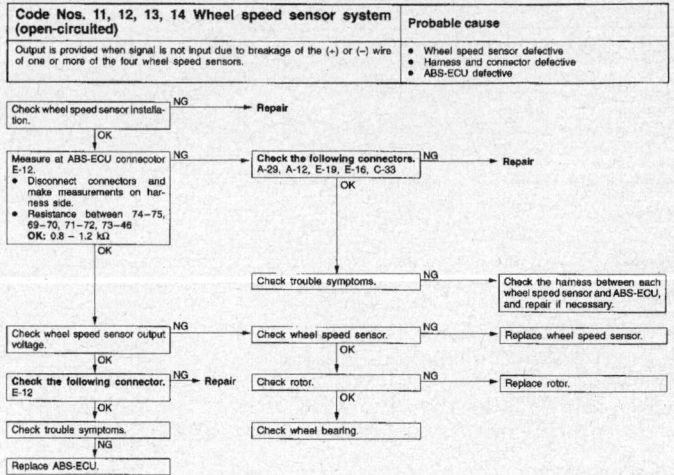

MT4029600251000X

Fig. 217   Codes 11, 12, 13 & 14: Wheel Speed Sensor System Open Circuit. 1996 3000GT

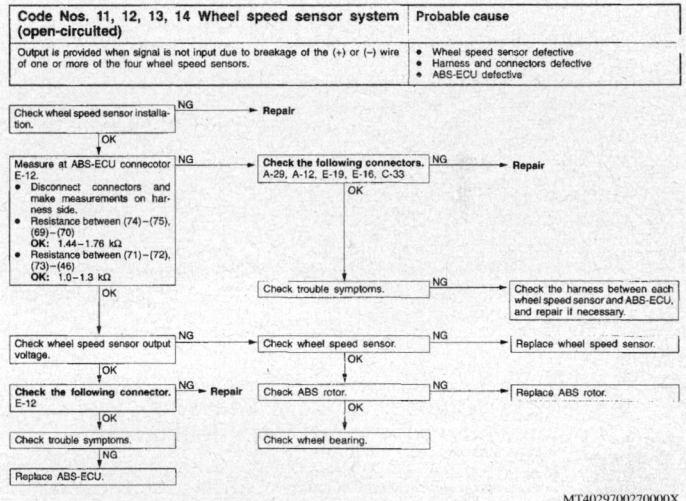

MT4029700270000X

Fig. 219   Codes 11, 12, 13 & 14: Wheel Speed Sensor System Open Circuit. 1997 3000GT FWD

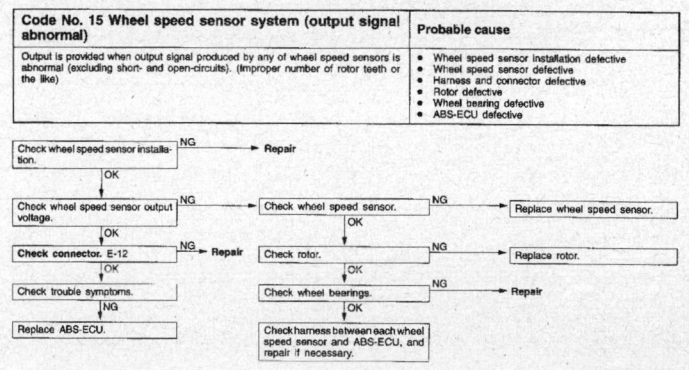

MT4029600252000X

Fig. 220   Code 15: Wheel Speed Sensor System Output Signal Abnormal. 1996–97 3000GT

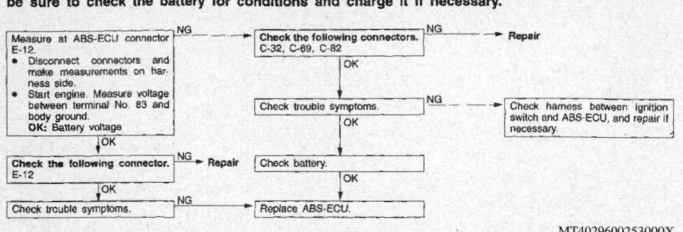

Code No. 16 ABS-ECU power supply system (voltage abnormally low or high)

	Probable cause
Output is provided when ABS-ECU power supply voltage drops below or rises above the normal value. Output is not provided if power supply voltage returns to normal voltage.	• Harness and connector defective • ABS-ECU defective

Caution

If battery voltage drops or rises while making this check, this code is output as an existing trouble, making it impossible to perform correct trouble diagnosis. Before carrying out the following check, be sure to check the battery for conditions and charge it if necessary.

Fig. 221   Code 16: ABS ECU Power Supply System Voltage Abnormally Low Or High. 1996–97 3000GT

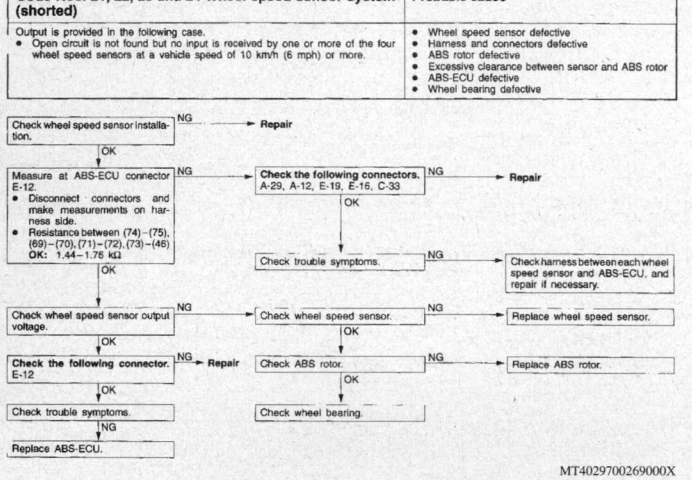

Code Nos. 21, 22, 23 and 24 Wheel speed sensor system (shorted)

	Probable cause
Output is provided in the following case. • Open circuit is not found but no input is received by one or more of the four wheel speed sensors at a vehicle speed of 10 km/h (6 mph) or more.	• Wheel speed sensor defective • Harness and connectors defective • ABS rotor defective • Excessive clearance between sensor and ABS rotor • ABS-ECU defective • Wheel bearing defective

Fig. 223   Codes 21, 22, 23 & 24: Wheel Speed Sensor System Shorted. 1997 3000GT AWD

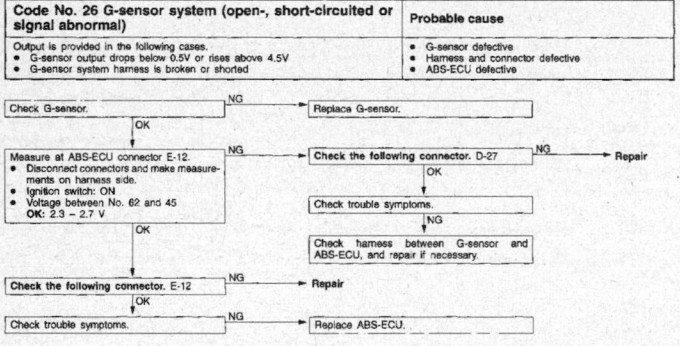

Code No. 26 G-sensor system (open-, short-circuited or signal abnormal)

	Probable cause
Output is provided in the following cases. • G-sensor output drops below 0.5V or rises above 4.5V • G-sensor system harness is broken or shorted	• G-sensor defective • Harness and connector defective • ABS-ECU defective

Fig. 225   Code 26: G-Sensor System Open, Shorted Or Signal Abnormal. 1996 3000GT

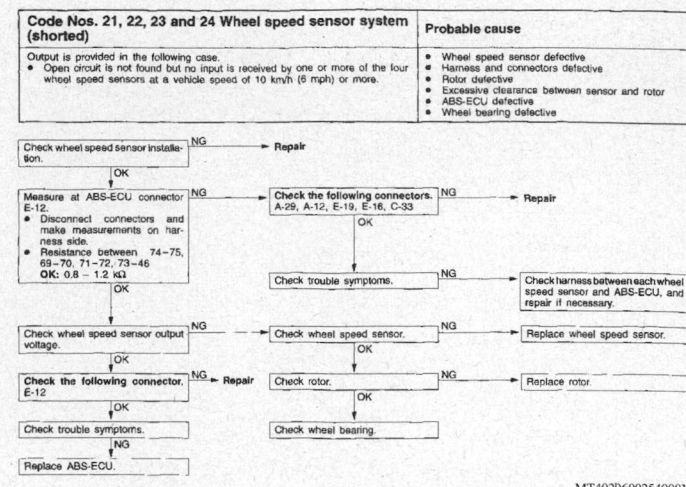

Code Nos. 21, 22, 23 and 24 Wheel speed sensor system (shorted)

	Probable cause
Output is provided in the following case. • Open circuit is not found but no input is received by one or more of the four wheel speed sensors at a vehicle speed of 10 km/h (6 mph) or more.	• Wheel speed sensor defective • Harness and connectors defective • Rotor defective • Excessive clearance between sensor and rotor • ABS-ECU defective • Wheel bearing defective

Fig. 222   Codes 21, 22, 23 & 24: Wheel Speed Sensor System Shorted. 1996 3000GT

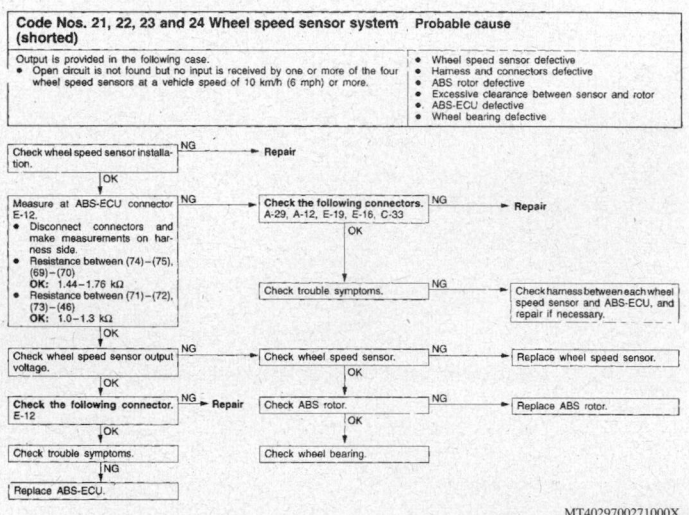

Code Nos. 21, 22, 23 and 24 Wheel speed sensor system (shorted)

	Probable cause
Output is provided in the following case. • Open circuit is not found but no input is received by one or more of the four wheel speed sensors at a vehicle speed of 10 km/h (6 mph) or more.	• Wheel speed sensor defective • Harness and connectors defective • ABS rotor defective • Excessive clearance between sensor and rotor • ABS-ECU defective • Wheel bearing defective

Fig. 224   Codes 21, 22, 23 & 24: Wheel Speed Sensor System Shorted. 1997 3000GT FWD

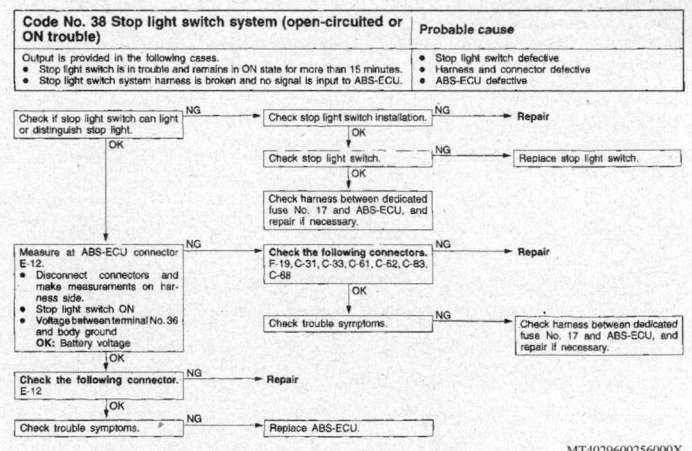

Code No. 38 Stop light switch system (open-circuited or ON trouble)

	Probable cause
Output is provided in the following cases. • Stop light switch is in trouble and remains in ON state for more than 15 minutes. • Stop light switch system harness is broken and no signal is input to ABS-ECU.	• Stop light switch defective • Harness and connector defective • ABS-ECU defective

Fig. 226   Code 38: Stop Light Switch System Open Circuit Or ON Trouble. 1996 3000GT

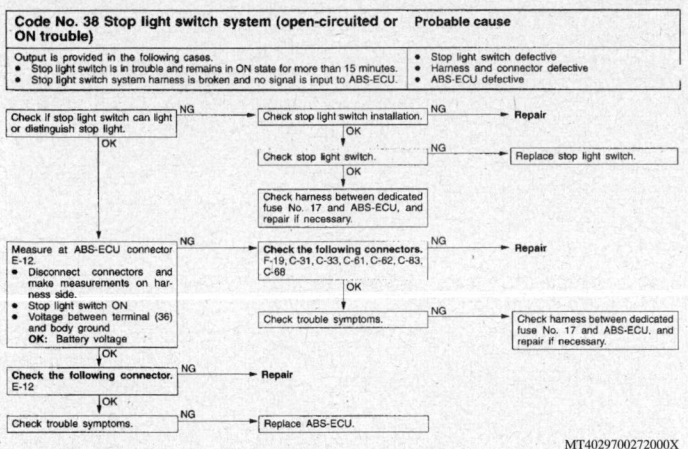

Fig. 227   Code 38: Stop Light Switch System Open Circuit Or ON Trouble. 1997 3000GT

MT4029700272000X

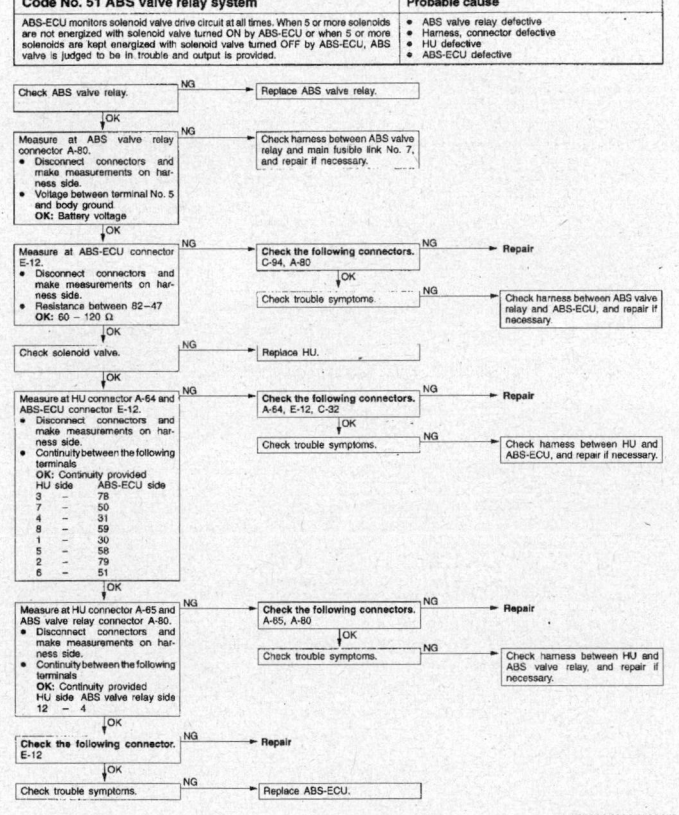

Fig. 229   Code 51: ABS Valve Relay System. 1996–97 3000GT

MT4029600258000X

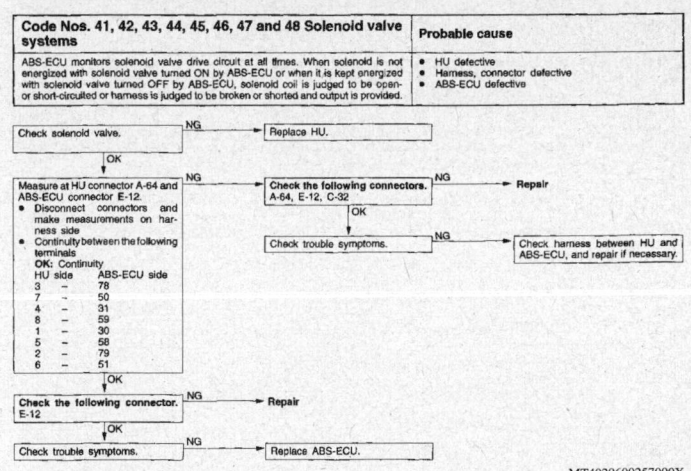

Fig. 228   Codes 41, 42, 43, 44, 45, 46, 47 & 48: Solenoid Valve Systems. 1996–97 3000GT

MT4029600257000X

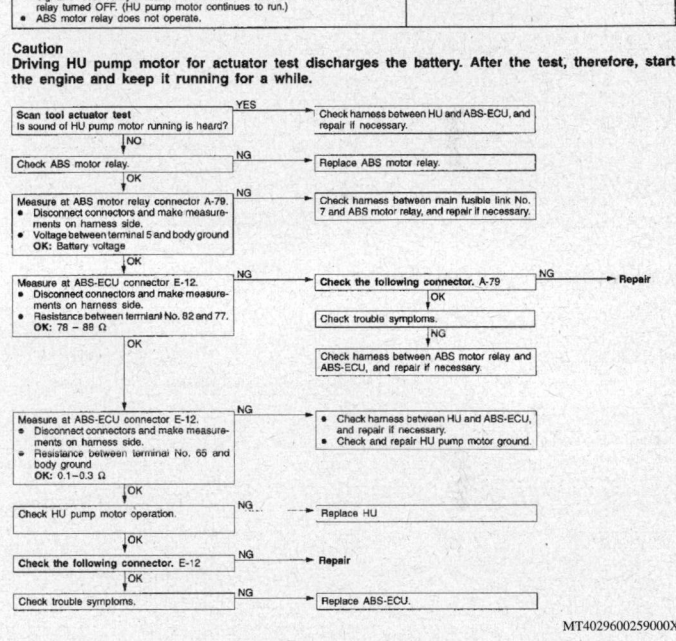

Fig. 230   Code 53: HU Pump Motor Or ABS Motor Relay System. 1996–97 3000GT

MT4029600259000X

Code No.	Diagnostic Item
11	F.R. wheel speed sensor system (open-circuited)
12	F.L. wheel speed sensor system (open-circuited)
13	R.R. wheel speed sensor system (open-circuited)
14	R.L. wheel speed sensor system (open-circuited)
15	Wheel speed sensor system (output signal abnormal)
16	ABS-ECU power supply system (voltage abnormally low or high)
21	F.R. wheel speed sensor system (shorted)
22	F.L. wheel speed sensor system (shorted)
23	R.R. wheel speed sensor system (shorted)
24	R.L. wheel speed sensor system (shorted)
38	Stop light switch system (open-circuited or ON trouble)
41	F.R. solenoid valve IN system
42	F.L. solenoid valve IN system
43	R.R. solenoid valve IN system
44	R.L. solenoid valve IN system
45	F.R. solenoid valve OUT system
46	F.L. solenoid valve OUT system
47	R.R. solenoid valve OUT system
48	R.L. solenoid valve OUT system
51	ABS valve relay system
53	HU pump motor or ABS motor relay system
63	ABS-ECU system

MT4029900331000X

Fig. 231   Diagnostic Trouble Code Inspection Chart. 1998–99 3000GT

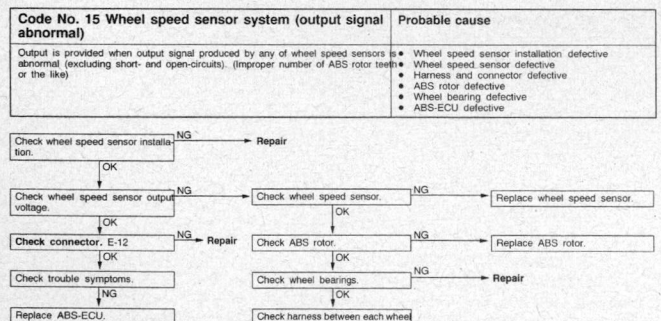

Code No. 15 Wheel speed sensor system (output signal abnormal)	Probable cause
Output is provided when output signal produced by any of wheel speed sensors is abnormal (excluding short- and open-circuits). (Improper number of ABS rotor teeth or the like)	• Wheel speed sensor installation defective • Wheel speed sensor defective • Harness and connector defective • ABS rotor defective • Wheel bearing defective • ABS-ECU defective

MT4029900333000X

Fig. 233   Code 15: Wheel Speed Sensor Output Signal Abnormal. 1998–99 3000GT

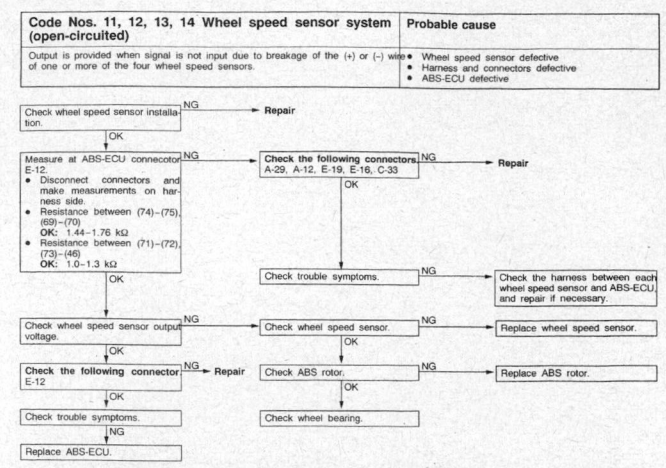

Code Nos. 11, 12, 13, 14 Wheel speed sensor system (open-circuited)	Probable cause
Output is provided when signal is not input due to breakage of the (+) or (–) wire of one or more of the four wheel speed sensors.	• Wheel speed sensor defective • Harness and connectors defective • ABS-ECU defective

MT4029900332000X

Fig. 232   Codes 11, 12, 13 & 14: Wheel Speed Sensor Open Circuit. 1998–99 3000GT

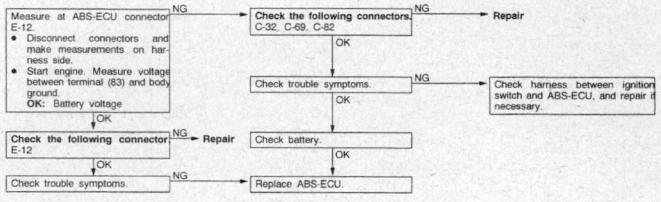

Code No. 16 ABS-ECU power supply system (voltage abnormally low or high)	Probable cause
Output is provided when ABS-ECU power supply voltage drops below or rises above the normal value. Output is not provided if power supply voltage returns to normal voltage.	• Harness and connector defective • ABS-ECU defective

Caution
If battery voltage drops or rises while making this check, this code is output as an existing trouble, making it impossible to perform correct trouble diagnosis. Before carrying out the following check, be sure to check the battery for conditions and charge it if necessary.

MT4029900334000X

Fig. 234   Code 16: ABS-ECU Voltage Low Or High. 1998–99 3000GT

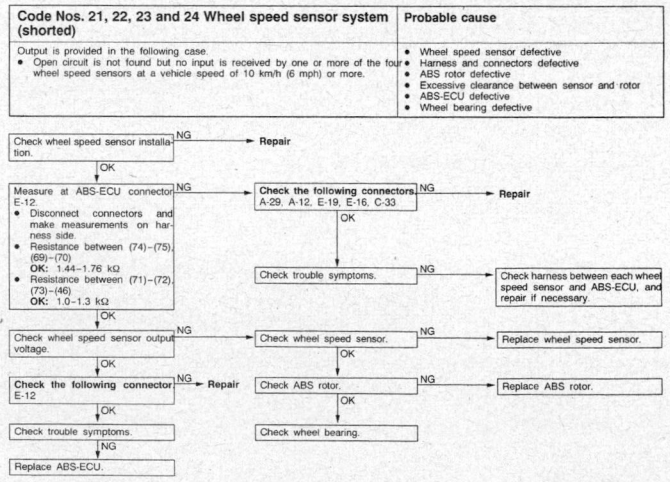

Code Nos. 21, 22, 23 and 24 Wheel speed sensor system (shorted)	Probable cause
Output is provided in the following case. • Open circuit is not found but no input is received by one or more of the four wheel speed sensors at a vehicle speed of 10 km/h (6 mph) or more.	• Wheel speed sensor defective • Harness and connectors defective • ABS rotor defective • Excessive clearance between sensor and rotor • ABS-ECU defective • Wheel bearing defective

MT4029900335000X

Fig. 235   Codes 21, 22, 23 & 24: Wheel Speed Sensor Shorted. 1998–99 3000GT

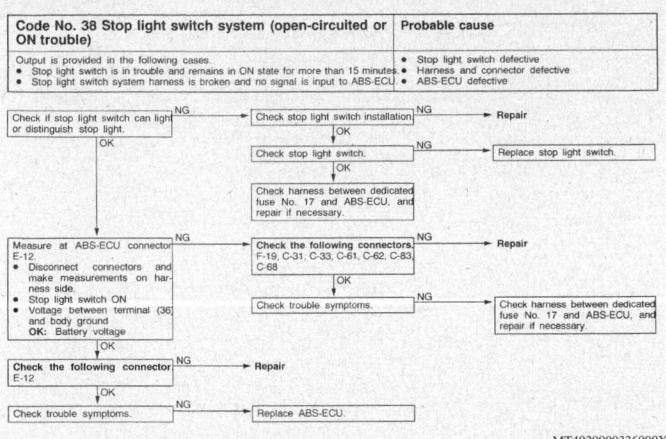

Fig. 236   Code 38: Stop Lamp Switch System. 1998–99 3000GT

MT4029900336000X

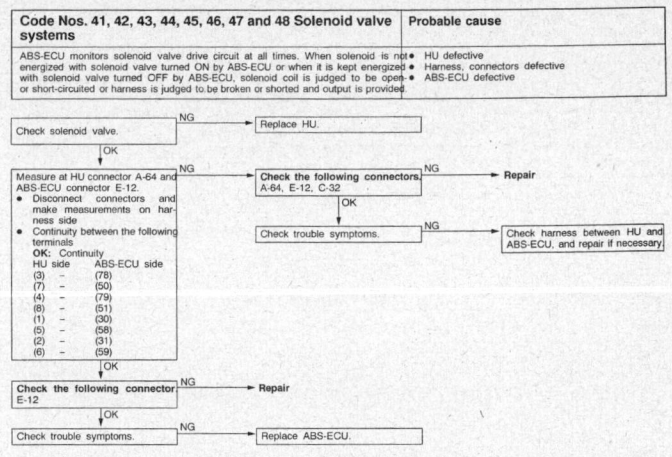

Fig. 237   Codes 41, 42, 43, 44, 45, 46, 47 & 48: Solenoid Valve. 1998–99 3000GT

MT4029900337000X

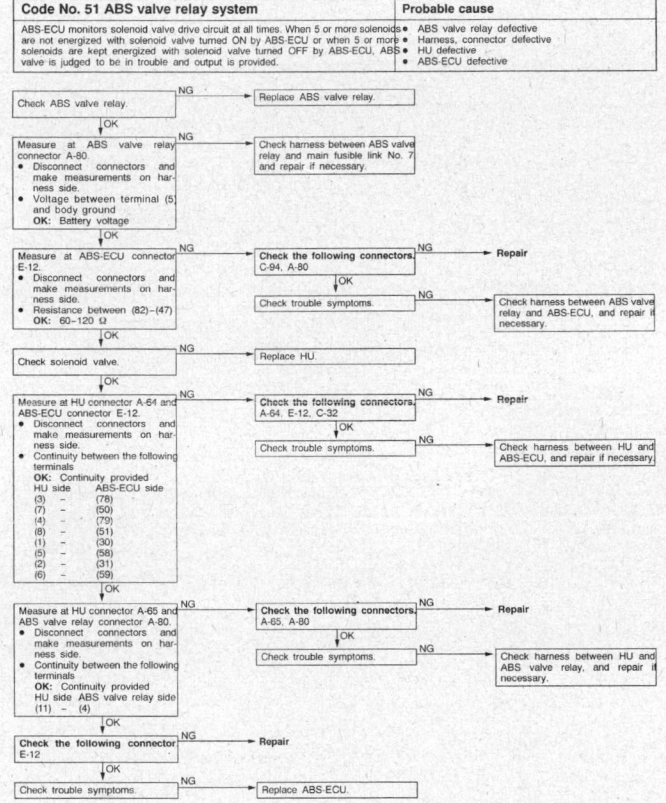

Fig. 238   Code 51: ABS Valve Relay System. 1998–99 3000GT

MT4029900338000X

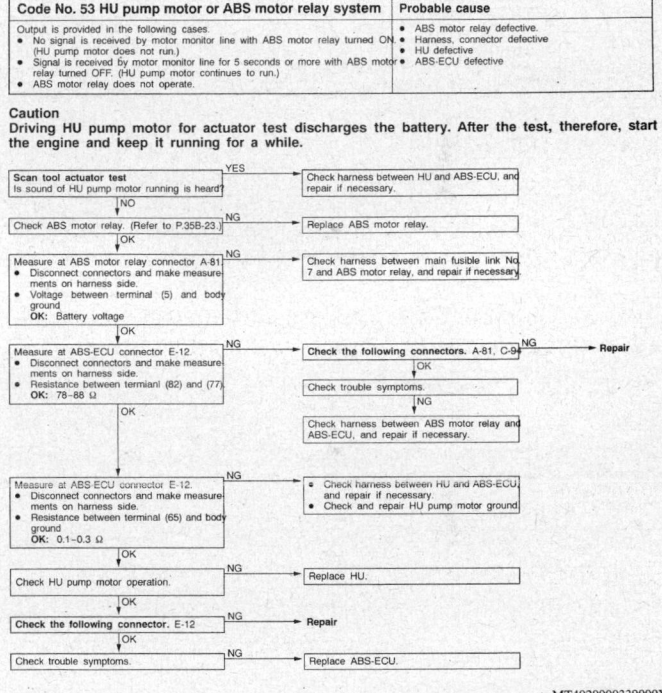

Fig. 239   Code 53: HU Pump Or ABS Motor Relay System. 1998–99 3000GT

MT4029900339000X

Trouble Symptom	Check Procedure No.
No communication is possible between scan tool and any of control systems.	1
No communication is possible between scan tool and ABS-ECU.	2
ABS warning light is not lighted with the ignition key turned ON (stationary engine).	3
ABS warning light does not go out after turning ON of the ignition switch.	4
Brakes operate abnormally.	5

MT4029900340000X

Fig. 240   Inspection Procedure Chart. 1998–99 3000GT

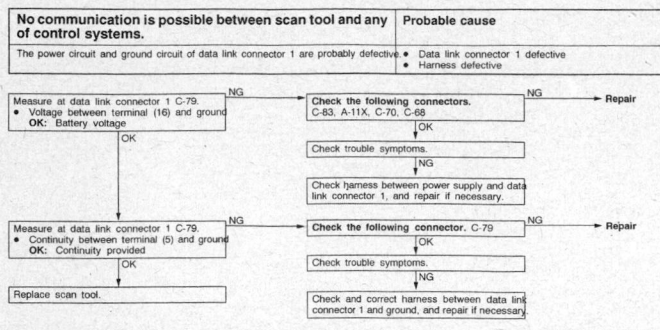

Fig. 241   Inspection Procedure 1: Communication w/Scan Tool Not Possible. 1998–99 3000GT

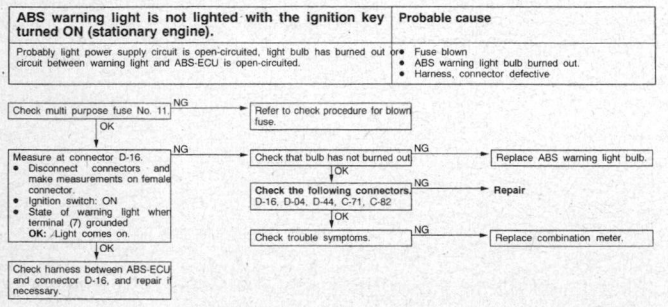

Fig. 243   Inspection Procedure 3: ABS Warning Lamp Does Not Illuminate w/Key ON. 1998–99 3000GT

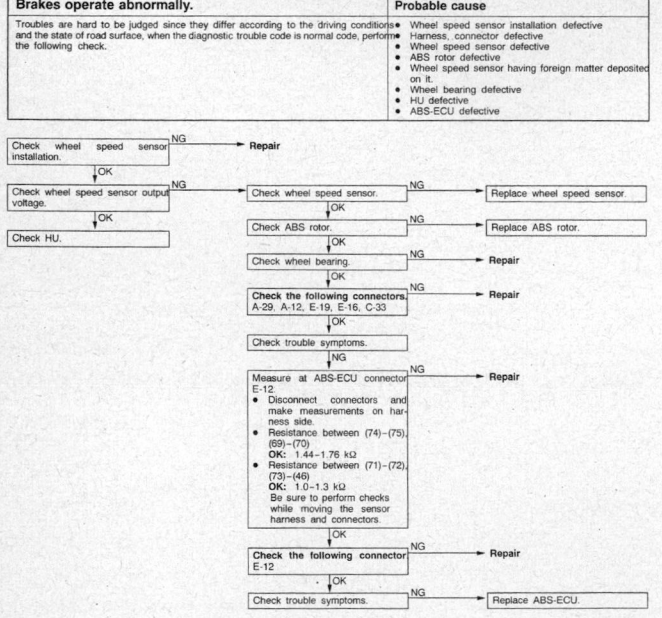

Fig. 245   Inspection Procedure 5: Brake Operation Abnormal. 1998–99 3000GT

No communication is possible between scan tool and ABS-ECU.	Probable cause
ABS-ECU power supply circuit or diagnosis output circuit is probably open-circuited.	• Fuse blown • Harness, connector defective • ABS-ECU defective

Fig. 242   Inspection Procedure 2: Communication Between Scan Tool & ABS-ECU Not Possible. 1998–99 3000GT

ABS warning light does not go out after turning ON of the ignition switch.	Probable cause
ABS warning light lighting circuit is probably short-circuited.	• Combination meter defective • ABS-ECU defective • Harness defective (shorted)

NOTE
This trouble symptom is limited to the case where communication with scan tool is possible (ABS-ECU power supply is normal) and diagnostic code is normal code.

Fig. 244   Inspection Procedure 4: ABS Warning Lamp Remains Illuminated w/Key ON. 1998–99 3000GT

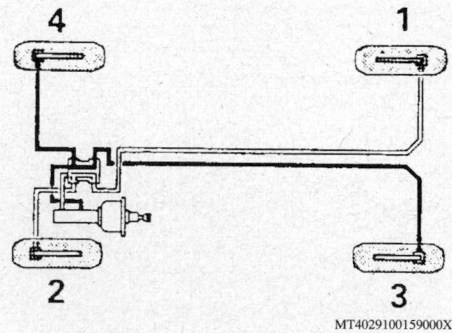

Fig. 246   Brake line bleed sequence. Diamante, Eclipse, Galant, Mirage & 3000GT

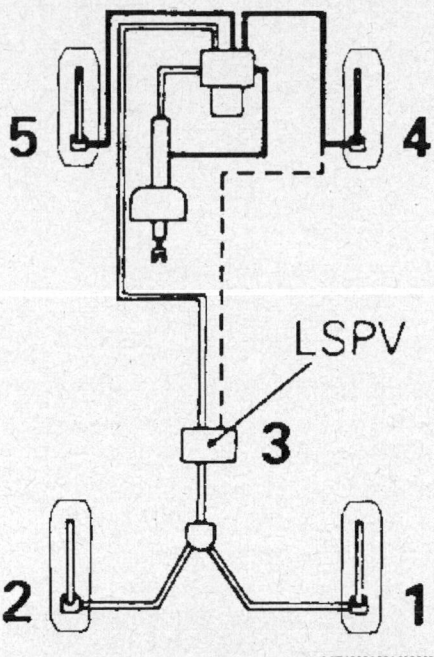

Fig. 247 Brake line bleed sequence. Montero & Montero Sport

MT4029100160000X

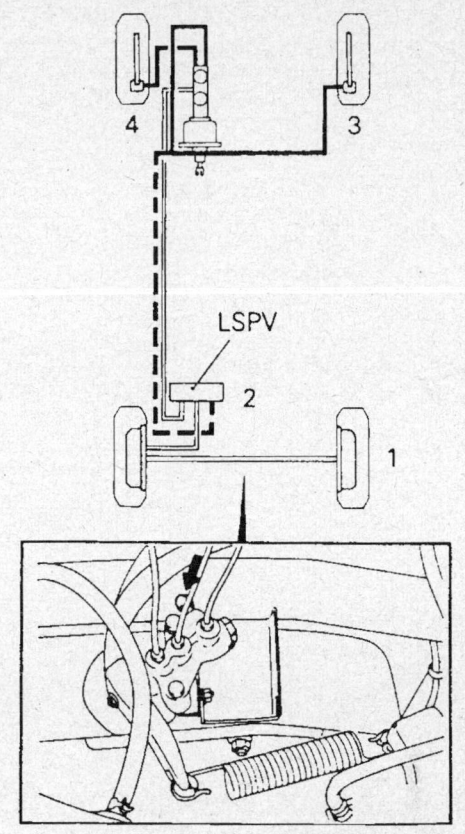

Fig. 248 Brake line bleed sequence. Pickup

MT4029100161000X

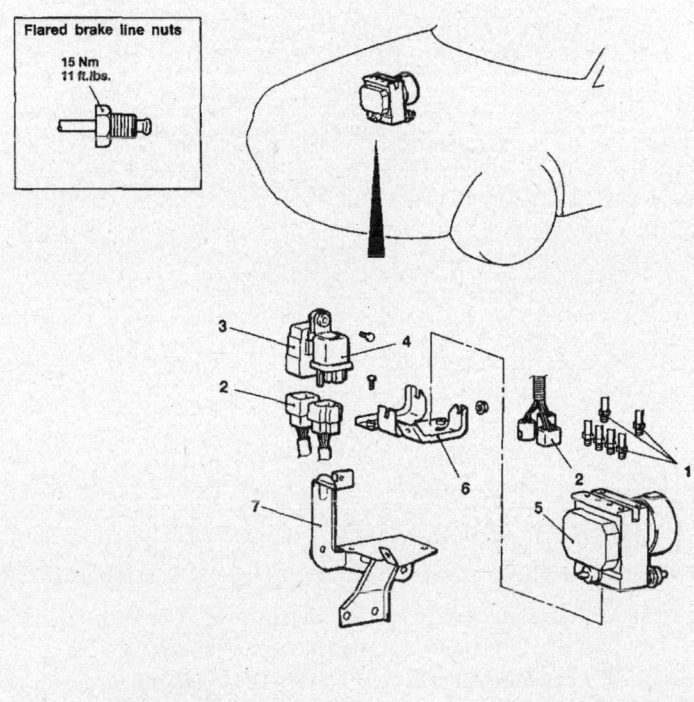

Removal steps
1. Connection for brake pipe
2. Connection for harness connector
3. Motor relay
4. Valve relay
5. Connection for brake hose
6. Bracket
7. Hydraulic unit assembly
8. Hydraulic unit
9. Hydraulic unit bracket (A)
10. Hydraulic unit bracket (B)

MT4029400260000X

Fig. 249 Hydraulic unit replacement. 1996–98 Galant

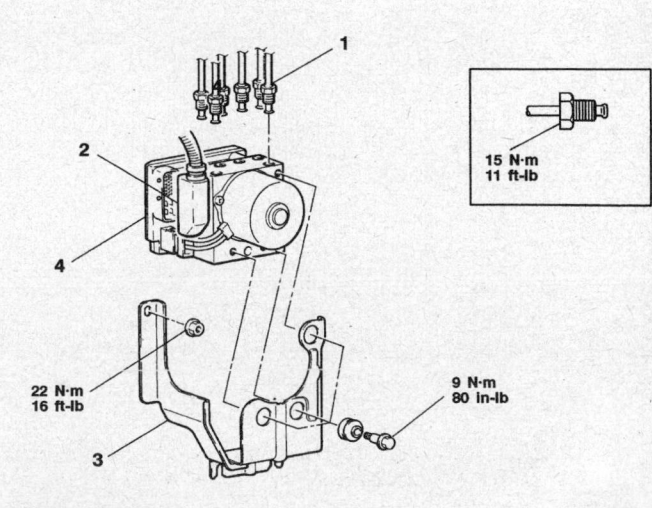

1. BRAKE TUBE
2. HARNESS CONNECTOR
3. BRACKET ASSEMBLY
4. HYDRAULIC UNIT

MT4029900439000X

Fig. 250 Hydraulic unit replacement. 1999 Galant

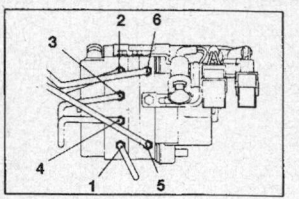

1. Hydraulic unit – Front brake (L.H.)
2. Hydraulic unit – Rear brake (R.H.)
3. Hydraulic unit – Front brake (R.H.)
4. Hydraulic unit – Rear braker (L.H.)
5. Hydraulic unit – Master cylinder
   (for left front and right rear)
6. Hydraulic unit – Master cylinder
   (for right front and left rear)

MT4029400261000X

Fig. 251 Brake line connections at hydraulic unit. 1996–98 Galant

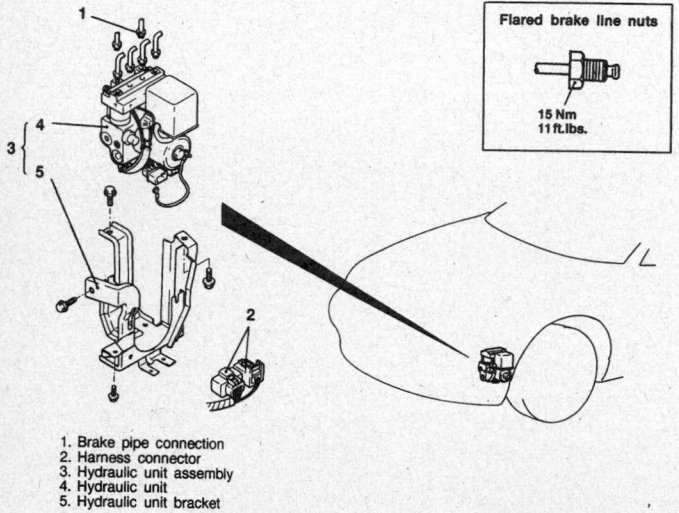

MT4029500262000X

Fig. 253 Hydraulic unit replacement. Eclipse

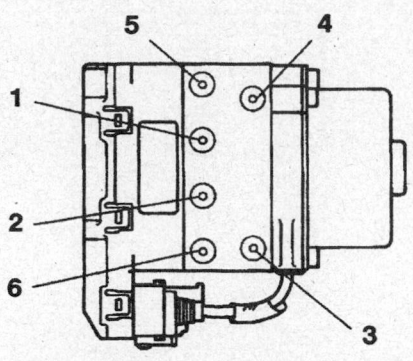

1. To LH rear proportioning valve.
2. to RH rear proportioning valve.
3. From master cylinder (Primary).
4. From master cylinder (Secondary).
5. To RH front brake.
6. To LH front brake.

MT4029900440000X

Fig. 252 Brake line connections at hydraulic unit. 1999 Galant

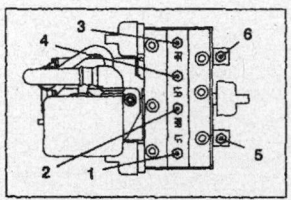

1. Hydraulic unit – Front brake (L.H.)
2. Hydraulic unit – Rear brake (R.H.)
3. Hydraulic unit – Front brake (R.H.)
4. Hydraulic unit – Rear braker (L.H.)
5. Hydraulic unit – Master cylinder (Secondary)
6. Hydraulic unit – Master cylinder (Primary)

MT4029500263000X

Fig. 254 Brake pipe connections at hydraulic unit. Eclipse

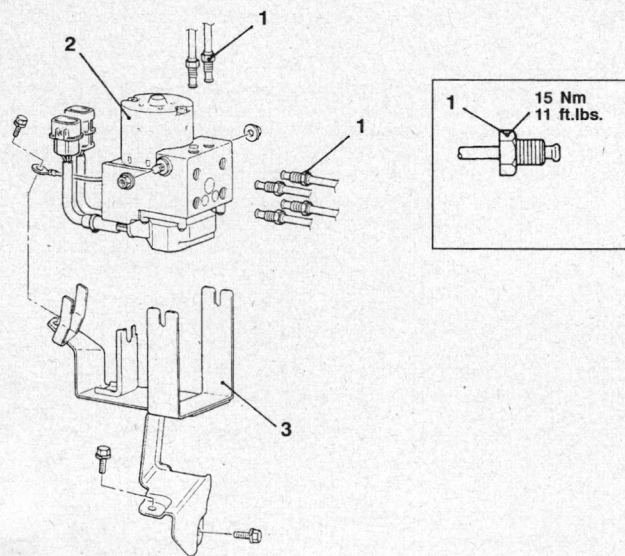

1. Brake pipe connection
2. Hydraulic unit assembly
3. Hydraulic unit bracket

MT4029900441000X

Fig. 255 Hydraulic unit replacement. Mirage

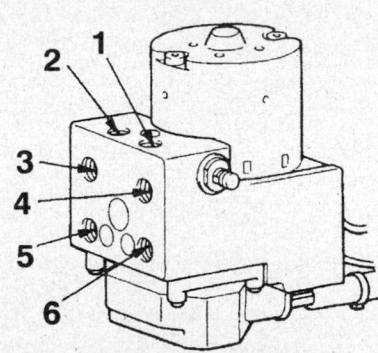

1. To RH proportioning valve.
2. to LH proportioning valve.
3. From master cylinder (Primary).
4. From master cylinder (Secondary).
5. To RH front brake.
6. To LH front brake.

MT4029900442000X

Fig. 256 Brake pipe installation. Mirage

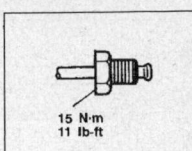

15 N·m
11 lb-ft

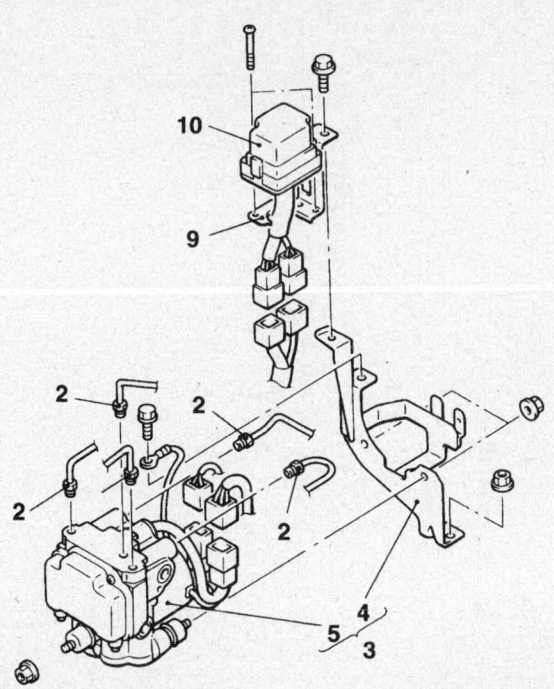

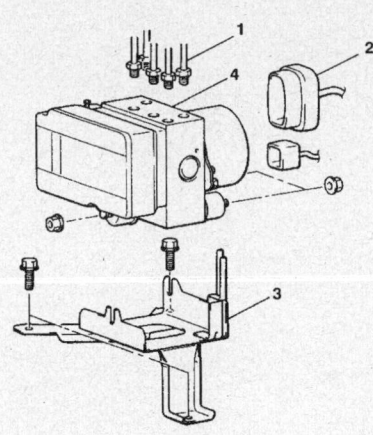

REMOVAL STEPS
1. BRAKE TUBE
2. HARNESS CONNECTOR
3. BRACKET ASSEMBLY
4. HYDRAULIC UNIT

MT4029700308000X

Fig. 258 Hydraulic unit replacement. Montero Sport

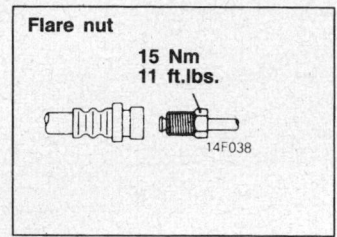

Flare nut

15 Nm
11 ft.lbs.

14F038

Hydraulic unit removal steps

1. Connector bracket
2. Brake pipe
3. Hydraulic unit assembly
4. Hydraulic unit bracket
5. Hydraulic unit
6. Relay box cover
7. Valve relay
8. Motor relay
9. Relay box bracket
10. ABS relay box

MT4029100164000X

Fig. 257 Hydraulic unit replacement. Montero

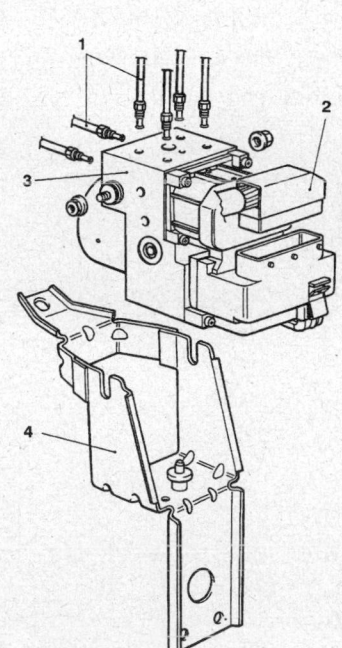

Flared brake line nuts

15 Nm
11 ft.lbs.

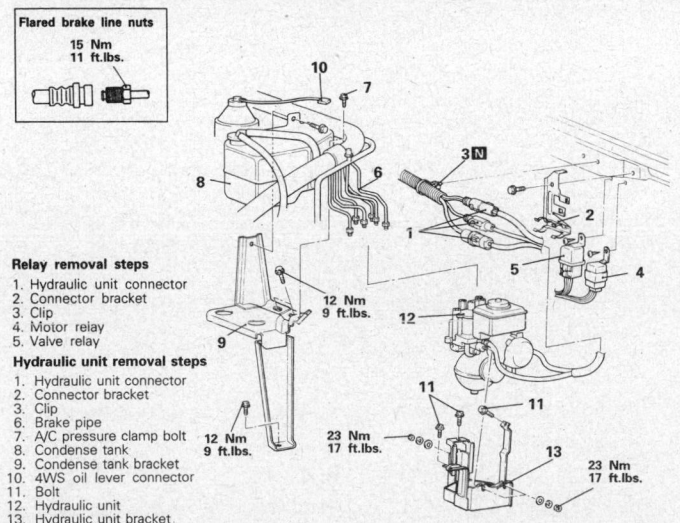

Flared brake line nuts

15 Nm
11 ft.lbs.

Relay removal steps
1. Hydraulic unit connector
2. Connector bracket
3. Clip
4. Motor relay
5. Valve relay

Hydraulic unit removal steps
1. Hydraulic unit connector
2. Connector bracket
3. Clip
6. Brake pipe
7. A/C pressure clamp bolt
8. Condense tank
9. Condense tank bracket
10. 4WS oil lever connector
11. Bolt
12. Hydraulic unit
13. Hydraulic unit bracket

12 Nm
9 ft.lbs.

12 Nm
9 ft.lbs.

23 Nm
17 ft.lbs.

23 Nm
17 ft.lbs.

MT4029100165000X

Fig. 259 Hydraulic unit replacement. 1996 Diamante

REMOVAL STEPS
1. CONNECTION FOR BRAKE PIPE
2. ABS-ECU CONNECTOR
3. ABS-HU/ECU
4. HYDRAULIC UNIT BRACKET

MT4029900443000X

Fig. 260 Hydraulic unit replacement. 1997–99 Diamante

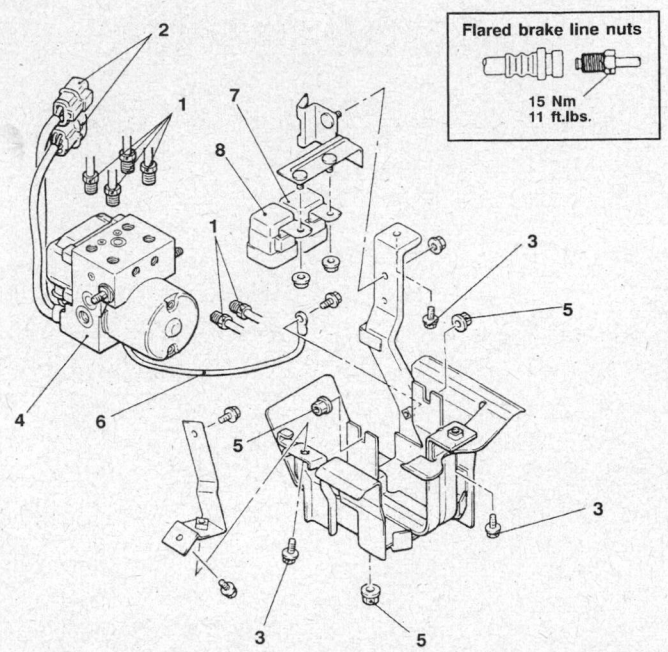

Hydraulic unit removal steps

1. Brake tube
2. Harness connector
3. Bracket nut
4. Hydraulic unit (HU) (with bracket)
5. Hydraulic unit (HU) nut
6. Grounding wire

Relay removal steps

7. ABS valve relay
8. ABS motor relay

MT4029900444000X

Fig. 261 Hydraulic unit replacement. 3000GT

Automatic
Transmissions/Transaxles

TABLE OF CONTENTS

Application Chart

Model	Transaxle/Transmission
1996	
Diamante	F4A33
Eclipse	F4AC1, F4A23, F4A33, W4A33
Galant	F4A23, F4A33, F4AC1
Mirage	F3A21, F4A22
Montero	V4AW2, V4AW3
Pickup	R4AC1
3000GT	F4A33
1997	
Diamante	F4A33
Eclipse	F4AC1, F4A23, F4A33, W4A33
Galant	F4A23, F4A33, F4AC1
Mirage	F4A22
Montero	W4A33
Montero Sport	R4AW3, W4A33
3000GT	F4A33
1998	
Diamante	F4A51
Eclipse	F4A23, F4A33, W4A33 & F5MC1
Galant	F4A23
Mirage	F4A41 & F4A42
Montero	V4AW3
Montero Sport	R4AW3 & V4AW3
3000GT	F4A33
1999	
Diamante	F4A51
Eclipse	F4A23, F4A33, W4A33 & F5MC1
Galant	F4A42 & F4A51
Mirage	F4A41 & F4A42
Montero	V4AW3
Montero Sport	R4A51 & V4A51
3000GT	F4A33

Mitsubishi R4AC1 Automatic Transmission

NOTE: On Air Bag Equipped Models, Refer To "Air Bag System Precautions" Located In The Front Of This Manual For System Disarming & Arming Procedures.

INDEX

PRECAUTIONS

BATTERY GROUND CABLE

Prior to service, disconnect battery ground cable and isolate as required.

IDENTIFICATION

The transmission identification number is located on the vehicle information code plate that is riveted to the firewall in the engine compartment, **Fig. 1.**

DESCRIPTION

This transmission is a four speed fully automatic units. The R4AC1 transmission uses a three element torque converter with a lock-up clutch system.

TROUBLESHOOTING

Refer to **Figs. 2 through 5** when troubleshooting the transmission.

MAINTENANCE

FLUID CHECK

With vehicle on a level surface, start engine and operate at idle. With parking brake applied, place selector lever in Neutral and check fluid level. When checking fluid level, transmission should be at operating temperature (approximately 170°F). Fluid level should be between the Add and Full notches on the dipstick. When adding fluid, use only that labeled Dexron II.

FLUID CHANGE

Under normal operating conditions, automatic transmission fluid change is required at 37,500 miles. Under severe conditions, such as trailer towing, prolonged operation in city traffic or commer-

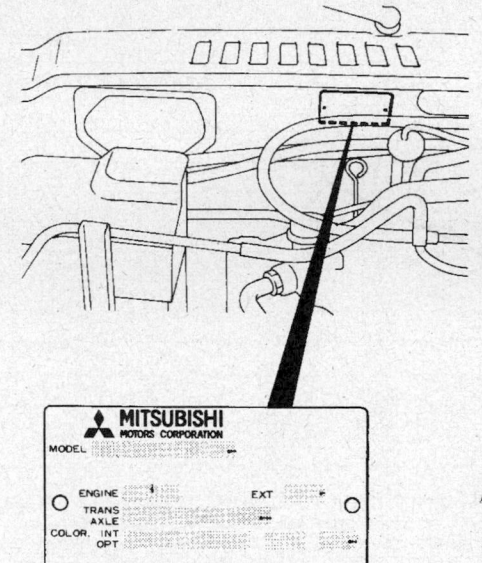

Fig. 1 Vehicle information code plate

cial use, fluid and filter should be changed and bands adjusted every 12,000 miles. When refilling transmission, use only Dexron II.

1. Raise and support front of vehicle, then position a drain pan under transmission oil pan.
2. Loosen transmission oil pan attaching bolts, then tap pan at one corner to loosen. Allow fluid to drain and remove pan.
3. Adjust low-reverse band, if necessary.
4. Install replacement transmission filter on bottom of valve body and tighten to specifications.
5. Clean transmission oil pan, then install pan and gasket on transmission. Tight-

en pan attaching bolts to specifications.
6. Add four quarts of Dexron II type automatic transmission fluid through transmission dipstick tube.
7. Start engine and operate at idle speed for approximately two minutes, then with parking brake applied, move selector lever through all detent positions.
8. Place selector lever in Drive, then check transmission fluid level. Fluid level should be at lower notch on dipstick. Add fluid as necessary.
9. After transmission has reached operating temperature, recheck fluid level. Fluid level should be between the Add and Full notches on the dipstick. Add fluid as necessary.

ADJUSTMENTS

SHIFT LOCK CABLE

1. Place selector lever in Park position and the ignition key in the Lock position.
2. Adjust shift lock cable so amount of protrusion (A) is .02–.18 inch and cable end and clearance (B) between cable end and slider is .02–.06 inch, **Fig. 6.**
3. Ensure proper operation of interlock mechanism.

KEY INTERLOCK

With selector lever in the Park position and the detent pin attached to the wall in the side of R position of detent groove, dimension (D) should be .04–.08 inch, **Fig. 7.**

KICKDOWN CABLE

1. Fix kickdown cable to bell crank lever.
2. Pull inner cable lightly with throttle lever being maintained in idle position.
3. With inner cable being pulled, caulk

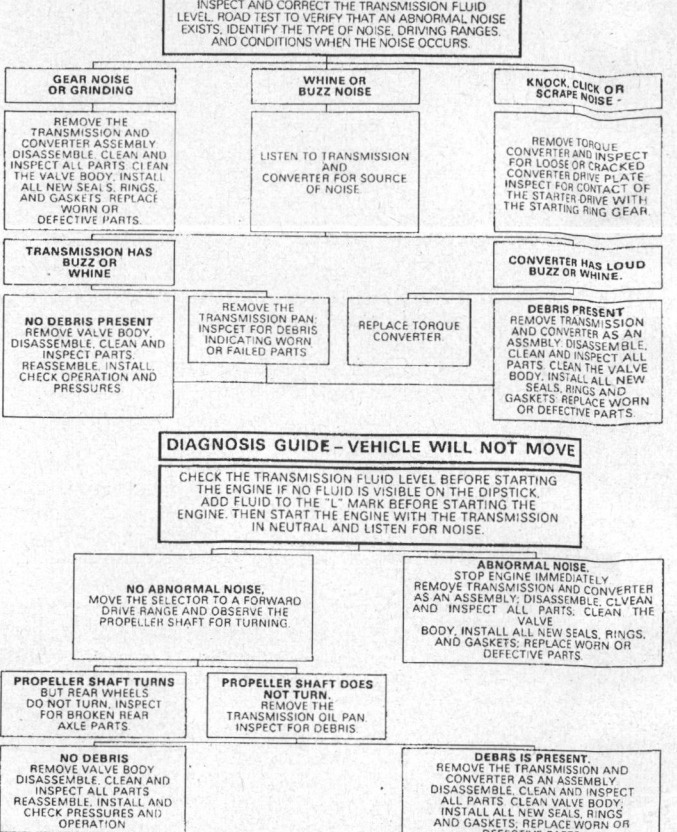

DIAGNOSIS GUIDE – ABNORMAL NOISE

INSPECT AND CORRECT THE TRANSMISSION FLUID LEVEL. ROAD TEST TO VERIFY THAT AN ABNORMAL NOISE EXISTS, IDENTIFY THE TYPE OF NOISE, DRIVING RANGES, AND CONDITIONS WHEN THE NOISE OCCURS.

GEAR NOISE OR GRINDING — REMOVE THE TRANSMISSION AND CONVERTER ASSEMBLY. DISASSEMBLE, CLEAN AND INSPECT ALL PARTS. CLEAN THE VALVE BODY, INSTALL ALL NEW SEALS, RINGS, AND GASKETS. REPLACE WORN OR DEFECTIVE PARTS.

WHINE OR BUZZ NOISE — LISTEN TO TRANSMISSION AND CONVERTER FOR SOURCE OF NOISE.

KNOCK, CLICK OR SCRAPE NOISE — REMOVE TORQUE CONVERTER AND INSPECT FOR LOOSE OR CRACKED CONVERTER DRIVE PLATE. INSPECT FOR CONTACT OF THE STARTER DRIVE WITH THE STARTING RING GEAR.

TRANSMISSION HAS BUZZ OR WHINE

CONVERTER HAS LOUD BUZZ OR WHINE.

NO DEBRIS PRESENT REMOVE VALVE BODY. DISASSEMBLE, CLEAN AND INSPECT PARTS. REASSEMBLE, INSTALL, CHECK OPERATION AND PRESSURES

REMOVE THE TRANSMISSION PAN. INSPECT FOR DEBRIS INDICATING WORN OR FAILED PARTS

REPLACE TORQUE CONVERTER

DEBRIS PRESENT REMOVE TRANSMISSION AND CONVERTER AS AN ASSEMBLY. DISASSEMBLE, CLEAN AND INSPECT ALL PARTS. CLEAN THE VALVE BODY, INSTALL ALL NEW SEALS, RINGS AND GASKETS. REPLACE WORN OR DEFECTIVE PARTS.

DIAGNOSIS GUIDE – VEHICLE WILL NOT MOVE

CHECK THE TRANSMISSION FLUID LEVEL BEFORE STARTING THE ENGINE IF NO FLUID IS VISIBLE ON THE DIPSTICK. ADD FLUID TO THE "L" MARK BEFORE STARTING THE ENGINE. THEN START THE ENGINE WITH THE TRANSMISSION IN NEUTRAL AND LISTEN FOR NOISE.

NO ABNORMAL NOISE. MOVE THE SELECTOR TO A FORWARD DRIVE RANGE AND OBSERVE THE PROPELLER SHAFT FOR TURNING.

ABNORMAL NOISE. STOP ENGINE IMMEDIATELY. REMOVE TRANSMISSION AND CONVERTER AS AN ASSEMBLY. DISASSEMBLE, CLEAN AND INSPECT ALL PARTS. CLEAN THE VALVE BODY. INSTALL ALL NEW SEALS, RINGS, AND GASKETS; REPLACE WORN OR DEFECTIVE PARTS.

PROPELLER SHAFT TURNS BUT REAR WHEELS DO NOT TURN. INSPECT FOR BROKEN REAR AXLE PARTS.

PROPELLER SHAFT DOES NOT TURN. REMOVE THE TRANSMISSION OIL PAN. INSPECT FOR DEBRIS.

NO DEBRIS REMOVE VALVE BODY. DISASSEMBLE, CLEAN AND INSPECT ALL PARTS. REASSEMBLE, INSTALL, AND CHECK PRESSURES AND OPERATION

DEBRIS IS PRESENT. REMOVE THE TRANSMISSION AND CONVERTER AS AN ASSEMBLY. DISASSEMBLE, CLEAN AND INSPECT ALL PARTS. CLEAN VALVE BODY; INSTALL ALL NEW SEALS, RINGS AND GASKETS; REPLACE WORN OR DEFECTIVE PARTS.

MT5029100513010X

Fig. 2 Troubleshooting chart: Abnormal noise, vehicle will not move & fluid leaks (Part 1 of 2)

DIAGNOSIS GUIDE – FLUID LEAKS

VISUALLY INSPECT FOR SOURCE OF LEAK. IF THE SOURCE OF LEAK CANNOT BE READILY DETERMINED, CLEAN THE EXTERIOR OF THE TRANSMISSION. CHECK TRANSMISSION FLUID LEVEL. CORRECT IF NECESSARY

THE FOLLOWING LEAKS MAY BE CORRECTED WITHOUT REMOVING THE TRANSMISSION. MANUAL LEVER SHAFT OIL SEAL FILLER TUBE "O" RING PRESSURE GAUGE PLUG NEUTRAL START SWITCH PAN GASKET OIL COOLER FITTINGS EXTENSION HOUSING TO CASE GASKET EXTENSION HOUSING TO CASE BOLTS EXTENSION HOUSING YOKE SEAL SPEEDOMETER ADAPTER "O" RING FRONT BAND ADJUSTING SCREW

THE FOLLOWING LEAKS REQUIRE REMOVAL OF THE TRANSMISSION AND TORQUE CONVERTER FOR CORRECTION. TRANSMISSION FLUID LEAKING FROM THE LOWER EDGE OF THE CONVERTER HOUSING, CAUSED BY FRONT PUMP SEAL, PUMP TO CASE SEAL, OR TORQUE CONVERTER WELD. CRACKED OR POROUS TRANSMISSION CASE

MT5029100513020X

Fig. 2 Troubleshooting chart: Abnormal noise, vehicle will not move & fluid leaks (Part 2 of 2)

wise increases pressure and clockwise turn decreases pressure.

THROTTLE PRESSURE

Throttle pressure cannot be tested accurately, therefore adjustment should be measured if a malfunction is evident.

1. Insert gauge pin of tool No. C-3763, or equivalent, between throttle lever cam and kickdown lever.
2. By pushing in on tool, compress kickdown valve against its spring so throttle valve is completely bottomed inside the valve body.
3. As force is exerted to compress spring, turn throttle lever stop screw with hex wrench until head of screw touches throttle lever tang with throttle lever cam touching tool and the throttle valve bottomed, **Fig. 14.** Be sure adjustment is made with spring fully compressed and valve bottomed in valve body.

IN-VEHICLE REPAIRS

SPEEDOMETER PINION GEAR REPLACEMENT

1. Remove bolt and clamp retaining speedometer pinion adapter in extension housing.
2. With cable housing connected, carefully work adapter and pinion out of extension housing.
3. If there is transmission fluid in cable housing, replace seal in adapter, **Fig. 15.**
4. Note number of gear teeth and install speedometer pinion gear into adapter, then fit O-ring over adapter.
5. Rotate speedometer pinion gear and adapter assembly so number on adapter, corresponding to number of teeth on gear, is in six o'clock position as assembly is installed.
6. Install clamp and bolt with clamp tangs in adapter positioning slots, then tap adapter firmly into extension housing and tighten sleeve clamp screw to specifications.

OVERDRIVE HOUSING YOKE SEAL REPLACEMENT

1. Mark then remove propeller shaft assembly.

inner cable stopper so space between stopper and outer cable becomes .031–.059 inch, **Fig. 8.**

4. Pull inner cable and put throttle lever to full open position. Loosen and adjust length of bell crank lever arm so that space between inner cable stopper and cable becomes 1.46–2.50 inches, **Fig. 9.**
5. After adjusting engine to regular idling position, fix inner cable to throttle lever. At this time, fasten outer cable with adjustment nuts so that space between inner cable stopper and outer cable becomes .031–.050 inch, **Fig. 10.**
6. With throttle lever being full open, confirm that space between outer cable and inner cable is 1.30–1.38 inches.

KICKDOWN BAND

The kickdown band adjustment screw is located on the left side of the transmission case, **Fig. 11.**

1. Loosen locknut, then back off adjustment screw approximately five turns.
2. Using wrench tool No. C-3380-A and adapter tool No. C3705, or equivalents, **torque** band adjustment screw to 6 ft. lbs.
3. Back off adjustment screw 1⅞ turns, then tighten locknut to specifications while holding adjustment screw.

LOW & REVERSE BAND

1. Raise and support front of vehicle, then drain transmission fluid and remove transmission oil pan.
2. Remove locknut, then **torque** adjustment screw to 30 inch lbs., **Fig. 12.**
3. Back off adjustment screw six turns, then tighten locknut to specifications while holding adjustment screw.
4. Install oil pan and gasket, then tighten bolts to specifications.
5. Fill transmission with Dexron or Dexron II automatic transmission fluid.

LINE PRESSURE

An incorrect throttle pressure setting will cause incorrect line pressure readings even though the pressure adjustment is correct. Always inspect and correct throttle pressure adjustment before adjusting line pressure.

The approximate adjustment is 1 5/16 inch, measured from valve body to inner edge of adjustment nut, **Fig. 13.** However, due to manufacturing tolerances, the adjustment can be varied to obtain specified line pressure.

The adjustment screw may be turned with a suitable hex wrench. One complete turn of adjustment screw changes closed throttle line pressure approximately 1⅔ psi. Turning adjustment screw counterclock-

POSSIBLE CAUSE

#	Possible Cause
35	Faulty TCC.
34	Overrunning clutch inner race damaged.
33	Overruning clutch worn, broken or seized.
32	Planetary gear sets broken or seized.
31	Rear clutch dragging.
30	Worn or faulty rear clutch.
29	Insufficient clutch plate clearance.
28	Faulty cooling system.
27	Kickdown band adjustment too tight.
26	Hydraulic pressure too high.
25	Breather clogged.
24	High fluid level.
23	Worn or faulty front clutch.
22	Kickdown servo band or linkage malfunction.
21	Governor malfunction.
20	Worn or broken reaction shaft support seal rings.
19	Governor support seal rings broken or worn.
18	Intermediate shaft bearing and/or bushing damaged.
17	Overrunning clutch not holding.
16	Kickdown band out of adjustment.
15	Incorrect throttle linkage adjustment.
14	Engine idle speed too low.
13	Aerated fluid.
12	Worn or broken input shaft seal rings.
11	Faulty oil pump.
10	Oil filter clogged.
9	Incorrect gearshift control linkage adjustment.
8	Low fluid level.
7	Low-reverse servo, band or linkage malfunction.
6	Valve body malfunction or leakage.
5	Low-reverse band out of adjustment.
4	Hydraulic pressures too low.
3	Engine idle speed too high.
2	Stuck TCC valve.
1	Stuck switch valve.

CONDITION (chart columns)

- HARSH ENGAGEMENT FROM NEUTRAL TO D OR R
- DELAYED ENGAGEMENT FROM NEUTRAL TO D OR R
- RUNAWAY UPSHIFT
- NO UPSHIFT
- 3-2 KICKDOWN RUNAWAY
- NO KICKDOWN OR NORMAL DOWNSHIFT
- SHIFTS ERRATIC
- SLIPS IN FORWARD DRIVE POSITIONS
- SLIPS IN REVERSE ONLY
- SLIPS IN ALL POSITIONS
- NO DRIVE IN ANY POSTION
- NO DRIVE IN FORWARD DRIVE POSITIONS
- NO DRIVE IN REVERSE
- DRIVES IN NEUTRAL
- DRAGS OF LOCKS
- GRATING, SCRAPING GROWLING NOISE
- BUZZING NOISE
- HARD TO FILL, OIL BLOWS OUT FILLER HOLE
- TRANSMISSION OVERHEATS
- HARSH UPSHIFT
- DELAYED UPSHIFT
- SLIPS IN REVERSE OR MANUAL LOW

MT5029100514000X

Fig. 3   Troubleshooting chart: General diagnosis

2. Remove overdrive housing yoke seal using seal remover tool No. C-3985, or equivalent.
3. Position new seal in opening of housing and drive it into housing using seal installer tool No. C-3995, or equivalent.
4. Install propeller shaft assembly using marks made during removal.

VALVE BODY & ACCUMULATOR PISTON REPLACEMENT

1. Raise and support vehicle.
2. Loosen oil pan bolts. Tap pan to break loose and allow transmission fluid to drain, then remove oil pan.
3. Remove gearshift control rod and throttle rod A from respective levers of transmission, then loosen clamp bolts to remove throttle lever and manual control lever from transmission.
4. While holding valve body in position, remove valve body to transmission attaching bolts.
5. Lower valve body and pull forward out of case. It may be necessary to rotate propeller shaft to align parking gear and sprag to permit cam on end of parking sprag rod to pass sprag.
6. Remove accumulator piston and spring from transmission case.
7. Inspect piston for nicks, scores or wear, spring for distortion, and rings for freedom in piston grooves and wear or breakage. Replace parts as necessary.
8. If valve body manual lever shaft seal must be replaced, drive it out of case with suitable punch, then drive new seal into case using a $^{15}/_{16}$ inch socket and hammer.
9. Place valve body manual lever in low position.
10. Use screwdriver to push park sprag into engagement with parking gear, turning output shaft to verify engagement.
11. Install accumulator piston in transmission case.
12. Position accumulator spring between piston and valve body.
13. Place valve body in position, working park sprag rod through opening and past sprag, then install bolts finger tight and tighten evenly to specifications.
14. Install manual control lever to shaft portion of manual lever and tighten clamp bolt, then move lever to all detent positions to check for smooth operation. Loosen valve body attaching bolts, relocate and adjust as necessary.
15. Install throttle lever and tighten clamp bolt, then connect throttle and control rod and adjust as necessary.
16. Install oil pan and new gasket, then fill transmission fluid to specifications.

TRANSMISSION
REPLACE

1. Remove engine undercover.
2. Remove front exhaust pipe.
3. Scribe alignment marks on propeller shaft and axle flange then remove propeller shaft.
4. Remove transmission in numbered sequence shown in **Fig. 16,** noting the following:
   a. Tilt transmission so rear is lower than front to remove bolt that fastens the starter motor and bell crank bracket.
   b. Pull transmission rearward to disconnect transmission from engine then lower transmission from vehicle. **Ensure torque converter does not remain on the engine side, damage to the transmission oil pump could result.**
5. Reverse numbered sequence shown in **Fig. 16** to install transmission, noting the following:
   a. Align centering locations when installing transmission, **Fig. 17.**
   b. Install special bolts so that the paint applied to the torque converter can be seen through check hole in driveplate, **Fig. 18.**

POSSIBLE CAUSE

	NO LOCKUP	WILL NOT UNLOCK	STAYS LOCKED UP TO TOO LOW A SPEED IN DIRECT	LOCKS UP OR DRAGS IN LOW OR SECOND	STALLS OR IS SLUGGISH IN REVERSE	LOUD CHATTER DURING LOCKUP ENGAGEMENT – (COLD)	VIBRATION OR SHUDDER DURING LOCKUP ENGAGEMENT	VIBRATIONS AFTER LOCKUP ENGAGEMENT	VIBRATION WHEN "REVED" IN NEUTRAL	OVERHEATING, OIL BLOWING OUT DIPSTICK OR PUMP SEAL	SHUDDER AFTER LOCKUP ENGAGEMENT
FAULTY OIL PUMP	x			x	x		x				x
STICKING GOVERNOR VALVE	x	x	x								
PLUGGED COOLER, LINES OR FITTINGS					x					x	x
VALVE BODY MALFUNCTION	x	x	x	x	x		x				x
STUCK SWITCH VALVE	x	x	x	x	x					x	
STUCK TCC VALVE	x	x	x								
STUCK TCC TIMING VALVE	x	x	x	x							
STUCK TCC SOLENOID	x		x								
SOLENOID WIRING DISCONNECTED	x										
FAILED TCC SOLENOID	x										
FAILED TRANSMISSION CONTROL UNIT	x	x									
FAULTY TORQUE CONVERTER:	x					x	x	x			x
OUT OF BALANCE									x		
FAILED TCC	x					x					x
LEAKING TURBINE HUB SEAL	x					x					
ALIGN EXHAUST SYSTEM								x			x
TUNE ENGINE							x	x			x
FAULTY INPUT SHAFT OR SEAL RING	x				x						
THROTTLE LINKAGE MISADJUSTED								x			x

NOTE
TCC Torque Converter Clutch

MT5029100515000X

Fig. 4 Troubleshooting chart: Electronic lockup torque converter

POSSIBLE CAUSE

	NO REVERSE OR SLIPS IN REVERSE	NO OVERDRIVE SHIFT	RUNAWAY OVERDRIVE SHIFT	OVERDRIVE SHIFT OCCURS IMMEDIATELY AFTER 2-3 SHIFT	EXCESSIVELY DELAYED OVERDRIVE SHIFT	NO 4-3 DOWNSHIFT	NO 4-3 DOWNSHIFT WITH OVERDRIVE OFF SWITCH	TORQUE CONVERTER LOCKS UP IN 2ND AND 3RD GEARS	HARSH SHIFTS 1-2, 2-3, AND 3-2	LOW GOVERNOR PRESSURE	NOISY
FAILED DIRECT CLUTCH	x										
OVERDRIVE SPRING LOST LOAD	x										
INCORRECT OVERDRIVE PISTON BEARING SPACER	x	x			x						
BLOWN FUSE		x									
FAULTY OVERDRIVE SOLENOID		x		x							
FAULTY WIRING OR CONNECTORS		x		x			x	x			
FAULTY OVERDRIVE OFF SWITCH		x						x			
FAULTY TRANSMISSION CONTROL UNIT		x		x			x	x			
LOW OVERDRIVE PRESSURE		x									
LOWER VALVE BODY MALFUNCTION		x		x		x					
FAILED OVERDRIVE OVERRUNNING CLUTCH			x								x
FAULTY THROTTLE POSITION SENSOR				x							
FAULTY TCC SOLENOID - NOT VENTING						x	x	x	x		
LEAKING GOVERNOR TUBES - BENT										x	
LEAKING GOVERNOR TUBES - LOOSE FIT										x	
GOVERNOR SEAL RINGS BROKEN OR WORN										x	
FAILED OVERDRIVE PISTON BEARING											x
FAILED GEAR TRAIN NEEDLE THRUST BEARINGS											x
FAILED OVERDRIVE PLANETARY GEAR											x

NOTE
TCC Torque Converter Clutch

MT5029100516000X

Fig. 5 Troubleshooting chart: Overdrive unit

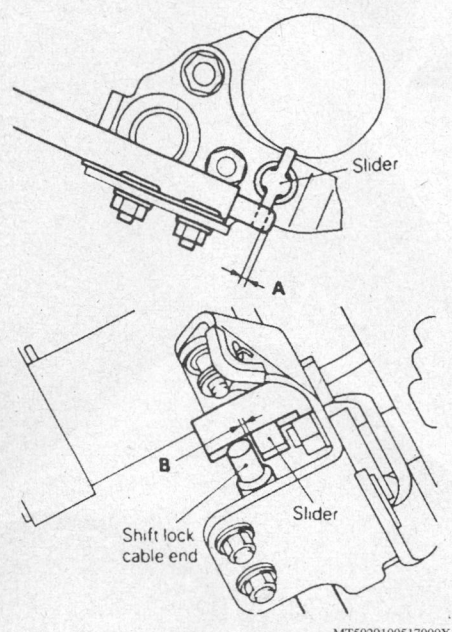

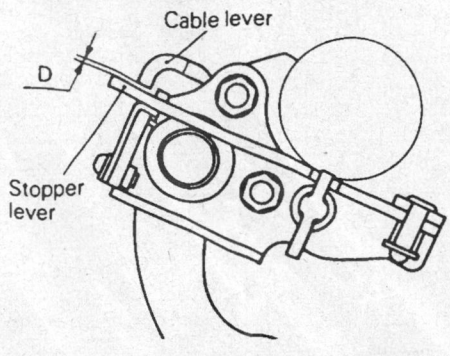

Fig. 7 Key interlock cable adjustment

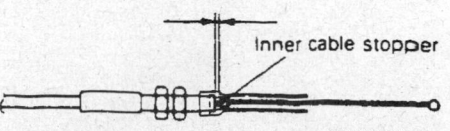

Fig. 8 Inner cable stopper to outer cable measurement

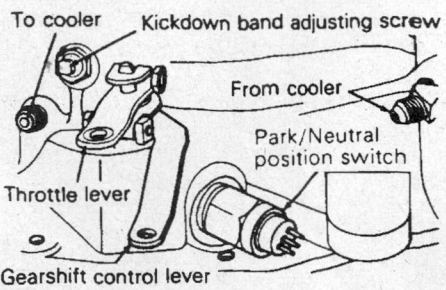

Fig. 11 Kickdown band adjustment screw location

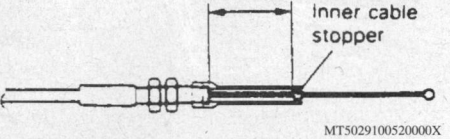

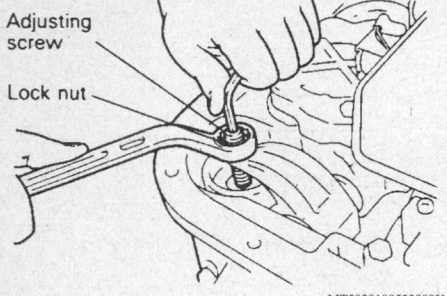

Fig. 6 Shift lock cable adjustment

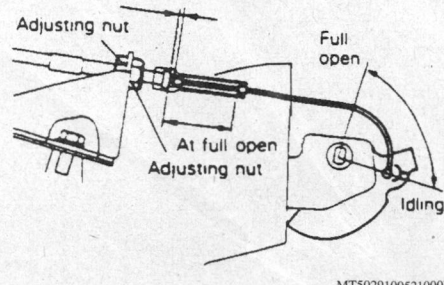

Fig. 10 Outer cable adjustment

Fig. 9 Inner cable stopper to outer cable w/throttle lever at full open measurement

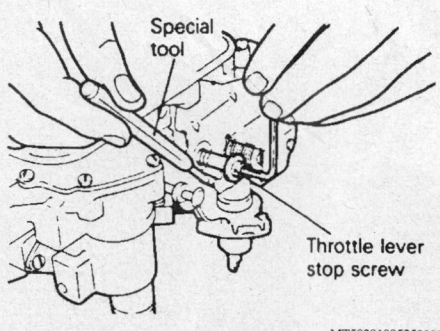

Fig. 14 Throttle pressure adjustment

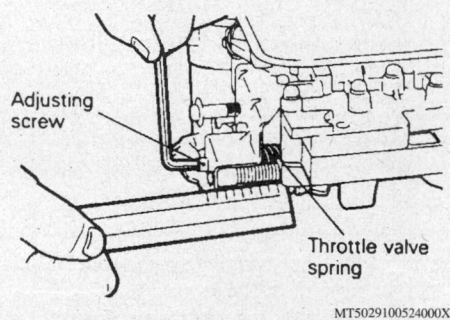

Fig. 13 Line pressure adjustment

Fig. 12 Low-reverse band adjustment

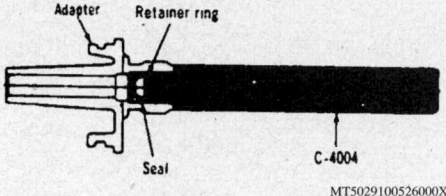

Fig. 15 Speedometer adapter seal installation

MT5029100526000X

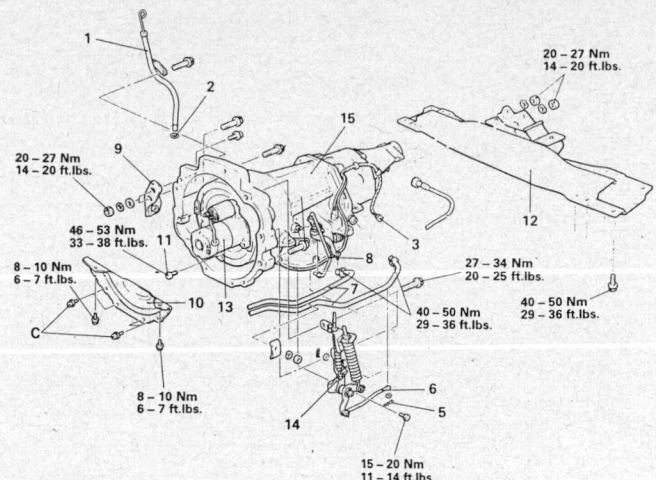

20 – 27 Nm
14 – 20 ft.lbs.

20 – 27 Nm
14 – 20 ft.lbs.

46 – 53 Nm
33 – 38 ft.lbs.

8 – 10 Nm
6 – 7 ft.lbs.

8 – 10 Nm
6 – 7 ft.lbs.

27 – 34 Nm
20 – 25 ft.lbs.

40 – 50 Nm
29 – 36 ft.lbs.

40 – 50 Nm
29 – 36 ft.lbs.

15 – 20 Nm
11 – 14 ft.lbs.

1. Oil filler tube
2. O-ring
3. Transmission harness conector
4. Speedometer cable
5. Cotter pin
6. Transmission control rod (Transmission side)
7. Automatic transmission cooler tube
8. Transmission throttle lever (Bell crank bracket side)
9. Exhaust pipe mounting bracket
10. Bell housing cover
11. Special bolt
12. No.2 crossmember
13. Starter motor
14. Bell crank bracket assembly
15. Transmission assembly

	Nm	ft.lbs.	O.D.×Length mm(in.)	Bolt identification
A	43 – 55	31 – 40	⑦ 10×50(.4×2.0)	⑦ D×L
B	43 – 55	31 – 40	⑦ 10×70(.4×2.8)	;D
C	30 – 42	21 – 30	⑦ 10×16(.4×:6)	L

MT5029100527000X

Fig. 16 Transmission replacement

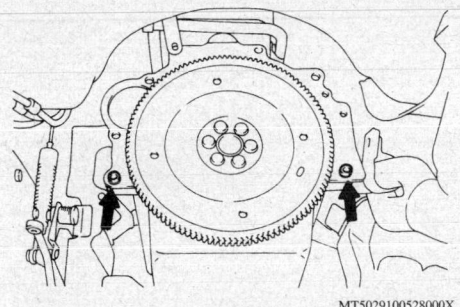

MT5029100528000X

Fig. 17 Transmission alignment pins

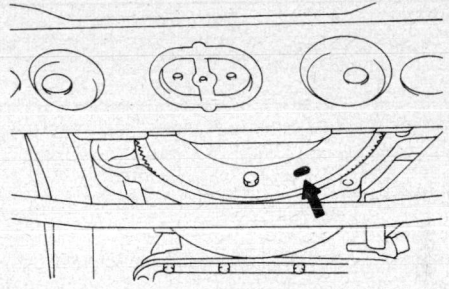

MT5029100529000X

Fig. 18 Transmission driveplate check hole

TIGHTENING SPECIFICATIONS

Component	Torque/Ft. Lbs.
Bell Crank Bracket	20–25
Bellhousing Cover	6–7
Driveplate To Torque Converter	23
Exhaust Pipe Mounting Bracket	14–20
Kickdown Band Adjusting Screw Locknut	30
Low/Reverse Band Adjusting Screw Locknut	25
No. 2 Crossmember To Frame	29–40
No. 2 Crossmember To Transmission	14–18
Overdrive Unit To Transmission Case	25
Park/Neutral Position Switch	25
Pressure Test Take-Off Plug	10
Selector Lever Rod	7–10
Shift Lock Cable	36–48①
Shift Lock Cable Locknut	7–10
Speedometer Sleeve Clamp Screw	8
Transmission Control Arm	14–20
Transmission Control Cable Locknut	12–19
Transmission Control Rod	11–14
Transmission Filter To Valve Body	35①
Transmission Mounting Bolt (.6 Inch)	21–30
Transmission Mounting Bolt (2.0 & 2.8 Inch)	31–40
Transmission Oil Cooler Eye Bolt	22–25
Transmission Oil Cooler Flare Nut	29–36
Transmission Oil Pan	13
Valve Body Screw	36①
Valve Body To Transmission Case	9

① — Inch Lbs.

Mitsubishi F3A21 Automatic Transaxle

NOTE: On Air Bag Equipped Models, Refer To "Air Bag System Precautions" Located In The Front Of This Manual For System Disarming & Arming Procedures.

INDEX

PRECAUTIONS

AIR BAG SYSTEMS

Refer to "Air Bag System Precautions" in the front of this manual for system disarming and arming procedures.

BATTERY GROUND CABLE

Prior to service, disconnect battery ground cable and isolate as required.

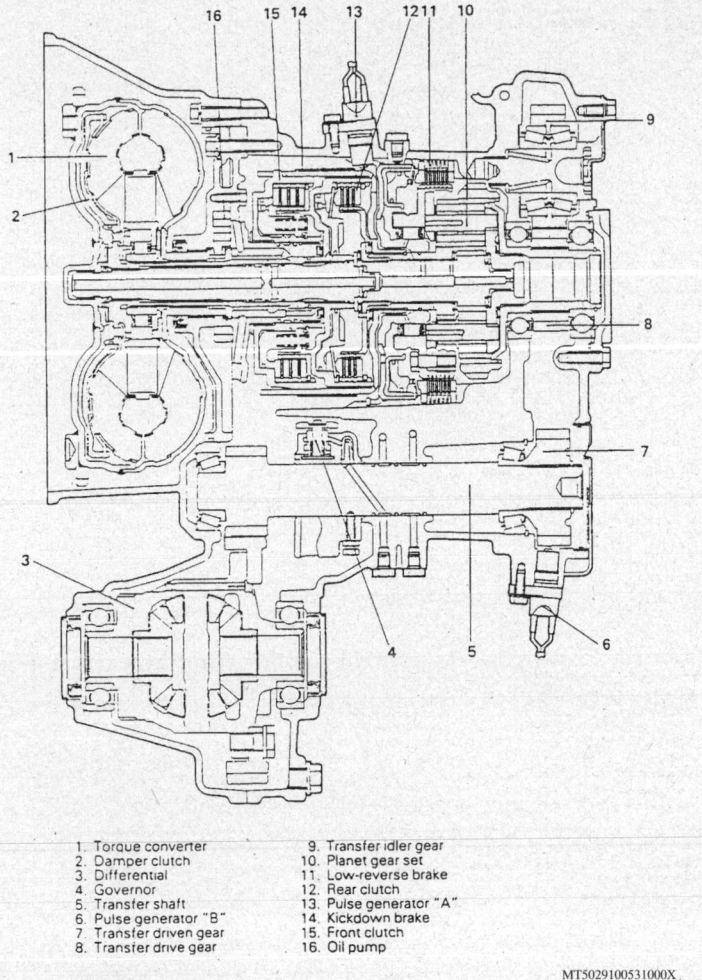

1. Torque converter
2. Damper clutch
3. Differential
4. Governor
5. Transfer shaft
6. Pulse generator "B"
7. Transfer driven gear
8. Transfer drive gear
9. Transfer idler gear
10. Planet gear set
11. Low-reverse brake
12. Rear clutch
13. Pulse generator "A"
14. Kickdown brake
15. Front clutch
16. Oil pump

MT5029100531000X

Fig. 1 Cross-sectional view of transaxle

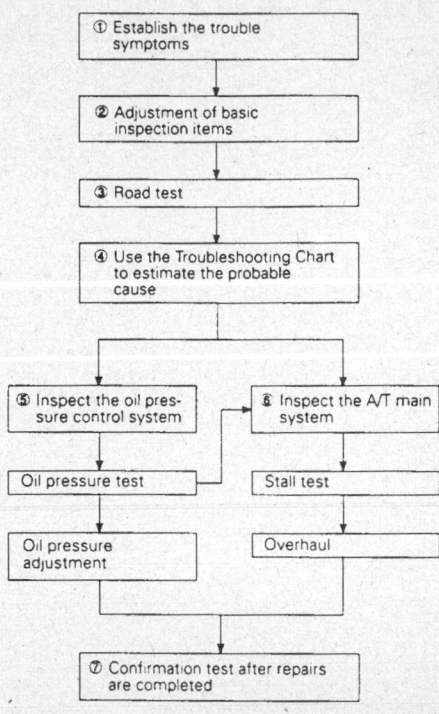

① Establish the trouble symptoms
② Adjustment of basic inspection items
③ Road test
④ Use the Troubleshooting Chart to estimate the probable cause
⑤ Inspect the oil pressure control system — Oil pressure test — Oil pressure adjustment
⑥ Inspect the A/T main system — Stall test — Overhaul
⑦ Confirmation test after repairs are completed

MT5029300534000X

Fig. 2 Troubleshooting flow chart

IDENTIFICATION

The transaxle identification number is located on the vehicle information code plate that is attached on the fender shield in the engine compartment. The plate shows model and body code and engine and transaxle model numbers.

DESCRIPTION

These transaxles are three speed, fully automatic units using an internal damper clutch style torque converter, **Fig. 1.**

TROUBLESHOOTING

TRANSAXLE

Refer to **Figs. 2 and 3** when troubleshooting the transaxle.

MAINTENANCE

FLUID CHECK

The vehicle on level surface, start engine and operate at idle speed. With parking brake applied, place selector lever in Neutral, then remove dipstick and check fluid level. Transaxle should be at operating temperature when checking fluid level (120–180°F). Fluid level should be between Add and Full lines on dipstick. If necessary, add Dexron II fluid to bring fluid level within Add and Full lines on dipstick.

FLUID CHANGE

The automatic transaxle fluid should be changed every 30,000 miles on these units. When refilling transaxle, add only Dexron II automatic transaxle fluid.
1. Raise and support front of vehicle, then position drain pan under transaxle and remove drain located at bottom of differential and allow transaxle to drain.
2. Install drain plug, then add 4.2 quarts of the specified automatic transaxle fluid through transaxle dipstick hole.
3. Start engine and check fluid level as described under " Fluid Check" in this section.

ADJUSTMENTS

SHIFT LOCK CABLE

1. Place selector lever in Park position.
2. Fasten the shift lock cable at a position where end of shift lock cable is positioned above the red marking as shown in **Fig. 4.**

THROTTLE CONTROL CABLE

1. Place throttle lever in curb idle position.
2. Raise throttle cable cover B upward, then loosen cable lower mounting bracket bolt, **Fig. 5.**
3. Move cable lower mounting bracket until clearance between nipple and top of cable cover A is .02–.06 inch, then **torque** cable lower mounting bracket bolt to 9–10.5 ft. lbs.
4. With throttle lever in wide open position, pull throttle cable upward to ensure cable has freedom of movement.

LINE PRESSURE

1. Drain transaxle fluid by removing oil pan drain plug.
2. Remove oil pan.
3. Disconnect throttle control cable from throttle cam.
4. Remove oil filter and filter plate.
5. Remove valve body assembly, being careful not to drop manual valve.
6. Adjust line pressure by turning adjustment screw at regulator valve, **Fig. 6,** counterclockwise to increase line pressure or clockwise to decrease line pressure. One complete rotation of adjustment screw will change line pressure approximately 3.7 psi for wide open condition of throttle cable.
7. Ensure O-ring is properly installed in top of valve body, **Fig. 7.**
8. Install valve body assembly, fitting groove of manual valve on manual control shaft detent plate pin.
9. Install valve body attaching bolts in proper positions, **Fig. 8,** and **torque** to 8 ft. lbs. Bolt (A) is .709 inch long, bolt (B) is .984 inch long and bolt (C) is 1.576 inches long.

Problem symptom	Probable cause number
Starter motor does not operate in P and N positions	1
Movement impossible (in D, 2, L and R positions)	3, 4, 11, 14, 15, 21
Movement impossible (in D, 2 and L positions)	8, 23
Movement impossible (in D and 2 positions)	6
Movement impossible (in R position)	7, 9, 11, 17
Engine stalls when shifting from N to R, D	2, 11, 14, 23, 21
Vehicle starts to move in P position	26
High creeping in N position	7, 8
Poor acceleration in 2nd gear	3, 4, 5, 8, 10, 11, 14, 17, 23, 24
Poor acceleration in 3rd gear	3, 4, 5, 11, 17, 18, 23
Shift point displacement when shifting from 1st and 2nd	3, 4, 12, 13, 14, 17, 24
Flare shift 1 → 2	3, 4, 5, 11, 12, 13, 14, 17, 20, 24
Harsh 1 → 2 upshift	11, 12, 13, 14, 17, 20, 24
Shifting up from 1st to 2nd impossible	3, 4, 10, 11, 12, 13, 14, 24
Shift point displacement when shifting from 2nd and 3rd	3, 4, 11, 12, 13, 14, 18
Engine running up when shifting from 2nd to 3rd	3, 4, 5, 11, 14, 17, 18
Harsh 2 → 3 upshift	7, 10, 11, 12, 13, 14
Shifting up from 2nd to 3rd impossible	3, 4, 7, 10, 11, 12, 13, 14
Time lag during kickdown in D range	3, 4, 11, 12, 18, 22
Shock during kickdown in D range	7, 10, 14
No kickdown in D range	12, 13, 18, 22
Large shock felt when shifting from 3rd to 2nd	10, 12, 13, 14, 18, 19
Large shock felt when shifting from 3rd to 1st	12, 13, 14, 24
Large shock felt when shifting from 2nd to 1st	10, 12, 13, 14, 24
Shifting down from 3rd to 2nd impossible	12, 13, 18
Shifting down from 3rd to 1st impossible	12, 13, 18, 19
Shifting down from 2nd to 1st impossible	12, 13, 19
Shifting up to 3rd in 2 range	11, 18, 19, 25
Shifting up in L range	11, 17, 18, 19, 24
Engine braking ineffective in L range	9, 11, 14, 16
Stall r/min too high in R range	3, 4, 7, 9, 11, 14
Stall r/min too high in D range	3, 4, 6, 8, 11, 14
Stall r/min too low	2, 5

MT5029300535010X

Fig. 3   Transaxle troubleshooting chart (Part 1 of 2)

PROBABLE CAUSE

1. Engine starting system
2. Insufficient engine output
3. Poor oil pump discharge pressure
4. Clogged oil filter
5. Torque converter
   a. Malfunction of stator one-way clutch
   b. Burned out stator one-way clutch
6. One-way clutch
   a. Malfunction
   b. Burn out
7. Front clutch
   a. Sticking of piston
   b. Foreign material caught in check valve
   c. Damaged seal ring
   d. Worn disc
   e. Deformed return spring
   f. Excessive clutch clearance
8. Rear clutch
   a. Sticking of piston
   b. Foreign material caught in check valve
   c. Damaged seal ring
   d. Worn disc
   e. Deformed return spring
   f. Excessive clutch clearance
9. Low-reverse brake
   a. Sticking of piston
   b. Damaged seal ring
   c. Worn disc
   d. Deformed return spring
   e. Excessive clutch clearance
10. Kickdown brake
    a. Sticking of piston
    b. Damaged seal ring
    c. Kickdown servo poorly adjusted
    d. Malfunction of anchor rod
    e. Burned out kickdown band
    f. Worn kickdown band
    g. Deformed return spring
    h. Kickdown servo bore worn
    i. Kickdown servo bore check valve malfunction

11. Valve body
    a. Improper installation
    b. Damaged O-ring at installation surfaces
    c. Sticking of check ball
12. Malfunction of throttle valve
13. Governor
    a. Damaged weight
    b. Clogged filter
14. Regulator valve
    a. Improper adjustment
    b. Malfunction
15. Line pressure relief valve
    a. Sticking of ball
    b. Deformed or damaged spring
16. Low-relief valve
    a. Sticking of ball
    b. Deformed or damaged spring
17. Malfunction of 1-2 shift valve
18. Malfunction of 2-3 shift valve
19. Malfunction of 2-3 control-valve
20. Malfunction of range control valve
21. Malfunction of torque converter control valve
22. Malfunction of kickdown valve
23. Malfunction of N-D accumulator valve
24. Malfunction of 1-2 accumulator valve
25. Malfunction of 1-2 engine brake valve
26. Parking mechanism failure

MT5029300535020X

Fig. 3   Transaxle troubleshooting chart (Part 2 of 2)

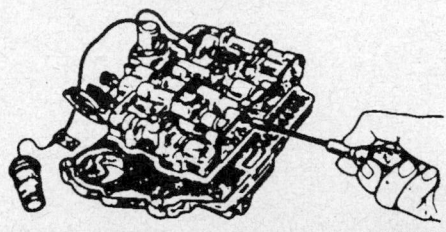

MT5029100540000X

Fig. 6   Line pressure adjustment

coupling nut to 8 ft. lbs.
6. Ensure gear selector lever is still in Neutral position, then apply service brakes.
7. Attempt to start engine in all selector lever positions; ensure starting occurs only in Park or Neutral positions.

IN-VEHICLE REPAIRS

CONTROL CABLE REPLACEMENT

1. Remove air cleaner assembly.
2. Service transaxle controls in numbered sequence shown in **Fig. 10**, as follows:
   a. Place gear selector in Neutral position.
   b. Install adjusting nut loosely on adjuster stud.
   c. Gently pull transaxle control cable in direction shown in **Fig. 11** and tighten nut.

TRANSAXLE

REPLACE

Replace transaxle assembly in numbered sequence shown in **Fig. 12**, noting the following:
1. Remove starter motor assembly leaving electrical harness connected.

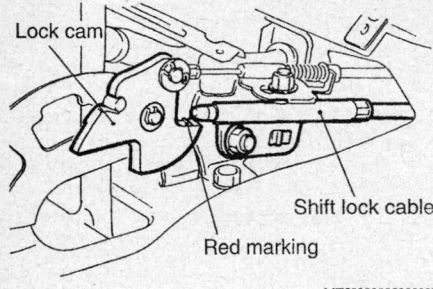

MT5029300538000X

Fig. 4   Shift lock cable adjustment

10. Install filter plate, gasket, and oil filter. **Torque** attaching bolts to 48–60 inch lbs.
11. Connect throttle cable to throttle cam.
12. Install new oil pan gasket, oil pan, washers, and bolts. **Torque** bolts to 7.5–8.5 ft. lbs.
13. Fill transaxle to specifications with Dexron II automatic transaxle fluid.

PARK/NEUTRAL POSITION SWITCH

The following procedure has been revised by a Technical Service Bulletin.
1. Set parking brake and place gear selector lever in Neutral position.
2. Loosen transaxle control cable to manual control lever coupling nut to allow lever to move freely.
3. Place manual control lever in its neu-

MT5029100539000X

Fig. 5   Throttle control cable adjustment

tral position, then loosen park/neutral position switch mounting bolts.
4. Rotate switch body until holes in flange and manual control lever are aligned, **Fig. 9**, then **torque** switch mounting bolts to 8 ft. lbs.
5. Pull transaxle control cable gently away from cable housing, then **torque**

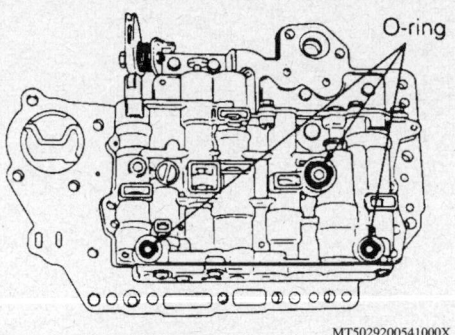

Fig. 7 O-ring installation in top of valve body

MT5029200541000X

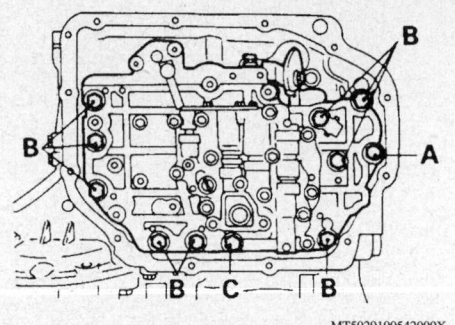

Fig. 8 Valve body attaching bolt locations

MT5029100542000X

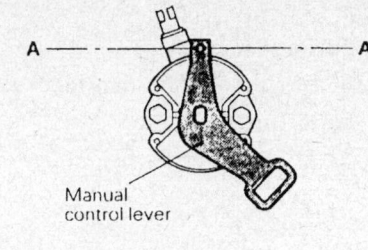

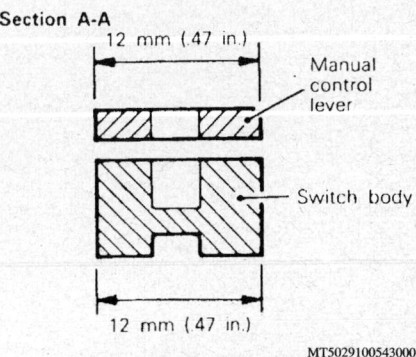

MT5029100543000X

Fig. 9 Park/Neutral position switch installation

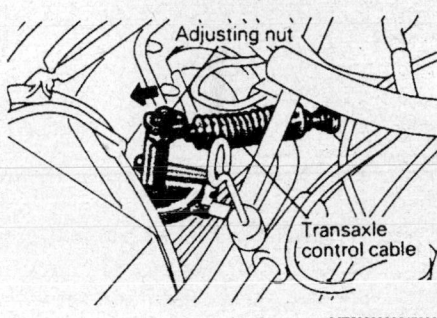

Fig. 11 Control cable adjustment

MT5029300547000X

Transaxle control cable assembly removal steps

1. Nut
2. Clip
3. Rear floor console
4. Front floor console
5. Clip
6. Nut
7. Bolt
8. Cover
9. Transaxle control module
10. Connection for the transaxle control cable assembly
11. Nut
12. Transaxle control cable assembly
13. Adjuster

Selector lever assembly removal steps

3. Rear floor console
4. Front floor console
10. Connection for the transaxle control cable assembly
14. Connection of key interlock cable
15. Connection of shift lock cable
16. Clip
17. Selector lever assembly

MT5029300546000X

Fig. 10 Transaxle control cable replacement

2. Raise transaxle enough to remove weight off transaxle mount, then remove transaxle mounting bolts.

3. Support engine assembly using engine support tool No. MZ203827, or equivalent.

4. Remove tie rod end and lower ball joint using ball joint remover tool No. MB991193, or equivalent.

5. Insert a suitable pry bar between the driveshaft and transaxle case and pry driveshaft out of transaxle. Support

driveshaft and do not allow to hang from driveshaft boot.

6. Remove three bolts connecting the torque converter to the driveplate.

7. After removing converter bolts push torque converter toward transaxle so that it does not remain on the engine.

8. Support transaxle using a suitable transaxle jack and remove from vehicle by moving assembly to the right and then lowering out of vehicle.

9. After securely inserting torque converter into transaxle, slide it so that value marked A is approximately .472 inch, **Fig. 13**, then install transaxle assembly on to engine.

10. Install driveshaft so that inboard joint of driveshaft is straight and not bent relative to the transaxle.

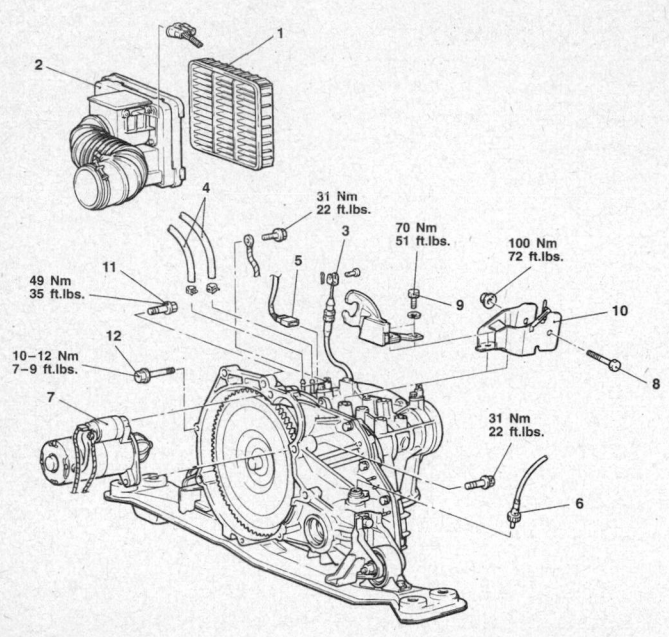

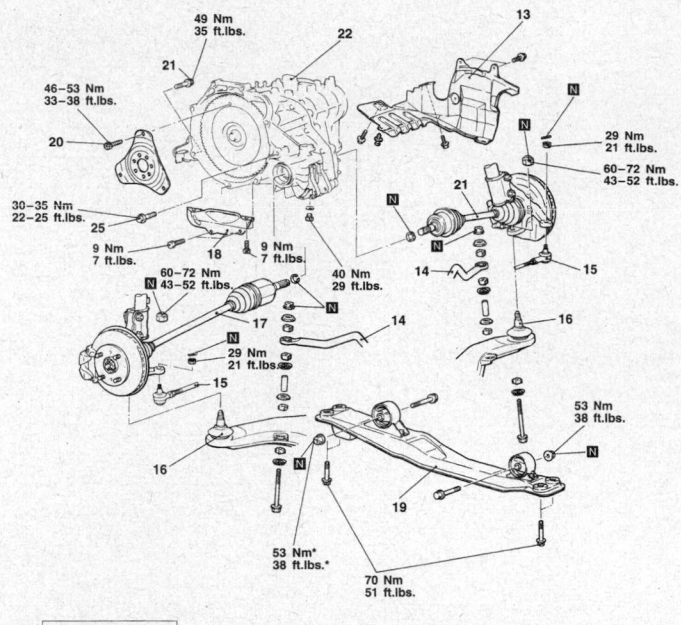

Removal steps

1. Air cleaner element
2. Air cleaner cover and hose assembly
3. Manual control lever connection
4. Transaxle oil cooler hoses connection
5. Park/Neutral position switch connector
6. Speedometer cable connection
7. Starter motor
8. Transaxle mount bolt
9. Bolt
10. Transaxle mount bracket
11. Transaxle assembly upper part coupling bolt
12. Bolt
● Support of engine assembly

MT5029300549010X

Fig. 12 Transaxle replacement (Part 1 of 2)

From under vehicle

● Draining of the transaxle fluid
13. Under cover (RH)
14. Connection for stabilizer bar
15. Connection for tie rod end
16. Connection for lower arm ball joint
17. Connection for drive shaft
18. Bell housing cover
19. Center member assembly
20. Drive plate connecting bolt
21. Transaxle assembly lower part coupling bolt
22. Transaxle assembly

NOTE
For tightening locations indicated by the * symbol, first tighten temporarily, and then make the final tightening with the entire weight of the engine applied to the vehicle body.

MT5029300549020X

Fig. 12 Transaxle replacement (Part 2 of 2)

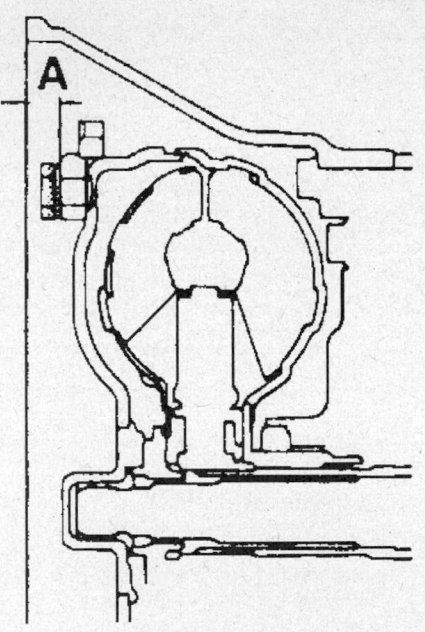

MT5029300550000X

Fig. 13 Torque converter installation inspection

TIGHTENING SPECIFICATIONS

Component	Torque/Ft. Lbs.
Bearing Retainer Attaching Bolt	11–15
Bellhousing Cover Mounting Bolt	7–9
Cable Clip Mounting Bolt	36–48①
Control Cable To Body	7–10
Converter Housing Mounting Bolt	14–16
Differential Drive Gear Bolt	95–101
Driveplate To Torque Converter	34–38
Driveshaft Attaching Nut	144–188
Governor Setscrew	36–48①
Idler Shaft Lock Plate	15–19
Inhibitor Switch Attaching Bolt	8–9
Key Interlock Cable Mounting Nut	36–48①
Lever Assembly To Body	7–10
Lever To Bracket Assembly	10–14
Lower Arm Ball Joint To Knuckle	43–52
Manual Control Lever Attaching Bolt	13–16
Manual Control Lever Setscrew	72–84①
Oil Filter Mounting Bolt	48–60①
Oil Pan Mounting Bolt	96–108①
Oil Pump Housing Bolt	96–108①
Oil Pump Mounting Bolt	18–23
Planetary Carrier Bolt	25–32
Pulse Generator Attaching Bolt	96–108①
Shift Lock Cable Mounting Nuts (Brake Pedal Side)	7–10
Shift Lock Cable Mounting Nuts (Lever Assembly Side)	36–48①
Sprag Rod Support Bolt	15–19
Starter Motor Mounting Bolt	20–25
Throttle Cam Attaching Bolt	6–7
Tie Rod End To Knuckle	11–25
Transaxle Mounting Bolts (.47 Inch Diameter)	31–40
Transaxle Mounting Bolts (.40 Inch Diameter)	22–25
Transaxle Mounting Bolts (.31 Inch Diameter)	7–8
Transaxle Mounting Bracket To Body	43–58
Transaxle Mounting Bracket To Transaxle	43–58
Valve Body Assembly Bolts	36–48①
Valve Body To Transaxle Case	8

① — Inch lbs.

Mitsubishi F4AC1, F4A22, F4A23, F4A33 & W4A33 Automatic Transaxles

---

NOTE: On Air Bag Equipped Models, Refer To "Air Bag System Precautions" Located In The Front Of This Manual For System Disarming & Arming Procedures.

NOTE: Prior To Performing Any Service Operations Listed In This Section, Consult The "Technical Service Bulletins" Section For Related Information.

INDEX

PRECAUTIONS

AIR BAG SYSTEMS

Refer to "Air Bag System Precautions" in the front of this manual for system disarming and arming procedures.

BATTERY GROUND CABLE

Prior to service, disconnect battery ground cable and isolate as required.

IDENTIFICATION

The transaxle identification number is located at the top of the bellhousing as shown in **Figs. 1 and 2.**

DESCRIPTION

F4A22, F4A23, F4A33 & W4A33 TRANSAXLES

The Mitsubishi F4A22, F4A23, F4A33 and W4A33 transaxles, **Figs. 3 through 6,** are four speed, fully automatic transaxles using a three element damper clutch torque converter. Two shift patterns are stored in the control unit of these transaxles. One is the power pattern and the other is the economy pattern. The driver can select and switch to the desired pattern by using the power/economy select switch on the center console.

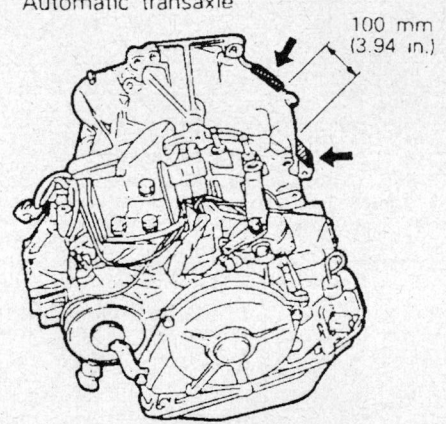

■ : for original equipment parts
▨ : for replacement parts

Automatic transaxle

100 mm
(3.94 in.)

MT5029100561000X

Fig. 1 F4A22, F4A23, F4A33, W4A32 & W4A33 transaxle identification

F4AC1 TRANSAXLE

The F4AC1 automatic transaxle, **Fig. 7,** is a fully adaptive, electronically controlled four speed full automatic transaxle. The F4AC1 transaxle uses a three element type torque converter with torque converter clutch.

The F4AC1 provides four forward speeds with ratios of 2.84:1, 1.57:1, 1.00:1 and .069:1. Reverse ratio is 2.21:1 and the final gear ratio is 4.08:1. It includes damper, underdrive, reverse, 2/4, and low/reverse clutches. It is also equipped with output and input speed sensors.

TROUBLESHOOTING

TRANSAXLE

Refer to **Figs. 8 and 9** when troubleshooting these transaxles.

SHIFT LOCK SYSTEM

Refer to **Fig. 10** when troubleshooting the shift lock system.

MAINTENANCE

FLUID CHECK

Place vehicle on level surface, start engine and operate at idle speed. Shift transaxle through all gear ranges and return to Park. With parking brake applied, place selector lever in Neutral, then remove dipstick and check fluid level. Transaxle should be at operating temperature when checking fluid level (160–180°F). Fluid level should be between ADD and FULL lines on dipstick. If necessary, add Dexron II automatic transaxle fluid to bring fluid level within ADD and FULL lines on dipstick.

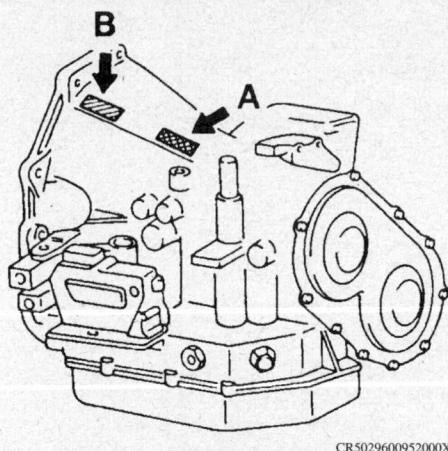

Fig. 2   F4AC1 transaxle identification

FLUID CHANGE

Except F4AC1 Transaxle

The automatic transaxle fluid should be changed every 30,000 miles. When refilling transaxle, add only Dexron II automatic transaxle fluid.

1. Remove drain plug from bottom of differential and drain fluid into a suitable container.
2. Loosen transaxle oil pan attaching bolts, then tap pan at one corner to break loose and drain fluid into a suitable container.
3. Remove oil pan and drain residual fluid.
4. Inspect oil filter for damage or obstructions and replace if necessary.
5. Install drain plug with a new gasket and tighten to specifications.
6. Clean transaxle case and oil pan mating surfaces, then install oil pan with a new gasket and **torque** attaching bolts to 7–9 ft. lbs.
7. Add 4.2 quarts Dexron II automatic transaxle fluid to transaxle through dipstick hole.
8. Run engine at idle for at least two minutes, then shift transaxle through all ranges and recheck fluid level.
9. Add sufficient fluid to bring level to lower mark on dipstick, then run engine until normal operating temperature is reached. Recheck dipstick and ensure fluid level is within Hot range.

F4AC1 Transaxle

The automatic transaxle fluid should be changed every 30,000 miles on these units. When refilling transaxle, add only Mopar ATF Plus (Type 7176), or equivalent.

1. Raise and support front of vehicle, then position drain pan under transaxle.
2. Loosen the transaxle oil pan bolts and tap pan at one corner to break it loose allowing fluid to drain.
3. Install a new filter and O-ring on bottom of valve body and clean oil pan and magnet.
4. Install oil pan and **torque** mounting

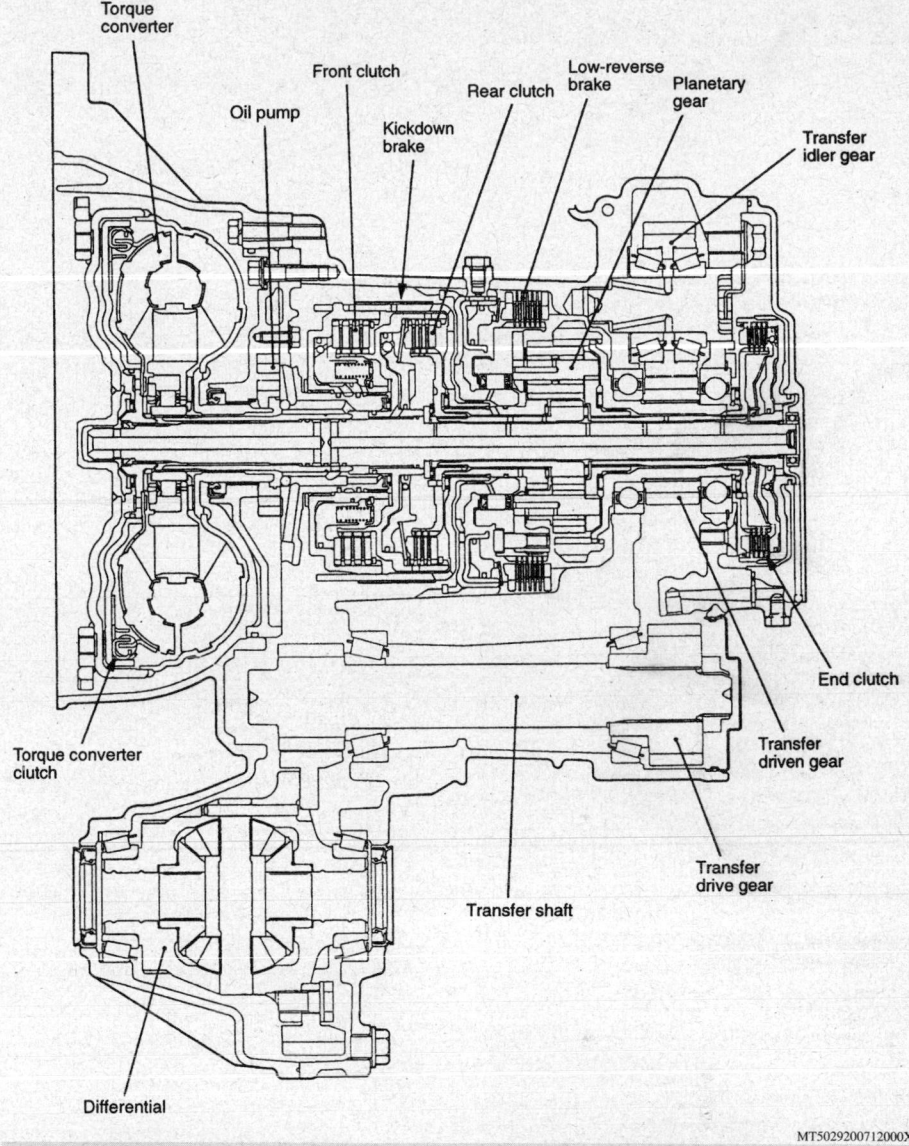

Fig. 3   Cross-sectional view of F4A23 automatic transaxle

bolts to 14 ft. lbs.
5. Add 4.0 qts. of transaxle fluid through filler tube.
6. Start engine and check fluid level as outlined under " Fluid Check" in this section.

ADJUSTMENTS

PARK/NEUTRAL POSITION SWITCH

1. Place selector lever in Neutral position.
2. Place manual control lever in Neutral position.
3. Rotate switch body so that manual control lever and switch body holes are aligned, **Fig. 11.**
4. **Torque** park/neutral position switch mounting bolts 7–9 ft. lbs. Do not drop switch body.

5. Loosen transaxle control cable nut and lightly pull end of cable as shown in **Fig. 12.**
6. **Torque** nut to 7–10 ft. lbs.
7. Ensure selector lever is in Neutral position.
8. Ensure selector lever operates on transaxle side in range which corresponds to each position of selector lever.

SHIFT LOCK CABLE

Mirage

1. Place selector lever in Park position.
2. Fasten shift lock cable in position at which cable end is above red mark, **Fig. 13.**

Diamante & 3000GT

1. With vehicle stopped and engine off, remove floor console and place selector lever in Park position.
2. Place ignition key in Lock position,

then loosen key interlock cable nut, **Fig. 14.**

3. While pressing gently upon lock cam in direction of arrow, **Fig. 14,** press on cable to remove slack, then tighten nut.
4. Install console, then inspect key interlock system as follows:
   a. Ensure selector lever cannot be moved out of Park position with ignition key in Lock position or removed and brake pedal depressed.
   b. Ensure selector lever can be moved out of Park position with ignition key in Accessory position, brake pedal depressed and selector lever button pressed.
   c. Ensure ignition key cannot be turned to Lock position with selector lever in any position other than Park.
   d. Ensure ignition key can be smoothly turned to Lock position with selector lever in Park position and lever button released.

KICKDOWN SERVO

1. Clean area around kickdown servo switch.
2. Remove snap ring.
3. Remove kickdown servo switch.
4. To prevent rotation of piston, engage pawl of kickdown servo wrench tool No. MD998918, or equivalent, into notch of piston and attach wrench using adapter tool No. MD998916-1-01, or equivalent, **Fig. 15. Do not press in piston with special tool. When mounting adapter on transaxle case, tighten by hand only. Do not over-tighten.**
5. Loosen locknut to before the V groove of adjusting rod and tighten kickdown adjustment inner tool No. MD998916-3-01, or equivalent, until it contacts locknut, **Fig. 16.**
6. Engage kickdown adjustment outer tool No. MD998916-2-01, or equivalent, on locknut. Rotating outer cylinder counterclockwise and inner cylinder clockwise, lock the locknut and inner tool.
7. Attach torque wrench to inner tool and repeat tightening and returning at a **torque** of 7.2 ft. lbs. two times, then **torque** to 3.6 ft. lbs. Loosen inner tool 2–2¾ turns.
8. Unlock inner tool from locknut by rotating outer cylinder clockwise and the inner cylinder counterclockwise. **When unlocking, apply equal force to both tools.**
9. Tighten locknut by hand until locknut contacts piston. **Torque** locknut to 18–23 ft. lbs.
10. Remove kickdown servo wrench and adapter and install a plug at the low-reverse pressure port.

LINE PRESSURE

1. Drain fluid and remove oil pan and filter assembly.
2. Remove oil temperature sensor.
3. Press solenoid valve harness grommet and connector into transaxle case.

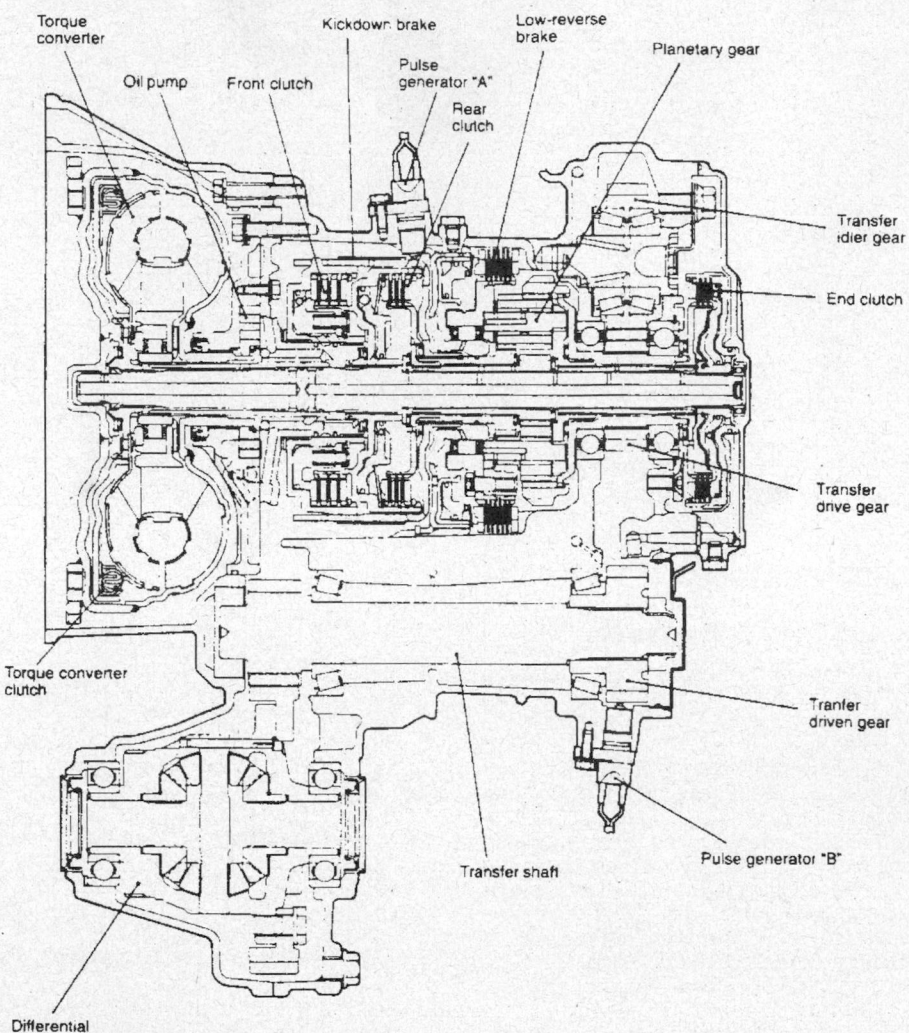

Fig. 4   Cross-sectional view of F4A22 automatic transaxle

MT5029200711000X

4. Remove valve body assembly. **Use care not to drop manual valve.**
5. **On all models except Eclipse and Galant,** turn regulator valve adjustment screw and adjust so that line pressure is 124–127 psi, **Fig. 17.** When adjustment screw is turned clockwise with the solenoid valves pointed up, the line pressure is lowered; when adjustment screw is turned counterclockwise with the solenoid valves pointed up, the line pressure is raised. **Each 360° turn of adjustment screw adjusts line pressure approximately 5 psi.**
6. **On Eclipse and Galant models,** turn regulator valve adjustment screw and adjust so that line pressure is 126.2–129.1 psi, **Fig. 17.** When adjustment screw is turned clockwise with the solenoid valves pointed up, the line pressure is lowered; when adjustment screw is turned counterclockwise with the solenoid valves pointed up, the line pressure is raised. **Each 360° turn of adjustment screw adjusts line pressure approximately 5.4 psi.**

7. **On all models,** ensure O-ring is installed on upper surface of valve body as shown, **Fig. 18.**
8. Install new solenoid valve harness grommet O-ring.
9. Install harness grommet into case.
10. **On all models except those equipped with F4AC1 transaxle,** install valve body and oil temperature sensor. Tighten valve body bolts to specifications, referring to **Figs. 19 and 20** for correct bolt length position.
    a. Positions marked A use .709 inch long bolts.
    b. Positions marked B use .984 inch long bolts.
    c. Positions marked C use 1.575 inch long bolts.
11. **On models equipped with F4AC1 transaxle,** install valve body and oil temperature sensor.
12. **On all models,** install oil filter, new oil pan gasket, oil pan and ATF as outlined under "Fluid Change" in "Maintenance" section.
13. Ensure transaxle oil pressure is correct. Readjust as necessary.

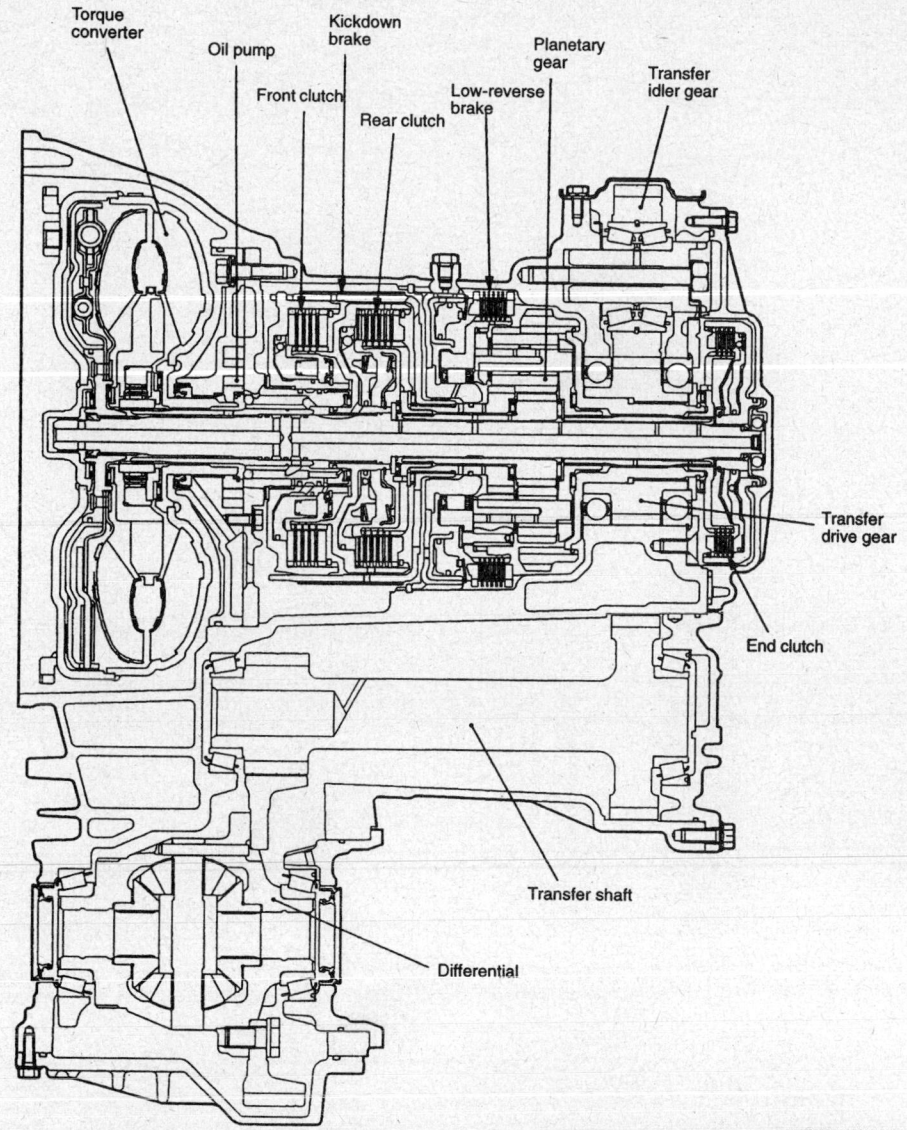

Fig. 5 Cross-sectional view of F4A33 automatic transaxle

MT5029200713000X

REDUCING PRESSURE

Less Multi-Use Tester

1. Drain transaxle fluid, remove oil pan and filter.
2. Turn adjustment screw of lower valve body and adjust so that reducing pressure is 59–61 psi with a preferred of 60 psi, **Fig. 21.** When adjustment screw is turned clockwise, the reducing pressure becomes lower; when adjustment screw is turned counterclockwise the reducing pressure becomes higher.
3. Each 360° turn of the adjustment screw adjusts pressure approximately 6.4 psi.
4. Install oil filter, new oil pan gasket, oil pan and ATF as outlined under "Fluid Change" in "Maintenance" section.
5. Ensure oil pressure is correct. Readjust as necessary.
6. Install oil filter, new oil pan gasket, oil pan and ATF as outlined under "Fluid Change" in "Maintenance" section.

7. Ensure transaxle oil pressure is correct. Readjust as necessary.

With Multi-Use Tester

1. Adjust screw to obtain the following kickdown brake pressures when pressure control solenoid is activated at 50 percent duty ratio with diagnostic scan tool:
   a. **On Mirage models equipped with F4A22 transaxle, Eclipse and Galant models,** correct kickdown brake pressure is 35–43 psi.
   b. **On Diamante and 3000GT models,** correct kickdown brake pressure is 39 psi.
2. Ensure reducing pressure is 51–68 psi after adjustment. **This adjustment must be made with oil temperature at 158–176°F. Higher oil temperatures result in lower line pressure at idle, making accurate adjustment difficult.**

THROTTLE POSITION SENSOR

Less Multi-Use Tester

1. Disconnect throttle position sensor connector.
2. Connect test harness tool No. MB991348, or equivalent, inline.
3. Connect a digital voltmeter between sensor output terminal 2 and sensor ground terminal 4, **Fig. 22.**
4. Turn ignition switch to Run position. **Do not start engine.**
5. Ensure throttle position sensor output voltage is .48–.52 volts.
6. If voltage is not as specified, adjust throttle position sensor as follows:
   a. Loosen throttle position sensor screws and rotate throttle position sensor body clockwise to increase output voltage.
   b. Loosen throttle position sensor screws and rotate throttle position sensor body counterclockwise to decrease output voltage.
7. Tighten throttle position screws and recheck output voltage.

With Multi-Use Tester

1. Connect multi-use tester to diagnosis connector.
2. Select item No. 14 to read throttle position sensor output voltage. Standard voltage is .48–.52 volts.
3. If voltage is not as specified, adjust throttle position sensor as follows:
   a. Loosen throttle position sensor screws and rotate throttle position sensor body clockwise to increase output voltage.
   b. Loosen throttle position sensor screws and rotate throttle position sensor body counterclockwise to decrease output voltage.
4. Tighten throttle position screws and recheck output voltage.

IN-VEHICLE REPAIRS

CONTROL CABLE REPLACEMENT

Refer to **Figs. 23 through 27** when replacing transaxle control cables.

DRIVESHAFT OIL SEAL REPLACEMENT

Diamante, Mirage & 3000GT

1. Raise and support vehicle, then remove front wheels.
2. Remove cotter pin, wheel bearing nut and washer.
3. Disconnect lower control arm ball joint from knuckle using tool No. MB991113, or equivalent.
4. Disconnect tie rod end from knuckle using tool No. MB991113, or equivalent.
5. Disconnect center bearing snap ring if equipped.
6. **On models without center bearing,** proceed as follows:
   a. Insert pry bar between transaxle

case and driveshaft, then pry drive-shaft from transaxle. **Do not pull on driveshaft, or insert pry bar deep enough to damage oil seal.**

   b. Remove driveshaft from hub using tool No. MB990241-01, or equivalent, then the circlip from driveshaft.

7. **On models with center bearing,** proceed as follows:

   a. Remove driveshaft from transaxle by lightly tapping driveshaft outer race with a plastic hammer. **Do not pull on driveshaft or insert pry bar between transaxle case and driveshaft.**

   b. Remove driveshaft from hub by lightly tapping driveshaft end with plastic hammer.

   c. Remove center bearing bracket attaching bolts, then the center bearing bracket and spacers. Remove seal.

8. **On all models,** reverse procedure to install, noting the following:

   a. **On models with center bearing,** press in driveshaft until center bearing comes in contact with center bearing bracket, then install snap ring into center bearing bracket.

   b. **On all models,** lower vehicle to ground, then attach and adjust driveshaft nut. Tighten nut to specifications.

   c. If cotter pin hole does not line up, tighten bolt until hole lines up. **Do not exceed maximum tightening specification.**

TRANSAXLE

REPLACE

F4AC1, F4A22, F4A23 & F4A33 TRANSAXLES

1. Remove battery and battery tray.
2. Remove air cleaner assembly and, if necessary, engine undercover.
3. Drain transaxle fluid as outlined under "Fluid Change" in "Maintenance" section.
4. Remove transaxle assembly in numbered sequence shown in **Figs. 28 through 33,** noting the following:

   a. Support engine using suitable floor jack.

   b. **On models equipped with Electronic Controlled Suspension (ECS),** remove ECS compressor leaving hoses attached and secure to body.

   c. **On models equipped with Four Wheel Steering (4WS),** remove 4WS oil pump with hoses attached and secure to body.

   d. **On all models,** loosen, but do not remove, tie rod end assembly nut using steering linkage puller tool No. MB991113, or equivalent. **Tie cord of special tool to nearby part to prevent slippage.**

   e. Loosen, but do not remove, lower ball joint nut using steering linkage puller tool No. MB991113, or equiv-

alent. **Tie cord of special tool to nearby parts to prevent slippage.**

   f. Insert a pry bar between transaxle case and driveshaft and pry driveshaft from transaxle, **Fig. 34.**

   g. **On models equipped with F4A33 transaxle,** use puller tool No. MB990241-01, or equivalent, to push out righthand driveshaft from front hub. **Do not pull on driveshaft as damage to the joint will result.**

   h. **On all models,** secure driveshaft away from the transaxle case using suitable rope to prevent damage.

   i. Remove torque converter driveplate bolts prior to removal of transaxle.

   j. After removing torque converter bolts, push torque converter toward transaxle so it does not remain on the engine side.

   k. Support transaxle assembly using a suitable jack stand; then, after moving transaxle to the right, lower transaxle from vehicle.

5. Reverse numbered sequence shown in **Figs. 28 through 33** to install transaxle, noting the following:

   a. Ensure all electrical and ground connections are clean and tight.

   b. Refill transaxle with fluid as outlined under "Fluid Change" in "Maintenance" section.

   c. Ensure proper operation of selector and control cables.

W4A32 & W4A33 TRANSAXLES

1. Remove battery and battery tray.
2. Remove air cleaner assembly.
3. Drain transaxle fluid as outlined under

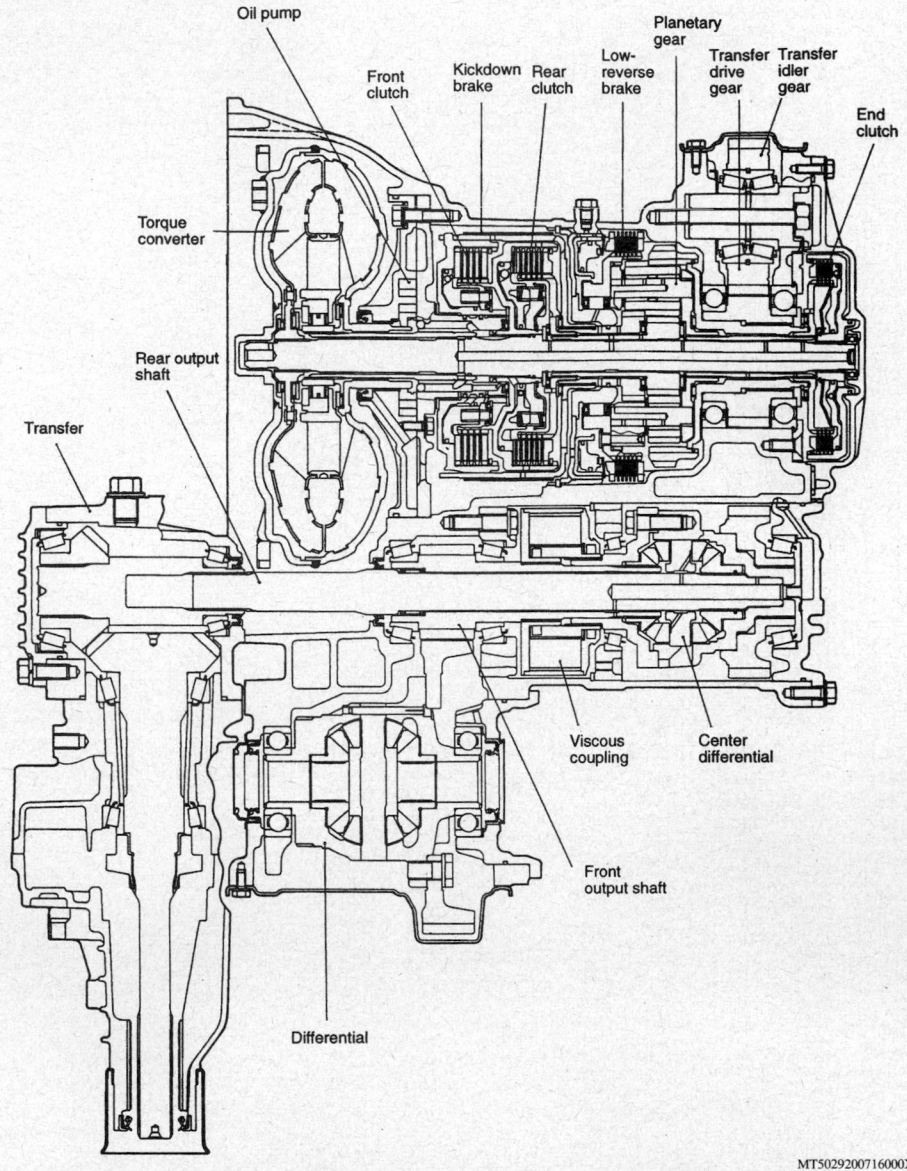

Fig. 6   Cross-sectional view of W4A33 automatic transaxle

MT5029200716000X

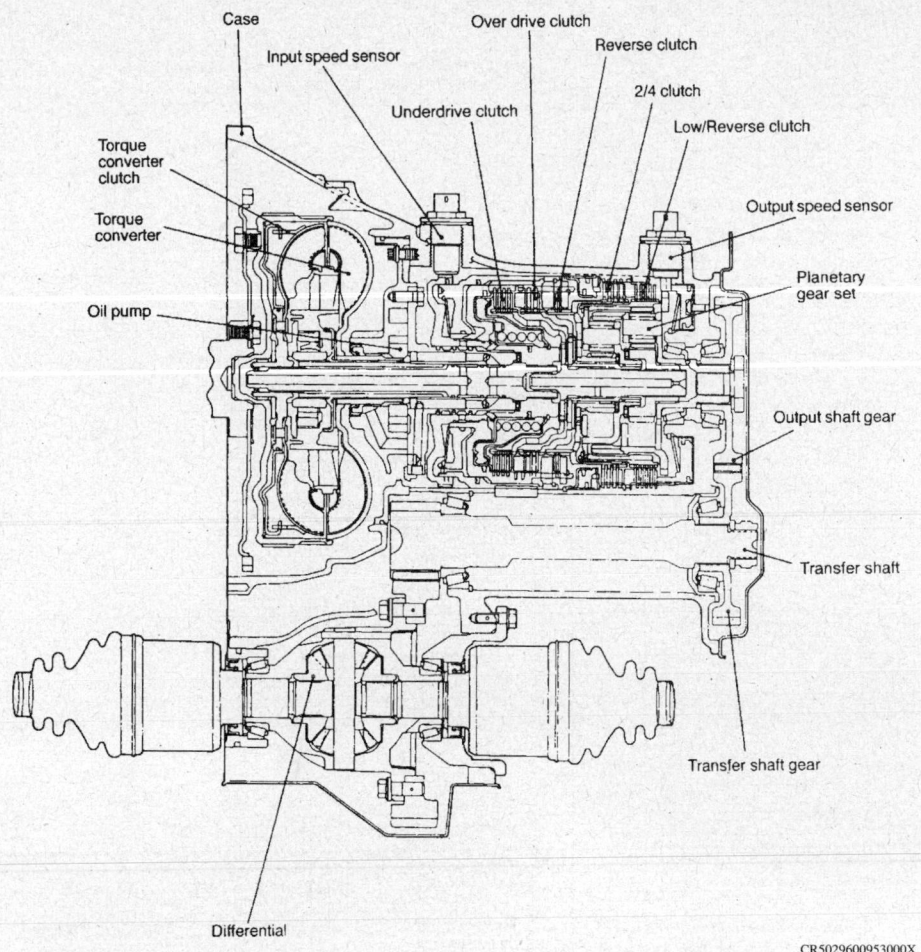

Fig. 7 Cross-sectional view of F4AC1 transaxle

Labels on figure: Case, Over drive clutch, Reverse clutch, Input speed sensor, 2/4 clutch, Underdrive clutch, Low/Reverse clutch, Torque converter clutch, Output speed sensor, Torque converter, Oil pump, Planetary gear set, Output shaft gear, Transfer shaft, Transfer shaft gear, Differential

CR5029600953000X

"Fluid Change" in "Maintenance" section.

4. Remove transaxle assembly in numbered sequence shown in **Fig. 35** noting the following:

a. Loosen, but do not remove, tie rod end assembly nut using steering linkage puller tool No. MB991113, or equivalent. **Ensure special tool cord is tied to nearby parts to prevent slippage.**

b. Loosen, but do not remove, lower ball joint nut using steering linkage puller tool No. MB991113, or equivalent. **Tie cord of special tool to nearby parts to prevent slippage.**

c. Use puller tool No. MB990241-01, or equivalent, to push righthand driveshaft from front hub.

d. Insert a pry bar between transaxle case and driveshaft and pry driveshafts from transaxle. **Do not pull on driveshaft as damage to the joint will result.**

e. Remove lefthand driveshaft by lightly tapping driveshaft joint case with a plastic hammer.

f. Secure driveshaft away from the transaxle case using suitable rope to prevent damage.

g. Mark location of propeller shaft on rear axle flange, then remove attaching bolts from propeller shaft at rear axle flange.

h. Disconnect propeller shaft center support bearing and bracket.

i. Pull propeller shaft from transfer assembly.

j. Remove transfer assembly attaching bolts then the transfer assembly.

5. Reverse numbered sequence shown in **Fig. 35,** to install transaxle, noting the following:

a. After installing wheel, lower vehicle to ground and finally tighten wheel bearing nut. If position of cotter pin holes do not match, **torque** nut to 188 ft. lbs. maximum to align holes.

b. Ensure all electrical connections and ground connections are clean and tight.

c. Refill transaxle with fluid as outlined under "Fluid Change" in "Maintenance" section.

d. Ensure proper operation of selector and control cables. Adjust, if necessary.

Troubleshooting chart — Driving impossible or abnormal (before start-off)

Category	No.	Presumed cause	Starter motor won't function	Forward/backward movement impossible	Forward movement impossible	Backward movement impossible	Engine stalls when N → D or R	Clutch slips at D (stall rpm too high)	Clutch slips at R (stall rpm too high)	Stall rpm too low	Vehicle moves at P or N	Engine starts, or vehicle moves, between N-R or N-D	Parking doesn't hold	Abnormal vibration-shock when shift to D-2-L-R
Engine	1	Abnormal idling rpm					⊗							×
Engine	2	Performance malfunction						×		×				
Transaxle (power train)	3	Improper adjustment of manual linkage	×	⊗	⊗	⊗		⊗	⊗			⊗	⊗	⊗
Transaxle (power train)	4	Malfunction of torque convertor		×	×	×				×				
Transaxle (power train)	5	Operation malfunction of oil pump		×	×	×		×	×					
Transaxle (power train)	6	Malfunction of one-way clutch				×		×						
Transaxle (power train)	7	Damaged or worn gear or other rotating part, or improper adjustment of the preload												
Transaxle (power train)	8	Malfunction of parking mechanism									×		×	
Transaxle (power train)	9	Cracked drive plate, or loose bolt		×										
Transaxle (power train)	10	Worn inside diameter of front clutch retainer				×	-		×					
Oil-pressure system (including friction elements)	11	Low fluid level		⊗	⊗	⊗		×	×					
Oil-pressure system (including friction elements)	12	Line pressure too low (seal damaged, leakage, looseness, etc.)		⊗	⊗	⊗		⊗	⊗					
Oil-pressure system (including friction elements)	13	Malfunction of valve body (sticking valve, working cavity, adjustment, etc.)		⊗	⊗	⊗	×	×	×			×	×	×
Oil-pressure system (including friction elements)	14	Malfunction of front clutch or piston				×			×					×
Oil-pressure system (including friction elements)	15	Malfunction of rear clutch or piston			⊗			×						×
Oil-pressure system (including friction elements)	16	Malfunction of kickdown band or piston												
Oil-pressure system (including friction elements)	17	Improper adjustment of kickdown servo												
Oil-pressure system (including friction elements)	18	Malfunction of low-reverse brake or piston		×		×			×					×
Oil-pressure system (including friction elements)	19	O-ring of low-reverse brake circuit between valve body and case not installed				×			×					
Oil-pressure system (including friction elements)	20	Malfunction of end clutch or piston (check ball hole, other)												
Electronic-control system	21	Malfunction of inhibitors switch, damaged or disconnected wiring, or improper adjustment	×								×	×		×
Electronic-control system	22	Malfunction of TPS, or improper adjustment												×
Electronic-control system	23	Pulse generator (A) damaged or disconnected wiring, or short-circuit												
Electronic-control system	24	Pulse generator (B) damaged or disconnected wiring, or short-circuit				×								
Electronic-control system	25	Malfunction of kickdown servo switch												
Electronic-control system	26	SCSV-A or B damaged or disconnected wiring, or short-circuit or sticking (valve open)												
Electronic-control system	27	Malfunction of ignition signal system												
Electronic-control system	28	Incorrectly grounded ground strap												
Electronic-control system	29	PCSV damaged or disconnected wiring, or short-circuit												
Electronic-control system	30	PCSV damaged or disconnected wiring (valve open)		⊗	⊗	⊗		×	×					
Electronic-control system	31	DCCSV damaged or disconnecting wiring (valve closed)												
Electronic-control system	32	DCCSV short-circuit or sticking (valve open)					⊗							
Electronic-control system	33	Malfunction of overdrive control switch												
Electronic-control system	34	Malfunction of accelerator switch, or improper adjustment												×
Electronic-control system	35	Malfunction of oil-temperature sensor												
Electronic-control system	36	Malfunction of lead switch												
Electronic-control system	37	Poor contact of ignition switch												
Electronic-control system	38	Malfunction of transaxle control unit												×

NOTE: ⊗ indicates items of high priority during inspection.
Abbreviations: TPS = Throttle position sensor   SCSV = Shift control solenoid valve

CR5019000166010X

Fig. 8   Transaxle troubleshooting (Part 1 of 2). Except F4AC1 transaxle

	Won't shift from 2nd to 3rd	Won't shift to 4th	Overdrive control switch doesn't function	Doesn't shift according to shift pattern (shifting is possible)	Improper start-off (starts off from 2nd, etc.)	Excessive creeping or idling vibration	Excessive vibration-shock when shift 1-2 or 3-4	Excessive vibration-shock when shift 2-3 or 4-3	Excessive vibration-shock during upshift	Excessive vibration-shock during D-2 downshift	Sudden engine rpm increase during upshift	Sudden engine rpm increase during 3-2 shift, excessive vibration	Excessive vibration-shock only when cold	Excessive vibration-shock (other than already described)	Damper clutch won't function	Abnormal vibration in high-load region in low gear (approx. 1 Hz)	Abnormal noise from convertor housing together with engine rpm	Mechanical noise (clatter noise) from convertor housing	Abnormal noise inside transaxle case	3rd gear is held
	Transaxle malfunction of shift-shock (after start-off)																Abnormal noise, other			
1						×														
2					×		×	×	×	×			×	×		×				
3		×			×															×
4					×												×	×		
5												×						×		
6																				
7																			×	
8																				
9																			×	
10	×	×									×	×								×
11												×								×
12											⊗	⊗		×						×
13	×			×	×		×	×	×	×	×	×	×	×		×				×
14	×							×	×		×									×
15																				×
16							×				×	×								×
17							×				×	×			×					×
18											×									×
19																				×
20		⊗					×													×
21		×			×															×
22			⊗				×	×	⊗	×	⊗	×		×	×					×
23							×	×	×	×	×	×		×	×					×
24			×											×	×					
25							×					×								×
26																				×
27							×	×	×	×	×	×		×	×					×
28																				×
29																				×
30	×	×									×	×								×
31															×					
32																	×			
33		×	×																	
34				×	×										×					
35															×	×	×			
36																				×
37					×															×
38	×	×	×	×	×	×	×	×	×	×	×	×	×	×	×	×	×	×	×	×

PSCV = Pressure control solenoid valve
DCCSV = Damper clutch control solenoid valve

CR5019000166020X

Fig. 8   Transaxle troubleshooting (Part 2 of 2). Except F4AC1 transaxle

Probable cause	Trouble symptom	Harsh engagement from Neutral(N) to Drive(D)	Harsh engagement from Neutral(N) to Reverse(R)	Delayed engagement from Neutral(N) to Drive(D)	Delayed engagement from Neutral(N) to Reverse(R)	Poor shift quality	Shifts erratically	Dives in Neutral(N)	Drags or locks	Grating, scraping, growling noise	Knocking noise	Buzzing noise during shifts only	Hard to fill oil blows out filler tube	Transaxle overheats	Harsh upshift	No upshift into overdrive	No torque converter control	Harsh downshifts	High shift efforts	Harsh torque converter control shift
Engine performance						X								X					X	X
Worn or faulty clutch(es)	Underdrive clutch	X												X	X	X		X		
	Overdrive clutch			X	X									X	X	X				
	Reverse clutch													X	X		X	X		
	2-4 clutch	X				X								X	X					
	Low/Reverse clutch	X												X	X				X	X
Clutch(es) dragging														X						
Insufficient clutch plate clearance							X							X						
Damaged clutch seal		X															X	X		
Worn or damaged accumulator sealing(s)		X													X	X	X	X		
Faulty cooling system							X													
Engine coolant temperature too low				X	X															
Incorrect gear shift control linkage adjustment							X													
Shift linkage damaged		X																		
Chipped or damaged gear teeth										X	X									
Planetary gear sets broken or seized										X	X									
Bearings worn or damaged										X	X									
Driveshaft(s) bushing(s) worn or damaged										X										
Worn or broken reaction shaft support sealing		X													X	X	X	X		
Worn or damaged input shaft sealing						X										X	X			
Valve body malfunction or leakage		X	X	X	X				X					X	X	X	X	X	X	X
Hydraulic pressures too low				X		X	X							X	X	X	X			
Hydraulic pressures too high		X				X													X	X
Faulty oil pump						X		X						X	X	X				
Oil filter clogged									X					X	X	X	X			
Low fluid level		X	X			X			X		X			X	X	X	X			
High fluid level								X	X											
Aerated fluid		X	X			X	X		X		X			X	X	X	X			
Engine idle too low																		X	X	
Engine idle too high		X				X													X	X
Normal solenoid operation												X								
Solenoid sound cover loose												X								
Sticking lockup piston		X																		
Torque converter failure						X		X												X

CR5029500782000X

Fig. 9 Inspection matrix for trouble symptoms. F4AC1 transaxle

Symptom	Probable cause	Remedy
Selector lever cannot be shifted from R to P.	Defective selector lever assembly	Check and replace selector lever assembly.
	Improperly adjusted transaxle control cable	Adjust transaxle control cable.
Ignition key cannot be turned to LOCK position with selector lever in P.	Foreign matter wedged in lock cams A and B	Check and replace lock cams A and B.
	Improperly adjusted key interlock cable, sticking inner cable	Check, adjust, and replace key interlock cable.
	Binding slide lever inside key cylinder	Check slide lever.
Ignition key can be turned to LOCK position even with selector lever in position other than P.	Damaged lock cam A	Check and replace lock cam A.
	Loose key cylinder cover	Check and retighten cover.
	Broken key interlock cable, loose connections, elongated inner cable	Check and replace key interlock cable.
	Damaged cam lever inside key cylinder	Check and replace cam lever.
Buzzer does not sound even when selector lever is placed in R position.	Defective buzzer	Check and replace buzzer.
	Open-circuited buzzer circuit harness	Check or correct harness.
	Defective inhibitor switch	Check and replace inhibitor switch.
	Improperly adjusted transaxle control cable	Adjust transaxle control cable.

CR5019000167020X

Fig. 10 Shift lock system troubleshooting (Part 2 of 2)

Symptom	Probable cause	Remedy
Selector lever can be selected into R from P without depressing brake pedal with ignition key in a position other than LOCK.	Damaged lock cam B	Check and replace lock cam B.
	Improperly adjusted shift lock cable, broken inner cable, loose or off connections	Check, adjust or replace the shift lock cable.
	Broken or sagging outer cable (shift lock cable) return spring	Check and replace shift lock cable.
Selector lever cannot be selected into R from P by depressing brake pedal with ignition key in position other than LOCK.	Defective selector lever assembly	Check and replace selector lever assembly.
	Sticking shift lock cable, key interlock cable, and transaxle control cable	Check and replace shift lock cable, key interlock cable, and transaxle control cable.
	Foreign matter wedged in lock cams A and B	Check and adjust lock cams A and B.
	Improperly adjusted shift lock cable, elongated inner cable	Check, adjust, and replace shift lock cable.
	Sticking slide lever and cam lever inside key cylinder	Check and adjust slide lever and cam lever.
Selector lever can be selected into R from P when brake pedal is depressed even though the ignition key is in the LOCK position.	Damaged lock cam A	Check and replace lock cam A.
	Broken or disconnected key interlock cable	Check and replace key interlock cable.
	Damaged slide lever and cam lever inside key cylinder	Check and replace slide lever and cam lever.
Selector lever operation from P to R is not smooth.	Improperly adjusted key interlock cable	Check and adjust key interlock cable.
	Improperly adjusted shift lock cable, elongated inner cable	Check, adjust, and replace shift lock cable.
	Binding lock cams A and B (in rotation)	Check rotating parts of lock cams A and B.
	Defective selector lever assembly	Check and replace selector lever assembly.
	Binding slide lever inside key cylinder	Check slide lever and cam lever.

CR5019000167010X

Fig. 10 Shift lock system troubleshooting (Part 1 of 2)

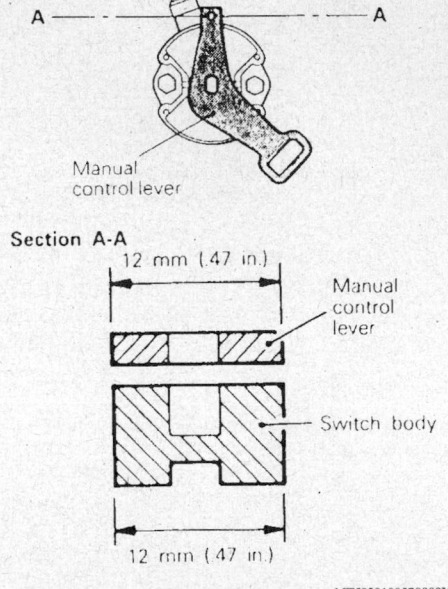

Section A-A

12 mm (.47 in.)

12 mm (.47 in.)

Manual control lever

Switch body

MT5029100570000X

Fig. 11 Lever & switch hole alignment

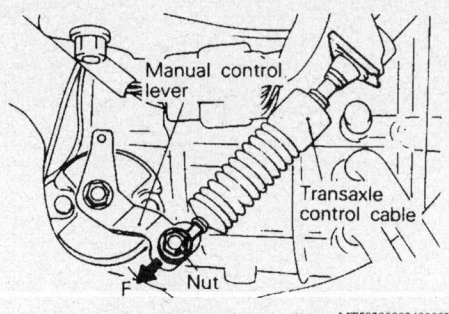

Fig. 12 Control cable adjustment

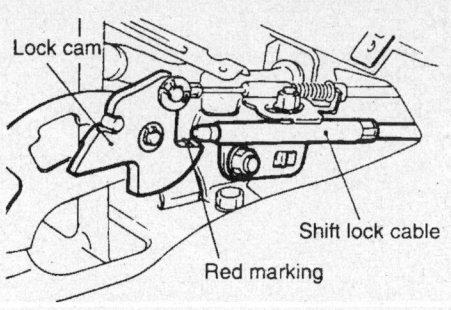

Fig. 13 Shift lock cable adjustment. Mirage

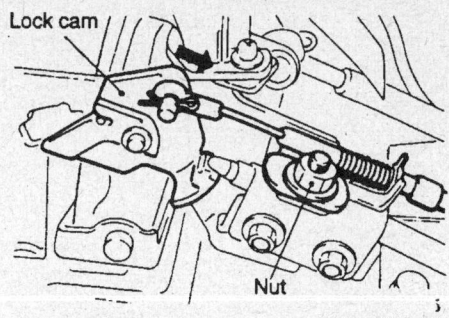

Fig. 14 Shift lock cable adjustment. Diamante & 3000GT

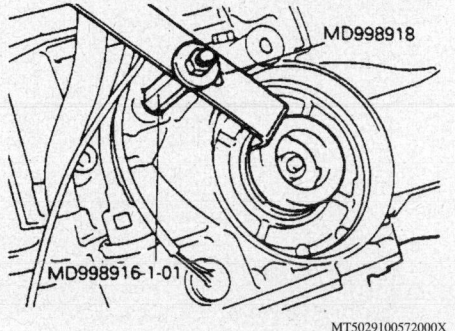

Fig. 15 Kickdown servo tool

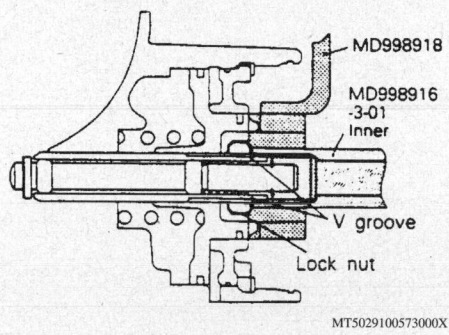

Fig. 16 Inner & outer adjustment tool installation

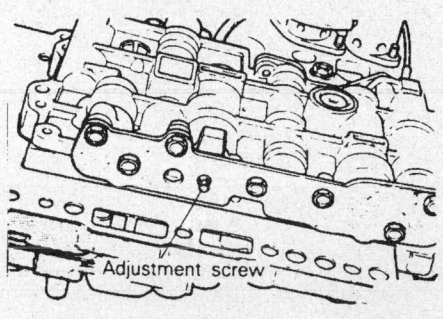

Fig. 17 Regulator valve adjustment screw

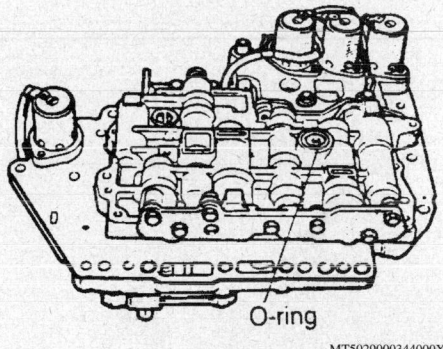

Fig. 18 Valve body O-ring position

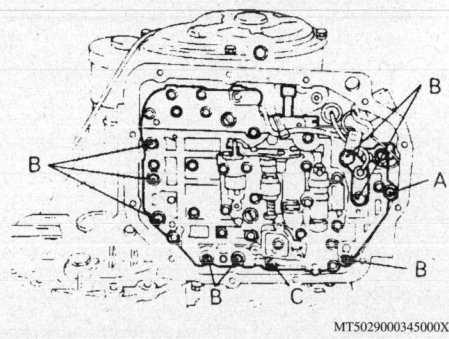

Fig. 19 Valve body bolt location. F4A22 & F4A23 transaxles

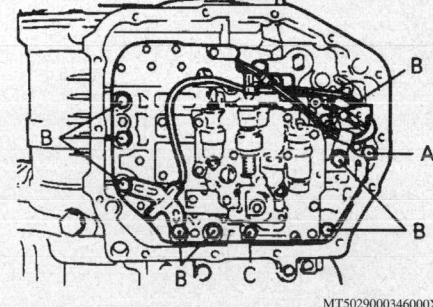

Fig. 20 Valve body bolt location. F4A33, W4A32 & W4A33 transaxles

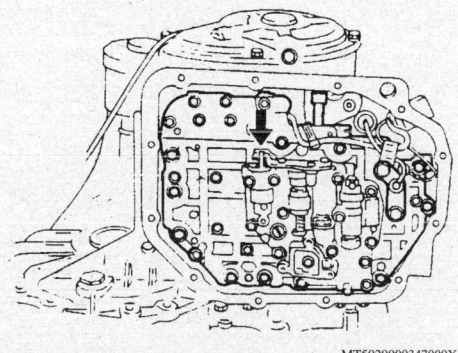

Fig. 21 Reducing pressure adjustment screw

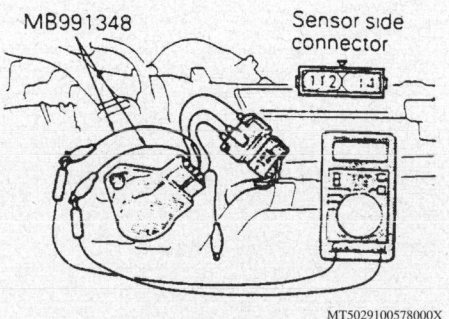

Fig. 22 Throttle position sensor adjustment

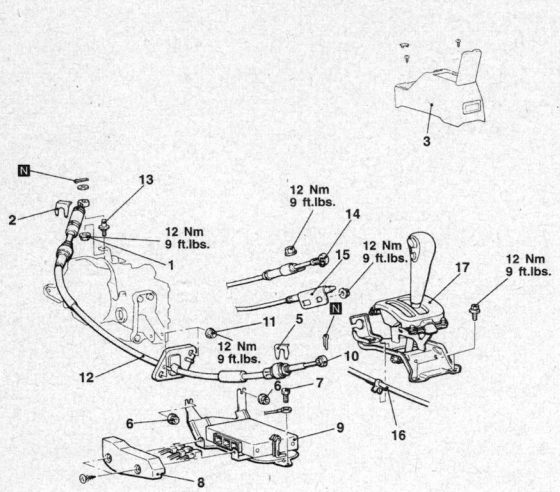

Transaxle control cable assembly removal steps

1. Nut
2. Clip
3. Rear floor console
4. Front floor console
5. Clip
6. Nut
7. Bolt
8. Cover
9. Transaxle control module
10. Connection for the transaxle control cable assembly
11. Nut
12. Transaxle control cable assembly
13. Adjuster

Selector lever assembly removal steps

3. Rear floor console
4. Front floor console
10. Connection for the transaxle control cable assembly
14. Key interlock cable connection
15. Shift lock cable connection
16. Clip
17. Selector lever assembly

MT5029300994000X

Fig. 23 Control cable replacement. Mirage

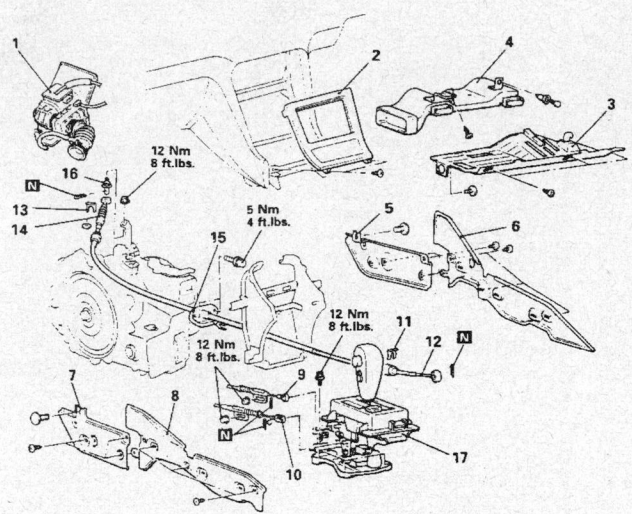

Removal steps of transaxle control cable assembly

1. Air cleaner cover, air intake hose
2. Audio panel
3. Passenger side under cover
4. Foot shower duct
5. Front center reinforcement (right side)
6. Rear center reinforcement (right side)
11. Clip
12. Connector of transaxle control cable assembly (selector lever assembly side)
13. Clip
14. Connection of transaxle control cable assembly (transaxle side)
15. Transaxle control cable assembly
16. Adjuster

Removal steps of select lever assembly

1. Air cleaner cover, air intake hose
2. Audio panel
3. Passenger side under cover
4. Foot shower duct
5. Front center reinforcement (right side)
6. Rear center reinforcement (right side)
7. Front center reinforcement (left side)
8. Rear center reinforcement (left side)
9. Connection of key interlock cable (selector lever assembly side)
10. Connection of shift lock cable (selector lever assembly side)
11. Clip
12. Connection of transaxle control cable assembly (selector lever assembly side)
17. Selector lever assembly

MT5029200996000X

Fig. 24 Control cable replacement. Diamante

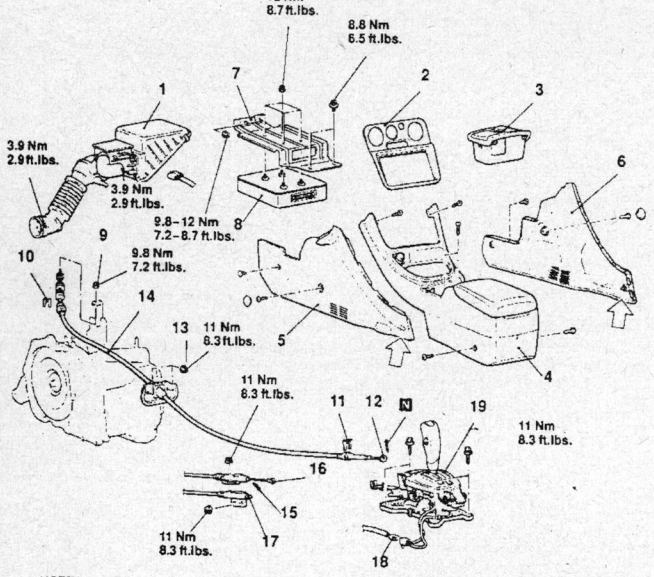

NOTE
⟳ : Resin clip position

Transaxle control cable assembly removal steps

1. Air cleaner and air intake hose assembly
2. Center panel
3. Cup holder assembly
4. Floor console assembly
5. Console side cover LH
6. Console side cover RH
7. TCM bracket
8. Transaxle control module (TCM)
9. Nut
10. Clip
11. Clip
12. Transaxle control cable connection
13. Nut
14. Transaxle control cable assembly

Selector lever assembly removal steps

2. Center panel
3. Cup holder assembly
4. Floor console assembly
5. Console side cover LH
6. Console side cover RH
11. Clip
12. Transaxle control cable connection
15. Snap pin
16. Key interlock cable connection
17. Shift lock cable connection
18. Overdrive switch/position indicator light connector
19. Selector lever assembly

MT5029500998000X

Fig. 25 Control cable replacement. Eclipse

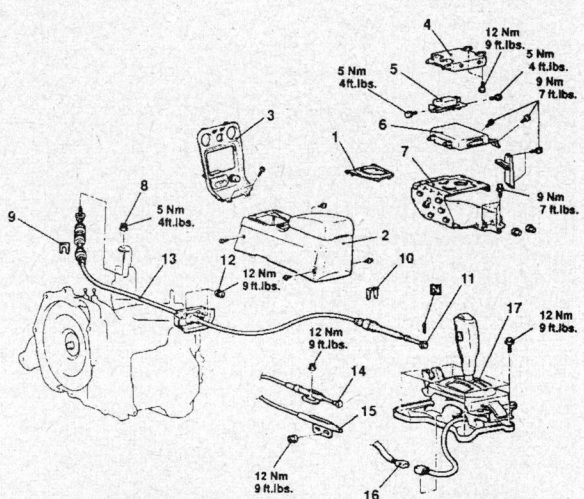

Transaxle control cable assembly removal steps

1. Selector lever panel
2. Floor console box
3. Center console panel
4. Engine control module
5. Fuel pump relay module (From 1995 models for California)
6. Transaxle control module (TCM)
7. TCM bracket
8. Nut
9. Clip (engine compartment side)
10. Clip (passenger compartment side)
11. Transaxle control cable connection (selector lever side)
12. Nut
13. Transaxle control cable assembly

Selector lever assembly removal steps

1. Selector lever panel
2. Floor console box
3. Center console panel
10. Clip (passenger compartment side)
11. Transaxle control cable connection (selector lever side)
14. Key interlock cable connection
15. Shift lock cable connection
16. Overdrive switch / position indicator light connector
17. Selector lever assembly

MT5029401000000X

Fig. 26 Control cable replacement. Galant

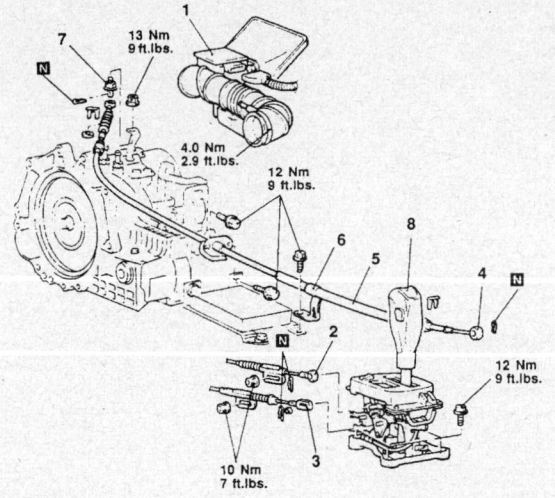

Transaxle control cable removal steps

1. Air cleaner cover, Air intake hose
4. Transaxle control cable assembly connection (Select lever assembly side)
5. Transaxle control cable assembly
6. Clamp
7. Adjuster

Selector lever assembly removal steps

1. Air cleaner cover, Air intake hose
2. Key-interlock cable connection (Selector lever assembly side)
3. Shift-lock cable connection (Selector lever assembly side)
4. Transaxle control cable connection (Selector lever assembly side)
8. Selector lever assembly

MT5029201001000X

Fig. 27 Control cable replacement. 3000GT

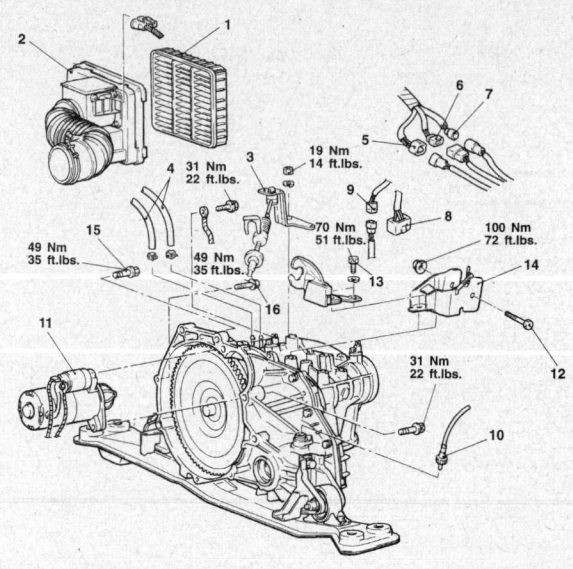

Removal steps

1. Air cleaner element
2. Air cleaner cover and hose assembly
3. Manual control lever connection
4. Transaxle oil cooler hoses connection
5. Oil temperature sensor connector
6. Pulse generator connector
7. Kickdown servo switch connector
8. Park/Neutral position switch connector
9. Solenoid valve connector
10. Speedometer cable connection
11. Starter motor
12. Transaxle mount bolt
13. Bolt
14. Transaxle mount bracket
15. Transaxle assembly upper part coupling bolt
16. Bolt
• Support of engine assembly

MT5029000349010X

Fig. 28 Transaxle replacement (Part 1 of 2). Mirage

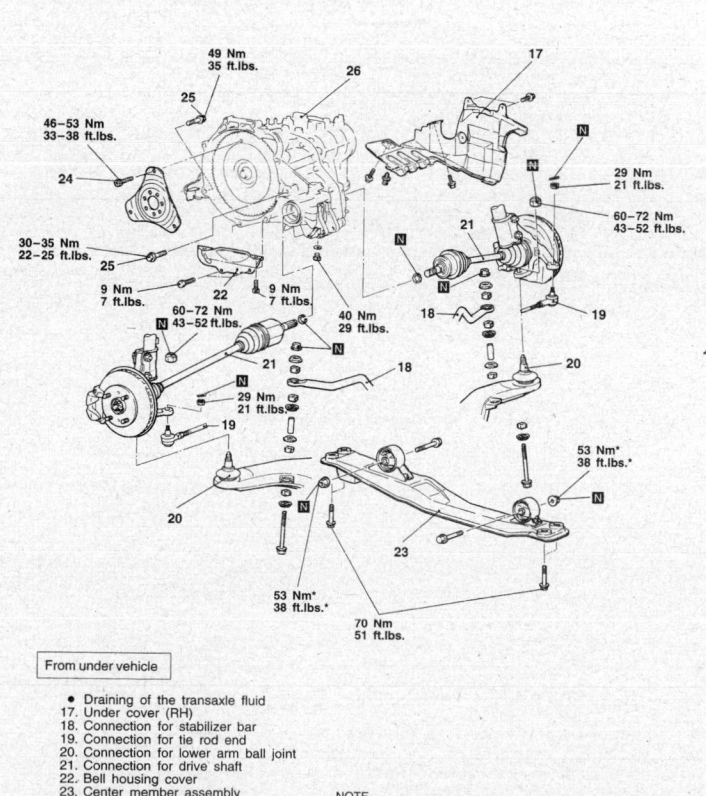

From under vehicle

• Draining of the transaxle fluid
17. Under cover (RH)
18. Connection for stabilizer bar
19. Connection for tie rod end
20. Connection for lower arm ball joint
21. Connection for drive shaft
22. Bell housing cover
23. Center member assembly
24. Drive plate connecting bolt
25. Transaxle assembly lower part coupling bolt
26. Transaxle assembly

NOTE
For tightening locations indicated by the * symbol, first tighten temporarily, and then make the final tightening with the entire weight of the engine applied to the vehicle body.

MT5029000349020X

Fig. 28 Transaxle replacement (Part 2 of 2). Mirage

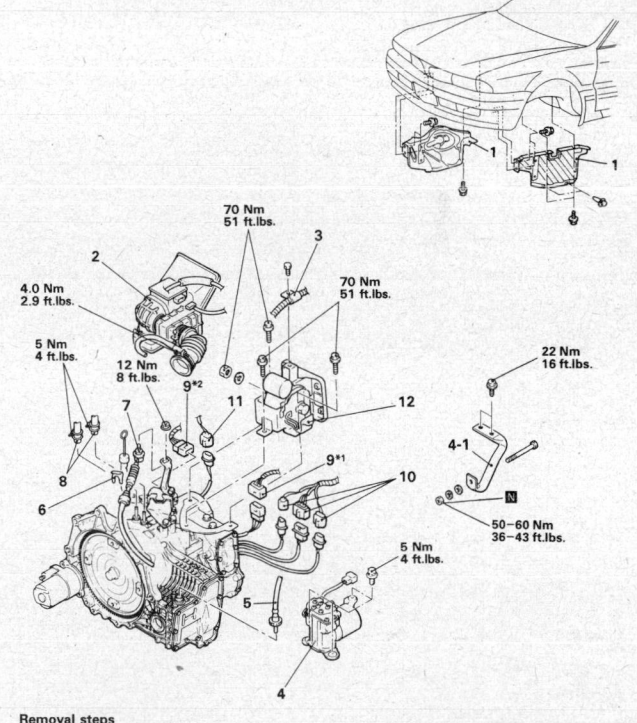

Removal steps

1. Side under cover
2. Air cleaner cover, air intake hose
3. Engine harness connection
4. Compressor assembly
   <Vehicles with ACTIVE-ECS>
4-1. Roll stopper stay
   <SOHC–For California from 1994 models>
5. Speedometer cable connection
6. Clip
7. Transaxle control cable connection
8. Connection for transmission fluid cooler hose
9. Park/neutral position switch connector
10. Kick down servo switch connector, pulse generator connector, oil temperature sensor connector
11. Shift control solenoid valve connector
12. Connection for transaxle mounting bracket

MT5029200350010X

Fig. 29 Transaxle replacement (Part 1 of 2). Diamante

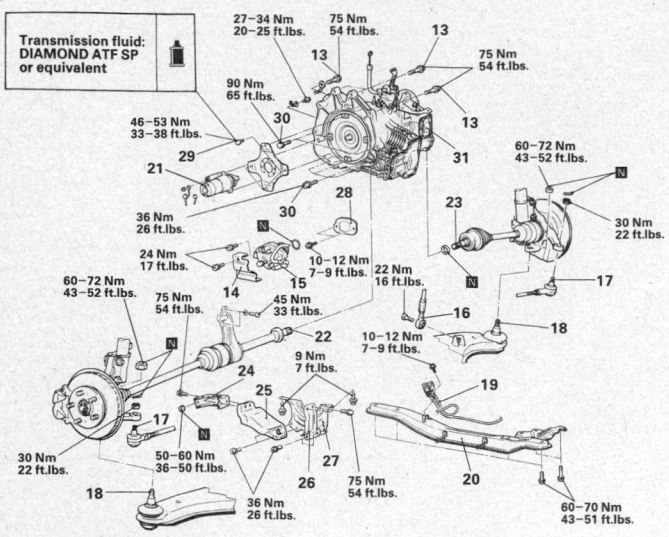

Transmission fluid: DIAMOND ATF SP or equivalent

Fig. 29 Transaxle replacement (Part 2 of 2). Diamante

MT5029200350020X

13. Transaxle assembly upper connection bolt
14. Heat protector <Vehicles with 4WS>
15. Oil pump assembly <Vehicles with 4WS>
16. Front height sensor rod <Vehicles with ACTIVE-ECS>
17. Connection for tie rod end and knuckle
18. Connection for lower arm ball joint and knuckle
19. Oxygen sensor <For California from 1994 models>
20. Right member
21. Starter
22. Drive shaft (left side), inner shaft assembly
23. Drive shaft (right side)
24. Roll stopper stay A
25. Transaxle stay (Front bank side)
26. Transaxle stay (Rear bank side)
27. Bell housing cover
28. Oil pan cover
29. Torque converter connection bolt
30. Transaxle assembly lower connection bolt
31. Transaxle assembly

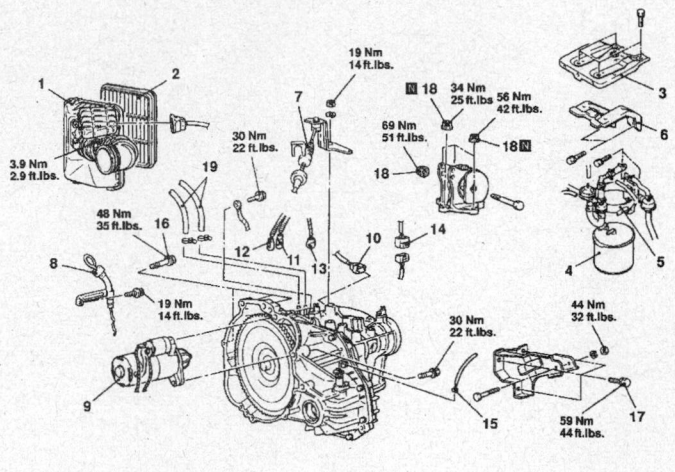

Fig. 30 Transaxle replacement (Part 1 of 2). Eclipse FWD w/2.4L engine

MT5029501083010X

Removal steps

1. Air cleaner cover and air intake hose assembly
2. Air cleaner element
3. Battery tray
4. Evaporative emission canister
5. Evaporative emission canister holder
6. Battery tray stay
7. Transaxle control cable connection
8. Oil dipstick and guide assembly
9. Starter motor
10. Park/Neutral position switch connector
11. Oil temperature sensor connector
12. Kick down servo switch connector
13. Solenoid valve connector
14. Pulse generator connector
15. Speedometer connector
16. Transaxle assembly mounting bolts
17. Rear roll stopper bracket mounting bolts
18. Transaxle mounting bracket mounting nuts
19. Transaxle oil cooler hoses connection
• Supporting engine assembly

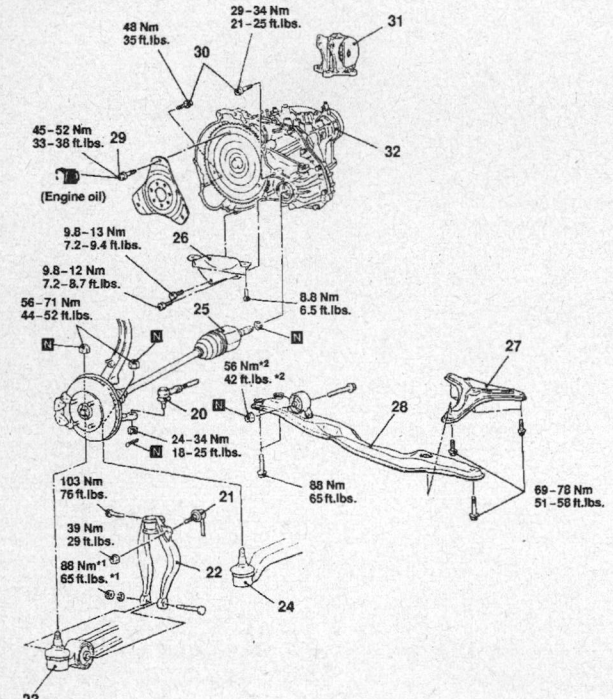

Fig. 30 Transaxle replacement (Part 2 of 2). Eclipse FWD w/2.4L engine

MT5029501083020X

From under vehicles

20. Tie rod end ball joint and knuckle connection
21. Stabilizer link connection
22. Damper fork
23. Lateral lower arm ball joint and knuckle connection
24. Compression lower arm ball joint and knuckle connection
25. Drive shaft connection
26. Bell housing cover
27. Stay (R.H.)
28. Centermember assembly
29. Drive plate connecting bolts
30. Transaxle assembly mounting bolts
31. Transaxle mounting bracket
32. Transaxle assembly

Caution
*1: The fasteners marked * should be temporally tightened before they are finally tightened once the total weight of the engine has been placed on the vehicle body.
*2: For tightening locations indicated by the symbol, first tighten temporarily, and then make the final tightening with the entire weight of the engine applied to the vehicle body.

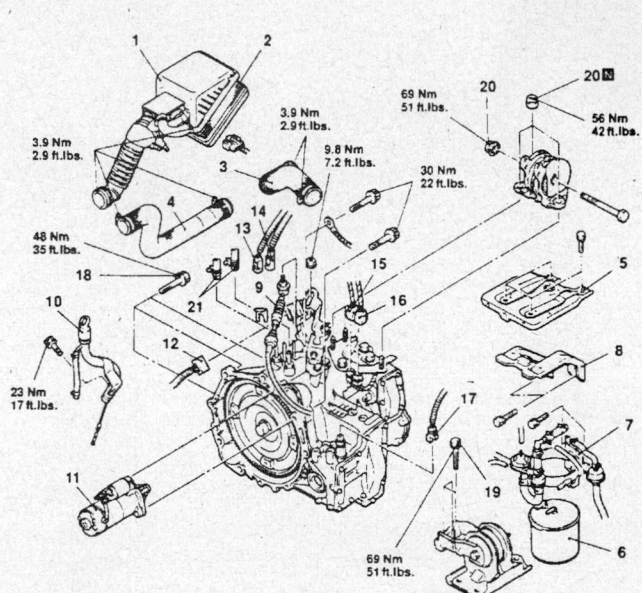

Fig. 31 Transaxle replacement (Part 1 of 2). Eclipse FWD w/2.0L turbocharged engine

MT5029501002010X

Removal steps

1. Air cleaner cover and air intake hose assembly
2. Air cleaner element
3. Air hose C
4. Air hose A
5. Battery tray
6. Evaporative emission canister
7. Evaporative emission canister holder
8. Battery tray stay
9. Transaxle control cable connection
10. Oil level gauge and guide assembly
11. Starter motor
12. Park/Neutral position switch connector
13. Oil temperature sensor connector
14. Kick down servo switch connector
15. Solenoid valve connector
16. Pulse generator connector
17. Speedometer connector
18. Transaxle assembly mounting bolts
19. Rear roll stopper bracket mounting bolts
20. Transaxle mounting bracket mounting nuts
21. Transaxle oil cooler hoses connection
• Engine assembly supporting

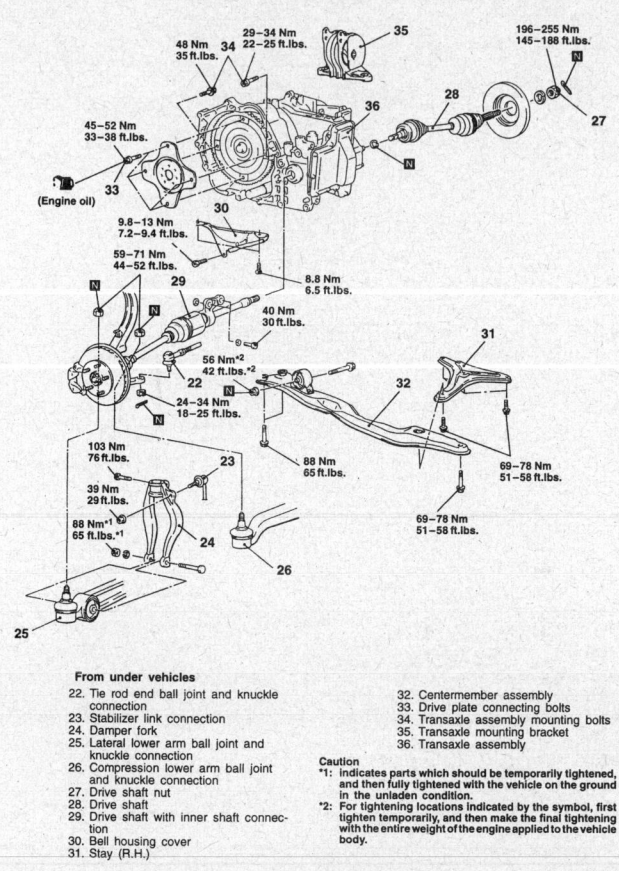

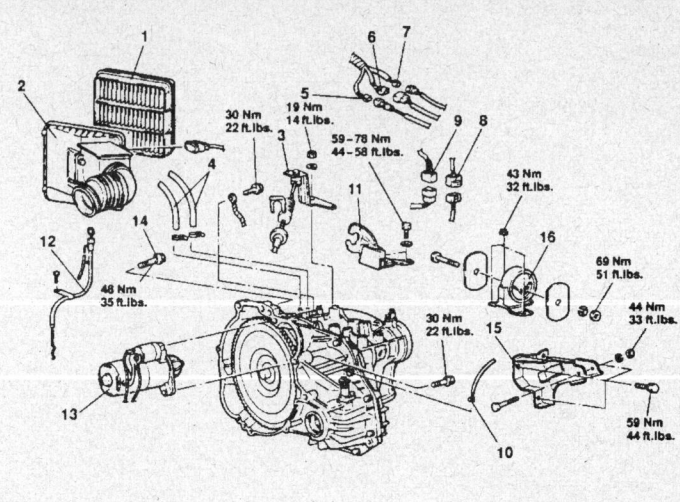

Fig. 32   Transaxle replacement (Part 1 of 2). Galant

Removal steps

1. Air cleaner element
2. Air cleaner cover and hose assembly
3. Manual control lever connection
4. Connection for transaxle oil cooler hoses
5. Oil temperature sensor connector
6. Pulse generator connector
7. Kickdown servo switch connector
8. Park/ Neutral position switch connector
9. Solenoid valve connector
10. Speedometer connector
11. Shift cable bracket
12. Oil level gauge and guide assembly
13. Starter motor
14. Transaxle assembly upper part coupling bolts
15. Rear roll stopper bracket
16. Transaxle mounting
• Supporting engine assembly

From under vehicles

22. Tie rod end ball joint and knuckle connection
23. Stabilizer link connection
24. Damper fork
25. Lateral lower arm ball joint and knuckle connection
26. Compression lower arm ball joint and knuckle connection
27. Drive shaft nut
28. Drive shaft
29. Drive shaft with inner shaft connection
30. Bell housing cover
31. Stay (R.H.)

32. Centermember assembly
33. Drive plate connecting bolts
34. Transaxle assembly mounting bolts
35. Transaxle mounting bracket
36. Transaxle assembly

Caution
*1: indicates parts which should be temporarily tightened, and then fully tightened with the vehicle on the ground in the unladen condition.
*2: For tightening locations indicated by the symbol, first tighten temporarily, and then make the final tightening with the entire weight of the engine applied to the vehicle body.

MT5029501002020X

Fig. 31   Transaxle replacement (Part 2 of 2). Eclipse FWD w/2.0L turbocharged engine

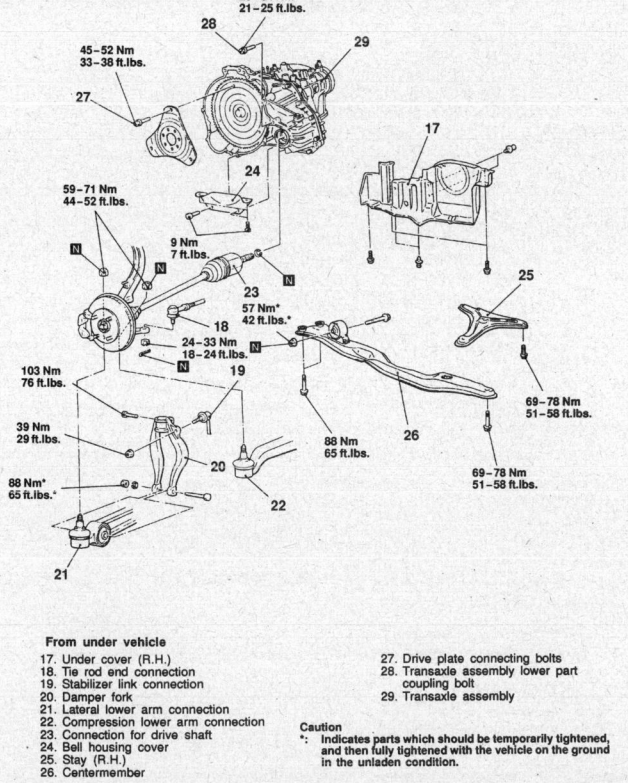

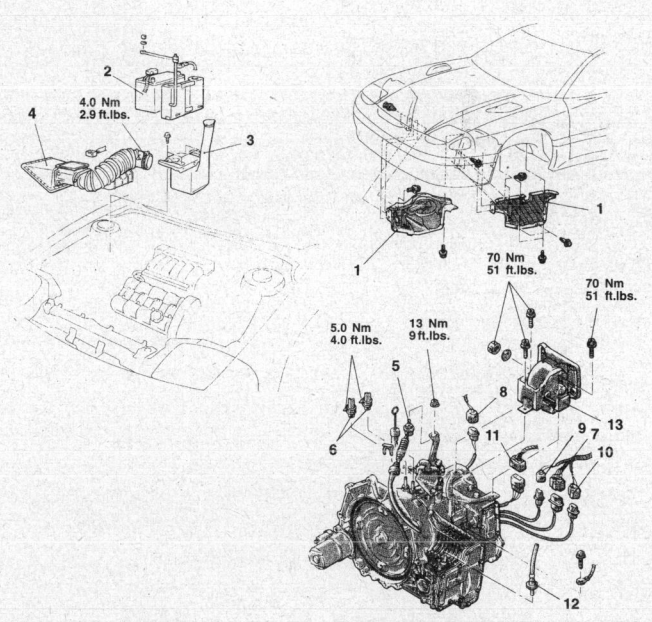

From under vehicle

17. Under cover (R.H.)
18. Tie rod end connection
19. Stabilizer link connection
20. Damper fork
21. Lateral lower arm connection
22. Compression lower arm connection
23. Connection for drive shaft
24. Bell housing cover
25. Stay (R.H.)
26. Centermember

27. Drive plate connecting bolts
28. Transaxle assembly lower part coupling bolt
29. Transaxle assembly

Caution
*: Indicates parts which should be temporarily tightened, and then fully tightened with the vehicle on the ground in the unladen condition.

MT5029401003020X

Fig. 32   Transaxle replacement (Part 2 of 2). Galant

Removal steps

1. Side under cover
2. Battery
3. Battery seat, Washer tank
4. Air cleaner cover, Air intake hose
5. Transaxle control cable connection
6. Oil cooler hose connection
7. Park/neutral position switch connector
8. Kickdown servo switch connector
9. Pulse generator connector
10. Oil temperature sensor connector
11. Shift control solenoid valve connector
12. Speedometer cable or speedometer connector connection
13. Transaxle mount bracket connection

MT5029201004010X

Fig. 33   Transaxle replacement (Part 1 of 2). 3000GT

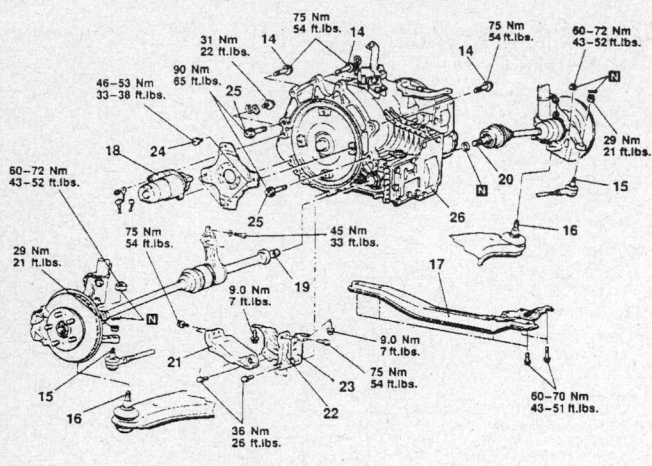

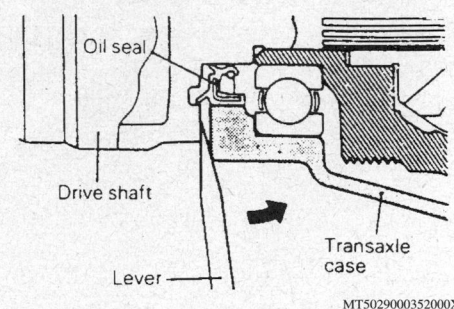

Fig. 34 Driveshaft removal

14. Transaxle assembly upper part coupling bolt
15. Tie rod end connection
16. Lower arm ball joint connection
17. Right member
18. Starter
19. Drive shaft (left side), Inner shaft assembly
20. Drive shaft (right side)
21. Transaxle stay (front bank side)
22. Transaxle stay (rear bank side)
23. Bell housing cover
24. Special bolts
25. Transaxle assembly lower part coupling bolt
26. Transaxle assembly

MT5029201004020X

Fig. 33 Transaxle replacement (Part 2 of 2). 3000GT

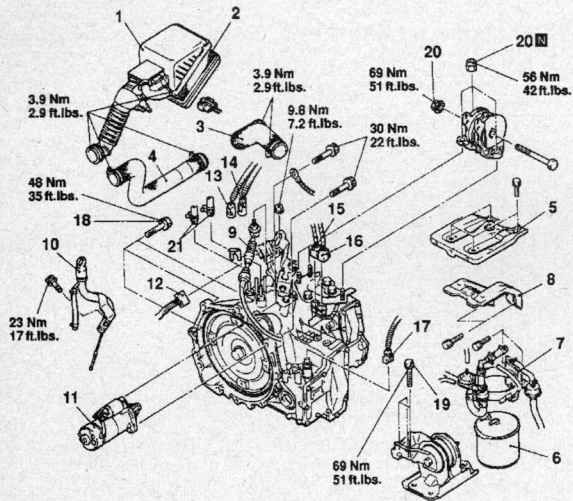

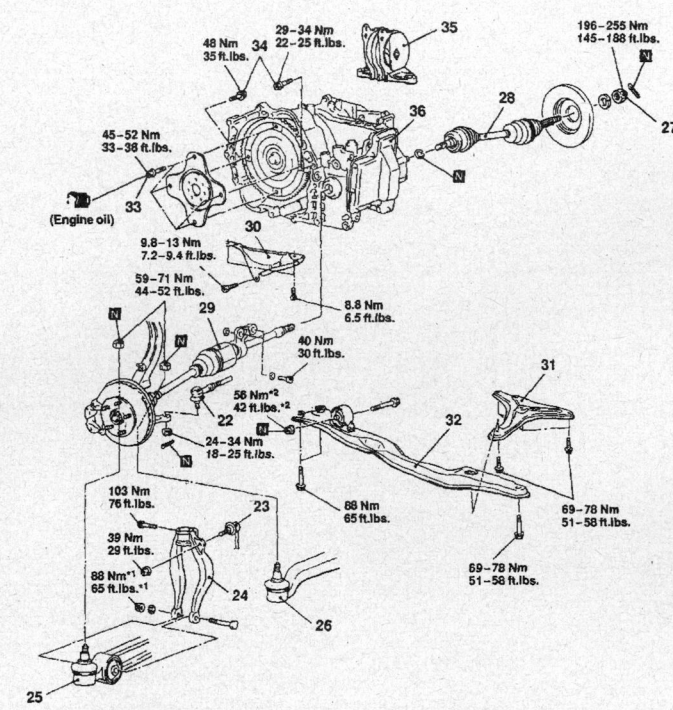

Removal steps
1. Air cleaner cover and air intake hose assembly
2. Air cleaner element
3. Air hose C
4. Air hose A
5. Battery tray
6. Evaporative emission canister
7. Evaporative emission canister holder
8. Battery tray stay
9. Transaxle control cable connection
10. Oil dipstick and guide assembly
11. Starter motor
12. Park/Neutral position switch connector
13. Oil temperature sensor connector
14. Kick down servo switch connector
15. Solenoid valve connector
16. Pulse generator connector
17. Speedometer connector
18. Transaxle assembly mounting bolts
19. Rear roll stopper bracket mounting bolts
20. Transaxle mounting bracket mounting nuts
21. Transaxle oil cooler hoses connection
● Supporting engine assembly

MT5029501084010X

Fig. 35 Transaxle replacement (Part 1 of 2). Eclipse w/W4A32 transaxle

From under vehicles
22. Tie rod end ball joint and knuckle connection
23. Stabilizer link connection
24. Damper fork
25. Lateral lower arm ball joint and knuckle connection
26. Compression lower arm ball joint and knuckle connection
27. Drive shaft nut
28. Drive shaft
29. Drive shaft with inner shaft connection
30. Bell housing cover
31. Stay (R.H.)
32. Centermember assembly
33. Drive plate connecting bolts
34. Transaxle assembly mounting bolts
35. Transaxle mounting bracket
36. Transaxle assembly

Caution
*1: Indicates parts which should be temporarily tightened, and then fully tightened with the vehicle on the ground in the unladen condition.
*2: For tightening locations indicated by the symbol, first tighten temporarily, and then make the final tightening with the entire weight of the engine applied to the vehicle body.

MT5029501084020X

Fig. 35 Transaxle replacement (Part 2 of 2). Eclipse w/W4A33 transaxle

TIGHTENING SPECIFICATIONS

Component	Torque/Ft. Lbs.
F4AC1 TRANSAXLE	
Differential Cover	14
Differential Ring Gear	70
Differential Retainer	20
Extension Housing	20
Oil Dipstick & Guide Assembly	9
Oil Pan	14
Output Gear	200
Pump	16
Rear Cover	14
Rear Roll Stopper Bracket	54
Starter To Bellhousing	40
Transaxle Control Cable To Bell Crank	7
Transaxle Mounting Bracket Flange	42
Transaxle Mounting Bracket Through Bolt	51
Transaxle To Engine	70
Transfer Shaft Gear	200
Valve Body	43①
F4A22, F4A23, F4A33, W4A32 & W4A33 TRANSAXLES	
Air Cleaner Mounting Bolt	6
Axle Nut	144–188
Bearing Bracket To Engine	29–36
Bearing Retainer Screw	12–15
Bellhousing Cover To Engine	6
Center Support Bolt	18–25
Control Cable Adjusting Nut	7–10
Converter Housing Bolt	7.5–8.5
Differential Drive Gear Bolt	94–101
Drain Plug	24
Driveplate To Converter	34–38
Driveshaft Nut	144–188
Hub Nut	144–188
Inhibitor Switch	7.5–8.5
Kickdown Servo Piston Plate Screw	5
Lock Plate	35–43
Lower Arm Ball Joint To Knuckle	43–52
Manual Control Lever	13–15
Manual Control Shaft Setscrew	6
Oil Cooler Connector	11–15
Oil Filter	52①
Oil Pan	5–6
Oil Pump Assembly	11–15
One-Way Clutch Outer Race Bolt	18–25
Pressure Check Plug	6
Pulse Generator	8
Pump Housing To Reaction Shaft Support	8
Selector Lever	10–14
Speedometer Sleeve Locking Plate Bolt	36
Sprag Rod Support Bolt	15–19
Starter Motor Mounting Bolt	20–24
Tie Rod End To Knuckle	17–25
Torque Converter To Driveplate	53–55
Transaxle Flange Mounting Bolt	58–72
Transaxle Mounting Bolt & Washer Assembly	47–61
Transaxle Mounting Bracket To Body	29–36

Continued

TIGHTENING
SPECIFICATIONS—Continued

Component	Torque/Ft. Lbs.
F4A22, F4A23, F4A33, W4A32 & W4A33 TRANSAXLES	
Transaxle Mounting Bracket To Transaxle	43–57
Transaxle Stay To Engine	47–61
Transaxle Stay To Transaxle	22–30
Valve Body Assembly Mounting Bolt	7.5–8.5
Valve Body Bolt	40①

① — Inch lbs.

Mitsubishi R4AW3, V4AW2 & V4AW3 Automatic Transmissions

NOTE: On Air Bag Equipped Models, Refer To "Air Bag System Precautions" Located In The Front Of This Manual For System Disarming & Arming Procedures.

INDEX

PRECAUTIONS

AIR BAG SYSTEMS

Refer to "Air Bag System Precautions" in the front of this manual for system disarming and arming procedures.

BATTERY GROUND CABLE

Prior to service, disconnect battery ground cable and isolate as required.

IDENTIFICATION

The vehicle information code plate is riveted to the bulkhead or to the front end upper bar in the engine compartment. The information code plate displays model, engine, transmission and body color code.

DESCRIPTION

These transmissions, **Figs. 1 through 3,** are both fully automatic four-speed units with a three element type torque converter. The R4AW3 & V4AW3, however, are controlled electronically and have on-board diagnostic capabilities.

MAINTENANCE

FLUID CHECK

With vehicle on a level surface, start engine and operate at idle speed until normal operating temperature is reached. With parking brake applied, shift transmission through all ranges, then return to Neutral. Remove dipstick and check fluid level. Fluid level should be within the " HOT" range on dipstick. If necessary, add Dexron II fluid to raise fluid level as specified.

FLUID CHANGE

On 4WD models and models operated under severe conditions, the transmission fluid should be changed every 30,000 miles. When refilling transmission, add only Dexron II automatic transmission fluid.
1. Remove drain plug and drain differential into a suitable container.
2. Install drain plug using a new gasket.
3. Refill automatic transmission fluid through oil level tube until it reaches "COLD" lower limit on dipstick.
4. Run engine at least two minutes, then shift transmission through all ranges and recheck fluid level.
5. Ensure fluid level is between the "HOT" upper and lower limits with transmission fluid at normal operating temperature. Add or remove fluid as necessary.

ADJUSTMENTS

THROTTLE CONTROL CABLE

3.0L Engine
1. Ensure throttle lever and bracket are in good condition, then remove outer cable boot to access inner cable stopper.
2. With throttle lever fully opened, measure distance between inner and outer cable stoppers, **Fig. 4.** Distance should be 1.34–1.38 inches.
3. If distance is not as specified, adjust nut until specification is reached.

3.5L Engine
1. Check engine idle speed and adjust as necessary.
2. Ensure throttle lever and throttle cable bracket are not bent or deformed.
3. Measure distance between inner cable stopper and cover end, **Fig. 5,** with accelerator pedal fully depressed. Distance should be .4 inch or less.
4. If distance is not as specified, adjust nut until specification is reached.

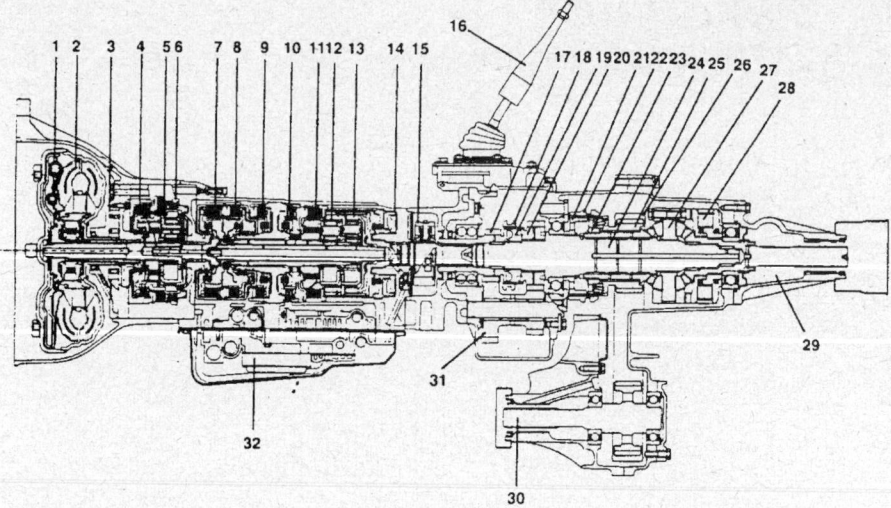

1. Lockup clutch
2. Torque converter
3. Oil pump
4. Overdrive clutch
5. Overdrive brake
6. Overdrive planetary gear
7. Forward clutch
8. Direct clutch
9. Brake No. 1
10. Brake No. 2
11. Brake No. 3
12. Front planetary gear
13. Rear planetary gear
14. Brake No. 3 piston
15. Governor
16. Transfer control lever

17. Input gear
18. High-low sleeve
19. High-low hub
20. Low speed gear
21. Differential lock hub
22. 2WD-4WD synchronizer sleeve
23. 2WD-4WD hub
24. Transfer drive shaft
25. Drive sprocket
26. Chain
27. Center differential
28. Viscous coupling
29. Rear output shaft
30. Front output shaft
31. Counter gear
32. Valve body

MT5029200596000X

Fig. 1   Cross-sectional view of V4AW2 automatic transmission

PARK/NEUTRAL POSITION SWITCH

1. Place selector lever in Neutral position, then loosen control cable adjustment nut and park/neutral position switch mounting bolt.
2. Rotate park/neutral position switch until Neutral position bosses on switch and adjustment lever are aligned, then tighten switch bolt.
3. Pull transmission control cable gently in direction of arrow, **Fig. 6,** then tighten adjustment nut.
4. Ensure selector lever is in Neutral position and corresponding with transmission lever.

SHIFT INTERLOCK

1. Remove floor console as shown in **Figs. 7 and 8.**
2. Ensure selector lever is in "P."
3. Loosen nut clamping shift lock cable, adjust shift lock cable so that end of cable with red mark comes between lobe of lock cam, **Figs. 9 and 10,** then tighten nut.
4. Reinstall floor console.

TRANSMISSION
REPLACE

1. Remove transfer control lever assembly, transfer case protector and front exhaust pipe.
2. Drain transmission and transfer case fluid into a suitable container, then remove front and rear driveshafts.
3. Remove transmission in numbered sequences shown, **Figs. 11 and 12,** noting the following:
   a. Before removing transmission roll stopper, transmission and transfer case assembly must be supported with a suitable jack.
   b. Move transmission away from engine carefully. When transmission and engine have been separated slightly, push torque converter assembly onto transmission side so that it can be removed with transmission.
   c. Note control housing bolt lengths and positions for installation reference.
4. Reverse procedure to install, noting the following:
   a. Remove all old adhesive from control housing and bolts, then apply 3M Stud Locking Compound No. 4170, or equivalent, to bolt threads.
   b. Refer to **Figs. 11 and 12** for transmission to engine bolt tightening specifications. **Specifications vary according to bolt size and location.**
   c. Adjust control cables as necessary when installation is complete.

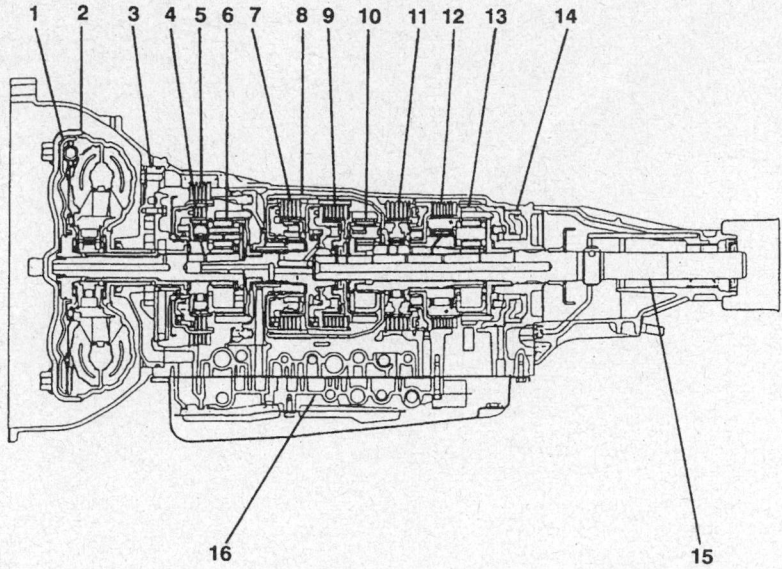

1. TORQUE CONVERTER CLUTCH
2. TORQUE CONVERTER
3. OIL PUMP
4. OVERDRIVE CLUTCH
5. OVERDRIVE BRAKE
6. OVERDRIVE PLANETARY GEAR
7. FORWARD CLUTCH
8. DIRECT CLUTCH

9. SECOND COAST BRAKE
10. SECOND BRAKE
11. FIRST & REVERSE BRAKE
12. FRONT PLANETARY GEAR
13. REAR PLANETARY GEAR
14. FIRST & REVERSE BRAKE PISTON
15. OUTPUT SHAFT
16. VALVE BODY

MT5029701085000X

Fig. 2   Cross-sectional veiw of R4AW3 automatic transmission

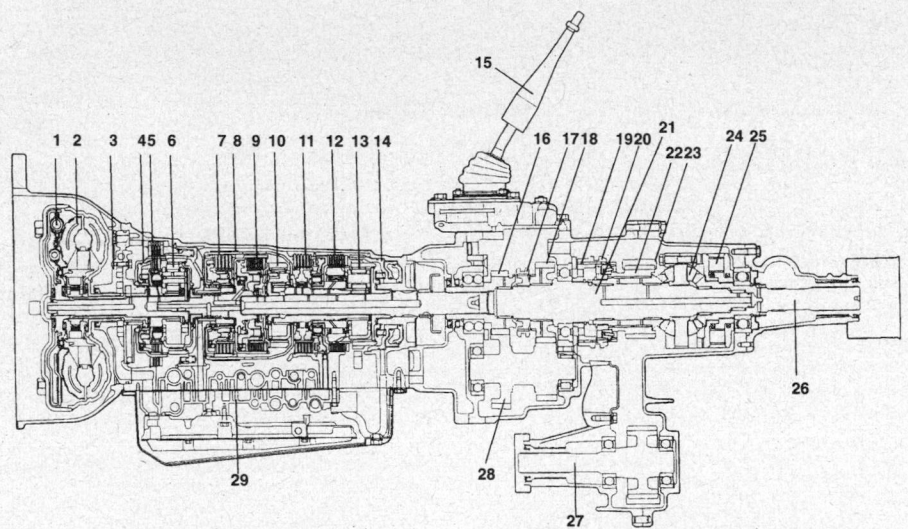

1. Torque converter clutch
2. Torque converter
3. Oil pump
4. Overdrive clutch
5. Overdrive brake
6. Overdrive planetary gear
7. Direct clutch
8. Second coast brake
9. Forward clutch
10. Front planetary gear
11. Second brake
12. First & reverse brake
13. Rear planetary gear
14. First & reverse brake piston
15. Transfer control lever

16. Input gear
17. High-low clutch
18. Low speed gear
19. Differential lock hub
20. 2-4WD synchronizer sleeve
21. Transfer drive shaft
22. Drive sprocket
23. Chain
24. Center differential
25. Viscous coupling
26. Rear output shaft
27. Front output shaft
28. Counter gear
29. Valve body

MT5029400597000X

Fig. 3   Cross-sectional view of V4AW3 automatic transmission

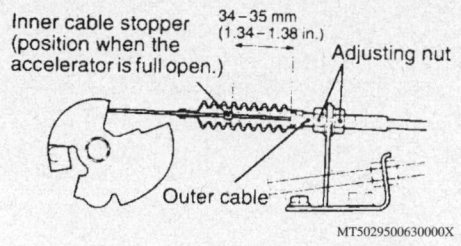

Inner cable stopper (position when the accelerator is full open.)
34 – 35 mm (1.34 – 1.38 in.)
Adjusting nut
Outer cable

MT5029500630000X

Fig. 4 Throttle control cable measurement. 3.0L engine

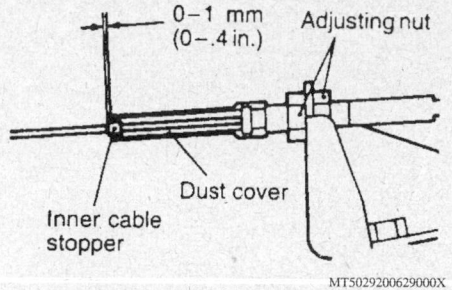

0 – 1 mm (0 –.4 in.)
Adjusting nut
Dust cover
Inner cable stopper

MT5029200629000X

Fig. 5 Throttle control cable measurement. 3.5L engine

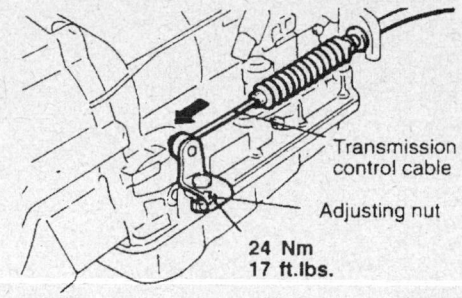

Transmission control cable
Adjusting nut
24 Nm
17 ft.lbs.

MT5029200631000X

Fig. 6 Transmission control cable adjustment

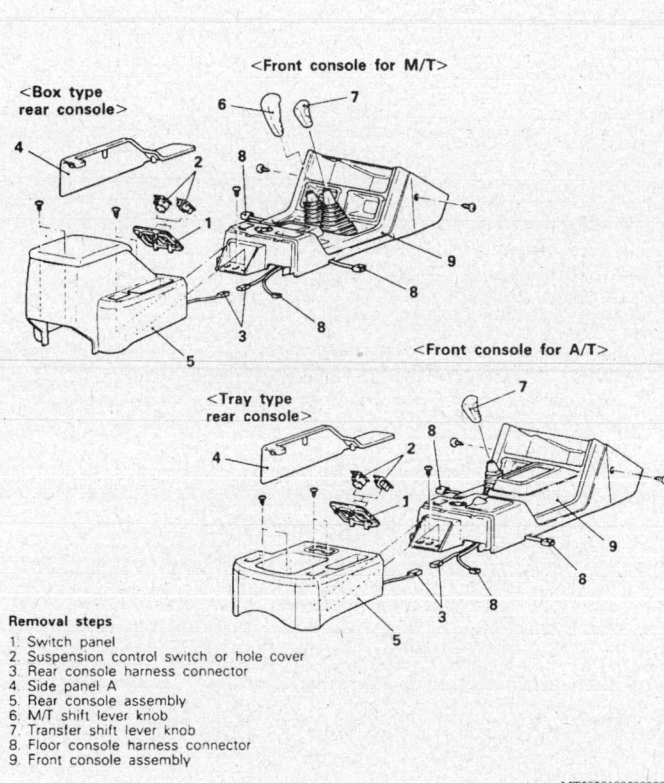

<Box type rear console>
<Front console for M/T>
<Tray type rear console>
<Front console for A/T>

Removal steps
1. Switch panel
2. Suspension control switch or hole cover
3. Rear console harness connector
4. Side panel A
5. Rear console assembly
6. M/T shift lever knob
7. Transfer shift lever knob
8. Floor console harness connector
9. Front console assembly

MT5029100590000X

Fig. 7 Floor console replacement. Montero

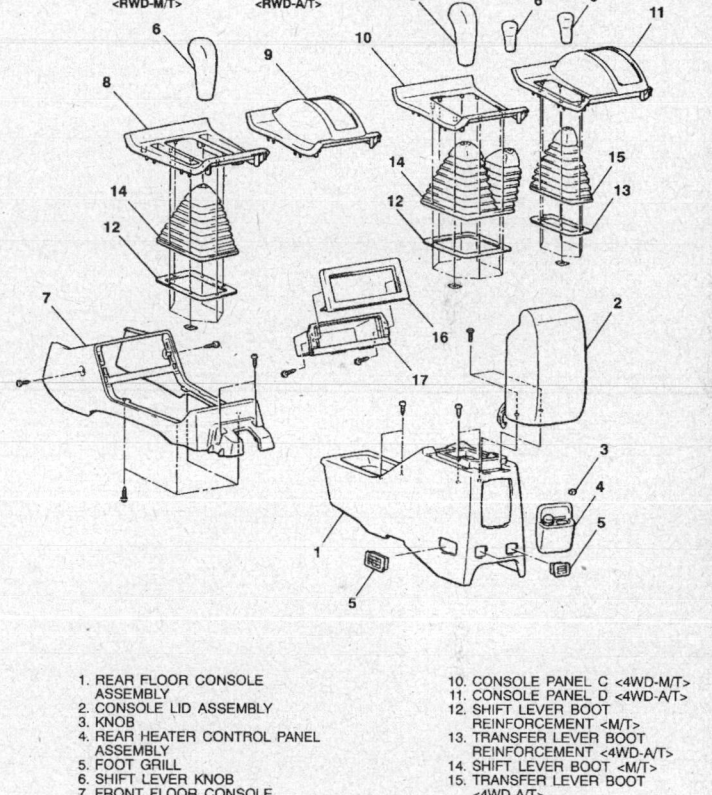

<RWD-M/T> <RWD-A/T> <4WD-M/T> <4WD-A/T>

1. REAR FLOOR CONSOLE ASSEMBLY
2. CONSOLE LID ASSEMBLY
3. KNOB
4. REAR HEATER CONTROL PANEL ASSEMBLY
5. FOOT GRILL
6. SHIFT LEVER KNOB
7. FRONT FLOOR CONSOLE ASSEMBLY
8. CONSOLE PANEL A <RWD-M/T>
9. CONSOLE PANEL B <RWD-A/T>
10. CONSOLE PANEL C <4WD-M/T>
11. CONSOLE PANEL D <4WD-A/T>
12. SHIFT LEVER BOOT REINFORCEMENT <M/T>
13. TRANSFER LEVER BOOT REINFORCEMENT <4WD-A/T>
14. SHIFT LEVER BOOT <M/T>
15. TRANSFER LEVER BOOT <4WD-A/T>
16. CONSOLE PANEL
17. BOX

MT5029701279000X

Fig. 8 Floor console replacement. Montero Sport

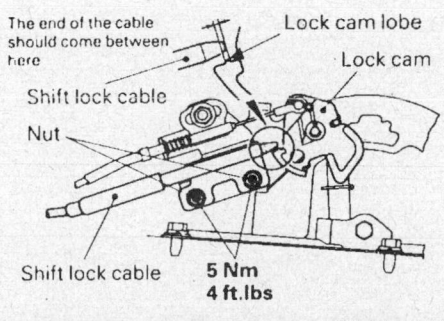

The end of the cable should come between here
Lock cam lobe
Lock cam
Shift lock cable
Nut
Shift lock cable
5 Nm
4 ft.lbs

MT5029100591000X

Fig. 9 Shift lock adjustment. Montero

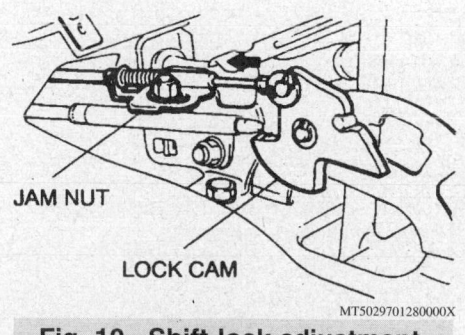

JAM NUT
LOCK CAM

MT5029701280000X

Fig. 10 Shift lock adjustment. Montero Sport

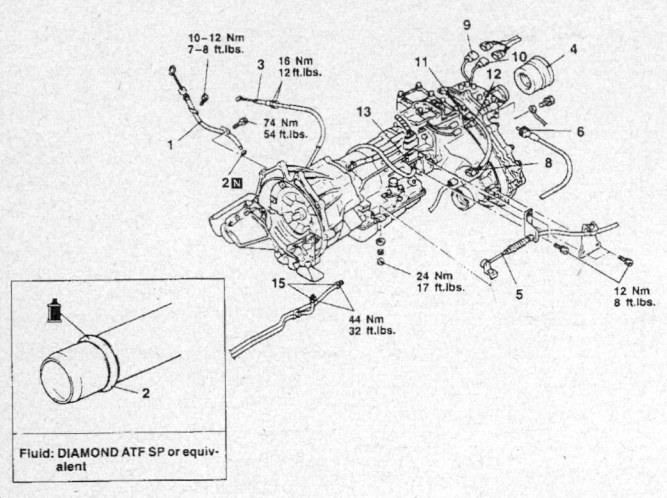

Fluid: DIAMOND ATF SP or equivalent

Removal steps
1. Fluid filler pipe
2. O-ring
3. Connection for throttle control cable
4. Dust seal guard
5. Connection for transmission control cable
6. Connection for speedometer cable
8. HI/LO detection switch connector
9. 4WD operation detection switch connector
10. Center differential lock operation detection switch connector
11. Center differential lock detection switch connector
12. 2WD/4WD detection switch connector
13. Park/Neutral position switch connector
15. Connection for fluid cooler pipe

MT5029200632010X

**Fig. 11 Transmission replacement (Part 1 of 2).
3.0L 12 valve engine**

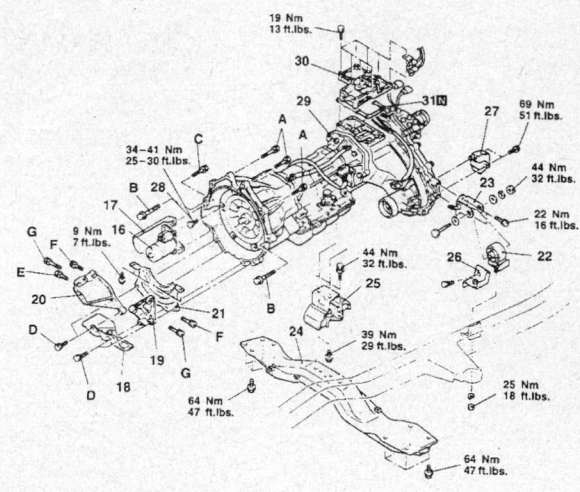

	Nm	ft.lbs.	O.D.×Length mm (in.)	Bolt identification
A	74	54	"7" 12×40 (.5×1.6)	
B	88	65	"7" 12×55 (.5×2.2)	
C	30	22	"7" 10×55 (.4×2.2)	"7" D X L
D	35	26	"7" 10×40 (.4×1.6)	
E	74	54	"7" 12×35 (.5×1.4)	L
F	41	31	"7" 10×30 (.4×1.2)	
G	74	54	"7" 12×30 (.5×2.0)	

Sealant: 3M ATD Part No. 8663 or equivalent

16. Starter motor
17. Starter cover
18. Heat protector
19. Transmission stay (L.H.)
20. Transmission stay (R.H.)
21. Bell housing cover
22. Transfer roll stopper
23. Transfer mounting bracket
24. No. 2 crossmember
25. Engine mount rear insulator
26. Transfer case protector bracket
27. Mass damper
28. Torque converter connecting bolt
29. Transmission and transfer assembly
31. Gasket
31. Gasket

MT5029200632020X

**Fig. 11 Transmission replacement (Part 2 of 2).
3.0L 12 valve engine**

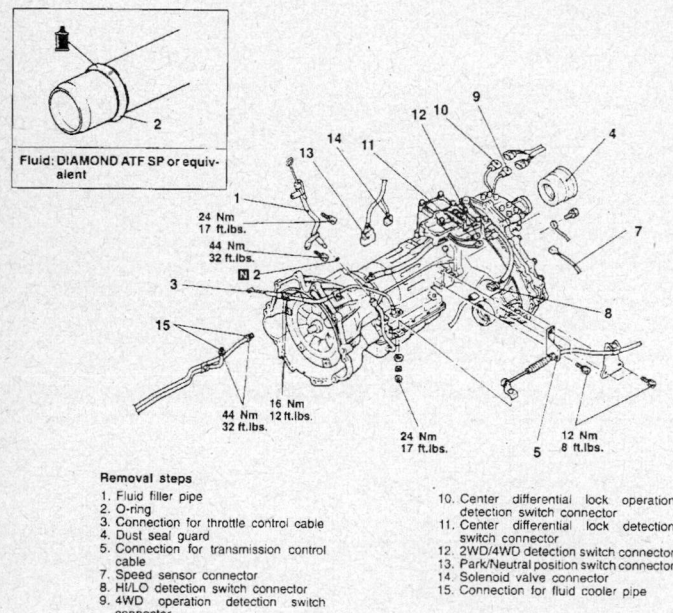

Fluid: DIAMOND ATF SP or equivalent

Removal steps
1. Fluid filler pipe
2. O-ring
3. Connection for throttle control cable
4. Dust seal guard
5. Connection for transmission control cable
7. Speed sensor connector
8. HI/LO detection switch connector
9. 4WD operation detection switch connector
10. Center differential lock operation detection switch connector
11. Center differential lock detection switch connector
12. 2WD/4WD detection switch connector
13. Park/Neutral position switch connector
14. Solenoid valve connector
15. Connection for fluid cooler pipe

MT5029200633010X

**Fig. 12 Transmission replacement (Part 1 of 2).
3.0L 24-valve & 3.5L engines**

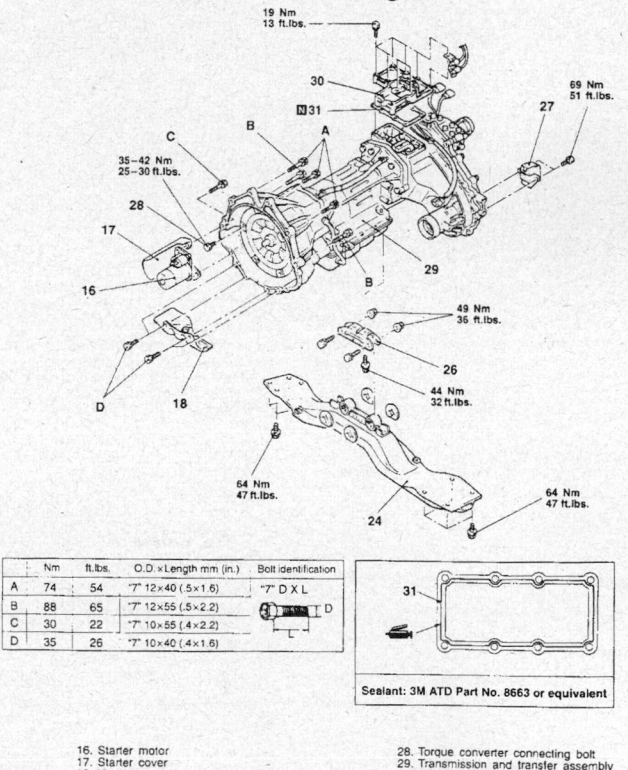

	Nm	ft.lbs.	O.D.×Length mm (in.)	Bolt identification
A	74	54	"7" 12×40 (.5×1.6)	"7" D X L
B	88	65	"7" 12×55 (.5×2.2)	
C	30	22	"7" 10×55 (.4×2.2)	
D	35	26	"7" 10×40 (.4×1.6)	

Sealant: 3M ATD Part No. 8663 or equivalent

16. Starter motor
17. Starter cover
18. Heat protector
24. No. 2 crossmember
26. Engine rear mount bracket
27. Mass damper
28. Torque converter connecting bolt
29. Transmission and transfer assembly
30. Control housing
31. Gasket

MT5029200633020X

**Fig. 12 Transmission replacement (Part 2 of 2).
3.0L 24-valve & 3.5L engines**

TIGHTENING SPECIFICATIONS

Component	Torque/Ft. Lbs.
Center Support	19
Control Housing Bolt	11–15
Control Lever Assembly To Control Housing	60–84②
Control Shaft Setscrew	60–84②
Converter Housing Installation Bolt (.39 Inch Diameter)	20–30
Converter Housing Installation Bolt (.47 Inch Diameter)	20–30
Cover Bolt	11–15
Cover Plate Installation Screw	43–52②
Cross Shaft Bracket (A) To Body	84–108②
Elbow Connector	48–84②
Inhibitor Switch Attaching Bolt	33–48②
Locking Plate Bolt	11–15
Manual Lever Installation Nut	10–13
No. 2 Crossmember To Frame	40–54
No. 2 Crossmember To Transmission	13–18
Oil Filler Plug	22–25
Oil Filler Tube To Transmission	84–108②
Oil Pan Drain Plug	13–17
Oil Pan Installation Bolt	14–21
Oil Pump Assembly Installation Bolt	13–18
Oil Pump Body & Cover-Tightening Bolt	48–84②
Oil Screen Installation Bolt	43–52②
Overdrive Solenoid Valve Installation Bolt	7–12
Parking Cam Plate Installation	48–84②
Plug (Hydraulic Test)	7–12
Rear Cover Bolt	11–15
Rear Engine Support Member To Frame	7–9
Rear Output Shaft Locknut	72–94
Seal Plug	22–30
Select Plug	22–25
Selector Handle Mounting Screw	5②
Side Cover Bolt	60–84②
Speedometer Sleeve Clamp Bolt	13–19②
Throttle Cam Installation Bolt	52–78②
Torque Converter To Driveplate	25–30
Transfer Case Chain Cover	26
Transfer Case Mounting Bolts & Nuts	26
Transfer Case Oil Drain Plug	24
Transfer Case Oil Filler Plug	24
Transmission Control Arm Bracket	13–17
Transmission Control Rod (B) To Pin	108②
Transmission Oil Cooler Eye Bolts	22–25
Transmission Oil Cooler Tube Flare Nut	29–36
Transmission To Engine	①
Transmission To Starter	20–25
Union	14–21
Valve Body Assembly Bolts	48②
Valve Body Mounting Bolts	7
4WD Switch	22–30

① — Refer to "Transmission, Replace" in this section for tightening specifications.
② — Inch lbs.

Mitsubishi F4A41, F4A42 & F4A51 Automatic Transaxles

NOTE: On Air Bag Equipped Models, Refer To "Air Bag System Precautions" Located In The Front Of This Manual For System Disarming & Arming Procedures.

INDEX

PRECAUTIONS

AIR BAG SYSTEMS

Refer to "Air Bag System Precautions" in the front of this manual for system disarming and arming procedures.

BATTERY GROUND CABLE

Prior to service, disconnect battery ground cable and isolate as required.

IDENTIFICATION

There are two transaxle identification plates mounted on the transaxle, **Fig. 1.** The identification plate indicated by the letter "A" is for original equipment parts. The identification plate indicated by the letter "B" is for replacement parts.

DESCRIPTION

These are four speed electronically controlled transaxles incorporating the Innovative Vehicle Electronic Control System-II (INVEC-II).

MAINTENANCE

FLUID CHECK

1. Drive vehicle until fluid temperature reaches normal operating temperature (158–176°F).
2. Park vehicle on level surface.
3. Move selector lever sequentially to every position to fill torque converter and hydraulic circuit with fluid, then place selector lever in neutral position.
4. Wipe all dirt and debris from around dipstick, then remove dipstick from transaxle.
5. If fluid smells burnt, color is brown or black, or if metal particles can be seen or felt on dipstick, transaxle will need to be disassembled for further diagnosis.
6. Check to see if fluid level is at Hot range on dipstick.

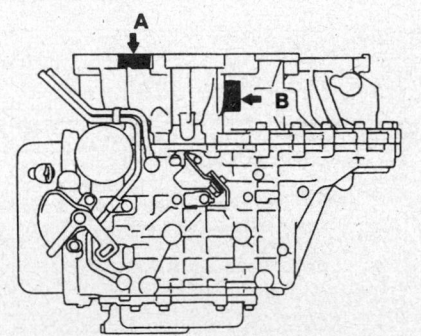

MT5029801888000X

Fig. 1   Transaxle identification

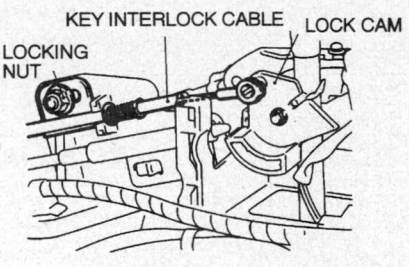

MT5029901905000X

Fig. 2   Key interlock cable adjustment

7. If fluid level is low add fluid until level reaches Hot range on dipstick.
8. Do not overfill transaxle. Refer to "Lubricant Data & Maintenance Charts" for fluid type and amount.

FLUID CHANGE

1. Drain fluid and inspect for any evidence of contamination.
2. If fluid smells burnt, color is brown or black, or if metal particles can be seen or felt on dipstick, transaxle will need to be disassembled for further diagnosis.
3. Remove right hand hose connecting

transaxle oil cooler pipe to oil cooler (built in to bottom of radiator).
4. Connect a length of hose from radiator cooler pipe to a suitable oil drain receptacle.
5. Start engine in neutral and allow to idle. Discharge ATF.
6. Stop engine within one minute of starting. If ATF is discharged before one minute elapses, stop engine.
7. Approximate amount of ATF discharged is 6.8 quarts.
8. Remove drain plug from bottom of transaxle case and drain ATF. (Amount of ATF drained is approximately 2 quarts).
9. Inspect ATF oil filter and replace if necessary.
10. Install drain plug and gasket, tighten to specification.
11. Fill transaxle with new ATF through oil filler tube. Refer to "Lubricant Data & Maintenance Charts" for fluid type and amount.

ADJUSTMENTS

KEY INTERLOCK CABLE

1. Remove floor console.
2. Place selector lever in Park position.
3. Turn ignition key to Lock position.
4. Loosen key interlock cable locking nut, **Fig. 2.**
5. Push cable joint on lock cam gently toward arrow until cable stops.
6. Tight locking nut and install floor console.

SHIFT INTERLOCK CABLE

1. Remove floor console.
2. Place selector lever in Park position.
3. Loosen shift interlock cable locking nut, **Fig. 3.**
4. Tighten locking nut until end of shift interlock cable comes above red marking of lock cam.
5. Install floor console.

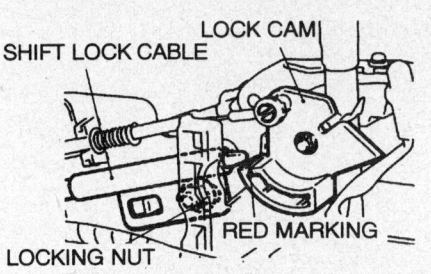

Fig. 3 Shift interlock cable adjustment

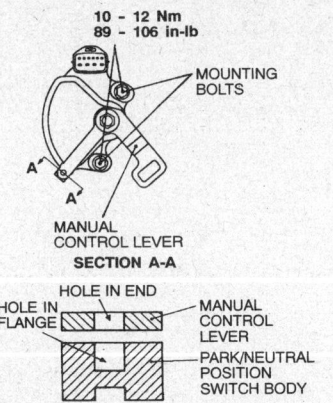

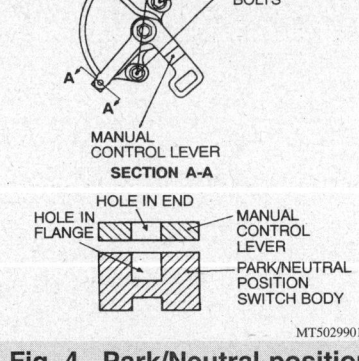

Fig. 4 Park/Neutral position switch adjustment

Fig. 5 Line pressure adjustment

body cover.
2. Turn adjusting screw until line pressure is 147–152 psi, **Fig. 5.**
3. Each full turn of adjusting screw changes line pressure 5.1 psi.
4. Install valve body cover and add fluid as necessary. Refer to "Lubricant Data & Maintenance Chart" for fluid type and amount.

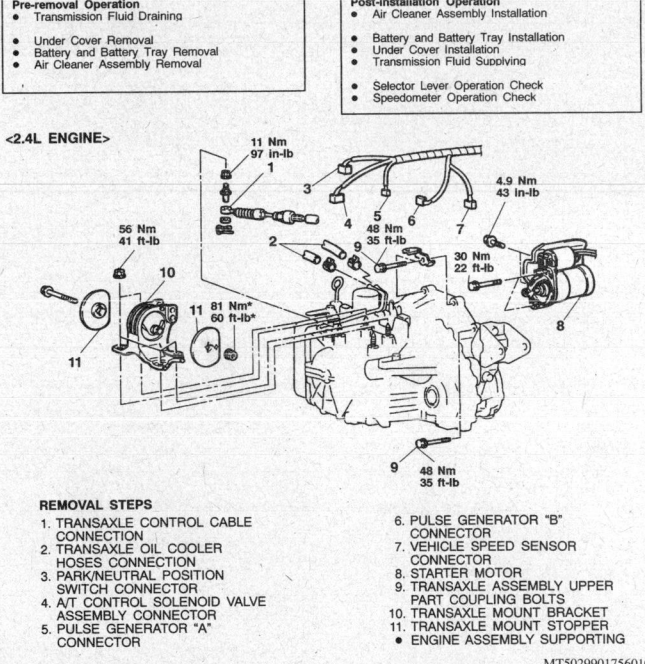

Fig. 6 Transaxle removal (Part 1 of 2). Mirage & Galant w/2.4L engine

PARK/NEUTRAL POSITION SWITCH & CONTROL CABLE ADJUSTMENT

1. Set selector lever to N position.
2. Loosen control cable to manual control lever coupling nut.
3. Set manual control lever to Neutral position.
4. Loosen Park/Neutral position switch body mounting bolts.
5. Turn switch body until hole in end of manual control lever and hole in cross section "A-A," in flange of switch body are aligned, **Fig. 4.**
6. Tighten switch body mounting bolt to specification. **Do not allow switch body to move during tightening.**
7. Gently pull transaxle control cable in direction of arrow until cable is taut, then tighten adjusting nut to specification.
8. Ensure selector lever and manual control lever match at each gear position.

LINE PRESSURE ADJUSTMENT

1. Drain automatic transaxle fluid into suitable container, then remove valve

TRANSAXLE

REPLACE

REMOVAL

Remove transaxle in numbered sequence, **Figs. 6 through 8,** noting the following:
1. Remove starter motor with harness attached and secure inside engine compartment.
2. Jack up transaxle assembly, then remove transaxle mounting.
3. Remove tie rod end with tie rod separator tool No. MD991113, or equivalent.
4. Insert pry bar between transaxle case and driveshaft, then remove driveshaft. **Do not remove hub and knuckle from driveshaft.**
5. Suspend removed drive shaft with wire so there are no sharp bends in any of joints.
6. Support transaxle assembly with a suitable transaxle jack.
7. Remove driveplate attaching bolts.
8. Press in torque converter to transaxle side so torque converter does not stay engaged to driveplate.
9. Remove transaxle lower bolts, then the transaxle.

INSTALLATION

Install transaxle in numbered sequence, **Figs. 6 through 8,** noting the following:
1. Insert torque converter into transaxle oil pump so that dimension, **Fig. 9,** measures approximately .48 inch for vehicles with 2.4L engine, and .37 inch for vehicles with 3.0L engine.
2. Install transaxle, then install transaxle mount stopper so arrow mark points in direction illustrated, **Fig. 10.**

MITSUBISHI UNIT REPAIR

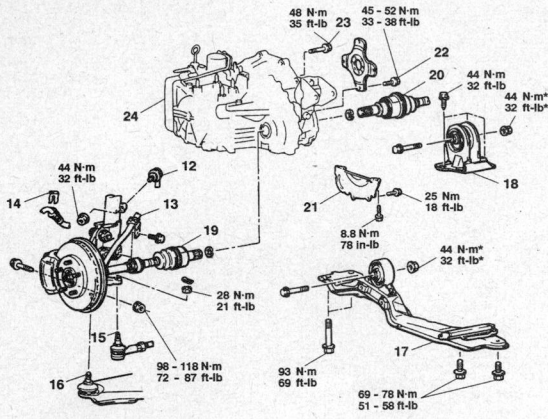

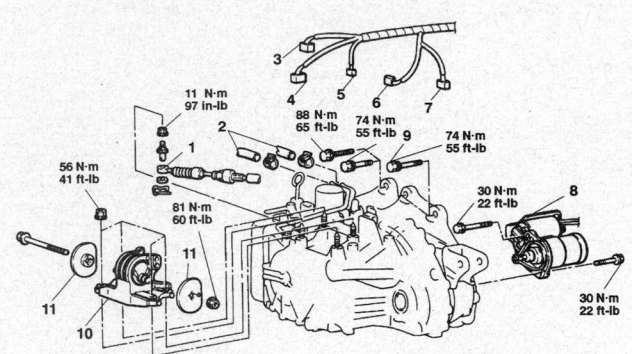

LIFTING UP OF THE VEHICLE

12. STABILIZER LINK CONNECTION <STRUT SIDE>
13. SPEED SENSOR CABLE CONNECTION <VEHICLES WITH ABS>
14. BRAKE HOSE CLAMP
15. TIE ROD END CONNECTION
16. LOWER ARM CONNECTION
17. CENTERMEMBER ASSEMBLY
18. REAR ROLL STOPPER

19. DRIVE SHAFT <LH> CONNECTION
20. DRIVE SHAFT <RH> CONNECTION
21. BELL HOUSING COVER
22. DRIVE PLATE BOLTS
23. TRANSAXLE ASSEMBLY LOWER PART COUPLING BOLTS
24. TRANSAXLE ASSEMBLY

Required Special Tools:
MB991113: Steering Linkage Puller
MB991453: Engine Hanger Assembly
MZ203827: Engine Lifter

MT5029901756020X

REMOVAL STEPS

1. TRANSAXLE CONTROL CABLE CONNECTION
2. TRANSAXLE OIL COOLER HOSES CONNECTION
3. PARK/NEUTRAL POSITION SWITCH CONNECTOR
4. A/T CONTROL SOLENOID VALVE ASSEMBLY CONNECTOR
5. PULSE GENERATOR "A" CONNECTOR

6. PULSE GENERATOR "B" CONNECTOR
7. VEHICLE SPEED SENSOR CONNECTOR
8. STARTER MOTOR
9. TRANSAXLE ASSEMBLY UPPER PART COUPLING BOLTS
10. TRANSAXLE MOUNT BRACKET
11. TRANSAXLE MOUNT STOPPER
• ENGINE ASSEMBLY SUPPORTING

MT5029901757010X

Fig. 6 Transaxle removal (Part 2 of 2). Mirage & Galant w/2.4L engine

Fig. 7 Transaxle removal (Part 1 of 2). Galant w/3.0L engine

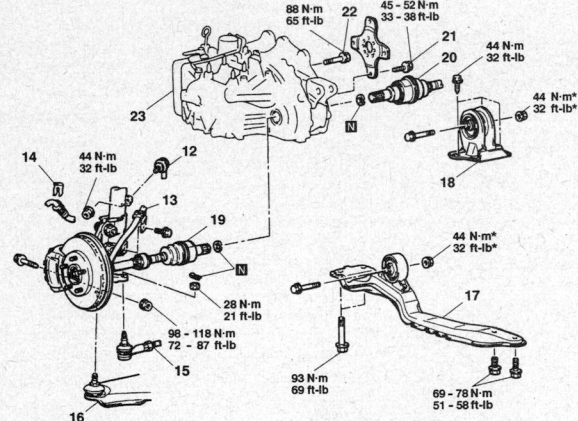

Pre-removal Operation
(1) Transaxle Fluid Draining
(2) Under Cover Removal
(3) Battery and Battery Tray Removal
(4) Air Cleaner Assembly Removal

Post-installation Operation
(1) Air Cleaner Assembly Installation
(2) Battery and Battery Tray Installation
(3) Under Cover Installation
(4) Transaxle Fluid Supplying
(5) Selector Lever Operation Check
(6) Speedometer Operation Check

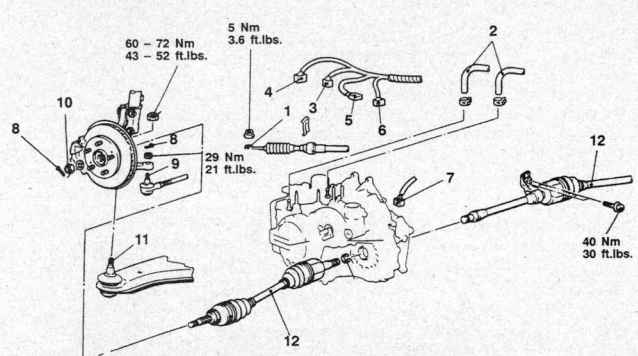

LIFTING UP OF THE VEHICLE

12. STABILIZER LINK CONNECTION <STRUT SIDE>
13. SPEED SENSOR CABLE CONNECTION <VEHICLES WITH ABS>
14. BRAKE HOSE CLAMP
15. TIE ROD END CONNECTION
16. LOWER ARM CONNECTION
17. CENTERMEMBER ASSEMBLY
18. REAR ROLL STOPPER

19. DRIVE SHAFT <LH> CONNECTION
20. DRIVE SHAFT <RH> CONNECTION
21. DRIVE PLATE BOLTS
22. TRANSAXLE ASSEMBLY LOWER PART COUPLING BOLTS
23. TRANSAXLE ASSEMBLY

Required Special Tools:
MB991113: Steering Linkage Puller
MB991453: Engine Hanger Assembly
MZ203827: Engine Lifter

MT5029901757020X

REMOVAL STEPS

1. TRANSAXLE CONTROL CABLE CONNECTION
2. TRANSAXLE OIL COOLER HOSES CONNECTION
3. PNP SWITCH CONNECTOR
4. A/T CONTROL SOLENOID VALVE CONNECTOR
5. INPUT SHAFT SPEED SENSOR CONNECTOR
6. OUTPUT SHAFT SPEED SENSOR CONNECTOR
7. VEHICLE SPEED SENSOR CONNECTOR
8. SPLIT PIN

9. CONNECTION OF THE TIE ROD END
10. DRIVE SHAFT NUT
11. CONNECTION FOR THE LOWER ARM BALL JOINT
12. DRIVE SHAFT AND INNER SHAFT ASSEMBLY (RH) AND THE DRIVE SHAFT (LH)

CAUTION: Mounting locations marked by * should be provisionally tightened, and then fully tightened when the body is supporting the full weight of the engine.

MT5029901758010X

Fig. 7 Transaxle removal (Part 2 of 2). Galant w/3.0L engine

Fig. 8 Transaxle removal (Part 1 of 2). Diamante

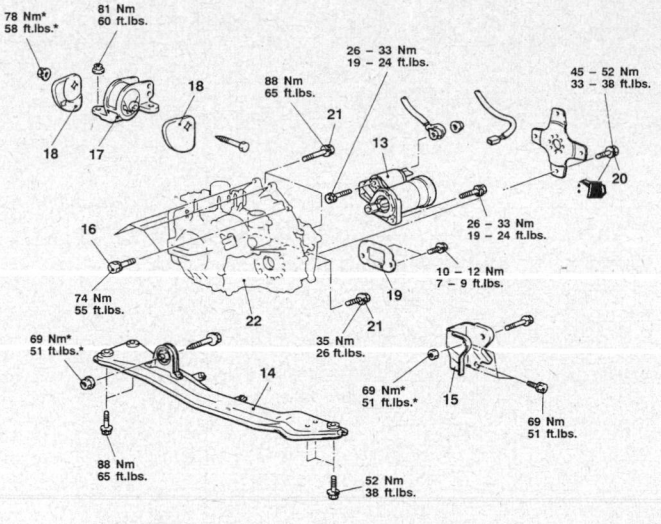

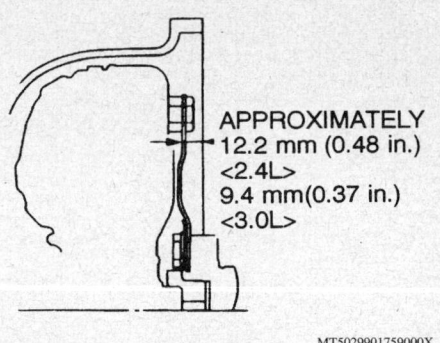

Fig. 9 Torque converter installation

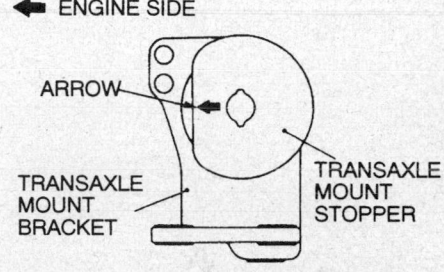

Fig. 10 Transaxle mount stopper installation

LIFTING UP OF THE VEHICLE
13. STARTER MOTOR
14. CENTER MEMBER ASSEMBLY
15. REAR ROLL STOPPER BRACKET
16. TRANSAXLE UPPER PORTION FIXING BOLT
17. TRANSAXLE MOUNTING BRACKET
18. TRANSAXLE MOUNT STOPPER
● SUPPORT THE ENGINE AND TRANSAXLE ASSEMBLY

19. BELL HOUSING COVER
20. DRIVE PLATE ATTACHING BOLT
21. TRANSAXLE LOWER PORTION FIXING BOLT
22. TRANSAXLE ASSEMBLY

Fig. 8 Transaxle removal (Part 2 of 2). Diamante

TIGHTENING SPECIFICATIONS

Year	Component	Torque Ft, Lbs
1998–99	Control Cable Bracket	17
	Differential Drive Gear	98
	Eye bolt	22
	Fluid Temperature Sensor	8
	Input Shaft Speed Sensor	8
	Manual Control Lever	16
	Manual Control Shaft Detent	4.5
	Oil Cooler Feed Tube	8
	Oil Filter	9
	Oil Pump	17
	Output Shaft Bearing Retainer (F4A41 & F4A42)	17
	Output Shaft Bearing Retainer (F4A51)	40
	Output Shaft Jam Nut	125
	Output Shaft Speed sensor	8
	Park/Neutral Position Switch	8
	Rear Cover	17
	Roll Stopper Bracket	52
	Speedometer Gear	3.5
	Torque Converter Housing	35
	Transfer Drive Gear (F4A41 & F4A42)	14
	Transfer Drive Gear (FA51)	25
	Valve Body Cover	8
	Valve Body mounting bolt	8
	Wiring harness Bracket	17

Mitsubishi R4A51 & V4A51 Automatic Transmissions

NOTE: On Air Bag Equipped Models, Refer To "Air Bag System Precautions" Located In The Front Of This Manual For System Disarming & Arming Procedures.

NOTE: Electrical Symbol & Wire Color Code Identification Located In The Front Of This Manual May Be Used As An Aid When Using Wiring Circuits Found In This Section.

NOTE: Refer To "Computer Relearn Procedures" Located In The Front Of This Manual For Computer Relearn Procedures.

INDEX

PRECAUTIONS

AIR BAG SYSTEMS

Refer to "Air Bag System Precautions" in the front of this manual for system disarming and arming procedures.

BATTERY GROUND CABLE

Prior to service, disconnect battery ground cable and isolate as required.

IDENTIFICATION

The vehicle information code plate is riveted to the cowl top outer panel in the engine compartment. The plate shows the model code, engine model, transmission model, and body color code.

DESCRIPTION

These transmissions, **Figs. 1 and 2** are the newly developed 4 speed automatics that merge advanced electronic and mechanical technology. The weight has been reduced by using precision sheet metal stampings and aluminum die casting throughout.

MAINTENANCE

FLUID CHECK

1. Drive vehicle until fluid reaches normal operating temperature of 158–176°F.
2. Park vehicle on a level surface.
3. Move gear selector through all positions to fill torque converter and hy-draulic circuits with fluid, then move selector to N position.
4. If fluid smells burnt, fluid has been contaminated by fine particles from bushing and friction materials, transmission flushing and/or overhaul will be necessary.
5. Remove dipstick and check that fluid level is at Hot mark.
6. If fluid is below specified level, top up fluid. refer to " Lubricant Data & Maintenance Charts" for proper quantities and types.

FLUID CHANGE

The following procedure should be followed when contaminated fluid has been encountered.
1. Disconnect hose between transmission and transmission oil cooler.
2. Place a suitable container under hose to collect fluid.
3. Start engine and run in N at idle, allow fluid to drain out.
4. Engine should be stopped when all fluid has been drained out (or within one minute of starting).
5. Remove drain plug from bottom of transmission, and drain fluid into suitable container.
6. Reinstall drain plug with a new gasket, tighten to specification.
7. Pour new ATF in through oil filler tube.
8. Repeat procedure to purge remaining contaminated fluid.
9. Reconnect hose that was disconnect previously and replace dipstick.
10. Start engine and run at idle for 1–2 minutes. Move selector through all po-sitions, then move to N position.
11. Check that fluid is at Cold mark on dipstick. If level is lower than this, add ATF to transmission.
12. Drive vehicle until fluid reaches normal operating temperature (158–176°F), then check fluid level again. Level must be at Hot mark on dipstick.
13. Cold level on dipstick is used for reference only, Hot level should be regarded as standard level.

ADJUSTMENTS

KEY INTERLOCK MECHANISM

1. Remove floor console.
2. Shift selector lever to P position.
3. Turn ignition key to Lock.
4. Loosen jam nut of key interlock cable.
5. Push cable joint on lock cam toward arrow, **Fig. 3,** then tighten jam nut to specification.
6. Install floor console.

PARK/NEUTRAL POSITION SWITCH & CONTROL CABLE

1. Set selector lever to N position.
2. Loosen control cable to manual control lever coupling nut to free cable and lever.
3. Set manual control lever to neutral position.
4. Loosen park/neutral position switch body mounting bolts and turn park/neutral position switch so hole in end of manual control lever and hole " AA"

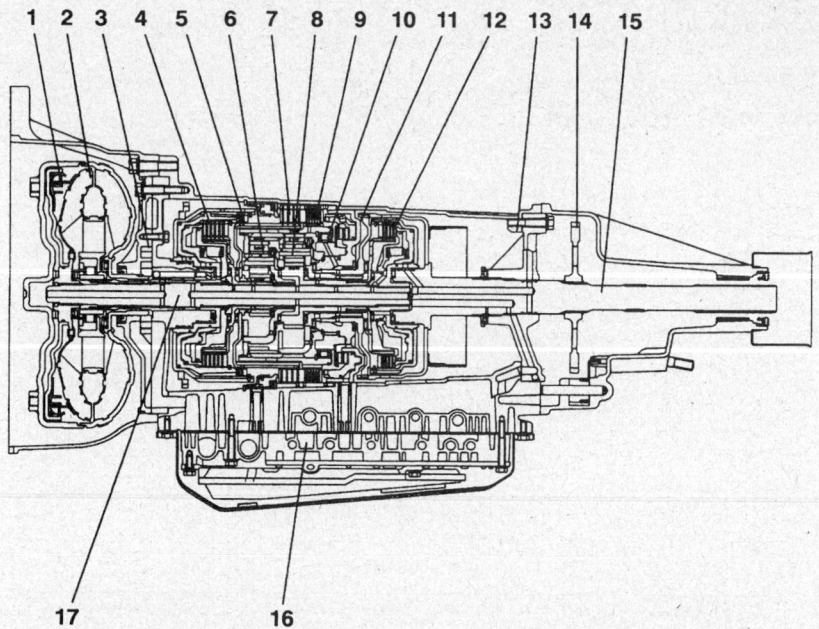

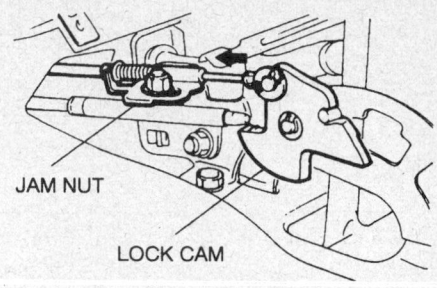

MT5029901411000X

Fig. 3 Key interlock cable adjustment

Fig. 4, in flange of park/neutral position switch body flange are aligned. Tighten park/neutral position switch body mounting bolts to specification. Ensure body does not move during tightening.

5. Pull transmission control cable in direction of arrow **Fig. 4,** until cable is taut. Tighten adjusting nut to specified value.
6. Check that selector lever is in N position.
7. Check that each position of manual control lever matches each position of selector lever.

SHIFT INTERLOCK MECHANISM

1. Remove floor console assembly.
2. Move selector lever to P position.
3. Loosen jam nut clamping shift interlock cable.
4. Tighten jam nut to specified torque at position where end of shift interlock cable comes to above red marking on lock cam.
5. Install floor console.

TRANSMISSION
REPLACE

1. Raise and support vehicle.
2. Remove lower shields (if applicable).
3. Remove transmission control cable.
4. Drain automatic transmission fluid, then remove propeller shaft.
5. Remove catalytic converter and front exhaust pipe.
6. Remove remaining components in numbered sequence, **Figs. 5 and 6.**

1. TORQUE CONVERTER CLUTCH
2. TORQUE CONVERTER
3. OIL PUMP
4. OVERDRIVE CLUTCH
5. REVERSE CLUTCH
6. OVERDRIVE PLANETARY CARRIER
7. SECOND BRAKE
8. OUTPUT PLANETARY CARRIER
9. LOW/REVERSE BRAKE
10. ONE-WAY CLUTCH
11. CENTER SUPPORT
12. UNDERDRIVE CLUTCH
13. OUTPUT SHAFT SUPPORT
14. PARKING GEAR
15. OUTPUT SHAFT
16. VALVE BODY
17. INPUT SHAFT

MT5029901368000X

Fig. 1 Cross-sectional view of R4A51 automatic transmission

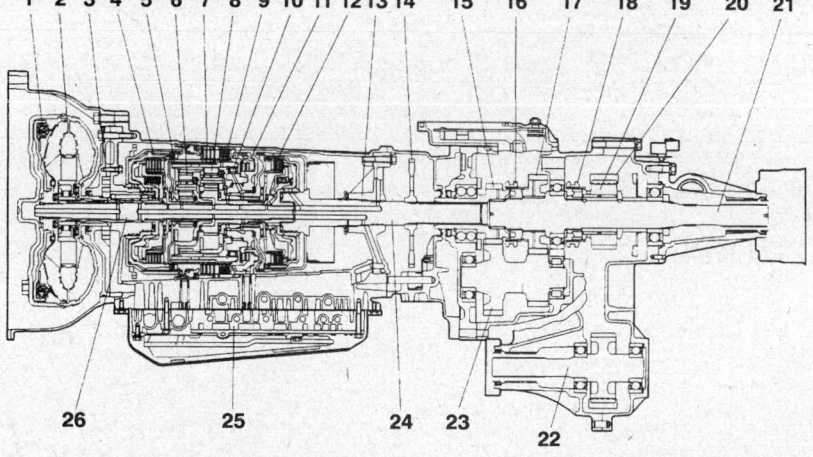

1. TORQUE CONVERTER CLUTCH
2. TORQUE CONVERTER
3. OIL PUMP
4. OVERDRIVE CLUTCH
5. REVERSE CLUTCH
6. OVERDRIVE PLANETARY CARRIER
7. SECOND BRAKE
8. OUTPUT PLANETARY CARRIER
9. LOW/REVERSE BRAKE
10. ONE-WAY CLUTCH
11. CENTER SUPPORT
12. UNDERDRIVE CLUTCH
13. OUTPUT SHAFT SUPPORT
14. PARKING GEAR
15. TRANSFER INPUT GEAR
16. H-L CLUTCH
17. LOW SPEED GEAR
18. 2-4WD SYNCHRONIZER SLEEVE
19. DRIVE SPROCKET
20. CHAIN
21. REAR OUTPUT SHAFT
22. FRONT OUTPUT SHAFT
23. TRANSFER COUNTER GEAR
24. OUTPUT SHAFT
25. VALVE BODY
26. INPUT SHAFT

MT5029901369000X

Fig. 2 Cross-sectional view of V4A51 automatic transmission

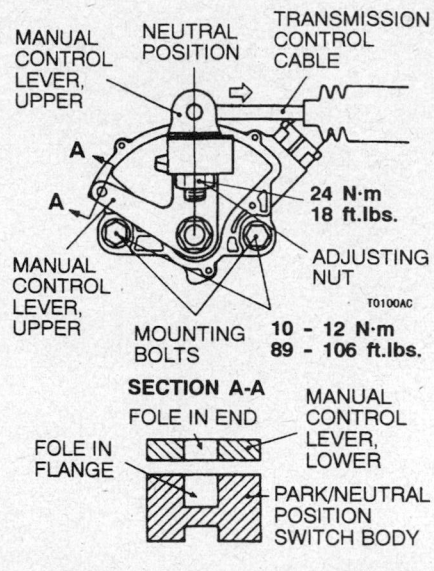

Fig. 4 Park/neutral position switch & control cable adjustment

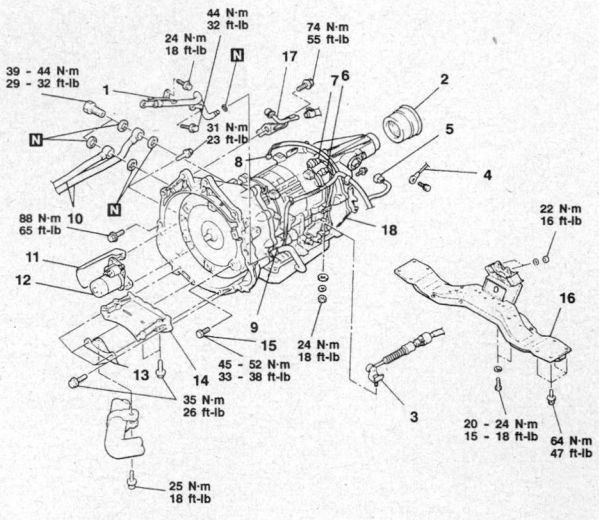

1. FILLER TUBE ASSEMBLY
2. DUST SHIELD COVER
3. TRANSMISSION CONTROL CABLE CONNECTION
4. GROUND CABLE
5. SPEED SENSOR CONNECTION
6. PARK/NEUTRAL POSITION SWITCH CONNECTION
7. SOLENOID VALVE CONNECTION
8. OUTPUT SHAFT SPEED SENSOR CONNECTION
9. INPUT SHAFT SPEED SENSOR CONNECTION
10. OIL COOLER TUBE
11. STARTER COVER
12. STARTER MOTOR
13. EXHAUST PIPE BRACKET
14. TRANSMISSSION STAY <3.0L>
15. TORQUE CONVERTER AND DRIVE PLATE CONNECTION BOLTS
• SUPPORT THE TRANSMISSION WITH A TRANSMISSION JACK
16. NO.2 CROSSMEMBER
17. AIR BREATHER PIPE ASSEMBLY
18. TRANSMISSION ASSEMBLY

Fig. 5 Transmission replacement. R4A51 transmission

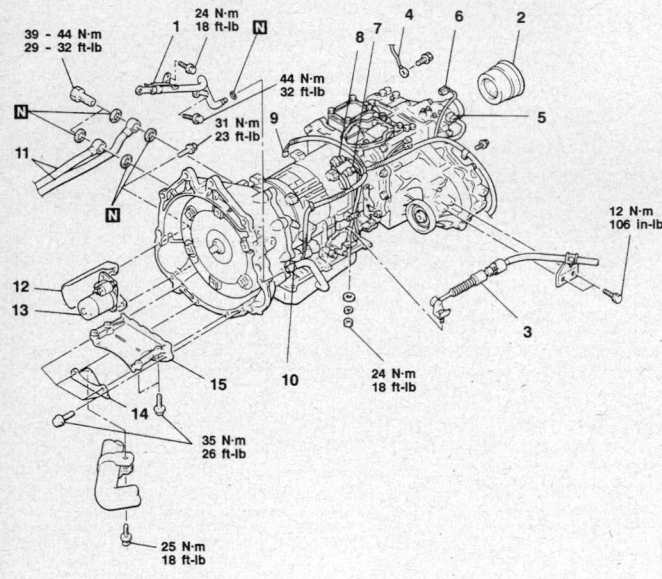

1. FILLER TUBE ASSEMBLY
2. DUST SHIELD COVER
3. TRANSMISSION CONTROL CABLE
4. GROUND CABLE CONNECTION
5. SPEED SENSOR CONNECTION
6. HIGH/LOW DETECTION SWITCH CONNECTION
7. PARK/NEUTRAL POSITION SWITCH CONNECTION
8. SOLENOID VALVE CONNECTION
9. OUTPUT SHAFT SPEED SENSOR CONNECTION
10. INPUT SHAFT SPEED SENSOR CONNECTION
11. OIL COOLER TUBE
12. STARTER COVER
13. STARTER MOTOR
14. EXHAUST PIPE BRACKET
15. TRANSMISSION STAY <3.0L>

Fig. 6 Transmission replacement (Part 1 of 2). V4A51 transmission

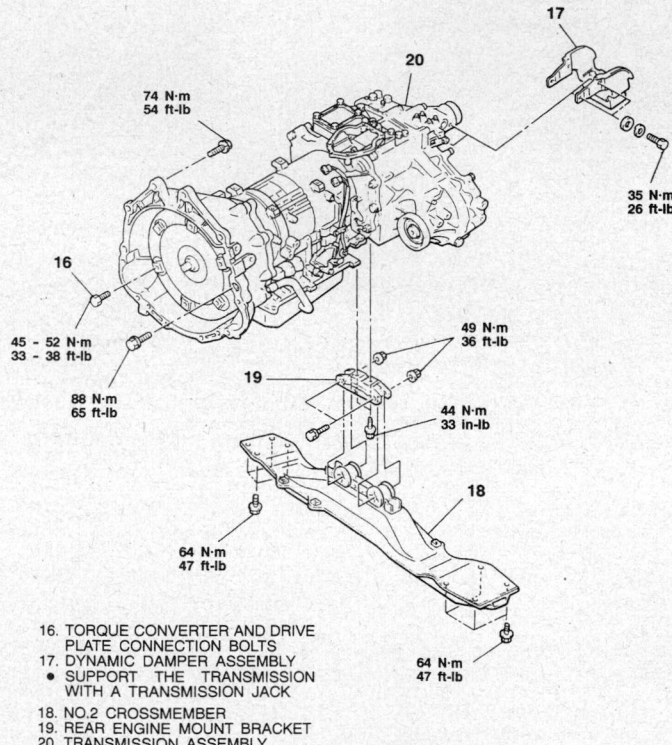

16. TORQUE CONVERTER AND DRIVE PLATE CONNECTION BOLTS
17. DYNAMIC DAMPER ASSEMBLY
• SUPPORT THE TRANSMISSION WITH A TRANSMISSION JACK
18. NO.2 CROSSMEMBER
19. REAR ENGINE MOUNT BRACKET
20. TRANSMISSION ASSEMBLY

Fig. 6 Transmission replacement (Part 2 of 2). V4A51 transmission

TIGHTENING SPECIFICATIONS

33-315

Year	Component	Torque/ Ft. Lbs.
1998–99	Air Breather Pipe Assembly	55
	Converter Housing To Transmission	35
	Cable Bracket	9
	Cable End Bracket	18
	Detent Spring Mounting	52①
	Dynamic Damper (V4A51)	26
	Exhaust Pipe Connection Bolt	18
	Entension Housing Mounting Bolt (R4A51)	35
	Filler Tube Assembly (Engine Side)	18
	Filler Tube Assembly (transmission Side)	32
	Indicator Assembly	13①
	Key Interlock Cable	9
	Lower Valve Body Mounting Bolt	8
	Lower Valve Body Cover	8
	Manual Control Lever Mounting Nut	16
	No. 2 Crossmember	47
	Oil Filter	52①
	Oil Pan Mounting Bolt	8
	Oil Pump	17
	Output Shaft Speed Sensor	8
	Output Shaft Support Mounting Bolt	17
	Park/Neutral Position Switch Mounting	8
	Rear Engine Mount Bracket	33
	Rear Engine Support Insulator	15–18
	Selector Lever Assembly	9
	Selector Lever To Bracket	9
	Shift Knob Attaching Screw	18①
	Shift Lock Cable	9
	Speedometer Sleeve Clamp (R4A51)	13
	Starter	23
	Stopper Plate	14
	Torque Converter & Drive Plate Connection Bolt	33–38
	Transmission Assembly (Engine To Transmission)	65
	Transmission Assembly (Transmission To Engine)	55
	Transmission Assembly To No. 2 Crossmember (R4A51)	16
	Transmission Assembly To No. 2 Crossmember (V4A51)	36
	Transmission Control Upper Lever	18
	Transmission Stay	26
	Transmission Oil Cooler	29–32
	Upper Valve Body Mounting Bolt	8
	Selector Lever Assembly	9
	Selector Lever To Bracket	9
	Shift Lock Cable	9
	Shift Boot Retainer Plate	44①
	Stopper Plate	14
	Shift Knob Attaching Screw	18①
	Transmission Control Upper lever	18

① — Inch lbs.

Front Wheel Drive Axles

INDEX

PRECAUTIONS

BATTERY GROUND CABLE

Prior to service, disconnect battery ground cable and isolate as required.

TROUBLESHOOTING

When troubleshooting front wheel drive vehicles, refer to **Fig. 1.**

DRIVESHAFT

REPLACE

DIAMANTE & 3000GT

1. Raise and support vehicle, then remove front wheel.
2. Remove dust cover, cotter pin and driveshaft nut.
3. Drain transmission oil.
4. Disconnect lower arm ball joint from knuckle, then remove stabilizer and strut bars from lower arm.
5. **On models with driveshaft center bearing,** remove bearing bracket attaching bolts.
6. **On all models,** insert suitable pry bar between transmission case and driveshaft, then pry driveshaft from transmission. **Do not pull on driveshaft and do not insert pry bar deep enough to damage oil seal.**
7. Using tool No. MB990767, or equivalent, remove driveshaft from hub.
8. Reverse procedure to install, noting the following:
   a. Ensure driveshaft washer is correctly installed.
   b. Lower vehicle to ground, then attach and adjust driveshaft nut. **Torque** to 144–188 ft. lbs.
   c. If cotter pin holes do not line up, tighten bolt, without exceeding **torque** of 188 ft. lbs., until holes line up.
   d. Install new cotter pin.
   e. Refill transaxle to proper level.

GALANT, ECLIPSE

1. Raise and support vehicle, then remove front wheel.
2. Remove cotter pin and driveshaft nut, noting the following:
   a. **Do not allow vehicle weight to rest upon wheel bearing unless absolutely necessary. If weight must be applied to bearing during removal, secure with tool No.**

Fig. 1 Front wheel drive troubleshooting chart

Symptom	Probable cause	Remedy
Vehicle pulls to one side	Seizure of drive shaft ball joint	Replace
	Abnormal wear, play or seizure of wheel bearing	Replace
	Malfunction of front suspension or steering	Adjust or replace
Vibration	Bend, damage or abnormal wear of drive shaft	Replace
	Play in drive shaft and hub serration	Replace
	Abnormal wear, play or seizure of wheel bearing	Replace
Shimmy	Improper wheel alignment	Adjust or replace
	Malfunction of front suspension or steering	Adjust or replace
Excessive noise	Broken boot, grease leakage	Replace, repack grease
	Bend, damage or abnormal wear of drive shaft	Replace
	Play of drive shaft and hub serration	Replace
	Abnormal wear, play or seizure of center bearing	Replace
	Abnormal wear, play or seizure of wheel bearing	Replace
	Loose wheel nut	Retighten
	Malfunction of front suspension and steering	Adjust or replace

MT3039100009000X

MB990998, or equivalent.
   b. Tool No. MB990767, or equivalent, can be used to prevent hub from rotating while nut is being removed.
3. Loosen, but do not remove, nut securing tie rod end to steering knuckle.
4. Using ball joint separator tool No. MB991113, or equivalent, separate tie rod end ball joint from steering knuckle. Support tool with a suitable cord to keep it in place during ball joint separation.
5. Separate damper fork from stabilizer link ball joint, then remove fork.
6. Using ball joint separator tool No. MB991113, or equivalent, separate lateral and compression lower arm ball joints from steering knuckle. Support tool with a suitable cord to keep it in place during ball joint separation.
7. **On Galant models,** use tool Nos. MB990241 and MB990767, or equivalents, to press driveshaft out of hub assembly.
8. **On all models,** use a suitable pry bar to separate driveshaft from transaxle case. **Do not insert pry bar farther than necessary to remove shaft, as oil seal may be damaged.**
9. Insert cover tool No. MB991461, or equivalent, into transaxle case driveshaft hole to prevent entry of foreign matter.
10. Reverse procedure to install, noting the following:
    a. Install driveshaft washer with con-

vex portion facing outward.
   b. Use tool No. MB990767, or equivalent, to secure hub and **torque** driveshaft nut to 144–188 ft. lbs.
   c. If cotter pin holes do not align, turn driveshaft nut until pin can be inserted. **Do not exceed maximum torque of 188 ft. lbs.**

MIRAGE

1. Raise and support vehicle, then remove front wheels.
2. Remove cotter pin, wheel bearing nut and washer.
3. Disconnect lower control arm ball joint from knuckle using tool No. MB991113, or equivalent.
4. Disconnect tie rod end from knuckle using tool No. MB991113, or equivalent.
5. Disconnect center bearing snap ring if equipped.
6. **On models without center bearing,** proceed as follows:
   a. Insert pry bar between transaxle case and driveshaft, then pry driveshaft from transaxle. **Do not pull on driveshaft, or insert pry bar deep enough to damage oil seal.**
   b. Remove driveshaft from hub using tool No. MB990241-01, or equivalent, then the circlip from driveshaft.
7. **On models with center bearing,** proceed as follows:

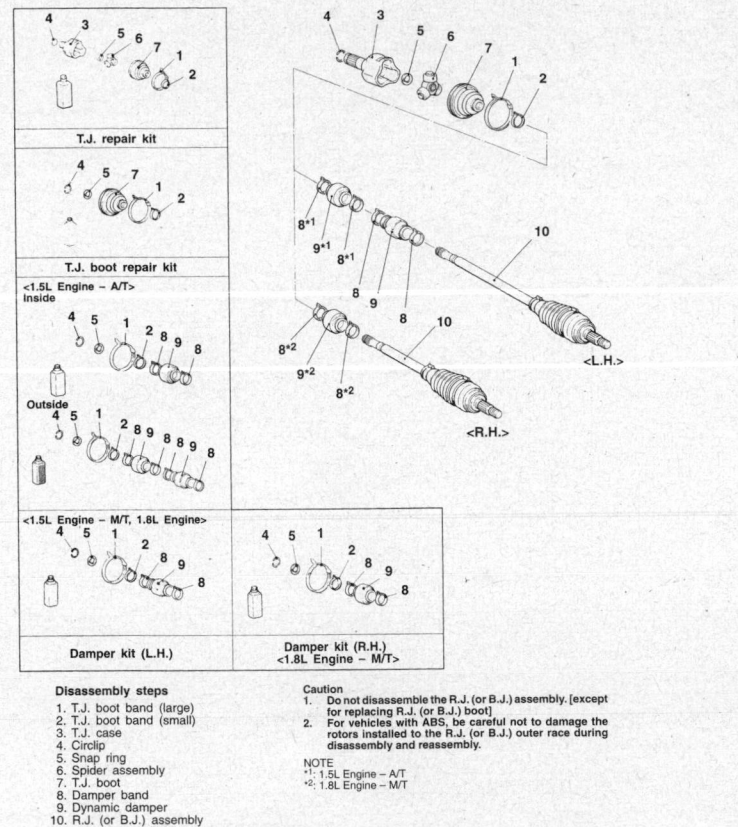

T.J. repair kit

T.J. boot repair kit

<1.5L Engine – A/T>
Inside

Outside

<1.5L Engine – M/T, 1.8L Engine>

Damper kit (L.H.)

Damper kit (R.H.)
<1.8L Engine – M/T>

Disassembly steps
1. T.J. boot band (large)
2. T.J. boot band (small)
3. T.J. case
4. Circlip
5. Snap ring
6. Spider assembly
7. T.J. boot
8. Damper band
9. Dynamic damper
10. R.J. (or B.J.) assembly

Caution
1. Do not disassemble the R.J. (or B.J.) assembly. [except for replacing R.J. (or B.J.) boot]
2. For vehicles with ABS, be careful not to damage the rotors installed to the R.J. (or B.J.) outer race during disassembly and reassembly.

NOTE
*1: 1.5L Engine – A/T
*2: 1.8L Engine – M/T

MT3039300013000X

Fig. 2 Exploded view of driveshaft. 1996 Mirage

T.J. boot repair kit

T.J. repair kit

R.J. boot repair kit

Disassembly steps
1. T.J. boot band (large)
2. T.J. boot band (small)
3. T.J. case
4. Circlip
5. Snap ring
6. Spider assembly
7. T.J. boot
8. Damper band
9. Dynamic damper
10. R.J. assembly
11. R.J. boot band (small)
12. R.J. boot band (large)
13. R.J. boot
14. Front axle shim

Caution
1. Never disassemble the R.J. assembly except when replacing the R.J. boot.
2. On vehicles with ABS, be sure not to damage the rotor attached to the R.J. outer race.

MT3039900074000X

Fig. 3 Exploded view of driveshaft. 1997–99 Mirage

a. Remove driveshaft from transaxle by lightly tapping driveshaft outer race with a plastic hammer. **Do not pull on driveshaft or insert pry bar between transaxle case and driveshaft.**

b. Remove driveshaft from hub by lightly tapping driveshaft end with plastic hammer.

c. Remove center bearing bracket attaching bolts, then the center bearing bracket and spacers.

8. **On all models,** reverse procedure to install, noting the following:

a. **On models with center bearing,** press in driveshaft until center bearing comes in contact with center bearing bracket, then install snap ring into center bearing bracket.

b. **On all models,** lower vehicle to ground, then attach and adjust driveshaft nut. **Torque** nut to 144–188 ft. lbs.

c. If cotter pin hole does not line up, tighten bolt without exceeding **torque** of 188 ft. lbs., until hole lines up.

MONTERO & MONTERO SPORT

1. Raise and support vehicle, then remove wheel.
2. Remove ABS wheel speed sensor.
3. Remove caliper assembly without disconnecting brake hose. Support cali-

per out of way. Do not strain brake hose.

4. Remove freewheeling hub cover assembly, then the snap ring from driveshaft.

5. Remove knuckle and front hub assembly as an assembly.

6. Pull left driveshaft out of differential carrier assembly, without damaging oil seal.

7. Remove right driveshaft to differential carrier inner shaft attaching bolts, then pull driveshaft from differential assembly.

8. Reverse procedure to install, noting the following:

a. Install left driveshaft into front differential carrier using a plastic hammer.

b. **Torque** right driveshaft to inner shaft attaching bolts to 36–43 ft. lbs.

PICKUP

1. Raise and support vehicle, then remove wheel.

2. Remove caliper assembly without disconnecting brake hose. Support caliper out of way. Do not strain brake hose.

3. Remove freewheeling hub cover assembly and remove snap ring from driveshaft.

4. Remove knuckle and front hub assembly.

5. Pull left driveshaft out of differential

carrier assembly without damaging oil seal.

6. Using suitable jack, raise the lower arm.

7. Remove upper mounting nuts from right shock absorber, then the shock absorber from arm post of side frame. **Do not lower jack while disconnecting shock absorber or while it is disconnected. Do not remove jack until upper part of shock absorber has been reconnected to arm post of side frame.**

8. Detach right driveshaft from inner shaft assembly, then remove right driveshaft.

9. Using tool Nos. MB990211 and MB990906, or equivalents, pull inner shaft out of differential carrier without damaging oil seal.

10. Using screwdriver, remove dust seal from housing tube assembly.

11. Reverse procedure to install, noting the following:

a. **Torque** upper knuckle to ball joint bolts to 44–65 ft. lbs., lower knuckle at ball joints to 87–130 ft. lbs. and freewheeling hub assembly bolts to 8–10 ft. lbs.

b. Apply multi-purpose grease to lip of dust seal; then, using tool Nos. MB990938 and MB990985, or equivalents, drive dust seal into housing tube end.

c. Using tool Nos. MB990211 and MB990906, or equivalents, drive

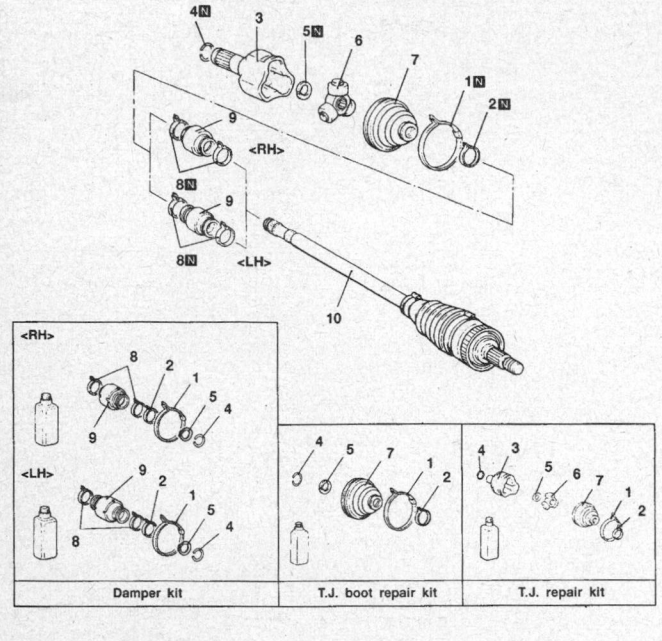

Fig. 4 Exploded view of driveshaft. 1996–98 Galant

Disassembly steps
1. T.J. boot band (large)
2. T.J. boot band (small)
3. T.J. case
4. Circlip
5. Snap ring
6. Spider assembly
7. T.J. boot
8. Damper band
9. Dynamic damper
10. B.J. assembly

Caution
Do not disassemble the B.J. assembly.

MT3039400058000X

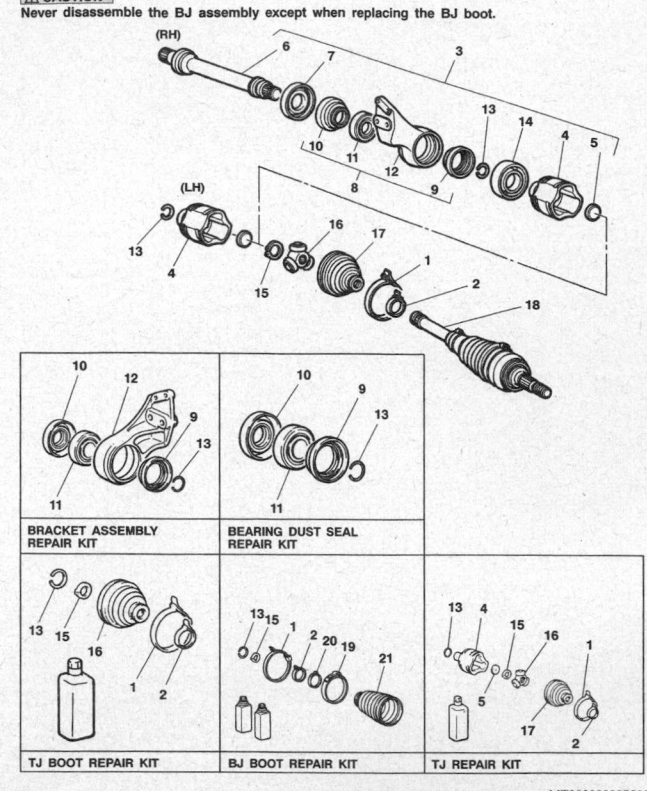

> **⚠ CAUTION**
> Never disassemble the BJ assembly except when replacing the BJ boot.

Fig. 5 Exploded view of driveshaft. 1999 Galant

MT3039900075000X

DRIVESHAFT SERVICE
FWD MODELS
ECLIPSE, GALANT & MIRAGE

Refer to **Figs. 2 through 6** when disassembling the front driveshafts, noting the following:
1. Wrap masking tape on splined end of driveshaft prior to removing joint boot.
2. **On models equipped with a Double Offset Joint (DOJ),** proceed as follows:

inner shaft assembly into differential carrier assembly. Do not damage oil seal.
d. Replace circlip which is attached to Birfield Joint (BJ) side spline with new one.
e. Install right driveshaft to inner shaft assembly, then **torque** bolts to 37–43 ft. lbs.
f. Attach shock absorber to arm post of side frame by installing double nuts. Install first nut so that distance between base of nut and end of strut is .81 inch, then **torque** second nut to 9–13 ft. lbs.
g. Using plastic mallet, drive left driveshaft into differential carrier assembly. Do not damage oil seal.
h. Install new circlip on BJ side spline.
i. Mount knuckle and front hub assembly, then adjust driveshaft axial play as necessary.

a. Make alignment marks on DOJ inner race and cage.
b. Remove DOJ cage from inner race by turning cage in a clockwise direction looking at end of driveshaft.
c. Using a suitable brass drift, tap DOJ inner race off driveshaft.
3. **On all models,** reverse procedure to assemble, noting the following:
a. Align mating marks made during disassemble.
b. When installing joint boots, ensure distance between clamps is as shown in **Fig. 7.**
c. Install dynamic damper, if equipped at distance from outer joint shown in **Fig. 8.**

DIAMANTE & 3000GT

Refer to **Fig. 9** when disassembling the front driveshafts, noting the following:
1. Press off inner shaft using suitable press and bearing remover tool Nos. MB991248 or MD998801, or equivalent.
2. Remove center bearing using bearing remover tool Nos. MB990938 and MB990930, or equivalent.
3. Wrap masking tape on splined end of driveshaft prior to removing joint boot.
4. Reverse procedure to assemble, noting the following:
a. Install center bearing using bearing installation tool Nos. MB990938 and MB990932, or equivalent.
b. Apply grease to rear surface of all dust seals.

c. Install oil seals using oil seal installer tool No. MB990890, or equivalent.
d. Install inner shaft using bearing installation tool No. MB991172, or equivalent.
e. Assemble TJ case and inner shaft using shaft installation tool Nos. MB991248 or MD998801, or equivalent.
f. When installing joint boots ensure distance between clamps is as shown in **Fig. 7.**

AWD MODELS
ECLIPSE

Refer to **Fig. 10** when disassembling the front driveshafts, noting the following:
1. Remove inner driveshaft using bearing remover tool Nos. MB991248 and MD998801, or equivalents.
2. Remove center bearing using bearing remover tool No. MB990938-01, or equivalent.
3. Reverse procedure to assemble, noting the following:
a. Install center bearing using bearing installation tool No. MB990938-01, or equivalent.
b. Apply grease to all dust seals.
c. Install dust seals using seal installation tool No. MB990938-01, or equivalent.
d. Assemble TJ case and inner shaft using shaft installation tool No. MB991248, or equivalent.
e. When installing joint boots, ensure

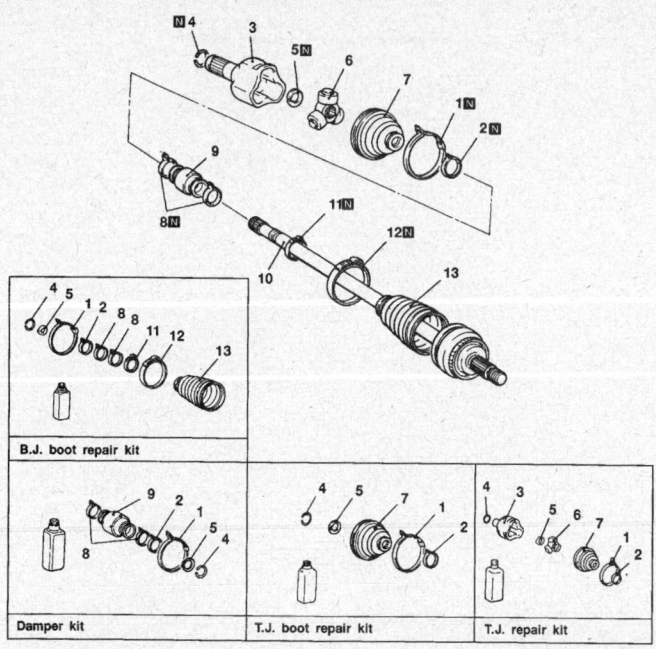

B.J. boot repair kit

Damper kit

T.J. boot repair kit

T.J. repair kit

Disassembly steps
1. T.J. boot band (large)
2. T.J. boot band (small)
3. T.J. case
4. Circlip
5. Snap ring
6. Spider assembly
7. T.J. boot
8. Damper band
9. Dynamic damper

10. B.J. assembly
11. B.J. boot band (small)
12. B.J. boot band (large)
13. B.J. boot

Caution
Do not disassemble the B.J. assembly except replacement of the B.J. boot.

MT3039500059000X

Fig. 6 Exploded view of driveshaft. Eclipse

Engine	Drive Joint Type	Distance, Inch	
		LH Driveshaft	RH Driveshaft
DIAMANTE			
All	All	2.83–3.07	2.83–3.07
ECLIPSE			
1.8L	TJ & BJ	2.95	3.35
2.0L & 2.4L	TJ & BJ	3.15	3.15
GALANT			
All	TJ & RJ	3.23	3.35
All	TJ & BJ	3.15	3.15
MIRAGE			
All	All	3.35	3.35
3000GT			
All	All	2.95	2.95

TJ: Tripod Joint RJ: Rzeppa Joint BJ: Birfield Joint

Fig. 7 Boot clamp installation dimension chart

Model	Year	Engine	Dimension	
			LH Driveshaft	RH Driveshaft
Eclipse	1996–99	2.0L Non-Turbo①	—	14.72
		2.0L Non-Turbo②	7.64	14.72
		2.0L Turbo	14.72	—
		2.4L	14.37	8.70
Galant	1996–98	2.4L	14.37	8.70
Mirage	1996–99	1.5L	13.82	13.82
		1.8L	14.37	7.89

① — Automatic transaxle.
② — Manual transaxle.

Fig. 8 Dynamic damper installation dimension

distance between clamps is 3.35 inches.

3000GT

Refer to the "FWD Models" section when servicing the front driveshaft on these models.

4WD MODELS

DISASSEMBLE
Driveshaft

1. Using a suitable screwdriver, remove boot bands, **Fig. 11.**
2. Use screwdriver to remove circlip from Double Offset Joint (DOJ) outer race.
3. Remove driveshaft from DOJ outer race, then wipe away grease.
4. Using screwdriver, remove balls from DOJ cage.
5. Remove DOJ cage from DOJ inner race in direction of Birfield Joint (BJ) by turning DOJ cage 30° from position at which balls were removed.
6. Using pliers, remove snap ring from driveshaft, then the DOJ inner race from driveshaft.
7. Remove circlip from driveshaft.
8. Remove DOJ and BJ boots from driveshaft. Wrap vinyl tape around spline on DOJ side of driveshaft so that boots are not damaged when removed.
9. Using a screwdriver, remove dust cover.
10. Inspect all parts and replace as necessary. **Do not disassemble BJ.**

Inner Shaft

1. Using a suitable hammer, bend down outer circumference of dust cover.
2. Install tool No. MB990560, or equivalent, then press bearing from shaft.
3. Using a suitable screwdriver, remove dust cover.
4. Inspect all parts and replace as necessary.

ASSEMBLE
Inner Shaft

1. Using a suitable pipe with an outside diameter of 2.95 inches and metal thickness of .16 inch, press dust cover onto inner shaft.
2. Using tool No. MB990560, equivalent, press bearing onto shaft.

Driveshaft

1. Using a suitable pipe with an outside diameter of 2.71 inches and metal thickness of .09 inch, press dust cover onto Birfield Joint (BJ) side.
2. Using a suitable pipe with an outside diameter of 2.24 inches and metal thickness of .24 inch, press dust cover

onto Double Offset Joint (DOJ) side.
3. Wrap vinyl tape around driveshaft splines to prevent damage to boots.
4. Using grease supplied with repair kit, lubricate driveshaft.
5. Install BJ boot, new boot bands, DOJ boot on driveshaft, then BJ in that order. **BJ and DOJ boots are of different size and shape and must be installed correctly.**
6. Install DOJ cage, small diameter side first, onto driveshaft, then install circlip on driveshaft.
7. Install DOJ inner race onto driveshaft and secure with snap ring.
8. Using grease supplied with repair kit, lubricate DOJ inner race and DOJ cage, then fit balls into cage.
9. Using grease supplied with repair kit, apply 1.8–2.8 ounces to DOJ outer race, then install on driveshaft.
10. Apply an additional 1.8–2.5 ounces of grease to DOJ outer race and install circlip.
11. Using grease supplied with repair kit, lubricate BJ side, then install BJ boot.
12. Ensure distance of 3.1 inches exists between boot bands, then tighten bands securely.

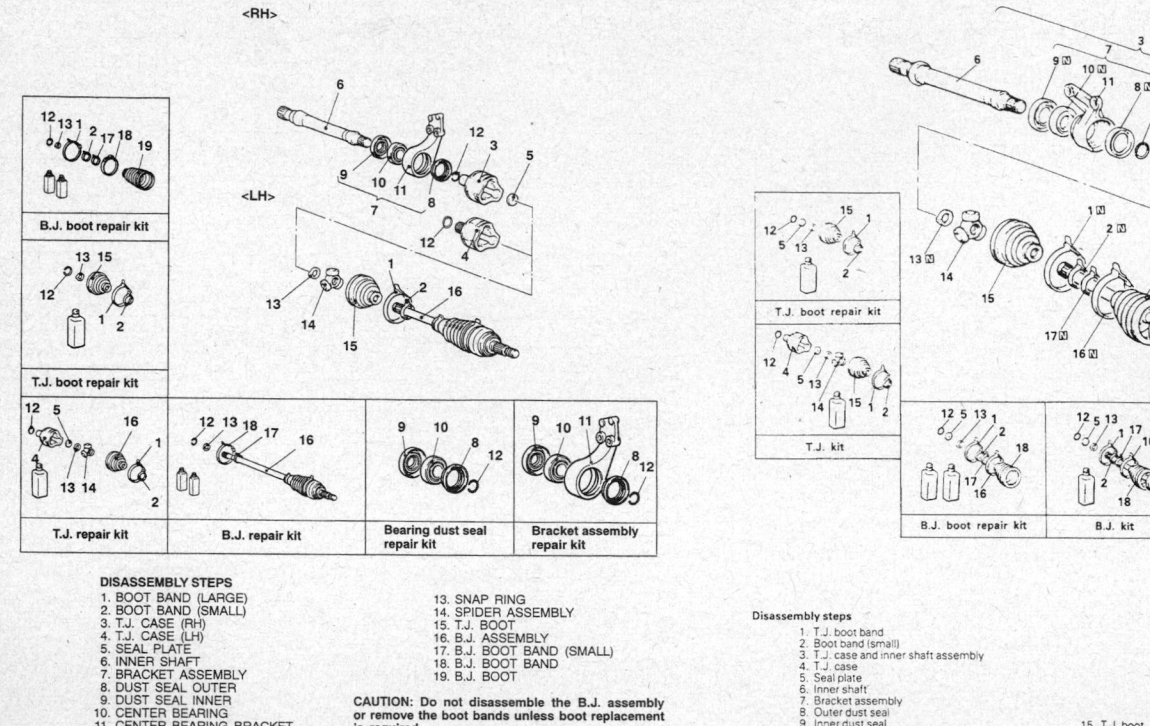

<RH>

<LH>

B.J. boot repair kit

T.J. boot repair kit

T.J. repair kit

B.J. repair kit

Bearing dust seal repair kit

Bracket assembly repair kit

DISASSEMBLY STEPS
1. BOOT BAND (LARGE)
2. BOOT BAND (SMALL)
3. T.J. CASE (RH)
4. T.J. CASE (LH)
5. SEAL PLATE
6. INNER SHAFT
7. BRACKET ASSEMBLY
8. DUST SEAL OUTER
9. DUST SEAL INNER
10. CENTER BEARING
11. CENTER BEARING BRACKET
12. CIRCLIP

13. SNAP RING
14. SPIDER ASSEMBLY
15. T.J. BOOT
16. B.J. ASSEMBLY
17. B.J. BOOT BAND (SMALL)
18. B.J. BOOT BAND
19. B.J. BOOT

CAUTION: Do not disassemble the B.J. assembly or remove the boot bands unless boot replacement is required.

MT3039900076000X

Fig. 9   Exploded view of front driveshaft assembly. Diamante & 3000GT FWD

T.J. boot repair kit

T.J. kit

B.J. boot repair kit

B.J. kit

Bearing dust seal kit

Bracket assembly kit

Disassembly steps
1. T.J. boot band
2. Boot band (small)
3. T.J. case and inner shaft assembly
4. T.J. case
5. Seal plate
6. Inner shaft
7. Bracket assembly
8. Outer dust seal
9. Inner dust seal
10. Center bearing
11. Center bearing bracket
12. Circlip
13. Snap ring
14. Spider assembly

15. T.J. boot
16. B.J. boot band
17. Boot band (small)
18. B.J. boot
19. B.J. assembly
20. Dust cover

MT3039100017000X

Fig. 10   Exploded view of front driveshaft. Eclipse

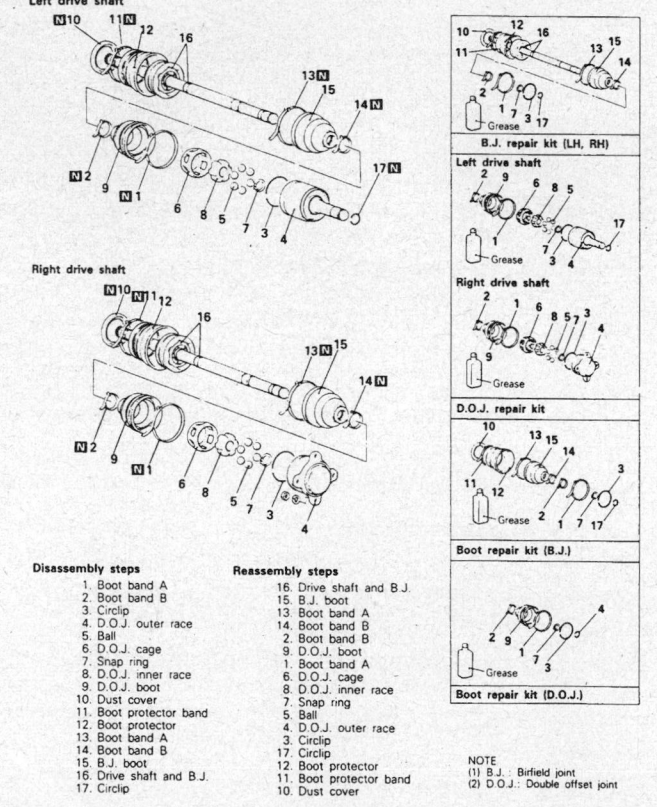

Left drive shaft

Right drive shaft

Disassembly steps
1. Boot band A
2. Boot band B
3. Circlip
4. D.O.J. outer race
5. Ball
6. D.O.J. cage
7. Snap ring
8. D.O.J. inner race
9. D.O.J. boot
10. Dust cover
11. Boot protector band
12. Boot protector
13. Boot band A
14. Boot band B
15. B.J. boot
16. Drive shaft and B.J.
17. Circlip

Reassembly steps
16. Drive shaft and B.J.
15. B.J. boot
13. Boot band A
14. Boot band B
2. Boot band B
9. D.O.J. boot
1. Boot band A
6. D.O.J. cage
8. D.O.J. inner race
7. Snap ring
5. Ball
4. D.O.J. outer race
3. Circlip
17. Circlip
12. Boot protector
11. Boot protector band
10. Dust cover

B.J. repair kit (LH, RH)

Left drive shaft

Right drive shaft

D.O.J. repair kit

Boot repair kit (B.J.)

Boot repair kit (D.O.J.)

NOTE
(1) B.J. : Birfield joint
(2) D.O.J. : Double offset joint

MT3039100020000X

Fig. 11   Exploded view of front driveshaft. Montero, Montero Sport & Pickup

All-Wheel Drive Systems

NOTE: Refer To The "Front Wheel Drive Axles" Section For Front Driveshaft Service Procedures.

INDEX

DESCRIPTION

The All-Wheel Drive (AWD) system is based upon a front wheel drive design. A transversely mounted transaxle delivers torque to front driveshafts, as well as to an integral transfer assembly. The transfer, in turn, operates the rear wheels via a propeller shaft and rear axle differential.

DRIVESHAFT

REPLACE

3000GT

Replace driveshaft in numbered sequence shown in **Fig. 1,** noting the following:

1. Using a suitable pry bar, remove driveshaft from differential carrier, **Fig. 2.**
2. Install driveshaft oil seal using oil seal installer tool Nos. MB990938-01 and MB991115, or equivalents.
3. When installing driveshaft, ensure splines of driveshaft do not damage oil seal lip.

ECLIPSE

1. Raise and support vehicle, then remove rear wheel.
2. Remove driveshaft in numbered sequence shown, **Fig. 3,** noting the following:
   a. Use tool No. MB990767, or equivalent, to prevent hub from turning while removing driveshaft nut.
   b. Remove shaft from vehicle by pushing lower portion of knuckle outward while prying shaft away from differential carrier with a suitable pry bar.
   c. Insert tool No. MB991460, or equivalent, into carrier to prevent entry of foreign matter while driveshaft is removed.
   d. If both shafts are to be removed, distinguish lefthand from righthand side for installation reference.
3. Reverse numbered sequence to install, noting the following:
   a. Do not allow driveshaft splines to

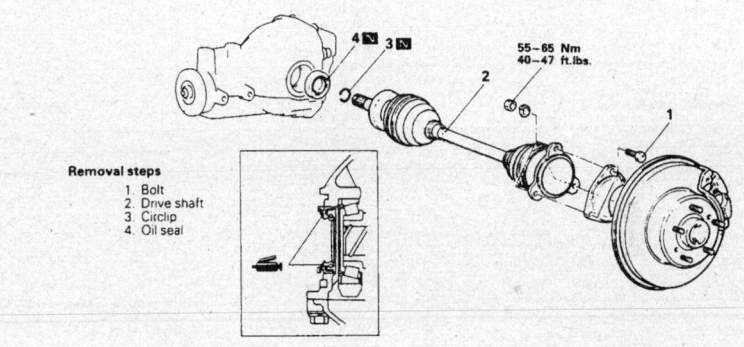

Fig. 1   Driveshaft replacement. 3000GT

Removal steps
1. Bolt
2. Drive shaft
3. Circlip
4. Oil seal

55~65 Nm
40~47 ft.lbs.

MT3039100021000X

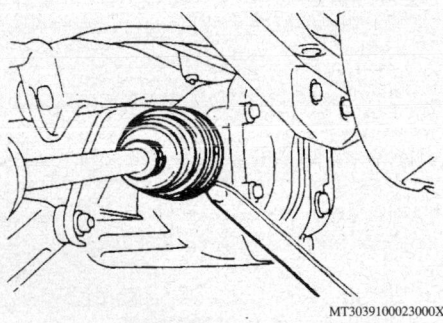

Fig. 2   Driveshaft separation. 3000GT

MT3039100023000X

damage differential carrier oil seal during installation.
   b. Tighten driveshaft nut using tool No. MB990767, or equivalent. If cotter pin holes do not align, tighten nut until pin can be inserted. **Do not exceed torque of 188 ft. lbs.**
   c. Bleed brake system as outlined in "Hydraulic Brake Systems" section.
   d. Adjust parking brake as outlined in "Disc Brakes " or "Drum Brakes" section.

DRIVESHAFT SERVICE

Disassemble driveshaft in numbered sequence shown in **Fig. 4,** noting the following:

1. Remove snap ring from driveshaft.
2. Remove spider assembly from driveshaft. **Do not disassemble spider assembly. If Tripod Joint (TJ) of driveshaft assembly is bent, joint may be damaged.**
3. Clean spider assembly.
4. Wrap tape around splines of driveshaft so boot are not damaged when removed.
5. Remove TJ and Birfield Joint (BJ) boots off driveshaft.
6. Wipe grease off BJ. **Do not disassemble.**
7. Reverse numbered sequence to assemble, noting the following:
   a. Wrap tape around splines of driveshaft.
   b. Install BJ boot, bands, TJ boot and bands in that sequence.
   c. Fill inside of BJ and BJ boot with special grease.
   d. Secure BJ boot bands ensuring

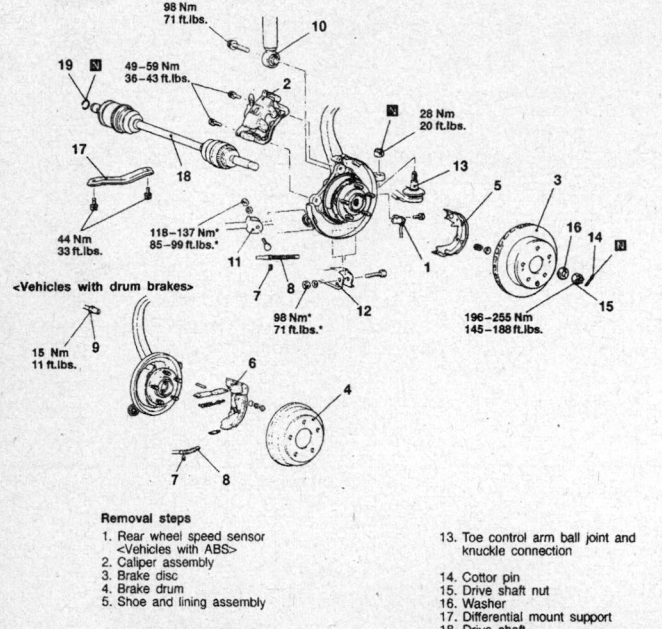

Removal steps
1. Rear wheel speed sensor <Vehicles with ABS>
2. Caliper assembly
3. Brake disc
4. Brake drum
5. Shoe and lining assembly

6. Shoe and lever assembly
7. Clip
8. Parking brake cable
9. Brake pipe connection
10. Shock absorber connection
11. Trailing arm connection
12. Lower arm connection

13. Toe control arm ball joint and knuckle connection
14. Cotter pin
15. Drive shaft nut
16. Washer
17. Differential mount support
18. Drive shaft
19. Circlip

Caution
1. For vehicles with ABS, be careful not to damage the drive shaft rotor.
2. *: Indicates parts which should be temporarily tightened, and then fully tightened with the vehicle on the ground in the unladen condition.

MT3039500061000X

Fig. 3   Driveshaft replacement. Eclipse

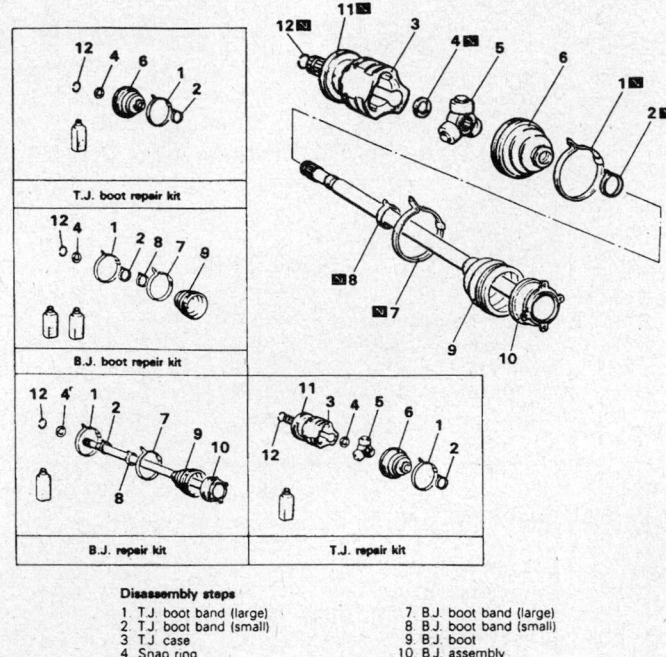

Disassembly steps
1. T.J. boot band (large)
2. T.J. boot band (small)
3. T.J. case
4. Snap ring
5. Spider assembly
6. T.J. boot

7. B.J. boot band (large)
8. B.J. boot band (small)
9. B.J. boot
10. B.J. assembly
11. Dust cover
12. Circlip

MT3039200028000X

Fig. 4   Driveshaft assembly service

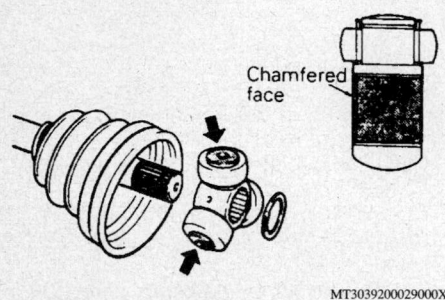

MT3039200029000X

Fig. 5   Spider assembly installation

that driveshaft is at 0° angle to the BJ.
e. Apply special grease to the spider assembly.
f. Install spider assembly with chamfered spline end first, **Fig. 5**.
g. Set TJ boot bands 3.23–3.47 inches apart in order to adjust amount of air inside TJ boot then tighten TJ boot band securely.

DIFFERENTIAL SERVICE

INSPECTION BEFORE DISASSEMBLE

With differential carrier assembly properly supported, perform the following inspections:
1. Measure final drive gear backlash as follows:
   a. With drive pinion locked into place, measure final drive gear backlash using a suitable dial indicator, **Fig. 6.**
   b. Measure at four points or more in

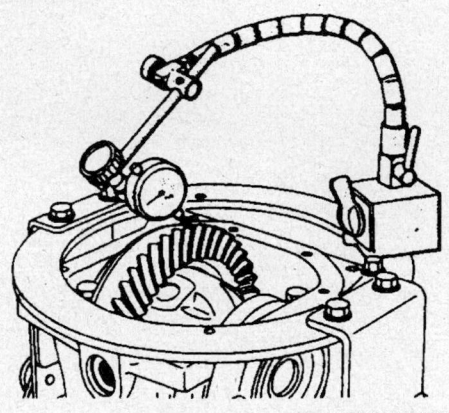

MT3019100006000X

Fig. 6   Final drive gear backlash measurement

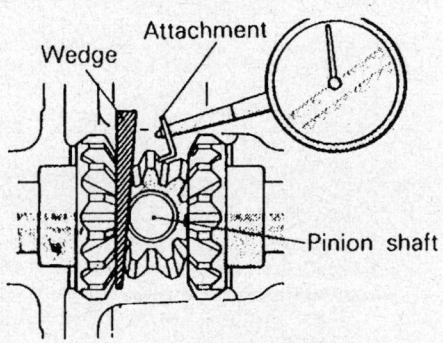

MT3019100008000X

Fig. 8   Differential gear backlash measurement

the circumference on the drive gear and ensure backlash is .004–.006 inch.

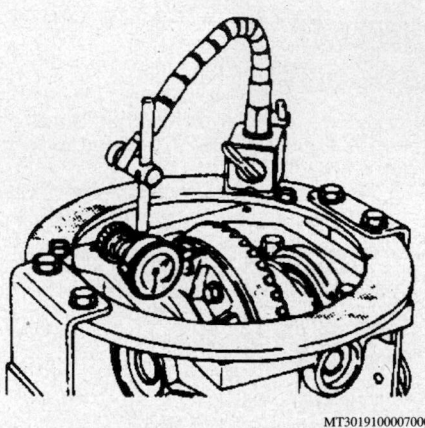

MT3019100007000X

Fig. 7   Drive gear runout measurement

2. Measure gear runout as follows:
   a. Measure drive gear runout at the shoulder on reverse side of drive gear, **Fig. 7**.
   b. Ensure runout is a maximum of .002 inch.
3. Measure differential gear backlash as follows:
   a. While locking side gear with wedge, measure differential gear backlash with a suitable dial indicator on pinion gear, **Fig. 8**.
   b. Ensure backlash is within the 0–.003 inch limit.
4. Inspect final drive gear tooth contact as follows:
   a. Apply a thin, uniform coat of machine blue to both surfaces of the drive gear teeth.
   b. Insert a brass rod between differential carrier and differential case, then rotate companion flange by

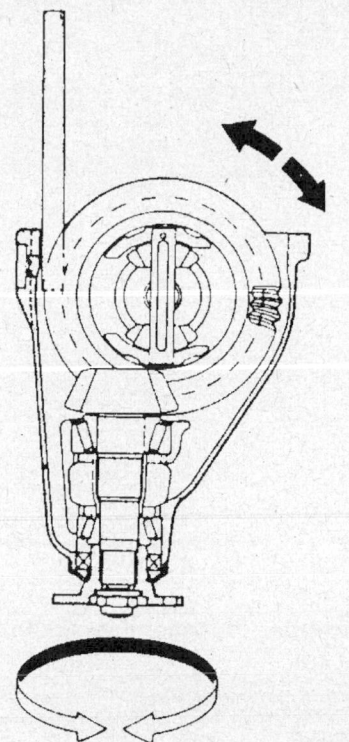

MT3019100009000X

Fig. 9　Tooth contact inspection

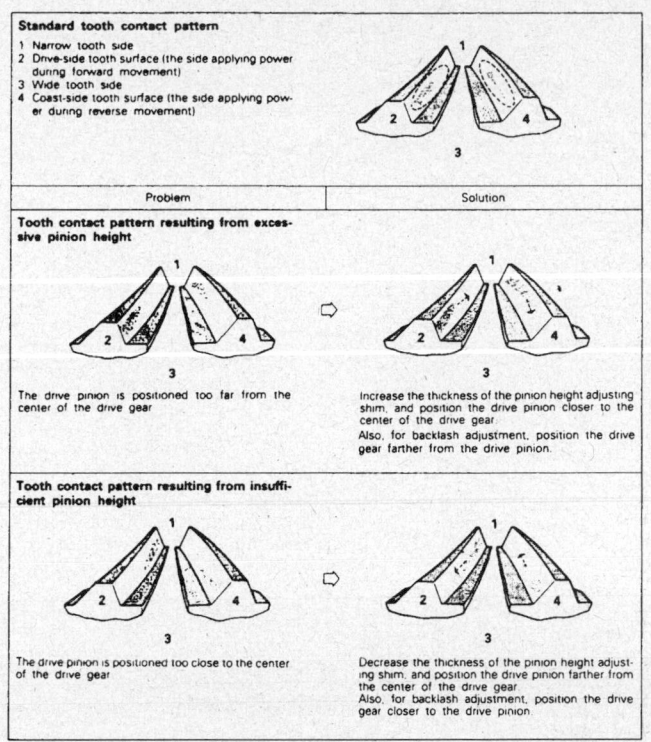

MT3019100010000X

Fig. 10　Differential carrier tooth contact

hand once in each direction while applying a load to the drive gear, so that revolution **torque** of approximately 28–32 inch lbs. is applied to drive pinion, **Fig. 9.**

c. Check tooth contact condition of drive gear and pinion, **Fig. 10.**

DISASSEMBLE

Disassemble differential assembly in numbered sequence shown in **Figs. 11 and 12,** noting the following:

1. **On Eclipse models,** proceed as follows:
   a. Slowly and carefully pry out differential case assembly using hammer handles, **Fig. 13. When removing differential case assembly, ensure side bearing outer race is not dropped. Keep right and left side bearing separate.**
   b. Place nut on top of differential case, then use removal tool, **Fig. 14,** to remove side bearing inner race.
   c. **On all models,** scribe alignment marks on differential case and drive gear. Loosen drive gear bolts in diagonal sequence to remove drive gear.
   d. Drive out lockpin with a punch and remove pinion gears and washers, side gears and spacers.
   e. Using end yoke holder tool No. MB990850, or equivalent, remove companion flange self-locking nut.
   f. Scribe alignment marks on drive pinion and companion flange. Remove out drive pinion together with drive pinion spacer and shims. **Marks should not be made on**

contact surfaces of companion flange and shaft.
   g. Pull out drive pinion bearing inner races by using insert tool, pinion carrier bearing puller tool, and side bearing cup remover step plate tool, or equivalent.
   h. Drive out drive pinion front and rear bearing from gear carrier.

2. **On 3000GT models,** proceed as follows:
   a. Using spanner wrench tool No. MB991367 and pin tool No. MB991385, or equivalents, remove side bearing nut.
   b. Using a suitable press, push differential case until it is pressed against the carrier.
   c. Remove differential case from press. Insert two spacers in diagonally opposite positions between side bearing outer race to be removed and inner race. Using a press, remove outer race. **Do not allow side bearing to drop. Keep right and left bearings separate. Use a spacer 1.18 inches long, .39 inch wide and .04–.08 inch high made of copper to prevent damage to bearings.**
   d. Pull out side bearing inner races using insert tool No. MT303173, pinion carrier bearing puller tool No. MB990339-01 and side bearing cup remover step plate tool No. MB990811-01, or equivalents, **Fig. 15.**
   e. Scribe alignment marks on differential case and drive gear. Loosen drive gear bolts in diagonal sequence to remove drive gear.

f. Using end yoke holder tool No. MB990850, or equivalent, remove companion flange self-locking nut.
   g. Scribe alignment marks on drive pinion and companion flange. Remove out drive pinion together with drive pinion spacer and shims. **Marks should not be made on contact surfaces of companion flange and shaft.**
   h. Pull out drive pinion bearing inner races by using insert tool, pinion carrier bearing puller tool, and side bearing cup remover step plate tool, or equivalent.
   i. Drive out drive pinion front and rear bearing from gear carrier.

ASSEMBLE

Assemble differential carrier in numbered sequence shown in **Figs. 16 and 17,** noting the following:

1. **On Eclipse models,** apply grease to oil seal lip; then, using oil seal installer tool No. MB991115 and handle tool No. MB990938-01, or equivalents, press fit oil seal until it is flush with end of gear carrier.

2. **On 3000GT models with 4WS,** tap spring pin into differential case to position shown in **Fig. 18,** before press fitting rear wheel oil pump drive gear. Notch on spring should be in position shown.

3. **On 3000GT models,** with beveled part of rear wheel oil pump drive gear at inner side, press in drive gear, using rear suspension bushing base tool No. MB990890-01, or equivalent, until drive gear contacts end surface of differential case. Ensure drive gear and

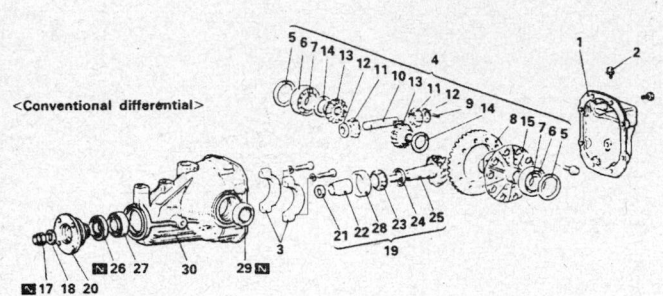

<Conventional differential>

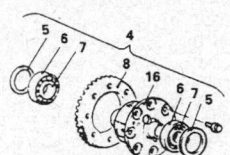

<Limited slip differential>

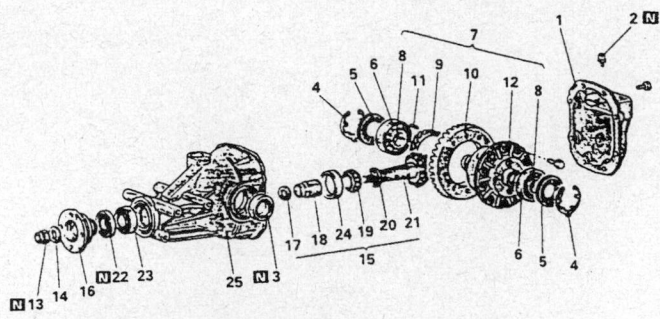

Disassembly steps

1. Differential cover assembly
2. Vent plug
3. Oil seal
4. Snap ring
5. Side bearing nut
6. Side bearing outer race
7. Differential case assembly
8. Side bearing inner race
9. Drive gear (for 4WS)
10. Drive gear
11. Spring pin (for 4WS)
12. LSD case
13. Self-locking nut
14. Washer

15. Drive pinion assembly
16. Companion flange
17. Drive pinion front shim (for preload adjustment)
18. Drive pinion spacer
19. Drive pinion rear bearing inner race
20. Drive pinion rear shim (for pinion height adjustment)
21. Drive pinion
22. Oil seal
23. Drive pinion front bearing
24. Drive pinion rear bearing outer race
25. Differential carrier

MT3019100012000X

Fig. 12 Rear differential disassemble. 3000GT

Disassembly steps

1. Differential cover
2. Vent plug
3. Bearing caps
4. Differential case assembly
5. Side bearing spacers
6. Side bearing outer race
7. Side bearing inner race
8. Drive gear
9. Lock pin
10. Pinion shaft
11. Pinion gears
12. Pinion washers
13. Side gears
14. Side gear spacers
15. Differential case
16. Limited slip differential case assembly
17. Self-locking nut
18. Washer
19. Drive pinion assembly

20. Companion flange
21. Drive pinion front shim (for preload adjustment)
22. Drive pinion spacer
23. Drive pinion rear bearing inner race
24. Drive pinion rear shim (for pinion height adjustment)
25. Drive pinion
26. Oil seal
27. Drive pinion front bearing
28. Drive pinion rear bearing outer race
29. Oil seal
30. Gear carrier

MT3019100011000X

Fig. 11 Rear differential disassemble. Eclipse

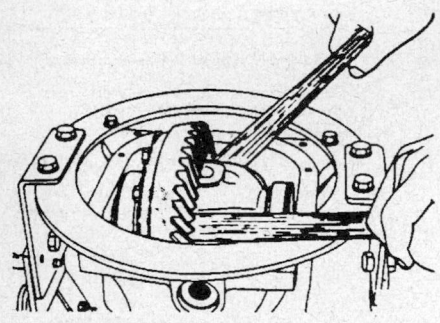

MT3019100013000X

Fig. 13 Differential case replacement. Eclipse

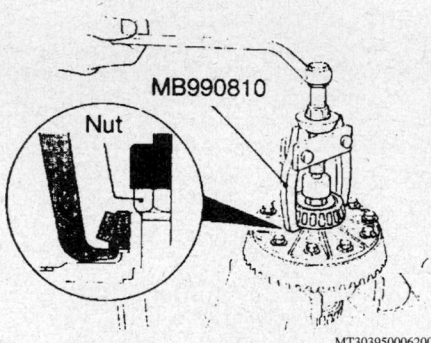

MT3039500062000X

Fig. 14 Side bearing inner race removal. Eclipse

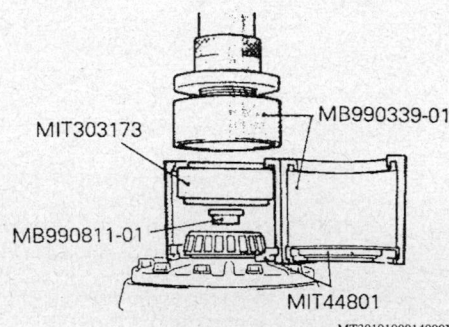

MT3019100014000X

Fig. 15 Side bearing inner race removal. 3000GT

spring pin are flush.

4. **On 3000GT models,** press fit drive pinion rear and front bearing outer races onto gear carrier using handle tool and bearing and oil seal installer set tool No. MB990925, or equivalent. **Use care not to press in outer race at an angle.**

5. **On Eclipse models,** press fit drive pinion front bearing outer race using tool Nos. MB990932 and MB990938, or equivalents, and rear bearing outer race using tool Nos. MB990935 and MB990938, or equivalents.

6. **On 3000GT models,** adjust pinion height as follows:
   a. Install special tools as shown in **Fig. 19.**
   b. Tighten handle of tool until the standard drive pinion turning torque

value shown in **Figs. 20 and 21** is obtained.
   c. Measure drive pinion turning torque without oil seal installed.
   d. Position gauge tube tool No. MB990392-01, or equivalent, in side bearing seat of gear carrier, then select a drive pinion rear shim of thickness which corresponds to gap between special tools.
   e. Install selected shim on drive pinion and press fit rear bearing inner race using bearing installer tool No. MT215013, or equivalent.

7. **On Eclipse models,** adjust pinion height as follows:
   a. Apply a thin film of suitable multipurpose grease to mating face of tool washer, **Fig. 22,** then install tools and drive pinion front and rear

bearing inner races on gear carrier.
   b. Gradually tighten nut on tool until standard drive pinion turning torque value shown in **Fig. 20** is obtained.
   c. Thoroughly clean side bearing seat, then install tools, **Fig. 23,** and bearing cap. **Ensure tool cutout sections are positioned as shown in Fig. 23** and tool contacts side bearing seat.
   d. Use a suitable feeler gauge to measure clearance (dimension A) between tools, **Fig. 23,** then remove tools.
   e. Use a suitable micrometer to measure tool dimensions B and C, **Fig. 24.**
   f. Install bearing cap, then use a suitable cylinder gauge and micrometer to measure inside diameter of bearing bore (dimension D), **Fig. 25.**
   g. Calculate drive pinion rear shim thickness. Thickness is equal to dimension $A + B + C - \frac{1}{2}D - 3.39$ inches.
   h. Select a shim that is as close to calculated thickness as possible, then fit shim on drive pinion and press fit rear bearing inner race using tool

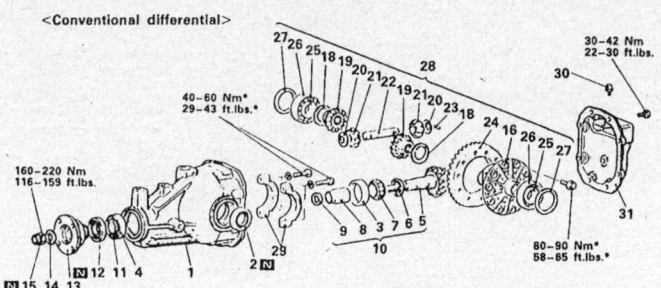

<Conventional differential>

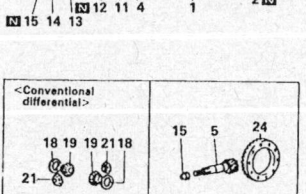

<Conventional differential>

Differential gear set	Final drive gear set
21 18 19 19 21 18	15 5 24

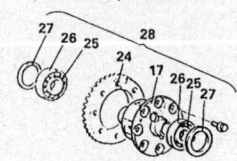

<Limited slip differential>

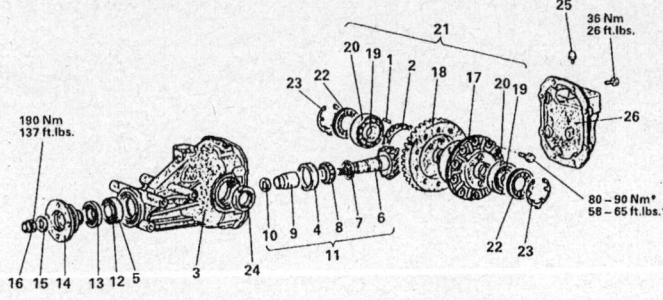

Reassembly steps

1. Gear carrier
   Oil seal
3. Drive pinion rear bearing outer race
4. Drive pinion front bearing outer race
   Adjustment of pinion height
5. Drive pinion
6. Drive pinion rear shim
   (for pinion height adjustment)
7. Drive pinion rear bearing inner race
8. Drive pinion spacer
   Adjustment of drive pinion preload
9. Drive pinion front shim
   (for preload adjustment)
10. Drive pinion assembly
11. Drive pinion front bearing inner race
12. Oil seal
13. Companion flange
14. Washer
15. Self-locking nut
16. Differential case

17. Limited slip (viscous coupling) differential case
    Adjustment of differential gear backlash
18. Side gear spacers
19. Side gears
20. Pinion washers
21. Pinion gears
22. Pinion shaft
23. Lock pin
24. Drive gear
25. Side bearing inner race
26. Side bearing outer race
    Adjustment of final drive gear backlash
27. Side bearing spacers
28. Differential case assembly
29. Bearing caps
30. Vent plug
31. Differential cover

NOTE
* : Tightening torque with oil applied.

MT3019100015000X

Fig. 16   Rear differential assembly. Eclipse

Reassembly steps

1. Spring pin (for 4WS)
2. Drive gear (for 4WS)
3. Differential carrier
4. Drive pinion rear bearing outer race
5. Drive pinion front bearing outer race
   Drive pinion height adjustment
6. Drive pinion
7. Drive pinion rear shim
   (for drive pinion height adjustment)
8. Drive pinion rear bearing inner race
9. Drive pinion spacer
   Drive pinion preload adjustment
10. Drive pinion front shim
11. Drive pinion assembly
12. Drive pinion front bearing inner race
13. Oil seal
14. Companion flange

15. Washer
16. Self-locking nut
17. LSD case
18. Drive gear
19. Side bearing inner race
20. Side bearing outer race
    Final drive gear backlash adjustment
21. Differential case assembly
22. Side bearing nut
23. Snap ring
24. Oil seal
25. Vent plug
26. Differential cover assembly

NOTE
* : Tightening torque with oil applied.

MT3019100016000X

Fig. 17   Rear differential assembly. 3000GT

Bearing classification	Bearing lubrication	Rotation torque (starting friction torque) Nm – (in.lbs.)
New	None (with rust-prevention oil)	0.9–1.2 (8–10)
New/reused	Oil application	0.4–0.5 (3–4)

NOTE
(1) Gradually tighten the handle of the special tool while checking the drive pinion turning torque.
(2) Because the special tool cannot be turned one turn, turn it several times within the range that it can be turned; then, after fitting to the bearing, measure the rotation torque.

MT3019100020000X

Fig. 20   Pinion turning torque. Eclipse

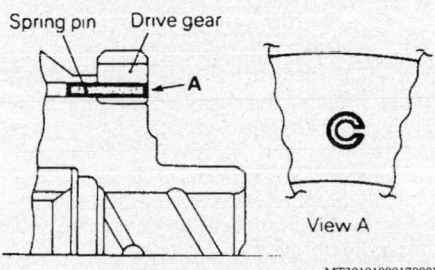

Spring pin   Drive gear

View A

MT3019100017000X

Fig. 18   Spring pin installation. 3000GT w/4WS

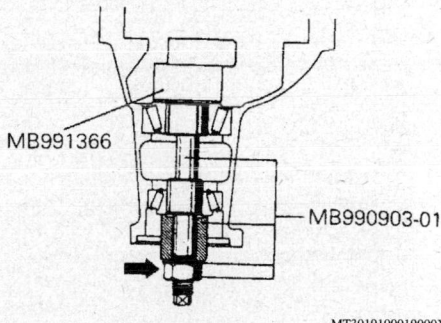

MB991366

MB990903-01

MT3019100019000X

Fig. 19   Pinion height adjustment. 3000GT

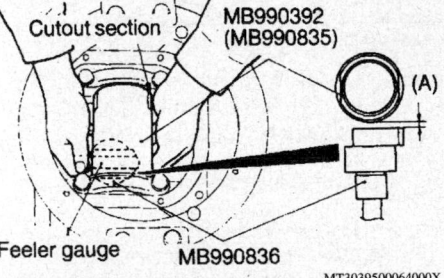

Cutout section   MB990392 (MB990835)

(A)

Feeler gauge   MB990836

MT3039500064000X

Fig. 23   Side bearing tool orientation. Eclipse

Bearing classification	Bearing lubrication	Rotation torque Nm (in.lbs.)
New	None (with rust-prevention oil)	0.3–0.5 (3–4)
New/reused	Gear oil application	0.15–0.25 (1–2)

NOTE
(1) Gradually tighten the nut of the special tool while checking the drive pinion rotation torque.
(2) Because the special tool cannot be turned one turn, turn it several times within the range that it can be turned; then, after fitting to the bearing, measure the rotation torque.

MT3019100021000X

Fig. 21   Pinion turning torque. 3000GT

No. MB990728, or equivalent.

8. **On all models,** adjust drive pinion preload as follows:
   a. Install drive pinion front shim(s) between pinion spacer and pinion front bearing inner race.

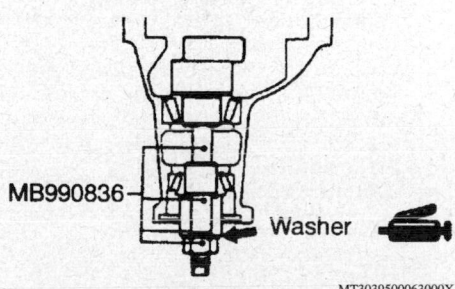

MB990836   Washer

MT3039500063000X

Fig. 22   Drive pinion front & rear bearing inner race installation. Eclipse

   b. **On 3000GT models, torque** companion flange to 135 ft. lbs., using

end yoke holder tool to prevent yoke rotation. Do not install oil seal.

   c. **On Eclipse models, torque** companion flange to 137 ft. lbs., using end yoke holder tool to prevent yoke rotation. Do not install oil seal.

   d. **On all models,** ensure drive pinion turning torque is as shown in **Figs. 20 and 21.**

   e. If drive pinion turning torque is not

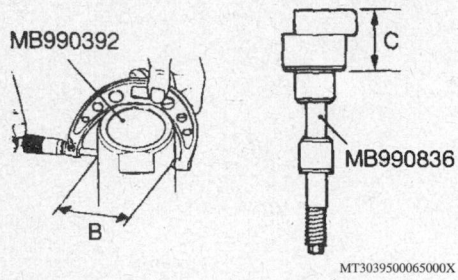

Fig. 24 Side bearing clearance measurements. Eclipse

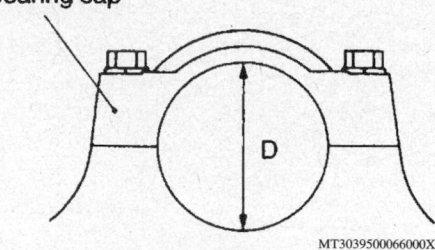

Fig. 25 Bearing cap clearance measurement. Eclipse

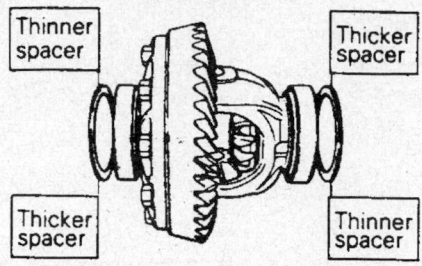

Fig. 26 Gear backlash adjustment. Eclipse

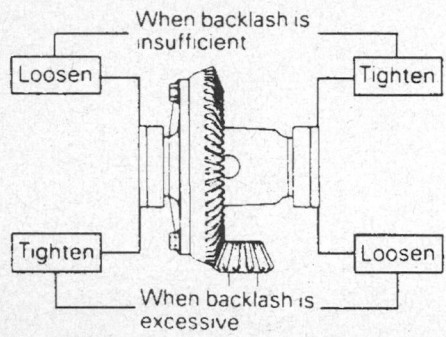

Fig. 27 Gear backlash adjustment. 3000GT

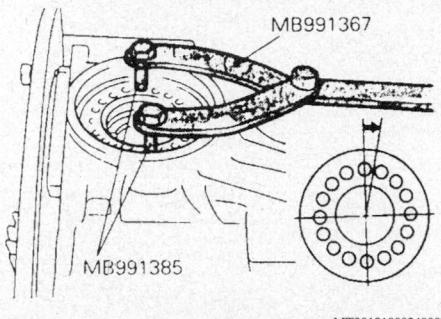

Fig. 28 Side bearing adjustment. 3000GT

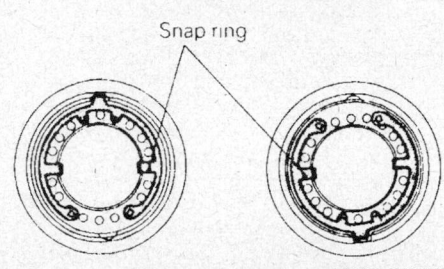

Fig. 29 Bearing nut snap ring installation. 3000GT

within specified range, adjust by replacing drive pinion front shims(s) or drive pinion spacer.
f. Remove companion flange and drive pinion.
g. Install oil seal using suitable oil seal installation tool.
h. Install drive pinion and companion flange aligning marks made during disassemble then tighten companion flange self-locking nut to specification.
i. Measure pinion turning torque with oil seal installed and ensure turning torque is no more than one inch lb. greater than what is shown in **Figs. 20 and 21.**

9. **On models with conventional differential,** adjust differential gear backlash as follows:
a. Assemble side gears and spacers, pinion gears and washers into differential case.
b. Temporarily install pinion shaft.
c. While locking side gear with wedge, measure differential gear backlash with a dial indicator on pinion gear. **The measurement should be made for both pinion gears individually.**
d. If differential gear backlash exceeds .008 inch, adjust backlash by installing thicker side gear spacers.
e. Measure differential gear backlash again and confirm it is within the specification.
f. After adjustment, ensure backlash is less than limit and differential gear rotates smoothly.
g. When adjustment is impossible, replace side gear pinion gears as a set.

h. Align pinion shaft lockpin hole with differential case and install lockpin.
i. Stake lockpin at two points.
10. **On all models,** clean drive gear attaching bolts.
11. Use a 10 mm x 1.25 tap to remove adhesive from threaded holes of drive gear.
12. Install drive gear onto differential case aligning marks made during disassemble. Tighten bolts in a diagonal sequence.
13. Press side bearing inner races onto differential case.
14. **On Eclipse models,** adjust final drive gear backlash as follows:
a. Install side bearing spacers, which are thinner than those removed, and mount the differential case assembly into the gear carrier.
b. Push differential case to one side and measure clearance between gear carrier and side bearing.
c. Measure thickness of side bearing spacers on one side, select two pairs of spacers which correspond to thickness plus one half of clearance plus .002 inch. Install one pair each to drive pinion side and drive gear side.
d. Install side bearing spacers and differential case assembly into gear carrier.
e. Tap side bearing spacers with a suitable brass bar to fit them to side bearing outer race.
f. Align marks made during disassembling then tighten bearing cap.
g. With drive pinion locked in place, measure final drive gear backlash.
h. If backlash is not .004–.006 inch, change bearing spacers as shown in **Fig. 26** to obtain correct backlash.

i. Check tooth contact as outlined under "Inspection Before Disassemble."
j. Measure drive gear runout at shoulder on reverse side of drive gear.
k. If runout exceeds .002 inch, reinstall by changing phase of drive gear and differential case and measure again.
15. **On 3000GT models,** adjust final drive gear backlash as follows:
a. Using spanner wrench tool No. MB991367 and pin tool No. MB991385, or equivalents, temporarily tighten side bearing nut until just before preloading.
b. Measure final drive gear backlash at four or more points on drive gear.
c. Using spanner wrench and pin tools, adjust backlash until a .004–.006 inch value is reached by turning side bearing nut as shown, **Fig. 27.**
d. Using the spanner wrench to apply preload, turn down both right and left side bearing nuts on half the distance between centers of two neighboring holes, **Fig. 28.**
e. Install snap ring at either position shown to lock side bearing nut, **Fig. 29.**
f. Check drive gear and pinion tooth contact as outlined under "Inspection Before Disassemble."
g. Measure drive gear runout at shoulder on reverse side of drive gear.
h. If runout exceeds .002 inch, reinstall by changing phase of drive gear and differential case and measure again.
i. Using suitable oil seal installer, install oil seal flush with gear carrier end face.

DIFFERENTIAL CARRIER
REPLACE

Refer to appropriate chassis section under "Rear Axle & Suspension" for differential carrier replacement procedure.

DIFFERENTIAL CARRIER SERVICE

LIMITED SLIP DIFFERENTIAL

Inspection Before Service

1. Secure differential case assembly in a vise so that differential right side gear is facing upward. **When securing in vise, ensure not to hold differential case assembly to tightly.**
2. Insert a .0012 inch feeler gauge at two places between differential case B and right thrust washer, **Fig. 30. Do not insert a feeler gauge in oil groove of differential case B.**
3. Insert tool A of tool kit No. MB990988, or equivalent, at spline part of differential right side gear and ensure right side gear rotates, **Fig. 31.**
4. Replace on of the .0012 inch feeler gauge with a .0035 inch feeler gauge.
5. Insert tool A of tool kit No. MB990988, or equivalent, at spline part of differential right side gear and ensure right side gear does not rotate, **Fig. 31.**
6. If clearance in thrust direction of side gear is within .0012–.0035 inch, backlash of differential gear is normal.
7. If clearance in thrust direction of side gear is not .0012–.0035 inch, remove differential case A and make adjustment by adjusting thickness of left thrust washer.

Disassemble

Disassemble limited slip differential carrier in numbered sequence shown in **Fig. 32.** Right and left thrust washers are of different thickness, and should be identified in some way for reference during assemble.

Assemble

Assemble limited slip differential carrier in reverse numbered sequence shown in **Fig. 32,** noting the following:
1. Align mating marks of differential case A and B when assembling.
2. With pinion mate washers in position, install to differential pinion shaft, then to differential case B, **Fig. 33.**
3. If differential side gear and pinion mate gear have been replaced, select left thrust washer as follows:
   a. Wash differential gear and pinion mate gears in unleaded gasoline.
   b. Install old thrust washer together with gears, viscous unit, pinion mate washer and pinion shaft into differential cases A and B then temporarily tighten screws.
   c. Perform "Inspection Before Disassemble" procedure.
   d. If clearance in thrust direction of side gear is not within .0012–.0035 inch, remove differential case A and

make adjustment by changing thickness of left thrust washer. Select one left thrust washer from 11 types in thrust washer kit tool No. MB569243, or equivalent, **Fig. 34.**
4. Reassemble case halves and install into differential.

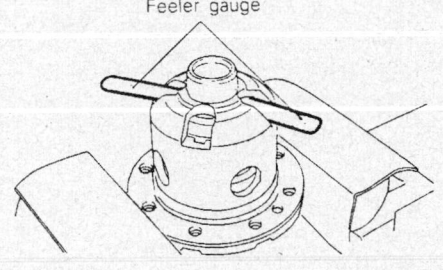

Fig. 30 Feeler gauge insertion

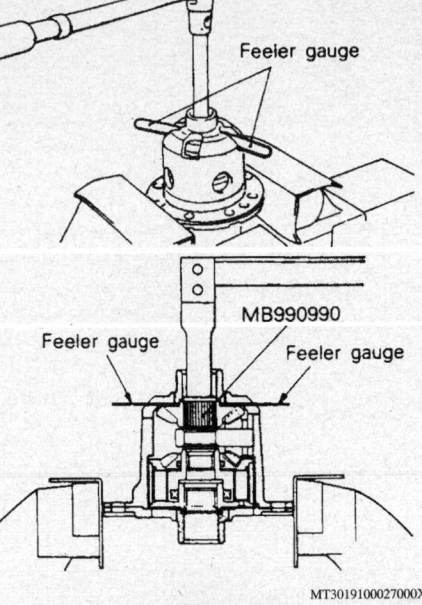

Fig. 31 Right side gear inspection

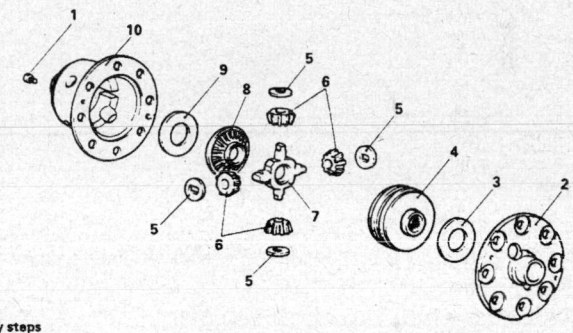

Disassembly steps
1. Screw
2. Differential case A
3. Thrust washer (L.H.)
4. Viscous unit
5. Pinion mate washer
6. Differential pinion mate
7. Differential pinion shaft
8. Differential side gear (R.H.)
9. Thrust washer (R.H.)
10. Differential case B

Fig. 32 Limited slip differential carrier disassemble

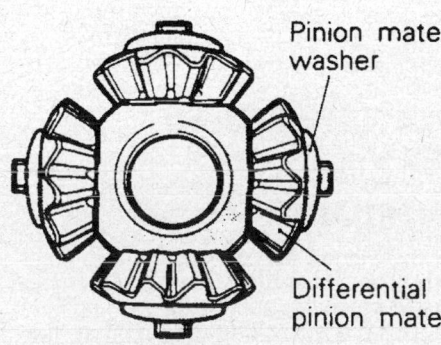

Pinion mate washer

Differential pinion mate

Fig. 33 Differential pinion mate installation

PROPELLER SHAFT
REPLACE

1. Remove propeller shaft in numbered sequence, **Figs. 35 and 36,** noting the following:
   a. Place mating marks on companion flange and flange yoke for installation reference.
   b. Number of spacers used may vary between models. Note number of spacers for installation reference.
2. Reverse numbered sequence in **Figs. 35 and 36** to install, noting the following:
   a. Do not damage transfer case oil seal lip during installation.

Thrust washer (left)	
Part No.	Thickness mm (in.)
MB569243	0.8 (.031)
	0.9 (.035)
	1.0 (.039)
	1.1 (.043)
	1.15 (.045)
	1.2 (.047)
	1.25 (.049)
	1.3 (.051)
	1.35 (.053)
	1.4 (.055)
	1.5 (.059)

MT3019100030000X

Fig. 34 Left thrust washer chart

Gear Oil:
API Classification GL-4
SAE 75W-90 or
75W-85W

29-34 Nm
22-25 ft.lbs.

29 Nm
22 ft.lbs.

29 Nm
22 ft.lbs.

11 Nm
8 ft.lbs.

Removal steps
1. Self-locking nut
2. Insulator
3. Spacer
4. Propeller shaft assembly
5. Spacer
6. Heat protector

MT3039300067000X

Fig. 35 Propeller shaft replacement. Eclipse

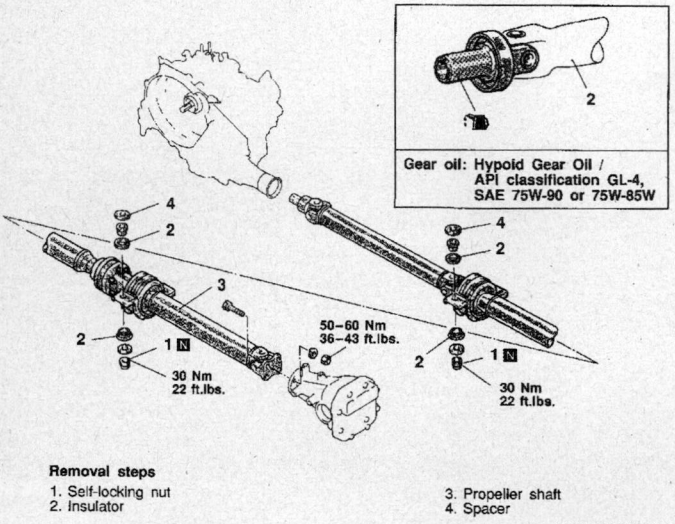

Gear oil: Hypoid Gear Oil /
API classification GL-4,
SAE 75W-90 or 75W-85W

50-60 Nm
36-43 ft.lbs.

30 Nm
22 ft.lbs.

30 Nm
22 ft.lbs.

Removal steps
1. Self-locking nut
2. Insulator
3. Propeller shaft
4. Spacer

MT3039300069000X

Fig. 36 Propeller shaft replacement. 3000GT

b. Using a suitable dial indicator, inspect shaft runout after installation; runout should not exceed .024 inch at any point.

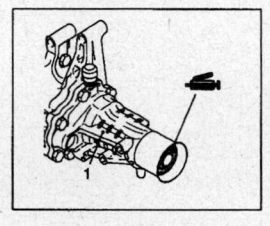

Sleeve yoke

Gear oil:
API classification GL-4 SAE 75W-90
or 75W-85W

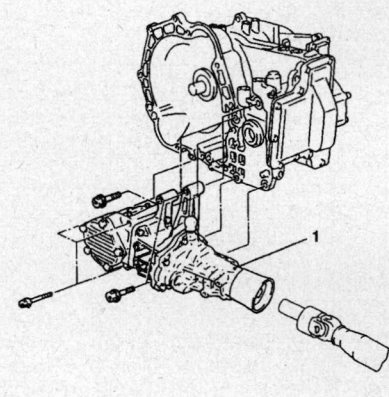

1. Transfer assembly

MT3049100027000A

Fig. 37 Transfer case assembly replacement

TRANSFER CASE

REPLACE

1. Drain transfer oil into a suitable container.
2. Remove transfer case assembly as shown, **Fig. 37,** noting the following:
   a. It may be necessary to disconnect front exhaust pipe to gain working clearance.
   b. Move the transfer case to the left and lower the front side, then remove it from the propeller shaft.
   c. Suspend the propeller shaft so that it can not be sharply bent.
   d. Cover the transfer opening with tool No. MB991193, or equivalent, to prevent transaxle oil discharge and the entry of foreign objects.
3. Reverse procedure to install. Refill transfer oil.

TRANSFER CASE SERVICE

OVERHAUL

Disassemble transfer assembly in numbered sequence, **Fig. 38.** Reverse procedure to assemble, noting the following:

1. Using a suitable brush, apply a thin, even coat of machine blue, **Fig. 39,** to both tooth surfaces of the driven bevel gear.
2. Install the old spacer.
3. Tighten transfer case adapter subassembly on transfer case subassembly.
4. Using tool No. MB99088, or equiva-

lent, turn the drive bevel gear shaft, **Fig. 40,** one turn in the direction of normal and reverse rotation, ensuring contact pattern of driven bevel gear is correct.
5. Ensure backlash between the drive and driven bevel gears is .0031-.0050 inch.

SUBASSEMBLY SERVICE

Transfer Case

Disassemble transfer case subassembly in numbered sequence, **Fig. 41.** Reverse procedure to assemble, noting the following:

1. Using tool No. MD998323-01, or

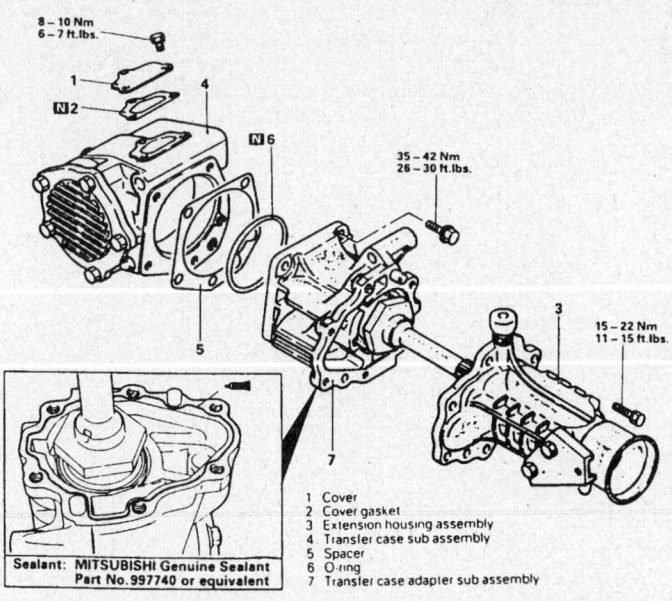

1 Cover
2 Cover gasket
3 Extension housing assembly
4 Transfer case sub assembly
5 Spacer
6 O-ring
7 Transfer case adapter sub assembly

Sealant: MITSUBISHI Genuine Sealant
Part No. 997740 or equivalent

8 – 10 Nm
6 – 7 ft.lbs.

35 – 42 Nm
26 – 30 ft.lbs.

15 – 22 Nm
11 – 15 ft.lbs.

MT3049100028000X

Fig. 38 Exploded view of transfer assembly

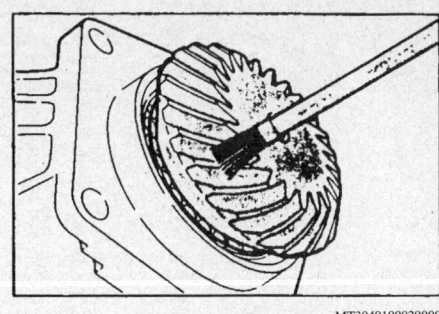

MT3049100029000X

Fig. 39 Drive bevel gear

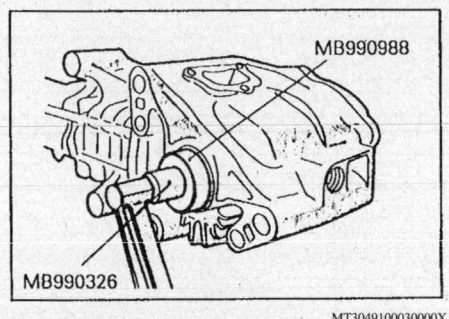

MB990988

MB990326

MT3049100030000X

Fig. 40 Drive bevel gear shaft

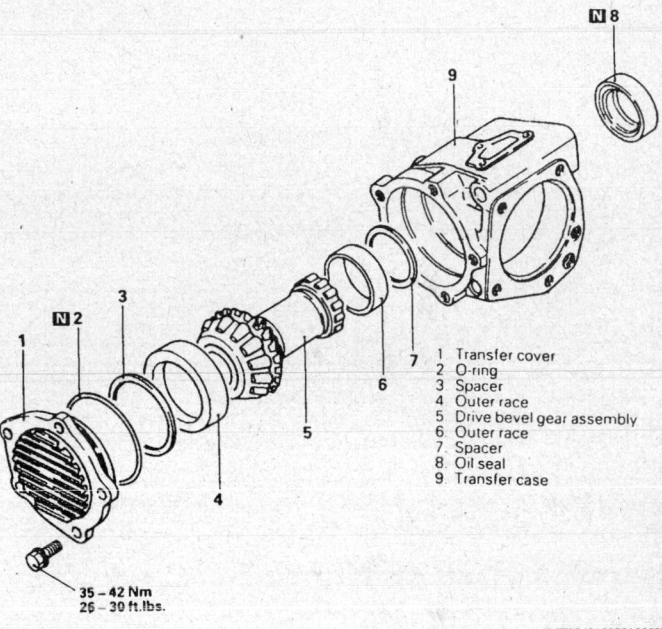

1 Transfer cover
2 O-ring
3 Spacer
4 Outer race
5 Drive bevel gear assembly
6 Outer race
7 Spacer
8 Oil seal
9 Transfer case

35 – 42 Nm
26 – 30 ft.lbs.

MT3049100031000X

**Fig. 41 Exploded view of transfer case
subassembly**

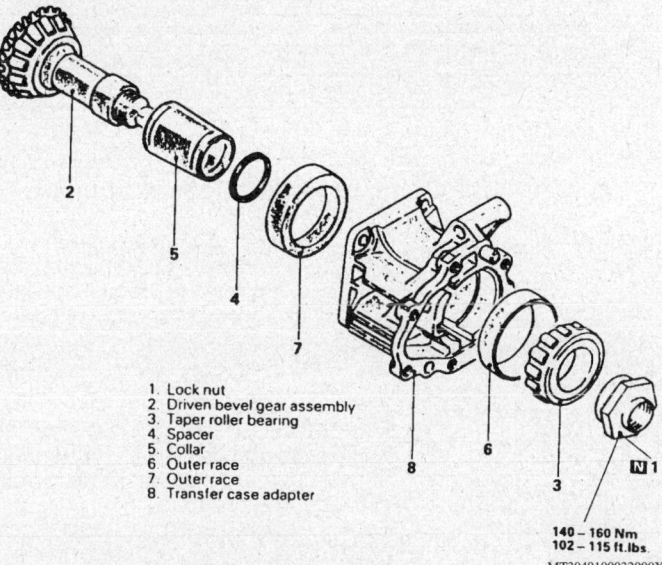

1 Lock nut
2 Driven bevel gear assembly
3 Taper roller bearing
4 Spacer
5 Collar
6 Outer race
7 Outer race
8 Transfer case adapter

140 – 160 Nm
102 – 115 ft.lbs.

MT3049100032000X

**Fig. 42 Exploded view of transfer case adapter
subassembly**

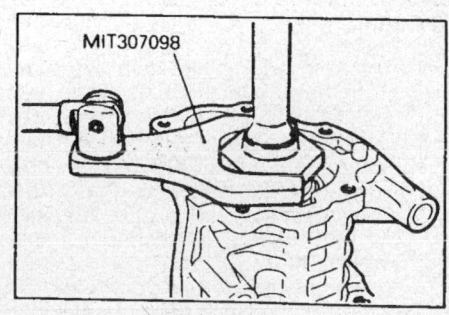

MIT307098

MT3049100033000X

**Fig. 43 Driven gear locknut
removal**

equivalent, install the oil seal.
2. Install old spacers which were used previously.
3. Inspect drive bevel gear assembly using tool Nos. MB990988 and MB990326, or equivalents. Drive bevel gear **torque** should be 1.23–1.81 ft. lbs.

Transfer Case Adapter

Disassemble transfer case adapter subassembly in numbered sequence, **Fig. 42**, noting the following:
1. Unstake locknut before removal.
2. Remove the locknut using tool No. MIT 307098, or equivalent, **Fig. 43**.

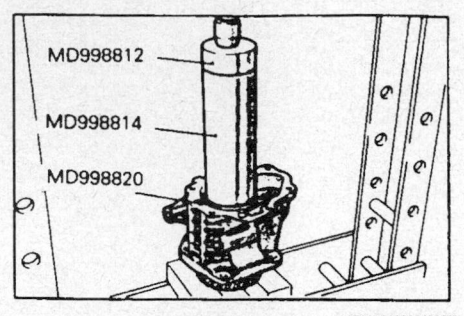

MD998812
MD998814
MD998820

MT3049100034000X

Fig. 44 Taper roller bearing installation

3. Using a press, remove driven bevel gear assembly.
4. Using a screwdriver, remove spacer.
5. Reverse procedure to assemble, noting the following:
   a. Install spacer that was used previously.
   b. Using special tools, **Fig. 44**, install tapered roller bearing.
   c. Tighten driven bevel gear locknut, then stake locknut at two places to lock.

Drive Axles

INDEX

IDENTIFICATION

Refer to **Fig. 1** to identify drive axles by ratio or number of ring gear teeth.

DISASSEMBLE

DIFFERENTIAL CASE ASSEMBLY

Except Limited Slip & Rear Differential Lock

1. If rear differential is being serviced, remove lock plate and side bearing nuts using tool No. MB990201, or equivalent.
2. Remove the carrier cap (bearing cap), **Figs. 2 and 3**.
3. Remove differential case assembly using the wooden handles of two hammers to avoid damaging the gears.
4. Using puller tool No. MB990810 and adapter tool No. MB9990811, or equivalents, remove side bearings. Keep side bearings, nuts and adjusting spacers together for assembly reference.
5. Scribe alignment mark on differential case and drive gear, then remove drive gear attaching bolts and drive gear. Loosen bolts alternately in a diagonal pattern.
6. Remove lockpin with a punch, then remove pinion shaft, pinion gears, side gears and side gear thrust spacers. Keep left and right side components separate for identification during reassemble.

Year	Model	No. Of Ring Gear Teeth	Gear Ratio
REAR			
1996	Pickup	①	②
	Montero④	—	③
	Montero⑤	—	4.636
1997–99	Montero	—	4.272
	Montero Sport	—	⑥
FRONT			
1996	Pickup	38	4.222
	Montero④	—	③
	Montero⑤	—	4.636
1997–99	Montero	—	4.272
	Montero Sport	—	⑥

① — Except light duty 2WD models, 38 teeth; light duty 2WD models, 43 teeth.
② — Except light duty 2WD models, 4.222; light duty 2WD models, 3.909.
③ — Models less wide fenders, 4.625; models w/wide fenders, 4.875.
④ — 3.0L 12 valve engine.
⑤ — 3.0L 24 valve & 3.5L engines.
⑥ — Models less wide fenders, 4.272; models w/wide fenders & 3.0L engine, 4.636; models w/wide fenders & 3.5L engine, 4.272.

Fig. 1 Drive axle identification

Limited Slip & Rear Differential Lock

1. Remove case from gear carrier, **Fig. 4**, as described under conventional differential.
2. Remove side bearing using tool Nos. MB990339-01, MIT303173 and MB990811-01, or equivalents, **Fig. 5**. Keep adjusting spacers separate to facilitate reassembly.

3. Mark relative position between differential case and drive gear, then loosen and remove drive gear mounting bolts in a diagonal sequence.
4. Evenly loosen differential case attaching bolts A and B, separate the two halves, then remove components from case B. **Separate right and left thrust washers, spring plates, spring discs, friction plates and friction discs to facilitate assemble.**

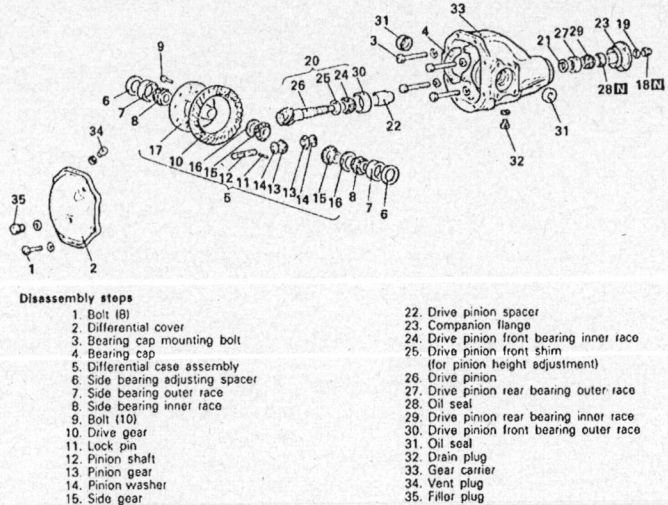

Disassembly steps

1. Bolt (8)
2. Differential cover
3. Bearing cap mounting bolt
4. Bearing cap
5. Differential case assembly
6. Side bearing adjusting spacer
7. Side bearing outer race
8. Side bearing inner race
9. Bolt (10)
10. Drive gear
11. Lock pin
12. Pinion shaft
13. Pinion gear
14. Pinion washer
15. Side gear
16. Side gear thrust spacer
17. Differential case
18. Companion flange self-locking nut
19. Washer
20. Drive pinion assembly
21. Drive pinion rear shim
(for preload adjustment)

22. Drive pinion spacer
23. Companion flange
24. Drive pinion front bearing inner race
25. Drive pinion front shim
(for pinion height adjustment)
26. Drive pinion
27. Drive pinion rear bearing outer race
28. Oil seal
29. Drive pinion rear bearing inner race
30. Drive pinion front bearing outer race
31. Oil seal
32. Drain plug
33. Gear carrier
34. Vent plug
35. Filler plug

MT3039100036000X

Fig. 2 Exploded view of front differential. Except limited slip & rear differential lock

DRIVE PINION

1. Hold end yoke with tool No. MB990850, or equivalent, on rear differentials, or No. MB990767, or equivalent, on front differentials. Remove mounting nut and end yoke.
2. Scribe alignment mark on end yoke and drive pinion, then tap or push out drive pinion with height adjustment shim, rear bearing inner race, spacer and preload adjustment shim still installed on shaft.
3. Using tool Nos. MB990339 and MB990648, or equivalents, remove drive pinion rear bearing inner race and height adjustment shim from shaft.
4. Remove front and rear pinion bearing outer races. **When removing front outer race, remove and discard oil seal, then remove front bearing inner race.**

CLEANING & INSPECTION

1. Check differential gear tooth contact and replace any gear that is worn or damaged.
2. Check bearings and races and replace if worn, damaged or discolored.
3. Install side gear (with circlip on front differentials), onto splined end of axle shaft. Install assembly in vise, **Fig. 6.** Freeplay should not exceed .020 inch on rear differential or .024 inch on front differential.
4. Inspect differential pinion and pinion shaft; replace if worn or seized.
5. **On models equipped with limited slip differential,** proceed as follows:
   a. Clean all components in solvent.
   b. Inspect sliding and mating surfaces of clutch plate and pressure ring for pitting or damage.
   c. Inspect contact surfaces of friction

plates, friction discs, spring plates and spring discs. If any signs of seizure, severe friction or discoloration from heat damage are present, replace damaged components. **Worn area around circumference of friction surfaces is due to spring plate and spring disc; wear is normal.**

   d. Check the six projections on the inner circumference of the friction disc for nicks and dents. Repair using an oil stone, or replace as necessary.
   e. Check the four projections on the outer circumference of friction disc for nicks and dents, then repair using an oil stone, or replace as necessary.
   f. Inspect the sliding surfaces of the thrust washers and differential case, spring contacting surfaces of differential case, contacting surfaces of pressure rings, sliding surface of thrust washers and sliding surface of hole in side gears and repair as necessary using an oil stone.
   g. Check spherical surface of pinion gears and I.D. of pressure rings, then the V-shaped groove in the pressure rings and pinion shaft. Check O.D. of pinion shaft and hole in pinion gear, then the outer and inner circumference of differential case. Inspect sliding surface of thrust block. If any damage is found on these components, repair using an oil stone, or replace as necessary.
   h. Inspect friction plates, friction discs,

Disassembly steps

1. Lock plate
2. Side bearing nut
3. Bolt
4. Bearing cap
5. Differential case assembly
6. Hose
7. Air pipe assembly (A) <Vehicles with
8. Eye bolt   rear differential
9. Air pipe assembly (B) lock>
10. Gasket
11. Actuator assembly
12. Pressure plate
13. Side bearing outer race
14. Side bearing inner race
15. Drive gear
16. Lock pin
17. Pinion shaft
18. Pinion gear
19. Pinion washer
20. Side gear
21. Side gear spacer
22. Differential case
23. Differential case
24. Self-locking nut
25. Washer
26. Drive pinion assembly

27. Drive pinion front shim (For adjusting of drive pinion bearing preload)
28. Drive pinion spacer
29. Drive pinion rear bearing inner race
30. Drive pinion rear shim
(For adjusting drive pinion height)
31. Drive pinion
32. Companion flange
33. Oil seal
34. Drive pinion front bearing inner race
35. Drive pinion front bearing outer race
36. Drive pinion rear bearing outer race
37. Rear differential   <Vehicles with rear
lock detection switch differential lock>
38. Gasket
39. Differential carrier

MT3039100037000X

Fig. 3 Exploded view of rear differential. Except limited slip & rear differential lock

spring discs and spring plates for flatness using a dial indicator. If found to be worn more than .003 inch on friction plate, or .004 inch on clutch plate, replace worn components.

ASSEMBLE

DIFFERENTIAL CASE ASSEMBLY

Except Limited Slip & Rear Differential Lock

1. Install side gear thrust washers and side gears into differential case.
2. Install pinion gears with washers into case. Rotate pinion gears to mesh with side gears.
3. Install pinion shaft. Do not install lockpin at this time.
4. Insert a wedge between side gear and pinion shaft to prevent side gear from turning, then install dial indicator to gear and measure gear backlash. Backlash must not exceed .005 inch on rear differentials, or .006 inch on front differentials. If backlash is not within specifications, replace side gear thrust spacers as needed, then recheck backlash.
5. Align pinion shaft lockpin hole with differential case lockpin hole, then drive lockpin into hole. **Stake the lockpin in position in two places, using a punch.**
6. Remove adhesive tape from drive gear attaching bolts and the internal threads in gear.

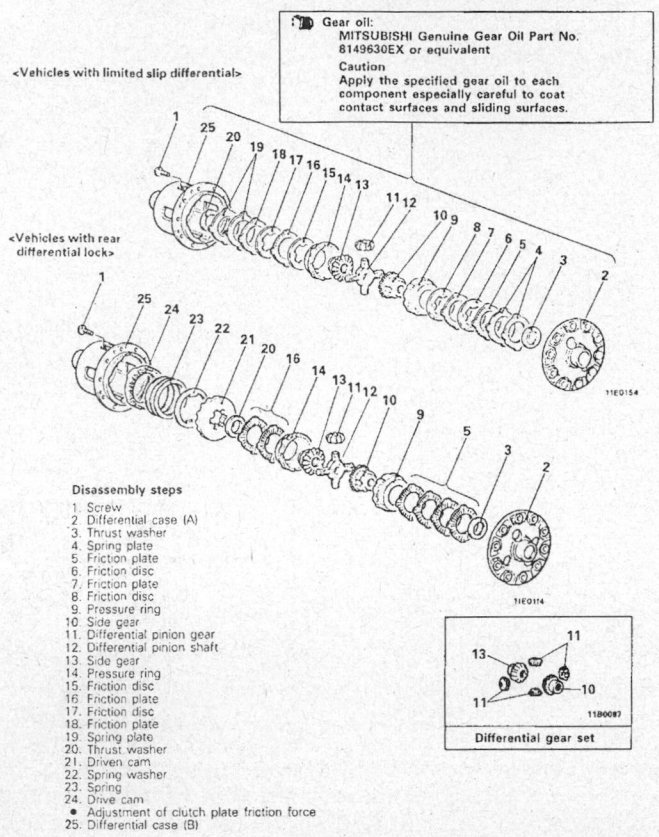

Fig. 4   Exploded view of differential. Limited slip & rear differential lock

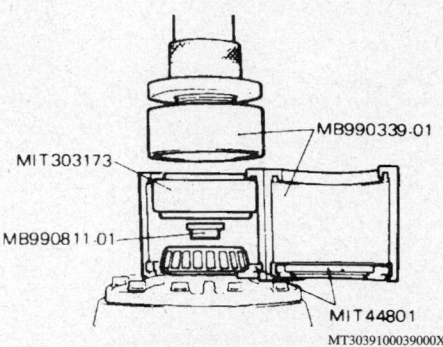

Fig. 5   Differential side bearing removal. Limited slip & rear differential lock

contacting surfaces.

13. Assemble differential clutch and pinion assembly as shown, **Fig. 12.**
14. After assembly, measure rotating torque of assemble using tool No. MB990988, or equivalent. Turning **torque** should be 25–72 ft. lbs. for used clutch plates or 47–72 ft. lbs. for new clutch plates.
15. Remove old adhesive from drive gear attaching bolts, then apply sealer to bolts.
16. Install and finger tighten bolts, then alternately **torque** to 58–65 ft. lbs.

DRIVE PINION

1. Press drive front and rear bearing outer races into gear carrier using tool Nos. MB990934, MB990936 and MB990938, or equivalents.
2. Adjust drive pinion height as follows:
   a. Install tool No. MB990819, or equivalent, and the drive pinion bearings into gear carrier. Apply a thin coat of grease to washer on tool.
   b. Gradually tighten nut on tool until drive pinion preload is 3.5–4.3 inch lbs.
   c. Position cylinder of tool No. MB990552, or equivalent, in side bearing seat of gear carrier, **Fig. 13.**
   d. Using a feeler gauge, measure clearance between the two tools, then select drive pinion rear adjusting shim(s) corresponding to this measurement.
   e. Install shim(s) between pinion and rear bearing, then press rear bearing onto pinion.
   f. If the gear set is being replaced, install new shims of the same thickness as those previously used on the drive pinion. **In determining thickness of shim pack to be used, the amount of compression of the shim pack and wear of the bearing, if the old bearing is reused, should be taken into consideration.**
3. Adjust drive pinion preload as follows:
   a. Install pinion preload adjustment shim between pinion spacer and front bearing. **Torque** end yoke to 138–180 ft. lbs. on rear differential or 116–159 ft. lbs. on front differential.

---

7. Apply Loctite No. 271, or equivalent, to drive gear threaded holes, then install gear onto case with reference marks aligned. **Torque** attaching bolts alternately, in a diagonal pattern, to 58–65 ft. lbs.

Limited Slip & Rear Differential Lock

1. Measure differential case depth (A), **Fig. 7,** using formula A = E – F + G.
2. Measure spring disc and plate thickness with both extended in the same direction and one placed over the other as shown, **Fig. 8.** Arrange them so that the difference between left and right is minimized, then measure thicknesses of friction plates and discs in the same manner. **Right side (Lr) and left side (Ll).**
3. Measure thickness of left and right clutch plate assemblies, then find the difference of the two. Difference should not exceed .002 inch. **Clutch plate assembly thickness is thickness of spring, disc, spring plate, friction disc and friction plate.**
4. Assemble right and left friction plates, friction discs, pinion shafts and pressure rings, then measure total width (B), **Fig. 9. Measure distance between clutch plates on a line with V-shaped groove in the pressure ring while pressing from both sides, ensuring groove is secured against pinion shaft. All parts should be dry.**

5. Measure clearance between clutch plate and differential (S), then use the following formula: A(B+Lr+Ll).
6. If the difference (S) between the depth (A) of differential case and the overall width (B) obtained previously, plus the spring plate and spring disc assembly thickness, is not .002–.008 inch, replace friction discs to adjust.
7. Measure distance (A), **Fig. 10,** then the depths of thrust washer contact surfaces, dimensions (C) and (D), in differential cases A and B.
8. Assemble pressure rings, pinion gears, side gears, pinion shafts and thrust washers.
9. Measure distance from back of left pressure ring to edge of thrust washer and ensure difference between the two does not exceed .002 inch. **Measure distance between clutch plates on a line with V-shaped groove in the pressure ring while pressing from both sides, ensuring groove is secured against pinion shaft. All parts should be dry.**
10. Measure overall width shown in **Fig. 11,** as dimension "R."
11. Using width of assembled differential unit and depth of differential case, measure clearance of side gear in axial direction. If clearance is not .002–.007 inch, replace thrust washers to adjust. **Find clearance of side gear in axial direction using formula: A + C + DR.**
12. Before assemble, apply lubricant to all

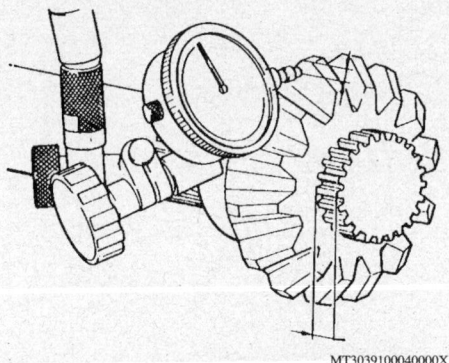

MT3039100040000X

Fig. 6 Driveshaft spline freeplay measurement

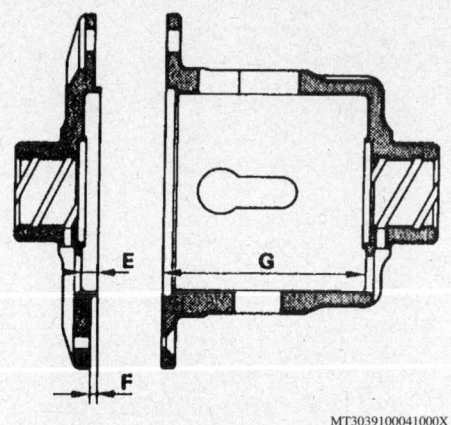

MT3039100041000X

Fig. 7 Differential case depth measurement. Limited slip & rear differential lock

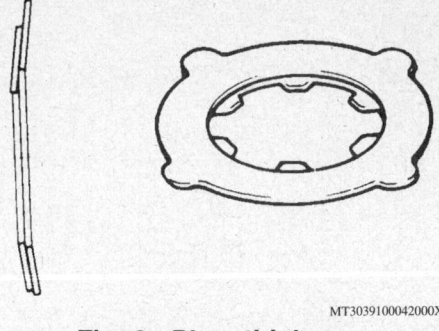

MT3039100042000X

Fig. 8 Plate thickness measurement. Limited slip & rear differential lock

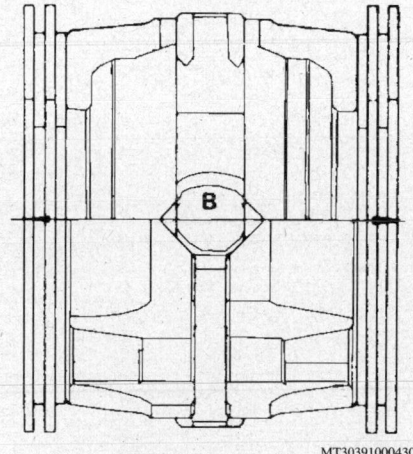

MT3039100043000X

Fig. 9 Total width measurement. Limited slip & rear differential lock

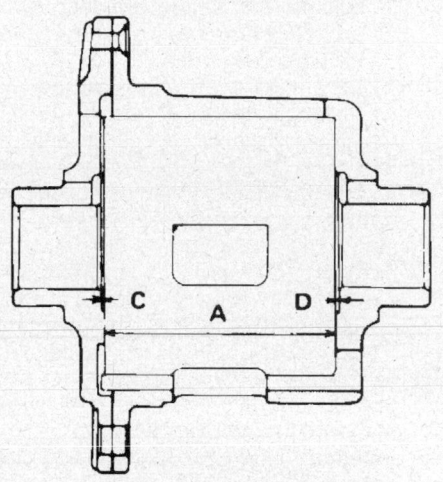

MT3039100044000X

Fig. 10 Thrust washer thickness measurement. Limited slip & rear differential lock

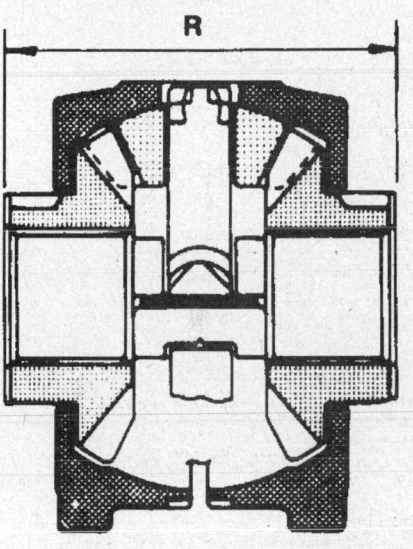

MT3039100045000X

Fig. 11 Dimension "R"

b. Measure drive pinion preload. Preload should measure 3.5–4.3 inch lbs. without oil seal installed.

c. Adjust preload as necessary by replacing adjustment shims or drive pinion spacers.

4. Remove end yoke, then apply a thin coat of grease to lip of oil seal. Drive seal into gear carrier using tool No. MB990031, or equivalent.

5. Apply grease to end yoke mating surface of seal, then install the end yoke. **Torque** attaching nut to 138–180 ft. lbs. on rear differential or 116–159 ft. lbs. on front differential.

SIDE BEARING & DRIVE GEAR

1. Install side bearing inner race into differential case using tool No. MB990802, or equivalent.

2. For front differentials, adjust drive gear backlash as follows:

a. Install side bearing adjustment spacers, thinner than those removed, to the side gear bearings, then install differential case assembly into gear carrier. **Select adjustment spacers of the same thickness for both the drive pinion side and the drive gear side.**

b. Push differential case to one side, then measure clearance between gear carrier and side bearing adjustment space using two feeler gauges.

c. Remove, then measure the thickness of side bearing adjustment spacers from one side.

d. To determine proper thickness spacer to be used, add .002 inch to thickness measured in preceding step and ½ the clearance measured between gear carrier and side bearing adjustment space.

e. Install one pair of the correct spacers each to the drive pinion side and drive gear side.

f. Install differential case assembly, with side bearing adjustment spacers, into gear carrier. Gently tap spacers with a brass drift to seat them on bearing outer race.

g. Install bearing cap with reference marks aligned. **Torque** cap bolts to 40–47 ft. lbs.

h. With drive pinion locked in place, measure drive gear backlash, **Fig. 14,** at four different points on the drive gear. Backlash should measure .005–.007 inch. If not, replace spacers as necessary to bring within

in specifications, **Fig. 15.**

i. Check drive gear and drive pinion for proper tooth contact by applying marking compound to both surfaces of drive gear teeth. Insert a brass rod between carrier and case and rotate spline coupling by hand one revolution in each direction, **Fig. 16,** while applying a load of approximately 2 ft. lbs. to the drive pinion. Adjust pinion height and backlash as needed until tooth contact pattern resembles standard pattern, **Fig. 17.**

3. For rear differential, proceed as follows:

a. Position differential case assembly into gear carrier, then install carrier cap and cap nuts. **Tighten** cap nuts finger tight only.

b. Install side bearing nut to carrier cap, then **torque** to 40–47 ft. lbs.

c. Install side bearing nut on each side of drive gear using tool No. MB990201, or equivalent, then **torque** to 11 ft. lbs. Turn bearing nuts in and out several times until they operate smoothly before final tightening.

d. Measure drive gear backlash, **Fig. 18.** Backlash should measure .005–.007 inch. If backlash is less

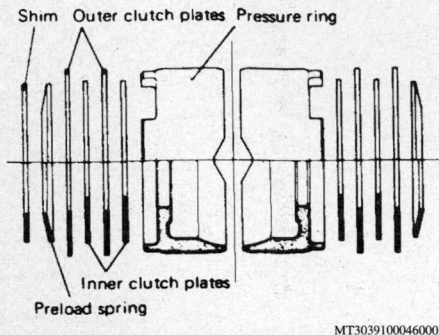

Fig. 12 Differential clutch component assembly. Limited slip & rear differential lock

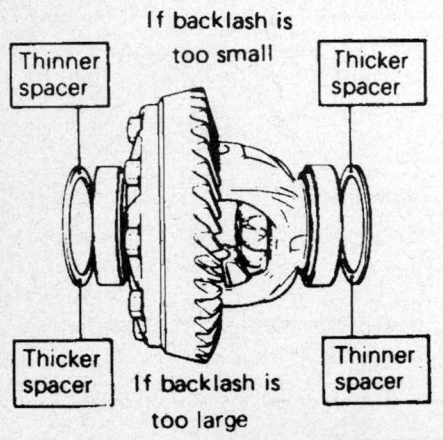

Fig. 15 Drive gear backlash adjustment

than .005 inch, loosen side bearing nut on back side of drive gear and tighten nut on front side of gear by the same amount.
e. When backlash has been adjusted within specifications, tighten both

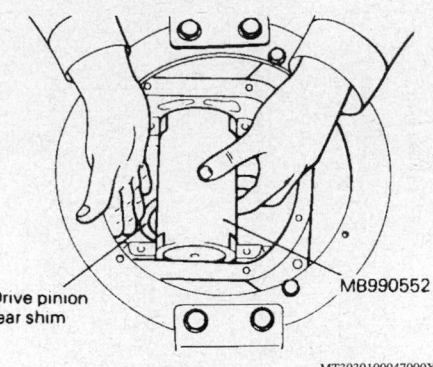

Fig. 13 Drive pinion height measurement

side bearing nuts by a half pitch to preload side bearings. **One pitch equals the space between two adjacent holes on the side of the side bearing nuts.**
f. Install lock plate, then **torque** attaching nut to 11–15 ft. lbs.
4. On all differentials, check drive gear and drive pinion for proper tooth contact by applying marking compound to both surfaces of drive gear teeth. Insert a brass rod between carrier and case and rotate yoke end by hand one revolution in each direction, **Fig. 16,** while applying a load of approximately 2 ft. lbs., to the drive pinion. Adjust pinion height and backlash as needed until tooth contact pattern resembles standard pattern, **Fig. 17.**
5. Measure drive gear runout using dial indicator, **Fig. 19.** If runout exceeds .002 inch, change position of drive gear in differential and recheck. If runout still exceeds specification, replace drive gear or differential case as needed.

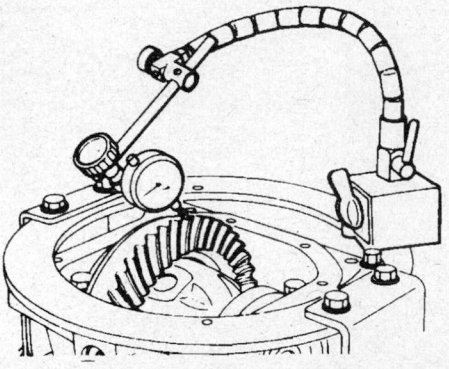

Fig. 14 Drive gear backlash measurement

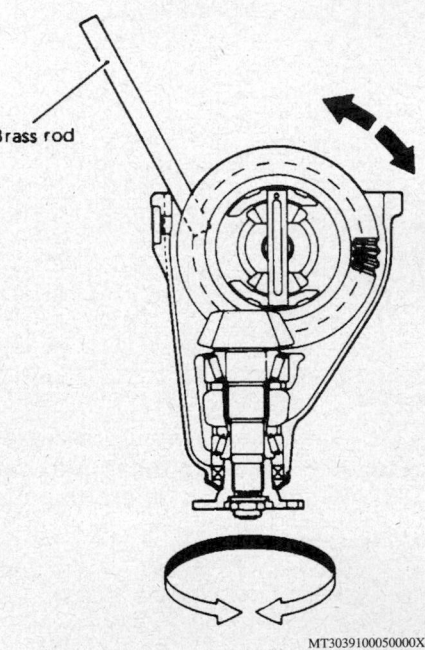

Fig. 16 Gear tooth contact inspection

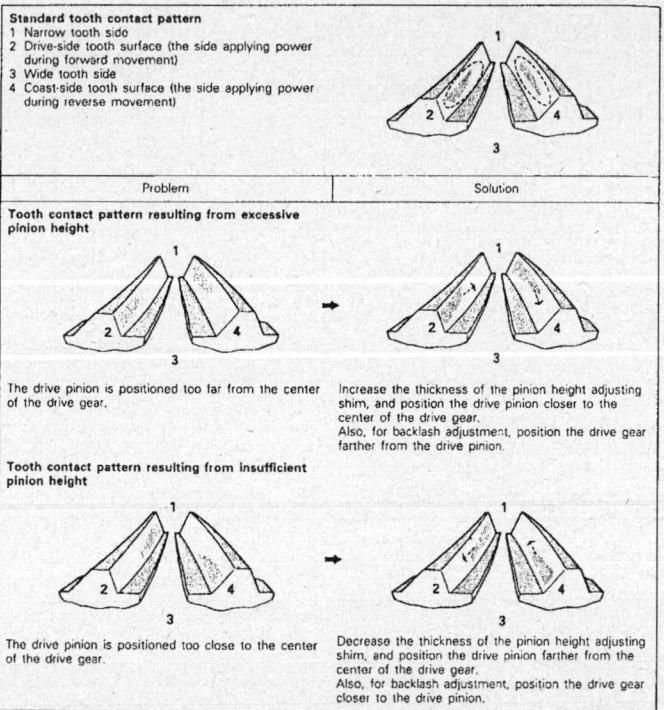

Standard tooth contact pattern
1 Narrow tooth side
2 Drive-side tooth surface (the side applying power during forward movement)
3 Wide tooth side
4 Coast-side tooth surface (the side applying power during reverse movement)

Problem	Solution
Tooth contact pattern resulting from excessive pinion height	
The drive pinion is positioned too far from the center of the drive gear.	Increase the thickness of the pinion height adjusting shim, and position the drive pinion closer to the center of the drive gear. Also, for backlash adjustment, position the drive gear farther from the drive pinion.
Tooth contact pattern resulting from insufficient pinion height	
The drive pinion is positioned too close to the center of the drive gear.	Decrease the thickness of the pinion height adjusting shim, and position the drive pinion farther from the center of the drive gear. Also, for backlash adjustment, position the drive gear closer to the drive pinion.

MT3039100051000X

Fig. 17 Gear tooth contact pattern chart

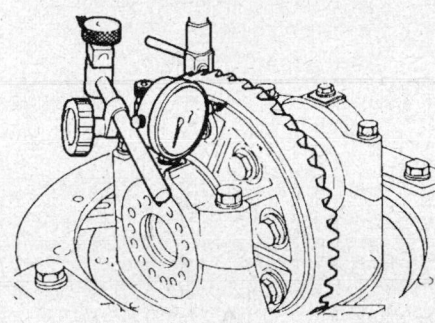

MT3039100052000X

Fig. 18 Rear differential drive gear backlash measurement

MT3039100053000X

Fig. 19 Drive gear runout measurement

MITSUBISHI UNIT REPAIR

DRIVE AXLE SPECIFICATIONS

Model	Axle	Ring Gear & Pinion Backlash		Pinion Bearing Preload			Differential Bearing Preload	
		Method	Adjustment, Inch	Method	With Seal, Inch Lbs.	Less Seal, Inch Lbs.	Method	Adjustment
Montero & Montero Sport	Rear	①	.005–.007	Shims	7.4–10.0	5.2–7.8	①	②
	Front	Shims	.004–.006	Shims	4.3–6.1	2.6–4.3	Shims	②
Pickup 2WD	Rear	①	.004–.006	Shims	5.6–6.5	3.5–4.3	①	②
Pickup 4WD	Rear	①	.005–.007	Shims	5.6–6.5	3.5–4.3	①	②
	Front	Shims	.004–.006	Shims	5.2–6.1	3.5–4.3	Shims	②

① — Adjustment is obtained by loosening or tightening differential side bearing adjustment nut.

② — Preload is correct when ring gear and pinion backlash is properly adjusted.

Engine Rebuilding Specifications

INDEX

CYLINDER HEAD, VALVE GUIDE & VALVE SEATS

All Measurements Given In Inches, Unless Otherwise Specified.

Engine	Year	Cylinder Head Warpage Limit	Cylinder Head Overall Thickness[5]	Valve Stem To Guide Clearance		Valve Seats			
				Intake	Exhaust	Seat Angle, °	Seat Width		
							Intake	Exhaust	
1.5L	1996–99	.008	4.209–4.217	.0008–.0020	.0020–.0035	45–45.5	.035–.051	.035–.051	
1.8L	1996–99	.008	4.720–4.728	.0008–.0016	.0012–.0024	—	.035–.051	.035–.051	
2.0L	1996–99[6]	.008	5.193–5.201	.0008–.0020	.0020–.0035	45–45.5	.035–.051	.035–.051	
	1996–99[7]	.004	—	.0019–.0026	.0029–.0037	45	.035–.051	.035–.051	
2.4L SOHC	1996–99[1]	.008	4.720–4.728	.0008–.0020	.0008–.0028	43.5–44.0	.035–.051	.035–.051	
	1996–99[4]	.008	3.539–3.547	.0008–.0024	.0020–.0035	43.5–44.0	.035–.051	.035–.051	
3.0L DOHC	1996–99	.008	5.200	.0008–.0020	.0020–.0035	45	.035–.051	.035–.051	
3.0L SOHC	1996–99[2]	.008	3.310	.0012–.0024	.0020–.0035	45	.035–.051	.035–.051	
	1996–99[3]	.008	4.720	.0008–.0020	.0016–.0028	45	.035–.051	.035–.051	
3.5L	1996–99	.008	5.200	.0008–.0020	.0020–.0035	45	.035–.051	.035–.051	

DOHC: Dual Overhead Cam
SOHC: Single Overhead Cam
① — 4 valves per cylinder.
② — Montero w/12 valve engine, Diamante & Pickup.
③ — Montero w/24 valve engine.

④ — 2 valves per cylinder.
⑤ — Minimum thickness is overall thickness, less warpage limit, combined with amount of grinding of cylinder block gasket surface.

⑥ — Except Eclipse w/non-turbocharged engine.
⑦ — Eclipse w/non-turbocharged engine.

VALVE SPRINGS
All Measurements Given In Inches, Unless Otherwise Specified.

Engine	Year	Free Length		Installed Height	Seated Pressure, Lbs.		Out Of Square Limit, °
		Intake	Exhaust		Intake	Exhaust	
1.5L	1996–99	1.820	1.840	1.570	51.0	64.0	4
1.8L	1996–99	2.000	2.000	1.740	49.0	49.0	4
2.0L	1996–99②	1.850	1.850	1.570	54.0	54.0	4
	1996–99④	1.811	1.811	1.496	55.0–60.0	55.0–60.0	—
2.4L SOHC	1996③	1.960	1.960	1.590	73.0	73.0	4
	1996–99①	2.010	2.010	1.740	60.0	60.0	4
3.0L DOHC	1996–99	1.830	1.830	1.492	52.9	52.9	4
3.0L SOHC	1996–99⑤	1.960	1.960	1.591	72.5	72.5	4
	1996–99⑥	2.010	2.010	1.740	60.0	60.0	4
3.5L	1996–99	1.830	1.830	1.492	52.9	52.9	4

DOHC: Dual Overhead Cam
SOHC: Single Overhead Cam
① — 4 valves per cylinder.
② — Except Eclipse w/non-turbocharged engine.

③ — 2 valves per cylinder.
④ — Eclipse w/non-turbocharged engine.
⑤ — Montero w/12 valve engine, Diamante & Pickup.

⑥ — Montero w/24 valve engine.

VALVES
All Measurements Given In Inches, Unless Otherwise Specified.

Engine	Year	Stem Diameter		Face Angle, °	Margin		Clearance[3]	
		Intake	Exhaust		Intake	Exhaust	Intake	Exhaust
1.5L	1996–99	.260	.256	45.0–45.5	.039	.059	.004	.007
1.8L	1996–99	.236	.236	45.0–45.5	.039	.051	.004	.008
2.0L	1996–99[2]	.315	.311	45.0–45.5	.039	.059	[8]	[8]
	1996–99[4]	.233–.234	.233	44.5–45.0	.050–.063	.038–.050	[8]	[8]
2.4L SOHC	1996[6]	.236	.232	45.0–45.5	.047	.079	[8]	[8]
	1996–99[1]	.260	.256	45.0–45.5	.039	.047	[8]	[8]
3.0L DOHC	1996–99	.260	.256	45.0–45.5	.039	.059	[8]	[8]
3.0L SOHC	1996–99[5]	.315	.311	45.0–45.5	.047	.079	[8]	[8]
	1996–99[7]	.236	.236	45.0–45.5	.039	.047	[8]	[8]
3.5L	1996–99	.260	.256	45.0–45.5	.039	.059	[8]	[8]

DOHC: Dual Overhead Cam
SOHC: Single Overhead Cam
[1] — 4 valves per cylinder.
[2] — Except Eclipse w/non-turbocharged engine.

[3] — Cold engine.
[4] — Eclipse w/non-turbocharged engine.
[5] — Montero w/12 valve engine, Diamante & Pickup.

[6] — 2 valves per cylinder.
[7] — Montero w/24 valve engine.
[8] — Equipped w/hydraulic lash adjusters. No provision for adjustment.

CAMSHAFT
All Measurements Given In Inches, Unless Otherwise Specified.

Engine	Year	Camshaft Endplay	Bearing Bore Diameter	Bearing Clearance	Cam Height		Journal Diameter
					Intake	Exhaust	
1.5L	1996–99	—	—	—	1.53	1.54	1.8100
1.8L	1996–99①③	—	—	—	1.48	1.77	1.7700
2.0L	1996–99⑤	—	—	—	⑦	⑧	1.0200
	1996–99⑥	.006	1.024–1.025	.0027–.0028	—	—	1.0217–1.0224
2.4L SOHC	1996–99④	—	—	—	1.67	1.67	1.3400
	1996–99①	—	—	—	1.47	1.48	1.7700
3.0L DOHC	1996–99	—	—	—	1.37	1.37	1.0200
3.0L SOHC	1996–99⑨	—	—	—	1.62	1.60	1.3400
	1996–99②	—	—	—	1.48	1.45	1.7700
3.5L	1996–99	—	—	—	1.37	1.39	1.0200

DOHC: Dual Overhead Cam
SOHC: Single Overhead Cam
① — 4 valves per cylinder.
② — Montero w/24 valve engine.
③ — Mirage.
④ — 2 valves per cylinder.
⑤ — Except Eclipse w/2.0L non-turbocharged engine.

⑥ — Eclipse w/2.0L non-turbocharged engine.

⑦ — Identification marks A & D, 1.40 inch; marks B, E & K, 1.39 inch; mark J, 1.37 inch.

⑧ — Identification mark A, 1.39 inch; mark C, 1.40 inch; marks H & J, 1.37 inch.

⑨ — Montero w/12 valve engine, Diamante & Pickup.

CRANKSHAFT, BEARINGS & RODS
All Measurements Given In Inches, Unless Otherwise Specified.

Engine	Year	Crankshaft		Out of Round (All)	Taper (All)	Bearing Clearance		Connecting Rod Side Clearance
		Standard Journal Diameter				Main Bearing	Connecting Rod Bearings	
		Main Bearing	Crank Pin					
1.5L	1996–99	1.8900	1.6500	.0002	.0002	.0008–.0020	.0008–.0020	.0039–.0098
1.8L	1996–99	1.9700	1.7700	.0002	.0002	.0008–.0016	.0008–.0020	.0039–.0098
2.0L	1996–99②	2.2400	1.7700	.0004	.0004	.0008–.0020	.0008–.0020	.0039–.0098
	1996–99①	2.0469–2.0475	1.8894–1.8900	.0001	.0001	.0008–.0024	.0010–.0023	.0051–.0150
2.4L	1996–99	2.2400	1.7700	.0004	.0004	.0008–.0020	.0008–.0020	.0039–.0098
3.0L DOHC	1996–99	2.3600	1.9700	.0001	.0001	.0008–.0020	.0008–.0020	.0039–.0098
3.0L SOHC	1996–99	2.3600	1.9700	.0002	.0002	.0008–.0020	.0008–.0020	.0039–.0098
3.5L	1996–99	2.5200	2.1700	.0001	.0001	.0008–.0020	.0012–.0020	.0039–.0098

DOHC: Dual Overhead Cam
SOHC: Single Overhead Cam

① — Eclipse w/2.0L non-turbocharged engine.

② — Except Eclipse w/2.0L non-turbocharged engine.

PISTONS, PINS & RINGS
All Measurements Given In Inches, Unless Otherwise Specified.

Engine	Year	Piston Diameter (Std.)	Piston Clearance	Piston Ring End Gap			Compression Ring Side Clearance	
				Compression		Oil	No. 1	No. 2
				No. 1	No. 2			
1.5L	1996–99	2.9700	.0008–.0016	.0079–.0157	.0079–.0138	.0079–.0276	.0012–.0028	.0008–.0024
1.8L	1996–99	3.1900	.0008–.0016	.0098–.0157	.0157–.0217	.0079–.0236	.0012–.0028	.0008–.0024
2.0L	1996–99①⑤	3.3500	.0008–.0016	.0098–.0157	.0177–.0236	.0051–.0150	.0008–.0024	.0008–.0024
	1996–99⑥	3.3500	.0012–.0020	.0098–.0138	.0157–.0217	.0039–.0157	.0016–.0031	.0008–.0024
	1996–99①③	3.4434–3.4441	.0005–.0017	.0090–.0200	.0190–.0310	.0090–.0260	.0010–.0026	.0010–.0026
2.4L SOHC	1996–99②	3.4100	.0008–.0016	.0098–.0157	.0157–.0236	.0079–.0236	.0012–.0028	.0012–.0028
	1996–99④	3.4100	.0008–.0016	.0098–.0138	.0157–.0236	.0079–.0236	.0012–.0028	.0012–.0028
3.0L	1996–99	3.5800	.0008–.0020	.0118–.0177	.0177–.0236	.0079–.0236	.0012–.0028	.0008–.0024
3.5L	1996–99	3.6600	.0012–.0020	.0118–.0177	.0177–.0236	.0039–.0137	.0012–.0028	.0008–.0024

DOHC: Dual Overhead Cam
SOHC: Single Overhead Cam
① — Non-turbocharged.

② — 2 valves per cylinder.
③ — Eclipse.
④ — 4 valves per cylinder.

⑤ — Except Eclipse.
⑥ — Turbocharged.

ENGINE REBUILDING SPECIFICATIONS

CYLINDER BLOCK

All Measurements Given In Inches, Unless Otherwise Specified.

Engine	Year	Cylinder Bore Diameter (Std.)	Cylinder Bore Taper (Max.)	Cylinder Bore Out of Round (Max.)
1.5L	1996–99	2.9700	.0004	.0004
1.8L	1996–99	3.1900	.0004	.0004
2.0L	1996–99②	3.3500	.0004	.0004
	1996–99①	3.4450	.0020	.0020
2.4L	1996–99	3.4100	.0004	.0004
3.0L	1996–99	3.5900	.0004	.0004
3.5L	1996–99	3.6600	.0004	.0004

DOHC: Dual Overhead Cam
SOHC: Single Overhead Cam
① — Eclipse w/non-turbocharged engine.
② — Except Eclipse w/non-turbocharged engine.

OIL PUMP

All Measurements Given In Inches, Unless Otherwise Specified.

Engine	Year	Tip Clearance	Side Clearance		Body Clearance
			Drive Gear	**Driven Gear**	
1.5L	1996–99	.0024–.0071	.0016–.0039	.0016–.0039	.0039–.0071
1.8L	1996–99	.0024–.0071	.0016–.0039	.0016–.0039	.0039–.0071
2.0L	1996–99①	—	.0031–.0055	.0024–.0047	
	1996–99②	.0008③	—	—	—
2.4L	1996–99	—	.0031–.0055	.0024–.0047	—
3.0L	1996–99	.0024–.0071	.0016–.0039	.0016–.0039	.0039–.0071
3.5L	1996–99	.0024–.0071	.0016–.0039	.0016–.0039	.0039–.0071

① — Except Eclipse w/non-turbocharged engine.

② — Eclipse w/non-turbocharged engine.

③ — Limit.

NISSAN:

GENERAL INFORMATION

GENERAL INFORMATION

Manual Information Locator, Inside Rear Cover

Specifications

GENERAL ENGINE SPECIFICATIONS

Year	Engine	Fuel System	Displace-ment Liters	Bore x Stroke, Inches	Comp-ression Ratio	Maximum H.P. @ RPM	Maximum Torque, Ft. Lbs. @ RPM	Normal Oil Pressure, psi①
1996–99	KA24DE	Fuel Inj.	2.4L	3.50 x 3.78	9.2	150 @ 5600	154 @ 4400	60–70

① — At 3000 RPM.

TUNE UP SPECIFICATIONS

Year & Engine	Spark Plug Gap, Inch	Ignition Timing			Curb Idle Speed①		Fast Idle Speed		Fuel Pump Pressure, psi	Valve Lash
		Firing Order②	Timing, °BTDC③	Timing Mark	Man. Trans.	Auto. Trans.	Man. Trans.	Auto. Trans.		
1996–99										
KA24DE	.041	③	⑤	④	700	700N	⑤	⑤	43	⑥

BTDC — Before Top Dead Center
N — Neutral
① — When adjusting idle speed, set parking brake & chock drive wheels.
② — Before disconnecting spark plug wires from distributor cap, deter-mine location of No. 1 wire in cap, as distributor position may have been altered.
③ — No. 1 located front of engine. Firing order 1-3-4-2.
④ — Mark located on pulley.
⑤ — Controlled by ECCS.
⑥ — Refer to "Valve Clearance Specifi-cations."

FRONT WHEEL ALIGNMENT SPECIFICATIONS

Year	Caster Angle, Deg.		Camber Angle, Deg.		King Pin Inclin-ation, Deg.	Toe-In, Inch①	Toe-Out On Turns, Deg.②		Ball Joint Wear
	Limits	Desired	Limits	Desired			Inner Wheel	Outer Wheel	
1996–99	+1¹¹⁄₁₂ to +3⁵⁄₁₂	+2⅔	−⅚ to +⅔	−¹⁄₁₂	13⅓ to 14⅚	0 to +.08	32¹⁄₁₀ to 36¹⁄₁₀	26³⁄₁₀ to 30³⁄₁₀	③

① — Toe-in (+); toe-out (-).
② — Measure w/wheels at full lock positions.
③ — Refer to "Ball Joint Inspection" section under "Front Suspension & Steering."

REAR WHEEL ALIGNMENT SPECIFICATIONS

Year	Camber Angle, Deg.		Toe, Inch①
	Limits	Desired	
1996–99	−2 to −½	−1¼	+.04 to +.12

① — Toe-in (+); toe-out (-).

FLUID CAPACITIES & COOLING SYSTEM DATA

Year	Cooling Capacity, Qts.	Radiator Cap Relief Pressure, Lbs.	Thermo. Opening Temp., °F	Fuel Tank, Gals.	Engine Oil Refill, Qts.①	Transmission Oil		Differential Oil, Pts.
						Man. Trans., Pts.	Auto. Trans., Qts.②	
1996–99	8¼	11–14	170	15⅞	4⅛	10	10	—

① — Includes filter.

② — Approximate, make final check w/dipstick.

LUBRICANT DATA

Year	Lubricant Type					
	Transmission		Transfer Case	Rear Axle	Power Steering	Brake System
	Manual	Automatic				
1996–99	80W-90 GL-4	Nissan Matic D ①	—	—	Dexron IIE/III	DOT 3

① — Dexron III/Mercon, or equivalent, automatic transmission fluid may also be used.

Electrical

NOTE: On Air Bag Equipped Models, Refer To "Air Bag System Precautions" Located In The Front Of This Manual For System Disarming & Arming Procedures.

NOTE: Refer To "Computer Relearn Procedures" Located In The Front Of This Manual For Computer Relearn Procedures.

INDEX

PRECAUTIONS

BATTERY GROUND CABLE

Prior to service, disconnect battery ground cable and isolate as required.

AIR BAG SYSTEMS

Refer to "Air Bag System Precautions" in the front of this manual for system disarming and arming procedures.

FUSE PANEL & FLASHER LOCATION

The fuse panel is located behind the lower lefthand side of the instrument panel, left of the steering column.

The combination flasher unit is located behind the center of the instrument panel, near the time control module.

RELAY CENTER LOCATION

Relay box No. 1 is located on the right-hand side of the engine compartment. Relay box No. 2 is located on the front right-hand side of the engine compartment, near the battery.

FUEL PUMP RELAY LOCATION

The fuel pump relay is located on the front righthand side of the engine compartment, in relay box No. 2.

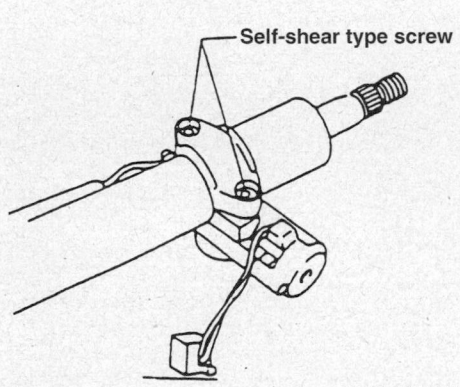

Fig. 1 Ignition lock replacement

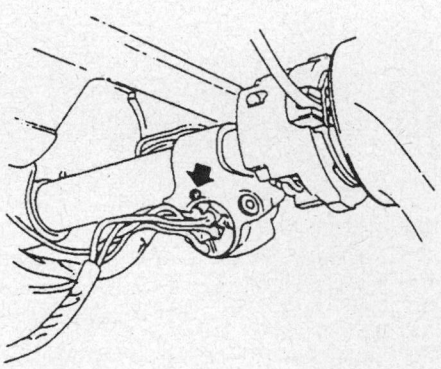

Fig. 2 Ignition switch replacement

STARTER
REPLACE

1. Disconnect starter wiring from starter.
2. Remove starter retaining bolts, then the starter.
3. Reverse procedure to install.

DISTRIBUTOR
REPLACE

1. Remove distributor cap and spark plug cables as an assembly.
2. Disconnect distributor electrical connections.
3. Remove distributor retaining bolt.
4. Remove distributor assembly.
5. Reverse procedure to install.

IGNITION LOCK
REPLACE

1. Remove steering wheel as outlined under "Steering Wheel, Replace."
2. Drill out two shear type ignition lock retaining screws, **Fig. 1.**
3. Remove ignition lock from steering column.
4. Reverse procedure to install, using shear type screws.

IGNITION SWITCH
REPLACE

1. Remove four upper and lower shell cover retaining screws, then the shell covers.
2. Disconnect electrical connectors from switch.
3. Remove switch retaining screw from steering lock, **Fig. 2.**
4. Remove switch.
5. Reverse procedure to install.

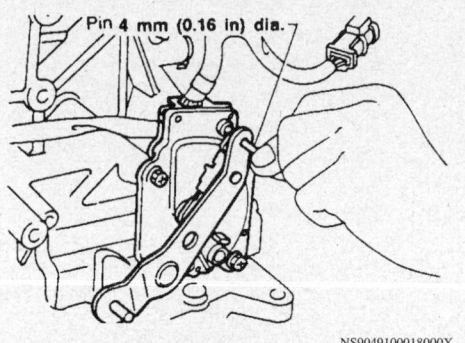

NS9049100018000X

Fig. 3 Neutral safety switch adjustment

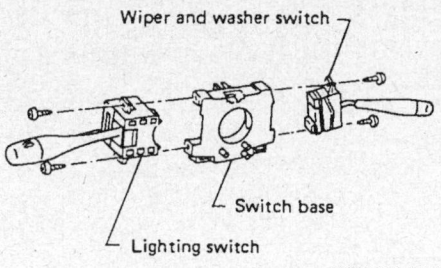

Wiper and washer switch

Switch base

Lighting switch

NS9049100019000X

Fig. 4 Headlamp, turn signal & wiper switch removal

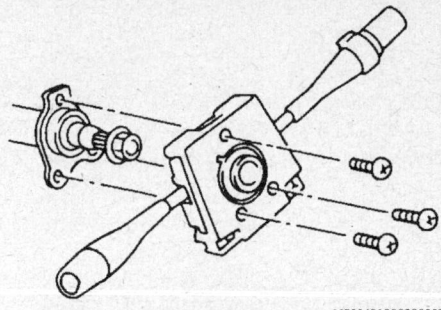

NS9049100020000X

Fig. 5 Combination switch replacement

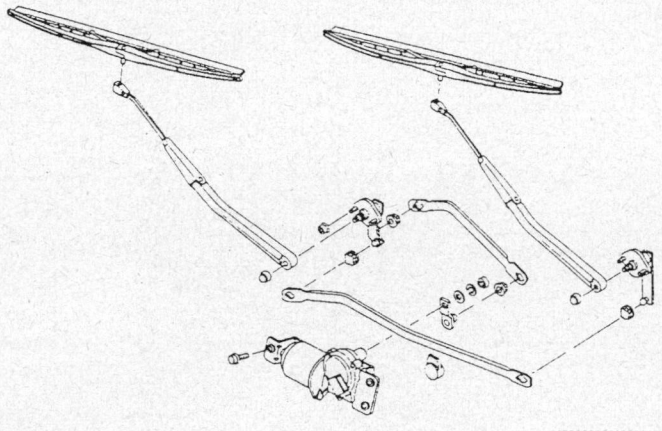

NS9029100003000X

Fig. 6 Exploded view of windshield wiper system

NEUTRAL SAFETY SWITCH

ADJUST

1. Remove control cable from manual shaft.
2. Set selector lever manual shaft at Neutral position.
3. Loosen neutral safety switch attaching screws.
4. Insert suitable pin into adjustment holes in both neutral safety switch and switch lever as near vertical as possible, **Fig. 3.**
5. Tighten neutral safety switch screws.
6. Connect control cable, the check switch for continuity.

HEADLAMP SWITCH

REPLACE

1. Remove steering column covers.
2. Disconnect light switch electrical connections.
3. Remove switch retaining screws, then the light switch, **Fig. 4.** It is not necessary to remove combination switch base when replacing light switch.

STOP LIGHT SWITCH

REPLACE

The stop lamp switch is located on the brake pedal support.

1. Disconnect switch electrical connectors.
2. Loosen switch retaining locknut and remove switch.
3. Reverse procedure to install.

COMBINATION SWITCH

REPLACE

1. Remove horn cover and steering wheel as outlined under " Steering Wheel, Replace."
2. Remove steering column shell covers.
3. Disconnect switch electrical connections.
4. Remove switch base retaining screws and switch, **Fig. 5.**
5. Reverse procedure to install.

TURN SIGNAL SWITCH

REPLACE

Refer to "Headlamp Switch, Replace" for replacement procedure.

STEERING WHEEL

REPLACE

1. Ensure ignition switch is OFF, then disconnect battery cables and wait for at least ten minutes.
2. Remove lower lid from steering wheel and disconnect air bag module connector.
3. Remove air bag module as follows:

   a. Remove left and right air bag module retaining bolts. **Discard bolts.**
   b. Remove air bag module from steering wheel.
   c: **Always place air bag module with pad side facing upward.**
   d. **Do not attempt to disassemble air bag module.**
   e. **Do not drop or impact air bag module. If any portion is deformed or cracked, replace module.**
   f. **Do not allow oil, grease or water to come in contact with the air bag module.**
4. Remove steering wheel using puller tool No. J25726-A, or equivalent.
5. Reverse procedure to install, noting the following:
   a. Apply suitable grease to entire surface of turn signal cancel pin and horn contact slip ring.
   b. Air bag module retaining bolts are coated with a special bonding agent. Always discard old bolts and replace with new ones.

INSTRUMENT CLUSTER

REPLACE

1. Remove steering column cover and steering wheel, if necessary, as outlined under "Steering Wheel, Replace."
2. Remove instrument panel cover, if necessary, as outlined under "Dash Panel Service."
3. Remove cluster lid retaining screws, then the cluster lid.
4. Disconnect speedometer cable, cluster retaining nuts and electrical connectors as necessary. The cluster may have to be pulled slightly forward after removing the retaining screws to allow access to the electrical connectors.
5. Reverse procedure to install.

RADIO

REPLACE

1. Remove cluster lid or instrument panel fascia as necessary to gain access to brackets, as outlined under "Dash Panel Service."
2. Remove radio bracket to instrument panel attaching screw.
3. Disconnect electrical leads from radio.
4. Remove radio from vehicle.

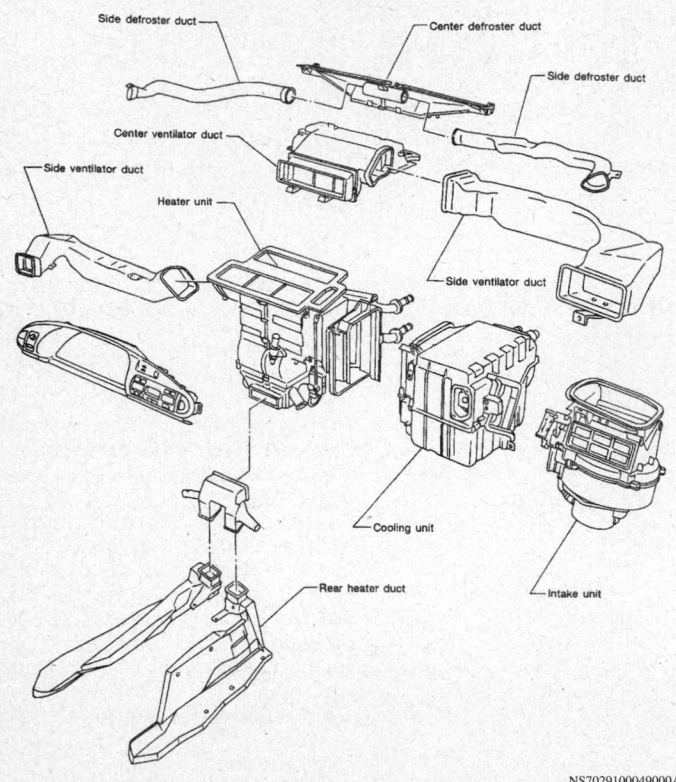

Fig. 7 Exploded view of heater system. 1996–97

NS7029100049000A

5. Reverse procedure to install.

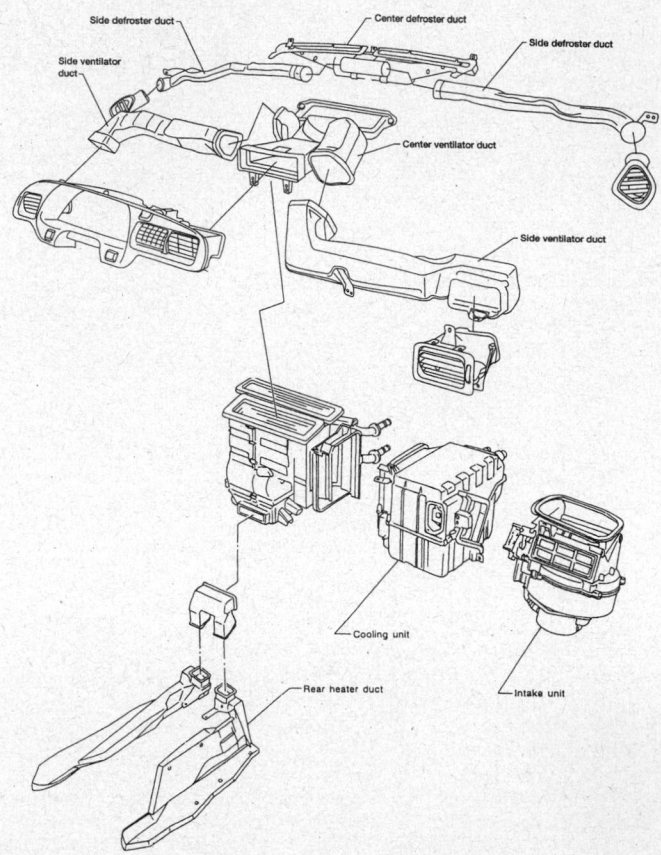

NS7029900486000X

Fig. 8 Exploded view of heater system. 1998–99

WIPER MOTOR

REPLACE

Refer to **Fig. 6** for wiper system exploded view.
1. Remove wiper arms.
2. Disconnect electrical connector from motor, then remove top grille retaining screws and top grille, where possible, to gain access to wiper linkage.
3. Remove wiper motor mounting bolts and pull motor away from firewall if necessary to gain access. Disconnect motor shaft from linkage taking care not to bend linkage.
4. Remove cowl top grille.
5. Remove flange nuts retaining pivot to cowl top, then the wiper motor linkage.
6. Reverse procedure to install.

WIPER SWITCH

REPLACE

1. Remove steering column covers.
2. Disconnect wiper switch electrical connections.
3. Remove switch retaining screws, then the light switch, **Fig. 4.** It is not necessary to remove combination switch base when replacing wiper switch.

BLOWER MOTOR

REPLACE

1. Recover refrigerant.
2. Remove passenger side instrument lower cover and glove compartment.
3. Disconnect wiring harness connectors to intake unit, **Figs. 7 and 8.**
4. Remove intake unit.
5. Remove blower motor from intake unit.
6. Reverse procedure to install.

HEATER CORE

REPLACE

1. Drain cooling system.
2. Disconnect heater inlet and outlet coolant pipes from heater unit.
3. Remove instrument panel as outlined in "Dash Panel Service."
4. Disconnect heater ducts, **Figs. 7 and 8.**
5. Disconnect wiring harness connectors to heater unit.
6. **On 1998–99 models,** remove steering member assembly.
7. **On all models,** remove heater unit.
8. **On 1996–97 models,** separate heater

unit case halves and remove heater core.
9. **On 1998–99 models,** remove heater core from heater unit by sliding out from side.
10. **On all models,** reverse procedure to install.

EVAPORATOR CORE

REPLACE

1. Recover A/C system refrigerant.
2. Disconnect two refrigerant lines from engine compartment. **Cap lines to prevent moisture from entering system.**
3. Remove passenger side instrument lower cover and glove compartment.
4. **On 1996–97 models,** disconnect wiring harness connectors to intake unit, then remove intake unit.
5. **On all models,** disconnect wiring harness connectors to evaporator, then remove cooling unit.
6. Separate cooling unit case halves and remove evaporator, **Figs. 7 and 8.**
7. Reverse procedure to install.

KA24DE Engine

NOTE: On Air Bag Equipped Models, Refer To "Air Bag System Precautions" Located In The Front Of This Manual For System Disarming & Arming Procedures.

NOTE: Refer To "Computer Relearn Procedures" Located In The Front Of This Manual For Computer Relearn Procedures.

NOTE: For Procedures Not Found In This Section, Refer To KA24DE Engine Section In The "Nissan 240SX" Chapter.

INDEX

PRECAUTIONS

BATTERY GROUND CABLE

Prior to service, disconnect battery ground cable and isolate as required.

AIR BAG SYSTEMS

Refer to "Air Bag System Precautions" in the front of this manual for system disarming and arming procedures.

FUEL SYSTEM PRESSURE RELIEF

1. Remove fuel pump fuse from fuse panel.
2. Start engine.
3. Run engine until it stalls.
4. After engine stalls, crank engine two or three times to ensure fuel pressure is released.
5. Turn ignition switch off and install fuse for fuel pump.

COMPRESSION PRESSURE

1. Start engine and run until engine reaches operating temperature.
2. Turn ignition switch off.
3. Release fuel pressure. Refer to "Precautions" for fuel system pressure release procedure.
4. Remove all spark plugs.
5. Disconnect distributor center cable.
6. Attach a compression tester to cylinder No. 1.
7. Depress accelerator pedal fully to keep throttle valve wide open.

8. Crank engine and record highest gauge indication.
9. Repeat measurement on each cylinder.
10. Standard compression is 178 psi at 300 RPM, minimum pressure is 149 psi at 300 RPM and compression difference limit between cylinders is 14 psi.
11. If compression in one or more cylinders is low, pour a small amount of engine oil into cylinders through spark plug holes, then retest compression.
12. If adding oil helps compression, then piston rings may be at fault. If adding oil does not help compression, then valves may be at fault.
13. If compression stays low in two cylinders that are next to each other, then cylinder head gasket may be leaking or both cylinders have valve component damage.
14. Repair as necessary.

ENGINE MOUNT

REPLACE

Refer to **Fig. 1** for engine mount replacement.

ENGINE

REPLACE

1. Drain engine coolant.
2. Remove engine undercover and hood.
3. Drain engine coolant.
4. Release fuel system pressure as outlined under " Precautions."
5. Disconnect necessary electrical connections and vacuum hoses.

6. Remove drive belts, power steering pump, A/C compressor, alternator and driveshafts.
7. Remove front exhaust pipe.
8. Attach suitable engine lift and raise engine slightly.
9. Remove right, left, front and rear engine mounts, then center member, **Fig. 1.**
10. Place suitable jack under transaxle and engine, then lower engine and transaxle assembly.
11. Remove engine to transaxle attaching bolts, then remove engine.
12. Reverse procedure to install.

VALVE CLEARANCE SPECIFICATIONS

Intake, Inch①	Exhaust, Inch①
.0012–.0015	.0013–.0016

① — Engine @ operating temperature.

VALVE ADJUSTMENT

1. Remove rocker cover.
2. Remove spark plugs and set No. 1 piston to TDC of compression stroke.
3. Use feeler gauge to measure and record clearance between valve lifter and camshaft on No. 1 and No. 2 intake valves, and No. 1 and No. 3 exhaust valves.
4. Turn crankshaft 360° and align crankshaft pulley mark with point.
5. Use feeler gauge to measure and record clearance between valve lifter and camshaft on Nos. 3 and 4 intake valves, and Nos. 2 and 4 exhaust valves.

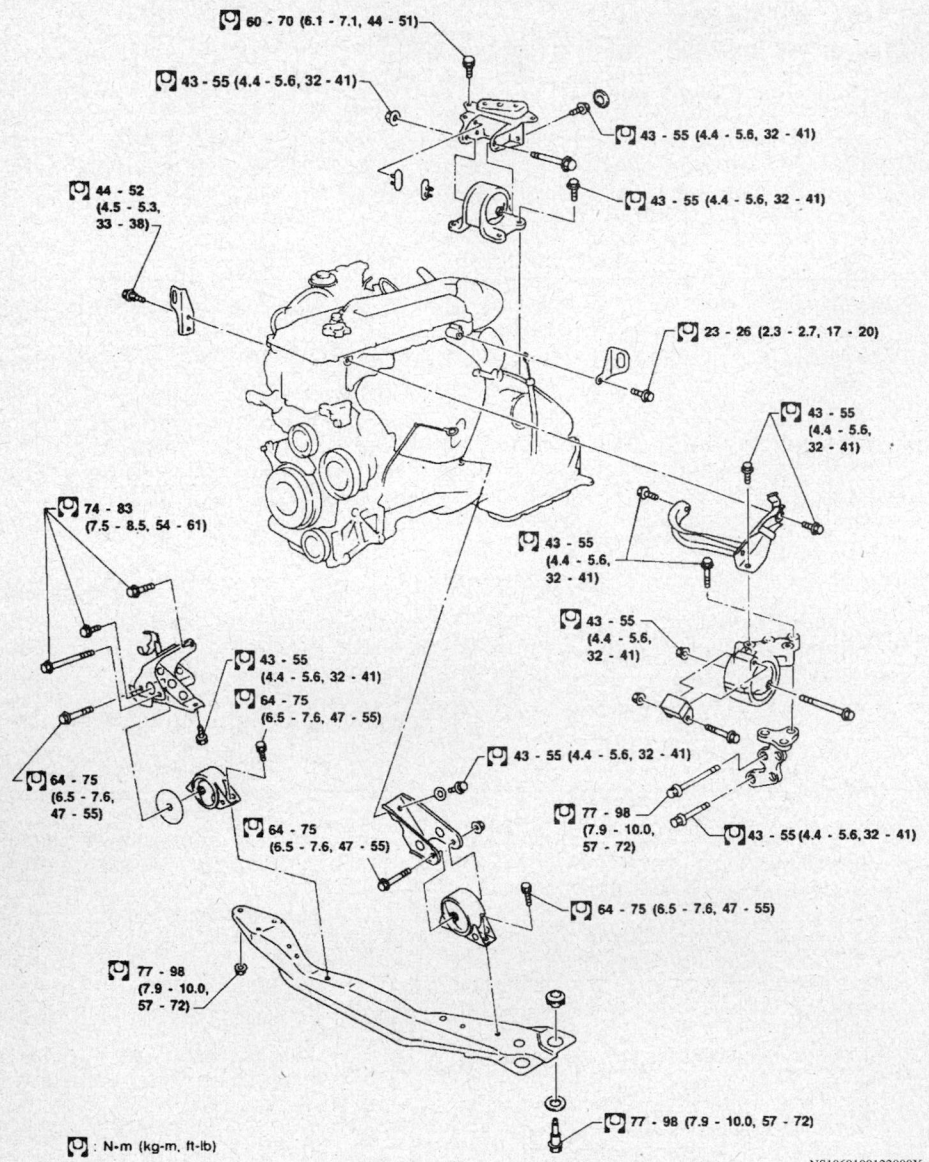

Fig. 1 Engine mount replacement

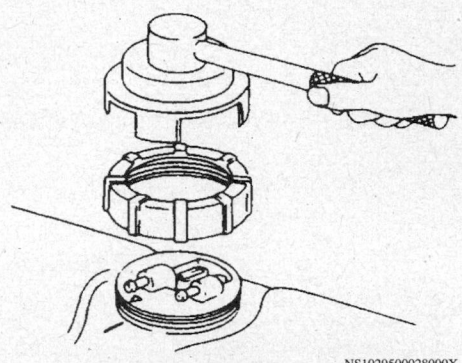

	Used belt deflection		Deflection of new belt
	Limit	Deflection after adjustment	
Generator & Power steering oil pump	8 (0.31)	6 - 7 (0.24 - 0.28)	5 - 6 (0.20 - 0.24)
Air conditioning compressor	10 (0.39)	7 - 8 (0.28 - 0.31)	6 - 7 (0.24 - 0.28)
Applied pushing force	98 N (10 kg, 22 lb)		

Unit: mm (in)

NS1069100124000X

Fig. 2 Belt deflection specifications

Fig. 4 Fuel tank lock ring removal

6. Turn crankshaft to position cam lobe on valve to be adjusted.
7. Place suitable camshaft pliers around camshaft and rotate so lifter is pushed down.
8. Place suitable lifter stopper between camshaft and edge of lifter and remove pliers.
9. Blow air into hole to separate adjusting shim from valve lifter, then remove shim with small screwdriver and magnetic finger.
10. Measure removed shim and calculate thickness of new shim necessary to obtain specified clearance. New intake shim size equals removed shim size plus measured clearance minus (.0146 inch). New exhaust shim size equals removed shim size plus measured clearance minus (.0146 inch). Shims are available from .0772 inch to .1055 inch, in .0008 inch steps.
11. Install new shim, attach pliers, rotate, then remove stopper and pliers.
12. Recheck valve clearance.
13. Repeat shim removal and replacement procedure as necessary.
14. Reverse procedure to install.

BELT TENSION DATA

Refer to **Fig. 2** for belt deflection specifications.

RADIATOR
REPLACE

1. Drain engine coolant.
2. Disconnect radiator upper and lower hoses, **Fig. 3**.
3. **On models equipped with automatic transmission,** remove automatic transmission oil cooler lines.

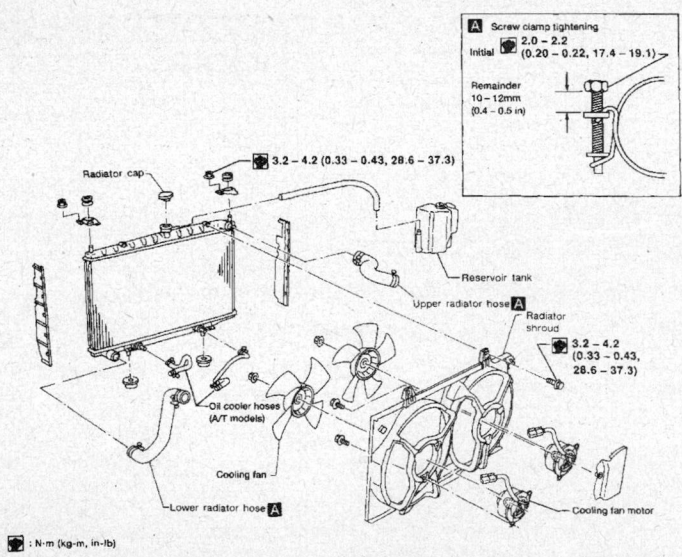

Fig. 3 Radiator replacement

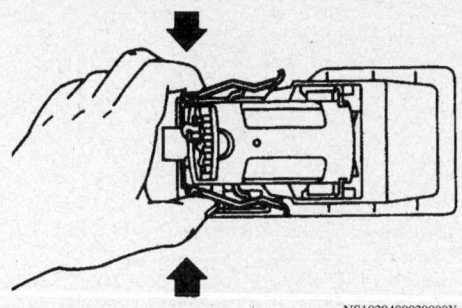

Fig. 5 Fuel pump removal

4. **On all models,** remove radiator shroud.
5. Disconnect reservoir tank hose.
6. Lift radiator out of vehicle carefully to avoid damage.
7. Reverse procedure to install.

FUEL PUMP
REPLACE

1. Release fuel pump pressure as outlined under "Precautions."
2. Remove rear seat back and bottom.
3. Remove inspection hole cover located under rear seat.
4. Disconnect necessary fuel lines and electrical connectors.
5. Remove lock ring using tool No. KV999G0010 (J38879), or equivalent, **Fig. 4.**
6. Remove fuel pump by pinching two tabs together while lifting out of fuel tank, **Fig. 5.**
7. Reverse procedure to install.

FUEL FILTER
REPLACE

1. Release fuel system pressure as out-

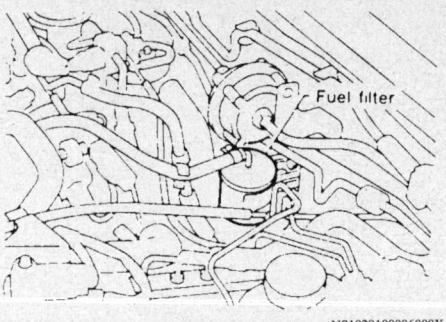

Fig. 6 Fuel filter location

lined under "Precautions."
2. Loosen two fuel filter hose clamps, **Fig. 6.**
3. Remove fuel filter. **Wrap filter with a rag to prevent fuel spillage.**
4. Reverse procedure to install.

TIGHTENING SPECIFICATIONS

Year	Component	Torque, Ft. Lbs.
1996–99	Aluminum Oil Pan Bolts	60–72①
	Crankshaft Pulley	105–112
	Driveplate	105–112
	Engine Crossmember	57–72
	Flywheel	105–112
	Front Exhaust Pipe	22–27
	Lefthand Camshaft Sprocket	123–130
	Lower Chain Guide	9–14
	Oil Drain Plug	22–29
	Righthand Camshaft Sprocket	48–61
	Steel Oil Pan Bolts	12–14
	Upper Chain Guide	12–14
	Upper Engine Mount	32–41
	Upper Timing Chain Tensioner	12–14

① — Inch lbs.

Clutch & Manual Transaxle

INDEX

PRECAUTIONS
BATTERY GROUND CABLE

Prior to service, disconnect battery ground cable and isolate as required.

ADJUSTMENTS
CLUTCH PEDAL

The clutch hydraulic system must be bled whenever a clutch line has been disconnected or when air has entered the system. The bleed valve is located on the clutch operating cylinder.

1. Adjust clutch pedal height "H," **Fig. 1,** to 6.6–6.9 inches by turning clutch switch or pedal stopper, then **torque** clutch switch locknut to 9–11 ft. lbs. or pedal stopper locknut to 14–16 ft. lbs.
2. Adjust pedal freeplay "A," **Fig. 1,** to .04–.12 inch (1–3mm) by turning pushrod, then **torque** pushrod locknut to 6–8 ft. lbs.
3. Adjust clearance "C," **Fig. 2,** between pedal stopper rubber and threaded end of clutch interlock switch, to .004–.039 inch, while depressing clutch pedal fully.

HYDRAULIC SYSTEM SERVICE
CLUTCH SLAVE CYLINDER

1. Disconnect brake line from slave cylinder. **Do not bend brake line.**

2. Remove cylinder attaching bolts, then the slave cylinder.
3. Reverse procedure to install, then bleed clutch hydraulic system as outlined under "Clutch System Bleed."

CLUTCH SYSTEM BLEED

The clutch hydraulic system must be bled whenever a clutch line has been disconnected or when air has entered the system. The bleed valve is located on the clutch operating cylinder. Carefully monitor fluid level at master cylinder during bleeding operation.

1. Fill up reservoir with recommended brake fluid.
2. Connect a transparent vinyl tube to air bleeder valve.
3. Fully depress clutch pedal several times.
4. With clutch pedal depressed, open bleeder valve to release air.
5. Close bleeder valve.
6. Repeat steps 3 through 5 until brake fluid flows from air bleeder valve without air bubbles.

CLUTCH
REPLACE

1. Remove transaxle as outlined in "Transaxle Replace" in this section.
2. Insert a dummy shaft into clutch disc hub.
3. Loosen clutch cover attaching bolts alternately.

4. Remove clutch disc and cover assembly.
5. Remove release bearing.
6. Reverse procedure to install.

TRANSAXLE
REPLACE

1. Remove battery and battery support bracket from vehicle.
2. Remove air cleaner assembly and air flow meter as necessary.
3. Raise and support vehicle.
4. Remove both driveshafts.
5. Remove front exhaust pipe retaining bolts.
6. Disconnect all cables and electrical connectors from transaxle.
7. Using a suitable jack, support engine with a wooden block placed between oil pan and jack.
8. Remove starter motor, if necessary.
9. Remove engine mount retaining bolts.
10. Remove engine to transaxle retaining bolts, then separate engine from transaxle and lower transaxle assembly from vehicle.
11. Reverse procedure to install.

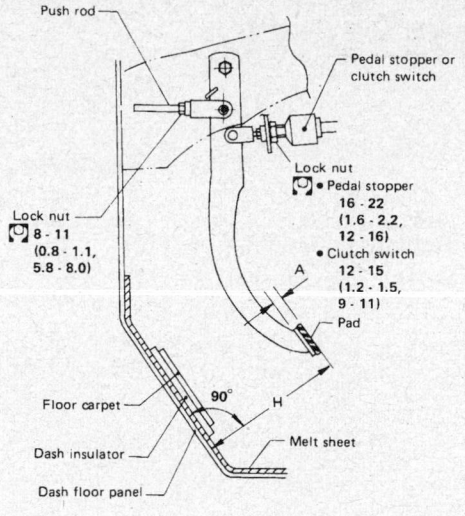

Fig. 1 Clutch pedal height & freeplay adjustment

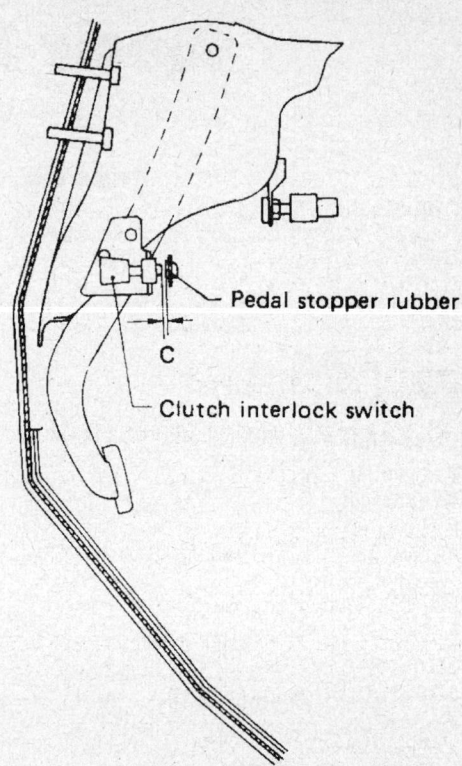

Fig. 2 Clutch interlock switch adjustment

TIGHTENING SPECIFICATIONS

Year	Component	Torque, Ft. Lbs.
1996–99	Bleeder Screw	48–84 ①
	Clutch Cover Attaching Bolts	16–22
	Clutch Interlock Switch Attaching Nut	9–11
	Clutch Master Cylinder Attaching Nuts	72–96 ①
	Clutch Slave Cylinder Attaching Bolts	22–30
	Flywheel	105–112
	Transaxle (45 & 48 mm Bolts)	29–36
	Transaxle (Except 45 & 48 mm Bolts)	22–30

① — Inch lbs.

Rear Axle & Suspension

INDEX

REAR AXLE

REPLACE

1. Raise and support vehicle, then remove rear wheels.
2. **On models equipped with drum brakes,** disconnect brake hydraulic line, parking brake cable at equalizer, then remove parking brake cable attaching bolts.
3. **On models equipped with disc brakes,** disconnect parking brake cable from caliper, then remove caliper assembly. **Brake hydraulic hose does not have to be disconnected.**
4. **On all models,** remove stabilizer and suspension member attaching bolts, **Fig. 1.**
5. Lower vehicle, then remove rear seat and parcel shelf.
6. Remove upper strut retaining nuts, then the rear axle.
7. Reverse procedure to install.

STRUT

REPLACE

Refer to "Rear Axle, Replace" procedure for strut replacement.

STRUT SERVICE

DISASSEMBLE

1. Position strut assembly into a suitable vise, then loosen piston rod locknut. **Do not remove piston rod locknut at this time.**
2. Using spring compressor tool No. HT71780000, or equivalent, compress coil spring until the strut mounting insulator can be turned by hand.
3. Remove piston rod locknut.
4. Using gland packing removal tool No. ST35490000, or equivalent, remove gland packing.
5. Retract piston rod by pushing it down until it bottoms, then slowly withdraw piston rod from cylinder together with piston guide.

ASSEMBLE

1. Install gland packing.
2. Place spring on strut assembly, then install dust cover and upper spring rubber seat.
3. Install upper spring seat, **Fig. 2.**
4. Install strut mounting insulator, spacer and strut mounting collar.

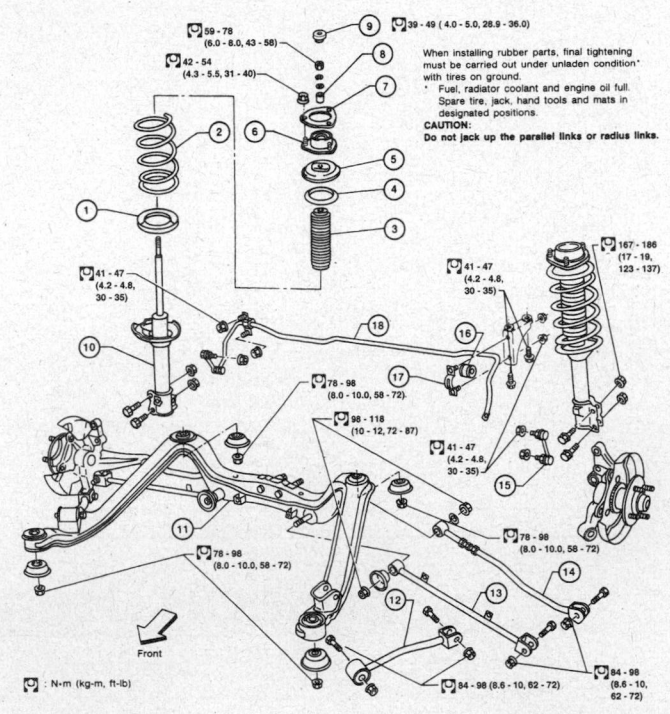

①	Lower spring rubber seat	⑦	Spacer	⑬	Front parallel link
②	Coil spring	⑧	Strut mounting collar	⑭	Rear parallel link
③	Bound bumper with dust cover	⑨	Strut damper	⑮	Connecting rod
④	Upper spring rubber seat	⑩	Strut assembly	⑯	Bushing
⑤	Upper spring seat	⑪	Suspension member	⑰	Clamp
⑥	Strut mounting insulator	⑫	Radius link	⑱	Stabilizer bar

NS2039100009000X

Fig. 1   Exploded view of rear suspension

5. Install piston rod locknut.
6. After placing coil spring in position on lower spring seat, release spring compressor gradually.
7. Tighten piston rod locknut to specifications.

COIL SPRING

REPLACE

Refer to "Strut, Replace" for procedure.

STABILIZER BAR

REPLACE

1. Raise and support vehicle.
2. Remove stabilizer bar, **Fig. 3.**
3. Reverse procedure to install, noting the following:
   a. Ensure paint marks are positioned as shown in **Fig. 4.**
   b. Ensure stabilizer ball joint socket is properly placed, **Fig. 5.**

PARALLEL & RADIUS LINK

REPLACE

1. Raise and support vehicle.
2. Remove parallel and radius link, **Fig. 6.**
3. Reverse procedure to install, noting the following:
   a. When installing front parallel link, ensure paint mark faces in the correct direction, **Fig. 7.**
   b. Final tightening of the parallel and radius link must be done with tires on ground.
   c. Check rear wheel alignment.

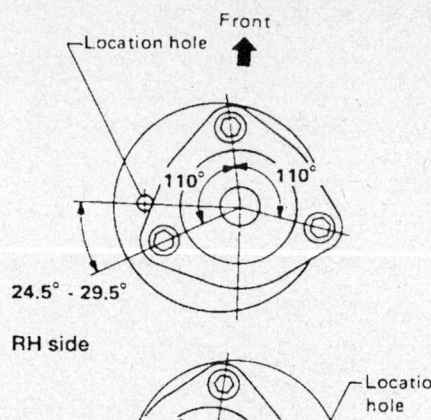

Fig. 2 Upper spring seat positioning

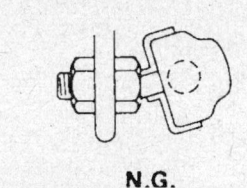

O.K.   N.G.

Fig. 5 Stabilizer bar ball joint socket position

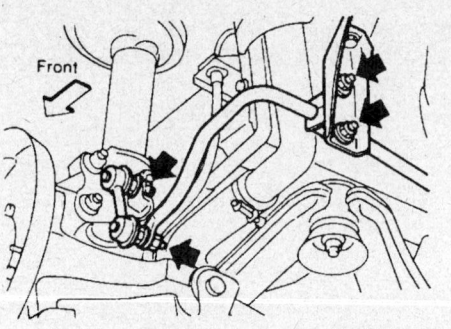

Fig. 3 Stabilizer bar removal

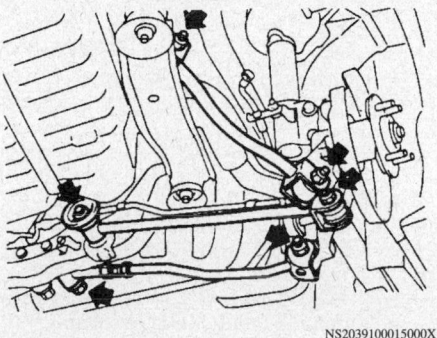

Fig. 6 Parallel & radius link removal

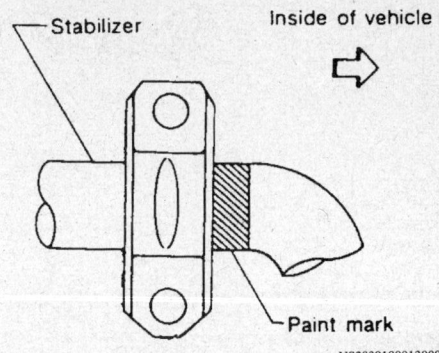

Fig. 4 Stabilizer bar installation

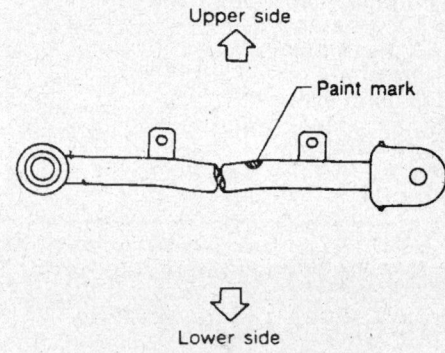

Fig. 7 Front parallel link installation

TIGHTENING SPECIFICATIONS

Year	Component	Torque, Ft. Lbs.
1996–99	Axle Nut	137–188
	Driveshaft Nut	137–188
	Front Parallel Link To Suspension Crossmember	72–87
	Hub Nut	137–188
	Lower Strut Mounting Bolts	87–108
	Piston Rod Locknut	43–58
	Radius Link To Suspension Crossmember	62–72
	Rear Parallel Link To Suspension Crossmember	72–87
	Stabilizer Bar Clamps	30–35
	Stabilizer Bar Connecting Rod	30–35
	Suspension Member	62–72
	Upper Strut Securing Nuts	31–40
	Wheel Lug Nut	72–87

Front Suspension & Steering

NOTE: On Air Bag Equipped Models, Refer To "Air Bag System Precautions" Located In The Front Of This Manual For System Disarming & Arming Procedures.

NOTE: Refer To "Computer Relearn Procedures" Located In The Front Of This Manual For Computer Relearn Procedures.

INDEX

PRECAUTIONS

AIR BAG SYSTEMS

Refer to "Air Bag System Precautions" in the front of this manual for system disarming and arming procedures.

BATTERY GROUND CABLE

Prior to service, disconnect battery ground cable and isolate as required.

WHEEL BEARING INSPECTION

1. Raise and support vehicle.
2. Remove brake pads.
3. Ensure wheel bearing is tightened to the correct specification.
4. Ensure wheel bearing operates smoothly.
5. Check axial endplay.
6. If axial endplay is not .0020 inch or less, replace wheel bearing.

WHEEL HUB & STEERING KNUCKLE

REPLACE

1. Raise and support vehicle, then remove wheel.
2. Remove wheel bearing locknut, **Fig. 1,** then the brake caliper. **Brake hose need not be disconnected from brake caliper. Do not depress brake pedal with caliper removed.**
3. Separate tie rod from knuckle using a suitable tool.
4. Separate driveshafts from knuckle by lightly tapping end of driveshaft.
5. Remove knuckle attaching bolts as shown in **Fig. 2,** then the knuckle.
6. To remove wheel bearing assembly from knuckle, proceed as follows:

a. Drive hub with inner race from knuckle using suitable tool.
b. Remove bearing inner race, then the grease seal.
c. Using a screwdriver, remove inner grease seal from knuckle.
d. Remove inner and outer snap rings.
e. Using a suitable tool, press out bearing outer race.
7. To install wheel bearing assembly into knuckle, proceed as follows:
a. Install inner snap ring into groove of knuckle.
b. Using a suitable press, press new wheel bearing assembly into knuckle. **Do not press inner race of wheel bearing assembly. Do not apply oil or grease to mating surfaces of wheel bearing outer race and knuckle.**
c. Install outer snap ring into groove of knuckle.
d. Pack grease seal lip with multipurpose grease, then install outer grease seal.
e. Install inner grease seal, then press hub into knuckle.
8. Reverse steps 1 through 5 to install wheel hub and steering knuckle assembly.

BALL JOINT INSPECTION

1. Raise front of vehicle and support with suitable jack stands.
2. Clamp dial indicator onto transverse link and place dial indicator tip on lower edge of brake caliper, **Fig. 3.**
3. Ensure front wheels are straight ahead and brake pedal is depressed.
4. Place a suitable pry bar between transverse link and inner rim of wheel.
5. While raising and releasing pry bar, observe dial indicator.

6. There should not be any vertical end play indicated.

BALL JOINT

REPLACE

LOWER

1. Raise and support vehicle, then remove wheel.
2. Remove stabilizer connecting rod from transverse link.
3. Remove cotter pin and locknut securing lower ball joint to knuckle.
4. Strike knuckle with a hammer to separate lower ball joint from knuckle.
5. Remove bolts and nuts shown in **Fig. 4.**
6. Remove transverse link and lower ball joint.
7. Reverse procedure to install, noting the following:
a. Final tightening of bolts and nuts must be done with vehicle at curb height and tires on the ground.
b. Check wheel alignment.

STRUT

REPLACE

1. Raise and support front of vehicle, then remove wheels.
2. Disconnect brake line from strut if necessary.
3. Remove strut to steering knuckle attaching nuts and bolts, **Fig. 5.**
4. Remove strut to strut tower attaching nuts, then the strut assembly from the vehicle.
5. Reverse procedure to install.

STRUT SERVICE

DISASSEMBLE

1. Secure strut assembly in a vise.

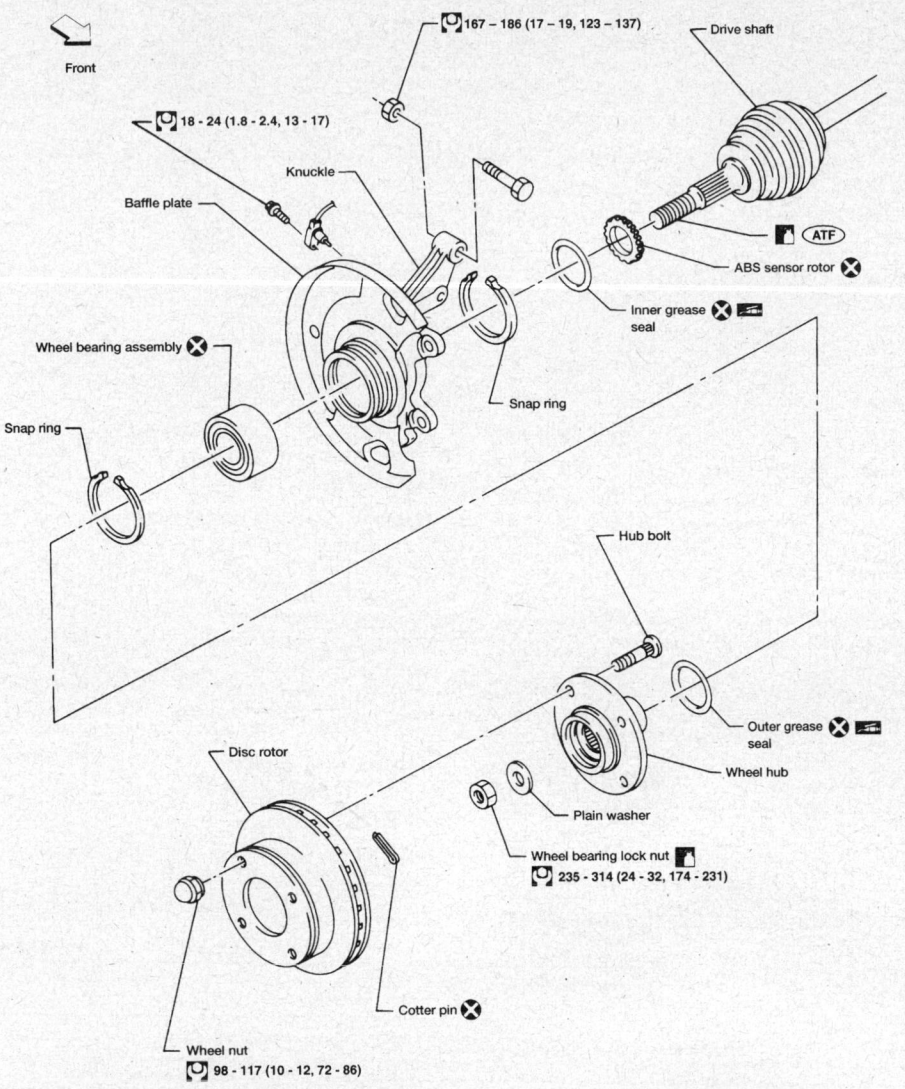

Fig. 1 Exploded view of wheel hub & steering knuckle

NS2049100022000X

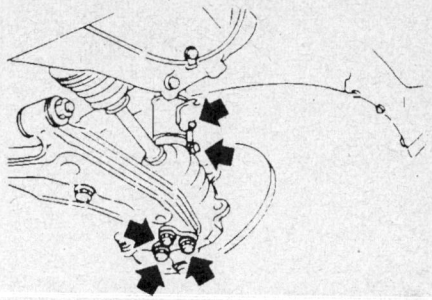

NS2049100023000X

Fig. 2 Knuckle & hub assembly removal

4. Remove bolt securing lower joint to steering gear pinion and remove lower joint from pinion. Refer to **Fig. 8,** when replacing power steering gear.
5. Remove steering gear attaching bolts.
6. Remove steering gear and linkage assembly from vehicle.
7. Reverse procedure to install.

POWER STEERING PUMP
REPLACE

1. Remove air conditioning compressor drive belt.
2. Loosen idler pulley locknut.
3. Turn adjusting nut counterclockwise and remove power steering pump drive belt.
4. Loosen power steering hoses at pump and remove bolts securing power steering pump to brackets.
5. Raise pump and disconnect power steering hoses. Catch fluid in a suitable container, plug hose ends and ports in power steering pump, and remove pump from vehicle.
6. Reverse procedure to install, then bleed system as follows:
   a. Raise and support front of vehicle.
   b. Run engine for three to five seconds, stop engine, check and fill power steering pump reservoir as needed.
   c. Quickly turn steering wheel all the way to right and left ten times.
   d. Start engine and idle for three to five seconds. Stop engine, check and fill power steering pump reservoir as needed.
   e. With steering wheel all the way to the right, open bleeder screw, to expel air and tighten bleeder screw.
   f. Repeat procedure until all air has been bled from system.
   g. If air cannot be bled completely after repeated attempts, repeat step "e" with engine running.

2. Loosen piston rod locknut. **Do not remove piston rod locknut at this time.**
3. Using spring compressor tool No. HT71780000, or equivalent, compress coil spring until strut mounting insulator can be turned by hand.
4. Remove piston rod locknut.
5. Remove remaining parts from strut assembly.

ASSEMBLE

1. Install bound bumper and dust cover.
2. Install spring, position spring as shown in **Figs. 6.**
3. Install upper spring seat, ensure it is positioned as shown in **Fig. 7.**

4. Install strut lock washer, then the strut mounting insulator.
5. Install piston rod locknut and tighten to specifications.
6. Install cap and spacer.

POWER STEERING GEAR
REPLACE

1. Raise and support front of vehicle, then remove wheels.
2. Disconnect power steering hose clamp, then the hose at steering gear and drain fluid into a suitable container.
3. Disconnect tie rod studs from steering knuckles.

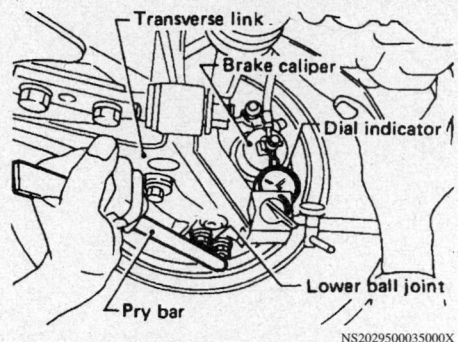

Fig. 3 Ball joint inspection

NS2029500035000X

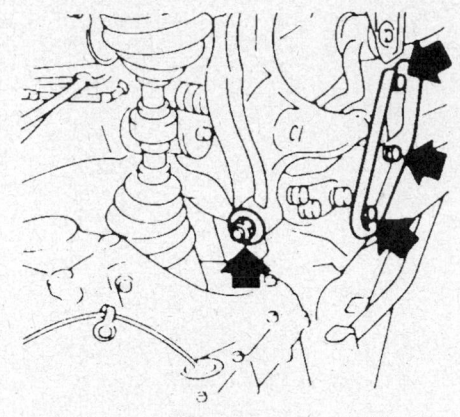

NS2029100019000X

Fig. 4 Transverse link & lower
ball joint removal

When installing rubber parts, final tightening
must be carried out under unladen condition*
with tires on ground.
* Fuel, radiator coolant and engine oil full.
  Spare tire, jack, hand tools and mats in
  designated positions.

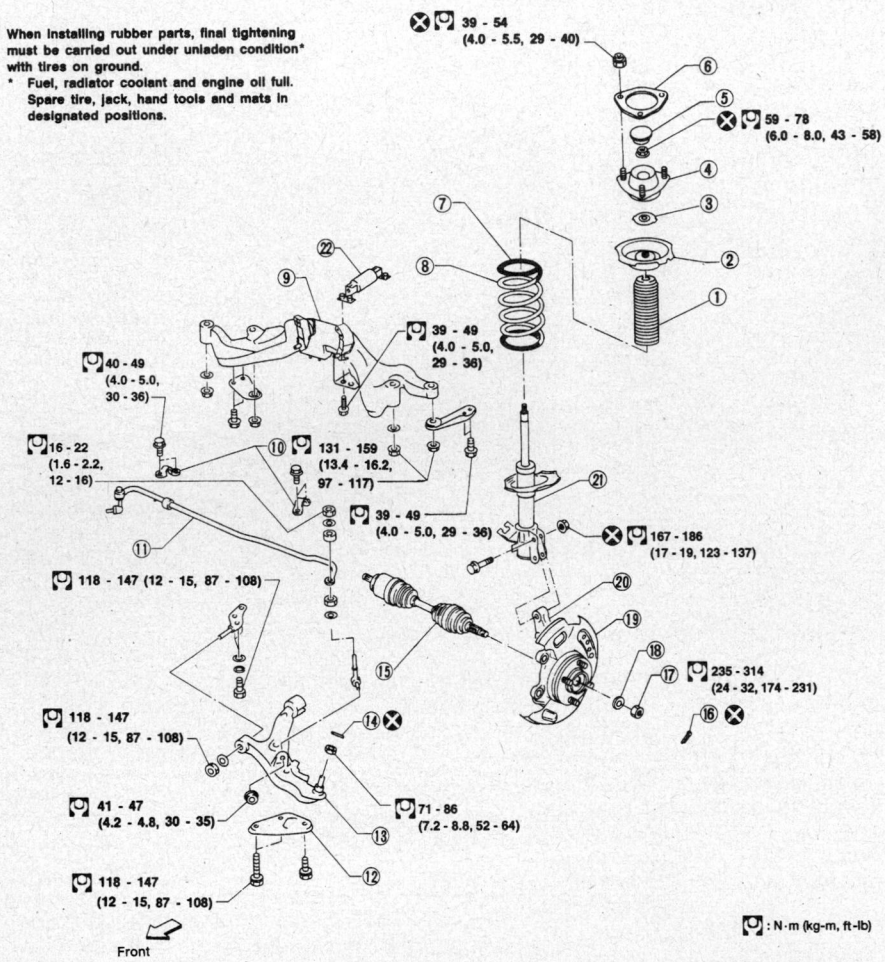

39 - 54
(4.0 - 5.5, 29 - 40)

59 - 78
(6.0 - 8.0, 43 - 58)

40 - 49
(4.0 - 5.0,
30 - 36)

16 - 22
(1.6 - 2.2,
12 - 16)

131 - 159
(13.4 - 16.2,
97 - 117)

39 - 49
(4.0 - 5.0, 29 - 36)

39 - 49
(4.0 - 5.0, 29 - 36)

167 - 186
(17 - 19, 123 - 137)

118 - 147 (12 - 15, 87 - 108)

118 - 147
(12 - 15, 87 - 108)

235 - 314
(24 - 32, 174 - 231)

41 - 47
(4.2 - 4.8, 30 - 35)

71 - 86
(7.2 - 8.8, 52 - 64)

118 - 147
(12 - 15, 87 - 108)

Front

: N·m (kg-m, ft-lb)

① Bound bumper with dust cover
② Upper spring seat
③ Dust seal
④ Strut insulator
⑤ Cap
⑥ Spacer
⑦ (Polyurethane tube)
⑧ Coil spring

⑨ Front suspension member
⑩ Stabilizer clamp
⑪ Stabilizer
⑫ Compression rod clamp
⑬ Transverse link
⑭ Cotter pin
⑮ Drive shaft
⑯ Cotter pin

⑰ Wheel bearing lock nut
⑱ Plain washer
⑲ Baffle plate
⑳ Knuckle
㉑ Strut assembly
㉒ Front suspension damper
   assembly
   (A/T models except XE)

NS2029100015000X

Fig. 5 Exploded view of front suspension

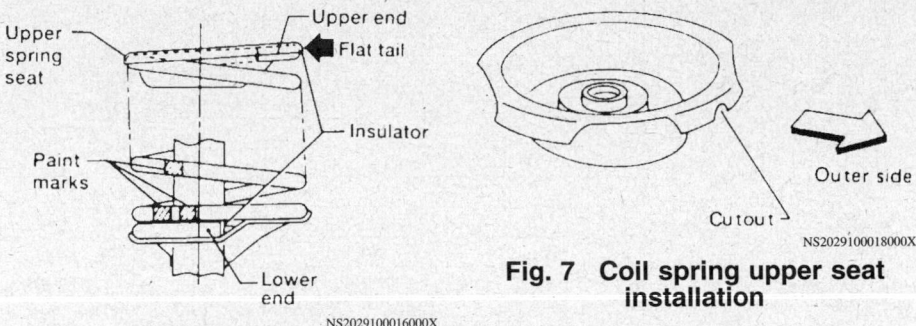

Fig. 7 Coil spring upper seat installation

Fig. 6 Coil spring installation

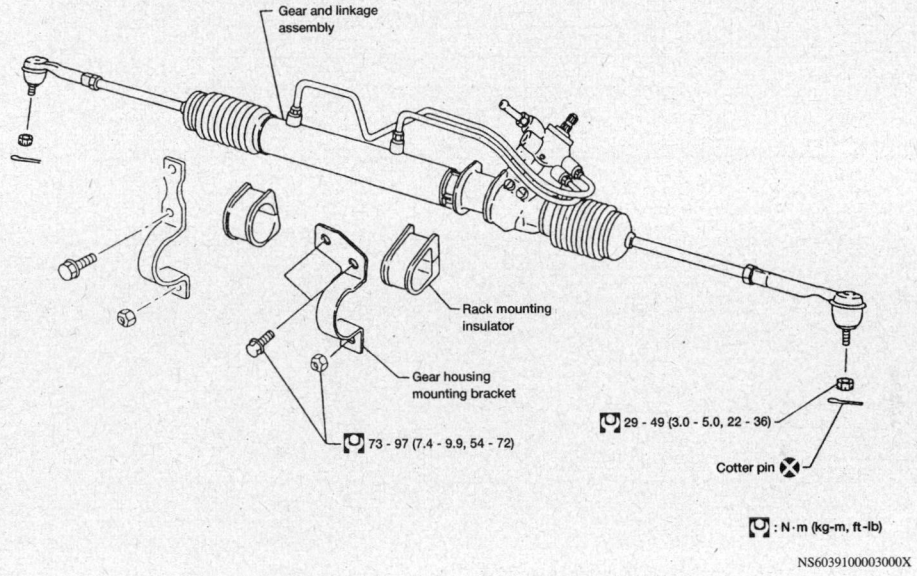

73 - 97 (7.4 - 9.9, 54 - 72)

29 - 49 (3.0 - 5.0, 22 - 36)

Cotter pin

: N·m (kg-m, ft-lb)

NS6039100003000X

Fig. 8 Power steering gear replacement

TIGHTENING SPECIFICATIONS

Year	Component	Torque, Ft. Lbs.
1996–99	Axle Nut	174–231
	Ball Joint Attaching Nut	56–80
	Driveshaft Nut	174–231
	Hub Nut	174–231
	Piston Rod Locknut	43–58
	Steering Gear Attaching Bolts	54–72
	Steering Knuckle Upper Attaching Bolt	82–91
	Strut To Lower Knuckle Arm Attaching Bolts	82–91
	Tie Rod Attaching Nut	22–29
	Transverse Link Attaching Nuts	65–87
	Transverse Link Bracket Attaching Nuts	87–108
	Upper Strut Attaching Bolts	43–53
	Wheel Bearing Locknut	174–231
	Wheel Lug Nut	72–87

Wheel Alignment

INDEX

PRELIMINARY INSPECTION

1. Check tire pressures and adjust as needed.
2. Ensure tires are of the proper size and are properly matched.
3. Check steering gear adjustment and ensure steering gear is properly secured to frame.
4. Inspect steering linkage and suspension components for damage and wear, and repair or replace components as needed.
5. Measure vehicle ride height with vehicle unloaded and ensure springs are not collapsed.
6. Place vehicle on suitable alignment rack following manufacturer's instructions, then jounce vehicle several times to settle suspension.
7. Check and correct rear wheel camber and toe first, if applicable, then check and correct front suspension angles in the following order: caster and kingpin inclination, camber, toe setting and turning angle (toe-out on turns).

FRONT WHEEL ALIGNMENT

Correct front wheel alignment is necessary to provide proper handling and to prevent uneven tire wear. To ensure correct alignment, angles should be checked, and if necessary corrected, in the following sequence: caster and kingpin inclination, camber, toe-setting, and the turning angle and toe-out on turns. Front wheel alignment should only be checked after ensuring the rear wheels are properly aligned in relation to the vehicle centerline, as most equipment uses the rear wheels as reference for correct front wheel alignment. Front wheel alignment should be checked with the vehicle at normal ride height, and following equipment manufacturer's instructions.

CASTER & KINGPIN INCLINATION

Kingpin inclination is a function of the steering knuckle design and cannot be adjusted. Caster, the alignment angle which provides the self-centering steering effect, is not adjustable. If caster or kingpin angle are not within specifications, check suspension components and sheet metal for damage, distortion and excessive wear, repair or replace as necessary.

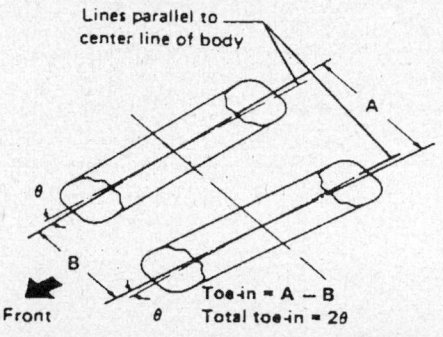

Fig. 1   Toe-in measurement

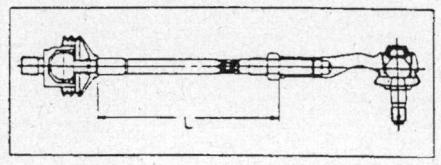

Fig. 2   Tie rod length measurement

CAMBER

Camber cannot be adjusted. If camber is not within specifications, inspect suspension and sheet metal for damage, distortion and excessive wear, and repair or replace components as needed.

TOE-IN

The toe setting is the measurement of the wheels in relation to the vehicle centerline, **Fig. 1.** The leading edge of each wheel should toe-in or toe-out slightly in relation to the vehicle centerline to ensure proper vehicle tracking. Toe should be inspected using suitable alignment gauges, following manufacturer's instructions. When checking or adjusting toe, always ensure the setting of the left and right wheels is as equal as possible.

Toe is adjusted by loosening the tie rod locknuts or adjusting sleeve bolts and equally altering the length of the tie rods. After toe has been adjusted to specifications, the lengths of the left and right tie rods, **Fig. 2,** should be nearly equal. If tie rod lengths are incorrect, tie rods should be disassembled and adjusted to equal lengths, and the toe setting should be readjusted before checking steering angles. Incorrect tie rod length will adversely affect steering angles and toe-out on turns.

STEERING ANGLE

1. Set wheel in a straight ahead position.
2. Position front wheel on turning radius gauge.
3. Rotate fully steering wheel to right and left.
4. Ensure turning angle is as specified in "Front Wheel Alignment Specifications."

REAR WHEEL ALIGNMENT

The proper alignment of the rear suspension and wheels is essential for proper handling and to providing a reference for front wheel alignment. Always ensure rear wheel alignment is within specifications prior to checking and adjusting front wheel alignment.

CAMBER

Rear camber cannot be adjusted. If rear camber is not within specifications, check for damaged or worn suspension components and deformed sheet metal, and repair as needed.

TOE-IN

On models equipped with independent rear suspension, rear toe is the measurement of the rear wheels in relation to the vehicle centerline, **Fig. 1.** The leading edge of each rear wheel should toe-in slightly toward the vehicle centerline to ensure proper vehicle tracking. Rear toe should be inspected using suitable alignment gauges, following manufacturer's instructions. When checking or adjusting rear toe, always ensure the amount that the left and right wheels toe-in is as equal as possible.

Rear toe-in is adjusted by varying the length of the rear parallel links, **Fig. 3.**

1. Measure total toe-in and toe-in for each wheel following equipment manufacturer's instructions.
2. Loosen locknuts and adjust parallel link length to obtain specified toe-in, noting the following:
   a. Adjust left and right rear parallel links to the same length A, **Fig. 4.**
   b. Standard length is 1.97–2.17 inches. If toe-in cannot be properly adjusted with links at equal length, and at or near specified standard length, check rear suspension for damage and wear, and repair as needed.

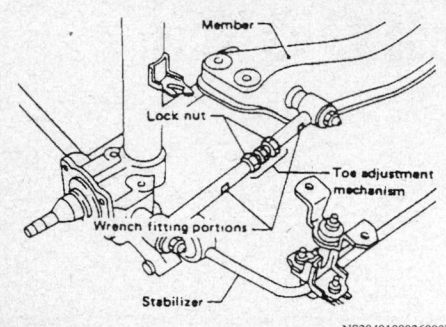

Fig. 3 Rear toe-in adjustment

3. After adjustment, hold link with suitable wrench to prevent bushing from twisting, then **torque** locknuts to 58–72 ft. lbs.

VEHICLE RIDE HEIGHT

1. Park vehicle on a level surface, then ensure tires are inflated to proper air pressure, fluid levels are to specified level and spare tire and jack are in their correct locations.
2. Bounce vehicle up and down several times, then measure vehicle height from top of wheelwell to ground.
3. Vehicle ride heights should be as follows:
   a. **On SE models,** 27.17 inches in the front and 26.69 inches in the rear.
   b. **On XE/GLE/GXE models,** vehicle ride height should be 27.20 inches in the front of vehicle and 26.77 inches in the rear of vehicle.
4. **On all models,** vehicle height is not

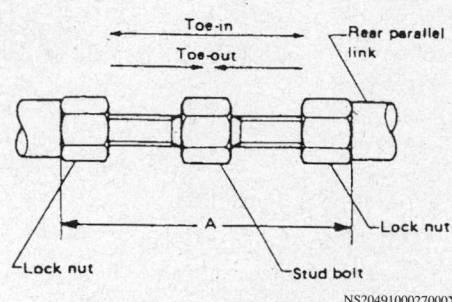

Fig. 4 Parallel link length measurement

adjustable. If vehicle height is not as specified, check for worn springs or suspension parts.

NISSAN MAXIMA & 300ZX

INDEX OF SERVICE OPERATIONS

Specifications

GENERAL ENGINE SPECIFICATIONS

Year	Engine Model	Fuel System	Displacement Liters	Bore x Stroke, Inches	Compression Ratio	Maximum HP @ RPM	Maximum Torque @ RPM	Normal Oil Pressure, psi①
1996	VG30DE	Fuel Inj.	3.0L	3.43 x 3.27	10.5	222 @ 6400	198 @ 4800	51–65
	VG30DETT	Fuel Inj.	3.0L	3.43 x 3.27	8.5	②	283 @ 3600	51–65
	VQ30DE	Fuel Inj.	3.0L	3.66 x 2.89	10.0	190 @ 5600	205 @ 4000	63–80
1997–99	VQ30DE	Fuel Inj.	3.0L	3.66 x 2.89	10.0	190 @ 5600	205 @ 4000	63–80

① — 3000 RPM.

② — Manual transmission, 300 HP @ 6400 RPM; automatic transmission, 280 HP @ 6400 RPM.

TUNE UP SPECIFICATIONS

Year	Engine Model	Spark Plug Gap, Inch	Ignition Firing Order	Ignition Timing, °BTDC	Curb Idle Speed Man. Trans.	Curb Idle Speed Auto. Trans.	Fuel Pump Pressure, psi	Valve Lash
1996	VG30DE	.041	1-2-3-4-5-6	15	650–750	650–750N	43	①
	VG30DETT	.041	1-2-3-4-5-6	15	720–820	700–800N	43	①
	VQ30DE	.041	1-2-3-4-5-6	15	600–700	650–750N	36	①
1997–99	VQ30DE	.041	1-2-3-4-5-6	15	525–625	600–700N	43	①

BTDC — Before Top Dead Center
N — Neutral

① — Refer to "Valve Adjustment" under specific engine section.

FRONT WHEEL ALIGNMENT SPECIFICATIONS

Year	Model	Caster Angle, ° Limits	Caster Angle, ° Desired	Camber Angle, ° Limits	Camber Angle, ° Desired	Kingpin Inclination, °	Toe-In, Inch①	Toe-Out On Turns, °② Inner Wheel	Toe-Out On Turns, °② Outer Wheel	Ball Joint Wear
1996	300ZX	+8 11/12 to +10 5/12	+9 2/3	−1 7/12 to −1/12	−5/6	12 1/6 to 13 2/3	0 to +.08	32 1/2 to 36 1/2	26 1/2 to 30 1/2	③
1997–99	Maxima	+2 to +3 1/2	+2 3/4	−1 to +1/2	−1/4	13 1/2 to 15	+.04 to +.12	37 to 41	28 7/10 to 32 7/10	③

① — Toe-in (+); toe-out (−).
② — Measure w/wheels at full lefthand & righthand turn positions.

③ — Refer to "Ball joint Inspection" in "Front Suspension & Steering" section.

REAR WHEEL ALIGNMENT SPECIFICATIONS

Year	Model	Camber Angle, ° Limits	Camber Angle, ° Desired	Toe, Inch①
1996	300ZX	−1 1/2 to −1/2	−1	+.016 to +.173
1997–99	Maxima	−1 3/4 to −1/4	−1	−.12 to +.20

① — Toe-in (+); toe-out (−).

FLUID CAPACITIES & COOLING SYSTEM DATA

Model	Coolant Capacity, Qts.	Radiator, Cap Relief Pressure, Lbs.	Thermo. Opening Temp., °F	Fuel Tank, Gals.	Engine Oil Refill, Qts.①	Transmission Oil		Differential Oil, Pts.
						Man. Trans., Pts.	Auto. Trans., Qts.②	
1996								
Maxima	11¼	11–14	180	18½	4½	③	10⅛	—
300ZX Non Turbo	9½	16–18	170	19	3⅝	5⅞	8¾	2¾
300ZX Turbo	9½	16–18	170	19	3⅝	5⅞	8⅝	3⅞
1997–99								
Maxima	9	11–14	180	18½	4¼	④	10	—

① — Includes filter.
② — Approximate, make final check w/dipstick.

③ — RS5F50A, 8 pts.; RS5F50V, 7 ⅝ pts.

④ — RS5F50A, 9⅛–9½ pts.; RS5F50V, 9½–10⅛ pts.

LUBRICANT DATA

Year	Model	Lubricant Type				
		Transmission		Rear Axle	Power Steering	Brake System
		Manual	Automatic			
1996	300ZX	75W-90 GL-4	Nissan Matic D ①	80W-90 GL-5	Dexron II/IIE/III	DOT 3
1997–99	Maxima	80W-90 GL-4	Nissan Matic D ①	—	Dexron II/IIE/III	DOT 3

① — Dexron III/Mercon, or equivalent automatic transmission fluid, may also be used.

Electrical

NOTE: On Air Bag Equipped Models, Refer To " Air Bag System Precautions" Located In Front Of This Manual For System Disarming & Arming Procedures.

INDEX

PRECAUTIONS

AIR BAG SYSTEMS

Refer to "Air Bag System Precautions" in front of this manual for system disarming and arming procedures.

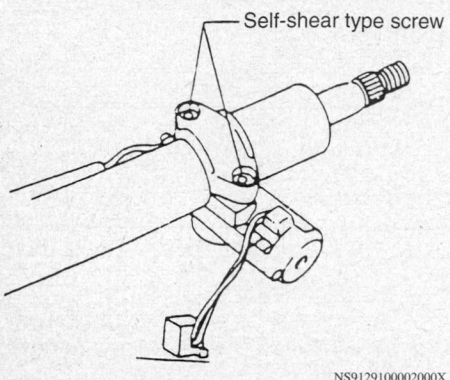

Self-shear type screw

NS9129100002000X

Fig. 1 Ignition lock replacement

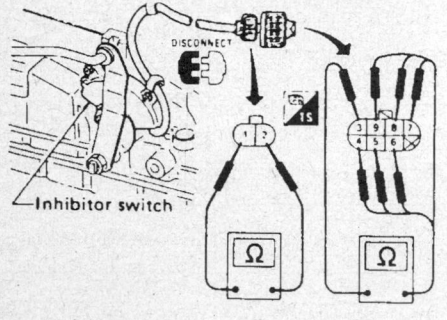

DISCONNECT

Inhibitor switch

NS9049100009000X

Fig. 4 Inhibitor switch continuity inspection. 300ZX

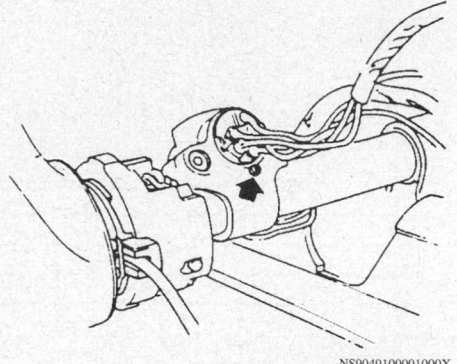

NS9049100001000X

Fig. 2 Ignition switch replacement

Lever position	Terminal No.	
P	① — ②	③ — ④
R	③ — ⑤	
N	① — ②	③ — ⑥
D	③ — ⑦	
2	③ — ⑧	
1	③ — ⑨	

NS9049100010000X

Fig. 5 Inhibitor switch continuity specifications. Maxima w/RE4F04V transaxle & 300ZX

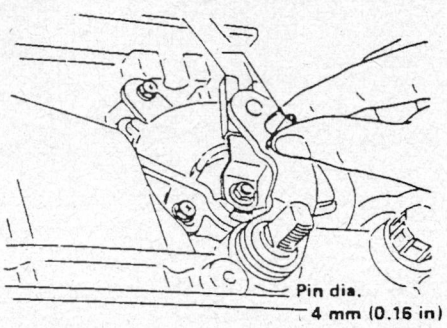

Pin dia. 4 mm (0.16 in)

NS9049100008000X

Fig. 3 Inhibitor switch adjustment. 300ZX

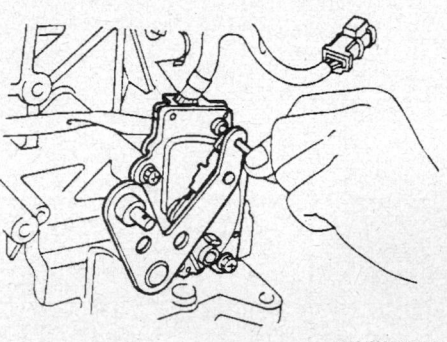

NS9049200012000X

Fig. 6 Inhibitor switch adjustment. Maxima w/VQ30DE engine

BATTERY GROUND CABLE

Prior to service, disconnect battery ground cable and isolate as required.

FUSE PANEL & FLASHER LOCATION

300ZX

The fuse panel is located behind the lefthand side kick panel. The combination flasher unit is located under the center of the instrument panel.

MAXIMA

The fuse panel is located behind the lefthand side of the instrument panel, to the left of the steering column. The combination flasher unit is located behind the center of the instrument panel.

FUEL PUMP RELAY LOCATION

The fuel pump relay is located behind the lefthand side kick panel.

RELAY CENTER LOCATION

The relay center is located in the front lefthand corner of the engine compartment.

STARTER
REPLACE

1. Remove air intake duct, if required.
2. Disconnect starter wiring from starter.
3. Remove starter motor mounting bolts, then the starter.
4. Reverse procedure to install.

COIL PACK
REPLACE

1. Remove ornament covers.
2. Disconnect coil electrical connectors from each coil.
3. Remove individual coil attaching bolts.
4. Disconnect coils from spark plugs.
5. Reverse procedure to install.

IGNITION LOCK
REPLACE

1. Drill out two shear type retaining screws, **Fig. 1**.
2. Remove ignition lock from steering tube.
3. Reverse procedure to install. Ensure shear type screws are used.

IGNITION SWITCH
REPLACE

1. Remove four upper and lower shell cover retaining screws, then the shell covers.
2. Disconnect electrical connectors from switch.
3. Remove switch retaining screw from steering lock, **Fig. 2**.
4. Reverse procedure to install.

NEUTRAL SAFETY SWITCH
REPLACE

300ZX

1. Place manual valve in Neutral (vertical position).
2. Remove adjustment cover screw.
3. Loosen switch attaching screws.
4. Using suitable alignment pin, move switch until pin falls into hole in rotor, **Fig. 3**.
5. Tighten attaching bolts. Then, while moving selector lever through all gear ranges, check switch for continuity as shown in **Fig. 4**.
6. Compare results with **Fig. 5**.
7. If switch does not operate as specified, replace switch.

MAXIMA

1. Remove control cable from manual lever, then set selector lever manual lever to Neutral position.
2. Loosen inhibitor switch attaching screws.
3. Insert suitable pin into adjustment holes in both inhibitor switch and switch lever as near vertical as possible, **Fig. 6**.
4. Tighten attaching bolts. Then, while moving selector lever through all gear ranges, check switch for continuity as shown in **Figs. 7 and 8**.
5. Compare results with **Figs. 5 and 9**.
6. If switch does not operate as specified, replace switch.

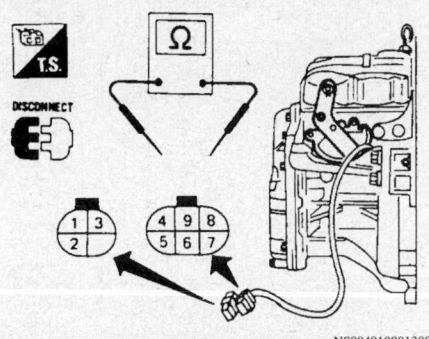

Fig. 7 Inhibitor switch continuity inspection. Maxima w/RE4F02A transaxle

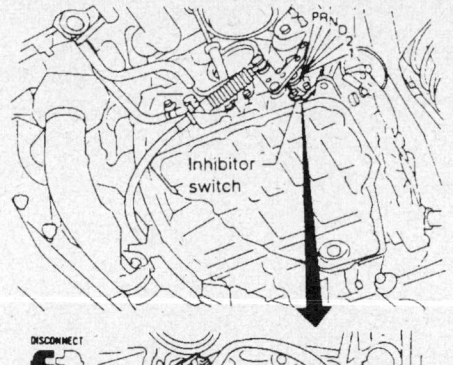

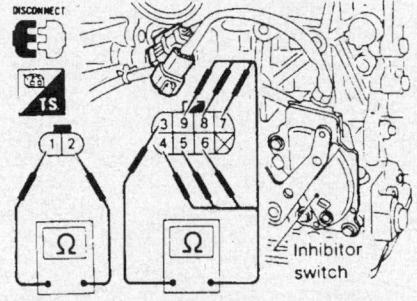

Fig. 8 Inhibitor switch continuity inspection. Maxima w/RE4F04V transaxle

Lever position	Terminal No.			
P	① — ③		④ — ⑥	
R	④ — ⑦			
N	① — ③		② — ④	
D	④ — ⑤			
2	④ — ⑧			
1	④ — ⑨			

Fig. 9 Inhibitor switch continuity specifications. Maxima w/RE4F02A transaxle

4. Disconnect switch electrical connectors from switch base, then remove switch.
5. Remove switch base, if necessary.
6. Reverse procedure to install.

TURN SIGNAL SWITCH
REPLACE

Refer to "Combination Switch, Replace" for turn signal switch replacement.

STEERING WHEEL
REPLACE

1. Place steering wheel in neutral position.
2. Remove lefthand and righthand side lids, **Fig. 10.**
3. Using special Torx bit No. T50H, or equivalent, remove lefthand and righthand special bolts.
4. Remove air bag module from steering wheel. **Always place air bag module with pad side facing upward. Do not attempt to disassemble air bag module. Special bolts are coated with a bonding agent, discard after removal and replace. If any portion of air bag module is damaged or cracked, replace module. Do not allow oil, grease or water to come into contact with air bag module.**
5. Ensure steering wheel is in neutral position, then disconnect horn electrical connector and remove steering wheel attaching nut.
6. Remove steering wheel using puller tool No. J25726-A, or equivalent.
7. Reverse procedure to install, noting the following:
   a. Install steering wheel aligning spiral cable pin guides, and pull spiral cable connector through steering wheel, **Fig. 11.**
   b. Connect horn connector and secure spiral cable harness with pawls in steering wheel.
   c. **Torque** steering wheel retaining nut to 22–29 ft. lbs.
   d. Position air bag module and install new special bolts. **Torque** bolts to 11–18 ft. lbs.

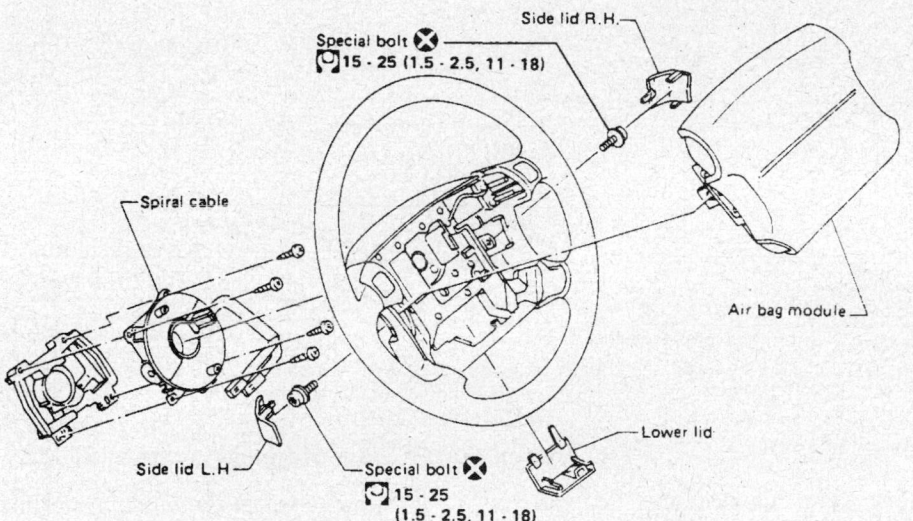

Fig. 10 Air bag module & spiral cable replacement

HEADLAMP SWITCH
REPLACE
MAXIMA

Refer to "Combination Switch, Replace." It is not necessary to remove combination switch base to replace light switch.

300ZX

1. Remove retaining screw from lower side of switch assembly on lefthand side of instrument cluster.
2. Pull switch assembly out of instrument panel, then remove switch to switch assembly attaching screws.
3. Reverse procedure to install.

STOP LIGHT SWITCH
REPLACE

Stop lamp switch is located on brake pedal support.
1. Disconnect switch electrical connectors.
2. Loosen switch retaining locknut and remove switch.
3. Reverse procedure to install.

COMBINATION SWITCH
REPLACE

1. Remove steering wheel as outlined under "Steering Wheel, Replace."
2. Remove steering column shell covers.
3. Remove switch retaining screws.

INSTRUMENT CLUSTER
REPLACE

1. Remove steering column cover, steering wheel and combination switch, if necessary.
2. Remove instrument panel cover, if necessary.

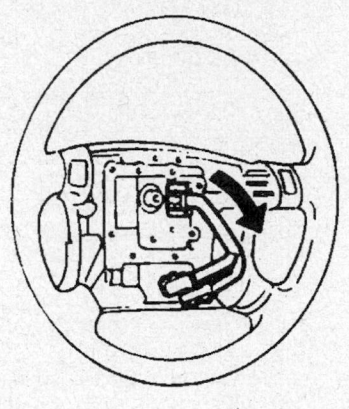

NS6049100003000X

Fig. 11 Spiral cable alignment

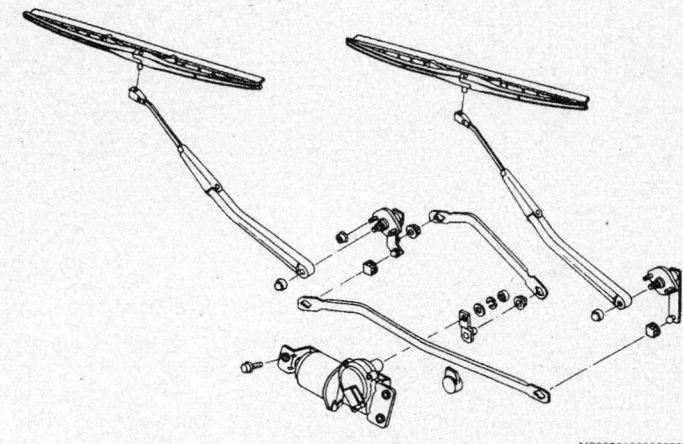

NS9029100002000X

Fig. 12 Exploded view of wiper system

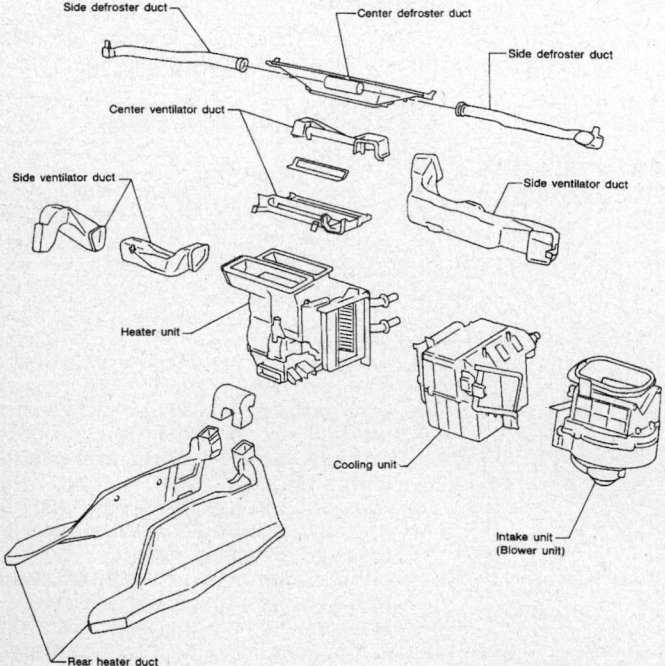

NS7029600009000X

Fig. 13 Exploded view of heater system. Maxima

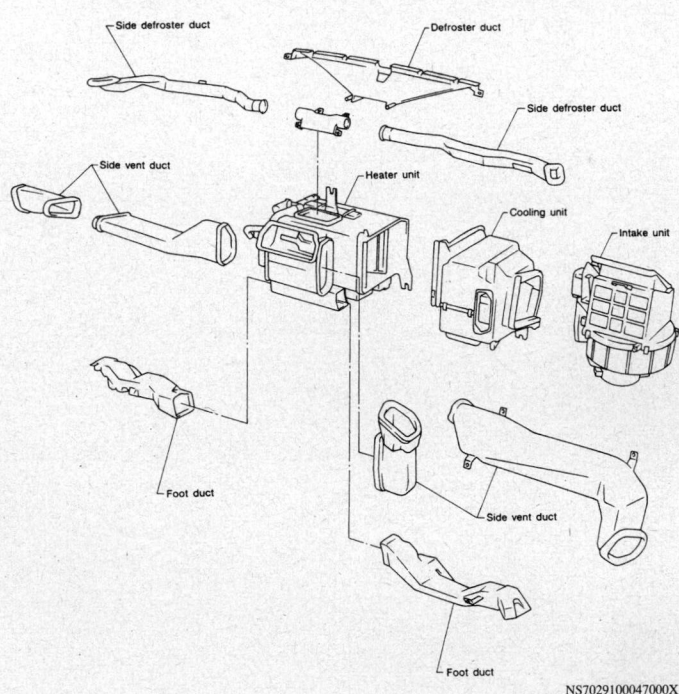

NS7029100047000X

Fig. 14 Exploded view of heater system. 300ZX

3. Remove cluster lid retaining screws, then the cluster lid.
4. Remove cluster retaining screws and nuts.
5. Disconnect speedometer cable and electrical connectors.
6. Reverse procedure to install.

RADIO
REPLACE

1. Remove cluster lid or instrument panel fascia.
2. Remove radio bracket to instrument panel attaching screws.
3. Disconnect radio electrical connectors, then remove radio from vehicle.
4. Reverse procedure to install.

WIPER MOTOR
REPLACE
FRONT

1. Remove wiper arms, then disconnect electrical connector from motor, **Fig. 12.**
2. Remove top grille retaining screws and top grille.
3. Remove wiper motor mounting bolts and pull motor away from firewall.
4. Disconnect motor shaft from linkage, taking care not to bend linkage.
5. Remove pivot to cowl top retaining nuts, then the wiper motor linkage.
6. Reverse procedure to install.

REAR

1. Raise rear wiper arm off glass and remove retaining nut.

2. Remove tailgate inner trim panel, disconnect electrical connector at motor.
3. Remove wiper motor retaining bolts, then the motor.
4. Reverse procedure to install.

WIPER SWITCH
REPLACE
FRONT
Maxima

Refer to "Combination Switch, Replace" for wiper switch replacement. It is not necessary to remove combination switch base to remove windshield wiper switch.

300ZX

1. Remove retaining screw from lower

side of switch assembly on righthand side of instrument cluster.
2. Pull switch assembly out of instrument panel, then remove switch to switch assembly attaching screws.
3. Reverse procedure to install.

REAR

300ZX

1. Remove retaining screw from lower side of switch assembly on righthand side of instrument cluster.
2. Pull switch assembly out of instrument

panel, then remove switch to switch assembly attaching screws.
3. Reverse procedure to install.

BLOWER MOTOR
REPLACE

Refer to **Figs. 13 and 14** for replacement.

HEATER CORE
REPLACE

1. Remove instrument panel as outlined

under "Dash Panel Service."
2. Refer to **Fig. 14** for heater core replacement.

EVAPORATOR CORE
REPLACE

1. Recover A/C system.
2. Remove passenger side instrument lower cover and glove compartment.
3. Disconnect wiring harness connectors to evaporator.
4. Separate cooling unit case halves and remove evaporator, **Fig. 14**.
5. Reverse procedure to install.

VG30DE & VG30DETT Engines

NOTE: On Air Bag Equipped Models, Refer To " Air Bag System Precautions" Located In Front Of This Manual For System Disarming & Arming Procedures.

INDEX

PRECAUTIONS
AIR BAG SYSTEMS

Refer to "Air Bag System Precautions" in front of this manual for system disarming and arming procedures.

BATTERY GROUND CABLE

Prior to service, disconnect battery ground cable and isolate as required.

FUEL SYSTEM PRESSURE RELIEF

1. Disconnect fuel pump relay, which is located behind lefthand side kick panel.
2. Start and run engine until it stalls.
3. Try to start engine two or three more times to ensure fuel pressure is released.
4. Turn ignition switch off.
5. Reconnect fuel pump relay.

COMPRESSION PRESSURE

1. Start and run engine until it reaches

operating temperature.
2. Turn ignition switch off.
3. Release fuel pressure as outlined under "Precautions. "
4. Remove all spark plugs.
5. Disconnect camshaft position sensor electrical connector.
6. Attach a compression tester to cylinder No.1.
7. Depress accelerator pedal fully to keep throttle valve wide open.
8. Crank engine and record highest gauge indication.
9. Repeat measurement on each cylinder.
10. **On models equipped with VG30DE engine,** at 300 RPM, standard compression is 186 psi and minimum pressure is 142 psi. Maximum difference between cylinders is 14 psi.
11. **On models equipped with VG30DETT engine,** at 300 RPM, standard compression is 171 psi and minimum pressure is 128 psi. Maximum difference between cylinders is 14 psi.
12. **On all models,** if compression in one or more cylinders is low, pour a small amount of engine oil into cylinders through spark plug holes, then retest

compression.
13. If adding oil helps compression, then piston rings may be at fault. If adding oil does not help compression, then valves may be at fault.
14. If compression stays low in two cylinders that are next to each other, then cylinder head gasket may be leaking or both cylinders have valve component damage.
15. Repair as necessary.

ENGINE MOUNT
REPLACE

Refer to **Fig. 1** to replace engine mounts.

ENGINE
REPLACE

1. Release fuel system pressure as outlined under " Precautions."
2. Remove hood.
3. Drain engine coolant from cylinder block and radiator.
4. Disconnect vacuum and fuel hoses, wires, harnesses, electrical connectors and linkages. **Mark hoses and**

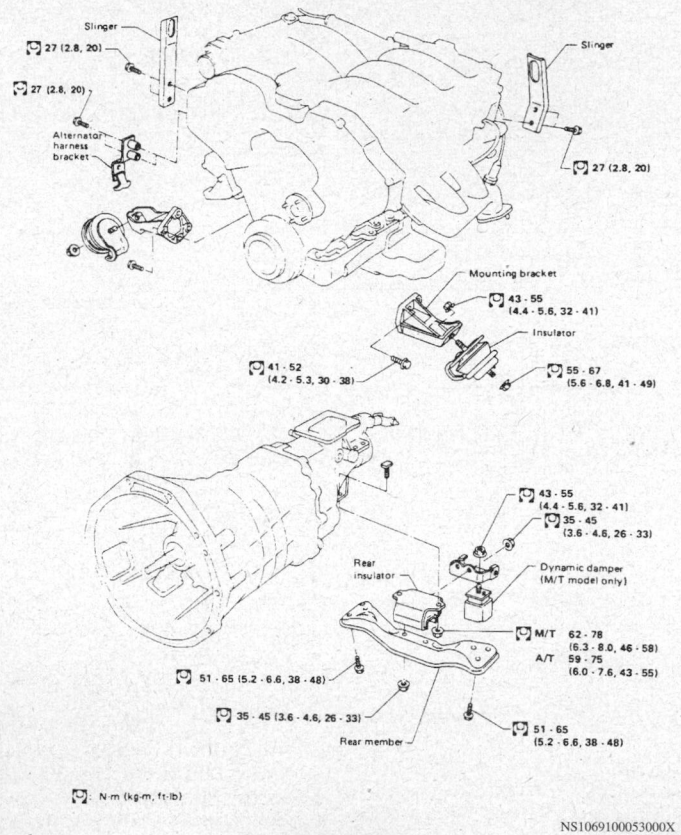

Fig. 1   Engine mounts

NS1069100053000X

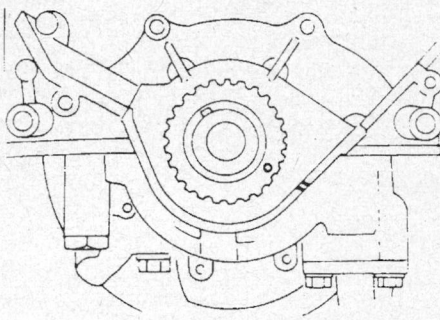

NS1069100149000X

Fig. 2   Crankshaft sprocket & oil pump alignment marks

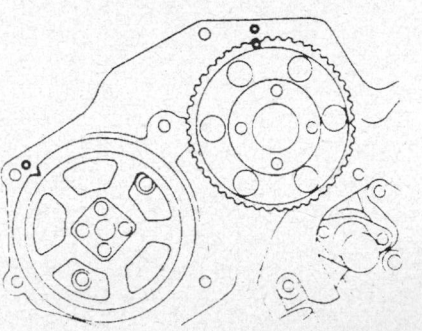

NS1069100150000X

Fig. 3   Camshaft sprocket & timing belt rear cover alignment marks

electrical connectors for installation reference.

5. Remove radiator, fans and coupling, then the drive belts.
6. Remove alternator, then the air conditioning compressor and power steering pump without disconnecting pressure hoses. Position compressor and pump aside.
7. Raise and support vehicle, remove engine undercover and drain engine oil.
8. Remove exhaust pipes and drive shafts, as necessary.
9. **On models equipped with manual transmission,** proceed as follows:
   a. Remove starter motor and clutch cylinder, then disconnect air conditioning tube clamps.
   b. Disconnect steering column lower joint, then remove tension rod fixing bolts.
   c. Loosen transverse link bolts.
   d. Attach suitable lifting equipment to engine and support suspension member with suitable jack.
   e. Remove suspension member and engine mounting bolts.
   f. Slowly lower jack and remove engine with transmission from vehicle.
10. **On models equipped with automatic transmission,** proceed as follows:
   a. Remove starter motor.
   b. Remove transmission.
   c. Attach suitable lifting equipment to engine.
   d. Remove engine mounting bolts.
   e. Lift engine from vehicle.

11. **On all models,** reverse procedure to install.

INTAKE MANIFOLD
REPLACE

1. Release fuel system pressure as outlined under "Precautions."
2. Remove intake manifold collector, then the injector pipe assembly.
3. Remove valve covers.
4. Remove timing belt as outlined under "Timing Belt, Replace."
5. Remove idler pulley and stud bolt.
6. Remove intake manifold.
7. Reverse procedure to install. Tighten bolts to specifications.

CYLINDER HEAD
REPLACE
REMOVAL

1. Removal intake manifold as outlined under "Intake Manifold, Replace."
2. Disconnect exhaust manifold front tube.
3. Remove cylinder head bolts in two or three steps, then the cylinder head.

INSTALLATION

1. Set No. 1 piston at TDC on compression stroke by aligning crankshaft sprocket alignment mark with oil pump body mark, Fig. 2.
2. Align camshaft sprocket alignment mark with timing belt rear cover mark, Fig. 3.

3. Install cylinder head with new gaskets and washers between bolts and head.
4. Tighten cylinder head bolts in order shown in Fig. 4 as follows:
   a. Install shorter bolts in positions 1 and 6.
   b. **Torque** bolts to 29 ft. lbs.
   c. **Torque** bolts to 90 ft. lbs.
   d. Loosen bolts completely.
   e. **Torque** bolts to 25–33 ft. lbs.
   f. Use angle wrench and turn long bolts 70–75° clockwise and short bolts 65–70.°
   g. If angle wrench is not available, **torque** bolts to 90 ft. lbs.
   h. **Torque** outside cylinder head bolts to 7–9 ft. lbs.
5. Install exhaust manifold front tube.
6. Install intake manifold as outlined under "Intake Manifold, Replace."

ENGINE DISASSEMBLE

1. Place engine on a work stand, then ensure coolant and oil have drained.
2. Remove timing belt as outlined under "Timing Belt, Replace."
3. Remove water pump as outlined under "Water Pump, Replace."
4. Remove oil pan as outlined under "Oil Pan, Replace."
5. Remove oil pump as outlined under "Oil Pump, Replace."
6. Remove rear oil seal retainer.
7. Remove intake manifold as outlined under "Intake Manifold, Replace."

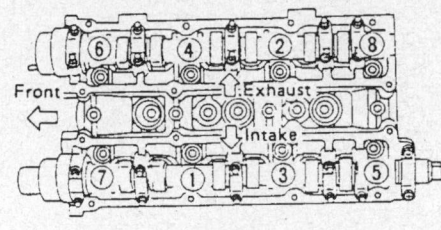

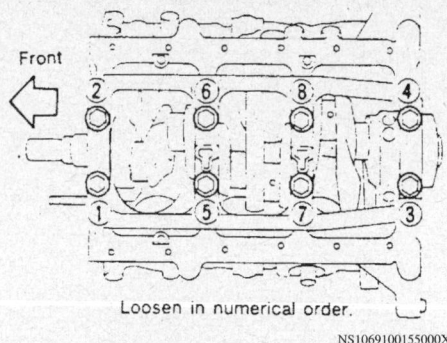

Loosen in numerical order.

NS1069100155000X

Fig. 5 Main bearing cap bolt loosening sequence

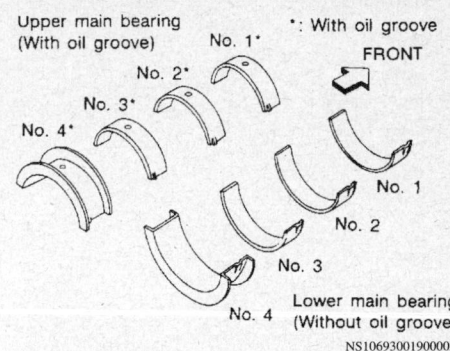

NS1069300190000X

Fig. 6 Main bearing identification

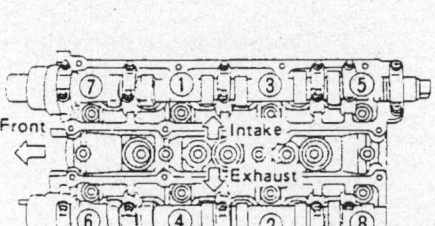

NS1069100117000X

Fig. 4 Cylinder head bolt tightening sequence

8. Remove cylinder heads as outlined under "Cylinder Head, Replace."
9. Remove pistons with connecting rod.
10. Before removing bearing cap, measure crankshaft end play.
11. Loosen main bearing beam and crankshaft retaining bolts in sequence shown in **Fig. 5** in two or three steps, then remove.

ENGINE ASSEMBLE

1. Install main bearings, **Fig. 6,** crankshaft and bearing cap. Tighten bearing cap attaching bolts to specifications in sequence shown in **Fig. 7** in two or three steps.
2. Install piston assemblies with rings properly positioned, **Fig. 8.**
3. Reverse remainder of "Engine Disassemble" procedure to complete assembly, noting the following:
   a. Tighten cylinder head attaching bolts to specifications using sequence shown in **Fig. 4.**
   b. Tighten intake manifold attaching bolts to specifications using sequence shown in **Fig. 9** in two or three steps.

VALVE CLEARANCE SPECIFICATIONS

Engine	Stem-To-Guide Clearance, Inch①	
	Intake	Exhaust
VG30DE & VG30DETT	.0008–.0021	.0016–.0029

① — Cold.

VALVE ADJUSTMENT

These engines are equipped with hydraulic lash adjusters. No adjustments are required.

TIMING BELT
REPLACE
REMOVAL

1. Raise and support vehicle.
2. Remove engine undercover.
3. Drain engine coolant, then remove radiator.
4. Remove drive belts, cooling fan and coupling.
5. Remove starter motor, then use screwdriver or other suitable tool to keep crankshaft from turning and remove crankshaft pulley bolt, **Fig. 10.**
6. Remove crankshaft pulley with suitable puller.
7. Remove water inlet and outlet, then the front timing belt covers.
8. Install suitable stopper bolt into tensioner arm of auto tensioner, **Fig. 11.**
9. Place No. 1 cylinder at TDC of compression stroke, then remove auto tensioner and timing belt.

INSTALLATION

1. Ensure No. 1 cylinder at TDC of compression stroke.
2. Align mark on camshaft and crankshaft sprocket with aligning marks on rear belt cover and oil pump housing, **Fig. 12,** then remove spark plugs.
3. Install timing belt white aligning marks on timing belt with matching marks on crankshaft and camshaft sprockets, with arrow on timing belt facing forward, **Fig. 13.**
4. With auto tensioner in suitable vise, adjust arm to .16 inch clearance with pusher, then install stopper bolt into tensioner arm, **Fig. 14. Do not push tensioner bolt arm with stopper bolt installed. Possible damage to threaded portion could result.**
5. Install auto tensioner, then tighten nut 1 and bolts 2 and 3 by hand slightly, **Fig. 15.**
6. Push tensioner toward timing belt until slight tension on belt is felt, then turn crankshaft clockwise 10° and **torque** nut 1 and bolts 2 and 3 to 12–15 ft. lbs., **Fig. 15.**
7. Turn crankshaft 120° counterclockwise, then loosen nut 1 and bolts 2 and 3 ½ turns to set tensioner body back as far as it will go.
8. Turn crankshaft clockwise and set No.

1 cylinder at TDC of compression stroke.
9. Attach special push-pull gauge tool No. EG14860000, or equivalent, and push pusher end with approximately 13.2 lbs. pressure, then **torque** nut 1 and bolts 2 and 3 to 12–15 ft. lbs.
10. Turn crankshaft 120° clockwise, then 120° counterclockwise and set No. 1 cylinder on TDC of compression stroke.
11. Use a suitable steel plate, **Fig. 16,** to measure belt deflection.
12. Set plate and use push-pull tool to push with 11 lbs. pressure at four points, **Fig. 17,** measuring deflection at each point. Add measurements together, then divide by four. This should equal an average deflection of .24–.28 inch.
13. If not within specification, adjust auto tensioner.
14. Remove auto tensioner stopper bolt. After five minutes, ensure rod projection between tensioner arm and pusher stays between .138 and .205 inch.
15. Install timing belt cover.

PISTON & ROD ASSEMBLY

DISASSEMBLE

1. Remove piston rings with a ring remover.
2. Remove snap ring, then press out piston pin using piston pin press or heat piston to 140–150°F and remove piston pin. **Keep disassembled parts in order.**

ASSEMBLE

1. Assemble pistons, piston pins and connecting rods of designated cylinders.
2. Install new snap ring on one side of piston pin.
3. Align piston and connecting rod direction.
4. Ensure stamped numbers on connecting rod and cap correspond to each cylinder.
5. Heat piston to 140–150°F and assemble piston, piston pin, connecting rod and new snap ring.
6. Install piston rings.

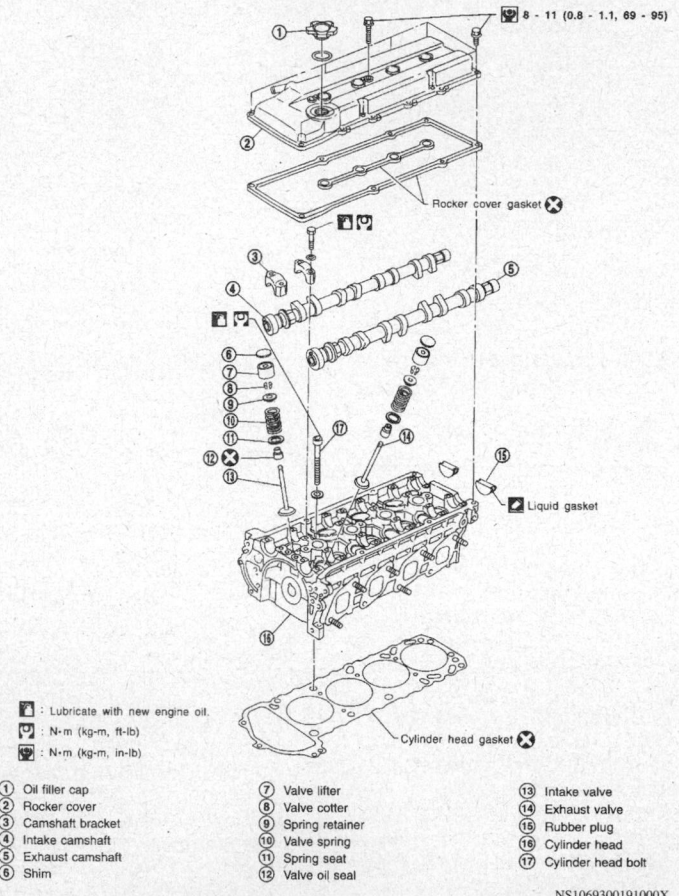

8 - 11 (0.8 - 1.1, 69 - 95)

Rocker cover gasket ⊗

Liquid gasket

: Lubricate with new engine oil.
N·m (kg-m, ft-lb)
N·m (kg-m, in-lb)

Cylinder head gasket ⊗

① Oil filler cap
② Rocker cover
③ Camshaft bracket
④ Intake camshaft
⑤ Exhaust camshaft
⑥ Shim
⑦ Valve lifter
⑧ Valve cotter
⑨ Spring retainer
⑩ Valve spring
⑪ Spring seat
⑫ Valve oil seal
⑬ Intake valve
⑭ Exhaust valve
⑮ Rubber plug
⑯ Cylinder head
⑰ Cylinder head bolt

NS1069300191000X

Fig. 7 Main bearing cap bolt tightening sequence

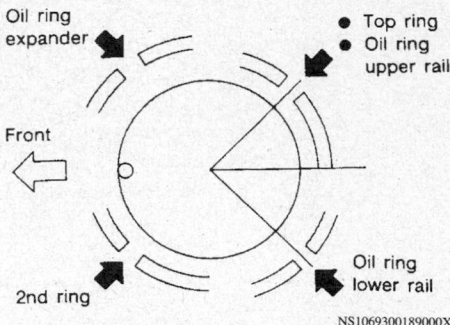

Oil ring expander

Front

Top ring
Oil ring upper rail

2nd ring

Oil ring lower rail

NS1069300189000X

Fig. 8 Piston ring positioning

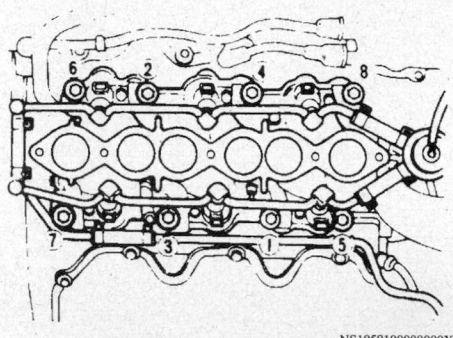

NS1059100008000X

Fig. 9 Intake manifold bolt tightening sequence

CRANKSHAFT SEAL

REPLACE

1. Remove timing belt as outlined under "Timing Belt, Replace."
2. Remove crankshaft sprocket.
3. Remove oil pump assembly as outlined under "Oil Pump, Replace."
4. Remove front oil seal from oil pump body.
5. Apply engine oil to new oil seal and install using suitable oil seal installation tool.

CRANKSHAFT REAR OIL SEAL

REPLACE

1. Remove flywheel or driveplate.
2. Remove rear oil seal retainer.
3. Remove rear oil seal.
4. Apply engine oil to new seal and install with suitable seal installation tool.

OIL PAN

REPLACE

1. Raise and support vehicle, then drain engine oil and remove engine undercover.
2. Remove oil filter and bracket, then the engine rear gussets.
3. Disconnect A/C tube clamps, then the steering column lower joint.
4. Remove tension rod attaching bolts, then the transverse link bolts.
5. Place a suitable transmission jack under suspension member, then hoist engine with slingers.
6. Remove suspension member attaching bolts, engine mounting bolts, then slowly lower transmission jack.
7. Remove oil pan bolts, then the oil pan.
8. Reverse procedure to install, noting the following:
   a. Remove all liquid gasket from oil pan and cylinder block mating surfaces.
   b. Apply sealant to front cover gasket and rear oil seal retainer gasket.
   c. Apply a continuous bead of liquid gasket to mating surface of oil pan.
   d. **Torque** bolts 1–12 to 12–15 ft. lbs. and bolts 13–18 to 55–77 inch lbs. in sequence shown in **Fig. 18.**
   e. Wait at least 30 minutes before refilling engine oil.

OIL PUMP

REPLACE

1. Drain oil.
2. Remove oil pan as outlined under "Oil Pan, Replace."
3. Remove oil pump assembly.
4. Reverse procedure to install.

BELT TENSION DATA

Refer to **Fig. 19** for belt tension data.

COOLING SYSTEM BLEED

These engines do not require a specified bleed procedure. After filling cooling system, run engine to operating temperature with radiator/pressure cap off. Air will then be automatically bled through cap opening.

THERMOSTAT

REPLACE

1. Drain engine and radiator coolant.
2. Remove engine undercover and radiator upper hose.
3. Remove radiator shroud, fan belt, cooling fan and coupling.
4. Remove water inlet, then the thermostat, **Fig. 20.**
5. Reverse procedure to install.

WATER PUMP

REPLACE

1. Drain engine and radiator coolant.
2. Remove undercover, radiator, drive belts, cooling fan and coupling, water inlet and outlet, crank pulley and timing belt cover.
3. Remove water pump, **Fig. 21.**
4. Reverse procedure to install.

RADIATOR

REPLACE

1. Remove undercover, then drain coolant.
2. Disconnect upper and lower radiator hoses, **Fig. 22.**

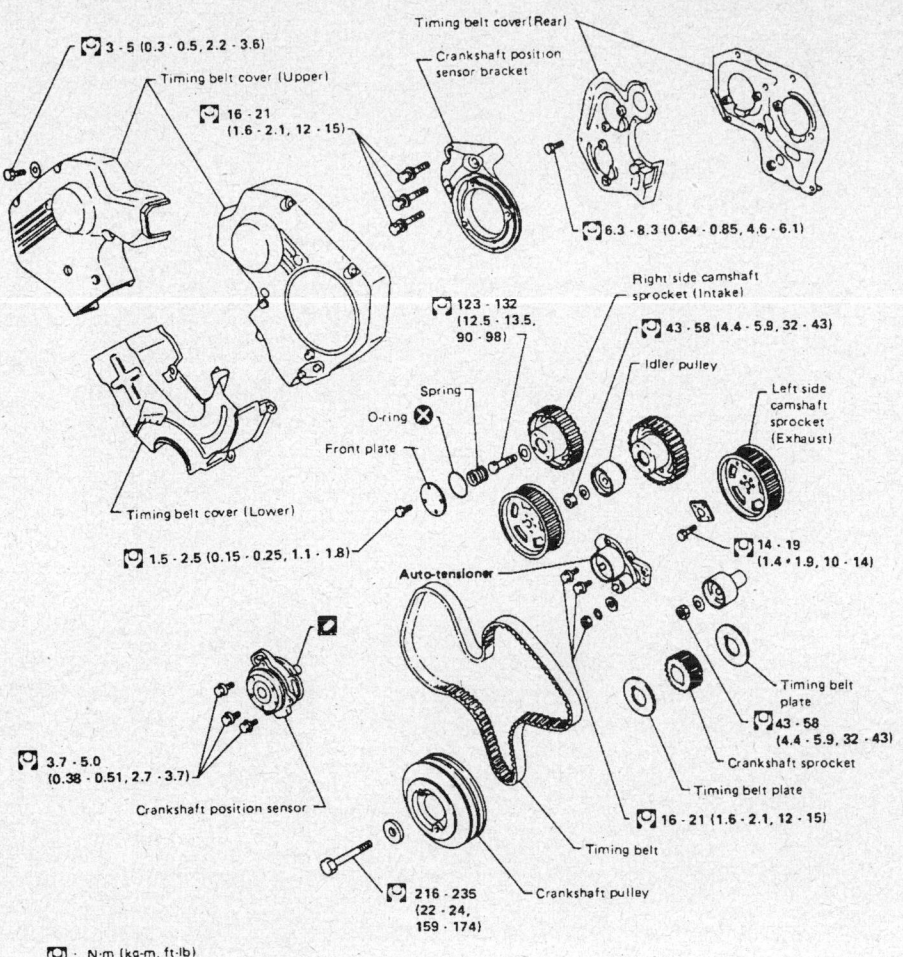

Fig. 10 Timing belt replacement

NS1069100059000X

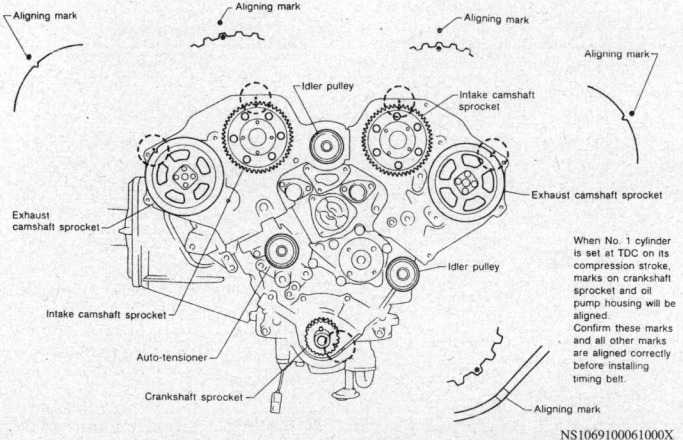

When No. 1 cylinder is set at TDC on its compression stroke, marks on crankshaft sprocket and oil pump housing will be aligned. Confirm these marks and all other marks are aligned correctly before installing timing belt.

NS1069100061000X

Fig. 12 Alignment of camshaft & crankshaft sprockets

3. **On models equipped with automatic transaxle,** remove ATF cooler hoses.
4. **On all models,** remove lower shroud.
5. Remove radiator.
6. Reverse procedure to install.

FUEL PUMP

REPLACE

1. Release fuel pump pressure as outlined under "Precautions."

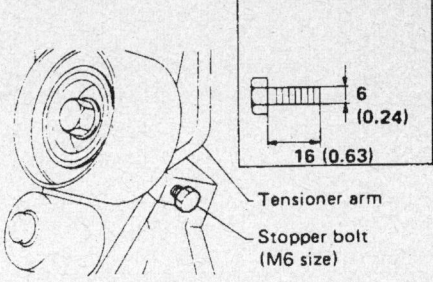

Unit: mm (in)

NS1069100060000X

Fig. 11 Stopper bolt installation

2. Drain fuel into suitable container.
3. Disconnect necessary fuel lines and electrical connectors.
4. Disconnect fuel tank attaching bolts, then lower tank.
5. Remove fuel pump attaching bolts, then the fuel pump.
6. Reverse procedure to install.

FUEL FILTER

REPLACE

1. Relieve fuel system pressure as outlined under "Precautions."
2. Loosen two fuel filter hose clamps, **Fig. 23.**
3. Disconnect fuel hoses from fuel filter. **Do not allow gasoline to spill over engine compartment.**
4. Reverse procedure to install.

TURBOCHARGER

REPLACE

RIGHT SIDE

1. Remove battery.
2. Remove right part of cowl top, then the air inlet hose and pipe.
3. Disconnect lower exhaust pipe from turbo unit, then remove wiper motor bracket.
4. Disconnect exhaust gas sensor, remove turbochargers water hoses, then the oil inlet tube.
5. Remove pre-catalyst attaching bolts, then the pre-catalyst.
6. Remove front exhaust tube, oil return tube, oil filter, then the oil pressure switch.
7. Remove rod pin from wastegate valve actuator, then the oil filter bracket.
8. Remove turbocharger attaching nuts, then the turbocharger.
9. Reverse procedure to install.

LEFT SIDE

1. Remove brake master cylinder, then the brake booster.
2. Disconnect exhaust gas sensor, then remove air inlet hose and pipe.
3. Disconnect lower exhaust pipe from turbo unit.

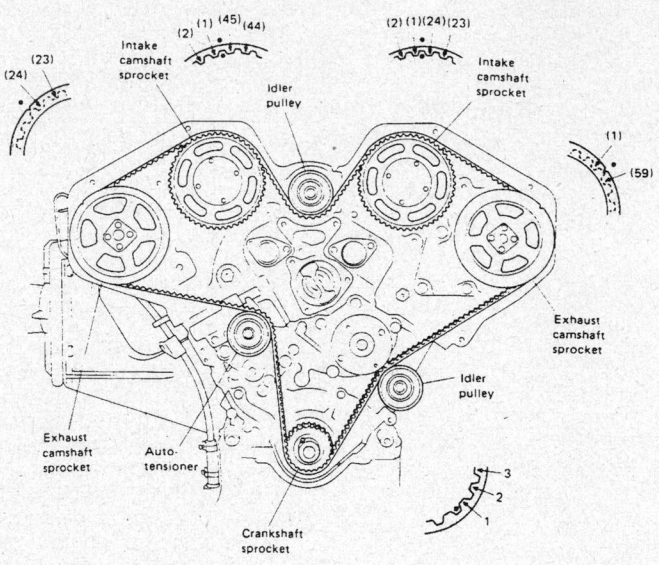

Fig. 13 Timing belt installation

Fig. 14 Auto tensioner adjustment

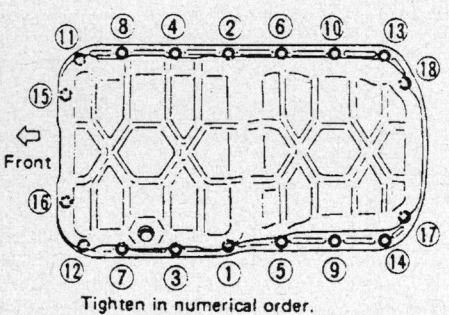

Fig. 15 Auto tensioner attaching nut & bolts

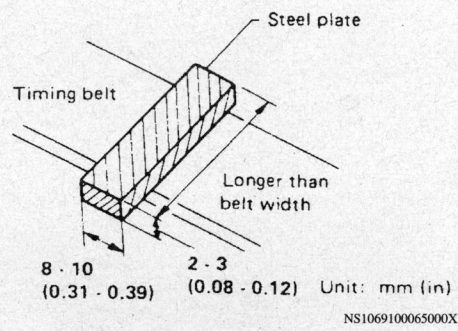

Fig. 16 Steel plate used to measure belt deflection

Fig. 17 Belt deflection inspection

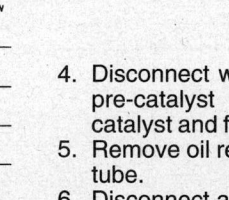

Fig. 18 Oil pan bolt tightening sequence

Tighten in numerical order.

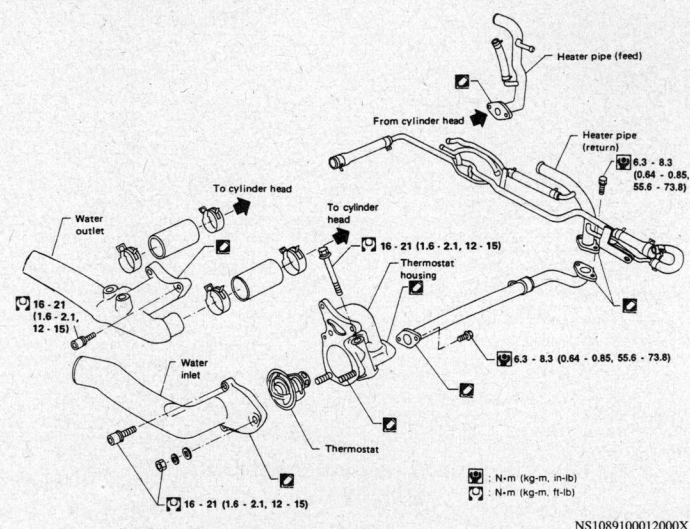

Fig. 20 Thermostat replacement

Unit: mm (in)

	Used belt deflection		Deflection of new belt
	Limit	Deflection after adjustment	
Alternator	11.5 (0.453)	7 - 8 (0.28 - 0.31)	6.5 - 7.5 (0.256 - 0.295)
Air conditioner compressor	12.5 (0.492)	8 - 9 (0.31 - 0.35)	7 - 8 (0.28 - 0.31)
Power steering oil pump	19 (0.75)	12 - 13.5 (0.472 - 0.531)	10.5 - 11.5 (0.413 - 0.453)
Applied pushing force	98 N (10 kg, 22 lb)		

Fig. 19 Belt tension data

4. Disconnect water tubes, then remove pre-catalyst attaching bolts, pre-catalyst and front exhaust pipe.
5. Remove oil return tube, then the water tube.
6. Disconnect actuator bracket and EGR tube form turbo unit.
7. Remove manifold cover, manifold at-taching nuts, then the exhaust manifold with turbocharger.
8. Reverse procedure to install.

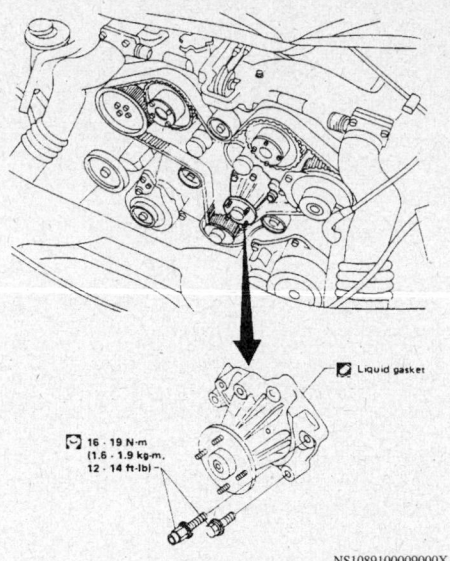

Fig. 21 Water pump replacement

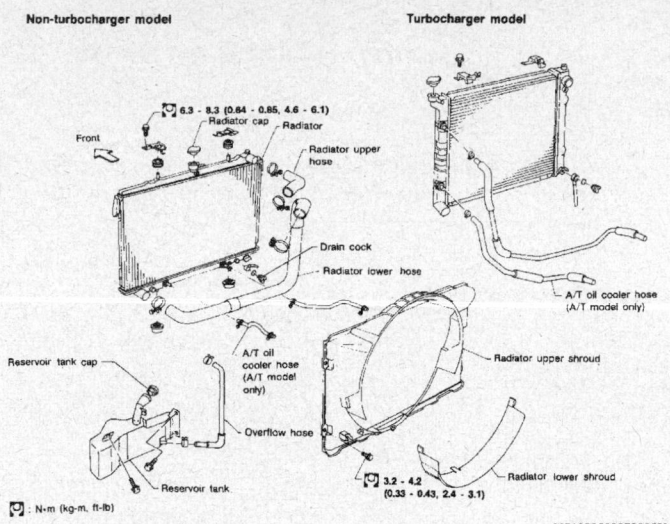

Fig. 22 Radiator replacement

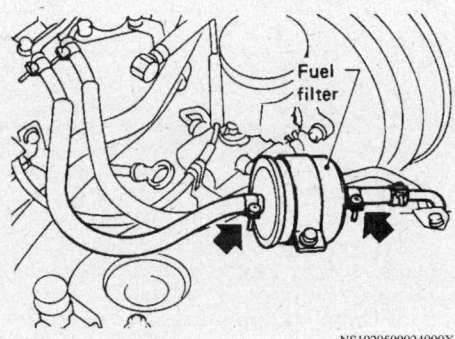

Fig. 23 Fuel filter replacement

TIGHTENING SPECIFICATIONS

Year	Component	Torque, Ft. Lbs.
1996	Camshaft Bracket Attaching Bolts	84–108④
	Camshaft Sprocket Bolt (Exhaust)	10–14
	Camshaft Sprocket Bolt (Intake)	90–98
	Connecting Rod Bearing Caps	①
	Crankshaft Pulley	159–174
	Cylinder Head	②
	Exhaust Manifold	13–17
	Flywheel	61–69
	Intake Manifold	12–17
	Main Bearing Cap	67–74
	Oil Pan Bolts	43–61④
	Starter Motor	22–27
	Timing Belt Tensioner	③
	Water Pump	12–15

① — Tighten to 12 ft. lbs.; then to 28–33 ft. lbs.
② — Refer to "Cylinder Head, Replace" in this section.
③ — Refer to "Timing Belt, Replace." in this section.
④ — Inch lbs.

VQ30DE Engine

NOTE: On Air Bag Equipped Models, Refer To " Air Bag System Precautions" Located In Front Of This Manual For System Disarming & Arming Procedures.

INDEX

PRECAUTIONS

AIR BAG SYSTEMS

Refer to "Air Bag System Precautions" in front of this manual for system disarming and arming procedures.

BATTERY GROUND CABLE

Prior to service, disconnect battery ground cable and isolate as required.

FUEL SYSTEM PRESSURE RELIEF

1. Remove fuel pump fuse from fuse panel.
2. Start and run engine until it stalls.
3. Try to start engine two or three more times to ensure fuel pressure is released.
4. Turn ignition switch off.
5. Install fuel pump fuse.

COMPRESSION PRESSURE

1. Start and run engine until it reaches operating temperature.
2. Turn ignition switch off.
3. Release fuel pressure as outlined under "Precautions."
4. Disconnect ignition coil with power transistor harness connectors, then remove ignition coils.
5. Remove all spark plugs.
6. Disconnect all injector harness connectors.
7. Attach a compression tester to cylinder No. 1.
8. Depress accelerator pedal fully to keep throttle valve wide open.
9. Crank engine and record highest gauge indication.

10. Repeat measurement on each cylinder.
11. At 300 RPM, standard compression is 185 psi and minimum pressure is 142 psi. Maximum difference between cylinders is 14 psi.
12. If compression in one or more cylinders is low, pour a small amount of engine oil into cylinders through spark plug holes, then retest compression.
13. If adding oil helps compression, then piston rings may be at fault. If adding oil does not help compression, then valves may be at fault.
14. If compression stays low in two cylinders that are next to each other, then cylinder head gasket may be leaking or both cylinders have valve component damage.
15. Repair as necessary.

ENGINE MOUNT

REPLACE

Refer to **Fig. 1** to replace engine mounts.

ENGINE

REPLACE

1. Release fuel system pressure as outlined under "Precautions."
2. Drain engine coolant from cylinder block and radiator, then drain engine oil.
3. Recover air conditioning coolant.
4. Remove engine undercover and hood.
5. Disconnect vacuum hoses, fuel hoses, electrical wires, harnesses and connectors. **Mark hoses and connectors for installation reference.**
6. Remove front exhaust pipe at manifold.
7. Disconnect ball joints and drive shafts.
8. Remove radiator and electric cooling fans.

9. Remove drive belts.
10. Remove alternator, A/C compressor and power steering pump from engine.
11. Raise and support vehicle and set a suitable transmission jack under transaxle.
12. Lift engine with engine hoist enough to take pressure off of engine mounts.
13. Remove rear engine mounting.
14. **On models equipped with manual transaxle,** disconnect control rod and support rod from transaxle.
15. **On models equipped with automatic transaxle,** disconnect control cable from transaxle.
16. **On all models,** remove front engine mounting.
17. Remove center member, then slowly lower transmission jack.
18. Remove engine with transaxle from under vehicle with transmission jack.
19. Reverse procedure to install.

INTAKE MANIFOLD

REPLACE

1. Release fuel system pressure as outlined under " Precautions."
2. Drain engine and radiator coolant, then remove lefthand rocker cover ornament.
3. Remove intake manifold air duct, collector, fuel hoses, wires, harness and connectors.
4. Remove vacuum, water, canister purge and blow-by hoses.
5. Remove ignition coils and EGR guide tube.
6. Remove righthand cylinder head intake manifold collector supports and intake manifold collector.
7. Remove fuel tube assembly.
8. Remove intake manifold bolts in reverse order of installation, **Fig. 2,** and intake manifold.

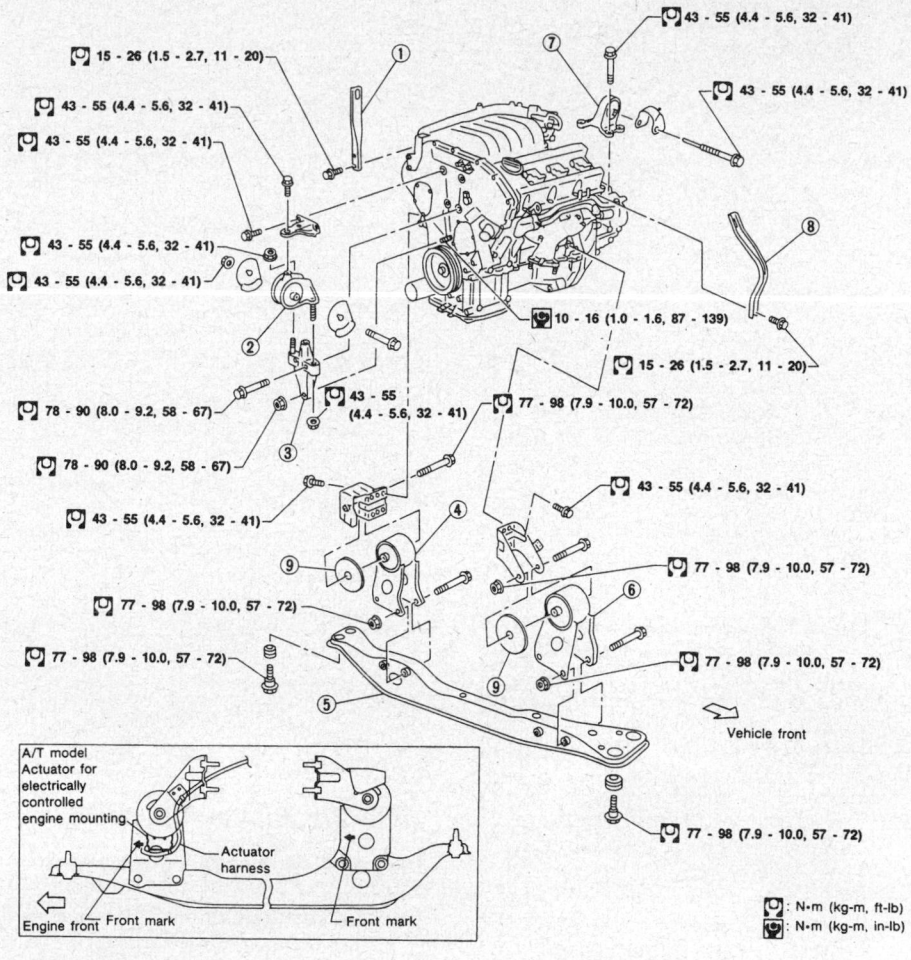

Fig. 1 Engine mounts

① Front upper engine slinger
② RH engine mounting
③ Mounting bracket
④ Rear engine mounting (Fluid type)
⑤ Center member
⑥ Front engine mounting (Fluid type)
⑦ LH engine mounting
⑧ Rear engine slinger
⑨ Insulator

NS1069500147000X

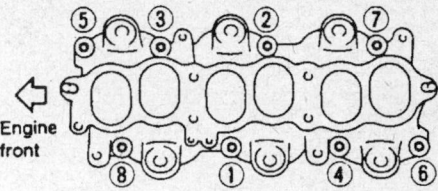

Tighten in numerical order.

NS1059500017000X

Fig. 2 Intake manifold tightening sequence

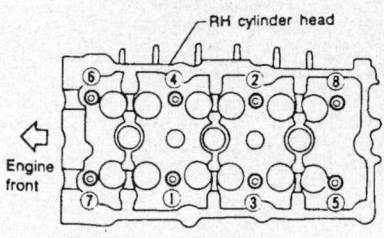

Tighten in numerical order.

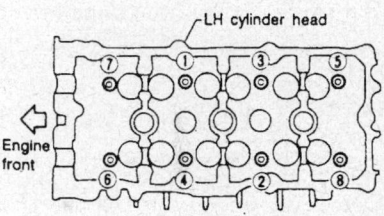

Tighten in numerical order.

NS1069500152000X

Fig. 4 Cylinder head bolt tightening sequence

Cylinder head bolt

(Measuring point) (Measuring point)

d2   d1

11 mm (0.43 In)
48 mm (1.89 In)

NS1069500151000X

Fig. 3 Cylinder head bolt measurement

9. Reverse procedure to install. **Torque** intake manifold bolts and nuts in order to 4–7 ft. lbs., then **torque** bolts to 14–18 ft. lbs. and nuts to 16–20 ft. lbs.

CYLINDER HEAD

REPLACE

REMOVAL

1. Remove intake manifold as outlined under "Intake Manifold, Replace."
2. Remove timing chain as outlined under "Timing Chain, Replace."
3. Remove cylinder heads.

INSTALLATION

Before installing rear timing chain case or cam bracket, removal all traces of liquid gasket. Remove all traces of liquid gasket from cylinder block mating surfaces and remove O-rings.

1. Turn crankshaft until No. 1 piston is set 240° before TDC on compression stroke.
2. Install cylinder heads with new gaskets. **Do not rotate crankshaft and camshaft separately or valves will strike pistons.**
3. Cylinder head bolts are tightened by plastic zone tightening. Measure all bolts, **Fig. 3.** If diameter "d1" minus "d2" exceeds .0043 inch, replace bolt.
4. Tighten cylinder head bolts in sequence shown in **Fig. 4** as follows:
   a. First, **torque** bolts to 72 ft. lbs., then loosen bolts completely.
   b. Second, **torque** bolts to 25–33 ft.

lbs., then turn bolts 90–95° clockwise.
   c. Finally, turn bolts an additional 90–95° clockwise.
5. Install cylinder head outside bolts. **Torque** to 7 ft. lbs., loosen completely, then **torque** to 7 ft. lbs. in three steps.
6. Install cam tensioners and apply sealant to No. 1 journal head mating surface.
7. Install exhaust and intake camshafts.
8. Install camshaft brackets in original positions and tighten bolts in three steps as follows:
   a. First, **torque** bolts in order of 7 to 10, then 1 to 6, to 17 inch lbs., **Fig. 5.**
   b. Second, **torque** bolts in numerical order to 52 inch lbs.
   c. Finally, **torque** bolts in numerical order to 7–9 ft. lbs.
9. If any part of valve or camshaft assembly has been replaced, check valve clearance as outlined under "Valve Adjustment."
10. Install cylinder block O-rings and apply sealant to hatched portions of rear timing chain case.
11. Align rear timing chain case with dowel pins, then install on cylinder head and block.
12. Tighten bolts to specifications in sequence shown in **Fig. 6.**

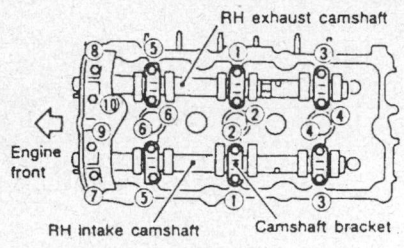

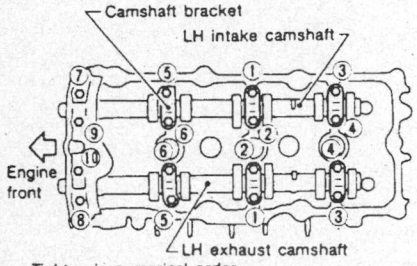

Fig. 5 Camshaft bracket tightening sequence

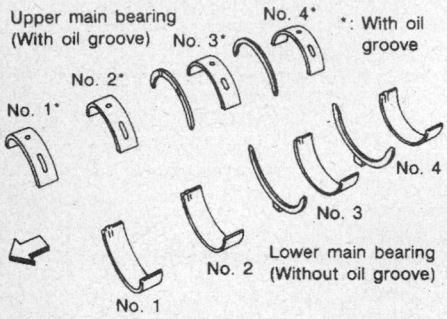

Fig. 8 Main bearing identification

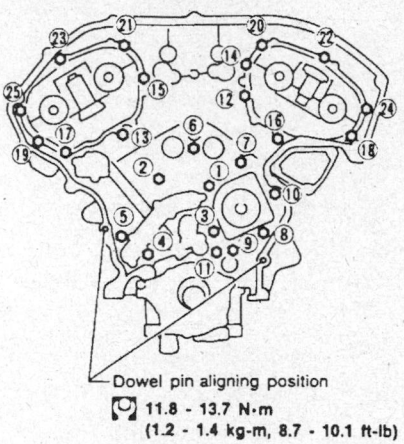

Dowel pin aligning position
⟦⟧ 11.8 - 13.7 N·m
(1.2 - 1.4 kg-m, 8.7 - 10.1 ft-lb)

NS1069500154000X

Fig. 6 Rear timing chain case tightening sequence

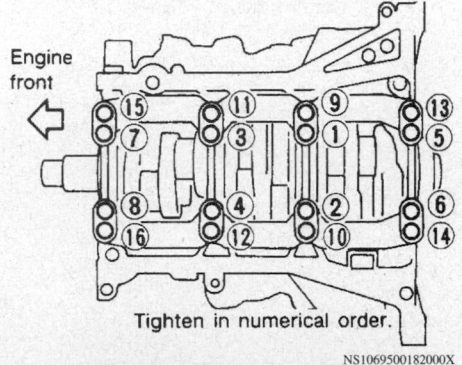

Tighten in numerical order.

NS1069500182000X

Fig. 9 Main bearing bolt tightening sequence

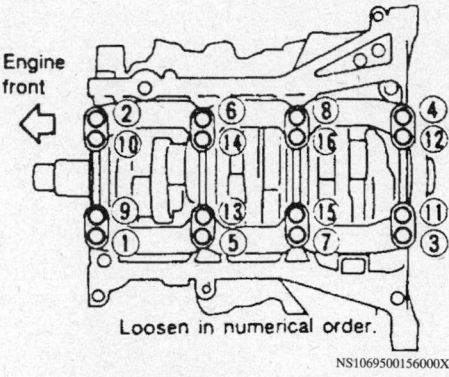

NS1069500156000X

Fig. 7 Main bearing cap bolt loosening sequence

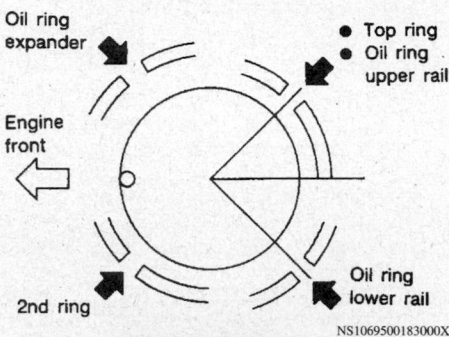

NS1069500183000X

Fig. 10 Piston ring position

ENGINE DISASSEMBLE

Prior to performing any service operations listed in this section, consult the "Technical Service Bulletins" section for related information.

1. Place engine on a work stand, then ensure coolant and oil have drained.
2. Remove cylinder heads as outlined under "Cylinder Head, Replace."
3. Remove oil pan as outlined under "Oil Pan, Replace."
4. Remove timing chain as outlined under "Timing Chain, Replace."
5. Remove pistons with connecting rod.
6. Remove rear oil seal retainer.
7. Before removing bearing cap, measure crankshaft end play.
8. Loosen main bearing beam and crankshaft retaining bolts in two or three steps using sequence shown in **Fig. 7**, then remove.

ENGINE ASSEMBLE

1. Install main bearings, **Fig. 8**, crankshaft and bearing caps. Using sequence shown in **Fig. 9**, **torque** attaching bolts to 24–28 ft. lbs.

2. Tighten all bolts an additional 90–95° clockwise using suitable angle wrench.
3. Measure crankshaft endplay, which should be .0039–.0098 inch.
4. Install piston assemblies with rings properly positioned, **Fig. 10**.
5. **Torque** connecting rod bearing caps 14–15 ft. lbs., then turn all nuts an additional 90–95.°
6. Reverse remainder of "Engine Disassemble" procedure to complete assembly, noting the following:
   a. Tighten cylinder head attaching bolts to specifications using sequence shown in **Fig. 4**.
   b. Tighten intake manifold attaching bolts to specifications using sequence shown in **Fig. 2** in two or three steps.

VALVE CLEARANCE SPECIFICATIONS

Engine	Stem-To-Guide Clearance, Inch①	
	Intake	Exhaust
VQ30DE	.0100–.0130	.0110–.0150

① — Cold.

VALVE ADJUSTMENT

1. Remove intake manifold collector and rocker cover ornaments, then the rocker covers.
2. Remove spark plugs and set No. 1 piston to TDC on compression stroke.
3. Use feeler gauge to measure and record clearance between valve lifter and camshaft on No. 1 and No. 6 intake valves, and No. 2 and 3 exhaust valves.
4. Turn crankshaft 240° and set No. 3 piston to TDC on compression stroke.
5. Use feeler gauge to measure and record clearance between valve lifter and camshaft on No. 2 and No. 3 intake valves, and No. 4 and 5 exhaust valves.
6. Turn crankshaft 240° and set No. 5 piston to TDC on compression stroke.
7. Use feeler gauge to measure and record clearance between valve lifter and camshaft on No. 4 and No. 5 intake valves, and No. 1 and 6 exhaust valves.
8. Turn crankshaft to position cam lobe on valve to be adjusted.
9. Place suitable camshaft pliers around camshaft and rotate so lifter is pushed down.
10. Place suitable lifter stopper between camshaft and edge of lifter and remove pliers.
11. Blow air into hole to separate adjusting shim from valve lifter, then remove shim with small screwdriver and magnetic finger.
12. Measure removed shim and calculate thickness of new shim necessary to

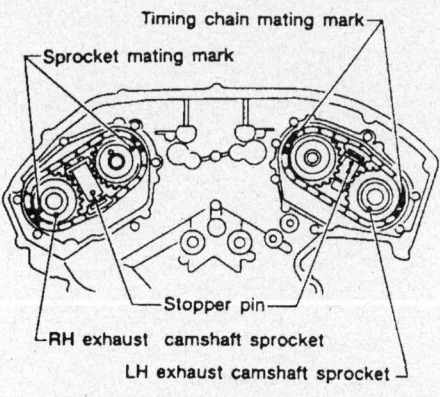

Fig. 11 Second timing chain alignment

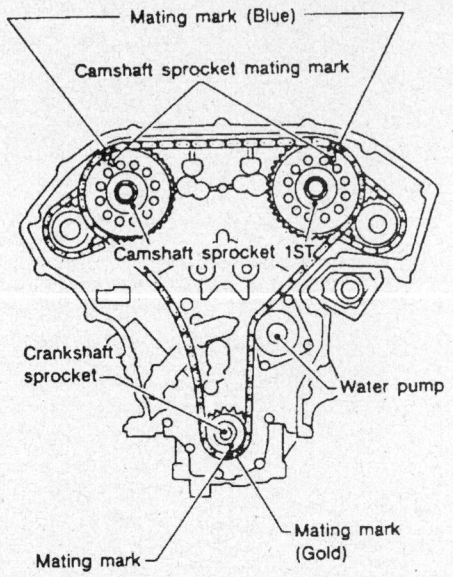

Fig. 12 Timing chain matchmark align

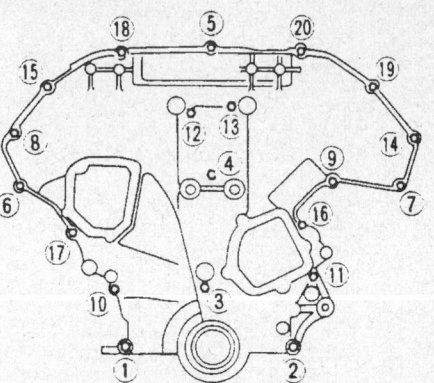

Fig. 13 Timing chain case bolt tightening sequence

1 - 2 8 mm dia. bolts
25.5 - 31.4 N·m
(2.6 - 3.2 kg-m, 18.8 - 23.1 ft-lb)
3 - 20 6 mm dia. bolts
11.8 - 13.7 N·m
(1.2 - 1.4 kg-m, 8.7 - 10.1 ft-lb)

obtain specified clearance. New intake shim size equals removed shim size plus measured clearance minus .0118 inch. New exhaust shim size equals removed shim size plus measured clearance minus .0130 inch. Shims are available from .0913 inch to .1161 inch, in .0004 inch steps.

13. Install new shim, attach pliers, rotate, then remove stopper and pliers.
14. Recheck valve clearance.
15. Repeat shim removal and replacement procedure as necessary.
16. Install spark plugs.
17. Install intake rocker covers, rocker cover ornaments and manifold collector.

TIMING CHAIN
REPLACE
REMOVAL

1. Remove intake manifold as outlined under "Intake Manifold, Replace."
2. Remove rocker covers, then raise and support vehicle.
3. Remove engine undercover, righthand front wheel and engine side cover.
4. Remove drive belts, idler pulley bracket and power steering pump.
5. Remove camshaft and crankshaft position sensors, then set No. 1 piston at TDC of compression stroke.
6. Loosen crankshaft pulley bolt, then remove oil pan rear cover plate and set screwdriver or other suitable tool in ring gear to stop crankshaft rotation.
7. Remove crankshaft pulley with suitable puller, then the air conditioning compressor and bracket.
8. Remove front exhaust tube and support.
9. Support right and left sides of engine with suitable hoist, and remove righthand engine mounting, bracket and nuts.
10. Remove center member, then the upper and lower oil pans as outlined under "Oil Pan, Replace."
11. Remove water pump cover, then the front timing chain case bolts and case.
12. Remove internal timing and upper chain guides, then the timing chain tensioner and slack side chain guide.

13. Remove first chain camshaft sprocket bolts, then the first chain camshaft sprockets, crankshaft sprocket and timing chain.
14. Insert suitable stopper pin into camshaft tensioners, then remove second chain exhaust camshaft sprocket bolts and exhaust sprockets.
15. Remove second chain intake camshaft sprocket bolts and intake sprockets.
16. Remove lower chain guide, then scrape all traces of liquid gasket from timing chain case and water pump cover.

INSTALLATION

1. Install crankshaft sprocket, then set No. 1 piston to TDC on compression stroke.
2. Install lower chain guide on dowel pin with front mark on guide facing upside.
3. Align marks on second chain intake and exhaust camshaft sprockets, and second camshaft chain, Fig. 11.
4. Install intake and exhaust camshaft sprockets. **Exhaust sprocket is thicker than intake.**
5. Remove camshaft tensioner stopper pins.
6. Align crankshaft sprocket mating mark with chain gold matchmark, Fig. 12.
7. Attach lower timing chain on water pump sprocket.
8. Install first chain camshaft sprockets onto timing chain by matching sprocket dowel grooves with camshaft and tighten bolts to specifications.
9. Install timing chain, ensuring mating marks and matchmarks are aligned.
10. Install internal and upper chain guides, then the tensioner and slack side guide.
11. Apply liquid gasket to front timing chain case and install rear case pin into dowel pin hole of front timing case.
12. **Torque** bolts 1 and 2 to 18.8–23.1 ft.

lbs. and bolts 3–20 to 8.7–10.1 ft. lbs. in sequence shown in **Fig. 13.**
13. Apply liquid gasket to water pump cover and install.
14. Apply liquid gasket to rocker covers and install.
15. **Torque** rocker cover bolts to .7–2.2 ft. lbs. in sequence shown in **Figs. 14 and 15,** then **torque** bolts to 4.3–5.8 ft. lbs.

PISTON & ROD ASSEMBLY
DISASSEMBLE

1. Remove piston rings with a ring remover.
2. Remove snap ring, then press out piston pin using piston pin press or heat piston to 140–150°F and remove piston pin. **Keep disassembled parts in order.**

ASSEMBLE

1. Assemble pistons, piston pins and connecting rods of designated cylinders.
2. Install new snap ring on one side of piston pin.
3. Align piston and connecting rod direction.
4. Ensure stamped numbers on connecting rod and cap correspond to each cylinder.
5. Heat piston to 140–150°F and assemble piston, piston pin, connecting rod and new snap ring.
6. Install piston rings.

CRANKSHAFT SEAL
REPLACE

1. Raise and support vehicle, then remove engine undercover.
2. Remove righthand front wheel and engine side cover.

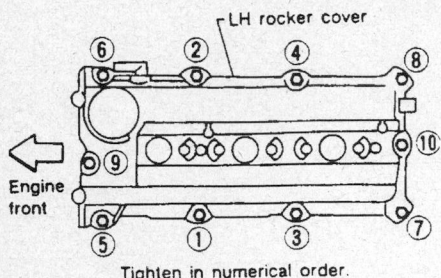

Fig. 14 Lefthand rocker cover bolt tightening sequence

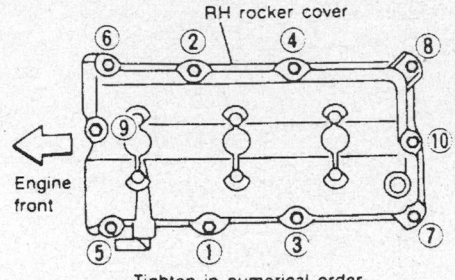

Fig. 15 Righthand rocker cover bolt tightening sequence

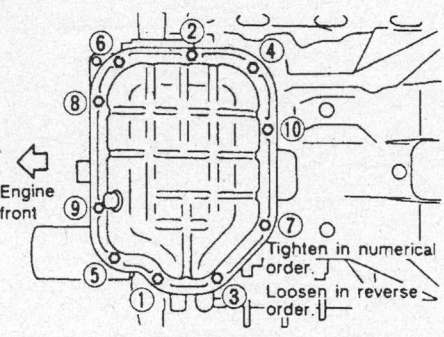

Fig. 16 Steel oil pan bolt tightening sequence

3. Remove drive belts.
4. Remove crankshaft position sensor.
5. Remove crankshaft pulley.
6. Remove front oil seal being careful not to scratch front cover.
7. Apply engine oil to new oil seal and install using suitable oil seal installation tool.

CRANKSHAFT REAR OIL SEAL

REPLACE

1. Remove flywheel or driveplate.
2. Remove oil pan as outlined under "Oil Pan, Replace."
3. Remove rear oil seal retainer.
4. Remove rear oil seal.
5. Apply engine oil to new seal and install with suitable seal installation tool.

OIL PAN

REPLACE

REMOVAL

1. Remove engine undercover and drain engine oil.
2. Remove steel oil pan bolts in reverse order, **Fig. 16.**
3. Insert suitable tool between steel and aluminum oil pans, then slide tool by tapping slide with hammer and remove steel oil pan. **Do not use screwdriver and be careful not to damage aluminum mating surface.**
4. Remove oil strainer, then the front exhaust tube and support.
5. Place suitable transmission jack under transaxle and lift engine with slinger.
6. Remove crankshaft position sensors.
7. Remove front and rear engine mounting nuts and bolts, then the center member.
8. Remove drive belts, then the A/C compressor and bracket.
9. Remove rear cover plate.
10. Remove aluminum oil pan bolts in reverse order, **Fig. 17.**
11. Remove transaxle bolts.
12. Insert suitable tool between cylinder block and aluminum oil pans, then slide tool by tapping slide with hammer and remove aluminum oil pan. **Do not use screwdriver and be careful not to damage aluminum mating surface.**
13. Remove baffle plate and cylinder block O-rings.

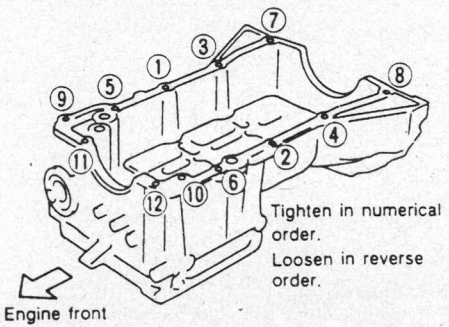

Fig. 17 Aluminum oil pan bolt tightening sequence

INSTALLATION

1. Remove all traces of liquid gasket on oil pans and cylinder block mating surfaces.
2. Install baffle plate, then apply sealant to front cover and rear oil seal gaskets.
3. Apply continuous liquid gasket bead to aluminum oil pan mating surface and inner sealing surface.
4. Install O-rings and install aluminum oil pan, tightening bolts in order to specifications, **Fig. 17.**
5. Install transaxle bolts, rear cover plate, A/C compressor and bracket, drive belts, center member, front and rear engine mounting insulator nuts and bolts, crankshaft position sensors, front exhaust tube and support, and oil strainer.
6. Apply continuous liquid gasket bead to steel oil pan mating surface and install steel oil pan.
7. Tighten bolts in order to specifications, **Fig. 16.**
8. Wait at least 30 minutes before filling with engine oil.

OIL PUMP

REPLACE

1. Drain engine oil and remove drive belts.
2. Remove oil pan as outlined under "Oil Pan, Replace."
3. Remove water pump and front covers.
4. Remove timing chain as outlined under "Timing Chain, Replace."
5. Remove oil pump assembly.
6. Reverse procedure to install.

BELT TENSION DATA

Refer to **Fig. 18** for belt tension data.

COOLING SYSTEM BLEED

These engines do not require a specified bleed procedure. After filling cooling system, run engine to operating temperature with radiator/pressure cap off. Air will then be automatically bled through cap opening.

THERMOSTAT

REPLACE

1. Drain engine and radiator coolant.
2. Remove lower radiator hose, then the water inlet, **Fig. 19.**
3. Remove thermostat from thermostat housing.
4. Reverse procedure to install.

WATER PUMP

REPLACE

1. Drain engine and radiator coolant.
2. Remove cylinder block drain plug, then the right engine mounting, mounting bracket and nuts.
3. Remove drive belts and idler pulley bracket.
4. Remove chain tensioner cover and water pump cover, **Fig. 20.**
5. Push timing chain tensioner sleeve, install stopper pin and remove chain tensioner assembly.
6. Remove three water pump attaching bolts, then turn crankshaft 20° counterclockwise to create gap between water pump gear and timing chain.
7. Put two M8 bolts in opposing water pump mounting holes, then alternately turn bolts ½ turn until they reach timing chain rear case.
8. Lifting up, remove water pump without hitting timing chain.
9. Reverse procedure to install.

RADIATOR

REPLACE

1. Remove undercover, then drain coolant.
2. Disconnect upper and lower radiator hoses, **Fig. 21.**

Drive belts	Used belt deflection		Deflection of new belt
	Limit	Deflection after adjustment	
Alternator			
With air conditioner compressor	7 (0.28)	4.2 - 4.6 (0.165 - 0.181)	3.8 - 4.1 (0.150 - 0.161)
Without air conditioner compressor	10 (0.39)	6.3 - 6.9 (0.248 - 0.272)	5.8 - 6.2 (0.228 - 0.244)
Power steering oil pump	11 (0.43)	7.3 - 8 (0.287 - 0.315)	6.5 - 7 (0.256 - 0.276)
Applied pushing force	98 N (10 kg, 22 lb)		

Unit: mm (in)

NS1069500162000X

Fig. 18 Belt tension data

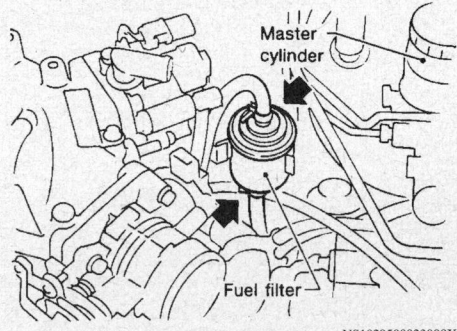

Gasket ⊗

Water inlet & Thermostat

8.34 - 11.28
(0.851 - 1.151, 6.152 - 8.320)

N·m (kg-m, ft-lb)

NS1089500069000X

Fig. 19 Thermostat replacement

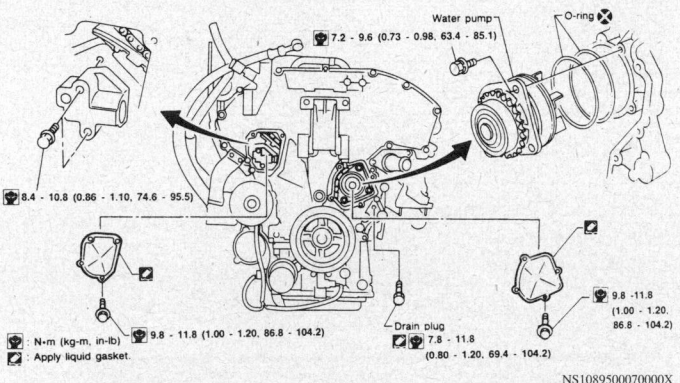

Water pump

O-ring ⊗

7.2 - 9.6 (0.73 - 0.98, 63.4 - 85.1)

8.4 - 10.8 (0.86 - 1.10, 74.6 - 95.5)

9.8 -11.8 (1.00 - 1.20, 86.8 - 104.2)

N·m (kg-m, in-lb)
9.8 - 11.8 (1.00 - 1.20, 86.8 - 104.2)
Apply liquid gasket.

Drain plug

7.8 - 11.8
(0.80 - 1.20, 69.4 - 104.2)

NS1089500070000X

Fig. 20 Water pump replacement

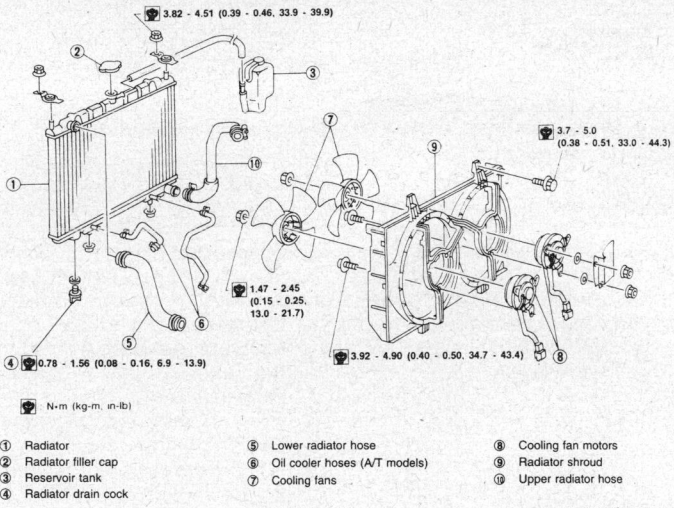

3.82 - 4.51 (0.39 - 0.46, 33.9 - 39.9)

3.7 - 5.0 (0.38 - 0.51, 33.0 - 44.3)

1.47 - 2.45 (0.15 - 0.25, 13.0 - 21.7)

0.78 - 1.56 (0.08 - 0.16, 6.9 - 13.9)

3.92 - 4.90 (0.40 - 0.50, 34.7 - 43.4)

N·m (kg-m, in-lb)

① Radiator	⑤ Lower radiator hose	⑧ Cooling fan motors
② Radiator filler cap	⑥ Oil cooler hoses (A/T models)	⑨ Radiator shroud
③ Reservoir tank	⑦ Cooling fans	⑩ Upper radiator hose
④ Radiator drain cock		

NS1089500074000X

Fig. 21 Radiator replacement

3. Remove shroud.
4. **On models equipped with automatic transaxle,** remove ATF cooler hoses.
5. **On all models,** disconnect reservoir tank hose.
6. Remove radiator mounting bracket attaching bolts.
7. Remove radiator.
8. Reverse procedure to install.

FUEL PUMP
REPLACE

1. Release fuel pump pressure as outlined under "Precautions."

Master cylinder

Fuel filter

NS1029500023000X

Fig. 22 Fuel filter replacement

2. Drain fuel into suitable container.
3. Disconnect necessary fuel lines and electrical connectors.
4. Disconnect fuel tank attaching bolts, then lower tank.
5. Remove fuel pump attaching bolts, then the fuel pump.
6. Reverse procedure to install.

FUEL FILTER
REPLACE

1. Relieve fuel system pressure as outlined under " Precautions."
2. Loosen two fuel filter hose clamps, **Fig. 22.**
3. Disconnect fuel hoses from fuel filter. **Do not allow gasoline to spill over engine compartment.**
4. Reverse procedure to install.

TECHNICAL SERVICE BULLETINS
OIL FILTER

The oil filter used on this engine is different than filters used on previous engines. It is smaller and has metric threads and an internal relief valve. This filter is not interchangeable with previous engines. Use correct filter for application.

TIGHTENING SPECIFICATIONS

Year	Component	Torque, Ft. Lbs.
1996–99	Camshaft Sprocket	88–95
	Connecting Rod Nuts	④
	Cylinder Head	①
	Exhaust Manifold	②
	Intake Manifold	③
	Intake Manifold Collector	③
	Main Bearing Cap Bolts	④
	Oil Pan Bolts (Aluminum)	12–14
	Oil Pan Bolts (Steel)	60–72⑤
	Oil Pump Cover Bolt	60⑤
	Oil Pump Cover Screw	36–48⑤
	Rear Timing Chain Case Bolts	9–10
	Thermostat Housing	72–96⑤
	Timing Chain Case (6 mm)	9–10
	Timing Chain Case (8 mm)	19–23
	Timing Chain Sprockets	84–108⑤
	Water Pump	60–84⑤

① — Refer to "Cylinder Head, Replace" in this section.
② — Refer to "Exhaust Manifold, Replace" in this section.
③ — Refer to "Intake Manifold, Replace" in this section.
④ — Refer to "Engine Assemble" in this section.
⑤ — Inch lbs.

Clutch & Manual Transmission

INDEX

ADJUSTMENTS
CLUTCH PEDAL

The clutch hydraulic system must be bled whenever a clutch line has been disconnected or when air has entered the system. The bleed valve is located on the clutch operating cylinder.
1. Adjust clutch pedal height, dimension "H" in **Figs. 1 and 2,** to specifications shown in **Fig. 3.**
2. Measure clutch pedal freeplay as shown in **Figs. 1 and 4,** dimension "A." Adjust clutch pedal freeplay by rotating clutch master cylinder pushrod inward or outward until specified freeplay is obtained. After completing freeplay adjustment, tighten locknut. Clutch pedal freeplay is sum of play between piston and piston rod.
3. Adjust dimension "C," **Fig. 5,** to specifications, with clutch pedal fully depressed.
4. After above adjustments have been completed, cycle clutch pedal several times to ensure clutch linkage operates smoothly without binding.

HYDRAULIC SYSTEM SERVICE
CLUTCH OPERATING CYLINDER, REPLACE

1. Disconnect brake line from operating cylinder. **Do not bend brake line.**
2. Remove cylinder attaching bolts, **Figs. 6 through 8.**
3. Remove operating cylinder.
4. Reverse procedure to install, bleed clutch hydraulic system as outlined under "Clutch Bleeding Procedure."

CLUTCH BLEED PROCEDURE

The clutch hydraulic system must be bled whenever a clutch line has been disconnected or when air has entered the system. The bleed valve is located on the clutch operating cylinder. Carefully monitor the fluid level at the master cylinder during the bleeding operation.
1. Fill up reservoir with recommended brake fluid.
2. Connect a transparent vinyl tube to air bleeder valve.
3. Fully depress clutch pedal several times.
4. With clutch pedal depressed, open bleeder valve to release air.
5. Close bleeder valve.
6. Repeat steps 3 through 5 until brake fluid flows from air bleeder valve without air bubbles.

CLUTCH
REPLACE

1. Remove transmission as outlined under "Manual Transmission Replace," in this section.
2. Insert a dummy shaft into clutch disc hub.

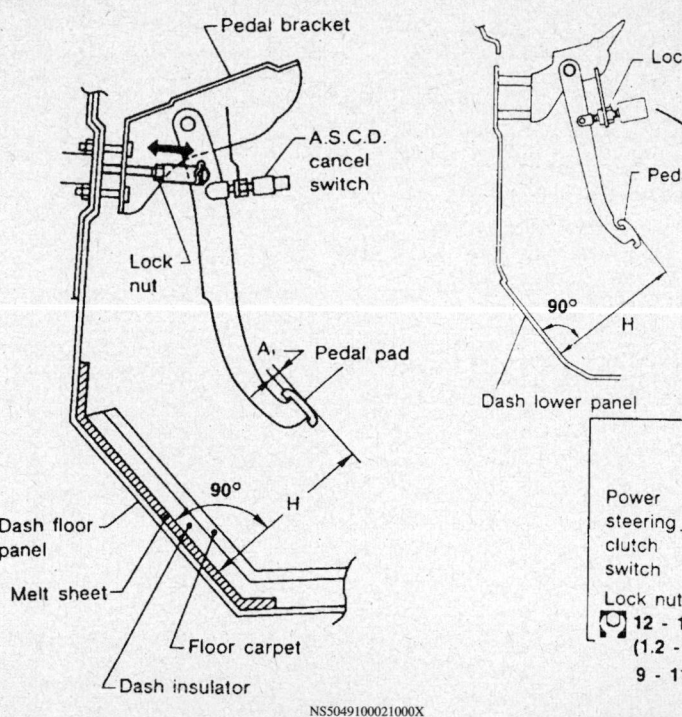

Fig. 1 Clutch pedal free travel & height adjustment. Maxima

Fig. 2 Clutch pedal height adjustment. 300ZX

Year	Model	Pedal Height, Inch	Pedal Freeplay, Inch	Pedal Stop Clearance, Inch
1996–99	Maxima	6.61–6.89	.039–.118	.012–.039
	300ZX Less Turbo	7.76–8.15	.039–.118	.039–.079
	300ZX With Turbo	7.20–7.60	.039–.118	.039–.079

Fig. 3 Clutch pedal height & freeplay specifications

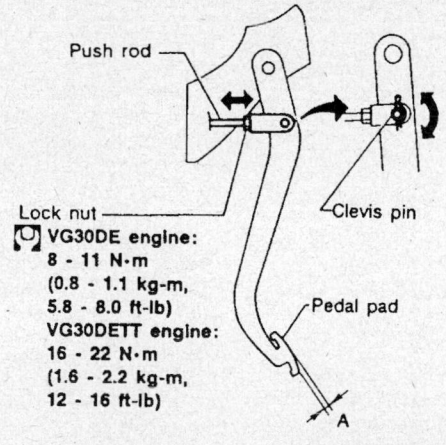

Fig. 4 Clutch pedal free travel adjustment. 300ZX

3. Loosen clutch cover attaching bolts alternately.
4. Remove clutch disc and cover assembly.
5. Remove release bearing.
6. Reverse procedure to install.

TRANSMISSION
REPLACE

300ZX

1. Remove accelerator linkage.
2. Raise and support vehicle.
3. Remove front exhaust pipe, catalytic converter and exhaust manifold connecting tube.
4. Remove control rod from shift lever.
5. Disconnect all cables and electrical connectors from transmission case.
6. Remove propeller shaft. **Install a plug in extension housing rear opening to prevent fluid spillage.**
7. Remove clutch operating cylinder from clutch housing.
8. Using a suitable jack support engine with a wooden block placed betweenoil pan and jack. **Do not place jack under oil pan drain plug.**
9. Place transmission control lever in Neutral, then remove E-ring and control lever.
10. Remove rear engine mount and crossmember attaching bolts.
11. Remove starting motor.
12. Remove bolts attaching transmission to engine, then move transmission rearward and lower from vehicle.
13. Reverse procedure to install.

MAXIMA

1. Remove battery and battery support bracket from vehicle as necessary.
2. Remove air cleaner assembly and air flow meter, as necessary.
3. Raise and support vehicle.
4. Remove both front propeller shafts. **When disconnecting driveshafts, use care not to damage oil seals. After disconnecting driveshafts, insert a suitable bar so that side gears will not rotate and fall into differential case.**
5. Disconnect control and support rods from transmission as necessary.
6. Remove front exhaust pipe attaching bolts.
7. Disconnect all cables and electrical connectors from transaxle.
8. Using a suitable jack, support engine with a wooden block placed between oil pan and jack.
9. Remove starter motor, as necessary.
10. Remove engine mount attaching bolts.
11. Remove engine to transaxle attaching bolts, then separate engine from transaxle and lower transaxle assembly from vehicle.
12. Reverse procedure to install.

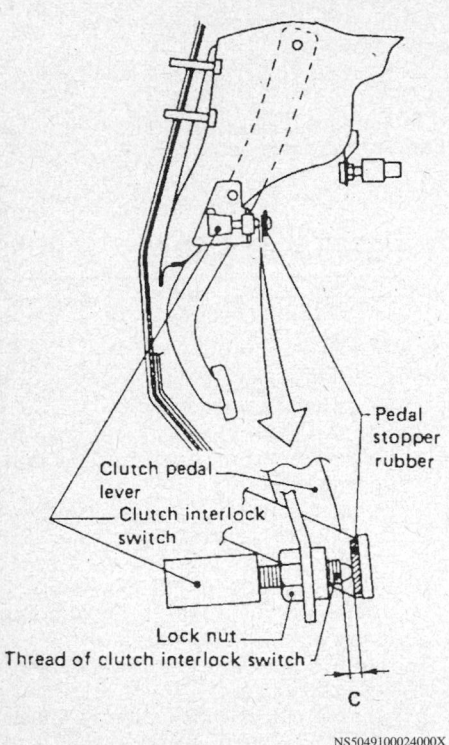

Fig. 5 Clutch interlock switch adjustment

NS5049100024000X

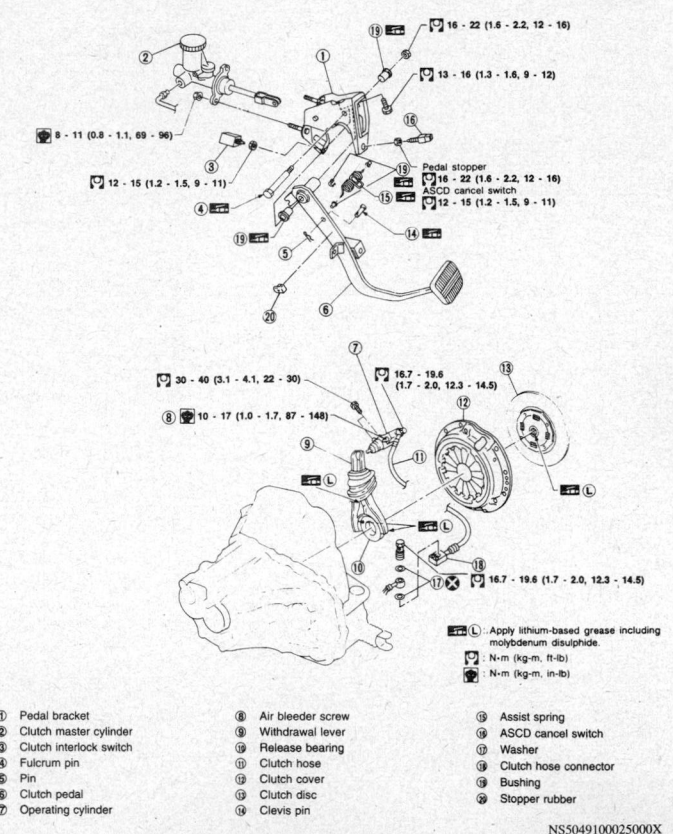

Apply lithium-based grease including molybdenum disulphide.
N·m (kg-m, ft-lb)
N·m (kg-m, in-lb)

① Pedal bracket
② Clutch master cylinder
③ Clutch interlock switch
④ Fulcrum pin
⑤ Pin
⑥ Clutch pedal
⑦ Operating cylinder
⑧ Air bleeder screw
⑨ Withdrawal lever
⑩ Release bearing
⑪ Clutch hose
⑫ Clutch cover
⑬ Clutch disc
⑭ Clevis pin
⑮ Assist spring
⑯ ASCD cancel switch
⑰ Washer
⑱ Clutch hose connector
⑲ Bushing
⑳ Stopper rubber

NS5049100025000X

Fig. 6 Exploded view of clutch assembly. Maxima

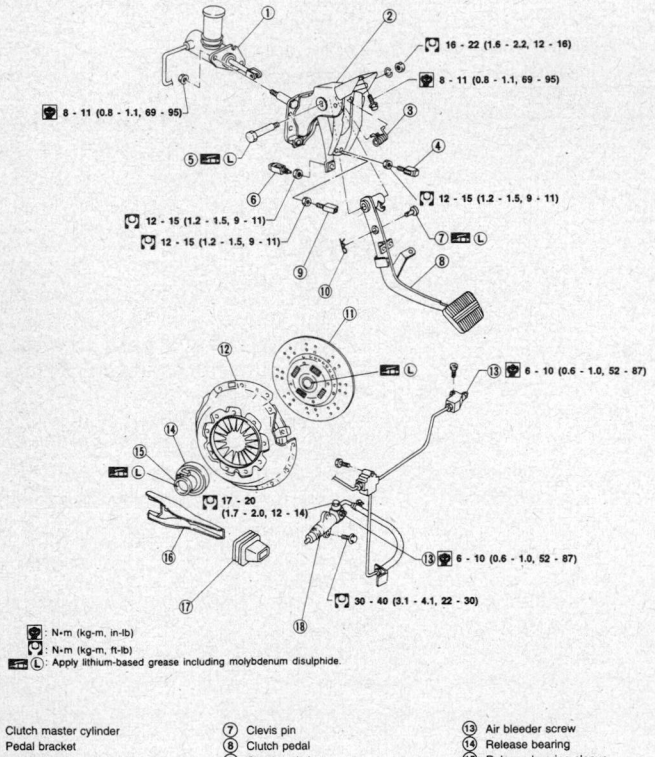

N·m (kg-m, in-lb)
N·m (kg-m, ft-lb)
Apply lithium-based grease including molybdenum disulphide.

① Clutch master cylinder
② Pedal bracket
③ Assist spring
④ ASCD cancel switch
⑤ Fulcrum pin
⑥ Clutch interlock switch
⑦ Clevis pin
⑧ Clutch pedal
⑨ Clutch switch
⑩ Snap pin
⑪ Clutch disc
⑫ Clutch cover
⑬ Air bleeder screw
⑭ Release bearing
⑮ Release bearing sleeve
⑯ Withdrawal lever
⑰ Dust cover
⑱ Operating cylinder

NS5049100026000X

Fig. 7 Exploded view of clutch assembly. 300ZX w/VG30DE engine

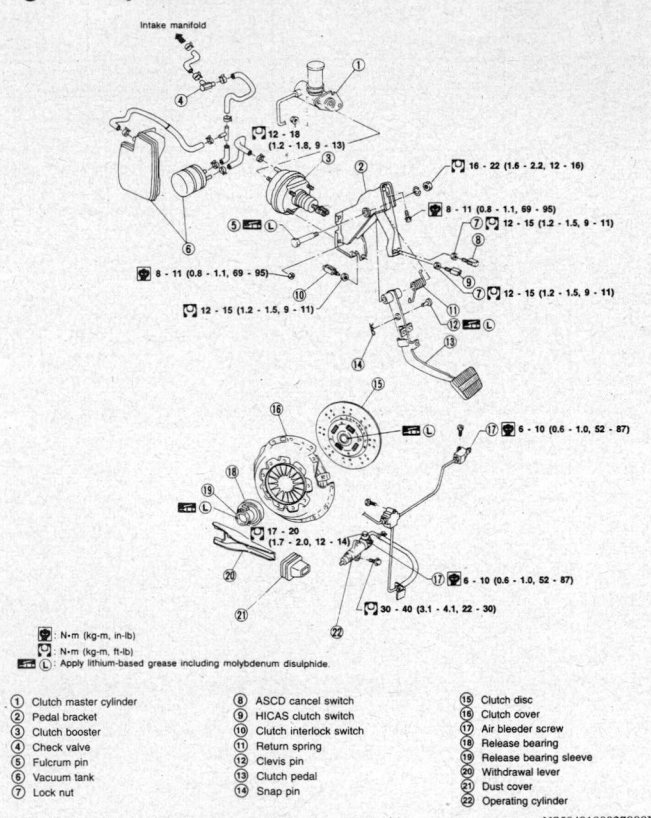

N·m (kg-m, in-lb)
N·m (kg-m, ft-lb)
Apply lithium-based grease including molybdenum disulphide.

① Clutch master cylinder
② Pedal bracket
③ Clutch booster
④ Check valve
⑤ Fulcrum pin
⑥ Vacuum tank
⑦ Lock nut
⑧ ASCD cancel switch
⑨ HICAS clutch switch
⑩ Clutch interlock switch
⑪ Return spring
⑫ Clevis pin
⑬ Clutch pedal
⑭ Snap pin
⑮ Clutch disc
⑯ Clutch cover
⑰ Air bleeder screw
⑱ Release bearing
⑲ Release bearing sleeve
⑳ Withdrawal lever
㉑ Dust cover
㉒ Operating cylinder

NS5049100027000X

Fig. 8 Exploded view of clutch assembly. 300ZX w/VG30DETT engine

TIGHTENING SPECIFICATIONS

Year	Component	Torque, Ft. Lbs.
1996–99	Air Bleeder Screw	48–84②
	Clutch Cover Assembly Attaching Bolts	①
	Clutch Interlock Switch Locknut	9–11
	Clutch Switch	9–11
	Clutch Tube Flare Nuts	11–13
	Flywheel Bolts	61–69
	Master Cylinder Attaching Nuts	72–96②
	Master Cylinder Pushrod Locknut	72–96②
	Pedal Stopper Locknut	12–16
	Slave Cylinder Attaching Bolts	22–30
	Supply Valve Stopper	12–24②

① — 300ZX, 25–33 ft. lbs.; Maxima, 16–22 ft. lbs.
② — Inch lbs.

Rear Axle & Suspension

INDEX

REAR AXLE

REPLACE

MAXIMA

Removal

1. Raise and support vehicle, then disconnect ABS wheel sensor, **Fig. 1.**
2. Remove brake caliper assemblies and suspend with wire, then the rotors.
3. Support torsion beam with suitable transmission jack, then raise slightly and remove suspension attaching nuts and bolts.
4. Remove luggage compartment trim, then upper strut mounting nuts and strut assembly.

Installation

1. Temporarily attach torsion beam to vehicle.
2. Place lateral link and control rod horizontally against torsion beam, then tighten lateral link bolts to specifications.
3. Attach shock absorber to vehicle, then tighten lower shock absorber nut to specifications.
4. Tighten torsion beam to specifications with suspension in full rebound position.

300ZX

Refer to **Figs. 2 and 3** for replacement, noting the following:

1. Disconnect parking brake cable, then remove brake caliper assembly.
2. Remove rear exhaust pipe.
3. Remove upper strut attaching bolts.
4. Disconnect propeller shaft.
5. Remove suspension attaching nuts, then the rear suspension assembly.
6. Reverse procedure to install.

REAR HALFSHAFT

REPLACE

300ZX

1. Raise and support vehicle, then remove rear wheels.
2. Remove wheel bearing attaching nut, then the side flange attaching nuts and bolts.
3. Remove driveshafts by lightly tapping inward on shafts with a copper hammer.

HUB & BEARING

REPLACE

MAXIMA

1. Raise and support vehicle, then remove rear wheel.
2. Remove rear caliper assembly and support with wire.
3. Remove rear wheel bearing locknut, **Fig. 4.**
4. Remove rear wheel hub bearing.

5. Reverse procedure to install. Ensure wheel bearing axial endplay is .0020 inch or less.

REAR SUSPENSION

REPLACE

300ZX

1. Before removal of lower arm mark adjusting pin for reference when installing.
2. Refer to "Rear Axle, Replace" for removal of lower arm.
3. Check ball joint for swing force, turning torque, then vertical endplay as shown in **Fig. 5.**
4. If any of ball joint checks are not within specifications, replace lower arm and ball joint as an assembly.

STRUT

REPLACE

MAXIMA

1. Remove rear axle as outlined under "Rear Axle, Replace."
2. Remove strut from rear axle.
3. Reverse procedure to install.

300ZX

1. Raise and support vehicle.
2. Remove upper and lower strut attaching nuts and/or bolts, then the strut assembly.

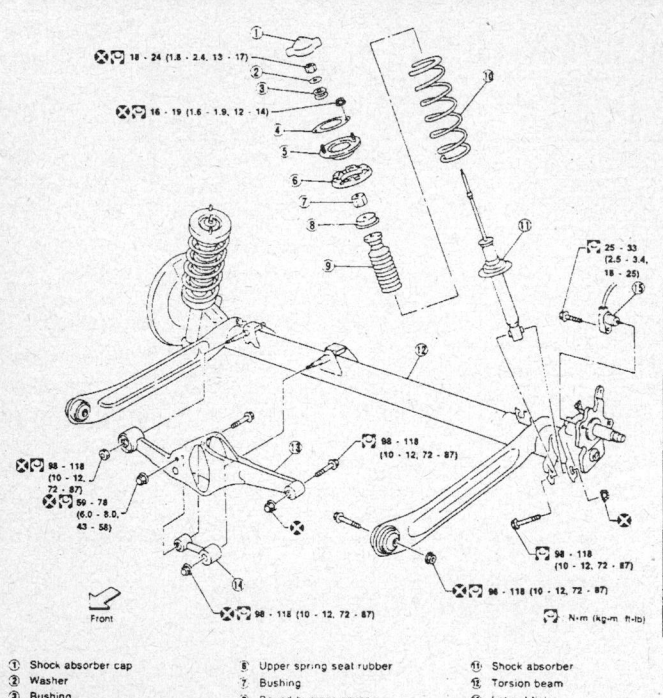

Fig. 1 Exploded view of rear suspension. Maxima

① Shock absorber cap
② Washer
③ Bushing
④ Shock absorber mounting seal
⑤ Shock absorber mounting bracket
⑥ Upper spring seat rubber
⑦ Bushing
⑧ Bound bumper cover
⑨ Bound bumper
⑩ Coil spring
⑪ Shock absorber
⑫ Torsion beam
⑬ Lateral link
⑭ Control rod
⑮ ABS sensor

NS2039500024000X

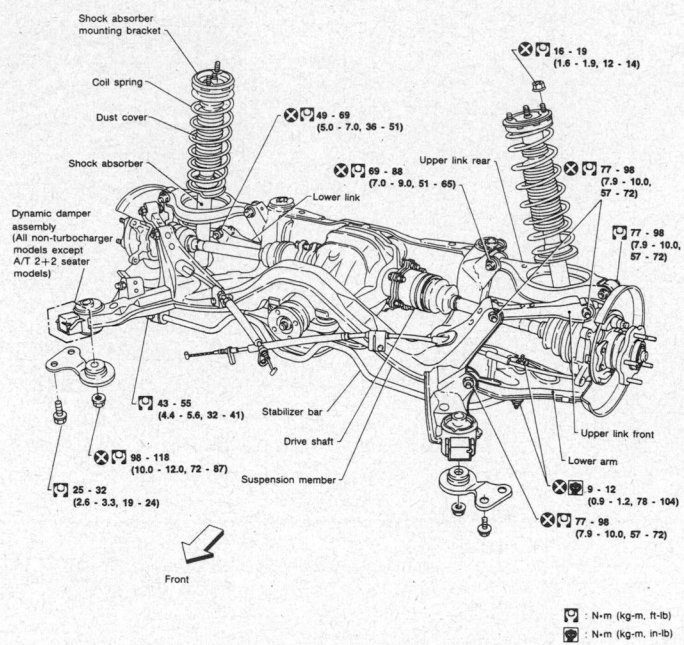

Fig. 2 Rear suspension. 300ZX

NS2039100007000X

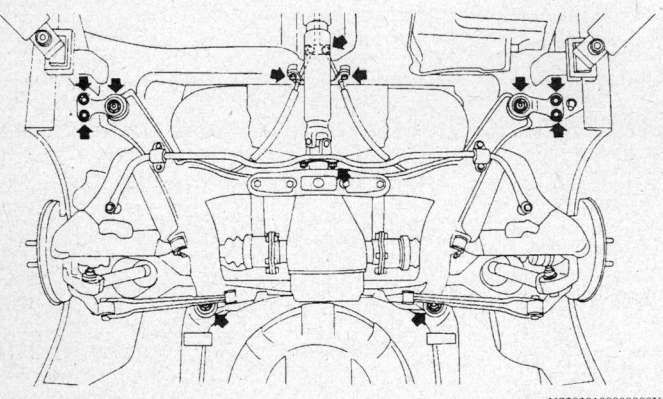

Fig. 3 Axle & suspension assembly removal. 300ZX

NS2039100008000X

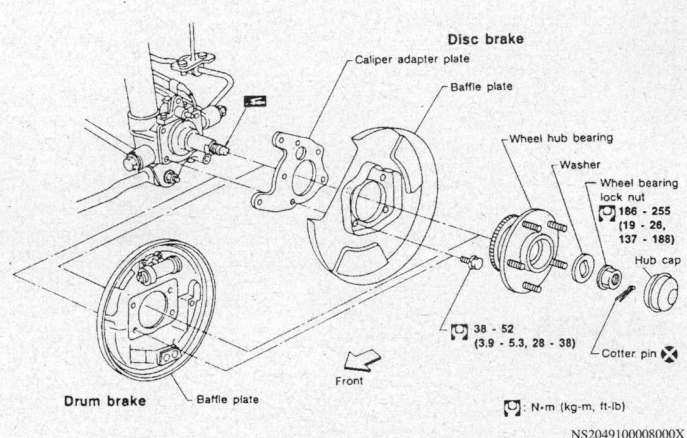

Fig. 4 Wheel hub assembly. Maxima

NS2049100008000X

3. Reverse procedure to install.

STRUT SERVICE

1. Set strut assembly in vise.
2. **Loosen, but do not remove, piston rod locknut.**
3. Compress spring using suitable spring compressor tool until strut upper spring seat can be turned by hand.
4. Remove piston locknut.
5. Remove strut assembly components.
6. Reverse procedure to assemble, noting the following:
   a. When installing coil spring, use care not to reverse top and bottom direction, **Fig. 6.**
   b. When installing spring on strut, position as shown in **Fig. 7.**

KNUCKLE

REPLACE

300ZX

1. Raise and support vehicle.
2. Remove wheel bearing locknut.
3. Remove brake caliper assembly and support by frame using suitable wire.
4. Separate driveshaft from axle housing (knuckle) by slightly tapping with a suitable soft face hammer, **Fig. 8.**
5. Remove axle housing attaching bolts then axle housing, **Fig. 9.**

6. Remove wheel bearing with flange and wheel hub from axle housing.
7. Using a suitable press, press off wheel bearing from wheel hub.
8. Reverse procedure to install, noting the following:
   a. Install wheel bearing as shown in **Fig. 10.**
   b. Ensure wheel bearing axial end-play is .0020 inch or less.

STABILIZER BAR

REPLACE

1. Raise and support vehicle.
2. Remove exhaust assembly as necessary.
3. Disconnect stabilizer bar from bushing brackets and locating bolts, then remove stabilizer bar.
4. Reverse procedure to install.

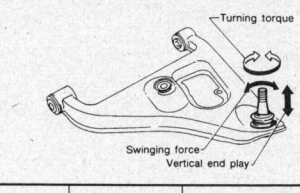

Ball joint specifications	Swinging force	7.8 - 54.9 N (0.8 - 5.6 kg, 1.8 - 12.3 lb)
	Turning torque	0.5 - 3.4 N·m (5 - 35 kg-cm, 4.3 - 30.4 in-lb)
	Vertical end play	0 mm (0 in)

NS2049100015000X

Fig. 5   Lower ball joint inspection. 300ZX

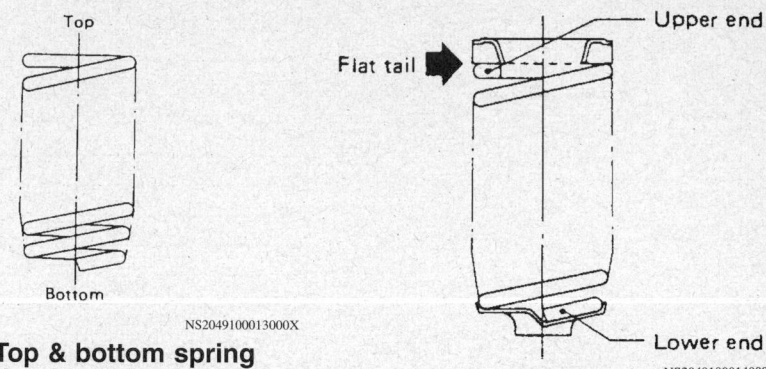

NS2049100013000X

Fig. 6   Top & bottom spring position identification

NS2049100014000X

Fig. 7   Spring installation position

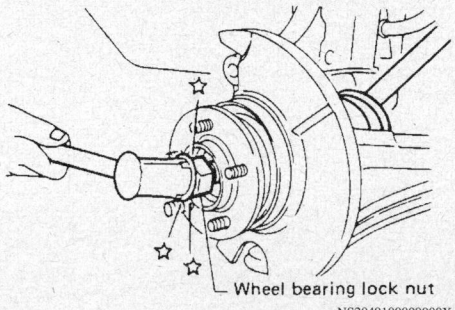

NS2049100009000X

Fig. 8   Driveshaft removal. 300ZX

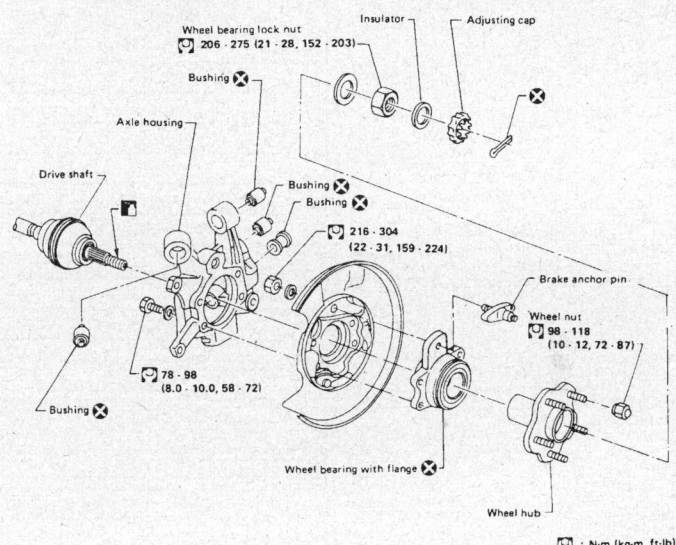

Wheel bearing lock nut
⟲ 206 - 275 (21 - 28, 152 - 203)

Insulator

Adjusting cap

Bushing ⊠

Axle housing

Drive shaft

Bushing ⊠

Bushing ⊠

⟲ 216 - 304 (22 - 31, 159 - 224)

Brake anchor pin

Wheel nut
⟲ 98 - 118 (10 - 12, 72 - 87)

⟲ 78 - 98 (8.0 - 10.0, 58 - 72)

Bushing ⊠

Wheel bearing with flange ⊠

Wheel hub

⟲ : N·m (kg-m, ft-lb)

NS2049100010000X

Fig. 9   Exploded view of wheel hub & axle housing assembly. 300ZX

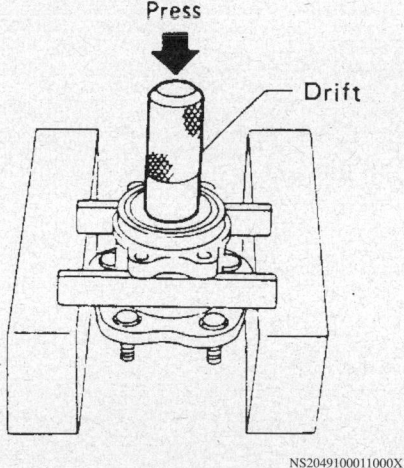

Press

Drift

NS2049100011000X

Fig. 10   Wheel bearing installation. 300ZX

TIGHTENING SPECIFICATIONS

Year	Component	Torque, Ft. Lbs.
MAXIMA		
1996–99	Axle Nut	137–188
	Baffle Plate Bolts	28–38
	Control Rod Bolt	43–58
	Driveshaft Nut	137–188
	Gland Packing	51–94
	Hub Nut	137–188
	Lateral Link Bolts	72–87
	Parallel Link Adjustment Nut	58–72
	Parallel Link Fixing Bolt	65–87
	Piston Rod Locknut	②
	Radius Rod Fixing Bolt	65–80
	Stabilizer Bar Fixing Bolts	43–58
	Stabilizer Bar Nuts	30–35
	Torsion Beam Bolt	72–87
	Upper Strut Mounting Nuts	①
	Wheel Bearing Locknut	137–188
	Wheel Lug Nut	72–87
300ZX		
1996	Axle Nut	152–203
	Axle Housing Bolts	58–72
	Brake Anchor Pin Nut	159–224
	Driveshaft Nut	152–203
	Driveshaft To Side Flange Bolt	25–33
	Front Upper Link Nuts	57–72
	Hub Nut	152–203
	Lower Control Arm Bolts	57–72
	Lower Shock Absorber Nut	57–72
	Stabilizer Bar To Connecting Rod	84–108③
	Strut To Body	18–22
	Strut To Knuckle	72–87
	Suspension Crossmember	65–80
	Upper Link Front To Suspension Member	57–72
	Upper Link Rear To Knuckle	57–72
	Wheel Bearing Locknut	152–203
	Wheel Lug Nut	72–87

① — 1996, 12–14 ft. lbs.

② — 1996, 13–17 ft. lbs.

③ — Inch lbs.

Front Suspension & Steering

INDEX

WHEEL BEARING

ADJUST

300ZX

1. Raise and support vehicle.
2. Remove brake pads.
3. Ensure wheel bearing is tightened to correct specifications.
4. Ensure wheel bearing operates smoothly.
5. Using a dial indicator, check axial end-play.
6. If axial endplay is more than .0020 inch, replace wheel bearing.

HUB & BEARING

REPLACE

300ZX

1. Raise and support vehicle, remove wheels.
2. Remove caliper without disconnecting brake line.
3. Using ball joint remover tool No. HT72750000, or equivalent, remove tie rod ball joint and lower ball joint from steering knuckle.
4. Remove kingpin lower attaching nut, then the steering knuckle assembly.
5. Reverse procedure to install.

WHEEL HUB & STEERING KNUCKLE

REPLACE

MAXIMA

1. Raise and support vehicle, then remove wheels.
2. Remove wheel bearing locknut, **Fig. 1.**
3. Remove brake caliper. **Do not disconnect brake lines.**
4. Separate tie rod from knuckle using suitable tool.
5. Remove nuts and bolts as shown in **Fig. 2,** then knuckle assembly.
6. Reverse procedure to install, noting the following:
   a. Tighten wheel bearing to specifications.
   b. Ensure wheel bearing axial end-play is not more than .0020 inches.

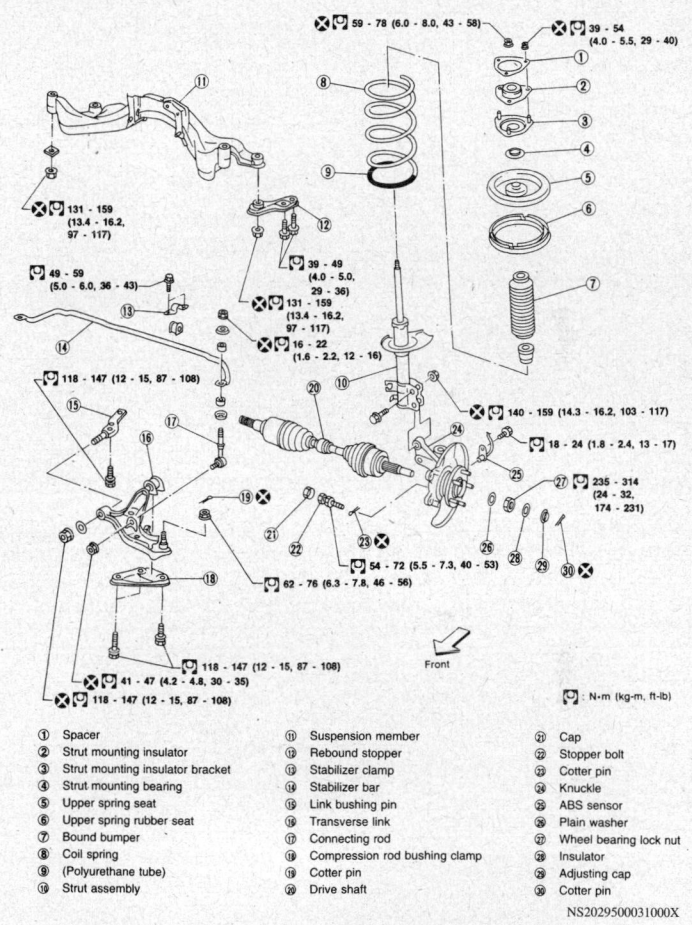

① Spacer
② Strut mounting insulator
③ Strut mounting insulator bracket
④ Strut mounting bearing
⑤ Upper spring seat
⑥ Upper spring rubber seat
⑦ Bound bumper
⑧ Coil spring
⑨ (Polyurethane tube)
⑩ Strut assembly
⑪ Suspension member
⑫ Rebound stopper
⑬ Stabilizer clamp
⑭ Stabilizer bar
⑮ Link bushing pin
⑯ Transverse link
⑰ Connecting rod
⑱ Compression rod bushing clamp
⑲ Cotter pin
⑳ Drive shaft
㉑ Cap
㉒ Stopper bolt
㉓ Cotter pin
㉔ Knuckle
㉕ ABS sensor
㉖ Plain washer
㉗ Wheel bearing lock nut
㉘ Insulator
㉙ Adjusting cap
㉚ Cotter pin

N·m (kg-m, ft-lb)

NS2029500031000X

Fig. 1 Front suspension. Maxima

BALL JOINT INSPECTION

Check ball joint for play. If ball stud is worn, play in axial direction (C) is more than zero inches, ball joint swing force (A) is not 1.8–17.4 lbs. or ball joint turning torque (B) is not 4.3–43.4 inch lbs., replace ball joint, **Fig. 3.** Before checking, turn ball joint at least 10 revolutions.

BALL JOINT

REPLACE

MAXIMA

1. Remove driveshaft as outlined under "Driveshaft, Replace" in "Front Wheel Drive" section, as necessary.
2. Remove ball joint attaching nuts/bolts and ball joint.
3. Reverse procedure to install.

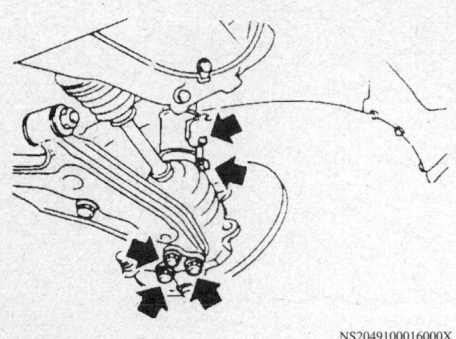

NS2049100016000X

Fig. 2 Knuckle assembly removal. Maxima

STRUT

REPLACE

MAXIMA

1. Raise and support front of vehicle and remove wheel.
2. Disconnect brake line from strut.
3. Remove strut to steering knuckle attaching bolts, then separate strut from knuckle.
4. Remove strut to strut tower attaching nuts, then the strut assembly from vehicle.
5. Reverse procedure to install.

300ZX

1. Raise and support front of vehicle and remove wheel.
2. Remove brake caliper assembly. **Do not disconnect brake line.**
3. Remove brake hose locking spring.
4. Remove brake hose from strut bracket, remove brake assembly if necessary.
5. **On models equipped with adjustable shocks,** disconnect shock electrical connectors.
6. **On all models,** remove strut to steering knuckle attaching bolts, **Fig. 4.**
7. Disconnect knuckle arm from bottom of strut.
8. Remove strut to strut tower attaching nuts, then the strut.
9. Reverse procedure to install.

STABILIZER BAR

REPLACE

1. Raise and support vehicle.
2. Remove stabilizer bar attaching bolts, **Figs. 5 and 6,** then stabilizer bar.
3. Reverse procedure to install, noting the following:
   a. When installing bar, ensure paint mark and clamp face are in their correct positions, **Fig. 7.**

b. **On Maxima models,** install stabilizer bar with ball joint sockets positioned as shown in **Fig. 8.**

TRANSVERSE LINK

REPLACE

MAXIMA

1. Raise and support vehicle.
2. Remove stabilizer bar attaching bolts.
3. Remove transverse link attaching bolts, then the transverse link.
4. Reverse procedure to install, noting the following:
   a. Final tightening must be made with vehicle on ground.
   b. Check wheel alignment after installing transverse link.

300ZX

1. Raise and support vehicle and remove wheels.
2. Remove tension rod and stabilizer bar, **Fig. 4.**
3. Remove ball joint and transverse link mounting nut/bolts, then separate link from crossmember.
4. Reverse procedure to install.

POWER STEERING GEAR

REPLACE

MAXIMA

Refer to **Fig. 9** for power steering gear replacement procedure, noting the following:
1. Detach tie rod ball studs from steering knuckle arms using suitable tool.
2. Remove carbon canister, engine mounting and front stabilizer bar.
3. Remove hole cover mounting nuts.
4. Remove manual transaxle control linkage or automatic transaxle control cable as necessary.

300ZX

Refer to **Fig. 10** for power steering gear replacement procedure, noting the following.
1. When removing power steering hoses plug ports and lines.
2. Set wheels straight ahead before removing lower joint.
3. After removing lower joint put matching mark on pinion shaft and pinion housing.

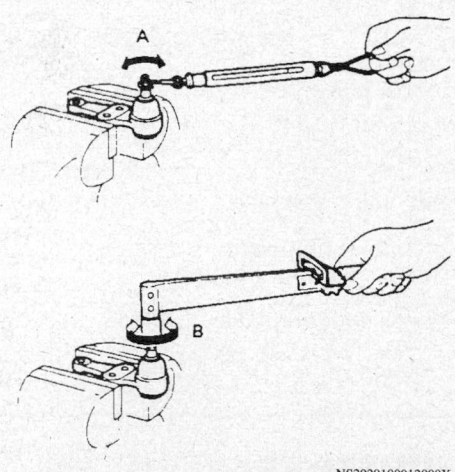

NS2029100012000X

Fig. 3 Ball joint inspection

POWER STEERING PUMP

REPLACE

1. Loosen idler pulley locknut, turn adjusting nut counterclockwise, and remove power steering pump drive belt.
2. **On some air conditioned models,** remove air conditioning compressor drive belt.
3. **On all models,** loosen power steering hoses at pump and remove bolts securing power steering pump to brackets.
4. Raise pump and disconnect power steering hoses. Catch fluid in a suitable container, plug hose ends and ports in power steering pump, and remove pump from vehicle.
5. Re-install power steering pump by reversing procedure and bleed system as follows:
   a. Raise and support front of vehicle.
   b. Run engine for 3–5 seconds, stop engine, check and fill power steering pump reservoir as needed.
   c. Quickly turn steering wheel all way to right and left 10 times.
   d. Start engine and idle for 3–5 seconds. Stop engine, check and fill power steering pump reservoir as needed.
   e. With steering wheel all way to right, open bleeder screw, to expel air and tighten bleeder screw.
   f. Repeat procedure until all air has been bled from system.
   g. If air cannot be bled completely after repeated attempts, repeat step e with engine running.

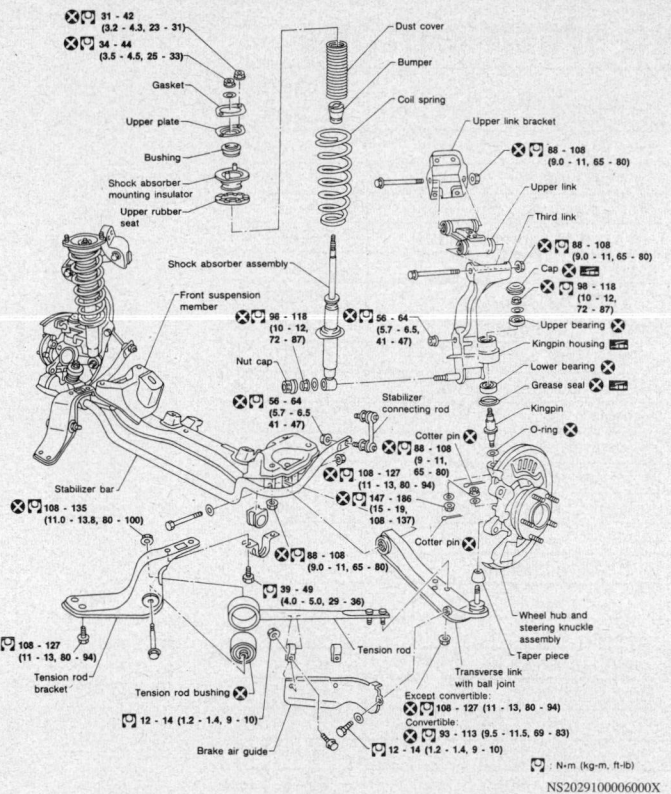

Fig. 4 Front suspension. 300ZX

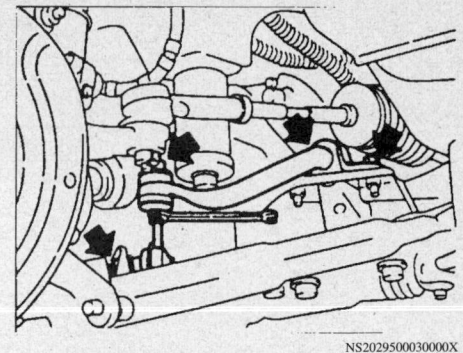

Fig. 5 Stabilizer bar removal. Maxima

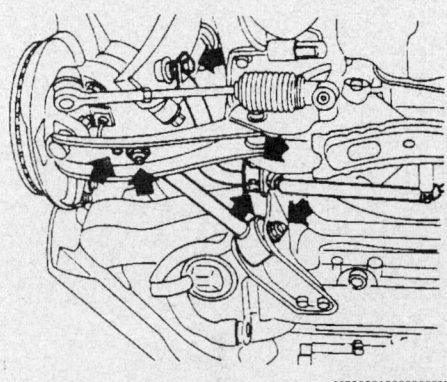

Fig. 6 Stabilizer bar removal. 300ZX

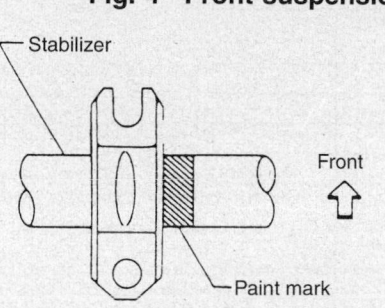

Fig. 7 Stabilizer & bushing installation

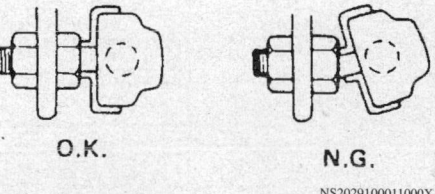

O.K.   N.G.

Fig. 8 Ball joint position. Maxima

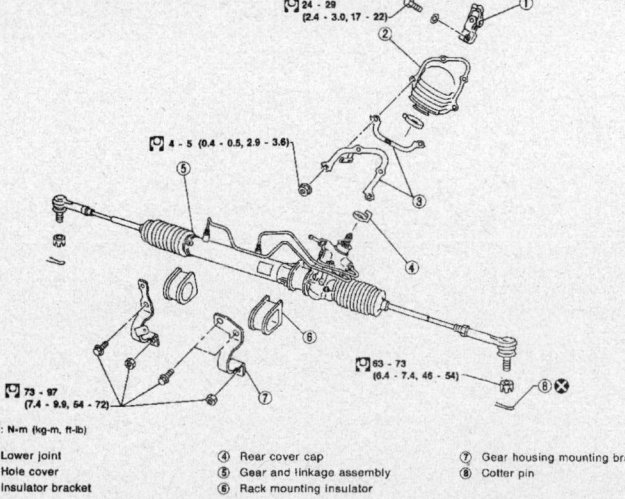

① Lower joint
② Hole cover
③ Insulator bracket
④ Rear cover cap
⑤ Gear and linkage assembly
⑥ Rack mounting insulator
⑦ Gear housing mounting bracket
⑧ Cotter pin

Fig. 9 Power steering gear replacement. Maxima

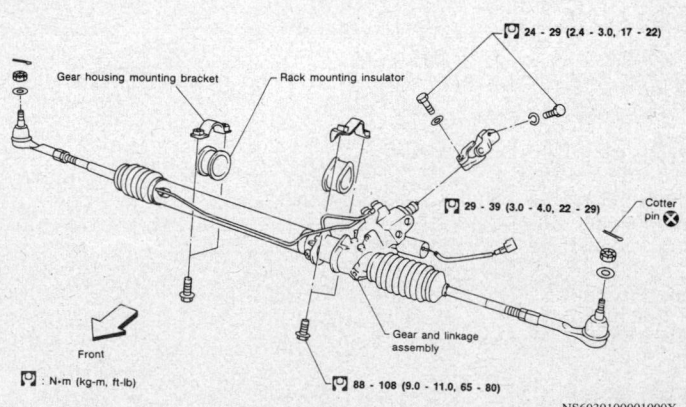

Fig. 10 Power steering gear replacement. 300ZX

TIGHTENING SPECIFICATIONS

Year	Component	Torque, Ft. Lbs.
MAXIMA		
1996–99	Axle Nut	174–231
	Ball Joint To Knuckle Nut	52–64
	Ball Joint To Transverse Link Nut	56–80
	Driveshaft Nut	174–231
	Hub Nut	174–231
	Piston Rod Locknut	43–58
	Stabilizer Bar Clamp	23–31
	Stabilizer Bar To Connecting Rod	30–38
	Stopper Bolt	40–53
	Strut To Inner Fender Mounting Nut	29–40
	Strut To Knuckle Bolt	116–123
	Transverse Link Bushing Clamp	87–108
	Transverse Link To Gusset Nut	65–87
	Wheel Bearing Locknut	174–231
300ZX		
1996	Axle Nut	152–210
	Ball Joint To Knuckle	65–80
	Driveshaft Nut	152–210
	Hub Nut	152–210
	Kingpin Lower Nut	108–137
	Kingpin Upper Nut	72–87
	Piston Rod Locknut	25–33
	Stabilizer Connecting Rod To Front Suspension Member	41–47
	Strut Lower Nut	72–87
	Strut To Inner Fender Attaching Nut	23–31
	Tension Rod Bushing	80–100
	Tension Rod To Transverse Link	80–83
	Third Link Bolt	65–80
	Transverse Link To Front Suspension Member	80–94
	Upper Link Bolt	65–80
	Wheel Bearing Locknut	152–210

Wheel Alignment

INDEX

PRELIMINARY INSPECTION

1. Check tire pressures and adjust as needed.
2. Ensure tires are of proper size and are properly matched.
3. Ensure wheel bearings (front and rear) are properly adjusted.
4. Check steering gear for correct adjustment and that it is properly secured to frame.
5. Inspect steering linkage and suspension components for damage and wear, repair or replace components as needed.
6. Measure vehicle ride height with vehicle unloaded.
7. Place vehicle on suitable alignment rack following manufacturer's instructions, then jounce vehicle several times to settle suspension.
8. Check and correct rear wheel camber and toe first, if applicable, then check and correct front suspension angles in following order: caster and kingpin inclination, camber, toe setting and turning angle (toe-out on turns).

FRONT WHEEL ALIGNMENT

To ensure correct alignment, angles should be checked, and if necessary corrected, in following sequence: caster and kingpin inclination, camber, toe-setting, and turning angle and toe-out on turns. Front wheel alignment should only be checked after ensuring rear wheels are properly aligned in relation to vehicle centerline, as most equipment uses rear wheels as reference for correct front wheel alignment. Front wheel alignment should be checked with vehicle at normal ride height, and following equipment manufacturer's instructions.

CASTER & KINGPIN INCLINATION

If caster or kingpin angle are not within specifications, check suspension components and sheet metal for damage, distortion and excessive wear, repair or replace components as necessary.

CAMBER

Camber cannot be adjusted. If camber is not within specifications, inspect suspen-

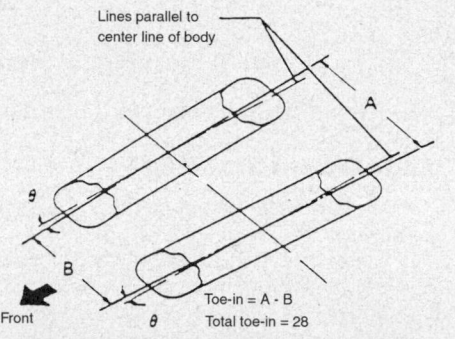

Fig. 1   Toe-in measurement

Toe-in = A - B
Total toe-in = 2θ

NS2049100017000X

Year	Model	Standard Tie Rod Length, Inch
1996–99	Maxima	7.98
	300ZX	6.10

Fig. 3   Tie rod length specifications

sion and sheet metal for damage, distortion and excessive wear, repair or replace components as necessary.

TOE-IN

Toe setting is measurement of wheels in relation to vehicle centerline, **Fig. 1**. Leading edge of each wheel should toe-in or toe-out slightly in relation to vehicle centerline to ensure proper vehicle tracking. Toe should be inspected using suitable alignment gauges, following manufacturer's instructions. When checking or adjusting toe, always ensure setting of left and right wheels is as equal as possible.

Toe is adjusted by loosening tie rod locknuts or adjusting sleeve bolts and equally altering length of tie rods. After toe has been adjusted to specifications, lengths of left and right tie rods, **Figs. 2 and 3**, should be nearly equal and close to length specified. Incorrect tie rod length will adversely affect steering angles and toe-out on turns.

STEERING ANGLE

When a vehicle negotiates a turn, inner wheel must turn at a sharper angle than outer wheel, and outer wheel must travel farther than inner wheel. Vehicle steering geometry is calculated to allow for these variations, causing outer wheel to toe-out by a calibrated amount. This toe-out on

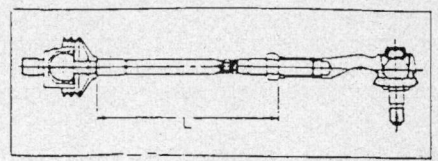

NS2049100020000X

Fig. 2   Typical tie rod length measurement

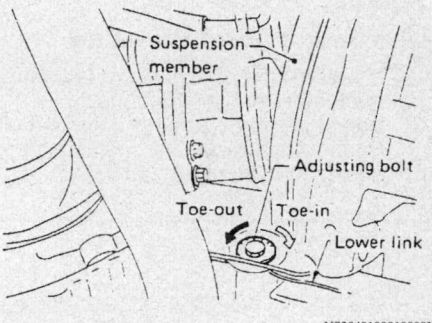

NS2049100019000X

Fig. 4   Rear toe-in adjustment. 300ZX

turns is also referred to as steering angle and on these models, is generally checked at two positions. first position is at a reference point on inner wheel travel while second position of measurement is at full steering lock. To check steering angles, proceed as follows:

1. Turn steering to full lock and measure inner and outer wheel turning angles.
2. If "Turning Angles" at full lock are not within specifications, check for damaged steering linkage or improperly adjusted tie rods.
3. If steering linkage and tie rods are satisfactory, check for improper rack or rack piston stroke and repair steering gear as needed.

REAR WHEEL ALIGNMENT

CAMBER

Rear camber cannot be adjusted. If rear camber is not within specifications, check for damaged or worn suspension components and deformed sheet metal, repair as necessary.

TOE-IN

On models equipped with independent rear suspension, rear toe is measurement

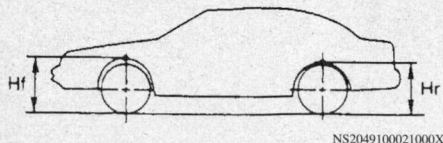

NS2049100021000X

Fig. 5 Vehicle ride height inspection

of rear wheels in relation to vehicle center-line, **Fig. 1**. leading edge of each rear wheel should toe-in slightly toward vehicle center-line to ensure proper vehicle tracking. Rear toe should be inspected using suitable alignment gauges, following manufacturer's instructions. When checking or adjusting rear toe, always ensure amount that left and right wheel toe-in is as equal as possible.

MAXIMA

Toe-in is preset and cannot be adjusted. If out of specification, inspect and replace damaged or worn rear suspension parts.

300ZX

Less Four Wheel Steering

1. Measure toe-in following equipment manufacturer's instructions.
2. Adjust toe-in by turning adjusting pin. Each graduation of adjusting pin equals .059 inch, **Fig. 4**.

3. **Torque** adjusting bolt to 51–65 ft. lbs.

Four Wheel Steering

Rear toe-in can be adjusted by adjusting power cylinder lower links.
1. Measure toe-in for each wheel following equipment manufacturer's instructions.
2. Adjust toe in by adjusting lengths of power cylinder lower links.
3. After adjustment is complete, ensure both lower links are same length.

Year	Model	Vehicle Ride Height Inch, Unladen①	
		Front	Rear
MAXIMA			
1996–99	GXE & GLE	28.07	28.15
	SE	28.07	28.07
300ZX			
1996	Two-Seater Less Turbo	26.57	26.61
	Two-Seater w/Turbo	26.57	26.57
	2+2	26.65	26.57

① — Measured @ top of wheel arch.

Fig. 6 Vehicle ride height

VEHICLE RIDE HEIGHT

When checking ride height vehicle must be parked on a level surface and tires inflated to proper air pressure. Ensure all fluid levels are to specified level, spare tire and jack are in proper locations.

Bounce vehicle up and down several times, then measure vehicle height from top of wheelwell to ground, **Fig. 5**. Vehicle height is not adjustable. If vehicle height is not as specified, check for worn springs or suspension parts. Vehicle ride heights are shown in **Fig. 6**.

NISSAN FRONTIER, PATHFINDER & PICKUP

INDEX OF SERVICE OPERATIONS

Specifications

GENERAL ENGINE SPECIFICATIONS

Year	Engine	Fuel System	Displacement, Liters	Bore x Stroke, Inches (mm)	Compression Ratio	Maximum H.P. @ RPM	Maximum Torque @ RPM	Normal Oil Pressure, psi
1996	KA24E	Fuel Inj.	2.4L	3.50 x 3.78 (89 x 96)	8.6	140 @ 5600	152 @ 4400	60–70①
	VG33E	Fuel Inj.	3.3L	3.60 x 3.27 (92 x 83)	8.9	168 @ 4800	196 @ 2800	60–65①
1997	KA24E	Fuel Inj.	2.4L	3.50 x 3.78 (89 x 96)	8.6	134 @ 5200	154 @ 3600	60–70①
	VG33E	Fuel Inj.	3.3L	3.60 x 3.27 (92 x 83)	8.9	168 @ 4800	196 @ 2800	60–70①
1998	KA24E	Fuel Inj.	2.4L	3.50 x 3.78 (89 x 96)	8.9	143 @ 5200	154 @ 4000	60–70①
	VG33E	Fuel Inj.	3.3L	3.60 x 3.27 (91.5 x 83)	8.9	168 @ 4800	196 @ 2800	60–70①
1999	KA24E	Fuel Inj.	2.4L	3.50 x 3.78 (89 x 96)	9.2	143 @ 5200	154 @ 4000	60–70①
	VG33E	Fuel Inj.	3.3L	3.60 x 3.27 (91.5 x 83)	8.9	168 @ 4800	196 @ 2800	60–70①

① — 3000 RPM.

TUNE UP SPECIFICATIONS

Year, Model & Engine	Spark Plug Gap, Inch	Ignition Timing			Curb Idle Speed②		Fast Idle Speed		Fuel Pressure, psi	Valve Lash
		Firing Order Fig.①	Timing, °BTDC	Timing Mark Fig.	Man. Trans.	Auto. Trans.	Man. Trans.	Auto. Trans.		
1996										
Pathfinder VG33E	.033	⑤	15	C	750	750N	③	③	43	④
Pickup KA24E	.041	⑥	10	A	800	800N	③	③	43	④
1997										
Pathfinder VG33E	.041	⑤	15	C	750	750N	③	③	43	④
Pickup KA24E	.041	⑥	10	A	750	750N	③	③	43	④
1998–99										
Pathfinder VG33E	.041	⑤	15	B	750	750N	③	③	43	④
Frontier KA24E	.041	⑥	20	C	800	800N	③	③	43	④

BTDC — Before Top Dead Center.
N — Neutral.
① — Before disconnecting spark plug wires from distributor cap, determine location of No. 1 wire in cap, as distributor position may have been altered from that shown.

② — When adjusting idle speed, set parking brake & chock drive wheels.
③ — Controlled by ECCS.
④ — Refer to "Valve Adjustment" in specific engine section.

⑤ — Cylinder number from front of engine to rear; right bank 1, 3, 5; left bank 2, 4, 6. Firing order, 1-2-3-4-5-6.
⑥ — No. 1 located front of engine. Firing order, 1-3-4-2.

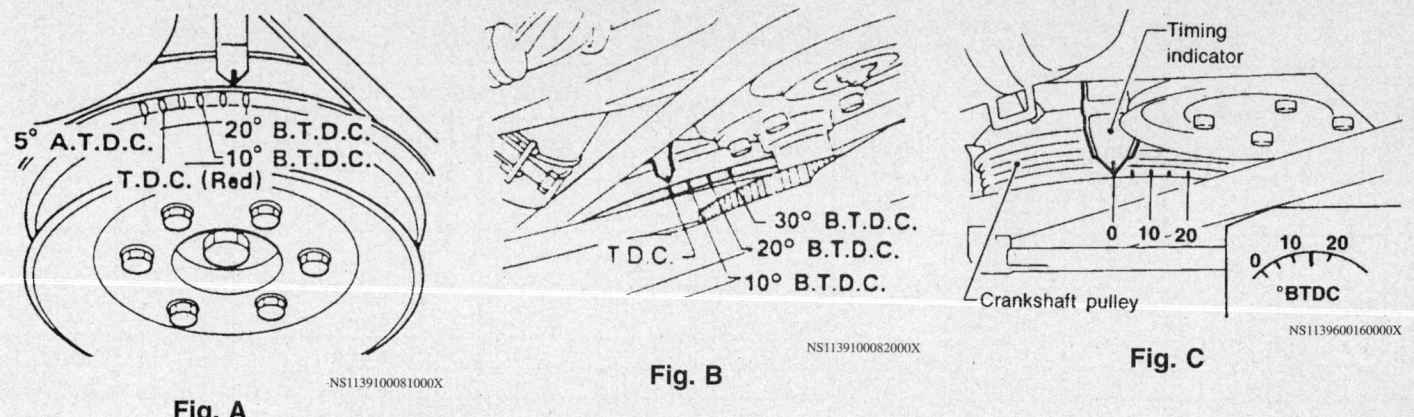

-NS1139100081000X

Fig. A

NS1139100082000X

Fig. B

NS1139600160000X

Fig. C

FRONT WHEEL ALIGNMENT SPECIFICATIONS

Year	Model	Caster Angle, Deg.		Camber Angle, Deg.		Kingpin Inclin-ation, Deg.	Toe-In, Inch①	Toe-Out On Turns, Deg.②		Ball Joint Wear
		Limits	Desired	Limits	Desired			Inner Wheel	Outer Wheel	
1996–97	Pathfinder	+2.25 to +3.75	+3	-.58 to +.92	+.17	13.58 to 15.08	+.04 to +.12	③	④	⑤
	Pickup 2WD	-.13 to +.87	+.22	-.08 to +.+92	+.42	8.58 to 9.58	+.08 to _.16	36 to 38	33 to 35	⑤
	Pickup 4WD	+.8 to +1.8	+1.3	+.17 to +1.17	+.67	7.6 to 8.6	+.12 to +.20	33 to 35	31 to 33	⑤
1998–99	Pathfinder	+2.25 to +3.75	+3	-.58 to +.92	+.17	13.58 to 15.08	+.04 to +.12	③	④	⑤
	Frontier 2WD	+.1 to +1.1	+.6	-.08 to +.92	+.42	8.58 to 9.58	+.08 to +.16	⑥	⑦	⑤
	Frontier 4WD	+1.67 to +2.67	+2.17	+.1 to +1.1	+.6	10.3 to 11.3	+.12 to +.20	⑧	⑨	⑤

2WD — 2 Wheel Drive.
4WD — 4 Wheel Drive.
① — Toe-in (+); toe-out (-).
② — Measure w/wheels @ full lefthand & righthand turn positions.
③ — Models w/235/70 R 15 tires, 32 to 36; models w/265/70 R 15 tires, 30 to 34.
④ — Models w235/70 R 15 tires, 30 to 34; models w/265/70 R15 tires, 28 to 32.

⑤ — Refer to "Ball Joint Inspection" section under "Front Suspension & Steering."
⑥ — Except P215/65 R125 tires, 36 to 38; w/P215/65 R15 tires, 35 to 37.
⑦ — Except P215/65 R15 tires, 32.6 to 34.6; w215/65 R15 tires, 31.6 to 33.6.

⑧ — Except P265/70 R15 tires, 33.1 to 35.1; w/P265/70 R15 tires, 31 to 33.
⑨ — Except P265/70 R15 tires, 31.2 to 33.2; wP265/70 R15 tires, 29 to 31.

FLUID CAPACITIES & COOLING SYSTEM DATA

Year	Model	Coolant Capacity, Qts.	Radiator Cap Relief Pressure, Lbs.	Thermo Opening Temp., °F	Fuel Tank, Gals.	Engine Oil Refill, Qts.①	Transmission Oil		Transfer Case Oil, Pts.	Differential Oil, Pts.	
							Man. Trans., Pts.	Auto. Trans., Qts.②		Front	Rear
1996	Pathfinder 2WD	11⅜	11–14	170	21⅛	4¼	5⅛	8⅜	—	—	5⅞
	Pathfinder 4WD	12⅜	11–14	170	21⅛	4⅛	10¾	9	4¾	4⅜	5⅞
	Pickup 2WD	8⅝	11–14	170	15⅞	4⅛	4¼	8⅜	—	—	3⅛
	Pickup 4WD	9½	11–14	170	15⅞	4⅜	10⅜	8⅜	4¾	2¾	5⅞

Continued

FLUID CAPACITIES & COOLING SYSTEM DATA—Continued

Year	Model	Coolant Capacity, Qts.	Radiator Cap Relief Pressure, Lbs.	Thermo Opening Temp., °F	Fuel Tank, Gals.	Engine Oil Refill, Qts.①	Transmission Oil		Transfer Case Oil, Pts.	Differential Oil, Pts.	
							Man. Trans., Pts.	Auto. Trans., Qts.②		Front	Rear
1997	Pathfinder 2WD	11¼	11–14	170	21⅛	3⅞	5⅛	8¾	—	—	5⅞
	Pathfinder 4WD	11¼	11–14	170	21⅛	3⅞	10¾	9	2⅜	4⅜	5⅞
	Pickup 2WD	8⅝	11–14	170	15⅞	3⅞	4¼	8⅜	—	—	④
	Pickup 4WD	9½	11–14	170	15⅞	4⅜	10⅜	8⅜	4¾	2¾	5⅞
1998	Pathfinder 2WD	11¼	11–14	180	21¹/₁₀	3⅞	5⅛	8¾	—	—	5⅞
	Pathfinder 4WD	11¼	11–14	180	21¹/₁₀	3⅞	10¾	9	4¾	4⅜	5⅞
	Frontier 2WD	8⅝	11–14	170	15⁹/₁₀	3¾	4¼	8⅜	—	—	④
	Frontier 4WD	9½	11–14	170	15⁹/₁₀	4⅛	10⅜	8⅜	4¾	2¾	④
1999	Pathfinder 2WD	11¼	11–14	180	21¹/₁₀	3⅞	5⅛	8¾	—	—	5⅞
	Pathfinder 4WD	11¼	11–14	180	21¹/₁₀	3⅞	10¾	9	4¾	3⅞	5⅞
	Frontier 2WD	⑤	11–14	170	15⁹/₁₀	⑥	⑦	8⅜	4¾	2¾	④
	Frontier 4WD	11⅝	11–14	180	③	3½	10¾	9	4¾	3⅛	5⅞

2WD — Two wheel drive.
4WD — Four wheel drive.
① — Includes filter.
② — Approximate, make final check w/dipstick.
③ — Regular cab models, 15⁹/₁₀ gals.; King cab models, 19²/₅ gals.

④ — Model H190A, 3⅛; model C200, 2¾; model H233B, 5⅞.
⑤ — 2WD models w M/T, 9⅝ qts.; w A/T, 9½ qts. 4WD models, 9¾ qts.

⑥ — 2WD models, 3¾ qts.; 4WD 4⅛qts.
⑦ — 2WD models, 4¼ pts.; 4WD models, 10⅜ pts.

LUBRICANT DATA

Year	Model	Lubricant Type					
		Transmission		Transfer Case	Rear Axle	Power Steering	Brake System
		Manual	Automatic				
1996–97	Pathfinder & Pickup	75W-90 GL-4	Nissan Matic D①	Dexron IIE	80W-90 GL-5②	Dexron IIE/III	DOT 3
1998–99	Pathfinder & Frontier	75W-90 GL-4	Nissan Matic D①	75W-90 GL-4	80W-90 GL-4②	Dexron III	DOT 3

① — Dexron III/Mercon automatic transmission fluid, or equivalent, may also be used.

② — With limited slip differential, use gear oil approved for Nissan LSD.

NOTE: Refer To "Computer Relearn Procedures" Located In The Front Of This Manual For Computer Relearn Procedures.

NOTE: On Air Bag Equipped Models, Refer To "Air Bag System Precautions" Located In The Front Of This Manual For System Disarming & Arming Procedures.

INDEX

PRECAUTIONS

BATTERY GROUND CABLE

Prior to service, disconnect battery ground cable and isolate as required.

AIR BAG SYSTEMS

Refer to "Air Bag System Precautions" in the front of this manual for system disarming and arming procedures.

FUSE PANEL & FLASHER LOCATION

The fuse panel is located under the left-hand side of the instrument panel.

The combination flasher unit is located behind the lefthand side of the instrument panel, near the top of the clutch pedal.

FUEL PUMP RELAY LOCATION

The fuel pump relay is located in the engine compartment relay block on the right-hand side of the engine compartment, behind the battery.

RELAY CENTER LOCATION

The relay center is located in the rear righthand side of the engine compartment.

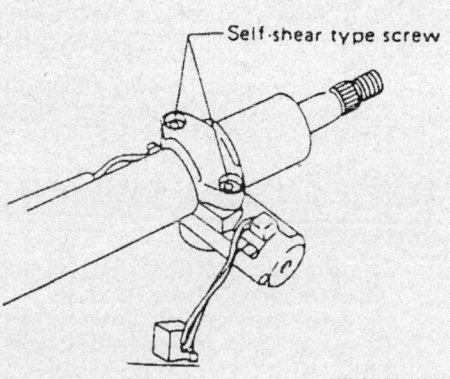

NS9129100004000X

Fig. 1 Ignition lock replacement

STARTER

REPLACE

1. Remove engine undercover.
2. Disconnect starter wiring from starter.
3. Remove starter retaining bolts, then the starter.
4. Reverse procedure to install.

ALTERNATOR

REPLACE

1. Remove engine under cover.
2. Remove side splash shield
3. Loosen alternator adjusting bolt.
4. Remove alternator drive belt.
5. Remove two alternator retaining bolts, then disconnect alternator electrical connector.
6. Remove alternator from the vehicle.

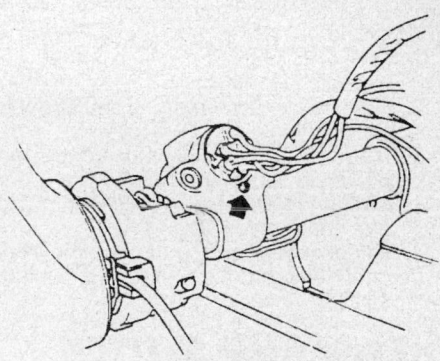

NS9049100021000X

Fig. 2 Ignition switch replacement

7. Reverse procedure to install.

DISTRIBUTOR

REPLACE

1. Rotate engine to TDC.
2. Disconnect spark plug wires and all electrical connectors.
3. Remove distributor mounting bolt and distributor.
4. Reverse procedure to install.

IGNITION LOCK

REPLACE

The ignition lock is retained by two shear type screws, **Fig. 1.** It is necessary to drill

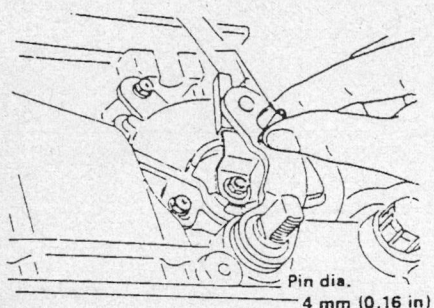

Pin dia.
4 mm (0.16 in)

NS9049100022000X

Fig. 3 Inhibitor switch adjustment

out these screws to remove ignition lock from steering tube. When installing, ensure new shear type screws are used.

IGNITION SWITCH
REPLACE

1. Remove the four upper and lower shell cover retaining screws, then the shell covers.
2. Disconnect electrical connectors from switch.
3. Remove switch retaining screw from steering lock, **Fig. 2.**
4. Remove switch.
5. Reverse procedure to install.

NEUTRAL SAFETY SWITCH
ADJUST

1. Loosen inhibitor switch attaching screws, **Fig. 3.**
2. Set selector lever manual shaft at Neutral position.
3. Insert suitable pin into adjustment holes in both inhibitor switch and switch lever as near vertical as possible, then tighten screws.
4. Check switch for continuity, **Fig. 4.** If continuity is not as specified, replace switch.

HEADLAMP SWITCH
REPLACE

1. Remove steering wheel as outlined under "Steering Wheel, Replace."
2. Remove steering column shell covers.
3. Disconnect switch electrical connections.
4. Remove headlamp switch attaching screw and the switch from combination switch base, **Fig 5.**
5. Reverse procedure to install.

STOP LIGHT SWITCH
REPLACE

The stop lamp switch is located on the brake pedal support.
1. Disconnect switch electrical connectors.
2. Loosen switch retaining locknut and remove switch.

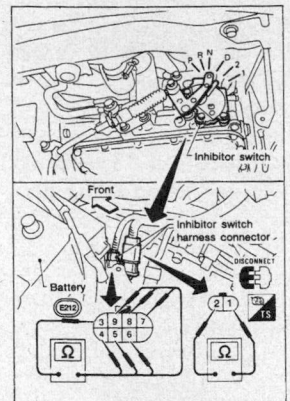

Lever position	Terminal No.	
P	①—②	③—④
R	③—⑤	
N	①—②	③—⑥
D	③—⑦	
2	③—⑧	
1	③—⑨	

NS9049100023000X

Fig. 4 Inhibitor switch continuity check

3. Reverse procedure to install.

COMBINATION SWITCH
REPLACE

1. Remove steering wheel as outlined under "Steering Wheel, Replace."
2. Remove steering column shell covers.
3. Disconnect switch electrical connections.
4. Remove combination switch base attaching screws, then the switch **Fig 6.**
5. Reverse procedure to install.

TURN SIGNAL SWITCH
REPLACE

1. Remove steering wheel as outlined under "Steering Wheel, Replace."
2. Remove steering column shell covers.
3. Disconnect switch electrical connections.
4. Remove turn signal switch attaching screw and the switch from combination switch base, **Fig 6.**
5. Reverse procedure to install.

STEERING WHEEL
REPLACE

1. Turn ignition switch OFF, wait at least three minutes with battery cables disconnected before continuing work
2. Remove lower lid from steering wheel, then disconnect air bag module connector, **Fig. 7.**
3. Remove lefthand and righthand side lids.
4. Remove left and right TORX bolts from air bag module, then the air bag module.
5. Set steering wheel in the straight ahead position.

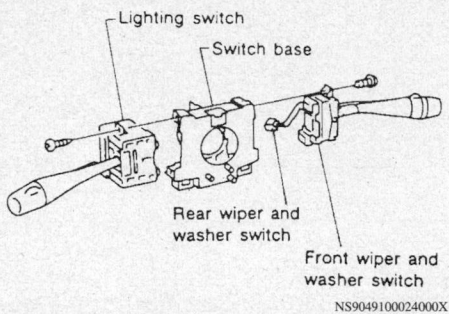

NS9049100024000X

Fig. 5 Headlamp & turn signal switch replacement

6. Disconnect horn connector and remove steering wheel nut.
7. Using suitable puller, remove steering wheel.
8. Reverse procedure to install.

INSTRUMENT CLUSTER
REPLACE

1. Remove steering wheel as outlined under "Steering Wheel, Replace."
2. Remove steering column cover.
3. Remove left side lower instrument panel.
4. Remove instrument cluster bezel.
5. Remove four screws, then the instrument cluster.
6. Reverse procedure to install.

RADIO
REPLACE

1. Remove cluster lid or instrument panel fascia as necessary to gain access to brackets.
2. Remove radio bracket to instrument panel attaching screws.
3. Disconnect electrical leads from radio.
4. Remove radio from vehicle.
5. Reverse procedure to install.

WIPER MOTOR
REPLACE
FRONT

1. Remove wiper arms, **Fig. 8.**
2. Remove cowl top grille.
3. Remove stop ring connecting wiper motor arm to connecting rod, then disconnect wiper motor electrical connector from beneath instrument panel.
4. Remove wiper motor retaining bolts and the wiper motor.
5. Remove flange nuts retaining pivot to cowl top, then remove wiper motor linkage.
6. Reverse procedure to install.

REAR

1. Raise rear wiper arm off glass and remove retaining nut.
2. Remove rear wiper arm.
3. Remove tailgate inner trim panel and disconnect electrical connector at motor.

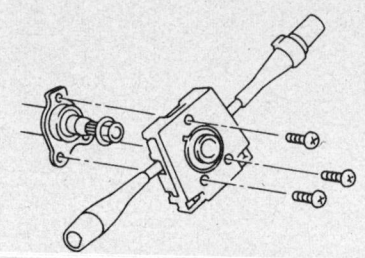

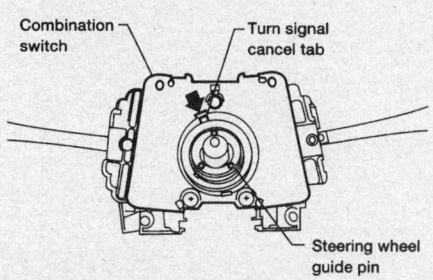

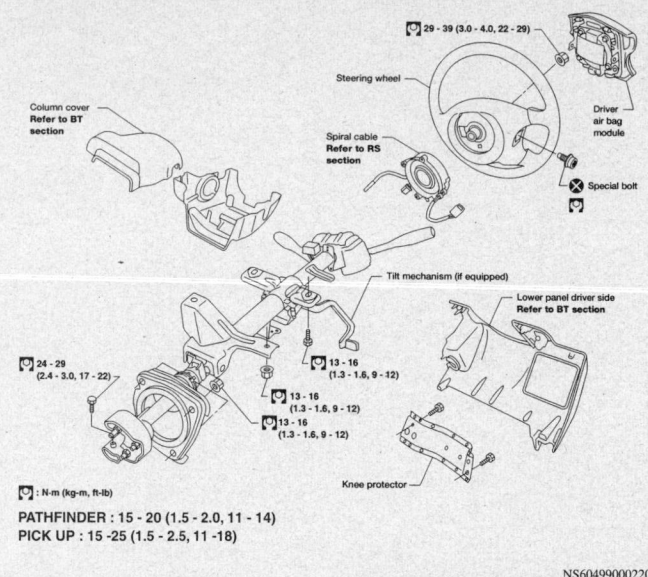

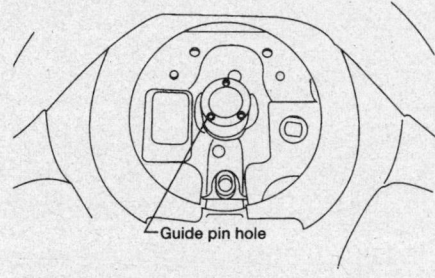

PATHFINDER : 15 - 20 (1.5 - 2.0, 11 - 14)
PICK UP : 15 -25 (1.5 - 2.5, 11 -18)

NS6049900022000X

Fig. 7   Steering wheel replacement

NS9049900095000X

Fig. 6   Combination switch replacement

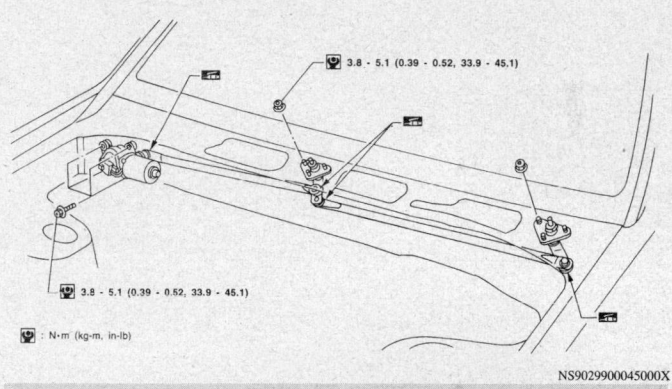

NS9029900045000X

Fig. 8   Wiper motor replacement

4. Remove wiper motor retaining bolts, then the wiper motor.
5. Reverse procedure to install.

WIPER SWITCH

REPLACE

FRONT

Refer to the "Combination Switch, Replace" procedure for wiper switch replacement. It is not necessary to remove combination switch base to remove windshield wiper switch.

REAR

1. Disconnect electrical connector from switch.

2. Remove switch knob by depressing and/or twisting as necessary.
3. Remove any switch retaining nuts or clips, then remove the switch.
4. Reverse procedure to install.

BLOWER MOTOR

REPLACE

Refer to **Figs. 9 and 10** for blower motor replacement.

HEATER CORE

REPLACE

Refer to **Figs. 9 and 10** for heater core replacement.

EVAPORATOR CORE

REPLACE

1. Recover A/C system refrigerant.
2. Remove passenger side instrument lower cover and glove compartment.
3. Disconnect wiring harness connectors to evaporator.
4. Separate cooling unit case halves and remove evaporator, **Fig. 9 and 10**.
5. Reverse procedure to install.

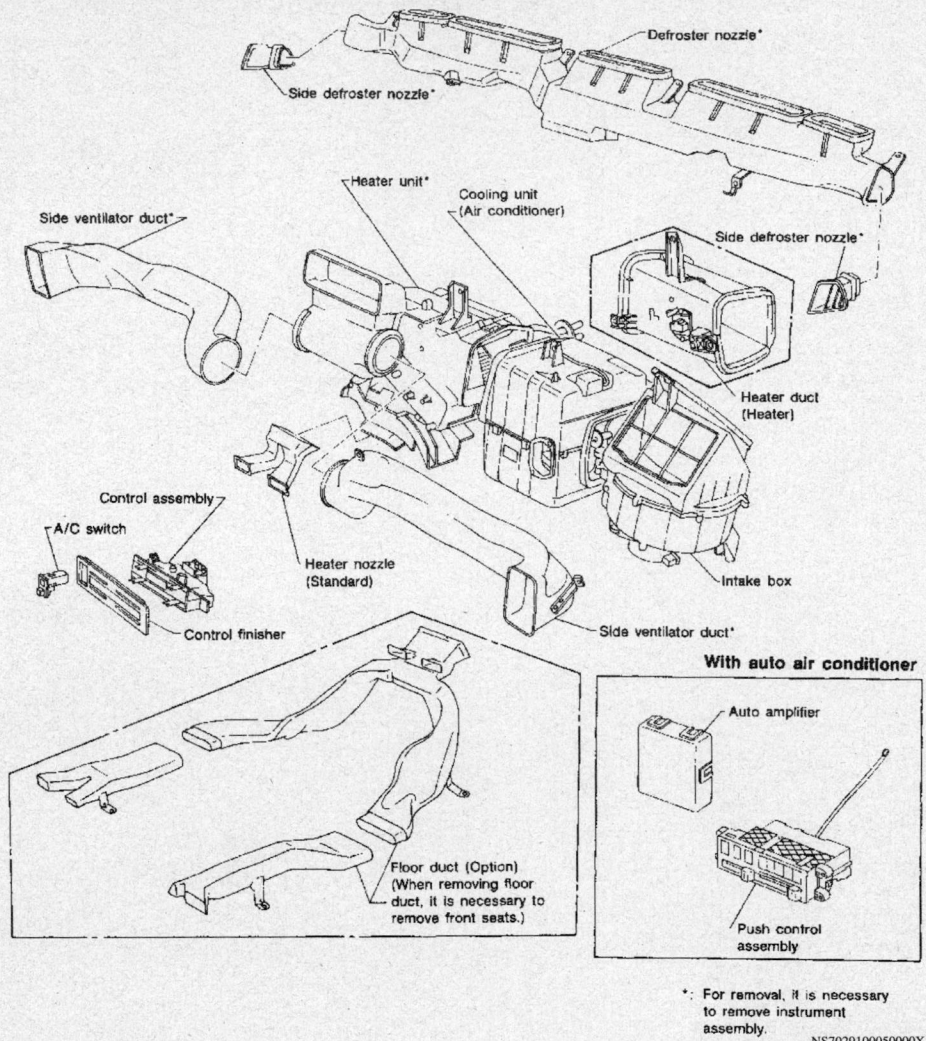

Fig. 9 Exploded view of A/C & heater system. 1996–97

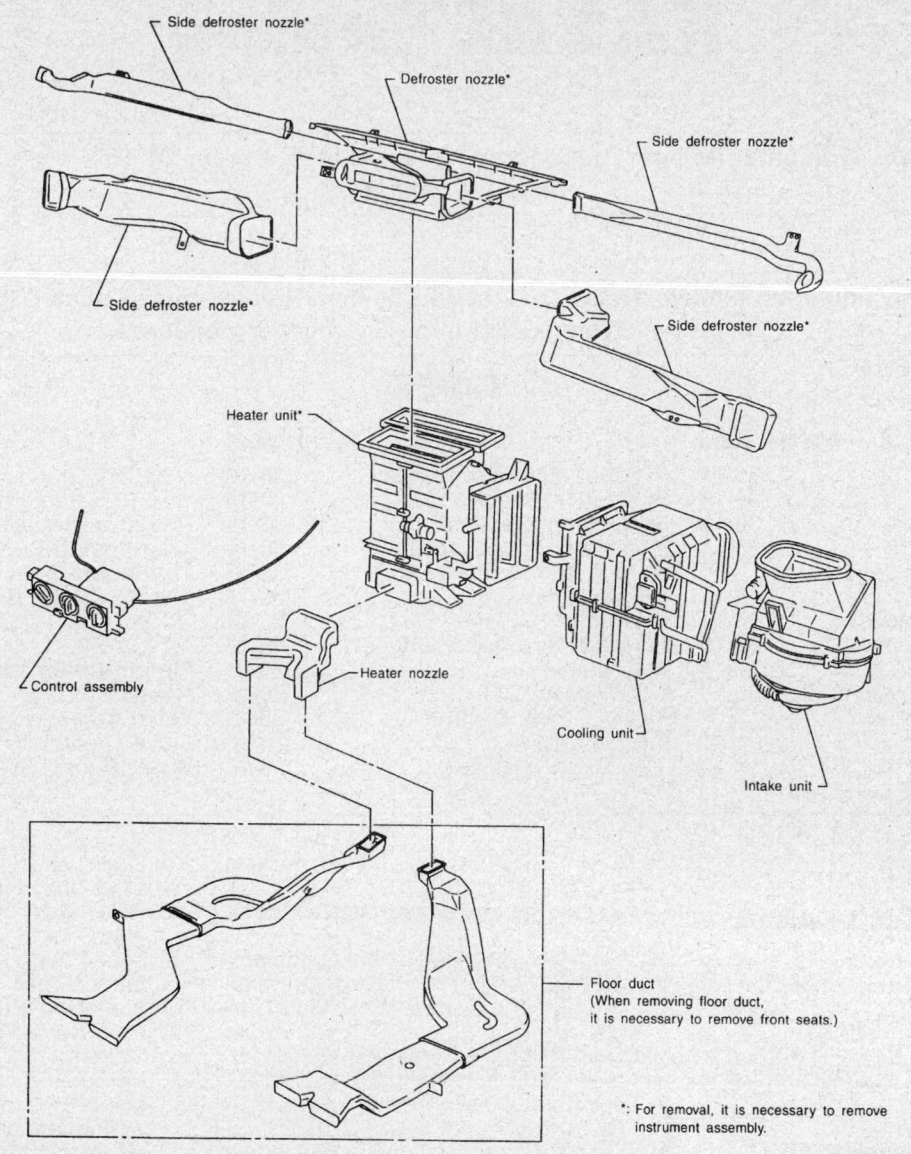

Side defroster nozzle*

Defroster nozzle*

Side defroster nozzle*

Side defroster nozzle*

Side defroster nozzle*

Heater unit*

Control assembly

Heater nozzle

Cooling unit

Intake unit

Floor duct
(When removing floor duct,
it is necessary to remove front seats.)

*: For removal, it is necessary to remove
instrument assembly.

NS7029900485000X

Fig. 10 Exploded view of A/C & heater system. 1998–99

KA24E Engine

NOTE: Refer To "Computer Relearn Procedures" Located In The Front Of This Manual For Computer Relearn Procedures.

NOTE: On Air Bag Equipped Models, Refer To "Air Bag System Precautions" Located In The Front Of This Manual For System Disarming & Arming Procedures.

INDEX

PRECAUTIONS

BATTERY GROUND CABLE

Prior to service, disconnect battery ground cable and isolate as required.

AIR BAG SYSTEMS

Refer to "Air Bag System Precautions" in the front of this manual for system disarming and arming procedures.

FUEL SYSTEM PRESSURE RELEASE

1. Remove fuel pump fuse from fuse panel.
2. Start engine.
3. Run engine until it stalls.
4. After engine stalls, crank engine two or three times to ensure fuel pressure is released.
5. Turn ignition switch off and install fuse for fuel pump.

COMPRESSION PRESSURE

1. Start engine and run until engine reaches operating temperature.
2. Turn ignition switch off.
3. Release fuel pressure. Refer to "Precautions" for fuel system pressure release procedure.
4. Remove all spark plugs.
5. Disconnect distributor coil cable.
6. Attach a compression tester to cylinder No. 1.
7. Depress accelerator pedal fully to keep throttle valve wide open.
8. Crank engine and record highest gauge indication.
9. Repeat measurement on each cylinder.
10. **On 1996–97 models,** standard compression is 192–142 psi, compression difference limit between cylinders is 14 psi.
11. **On 1998–99 models,** standard compression is 178–149 psi, compression difference limit between cylinders is 14 psi.
12. **On all models,** if compression in one or more cylinders is low, pour a small amount of engine oil into cylinders through spark plug holes, then retest compression.
13. If adding oil helps compression, then piston rings may be at fault. If adding oil does not help compression, then valves may be at fault.
14. If compression stays low in two cylinders that are next to each other, then cylinder head gasket may be leaking or both cylinders have valve component damage.
15. Repair as necessary.

ENGINE MOUNT

REPLACE

Refer to **Fig. 1,** when replacing engine mounts.

ENGINE

REPLACE

1. Release fuel system pressure as outlined under " Precautions."

2. Drain engine coolant from cylinder block and radiator.
3. Disconnect or remove all hoses, linkages, electrical connectors and accessories necessary for engine removal. **Mark hoses and connectors for installation reference.**
4. Remove radiator with shroud and cooling fan.
5. Remove drive belts, then the power steering pump and A/C compressor. **Do not disconnect power steering hydraulic lines or A/C compressor refrigerant lines.**
6. Remove front exhaust tube.
7. Remove transmission.
8. Attach suitable lifting equipment to engine.
9. Remove engine mounting bolts, **Fig. 1.**
10. Remove engine from vehicle.
11. Reverse procedure to install.

INTAKE MANIFOLD

REPLACE

Refer to "Cylinder Head, Replace" for intake manifold replacement.

EXHAUST MANIFOLD

REPLACE

Refer to "Cylinder Head, Replace" for exhaust manifold replacement.

CYLINDER HEAD

REPLACE

1. Release fuel system pressure as outlined under " Precautions."

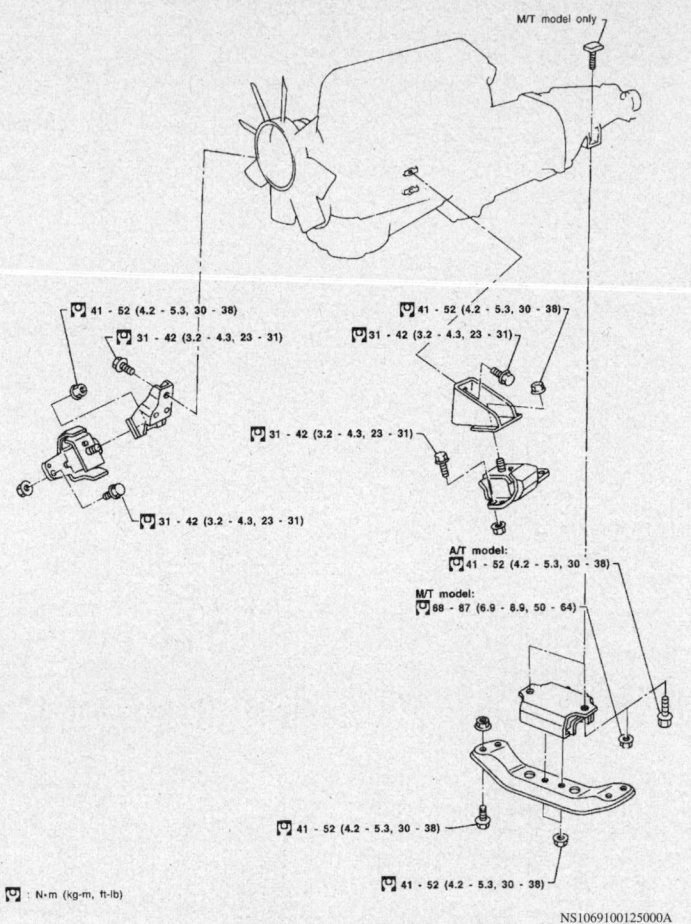

Fig. 1 Engine mount replacement

2. Drain engine coolant from cylinder block and radiator.
3. Remove power steering drive belt, pump, idler pulley and brackets.
4. Disconnect vacuum hoses for swirl control valve and pressure control solenoid valve.
5. Remove accelerator wire bracket.
6. Disconnect EGR tube from exhaust manifold.
7. Remove bolts which hold intake manifold collector to intake manifold.
8. Remove bolts which hold intake manifold to cylinder head while raising collector upwards.
9. Remove exhaust manifold attaching bolts and manifold.
10. Remove rocker cover.
11. Set No. 1 piston at TDC on its compression stroke. Check position by looking at distributor rotor position.
12. Loosen camshaft sprocket bolt and support timing chain by using chain stopper tool No. KV10105800, or equivalent.
13. Remove camshaft sprocket.
14. Remove front timing cover to cylinder head bolts.
15. Remove cylinder head attaching bolts in numerical order in two or three steps, **Fig. 2.**
16. Reverse procedure to install, noting the following:
    a. Install cylinder head with new gasket and tighten cylinder head bolts

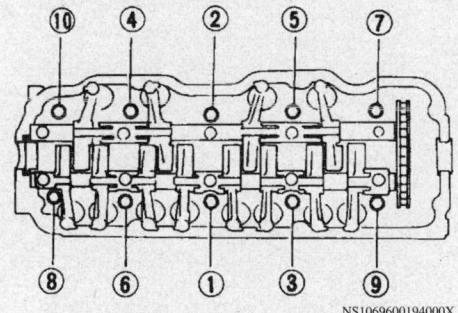

Fig. 3 Cylinder head bolt tightening sequence

to specifications in numerical order, **Fig. 3.**
b. **Torque** all cylinder head bolts to 22 ft. lbs., then to 58 ft. lbs.
c. Loosen all bolts completely.
d. **Torque** all cylinder head bolts to 22 ft. lbs. Using an angle wrench, or equivalent, turn all cylinder head bolts 80–85° clockwise. If an angle wrench is not available, **torque** all bolts to 54–61 ft. lbs.
e. Tighten all remaining fasteners to specifications.

ENGINE DISASSEMBLE

1. Place engine on work stand.
2. Drain oil and remaining coolant.

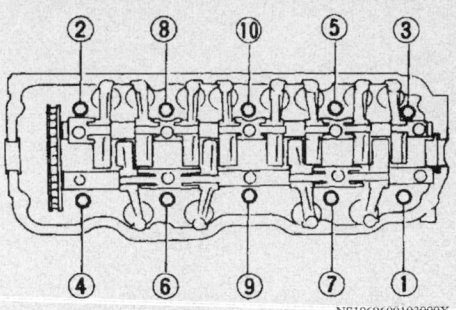

Fig. 2 Cylinder head bolt loosening sequence

3. Remove oil pan as outlined under "Oil Pan, Replace."
4. Remove timing chain as outlined under "Timing Chain, Replace."
5. Remove water pump as outlined under "Water Pump, Replace."
6. Remove cylinder head as outlined under "Cylinder Head, Replace."
7. Remove pistons with connecting rod.
8. Remove bearing caps and crankshaft. **Bearing cap bolts should be loosened in two or three steps.**
9. Reverse procedure to install, noting to tighten to specifications.

VALVE CLEARANCE SPECIFICATIONS

Year	Stem-To-Guide Clearance, Inch①	
	Intake	Exhaust
1996–97	.0008–.0021	.0016–.0028
1998–99	.012–.015	.013–.016

① — Cold.

VALVE ADJUSTMENT

These engines are equipped with hydraulic lash adjusters. No adjustments are required.

TIMING CHAIN
REPLACE
1996–97

1. Drain engine coolant from radiator.
2. Remove radiator shroud and cooling fan.
3. Remove power steering, compressor and generator drive belts.
4. Remove all spark plugs.
5. Set No. 1 piston at TDC on its compression stroke.
6. Remove power steering pump, idler pulley and power steering pump brackets.
7. Remove compressor idler pulley.
8. Remove crankshaft pulley with a suitable puller, **Fig. 4.**
9. Remove oil pump with pump drive spindle.
10. Remove rocker cover.
11. Remove oil pan. Refer to "Oil Pan, Replace."
12. Remove front cover.

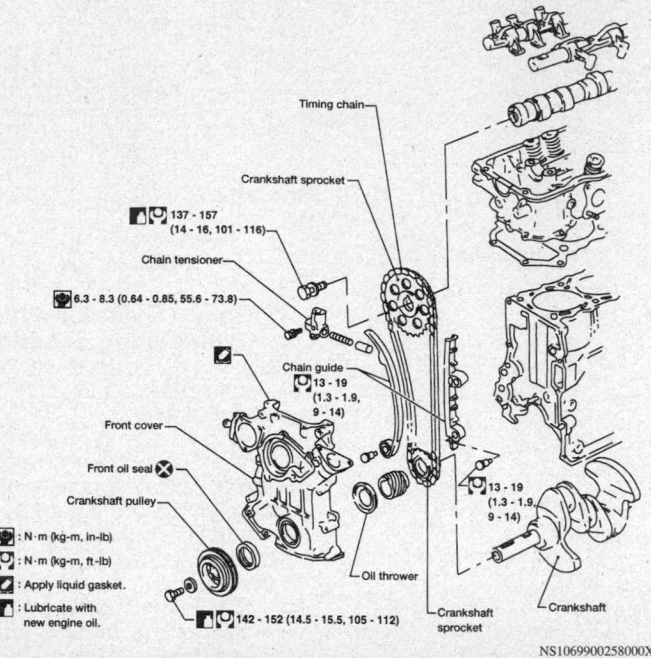

Fig. 4   Timing chain removal. 1996–97

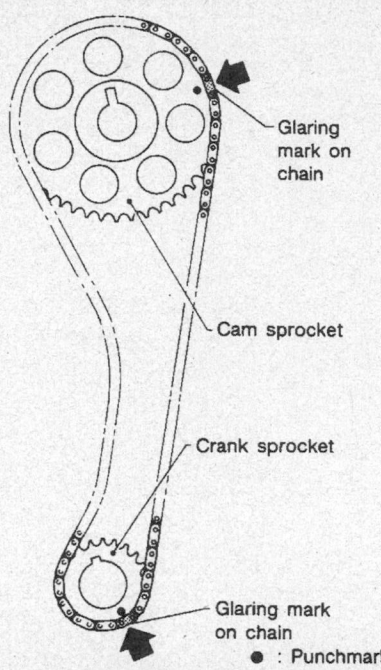

Fig. 5   Timing chain alignment. 1996–97

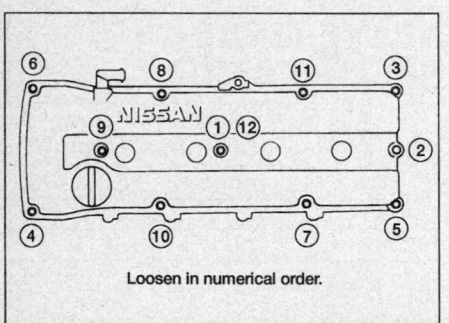

Fig. 6   Rocker cover replacement. 1998–99

13. Remove chain tensioner and guides.
14. Remove timing chain and camshaft sprocket.
15. Remove oil thrower, oil pump drive gear and crankshaft sprocket.
16. Reverse procedure to install, noting the following:
    a. Refer to **Fig. 5** for timing chain and sprocket alignment marks.
    b. Using suitable scraper, clean mating surface of front cover, then apply ⅛ inch bead of liquid gasket, or equivalent, around inside of bolt holes.
    c. Tighten to specifications.

1998–99
Upper

1. Drain coolant from both cylinder block and radiator.
2. Remove vacumn hoses, fuel tubes, wires, harness and connectors.
3. Remove exhaust manifold cover and front exhaust tube.

4. Remove exhaust manifold.
5. Remove air duct, cooling fan with coupling and radiator shroud.
6. Disconnect injector harness connector and remove injector tube assembly with injectors.
7. Remove spark plugs.
8. Remove intake cam sprocket
9. Set No. 1 piston at TDC on its compression stroke.
10. Remove distributor.
11. Remove rocker cover as outlined in **Fig. 6. R**
12. Remove cam brackets and camshafts as outlined in **Fig. 7.**
13. Remove camshaft sprocket cover as outlined in **Fig. 8**
14. Remove upper chain tensioner and idler sprocket bolt.
15. Loosen cylinder head bolts as outlined in **Fig. 2.**
16. Remove cylinder head and gasket.
17. Reverse procedure to install.

Lower

1. Remove oil pan and oil strainer.
2. Remove P/S, alternator and A/C drive belts.
3. Remove A/C compressor idler pulley.
4. Remove oil pump.
5. Remove front cover.
6. Remove timing chain tensioner, chain tensioner arm and lower timing chain guide.
7. Remove lower timing chain and idler sprocket.
8. Reverse procedures to install noting the following:
    a. Set upper and lower timgin chain on sprockets, aligning mating marks.
    b. Insert a suitable pin into pin hole to stop piston, after installed, remove pin.

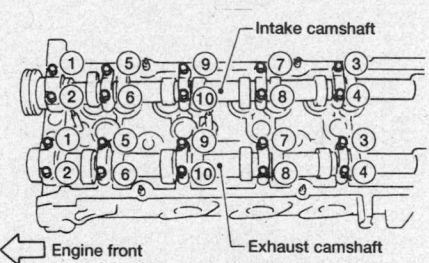

Fig. 7   Camshaft replacement. 1998–99

c. **Torque** all cylinder head bolts to 22 ft. lbs.
d. **Torque** all cylinder head bolts to 59 ft. lbs.
e. Loosen all bolts completely.
f. **Torque** all cylinder head bolts 18–25 ft. lbs.
g. **Torque** all cylinder head bolts additional 55–62 ft. lbs.

TIMING CHAIN TENSIONER
REPLACE

Refer to "Timing Chain, Replace" for timing chain tensioner replacement.

CAMSHAFT
REPLACE

1. Remove valve cover.
2. Remove rocker shaft assembly in sequence, **Figs.9 and 10,** in two or three steps.

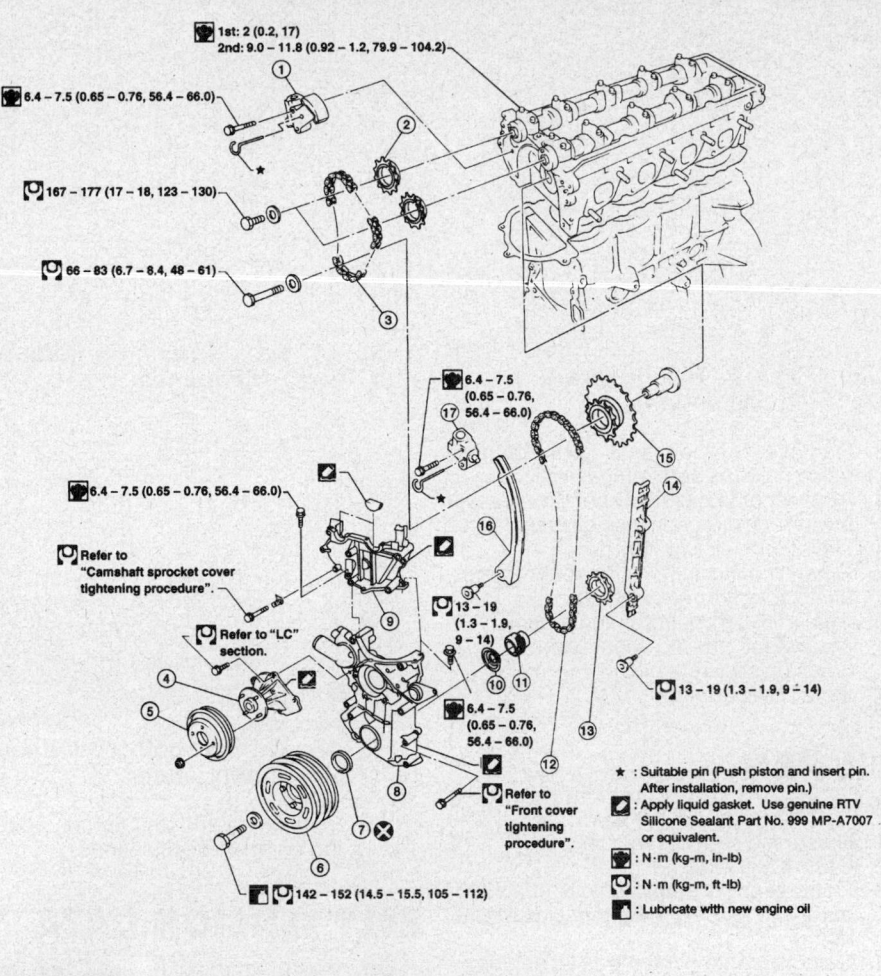

1st: 2 (0.2, 17)
2nd: 9.0 – 11.8 (0.92 – 1.2, 79.9 – 104.2)

6.4 – 7.5 (0.65 – 0.76, 56.4 – 66.0)

167 – 177 (17 – 18, 123 – 130)

66 – 83 (6.7 – 8.4, 48 – 61)

6.4 – 7.5 (0.65 – 0.76, 56.4 – 66.0)

6.4 – 7.5 (0.65 – 0.76, 56.4 – 66.0)

Refer to "Camshaft sprocket cover tightening procedure".

Refer to "LC" section.

13 – 19 (1.3 – 1.9, 9 – 14)

13 – 19 (1.3 – 1.9, 9 – 14)

6.4 – 7.5 (0.65 – 0.76, 56.4 – 66.0)

Refer to "Front cover tightening procedure".

142 – 152 (14.5 – 15.5, 105 – 112)

★ : Suitable pin (Push piston and insert pin. After installation, remove pin.)
⬚ : Apply liquid gasket. Use genuine RTV Silicone Sealant Part No. 999 MP-A7007 or equivalent.
: N·m (kg-m, in-lb)
: N·m (kg-m, ft-lb)
: Lubricate with new engine oil

① Upper timing chain tensioner
② Cam sprocket
③ Upper timing chain
④ Water pump
⑤ Water pump pulley
⑥ Crankshaft pulley
⑦ Front oil seal
⑧ Front cover
⑨ Camshaft sprocket cover
⑩ Oil slinger
⑪ Oil pump drive gear
⑫ Lower timing chain
⑬ Crankshaft sprocket
⑭ Chain guide
⑮ Idler sprocket
⑯ Chain tension arm
⑰ Lower timing chain tensioner

NS1069900259000X

Fig. 8   Timing chain removal. 1998–99

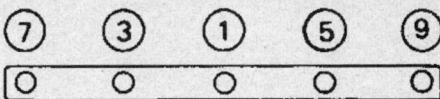
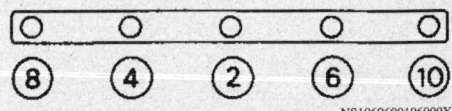

NS1069600196000X

Fig. 9   Rocker shaft assembly loosening sequence. 1996–97

Punchmark side up if present

NS1069600197000X

Fig. 11   Piston ring arrangement

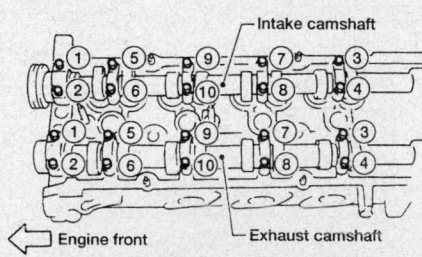

Intake camshaft

Engine front — Exhaust camshaft

Tighten in numerical order.
Loosen in reverse order.

NS1069900262000X

Fig. 10   Rocker shaft assembly loosening sequence. 1998–99

3. Measure camshaft endplay. Endplay should be between .0028–.0059 inch.
4. Remove and support camshaft sprocket.
5. Remove camshaft.
6. Remove valve components using valve spring compressor tool No. KV10109210, or equivalent. **Set piston concerned to TDC to prevent valve from falling.**
7. Remove valve oil seals using valve oil seal removal tool No. J36467, or equivalent.
8. Reverse procedure to install.

PISTON & ROD ASSEMBLY

DISASSEMBLE

1. Remove piston rings with a ring remover.
2. Remove snap ring, then press out piston pin using piston pin press or heat piston to 140–150°F and remove piston pin. **Keep disassembled parts in order.**

ASSEMBLE

1. Assemble pistons, piston pins and

connecting rods of designated cylinders.
2. Install new snap ring on one side of piston pin.
3. Align piston and connecting rod direction.
4. Ensure stamped numbers on connecting rod and cap correspond to each cylinder.
5. Heat piston to 140–150°F and assemble piston, piston pin, connecting rod and new snap ring.
6. Install piston rings.

PISTONS, PINS & RINGS

1. Heat piston to 140–158°F and assemble piston, piston pin and connecting rod using piston pin press stand assembly tool No. KV10110300, or equivalent. **After assembly, ensure connecting rod swings smoothly.**
2. Set piston rings as shown, **Fig. 11.**
3. Align piston rings so end gaps are positioned properly, **Fig. 12.**

MAIN & ROD BEARINGS

1. Set main bearings in their proper positions on cylinder block and main bearing beam, **Fig. 13,** then apply engine oil to bearing surfaces.
2. Install crankshaft and main bearing beam and tighten to specifications in two or three steps in sequence, **Fig. 14.**
3. After installing bearing cap bolts, ensure crankshaft turns smoothly, then

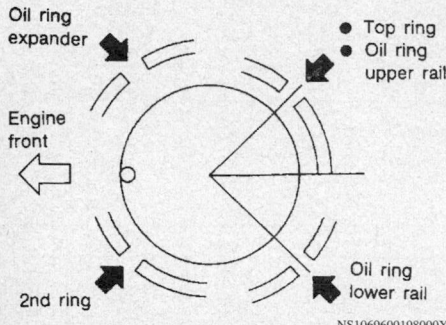

Fig. 12   Piston ring alignment

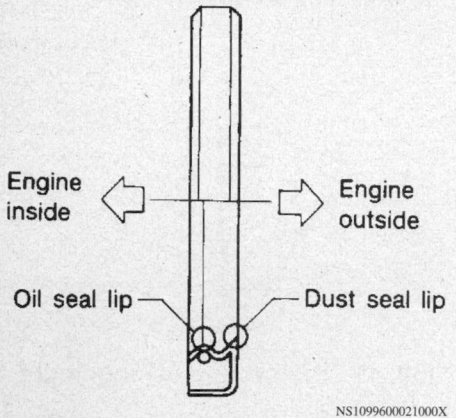

Fig. 15   Oil seal installation direction

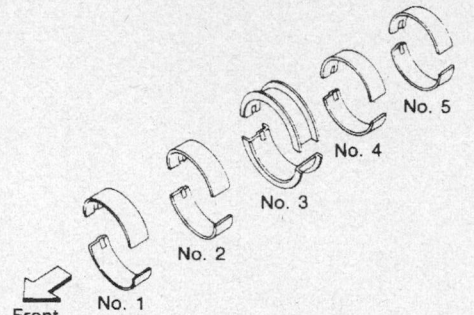

Fig. 13   Main bearing arrangement

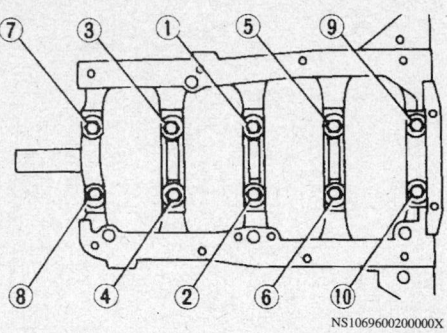

Fig. 14   Bearing cap tightening sequence

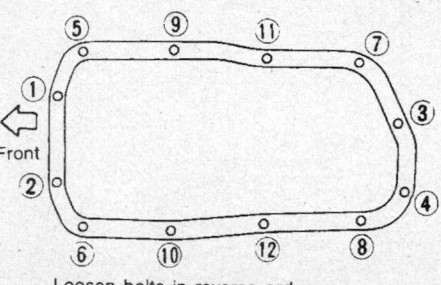

Loosen bolts in reverse order.

Fig. 16   Oil pan bolt loosening sequence

measure crankshaft endplay. Endplay should be between .0020–.0071 inch.
4. Install connecting rod bearings in connecting rods and caps. Align oil hole in rod and bearing, then apply engine oil to bearing surface, bolt threads and seating surfaces.
5. Install piston and connecting rod assemblies with mark on piston head facing toward front of engine, using piston installation tool No. EM03470000 (J8037), or equivalent.
6. Install connecting rod bearing caps by first tightening to a **Torque** of 10–12 ft. lbs., then tighten bolts an additional 60–65° clockwise with suitable angle wrench.

CRANKSHAFT SEAL
REPLACE

1. Remove radiator shroud.
2. Remove drive belts.
3. Remove crankshaft pulley with suitable puller.
4. Remove front oil seal using screw driver, or equivalent. While prying out seal, be careful not to scratch front cover.
5. Apply engine oil to new seal and install in correct direction using suitable tool, **Fig. 15.**

CRANKSHAFT REAR OIL SEAL
REPLACE

1. Remove flywheel or driveplate.
2. Remove rear oil seal retainer.

3. Remove rear oil seal from retainer using suitable seal removal tool.
4. Apply engine oil to new seal and install in correct direction using suitable installation tool, **Fig. 15.**
5. Clean mating surface of seal retainer using scraper or equivalent.
6. Apply ⅛ inch bead of liquid gasket or equivalent around inner side of bolt holes on seal retainer.
7. Install seal retainer.

OIL PAN
REPLACE

1. Raise and support vehicle.
2. Drain engine oil.
3. Remove front stabilizer bar attaching bolts and nuts from bottom side member.
4. Using suitable equipment, lift engine.
5. Remove oil pan bolts in order, **Fig. 16.**
6. Insert seal cutter tool No. KV10111100 (J37228), or equivalent, between cylinder block and oil pan. **Do not insert screwdriver, or oil pan flange will be damaged.**
7. Slide tool by tapping on side of tool with a suitable hammer.
8. Pull out oil pan from front side.
9. Reverse procedure to install, noting the following:
   a. Clean oil pan mating surface with a suitable scraper tool.
   b. Apply ⅛ inch bead of liquid gasket or equivalent to mating surface of oil pan.
   c. Tighten oil pan mounting bolts to specifications in reverse order of loosening sequence, **Fig. 16.**

OIL PUMP
REPLACE

1. Raise and support vehicle.
2. Drain engine oil.
3. Turn crankshaft so that No. 1 cylinder is at TDC on its compression stroke.
4. Remove oil pump attaching bolts.
5. Remove oil pump, oil seal and gasket.
6. Reverse procedure to install, noting the following:
   a. Apply engine oil to gears, then align punch mark on drive spindle and oil hole on oil pump.
   b. Install new oil seal and gasket.

   c. Install oil pump and tighten attaching bolts to specifications.

BELT TENSION DATA

On 1998–99 models, P/S oil pump used belt deflection; limit: 0.67 inch, adjustment: 0.39–0.51 inch, new belt: 0.31–0.39 inch.
On all models, refer to **Fig. 17,** for belt tension data.

COOLING SYSTEM BLEED

1. Open radiator cap and air relief plug.
2. Fill radiator with coolant to specified level.
3. Close air relief plug.
4. Run engine and bring to operating temperature.
5. Race engine two or three times under no-load.
6. Stop engine and let cool, then add coolant as necessary.

THERMOSTAT
REPLACE

1. Drain engine and radiator coolant.
2. Remove air cleaner and air duct assembly.
3. Remove radiator hose, then the water inlet housing.
4. Remove thermostat from thermostat housing.
5. Reverse procedure to install. Clean mating surface of water inlet and apply ⅛ inch bead of liquid gasket, or equivalent, to mating surface of water inlet.

	Used belt deflection		Deflection of new belt
	Limit	Deflection after adjustment	
Generator	17 (0.67)	10 - 12 (0.39 - 0.47)	8 - 10 (0.31 - 0.39)
Air conditioner compressor	16 (0.63)	10 - 12 (0.39 - 0.47)	8 - 10 (0.31 - 0.39)
Power steering oil pump	15 (0.59)	9 - 11 (0.35 - 0.43)	7 - 9 (0.28 - 0.35)
Applied pushing force	98 N (10 kg, 22 lb)		

Unit: mm (in)

NS1139600161000X

Fig. 17   Belt deflection. 1996–97

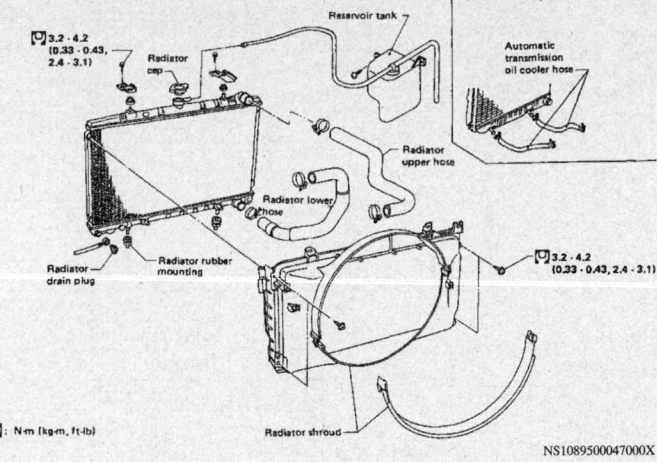

NS1089500047000X

Fig. 18   Radiator removal

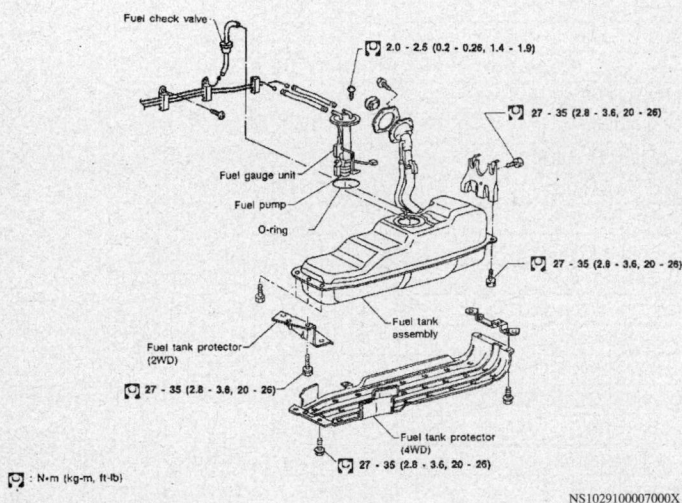

NS1029100007000X

Fig. 19   Fuel pump removal

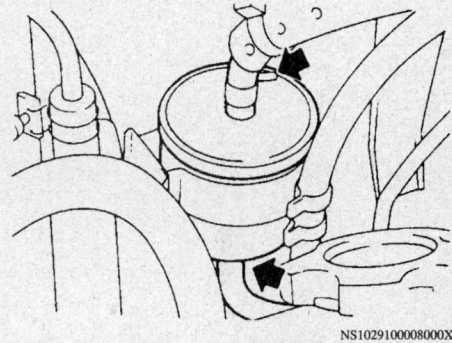

NS1029100008000X

Fig. 20   Fuel filter

WATER PUMP
REPLACE

1. Drain engine coolant from engine.
2. Remove fan coupling with fan.
3. Remove power steering, generator and A/C compressor drive belts.
4. Remove water pump attaching bolts and pump.
5. Reverse procedure to install, noting to clean mating surface of water pump and apply ⅛ inch bead of liquid gasket, or equivalent, to mating surface of water pump.

RADIATOR
REPLACE

1. Remove undercover panel and drain coolant.
2. Disconnect radiator upper and lower hoses, **Fig. 18.**
3. **On models equipped with automatic transmission,** remove automatic transmission oil cooler lines.
4. **On all models,** remove radiator lower shroud.
5. Disconnect reservoir tank hose.
6. Lift radiator out of vehicle, using care to avoid damage.
7. Reverse procedure to install.

FUEL PUMP
REPLACE

1. Release fuel system pressure as outlined under " Precautions."
2. Remove fuel filler tube attaching bolts, **Fig. 19.**
3. Remove fuel tank protector.
4. Support fuel tank with a suitable jack, then remove fuel tank to frame attaching bolts.
5. Lower tank to gain access to fuel lines, then disconnect fuel lines and electrical connector at fuel pump.
6. Lower tank and remove fuel pump from fuel tank.
7. Reverse procedure to install.

FUEL FILTER
REPLACE

1. Release fuel system pressure as outlined under " Precautions."
2. Loosen fuel filter hose clamps, **Fig. 20.**
3. Remove fuel filter from vehicle. **Be careful not to spill fuel over engine compartment.**
4. Reverse procedure to install.

TIGHTENING SPECIFICATIONS

Year	Component	Torque/ Ft. Lbs.
1996–99	Alternator Adjusting Bar Bolt	12–15
	Alternator Bracket To Engine Bolts	33–43
	Alternator Through Bolt	33–44
	Camshaft Sprocket	105–112
	Connecting Rod Bearing Caps	①
	Crank Pulley Bolts	105–112
	Crank Pulley Dampner Bolt	105–112
	Cylinder Head Bolt	②
	Distributor Mounting Bolt	83–96④
	Driveplate Bolt	③
	Engine Mount Through Bolt	30–38
	Engine Mount To Engine	23–31
	Engine Mount To Frame	23–31
	Exhaust Gas Sensor	30–37
	Exhaust Manifold Bolts	28–36
	Exhaust Manifold Cover Bolts	45–57④
	Main Bearing Cap Bolts	34–38
	Oil Filter	11–15
	Oil Filter Bracket	12–15
	Oil Pan Bolts	52–61④
	Oil Pan Drain Plug	22–29
	Oil Pressure Sender	12–15
	Oil Strainer Bolts	12–15
	Radiator Support	29–37④
	Rear Oil Seal Retainer	61–70④
	Rocker Shaft Bolt	27–30
	Timing Chain Guide Bolts	9–14
	Timing Chain Tensioner Bolt	56–66④
	Valve Rocker Cover	69-95④
	Water Inlet Bolts	12–15
	Water Pump Bolts	12–15
	Water Pump Pulley Nuts	52–87④

① — Refer to "Main & Rod Bearings."

② — Refer to "Cylinder Head, Replace."

③ — Automatic transmission, 69–76 ft. lbs.; manual transmission, 105–112 ft. lbs.

④ — Inch lbs.

NOTE: Refer To "Computer Relearn Procedures" Located In The Front Of This Manual For Computer Relearn Procedures.

NOTE: On Air Bag Equipped Models, Refer To "Air Bag System Precautions" Located In The Front Of This Manual For System Disarming & Arming Procedures.

INDEX

PRECAUTIONS

BATTERY GROUND CABLE

Prior to service, disconnect battery ground cable and isolate as required.

AIR BAG SYSTEMS

Refer to "Air Bag System Precautions" in the front of this manual for system disarming and arming procedures.

FUEL SYSTEM PRESSURE RELEASE

1. Remove fuel pump fuse from fuse panel.
2. Start engine.
3. Run engine until it stalls.
4. After engine stalls, crank engine two or three times to ensure fuel pressure is released.
5. Turn ignition switch off and install fuse for fuel pump.

COMPRESSION PRESSURE

1. Start engine and run until engine reaches operating temperature.
2. Turn ignition switch off.
3. Release fuel pressure. Refer to "Precautions" for fuel system pressure release procedure.
4. Remove all spark plugs.
5. Disconnect distributor coil cable.
6. Attach a compression tester to cylinder No. 1.
7. Depress accelerator pedal fully to keep throttle valve wide open.
8. Crank engine and record highest gauge indication.
9. Repeat measurement on each cylinder.

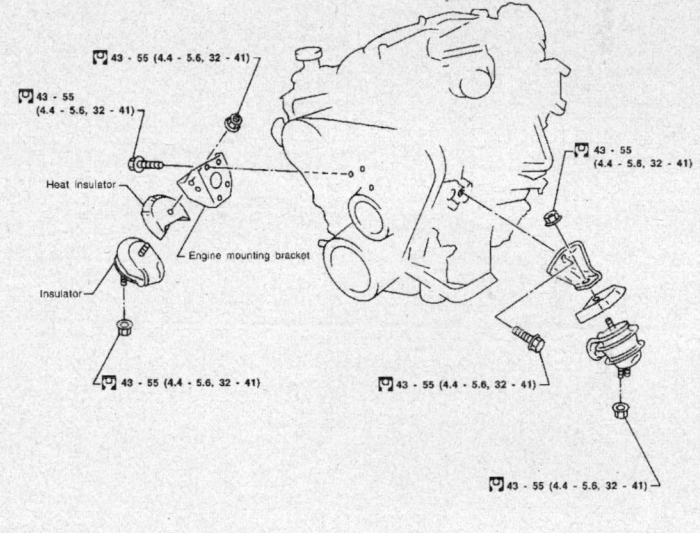

Fig. 1   Front engine mount replacement

10. Standard compression is 173 psi at 300 RPM, minimum pressure is 128 psi at 300 RPM and compression difference limit between cylinders is 14 psi.
11. If compression in one or more cylinders is low, pour a small amount of engine oil into cylinders through spark plug holes, then retest compression.
12. If adding oil helps compression, then piston rings may be at fault. If adding oil does not help compression, then valves may be at fault.
13. If compression stays low in two cylinders that are next to each other, then cylinder head gasket may be leaking or

both cylinders have valve component damage.
14. Repair as necessary.

ENGINE MOUNT
REPLACE

Refer to **Figs. 1 and 2,** when replacing engine mounts.

ENGINE
REPLACE

1. Release fuel system pressure as outlined under " Precautions."
2. Remove engine undercover and hood.

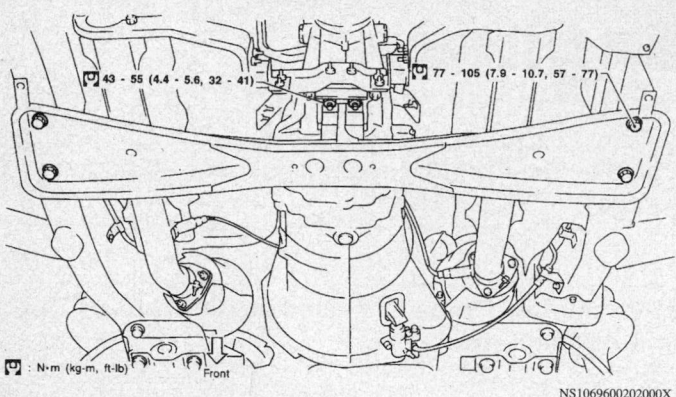

Fig. 2 Rear engine mount replacement

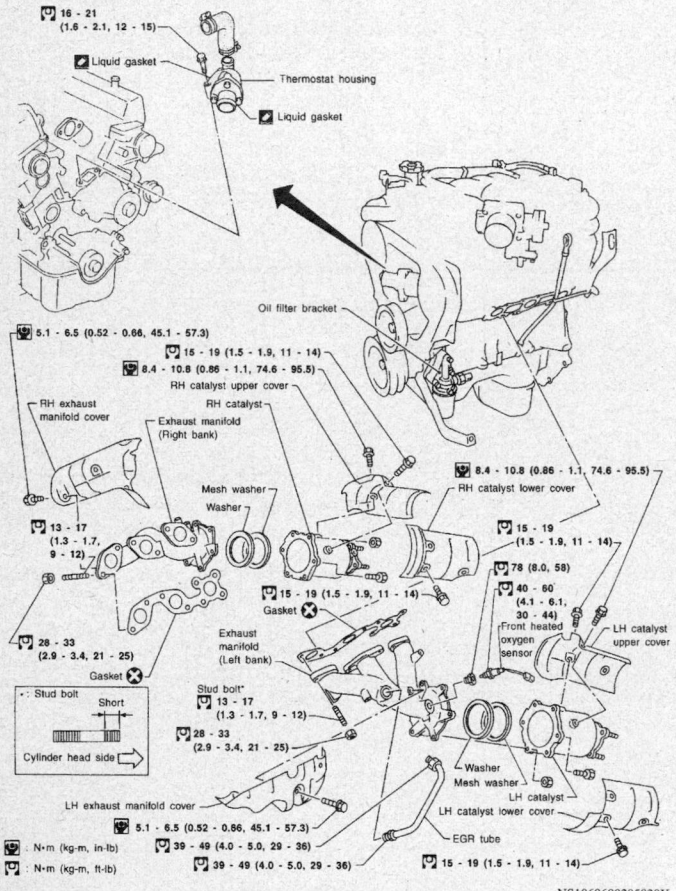

Fig. 3 Outer components (Part 2 of 2)

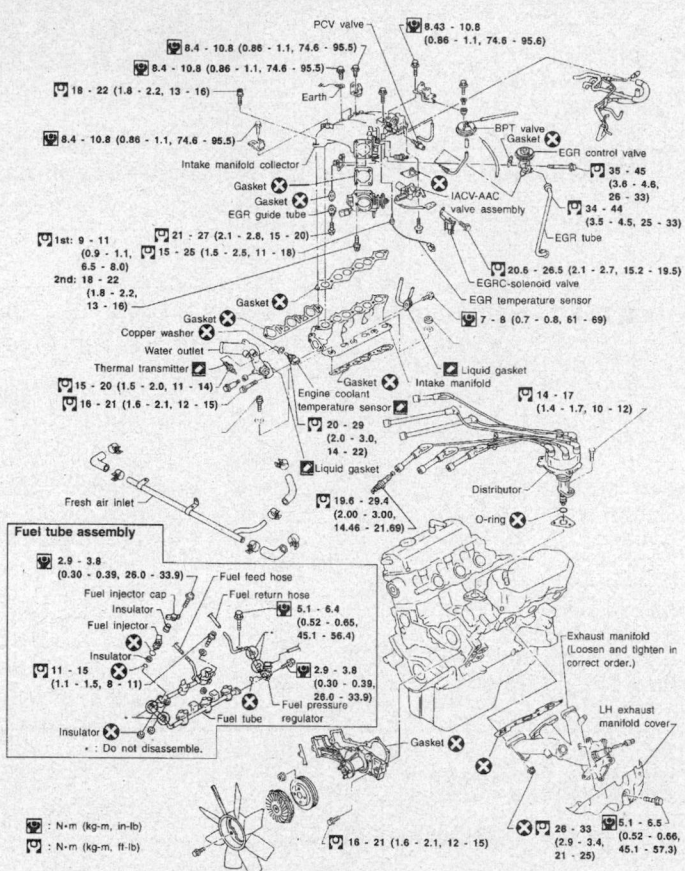

Fig. 3 Outer components (Part 1 of 2)

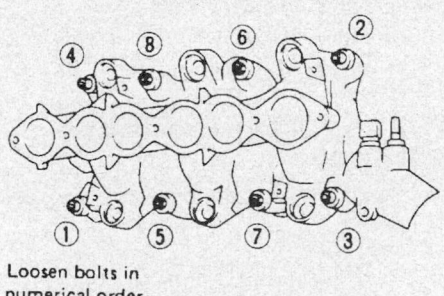

Loosen bolts in numerical order.

Fig. 4 Intake manifold bolt loosening sequence

3. Drain engine coolant from cylinder block and radiator.
4. Disconnect or remove all hoses, linkages, electrical connectors and accessories necessary for engine removal. **Mark hoses and connectors for installation reference.**
5. Remove radiator with shroud and cooling fan.
6. Remove drive belts, then the power steering pump and A/C compressor. **Do not disconnect power steering hydraulic lines or A/C compressor refrigerant lines.**
7. Remove front exhaust tube.

8. Remove transmission.
9. Attach suitable lifting equipment to engine.
10. Remove engine mounting bolts, **Fig. 1.**
11. Remove engine from vehicle.
12. Reverse procedure to install.

INTAKE MANIFOLD
REPLACE

1. Release fuel system pressure as outlined under " Precautions."
2. Remove timing belt.

3. Drain coolant from engine and radiator.
4. Separate automatic speed control and accelerator control cable from intake manifold collector, **Fig. 3.**
5. Remove the following from the intake manifold collector:
   a. Harness connectors for IACV-AAC valve.
   b. Throttle position sensor and throttle position switch.
   c. Ignition coil and power transistor.
   d. EGRC-solenoid valve and IACV-air regulator.
   e. **On California models,** EGR temperature sensor.

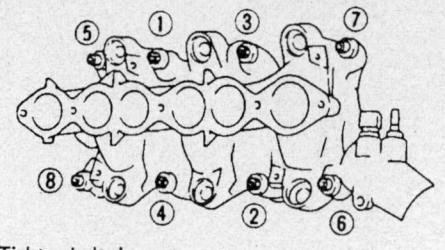

Tighten bolts in numerical order.

NS1059100011000X

Fig. 5 Intake manifold bolt tightening sequence

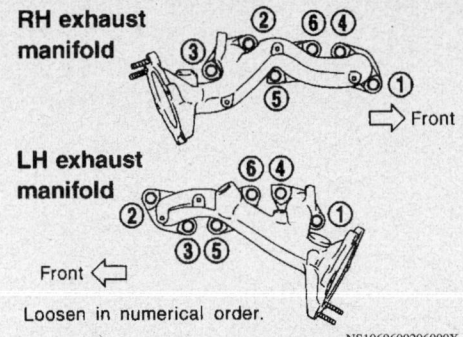

RH exhaust manifold

LH exhaust manifold

Front

Loosen in numerical order.

NS1069600206000X

Fig. 6 Exhaust manifold bolt loosening sequence

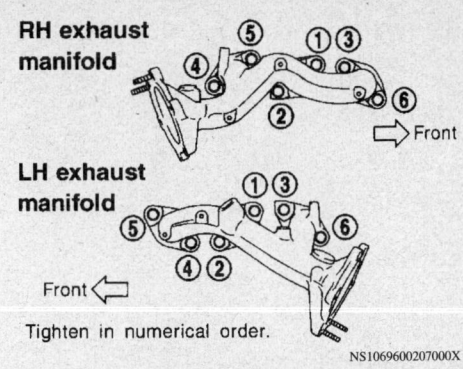

RH exhaust manifold

LH exhaust manifold

Front

Tighten in numerical order.

NS1069600207000X

Fig. 7 Exhaust manifold bolt tightening sequence

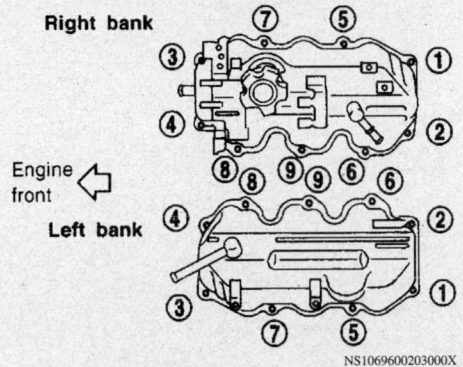

Right bank

Engine front

Left bank

NS1069600203000X

Fig. 8 Valve cover bolt sequence

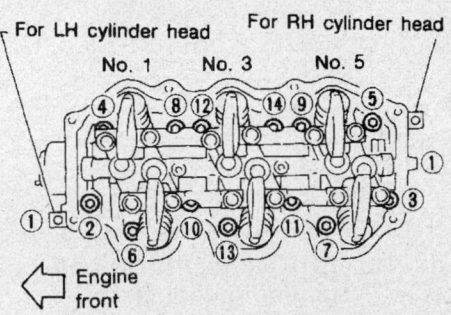

For LH cylinder head   For RH cylinder head

No. 1   No. 3   No. 5

Engine front

Loosen in numerical order.

NS1069600204000X

Fig. 9 Cylinder head bolt loosening sequence

f. **On all models,** water and heater hoses.
g. PCV hose and righthand rocker cover.
h. Vacuum hoses for canister, brake master cylinder and pressure regulator.
i. EGR tube, ground harness and air duct hose.
j. **Mark all vacuum hoses and electrical connectors for installation reference.**

6. Remove fuel feed and fuel return hoses from injector tube assembly.
7. Disconnect all injector harness connectors.
8. Remove injector fuel tube assembly.
9. Disconnect coolant temperature switch and thermal switch harness connectors.
10. Remove water hose from thermostat housing.
11. Using loosening sequence, **Fig. 4,** remove intake manifold.
12. Reverse procedure to install. Using sequence shown in **Fig. 5,** tighten intake manifold bolts as follows:
   a. **Torque** all nuts and bolts to 2.9 ft. lbs.
   b. **Torque** all nuts and bolts to 6.5 ft. lbs.
   c. **Torque** all nuts and bolts to 7 ft. lbs.

EXHAUST MANIFOLD
REPLACE

1. Remove exhaust pipe to exhaust manifold attaching nuts.
2. Disconnect any vacuum hoses or electrical connectors that interfere with

manifold removal, **Fig. 3.** Mark hoses and connectors for installation reference.
3. Remove A/C compressor from its bracket and position aside. **Do not disconnect refrigerant lines.**
4. Remove alternator from its bracket and position aside.
5. Remove compressor and alternator brackets.
6. Using sequence shown in **Fig. 6,** remove exhaust manifold attaching bolts.
7. Remove manifolds from engine.
8. Reverse procedure to install. Tighten manifold attaching bolts to specifications using sequence shown in **Fig. 7.**

CYLINDER HEAD
REPLACE

1. Release fuel system pressure as outlined under " Precautions."
2. Remove timing belt as outlined under "Timing Belt, Replace."
3. Drain engine coolant from cylinder block and radiator.
4. Separate ASCD and accelerator control wire from intake manifold collector.
5. Remove intake manifold collector from engine as follows:
   a. Disconnect connectors for IACV-AAC valve, throttle position sensor, throttle position switch, ignition coil, power transistor, EGRC solenoid valve and EGR temperature sensor.
   b. Disconnect water hoses from collector.
   c. Disconnect heater hoses.
   d. Disconnect PCV hose from righthand rocker cover.
   e. Disconnect vacuum hoses for EVAP canister, master brake cylinder and pressure regulator.
   f. Disconnect purge hose from EVAP canister
   g. Disconnect EGR tube.
   h. Disconnect ground harnesses.
   i. Disconnect air duct hose.
   j. Remove intake manifold collector.
6. Remove fuel feed and fuel return hoses from injector fuel tube assembly.
7. Disconnect all injector harness connectors.
8. Remove injector fuel tube assembly.

9. Remove intake manifold from engine as follows:
   a. Disconnect engine coolant temperature switch harness connector.
   b. Disconnect thermal transmitter harness connector.
   c. Disconnect water hose from thermostat housing.
   d. Remove intake manifold.
10. Remove both camshaft sprockets.
11. Remove rear timing belt cover.
12. Remove distributor and ignition wires.
13. Remove harness clamp from righthand rocker cover.
14. Remove front exhaust tube from exhaust manifold.
15. Remove compressor and power steering pump.
16. Remove alternator.
17. Remove compressor and alternator bracket.
18. Remove valve cover bolts in sequence, **Fig. 8,** then remove both valve covers.
19. Remove cylinder head bolts in sequence, **Fig. 9,** then the cylinder head with exhaust manifold.
20. Remove exhaust manifold from cylinder head. Refer to " Exhaust Manifold, Replace."
21. Reverse procedure to install. Using sequence shown in **Fig. 10,** tighten cylinder head bolts. Install cylinder head and intake manifold at same time.
   a. **Torque** cylinder head bolts to 22 ft. lbs.
   b. **Torque** cylinder head bolts to 43 ft. lbs.
   c. Loosen all bolts completely.

RH side

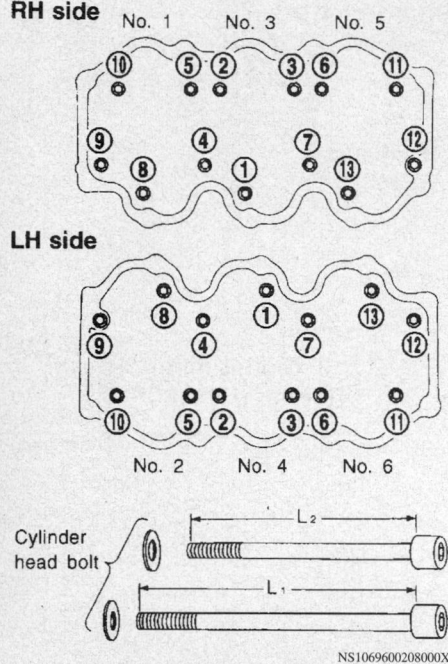

LH side

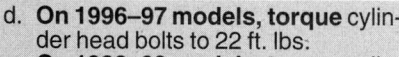

Fig. 10 Cylinder head bolt tightening sequence

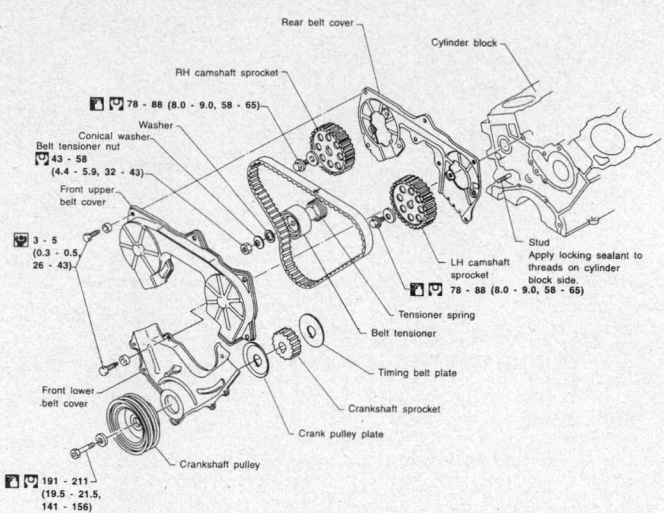

Fig. 11 Timing belt components

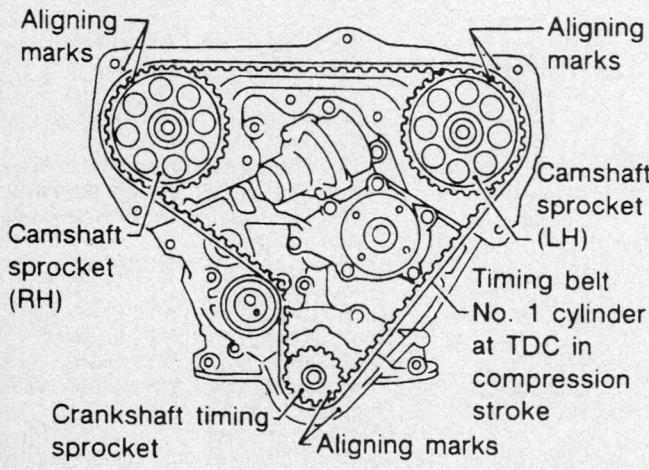

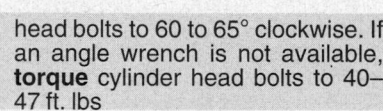

Fig. 12 Crankshaft & camshaft sprocket timing marks

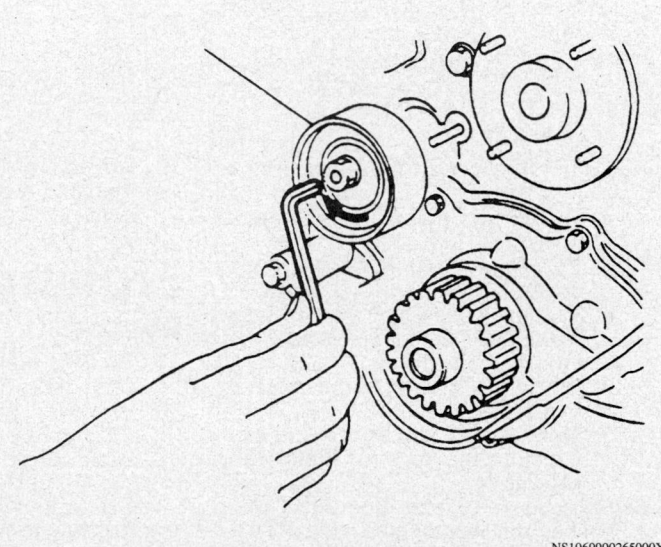

Fig. 13 Positioning timing belt tensioner

d. **On 1996–97 models, torque** cylinder head bolts to 22 ft. lbs:

e. **On 1998–99 models, torque** cylinder head bolts to 7 ft. lbs.

f. **On 1998–99 models, torque** intake manifold bolts and nuts to 2.9 ft. lbs.

g. **On 1998–99 models, torque** intake manifold bolts and nuts to 13 ft. lbs.

h. **On 1998–99 models,** loosen manifold bolts and nuts completely.

i. **On 1998–99 models, torque** cylinder head bolts 2.2 ft. lbs.

j. **On 1998–99 models, torque** intake manifold bolts and nuts as outlined under "Intake Manifold, Replace."

k. **On all models,** tighten cylinder head bolts to 60 to 65° clockwise. If an angle wrench is not available, **torque** cylinder head bolts to 40–47 ft. lbs

VALVE CLEARANCE SPECIFICATIONS

Refer to "Tune Up Specifications" for valve clearance.

VALVE ADJUSTMENT

These engines are equipped with hydraulic lash adjusters. No adjustments are required.

TIMING BELT

REPLACE

REMOVAL

1. Disconnect and isolate battery ground cable.
2. Remove engine compartment under cover.
3. Drain engine coolant into suitable container.
4. Remove radiator assembly.
5. Remove engine cooling fan and water pump pulley.
6. Remove engine drive belts.
7. Disconnect spark plug leads, after marking for installation.
8. Remove spark plugs.
9. Remove distributor protector.
10. Remove A/C compressor drive belt idler pulley bracket.
11. Remove fresh air intake tube from rocker arm cover.

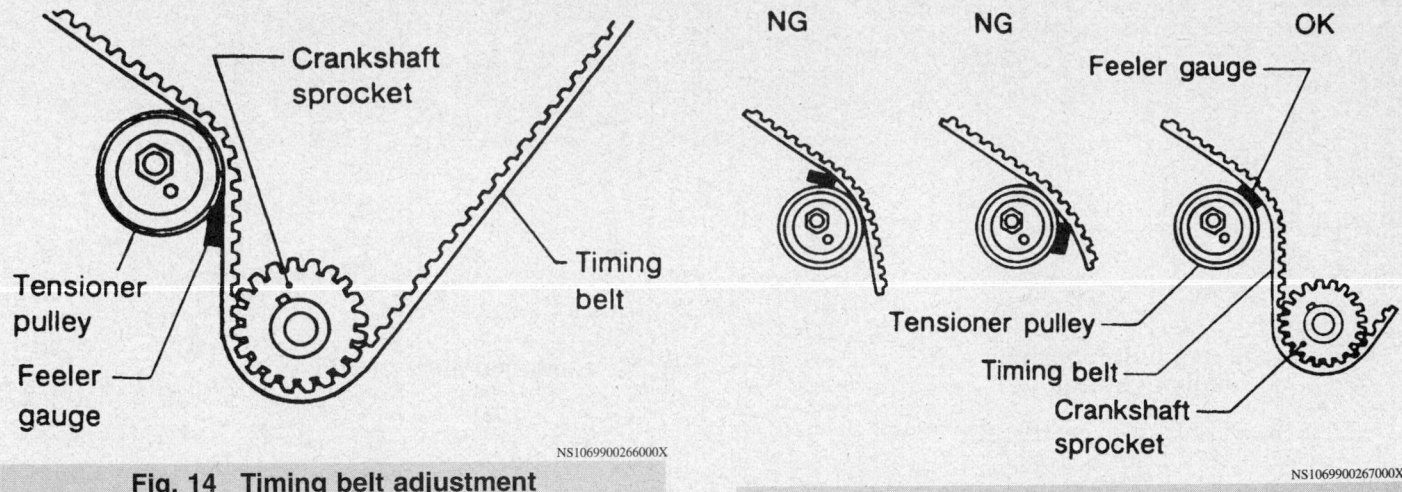

Fig. 14 Timing belt adjustment

NS1069900266000X

Fig. 15 Feeler gauge positioning

NS1069900267000X

12. Remove coolant hose from thermostat housing.
13. Rotate crankshaft clockwise until No. 1 cylinder reaches TDC mark.
14. Remove crankshaft pulley bolt, **Fig. 11.**
15. Remove crankshaft pulley using suitable puller.
16. Remove timing belt upper and lower covers.
17. Align lefthand camshaft sprocket punch mark with punch mark on timing belt upper rear cover, **Fig. 12**
18. Align crankshaft sprocket punch mark with oil pump housing notch, **Fig. 12.**
19. Temporarily install crankshaft pulley bolt so crankshaft can be rotated.
20. Loosen timing belt tensioner nut, turn tensioner outward, then remove timing belt, **Fig. 11.**
21. Inspect timing belt tensioner. Ensure it rotates freely, and spring is in good condition.

INSTALLATION

1. Ensure No. 1 piston is set at TDC on its compression stroke, **Fig. 12.**
2. If tensioner was removed, apply threads lock sealer to tensioner spring and stud threads which enter engine block, then install the stud, tensioner and spring.
3. Turn tensioner completely outward using a hex wrench, then temporarily tighten locknut.
4. Install new timing belt as follows:
   a. Arrow on timing belt should face toward front cover.
   b. On timing belts equipped with markings, align white lines on timing belt with punch marks on camshaft sprockets and crankshaft sprocket.
   c. Belt has 133 teeth. When properly installed, there should be 40 teeth between the lefthand and righthand camshaft sprockets, and 43 teeth between the lefthand camshaft sprocket and the crankshaft sprocket.
5. Loosen tensioner locknut while steadying tensioner with hex wrench.

6. Turn tensioner 70–80° clockwise, then temporarily tighten locknut, **Fig. 13.**
7. Turn crankshaft clockwise at least twice, then slowly set No. 1 piston at TDC, **Fig. 12.**
8. Push in middle of timing belt between righthand camshaft sprocket and tensioner pulley with force of 22 lbs.
9. Loosen tensioner locknut while steadying tensioner with hex wrench.
10. Install a .0138 inch thick by .50 inch wide feeler gauge as outlined in **Fig. 14.**
11. Turn crankshaft clockwise until feeler gauge is positioned as outlined in **Fig. 15.** Timing belt will move approximately 2.5 teeth.
12. Tighten tensioner locknut specification.
13. Turn crankshaft as needed to remove feeler gauge.
14. Turn crankshaft in clockwise direction twice, then slowly set No. 1 piston at TDC, **Fig. 12.**
15. Measure timing belt deflection midway between camshaft pulleys while applying a force of 22 lbs.
16. If deflection is not within 0.51–0.59 inch, adjust tensioner as needed to bring into proper range.
17. Tighten mounting bolts for upper and lower timing chain covers to specification.
18. **Torque** crankshaft pulley to 141–156 ft. lbs.
19. Install coolant hose at thermostat housing.
20. Install fresh air tube at rocker cover.
21. Install A/C compressor drive belt idler bracket.
22. Install distributor protector.
23. Install spark plug, then connect leads.
24. Install water pump pulley and engine cooling fan.
25. Install engine drive belts.
26. After ensuring drain plug is securely in place, install radiator.
27. Install engine undercover.
28. Start engine, inspect and adjust timing as necessary.

OIL PAN
REPLACE

1. Remove undercover, then drain engine oil.
2. **On 2WD models,** remove stabilizer bracket bolts.
3. **On 4WD models,** proceed as follows:
   a. Disconnect front propeller shaft from differential carrier.
   b. Remove front driveshaft attaching bolts.
   c. Remove front differential carrier member bolts.
   d. Support front differential carrier with suitable jack and remove attaching fixing bolts.
   e. Remove front differential carrier bleeder hose.
4. **On 2WD models,** remove front suspension crossmember.
5. **On 4WD models,** proceed as follows:
   a. Remove differential front mounting bolts.
   b. Remove front differential carrier.
   c. Remove front differential carrier mounting bracket.
6. **On all models,** remove idler arm.
7. Remove starter motor.
8. **On 4WD models,** proceed as follows:
   a. Remove transmission to rear engine mounting bracket attaching nuts.
   b. Remove engine mounting bolts or nuts.
9. **On all models,** remove engine gussets.
10. **On 4WD models,** raise engine if necessary and disconnect exhaust tube.
11. **On all models,** loosen oil pan attaching bolts using sequence shown in **Fig. 16.**
12. Remove oil pump assembly.
13. Remove dipstick. **If dipstick is left in engine, the end of it may be caught between main bearing beam and windage tray of oil pan during oil pan installation.**
14. Reverse procedure to install, noting the following:
    a. Apply a continuous bead of suitable

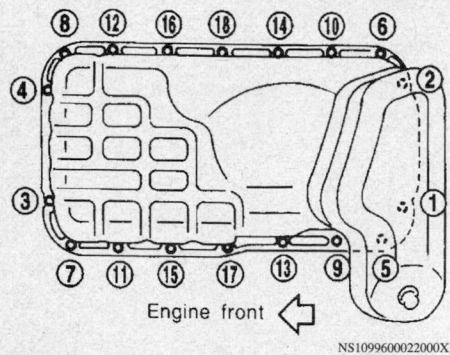

Fig. 16 Oil pan bolt loosening sequence

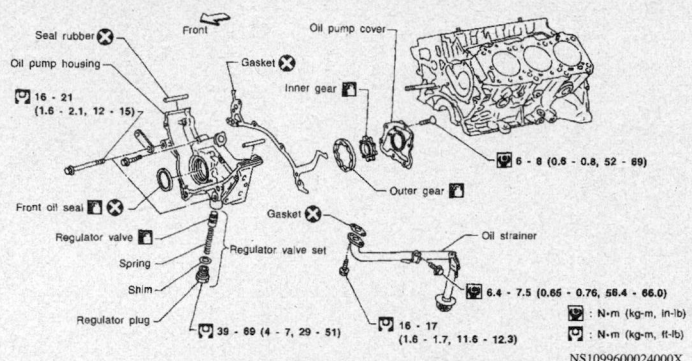

Fig. 17 Exploded view of oil pump

	Used belt deflection		Deflection of new belt
	Limit	Deflection after adjustment	
Alternator	10.5 (0.413)	6 - 7 (0.24 - 0.28)	5.5 - 6.5 (0.217 - 0.256)
Air conditioner compressor	16.5 (0.650)	9 - 11 (0.35 - 0.43)	9 - 10 (0.35 - 0.39)
Power steering oil pump	18 (0.71)	9 - 10 (0.35 - 0.39)	9 - 11 (0.35 - 0.43)
Applied pushing force	98 N (10 kg, 22 lb)		

Unit: mm (in)

NS1069600209000X

Fig. 18 Belt deflection

sealant .138–.177 inch wide to oil pan mating surface.
  b. Tighten bolts in reverse order of removal.

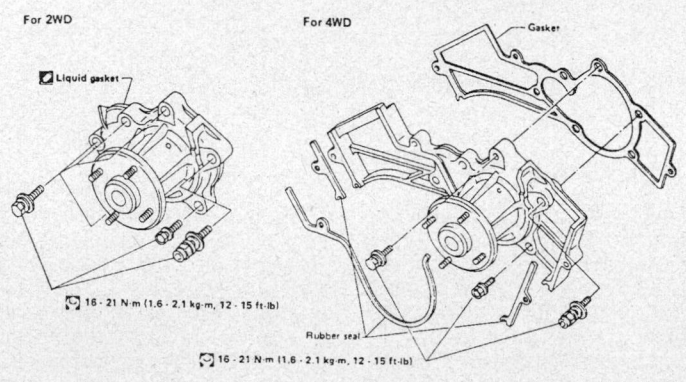

Fig. 19 Water pump replacement

OIL PUMP
REPLACE

1. Drain oil from engine and coolant from radiator.
2. Remove air duct from engine compartment.
3. Remove cooling fan.
4. Disconnect upper and lower radiator hoses.
5. Remove fan shroud.
6. Remove drive belts.
7. Remove crankshaft pulley and front and lower belt covers.
8. Remove oil pan.
9. Remove oil strainer, **Fig. 17.**
10. Remove oil pump assembly.
11. Reverse procedure to install, noting the following:
    a. Install new oil seal and gasket.
    b. Apply engine oil to inner and outer gears of pump.
    c. Tighten to specifications.

BELT TENSION DATA

Refer to **Fig. 18,** for belt deflection specifications. Check drive belt tension when engine is cold.

WATER PUMP
REPLACE

1. Drain coolant from drain cocks on both sides of cylinder block and radiator.
2. Remove drive belts.
3. Remove water pump attaching bolts, **Fig. 19.**
4. Remove water pump from engine. **Do not spill coolant on timing belt.**
5. Reverse procedure to install.

RADIATOR
REPLACE

1. Remove undercover panel and drain coolant.
2. Remove air duct.
3. Disconnect radiator upper and lower hoses, **Fig20.**
4. **On models equipped with automatic transmission,** remove automatic transmission oil cooler lines.
5. **On all models,** remove radiator lower shroud.
6. Disconnect reservoir tank hose.
7. Carefully lift radiator out of vehicle to avoid damage.
8. Reverse procedure to install.

FUEL PUMP
REPLACE

1. Release fuel system pressure as outlined under " Precautions."
2. Remove inspection hole cover located behind rear seat, **Fig. 21.**
3. Disconnect harness connectors and fuel tubes from upper plate of fuel gauge. **Put mating marks on tubes for correct installation.**
4. Remove fuel gauge retainer and fuel gauge.
5. Remove fuel pump with bracket while lifting pawl of fuel pump bracket upward.
6. Reverse procedure to install.

FUEL FILTER
REPLACE

1. Release fuel system pressure as outlined under " Precautions."
2. Loosen fuel filter hose clamps, **Fig. 22.**
3. Remove fuel filter from vehicle. **Be careful not to spill fuel over engine compartment.**
4. Reverse procedure to install.

NS1089600078000X

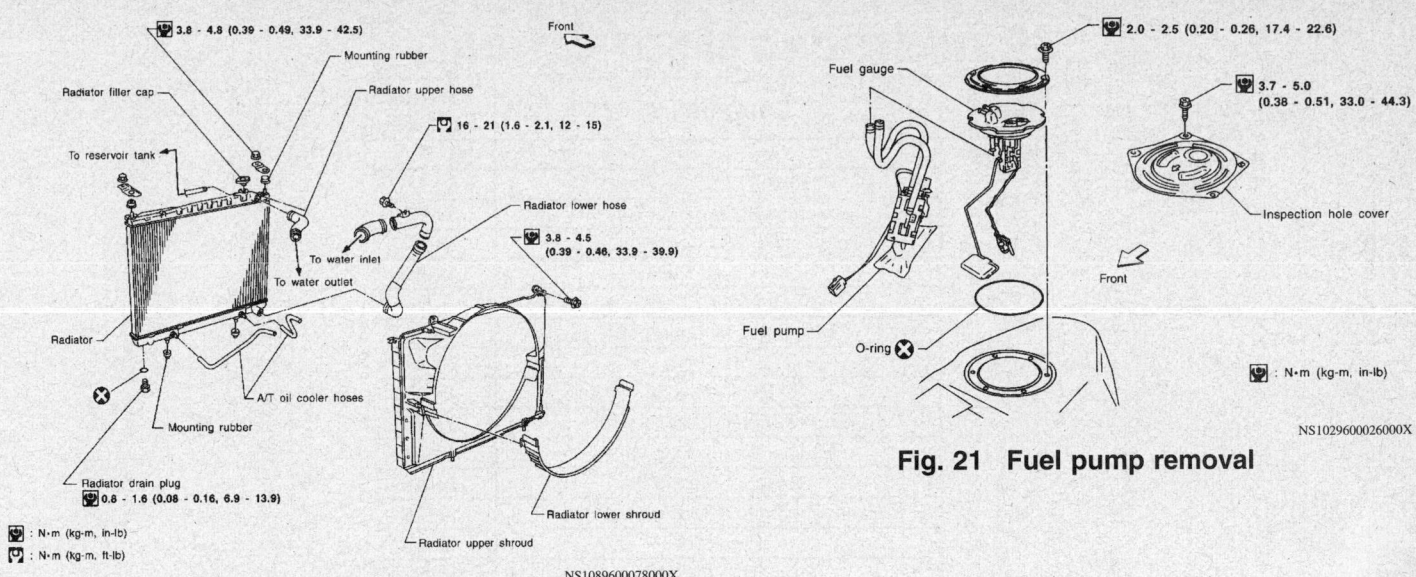

Fig. 20 Radiator removal

NS1029600026000X

Fig. 21 Fuel pump removal

NS1029600027000X

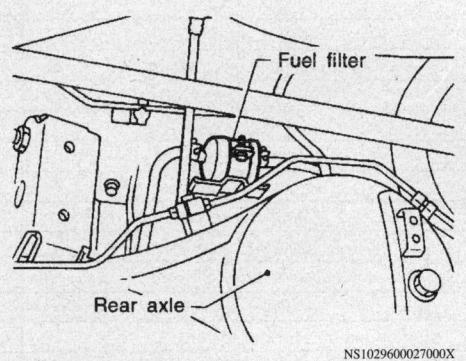

Fig. 22 Fuel filter replacement

TIGHTENING SPECIFICATIONS

Year	Component	Torque/ Ft. Lbs.
1996–99	Air Regulator	74–96③
	Camshaft Locate Plate	58–65
	Camshaft Sprocket Bolt	58–65
	Connecting Rod Bearing Caps	33–40
	Crankshaft Pulley	141–156
	Cylinder Head	①
	Distributor Mounting Bolt	10–12
	EGR Tube	25–33
	EGR Valve	9–12
	Engine Mount Through Bolt	30–38
	Engine Mount To Engine	23–31
	Exhaust Manifold	13–16
	Exhaust Manifold To Exhaust Pipe	16–20
	Flywheel	72–80
	Front Engine Slinger	16–22
	Fuel Tube Hold-Down Bolt	12–15
	Ignition Coil	61–70③
	Intake Manifold	②
	Intake Manifold Collector Bolt	13–16
	Main Bearing Cap	67–74
	Oil Pan Bolts	43–61③
	Oil Pan Drain Plug	22–29
	Oil Strainer	12–15
	Power Transistor	36–48③
	Radiator Support	30–36③
	Rear Engine Slinger	16–22
	Rocker Cover	8–26③
	Rocker Shaft	13–16
	Thermostat Housing	12–15
	Timing Belt Covers	26–43③
	Timing Belt Tensioner	32–43
	Water Outlet Bolt	12–15

① — Refer to "Cylinder Head, Replace."

② — Refer to "Intake Manifold, Replace."

③ — Inch lbs.

Clutch & Manual Transmission

INDEX

ADJUSTMENTS

CLUTCH PEDAL

1. Adjust clutch pedal height, dimension "H" in **Fig. 1**, as follows:
   a. **On 1996 models with KA24E engine,** 7.13–7.52 inches.
   b. **On 1997 models with KA 24E engine,** 9.29–9.69 inches.
   c. **On 1998–99 models, with KA24E engine,** 8.70–9.09 inches.
   d. **On 1996–97 models with VG33E engine,** 7.13–7.52 inches.
   e. **On 1998–99 models with VG33E engine,** 8.94–9.33 inches.
2. **On all models,** adjust clearance between pedal stopper bracket and threaded end of clutch interlock switch with clutch pedal fully depressed. Clearance should be .012–.039 inch.
3. Measure clutch pedal freeplay as shown in **Fig. 1,** dimension "A." Clutch pedal freeplay is the sum of play between piston and piston rod. Clutch pedal freeplay should be as follows:
   a. **On models equipped with KA24E engines,** freeplay should be between .039–.059 inch.
   b. **On models equipped with VG33E engine,** freeplay should be between .350–.630 inch.
4. **On all models,** adjust clutch pedal freeplay by rotating the clutch master cylinder pushrod inward or outward until the specified freeplay is obtained. After completing freeplay adjustment, tighten locknut.
5. After the above adjustments have been completed, cycle clutch pedal several times to ensure clutch linkage operates smoothly without binding.

HYDRAULIC SYSTEM SERVICE

CLUTCH MASTER CYLINDER, REPLACE

The clutch hydraulic system must be bled whenever a clutch line has been disconnected or when air has entered the system.
1. Disconnect clutch master cylinder pushrod from clutch pedal.
2. Disconnect clutch hydraulic line from clutch master cylinder.
3. Remove master cylinder mounting nuts and master cylinder.

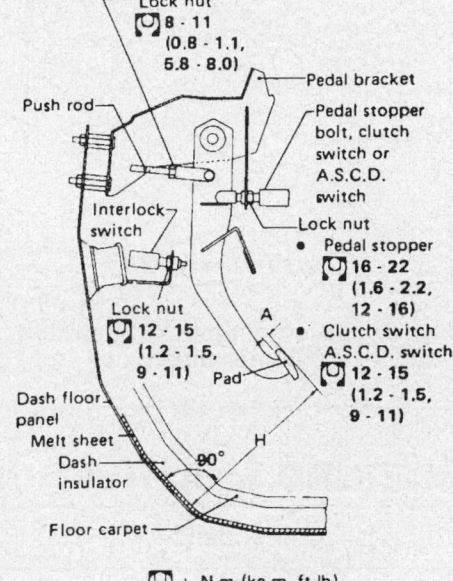

Lock nut
8 - 11
(0.8 - 1.1, 5.8 - 8.0)

Push rod

Pedal bracket

Pedal stopper bolt, clutch switch or A.S.C.D. switch

Interlock switch

Lock nut
Pedal stopper
16 - 22
(1.6 - 2.2, 12 - 16)

Lock nut
12 - 15
(1.2 - 1.5, 9 - 11)

Clutch switch A.S.C.D. switch
12 - 15
(1.2 - 1.5, 9 - 11)

Dash floor panel
Melt sheet
Dash insulator

A
Pad
90°
H

Floor carpet

: N·m (kg-m, ft-lb)

NS5049100032000X

Fig. 1 Clutch pedal free travel & height adjustment

4. Reverse procedure to install.

CLUTCH OPERATING CYLINDER, REPLACE

The clutch hydraulic system must be bled whenever a clutch line has been disconnected or when air has entered the system.
1. Disconnect hydraulic hose from clutch operating cylinder.
2. Remove mounting bolts and clutch operating cylinder.
3. Reverse procedure to install.

CLUTCH SYSTEM BLEED

Carefully monitor fluid level at master cylinder during bleeding operation.
1. Fill reservoir with recommended brake fluid.
2. Connect transparent vinyl tube to air bleeder valve, **Fig. 2.**
3. Fully depress clutch pedal several times.
4. With clutch pedal fully depressed, open bleeder valve to release air.
5. Close bleeder valve.
6. Repeat steps three through five until clear brake fluid comes out of bleeder valve.

CLUTCH

REPLACE

1. Remove transmission as outlined under "Transmission, Replace."
2. Insert a dummy shaft into the clutch disc hub.
3. Loosen clutch cover attaching bolts alternately.
4. Remove clutch disc and cover assembly.
5. Remove release bearing.
6. Reverse procedure to install.

TRANSMISSION

REPLACE

1. Raise and support vehicle.
2. **On 4WD models,** remove primary propeller shaft, then the front propeller shaft.
3. **On 2WD models,** remove propeller shaft.
4. **On all models,** disconnect front exhaust pipe.
5. **On 4WD models,** remove torsion bar springs as follows:
   a. Remove adjusting nut, then move the dust cover and remove snap ring from anchor arm.
   b. Remove torque arm fixing nuts, then the torsion bar spring with torque arm.
6. **On all models,** remove second crossmember.
7. Disconnect wiring of back-up lamp, neutral, top and overdrive switches as equipped.
8. Disconnect speedometer cable.
9. Remove starter motor, if necessary.
10. Support transmission with suitable jack.
11. Remove console box, if equipped.
12. Place selector lever in neutral, then remove snap ring and selector lever.
13. Remove transmission to engine retaining bolts.
14. Slide transmission rearward and lower from vehicle.
15. Reverse procedure to install. Tighten retaining bolts as follows:
    a. **Torque** 60 mm and 65 mm bolts to 29–36 ft. lbs.
    b. **On models equipped with KA24E engine, torque** 25 mm and 16 mm bolts to 22–29 ft. lbs.
    c. **On models equipped with VG33E engine, torque** 30 mm and 25 mm bolts to 22–29 ft. lbs.

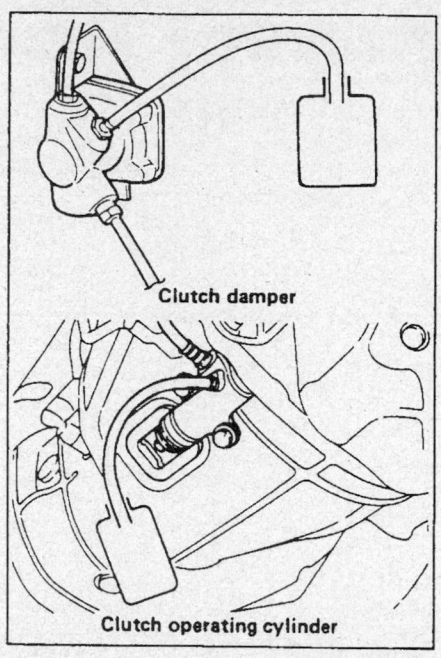

NS5049100033000X

Fig. 2 Clutch damper & operating cylinder bleed

TIGHTENING SPECIFICATIONS

Year	Component	Torque/Ft. Lbs.
1996–99	Air Bleeder	61–78③
	Clutch Cover Bolt	16–22
	Clutch Hose Eye Bolt	12–14
	Clutch Hose Mounting Bracket	69–96③
	Clutch Hose To Operating Cylinder	12–14
	Clutch Pedal Bracket	69–96③
	Clutch Switch Locknut	9–11
	Damper Cover To Cylinder Body	32–44③
	Flywheel①	72–80
	Flywheel②	105–112
	Fulcrum Pin	12–16
	Hydraulic Tube Flare Nuts	11–13
	Master Cylinder Nuts	69–96③
	Master Cylinder Pushrod Adjusting Locknut	69–96③
	Operating Cylinder Bolts	22–30
	Pedal Stopper	12–16
	Reservoir Band	21–35③
	Valve Stopper	13–26③

① — VG30E & VG33E engines.

② — KA24E engine.

③ — Inch lbs.

Rear Axle & Suspension

INDEX

REAR AXLE

REPLACE

PATHFINDER

1. Raise and support vehicle.
2. Disconnect brake hydraulic line and parking brake cable.
3. Support axle with suitable jack.
4. Disconnect stabilizer rod, upper and lower links and the panhard rod from body, **Fig. 1.**
5. Disconnect propeller shaft.
6. Remove upper shock absorber attaching nuts.
7. Lower jack slowly until coil spring are extended fully.
8. Reverse procedure to install. When tightening rubber parts, vehicle should be in unloaded condition with tires on ground.

FRONTIER

1. Raise and support vehicle.
2. Disconnect brake hydraulic line and parking brake cable.
3. Support axle with suitable jack.
4. Disconnect propeller shaft.
5. Remove upper shock absorber attaching nuts.
6. Remove front and rear leaf spring attaching bolts and nuts.
7. Lower axle assembly with jack.
8. Reverse procedure to install. When tightening rubber parts, vehicle should be in unloaded condition with tires on ground.

REAR AXLE SHAFT

REPLACE

DRUM BRAKES

1. Raise and support rear of vehicle and remove rear wheel.
2. Disconnect parking brake cable and brake hydraulic line. Plug end of hydraulic line to prevent fluid loss and entrance of dirt.
3. Remove wheel bearing cage to baffle plate attaching nuts, **Figs. 2 and 3.**
4. Using axle shaft puller tool No. KV40101000 and slide hammer tool No. ST36230000, or equivalents, remove axle shaft assembly from rear axle case, **Fig. 4.**
5. Replace oil seal in axle case.
6. Support axle assembly in a vise, and unbend lock washer away from bearing locknut.

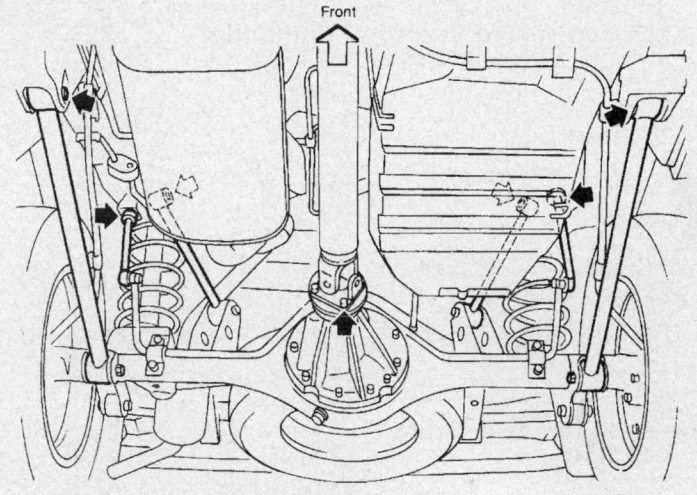

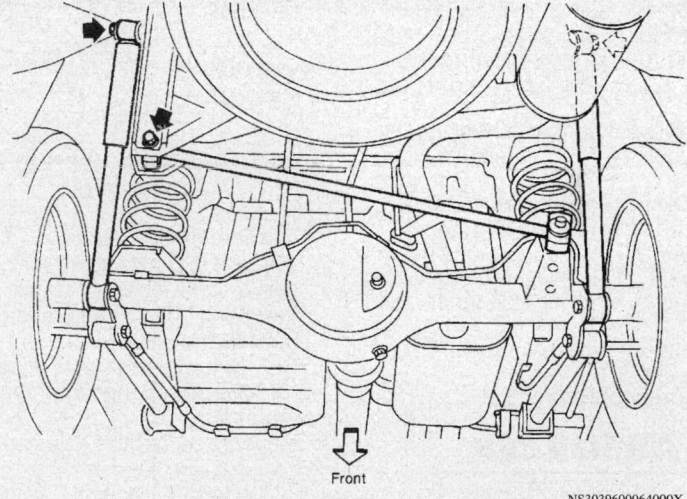

NS3039600064000X

Fig. 1   Rear axle replacement. Pathfinder

7. Remove bearing locknut as shown in **Fig. 5.**
8. Remove wheel bearing, bearing cage and baffle plate from axle shaft using bearing puller tool No. HT72480000 (J25852–B), or equivalent, **Fig. 6.**
9. Remove grease seal in bearing cage with screwdriver or equivalent.
10. Remove wheel bearing assembly with a brass drift or equivalent.
11. Reverse procedure to install, noting the following:
    a. When installing new oil seal, coat sealing lip with multi-purpose grease.
    b. Apply gear oil to spline of axle shaft and multi-purpose grease to seal surface of axle shaft.
    c. Adjust axle endplay to specification in "Drive Axles" section.

DISC BRAKES

1. Raise and support rear of vehicle and remove rear wheels.
2. Remove brake caliper assembly and rotor.

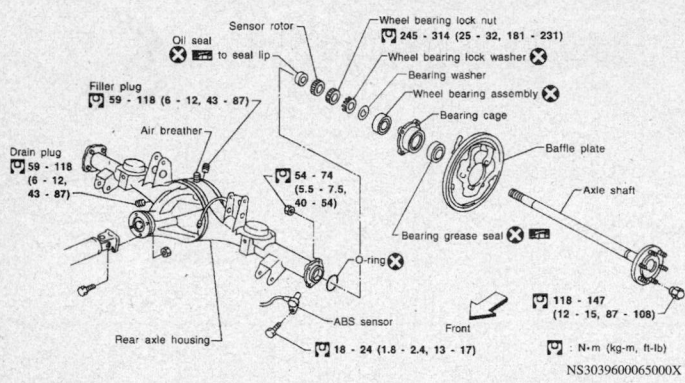

Fig. 2   Exploded view of rear axle. Pathfinder w/drum brakes

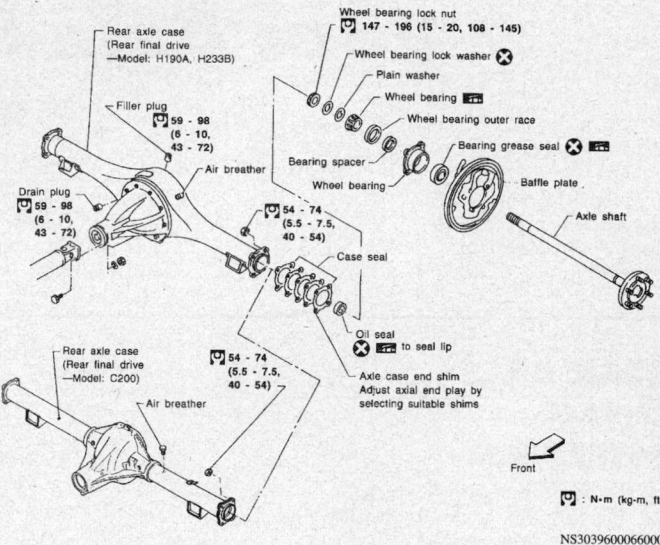

Fig. 3   Exploded view of rear axle. Pickup w/drum brakes

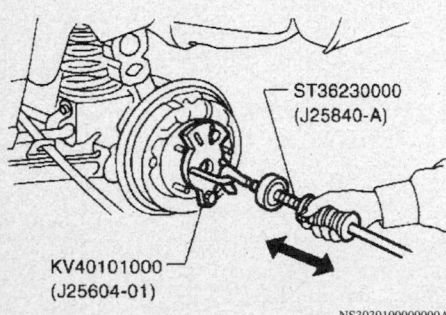

Fig. 4   Axle shaft removal. Drum brakes

3. Disconnect parking brake cable and brake tube.
4. Remove nuts securing bearing housing to baffle plate, **Fig. 7.**
5. Using sliding hammer tool No. ST36230000 and axle stand tool No. KV40101000, or equivalents, pull out axle shaft, **Fig. 8.**
6. Remove oil seal from axle housing.
7. Mount axle shaft in a suitable vise, then using a screwdriver, unbend lock washer. **Do not reuse lock washer.**
8. Remove bearing locknut, **Fig. 5.**
9. Remove wheel bearing, bearing housing and baffle plate from axle shaft.
10. Remove bearing outer side inner race from axle shaft.
11. Remove bearing outer race with suitable tool, **Fig. 9.**
12. Reverse procedure to install.

SHOCK ABSORBER
REPLACE

1. Raise and support rear of vehicle.
2. Disconnect shock absorber at upper and lower mountings, **Figs. 10 through 12.**
3. Remove shock absorber from vehicle.
4. Reverse procedure to install.

COIL SPRING
REPLACE

1. Raise vehicle and support underbody

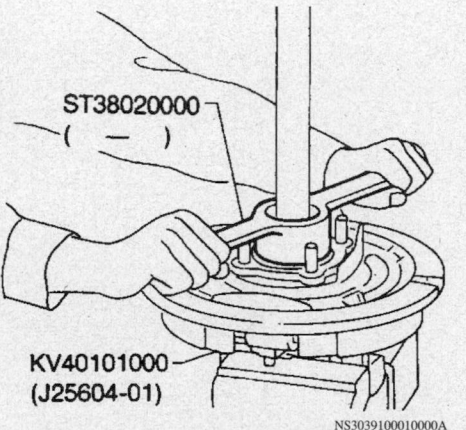

Fig. 5   Rear axle bearing locknut removal

member on both sides.
2. Support rear axle with floor jack and remove both lower shock absorber mounting bolts. Remove rear wheels if necessary.
3. Slowly lower rear axle assembly and remove coil springs after they are fully extended.
4. Reverse procedure to install.

LEAF SPRING
REPLACE

1. Raise and support rear of vehicle at chassis. Support rear axle to relieve

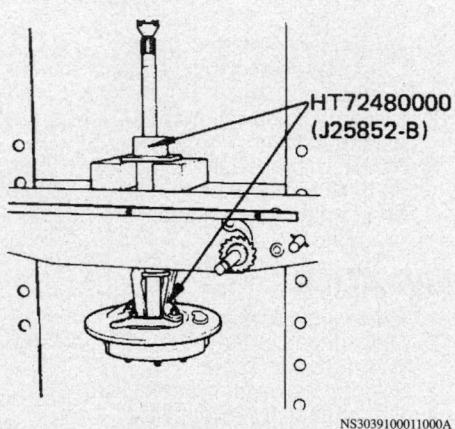

Fig. 6   Wheel bearing removal. Drum brakes

tension from spring.
2. Disconnect shock absorber at lower mounting and remove U-bolts and spring plates.
3. Disconnect spring from rear shackle, **Figs. 10 and 11.**
4. Disconnect spring from front body attachment.
5. Remove spring from vehicle.
6. Reverse procedure to install.

STABILIZER BAR
REPLACE

1. Raise and support vehicle.
2. Remove exhaust assembly as necessary.
3. Disconnect stabilizer bar from bushing brackets and locating bolts, then remove stabilizer bar.
4. Reverse procedure to install.

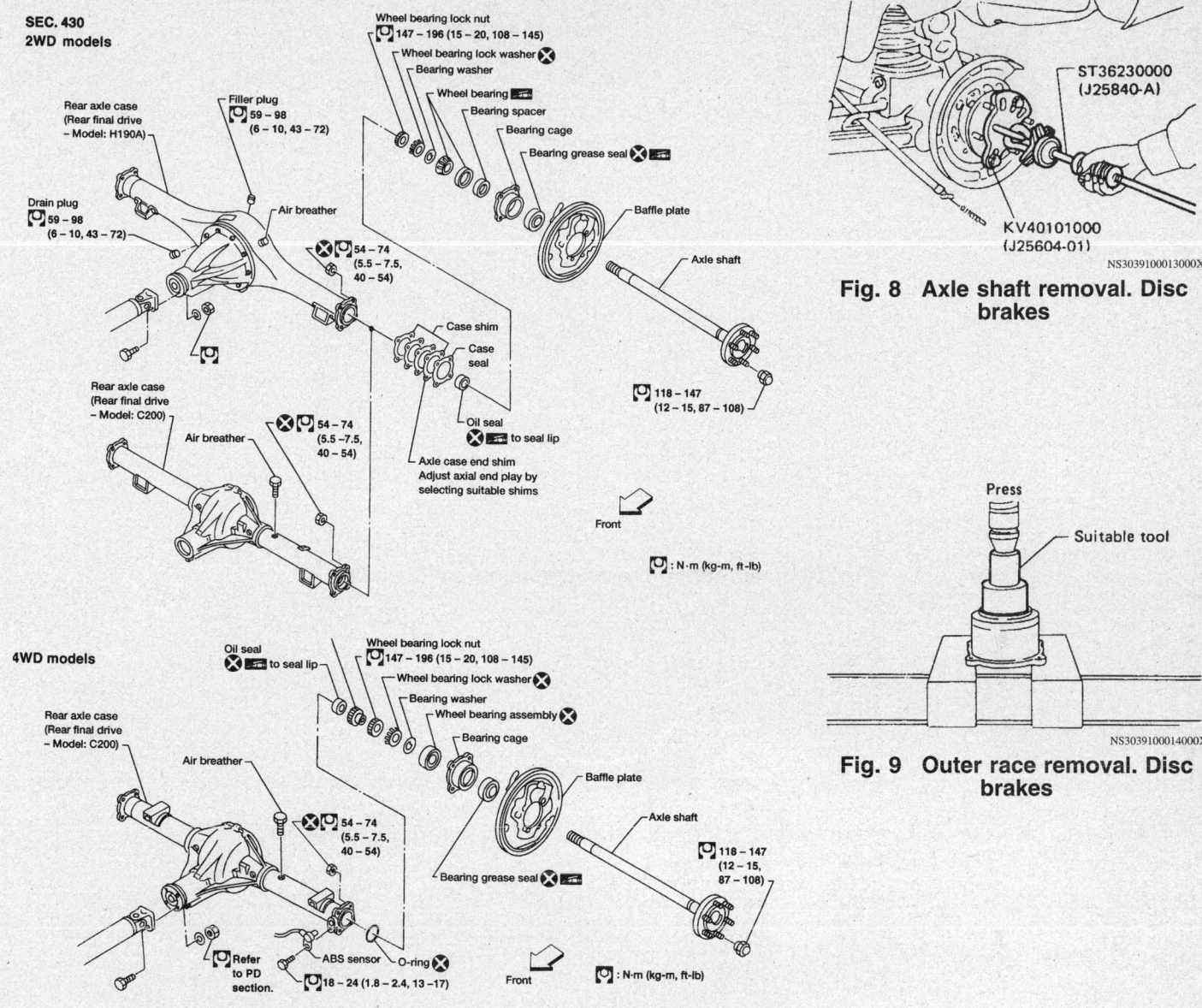

SEC. 430
2WD models

Wheel bearing lock nut
147 – 196 (15 – 20, 108 – 145)
Wheel bearing lock washer
Bearing washer
Wheel bearing
Bearing spacer
Bearing cage
Bearing grease seal to seal lip

Rear axle case
(Rear final drive
– Model: H190A)

Filler plug
59 – 98
(6 – 10, 43 – 72)

Drain plug
59 – 98
(6 – 10, 43 – 72)

Air breather

Baffle plate

Axle shaft

54 – 74
(5.5 – 7.5,
40 – 54)

Case shim
Case seal

Rear axle case
(Rear final drive
– Model: C200)

Air breather

54 – 74
(5.5 – 7.5,
40 – 54)

Oil seal
to seal lip

Axle case end shim
Adjust axial end play by
selecting suitable shims

118 – 147
(12 – 15, 87 – 108)

Front

: N·m (kg-m, ft-lb)

ST36230000
(J25840-A)

KV40101000
(J25604-01)

NS3039100013000X

Fig. 8   Axle shaft removal. Disc brakes

4WD models

Oil seal
to seal lip

Wheel bearing lock nut
147 – 196 (15 – 20, 108 – 145)
Wheel bearing lock washer
Bearing washer
Wheel bearing assembly
Bearing cage

Rear axle case
(Rear final drive
– Model: C200)

Air breather

54 – 74
(5.5 – 7.5,
40 – 54)

Baffle plate

Axle shaft

Bearing grease seal

Refer
to PD
section.

ABS sensor   O-ring

18 – 24 (1.8 – 2.4, 13 – 17)

Front

118 – 147
(12 – 15,
87 – 108)

: N·m (kg-m, ft-lb)

NS3039100012000A

Fig. 7   Exploded view of rear axle. Disc brakes

Press
Suitable tool

NS3039100014000X

Fig. 9   Outer race removal. Disc brakes

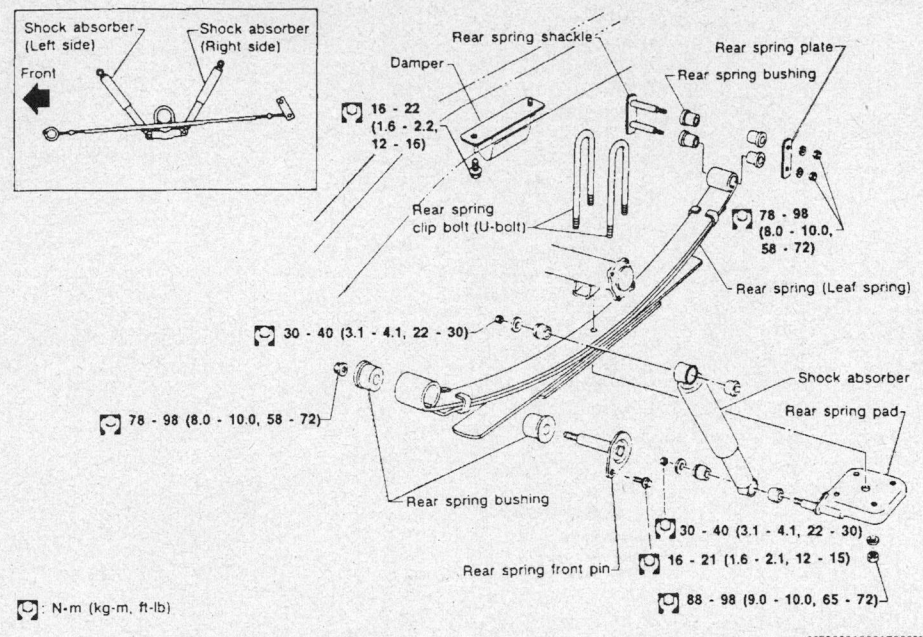

Fig. 10 Leaf spring rear suspension. 2WD models

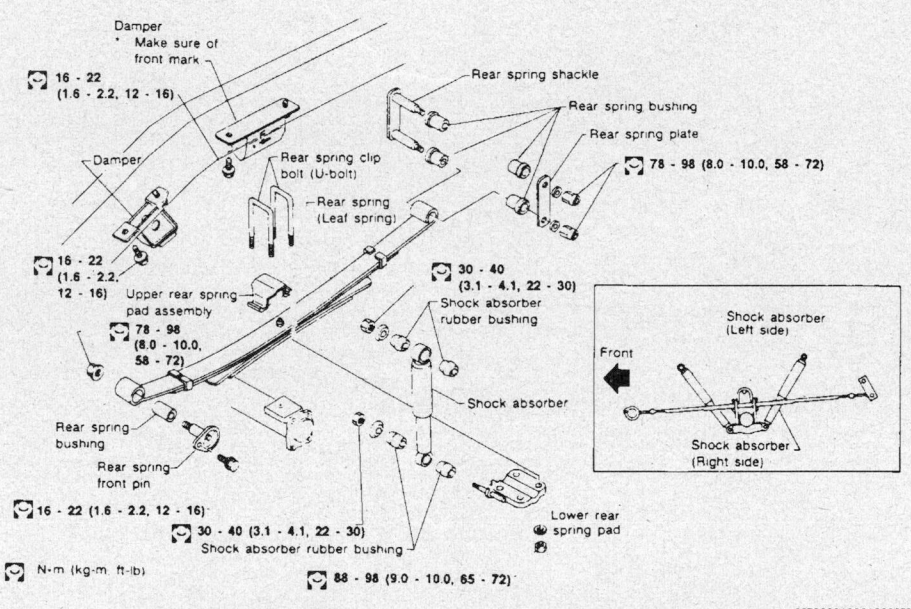

Fig. 11 Leaf spring rear suspension. 4WD models

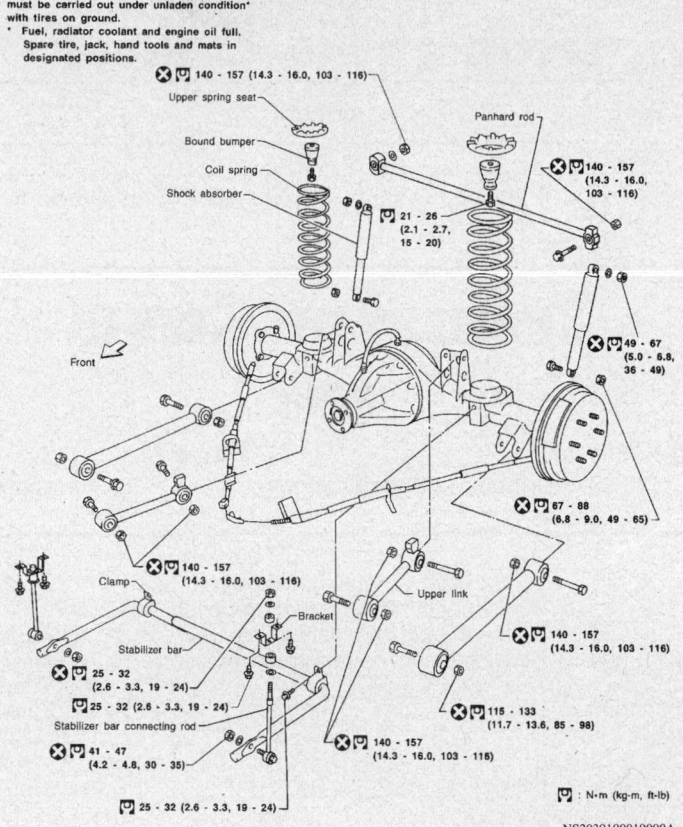

When installing rubber parts, final tightening must be carried out under unladen condition* with tires on ground.
* Fuel, radiator coolant and engine oil full. Spare tire, jack, hand tools and mats in designated positions.

Fig. 12 Coil spring rear suspension

TIGHTENING SPECIFICATIONS

Year	Component	Torque/Ft. Lbs.
1996–99	Axle Nut	181–231
	Axle Shaft To Wheel Hub	42–55
	Backing Plate Mounting Bolt	39–46
	Brake Tube Flare Nut	11–13
	Bumper Rubber Fixing Bolt	12–15
	Connecting Rod To Body	19–24
	Driveshaft Nut	181–231
	Driveshaft To Companion Flange	①
	Hub Nut	181–231
	Leaf Spring U-bolt	65–72
	Left Side Panhard Rod Nut	36–51
	Lower Link Bolt	80–108
	Right Side Panhard Rod Bolt	80–108
	Shock Absorber Lower Nut	22–30
	Shock Absorber Upper Nut	22–30
	Spring Front Pin Bolt To Frame	12–15
	Spring Front Pin Nut	58–72
	Spring Shackle	58–72
	Stabilizer Bar Bracket To Axle Case	19–24
	Stabilizer Bar To Connecting Rod	30–35
	Upper Link Bolt	80–108
	Wheel Bearing Locknut	181–231
	Wheel Cylinder Air Breather	61–78②
	Wheel Lug Nut	87–108

TIGHTENING SPECIFICATIONS—Continued

Year	Component	Torque/Ft. Lbs.
1996–99	Yoke Nut	145–210

① — KA24E engine, 29–33 ft. lbs.; VG30E engines, 58–65 ft. lbs.
② — Inch lbs.

Transfer Case

INDEX

FLUID CHANGE

1. Raise and support vehicle.
2. Remove transfer case drain plug and drain oil from transfer case.
3. Refill transfer case with recommended fluid, **torque** drain plug 18–25 ft. lbs.

TRANSFER CASE
REPLACE

1. Raise and support vehicle.
2. Drain oil from transfer case and transmission.
3. Remove exhaust front and rear tubes.
4. Remove front and rear propeller shaft.
5. Insert plug into rear oil seal.
6. Disconnect neutral safety position and 4WD switch harness connectors.
7. Remove transfer control lever from transfer outer shift lever.
8. Carefully remove transfer case from transmission. Support transfer case while removing.
9. Reverse procedure to install. Apply Nissan sealant part No. KP610-00250, or equivalent, to mating surfaces and tighten transfer case mounting bolts to specifications.

TIGHTENING SPECIFICATIONS

Year	Component	Torque/Ft. Lbs.
1996–99	Anchor Bolt Locknut	22–30
	Drain Plug	18–25
	Front Propeller Shaft Flange Nut	29–33
	Rear Propeller Shaft Locknut	181–217
	Transfer Case Mounting Bolts	23–30
	Transfer Control Lever Bracket Screws	12–15

Front Suspension & Steering

INDEX

WHEEL BEARING

ADJUST

2WD MODELS

Adjust wheel bearing preload after wheel bearing has been replaced or front axle has been reassembled.
1. Before adjustment, thoroughly clean all parts to prevent dirt entry.
2. Apply multi-purpose grease to the following parts:
   a. Rubbing surface of spindle.
   b. Contact surface between lock washer and outer wheel bearing.
   c. Grease seal lip and hub cap.
3. **Torque** wheel bearing lock nut to 25–29 ft. lbs.
4. Turn wheel hub several times in both directions to seat wheel bearing correctly.
5. **Torque** wheel bearing lock nut to 25–29 ft. lbs.
6. Turn back wheel lock nut 45°.
7. Fit adjusting cap and new cotter pin loosening nut 15° or less.
8. Connect spring scale to wheel stud, measure bearing preload. Wheel bearing preload as measured at wheel hub bolt 2.2–6.4 lbs.

4WD MODELS

Prior to adjusting wheel bearing preload, ensure bearings are in satisfactory condition and properly lubricated. Apply suitable grease to threaded portion of spindle and the contact surface of the outer bearing to ensure proper adjustment.
1. Raise and support front of vehicle, then remove wheel and locking hub assembly.
2. Remove caliper retaining bolts and secure caliper aside. **Do not allow caliper to hang from brake hose.**
3. Tighten wheel bearing locknut to specification, then rotate hub several revolutions in both directions to seat bearings.
4. Loosen wheel bearing nut until torque on nut is zero and bearing axial play is zero.
5. **Torque** bearing locknut to 10–16 inch. lbs., then rotate hub several revolutions to seat bearings, then **torque**

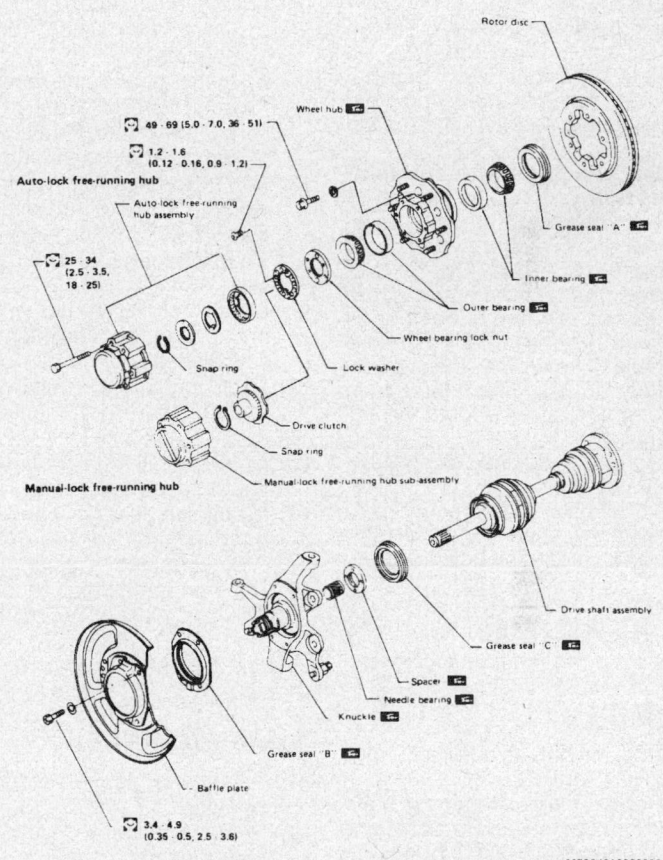

Fig. 1 Exploded view of front axle. 4WD Pickup & Frontier

NS2049100028000X

locknut an additional 10–16 inch. lbs.
6. Connect spring scale to wheel stud, measure hub starting torque through 90° of rotation and record measurement as "A."
7. Install lock washer and retaining screw, if equipped, tightening bearing locknut up to an additional 30° to align washer and nut.
8. Rotate hub several turns in each direction to seat bearings, then connect spring scale to wheel stud, measure hub starting torque through 90° of rotation and record measurement as "B."
9. Calculate wheel bearing preload by subtracting measurement A from measurement B. If remainder is not 1.59–4.72 lbs., repeat steps 3–8 until correct preload is obtained.
10. If bearings do not operate smoothly, or if preload cannot be properly adjusted as outlined, remove hub and inspect bearings.

LOCKING HUB SERVICE

1. Place locking hub in free position, raise and support front of vehicle, and remove wheel.

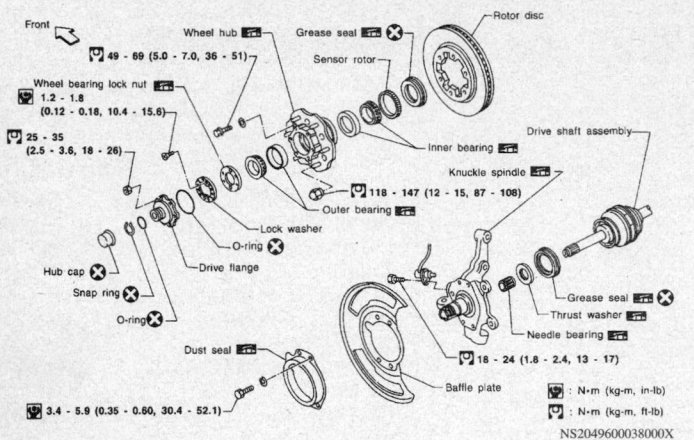

Fig. 2 Exploded view of front axle. 4WD Pathfinder

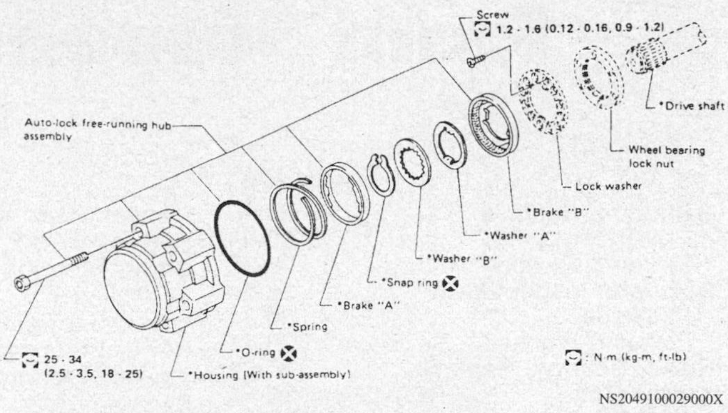

Fig. 3 Exploded view of automatic locking hub assembly

2. Remove bolts securing locking hub housing.
3. With brake pedal depressed, remove housing assembly, **Figs. 1 and 2.**
4. **On models equipped with manual locking hub,** remove snap ring from drive axle, then withdraw drive clutch from hub.
5. **On models equipped with automatic locking hub,** proceed as follows:
   a. Remove snap ring from drive axle, then withdraw washer A, washer B and brake B from hub, **Fig. 3.**
   b. Remove brake A from housing, assemble brakes A and B together as shown in **Fig. 3,** then measure thickness of assembly. If assembly thickness is less than .606 inch (15.4 mm), brakes should be replaced.
   c. Reassemble housing using new O-ring.
6. **On all models,** reverse procedure to install, using new snap rings and tighten locking hub mounting bolts to specification.

HUB & BEARING
REPLACE
4WD MODELS

1. Remove locking hub as outlined under "Locking Hub Service."
2. Remove brake caliper retaining bolts and secure caliper aside. **Do not allow caliper to hang from brake hose.**
3. Remove retaining screw and lock washer, then remove bearing locknut using suitable puller.
4. Remove hub assembly from steering knuckle, taking care not to drop outer bearing.
5. Remove outer bearing, pry seal from rear of hub, then remove inner bearing.
6. Scribe matching marks between hub and rotor, then separate rotor from hub.
7. Clean hub and bearings with suitable solvent and blow dry with compressed air.
8. Inspect bearings for damage scoring and wear, and replace as needed.

9. If bearings are to be replaced, replace bearing outer races as follows:
   a. Drive outer races from hub using suitable drift.
   b. Install new outer races using suitable driver. Ensure races are fully seated in hub. Replace hub if bearing outer races are loose in hub.
10. Pack bearings with suitable grease, working grease through rollers from wide end of bearing with palm of hand. Keep bearings covered until installation.
11. Mount rotor on hub with matching marks aligned and tighten bolts to specification.
12. Pack center of hub with suitable grease, then install inner bearing in hub.
13. Coat seal lip with grease, then install seal in rear of hub using suitable driver.
14. Install hub assembly and adjust wheel bearing preload as outlined under "Wheel Bearing, Adjust."
15. Reverse remaining procedure to complete installation. When installing locking hub, select snap ring that will provide .004–.012 endplay at drive axle.

2WD MODELS

1. Raise and support vehicle, remove wheels.
2. Remove caliper without disconnecting brake line.
3. Remove wheel hub cap, cotter pin, wheel bearing locknut.
4. Remove wheel hub, rotor and wheel bearings from spindle, **Fig. 4 and 5.**
5. Remove rotor and bearings from hub. **Inspect components for wear and/ or damage, replace as necessary.**
6. Using a suitable tool, remove bearing races, if necessary, from hub assembly.
7. Reverse procedure to install.

BALL JOINT INSPECTION
PICKUP & FRONTIER
Upper

1. Raise and support front of vehicle.
2. Clamp dial indicator onto transverse link and place indicator tip on lower edge of brake caliper.
3. Ensure front wheels are straight and brake pedal is depressed.
4. Place a pry bar between transverse link and inner rim of wheel.
5. While pushing and releasing pry bar, observe maximum dial indicator value.
6. **On 1996–97 models,** movement should not exceed .021 inch.
7. **On 1998–99 models,** movement should not be indicated.
8. **On all models,** if ball joint movement is beyond specifications, replace ball joint as necessary.

Lower

1. Raise and support front of vehicle.
2. Remove tire and wheel assembly.
3. Clamp dial indicator onto upper link and place indicator tip on knuckle near ball joint.
4. Jack up lower link approximately .79 inch.
5. Place a pry bar between upper link and upper link spindle.
6. While pushing and releasing pry bar, observe maximum dial indicator value.
7. Movement should not exceed .018 inch for 2WD models and .008 for 4WD models.
8. If ball joint movement is beyond specifications, replace ball joint as necessary.

PATHFINDER
Transverse Link & Lower

1. Raise and support front of vehicle.
2. Remove tire and wheel assembly.
3. Check transverse link for damage,

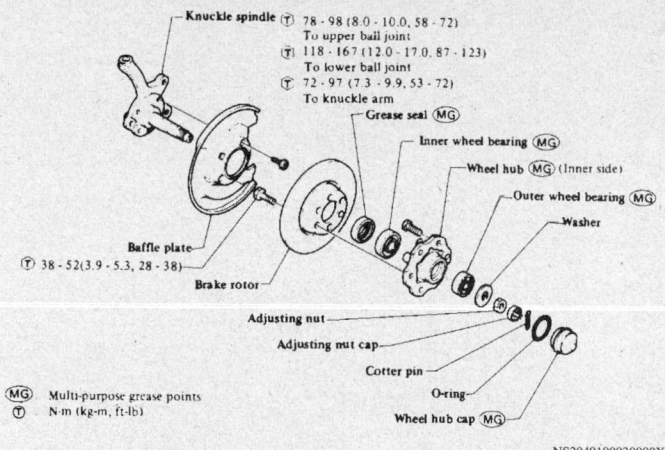

Fig. 4 Exploded view of wheel hub assembly. 2WD Pickup & Frontier

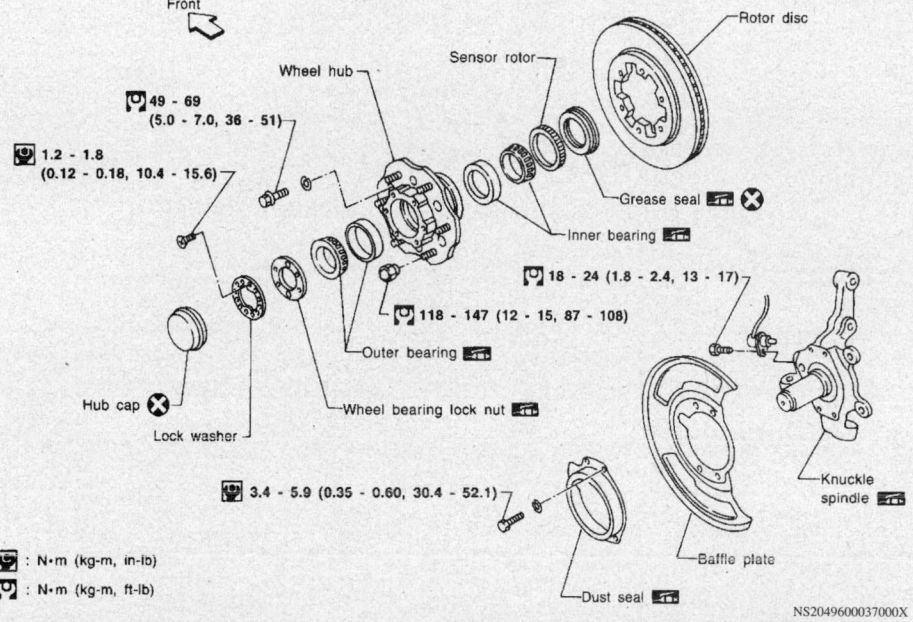

Fig. 5 Exploded view of wheel hub assembly. 2WD Pathfinder

cracks or deformation.
4. Check transverse link rubber bushing for damage.
5. Check ball joint for excessive play.
6. Replace lower ball joint assembly if any of the following exists:
  a. Ball stud is worn.
  b. Joint is hard to swing.
  c. Play in axial direction is excessive.
  d. Any vertical endplay.
7. Check dust cover for damage.

BALL JOINT

REPLACE

PICKUP & FRONTIER

Upper

1. Raise and support front of vehicle and remove wheel. **Do not raise on lower link assembly.**
2. Remove shock absorber upper attaching bolt, if necessary.
3. Using suitable jack, raise lower link

and remove upper ball joint tightening nut, then press ball joint out of knuckle.
4. Remove the upper link spindle attaching bolts and upper link. **Adjusting shims are behind spindle.**
5. Remove ball joint attaching nuts, then the ball joint, **Figs. 6 and 7.**
6. Remove nuts and washers from both ends of upper link spindle, then press spindle and bushings out of link.
7. Reverse procedure to install.

Lower

1. Raise and support front of vehicle and remove wheel.
2. Remove torsion bar, refer to "Torsion Bar, Replace."
3. Remove lower shock absorber attaching bolt, **Figs. 7 and 6.**
4. Disconnect stabilizer connecting rod and tension or compression rod from lower link.
5. Remove ball joint tightening nut, then press ball joint from knuckle spindle.
6. Remove the lower link spindle and

lower link assembly.
7. Remove ball joint attaching nuts, then the ball joint.
8. Remove nuts and washers from both ends of lower link spindle, then press spindle and bushings out of link.
9. Reverse procedure to install.

PATHFINDER

Transverse Link & Lower

1. Raise and support front of vehicle and remove wheel.
2. **On 4WD models,** separate drive shaft from knuckle.
3. **On all models,** separate lower ball joint stud from knuckle, **Figs. 8 and 9.**
4. Remove lower ball joint assembly from transverse link.
5. Remove transverse link.
6. Reverse procedure to install, noting that final tightening must be carried out at curb weight with tires on ground.

SHOCK ABSORBER

REPLACE

PICKUP, FRONTIER & PATHFINDER

1. Raise and support vehicle.
2. Remove wheel.
3. Disconnect shock absorber from upper mounting, **Figs. 7 and 9.**
4. Disconnect shock absorber from lower mounting.
5. Remove shock absorber from vehicle.
6. Reverse procedure to install.

TORSION BAR

REPLACE

PICKUP & FRONTIER

1. Raise and support vehicle.
2. Remove wheel.
3. Remove anchor arm bolt, **Figs. 6 through 7.**
4. Remove dust cover, then disconnect snap ring from anchor arm.
5. **On 2WD models,** pull anchor arm rearward, then remove torsion bar spring rearward. Remove torque arm.
6. **On 4WD models,** remove torque arm attaching nuts, then pull torsion bar spring forward and remove with torque arm.
7. **On all models,** reverse procedure to install.

STABILIZER BAR

REPLACE

Refer to **Figs. 7 through 9** for stabilizer bar replacement.

STRUT DAMPNER

REPLACE

PATHFINDER

Refer to **Fig. 10** for strut damper replacement.

POWER STEERING GEAR
REPLACE
PICKUP & FRONTIER

Refer to **Fig. 11** for power steering gear replacement.

PATHFINDER

Refer to **Fig. 12** for power steering gear replacement.

POWER STEERING TRANSFER GEAR
REPLACE
PATHFINDER

1. Set wheels in straight forward position. Straight forward position is indicated by a protrusion on surface of power steering gear rear cover cap and matching mark on rear housing.
2. Remove steering column upper and lower joint from transfer gear, **Fig. 13.**
3. Remove transfer gear assembly.
4. Reverse procedure to install.

POWER STEERING PUMP
REPLACE

1. Loosen idler pulley locknut, turn adjusting nut counterclockwise, and remove power steering pump drive belt.
2. **On models equipped with A/C,** remove air conditioning compressor drive belt.
3. **On all models,** loosen power steering hoses at pump and remove bolts securing power steering pump to brackets.
4. Raise pump and disconnect power steering hoses. Catch fluid in a suitable container, plug hose ends and ports in power steering pump, and remove pump from vehicle.
5. Reinstall power steering pump by reversing procedure and bleed system as follows:
   a. Raise and support front of vehicle.
   b. Run engine for three to five seconds, stop engine, check and fill power steering pump reservoir as needed.
   c. Quickly turn steering wheel all the way to right and left 10 times.
   d. Start engine and idle for three to five seconds. Stop engine, check and fill power steering pump reservoir as needed.
   e. With steering wheel all the way to the right, open bleeder screw, to expel air and tighten bleeder screw.
   f. Repeat procedure until all air has been bled from system.
   g. If air cannot be bled completely after repeated attempts, repeat

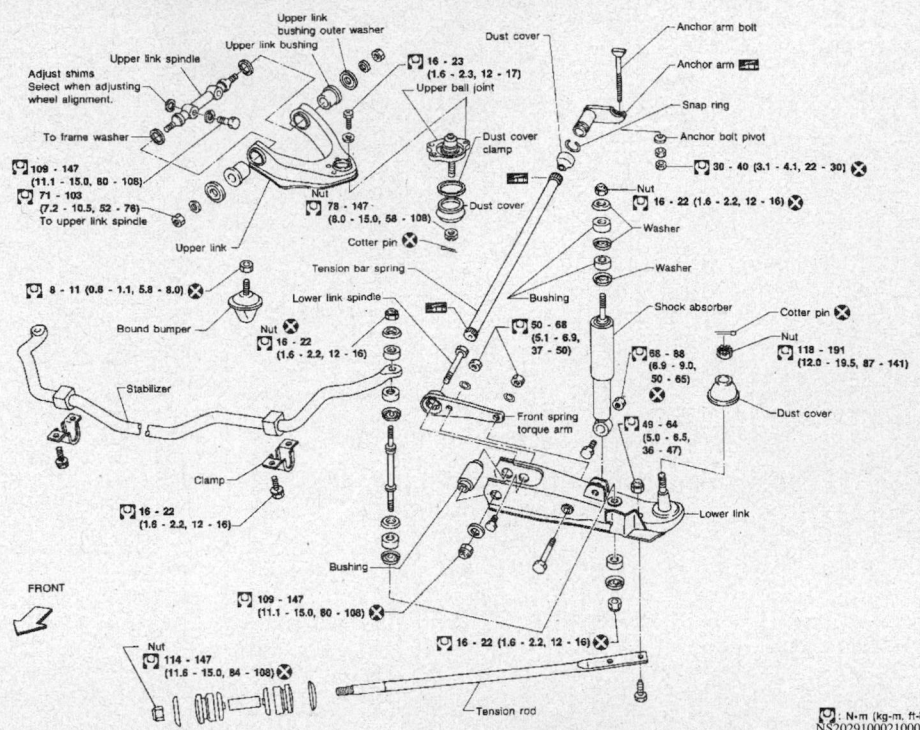

Fig. 6   Front suspension. 2WD Pickup Frontier

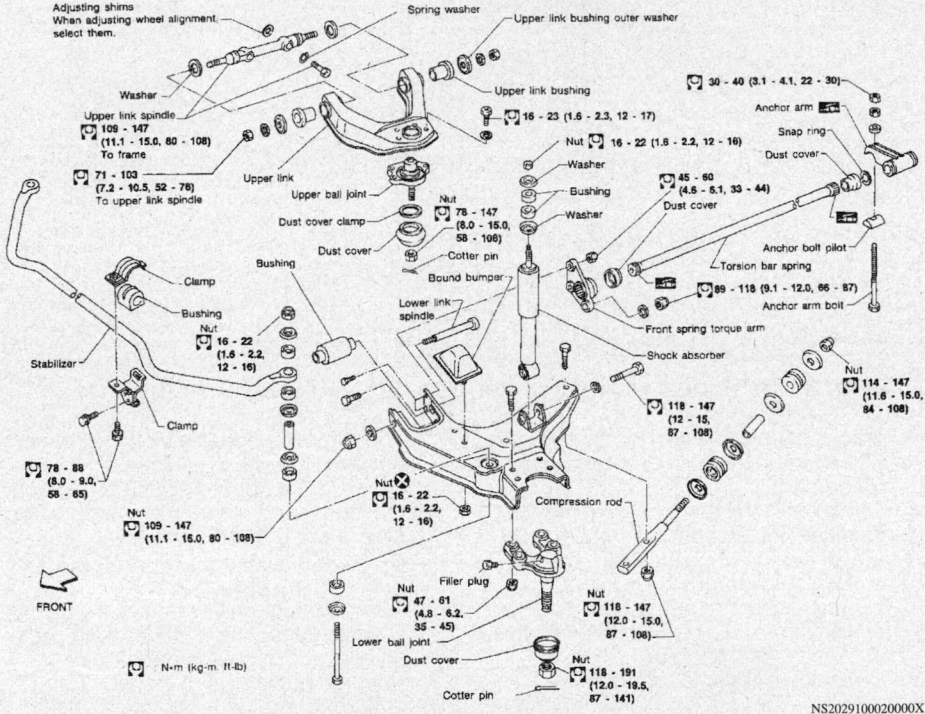

Fig. 7   Front suspension. 4WD Pickup & Frontier

step e with engine running.

MANUAL STEERING GEAR
REPLACE

Refer to **Fig. 14** for manual steering gear replacement procedure.

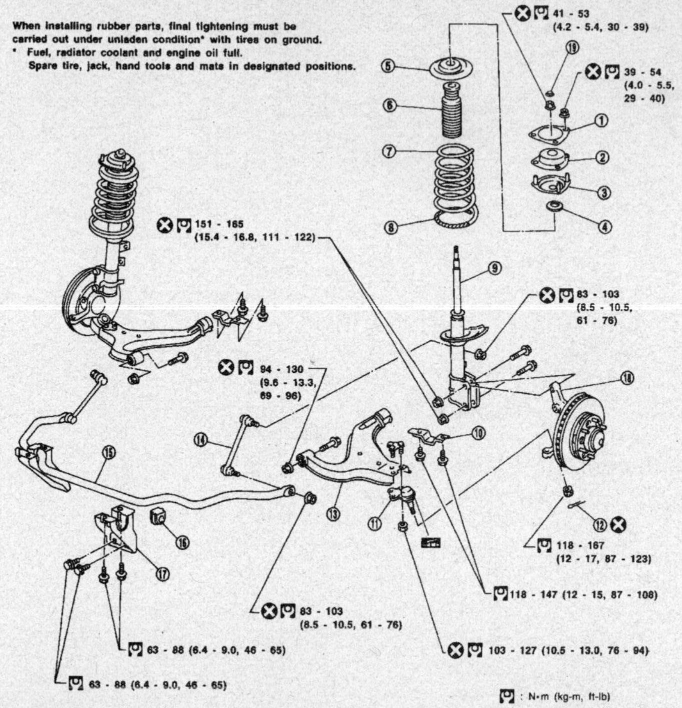

When installing rubber parts, final tightening must be carried out under unladen condition* with tires on ground.
* Fuel, radiator coolant and engine oil full.
  Spare tire, jack, hand tools and mats in designated positions.

41 - 53
(4.2 - 5.4, 30 - 39)

39 - 54
(4.0 - 5.5, 29 - 40)

151 - 165
(15.4 - 16.8, 111 - 122)

83 - 103
(8.5 - 10.5, 61 - 76)

94 - 130
(9.6 - 13.3, 69 - 96)

118 - 167
(12 - 17, 87 - 123)

118 - 147 (12 - 15, 87 - 108)

83 - 103
(8.5 - 10.5, 61 - 76)

63 - 88 (6.4 - 9.0, 46 - 65)

103 - 127 (10.5 - 13.0, 76 - 94)

63 - 88 (6.4 - 9.0, 46 - 65)

: N·m (kg-m, ft-lb)

① Spacer
② Strut mounting insulator
③ Bracket
④ Strut mounting bearing
⑤ Spring upper seat
⑥ Bound bumper
⑦ Coil spring
⑧ (Polyurethane tube)
⑨ Strut assembly
⑩ Bracket
⑪ Lower ball joint assembly
⑫ Cotter pin
⑬ Transverse link
⑭ Stabilizer connecting rod
⑮ Stabilizer bar
⑯ Bushing
⑰ Bracket
⑱ Knuckle spindle
⑲ Cap

NS2029600032000X

Fig. 8 Front suspension. 2WD Pathfinder

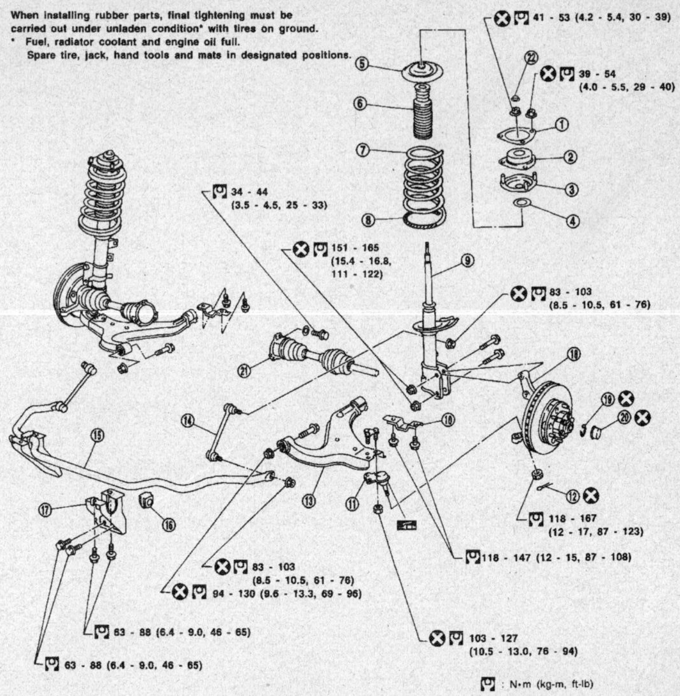

When installing rubber parts, final tightening must be carried out under unladen condition* with tires on ground.
* Fuel, radiator coolant and engine oil full.
  Spare tire, jack, hand tools and mats in designated positions.

41 - 53 (4.2 - 5.4, 30 - 39)

39 - 54
(4.0 - 5.5, 29 - 40)

34 - 44
(3.5 - 4.5, 25 - 33)

151 - 165
(15.4 - 16.8,
111 - 122)

83 - 103
(8.5 - 10.5, 61 - 76)

118 - 167
(12 - 17, 87 - 123)

118 - 147 (12 - 15, 87 - 108)

83 - 103
(8.5 - 10.5, 61 - 76)

94 - 130 (9.6 - 13.3, 69 - 96)

63 - 88 (6.4 - 9.0, 46 - 65)

103 - 127
(10.5 - 13.0, 76 - 94)

63 - 88 (6.4 - 9.0, 46 - 65)

: N·m (kg-m, ft-lb)

① Spacer
② Strut mounting insulator
③ Bracket
④ Strut mounting bearing
⑤ Spring upper seat
⑥ Bound bumper
⑦ Coil spring
⑧ (Polyurethane tube)
⑨ Strut assembly
⑩ Bracket
⑪ Lower ball joint assembly
⑫ Cotter pin
⑬ Transverse link
⑭ Stabilizer connecting rod
⑮ Stabilizer bar
⑯ Bushing
⑰ Bracket
⑱ Knuckle spindle
⑲ Snap ring
⑳ Hub cap
㉑ Drive shaft
㉒ Cap

NS2029600033000X

Fig. 9 Front suspension. 4WD Pathfinder

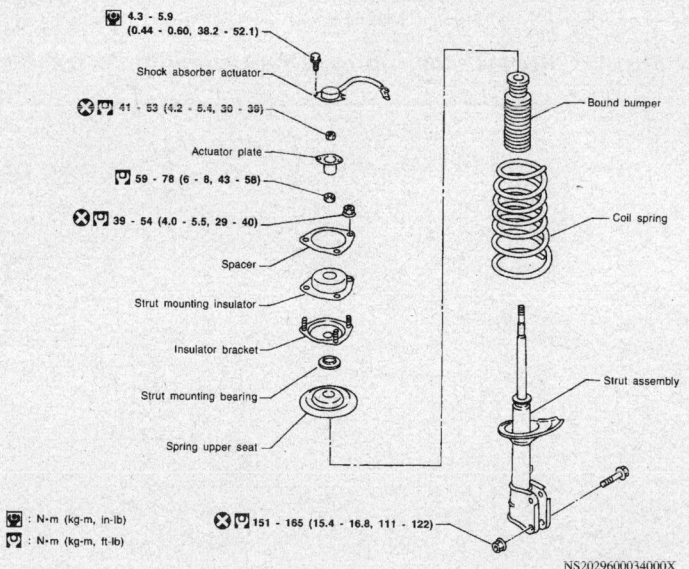

4.3 - 5.9
(0.44 - 0.60, 38.2 - 52.1)

Shock absorber actuator

41 - 53 (4.2 - 5.4, 30 - 39)

Actuator plate

59 - 78 (6 - 8, 43 - 58)

39 - 54 (4.0 - 5.5, 29 - 40)

Spacer

Strut mounting insulator

Insulator bracket

Strut mounting bearing

Spring upper seat

Bound bumper

Coil spring

Strut assembly

: N·m (kg-m, in-lb)

: N·m (kg-m, ft-lb)

151 - 165 (15.4 - 16.8, 111 - 122)

NS2029600034000X

Fig. 10 Exploded view of strut damper. Pathfinder

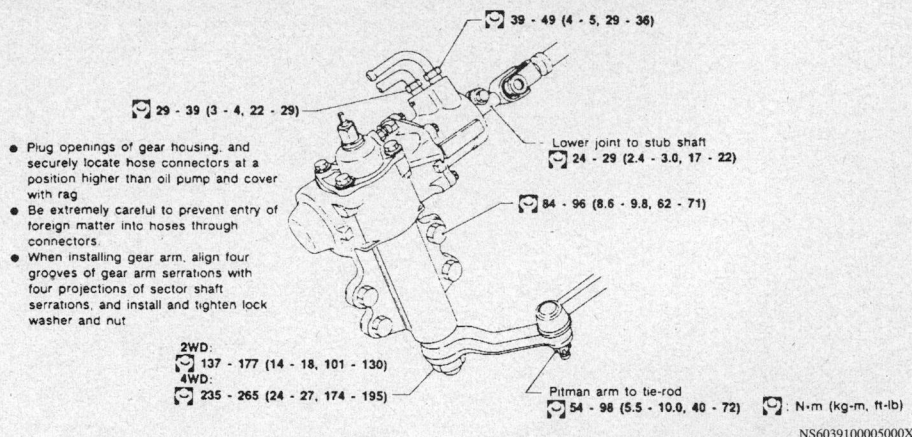

* Plug openings of gear housing, and securely locate hose connectors at a position higher than oil pump and cover with rag
* Be extremely careful to prevent entry of foreign matter into hoses through connectors
* When installing gear arm, align four grooves of gear arm serrations with four projections of sector shaft serrations, and install and tighten lock washer and nut

39 - 49 (4 - 5, 29 - 36)

29 - 39 (3 - 4, 22 - 29)

Lower joint to stub shaft
24 - 29 (2.4 - 3.0, 17 - 22)

84 - 96 (8.6 - 9.8, 62 - 71)

2WD:
137 - 177 (14 - 18, 101 - 130)
4WD:
235 - 265 (24 - 27, 174 - 195)

Pitman arm to tie-rod
54 - 98 (5.5 - 10.0, 40 - 72)   N·m (kg-m, ft-lb)

NS6039100005000X

Fig. 11   Power steering gear replacement. Pickup & Frontier

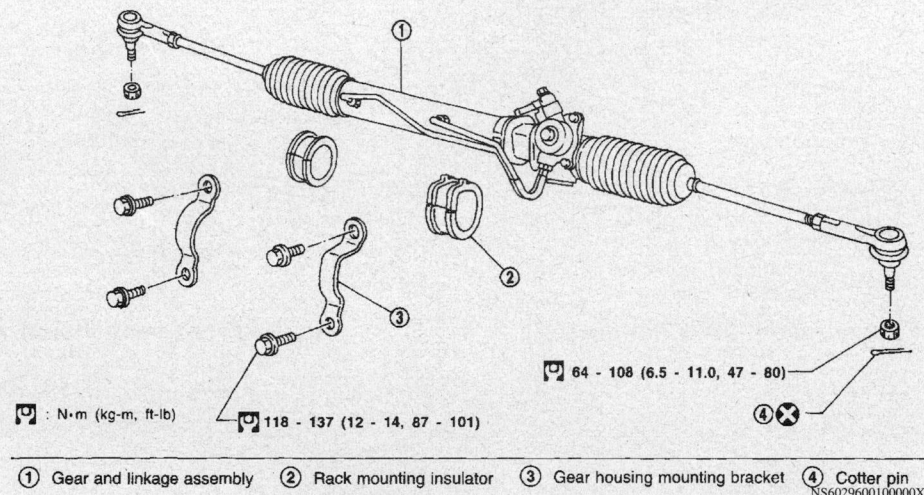

N·m (kg-m, ft-lb)

118 - 137 (12 - 14, 87 - 101)

64 - 108 (6.5 - 11.0, 47 - 80)

① Gear and linkage assembly   ② Rack mounting insulator   ③ Gear housing mounting bracket   ④ Cotter pin

NS6029600100000X

Fig. 12   Power steering gear replacement. Pathfinder

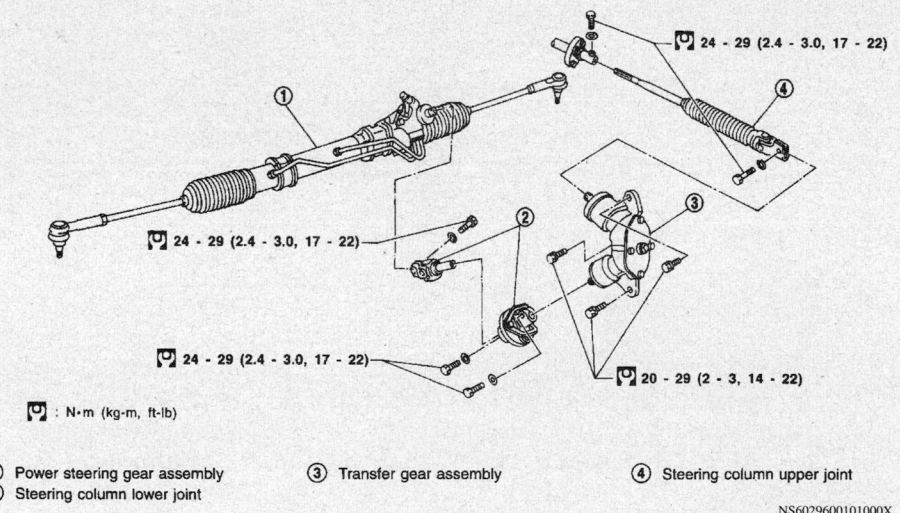

24 - 29 (2.4 - 3.0, 17 - 22)

24 - 29 (2.4 - 3.0, 17 - 22)

24 - 29 (2.4 - 3.0, 17 - 22)

20 - 29 (2 - 3, 14 - 22)

N·m (kg-m, ft-lb)

① Power steering gear assembly   ③ Transfer gear assembly   ④ Steering column upper joint
② Steering column lower joint

NS6029600101000X

Fig. 13   Power steering transfer gear replacement. Pathfinder

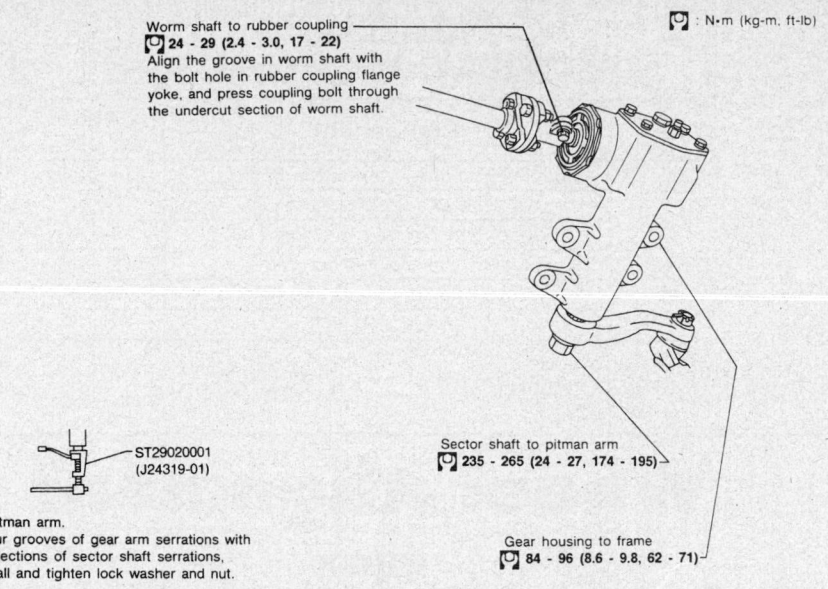

Worm shaft to rubber coupling
🔧 24 - 29 (2.4 - 3.0, 17 - 22)
Align the groove in worm shaft with
the bolt hole in rubber coupling flange
yoke, and press coupling bolt through
the undercut section of worm shaft.

🔧 : N·m (kg-m, ft-lb)

ST29020001
(J24319-01)

● Install pitman arm.
Align four grooves of gear arm serrations with
four projections of sector shaft serrations,
and install and tighten lock washer and nut.

Sector shaft to pitman arm
🔧 235 - 265 (24 - 27, 174 - 195)

Gear housing to frame
🔧 84 - 96 (8.6 - 9.8, 62 - 71)

NS6039100004000A

Fig. 14 Manual steering gear replacement

TIGHTENING SPECIFICATIONS

Year	Component	Torque/ Ft. Lbs.
1996–99	Anchor Adjusting Bolt Locknut	22–30
	Axle Nut①	58–72
	Axle Nut②	25–29
	Bound Bumper To Frame②	69–96③
	Bound Bumper To Lower Link①	12–16
	Compression Rod To Body①	87–116
	Compression Rod To Lower Link①	87–108
	Driveshaft Nut①	58–72
	Driveshaft Nut②	25–29
	Driveshaft To Differential Carrier①	25–33
	Hub Nut①	58–72
	Hub Nut②	25–29
	Knuckle Arm To Knuckle Spindle	53–72
	Knuckle Arm To Tie Rod	40–72
	Knuckle Spindle To Caliper	53–72
	Locking Hub Mounting Bolts	18–25
	Lower Ball Joint To Knuckle Spindle	87–141
	Lower Ball Joint To Lower Link①	35–45
	Lower Link To Frame	80–108
	Shock Absorber Lower Bolt	43–58
	Shock Absorber Upper Bolt	12–16
	Stabilizer Bar To Frame	12–16
	Stabilizer Bar To Lower Link	12–16
	Steering Stopper Bolt Locknut①	56–72
	Steering Stopper Bolt Locknut②	20–27
	Tension Rod To Frame	87–116
	Tension Rod To Lower Link	36–47
	Torque Arm To Lower Link Inside①	66–87
	Torque Arm To Lower Link Inside②	37–50
	Torque Arm To Lower Link Outside①	66–87
	Torque Arm To Lower Link Outside②	37–50

Continued

TIGHTENING SPECIFICATIONS—Continued

Year	Component	Torque/Ft. Lbs.
1996–99	Upper Ball Joint To Knuckle Spindle	58–108
	Upper Ball Joint To Upper Link	12–15
	Upper Link Spindle To Upper Link¹	52–76
	Upper Link Spindle To Frame	80–108
	Wheel Hub To Disc Brake Rotor	36–51
	Wheel Lug Nut	87–108

① — 4WD models.
② — 2WD models.
③ — Inch lbs.

Wheel Alignment

INDEX

PRELIMINARY INSPECTION

1. Check tire pressures and adjust as needed.
2. Ensure tires are of the proper size and tires are properly matched.
3. Ensure wheel bearings (front and rear) are properly adjusted.
4. Check steering gear adjustment and ensure steering gear is properly secured to frame.
5. Inspect steering linkage and suspension components for damage and wear, and repair or replace components as needed.
6. Measure vehicle ride height with vehicle unloaded, and ensure springs are not collapsed.
7. Place vehicle on suitable alignment rack following manufacturer's instructions, then jounce vehicle several times to settle suspension.
8. Check and correct rear wheel camber and toe first, if applicable, then check and correct front suspension angles in the following order: caster and kingpin inclination, camber, toe setting and turning angle (toe-out on turns).

FRONT WHEEL ALIGNMENT

Correct front wheel alignment is necessary to provide proper handling and to prevent uneven tire wear. To ensure correct alignment, angles should be checked, and if necessary corrected, in the following sequence: caster and kingpin inclination, camber, toe-setting, and the turning angle and toe-out on turns. Front wheel align-

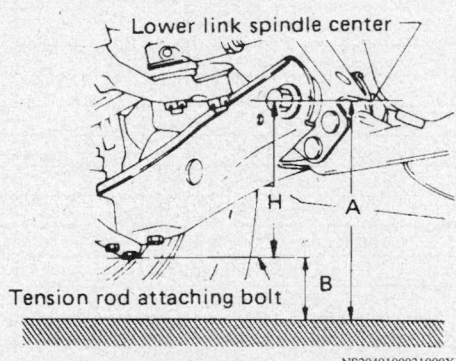

Fig. 1 Front suspension height measurement. 2WD Pickup

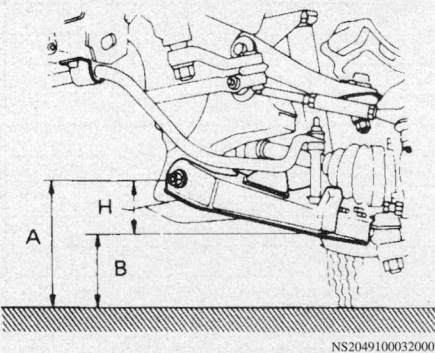

Fig. 2 Front suspension height measurement. 4WD Pickup

ment should only be checked after ensuring rear wheels are properly aligned in relation to the vehicle centerline, as most equipment uses the rear wheels as reference for correct front wheel alignment.

Front wheel alignment should be checked with the vehicle at normal ride height, and following equipment manufacturer's instructions.

CASTER & KINGPIN INCLINATION

Kingpin inclination is a function of the steering knuckle design and cannot be adjusted. Caster is the alignment angle which provides the self-centering steering effect. For caster adjustment, refer to camber adjustment, as the caster and camber are both adjusted by inserting shims between the upper control arm spindle and the crossmember.

CAMBER

Pickup

Caster and camber are adjusted together by varying the thickness of shims between the upper control arm shaft and crossmember. To check and adjust caster and camber, proceed as follows:

1. Prior to checking and adjusting caster and camber, ensure front suspension height is within specifications as follows:
   a. Measure suspension height of suspension arm pivot (A) and height of tension rod attaching bolt or steering stopper bracket (B), **Figs. 1 and 2.**
   b. Subtract measurement (B) from measurement (A) to determine suspension height (H). 2WD models should measure 4.37–4.53 inches and 4WD models should measure 1.73–1.89 inches.

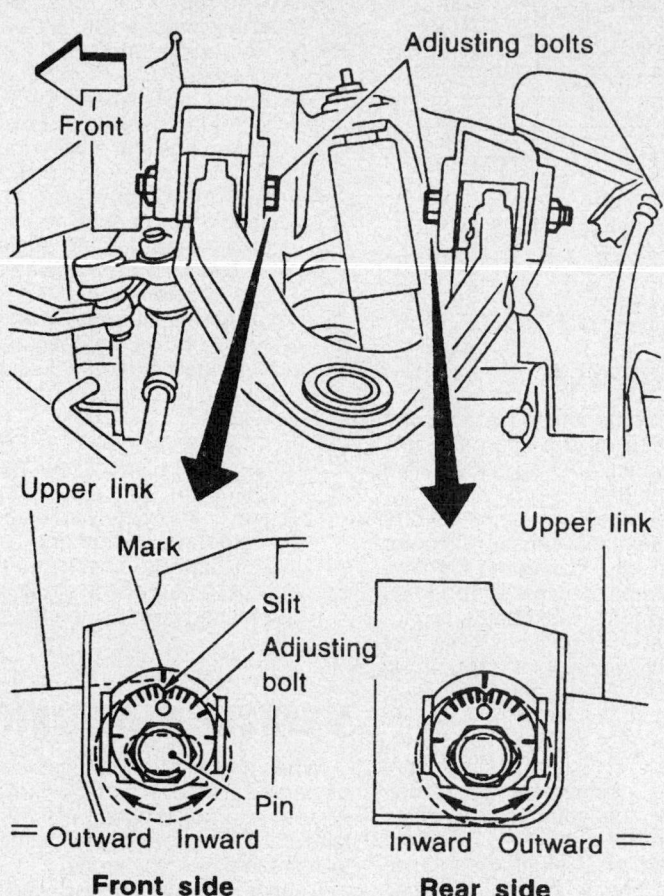

Fig. 3 Front suspension camber adjustment. Frontier

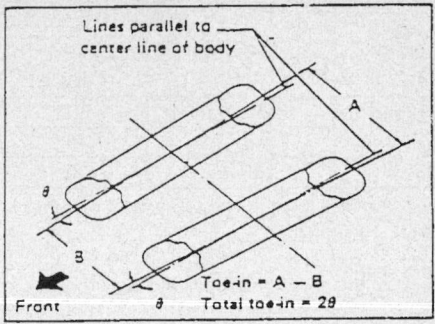

Fig. 4 Toe-in measurement

Model	Manual Steering	Power Steering
Pathfinder	11.06	11.06
Pickup 2WD	13.54	13.54
Pickup 4WD	11.06	11.06

Fig. 6 Tie rod length specifications

varying shim thickness to perform caster adjustment. Always adjust caster angle first, then reduce or increase shim thickness equally at front and rear positions to adjust camber.

d. To adjust camber, add shims of equal thickness to both front and rear positions to move camber toward a more positive value, or decrease shim thickness equally at front and rear positions to move camber toward a more negative value.

5. Tighten upper control arm nuts and ensure caster and camber are still within specifications.

Frontier

1. Measure camber, caster and kingpin inclination of both right and left front wheels with a suitable alignment gauge and adjust in accordance with the following:
2. Temporarily tighten adjusting bolts while aligning matching marks with slits shown in **Fig. 3,** measure the camber, caster and kingpin inclination.
   a. When replacing upper link or other suspension parts with new ones.
   b. When matching marks were not painted on adjusting bolts before suspension disassembly procedures.
3. If matching marks were already painted during suspension disassembly, align matching marks with slits, then temporarily tighten adjusting bolts. Measure camber, caster and kingpin inclination.

Pathfinder

1. Measure camber, caster and kingpin inclination of both right and left wheels with a suitable alignment gauge.
2. If camber, caster or kingpin inclination is not within specification, inspect front suspension parts. Replace damaged

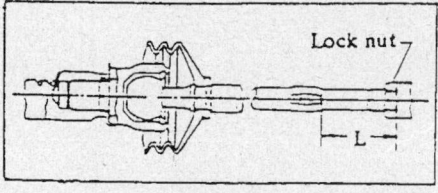

Fig. 5 Tie rod length measurement

c. If camber, caster or kingpin inclination is not within specification, inspect front suspension parts. Replace damaged or worn out parts.
d. If vehicle height is not within specifications, jounce vehicle several times to settle suspension. If height is still not within specifications, check suspension and repair or replace component as needed before continuing with alignment procedure.
2. Check caster and camber and refer to wheel alignment specifications.
3. If caster and or camber are not within

specifications, place suitable jack under lower control arm, raise arm to remove tension from upper control arm and loosen nuts securing upper control arm to crossmember.

4. Replace shims between upper control arm shaft and crossmember, noting the following:
   a. Do not use more than three shims at any one position, and ensure shim thickness does not exceed .315 inch (8 mm).
   b. When installing shims with a right angle tab at the top, ensure tab faces control arm shaft, insert shim from bracket side and only use one shim of this type at any one position.
   c. To adjust caster, vary thickness of shims between front and rear positions. When thickness of front shim is increased, caster decreases. When increasing shim thickness at the rear position, caster increases. When performing adjustment, ensure difference in shim thickness between front and rear positions does not exceed .079 inch (2 mm).

Camber angle is affected by

Year	Model	Toe-Out On Turns		Turning Angle①	
		Inner Wheel	Outer Wheel	Inner Wheel	Outer Wheel
1996–99	Pathfinder	22°	20°	32–36°	30–33°
	Pickup 2WD	22°	20°	36–38°	33–35°
	Pickup 4WD	22°	20°	②	②

2WD: 2 Wheel Drive WD: 4 Wheel Drive
① — At full lock.
② — Except 31 X 10.5 R15 tires: inner wheel, 33–35°; outer wheel, 31–33°. 31 X 10.5 R15 tires: inner wheel, 27–29°; outer wheel 25–27°.

Fig. 7 Turning angle specifications

or worn out parts.

TOE-IN SETTING

The toe setting is the measurement of the wheels in relation to the vehicle centerline, **Fig. 4.** The leading edge of each wheel should toe-in or toe-out slightly in relation to the vehicle centerline to ensure proper vehicle tracking. Toe should be inspected using suitable alignment gauges, following manufacturer's instructions. When checking or adjusting toe, always ensure the setting of the left and right wheels is as equal as possible.

Toe is adjusted by loosening the tie rod locknuts or adjusting sleeve bolts and equally altering the length of the tie rods. After toe has been adjusted to specifications, the lengths of the left and right tie rods, **Fig. 5,** should be nearly equal and close to the length specified in **Fig. 6.** If tie rod lengths are incorrect, tie rods should be disassembled and adjusted to specifications, and the toe setting should be readjusted before checking steering angles. Incorrect tie rod length will adversely affect steering angles and toe-out on turns.

STEERING ANGLE

When a vehicle negotiates a turn, the inner wheel must turn at a sharper angle than the outer wheel, and the outer wheel must travel farther than the inner wheel. Vehicle steering geometry is calculated to allow for these variations, causing the outer wheel to toe-out by a calibrated amount. This toe-out on turns is also referred to as steering angle and on these models, is generally checked at two positions. The first position is at a reference point on the inner wheel travel while the second position of measurement is at full steering lock. To check steering angles, proceed as follows:

1. Place vehicle on suitable alignment rack and ensure kingpin angle, caster, camber and toe settings are within specifications.
2. Turn wheels from straight-ahead position until the inner wheel is at the position specified for "Toe-Out On Turns" shown in **Fig. 7.** If the outer wheel reference angle is incorrect, check for damaged or improperly adjusted tie rods. Perform check in both left and right directions.
3. **On models less rack and pinion steering,** proceed as follows:
   a. Rotate steering to full lock in each direction.
   b. Adjust inner wheel "Turning Angle" to value specified in **Fig. 7,** by adjusting position of steering stop.
   c. With inner wheel adjusted to specifications, outer wheel turning angle should be as specified in **Fig. 7.** If outer wheel turning angle is incorrect, repair or replace steering linkage as needed.
4. **On models equipped with rack and pinion steering,** proceed as follows:
   a. Turn steering to full lock and measure inner and outer wheel turning angles.
   b. If "Turning Angles" at full lock are not within specifications, **Fig. 7,** check for damaged steering linkage or improperly adjusted tie rods.
   c. If steering linkage and tie rods are satisfactory, check for improper rack or rack piston stroke and repair steering gear as needed.

VEHICLE RIDE HEIGHT

When checking ride height vehicle must be parked on a level surface and tires inflated to proper air pressure. Ensure all fluid levels are to specified level, spare tire and jack are in proper locations.

Bounce vehicle up and down several times, then measure vehicle height as outlined in "Camber" under "Front Wheel Alignment." If vehicle height is not as specified, Readjust vehicle posture using anchor arm adjusting nut.

NISSAN QUEST
INDEX OF SERVICE OPERATIONS

Specifications

GENERAL ENGINE SPECIFICATIONS

Year	Model	Engine	Fuel System	Bore & Stroke, Inches	Compress-ion Ratio	Horsepower @ RPM	Torque, Ft. Lbs. @ RPM	Normal Oil Pressure, psi
1996–99	VG30E	3.0L	MFI	3.43 x 3.27	9.0	151 @ 4800	174 @ 4400	57–70①
	VG33E	3.3L	MFI	3.60 x 3.27	8.9	168 @ 4800	196 @ 2800	60–65①

① — At 3200 RPM.

TUNE UP SPECIFICATIONS

| Year | Model | Engine | Spark Plug Gap, Inch | Ignition Timing, °BTDC | | | Curb Idle Speed, RPM | Fast Idle Speed, RPM | Fuel Pump Pressure, psi② | Valve Lash |
				Firing Order	Auto. Trans.	Mark Location, Fig.				
1996–99	VG30E	3.0L	.033	④	15	A	750N	①	36–38	③
	VG33E	3.3L	.041	④	15	B	750N	①	43	③

BTDC — Before Top Dead Center
① — Controlled by idle control system.
② — With engine running.
③ — Refer to "Valve Clearance Specifi-

cations." section under "VG30E & VG33E Engines."

④ — Cylinder number from front of

engine to rear; right bank 1, 3, 5; left bank 2, 4, 6. Firing order, 1-2-3-4-5-6.

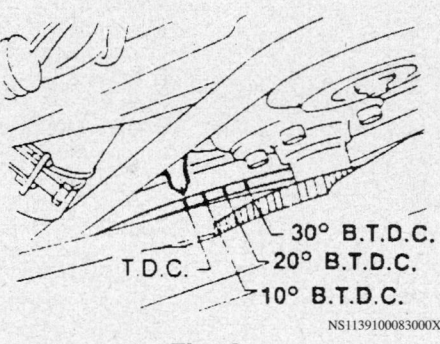

Fig. A

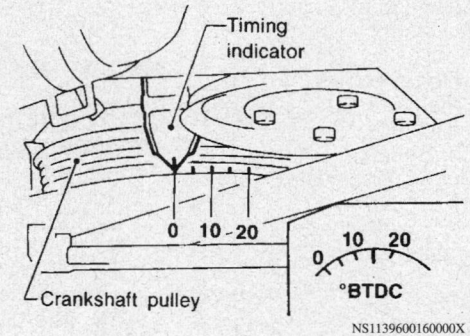

Fig. B

FRONT WHEEL ALIGNMENT SPECIFICATIONS

Year	Caster Angle, °		Camber Angle, °		Front Turning Angle, °		Toe-In, Inch	Kingpin Inclination, °	Ball Joint
	Limits	Desired	Limits	Desired	Inside	Outside			
1996–99	+1/20 to +11/20	+4/5	+9/20 to +11/20	+3/4	36–40	28–32	—	12 5/6 to 14 1/3	①

① — Refer to "Ball Joint Inspection" section under "Front Suspension & Steering."

REAR WHEEL ALIGNMENT SPECIFICATIONS

Year	Camber Angle, °		Toe-In, °
	Limits	Desired	
1996–99	−1/4 to +1/4	0	−.16 to +.16

FLUID CAPACITIES & COOLING SYSTEM DATA

Year	Engine	Coolant Capacity, Qts.		Radiator Cap Relief Pressure, psi	Thermo Opening, Temp. °F	Fuel Tank, Gals.	Engine Oil Refill, Qts.①	Transaxle Oil, Qts.
		Less A/C	With A/C					
1996–99	3.0L	②	②	12–16	180	20	4.25③	10
	3.3L	②	②	12–16	180	20	4.00③	10

① — Approximate, make final check w/dipstick.

② — With trailer package, less rear heater, 11.6 qts., w/rear heater, 13 qts.; less trailer package, less rear heater, 10.7 qts., w/rear heater, 12.1 qts.

③ — Includes filter.

LUBRICANT DATA

Year	Model	Lubricant Type				
		Transaxle	Transfer Case	Rear Axle	Power Steering	Brake System
1996–99	All	Nissan Matic D ①	—	—	Ford Premium Power Steering Fluid	DOT 3

① — Dexron III/Mercon, or equivalent automatic transmission fluid, may also be used.

Electrical

NOTE: On Air Bag Equipped Models, Refer To "Air Bag System Precautions" Located In Front Of This Manual For System Disarming & Arming Procedures.

NOTE: Refer To "Computer Relearn Procedures" Located In The Front Of This Manual For Computer Relearn Procedures.

INDEX

PRECAUTIONS

AIR BAG SYSTEMS

Refer to "Air Bag System Precautions" in front of this manual for system disarming and arming procedures.

BATTERY GROUND CABLE

Prior to service, disconnect battery ground cable and isolate as required.

FUSE PANEL & FLASHER LOCATION

Fuse panel is located on lefthand side of instrument panel above hood release lever behind fuse panel cover. Flasher module is located behind lefthand side of instrument panel, on righthand side of steering column.

FUEL PUMP RELAY LOCATION

The fuel pump relay is located in the lefthand engine compartment relay box.

RELAY CENTER LOCATION

The lefthand relay box is located in front lefthand corner of engine compartment, in front of battery. The righthand relay box is located on the front righthand side of engine compartment, along inner fender.

STARTER
REPLACE

1. Remove air intake system.
2. Disconnect battery cable from starter motor.
3. Disconnect brush cable from magnetic switch assembly.
4. Disconnect harness connector from starter motor harness.
5. Remove starter motor attaching bolts, then starter.
6. Reverse procedure to install.

ALTERNATOR
REPLACE

1. Loosen idler pulley adjusting bolt, then remove A/C compressor belt.
2. Remove engine undercover.
3. Disconnect alternator harness and remove harness bracket.
4. Loosen alternator mounting bolt, then remove drive belt.
5. Remove alternator from vehicle.
6. Reverse procedure to install.

DISTRIBUTOR
REPLACE

1. Remove distributor cover.
2. Loosen three distributor cap attaching screws, then position cap and spark plug wires aside.
3. Disconnect distributor ground connector from housing.

4. Disconnect electrical connector from distributor.
5. Remove distributor electrical connector from bracket.
6. Rotate engine until No. 1 piston is at TDC of compression stroke, ensure crankshaft pulley yellow timing mark and lower timing belt cover timing pointer are aligned.
7. Mark installation alignment between rotor and engine.
8. Remove distributor attaching bolt, then distributor.
9. Reverse procedure to install.

IGNITION LOCK
REPLACE

1. Remove steering wheel as outlined under "Steering Wheel, Replace."
2. Drill out two shear type ignition lock retaining screws, **Fig. 1.**
3. Remove ignition lock from steering column.
4. Reverse procedure to install, using shear type screws.

IGNITION SWITCH
REPLACE

1. Remove lower dash panel attaching screw, then pull panel rearward to disengage.
2. Remove four lefthand knee reinforcement plate attaching bolts, then plate.
3. Remove ignition switch harness attaching bolts, then disconnect harness from switch.

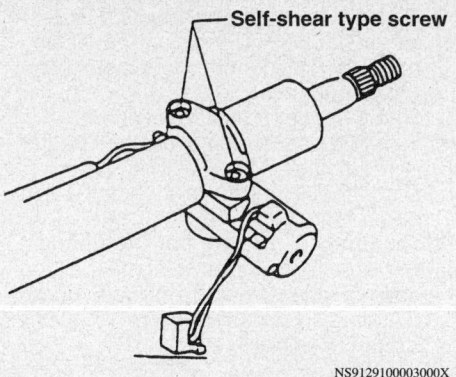

Self-shear type screw

NS9129100003000X

Fig. 1   Ignition lock replacement

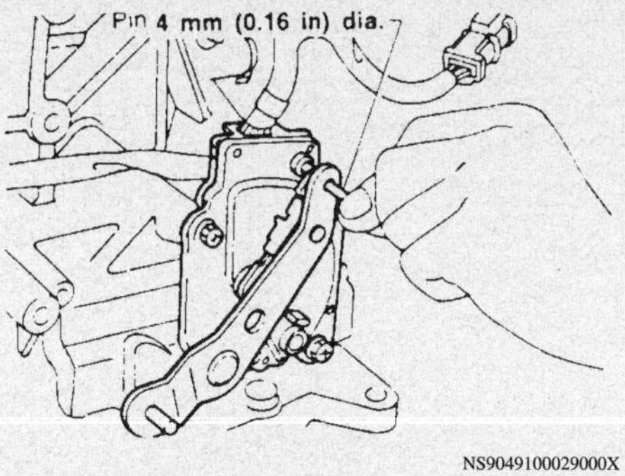

Pin 4 mm (0.16 in) dia.

NS9049100029000X

Fig. 2   Inhibitor switch adjustment

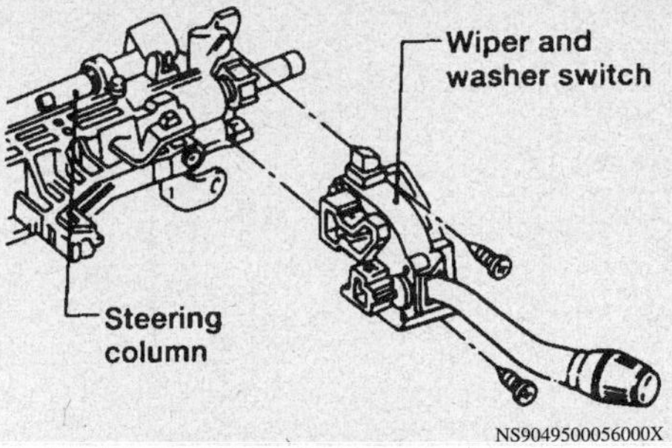

Wiper and washer switch

Steering column

NS9049500056000X

Fig. 3   Combination switch replacement

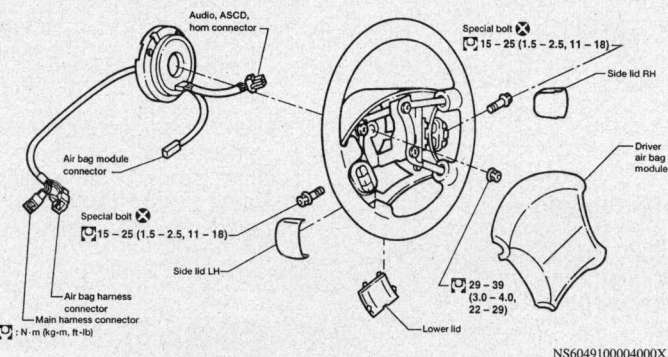

Audio, ASCD, horn connector

Special bolt ✖
☐ 15 – 25 (1.5 – 2.5, 11 – 18)

Side lid RH

Air bag module connector

Driver air bag module

Special bolt ✖
☐ 15 – 25 (1.5 – 2.5, 11 – 18)

Side lid LH

Air bag harness connector
Main harness connector
☐ : N·m (kg-m, ft-lb)

☐ 29 – 39
(3.0 – 4.0, 22 – 29)

Lower lid

NS6049100004000X

Fig. 4   Steering wheel replacement

4. Remove two ignition switch attaching screws, then switch assembly.
5. Reverse procedure to install.

NEUTRAL SAFETY SWITCH
REPLACE
1. Remove control cable from manual shaft.
2. Set manual shaft to "N" position, then loosen inhibitor switch fixing bolts.
3. Insert pin into adjustment holes in both inhibitor switch and manual shaft as near vertical as possible, **Fig. 2.**
4. Tighten inhibitor switch fixing bolts and remove pin from adjustment holes.
5. Attach control cable to manual shaft.

HEADLAMP SWITCH
REPLACE
1. Pull headlamp switch, autolamp and instrument panel dimmer switch from instrument cluster bezel.
2. Disconnect headlamp switch electrical connector, then autolamp, instrument panel dimmer switch assembly electrical connector.
3. Remove two headlamp switch attaching screws, then remove switch.
4. Reverse procedure to install.

STOP LIGHT SWITCH
REPLACE
1. Depress switch electrical connector tabs, then disconnect electrical connector.

2. Loosen switch locknut, then remove switch.
3. Reverse procedure to install, Adjust switch height as follows:
   a. Measure distance between brake pedal stopper and threaded end of switch, .012–.039 inch should be indicated.
   b. If not as indicated, loosen switch locknut and adjust switch until height is within specification.
   c. **Torque** switch locknut to 9–11 ft. lbs.

COMBINATION SWITCH
REPLACE
Refer to **Fig. 3** for combination switch replacement.

STEERING WHEEL
REPLACE
1. Remove lefthand and righthand steering wheel side lids to expose special bolts, **Fig 4.**
2. Using a T50H Torx bit, remove and discard lefthand and righthand special bolts, then remove air bag module. **Always place air bag module with pad facing upward.**
3. Set steering wheel in neutral position.
4. Remove steering wheel bolt, then disconnect horn connector.
5. Using steering wheel puller, remove steering wheel.
6. Reverse procedure to install, using new special bolts to secure air bag module.

INSTRUMENT CLUSTER
REPLACE
1. Remove lower console center cover, then lower instrument cover.
2. Disconnect lamp harness connector.
3. Remove lefthand side lower instrument panel.
4. Remove lefthand side knee reinforcement plate.
5. Remove steering column to instrument panel mounting nuts, then lower steering column.
6. Remove instrument cluster lid.
7. Remove instrument cluster to instrument panel attaching screws.
8. Pull cluster rearward and disconnect cluster harness connectors.
9. Remove cluster from vehicle.
10. Reverse procedure to install.

RADIO
REPLACE
1. Pull ashtray assembly rearward to remove.
2. Remove control console bezel attaching screw, then remove bezel.
3. Remove climate control panel attaching screws, then control panel.
4. Disconnect climate control panel from rear of radio and tape chassis.
5. Remove four radio attaching screws.
6. Pull radio assembly rearward, then disconnect radio electrical connectors and antenna cables.
7. Remove radio to bracket attaching screws, then remove radio from bracket.
8. Reverse procedure to install.

WIPER MOTOR
REPLACE
FRONT
1. Remove wiper arm and blade assembly.
2. Remove ten lower windshield molding attaching plastic screws.
3. Remove five windshield side trim attaching screws from each side.
4. Disconnect washer hose from lower windshield molding Y connector.
5. Remove windshield molding.
6. Disconnect wiper motor electrical connector.
7. Remove wiper motor assembly attaching bolts, then motor assembly.

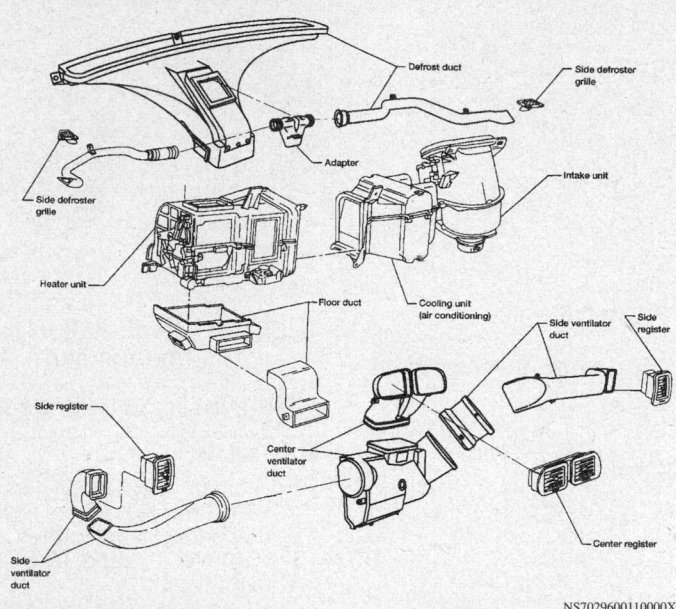

NS7029600110000X

Fig. 5 Exploded view of front A/C & heater unit

8. Remove four bracket to motor attaching locknuts and bolts, then separate motor from bracket.
9. Reverse procedure to install. **Torque** wiper motor attaching bolts to 52–68 inch lbs.

REAR

1. Remove rear wiper arm and blade assembly.
2. Remove rear wiper motor shaft nut cover, then attaching nut.
3. Remove outer collar and seal from liftgate.
4. Remove liftgate trim panel.
5. **On models equipped with opening liftgate glass,** remove liftgate glass latch cover.
6. **On all models,** remove rear courtesy lamps.
7. Carefully remove plastic weather barrier at adhesive areas.
8. Disconnect rear wiper electrical connector.
9. Remove three wiper motor attaching bracket bolts.
10. Remove wiper motor shaft inner collar, then two wiper motor to bracket attaching bolts.
11. Slide wiper motor connector from bracket, then remove motor.
12. Reverse procedure to install, noting the following:
    a. **Torque** wiper motor shaft to 53–71 inch. lbs.
    b. **Torque** wiper motor bracket bolts to 52–68 inch. lbs.
    c. **Torque** wiper motor to bracket bolts to 45 inch. lbs.

WIPER TRANSMISSION
REPLACE

1. Mark installation alignment on end of wiper linkage. Remove front wiper motor as outlined under "Wiper Motor, Replace."

2. Using suitable screwdrivers, remove each end of wiper linkage.
3. Remove two dust covers.
4. Remove motor pivot shaft attaching nut.
5. Using suitable screwdrivers, remove pivot arm and dust cover.
6. Reverse procedure to install.

BLOWER MOTOR
REPLACE
FRONT

1. Remove one plastic rivet and four righthand instrument trim panel attaching screws, then remove trim panel.
2. Disconnect blower motor electrical connector.
3. Remove blower motor air vent tubes.
4. Remove three blower motor attaching screws, then remove blower motor.
5. Remove blower motor fan from motor as required.
6. Reverse procedure to install. **Torque** righthand instrument trim panel attaching screws to 23–32 inch lbs.

REAR

1. Remove driver's side trim panel.
2. Disconnect blower motor electrical connector.
3. Remove three blower motor attaching screws, then the blower motor.
4. Remove blower motor fan from motor.
5. Reverse procedure to install.

HEATER CORE
REPLACE
FRONT

1. Drain engine coolant.
2. Disconnect heater hoses from heater core in engine compartment.
3. Remove instrument panel as outlined in "Dash Panel Service" section.

4. Disconnect heater unit ducts, **Fig. 5.**
5. Remove two heater unit attaching bolts, then disconnect door motor electrical connectors.
6. Remove heater unit from vehicle.
7. Remove heater pipe plate, then heater core retainer.
8. Disconnect heater core shutoff valve control rod.
9. Remove heater core from heater unit.
10. Reverse procedure to install, bleed cooling system as outlined under "Cooling System Bleed" in "VG30E & VG33E Engines" section.

REAR

1. Drain cooling system.
2. Remove driver's side trim panel, then loosen rear housing attaching bolts.
3. Remove upper housing and outer housing, **Fig. 6.**
4. Remove heater core from housing.
5. Reverse procedure to install, bleed cooling system as outlined under "Cooling System Bleed" in "VG30E & VG33E Engines" section.

EVAPORATOR CORE
REPLACE
FRONT

1. Recover A/C system refrigerant.
2. Using A/C spring lock coupling disconnect tool No. T84L-19623-B, or equivalent, disconnect evaporator inlet and outlet line spring lock couplings inside engine compartment.
3. Remove one plastic rivet and four righthand instrument trim panel attaching screws, then remove trim panel.
4. Remove heater unit to righthand register duct, **Fig. 5.**
5. Disconnect blower motor, blower motor resistor and blower case door actuator electrical connectors.
6. Remove evaporator blower assembly attaching bolts, then remove assembly.
7. Remove evaporator blower assembly screws, then separate case halves.
8. Remove evaporator core.
9. Reverse procedure to install.

REAR

1. Recover A/C system refrigerant.
2. Remove driver's side trim panel, then loosen rear housing attaching bolts.
3. Remove upper housing and outer housing, **Fig. 6.**
4. Remove evaporator core from housing.
5. Reverse procedure to install, recharge A/C system.

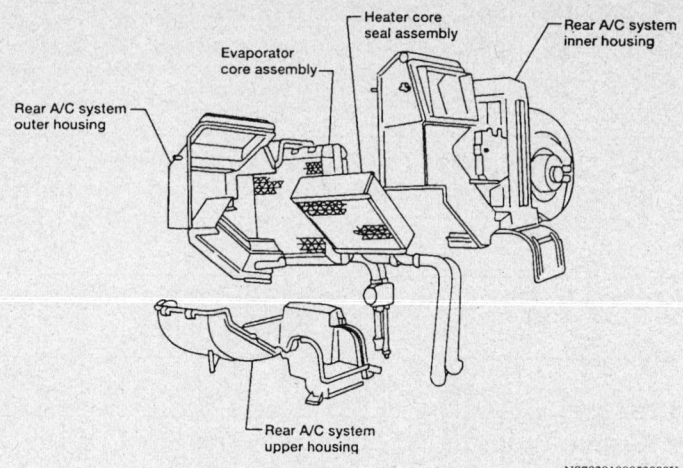

Heater core
seal assembly

Evaporator
core assembly

Rear A/C system
inner housing

Rear A/C system
outer housing

Rear A/C system
upper housing

NS7029100053000X

Fig. 6 Exploded view of rear A/C & heater unit

VG30E & VG33E Engines

NOTE: On Air Bag Equipped Models, Refer To "Air Bag System Precautions" Located In Front Of This Manual For System Disarming & Arming Procedures.

NOTE: For Procedures Not Found In This Section, Refer To VG30E & VG33E Engines Section In Nissan Frontier, Pathfinder & Pickup Chapter.

NOTE: Refer To "Computer Relearn Procedures" Located In The Front Of This Manual For Computer Relearn Procedures.

INDEX

PRECAUTIONS

AIR BAG SYSTEMS

Refer to "Air Bag System Precautions" in front of this manual for system disarming and arming procedures.

BATTERY GROUND CABLE

Prior to service, disconnect battery ground cable and isolate as required.

FUEL SYSTEM PRESSURE RELIEF

1. Remove fuel pump fuse from fuse panel, then start engine.
2. After engine stalls, crank engine over two more times to ensure all pressure has been relieved, then turn ignition switch Off and install fuel pump fuse.

COMPRESSION PRESSURE

1. Start engine and run until engine reaches operating temperature.
2. Turn ignition switch off.
3. Release fuel pressure as outlined under "Precautions."
4. Remove all spark plugs.
5. Disconnect distributor center cable.
6. Attach a compression tester to cylinder No. 1.
7. Depress accelerator pedal fully to keep throttle valve wide open.
8. Crank engine and record highest gauge indication.
9. Repeat measurement on each cylinder.
10. Standard compression is 173 psi at 300 RPM, minimum pressure is 128 psi at 300 RPM and compression difference limit between cylinders is 14 psi.
11. If compression in one or more cylinders is low, pour a small amount of engine oil into cylinders through spark plug holes, then retest compression.
12. If adding oil helps compression, then piston rings may be at fault. If adding oil does not help compression, then valves may be at fault.
13. If compression stays low in two cylinders that are next to each other, then cylinder head gasket may be leaking or both cylinders have valve component damage.
14. Repair as necessary.

ENGINE MOUNT

REPLACE

Refer to **Fig. 1** when replacing engine mounts.

ENGINE

REPLACE

1. Relieve fuel system pressure as outlined under " Precautions," then drain cooling system.
2. Raise and support vehicle.
3. Remove front wheels, engine undercovers and side cover.
4. Remove vacuum hoses, fuel hoses, wires, harnesses and connectors. **Mark vacuum hoses, wires and connectors, for installation reference.**
5. Remove front exhaust pipes, ball joints and driveshafts.
6. Lower vehicle and remove drive belts, alternator, A/C compressor and power steering oil pump from engine.
7. Raise and support vehicle, and position a suitable engine lifting device under engine and transaxle.
8. Remove lefthand side rear engine mounting bolts, **Fig. 1.**
9. Remove righthand side rear engine mounting.
10. Remove center member mounting bolts, **Fig. 1.**
11. Slowly lower engine and transaxle from vehicle.
12. Remove upper transaxle to engine bolts, then exhaust bracket.
13. Remove front and rear transaxle to engine brace bolts, then lower transaxle to engine bolt.
14. Remove torque converter to flexplate bolts, then separate transaxle from engine assembly.
15. Reverse procedure to install. Tighten fasteners to specifications.

VALVE CLEARANCE SPECIFICATIONS

Engine	Stem-To-Guide Clearance, Inch①	
	Intake	Exhaust
VG30E & VG33E	.0008–.0021	.0016–.0029

① — Cold.

VALVE ADJUSTMENT

These engines are equipped with hydraulic lash adjusters. No adjustments are required.

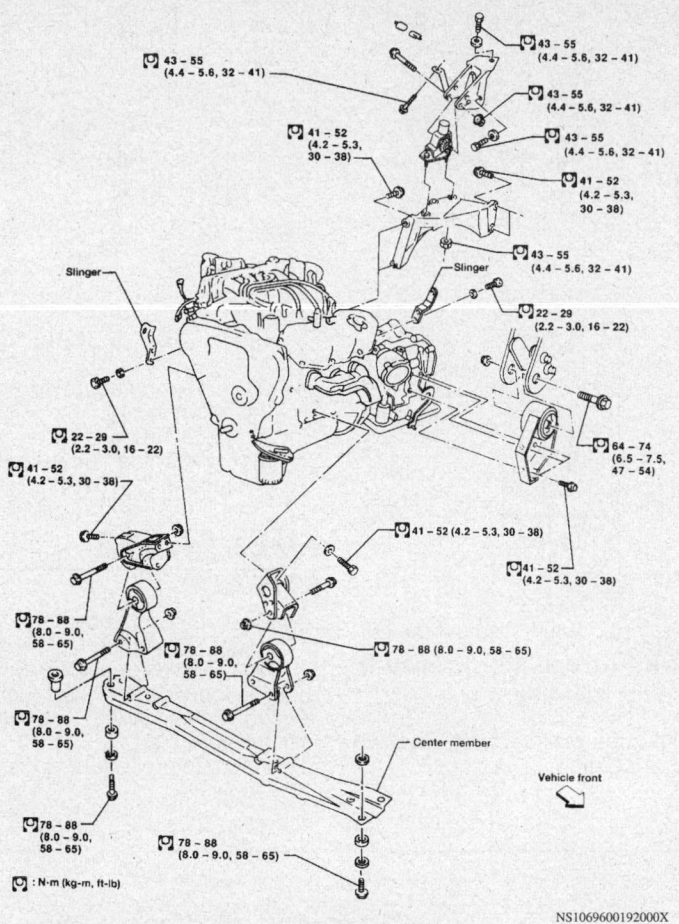

Fig. 1 Engine & transaxle mounts

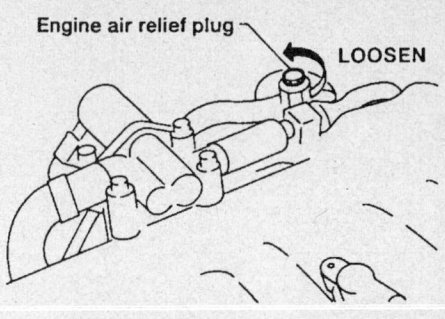

NS1069100143000X

Fig. 2 Engine air relief plug location

CRANKSHAFT REAR OIL SEAL
REPLACE

1. Remove transaxle assembly as outlined under "Transaxle, Replace" in "Automatic Transmissions" section.
2. Remove flexplate, then use seal remover tool No. T92C-6700-CH, or equivalent, to remove rear main seal from housing.
3. Apply a small amount of clean engine oil to lip of new seal, then use rear crankshaft seal replacer tool No. T92P-6701-AH, or equivalent, to install rear main seal until it is flush with edge of rear main seal housing.
4. Install flexplate, then transaxle assembly as outlined under " Transaxle, Replace" in "Automatic Transmissions" section.

COOLING SYSTEM BLEED

1. Turn ignition switch On and set front temperature control knob to full warm position. **On vehicles with rear heater, ensure rear blower switch is in any position except Off.**
2. Loosen engine air relief plug, **Fig. 2,** then radiator air relief plug three turns. **Do not remove radiator air relief plug.**

3. Remove air duct, then loosen heater pipe air relief clamp and remove cap, **Fig. 3.**
4. Install a hose to heater pipe air relief tube, then add a 50/50 mixture of coolant and water to MAX mark on coolant reservoir.
5. Install other end of hose in coolant reservoir. **Ensure hose end is submerged in coolant at all times.**
6. Place a drain pan under radiator relief plug opening, then slowly pour a 50/50 mixture of coolant into radiator, allowing several minutes for air to escape.
7. Fill radiator with coolant until coolant starts to drip from radiator air relief plug opening, then close plug, tightening to specifications.
8. Pour more coolant into radiator while gently moving upper radiator hose up and down.
9. Install a wire under radiator pressure cap negative pressure valve, **Fig. 4,** to allow flow of air and coolant regardless of pressure. Do not install cap at this time.
10. With engine air relief plug open, radiator filler cap off, and selector lever in P position, start and run engine at 2000 RPM until lower radiator hose becomes hot, indicating thermostat has opened. **If coolant comes out of engine air relief plug, close it. If coolant level in radiator filler neck lowers, add coolant, If coolant over-**

flows from radiator filler neck, install radiator pressure cap (with wire installed).
11. Close engine air relief plug if it is not already closed, then stop engine and allow to cool down completely.
12. Refill radiator and coolant reservoir as necessary, then install radiator pressure cap (with wire installed) and again warm engine to normal operating temperature.
13. Observe temperature gauge closely. If gauge begins to rise above normal, stop engine and allow to cool down completely, then refill radiator and coolant reservoir as necessary.
14. **On models less rear heater,** run engine at 3000 RPM with temperature control knob in full warm position for five minutes or until outlet air is hot. **Keep coolant reservoir at MAX level. Repeat procedure three times to ensure no air is trapped in system.**
15. **On models equipped with rear heater,** proceed as follows
    a. Run engine at 3000 RPM with front temperature control knob in full cool position, and front and rear blower switches in any position but Off, for five minutes or until rear outlet air is hot.
    b. Repeat procedure three times to ensure no air is trapped in system.
    c. Turn rear blower switch to Off position, front temperature control knob to full warm position until front outlet air is hot.
16. **On all models,** stop engine, then pour coolant mixture into coolant reservoir to MAX level.
17. Allow engine to cool down, then remove radiator pressure cap.
18. Remove wire and reinstall radiator pressure cap, then remove hose from heater pipe air relief tube and quickly reinstall cap and clamp.
19. Install air duct.

RADIATOR
REPLACE

1. Remove under cover and drain coolant.
2. Disconnect upper and lower radiator hoses, then remove ATF cooler hoses.
3. Disconnect reservoir tank hose, then

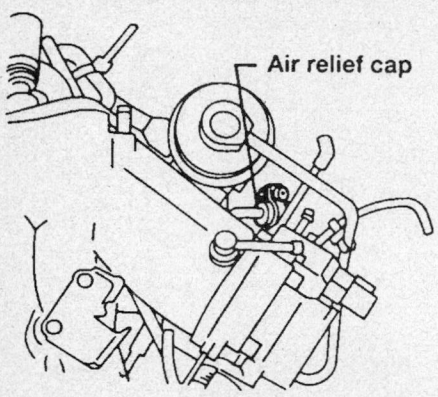

Fig. 3 Air relief cap location

remove right hand bolt from fuse box and place fuse box aside.
4. Disconnect cooling fan harness connects and remove radiator.
5. Reverse procedure to install.

FUEL PUMP
REPLACE

1. Relieve fuel pressure as outlined under "Precautions," then remove fuel tank.
2. Clean area of fuel tank around fuel pump, then remove fuel pump bolts.

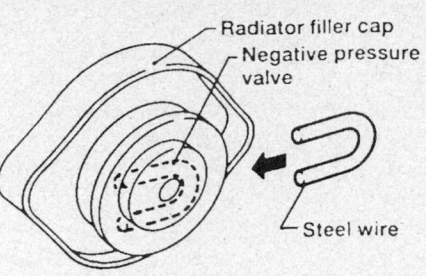

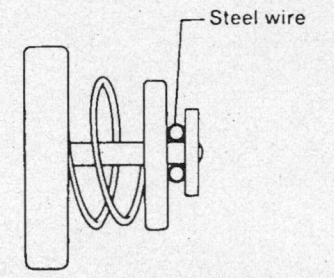

Fig. 4 Wire on radiator pressure cap installation

3. Lift fuel pump from fuel tank. Remove and discard O-ring.

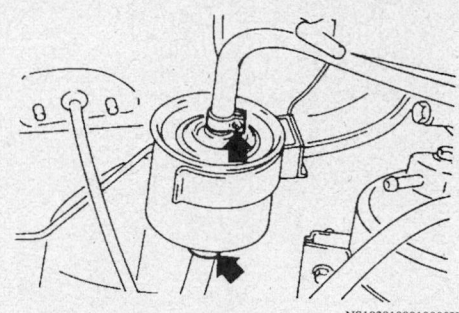

Fig. 5 Fuel filter

4. Reverse procedure to install, noting the following:
   a. Install new O-ring.
   b. Tighten fuel pump bolts to specifications.

FUEL FILTER
REPLACE

1. Relieve fuel pressure as outlined under "Precautions," then loosen fuel filter hose clamps, **Fig. 5.**
2. Disconnect and plug fuel filter hoses from filter, then remove filter from bracket.
3. Reverse procedure to install.

TIGHTENING SPECIFICATIONS

Year	Component	Torque, Ft. Lbs.
1996–99	A/C Compressor Drive Belt Tensioner	15
	A/C Compressor To Accessory Bracket	33–44
	Alternator Bracket To Oil Pump	15
	Alternator Lock Bolt	12–15
	Alternator To Accessory Bracket	17–19
	Converter Inlet Pipe To Exhaust Bracket	32
	Converter Inlet To Three-Way Catalytic Converter	32–40
	Distributor Hold-Down	10–12
	Engine Mount Bracket	30–38
	Engine Mount Through Bolt	57–72
	Exhaust Bracket To Transaxle	22–30
	Exhaust Manifold To Converter Inlet	32–40
	Flexplate	61–69
	Front Exhaust Manifold Flange Cover	48–59①
	Front Lefthand Transaxle Mount	30–38
	Front Transaxle To Engine	22–30
	Oil Drain Plug	22–29
	Oil Filter Adapter	12–15
	Power Steering Pump To Bracket	11–15
	Power Transistor Bracket To Cylinder Head Bolt	18
	Pressure Regulator Cap	29–51
	Radiator/Heater Pipe Bracket	15
	Rear Main Seal Housing	6
	Rear Righthand Transaxle Mount	32–41
	Rear Transaxle To Engine	22–30
	Thermostat Housing	12–15
	Torque Converter To Flexplate	33–43
	Transaxle To Engine Brace	22–30
	Transverse Member	57–72
	Upper Radiator Hose Bracket	34–48
	Upper Radiator Hose Clamps	14–17
	Upper Transaxle To Engine	29–36
	Wheel Lug Nut	72–87

① — Inch lbs.

Rear Axle & Suspension

INDEX

REAR AXLE
REPLACE

Refer to **Fig. 1** during replacement procedures.
1. Raise and support vehicle.
2. Support axle with jack stands or hoist.
3. Remove rear wheel and tire assemblies.
4. If equipped, remove stabilizer bar as outlined under " Stabilizer Bar, Replace."
5. Remove hub/bearing assemblies as outlined under " Hub & Bearing, Replace."
6. Remove wheel speed sensor bolts, sensor and sensor cable to axle bracket bolt.
7. Remove brake lines from axle.
8. Remove backing plate, then wire backing plate aside.
9. Remove spindle as outlined under "Rear Wheel Spindle, Replace."
10. Remove dual-load spring valve.
11. Remove shock absorber nuts and washers, then shock absorber.
12. Remove U-bolt nuts and washers, then U-bolts.
13. Remove alignment bolt cover plates and U-bolt alignment plates.
14. Remove axle from vehicle.
15. Reverse procedure to install. Tighten bolts to specifications.

HUB & BEARING
REPLACE

1. Raise and support vehicle.
2. Remove wheel and tire assembly.
3. Remove brake drum, grease cap and cotter pin, **Fig. 2.** Discard and replace cotter pin.
4. Remove hub/bearing assembly nut and washer, then hub/bearing assembly.
5. Reverse procedure to install. Tighten bolts to specifications.

HUB & BEARING SERVICE

Refer to **Fig. 2** during service procedures.
1. Remove hub/bearing assembly as outlined under "Hub & Bearing, Replace."
2. Remove snap ring, then using press and suitable bearing cup removal tool, press bearing from hub.
3. Using a press and suitable pinion bearing pressing tool, press bearing into hub.

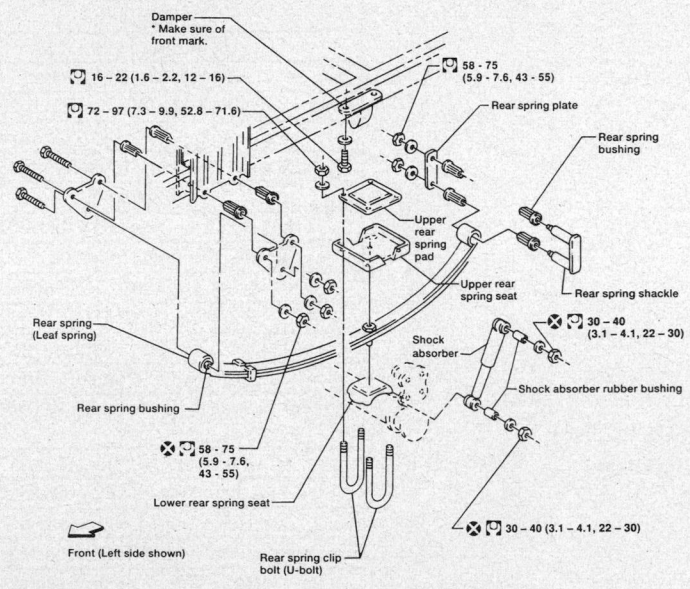

Fig. 1 Rear suspension

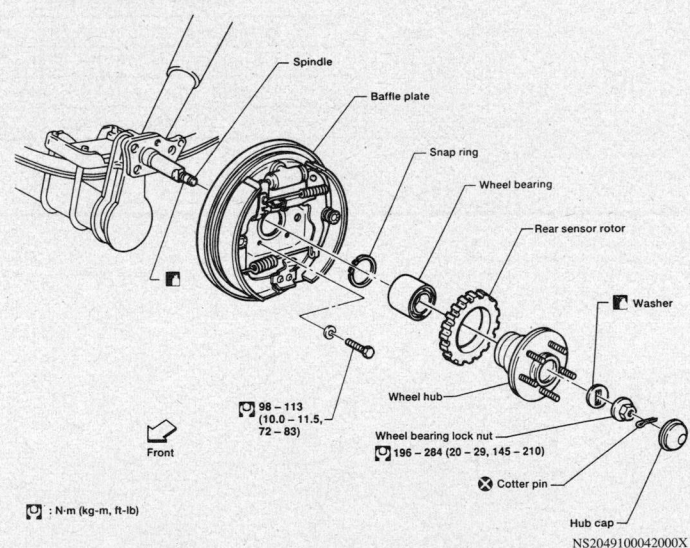

Fig. 2 Hub & bearing assembly

4. Install snap ring and hub/bearing assembly. Tighten bolts to specifications.

REAR WHEEL SPINDLE
REPLACE

1. Remove backing plate.
2. Remove spindle.

3. Reverse procedure to install. Tighten bolts to specifications.

SHOCK ABSORBER
REPLACE

1. Raise and support vehicle.

2. Remove upper and lower shock absorber nuts and washers, then shock absorber.
3. Reverse procedure to install. Tighten bolts to specifications.

LEAF SPRING
REPLACE

Refer to **Fig. 1** during replacement procedures.
1. Raise and support vehicle.
2. Support axle with a floor jack or hoist.
3. Remove U-bolt nuts, washers, U-bolts, alignment bolt cover plate and U-bolt alignment cover plate.
4. Remove shackle nuts, shackle end plate and shackle.

5. Remove leaf spring front nut and bolt. Raise vehicle until weight is off axle enough to easily remove leaf spring.
6. Reverse procedure to install, noting the following:
   a. When installing left leaf spring, ensure leaf spring front bolt is installed with head of bolt on front mounting plate marked INNER and threaded end of bolt on front mounting plate marked OUTER.
   b. When installing right leaf spring, ensure leaf spring front bolt is installed with head of bolt on front mounting plate marked OUTER and threaded end of bolt on front mounting plate marked INNER.

STABILIZER BAR
REPLACE

1. Raise and support vehicle.
2. Hold stabilizer bar link studs with a wrench and remove stabilizer bar to link nuts.
3. Disconnect stabilizer bar from link studs.
4. Loosen, but do not remove, upper stabilizer bar to axle bolts.
5. Remove lower stabilizer bar to axle bolts.
6. Slide stabilizer bar down until stabilizer bar mounting brackets clear loosened bolts, then remove bar from rear axle.
7. Reverse procedure to install. Tighten bolts to specifications.

TIGHTENING SPECIFICATIONS

Year	Component	Torque, Ft. Lbs.
1996–99	Axle Bumper Stop	12–16
	Axle Nut	145–210
	Driveshaft Nut	145–210
	Front Mounting Plate	37–50
	Hub Nut	145–210
	Leaf Spring	37–50
	Shackle Nuts	37–50
	Shock Absorber	22–30
	Stabilizer Bar To Axle	23–31
	Stabilizer Bar To Link	29–33
	Stabilizer Link To Chassis	12–16
	U-Bolt Nuts	53–72
	Wheel Lug Nuts	72–87
	Wheel Speed Sensor	16–21①
	Wheel Speed Sensor Cable Bracket To Axle	35–44①

① — Inch lbs.

Front Suspension & Steering

NOTE: On Air Bag Equipped Models, Refer To "Air Bag System Precautions" Located In The Front Of This Manual For System Disarming & Arming Procedures.

INDEX

PRECAUTIONS

AIR BAG SYSTEMS

Refer to "Air Bag System Precautions" in the front of this manual for system disarming and arming procedures.

BATTERY GROUND CABLE

Prior to service, disconnect battery ground cable and isolate as required.

DESCRIPTION

The independent front suspension consists of McPherson struts riding in a heavy rubber spring seat. A forged steering knuckle bolts to bottom end of strut and also locates ball joint. A stabilizer bar connected to both control arms via stabilizer bar links controls vehicle's body lean while cornering. Each control arm attaches to a control arm gusset which is attached directly to chassis.

WHEEL BEARING

ADJUST

Bearing is not adjustable. If Abnormal noise is indicated, bearing may require replacement. Noise will occur if bearing is dirty, worn or dry. bearings are sealed and can not be cleaned or greased.

WHEEL HUB & STEERING KNUCKLE

REPLACE

Refer to **Fig. 1** during replacement procedures.
1. Raise and support vehicle.
2. Remove wheel and tire assembly.
3. Remove wheel bearing locknut.
4. Remove front brake caliper and wire aside. It is not necessary to disconnect brake line. **Do not touch brake pedal, or piston may pop out.**
5. Remove brake rotor.
6. Using ball joint remover tool No.

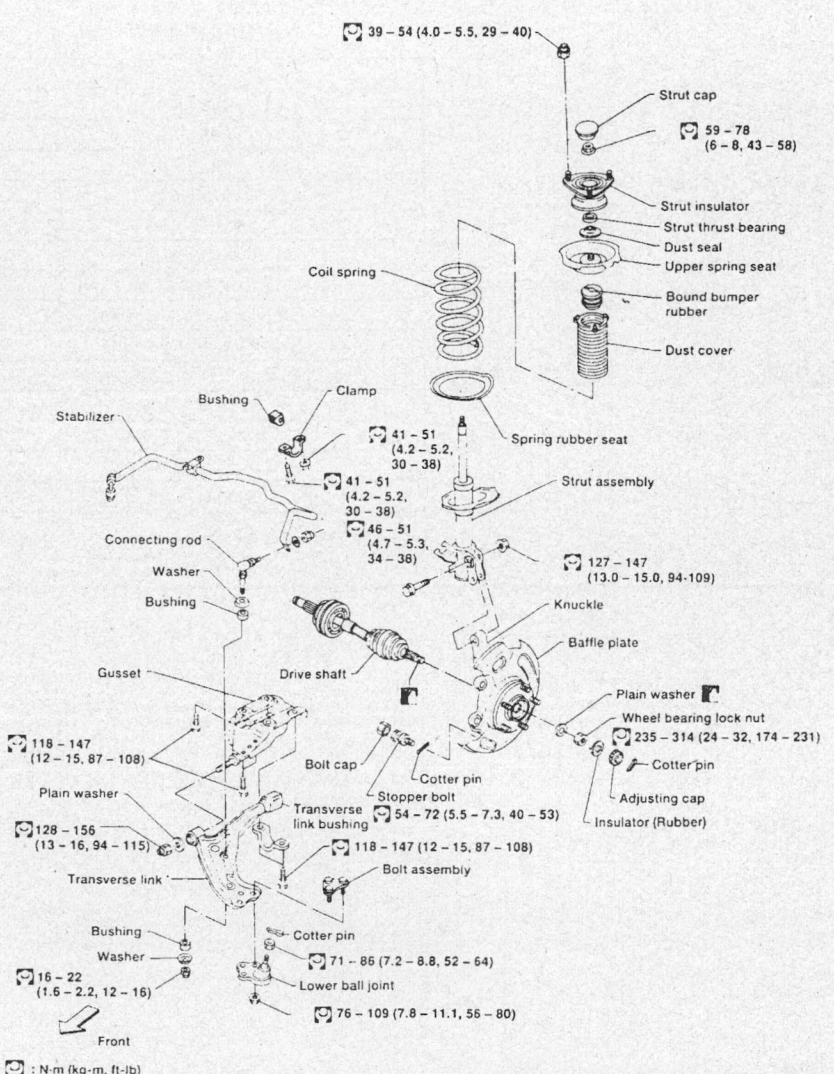

Fig. 1   Exploded view of front suspension

J25730-A, or equivalent, separate tie rod ball joint from knuckle.
7. Remove strut to steering knuckle/ wheel hub assembly nuts and bolts.
8. Remove ball joint cotter pin from ball joint shaft. Loosen ball joint nut until it contacts outer CV joint.
9. Strike steering knuckle with a hammer

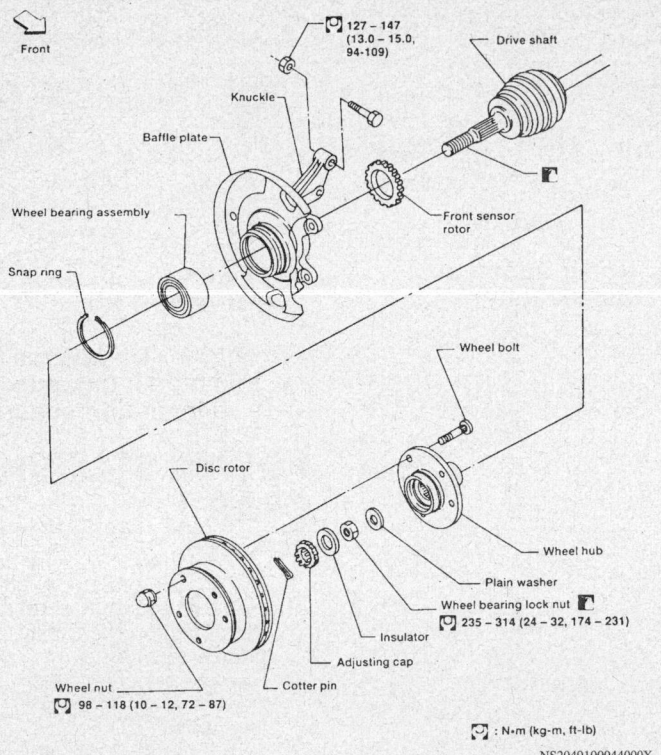

Fig. 2 Exploded view of hub & wheel bearing assembly

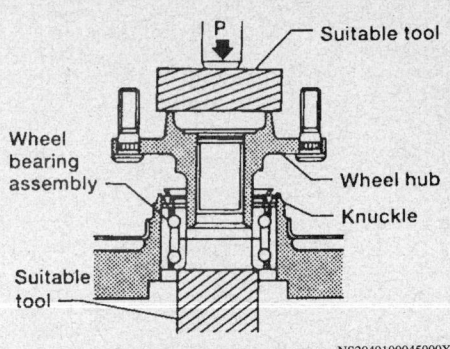

Fig. 3 Pressing wheel hub into knuckle

8. Reverse procedure to install. Tighten bolts to specifications.

COIL SPRING
REPLACE

Refer to **Fig. 1** during replacement procedures.
1. Use a grease pencil or suitable marking device and put an alignment mark on inside of strut mounting block and chassis strut tower.
2. Raise and support vehicle.
3. Remove wheel and tire assembly.
4. Remove wheel speed sensor cable bracket bolts and position cable aside.
5. Remove brake hose U-clip and position aside.
6. Remove strut to steering knuckle/wheel hub assembly nuts and bolts.
7. Separate strut from steering knuckle.
8. Remove mounting locknuts.
9. Remove coil spring/strut assembly from vehicle.
10. Reverse procedure to install. Tighten bolts to specifications.

STRUT
REPLACE

Refer to "Coil Spring, Replace" for procedure.

COIL SPRING & STRUT SERVICE

Refer to **Fig. 1** during service procedures.
1. Remove coil spring/strut assembly as outlined under "Coil Spring, Replace."
2. Place assembly in suitable vise and remove strut nut cover.
3. Loosen, but do not remove, piston rod locknut.
4. Use spring compressor tool No. HT1780000, or equivalent to compress coil spring.
5. Remove piston rod locknut and rubber mounting block.
6. Remove strut insulator, strut thrust bearing, dust seal, upper spring seat, bound bumper rubber and coil spring.
7. Slowly release tension from strut compressor.
8. Reverse procedure to install, noting the following:

---

while pulling down on control arm until ball joint breaks free from steering knuckle.
10. Remove ball joint nut. Separate ball joint from steering knuckle/wheel hub assembly.
11. Remove wheel speed sensor bolt.
12. Separate driveshaft from knuckle by lightly tapping it. If it is hard to remove, use a puller.
13. Remove steering knuckle/wheel hub assembly from vehicle.
14. Reverse procedure to install, noting the following:
    a. Before tightening wheel bearing locknut, apply oil to threaded portion of driveshaft and to both sides of plain washer.
    b. Ensure wheel bearing operates smoothly.
    c. Check wheel bearing axial endplay.

HUB & BEARING SERVICE

Refer to **Fig. 2** during service procedures.
1. Remove steering knuckle/wheel hub assembly as outlined under "Steering Knuckle & Hub Assembly, Replace."
2. Using a hammer, drive wheel hub from knuckle.
3. Remove snap ring.
4. Using a suitable pressing tool, press wheel bearing from steering knuckle.
5. Reverse procedure to install, noting the following:
    a. **Do not press inner race of wheel bearing, press only on outer race.**

---

b. **Do not apply oil or grease to mating surfaces of wheel bearing outer race and knuckle.**
c. When pressing wheel hub into knuckle, wheel bearing inner race must be held as shown in **Fig. 3**.
d. Ensure wheel bearing operates smoothly.
e. Check wheel bearing axial endplay.

BALL JOINT INSPECTION

Raise and support vehicle. Grasp tire and rock wheel up and down, inspect ball joint in control arm at bottom of steering knuckle. If movement is indicated, replace ball joint.

BALL JOINT
REPLACE

Refer to **Fig. 1** during replacement procedures.
1. Raise and support vehicle.
2. Remove wheel and tire assembly.
3. Remove and discard cotter pin from ball joint shaft. Cotter pin must be replaced.
4. Loosen ball joint nut until it contacts outer CV joint.
5. Strike steering knuckle with a hammer while pulling down on control arm until ball joint breaks free from steering knuckle.
6. Remove ball joint nut, then ball joint to control arm nuts.
7. Remove ball joint and three-stud shackle from control arm.

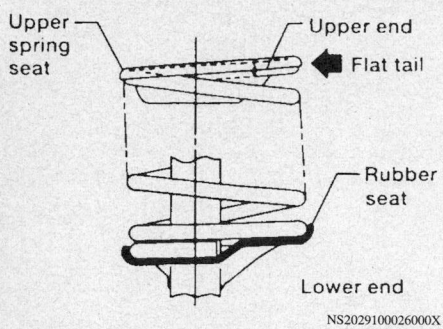

Fig. 4 Coil spring installation

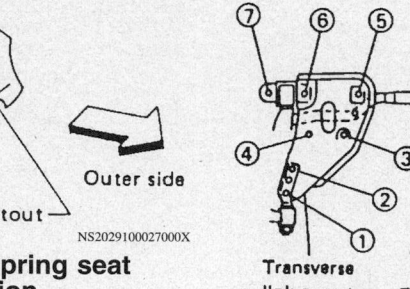

Fig. 5 Upper spring seat installation

Fig. 6 Transverse link & transverse link gusset bolt installation sequence

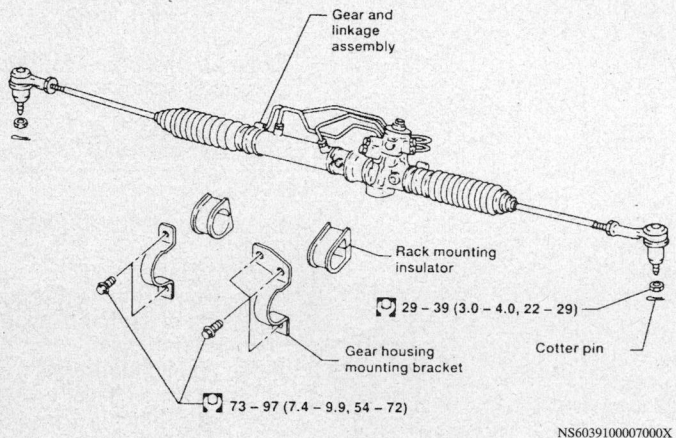

Fig. 7 Power steering gear

a. Position coil spring on strut assembly as shown in **Fig. 4.**
b. When installing upper spring seat, ensure its cutout portion is facing outer side of vehicle, inline with strut to knuckle attachment point, **Fig. 5.**
c. Tighten bolts to specifications.

CONTROL ARM
REPLACE

Refer to **Fig. 1** during replacement procedures.
1. Raise and support vehicle.
2. Remove wheel and tire assembly.
3. Remove ball joint as outlined under "Ball Joint, Replace."
4. Remove stabilizer link to control arm nut.
5. Remove stabilizer link shaft from control arm.
6. Remove rear control arm bolts and mounting bracket.
7. Remove control arm, then pull rear of control arm down and gently pry control arm forward and off gusset.
8. Reverse procedure to install. Tighten bolts to specifications.

CONTROL ARM BUSHING
REPLACE

1. Remove control arm as outlined under "Control Arm, Replace."
2. Using a suitable pressing tool, press bushing out of control arm.

3. Reverse procedure to install. Tighten bolts to specifications.

STABILIZER BAR
REPLACE

Refer to **Fig. 1** during replacement procedures.
1. Raise and support vehicle.
2. Remove stabilizer bar to stabilizer link nuts.
3. Remove stabilizer bar to control arm gusset nuts and bolts.
4. Remove stabilizer bar mounting brackets.
5. Gently pry stabilizer bar ends off stabilizer links and remove bar.
6. Reverse procedure to install. Tighten bolts to specifications.

TRANSVERSE LINK
REPLACE

1. Remove stabilizer bar as outlined under "Stabilizer Bar, Replace."
2. Remove transverse link and transverse link gusset attaching bolts.
3. Remove transverse link and transverse link gusset.
4. Reverse procedure to install, noting the following:
   a. Install attaching bolts in order shown in **Fig. 6.**
   b. Final tightening of bolts must be done with vehicle at curb weight and tires on ground.
   c. Check wheel alignment.

POWER STEERING GEAR
REPLACE

1. Place drain pan under steering gear.
2. Remove brake fluid reservoir screws, then position reservoir aside and suspend with wire.
3. Remove junction block high-pressure line from steering gear and position line aside.
4. Raise and support vehicle.
5. Remove front tire and wheel assemblies.
6. Remove stabilizer bar as outlined under "Stabilizer Bar, Replace."
7. Separate tie rod ends from steering knuckles, **Fig. 7.**
8. Pull steering gear dust boot back and have an assistant turn steering column shaft until clamp bolt is accessible, then lock steering column.
9. Remove clamp bolt from intermediate shaft lower universal joint.
10. Loosen low-pressure hose clamp and disconnect hose from steering gear. Position line out of way.
11. Remove five steering gear mounting bolts.
12. Remove mounting brackets.
13. Carefully slide steering gear to left and remove from vehicle.
14. Reverse procedure to install, noting the following:
    a. Slide steering gear in from left and position pinion shaft just below intermediate shaft lower universal joint.
    b. Raise gear so plastic aligning tab on pinion shaft enters clamp bolt gap on intermediate shaft universal joint.
    c. Mounting brackets are marked UP with arrows pointing to one end of bracket. Ensure brackets are installed correctly.
    d. Tighten bolts to specifications.

POWER STEERING PUMP
REPLACE

1. Raise and support vehicle.
2. Remove power steering pump pulley as follows:

a. Remove water pump and power steering pump drive belt.
b. Use strap wrench tool No. D85L-6000-A, or equivalent, and hold pulley while removing pulley nut.

3. Place drain pan under pump.
4. Remove hose connection bolt from pump, position high-pressure hose and connection out of way.
5. Remove pump inlet hose bolts and position hose out of way.
6. Remove front bolts, then rear bolt.
7. Remove pump from vehicle.
8. Reverse procedure to install. Tighten bolts to specifications.

TIGHTENING SPECIFICATIONS

Year	Component	Torque, Ft. Lbs.
1996–99	Axle Nut	174–231
	Clamp Bolt	17–22
	Driveshaft Nut	174–231
	Front Steering Pump Bolt	11–15
	Hub Nut	174–231
	Junction Block Bolt	18–26①
	Junction Block/High-Pressure Line	11–18
	Power Steering Pump Inlet Hose Bolts	10–13
	Power Steering Pump Pulley Nut	40–50
	Rear Housing Bolts	23–31
	Rear Steering Pump Bolt	11–15
	Steering Gear Bolts	54–72
	Upper High-Pressure Hose Bolt	36–51
	Upper Right Cooling Line Bolt	18–26①
	Wheel Lug Nuts	72–87

① — Inch lbs.

Wheel Alignment

INDEX

PRELIMINARY INSPECTION

1. Inflate tires to cold specifications.
2. Ensure tires are of same size, ply rating and load rating.
3. Inspect for excessive wheel bearing endplay.
4. Inspect for worn or damaged ball joints.
5. Inspect steering gear mounting bolts for proper torque.
6. Inspect control arm for bent or damaged condition.
7. Inspect control arm to frame bushings for looseness or wear.
8. Inspect suspension components for wear or damage.
9. Inspect vehicle ride height as outlined under "Vehicle Ride Height."

FRONT WHEEL ALIGNMENT

CASTER & CAMBER

Caster and camber are preset at factory and are not adjustable. If caster or camber angles are not within specifications, replace suspension components responsible for incorrect angles.

TOE-IN

1. Loosen jam nuts at tie rod ends and release clips at small ends of steering gear boots. **Ensure boots are free on tie rods to prevent twisting.**
2. Adjust toe-in to specification by turning tie rod ends in or out an equal amount on each side to keep steering wheel centered, **Fig. 1.**
3. Check front tracking. **Follow equipment manufacturers instructions.**
4. **Torque** tie rod end jam nuts to 58–72 ft. lbs. and install clips.

REAR WHEEL ALIGNMENT

Rear camber and toe-in are preset at factory and are not adjustable. If camber or toe-in angles are not within specifications, replace suspension components responsible for incorrect angles.

KINGPIN
ADJUST

Kingpin inclination is preset at factory and is not adjustable. If kingpin inclination is not within specifications, replace suspension components responsible for incorrect angles.

VEHICLE RIDE HEIGHT

Refer to **Fig. 2** for vehicle ride height measurement locations and specifications.

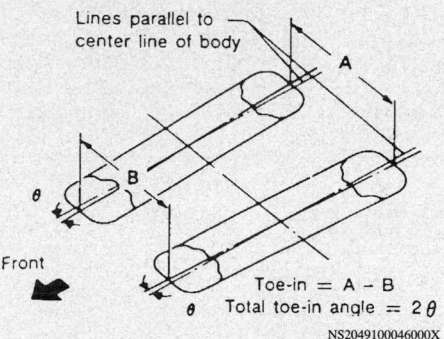

Toe-in = A - B
Total toe-in angle = 2θ

NS2049100046000X

Fig. 1   Toe-in measurement

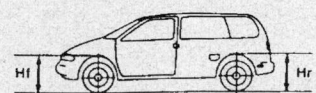

	Applied model	All
Front (Hf)	mm (in)	
Standard/Optional suspension		772 ± 10 (30.39 ± 0.39)
Rear (Hr)	mm (in)	
Standard suspension		793 ± 10 (31.22 ± 0.39)
Optional suspension		793 ± 10 (31.22 ± 0.39)

: Fuel, radiator coolant and engine oil full. Spare tire, jack, hand tools and mats in designated positions.

NS2049100047000X

Fig. 2   Vehicle ride height measurement locations & specifications

NISSAN SENTRA & 200SX

INDEX OF SERVICE OPERATIONS

Specifications

GENERAL ENGINE SPECIFICATIONS

Year	Engine Model	Fuel System	Displace- ment, Liters	Bore x Stroke, Inches (mm)	Compres- sion Ratio	Maximum H.P. @ RPM	Maximum Torque, Ft. Lbs. @ RPM	Normal Oil Pressure, psi
1996–99	GA16DE	MFI	1.6L	2.99 x 3.47 (76 x 88)	9.9	115 @ 6000	108 @ 4000	②
	SR20DE	MFI	2.0L	3.39 x 3.39 (86 x 86)	9.5	140 @ 6400	132 @ 4800	①

① — 46–57 psi @ 3200 RPM.   ② — 50–64 psi @ 3000 RPM.

TUNE UP SPECIFICATIONS

Year	Engine Model	Spark Plug Gap, Inch	Ignition Timing		Curb Idle Speed		Fuel Pump Pressure, psi	Valve Lash
			Firing Order	Timing, °BTDC	Man. Trans.	Auto. Trans.①		
1996–99	GA16DE	.041	1-3-4-2	8	675	800N	36	②
	SR20DE	.033	1-3-4-2	15	800	800N	36	②

BTDC — Before Top Dead Center
D — Drive
N — Neutral

① — When adjusting idle speed, set parking brake & chock drive wheels.

② — Refer to "Valve Adjustment" under specific engine section for valve lash adjustment procedure.

FRONT WHEEL ALIGNMENT SPECIFICATIONS

Year	Model	Caster Angle, °		Camber Angle, °		Kingpin Inclination, °	Toe-In, Inch①	Toe-Out On Turns, °②		Ball Joint
		Limits	Desired	Limits	Desired			Inner Wheel	Outer Wheel	
1996–99	All	+²⁄₃ to +2¹⁄₆	+1⁵⁄₁₂	-1¹⁄₃ to +¹⁄₆	-⁷⁄₁₂	+14 to +15¹⁄₂	0 to +.16	③	④	⑤

① — Toe-in (+); toe-out (-).
② — Measure w/wheels @ full lefthand & righthand turn positions.
③ — Models w/manual steering, +38 to +42; models w/power steering, +34 to +38.

④ — Models w/manual steering, +34; models w/power steering, +31.
⑤ — Refer to "Front Suspension &

Steering" under "Ball Joint Inspec- tion" for inspection procedure.

REAR WHEEL ALIGNMENT SPECIFICATIONS

Year	Model	Camber Angle, °		Toe, Inch①
		Limits	Desired	
1996–99	All	-1³⁄₄ to -¹⁄₄	-1	-.15 to +.25

① — Toe-in (+); toe-out (-).

FLUID CAPACITIES & COOLING SYSTEM DATA

Year	Engine	Coolant Capacity, Qts.	Radiator Cap Relief Pressure, Lbs.	Thermo. Opening Temp., °F	Fuel Tank, Gals.	Engine Oil Refill, Qts.①	Transmission Oil		Differential Oil, Pts.
							Man. Trans., Pts.	Auto. Trans., Qts.②	
1996	GA16DE	③	11–14	170	14	3⅜	6⅜	7⅜	—
	SR20DE	④	11–14	170	14	3⅝	8	7⅜	—
1997–99	GA16DE	⑤	11–14	170	13.2	3⅜	6⅜	7⅜	—
	SR20DE	6½	11–14	170	13.2	3⅝	8	7⅜	—

① — Includes filter.
② — Approximate, make final check w/dipstick.
③ — Man. trans., 6¼ qts.; auto. trans., 5⅝ qts.
④ — Man. trans., 6½ qts.; auto. trans., 7 qts.
⑤ — Man. trans., 5½ qts.; auto. trans., 6 qts.

LUBRICANT DATA

Year	Model	Lubricant Type					
		Transaxle		Transfer Case	Rear Axle	Power Steering	Brake System
		Manual	Automatic				
1996–99	All	80W-90 API GL-4	Nissan Matic D①	—	—	Dexron II/IIE/III	DOT 3

① — Dexron III/Mercon, or equivalent automatic transmission fluid, may also be used.

Electrical

NOTE: On Air Bag Equipped Models, Refer To "Air Bag System Precautions" Located In The Front Of This Manual For System Disarming & Arming Procedures.

NOTE: Refer To "Computer Relearn Procedures" Located In The Front Of This Manual For Computer Relearn Procedures.

INDEX

PRECAUTIONS
AIR BAG SYSTEMS

Refer to "Air Bag System Precautions" in the front of this manual for system disarming and arming procedures.

BATTERY GROUND CABLE

Prior to service, disconnect battery ground cable and isolate as required.

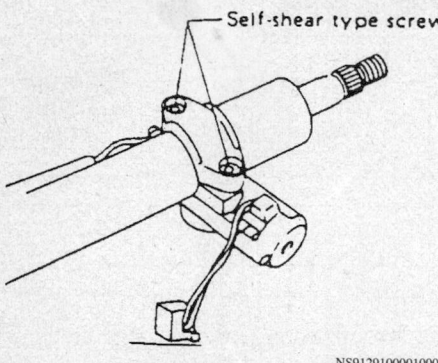

Fig. 1 Ignition lock replacement

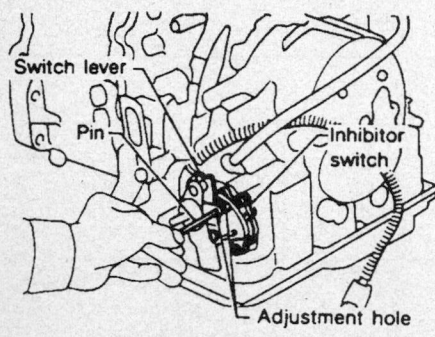

Fig. 4 Inhibitor switch adjustment

FUSE PANEL & FLASHER LOCATION

The fuse panel is located under the lefthand side of the instrument panel, to the left of the steering column.

The combination flasher unit is located behind the center of the instrument panel, to the left of the radio.

FUEL PUMP RELAY LOCATION

The fuel pump relay is located behind the lefthand side of the instrument panel, to the left of the steering column.

RELAY CENTER LOCATION

The primary engine compartment relay box is located on the righthand side of the engine compartment, near the washer fluid reservoir. Two secondary relay boxes are located in the front lefthand side of the engine compartment, on either side of the battery.

STARTER
REPLACE

1. Remove air intake duct.
2. Disconnect starter wiring from starter.
3. Remove starter retaining bolts, then the starter as follows:
   a. **On models equipped with**

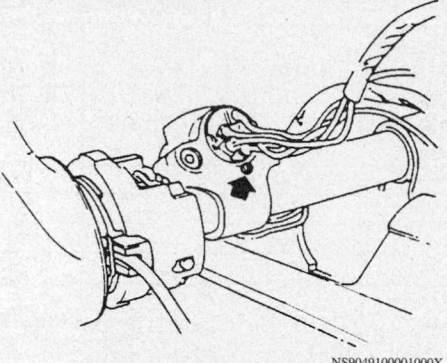

Fig. 2 Ignition switch replacement

GA16DE engine and automatic transaxle, remove starter from engine side.
   b. **On models equipped with GA16DE engine and manual transaxle,** remove starter from transaxle side.
   c. **On models equipped with SR20DE engine,** raise and support vehicle and remove starter from under vehicle.
4. **On all models,** reverse procedure to install. **Torque** starter motor mounting bolts to 23–31 ft. lbs.

DISTRIBUTOR
REPLACE

1. Position engine No. 1 cylinder at TDC.
2. Remove distributor cap and cables, then position aside.
3. Disconnect distributor electrical connections.
4. Remove distributor flange retaining nuts.
5. Remove distributor.
6. Reverse procedure to install. Ensure distributor rotor is pointing toward No. 1 cylinder spark position.

IGNITION LOCK
REPLACE

1. Break ignition lock shear type retaining screws with drill or other suitable tool, **Fig. 1.**
2. Remove ignition lock.
3. Drill out remaining part of screws.
4. Reverse procedure to install, using shear type screws.

IGNITION SWITCH
REPLACE

1. Remove four upper and lower shell cover retaining screws, then the shell covers.
2. Disconnect electrical connectors from switch.
3. Remove switch retaining screw from steering lock, **Fig. 2.**
4. Remove switch.
5. Reverse procedure to install.

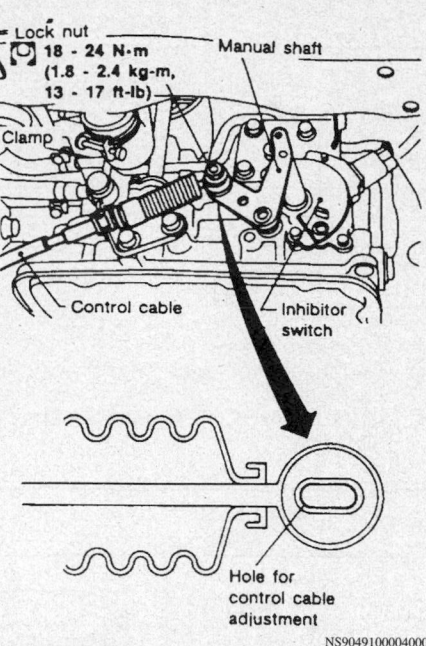

Fig. 3 Control cable adjustment

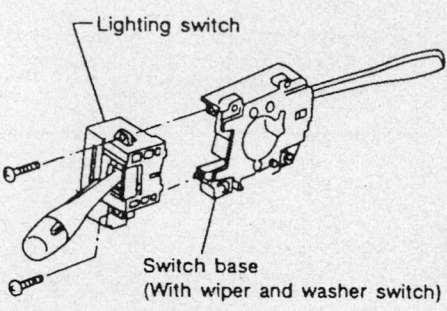

Fig. 5 Headlamp switch replacement

NEUTRAL SAFETY SWITCH
REPLACE

1. Remove control cable end from manual shaft, **Fig. 3.**
2. Set manual shaft in "N" range, then loosen inhibitor switch fixing bolts.
3. Insert a .157 inch (3.9 mm) pin into adjustment hole in both inhibitor switch and manual shaft as vertically as possible, **Fig. 4.**
4. Tighten inhibitor switch fixing bolts.
5. Remove pin from adjustment hole, then adjust control cable as follows:
   a. Place selector in "P" position.
   b. Loosen control cable locknut, then place manual shaft in "P" position.
   c. Adjust using long hole in control cable at transaxle end, **Fig. 3.**
   d. **Torque** locknut to 13–17 ft. lbs.
   e. Move selector lever from "P" range to "1" range, ensuring selector lever moves smoothly.

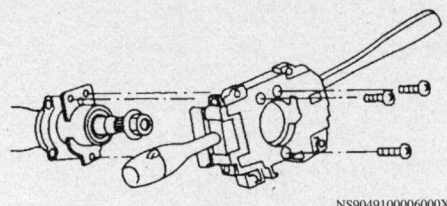

Fig. 6 Combination switch replacement

f. Apply a suitable grease to contacting areas of selector lever and control cable.

HEADLAMP SWITCH
REPLACE

1. Remove steering column covers.
2. Disconnect headlamp switch electrical connector, then remove switch retaining screws and switch, **Fig. 5.** It is not necessary to remove combination switch base to replace headlamp switch.

STOP LIGHT SWITCH
REPLACE

The stop lamp switch is located on the brake pedal support.
1. Disconnect switch electrical connectors.
2. Loosen switch retaining locknut and remove switch.
3. Reverse procedure to install.

COMBINATION SWITCH
REPLACE

1. Remove horn cover and steering wheel as outlined under "Steering Wheel, Replace."
2. Remove steering column shell covers.
3. Disconnect switch electrical connectors.
4. Remove retaining screws, then the switch, **Fig. 6.**
5. Reverse procedure to install.

TURN SIGNAL SWITCH
REPLACE

1. Remove steering column covers.
2. Disconnect turn signal switch electrical connections, then remove switch retaining screws and turn signal switch, **Fig. 5.** It is not necessary to remove combination switch base to replace turn signal switch.

STEERING WHEEL
REPLACE

1. Place steering wheel in Neutral position.
2. Remove lower lid from steering wheel, then disconnect air bag module electrical connector, **Fig. 7.**
3. Remove side lids.
4. Using a Tea Torx bit, remove left and right special securing bolts.

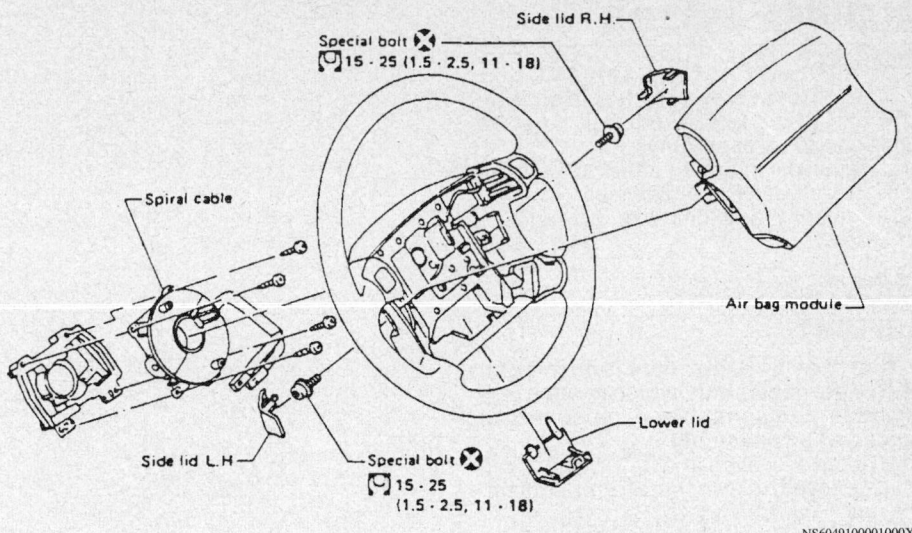

Fig. 7 Air bag module replacement

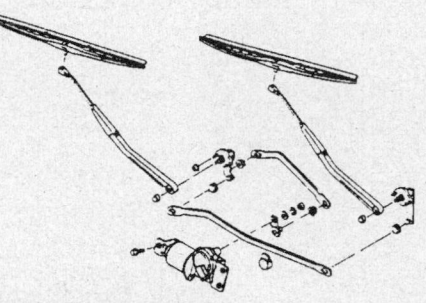

Fig. 8 Exploded view of windshield wiper system

5. Remove air bag module and observe the following precautions:
   a. **Always place air bag module with pad side facing upward.**
   b. **Do not attempt to disassemble air bag module.**
   c. **Special bolts are coated with a bonding agent. Discard after removal and replace.**
   d. **If any portion of air bag module is damaged or cracked, replace module.**
   e. **Do not allow oil, grease or water to come in contact with air bag module.**
6. Set steering wheel to Neutral position, then disconnect horn electrical connector and remove steering wheel attaching nut.
7. Using puller tool No. J25726-A, or equivalent, remove steering wheel.
8. Reverse procedure to install, noting the following:
   a. **Torque** steering wheel retaining nut to 22–29 ft. lbs.
   b. Position air bag module and **torque** new bolts to 11–18 ft. lbs.

INSTRUMENT CLUSTER
REPLACE

1. Remove steering column cover and steering wheel, if necessary.

2. Remove instrument panel cover, if necessary.
3. Remove cluster lid retaining screws, then the cluster lid.
4. Disconnect speedometer cable, cluster retaining nuts and electrical connectors as necessary. Cluster may have to be pulled slightly forward after removing retaining screws to allow access to electrical connectors in rear.
5. Reverse procedure to install.

RADIO
REPLACE

1. Remove cluster lid or instrument panel cover as necessary to gain access to brackets.
2. Remove radio bracket to instrument panel attaching screw, then disconnect electrical leads from radio.
3. Remove radio from vehicle.
4. Reverse procedure to install.

WIPER MOTOR
REPLACE

1. Remove wiper arms, **Fig. 8.**
2. Disconnect electrical connector from motor, then remove top grille retaining screws and top grille, where possible, to gain access to wiper linkage.
3. Remove wiper motor mounting bolts and pull motor away from firewall.
4. Disconnect motor shaft from linkage, taking care not to bend linkage.
5. Remove cowl top grille.
6. Remove flange nuts retaining pivot to cowl top.
7. Remove wiper motor linkage.
8. Reverse procedure to install.

WIPER SWITCH
REPLACE

The wiper switch is an integrated part of the combination switch and must be replaced as a unit. Refer to "Combination Switch, Replace."

BLOWER MOTOR
REPLACE

Note that the blower motor is an integral part of the intake unit and must be replaced as an assembly.
1. Remove instrument panel as outlined under "Dash Panel Service."
2. Refer to **Fig. 9** for intake unit replacement.

HEATER CORE
REPLACE

Note that the heater core is an integral part of the heater unit, which is not a serviceable component and must be replaced as an assembly.
1. Recover cooling and A/C systems into approved recovery/recycling containers.
2. Remove instrument panel as outlined under "Dash Panel Service."
3. Remove instrument panel reinforcement.
4. Remove cooling unit, **Fig. 9**.
5. Remove heater unit.
6. Reverse procedure to install.

EVAPORATOR CORE
REPLACE

Note that the evaporator core is an integral part of the cooling unit, which is not a serviceable component and must be replaced as an assembly.
1. Discharge A/C system into an approved recovery/recycling container.
2. Remove instrument panel as outlined under "Dash Panel Service."
3. Remove cooling unit, **Fig. 9**.
4. Reverse procedure to install.

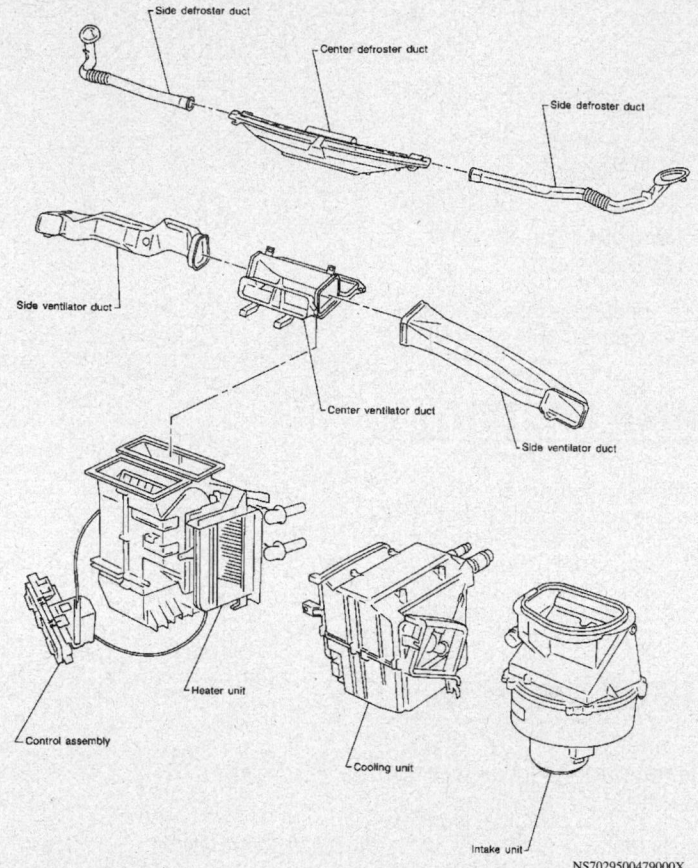

Fig. 9 Exploded view of HVAC system

GA16DE Engine

NOTE: On Air Bag Equipped Models, Refer To "Air Bag System Precautions" Located In The Front Of This Manual For System Disarming & Arming Procedures.

NOTE: Refer To "Computer Relearn Procedures" Located In The Front Of This Manual For Computer Relearn Procedures.

INDEX

PRECAUTIONS

AIR BAG SYSTEMS

Refer to "Air Bag System Precautions" in the front of this manual for system disarming and arming procedures.

BATTERY GROUND CABLE

Prior to service, disconnect battery ground cable and isolate as required.

FUEL SYSTEM PRESSURE RELEASE

1. Remove fuel pump fuse from fuse panel.
2. Start engine.
3. After engine stalls, crank engine two or three times to ensure pressure is released.
4. Turn ignition switch to off position.
5. After fuel system operations are complete, replace fuel pump fuse.

COMPRESSION PRESSURE

1. Start engine and run until engine reaches operating temperature.
2. Turn ignition switch off.
3. Release fuel pressure. Refer to "Precautions" for fuel system pressure release procedure.
4. Remove all spark plugs.
5. Disconnect distributor coil connector.
6. Attach a compression tester to cylinder No. 1.

7. Depress accelerator pedal fully to keep throttle valve wide open.
8. Crank engine and record highest gauge indication.
9. Repeat measurement on each cylinder.

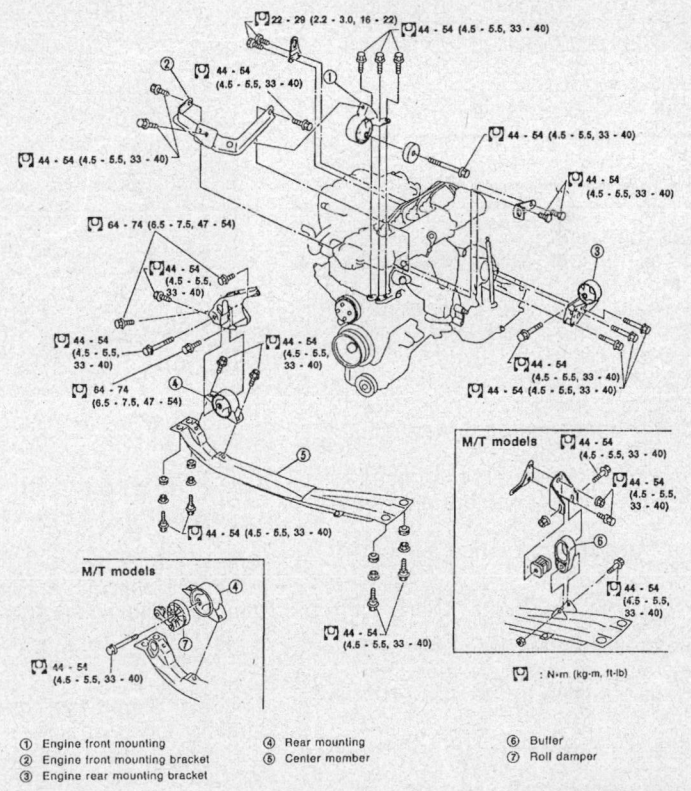

① Engine front mounting
② Engine front mounting bracket
③ Engine rear mounting bracket
④ Rear mounting
⑤ Center member
⑥ Buffer
⑦ Roll damper

NS1069100001000X

Fig. 1 Exploded view of engine mounting brackets

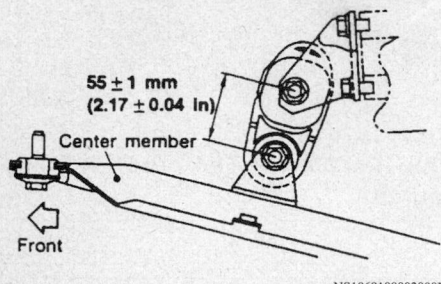

Fig. 2 Buffer rod installation

10. Standard compression is 178 psi, minimum pressure is 149 psi and compression difference limit between cylinders is 14 psi.
11. If compression in one or more cylinders is low, pour a small amount of engine oil into cylinders through spark plug holes, then retest compression.
12. If adding oil helps compression, then piston rings may be at fault. If adding oil does not help compression, then valves may be at fault.
13. If compression stays low in two cylinders that are next to each other, then cylinder head gasket may be leaking or both cylinders may have valve component damage.
14. Repair as necessary.

ENGINE MOUNT

REPLACE

Refer to **Fig. 1** for engine mount replacement.

ENGINE

REPLACE

1. Release fuel system pressure as outlined under "Precautions."
2. Drain cooling system.
3. Mark hood for installation reference, then remove hood.
4. Remove battery, then the engine coolant reservoir tank and brackets.
5. Remove drive belts.
6. Remove alternator, compressor and power steering pump from engine. Position components out of the way without disconnecting hoses.
7. Disconnect fuel lines, vacuum hoses, wire harness and connectors as necessary.
8. Remove front tire and wheel assemblies.
9. Remove engine undercover and splash shields.
10. Remove brake caliper assembly without disconnecting hydraulic lines, then support caliper from frame using suitable wire.
11. Disconnect tie rod ball joint from knuckle.
12. **On models equipped with manual transaxle,** disconnect control rod and support rod from transaxle.
13. **On models equipped with automatic transaxle,** disconnect control cable.
14. **On all models,** support engine with suitable lifting device.

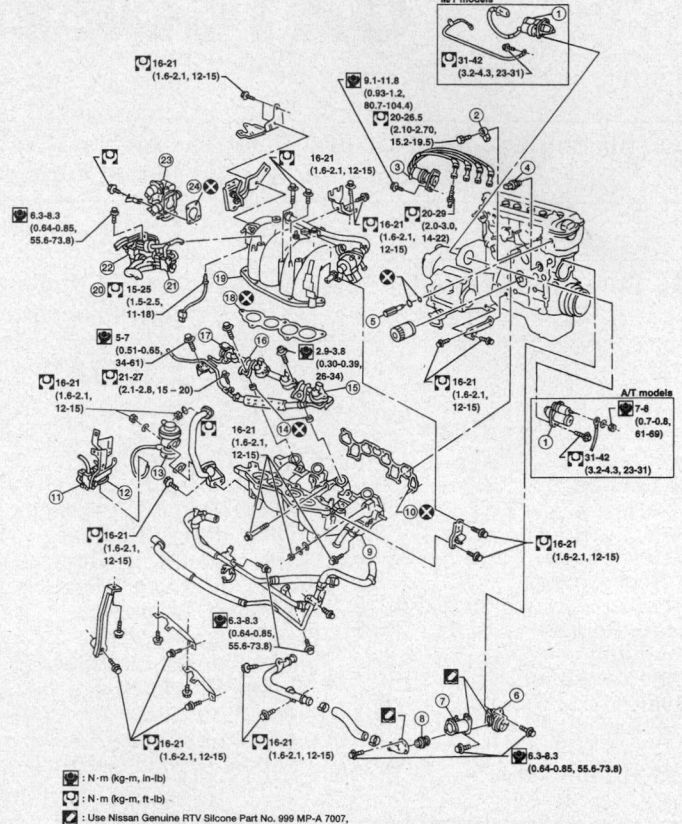

Fig. 3 Exploded view of intake manifold

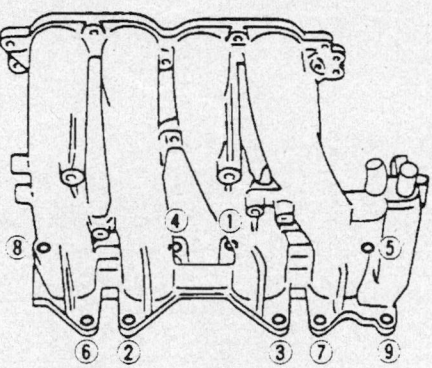

Tighten in numerical order.

Fig. 4 Intake manifold bolt tightening sequence

15. Remove center member, front exhaust tube and stabilizer bar, **Fig. 1.**
16. Remove radiator fan and radiator assembly.
17. Disconnect front mounting bracket.
18. Remove air duct, then disconnect or remove all engine mounts.
19. Carefully lower engine and transaxle assembly out of engine compartment.
20. Reverse procedure to install, adjusting buffer rod as shown in **Fig. 2.**

INTAKE MANIFOLD

REPLACE

For intake manifold replacement procedure, refer to **Figs. 3 through 5** and the cylinder head section of "Engine, Disassemble."

EXHAUST MANIFOLD

REPLACE

For exhaust manifold replacement procedure, refer to **Fig. 6** and the cylinder head section of the "Engine, Disassemble."

CYLINDER HEAD

REPLACE

Refer to "Timing Chain, Replace" for cylinder head replacement procedure.

ENGINE DISASSEMBLE

CYLINDER HEAD

Refer to **Fig. 7** when performing the following procedure.
1. Remove intake and exhaust manifolds from cylinder head.
2. Remove valve components using valve spring compression and attachment tool Nos. KV10116200 (J26339-A) and KV10115900 (J26336-20), or equivalents.
3. Remove valve oil seals using seal puller tool No. KV10107902 (J38959), or equivalent.

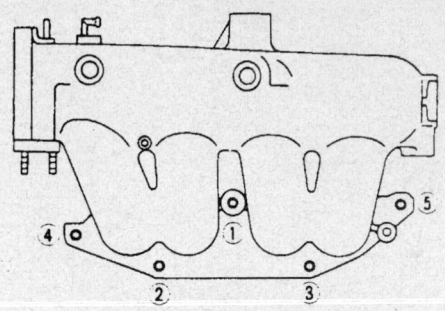

Tighten in numerical order.

NS1069200178000X

Fig. 5   Intake manifold cover bolt tightening sequence

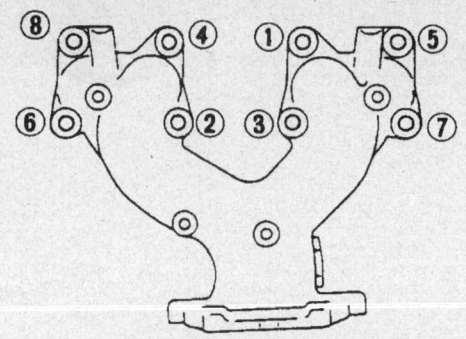

Tighten in numerical order.

NS1069200179000X

Fig. 6   Exhaust manifold bolt tightening sequence

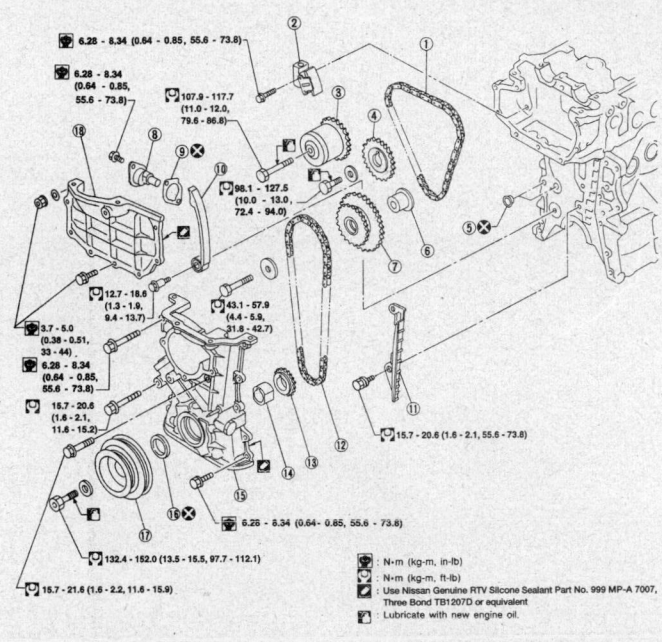

① Upper timing chain
② Upper timing chain tensioner
③ Camshaft sprocket (Intake)
④ Camshaft sprocket (Exhaust)
⑤ O-ring
⑥ Idler shaft
⑦ Idler sprocket
⑧ Lower chain tensioner
⑨ Gasket
⑩ Timing chain guide
⑪ Timing chain guide
⑫ Lower timing chain
⑬ Crankshaft sprocket
⑭ Oil pump drive spacer
⑮ Front cover
⑯ Oil seal
⑰ Crankshaft pulley
⑱ Cylinder head front cover

NS1069100005010X

Fig. 7   Exploded view of timing chain & cylinder head components (Part 1 of 2)

PISTON, ROD & CRANKSHAFT

Refer to **Fig. 8** when performing the following procedure.
1. Place engine on a suitable work stand.
2. Drain coolant and oil, then remove timing chain and cylinder head.
3. Remove oil pan and pump.
4. Remove piston, then the snap rings from the piston assembly.
5. Heat piston and rod assemblies to 140–158°F and push out piston pin. If heat method is not used, piston pins can be pressed out using a suitable press at room temperature.
6. Measure crankshaft endplay using a dial indicator. Endplay should be .0024–.0071 inch.

7. Using sequence shown in **Fig. 9**, remove main bearing caps by loosening bolts in two or three steps.
8. Remove crankshaft.

COMPONENT SERVICE
VALVE OIL SEAL

When removing valve oil seals, ensure piston under valve set being serviced is at TDC. This will prevent valves from falling into cylinder.
1. Remove rocker cover, camshaft, valve spring and valve oil seal.
2. Coat new oil seal with clean engine oil and install.

ENGINE ASSEMBLE
CYLINDER HEAD

Refer to **Fig. 7** when performing the following procedure.
1. Install valve oil seals using seal drift tool No. KV10115600 (J38958), or equivalent.
2. Install valve components using valve spring compression and attachment tool Nos. KV10116200 (J26339-A) and KV10115900 (J26336-20), or equivalents. When installing valve springs, ensure narrow pitch of spring is pointed toward cylinder head.
3. Install intake and exhaust manifolds to cylinder head. Refer to "Intake Manifold, Replace" and "Exhaust Manifold, Replace."

PISTON, ROD & CRANKSHAFT

When performing the following piston, rod and crankshaft repair procedures, refer to **Fig. 8**.
1. Install crankshaft main bearings and caps, then tighten bolts to specifications using sequence shown in **Fig. 10**.
2. If crankshaft endplay was not within specification, replace thrust bearing.
3. Install snap ring on one side of piston pin hole.
4. Heat piston to 140–158°F, then assemble piston, piston pin, connecting rod and new snap ring.
5. Install piston rings. **Figs. 11 and 12**.
6. Install connecting rod bearings with oil holes aligned, **Fig. 13**.
7. Install piston and rod assemblies into proper cylinder, then **torque** rod bolts to 10–12 ft. lbs. plus an additional 35–40° or 17–21 ft. lbs.
8. Piston skirt diameter (A) should be 2.9911–2.9915 inches standard piston and dimension (a) .390 inch, **Fig. 14**.
9. Connecting rod side clearance should be .0079–.0185 inch. If not, replace connecting rod or crankshaft.

VALVE CLEARANCE SPECIFICATIONS

Refer to "Valve Adjustment" for valve clearance specifications

VALVE ADJUSTMENT

1. Remove rocker cover and all spark plugs.
2. Set No. 1 cylinder at TDC on its compression stroke.
3. Align pointer with TDC mark on crankshaft pulley.
4. Valve lifters on No. 1 cylinder should be loose and valve lifters on No. 4 cylinder should be tight. If lifters are as specified, proceed to step 5. If lifters are not as specified, turn crankshaft 360° and realign pointer with TDC mark on crankshaft pulley, then proceed to step 5.
5. With engine at operating temperature,

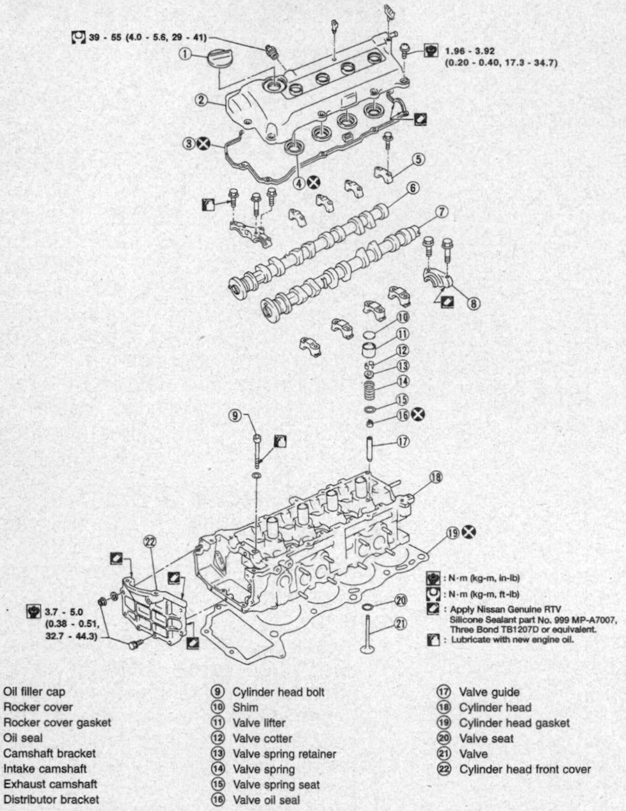

SEC. 110 • 120

Fig. 7 Exploded view of timing chain & cylinder head components (Part 2 of 2)

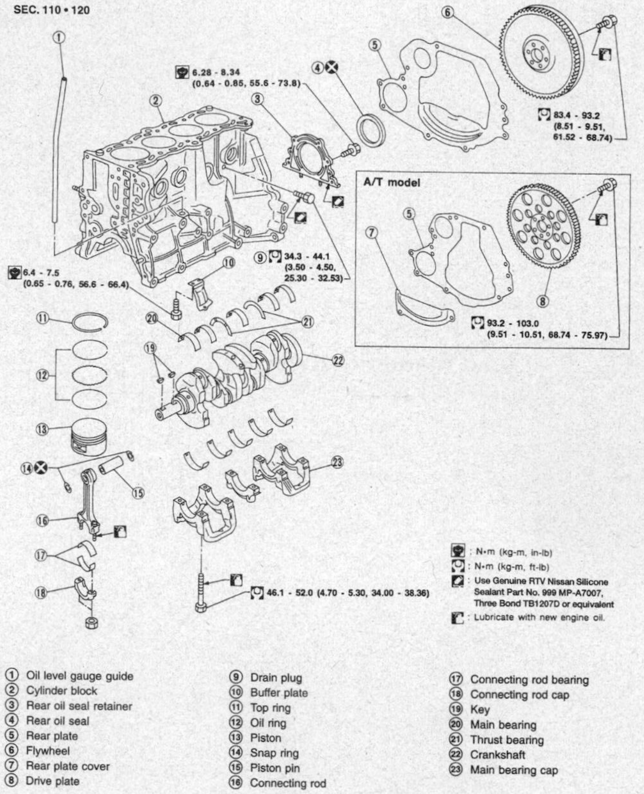

① Oil filler cap
② Rocker cover
③ Rocker cover gasket
④ Oil seal
⑤ Camshaft bracket
⑥ Intake camshaft
⑦ Exhaust camshaft
⑧ Distributor bracket
⑨ Cylinder head bolt
⑩ Shim
⑪ Valve lifter
⑫ Valve cotter
⑬ Valve spring retainer
⑭ Valve spring
⑮ Valve spring seat
⑯ Valve oil seal
⑰ Valve guide
⑱ Cylinder head
⑲ Cylinder head gasket
⑳ Valve seat
㉑ Valve
㉒ Cylinder head front cover

N∙m (kg-m, in-lb)
N∙m (kg-m, ft-lb)
Apply Nissan Genuine RTV Silicone Sealant part No. 999 MP-A7007, Three Bond TB1207D or equivalent.
Lubricate with new engine oil.

NS1069100005020X

Fig. 8 Exploded view of cylinder block

A/T model

① Oil level gauge guide
② Cylinder block
③ Rear oil seal retainer
④ Rear oil seal
⑤ Rear plate
⑥ Flywheel
⑦ Rear plate cover
⑧ Drive plate
⑨ Drain plug
⑩ Buffer plate
⑪ Top ring
⑫ Oil ring
⑬ Piston
⑭ Snap ring
⑮ Piston pin
⑯ Connecting rod
⑰ Connecting rod bearing
⑱ Connecting rod cap
⑲ Key
⑳ Main bearing
㉑ Thrust bearing
㉒ Crankshaft
㉓ Main bearing cap

N∙m (kg-m, in-lb)
N∙m (kg-m, ft-lb)
Use Genuine RTV Nissan Silicone Sealant No. 999 MP-A7007, Three Bond TB1207D or equivalent.
Lubricate with new engine oil.

NS1069100003000X

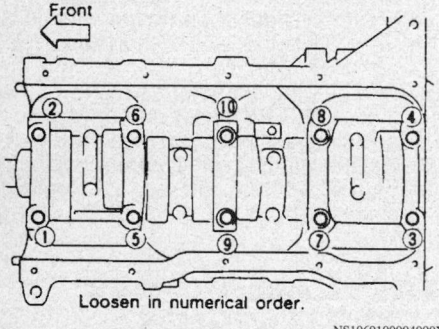

Loosen in numerical order.

NS1069100004000X

Fig. 9 Crankshaft bearing cap bolt removal sequence

use a feeler gauge to measure clearance between valve lifter and camshaft as follows:

a. Check clearance on No. 1 and No. 2 intake valves. Clearance should be .008–.019 inch.
b. Check clearance on No. 1 and No. 3 exhaust valves. Clearance should be .012–.023 inch.
c. Turn crankshaft 360° and align pointer with TDC mark on crankshaft pulley.
d. Check clearance on No. 3 and No. 4 intake valves. Clearance should be .008–.019 inch.
e. Check clearance on No. 2 and No. 4 exhaust valves. Clearance should be .012–.023 inch.

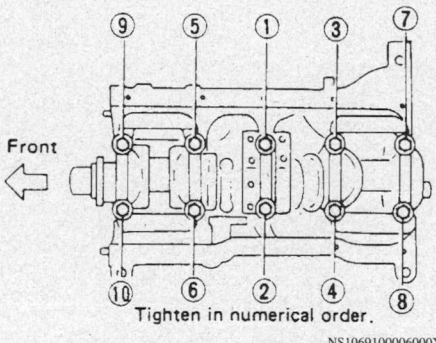

Front

Tighten in numerical order.

NS1069100006000X

Fig. 10 Main bearing cap bolt tightening sequence

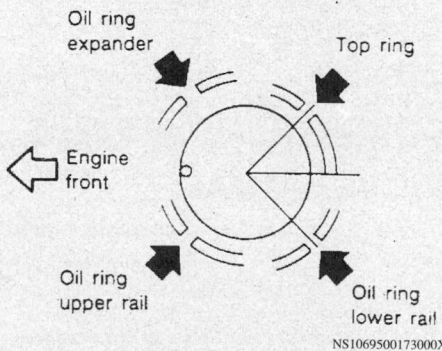

Oil ring expander
Top ring
Engine front
Oil ring upper rail
Oil ring lower rail

NS1069500173000X

Fig. 12 Piston ring alignment

6. Adjust valves while engine is cold using cam turning tool (A) No.

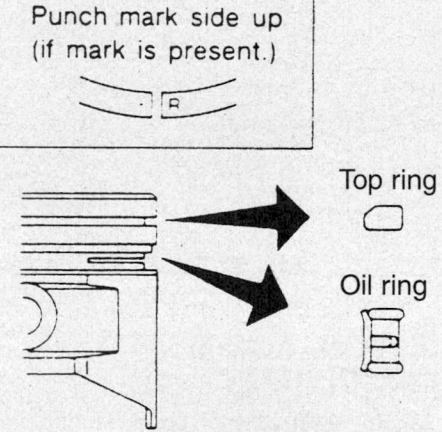

Top and second ring Punch mark side up (if mark is present.)

R

Top ring

Oil ring

NS1069500172000X

Fig. 11 Piston ring punch mark identification

KV10115110 and valve lifter holding tool (B) No. KV10115120, or equivalents, **Fig. 15.**
7. Turn crankshaft to position cam lobe on camshaft of valve to be adjusted upward.
8. Install tool (A) around camshaft, **Fig. 16.**
9. Rotate tool (A) so that lifter is pushed down.
10. Place tool (B) between camshaft and

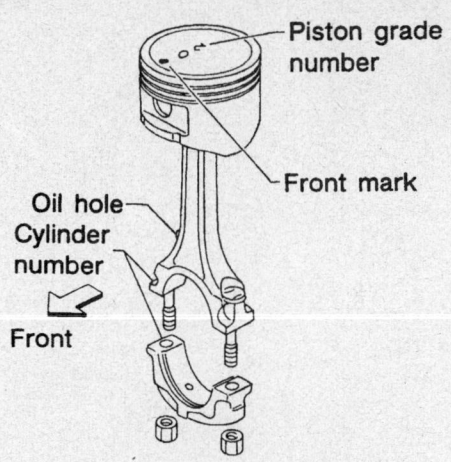

Fig. 13   Connecting rod oil hole alignment

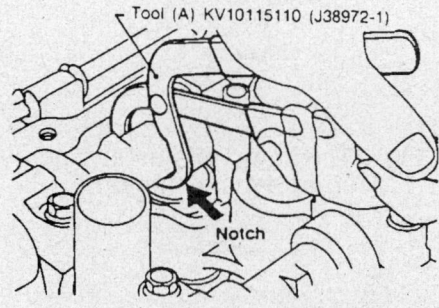

Fig. 16   Cam tool (A) installation

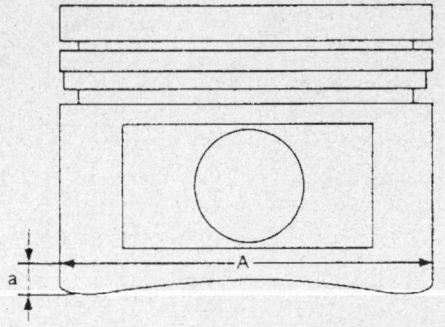

Fig. 14   Piston dimensions

Valve clearance specifications

Unit: mm (in)

	For adjusting		For checking
	Hot	Cold*	Hot
Intake	0.32 - 0.40 (0.013 - 0.016)	0.25 - 0.33 (0.010 - 0.013)	0.21 - 0.49 (0.008 - 0.019)
Exhaust	0.37 - 0.45 (0.015 - 0.018)	0.32 - 0.40 (0.013 - 0.016)	0.30 - 0.58 (0.012 - 0.023)

*: At a temperature of approximately 20°C (68°F)
Whenever valve clearances are adjusted to cold specifications, check that the clearances satisfy hot specifications and adjust again if necessary.

Fig. 17   Valve clearance specifications

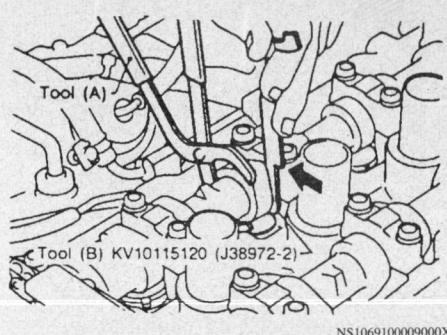

Fig. 15   Valve adjusting tools

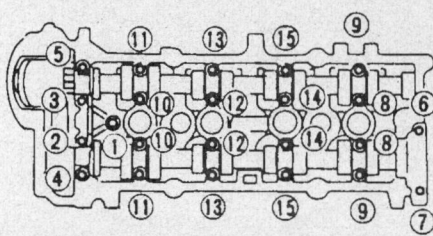

Loosen in numerical order.

Fig. 18   Camshaft bracket bolt removal sequence

edge of valve filter to retain lifter.
11. Remove tool (A).
12. Remove adjusting shim using a screwdriver and a magnet.
13. Determine replacement adjusting shim size for intake valves using the following formula:
   a. Use a micrometer to determine thickness of removed shim.
   b. Calculate thickness of new shim so valve clearance becomes .010–.013 inch by subtracting .0146 inch from measured valve clearance (M). Then add value of thickness of removed shim (R) to give thickness of new shim (N). N = R + (M − .0146 inch).
14. Determine replacement adjusting shim size for exhaust valves using the following formula:
   a. Use a micrometer to determine thickness of removed shim.
   b. Calculate thickness of new shim so valve clearance becomes .013–.016 inch by subtracting .0157 inch from measured valve clearance (M). Then add value of thickness of removed shim (R) to give thickness of new shim (N). N = R + (M − .0157 inch).
15. Select new shim with thickness as close as possible to calculated value.
16. Install selected shim and check valve clearance, **Fig. 17.**

FRONT COVER SEAL
REPLACE
1. Remove front cover as outlined under "Timing Chain, Replace."
2. Remove front oil seal from front cover.
3. Apply clean engine oil to new front oil seal.
4. Install oil seal into front cover.
5. Install front cover as outlined under "Timing Chain, Replace."

TIMING CHAIN
REPLACE
After removing timing chain, do not turn crankshaft and camshaft separately, or damage to the valves may occur.
Refer to **Fig. 7** when servicing the timing chain.

REMOVAL
1. Drain coolant from radiator and block.
2. Release fuel system pressure as outlined under "Precautions."
3. Remove power steering pump, alternator and A/C drive belts.
4. Remove power steering pump bracket.
5. Remove air duct to intake manifold collector.
6. Remove wheels and splash shields.
7. Remove engine undercover, then the front exhaust pipe.
8. Support engine with a suitable jack or lifting device, then remove engine mount bracket.
9. Remove valve cover, distributor cap, ignition wires and spark plugs.
10. Remove intake manifold support.
11. Set No. 1 piston at TDC on its compression stroke.
12. Remove distributor assembly.

13. Remove camshaft sprocket cover and gusset.
14. Remove water pump pulley, then the thermostat housing.
15. Remove timing chain tensioners and chain guide.
16. Loosen idler sprocket bolt.
17. Remove camshaft sprocket bolts, then the sprockets.
18. Using sequence shown in **Fig. 18,** loosen camshaft bracket bolts in two or three steps.
19. Remove camshaft brackets, distributor bracket and camshafts. **Note position of these parts prior to removal. Parts should be reassembled in their original positions.**
20. Remove idler sprocket bolt.
21. Using sequence shown in **Fig. 19,** remove cylinder head bolts in two or three steps.
22. Remove cylinder head and gasket with manifolds attached.
23. Remove idler sprocket shaft from rear side of engine.
24. Remove upper timing chain, then raise and support vehicle.
25. Remove center member, then the oil pan as outlined under "Oil Pan, Replace."
26. Remove oil strainer, then the crankshaft pulley.
27. Support engine using a suitable jack or lifting device, then remove engine front mounting bracket.
28. Remove front cover bolts and front cover.
29. Remove idler sprocket, lower timing chain, oil pump drive spacer, chain guide and crankshaft sprocket.

INSTALLATION
1. Confirm No. 1 cylinder is at TDC on its

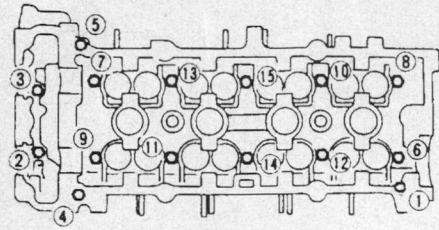

Fig. 19 Cylinder head bolt removal sequence

Loosen in numerical order.

NS1069100013000X

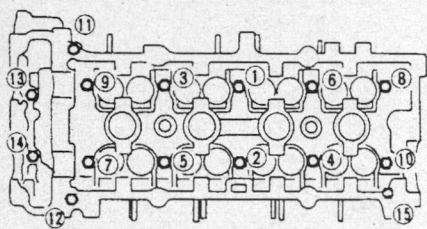

Fig. 22 Cylinder head bolt tightening sequence

Tighten in numerical order.

NS1069100016000X

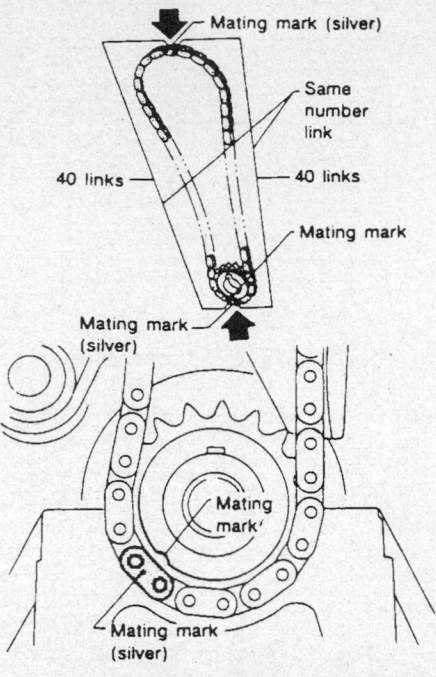

Fig. 20 Lower timing chain installation

NS1069100014000X

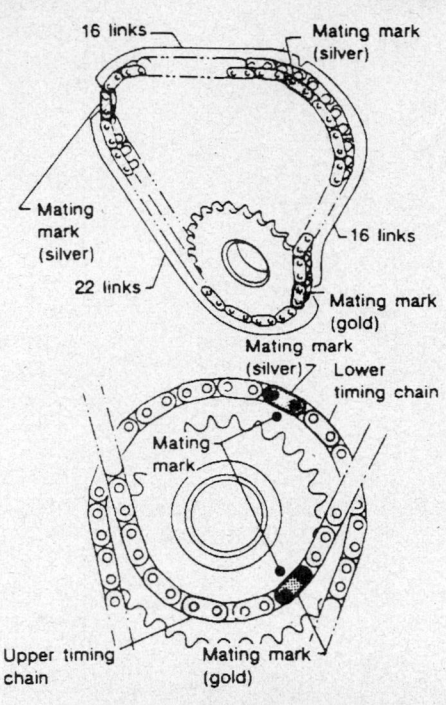

Fig. 21 Timing chains on idler sprocket installation

NS1069100015000X

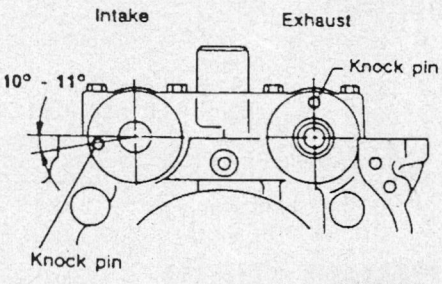

Fig. 23 Camshaft installation

NS1069100017000X

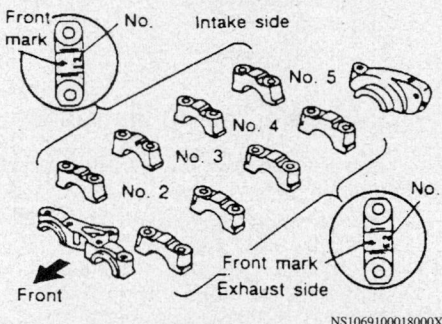

Fig. 24 Camshaft bracket installation

NS1069100018000X

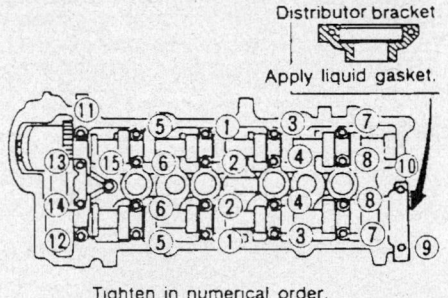

Fig. 25 Camshaft bracket bolt tightening sequence

Tighten in numerical order.

NS1069100019000X

compression stroke.
2. Install chain guide and crankshaft sprocket.
3. Install lower timing chain as shown in **Fig. 20.**
4. Apply liquid gasket to front cover.
5. Check alignment of mating marks on chain and crankshaft sprocket.
6. Align oil drive spacer with oil pump.
7. Ensure two O-rings are present in rear of front cover.
8. Put chain to side of chain guide so chain does not make contact with water seal area of front cover. **Be careful not to damage oil seal when installing front cover.**
9. Install engine front mounting bracket.
10. Install oil strainer and pan assembly as outlined under "Oil Pan, Replace."
11. Install crankshaft pulley.
12. Install center member, then lower vehicle.
13. Install idler sprocket by aligning mating mark on larger sprocket with silver mating mark on lower timing chain, **Fig. 21.**
14. Install upper timing chain by aligning mating mark on smaller sprocket with silver mating mark on upper timing chain. **Ensure sprocket's mating mark faces front of engine.**
15. Install idler sprocket shaft from rear side of engine.
16. Install cylinder head with new gasket. **Ensure head bolt washers are installed with beveled edge pointed away from head. Do not rotate crankshaft and camshaft separately, or valves will strike piston heads.**
17. Using sequence shown in **Fig. 22,** tighten cylinder head bolts 1 through 10 as follows:
   a. **Torque** bolts to 22 ft. lbs.
   b. **Torque** bolts to 43 ft. lbs.

c. Loosen bolts completely.
d. **Torque** bolts to 22 ft. lbs.
e. Tighten bolts an additional 50–55.°
18. Using sequence shown in **Fig. 22,** torque cylinder head bolts 11 through 15 to 4.6–6.1 ft. lbs.
19. Install idler sprocket bolt.
20. Install and align camshafts shown in **Fig. 23.** Intake and exhaust identifica-

tion marks are present in center of camshaft.
21. Install and align camshaft and distributor brackets as shown in **Fig. 24.**
22. Apply liquid gasket to distributor bracket, then tighten bolts in two or three steps as shown in **Fig. 25.**
23. If any part of valve assembly or camshaft has been replaced, check and adjust valve clearance as outlined under "Valve Adjustment."
24. Assemble camshaft sprocket with chain and align mating marks as shown in **Fig. 26.**
25. Install camshaft sprocket bolts.
26. Install upper chain tensioner and chain guide. **Ensure hook used to retain chain tensioner is released.**
27. Install lower chain tensioner, then rotate engine and ensure no problems occur.
28. Ensure No. 1 piston is set at TDC on its compression stroke.

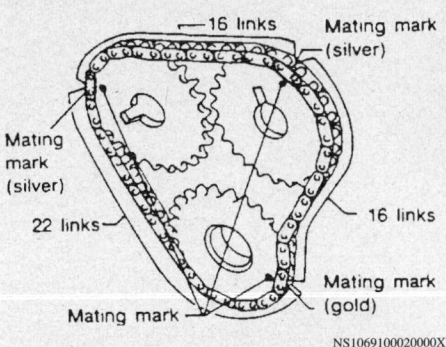

Fig. 26 Upper timing chain installation

NS1069100020000X

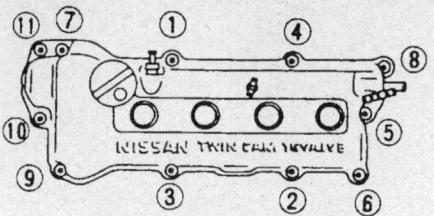

Tighten in numerical order.

NS1069100021000X

Fig. 27 Valve cover bolt tightening sequence

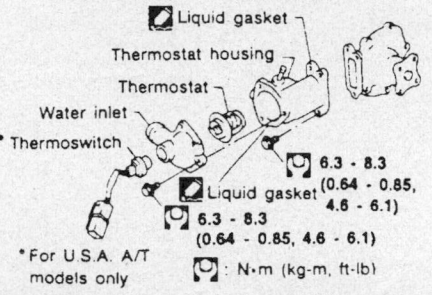

* For U.S.A. A/T models only

NS1089100001000X

Fig. 30 Thermostat replacement

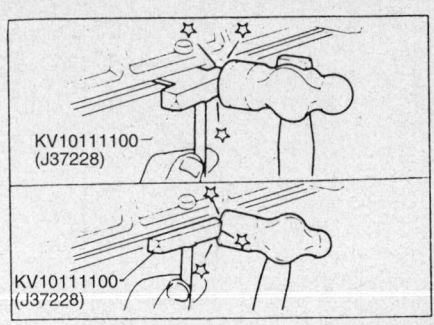

KV10111100 (J37228)

KV10111100 (J37228)

NS1069100022000X

Fig. 28 Oil pan removal

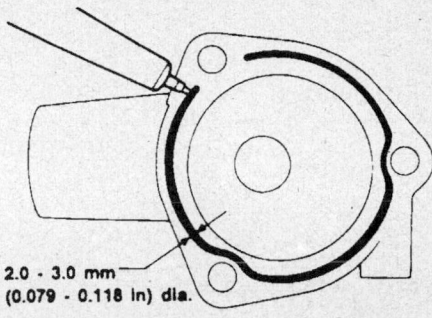

2.0 - 3.0 mm (0.079 - 0.118 in) dia.

NS1089100002000X

Fig. 31 Thermostat housing sealant application

	Used belt deflection		Deflection of new belt
	Limit	Deflection after adjustment	
Generator			
With air conditioner compressor	11.5 - 12.5 (0.453 - 0.492)	7 - 8 (0.28 - 0.31)	6.5 - 7.5 (0.256 - 0.295)
Without air conditioner compressor	12 - 13 (0.47 - 0.51)	8 - 9 (0.31 - 0.35)	7 - 8 (0.28 - 0.31)
Power steering pump	6 - 7 (0.24 - 0.28)	4 - 5 (0.16 - 0.20)	3.5 - 4.5 (0.138 - 0.177)
Applied pushing force	98 N (10 kg, 22 lb)		

Unit: mm (in)

NS1069100023000X

Fig. 29 Drive belt deflection specifications

29. Apply liquid gasket to thermostat housing, then install thermostat housing.
30. Install water pump pulley.
31. Install distributor and ensure distributor rotor is pointing toward No. 1 cylinder spark position.
32. Apply liquid gasket to cam sprocket cover gusset and cam sprocket cover.
33. Install cam sprocket gusset and cam sprocket cover.
34. Apply liquid gasket to valve cover and cylinder head mating surfaces.
35. Install valve cover, then tighten valve cover retaining bolts using sequence shown in **Fig. 27**.
36. Install spark plugs, then raise and support vehicle.
37. Install front exhaust pipe, engine undercover, splash shields and wheels.
38. Lower vehicle, then install air cleaner and power steering pump bracket.
39. Install alternator, power steering pump and A/C compressor drive belts.

CRANKSHAFT REAR OIL SEAL

REPLACE

1. Remove flywheel or driveplate, then the rear oil seal retainer.
2. Remove rear oil seal from retainer.
3. Clean mating surfaces, coat new oil seal with clean engine oil and install into retainer.
4. Apply liquid gasket to retainer and install.

OIL PAN

REPLACE

1. Raise and support vehicle, then remove engine undercovers.
2. Drain oil, then remove center member and front exhaust tube.
3. Using pan removal tool No. KV10111100, or equivalent, and a hammer, carefully remove oil pan as shown in **Fig. 28**.
4. Clean any remaining liquid gasket from oil pan and cylinder block mating surfaces.
5. Apply a continuous bead of liquid gasket to pan mating surface, then install oil pan within five minutes of gasket application.
6. Install front exhaust tube, center member, and engine undercovers, then lower vehicle.
7. Allow liquid gasket to set at least 30 minutes before refilling engine oil.

BELT TENSION DATA

Refer to **Fig. 29** for belt deflection specifications.

COOLING SYSTEM BLEED

Refer to "Cooling System Bleed" in "SR20DE Engine" section.

THERMOSTAT

REPLACE

1. Disconnect thermoswitch electrical connector, then remove thermoswitch from water inlet, **Fig. 30**.
2. Remove water inlet to thermostat housing attaching bolts.

3. Remove thermostat from thermostat housing.
4. Reverse procedure to install. Apply a suitable liquid gasket to water inlet as shown in **Fig. 31**.

WATER PUMP

REPLACE

1. Drain cooling system.
2. Remove drive belts from compressor, power steering and alternator.
3. Remove water pump pulley, then the water pump, **Fig. 32**.
4. Clean any traces of liquid gasket from water pump and cylinder block mating surfaces.
5. Reverse procedure to install. Apply liquid gasket to mating surface of pump housing.

RADIATOR

REPLACE

1. When performing radiator replacement, refer to **Fig. 33**.
2. Refer to "Cooling System Bleed" in "SR20DE Engine" section.

FUEL PUMP

REPLACE

1. Remove rear seat assembly.
2. Remove fuel pump inspection cover.
3. Disconnect fuel outlet, return tube and electrical connectors.
4. Remove fuel pump screws.
5. Remove fuel gauge assembly and disconnect tubes and connectors, **Fig. 34**.

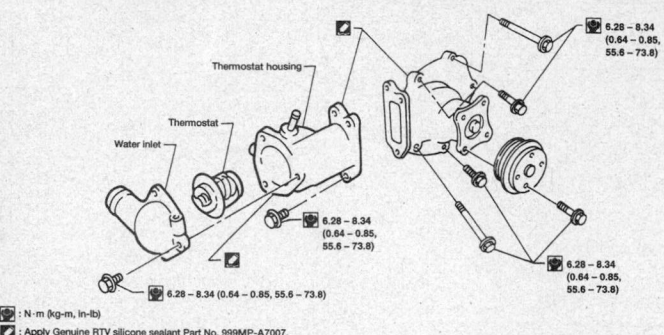

: N·m (kg-m, in-lb)

: Apply Genuine RTV silicone sealant Part No. 999MP-A7007, Three Bond TB1207D or equivalent.

NS1089100003000X

Fig. 32 Water pump replacement

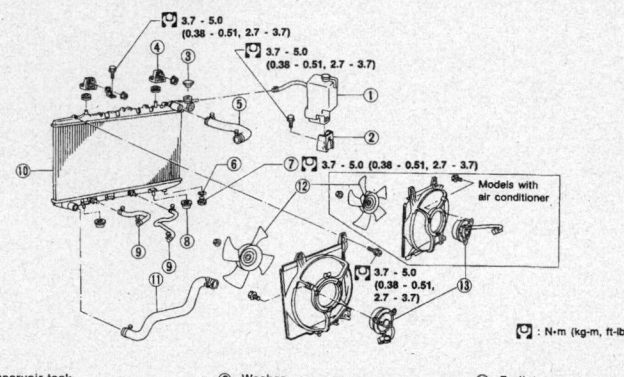

① Reservoir tank	⑥ Washer	⑩ Radiator
② Reservoir tank bracket	⑦ Drain plug	⑪ Lower hose
③ Radiator cap	⑧ Mounting rubber	⑫ Fan
④ Mounting bracket	⑨ Oil cooler hose (A/T models)	⑬ Fan motor
⑤ Upper hose		

: N·m (kg-m, ft-lb)

NS1089500075000X

Fig. 33 Radiator replacement

6. Remove fuel pump assembly.
7. Reverse procedure to install.

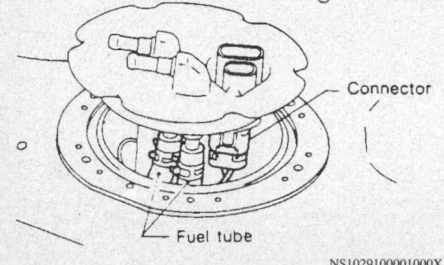

NS1029100001000X

Fig. 34 Fuel pump removal

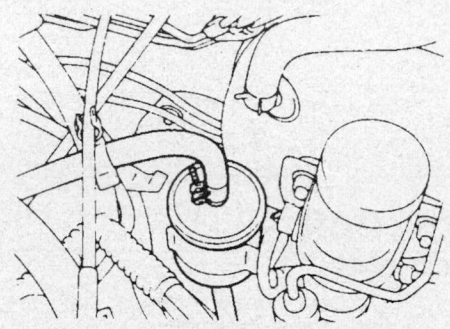

NS1029100002000X

Fig. 35 Fuel filter replacement

Description	Part No.	Quantity
Chain Tensioner Guide	13085-0M300	1
Bolt	08120-8161E or 08120-81628	2

Fig. 36 Timing chain tensioner chart

FUEL FILTER

REPLACE

1. Relieve fuel system pressure as outlined under "Precautions."
2. Loosen fuel filter hose clamps, **Fig. 35.**
3. Remove fuel filter. **Be careful not to spill fuel over engine compartment.**
4. Reverse procedure to install.

TECHNICAL SERVICE BULLETINS

TIMING CHAIN TENSIONER GUIDE BROKEN

Some vehicles may exhibit engine noise from the timing chain area. This condition may be caused by a broken timing chain tensioner guide.

The chain tensioner guide has been improved with a steel backing. Due to the improvement made to the chain tensioner guide, new style bolts are also required. Refer to **Fig. 36.**

TIGHTENING SPECIFICATIONS

Year	Component	Torque, Ft. Lbs.
1996–99	Air Regulator	12–15
	Alternator Adjusting Bracket	12–15
	Alternator Mounting Bracket	29–33
	BPT Valve Nut	36–48②
	Buffer Mounting Bolt	33–40
	Camshaft Brackets	84–108②
	Camshaft Sprocket (Exhaust)	72–94
	Cam Sprocket Cover Bolt	36–48②
	Cam Sprocket Cover Gusset	48②
	Cam Sprocket Cover Nut	36–48②
	Center Member	33–40
	Compressor Bracket	27–37
	Connecting Rod Caps	①
	Crank Angle Sensor/Distributor	84–108②
	Crankshaft Pulley	98–112
	Cylinder Head	①
	Distributor Bracket	84–108②
	Driveplate To Crankshaft Bolt	69–76
	EGR & Canister Control Solenoid Valve	36–48②
	EGR Control Valve Securing Nut	12–15
	Engine Front Mounting	33–40
	Engine Front Mounting Bracket	33–40
	Engine Rear Mounting Bracket	33–40
	Engine Temperature Sensor	14–22
	Exhaust Gas Sensor	30–37
	Exhaust Manifold To Exhaust Pipe Nuts	21–25
	Exhaust Manifold	12–15
	Flywheel To Crankshaft Bolts	61–69
	Fuel Gallery Assembly	12–15
	Fuel Pressure Regulator	24–36②
	Gusset	12–15
	Idle Air Adjusting Unit	60–72②
	Idler Sprocket	32–43
	Ignition Coil	60–72②
	Intake Manifold Collector	12–15
	Intake Manifold Mounting Nut	12–15
	Lower Timing Chain Guide	9–14
	Main Bearing Cap	34–38
	Oil Pan	60–72②
	Oil Pan Drain Plug	22–29
	Oil Pressure Switch	23–31
	Rear Mounting	33–40
	Rear Oil Seal Retainer	60–72②
	Rocker Cover Securing Bolt	24–36②
	Roll Damper Bolt	33–40
	Starter Motor Mounting Bolt	23–31
	Thermostat Housing Securing Bolt	60–72②
	Throttle Chamber	13–16
	Timing Chain Tensioner	60–72②
	Upper Timing Chain Guide	84–108②
	VTC Camshaft Sprocket (Intake)	72–94
	Water Inlet	60–72②
	Water Outlet Bolt	60–72②

① — Refer to "Timing Chain, Replace."
② — Inch lbs.

SR20DE Engine

NOTE: On Air Bag Equipped Models, Refer To "Air Bag System Precautions" Located In The Front Of This Manual For System Disarming & Arming Procedures.

NOTE: Refer To "Computer Relearn Procedures" Located In The Front Of This Manual For Computer Relearn Procedures.

INDEX

PRECAUTIONS

AIR BAG SYSTEMS

Refer to "Air Bag System Precautions" in the front of this manual for system disarming and arming procedures.

BATTERY GROUND CABLE

Prior to service, disconnect battery ground cable and isolate as required.

FUEL SYSTEM PRESSURE RELEASE

1. Remove fuel pump fuse from fuse panel.
2. Start engine.
3. After engine stalls, crank engine two or three times to ensure pressure is released.
4. Turn ignition switch to off position.
5. After fuel system operations are complete, replace fuel pump fuse.

COMPRESSION PRESSURE

1. Start engine and run until engine reaches operating temperature.
2. Turn ignition switch off.
3. Release fuel pressure. Refer to "Precautions" for fuel system pressure release procedure.
4. Remove all spark plugs.
5. Disconnect distributor coil connector.
6. Attach a compression tester to cylinder No. 1.

7. Depress accelerator pedal fully to keep throttle valve wide open.
8. Crank engine and record highest gauge indication.
9. Repeat measurement on each cylinder.
10. Standard compression is 178 psi, minimum pressure is 149 psi and compression difference limit between cylinders is 14 psi.
11. If compression in one or more cylinders is low, pour a small amount of engine oil into cylinders through spark plug holes, then retest compression.
12. If adding oil helps compression, then piston rings may be at fault. If adding oil does not help compression, then valves may be at fault.
13. If compression stays low in two cylinders that are next to each other, then cylinder head gasket may be leaking or both cylinders may have valve component damage.
14. Repair as necessary.

ENGINE MOUNT
REPLACE

Refer to **Fig. 1** when replacing the engine mounts.

ENGINE
REPLACE

Refer to **Figs. 1 and 2** when removing the engine.
1. Place vehicle on level ground and block wheels.

2. Release fuel system pressure as outlined under "Precautions."
3. Remove engine undercover.
4. Mark hood for installation reference, then remove hood.
5. Drain cooling system and engine oil.
6. Disconnect fuel and vacuum hoses, wire harness and connectors as necessary. **Label hoses and connectors for installation reference.**
7. Remove front exhaust tube, ball joints and driveshafts.
8. Remove radiator fan and radiator assembly.
9. Remove drive belts.
10. Remove alternator, compressor and power steering pump from engine. Position component out of the way without disconnecting hoses.
11. Support engine with a suitable lifting device or jack, then remove center member.
12. Carefully lower engine and transaxle out of engine compartment.
13. Reverse procedure to install, noting the following:
    a. Install engine mount insulators as shown in **Fig. 3**.
    b. **On models equipped with manual transaxle**, adjust height of engine mounting as shown in **Fig. 4**.

INTAKE MANIFOLD
REPLACE

Refer to "Cylinder Head" under "Engine

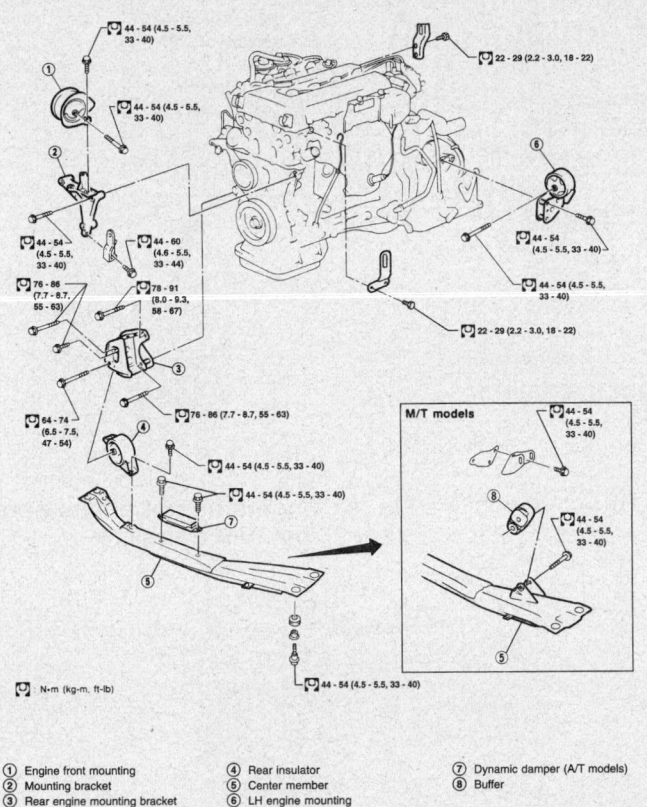

Fig. 1 Engine mount replacement

① Engine front mounting
② Mounting bracket
③ Rear engine mounting bracket
④ Rear insulator
⑤ Center member
⑥ LH engine mounting
⑦ Dynamic damper (A/T models)
⑧ Buffer

NS1069100024000X

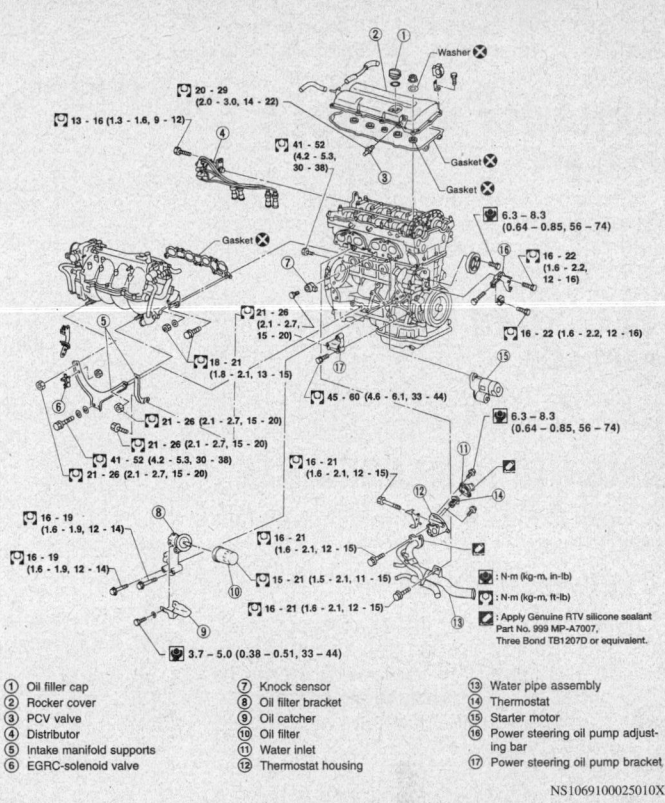

Fig. 2 Exploded view of engine outer components (Part 1 of 3)

① Oil filler cap
② Rocker cover
③ PCV valve
④ Distributor
⑤ Intake manifold supports
⑥ EGRC-solenoid valve
⑦ Knock sensor
⑧ Oil filter bracket
⑨ Oil catcher
⑩ Oil filter
⑪ Water inlet
⑫ Thermostat housing
⑬ Water pipe assembly
⑭ Thermostat
⑮ Starter motor
⑯ Power steering oil pump adjusting bar
⑰ Power steering oil pump bracket

NS1069100025010X

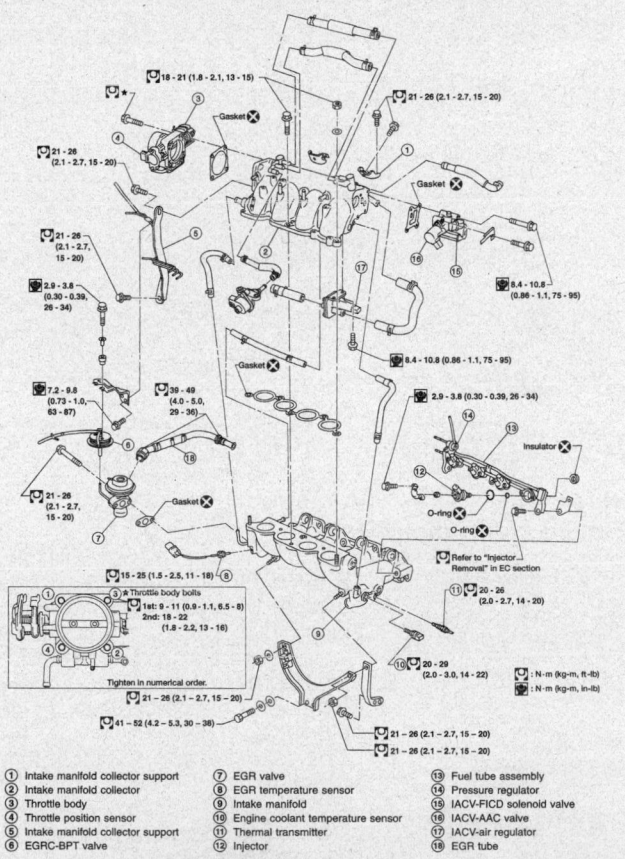

Fig. 2 Exploded view of engine outer components (Part 2 of 3)

① Intake manifold collector support
② Intake manifold collector
③ Throttle body
④ Throttle position sensor
⑤ Intake manifold collector support
⑥ EGRC-BPT valve
⑦ EGR valve
⑧ EGR temperature sensor
⑨ Intake manifold
⑩ Engine coolant temperature sensor
⑪ Thermal transmitter
⑫ Injector
⑬ Fuel tube assembly
⑭ Pressure regulator
⑮ IACV-FICD solenoid valve
⑯ IACV-AAC valve
⑰ IACV-air regulator
⑱ EGR tube

NS1069100025020X

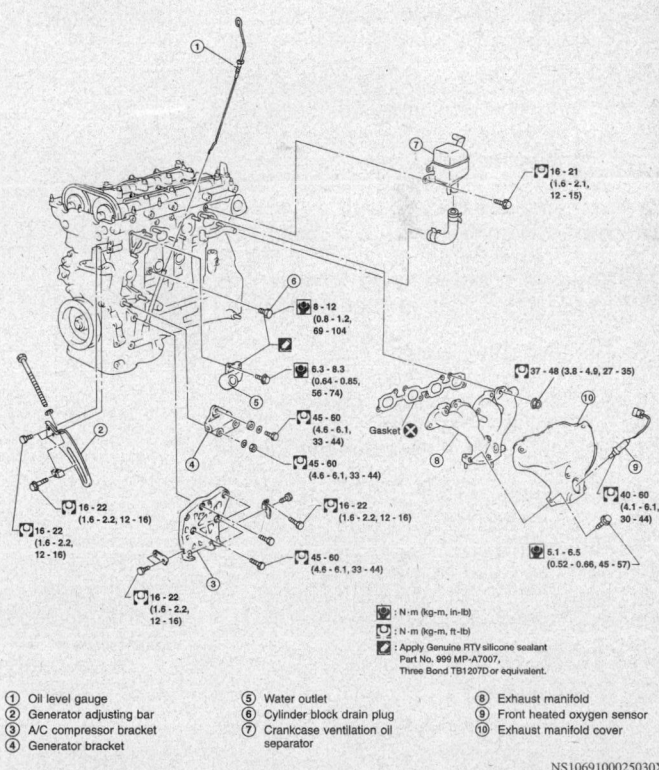

Fig. 2 Exploded view of engine outer components (Part 3 of 3)

① Oil level gauge
② Generator adjusting bar
③ A/C compressor bracket
④ Generator bracket
⑤ Water outlet
⑥ Cylinder block drain plug
⑦ Crankcase ventilation oil separator
⑧ Exhaust manifold
⑨ Front heated oxygen sensor
⑩ Exhaust manifold cover

NS1069100025030X

Disassemble" to remove the intake manifold and "Engine Assemble" to install the intake manifold.

EXHAUST MANIFOLD
REPLACE

Refer to "Cylinder Head" under "Engine Disassemble" to remove the exhaust manifold and "Engine Assemble" to install the exhaust manifold.

CYLINDER HEAD
REPLACE

Refer to "Timing Chain, Replace" for cylinder head replacement procedure.

ENGINE DISASSEMBLE

Refer to **Figs. 5 and 6** when disassembling engine.

CYLINDER HEAD

1. Remove rocker cover, rocker arms, shim rocker arm guides and hydraulic lash adjusters. **Keep components in order in which they were removed.**
2. Remove throttle chamber with throttle drum unit.
3. Remove EGR tube.
4. Remove exhaust manifold cover, then the exhaust manifold. Remove bolts in sequence shown in **Fig. 7.**
5. Remove fuel tube assembly as follows:
   a. Release fuel system pressure as outlined under "Precautions."
   b. Disconnect injector harness connectors.
   c. Disconnect vacuum hose from pressure regulator.
   d. Disconnect fuel hoses from fuel tube assembly.
   e. Remove injectors with fuel tube assembly.
6. Remove intake manifold bolts and manifold in sequence shown in **Fig. 8.**
7. Remove intake manifold collector from intake manifold in sequence shown in **Fig. 9.**
8. Remove water outlet.
9. Remove water connector.
10. Remove thermostat housing with water pipe.
11. Remove valve components using valve spring compression and attachment tool Nos. KV10116200 (J26339-A) and KV10115900 (J26336-20), or equivalents.
12. Remove valve oil seals using seal puller tool No. KV10107902 (J38959), or equivalent.

PISTON, ROD & CRANKSHAFT

1. Remove engine as outlined under "Engine, Replace."
2. Remove cylinder head and timing chain as outlined under "Timing Chain, Replace."
3. Remove oil pan as outlined under "Oil Pan, Replace."

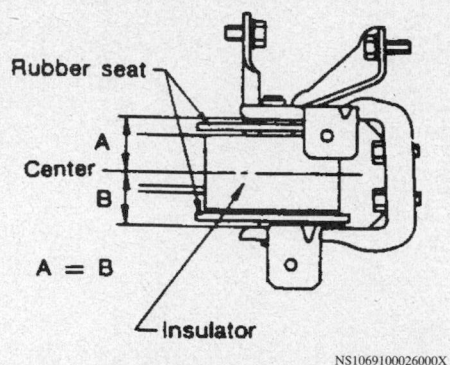

Fig. 3 Engine mount insulators installation

NS1069100026000X

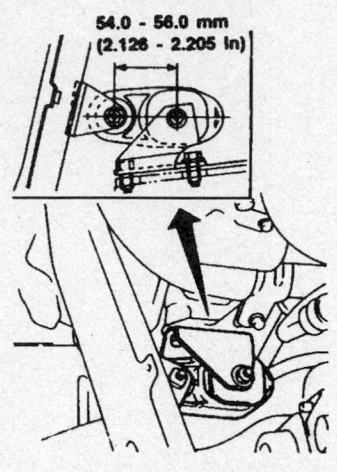

NS1069100027000X

Fig. 4 Engine height adjustment. manual transaxle

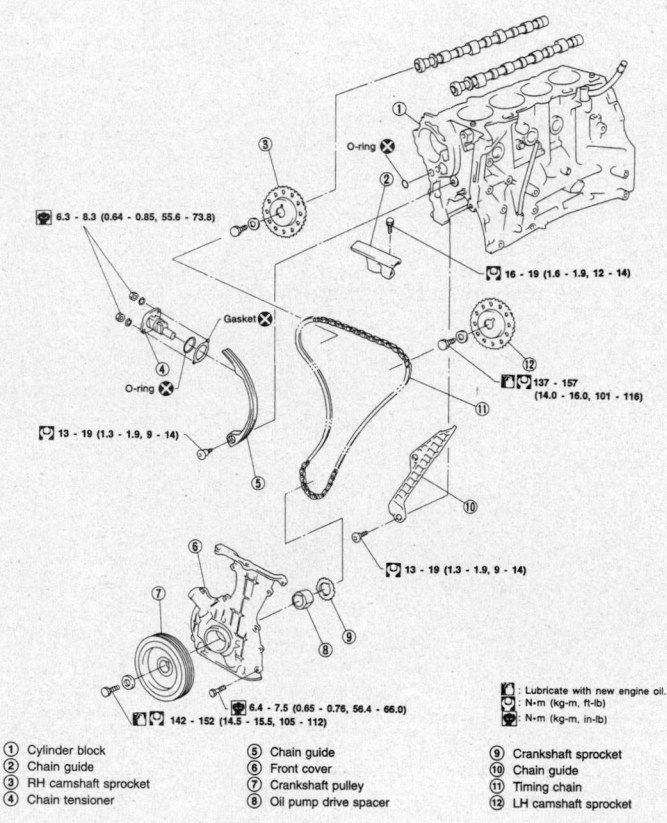

NS1069100028010X

Fig. 5 Timing chain replacement (Part 1 of 2)

① Cylinder block
② Chain guide
③ RH camshaft sprocket
④ Chain tensioner
⑤ Chain guide
⑥ Front cover
⑦ Crankshaft pulley
⑧ Oil pump drive spacer
⑨ Crankshaft sprocket
⑩ Chain guide
⑪ Timing chain
⑫ LH camshaft sprocket

4. Remove pistons with connecting rods attached.
5. Remove rear oil seal retainer.
6. Using sequence shown in **Fig. 10**, remove bearing beam bolts in two or three steps.

COMPONENT SERVICE
VALVE OIL SEAL, REPLACE

1. Remove accelerator cable.
2. Remove valve cover and oil separator.

3. Remove camshafts and sprockets as outlined under "Timing Chain, Replace."
4. Remove spark plugs and cables.
5. Install air hose adapter into spark plug hole and apply pressure of 71 psi to hold valves in place.
6. Remove rocker arm, rocker arm guide and shim.
7. Remove valve spring using suitable valve spring compression tool.
8. Remove valve oil seal.

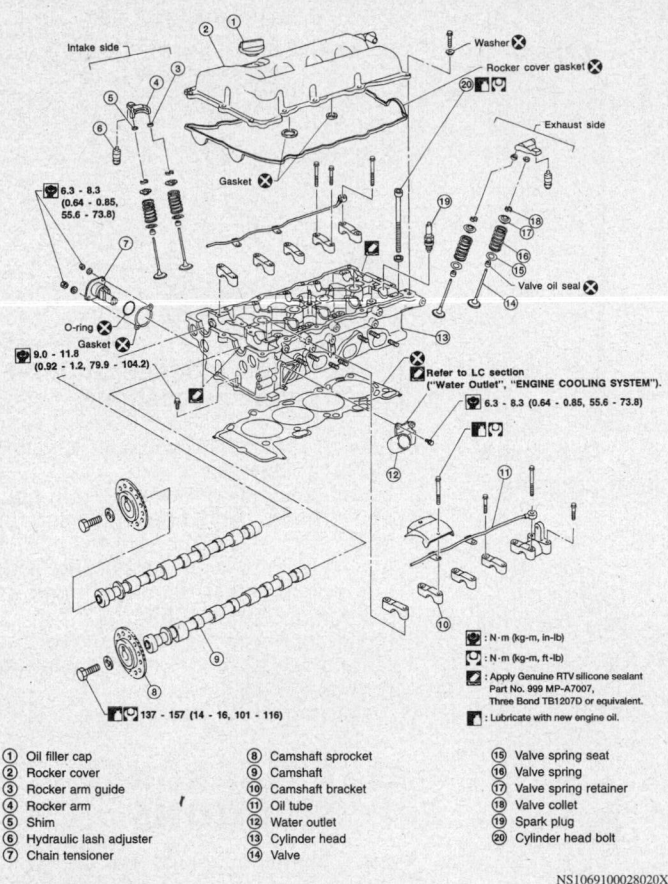

Fig. 5 Timing chain replacement (Part 2 of 2)

① Oil filler cap
② Rocker cover
③ Rocker arm guide
④ Rocker arm
⑤ Shim
⑥ Hydraulic lash adjuster
⑦ Chain tensioner
⑧ Camshaft sprocket
⑨ Camshaft
⑩ Camshaft bracket
⑪ Oil tube
⑫ Water outlet
⑬ Cylinder head
⑭ Valve
⑮ Valve spring seat
⑯ Valve spring
⑰ Valve spring retainer
⑱ Valve collet
⑲ Spark plug
⑳ Cylinder head bolt

NS1069100028020X

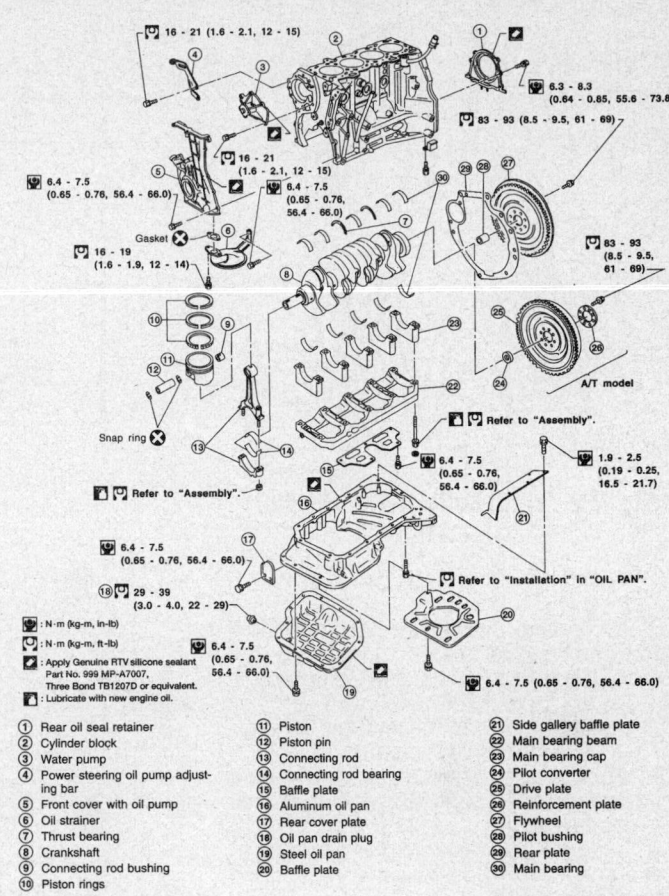

Fig. 6 Exploded view of cylinder block

① Rear oil seal retainer
② Cylinder block
③ Water pump
④ Power steering oil pump adjusting bar
⑤ Front cover with oil pump
⑥ Oil strainer
⑦ Thrust bearing
⑧ Crankshaft
⑨ Connecting rod bushing
⑩ Piston rings
⑪ Piston
⑫ Piston pin
⑬ Connecting rod
⑭ Connecting rod bearing
⑮ Baffle plate
⑯ Aluminum oil pan
⑰ Rear cover plate
⑱ Oil pan drain plug
⑲ Steel oil pan
⑳ Baffle plate
㉑ Side gallery baffle plate
㉒ Main bearing beam
㉓ Main bearing cap
㉔ Pilot converter
㉕ Drive plate
㉖ Reinforcement plate
㉗ Flywheel
㉘ Pilot bushing
㉙ Rear plate
㉚ Main bearing

NS1069100029000X

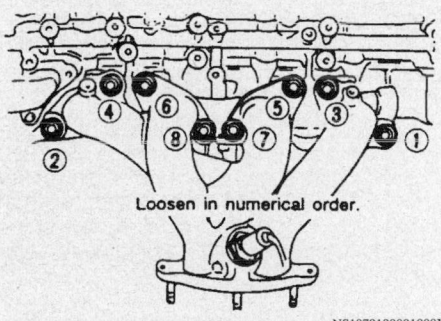

Fig. 7 Exhaust manifold bolt removal sequence

NS1079100001000X

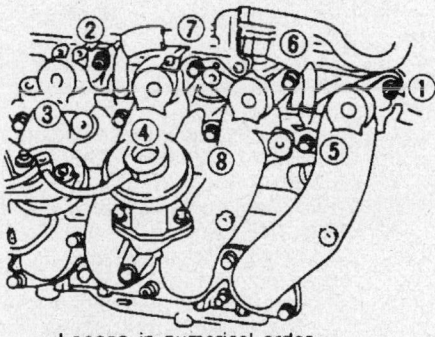

Fig. 8 Intake manifold bolt removal sequence

NS1059100001000X

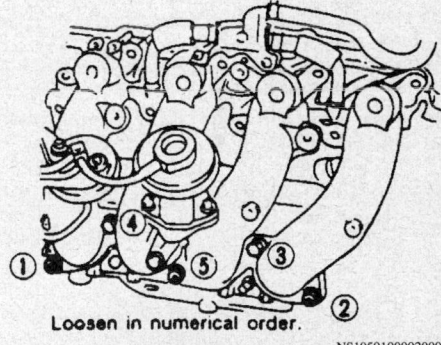

Fig. 9 Intake manifold collector bolt removal sequence

NS1059100002000X

9. Reverse procedure to install. Apply engine oil to new seal before installation.

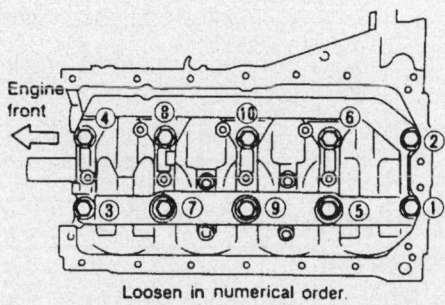

Fig. 10 Crankshaft bearing beam bolt removal sequence

NS1069100030000X

ENGINE ASSEMBLE
CYLINDER HEAD

1. Apply a bead of liquid gasket to water connector mating surface.
2. Using bolt tightening sequence shown in **Fig. 11**, install thermostat housing with water pipe as follows:
   a. **Torque** thermostat housing bolt A to 1.4–3.6 ft. lbs.

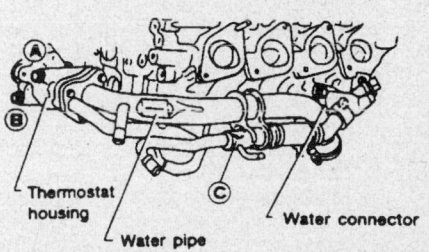

Fig. 11 Thermostat housing & water pipe bolt tightening sequence

NS1069100031000X

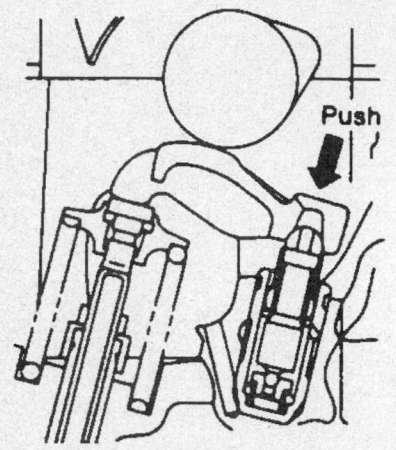

NS1069100032000X

Fig. 12 Hydraulic lash adjuster inspection

b. **Torque** water pipe bolt C to 12–15 ft. lbs.
c. **Torque** thermostat housing bolt A to 12–15 ft. lbs.
d. **Torque** thermostat housing bolt B to 12–15 ft. lbs.
e. Repeat steps "b" through "d" after installing cylinder head.
3. Apply a bead of liquid gasket to mating surface of water outlet, then install water outlet.
4. Install intake manifold collector bolts to intake manifold in reverse sequence shown in **Fig. 9.**
5. Install intake manifold bolts in reverse sequence shown in **Fig. 8.**
6. Install injector tube assembly in reverse order of removal.
7. Install exhaust manifold bolts in reverse sequence shown in **Fig. 7.**
8. Install exhaust manifold cover.
9. Install EGR tube.
10. Install throttle chamber with throttle drum unit. Adjust throttle drum unit.
11. Install valve oil seals using seal drift tool No. KV10115600 (J38958), or equivalent.
12. Install valve components in order of removal (except shim), using valve spring compression and attachment tool Nos. KV10116200 (J26339-A) and KV10115900 (J26336-20), or equivalents. When installing valve springs, ensure narrow pitch of spring is pointed toward cylinder head.
13. When replacing valve, cylinder head, shim, rocker arm guide and/or valve seat, select a new valve adjustment shim as follows:
    a. Install dial gauge stand tool No. KV10115700, or equivalent, and a suitable dial indicator onto cylinder head.
    b. Measure distance between sliding surface of rocker arm guide and valve stem end. **When measuring, pull lightly on dial gauge stand tool to eliminate any play in tool.**
    c. Shims are available in 17 different thicknesses ranging from .1102 inch to .1260 inch. Select a suitable shim to obtain a zero clearance ±

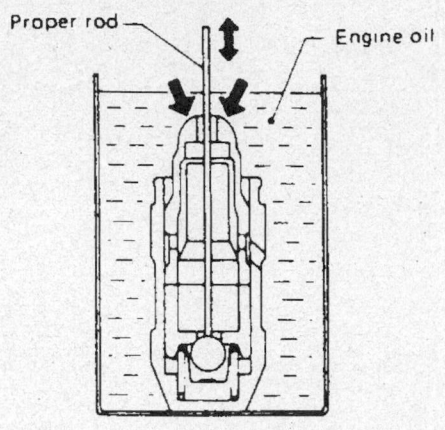

NS1069100033000X

Fig. 13 Hydraulic lash adjuster bleed

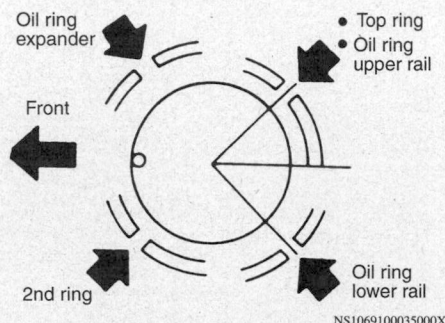

NS1069100035000X

Fig. 15 Piston rings installation

.0010 inch between valve shim and rocker arm guide.
14. Check hydraulic lash as follows:
    a. Push on rocker arm assembly, **Fig. 12.**
    b. If rocker arm can be moved .04 inch, air is trapped in high pressure chamber.
    c. Remove hydraulic lash adjuster and dip in a container of clean engine oil.
    d. While pushing plunger, lightly push check ball using a thin rod. Air is completely bled when plunger no longer moves, **Fig. 13.**
15. Install hydraulic lash adjusters, rocker arm guides, rocker arms, shims and rocker cover.

PISTON, ROD & CRANKSHAFT

1. Install piston on rod as shown in **Fig. 14.**
2. Install piston rings on piston as shown in **Fig. 15.**
3. Install main bearing in proper position on cylinder block and main bearing caps.
4. Install crankshaft, main bearing caps and beam.
5. Using reverse sequence shown in **Fig. 10,** tighten bolts as follows:
    a. **Torque** bolts to 20–24 ft. lbs.
    b. Tighten all bolts 75–80° clockwise.
    c. Loosen all bolts completely.
    d. **Torque** bolts to 24–28 ft. lbs.
    e. Tighten all bolts 45–50° clockwise.

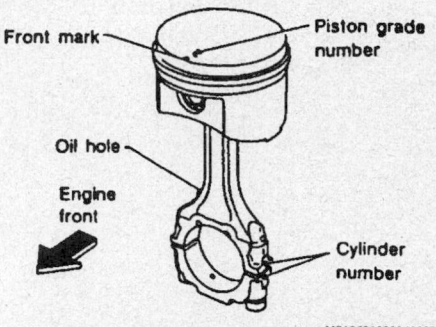

NS1069100034000X

Fig. 14 Piston & connecting rod front mark location

6. Ensure crankshaft endplay is within .0039–.0102 inch.
7. Install connecting rod bearing in connection rods and caps, aligning oil hole.
8. Install pistons with connecting rods into cylinder block with front mark toward front of engine, **Fig. 14.**
9. Install connecting rod caps and **torque** nuts to 10–12 ft. lbs., then tighten all nuts 60–65° clockwise.
10. Install rear oil seal retainer.

VALVE CLEARANCE SPECIFICATIONS

Valve clearance should be -.0010 to .0010 inch. Hydraulic lash adjuster guide inner diameter should be .6693–.6701 inch. Standard clearance between hydraulic lash adjuster and adjuster guides is .0003–.0016 inch.

VALVE ADJUSTMENT

This engine uses hydraulic lash adjusters to maintain a valve clearance of -.0010 to .0010 inch. If clearance between rocker arm guide and valve shim is greater than .0010 inch, select and install a new shim. Refer to "Cylinder Head" in "Engine Assemble" for procedure.

FRONT COVER SEAL
REPLACE

1. Remove engine undercover.
2. Remove righthand wheel and engine side cover.
3. Remove drive belts, then the crankshaft pulley.
4. Remove front oil seal.
5. Reverse procedure to install. Apply engine oil to seal prior to installation.

TIMING CHAIN
REPLACE

Refer to **Fig. 5** when replacing timing chain.

REMOVAL

1. Release fuel system pressure as outlined under "Precautions."
2. Remove engine undercover.

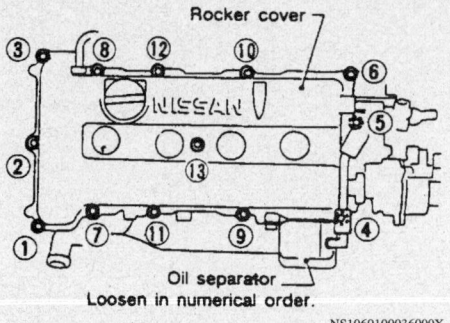

Fig. 16   Valve cover bolt removal sequence

NS1069100036000X

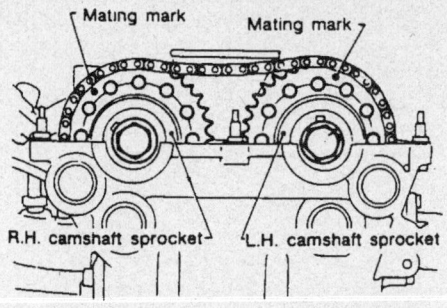

Fig. 17   Camshaft timing mark alignment

NS1069100037000X

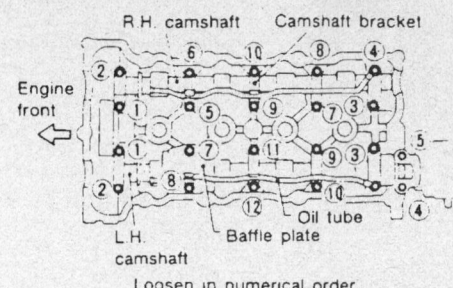

Fig. 18   Camshaft bracket bolt removal sequence

NS1069100038000X

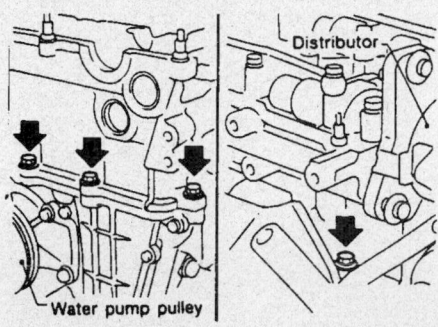

Fig. 19   Cylinder head outer bolts removal

NS1069100039000X

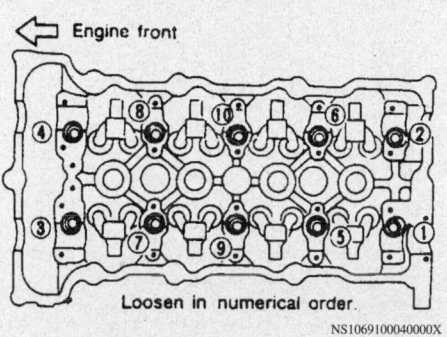

Fig. 20   Cylinder head bolt removal sequence

NS1069100040000X

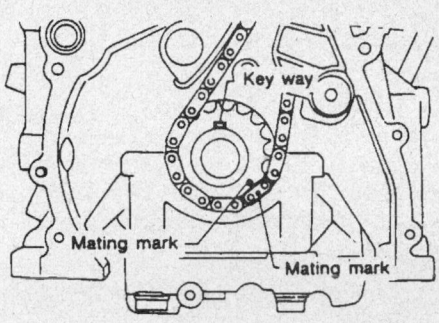

Fig. 21   Crankshaft timing mark alignment

NS1069100041000X

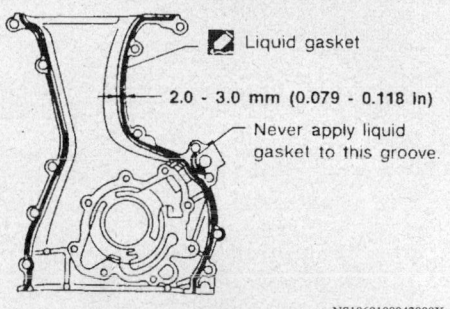

Fig. 22   Front cover liquid gasket application

NS1069100042000X

3. Remove righthand wheel and engine side cover.
4. Drain engine coolant and oil.
5. Remove radiator and shroud assembly.
6. Remove air duct to intake manifold.
7. Remove drive belts.
8. Remove water pump pulley, alternator and power steering pump.
9. Remove necessary vacuum, fuel and electrical connections. **Label hoses and connectors for installation reference.**
10. Remove spark plugs and cables.
11. Remove valve cover and oil separator, **Fig. 16.**
12. Remove intake manifold supports.
13. Remove oil filter and power steering pump brackets.
14. Set No. 1 cylinder at TDC on its compression stroke, then rotate crankshaft until mating marks on camshaft sprockets are aligned as shown in **Fig. 17.**
15. Remove chain tensioner.
16. Remove distributor, then the timing chain guide.
17. Remove camshaft sprockets.
18. Using sequence shown in **Fig. 18,** remove camshaft brackets.
19. Remove camshafts, oil tube and baffle plate.
20. Remove water hose for cylinder block and hose from heater.
21. Remove starter motor, then the water pipe bolt.
22. Disconnect knock sensor harness connector.
23. Remove EGR tube.

24. Remove cylinder head outside bolts, **Fig. 19.**
25. Using sequence shown in **Fig. 20,** remove cylinder head bolts in two or three steps.
26. Remove cylinder head with manifolds attached.
27. Remove oil pan as outlined under "Oil Pan, Replace."
28. Remove oil pan strainer and baffle plate.
29. Remove crankshaft pulley.
30. Set a suitable transmission jack under main bearing beam.
31. Remove righthand engine mounting.
32. Remove front cover and oil pump drive spacer.
33. Remove timing chain guides and timing chain.

INSTALLATION

1. Install crankshaft sprocket on crankshaft.
2. Position crankshaft so that No. 1 cylinder is at TDC.

3. Align gold mating mark on timing chain to crankshaft sprocket, then install timing chain on crankshaft sprocket, **Fig. 21.**
4. Install timing chain guides.
5. Before installing front cover, remove all traces of gasket material on all mounting surfaces.
6. Apply a bead of liquid gasket to mounting surface of front cover, **Fig. 22.**
7. Install oil pump drive spacer and front cover. **Ensure mating marks on timing chain and crankshaft sprocket align.**
8. Remove excess liquid gasket.
9. Install front engine mounting bracket.
10. Install crankshaft pulley and set No. 1 cylinder at TDC on its compression stroke.
11. Install oil strainer and oil pan baffle plate.
12. Install oil pan as outlined under "Oil Pan, Replace."
13. Remove all traces of gasket material from mating surfaces of cylinder head and cylinder block.
14. Prior to installing cylinder head bolts, ensure dimension "A" shown in **Fig. 23** is less than 6.23 inches.
15. Install cylinder head bolts, then using sequence shown in **Fig. 24,** tighten as follows:
    a. **Torque** bolts to 29 ft. lbs.
    b. **Torque** bolts to 58 ft. lbs.
    c. Loosen bolts completely.
    d. **Torque** bolts to 25–33 ft. lbs.
    e. Turn bolts 90–100° clockwise.
    f. Turn bolts an additional 90–95° clockwise.
16. Install cylinder head outside bolts, **Fig. 19.**

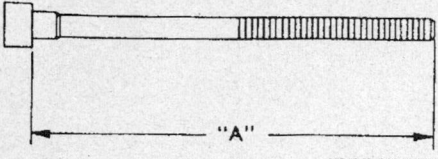

Fig. 23 Cylinder head bolt measurement

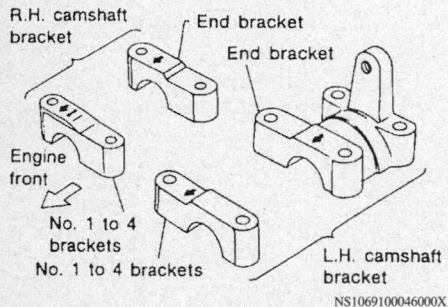

Fig. 26 Camshaft bracket installation direction

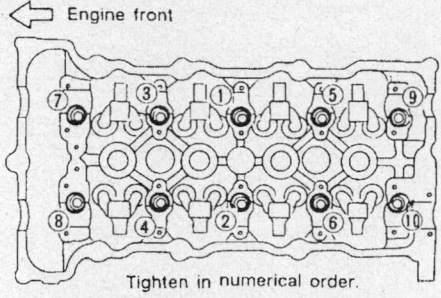

Tighten in numerical order.

Fig. 24 Cylinder head bolt tightening sequence

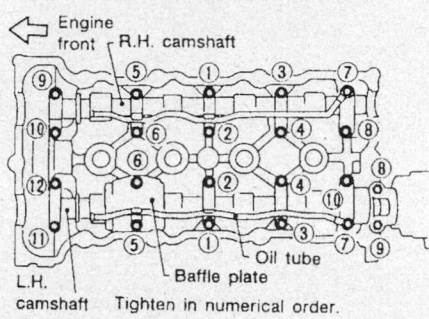

Tighten in numerical order.

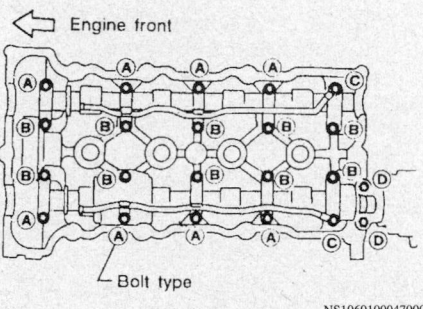

Fig. 27 Camshaft bracket bolt tightening sequence

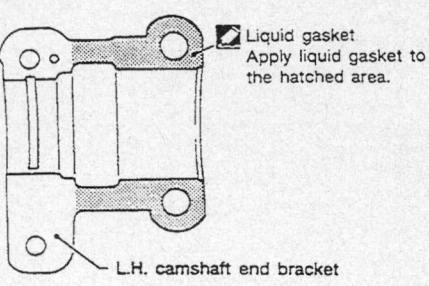

Liquid gasket
Apply liquid gasket to the hatched area.

L.H. camshaft end bracket

Fig. 25 Lefthand camshaft end bracket liquid gasket application

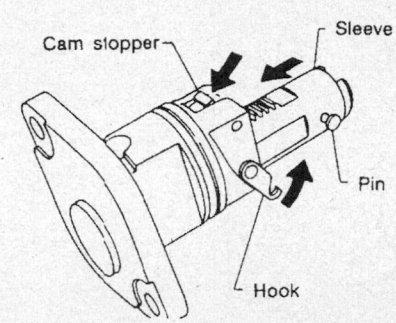

Fig. 28 Chain tensioner installation

17. Install EGR tube.
18. Connect knock sensor harness connector.
19. Install water pipe bolt.
20. Install starter motor.
21. Install water hoses.
22. Remove all traces of gasket material from lefthand camshaft end bracket and apply a bead of liquid gasket to area shown in **Fig. 25.**
23. Install camshafts by positioning lefthand camshaft keyway at about the 12 o'clock position and righthand camshaft keyway at about the 10 o'clock position. Install oil tube and baffle plate.
24. Install camshaft brackets as shown in, **Fig. 26.**
25. Using sequence shown in **Fig. 27,** tighten bolts as follows:
   a. **On righthand camshaft, torque** bolts 9 and 10 to 1.4 ft. lbs., then bolts 1 through 8 to 1.4 ft. lbs.
   b. **On lefthand camshaft, torque** bolts 11 and 12 to 1.4 ft. lbs., then bolts 1 through 10 to 1.4 ft. lbs.
   c. **On both camshafts, torque** bolts described in steps "a" or "b" to 4.3 ft. lbs.
   d. **Torque** bolts marked A, B and C to 8.7 ft. lbs.
   e. **Torque** bolts marked D to 13–19 ft. lbs.
26. Align silver mating mark on timing chain with marks on camshaft sprockets, then install camshaft sprockets.
27. Lock camshaft using a suitable wrench on flats of camshaft and **torque** camshaft bolts in two steps to 101–116 ft. lbs.
28. Install timing chain guide.
29. Install distributor. **Ensure after installing distributor, distributor rotor is positioned at No. 1 cylinder spark position.**
30. Press cam stopper down and press in

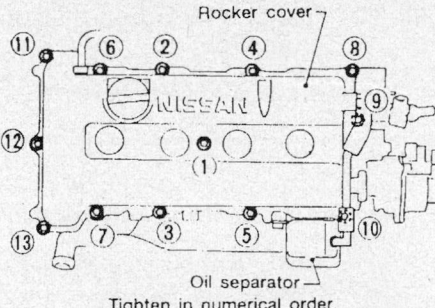

Tighten in numerical order.

Fig. 29 Valve cover bolt tightening sequence

sleeve until hook of chain tensioner can be engaged on pin, **Fig. 28.** Ensure arrow marked A faces front of engine.
31. Install filter and power steering pump bracket.
32. Install intake manifold supports.
33. Install valve cover, then using se-

quence shown in **Fig. 29,** tighten nuts as follows:
   a. **Torque** nuts 1, 10, 11 and 8 to 2.9 ft. lbs.
   b. **Torque** nuts 1 through 13 to 7.2 ft. lbs.
34. Reverse remaining removal steps.

CRANKSHAFT REAR OIL SEAL
REPLACE

1. **On models equipped with manual transaxle,** remove transaxle assembly as outlined under "Transaxle, Replace" in "Clutch & Manual Transmission."
2. **On models equipped with automatic transaxles,** remove transaxle assembly as outlined in "Automatic Transmissions/Transaxles."
3. **On all models,** remove flywheel or driveplate.
4. Remove rear oil seal.

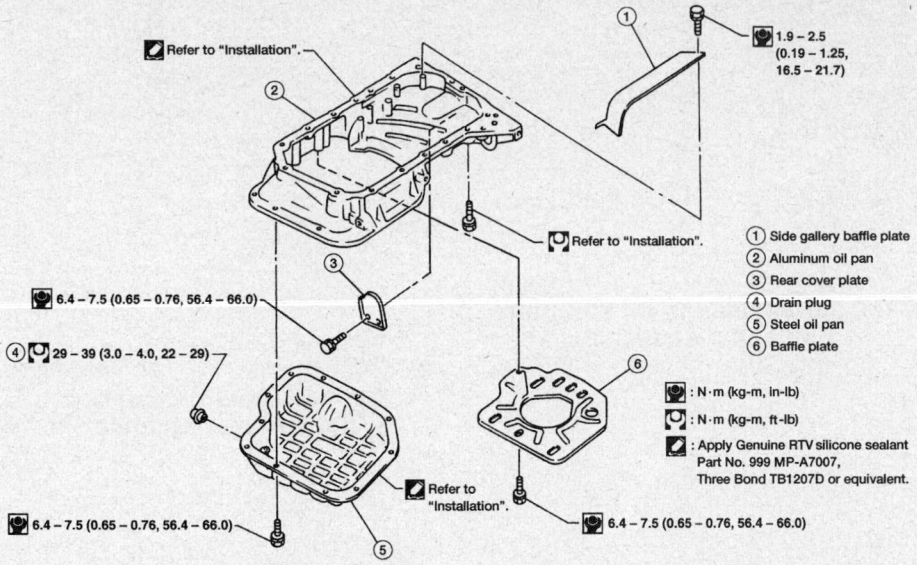

① Side gallery baffle plate
② Aluminum oil pan
③ Rear cover plate
④ Drain plug
⑤ Steel oil pan
⑥ Baffle plate

🔧 : N·m (kg-m, in-lb)
🔧 : N·m (kg-m, ft-lb)
🔧 : Apply Genuine RTV silicone sealant Part No. 999 MP-A7007, Three Bond TB1207D or equivalent.

NS1099100001000X

Fig. 30   Exploded view of oil pan

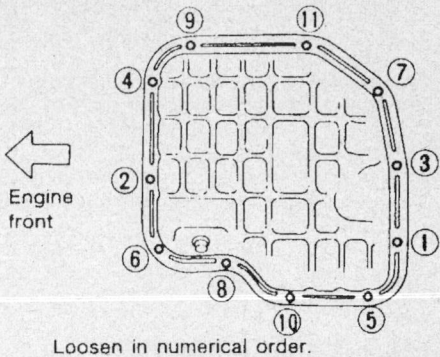

Loosen in numerical order.

NS1099100002000X

Fig. 31   Steel oil pan bolt removal sequence

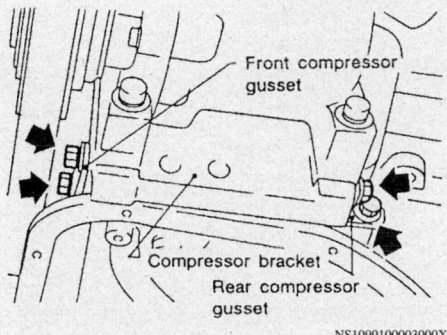

NS1099100003000X

Fig. 32   Compressor gussets replacement

5. Reverse procedure to install. Apply engine oil to new seal before installation.

OIL PAN

REPLACE

Refer to **Fig. 30** when replacing oil pan assembly.

REMOVAL

1. Remove engine undercover.
2. Drain engine oil into a suitable container.
3. Using sequence shown in **Fig. 31**, remove steel oil pan bolts.
4. Insert oil pan remover tool No. KV10111100, or equivalent, between steel oil pan and aluminum oil pan, then using a hammer, remove steel oil pan. **Use care not to damage aluminum oil pan when inserting oil pan remover tool.**
5. Remove oil baffle plate.
6. Remove front exhaust tube.
7. Support engine with a suitable lifting device or jack, then remove center member.
8. **On models equipped with automatic transaxles,** remove shift control cable.

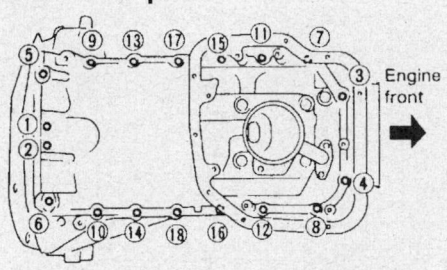

Loosen in numerical order.

NS1099100004000X

Fig. 33   Aluminum oil pan bolt removal sequence

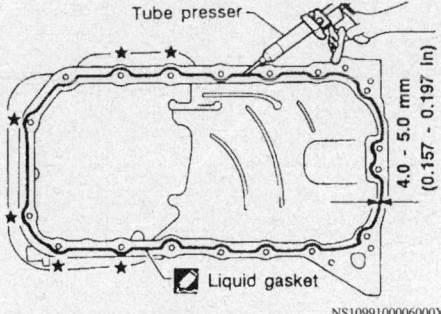

NS1099100006000X

Fig. 35   Oil pan liquid gasket application

9. **On all models,** remove compressor gussets, **Fig. 32.**
10. Remove oil pan rear cover plate.
11. Using sequence shown in **Fig. 33**, remove aluminum oil pan bolts.
12. Remove two engine to transaxle bolts and install them into vacant holes, **Fig. 34.**
13. Tighten bolts to release aluminum oil pan from cylinder block.
14. Insert oil pan remover tool No. KV10111100, or equivalent, between aluminum oil pan and cylinder block, then using a hammer, remove aluminum oil pan. **Use care not to damage aluminum oil pan when inserting oil pan remover tool.**

NS1099100005000X

Fig. 34   Transaxle bolts placement

15. Remove two engine to transaxle bolts, used to remove aluminum oil pan.

INSTALLATION

1. Remove all traces of gasket material from mating surfaces of oil pans and cylinder block.
2. Apply a bead of liquid gasket to cylinder block mating surface as shown, **Fig. 35. On areas marked with a star, apply gasket to outer side of bolt hole.**
3. Install aluminum oil pan and oil pan bolts, then using sequence shown in **Fig. 36, torque** bolts 1 through 16 to 12–14 ft. lbs. and bolts 17 and 18 to 4.7–5.5 ft. lbs.
4. Install two engine to transaxle bolts.
5. Install rear cover plate.
6. Install compressor gussets.
7. **On models equipped with automatic transaxles,** install shift control cable.
8. **On all models,** install center member.
9. Install front exhaust tube.
10. Install oil pan baffle plate.
11. Apply a bead of liquid gasket to steel oil pan.
12. Install steel oil pan and oil pan bolts, then using sequence shown in **Fig. 37,** tighten bolts to specifications.
13. Wait at least 60 minutes before refilling engine with oil.

OIL PUMP

REPLACE

1. Remove drive belts.
2. Remove cylinder head as outlined

under "Cylinder Head, Replace."

3. Remove oil pans as outlined under "Oil Pan, Replace."
4. Remove oil strainer and baffle plate.
5. Remove front cover assembly, **Fig. 38.**
6. Reverse procedure to install, noting the following:
   a. Prior to installation, remove all traces of gasket material from mating surfaces.
   b. Apply a bead of liquid gasket to mating surface of front cover assembly.

BELT TENSION DATA

Refer to **Fig. 39** for drive belt deflection specifications.

COOLING SYSTEM BLEED

1. Set heater temperature control lever to Max Hot position.
2. Remove radiator fill cap, air relief plug and bleeder cap, **Fig. 40.**
3. Fill radiator and reservoir tank with coolant. Air relief plug should be installed once coolant spills from hole during filling.
4. Reinstall air bleeder cap.
5. Install a suitable steel wire under radiator fill cap to allow coolant to pass into reservoir tank regardless of system pressure.
6. Start engine and raise engine temperature to normal operating temperature.
7. Run engine at 2500 RPM for ten seconds and return to idle. Repeat two or three times. **Watch engine coolant temperature gauge so engine does not overheat.**
8. Stop engine and allow to cool.
9. Fill radiator and reservoir as necessary.
10. Repeat steps 7 through 9 two or three times.
11. Remove steel wire and reinstall filler cap.
12. Raise engine temperature to normal and check for sounds of coolant flow while running engine from idle to 4000 RPM.
13. If sound is heard, bleed air from system as follows:
    a. Allow engine to cool.
    b. Remove air bleeder cap on heater inlet hose.
    c. Attach a suitable transparent hose at air bleeder pipe and place other end into coolant reservoir tank.
    d. Start engine and check for bubbles in reservoir tank.
    e. Set heater temperature control lever to Max Cool position.
    f. Run engine at 2300 RPM until bubbles disappear. **Do not run engine over 2300 RPM because engine damage may occur due to reduced coolant flow.**
    g. Set heater temperature control lever to Max Hot position and check for coolant flow sounds.
    h. If sounds are present, repeat steps "e" through "g."

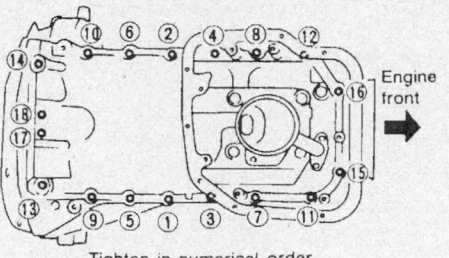

Fig. 36 Aluminum oil pan bolt tightening sequence

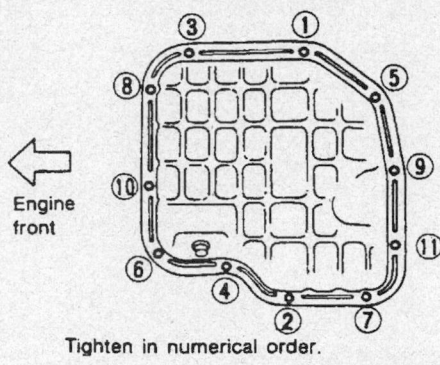

Fig. 37 Steel oil pan bolt tightening sequence

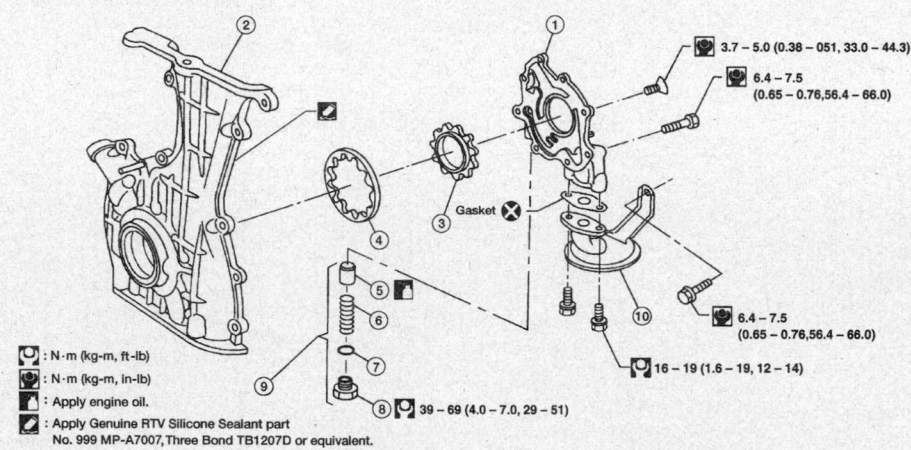

- N·m (kg-m, ft-lb)
- N·m (kg-m, in-lb)
- Apply engine oil.
- Apply Genuine RTV Silicone Sealant part No. 999 MP-A7007, Three Bond TB1207D or equivalent.

① Oil pump cover	④ Outer gear	⑦ Shim
② Front cover	⑤ Regulator valve	⑧ Plug
③ Inner gear	⑥ Spring	⑨ Regulator valve assembly
		⑩ Oil strainer

Fig. 38 Exploded view of oil pump assembly

Fig. 39 Drive belt deflection specifications

Unit: mm (in)

	Used belt deflection		Deflection of new belt
	Limit	Deflection after adjustment	
Generator			
With air conditioner compressor	11.5 - 12.5 (0.453 - 0.492)	7 - 8 (0.28 - 0.31)	6.5 - 7.5 (0.256 - 0.295)
Without air conditioner compressor	12 - 13 (0.47 - 0.51)	8 - 9 (0.31 - 0.35)	7 - 8 (0.28 - 0.31)
Power steering pump	6 - 7 (0.24 - 0.28)	4 - 5 (0.16 - 0.20)	3.5 - 4.5 (0.138 - 0.177)
Applied pushing force	98 N (10 kg, 22 lb)		

i. If sounds are not present, allow engine to cool, remove steel wire and hose attached to air bleeder, then install air bleeder cap.

THERMOSTAT

REPLACE

1. Drain engine coolant.
2. Remove water inlet attaching bolts, then the water inlet, **Fig. 41.**
3. Remove thermostat from thermostat housing.
4. Reverse procedure to install. Apply suitable liquid sealant to water inlet.

WATER PUMP

REPLACE

1. Drain cooling system into a suitable container.
2. Remove drive belts.
3. Remove water pump, **Fig. 42.**
4. Reverse procedure to install.

RADIATOR

REPLACE

1. When performing radiator replacement, refer to **Fig. 43.**
2. Refer to "Cooling System Bleed."

FUEL PUMP

REPLACE

1. Remove rear seat assembly.
2. Remove fuel pump inspection cover.
3. Disconnect fuel outlet, return tube and electrical connectors.

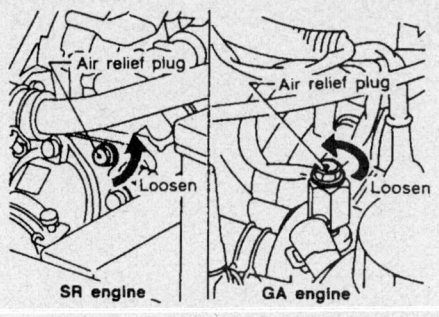

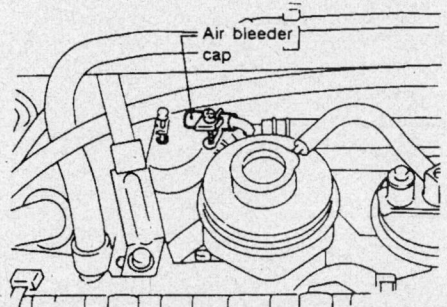

Fig. 40 Bleeding cooling system

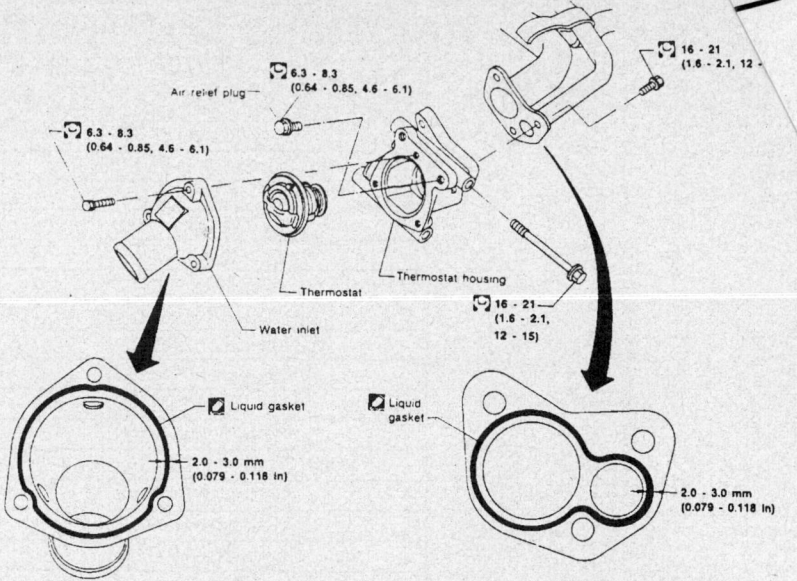

Fig. 41 Thermostat replacement

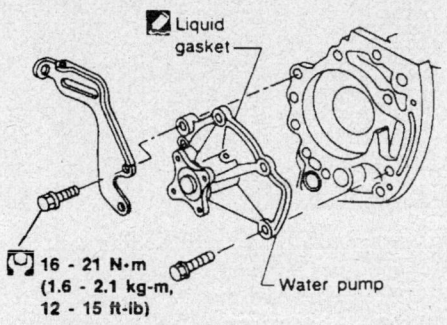

Fig. 42 Water pump replacement

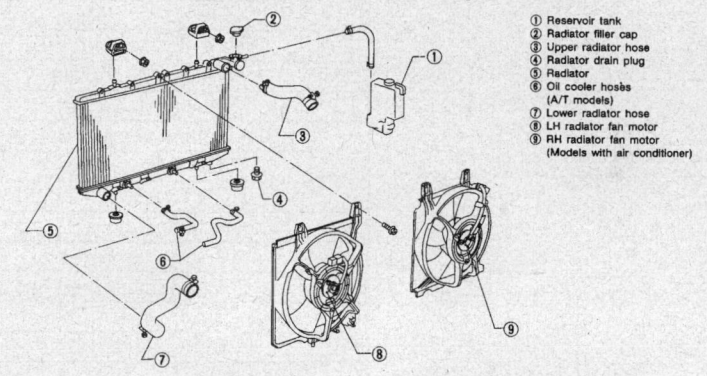

① Reservoir tank
② Radiator filler cap
③ Upper radiator hose
④ Radiator drain plug
⑤ Radiator
⑥ Oil cooler hoses (A/T models)
⑦ Lower radiator hose
⑧ LH radiator fan motor
⑨ RH radiator fan motor (Models with air conditioner)

Fig. 43 Radiator replacement

4. Remove fuel pump screws.
5. Remove fuel gauge assembly, then disconnect tubes and connectors, **Fig. 44.**
6. Remove fuel pump assembly.
7. Reverse procedure to install.

FUEL FILTER
REPLACE

1. Relieve fuel system pressure as outlined under "Precautions."
2. Loosen fuel filter hose clamps, **Fig. 45.**
3. Remove fuel filter. **Be careful not to spill fuel over engine compartment.**
4. Reverse procedure to install.

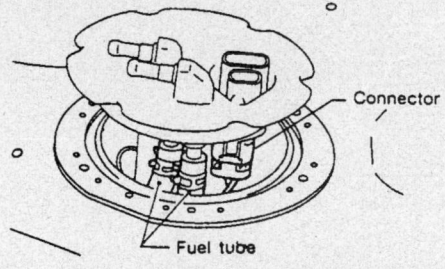

Fig. 44 Fuel pump replacement

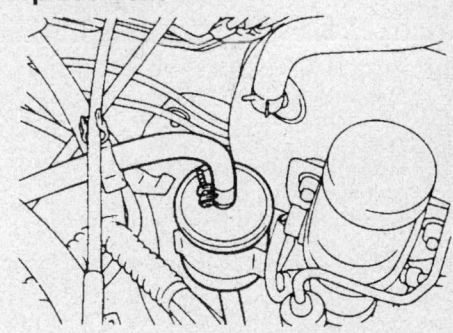

Fig. 45 Fuel filter

TIGHTENING SPECIFICATIONS

Year	Component	Torque, Ft. Lbs.
1996–99	AAC Valve	13–74⑤
	AIV Control Solenoid Valve	26–37⑤
	AIV Tube Mounting	55–73⑤
	AIV Unit Mounting	12–15
	Accel-Drum Unit	13–16
	Air Regulator	74–96⑤
	Alternator Adjusting Bar	12–16
	Alternator Bracket	33–44
	Alternator Fixing Bolt	12–16
	Aluminum Oil Pan	②
	BPT Valve	26–37⑤
	Buffer To Center Member (M/T)	33–40
	Camshaft Bracket	①
	Camshaft Sprocket Bolt	101–116
	Compressor Bracket	33–44
	Connecting Rod Bearing Cap Nut	③
	Crank Angle Sensor/Distributor	9–12
	Crankshaft Pulley	105–112
	Cylinder Block Drain Plug	56–104⑤
	Cylinder Head Bolts	①
	Detonation Sensor	15–20
	EGR Control Mounting Bracket	15–20
	EGR Control Valve	80–104⑤
	EGR Tube Mounting	13–15
	Engine Temperature Sensor	14–22
	Exhaust Gas Sensor	13–17
	Exhaust Gas Temperature Sensor	11–18
	Exhaust Manifold Cover	45–57⑤
	Exhaust Manifold Nuts	27–35
	Flywheel To Crankshaft	61–69
	Front Cover	12–15
	Front Engine Mounting (Fluid Type)	33–40
	Front Engine Mounting To Mounting Bracket	33–40
	Front Engine Slinger	16–22
	Ignition Coil	12–15
	Injector Mounting Bracket	26–37⑤
	Intake Manifold Collector To Intake Manifold	13–15
	Intake Manifold Nuts	13–15
	Intake Manifold Supports	12–15
	Lefthand Camshaft Sprocket	101–116
	Lower Crankcase Oil Pan Drain Plug	56–66⑤
	Main Bearing Cap	③
	Mounting Bracket	33–40
	Mounting Bracket To Buffer	33–40
	Oil Catcher	32–44⑤
	Oil Filter Bracket	12–14
	Oil Pan Baffle Plate	56–66⑤
	Oil Pan Drain Plug	22–29
	Oil Separator Mounting	12–15
	Oil Strainer To Crankcase	56–66⑤
	Oil Strainer To Front Cover	56–66⑤
	Power Steering Pump Adjusting Bar	12–15
	Power Steering Pump Bracket	33–44
	Power Transistor	32–44⑤
	Rear Engine Mounting	33–40

Continued

SR20DE ENGINE

TIGHTENING
SPECIFICATIONS—Continued

Year	Component	Torque, Ft. Lbs.
1996–99	Rear Engine Slinger	16–22
	Rear Insulator To Center Member	33–40
	Rear Insulator To Mounting Bracket	47–54
	Rear Oil Seal Retainer	55–72 ⑤
	Resonator Mounting Bolt	12–15
	Righthand Camshaft Sprocket	55–72 ⑤
	Rocker Cover	①
	Side Gallery Baffle Plate	17–21 ⑤
	Steel Oil Pan	56–66 ⑤
	Thermal Transmitter	55–72 ⑤
	Thermostat Housing	12–15
	Throttle Chamber	④
	Timing Chain Guide	9–14
	Timing Chain Guide	12–14
	Timing Chain Tensioner	①
	Timing Chain	①
	Water Inlet	55–72 ⑤
	Water Outlet	55–72 ⑤

① — Refer to "Timing Chain, Replace."
② — Refer to "Oil Pan, Replace."
③ — Refer to "Piston, Rod & Crankshaft" under "Engine Assemble."
④ — Torque throttle chamber in two steps; first to 6.5–8.0 ft. lbs., then to 13–16 ft. lbs.
⑤ — Inch lbs.

Clutch & Manual Transaxle

INDEX

ADJUSTMENTS

CLUTCH PEDAL

1. Adjust clutch pedal height, dimension "H" in **Fig. 1,** to 6.02–6.42 inches using pedal stop or clutch switch.
2. Adjust withdrawal lever play, dimension "B" in **Fig. 2,** to .098–.138 inch using adjuster or locknuts.
3. Adjust dimension "C" in **Fig. 3,** to .012–.039 inch with clutch pedal fully depressed.
4. Measure clutch pedal freeplay as shown in **Fig. 1,** dimension "A." Clutch pedal freeplay should be .425–.594 inch. Clutch pedal freeplay is the sum of play between clevis pin and clevis pin hole.
5. After above adjustments have been completed, cycle clutch pedal several times to ensure clutch linkage operates smoothly without binding.

CLUTCH
REPLACE

1. Remove transaxle as outlined under "Transaxle, Replace."
2. Insert a dummy shaft into clutch disc hub.
3. Alternately loosen clutch cover attaching bolts.
4. Remove clutch disc and cover assembly.
5. Remove release bearing.
6. Reverse procedure to install.

TRANSAXLE
REPLACE

1. Remove battery and battery support bracket from vehicle, as necessary.
2. Remove air cleaner assembly and air flow meter, as necessary.
3. Raise and support vehicle.
4. Remove both front propeller shafts. **When disconnecting driveshafts, use care not to damage oil seals. After disconnecting driveshafts, insert a suitable bar so side gears will not rotate and fall into differential case.**
5. Disconnect control and support rods from transaxle, as necessary.
6. Remove front exhaust pipe attaching bolts.
7. Disconnect all cables and electrical connectors from transaxle.
8. Using a suitable jack, support engine with a wooden block placed between oil pan and jack.
9. Remove starter motor, as necessary.
10. Remove engine mount attaching bolts.
11. Remove engine to transaxle attaching bolts, then separate engine from transaxle and lower transaxle assembly from vehicle.
12. Reverse procedure to install.

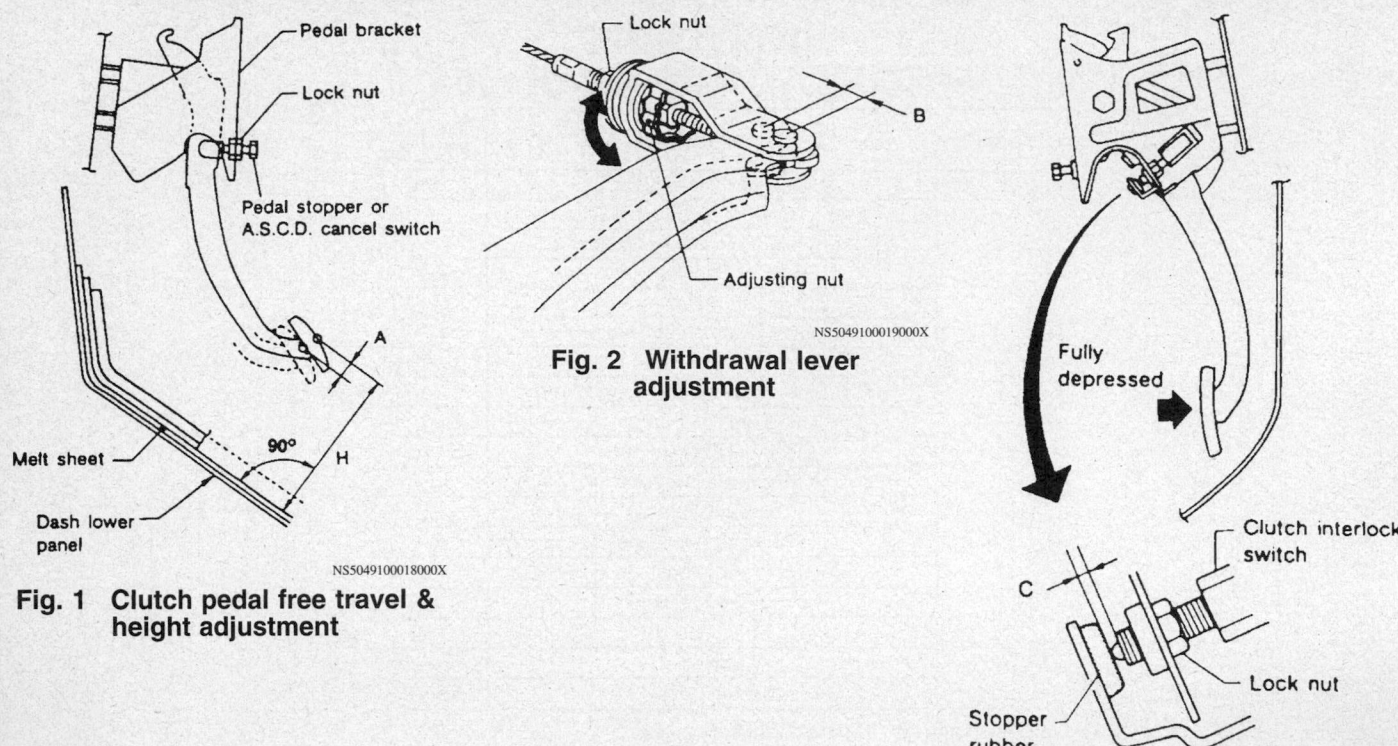

Fig. 1   Clutch pedal free travel &
height adjustment

Fig. 2   Withdrawal lever
adjustment

Fig. 3   Clutch interlock switch
adjustment

CLUTCH PEDAL ADJUSTMENT SPECIFICATIONS

Pedal Height, Inch (mm)	Withdrawal Lever Play, Inch (mm)	Pedal Freeplay, Inch (mm)
6.02–6.42 (150–160)	.098–.138 (2.5–3.5)	.425–.594 (10.8–15.1)

TIGHTENING SPECIFICATIONS

Year	Component	Torque, Ft. Lbs.
1996–99	Bleeder Screw	48–84①
	Clutch Cable Locknut	24–36①
	Clutch Cover Securing Bolt	16–22
	Clutch Cover To Flywheel	16–22
	Clutch Hose Clamp To Body	6–10
	Clutch Hose To Operating Cylinder Or Clutch Tube	12–14
	Clutch Interlock Switch Locknut	9–11
	Clutch Master Cylinder To Dash Panel	72–96①
	Clutch Operating Cylinder	22–30
	Clutch Pedal Bracket Securing Nut	72–96①
	Clutch Switch Locknut	9–11
	Clutch Tube Flare Nut	11–13
	Control Lever Socket To Support Rod	72–96①
	Control Lever To Control Rod	12–15
	Control Rod To Transaxle	12–16
	Engine Gusset To Engine	22–30
	Engine Mounting Bracket	15–20
	Engine Rear Gusset To Engine	12–15
	Flywheel To Crankshaft	61–69
	Fulcrum Pin Securing Nut	12–16
	Holder Bracket Fixing Bolt	72–96①
	Holder Bracket To Support Rod	14–19
	Interlock Switch Locknut	9–11
	Master Cylinder Securing Nut	72–96①
	Operating Cylinder Securing Nut	22–30
	Pedal Stopper Locknut	12–16
	Reservoir Band	24–36①
	Support Rod Bracket To Transaxle	20–27
	Support Rod To Bracket	23–30
	Support Rod To Engine Mount Bracket	23–30
	Valve Stopper	12–24①

① — Inch lbs.

Rear Axle & Suspension

INDEX

PRECAUTIONS

Prior to removal of rear suspension assembly, disconnect ABS wheel sensor wiring from sensors. Failure to do so may result in damage to sensor wiring causing sensors to become inoperative.

REAR AXLE

REPLACE

Refer to "Rear Axle & Suspension" section found in "Maxima" chapter.

HUB & BEARING

REPLACE

1. Raise and support vehicle.
2. Remove wheel bearing locknut, **Fig. 1.**
3. Remove brake caliper and rotor, then position aside.
4. Remove hub assembly.
5. Reverse procedure to install noting to **Torque** wheel bearing to 137–188 ft. lbs. on 2WD models or 174–231 ft. lbs. on 4WD models, then refer to "Wheel Bearing Inspection."

WHEEL BEARING INSPECTION

1. Check wheel bearing torque. **Torque** should measure 137–188 ft. lbs. on 2WD models or 174–231 ft. lbs. on 4WD models.
2. Ensure wheel bearing operates smoothly.
3. Ensure axial play is .0020 inch or less.
4. If axial endplay is more than specified or bearing does not operate smoothly, replace wheel bearing assembly.

STRUT

REPLACE

Refer to "Coil Spring, Replace."

COIL SPRING

REPLACE

1. Raise and support vehicle.
2. Remove upper and lower strut attaching nuts and/or bolts, **Fig. 2,** then the strut assembly.
3. Place strut assembly in a suitable vise, then loosen piston rod locknut. **Loosen but do not remove.**
4. Compress coil spring using a suitable coil spring compression tool.
5. Remove piston rod locknut.

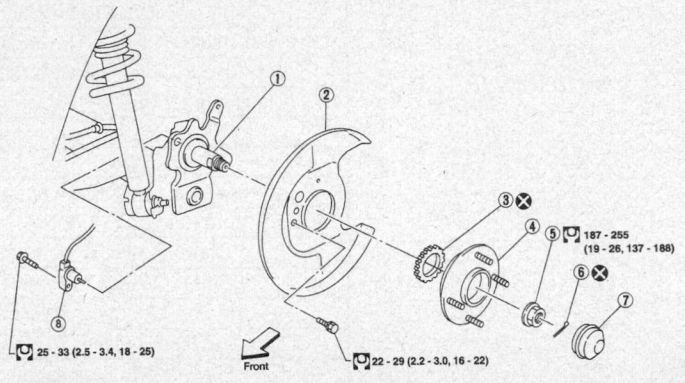

**: N·m (kg-m, ft-lb)

① Spindle
② Baffle plate
③ ABS sensor rotor
④ Wheel hub bearing
⑤ Wheel bearing lock nut
⑥ Cotter pin
⑦ Hub cap
⑧ ABS sensor

NS2049100001000X

Fig. 1 Exploded view of wheel hub assembly

When installing each rubber part, final tightening must be carried out under unladen condition* with tires on ground.
* Fuel, radiator coolant and engine oil full. Spare tire, jack, hand tools and mats in designated positions.

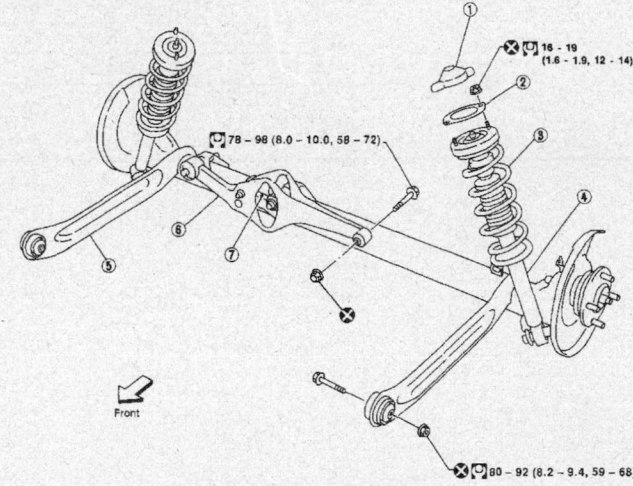

**: N·m (kg-m, ft-lb)

① Shock absorber cap
② Shock absorber mounting seal
③ Coil spring
④ Shock absorber
⑤ Torsion beam
⑥ Lateral link
⑦ Control rod

NS2039100001000A

Fig. 2 Exploded view of rear suspension

6. Remove spring components from strut.

7. Reverse procedure to install, noting the following:

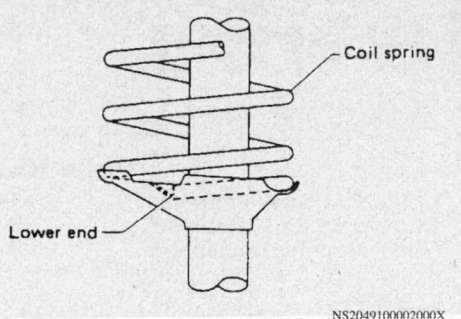

NS2049100002000X

Fig. 3 Spring installation direction

a. Install coil spring in correct direction, **Fig. 3.**
b. Position coil spring in lower spring seat as shown in **Figs. 3 and 4.**

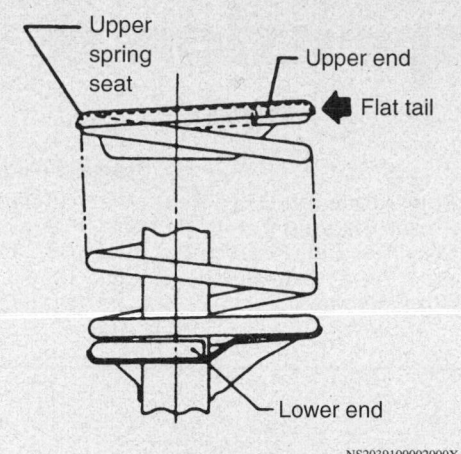

NS2039100002000X

Fig. 4 Coil spring installation

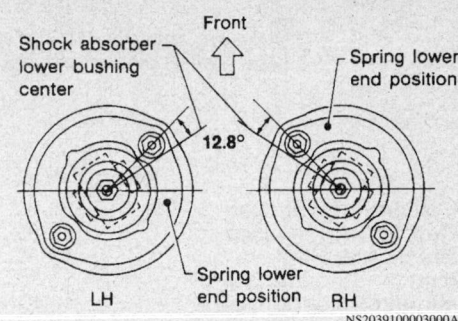

NS2039100003000A

Fig. 5 Upper spring seat installation direction

c. Install upper spring seat as shown in **Fig. 5.**

TIGHTENING SPECIFICATIONS

Year	Component	Torque, Ft. Lbs.
1996–99	Axle Nut	133–188
	Backing Plate (Drum Brake)	28–38
	Baffle Plate (Disc Brake) To Knuckle	7–10
	Connecting Rod To Strut	14–22
	Driveshaft Nut	133–188
	Hub Nut	133–188
	Parallel Link To Crossmember	72–87
	Parallel Link To Knuckle	72–87
	Radius Rod To Bracket	72–87
	Radius Rod To Knuckle	72–87
	Strut Mounting Insulator To Body	18–22
	Strut Piston Self-Locking Nut	46–53
	Wheel Bearing Self-Locking Nut	137–188
	Wheel Lug Nuts	72–87

Front Suspension & Steering

INDEX

WHEEL BEARING INSPECTION

Ensure wheel bearing operates smoothly and has an axial endplay of .0020 inch or less. If not as specified, replace wheel bearing.

WHEEL HUB & STEERING KNUCKLE

REPLACE

1. While depressing brake pedal, remove wheel bearing locknut.
2. Remove brake caliper assembly, then support caliper assembly to frame using suitable wire.
3. Remove tie rod end from knuckle, **Fig. 1.**
4. Separate driveshaft from knuckle by slightly tapping on end. **Cover boots with a cloth to prevent damage.**
5. Remove strut lower mounting bolts, **Fig. 2.**
6. Loosen lower ball joint nut, then separate lower ball joint from knuckle.
7. Using a suitable tool, drive out hub with inner race from knuckle.
8. Remove wheel bearing inner race, inner and outer grease seals, then the outer bearing race.
9. Reverse procedure to install, checking wheel bearing axial play as outlined under "Wheel Bearing Inspection."

DRIVESHAFT

REPLACE

1. While depressing brake pedal, remove wheel bearing locknut.
2. Remove brake caliper assembly and support to frame using suitable wire. **Brake hose does not need to be disconnected. Ensure there is no tension on brake hose.**
3. Remove tie rod end from knuckle, **Fig. 1.**
4. Separate driveshaft from knuckle by slightly tapping on end. **Cover boots with a cloth to prevent damage. Be careful not to damage threads on end of driveshaft.**
5. Remove strut lower mounting bolts, **Fig. 2.**
6. Loosen lower ball joint nut, then separate lower ball joint from knuckle.

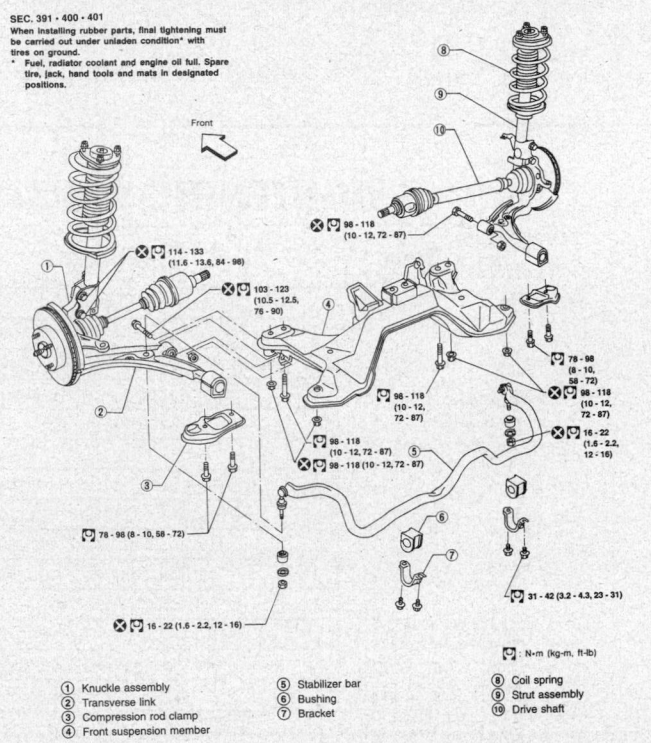

SEC. 391 · 400 · 401
When installing rubber parts, final tightening must be carried out under unladen condition* with tires on ground.
* Fuel, radiator coolant and engine oil full. Spare tire, jack, hand tools and mats in designated positions.

⊗ Ⓟ 114 - 133 (11.6 - 13.6, 84 - 98)
⊗ Ⓟ 103 - 123 (10.5 - 12.5, 76 - 90)
⊗ Ⓟ 98 - 118 (10 - 12, 72 - 87)
Ⓟ 78 - 98 (8 - 10, 58 - 72)
⊗ Ⓟ 98 - 118 (10 - 12, 72 - 87)
⊗ Ⓟ 16 - 22 (1.6 - 2.2, 12 - 16)
Ⓟ 98 - 118 (10 - 12, 72 - 87)
Ⓟ 98 - 118 (10 - 12, 72 - 87)
Ⓟ 78 - 98 (8 - 10, 58 - 72)
⊗ Ⓟ 16 - 22 (1.6 - 2.2, 12 - 16)
Ⓟ 31 - 42 (3.2 - 4.3, 23 - 31)

Ⓟ : N·m (kg-m, ft-lb)

① Knuckle assembly
② Transverse link
③ Compression rod clamp
④ Front suspension member
⑤ Stabilizer bar
⑥ Bushing
⑦ Bracket
⑧ Coil spring
⑨ Strut assembly
⑩ Drive shaft

NS3039100001000X

Fig. 1 Exploded view of front axle & suspension

7. Remove right driveshaft as shown in **Figs. 3 and 4.**
8. **On models equipped with manual transaxle,** remove left driveshaft as shown in **Fig. 5.**
9. **On models equipped with automatic transaxle,** remove left driveshaft using a suitable tool placed on driveshaft end through differential housing, as shown in **Fig. 6. Do not damage pinion mate shaft and side gear.**
10. **On all models,** reverse procedure to install, noting the following:
    a. Install new oil seals.
    b. Protect oil seal using seal protector tool No. KV38106700, or equivalent.
    c. Ensure to properly align serrations when installing driveshaft.
    d. Ensure circular clip engages into clip groove of side gear.
    e. Tighten wheel bearing locknut to specifications, then check axial endplay as outlined under "Wheel Bearing, Inspection."

BALL JOINT INSPECTION

Check ball joint for play. If ball stud is worn, there is excessive play in axial direction or joint is hard to swing, replace lower ball joint.

COIL SPRING

REPLACE

1. Raise and support front of vehicle and remove wheel.
2. Disconnect brake line from strut.
3. Place alignment marks on strut lower bracket and camber adjusting pin.
4. Remove strut to steering knuckle attaching bolts, then separate strut from knuckle, **Fig. 7.**
5. Remove strut to strut tower attaching nuts, then strut assembly from vehicle.
6. Install strut assembly in a vise, then

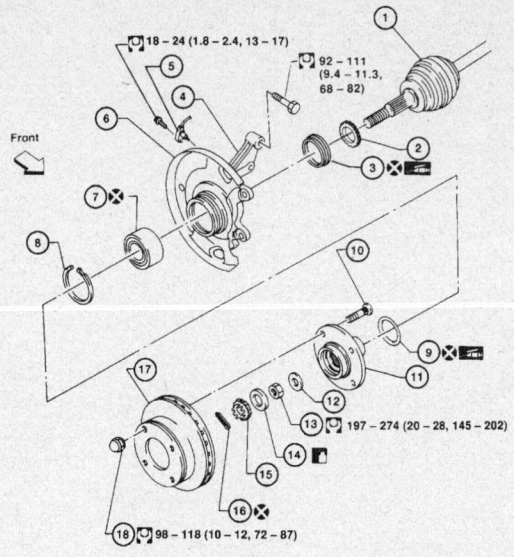

18 – 24 (1.8 – 2.4, 13 – 17)
92 – 111 (9.4 – 11.3, 68 – 82)

197 – 274 (20 – 28, 145 – 202)

98 – 118 (10 – 12, 72 – 87)

 : N·m (kg-m, ft-lb)

① Drive shaft
② ABS sensor rotor
③ Inner grease seal
④ Knuckle
⑤ ABS sensor
⑥ Baffle plate

⑦ Wheel bearing assembly
⑧ Snap ring
⑨ Outer grease seal
⑩ Wheel bolt
⑪ Wheel hub
⑫ Plain washer

⑬ Wheel bearing lock nut
⑭ Insulator
⑮ Adjusting cap
⑯ Cotter pin
⑰ Disc rotor
⑱ Wheel nut

NS3039100002000A

Fig. 2 Exploded view of wheel hub & knuckle

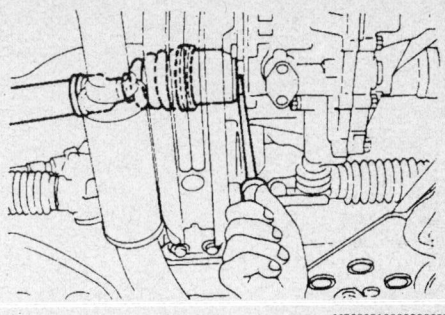

NS3039100003000X

Fig. 3 Right driveshaft removal. Less support bearing

A/T model

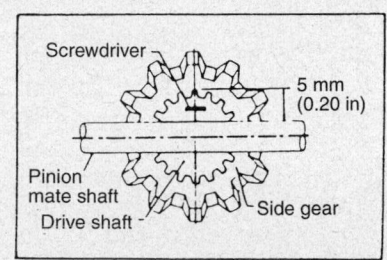

Screwdriver

5 mm (0.20 in)

Pinion mate shaft

Drive shaft

Side gear

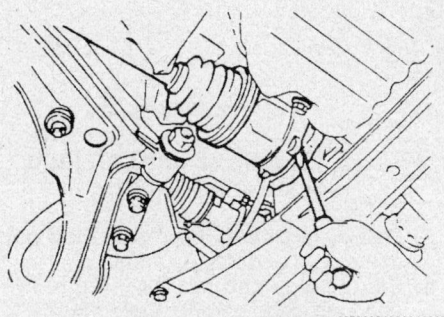

NS3039100004000X

Fig. 4 Right driveshaft removal. With support bearing

loosen strut rod locknut. **Loosen but do not remove.**

7. Compress coil spring using a suitable coil spring compression tool.
8. Remove piston rod locknut.
9. Remove spring components from strut.
10. Reverse procedure to install, noting the following:
    a. Install coil spring in correct direction, **Fig. 8.**
    b. Position coil spring in lower spring seat as shown in **Fig. 9.**
    c. Install upper spring seat as shown in **Fig. 10.**

STRUT

REPLACE

Refer to "Coil Spring, Replace" for strut replacement procedure.

STABILIZER BAR

REPLACE

1. Raise and support vehicle.
2. Remove front exhaust tube.

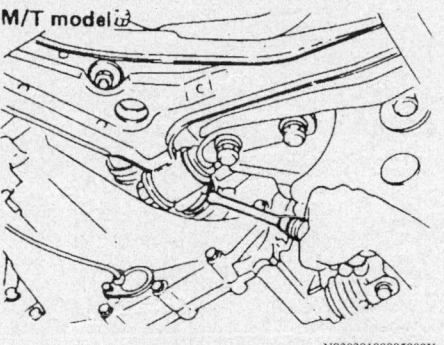

M/T model

NS3039100005000X

Fig. 5 Left driveshaft removal. Manual transaxle

3. Remove stabilizer bar attaching bolts and nuts, then the stabilizer bar.
4. Reverse procedure to install, noting the following:
   a. Install stabilizer rear side bushing, then the front bushings.
   b. Install stabilizer bar with ball joint socket, as shown in **Fig. 11.**

TRANSVERSE LINK

REPLACE

1. Raise and support vehicle.
2. Remove tie rod ball joint.
3. Remove wheel bearing locknut.
4. Separate driveshaft from knuckle by tapping driveshaft end with a suitable hammer. **Cover boots with a cloth to prevent damage. Be careful not to damage threads on end of driveshaft.**
5. Remove stabilizer bar attaching bolt from transverse link.
6. Separate lower ball joint stud from

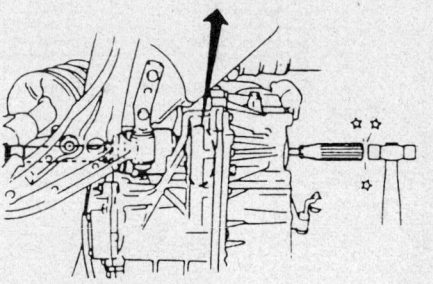

NS3039100006000X

Fig. 6 Left driveshaft removal. Automatic transaxle

knuckle using ball joint separating tool No. HT72520000, or equivalent.
7. Remove transverse link bracket attaching bolts, then the transverse link bracket.
8. Remove remaining transverse link assembly attaching bolt, then the transverse link and ball joint assembly.
9. Reverse procedure to install.

POWER STEERING GEAR

REPLACE

1. Raise and support front of vehicle and remove wheels.
2. Disconnect power steering hose clamp, then the hose at steering gear and drain fluid into a suitable container.
3. Disconnect tie rod studs from steering knuckles.
4. **On Sentra models,** support transaxle with a suitable jack, then remove exhaust pipe and rear engine mounts, if necessary.
5. **On all models,** remove bolt securing

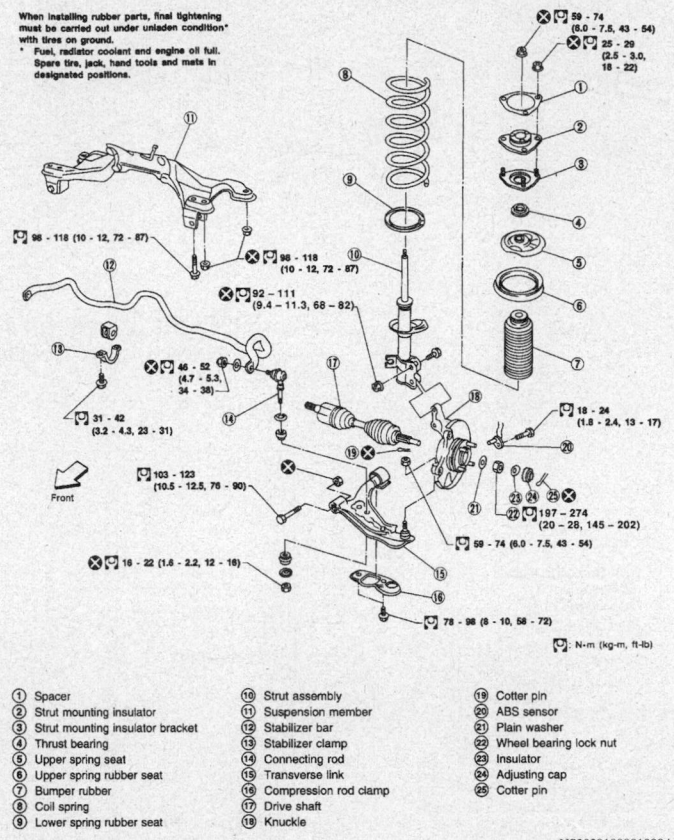

When installing rubber parts, final tightening must be carried out under unladen condition* with tires on ground.
* Fuel, radiator coolant and engine oil full. Spare tire, jack, hand tools and mats in designated positions.

96 - 118 (10 - 12, 72 - 87)
96 - 118 (10 - 12, 72 - 87)
92 - 111 (9.4 - 11.3, 68 - 82)
46 - 52 (4.7 - 5.3, 34 - 38)
31 - 42 (3.2 - 4.3, 23 - 31)
103 - 123 (10.5 - 12.5, 76 - 90)
16 - 22 (1.6 - 2.2, 12 - 16)
78 - 98 (8 - 10, 58 - 72)
59 - 74 (6.0 - 7.5, 43 - 54)
25 - 29 (2.5 - 3.0, 18 - 22)
18 - 24 (1.8 - 2.4, 13 - 17)
197 - 274 (20 - 28, 145 - 202)
59 - 74 (6.0 - 7.5, 43 - 54)

: N·m (kg-m, ft-lb)

Front

① Spacer	⑩ Strut assembly	⑲ Cotter pin
② Strut mounting insulator	⑪ Suspension member	⑳ ABS sensor
③ Strut mounting insulator bracket	⑫ Stabilizer bar	㉑ Plain washer
④ Thrust bearing	⑬ Stabilizer clamp	㉒ Wheel bearing lock nut
⑤ Upper spring seat	⑭ Connecting rod	㉓ Insulator
⑥ Upper spring rubber seat	⑮ Transverse link	㉔ Adjusting cap
⑦ Bumper rubber	⑯ Compression rod clamp	㉕ Cotter pin
⑧ Coil spring	⑰ Drive shaft	
⑨ Lower spring rubber seat	⑱ Knuckle	

NS2029100001000A

Fig. 7 Exploded view of front suspension

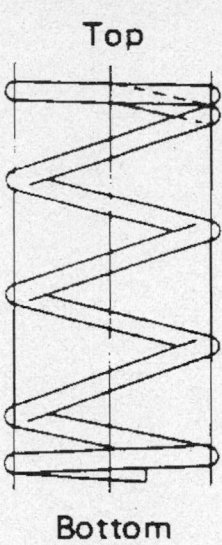

Top

Bottom

NS2029100002000X

Fig. 8 Spring installation direction

View from B

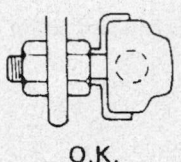 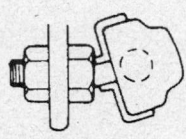

O.K.   N.G.

NS2029100005000X

Fig. 11 Stabilizer bar ball joint socket installation

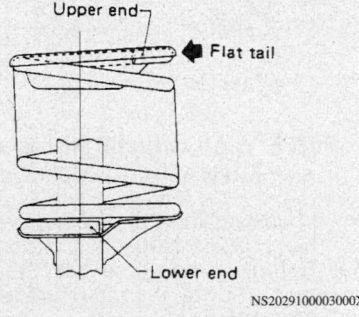

Upper end
Flat tail
Lower end

NS2029100003000X

Fig. 9 Coil spring installation

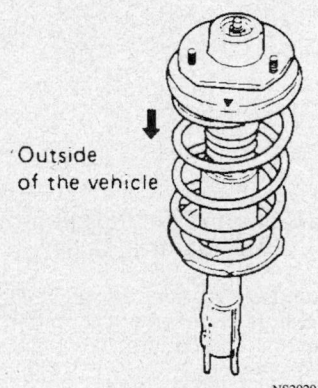

Outside of the vehicle

NS2029100004000X

Fig. 10 Upper spring seat installation direction

lower joint to steering gear pinion and remove lower joint from pinion.
6. Remove steering gear attaching bolts.
7. Remove steering gear and linkage assembly from vehicle.
8. Reverse procedure to install.

POWER STEERING PUMP

REPLACE

1. Remove A/C compressor drive belt.
2. Loosen idler pulley locknut, then turn adjusting nut counterclockwise and remove power steering pump drive belt.
3. Loosen power steering hoses at pump and remove bolts securing power steering pump to brackets.
4. Raise pump and disconnect power steering hoses. Catch fluid in a suitable container, plug hose ends and ports in power steering pump, and remove pump from vehicle.
5. Reverse procedure to install, then bleed system.

STEERING SYSTEM BLEED

1. Raise and support front of vehicle.
2. Run engine for three to five seconds, stop engine, then check and fill power steering pump reservoir as necessary.
3. Quickly turn steering wheel all the way to the right and left ten times.
4. Start engine and idle for three to five seconds. Stop engine, then check and fill power steering pump reservoir as necessary.
5. With steering wheel all the way to the right, open bleeder screw to expel air, then tighten bleeder screw.
6. Repeat procedure until all air has been bled from system.
7. If air cannot be bled completely after repeated attempts, repeat step "e" with engine running.

MANUAL STEERING GEAR

REPLACE

1. Raise and support front of vehicle and remove wheels.
2. Disconnect tie rod from steering knuckle.
3. Loosen steering gear attaching bolts, then remove bolt securing lower joint to steering gear pinion and remove lower joint from pinion.
4. Remove steering gear housing to body attaching bolts, then the steering gear and linkage assembly from vehicle.
5. Reverse procedure to install.

TIGHTENING SPECIFICATIONS

Year	Component	Torque, Ft. Lbs.
1996–99	ABS Speed Sensor Bolt	13–17
	Axle Nut	145–203
	Axle To Caliper	40–47
	Connecting Rod To Transverse Link	12–16
	Driveshaft Nut	145–203
	Hub Nut	145–203
	Lower Ball Joint Stud Nut	43–54
	Stabilizer Bar Clamp To Body	12–15
	Stabilizer Bar To Ball Joint	25–33
	Strut Assembly Piston Rod Self-Locking Nut	46–53
	Strut Assembly To Body	18–22
	Strut Assembly To Knuckle	84–98
	Tie Rod Locknut	27–34
	Tie Rod Stud Nut	22–29
	Transverse Link Securing Bolt	58–72
	Transverse Securing Nut	72–87
	Wheel Bearing Locknut	145–203
	Wheel Lug Nut	72–87

Wheel Alignment

INDEX

PRELIMINARY INSPECTION

1. Check tire pressure and adjust as necessary.
2. Ensure tires are properly sized and matched.
3. Ensure wheel bearings (front and rear) are properly adjusted.
4. Check steering gear adjustment and ensure steering gear is properly secured to frame.
5. Inspect steering linkage and suspension components for damage and wear. Repair or replace components as necessary.
6. Measure vehicle ride height with vehicle unloaded, and ensure springs are not collapsed.
7. Place vehicle on suitable alignment rack following manufacturer's instructions, then bounce vehicle several times to settle suspension.
8. Check and correct rear wheel camber and toe first, then check and correct front suspension angles in the following order: caster and kingpin inclination, camber, toe setting and turning angle (toe-out on turns).

FRONT WHEEL ALIGNMENT

Correct front wheel alignment is necessary to provide proper handling and to prevent uneven tire wear. To ensure correct alignment, angles should be checked, and if necessary corrected, in the following sequence: caster and kingpin inclination, camber, toe-setting, and the turning angle and toe-out on turns. Front wheel alignment should only be checked after the rear wheels are properly aligned in relation to the vehicle centerline, as most equipment uses the rear wheels as reference for correct front wheel alignment. Front wheel alignment should be checked with the vehicle at normal ride height, and following equipment manufacturer's instructions.

CASTER & KINGPIN INCLINATION

If caster or kingpin angles are not within specifications, check suspension components and sheet metal for damage, distortion and excessive wear. Repair or replace components as necessary.

CAMBER

Camber cannot be adjusted. If camber is not within specifications, inspect suspension and sheet metal for damage, distortion and excessive wear, and repair or replace components as necessary.

TOE SETTING

The toe setting is the measurement of the wheels in relation to the vehicle centerline, **Fig. 1.** The leading edge of each wheel should toe-in or toe-out slightly in relation to the vehicle centerline to ensure proper vehicle tracking. Toe should be inspected using suitable alignment gauges, following manufacturer's instructions. When checking or adjusting toe, always ensure the setting of the left and right wheels is as equal as possible.

Toe is adjusted by loosening the tie rod locknuts or adjusting sleeve bolts and equally altering the length of the tie rods. After toe has been adjusted to specifications, the lengths of the left and right tie rods, **Fig. 2,** should be nearly equal. If tie rod lengths are incorrect, tie rods should be disassembled and adjusted to equal

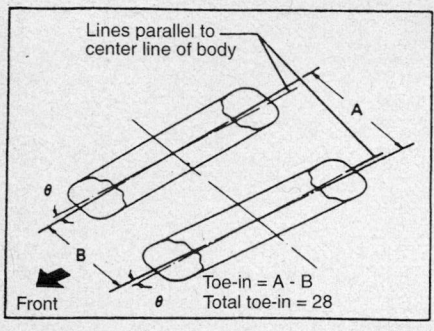

Fig. 1   Toe-in measurement

lengths, and the toe setting should be readjusted before checking steering angles. Incorrect tie rod length will adversely affect steering angles and toe-out on turns.

STEERING ANGLE

When a vehicle negotiates a turn, the inner wheel must turn at a sharper angle than the outer wheel, and the outer wheel must travel farther than the inner wheel. Vehicle steering geometry is calculated to allow for these variations, causing the outer wheel to toe-out by a calibrated amount. This toe-out on turns is also referred to as steering angle and on these models, is generally checked at two positions. The first position is at a reference point on the inner wheel travel, while the second position of measurement is at full steering lock. To check steering angles, proceed as follows:

1. Place vehicle on suitable alignment rack and ensure kingpin angle, caster, camber and toe settings are within specifications.
2. Turn steering to full lock and measure inner and outer wheel turning angles.

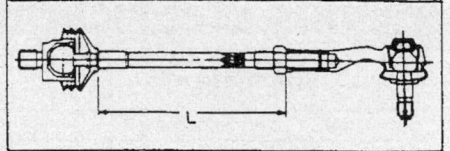

Fig. 2   Tie rod length measurement

3. If "turning angles" at full lock are not within specifications, check for damaged steering linkage or improperly adjusted tie rods.
4. If steering linkage and tie rods are satisfactory, check for improper rack or rack piston stroke. Repair steering gear as necessary.

REAR WHEEL ALIGNMENT

The proper alignment of the rear suspension and wheels is essential for proper handling and to providing a reference for front wheel alignment. Always ensure rear wheel alignment is within specifications prior to checking and adjusting front wheel alignment.

CAMBER

The rear wheel camber must be within specifications for proper vehicle handling and to prevent uneven tire wear. Rear camber cannot be adjusted. If rear camber is not within specifications, check for damaged or worn suspension components and deformed sheet metal. Repair as necessary.

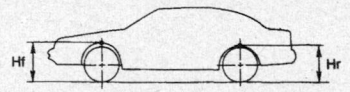

Applied model	155SR13	175/70R13	175/65/R14	195/55R15
Front (Hf) mm (in)	659 (25.94)		666 (26.22)	669 (26.34)
Rear (Hr) mm (in)	640 (25.20)	642 (25.28)	648 (25.51)	650 (25.59)

*: Fuel, radiator coolant and engine oil full. Spare tire, jack, hand tools and mats in designated positions.

NS2049500035000X

Fig. 3   Vehicle ride height measurement

TOE-IN

The rear wheel toe-in must be within specifications for proper vehicle handling and to prevent uneven tire wear. Rear toe-in cannot be adjusted. If rear toe-in is not within specifications, check for damaged or worn suspension components. Repair as necessary.

VEHICLE RIDE HEIGHT

When checking ride height, vehicle must be parked on a level surface and tires inflated to proper air pressure. Ensure all fluid levels are to specified level, spare tire and jack are in proper locations.

Bounce vehicle up and down several times, then measure vehicle height from top of wheelwell to ground, **Fig. 3.** Vehicle height is not adjustable. If vehicle height is not as specified, check for worn springs or suspension parts.

NISSAN 240SX
INDEX OF SERVICE OPERATIONS

Specifications

GENERAL ENGINE SPECIFICATIONS

Year	Engine Model	Fuel System	Displacement Liters	Bore x Stroke, Inches	Compression Ratio	Maximum HP @ RPM	Maximum Torque, Ft. Lbs. @ RPM	Normal Oil Pressure, psi
1996–97	KA24DE	Fuel Inj.	2.4L	3.50 X 3.78	9.5	155 @ 5600	160 @ 4400	60–70

TUNE UP SPECIFICATIONS

Year	Engine Model	Spark Plug Gap, Inch	Ignition Timing		Curb Idle Speed①		Fast Idle Speed		Fuel Pump Pressure, psi	Valve Lash
			Firing Order	Timing, °BTDC	Man. Trans.	Auto. Trans.	Man. Trans.	Auto. Trans.		
1996–97	KA24DE	.041	1-3-4-2	③	700	700N	—	—	34	②

BTDC — Before Top Dead Center
N — Neutral
① — When adjusting idle speed, set parking brake & chock drive wheels.
② — Refer to "Valve Adjustment" under "KA24E Engine."
③ — Controlled by ECCS control module.

FRONT WHEEL ALIGNMENT SPECIFICATIONS

Year	Caster Angle, °		Camber Angle, °		King Pin Inclination, °	Toe-In, Inch①	Toe-Out On Turns, °②		Ball Joint Wear
	Limits	Desired	Limits	Desired			Inner Wheel	Outer Wheel	
1996–97	+6 to +7½	+6¾	−1½ to 0	−¾	12½ to 14	+.012 to +.091	39 to 43	33	③

① — Toe-in (+); toe-out (-).
② — Measure w/wheels at full lefthand & righthand turn positions.
③ — Refer to "Ball Joint Inspection" under "Front Suspension & Steering."

REAR WHEEL ALIGNMENT SPECIFICATIONS

Year	Camber Angle, °		Toe, Inch①
	Limits	Desired	
1996–97	−1⅔ to −⅔	−1⅙	0 to +.197

① — Toe-in (+); toe-out (-).

FLUID CAPACITIES & COOLING SYSTEM DATA

Year	Coolant Capacity, Qts.	Radiator, Cap Relief Pressure, Lbs.	Thermo. Opening Temp., °F	Fuel Tank, Gals.	Engine Oil Refill, Qts.①	Transmission Oil		Differential Oil, Pts.
						Man. Trans., Pts.	Auto. Trans., Qts.②	
1996–97	7 ¼	11–14	170	17 ⅛	4	5 ⅛	8 ¾	2 ¾

① — Includes filter.
② — Approximate, make final check w/dipstick.

LUBRICANT DATA

Year	Lubricant Type					
	Transmission		Transfer Case	Rear Axle	Power Steering	Brake System
	Manual	Automatic				
1996–97	75W-90 GL-4	Nissan Matic D ①	—	80W-90 GL-5	Dexron II/IIE/III	DOT 3

① — Dexron III/Mercon, or equivalent automatic transmission fluid, may also be used.

Electrical

NOTE: On Air Bag Equipped Models, Refer To "Air Bag System Precautions" Located In Front Of This Manual For System Disarming & Arming Procedures.

NOTE: Refer To "Computer Relearn Procedures" Located In The Front Of This Manual For Computer Relearn Procedures.

INDEX

PRECAUTIONS

AIR BAG SYSTEMS

Refer to "Air Bag System Precautions" in front of this manual for system disarming and arming procedures.

BATTERY GROUND CABLE

Prior to service, disconnect battery ground cable and isolate as required.

FUSE PANEL & FLASHER LOCATION

The fuse panel is located under the lefthand side of the instrument panel, to the left of the steering column.

The combination flasher unit is located behind the lefthand side of the instrument panel, near the steering column.

FUEL PUMP RELAY LOCATION

The fuel pump relay is located behind the driver's side kick panel near the fuse panel.

RELAY CENTER LOCATION

Relay center No. 1 is located at the front lefthand side of the engine compartment. Relay center No. 2 is located on the righthand side of the engine compartment, to the rear of the battery.

STARTER

REPLACE

1. **On models equipped with automatic transmission,** proceed as follows:
   a. Support transmission with suitable jack.
   b. Remove four rear mounting bracket bolts.
   c. Slightly lower transmission.
   d. Remove ATF level gauge pipe.
2. **On all models,** disconnect starter wiring from starter.
3. Remove starter retaining bolts and starter.
4. Reverse procedure to install.

DISTRIBUTOR

REPLACE

1. Remove distributor cap and spark plug cables as an assembly.
2. Disconnect distributor electrical connections.
3. Remove distributor retaining bolt.
4. Remove distributor assembly.

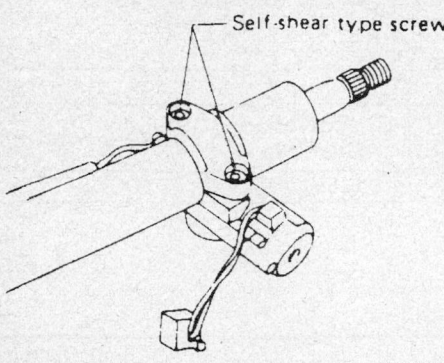

NS9129100005000X

Fig. 1   Ignition lock replacement

5. Reverse procedure to install. **Torque** distributor retaining bolt to 12–14 ft. lbs.

IGNITION LOCK
REPLACE

Ignition lock is retained by two shear type screws, **Fig. 1.** It is necessary to drill out these screws to remove ignition lock from steering tube. When installing, ensure shear type screws are used.

IGNITION SWITCH
REPLACE

1. Remove four upper and lower shell cover retaining screws, then shell covers.
2. Disconnect electrical connectors from switch.
3. Remove switch retaining screw from steering lock, **Fig. 2.**
4. Remove switch.
5. Reverse procedure to install.

NEUTRAL SAFETY SWITCH
REPLACE

1. Loosen inhibitor switch attaching screws, **Fig. 3.**
2. Set selector lever manual shaft at Neutral position.
3. Insert suitable pin into adjustment holes in both inhibitor switch and switch lever as near vertical as possible, then tighten screws.
4. Check switch for continuity, and replace as necessary.

HEADLAMP SWITCH
REPLACE

1. Remove steering column covers.
2. Disconnect light switch electrical connectors.
3. Remove switch retaining screws and light switch. It is not necessary to remove combination switch base to replace light switch.
4. Reverse procedure to install.

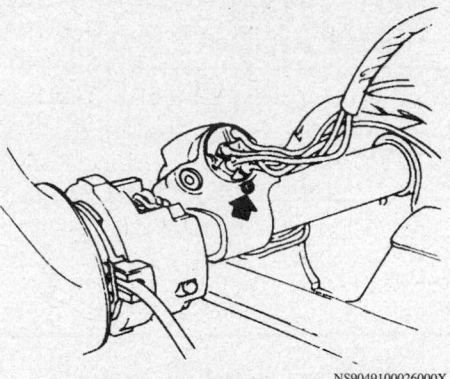

NS9049100026000X

Fig. 2   Ignition switch replacement

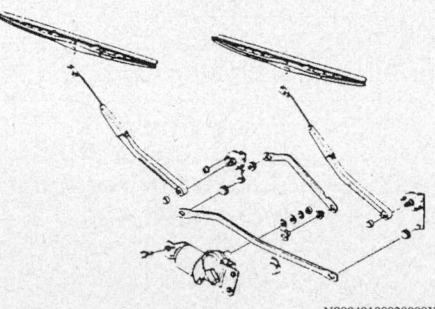

NS9049100028000X

Fig. 4   Windshield wiper system

STOP LIGHT SWITCH
REPLACE

Stop lamp switch is located on brake pedal support.
1. Disconnect switch electrical connectors.
2. Loosen switch retaining locknut and remove switch.
3. Reverse procedure to install.

COMBINATION SWITCH
REPLACE

1. Remove horn cover and steering wheel as outlined under " Steering Wheel, Replace."
2. Remove steering column shell covers.
3. Disconnect switch electrical connections.
4. Remove retaining screws.
5. Push switch toward instrument panel, then turn switch clockwise and remove combination switch base assembly.
6. Reverse procedure to install.

TURN SIGNAL SWITCH
REPLACE

1. Remove steering column covers.
2. Disconnect turn signal switch electrical connections.
3. Remove switch retaining screws, then turn signal switch. It is not necessary to remove combination switch base to replace turn signal switch.
4. Reverse procedure to install.

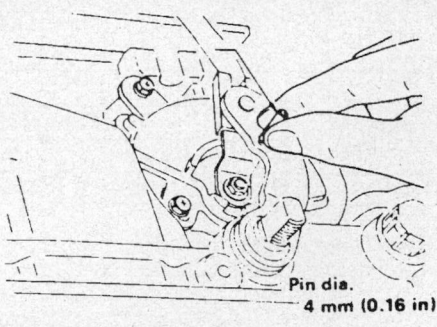

Pin dia.
4 mm (0.16 in)

NS9049100027000X

Fig. 3   Inhibitor switch adjustment

STEERING WHEEL
REPLACE

1. Remove driver side air bag as outlined under "Passive Restraints."
2. Remove steering wheel retaining nut.
3. Use suitable steering wheel puller and remove steering wheel.
4. Reverse procedure to install, noting the following:
   a. Apply suitable grease to entire surface of turn signal cancel pin and horn contact slip ring.
   b. **Torque** steering wheel retaining nut to 22–29 ft. lbs.

INSTRUMENT CLUSTER
REPLACE

Refer to "Instrument Panel, Replace" in "Dash Panel Service" when replacing instrument cluster.
1. Remove steering column cover and steering wheel.
2. Remove gear shift boot.
3. Remove instrument panel cover.
4. Remove cluster lid retaining screws, then the cluster lid.
5. Disconnect speedometer cable, cluster retaining nuts and electrical connectors. Cluster may have to be pulled slightly forward after removing retaining screws to allow access to electrical connectors.
6. Reverse procedure to install.

RADIO
REPLACE

Refer to "Instrument Panel, Replace" in "Dash Panel Service" when replacing radio.
1. Remove cluster lid or instrument panel fascia to gain access to brackets.
2. Remove radio bracket to instrument panel attaching screw.
3. Disconnect electrical leads from radio.
4. Remove radio from vehicle.
5. Reverse procedure to install.

WIPER MOTOR
REPLACE

Refer to **Fig. 4** for typical wiper system exploded view.
1. Remove wiper arms.
2. Disconnect electrical connector from

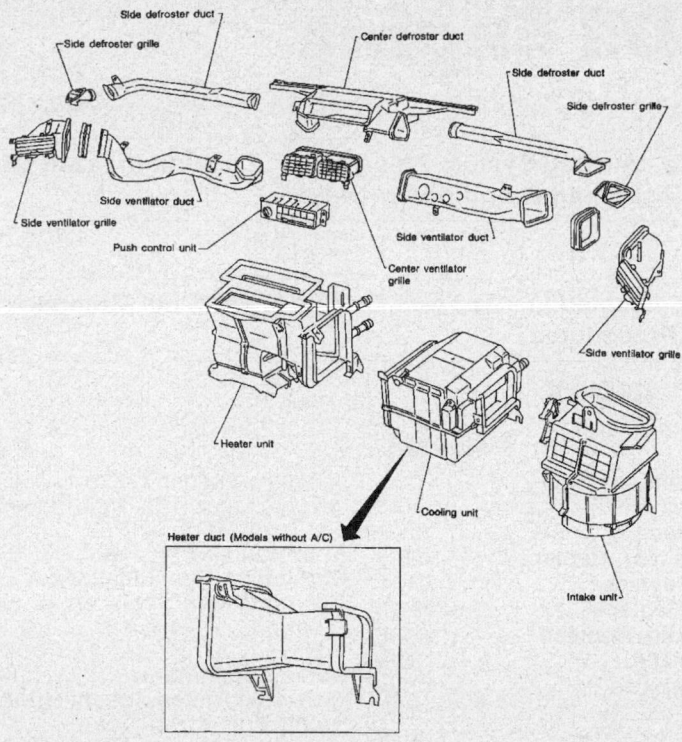

Fig. 5   Exploded view of heater system

BLOWER MOTOR
REPLACE

1. Recover refrigerant as outlined under "Air Conditioning."
2. Remove passenger side instrument lower cover and glove compartment.
3. Disconnect wiring harness connectors from intake unit, **Fig. 5.**
4. Remove intake unit.
5. Remove blower motor from intake unit.
6. Reverse procedure to install.

HEATER CORE
REPLACE

1. Drain cooling system.
2. Disconnect heater inlet and outlet coolant pipes from heater unit.
3. Remove instrument panel as outlined under "Dash Panel Service."
4. Disconnect heater ducts, **Fig. 5.**
5. Disconnect wiring harness connectors from heater unit.
6. Remove heater unit.
7. Separate heater unit case halves and remove heater core.
8. Reverse procedure to install.

EVAPORATOR CORE
REPLACE

1. Recover refrigerant as outlined under "Air Conditioning."
2. Remove passenger side instrument lower cover and glove compartment.
3. Disconnect wiring harness connectors from intake unit.
4. Remove intake unit.
5. Disconnect wiring harness connectors from evaporator.
6. Remove cooling unit.
7. Separate cooling unit case halves and remove evaporator, **Fig. 5.**
8. Reverse procedure to install.

motor, then remove top grille retaining screws and top grille.
3. Remove wiper motor mounting bolts and pull motor away from firewall.
4. Disconnect motor shaft from linkage taking care not to bend linkage.
5. Remove cowl top grille.
6. Remove flange nuts retaining pivot to cowl top.
7. Remove wiper motor linkage.
8. Reverse procedure to install.

WIPER SWITCH
REPLACE

1. Remove steering column covers.
2. Disconnect wiper switch electrical connections.
3. Remove switch retaining screws, then the switch. It is not necessary to remove combination switch base to replace wiper switch.
4. Reverse procedure to install.

WIPER TRANSMISSION
REPLACE

Refer to "Wiper Motor, Replace" for wiper transmission replacement.

KA24DE Engine

NOTE: On Air Bag Equipped Models, Refer To "Air Bag System Precautions" Located In Front Of This Manual For System Disarming & Arming Procedures.

NOTE: Refer To "Computer Relearn Procedures" Located In The Front Of This Manual For Computer Relearn Procedures.

INDEX

PRECAUTIONS

AIR BAG SYSTEMS

Refer to "Air Bag System Precautions" in front of this manual for system disarming and arming procedures.

BATTERY GROUND CABLE

Prior to service, disconnect battery ground cable and isolate as required.

FUEL SYSTEM PRESSURE RELEASE

1. Remove fuel pump fuse from fuse panel.
2. Start engine.
3. After engine stops, crank engine two or three times to release all fuel pressure.
4. Turn ignition switch to the Off position.
5. After fuel system service is complete, replace fuel pump fuse.

COMPRESSION PRESSURE

1. Start engine and run until engine reaches operating temperature.
2. Turn ignition switch off.
3. Release fuel pressure as outlined under "Precautions."
4. Remove all spark plugs.
5. Disconnect distributor center cable.
6. Attach a compression tester to cylinder No. 1.
7. Depress accelerator pedal fully to keep throttle valve wide open.
8. Crank engine and record highest gauge indication.

9. Repeat measurement on each cylinder.
10. Standard compression pressure is 179 psi, minimum pressure is 151 psi. Difference between cylinders should not exceed 14 psi.
11. If compression in one or more cylinders is low, pour a small amount of engine oil into cylinders through spark plug holes, then retest compression.
12. If adding oil helps compression, then piston rings may be at fault. If adding oil does not help compression, then the valves may be at fault.
13. If compression stays low in two cylinders that are next to each other, then cylinder head gasket may be leaking or both cylinders have valve component damage.
14. Repair as necessary.

ENGINE MOUNT

REPLACE

Refer to **Fig. 1** for engine mount replacement.

ENGINE

REPLACE

1. Place vehicle on level ground and block wheels.
2. Release fuel pressure as outlined under "Precautions."
3. **On models equipped with automatic transmission,** remove transmission as outlined under "Transmission, Replace" in "RE4R01A, RE4R03A & RL4R01A Automatic Transmissions."
4. **On models equipped with manual transmission,** remove transmission

as outlined under "Transmission, Replace" in "Clutch & Manual Transmission."
5. **On all models,** remove engine undercover and hood.
6. Drain coolant from engine and radiator.
7. Drain engine oil.
8. Remove vacuum hoses, fuel tubes, wires, harnesses and connectors. **Mark vacuum hoses, wires and connectors for installation reference.**
9. Remove front exhaust pipes from exhaust manifolds.
10. Remove radiator and shroud, then drive belts.
11. Remove A/C pump and power steering pump from engine.
12. Install a suitable engine lifting device to cylinder head.
13. Remove engine mounting bolts from both sides, then slowly raise engine.
14. Reverse procedure to install.

INTAKE MANIFOLD

REPLACE

Refer to **Figs. 2 through 4** for intake manifold service.

EXHAUST MANIFOLD

REPLACE

Refer to **Figs. 5 and 6** for exhaust manifold service.

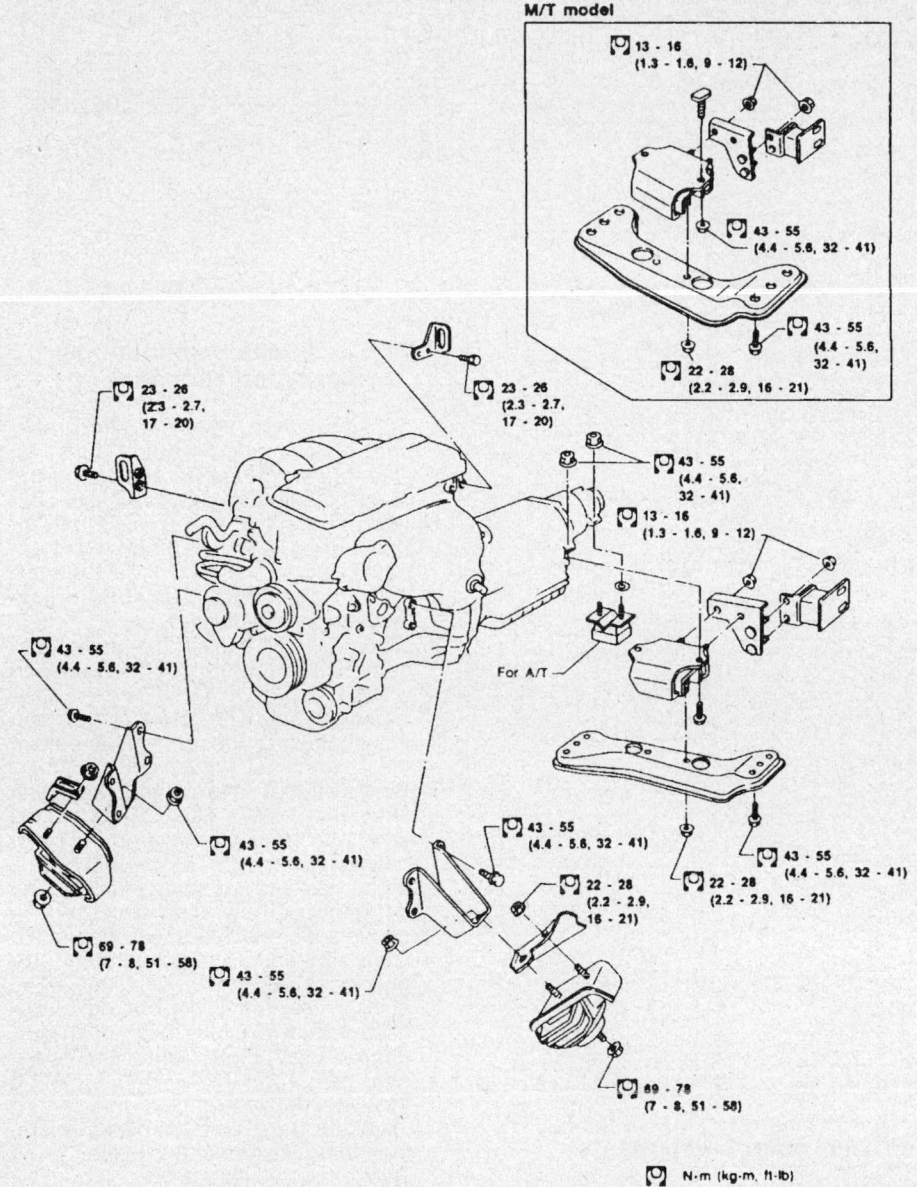

Fig. 1 Engine mounting brackets

INSTALLATION

1. Install idler shaft, cylinder head gasket and cylinder head.
2. Temporarily finger tighten cylinder head bolts.
3. Align gold marking on upper timing chain with mark on idler sprocket, **Fig. 9,** then install upper timing chain, chain tensioner and chain guide. **Remove pin to release tensioner piston.**
4. Apply a bead of liquid gasket to mating surfaces of front cover.
5. Ensure mating marks on timing chain and idler sprocket are aligned, then install camshaft sprocket cover.
6. Using sequence shown in **Fig. 10,** tighten cylinder head bolts as follows:
   a. **Torque** bolts to 22 ft. lbs.
   b. **Torque** bolts to 59 ft. lbs.
   c. Loosen all bolts completely.
   d. **Torque** bolts 18–25 ft. lbs.
   e. If using an angle wrench, turn head bolts 86–91° clockwise.
   f. If using a torque wrench, **torque** head bolts to 55–62 ft. lbs.
7. Install camshaft and camshaft brackets, then using sequence shown in **Fig. 11,** tighten bolts as follows:
   a. **Torque** bolts to 16.8 inch lbs.
   b. **Torque** bolts to 7–9 ft. lbs.
8. Align gold marking on chain with mark on camshaft sprockets, then install sprocket on camshaft, **Fig. 12.**
9. Install chain guide between both camshaft sprockets.
10. Apply liquid gasket to rubber plugs and install rubber plugs, then move them by hand to evenly spread liquid gasket and install plugs flush with cylinder head surface.
11. Ensure No. 1 cylinder is at TDC, and distributor rotor is set at No. 1 cylinder spark position, then install distributor. **Ensure distributor shaft marks align with housing indent mark.**
12. Install rocker cover using tightening sequence shown in **Fig. 13.**
13. Install spark plugs and wires.
14. Connect injector harness, then install injector tube assembly and injectors.
15. Install radiator shroud, cooling fan with coupling and air duct.
16. Install vacuum hoses, fuel tubes, wires and harness connectors.

ENGINE DISASSEMBLE

1. Place engine on work stand.
2. Remove timing chain as outlined under "Timing Chain, Replace."
3. Remove pistons with connecting rods.
4. Remove main bearing beam and crankshaft, loosening bolts in two or three steps using sequence shown in **Fig. 14.**

ENGINE ASSEMBLE

1. Install new snap ring on one side of piston pin hole, heat piston to 140–158°F and assemble piston, pin, connecting rod and snap ring.
2. Install piston rings with punch mark side of compression rings facing up.
3. Install main bearings and bearing

CYLINDER HEAD
REPLACE
REMOVAL

1. Release fuel system pressure as outlined under "Precautions."
2. Drain engine oil and coolant.
3. Remove vacuum hoses, fuel tubes, wires, harness and electrical connectors from cylinder head and front covers. **Mark vacuum hoses, wires and electrical connectors for installation reference.**
4. Remove exhaust manifold cover and front exhaust pipe.
5. Remove air duct, cooling fan with coupling and radiator shroud.
6. Disconnect injector harness connector, then remove injector tube assembly with injectors.
7. Remove spark plugs and cables.
8. Turn crankshaft and set No. 1 piston at TDC on compression stroke.
9. Remove rocker cover and gasket, **Fig. 7.**
10. Remove distributor.
11. Hold camshaft with a suitable wrench and remove camshaft sprockets.
12. Remove camshaft brackets and camshaft. **Place brackets and camshaft aside in order of removal. These components must be installed in original position.**
13. Using numbered sequence shown in **Fig. 8,** loosen cylinder head bolts in two or three steps.
14. Remove camshaft sprocket cover.
15. Push upper chain tensioner piston and insert suitable pin into pin hole, then remove tensioner, upper chain guides and upper timing chain.
16. Remove idler sprocket bolt.
17. Remove cylinder head with intake and exhaust manifolds as an assembly.
18. Remove cylinder head gasket.

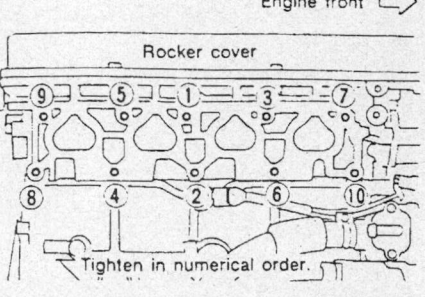

Fig. 3 Intake manifold bolt tightening sequence

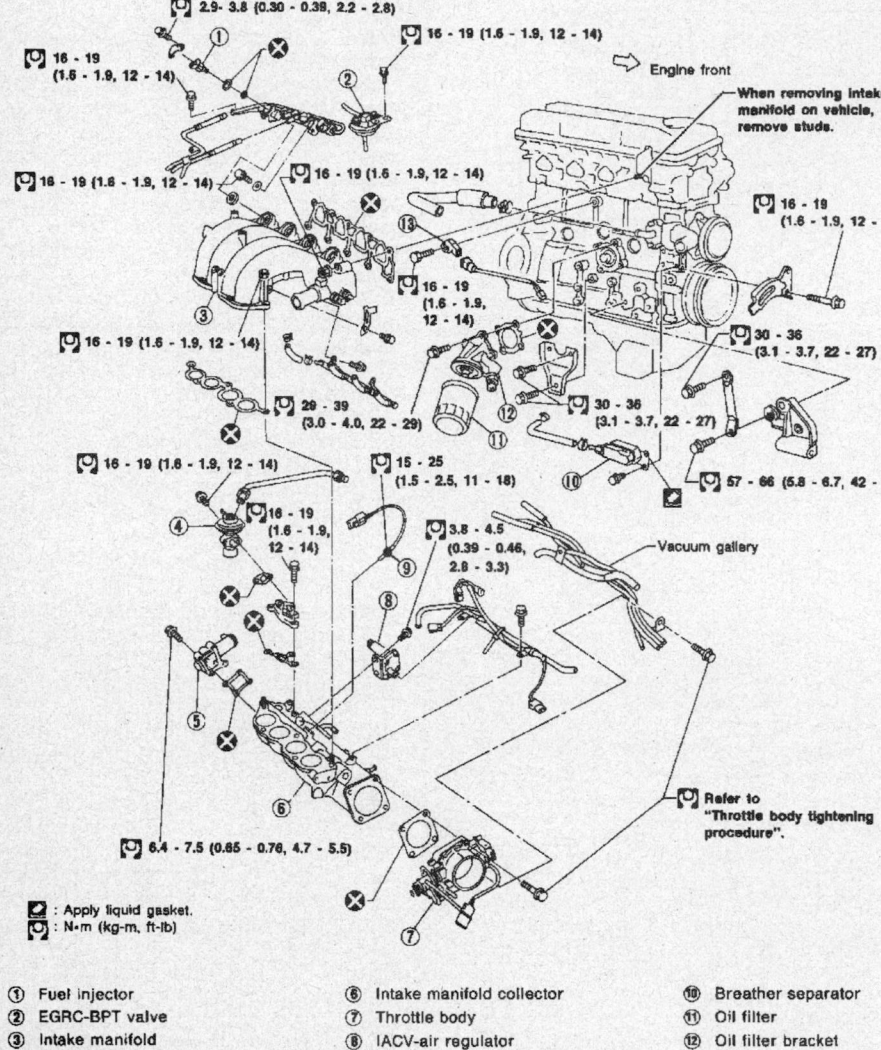

① Fuel injector
② EGRC-BPT valve
③ Intake manifold
④ EGR valve
⑤ IAA unit
⑥ Intake manifold collector
⑦ Throttle body
⑧ IACV-air regulator
⑨ EGR temperature sensor
⑩ Breather separator
⑪ Oil filter
⑫ Oil filter bracket
⑬ Knock sensor

NS1069500163000X

Fig. 2 Exploded view of engine lefthand outer components

beam. **Torque** bolts in two or three steps using sequence shown in **Fig. 15.**

4. Install connecting rod bearings on connecting rods. Ensure oil hole in rod and bearing match.
5. Install piston and rod assemblies, ensure mark on piston faces front.
6. Install connecting rod bearing caps. **Torque** nuts to 10–12 ft. lbs., noting the following:
   a. If using an angle wrench, turn an additional 60–65° clockwise.
   b. If angle wrench is not available, **torque** to 28–33 ft. lbs.

VALVE CLEARANCE SPECIFICATIONS

Year	Stem-To-Guide Clearance, Inch①	
	Intake	Exhaust
1996–97	.0008–.0021	.0016–.0029

① — Engine at operating temperature.

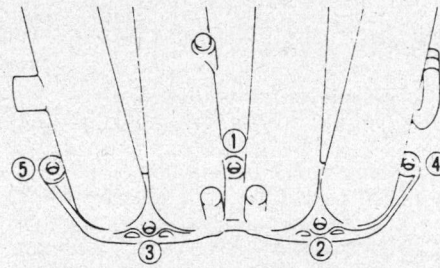

Tighten in numerical order.

NS1069500166000X

Fig. 4 Intake manifold collector bolt tightening sequence

VALVE ADJUSTMENT

1. Remove rocker cover.
2. Remove spark plugs and set No. 1 piston to TDC on compression stroke.
3. Use feeler gauge to measure and record clearance between valve lifter and camshaft on No. 1 and No. 2 intake valves, and No. 1 and No. 3 exhaust valves.

4. Turn crankshaft 360° and align crankshaft pulley mark with point.
5. Use feeler gauge to measure and record clearance between valve lifter and camshaft on No. 3 and No. 4 intake valves, and No. 2 and No. 4 exhaust valves.
6. Turn crankshaft to position cam lobe on valve to be adjusted.
7. Place suitable camshaft pliers around camshaft and rotate so lifter is pushed down.
8. Place suitable lifter stopper between camshaft and edge of lifter and remove pliers.
9. Blow air into hole to separate adjusting shim from valve lifter, then remove shim with small screwdriver and magnetic finger.
10. Measure removed shim and calculate thickness of new shim necessary to obtain specified clearance. New intake shim size equals removed shim size plus measured clearance minus .0146 inch. New exhaust shim size equals removed shim size plus measured clearance minus .0146 inch. Shims are available from .0772 inch to .1055 inch, in .0008 inch steps.
11. Install new shim, attach pliers, rotate, then remove stopper and pliers.
12. Recheck valve clearance.
13. Repeat shim removal and replacement procedure as necessary.
14. Reverse procedure to install.

TIMING CHAIN
REPLACE
UPPER

For upper timing chain service, refer to "Cylinder Head, Replace," **Fig. 16.**

LOWER
Removal

1. Remove cylinder head as outlined under "Cylinder Head, Replace."
2. Remove oil pan as outlined under "Oil Pan, Replace."
3. Remove oil strainer.
4. Remove power steering pump, alternator and air conditioning compressor drive belts, then air conditioning compressor idler pulley.
5. Remove crankshaft pulley using suitable puller.

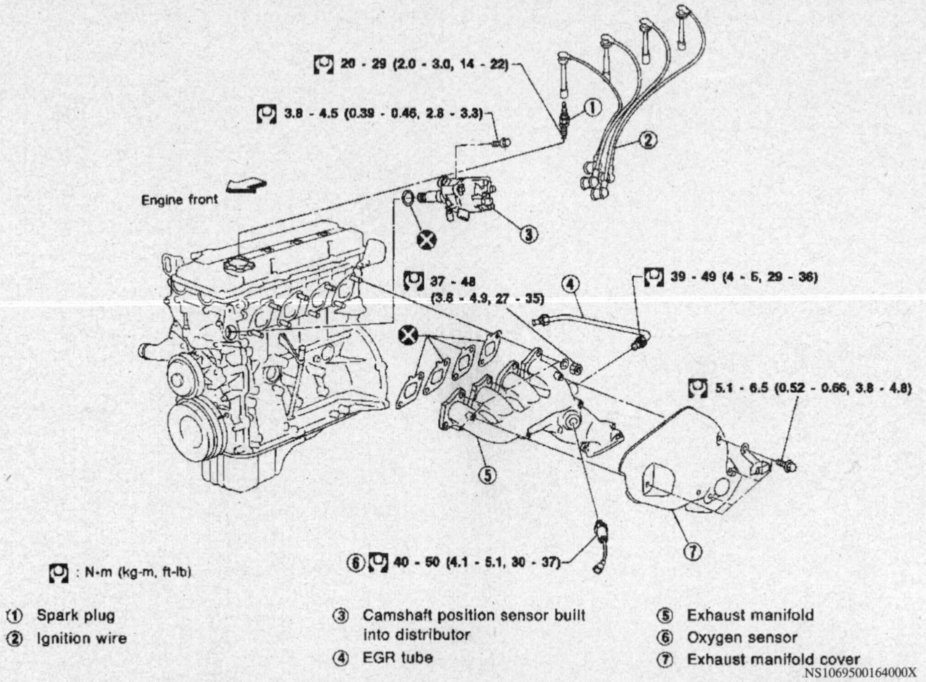
20 - 29 (2.0 - 3.0, 14 - 22)
3.8 - 4.5 (0.39 - 0.46, 2.8 - 3.3)
Engine front
37 - 48
(3.8 - 4.9, 27 - 35)
39 - 49 (4 - 5, 29 - 36)
5.1 - 6.5 (0.52 - 0.66, 3.8 - 4.8)
40 - 50 (4.1 - 5.1, 30 - 37)
: N·m (kg-m, ft-lb)
① Spark plug
② Ignition wire
③ Camshaft position sensor built into distributor
④ EGR tube
⑤ Exhaust manifold
⑥ Oxygen sensor
⑦ Exhaust manifold cover
NS1069500164000X

Fig. 5 Exploded view of engine righthand outer components

6. Remove front cover.
7. Push timing chain tensioner piston in and insert suitable pin into pin hole, then remove tensioner, tensioner arm and chain guide.
8. Remove lower timing chain and idler sprocket.

Installation

1. Install crankshaft sprocket. **Ensure mating marks on crankshaft sprocket face toward front of engine.**
2. Position No. 1 cylinder at TDC on compression stroke.
3. Align silver mark on timing chain with mark on crankshaft and idler sprockets, then install idler sprocket and lower timing chain, **Fig. 17.**
4. Install chain tensioner arm and chain guide.
5. Install lower timing chain tensioner and remove pin to release piston.
6. Apply continuous liquid gasket bead to front cover and install.
7. Install crankshaft pulley, oil strainer and oil pan.
8. Install component parts below engine.
9. Install air compressor idler pulley.
10. Install new cylinder head as outlined under "Cylinder Head, Replace."

CRANKSHAFT SEAL

REPLACE

1. Remove radiator shroud attaching screws and shroud.
2. Remove crankshaft pulley attaching bolt and pulley, then remove front oil seal using screw driver, or equivalent, to pry out seal.
3. Apply engine oil to new seal and use suitable oil seal tool to install.

CRANKSHAFT REAR OIL SEAL

REPLACE

1. **On models equipped with manual transmission,** remove transmission as outlined under "Clutch & Manual Transmission."
2. **On models equipped with automatic transmission,** remove transmission as outlined under "Automatic Transmission/Transaxles."
3. **On all models,** remove flywheel or driveplate, then the rear oil seal retainer.
4. Using a suitable scraper, remove all traces of liquid gasket from matting surface.
5. Remove rear oil seal from rear oil seal retainer.
6. Coat new seal with engine oil and use suitable seal tool to install into retainer.
7. Apply liquid gasket, or equivalent, to retainer and install.

OIL PAN

REPLACE

1. Raise and support vehicle, then drain engine oil.
2. Remove power steering tube, then front stabilizer bar mounting bolts.
3. Use suitable hoist to hold engine with slingers attached to cylinder head.
4. Remove tension rod bolts at transverse links, then front stabilizer bar mounting bolts and nuts from side member.
5. Remove left and right side engine mounting bolts.
6. Remove gussets, then disconnect steering shaft lower joint.

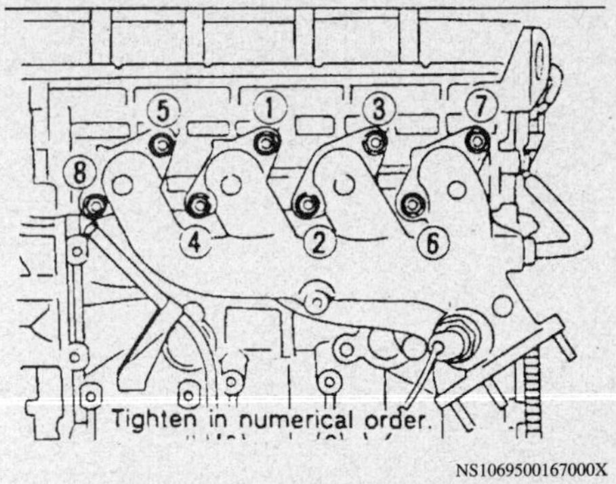
Tighten in numerical order.
NS1069500167000X

Fig. 6 Exhaust manifold nut tightening sequence

7. Remove power steering tube bracket mounting bolts at left tension rod bracket.
8. Support front suspension member with suitable jack and lower approximately 2 ½ inches, then remove pan bolts.
9. Insert a suitable tool between cylinder block and oil pan, then tap tool side with hammer and remove oil pan. **Do not use a screwdriver; oil pan flange will be deformed. Be careful not to damage aluminum mating surface of cylinder block.**
10. Pull pan from front while lowering front suspension member. Use care when separating pan from block.
11. Reverse procedure to install, noting the following:
    a. Remove all remaining liquid gasket from pan and cylinder block mating surfaces.
    b. Apply a continuous bead of liquid gasket to oil pan mating surface.
    c. Install pan within five minutes of applying gasket.
    d. Wait at least 30 minutes before refilling engine with oil.

OIL PUMP

REPLACE

1. Remove front cover as outlined under "Timing Chain, Replace."
2. Turn front cover over and remove oil pump cover, **Fig. 18.**
3. Reverse procedure to install.

BELT TENSION DATA

Refer to **Fig. 19** for drive belt deflection specifications. Measure drive belt deflection when engine is cold.

COOLING SYSTEM BLEED

This engines does not require a specified bleed procedure. After filling cooling system, run engine to operating temperature with radiator/pressure cap off. Air will then be automatically bled through cap opening.

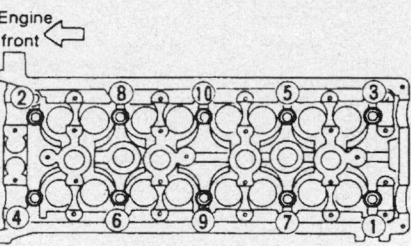

Loosen in numerical order.

NS1069100135000X

Fig. 8 Cylinder head bolt loosening sequence

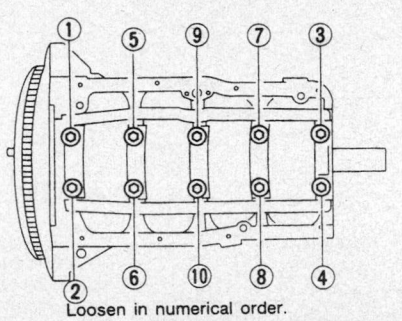

Loosen in numerical order.

NS1069500168000X

Fig. 11 Camshaft tightening sequence

THERMOSTAT
REPLACE

1. Drain cooling system, then disconnect radiator hose from thermostat housing.
2. Remove thermostat housing attaching bolts, then housing.
3. Remove thermostat from housing.
4. Reverse procedure to install.

WATER PUMP
REPLACE

1. Drain cooling system.
2. Remove fan coupling with fan, then power steering, alternator and air conditioning compressor drive belts.
3. Remove water pump and gasket, **Fig. 20**.
4. Reverse procedure to install, using new gasket.

RADIATOR
REPLACE

To service radiator, refer to **Fig. 21**.

FUEL PUMP
REPLACE

1. Release fuel system pressure as outlined under " Precautions."
2. Remove inspection hole cover located behind rear seat.
3. Disconnect fuel lines and harness connectors on upper plate.
4. Remove fuel tank lock ring using tool No. SST J38879-A, or equivalent.
5. Remove fuel pump by pulling top end of fuel pump bracket upward.

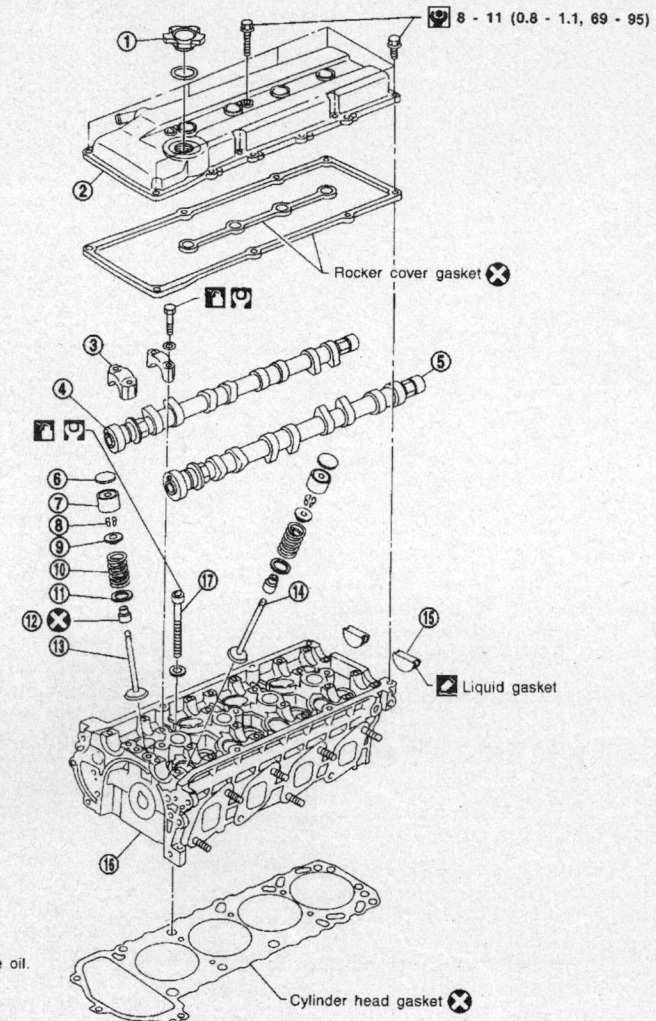

$\boxed{\text{⚙}}$ 8 - 11 (0.8 - 1.1, 69 - 95)

Rocker cover gasket ⊗

Liquid gasket

🛢 : Lubricate with new engine oil.
🔧 : N·m (kg-m, ft-lb)
⚙ : N·m (kg-m, in-lb)

① Oil filler cap
② Rocker cover
③ Camshaft bracket
④ Intake camshaft
⑤ Exhaust camshaft
⑥ Shim
⑦ Valve lifter
⑧ Valve cotter
⑨ Spring retainer
⑩ Valve spring
⑪ Spring seat
⑫ Valve oil seal
⑬ Intake valve
⑭ Exhaust valve
⑮ Rubber plug
⑯ Cylinder head
⑰ Cylinder head bolt

Cylinder head gasket ⊗

NS1069300191000X

Fig. 7 Exploded view of cylinder head

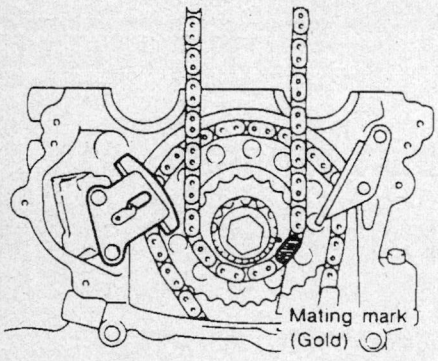

Mating mark (Gold)

NS1069100136000X

Fig. 9 Upper timing chain on idler pulley alignment

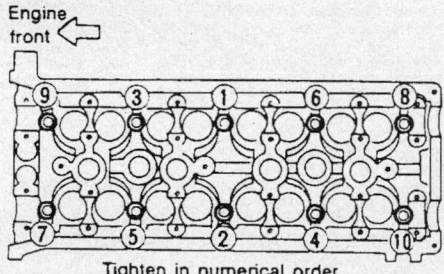

Engine front ⇦

Tighten in numerical order.

NS1069100137000X

Fig. 10 Cylinder head bolt tightening sequence

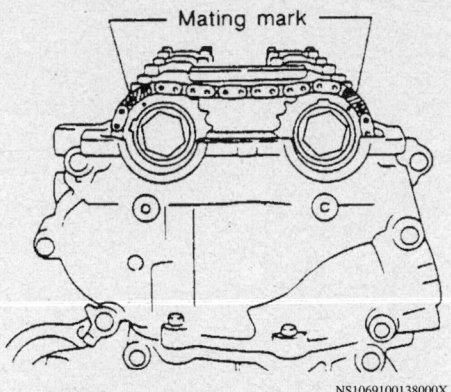

Fig. 12 Upper timing chain on camshafts alignment

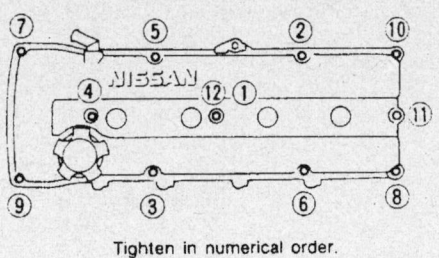

Tighten in numerical order.

Fig. 13 Rocker cover tightening sequence

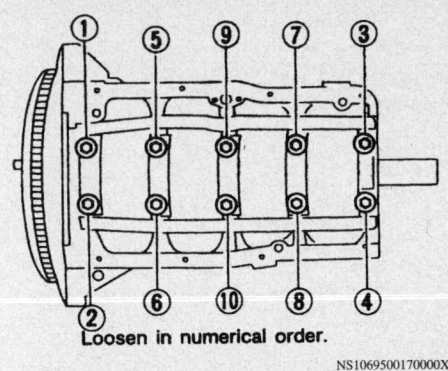

Loosen in numerical order.

Fig. 14 Main bearing cap bolt loosening sequence

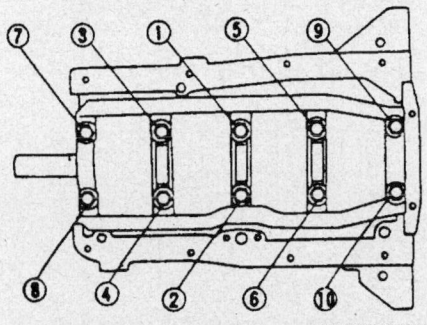

Fig. 15 Main bearing cap bolt tightening sequence

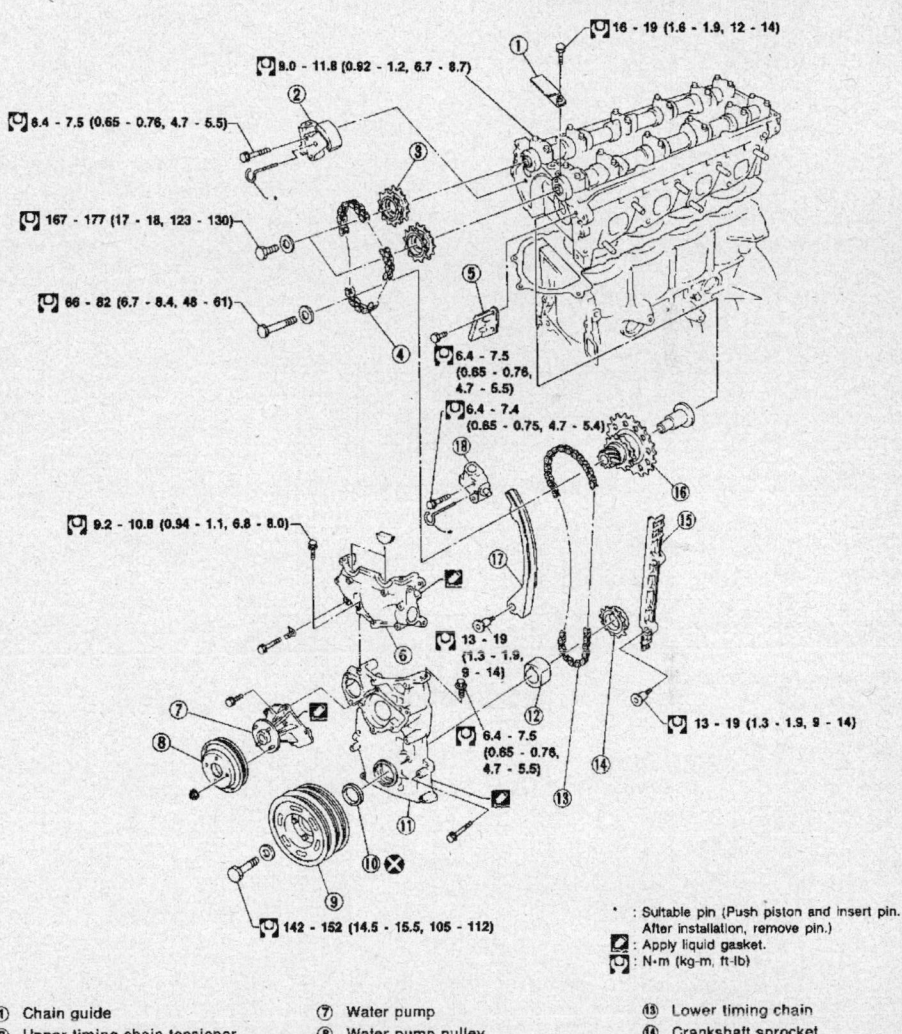

① Chain guide
② Upper timing chain tensioner
③ Cam sprocket
④ Upper timing chain
⑤ Chain guide
⑥ Upper front cover
⑦ Water pump
⑧ Water pump pulley
⑨ Crankshaft pulley
⑩ Front oil seal
⑪ Front cover
⑫ Oil pump drive spacer
⑬ Lower timing chain
⑭ Crankshaft sprocket
⑮ Chain guide
⑯ Idler sprocket
⑰ Chain tension arm
⑱ Lower timing chain tensioner

Fig. 16 Exploded view of timing chain components

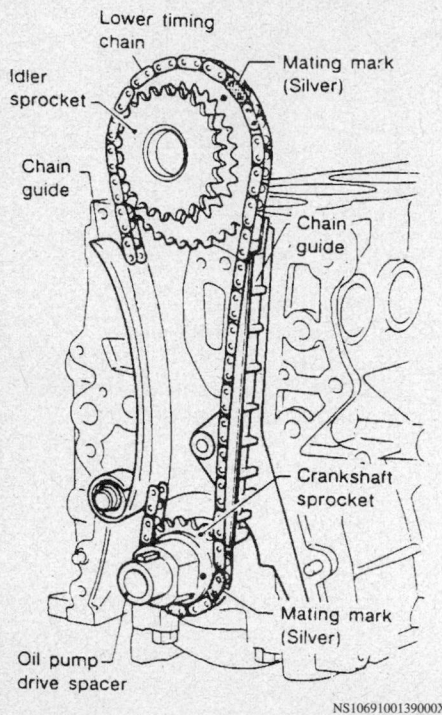

Fig. 17 Lower timing chain alignment

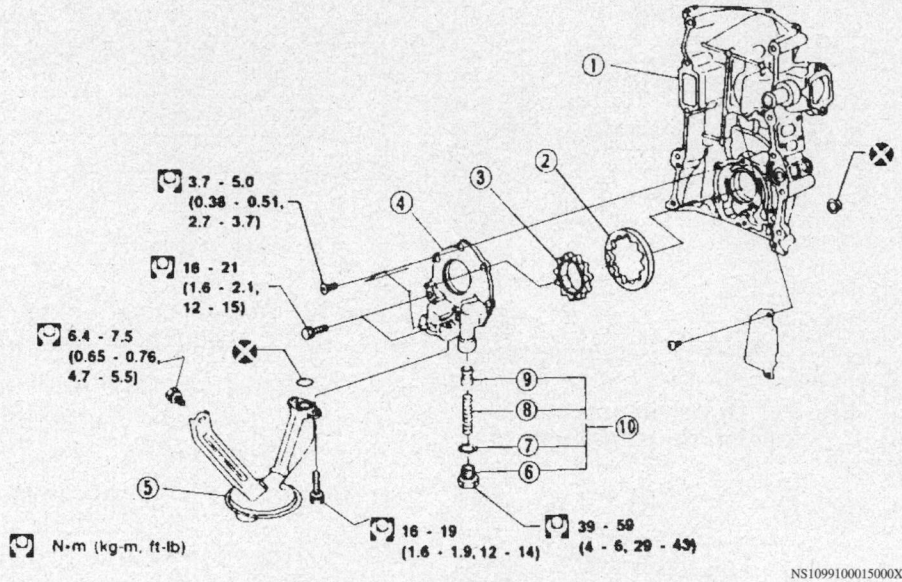

Fig. 18 Exploded view of oil pump assembly

NS1099100015000X

	Used belt deflection		Deflection of new belt
	Limit	Deflection after adjustment	
Alternator	11 (0.43)	7 - 8 (0.28 - 0.31)	6 - 7 (0.24 - 0.28)
Air conditioner compressor	12 (0.47)	7.5 - 8.5 (0.295 - 0.335)	6.5 - 7.5 (0.256 - 0.295)
Power steering oil pump	13 (0.51)	7.5 - 8.5 (0.295 - 0.335)	6.5 - 7.5 (0.256 - 0.295)
Applied pushing force	98 N (10 kg, 22 lb)		

Unit: mm (in)

NS1069100141000X

Fig. 19 Belt tightening specifications

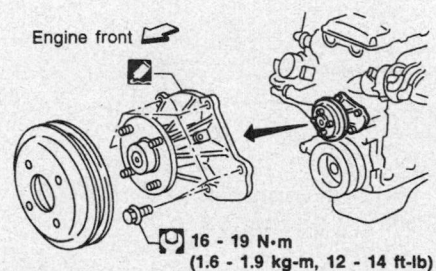

16 - 19 N·m (1.6 - 1.9 kg-m, 12 - 14 ft-lb)

: Apply liquid gasket.

NS1089100015000X

Fig. 20 Water pump replacement

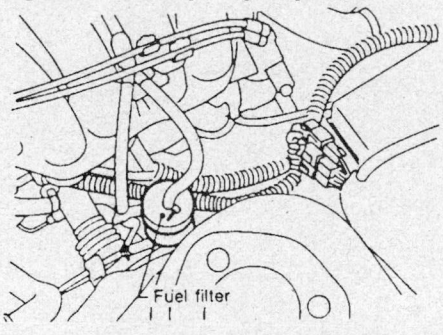

NS1029100009000X

Fig. 22 Fuel filter

6. Reverse procedure to install.

FUEL FILTER
REPLACE

1. Release fuel system pressure as outlined under " Precautions."
2. Loosen fuel filter hose clamps, **Fig. 22.**
3. Remove fuel filter. **Be careful not to spill fuel in engine compartment.**
4. Reverse procedure to install.

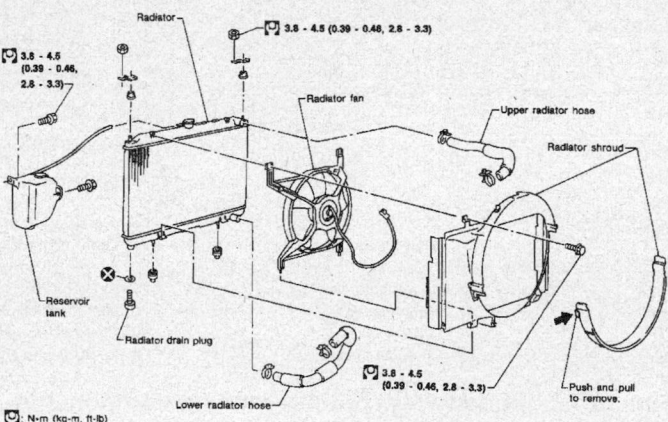

NS1089500077000X

Fig. 21 Radiator replacement

TIGHTENING SPECIFICATIONS

Year	Component	Torque/Ft. Lbs.
1996–97	Camshaft Sprocket Bolt	123–130
	Connecting Rod Bearing Caps	34–41
	Crankshaft Pulley	105–112
	Cylinder Head	①
	Exhaust Manifold	27–35
	Flywheel	105–112
	Main Bearing	34–38
	Oil Pan Bolts	56–66②
	Oil Pan Drain Plug	22–29
	Water Pump	12–14

① — Refer to "Cylinder Head, Replace" for procedure.
② — Inch lbs.

Clutch & Manual Transmission

INDEX

ADJUSTMENTS

CLUTCH PEDAL

Clutch hydraulic system must be bled whenever a clutch line has been disconnected or when air has entered system. Bleed valve is located on clutch operating cylinder.

1. Adjust clutch pedal height dimension "H ," **Fig. 1**, to specifications, **Fig. 2**, using pedal stop or clutch switch.
2. Adjust dimension "C," **Fig. 3**, to specifications, **Fig. 2**, with clutch pedal fully depressed.
3. Adjust clutch pedal freeplay dimension "A," **Fig. 1**, to specifications, **Fig. 2**. Adjust clutch pedal freeplay by rotating clutch master cylinder pushrod inward or outward until specified freeplay is obtained. After completing freeplay adjustment, tighten locknut. Clutch pedal freeplay is sum of play between piston and piston rod.
4. After above adjustments have been completed, cycle clutch pedal several times to ensure clutch linkage operates smoothly without binding.

HYDRAULIC SYSTEM SERVICE

CLUTCH SLAVE CYLINDER, REPLACE

1. Drain fluid from clutch system into a suitable container.
2. Disconnect clutch hose from clutch tube.

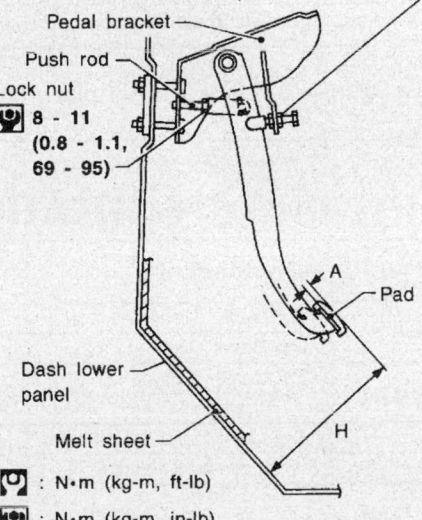

ASCD cancel switch or pedal stopper lock nut

● ASCD cancel switch
12 - 15 (1.2 - 1.5, 9 - 11)
● Pedal stopper
16 - 22 (1.6 - 2.2, 12 - 16)

Pedal bracket
Push rod
Lock nut
8 - 11 (0.8 - 1.1, 69 - 95)

A
Pad

Dash lower panel
Melt sheet
H

: N•m (kg-m, ft-lb)
: N•m (kg-m, in-lb)

NS5049100034000A

Fig. 1 Clutch pedal free travel & height adjustment

3. Remove clutch slave cylinder mounting bolt, then the clutch slave cylinder.
4. Reverse procedure to install. Bleed hydraulic system as outlined under "Clutch Bleed Procedure."

CLUTCH BLEED PROCEDURE

1. Fill reservoir to full level with brake fluid.
2. Connect a transparent vinyl tube to air bleeder valve, **Fig. 4.**
3. Fully depress clutch pedal several times.
4. With clutch fully depressed, open bleeder valve to release air.
5. Close bleeder valve when pedal reaches floor.
6. Repeat steps 3 through 5 until all air is bleed from clutch system.
7. Bleed air from clutch piping connector according to steps 3 through 6.
8. Repeat procedure several times to ensure all air is removed from clutch system.
9. If clutch is still not fully operational (offers very little resistance), proceed as follows:
   a. Raise and support front of vehicle two feet.
   b. Continue pumping fluid through both air bleeder valves in an alternating fashion one valve at a time.
   c. Ensure transparent tubes are submerged in container fluid.
   d. Frequently check reservoir fluid level.
   e. If air pockets continue to prevent full clutch operation, flush entire system and refill reservoir with approximately 20 oz. of fluid.

CLUTCH

REPLACE

1. Remove transmission as outlined

Year	Clutch Pedal Adjustment Specifications, Inches		
	Height	Freeplay	Stop Clearance
1996–97	7.56–7.95	.039–.118	.012–.039

Fig. 2 Clutch pedal specifications

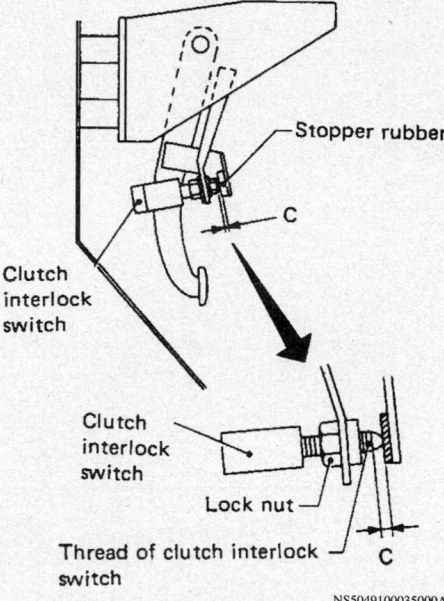

Fig. 3 Clutch interlock switch adjustment

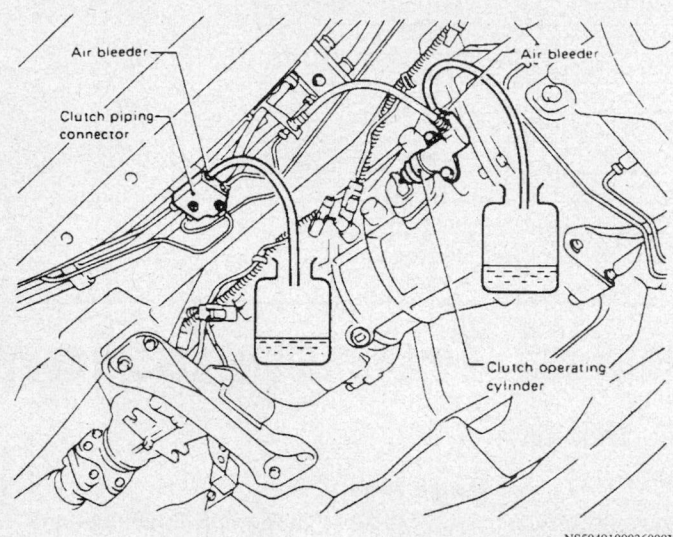

Fig. 4 Clutch bleed procedure

under "Transmission, Replace."
2. Insert a pilot tool into the clutch disc hub.
3. Loosen clutch cover retaining bolts one turn at a time in criss-cross pattern until all pressure is released.
4. Remove clutch disc and cover assembly.
5. Remove release bearing.
6. Reverse procedure to install, noting the following:
   a. Tighten clutch cover retaining bolts one turn at a time, until a final **torque** of 16–22 ft. lbs. is reached.

TRANSMISSION
REPLACE

1. Raise and support vehicle.
2. Disconnect transmission switch wiring.
3. Disconnect speedometer cable from extension housing, if equipped.
4. Remove propeller shaft. **Install a plug in extension housing rear opening to prevent fluid spillage.**
5. Using a suitable jack, support engine with a wooden block placed between oil pan and jack. **Do not place jack**

under oil pan drain plug.
6. Support transmission with suitable jack.
7. Remove console, if necessary.
8. Place transmission control lever in Neutral, then remove snap ring and control lever.
9. Remove rear engine mount and crossmember retaining bolts.
10. Remove bolts retaining transmission to engine, then move transmission rearward and lower from vehicle.
11. Reverse procedure to install, noting the following.
    a. **Torque** 25 mm, 60 mm and 70 mm bolts to 29–36 ft. lbs.
    b. **Torque** 30 mm bolts to 22–29 ft. lbs.

TIGHTENING SPECIFICATIONS

Year	Component	Torque/Ft. Lbs.
1996–97	Air Bleeder Screw	48–84②
	Clutch Cover Cylinder	16–22
	Clutch Master Cylinder	60–96②
	Flywheel	105–112
	Slave Cylinder Mounting Bolt	22–30
	Transmission To Engine	①

① — Refer to "Transmission, Replace" for procedure.

② — Inch lbs.

Rear Axle & Suspension

INDEX

HUB & BEARING
REPLACE

1. Raise and support vehicle.
2. Remove wheel bearing locknut.
3. Remove brake caliper assembly and support by frame using suitable wire.
4. Separate driveshaft from axle housing by slightly tapping with a suitable soft face hammer, **Fig. 1.**
5. Remove axle housing attaching bolts then axle housing, **Fig. 2.**
6. Remove wheel bearing with flange and wheel hub from axle housing.
7. Using a suitable press, press off wheel bearing from wheel hub.
8. Reverse procedure to install, noting the following:
   a. Install wheel bearing as shown in **Fig. 3.**
   b. Check and ensure wheel bearing axial endplay is .0020 inch or less.

REAR SUSPENSION
REPLACE

1. Disconnect ABS sensor and move away from rear suspension assembly, then remove exhaust pipe, propeller shaft rear end and disconnect parking brake cable.
2. Remove brake caliper assembly and suspend on wire.
3. Remove rear parcel shelf, then remove upper shock absorber nuts. **Do not remove piston rod lock nut.**
4. Remove suspension member mounting nuts, **Fig. 4.**
5. Draw out rear axle and suspension assembly.
6. Before removing any suspension component, put matchmarks on adjusting pin.
7. Reverse procedure to install, noting the following:
   a. Final tightening must be done with curb weight on wheels, on ground.
   b. After installation, check wheel alignment.

STRUT
REPLACE

1. Raise and support vehicle.

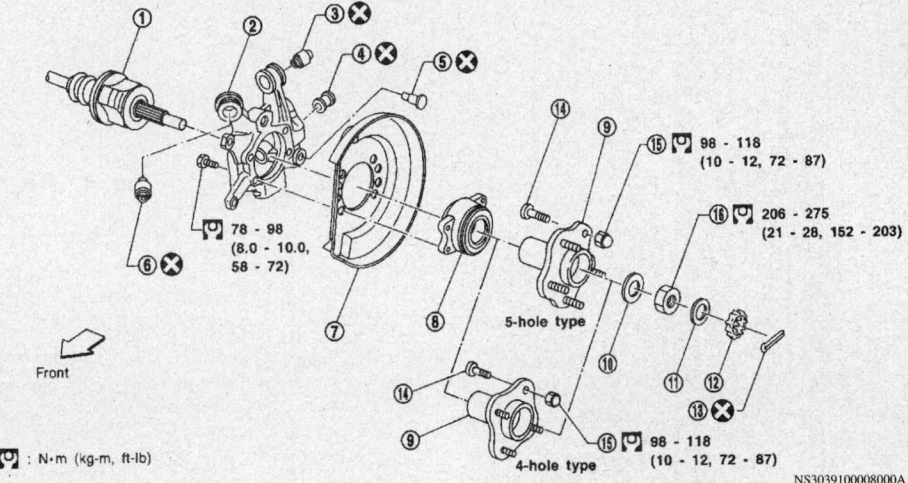

Fig. 1 Wheel hub & axle housing

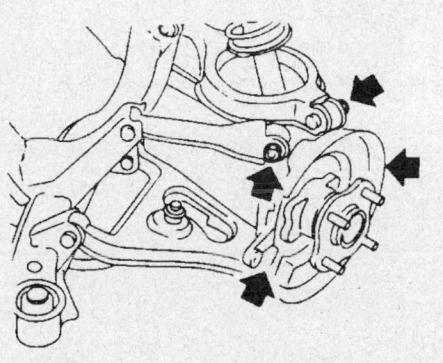

Fig. 2 Axle housing removal

2. Remove upper and lower strut attaching nuts and bolts, **Fig. 5.**
3. Remove coil spring and strut assembly.
4. Reverse procedure to install.

STRUT SERVICE

1. Set strut assembly in vise using suitable holding tool.
2. Compress spring using suitable spring compressor until strut upper spring seat can be turned by hand.
3. Loosen, but do not remove, piston rod locknut.
4. Remove piston locknut.
5. Remove strut assembly components.
6. Reverse procedure to assemble, noting the following:
   a. When installing coil spring, use care not to reverse top and bottom direction, **Fig. 6.**
   b. When installing spring on strut, position as shown in **Fig. 6.**
   c. When installing upper spring seat, position as shown in **Fig. 7.**

STABILIZER BAR
REPLACE

1. Raise and support vehicle.
2. Remove exhaust assembly as necessary.
3. Disconnect stabilizer bar from bushing brackets and locating bolts, then remove stabilizer bar.
4. Reverse procedure to install.

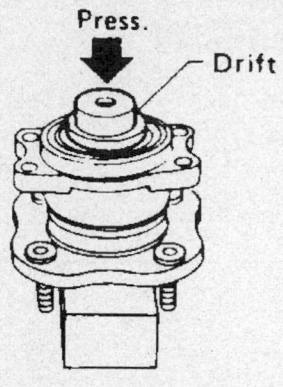

Press.

Drift

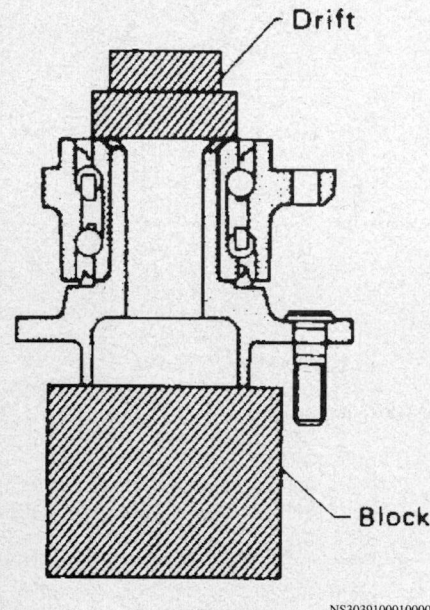

Drift

Block

Fig. 3 Wheel hub bearing installation

NS3039100010000X

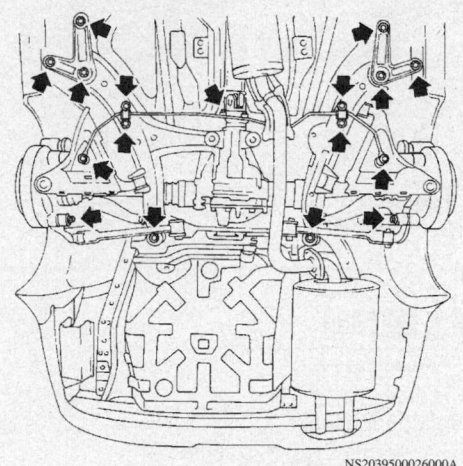

NS2039500026000A

Fig. 4 Rear suspension assembly replacement

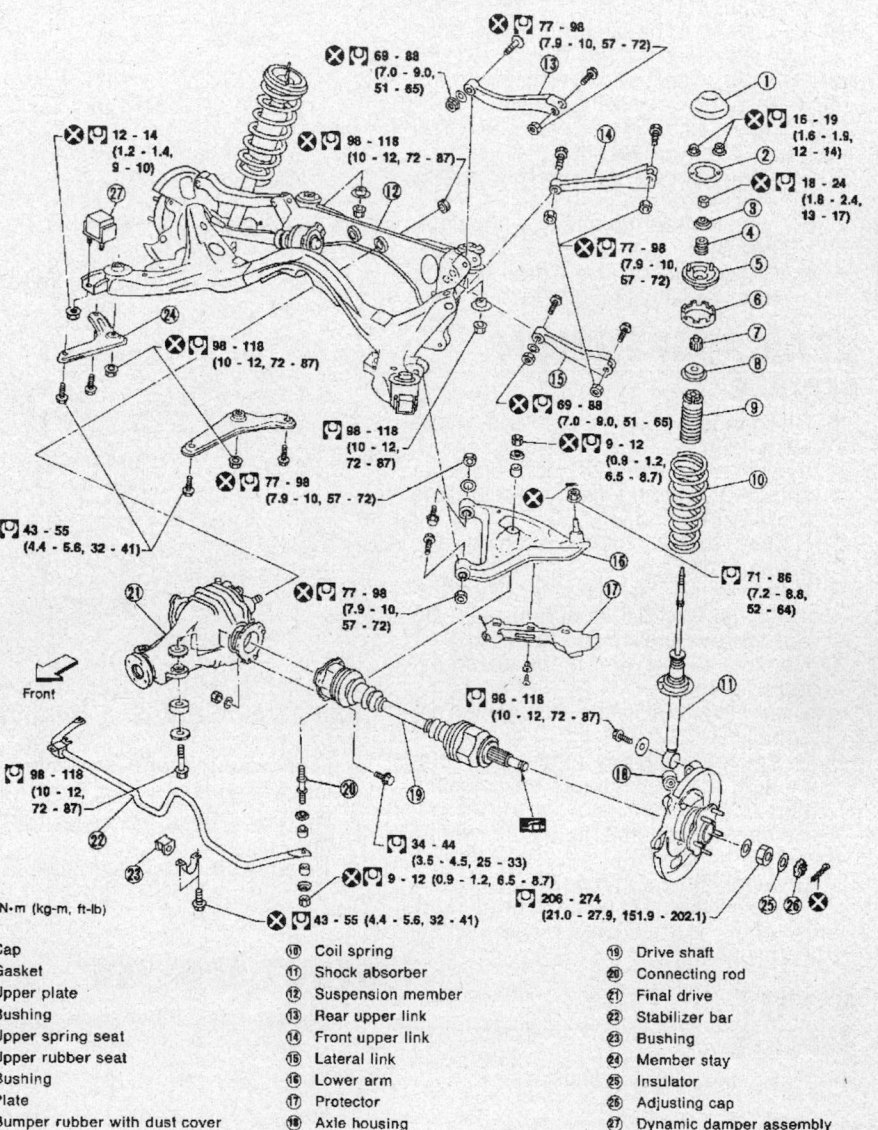

NS2039500027000X

Fig. 5 Exploded view of rear suspension.

① Cap	⑩ Coil spring	⑲ Drive shaft
② Gasket	⑪ Shock absorber	⑳ Connecting rod
③ Upper plate	⑫ Suspension member	㉑ Final drive
④ Bushing	⑬ Rear upper link	㉒ Stabilizer bar
⑤ Upper spring seat	⑭ Front upper link	㉓ Bushing
⑥ Upper rubber seat	⑮ Lateral link	㉔ Member stay
⑦ Bushing	⑯ Lower arm	㉕ Insulator
⑧ Plate	⑰ Protector	㉖ Adjusting cap
⑨ Bumper rubber with dust cover	⑱ Axle housing	㉗ Dynamic damper assembly

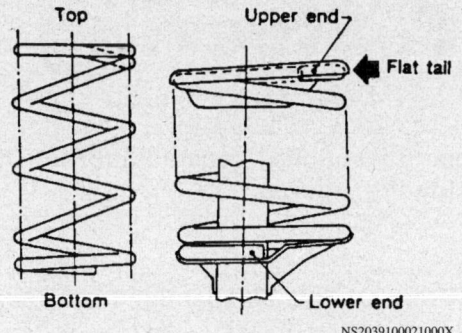

NS2039100021000X

Fig. 6 Coil spring installation

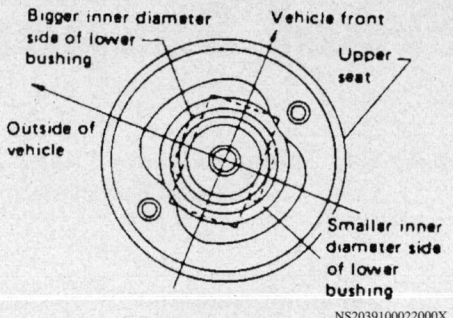

NS2039100022000X

Fig. 7 Upper spring seat installation

TIGHTENING SPECIFICATIONS

Year	Component	Torque/Ft. Lbs.
1996–97	Axle Nut	152–203
	Driveshaft Nut	152–203
	Hub Nut	152–203
	Parallel Link To Strut	65–87
	Parallel Link To Suspension Member	65–87
	Parking Brake Adjuster Locknut	28–38①
	Parking Brake Control Lever To Body	70–96①
	Radius Rod Bracket To Strut	43–58
	Radius Rod To Body	65–80
	Radius Rod To Knuckle	47–61
	Strut To Body	18–22
	Strut To Knuckle	72–87
	Suspension Crossmember	65–80
	Wheel Bearing Locknut	18–25
	Wheel Lug Nut	72–87

① — Inch lbs.

Front Suspension & Steering

NOTE: On Air Bag Equipped Models, Refer To "Air Bag System Precautions" Located In Front Of This Manual For System Disarming & Arming Procedures.

NOTE: Refer To "Computer Relearn Procedures" Located In The Front Of This Manual For Computer Relearn Procedures.

INDEX

WHEEL BEARING
ADJUST

1. Raise and support vehicle.
2. Remove brake pads.
3. Ensure wheel bearing is tightened to specifications.
4. Ensure wheel bearing operates smoothly.
5. Check axial endplay.
6. If axial endplay is more than .0020 inch, replace wheel bearing.

WHEEL HUB & STEERING KNUCKLE
REPLACE

1. Raise and support vehicle, then remove wheel.
2. Remove brake caliper assembly and support from frame using suitable wire.
3. Remove brake rotor.
4. Remove wheel bearing locknut, **Fig. 1.**
5. Remove wheel hub from spindle.
6. Separate tie rod ball joint and lower ball joint from knuckle.
7. Remove strut to knuckle attaching bolts.
8. Remove knuckle assembly from vehicle.
9. Reverse procedure to install, checking bearing axial endplay as outlined under "Wheel Bearing, Adjust."

BALL JOINT INSPECTION

Before checking, turn ball joint at least 10 revolutions. Check ball joint for play. If ball stud is worn, play in axial direction (C) is more than zero inch, ball joint swing force (A) is not 1.8–12.3 lbs. or ball joint turning torque (B) is not 4.3–30.4 inch lbs., replace ball joint, **Fig. 2.**

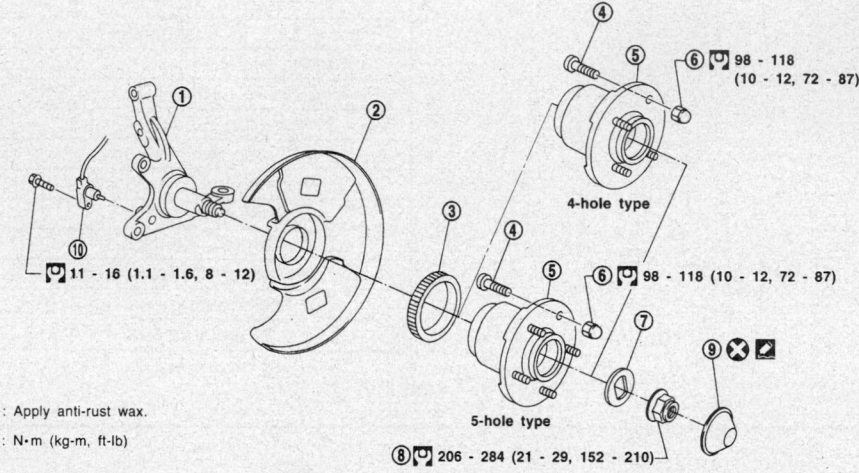

: Apply anti-rust wax.

: N•m (kg-m, ft-lb)

① Knuckle spindle
② Baffle plate
③ ABS ring
④ Hub bolt
⑤ Wheel hub bearing
⑥ Wheel nut
⑦ Lock washer
⑧ Wheel bearing lock nut
⑨ Hub cap
⑩ ABS sensor

98 - 118 (10 - 12, 72 - 87)

4-hole type

11 - 16 (1.1 - 1.6, 8 - 12)

98 - 118 (10 - 12, 72 - 87)

5-hole type

⑧ 206 - 284 (21 - 29, 152 - 210)

NS2049100035000X

Fig. 1   Exploded view of wheel hub assembly

BALL JOINT
REPLACE

For ball joint service, refer to "Transverse Link, Replace."

STRUT
REPLACE

1. Raise and support front of vehicle, then remove wheel.
2. Disconnect brake line from strut.
3. Place alignment marks on strut lower bracket and camber adjusting pin.
4. Remove strut to steering knuckle attaching bolts, then separate strut from knuckle, **Fig. 3.**
5. Remove strut to strut tower attaching nuts, then strut assembly from vehicle.

6. Reverse procedure to install.

TRANSVERSE LINK
REPLACE

1. Raise and support vehicle and remove wheels.
2. Remove tension rod and stabilizer bar, **Fig. 3.**
3. Remove ball joint and transverse link mounting nut/bolts, then separate link from crossmember.
4. Reverse procedure to install.

TENSION STRUT
REPLACE

1. Raise and support vehicle.
2. Remove tension rod and stabilizer bar attaching bolts, **Fig. 4.**

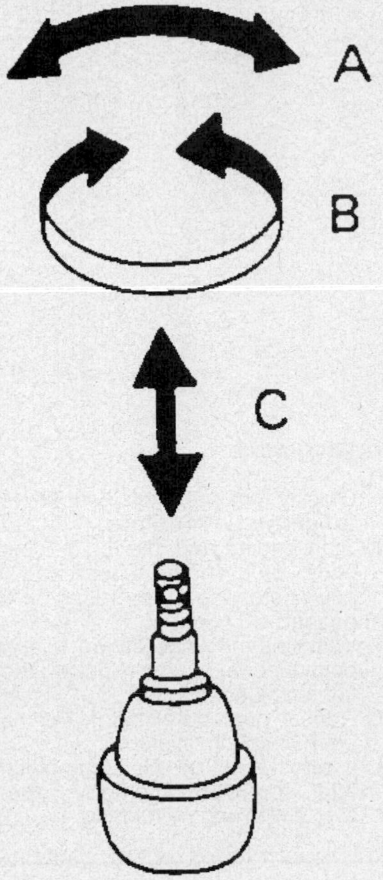

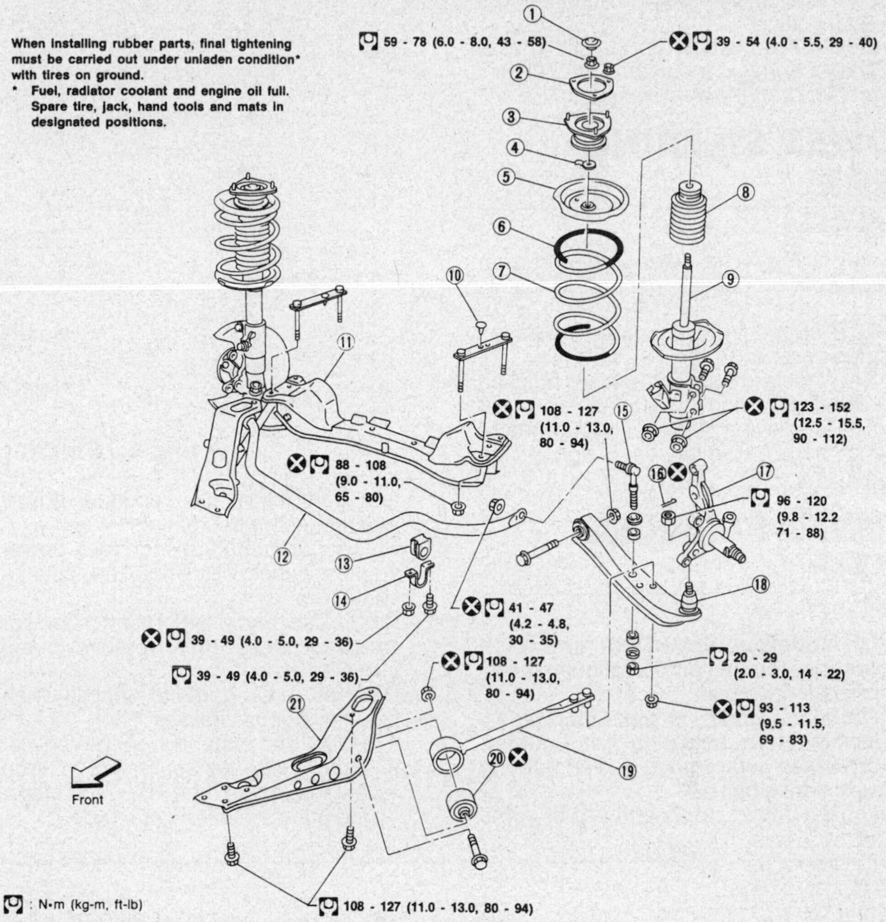

When installing rubber parts, final tightening must be carried out under unladen condition* with tires on ground.

* Fuel, radiator coolant and engine oil full. Spare tire, jack, hand tools and mats in designated positions.

Ⓧ 🔧 59 - 78 (6.0 - 8.0, 43 - 58) Ⓧ 🔧 39 - 54 (4.0 - 5.5, 29 - 40)

🔧 108 - 127 (11.0 - 13.0, 80 - 94)

🔧 123 - 152 (12.5 - 15.5, 90 - 112)

Ⓧ 🔧 88 - 108 (9.0 - 11.0, 65 - 80)

🔧 96 - 120 (9.8 - 12.2 71 - 88)

Ⓧ 🔧 41 - 47 (4.2 - 4.8, 30 - 35)

🔧 20 - 29 (2.0 - 3.0, 14 - 22)

Ⓧ 🔧 39 - 49 (4.0 - 5.0, 29 - 36)

Ⓧ 🔧 93 - 113 (9.5 - 11.5, 69 - 83)

Ⓧ 🔧 39 - 49 (4.0 - 5.0, 29 - 36)

🔧 108 - 127 (11.0 - 13.0, 80 - 94)

Front

🔧 : N·m (kg-m, ft-lb)

🔧 108 - 127 (11.0 - 13.0, 80 - 94)

Fig. 2 Ball joint inspection

NS2029100025000X

①	Cap	⑧	Bound bumper	⑮	Stabilizer connecting rod
②	Gasket	⑨	Strut assembly	⑯	Cotter pin
③	Strut mounting insulator	⑩	Plastic clip	⑰	Knuckle spindle
④	Lock washer	⑪	Front suspension member	⑱	Transverse link with ball joint
⑤	Upper seat	⑫	Stabilizer bar	⑲	Tension rod
⑥	(Polyurethane tube)	⑬	Bushing	⑳	Tension rod bushing
⑦	Coil spring	⑭	Clamp	㉑	Tension rod bracket

NS2029100022000X

Fig. 3 Exploded view of front suspension

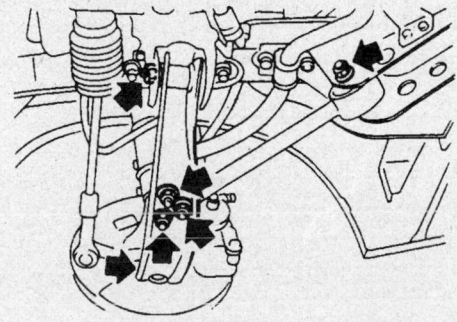

NS2029100023000X

Fig. 4 Tension rod & stabilizer bar removal

View from B

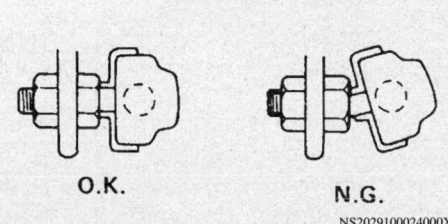

O.K.   N.G.

NS2029100024000X

Fig. 5 Stabilizer bar installation

3. Remove tension rod and stabilizer bar from vehicle.
4. Reverse procedure to install, ensure stabilizer bar is installed with ball joint socket properly placed, **Fig. 5.**

POWER STEERING GEAR

REPLACE

Refer to **Fig. 6** for power steering gear replacement procedure, noting the following.
1. When removing power steering hoses plug ports and lines.
2. Set wheels in a straight-ahead position before removing lower joint.
3. After removing lower joint, put matching mark on pinion shaft and pinion housing.

POWER STEERING PUMP

REPLACE

1. **On models equipped with air conditioning,** remove air conditioning compressor drive belt.
2. **On all models,** loosen idler pulley locknut, turn adjusting nut counterclockwise and remove power steering pump drive belt.
3. Loosen power steering hoses at pump

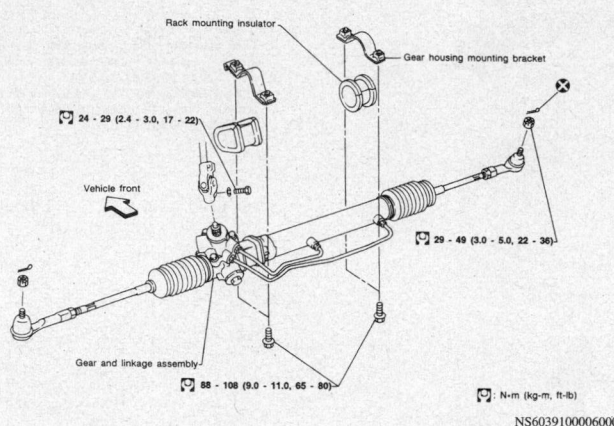

Fig. 6   Steering gear replacement

NS6039100006000X

and remove bolts securing power steering pump to brackets.
4. Raise pump and disconnect power steering hoses, catch fluid in a suitable container.
5. Plug hose ends and ports in power steering pump, then remove pump from vehicle.
6. Reverse procedure to install, then bleed system as follows:
   a. Raise and support front of vehicle.
   b. Run engine for 3–5 seconds, stop engine, check and fill power steering pump reservoir as needed.
   c. Quickly turn steering wheel all way to right and left 10 times.
   d. Start engine and idle for 3–5 seconds. Stop engine, check and fill power steering pump reservoir as needed.
   e. With steering wheel all way to right, open bleeder screw, expel air, then tighten bleeder screw.
   f. Repeat procedure until all air has been bled from system.
   g. If air cannot be bled completely after repeated attempts, repeat step e with engine running.

TIGHTENING SPECIFICATIONS

Year	Component	Torque/Ft. Lbs.
1996–97	Axle Nut	152–210
	Brake Caliper	53–72
	Driveshaft Nut	152–210
	Front Suspension Member To Body	65–80
	Hub Nut	152–210
	Stabilizer Bar To Body	29–36
	Stabilizer Bar To Link	34–38
	Stabilizer Link To Transverse Link	14–22
	Steering Column Coupling To Gear	17–22
	Steering Gear Mounting Bracket	65–80
	Steering Pump To Bracket	23–31
	Strut Piston Nut	43–58
	Strut To Body	29–40
	Strut To Knuckle	84–89
	Tension Rod Bracket Bolts	29–36
	Tension Rod To Tension Bracket	65–80
	Tension Rod To Transverse Link	65–80
	Tie Rod End To Knuckle	22–36
	Transverse Link To Front Suspension Member	65–80
	Wheel Bearing Locknut	108–159
	Wheel Lug Nut	72–87

Wheel Alignment

INDEX

PRELIMINARY INSPECTION

Before checking and adjusting wheel alignment angles, perform following checks:

1. Check tire pressures and adjust as needed.
2. Ensure tires are of proper size and are properly matched.
3. Check steering gear adjustment and ensure steering gear is properly secured to frame.
4. Inspect steering linkage and suspension components for damage and wear, and repair or replace components as needed.
5. Measure vehicle ride height with vehicle unloaded, ensure springs are not collapsed.
6. Place vehicle on suitable alignment rack following manufacturer's instructions, then jounce vehicle several times to settle suspension.
7. Check and correct rear wheel camber and toe first, if applicable, then check and correct front suspension angles in following order: caster and kingpin inclination, camber, toe setting and turning angle (toe-out on turns).

FRONT WHEEL ALIGNMENT

Front wheel alignment should only be checked after rear wheels are properly aligned in relation to vehicle centerline, as most equipment uses rear wheels as reference for correct front wheel alignment. Front wheel alignment should be checked with vehicle at normal ride height and following equipment manufacturer's instructions.

CASTER & KINGPIN INCLINATION

Caster and kingpin inclination cannot be adjusted. If caster or kingpin angle are not within specifications, check suspension components and sheet metal for damage, distortion and excessive wear, repair or replace as necessary.

CAMBER

Camber cannot be adjusted. If camber is not within specifications, inspect suspension and sheet metal for damage, distortion and excessive wear. Repair or replace components as necessary.

TOE-IN

1. Jounce front end several times to eliminate friction, then set steering wheel in straight-ahead position.
2. Ensure tie rods are same length.
3. Loosen lock nuts, then adjust toe-in by turning tie rods.
4. Tighten lock nuts to specifications.

STEERING ANGLE

1. Set wheels in a straight-ahead position.
2. Position front wheels on turning radius gauge.
3. Rotate steering wheel fully to right and left.
4. Ensure inner turning angle is within specifications.

REAR WHEEL ALIGNMENT

CAMBER

1. Measure camber for each wheel following equipment manufacturer's instructions.
2. Scribe matching mark between cam and upper rear link, then loosen nut securing link bushing bolt.
3. Rotate cam bolt, **Fig. 1,** to bring camber within specifications. Each graduation represents 4° camber change.
4. When camber is within specifications, hold position of cam bolt and **torque** nut to 51–65 ft. lbs.
5. Ensure camber is still within specifications.

TOE-IN

1. Draw a base line across tire tread.
2. Measure toe-in for each wheel following equipment manufacturer's instructions.
3. Rotate bolt, **Fig. 2,** to bring toe-in within specifications. Each graduation of bolt will change toe-in on one side approximately .051 inch.
4. When toe-in is within specifications, hold position of bolt and **torque** nut to 51–65 ft. lbs.
5. Ensure toe-in is still within specifications.

VEHICLE RIDE HEIGHT

1. Parked on a level surface and tires inflated to proper air pressure.
2. Ensure all fluid levels are to specified level, spare tire and jack are in proper locations.
3. Bounce vehicle up and down several times, then measure vehicle height from top of wheelwell to ground, **Fig. 3.**
4. Vehicle ride height is not adjustable. If vehicle height is not within specifications, check for worn springs or suspension parts.
5. **On models equipped with 205/55R16 tires,** front wheel arch height should be 27.32 inches and rear 26.38 inches.
6. **On models equipped with 195/60R15 tires,** front wheel arch height should be 27.05 inches and rear 26.10 inches.

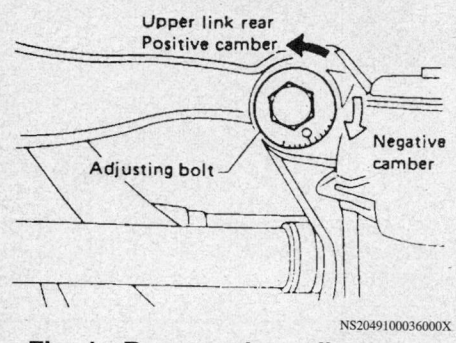

Fig. 1 Rear camber adjustment

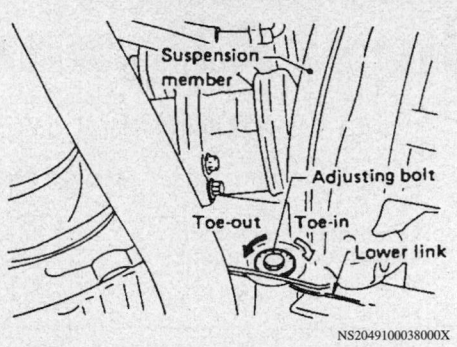

Fig. 2 Rear toe-in adjustment

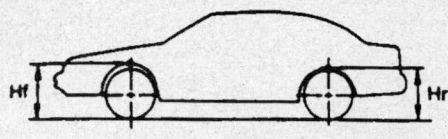

Fig. 3 Measuring vehicle ride
height

NISSAN UNIT REPAIR

TABLE OF CONTENTS

Air Conditioning

INDEX

PRECAUTIONS

R134A REFRIGERANT

1. R-12 and R-134a refrigerant must never be mixed. If refrigerants are mixed, compressor failure will probably occur.
2. When filling system with oil, use specified A/C System lubricant. If specified oil is not used, compressor failure will probably occur.
3. Nissan A/C System Type R Part No. KLH00-PAGR0 or equivalent refrigerant oil absorbs moisture from the atmosphere at a rapid rate, the following precautions must be followed when using this lubricant:
   a. When removing components from the vehicle, immediately cap component to minimize the entry of moisture from the atmosphere.
   b. When installing components on a vehicle, do not remove cap until just before connecting components. Complete connection of all refriger-

ant loop components as quickly as possible to minimize entry of moisture into system.
   c. Use specified lubrication oil from a sealed container only. Containers must be sealed immediately after dispensing lubrication oil. Lubrication oil in containers which are not properly sealed will become moisture saturated.
   d. **Avoid breathing A/C refrigerant and lubricant vapor or mist. Exposure may irritate eyes, nose and throat.**
   e. When removing refrigerant from the system, always use service equipment certified by the requirements of SAE J2210 (R-134a recycling equipment) or J2209 (R-134a recovery equipment). If accidental system discharge does occur, ventilate work area before resuming system service.
   f. Do not allow lubrication oil to come in contact with styrofoam parts. Damage may result.

PERFORMANCE TEST

Refer to **Figs. 1 through 16** for recirculating to discharge air temperature and ambient temperature to compressor pressure test readings.

ALTIMA, MAXIMA, SENTRA, 200SX & 240SX

1. The following system performance test must be performed as follows:
   a. Vehicle must be parked indoors or in the shade and in a well ventilated place.
   b. Vehicle doors must be closed, door windows open and hood open.
   c. Temperature lever position must be set to maximum cold.
   d. Air control lever position set to FACE.
   e. Intake lever position set to RE-CIRC.
   f. Fan lever set at MAX.
   g. Engine speed at 1500 RPM.
2. The time required to start the test after the air conditioner starts operating

Inside air at blower assembly inlet for recirculation*		Discharge air temperature at center ventilator °C (°F)
Relative humidity %	Air temperature °C (°F)	
50 - 60	20 (68)	4.0 - 5.4 (39 - 42)
	25 (77)	4.2 - 5.6 (40 - 42)
	30 (86)	8.5 - 11.1 (47 - 52)
	35 (95)	13.5 - 16.7 (56 - 62)
	40 (104)	18.5 - 22.3 (65 - 72)
60 - 70	20 (68)	5.4 - 6.8 (42 - 44)
	25 (77)	5.6 - 8.0 (42 - 46)
	30 (86)	11.1 - 14.1 (52 - 57)
	35 (95)	16.7 - 20.3 (62 - 69)
	40 (104)	22.3 - 26.5 (72 - 80)

* Thermometer should be placed at intake unit under RH side of instrument panel.

NS7029600417000X

Fig. 1 A/C Performance Test, recirculating to discharge air temperature. Altima

Inside air (Recirculating air) at blower assembly inlet		Discharge air temperature at center ventilator °C (°F)
Relative humidity %	Air temperature °C (°F)	
50 - 60	20 (68)	1.5 - 2.6 (35 - 37)
	25 (77)	3.7 - 5.7 (39 - 42)
	30 (86)	7.6 - 10.0 (46 - 50)
	35 (95)	12.4 - 15.2 (54 - 59)
60 - 70	20 (68)	2.6 - 3.6 (37 - 38)
	25 (77)	5.7 - 7.6 (42 - 46)
	30 (86)	10.0 - 12.4 (50 - 54)
	35 (95)	15.2 - 18.0 (59 - 64)

NS7029600419000X

Fig. 3 A/C Performance Test, recirculating to discharge air temperature. Maxima

Inside air (Recirculating air) at blower assembly inlet		Discharge air temperature at center ventilator °C (°F)
Relative humidity %	Air temperature °C (°F)	
50 - 60	25 (77)	6.0 - 9.0 (43 - 48)
	30 (86)	10.0 - 13.6 (50 - 56)
	35 (95)	15.2 - 19.5 (59 - 67)
	40 (104)	22.5 - 27.1 (73 - 81)
60 - 70	25 (77)	9.0 - 12.2 (48 - 54)
	30 (86)	13.6 - 17.2 (56 - 63)
	35 (95)	19.5 - 23.7 (67 - 75)
	40 (104)	27.1 - 32.3 (81 - 90)

NS7029600421000X

Fig. 5 A/C Performance Test, recirculating to discharge air temperature. Pathfinder

Ambient air		High-pressure (Discharge side) kPa (kg/cm², psi)	Low-pressure (Suction side) kPa (kg/cm², psi)
Relative humidity %	Air temperature °C (°F)		
50 - 70	20 (68)	834 - 1,098 (8.5 - 11.2, 121 - 159)	122.6 - 161.8 (1.25 - 1.65, 17.8 - 23.5)
	25 (77)	1,049 - 1,363 (10.7 - 13.9, 152 - 198)	137.3 - 181.4 (1.4 - 1.85, 19.9 - 26.3)
	30 (86)	1,226 - 1,618 (12.5 - 16.5, 178 - 235)	152.0 - 201.0 (1.55 - 2.05, 22.0 - 29.2)
	35 (95)	1,255 - 1,716 (12.8 - 17.5, 182 - 249)	166.7 - 230.5 (1.7 - 2.35, 24.2 - 33.4)
	40 (104)	1,540 - 2,030 (15.7 - 20.7, 223 - 294)	201.0 - 289.3 (2.05 - 2.95, 29.2 - 41.9)

NS7029600418000X

Fig. 2 A/C Performance Test, ambient air temperature to operating pressure. Altima

Ambient air		High-pressure (Discharge side) kPa (kg/cm², psi)	Low-pressure (Suction side) kPa (kg/cm², psi)
Relative humidity %	Air temperature °C (°F)		
50 - 70	20 (68)	785 - 1,040 (8.0 - 10.6, 114 - 151)	137 - 167 (1.4 - 1.7, 20 - 24)
	25 (77)	981 - 1,304 (10.0 - 13.3, 142 - 189)	137 - 167 (1.4 - 1.7, 20 - 24)
	30 (86)	1,167 - 1,550 (11.9 - 15.8, 169 - 225)	147 - 177 (1.5 - 1.8, 21 - 26)
	35 (95)	1,373 - 1,804 (14.0 - 18.4, 199 - 262)	157 - 186 (1.6 - 1.9, 23 - 27)
	40 (104)	1,550 - 2,059 (15.8 - 21.0, 225 - 299)	167 - 206 (1.7 - 2.1, 24 - 30)

NS7029600420000X

Fig. 4 A/C Performance Test, ambient air temperature to operating pressure. Maxima

Ambient air		High-pressure (Discharge side) kPa (kg/cm², psi)	Low-pressure (Suction side) kPa (kg/cm², psi)
Relative humidity %	Air temperature °C (°F)		
50 - 70	25 (77)	1,226 - 1,638 (12.5 - 16.7, 178 - 237)	172 - 250 (1.75 - 2.55, 25 - 36)
	30 (86)	1,422 - 1,883 (14.5 - 19.2, 206 - 273)	196 - 275 (2.0 - 2.8, 28 - 40)
	35 (95)	1,657 - 2,187 (16.9 - 22.3, 240 - 317)	231 - 309 (2.35 - 3.15, 33 - 45)
	40 (104)	1,922 - 2,501 (19.6 - 25.5, 279 - 363)	280 - 373 (2.85 - 3.8, 41 - 54)

NS7029600422000X

Fig. 6 A/C Performance Test, ambient air temperature to operating pressure. Pathfinder

should exceed 10 minutes.

3. **On 240SX models,** ensure condenser fan motor does not operate during test.

300ZX

1. The system performance test must be performed as follows:
   a. Vehicle must be parked indoors or in the shade and in a well ventilated place.
   b. Vehicle doors must be closed with door windows and hood open.
   c. Temperature lever position must be in the maximum cold position and mode switch position on FACE.
   d. The recirculation switch position be on RECIRC and fan speed set at MAX HI.
   e. Engine speed at 1500 RPM.
2. The time required before testing the system after the air conditioner starts operating should exceed 10 minutes.

PATHFINDER & PICKUP

1. The system performance test must be performed as follows:
   a. Vehicle must be parked indoors or in the shade and in a well ventilated place.
   b. Vehicle doors must be closed with door windows and hood open.

   c. Temperature control lever must be in MAX cold position with mode lever in vent position.
   d. Air intake lever must be in recirc position and the fan control lever must be in MAX position.
   e. Engine speed at 1500 RPM.
2. The time required before testing the system after the air conditioner starts operating should exceed 10 minutes.
3. Measure discharge air temperature at center outlet grille, inside air relative humidity and temperature at blower assembly inlet and the ambient air relative humidity and temperature at a point 3.3 feet in front of condenser.

QUEST

1. The system performance test must be performed under the following conditions:
   a. Run engine at 1500 RPM for at least 10 minutes.
   b. Operate A/C system on MAX recirculating air.
   c. Run blower at high speed.
   d. Stabilize temperature at 70–80°F.
2. Use the following procedure to perform pressure test:
   a. Connect manifold gauge set to system.

b. Run engine with A/C on.
c. As soon as system stabilizes, record high and low refrigerant pressures as indicated by the manifold gauges.
d. Low side pressure should cycle between 24.5–44 psi.
e. Determine clutch cycle rate per minute.
f. Record clutch Off time in seconds, then On time in seconds.
g. Record center register discharge temperature and ambient temperature.
h. Compare test readings with applicable chart, **Figs. 9 and 10.**

OIL CHARGE

Refer to "Precautions" before adding oil to refrigerant systems.

ALTIMA, FRONTIER, MAXIMA, PATHFINDER, PICKUP, SENTRA, 200SX, 240SX & 300ZX

Refer to "R-134a Refrigerant" under "Precautions" before adjusting oil level. Adjust oil quantity according to the charts in Figs. 17 and 18.

QUEST

When replacing any other A/C system component, refer to **Fig. 19** for amount of oil that needs to be added.

Inside air (Recirculating air) at blower assembly inlet		Discharge air temperature at center ventilator °C (°F)
Relative humidity %	Air temperature °C (°F)	
50 - 60	20 (68)	6.6 - 8.3 (44 - 47)
	25 (77)	10.4 - 12.4 (51 - 54)
	30 (86)	14.2 - 16.7 (58 - 62)
	35 (95)	18.2 - 21.0 (65 - 70)
	40 (104)	22.0 - 25.2 (72 - 77)
60 - 70	20 (68)	8.3 - 9.8 (47 - 50)
	25 (77)	12.4 - 14.4 (54 - 58)
	30 (86)	16.7 - 18.9 (62 - 66)
	35 (95)	21.0 - 23.6 (70 - 74)
	40 (104)	25.2 - 28.1 (77 - 83)

NS7029600423000X

Fig. 7 A/C Performance Test, recirculating to discharge air temperature. Frontier & Pickup

Ambient air		High-pressure (Discharge side) kPa (kg/cm², psi)	Low-pressure (Suction side) kPa (kg/cm², psi)
Relative humidity %	Air temperature °C (°F)		
50 - 70	20 (68)	961 - 1,187 (9.8 - 12.1, 139 - 172)	108 - 157 (1.1 - 1.6, 16 - 23)
	25 (77)	1,295 - 1,599 (13.2 - 16.3, 188 - 232)	161.8 - 215.8 (1.65 - 2.2, 23.5 - 31.3)
	30 (86)	1,285 - 1,569 (13.1 - 16, 186 - 228)	167 - 216 (1.7 - 2.2, 24 - 31)
	35 (95)	1,520 - 1,863 (15.5 - 19, 220 - 270)	235 - 284 (2.4 - 2.9, 34 - 41)
	40 (104)	1,765 - 2,158 (18 - 22, 256 - 313)	289.3 - 353.1 (2.95 - 3.6, 41.9 - 51.2)

NS7029600424000X

Fig. 8 A/C Performance Test, ambient air temperature to operating pressure. Frontier & Pickup

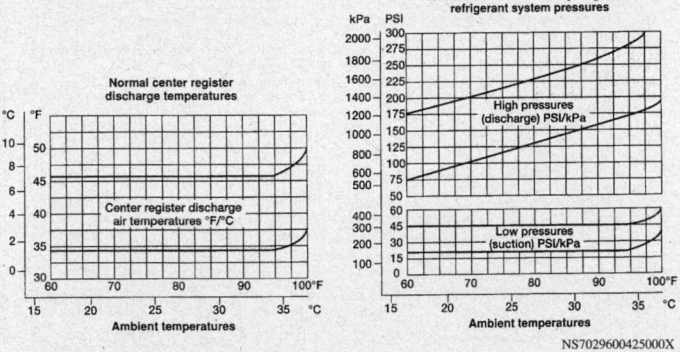

Fig. 9 A/C Performance Test, normal fixed orifice tube refrigerant system pressure/temperature relationships. Quest

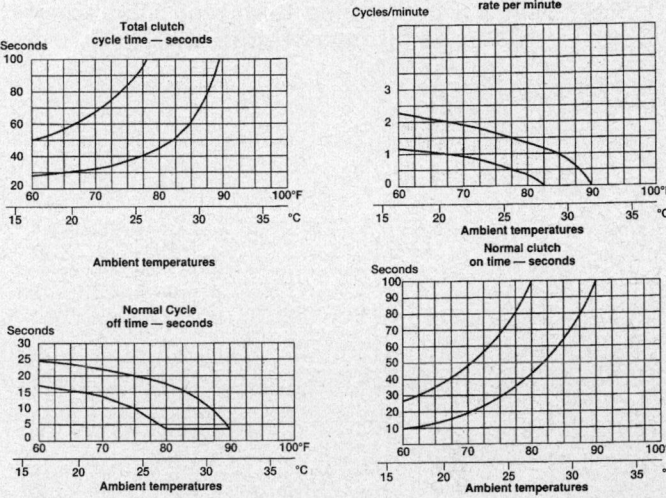

NS7029600426000X

Fig. 10 A/C Performance Test, normal fixed orifice tube refrigerant system clutch cycle timing rates. Quest

Inside air (Recirculating air) at blower assembly inlet		Discharge air temperature at center ventilator °C (°F)
Relative humidity %	Air temperature °C (°F)	
50 - 60	20 (68)	4.4 - 7.0 (40 - 45)
	25 (77)	7.9 - 11.1 (46 - 52)
	30 (86)	11.6 - 15.8 (53 - 60)
	35 (95)	15.4 - 20.4 (60 - 69)
	40 (104)	19.6 - 26.0 (67 - 79)
60 - 70	20 (68)	7.0 - 9.3 (45 - 49)
	25 (77)	11.1 - 14.5 (52 - 58)
	30 (86)	15.8 - 20.2 (60 - 68)
	35 (95)	20.4 - 26.2 (69 - 79)
	40 (104)	26.0 - 33.6 (79 - 92)

NS7029600427000X

Fig. 11 A/C Performance Test, recirculating to discharge air temperature. Sentra & 200SX

Ambient air		High-pressure (Discharge side) kPa (kg/cm², psi)	Low-pressure (Suction side) kPa (kg/cm², psi)
Relative humidity %	Air temperature °C (°F)		
50 - 70	20 (68)	1,010 - 1,314 (10.3 - 13.4, 146 - 191)	108 - 206 (1.1 - 2.1, 16 - 30)
	25 (77)	1,236 - 1,599 (12.6 - 16.3, 179 - 232)	118 - 226 (1.2 - 2.3, 17 - 33)
	30 (86)	1,471 - 1,883 (15.0 - 19.2, 213 - 273)	137 - 265 (1.4 - 2.7, 20 - 38)
	35 (95)	1,893 - 2,167 (19.3 - 22.1, 274 - 314)	157 - 324 (1.6 - 3.3, 23 - 47)
	40 (104)	1,922 - 2,452 (19.6 - 25.0, 279 - 356)	196 - 392 (2.0 - 4.0, 28 - 57)

NS7029600428000X

Fig. 12 A/C Performance Test, ambient air temperature to operating pressure. Sentra & 200SX

Inside air at blower assembly inlet for recirculation*		Discharge air temperature at center ventilator °C (°F)
Relative humidity %	Air temperature °C (°F)	
50 - 60	20 (68)	3.7 - 6.3 (39 - 43)
	25 (77)	8.3 - 11.5 (47 - 53)
	30 (86)	13.0 - 16.6 (55 - 62)
	35 (95)	17.6 - 21.8 (64 - 71)
	40 (104)	22.2 - 27.0 (72 - 81)
60 - 70	20 (68)	6.3 - 9.2 (43 - 49)
	25 (77)	11.5 - 14.9 (53 - 59)
	30 (86)	16.6 - 20.5 (62 - 69)
	35 (95)	21.8 - 26.1 (71 - 79)
	40 (104)	27.0 - 31.8 (81 - 89)

* Thermometer should be placed at intake unit under RH side of instrument panel.

NS7029600429000X

Fig. 13 A/C Performance Test, recirculating to discharge air temperature. 240SX

Ambient air		High-pressure (Discharge side) kPa (kg/cm², psi)	Low-pressure (Suction side) kPa (kg/cm², psi)
Relative humidity %	Air temperature °C (°F)		
50 - 70	20 (68)	736 - 892 (7.5 - 9.1, 107 - 129)	147 - 226 (1.5 - 2.3, 21 - 33)
	25 (77)	922 - 1,118 (9.4 - 11.4, 134 - 162)	147 - 226 (1.5 - 2.3, 21 - 33)
	30 (86)	1,157 - 1,393 (11.8 - 14.2, 168 - 202)	147 - 226 (1.5 - 2.3, 21 - 33)
	35 (95)	1,393 - 1,687 (14.2 - 17.2, 202 - 245)	157 - 265 (1.6 - 2.7, 23 - 38)
	40 (104)	1,638 - 2,001 (16.7 - 20.4, 237 - 290)	196 - 324 (2.0 - 3.3, 28 - 47)

NS7029600430000X

Fig. 14 A/C Performance Test, ambient air temperature to operating pressure. 240SX

Inside air(Recirculating air) at blower assembly inlet		Discharge air temperature at center ventilator °C (°F)
Relative humidity %	Air temperature °C (°F)	
50 - 60	20 (68)	5.8 - 7.5 (42 - 46)
	25 (77)	9.3 - 11.0 (49 - 52)
	30 (86)	13.9 - 15.8 (57 - 60)
	35 (95)	18.8 - 20.9 (66 - 70)
	40 (104)	23.3 - 25.5 (74 - 78)
60 - 70	20 (68)	7.5 - 9.0 (46 - 48)
	25 (77)	11.0 - 13.0 (52 - 55)
	30 (86)	15.8 - 17.0 (60 - 63)
	35 (95)	20.9 - 22.6 (70 - 73)
	40 (104)	22.5 - 27.3 (73 - 81)

NS7029600431000X

Fig. 15 A/C Performance Test, recirculating to discharge air temperature. 300ZX

Ambient air		High-pressure (Discharge side) kPa (kg/cm², psi)	Low-pressure (Suction side) kPa (kg/cm², psi)
Relative humidity %	Air temperature °C (°F)		
50 - 70	20 (68)	1,030 - 1,245 (10.5 - 12.7, 149 - 181)	181.4 - 221.6 (1.85 - 2.26, 26.3 - 32.1)
	25 (77)	1,118 - 1,373 (11.4 - 14.0, 162 - 199)	185.4 - 226.5 (1.89 - 2.31, 26.9 - 32.8)
	30 (86)	1,344 - 1,638 (13.7 - 16.7, 195 - 237)	220.7 - 269.7 (2.25 - 2.75, 32.0 - 39.1)
	35 (95)	1,569 - 1,922 (16.0 - 19.6, 228 - 279)	269.7 - 328.5 (2.75 - 3.35, 39.1 - 47.6)
	40 (104)	1,814 - 2,207 (18.5 - 22.5, 263 - 320)	314 - 382 (3.2 - 3.9, 46 - 55)

NS7029600432000X

Fig. 16 A/C Performance Test, ambient air temperature to operating pressure. 300ZX

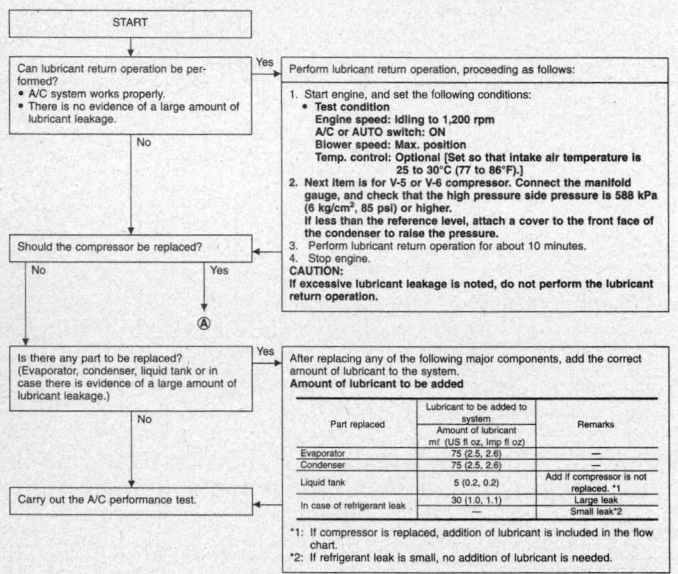

Fig. 17 Refrigerant oil replacement flow chart (Part 1 of 2). Frontier, Maxima, Pathfinder, Pickup, Sentra, 200SX & 300ZX

NS7029300070010A

Ⓐ

1. Discharge refrigerant into the refrigerant recovery/recycling equipment. Measure lubricant discharged into the recovery/recycling equipment.
2. Remove the drain plug of the "old" (removed) compressor (applicable only to V-5, V-6 and DKS-16H compressor). Drain the lubricant into a graduated container and record the amount of drained lubricant.
3. Remove the drain plug and drain the lubricant from the "new" compressor into a separate, clean container.
4. Measure an amount of new lubricant installed equal to amount drained from "old" compressor. Add this lubricant to "new" compressor through the suction port opening.
5. Measure an amount of new lubricant equal to the amount recovered during discharging. Add this lubricant to "new" compressor through the suction port opening.
6. Torque the drain plug.
   V-5 or V-6 compressor: 18 - 19 N·m (1.8 - 1.9 kg-m, 13 - 14 ft-lb)
   DKS-16H compressor: 14 - 16 N·m (1.4 - 1.6 kg-m, 10 - 12 ft-lb)
7. If the liquid tank also needs to be replaced, add an additional 5 mℓ (0.2 US fl oz, 0.2 Imp fl oz) of lubricant at this time.
   Do not add this 5 mℓ (0.2 US fl oz, 0.2 Imp fl oz) of lubricant if only replacing the compressor.

Lubricant adjusting procedure for compressor replacement

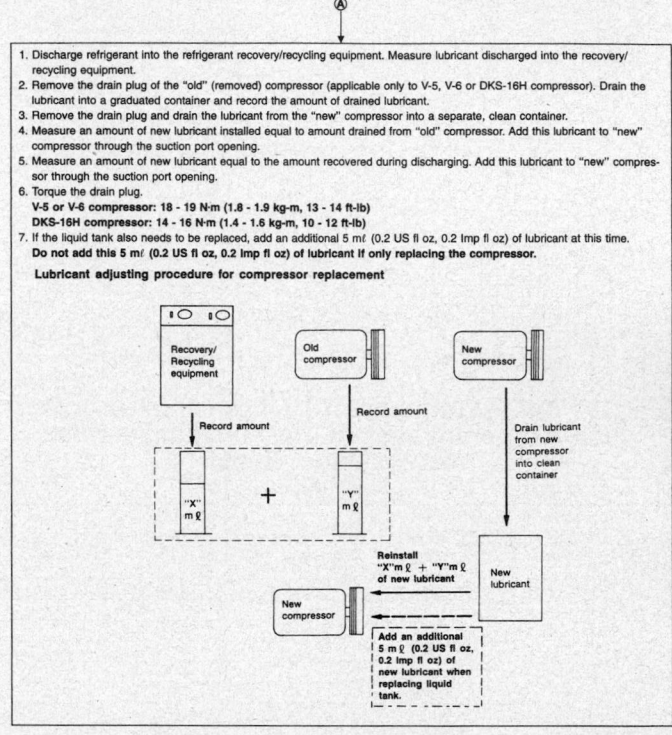

NS7029300070020A

Fig. 17 Refrigerant oil replacement flow chart (Part 2 of 2). Frontier, Maxima, Pathfinder, Pickup, Sentra, 200SX & 300ZX

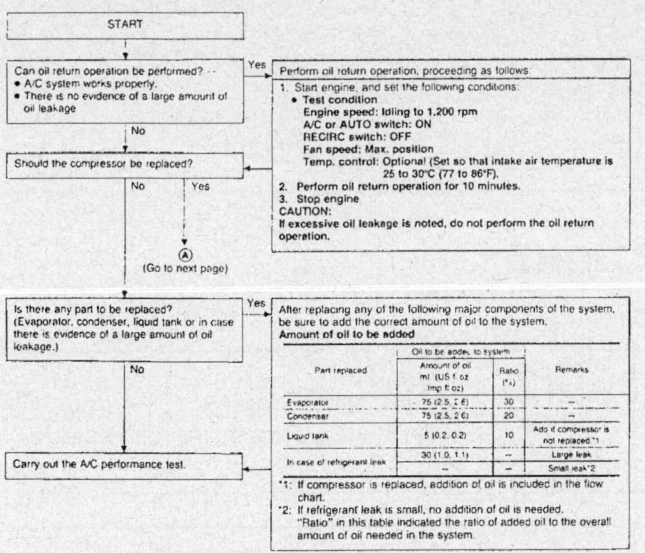

Fig. 18   Refrigerant oil replacement flow chart (Part 1 of 2). Altima & 240SX

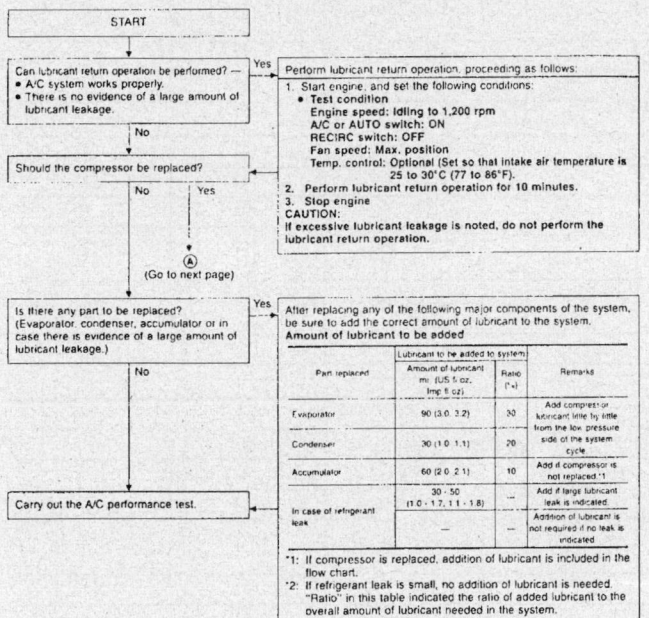

Fig. 19   Refrigerant oil replacement chart (Part 1 of 2). Quest

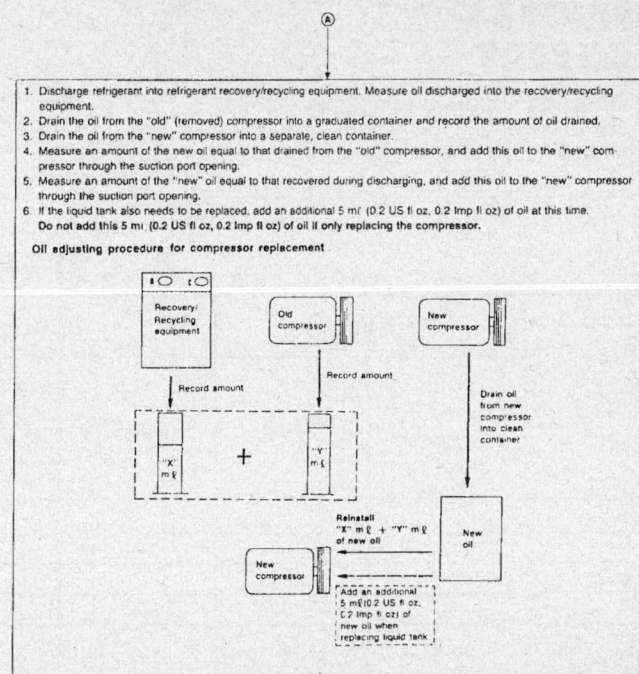

Fig. 18   Refrigerant oil replacement flow chart (Part 2 of 2). Altima & 240SX

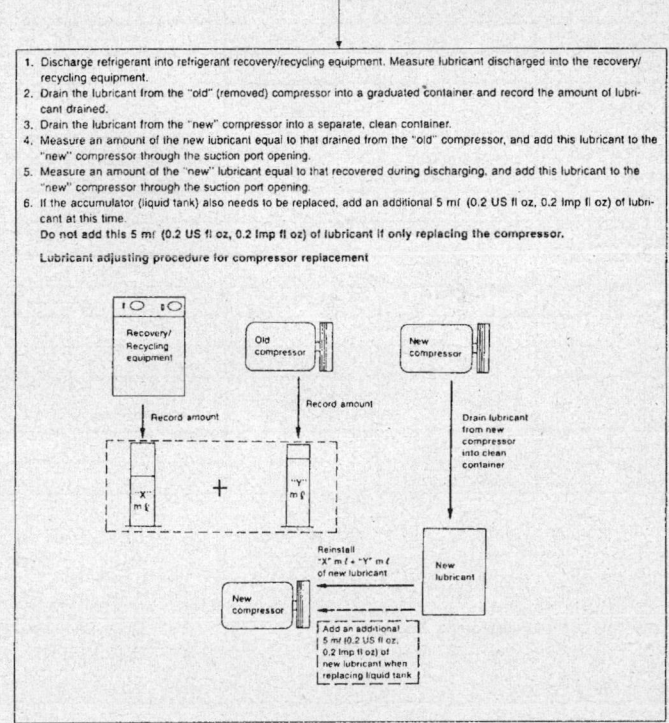

Fig. 19   Refrigerant oil replacement chart (Part 2 of 2). Quest

REFRIGERANT RECOVERY

Connect and operate refrigerant recovery system according to the manufacturers instructions.

A/C SPECIFICATIONS

Model	Refrigerant		Refrigerant Oil			Compressor Clutch Air Gap, Inch	Charging Valve Locations	
	Capacity, Lbs.	Type	Viscosity	Total System Capacity, Ounces	Compressor Oil Level Check, Inches		High Pressure	Low Pressure
1996								
Altima	1.54–1.76	R-134a	⑥	6.8	②	.012–.024	③	④
Maxima	1.71–1.82	R-134a	⑦	8.5	②	.012–.024	③	④
Quest	①	R-134a	⑧	⑤	②	.018–.034	③	④
Sentra & 200SX	1.32–1.54	R-134a	⑥	6.8	②	.012–.024	③	④
Pathfinder & Pickup	1.65–1.87	R-134a	⑥	7.0	②	.012–.024	③	④
240SX	1.32–1.54	R-134a	⑦	8.5	②	.012–.024	③	④
300ZX	1.21–1.43	R-134a	⑦	6.8	②	.012–.024	③	④
1997								
Altima	1.54–1.76	R-134a	⑥	6.8	②	.012–.024	③	④
Maxima	1.32–1.54	R-134a	⑦	7.0	②	.012–.024	③	④
Quest	①	R-134a	⑧	⑤	②	.018–.034	③	④
Sentra & 200SX	1.32–1.54	R-134a	⑥	6.8	②	.012–.024	③	④
Pathfinder & Pickup	1.32–1.54	R-134a	⑥	7.0	②	.012–.024	③	④
240SX	1.32–1.54	R-134a	⑦	8.5	②	.012–.024	③	④
1998-99								
Altima	1.54–1.76	R-134a	⑥	6.8	②	.012–.024	③	④
Frontier	1.32–1.54	R-134a	⑥	6.8	②	.012–.024	③	④
Maxima	1.32–1.54	R-134a	⑦	7.0	②	.012–.024	③	④
Quest	①	R-134a	⑧	⑤	②	.018–.034	③	④
Sentra & 200SX	1.32–1.54	R-134a	⑥	6.8	②	.012–.024	③	④
Pathfinder	1.32–1.54	R-134a	⑥	7.0	②	.012–.024	③	④
240SX	1.32–1.54	R-134a	⑦	8.5	②	.012–.024	③	④

① — Less rear A/C, 2.0 lbs.; w/rear A/C, 3.25 lbs.
② — Oil level inches cannot be checked.
③ — On high pressure line.
④ — On low pressure line.

⑤ — Less rear A/C, 7 ounces; w/rear A/C, 10 ounces.
⑥ — Nissan A/C System Oil Type R, part No. KLH00-RAGR0, or equivalent.

⑦ — Nissan A/C System Oil Type S, part No. KLH00-PAGS0, or equivalent.
⑧ — Nissan A/C System Oil Type F or equivalent.

BELT TENSION

ALTIMA

Using 22 lbs. of force, belt deflection should be .24–.28 inch for a new belt and .28–.31 inch for a used belt.

MAXIMA

Alternator drive belt deflection on models with A/C is .165–.181 inch for a used belt and .15–.16 inch for a new belt.

FRONTIER, PATHFINDER & PICKUP

Using 22 ft. lbs. of force, belt deflection should be .28–.35 inch for a new belt and .35–.43 inch for a used belt.

SENTRA & 200SX

Alternator drive belt deflection on models with A/C is .28–.31 inch for a used belt and .256–.295 inch for a new belt.

QUEST

Using 22 ft. lbs. of force, belt deflection

should be .16–.24 inch for a new belt and .20–.28 inch for a used belt.

should be .26–.30 inch for a new belt and .30–.34 inch for a used belt.

should be .28–.31 inch for a new belt and .31–.35 inch for a used belt.

240SX

Using 22 ft. lbs. of force, belt deflection

300ZX

Using 22 ft. lbs. of force, belt deflection

Cooling Fans

NOTE: "Electrical Symbol & Wire Color Code Identification" Located In The Front Of This Manual May Be Used As An Aid When Using Wiring Circuits Found In This Section.

NOTE: Refer To "Computer Relearn Procedures" Located In The Front Of This Manual For Computer Relearn Procedures.

INDEX

DESCRIPTION

ALTIMA

These models use an engine coolant temperature sensor, vehicle speed sensor, A/C "ON" signal and A/C pressure signal to input signals to the ECM. The module uses these input signals to open and close the two coolant fan relays.

With vehicle speed below 12 mph, A/C switch off, A/C triple-pressure switch off and engine coolant temperature below 203°F, both relays will remain open and cooling fans should be off. With engine temperature between 203–221°F, relay No. 1 should close and low speed coolant fan should come on. With engine temperature 221°F or more, both relays should close and both cooling fans should come on.

With vehicle speed below 12 mph, A/C switch on, A/C triple-pressure off and engine coolant temperature below 221°F, the low coolant fan relay should close and low speed coolant fan should be on. With engine coolant temperature above 221°F, both coolant fan relays should close and both coolant fans should be on.

With vehicle speed below 12 mph, A/C switch on and A/C triple-pressure on, both coolant fan relays should close and both fans should be on regardless of engine temperature.

With vehicle speed between 12–50 mph, A/C switch off, A/C triple-pressure off and engine coolant temperature below 203°F, both relays will remain open and coolant fans should be off. With engine coolant temperature between 203–212°F, the low

coolant fan relay should close and low speed coolant fan should be on. With engine coolant temperature above 212°F, both coolant fan relays should close and both coolant fans should be on.

With vehicle speed between 12–50 mph, A/C switch on, A/C triple-pressure switch on or off and engine coolant temperature below 212°F, the low speed coolant fan relay should close and low speed coolant fan should be on. With engine coolant temperature over 212°F, both relays should close and both fans should be on.

With vehicle speed over 50 mph, A/C switch on or off, A/C triple-pressure switch on or off and engine coolant temperature below 203°F, both relays will remain open and both fans should be off. With engine coolant temperature between 203–212°F, the low speed coolant fan relay should close and low speed coolant fan should be on. With engine coolant temperature over 212°F, both relays should close and both fans should be on.

MAXIMA

These models use one thermo sensor and three relays to control cooling fan operation.

With A/C off and engine coolant temperature below 205°F, the cooling fans will not operate. When coolant temperature exceeds 207°F, relay No. 1 closes and cooling fan operates at low speed. When coolant temperature exceeds 225°F, relays No. 2 and 3 close and cooling fan operates at high speed.

With A/C switch on and engine coolant

below 201°F, relay No. 1 closes and cooling fan operates at low speed. When coolant temperature exceeds 203°F, relays No. 2 and 3 close and cooling fan operates at high speed.

SENTRA & 200SX

Manual Transaxle

These models use an engine temperature sensor, vehicle speed sensor and A/C "ON" signal to input signals to the ECM. The control unit uses these input signals to open and close the coolant fan relay.

With A/C off and engine coolant temperature below 201°F, the cooling fan relay should remain open and cooling fans should not operate.

With A/C off and coolant temperature is between 203–210°F and vehicle speed is below 12 mph, the cooling fan relay should remain open and cooling fans should not operate.

With A/C off and coolant temperature is between 203–210°F and vehicle speed is above 12 mph, the cooling fan relay should close and activate both cooling fans.

With A/C off and coolant temperature is over 212°F, the cooling fan relay should close and activate both cooling fans.

With A/C on, engine coolant temperature below 201°F and vehicle speed is over 50 mph, the cooling fan relay should remain open and cooling fans should not operate.

With A/C on, engine coolant temperature is below 201°F and vehicle speed is below 49 mph, the cooling fan relay should close and activate both cooling fans.

With A/C on and engine coolant temperature is over 202°F, the cooling fan relay should close and activate both cooling fans.

Automatic Transaxle

These models use an engine temperature sensor, vehicle speed sensor and A/C "ON" signal to input signals to the ECM. The control unit uses these input signals to open and close the three coolant fan relays.

With A/C off and engine coolant temperature below 202°F, the coolant fan relays will remain open and coolant fans should not operate.

With A/C off and engine coolant is between 203–210°F, the coolant fan relays should activate the low speed coolant fan.

With A/C off, engine coolant temperature is between 211–219°F and vehicle speed is 12 mph or less, the coolant fan relays should activate the low speed coolant fan.

With A/C off, engine coolant temperature is between 211–219°F and vehicle speed is more than 12 mph, the coolant fan relays should activate both the low and high speed coolant fans.

With A/C off and engine coolant temperature is 221°F or more, the coolant fan relays should activate both the low and high speed coolant fans.

With A/C on, engine coolant temperature below 202°F and vehicle speed is 50 mph or more, the coolant fan relays should remain open and coolant fans should not operate.

With A/C on, engine coolant temperature below 202°F and vehicle speed is 49 mph or less, the coolant fan relays should activate the low speed coolant fan.

With A/C on and engine coolant is between 203–210°F, the coolant fan relays should activate the low speed coolant fan.

With A/C on, engine coolant temperature is between 211–219°F and vehicle speed is 12 mph or less, the coolant fan relays should activate the low speed coolant fan.

With A/C on, engine coolant temperature is between 211–219°F and vehicle speed is more than 12 mph, the coolant fan relays should activate both the low and high speed coolant fans.

With A/C on and engine coolant temperature is 221°F or more, the coolant fan relays should activate both the low and high speed coolant fans.

QUEST

These models use an engine coolant temperature sensor, vehicle speed sensor and A/C switch to input signals to the ECM. The module uses these input signals to open and close the coolant fan relays.

With engine coolant temperature below 201°F and A/C switch off, the coolant fan relays should be open and coolant fan should not be on. With engine coolant temperature between 203–210°F and A/C switch off, the low speed coolant fan relay should close and coolant fan should be running at low speed. With engine coolant temperature between 212–219°F, A/C switch off and vehicle speed is less than 12 mph, the low speed coolant fan relay should close and coolant fan should be running at

low speed. With engine coolant temperature between 212–219°F, A/C switch off and vehicle speed is more than 12 mph, the high speed coolant fan relay should close and coolant fan should be running at high speed. With engine coolant temperature over 221°F and A/C switch off, the high speed coolant fan relay should close and coolant fan should be running at high speed.

With engine coolant temperature 201°F or less, A/C switch on and vehicle speed is 68 mph or more, the coolant fan relays should be open and the coolant fan should be off. With engine coolant temperature 201°F or less, A/C switch on and vehicle speed is less than 68 mph, the low speed coolant fan relay should close and the coolant fan should run at low speed. With engine coolant temperature between 203–219°F, A/C switch on and vehicle speed is 12 mph or less, the low speed coolant fan relay should be closed and coolant fan should be running at low speed. With engine coolant temperature between 203–219°F, A/C switch on and vehicle speed is more than 12 mph, the high speed coolant fan relay should be closed and coolant fan should be running at high speed. With engine coolant temperature more than 221°F and A/C switch on, the high speed coolant fan relay should be closed and coolant fan should be running, regardless of vehicle speed.

240SX

These models use an engine coolant temperature sensor, vehicle speed sensor, A/C On signal and A/C pressure signal to input signals to the ECM. The module uses these input signals to open and close the two coolant fan relays.

With vehicle speed below 12 mph, A/C switch off and engine coolant temperature below 203°F, both relays will remain open and cooling fans should be off. With engine temperature between 203–212°F, relay No. 1 should close and low speed coolant fan should come on. With engine temperature 212°F or more, both relays should close and both cooling fans should be on.

With vehicle speed below 12 mph, A/C switch on, A/C triple-pressure off and engine coolant temperature below 212°F, the low coolant fan relay should close and the low speed coolant fan should be on. With engine coolant temperature above 212°F, both coolant fan relays should close and both coolant fans should be on.

With vehicle speed below 12 mph, A/C switch on and A/C triple-pressure on, both coolant fan relays should close and both fans should be on regardless of engine temperature.

300ZX

These models use an engine temperature sensor, vehicle speed sensor and A/C "ON" signal to input signals to the ECM. The control unit uses these input signals to open and close the two coolant fan relays.

With A/C switch off and engine coolant temperature 219°F or below, cooling fan relay will be open and coolant fan should not come on. With engine coolant tempera-

ture 221°F or over, cooling fan relays will be closed and cooling fan should come on.

On non-turbo models, A/C switch on, engine coolant temperature below 201°F and vehicle speed less than 24 mph, cooling fan relay should be open and coolant fan should not be on. With engine coolant temperature 203°F or more and vehicle speed less than 24 mph, cooling fan relays should be closed and cooling fan should operate at high speed. With engine coolant temperature below 219°F and vehicle speed more than 25 mph, cooling fan relays should be open and cooling fan should not come on. With engine coolant temperature 221°F or more and vehicle speed more than 25 mph, cooling fan relays should be closed and cooling fan should operate at high speed.

On turbo models, A/C switch on, engine coolant temperature below 192°F and vehicle speed less than 24 mph, cooling fan relay should be open and coolant fan should not be on. With engine coolant temperature between 194–210°F and vehicle speed less than 24 mph, low speed cooling fan relay should be closed and cooling fan should operate at low speed. With engine coolant temperature below 219°F and vehicle speed more than 25 mph, cooling fan relays should be open and cooling fan should not come on. With engine coolant temperature 221°F or more and vehicle speed more than 25 mph, cooling fan relays should be closed and cooling fan should operate at high speed.

SYSTEM DIAGNOSIS & TESTING

MAXIMA

Refer to diagnosis charts, **Fig. 1** to diagnose the cooling fan system.

SENTRA & 200SX

Refer to diagnosis charts, **Figs. 2 and 3** to diagnose cooling fan system.

QUEST

Refer to diagnosis chart in **Figs. 4 through 7** to diagnose the cooling fan system.

240SX

Refer to diagnosis chart in **Fig. 8** to diagnose the cooling fan system.

300ZX

Refer to diagnosis chart in **Fig. 9** to diagnose the cooling fan system.

COMPONENT DIAGNOSIS & TESTING

RADIATOR FAN RELAYS

Altima & Maxima

Refer to **Figs. 10 and 11** for fan relay testing, if test results are not as specified, replace relay.

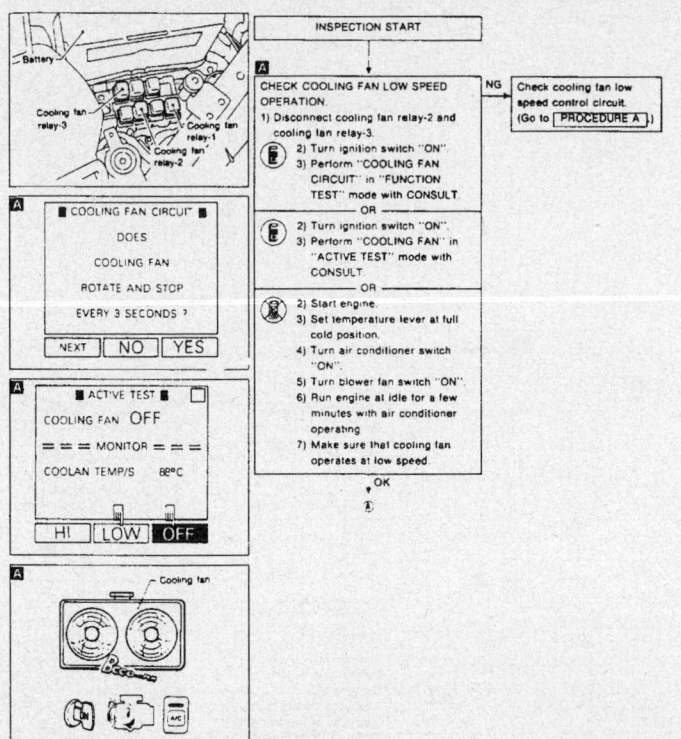

NS1089500056010X

Fig. 1   Cooling fan diagnosis (Part 1 of 5). Maxima

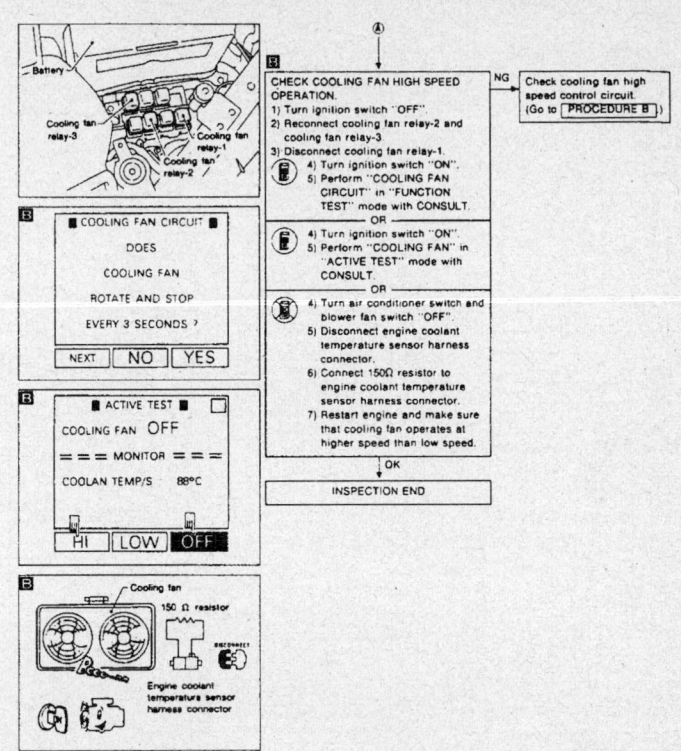

NS1089500056020X

Fig. 1   Cooling fan diagnosis (Part 2 of 5). Maxima

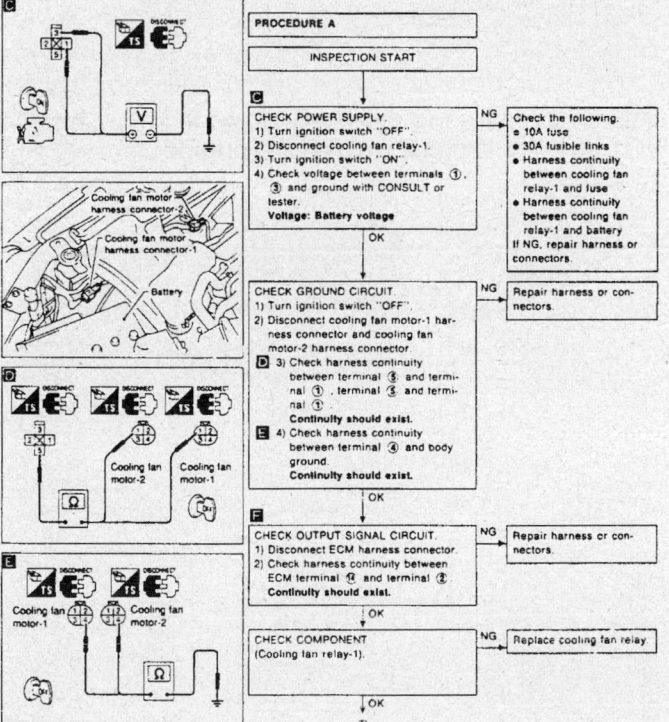

NS1089500056030X

Fig. 1   Cooling fan diagnosis (Part 3 of 5). Maxima

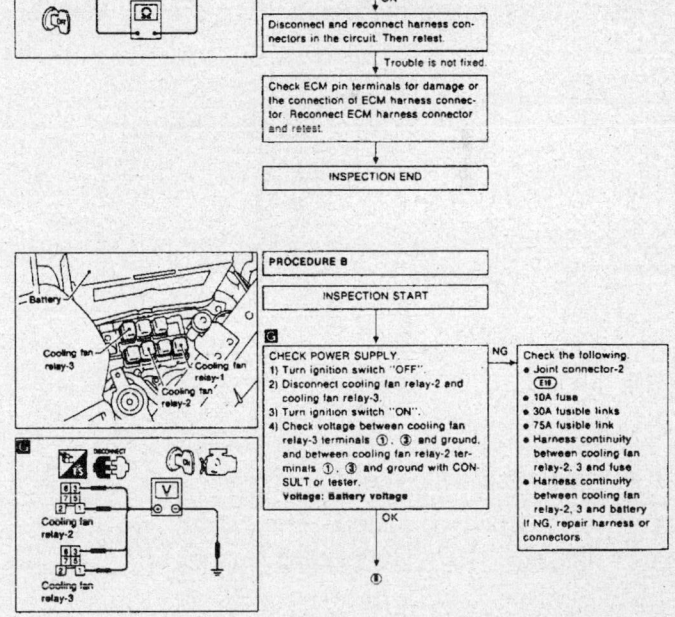

NS1089500056040X

Fig. 1   Cooling fan diagnosis (Part 4 of 5). Maxima

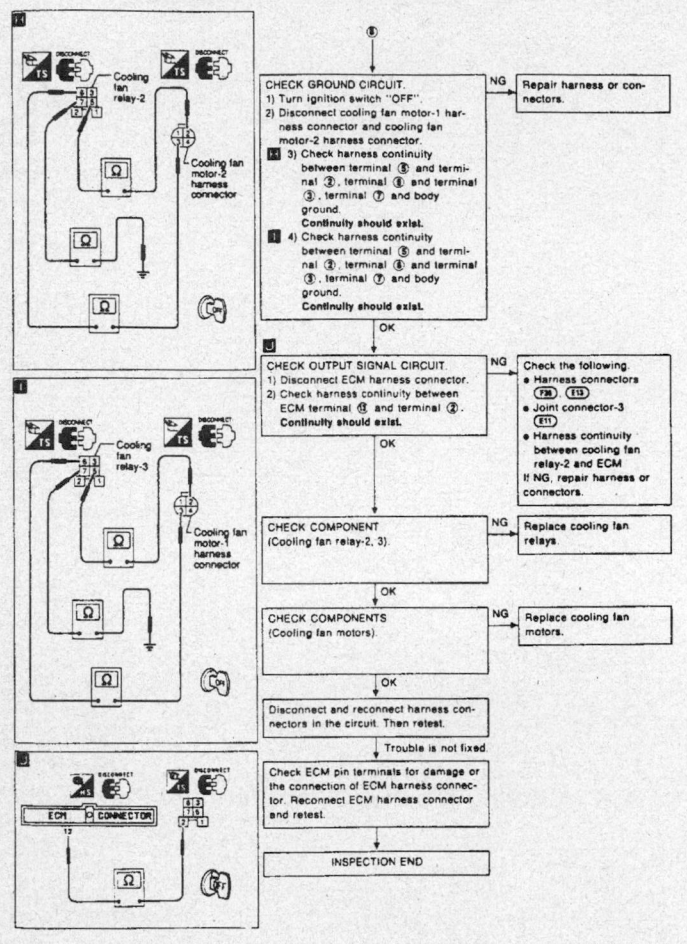

CHECK GROUND CIRCUIT.
1) Turn ignition switch "OFF".
2) Disconnect cooling fan motor-1 harness connector and cooling fan motor-2 harness connector.
3) Check harness continuity between terminal ⑥ and terminal ③, terminal ④ and terminal ③, terminal ⑦ and body ground.
Continuity should exist.
4) Check harness continuity between terminal ② and terminal ①, terminal ④ and terminal ③, terminal ⑦ and body ground.
Continuity should exist.

NG → Repair harness or connectors.

OK ↓

CHECK OUTPUT SIGNAL CIRCUIT.
1) Disconnect ECM harness connector.
2) Check harness continuity between ECM terminal ⑱ and terminal ②.
Continuity should exist.

NG → Check the following.
● Harness connectors (73M) (T13)
● Joint connector-3 (E11)
● Harness continuity between cooling fan relay-2 and ECM
If NG, repair harness or connectors.

OK ↓

CHECK COMPONENT
(Cooling fan relay-2, 3).

NG → Replace cooling fan relays.

OK ↓

CHECK COMPONENTS
(Cooling fan motors).

NG → Replace cooling fan motors.

OK ↓

Disconnect and reconnect harness connectors in the circuit. Then retest.

Trouble is not fixed. ↓

Check ECM pin terminals for damage or the connection of ECM harness connector. Reconnect ECM harness connector and retest.

↓

INSPECTION END

NS1089500056050X

Fig. 1 Cooling fan diagnosis (Part 5 of 5). Maxima

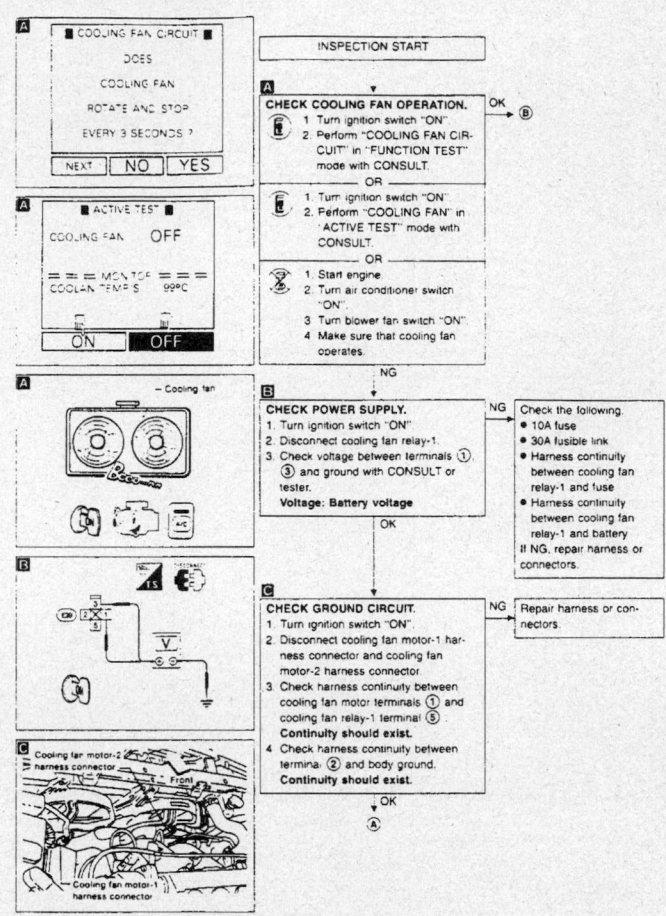

CHECK COOLING FAN OPERATION.
1) Turn ignition switch "ON".
2) Perform "COOLING FAN CIRCUIT" in "FUNCTION TEST" mode with CONSULT.
— OR —
1) Turn ignition switch "ON".
2) Perform "COOLING FAN" in "ACTIVE TEST" mode with CONSULT.
— OR —
1) Start engine.
2) Turn air conditioner switch "ON".
3) Turn blower fan switch "ON".
4) Make sure that cooling fan operates.

OK → B

NG ↓

CHECK POWER SUPPLY.
1) Turn ignition switch "ON".
2) Disconnect cooling fan relay-1.
3) Check voltage between terminals ① ③ and ground with CONSULT or tester.
Voltage: Battery voltage

NG → Check the following.
● 10A fuse
● 30A fusible link
● Harness continuity between cooling fan relay-1 and fuse
● Harness continuity between cooling fan relay-1 and battery
If NG, repair harness or connectors.

OK ↓

CHECK GROUND CIRCUIT.
1) Turn ignition switch "ON".
2) Disconnect cooling fan motor-1 harness connector and cooling fan motor-2 harness connector.
3) Check harness continuity between cooling fan motor terminals ① and cooling fan relay-1 terminal ⑤.
Continuity should exist.
4) Check harness continuity between terminal ② and body ground.
Continuity should exist.

NG → Repair harness or connectors.

OK ↓

Ⓐ

NS1089500057010X

Fig. 2 Cooling fan diagnosis (Part 1 of 3). Sentra & 200SX w/GA16DE engine

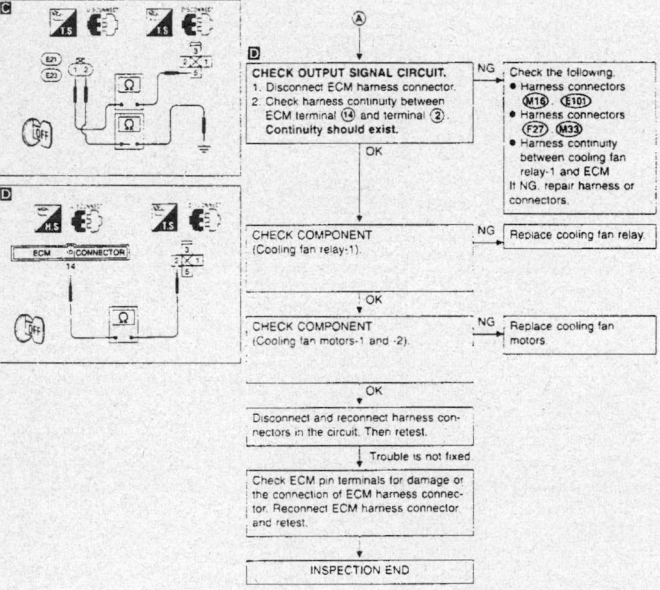

CHECK OUTPUT SIGNAL CIRCUIT.
1. Disconnect ECM harness connector.
2. Check harness continuity between ECM terminal ⑭ and terminal ②.
Continuity should exist.

NG → Check the following.
● Harness connectors (M16) (E101)
● Harness connectors (F27) (M33)
● Harness continuity between cooling fan relay-1 and ECM
If NG, repair harness or connectors.

OK ↓

CHECK COMPONENT
(Cooling fan relay-1).

NG → Replace cooling fan relay.

OK ↓

CHECK COMPONENT
(Cooling fan motors-1 and -2).

NG → Replace cooling fan motors.

OK ↓

Disconnect and reconnect harness connectors in the circuit. Then retest.

Trouble is not fixed. ↓

Check ECM pin terminals for damage or the connection of ECM harness connector. Reconnect ECM harness connector and retest.

↓

INSPECTION END

NS1089500057020X

Fig. 2 Cooling fan diagnosis (Part 2 of 3). Sentra & 200SX w/GA16DE engine

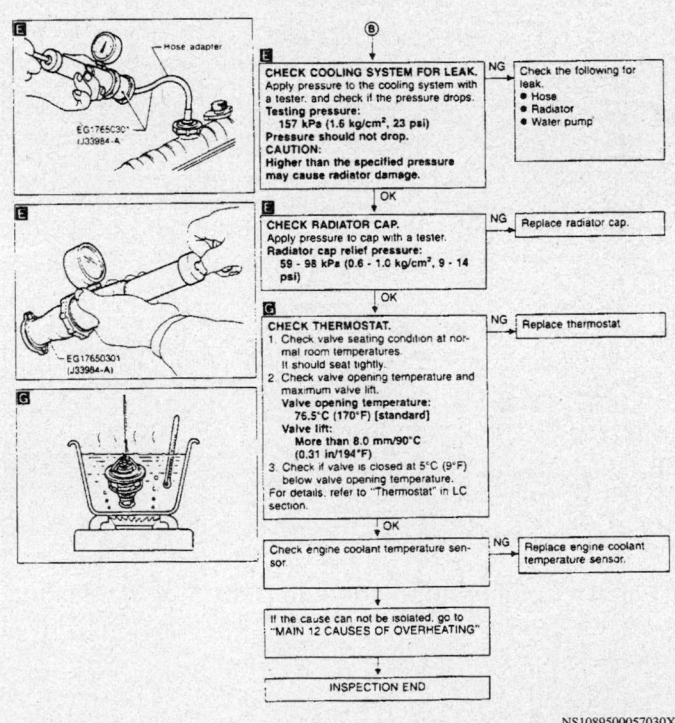

CHECK COOLING SYSTEM FOR LEAK.
Apply pressure to the cooling system with a tester, and check if the pressure drops.
Testing pressure:
157 kPa (1.6 kg/cm², 23 psi)
Pressure should not drop.
CAUTION:
Higher than the specified pressure may cause radiator damage.

NG → Check the following for leak.
● Hose
● Radiator
● Water pump

OK ↓

CHECK RADIATOR CAP.
Apply pressure to cap with a tester.
Radiator cap relief pressure:
59 - 98 kPa (0.6 - 1.0 kg/cm², 9 - 14 psi)

NG → Replace radiator cap.

OK ↓

CHECK THERMOSTAT.
1. Check valve seating condition at normal room temperatures.
It should seat tightly.
2. Check valve opening temperature and maximum valve lift.
Valve opening temperature:
76.5°C (170°F) [standard]
Valve lift:
More than 8.0 mm/90°C
(0.31 in/194°F)
3. Check if valve is closed at 5°C (9°F) below valve opening temperature.
For details, refer to "Thermostat" in LC section.

NG → Replace thermostat.

OK ↓

Check engine coolant temperature sensor.

NG → Replace engine coolant temperature sensor.

OK ↓

If the cause can not be isolated, go to "MAIN 12 CAUSES OF OVERHEATING".

↓

INSPECTION END

NS1089500057030X

Fig. 2 Cooling fan diagnosis (Part 3 of 3). Sentra & 200SX w/GA16DE engine

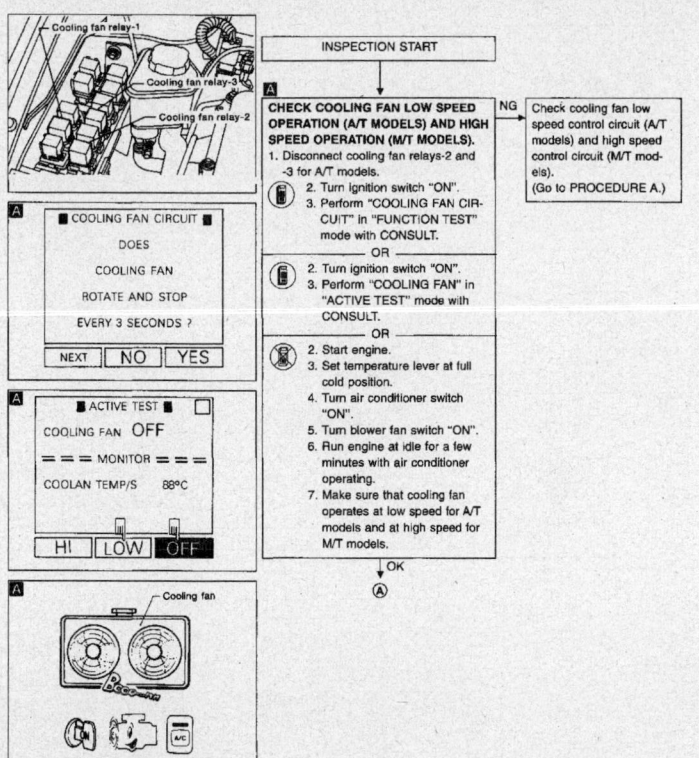

Fig. 3   Cooling fan diagnosis (Part 1 of 6). Sentra & 200SX w/SR20DE engine

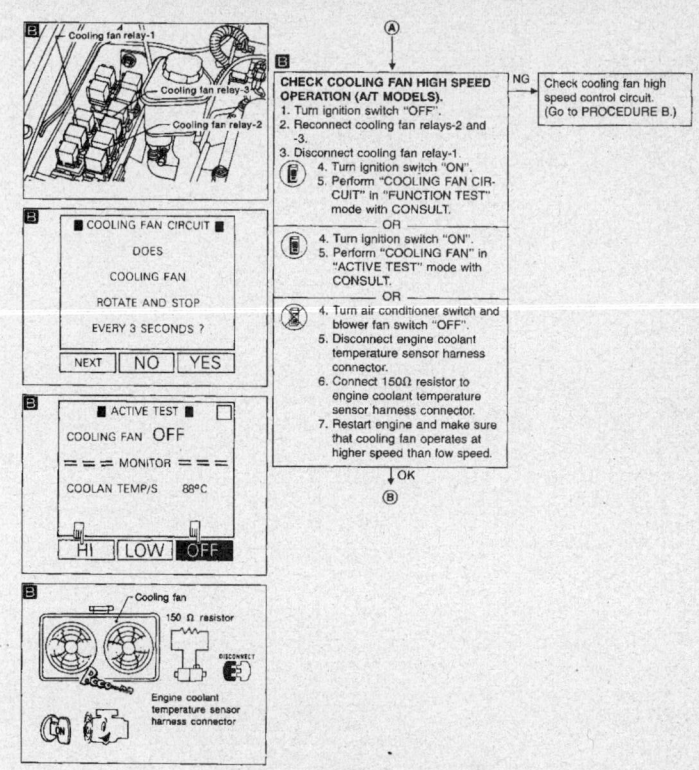

Fig. 3   Cooling fan diagnosis (Part 2 of 6). Sentra & 200SX w/SR20DE engine

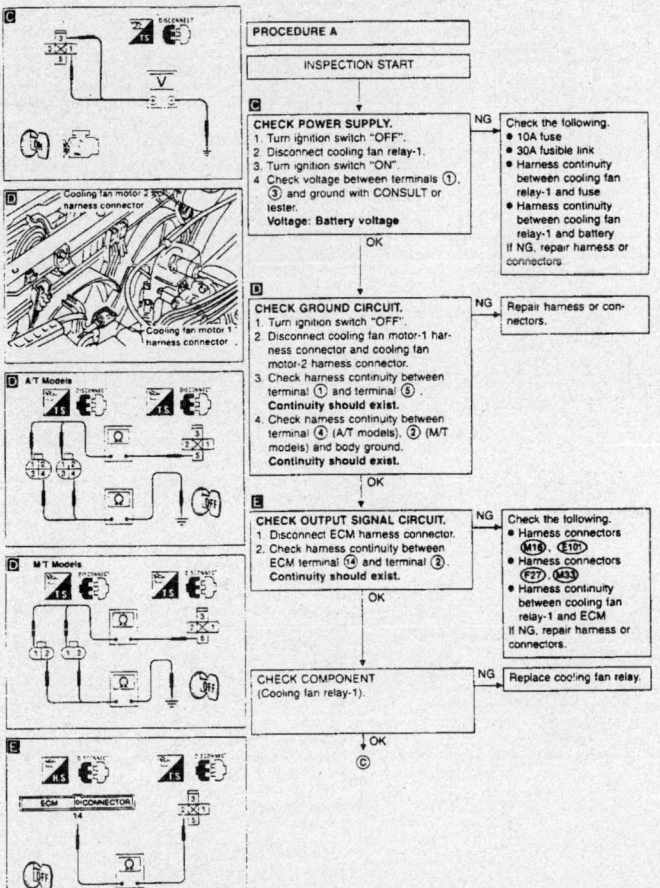

Fig. 3   Cooling fan diagnosis (Part 3 of 6). Sentra & 200SX w/SR20DE engine

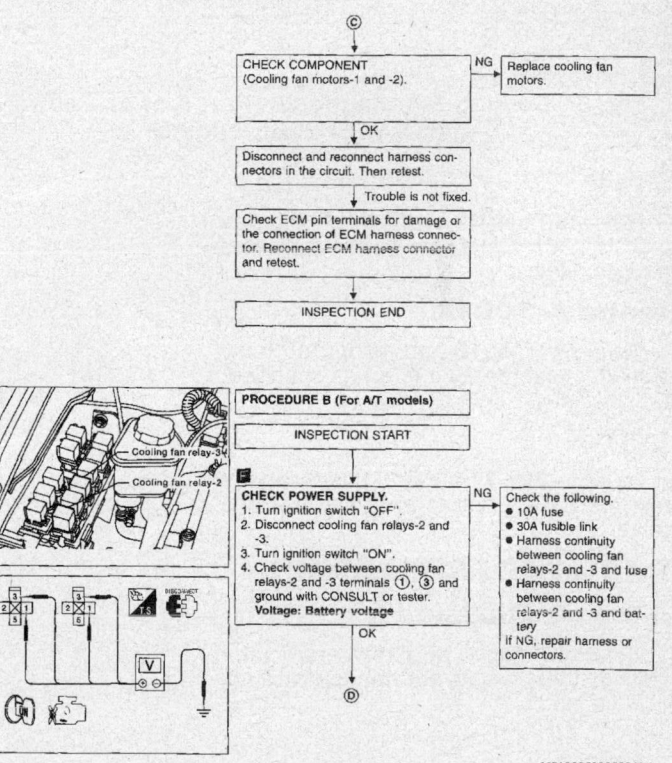

Fig. 3   Cooling fan diagnosis (Part 4 of 6). Sentra & 200SX w/SR20DE engine

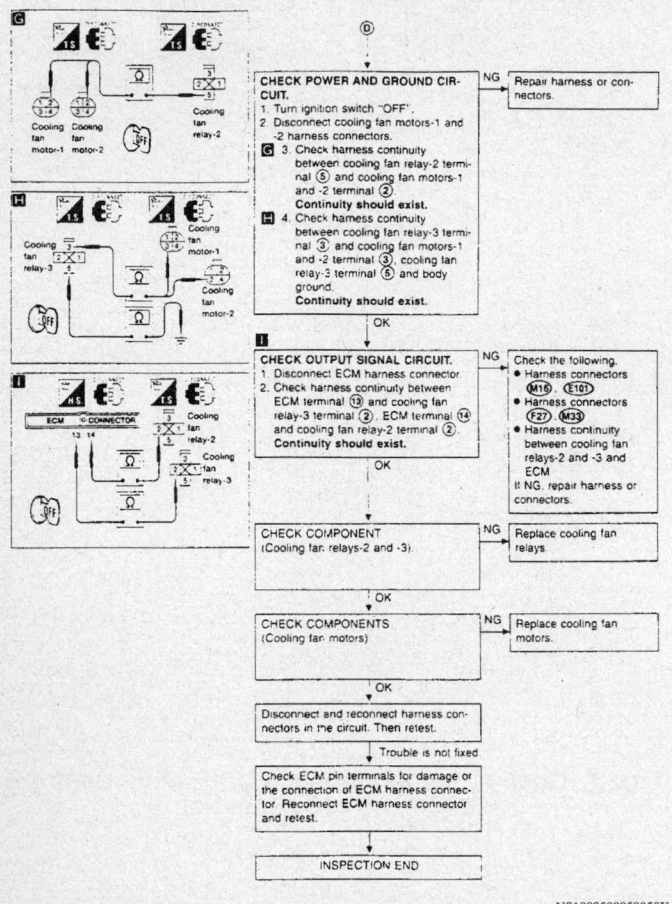

CHECK POWER AND GROUND CIRCUIT.
1. Turn ignition switch "OFF".
2. Disconnect cooling fan motors-1 and -2 harness connectors.
3. Check harness continuity between cooling fan relay-2 terminal ⑤ and cooling fan motors-1 and -2 terminal ②. Continuity should exist.
4. Check harness continuity between cooling fan relay-3 terminal ③ and cooling fan motors-1 and -2 terminal ③, cooling fan relay-3 terminal ⑤ and body ground. Continuity should exist.

NG → Repair harness or connectors.

OK ↓

CHECK OUTPUT SIGNAL CIRCUIT.
1. Disconnect ECM harness connector.
2. Check harness continuity between ECM terminal ⑬ and cooling fan relay-3 terminal ②, ECM terminal ⑭ and cooling fan relay-2 terminal ②. Continuity should exist.

NG → Check the following.
• Harness connectors M16, E101
• Harness connectors F27, M33
• Harness continuity between cooling fan relays-2 and -3 and ECM
If NG, repair harness or connectors.

OK ↓

CHECK COMPONENT (Cooling fan relays-2 and -3).

NG → Replace cooling fan relays.

OK ↓

CHECK COMPONENTS (Cooling fan motors).

NG → Replace cooling fan motors.

OK ↓

Disconnect and reconnect harness connectors in the circuit. Then retest.

Trouble is not fixed. ↓

Check ECM pin terminals for damage or the connection of ECM harness connector. Reconnect ECM harness connector and retest.

↓

INSPECTION END

NS1089500058050X

Fig. 3 Cooling fan diagnosis (Part 5 of 6). Sentra & 200SX w/SR20DE engine

Quest

Refer to **Figs. 12 and 13** for fan relay testing, if test results are not as specified, replace relay.

Sentra & 200SX

Refer to **Figs. 10 and 12** for fan relay testing, if test results are not as specified, replace relay.

300ZX

Refer to **Fig. 12** for fan relay testing, if test results are not as specified, replace relay.

RADIATOR FAN MOTORS

Altima & Maxima

Refer to **Figs. 14 and 15** for fan motor testing, if test results are not as specified, replace motor.

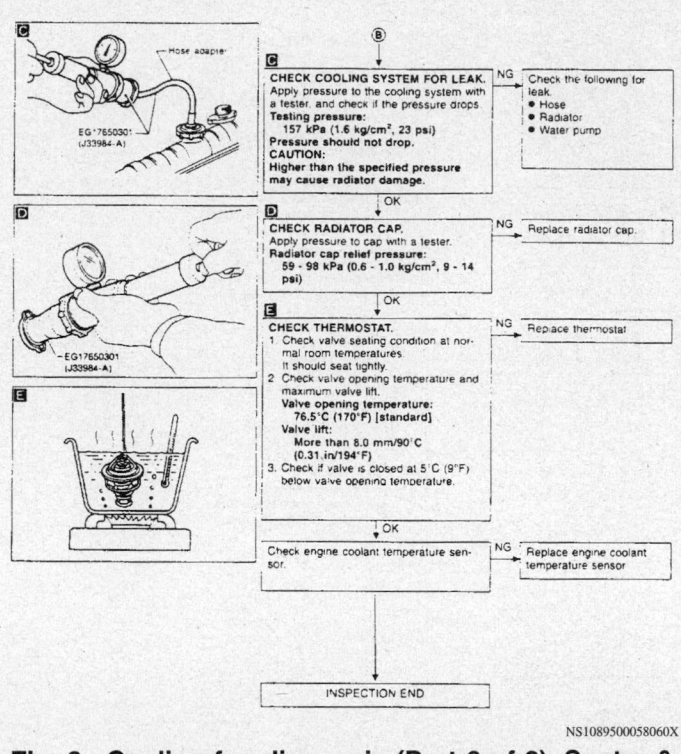

CHECK COOLING SYSTEM FOR LEAK.
Apply pressure to the cooling system with a tester, and check if the pressure drops.
Testing pressure:
157 kPa (1.6 kg/cm², 23 psi)
Pressure should not drop.
CAUTION:
Higher than the specified pressure may cause radiator damage.

NG → Check the following for leak.
• Hose
• Radiator
• Water pump

OK ↓

CHECK RADIATOR CAP.
Apply pressure to cap with a tester.
Radiator cap relief pressure:
59 - 98 kPa (0.6 - 1.0 kg/cm², 9 - 14 psi)

NG → Replace radiator cap.

OK ↓

CHECK THERMOSTAT.
1. Check valve seating condition at normal room temperatures.
It should seat tightly.
2. Check valve opening temperature and maximum valve lift.
Valve opening temperature:
76.5°C (170°F) [standard]
Valve lift:
More than 8.0 mm/90°C (0.31 in/194°F)
3. Check if valve is closed at 5°C (9°F) below valve opening temperature.

NG → Replace thermostat

OK ↓

Check engine coolant temperature sensor.

NG → Replace engine coolant temperature sensor

↓

INSPECTION END

NS1089500058060X

Fig. 3 Cooling fan diagnosis (Part 6 of 6). Sentra & 200SX w/SR20DE engine

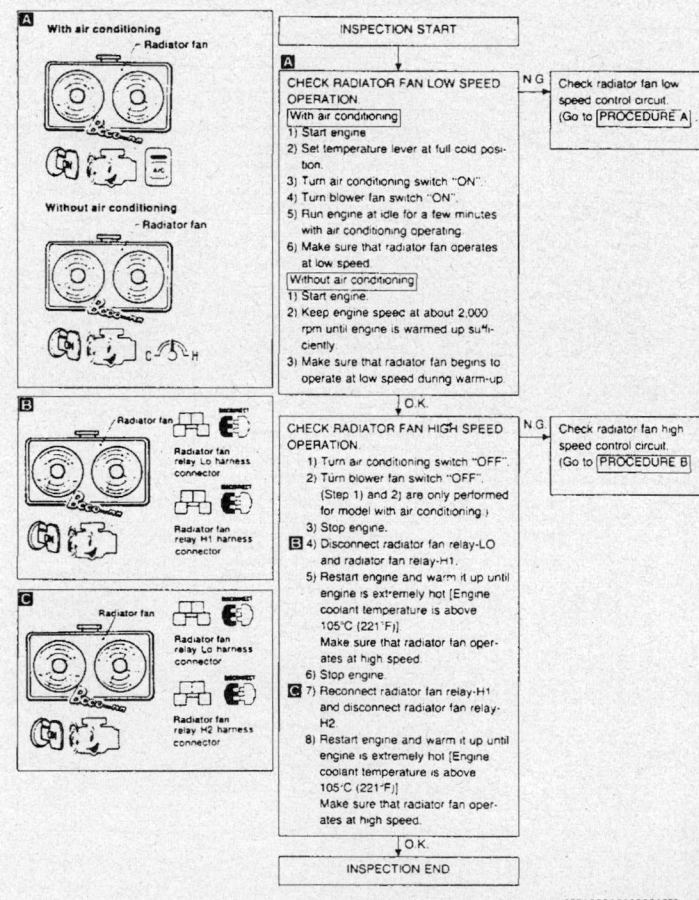

INSPECTION START

↓

CHECK RADIATOR FAN LOW SPEED OPERATION.
With air conditioning
1) Start engine
2) Set temperature lever at full cold position.
3) Turn air conditioning switch "ON".
4) Turn blower fan switch "ON".
5) Run engine at idle for a few minutes with air conditioning operating.
6) Make sure that radiator fan operates at low speed.
Without air conditioning
1) Start engine.
2) Keep engine speed at about 2,000 rpm until engine is warmed up sufficiently.
3) Make sure that radiator fan begins to operate at low speed during warm-up.

NG → Check radiator fan low speed control circuit. (Go to PROCEDURE A)

O.K. ↓

CHECK RADIATOR FAN HIGH SPEED OPERATION.
1) Turn air conditioning switch "OFF".
2) Turn blower fan switch "OFF".
(Step 1) and 2) are only performed for model with air conditioning.)
3) Stop engine.
4) Disconnect radiator fan relay-LO and radiator fan relay-H1.
5) Restart engine and warm it up until engine is extremely hot [Engine coolant temperature is above 105°C (221°F)].
Make sure that radiator fan operates at high speed.
6) Stop engine.
7) Reconnect radiator fan relay-H1 and disconnect radiator fan relay-H2.
8) Restart engine and warm it up until engine is extremely hot [Engine coolant temperature is above 105°C (221°F)].
Make sure that radiator fan operates at high speed.

NG → Check radiator fan high speed control circuit. (Go to PROCEDURE B)

O.K. ↓

INSPECTION END

NS1089100030010X

Fig. 4 Cooling fan diagnosis (Part 1 of 6). 1996–98 Quest

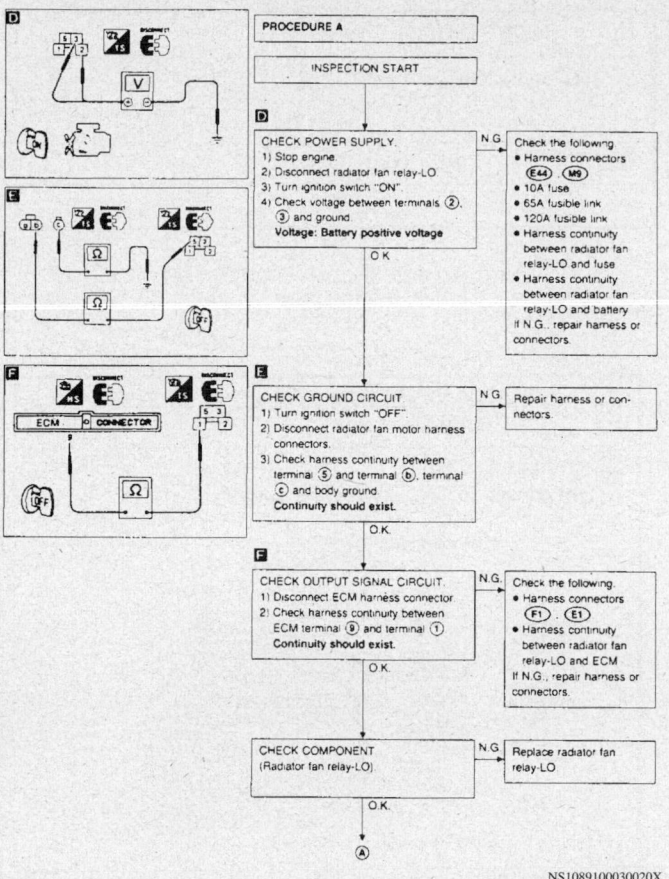

Fig. 4 Cooling fan diagnosis (Part 2 of 6). 1996—98 Quest

NS1089100030020X

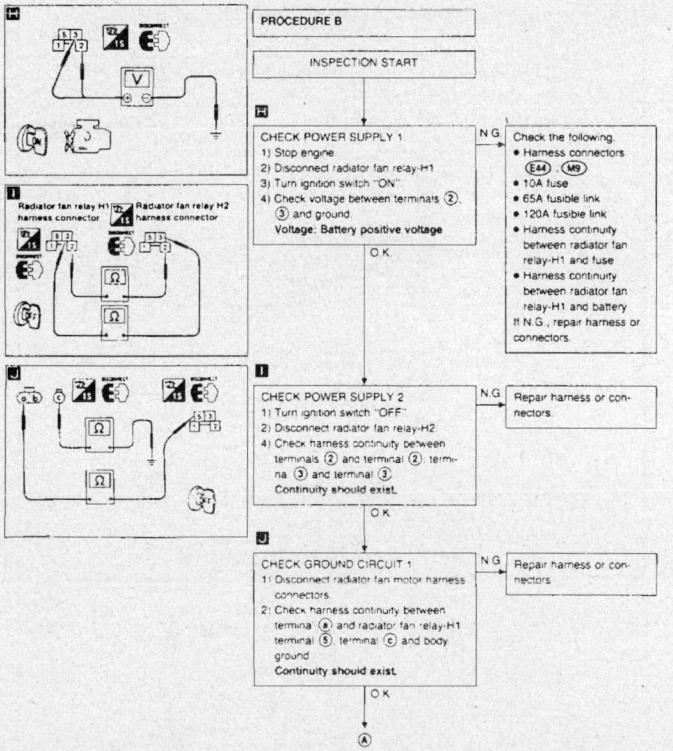

Fig. 4 Cooling fan diagnosis (Part 4 of 6). 1996—98 Quest

NS1089100030040X

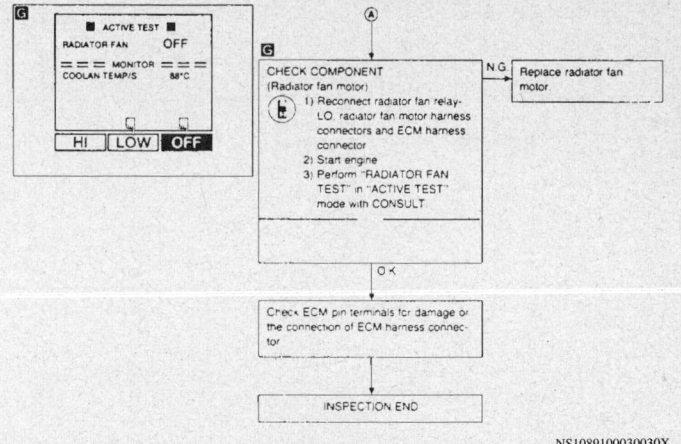

Fig. 4 Cooling fan diagnosis (Part 3 of 6). 1996—98 Quest

NS1089100030030X

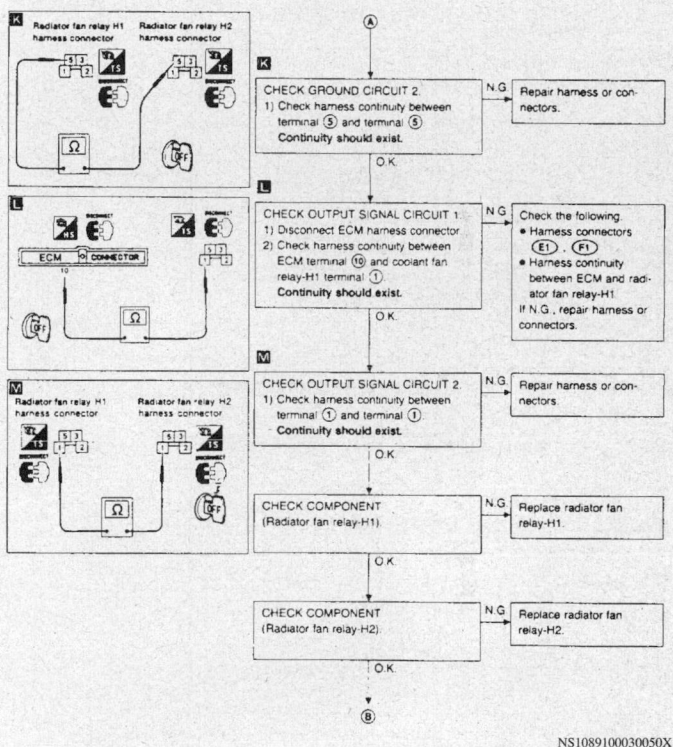

Fig. 4 Cooling fan diagnosis (Part 5 of 6). 1996—98 Quest

NS1089100030050X

Quest

Refer to **Figs. 16 and 17** for fan motor testing, if test results are not as specified, replace motor.

Sentra & 200SX

Refer to **Fig. 18** for fan motor testing, if test results are not as specified, replace motor.

240SX

Refer to **Fig. 19** for fan motor testing, if test results are not as specified, replace motor.

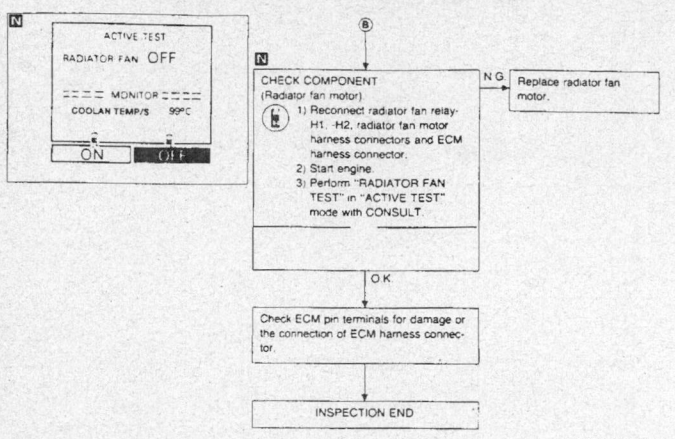

Fig. 4 Cooling fan diagnosis (Part 6 of 6). 1996–98 Quest

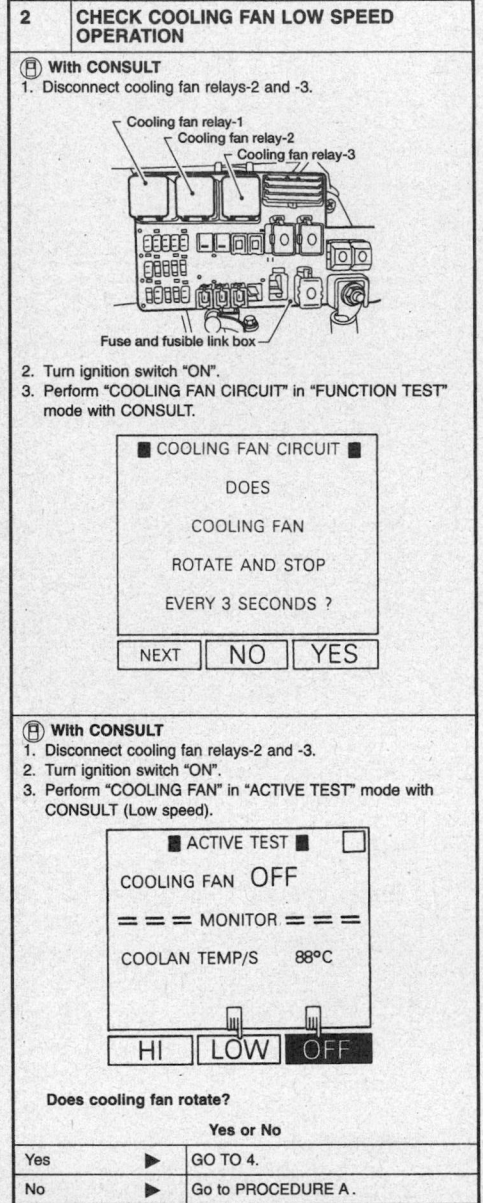

Fig. 5 Cooling fan diagnosis (Part 2 of 7). 1999 Quest

1	INSPECTION START

Do you have CONSULT?

Yes or No

Yes	▶	GO TO 2.
No	▶	GO TO 3.

NS1089900083010X

Fig. 5 Cooling fan diagnosis (Part 1 of 7). 1999 Quest

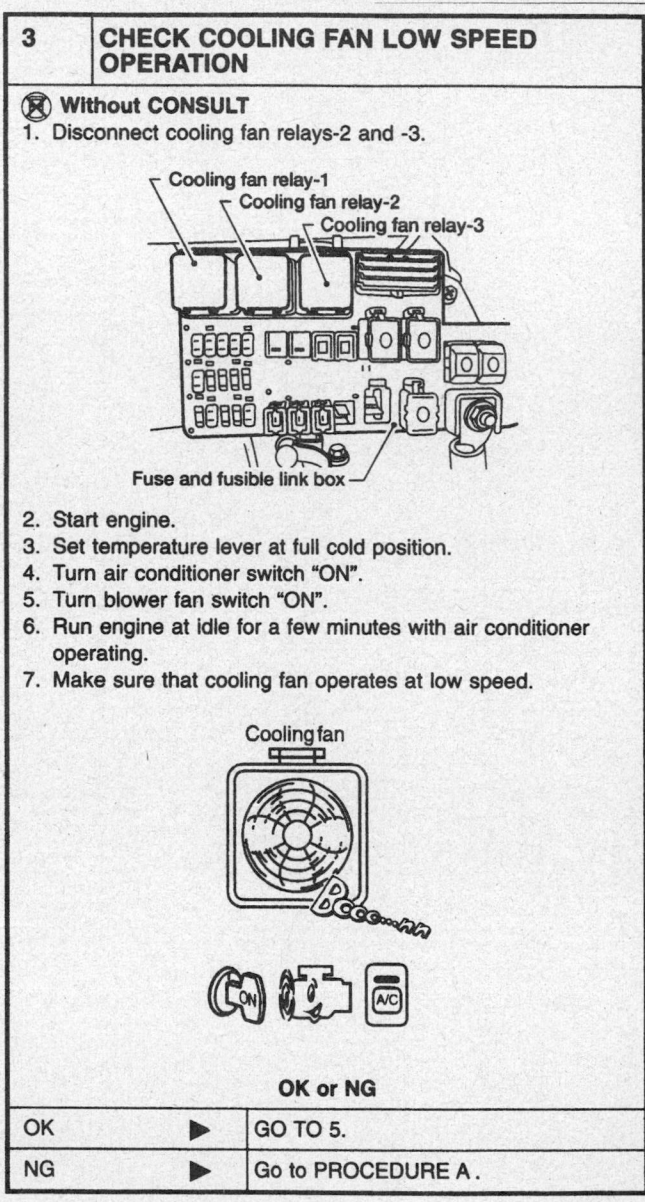

Fig. 5 Cooling fan diagnosis (Part 3 of 7). 1999 Quest

4	CHECK COOLING FAN HIGH SPEED OPERATION

With CONSULT

1. Turn ignition switch "OFF".
2. Reconnect cooling fan relays-2 and -3.
3. Disconnect cooling fan relay-1.
4. Turn ignition switch "ON".
5. Perform "COOLING FAN CIRCUIT" in "FUNCTION TEST" mode with CONSULT.

```
■ COOLING FAN CIRCUIT ■

        DOES

     COOLING FAN

   ROTATE AND STOP

   EVERY 3 SECONDS ?

  NEXT  │   NO  │   YES
```

With CONSULT

1. Turn ignition switch "OFF".
2. Reconnect cooling fan relays-2 and -3.
3. Disconnect cooling fan relay-1.
4. Turn ignition switch "ON".
5. Perform "COOLING FAN" in "ACTIVE TEST" mode with CONSULT (High speed).

```
  ■ ACTIVE TEST ■   □

 COOLING FAN  OFF

 = = = MONITOR = = =

 COOLAN TEMP/S    88°C



  HI  │  LOW  │  OFF
```

Does cooling fan rotate?

Yes or No

Yes	►	GO TO 6.
No	►	Go to PROCEDURE B.

NS1089900083040X

Fig. 5 Cooling fan diagnosis (Part 4 of 7). 1999 Quest

5	CHECK COOLING FAN HIGH SPEED OPERATION

Without CONSULT

1. Turn ignition switch "OFF".
2. Reconnect cooling fan relays-2 and -3.
3. Disconnect cooling fan relay-1.
4. Turn air conditioner switch and blower fan switch "OFF".
5. Disconnect engine coolant temperature sensor harness connector.
6. Connect 150Ω resistor to engine coolant temperature sensor harness connector.
7. Restart engine and make sure that cooling fan operates at higher speed than low speed.

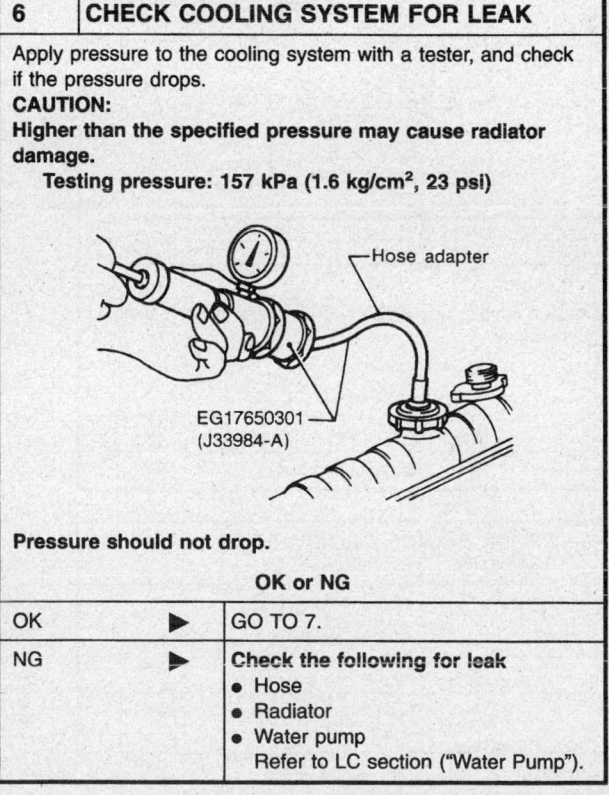

Cooling fan

Engine coolant temperature sensor harness connector

DISCONNECT

150Ω resistor

OK or NG

OK	►	GO TO 6.
NG	►	Go to PROCEDURE B, EC-447.

6	CHECK COOLING SYSTEM FOR LEAK

Apply pressure to the cooling system with a tester, and check if the pressure drops.

CAUTION:
Higher than the specified pressure may cause radiator damage.

Testing pressure: 157 kPa (1.6 kg/cm², 23 psi)

Hose adapter

EG17650301
(J33984-A)

Pressure should not drop.

OK or NG

OK	►	GO TO 7.
NG	►	Check the following for leak ● Hose ● Radiator ● Water pump Refer to LC section ("Water Pump").

NS1089900083050X

Fig. 5 Cooling fan diagnosis (Part 5 of 7). 1999 Quest

7	CHECK RADIATOR CAP

Apply pressure to radiator cap with a tester and check radiator cap relief pressure.

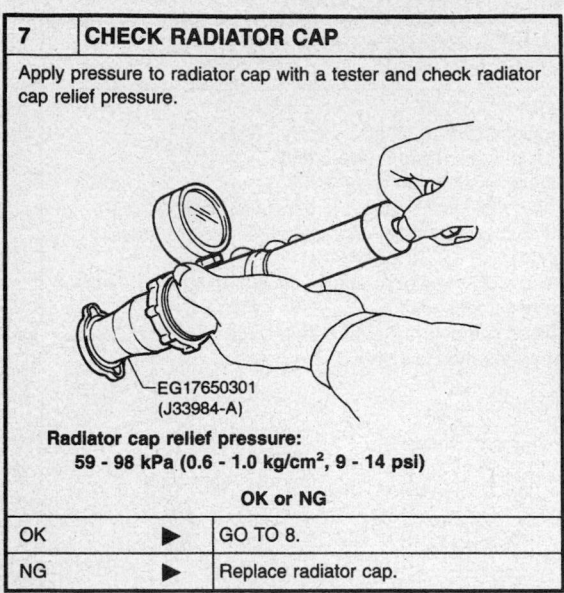

EG17650301
(J33984-A)

Radiator cap relief pressure:
59 - 98 kPa (0.6 - 1.0 kg/cm², 9 - 14 psi)

OK or NG

OK	▶	GO TO 8.
NG	▶	Replace radiator cap.

8	CHECK THERMOSTAT

1. Check valve seating condition at normal room temperatures.
   It should seat tightly.
2. Check valve opening temperature and valve lift.

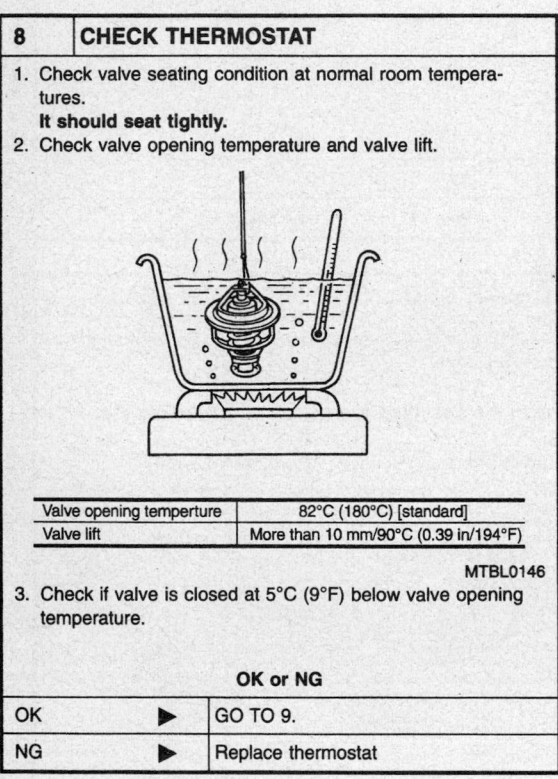

Valve opening temperture	82°C (180°C) [standard]
Valve lift	More than 10 mm/90°C (0.39 in/194°F)

MTBL0146

3. Check if valve is closed at 5°C (9°F) below valve opening temperature.

OK or NG

OK	▶	GO TO 9.
NG	▶	Replace thermostat

9	CHECK ENGINE COOLANT TEMPERATURE SENSOR

OK or NG

OK	▶	GO TO 10.
NG	▶	Replace engine coolant temperature sensor.

NS1089900083060X

Fig. 5 Cooling fan diagnosis (Part 6 of 7). 1999 Quest

10	CHECK "MECHANICAL CONDITION"

▶	INSPECTION END

NS1089900083070X

Fig. 5 Cooling fan diagnosis (Part 7 of 7). 1999 Quest

THERMO SWITCH/SENSOR

300ZX

1. Remove thermo switch/sensor as outlined under "Component Replacement."
2. Connect suitable ohmmeter across switch terminals, then immerse lower part of switch in water. Ohmmeter should indicate an open circuit.
3. Heat water until temperature reaches approximately 212°F. Switch contacts should close and the ohmmeter should indicate continuity.
4. If switch does not operate properly, replace it.

COMPONENT REPLACEMENT

THERMO SWITCH/SENSOR

300ZX

The thermo switch is located on left side of engine.
1. Drain cooling system into suitable container.
2. Disconnect thermo switch wiring, then remove switch.
3. Reverse procedure to install.

COOLING FAN MOTOR

Altima

Refer to **Fig. 20** for cooling fan motor replacement.

Maxima

Refer to **Fig. 21** for cooling fan motor replacement.

Sentra & 200SX

Refer to **Figs. 22 and 23** for cooling fan motor replacement.

Quest

Refer to **Figs. 24 and 25** for cooling fan motor replacement.

240SX

Refer to **Fig. 26** for cooling fan motor replacement.

300ZX

1. Disconnect fan motor electrical connector.
2. Remove fan motor assembly attaching bolts, then the fan motor assembly.
3. Reverse procedure to install.

1	**CHECK POWER SUPPLY**

1. Turn ignition switch "OFF".
2. Disconnect cooling fan relay-1.
3. Turn ignition switch "ON".
4. Check voltage between terminals 1, 5 and ground with CONSULT or tester.

Voltage: Battery voltage

OK or NG

OK	▶	GO TO 3.
NG	▶	GO TO 2.

2	**DETECT MALFUNCTIONING PART**

Check the following.
- Harness connectors M1, E101
- Joint connector-4
- 10A fuse
- 75A fusible link
- Harness for open or short between cooling fan relay-1 and fuse
- Harness for open or short between cooling fan relay-1 and battery

	▶	Repair open circuit or short to ground or short to power in harness or connectors.

NS1089900084010X

Fig. 6 Inspection procedure A (Part 1 of 4). 1999 Quest

3	**CHECK GROUND CIRCUIT**

1. Turn ignition switch "OFF".
2. Disconnect cooling fan motor harness connector.

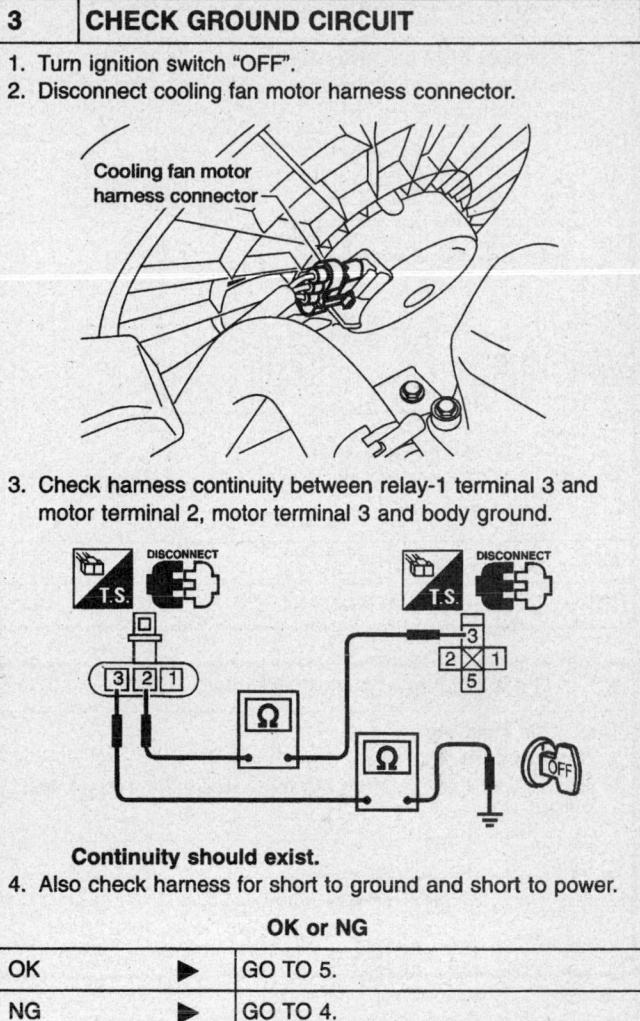

Cooling fan motor harness connector

3. Check harness continuity between relay-1 terminal 3 and motor terminal 2, motor terminal 3 and body ground.

Continuity should exist.
4. Also check harness for short to ground and short to power.

OK or NG

OK	▶	GO TO 5.
NG	▶	GO TO 4.

4	**DETECT MALFUNCTIONING PART**

Check the following.
- Joint connector-4
- Harness for open or short between cooling fan relay-1 and cooling fan motor
- Harness for open or short between cooling fan motor and body ground

	▶	Repair open circuit or short to ground or short to power in harness or connectors.

NS1089900084020X

Fig. 6 Inspection procedure A (Part 2 of 4). 1999 Quest

5 | CHECK OUTPUT SIGNAL CIRCUIT

1. Disconnect ECM harness connector.
2. Check harness continuity between ECM terminal 38 and relay-1 terminal 2.

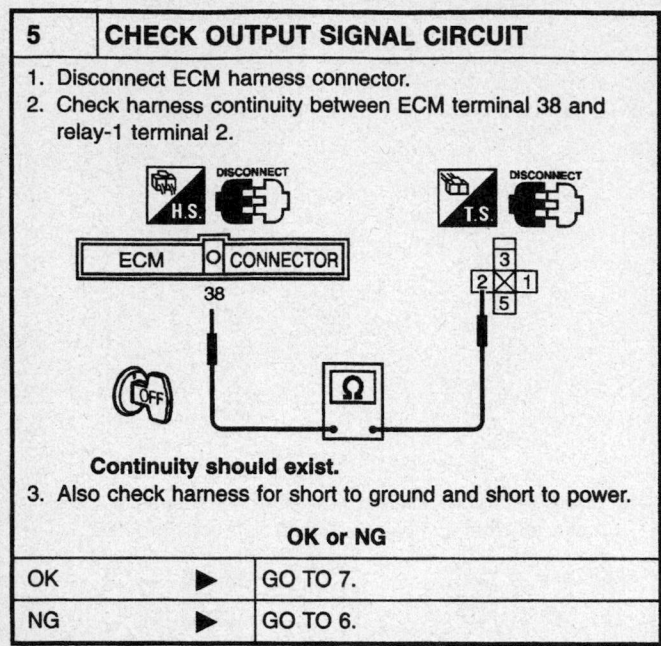

Continuity should exist.

3. Also check harness for short to ground and short to power.

OK or NG

OK	▶	GO TO 7.
NG	▶	GO TO 6.

6 | DETECT MALFUNCTIONING PART

Check the following.
- Harness connectors E54, F3
- Harness for open or short between cooling fan relay-1 and ECM

	▶	Repair open circuit or short to ground or short to power in harness or connectors.

NS1089900084030X

Fig. 6   Inspection procedure A (Part 3 of 4). 1999 Quest

7 | CHECK COOLING FAN RELAY-1

OK or NG

OK	▶	GO TO 8.
NG	▶	Replace cooling fan relay.

8 | CHECK COOLING FAN MOTOR

OK or NG

OK	▶	GO TO 9.
NG	▶	Replace cooling fan motor.

9 | CHECK INTERMITTENT INCIDENT

	▶	INSPECTION END

NS1089900084040X

Fig. 6   Inspection procedure A (Part 4 of 4). 1999 Quest

1	CHECK POWER SUPPLY

1. Turn ignition switch "OFF".
2. Disconnect cooling fan relays-2 and -3.
3. Turn ignition switch "ON".
4. Check voltage between cooling fan relays-2 and -3 terminals 1, 5 and ground with CONSULT or tester.

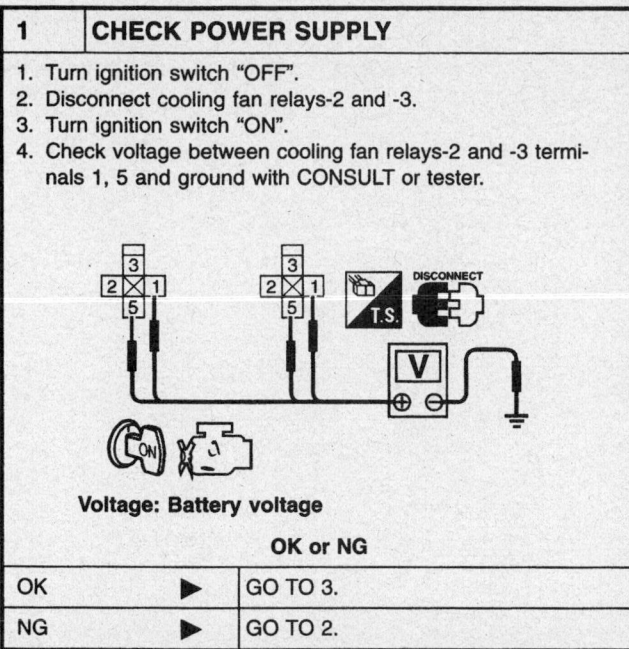

Voltage: Battery voltage

OK or NG

OK	▶	GO TO 3.
NG	▶	GO TO 2.

2	DETECT MALFUNCTIONING PART

Check the following.
● Joint connector-4
● Harness for open or short between cooling fan relays-2, -3 and joint connector-4

	▶	Repair harness or connectors.

3	CHECK POWER AND GROUND CIRCUIT

1. Turn ignition switch "OFF".
2. Disconnect cooling fan motor harness connector.
3. Check harness continuity between motor terminal 1 and relays-2, 3 terminal 3.

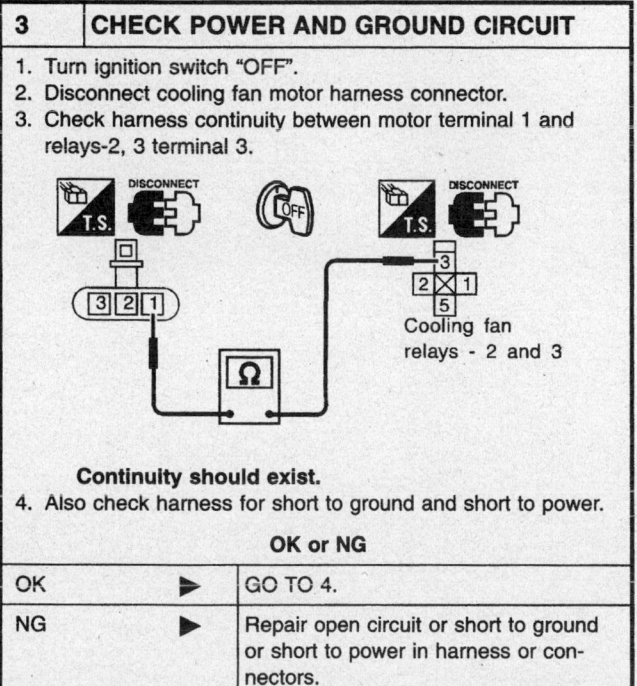

Cooling fan relays - 2 and 3

Continuity should exist.
4. Also check harness for short to ground and short to power.

OK or NG

OK	▶	GO TO 4.
NG	▶	Repair open circuit or short to ground or short to power in harness or connectors.

NS1089900085010X

Fig. 7   Inspection procedure B (Part 1 of 2). 1999 Quest

4	CHECK OUTPUT SIGNAL CIRCUIT

1. Disconnect ECM harness connector.
2. Check harness continuity between ECM terminal 36 and relays-2, 3 terminal 2.

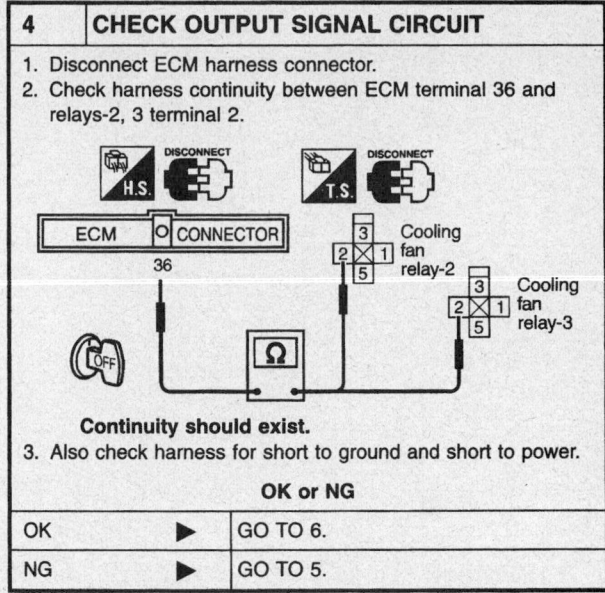

Continuity should exist.
3. Also check harness for short to ground and short to power.

OK or NG

OK	▶	GO TO 6.
NG	▶	GO TO 5.

5	DETECT MALFUNCTIONING PART

Check the following.
● Harness connectors E54, F3
● Harness for open or short between cooling fan relays-2, -3 and ECM

	▶	Repair open circuit or short to ground or short to power in harness or connectors.

6	CHECK COOLING FAN RELAYS-2 AND -3

OK or NG

OK	▶	GO TO 7.
NG	▶	Replace cooling fan relays.

7	CHECK COOLING FAN MOTOR

OK or NG

OK	▶	GO TO 8.
NG	▶	Replace cooling fan motor.

8	CHECK INTERMITTENT INCIDENT

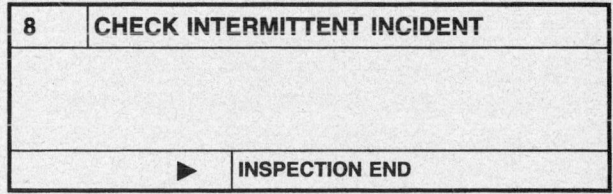

	▶	INSPECTION END

NS1089900085020X

Fig. 7   Inspection procedure B (Part 2 of 2). 1999 Quest

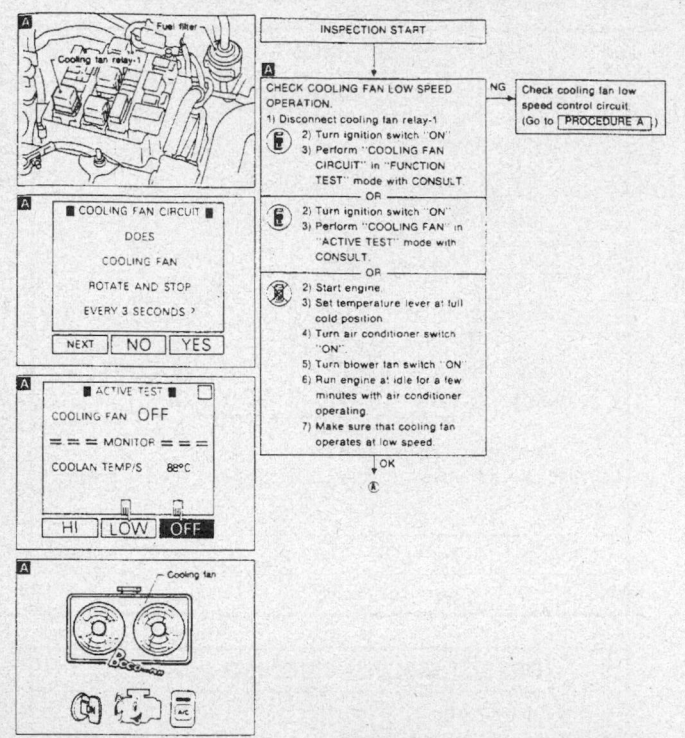

Fig. 8   Cooling fan diagnosis (Part 1 of 5). 240SX

NS1089500059010X

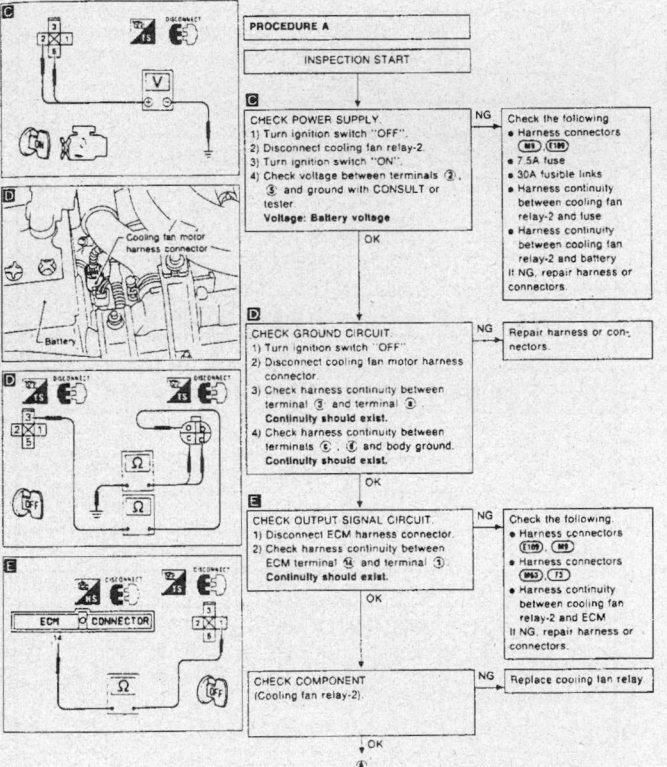

Fig. 8   Cooling fan diagnosis (Part 3 of 5). 240SX

NS1089500059030X

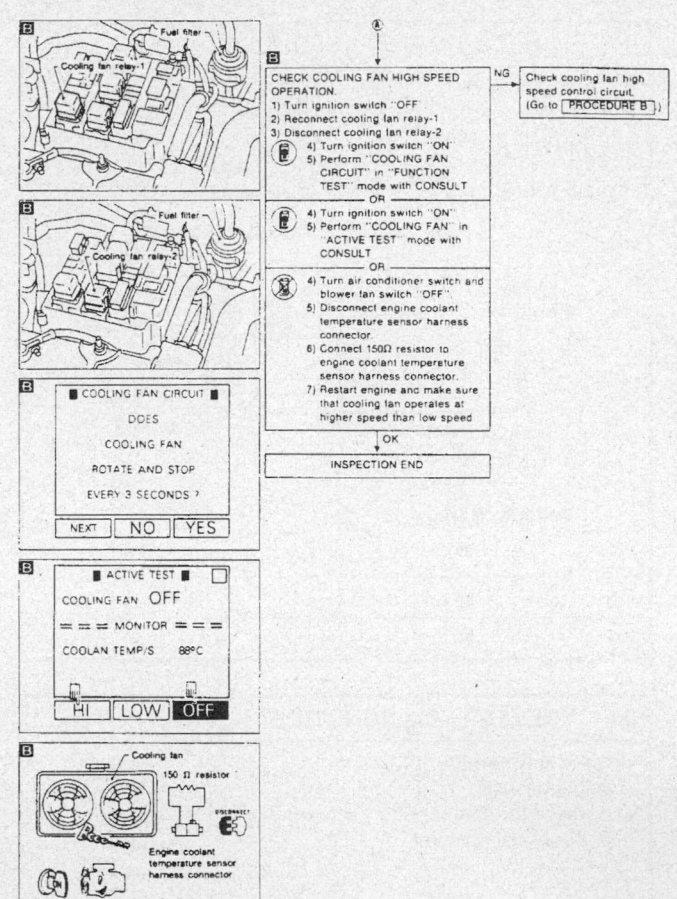

Fig. 8   Cooling fan diagnosis (Part 2 of 5). 240SX

NS1089500059020X

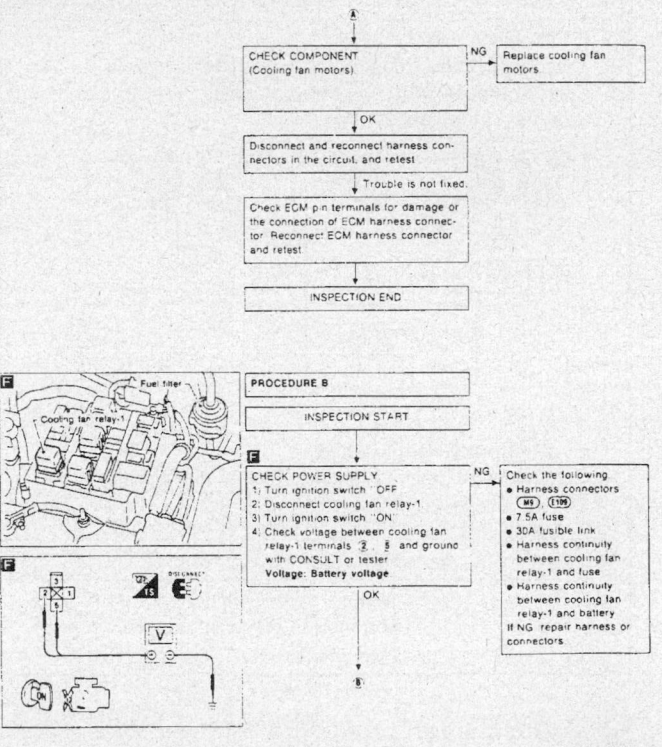

Fig. 8   Cooling fan diagnosis (Part 4 of 5). 240SX

NS1089500059040X

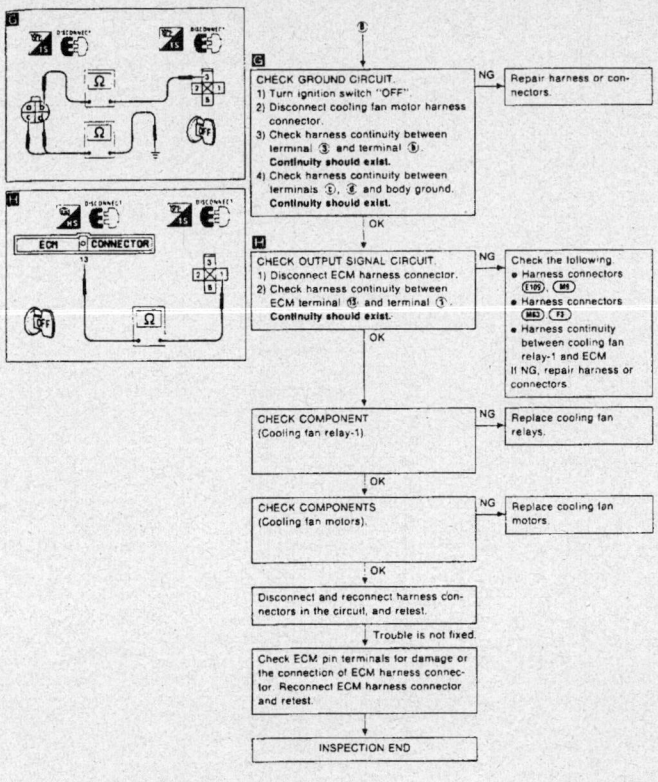

Fig. 8 Cooling fan diagnosis (Part 5 of 5). 240SX

NS1089500059050X

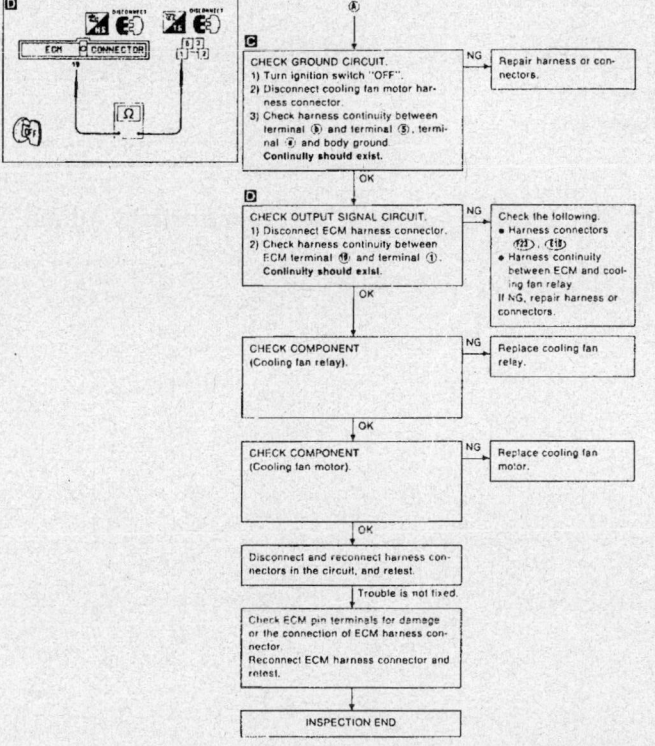

Fig. 9 Cooling fan diagnosis (Part 2 of 6). 300ZX

NS1089400033020X

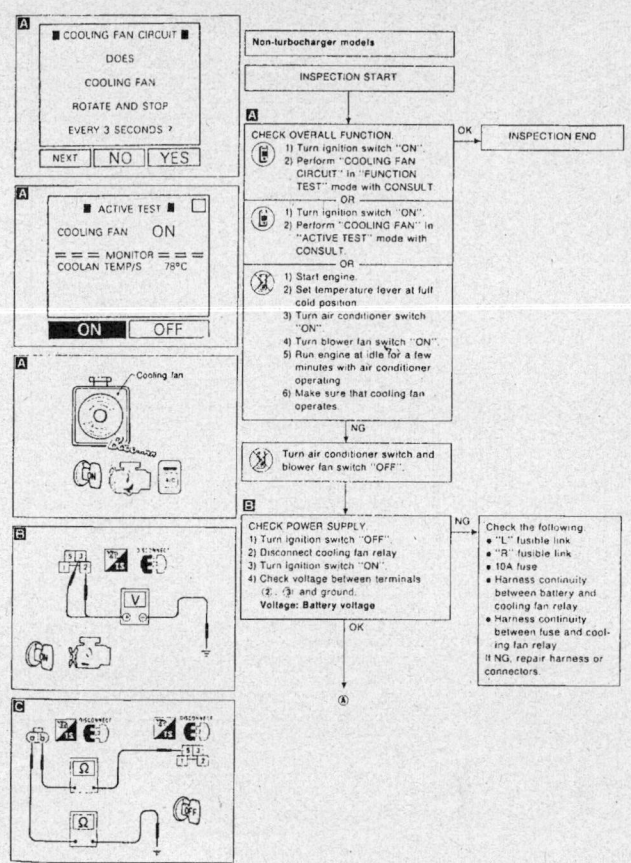

Fig. 9 Cooling fan diagnosis (Part 1 of 6). 300ZX

NS1089400033010X

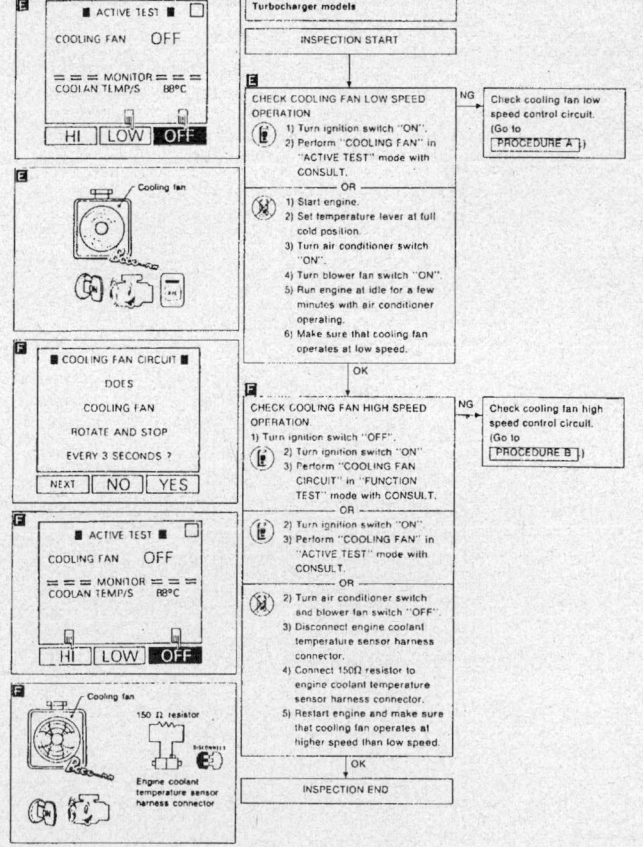

Fig. 9 Cooling fan diagnosis (Part 3 of 6). 300ZX

NS1089400033030X

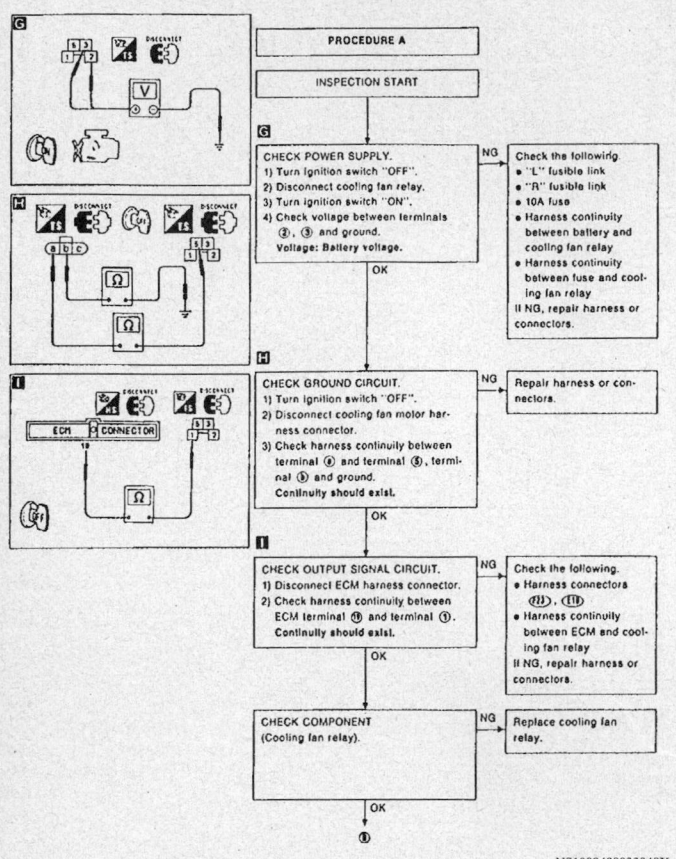

Fig. 9 Cooling fan diagnosis (Part 4 of 6). 300ZX

NS1089400033040X

PROCEDURE A

INSPECTION START

G CHECK POWER SUPPLY.
1) Turn ignition switch "OFF".
2) Disconnect cooling fan relay.
3) Turn ignition switch "ON".
4) Check voltage between terminals ②, ③ and ground.
Voltage: Battery voltage.

NG → Check the following.
- "L" fusible link
- "R" fusible link
- 10A fuse
- Harness continuity between battery and cooling fan relay
- Harness continuity between fuse and cooling fan relay
If NG, repair harness or connectors.

OK

H CHECK GROUND CIRCUIT.
1) Turn ignition switch "OFF".
2) Disconnect cooling fan motor harness connector.
3) Check harness continuity between terminal ⑥ and terminal ⑤, terminal ⑤ and ground.
Continuity should exist.

NG → Repair harness or connectors.

OK

I CHECK OUTPUT SIGNAL CIRCUIT.
1) Disconnect ECM harness connector.
2) Check harness continuity between ECM terminal ⑩ and terminal ①.
Continuity should exist.

NG → Check the following.
- Harness connectors
- Harness continuity between ECM and cooling fan relay
If NG, repair harness or connectors.

OK

CHECK COMPONENT
(Cooling fan relay).

NG → Replace cooling fan relay.

OK

Procedure B (right column)

CHECK COMPONENT
(Cooling fan motor).

NG → Replace cooling fan motor.

OK

Disconnect and reconnect harness connectors in the circuit, and retest.

Trouble is not fixed.

Check ECM pin terminals for damage or the connection of ECM harness connector. Reconnect ECM harness connector and retest.

PROCEDURE B

INSPECTION START

J CHECK POWER SUPPLY.
1) Turn ignition switch "OFF".
2) Disconnect cooling fan sub-relay.
3) Turn ignition switch "ON".
4) Check voltage between terminals ②, ③ and ground.
Voltage: Battery voltage.

NG → Check the following.
- Harness continuity between battery and cooling fan sub-relay
- Harness continuity between fuse and cooling fan sub-relay
If NG, repair harness or connectors.

OK

K CHECK GROUND CIRCUIT.
1) Turn ignition switch "OFF".
2) Disconnect cooling fan motor harness connector.
3) Check harness continuity between terminal ① and terminal ⑤.
Continuity should exist.

NG → Repair harness or connectors.

OK

Fig. 9 Cooling fan diagnosis (Part 5 of 6). 300ZX

NS1089400033050X

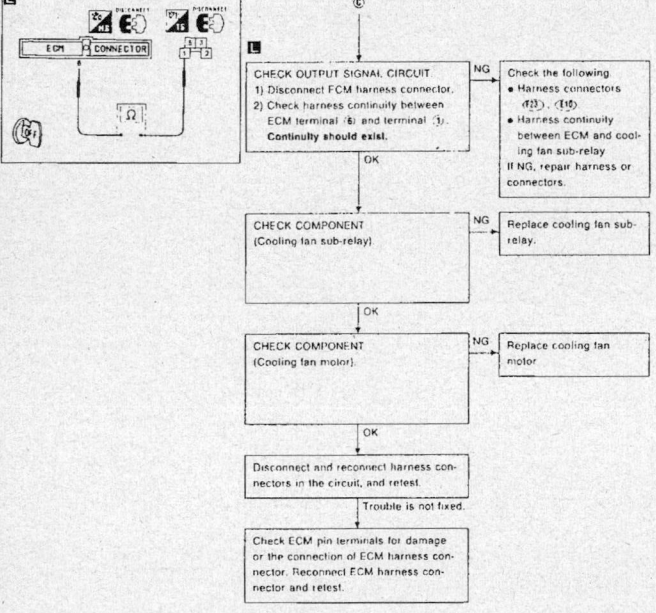

Fig. 9 Cooling fan diagnosis (Part 6 of 6). 300ZX

NS1089400033060X

L CHECK OUTPUT SIGNAL CIRCUIT.
1) Disconnect ECM harness connector.
2) Check harness continuity between ECM terminal ⑥ and terminal ①.
Continuity should exist.

NG → Check the following
- Harness connectors
- Harness continuity between ECM and cooling fan sub-relay
If NG, repair harness or connectors.

OK

CHECK COMPONENT
(Cooling fan sub-relay).

NG → Replace cooling fan sub-relay.

OK

CHECK COMPONENT
(Cooling fan motor).

NG → Replace cooling fan motor.

OK

Disconnect and reconnect harness connectors in the circuit, and retest.

Trouble is not fixed.

Check ECM pin terminals for damage or the connection of ECM harness connector. Reconnect ECM harness connector and retest.

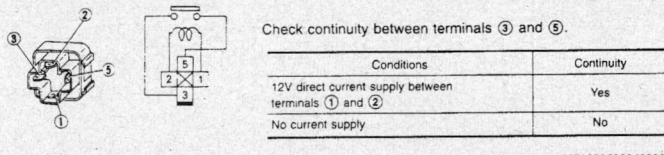

Check continuity between terminals ③ and ⑤.

Conditions	Continuity
12V direct current supply between terminals ① and ②	Yes
No current supply	No

NS1089500060000X

Fig. 10 Cooling fan relay No. 1 inspection. Altima, Maxima, 240SX & Sentra & 200SX

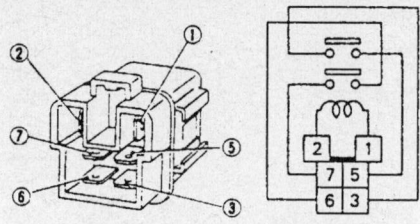

Check continuity between terminals ③ and ⑤, ⑥ and ⑦.

Conditions	Continuity
12V direct current supply between terminals ① and ②	Yes
No current supply	No

NS1089100035000X

Fig. 11 Cooling fan relay No. 2 & 3 inspection. Altima & Maxima

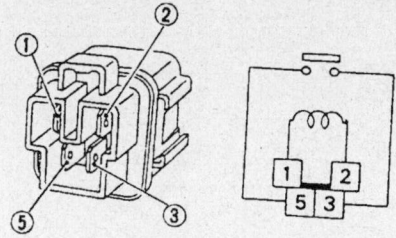

Check continuity between terminals ③ and ⑤.

Conditions	Continuity
12V direct current supply between terminals ① and ②	Yes
No current supply	No

NS1089100034000X

Fig. 12 Cooling fan relay inspection. 300ZX w/manual transaxle, Sentra, 200SX & 1996–98 Quest

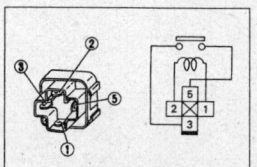

Check continuity between terminals 3 and 5.

Conditions	Continuity
12V direct current supply between terminals 1 and 2	Yes
No current supply	No

If NG, replace relay.

NS1089900086000X

Fig. 13 Cooling fan relay inspection. 1999 Quest

	Speed	Terminals	
		(⊕)	(⊖)
Cooling fan motor	Low	ⓐ	ⓓ
	High	ⓐ, ⓑ	ⓒ, ⓓ

NS1089500081000X

Fig. 14 Cooling fan motor inspection. Altima

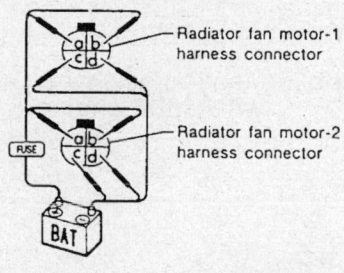

Radiator fan motor-1 harness connector

Radiator fan motor-2 harness connector

	Speed	Terminals	
		(⊕)	(⊖)
Radiator fan motor-1	Low	ⓑ	ⓒ
	High	ⓐ, ⓑ	ⓒ, ⓓ
Radiator fan motor-2	Low	ⓑ	ⓒ
	High	ⓐ, ⓑ	ⓒ, ⓓ

NS1089100037000X

Fig. 15 Cooling fan motor inspection. Maxima w/automatic transaxle

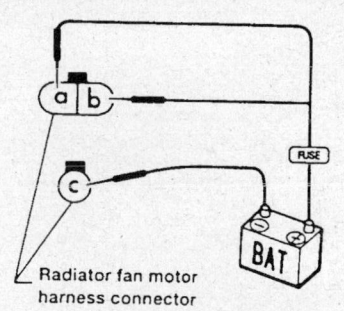

Radiator fan motor harness connector

	Speed	Terminals	
		(⊕)	(⊖)
Radiator fan motor	Low	ⓐ	ⓒ
	High	ⓑ	ⓒ

NS1089100038000X

Fig. 16 Cooling fan motor inspection. 1996–98 Quest

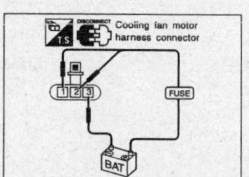

Cooling fan motor harness connector

1. Disconnect cooling fan motor harness connector.
2. Supply cooling fan motor terminals with battery voltage and check operation.

	Speed	Terminals	
		(+)	(−)
Cooling fan motor	Low	2	3
	High	1	3

Cooling fan motor should operate.
If NG, replace cooling fan motor.

NS1089900087000X

Fig. 17 Cooling fan motor inspection. 1999 Quest

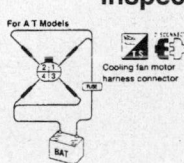

For A/T Models

Cooling fan motor harness connector

For M/T models

Cooling fan motor harness connector

1. Disconnect cooling fan motor harness connectors.
2. Supply cooling fan motor terminals with battery voltage and check operation.

	Speed	Terminals	
		(⊕)	(⊖)
Cooling fan motor	Low (A/T models)	①	④
	High (A/T models)	②	③
	High (M/T models)	①	②

Cooling fan motor should operate.
If NG, replace cooling fan motor.

NS1089500061000X

Fig. 18 Cooling fan motors inspection. Sentra & 200SX

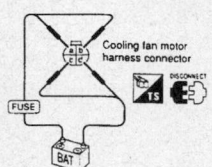

1. Disconnect cooling fan motor harness connectors.
2. Supply cooling fan motor terminals with battery voltage and check operation.

	Speed	Terminals	
		(⊕)	(⊖)
Cooling fan motor	Low	ⓐ	ⓓ
	High	ⓐ, ⓑ	ⓒ, ⓔ

Cooling fan motor should operate.
If NG, replace cooling fan motor.

NS1089500062000X

Fig. 19 Cooling fan motor inspection. 240SX

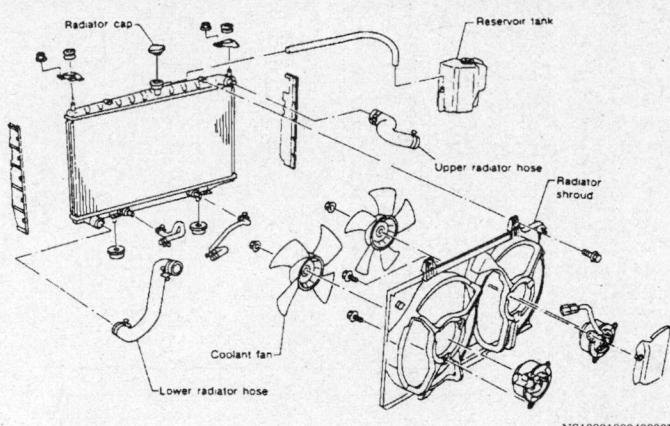

NS1089100040000X

Fig. 20 Cooling fan replacement. Altima

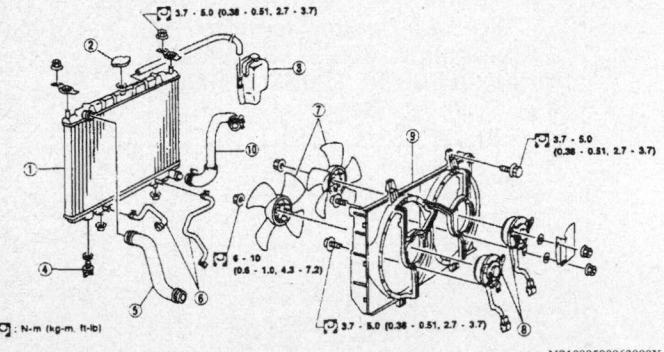

NS1089500063000X

Fig. 21 Cooling fan replacement. Maxima w/ VQ30DE engine

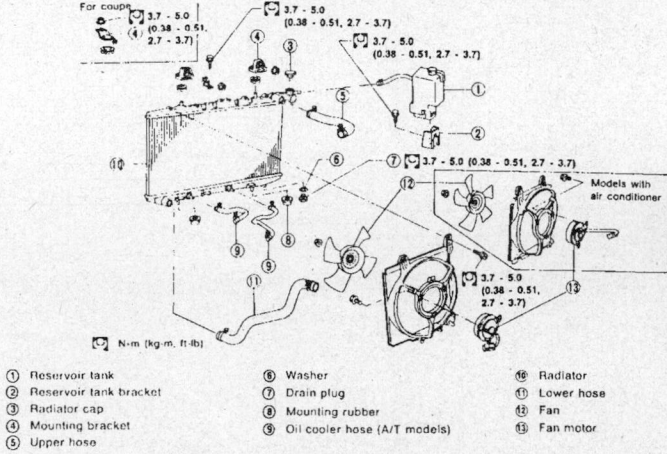

① Reservoir tank	⑥ Washer	⑩ Radiator
② Reservoir tank bracket	⑦ Drain plug	⑪ Lower hose
③ Radiator cap	⑧ Mounting rubber	⑫ Fan
④ Mounting bracket	⑨ Oil cooler hose (A/T models)	⑬ Fan motor
⑤ Upper hose		

NS1089100044000X

Fig. 22 Cooling fan replacement. Sentra & 200SX w/GA16DE engine

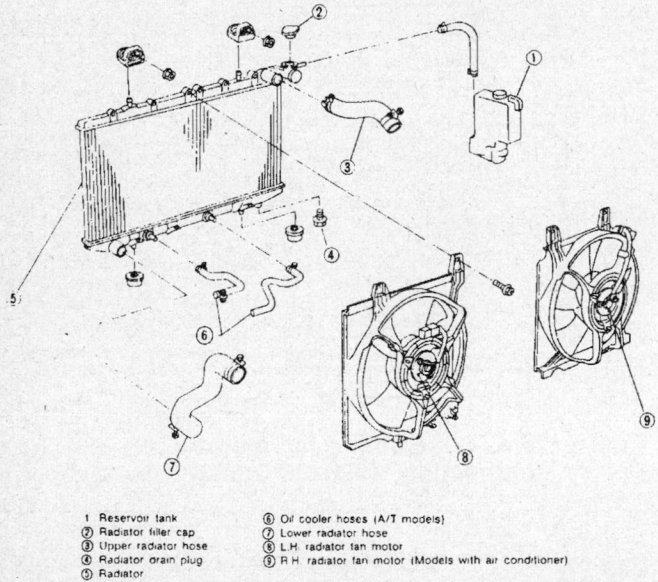

1 Reservoir tank
2 Radiator filler cap
3 Upper radiator hose
4 Radiator drain plug
5 Radiator
6 Oil cooler hoses (A/T models)
7 Lower radiator hose
8 L.H. radiator fan motor
9 R.H. radiator fan motor (Models with air conditioner)

NS1089100045000X

Fig. 23 Cooling fan replacement. Sentra & 200SX w/SR20DE engine

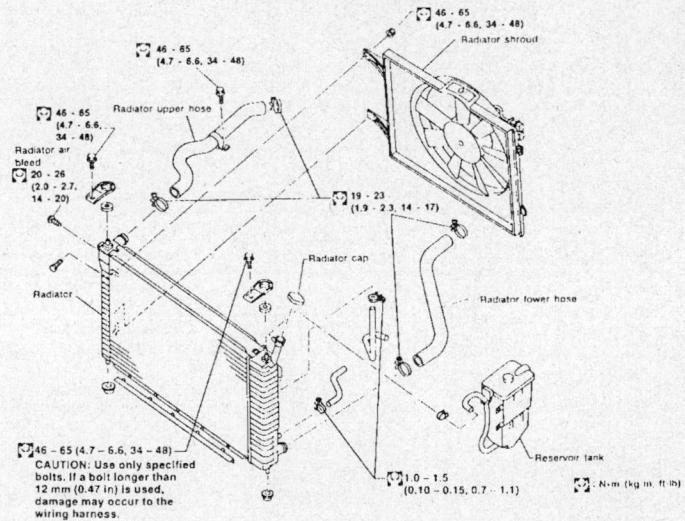

NS1089100046000X

Fig. 24 Cooling fan replacement. 1996–98 Quest

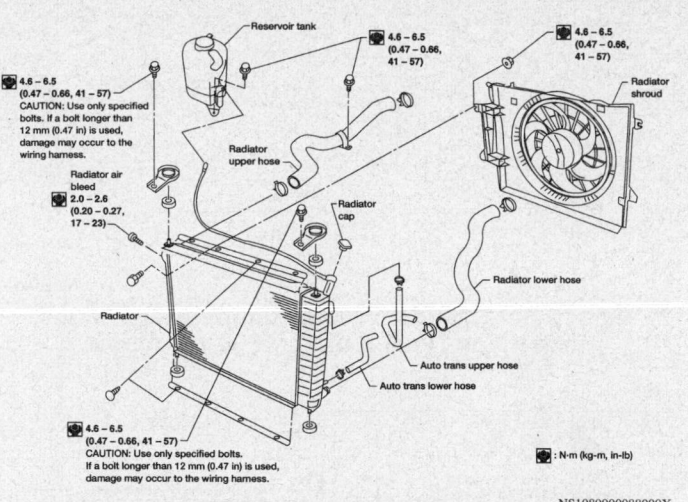

Fig. 25 Cooling fan replacement. 1999 Quest

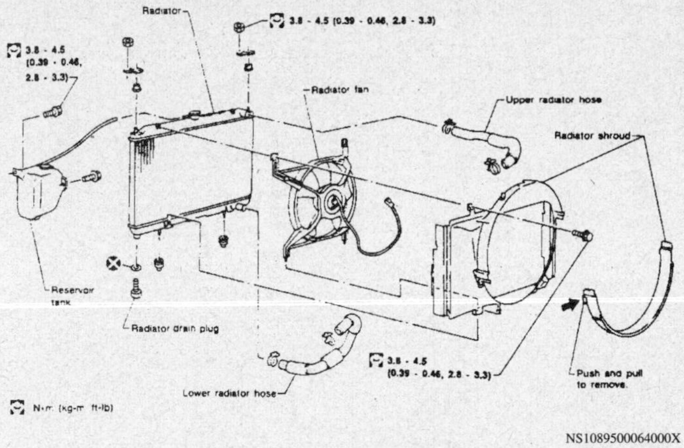

NS1089900088000X

Fig. 26 Cooling fan replacement. 240SX

NS1089500064000X

Dash Gauges

NOTE: Refer To The "Dash Panel Service" Section For Dash Panel Removal Procedures.

NOTE: Refer To The "Electronic Instrumentation" Section In "MOTOR's Imported Engine Performance & Driveability Manual" For Information Related To Electronic Instrumentation.

NOTE: On Air Bag Equipped Models, Refer To "Air Bag System Precautions" Located In The Front Of This Manual For System Disarming & Arming Procedures.

NOTE: Refer To "Computer Relearn Procedures" Located In The Front Of This Manual For Computer Relearn Procedures.

INDEX

GAUGES
INSPECTION
Fuel Gauge & Water Temperature Gauge

Refer to **Figs. 1 through 20** for fuel and water temperature gauge diagnosis.

Fuel Tank Gauge Unit

Remove fuel tank gauge unit from the fuel tank, then connect an ohmmeter between terminals of the gauge unit connector as shown in **Figs. 21 through 32**. Compare results with specifications in **Figs. 33 through 41**. Repair or replace as necessary.

Oil Pressure Switch

Connect an ohmmeter as shown in **Fig. 42**, then compare results with **Figs. 43 and 44**.

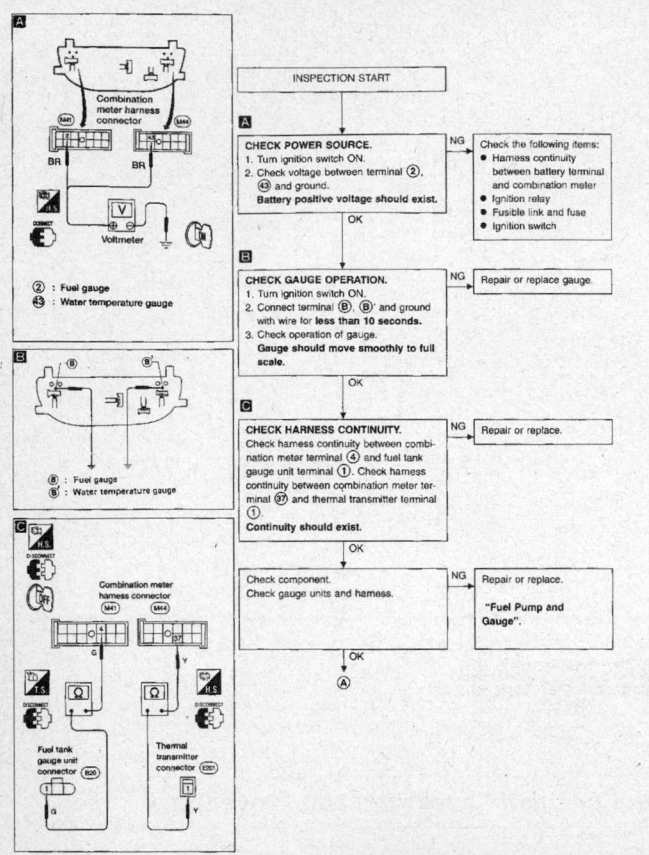

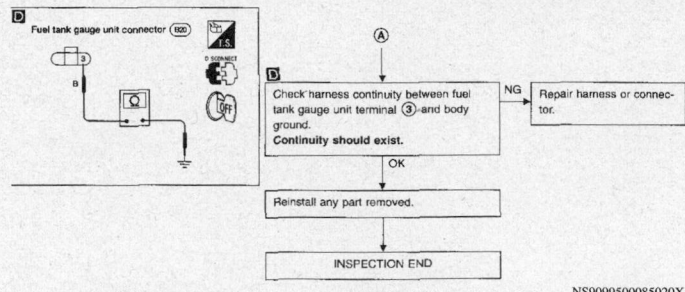

NS9099500085020X

Fig. 1 Fuel gauge & water temperature gauge inspection (Part 2 of 2). 1996–97 Altima

NS9099500085010X

Fig. 1 Fuel gauge & water temperature gauge inspection (Part 1 of 2). 1996–97 Altima

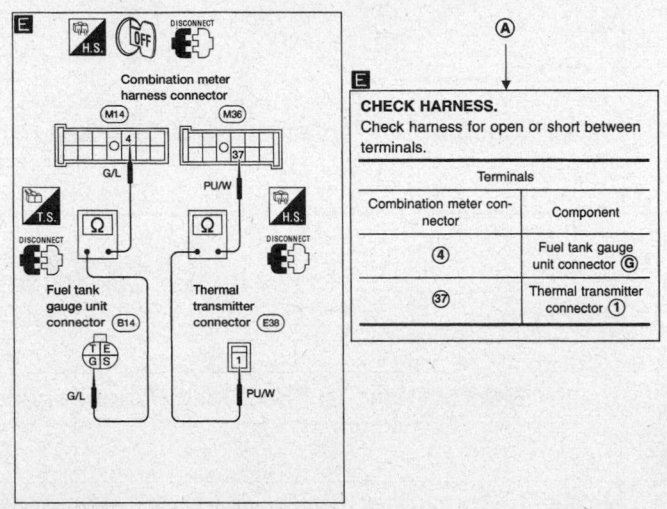

NS9099900092020X

Fig. 2 Fuel gauge & water temperature gauge inspection (Part 2 of 2). 1998–99 Altima

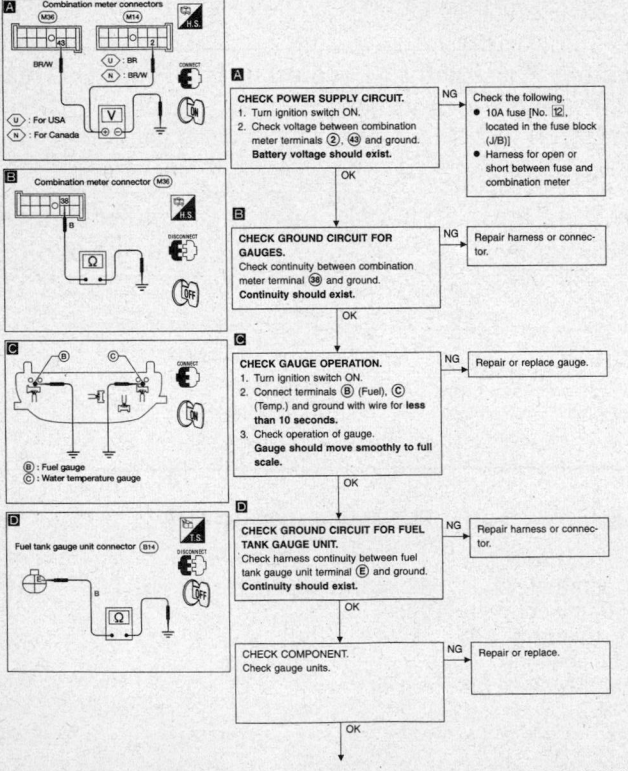

NS9099900092010X

Fig. 2 Fuel gauge & water temperature gauge inspection (Part 1 of 2). 1998–99 Altima

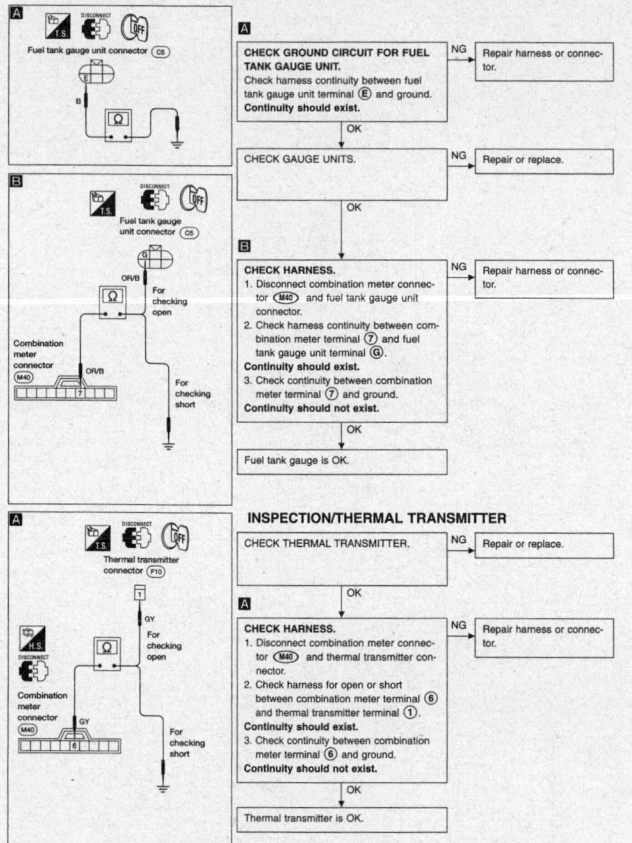

Fig. 3   Fuel gauge inspection. 1998-99 Frontier w/2.4L engine

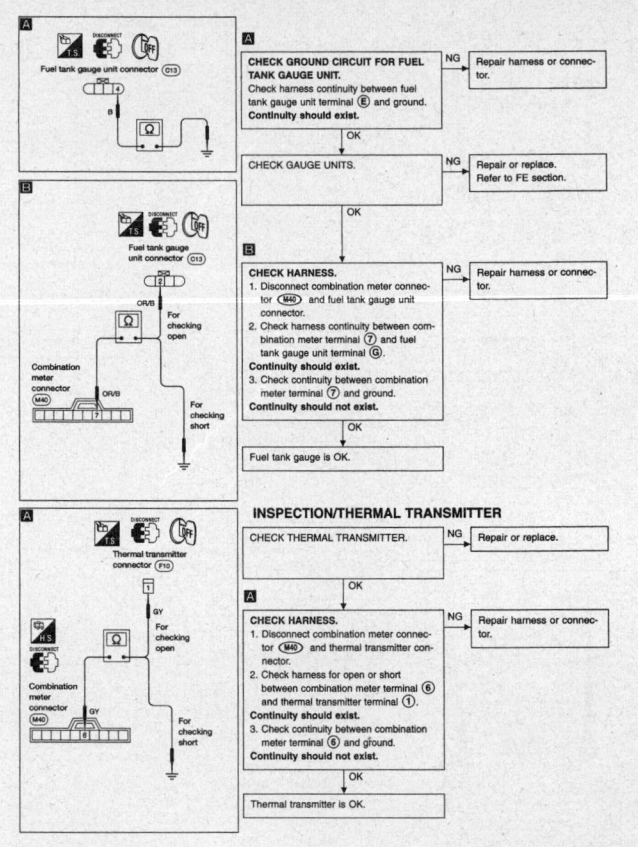

Fig. 4   Fuel gauge inspection. 1998-99 Frontier w/3.3L engine

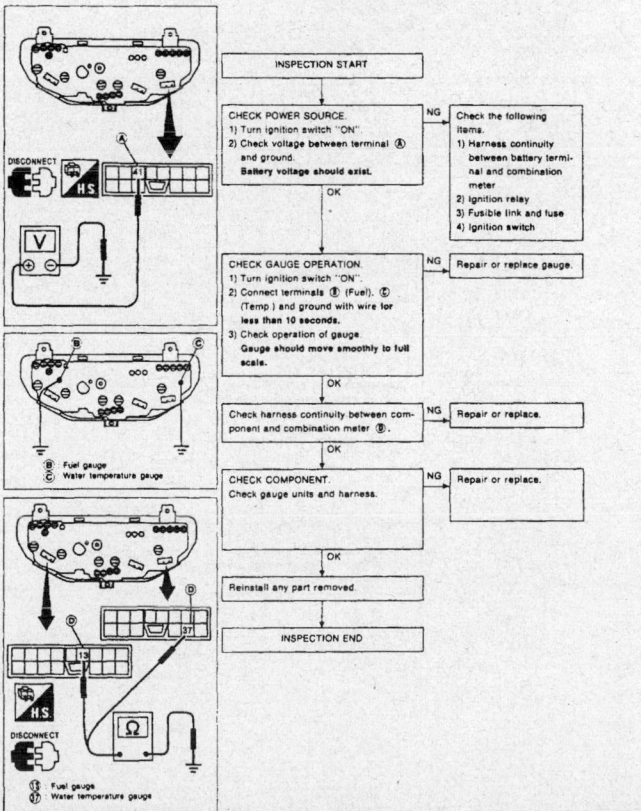

Fig. 5   Fuel gauge & water temperature gauge inspection. Maxima

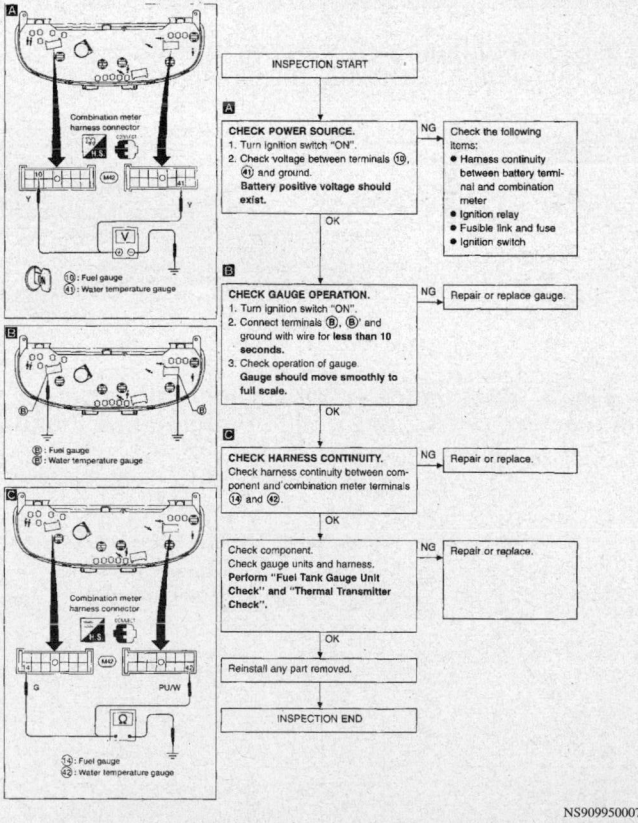

Fig. 6   Fuel gauge & water temperature gauge inspection. Sentra & 200SX less tachometer

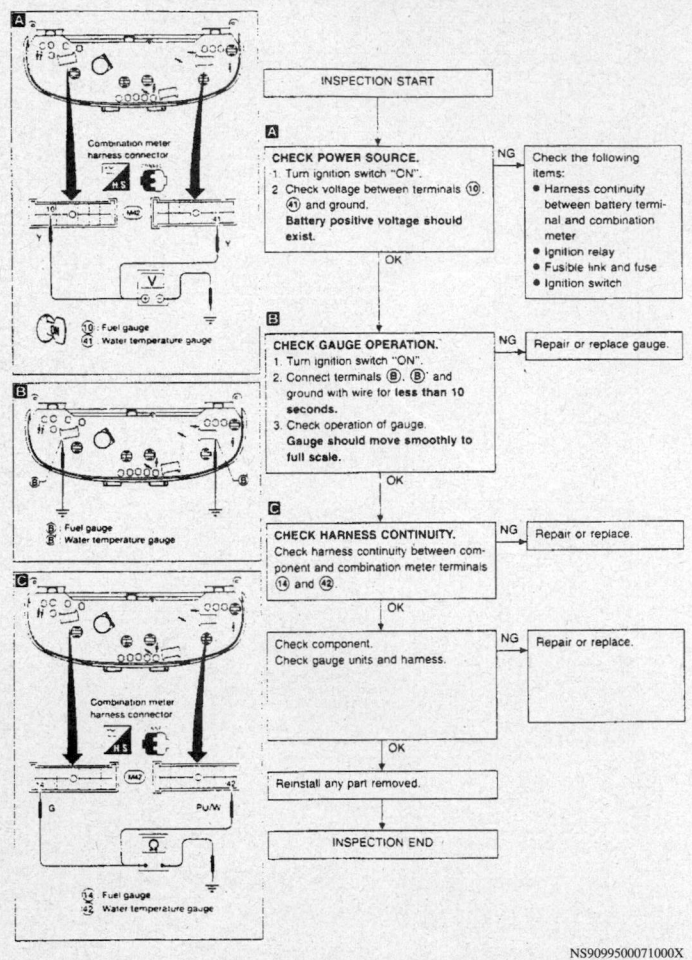

Fig. 7 Fuel gauge & water temperature gauge inspection. Sentra & 200SX w/tachometer

NS9099500071000X

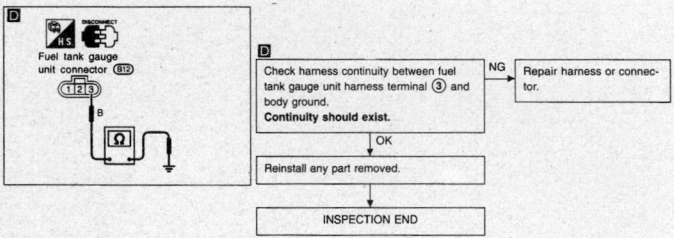

Fig. 8 Fuel gauge & water temperature gauge inspection (Part 2 of 2). 1996 Pathfinder & Pickup

NS9099600080020X

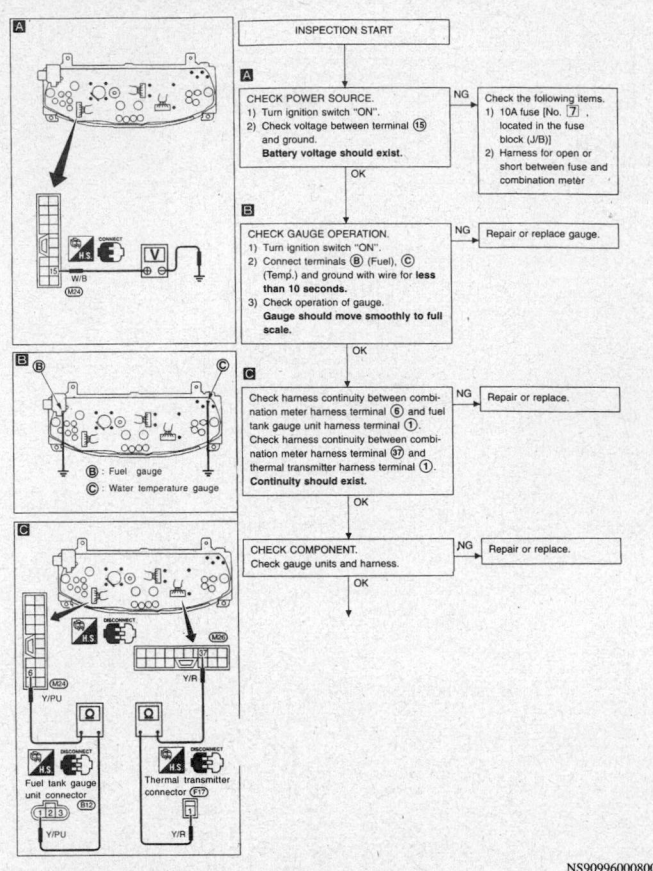

NS9099600080010X

Fig. 8 Fuel gauge & water temperature gauge inspection (Part 1 of 2). 1996 Pathfinder & Pickup

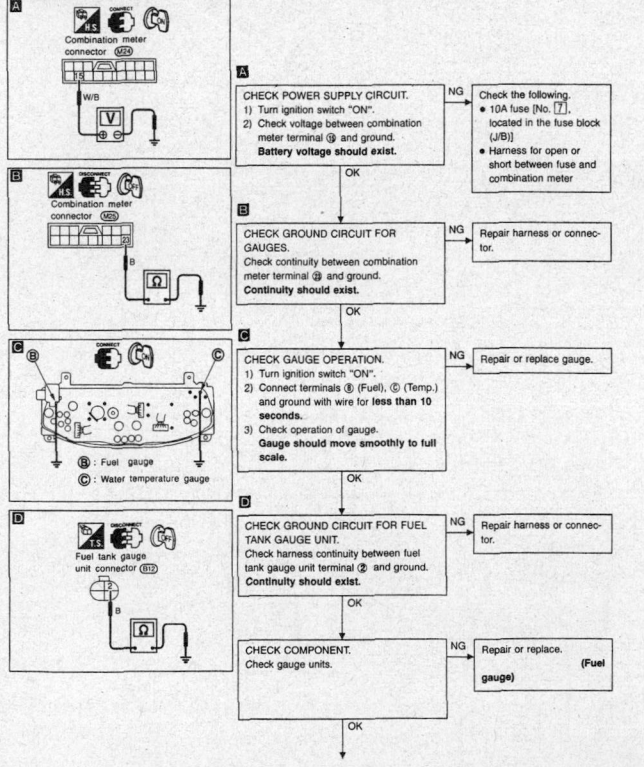

NS9099700089010X

Fig. 9 Fuel gauge & water temperature gauge inspection (Part 1 of 2). 1997–99 Pathfinder

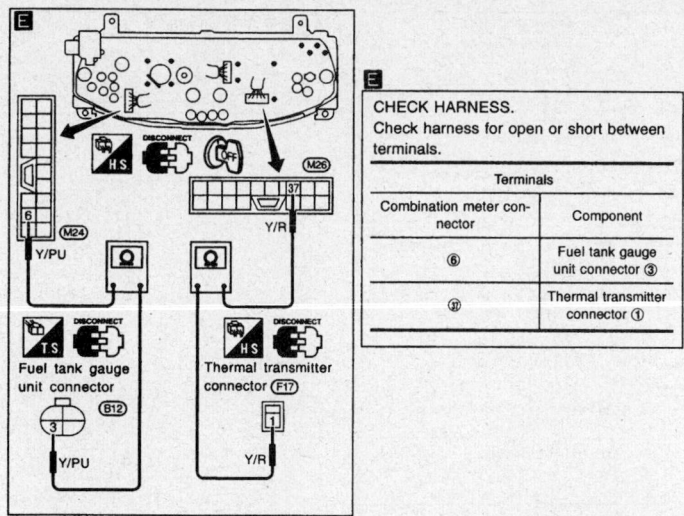

Fig. 9   Fuel gauge & water temperature gauge inspection (Part 2 of 2). 1997–99 Pathfinder

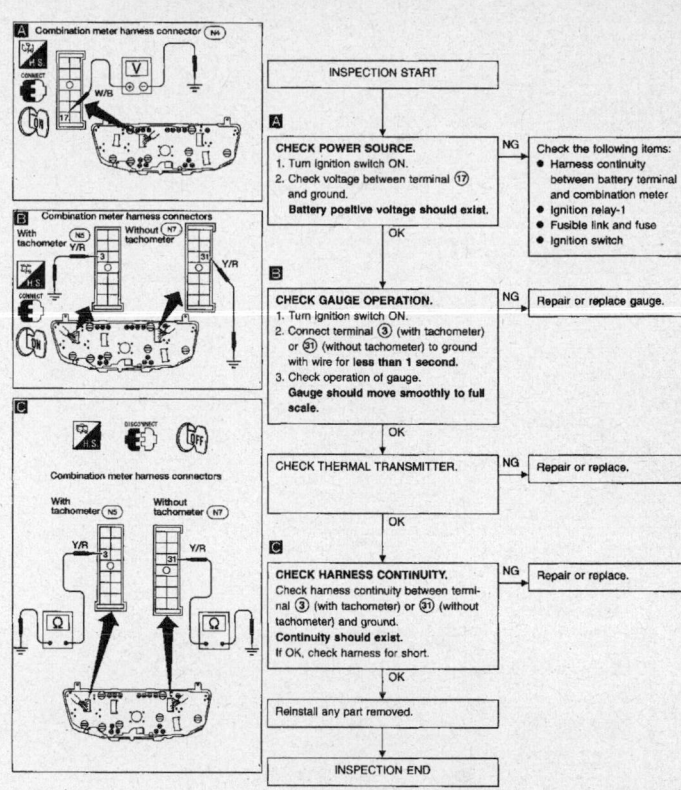

Fig. 10   Water temperature gauge inspection. 1997 Pickup

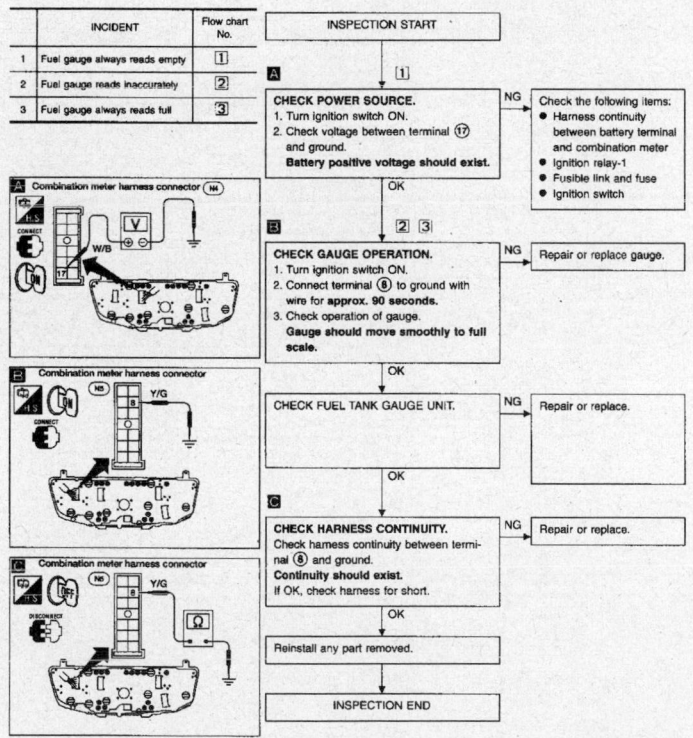

Fig. 11   Fuel gauge inspection. 1997 Pickup

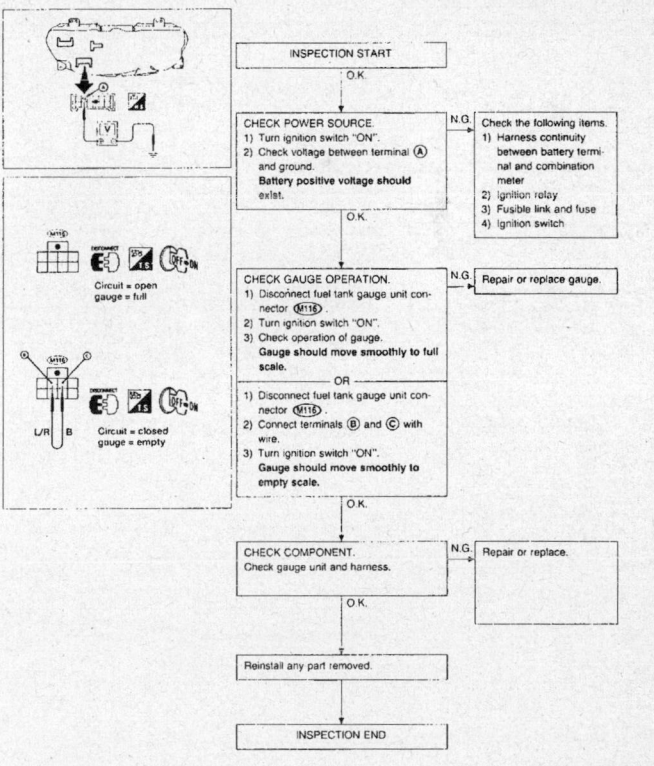

Fig. 12   Fuel gauge inspection. 1996 Quest

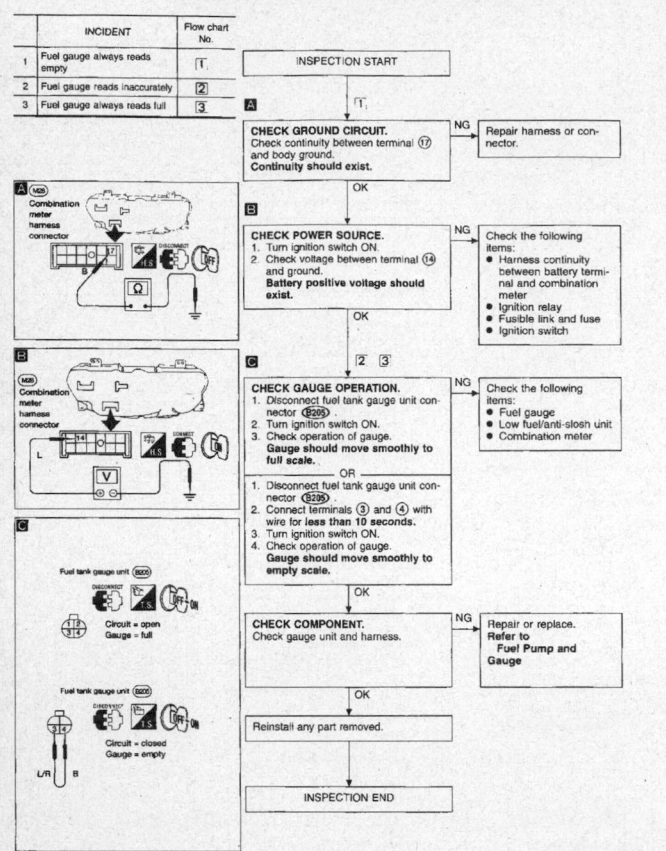

	INCIDENT	Flow chart No.
1	Fuel gauge always reads empty	1
2	Fuel gauge reads inaccurately	2
3	Fuel gauge always reads full	3

INSPECTION START

↓ 1

A

CHECK GROUND CIRCUIT.
Check continuity between terminal ⑰ and body ground.
Continuity should exist. → NG → Repair harness or connector.

↓ OK

B

CHECK POWER SOURCE.
1. Turn ignition switch ON.
2. Check voltage between terminal ⑭ and ground.
Battery positive voltage should exist. → NG → Check the following items:
● Harness continuity between battery terminal and combination meter
● Ignition relay
● Fusible link and fuse
● Ignition switch

↓ OK

C 2 3

CHECK GAUGE OPERATION.
1. Disconnect fuel tank gauge unit connector (B205).
2. Turn ignition switch ON.
3. Check operation of gauge.
Gauge should move smoothly to full scale.
OR
1. Disconnect fuel tank gauge unit connector (B205).
2. Connect terminals ③ and ④ with wire for **less than 10 seconds**.
3. Turn ignition switch ON.
4. Check operation of gauge.
Gauge should move smoothly to empty scale. → NG → Check the following items:
● Fuel gauge
● Low fuel/anti-slosh unit
● Combination meter

↓ OK

CHECK COMPONENT.
Check gauge unit and harness. → NG → Repair or replace. Refer to Fuel Pump and Gauge

↓ OK

Reinstall any part removed.

↓

INSPECTION END

NS9099700087000X

Fig. 13 Fuel gauge inspection. 1997–98 Quest

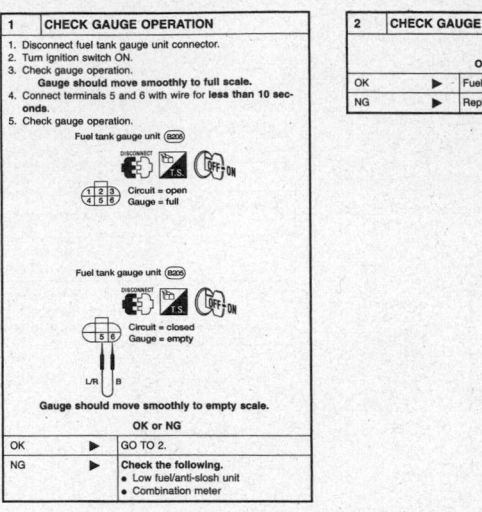

1	CHECK GAUGE OPERATION

1. Disconnect fuel tank gauge unit connector.
2. Turn ignition switch ON.
3. Check gauge operation.
   Gauge should move smoothly to full scale.
4. Connect terminals 5 and 6 with wire for **less than 10 sec-onds.**
5. Check gauge operation.

Fuel tank gauge unit (B205)

Circuit = open
Gauge = full

Fuel tank gauge unit (B205)

Circuit = closed
Gauge = empty

Gauge should move smoothly to empty scale.

OK or NG

| OK | ► | GO TO 2. |
| NG | ► | Check the following.
● Low fuel/anti-slosh unit
● Combination meter |

2	CHECK GAUGE UNITS
	OK or NG

| OK | ► | Fuel tank gauge is OK. |
| NG | ► | Replace fuel tank gauge unit. |

NS9099900095000X

Fig. 14 Fuel gauge inspection. 1999 Quest

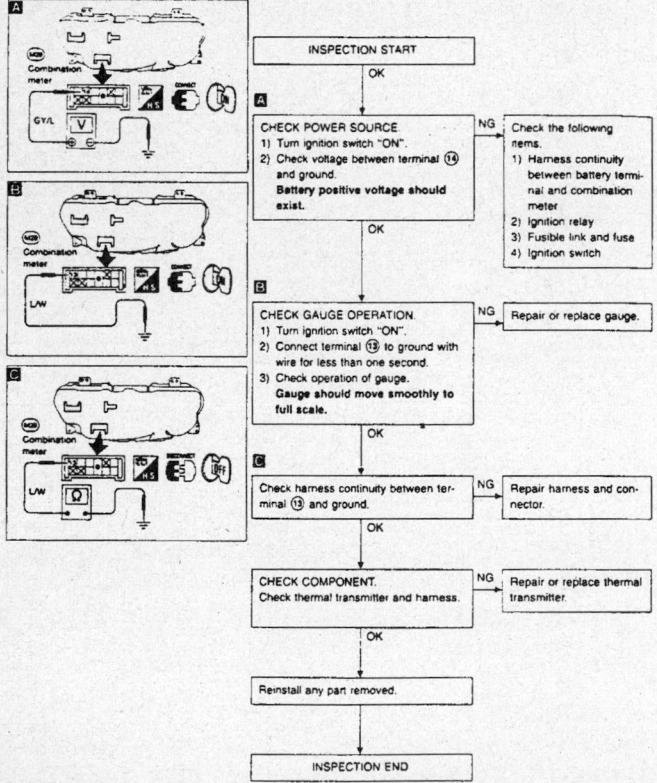

INSPECTION START

↓ OK

A

CHECK POWER SOURCE.
1) Turn ignition switch "ON".
2) Check voltage between terminal ⑭ and ground.
Battery positive voltage should exist. → NG → Check the following items:
1) Harness continuity between battery terminal and combination meter
2) Ignition relay
3) Fusible link and fuse
4) Ignition switch

↓ OK

B

CHECK GAUGE OPERATION.
1) Turn ignition switch "ON".
2) Connect terminal ⑬ to ground with wire for **less than one second.**
3) Check operation of gauge.
Gauge should move smoothly to full scale. → NG → Repair or replace gauge.

↓ OK

C

Check harness continuity between terminal ⑬ and ground. → NG → Repair harness and connector.

↓ OK

CHECK COMPONENT.
Check thermal transmitter and harness. → NG → Repair or replace thermal transmitter.

↓ OK

Reinstall any part removed.

↓

INSPECTION END

NS9099100015000X

Fig. 15 Water temperature gauge inspection. 1996 Quest

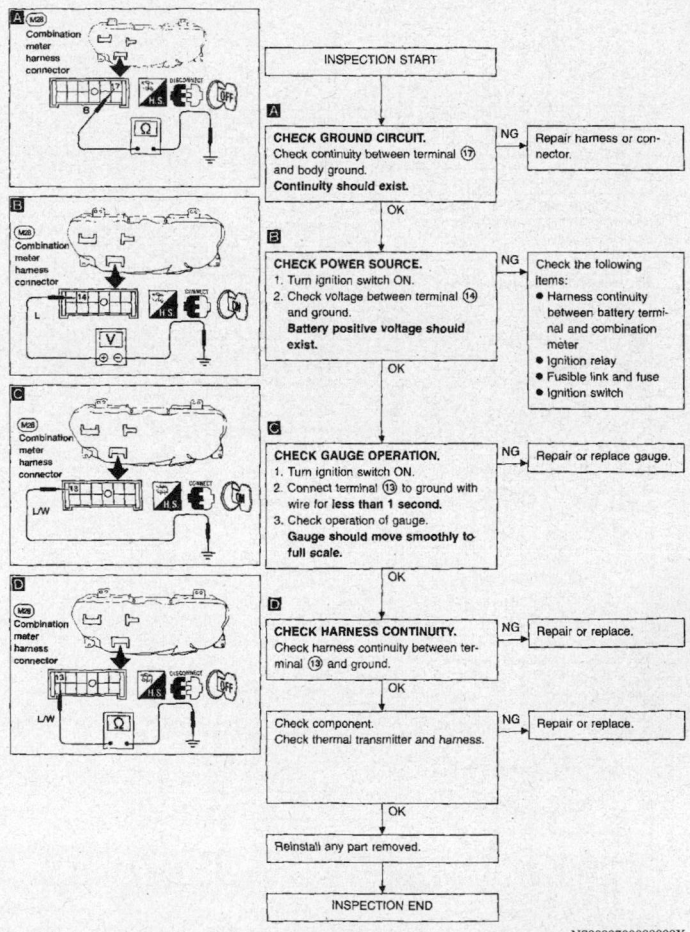

INSPECTION START

↓ OK

A

CHECK GROUND CIRCUIT.
Check continuity between terminal ⑰ and body ground.
Continuity should exist. → NG → Repair harness or connector.

↓ OK

B

CHECK POWER SOURCE.
1. Turn ignition switch ON.
2. Check voltage between terminal ⑭ and ground.
Battery positive voltage should exist. → NG → Check the following items:
● Harness continuity between battery terminal and combination meter
● Ignition relay
● Fusible link and fuse
● Ignition switch

↓ OK

C

CHECK GAUGE OPERATION.
1. Turn ignition switch ON.
2. Connect terminal ⑬ to ground with wire for **less than 1 second.**
3. Check operation of gauge.
Gauge should move smoothly to full scale. → NG → Repair or replace gauge.

↓ OK

D

CHECK HARNESS CONTINUITY.
Check harness continuity between terminal ⑬ and ground. → NG → Repair or replace.

↓ OK

Check component.
Check thermal transmitter and harness. → NG → Repair or replace.

↓ OK

Reinstall any part removed.

↓

INSPECTION END

NS9099700088000X

Fig. 16 Water temperature gauge inspection. 1997–98 Quest

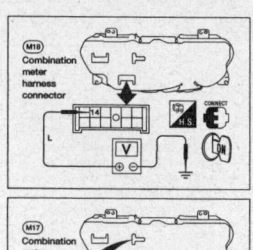

Terminals		Ignition switch position		
(+)	(−)	OFF	ON	START
14	Ground	0 V	Battery voltage	Battery voltage
33	Ground	0 V	Battery voltage	Battery voltage

If NG, check the following
- 10A fuse (No. 29, located in fuse block)
- Harness for open or short between fuse and combination meter.

NS9099900096000X

Fig. 17 Water temperature gauge inspection. 1999 Quest

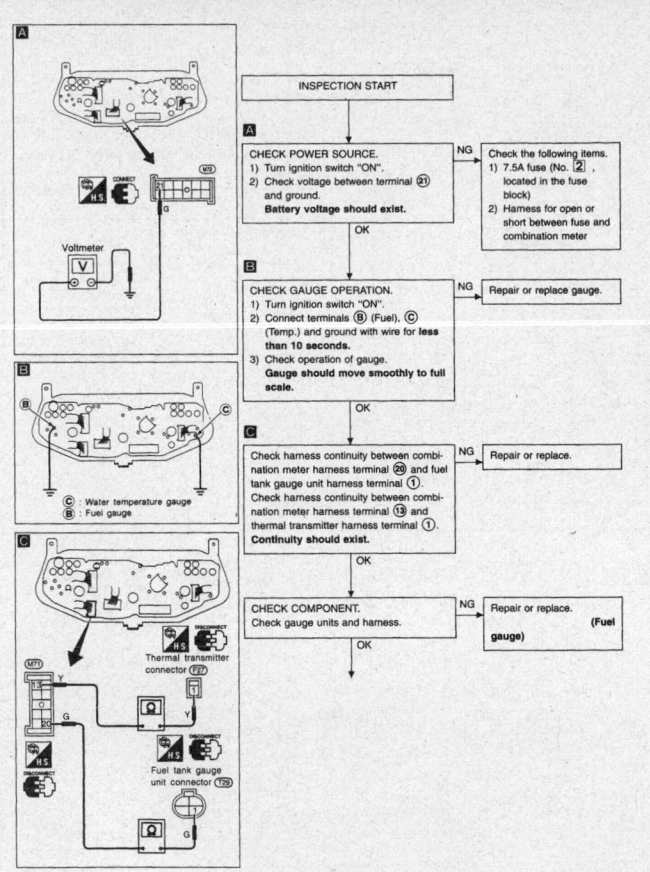

NS9099500072010X

Fig. 18 Fuel gauge & water temperature gauge inspection (Part 1 of 2). 1996 240SX

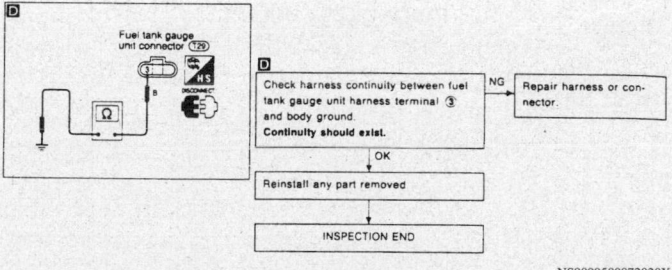

NS9099500072020X

Fig. 18 Fuel gauge & water temperature gauge inspection (Part 2 of 2). 1996 240SX

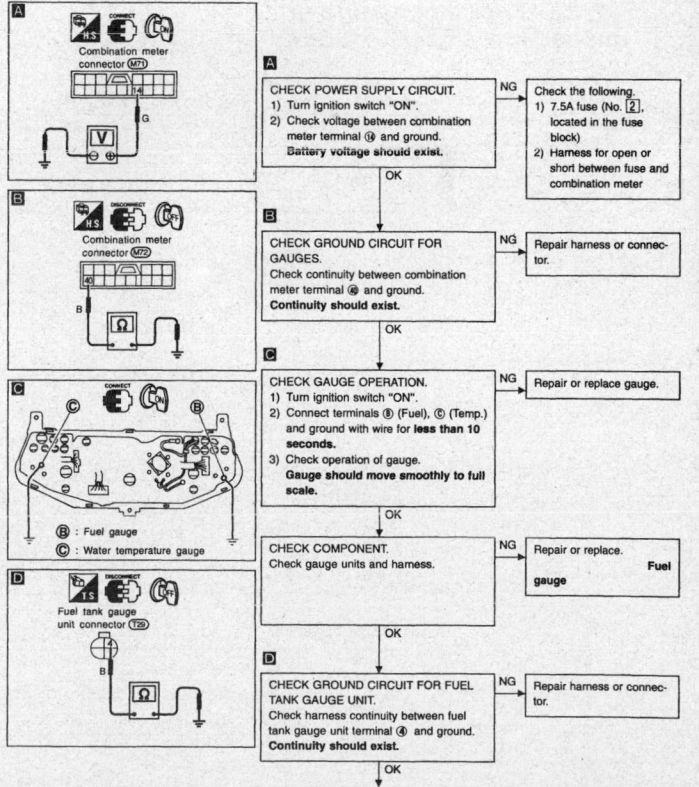

NS9099700086010X

Fig. 19 Fuel gauge & water temperature gauge inspection (Part 1 of 2). 1997–98 240SX

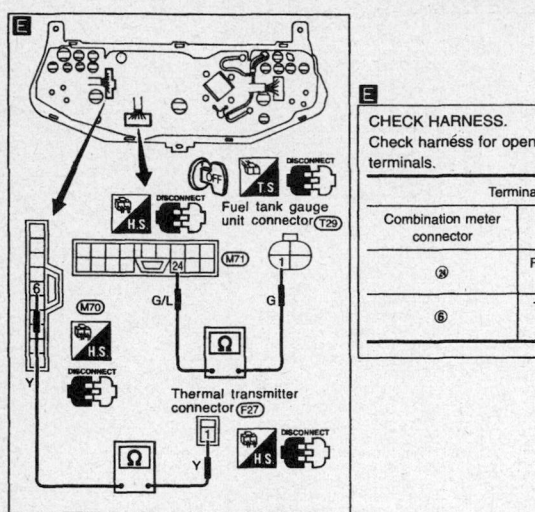

CHECK HARNESS.
Check harness for open or short between terminals.

Terminals	
Combination meter connector	Component
N	Fuel tank gauge unit connector ①
S	Thermal transmitter connector ①

NS9099700086020X

Fig. 19   Fuel gauge & water temperature gauge inspection (Part 2 of 2). 1997–98 240SX

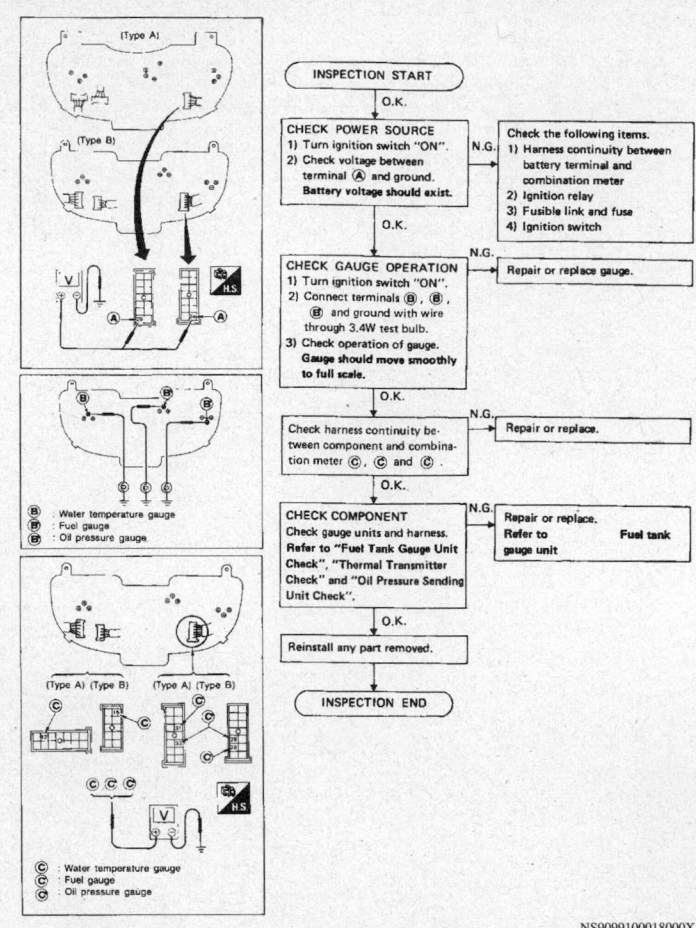

INSPECTION START

O.K.

CHECK POWER SOURCE
1) Turn ignition switch "ON".
2) Check voltage between terminal Ⓐ and ground.
Battery voltage should exist.

N.G. → Check the following items.
1) Harness continuity between battery terminal and combination meter
2) Ignition relay
3) Fusible link and fuse
4) Ignition switch

O.K.

CHECK GAUGE OPERATION
1) Turn ignition switch "ON".
2) Connect terminals Ⓑ, Ⓑ, Ⓑ and ground with wire through 3.4W test bulb.
3) Check operation of gauge.
Gauge should move smoothly to full scale.

N.G. → Repair or replace gauge.

O.K.

Check harness continuity between component and combination meter Ⓒ, Ⓒ and Ⓒ.

N.G. → Repair or replace.

O.K.

CHECK COMPONENT
Check gauge units and harness. Refer to "Fuel Tank Gauge Unit Check", "Thermal Transmitter Check" and "Oil Pressure Sending Unit Check".

N.G. → Repair or replace. Refer to "Fuel Tank Gauge Unit".

O.K.

Reinstall any part removed.

O.K.

INSPECTION END

Ⓑ : Water temperature gauge
Ⓑ : Fuel gauge
Ⓑ : Oil pressure gauge

(Type A) (Type B)   (Type A) (Type B)

Ⓒ : Water temperature gauge
Ⓒ : Fuel gauge
Ⓒ : Oil pressure gauge

NS9099100018000X

Fig. 20   Fuel gauge & water temperature gauge inspection. 300ZX

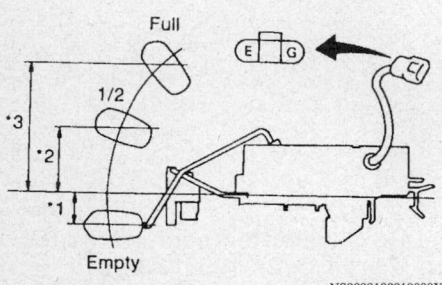

NS9099100019000X

Fig. 21   Fuel tank gauge unit inspection. 1996–97 Altima

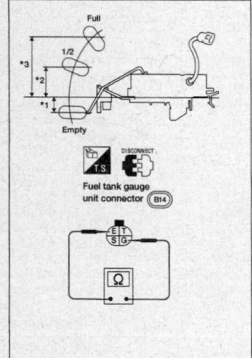

Check the resistance between terminals Ⓖ and Ⓔ.

Ohmmeter (+)	Ohmmeter (−)		Float position mm (in)		Resistance value (Ω)
G	E	*3	Full	80.5 (3.169)	Approx. 4.5 - 6
		*2	1/2	29.4 (1.157)	31.5 - 33.5
		*1	Empty	19 (0.748)	80 - 83

*1 and *3: When float rod is in contact with stopper.

NS9099900097000X

Fig. 22   Fuel tank gauge unit inspection. 1998–99 Altima

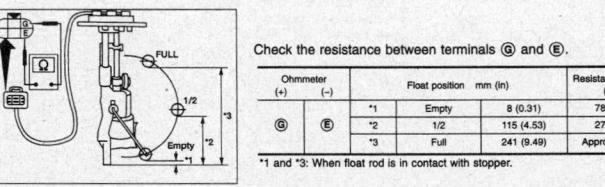

Check the resistance between terminals Ⓖ and Ⓔ.

Ohmmeter (+)	Ohmmeter (−)		Float position	mm (in)	Resistance value (Ω)
G	E	*1	Empty	8 (0.31)	78 - 85
		*2	1/2	115 (4.53)	27 - 35
		*3	Full	241 (9.49)	Approx. 4 - 6

*1 and *3: When float rod is in contact with stopper.

NS9099900098000X

Fig. 23   Fuel tank gauge unit inspection. Frontier w/2.4L engine

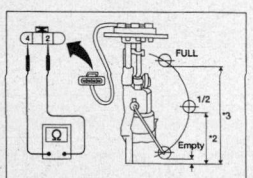

Check the resistance between terminals Ⓖ and Ⓔ.

Ohmmeter (+)	Ohmmeter (−)		Float position	mm (in)	Resistance value (Ω)
②	④	*1	Empty	8 (0.31)	78 - 85
		*2	1/2	115 (4.53)	27 - 35
		*3	Full	241 (9.49)	Approx. 4 - 6

*1 and *3: When float rod is in contact with stopper.

NS9099900099000X

Fig. 24   Fuel tank gauge unit inspection. Frontier w/3.3L engine

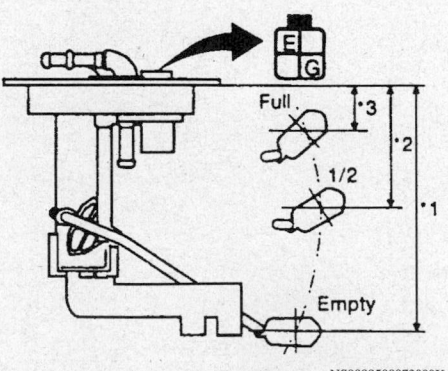

NS9099500073000X

Fig. 25   Fuel tank gauge unit inspection. Maxima

Fuel tank gauge connector

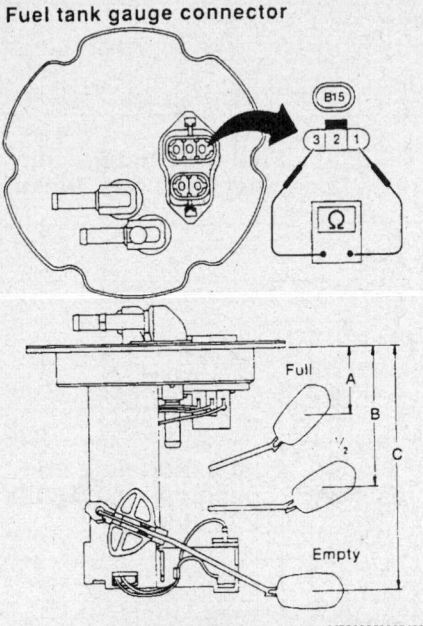

Fig. 26 Fuel tank gauge unit inspection. Sentra & 200SX

NS9099500074000X

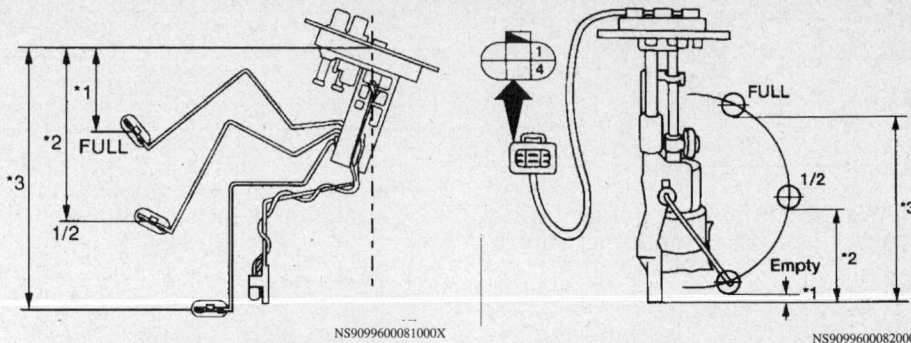

NS9099600081000X

Fig. 27 Fuel tank gauge unit inspection. Pathfinder

NS9099600082000X

Fig. 28 Fuel tank gauge unit inspection. Pickup

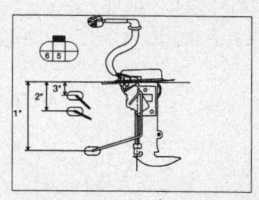

Check the resistance between terminals 5 and 6.

Ohmmeter		Float position mm (in)		Resistance value (Ω)
(+)	(−)			
5	6	*3	Full	15 (0.59)	Approx. 150
		*2	1/2	73 (2.87)	84
		*1	Empty	151 (5.94)	15

NS9099900100000X

Fig. 30 Fuel tank gauge unit inspection. 1999 Quest

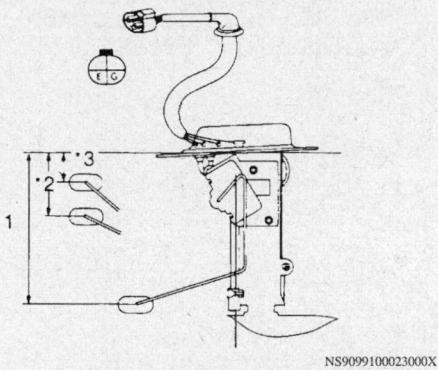

Fig. 29 Fuel tank gauge unit inspection. 1996–98 Quest

NS9099100023000X

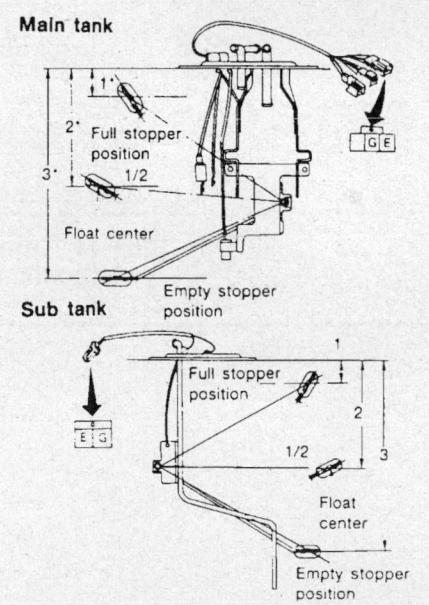

Main tank

Sub tank

NS9099100026000X

Fig. 32 Fuel tank gauge unit inspection. 300ZX

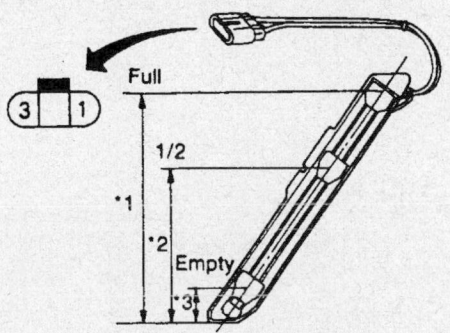

Fig. 31 Fuel tank gauge unit inspection. 240SX

NS9099500075000X

Ohmmeter		Float position mm (in)		Resistance value (Ω)
(−)	(−)			
G	E	*3	Full	80 5 (3 169)	Approx. 4 5 - 6
		*2	1/2	29 4 (1 157)	Approx. 31 5 - 33 5
		*1	Empty	19 0 (0 748)	Approx. 80 - 83

NS9099100027000X

Fig. 33 Fuel tank gauge unit resistance specifications. Altima

Ohmmeter		Float position mm (in)		Resistance value (Ω)
(+)	(−)			
G	E	*3	Full	33 (1.30)	Approx. 5 - 8
		*2	1/2	91 (3.58)	32 - 35
		*1	Empty	159 (6.26)	80 - 83

*1 and *3: When float rod is in contact with stopper.

NS9099500076000X

Fig. 34 Fuel tank gauge unit resistance specifications. Maxima

Ohmmeter (+)	(-)	Float position mm (in)			Resistance value (Ω)
①	③	A	Full	35.8 (1.409)	Approx. 4.5 - 6
		B	1/2	85.9 (3.382)	Approx. 31.5 - 33.5
		C	Empty	128.8 (5.071)	Approx. 80 - 83

NS9099100077000X

Fig. 35 Fuel tank gauge unit resistance specifications. Sentra & 200SX

Ohmmeter (-)	(-)	Float position mm (in)		Resistance value (Ω)
G	E	*3	Full	23 (0.91)	Approx 160
		*2	1/2	93 (3.66)	78
		*1	Empty	151 (5.94)	15

NS9099100032000X

Fig. 38 Fuel tank gauge unit resistance specifications. 1996–98 Quest

Ohmmeter (-)	(-)	Float position mm (in)		Resistance value (Ω)
G	E	1*	Full	21.0 (0.827)	4.3 - 5.8
		2*	1/2	115.0 (4.53)	27.7 - 34.3
		3*	Empty	207.0 (8.15)	78.3 - 84.8

1* and 3*: When float rod is in contact with stopper.

NS9099100036000X

Fig. 41 Fuel tank gauge unit resistance specifications. 300ZX 4 seater

Ohmmeter (+)	(-)	Float position mm (in)		Resistance value (Ω)
①	③	*1	Full	96 (3.78)	Approx. 4 - 6
		*2	1/2	188 (7.40)	30 - 34
		*3	Empty	257 (10.12)	80 - 83

*1 and *3: When float rod is in contact with stopper.

NS9099600083000X

Fig. 36 Fuel tank gauge unit resistance specifications. Pathfinder

Ohmmeter (+)	(-)	Float position mm (in)		Resistance value (Ω)
①	③	*1	Full	356 (14.02)	Approx. 4 - 6
		*2	1/2	245 (9.65)	30 - 35
		*3	Empty	50 (1.97)	80 - 84

*1 and *3: When float rod is in contact with stopper.

NS9099500078000X

Fig. 39 Fuel tank gauge unit resistance specifications. 240SX

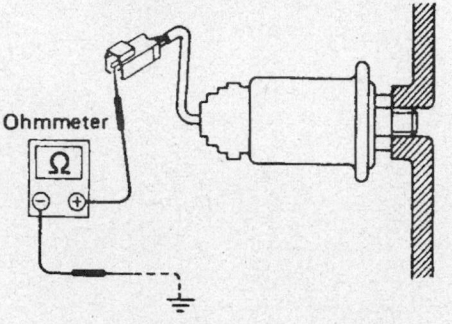

Ohmmeter

NS9099100040000X

Fig. 42 Oil pressure switch inspection. 300ZX

Oil pressure kPa (kg/cm² psi)	Resistance (Ω)
0 (0, 0) (Engine is stopped)	More than 83
392 (4, 57)	Approx. 26 - 37
588 (6, 85)	Approx. 18 - 26

NS9099100042000X

Fig. 44 Oil pressure switch specifications. 300ZX

Ohmmeter (+)	(-)	Float position mm (in)			Resistance value (Ω)
①	④	*3	Full	245.0 (9.646)	Approx. 4 - 7
		*2	1/2	119.0 (4.685)	Approx. 31 - 34
		*1	Empty	12.0 (0.472)	Approx. 79 - 84

NS9099600084000X

Fig. 37 Fuel tank gauge unit resistance specifications. Pickup

Ohmmeter (+)	(-)	Float position mm (in)			Resistance value (Ω)
G	E	1*	Full	Main	41.0 (1.614)	8.5 - 11.6
				Sub	40.0 (1.575)	
		2*	1/2	Main	137.0 (5.39)	55.4 - 68.6
				Sub	139.5 (5.49)	
		3*	Empty	Main	232.0 (9.13)	157.6 - 170.6
				Sub	261.0 (10.28)	

1* and 3*: When float rod is in contact with stopper.

NS9099100035000X

Fig. 40 Fuel tank gauge unit resistance specifications. 300ZX 2 seater

	Oil pressure kPa (kg/cm² psi)	Continuity
Engine start	More than 10 - 20 (0.1 - 0.2 1.4 - 2.8)	NO
Engine stop	Less than 10 - 20 (0.1 - 0.2 1.4 - 2.8)	YES

NS9099100041000X

Fig. 43 Oil pressure switch specifications. Except 300ZX

Starter Motors

INDEX

APPLICATION CHART

Year	Model	Engine	Starter Number
1996-97	Altima	KA24DE	M1T73881ZC
	Altima	KA24DE	S114-754A
	Maxima	VQ30DE	S114-801A
	Pathfinder	VG33E	MOT60181
	Pickup	KA24E	M000T60081ZC①
	Pickup	KA24E	M003T70381②
	Quest	VG30E	M001T64285
	Sentra & 200SX	GA16DE	M0T80281ZC
	Sentra & 200SX	GA16DE	M2T42983ZC
	Sentra & 200SX	GA16DE	S114-802A
	Sentra & 200SX	SR20DE	S114-701C
	Sentra & 200SX	SR20DE	M1T72985A
	240SX	KA24DE	M1T72781B
	300ZX	VG30DE, VG30DETT	M2T25282
1998	Altima	KA24DE	M000T85081ZC
	Frontier	KA24E	M003T70381ZC
	Frontier	VG33E	M000T60081ZC
	Maxima	VQ30DE	S114-801A
	Pathfinder	VG33E	MOT60181
	Quest	VG30E	M001T64285
	Sentra & 200SX	GA16DE	M0T80281ZC
		GA16DE	M2T42983ZC
		GA16DE	S114-802A
		SR20DE	S114-701C
		SR20DE	M1T72985A
	240SX	KA24DE	M1T72781B
1999	Altima	KA24DE	M00T85081ZC
	Frontier	KA24E	M003T70381ZC
			M000T60081AC
	Frontier	VG33E	M000T60185ZC
	Maxima	VQ30DE	S114-801A
	Pathfinder	VG33E	MOT60181
	Quest	—	M001T68081ZC
	Sentra	GA16DE	M0T80281ZC
	Sentra	GA16DE	M2T42983ZC
	Sentra	GA16DE	S114-802A
	Sentra	SR20DE	S114-701C
	Sentra	SR20DE	M1T72985A

① — Except California.
② — California.

DESCRIPTION

Nissan starters are of two types, direct drive and gear reduction. The direct drive starter **Fig. 1,** is equipped with an overrunning clutch type starter drive. A solenoid switch is mounted on the starter motor.

Gear reduction starters, **Figs. 2 and 3,** may use a planetary gear train or an idler gear train to transmit armature rotation to the pinion shaft. A solenoid switch is mounted on the starter motor.

DIAGNOSIS & TESTING

STARTER TEST

Refer to **Fig. 4** for starter in-vehicle testing.

STARTER SOLENOID TEST

1. Disconnect "M" terminal of starter motor, **Fig. 5**.
2. Using a suitable ohmmeter, check continuity between "S" terminal of starter motor and switch body. Continuity should exist. If continuity does not exist, starter solenoid is defective. Replace as necessary.
3. Check for continuity between "S" and "M" terminals of starter motor. Continuity should exist. If continuity does not exist, starter solenoid is defective. Replace as necessary.

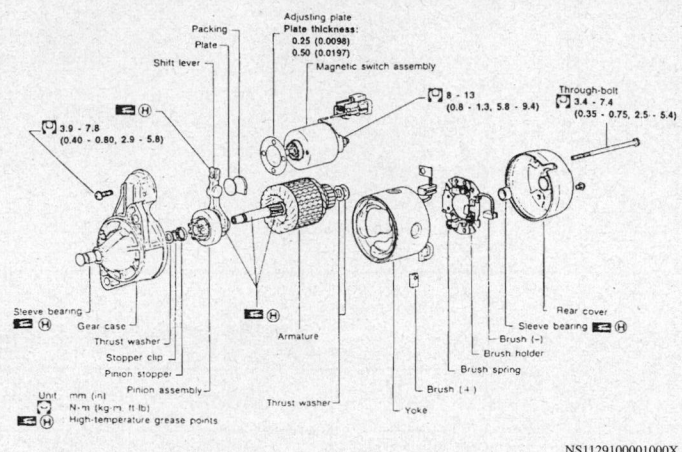

NS1129100001000X

Fig. 1 Exploded view of direct drive starter

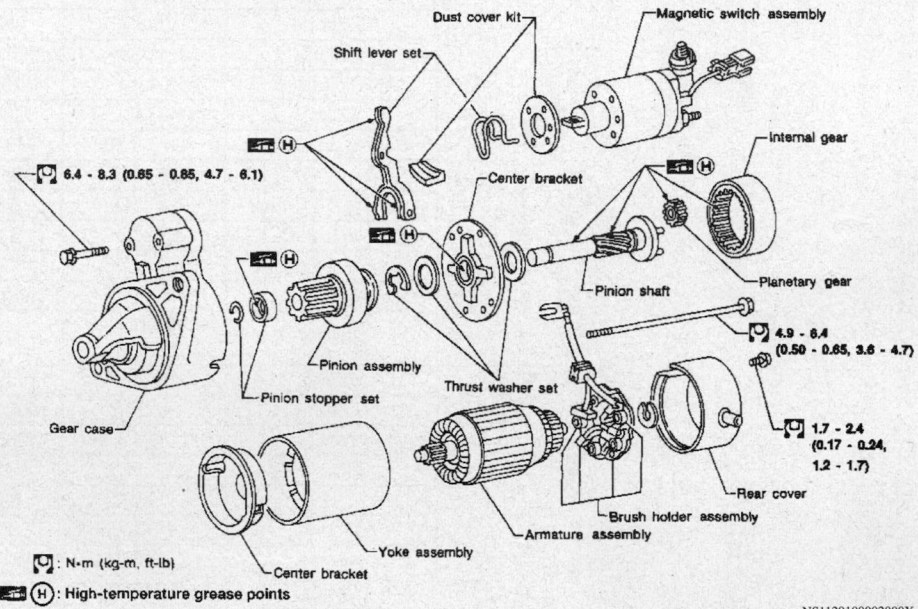

NS1129100002000X

Fig. 2 Exploded view of gear reduction starter

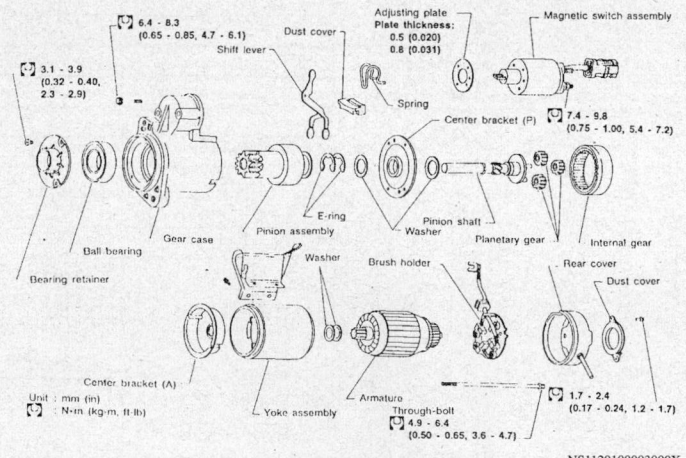

NS1129100003000X

Fig. 3 Exploded view of planetary gear reduction starter

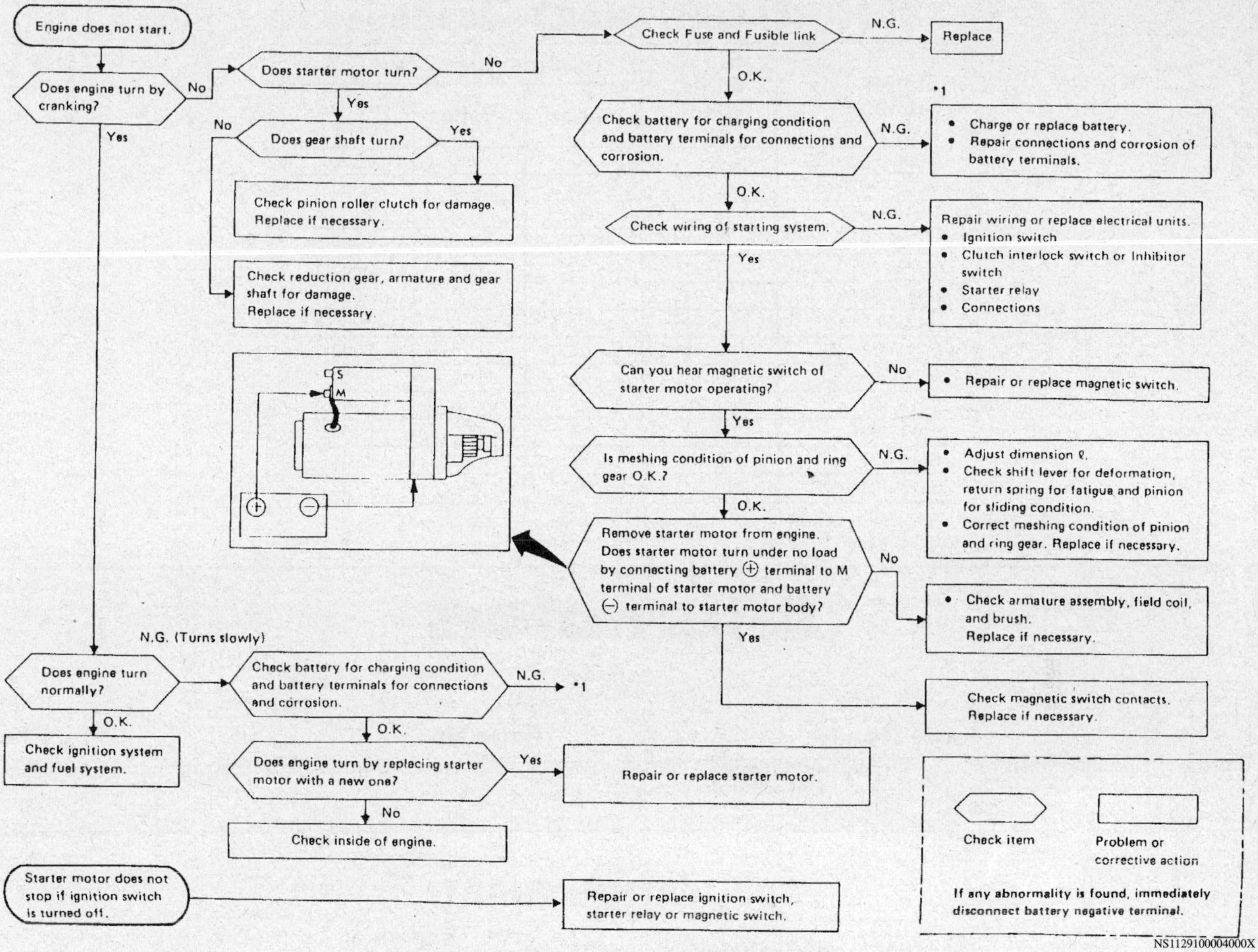

Fig. 4 Starting system diagnosis chart

Engine does not start.

Does engine turn by cranking? → No → Does starter motor turn? → No → Check Fuse and Fusible link → N.G. → Replace

Does starter motor turn? → Yes → Does gear shaft turn?

Does gear shaft turn? → No → Check reduction gear, armature and gear shaft for damage. Replace if necessary.

Does gear shaft turn? → Yes → Check pinion roller clutch for damage. Replace if necessary.

Check Fuse and Fusible link → O.K. → Check battery for charging condition and battery terminals for connections and corrosion. → N.G. → *1
- Charge or replace battery.
- Repair connections and corrosion of battery terminals.

Check battery for charging condition... → O.K. → Check wiring of starting system. → N.G. → Repair wiring or replace electrical units.
- Ignition switch
- Clutch interlock switch or Inhibitor switch
- Starter relay
- Connections

Check wiring of starting system. → Yes → Can you hear magnetic switch of starter motor operating? → No → Repair or replace magnetic switch.

Can you hear magnetic switch... → Yes → Is meshing condition of pinion and ring gear O.K.? → N.G. →
- Adjust dimension ℓ.
- Check shift lever for deformation, return spring for fatigue and pinion for sliding condition.
- Correct meshing condition of pinion and ring gear. Replace if necessary.

Is meshing condition... → O.K. → Remove starter motor from engine. Does starter motor turn under no load by connecting battery ⊕ terminal to M terminal of starter motor and battery ⊖ terminal to starter motor body? → No →
- Check armature assembly, field coil, and brush. Replace if necessary.

Remove starter motor from engine... → Yes → Check magnetic switch contacts. Replace if necessary.

Does engine turn by cranking? → Yes → Does engine turn normally? → N.G. (Turns slowly) → Check battery for charging condition and battery terminals for connections and corrosion. → N.G. → *1

Check battery for charging condition... → O.K. → Does engine turn by replacing starter motor with a new one? → Yes → Repair or replace starter motor.

Does engine turn by replacing starter motor... → No → Check inside of engine.

Does engine turn normally? → O.K. → Check ignition system and fuel system.

Starter motor does not stop if ignition switch is turned off. → Repair or replace ignition switch, starter relay or magnetic switch.

⬡ Check item   ▭ Problem or corrective action

If any abnormality is found, immediately disconnect battery negative terminal.

NS1129100004000X

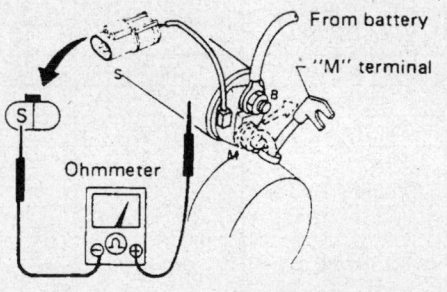

Fig. 5 Starter solenoid test

From battery
"M" terminal
Ohmmeter

NS1129100005000X

SPECIFICATION CHART

Starter Number	Brush Spring Tension, Oz.	Free Speed Test		
		Amps①	Volts	Starter RPM②
M000T60081AC	42-84	90	11	2500
M001T64285	64-78	90	11	2900
M001T68081ZC	—	90	11	2400

SPECIFICATION CHART—Continued

Starter Number	Brush Spring Tension, Oz.	Free Speed Test		
		Amps①	Volts	Starter RPM②
M000T85081ZC	—	90	11	2500
M003T70381ZC	50-91	60	11.5	6500
M0T80281ZC	43–85	90	11.0	2750
M1T60281	50–91	50–75	11.0	3000
M1T72781B	50–91	50–75	11.0	3000
M1T72985A	50–91	75	11.0	4000
M1T73881ZC	50–91	88	11.0	3000
M2T25282	49–91	70	11.0	2000
M2T42983ZC	50–91	53	11.5	6000
S114-701C	64–78	90	11.0	2950
S114-754A	53–64	85	11.0	2950
S114-801A	46–64	90	11.0	2900
S114-802A	46–64	90	11.0	2700

① — Maximum.
② — Minimum.

Alternators

INDEX

APPLICATION CHART

Year	Model	Engine	Alternator Number
1996–97	Altima	KA24DE	LR180-736B
	Maxima	VQ30DE	LR1125-702B①
			LR1110-705①
	Pathfinder	KA24E	LR190-729
	Pickup	VG30E	LR160-727
	Quest	VG30E	A4T02591ZC
	Sentra & 200SX	GA16DE	LR170-748①
			LR180-751①
		SR20DE	LR180-741H①
	240SX	KA24DE	LR180-742①
			LR190-724①
	300ZX	VG30DE	LR180-724C①
	300ZX	VG30DETT	A2T33593A②

APPLICATION CHART—Continued

Year	Model	Engine	Alternator Number
	Altima	KA24DE	LR1100-709B
	Frontier	KA24E	LR1100-757B
		VG33E	LR180-786
	Maxima	VQ30DE	LR1125-702B①
			LR1110-705①
	Pathfinder	KA24E	LR190-729
	Quest	VG30E	A4T02591ZC
	Sentra & 200SX	GA16DE	LR170-748①
			LR180-751①
	Sentra & 200SX	SR20DE	LR180-741H①
	240SX	KA24DE	LR180-742①
			LR190-724①
	Altima	KA24DE	LR1100-709B
	Frontier	KA24E	LR1100-757B
		VG33E	LR180-786
	Maxima	VQ30DE	LR1125-702B①
			LR1110-705①
	Pathfinder	KA24E	LR190-729
	Quest	VG30E	A3TA5691ZC①
	Sentra	GA16DE	LR170-748①
			LR180-751①
		SR20DE	LR180-741H①

① — Hitachi.
② — Mitsubishi.

DESCRIPTION

Alternators are composed of the same functional parts as the conventional D.C. generator but they operate differently. The field is called a rotor and is the turning portion of the unit. A generating part, called a stator, is the stationary member, comparable to the armature in a D.C. generator. The regulator, similar to those used in a D.C. system, regulates the output of the alternator-rectifier system, **Figs. 1 and 2.**

The power source of the system is the alternator. Current is transmitted from the field terminal of the regulator through a slip ring to the field coil and back to ground through another slip ring. The strength of the field regulates the output of the alternating current. This alternating current is then transmitted from the alternator to the rectifier where it is converted to direct current.

DIAGNOSIS & TESTING

1. Turn ignition switch to on position and note charge lamp.
2. If lamp lights proceed to step 7. If lamp does not light proceed to next step.
3. Disconnect two wire connectors labeled S and L, then using a jumper wire connect L terminal to a suitable ground.
4. If charge lamp lights proceed to next step. If lamp does not light the bulb in the instrument cluster is defective. **Steps 5 and 6 do not apply to models equipped with Mitsubishi alter-**

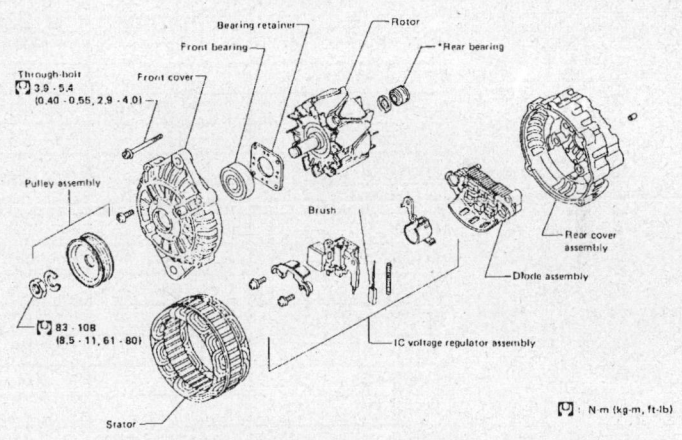

Fig. 1 Exploded view of Hitachi alternator

NS1129100006000X

nators. On these models, if charge lamp lights, the internal regulator or some other internal component is defective and the alternator must be removed for bench testing.

5. Reconnect two wire connectors, then insert a short stiff length of wire through the access hole at back of alternator until it contacts outer brush. Ground other end of wire to alternator case which will actually ground the F terminal internally, **Fig. 3.**
6. If charge lamp remains lit, the internal regulator is defective and will require disassembly of the alternator for re-

pair. If lamp goes out, some other internal component is defective therefore alternator must be removed for bench testing.

7. With engine idling if charge lamp is lit, a defective internal component exists in the alternator and requires removal for bench testing. If the charge lamp is not lit, proceed to next step.
8. With engine speed at 1500 RPM and headlights on, if charge lamp is not lit proceed to next step. If lamp is lit dimly, let engine idle and measure voltage across B and L terminals. If voltage is more than .5 volts a defective internal

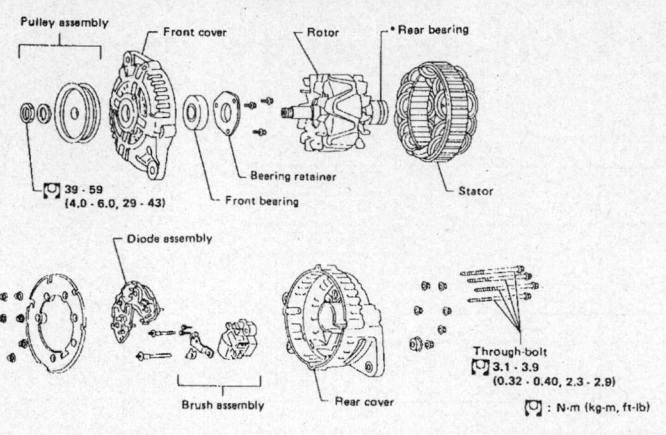

Fig. 2 Exploded view of Mitsubishi alternator

NS1129100007000X

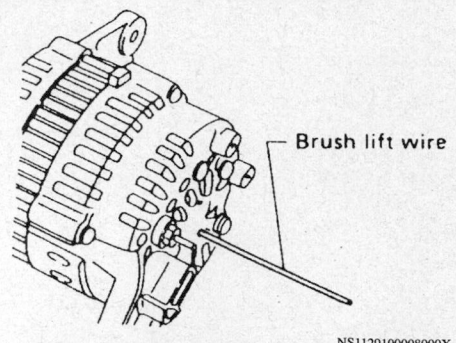

NS1129100008000X

Fig. 3 Alternator "F" terminal ground

component exists in the alternator and requires removal for bench testing. **If voltage is less than .5 volts, alternator if considered to be in satisfactory condition.**

9. With engine at 1500 RPM measure voltage at B terminal, making sure S terminal is properly connected.
10. If voltage reading is above 15.5 volts, the internal regulator is faulty and requires removal of alternator for replacement. If voltage reading is between 13 and 15 volts proceed to next step.
11. With engine idling and headlights on, if charge lamp is lit a defective internal component exists in the alternator and requires removal for bench testing. If charge lamp is not lit, alternator is considered to be in satisfactory condition.

ALTERNATOR SPECIFICATIONS

Model	Rated Hot Output Amps. Minimum	Hot Output Amps. Minimum @ 2500 RPM	Regulated Voltage
A2T33593A	90	61	14.1–14.7
A3TA5691ZC	36	90	14.1–14.7
A4T02591ZC	110	85	14.1–14.7
LR160-727	57	48	14.1–14.7
LR170-739	70	50	14.1–14.7
LR170-748	70	50	14.1–14.7
LR180-724	80	65	14.1–14.7
LR180-736B	80	63	14.1–14.7
LR180741H	90	63	14.1-14.7
LR180-742	77	65	14.1–14.7
LR180-751	77	63	14.1–14.7
LR180-786	23	77	14.1–14.7
LR190-724	87	65	14.1–14.7
LR190-729	87	65	14.1–14.7
LR1110-705	105	82	14.1–14.7
LR1100-709B	24	71	14.1–14.7
LR1100-757B	17	54	14.1–14.7
LR1125-702B	123	94	14.1–14.7

Speed Control Systems

NOTE: On Air Bag Equipped Models, Refer To "Air Bag System Precautions" Located In The Front Of This Manual For System Disarming & Arming Procedures.

NOTE: Refer To "Computer Relearn Procedures" Located In The Front Of This Manual For Computer Relearn Procedures.

INDEX

DESCRIPTION

The speed control system is composed of On-Off, Set-Accelerate, Coast, Resume (if equipped) switches. The system includes vacuum hoses, servo (throttle actuator) assembly, speed sensor, check valve assembly, and depending on model, a clutch switch and stop light switch.

To operate speed control system, the engine must be running and vehicle speed must exceed 30 mph. When the On-Off switch is actuated, the system is ready to accept a set speed signal. When vehicle speed stabilizes (exceeds 30 mph), and the On switch is engaged, the operator may depress or release the Set-Accelerate button. This speed will be maintained until a new speed has been set, brake pedal has been depressed, or the system is turned off.

ADJUSTMENTS

ASCD WIRE

1. Confirm adjustment of accelerator cable.
2. Loosen adjusting nut on the ASCD wire ½ to 1 turn from full closed position of throttle cable.
3. Tighten adjusting locknut.

SYSTEM DIAGNOSIS & TESTING

ALTIMA

1996

Refer to **Figs. 1 through 8** for diagnostic charts.

1997

Refer to **Fig. 9** for Fail-Safe system diagnostic check, then refer to " Component Diagnosis & Testing" for component diagnostic charts.

1998-99

Refer to **Figs. 10 through 19** for diagnostic charts.

FRONTIER

Refer to **Figs. 20 through 29** for diagnostic charts.

MAXIMA

Refer to **Fig. 30** for Fail-Safe system diagnostic check, then refer to " Component Diagnosis & Testing" for component diagnostic charts.

QUEST

1996-98

Refer to **Fig. 30** for Fail-Safe system diagnostic check, then refer to " Component Diagnosis & Testing" for component diagnostic charts.

1999

Refer to **Figs. 31 through 40** for diagnostic charts.

PATHFINDER & PICKUP

Refer to **Fig. 41** for Fail-Safe system diagnostic check, then refer to " Component Diagnosis & Testing" for component diagnostic charts.

SENTRA & 200SX

1996

Refer to **Figs. 42 through 49** for diagnostic charts.

1997-99

Refer to **Fig. 50** for Fail-Safe system diagnostic check, then refer to " Component Diagnosis & Testing" for component diagnostic charts.

240SX

Refer to **Fig. 51** for Fail-Safe system diagnostic check, then refer to " Component Diagnosis & Testing" for component diagnostic charts.

300ZX

Refer to **Figs. 52 through 59** for diagnostic charts.

COMPONENT DIAGNOSIS & TESTING

ALTIMA, SENTRA, 200SX & 300ZX

ELECTRICAL COMPONENT

Refer to **Figs. 60 through 65** for ASCD electrical component check procedures.

ASCD ACTUATOR

1996 Altima

Refer to **Fig. 66** for ASCD actuator test procedures.

1997 Altima

Refer to **Fig. 67** for ASCD actuator test procedures.

1996 Sentra & 200 SX

Refer to **Fig. 68** for ASCD actuator test procedures.

1997-99 Sentra & 200 SX

Refer to **Fig. 69** for ASCD actuator/pump circuit test procedures.

300ZX

Refer to **Fig. 70** for ASCD actuator test procedures.

ASCD POWER SUPPLY & GROUND CIRCUIT

1997 Altima

Refer to **Fig. 71** for ASCD power supply and ground circuit test.

1997-98 Sentra & 200SX

Refer to **Fig. 72** for ASCD power supply and ground circuit test.

ASCD MAIN SWITCH

1997 Altima

Refer to **Fig. 73** for ASCD main switch test procedures.

1997-98 Sentra & 200SX

Refer to **Fig. 74** for ASCD main switch test procedures.

ASCD HOLD RELAY

1997 Altima

Refer to **Fig. 75** for ASCD hold relay test procedures.

1997-99 Sentra & 200SX

Refer to **Fig. 76** for ASCD hold relay test procedures.

ASCD CANCEL SWITCH

1997 Altima

Refer to **Fig. 77** for ASCD cancel switch inpection.

ASCD CLUTCH & BRAKE SWITCH

1997-99 Sentra & 200SX

Refer to **Fig. 78** for ASCD clutch and brake switch inpection.

ASCD STEERING SWITCH

1997 Altima

Refer to **Fig. 79** for ASCD steering switch test procedures.

1997-99 Sentra & 200SX

Refer to **Fig. 80** for ASCD steering switch test procedures.

VEHICLE SPEED SENSOR

1997 Altima

Refer to **Fig. 81** for vehicle speed sensor test procedures.

1997-99 Sentra & 200SX

Refer to **Fig. 82** for vehicle speed sensor test procedures.

VACUUM HOSE & ACCEL WIRE

1997 Altima

Refer to **Figs. 83** for vacuum hose and ACCEL wire inspection procedures.

ASCD PUMP CIRCUIT

1997-99 Sentra & 200SX

Refer to **Figs. 84** for ASCD pump circuit check inspection procedures.

FRONTIER & 1999 QUEST

Refer to **Figs. 85 and 86** for ASCD electrical component check procedures.

MAXIMA, PATHFINDER, PICKUP, 240SX & 1996-98 QUEST

POWER SUPPLY & GROUND CIRCUIT CHECK

Refer to **Figs. 87 through 90** for diagnostic charts.

ASCD Main Switch Check

Refer to **Figs. 91 through 95** for diagnostic charts.

ASDC HOLD RELAY CIRCUIT

1996-97

Refer to **Figs. 96 through 100** for diagnostic charts.

ASCD CANCEL SWITCH

1996-97

Refer to **Figs. 101 through 104** for diagnostic charts.

ASCD STEERING SWITCH

1996-97

Refer to **Figs. 105 through 108** for diagnostic charts.

VEHICLE SPEED SENSOR

1996-97

Refer to **Figs. 109 through 113** for diagnostic charts.

ASCD ACTUATOR

1996-97

Refer to **Figs. 114 through 117** for diagnostic charts.

VACUUM HOSE & ACCEL WIRE

1996-97

Refer to **Figs. 118 through 121** for diagnostic charts.

DIAGNOSTIC CHART INDEX

Test	Description	Page No.	Fig. No.
1996 ALTIMA			
Test 1	ASCD Control Cannot Be Set	40-45	1
Test 2	Engine Hunts	40-46	2
Test 3	Large Difference Between Set Vehicle Speed & Actual Speed	40-46	3
Test 4	Deceleration Is Greatest Immediately After ASCD Has Been Set	40-46	4
Test 5	ACCEL Switch Will Not Operate	40-46	5
Test 6	RESUME Switch Will Not Operate	40-47	6
Test 7	Set Speed Cannot Be Cancelled	40-47	7
Test 8	"CRUISE" Indicator Lamp Blinks	40-47	8
—	Actuator Check	40-63	66
—	Electrical Component Check	40-61	60
1997 ALTIMA			
—	Fail Safe System Check	40-47	9
—	Electrical Component Check	40-61	61
—	Actuator Check	40-64	67

Continued

DIAGNOSTIC CHART INDEX—Continued

Test	Description	Page No.	Fig. No.
1997 ALTIMA			
—	Power Supply & Ground Circuit	40-65	71
—	ASCD Cancel Switch	40-66	77
—	ASCD Steering Switch	40-66	79
—	ASCD Hold Relay Circuit	40-65	75
—	ASCD Main Switch	40-65	73
—	Vehicle Speed Sensor	40-67	81
—	Vacuum Hose & ACCEL Wire Inspection	40-67	83
1998–99 ALTIMA			
—	Fail Safe System Check	40-48	10
—	Symptom Inspection	40-48	11
Diagnostic Procedure 1	Power & Ground Supply Inspection	40-48	12
Diagnostic Procedure 2	ASCD Main Switch Inspection	40-48	13
Diagnostic Procedure 3	ASCD Hold Relay Inspection	40-49	14
Diagnostic Procedure 4	Brake Lamp Switch Inspection	40-49	15
Diagnostic Procedure 5	Steering Switch Inspection	40-49	16
Diagnostic Procedure 6	Vehicle Speed Sensor Inspection	40-49	17
Diagnostic Procedure 7	Pump Circuit Inspection	40-50	18
Diagnostic Procedure 8	Actuator/Pump Inspection	40-50	19
—	Electrical Component Check	40-62	62
FRONTIER			
—	Diagnostic Symptom Chart	40-50	20
—	Fail Safe System Inspection	40-50	21
Diagnostic Procedure 1	Power Supply & Ground Circuit Inspection	40-51	22
Diagnostic Procedure 2	ASCD Main Switch Inspection	40-51	23
Diagnostic Procedure 3	ASCD Hold Relay Inspecton	40-51	24
Diagnostic Procedure 4	ASCD Brake Lamp Switch Inspection	40-51	25
Diagnostic Procedure 5	ASCD Steering Switch Inspection	40-52	26
Diagnostic Procedure 6	Vehicle Speed Sensor Inspection	40-52	27
Diagnostic Procedure 7	ASCD Pump Circuit Inspection	40-52	28
Diagnostic Procedure 8	ASCD Actuator/Pump Inspection	40-52	29
—	SCD Electrical Component Inspection	40-67	85
MAXIMA			
—	Fail-Safe System Check	40-53	30
Test 1	Power Supply & Ground Circuit Check	40-68	87
Test 2	ASCD Main Switch Check	40-69	91
Test 3	ASCD Hold Relay Circuit Check	40-69	96
Test 4	ASCD Cancel Switch Check	40-70	101
Test 5	ASCD Steering Switch Check	40-71	105
Test 6	Vehicle Speed Sensor Check	40-72	109
Test 7	ASCD Actuator Check	40-73	114
Test 8	Vacuum Hose & Accel Wire Check	40-74	118
PATHFINDER & PICKUP			
—	Fail-Safe System Check	40-55	41

Continued

DIAGNOSTIC CHART INDEX—Continued

Test	Description	Page No.	Fig. No.
PATHFINDER & PICKUP			
Test 1	Power Supply & Ground Circuit Check	40-68	88
Test 2	ASCD Main Switch Check	40-69	92
Test 2	ASCD Main Switch Check	40-69	93
Test 3	ASCD Hold Relay Circuit Check	40-69	97
Test 3	ASCD Hold Relay Circuit Check	40-70	98
Test 4	ASCD Cancel Switch Check	40-71	102
Test 5	ASCD Steering Switch Check	40-72	106
Test 6	Vehicle Speed Sensor Check	40-73	110
Test 6	Vehicle Speed Sensor Check	40-73	111
Test 7	ASCD Actuator Check	40-74	115
Test 8	Vacuum Hose & Accel Wire Check	40-74	119
1996–98 QUEST			
Test 1	Power Supply & Ground Circuit Check	40-68	89
Test 2	ASCD Main Switch Check	40-69	94
Test 3	ASCD Hold Relay Circuit Check	40-70	99
Test 4	ASCD Cancel Switch Check	40-71	103
Test 5	ASCD Steering Switch Check	40-72	107
Test 6	Vehicle Speed Sensor Check	40-73	112
Test 7	ASCD Actuator Check	40-74	116
Test 8	Vacuum Hose & Accel Wire Check	40-74	120
1999 QUEST			
—	Symptom Inspection Chart	40-53	31
—	Fail Safe System Check	40-53	32
—	Power Supply & Ground Circuit Inspection	40-53	33
—	AASCD Main Switch Inspection	40-54	34
—	SCD Hold Relay Inspection	40-54	35
—	ASCD Brake Lamp Switch Inspection	40-54	36
—	ASCD Steering Switch Inspection	40-54	37
—	Vehicle Speed Sensor Inspection	40-55	38
—	ASCD Actuator Circuit Inspection	40-55	39
—	ASCD Actuator Inspection	40-55	40
—	ASCD Electrical Component Inspection	40-68	86
1996 SENTRA & 200SX			
Test 1	Speed Control Cannot Be Set	40-56	42
Test 2	Engine Hunts	40-56	43
Test 3	Large Difference Between Set Vehicle Speed & Actual Speed	40-56	44
Test 4	Deceleration Is Greatest Immediately After ASCD Has Been Set	40-56	45
Test 5	ACCEL Switch Will Not Operate	40-57	46
Test 6	RESUME Switch Will Not Operate	40-57	47
Test 7	Set Speed Cannot Be Canceled	40-57	48
Test 8	CRUISE Indicator Lamp Blinks	40-57	49
—	Electrical Component Check	40-62	63
—	Actuator Check	40-64	68
1997–99 SENTRA & 200SX			
—	Fail Safe System Check	40-58	50
—	Electrical Component Check	40-63	64
—	Actuator/Pump Circuit Check	40-64	69
Test 1	Power Supply & Ground Circuit	40-65	72
Test 2	ASCD Main Switch	40-65	74
Test 3	ASCD Hold Relay Circuit	40-66	76
Test 4	ASCD Clutch & Brake Switch	40-66	78
Test 5	Vehicle Speed Sensor	40-67	82
Test 6	ASCD Pump Circuit	40-67	84
240SX			
Test 1	Power Supply & Ground Circuit Check	40-68	90

Continued

DIAGNOSTIC CHART INDEX—Continued

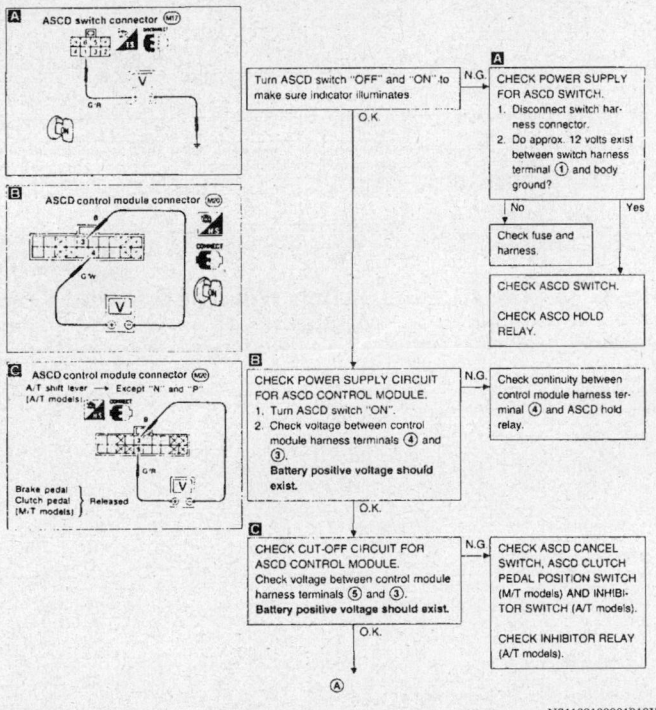

NS1109100001010X

Fig. 1 Test 1: ASCD Control Cannot Be Set (Part 1 of 2). 1996 Altima

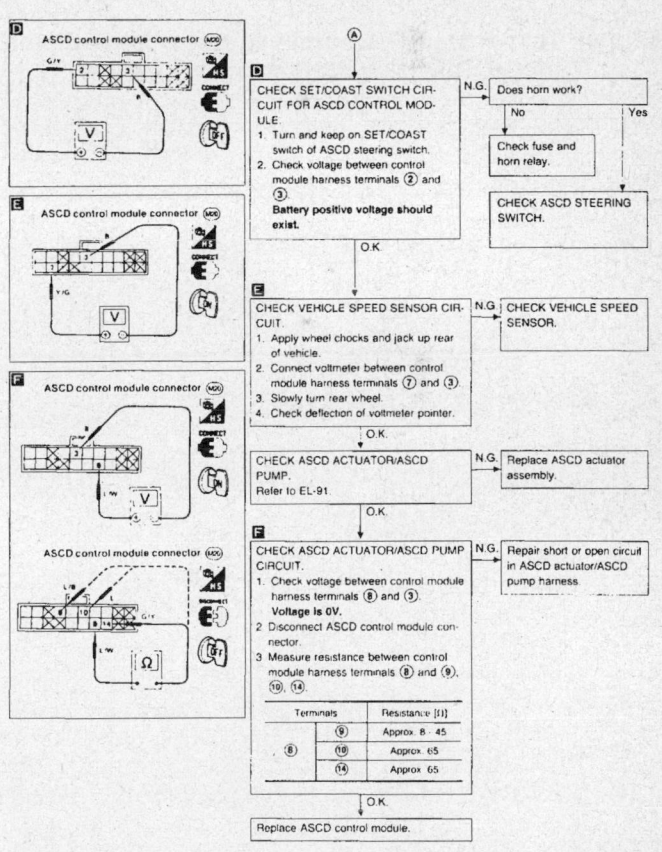

NS1109100001020X

Fig. 1 Test 1: ASCD Control Cannot Be Set (Part 2 of 2). 1996 Altima

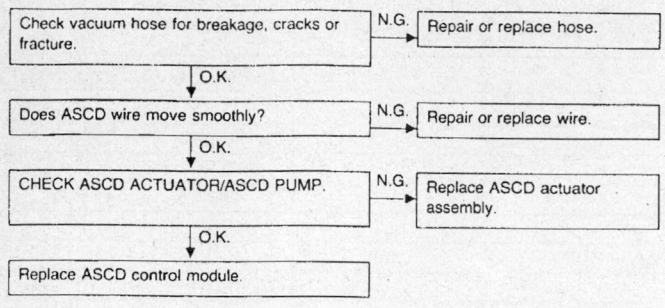

Check vacuum hose for breakage, cracks or fracture. → N.G. → Repair or replace hose.

↓ O.K.

Does ASCD wire move smoothly? → N.G. → Repair or replace wire.

↓ O.K.

CHECK ASCD ACTUATOR/ASCD PUMP. → N.G. → Replace ASCD actuator assembly.

↓ O.K.

Replace ASCD control module.

NS1109100002000X

Fig. 2   Test 2: Engine Hunts. 1996 Altima

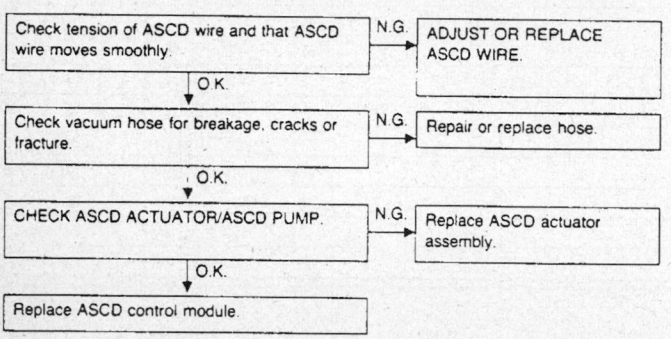

Check tension of ASCD wire and that ASCD wire moves smoothly. → N.G. → ADJUST OR REPLACE ASCD WIRE.

↓ O.K.

Check vacuum hose for breakage, cracks or fracture. → N.G. → Repair or replace hose.

↓ O.K.

CHECK ASCD ACTUATOR/ASCD PUMP. → N.G. → Replace ASCD actuator assembly.

↓ O.K.

Replace ASCD control module.

NS1109100004000X

Fig. 4   Test 4: Deceleration Is Greatest Immediately After ASCD Has Been Set. 1996 Altima

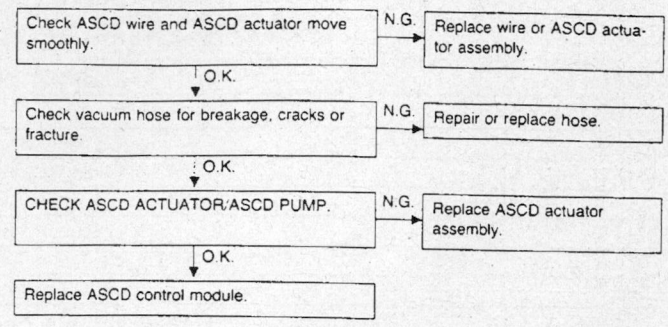

Check ASCD wire and ASCD actuator move smoothly. → N.G. → Replace wire or ASCD actuator assembly.

↓ O.K.

Check vacuum hose for breakage, cracks or fracture. → N.G. → Repair or replace hose.

↓ O.K.

CHECK ASCD ACTUATOR/ASCD PUMP. → N.G. → Replace ASCD actuator assembly.

↓ O.K.

Replace ASCD control module.

NS1109100003000X

Fig. 3   Test 3: Large Difference Between Set Vehicle Speed & Actual Speed. 1996 Altima

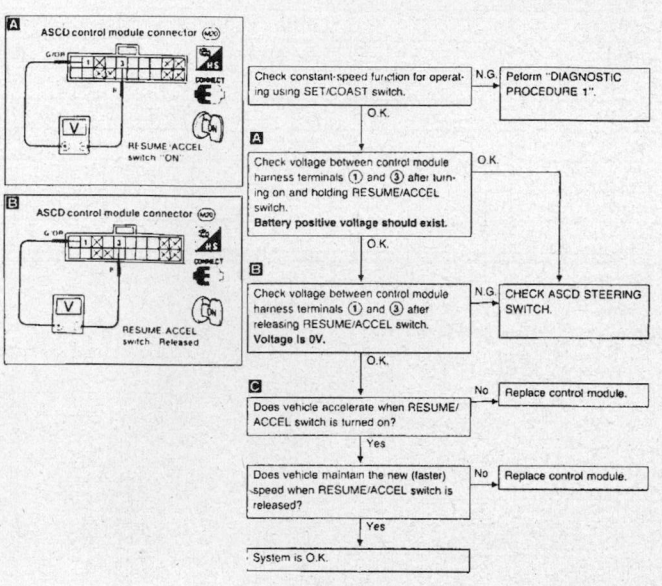

NS1109100005000X

Fig. 5   Test 5: ACCEL Switch Will Not Operate. 1996 Altima

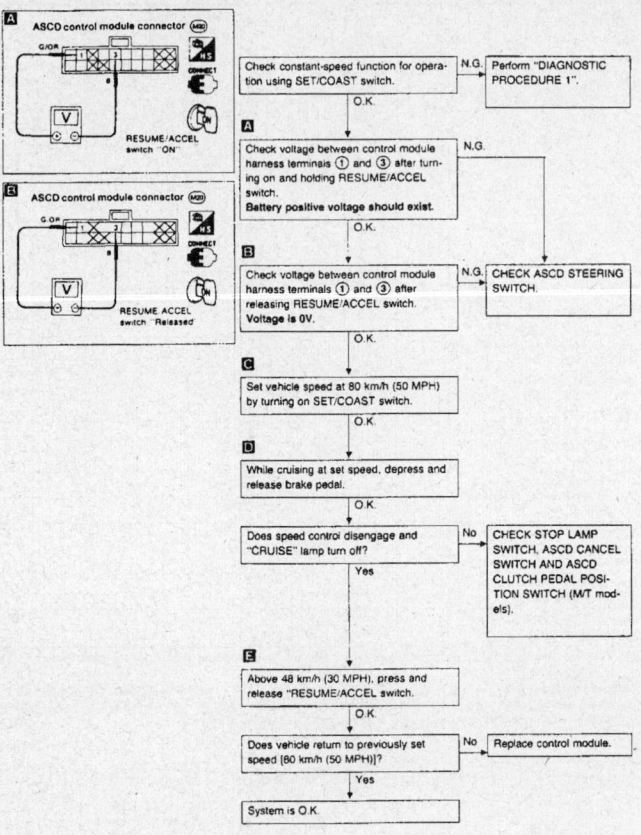

**Fig. 6 Test 6: RESUME Switch Will Not Operate.
1996 Altima**

Flowchart text (Fig. 6):
- Check constant-speed function for operation using SET/COAST switch. → N.G. → Perform "DIAGNOSTIC PROCEDURE 1".
- O.K.
- [A] Check voltage between control module harness terminals ① and ③ after turning on and holding RESUME/ACCEL switch. Battery positive voltage should exist. → N.G.
- O.K.
- [B] Check voltage between control module harness terminals ① and ③ after releasing RESUME/ACCEL switch. Voltage is 0V. → N.G. → CHECK ASCD STEERING SWITCH.
- O.K.
- [C] Set vehicle speed at 80 km/h (50 MPH) by turning on SET/COAST switch.
- O.K.
- [D] While cruising at set speed, depress and release brake pedal.
- O.K.
- Does speed control disengage and "CRUISE" lamp turn off? → No → CHECK STOP LAMP SWITCH, ASCD CANCEL SWITCH AND ASCD CLUTCH PEDAL POSITION SWITCH (M/T models).
- Yes
- [E] Above 48 km/h (30 MPH), press and release "RESUME/ACCEL switch.
- O.K.
- Does vehicle return to previously set speed [80 km/h (50 MPH)]? → No → Replace control module.
- Yes
- System is O.K.

NS1109100006000X

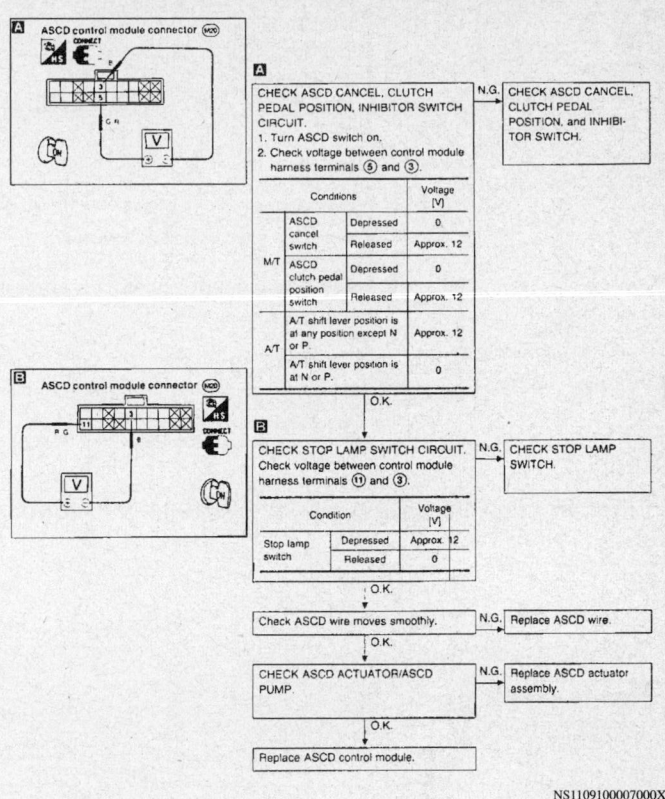

**Fig. 7 Test 7: Set Speed Cannot Be Cancelled.
1996 Altima**

Flowchart text (Fig. 7):
- [A] CHECK ASCD CANCEL, CLUTCH PEDAL POSITION, INHIBITOR SWITCH CIRCUIT.
  1. Turn ASCD switch on.
  2. Check voltage between control module harness terminals ⑤ and ③.
  → N.G. → CHECK ASCD CANCEL, CLUTCH PEDAL POSITION, AND INHIBITOR SWITCH.

	Conditions		Voltage [V]
M/T	ASCD cancel switch	Depressed	0
		Released	Approx. 12
	ASCD clutch pedal position switch	Depressed	0
		Released	Approx. 12
A/T	A/T shift lever position is at any position except N or P.		Approx. 12
	A/T shift lever position is at N or P.		0

- O.K.
- [B] CHECK STOP LAMP SWITCH CIRCUIT. Check voltage between control module harness terminals ⑪ and ③. → N.G. → CHECK STOP LAMP SWITCH.

	Condition	Voltage [V]
Stop lamp switch	Depressed	Approx. 12
	Released	0

- O.K.
- Check ASCD wire moves smoothly. → N.G. → Replace ASCD wire.
- O.K.
- CHECK ASCD ACTUATOR/ASCD PUMP. → N.G. → Replace ASCD actuator assembly.
- O.K.
- Replace ASCD control module.

NS1109100007000X

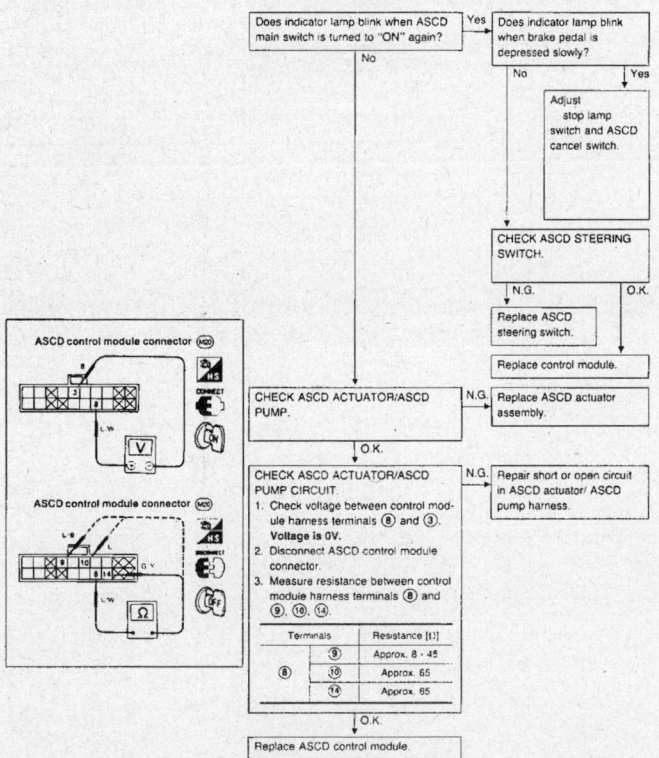

**Fig. 8 Test 8: "CRUISE" Indicator Lamp Blinks.
1996 Altima**

Flowchart text (Fig. 8):
- Does indicator lamp blink when ASCD main switch is turned to "ON" again? → Yes → Does indicator lamp blink when brake pedal is depressed slowly? → Yes → Adjust stop lamp switch and ASCD cancel switch.
- No → No → CHECK ASCD STEERING SWITCH. → N.G. → Replace ASCD steering switch. / O.K. → Replace control module.
- CHECK ASCD ACTUATOR/ASCD PUMP. → N.G. → Replace ASCD actuator assembly.
- O.K.
- CHECK ASCD ACTUATOR/ASCD PUMP CIRCUIT.
  1. Check voltage between control module harness terminals ⑧ and ③. Voltage is 0V.
  2. Disconnect ASCD control module connector.
  3. Measure resistance between control module harness terminals ⑧ and ⑨, ⑩, ⑭.
  → N.G. → Repair short or open circuit in ASCD actuator/ ASCD pump harness.

Terminals		Resistance [Ω]
⑧	⑨	Approx. 8 - 45
	⑩	Approx. 65
	⑭	Approx. 65

- O.K.
- Replace ASCD control module.

NS1109100008000X

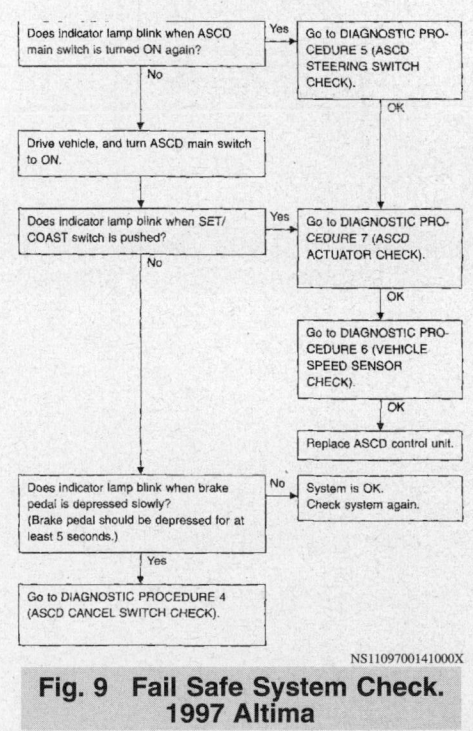

**Fig. 9 Fail Safe System Check.
1997 Altima**

Flowchart text (Fig. 9):
- Does indicator lamp blink when ASCD main switch is turned ON again? → Yes → Go to DIAGNOSTIC PROCEDURE 5 (ASCD STEERING SWITCH CHECK). → OK
- No
- Drive vehicle, and turn ASCD main switch to ON.
- Does indicator lamp blink when SET/COAST switch is pushed? → Yes → Go to DIAGNOSTIC PROCEDURE 7 (ASCD ACTUATOR CHECK). → OK
- No
- Go to DIAGNOSTIC PROCEDURE 6 (VEHICLE SPEED SENSOR CHECK). → OK
- Replace ASCD control unit.
- Does indicator lamp blink when brake pedal is depressed slowly? (Brake pedal should be depressed for at least 5 seconds.) → No → System is OK. Check system again.
- Yes
- Go to DIAGNOSTIC PROCEDURE 4 (ASCD CANCEL SWITCH CHECK).

NS1109700141000X

Fail-Safe System Check

1. Turn ignition switch ON.
2. Turn ASCD main switch to ON position and check if the "cruise indicator" blinks.
   If the indicator lamp blinks, check the following.
   - ASCD steering switch. Refer to "DIAGNOSTIC PROCE-DURE 5".

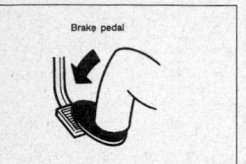

3. Drive the vehicle at more than 48 km/h (30 MPH) and push SET/COAST switch.
   If the indicator lamp blinks, check the following:
   - Vehicle speed sensor. Refer to "DIAGNOSTIC PROCE-DURE 6".
   - ASCD pump circuit. Refer to "DIAGNOSTIC PROCEDURE 7".
   - Replace control unit.

4. Depress brake pedal slowly (brake pedal should be depressed more than 5 seconds).
   If the indicator lamp blinks, check the following:
   - ASCD brake/stop lamp switch. Refer to "DIAGNOSTIC PROCEDURE 4".

NS1109900153000X

Fig. 10   Fail Safe System Check. 1998–99 Altima

PROCEDURE	—	Diagnostic procedure							
SYMPTOM	Fail-safe system check	DIAGNOSTIC PROCEDURE 1 (POWER SUPPLY AND GROUND CIRCUIT CHECK)	DIAGNOSTIC PROCEDURE 2 (ASCD MAIN SWITCH CHECK)	DIAGNOSTIC PROCEDURE 3 (ASCD HOLD RELAY CHECK)	DIAGNOSTIC PROCEDURE 4 (ASCD BRAKE/STOP LAMP SWITCH CHECK)	DIAGNOSTIC PROCEDURE 5 (ASCD STEERING SWITCH CHECK)	DIAGNOSTIC PROCEDURE 6 (VEHICLE SPEED SENSOR CHECK)	DIAGNOSTIC PROCEDURE 7 (ASCD PUMP CIRCUIT CHECK)	DIAGNOSTIC PROCEDURE 8 (ASCD ACTUATOR/PUMP CHECK)
ASCD cannot be set. ("CRUISE" indicator lamp does not blink.)		X	X	X		X	X		
ASCD cannot be set. ("CRUISE" indicator lamp blinks.★1)	X				X	X	X	X	
Vehicle speed does not decrease after SET/COAST switch has been pressed.						X			X
Vehicle speed does not return to the set speed after RESUME/ACCEL switch has been pressed.★2						X			X
Vehicle speed does not increase after RESUME/ACCEL switch has been pressed.						X			X
System is not released after CANCEL switch (steering) has been pressed.						X			X
Large difference between set speed and actual vehicle speed.									X
Deceleration is greatest immediately after ASCD has been set.									X

★1: It indicates that system is in fail-safe. After completing diagnostic procedures, perform "Fail-Safe System Check" to verify repairs.

★2: If vehicle speed is greater than 48 km/h (30 MPH) after system has been released, pressing RESUME/ACCEL switch returns vehicle speed to the set speed previously achieved. However, doing so when the ASCD main switch is turned to "OFF", vehicle speed will not return to the set speed since the memory is canceled.

NS1109900154000X

Fig. 11   Symptom Inspection. 1998–99 Altima

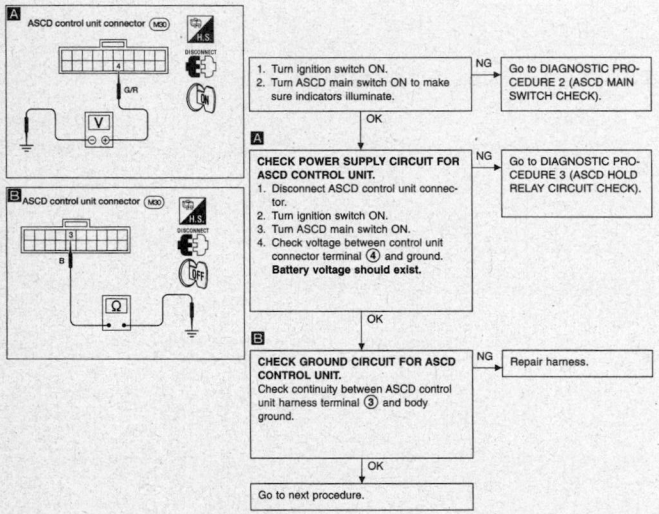

NS1109900155000X

Fig. 12   Diagnostic Procedure 1: Power & Ground Supply Inspection. 1998–99 Altima

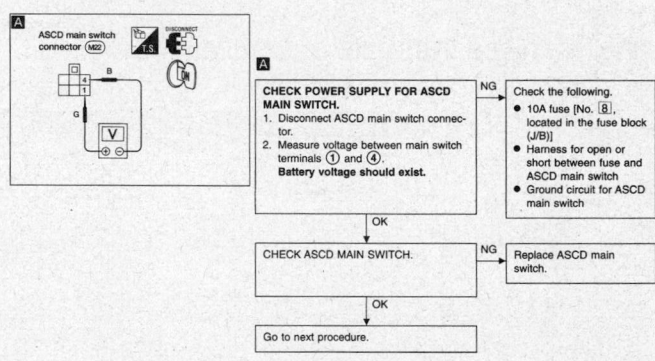

NS1109900156000X

Fig. 13   Diagnostic Procedure 2: ASCD Main Switch Inspection. 1998–99 Altima

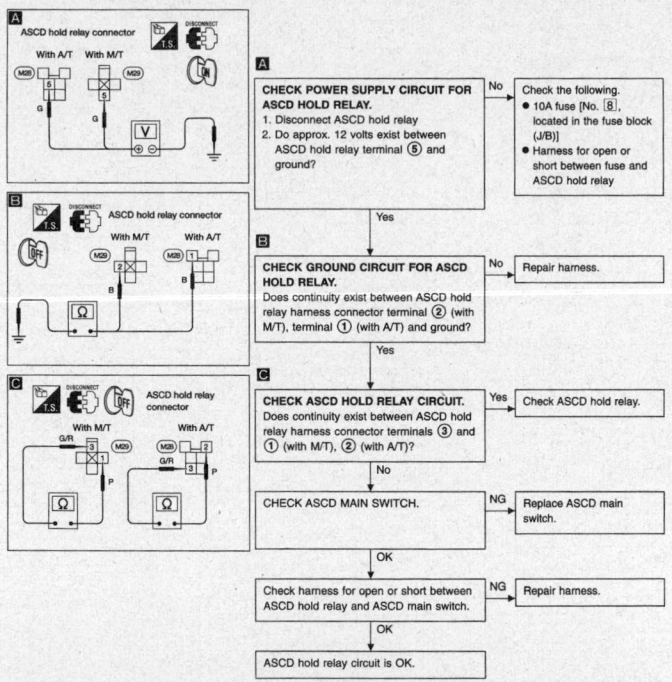

Fig. 14   Diagnostic Procedure 3: ASCD Hold Relay Inspection. 1998–99 Altima

NS1109900157000X

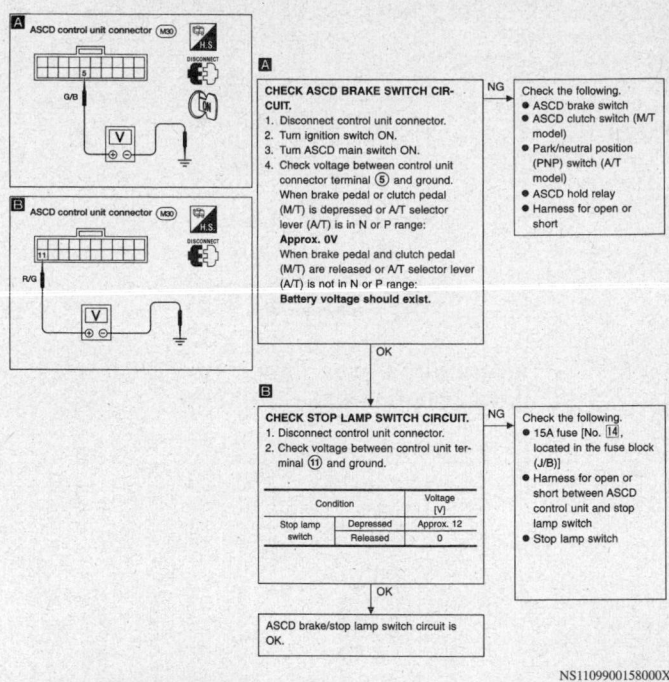

Fig. 15   Diagnostic Procedure 4: Brake Lamp Switch Inspection. 1998–99

NS1109900158000X

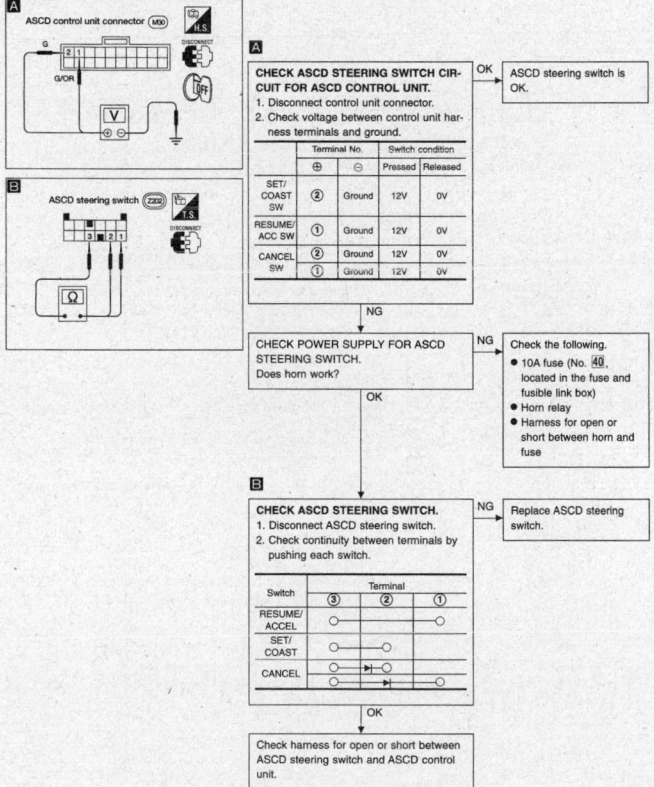

Fig. 16   Diagnostic Procedure 5: Steering Switch Inspection. 1998–99 Altima

NS1109900159000X

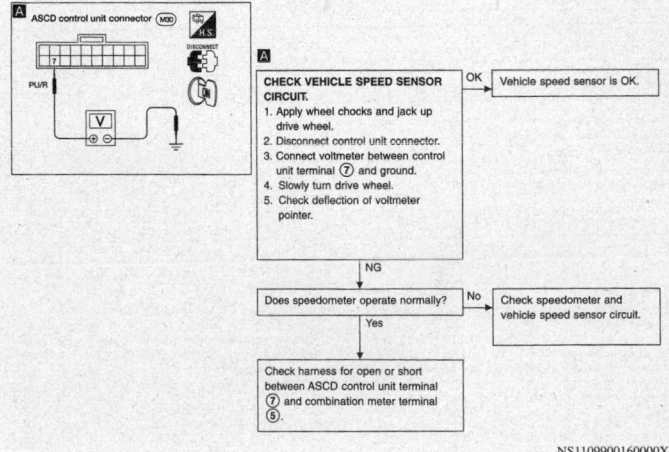

Fig. 17   Diagnostic Procedure 6: Vehicle Speed Sensor Inspection. 1998–99 Altima

NS1109900160000X

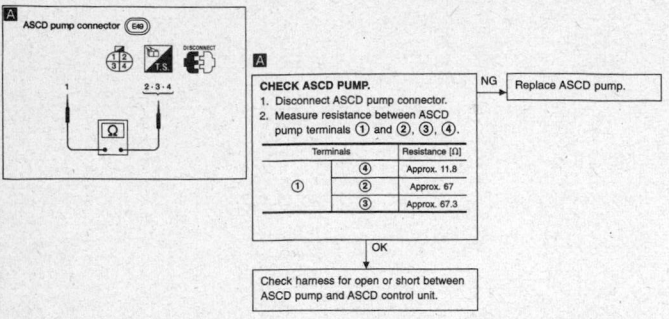

Fig. 18 Diagnostic Procedure 7: Pump Circuit Inspection. 1998–99 Altima

NS1109900161000X

PROCEDURE	—	Diagnostic procedure								
SYMPTOM	Fail-safe system check	DIAGNOSTIC PROCEDURE 1 (POWER SUPPLY AND GROUND CIRCUIT CHECK)	DIAGNOSTIC PROCEDURE 2 (ASCD MAIN SWITCH CHECK)	DIAGNOSTIC PROCEDURE 3 (ASCD HOLD RELAY CHECK)	DIAGNOSTIC PROCEDURE 4 (ASCD BRAKE/STOP LAMP SWITCH CHECK)	DIAGNOSTIC PROCEDURE 5 (ASCD STEERING SWITCH CHECK)	DIAGNOSTIC PROCEDURE 6 (VEHICLE SPEED SENSOR CHECK)	DIAGNOSTIC PROCEDURE 7 (ASCD PUMP CIRCUIT CHECK)	DIAGNOSTIC PROCEDURE 8 (ASCD ACTUATOR/PUMP CHECK)	
ASCD cannot be set. ("CRUISE" indicator lamp does not blink.)		X	X	X		X	X			
ASCD cannot be set. ("CRUISE" indicator lamp blinks.★1)	X				X	X	X	X		
Vehicle speed does not decrease after SET/COAST switch has been pressed.						X			X	
Vehicle speed does not return to the set speed after RESUME/ACCEL switch has been pressed.★2						X			X	
Vehicle speed does not increase after RESUME/ACCEL switch has been pressed.						X			X	
System is not released after CANCEL switch (steering) has been pressed.						X			X	
Large difference between set speed and actual vehicle speed.									X	
Deceleration is greatest immediately after ASCD has been set.									X	

X: Applicable

★1: It indicates that system is in fail-safe. After completing diagnostic procedures, perform "Fail-Safe System Check" to verify repairs.

★2: If vehicle speed is greater than 48 km/h (30 MPH) after system has been released, pressing RESUME/ACCEL switch returns vehicle speed to the set speed previously achieved. However, doing so when the ASCD main switch is turned to "OFF", vehicle speed will not return to the set speed since the memory is canceled.

NS1109900173000X

Fig. 20 Diagnostic Symptom Chart. Frontier

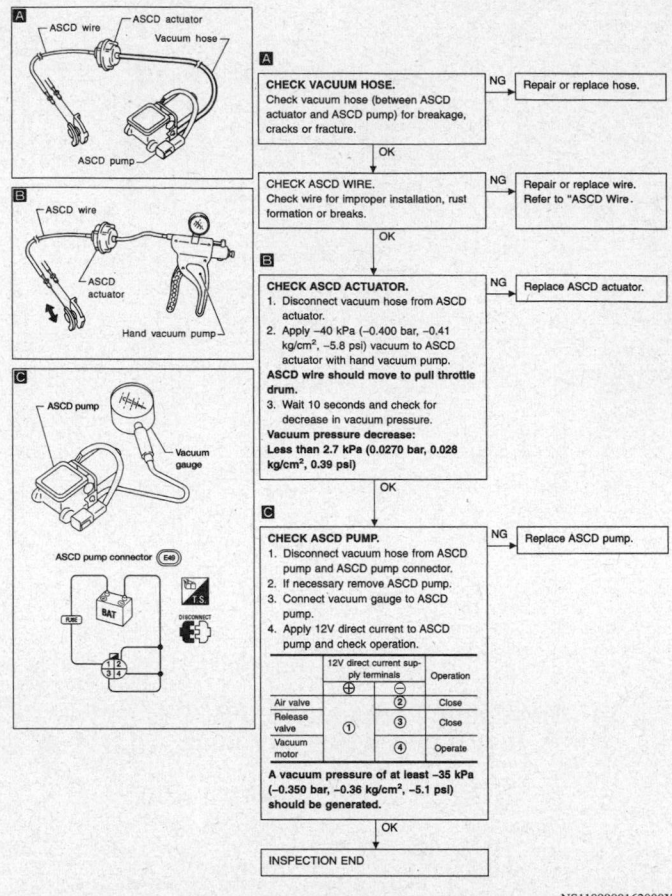

NS1109900162000X

Fig. 19 Diagnostic Procedure 8: Actuator/Pump Inspection. 1998–99 Altima

Fail-Safe System Check

1. Turn ignition switch ON.
2. Turn ASCD main switch to ON position and check if the "cruise indicator" blinks.
   If the indicator lamp blinks, check the following.
   - ASCD steering switch. Refer to "DIAGNOSTIC PROCEDURE 5".
3. Drive the vehicle at more than 48 km/h (30 MPH) and push SET/COAST switch.
   If the indicator lamp blinks, check the following:
   - Vehicle speed sensor. Refer to "DIAGNOSTIC PROCEDURE 6".
   - ASCD pump circuit. Refer to "DIAGNOSTIC PROCEDURE 7".
   - Replace control unit.
4. Depress brake pedal slowly (brake pedal should be depressed more than 5 seconds).
   If the indicator lamp blinks, check the following:
   - ASCD brake/stop lamp switch. Refer to "DIAGNOSTIC PROCEDURE 4".
5. END. (System is OK.)

NS1109900174000X

Fig. 21 Fail Safe System Inspection. Frontier

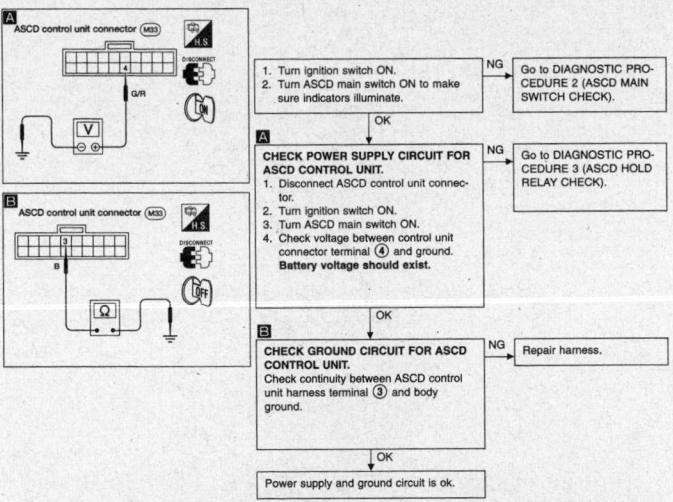

Fig. 22   Diagnostic Procedure 1: Power Supply &
Ground Circuit Inspection. Frontier

NS1109900175000X

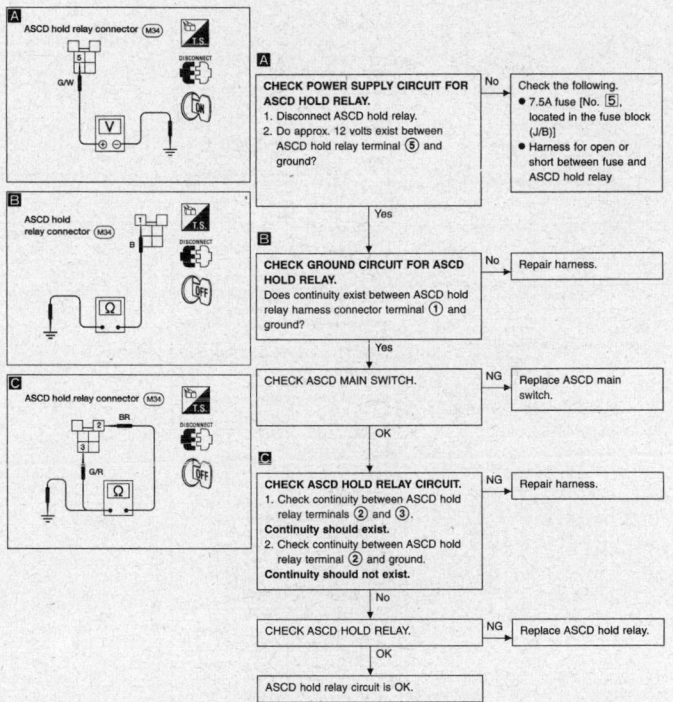

Fig. 24   Diagnostic Procedure 3: ASCD Hold Relay
Inspecton. Frontier

NS1109900177000X

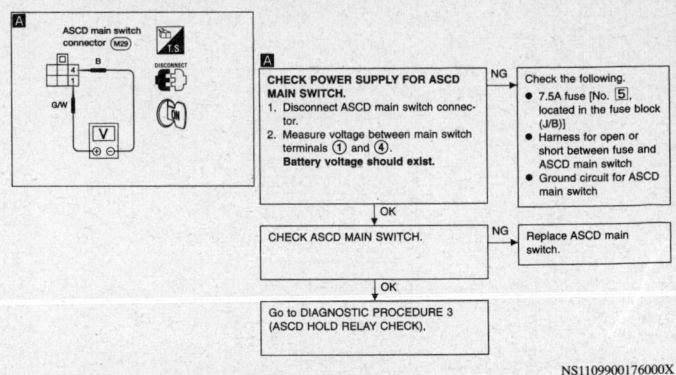

Fig. 23   Diagnostic Procedure 2: ASCD Main
Switch Inspection. Frontier

NS1109900176000X

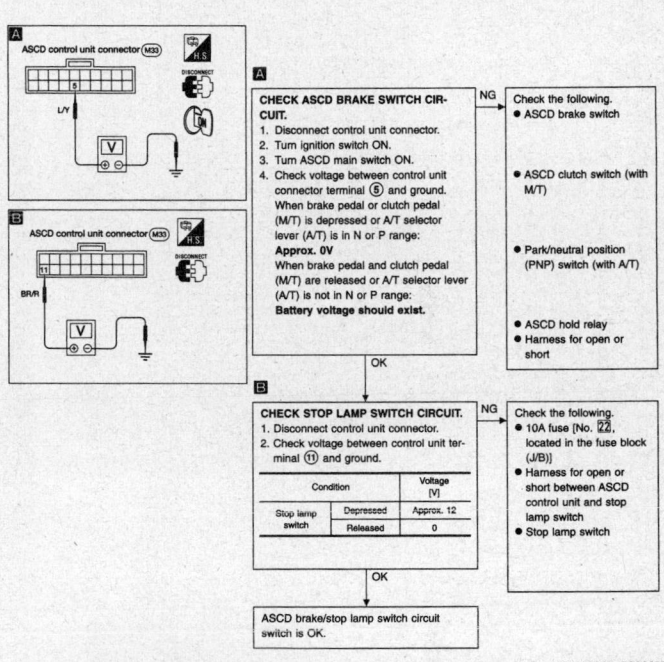

Fig. 25   Diagnostic Procedure 4: ASCD Brake
Lamp Switch Inspection. Frontier

NS1109900178000X

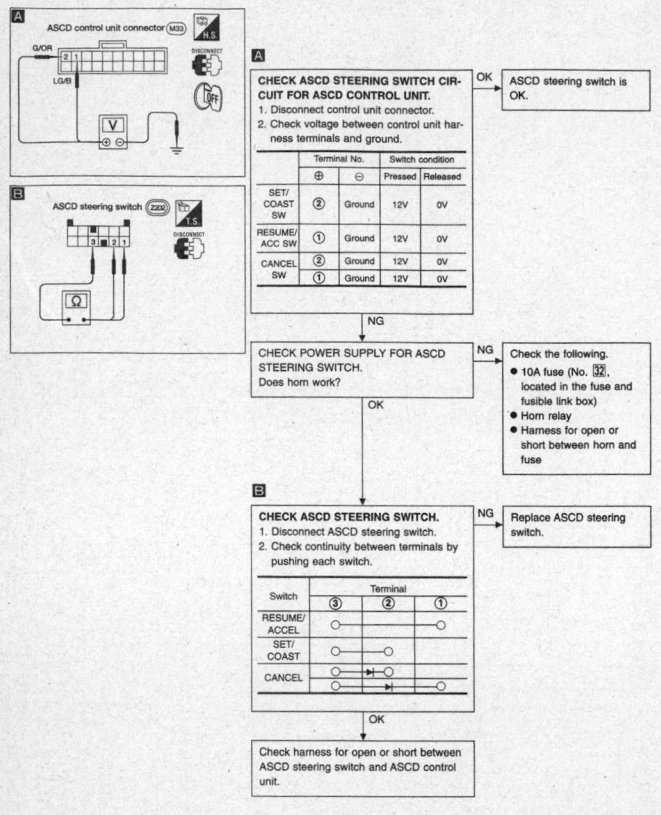

Fig. 26   Diagnostic Procedure 5: ASCD Steering Switch Inspection. Frontier

NS1109900179000X

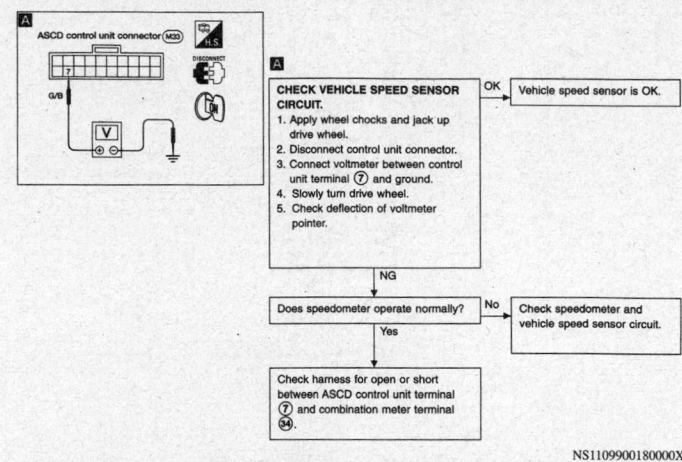

Fig. 27   Diagnostic Procedure 6: Vehicle Speed Sensor Inspection. Frontier

NS1109900180000X

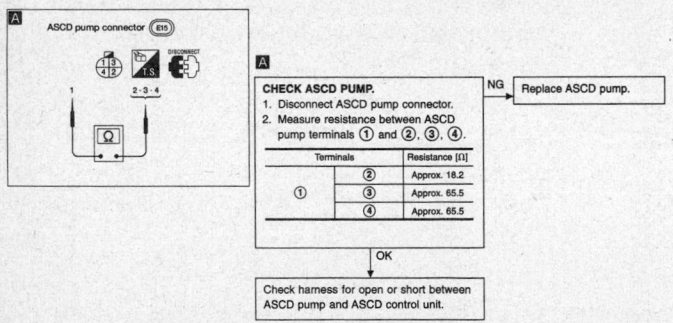

Fig. 28   Diagnostic Procedure 7: ASCD Pump Circuit Inspection. Frontier

NS1109900181000X

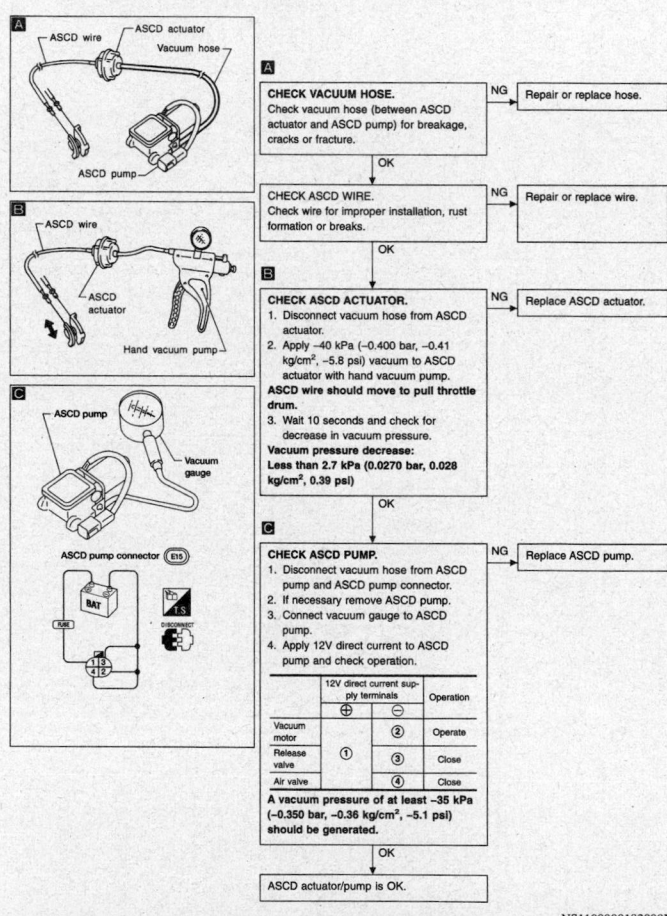

Fig. 29   Diagnostic Procedure 8: ASCD Actuator/ Pump Inspection. Frontier

NS1109900182000X

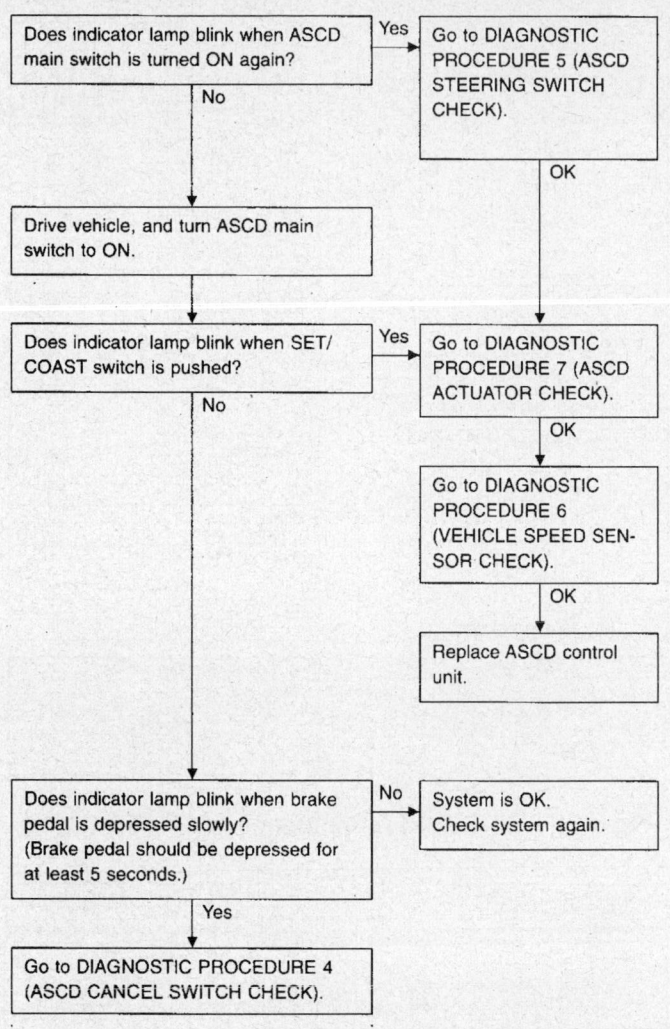

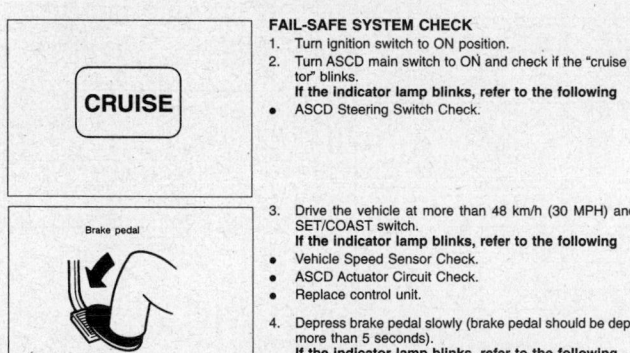

Fig. 30 Fail-Safe System Check. 1996–97 Maxima & 1996–98 Quest

FAIL-SAFE SYSTEM CHECK

1. Turn ignition switch to ON position.
2. Turn ASCD main switch to ON and check if the "cruise indicator" blinks.
   If the indicator lamp blinks, refer to the following
   - ASCD Steering Switch Check.

3. Drive the vehicle at more than 48 km/h (30 MPH) and push SET/COAST switch.
   If the indicator lamp blinks, refer to the following
   - Vehicle Speed Sensor Check.
   - ASCD Actuator Circuit Check.
   - Replace control unit.

4. Depress brake pedal slowly (brake pedal should be depressed more than 5 seconds).
   If the indicator lamp blinks, refer to the following
   - ASCD Brake/Stop Lamp Switch Check.

NS1109900164000X

Fig. 32 Fail Safe System Check. 1999 Quest

SYMPTOM	FAIL-SAFE SYSTEM CHECK	POWER SUPPLY AND GROUND CIRCUIT CHECK	ASCD MAIN SWITCH CHECK	ASCD HOLD RELAY CHECK	ASCD BRAKE/STOP LAMP SWITCH CHECK	ASCD STEERING SWITCH CHECK	VEHICLE SPEED SENSOR CHECK	ASCD ACTUATOR CIRCUIT CHECK	ASCD ACTUATOR CHECK
ASCD cannot be set. ("CRUISE" indicator lamp does not blink.		X	X	X		X	X		X★3
ASCD cannot be set. ("CRUISE" indicator lamp blinks.★1)	X				X	X	X	X	
Vehicle speed does not decrease after SET/COAST switch has been pressed.						X			X
Vehicle speed does not return to the set speed after RESUME/ACCEL switch has been pressed.★2						X			X
Vehicle speed does not increase after RESUME/ACCEL switch has been pressed.						X			X
System is not released after CANCEL switch (steering) has been pressed.						X			X
Large difference between set speed and actual vehicle speed.									X
Deceleration is greatest immediately after ASCD has been set.									X

★1: It indicates that system is in fail-safe. After completing diagnostic procedures, perform "FAIL-SAFE SYSTEM CHECK" to verify repairs.
★2: If vehicle speed is greater than 48 km/h (30 MPH) after system has been released, pressing RESUME/ACCEL switch returns vehicle speed to the set speed previously achieved. However, doing so when the ASCD main switch is turned to "OFF", vehicle speed will not return to the set speed since the memory is canceled.
★3: Verify that vacuum hose between ASCD vacuum tank and intake manifold collector or between ASCD vacuum tank and ASCD actuator has not come off.

NS1109900163000X

Fig. 31 Symptom Inspection Chart. 1999 Quest

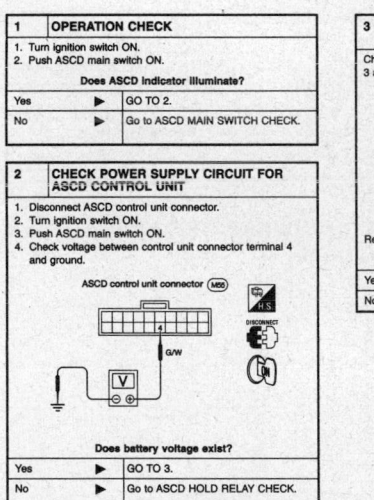

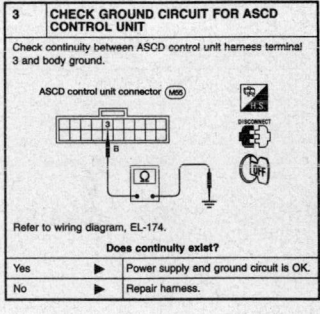

NS1109900165000X

Fig. 33 Power Supply & Ground Circuit Inspection. 1999 Quest

1	CHECK POWER SUPPLY FOR ASCD MAIN SWITCH

1. Disconnect main switch connector.
2. Check voltage between main switch terminals 1 and 4.

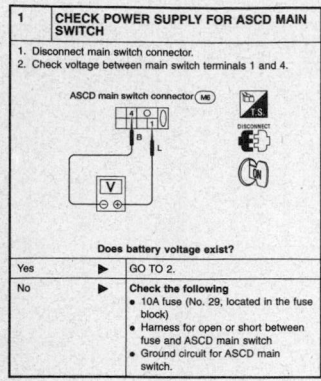

Does battery voltage exist?

Yes	▶	GO TO 2.
No	▶	Check the following • 10A fuse (No. 29, located in the fuse block) • Harness for open or short between fuse and ASCD main switch • Ground circuit for ASCD main switch

2	CHECK ASCD MAIN SWITCH

Check ASCD main switch.

	OK or NG	
OK	▶	Go to ASCD HOLD RELAY CHECK.
NG	▶	Replace ASCD main switch.

NS1109900166000X

Fig. 34 ASCD Main Switch Inspection. 1999 Quest

1	CHECK ASCD BRAKE SWITCH CIRCUIT

1. Disconnect control unit connector.
2. Turn ignition switch ON.
3. Push ASCD main switch ON.
4. Check voltage between control unit connector harness terminal 5 and body ground.

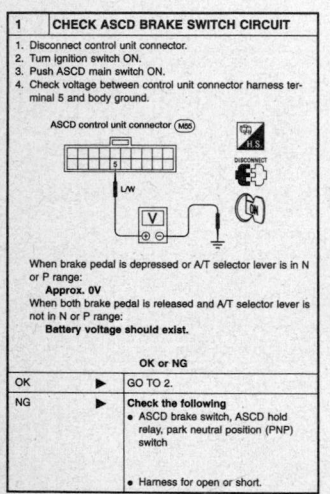

When brake pedal is depressed or A/T selector lever is in N or P range:
Approx. 0V
When both brake pedal is released and A/T selector lever is not in N or P range:
Battery voltage should exist.

	OK or NG	
OK	▶	GO TO 2.
NG	▶	Check the following • ASCD brake switch, ASCD hold relay, park neutral position (PNP) switch • Harness for open or short.

2	CHECK STOP LAMP SWITCH CIRCUIT

1. Disconnect control unit connector.
2. Check voltage between control unit harness terminal 11 and ground.

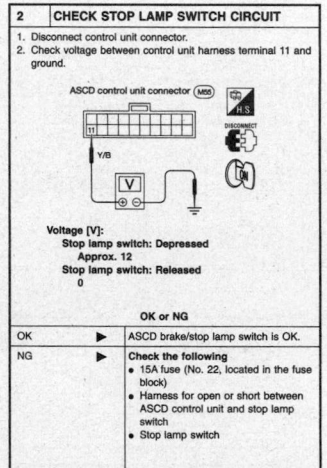

Voltage [V]:
Stop lamp switch: Depressed
Approx. 12
Stop lamp switch: Released
0

	OK or NG	
OK	▶	ASCD brake/stop lamp switch is OK.
NG	▶	Check the following • 15A fuse (No. 22, located in the fuse block) • Harness for open or short between ASCD control unit and stop lamp switch • Stop lamp switch

NS1109900168000X

Fig. 36 ASCD Brake Lamp Switch Inspection. 1999 Quest

1	CHECK POWER SUPPLY CIRCUIT FOR ASCD HOLD RELAY

1. Disconnect ASCD hold relay.
2. Check voltage between ASCD hold relay terminal 5 and body ground.

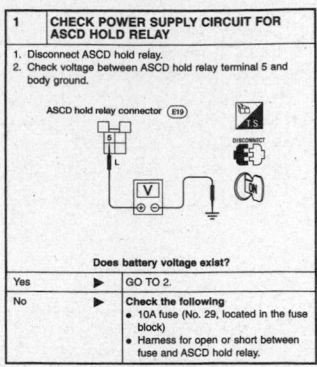

Does battery voltage exist?

Yes	▶	GO TO 2.
No	▶	Check the following • 10A fuse (No. 29, located in the fuse block) • Harness for open or short between fuse and ASCD hold relay.

2	CHECK GROUND CIRCUIT FOR ASCD HOLD RELAY

Check continuity between ASCD hold relay terminal 1 and body ground.

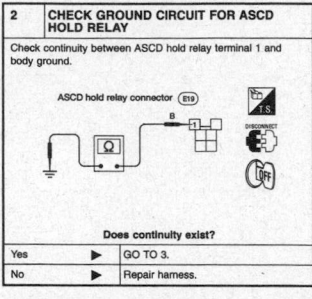

Does continuity exist?

Yes	▶	GO TO 3.
No	▶	Repair harness.

3	CHECK ASCD HOLD RELAY OPEN OR SHORT CIRCUIT

1. Check continuity between ASCD hold relay harness terminals 2 and 3.

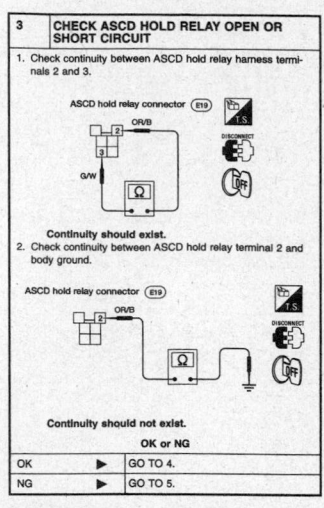

Continuity should exist.

2. Check continuity between ASCD hold relay terminal 2 and body ground.

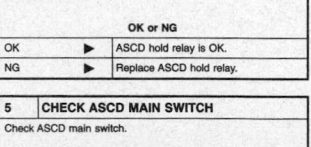

Continuity should not exist.

	OK or NG	
OK	▶	GO TO 4.
NG	▶	GO TO 5.

4	CHECK ASCD HOLD RELAY

Check ASCD hold relay.

	OK or NG	
OK	▶	ASCD hold relay is OK.
NG	▶	Replace ASCD hold relay.

5	CHECK ASCD MAIN SWITCH

Check ASCD main switch.

	OK or NG	
OK	▶	Repair harness.
NG	▶	Replace ASCD main switch.

NS1109900167000X

Fig. 35 ASCD Hold relay Inspection. 1999 Quest

1	CHECK ASCD STEERING SWITCH CIRCUIT FOR ASCD CONTROL UNIT

1. Disconnect control unit connector.
2. Check voltage between control unit harness terminals and ground.

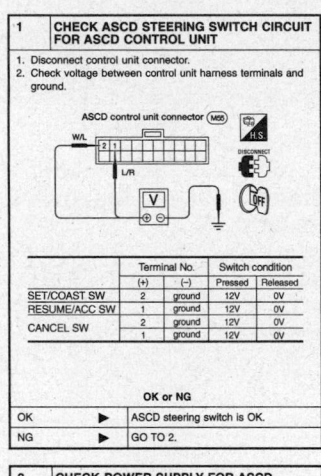

		Terminal No.		Switch condition	
		(+)	(-)	Pressed	Released
SET/COAST SW		2	ground	12V	0V
RESUME/ACC SW		1	ground	12V	0V
CANCEL SW		2	ground	12V	0V
		1	ground	12V	0V

	OK or NG	
OK	▶	ASCD steering switch is OK.
NG	▶	GO TO 2.

2	CHECK POWER SUPPLY FOR ASCD STEERING SWITCH

Does horn work?

Yes	▶	GO TO 3.
No	▶	Check the following • 15A fuse (No. 42, located in the fuse and fusible link box) • Horn relay • Harness for open or short between horn relay and fuse.

3	CHECK ASCD STEERING SWITCH

1. Disconnect ASCD steering switch.
2. Check continuity between terminals by pushing each switch.

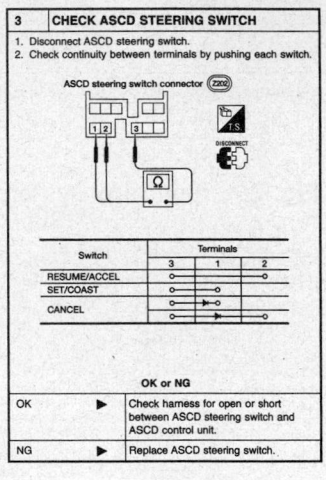

Switch	Terminals		
	3	1	2
RESUME/ACCEL		o—o	
SET/COAST	o——o		
CANCEL	o—	—o	

	OK or NG	
OK	▶	Check harness for open or short between ASCD steering switch and ASCD control unit.
NG	▶	Replace ASCD steering switch.

NS1109900169000X

Fig. 37 ASCD Steering Switch Inspection. 1999 Quest

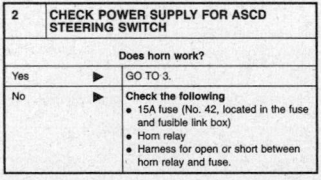

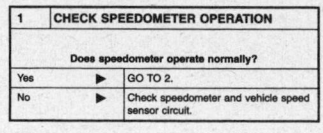

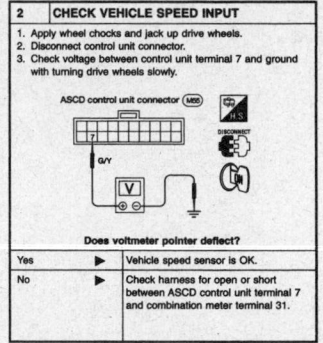

Fig. 38 Vehicle Speed Sensor Inspection. 1999 Quest

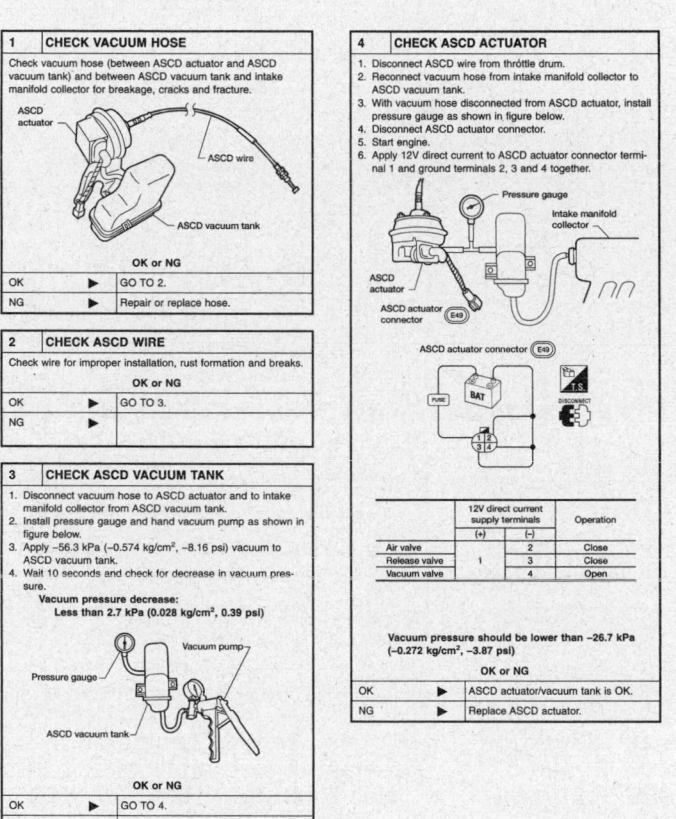

Fig. 40 ASCD Actuator Inspection. 1999 Quest

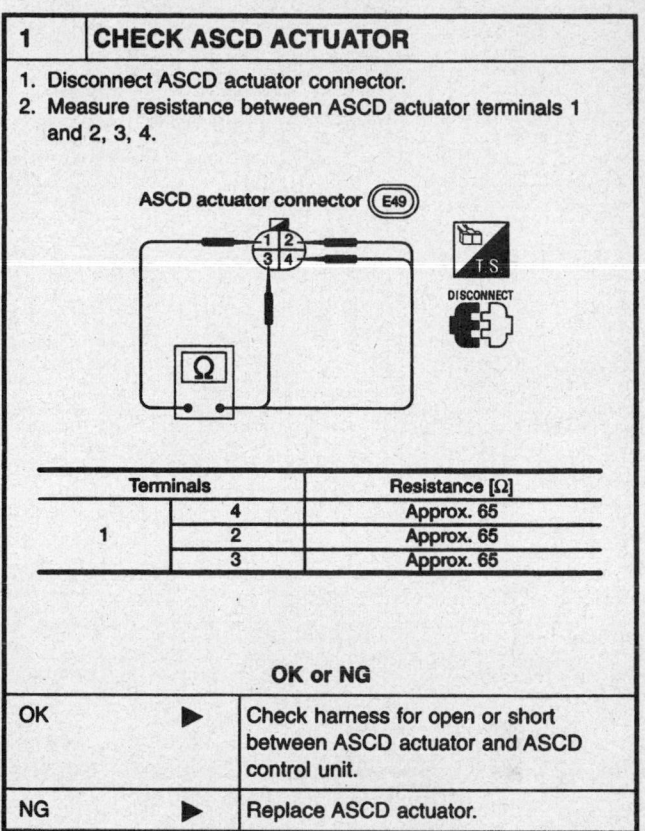

Terminals		Resistance [Ω]
1	4	Approx. 65
	2	Approx. 65
	3	Approx. 65

OK or NG

OK	▶	Check harness for open or short between ASCD actuator and ASCD control unit.
NG	▶	Replace ASCD actuator.

NS1109900171000X

Fig. 39 ASCD Actuator Circuit Inspection. 1999 Quest

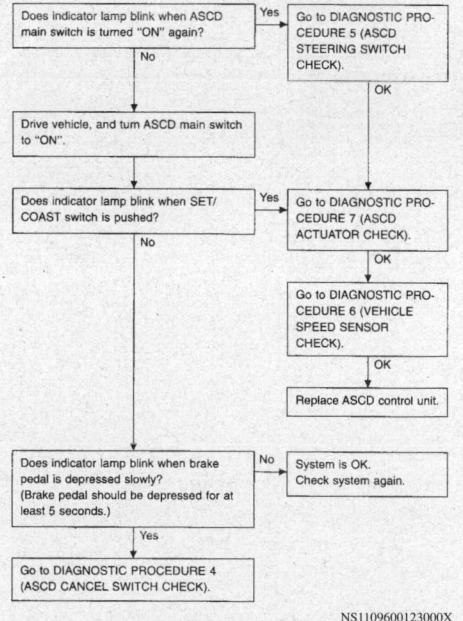

NS1109600123000X

Fig. 41 Fail-Safe System Check. 1996–97 Pathfinder & Pickup

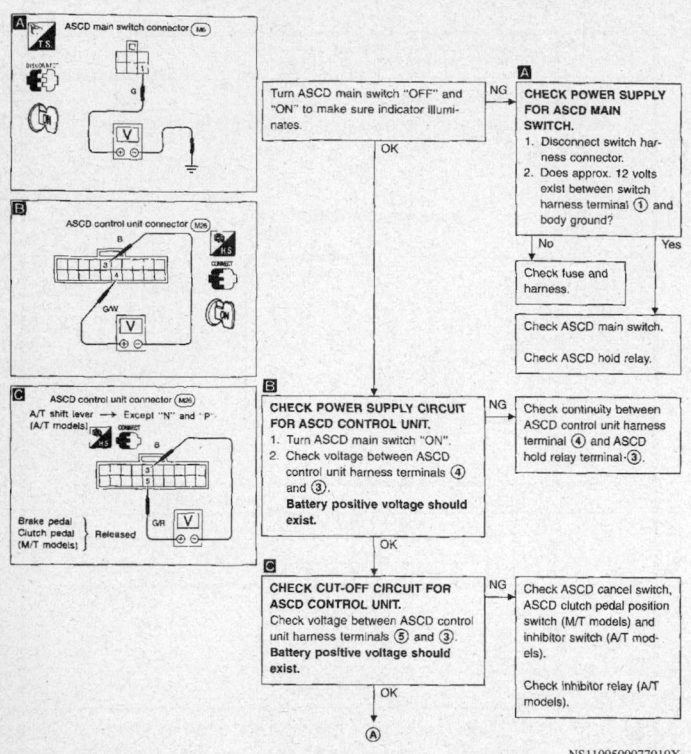

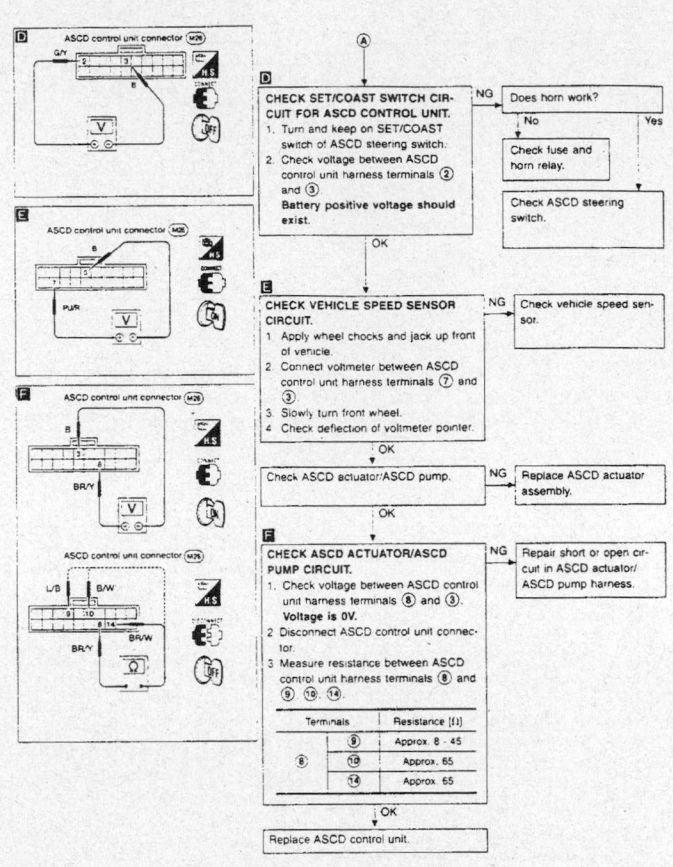

Fig. 42   Test 1: Speed Control Cannot Be Set (Part 1 of 2). 1996 Sentra & 200SX

NS1109500077010X

NS1109500077020X

Fig. 42   Test 1: Speed Control Cannot Be Set (Part 2 of 2). 1996 Sentra & 200SX

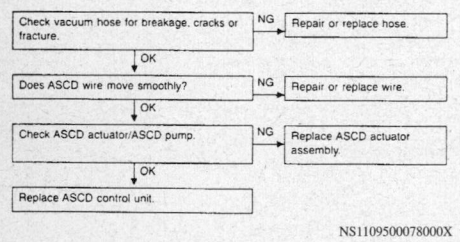

NS1109500078000X

Fig. 43   Test 2: Engine Hunts. 1996 Sentra & 200SX

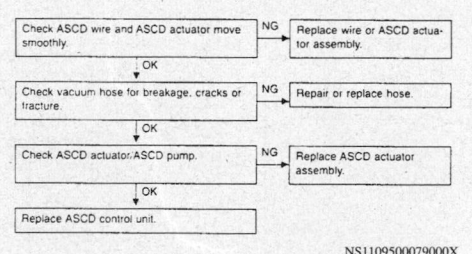

NS1109500079000X

Fig. 44   Test 3: Large Difference Between Set Vehicle Speed & Actual Speed. 1996 Sentra & 200SX

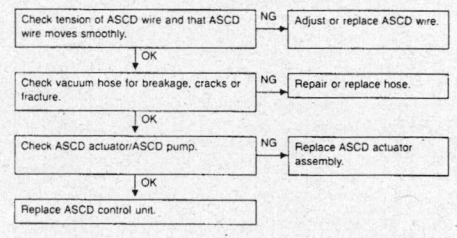

NS1109500080000X

Fig. 45   Test 4: Deceleration Is Greatest Immediately After ASCD Has Been Set. 1996 Sentra & 200SX

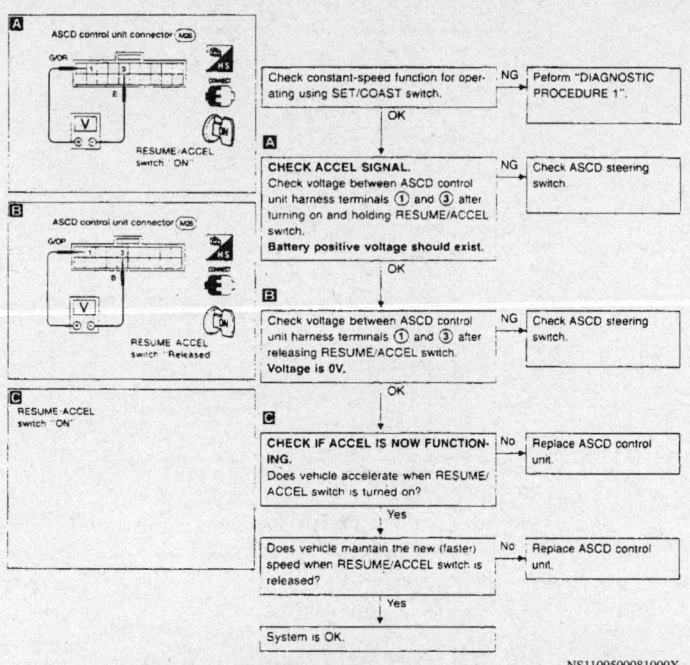

Fig. 46 Test 5: ACCEL Switch Will Not Operate. 1996 Sentra & 200SX

NS1109500081000X

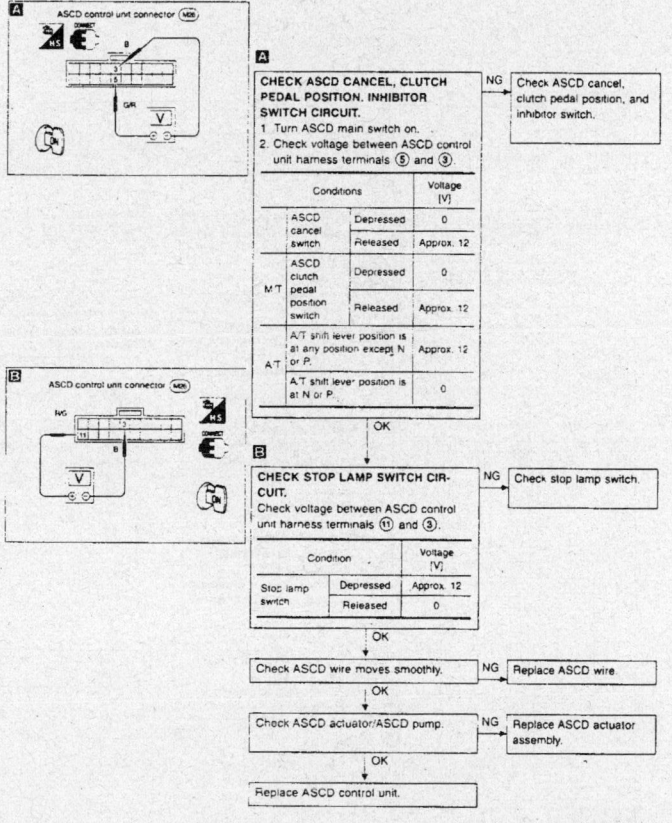

Fig. 48 Test 7: Set Speed Cannot Be Canceled. 1996 Sentra & 200SX

NS1109500083000X

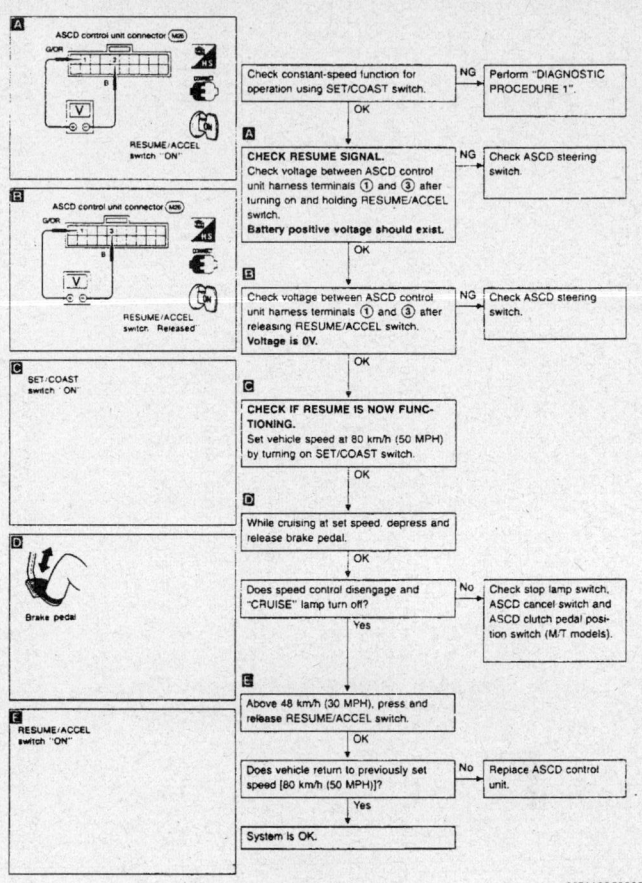

Fig. 47 Test 6: RESUME Switch Will Not Operate. 1996 Sentra & 200SX

NS1109500082000X

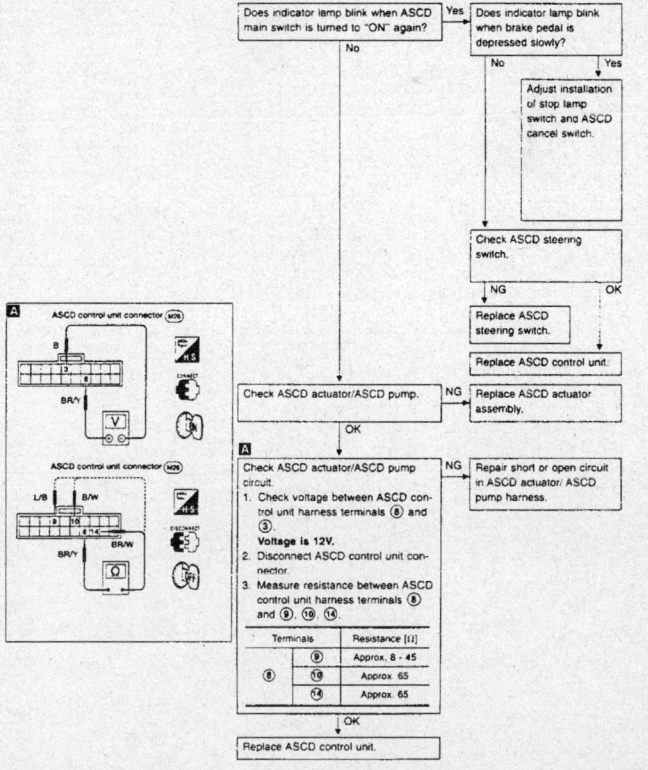

Fig. 49 Test 8: CRUISE Indicator Lamp Blinks. 1996 Sentra & 200SX

NS1109500084000X

Does indicator lamp blink when ASCD main switch is turned ON again? — Yes → Go to DIAGNOSTIC PROCEDURE 5 (ASCD STEERING SWITCH CHECK). → OK

No ↓

Drive vehicle, and turn ASCD main switch to ON.

↓

Does indicator lamp blink when SET/COAST switch is pushed? — Yes → Go to DIAGNOSTIC PROCEDURE 7 (ASCD ACTUATOR CHECK). → OK → Go to DIAGNOSTIC PROCEDURE 6 (VEHICLE SPEED SENSOR CHECK). → OK → Replace ASCD control unit.

No ↓

Does indicator lamp blink when brake pedal is depressed slowly? (Brake pedal should be depressed for at least 5 seconds.) — No → System is OK. Check system again.

Yes ↓

Go to DIAGNOSTIC PROCEDURE 4 (ASCD CLUTCH AND BRAKE SWITCH CHECK).

NS1109700143000X

Fig. 50   Fail Safe System Check. 1997–99 Sentra & 200SX

Does indicator lamp blink when ASCD main switch is turned "ON" again? — Yes → Go to DIAGNOSTIC PROCEDURE 5 (ASCD STEERING SWITCH CHECK). → OK

No ↓

Drive vehicle, and turn ASCD main switch to "ON".

↓

Does indicator lamp blink when SET/COAST switch is pushed? — Yes → Go to DIAGNOSTIC PROCEDURE 7 (ASCD ACTUATOR CHECK). → OK → Go to DIAGNOSTIC PROCEDURE 6 (VEHICLE SPEED SENSOR CHECK). → OK → Replace ASCD control unit.

No ↓

Does indicator lamp blink when brake pedal is depressed slowly? (Brake pedal should be depressed for at least 5 seconds.) — No → System is OK. Check system again.

Yes ↓

Go to DIAGNOSTIC PROCEDURE 4 (ASCD CANCEL SWITCH CHECK).

NS1109600124000X

Fig. 51   Fail-Safe System Check. 240SX

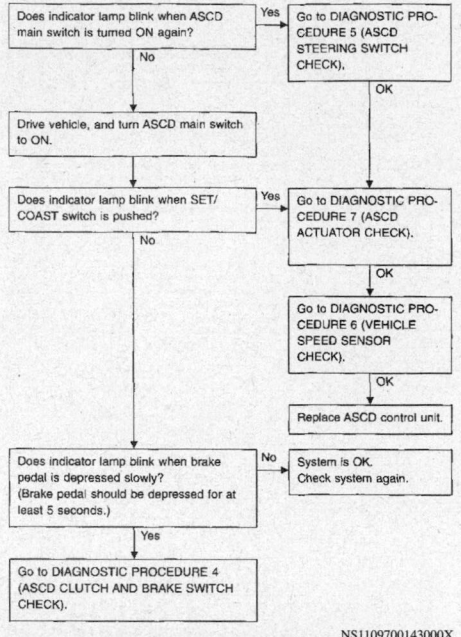

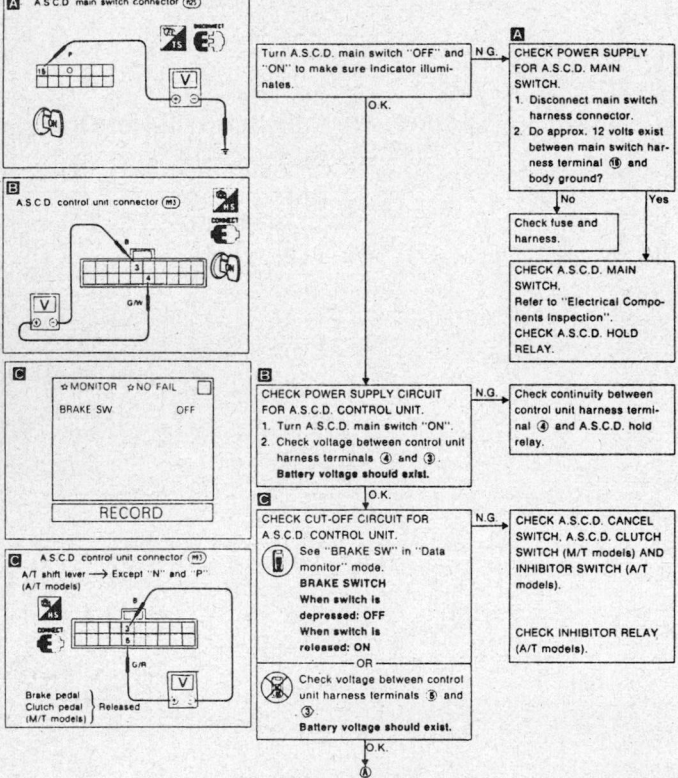

Fig. 52   Test 1: ASCD Control Unit Cannot Be Set (Part 1 of 3). 300ZX

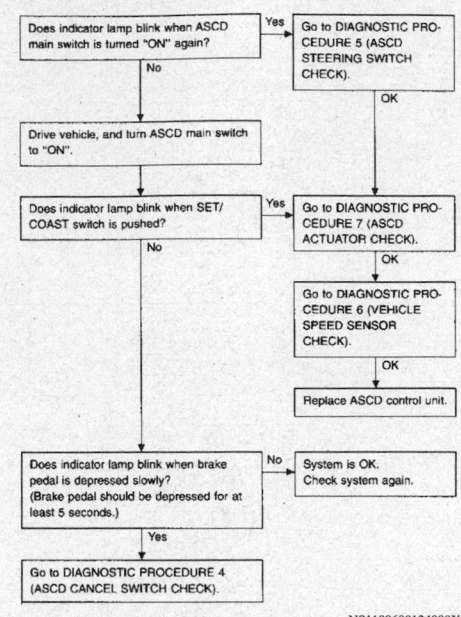

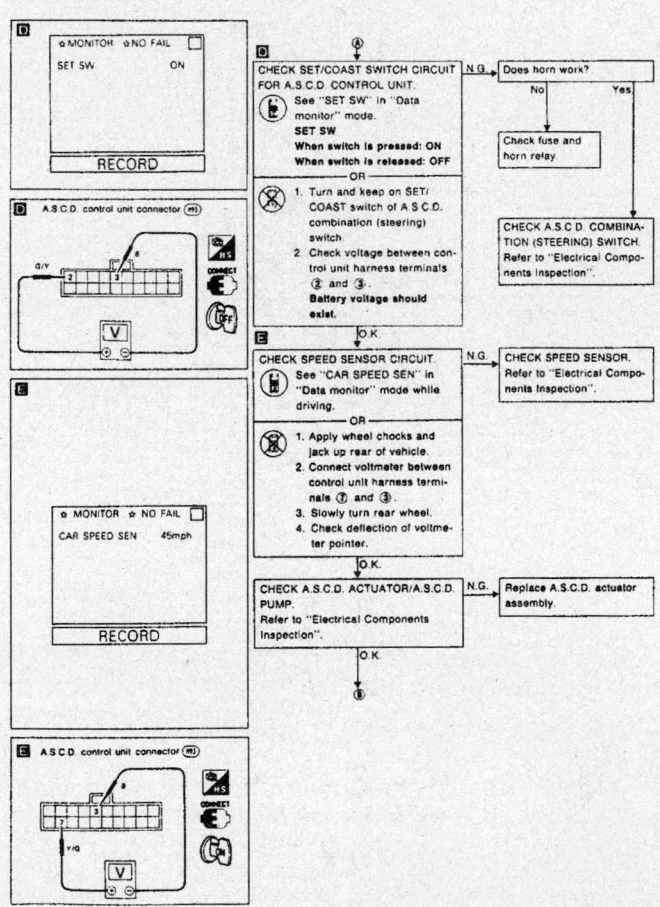

NS1109200053020X

Fig. 52   Test 1: ASCD Control Unit Cannot Be Set (Part 2 of 3). 300ZX

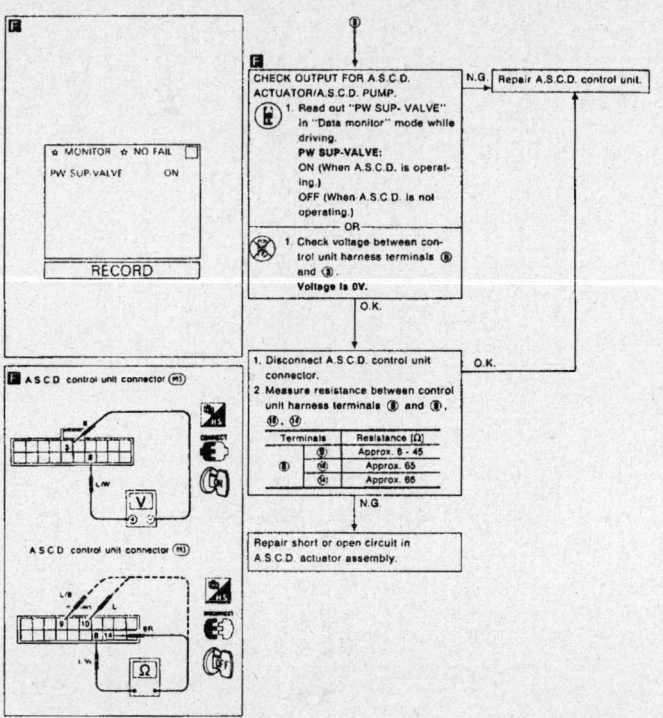

NS1109200053030X

Fig. 52   Test 1: ASCD Control Unit Cannot Be Set (Part 3 of 3). 300ZX

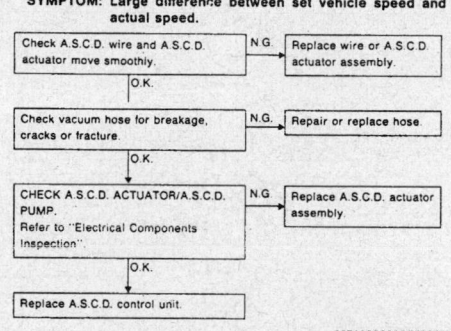

NS1109200055000X

Fig. 54   Test 3: Large Difference Between Set Vehicle Speed & Actual Speed. 300ZX

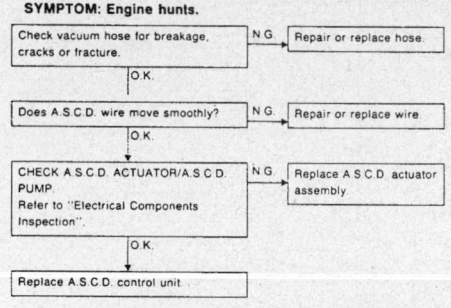

NS1109200054000X

Fig. 53   Test 2: Engine Hunts. 300ZX

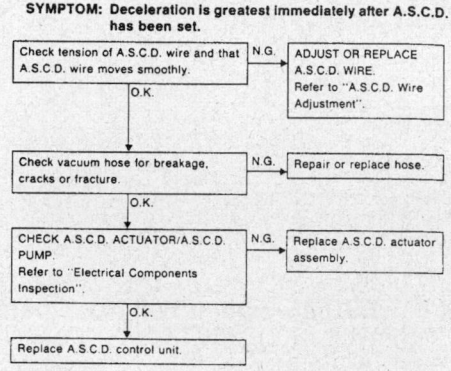

NS1109200056000X

Fig. 55   Test 4: Deceleration Is Greatest Immediately After ASCD Has Been Set. 300ZX

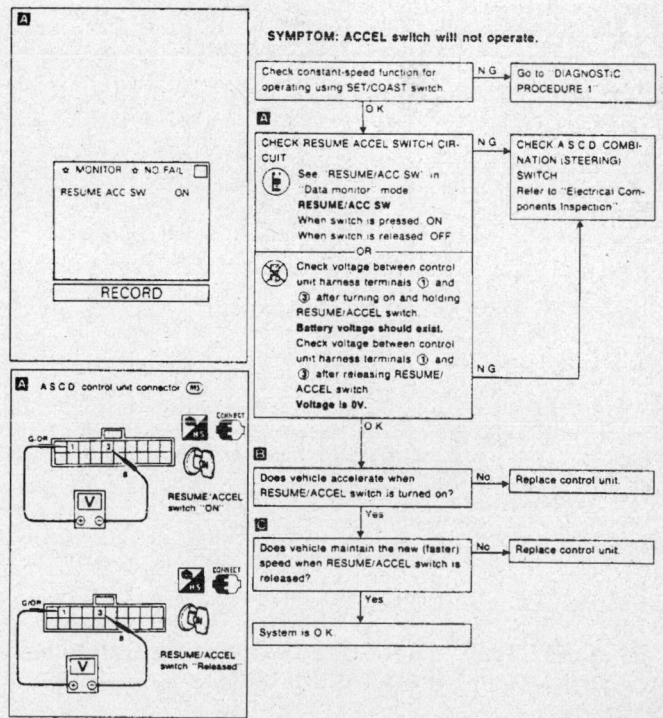

NS1109200057000X

Fig. 56   Test 5: ACCEL Switch Will Not Operate. 300ZX

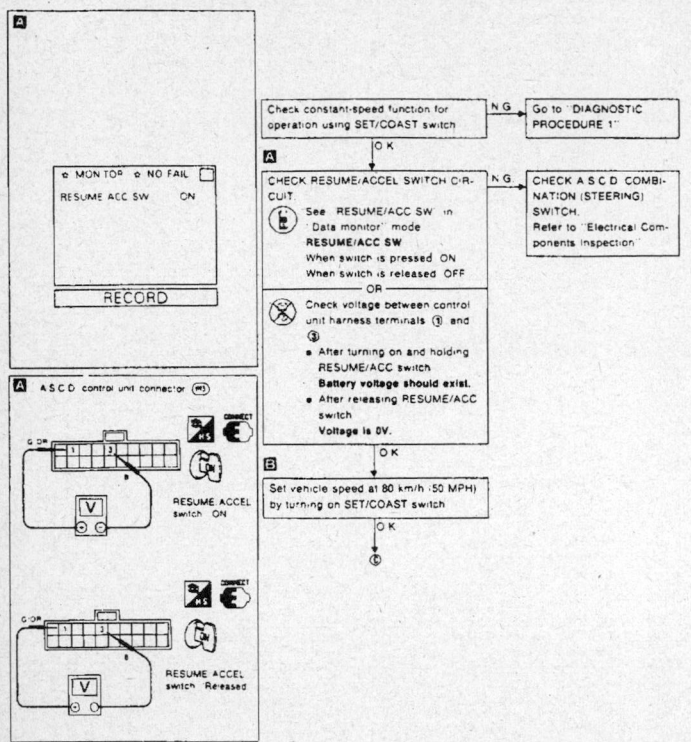

Fig. 57   Test 6: RESUME Switch Will Not Operate
(Part 1 of 2). 300ZX

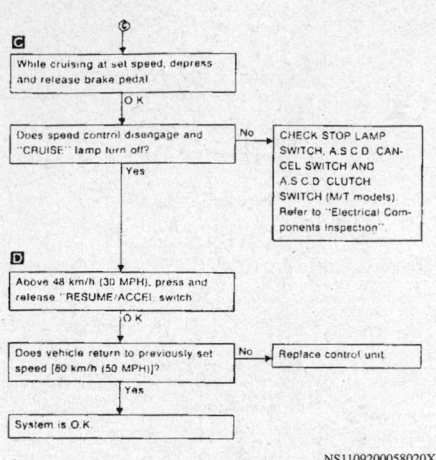

Fig. 57   Test 6: RESUME Switch
Will Not Operate (Part 2 of 2).
300ZX

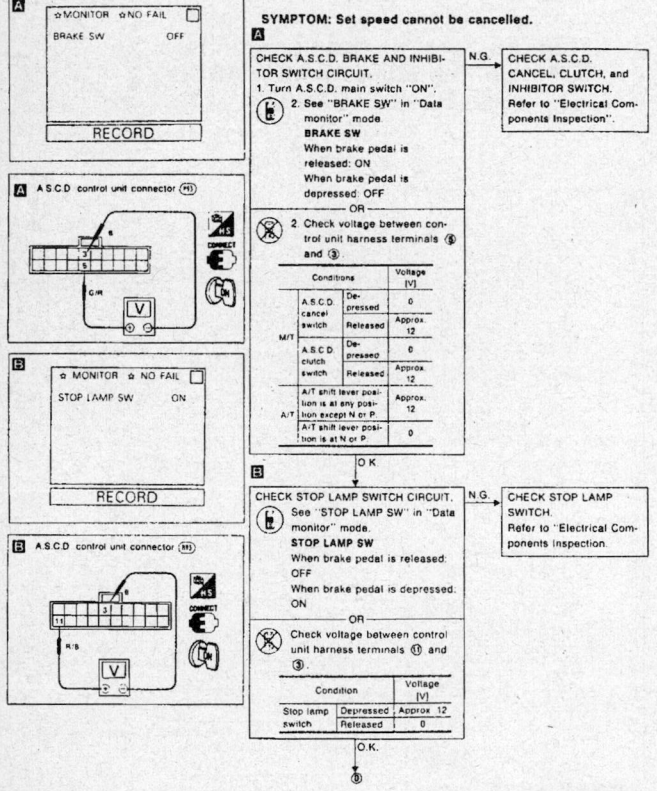

Fig. 58   Test 7: Set Speed Cannot Be Cancelled
(Part 1 of 2). 300ZX

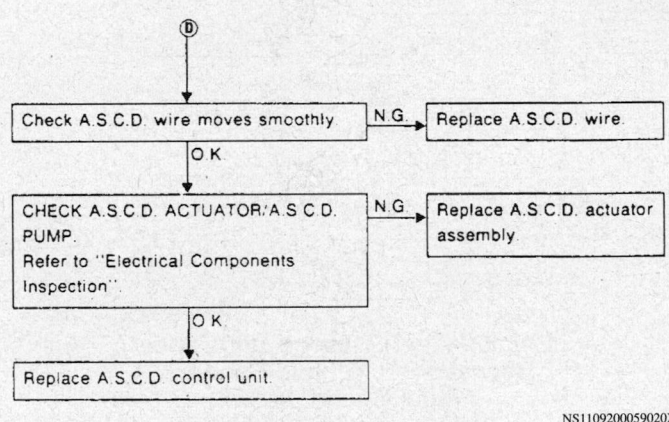

Fig. 58   Test 7: Set Speed Cannot Be Cancelled
(Part 2 of 2). 300ZX

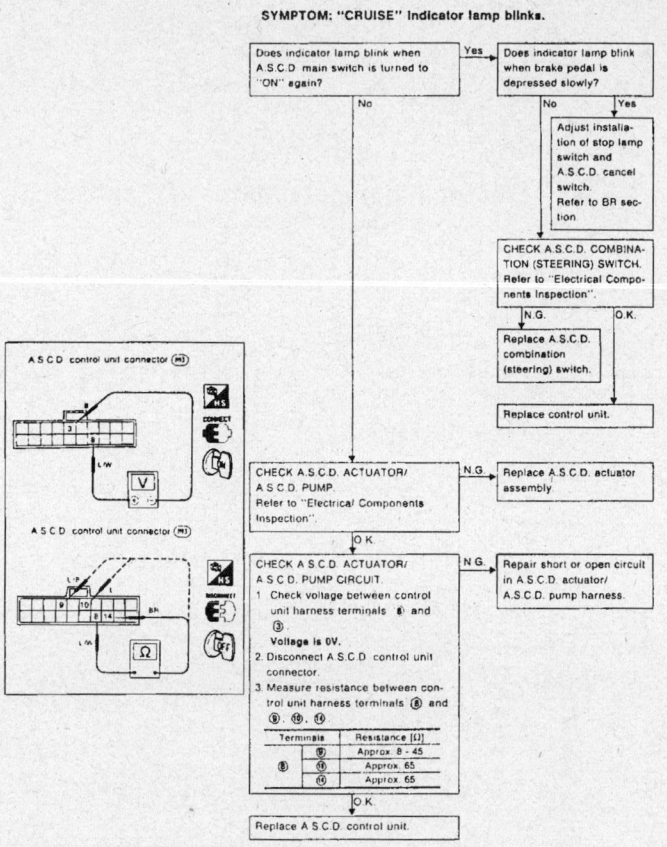

Fig. 59 Test 8: CRUISE Indicator Lamp Blinks. 300ZX

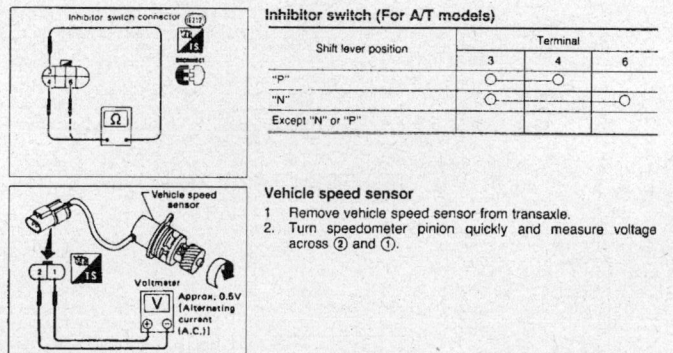

Inhibitor switch (For A/T models)

Shift lever position	Terminal		
	3	4	6
"P"	○—	—○	
"N"		○—	—○
Except "N" or "P"			

Vehicle speed sensor
1. Remove vehicle speed sensor from transaxle.
2. Turn speedometer pinion quickly and measure voltage across ② and ①.

Fig. 60 Electrical component check (Part 2 of 2). 1996 Altima

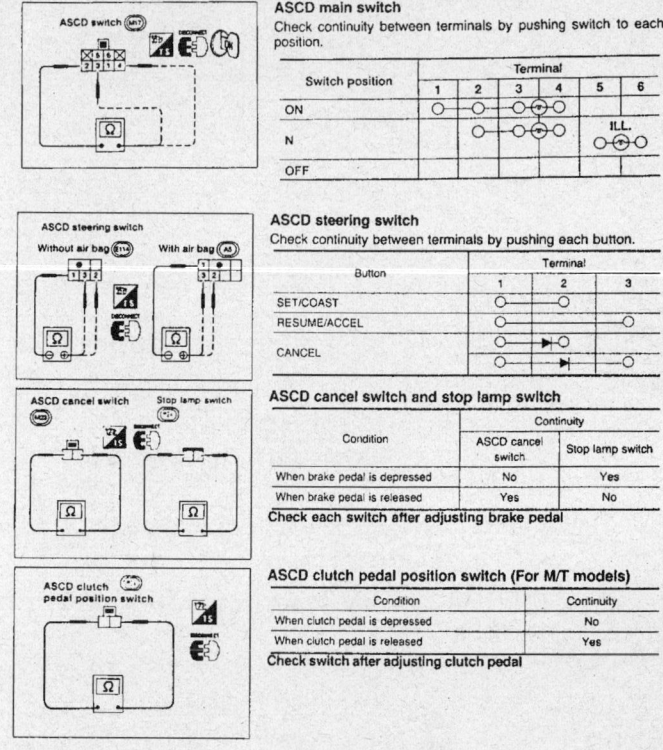

ASCD main switch
Check continuity between terminals by pushing switch to each position.

Switch position	Terminal					
	1	2	3	4	5	6
ON	○—	—○	○—(T)—○			
N		○—	—○	○—(T)—○		
OFF					○—ILL.—○	

ASCD steering switch
Check continuity between terminals by pushing each button.

Button	Terminal		
	1	2	3
SET/COAST	○—	—○	
RESUME/ACCEL	○—		—○
CANCEL	○—▶	—○	

ASCD cancel switch and stop lamp switch

Condition	Continuity	
	ASCD cancel switch	Stop lamp switch
When brake pedal is depressed	No	Yes
When brake pedal is released	Yes	No

Check each switch after adjusting brake pedal

ASCD clutch pedal position switch (For M/T models)

Condition	Continuity
When clutch pedal is depressed	No
When clutch pedal is released	Yes

Check switch after adjusting clutch pedal

Fig. 60 Electrical component check (Part 1 of 2). 1996 Altima

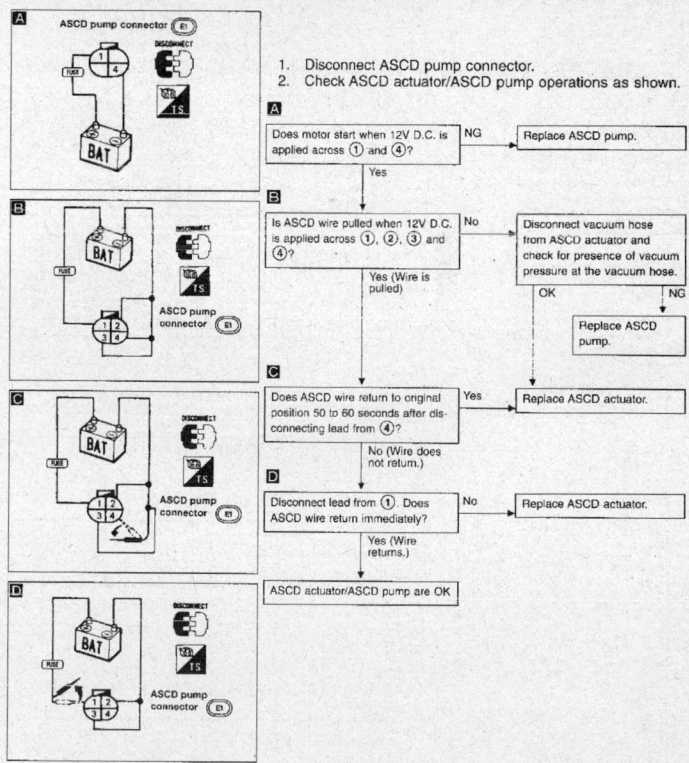

1. Disconnect ASCD pump connector.
2. Check ASCD actuator/ASCD pump operations as shown.

Fig. 61 Electrical component check (Part 1 of 3). 1997 Altima

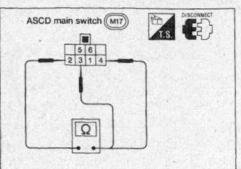

Check continuity between terminals by pushing switch to each position.

Switch position	Terminal					
	①	②	③	④	⑤	⑥
ON		○—⑪	○—⑪			
N		○—⑪	○—⑪		ILL.	
OFF					○—⑪	○

ASCD steering switch

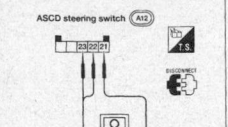
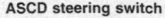

Check continuity between terminals by pushing each button.

Button	Terminal		
	㉑	㉒	㉓
SET/COAST	○	○	
RESUME/ACCEL	○		○
CANCEL	○—▶—○		
	○—▶		○

ASCD cancel switch and stop lamp switch

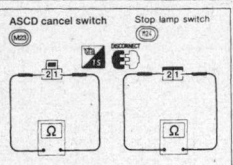

Condition	Continuity	
	ASCD cancel switch	Stop lamp switch
When brake pedal is depressed	No	Yes
When brake pedal is released	Yes	No

Check each switch after adjusting brake pedal.

ASCD cancel switch (For M/T models)

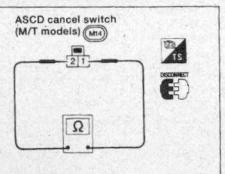

Condition	Continuity
When clutch pedal is depressed	No
When clutch pedal is released	Yes

Check switch after adjusting clutch pedal.

Inhibitor switch (For A/T models)

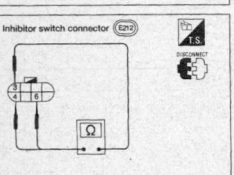

Shift lever position	Terminal		
	③	④	⑥
"P"	○	○	
"N"		○	○
Except "N" or "P"			

NS1109700142020X

Fig. 61 Electrical component check (Part 2 of 3). 1997 Altima

---

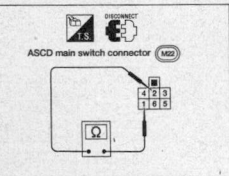

ASCD MAIN SWITCH

Check continuity between terminals by pushing switch to each position.

Switch position	Terminals					
	1	2	3	4	5	6
ON	○—○		○—○			
N		○—○		○—○		ILL.
OFF			○—⑪—○		○—⑪—○	

ASCD BRAKE SWITCH AND STOP LAMP SWITCH

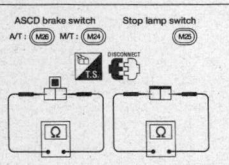

Condition	Continuity	
	ASCD brake switch	Stop lamp switch
When brake pedal is depressed	No	Yes
When brake pedal is released	Yes	No

Check each switch after adjusting brake pedal.

ASCD CLUTCH SWITCH (For M/T models)

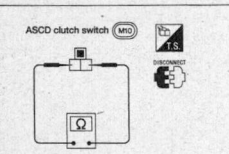

Condition	Continuity
When clutch pedal is depressed	No
When clutch pedal is released	Yes

PARK/NEUTRAL POSITION (PNP) SWITCH (For A/T models)

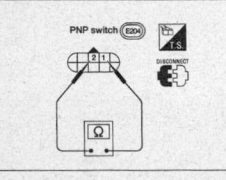

A/T selector lever position	Continuity
	Between terminals ① and ②
"P"	Yes
"N"	Yes
Except "P" and "N"	No

NS1109900183000X

Fig. 62 Electrical component check. 1998–99 Altima

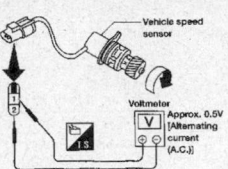

1. Remove vehicle speed sensor from transaxle.
2. Turn vehicle speed sensor pinion quickly and measure voltage across ② and ①.

NS1109700142030X

Fig. 61 Electrical component check (Part 3 of 3). 1997 Altima

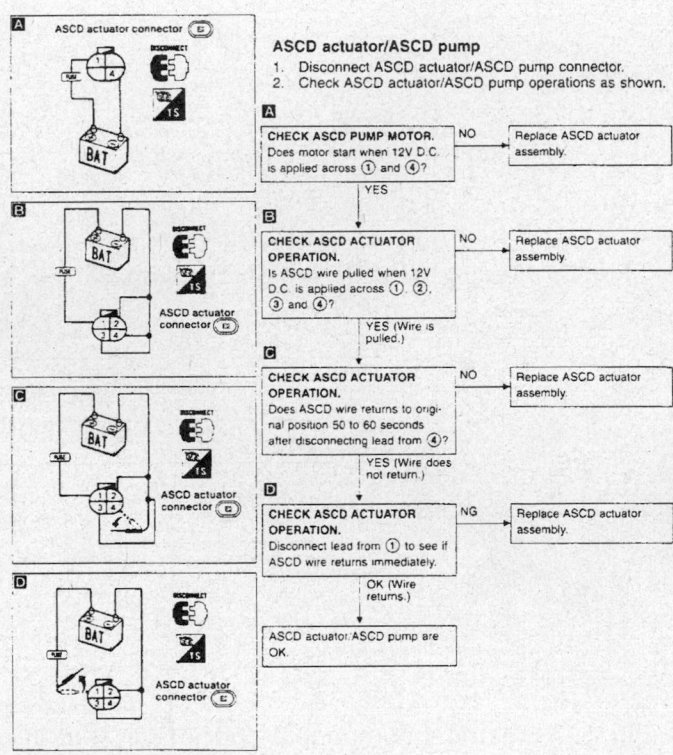

ASCD actuator/ASCD pump

1. Disconnect ASCD actuator/ASCD pump connector.
2. Check ASCD actuator/ASCD pump operations as shown.

Ⓐ CHECK ASCD PUMP MOTOR. Does motor start when 12V D.C. is applied across ① and ④? →NO→ Replace ASCD actuator assembly.

↓YES

Ⓑ CHECK ASCD ACTUATOR OPERATION. Is ASCD wire pulled when 12V D.C. is applied across ①, ②, ③ and ④? →NO→ Replace ASCD actuator assembly.

↓YES (Wire is pulled.)

Ⓒ CHECK ASCD ACTUATOR OPERATION. Does ASCD wire returns to original position 50 to 60 seconds after disconnecting lead from ④? →NO→ Replace ASCD actuator assembly.

↓YES (Wire does not return.)

Ⓓ CHECK ASCD ACTUATOR OPERATION. Disconnect lead from ① to see if ASCD wire returns immediately. →NG→ Replace ASCD actuator assembly.

↓OK (Wire returns.)

ASCD actuator/ASCD pump are OK.

NS1109500085000X

Fig. 63 Electrical component check. 1996 Sentra & 200SX

SPEED CONTROL SYSTEMS

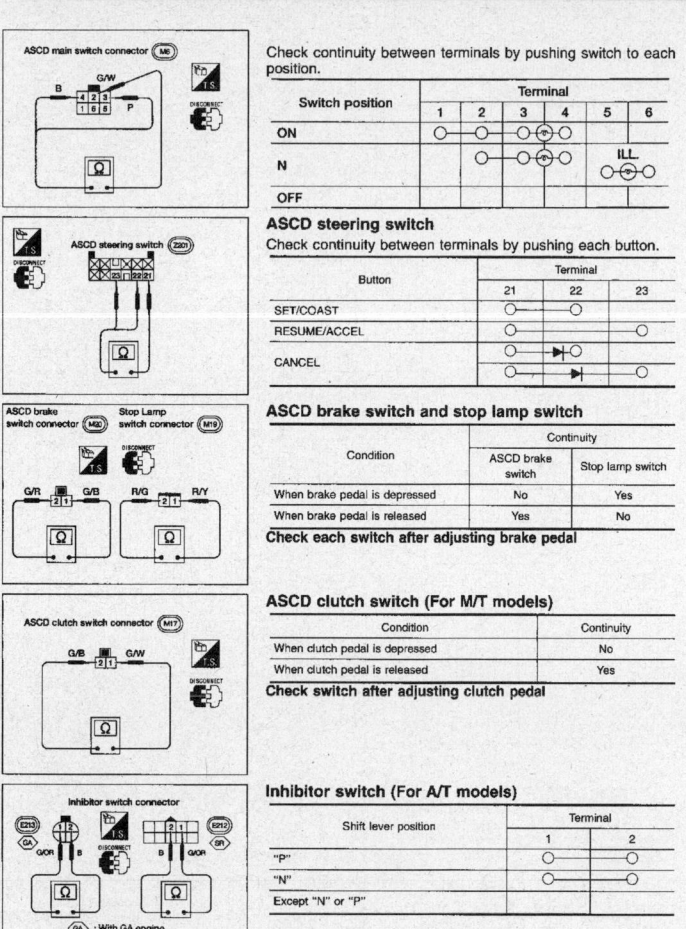

Check continuity between terminals by pushing switch to each position.

ASCD main switch connector (M6)

Switch position	Terminal					
	1	2	3	4	5	6
ON		○──○	○──(R)──○			
N			○──(R)──○		ILL.	○──(R)──○
OFF						

ASCD steering switch

Check continuity between terminals by pushing each button.

Button	Terminal		
	21	22	23
SET/COAST	○──────○		
RESUME/ACCEL	○───────────○		
CANCEL	○──▶|──○		

ASCD brake switch and stop lamp switch

Condition	Continuity	
	ASCD brake switch	Stop lamp switch
When brake pedal is depressed	No	Yes
When brake pedal is released	Yes	No

Check each switch after adjusting brake pedal

ASCD clutch switch (For M/T models)

Condition	Continuity
When clutch pedal is depressed	No
When clutch pedal is released	Yes

Check switch after adjusting clutch pedal

Inhibitor switch (For A/T models)

Shift lever position	Terminal	
	1	2
"P"	○──────○	
"N"	○──────○	
Except "N" or "P"		

(GA) : With GA engine
(SR) : With SR engine

NS1109700152000X

Fig. 64 Electrical Component Check. 1997–99 Sentra & 200SX

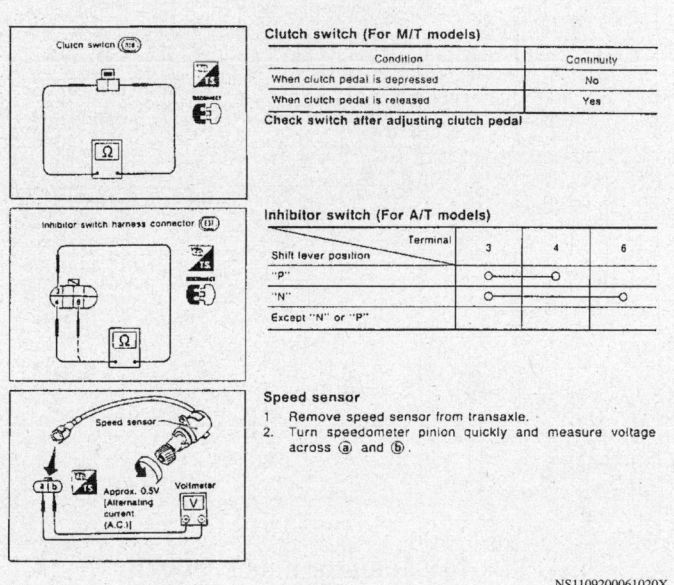

Clutch switch (For M/T models)

Condition	Continuity
When clutch pedal is depressed	No
When clutch pedal is released	Yes

Check switch after adjusting clutch pedal

Inhibitor switch (For A/T models)

Shift lever position	Terminal		
	3	4	6
"P"	○──────○		
"N"	○──────○		
Except "N" or "P"			

Speed sensor

1. Remove speed sensor from transaxle.
2. Turn speedometer pinion quickly and measure voltage across ⓐ and ⓑ.

Approx. 0.5V [Alternating current (A.C.)]

NS1109200061020X

Fig. 65 Electrical component check (Part 2 of 2). 300ZX

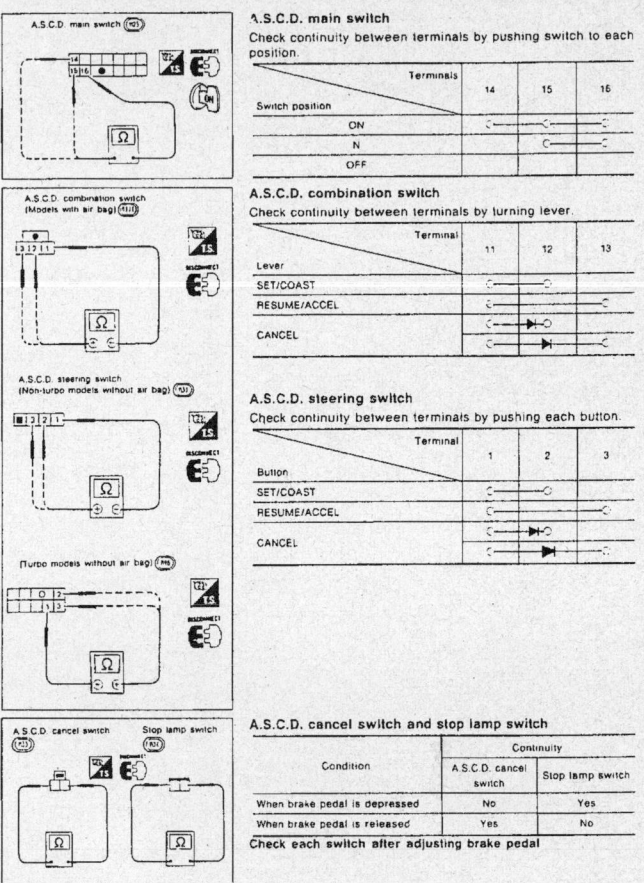

A.S.C.D. main switch

Check continuity between terminals by pushing switch to each position.

Switch position	Terminals		
	14	15	16
ON		○──○	
N		○──○	
OFF			

A.S.C.D. combination switch

Check continuity between terminals by turning lever.

Lever	Terminal		
	11	12	13
SET/COAST	○──────○		
RESUME/ACCEL	○───────────○		
CANCEL	○──▶|──○		

A.S.C.D. steering switch

Check continuity between terminals by pushing each button.

Button	Terminal		
	1	2	3
SET/COAST	○──────○		
RESUME/ACCEL	○───────────○		
CANCEL	○──▶|──○		

A.S.C.D. cancel switch and stop lamp switch

Condition	Continuity	
	A.S.C.D. cancel switch	Stop lamp switch
When brake pedal is depressed	No	Yes
When brake pedal is released	Yes	No

Check each switch after adjusting brake pedal

NS1109200061010X

Fig. 65 Electrical component check (Part 1 of 2). 300ZX

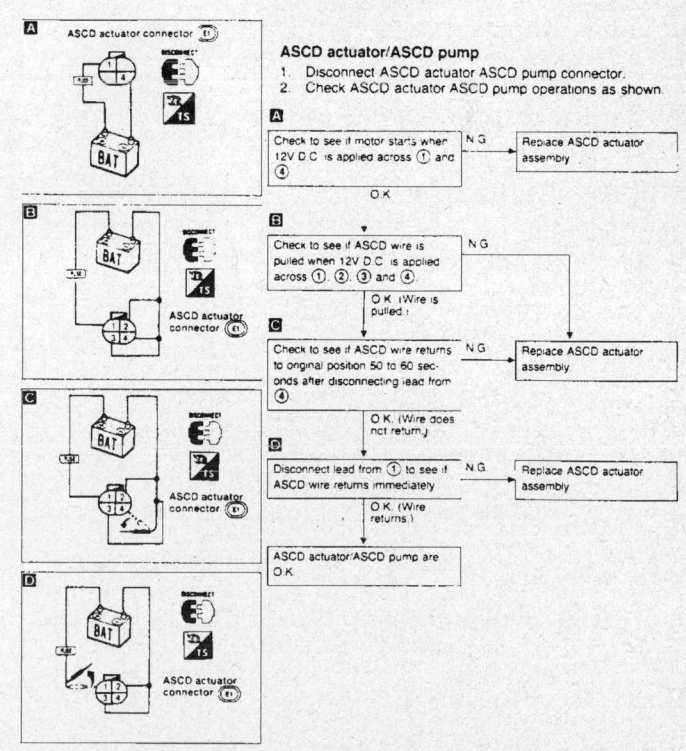

ASCD actuator/ASCD pump

1. Disconnect ASCD actuator ASCD pump connector.
2. Check ASCD actuator ASCD pump operations as shown.

A Check to see if motor starts when 12V D.C. is applied across ① and ④ — N.G → Replace ASCD actuator assembly
O.K

B Check to see if ASCD wire is pulled when 12V D.C. is applied across ①, ②, ③ and ④. — N.G → Replace ASCD actuator assembly
O.K. (Wire is pulled.)

C Check to see if ASCD wire returns to original position 50 to 60 seconds after disconnecting lead from ④. — N.G → Replace ASCD actuator assembly
O.K. (Wire does not return.)

D Disconnect lead from ① to see if ASCD wire returns immediately. — N.G → Replace ASCD actuator assembly
O.K. (Wire returns.)

ASCD actuator/ASCD pump are O.K.

NS1109100062000X

Fig. 66 Actuator Check. 1996 Altima

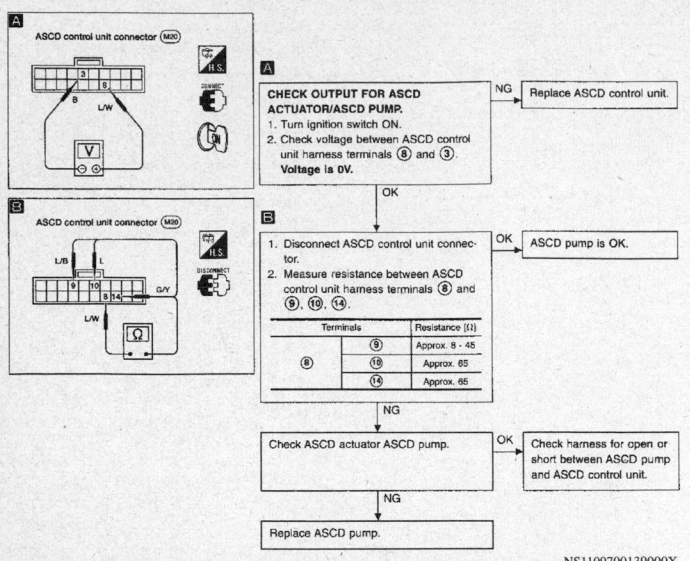

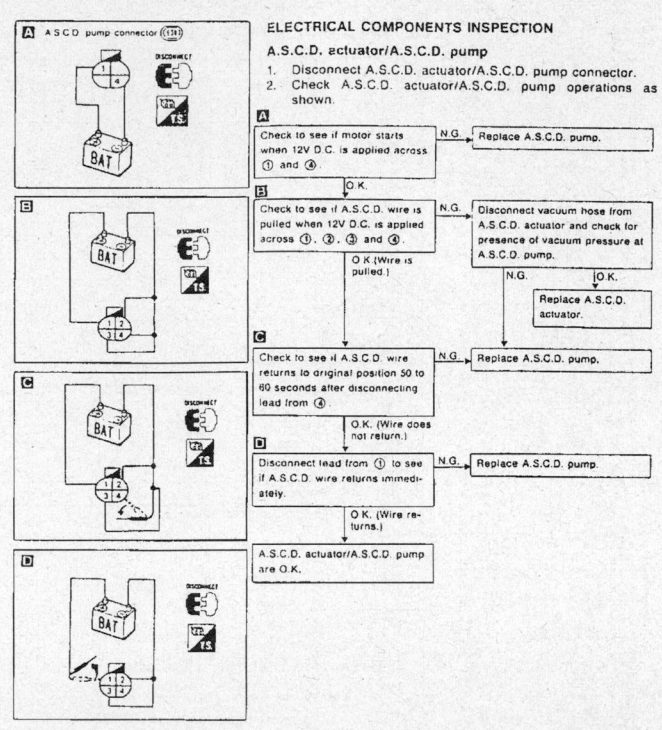

Fig. 68 Actuator Check. 1996 Sentra & 200SX

Fig. 67 Actuator Check. 1997 Altima

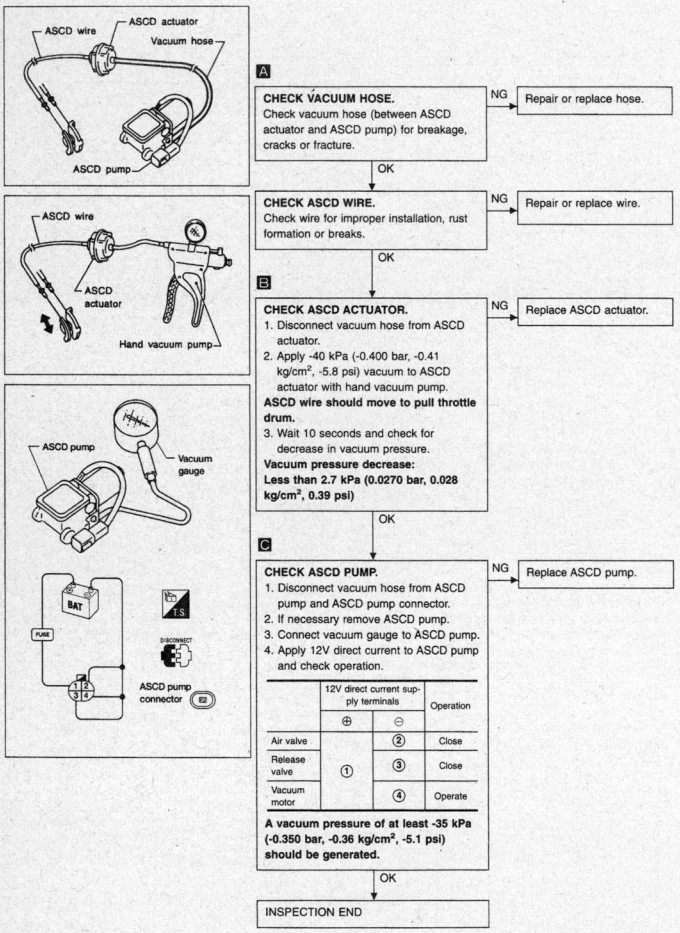

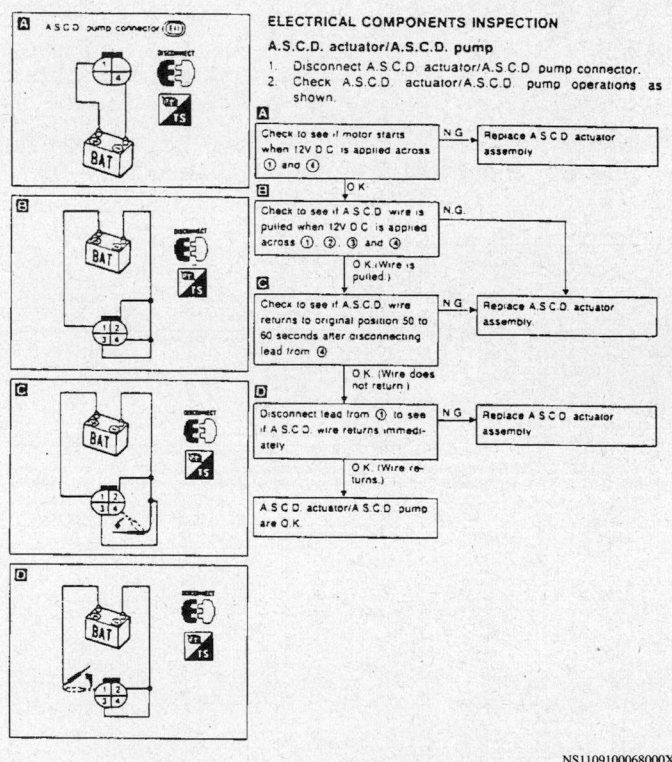

Fig. 69 Actuator/Pump Circuit Check. 1997–99
Sentra & 200SX

Fig. 70 Actuator check. 300ZX

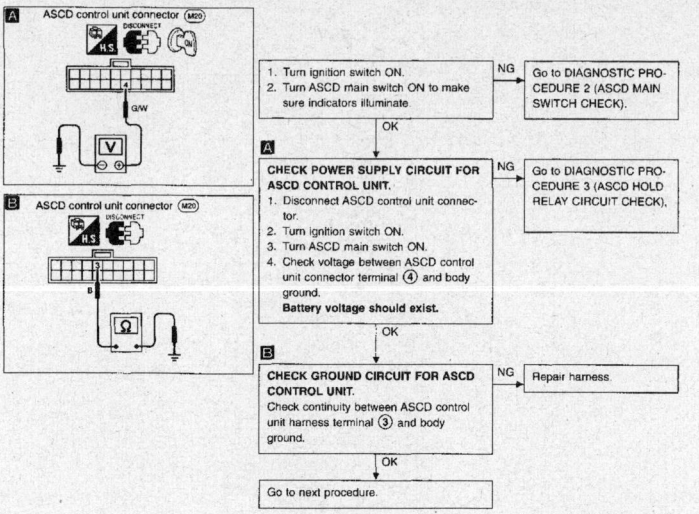

1. Turn ignition switch ON.
2. Turn ASCD main switch ON to make sure indicators illuminate.
NG → Go to DIAGNOSTIC PROCEDURE 2 (ASCD MAIN SWITCH CHECK).

OK

A
CHECK POWER SUPPLY CIRCUIT FOR ASCD CONTROL UNIT.
1. Disconnect ASCD control unit connector.
2. Turn ignition switch ON.
3. Turn ASCD main switch ON.
4. Check voltage between ASCD control unit connector terminal ④ and body ground.
Battery voltage should exist.
NG → Go to DIAGNOSTIC PROCEDURE 3 (ASCD HOLD RELAY CIRCUIT CHECK).

OK

B
CHECK GROUND CIRCUIT FOR ASCD CONTROL UNIT.
Check continuity between ASCD control unit harness terminal ③ and body ground.
NG → Repair harness.

OK

Go to next procedure.

NS1109700133000X

Fig. 71 Power Supply & Ground Circuit. 1997 Altima

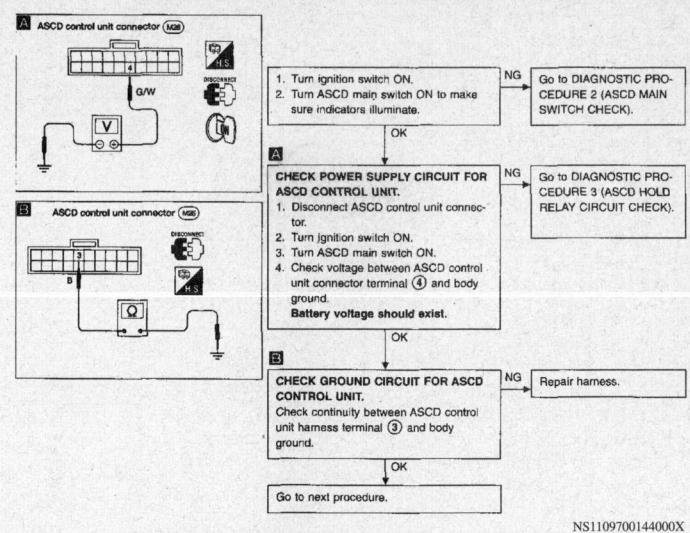

1. Turn ignition switch ON.
2. Turn ASCD main switch ON to make sure indicators illuminate.
NG → Go to DIAGNOSTIC PROCEDURE 2 (ASCD MAIN SWITCH CHECK).

OK

A
CHECK POWER SUPPLY CIRCUIT FOR ASCD CONTROL UNIT.
1. Disconnect ASCD control unit connector.
2. Turn ignition switch ON.
3. Turn ASCD main switch ON.
4. Check voltage between ASCD control unit connector terminal ④ and body ground.
Battery voltage should exist.
NG → Go to DIAGNOSTIC PROCEDURE 3 (ASCD HOLD RELAY CIRCUIT CHECK).

OK

B
CHECK GROUND CIRCUIT FOR ASCD CONTROL UNIT.
Check continuity between ASCD control unit harness terminal ③ and body ground.
NG → Repair harness.

OK

Go to next procedure.

NS1109700144000X

Fig. 72 Power Supply & Ground Circuit. 1997–98 Sentra & 200SX

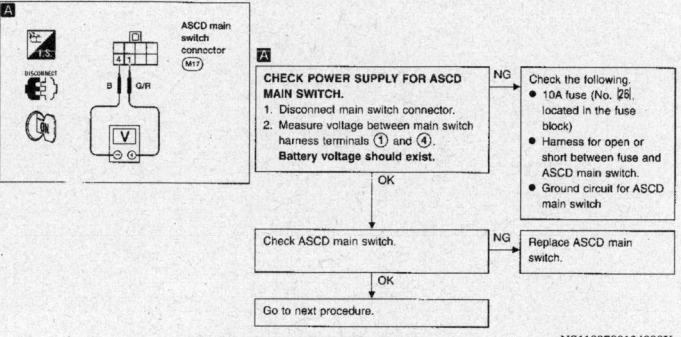

A
CHECK POWER SUPPLY FOR ASCD MAIN SWITCH.
1. Disconnect main switch connector.
2. Measure voltage between main switch harness terminals ① and ④.
Battery voltage should exist.
NG → Check the following.
● 10A fuse (No. 25), located in the fuse block)
● Harness for open or short between fuse and ASCD main switch.
● Ground circuit for ASCD main switch

OK

Check ASCD main switch.
NG → Replace ASCD main switch.

OK

Go to next procedure.

NS1109700134000X

Fig. 73 ASCD Main Switch. 1997 Altima

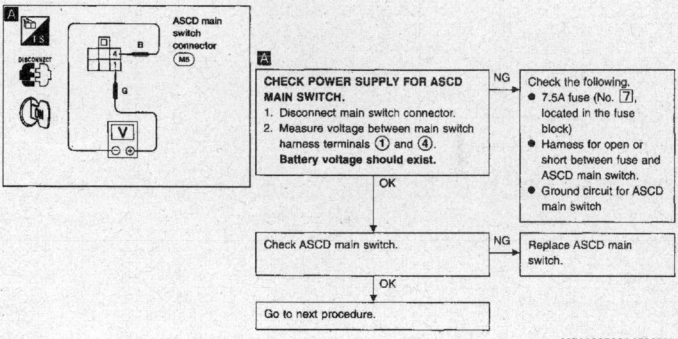

A
CHECK POWER SUPPLY FOR ASCD MAIN SWITCH.
1. Disconnect main switch connector.
2. Measure voltage between main switch harness terminals ① and ④.
Battery voltage should exist.
NG → Check the following.
● 7.5A fuse (No. 7), located in the fuse block)
● Harness for open or short between fuse and ASCD main switch.
● Ground circuit for ASCD main switch

OK

Check ASCD main switch.
NG → Replace ASCD main switch.

OK

Go to next procedure.

NS1109700145000X

Fig. 74 ASCD Main Switch. 1997–98 Sentra & 200SX

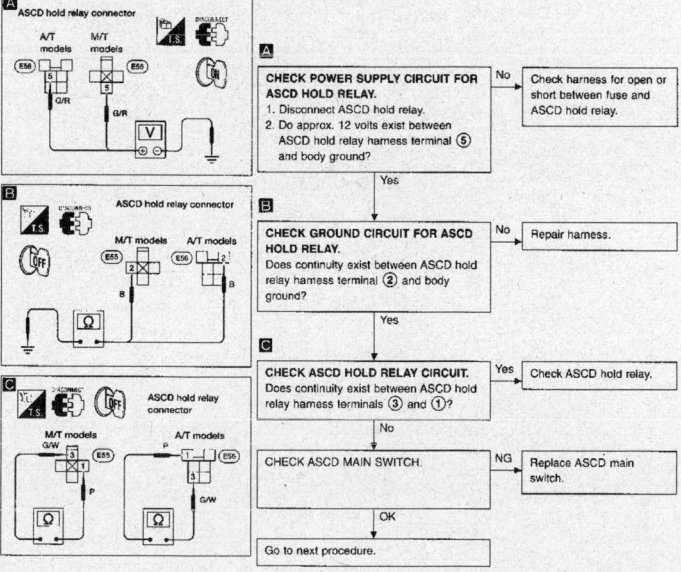

A
CHECK POWER SUPPLY CIRCUIT FOR ASCD HOLD RELAY.
1. Disconnect ASCD hold relay.
2. Do approx. 12 volts exist between ASCD hold relay harness terminal ⑤ and body ground?
No → Check harness for open or short between fuse and ASCD hold relay.

Yes

B
CHECK GROUND CIRCUIT FOR ASCD HOLD RELAY.
Does continuity exist between ASCD hold relay harness terminal ② and body ground?
No → Repair harness.

Yes

C
CHECK ASCD HOLD RELAY CIRCUIT.
Does continuity exist between ASCD hold relay harness terminals ③ and ①?
Yes → Check ASCD hold relay.

No

CHECK ASCD MAIN SWITCH.
NG → Replace ASCD main switch.

OK

Go to next procedure.

NS1109700135000X

Fig. 75 ASCD Hold Relay Circuit. 1997 Altima

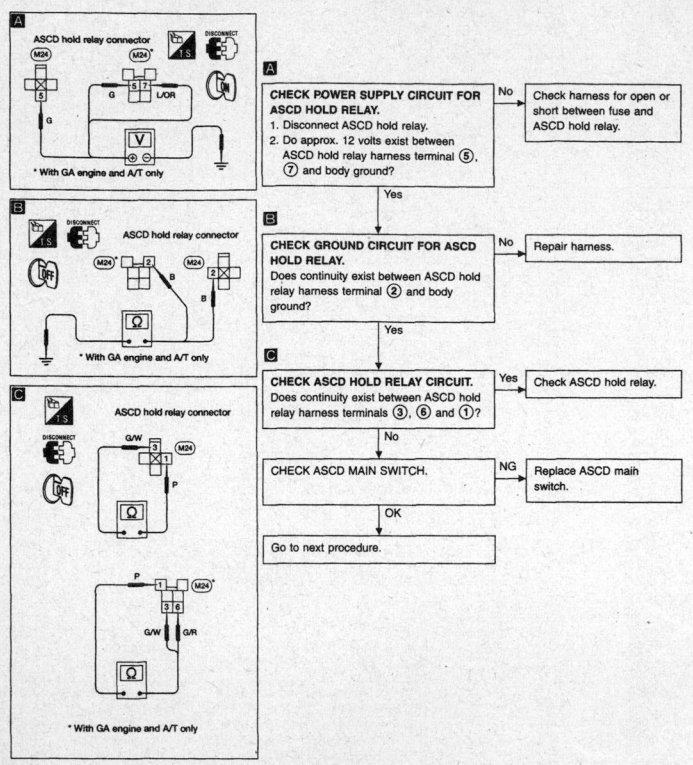

Fig. 76   ASCD Hold Relay Circuit. 1997–99 Sentra & 200SX

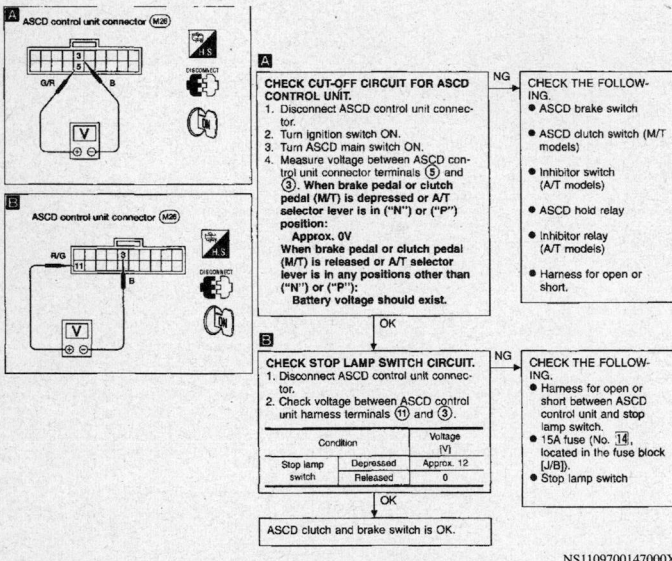

Fig. 78   ASCD Clutch & Brake Switch. 1997–99 Sentra & 200SX

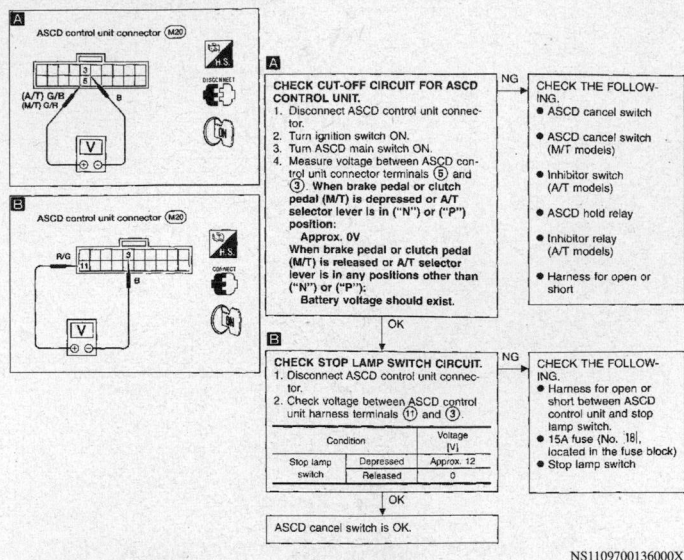

Fig. 77   ASCD Cancel Switch. 1997 Altima

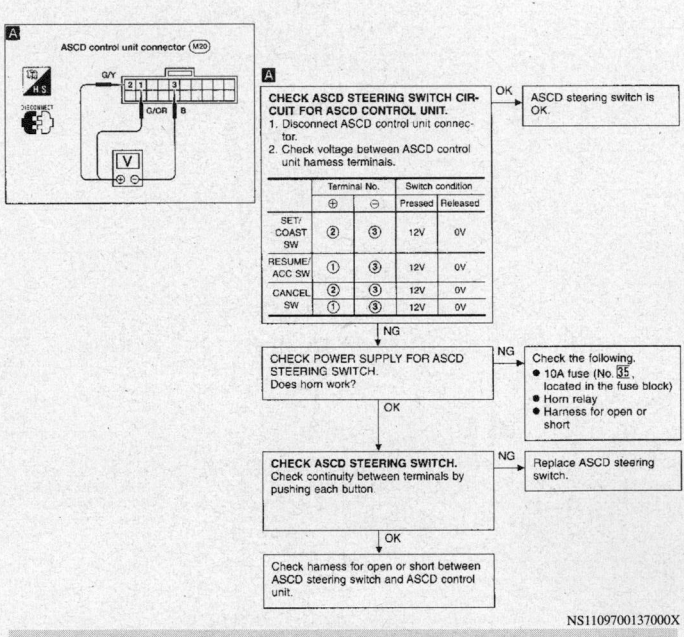

Fig. 79   ASCD Steering Switch. 1997 Altima

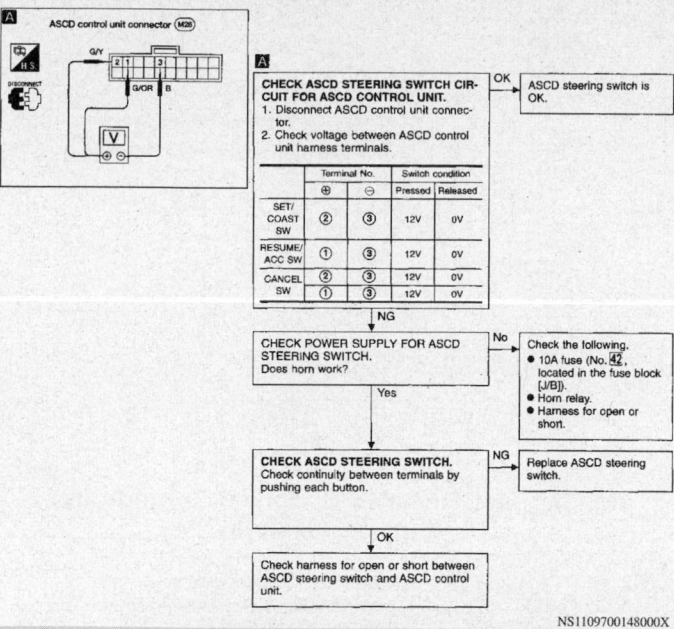

CHECK ASCD STEERING SWITCH CIRCUIT FOR ASCD CONTROL UNIT.
1. Disconnect ASCD control unit connector.
2. Check voltage between ASCD control unit harness terminals.

OK → ASCD steering switch is OK.

	Terminal No.		Switch condition	
	⊕	⊖	Pressed	Released
SET/COAST SW	②	③	12V	0V
RESUME/ACC SW	①	③	12V	0V
CANCEL SW	②	③	12V	0V
	①	③	12V	0V

↓ NG

CHECK POWER SUPPLY FOR ASCD STEERING SWITCH.
Does horn work?

No → Check the following.
- 10A fuse (No. 42, located in the fuse block [J/B]).
- Horn relay.
- Harness for open or short.

↓ Yes

CHECK ASCD STEERING SWITCH.
Check continuity between terminals by pushing each button.

NG → Replace ASCD steering switch.

↓ OK

Check harness for open or short between ASCD steering switch and ASCD control unit.

NS1109700148000X

Fig. 80 ASCD Steering Switch Check. 1997–99 Sentra & 200SX

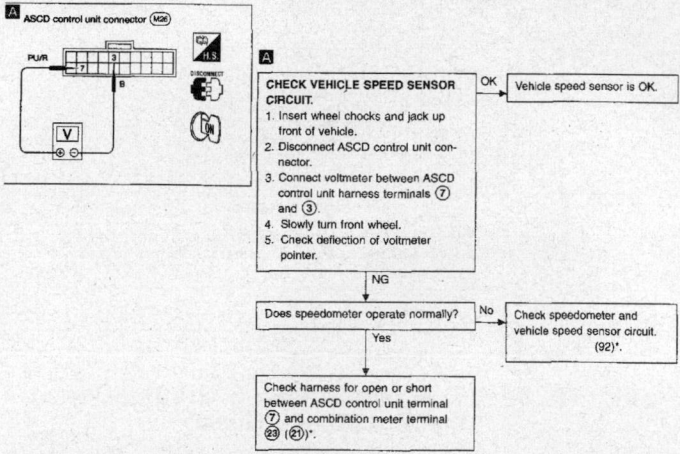

CHECK VEHICLE SPEED SENSOR CIRCUIT.
1. Insert wheel chocks and jack up front of vehicle.
2. Disconnect ASCD control unit connector.
3. Connect voltmeter between ASCD control unit harness terminals ⑦ and ③.
4. Slowly turn front wheel.
5. Check deflection of voltmeter pointer.

OK → Vehicle speed sensor is OK.

↓ NG

Does speedometer operate normally?

No → Check speedometer and vehicle speed sensor circuit. (92)*.

↓ Yes

Check harness for open or short between ASCD control unit terminal ⑦ and combination meter terminal ㉓ (㉑)*.

*: Terminal numbers in ( ) are for models without tachometer.

NS1109700149000X

Fig. 82 Vehicle Speed Sensor. 1997–99 Sentra & 200SX

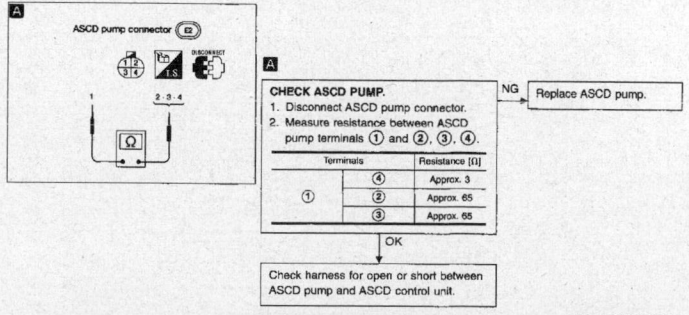

CHECK ASCD PUMP.
1. Disconnect ASCD pump connector.
2. Measure resistance between ASCD pump terminals ① and ②, ③, ④.

NG → Replace ASCD pump.

Terminals		Resistance [Ω]
①	④	Approx. 3
	②	Approx. 65
	③	Approx. 65

↓ OK

Check harness for open or short between ASCD pump and ASCD control unit.

NS1109700150000X

Fig. 84 ASCD Pump Circuit. 1997–99 Sentra & 200SX

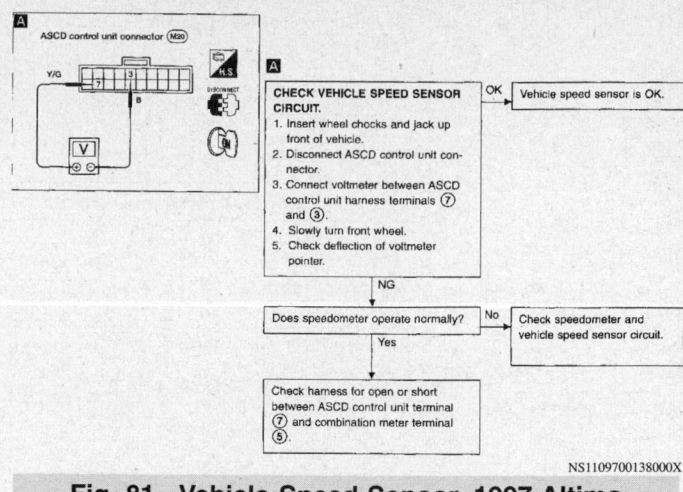

CHECK VEHICLE SPEED SENSOR CIRCUIT.
1. Insert wheel chocks and jack up front of vehicle.
2. Disconnect ASCD control unit connector.
3. Connect voltmeter between ASCD control unit harness terminals ⑦ and ③.
4. Slowly turn front wheel.
5. Check deflection of voltmeter pointer.

OK → Vehicle speed sensor is OK.

↓ NG

Does speedometer operate normally?

No → Check speedometer and vehicle speed sensor circuit.

↓ Yes

Check harness for open or short between ASCD control unit terminal ⑦ and combination meter terminal ⑤.

NS1109700138000X

Fig. 81 Vehicle Speed Sensor. 1997 Altima

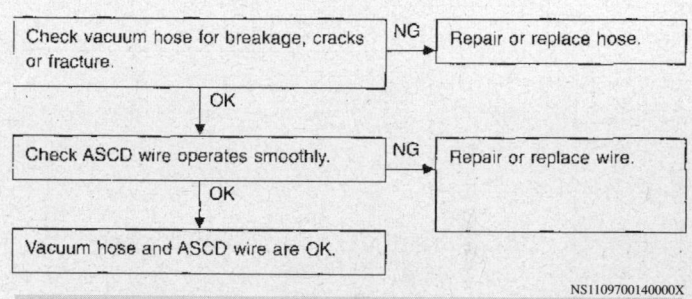

Check vacuum hose for breakage, cracks or fracture.

NG → Repair or replace hose.

↓ OK

Check ASCD wire operates smoothly.

NG → Repair or replace wire.

↓ OK

Vacuum hose and ASCD wire are OK.

NS1109700140000X

Fig. 83 Vacuum Hose & ACCEL Wire Inspection. 1997 Altima

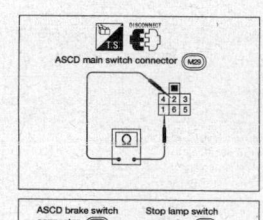

ASCD MAIN SWITCH
Check continuity between terminals by pushing switch to each position.

Switch position	Terminals					
	1	2	3	4	5	6
ON		○—○	○	○	ILL	
N			○—○		○—○	
OFF					○—○	

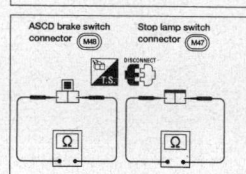

ASCD BRAKE SWITCH AND STOP LAMP SWITCH

Condition	Continuity	
	ASCD brake switch	Stop lamp switch
When brake pedal is depressed	No	Yes
When brake pedal is released	Yes	No

Check each switch after adjusting brake pedal.

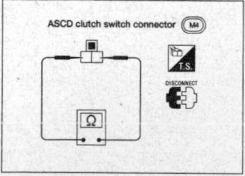

ASCD CLUTCH SWITCH (For M/T models)

Condition	Continuity
When clutch pedal is depressed	No
When clutch pedal is released	Yes

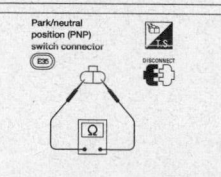

PARK/NEUTRAL POSITION (PNP) SWITCH (For A/T models)

A/T selector lever position	Continuity
	Between terminals
P	Yes
N	Yes
Except P and N	No

NS1109900184000X

Fig. 85 ASCD electrical component inspection. Frontier

Electrical Component Inspection

ASCD MAIN SWITCH

Check continuity between terminals by pushing switch to each position.

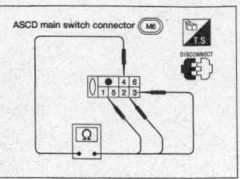

Switch position	Terminals	Illumination
ON	1 - 2 - 3 - 4	
N	2 - 3 - 4	5 - 6
OFF		

ASCD BRAKE SWITCH AND STOP LAMP SWITCH

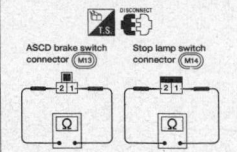

Condition	Continuity	
	ASCD brake switch	Stop lamp switch
When brake pedal is depressed	No	Yes
When brake pedal is released	Yes	No

Check each switch after adjusting brake pedal.

PARK NEUTRAL POSITION (PNP) SWITCH

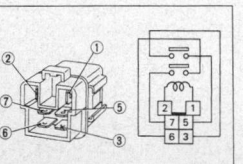

Selector lever position	Continuity
	Between terminals 1 and 2
P	Yes
N	Yes
Except P and N	No

ASCD HOLD RELAY

Check continuity between terminals 3 and 5, 6 and 7.

Condition	Continuity
12V DC direct current supply between terminals 1 and 2	Yes
No current supply	No

NS1109900185000X

Fig. 86   ASCD electrical component inspection. 1999 Quest

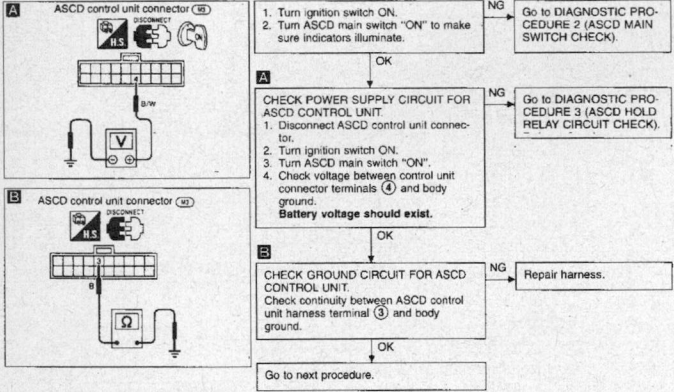

NS1109600095000X

Fig. 88   Test 1: Power Supply & Ground Circuit Check. Pathfinder & Pickup

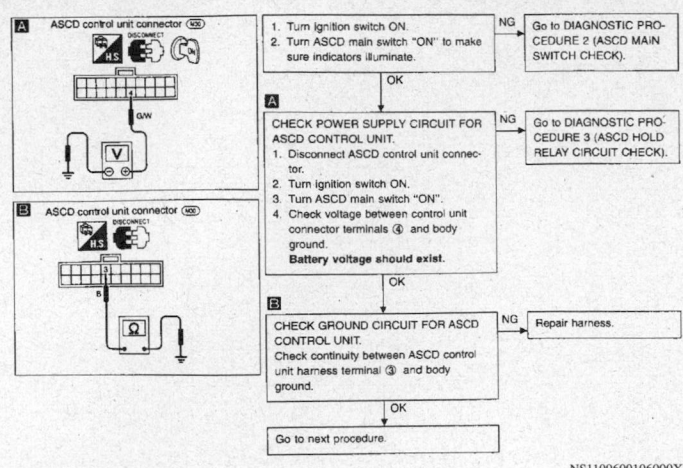

NS1109600106000X

Fig. 87   Test 1: Power Supply & Ground Circuit Check. Maxima

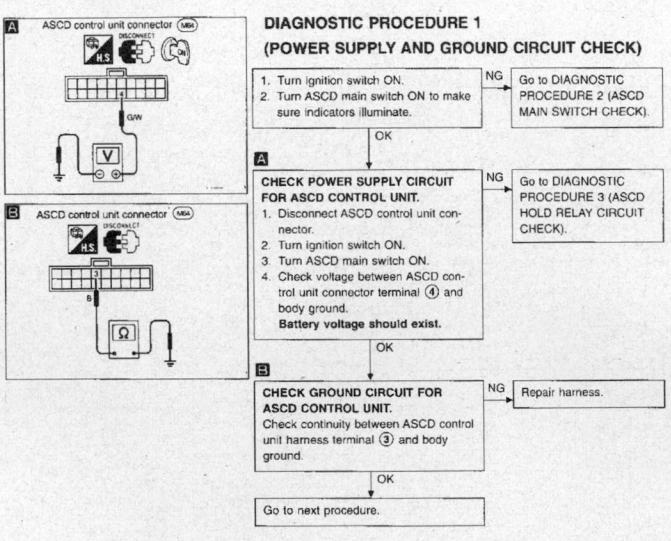

DIAGNOSTIC PROCEDURE 1
(POWER SUPPLY AND GROUND CIRCUIT CHECK)

NS1109600113000X

Fig. 89   Test 1: Power Supply & Ground Circuit Check. 1996–98 Quest

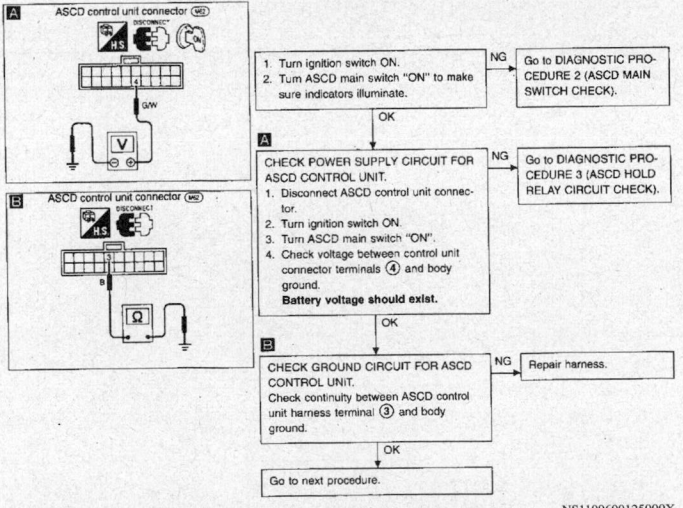

NS1109600125000X

Fig. 90   Test 1: Power Supply & Ground Circuit Check. 240SX

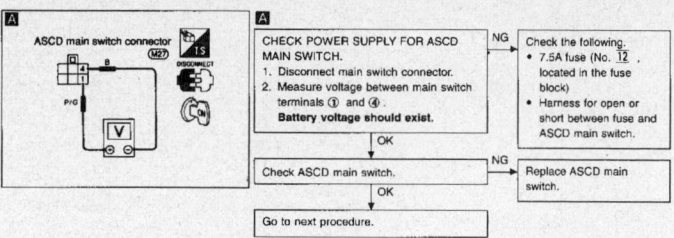

Fig. 91   Test 2: ASCD Main Switch Check. 1996–97 Maxima

NS1109600120000X

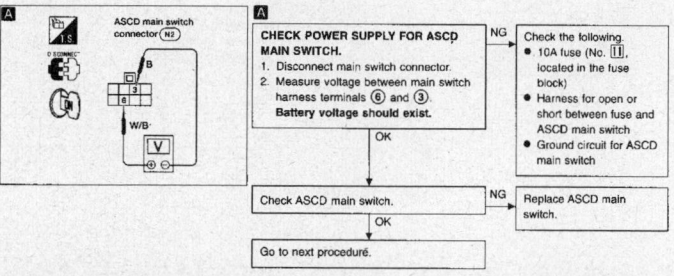

Fig. 93   Test 2: ASCD Main Switch Check. 1996–97 Pickup

NS1109600103000X

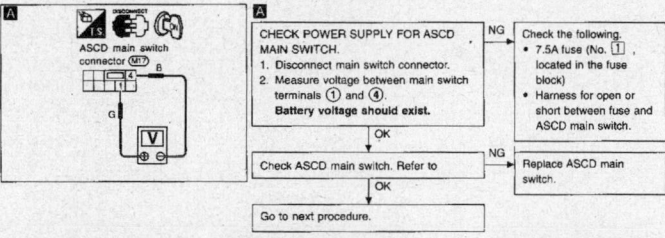

Fig. 95   Test 2: ASCD Main Switch Check. 1996–97 240SX

NS1109600126000X

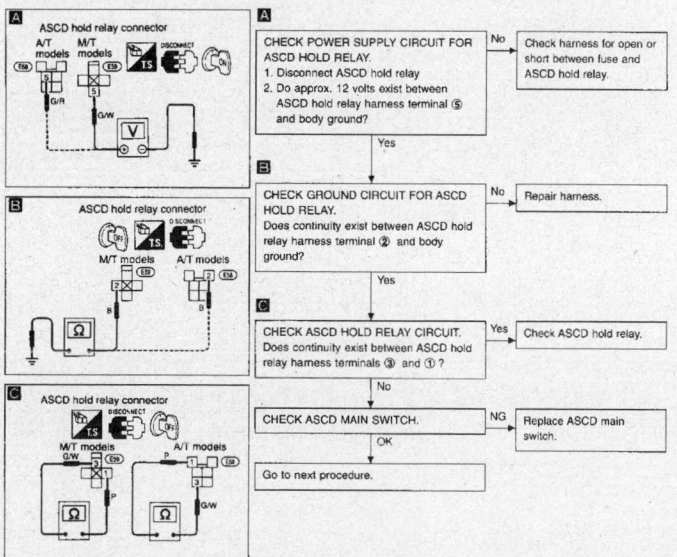

NS1109600107000X

Fig. 96   Test 3: ASCD Hold Relay Circuit Check. 1996–97 Maxima

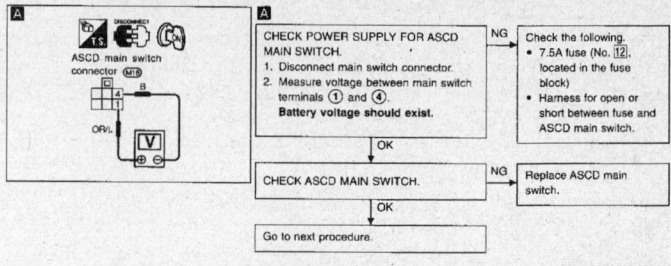

NS1109600096000X

Fig. 92   Test 2: ASCD Main Switch Check. 1996–97 Pathfinder

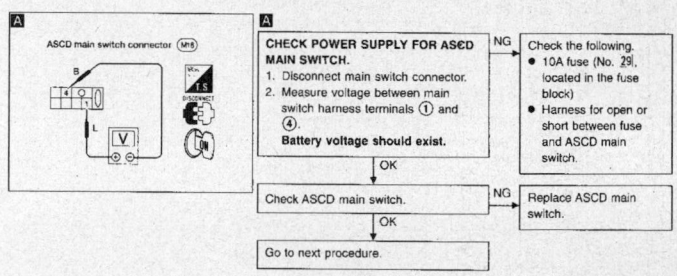

NS1109600121000X

Fig. 94   Test 2: ASCD Main Switch Check. 1996–97 Quest

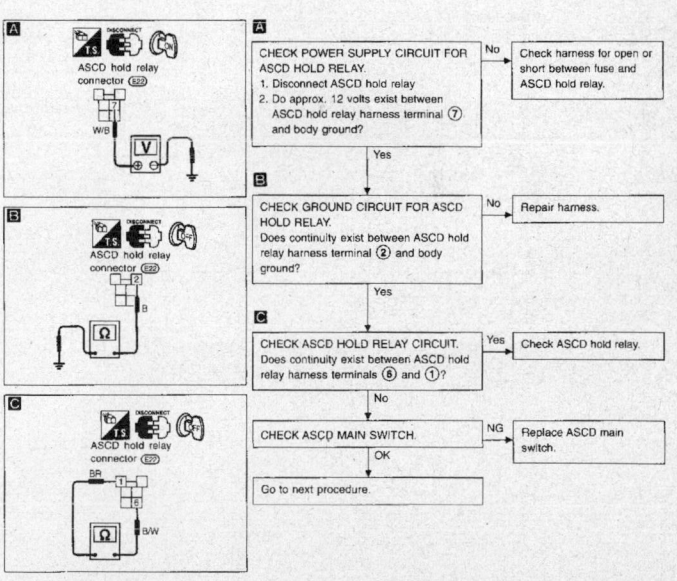

NS1109600097000X

Fig. 97   Test 3: ASCD Hold Relay Circuit Check. 1996–97 Pathfinder

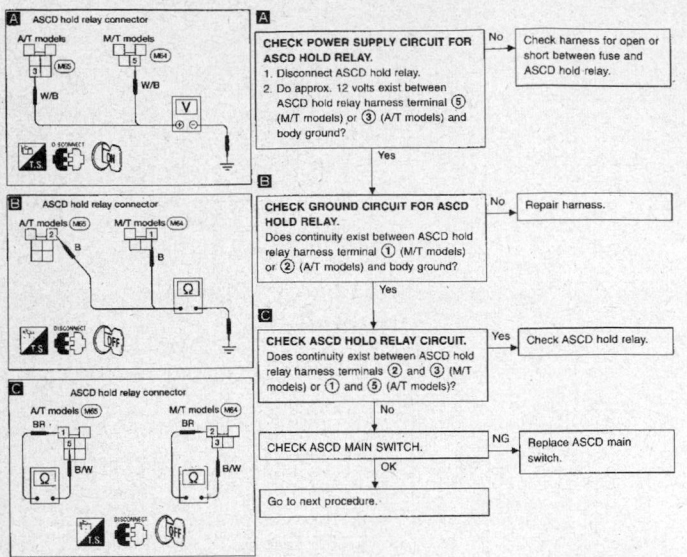

**Fig. 98   Test 3: ASCD Hold Relay Circuit Check.
1996–97 Pickup**

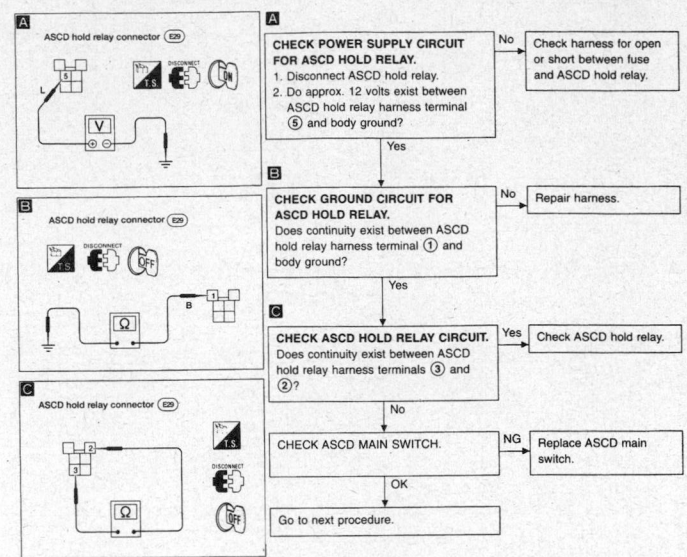

**Fig. 99   Test 3: ASCD Hold Relay Circuit Check.
1996–97 Quest**

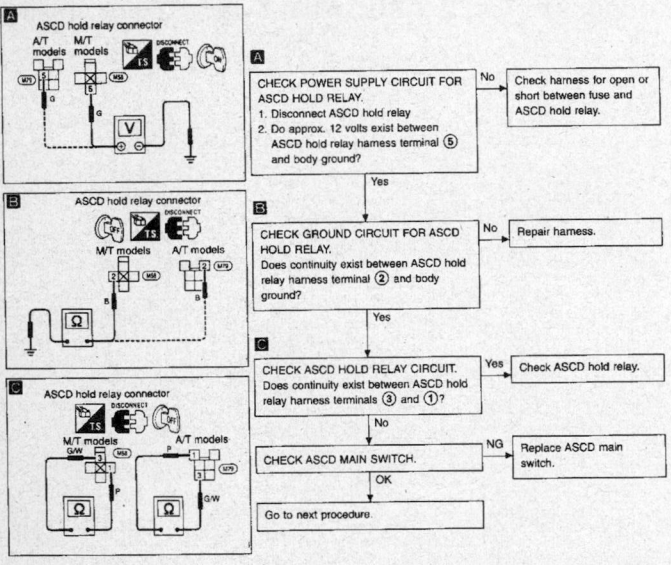

**Fig. 100   Test 3: ASCD Hold Relay Circuit Check.
1996–97 240SX**

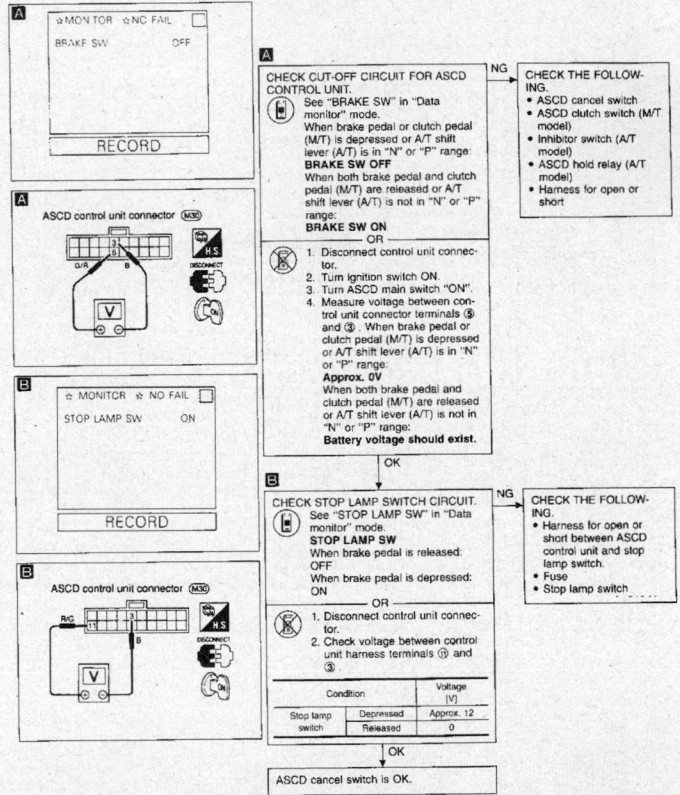

**Fig. 101   Test 4: ASCD Cancel Switch Check.
1996–97 Maxima**

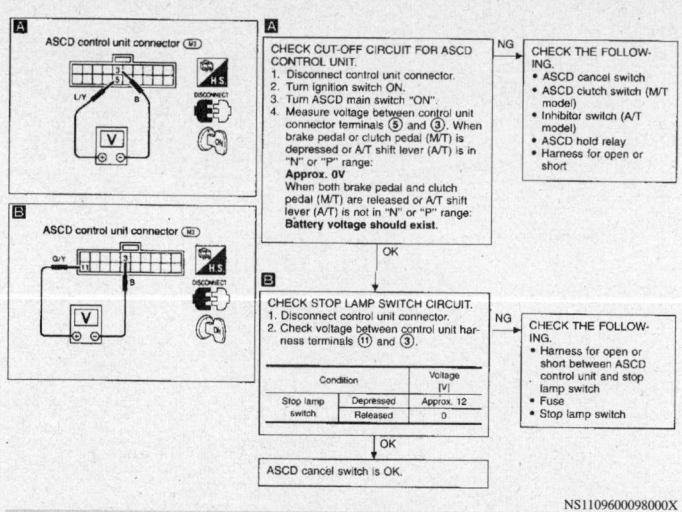

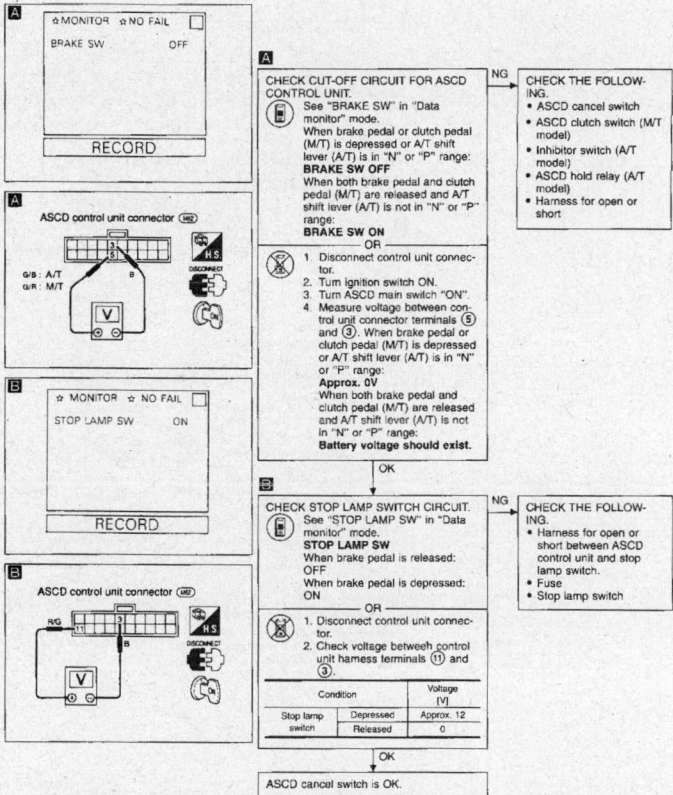

Fig. 102   Test 4: ASCD Cancel Switch Check. 1996–97 Pathfinder & Pickup

NS1109600098000X

Fig. 104   Test 4: ASCD Cancel Switch Check. 1996–97 240SX

NS1109600128000X

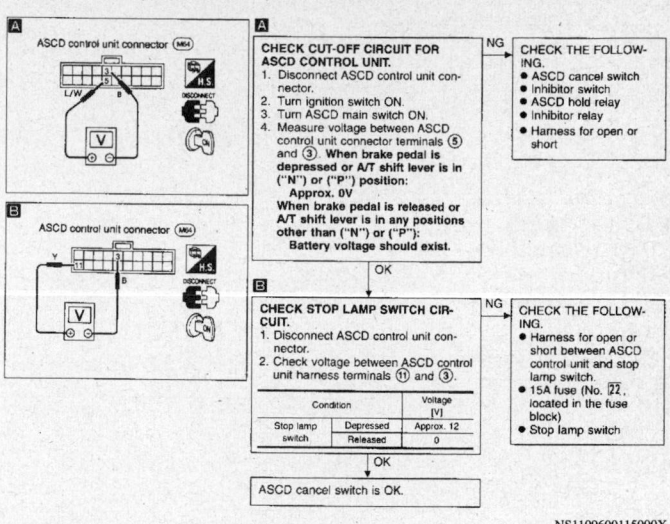

Fig. 103   Test 4: ASCD Cancel Switch Check. 1996–97 Quest

NS1109600115000X

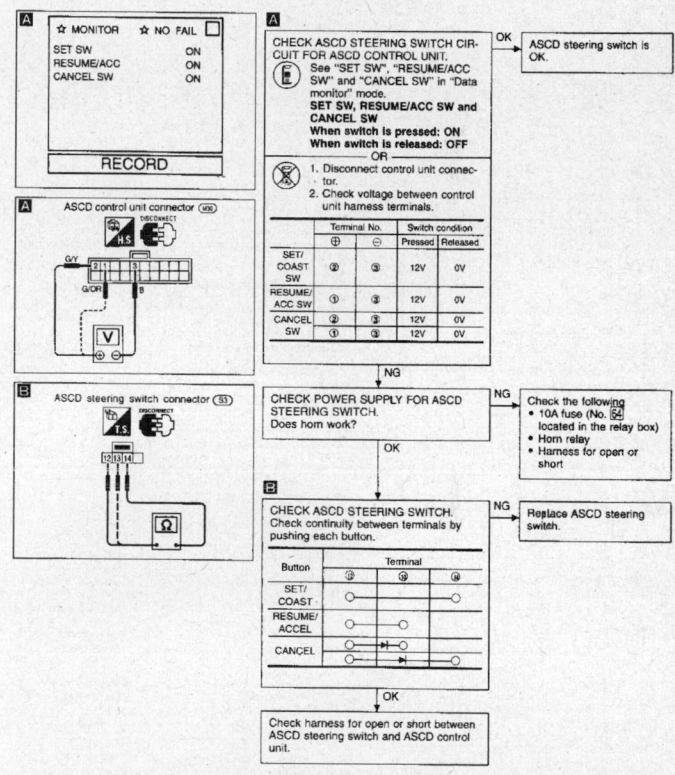

Fig. 105   Test 5: ASCD Steering Switch Check. 1996–97 Maxima

NS1109600109000X

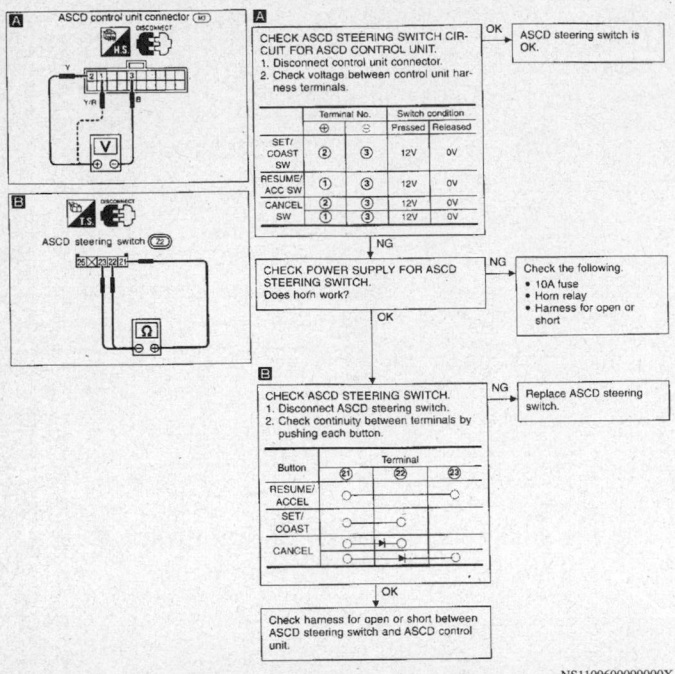

**Fig. 106 Test 5: ASCD Steering Switch Check.
1996–97 Pathfinder & Pickup**

NS1109600099000X

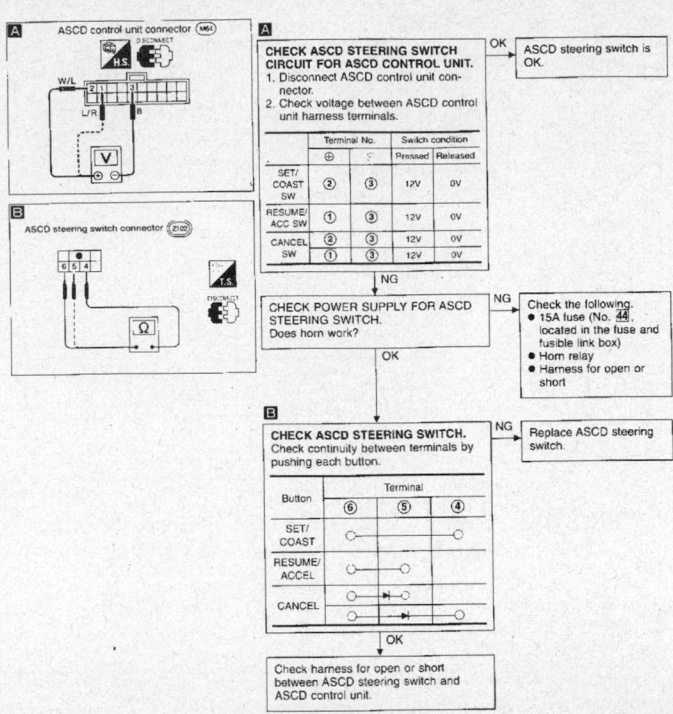

NS1109600116000X

**Fig. 107 Test 5: ASCD Steering Switch Check.
1996–97 Quest**

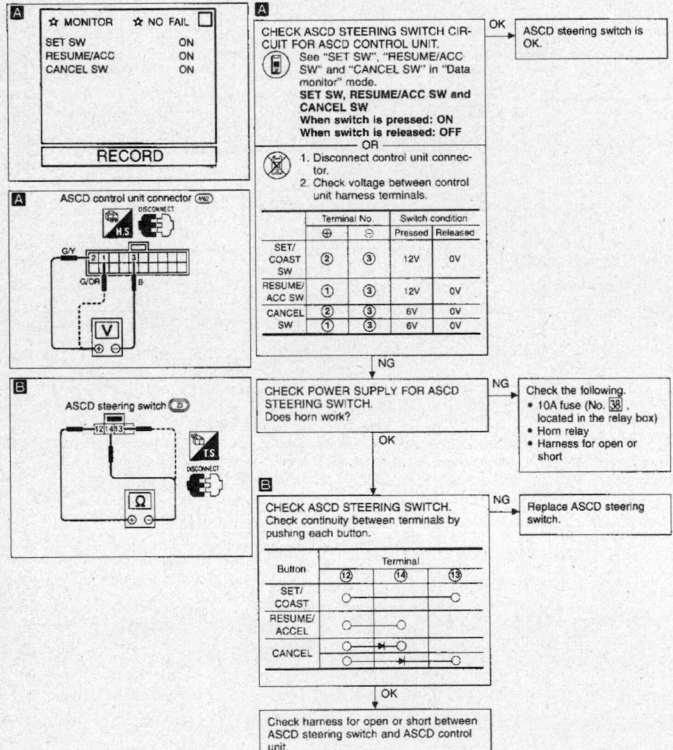

NS1109600129000X

**Fig. 108 Test 5: ASCD Steering Switch Check.
1996–97 240SX**

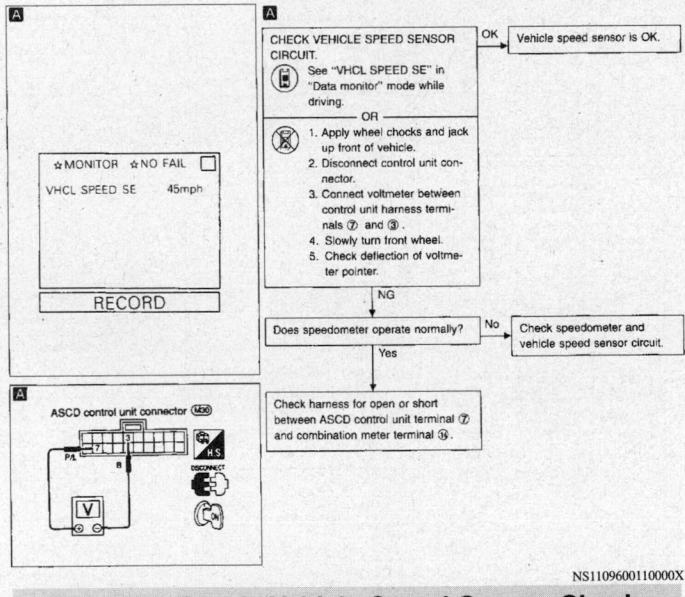

NS1109600110000X

**Fig. 109 Test 6: Vehicle Speed Sensor Check.
1996–97 Maxima**

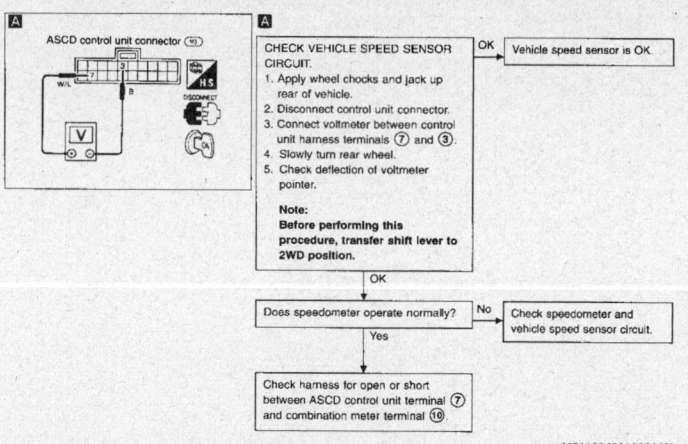

**Fig. 110   Test 6: Vehicle Speed Sensor Check.
1996–97 Pathfinder**

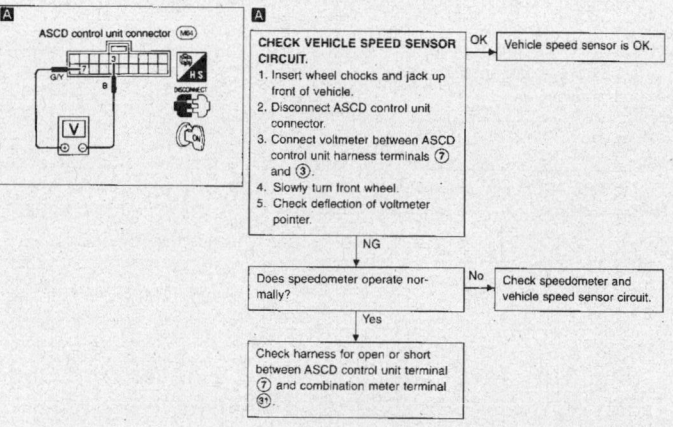

**Fig. 112   Test 6: Vehicle Speed Sensor Check.
1996–97 Quest**

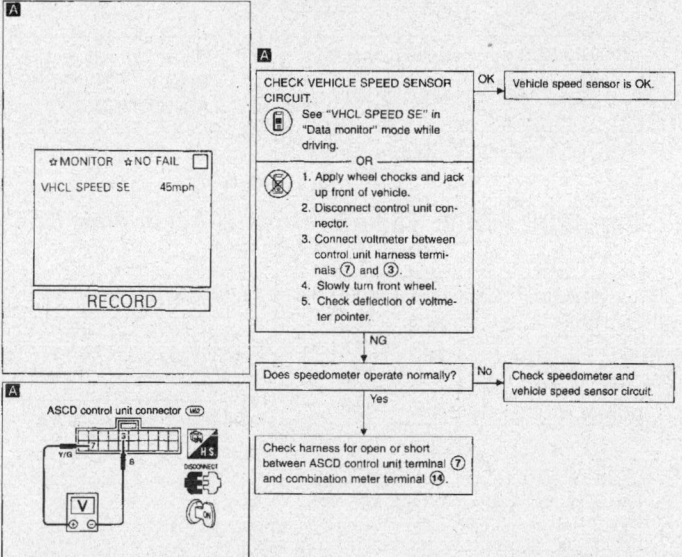

**Fig. 113   Test 6: Vehicle Speed Sensor Check.
1996–97 240SX**

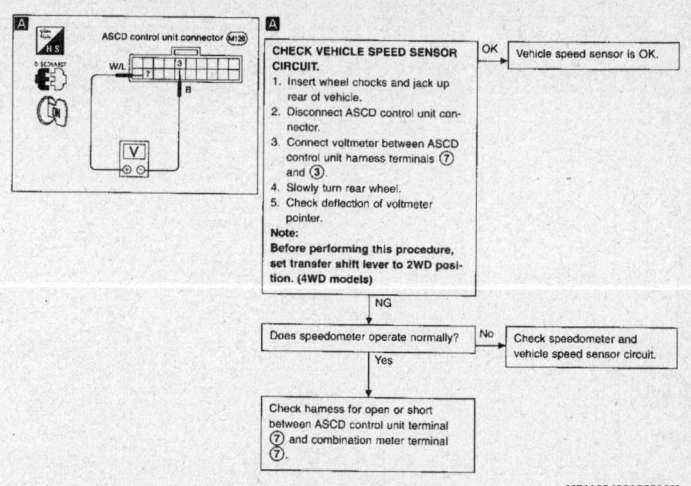

**Fig. 111   Test 6: Vehicle Speed Sensor Check.
1996–97 Pickup**

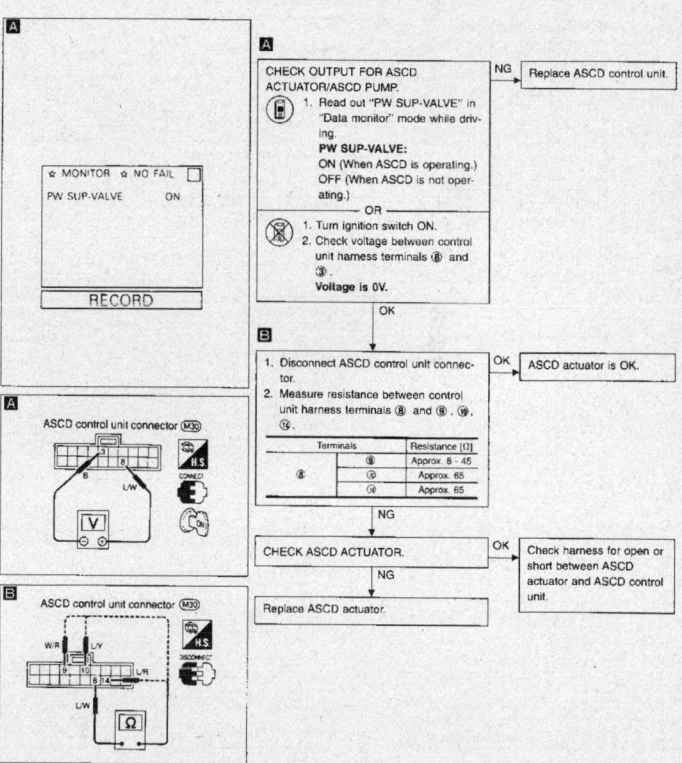

**Fig. 114   Test 7: ASCD Actuator Check. 1996–97
Maxima**

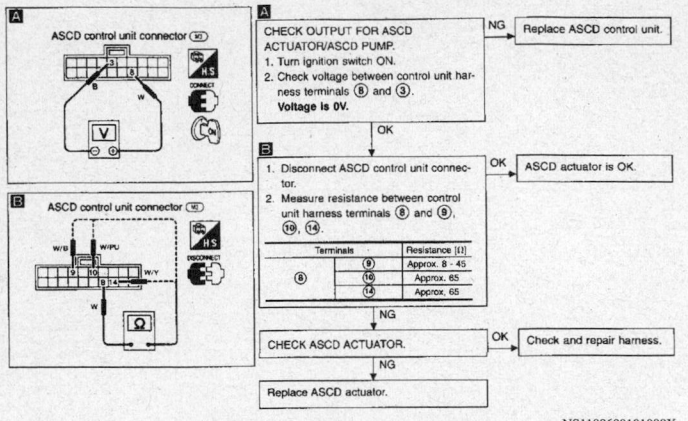

Fig. 115 Test 7: ASCD Actuator Check. 1996–97 Pathfinder & Pickup

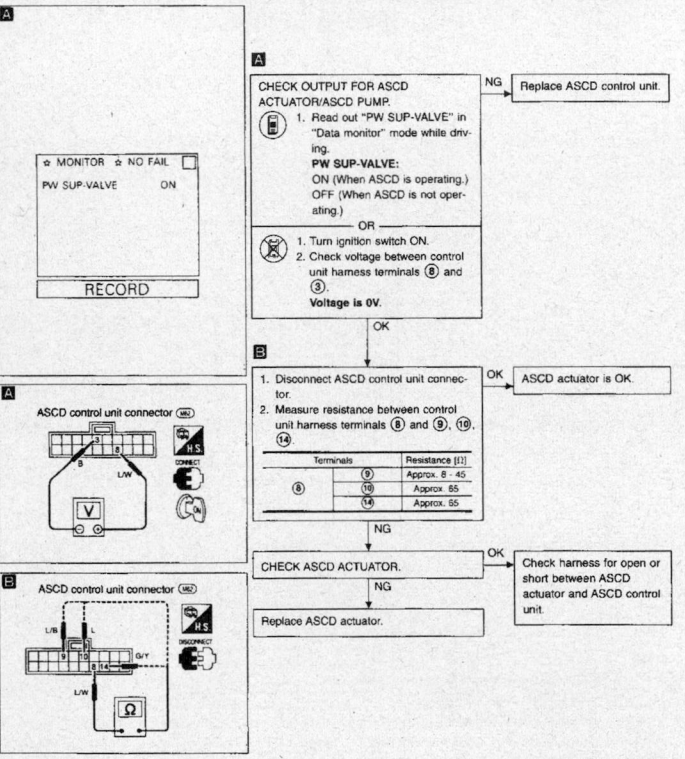

Fig. 117 Test 7: ASCD Actuator Check. 1996–97 240SX

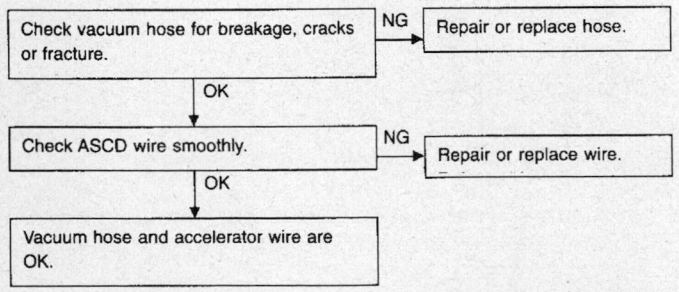

Fig. 119 Test 8: Vacuum Hose & Accel Wire Check. 1996–97 Pathfinder & Pickup

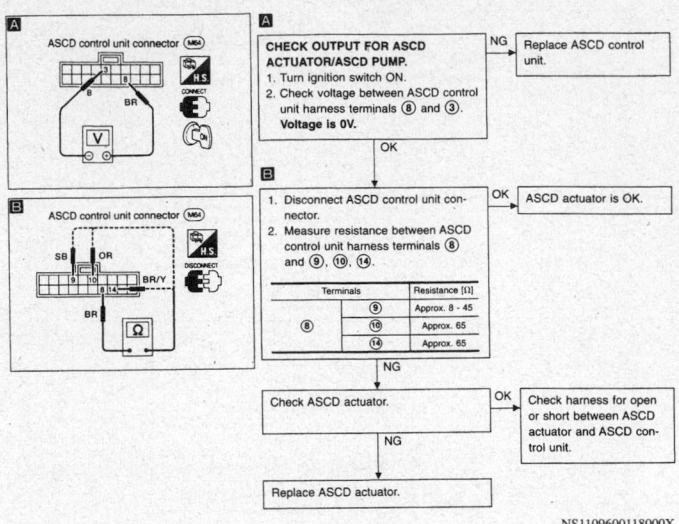

Fig. 116 Test 7: ASCD Actuator Check. 1996–97 Quest

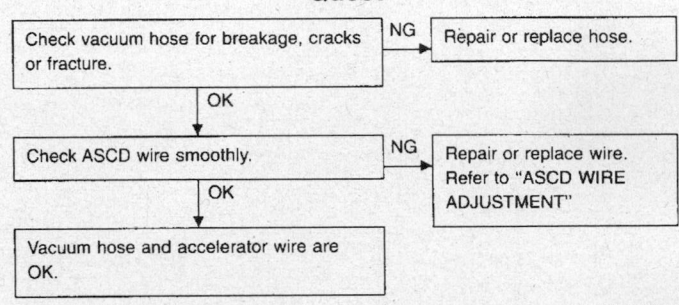

Fig. 118 Test 8: Vacuum Hose & Accel Wire Check. 1996–97 Maxima

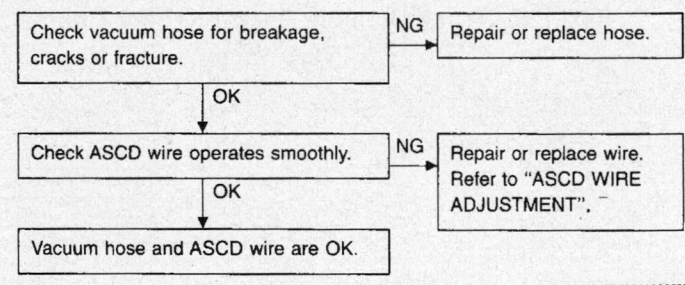

Fig. 120 Test 8: Vacuum Hose & Accel Wire Check. 1996–97 Quest

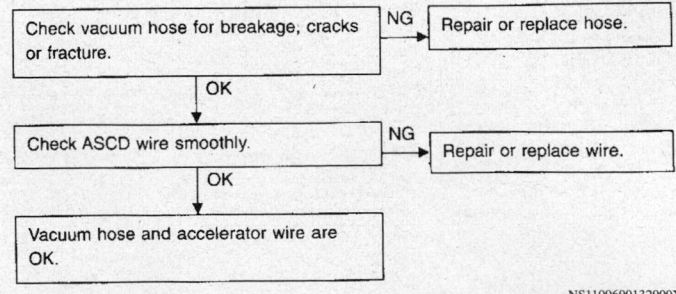

Fig. 121 Test 8: Vacuum Hose & Accel Wire Check. 1996–97 240SX

Wiper Systems

INDEX

SYSTEM DIAGNOSIS & TESTING

Refer to **Figs. 1 through 29** for system diagnosis and testing.

COMPONENT DIAGNOSIS & TESTING

WIPER AMPLIFIER & SWITCH

Pathfinder, Pickup & 300ZX

1. Connect a test lamp to wiper amplifier as shown in **Fig. 30**.
2. If test lamp comes on when connected to terminal (6) and battery ground, wiper amplifier is normal.

COMPONENT REPLACEMENT

Refer to appropriate chassis section for wiper system component replacement procedures.

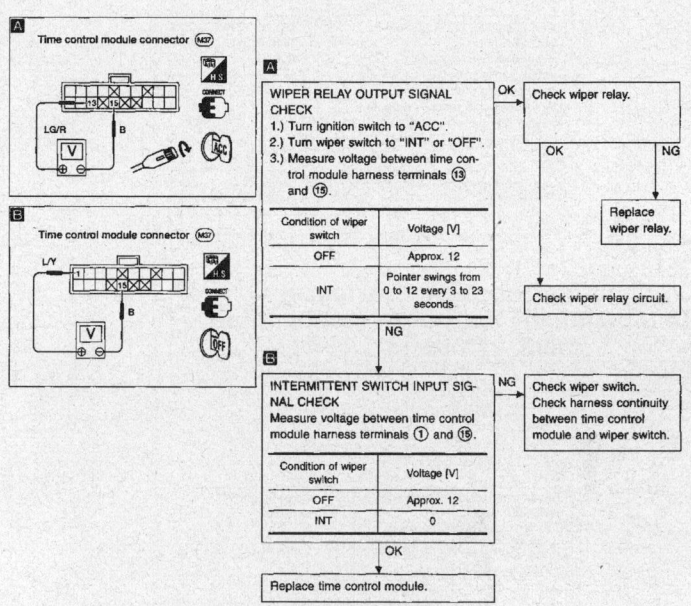

NS9029500029000X

Fig. 1   Diagnostic Procedure 1: Intermittent wiper does not operate. 1996–97 Altima

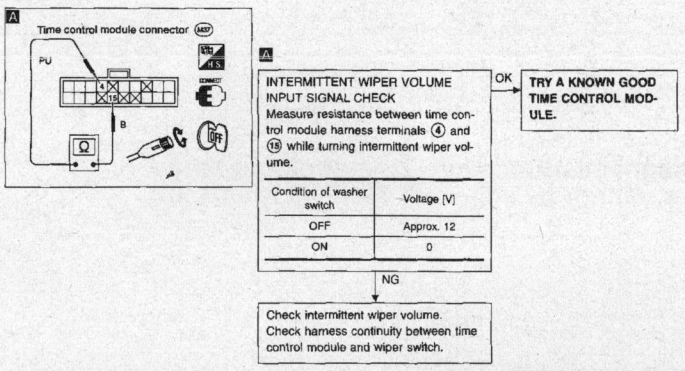

NS9029500030000X

Fig. 2   Diagnostic Procedure 2: Intermittent time of wiper cannot be adjusted. 1996–97 Altima

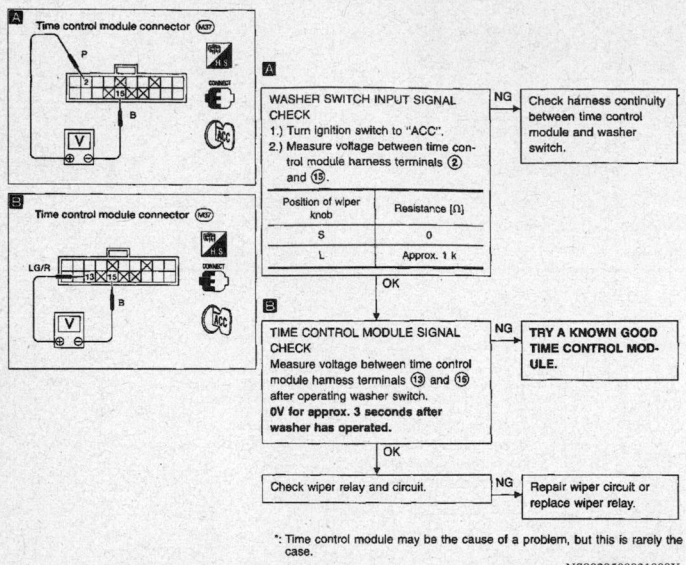

Fig. 3 Diagnostic Procedure 3: Wiper & washer activate individually but not in combination. 1996–97 Altima

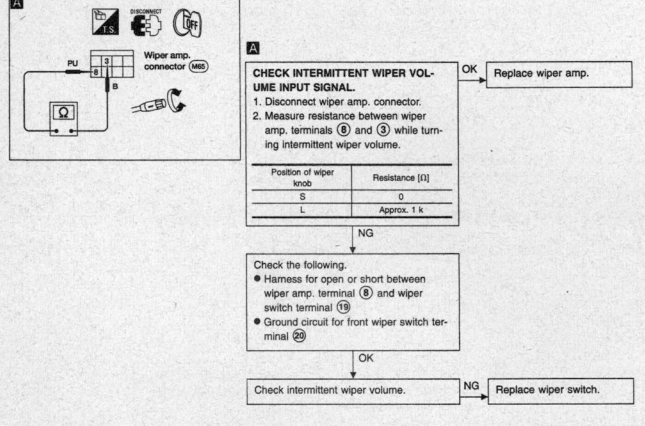

Fig. 5 Diagnostic Procedure 2: Intermittent time of wiper cannot be adjusted. 1998–99 Altima

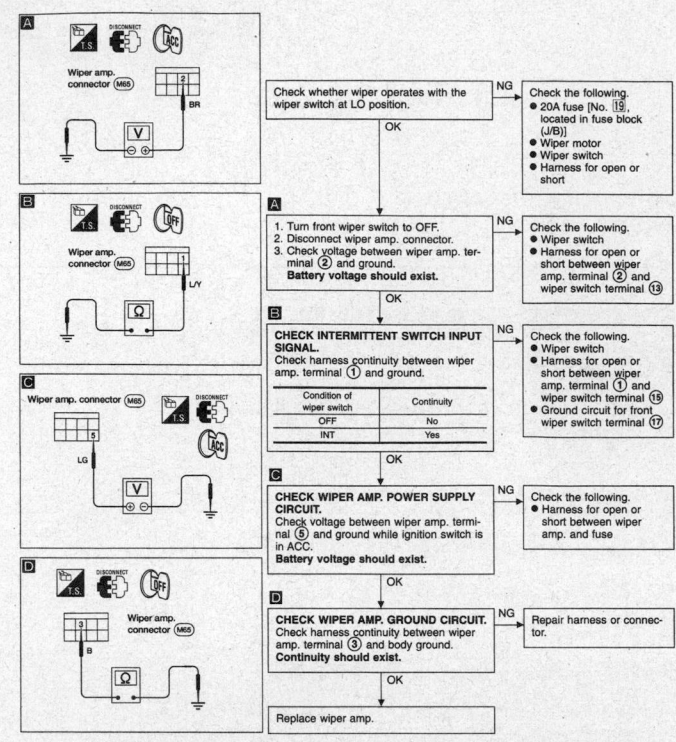

Fig. 4 Diagnostic Procedure 1: Intermittent wiper does not operate. 1998–99 Altima

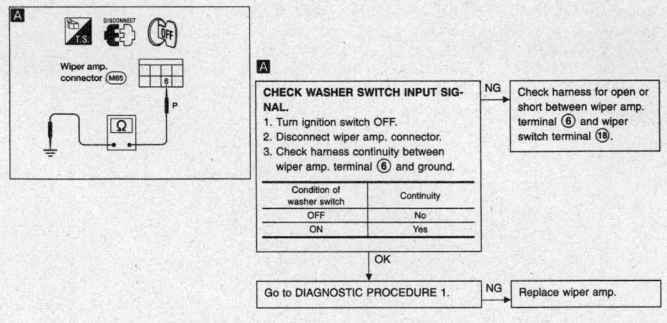

Fig. 6 Diagnostic Procedure 3: Wiper & washer activate individually but not in combination. 1998–99 Altima

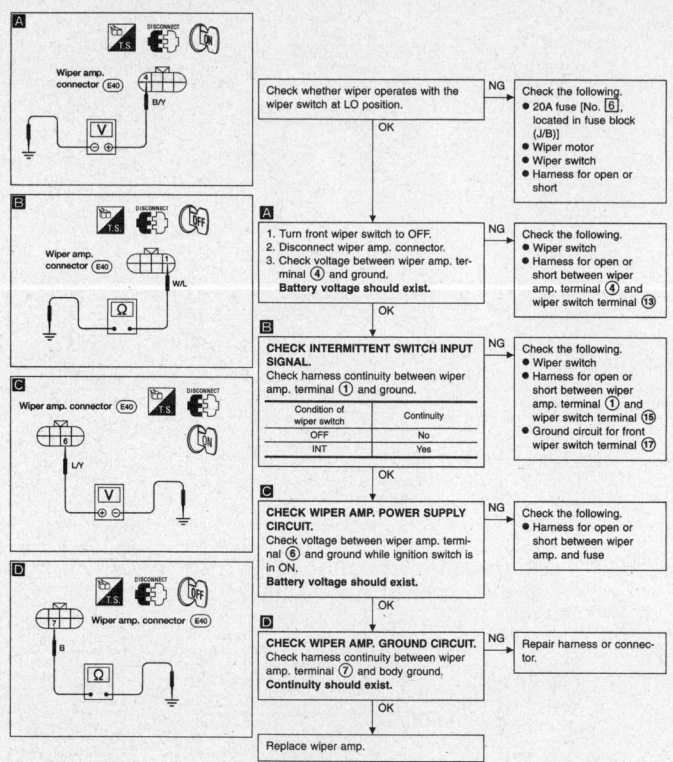

Check whether wiper operates with the wiper switch at LO position.

OK → (continues) / **NG** → Check the following.
- 20A fuse [No. 6], located in fuse block (J/B)]
- Wiper motor
- Wiper switch
- Harness for open or short

A
1. Turn front wiper switch to OFF.
2. Disconnect wiper amp. connector.
3. Check voltage between wiper amp. terminal ④ and ground.
Battery voltage should exist.

NG → Check the following.
- Wiper switch
- Harness for open or short between wiper amp. terminal ④ and wiper switch terminal ⑬

B CHECK INTERMITTENT SWITCH INPUT SIGNAL.
Check harness continuity between wiper amp. terminal ① and ground.

Condition of wiper switch	Continuity
OFF	No
INT	Yes

NG → Check the following.
- Wiper switch
- Harness for open or short between wiper amp. terminal ① and wiper switch terminal ⑮
- Ground circuit for front wiper switch terminal ⑰

C CHECK WIPER AMP. POWER SUPPLY CIRCUIT.
Check voltage between wiper amp. terminal ⑥ and ground while ignition switch is in ON.
Battery voltage should exist.

NG → Check the following.
- Harness for open or short between wiper amp. and fuse

D CHECK WIPER AMP. GROUND CIRCUIT.
Check harness continuity between wiper amp. terminal ⑦ and body ground.
Continuity should exist.

NG → Repair harness or connector.

OK → Replace wiper amp.

NS9029900040000X

Fig. 7 Diagnostic Procedure 1: Intermittent wiper does not operate. Frontier

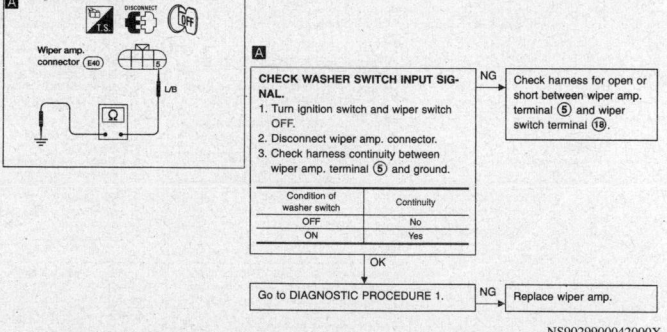

A CHECK WASHER SWITCH INPUT SIGNAL.
1. Turn ignition switch and wiper switch OFF.
2. Disconnect wiper amp. connector.
3. Check harness continuity between wiper amp. terminal ⑤ and ground.

Condition of washer switch	Continuity
OFF	No
ON	Yes

NG → Check harness for open or short between wiper amp. terminal ⑤ and wiper switch terminal ⑱.

OK → Go to DIAGNOSTIC PROCEDURE 1. **NG** → Replace wiper amp.

NS9029900042000X

Fig. 9 Diagnostic Procedure 3: Wiper & washer activate individually but not in combination. Frontier

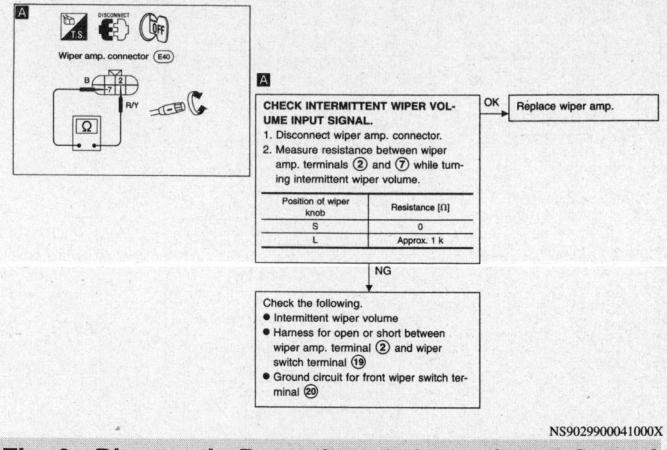

A CHECK INTERMITTENT WIPER VOLUME INPUT SIGNAL.
1. Disconnect wiper amp. connector.
2. Measure resistance between wiper amp. terminals ② and ⑦ while turning intermittent wiper volume.

Position of wiper knob	Resistance [Ω]
S	0
L	Approx. 1 k

OK → Replace wiper amp.

NG → Check the following.
- Intermittent wiper volume
- Harness for open or short between wiper amp. terminal ② and wiper switch terminal ⑲
- Ground circuit for front wiper switch terminal ⑳

NS9029900041000X

Fig. 8 Diagnostic Procedure 2: Intermittent time of wiper cannot be adjusted. Frontier

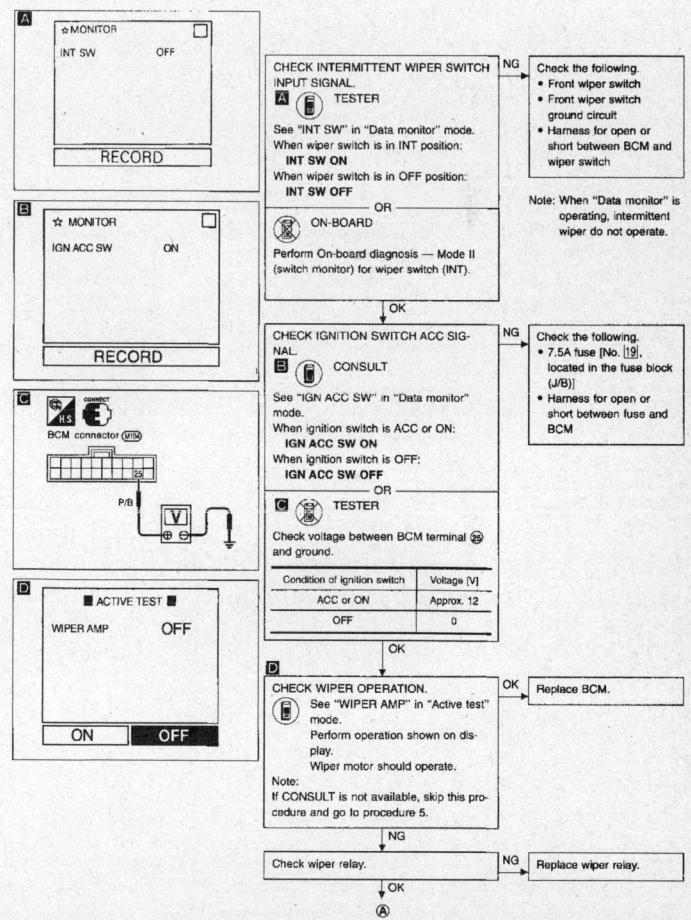

A CHECK INTERMITTENT WIPER SWITCH INPUT SIGNAL.
TESTER
See "INT SW" in "Data monitor" mode.
When wiper switch is in INT position:
INT SW ON
When wiper switch is in OFF position:
INT SW OFF
OR
ON-BOARD
Perform On-board diagnosis — Mode II (switch monitor) for wiper switch (INT).

NG → Check the following.
- Front wiper switch
- Front wiper switch ground circuit
- Harness for open or short between BCM and wiper switch

Note: When "Data monitor" is operating, intermittent wiper do not operate.

B CHECK IGNITION SWITCH ACC SIGNAL.
CONSULT
See "IGN ACC SW" in "Data monitor" mode.
When ignition switch is ACC or ON:
IGN ACC SW ON
When ignition switch is OFF:
IGN ACC SW OFF
OR
TESTER
Check voltage between BCM terminal ㉕ and ground.

Condition of ignition switch	Voltage [V]
ACC or ON	Approx. 12
OFF	0

NG → Check the following.
- 7.5A fuse [No. 19], located in the fuse block (J/B)]
- Harness for open or short between fuse and BCM

D CHECK WIPER OPERATION.
See "WIPER AMP" in "Active test" mode.
Perform operation shown on display.
Wiper motor should operate.
Note:
If CONSULT is not available, skip this procedure and go to procedure 5.

OK → Replace BCM.

NG → Check wiper relay. **NG** → Replace wiper relay.

OK → Ⓐ

NS9029700035010X

Fig. 10 Diagnostic Procedure 1: Intermittent wiper does not operate (Part 1 of 2). Maxima

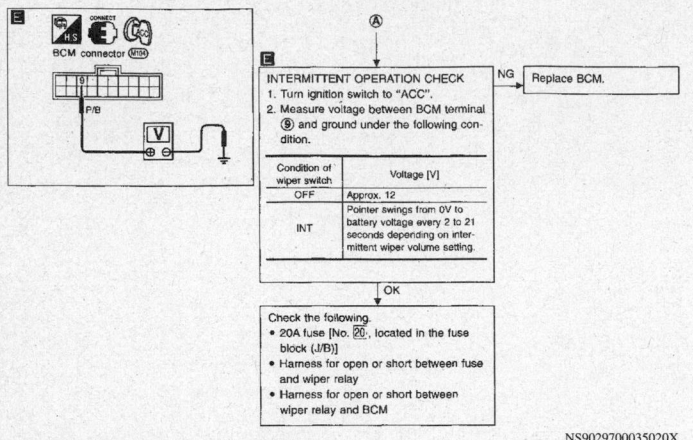

Fig. 10 Diagnostic Procedure 1: Intermittent wiper does not operate (Part 2 of 2). Maxima

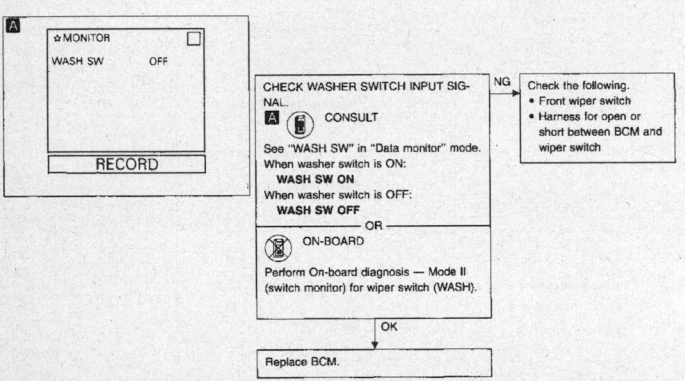

Fig. 12 Diagnostic Procedure 3: Wiper & washer activate individually but not in combination. Maxima

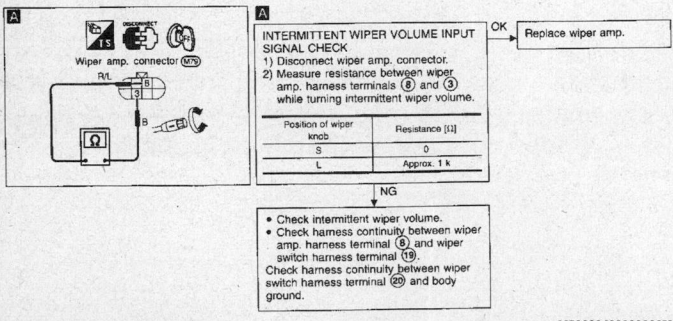

Fig. 14 Diagnostic Procedure 2: Intermittent time of wiper cannot be adjusted. Pathfinder

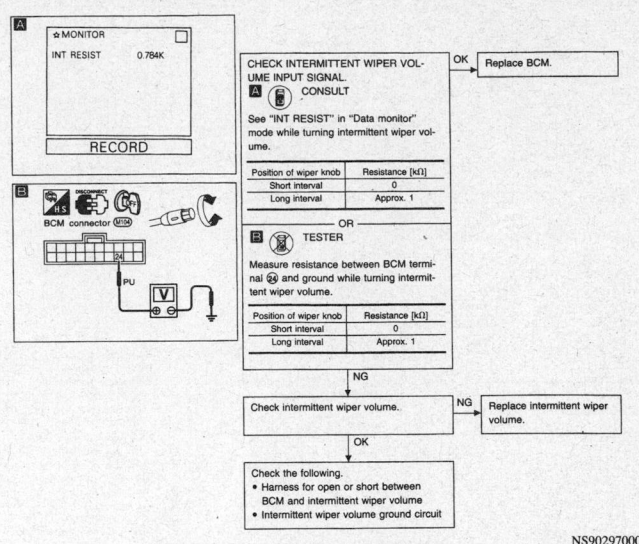

Fig. 11 Diagnostic Procedure 2: Intermittent time of wiper cannot be adjusted. Maxima

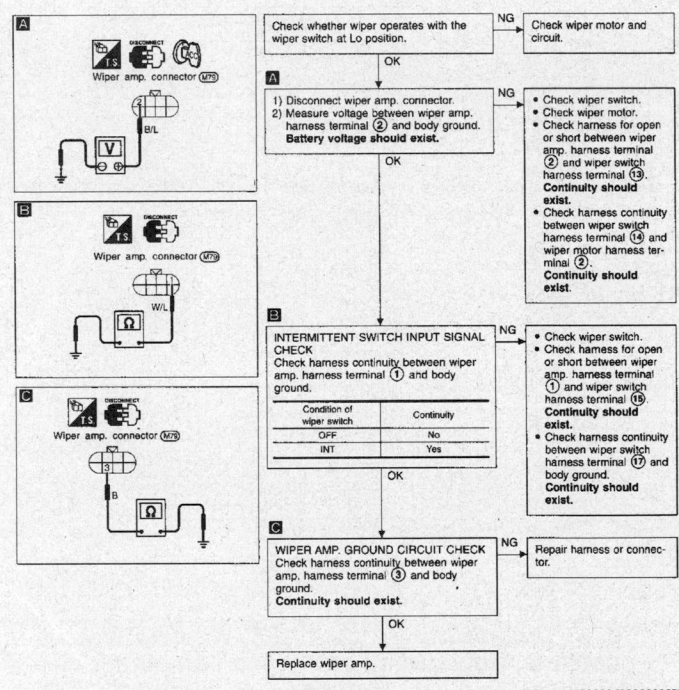

Fig. 13 Diagnostic Procedure 1: Intermittent wiper does not operate. Pathfinder

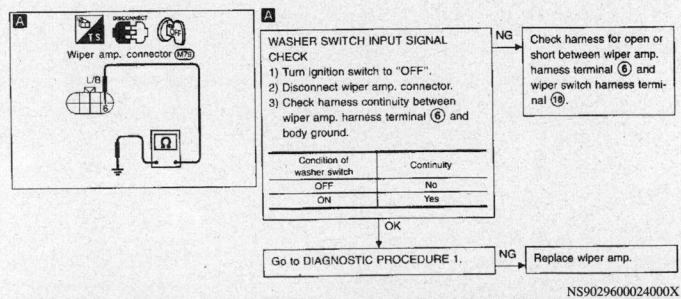

Fig. 15 Diagnostic Procedure 3: Wiper & washer activate individually but not in combination. Pathfinder

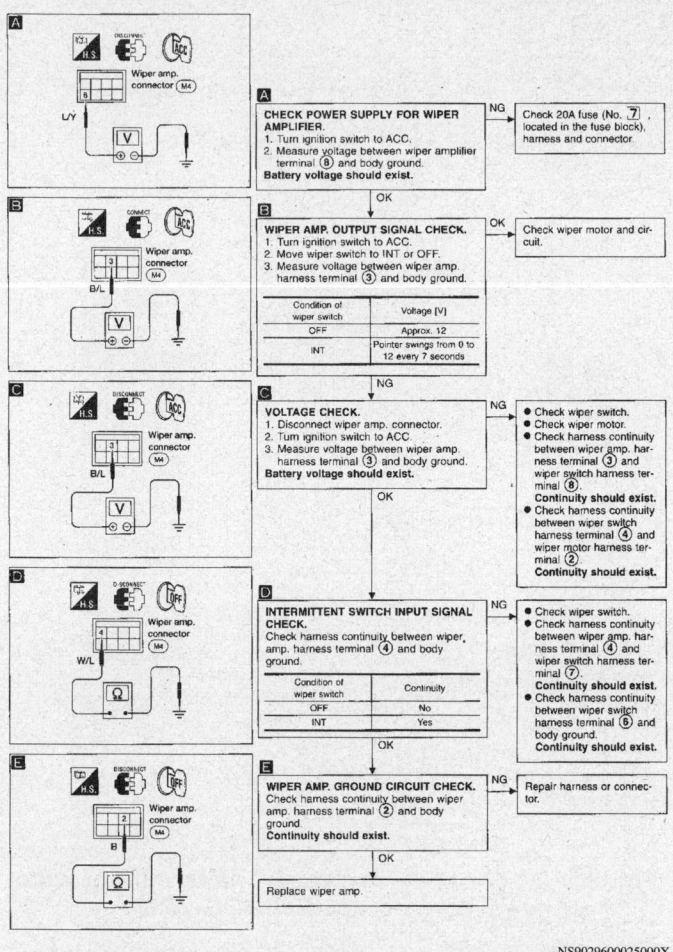

A

CHECK POWER SUPPLY FOR WIPER AMPLIFIER.
1. Turn ignition switch to ACC.
2. Measure voltage between wiper amplifier terminal ⑧ and body ground.
Battery voltage should exist.

NG → Check 20A fuse (No. ⑦), located in the fuse block), harness and connector.

OK

B

WIPER AMP. OUTPUT SIGNAL CHECK.
1. Turn ignition switch to ACC.
2. Move wiper switch to INT or OFF.
3. Measure voltage between wiper amp. harness terminal ③ and body ground.

Condition of wiper switch	Voltage [V]
OFF	Approx. 12
INT	Pointer swings from 0 to 12 every 7 seconds

OK → Check wiper motor and circuit.

NG

C

VOLTAGE CHECK.
1. Disconnect wiper amp. connector.
2. Turn ignition switch to ACC.
3. Measure voltage between wiper amp. harness terminal ③ and body ground.
Battery voltage should exist.

NG →
- Check wiper switch.
- Check wiper motor.
- Check harness continuity between wiper amp. harness terminal ③ and wiper switch harness terminal ⑧.
Continuity should exist.
- Check harness continuity between wiper switch harness terminal ④ and wiper motor harness terminal ②.
Continuity should exist.

OK

D

INTERMITTENT SWITCH INPUT SIGNAL CHECK.
Check harness continuity between wiper amp. harness terminal ④ and body ground.

Condition of wiper switch	Continuity
OFF	No
INT	Yes

NG →
- Check wiper switch.
- Check harness continuity between wiper amp. harness terminal ④ and wiper switch harness terminal ⑦.
Continuity should exist.
- Check harness continuity between wiper switch harness terminal ⑤ and body ground.
Continuity should exist.

OK

E

WIPER AMP. GROUND CIRCUIT CHECK.
Check harness continuity between wiper amp. harness terminal ② and body ground.
Continuity should exist.

NG → Repair harness or connector.

OK

Replace wiper amp.

NS9029600025000X

Fig. 16 Diagnostic Procedure 1: Intermittent wiper does not operate. Pickup

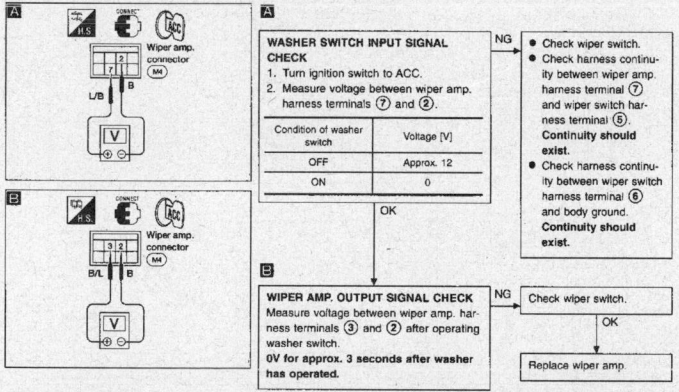

A

WASHER SWITCH INPUT SIGNAL CHECK
1. Turn ignition switch to ACC.
2. Measure voltage between wiper amp. harness terminals ⑦ and ②.

Condition of washer switch	Voltage [V]
OFF	Approx. 12
ON	0

NG →
- Check wiper switch.
- Check harness continuity between wiper amp. harness terminal ⑦ and wiper switch harness terminal ⑤.
Continuity should exist.
- Check harness continuity between wiper switch harness terminal ⑥ and body ground.
Continuity should exist.

OK

B

WIPER AMP. OUTPUT SIGNAL CHECK.
Measure voltage between wiper amp. harness terminals ③ and ② after operating washer switch.
0V for approx. 3 seconds after washer has operated.

NG → Check wiper switch.

OK

Replace wiper amp.

NS9029600027000X

Fig. 18 Diagnostic Procedure 3: Wiper & washer activate individually but not in combination. Pickup

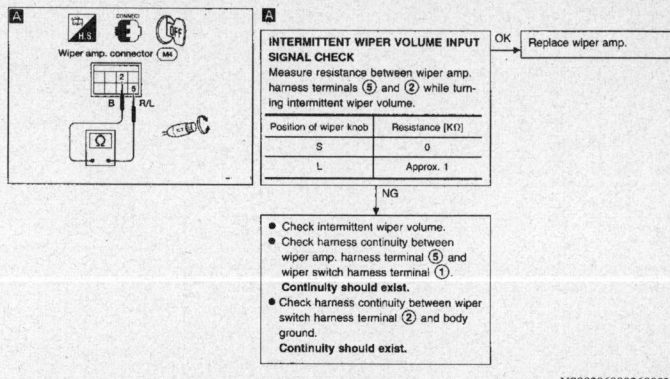

A

INTERMITTENT WIPER VOLUME INPUT SIGNAL CHECK
Measure resistance between wiper amp. harness terminals ⑤ and ② while turning intermittent wiper volume.

Position of wiper knob	Resistance [KΩ]
S	0
L	Approx. 1

OK → Replace wiper amp.

NG

- Check intermittent wiper volume.
- Check harness continuity between wiper amp. harness terminal ⑤ and wiper switch harness terminal ①.
Continuity should exist.
- Check harness continuity between wiper switch harness terminal ② and body ground.
Continuity should exist.

NS9029600026000X

Fig. 17 Diagnostic Procedure 2: Intermittent time of wiper cannot be adjusted. Pickup

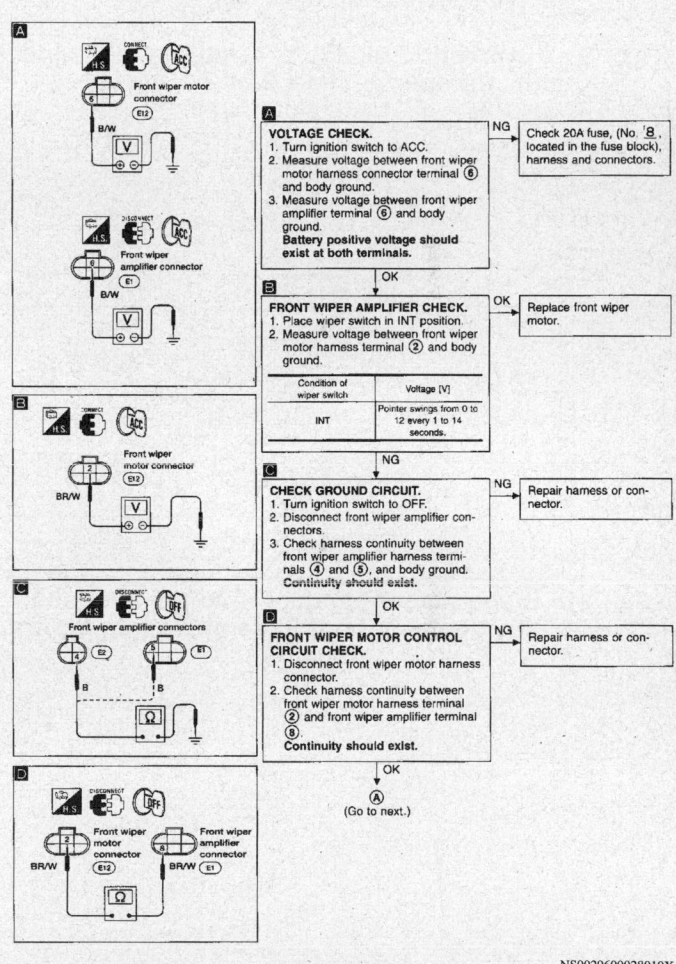

A

VOLTAGE CHECK.
1. Turn ignition switch to ACC.
2. Measure voltage between front wiper motor harness connector terminal ⑥ and body ground.
3. Measure voltage between front wiper amplifier terminal ⑥ and body ground.
Battery positive voltage should exist at both terminals.

NG → Check 20A fuse, (No. ⑧, located in the fuse block), harness and connectors.

OK

B

FRONT WIPER AMPLIFIER CHECK.
1. Place wiper switch in INT position.
2. Measure voltage between front wiper motor harness terminal ② and body ground.

Condition of wiper switch	Voltage [V]
INT	Pointer swings from 0 to 12 every 1 to 14 seconds.

OK → Replace front wiper motor.

NG

C

CHECK GROUND CIRCUIT.
1. Turn ignition switch to OFF.
2. Disconnect front wiper amplifier connectors.
3. Check harness continuity between front wiper amplifier harness terminals ④ and ⑤, and body ground.
Continuity should exist.

NG → Repair harness or connector.

OK

D

FRONT WIPER MOTOR CONTROL CIRCUIT CHECK.
1. Disconnect front wiper motor harness connector.
2. Check harness continuity between front wiper motor harness terminal ② and front wiper amplifier terminal ⑨.
Continuity should exist.

NG → Repair harness or connector.

OK

Ⓐ
(Go to next.)

NS9029600028010X

Fig. 19 Diagnostic Procedure 1: Intermittent wiper does not operate (Part 1 of 2). Quest

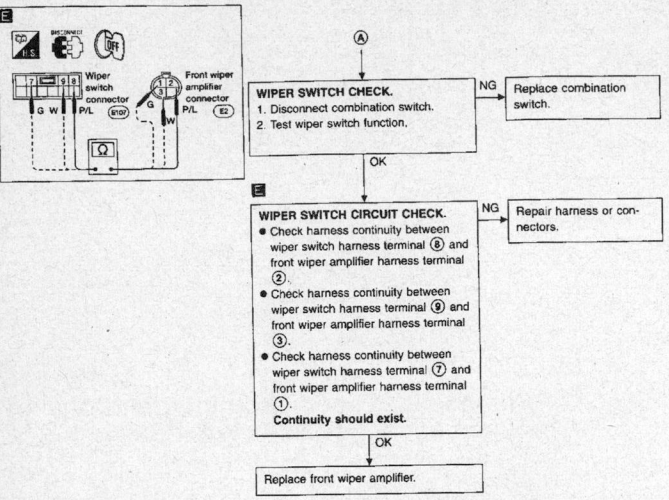

WIPER SWITCH CHECK.
1. Disconnect combination switch.
2. Test wiper switch function.

NG → Replace combination switch.

OK ↓

WIPER SWITCH CIRCUIT CHECK.
- Check harness continuity between wiper switch harness terminal ⑧ and front wiper amplifier harness terminal ②.
- Check harness continuity between wiper switch harness terminal ⑨ and front wiper amplifier harness terminal ③.
- Check harness continuity between wiper switch harness terminal ⑦ and front wiper amplifier harness terminal ①.
Continuity should exist.

NG → Repair harness or connectors.

OK ↓

Replace front wiper amplifier.

NS9029600028020X

Fig. 19 Diagnostic Procedure 1: Intermittent wiper does not operate (Part 2 of 2). Quest

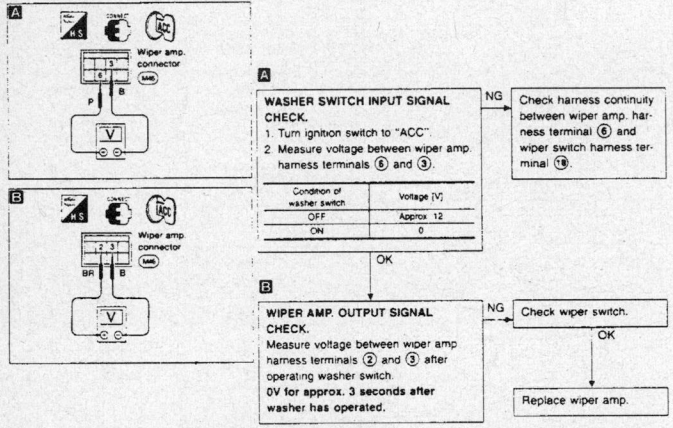

WASHER SWITCH INPUT SIGNAL CHECK.
1. Turn ignition switch to "ACC".
2. Measure voltage between wiper amp. harness terminals ⑥ and ③.

Condition of washer switch	Voltage [V]
OFF	Approx. 12
ON	0

NG → Check harness continuity between wiper amp. harness terminal ⑥ and wiper switch harness terminal ⑱.

OK ↓

WIPER AMP. OUTPUT SIGNAL CHECK.
Measure voltage between wiper amp. harness terminals ② and ③ after operating washer switch.
0V for approx. 3 seconds after washer has operated.

NG → Check wiper switch.

OK ↓

Replace wiper amp.

NS9029500021000X

Fig. 21 Diagnostic Procedure 2: Wiper & washer operate individually but not in combination. Sentra & 200SX

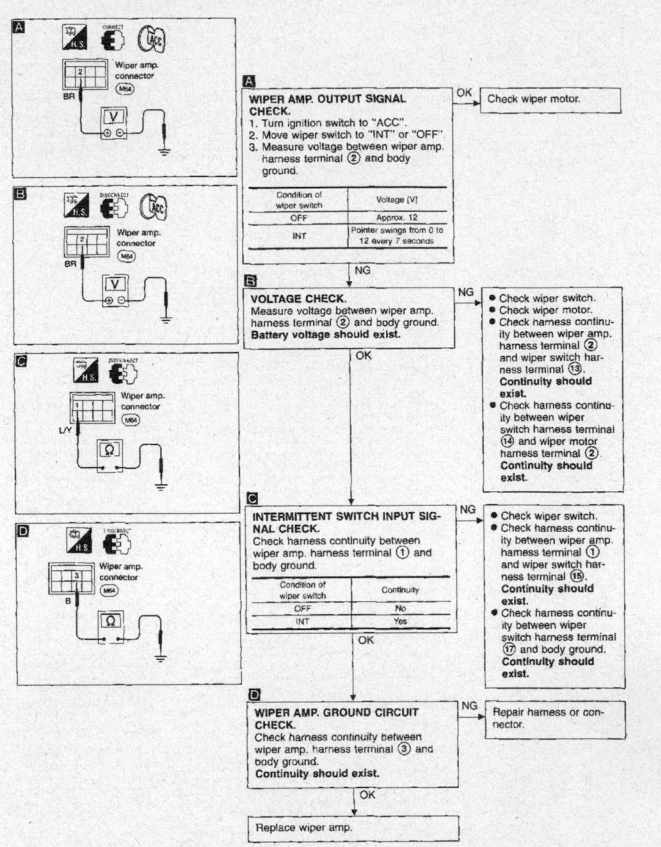

WIPER AMP. OUTPUT SIGNAL CHECK.
1. Turn ignition switch to "ACC".
2. Move wiper switch to "INT" or "OFF".
3. Measure voltage between wiper amp. harness terminal ② and body ground.

Condition of wiper switch	Voltage [V]
OFF	Approx. 12
INT	Pointer swings from 0 to 12 every 7 seconds

OK → Check wiper motor.

NG ↓

VOLTAGE CHECK.
Measure voltage between wiper amp. harness terminal ② and body ground.
Battery voltage should exist.

NG →
- Check wiper switch.
- Check wiper motor.
- Check harness continuity between wiper amp. harness terminal ② and wiper switch harness terminal ⑬. **Continuity should exist.**
- Check harness continuity between wiper switch terminal ⑭ and wiper motor harness terminal ②. **Continuity should exist.**

OK ↓

INTERMITTENT SWITCH INPUT SIGNAL CHECK.
Check harness continuity between wiper amp. harness terminal ① and body ground.

Condition of wiper switch	Continuity
OFF	No
INT	Yes

NG →
- Check wiper switch.
- Check harness continuity between wiper amp. harness terminal ① and wiper switch harness terminal ⑮. **Continuity should exist.**
- Check harness continuity between wiper switch harness terminal ⑰ and body ground. **Continuity should exist.**

OK ↓

WIPER AMP. GROUND CIRCUIT CHECK.
Check harness continuity between wiper amp. harness terminal ③ and body ground.
Continuity should exist.

NG → Repair harness or connector.

OK ↓

Replace wiper amp.

NS9029500020000X

Fig. 20 Diagnostic Procedure 1: Intermittent wiper does not operate. Sentra & 200SX

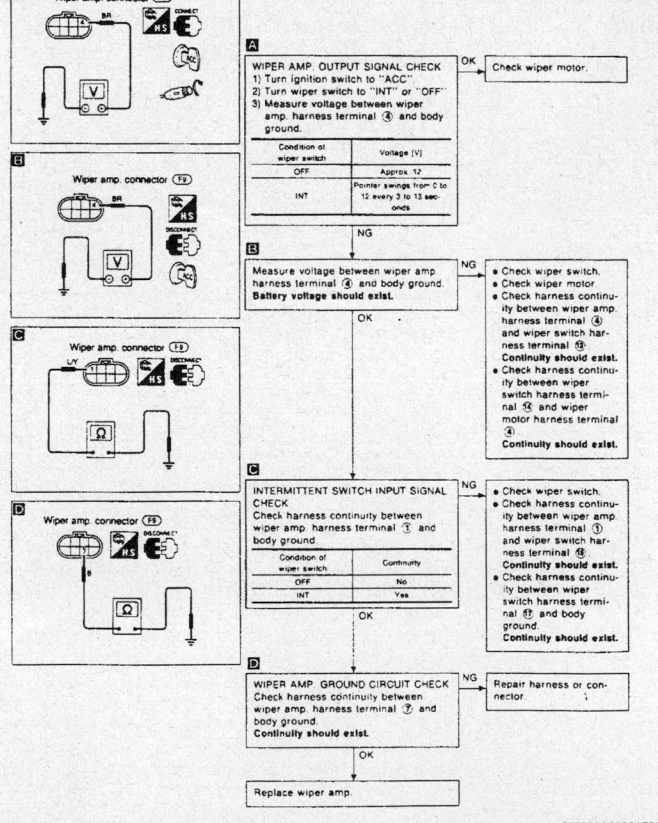

WIPER AMP. OUTPUT SIGNAL CHECK
1) Turn ignition switch to "ACC".
2) Turn wiper switch to "INT" or "OFF".
3) Measure voltage between wiper amp. harness terminal ④ and body ground.

Condition of wiper switch	Voltage [V]
OFF	Approx. 12
INT	Pointer swings from 0 to 12 every 3 to 13 seconds

OK → Check wiper motor.

NG ↓

Measure voltage between wiper amp harness terminal ④ and body ground.
Battery voltage should exist.

NG →
- Check wiper switch.
- Check wiper motor.
- Check harness continuity between wiper amp. harness terminal ④ and wiper switch harness terminal ⑫. **Continuity should exist.**
- Check harness continuity between wiper switch harness terminal ⑫ and wiper motor harness terminal ④. **Continuity should exist.**

OK ↓

INTERMITTENT SWITCH INPUT SIGNAL CHECK
Check harness continuity between wiper amp. harness terminal ③ and body ground.

Condition of wiper switch	Continuity
OFF	No
INT	Yes

NG →
- Check wiper switch.
- Check harness continuity between wiper amp. harness terminal ① and wiper switch harness terminal ⑭. **Continuity should exist.**
- Check harness continuity between wiper switch harness terminal ⑰ and body ground. **Continuity should exist.**

OK ↓

WIPER AMP. GROUND CIRCUIT CHECK
Check harness continuity between wiper amp. harness terminal ⑦ and body ground.
Continuity should exist.

NG → Repair harness or connector.

OK ↓

Replace wiper amp.

NS9029500017000X

Fig. 22 Diagnostic Procedure 1: Intermittent wiper does not operate. 1996 240SX

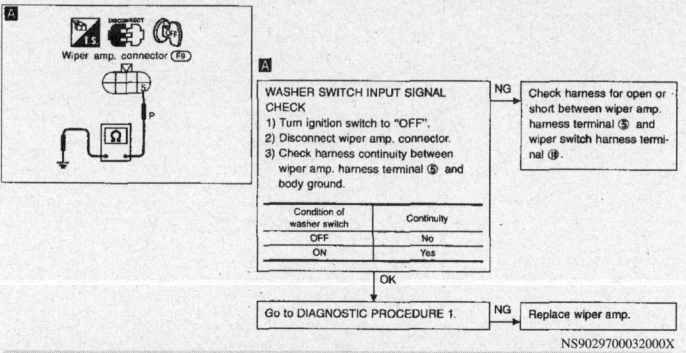

WASHER SWITCH INPUT SIGNAL CHECK
1) Turn ignition switch to "OFF".
2) Disconnect wiper amp. connector.
3) Check harness continuity between wiper amp. harness terminal ⑤ and body ground.

Condition of washer switch	Continuity
OFF	No
ON	Yes

NG → Check harness for open or short between wiper amp. harness terminal ⑤ and wiper switch harness terminal ⑱.

OK

Go to DIAGNOSTIC PROCEDURE 1. → NG → Replace wiper amp.

NS9029700032000X

Fig. 23 Diagnostic Procedure 1: Intermittent wiper does not operate. 1997–98 240SX

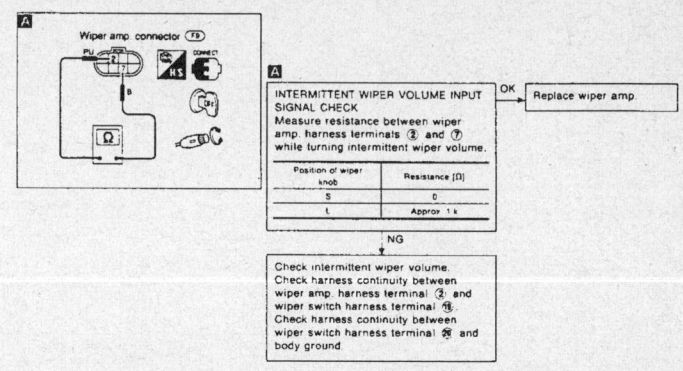

INTERMITTENT WIPER VOLUME INPUT SIGNAL CHECK
Measure resistance between wiper amp. harness terminals ② and ⑦ while turning intermittent wiper volume.

Position of wiper knob	Resistance [Ω]
S	0
L	Approx. 1 k

OK → Replace wiper amp.

NG

Check intermittent wiper volume.
Check harness continuity between wiper amp. harness terminal ② and wiper switch harness terminal ⑲.
Check harness continuity between wiper switch harness terminal ⑳ and body ground.

NS9029500018000X

Fig. 24 Diagnostic procedure 2: Intermittent time of wiper cannot be adjusted. 240SX

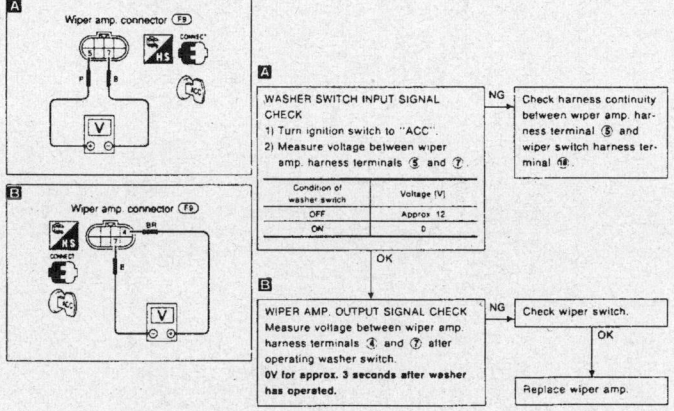

WASHER SWITCH INPUT SIGNAL CHECK
1) Turn ignition switch to "ACC".
2) Measure voltage between wiper amp. harness terminals ⑤ and ⑦.

Condition of washer switch	Voltage [V]
OFF	Approx. 12
ON	0

NG → Check harness continuity between wiper amp. harness terminal ⑤ and wiper switch harness terminal ⑱.

OK

WIPER AMP. OUTPUT SIGNAL CHECK
Measure voltage between wiper amp. harness terminals ④ and ⑦ after operating washer switch.
0V for approx. 3 seconds after washer has operated.

NG → Check wiper switch.

OK

Replace wiper amp.

NS9029500019000X

Fig. 25 Diagnostic procedure 3: Wiper & washer activate individually but not in combination. 1996 240SX

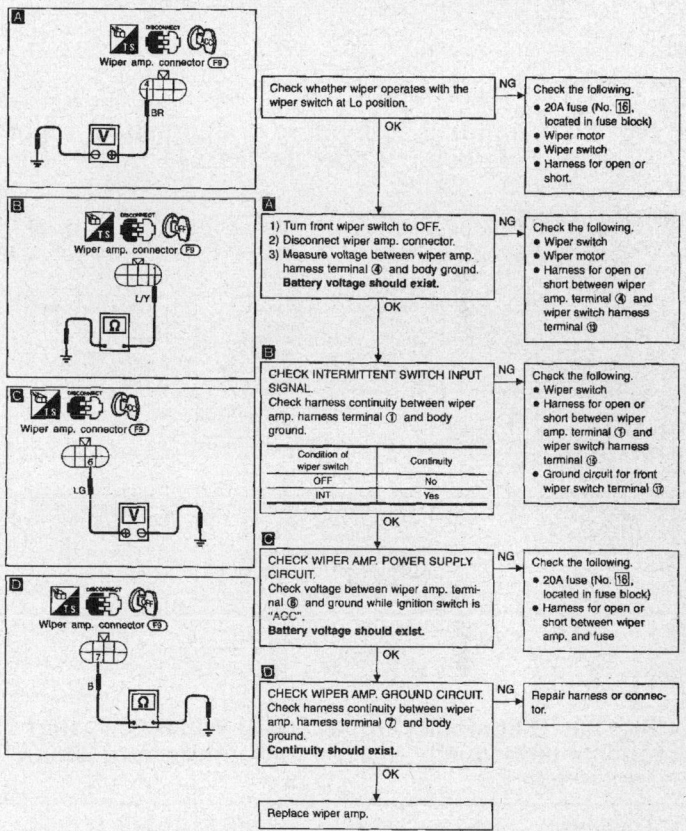

Check whether wiper operates with the wiper switch at Lo position.

NG → Check the following.
• 20A fuse (No. ⑯, located in fuse block)
• Wiper motor
• Wiper switch
• Harness for open or short.

OK

1) Turn front wiper switch to OFF.
2) Disconnect wiper amp. connector.
3) Measure voltage between wiper amp. harness terminal ④ and body ground.
Battery voltage should exist.

NG → Check the following.
• Wiper switch
• Wiper motor
• Harness for open or short between wiper amp. terminal ④ and wiper switch harness terminal ⑱

OK

CHECK INTERMITTENT SWITCH INPUT SIGNAL.
Check harness continuity between wiper amp. harness terminal ① and body ground.

Condition of wiper switch	Continuity
OFF	No
INT	Yes

NG → Check the following.
• Wiper switch
• Harness for open or short between wiper amp. terminal ① and wiper switch harness terminal ⑲
• Ground circuit for front wiper switch terminal ⑰

OK

CHECK WIPER AMP. POWER SUPPLY CIRCUIT.
Check voltage between wiper amp. terminal ⑥ and ground while ignition switch is "ACC".
Battery voltage should exist.

NG → Check the following.
• 20A fuse (No. ⑯, located in fuse block)
• Harness for open or short between wiper amp. and fuse

OK

CHECK WIPER AMP. GROUND CIRCUIT.
Check harness continuity between wiper amp. harness terminal ⑦ and body ground.
Continuity should exist.

NG → Repair harness or connector.

OK

Replace wiper amp.

NS9029700033000X

Fig. 26 Diagnostic procedure 3: Wiper & washer activate individually but not in combination. 1997–98 240SX

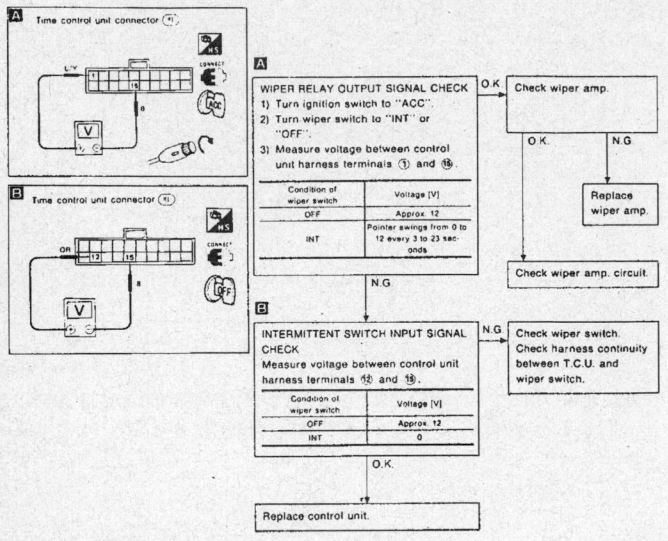

WIPER RELAY OUTPUT SIGNAL CHECK
1) Turn ignition switch to "ACC".
2) Turn wiper switch to "INT" or "OFF".
3) Measure voltage between control unit harness terminals ① and ⑯.

Condition of wiper switch	Voltage [V]
OFF	Approx. 12
INT	Pointer swings from 0 to 12 every 3 to 23 seconds

O.K. → Check wiper amp.

O.K. / N.G.

N.G. → Replace wiper amp.

Check wiper amp. circuit.

N.G.

INTERMITTENT SWITCH INPUT SIGNAL CHECK
Measure voltage between control unit harness terminals ⑫ and ⑯.

Condition of wiper switch	Voltage [V]
OFF	Approx. 12
INT	0

N.G. → Check wiper switch. Check harness continuity between T.C.U. and wiper switch.

O.K.

Replace control unit.

NS9029100011000X

Fig. 27 Diagnostic Procedure 1: Intermittent wiper does not operate. 300ZX

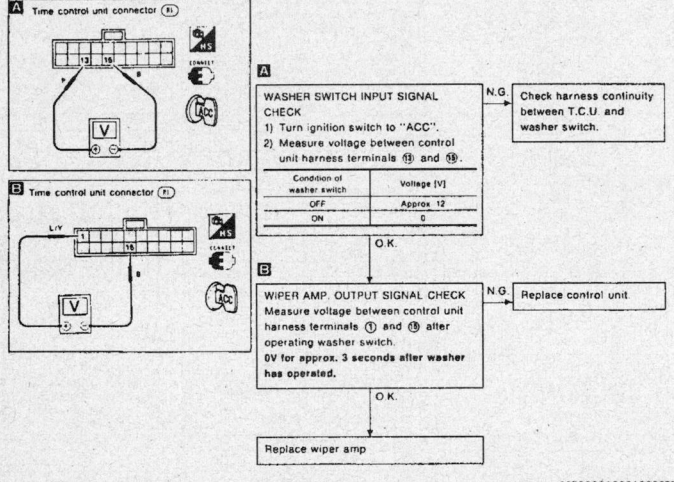

WASHER SWITCH INPUT SIGNAL CHECK
1) Turn ignition switch to "ACC".
2) Measure voltage between control unit harness terminals ⑬ and ⑯.

Condition of washer switch	Voltage [V]
OFF	Approx. 12
ON	0

N.G. → Check harness continuity between T.C.U. and washer switch.

O.K.

WIPER AMP. OUTPUT SIGNAL CHECK
Measure voltage between control unit harness terminals ① and ⑯ after operating washer switch.
0V for approx. 3 seconds after washer has operated.

N.G. → Replace control unit.

O.K.

Replace wiper amp.

NS9029100013000X

Fig. 29 Diagnostic Procedure 3: Wiper & washer activate individually but not in combination. 300ZX

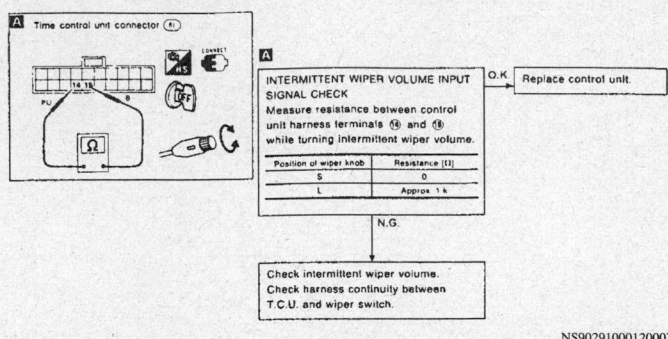

INTERMITTENT WIPER VOLUME INPUT SIGNAL CHECK
Measure resistance between control unit harness terminals ⑭ and ⑲ while turning intermittent wiper volume.

Position of wiper knob	Resistance [Ω]
S	0
L	Approx. 1 k

O.K. → Replace control unit.

N.G.

Check intermittent wiper volume.
Check harness continuity between T.C.U. and wiper switch.

NS9029100012000X

Fig. 28 Diagnostic Procedure 2: Intermittent time of wiper cannot be adjusted. 300ZX

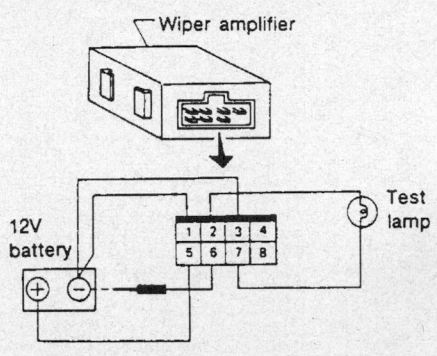

NS9029100014000X

Fig. 30 Wiper amplifier check. Pathfinder, Pickup & 300ZX

Air Bag System

NOTE: "Electrical Symbol & Wire Color Code Identification" Located In The Front Of This Manual May Be Used As An Aid When Using Wiring Circuits Found In This Section.

NOTE: Refer To "Computer Relearn Procedures" Located In The Front Of This Manual For Computer Relearn Procedures.

INDEX

AIR BAG SYSTEM DISARMING & ARMING

Disarming

1. Turn ignition switch to the OFF position, then disconnect both battery cables.
2. **Wait a minimum of 10 minutes for air bag system to discharge. The system will retain power for approximately 10 minutes after disconnecting the battery ground cable. It is possible for the air bag to deploy during this time.**
3. Remove steering wheel lower lid and disconnect air bag module electrical connector.

Arming

1. Ensure nobody is inside vehicle.
2. Connect battery positive cable, then the negative cable.
3. Turn ignition On and observe SRS warning lamp.
4. SRS lamp should light for approximately seven seconds, then go off. This indicates SRS is functioning properly.
5. If SRS warning lamp does not function as outlined, an SRS condition is indicated. Refer to "Diagnosis & Testing."

DESCRIPTION & OPERATION

On 300ZX, air bags will deploy if any

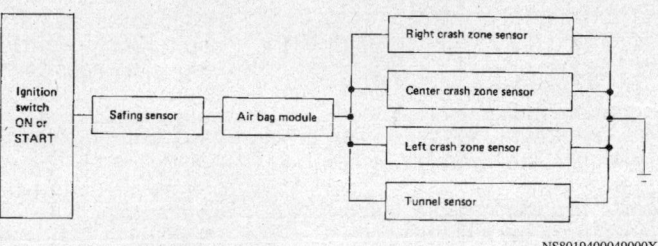

NS8019400049000X

Fig. 1 Supplemental Restraint System (SRS) operation. 300ZX

crash zone sensors (righthand, center, lefthand or tunnel) and safing sensor simultaneously activate while ignition is On, **Fig. 1.**

On Altima, Maxima, Sentra, 200SX, 240SX and Quest, air bag(s) will deploy if diagnosis sensor unit activates while ignition is in On or Start position, **Fig. 2.**

On Pathfinder and 2WD Frontier and Pickup, air bag(s) will deploy if diagnosis sensor unit activates while ignition is in On position, **Fig. 2.**

On 4WD Frontier and Pickups, air bag will deploy if G-sensor and/or crash zone sensor activates simultaneously with the safing sensor while the ignition switch is in the On position.

On all models, when ignition is turned to On or Start, the air bag warning lamp should light for about seven seconds, then go off. This indicates the Supplemental Restraint System (SRS) is operating normally. A failure is present if the lamp is illuminated for seven seconds and then flashing every half second, or if lamp does not light.

PRECAUTIONS

1. After disarming system, wait a minimum of 10 minutes for air bag system to discharge. System will retain power for approximately 10 minutes after disconnection. It is possible for air bag to deploy during this time.
2. All Supplemental Restraint System (SRS) harnesses and connectors are covered with yellow outer insulation.
3. Do not use electrical equipment on these circuits, as unwanted deployment or personal injury may result.
4. SRS sensors must always be installed with arrow mark facing toward front of vehicle.
5. Inspect sensors for cracks, deformities or rust before installation and replace as required.
6. The spiral cable must be aligned with neutral position since its rotations are limited. Do not attempt to turn steering wheel or column after steering gear removal.

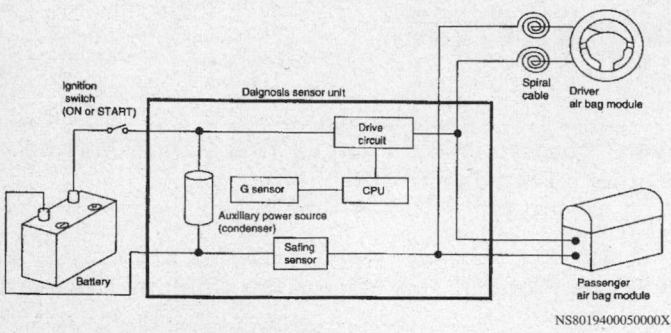

Fig. 2 Supplemental Restraint System (SRS) operation. Altima, Maxima, Sentra, 200SX, 240SX, Pathfinder, 2WD Frontier & Pickup & Quest

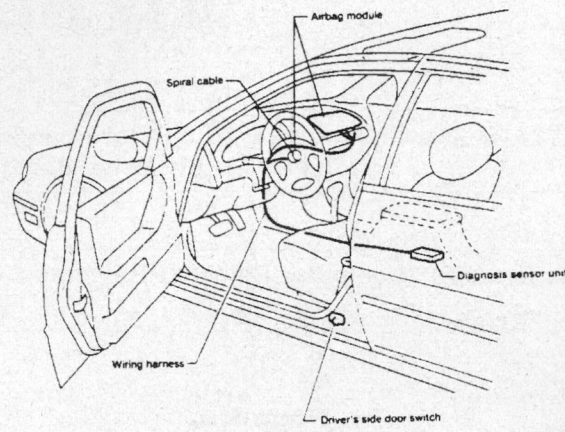

Fig. 3 Supplemental Restraint System (SRS) component locations. Altima

7. Handle air bag module carefully. Always place air bag with pad side facing upward.
8. After removing any Supplemental Restraint System (SRS) component, discard old retaining bolts and install replacements.
9. Conduct self-diagnosis as described in "Diagnosis & Testing" to ensure proper operation of entire Supplemental Restraint System (SRS).

SCHEDULED MAINTENANCE

The air bag system should be inspected every 10 years from date of manufacture as noted on certification label located on driver's door jam.

1. Ensure air bag warning lamp lights for seven seconds when ignition is turned to On or Start. After approximately seven seconds, the warning lamp should go off.
2. **On Frontier models,** ensure instrument panel passenger's air bag deactivation lamp lights for approximately seven seconds when ignition is turned to On or Start, then goes out. **This lamp will remain lit if deactivation switch is turned Off.**
3. **On all models,** visually inspect Supplemental Restraint System (SRS) sensors as follows:
   a. Inspect sensors to ensure arrow marks face toward front of vehicle.
   b. Inspect body, sensors and brackets for dents, cracks, deformities and/or rust.
   c. Inspect sensor harness for binds, connectors for damage and terminals for deformities.
4. Visually inspect Supplemental Restraint System (SRS) control/diagnostic/sensor unit as follows:
   a. Inspect case and bracket for dents, cracks or deformities.
   b. Inspect connectors for damage and terminals for deformities.
5. Visually inspect Supplemental Restraint System (SRS) main harness as follows:
   a. Inspect connectors for poor connections.
   b. Inspect harness for binds, connectors for damage and terminals for deformities.
6. Visually inspect Supplemental Restraint System (SRS) spiral cable as follows:
   a. Visually inspect lockpins and combination switch for damage.
   b. Inspect connectors, flat cable and protective tape for damage.
   c. Inspect steering wheel for noise, binds or difficult operation.
7. Visually inspect air bags and steering wheel as follows:
   a. Remove air bag(s) as described under "Component Service".
   b. Inspect harness cover and connectors for damage and terminals for deformities.
   c. Install air bag module to inspect fit or alignment with steering wheel.
   d. Inspect steering wheel for excessive freeplay.
   e. Install passenger air bag to inspect fit or alignment with instrument panel.

WIRE HARNESS & CONNECTOR REPAIR

SRS wiring is covered by yellow protective coating. Supplemental Restraint System (SRS) wiring should not be spliced, soldered or repaired. If wiring or connectors are found to be damaged or worn, SRS wiring harness should be replaced. When replacing SRS wiring harness, ensure harness is properly routed and all electrical connectors are securely installed.

COMPONENT LOCATIONS

Refer to **Figs. 3 through 11** for SRS component locations.

DIAGNOSIS & TESTING

Refer to **MOTOR's Air Bag Manual** for complete diagnosis and testing information.

COLLISION INSPECTION

When the SRS system has been activated in a collision, perform the following procedure:
1. Replace air bag diagnosis sensor unit.
2. Remove air bag modules.
3. Inspect all SRS system components and replace any component that shows visible signs of damage (dents, cracks and deformation).
4. Install new air bag modules.
5. Conduct self diagnosis as described in "Diagnosis & Testing."

When the SRS system has not been activated but the vehicle has been involved in a collision, perform the following:
1. Inspect all SRS system components and replace any component that shows visible signs of damage (dents, cracks or deformation).
2. Conduct self diagnosis as described in "Diagnosis & Testing."

COMPONENT SERVICE

Disarm air bag system as described under "Air Bag System Disarming and Arming."

Special bolts are coated with a bonding agent. Discard them and replace with new bolts. Tighten bolts to specifications.

Ensure all sensors, control units and brackets are free of deformities, dents, cracks and/or rust. Replace parts showing any visible signs of damage.

SENSORS, REPLACE

300ZX

Disarm SRS as described under "Air Bag System Disarming & Arming." Refer to **Figs. 12 through 14** to replace crash zone sensors, and **Fig. 15** to replace tunnel and safing sensor.

4WD FRONTIER & PICKUP

1. Disarm SRS as described under "Air Bag System Disarming & Arming."

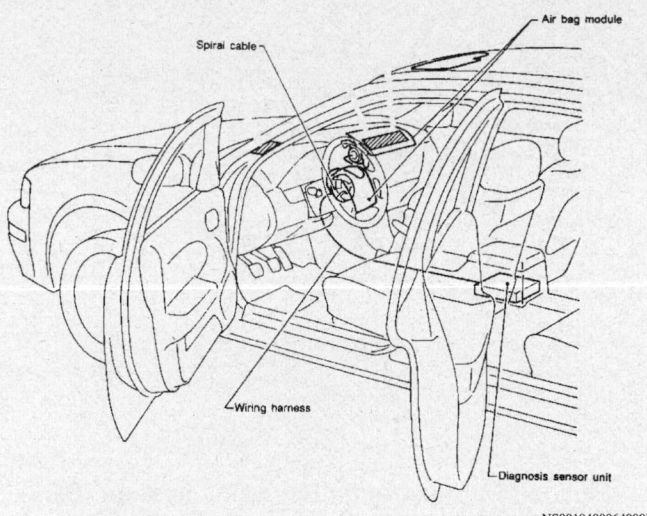

Fig. 4 Supplemental Restraint System (SRS) component locations. 1996–97 Maxima

NS8019400064000X

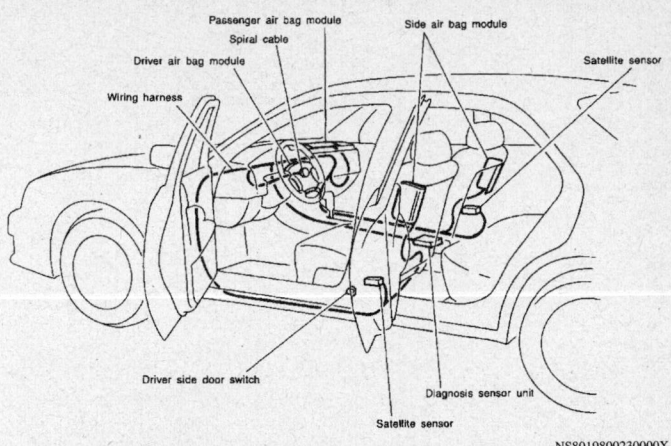

NS8019800230000X

Fig. 5 Supplemental Restraint System (SRS) component locations. 1998–99 Maxima

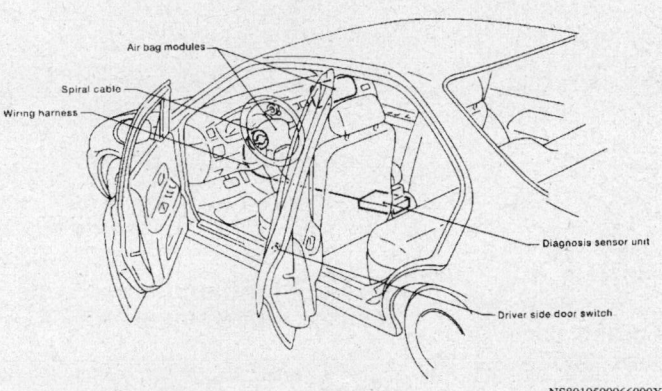

NS8019500066000X

Fig. 6 Supplemental Restraint System (SRS) component locations. Sentra & 200SX

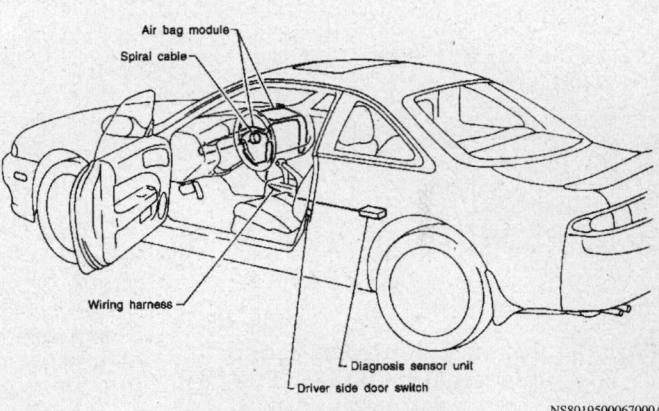

NS8019500067000A

Fig. 7 Supplemental Restraint System (SRS) component locations. 240SX

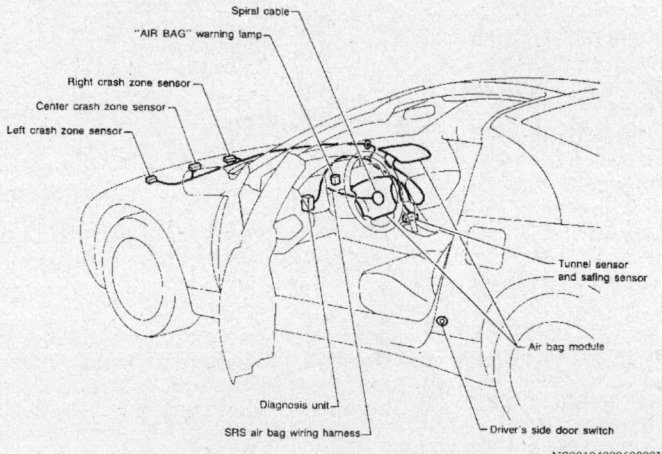

NS8019400068000X

Fig. 8 Supplemental Restraint System (SRS) component locations. 300ZX

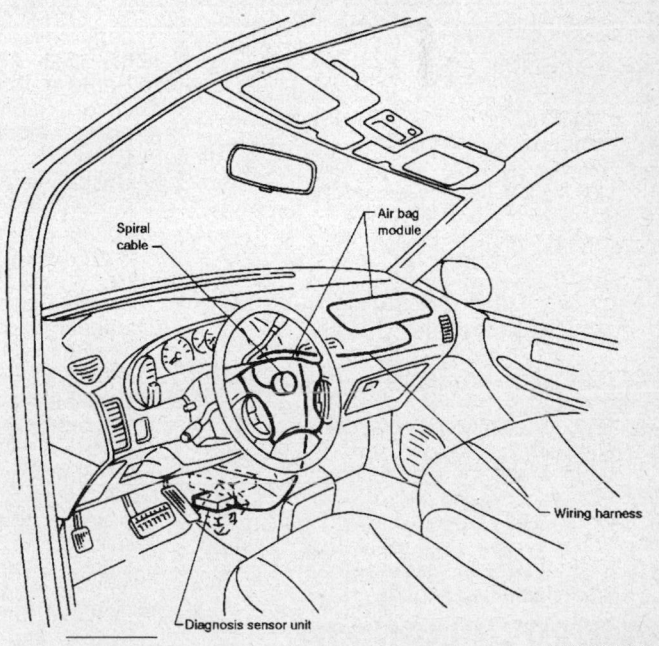

NS8019600124000X

Fig. 9 Supplemental Restraint System (SRS) component locations. Quest

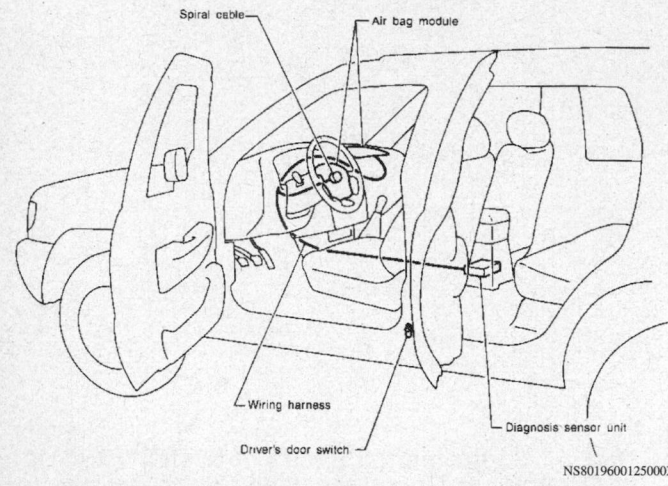

NS8019600125000X

Fig. 10   Supplemental Restraint System (SRS) component locations. Pathfinder

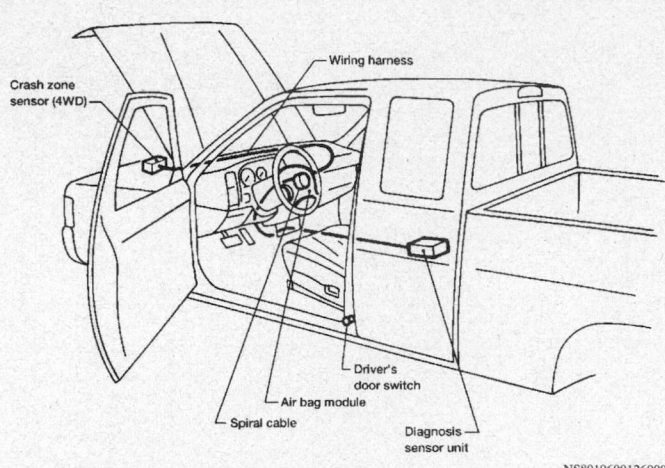

NS8019600126000X

Fig. 11   Supplemental Restraint System (SRS) component locations. Frontier & Pickup

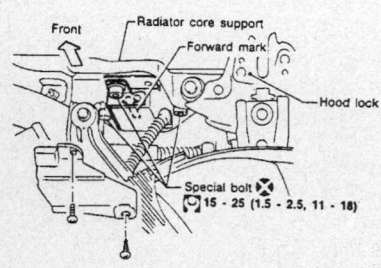

NS8019400096000X

Fig. 12   Center crash zone sensor replacement. 300ZX

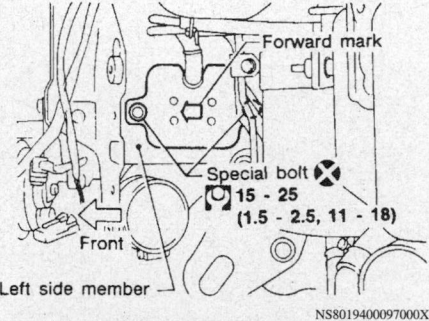

NS8019400097000X

Fig. 13   Lefthand crash zone sensor replacement. 300ZX

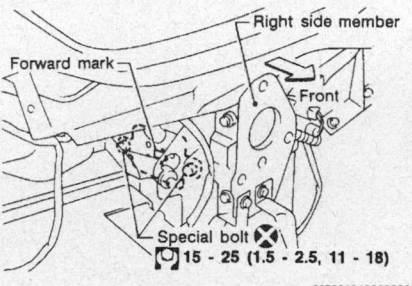

NS8019400098000X

Fig. 14   Righthand crash zone sensor replacement. 300ZX

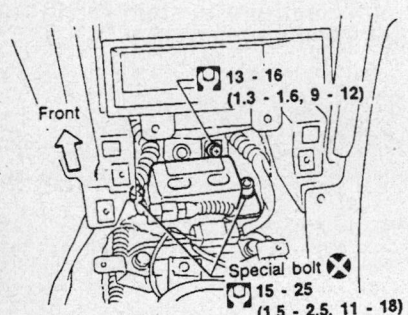

NS8019400099000X

Fig. 15   Tunnel & safing sensor replacement. 300ZX

2. Disconnect driver air bag module connector.
3. Disconnect crash zone connector.
4. Remove crash zone sensor attaching bolts, **Fig. 16,** then the sensor.
5. Reverse procedure to install. During installation, arrow marking on crash zone sensor unit must face toward front of vehicle. Use new coated bolts when installing sensor.

CONTROL/DIAGNOSIS SENSOR UNIT, REPLACE

ALTIMA

1. Disarm SRS as outlined under "Air Bag System Disarming & Arming."

2. Disconnect driver and passenger air bag module connectors.
3. Remove driver side lower instrument panel cover two attaching screws, then the cover.
4. Remove five instrument cluster trim cover attaching screws, then disconnect electrical connectors and remove cover.
5. Unsnap lefthand instrument finisher panel from instrument panel, then disconnect electrical connectors and remove panel.
6. Remove glove compartment from instrument panel.
7. Unsnap transaxle range selector lever boot.
8. Remove seven screws attaching front console cluster bezel to console, then the cluster bezel.
9. Remove righthand instrument finisher panel from instrument panel.
10. Remove audio and deck pockets.
11. Remove four HVAC control mounting screws.
12. Remove four rear console attaching screws, then the rear console.
13. Remove four front console attaching screws and two clips, then the front console.
14. Disconnect diagnosis sensor unit electrical connectors.
15. Remove control unit T50 mounting bolts using bit tool No. J38219, or

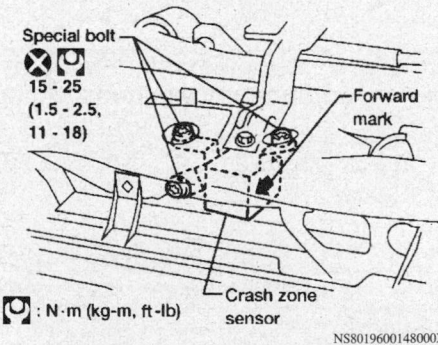

NS8019600148000X

Fig. 16   Crash zone sensor replacement. 4WD Pickup

equivalent, then the control unit.
16. Reverse procedure to install, noting the following:
   a. Arrow marking on diagnosis sensor unit must face toward front of vehicle.
   b. Use new coated bolts when installing diagnosis sensor unit.
   c. Tighten all attaching bolts to specifications.

FRONTIER

1. Disarm SRS as outlined under "Air Bag System Disarming & Arming."
2. Disconnect driver's and passenger's air bag module electrical connectors.

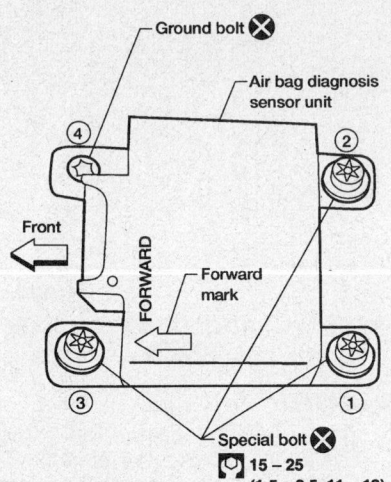

Tightening sequence: ①-②-③-④

NS8019900274000X

Fig. 17   Diagnosis sensor unit fastener tightening sequence. Frontier

3. Remove floor console.
4. Disconnect diagnosis sensor unit electrical connector.
5. Remove ground bolt, then using bit tool No. J38219, or equivalent, remove three T50 bolts and diagnosis sensor unit.
6. Reverse procedure to install, noting the following:
   a. Arrow marking on diagnosis sensor unit must face toward front of vehicle.
   b. Use new coated bolts when installing diagnosis sensor unit.
   c. Tighten all attaching bolts to specifications in sequence, **Fig. 17**.

MAXIMA

1. Disarm SRS as outlined under "Air Bag System Disarming & Arming."
2. Disconnect driver's, passenger's and side air bag module connectors.
3. Remove transmission shifter cover plate.
4. Remove ashtray.
5. Remove two center console attaching screws from under shifter cover plate.
6. Remove console attaching screws from under shifter cover plate and at rear sides of console, then the console.
7. Disconnect diagnosis sensor unit connectors.
8. Using bit tool No. J38219, or equivalent, remove T50 ground bolt and three special bolts securing diagnosis sensor unit, then the unit.
9. Reverse procedure to install, noting the following:
   a. Arrow marking on diagnosis sensor unit must face toward front of vehicle.
   b. Use new coated bolts when installing diagnosis sensor unit.
   c. Tighten all attaching bolts to specifications.

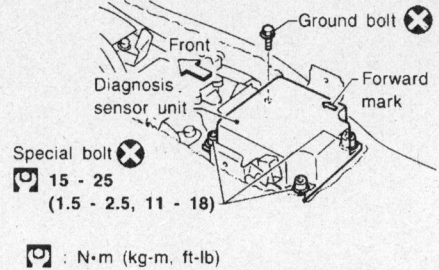

NS8019600150000X

Fig. 18   Diagnosis sensor unit replacement. Pathfinder

QUEST

1. Disarm SRS as outlined under "Air Bag System Disarming & Arming."
2. Disconnect driver's and passenger's air bag module connectors.
3. Remove console box or CD magazine, then disconnect foot lamp electrical connectors.
4. Disconnect diagnosis sensor unit electrical connector.
5. Remove diagnosis sensor unit ground nut.
6. Remove three special T50 bolts using bit tool No. J38219, or equivalent, then the diagnosis sensor unit.
7. Reverse procedure to install, noting the following:
   a. Arrow marking on diagnosis sensor unit must face toward front of vehicle.
   b. Use new coated bolts when installing diagnosis sensor unit.
   c. Tighten fasteners to specifications.

PATHFINDER

1. Disarm SRS as described under "Air Bag System Disarming & Arming."
2. Disconnect driver and passenger air bag module connectors.
3. Remove ash tray.
4. Remove transmission shift lever cover or boot.
5. Remove console attaching screws, then disconnect electrical connectors and remove console.
6. Disconnect diagnosis sensor unit connector, **Fig. 18**.
7. Remove ground bolt, then using a T50 Torx bit, remove three special bolts and diagnosis sensor unit.
8. Reverse procedure to install. During installation, arrow marking on diagnosis sensor unit must face toward front of vehicle. Use new coated bolts when installing diagnosis sensor unit.

PICKUP

1. Disarm SRS as described under "Air Bag System Disarming & Arming."
2. Disconnect driver's air bag module connectors.
3. Remove console attaching screws, then the console.
4. Disconnect diagnosis sensor unit connector, **Fig. 19**.
5. Remove ground bolt, then using a T50 Torx bit, remove three special bolts and diagnosis sensor unit.
6. Reverse procedure to install. During

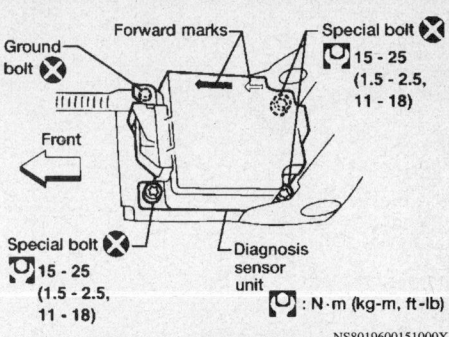

NS8019600151000X

Fig. 19   Diagnosis sensor unit replacement. Pickup

installation, arrow marking on diagnosis sensor unit must face toward front of vehicle. Use new coated bolts when installing diagnosis sensor unit.

SENTRA & 200SX

1. Disarm SRS as described under "Air Bag System Disarming & Arming."
2. Disconnect driver and passenger air bag module connectors.
3. Remove transmission shifter trim plate from console.
4. Remove four rear console attaching screws, then the rear console.
5. Remove four front console attaching screws, then the front console.
6. Disconnect diagnosis sensor unit connector, **Fig. 20**.
7. Remove ground bolt, then using a T50 Torx bit, remove three special bolts and diagnosis sensor unit.
8. Reverse procedure to install. During installation, arrow marking on diagnosis sensor unit must face toward front of vehicle. Use new coated bolts when installing diagnosis sensor unit.

240SX

1. Disarm SRS as described under "Air Bag System Disarming & Arming."
2. Disconnect driver and passenger air bag module connectors.
3. Remove rear seat assembly.
4. Remove diagnosis sensor unit cover.
5. Disconnect diagnosis sensor unit connector, **Fig. 21**.
6. Remove bolt, then use T50 Torx bit to remove special bolts and control unit.
7. Reverse procedure to install. During installation, arrow marking on diagnosis sensor unit must face toward front of vehicle. Use new coated bolts when installing diagnosis sensor unit.

300ZX

Disarm SRS as described under "Air Bag System Disarming & Arming." Refer to **Fig. 22** to replace control unit. Use new coated bolts when installing diagnosis sensor unit. After completing installation, arm SRS as described under " Air Bag System Disarming & Arming."

DRIVER'S AIR BAG MODULE, REPLACE

REMOVAL

1. Disarm SRS as described under "Air

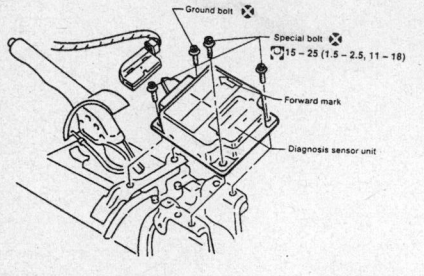

Fig. 20 Diagnosis sensor unit replacement. Sentra & 200SX

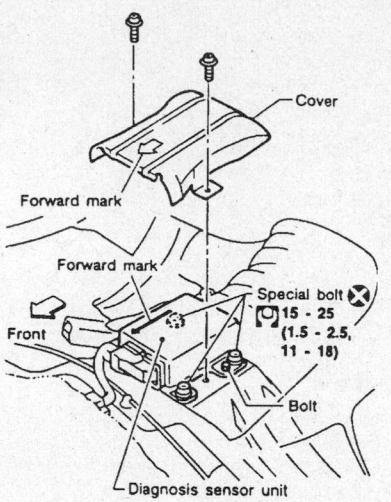

Fig. 21 Diagnosis sensor unit replacement. 240SX

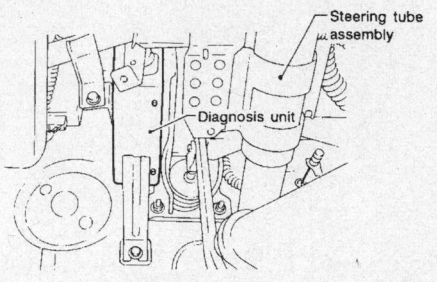

Fig. 22 Control unit replacement. 300ZX

FRONTIER

1. Disarm SRS as outlined under "Air Bag System Disarming & Arming."
2. Remove passenger's air bag module electrical connector clip from inside of glove compartment lid.
3. Disconnect air bag module electrical connector.
4. Remove glove compartment and instrument panel lower righthand side.
5. Remove two T50 bolts retaining air bag module to brackets using bit tool No. J38219, or equivalent.
6. Remove four air bag module mounting nuts.
7. Release retaining clips at upper portion of instrument panel.
8. Remove passenger's air bag module.
9. Reverse procedure to install, noting the following:
   a. Insert front edge of module first to ease installation.
   b. Ensure module wiring harness is properly routed between air bag module and mounting bracket.
   c. Install new module to bracket mounting bolts.
   d. Tighten all attaching fasteners to specifications.

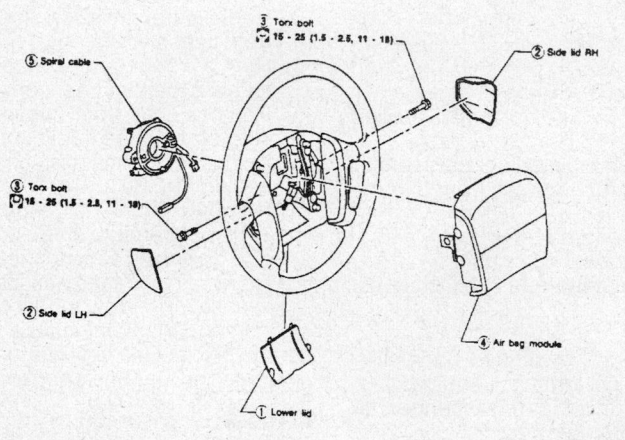

Fig. 23 Driver air bag & spiral cable replacement

Bag System Disarming & Arming."
2. Remove lower lid from steering wheel, then disconnect air bag module connector.
3. Set steering wheel in straight–ahead position, then remove side lids, **Fig. 23.**
4. Use Torx bit to remove left and right air bag module attaching bolts.
5. Remove air bag module from steering wheel.

INSTALLATION

1. Install air bag module and secure with new attaching bolts, then tighten to specified torque listed in "Tightening Specifications."
2. Connect air bag module electrical connector.
3. Install steering column covers and steering wheel lid.
4. Arm SRS as described under "Air Bag System Disarming & Arming."
5. Ensure entire SRS operates properly using Consult tool or warning lamp self–diagnosis. **Air bag warning lamp will light for about seven seconds**

when ignition is turned to On or Start. If lamp remains on or fails to light, refer to "Diagnosis and Testing."

PASSENGER'S AIR BAG MODULE, REPLACE

ALTIMA

1. Disarm SRS as described under "Air Bag System Disarming & Arming."
2. Remove glove compartment lid and glove compartment.
3. Disconnect passengers air bag module connector.
4. Remove two Torx 50 bolts retaining air bag module to brackets, **Fig. 24.**
5. Loosen screws at left and right side of passengers air bag module.
6. Remove passenger air bag module by releasing tabs at upper portion of instrument panel.
7. Reverse procedure to install. When installing, ensure module wiring harness is properly routed between air bag module and mounting bracket.

MAXIMA

1. Disarm SRS as described under "Air Bag System Disarming & Arming."
2. Open glove compartment door, then disconnect passenger inflator connect from body connector, **Fig. 25.**
3. Remove glove compartment lid and glove compartment.
4. Disconnect passenger's air bag module connector.
5. Remove A/C intake unit.
6. Remove passenger's air bag module attaching bolts, **Fig. 26.**
7. Remove passenger's air bag module from instrument panel.
8. Reverse procedure to install. When installing, ensure module wiring harness is properly routed between air bag module and mounting bracket.

SENTRA & 200SX

1. Disarm SRS as described under "Air Bag System Disarming & Arming."
2. Remove glove compartment lid and glove compartment.
3. Disconnect passenger's air bag module connector.
4. Remove two Torx 50 bolts retaining air bag module to brackets, **Fig. 27.**

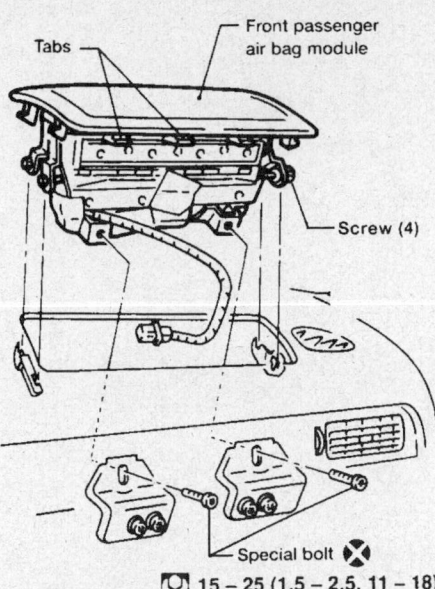

Fig. 24 Passenger's air bag module replacement. Altima

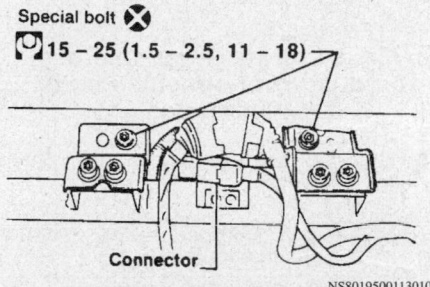

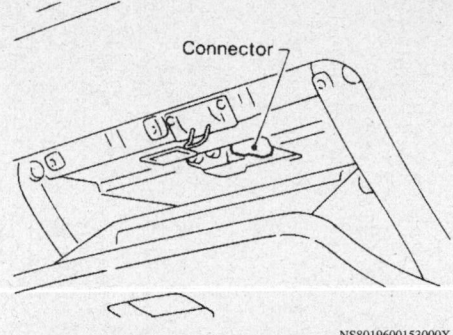

Fig. 25 Passenger's inflator connector location. Maxima

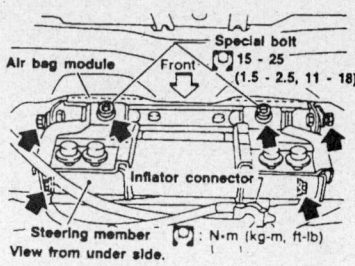

Fig. 26 Passenger air bag replacement. Maxima

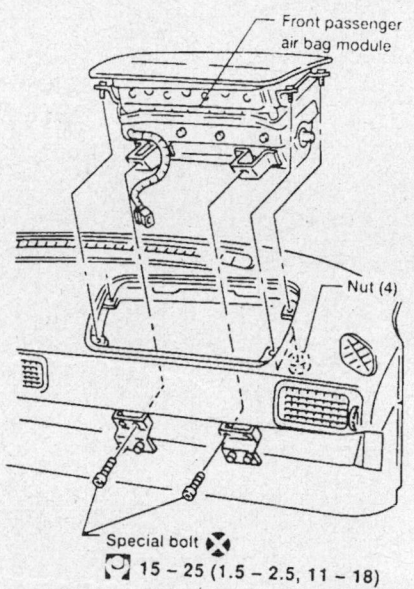

Fig. 27 Passenger air bag replacement (Part 1 of 2). Sentra & 200SX

5. Remove four passenger's air bag module to instrument panel attaching nuts.
6. Remove passenger's air bag module by releasing tabs at upper portion of instrument panel.
7. Reverse procedure to install. When installing, ensure module wiring harness is properly routed between air bag module and mounting bracket.

240SX

1. Disarm SRS as described under "Air Bag System Disarming & Arming."
2. Remove connector bracket from passenger air bag module, then disconnect electrical connector from body harness, **Fig. 28.**
3. Remove instrument panel.
4. Remove passenger's air bag module attaching bolts, **Fig. 29.**
5. Remove passenger's air bag module from instrument panel.
6. Reverse procedure to install. When installing, ensure module wiring harness is properly routed between air bag module and mounting bracket.

Fig. 27 Passenger air bag replacement (Part 2 of 2). Sentra & 200SX

300ZX

1. Disarm SRS as described under "Air Bag System Disarming & Arming."
2. Remove passenger side instrument panel lower cover.
3. Disconnect passenger's air bag module connector, **Fig. 30.**
4. Remove instrument panel.
5. Remove special bolts from left and right side of passenger's air bag module, **Fig. 31.**
6. Remove passenger's air bag module from instrument panel.
7. Reverse procedure to install. When installing, ensure module wiring harness is properly routed between air bag module and mounting bracket.

QUEST

1. Disarm SRS as described under "Air Bag System Disarming & Arming."
2. Remove access panel from behind glove compartment.
3. Disconnect passenger's air bag module connector, **Fig. 32.**
4. Remove glove compartment.

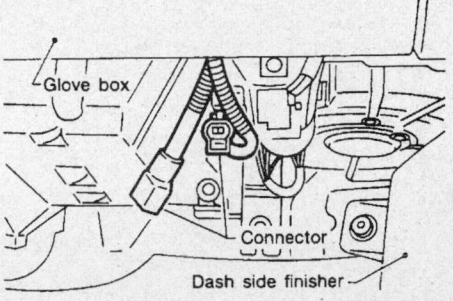

Fig. 28 Passenger's air bag module connector location. 240SX

5. Remove four passenger's air bag module attaching nuts, **Fig. 33.**
6. Remove passenger's air bag module from instrument panel.
7. Reverse procedure to install. When installing, ensure module wiring harness is properly routed between air bag module and mounting bracket.

PATHFINDER

1. Disarm SRS as described under "Air Bag System Disarming & Arming."
2. Remove glove compartment.
3. Disconnect passenger's air bag module connector from body harness.
4. Remove panel from lower passenger side of instrument panel.
5. Remove special bolt from front of passenger's air bag module, **Fig. 34.**
6. Remove instrument panel. Refer to "Dash Panel, Replace" section under "Dash Panel Service" for removal procedure.
7. Remove bolts from left and right side of passenger's air bag module.
8. Remove passenger's air bag module from instrument panel.
9. Reverse procedure to install. When installing, ensure module wiring harness is properly routed between air bag module and mounting bracket. Tighten bolts to specifications.

SPIRAL CABLE, REPLACE

REMOVAL

1. Disarm SRS as described under "Air Bag System Disarming & Arming."
2. Ensure steering wheel is in straight-ahead position.
3. Disconnect horn electrical connector,

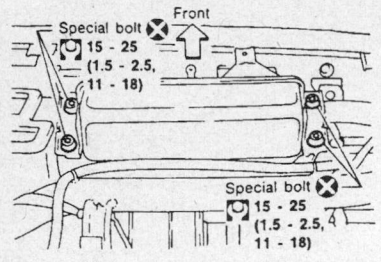

Fig. 29 Passenger air bag replacement. 240SX

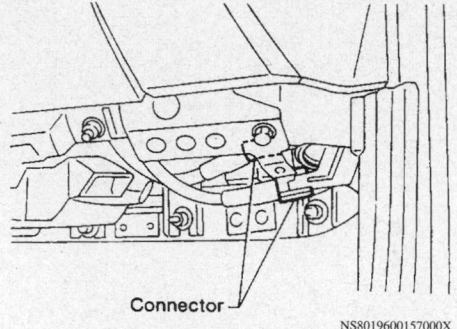

Fig. 30 Passenger's air bag module connector location. 300ZX

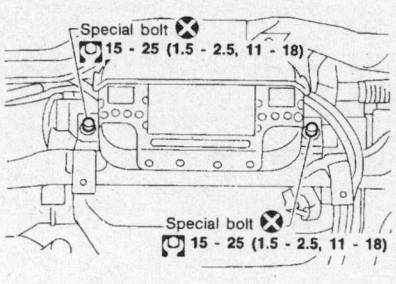

Fig. 31 Passenger air bag replacement. 300ZX

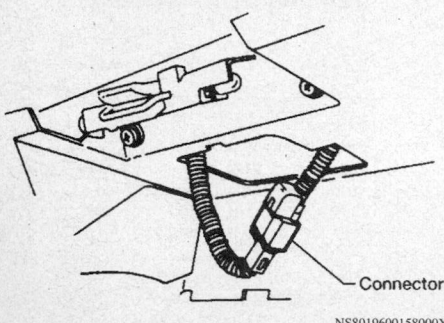

Fig. 32 Passenger's air bag module connector location. Quest

then remove steering wheel retaining nut.
4. Using suitable steering wheel puller, remove steering wheel.
5. Remove steering column upper and lower covers.
6. Attach spiral cable stopper to spiral cable or body with tape.
7. Disconnect electrical connector, then remove four attaching screws and spiral cable.

INSTALLATION
1. Ensure ignition is turned Off.
2. Install spiral cable, tighten attaching screws to specifications, then connect electrical connector.
3. Remove stopper by pulling two guide pins.
   a. Turn spiral cable clockwise until it contacts stopper. Turn cable back approximately two full turns until yellow alignment mark appears on lefthand gear.
   b. Align spiral cable's arrow mark with this yellow mark.
4. **On 1996 models except Quest,** if stopper is not used, align spiral cable to neutral position as follows:
   a. Turn spiral cable clockwise until it contacts stopper, then turn cable back 2.5 turns.
   b. Align cable arrow marks, **Fig. 35.**
5. **On Quest models,** if stopper is not used, align spiral cable to neutral position as follows:
   a. Turn spiral cable clockwise until it contacts stopper.
   b. Place alignment marks on inner and outer portions of spiral cable housing, **Fig. 36.**
   c. Rotate spiral cable three turns in the clockwise direction and align

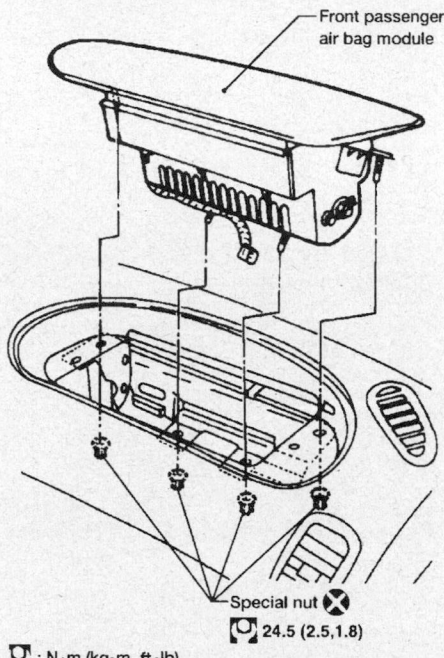

Fig. 33 Passenger's air bag module replacement. Quest

match marks. Use tape to hold spiral cable in position.
6. **On all models,** install steering wheel, aligning spiral cable guide pins, then pull spiral cable connector through wheel.
7. Connect horn electrical connector, then secure spiral cable harness with pawls in steering wheel.
8. Tighten steering wheel retaining nut to specifications.

SIDE AIR BAG MODULE, REPLACE

MAXIMA
1. Disarm SRS as outlined under "Air Bag System Disarming & Arming."
2. Remove seat back finisher. **Use caution when using a clip removal tool to avoid damaging air bag module wiring harness.**
3. Disconnect side air bag module electrical connector.
4. Remove side air bag module mounting nuts, then the module.

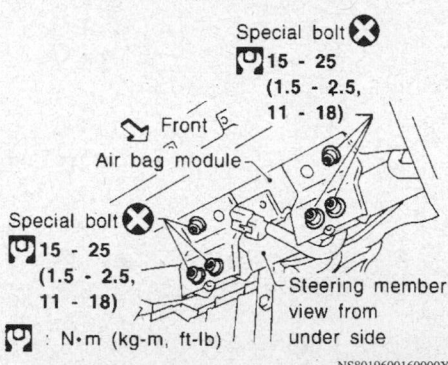

Fig. 34 Passenger's air bag module front attaching bolts. Pathfinder

5. Reverse procedure to install, noting the following:
   a. Install side air bag module to seat using new mounting nuts. Tighten to specifications.
   b. Install seat back finisher with new clips. **Ensure wiring harness is not pinched.**
   c. Perform Self-Diagnosis and ensure SRS operates properly.

SATELLITE SENSOR, REPLACE

MAXIMA
1. Remove seat belt pre-tensioner as outlined under " Seat Belt Pre-Tensioner, Replace."
2. Disconnect satellite sensor electrical connector, **Fig. 37.**
3. Remove satellite sensor mounting bolt and special nuts, then the sensor.
4. Reverse procedure to install, noting the following:
   a. Install new special nuts and bolts.
   b. Tighten all fasteners to specifications.
   c. Ensure all electrical connectors are securely in place.

SEAT BELT PRE-TENSIONER, REPLACE

MAXIMA
1. Disarm SRS as outlined under "Air Bag System Disarming & Arming."
2. Slide front seat as far forward as possible, then remove seat track to floor pan rear mounting covers and bolts.

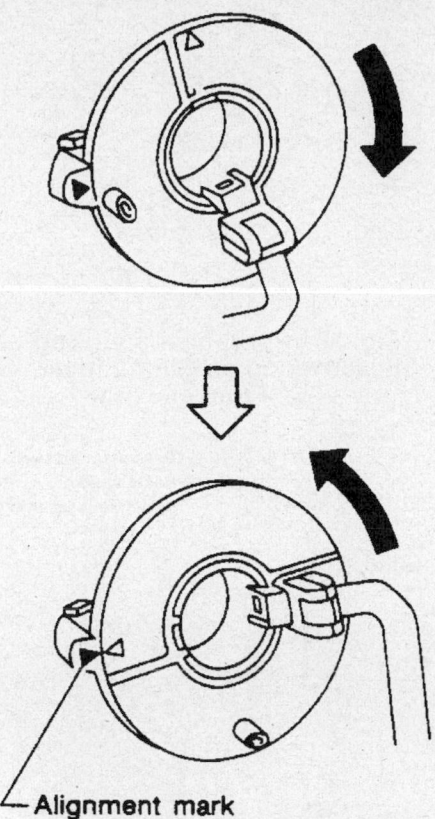

Alignment mark

NS8019600162000X

Fig. 35   Spiral cable alignment. 1996 models except Quest

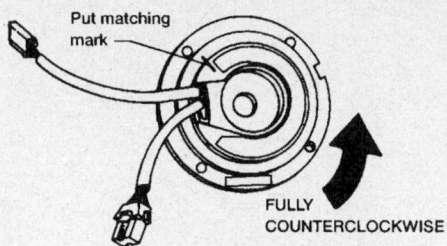

Put matching mark

FULLY COUNTERCLOCKWISE

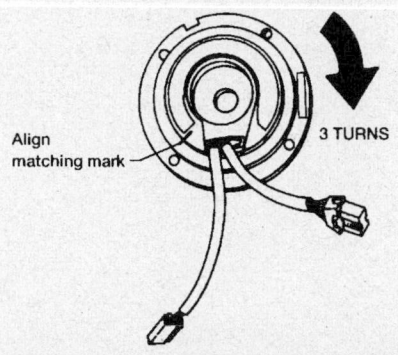

Align matching mark

3 TURNS

NS8019600163000X

Fig. 36   Spiral cable alignment. Quest

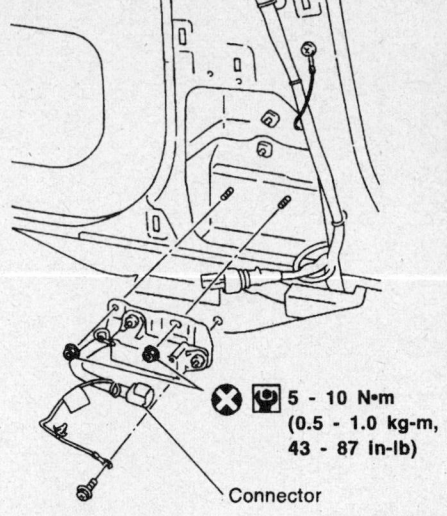

Connector

NS8019800242000X

Fig. 37   Satellite sensor removal. Maxima

3. Slide front seat as far rearward as possible, then remove seat track to floor pan front mounting bolts.
4. Remove front seat.
5. Remove shoulder belt anchor bolt.
6. Remove center pillar upper and lower moldings.
7. Remove seat belt retractor mounting bolts, **Fig. 38.**
8. Reverse procedure to install, noting the following:
   a. Install new special nuts and bolts.
   b. Tighten all fasteners to specifications.
   c. Ensure all electrical connectors are securely in place.

PASSENGER'S AIR BAG DEACTIVATION SWITCH

FRONTIER

1. Disarm SRS as outlined under "Air Bag System Disarming & Arming."
2. Remove instrument panel lower center trim panel.
3. Disconnect deactivation switch and cigar lighter electrical connectors.
4. Note deactivation switch and lock cylinder positioning.
5. Remove two deactivation switch mounting screws, then the switch, **Fig. 39.**
6. Reverse procedure to install, noting the following:
   a. The deactivation switch is keyed for proper installation. Improper positioning will result in switch damage.

b. Ensure deactivation switch and lock cylinder are positioned as noted during removal.
c. Ensure all electrical connectors are securely in place.

PASSENGER'S AIR BAG DEACTIVATION SWITCH INDICATOR LAMP

FRONTIER

1. Disarm SRS as outlined under "Air Bag System Disarming & Arming."
2. Remove driver's air bag module as outlined under " Driver's Air Bag Module, Replace."
3. Remove steering wheel.
4. Remove steering column cover.
5. Remove instrument panel lefthand lower trim panel.
6. Remove four instrument cluster bezel attaching screws, then the bezel.
7. Release deactivation indicator lamp tabs from rear side of instrument cluster bezel, **Fig. 40.**
8. Remove indicator lamp from front side of cluster bezel.
9. Reverse procedure to install.

PASSENGER'S AIR BAG DEACTIVATION SWITCH LOCK CYLINDER

FRONTIER

1. Disarm SRS as outlined under "Air Bag System Disarming & Arming."
2. Remove passenger's air bag deactivation switch as outlined.
3. Remove four screws and switch housing from instrument panel lower center trim panel.
4. Note deactivation switch and lock cylinder positioning, then remove cylinder retainer clip from bottom of housing,

Fig. 41.
5. Remove lock cylinder from front of housing.
6. Reverse procedure to install, noting the following:
   a. The deactivation switch is keyed for proper installation. Improper positioning will result in switch damage.
   b. Ensure deactivation switch and lock cylinder are positioned as noted during removal.
   c. Ensure cylinder retainer clip and all electrical connectors are securely in place.

AIR BAG MODULE DISPOSAL

   Before scrapping an air bag module or vehicle equipped with an air bag, the air bag must be deployed.

PRECAUTIONS

1. Vehicle should be placed outdoors with at least 20 feet of open space on all sides.
2. Remove battery from vehicle and position at least 15 feet from vehicle lefthand door.
3. Before deploying air bag, ensure no people, animals or objects are within 20 feet of vehicle.
4. Wear goggles when handling air bag modules.
5. Use care not to inhale gas produced by air bag deployment.
6. Do not handle deployed air bag for 30 minutes after deployment, due to extremely high temperatures. Never apply water to deployed air bag.
7. After disconnecting battery, wait at least 10–12 minutes before proceeding with disposal procedure.
8. Never disassemble an air bag. It cannot be used again.
9. Seal deployed air bag assemblies in heavy duty plastic bags, then dispose with other automotive scrap.
10. Wash hands after handling any deployed SRS components.

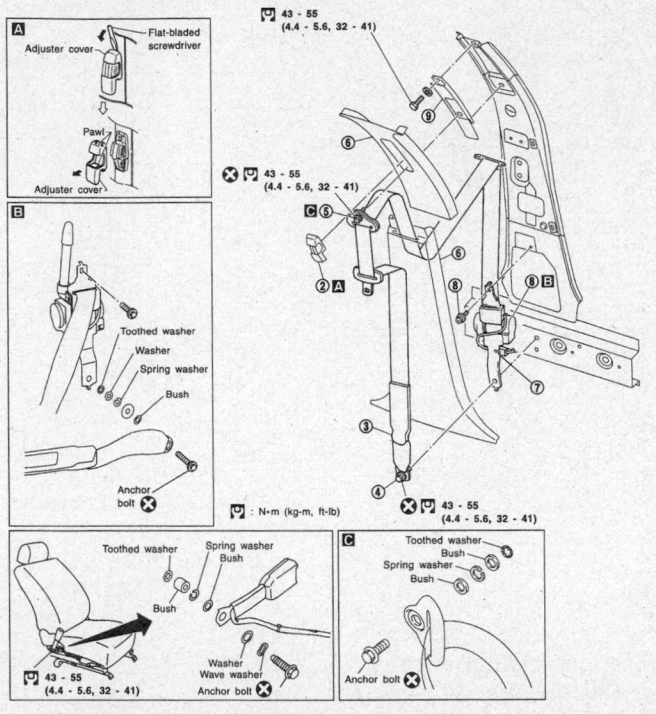

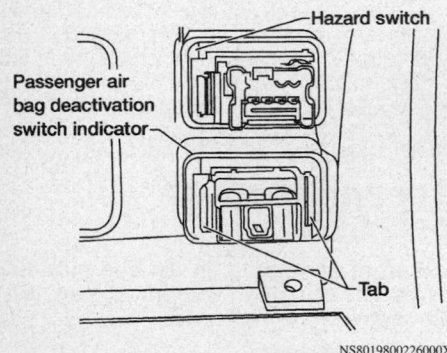

Fig. 38 Front seat belt removal. Maxima

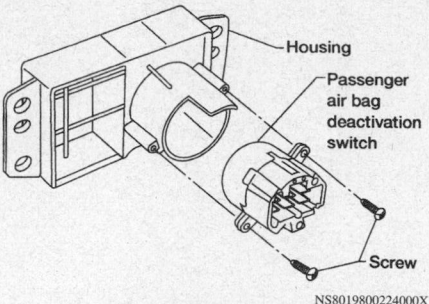

NS8019800224000X

Fig. 39 Passenger's air bag deactivation switch removal. Frontier

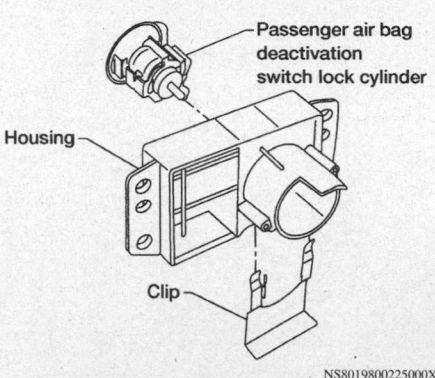

NS8019800225000X

Fig. 41 Passenger's air bag deactivation switch lock cylinder retainer clip removal. Frontier

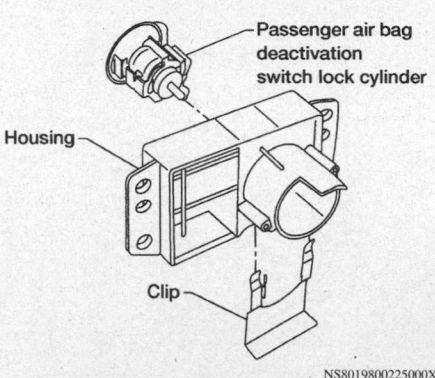

NS8019800226000X

Fig. 40 Passenger's air bag deactivation switch indicator lamp tabs. Frontier

DEPLOYMENT TOOL INSPECTION

1. Locate fully charged 12 volt battery at least 15 feet away from vehicle.
2. Connect special deployment tool No. J38381, or equivalent, to battery and ensure green lamp marked "Deployment Tool Power" on righthand side lights. If red lamp lights, reverse battery connections.
3. Connect deployment tool male and female check connectors.

4. Push tool switch to On position to ensure lefthand lamp marked "Air Bag Connector Voltage" lights. If lamp does not light, replace deployment tool.

DEPLOYING AIR BAG MODULE
Inside Vehicle

When vehicle is to be scrapped, deploy air bag module(s) while still mounted in vehicle.

1. Vehicle should be placed outdoors with at least 20 feet of open space on all sides.
2. Disarm SRS as described under "Air Bag System Disarming & Arming."
3. Remove battery from vehicle and position at least 15 feet from vehicle lefthand door.
4. **On models equipped with passenger air bag,** attach special deployment tool adapters No. J38382-30.
5. **On all models,** connect deployment tool connector to air bag module(s).
6. Connect deployment tool to battery. Ensure righthand lamp marked "Deployment Tool Power" lights.
7. Before deploying air bag, ensure no people, animals or objects are within 20 feet of vehicle.
8. Press deployment tool switch. Lefthand lamp marked "Air Bag Connector

Voltage" will light and air bag will deploy.
9. Dispose of air bag module.

Outside Vehicle

Activate only one air bag at a time.

1. Disarm SRS as described under "Air Bag System Disarming & Arming."
2. Remove air bag assembly from vehicle as described in, " Air Bag Assembly, Replace."
3. Securely anchor air bag module to vise.
4. Connect special deployment tool to air bag module connector.
5. At least 15 feet from air bag assembly, connect deployment tool to battery. Ensure righthand lamp marked "Deployment Tool Power" glows green.
6. Before beginning deployment, ensure no people, animals or objects are within 20 feet of air bag.
7. Press deployment tool button. Lefthand lamp marked "Air Bag Connector Voltage" will light and module will deploy.

TIGHTENING SPECIFICATIONS

Year	Component	Torque/ Ft. Lbs.
ALTIMA, MAXIMA, PATHFINDER, SENTRA, 200SX & 240SX		
1996–99	Control/Diagnosis Sensor Unit Bolts	11–18
	Driver's Air Bag Module to Steering Wheel Bolts	11–18
	Passenger's Air Bag Module Torx 50 Bolts	11–18
	Sensor Bolts	11–18
	Steering Wheel Nut	22–29
300ZX		
1996–98	Control Unit Bolts	11–18
	Driver's Air Bag Module Bolts	11–18
	Passenger's Air Bag Module Torx 50 Bolts	11–18
	Sensor Bolts	11–18
	Steering Wheel Nut	22–19
QUEST		
1996–99	Diagnosis Sensor Unit Special Bolts	11–18
	Diagnosis Sensor Unit Ground Bolts	43–52①
	Driver's Air Bag Module Bolts	11–18
	Steering Wheel Nut	22–29
FRONTIER & PICKUP		
1996–99	Crash Zone Sensor (4WD)	11–18
	Diagnosis Sensor Unit	11–18
	Driver's Air Bag Module Bolts	11–18
	Steering Wheel Nut	22–29

① — Inch lbs.

Dash Panel Service

NOTE: Refer To The "Dash Gauges" Section For Related Information.

NOTE: On Air Bag Equipped Models, Refer To "Air Bag System Precautions" Located In The Front Of This Manual For System Disarming & Arming Procedures.

NOTE: Refer To "Computer Relearn Procedures" Located In The Front Of This Manual For Computer Relearn Procedures.

INDEX

PRECAUTIONS
BATTERY GROUND CABLE

Prior to service, disconnect battery ground cable and isolate as required.

AIR BAG SYSTEMS

Refer to "Air Bag System Precautions" in the front of this manual for system disarming and arming procedures.

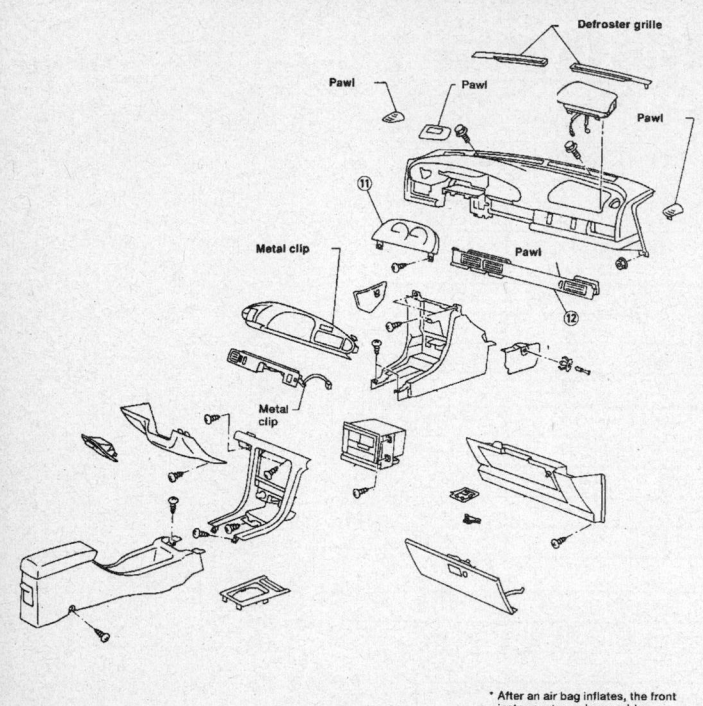

Fig. 1 Exploded view of instrument panel. 1996–97 Altima

* After an air bag inflates, the front instrument panel assembly should be replaced.

NS9149100001000A

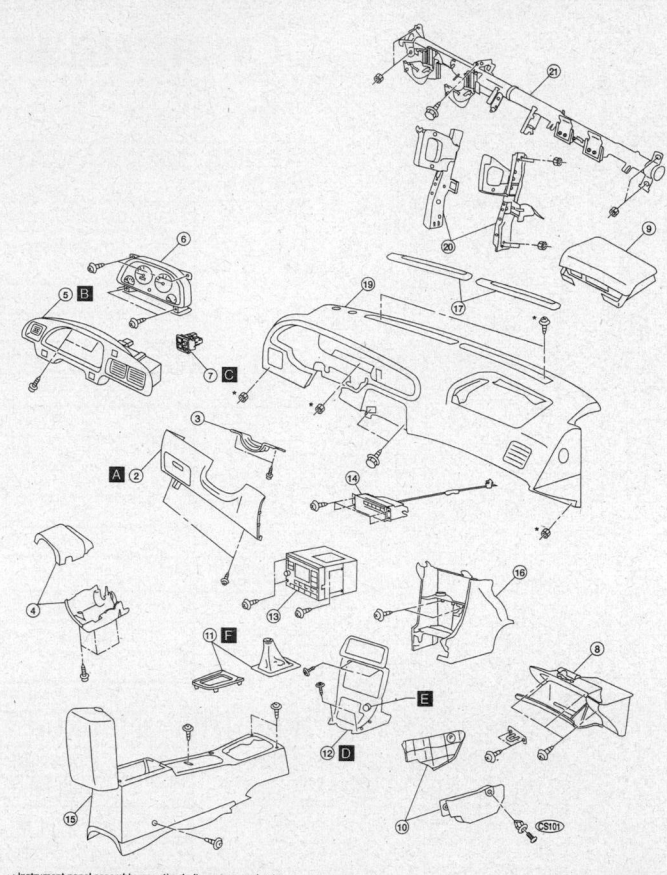

*: Instrument panel assembly mounting bolts, screws and nuts.

NS9149900015000X

Fig. 2 Exploded view of instrument panel. 1998–99 Altima

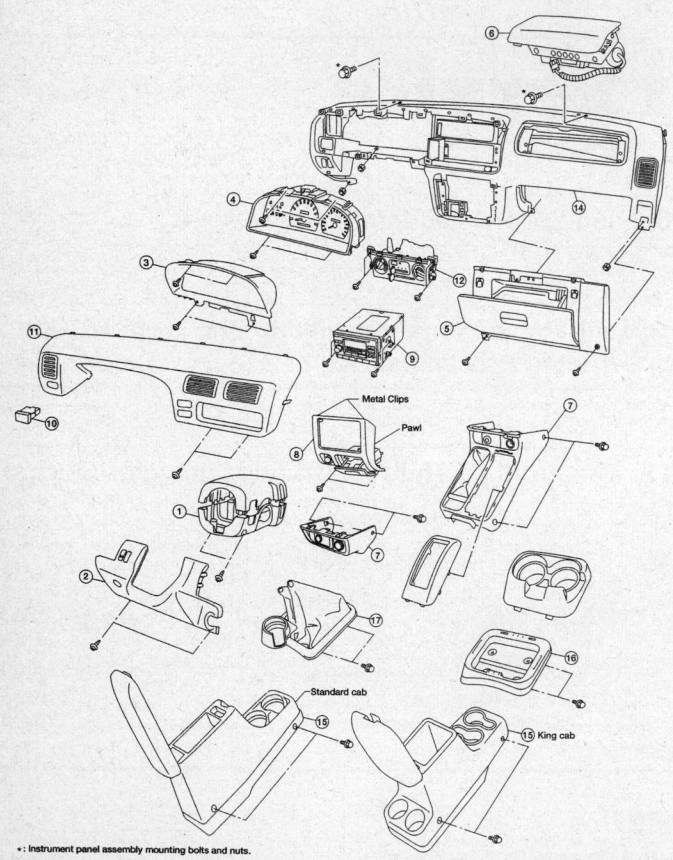

*: Instrument panel assembly mounting bolts and nuts.

NS9149900016000X

Fig. 3 Exploded view of instrument panel. Frontier

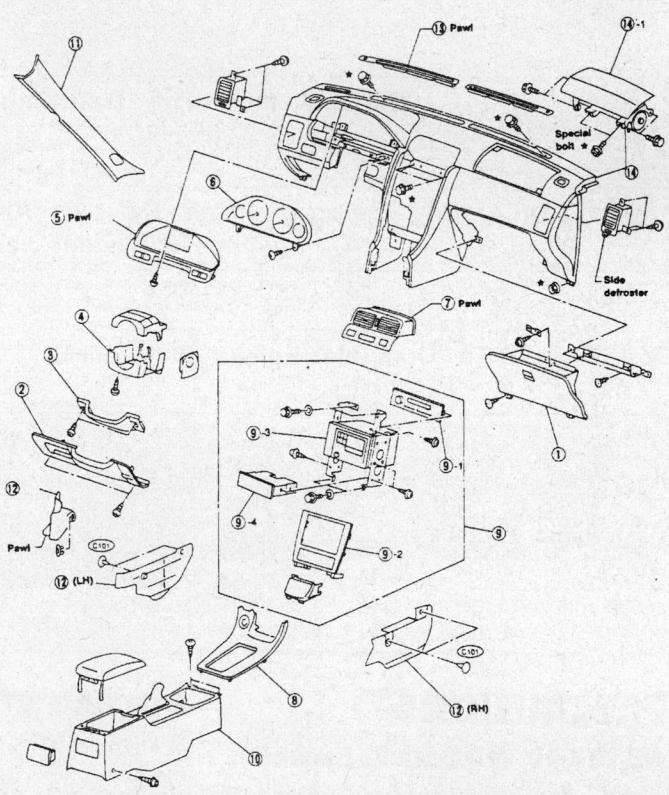

NS9149500010000X

Fig. 4 Exploded view of instrument panel. Maxima

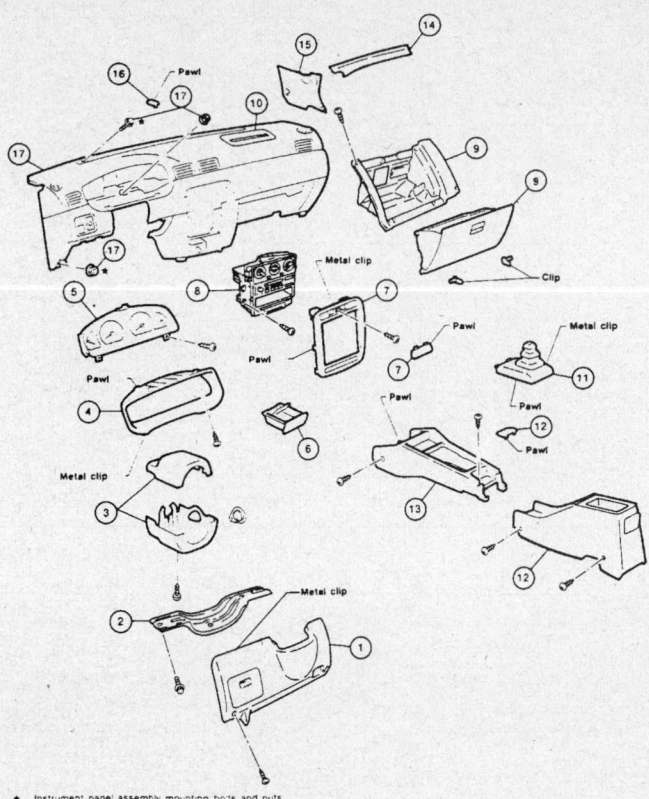

Fig. 5 Exploded view of instrument panel. Sentra & 200SX

NS9149500011000X

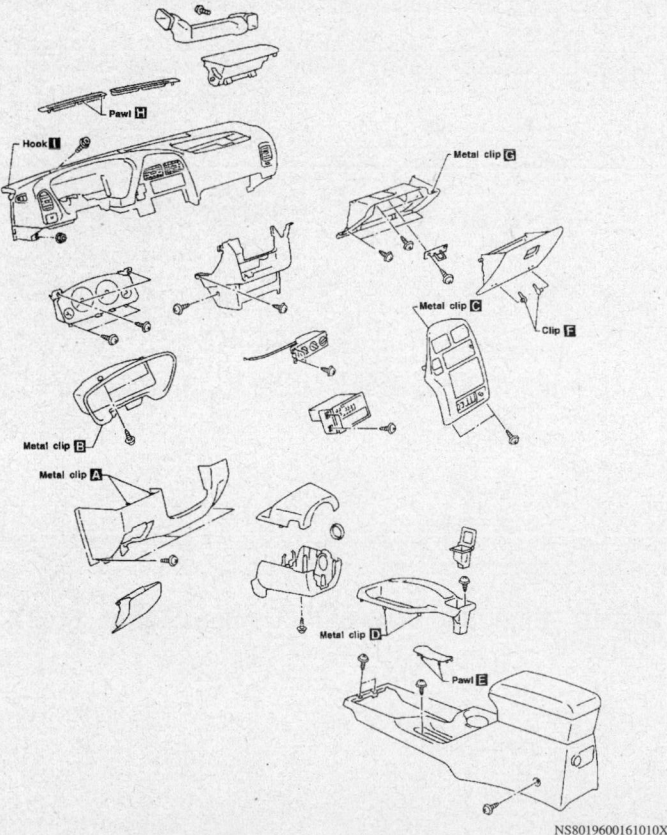

Fig. 7 Exploded view of instrument panel (Part 1 of 2). Pathfinder

NS8019600161010X

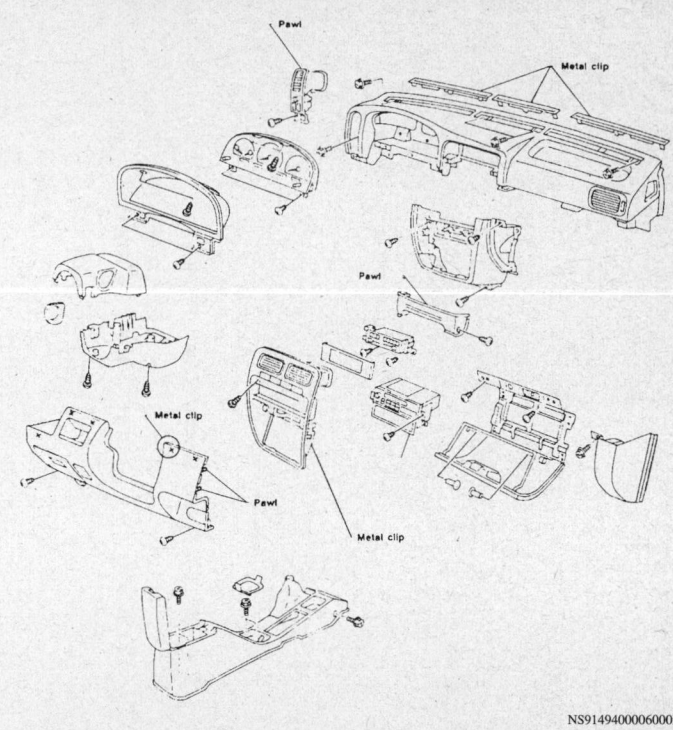

Fig. 6 Exploded view of instrument panel. Pickup

NS9149400006000X

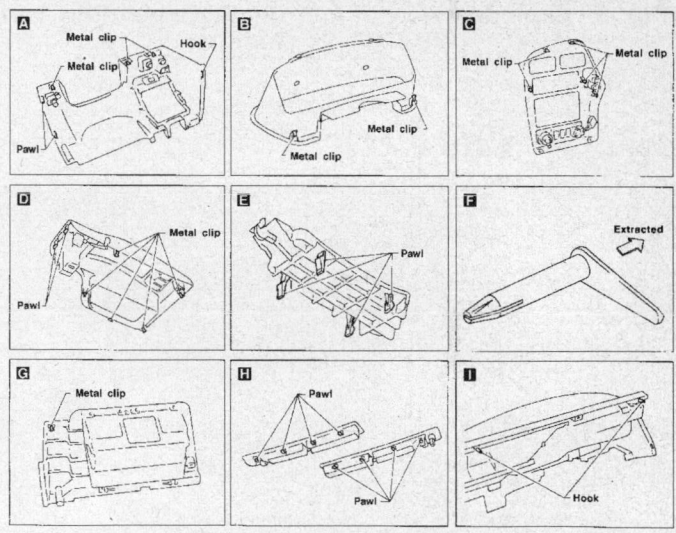

Fig. 7 Exploded view of instrument panel (Part 2 of 2). Pathfinder

NS8019600161020X

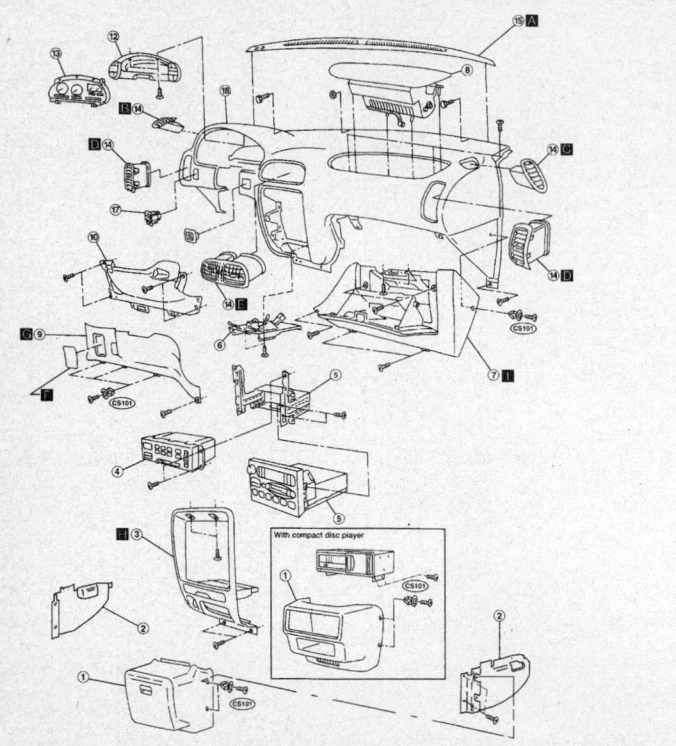

Fig. 8 Exploded view of instrument panel (Part 1 of 2). 1996–98 Quest

NS9149600014010X

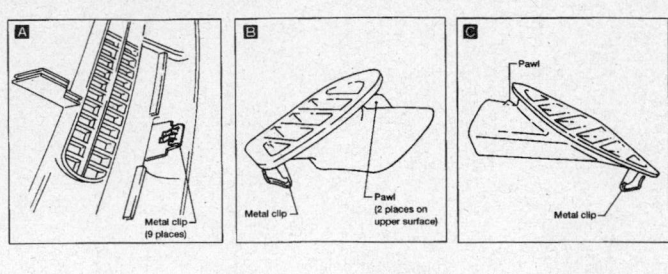

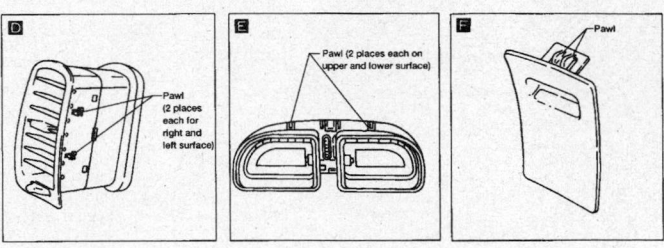

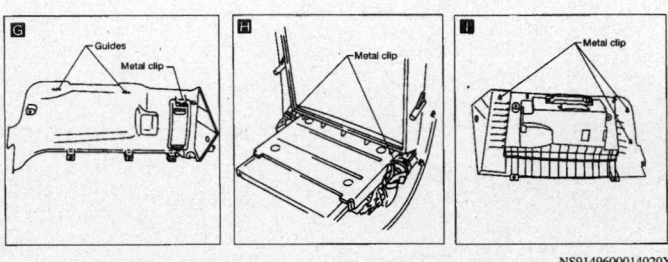

NS9149600014020X

Fig. 8 Exploded view of instrument panel (Part 2 of 2). 1996–98 Quest

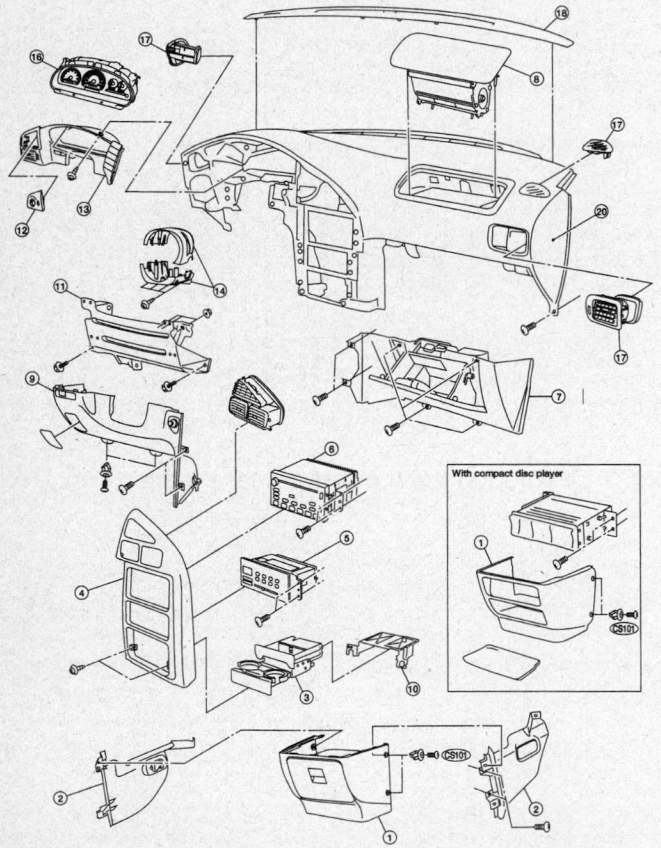

NS9149900017000X

Fig. 9 Exploded view of instrument panel. 1999 Quest

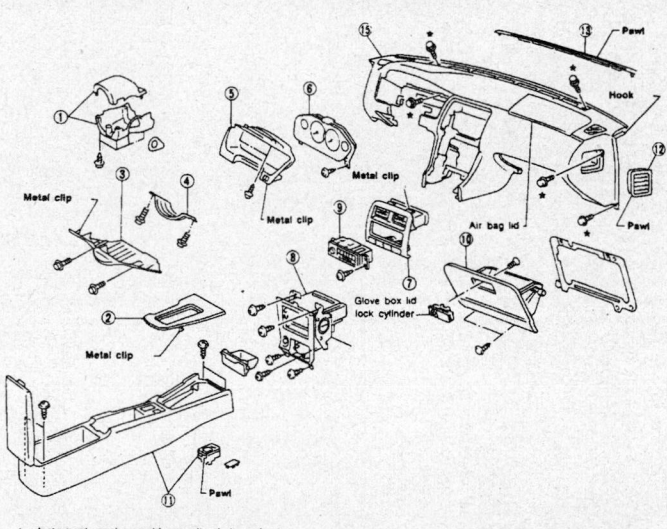

★ : Instrument panel assembly mounting bolts and nuts

NS9149500012000X

Fig. 10 Exploded view of instrument panel. 240SX

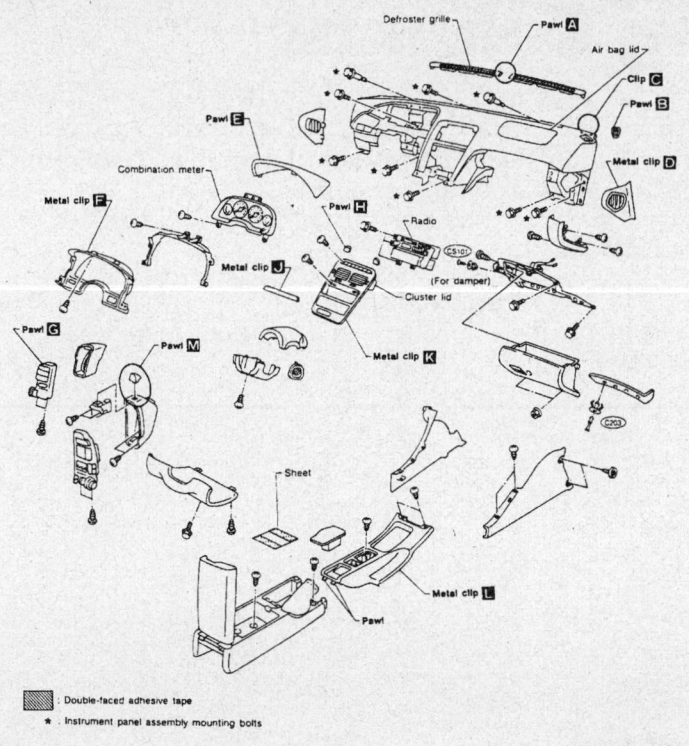

Fig. 11 Exploded view of instrument panel. 300ZX

NS9149500013000X

DASH PANEL
REPLACE
ALTIMA

Refer to **Figs. 1 and 2,** for instrument panel replacement.

FRONTIER

Refer to **Fig. 3** when replacing these dash panels.

MAXIMA

Refer to **Fig. 4** when replacing these dash panels.

SENTRA & 200SX

Refer to **Fig. 5** when replacing these dash panels.

PATHFINDER & PICKUP

Refer to **Figs. 6 and 7** when replacing these dash panels.

QUEST

Refer to **Figs. 8 and 9,** for instrument panel replacement.

240SX

Refer to **Fig. 10** when replacing this dash panel.

300ZX

Refer to **Fig. 11** when replacing these dash panels.

Steering Columns

NOTE: On Air Bag Equipped Models, Refer To "Air Bag System Precautions" Located In The Front Of This Manual For System Disarming & Arming Procedures.

INDEX

PRECAUTIONS

AIR BAG SYSTEMS

Refer to "Air Bag System Precautions" in the front of this manual for system disarming and arming procedures.

BATTERY GROUND CABLE

Prior to service, disconnect battery ground cable and isolate as required.

STEERING COLUMN SERVICE

For steering column service, refer to **Figs. 1 through 10.**

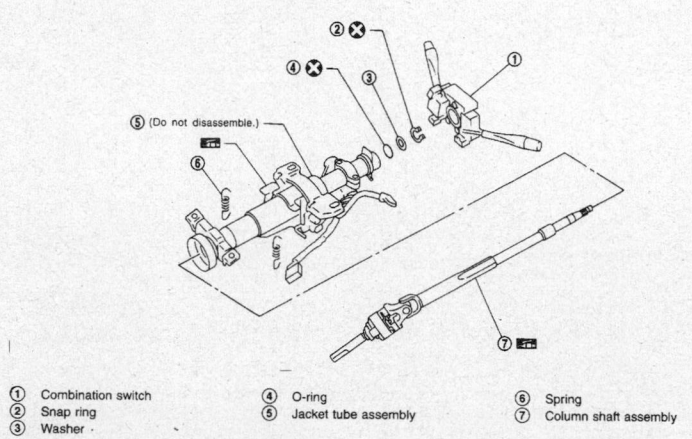

① Combination switch   ④ O-ring   ⑥ Spring
② Snap ring   ⑤ Jacket tube assembly   ⑦ Column shaft assembly
③ Washer

NS6049600015000X

Fig. 1 Exploded view of steering column. Altima

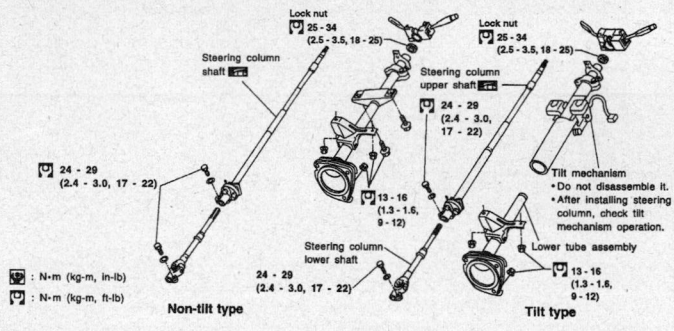

NS6049900020000X

Fig. 2 Exploded view of steering column. Frontier

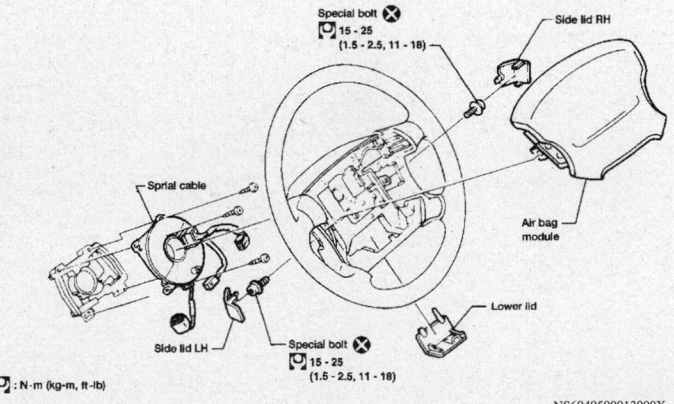

NS6049500013000X

Fig. 3 Exploded view of steering column. Maxima

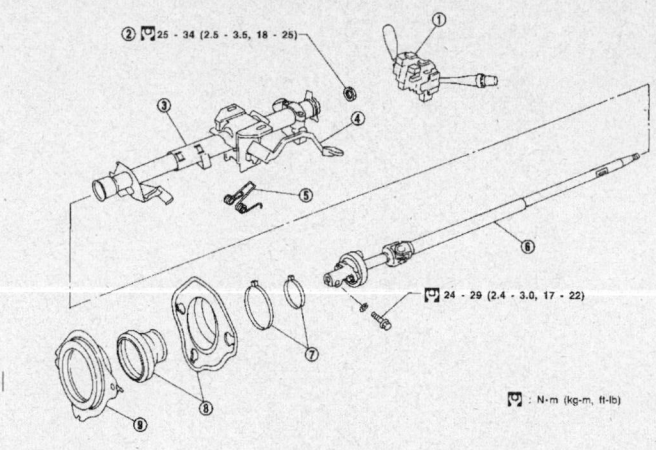

② ⎡25 - 34 (2.5 - 3.5, 18 - 25)

24 - 29 (2.4 - 3.0, 17 - 22)

⎡ : N·m (kg-m, ft-lb)

① Combination switch
② Lock nut
③ Jacket tube assembly
④ Tilt lever
⑤ Tilt spring
⑥ Steering column shaft assembly
⑦ Band
⑧ Jacket tube bracket insulator assembly
⑨ Hole cover

NS6049600016000X

Fig. 4 Exploded view of steering column. Pathfinder

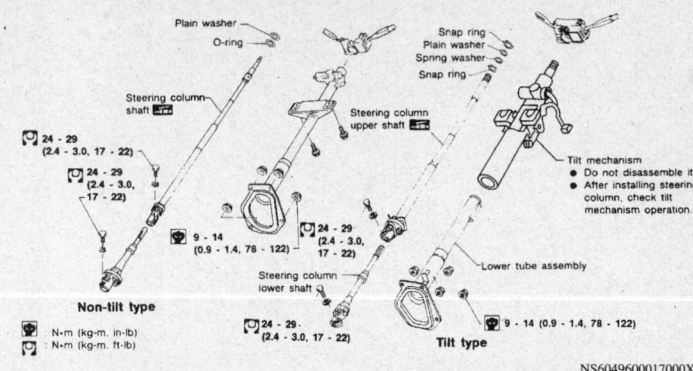

Plain washer
O-ring
Snap ring
Plain washer
Spring washer
Snap ring

Steering column shaft

Steering column upper shaft

Tilt mechanism
● Do not disassemble it.
● After installing steering column, check tilt mechanism operation.

24 - 29 (2.4 - 3.0, 17 - 22)
24 - 29 (2.4 - 3.0, 17 - 22)
9 - 14 (0.9 - 1.4, 78 - 122)
24 - 29 (2.4 - 3.0, 17 - 22)

Lower tube assembly

Non-tilt type

Steering column lower shaft

24 - 29 (2.4 - 3.0, 17 - 22)

⎡ : N·m (kg-m, in-lb)
⎡ : N·m (kg-m, ft-lb)

9 - 14 (0.9 - 1.4, 78 - 122)

Tilt type

NS6049600017000X

Fig. 5 Exploded view of steering column. Pickup

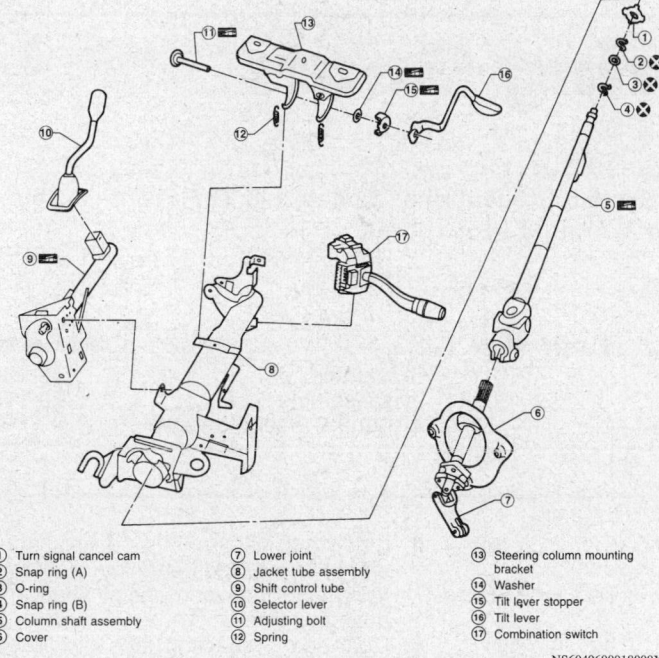

① Turn signal cancel cam
② Snap ring (A)
③ O-ring
④ Snap ring (B)
⑤ Column shaft assembly
⑥ Cover
⑦ Lower joint
⑧ Jacket tube assembly
⑨ Shift control tube
⑩ Selector lever
⑪ Adjusting bolt
⑫ Spring
⑬ Steering column mounting bracket
⑭ Washer
⑮ Tilt lever stopper
⑯ Tilt lever
⑰ Combination switch

NS6049600018000X

Fig. 6 Exploded view of steering column. 1996–98 Quest

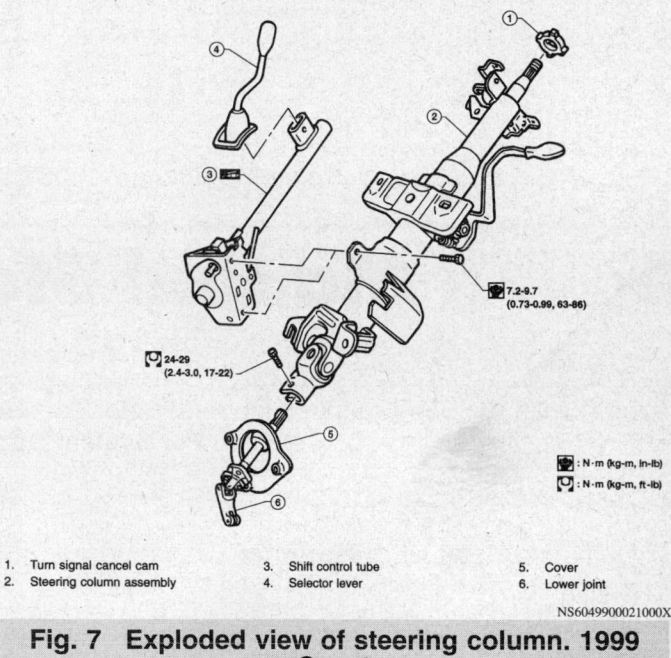

7.2-9.7 (0.73-0.99, 63-86)

24-29 (2.4-3.0, 17-22)

⎡ : N·m (kg-m, in-lb)
⎡ : N·m (kg-m, ft-lb)

1. Turn signal cancel cam
2. Steering column assembly
3. Shift control tube
4. Selector lever
5. Cover
6. Lower joint

NS6049900021000X

Fig. 7 Exploded view of steering column. 1999 Quest

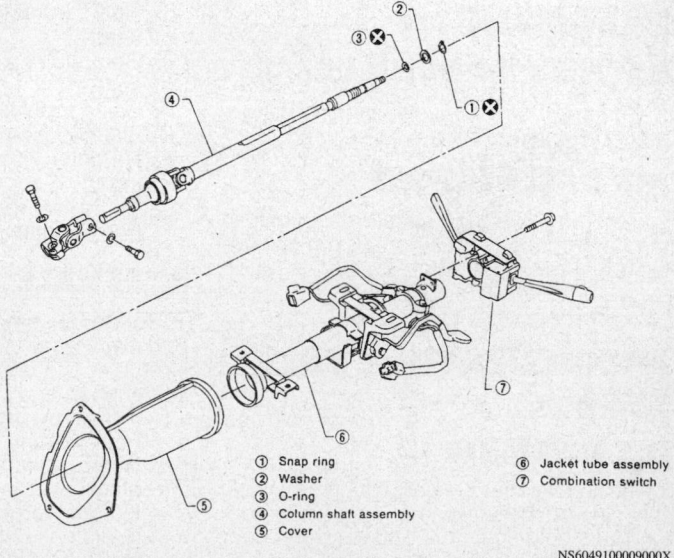

① Snap ring
② Washer
③ O-ring
④ Column shaft assembly
⑤ Cover
⑥ Jacket tube assembly
⑦ Combination switch

NS6049100009000X

Fig. 8 Exploded view of steering column. Sentra & 200SX

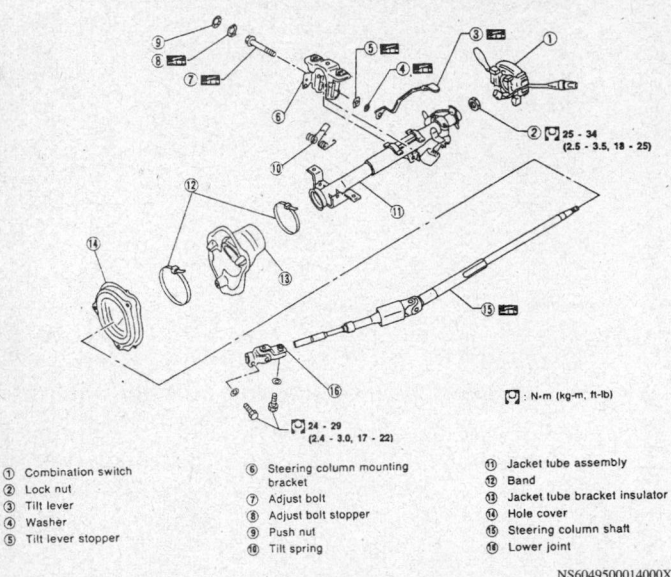

Fig. 9 Exploded view of steering column. 240SX

1. Combination switch
2. Lock nut
3. Tilt lever
4. Washer
5. Tilt lever stopper
6. Steering column mounting bracket
7. Adjust bolt
8. Adjust bolt stopper
9. Push nut
10. Tilt spring
11. Jacket tube assembly
12. Band
13. Jacket tube bracket insulator
14. Hole cover
15. Steering column shaft
16. Lower joint

NS6049500014000X

Fig. 10 Exploded view of steering column. 300ZX

NS6049100012000X

Manual Steering Gears

NOTE: On Air Bag Equipped Models, Refer To "Air Bag System Precautions" Located In The Front Of This Manual For System Disarming & Arming Procedures.

INDEX

PRECAUTIONS

BATTERY GROUND CABLE

Prior to service, disconnect battery ground cable and isolate as required.

AIR BAG SYSTEMS

Refer to "Air Bag System Precautions" in the front of this manual for system disarming and arming procedures.

RECIRCULATING BALL TYPE

DISASSEMBLE

1. Remove filler plug and drain oil.
2. Secure steering gear in vise with suitable holding fixture and set worm gear in straight ahead position.
3. Remove sector shaft cover attaching bolts, Fig. 1.
4. Remove sector shaft with sector shaft cover by pushing from opposite end.
5. Remove sector shaft cover from sector shaft.
6. Remove sector shaft oil seal, if necessary.
7. Using tool No. KV48101500, or equivalent, loosen adjusting plug locknut.
8. Remove worm gear with worm bearing.
9. Using suitable tools, remove oil seal from adjusting plug.

ASSEMBLE

Before assembling, lubricate all metal parts with gear oil and apply suitable lubricant in space between sealing lips of new sector shaft and adjusting plug oil seals.
1. Fit worm gear assembly with worm gear bearing in gear housing.
2. Using suitable tool, install adjusting plug.
3. Rotate worm shaft a few turns in both directions to settle worm bearing, then measure worm bearing preload. Preload should be 1.7–5.2 inch lbs.
4. Apply suitable sealant to locknut, install and tighten locknut, then ensure preload is still within specifications.
5. Select and install shaft adjusting screw shim that provides endplay of .0004–.0012 inch between sector shaft and adjusting screw.
6. Coat seal contacting face of oil seal with gear oil, then press oil seal into steering gear housing.
7. Install sector cover on adjusting screw with sector shaft.
8. Set worm gear in straight ahead position, then insert sector shaft and sector cover assembly with gasket into gear housing, being careful not to scratch oil seal.
9. **Torque** sector cover attaching bolts to 11–18 ft. lbs.
10. Fill assembly with gear oil and install filler plug.
11. Rotate worm gear a few turns in both directions to settle steering gear, then measure steering gear preload in straight ahead direction. Preload should be 7.4–10.9 inch lbs. **Backlash at gear arm top end should be 0–.004 inch.**
12. If steering gear preload is not within specifications, readjust adjusting

Fig. 1 Recirculating ball type steering gear

Lock nut

Filler plug

Sector shaft cover

Gasket

Adjusting shim

Sector shaft adjusting screw
When adjusting backlash, use it.

Sector shaft

Steering gear housing

Oil seal
Removed oil seal,
must not be used again.

Spring washer

Lock nut

Oil seal
Removed oil seal, must not be used again.

Adjusting plug
When adjust worm bearing
preload, use it.

Ball nut and worm assembly
- Be careful not to allow ball nut to run
  down to either end of worm.
  The ends of ball guides will be damaged
  if nut is rotated until it stops at the end
  of worm.
- Do not detach ball nut from worm shaft
  assembly.
  If necessary, replace ball nut and worm
  assembly with sector shaft.

NS6039100008000X

Fig. 1 Recirculating ball type steering gear

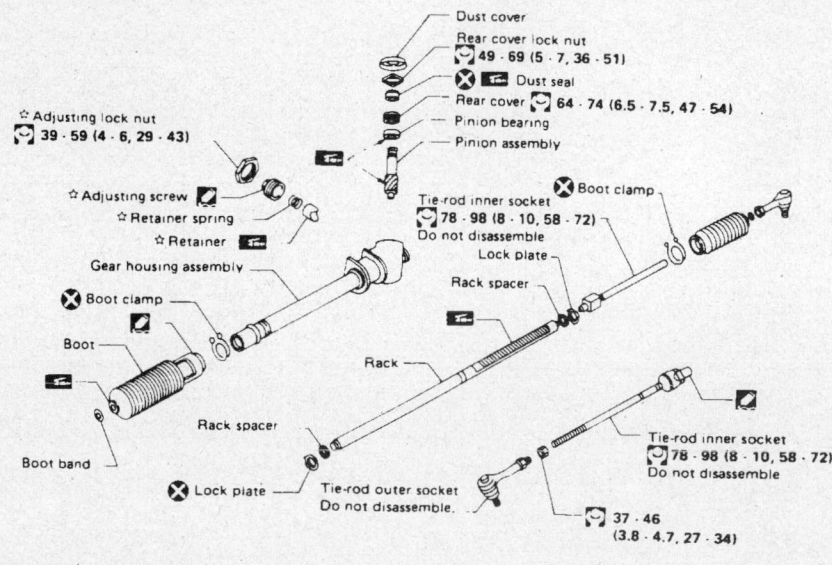

N·m (kg-m, ft-lb)

- Dust cover
- Rear cover lock nut
  49 - 69 (5 - 7, 36 - 51)
- Dust seal
- Rear cover 64 - 74 (6.5 - 7.5, 47 - 54)
- Pinion bearing
- Pinion assembly

☆ Adjusting lock nut
39 - 59 (4 - 6, 29 - 43)

☆ Adjusting screw

☆ Retainer spring

☆ Retainer

Gear housing assembly

Boot clamp

Boot

Rack spacer

Boot band

Lock plate

Boot clamp

Tie-rod inner socket
78 - 98 (8 - 10, 58 - 72)
Do not disassemble

Lock plate

Rack spacer

Rack

Tie-rod inner socket
78 - 98 (8 - 10, 58 - 72)
Do not disassemble

Tie-rod outer socket
Do not disassemble.

37 - 46
(3.8 - 4.7, 27 - 34)

NS6039100009000X

Fig. 2 Rack & pinion manual steering gear

screw to obtain correct preload. **Always adjust steering gear preload by turning adjusting screw in tightening direction.**

RACK & PINION TYPE
DISASSEMBLE

When disassembling manual steering gear, refer to **Fig. 2.**

ASSEMBLE

When assembling manual steering gear, refer to **Fig. 2,** noting the following:
1. Install rack gear from rack side, then place rack gear in neutral position.
2. Install pinion assembly, then with pinion rack held in place, install guide clip as shown in **Fig. 3.**
3. Apply suitable locking compound to threaded portion of rear cover, then install rear cover using a suitable tool.
4. Apply suitable grease to sealing lips of dust seal, then wrap suitable tape around pinion gear and install dust seal.
5. Apply suitable sealing compound to threaded portion of retainer cover, then install retainer, spring and retainer cover.
6. Adjust pinion rotating torque as follows:
   a. Place gear in neutral position and loosen locknut, then **torque** adjusting screw to 43 inch lbs.
   b. Loosen adjusting screw, then re to 1.74 inch lbs.
   c. Move rack over its entire stroke several times, then return to neutral position.
   d. Measure pinion rotating torque within a range of ±180° from neutral position. Find position where rotating torque is at its maximum.
   e. Loosen adjusting screw at position where rotating torque is at its maximum, then hand tighten adjusting screw until its end touches retainer.
   f. **Torque** locknut to 6–8 ft. lbs. while holding adjusting screw in position. **Ensure adjusting screw does not rotate.**
   g. While rotating pinion in the ±100° range from neutral position, ensure rotating **torque** is 6–10 inch lbs.
   h. If pinion rotating torque is not as specified, readjust as required. If correct adjustment can not be obtained, replace retainer spring.
7. Apply suitable locking compound to threaded portion of tie rod inner socket, then install inner socket into rack end together with new lock plate. **Ensure lock plate ratchet enters groove at end portion of rack.**
8. Tighten tie rod inner socket, then bend lock plate at two cutout portions of inner socket. **Remove burrs after bending lock plate to prevent damaging boot.**
9. Tighten outer socket locknut so tie rod length " L " is 6.94 inches and screwed length "I" is .98 inch or more, **Fig. 4.**
10. Measure rack stroke. Ensure stroke is 2.894 inches on both sides.

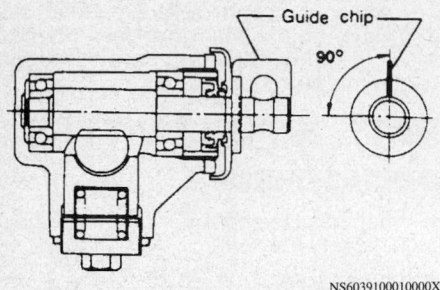

Fig. 3   Pinion guide clip installation

11. Apply suitable sealing compound to contact surfaces between boot and gear housing, then install boot and boot clamps. **Ensure boot clamps do not interfere with any other parts. Also, use caution not to twist boot.**

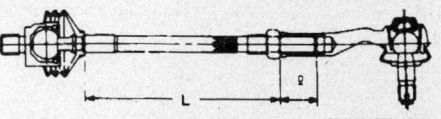

Fig. 4   Tie rod length adjustment

TIGHTENING SPECIFICATIONS

Year	Component	Torque/Ft. Lbs.
PATHFINDER & PICKUP		
1996–98	Adjusting Plug Locknut	166–188
	Gear Housing To Frame	62–71
	Pitman Arm To Sector Shaft	174–195
	Sector Shaft Adjusting Locknut	25–40
	Sector Shaft Cover Bolt	33–40
SENTRA & 200SX		
1996–99	Adjusting Screw Locknut	29–43
	Gear Housing Clamp Bolt	54–72
	Rear Cover Locknut	36–51
	Tie Rod Locknut	27–34
	Tie Rod To Gear	58–72
	Tie Rod To Knuckle	22–29

Power Steering

NOTE: On Air Bag Equipped Models, Refer To "Air Bag System Precautions" Located In The Front Of This Manual For System Disarming & Arming Procedures.

INDEX

APPLICATION CHART

Model	Year	Rack Id. No.
Altima	1996–99	PR26K
Frontier	1998–99	PB48S & PB59K
Maxima	1996–99	PR26AC
Pathfinder	1996–99	PR32K
Pickup	1996–97	PB48S & PB59K
Quest	1996–97	PR28T
Sentra & 200SX	1996–99	PR24T
240SX	1996–98	PR24AC
300ZX	1996	PR26AE

POWER STEERING PRESSURE SPECIFICATIONS

Year	Vehicle	Maximum Pressure At Idle, psi
1996	Altima	1109–1194
	Maxima	1180–1126
	Pathfinder	1251–1337
	Pickup	1109–1194
	Quest	1067–1209
	Sentra & 200SX	1038–1123
	240SX	1251–1337
	300ZX	1109–1194
1997–99	Altima	1109–1194
	Frontier	1109–1194
	Maxima	1180–1126
	Pathfinder	1221–1337
	Pickup	1109–1194
	Quest	1067–1209
	Sentra & 200SX	1038–1123
	240SX	1251–1337

PRECAUTIONS

BATTERY GROUND CABLE

Prior to service, disconnect battery ground cable and isolate as required.

AIR BAG SYSTEMS

Refer to "Air Bag System Precautions" in the front of this manual for system disarming and arming procedures.

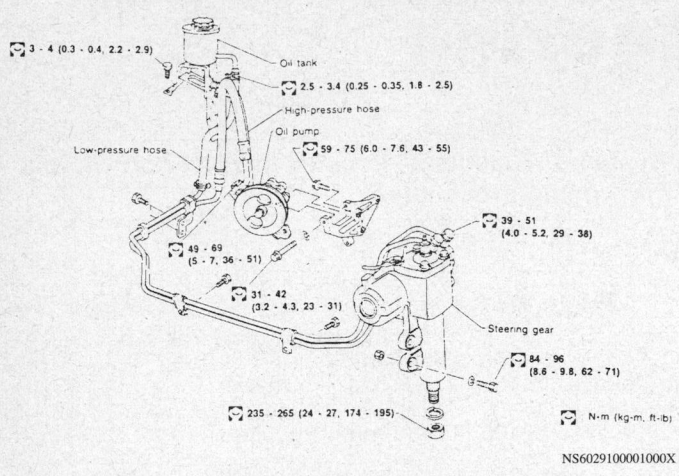

Fig. 1   Twin orifice steering system

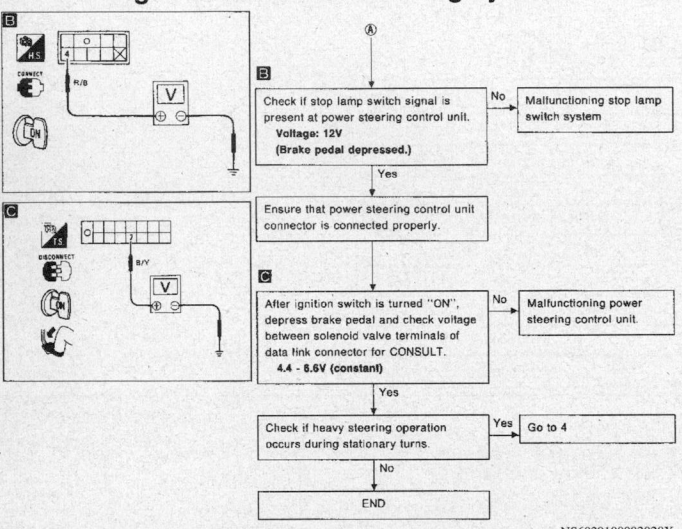

Fig. 2   Twin orifice steering system diagnosis (Part 2 of 10)

DESCRIPTION

TWIN ORIFICE POWER STEERING

The twin orifice power steering system, **Fig. 1,** uses a vehicle speed sensing electronic control design. Valve sensitivity is controlled in response to vehicle speed to achieve maximum steering effort.

When a vehicle speed signal is not entered into the control unit for about 10 seconds during normal operations, a fail safe system activates to maintain a steering effort similar to that of high speed operation. If a foot brake, parking brake or transmission position signal is not entered the steering system is held in a fail safe control state. This symptom is referred to as "Heavy Steering During Stationary Turns."

DIAGNOSIS & TESTING

TWIN ORIFICE POWER STEERING

When diagnosing the twin orifice power steering system refer to **Figs. 2 through 4** for diagnostic procedures.

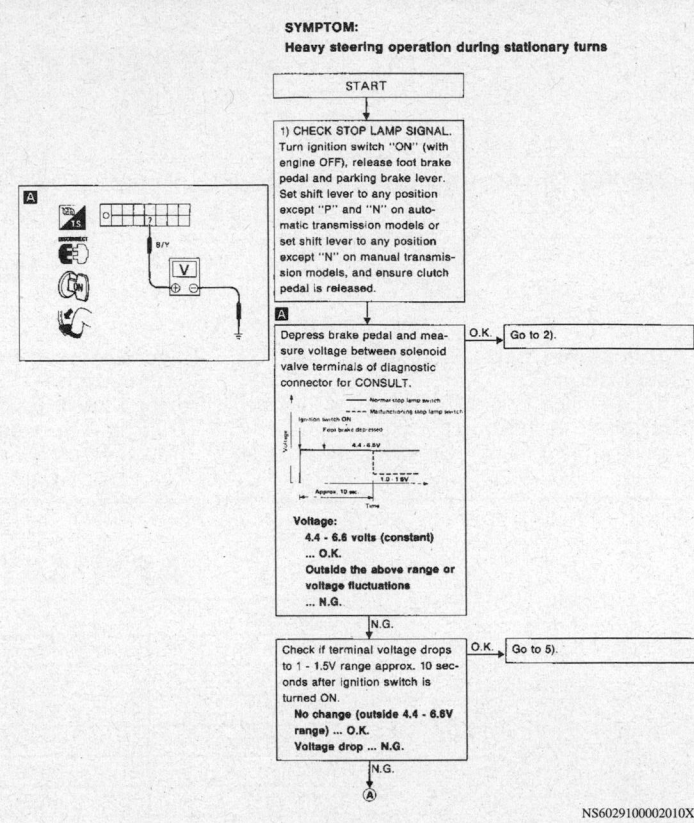

Fig. 2   Twin orifice steering system diagnosis (Part 1 of 10)

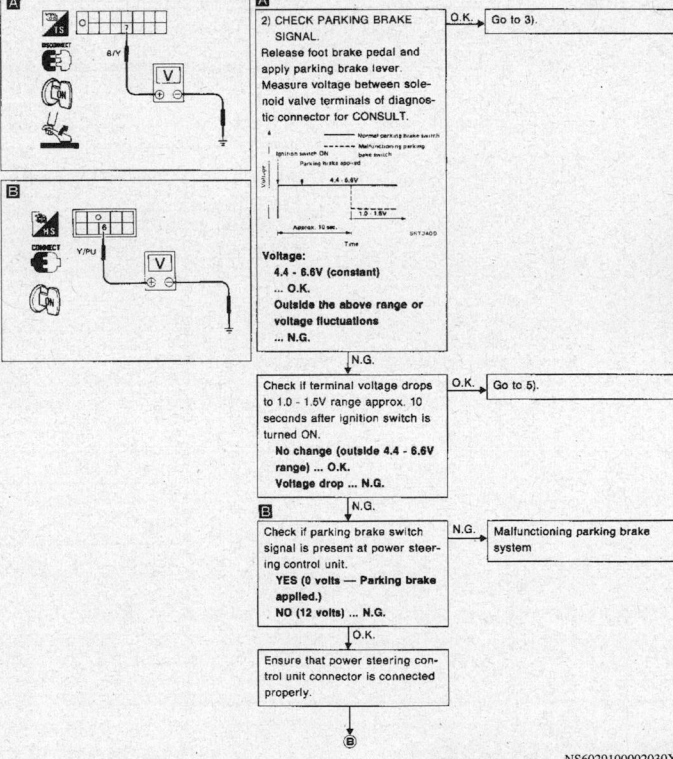

Fig. 2   Twin orifice steering system diagnosis (Part 3 of 10)

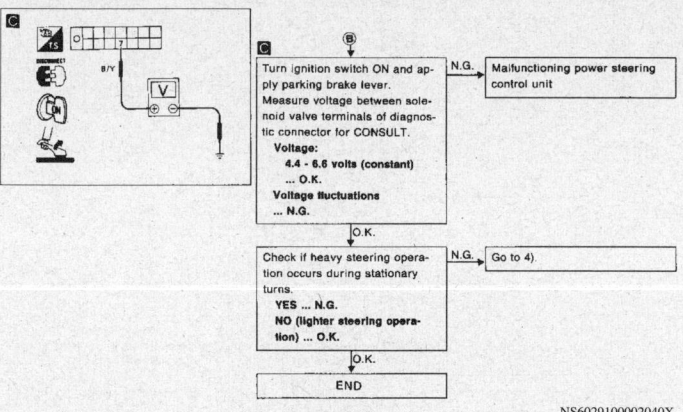

Turn ignition switch ON and apply parking brake lever. Measure voltage between solenoid valve terminals of diagnostic connector for CONSULT.

Voltage:
4.4 - 6.6 volts (constant) ... O.K.
Voltage fluctuations ... N.G.

→ N.G. → Malfunctioning power steering control unit

→ O.K.

Check if heavy steering operation occurs during stationary turns.

YES ... N.G.
NO (lighter steering operation) ... O.K.

→ N.G. → Go to 4).

→ O.K.

END

NS6029100002040X

Fig. 2 Twin orifice steering system diagnosis (Part 4 of 10)

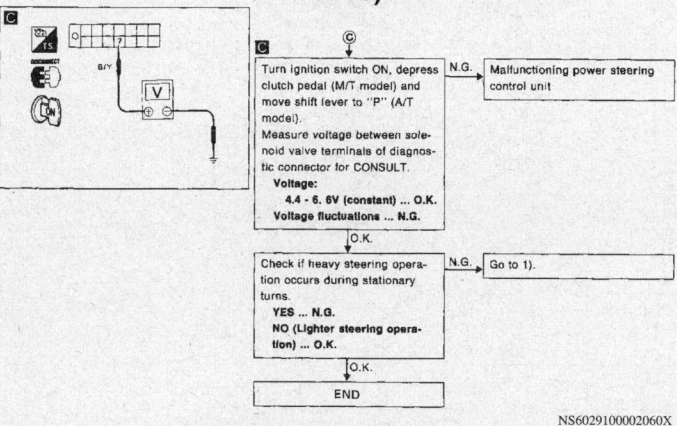

Turn ignition switch ON, depress clutch pedal (M/T model) and move shift lever to "P" (A/T model).
Measure voltage between solenoid valve terminals of diagnostic connector for CONSULT.

Voltage:
4.4 - 6.6V (constant) ... O.K.
Voltage fluctuations ... N.G.

→ N.G. → Malfunctioning power steering control unit

→ O.K.

Check if heavy steering operation occurs during stationary turns.

YES ... N.G.
NO (Lighter steering operation) ... O.K.

→ N.G. → Go to 1).

→ O.K.

END

NS6029100002060X

Fig. 2 Twin orifice steering system diagnosis (Part 6 of 10)

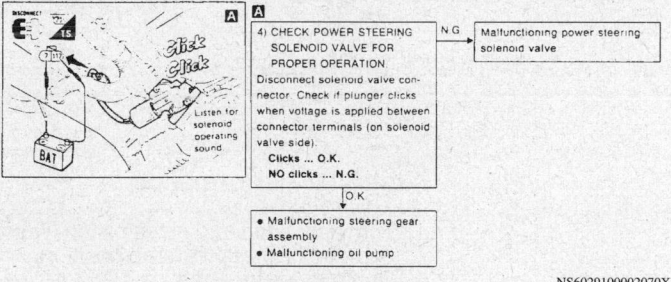

4) CHECK POWER STEERING SOLENOID VALVE FOR PROPER OPERATION
Disconnect solenoid valve connector. Check if plunger clicks when voltage is applied between connector terminals (on solenoid valve side).

Clicks ... O.K.
NO clicks ... N.G.

→ N.G. → Malfunctioning power steering solenoid valve

→ O.K.

• Malfunctioning steering gear assembly
• Malfunctioning oil pump

NS6029100002070X

Fig. 2 Twin orifice steering system diagnosis (Part 7 of 10)

POWER STEERING SYSTEM SERVICE

POWER RECIRCULATING BALL TYPE

PB48S & PB59K

Only the sealing parts of the gear assembly can be replaced, **Fig. 5.** The internal components of the steering gear must be replaced as an assembly.

Sector Shaft Oil Seal, Replace

1. Remove steering gear and set stub shaft in straight ahead position, which is 2.14 turns from lock position.
2. Remove bolts securing sector shaft cover and free sector shaft and cover

by lightly tapping sector shaft with a suitable mallet.
3. Place a roll of plastic film around the end of sector shaft, **Fig. 6,** and remove sector shaft from steering gear.
4. Remove dust cover, snap ring, dust cover special washer, back-up ring and oil seal, as required.
5. Replace O-ring seal on sector shaft cover.

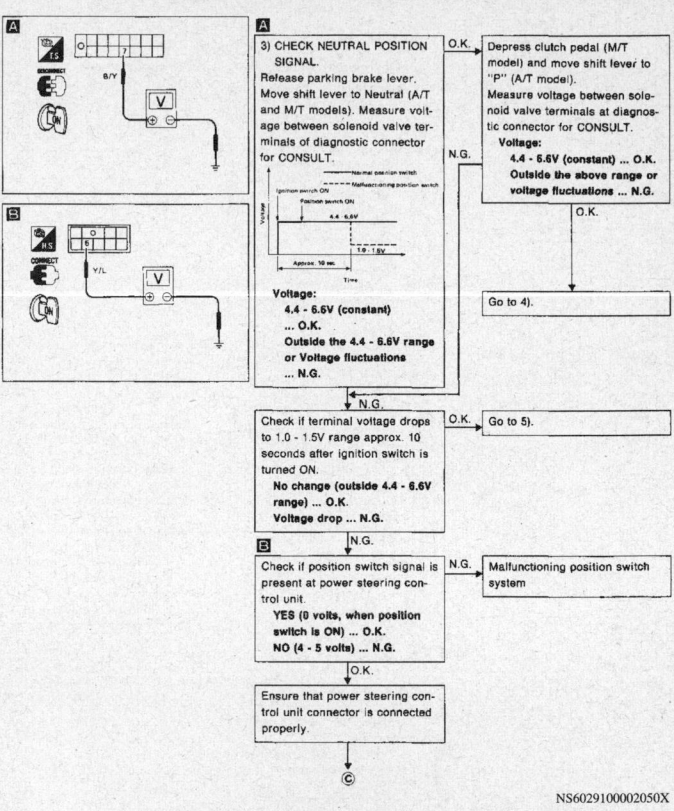

3) CHECK NEUTRAL POSITION SIGNAL.
Release parking brake lever.
Move shift lever to Neutral (A/T and M/T models). Measure voltage between solenoid valve terminals of diagnostic connector for CONSULT.

Voltage:
4.4 - 6.6V (constant) ... O.K.
Outside the 4.4 - 6.6V range or Voltage fluctuations ... N.G.

→ O.K. → Depress clutch pedal (M/T model) and move shift lever to "P" (A/T model).
Measure voltage between solenoid valve terminals at diagnostic connector for CONSULT.

Voltage:
4.4 - 6.6V (constant) ... O.K.
Outside the above range or voltage fluctuations ... N.G.

→ O.K. → Go to 4).

→ N.G.

Check if terminal voltage drops to 1.0 - 1.5V range approx. 10 seconds after ignition switch is turned ON.

No change (outside 4.4 - 6.6V range) ... O.K.
Voltage drop ... N.G.

→ O.K. → Go to 5).

→ N.G.

Check if position switch signal is present at power steering control unit.

YES (0 volts, when position switch is ON) ... O.K.
NO (4 - 5 volts) ... N.G.

→ N.G. → Malfunctioning position switch system

→ O.K.

Ensure that power steering control unit connector is connected properly.

→ ©

NS6029100002050X

Fig. 2 Twin orifice steering system diagnosis (Part 5 of 10)

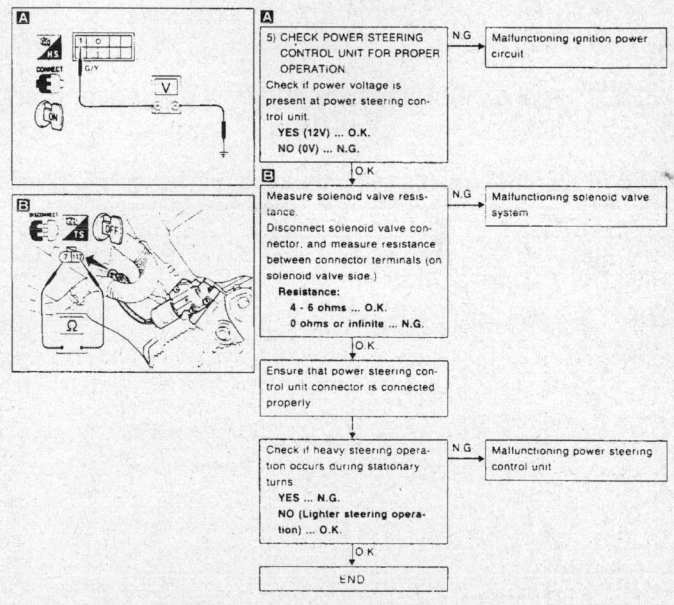

5) CHECK POWER STEERING CONTROL UNIT FOR PROPER OPERATION
Check if power voltage is present at power steering control unit.

YES (12V) ... O.K.
NO (0V) ... N.G.

→ N.G. → Malfunctioning ignition power circuit

→ O.K.

Measure solenoid valve resistance.
Disconnect solenoid valve connector, and measure resistance between connector terminals (on solenoid valve side).

Resistance:
4 - 6 ohms ... O.K.
0 ohms or infinite ... N.G.

→ N.G. → Malfunctioning solenoid valve system

→ O.K.

Ensure that power steering control unit connector is connected properly

→ O.K.

Check if heavy steering operation occurs during stationary turns

YES ... N.G.
NO (Lighter steering operation) ... O.K.

→ N.G. → Malfunctioning power steering control unit

→ O.K.

END

NS6029100002080X

Fig. 2 Twin orifice steering system diagnosis (Part 8 of 10)

6. Reverse procedure to assemble.

Rear Housing Seal, Replace. PB48S & PB59K

1. Remove steering gear from vehicle and mount in a suitable holding fixture.
2. Loosen but do not remove rear housing bolts.
3. Turn sector shaft slightly to raise intermediate cover through piston.

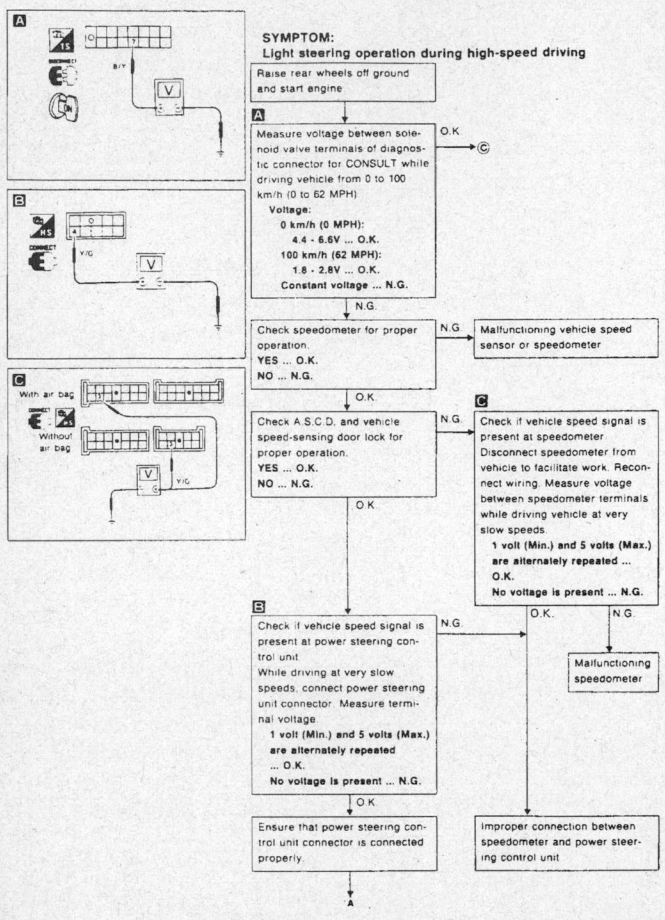

Fig. 2 Twin orifice steering system diagnosis (Part 9 of 10)

The standard values (voltage), measured with an analog tester in contact with the control unit terminal, are shown below:

Terminal No.	Application	Standard value
1	Power	Approx. 12V
2	Ground	0V
3	Vehicle speed sensor input	1 volt (min.) and 5 volts (max.) are alternately repeated when vehicle is driven at very slow speeds.
4	Stop lamp switch input	Pressed: Approx. 12V Released: 0V
5	Neutral switch input	0V (clutch engaged and shift lever in "N") ... M/T models 0V (selector lever in "N" or "P") ... A/T models 4 - 5V (except for the above)
6	Parking brake switch input	Applied: 0V Released: Approx. 12V
7	Power steering solenoid valve output	0 km/h 4.4 - 6.6V 100 km/h 1.8 - 2.8V Fail-safe 1.0 - 1.5V

NS6029100011000X

Fig. 3 Control unit inspection table

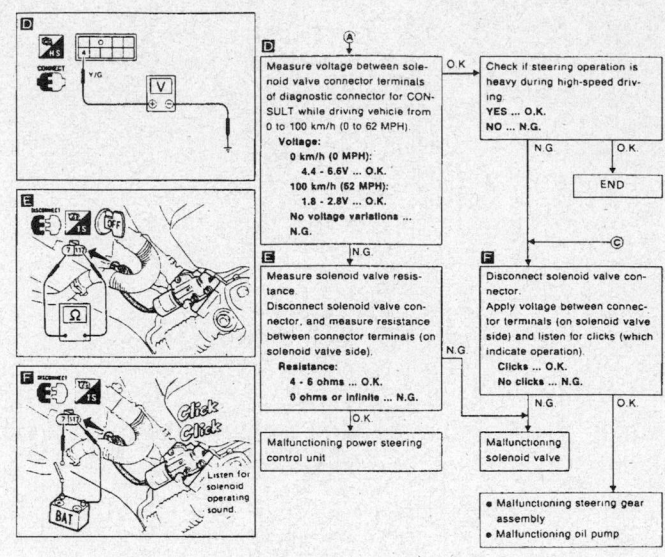

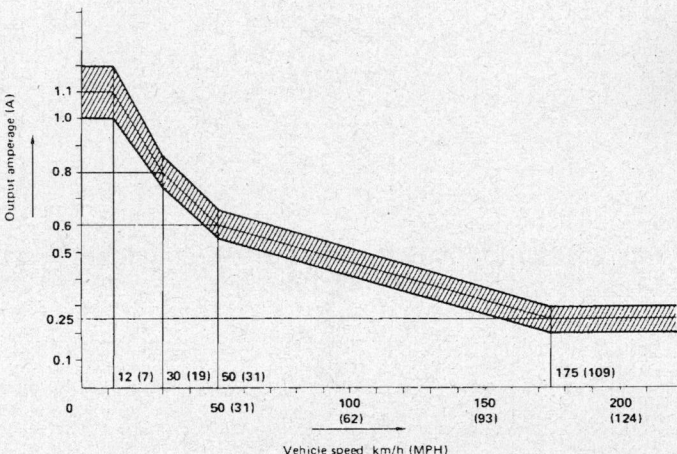

NS6029100002100X

Fig. 2 Twin orifice steering system diagnosis (Part 10 of 10)

NS6029100012000X

Fig. 4 Controller performance

4. Turn stub shaft and place piston (worm gear) in its straight ahead position.
5. Remove sector shaft.
6. Pull out rear housing, intermediate cover, and worm gear as an assembly, **Fig. 7.**
7. To remove rear housing, turn assembly with worm gear facing bench and tap lightly on stub shaft with a suitable mallet.
8. Remove rear housing seal and O-rings from both sides of intermediate cover.
9. To assemble, reverse procedure. Tighten rear housing attaching bolts in a criss-cross pattern.

POWER RACK & PINION TYPE

PR24AC, PR26K, PR26AC, PR26AE & PR32K

Disassemble

When disassembling power steering gears refer to **Figs. 8 through 11**, noting the following:

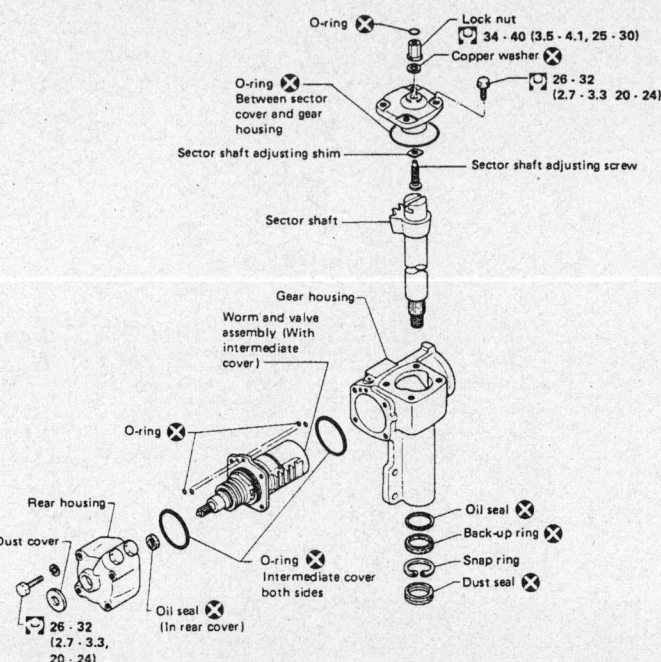

Fig. 5 Recirculating ball type power steering gear. PB48S & PB59K

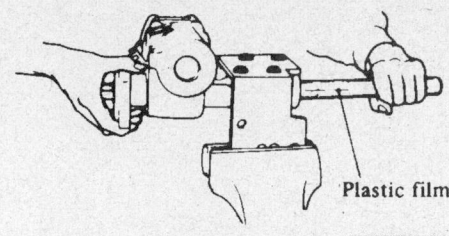

Fig. 6 Sector shaft removal. PB48S & PB59K

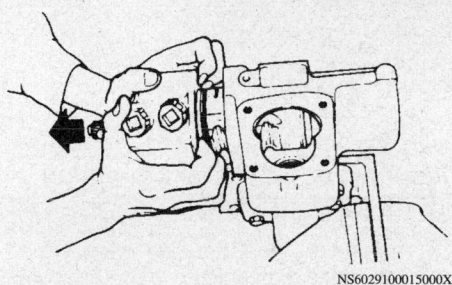

Fig. 7 Rear housing & worm gear removal. PB48S & PB59K

1. Before disassembling, measure pinion rotating torque and record, then drain fluid.
2. Remove pinion gear, tie rod outer sockets and boots.
3. Loosen tie rod inner socket by prying up staking, then remove retainer and pinion assembly.
4. Drill staked portion of the end cover with a .079–.098 inch drill bit, then remove gear housing end cover and draw rack out of tube.
5. Remove rack seal ring by heating with a heat gun, then replace with a new one by heating and installing by hand.
6. Remove center bushing and rack oil seal with a tape wrapped socket and extension bar.

Pinion Rotating Torque Adjustment

1. With gears at neutral without fluid, coat adjusting screw with locking sealant and install it.
2. Lightly tighten locknut, then **torque** adjusting screw to 43–52 inch lbs. Loosen it, then retorque to .43–1.74 inch lbs.

3. Move rack through entire stroke several times.
4. Measure pinion rotating torque within 180° from neutral and stop at point of greatest resistance.
5. Loosen adjusting screw, then **torque** to 43–52 inch lbs. Loosen adjusting screw 40–60°.
6. If steering gear rack sliding force is not 27.6–37.5 lbs. at neutral point, or 27.6–41.9 lbs. away from neutral point, repeat procedure from step 2. If still not within specifications, replace steering gear.
7. Measure pinion rotating within 100° of neutral point.
8. The maximum value allowable is 3.5 ft. lbs. and the minimum is 16 inch lbs.

Assemble

1. Using seal installation tool No. KV48104400, or equivalent, compress

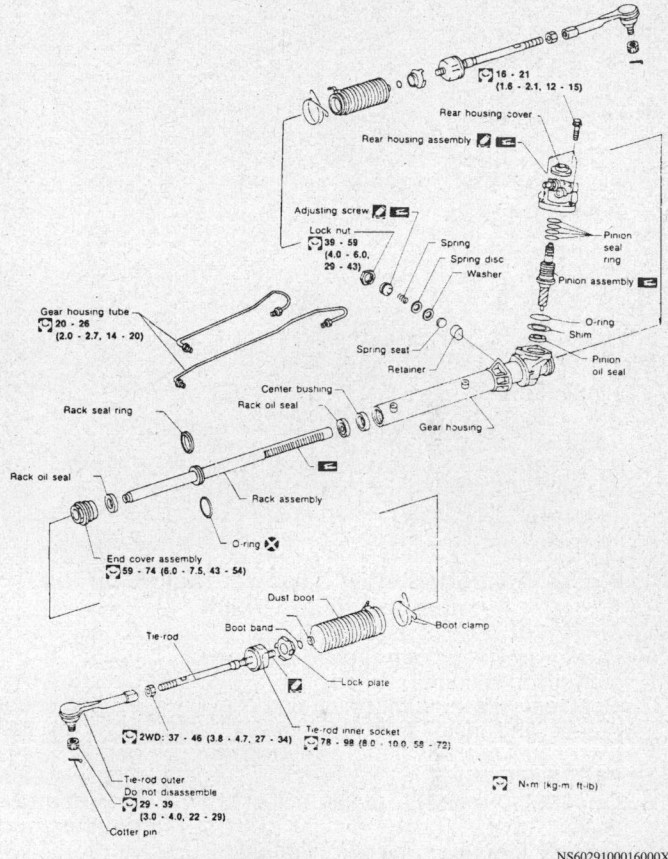

Fig. 8 Exploded view of power rack & pinion steering gear. PR24AC, PR24SC, PR26AC & PR26SC

the outside of rack seal ring to position and secure it on rack. **Insert tool on rack from the tooth side.**
2. Use a plastic film to protect rack oil seal from damage from rack teeth and install rack oil seal. Remove plastic film after installation. **Lips of rack oil seal face each other.**
3. Install center bushing and rack oil seal with rack assembly, then tighten cylinder end cover to specifications. Stake housing to secure end cover.
4. Set rack gear in neutral position so that dimension L, **Fig. 12,** is 2.697 inches, then coat pinion oil seal with multipurpose grease and install into pinion housing. Ensure lip of seal faces up.
5. Install new pinion bearing adjusting shim(s), then install pinion seal ring on pinion gear assembly using a heat gun to heat seal ring before installing.
6. Coat needle bearing roller and oil seal

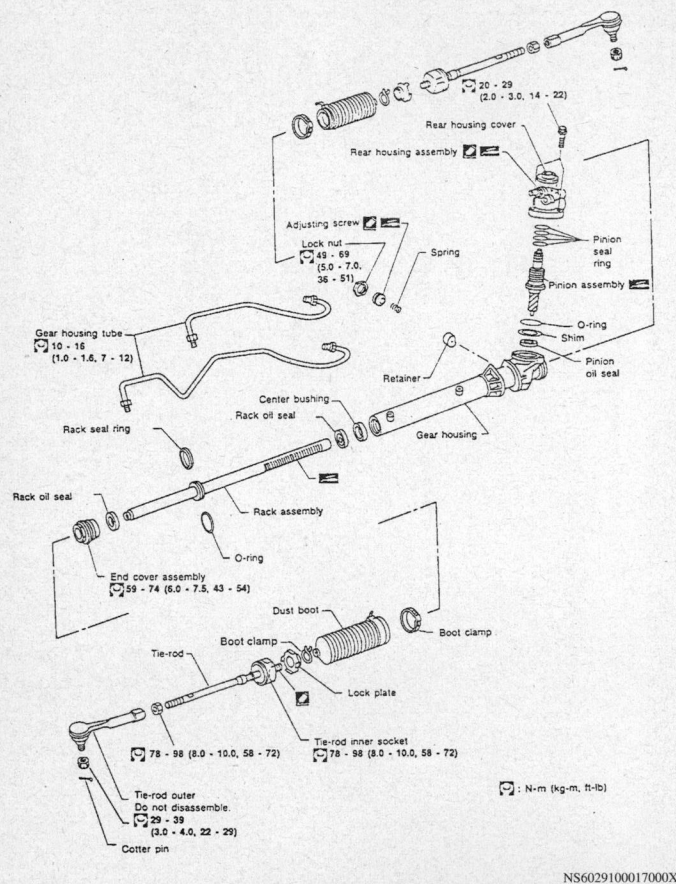

Fig. 9   Exploded view of power rack & pinion steering gear. PR26K

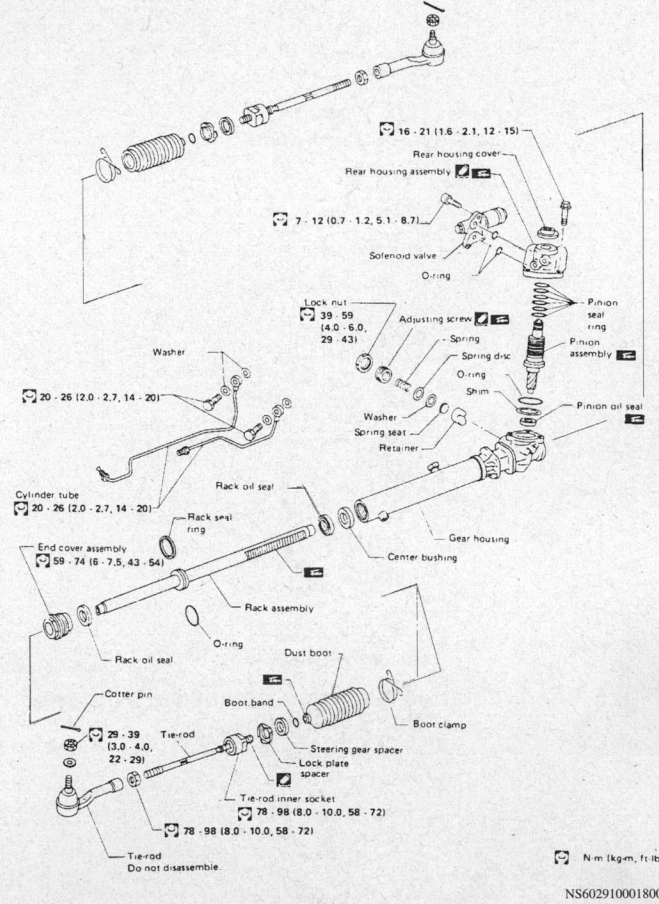

Fig. 10   Exploded view of power rack & pinion steering gear. PR26AE

lip with multi-purpose grease and install pinion assembly to housing.

7. Coat rear oil seal lip with multi-purpose grease and install into rear housing, then install rear cover cap as shown in **Fig. 13 and 14.**

8. **On 300ZX models,** install solenoid valve.

9. **On all models,** install diaphragm spring to retainer in the following order; retainer, spring washer, diaphragm spring.

10. Attach lock plate (2), to side rod inner socket (1), then apply locking sealant to inner socket threads and screw inner socket into rack and tighten to specifications. Bend lock plate at two cut out portions.

11. Tighten outer socket nut to specifications, after adjusting dimension L, **Fig. 15,** to 6.96 inches.

12. Measure and adjust rack stroke, then coat rubber boot contact surface with grease and install boot and clamps.

PR24T & PR28T

When performing repair procedures on this power steering rack, use a vise with soft jaws to hold the steering gear housing. Do not grip the cylinder in a vise.

Disassemble

1. Disconnect gear housing tube and drain fluid, **Fig. 16 and 17.**

2. Measure pinion rotating torque as described under "Adjustment."

3. Remove tie-rod outer sockets and boots.

4. Remove tie-rod inner sockets.

5. **Do not attempt to disassemble gear housing or cylinder.**

Inspection

Clean all parts in cleaning solvent or Type F automatic transmission fluid and blow dry with compressed air.

1. Check boot for cracks.

2. Check tie-rod ball joint swinging force as shown in **Fig. 18.** If outer ball joint swing force is not within .4–30.9 inch lbs.; replace tie-rod end. If inner ball joint swing force is not within .04–4.41 inch lbs; replace tie-rod end.

3. Check tie-rod end rotating torque as shown in **Fig. 19.** If rotating torque is not within 1.3–5.5 inch lbs; replace tie-rod end.

Assemble

1. Install tie-rod end inner and outer sockets.

2. Tighten outer socket locknut to specifications.

3. Measure rack stroke as shown in **Fig. 20,** rack stroke should be 2.83 inches. Adjust stroke as necessary.

4. To prevent interference with other parts. Install boot clamps so they are

behind the gear housing when it is attached to the vehicle.

Adjustment

1. Measure pinion rotating torque as shown, **Fig. 21.**

2. Pinion rotating torque should be 4.3–12.5 inch lbs. with a maximum deviation of 3.5 inch lbs. If torque is not within specifications, replace steering rack.

3. Check rack sliding force as follows:
   a. Disconnect tie-rod ends from knuckle assembly.
   b. Start engine and bleed air completely.
   c. Disconnect steering column lower joint from gear.
   d. Keep engine at idle speed and make sure steering fluid has reached normal operating temperature.
   e. While pulling tie-rod end slowly in the (±2.56 inch) range from the neutral position, ensure sliding force is less than 60 lbs., **Fig. 22.**
   f. Check rack outside of (±2.56 inch) range, sliding force should not be above 13 lbs.
   g. If sliding force is not within specifications, repeat adjustment procedure.

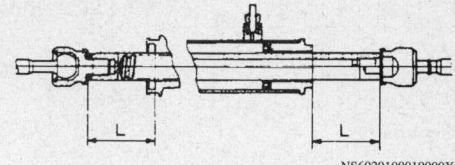

NS6029100019000X

Fig. 12   Rack gear neutral position. PR24AC, PR26AC & PR32K

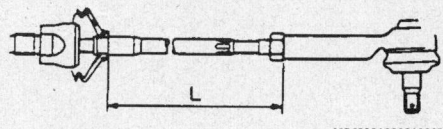

NS6029100021000X

Fig. 15   Tie rod length adjustment. PR24AC, PR26AC & PR32K

2. Using a screwdriver, remove oil seal.
3. Remove connector, then the control valve from front housing. **Do not drop control valve.**
4. Disassemble remaining parts as shown in **Fig. 23.**
5. Reverse procedure to assemble, noting the following:
   a. Use new seals and O-rings, ensure they are installed properly and in the correct direction.
   b. Cam ring, rotor and vanes must be replaced as a set.
   c. Coat all parts with automatic transmission fluid prior to assembly.
   d. When installing rotor, refer to **Fig. 24,** for correct direction.
   e. When inserting vanes into rotor, rounded surfaces of the vanes must be facing the cam ring side as shown in **Fig. 25.**
   f. **On models equipped with electronically controlled pump,** a wave washer is installed instead of the spring.
   g. **On all pumps,** insert pin into groove of front housing, then install the rotor and cam ring as shown in **Fig. 26.**

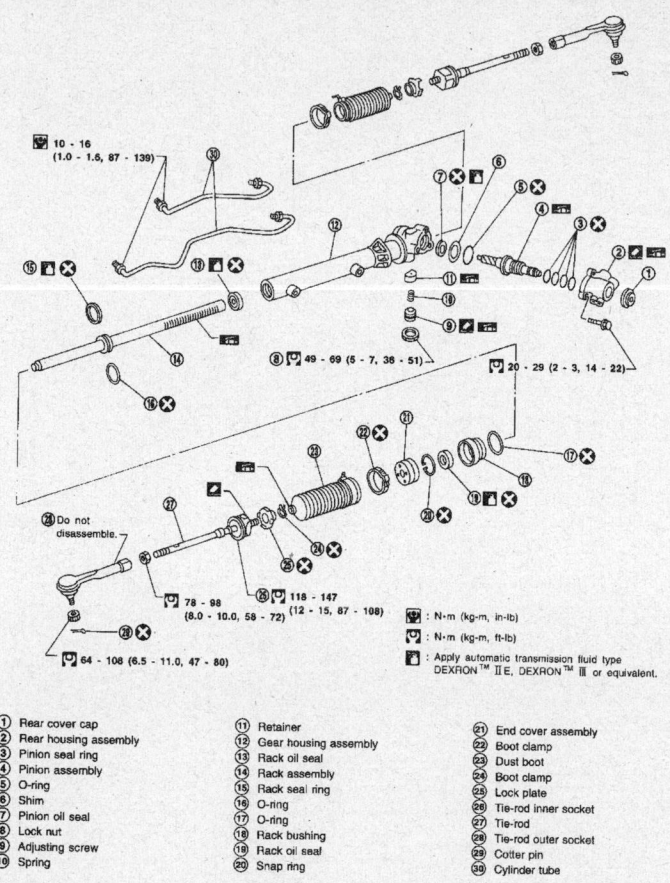

10 - 16 (1.0 - 1.6, 87 - 139)

8   49 - 69 (5 - 7, 38 - 51)

20 - 29 (2 - 3, 14 - 22)

② Do not disassemble.

78 - 98 (8.0 - 10.0, 58 - 72)

118 - 147 (12 - 15, 87 - 108)

64 - 108 (6.5 - 11.0, 47 - 80)

: N·m (kg-m, in-lb)

: N·m (kg-m, ft-lb)

: Apply automatic transmission fluid type DEXRON™ II E, DEXRON™ III or equivalent.

① Rear cover cap	⑪ Retainer	㉑ End cover assembly
② Rear housing assembly	⑫ Gear housing assembly	㉒ Boot clamp
③ Pinion seal ring	⑬ Rack oil seal	㉓ Dust boot
④ Pinion assembly	⑭ Rack assembly	㉔ Boot clamp
⑤ O-ring	⑮ Rack seal ring	㉕ Lock plate
⑥ Shim	⑯ O-ring	㉖ Tie-rod inner socket
⑦ Pinion oil seal	⑰ O-ring	㉗ Tie-rod
⑧ Lock nut	⑱ Rack bushing	㉘ Tie-rod outer socket
⑨ Adjusting screw	⑲ Rack oil seal	㉙ Cotter pin
⑩ Spring	⑳ Snap ring	㉚ Cylinder tube

NS6029600102000X

Fig. 11   Exploded view of power rack & pinion steering gear. PR32K

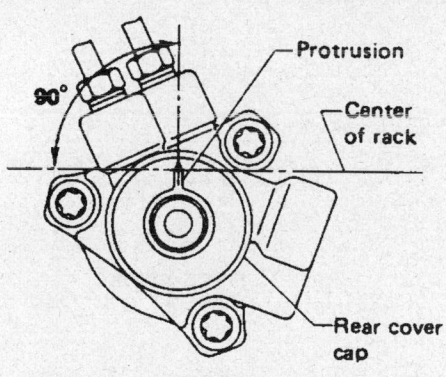

90°

Protrusion

Center of rack

Rear cover cap

NS6029100020000X

Fig. 13   Rear cover cap installation. PR24AC & PR26AC

OIL PUMP SERVICE

When performing this procedure ensure work area is clean. Do not use rags

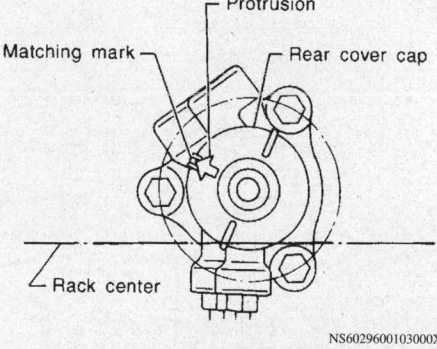

Protrusion

Matching mark

Rear cover cap

Rack center

NS6029600103000X

Fig. 14   Rear cover cap installation. PR32K

when cleaning parts, use nylon cloths or paper towels. Do not let foreign matter enter or contact parts.

1. Remove snap ring, then draw driveshaft out of pump, **Fig. 23.**

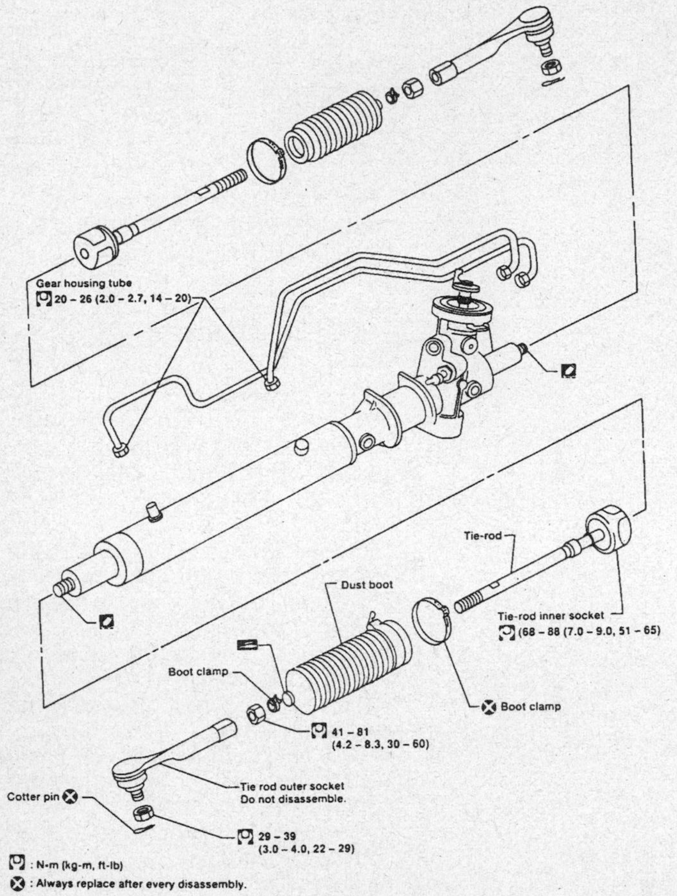

Gear housing tube
[U] 20 – 26 (2.0 – 2.7, 14 – 20)

Tie-rod

Dust boot

Tie-rod inner socket
[U] (68 – 88 (7.0 – 9.0, 51 – 65)

Boot clamp

[X] Boot clamp

41 – 81
(4.2 – 8.3, 30 – 60)

Cotter pin [X]

Tie rod outer socket
Do not disassemble.

[U] 29 – 39
(3.0 – 4.0, 22 – 29)

[U] : N·m (kg-m, ft-lb)
[X] : Always replace after every disassembly.

NS6029100022000X

Fig. 16 Exploded view of rack & pinion type power steering gear. PR28T

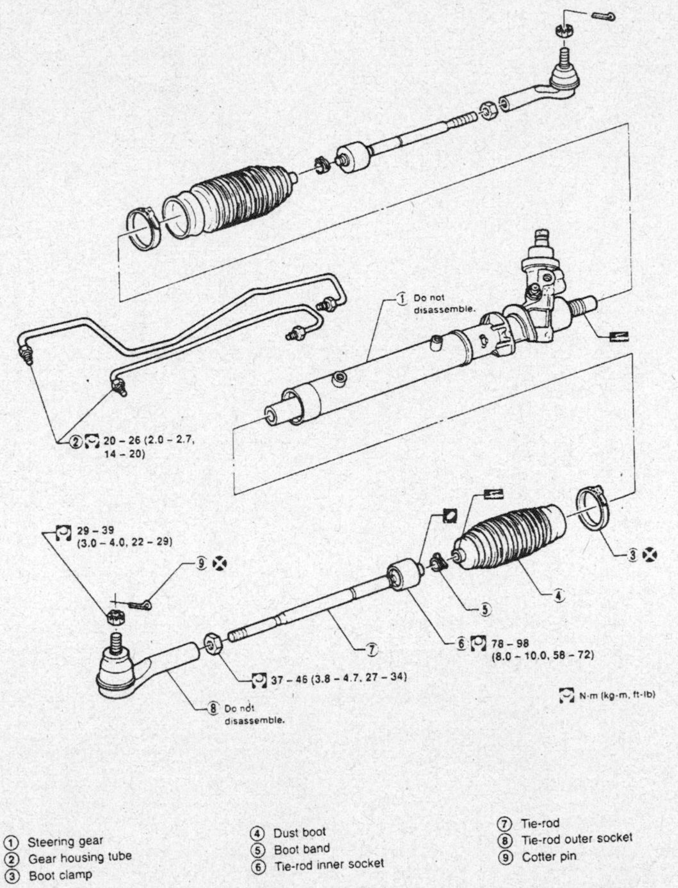

① Do not disassemble.

② [U] 20 – 26 (2.0 – 2.7, 14 – 20)

[U] 29 – 39 (3.0 – 4.0, 22 – 29) ⑨ [X]

③ [X]

④

⑤

⑥ [U] 78 – 98 (8.0 – 10.0, 58 – 72)

[U] 37 – 46 (3.8 – 4.7, 27 – 34) ⑦

⑧ Do not disassemble.

[U] : N·m (kg-m, ft-lb)

① Steering gear
② Gear housing tube
③ Boot clamp
④ Dust boot
⑤ Boot band
⑥ Tie-rod inner socket
⑦ Tie-rod
⑧ Tie-rod outer socket
⑨ Cotter pin

NS6029500099000X

Fig. 17 Exploded view of rack & pinion type power steering gear. PR24T

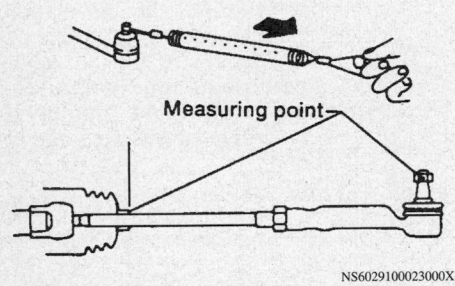

Measuring point

NS6029100023000X

Fig. 18 Tie-rod ball joint swinging force inspection. PR24T & PR28T

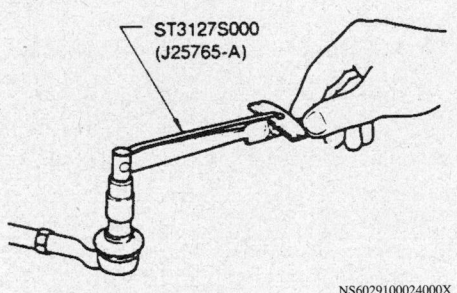

ST3127S000 (J25765-A)

NS6029100024000X

Fig. 19 Tie-rod end rotating torque inspection. PR24T & PR28T

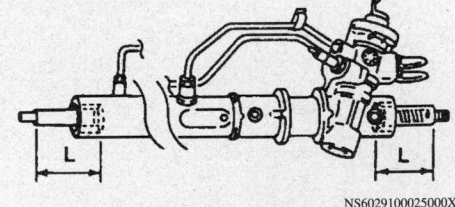

L   L

NS6029100025000X

Fig. 20 Rack stroke measurement. PR28T & PR24T

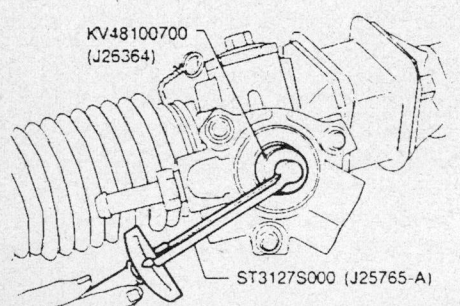

KV48100700 (J25364)

ST3127S000 (J25765-A)

NS6029100026000X

Fig. 21 Pinion rotating torque measurement. PR24T & PR28T

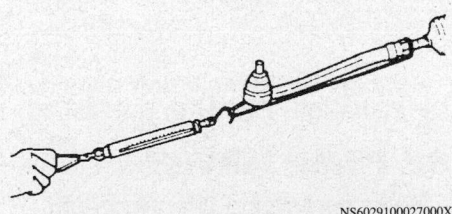

NS6029100027000X

Fig. 22 Rack sliding force measurement. PR24T & PR28T

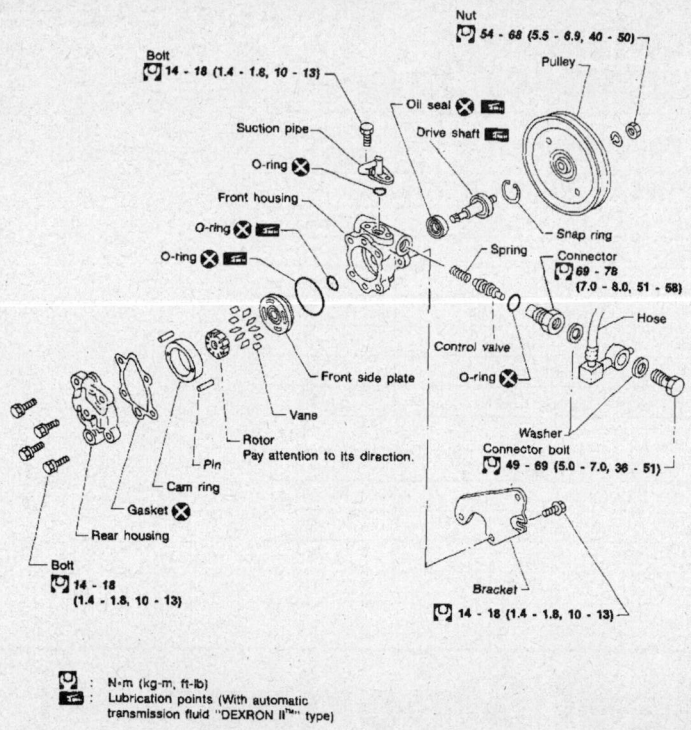

Fig. 23 Exploded view of oil pump assembly

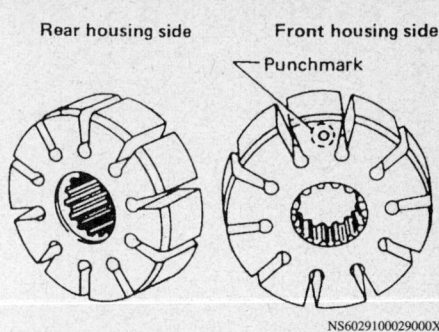

Fig. 24 Rotor installation

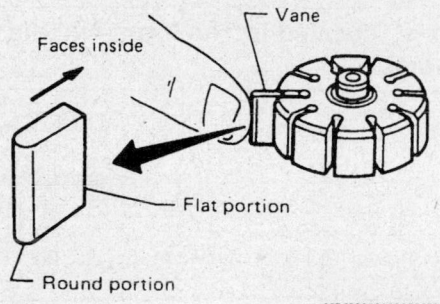

Fig. 25 Rotor vane installation

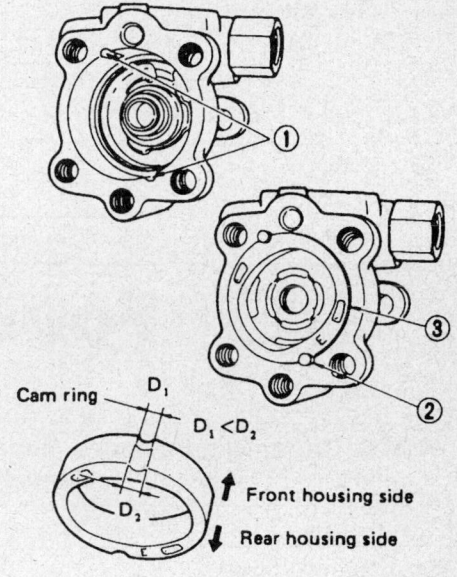

Fig. 26 Cam ring & rotor installation

TIGHTENING SPECIFICATIONS

Year	Component	Torque/Ft. Lbs.
PB48S & PB59K		
1996–99	Breather Screw	60–84①
	Cylinder Tube Flare Nuts	14–20
	Gear Housing Cover Bolts	20–24
	Rear Housing Bolts	20–24
	Sector Shaft Locknut	21–25
	Sector Shaft To Gear Arm	94–108
	Tie Rod End Locknut	27–34

TIGHTENING
SPECIFICATIONS—Continued

Year	Component	Torque/Ft. Lbs.
PR24AC, PR26AC, PR26AE, PR26K & PR32K		
1996–99	Adjusting Screw Locknut	29–43
	Cylinder Tube Flare Nuts	14–20
	Rack End Cover	43–54
	Rear Housing Bolts	12–15
	Tie Rod End Inner Socket	58–72
	Tie Rod End Locknut	27–34
	Tie Rod End To Spindle	22–29
PR24T & PR28T		
1996–99	Gear Housing Mounting Bracket	54–72
	Gear Housing Tube	14–20
	Tie Rod End Locknut	22–29
	Tie Rod Inner Socket	51–65
	Tie Rod Outer Socket Nut	30–60

① — Inch lbs.

Four Wheel Steering

NOTE: On Air Bag Equipped Models, Refer To "Air Bag System Precautions" Located In The Front Of This Manual For System Disarming & Arming Procedures.

INDEX

DESCRIPTION

The Super HICAS system is comprised of a steering angle sensor, power steering solenoid, control unit and actuator.

INSPECTION

FLUID LEVEL INSPECTION

Maintain fluid level so that the lower surface of the float is maintained between the L and H marks on the gauge rod. The fluid level should be checked when the engine is stopped and the fluid temperature is above 86°F. Recommended fluid is Dexron type automatic transmission fluid. **Never over fill.**

LEAK INSPECTION

Check lines for proper attachment, leaks, cracks, damage, loose connections, chafing and deterioration. Fluid leakage should be checked for when oil temperature in normal with engine idling.

HICAS SYSTEM OPERATION

Ensure shift lever is in the Park posi-

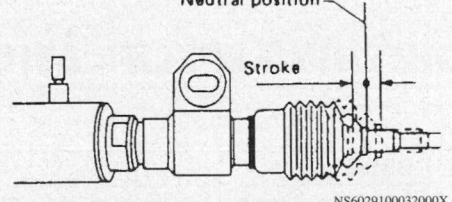

NS6029100032000X

Fig. 1 Rod stroke measurement

tion on models with automatic transmission or in Neutral position on models with manual transmissions before checking HICAS system operations.

Consult Tool

1. Have an assistant inside vehicle then raise and support vehicle in such a way to allow all four wheel to spin freely.
2. Connect consult tool to diagnostic connector and start engine.
3. Tough START on consult tool display.
4. Touch HICAS, ACTIVE TEST and SIMULATED DRIVE in that order.
5. Touch START when MAIN SIGNALS displayed is reversed.
6. Touch START. After simulated drive condition has continued for five minutes, it will automatically cancel and Consult tool will then show TEST IS INTERRUPTED TO AVOID OIL TEMP. RISE display. **To cancel this mode during self diagnosis, touch CANCEL.**
7. Operate engine at speeds greater than 2000 RPM and turn steering wheel 180° in one direction from the neutral position.
8. Measure extension value of one power cylinder rod and retraction value of the other, **Fig. 1.**
9. Turn steering wheel 180° in opposite direction from the neutral position and measure extension and retraction of power cylinder rod.
10. Determine strokes of respective power cylinder by adding measured extension and retraction values.
11. **Measure rod strokes in as short a period of time as possible.**
12. Specification for when steering wheel is turned to the right or left is .12 inch, with a total stroke of .24 inch.

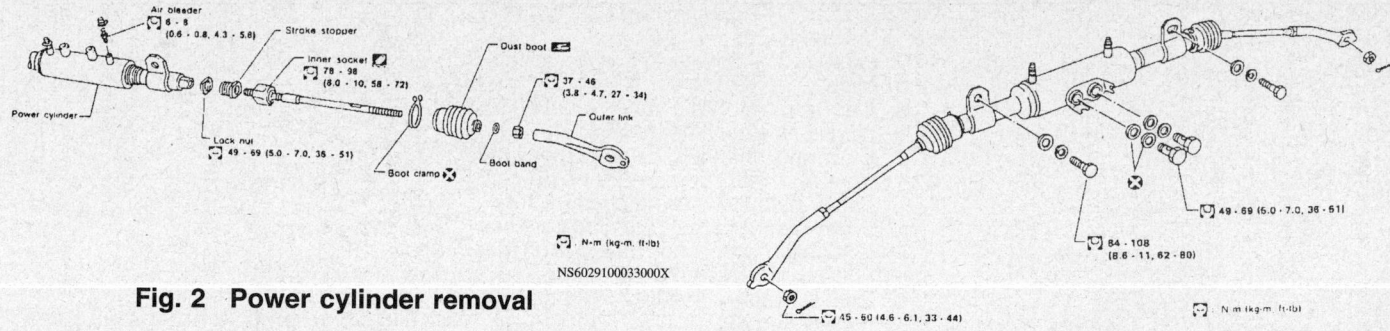

Fig. 2   Power cylinder removal

NS6029100033000X

Fig. 3   Exploded view of power cylinder

NS6029100034000X

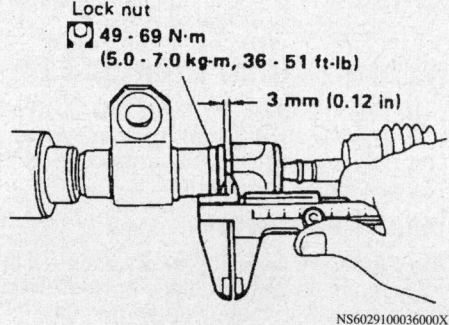

Fig. 4   Lower link removal

NS6029100035000X

Fig. 5   Stroke stopper removal

NS6029100036000X

power cylinder rod.

7. Determine strokes of respective power cylinder by adding measured extension and retraction values.

8. **Measure rod strokes in as short a period of time as possible.**

9. Specification for when steering wheel is turned to the right or left is .12 inch, with a total stroke of .24 inch.

DIAGNOSIS & TESTING

SYSTEM SERVICE

POWER CYLINDER SERVICE

Replacement

Detach power cylinder lower links from axle housing sockets using suitable tool, then disconnect oil pipes from power cylinder and remove power cylinders, **Fig. 2.**

Before installing power cylinder on suspension member, wipe power cylinder bracket and mating surface of suspension member. Using the left side of the bracket as a reference point, locate the right side oblong hole and install power cylinder. Install power cylinder and oil pipes. After installation check toe in and bleed hydraulic system.

Overhaul

1. Remove dust boot clamps and move boots toward outer links, **Fig. 3.**

2. Attach wrenches to left and right ball joint sockets and turn in direction shown in **Fig. 4.** Remove one of the loosened lower links.

3. Loosen stroke stopper nut from lower link assembly and remove stroke stopper.

4. While holding width across flats section of rod end from which stroke stopper was removed, remove other lower link assembly.

5. Reverse procedure to assemble, noting the following:
   a. Apply Loctite to inner ball joint threads.
   b. After installing stroke stopper, loosen locknut which secures stroke stopper.
   c. Turn stroke stopper until clearance between inner ball joint and stroke stopper is .12 inch on each side, **Fig. 5.**
   d. **Torque** locknut to 36–51 ft. lbs.

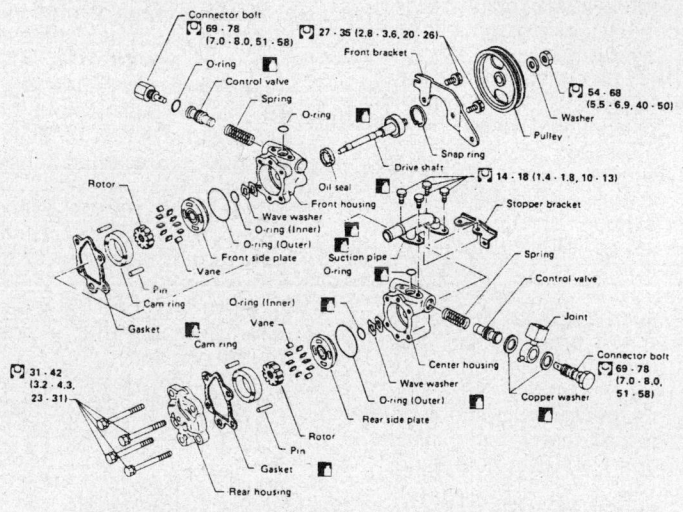

Fig. 6   Exploded view of oil pump

NS6029100038000X

HICAS Warning Light

1. Have an assistant inside vehicle then raise and support vehicle in such a way to allow all four wheel to spin freely.

2. Set HICAS system in self diagnosis as follows:
   a. Turn ignition switch to Off position.
   b. Position shift lever in Park or Neutral position on models with automatic transmission or Neutral on models with manual transmissions.
   c. Turn ignition switch to On position.
   d. Immediately start engine.
   e. Turn steering wheel from left to right at least 20° from the neutral position five times or more then depress foot brake pedal at least five times within 10 seconds after ignition

switch has been turned On. **Do not depress foot brake pedal during operation check, or operation will stop.**

3. Place steering wheel to a point approximately 10° from the neutral position and check to ensure rear wheels turn to the left and right alternately.

4. Operate engine at speeds greater than 2000 RPM and turn steering wheel 180° in one direction from the neutral position.

5. Measure extension value of one power cylinder rod and retraction value of the other, **Fig. 1.**

6. Turn steering wheel 180° in opposite direction from the neutral position and measure extension and retraction of

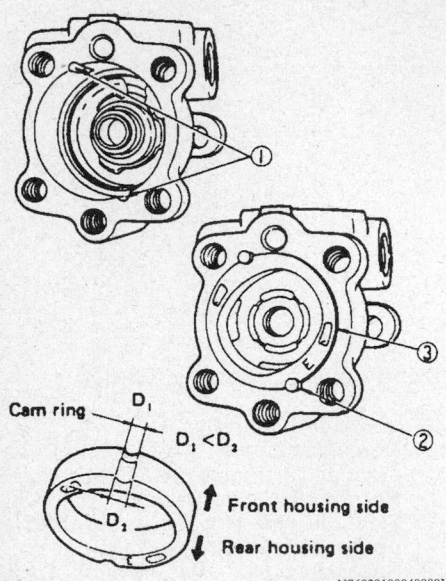

Fig. 7 Cam ring installation

e. Recheck clearance between inner ball joint and stroke stopper on each side.
f. Install dust boot using new boot band.

OIL PUMP SERVICE

Replacement

1. Remove oil pump drive belt.
2. Drain fluid into a suitable container.
3. Disconnect and plug oil pipes.
4. Remove oil pump mounting bolts then the oil pump.
5. Reverse procedure to install, bleeding hydraulic system.

Disassemble

Parts which can be disassembled are strictly limited. Never disassemble parts other than those specified. Refer to Fig. 6 to disassemble the oil pump assembly, noting the following:

1. Remove inlet and outlet connectors. The discharge connector incorporates a flow control valve. Ensure care is taken not to drop connector.
2. Remove end cover assembly then the driveshaft snap ring and the driveshaft.
3. Remove front cover oil seal.

Assemble

Refer to Fig. 6 to assemble the oil pump assembly, noting the following:

1. Ensure O-ring and oil seal are properly installed.
2. Coat each part with ATF when assembling.
3. Cam ring, rotor and vanes must be replaced as a set if necessary.
4. Cam ring shape is different between front and rear, ensure front side cam ring is installed with punch mark set on pulley side and that rear side cam ring is installed with punch mark set on rear housing side, Fig. 7.
5. Ensure rotor is installed in correct direction, Fig. 8.
6. When assembling vanes to rotor, rounded surface of vanes must face cam ring side.
7. Torque rear housing bolts in a diagonal sequence to 23–31 ft. lbs.

HYDRAULIC SYSTEM BLEED

Before bleeding air from HICAS system, ensure air is bleed from the power steering system as described in the "Power Steering" section.

Using Consult Tool

1. Place shift lever in Park on models with automatic transmissions or Neutral on models with manual transmissions.
2. Have an assistant inside vehicle then raise and support vehicle in such a way to allow all four wheel to spin freely.
3. Connect consult tool to diagnostic connector and start engine.
4. Tough START on consult tool display.
5. Touch HICAS, ACTIVE TEST and SIMULATED DRIVE in that order.
6. Touch START when MAIN SIGNALS displayed is reversed.
7. Connect a clear hose to the right and left power cylinder bleeder valve and place the other into a container of clean fluid.
8. Touch start.
9. Operate engine at speeds greater than 2000 RPM and turn steering wheel 180° to the right from the neutral position.
10. Loosen right power cylinder bleeder valve to bleed air, then retighten valve.
11. Return steering wheel to neutral position.
12. Repeat steps 9 through 11 turning steering wheel to left.
13. Repeat steps 9 through 12 until there are no air bubbles in fluid. While bleeding air from power cylinders, never allow fluid level to drop below inlet port of reservoir tank.
14. Tough CANCEL on Consult tool and

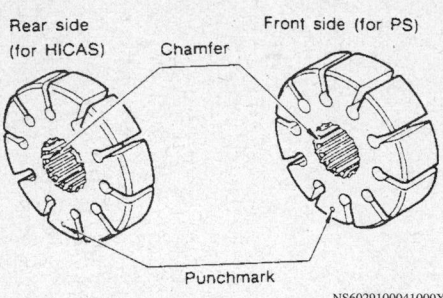

Fig. 8 Pump rotor installation

turn engine Off.

Using HICAS Warning Light

1. Have an assistant inside vehicle then raise and support vehicle in such a way to allow all four wheel to spin freely.
2. Place HICAS system in self diagnosis as follows:
   a. Turn ignition switch to Off position.
   b. Place shift lever in Park on models with automatic transmissions or Neutral on models with manual transmissions.
   c. Turn ignition switch to On position and immediately start engine.
   d. Turn steering wheel from left to right at least 20° from the neutral position five times or more then depress foot brake pedal at least five times within 10 seconds after ignition switch has been turned On.
3. Connect a clear hose to the right and left power cylinder bleeder valve and the other end into a container of clean fluid.
4. Place steering wheel within 10° from the neutral position and check to ensure rear wheels turn to the left and right alternately.
5. Operate engine at idle speeds and turn steering wheel 180° to right from the neutral position.
6. Loosen right power cylinder bleeder valve to bleed air, then retighten valve.
7. Return steering wheel to neutral position.
8. Repeat steps 4 through 7 turning steering wheel to left.
9. Repeat steps 4 through 8 until there are no air bubbles in fluid. While bleeding air from power cylinders, never allow fluid level to drop below inlet port of reservoir tank.
10. Turn ignition switch to Off position to complete self diagnosis operation.

Disc Brakes

INDEX

BRAKE SYSTEM BLEED

Refer to "Hydraulic Brake Systems" for brake bleed procedure.

BRAKE PAD SERVICE

FRONT

1. Raise and support front of vehicle and remove wheel.
2. Remove brake hose lock spring if necessary and lower pin bolt **Figs. 1 through 8,** then pivot caliper body upwards.
3. Remove pad retainers, inner and outer shims and the pads.
4. Install new inner pad and pivot caliper downward.
5. Compress piston(s) by inserting bar through caliper opening and prying against torque member.
6. Pivot caliper upwards, then install outer pad, inner and outer shims and pad retainers.
7. Position caliper body and install lower pin.

REAR

Except AD14VB & OPZ11V

1. Raise and support rear of vehicle and remove wheel.
2. Disconnect parking brake cable and remove spring retainer, if necessary.
3. Remove pin bolts, **Figs. 9 through 11.**
4. Remove pad springs, pads and pad shims.
5. Reverse procedure to install. Turn piston clockwise to retract it into cylinder body.

AD14VB

1. Raise and support rear of vehicle and remove wheels.
2. Remove caliper guide pin, then swing cylinder body upward.
3. Remove pad retainer, then the pads and shims, **Figs. 12 and 13.**
4. To install new pads, bring piston and yoke into position by turning outer piston clockwise until it retracts into caliper body.
5. Move yoke with lever until clearance to install inner and outer pads are equal.
6. Install pads and new shims, making sure tab on back of pad is aligned with groove in piston.

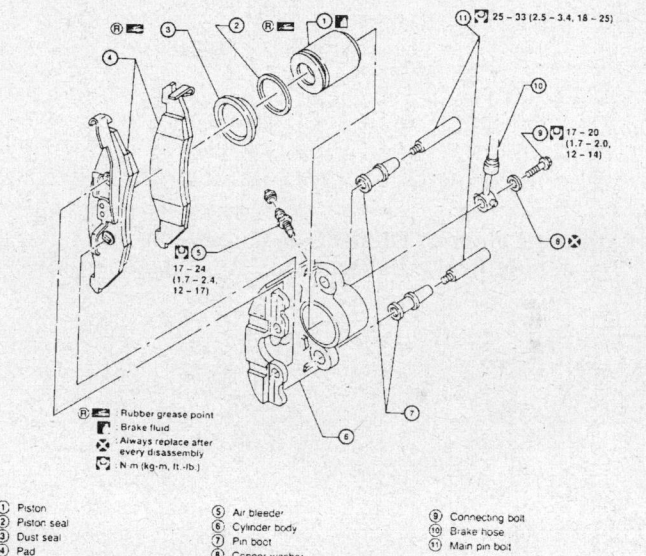

- Ⓡ ⮌ : Rubber grease point
- ⬛ : Brake fluid
- ⊗ : Always replace after every disassembly
- ⬜ : N·m (kg-m, ft.-lb.)

① Piston
② Piston seal
③ Dust seal
④ Pad
⑤ Air bleeder
⑥ Cylinder body
⑦ Pin boot
⑧ Copper washer
⑨ Connecting bolt
⑩ Brake hose
⑪ Main pin bolt

NS4079100004000X

Fig. 1 Exploded view of AD28VX front disc brake assembly

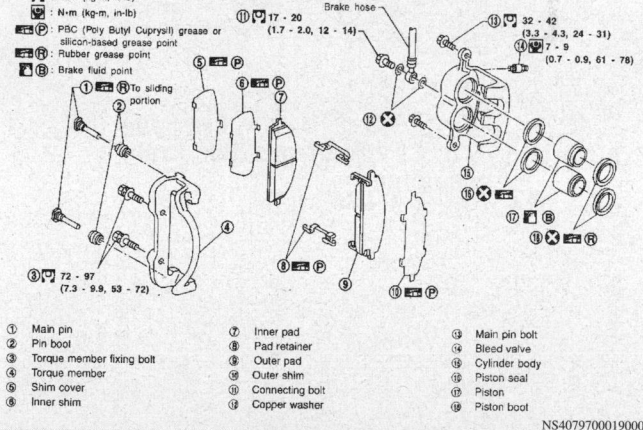

① Main pin
② Pin boot
③ Torque member fixing bolt
④ Torque member
⑤ Shim cover
⑥ Inner shim
⑦ Inner pad
⑧ Pad retainer
⑨ Outer pad
⑩ Outer shim
⑪ Connecting bolt
⑫ Copper washer
⑬ Main pin bolt
⑭ Bleed valve
⑮ Cylinder body
⑯ Piston seal
⑰ Piston
⑱ Piston boot

NS4079700019000X

Fig. 2 Exploded view of AD31VA front disc brake caliper

7. Install pad retainers.

OPZ11V

1. Raise and support rear of vehicle and remove wheels.
2. Remove clip from pad pin, **Fig. 13.**
3. Remove pad pin.
4. Remove cross spring.
5. Pull out outer pad.
6. Push back outer piston with suitable tool and install new pad.
7. Install cross spring, pad, pin and clip.

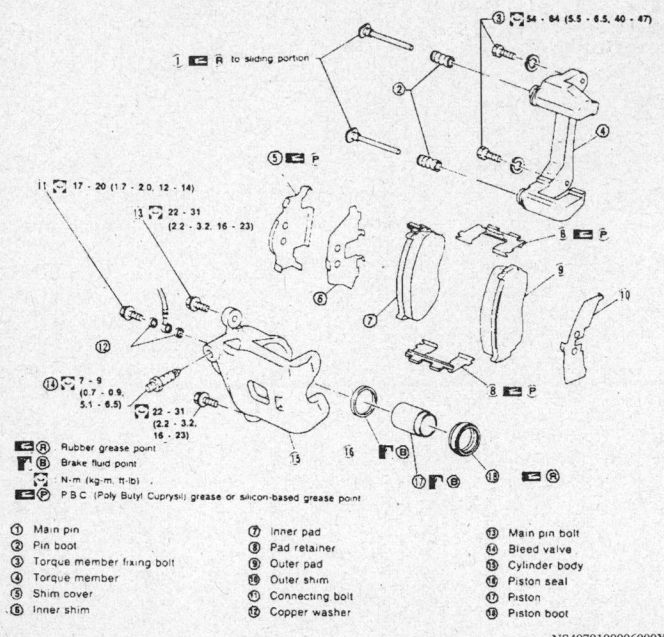

Fig. 3   Exploded view of CL22VD & CL22VE front
disc brake assembly

① Main pin
② Pin boot
③ Torque member fixing bolt
④ Torque member
⑤ Shim cover
⑥ Inner shim
⑦ Inner pad
⑧ Pad retainer
⑨ Outer pad
⑩ Outer shim
⑪ Connecting bolt
⑫ Copper washer
⑬ Main pin bolt
⑭ Bleed valve
⑮ Cylinder body
⑯ Piston seal
⑰ Piston
⑱ Piston boot

NS4079100006000X

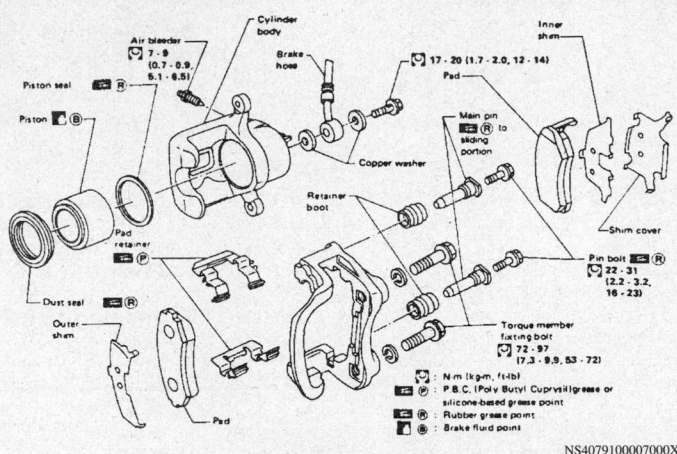

Fig. 4   Exploded view of CL22VB & CL22VF front
disc brake assembly

NS4079100007000X

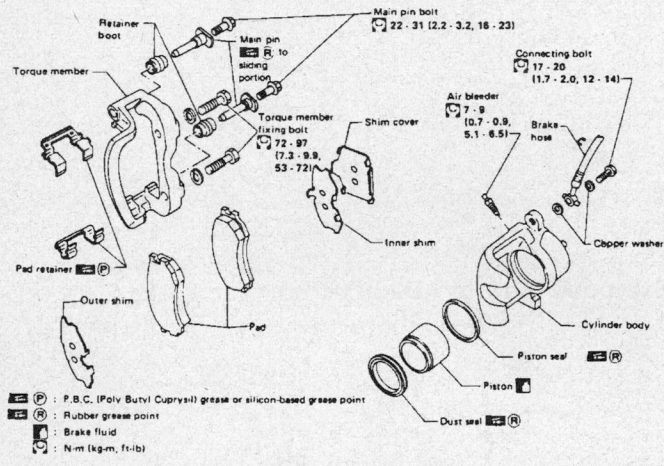

Fig. 5   Exploded view of CL25VA front disc brake
assembly

NS4079100008000X

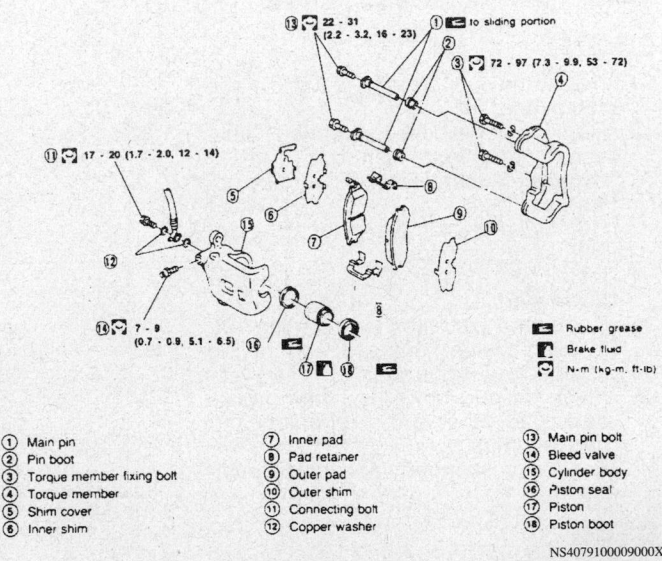

① Main pin
② Pin boot
③ Torque member fixing bolt
④ Torque member
⑤ Shim cover
⑥ Inner shim
⑦ Inner pad
⑧ Pad retainer
⑨ Outer pad
⑩ Outer shim
⑪ Connecting bolt
⑫ Copper washer
⑬ Main pin bolt
⑭ Bleed valve
⑮ Cylinder body
⑯ Piston seal
⑰ Piston
⑱ Piston boot

NS4079100009000X

Fig. 6   Exploded view of CL25VB front disc brake
assembly

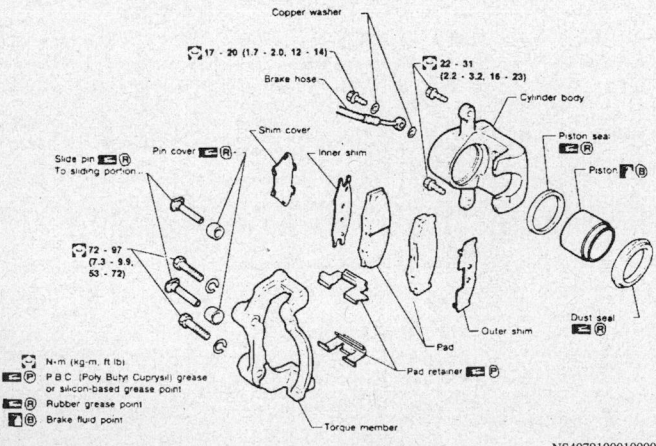

Fig. 7   Exploded view of CL28VA front disc brake
assembly

NS4079100010000X

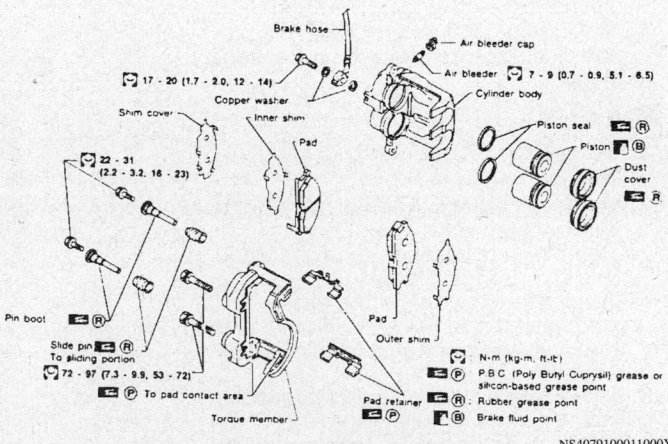

Fig. 8   Exploded view of CL28VD front disc brake
assembly

NS4079100011000X

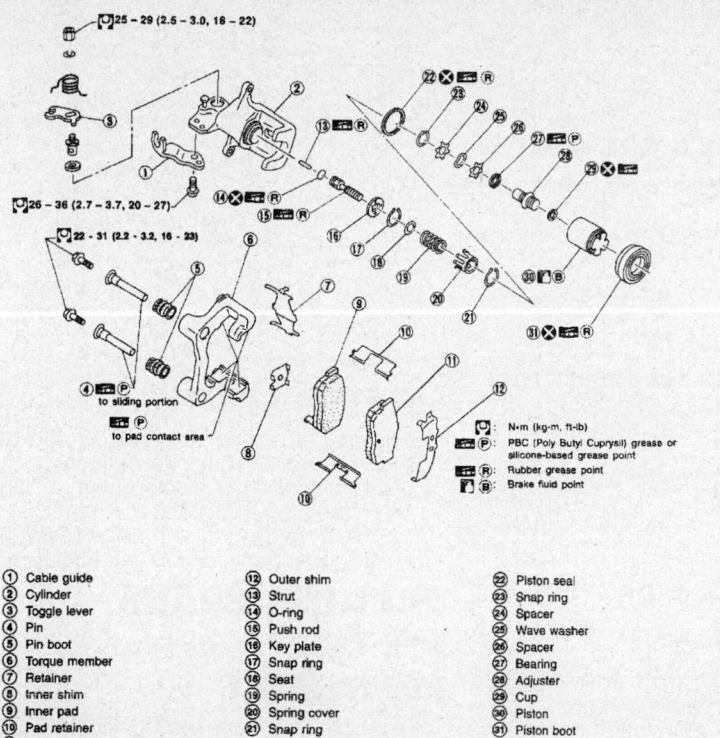

Parts list (Fig. 9):
1. Cable guide
2. Cylinder
3. Toggle lever
4. Pin
5. Pin boot
6. Torque member
7. Retainer
8. Inner shim
9. Inner pad
10. Pad retainer
11. Outer pad
12. Outer shim
13. Strut
14. O-ring
15. Push rod
16. Key plate
17. Snap ring
18. Seat
19. Spring
20. Spring cover
21. Snap ring
22. Piston seal
23. Snap ring
24. Spacer
25. Wave washer
26. Spacer
27. Bearing
28. Adjuster
29. Cup
30. Piston
31. Piston boot

N·m (kg-m, ft-lb)
PBC (Poly Butyl Cuprysil) grease or silicone-based grease point
Rubber grease point
Brake fluid point

NS4079500018000X

Fig. 9 Exploded view of CL7HB rear disc brake assembly

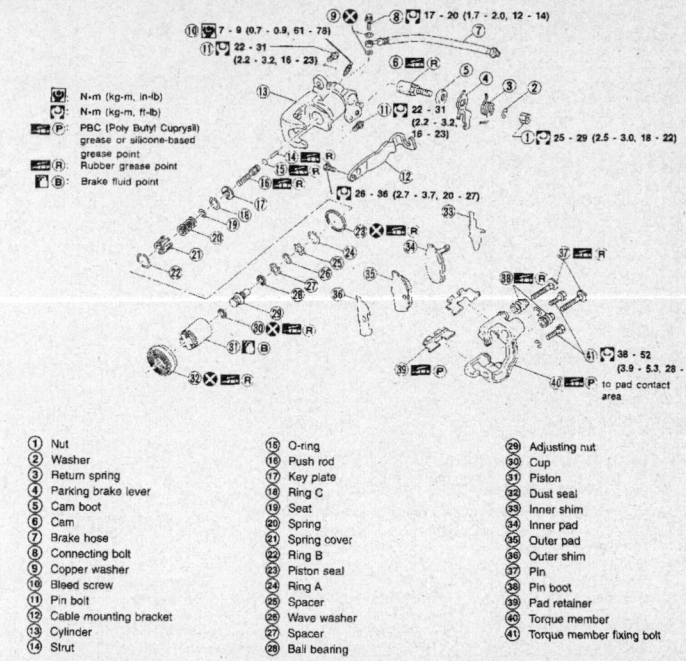

N·m (kg-m, in-lb)
N·m (kg-m, ft-lb)
PBC (Poly Butyl Cuprysil) grease or silicone-based grease point
Rubber grease point
Brake fluid point

Parts list (Fig. 10):
1. Nut
2. Washer
3. Return spring
4. Parking brake lever
5. Cam boot
6. Cam
7. Brake hose
8. Connecting bolt
9. Copper washer
10. Bleed screw
11. Pin bolt
12. Cable mounting bracket
13. Cylinder
14. Strut
15. O-ring
16. Push rod
17. Key plate
18. Ring C
19. Seat
20. Spring
21. Spring cover
22. Ring B
23. Piston seal
24. Ring A
25. Spacer
26. Wave washer
27. Spacer
28. Ball bearing
29. Adjusting nut
30. Cup
31. Piston
32. Dust seal
33. Inner shim
34. Inner pad
35. Outer pad
36. Outer shim
37. Pin
38. Pin boot
39. Pad retainer
40. Torque member
41. Torque member fixing bolt

NS4079100014000X

Fig. 10 Exploded view of CL11H rear disc brake assembly

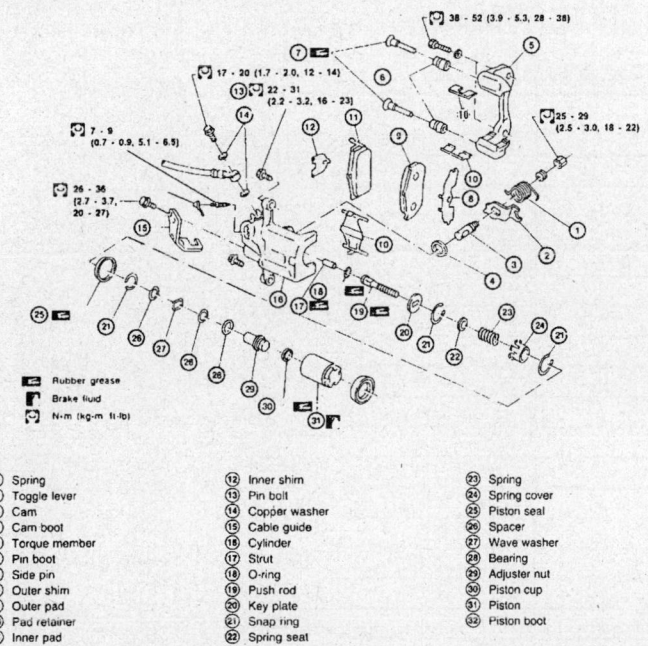

Rubber grease
Brake fluid
N·m (kg-m, ft-lb)

Parts list (Fig. 11):
1. Spring
2. Toggle lever
3. Cam
4. Cam boot
5. Torque member
6. Pin boot
7. Side pin
8. Outer shim
9. Outer pad
10. Pad retainer
11. Inner pad
12. Inner shim
13. Pin bolt
14. Copper washer
15. Cable guide
16. Cylinder
17. Strut
18. O-ring
19. Push rod
20. Key plate
21. Snap ring
22. Spring seat
23. Spring
24. Spring cover
25. Piston seal
26. Spacer
27. Wave washer
28. Bearing
29. Adjuster nut
30. Piston cup
31. Piston
32. Piston boot

NS4079100015000X

Fig. 11 Exploded view of CL9HB rear disc brake assembly

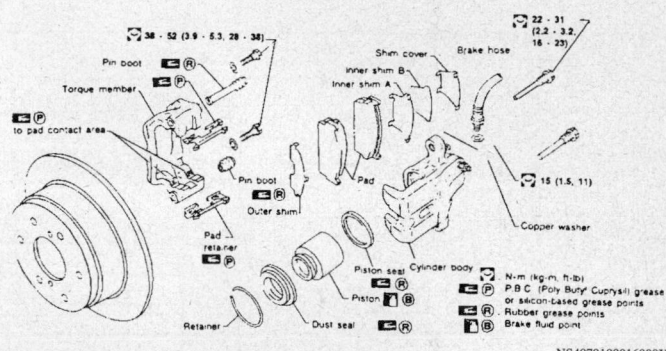

N·m (kg-m, ft-lb)
PBC (Poly Butyl Cuprysil) grease or silicone-based grease points
Rubber grease points
Brake fluid point

NS4079100016000X

Fig. 12 Exploded view of AD14VB rear disc brake assembly

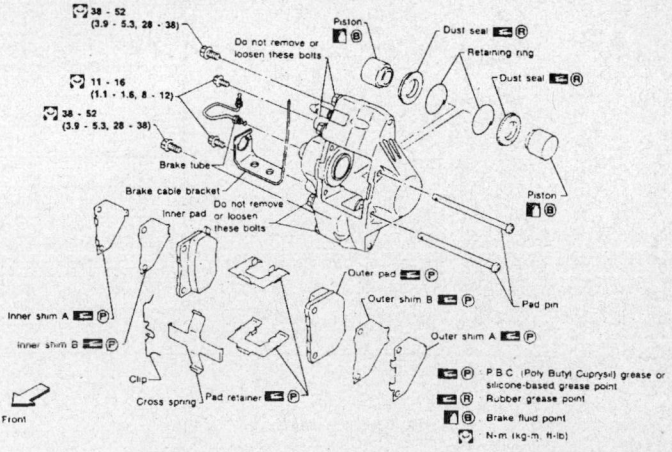

PBC (Poly Butyl Cuprysil) grease or silicone-based grease point
Rubber grease point
Brake fluid point
N·m (kg-m, ft-lb)

NS4079100017000X

Fig. 13 Exploded view of OPZ11V rear disc brake assembly

CALIPER SERVICE

FRONT

REPLACEMENT

1. Raise and support front of vehicle and remove wheel.
2. Disconnect brake hose from brake tube.
3. Remove caliper assembly from spindle.
4. Reverse procedure to install.

OVERHAUL

1. Remove pin bolts and separate cylinder body from torque member.
2. Remove pad retainers, shims and brake pads.
3. Feed compressed air gradually into caliper port and force out piston(s) with dust seals.
4. Remove piston seals, sub pins, main pins and dust seals.
5. Reverse procedure to assemble.

REAR

REPLACEMENT

Except AD14VB & OPZ11V

1. Disconnect parking brake cable and brake hose.
2. Remove caliper attaching bolts, then the caliper from vehicle.
3. Reverse procedure to install.

AD14VB & OPZ11V

1. Disconnect brake tube and hand brake cable from caliper assembly.
2. Remove caliper mounting bolts and the caliper.
3. To install, reverse procedure.

OVERHAUL

Except AD14VB & OPZ11V

1. Remove outer spring retainer, if equipped.
2. Remove pin bolts, then separate cylinder body and torque member.
3. Remove piston by rotating it counterclockwise with pliers.

4. Remove ring, adjusting nut, ball bearing, wave washer, spacers and cup from piston, as required.
5. Pry ring A, **Fig. 11,** off of cylinder body, then remove spring cover, spring and seat.
6. Pry ring B off of cylinder body, then remove key plate, pushrod and rod.
7. Remove O-ring from pushrod, then pry piston seal out of cylinder body.
8. Remove return spring, nut, spring washer and lever, then adjusting cam and cam boot.
9. Remove pins and pin boots.
10. Reverse procedure to assemble.

AD14VB & OPZ11V

Disassemble caliper assembly as shown in **Figs. 12 and 13,** noting the following:
1. Carefully remove piston retainer using a suitable screwdriver.
2. Apply compressed air to back side of piston to remove piston and dust seal.

PARKING BRAKE SERVICE

ADJUSTMENT

Refer to "Drum Brakes" for adjustment procedures.

DISC BRAKE SPECIFICATIONS

CALIPER SPECIFICATIONS

Year	Caliper	Caliper Bore Dia. Inch
1996–99	AD14VB①	1.6862
	AD28VX	2.3620
	AD31VA	1.7500
	CL7HB①	1.2500
	CL9HA①	1.3370
	CL9HB①	1.3370
	CL11H①	1.5030
	CL22VB	2.1260
	CL22VD	2.1260
	CL22VE	2.1260
	CL22VF	2.1260
	CL25VA	2.2520
	CL25VB	2.2520
	CL28VA	2.3860
	CL28VD	1.6850
	OPZ11V①	1.5000
	OPF25VA	1.5925

① — Rear disc.

ROTOR SPECIFICATIONS

Year	Model	Minimum Refinish Thickness. Inch	Lateral Runout (T.I.R.)
1996–99	Altima	②	.0028
	Frontier	1.024	.0028
	Maxima	③	.0028
	Pathfinder	1.024	.004
	Pickup	1.024	.0028
	Quest	.95	.0028
	Sentra & 200SX	⑤	.0028
	240SX	①	.0028
	300ZX	④	.0028

① — On 1996 models, front, .709 inch; 1997–99 models front, .787 inch; rear, .310 inch.
② — Front w/out ABS .709; front w/ABS, .787; rear, .315.
③ — Front, .787 inch; rear, .315 inch.
④ — Front: 1.102 inch. Rear, .630 inch.
⑤ — Front, .620 inch; rear, .236 inch.

TIGHTENING SPECIFICATIONS

ALTIMA

Year	Component	Torque/ Ft. lbs.
1996–99	Air Bleeder	60–72①
	Brake Pedal Mounting Bracket	72–96①
	Brake Fluid Line Connecting Bolt	12–14
	Caliper Pin Bolt	16–23
	Front Caliper Bracket	53–72
	Rear Caliper Bracket	28–38
	Stop Lamp Switch	9–11

① — Inch lbs.

MAXIMA

Year	Component	Torque/ Ft. Lbs.
1996–99	Baffle Plate & Adapter Plate Bolts	28–38
	Brake Booster To Body	72–96①
	Brake Booster To Master Cylinder	72–96①
	Brake Hose Connector	12–14
	Brake Pedal Bracket	72–96①
	Brake Tube Connector Mounting Bolt	11–13
	Brake Tube Flare Nut	11–13
	Caliper Bleeder	60–84②
	Caliper Pin Bolt	16–23
	Input Rod Locknut	12–16
	Parking Brake Adjuster Locknut	48–60②
	Parking Brake Cable Clamp	9–12
	Parking Brake Control Lever To Body	9–12
	Stop Lamp Switch Locknut	9–11
	Torque Member Fixing Bolt	①

① — Front, 53–72 ft. lbs.; rear, 28–38 ft. lbs.
② — Inch lbs.

FRONTIER, PATHFINDER & PICKUP

Year	Component	Torque/Ft. Lbs.
1996–99	Air Bleeder	60–72①
	Brake Booster To Body	72–84①
	Brake Hose Connector	12–14
	Brake Hose Connector	12–15
	Brake Pedal Bracket To Body	72–96①
	Brake Pedal Fulcrum Shaft	12–16
	Brake Tube Flare Nut	11–13
	Four Way Connector Fixing Bolt	45–60①
	Front Caliper Fixing Bolts	16–23
	Front Torque Member Fixing Bolts	53–72
	Load Sensing Valve Air Bleeder	60–72①
	Load Sensing Valve Fixing Bolt	12–15
	Master Cylinder To Brake Booster	72–84①
	Rear Caliper Fixing Bolts	16–23
	Rear Torque Member Fixing Bolts	28–38
	Stop Lamp Switch	9–11
	Three Way Connector Fixing Bolt	45–60
	Wheel Cylinder Fixing Bolts	60–96①

① — Inch lbs.

QUEST

Year	Component	Torque/Ft. lbs.
1996–99	Front Air Bleeder	12–17
	Front Caliper Main Pin Bolt	18–25
	Front Hydraulic Line Connecting Bolt	12–14

① — Inch lbs.

SENTRA & 200SX

Year	Component	Torque/Ft. Lbs.
1996–99	Air Bleeder	60–72①
	Brake Hose To Caliper Bolt	12–14
	Brake Tube To Connector	11–13
	Cable Guide Fixing Bolt	27–36
	Caliper Fixing Bolt	23–30
	Torque Member Fixing Bolt	40–47

① — Inch lbs.

240SX

Year	Component	Torque/ Ft. Lbs.
1996–99	Air Bleeder	60–72①
	Brake Booster To Body	9–12
	Brake Hose Connecting Bolt	12–14
	Brake Hose Connector Bolt	12–14
	Brake Pedal Bracket To Body	69–96①
	Brake Pedal Fulcrum Shaft	12–16
	Brake Tube Flare Nut	11–13
	Caliper Fixing Bolt	16–23
	Front Torque Member Fixing Bolt	53–72
	Master Cylinder To Brake Booster	72–96①
	Parking Brake Cable Stay	20–27
	Rear Torque Member Fixing Bolt	28–38
	Stop Lamp Switch Locknut	9–11

① — Inch lbs.

300ZX

Year	Component	Torque/ Ft. Lbs.
1996	Brake Booster To Master Cylinder	72–96①
	Brake Booster To Pedal Bracket	9–12
	Brake Pedal To Bracket	12–16
	Caliper Pin	60–84①
	Front Caliper Mounting Bolts	72–87
	Pedal Bracket To Body	72–96①
	Rear Caliper Mounting Bolts	28–38
	Speed Control Cancel Switch	9–11
	Stop Light Switch	9–11

① — Inch lbs.

Drum Brakes

INDEX

APPLICATION CHART

Year	Model	Type
1996–99	Altima	LT23E
	Frontier & Pickup	LT26B/LT30A
	Pathfinder	LT30C
	Quest	LT25X
	Sentra & 200SX	LT18C
	300ZX	DS17HD①

① — Parking drum brake.

BRAKE SERVICE

ALTIMA

1. Raise and support rear of vehicle, then remove rear wheel.
2. Fully release parking brake.
3. Remove brake drum, if drum is hard to remove, proceed as follows:
   a. Remove plug from rear side of backing plate.
   b. Using a suitable tool, push stopper towards backing plate to gain clearance between brake shoe and drum as shown in **Fig. 1.**
   c. Install two bolts into outside of brake drum as shown in **Fig. 2,** then gradually tighten the two bolts until drum separates from the brake shoes.
4. Push in shoe hold-down pins from behind backing plate, **Figs. 3 and 4.**
5. Pull out brake shoes.
6. Using pliers, remove lower return spring.
7. Separate shoes, one at a time, from wheel cylinder and remove from backing plate with adjuster assembly attached. **Be careful not to damage wheel cylinder boot.**
8. Disconnect parking brake cable from toggle lever, then remove adjuster return spring and shoe return spring.
9. Remove retainer ring, then separate toggle lever and brake shoe.
10. Reverse procedure to install, noting the following:
    a. Measure inside diameter of brake drum, replace if necessary.
    b. Apply grease to brake shoe contact areas shown in **Figs. 3 and 4.**
    c. Adjust parking brake and bleed brake hydraulic system.

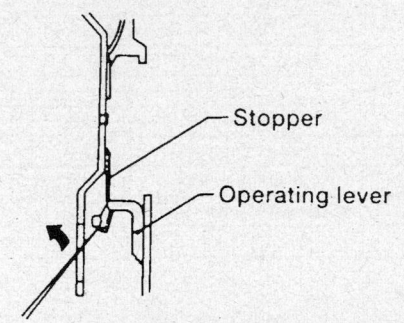

- Stopper
- Operating lever

NS4089100001000X

Fig. 1 Brake shoe & brake drum clearance adjustment. Altima

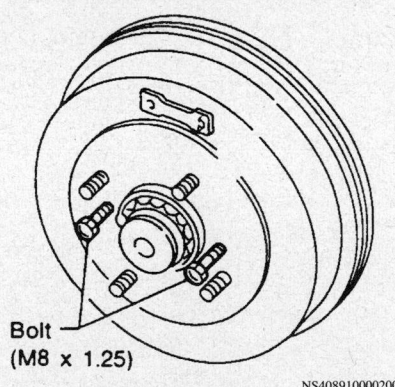

Bolt
(M8 x 1.25)

NS4089100002000X

Fig. 2 Brake drum removal

SENTRA & 200SX

1. Raise and support rear of vehicle.
2. Fully release parking brake.
3. Remove brake drum, if drum is difficult to remove, proceed as follows:
   a. Remove plug from rear of backing plate.

b. Shorten adjuster to increase clearance between brake shoe and drum.
c. Install two bolt into brake drum as shown in **Fig. 2,** then gradually tighten bolts until drum separates from the brake shoes.
4. Remove brake shoes retainers, **Fig. 5.**
5. Rotate brake shoes forward and remove lower return spring.
6. Disconnect parking brake cable from toggle lever.
7. Remove retainer ring, then separate toggle lever and brake shoe.
8. Reverse procedure to install, noting the following:
   a. Measure inside diameter of brake drum, replace if necessary.
   b. Apply grease to brake shoe contact areas shown in **Fig. 5.**
   c. Adjust parking brake and bleed brake hydraulic system.

FRONTIER, PATHFINDER & PICKUP

1. Fully release parking brake control lever.
2. Raise and support vehicle.
3. Remove brake drum.
4. Refer to **Figs. 6 and 7** to remove brake shoes.
5. Reverse procedure to install, noting the following:
   a. Measure inside diameter of brake drum, replace if necessary.
   b. Apply grease to brake shoe contact areas shown in **Figs. 6 and 7.**
   c. Adjust parking brake and bleed brake hydraulic system.

QUEST

1. Raise and support rear of vehicle, then remove rear wheel.
2. Fully release parking brake.
3. Remove brake drum, if drum is hard to

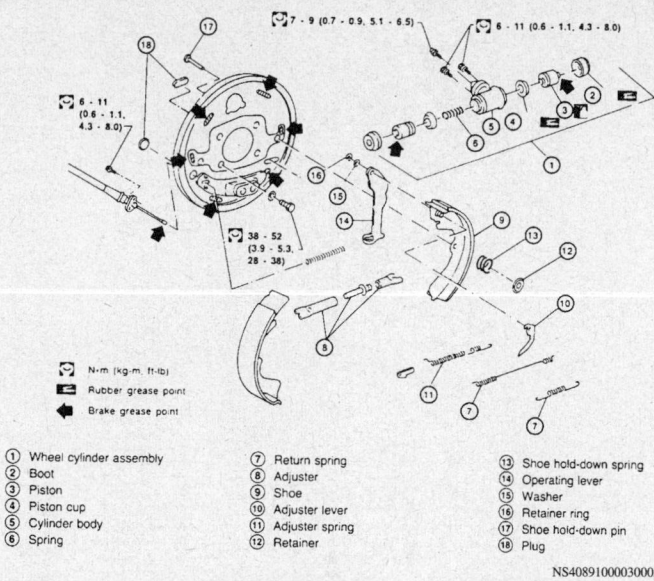

Fig. 3 Exploded view of drum brakes. 1996–97 Altima

① Wheel cylinder assembly
② Boot
③ Piston
④ Piston cup
⑤ Cylinder body
⑥ Spring
⑦ Return spring
⑧ Adjuster
⑨ Shoe
⑩ Adjuster lever
⑪ Adjuster spring
⑫ Retainer
⑬ Shoe hold-down spring
⑭ Operating lever
⑮ Washer
⑯ Retainer ring
⑰ Shoe hold-down pin
⑱ Plug

🔧 N·m (kg-m, ft-lb)
▣ Rubber grease point
◀ Brake grease point

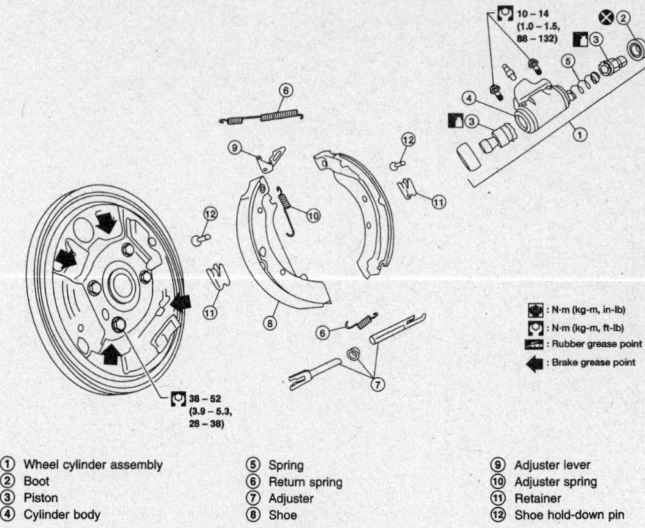

Fig. 4 Exploded view of drum brakes. 1998–99 Altima

① Wheel cylinder assembly
② Boot
③ Piston
④ Cylinder body
⑤ Spring
⑥ Return spring
⑦ Adjuster
⑧ Shoe
⑨ Adjuster lever
⑩ Adjuster spring
⑪ Retainer
⑫ Shoe hold-down pin

N·m (kg-m, in-lb)
N·m (kg-m, ft-lb)
▣ Rubber grease point
◀ Brake grease point

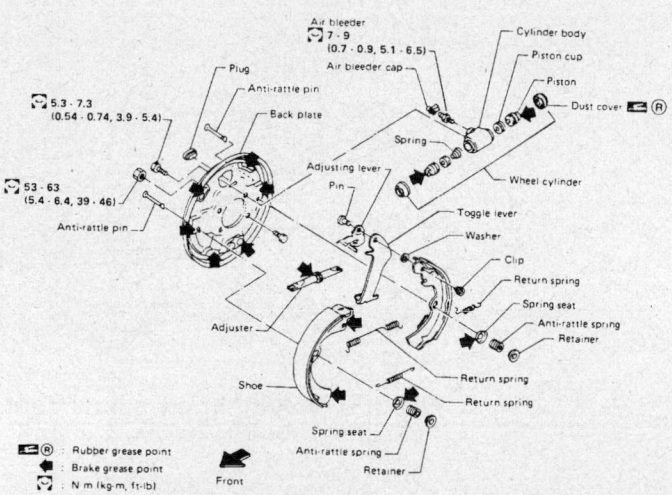

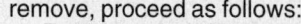

Fig. 5 Exploded view of drum brakes. Sentra & 200SX

▣ Rubber grease point
◀ Brake grease point
🔧 N·m (kg-m, ft-lb)

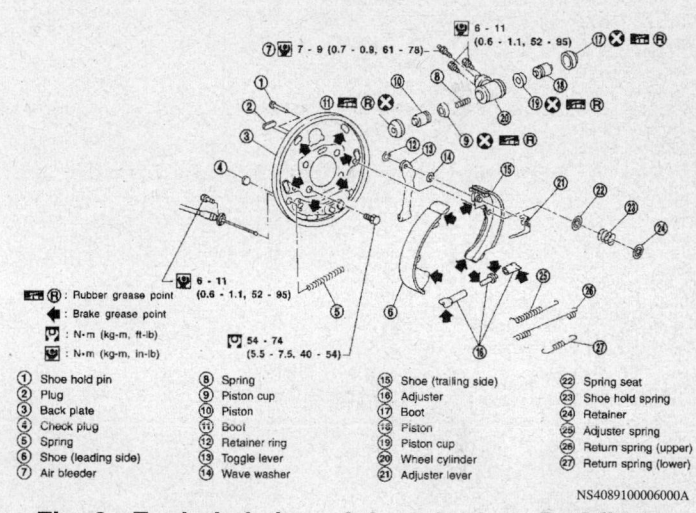

Fig. 6 Exploded view of drum brakes. Pathfinder

▣ Rubber grease point
◀ Brake grease point
🔧 N·m (kg-m, ft-lb)
🔧 N·m (kg-m, in-lb)

① Shoe hold pin
② Plug
③ Back plate
④ Check plug
⑤ Spring
⑥ Shoe (leading side)
⑦ Air bleeder
⑧ Spring
⑨ Piston cup
⑩ Boot
⑪ Boot
⑫ Retainer ring
⑬ Toggle lever
⑭ Wave washer
⑮ Shoe (trailing side)
⑯ Adjuster
⑰ Boot
⑱ Piston
⑲ Piston cup
⑳ Wheel cylinder
㉑ Adjuster lever
㉒ Spring seat
㉓ Shoe hold spring
㉔ Retainer
㉕ Adjuster spring
㉖ Return spring (upper)
㉗ Return spring (lower)

remove, proceed as follows:
a. Remove plug from rear side of backing plate.
b. Using a suitable tool, loosen adjuster to gain clearance between brake shoe and drum.
c. Install two bolts into outside of brake drum as shown in **Fig. 2,** then gradually tighten the two bolts until drum separates from the brake shoes.
4. Push in shoe hold-down pins from behind backing plate, **Fig. 8.**
5. Pull out brake shoes.
6. Using pliers, remove lower return spring.
7. Separate shoes, one at a time, from wheel cylinder and remove from backing plate with adjuster assembly attached. **Be careful not to damage wheel cylinder boot.**
8. Disconnect parking brake cable from toggle lever, then remove adjuster re-

turn spring and shoe return spring.
9. Remove retainer ring, then separate toggle lever and brake shoe.
10. Reverse procedure to install, noting the following:
a. Measure inside diameter of brake drum, replace if necessary.
b. Apply grease to brake shoe contact areas shown in **Fig. 8.**
c. Adjust parking brake and bleed brake hydraulic system.

ADJUSTMENTS
PARKING BRAKE
Altima

1. Prior to adjustment, check the following:
a. **On models equipped w/rear disc brakes,** ensure toggle lever returns to stopper when parking brake lever is released, **Fig. 9.**

b. **On all models,** ensure there is no drag when parking brake lever is released.
2. Release parking brake lever and loosen adjusting nut.
3. Start engine and depress brake pedal fully at least 10 times with engine running.
4. Pull parking brake control lever 4–5 notches, then adjust control lever by turning adjusting nut, **Fig. 10.**
5. Pull control lever using approximately 44 lbs. of force, parking brake should be engaged when lever stroke is 7–8 notches.
6. Bend parking brake warning lamp switch plate so that brake warning lamp comes on when parking brake lever is pulled one notch or less.

Maxima

1. Pull parking brake lever with a force of 44 lbs. and ensure lever travels 9–11 notches.
2. Rotate adjuster, **Fig. 11** until proper

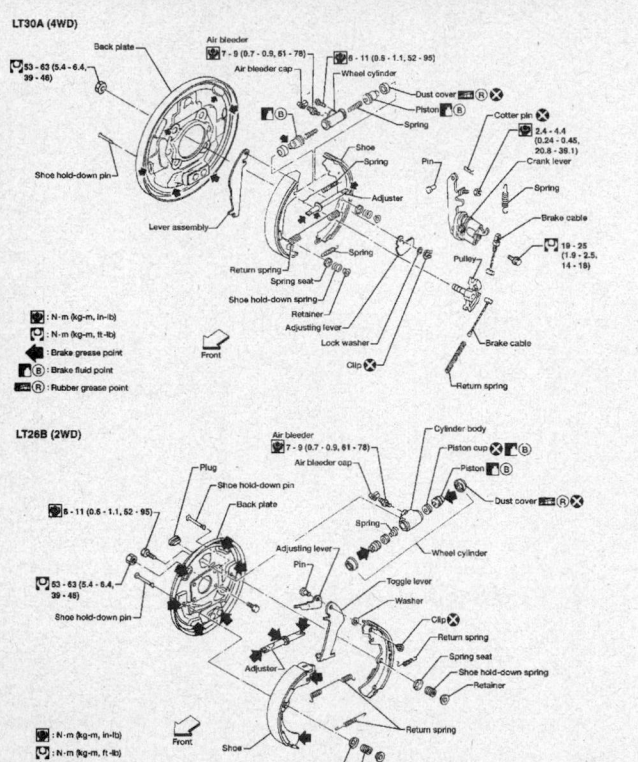

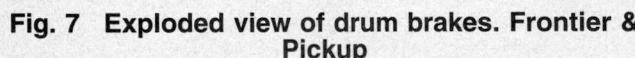

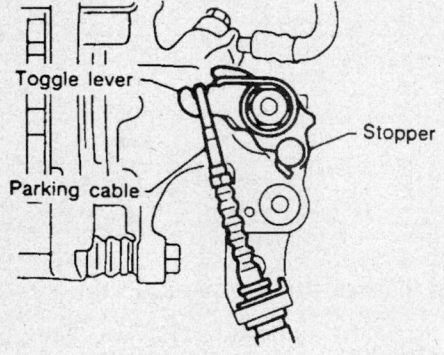

Fig. 7 Exploded view of drum brakes. Frontier & Pickup

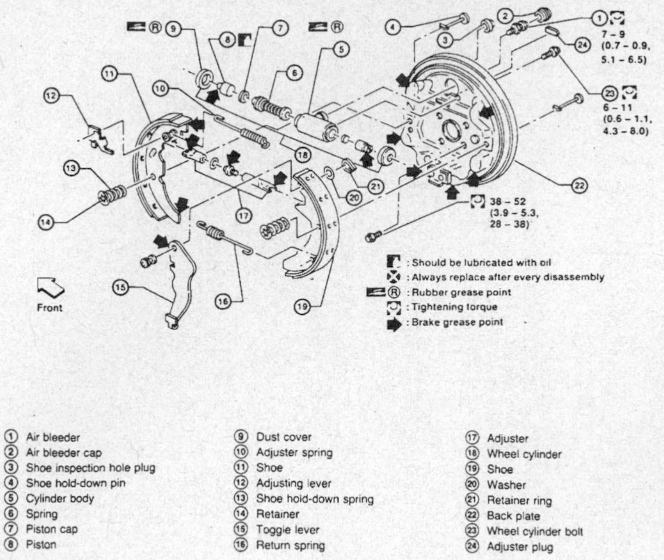

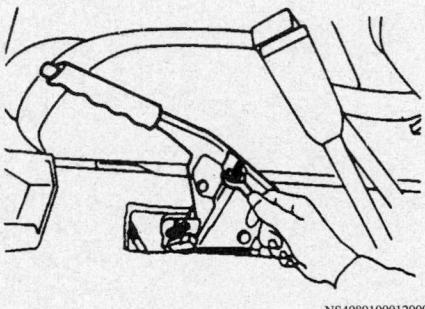

1. Air bleeder
2. Air bleeder cap
3. Shoe inspection hole plug
4. Shoe hold-down pin
5. Cylinder body
6. Spring
7. Piston cap
8. Piston
9. Dust cover
10. Adjuster spring
11. Shoe
12. Adjusting lever
13. Shoe hold-down spring
14. Retainer
15. Toggle lever
16. Return spring
17. Adjuster
18. Wheel cylinder
19. Shoe
20. Washer
21. Retainer ring
22. Back plate
23. Wheel cylinder bolt
24. Adjuster plug

◎ : Should be lubricated with oil
⊗ : Always replace after every disassembly
⊡ : Rubber grease point
◪ : Tightening torque
➡ : Brake grease point

NS4089100008000X

Fig. 8 Exploded view of drum brakes. Quest

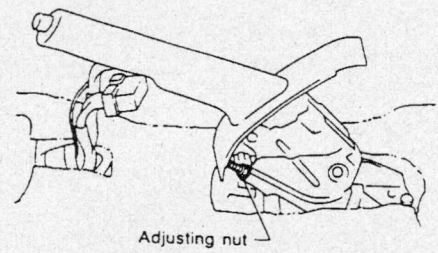

Fig. 9 Toggle lever inspection. Altima

NS4089100010000X

Fig. 10 Parking brake adjustment. Altima

NS4089100011000X

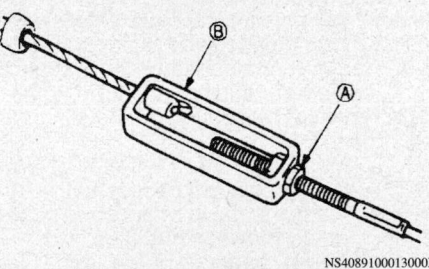

NS4089100013000X

Fig. 12 Parking brake adjustment. Frontier, Pathfinder & Pickup

Fig. 11 Parking brake adjustment. Maxima, Sentra, 200SX & 300ZX

NS4089100012000X

stroke is obtained, then tighten lock-nut.

Sentra, 200SX & 300ZX
1. Pull parking brake lever with a force of 44 lbs. and ensure lever travels is as follows:
   a. **On Sentra and 200SX models,** 7–11 notches.
   b. **On 300ZX models,** 6–9 notches.
2. Rotate adjuster, **Fig. 11** until proper stroke is obtained, then tighten lock-nut.

Frontier, Pathfinder & Pickup
1. Pull parking brake lever with a force of 44 lbs. and ensure lever travel is as follows:
   a. **On 2WD Frontier and Pickup models,** 10–12 notches.
   b. **On 4WD Frontier and Pickup models,** 9–11 notches.
   c. **On Pathfinder models,** 6–8 notches.
2. Rotate adjuster, **Fig. 12,** until proper

stroke is obtained, then tighten lock-nut.

Quest
1. Depress brake pedal several times until clicking sound from rear brakes stops.
2. Ensure there is no drag when parking brake pedal is released.
3. Loosen locknut, then rotate adjusting nut, **Fig. 13.**
4. Tighten locknut and adjusting nut.
5. Press down on parking brake pedal using approximately 44 lbs. of force, parking brake should be engaged when pedal is stroke is 11–12 notches.

240SX
1. Pull parking brake lever with a force of 44 lbs. and ensure lever travels 6–9 notches.
2. Rotate adjuster, **Fig. 14,** until proper stroke is obtained, then tighten lock-nut.

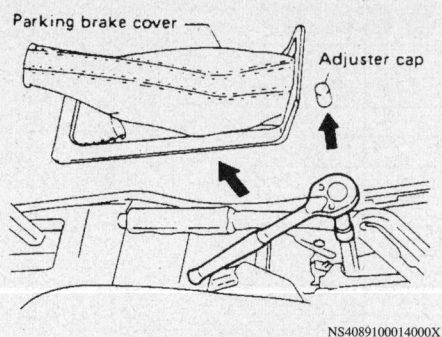

Fig. 13 Parking brake adjustment. Quest

NS4089100014000X

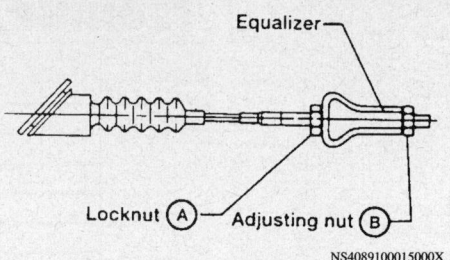

NS4089100015000X

Fig. 14 Parking brake adjustment. 240SX

DRUM BRAKE SPECIFICATIONS

Year	Model	Brake Drum Inside Dia., Inch	Maximum Refinish Dia., Inch
1996–99	Altima	9.00	9.06
	Pathfinder	③	—
	Frontier & Pickup①	10.24	10.30
	Frontier & Pickup②	11.61	11.67
	Quest	9.84	9.90
	Sentra	7.09	7.13
	200SX	7.09	7.13

① — Two wheel drive.
② — Four wheel drive.
③ — 1996, 10.24 inches; 1997–99, 11.61 inches.

TIGHTENING SPECIFICATIONS

ALTIMA

Year	Component	Torque/ Ft. lbs.
1996–99	Air Bleeder	60–72①
	Backing Plate To Axle	28–38
	Brake Pedal Mounting Bracket	72–96①
	Brake Fluid Line Connecting Bolt	12–14
	Stop Lamp Switch	9–11
	Wheel Cylinder To Backing Plate	60–96

① — Inch lbs.

FRONTIER, PATHFINDER & PICKUP

Year	Component	Torque/Ft. Lbs.
1996–99	Air Bleeder	60–72①
	Backing Plate Fixing Bolts	39–46
	Brake Booster To Body	72–96①
	Brake Hose Connector	12–14
	Brake Hose Connector	12–15
	Brake Pedal Bracket To Body	72–96①
	Brake Pedal Fulcrum Shaft	12–16
	Brake Tube Flare Nut	11–13
	Four Way Connector Fixing Bolt	44–60①
	Front Torque Member Fixing Bolts	53–72
	Load Sensing Valve Air Bleeder	60–72①
	Load Sensing Valve Fixing Bolt	12–15
	Master Cylinder To Brake Booster	72–96①
	Rear Torque Member Fixing Bolts	28–38
	Stop Lamp Switch	9–11
	Three Way Connector Fixing Bolt	44–60①
	Wheel Cylinder Fixing Bolts	60–96①

① — Inch lbs.

QUEST

Year	Component	Torque/Ft. lbs.
1996–99	Backing Plate To Axle	26–38
	Front Air Bleeder	12–17
	Front Hydraulic Line Connecting Bolt	12–14
	Rear Air Bleeder	60–72①
	Wheel Cylinder Bolt	60–96①

① — Inch lbs.

SENTRA & 200SX

Year	Component	Torque/Ft. Lbs.
1996–99	Air Bleeder	60–72①
	Backing Plate Fixing Bolt	28–38
	Brake Tube To Connector	11–13
	Cable Guide Fixing Bolt	27–36
	Parking Brake Cable To Backing Plate	39–55①
	Torque Member Fixing Bolt	40–47
	Wheel Cylinder Bolt	60–96①

① — Inch lbs.

Hydraulic Brake Systems

INDEX

ADJUSTMENTS

BRAKE BOOSTER OUTPUT ROD

Refer to "Output Rod Adjust" in the "Power Brake Units" section.

BRAKE PEDAL

1. Adjust brake pedal free height dimension "H" in **Fig. 1,** to specifications **Fig. 2,** using brake booster input rod **Fig. 3.** Ensure tip of input rod stays inside clevis pin.
2. With motor running, measure brake pedal depressed height dimension "D" in **Fig. 1,** is within specifications **Fig. 2.** If not within specifications check for leak in brake system, air in system, problem with master cylinder, wheel cylinder or brake caliper. Repair or replace as necessary.
3. Measure clearance dimension "C" **Fig. 1.** Clearance between pedal stopper and threaded end of brake light switch should be .012–0.39 inches. Clearance between pedal stopper and threaded end of ASCD switch if equipped, should be .012–0.39 inches.
4. Measure pedal freeplay dimension "A," **Fig. 1.** Pedal freeplay should be between .04–.12 inches.

COMPONENT REPLACEMENT

MASTER CYLINDER, REPLACE

Do not spill brake fluid on painted areas, it may cause paint damage.
1. Connect a vinyl tube to the bleeder screws.
2. Depress brake pedal, open bleeder valves and drain fluid into suitable container. Repeat until master cylinder is empty.
3. Disconnect brake lines, remove master cylinder attaching nuts, then master cylinder.
4. Reverse procedure to install, bleed brakes as outlined under " Brake Bleeding Procedure."

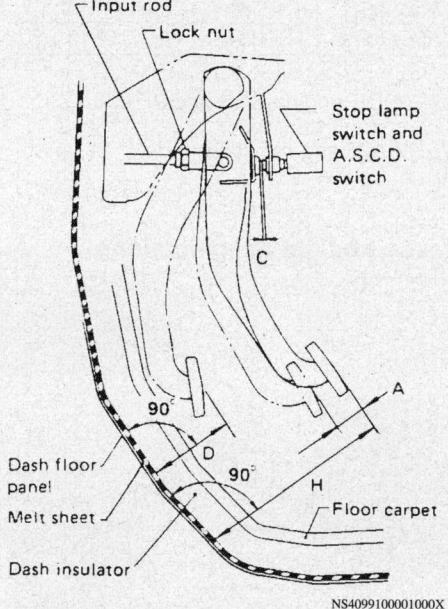

Fig. 1 Brake pedal adjustment

NS4099100001000X

COMPONENT SERVICE

MASTER CYLINDER OVERHAUL

OVERHAUL

Refer to **Figs. 4 through 11,** for master cylinder overhaul procedures, noting the following:
1. If piston assembly is stuck in cylinder bore, gradually apply air to fluid outlet port.
2. Replace stopper cap if claws are damaged. Bend claw inward when installing new stopper.

CLEANING & INSPECTION

Examine reservoirs for foreign matter and check all passages for restrictions. If there is any indication of contamination or evidence of corrosion, service the hydraulic system as needed.

When disassembled, wash all parts in denatured alcohol or clean brake fluid. Use an air hose to blow out all passages, orifices and valve holes. Air dry and place parts on clean paper or lint-free cloth.
1. Check components for wear, damage, or corrosion. Replace as needed.
2. Check master cylinder bore for scoring, rust, pitting or etching. Replace as necessary.

EXTERNAL PROPORTIONING VALVE

REPLACEMENT

Refer to **Figs. 12 through 14** for proportioning valve replacement.

TESTING

Altima, Sentra & 200SX

1. Check and fill brake fluid as required.
2. Connect pressure checking tool No. KV991V0010, or equivalent, to air bleeders of front and rear brakes on either left or right sides, **Fig. 15.**
3. Bleed air from tool.
4. Depress brake pedal and check fluid pressure.
5. Compare pressure readings to specifications in **Figs. 16 through 18**
6. If output pressure is not within specifications, replace proportioning valve.
7. Bleed brake system as described under "Brake System Bleed."

Frontier, Pathfinder & Pickup

If load sensing valve is damaged, replace as an assembly.
1. With one person sitting in drivers seat, set rear axle load to 221 lbs. by positioning weight in cargo area.
2. Install pressure gauge KV991V0010 as shown in **Fig. 19.** Then bleed air from front and rear brake lines.
3. Apply brakes, bring front brake pressure to 1422 psi and check rear brake pressure. Refer to **Fig. 20,** for specifications.
4. If brake pressure is not within specifications adjust bracket as follows:
   a. Adjust bracket in the direction of "R" when pressure is below specifications, **Fig. 21.**
   b. Adjust bracket in the direction of "L" when pressure is above specifications, **Fig. 21.**

Quest

1. Check length of dual load sensing valve spring in unladen condition, **Fig. 22.**
2. Spring length should be 5.945–6.063 inch. If spring length is not within specified length, adjust spring length by moving eye bracket while pushing lever toward "A" direction.
3. Connect pressure checking tool No. KV991V0010, or equivalent, to air bleeders of front and rear brakes on either left or right sides, **Fig. 15.**

Year	Model	Free Height, Inches		Depressed Height, Inches ①	
		Man. Trans.	Auto. Trans.	Man. Trans.	Auto. Trans.
1996–99	Altima	6.65–7.05	6.97–7.36	3.54	3.54
	Frontier & Pickup	8.23-8.62	8.35-8.74	4.72	4.72
	Maxima	6.22–6.50	6.57–6.85	2.76	2.95
	Pathfinder	6.50-6.89	6.89-7.28	2.56	2.76
	Quest	—	7.68-8.07	—	4.53-5.12
	Sentra & 200SX	5.83–6.22	6.18–6.57	②	③
	240SX	7.13–7.52	7.52–7.91	④	4.53
	300ZX	7.32–7.72	7.68–8.07	3.94	4.13

① — Minimum inches.
② — Man. trans. w/GA16DE engine 2.95; w/SR20DE engine 3.15 sedan; 2.95 & 200SX models.
③ — Auto. trans. w/GA16DE engine 3.15; w/SR20DE engine 3.35.
④ — Man. trans. less ABS 3.94; w/ABS 4.33.

Fig. 2 Brake pedal free & depressed height specifications

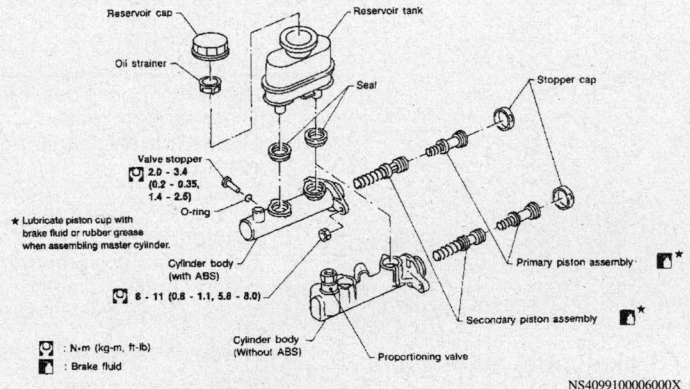

NS4099100006000X

Fig. 4 Exploded view of master cylinder. Altima

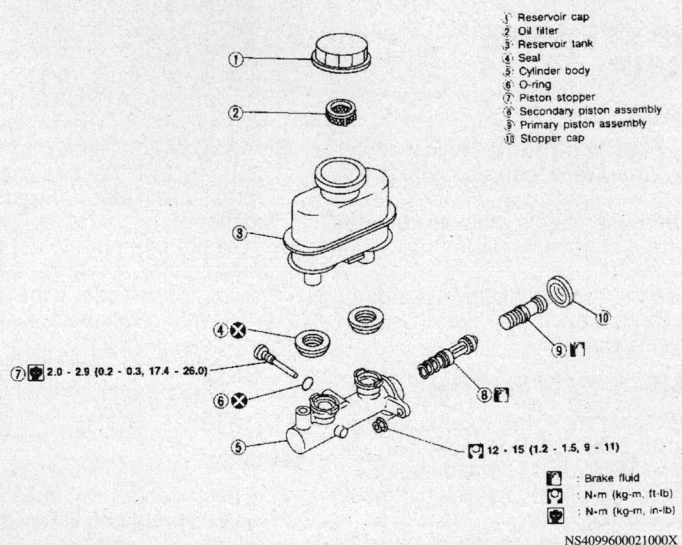

NS4099600021000X

Fig. 5 Exploded view of master cylinder. Maxima

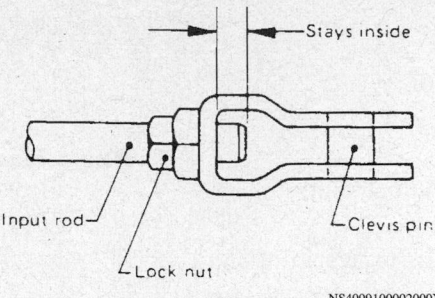

NS4099100002000X

Fig. 3 Input rod adjustment

specifications, replace dual load sensing valve.

BRAKE SYSTEM BLEED

LESS ANTI-LOCK BRAKES

Do not spill brake fluid on painted surfaces, it may cause damage to the paint. If brake fluid is spilled, wash immediately with water.
1. Place container under master cylinder to avoid spillage, then fill master cylinder with brake fluid.
2. Connect hose to bleeder valves, then depress brake pedal several times.
3. With pressure applied to pedal open bleeder valve to release air trapped in system.
4. Close bleeder, then release pedal slowly.
5. Repeat steps 3 and 4 as outlined above until all air is removed from system.
6. Bleed air from system in order as follows:
   a. Left rear wheel.
   b. Right front wheel.
   c. Right rear wheel.
   d. Left front wheel.

ANTI-LOCK BRAKES

Do not spill brake fluid on painted surfaces, it may cause damage to the paint. If brake fluid is spilled, wash immediately with water.
1. Place container under master cylinder to avoid spillage, then fill master cylinder with brake fluid.
2. Connect hose to bleeder valves, then depress brake pedal several times.
3. With pressure applied to pedal open bleeder valve to release air trapped in system.
4. Close bleeder, then release pedal slowly.
5. Repeat steps 3 and 4 as outlined above until all air is removed from system.
6. Bleed air from system in order as follows:
   a. Left rear wheel.
   b. Right rear wheel.
   c. Left front wheel.
   d. Right front wheel.
   e. Front air bleeder on ABS actuator.
   f. Rear air bleeder on ABS actuator.

4. Bleed air from tool.
5. Depress brake pedal until front brake fluid pressure reaches 853 psi. Hold pedal in that position and read rear brake pressure. Pressure should be 475–825 psi.

6. Depress brake pedal until front brake fluid pressure reaches 1706 psi. Hold pedal in that position and read rear brake pressure. Pressure should be 813–1064 psi.
7. If rear brake pressure is not within

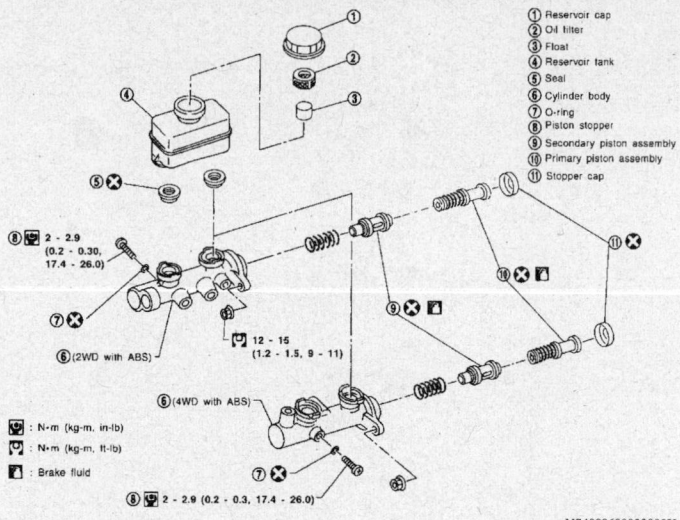

Fig. 6 Exploded view of master cylinder. Pathfinder

NS4099600022000X

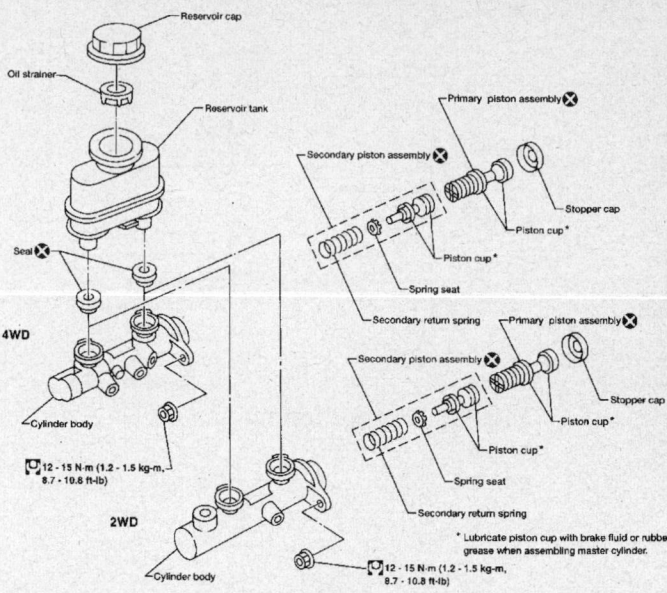

Fig. 7 Exploded view of master cylinder. Frontier & Pickup

NS4099600023000X

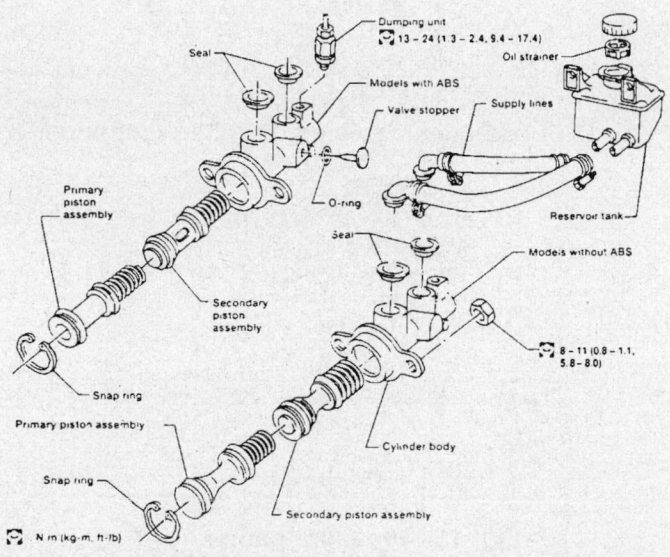

Fig. 8 Exploded view of master cylinder. Quest

NS4099100007000X

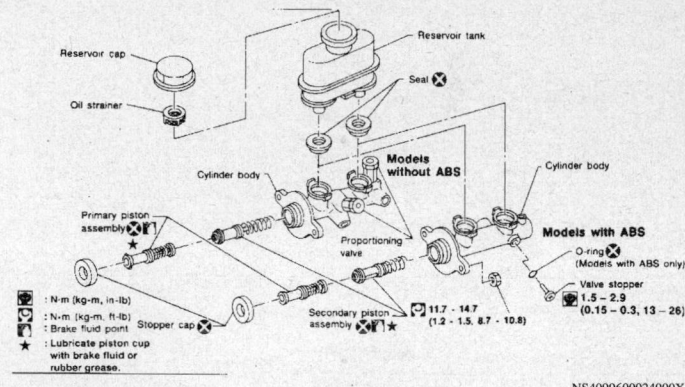

Fig. 9 Exploded view of master cylinder. Sentra & 200SX

NS4099600024000X

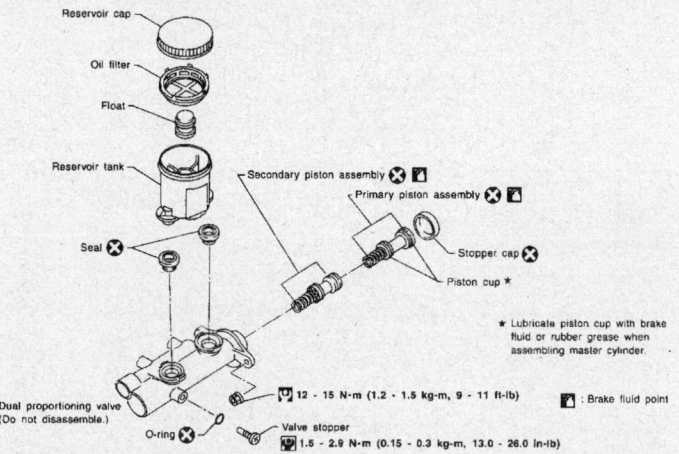

Fig. 10 Exploded view of master cylinder. 300ZX

NS4099100005000A

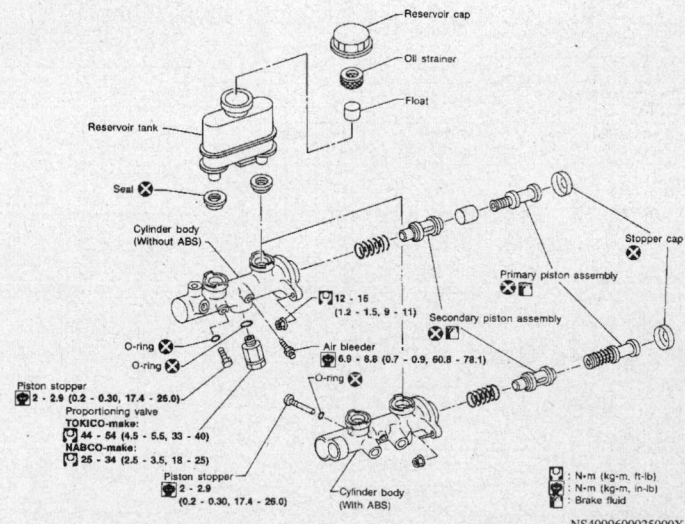

Fig. 11 Exploded view of master cylinder. 240SX

NS4099600025000X

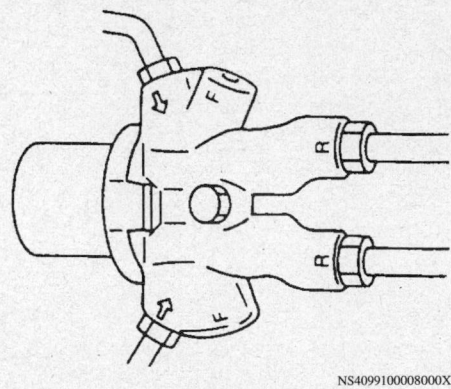

NS4099100008000X

Fig. 12   Proportioning valve. Sentra

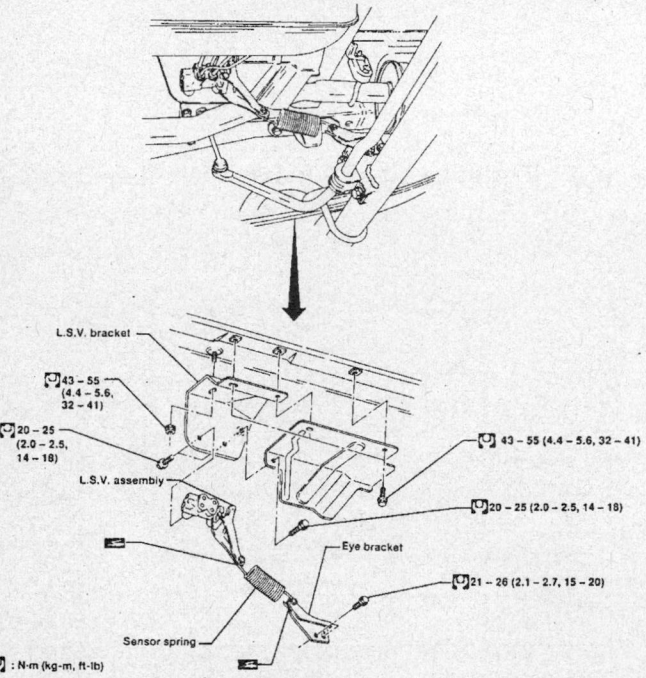

NS4099100011000X

Fig. 14   Dual load sensing valve. Quest

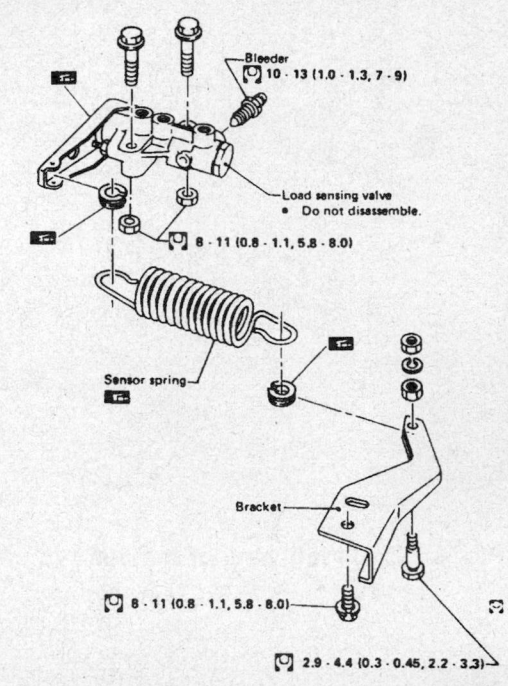

NS4099100010000X

Fig. 13   Load sensing valve. Frontier, Pathfinder & Pickup

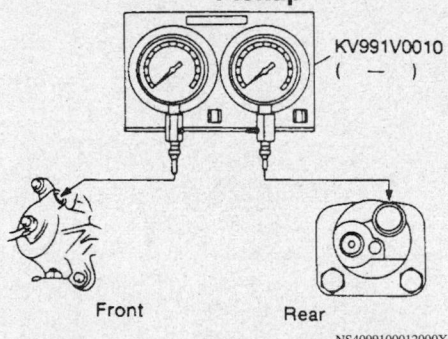

NS4099100012000X

Fig. 15   Pressure gauge installation. Altima, Sentra & 200SX

		Unit: kPa (kg/cm², psi)	
		Without ABS	With ABS
Applied pressure (Front brake)	D₁	5,394 (55, 782)	5,884 (60, 853)
Output pressure (Rear brake)	D₂	2,452 - 2,844 (25 - 29, 356 - 412)	3,334 - 3,727 (34 - 38, 483 - 540)

NS4099100013000X

Fig. 16   Pressure specification chart. 1996 Altima

		Unit: kPa (kg/cm², psi)		
		Without ABS		With ABS
Applied model		Except SE model	SE model	
Applied pressure (Front brake)	D₁	5,394 (55, 782)		6,375 (65, 924)
Output pressure (Rear brake)	D₂	2,452 - 2,844 (25 - 29, 356 - 412)		3,432 - 3,825 (35 - 39, 498 - 555)

NS4099700026000X

Fig. 17   Pressure specification chart. 1997–99 Altima

Applied model	GA16DE	SR20DE
Applied pressure (Front brake) kPa (kg/cm², psi)	7,355 (75, 1,067)	6,375 (65, 924)
Output pressure (Rear brake) kPa (kg/cm², psi)	5,100 - 5,492 (52 - 56, 739 - 796)	4,119 - 4,511 (42 - 46, 597 - 654)

NS4099100014000X

Fig. 18   Pressure specification chart. Sentra & 200SX

NS4099100017000X

Fig. 19   Pressure gauges connection. Frontier, Pathfinder & Pickup

	KA24E	VG30E	
		Except H.D. *	H.D. *
Without weight	2,942 - 3,727 (30 - 38, 427 - 540)	3,040 - 3,825 (31 - 39, 441 - 555)	3,040 - 3,825 (31 - 39, 441 - 555)
With weight	3,432 - 4,805 (35 - 49, 498 - 697)	4,119 - 5,492 (42 - 56, 587 - 796)	3,923 - 5,296 (40 - 54, 569 - 768)

*H.D.: Heavy duty models

NS4099200018000X

Fig. 20   Pressure specification chart. Frontier, Pathfinder & Pickup

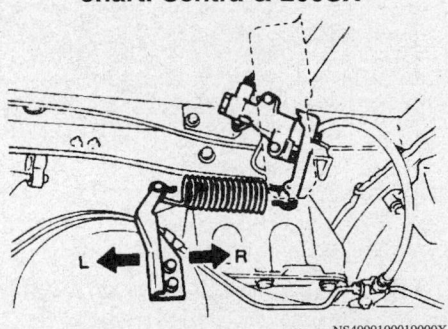

NS4099100019000X

Fig. 21   Sensor spring adjustment. Frontier, Pathfinder & Pickup

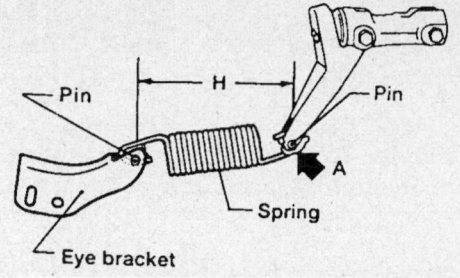

NS4099100020000X

Fig. 22 Dual load sensing valve spring adjustment. Quest

Power Brake Units

INDEX

DESCRIPTION

The vacuum assist diaphragm assembly multiplies the force exerted on the master cylinder piston in order to increase the hydraulic pressure delivered to the wheel calipers or cylinders, while decreasing the effort necessary to obtain acceptable stopping performance.

Vacuum assist units get their energy by opposing engine vacuum to atmospheric pressure. A piston, cylinder and flexible diaphragm utilize this energy to provide brake assistance. The diaphragm is balanced with engine vacuum until brake pedal is depressed, allowing atmospheric pressure to unbalance the unit and apply force to the brake system.

TROUBLESHOOTING

1. With engine off, depress brake pedal several times. There should be no change in pedal stroke.
2. With brake pedal depressed, start engine. Pedal should go down slightly.
3. Run engine for two minutes, then turn engine off. Depress brake pedal slowly several times.
4. Pedal should go down further the first time and rise gradually the second and third time **Fig. 1**. If this happens the booster is airtight.
5. With engine running and brake pedal depressed, stop engine.
6. If after 30 seconds there is no change

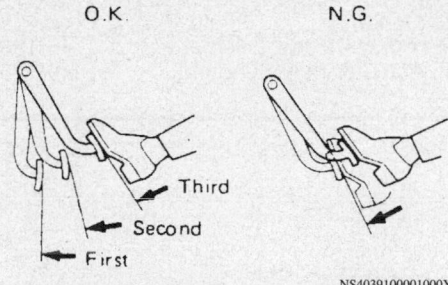

NS4039100001000X

Fig. 1 Brake booster inspection

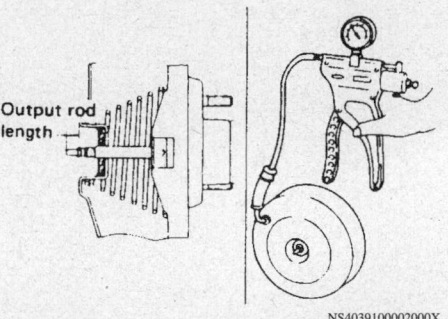

NS4039100002000X

Fig. 2 Output rod adjustment

in pedal movement, the booster is airtight.

ADJUSTMENTS
OUTPUT ROD

1. Apply 19.96 inch HG of vacuum to

brake booster using a suitable vacuum pump, **Fig. 2**.
2. Check output rod length as shown in **Fig. 2**.
3. Adjust output rod length to .4045–.4144 inch.

GENERAL SERVICE

BRAKE BOOSTER, REPLACE

1. Remove master cylinder as outlined in "Master Cylinder Replace" in the "Hydraulic Brake System" section.
2. Disconnect brake booster clevis pin on brake pedal.
3. Disconnect check valve hose at power booster.
4. Remove booster attaching nuts, then brake booster.
5. Reverse Procedure to install, noting the following:
   a. Check and adjust output rod as outlined in "Adjustments" in this section.
   b. Bleed system as outlined in "Hydraulic Brake System."

POWER BRAKE UNIT SERVICE

These units cannot be overhauled. They must be replaced if malfunctions occur.

Anti-Lock Brakes

NOTE: On Air Bag Equipped Models, Refer To "Air Bag System Precautions" Located In The Front Of This Manual For System Disarming & Arming Procedures.

NOTE: "Electrical Symbol & Wire Color Code Identification" Located In The Front Of This Manual May Be Used As An Aid When Using Wiring Circuits Found In This Section.

NOTE: Refer To "Computer Relearn Procedures" Located In The Front Of This Manual For Computer Relearn Procedures.

INDEX

PRECAUTIONS

BATTERY GROUND CABLE

Prior to service, disconnect battery ground cable and isolate as required.

AIR BAG SYSTEMS

Refer to "Air Bag System Precautions" in the front of this manual for system disarming and arming procedures.

BRAKE FLUID SAFETY

Do not allow brake fluid to contact painted areas, never reuse brake fluid and never use mineral oils such as gasoline or kerosene that will ruin rubber parts of hydraulic system.

DESCRIPTION

Both the four wheel and Rear wheel Anti-Lock Brake systems, **Figs. 1 through 11,** use a control unit, hydraulic actuator and wheel speed sensors to control brake fluid pressure and prevent wheel lock during severe braking conditions. With this system, directional stability is improved and steerability maintained even when panic braking on wet, sandy, snowy or icy road conditions.

TROUBLESHOOTING

The electronic control unit accepts input signals from sensors and drives actuators.

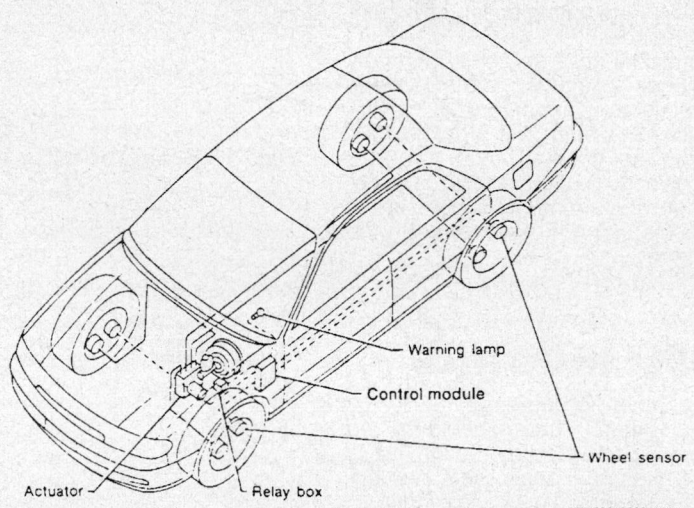

Fig. 1   Anti-Lock Brake System (ABS). Altima

NS4029100001000X

It is essential that both input and output signals are stable and accurate. Refer to **Figs. 12 through 14** for preliminary system checks.

DIAGNOSIS & TESTING

ACCESSING DIAGNOSTIC TROUBLE CODES

When a problem occurs in the ABS system, a warning light will flash on the instrument panel. To activate ABS self-diagnosis, ground the self diagnosis (check) terminal located on the data link connector. Refer to **Figs. 15 through 18** for self-diagnostic procedures and code identification.

DIAGNOSTIC TROUBLE CODE IDENTIFICATION

Refer to **Figs. 19 through 26** for diagnostic trouble code identification.

WIRING DIAGRAMS

When performing system diagnosis, refer to wiring circuits **Figs. 27 through 42.**

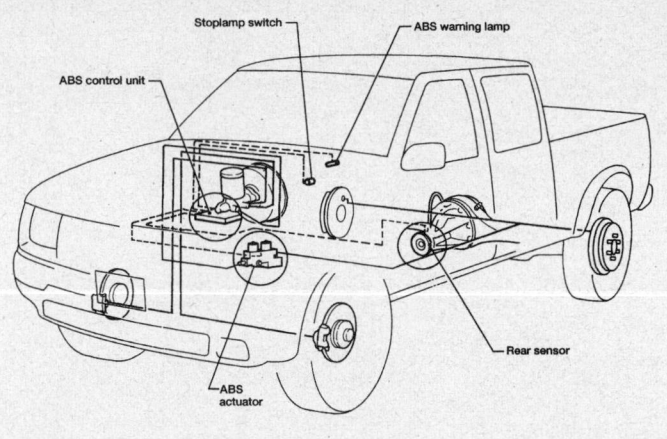

Fig. 2   Anti-Lock Brake System (ABS). 2WD Frontier

NS4029900300000X

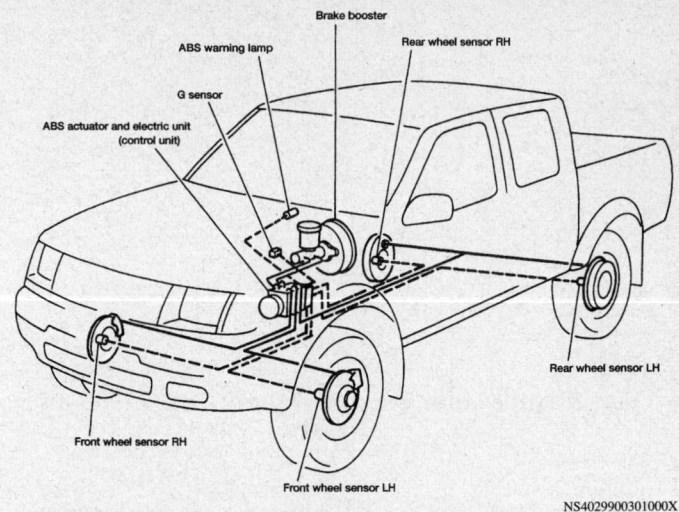

Fig. 3   Anti-Lock Brake System (ABS). 4WD Frontier

NS4029900301000X

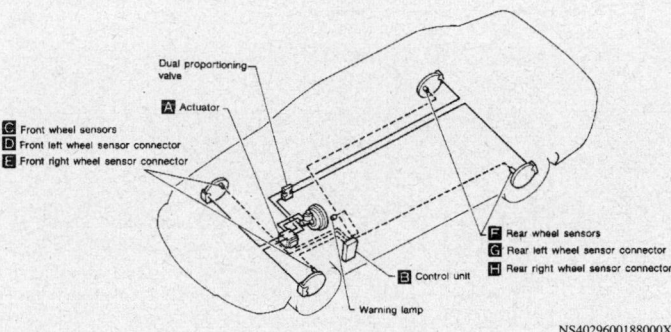

Fig. 4   Anti-Lock Brake System (ABS). Maxima

NS4029600188000X

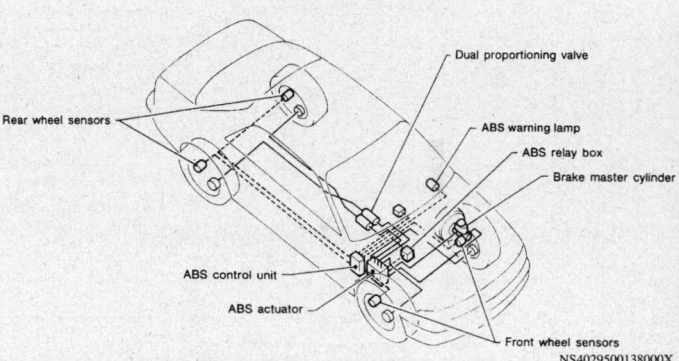

Fig. 5   Anti-Lock Brake System (ABS). Sentra & 200SX

NS4029500138000X

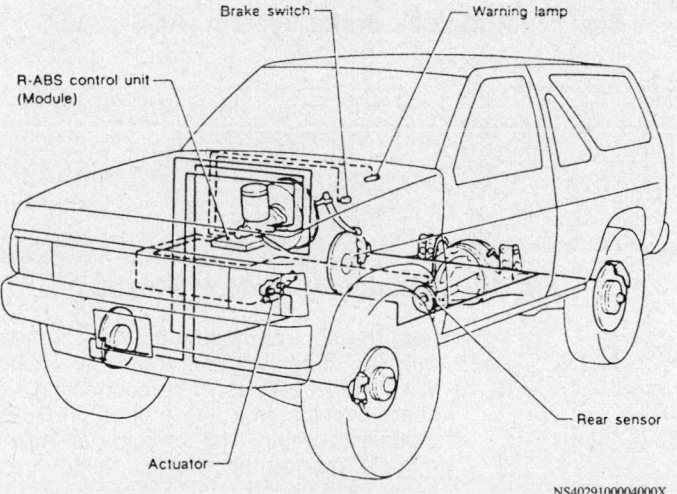

Fig. 6   Anti-Lock Brake System (ABS). Pickup

NS4029100004000X

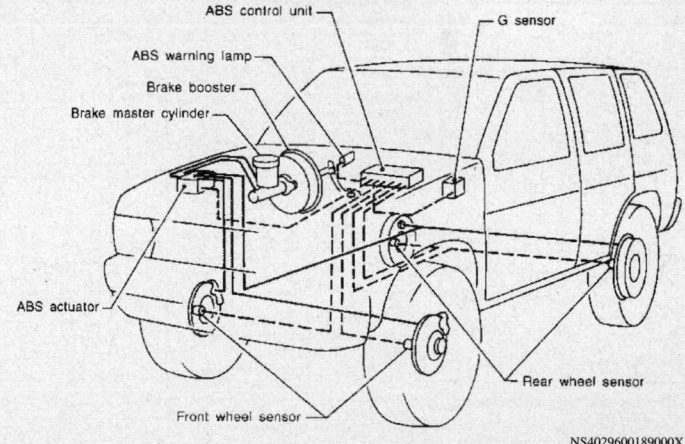

Fig. 7   Anti-Lock Brake System (ABS). Pathfinder

NS4029600189000X

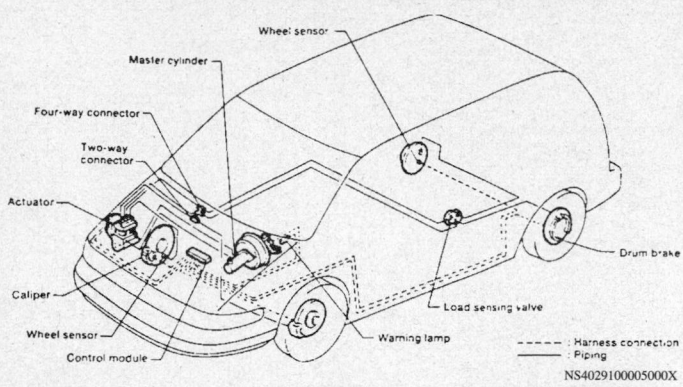

Fig. 8   Anti-Lock Brake System (ABS). 1996–98 Quest

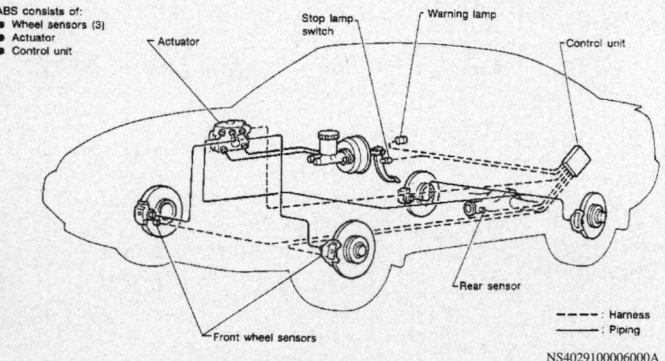

Fig. 10   Anti-Lock Brake System (ABS). 240SX

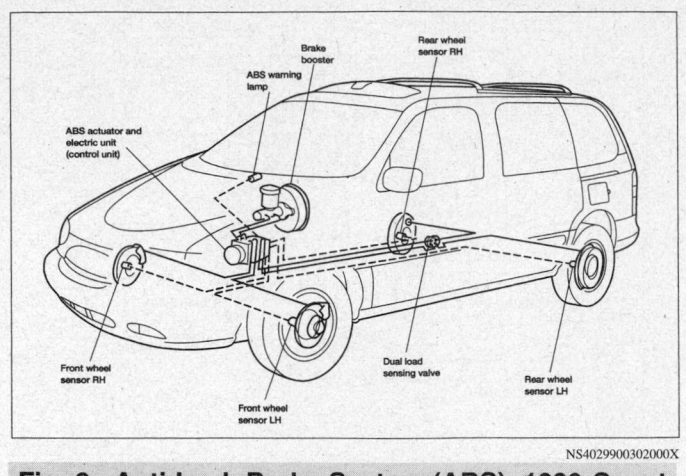

Fig. 9   Anti-Lock Brake System (ABS). 1999 Quest

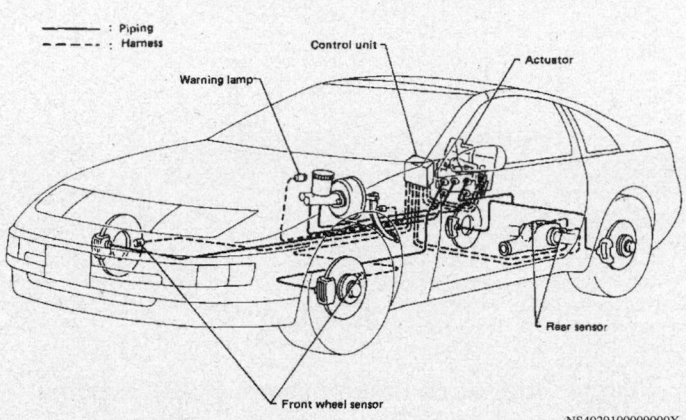

Fig. 11   Anti-Lock Brake System (ABS). 300ZX

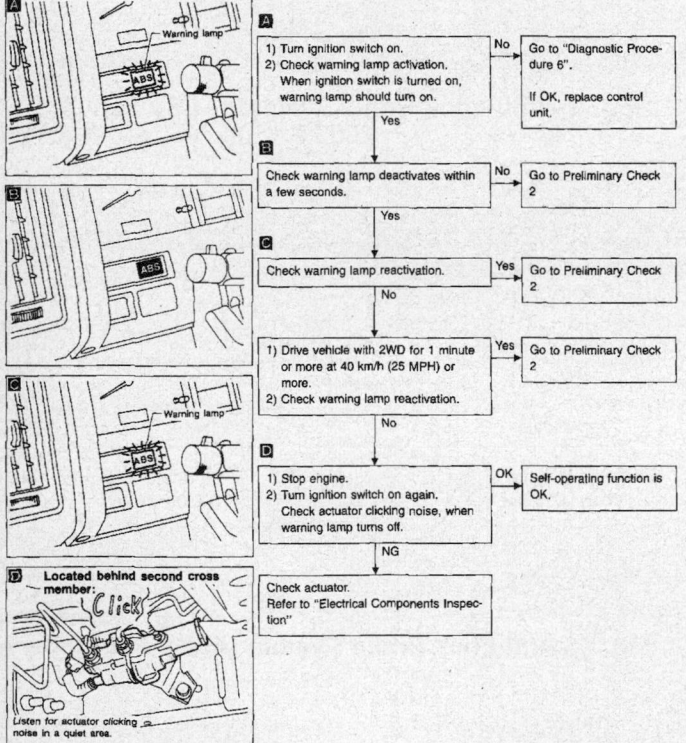

Fig. 12   Preliminary check 1. Pickup

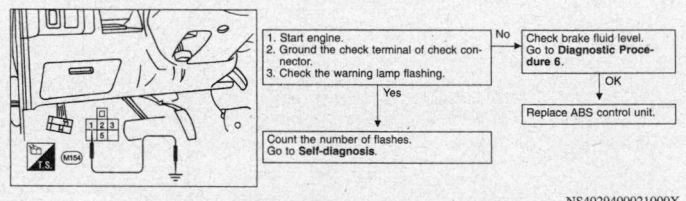

Fig. 13   Preliminary check 2. Pickup

from the control module memory, disconnect the check terminal from the ground. Within ten seconds of disconnecting the check terminal from the ground on Quest models or within 12.5 seconds on Altima models, ground the check terminal three times for a period of at least one second. The ABS warning lamp should remain on while erasing the malfunction (trouble) codes, and should go out after the erase mode has been completed. After erasing the malfunction (trouble) codes, rerun the self-diagnostic mode to verify that the malfunction (trouble) codes no longer appear.

DIAGNOSTIC TESTS

When performing system diagnosis, refer to diagnosis procedure charts **Figs. 43 through 246.**

CLEARING DIAGNOSTIC TROUBLE CODES

To erase malfunction (trouble) codes

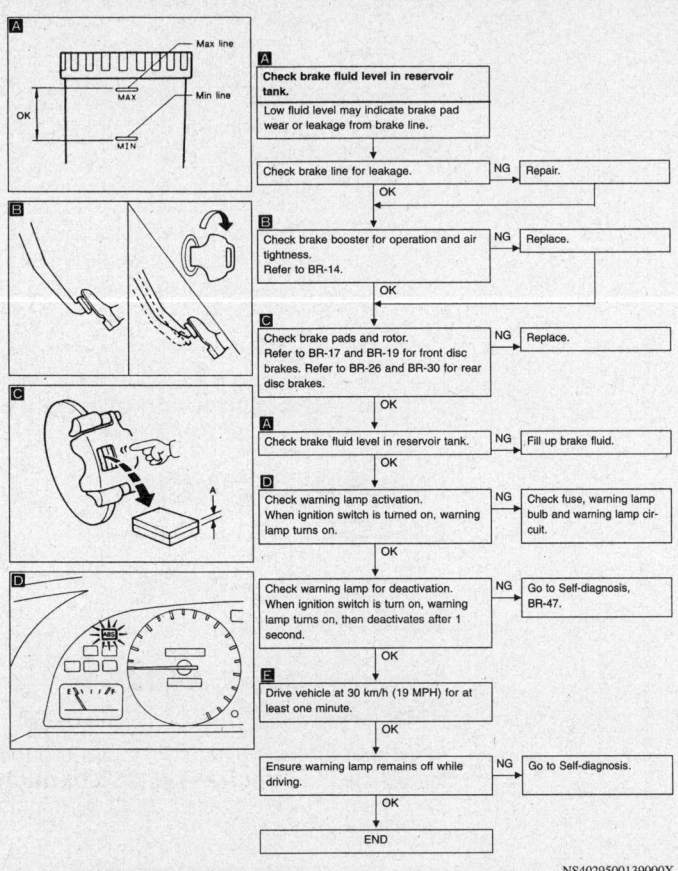

Fig. 14 Preliminary check. Except Pickup

ELECTRICAL COMPONENTS INSPECTION

ALTIMA, MAXIMA, SENTRA & 200SX

Wheel Sensors

Check resistance between wheel sensor connector terminals, **Fig. 247.** Resistance should be 1.0–1.25 K-ohms.

Actuator Motor Relay

Check continuity between motor relay terminals as shown in **Figs. 248 through 250.**

Solenoid Valve Relay

Check continuity between solenoid valve relay terminals as shown in **Figs. 251 and 252.**

240SX & 300ZX

Refer to **Figs. 253 through 255** for electrical component inspection.

FRONTIER, PATHFINDER & PICKUP

Refer to **Fig. 256** for electrical component inspection.

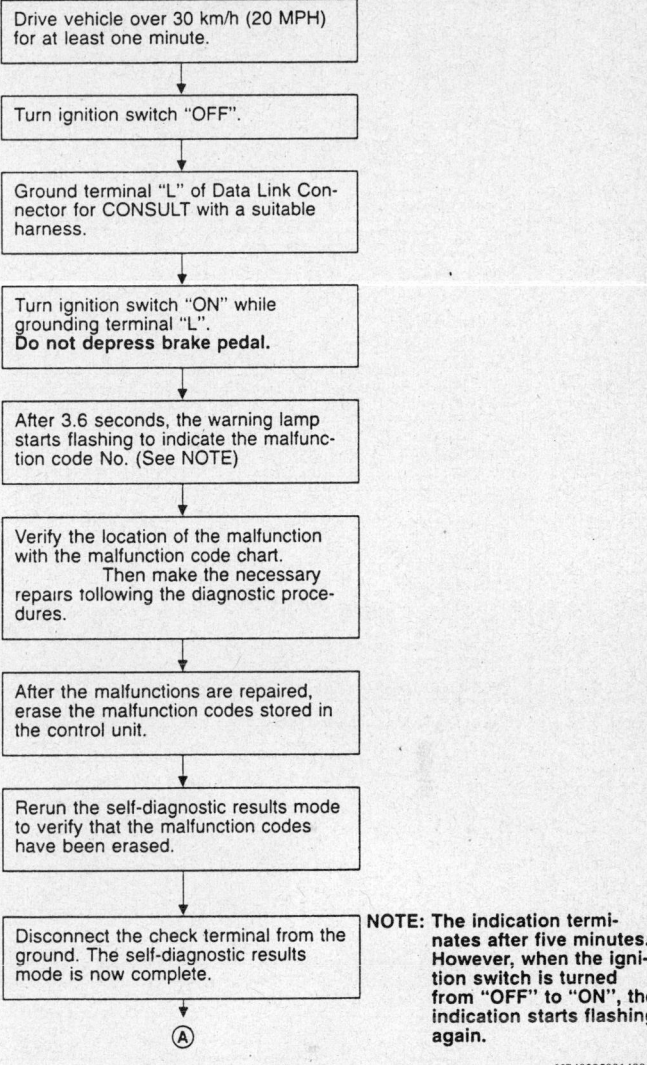

Fig. 15 Self-diagnostic procedure (Part 1 of 2). Altima, Frontier, Maxima, Pathfinder, Pickup, Sentra, 200SX & 300ZX

Fig. 15 Self-diagnostic procedure (Part 2 of 2). Altima, Frontier, Maxima, Pathfinder, Pickup, Sentra, 200SX & 300ZX

QUEST

Wheel Sensors

Check resistance between wheel sensor connector terminals, **Fig. 257.** Resistance should be .9–1.1 K-ohms.

Actuator Motor Relay

Check continuity between motor relay terminals as shown in **Figs. 258 and 259.**

Solenoid Valve Relay

Check continuity between solenoid valve relay terminals as shown in **Figs. 260 and 261.**

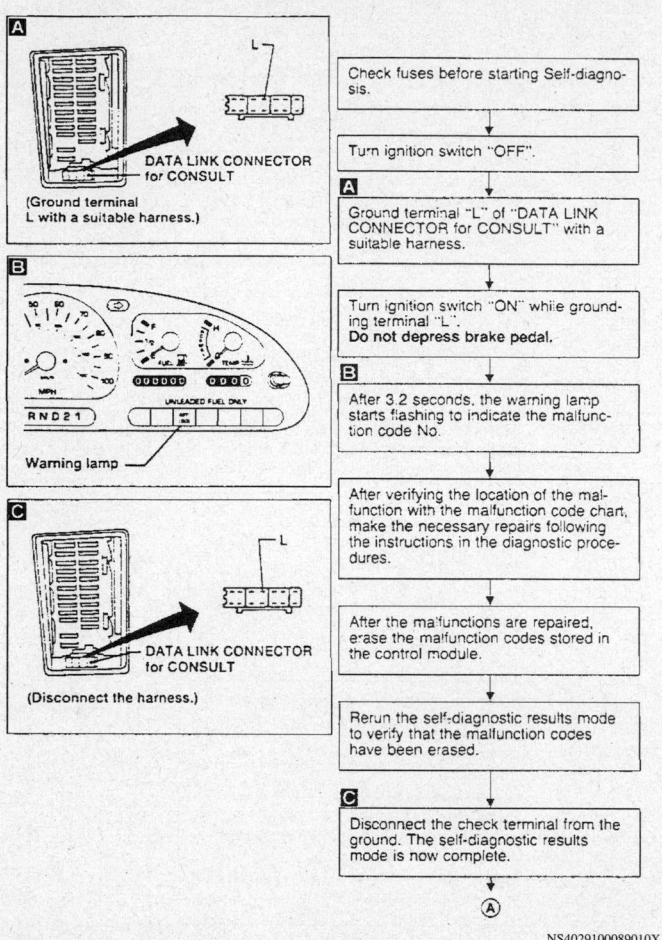

Fig. 16 Self-diagnostic procedure (Part 1 of 2). Quest

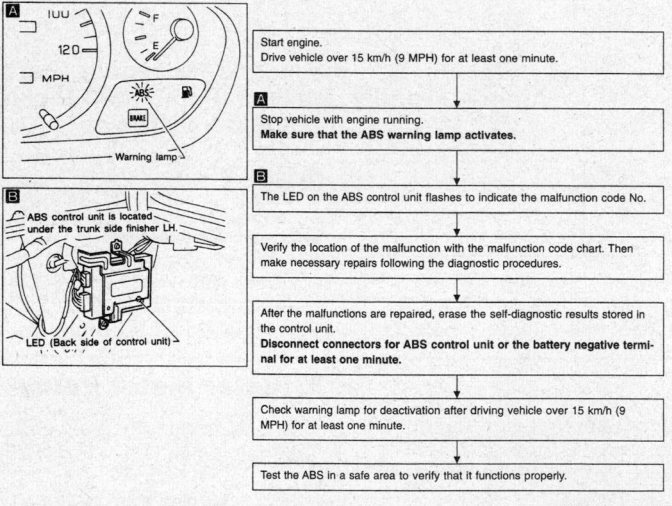

Fig. 17 Self-diagnostic procedure. 1996 240SX

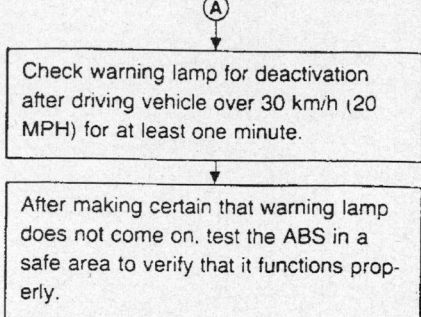

Fig. 16 Self-diagnostic procedure (Part 2 of 2). Quest

GROUND CIRCUIT CHECK

ACTUATOR MOTOR GROUND

Maxima, Quest, 240SX & 300ZX

When performing actuator motor ground circuit check, refer to **Figs. 262 through 265.** Resistance between both terminals should be zero ohms.

RELAY BOX GROUND

Altima

Check resistance between relay box harness connector terminal and ground, **Fig. 266.** Resistance should be zero ohms.

SYSTEM SERVICE

Brake System Bleed

Refer to "Hydraulic Brake Systems" for brake bleed procedure.

Component Replacement

When replacing components, refer to **Figs. 267 through 275,** for component location.

FUNCTION

- When a problem occurs in the ABS, the warning lamp on the instrument panel comes on. To start the self-diagnostic results mode, ground the self-diagnostic (check) terminal located on "Data Link Connector for CONSULT". The location of the malfunction is indicated by the warning lamp flashing.

SELF-DIAGNOSIS PROCEDURE

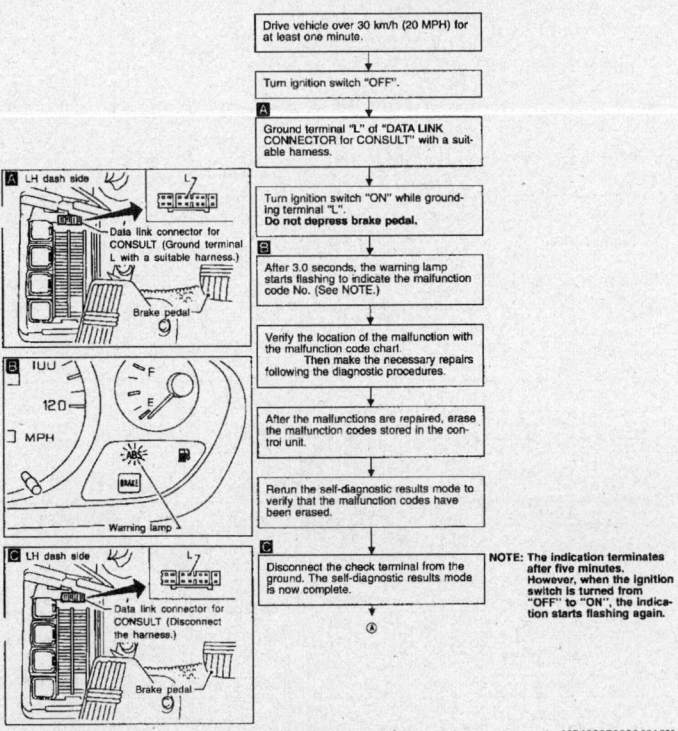

NS4029700236010X

Fig. 18 Self-diagnostic procedure (Part 1 of 2). 1997–98 240SX

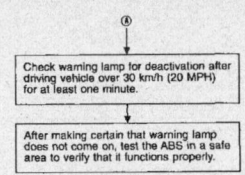

Check warning lamp for deactivation after driving vehicle over 30 km/h (20 MPH) for at least one minute.

After making certain that warning lamp does not come on, test the ABS in a safe area to verify that it functions properly.

HOW TO READ SELF-DIAGNOSTIC RESULTS (Malfunction codes)

- Determine the code No. by counting the number of times the warning lamp flashes on and off.
- When several malfunctions occur at one time, up to three code numbers can be stored; the latest malfunction will be indicated first.
- The indication begins with the start code 12. After that a maximum of three code numbers appear in the order of the latest one first. The indication then returns to the start code 12 to repeat (the indication will stay on for five minutes at the most).
- The malfunction code chart is given on the next page.

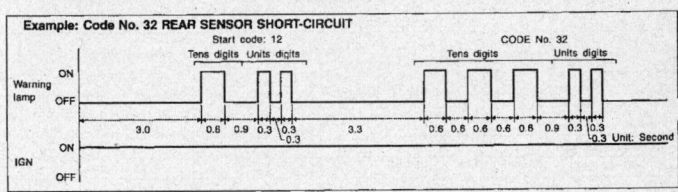

HOW TO ERASE SELF-DIAGNOSTIC RESULTS (Malfunction codes)

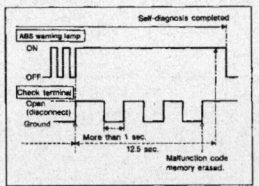

a. Under the self-diagnostic results mode, the malfunction memory erase mode starts when the check terminal is disconnected from the ground.
b. The self-diagnostic results (malfunction codes) can be erased by grounding the check terminal more than three times in succession within 12.5 seconds after the erase mode starts. (Each grounding must be longer than one second.) The ABS warning lamp stays on while the self-diagnosis is in the erase mode, and goes out after the erase operation has been completed.
c. The self-diagnosis is also completed at the same time.

After the erase operation is completed, it is necessary to rerun the self-diagnostic mode to verify that malfunction codes no longer appear. Only the start code (12) should be indicated when erase operation is completed and system is functioning normally.

NS4029700236020X

Fig. 18 Self-diagnostic procedure (Part 2 of 2). 1997–98 240SX

Code No. (No. of LED flashes)	Malfunctioning part	Diagnostic procedure
45	Actuator front left outlet solenoid valve	3
46	Actuator front left inlet solenoid valve	3
41	Actuator front right outlet solenoid valve	3
42	Actuator front right inlet solenoid valve	3
51	Actuator rear right outlet solenoid valve	3
52	Actuator rear right inlet solenoid valve	3
55	Actuator rear left inlet solenoid valve	3
56	Actuator rear left inlet solenoid valve	3
25	Front left sensor (open-circuit)	4
26	Front left sensor (short-circuit)	4
21	Front right sensor (open-circuit)	4
22	Front right sensor (short-circuit)	4
35	Rear left sensor (open-circuit)	4
36	Rear left sensor (short-circuit)	4
31	Rear right sensor (open-circuit)	4
32	Rear right sensor (short-circuit)	4
18	Sensor rotor	4
61	Actuator motor or motor relay	5
63	Solenoid valve relay	6
57	Power supply (Low voltage)	7
71	Control unit	8
Warning lamp stays on when ignition switch is turned on.	Control unit power supply circuit / Warning lamp bulb circuit / Control unit or control unit connector / Solenoid valve relay stuck / Power supply for solenoid valve relay coil	2
Warning lamp stays on, during self-diagnosis.	Control unit	—
Warning lamp does not come on when ignition switch is turned on.	Fuse, warning lamp bulb or warning lamp circuit / Control unit	1
Warning lamp does not come on during self-diagnosis.	Control unit	—
Pedal vibration and noise	—	9
Long stopping distance	—	10
Unexpected pedal action	—	11
ABS does not work.	—	12
ABS works frequently.	—	13

NS4029500142000X

Fig. 19 L.E.D. code identification. Maxima, Sentra & 200SX

Code No. (No. of LED flashes)	Malfunctioning part and circuit	Diagnostic procedure
01	Front right sensor (open-circuit)	4
02	Front left sensor (open-circuit)	4
03	Rear sensor (open-circuit)	4
05	Front right sensor (short-circuit)	4
06	Front left sensor (short-circuit)	4
07	Rear sensor (short-circuit)	4
11	Actuator front right inlet solenoid valve (open-circuit)	3
12	Actuator front left inlet solenoid valve (open-circuit)	3
13	Actuator rear inlet solenoid valve (open-circuit)	3
15	Actuator front right outlet solenoid valve (open-circuit)	3
16	Actuator front left outlet solenoid valve (open-circuit)	3
17	Actuator rear outlet solenoid valve (open-circuit)	3
21	Actuator front right inlet solenoid valve (short-circuit)	3
22	Actuator front left inlet solenoid valve (short-circuit)	3
23	Actuator rear inlet solenoid valve (short-circuit)	3
25	Actuator front right outlet solenoid valve (short-circuit)	3
26	Actuator front left outlet solenoid valve (short-circuit)	3
27	Actuator rear outlet solenoid valve (short-circuit)	3
41	Solenoid valve relay circuit (unable to turn off)	6
42	Solenoid valve relay circuit (unable to turn on)	6
43	Actuator motor or motor relay (unable to turn off)	5
44	Actuator motor or motor relay (unable to turn on)	5
47	Power supply (High voltage)	7
48	Power supply (Low voltage)	7
45, 46, 77 LED deactivation or continuous activation	Control unit / Ground circuit	2
Warning light does not come on when ignition switch is turned on.	Fuse, warning light bulb or warning light circuit / Control unit power supply circuit	1
Pedal vibration and noise	—	9
Long stopping distance	—	10
Unexpected pedal action	—	11
ABS does not work.	—	12
ABS works frequently.	—	13

NS4029500143000X

Fig. 20 L.E.D. code identification. 1996 240SX

Code No. (No. of warning lamp flashes)	Malfunctioning part	Diagnostic procedure
12	Self-diagnosis could not detect any malfunctions	—
21	Front right sensor (open-circuit)	1
22	Front right sensor (short-circuit)	1
25	Front left sensor (open-circuit)	1
26	Front left sensor (short-circuit)	1
31	Rear sensor (open-circuit)	1
32	Rear sensor (short-circuit)	1
41	Actuator front right outlet solenoid valve	2
42	Actuator front right inlet solenoid valve	2
45	Actuator front left outlet solenoid valve	2
46	Actuator front left inlet solenoid valve	2
55	Actuator rear outlet solenoid valve	2
56	Actuator rear inlet solenoid valve	2
57	Power supply (Low voltage)	5
61	Actuator motor or motor relay	4
63	Solenoid valve relay	3
71	Control unit	6
ABS works frequently	—	7
Unexpected pedal action	—	8
Long stopping distance	—	9
ABS does not work	—	10
Pedal vibration and noise	—	11
Warning lamp does not come on when engine is running	Fuse, warning lamp bulb or warning lamp circuit / Control unit	12
Warning lamp stays on when engine is running	Control unit power supply circuit / Warning lamp bulb circuit / Control unit or control unit connector / Solenoid valve relay stuck / Power supply for solenoid valve relay coil	13

NS4029700237000X

Fig. 21   Code/Symptom chart. 1997–98 240SX

Code No. (No. of LED flashes)	Malfunctioning part	Diagnostic procedure
45	Actuator front left outlet solenoid valve	1
46	Actuator front left inlet solenoid valve	1
41	Actuator front right outlet solenoid valve	1
42	Actuator front right inlet solenoid valve	1
51	Actuator rear right outlet solenoid valve	1
52	Actuator rear right inlet solenoid valve	1
55	Actuator rear left outlet solenoid valve	1
56	Actuator rear left inlet solenoid valve	1
25 *1	Front left sensor (open-circuit)	2
26 *1	Front left sensor (short-circuit)	2
21 *1	Front right sensor (open-circuit)	2
22 *1	Front right sensor (short-circuit)	2
35 *1	Rear left sensor (open-circuit)	2
36 *1	Rear left sensor (short-circuit)	2
31 *1	Rear right sensor (open-circuit)	2
32 *1	Rear right sensor (short-circuit)	2
18 *1	Sensor rotor	2
61 *3	Actuator motor or motor relay	3
63	Solenoid valve relay	4
57 *2	Power supply (Low voltage)	5
71	Control unit	6
Warning lamp stays on when ignition switch is turned ON.	Control unit power supply circuit / Warning lamp bulb circuit / Control unit or control unit connector / Solenoid valve relay stuck / Power supply for solenoid valve relay coil	13
Warning lamp stays on during self-diagnosis.	Control unit	—
Warning lamp does not come on when ignition switch is turned ON.	Fuse, warning lamp bulb or warning lamp circuit / Control unit	12
Warning lamp does not come on during self-diagnosis.	Control unit	—
Pedal vibration and noise	—	11
Long stopping distance	—	9
Unexpected pedal action	—	8
ABS does not work.	—	10
ABS works frequently.	—	7

*1: If one or more wheels spin on a rough or slippery road for 40 seconds or more, the ABS warning lamp will illuminate. This does not indicate a malfunction. Only in the case of the short-circuit (Code Nos. 26, 22, 32, and 36), after repair the ABS warning lamp also illuminates when the ignition switch is turned ON. In this case, drive the vehicle at speeds greater than 30 km/h (19 MPH) for approximately 1 minute as specified in "SELF-DIAGNOSIS PROCEDURE". Ensure that the ABS warning lamp goes out while the vehicle is being driven.
*2: The trouble code "57", which refers to a low power supply voltage, does not indicate that the ABS control unit is malfunctioning. Do not replace the ABS control unit with a new one.
*3: The trouble code "61" can sometimes appear when the ABS motor is not properly grounded. If it appears, be sure to check the condition of the ABS motor ground circuit connection.

NS4029900322000X

Fig. 23   L.E.D. code identification. 1997–99 Altima

Code No.	Malfunctioning part	Diagnostic procedure
45	Front left actuator solenoid valve	3
41	Front right actuator solenoid valve	3
55	Rear actuator solenoid valve	3
25	Front left sensor (open-circuit)	4
26	Front left sensor (short-circuit)	4
21	Front right sensor (open-circuit)	4
22	Front right sensor (short-circuit)	4
35	Rear left sensor (open-circuit)	4
36	Rear left sensor (short-circuit)	4
31	Rear right sensor (open-circuit)	4
32	Rear right sensor (short-circuit)	4
18	Sensor rotor	4
61	Actuator motor or motor relay	5
63	Solenoid valve relay circuit (except power supply for relay coil)	6
57	Power supply (Low voltage)	7
15	Stop lamp switch circuit	8
71	Control unit	9
Warning lamp stays on when ignition switch is turned on.	Control unit power supply circuit / Warning lamp bulb circuit / Control unit or control unit connector / Solenoid valve relay stuck / Power supply for solenoid valve relay coil	2
Warning lamp stays on only during self-diagnosis.	Control unit	—
Warning lamp does not come on when ignition switch is turned on	Fuse, warning lamp bulb or warning lamp circuit / Control unit	1
Warning lamp does not come on only during self-diagnosis.	Control unit	—

NS4029500144000X

Fig. 22   L.E.D. code identification. 300ZX & 1996 Altima

Code No. (No. of LED flashes)	Malfunctioning part	Diagnostic procedure
45*	Front left actuator solenoid	3
41*	Front right actuator solenoid	3
55*	Rear actuator solenoid	3
25	Front left sensor (open-circuit)	4
26	Front left sensor (frequency error)	4
21	Front right sensor (open-circuit)	4
22	Front right sensor (frequency error)	4
35	Rear left sensor (open-circuit)	4
36	Rear left sensor (frequency error)	4
31	Rear right sensor (open-circuit)	4
32	Rear right sensor (frequency error)	4
18	Sensor rotor (frequency error)	4
61	Actuator motor or motor relay	5
63*	Solenoid valve relay	6
71	Control unit	7
Warning lamp stays on when ignition switch is turned on	Control unit power supply circuit / Warning lamp bulb circuit / Control unit or control unit connector / Solenoid valve relay stuck / Power supply for solenoid valve relay coil	2
Warning lamp stays on during self-diagnosis	Control unit	—
Warning lamp does not come on when ignition switch is turned on	Fuse, warning lamp bulb or warning lamp circuit / Control unit	1
Warning lamp does not come on during self-diagnosis	Control unit	—
Pedal vibration and noise	—	8
Long stopping distance	—	9
Unexpected pedal action	—	10
ABS does not work	—	11
ABS works frequently	—	12

*: When these malfunctions occur, warning lamp stays on; does not blink. Remove the solenoid valve relay to obtain the malfunction code.

NS4029100091000B

Fig. 24   L.E.D. code identification. Quest

No. of warning lamp flashes	Detected items	Malfunctioning cause or part		Diagnostic Procedure
2	ABS actuator	ISO solenoid	Open	Diagnostic Procedure 7
7			Short circuit	Diagnostic Procedure 7
4			Blocked	Diagnostic Procedure 8
3		DUMP solenoid	Open	Diagnostic Procedure 9
8			Short circuit	Diagnostic Procedure 9
9	Rear sensor	Open		Diagnostic Procedure 10
10		Short circuit		Diagnostic Procedure 10
6		Erratic		Diagnostic Procedure 11
13, 14 or 15	ABS control unit			Diagnostic Procedure 12
5		Other		Diagnostic Procedure 13

NS4029100024000X

Fig. 25   L.E.D. code identification. Frontier & Pickup

Code No. (No. of warning lamp flashes)	Malfunctioning part	Diagnostic procedure
45	Actuator front left outlet solenoid valve	2
46	Actuator front left inlet solenoid valve	2
41	Actuator front right outlet solenoid valve	2
42	Actuator front right inlet solenoid valve	2
55	Actuator rear outlet solenoid valve	2
56	Actuator rear inlet solenoid valve	2
25 ★2	Front left sensor (open-circuit)	1
26 ★2	Front left sensor (short-circuit)	1
21 ★2	Front right sensor (open-circuit)	1
22 ★2	Front right sensor (short-circuit)	1
31 ★2	Rear right sensor (open-circuit)	1
32 ★2	Rear right sensor (short-circuit)	1
35 ★2	Rear left sensor (open-circuit)	1
36 ★2	Rear left sensor (short-circuit)	1
18 ★2	Sensor rotor	1
17 ★1	G sensor and circuit	6
61 ★4	Actuator motor or motor relay	4
63	Solenoid valve relay	3
57 ★3	Power supply (Low voltage)	5
71	Control unit	7
Warning lamp stays on when ignition switch is turned on	Control unit power supply circuit Warning lamp bulb circuit Control unit or control unit connector Solenoid valve relay stuck Power supply for solenoid valve relay coil	14
Warning lamp does not come on when ignition switch is turned on	Fuse, warning lamp bulb or warning lamp circuit Control unit	13
Pedal vibration and noise	—	12
Long stopping distance	—	10
Unexpected pedal action	—	9
ABS does not work	—	11
ABS works frequently	—	8

★1: 4WD model only.
★2: If one or more wheels spin on a rough or slippery road for 40 seconds or more, the ABS warning lamp will illuminate. This does not indicate a malfunction. Only in the case of the short-circuit (Code Nos. 26, 22, 32 and 36), after repair the ABS warning lamp also illuminates when the ignition switch is turned "ON". In this case, drive the vehicle at speeds greater than 30 km/h (19 MPH) for approximately 1 minute as specified in "SELF-DIAGNOSIS PROCEDURE". Check to ensure that the ABS warning lamp goes out while the vehicle is being driven.
★3: The trouble code "57", which refers to a low power supply voltage, does not indicate that the ABS control unit is malfunctioning. Do not replace the ABS control unit with a new one.
★4: The trouble code "61" can sometimes appear when the ABS motor is not properly grounded. If it appears, be sure to check the condition of the ABS motor ground circuit connection.

NS4029600190000A

Fig. 26 L.E.D. code identification. Pathfinder

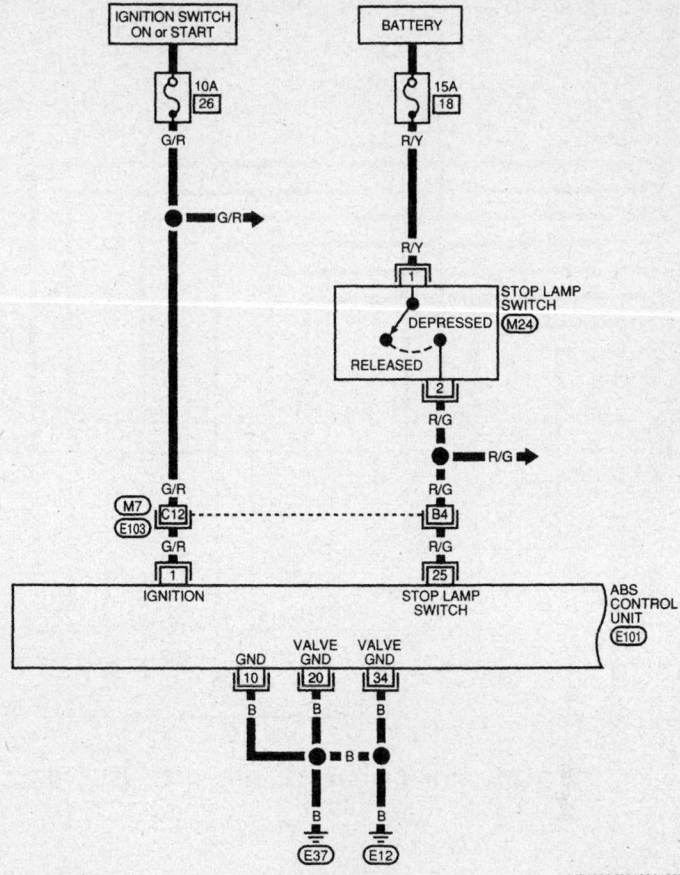

NS4029600192010X

Fig. 27 ABS wiring circuit (Part 1 of 4). 1996–97 Altima

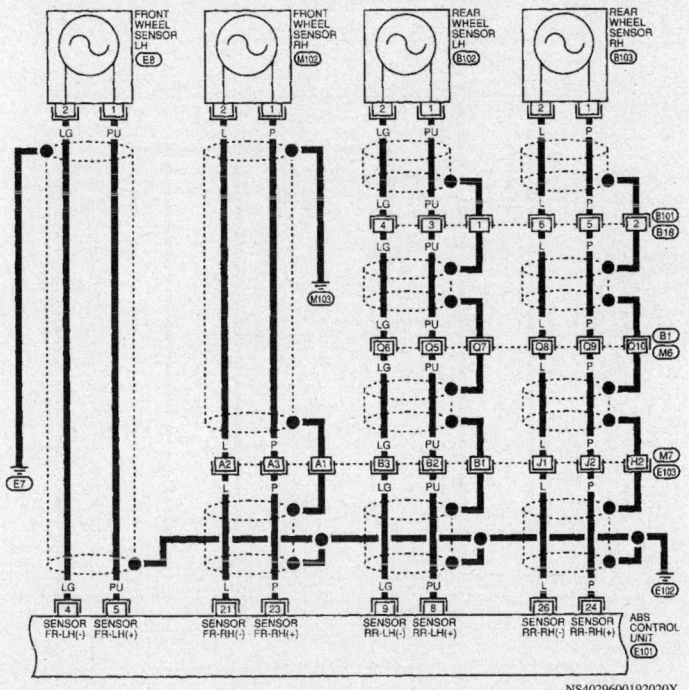

NS4029600192020X

Fig. 27 ABS wiring circuit (Part 2 of 4). 1996–97 Altima

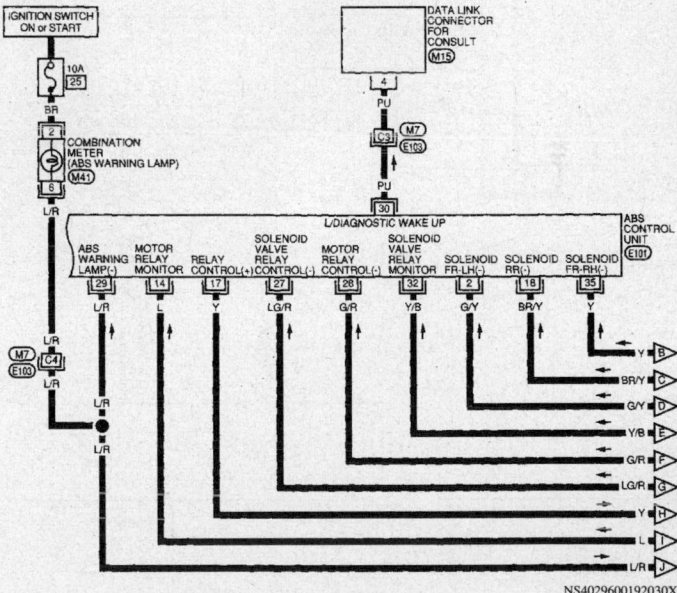

NS4029600192030X

Fig. 27 ABS wiring circuit (Part 3 of 4). 1996–97 Altima

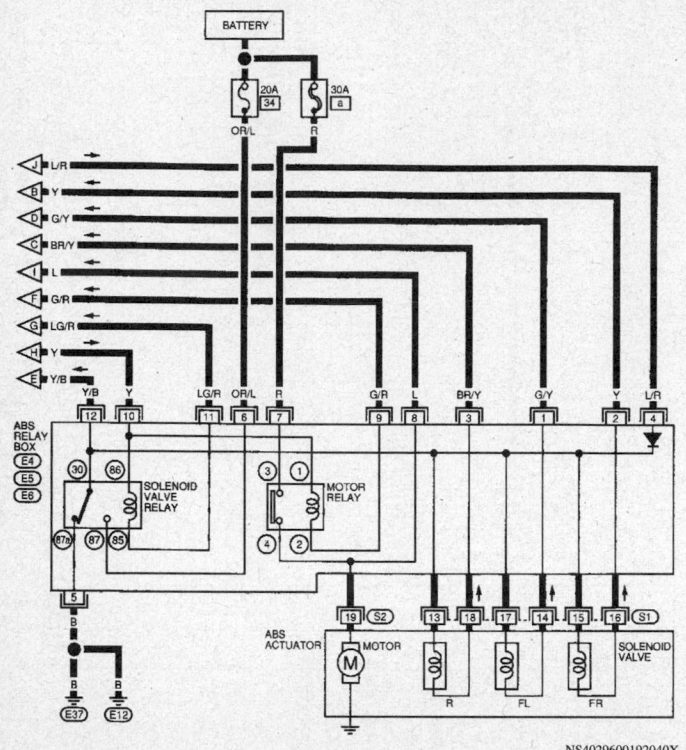

Fig. 27 ABS wiring circuit (Part 4 of 4). 1996–97 Altima

NS4029600192040X

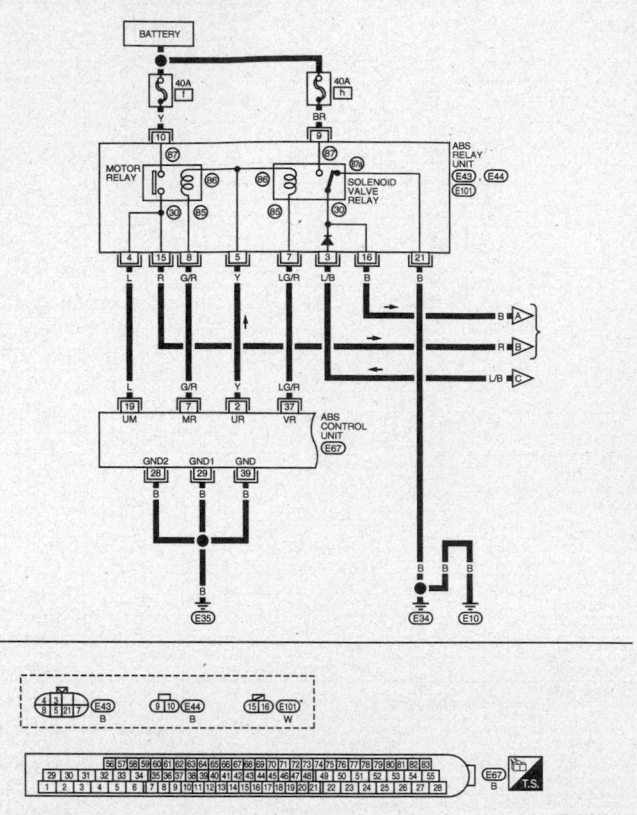

Fig. 28 ABS wiring circuit (Part 1 of 5). 1998–99 Altima

NS4029900303010X

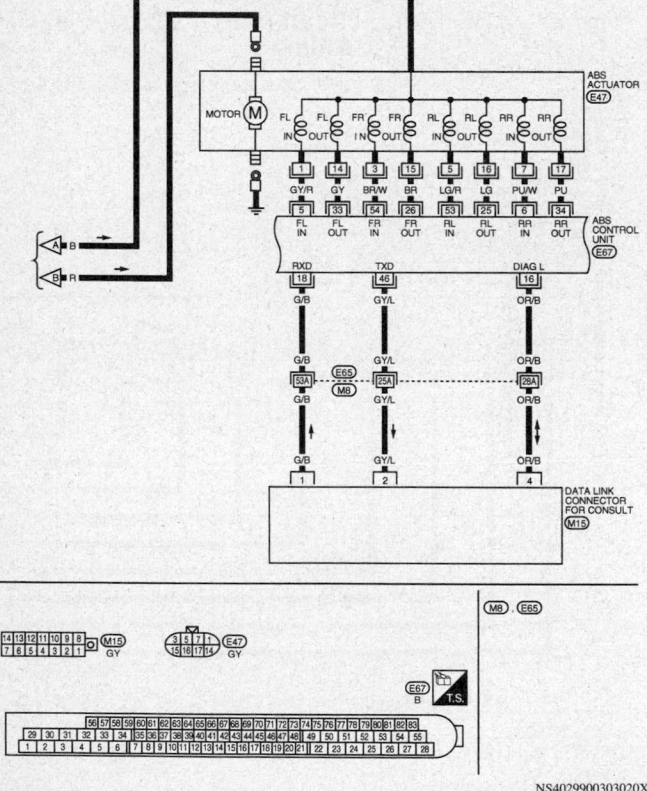

Fig. 28 ABS wiring circuit (Part 2 of 5). 1998–99 Altima

NS4029900303020X

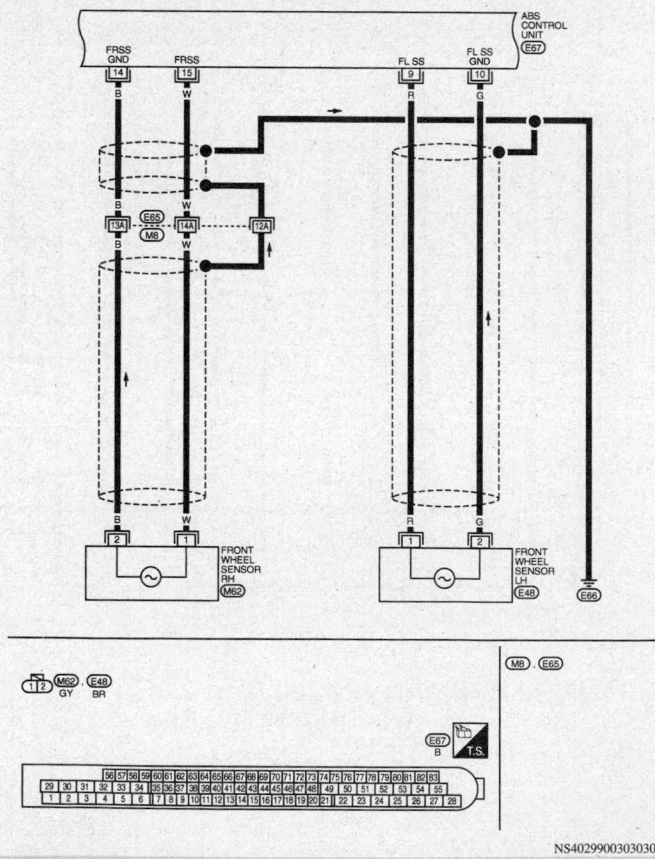

Fig. 28 ABS wiring circuit (Part 3 of 5). 1998–99 Altima

NS4029900303030X

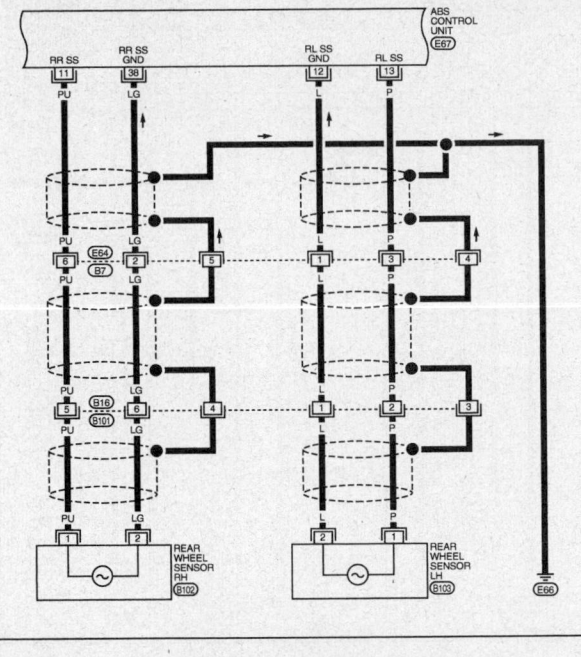

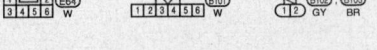

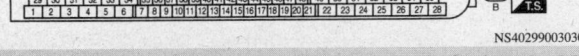

Fig. 28 ABS wiring circuit (Part 4 of 5). 1998–99 Altima

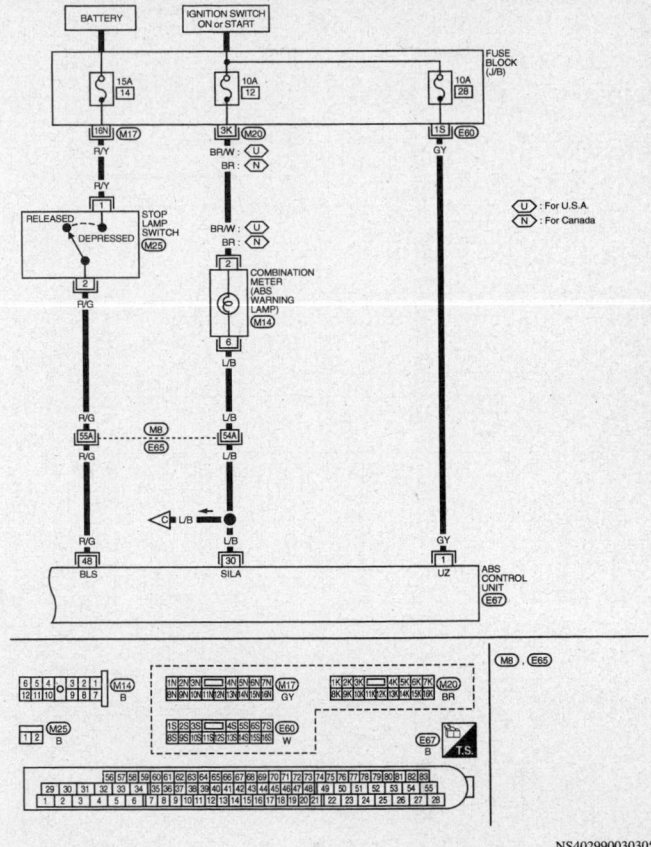

Fig. 28 ABS wiring circuit (Part 5 of 5). 1998–99 Altima

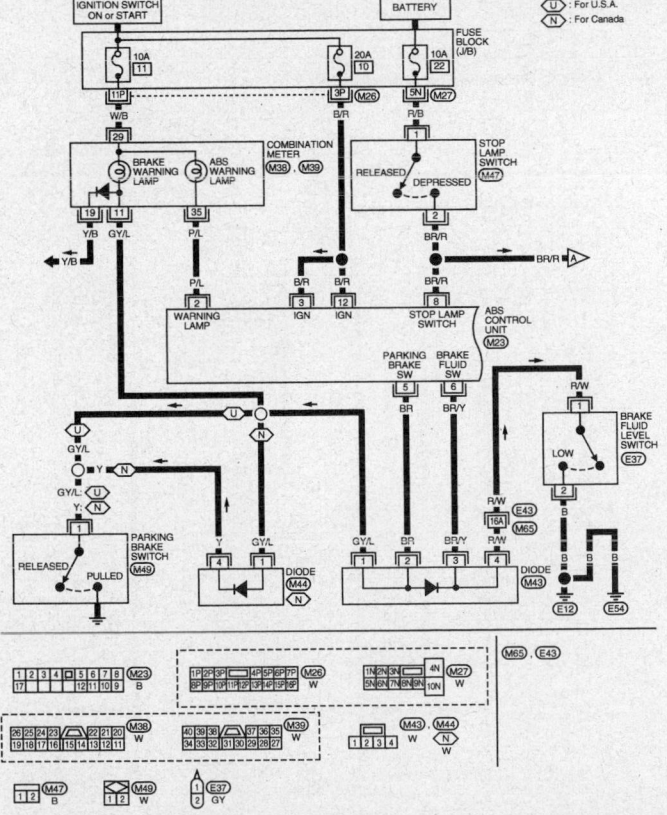

Fig. 29 ABS wiring circuit (Part 1 of 2). 2WD Frontier

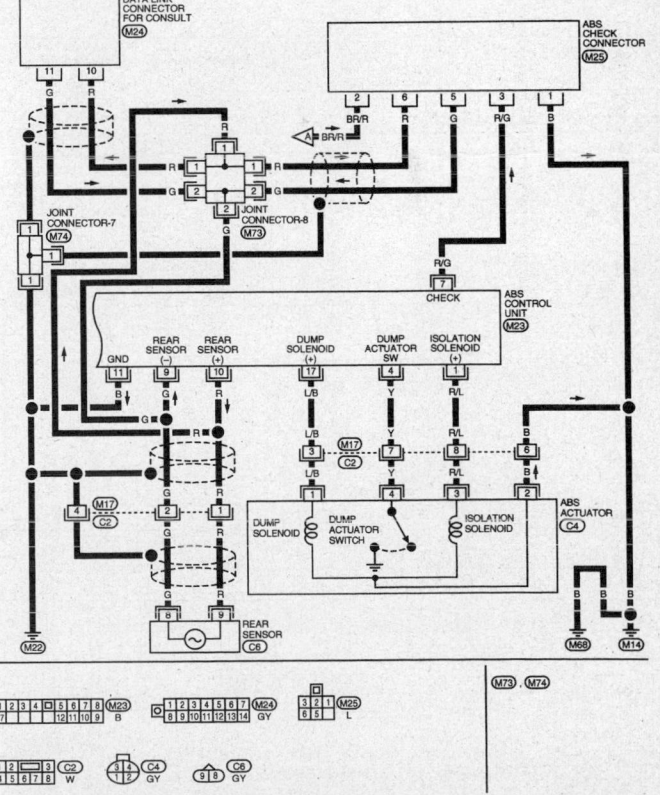

Fig. 29 ABS wiring circuit (Part 2 of 2). 2WD Frontier

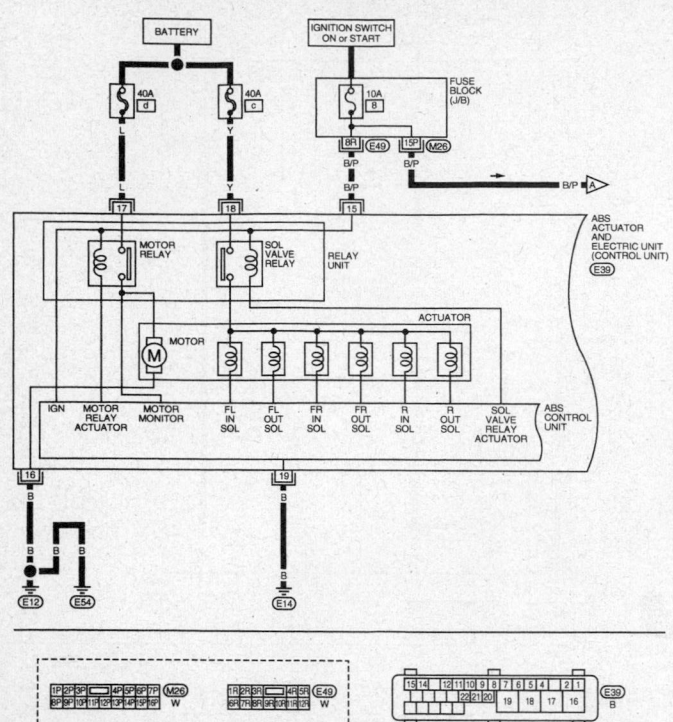

Fig. 30   ABS wiring circuit (Part 1 of 3). 4WD Frontier

NS4029900306010X

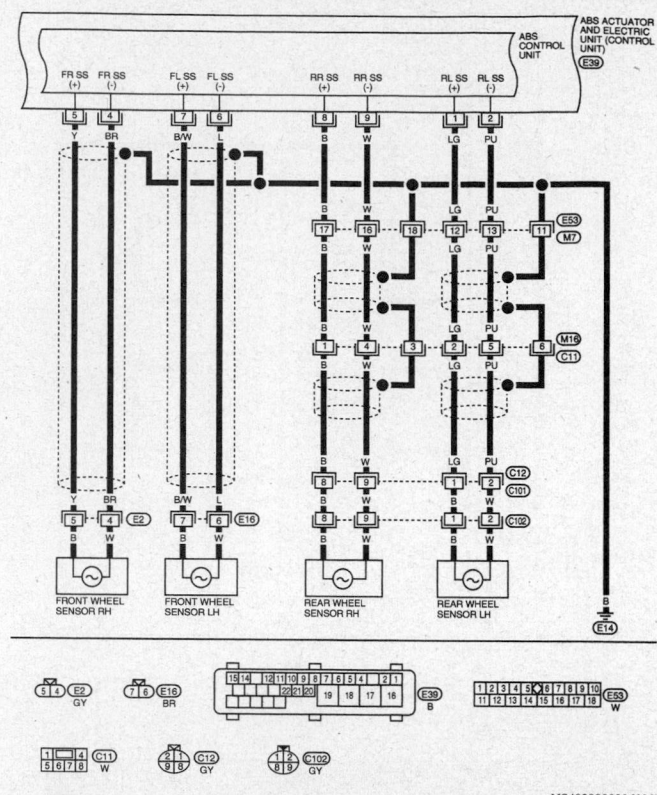

Fig. 30   ABS wiring circuit (Part 2 of 3). 4WD Frontier

NS4029900306020X

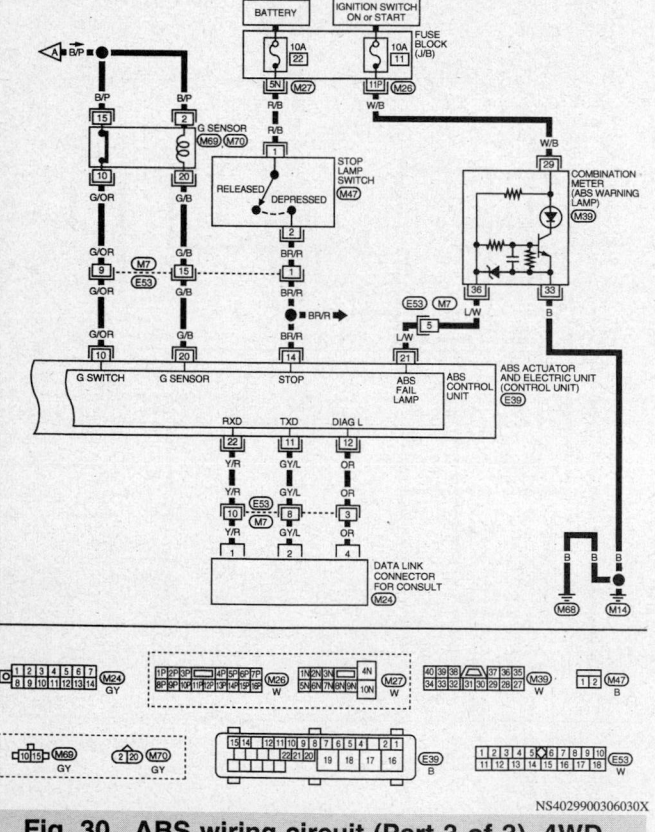

Fig. 30   ABS wiring circuit (Part 3 of 3). 4WD Frontier

NS4029900306030X

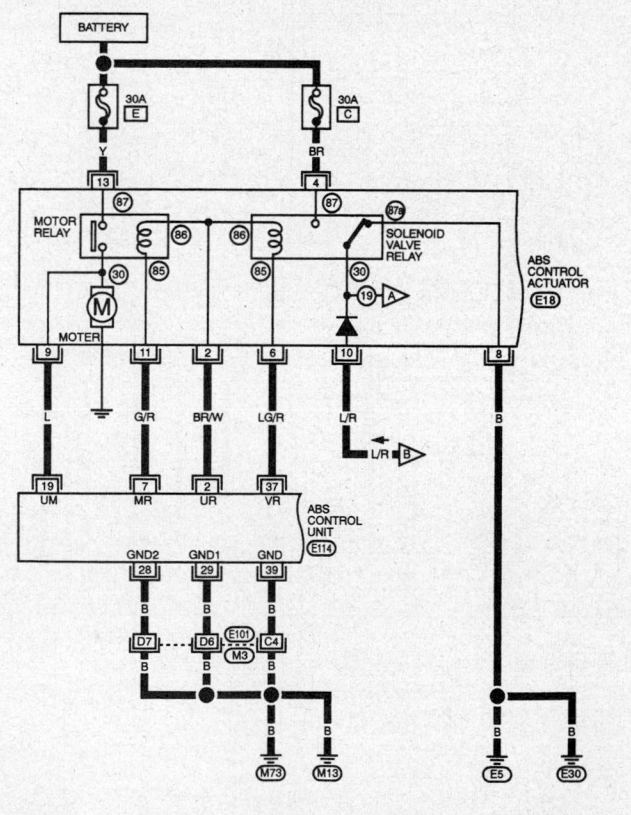

Fig. 31   ABS wiring circuit (Part 1 of 4). 1996 Maxima

NS4029500145010X

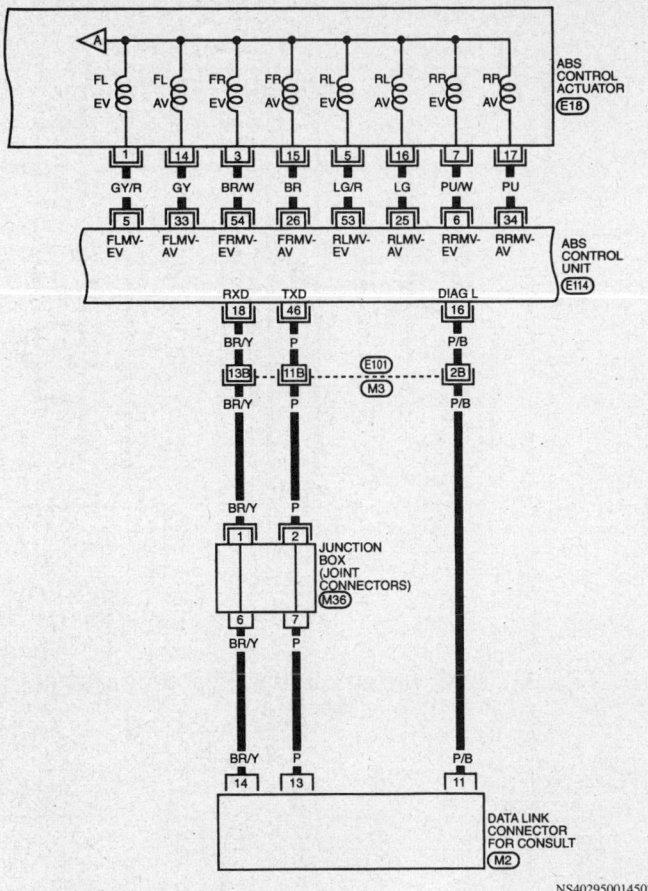

NS4029500145020X

Fig. 31   ABS wiring circuit (Part 2 of 4). 1996 Maxima

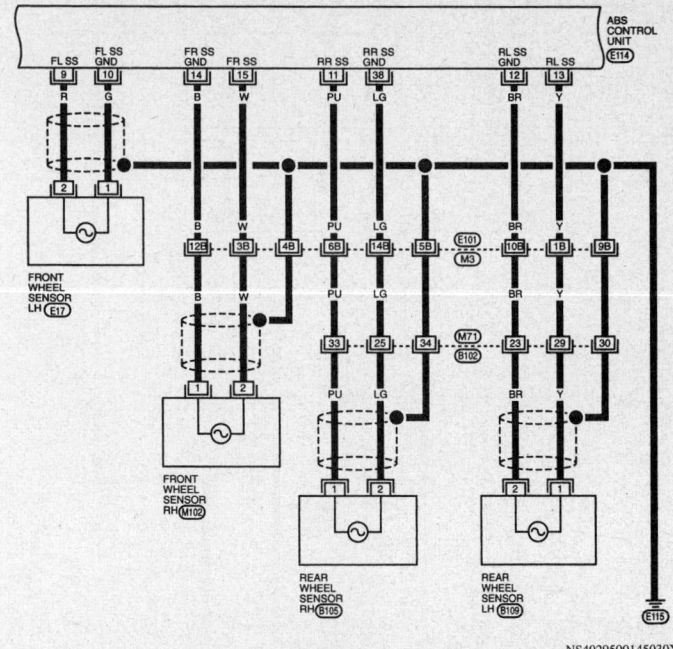

NS4029500145030X

Fig. 31   ABS wiring circuit (Part 3 of 4). 1996 Maxima

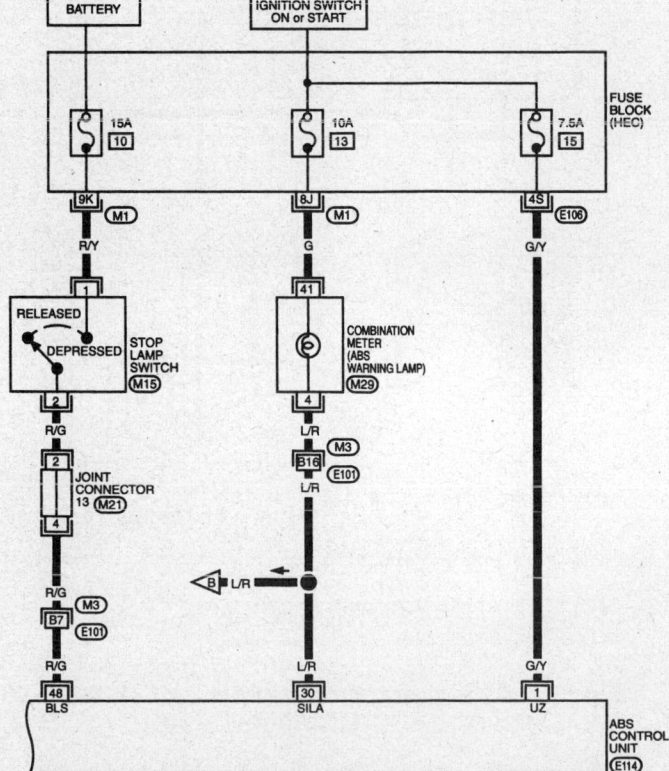

NS4029500145040X

Fig. 31   ABS wiring circuit (Part 4 of 4). 1996 Maxima

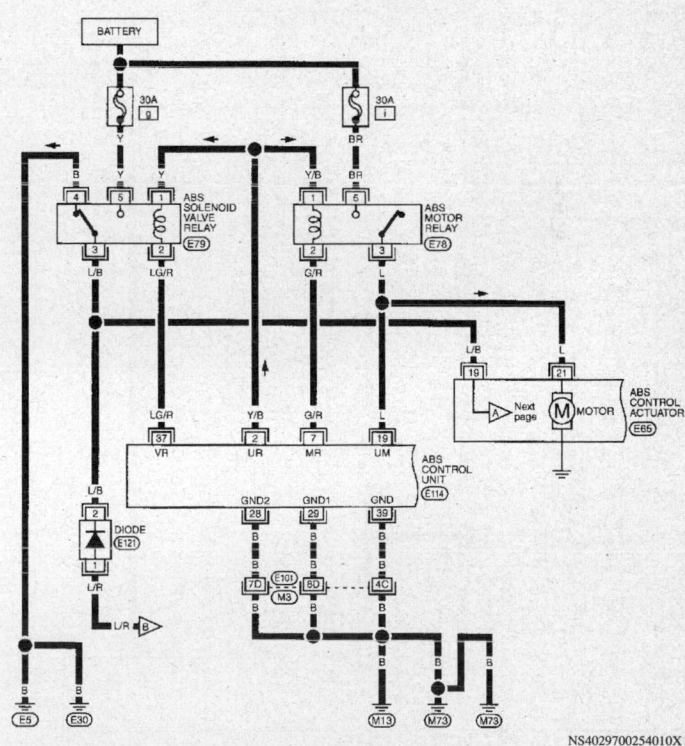

NS4029700254010X

Fig. 32   ABS wiring circuit (Part 1 of 4). 1997 Maxima

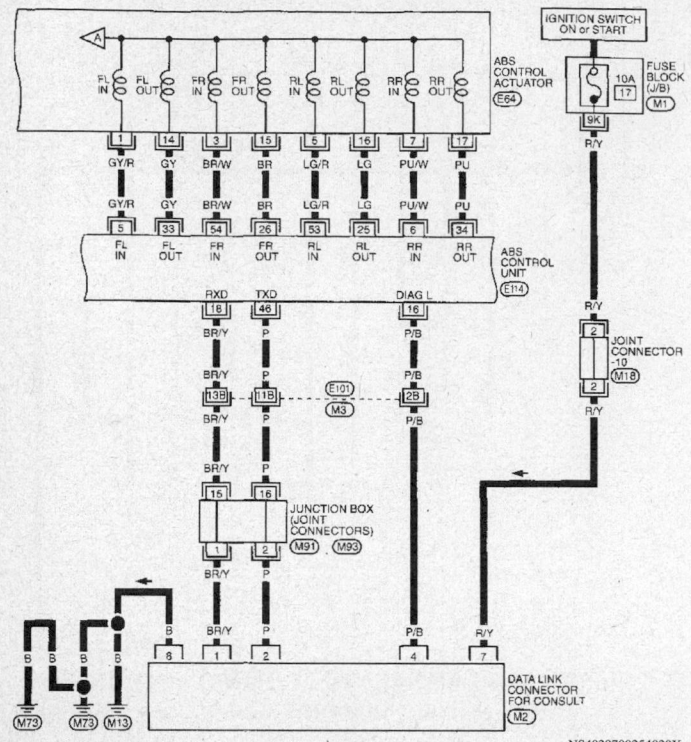

Fig. 32 ABS wiring circuit (Part 2 of 4). 1997
Maxima

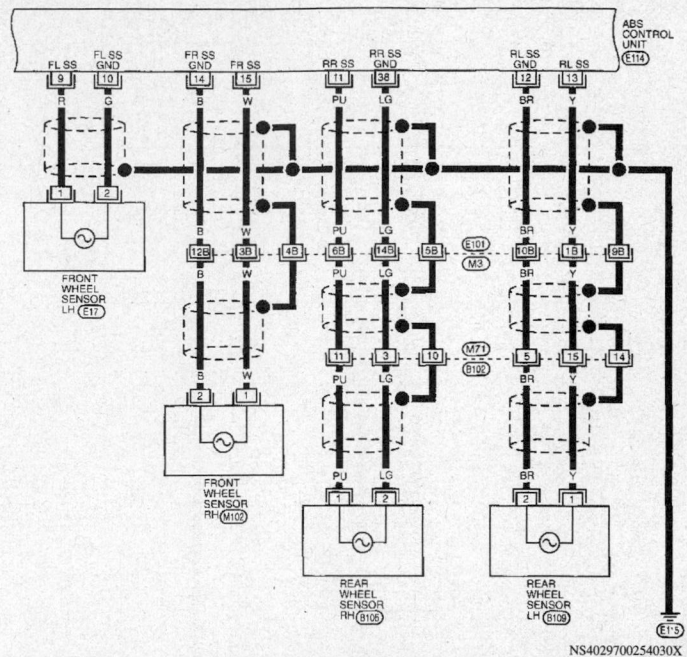

Fig. 32 ABS wiring circuit (Part 3 of 4). 1997
Maxima

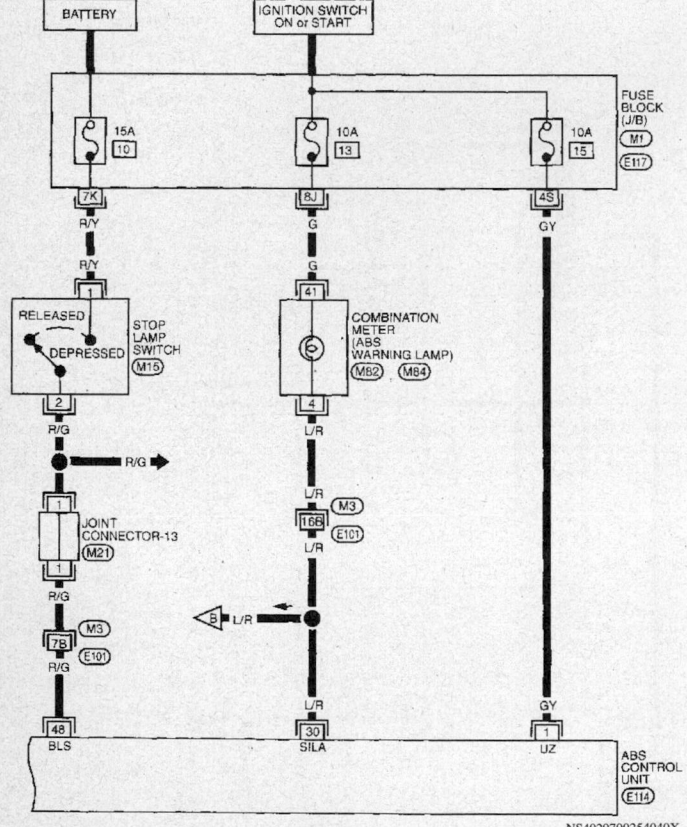

Fig. 32 ABS wiring circuit (Part 4 of 4). 1997
Maxima

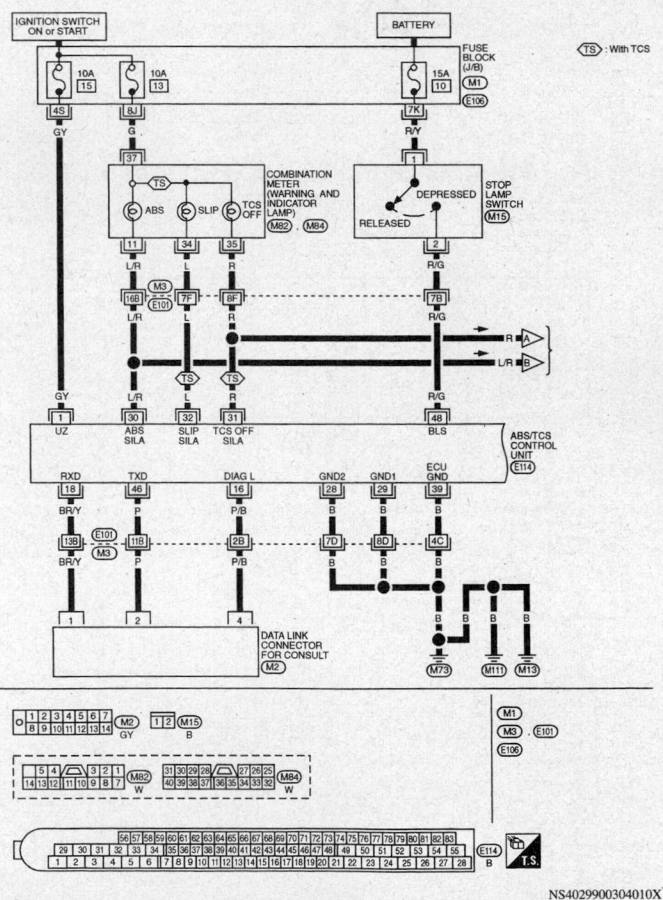

Fig. 33 ABS wiring circuit (Part 1 of 4). 1998–99
Maxima

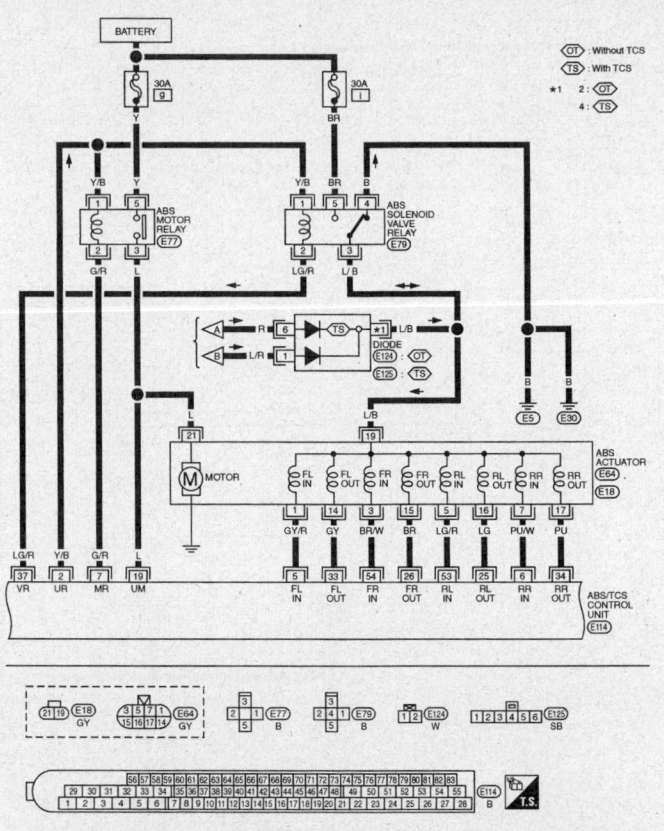

Fig. 33 ABS wiring circuit (Part 2 of 4). 1998–99 Maxima

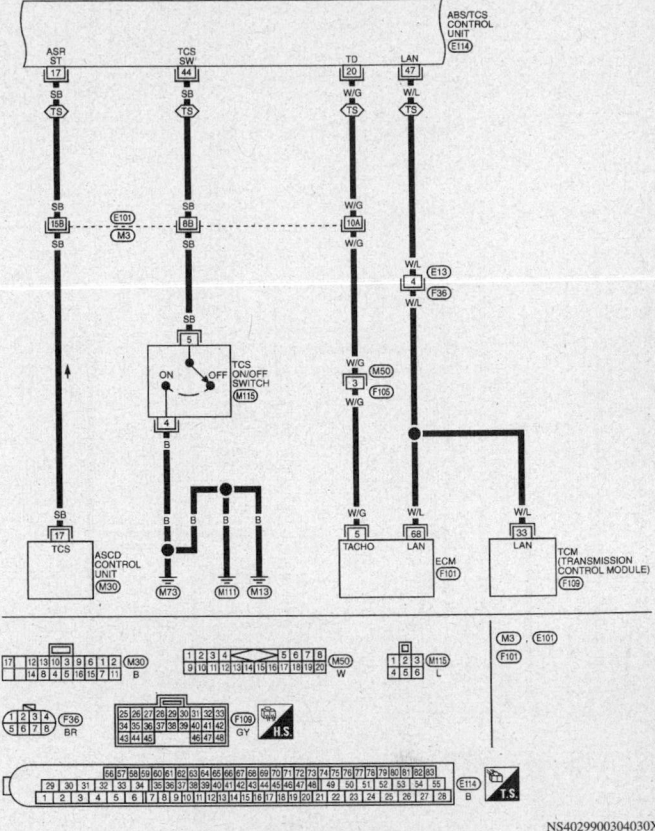

Fig. 33 ABS wiring circuit (Part 3 of 4). 1998–99 Maxima

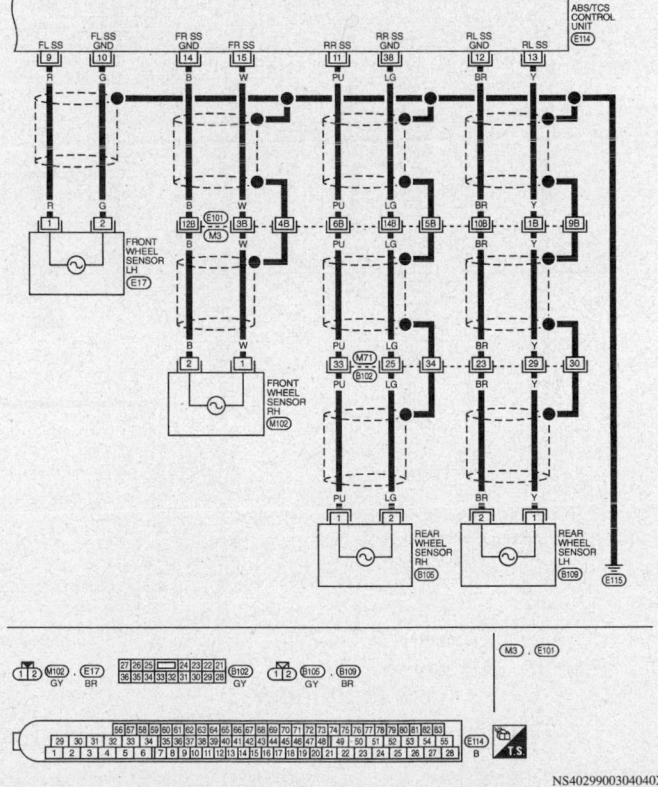

Fig. 33 ABS wiring circuit (Part 4 of 4). 1998–99 Maxima

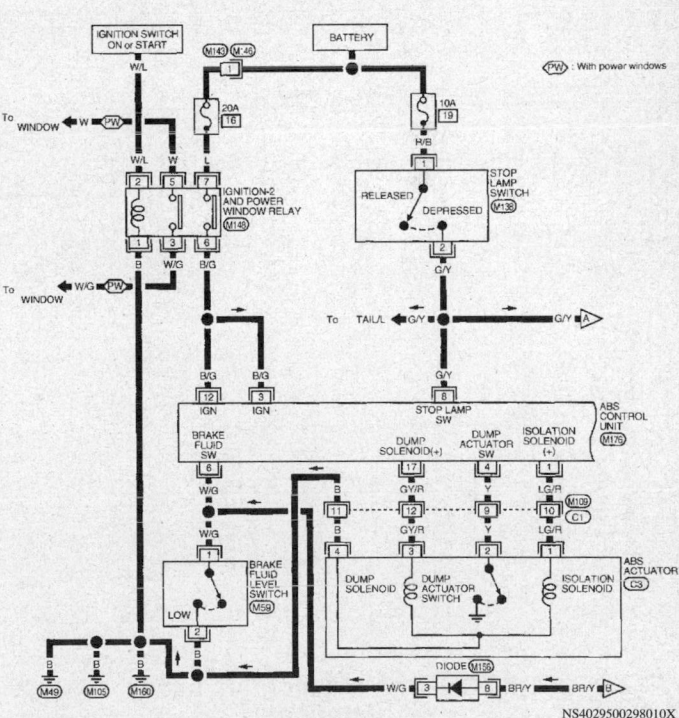

Fig. 34 ABS wiring circuit (Part 1 of 2). Pickup

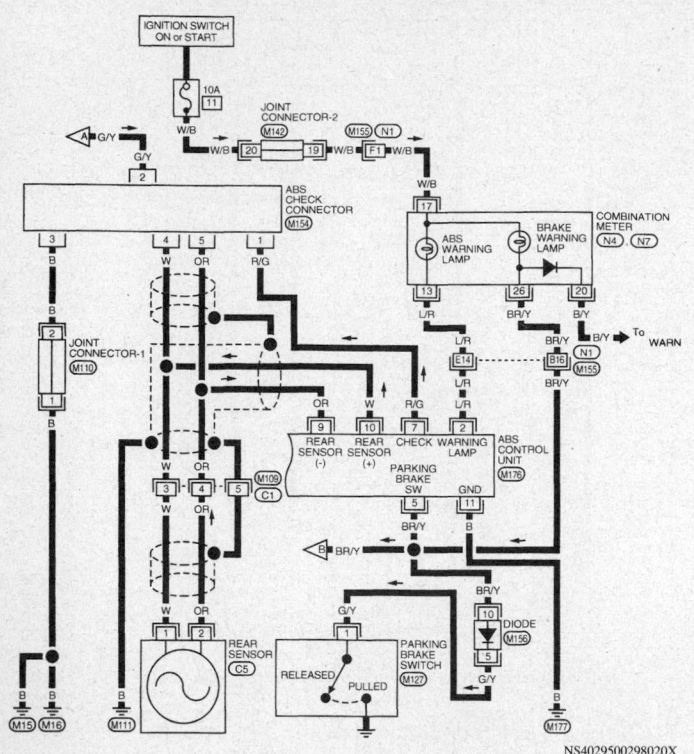

Fig. 34 ABS wiring circuit (Part 2 of 2). Pickup

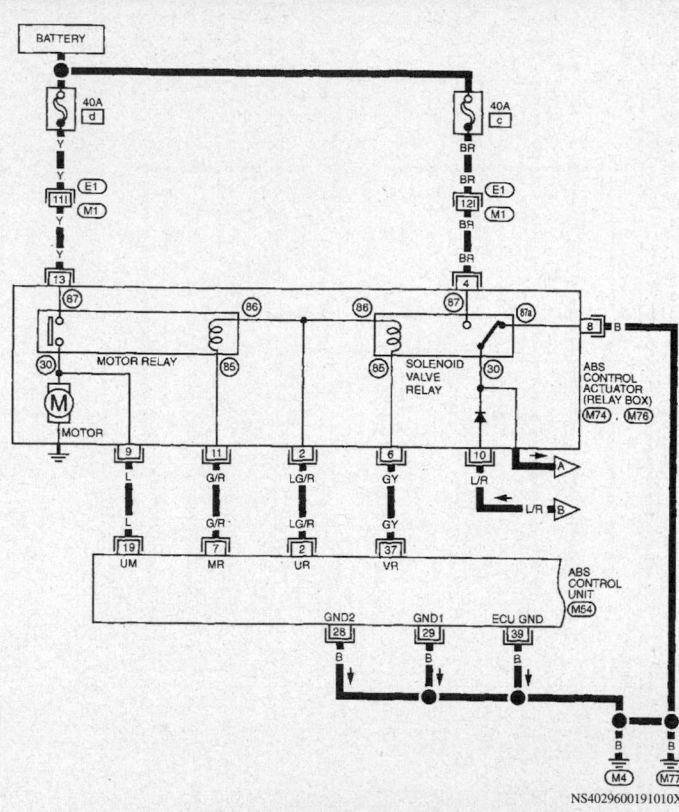

Fig. 35 ABS wiring circuit (Part 1 of 4). 1996 Pathfinder

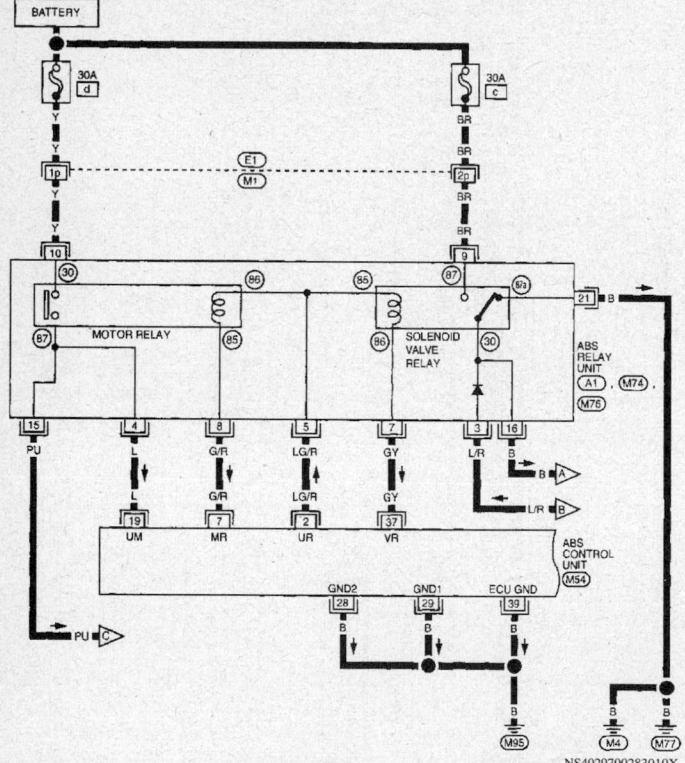

Fig. 35 ABS wiring circuit (Part 1 of 4). 1997–99 Pathfinder

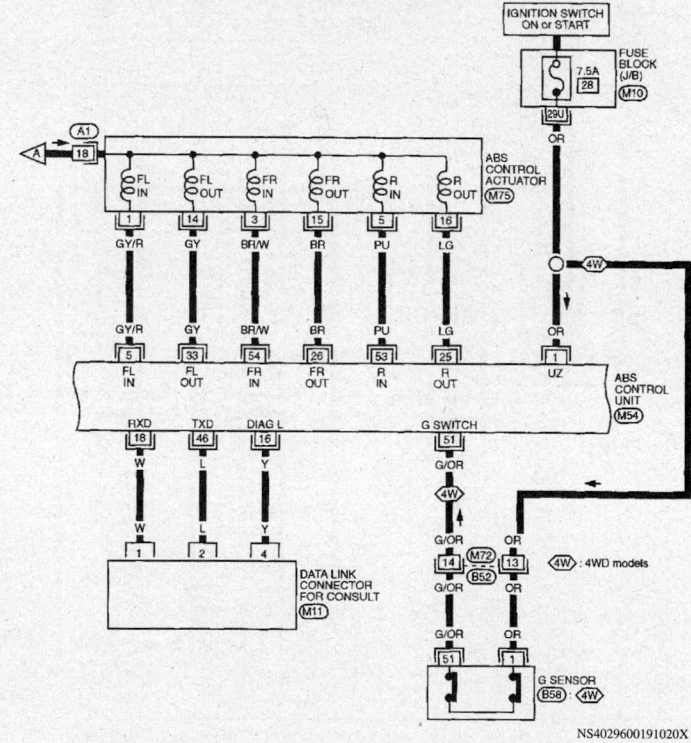

Fig. 35 ABS wiring circuit (Part 2 of 4). 1996 Pathfinder

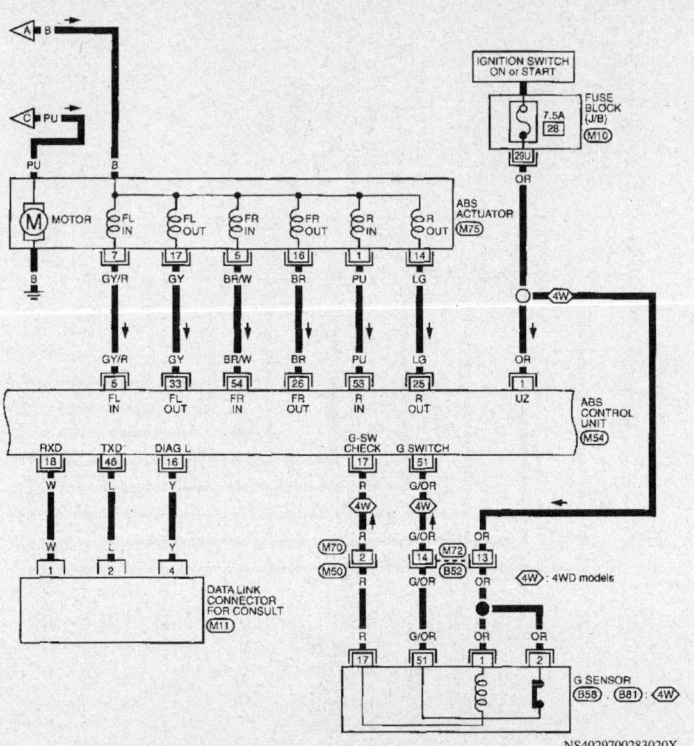

Fig. 35   ABS wiring circuit (Part 2 of 4). 1997–99 Pathfinder

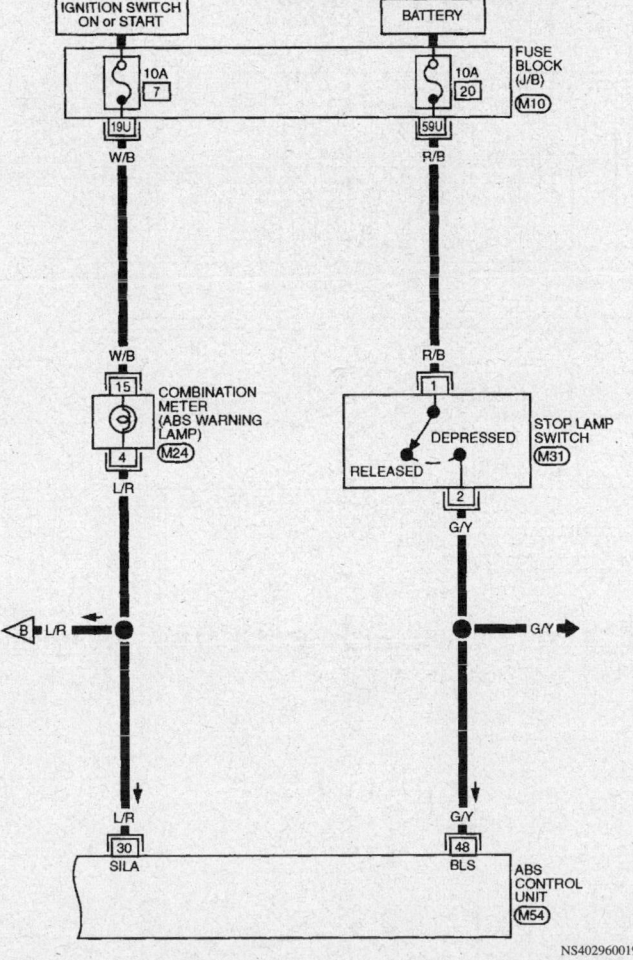

Fig. 35   ABS wiring circuit (Part 4 of 4). Pathfinder

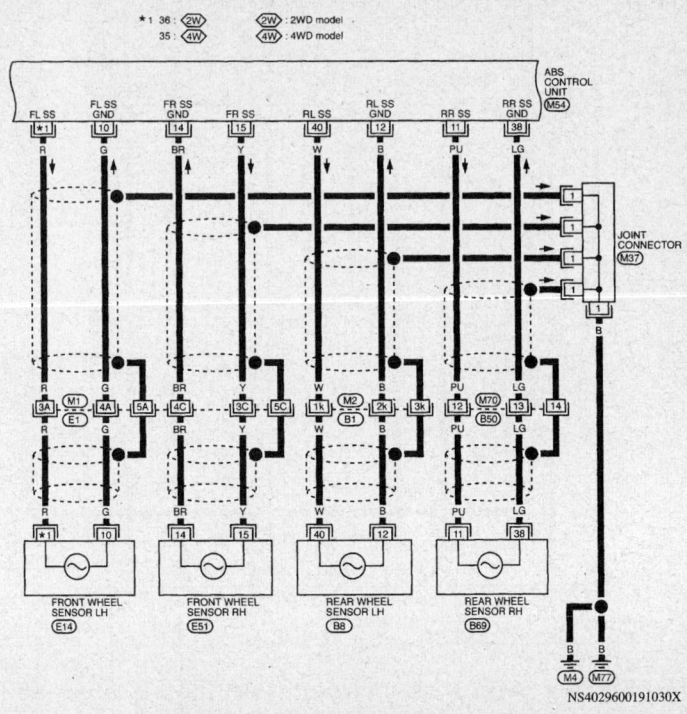

Fig. 35   ABS wiring circuit (Part 3 of 4). Pathfinder

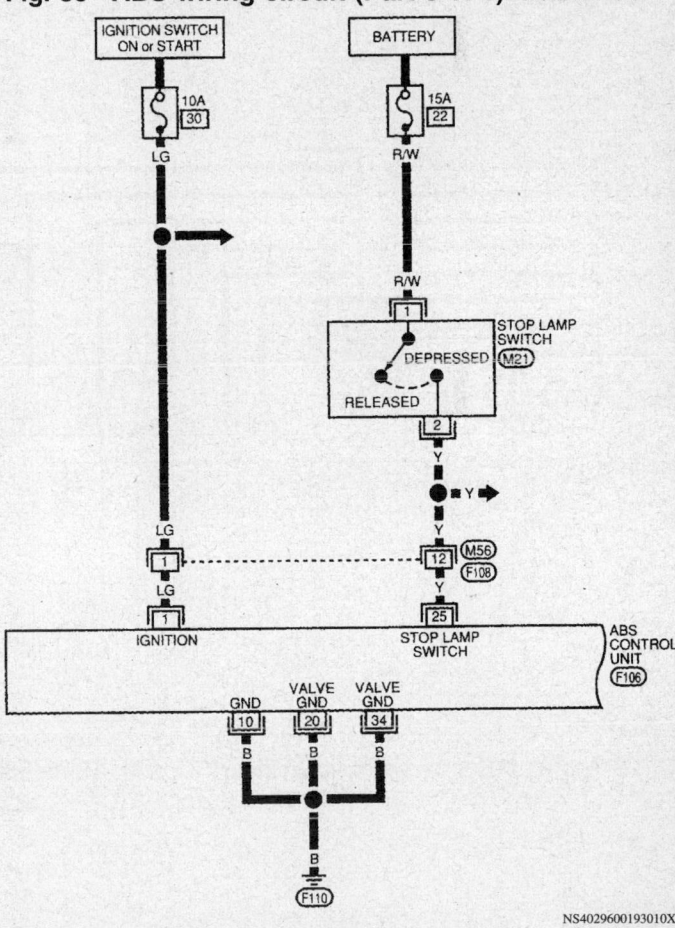

Fig. 36   ABS wiring circuit (Part 1 of 4). 1996–98 Quest

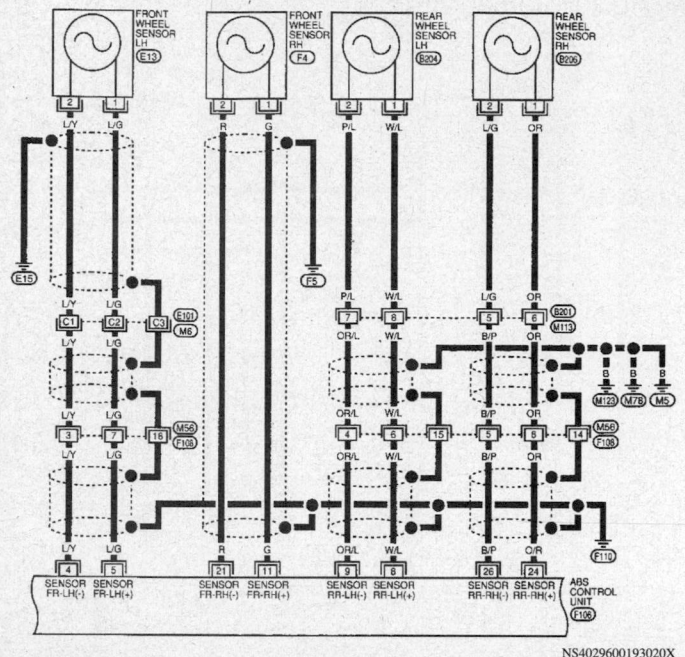

Fig. 36 ABS wiring circuit (Part 2 of 4). 1996–98 Quest

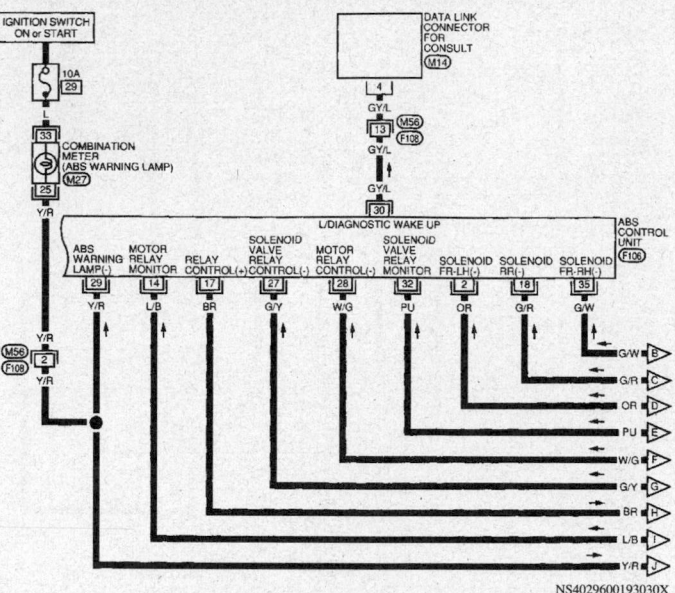

Fig. 36 ABS wiring circuit (Part 3 of 4). 1996–98 Quest

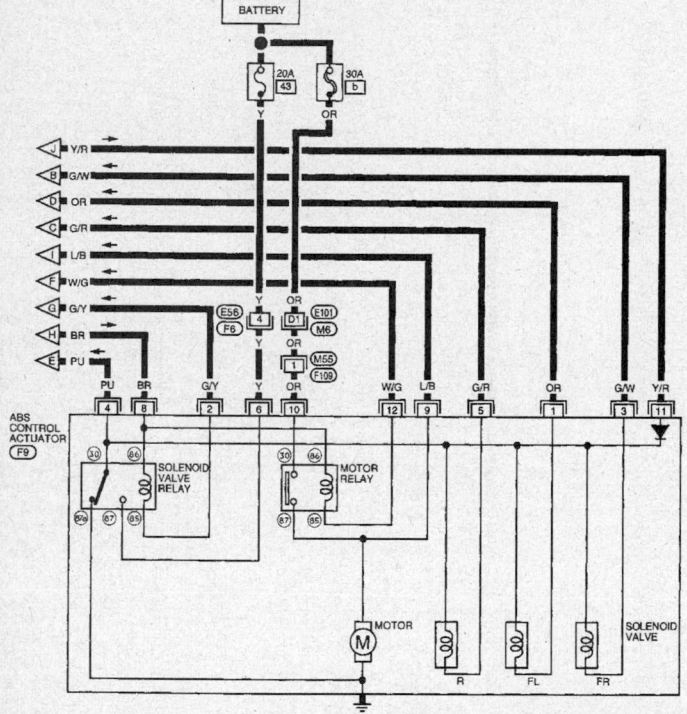

Fig. 36 ABS wiring circuit (Part 4 of 4). 1996–98 Quest

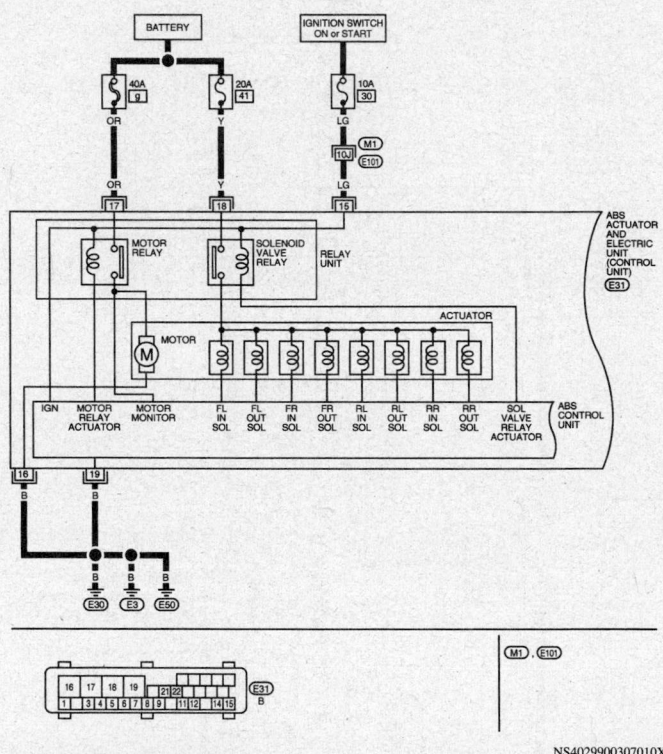

Fig. 37 ABS wiring circuit (Part 1 of 3). 1999 Quest

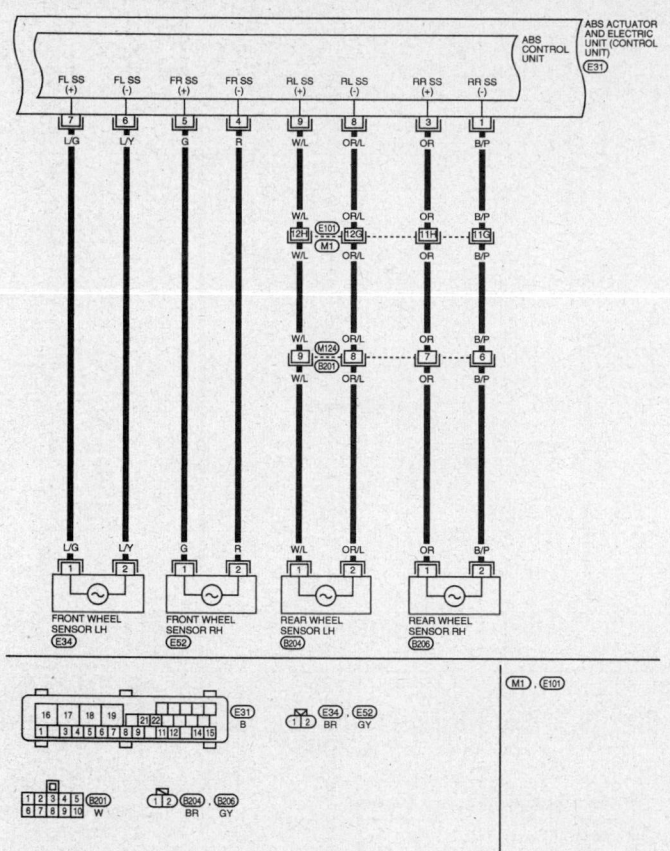

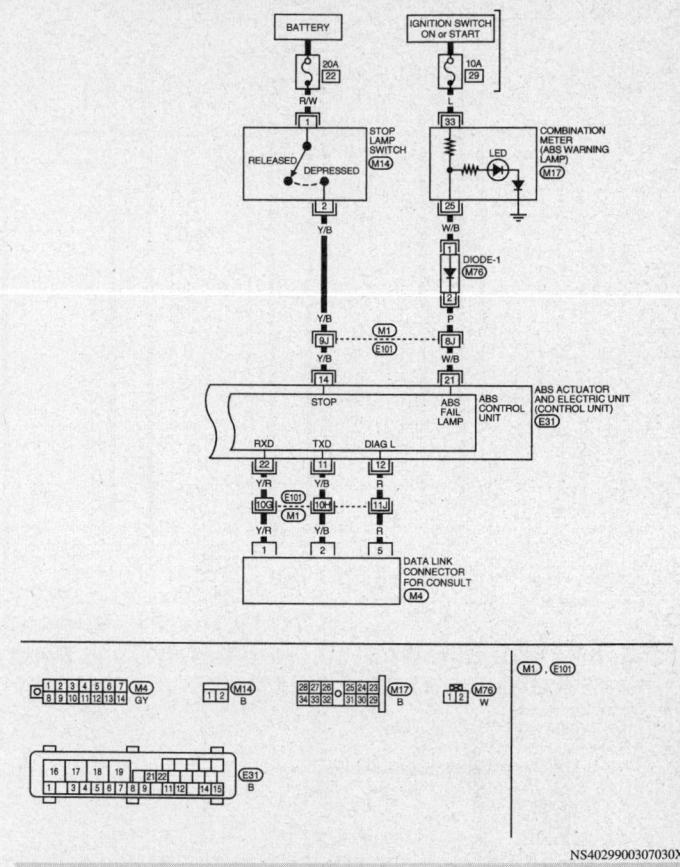

Fig. 37   ABS wiring circuit (Part 2 of 3). 1999 Quest

Fig. 37   ABS wiring circuit (Part 3 of 3). 1999 Quest

NS4029900307020X

NS4029900307030X

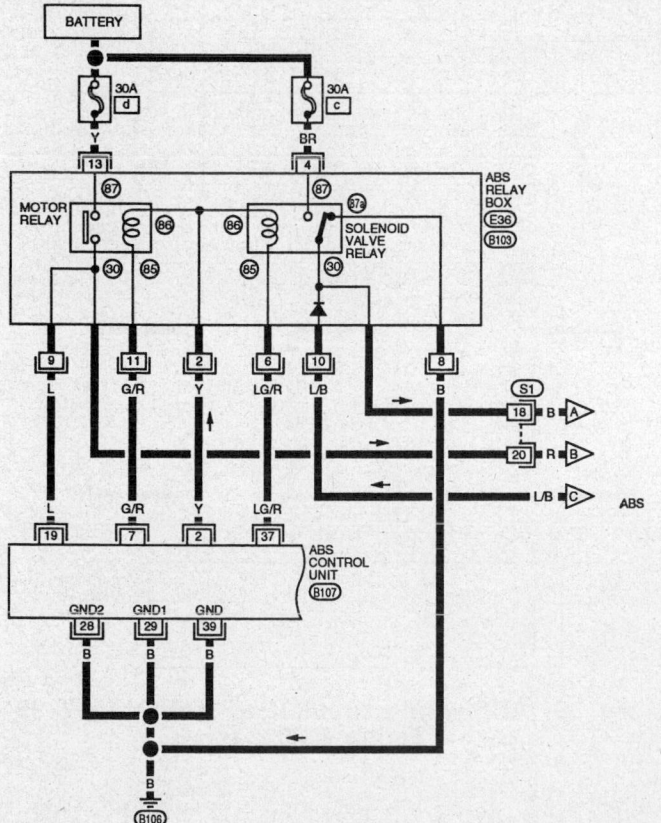

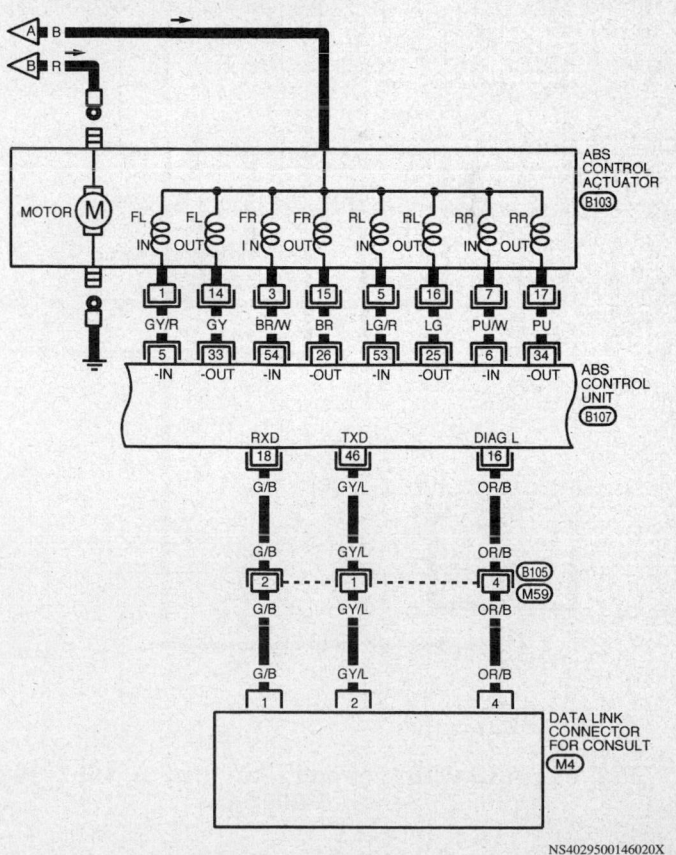

Fig. 38   ABS wiring circuit (Part 1 of 4). 1996 Sentra & 200SX

Fig. 38   ABS wiring circuit (Part 2 of 4). 1996 Sentra & 200SX

NS4029500146010X

NS4029500146020X

ANTI-LOCK BRAKES

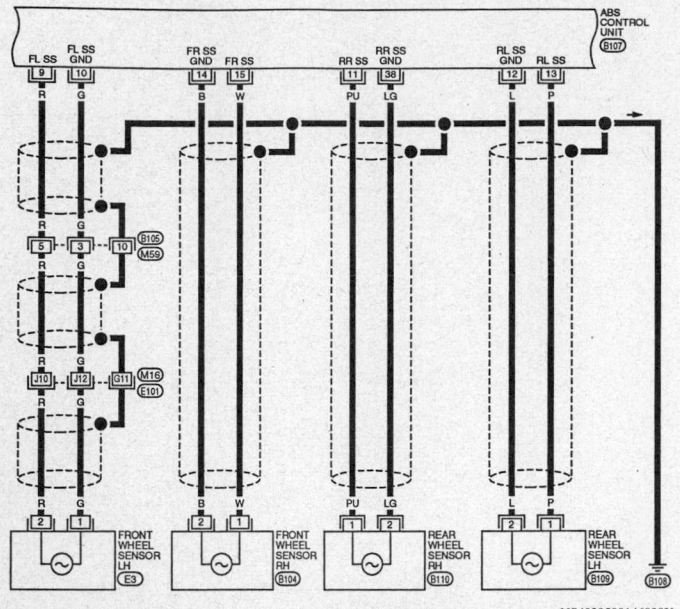

Fig. 38   ABS wiring circuit (Part 3 of 4). 1996 Sentra & 200SX

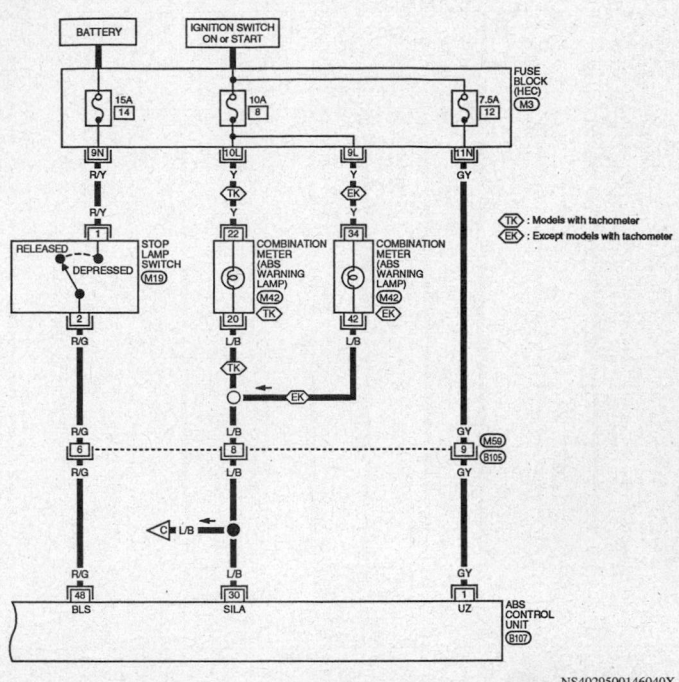

Fig. 38   ABS wiring circuit (Part 4 of 4). 1996 Sentra & 200SX

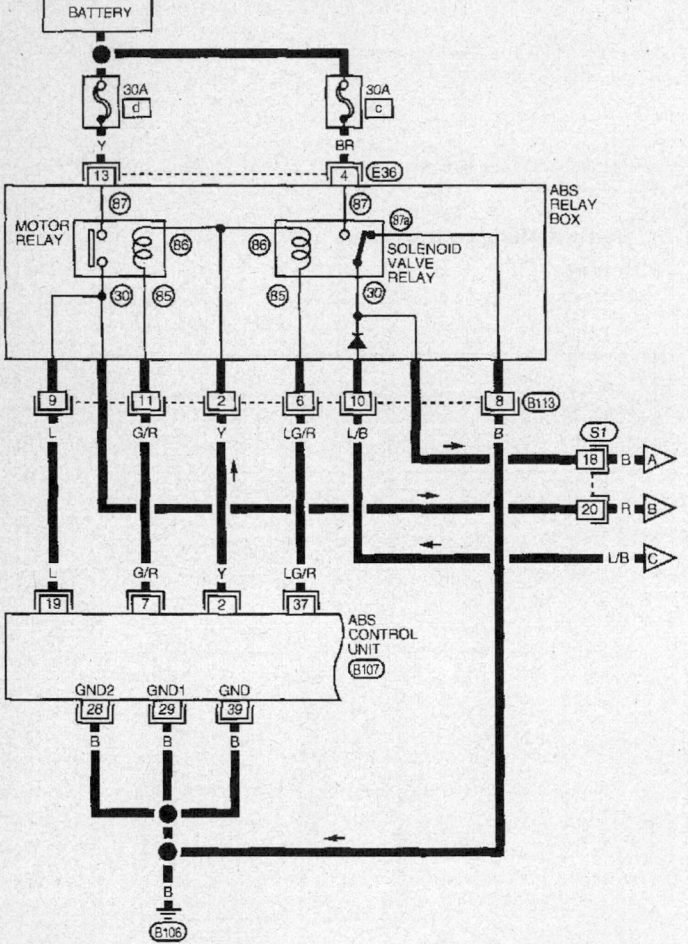

Fig. 39   ABS wiring circuit (Part 1 of 5). 1997–99 Sentra & 200SX

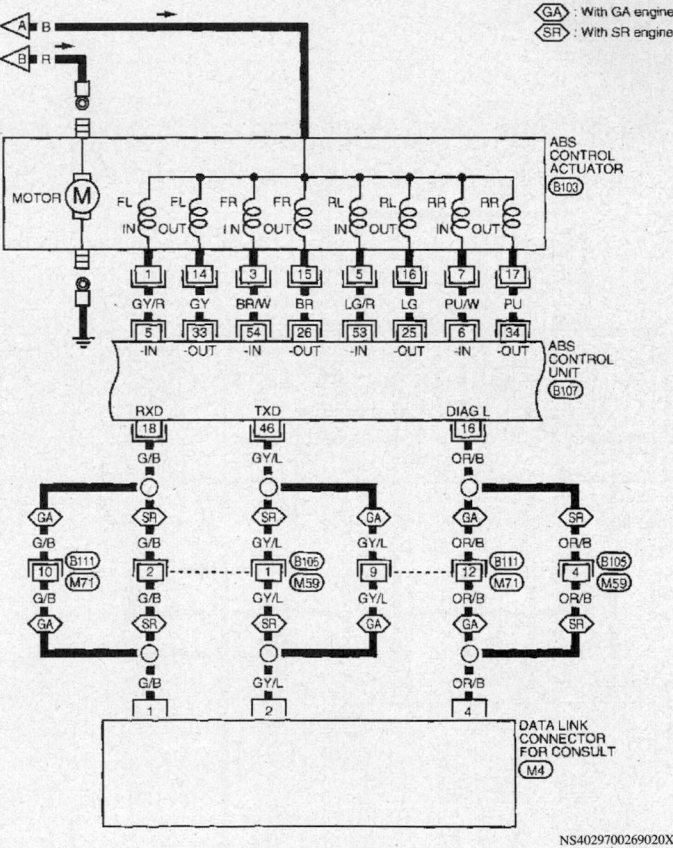

Fig. 39   ABS wiring circuit (Part 2 of 5). 1997–99 Sentra & 200SX

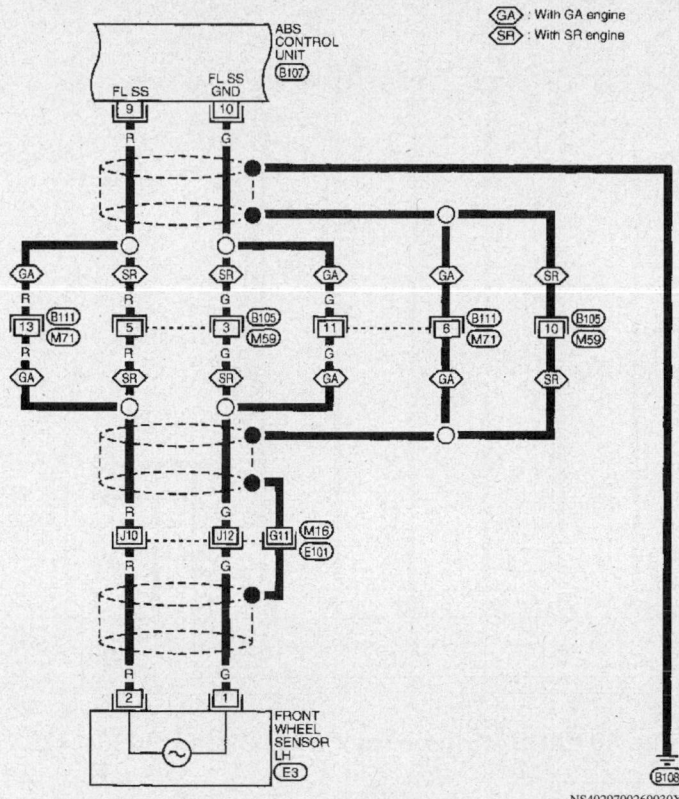

Fig. 39 ABS wiring circuit (Part 3 of 5). 1997–99 Sentra & 200SX

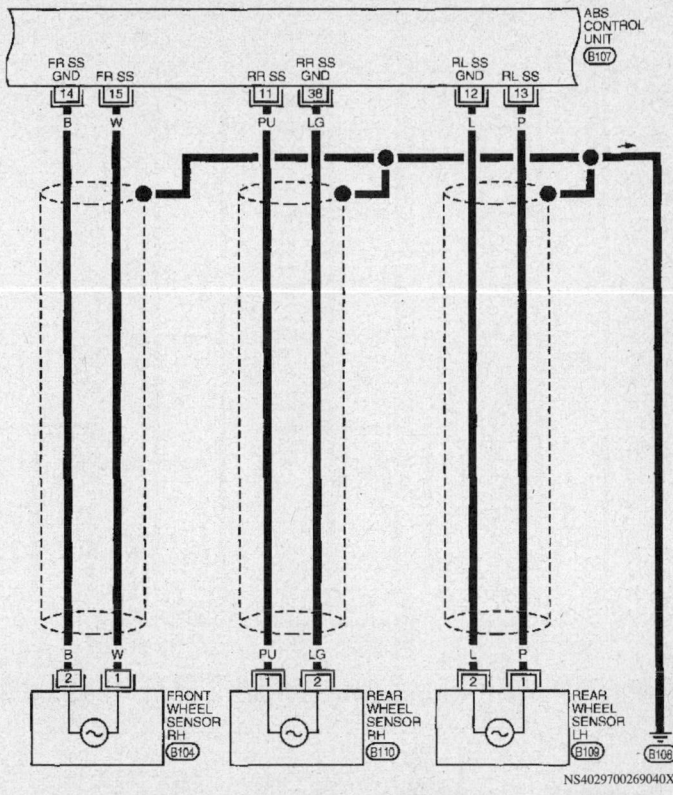

Fig. 39 ABS wiring circuit (Part 4 of 5). 1997–99 Sentra & 200SX

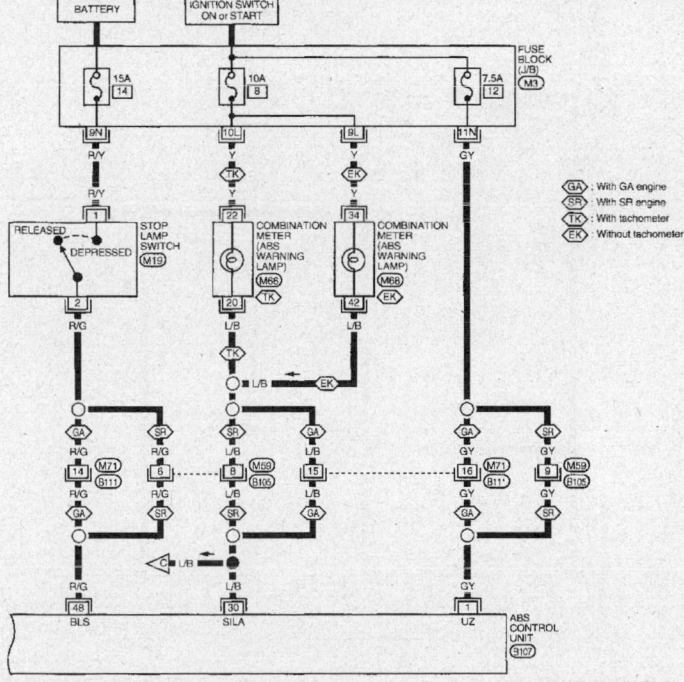

Fig. 39 ABS wiring circuit (Part 5 of 5). 1997–99 Sentra & 200SX

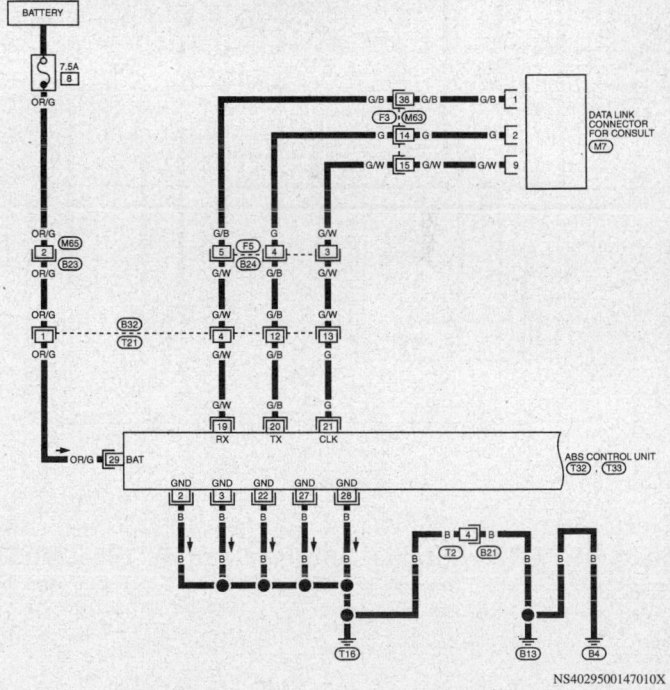

Fig. 40 ABS wiring circuit (Part 1 of 5). 1996 240SX

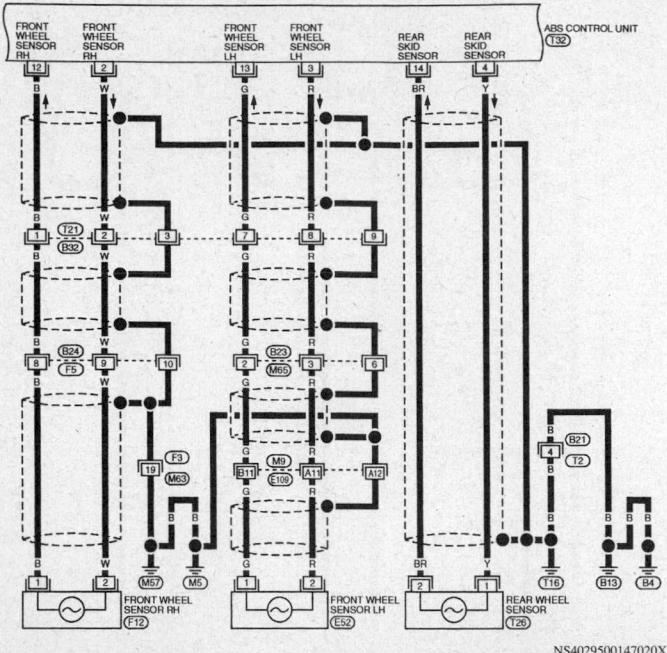

Fig. 40   ABS wiring circuit (Part 2 of 5). 1996 240SX

NS4029500147020X

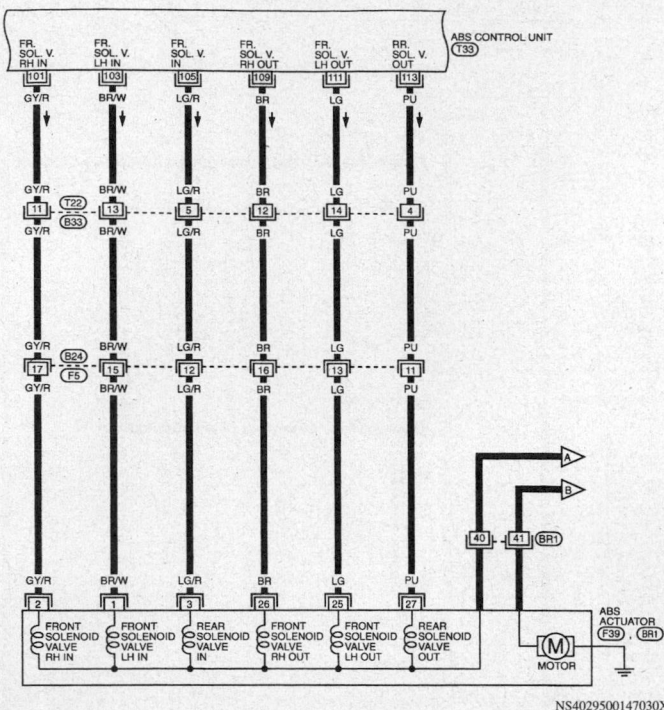

Fig. 40   ABS wiring circuit (Part 3 of 5). 1996 240SX

NS4029500147030X

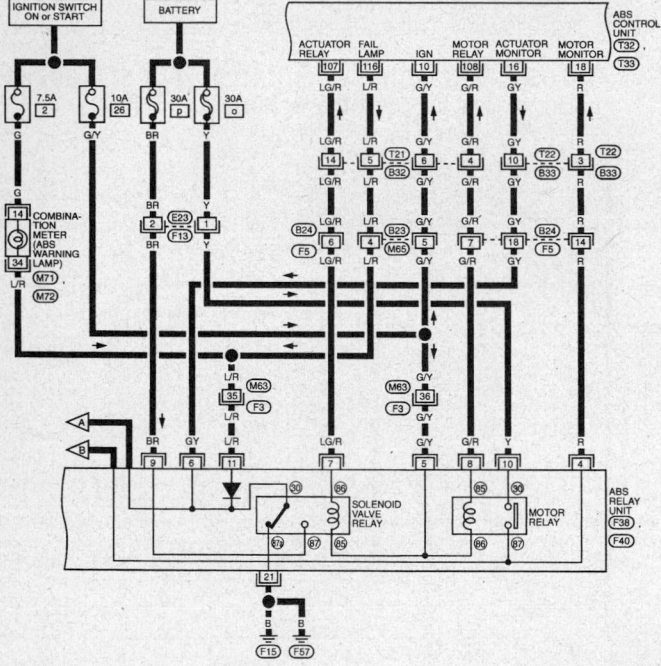

Fig. 40   ABS wiring circuit (Part 4 of 5). 1996 240SX

NS4029500147040X

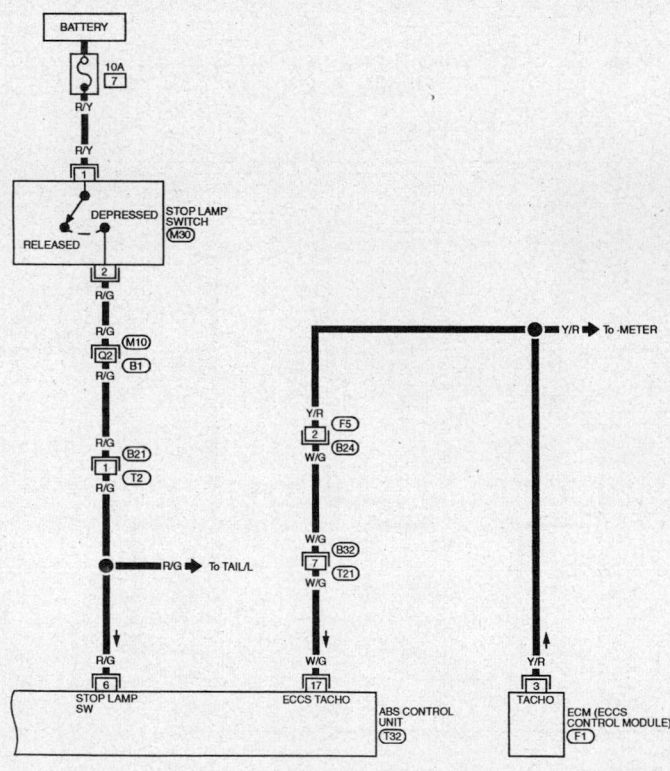

Fig. 40   ABS wiring circuit (Part 5 of 5). 1996 240SX

NS4029500147050X

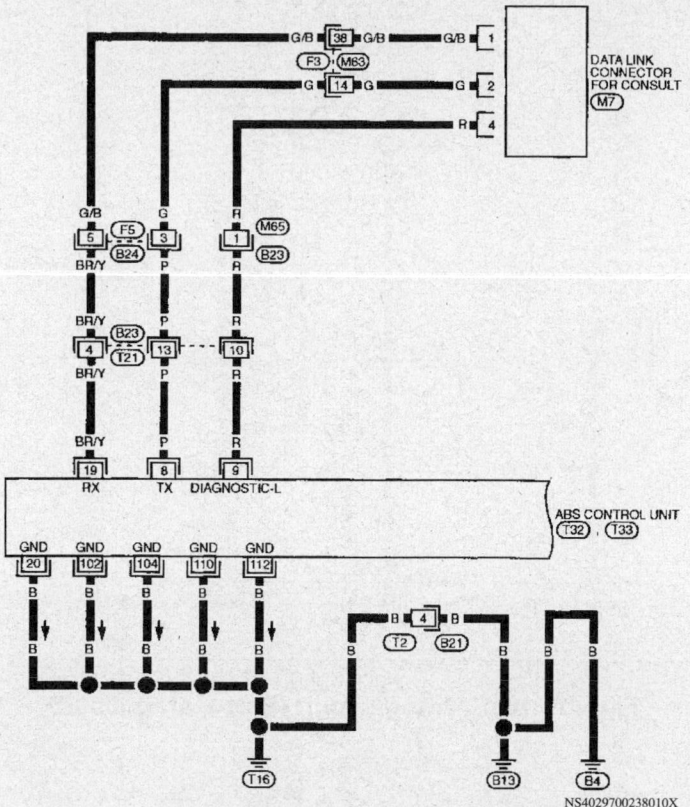

Fig. 41   ABS wiring circuit (Part 1 of 5). 1997–98 240SX

NS4029700238010X

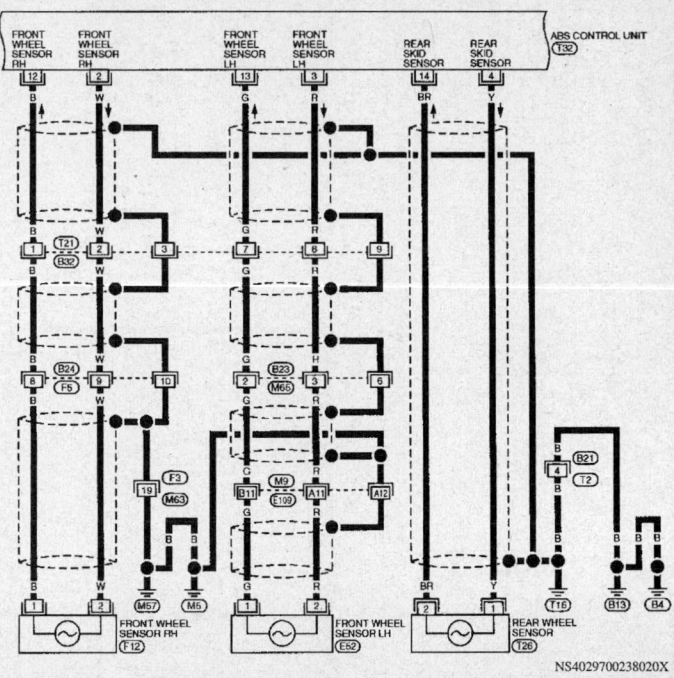

Fig. 41   ABS wiring circuit (Part 2 of 5). 1997–98 240SX

NS4029700238020X

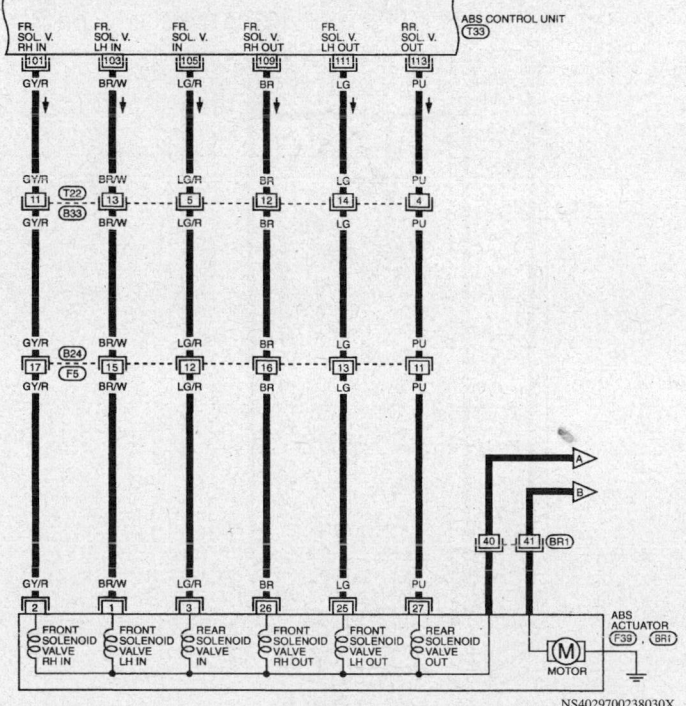

Fig. 41   ABS wiring circuit (Part 3 of 5). 1997–98 240SX

NS4029700238030X

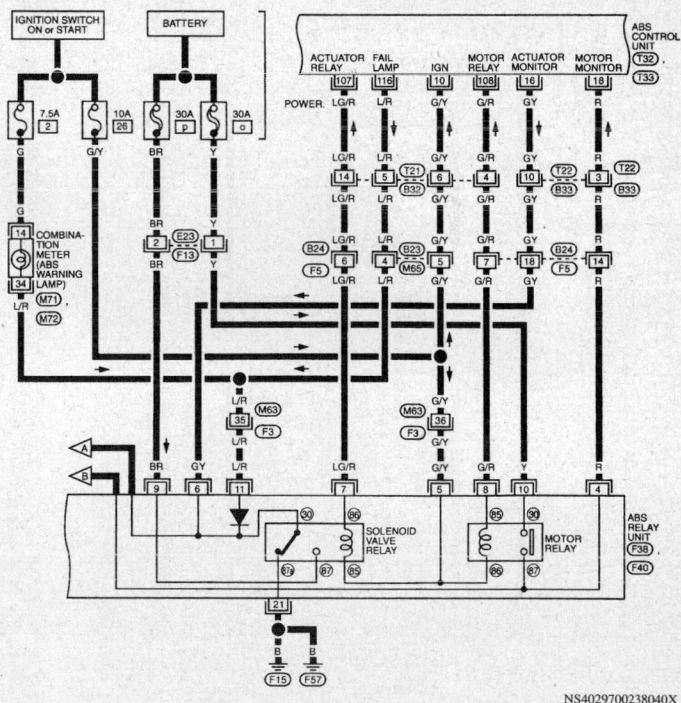

Fig. 41   ABS wiring circuit (Part 4 of 5). 1997–98 240SX

NS4029700238040X

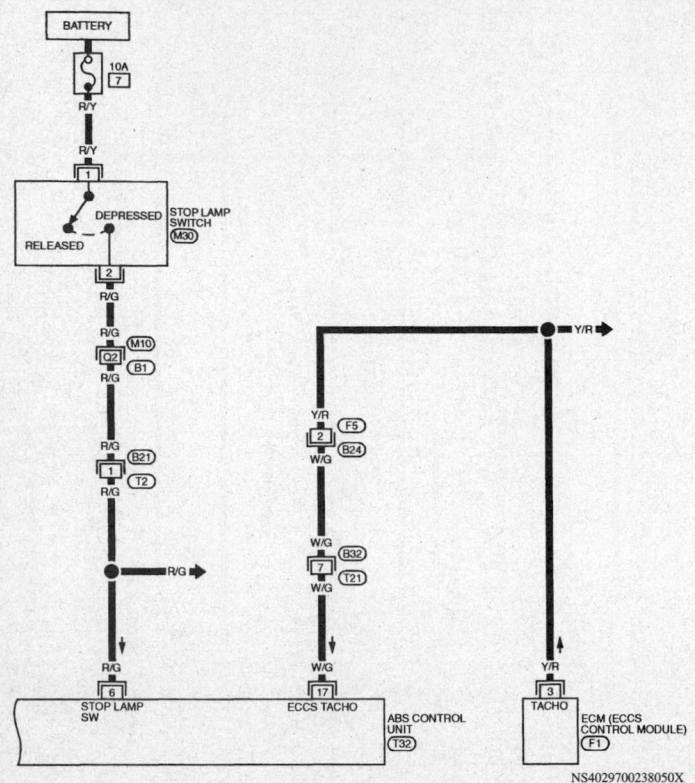

Fig. 41   ABS wiring circuit (Part 5 of 5). 1997–98 240SX

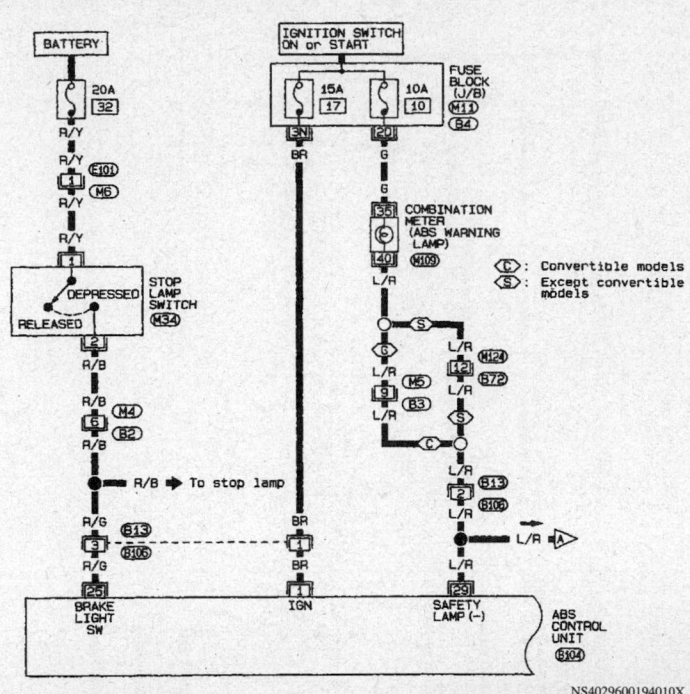

Fig. 42   ABS wiring circuit (Part 1 of 5). 300ZX

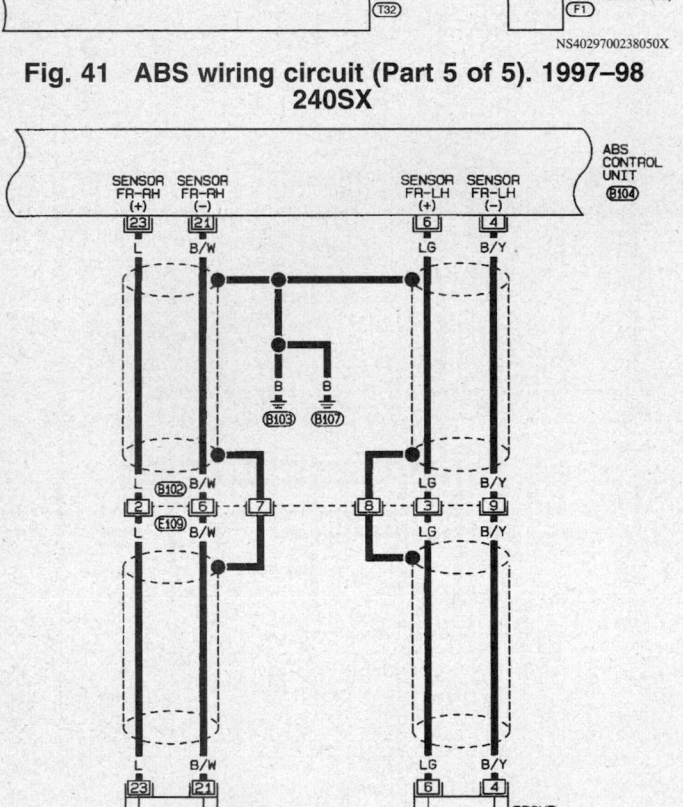

Fig. 42   ABS wiring circuit (Part 2 of 5). 300ZX

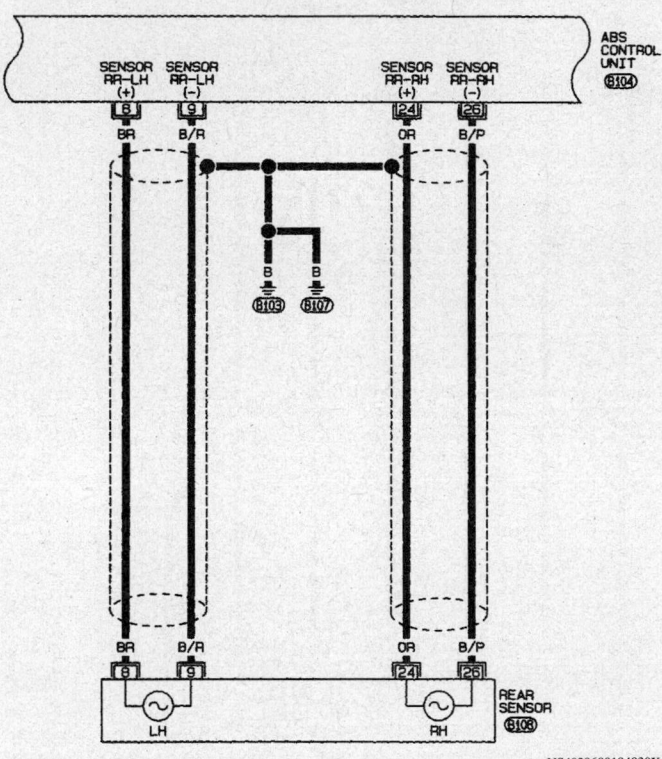

Fig. 42   ABS wiring circuit (Part 3 of 5). 300ZX

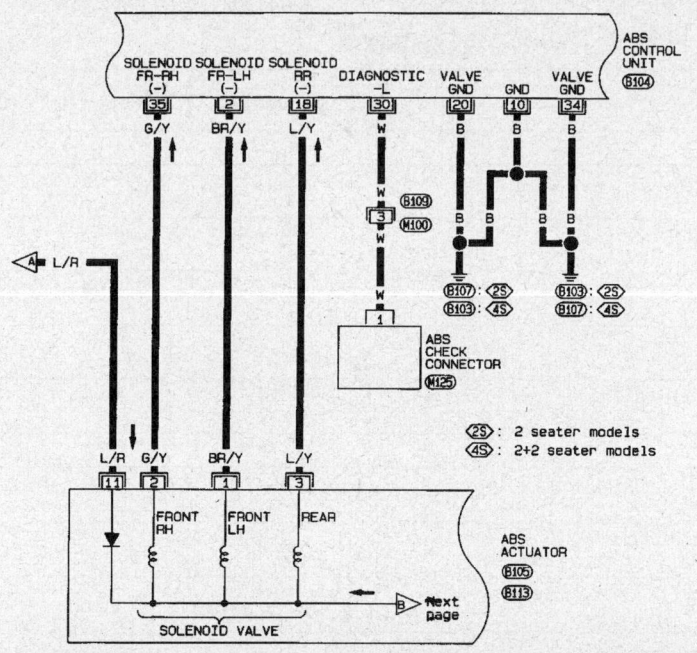

Fig. 42   ABS wiring circuit (Part 4 of 5). 300ZX

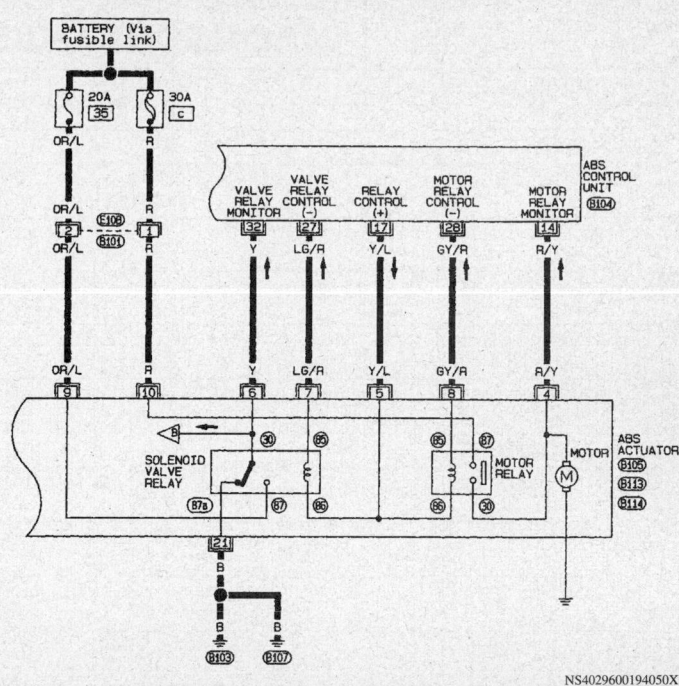

Fig. 42   ABS wiring circuit (Part 5 of 5). 300ZX

DIAGNOSTIC CHART INDEX

Test/Diagnostic Procedure	Description	Page No.	Fig. No.
1996–97 ALTIMA			
Test 1	Warning Lamp Does Not Work When Ignition Switch Is On	40-160	43
Test 2	Warning Lamp Stays On When Ignition Switch Is On	40-160	44
Test 3	Actuator Solenoid Valve	40-161	45
Test 4	Wheel Sensor Or Rotor	40-161	46
Test 5	Motor Relay Or Motor	40-162	47
Test 6	Solenoid Valve Relay	40-163	48
Test 7	Power Supply Low Voltage	40-163	49
Test 8	Stop Lamp Switch Circuit	40-163	50
Test 9	Control Unit	40-163	51
Test 10	Pedal Vibration & Noise	40-164	52
Test 11	Long Stopping Distance	40-164	53
Test 12	Unexpected Pedal Action	40-164	54
Test 13	ABS Does Not Work	40-164	55
Test 14	ABS Works Frequently	40-164	56
1998–99 ALTIMA			
Diagnostic Procedure 1	ABS Actuator Solenoid Valve	40-164	57
Diagnostic Procedure 2	Wheel Sensor Or Rotor	40-165	58
Diagnostic Procedure 3	Motor Relay Or Motor	40-165	59
Diagnostic Procedure 4	Solenoid Valve relay	40-166	60
Diagnostic Procedure 5	Low Voltage	40-167	61
Diagnostic Procedure 6	Control Unit	40-167	62
Diagnostic Procedure 7	ABS Works Frequently	40-167	63

Continued

DIAGNOSTIC CHART INDEX—Continued

Test/Diagnostic Procedure	Description	Page No.	Fig. No.
1998–99 ALTIMA			
Diagnostic Procedure 8	Unexpected Pedal Action	40-168	64
Diagnostic Procedure 9	Long Stopping Distance	40-168	65
Diagnostic Procedure 10	ABS Inoperative	40-168	66
Diagnostic Procedure 11	Pedal Vibration & Noise	40-168	67
Diagnostic Procedure 12	ABS Lamp Does Not Illuminate w/Key On	40-168	68
2WD FRONTIER			
Diagnostic Procedure 1	ABS Actuator Solenoid Short Circuit Or Open	40-170	70
Diagnostic Procedure 2	ABS Actuator ISO Solenoid Blocked	40-170	71
Diagnostic Procedure 3	ABS Actuator Dump Solenoid Short Circuit Or Open	40-170	72
Diagnostic Procedure 4	Rear Sensor Open Or Short Circuit	40-170	73
Diagnostic Procedure 5	Sensor Signal Erratic	40-170	74
Diagnostic Procedure 6	ABS Control Unit	40-171	75
Diagnostic Procedure 7	Warning Lamp Flashing	40-171	76
Diagnostic Procedure 8	ABS Works Frequently	40-171	77
Diagnostic Procedure 9	Brake Pedal Stroke Is Large	40-171	78
Diagnostic Procedure 10	Long Stopping Distance	40-171	79
Diagnostic Procedure 11	ABS Inoperative	40-171	80
Diagnostic Procedure 12	Pedal Vibration Or Noise	40-172	81
4WD FRONTIER			
Diagnostic Procedure 1	Wheel Sensor Or Rotor	40-172	82
Diagnostic Procedure 2	ABS Actuator Solenoid Valve Or relay	40-172	83
Diagnostic Procedure 3	Motor Relay Or Motor	40-173	84
Diagnostic Procedure 4	Low Voltage	40-173	85
Diagnostic Procedure 5	G Sensor	40-174	86
Diagnostic Procedure 6	Control Unit	40-174	87
Diagnostic Procedure 7	ABS Works Frequently	40-174	88
Diagnostic Procedure 8	Unexpected Pedal Action	40-174	89
Diagnostic Procedure 9	Long Stopping Distance	40-175	90
Diagnostic Procedure 10	ABS Does Not Work	40-175	91
Diagnostic Procedure 11	Pedal Vibration & Noise	40-175	92
Diagnostic Procedure 12	Warning Lamp Does Not Illuminate w/Key On	40-175	93

Continued

DIAGNOSTIC CHART INDEX—Continued

Continued

DIAGNOSTIC CHART INDEX—Continued

Test/Diagnostic Procedure	Description	Page No.	Fig. No.
1997-98 240SX			
Test 11	Pedal Vibration & Noise	40-193	144
Test 12	Warning Lamp Does Not Come On When Ignition Switch Is Turned On	40-194	145
Test 13	Warning Lamp Stays On When Ignition Switch Is Turned On	40-194	146
300ZX			
Test 1	Warning Lamp Does Not Work Before Engine Starts	40-195	147
Test 2	Warning Lamp Stays On Continuously	40-195	148
Test 3	Actuator Solenoid Valve	40-196	149
Test 4	Wheel Sensor Or Rotor	40-196	150
Test 5	Motor Relay Or Motor	40-197	151
Test 6	Solenoid Valve Relay	40-197	152
Test 7	Power Supply Low Voltage	40-198	153
Test 8	Stop Lamp Switch Circuit	40-198	154
Test 9	Control Unit	40-198	155
1996 SENTRA & 200SX			
Test 1	Warning Lamp Does Not Come On When Ignition Switch Is Turned On	40-198	156
Test 2	Warning Light Stays On When Ignition Switch Is Turned On	40-199	157
Test 3	ABS Actuator Solenoid Valve	40-199	158
Test 4	Wheel Sensor Or Rotor	40-200	159
Test 5	Motor Relay Or Motor	40-200	160
Test 6	Solenoid Valve Relay	40-201	161
Test 7	Power Supply Low Voltage	40-202	162
Test 8	Control Unit	40-202	163
Test 9	Pedal Vibration & Noise	40-202	164
Test 10	Long Stopping Distance	40-202	165
Test 11	Unexpected Pedal Action	40-202	166
Test 12	ABS Does Not Work	40-203	167
Test 13	ABS Works Frequently	40-203	168
1997-99 SENTRA & 200SX			
Test 1	ABS Actuator Solenoid Valve	40-203	169
Test 2	Wheel Sensor Or Rotor	40-204	170
Test 3	Motor Relay or Motor	40-204	171
Test 4	Solenoid Valve Relay	40-205	172
Test 5	Low Voltage	40-205	173
Test 6	Control Unit	40-206	174
Test 7	Warning Lamp Does Not Come On	40-206	175
Test 8	Warning Lamp Stays On	40-206	176
Test 9	Pedal Vibration & Noise	40-207	177
Test 10	Long Stopping Distance	40-207	178
Test 11	Unexpected Pedal Action	40-207	179
Test 12	ABS Does Not Work	40-207	180
Test 13	ABS Works Frequently	40-208	181
1996 PATHFINDER			
Test 1	Warning Lamp Does Not Work When Ignition Is On	40-209	195
Test 2	Warning Lamp Stays On When Ignition Switch Is On	40-210	196
Test 3	ABS Control Actuator Solenoid Valve	40-210	197
Test 4	Wheel Sensor Or Rotor	40-211	198
Test 5	Motor Relay Or Motor	40-211	199
Test 6	Solenoid Valve Relay	40-212	200
Test 7	Power Supply Low Voltage	40-212	201
Test 8	G Sensor	40-213	202
Test 9	Control Unit	40-213	203
Test 10	Pedal Vibration & Noise	40-213	204
Test 11	Long Stopping Distance	40-213	205
Test 12	Unexpected Pedal Action	40-213	206

Continued

DIAGNOSTIC CHART INDEX—Continued

Test/Diagnostic Procedure	Description	Page No.	Fig. No.
1996 PATHFINDER			
Test 13	ABS Does Not Work	40-214	207
Test 14	ABS Works Frequently	40-214	208
1997-99 PATHFINDER			
Test 1	Wheel Sensor or Rotor	40-214	209
Test 2	ABS Actuator Solenoid Valve	40-215	210
Test 3	Solenoid Valve Relay	40-215	211
Test 4	Motor Relay or Motor	40-216	212
Test 5	Low Voltage	40-217	213
Test 6	G Sensor	40-217	214
Test 7	Control Unit	40-217	215
Test 8	ABS Works Frequently	40-217	216
Test 9	Unexpected Pedal Action	40-217	217
Test 10	Long Stopping Distance	40-218	218
Test 11	ABS Does Not Work	40-218	219
Test 12	Pedal Vibration & Noise	40-218	220
Test 13	Warning Lamp Does Not Come On When Ignition Is Turned On	40-218	221
Test 14	Warning Lamp Stays On When Ignition Switch Is Turned On	40-219	222
PICKUP			
Test 1	Pedal Vibration Or Noise	40-208	182
Test 2	Long Stopping Distance	40-208	183
Test 3	Brake Pedal Stroke Is Abnormally Large	40-208	184
Test 4	ABS Doesn't Work	40-208	185
Test 5	ABS Works Frequently	40-208	186
Test 6	Main Power Supply & Ground circuit	40-208	187
Test 7	Actuator ISO Solenoid Short Circuit Or Open	40-208	188
Test 8	Actuator ISO Solenoid Blocked	40-208	189
Test 9	Actuator Dump Solenoid Short Circuit	40-209	190
Test 10	Sensor Open Or Short Circuit	40-209	191
Test 11	Sensor Signal Erratic	40-209	192
Test 12	Control Unit	40-209	193
Test 13	Other Problems	40-209	194
1996–98 QUEST			
Test 1	Warning Lamp Does Not Work When Ignition Is On	40-220	223
Test 2	Warning Lamp Stays On When Ignition Switch Is On	40-220	224
Test 3	ABS Control Actuator Solenoid Valve	40-221	225
Test 4	Wheel Sensor Or Rotor	40-221	226
Test 5	Motor Relay Or Motor	40-222	227
Test 6	Solenoid Valve Relay	40-222	228
Test 7	Control Unit	40-223	229
Test 8	Pedal Vibration & Noise	40-223	230
Test 9	Long Stopping Distance	40-223	231
Test 10	Unexpected Pedal Action	40-223	232
Test 11	ABS Does Not Work	40-224	233
Test 12	ABS Works Frequently	40-224	234
1999 QUEST			
Test 1	Wheel Sensor Or Rotor	40-224	235
Test 2	ABS Actuator Solenoid Valve Or Relay	40-225	236
Test 3	Motor Relay Or Motor	40-225	237
Test 4	Low Voltage	40-226	238
Test 5	Control Unit	40-226	239
Test 6	ABS Works Frequently	40-226	240
Test 7	Unexpected Pedal Action	40-227	241
Test 8	Long Stopping Distance	40-227	242
Test 9	ABS Inoperative	40-227	243

Continued

DIAGNOSTIC CHART INDEX—Continued

Test/Diagnostic Procedure	Description	Page No.	Fig. No.
1999 QUEST			
Test 10	Pedal Vibration & Noise	40-227	244
Test 11	Warning Lamp Does Not Illuminate w/Key On	40-227	245
Test 12	Warning Lamp Remains Illuminated w/Key On	40-227	246

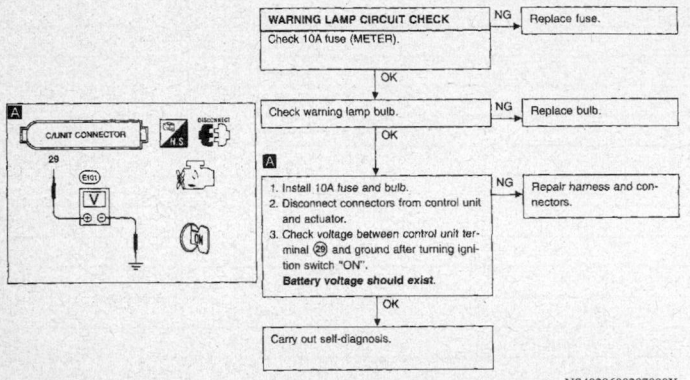

NS4029600207000X

Fig. 43   Test 1: Warning Lamp Does Not Work When Ignition Switch Is On. 1996–97 Altima

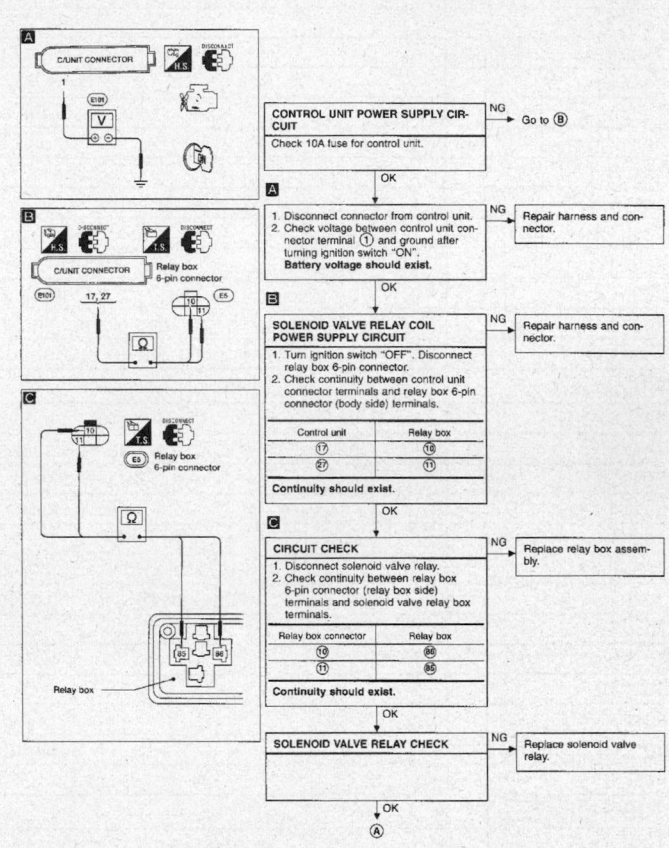

NS4029600208010X

Fig. 44   Test 2: Warning Lamp Stays On When Ignition Switch Is On (Part 1 of 3). 1996–97 Altima

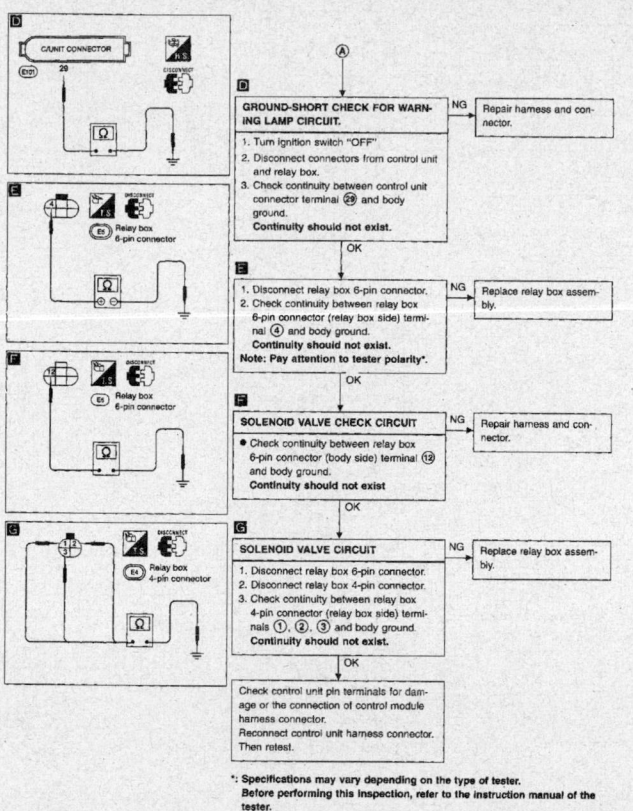

Fig. 44 Test 2: Warning Lamp Stays On When Ignition Switch Is On (Part 2 of 3). 1996–97 Altima

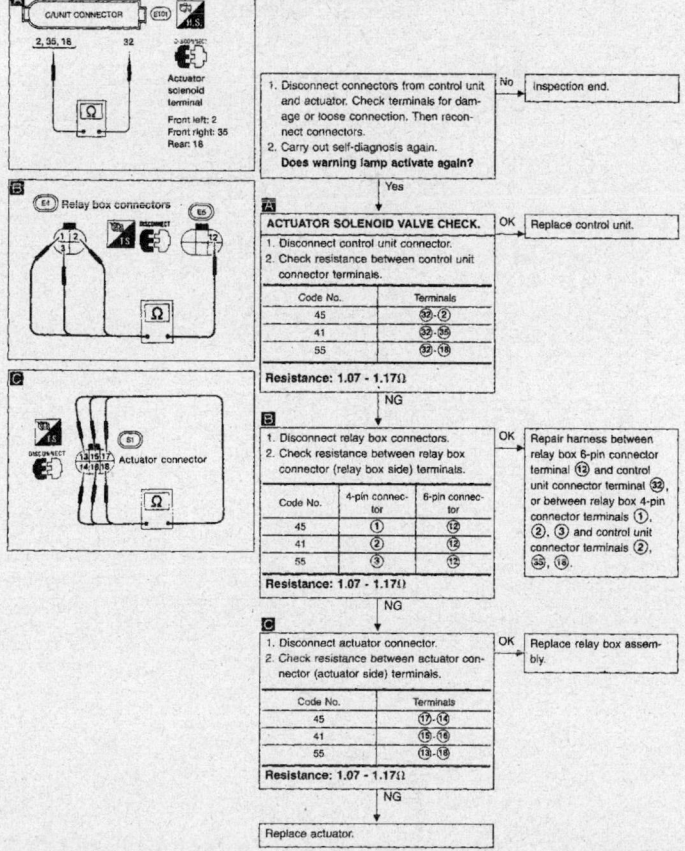

Fig. 45 Test 3: Actuator Solenoid Valve. 1996–97 Altima

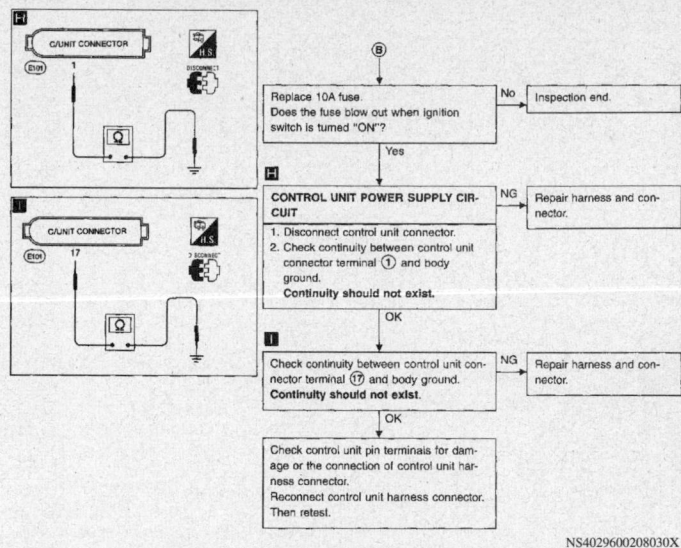

Fig. 44 Test 2: Warning Lamp Stays On When Ignition Switch Is On (Part 3 of 3). 1996–97 Altima

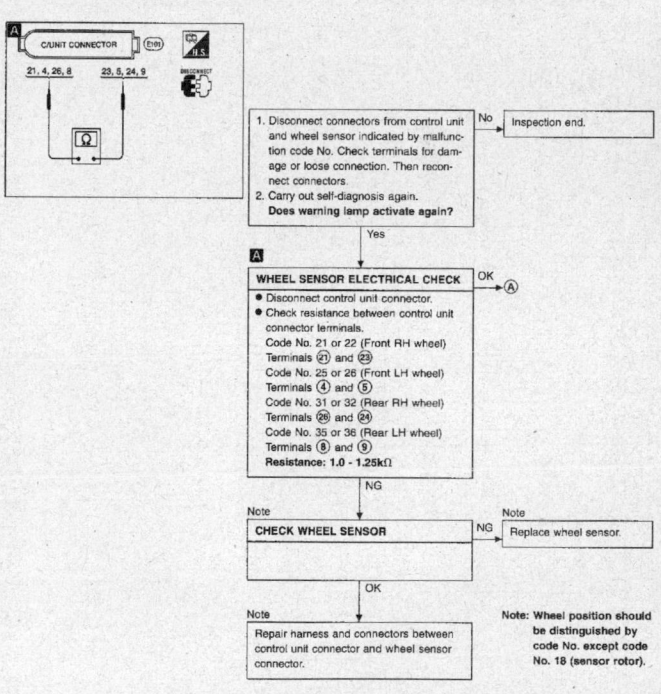

Fig. 46 Test 4: Wheel Sensor Or Rotor (Part 1 of 2). 1996–97 Altima

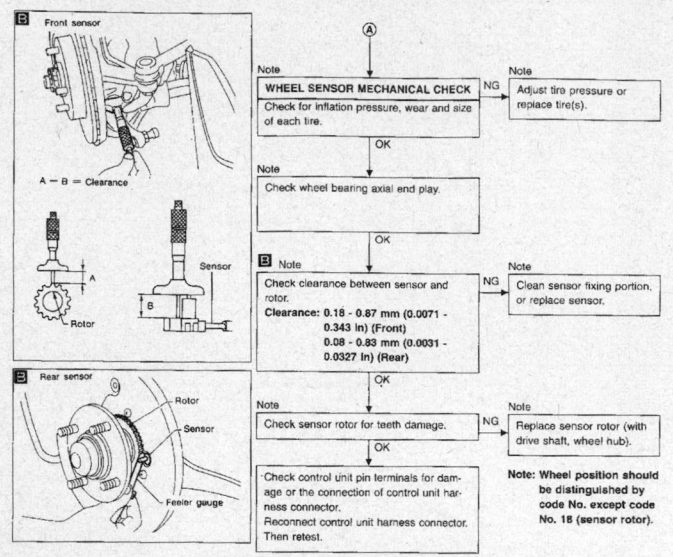

Fig. 46   Test 4: Wheel Sensor Or Rotor (Part 2 of 2). 1996–97 Altima

NS4029600210020X

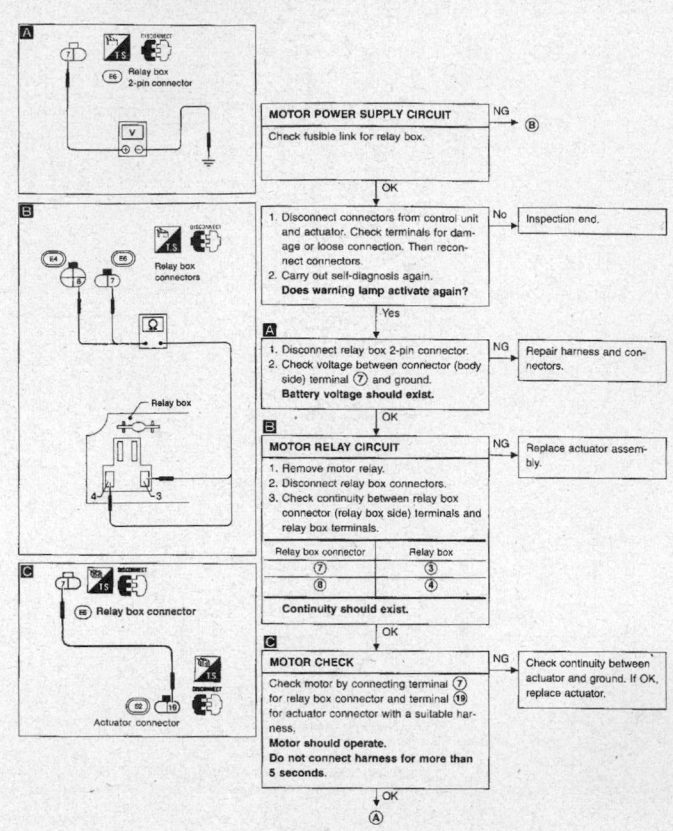

NS4029600211010X

Fig. 47   Test 5: Motor Relay Or Motor (Part 1 of 3). 1996–97 Altima

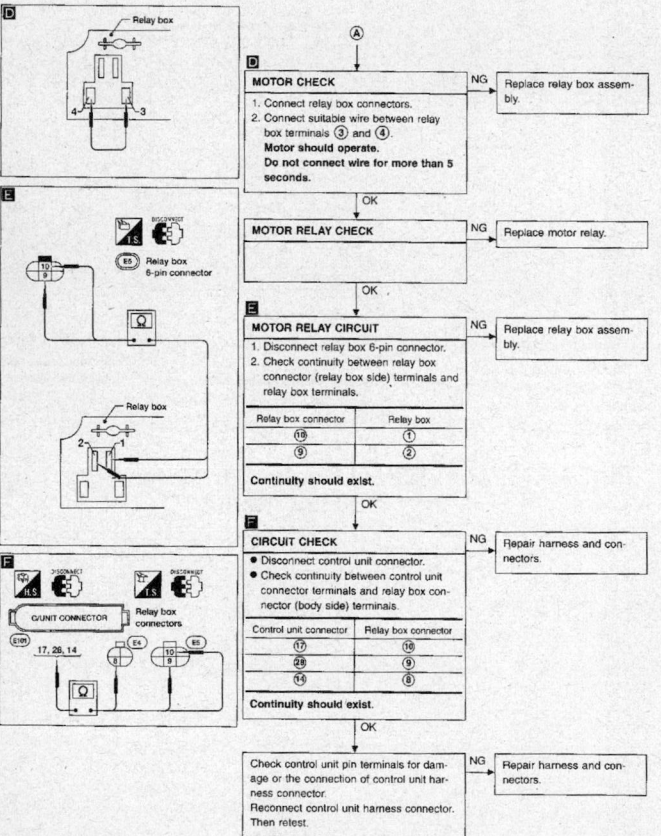

NS4029600211020X

Fig. 47   Test 5: Motor Relay Or Motor (Part 2 of 3). 1996–97 Altima

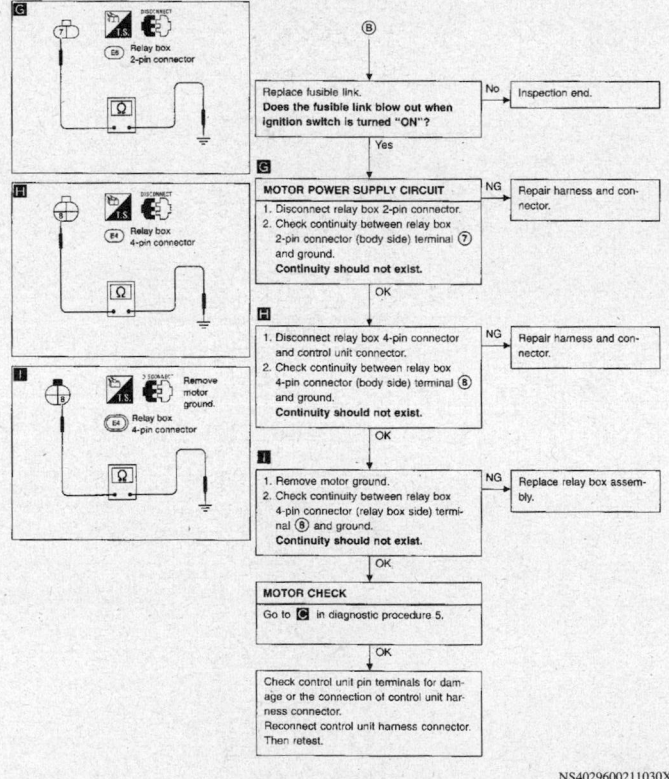

NS4029600211030X

Fig. 47   Test 5: Motor Relay Or Motor (Part 3 of 3). 1996–97 Altima

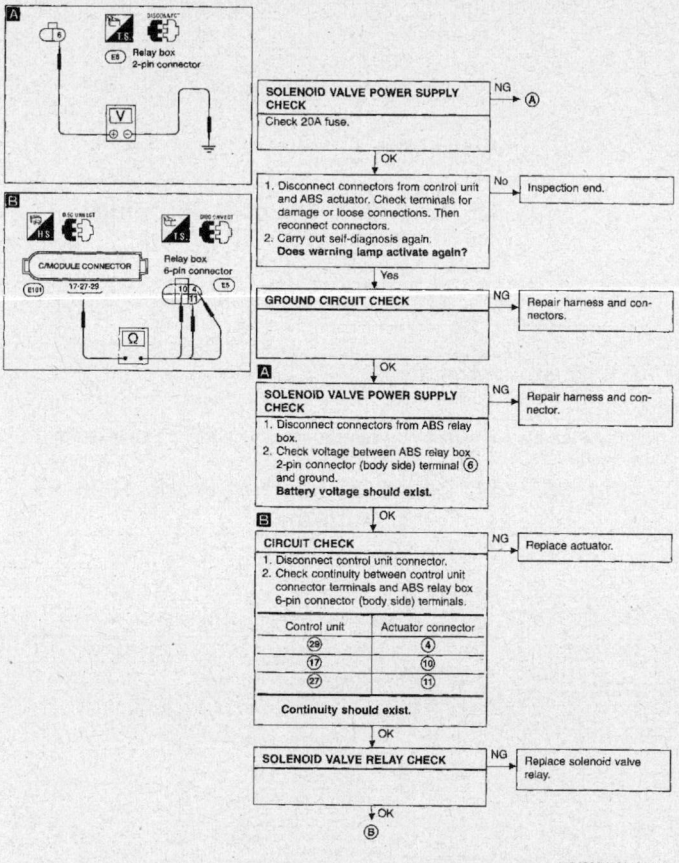

Fig. 48   Test 6: Solenoid Valve Relay (Part 1 of 2). 1996–97 Altima

NS4029600212010X

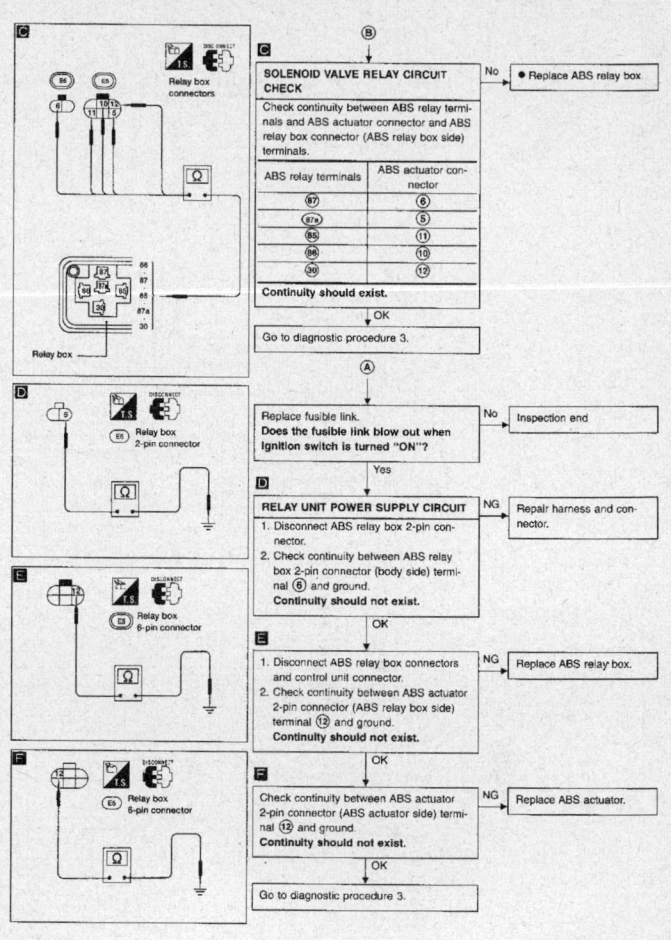

NS4029600212020X

Fig. 48   Test 6: Solenoid Valve Relay (Part 2 of 2). 1996–97 Altima

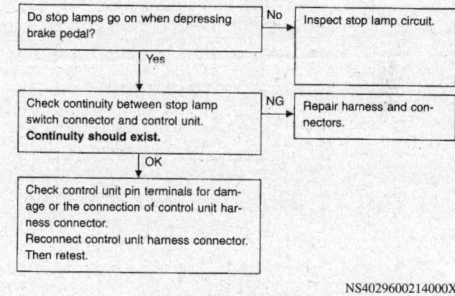

NS4029600214000X

Fig. 50   Test 8: Stop Lamp Switch Circuit. 1996–97 Altima

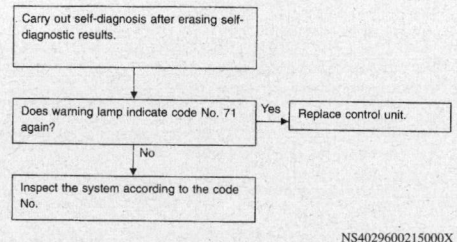

NS4029600215000X

Fig. 51   Test 9: Control Unit. 1996–97 Altima

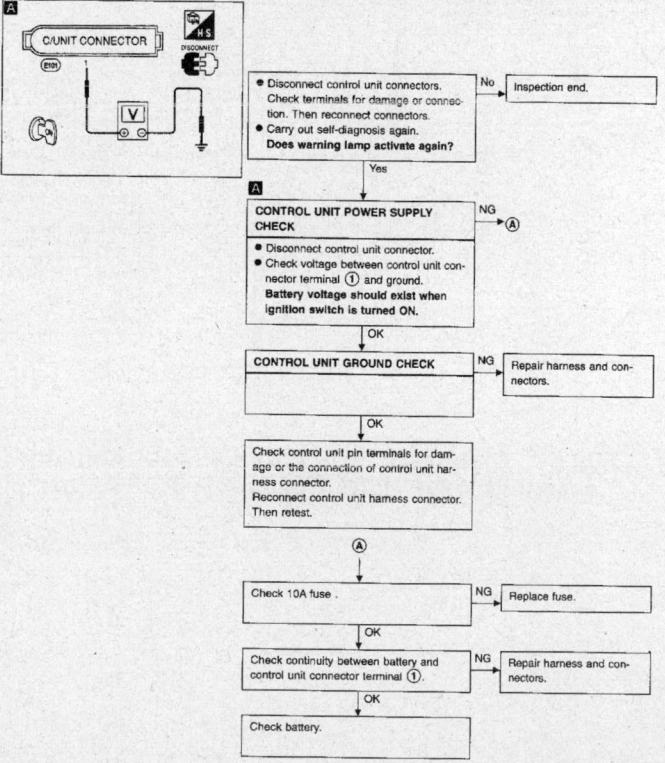

NS4029600213000X

Fig. 49   Test 7: Power Supply Low Voltage. 1996–97 Altima

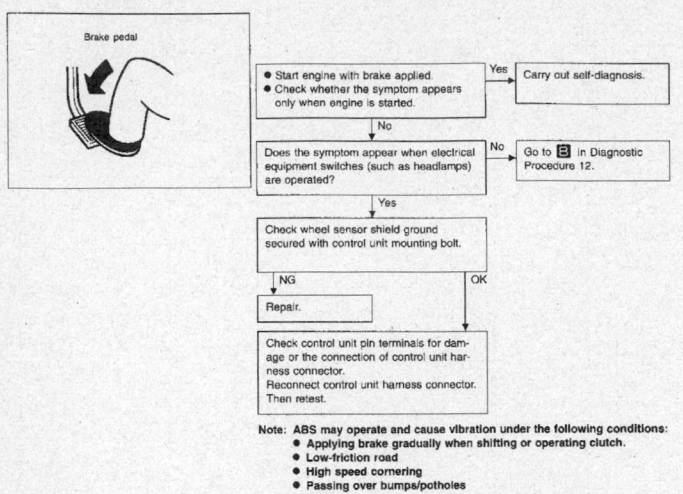

Fig. 52 Test 10: Pedal Vibration & Noise. 1996–97 Altima

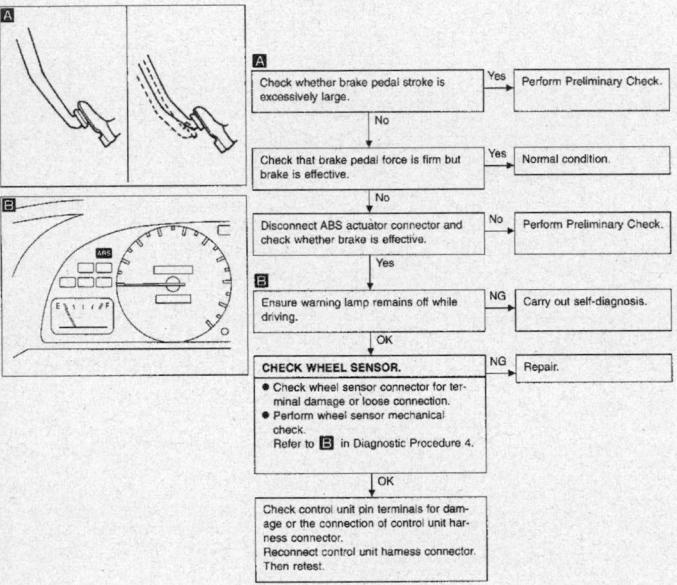

Fig. 54 Test 12: Unexpected Pedal Action. 1996–97 Altima

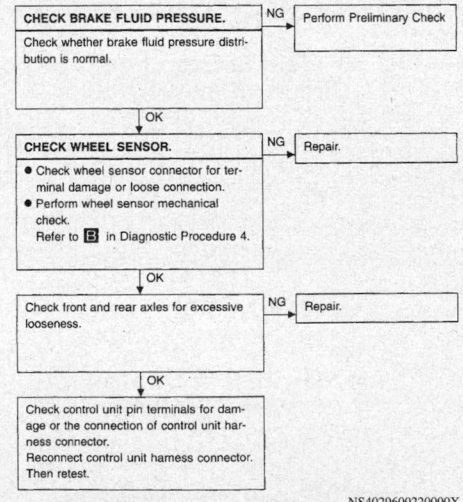

Fig. 56 Test 14: ABS Works Frequently. 1996–97 Altima

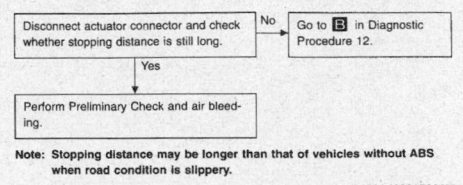

Note: Stopping distance may be longer than that of vehicles without ABS when road condition is slippery.

NS4029600217000X

Fig. 53 Test 11: Long Stopping Distance. 1996–97 Altima

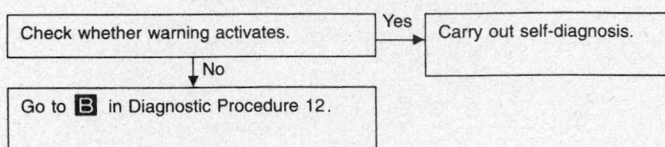

Note: ABS does not work when vehicle speed is under 10 km/h (6 MPH).

NS4029600219000X

Fig. 55 Test 13: ABS Does Not Work. 1996–97 Altima

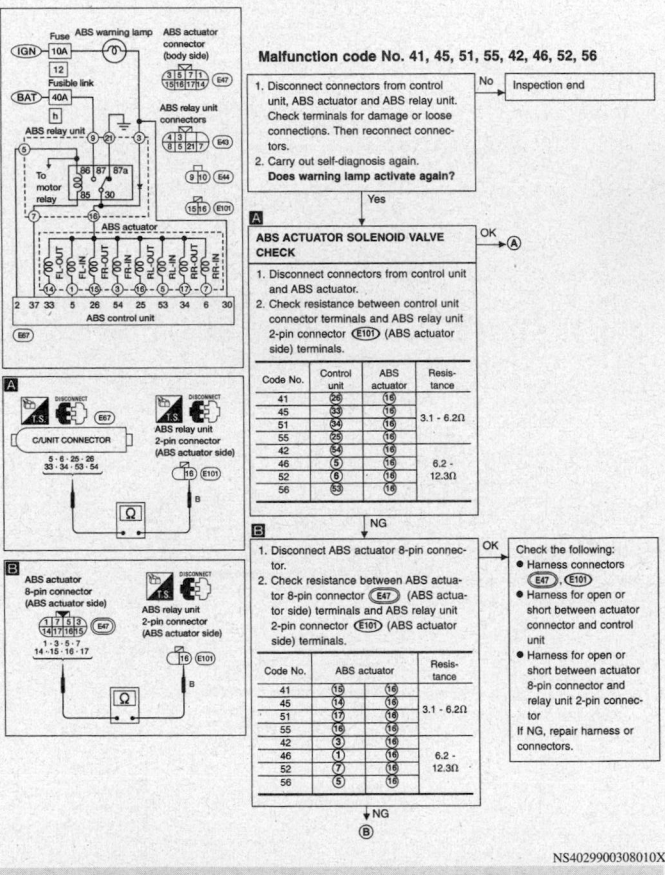

NS4029900308010X

Fig. 57 Diagnostic Procedure 1: ABS Actuator Solenoid Valve (Part 1 of 2). 1998–99 Altima

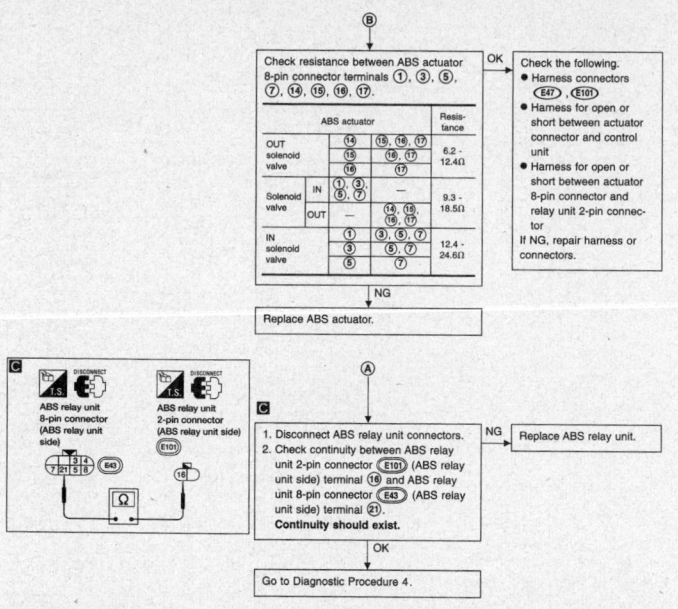

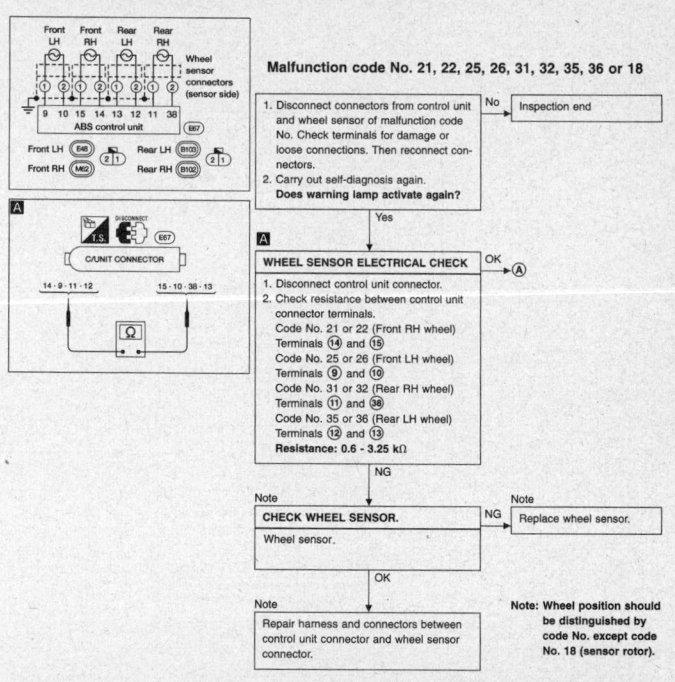

Fig. 57 Diagnostic Procedure 1: ABS Actuator Solenoid Valve (Part 2 of 2). 1998–99 Altima

NS4029900308020X

Fig. 58 Diagnostic Procedure 2: Wheel Sensor Or Rotor (Part 1 of 2). 1998–99 Altima

NS4029900309010X

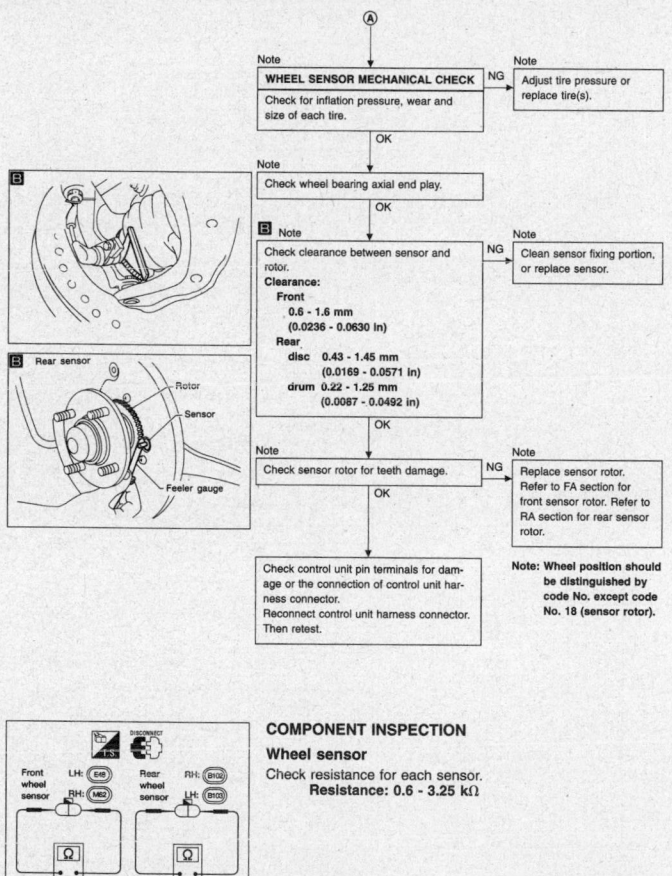

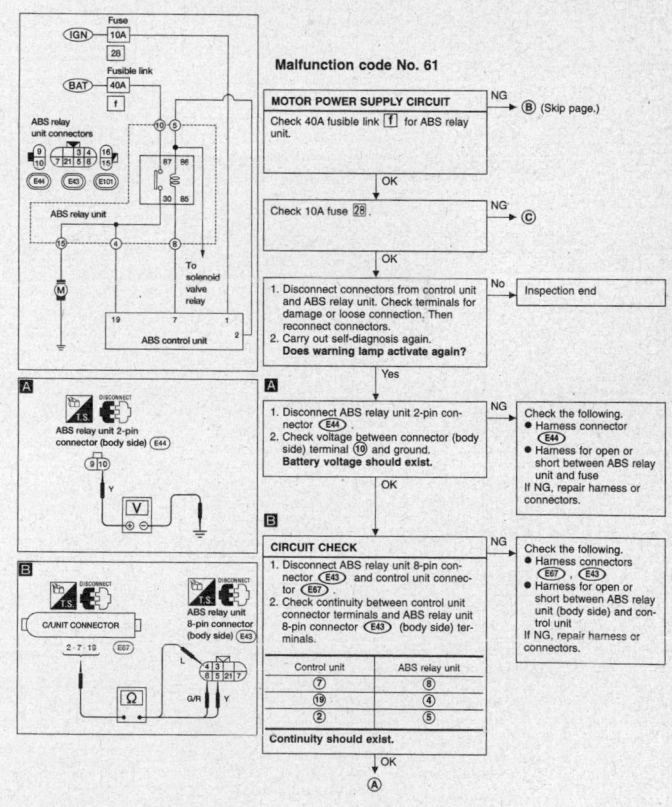

Fig. 58 Diagnostic Procedure 2: Wheel Sensor Or Rotor (Part 2 of 2). 1998–99 Altima

NS4029900309020X

Fig. 59 Diagnostic Procedure 3: Motor Relay Or Motor (Part 1 of 3). 1998–99 Altima

NS4029900310010X

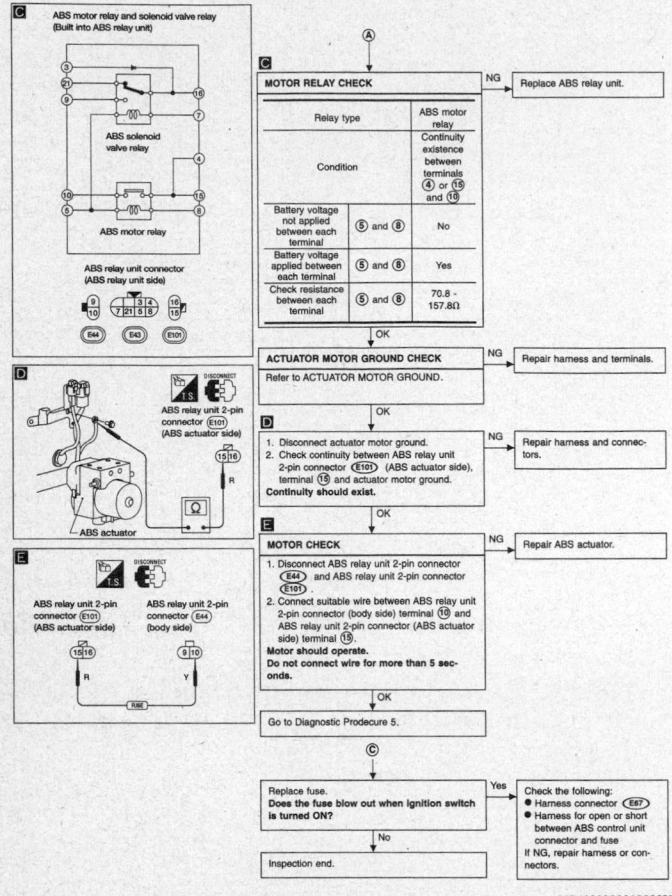

Fig. 59 Diagnostic Procedure 3: Motor Relay Or Motor (Part 2 of 3). 1998–99 Altima

NS4029900310020X

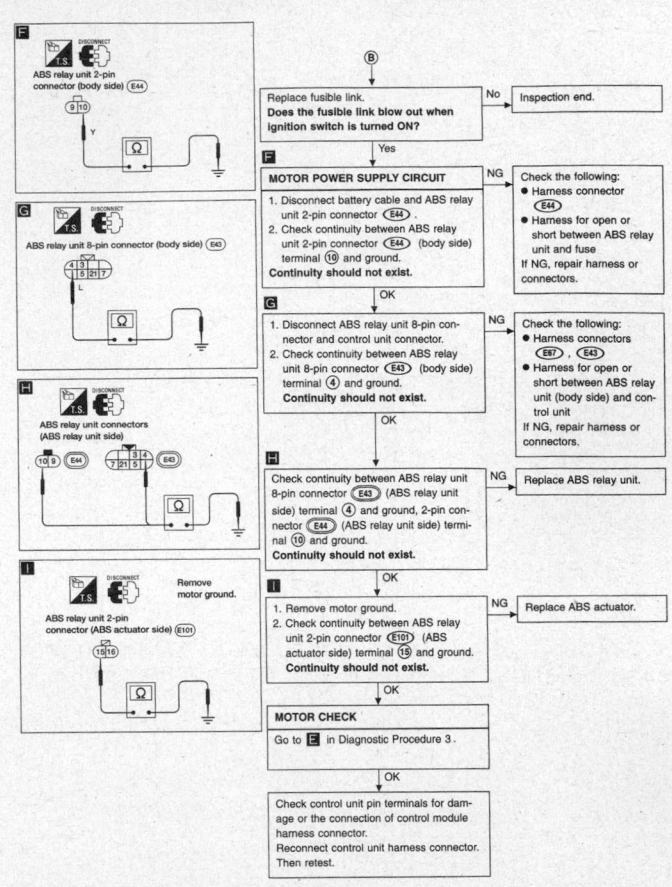

Fig. 59 Diagnostic Procedure 3: Motor Relay Or Motor (Part 3 of 3). 1998–99 Altima

NS4029900310030X

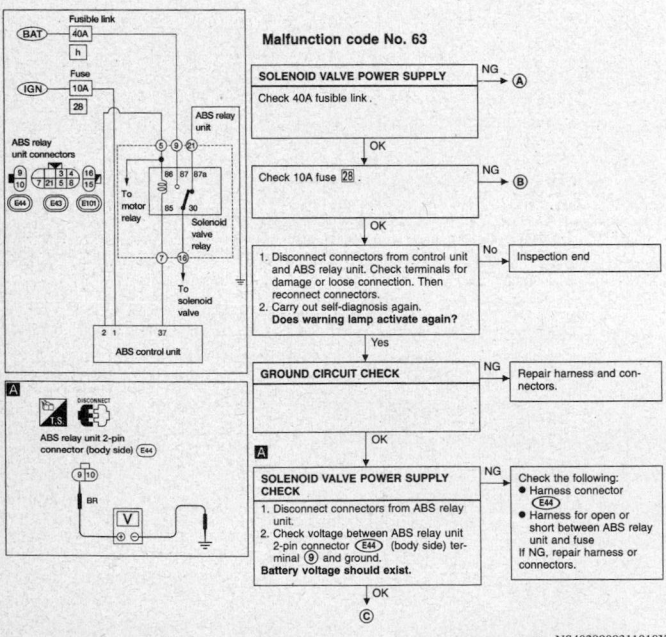

Fig. 60 Diagnostic Procedure 4: Solenoid Valve Relay (Part 1 of 3). 1998–99 Altima

NS4029900311010X

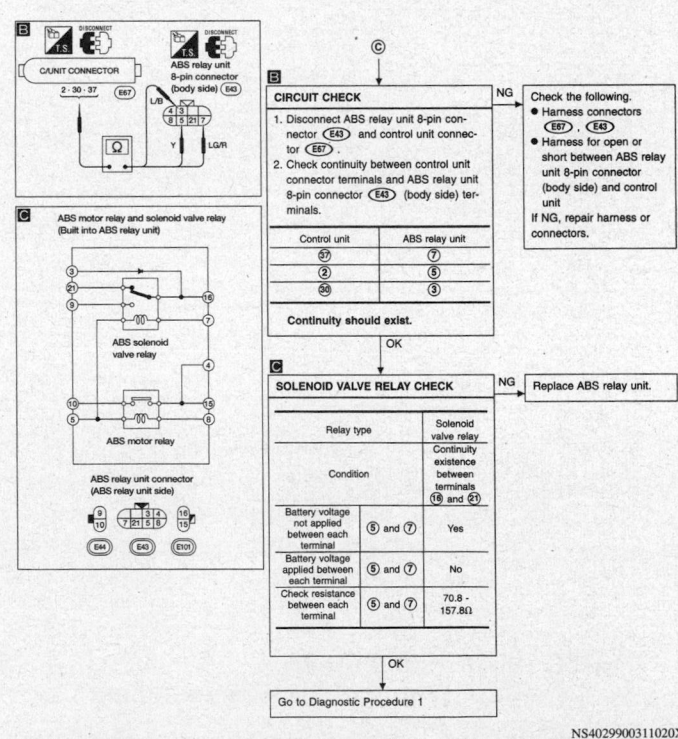

NS4029900311020X

Fig. 60 Diagnostic Procedure 4: Solenoid Valve Relay (Part 2 of 3). 1998–99 Altima

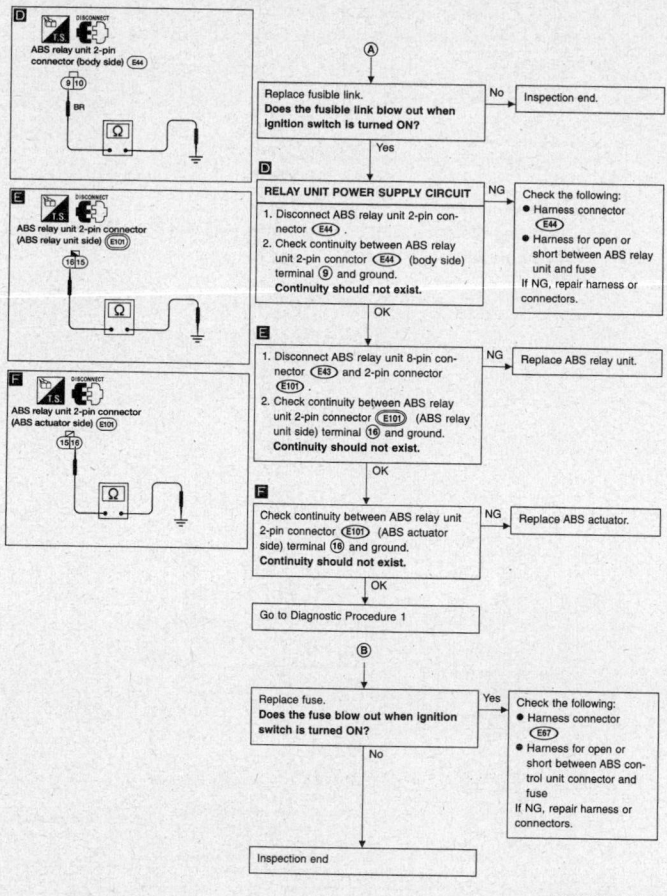

Fig. 60   Diagnostic Procedure 4: Solenoid Valve Relay (Part 3 of 3). 1998–99 Altima

NS4029900311030X

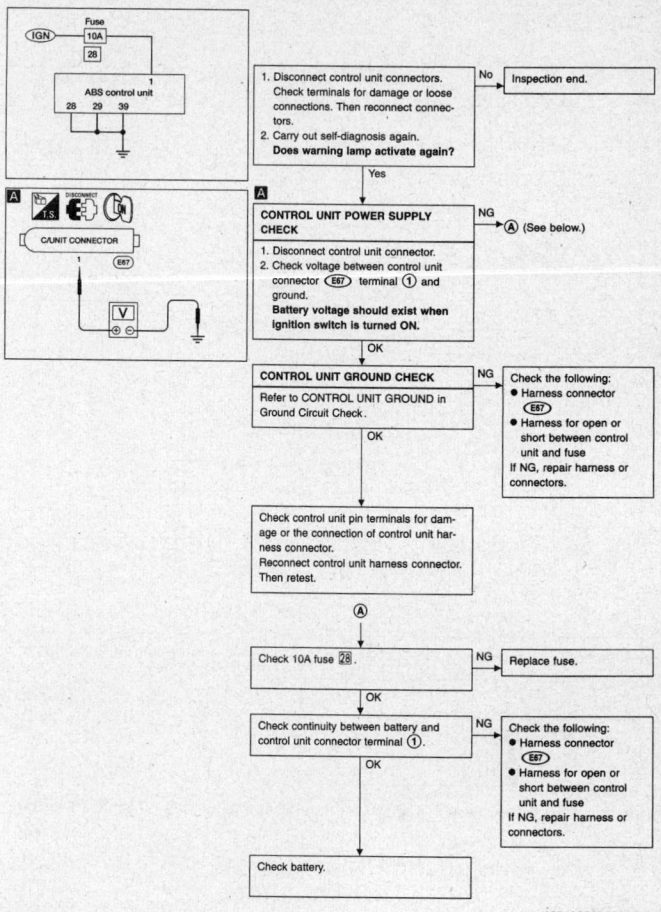

Fig. 61   Diagnostic Procedure 5: Low Voltage. 1998–99 Altima

NS4029900312000X

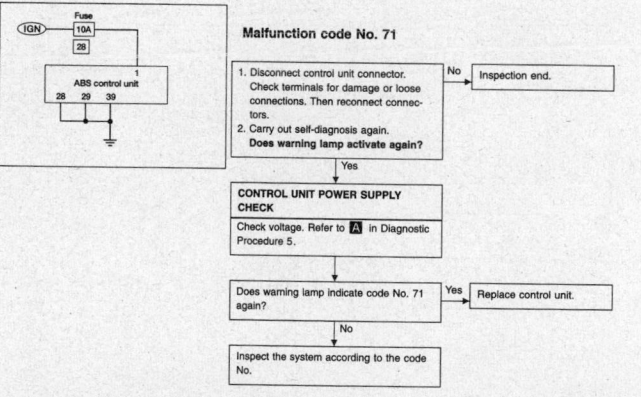

Fig. 62   Diagnostic Procedure 6: Control Unit. 1998–99 Altima

NS4029900313000X

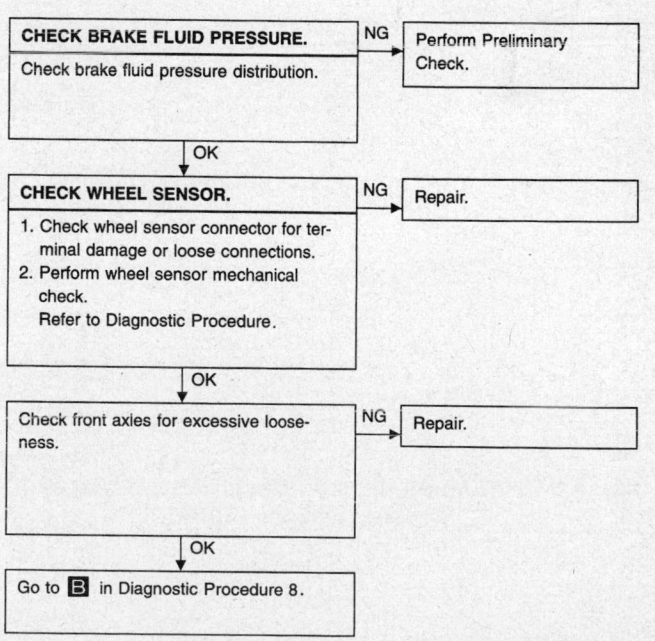

Fig. 63   Diagnostic Procedure 7: ABS Works Frequently. 1998–99 Altima

NS4029900314000X

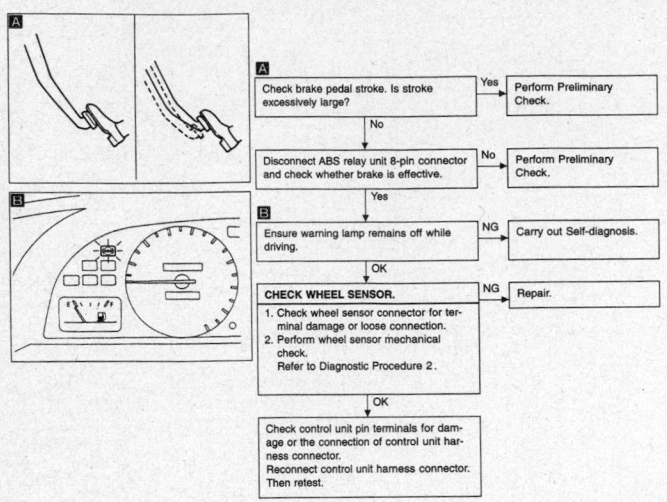

Fig. 64 Diagnostic Procedure 8: Unexpected Pedal Action. 1998–99 Altima

NS4029900315000X

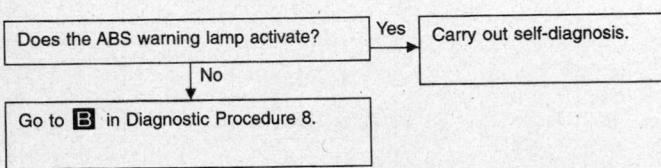

Note: ABS does not work when vehicle speed is under 10 km/h (6 MPH).

NS4029900317000X

Fig. 66 Diagnostic Procedure 10: ABS Inoperative. 1998–99 Altima

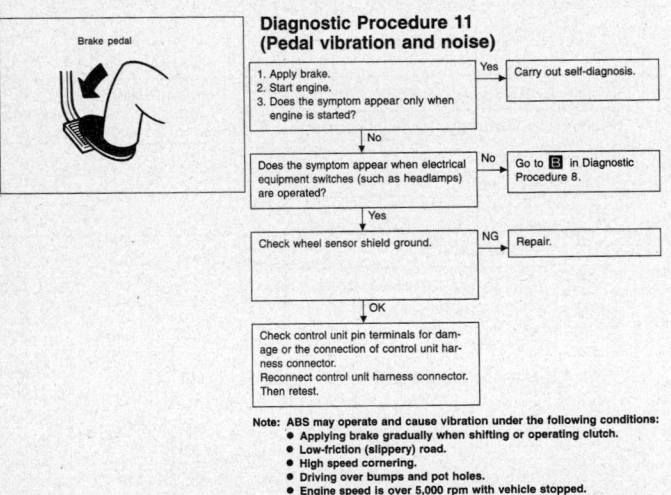

NS4029900318000X

Fig. 67 Diagnostic Procedure 11: Pedal Vibration & Noise. 1998–99 Altima

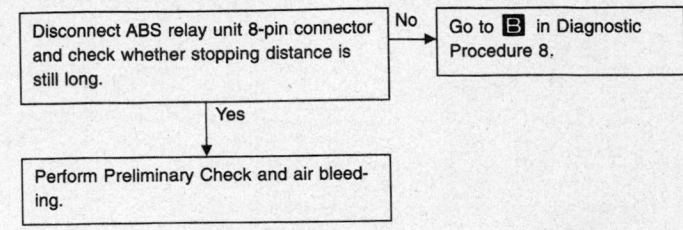

NS4029900316000X

Fig. 65 Diagnostic Procedure 9: Long Stopping Distance. 1998–99 Altima

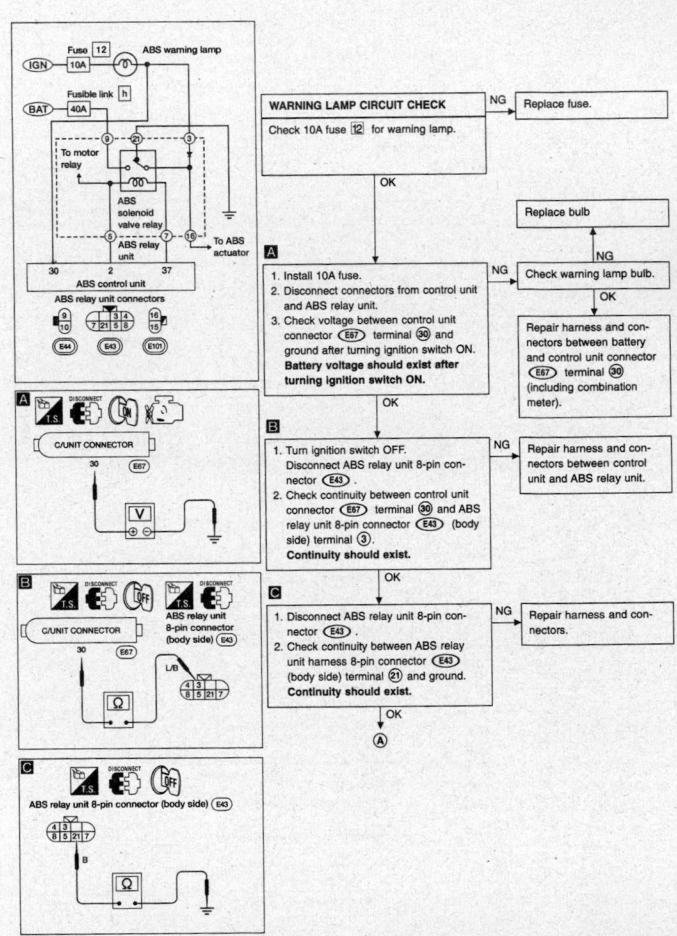

NS4029900319010X

Fig. 68 Diagnostic Procedure 12: ABS Lamp Does Not Illuminate w/Key On (Part 1 of 2). 1998–99 Altima

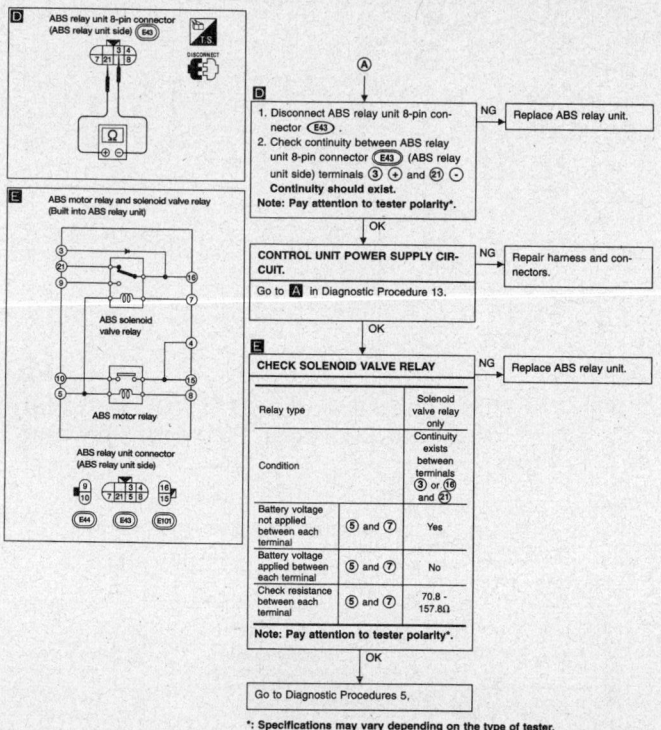

1. Disconnect ABS relay unit 8-pin connector E43.
2. Check continuity between ABS relay unit 8-pin connector E43 (ABS relay side) terminals ③ (+) and ㉑ (-)
Continuity should exist.
Note: Pay attention to tester polarity*.

NG → Replace ABS relay unit.

D

CONTROL UNIT POWER SUPPLY CIRCUIT.
Go to A in Diagnostic Procedure 13.

NG → Repair harness and connectors.

OK

E

CHECK SOLENOID VALVE RELAY

NG → Replace ABS relay unit.

Relay type		Solenoid valve relay only
Condition		Continuity exists between terminals ③ or ⑯ and ㉑
Battery voltage not applied between each terminal	⑤ and ⑦	Yes
Battery voltage applied between each terminal	⑤ and ⑦	No
Check resistance between each terminal	⑤ and ⑦	70.8 - 157.8Ω

Note: Pay attention to tester polarity*.

OK

Go to Diagnostic Procedures 5.

*: Specifications may vary depending on the type of tester. Before performing this inspection, refer to the instruction manual of the tester.

NS4029900319020X

Fig. 68 Diagnostic Procedure 12: ABS Lamp Does Not Illuminate w/Key On (Part 2 of 2). 1998–99 Altima

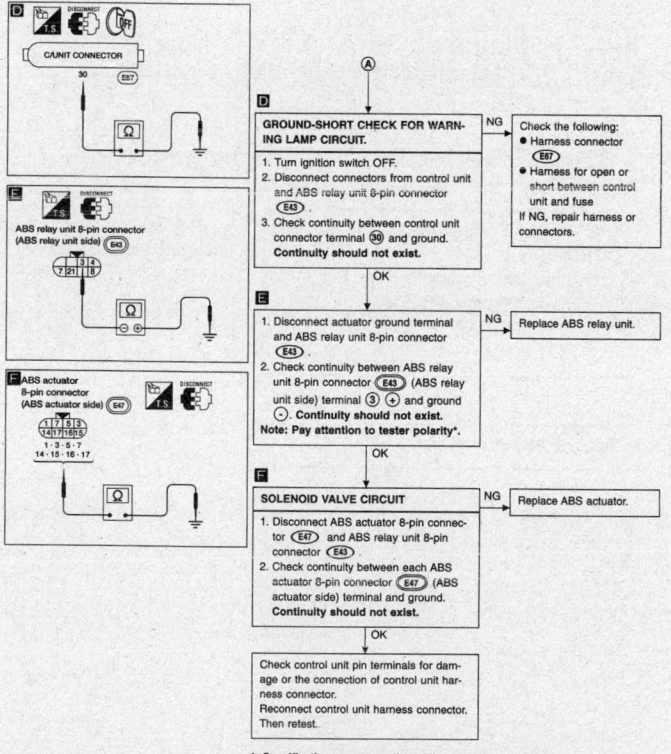

D

GROUND-SHORT CHECK FOR WARNING LAMP CIRCUIT.
1. Turn ignition switch OFF.
2. Disconnect connectors from control unit and ABS relay unit 8-pin connector E43.
3. Check continuity between control unit connector terminal ㉚ and ground.
Continuity should not exist.

NG → Check the following:
● Harness connector E67
● Harness for open or short between control unit and fuse
If NG, repair harness or connectors.

OK

E

1. Disconnect actuator ground terminal and ABS relay unit 8-pin connector E43.
2. Check continuity between ABS relay unit 8-pin connector E43 (ABS relay unit side) terminal ③ (+) and ground (-). Continuity should not exist.
Note: Pay attention to tester polarity*.

NG → Replace ABS relay unit.

OK

F

SOLENOID VALVE CIRCUIT
1. Disconnect ABS actuator 8-pin connector E47 and ABS relay unit 8-pin connector E43.
2. Check continuity between each ABS actuator 8-pin connector E47 (ABS actuator side) terminal and ground. Continuity should not exist.

NG → Replace ABS actuator.

OK

Check control unit pin terminals for damage or the connection of control unit harness connector.
Reconnect control unit harness connector. Then retest.

*: Specifications may vary depending on the type of tester. Before performing this inspection, refer to the instruction manual of the tester.

NS4029900320020X

Fig. 69 Diagnostic Procedure 13: ABS Lamp Remains Illuminated w/Key On (Part 2 of 3). 1998–99 Altima

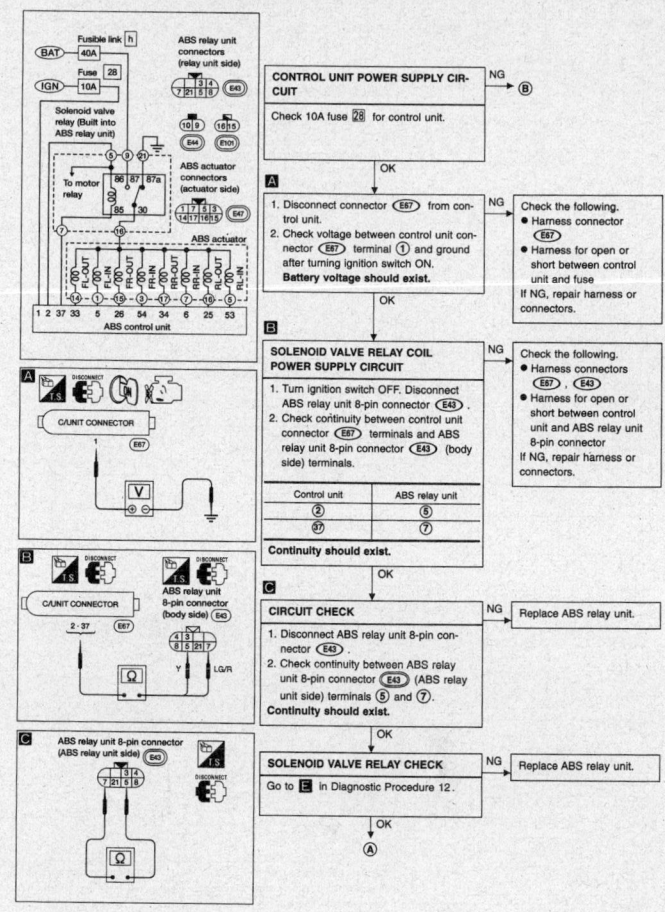

CONTROL UNIT POWER SUPPLY CIRCUIT
Check 10A fuse 28 for control unit.

NG → B

OK

A

1. Disconnect connector E67 from control unit.
2. Check voltage between control unit connector E67 terminal ① and ground after turning ignition switch ON.
Battery voltage should exist.

NG → Check the following.
● Harness connector E67
● Harness for open or short between control unit and fuse
If NG, repair harness or connectors.

OK

B

SOLENOID VALVE RELAY COIL POWER SUPPLY CIRCUIT
1. Turn ignition switch OFF. Disconnect ABS relay unit 8-pin connector E43.
2. Check continuity between control unit connector E67 terminals and ABS relay unit 8-pin connector E43 (body side) terminals.

NG → Check the following.
● Harness connectors E67, E43
● Harness for open or short between control unit and ABS relay unit 8-pin connector
If NG, repair harness or connectors.

Control unit	ABS relay unit
②	⑤
㊲	⑦

Continuity should exist.

OK

C

CIRCUIT CHECK
1. Disconnect ABS relay unit 8-pin connector E43.
2. Check continuity between ABS relay unit 8-pin connector E43 (ABS relay unit side) terminals ⑤ and ⑦.
Continuity should exist.

NG → Replace ABS relay unit.

OK

SOLENOID VALVE RELAY CHECK
Go to E in Diagnostic Procedure 12.

NG → Replace ABS relay unit.

OK

A

NS4029900320010X

Fig. 69 Diagnostic Procedure 13: ABS Lamp Remains Illuminated w/Key On (Part 1 of 3). 1998–99 Altima

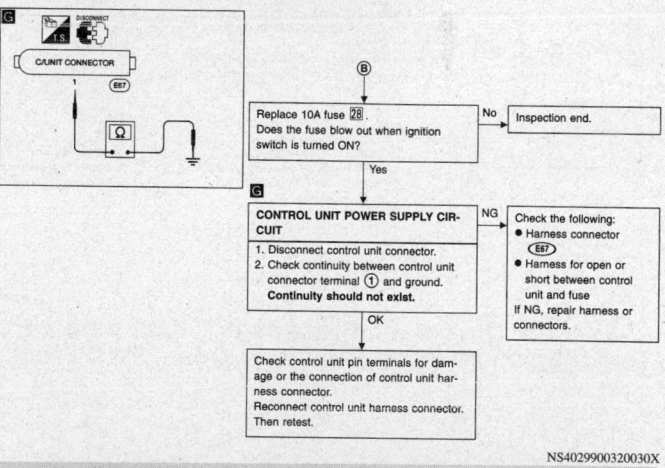

B

Replace 10A fuse 28.
Does the fuse blow out when ignition switch is turned ON?

No → Inspection end.

Yes

G

CONTROL UNIT POWER SUPPLY CIRCUIT
1. Disconnect control unit connector.
2. Check continuity between control unit connector terminal ① and ground.
Continuity should not exist.

NG → Check the following:
● Harness connector E67
● Harness for open or short between control unit and fuse
If NG, repair harness or connectors.

OK

Check control unit pin terminals for damage or the connection of control unit harness connector.
Reconnect control unit harness connector. Then retest.

NS4029900320030X

Fig. 69 Diagnostic Procedure 13: ABS Lamp Remains Illuminated w/Key On (Part 3 of 3). 1998–99 Altima

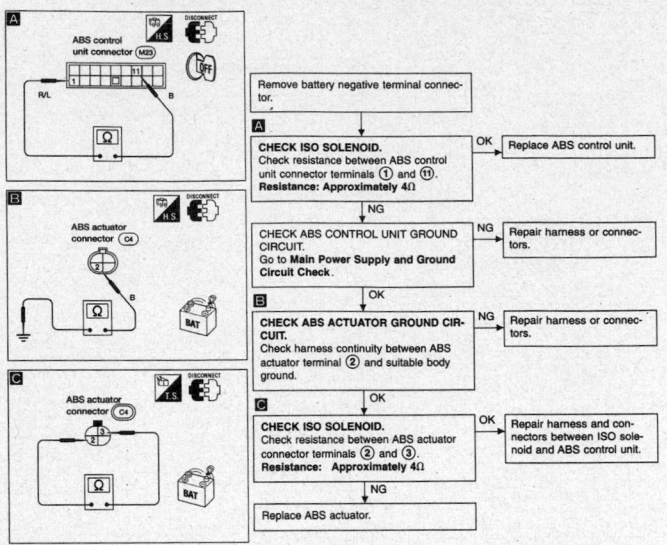

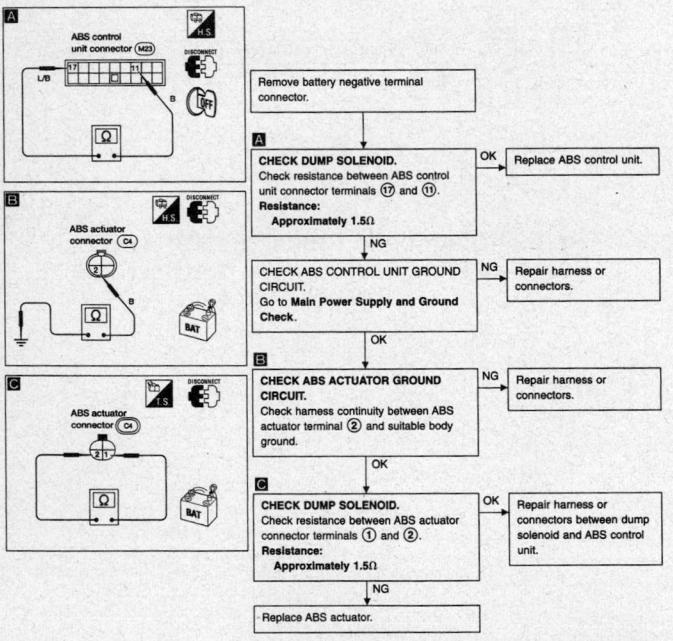

Fig. 70   Diagnostic Procedure 1: ABS Actuator Solenoid Short Circuit Or Open. 2WD Frontier

Fig. 72   Diagnostic Procedure 3: ABS Actuator Dump Solenoid Short Circuit Or Open. 2WD Frontier

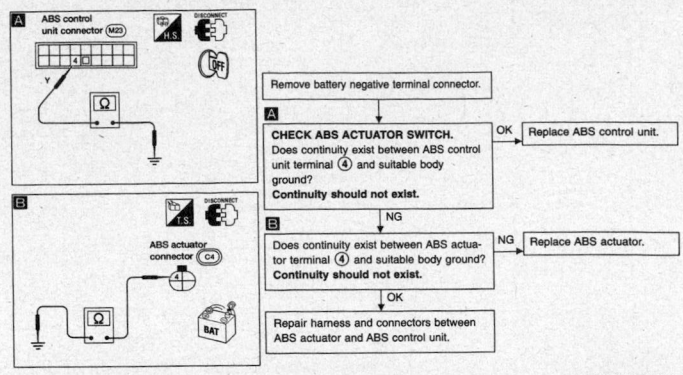

Fig. 71   Diagnostic Procedure 2: ABS Actuator ISO Solenoid Blocked. 2WD Frontier

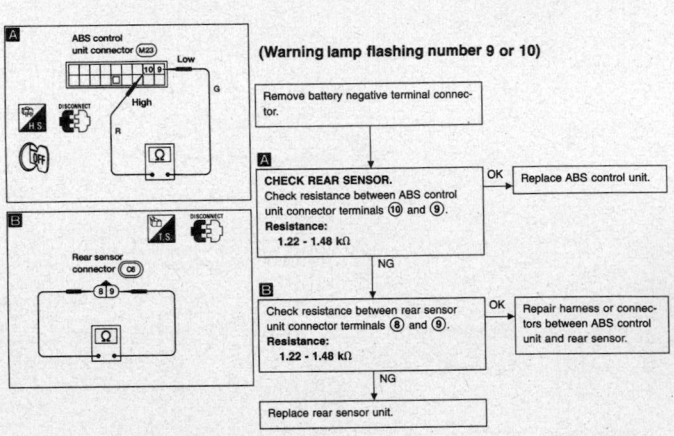

Fig. 73   Diagnostic Procedure 4: Rear Sensor Open Or Short Circuit. 2WD Frontier

SENSOR SIGNAL ERRATIC (Warning number 6)

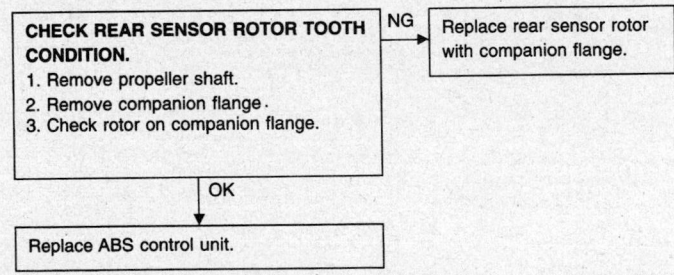

Fig. 74   Diagnostic Procedure 5: Sensor Signal Erratic. 2WD Frontier

(Warning lamp flashing 13, 14 or 15)

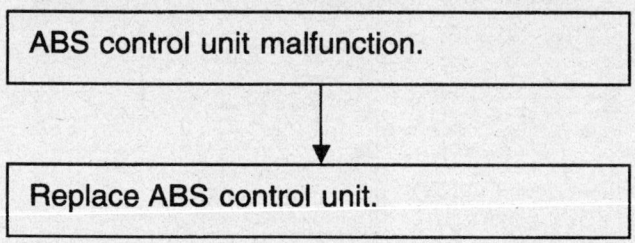

ABS control unit malfunction.

↓

Replace ABS control unit.

NS4029900340000X

Fig. 75   Diagnostic Procedure 6: ABS Control Unit. 2WD Frontier

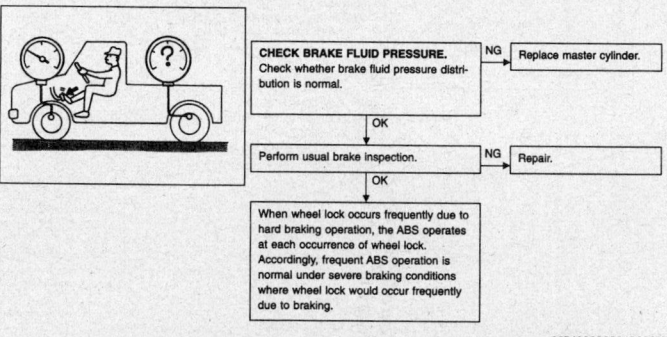

CHECK BRAKE FLUID PRESSURE. Check whether brake fluid pressure distribution is normal. — NG → Replace master cylinder.

OK ↓

Perform usual brake inspection. — NG → Repair.

OK ↓

When wheel lock occurs frequently due to hard braking operation, the ABS operates at each occurrence of wheel lock. Accordingly, frequent ABS operation is normal under severe braking conditions where wheel lock would occur frequently due to braking.

NS4029900342000X

Fig. 77   Diagnostic Procedure 8: ABS Works Frequently. 2WD Frontier

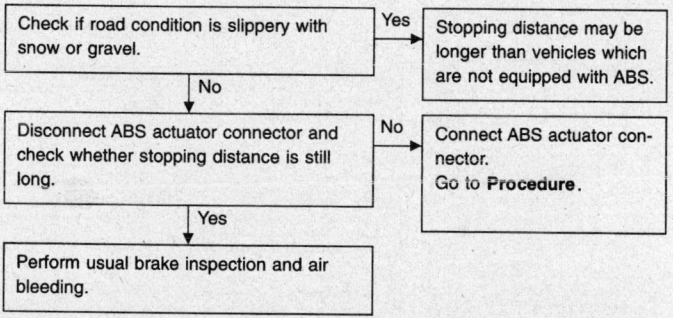

Check if road condition is slippery with snow or gravel. — Yes → Stopping distance may be longer than vehicles which are not equipped with ABS.

No ↓

Disconnect ABS actuator connector and check whether stopping distance is still long. — No → Connect ABS actuator connector. Go to **Procedure**.

Yes ↓

Perform usual brake inspection and air bleeding.

NS4029900344000X

Fig. 79   Diagnostic Procedure 10: Long Stopping Distance. 2WD Frontier

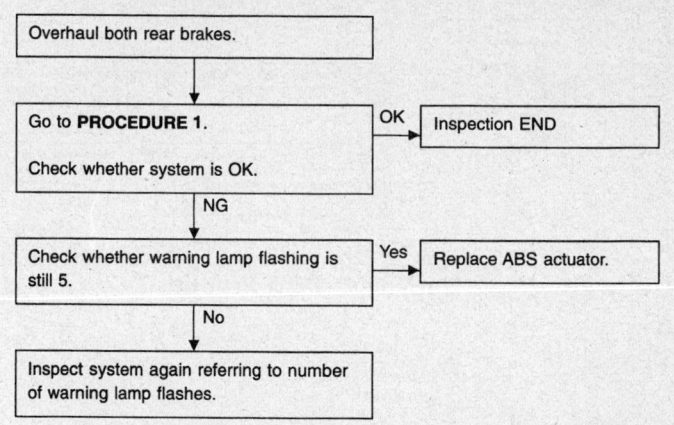

Overhaul both rear brakes.

↓

Go to **PROCEDURE 1**. Check whether system is OK. — OK → Inspection END

NG ↓

Check whether warning lamp flashing is still 5. — Yes → Replace ABS actuator.

No ↓

Inspect system again referring to number of warning lamp flashes.

NS4029900341000X

Fig. 76   Diagnostic Procedure 7: Warning Lamp Flashing. 2WD Frontier

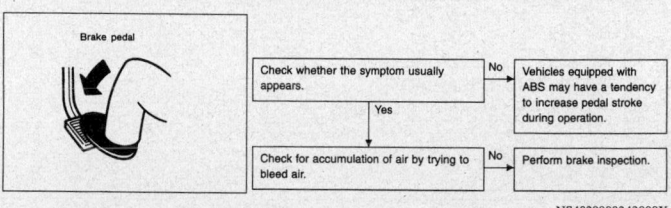

Brake pedal

Check whether the symptom usually appears. — No → Vehicles equipped with ABS may have a tendency to increase pedal stroke during operation.

Yes ↓

Check for accumulation of air by trying to bleed air. — No → Perform brake inspection.

NS4029900343000X

Fig. 78   Diagnostic Procedure 9: Brake Pedal Stroke Is Large. 2WD Frontier

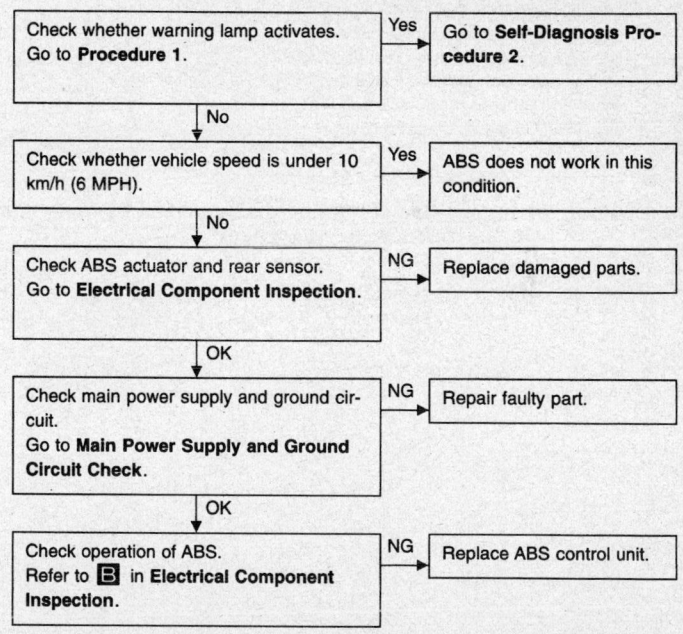

Check whether warning lamp activates. Go to **Procedure 1**. — Yes → Go to **Self-Diagnosis Procedure 2**.

No ↓

Check whether vehicle speed is under 10 km/h (6 MPH). — Yes → ABS does not work in this condition.

No ↓

Check ABS actuator and rear sensor. Go to **Electrical Component Inspection**. — NG → Replace damaged parts.

OK ↓

Check main power supply and ground circuit. Go to **Main Power Supply and Ground Circuit Check**. — NG → Repair faulty part.

OK ↓

Check operation of ABS. Refer to **B** in **Electrical Component Inspection**. — NG → Replace ABS control unit.

NS4029900345000X

Fig. 80   Diagnostic Procedure 11: ABS Inoperative. 2WD Frontier

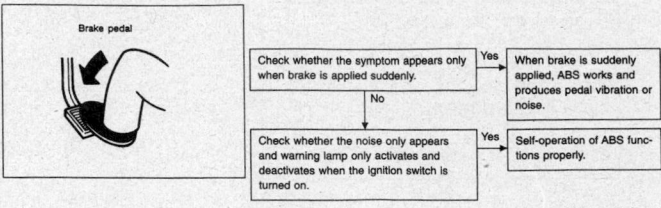

Fig. 81 Diagnostic Procedure 12: Pedal Vibration Or Noise. 2WD Frontier

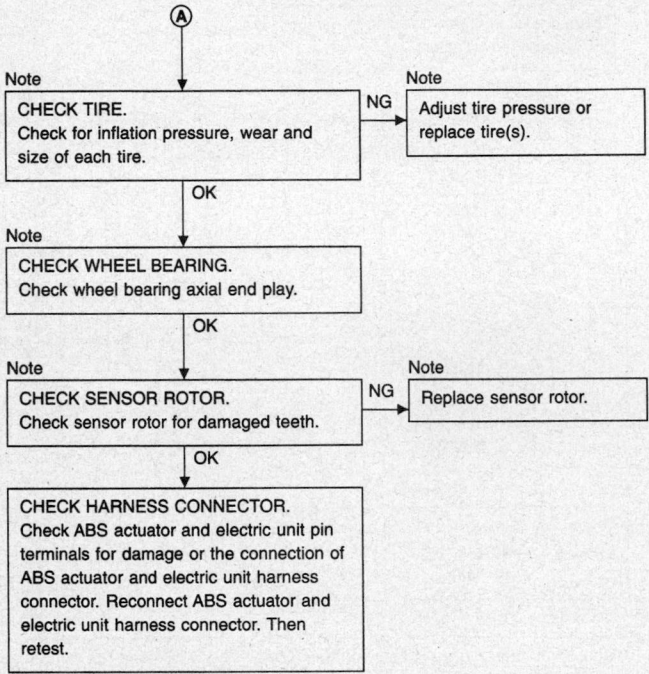

Note: Wheel position should be distinguished by code numbers except code No. 18 (sensor rotor).

NS4029900347020X

Fig. 82 Diagnostic Procedure 1: Wheel Sensor Or Rotor (Part 2 of 2). 4WD Frontier

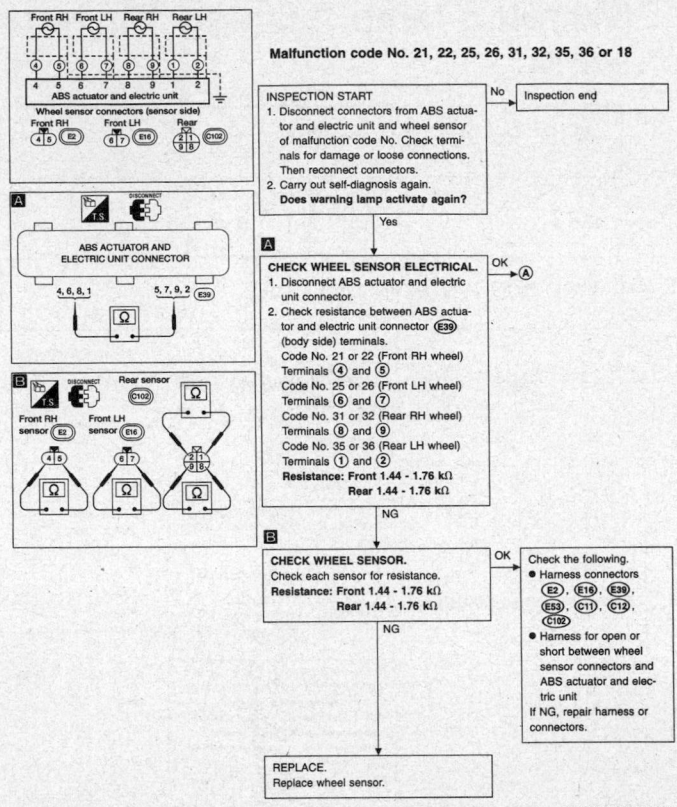

Fig. 82 Diagnostic Procedure 1: Wheel Sensor Or Rotor (Part 1 of 2). 4WD Frontier

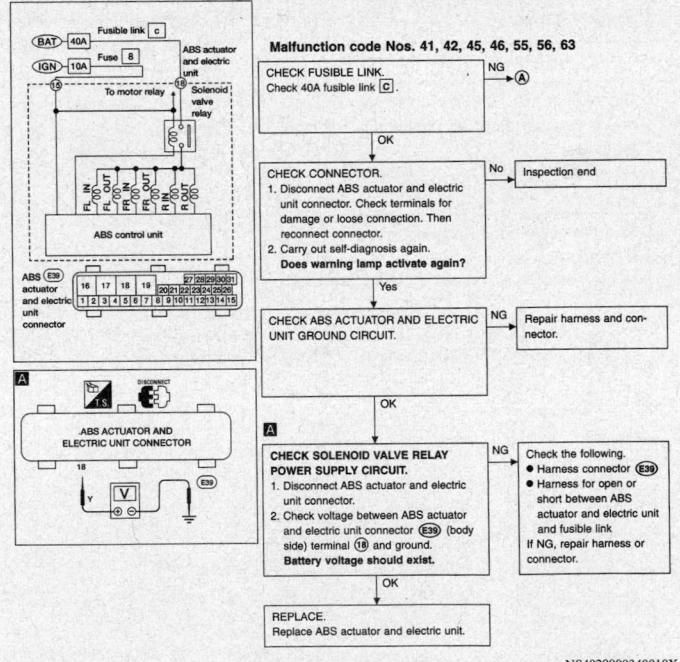

Fig. 83 Diagnostic Procedure 2: ABS Actuator Solenoid Valve Or relay (Part 1 of 2). 4WD Frontier

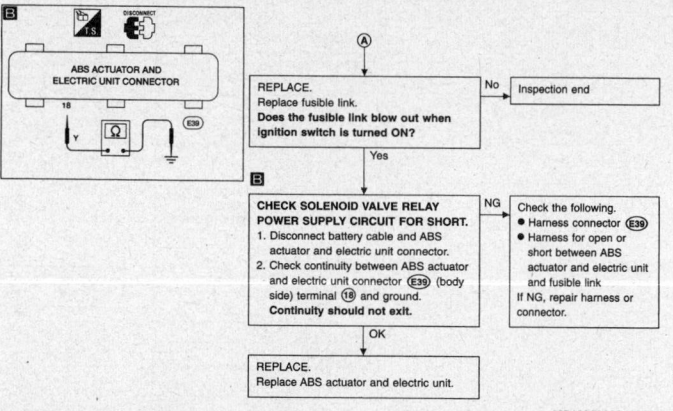

Fig. 83 Diagnostic Procedure 2: ABS Actuator Solenoid Valve Or relay (Part 2 of 2). 4WD Frontier

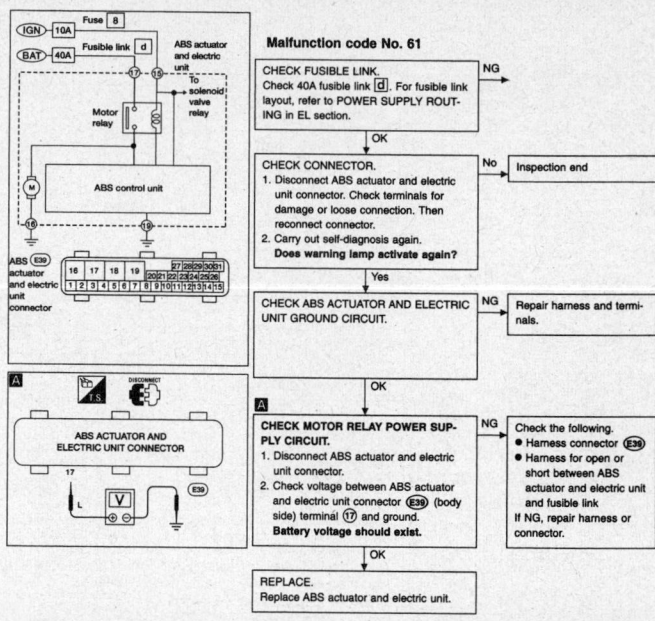

NS4029900349010X

Fig. 84 Diagnostic Procedure 3: Motor Relay Or Motor (Part 1 of 2). 4WD Frontier

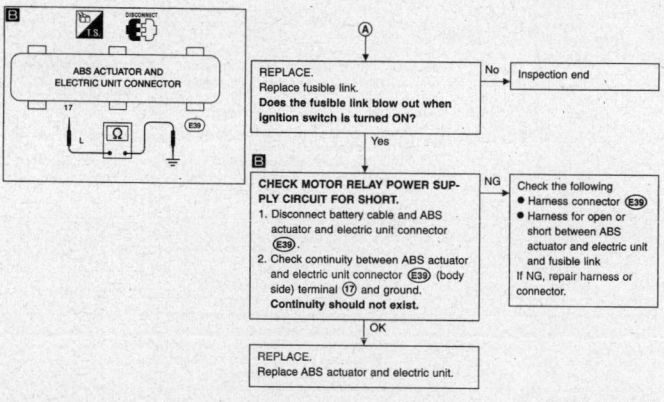

NS4029900348020X

Fig. 84 Diagnostic Procedure 3: Motor Relay Or Motor (Part 2 of 2). 4WD Frontier

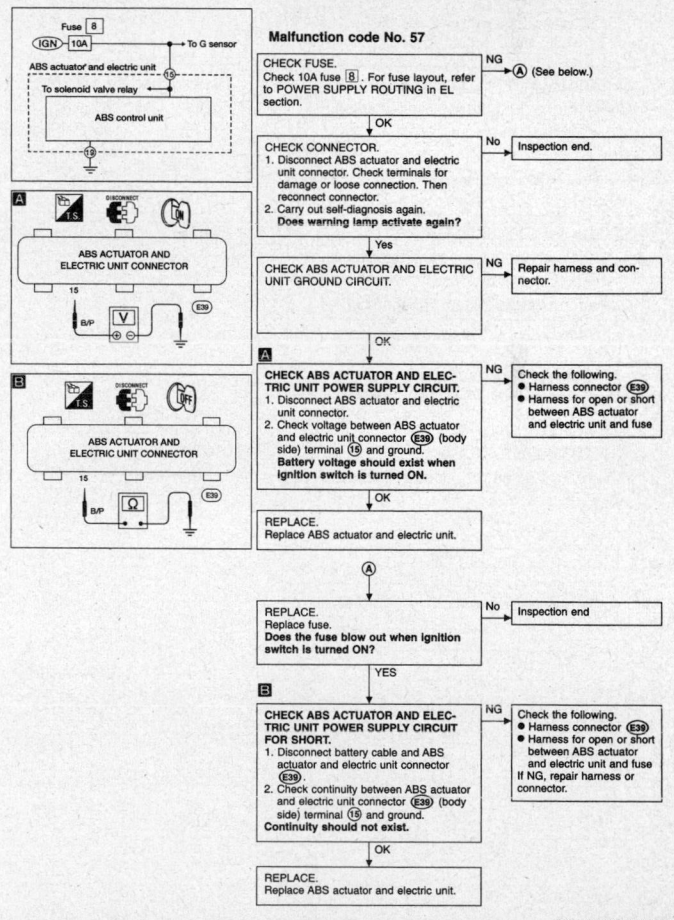

NS4029900350000X

Fig. 85 Diagnostic Procedure 4: Low Voltage. 4WD Frontier

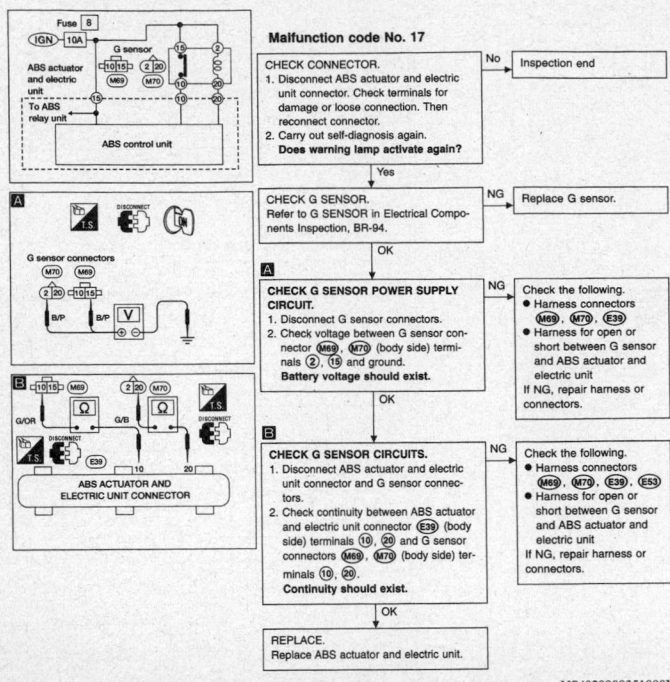

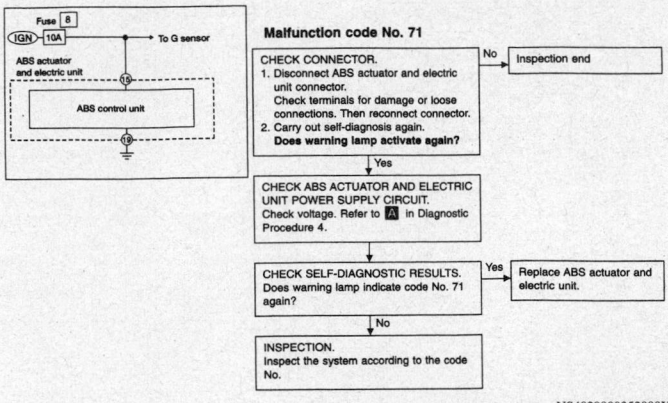

Fig. 87   Diagnostic Procedure 6: Control Unit. 4WD Frontier

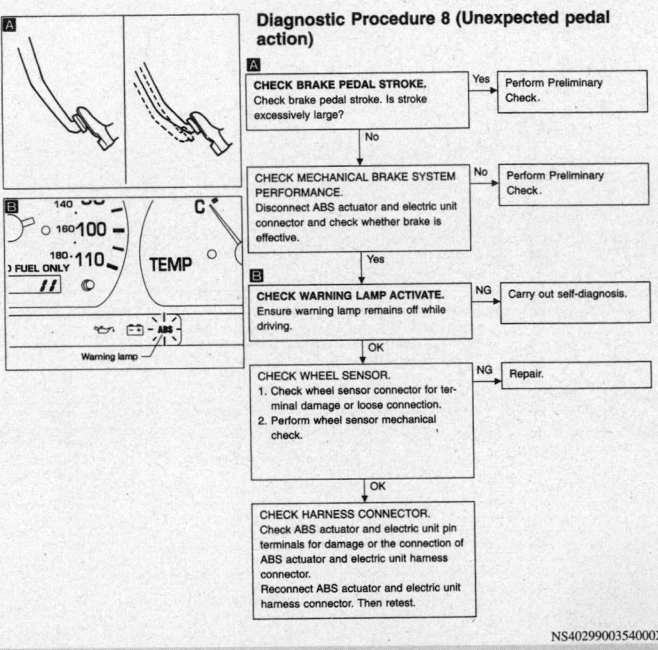

Fig. 89   Diagnostic Procedure 8: Unexpected Pedal Action. 4WD Frontier

NS4029900351000X

Fig. 86   Diagnostic Procedure 5: G Sensor. 4WD Frontier

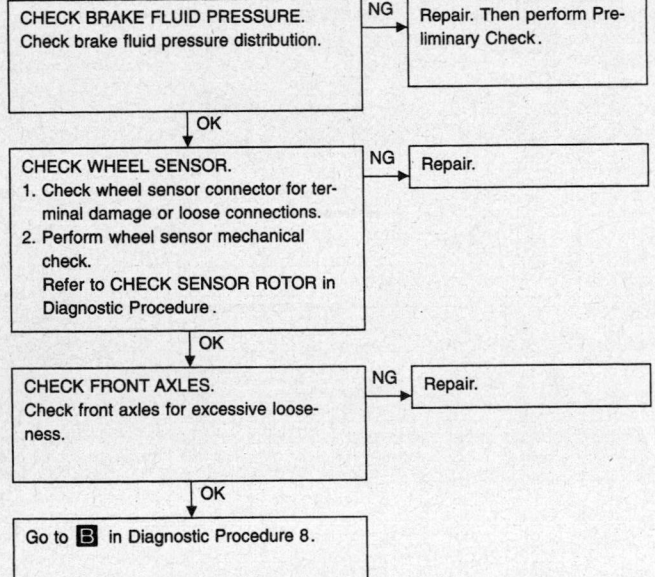

NS4029900353000X

Fig. 88   Diagnostic Procedure 7: ABS Works Frequently. 4WD Frontier

CHECK ABS PERFORMANCE.
Disconnect ABS actuator and electric unit connector and check whether stopping distance is still long. → No → Go to **B** in Diagnostic Procedure 8.

↓ Yes

Perform Preliminary Check and air bleeding (if necessary).

Note: Stopping distance may be longer for vehicles without ABS when road condition is slippery.

NS4029900355000X

Fig. 90 Diagnostic Procedure 9: Long Stopping Distance. 4WD Frontier

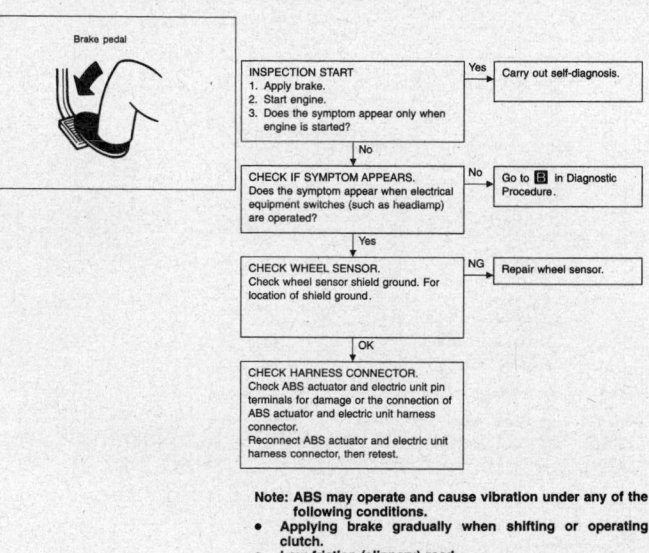

INSPECTION START
1. Apply brake.
2. Start engine.
3. Does the symptom appear only when engine is started? → Yes → Carry out self-diagnosis.

↓ No

CHECK IF SYMPTOM APPEARS.
Does the symptom appear when electrical equipment switches (such as headlamp) are operated? → No → Go to **B** in Diagnostic Procedure.

↓ Yes

CHECK WHEEL SENSOR.
Check wheel sensor shield ground. For location of shield ground. → NG → Repair wheel sensor.

↓ OK

CHECK HARNESS CONNECTOR.
Check ABS actuator and electric unit pin terminals for damage or the connection of ABS actuator and electric unit harness connector.
Reconnect ABS actuator and electric unit harness connector, then retest.

Note: ABS may operate and cause vibration under any of the following conditions.
- Applying brake gradually when shifting or operating clutch.
- Low friction (slippery) road.
- High speed cornering.
- Driving over bumps and pot holes.
- Engine speed is over 5,000 rpm with vehicle stopped.

NS4029900357000X

Fig. 92 Diagnostic Procedure 11: Pedal Vibration & Noise. 4WD Frontier

CHECK WARNING LAMP ACTIVATE.
Does the ABS warning lamp activate? → Yes → Carry out self-diagnosis.

↓ No

Go to **B** in Diagnostic Procedure 8.

Note: ABS does not work when vehicle speed is under 10 km/h (6 MPH).

NS4029900356000X

Fig. 91 Diagnostic Procedure 10: ABS Does Not Work. 4WD Frontier

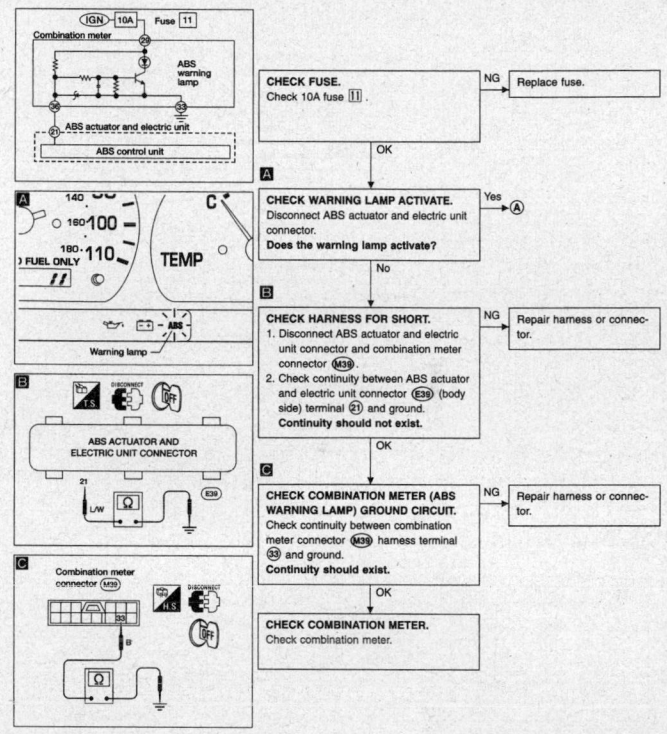

CHECK FUSE.
Check 10A fuse [11]. → NG → Replace fuse.

↓ OK

A

CHECK WARNING LAMP ACTIVATE.
Disconnect ABS actuator and electric unit connector.
Does the warning lamp activate? → Yes → **A**

↓ No

B

CHECK HARNESS FOR SHORT.
1. Disconnect ABS actuator and electric unit connector and combination meter connector (M39).
2. Check continuity between ABS actuator and electric unit connector (E39) (body side) terminal ㉑ and ground.
Continuity should not exist. → NG → Repair harness or connector.

↓ OK

C

CHECK COMBINATION METER (ABS WARNING LAMP) GROUND CIRCUIT.
Check continuity between combination meter connector (M39) harness terminal ㉝ and ground.
Continuity should exist. → NG → Repair harness or connector.

↓ OK

CHECK COMBINATION METER.
Check combination meter.

NS4029900358000X

Fig. 93 Diagnostic Procedure 12: Warning Lamp Does Not Illuminate w/Key On. 4WD Frontier

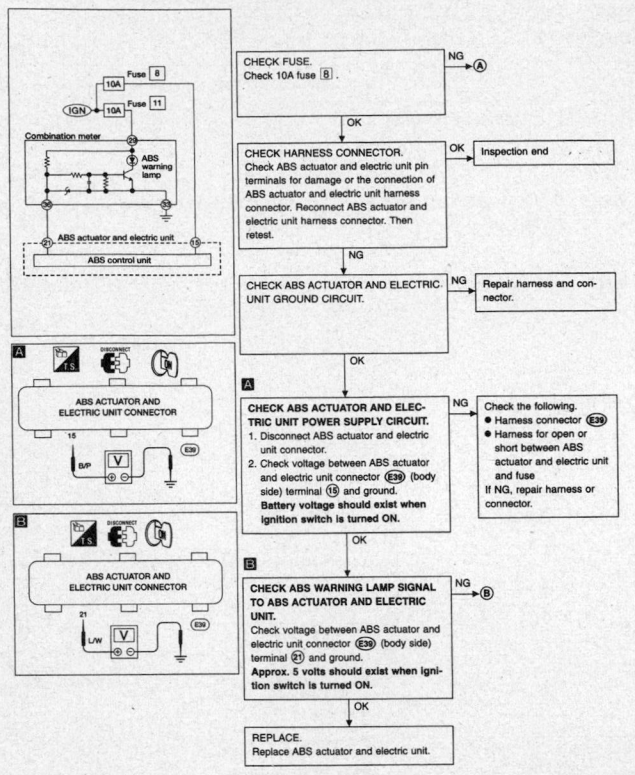

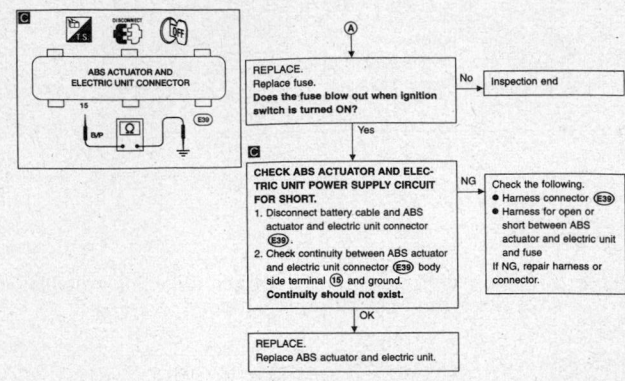

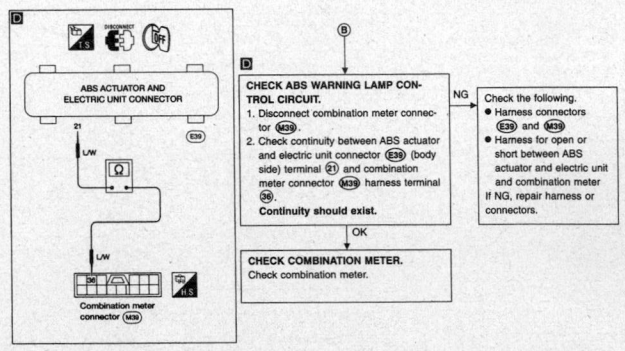

NS4029900359010X

Fig. 94 Diagnostic Procedure 13: Warning Lamp Remains Illuminated w/Key On (Part 1 of 2). 4WD Frontier

NS4029900359020X

Fig. 94 Diagnostic Procedure 13: Warning Lamp Remains Illuminated w/Key On (Part 2 of 2). 4WD Frontier

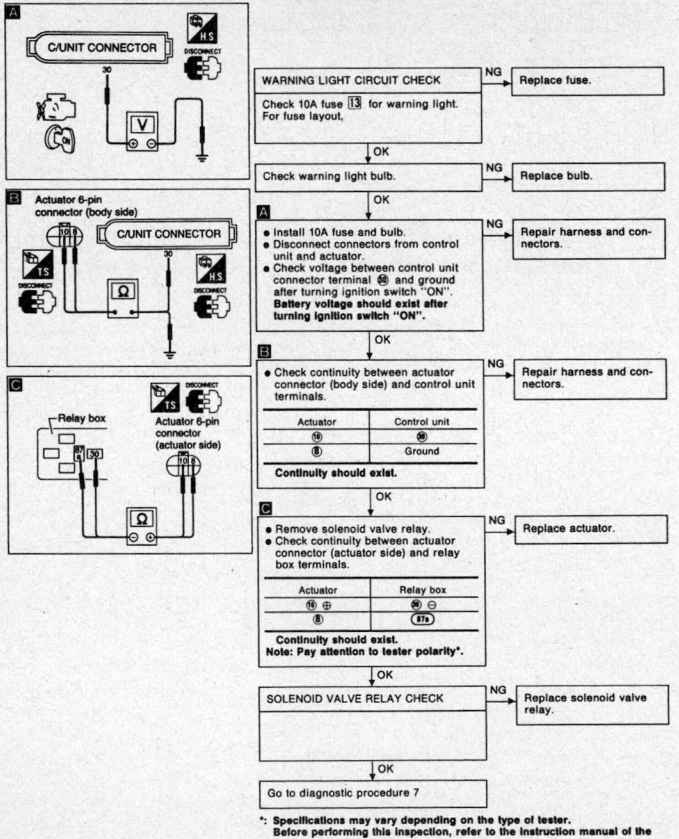

NS4029500148000X

Fig. 95 Test 1: Warning Light Does Not Work Before Engine Starts. 1996 Maxima

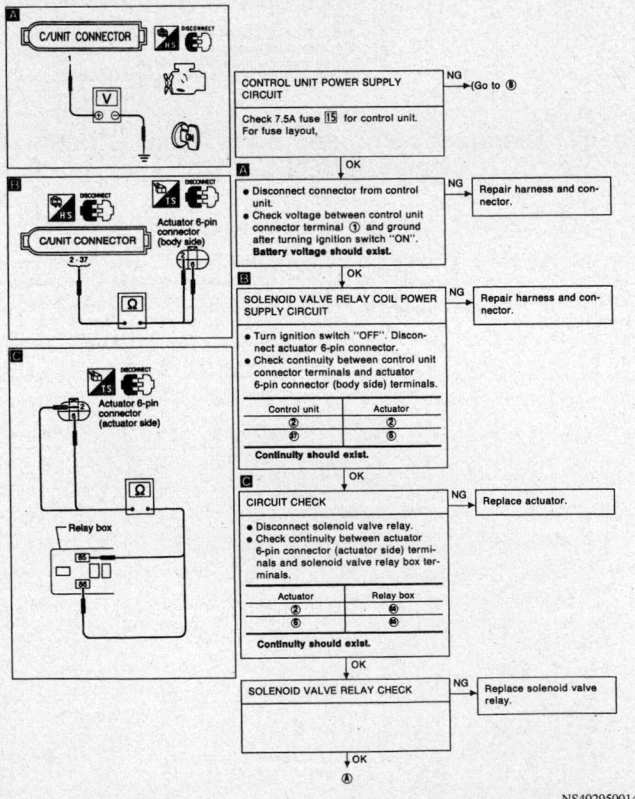

NS4029500149010X

Fig. 96 Test 2: Warning Light Stays On Continuously (Part 1 of 3). 1996 Maxima

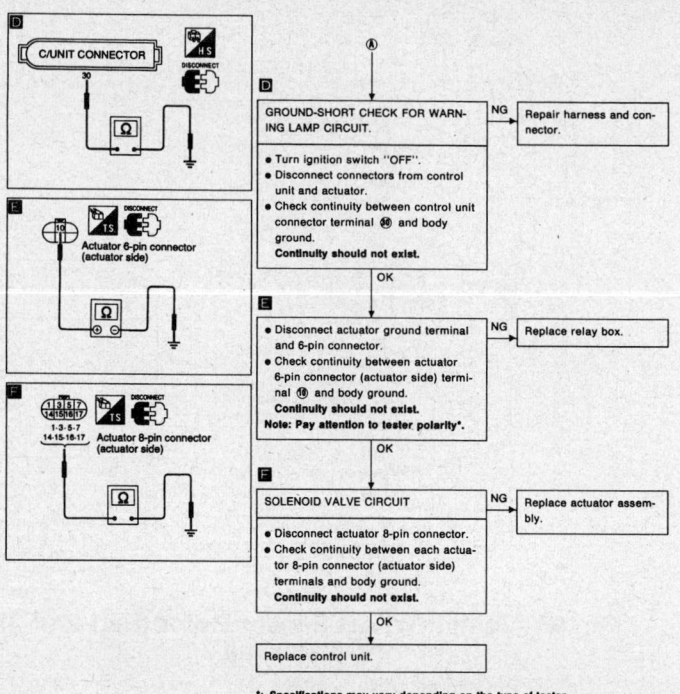

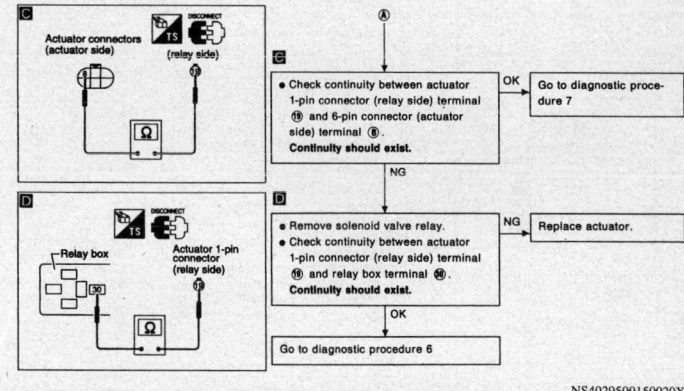

Fig. 96 Test 2: Warning Light Stays On Continuously (Part 3 of 3). 1996 Maxima

NS4029500149030X

*: Specifications may vary depending on the type of tester. Before performing this inspection, refer to the instruction manual of the tester.

NS4029500149020X

Fig. 96 Test 2: Warning Light Stays On Continuously (Part 2 of 3). 1996 Maxima

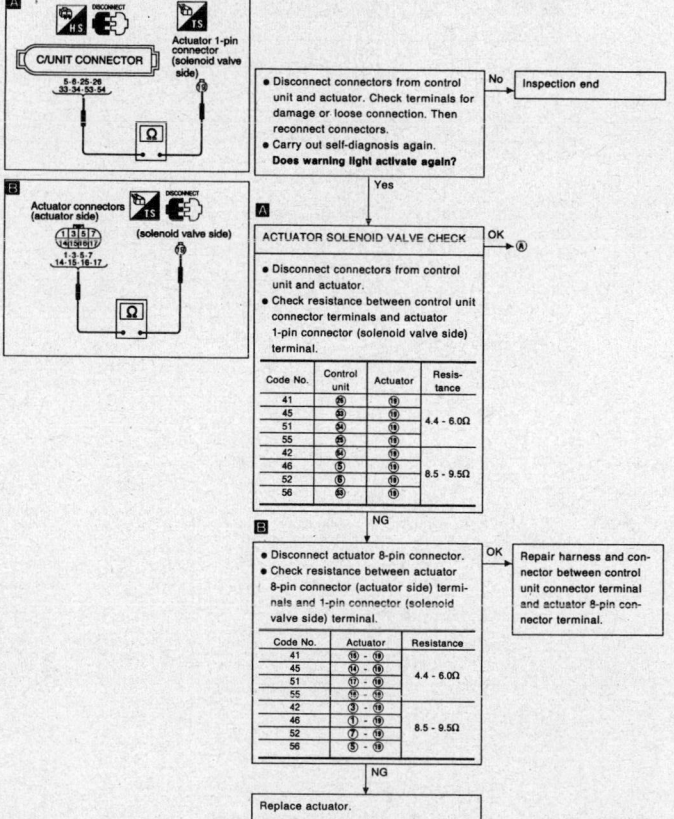

NS4029500150010X

Fig. 97 Test 3: Actuator Solenoid Valve (Part 1 of 2). 1996 Maxima

NS4029500150020X

Fig. 97 Test 3: Actuator Solenoid Valve (Part 2 of 2). 1996 Maxima

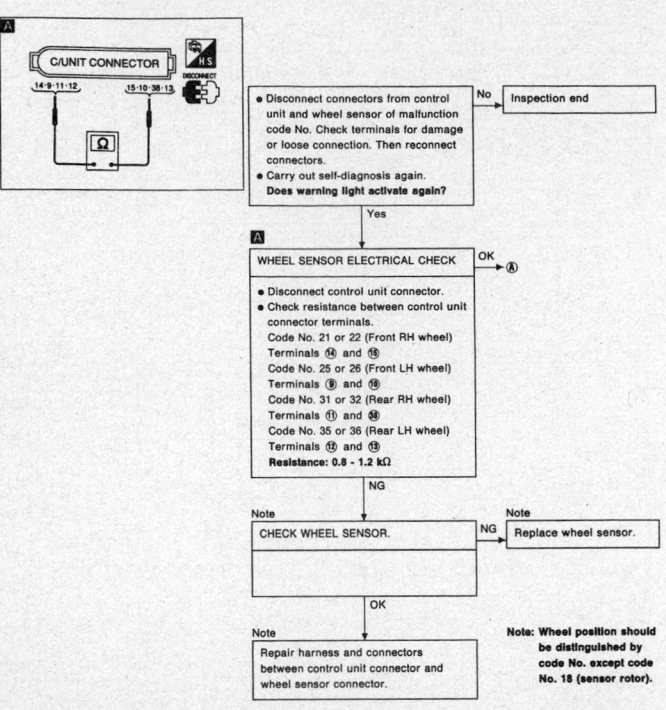

Fig. 98   Test 4: Wheel Sensor Rotor (Part 1 of 2).
1996 Maxima

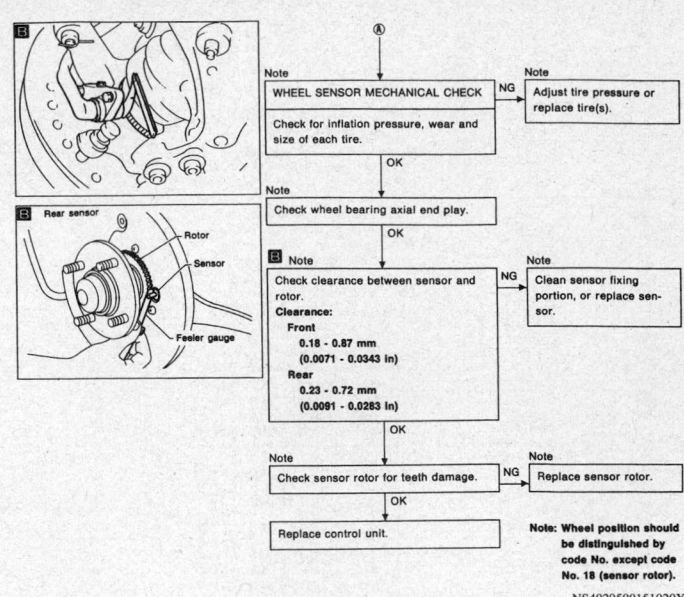

Fig. 98   Test 4: Wheel Sensor Rotor (Part 2 of 2).
1996 Maxima

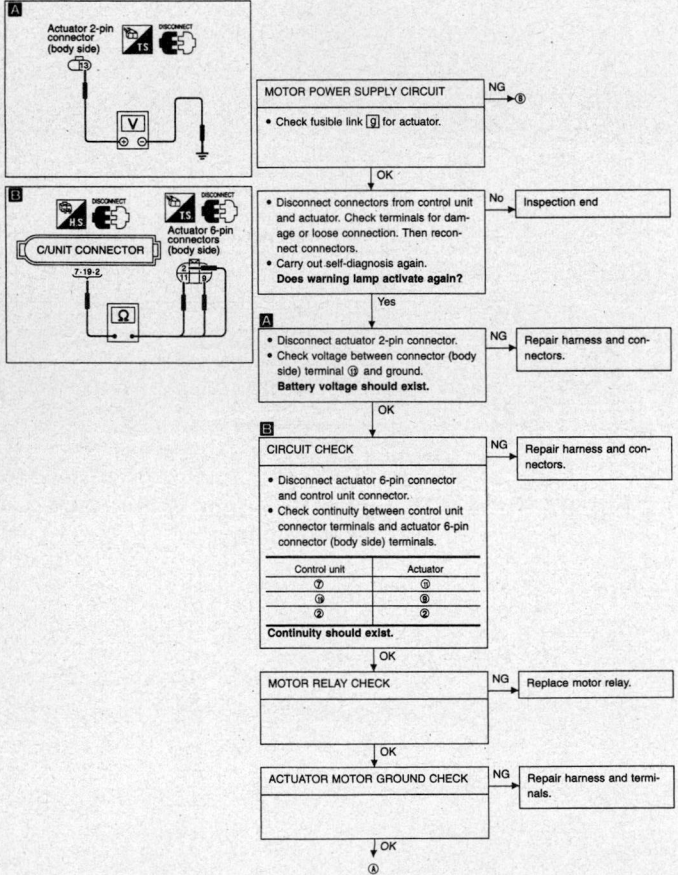

Fig. 99   Test 5: Motor Relay Or Motor (Part 1 of 3).
1996 Maxima

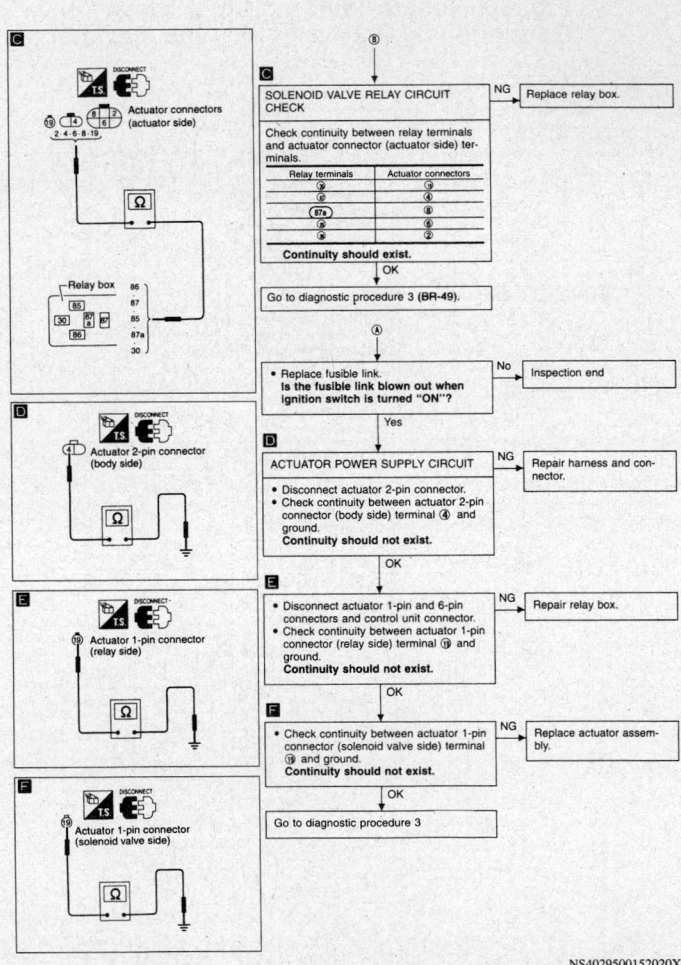

Fig. 99   Test 5: Motor Relay Or Motor (Part 2 of 3).
1996 Maxima

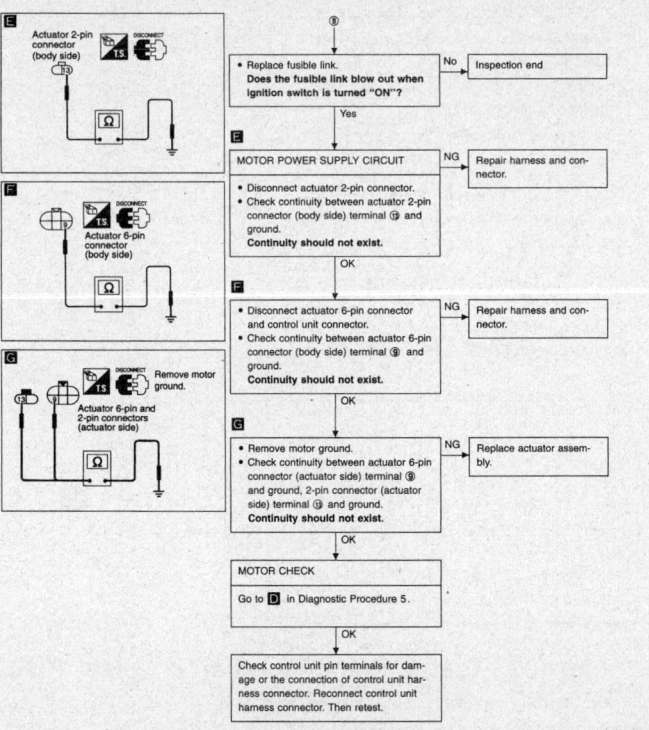

**Fig. 99   Test 5: Motor Relay Or Motor (Part 3 of 3).
1996 Maxima**

NS4029500152030X

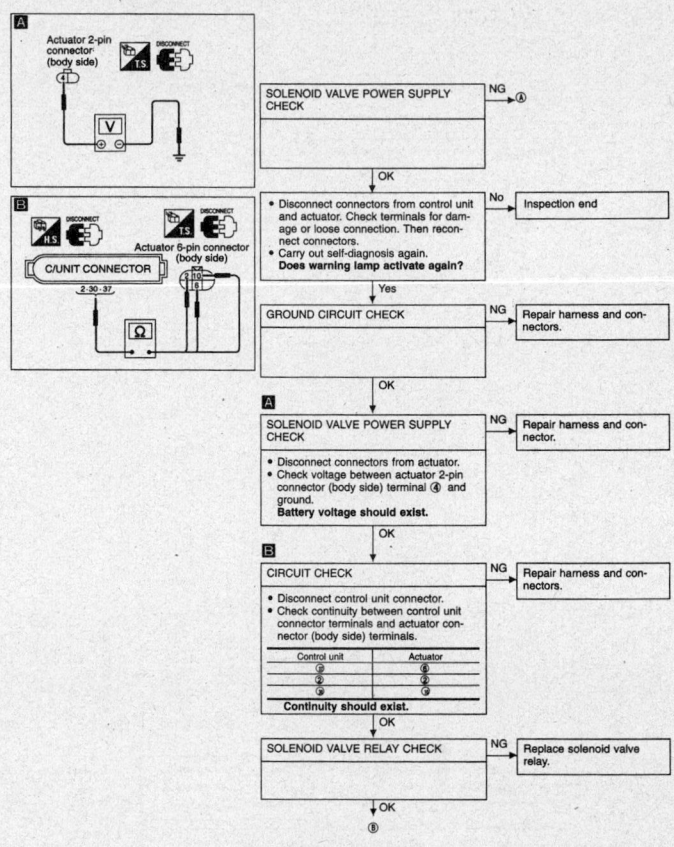

**Fig. 100   Test 6: Solenoid Valve Relay (Part 1 of 2).
1996 Maxima**

NS4029500153010X

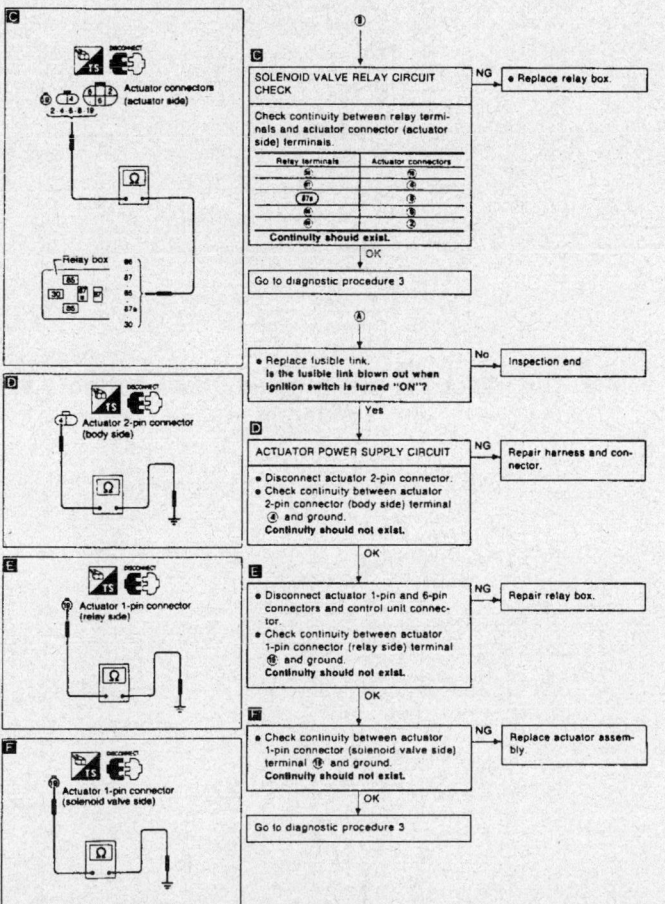

**Fig. 100   Test 6: Solenoid Valve Relay (Part 2 of 2).
1996 Maxima**

NS4029500153020X

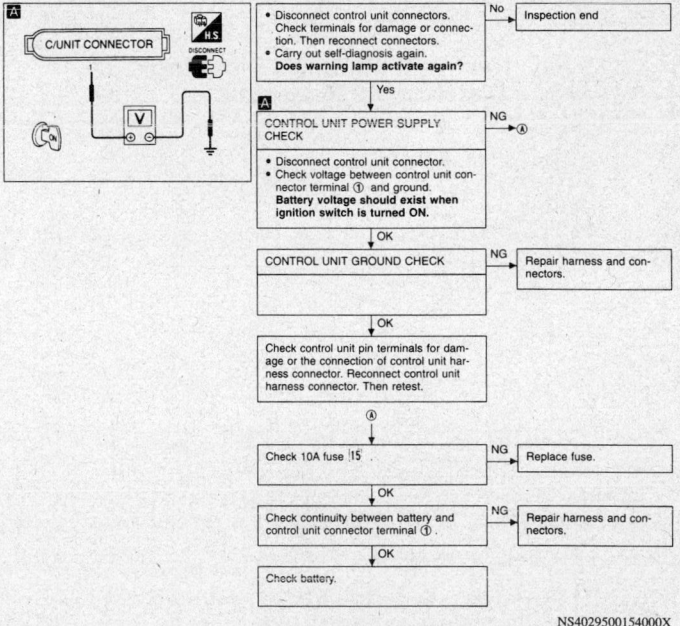

**Fig. 101   Test 7: Power Supply Low Voltage. 1996
Maxima**

NS4029500154000X

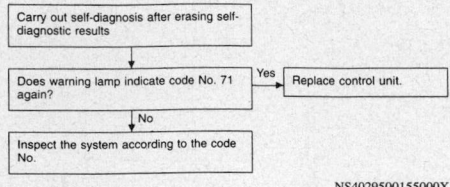

Carry out self-diagnosis after erasing self-diagnostic results

↓

Does warning lamp indicate code No. 71 again? — Yes → Replace control unit.

↓ No

Inspect the system according to the code No.

NS4029500155000X

Fig. 102   Test 8: Control Unit. 1996 Maxima

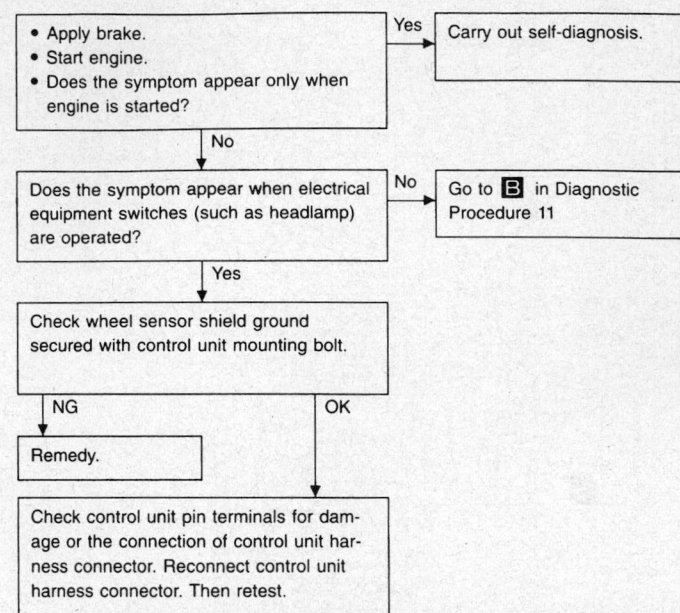

- Apply brake.
- Start engine.
- Does the symptom appear only when engine is started?

Yes → Carry out self-diagnosis.

↓ No

Does the symptom appear when electrical equipment switches (such as headlamp) are operated?

No → Go to **B** in Diagnostic Procedure 11

↓ Yes

Check wheel sensor shield ground secured with control unit mounting bolt.

NG ↓   ↓ OK

Remedy.

Check control unit pin terminals for damage or the connection of control unit harness connector. Reconnect control unit harness connector. Then retest.

NS4029500156000X

Fig. 103   Test 9: Pedal Vibration & Noise. 1996 Maxima

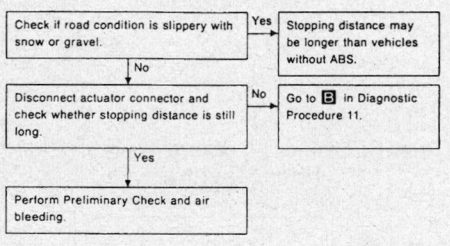

Check if road condition is slippery with snow or gravel. — Yes → Stopping distance may be longer than vehicles without ABS.

↓ No

Disconnect actuator connector and check whether stopping distance is still long. — No → Go to **B** in Diagnostic Procedure 11.

↓ Yes

Perform Preliminary Check and air bleeding.

NS4029500157000X

Fig. 104   Test 10: Long Stopping Distance. 1996 Maxima

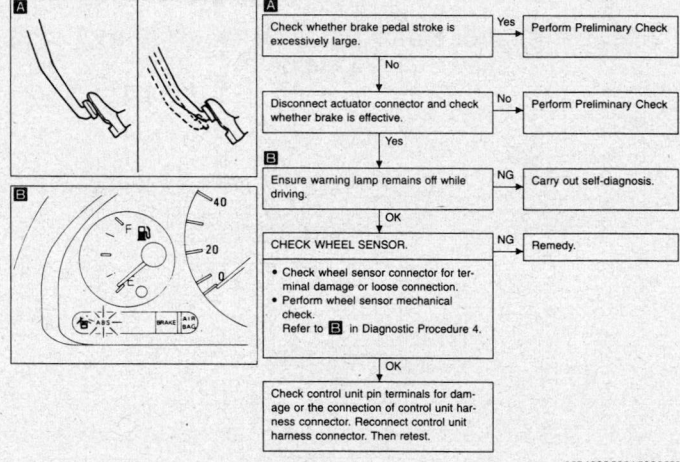

Check whether brake pedal stroke is excessively large. — Yes → Perform Preliminary Check

↓ No

Disconnect actuator connector and check whether brake is effective. — No → Perform Preliminary Check

↓ Yes

Ensure warning lamp remains off while driving. — NG → Carry out self-diagnosis.

↓ OK

CHECK WHEEL SENSOR. — NG → Remedy.
- Check wheel sensor connector for terminal damage or loose connection.
- Perform wheel sensor mechanical check.
  Refer to **B** in Diagnostic Procedure 4.

↓ OK

Check control unit pin terminals for damage or the connection of control unit harness connector. Reconnect control unit harness connector. Then retest.

NS4029500158000X

Fig. 105   Test 11: Unexpected Pedal Action. 1996 Maxima

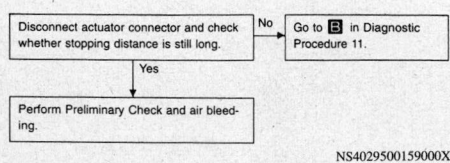

Disconnect actuator connector and check whether stopping distance is still long. — No → Go to **B** in Diagnostic Procedure 11.

↓ Yes

Perform Preliminary Check and air bleeding.

NS4029500159000X

Fig. 106   Test 12: ABS Does Not Work. 1996 Maxima

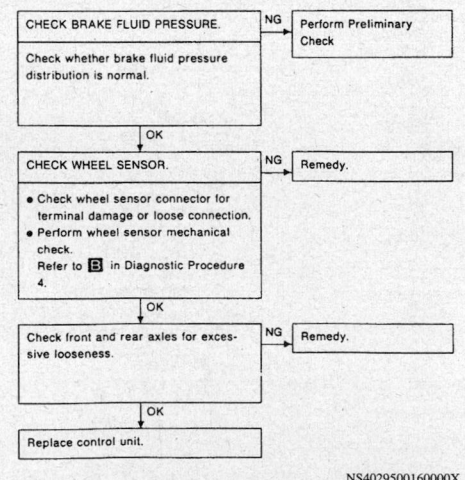

CHECK BRAKE FLUID PRESSURE.

Check whether brake fluid pressure distribution is normal. — NG → Perform Preliminary Check

↓ OK

CHECK WHEEL SENSOR. — NG → Remedy.
- Check wheel sensor connector for terminal damage or loose connection.
- Perform wheel sensor mechanical check.
  Refer to **B** in Diagnostic Procedure 4.

↓ OK

Check front and rear axles for excessive looseness. — NG → Remedy.

↓ OK

Replace control unit.

NS4029500160000X

Fig. 107   Test 13: ABS Works Frequently. 1996 Maxima

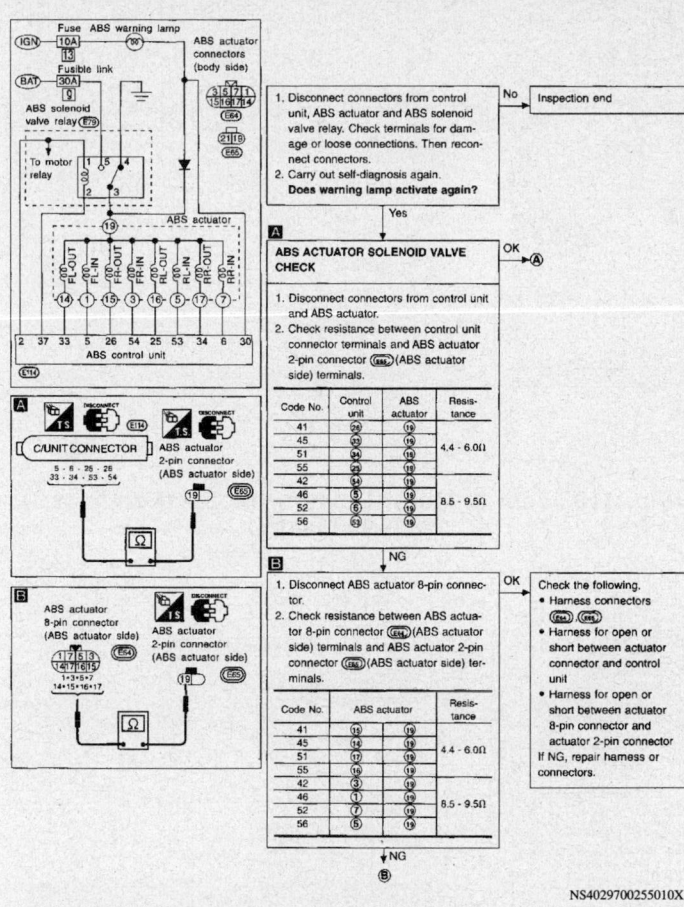

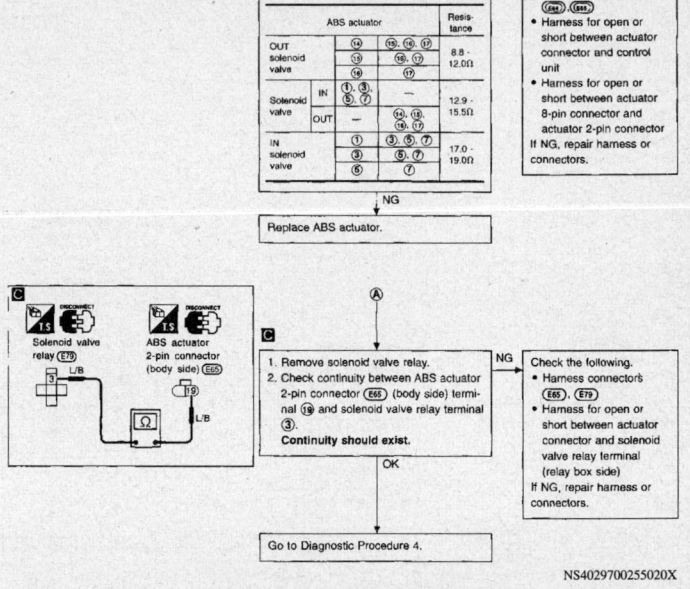

Fig. 108 Test 1: ABS Actuator Solenoid Valve (Part 1 of 2). 1997–99 Maxima

Fig. 108 Test 1: ABS Actuator Solenoid Valve (Part 2 of 2). 1997–99 Maxima

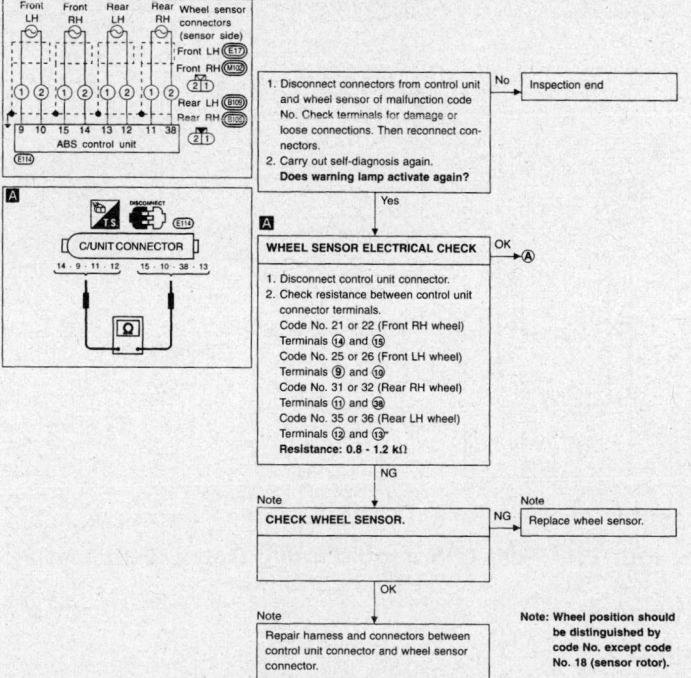

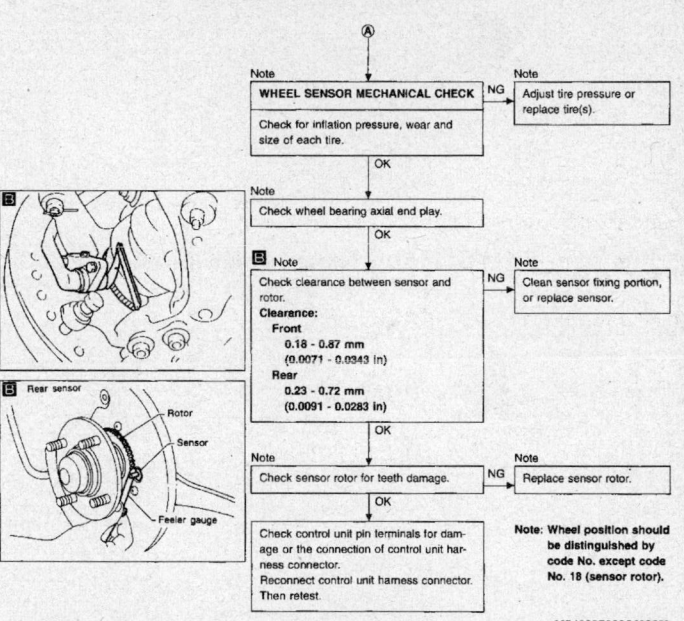

Fig. 109 Test 2: Wheel Sensor or Rotor (Part 1 of 2). 1997–99 Maxima

Fig. 109 Test 2: Wheel Sensor or Rotor (Part 2 of 2). 1997–99 Maxima

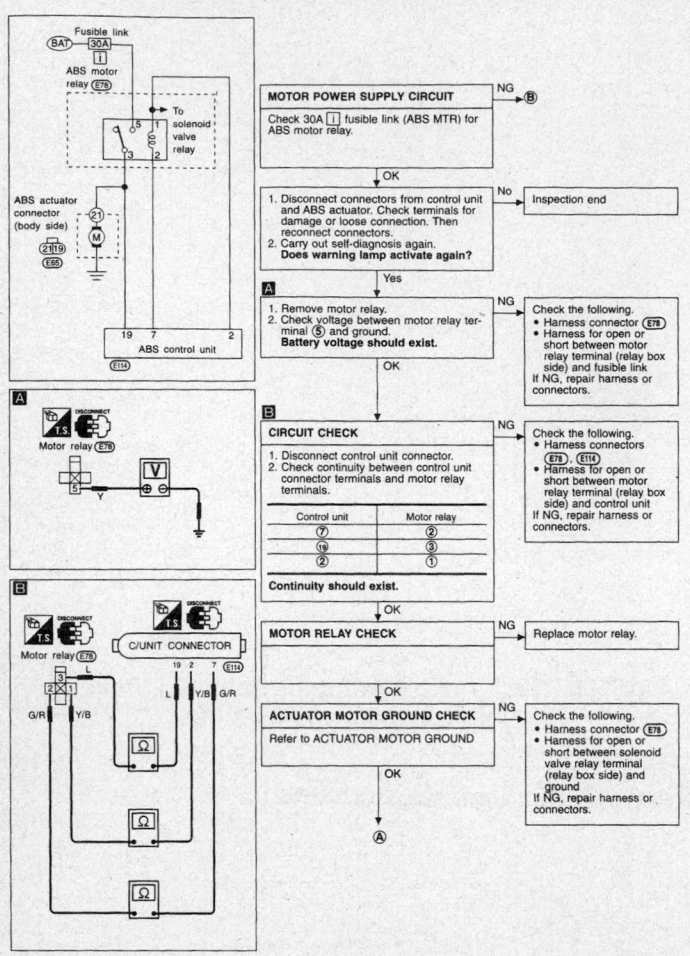

MOTOR POWER SUPPLY CIRCUIT

Check 30A 1 fusible link (ABS MTR) for ABS motor relay.

↓ OK

1. Disconnect connectors from control unit and ABS actuator. Check terminals for damage or loose connection. Then reconnect connectors.
2. Carry out self-diagnosis again.
   Does warning lamp activate again?

→ No → Inspection end

↓ Yes

A
1. Remove motor relay.
2. Check voltage between motor relay terminal ⑤ and ground.
   Battery voltage should exist.

→ Check the following.
- Harness connector (E78)
- Harness for open or short between motor relay terminal (relay box side) and fusible link
If NG, repair harness or connectors.

↓ OK

CIRCUIT CHECK → NG
1. Disconnect control unit connector.
2. Check continuity between control unit connector terminals and motor relay terminals.

Control unit	Motor relay
⑦	②
⑲	③
②	①

Continuity should exist.

→ Check the following.
- Harness connectors (E78) (E114)
- Harness for open or short between motor relay terminal (relay box side) and control unit
If NG, repair harness or connectors.

↓ OK

MOTOR RELAY CHECK → NG → Replace motor relay.

↓ OK

ACTUATOR MOTOR GROUND CHECK → NG
Refer to ACTUATOR MOTOR GROUND

→ Check the following.
- Harness connector (E78)
- Harness for open or short between solenoid valve relay terminal (relay box side) and ground
If NG, repair harness or connectors.

↓ OK
(A)

Fig. 110   Test 3: Motor Relay or Motor (Part 1 of 3). 1997–99 Maxima

NS4029700257010X

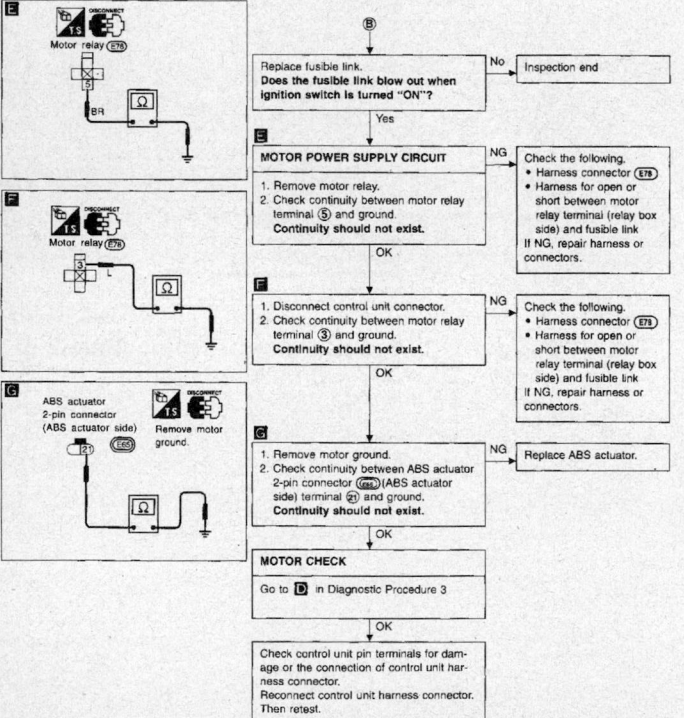

(B)

Replace fusible link.
Does the fusible link blow out when ignition switch is turned "ON"?

→ No → Inspection end

↓ Yes

E
MOTOR POWER SUPPLY CIRCUIT → NG
1. Remove motor relay.
2. Check continuity between motor relay terminal ⑤ and ground.
   Continuity should not exist.

→ Check the following.
- Harness connector (E78)
- Harness for open or short between motor relay terminal (relay box side) and fusible link
If NG, repair harness or connectors.

↓ OK

F
1. Disconnect control unit connector.
2. Check continuity between motor relay terminal ③ and ground.
   Continuity should not exist.

→ Check the following.
- Harness connector (E78)
- Harness for open or short between motor relay terminal (relay box side) and fusible link
If NG, repair harness or connectors.

↓ OK

G
1. Remove motor ground.
2. Check continuity between ABS actuator 2-pin connector (E65) (ABS actuator side) terminal ㉑ and ground.
   Continuity should not exist.

→ NG → Replace ABS actuator.

↓ OK

MOTOR CHECK
Go to D in Diagnostic Procedure 3.

↓ OK

Check control unit pin terminals for damage or the connection of control unit harness connector.
Reconnect control unit harness connector. Then retest.

NS4029700257030X

Fig. 110   Test 3: Motor Relay or Motor (Part 3 of 3). 1997–99 Maxima

---

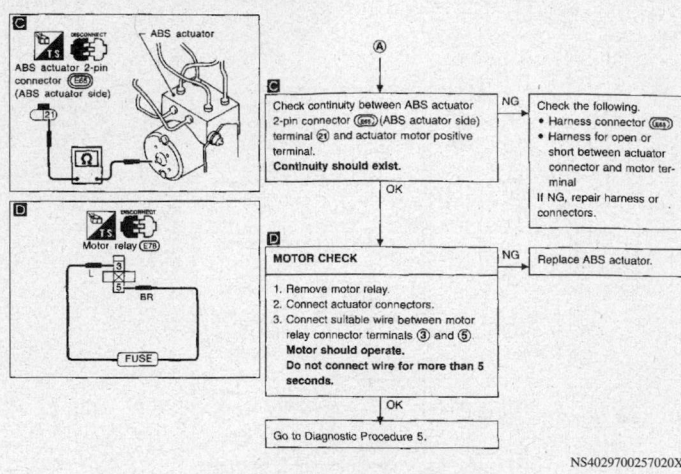

C
Check continuity between ABS actuator 2-pin connector (E65) (ABS actuator side) terminal ㉑ and actuator motor positive terminal.
Continuity should exist.

→ Check the following.
- Harness connector (E65)
- Harness for open or short between actuator connector and motor terminal
If NG, repair harness or connectors.

↓ OK

D
MOTOR CHECK → NG → Replace ABS actuator.
1. Remove motor relay.
2. Connect actuator connectors.
3. Connect suitable wire between motor relay connector terminals ③ and ⑤.
   Motor should operate.
   Do not connect wire for more than 5 seconds.

↓ OK

Go to Diagnostic Procedure 5.

NS4029700257020X

Fig. 110   Test 3: Motor Relay or Motor (Part 2 of 3). 1997–99 Maxima

---

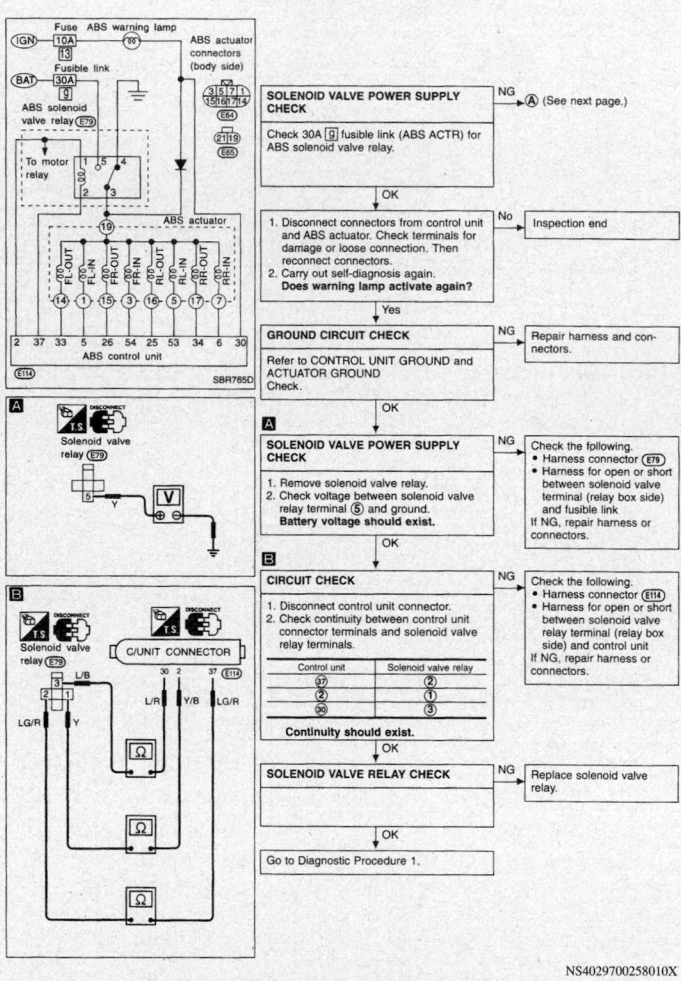

SOLENOID VALVE POWER SUPPLY CHECK → NG → (A) (See next page.)

Check 30A 9 fusible link (ABS ACTR) for ABS solenoid valve relay.

↓ OK

1. Disconnect connectors from control unit and ABS actuator. Check terminals for damage or loose connection. Then reconnect connectors.
2. Carry out self-diagnosis again.
   Does warning lamp activate again?

→ No → Inspection end

↓ Yes

GROUND CIRCUIT CHECK → NG → Repair harness and connectors.
Refer to CONTROL UNIT GROUND and ACTUATOR GROUND Check.

↓ OK

A
SOLENOID VALVE POWER SUPPLY CHECK → NG
1. Remove solenoid valve relay.
2. Check voltage between solenoid valve relay terminal ⑤ and ground.
   Battery voltage should exist.

→ Check the following.
- Harness connector (E79)
- Harness for open or short between solenoid valve terminal (relay box side) and fusible link
If NG, repair harness or connectors.

↓ OK

B
CIRCUIT CHECK → NG
1. Disconnect control unit connector.
2. Check continuity between control unit connector terminals and solenoid valve relay terminals.

Control unit	Solenoid valve relay
㊲	②
②	①
㉚	③

Continuity should exist.

→ Check the following.
- Harness connector (E114)
- Harness for open or short between solenoid valve relay terminal (relay box side) and control unit
If NG, repair harness or connectors.

↓ OK

SOLENOID VALVE RELAY CHECK → NG → Replace solenoid valve relay.

↓ OK

Go to Diagnostic Procedure 1.

NS4029700258010X

Fig. 111   Test 4: Solenoid Valve Relay (Part 1 of 2). 1997–99 Maxima

---

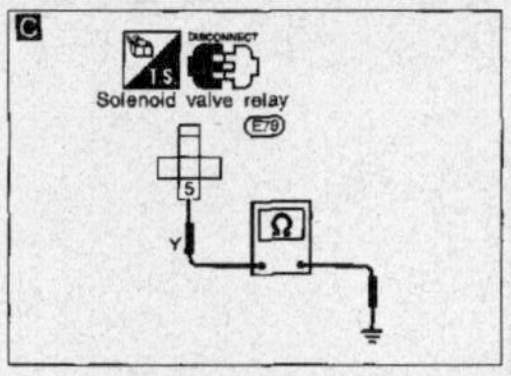

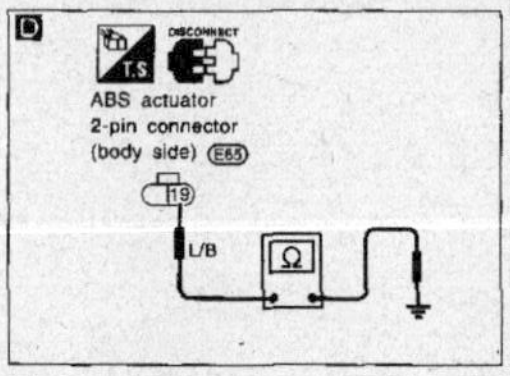

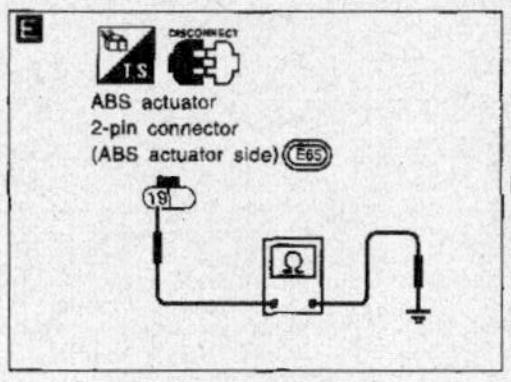

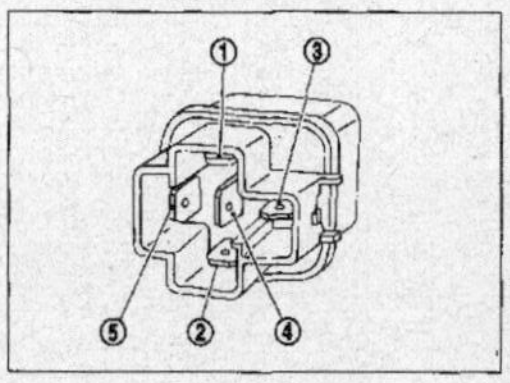

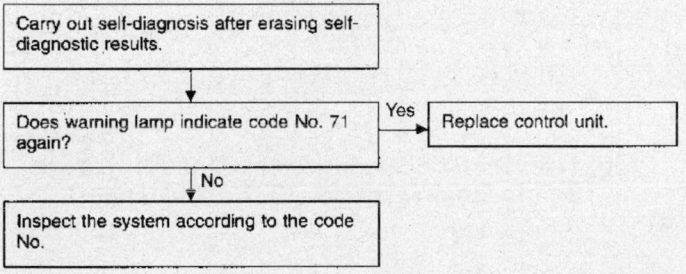

Fig. 111 Test 4: Solenoid Valve Relay (Part 2 of 2). 1997–99 Maxima

Solenoid valve relay

Condition	Continuity existence between terminals ③ and ④	Continuity existence between terminals ③ and ⑤
Battery voltage not applied between terminals ① and ②.	Yes	No
Battery voltage applied between terminals ① and ②.	No	Yes

While applying battery voltage to relay terminals, insert fuse into the circuit.

NS4029700258020X

Carry out self-diagnosis after erasing self-diagnostic results.

↓

Does warning lamp indicate code No. 71 again? — Yes → Replace control unit.

↓ No

Inspect the system according to the code No.

NS4029700260000X

Fig. 113 Test 6: Control Unit. 1997–99 Maxima

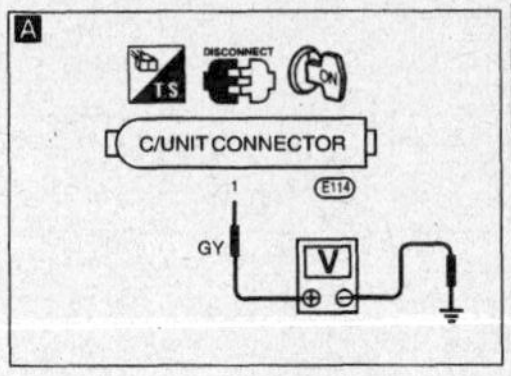

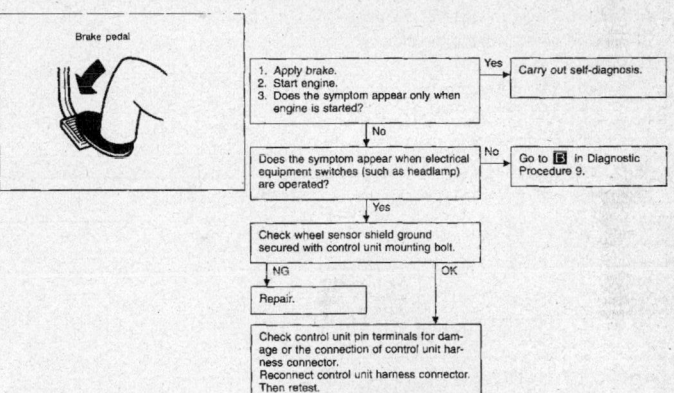

Fig. 112 Test 5: Low Voltage. 1997–99 Maxima

Fig. 114 Test 7: Pedal Vibration & Noise. 1997–99 Maxima

Note: ABS may operate and cause vibration under any of the following conditions.
- Applying brake gradually when shifting or operating clutch.
- Low friction (slippery) road.
- High speed cornering.
- Driving over bumps and pot holes.
- Engine speed is over 5,000 rpm with vehicle stopped.

NS4029700261000X

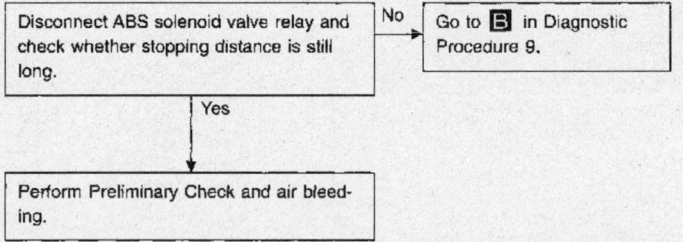

Disconnect ABS solenoid valve relay and check whether stopping distance is still long. — No → Go to **B** in Diagnostic Procedure 9.

↓ Yes

Perform Preliminary Check and air bleeding.

Note: Stopping distance may be larger than vehicles without ABS when road condition is slippery.

NS4029700262000X

Fig. 115 Test 8: Long Stopping Distance. 1997–99 Maxima

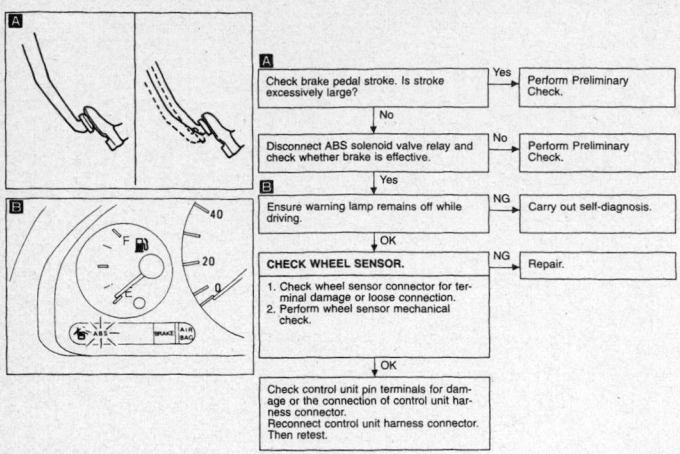

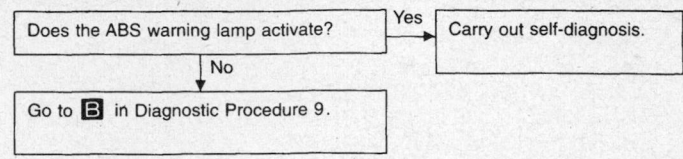

Does the ABS warning lamp activate?	Yes → Carry out self-diagnosis.

↓ No

Go to **B** in Diagnostic Procedure 9.

Note: ABS does not work when vehicle speed is under 10 km/h (6 MPH).

NS4029700264000X

Fig. 117   Test 10: ABS Does Not Work. 1997–99 Maxima

Fig. 116   Test 9: Unexpected Pedal Action. 1997–99 Maxima

NS4029700263000X

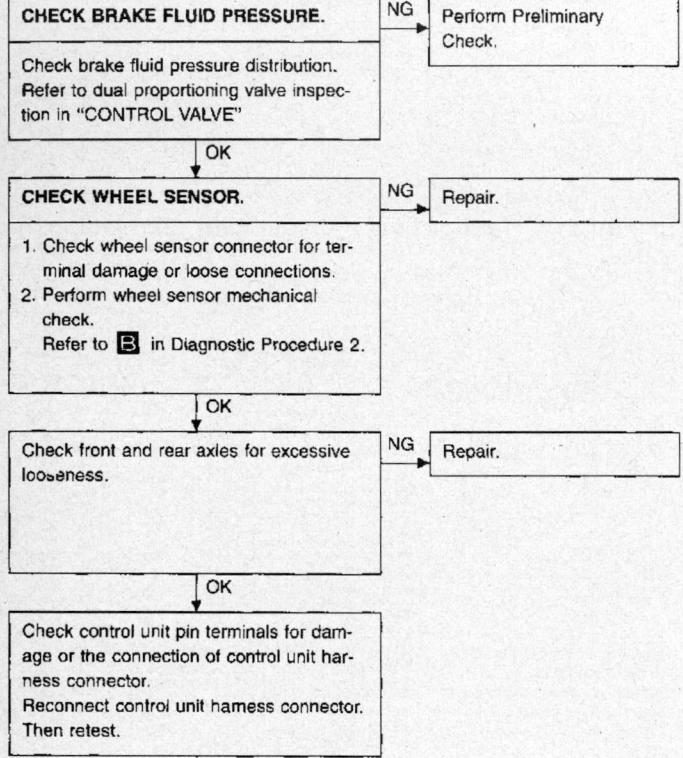

Fig. 118   Test 11: ABS Works Frequently. 1997–99 Maxima

NS4029700265000X

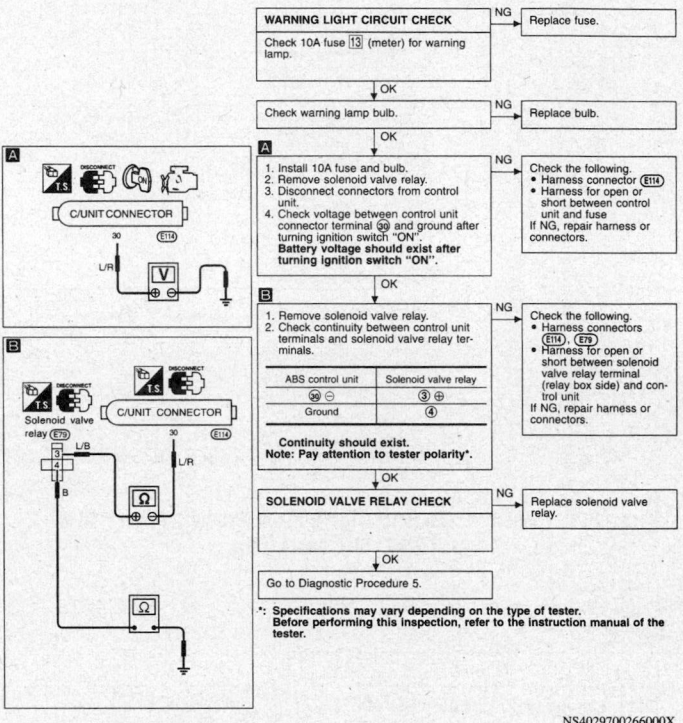

NS4029700266000X

Fig. 119   Test 12: Waring Lamp Does Not Work Before Engine Starts. 1997–99 Maxima

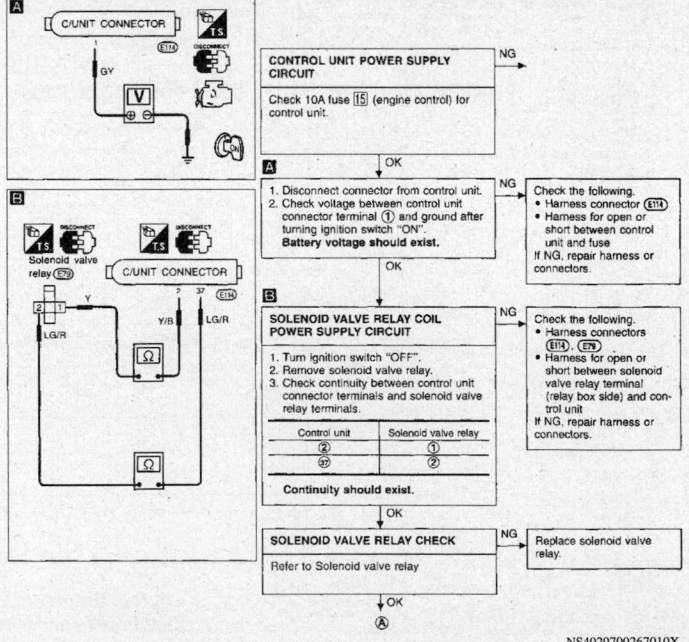

NS4029700267010X

Fig. 120   Test 13: Warning Lamp Stays On Continuously (Part 1 of 3). 1997–99 Maxima

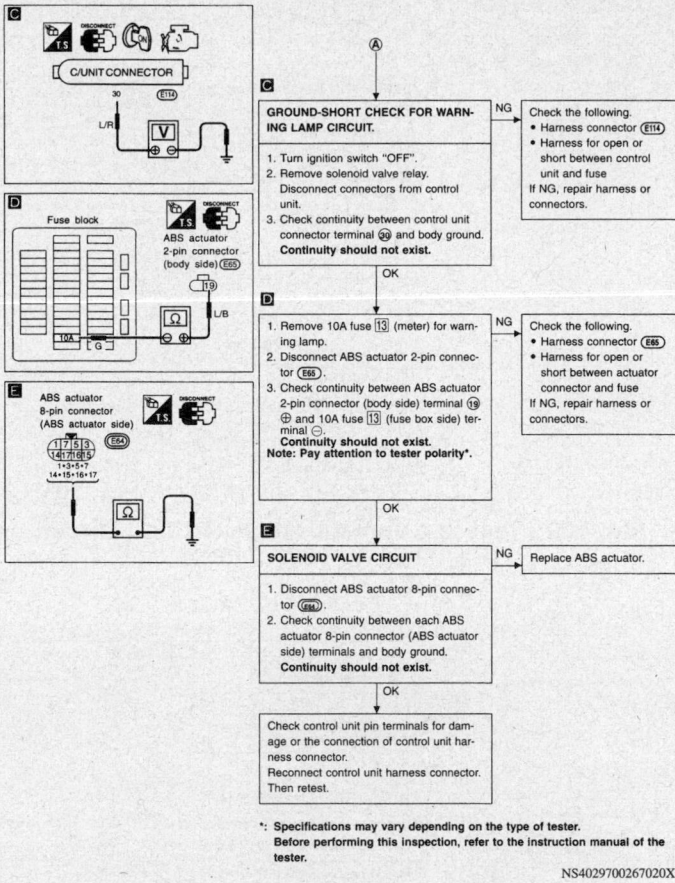

C

GROUND-SHORT CHECK FOR WARNING LAMP CIRCUIT.

1. Turn ignition switch "OFF".
2. Remove solenoid valve relay. Disconnect connectors from control unit.
3. Check continuity between control unit connector terminal ㉚ and body ground.
Continuity should not exist.

NG → Check the following.
• Harness connector (E114).
• Harness for open or short between control unit and fuse.
If NG, repair harness or connectors.

OK

D

1. Remove 10A fuse ⑬ (meter) for warning lamp.
2. Disconnect ABS actuator 2-pin connector (E65).
3. Check continuity between ABS actuator 2-pin connector (body side) terminal ⑲ ⊕ and 10A fuse ⑬ (fuse box side) terminal ⊖.
Continuity should not exist.
Note: Pay attention to tester polarity*.

NG → Check the following.
• Harness connector (E65)
• Harness for open or short between actuator connector and fuse
If NG, repair harness or connectors.

OK

E

SOLENOID VALVE CIRCUIT

1. Disconnect ABS actuator 8-pin connector (E54).
2. Check continuity between each ABS actuator 8-pin connector (ABS actuator side) terminals and body ground.
Continuity should not exist.

NG → Replace ABS actuator.

OK

Check control unit pin terminals for damage or the connection of control unit harness connector.
Reconnect control unit harness connector.
Then retest.

*: Specifications may vary depending on the type of tester.
Before performing this inspection, refer to the instruction manual of the tester.

NS4029700267020X

Fig. 120   Test 13: Warning Lamp Stays On Continuously (Part 2 of 3). 1997–99 Maxima

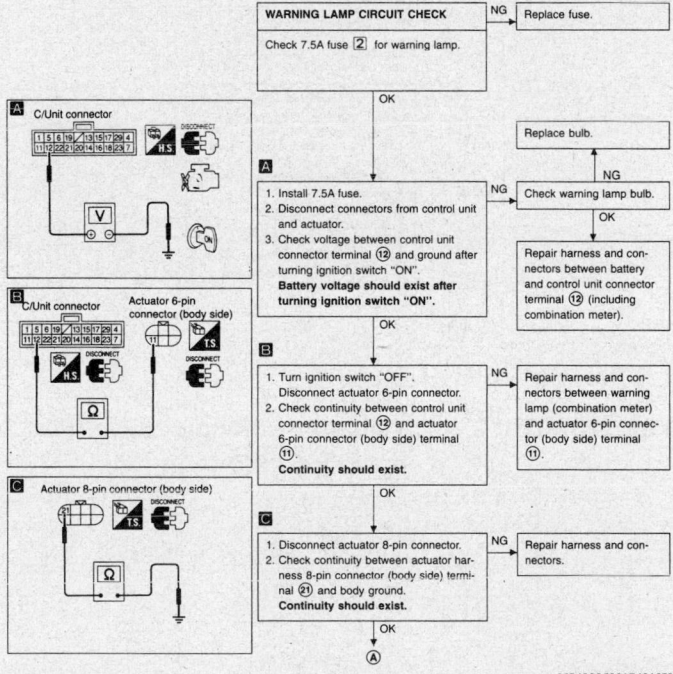

WARNING LAMP CIRCUIT CHECK

Check 7.5A fuse ② for warning lamp.

NG → Replace fuse.

OK

A

1. Install 7.5A fuse.
2. Disconnect connectors from control unit and actuator.
3. Check voltage between control unit connector terminal ⑫ and ground after turning ignition switch "ON".
Battery voltage should exist after turning ignition switch "ON".

NG → Check warning lamp bulb.

NG → Replace bulb.

OK → Repair harness and connectors between battery and control unit connector terminal ⑫ (including combination meter).

OK

B

1. Turn ignition switch "OFF". Disconnect actuator 6-pin connector.
2. Check continuity between control unit connector terminal ⑫ and actuator 6-pin connector (body side) terminal ⑪.
Continuity should exist.

NG → Repair harness and connectors between warning lamp (combination meter) and actuator 6-pin connector (body side) terminal ⑪.

OK

C

1. Disconnect actuator 8-pin connector.
2. Check continuity between actuator harness 8-pin connector (body side) terminal ㉑ and body ground.
Continuity should exist.

NG → Repair harness and connectors.

OK

Ⓐ

NS4029500174010X

Fig. 121   Test 1: Warning Lamp Does Not Work When Ignition Is Turned On (Part 1 of 2). 1996 240SX

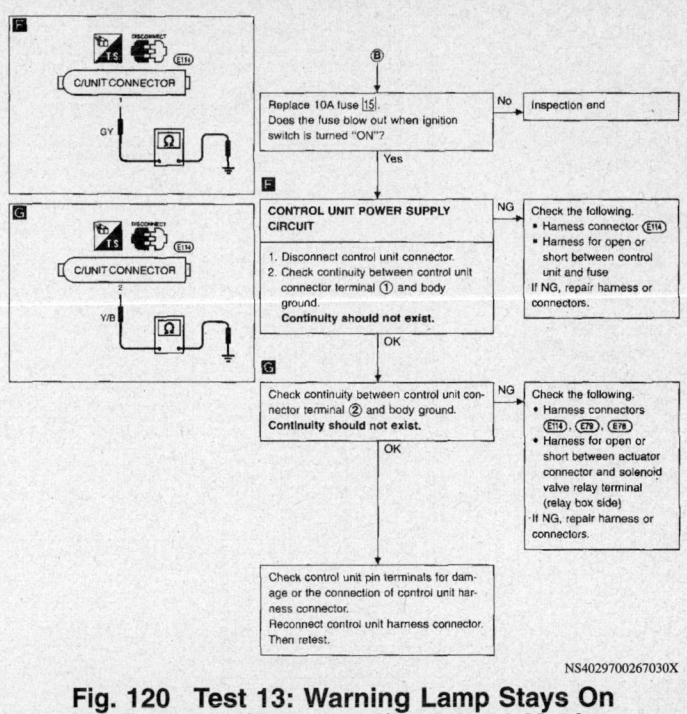

Ⓑ

Replace 10A fuse ⑮.
Does the fuse blow out when ignition switch is turned "ON"?

No → Inspection end

Yes

F

CONTROL UNIT POWER SUPPLY CIRCUIT

1. Disconnect control unit connector.
2. Check continuity between control unit connector terminal ① and body ground.
Continuity should not exist.

NG → Check the following.
• Harness connector (E114)
• Harness for open or short between control unit and fuse
If NG, repair harness or connectors.

OK

G

Check continuity between control unit connector terminal ② and body ground.
Continuity should not exist.

NG → Check the following.
• Harness connectors (E114), (C79), (E78)
• Harness for open or short between actuator connector and solenoid valve relay terminal (relay box side)
If NG, repair harness or connectors.

OK

Check control unit pin terminals for damage or the connection of control unit harness connector.
Reconnect control unit harness connector.
Then retest.

NS4029700267030X

Fig. 120   Test 13: Warning Lamp Stays On Continuously (Part 3 of 3). 1997–99 Maxima

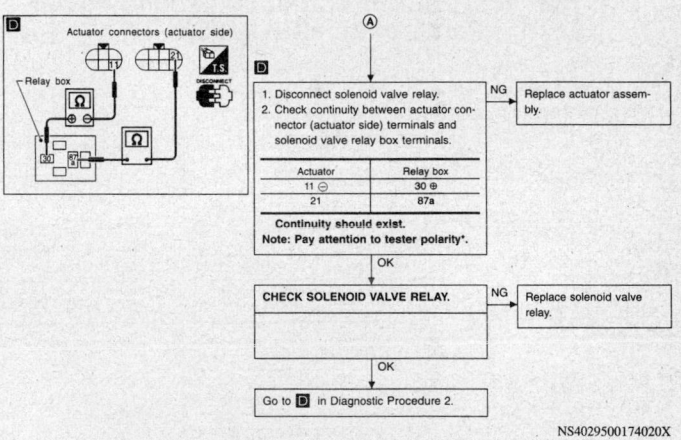

D

1. Disconnect solenoid valve relay.
2. Check continuity between actuator connector (actuator side) terminals and solenoid valve relay box terminals.

Actuator	Relay box
11 ⊖	30 ⊕
21	87a

Continuity should exist.
Note: Pay attention to tester polarity*.

NG → Replace actuator assembly.

OK

CHECK SOLENOID VALVE RELAY.

NG → Replace solenoid valve relay.

OK

Go to **D** in Diagnostic Procedure 2.

NS4029500174020X

Fig. 121   Test 1: Warning Lamp Does Not Work When Ignition Is Turned On (Part 2 of 2). 1996 240SX

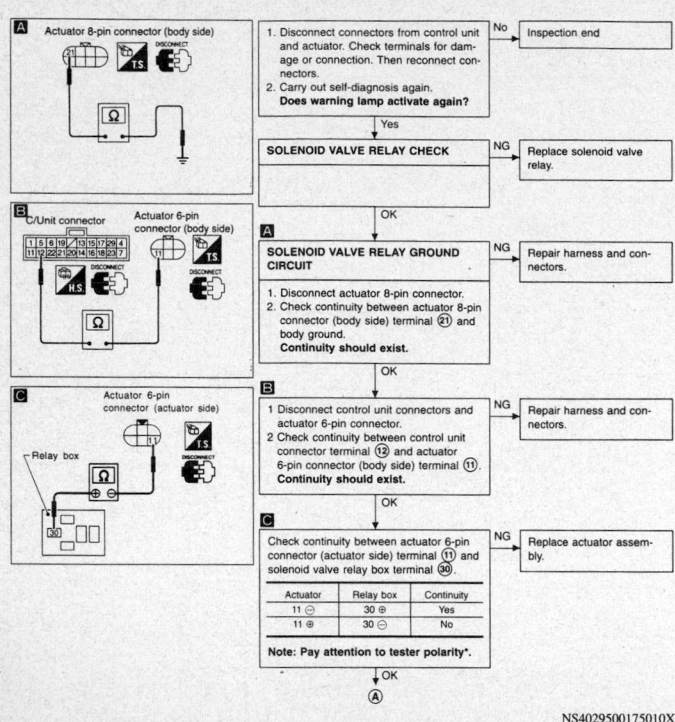

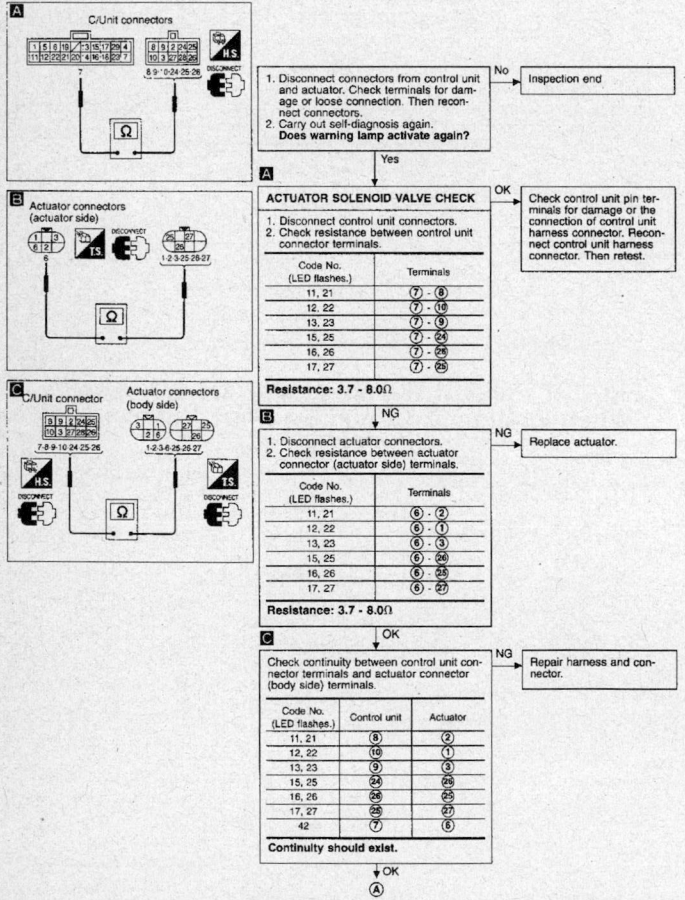

NS4029500175010X

Fig. 122 Test 2: Control Unit Or Ground Circuit (Part 1 of 2). 1996 240SX

NS4029500176010X

Fig. 123 Test 3: Actuator Solenoid Valve (Part 1 of 2). 1996 240SX

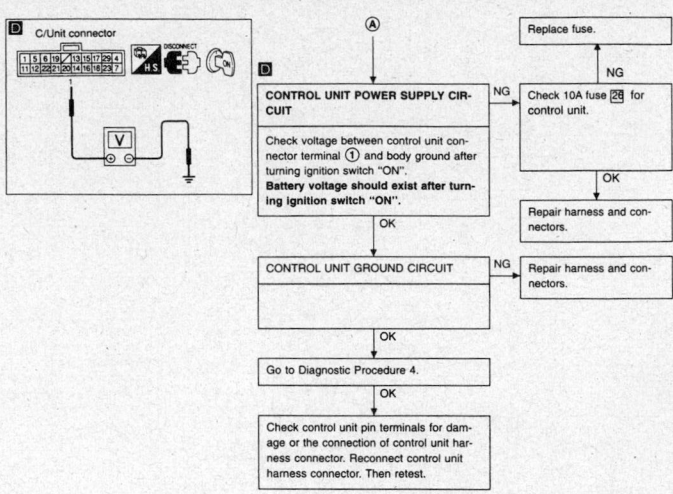

NS4029500175020X

Fig. 122 Test 2: Control Unit Or Ground Circuit (Part 2 of 2). 1996 240SX

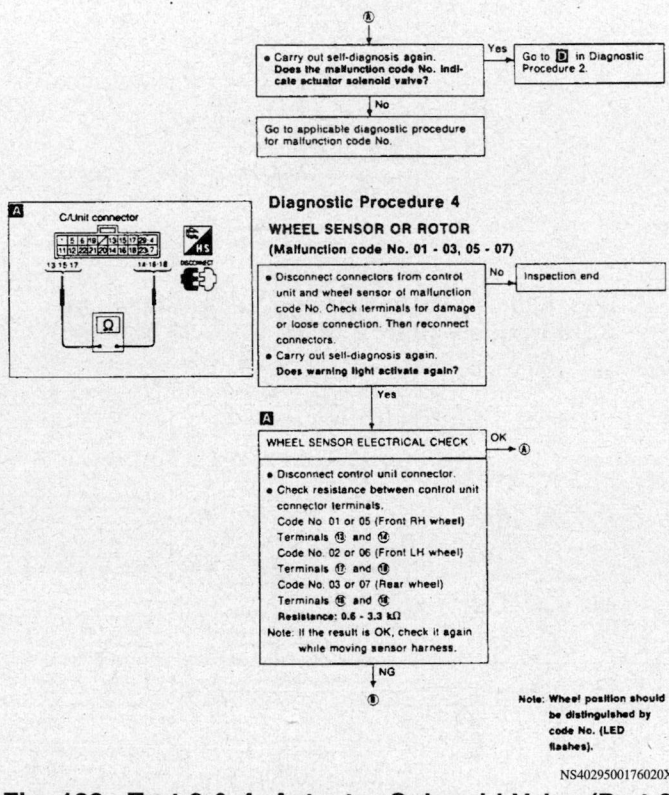

NS4029500176020X

Fig. 123 Test 3 & 4: Actuator Solenoid Valve (Part 2 of 2). 1996 240SX

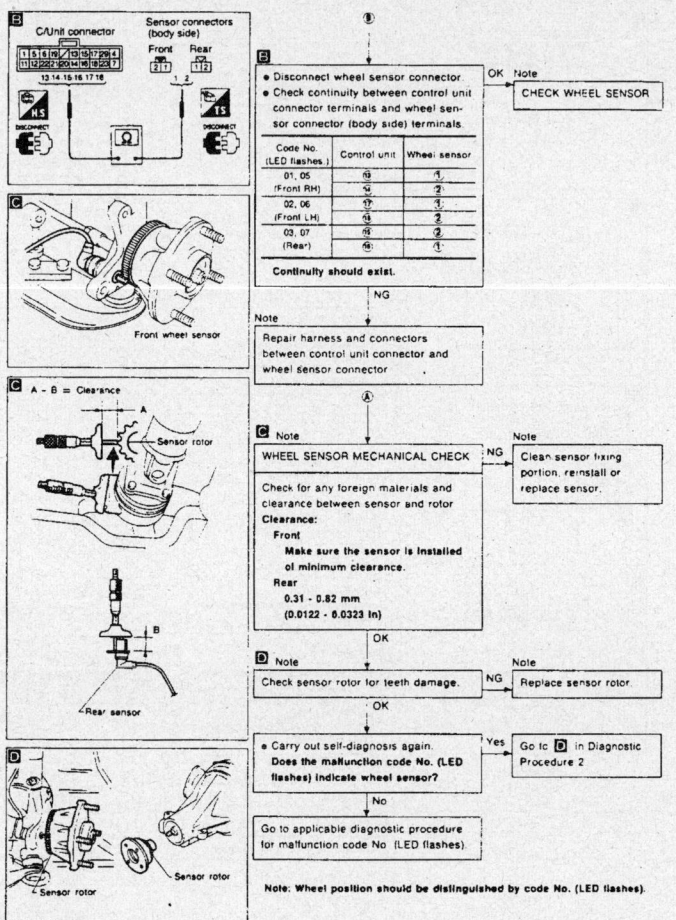

Fig. 124 Test 4: Wheel Sensor Or Rotor. 1996 240SX

NS4029500177000X

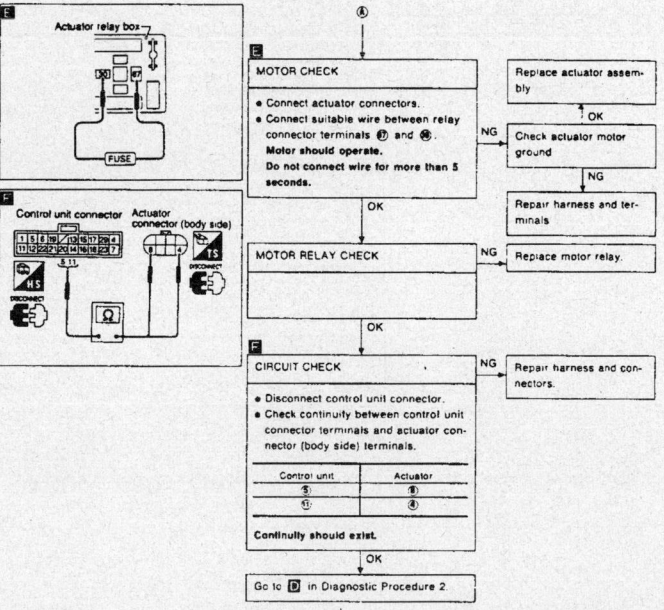

NS4029500178020X

Fig. 125 Test 5: Motor Relay Or Motor (Part 2 of 3). 1996 240SX

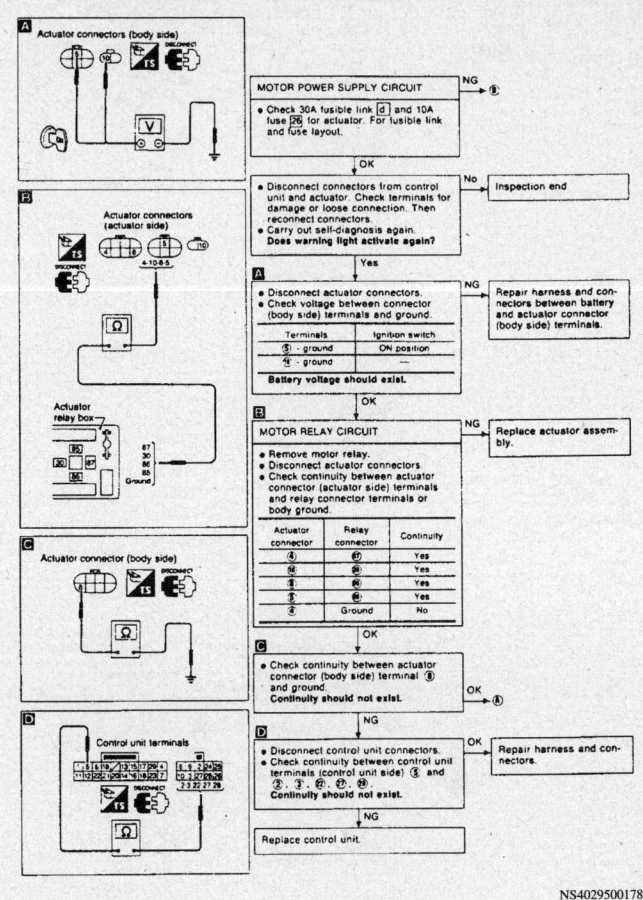

NS4029500178010X

Fig. 125 Test 5: Motor Relay Or Motor (Part 1 of 3). 1996 240SX

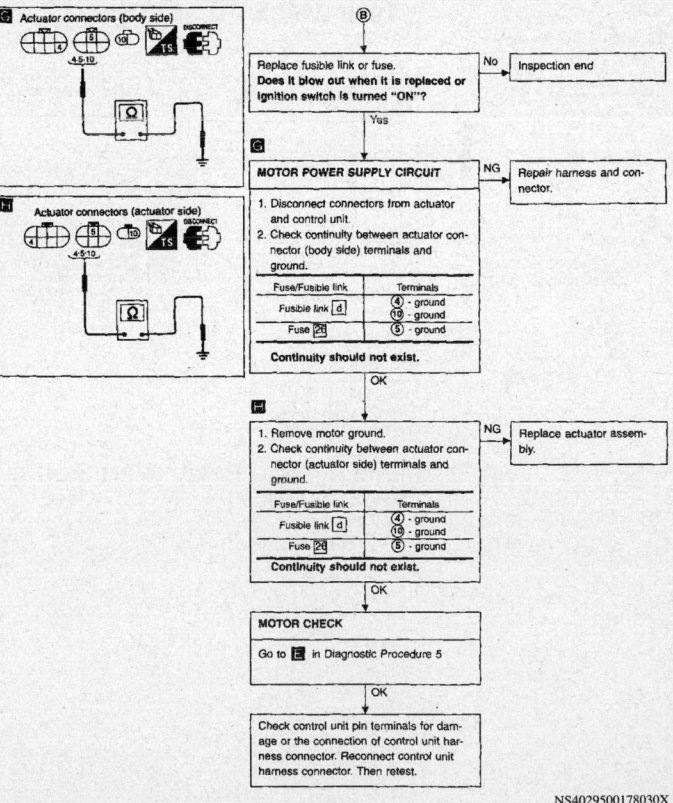

NS4029500178030X

Fig. 125 Test 5: Motor Relay Or Motor (Part 3 of 3). 1996 240SX

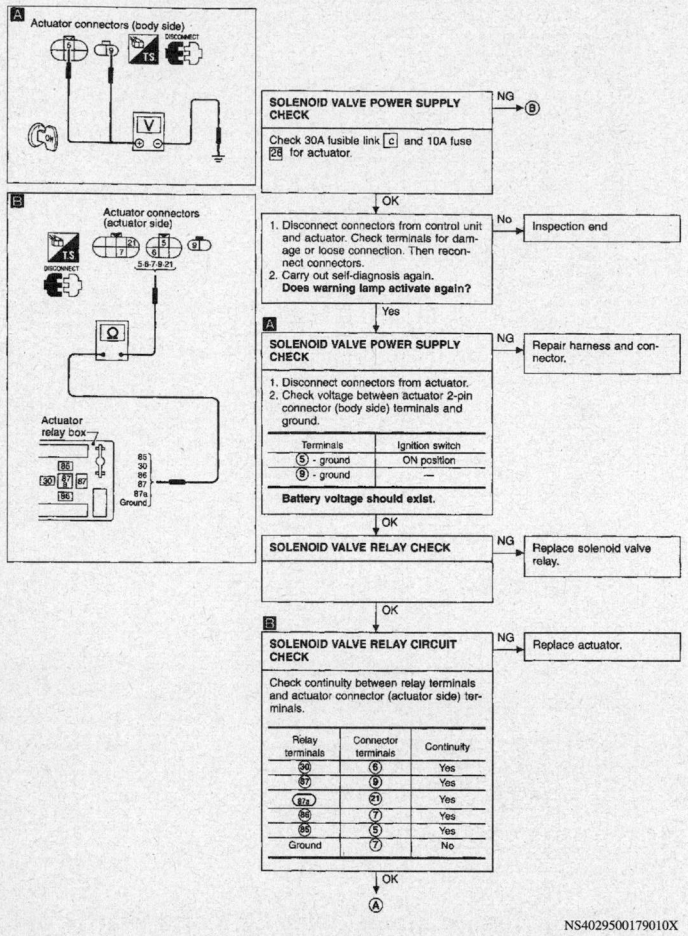

SOLENOID VALVE POWER SUPPLY CHECK — NG → Ⓑ

Check 30A fusible link [c] and 10A fuse 28 for actuator.

↓ OK

1. Disconnect connectors from control unit and actuator. Check terminals for damage or loose connection. Then reconnect connectors.
2. Carry out self-diagnosis again.
Does warning lamp activate again? — No → Inspection end

↓ Yes

Ⓐ **SOLENOID VALVE POWER SUPPLY CHECK** — NG → Repair harness and connector.

1. Disconnect connectors from actuator.
2. Check voltage between actuator 2-pin connector (body side) terminals and ground.

Terminals	Ignition switch
⑤ - ground	ON position
⑨ - ground	—

Battery voltage should exist.

↓ OK

SOLENOID VALVE RELAY CHECK — NG → Replace solenoid valve relay.

↓ OK

Ⓑ **SOLENOID VALVE RELAY CIRCUIT CHECK** — NG → Replace actuator.

Check continuity between relay terminals and actuator connector (actuator side) terminals.

Relay terminals	Connector terminals	Continuity
㉚	⑥	Yes
㊻	⑨	Yes
㉗ₐ	㉑	Yes
㉚	⑦	Yes
㉚	⑤	Yes
Ground	⑦	No

↓ OK

Ⓐ

NS4029500179010X

Fig. 126　Test 6: Solenoid Valve Relay (Part 1 of 3). 1996 240SX

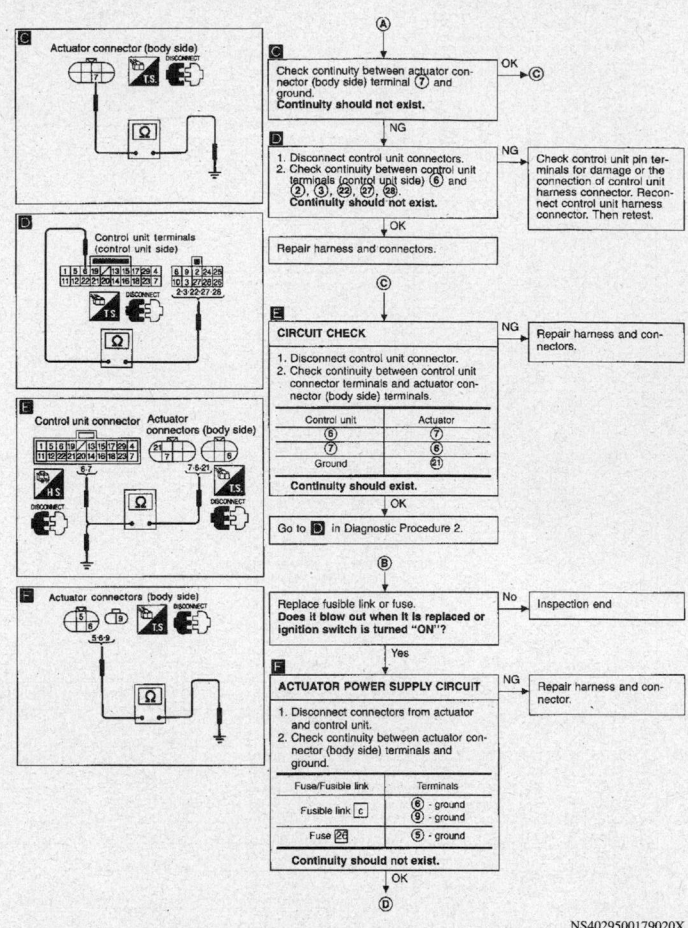

Ⓒ Check continuity between actuator connector (body side) terminal ⑦ and ground.
Continuity should not exist. — OK → Ⓒ

↓ NG

1. Disconnect control unit connectors.
2. Check continuity between control unit terminals (control unit side) ⑥ and ②, ③, ㉒, ㉗, ㉘.
Continuity should not exist. — NG → Check control unit pin terminals for damage or the connection of control unit harness connector. Reconnect control unit harness connector. Then retest.

↓ OK

Repair harness and connectors.

Ⓒ **CIRCUIT CHECK** — NG → Repair harness and connectors.

1. Disconnect control unit connector.
2. Check continuity between control unit connector terminals and actuator connector (body side) terminals.

Control unit	Actuator
⑥	⑦
⑦	⑥
Ground	㉑

Continuity should exist.

↓

Go to Ⓓ in Diagnostic Procedure 2.

Ⓑ Replace fusible link or fuse.
Does it blow out when it is replaced or ignition switch is turned "ON"? — No → Inspection end

↓ Yes

Ⓕ **ACTUATOR POWER SUPPLY CIRCUIT** — NG → Repair harness and connector.

1. Disconnect connectors from actuator and control unit.
2. Check continuity between actuator connector (body side) terminals and ground.

Fuse/Fusible link	Terminals
Fusible link [c]	⑥ - ground
	⑨ - ground
Fuse 26	⑤ - ground

Continuity should not exist.

↓ OK

Ⓓ

NS4029500179020X

Fig. 126　Test 6: Solenoid Valve Relay (Part 2 of 3). 1996 240SX

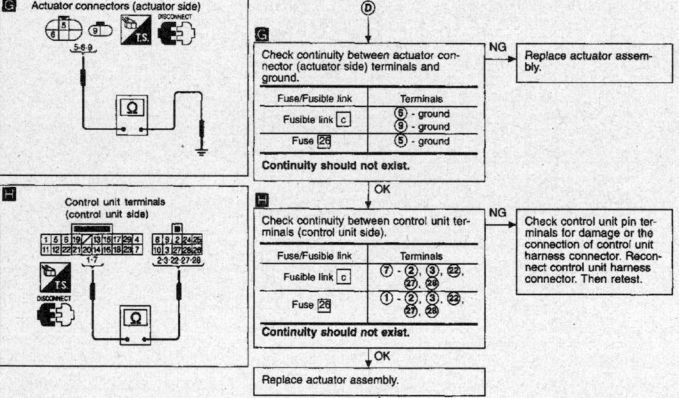

Ⓖ Check continuity between actuator connector (actuator side) terminals and ground. — NG → Replace actuator assembly.

Fuse/Fusible link	Terminals
Fusible link [c]	⑥ - ground
	⑨ - ground
Fuse 26	⑤ - ground

Continuity should not exist.

↓ OK

Ⓗ Check continuity between control unit terminals (control unit side). — NG → Check control unit pin terminals for damage or the connection of control unit harness connector. Reconnect control unit harness connector. Then retest.

Fuse/Fusible link	Terminals
Fusible link [c]	⑦ - ②, ③, ㉒, ㉗, ㉘
Fuse 26	①, ②, ③, ㉒, ㉗, ㉘

Continuity should not exist.

↓

Replace actuator assembly.

NS4029500179030X

Fig. 126　Test 6: Solenoid Valve Relay (Part 3 of 3). 1996 240SX

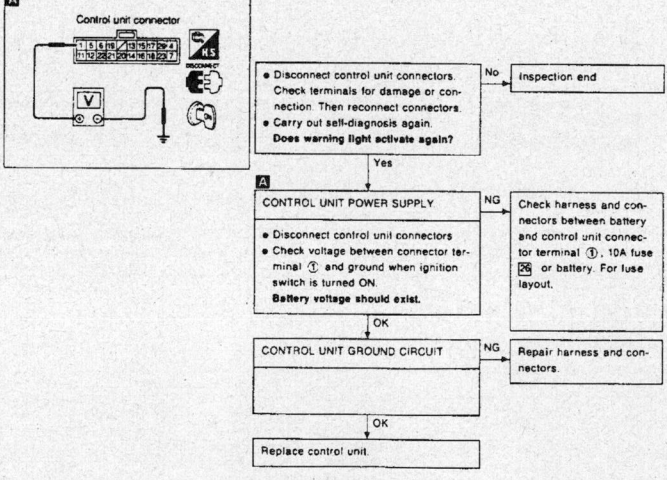

● Disconnect control unit connectors. Check terminals for damage or connection. Then reconnect connectors.
● Carry out self-diagnosis again.
Does warning light activate again? — No → Inspection end

↓ Yes

Ⓐ **CONTROL UNIT POWER SUPPLY** — NG → Check harness and connectors between battery and control unit connector terminal ①, 10A fuse 26 or battery. For fuse layout.

● Disconnect control unit connectors.
● Check voltage between connector terminal ① and ground when ignition switch is turned ON.
Battery voltage should exist.

↓ OK

CONTROL UNIT GROUND CIRCUIT — NG → Repair harness and connectors.

↓ OK

Replace control unit.

NS4029500180000X

Fig. 127　Test 7: Power Supply. 1996 240SX

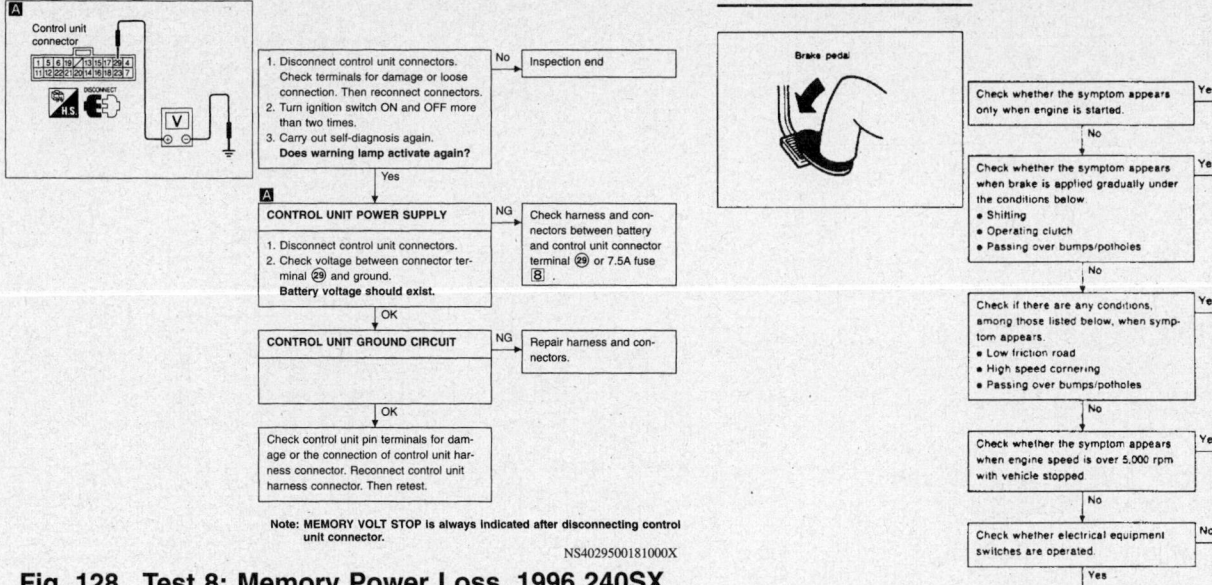

Fig. 128   Test 8: Memory Power Loss. 1996 240SX

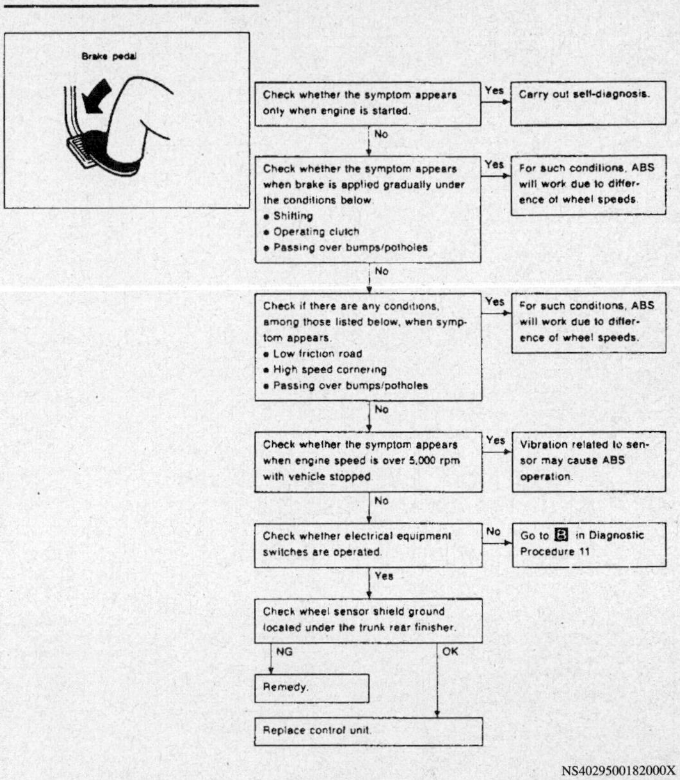

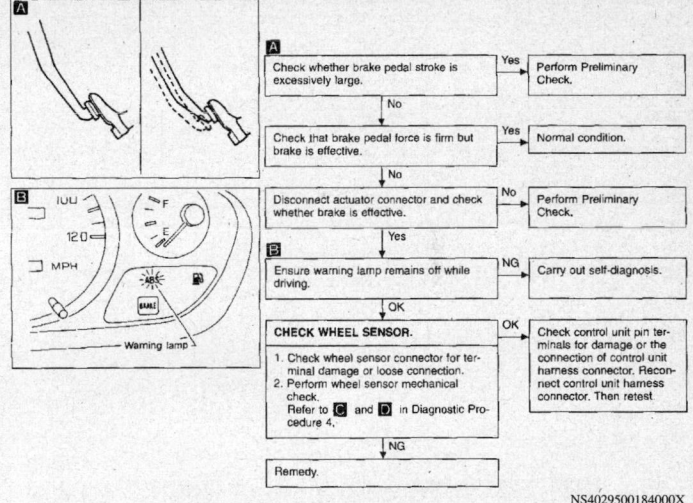

Fig. 129   Test 9: Pedal Vibration & Noise. 1996 240SX

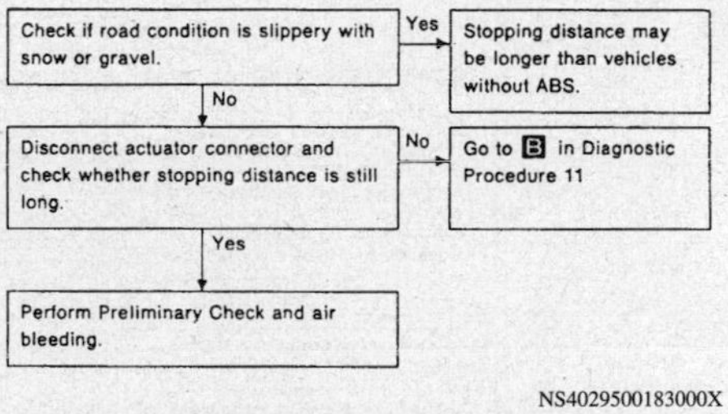

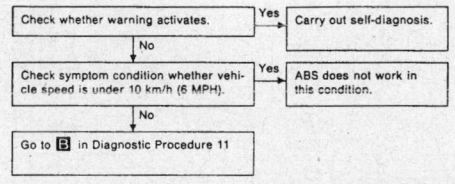

Fig. 130   Test 10: Long Stopping Distance. 1996 240SX

Fig. 131   Test 11: Unexpected Pedal Action. 1996 240SX

Fig. 132   Test 12: ABS Does Not Work. 1996 240SX

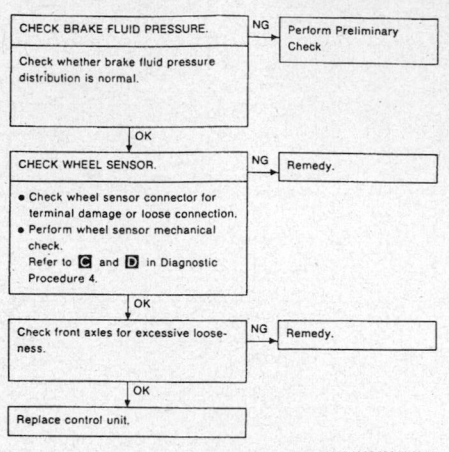

CHECK BRAKE FLUID PRESSURE.

Check whether brake fluid pressure distribution is normal.

→ NG → Perform Preliminary Check

↓ OK

CHECK WHEEL SENSOR.

- Check wheel sensor connector for terminal damage or loose connection.
- Perform wheel sensor mechanical check.
  Refer to C and D in Diagnostic Procedure 4.

→ NG → Remedy.

↓ OK

Check front axles for excessive looseness.

→ NG → Remedy.

↓ OK

Replace control unit.

NS4029500186000X

Fig. 133 Test 13: ABS Works Frequently. 1996 240SX

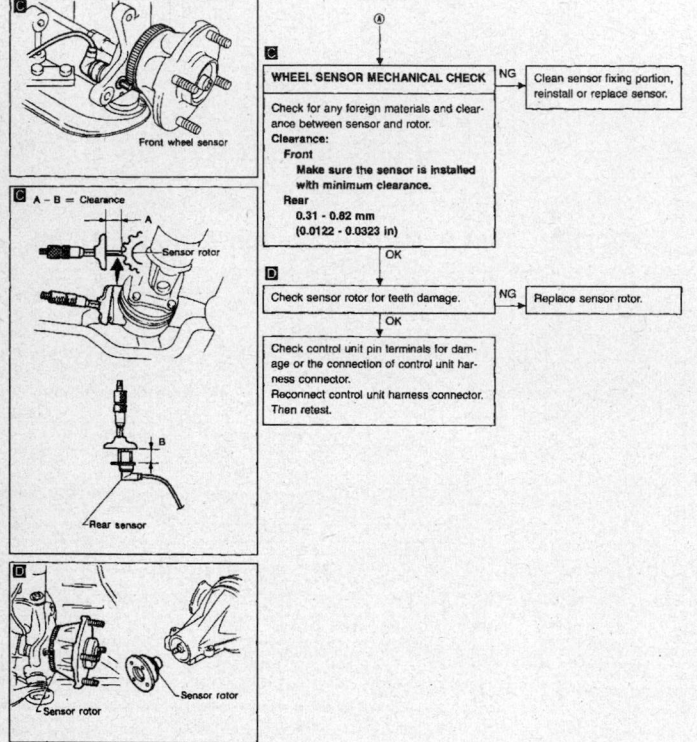

WHEEL SENSOR MECHANICAL CHECK

Check for any foreign materials and clearance between sensor and rotor.
Clearance:
Front
Make sure the sensor is installed with minimum clearance.
Rear
0.31 - 0.82 mm
(0.0122 - 0.0323 in)

→ NG → Clean sensor fixing portion, reinstall or replace sensor.

↓ OK

Check sensor rotor for teeth damage.

→ NG → Replace sensor rotor.

↓ OK

Check control unit pin terminals for damage or the connection of control unit harness connector.
Reconnect control unit harness connector. Then retest.

NS4029700239020X

Fig. 134 Test 1: Wheel Sensor or Rotor (Part 2 of 2). 1997-98 240SX

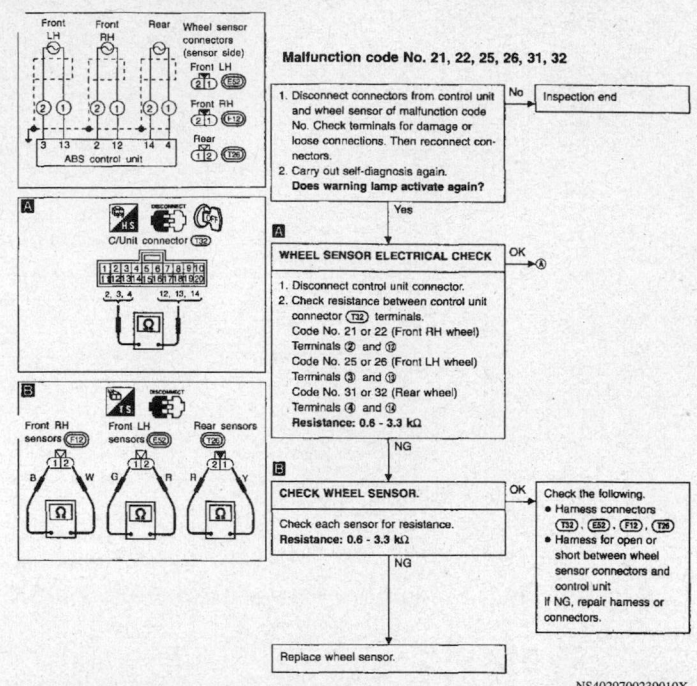

Malfunction code No. 21, 22, 25, 26, 31, 32

1. Disconnect connectors from control unit and wheel sensor of malfunction code No. Check terminals for damage or loose connections. Then reconnect connectors.
2. Carry out self-diagnosis again.
   Does warning lamp activate again?

→ No → Inspection end

↓ Yes

WHEEL SENSOR ELECTRICAL CHECK → OK → A

1. Disconnect control unit connector.
2. Check resistance between control unit connector (T32) terminals.
   Code No. 21 or 22 (Front RH wheel)
   Terminals ② and ⑫
   Code No. 25 or 26 (Front LH wheel)
   Terminals ③ and ⑬
   Code No. 31 or 32 (Rear wheel)
   Terminals ④ and ⑭
   Resistance: 0.6 - 3.3 kΩ

↓ NG

CHECK WHEEL SENSOR.

Check each sensor for resistance.
Resistance: 0.6 - 3.3 kΩ

→ OK → Check the following.
- Harness connectors (T32), (E52), (F12), (T26)
- Harness for open or short between wheel sensor connectors and control unit
If NG, repair harness or connectors.

↓ NG

Replace wheel sensor.

NS4029700239010X

Fig. 134 Test 1: Wheel Sensor or Rotor (Part 1 of 2). 1997-98 240SX

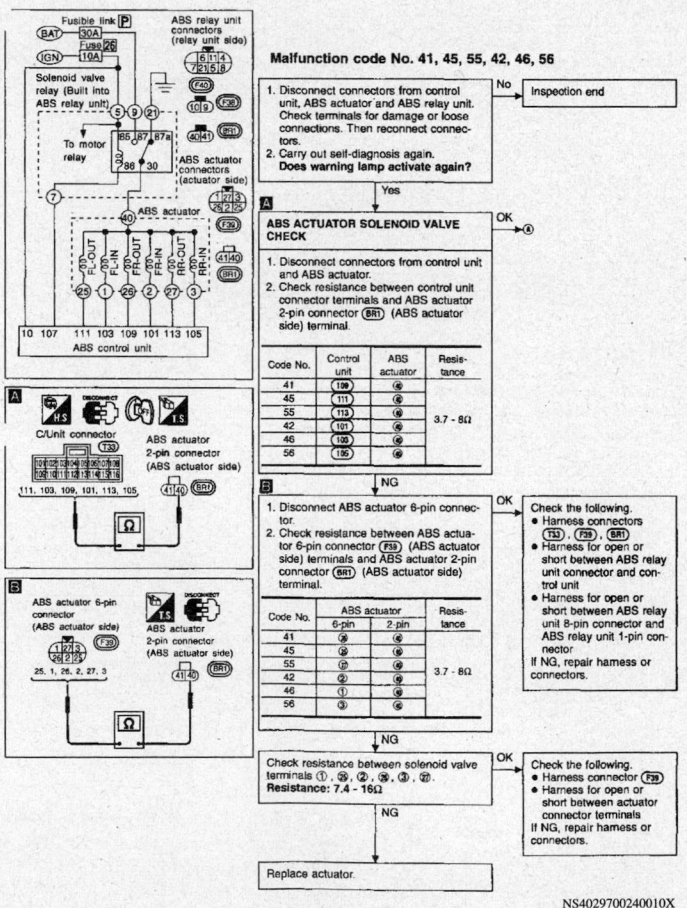

Malfunction code No. 41, 45, 55, 42, 46, 56

1. Disconnect connectors from control unit, ABS actuator and ABS relay unit. Check terminals for damage or loose connections. Then reconnect connectors.
2. Carry out self-diagnosis again.
   Does warning lamp activate again?

→ No → Inspection end

↓ Yes

ABS ACTUATOR SOLENOID VALVE CHECK → OK → A

1. Disconnect connectors from control unit and ABS actuator.
2. Check resistance between control unit connector terminals and ABS actuator 2-pin connector (BR1) (ABS actuator side) terminal.

Code No.	Control unit	ABS actuator	Resistance
41	109	④	
45	111	④	
55	113	④	3.7 - 8Ω
42	101	④	
46	105	④	
56	105	④	

↓ NG

1. Disconnect ABS actuator 6-pin connector.
2. Check resistance between ABS actuator 6-pin connector (F39) (ABS actuator side) terminals and ABS actuator 2-pin connector (BR1) (ABS actuator side) terminal.

Code No.	ABS actuator 6-pin	ABS actuator 2-pin	Resistance
41	④	④	
45	⑤	④	
55	⑦	④	3.7 - 8Ω
42	②	④	
46	①	④	
56	③	④	

→ OK → Check the following.
- Harness connectors (T33), (F39), (BR1)
- Harness for open or short between ABS relay unit connector and control unit
- Harness for open or short between ABS relay unit 8-pin connector and ABS relay unit 1-pin connector
If NG, repair harness or connectors.

↓ NG

Check resistance between solenoid valve terminals ①, ⑤, ②, ⑥, ③, ⑦.
Resistance: 7.4 - 16Ω

→ OK → Check the following.
- Harness connector (F39)
- Harness for open or short between actuator connector terminals
If NG, repair harness or connectors.

↓ NG

Replace actuator.

NS4029700240010X

Fig. 135 Test 2: ABS Actuator Solenoid Valve (Part 1 of 2). 1997-98 240SX

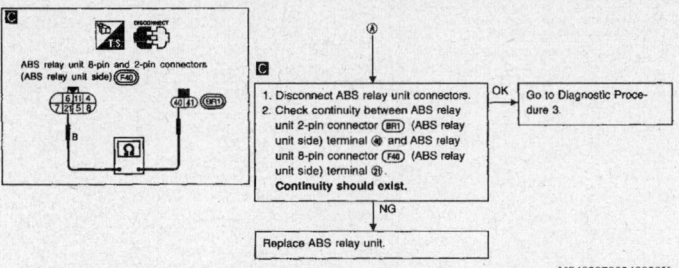

Fig. 135 Test 2: ABS Actuator Solenoid Valve (Part 2 of 2). 1997-98 240SX

NS4029700240020X

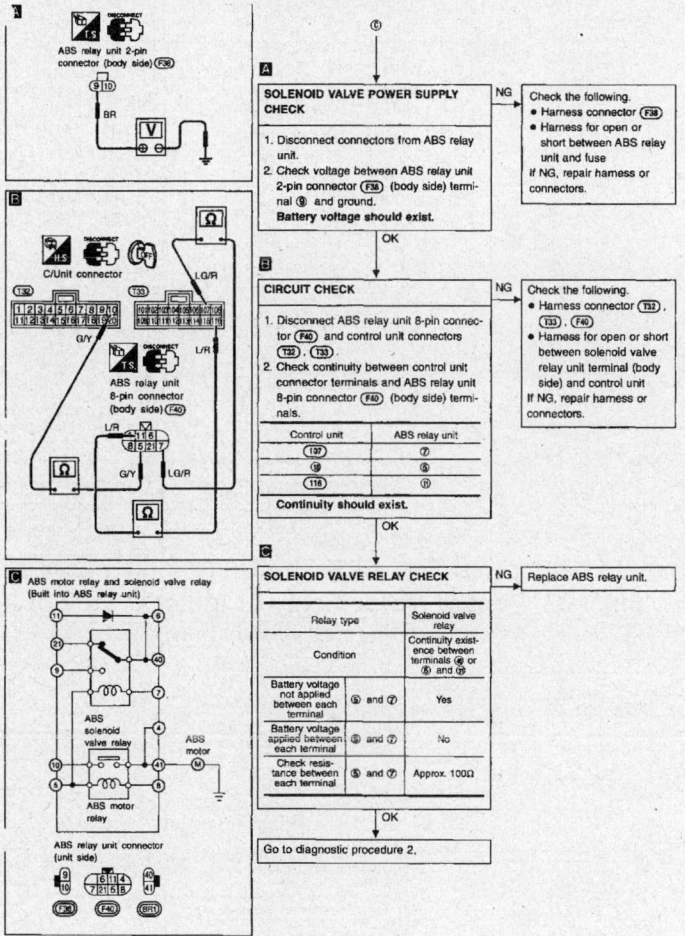

Fig. 136 Test 3: Solenoid Valve Relay (Part 2 of 3). 1997-98 240SX

NS4029700241020X

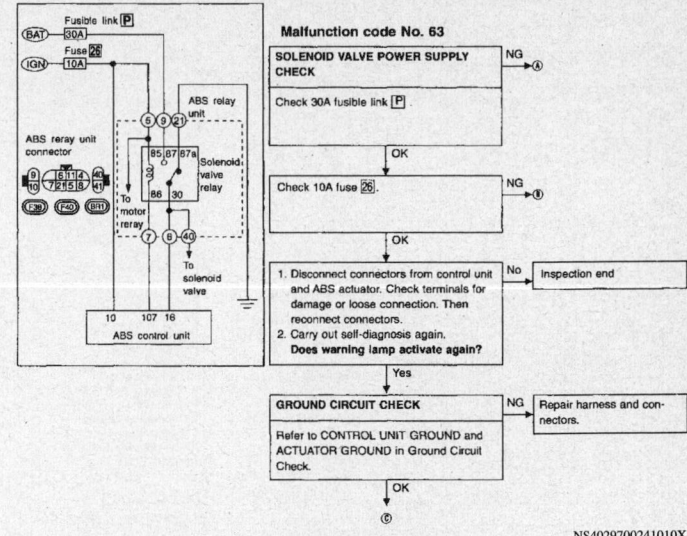

Fig. 136 Test 3: Solenoid Valve Relay (Part 1 of 3). 1997-98 240SX

NS4029700241010X

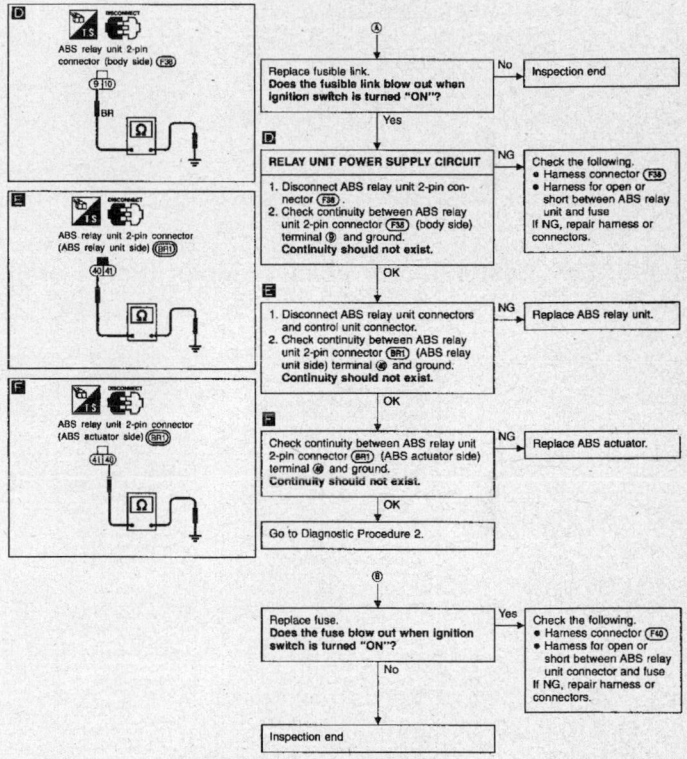

Fig. 136 Test 3: Solenoid Valve Relay (Part 3 of 3). 1997-98 240SX

NS4029700241030X

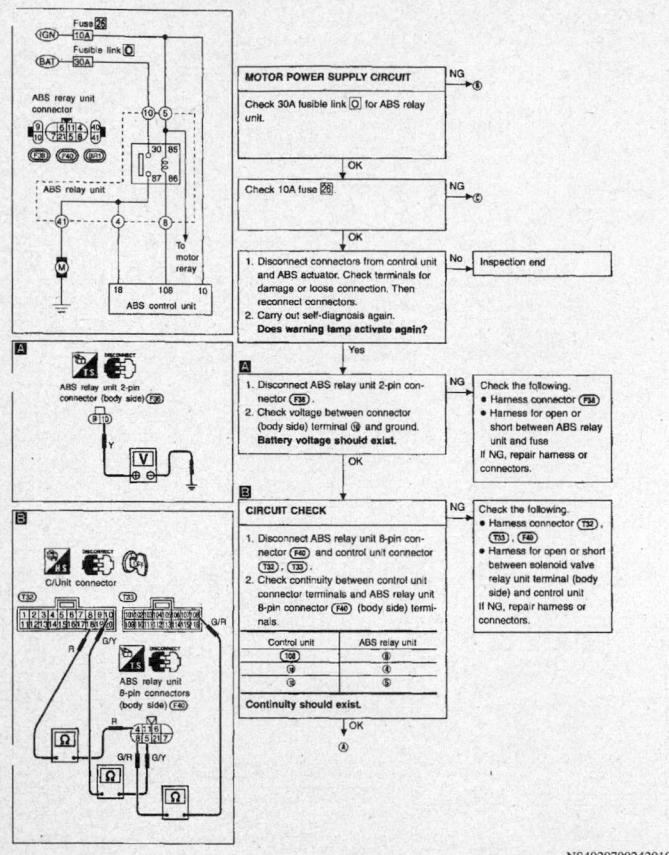

Fig. 137 Test 4: Motor Relay or Motor (Part 1 of 3). 1997–98 240SX

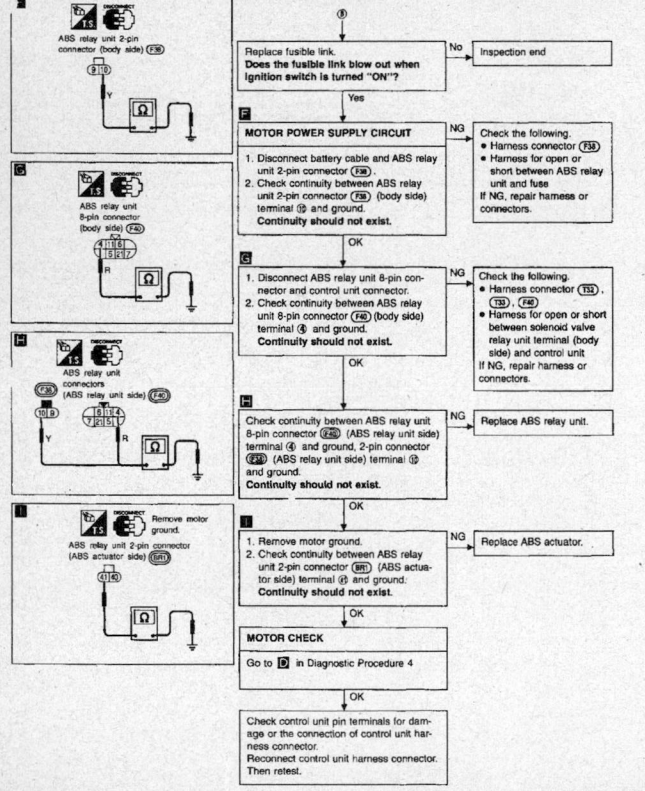

Fig. 137 Test 4: Motor Relay or Motor (Part 3 of 3). 1997–98 240SX

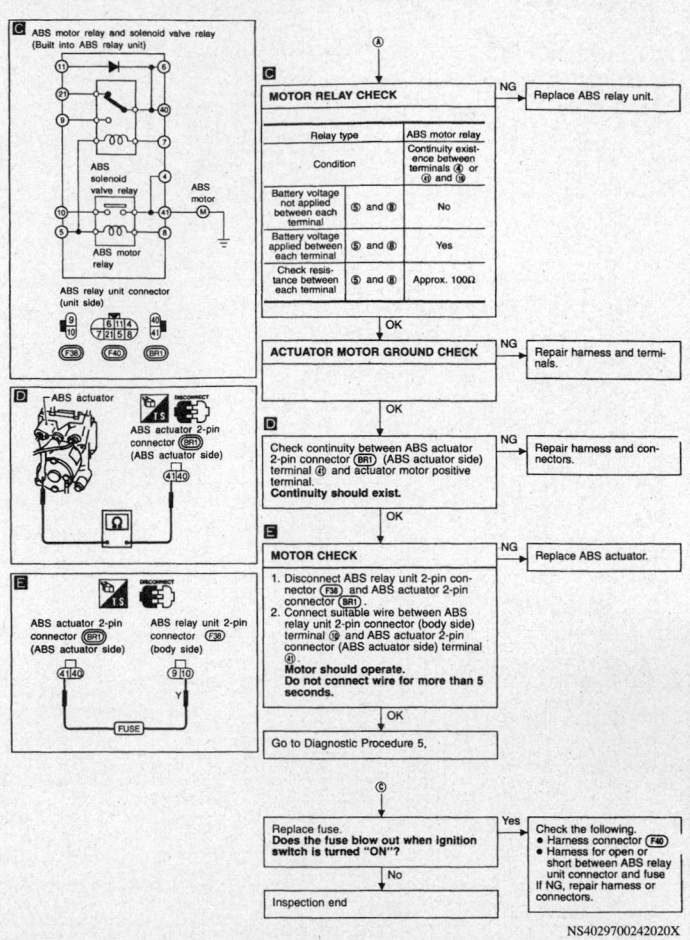

Fig. 137 Test 4: Motor Relay or Motor (Part 2 of 3). 1997–98 240SX

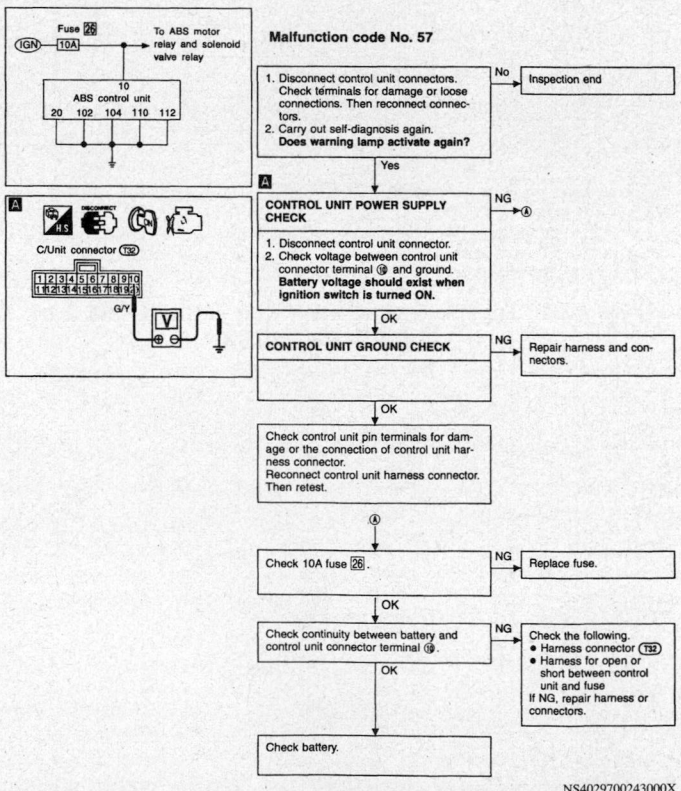

Fig. 138 Test 5: Low Voltage. 1997–98 240SX

ANTI-LOCK BRAKES

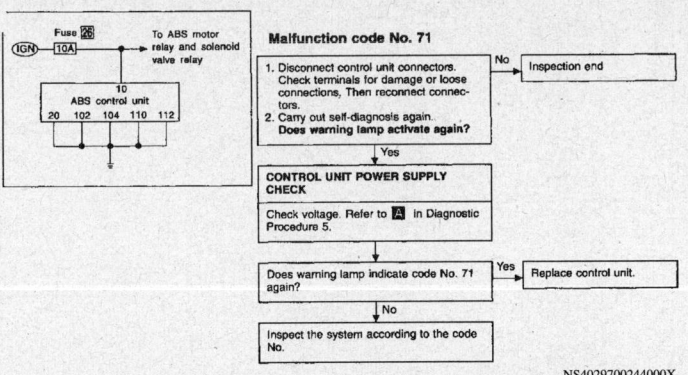

Fig. 139   Test 6: Control Unit. 1997–98 240SX

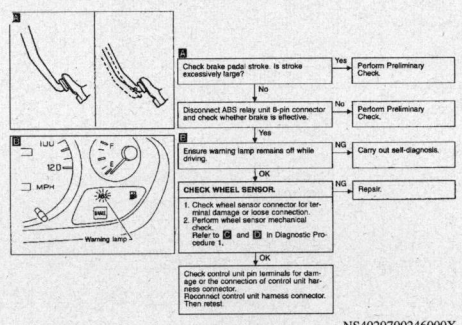

Fig. 141   Test 8: Unexpected
Pedal Action. 1997–98 240SX

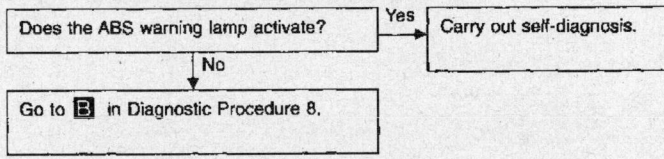

Does the ABS warning lamp activate? → Yes → Carry out self-diagnosis.

↓ No

Go to **B** in Diagnostic Procedure 8.

Note: ABS does not work when vehicle speed is under 10 km/h (6 MPH).

Fig. 143   Test 10: ABS Does Not Work. 1997–98
240SX

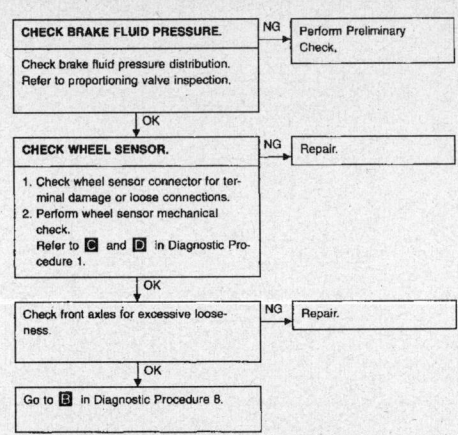

Fig. 140   Test 7: ABS Works
Frequently. 1997–98 240SX

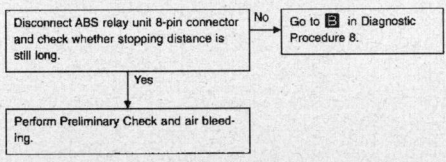

Note: Stopping distance may be larger than vehicles without
ABS when road condition is slippery.

Fig. 142   Test 9: Long Stopping
Distance. 1997–98 240SX

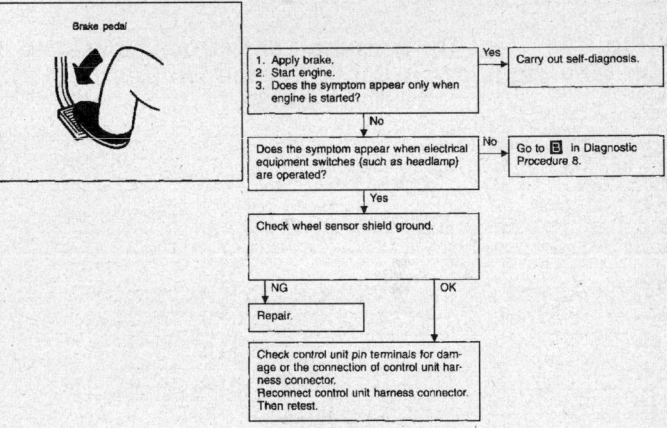

Note: ABS may operate and cause vibration under any of the
following conditions.
- Applying brake gradually when shifting or operating clutch.
- Low friction (slippery) road.
- High speed cornering.
- Driving over bumps and pot holes.
- Engine speed is over 5,000 rpm with vehicle stopped.

Fig. 144   Test 11: Pedal Vibration & Noise. 1997–98
240SX

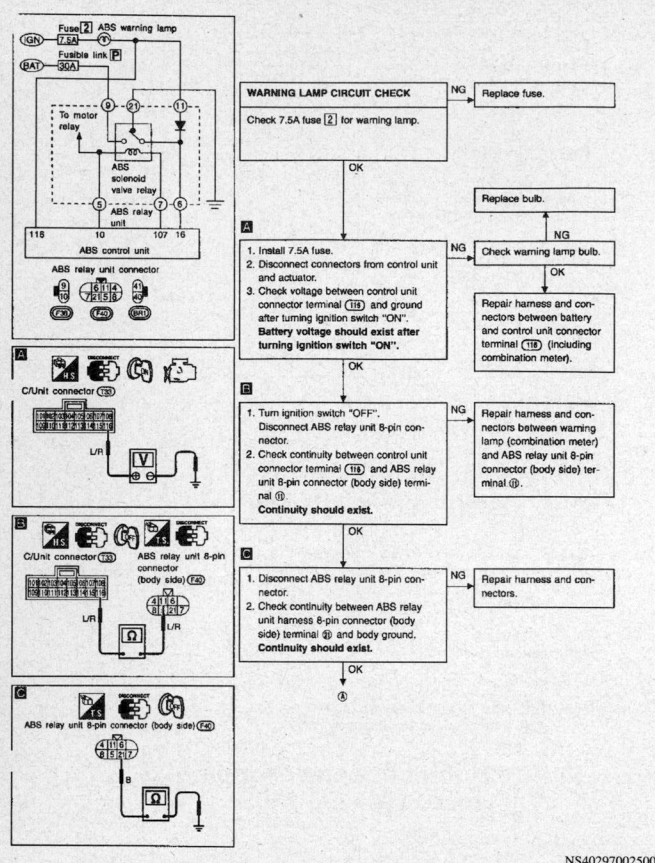

Fig. 145   Test 12: Warning Lamp Does Not Come
On When Ignition Switch Is Turned On (Part 1 of 2).
1997–98 240SX

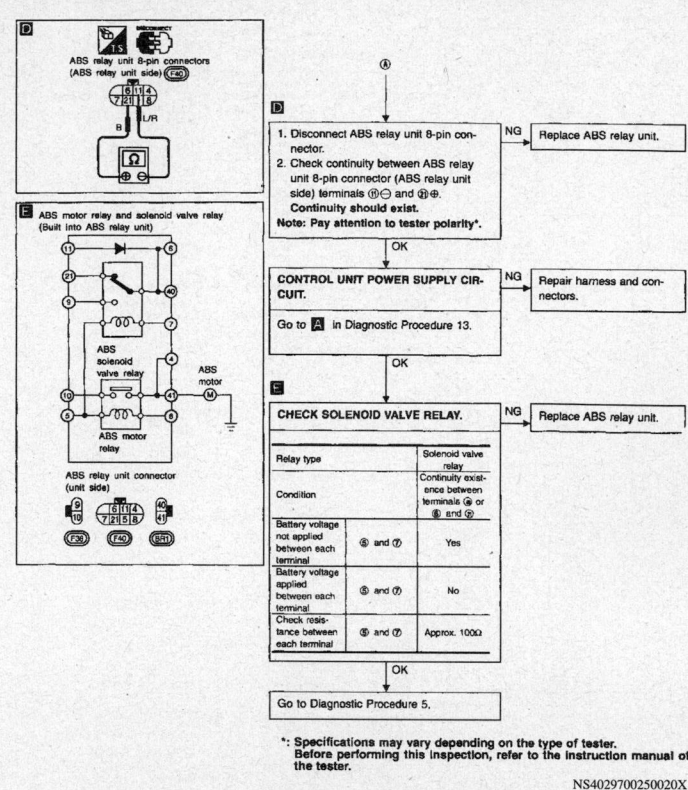

Fig. 145   Test 12: Warning Lamp Does Not Come
On When Ignition Switch Is Turned On (Part 2 of 2).
1997–98 240SX

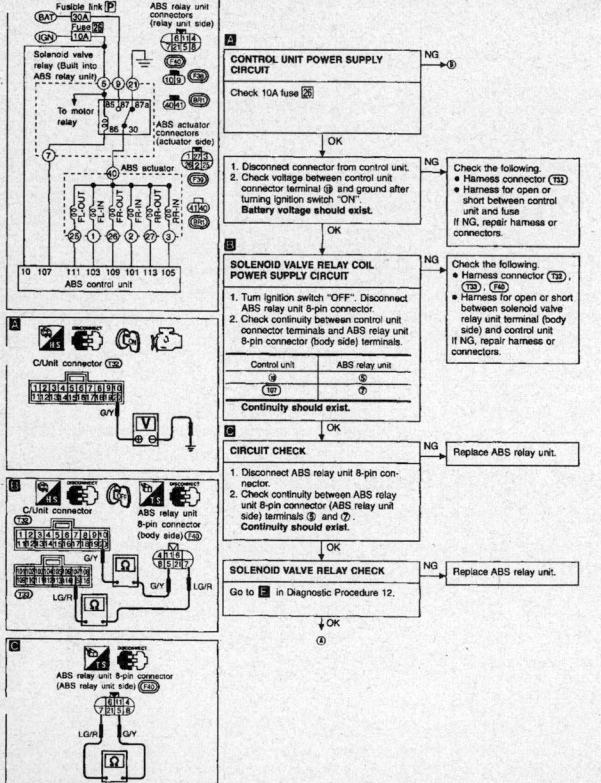

Fig. 146   Test 13: Warning Lamp Stays On When
Ignition Switch Is Turned On (Part 1 of 3). 1997–98
240SX

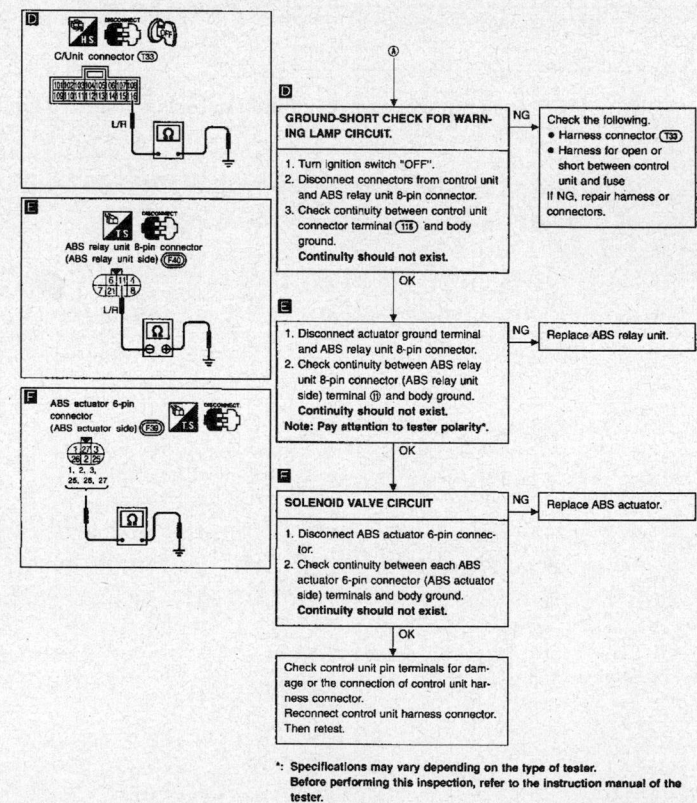

Fig. 146   Test 13: Warning Lamp Stays On When
Ignition Switch Is Turned On (Part 2 of 3). 1997–98
240SX

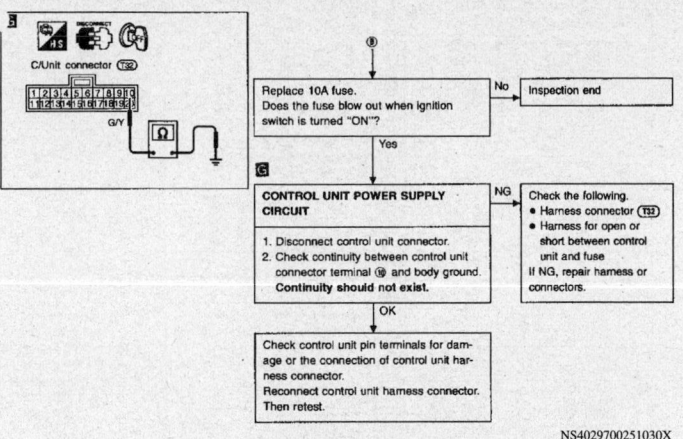

Fig. 146 Test 13: Warning Lamp Stays On When Ignition Switch Is Turned On (Part 3 of 3). 1997–98 240SX

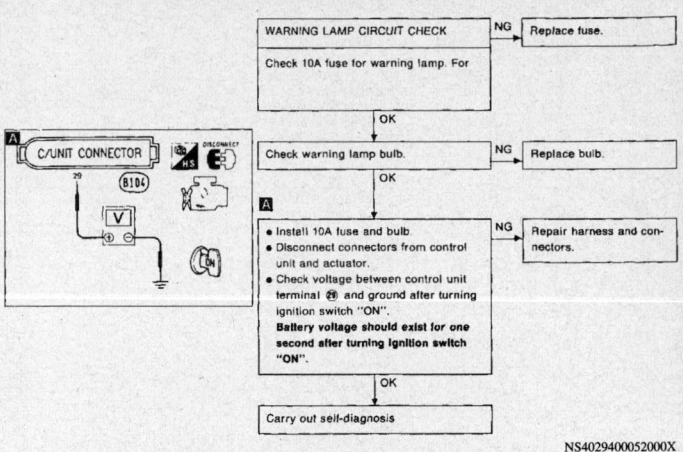

Fig. 147 Test 1: Warning Lamp Does Not Work Before Engine Starts. 300ZX

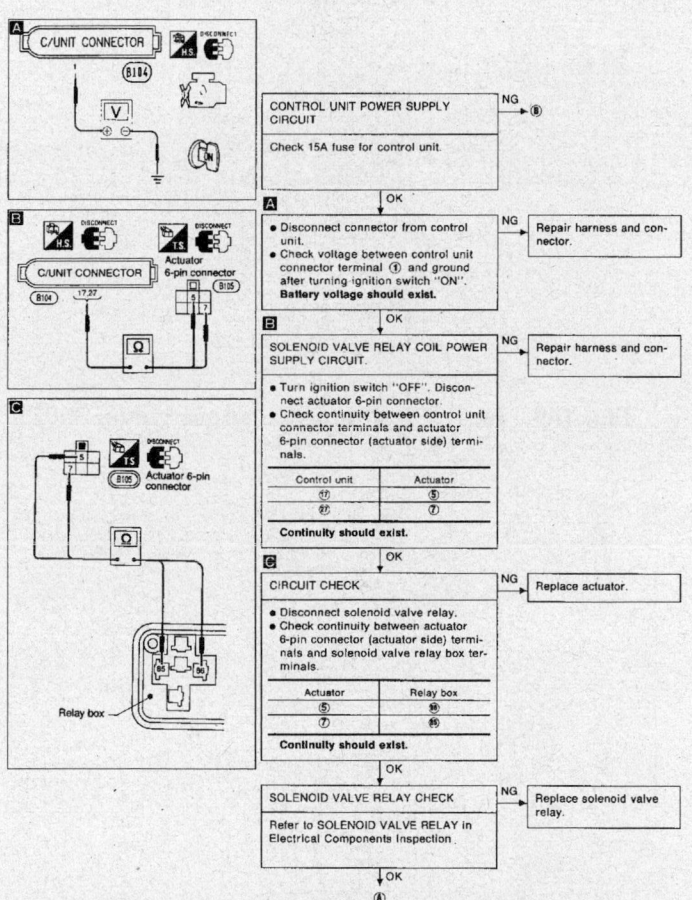

Fig. 148 Test 2: Warning Lamp Stays On Continuously (Part 1 of 3). 300ZX

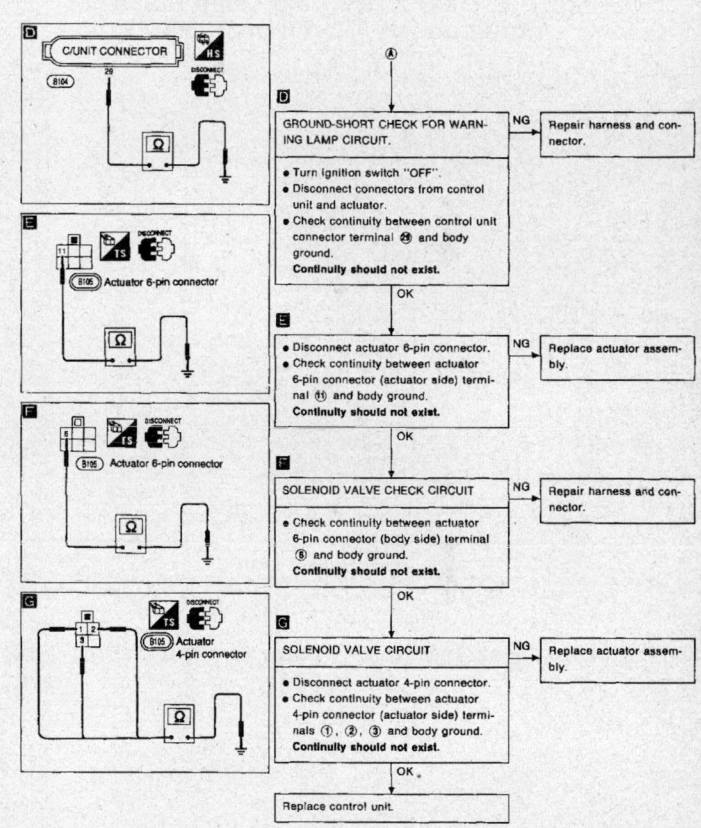

Fig. 148 Test 2: Warning Lamp Stays On Continuously (Part 2 of 3). 300ZX

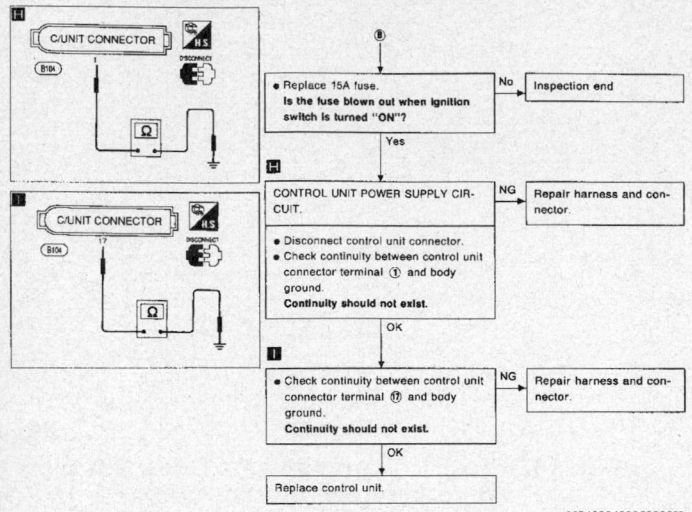

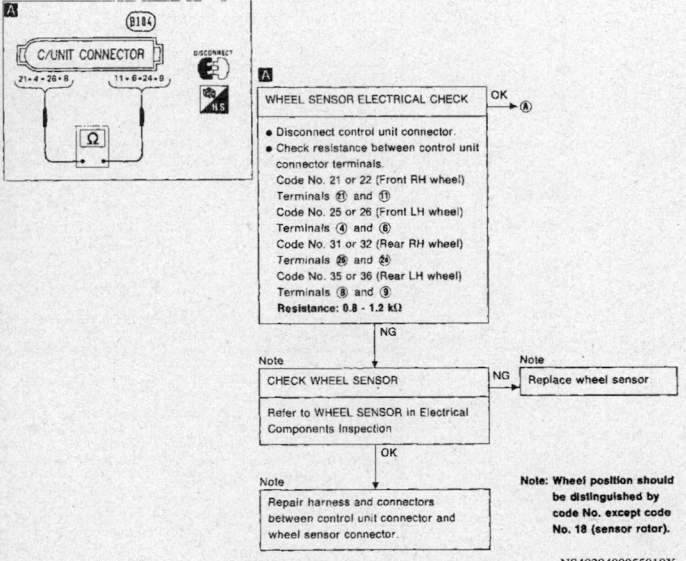

Fig. 148 Test 2: Warning Lamp Stays On Continuously (Part 3 of 3). 300ZX

NS4029400053030X

NS4029400055010X

Fig. 150 Test 4: Wheel Sensor Or Rotor (Part 1 of 2). 300ZX

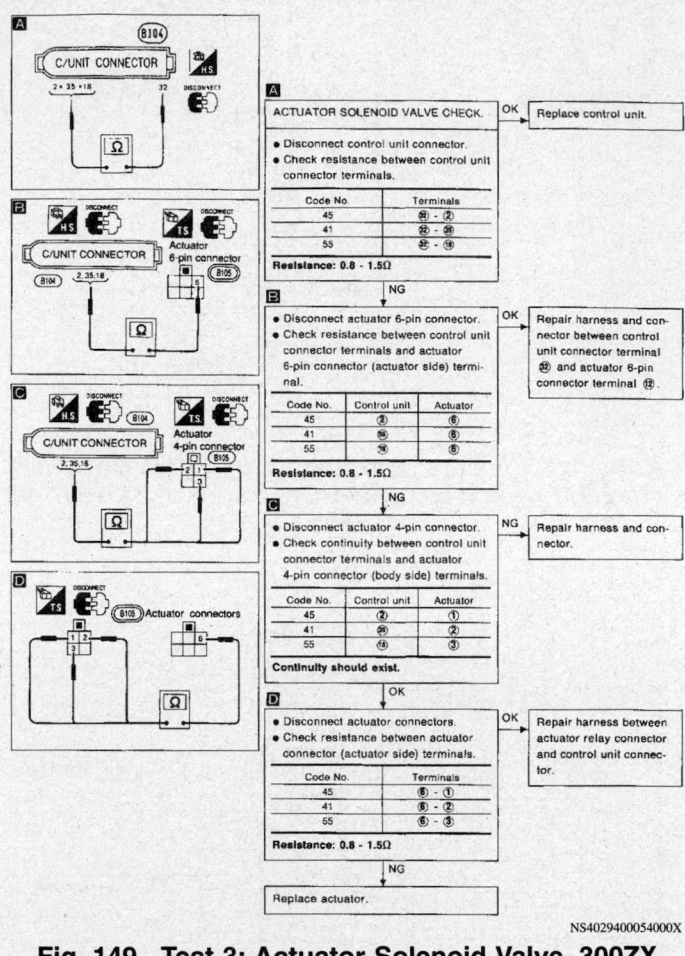

NS4029400054000X

Fig. 149 Test 3: Actuator Solenoid Valve. 300ZX

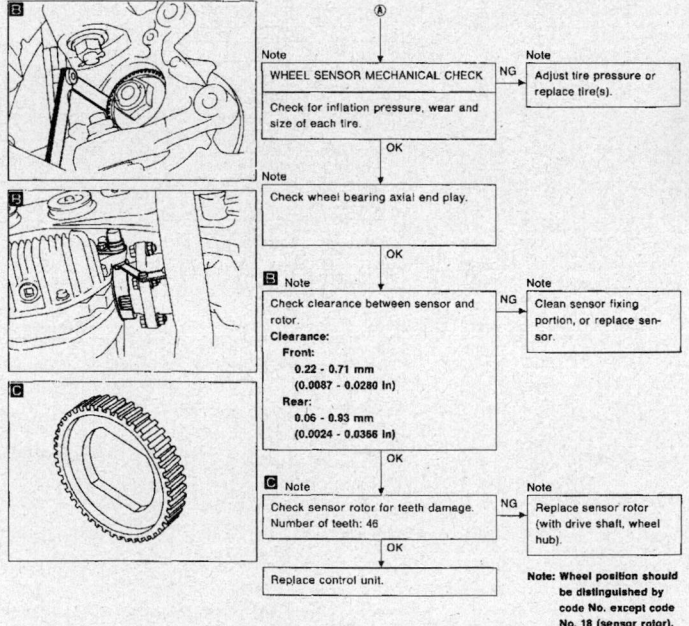

NS4029400055020X

Fig. 150 Test 4: Wheel Sensor Or Rotor (Part 2 of 2). 300ZX

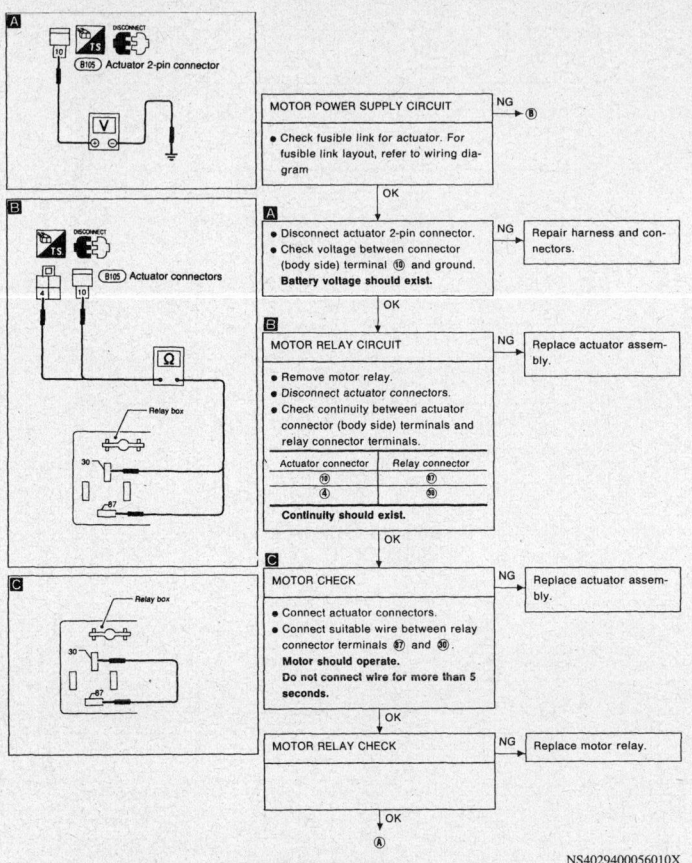

A

MOTOR POWER SUPPLY CIRCUIT → NG → B

- Check fusible link for actuator. For fusible link layout, refer to wiring diagram

↓ OK

A

- Disconnect actuator 2-pin connector.
- Check voltage between connector (body side) terminal ⑩ and ground. **Battery voltage should exist.** → NG → Repair harness and connectors.

↓ OK

B

MOTOR RELAY CIRCUIT → NG → Replace actuator assembly.

- Remove motor relay.
- Disconnect actuator connectors.
- Check continuity between actuator connector (body side) terminals and relay connector terminals.

Actuator connector	Relay connector
⑩	⑧⑦
④	⑤⑥

Continuity should exist.

↓ OK

C

MOTOR CHECK → NG → Replace actuator assembly.

- Connect actuator connectors.
- Connect suitable wire between relay connector terminals ⑧⑦ and ⑤⑥.
Motor should operate.
Do not connect wire for more than 5 seconds.

↓ OK

MOTOR RELAY CHECK → NG → Replace motor relay.

↓ OK

A

NS4029400056010X

Fig. 151   Test 5: Motor Relay Or Motor (Part 1 of 3). 300ZX

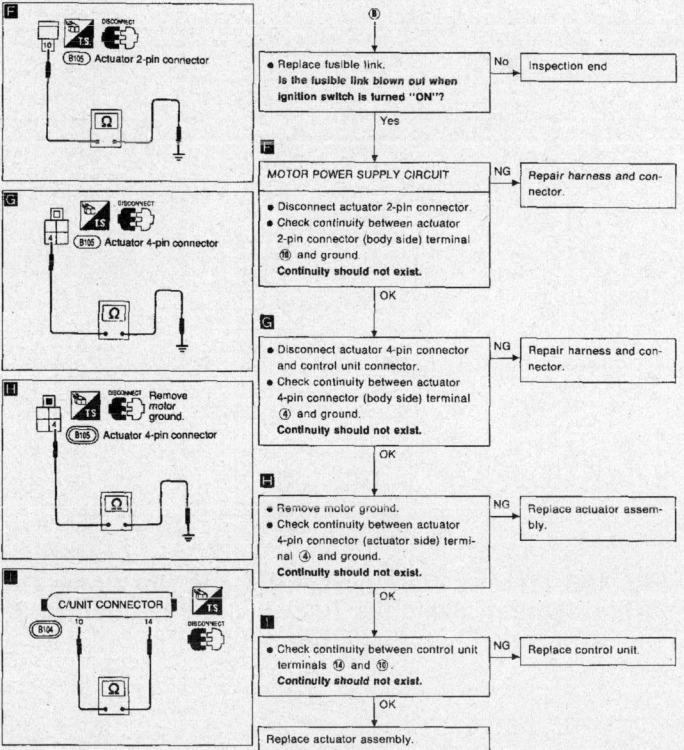

F

B

- Replace fusible link.
Is the fusible link blown out when ignition switch is turned "ON"? → No → Inspection end

↓ Yes

F

MOTOR POWER SUPPLY CIRCUIT → NG → Repair harness and connector.

- Disconnect actuator 2-pin connector.
- Check continuity between actuator 2-pin connector (body side) terminal ⑩ and ground.
Continuity should not exist.

↓ OK

G

- Disconnect actuator 4-pin connector and control unit connector.
- Check continuity between actuator 4-pin connector (body side) terminal ④ and ground.
Continuity should not exist. → NG → Repair harness and connector.

↓ OK

H

- Remove motor ground.
- Check continuity between actuator 4-pin connector (actuator side) terminal ④ and ground.
Continuity should not exist. → NG → Replace actuator assembly.

↓ OK

I

- Check continuity between control unit terminals ⑭ and ⑩.
Continuity should not exist. → NG → Replace control unit.

↓ OK

Replace actuator assembly.

NS4029400056030X

Fig. 151   Test 5: Motor Relay Or Motor (Part 3 of 3). 300ZX

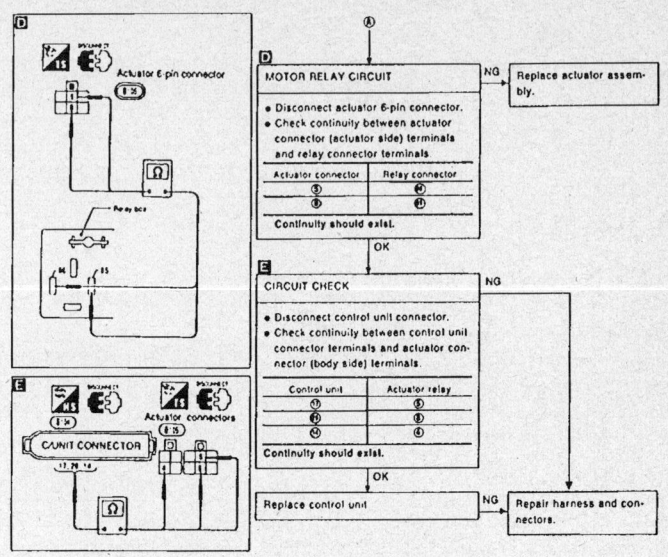

D

MOTOR RELAY CIRCUIT → NG → Replace actuator assembly.

- Disconnect actuator 6-pin connector.
- Check continuity between actuator connector (actuator side) terminals and relay connector terminals

Actuator connector	Relay connector
③	⑦

Continuity should exist.

↓ OK

E

CIRCUIT CHECK → NG →

- Disconnect control unit connector.
- Check continuity between control unit connector terminals and actuator connector (body side) terminals.

Control unit	Actuator relay
⑰	⑤
⑱	③

Continuity should exist.

↓ OK

Replace control unit → NG → Repair harness and connectors.

NS4029400056020X

Fig. 151   Test 5: Motor Relay Or Motor (Part 2 of 3). 300ZX

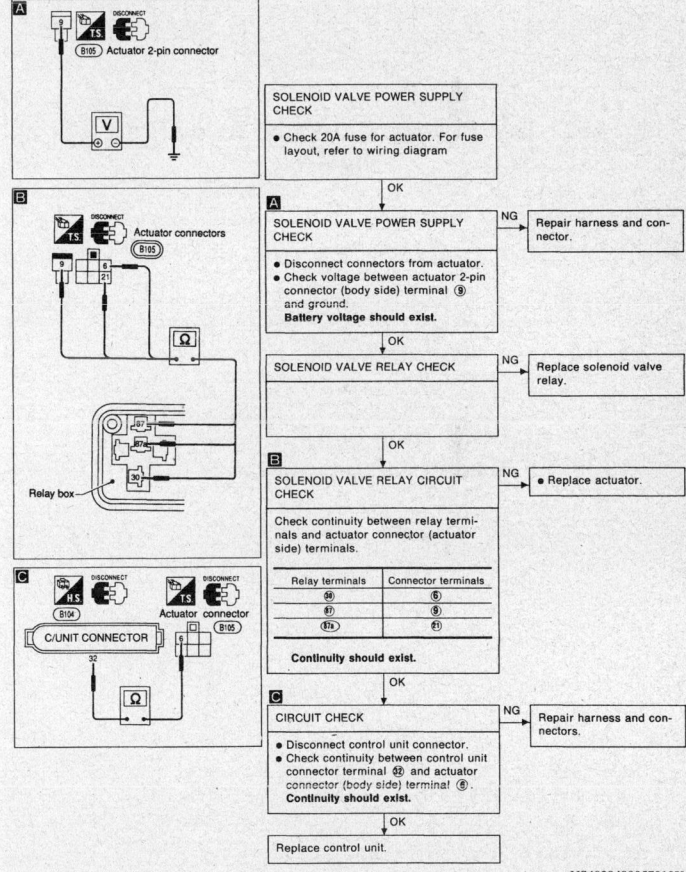

SOLENOID VALVE POWER SUPPLY CHECK

- Check 20A fuse for actuator. For fuse layout, refer to wiring diagram

↓ OK

A

SOLENOID VALVE POWER SUPPLY CHECK → NG → Repair harness and connector.

- Disconnect connectors from actuator.
- Check voltage between actuator 2-pin connector (body side) terminal ⑨ and ground.
Battery voltage should exist.

↓ OK

SOLENOID VALVE RELAY CHECK → NG → Replace solenoid valve relay.

↓ OK

B

SOLENOID VALVE RELAY CIRCUIT CHECK → NG → Replace actuator.

Check continuity between relay terminals and actuator connector (actuator side) terminals.

Relay terminals	Connector terminals
㉚	⑤
⑧⑦	⑨
㉚ₐ	㉑

Continuity should exist.

↓ OK

C

CIRCUIT CHECK → NG → Repair harness and connectors.

- Disconnect control unit connector.
- Check continuity between control unit connector terminal ㉜ and actuator connector (body side) terminal ⑤.
Continuity should exist.

↓ OK

Replace control unit.

NS4029400057010X

Fig. 152   Test 6: Solenoid Valve Relay (Part 1 of 2). 300ZX

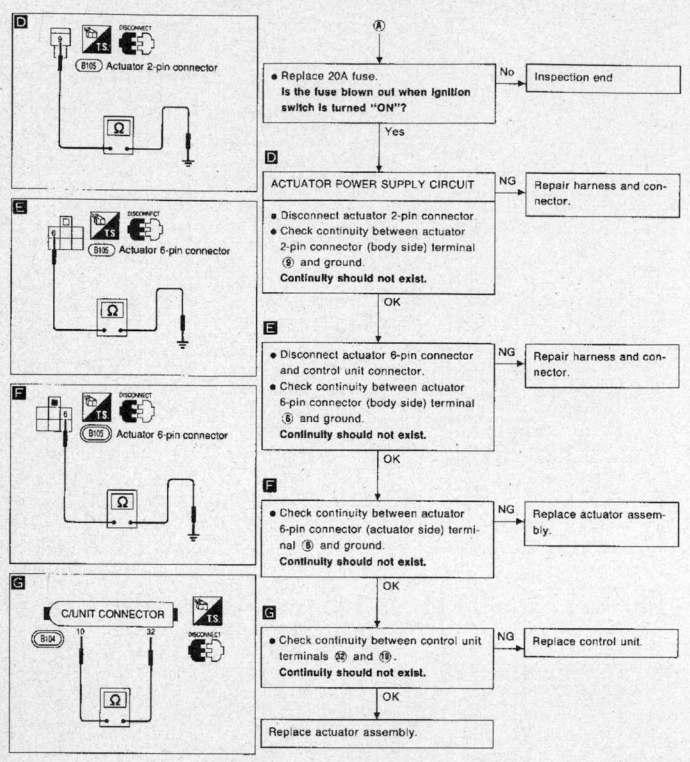

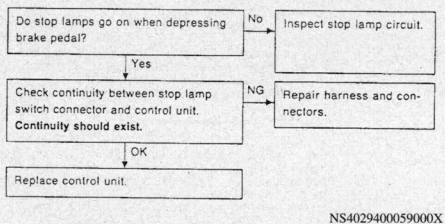

Fig. 152   Test 6: Solenoid Valve Relay (Part 2 of 2). 300ZX

Fig. 154   Test 8: Stop Lamp Switch Circuit. 300ZX

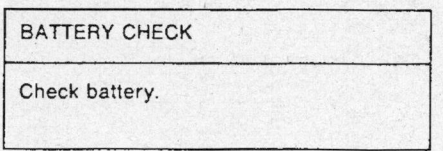

Fig. 153   Test 7: Power Supply Low Voltage. 300ZX

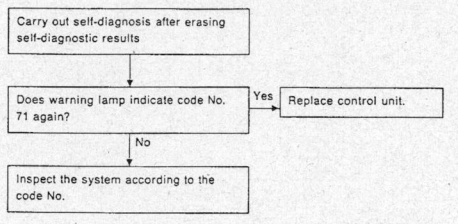

Fig. 155   Test 9: Control Unit. 300ZX

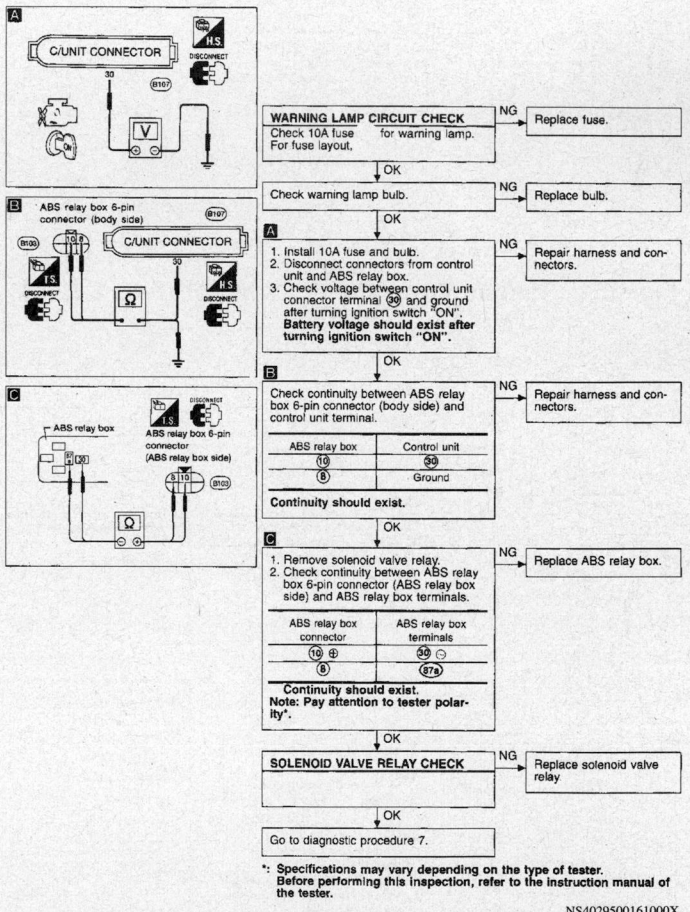

Fig. 156   Test 1: Warning Lamp Does Not Come On When Ignition Switch Is Turned On. 1996 Sentra & 200SX

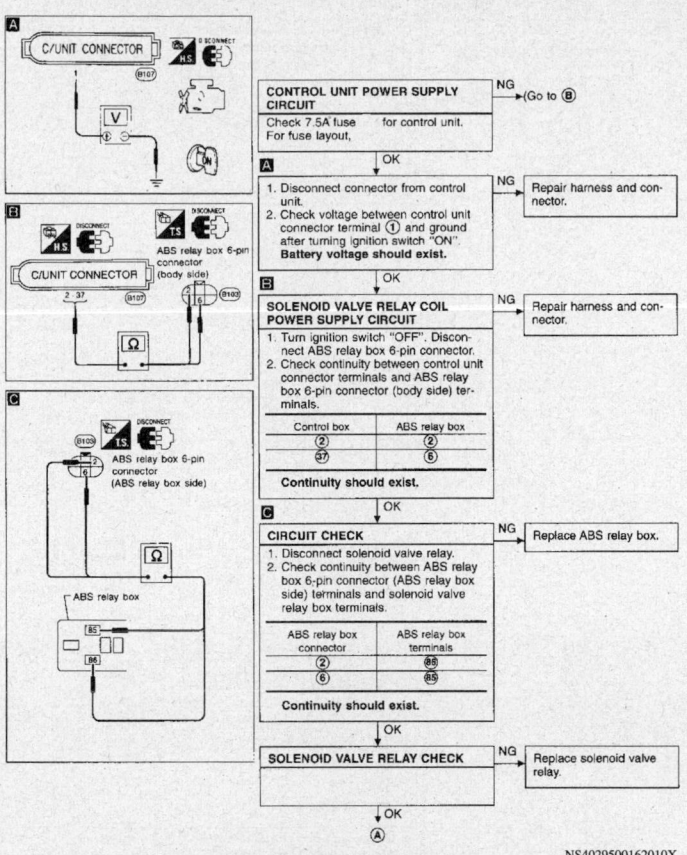

CONTROL UNIT POWER SUPPLY CIRCUIT

Check 7.5A fuse for control unit. For fuse layout,

→NG (Go to Ⓑ)

↓OK

Ⓐ
1. Disconnect connector from control unit.
2. Check voltage between control unit connector terminal ① and ground after turning ignition switch "ON". **Battery voltage should exist.**

→NG Repair harness and connector.

↓OK

Ⓑ **SOLENOID VALVE RELAY COIL POWER SUPPLY CIRCUIT**
1. Turn ignition switch "OFF". Disconnect ABS relay box 6-pin connector.
2. Check continuity between control unit connector terminals and ABS relay box 6-pin connector (body side) terminals.

Control box	ABS relay box
②	②
③⑦	⑥

Continuity should exist.

→NG Repair harness and connector.

↓OK

Ⓒ **CIRCUIT CHECK**
1. Disconnect solenoid valve relay.
2. Check continuity between ABS relay box 6-pin connector (ABS relay box side) terminals and solenoid valve relay box terminals.

ABS relay box connector	ABS relay box terminals
②	86
⑥	85

Continuity should exist.

→NG Replace ABS relay box.

↓OK

SOLENOID VALVE RELAY CHECK

→NG Replace solenoid valve relay.

↓OK

Ⓐ

NS4029500162010X

Fig. 157 Test 2: Warning Light Stays On When Ignition Switch Is Turned On (Part 1 of 3). 1996 Sentra & 200SX

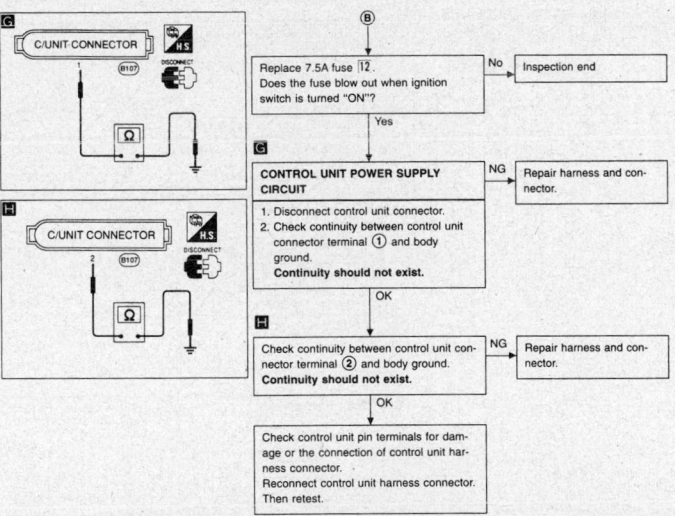

Ⓑ
Replace 7.5A fuse 12. Does the fuse blow out when ignition switch is turned "ON"?

→No Inspection end

↓Yes

Ⓖ **CONTROL UNIT POWER SUPPLY CIRCUIT**
1. Disconnect control unit connector.
2. Check continuity between control unit connector terminal ① and body ground. **Continuity should not exist.**

→NG Repair harness and connector.

↓OK

Ⓗ
Check continuity between control unit connector terminal ② and body ground. **Continuity should not exist.**

→NG Repair harness and connector.

↓OK

Check control unit pin terminals for damage or the connection of control unit harness connector. Reconnect control unit harness connector. Then retest.

NS4029500162030X

Fig. 157 Test 2: Warning Light Stays On When Ignition Switch Is Turned On (Part 3 of 3). 1996 Sentra & 200SX

Ⓐ

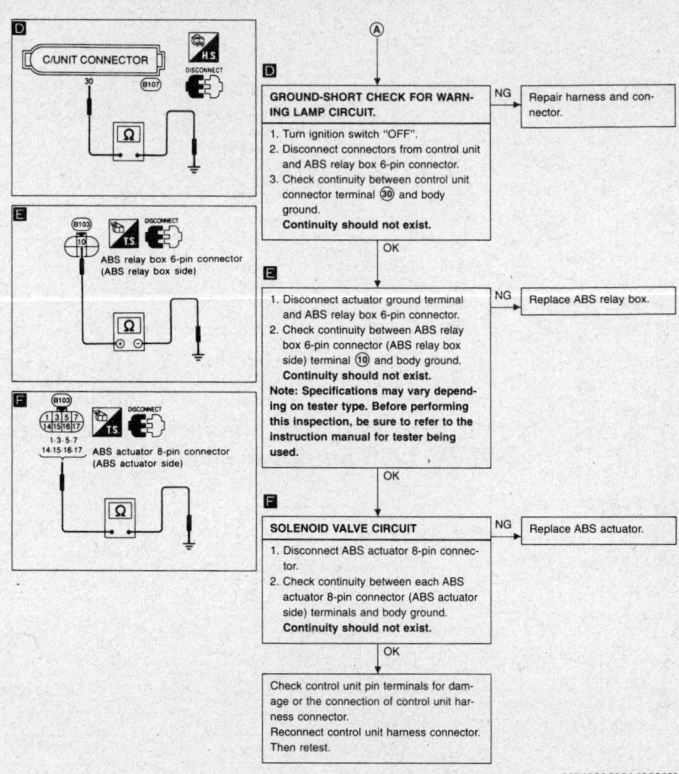

Ⓓ **GROUND-SHORT CHECK FOR WARNING LAMP CIRCUIT.**
1. Turn ignition switch "OFF".
2. Disconnect connectors from control unit and ABS relay box 6-pin connector.
3. Check continuity between control unit connector terminal ㉚ and body ground. **Continuity should not exist.**

→NG Repair harness and connector.

↓OK

Ⓔ
1. Disconnect actuator ground terminal and ABS relay box 6-pin connector.
2. Check continuity between ABS relay box 6-pin connector (ABS relay box side) terminal ⑩ and body ground. **Continuity should not exist.**
Note: Specifications may vary depending on tester type. Before performing this inspection, be sure to refer to the instruction manual for tester being used.

→NG Replace ABS relay box.

↓OK

SOLENOID VALVE CIRCUIT
1. Disconnect ABS actuator 8-pin connector.
2. Check continuity between each ABS actuator 8-pin connector (ABS actuator side) terminals and body ground. **Continuity should not exist.**

→NG Replace ABS actuator.

↓OK

Check control unit pin terminals for damage or the connection of control unit harness connector. Reconnect control unit harness connector. Then retest.

NS4029500162020X

Fig. 157 Test 2: Warning Light Stays On When Ignition Switch Is Turned On (Part 2 of 3). 1996 Sentra & 200SX

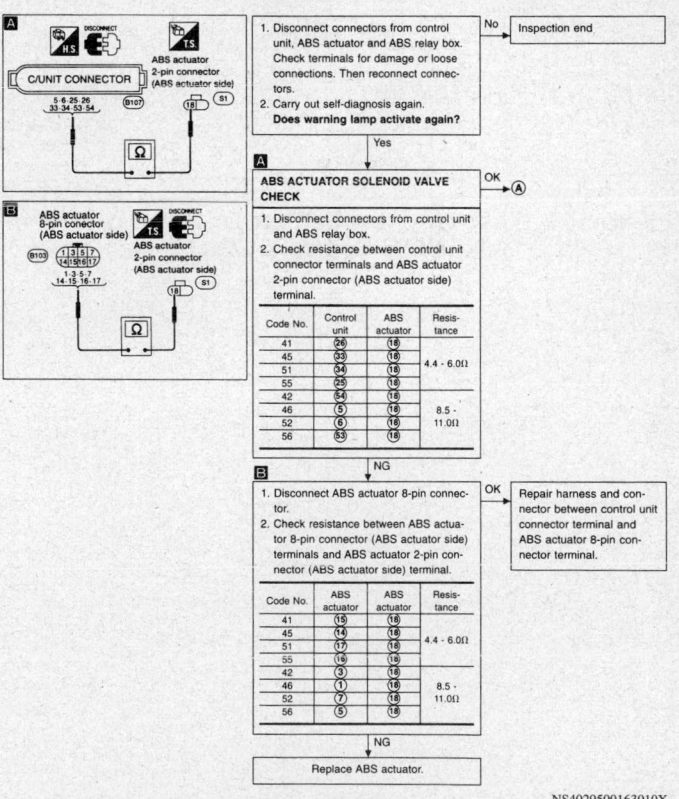

Ⓐ
1. Disconnect connectors from control unit, ABS actuator and ABS relay box. Check terminals for damage or loose connections. Then reconnect connectors.
2. Carry out self-diagnosis again. **Does warning lamp activate again?**

→No Inspection end

↓Yes

Ⓐ **ABS ACTUATOR SOLENOID VALVE CHECK**
1. Disconnect connectors from control unit and ABS relay box.
2. Check resistance between control unit connector terminals and ABS actuator 2-pin connector (ABS actuator side) terminal.

→OK ►Ⓐ

Code No.	Control unit	ABS actuator	Resistance
41	26	18	
45	33	18	
51	34	18	4.4 - 6.0Ω
55	25	18	
42	54	18	
46	5	18	
52	6	18	8.5 - 11.0Ω
56	53	18	

↓NG

Ⓑ
1. Disconnect ABS actuator 8-pin connector.
2. Check resistance between ABS actuator 8-pin connector (ABS actuator side) terminals and ABS actuator 2-pin connector (ABS actuator side) terminal.

→OK Repair harness and connector between control unit connector terminal and ABS actuator 8-pin connector terminal.

Code No.	ABS actuator	ABS actuator	Resistance
41	15	18	
45	14	18	
51	17	18	4.4 - 6.0Ω
55	16	18	
42	3	18	
46	1	18	
52	7	18	8.5 - 11.0Ω
56	5	18	

↓NG

Replace ABS actuator.

NS4029500163010X

Fig. 158 Test 3: ABS Actuator Solenoid Valve (Part 1 of 2). 1996 Sentra & 200SX

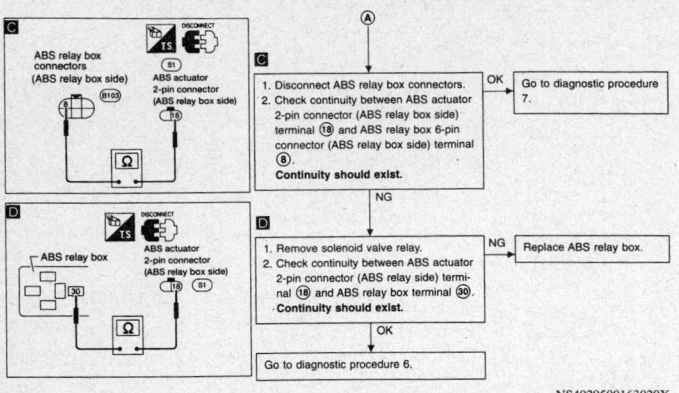

Fig. 158   Test 3: ABS Actuator Solenoid Valve (Part 2 of 2). 1996 Sentra & 200SX

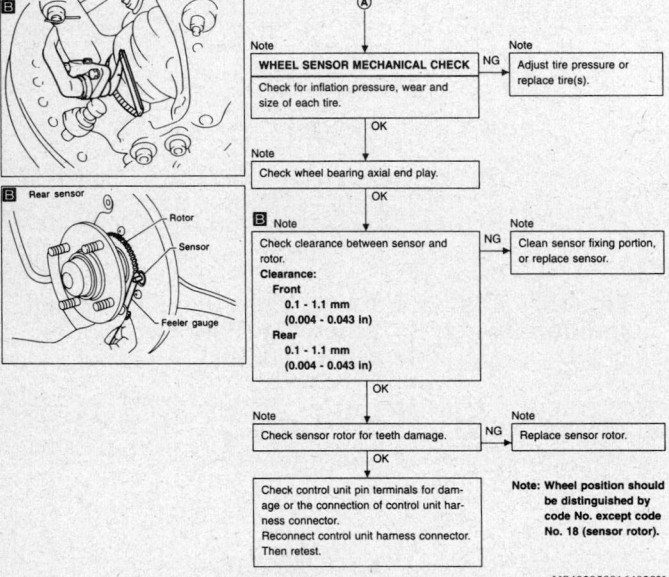

Fig. 159   Test 4: Wheel Sensor Or Rotor (Part 2 of 2). 1996 Sentra & 200SX

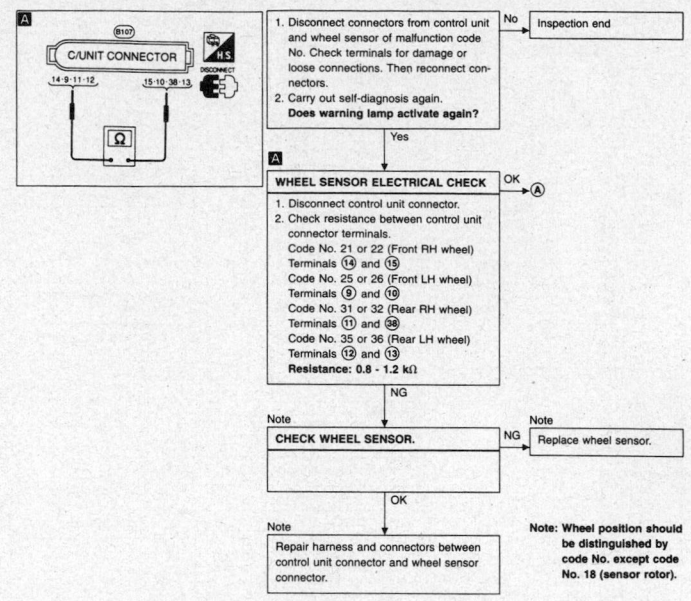

Fig. 159   Test 4: Wheel Sensor Or Rotor (Part 1 of 2). 1996 Sentra & 200SX

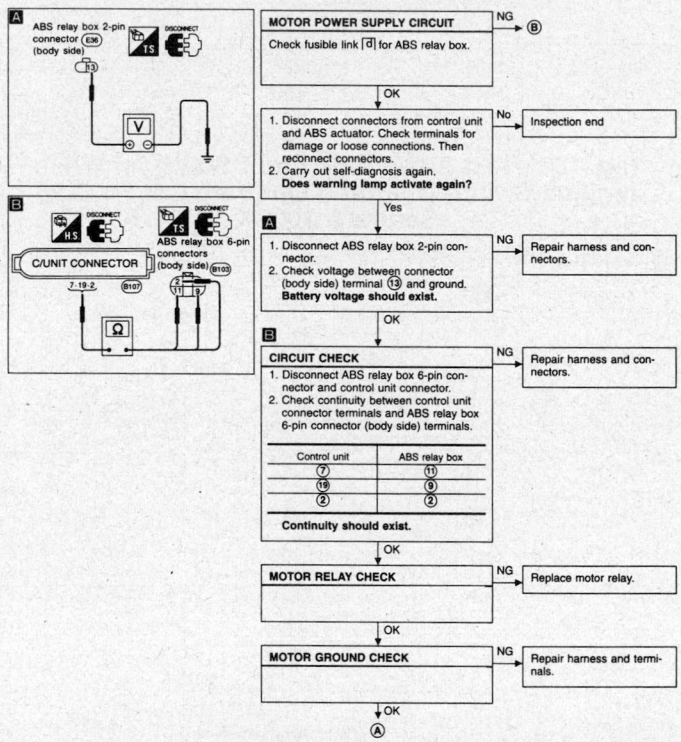

Fig. 160   Test 5: Motor Relay Or Motor (Part 1 of 3). 1996 Sentra & 200SX

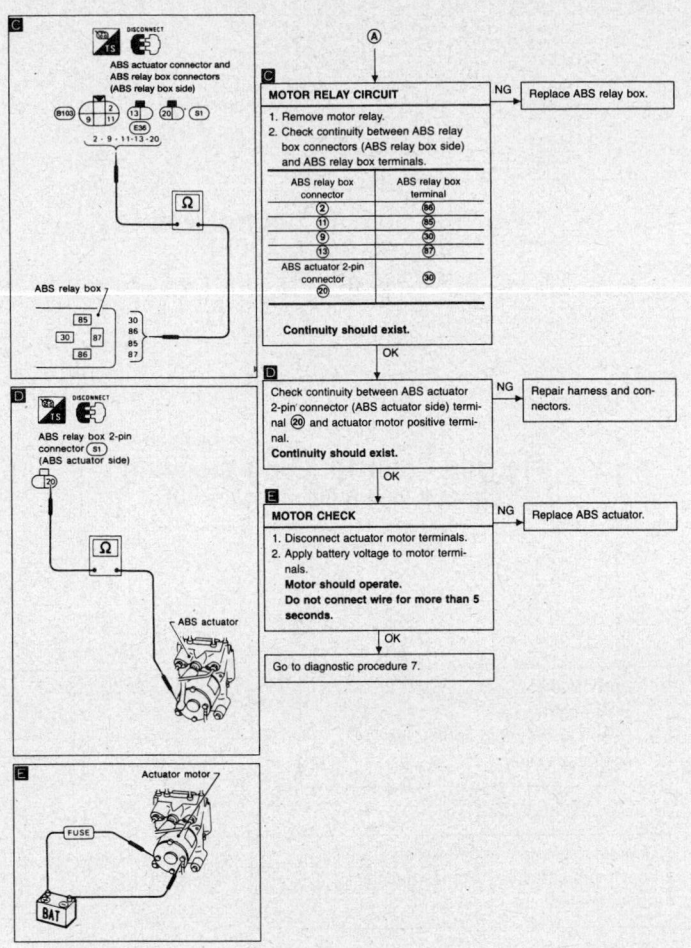

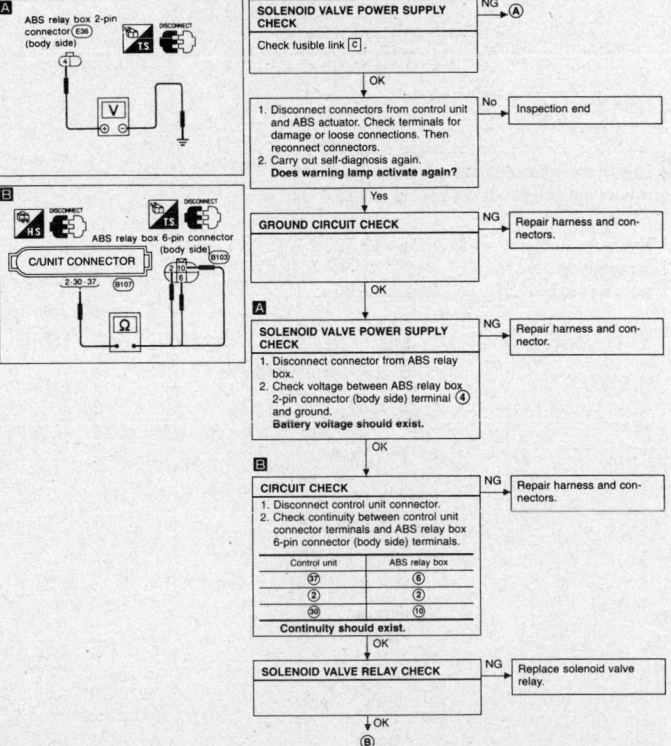

NS4029500165020X

**Fig. 160   Test 5: Motor Relay Or Motor (Part 2 of 3).
1996 Sentra & 200SX**

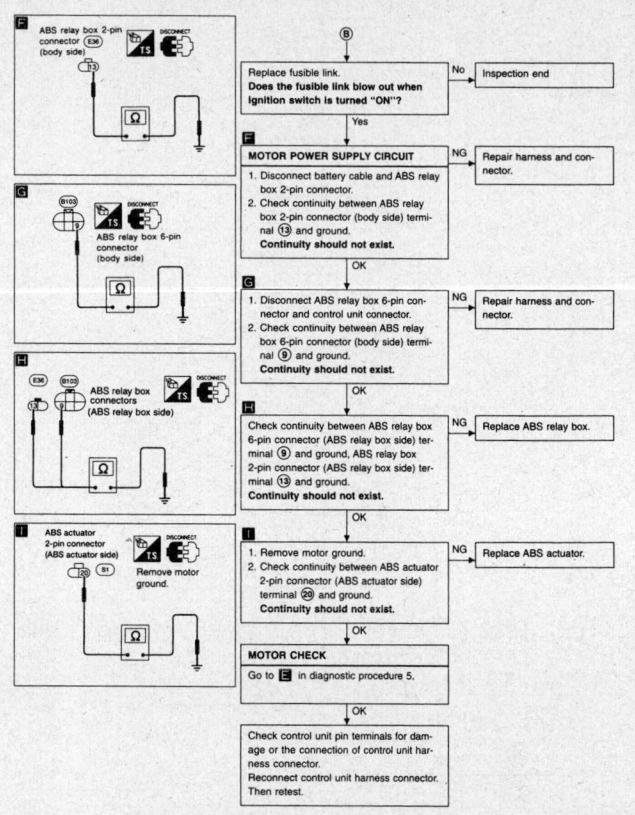

NS4029500165030X

**Fig. 160   Test 5: Motor Relay Or Motor (Part 3 of 3).
1996 Sentra & 200SX**

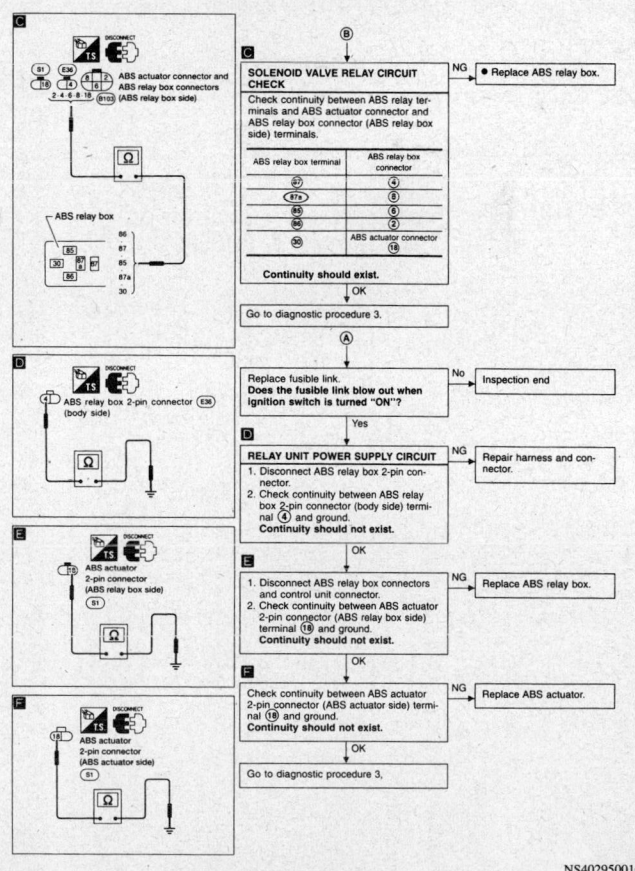

NS4029500166010X

**Fig. 161   Test 6: Solenoid Valve Relay (Part 1 of 2).
1996 Sentra & 200SX**

NS4029500166020X

**Fig. 161   Test 6: Solenoid Valve Relay (Part 2 of 2).
1996 Sentra & 200SX**

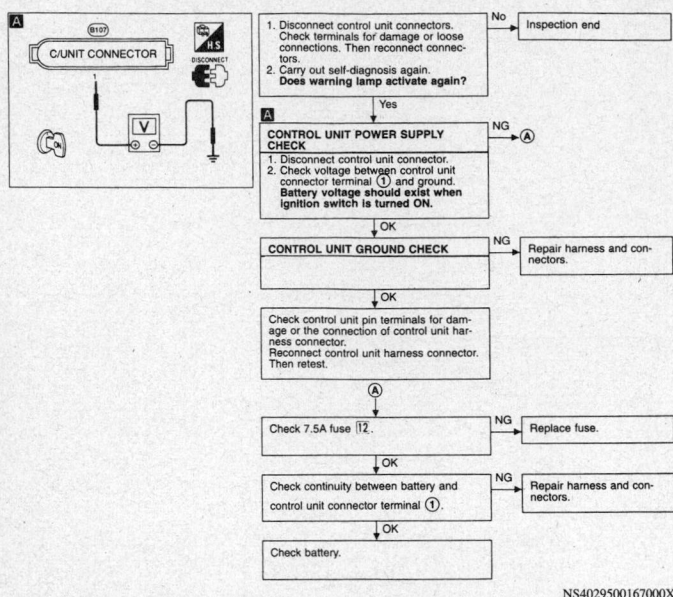

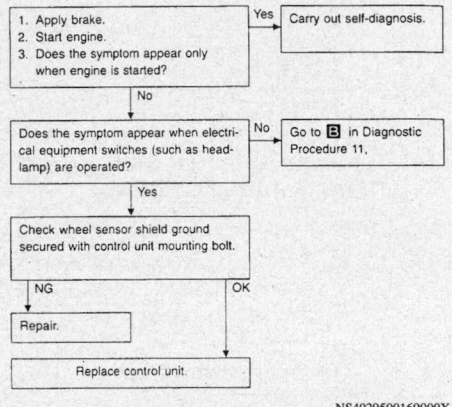

Fig. 162 Test 7: Power Supply Low Voltage. 1996 Sentra & 200SX

Test 9 flowchart:

1. Apply brake.
2. Start engine.
3. Does the symptom appear only when engine is started?

Yes → Carry out self-diagnosis.

No ↓

Does the symptom appear when electrical equipment switches (such as headlamp) are operated?

No → Go to **B** in Diagnostic Procedure 11,

Yes ↓

Check wheel sensor shield ground secured with control unit mounting bolt.

NG → Repair.

OK → Replace control unit.

NS4029500169000X

Fig. 164 Test 9: Pedal Vibration & Noise. 1996 Sentra & 200SX

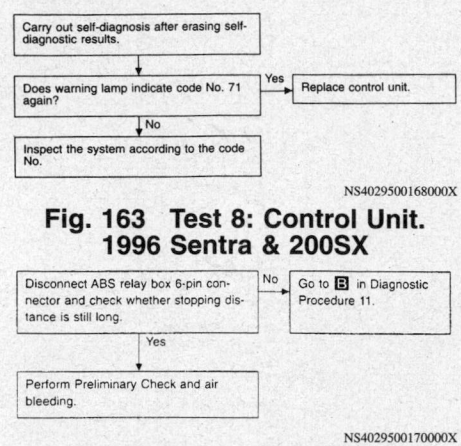

Fig. 163 Test 8: Control Unit. 1996 Sentra & 200SX

Test 10 flowchart:

Disconnect ABS relay box 6-pin connector and check whether stopping distance is still long.

No → Go to **B** in Diagnostic Procedure 11.

Yes ↓

Perform Preliminary Check and air bleeding.

NS4029500170000X

Fig. 165 Test 10: Long Stopping Distance. 1996 Sentra & 200SX

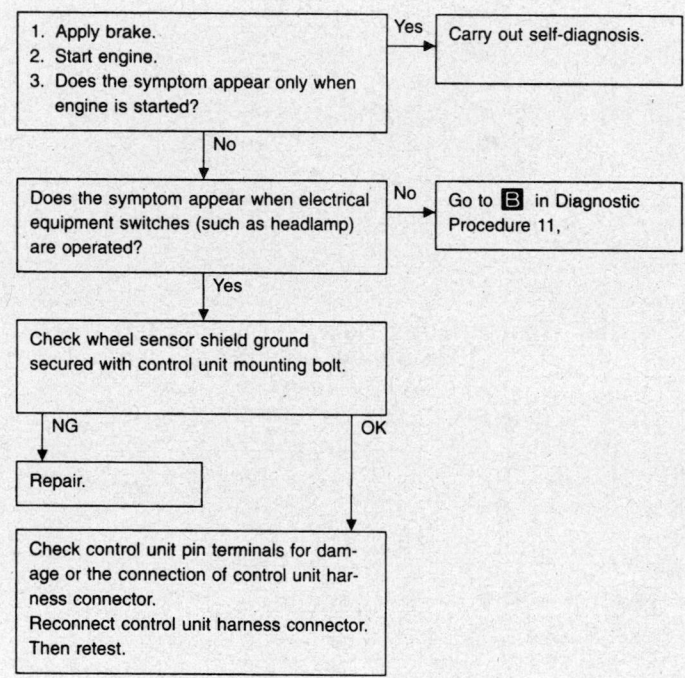

Fig. 166 Test 11: Unexpected Pedal Action. 1996 Sentra & 200SX

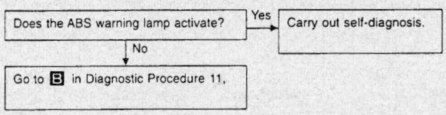

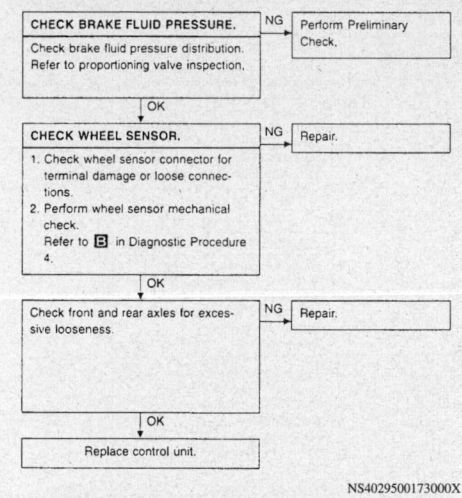

```
┌─────────────────────────────┐  Yes  ┌──────────────────────┐
│ Does the ABS warning lamp   ├──────►│ Carry out self-      │
│ activate?                   │       │ diagnosis.           │
└──────────┬──────────────────┘       └──────────────────────┘
           │ No
┌──────────▼──────────────────┐
│ Go to B in Diagnostic       │
│ Procedure 11,               │
└─────────────────────────────┘
```

NS4029500172000X

Fig. 167   Test 12: ABS Does Not Work. 1996 Sentra & 200SX

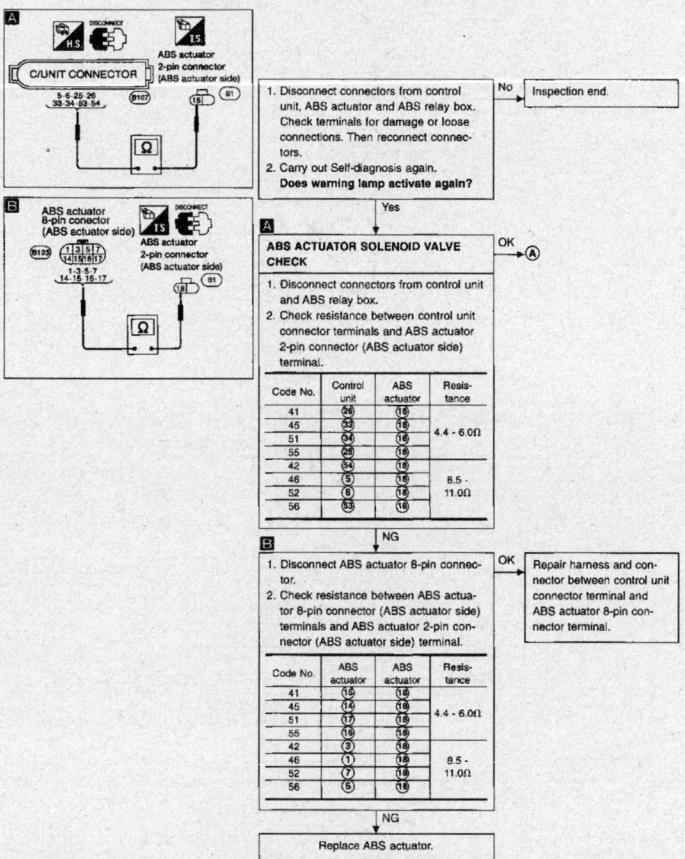

NS4029700270010X

Fig. 169   Test 1: ABS Actuator Solenoid Valve (Part 1 of 2). 1997–99 Sentra & 200SX

```
┌─────────────────────────────┐  NG   ┌──────────────────────┐
│ CHECK BRAKE FLUID PRESSURE.  ├──────►│ Perform Preliminary  │
│ Check brake fluid pressure   │       │ Check,               │
│ distribution. Refer to       │       └──────────────────────┘
│ proportioning valve          │
│ inspection,                  │
└──────────┬──────────────────┘
           │ OK
┌──────────▼──────────────────┐  NG   ┌──────────┐
│ CHECK WHEEL SENSOR.          ├──────►│ Repair.  │
│ 1. Check wheel sensor        │       └──────────┘
│    connector for terminal    │
│    damage or loose connec-   │
│    tions.                    │
│ 2. Perform wheel sensor      │
│    mechanical check.         │
│    Refer to B in Diagnostic  │
│    Procedure 4.              │
└──────────┬──────────────────┘
           │ OK
┌──────────▼──────────────────┐  NG   ┌──────────┐
│ Check front and rear axles   ├──────►│ Repair.  │
│ for excessive looseness.     │       └──────────┘
└──────────┬──────────────────┘
           │ OK
┌──────────▼──────────────────┐
│ Replace control unit.        │
└─────────────────────────────┘
```

NS4029500173000X

Fig. 168   Test 13: ABS Works Frequently. 1996 Sentra & 200SX

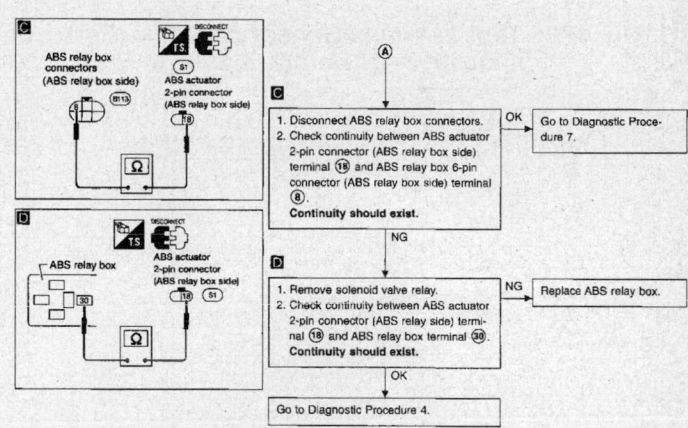

NS4029700270020X

Fig. 169   Test 1: ABS Actuator Solenoid Valve (Part 2 of 2). 1997–99 Sentra & 200SX

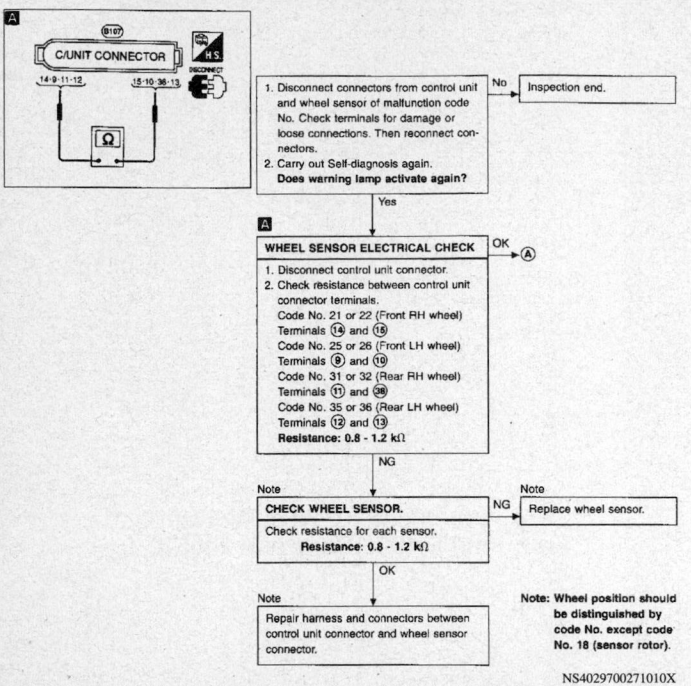

A — C/UNIT CONNECTOR — (B107) — 14·9·11·12 | 15·10·36·13 — Ω

1. Disconnect connectors from control unit and wheel sensor of malfunction code No. Check terminals for damage or loose connections. Then reconnect connectors.
2. Carry out Self-diagnosis again. **Does warning lamp activate again?**

→ No → Inspection end.

↓ Yes

A — **WHEEL SENSOR ELECTRICAL CHECK** → OK → (A)
1. Disconnect control unit connector.
2. Check resistance between control unit connector terminals.
   Code No. 21 or 22 (Front RH wheel)
   Terminals (14) and (15)
   Code No. 25 or 26 (Front LH wheel)
   Terminals (9) and (19)
   Code No. 31 or 32 (Rear RH wheel)
   Terminals (11) and (28)
   Code No. 35 or 36 (Rear LH wheel)
   Terminals (12) and (13)
   Resistance: 0.8 - 1.2 kΩ

↓ NG

Note — **CHECK WHEEL SENSOR.** → NG → Note — Replace wheel sensor.
Check resistance for each sensor.
Resistance: 0.8 - 1.2 kΩ

↓ OK

Note — Repair harness and connectors between control unit connector and wheel sensor connector.

Note: Wheel position should be distinguished by code No. except code No. 18 (sensor rotor).

NS4029700271010X

Fig. 170   Test 2: Wheel Sensor or Rotor (Part 1 of 2). 1997–99 Sentra & 200SX

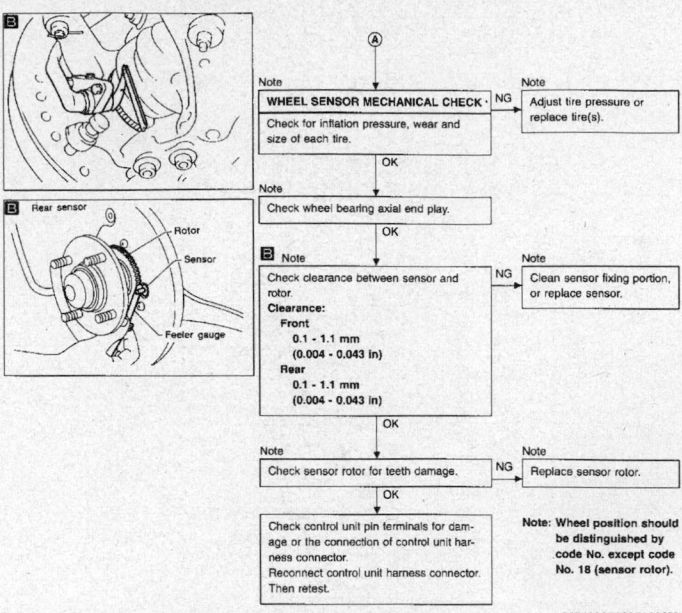

B (A)

B — Rear sensor — Rotor, Sensor, Feeler gauge

(A)
Note — **WHEEL SENSOR MECHANICAL CHECK** → NG → Note — Adjust tire pressure or replace tire(s).
Check for inflation pressure, wear and size of each tire.

↓ OK

Note — Check wheel bearing axial end play.

↓ OK

B Note — Check clearance between sensor and rotor. → NG → Note — Clean sensor fixing portion, or replace sensor.
Clearance:
Front
0.1 - 1.1 mm
(0.004 - 0.043 in)
Rear
0.1 - 1.1 mm
(0.004 - 0.043 in)

↓ OK

Note — Check sensor rotor for teeth damage. → NG → Note — Replace sensor rotor.

↓ OK

Check control unit pin terminals for damage or the connection of control unit harness connector. Reconnect control unit harness connector. Then retest.

Note: Wheel position should be distinguished by code No. except code No. 18 (sensor rotor).

NS4029700271020X

Fig. 170   Test 2: Wheel Sensor or Rotor (Part 2 of 2). 1997–99 Sentra & 200SX

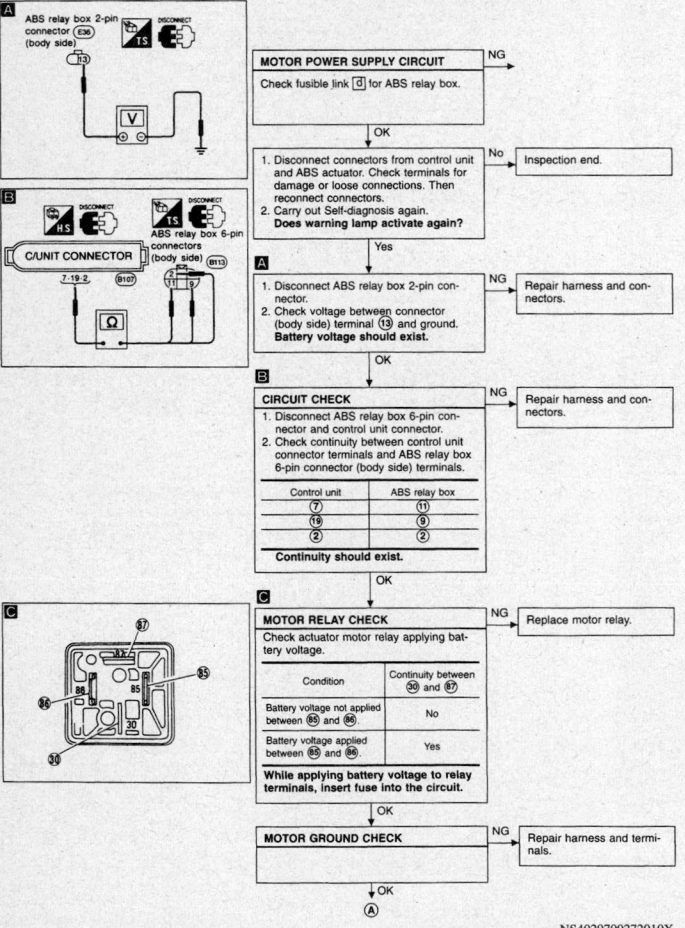

A — ABS relay box 2-pin connector (E36) (body side) — V

MOTOR POWER SUPPLY CIRCUIT → NG
Check fusible link (d) for ABS relay box.

↓ OK

1. Disconnect connectors from control unit and ABS actuator. Check terminals for damage or loose connections. Then reconnect connectors.
2. Carry out Self-diagnosis again. **Does warning lamp activate again?**
→ No → Inspection end.

↓ Yes

B — C/UNIT CONNECTOR (B107) 7·19·2 — ABS relay box 6-pin connectors (body side) (B113) — Ω

A
1. Disconnect ABS relay box 2-pin connector.
2. Check voltage between connector (body side) terminal (13) and ground.
   Battery voltage should exist.
→ NG → Repair harness and connectors.

↓ OK

B **CIRCUIT CHECK** → NG → Repair harness and connectors.
1. Disconnect ABS relay box 6-pin connector and control unit connector.
2. Check continuity between control unit connector terminals and ABS relay box 6-pin connector (body side) terminals.

Control unit	ABS relay box
(7)	(11)
(19)	(9)
(2)	(2)

Continuity should exist.

↓ OK

C — (87) (85) (86) (85) (30)

MOTOR RELAY CHECK → NG → Replace motor relay.
Check actuator motor relay applying battery voltage.

Condition	Continuity between (30) and (87)
Battery voltage not applied between (85) and (86)	No
Battery voltage applied between (85) and (86)	Yes

While applying battery voltage to relay terminals, insert fuse into the circuit.

↓ OK

MOTOR GROUND CHECK → NG → Repair harness and terminals.

↓ OK

(A)

NS4029700272010X

Fig. 171   Test 3: Motor Relay or Motor (Part 1 of 3). 1997–99 Sentra & 200SX

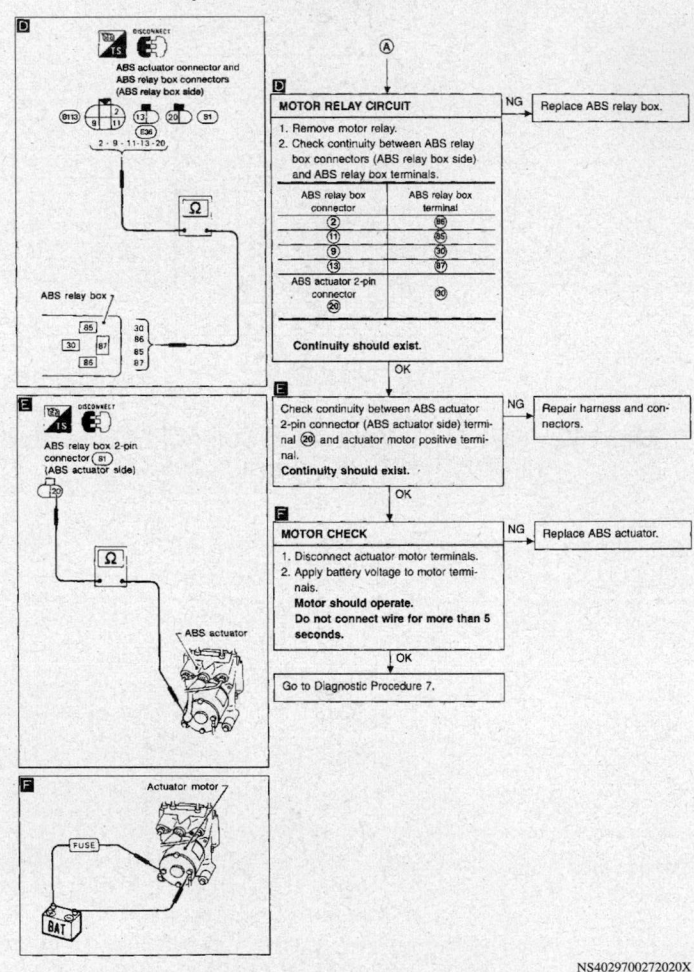

D — ABS actuator connector and ABS relay box connectors (ABS relay box side) — (B113) (E36) — 2·9·11·13·20 — Ω — ABS relay box — 85 30 87 85 86 87

(A)

D **MOTOR RELAY CIRCUIT** → NG → Replace ABS relay box.
1. Remove motor relay.
2. Check continuity between ABS relay box connectors (ABS relay box side) and ABS relay box terminals.

ABS relay box connector	ABS relay box terminal
(2)	(85)
(11)	(86)
(9)	(30)
(13)	(87)
ABS actuator 2-pin connector (20)	(30)

Continuity should exist.

↓ OK

E — ABS relay box 2-pin connector (B1) (ABS actuator side) — Ω — ABS actuator

E Check continuity between ABS actuator 2-pin connector (ABS actuator side) terminal (20) and actuator motor positive terminal. → NG → Repair harness and connectors.
Continuity should exist.

↓ OK

F **MOTOR CHECK** → NG → Replace ABS actuator.
1. Disconnect actuator motor terminals.
2. Apply battery voltage to motor terminals.
   Motor should operate.
   Do not connect wire for more than 5 seconds.

↓ OK

Go to Diagnostic Procedure 7.

F — Actuator motor — FUSE — BAT

NS4029700272020X

Fig. 171   Test 3: Motor Relay or Motor (Part 2 of 3). 1997–99 Sentra & 200SX

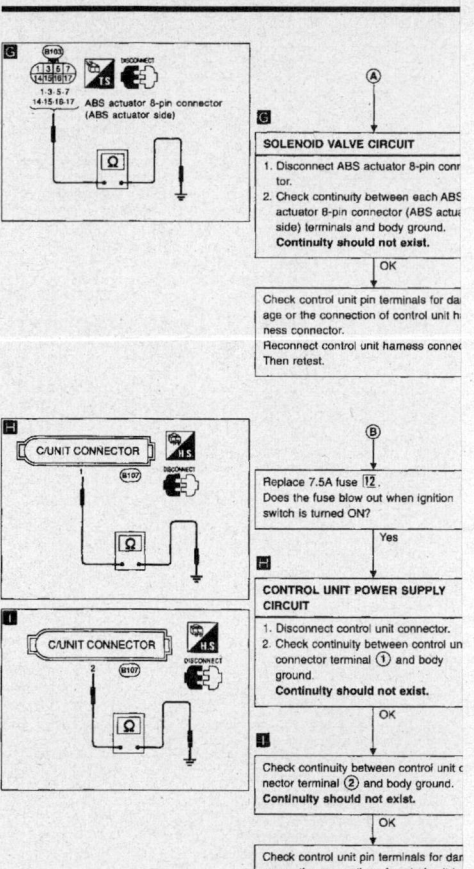

SOLENOID VALVE CIRCUIT
1. Disconnect ABS actuator 8-pin connector.
2. Check continuity between each ABS actuator 8-pin connector (ABS actuator side) terminals and body ground.
Continuity should not exist.

OK

Check control unit pin terminals for damage or the connection of control unit harness connector.
Reconnect control unit harness connector. Then retest.

B

Replace 7.5A fuse 12.
Does the fuse blow out when ignition switch is turned ON?

Yes

CONTROL UNIT POWER SUPPLY CIRCUIT
1. Disconnect control unit connector.
2. Check continuity between control unit connector terminal ① and body ground.
Continuity should not exist.

OK

Check continuity between control unit connector terminal ② and body ground.
Continuity should not exist.

Check control unit pin terminals for damage or the connection of control unit harness connector.
Reconnect control unit harness connector. Then retest.

Fig. 176 Test 8: Warning Lamp Sta... 3). 1997–99 Sentra & 20...

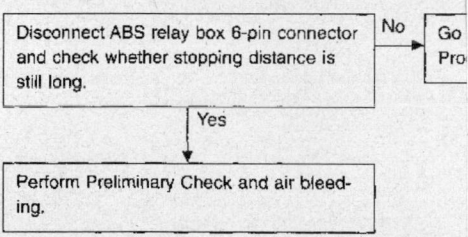

Disconnect ABS relay box 6-pin connector and check whether stopping distance is still long.

No → Go to ... Pro...

Yes

Perform Preliminary Check and air bleeding.

Note: Stopping distance may be larger ... out ABS when road condition is slipper...

Fig. 178 Test 10: Long Stopping Di... Sentra & 200SX

Does th...

Go to ...

Note...
km/h...

Fig...

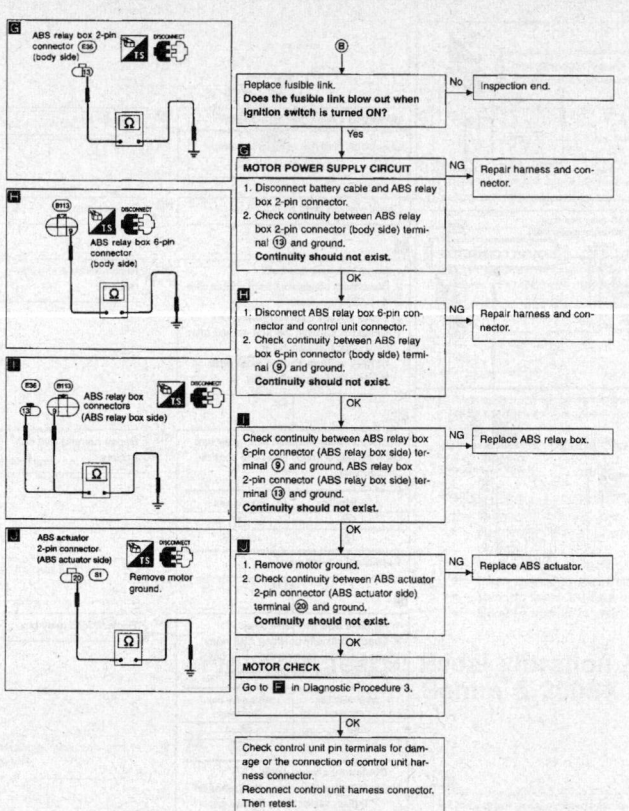

B

Replace fusible link.
Does the fusible link blow out when ignition switch is turned ON?

No → inspection end.

Yes

MOTOR POWER SUPPLY CIRCUIT
1. Disconnect battery cable and ABS relay box 2-pin connector.
2. Check continuity between ABS relay box 2-pin connector (body side) terminal ⑬ and ground.
Continuity should not exist.

OK

1. Disconnect ABS relay box 6-pin connector and control unit connector.
2. Check continuity between ABS relay box 6-pin connector (body side) terminal ⑨ and ground.
Continuity should not exist.

OK

Check continuity between ABS relay box 6-pin connector (ABS relay box side) terminal ⑨ and ground, ABS relay box 2-pin connector (ABS relay box side) terminal ⑬ and ground.
Continuity should not exist.

OK

1. Remove motor ground.
2. Check continuity between ABS actuator 2-pin connector (ABS actuator side) terminal ㉘ and ground.
Continuity should not exist.

OK

MOTOR CHECK
Go to ... in Diagnostic Procedure 3.

NG → inspection end.
NG → Repair harness and connector.
NG → Repair harness and connector.
NG → Replace ABS relay box.
NG → Replace ABS actuator.

Check control unit pin terminals for damage or the connection of control unit harness connector.
Reconnect control unit harness connector. Then retest.

NS4029700272030X

Fig. 171 Test 3: Motor Relay or Motor (Part 3 of 3). 1997–99 Sentra & 200SX

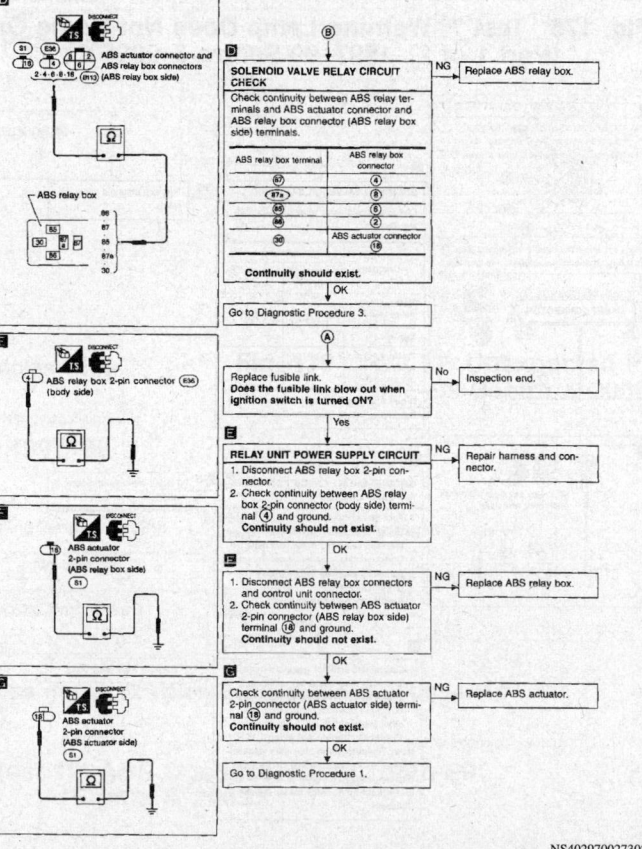

SOLENOID VALVE RELAY CIRCUIT CHECK
Check continuity between ABS relay box terminals and ABS actuator connector and ABS relay box connector (ABS relay box side) terminals.

ABS relay box terminal	ABS relay box connector
㉘	④
㉘	⑧
㉘	⑥
㉘	②
㉘	ABS actuator connector
	⑯

Continuity should exist.

OK

Go to Diagnostic Procedure 3.

NG → Replace ABS relay box.

A

Replace fusible link.
Does the fusible link blow out when ignition switch is turned ON?

No → Inspection end.

Yes

RELAY UNIT POWER SUPPLY CIRCUIT
1. Disconnect ABS relay box 2-pin connector.
2. Check continuity between ABS relay box 2-pin connector (body side) terminal ④ and ground.
Continuity should not exist.

OK

1. Disconnect ABS relay box connectors and control unit connector.
2. Check continuity between ABS actuator 2-pin connector (ABS relay box side) terminal ⑯ and ground.
Continuity should not exist.

OK

Check continuity between ABS actuator 2-pin connector (ABS actuator side) terminal ⑯ and ground.
Continuity should not exist.

OK

Go to Diagnostic Procedure 1.

NG → Repair harness and connector.
NG → Replace ABS relay box.
NG → Replace ABS actuator.

NS4029700273020X

Fig. 172 Test 4: Solenoid Valve Relay (Part 2 of 2). 1997–99 Sentra & 200SX

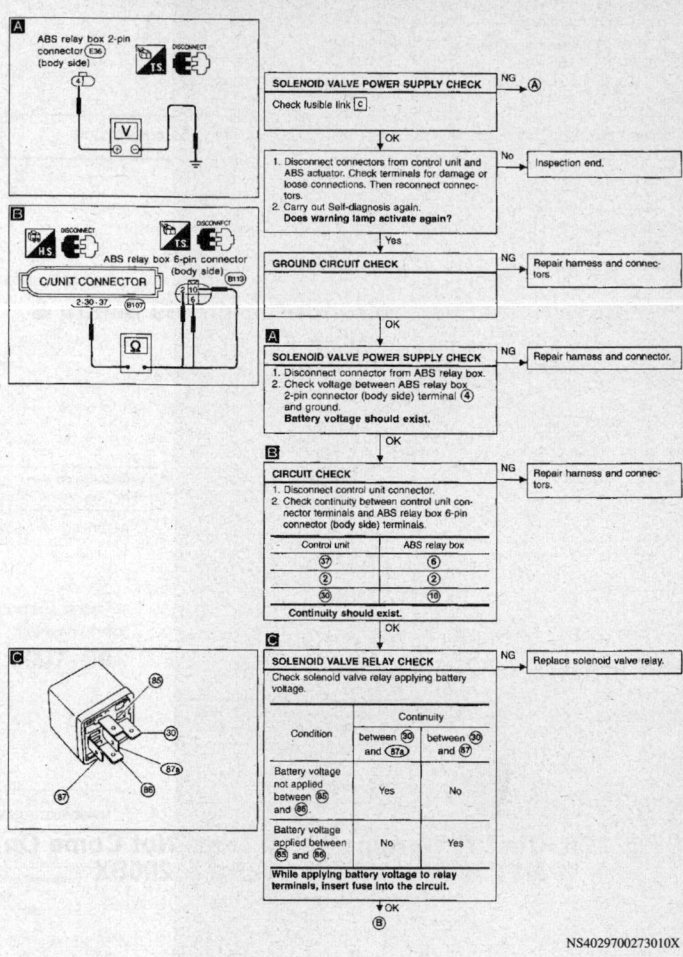

SOLENOID VALVE POWER SUPPLY CHECK
Check fusible link C.

NG → A

OK

1. Disconnect connectors from control unit and ABS actuator. Check terminals for damage or loose connections. Then reconnect connectors.
2. Carry out Self-diagnosis again.
Does warning lamp activate again?

NG → Inspection end.

Yes

GROUND CIRCUIT CHECK

NG → Repair harness and connectors.

OK

SOLENOID VALVE POWER SUPPLY CHECK
1. Disconnect connector from ABS actuator.
2. Check voltage between ABS relay box 2-pin connector (body side) terminal ④ and ground.
Battery voltage should exist.

NG → Repair harness and connector.

OK

CIRCUIT CHECK
1. Disconnect control unit connector.
2. Check continuity between control unit connector terminals and ABS relay box 6-pin connector (body side) terminals.

Control unit	ABS relay box
㊲	⑥
	⑧
㊱	⑩

Continuity should exist.

NG → Repair harness and connectors.

OK

SOLENOID VALVE RELAY CHECK
Check solenoid valve relay applying battery voltage.

NG → Replace solenoid valve relay.

Condition	Continuity	
	between ㉚ and 87a	between ㉚ and ㉘⑦
Battery voltage not applied between ㉘⑤ and ㉘⑥	Yes	No
Battery voltage applied between ㉘⑤ and ㉘⑥	No	Yes

While applying battery voltage to relay terminals, insert fuse into the circuit.

OK

B

NS4029700273010X

Fig. 172 Test 4: Solenoid Valve Relay (Part 1 of 2). 1997–99 Sentra & 200SX

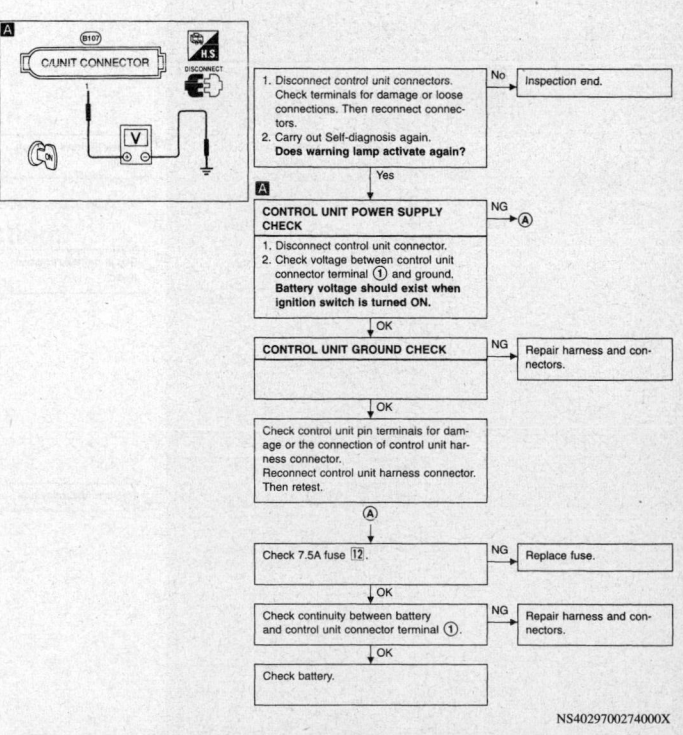

A

1. Disconnect control unit connectors. Check terminals for damage or loose connections. Then reconnect connectors.
2. Carry out Self-diagnosis again.
Does warning lamp activate again?

No → Inspection end.

Yes

CONTROL UNIT POWER SUPPLY CHECK
1. Disconnect control unit connector.
2. Check voltage between control unit connector terminal ① and ground.
Battery voltage should exist when ignition switch is turned ON.

NG → A

OK

CONTROL UNIT GROUND CHECK

NG → Repair harness and connectors.

OK

Check control unit pin terminals for damage or the connection of control unit harness connector.
Reconnect control unit harness connector. Then retest.

A

Check 7.5A fuse 12.

NG → Replace fuse.

OK

Check continuity between battery and control unit connector terminal ①.

NG → Repair harness and connectors.

OK

Check battery.

NS4029700274000X

Fig. 173 Test 5: Low Voltage. 1997–99 Sentra & 200SX

NISSAN UNIT REPA NISSAN UNIT REPAIR

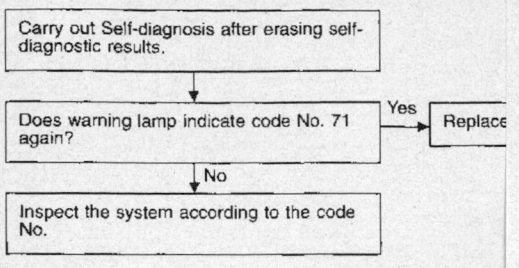

Carry out Self-diagnosis after erasing self-diagnostic results.

↓

Does warning lamp indicate code No. 71 again? → Yes → Replace

↓ No

Inspect the system according to the code No.

Fig. 174 Test 6: Control Unit. 1997–9 200SX

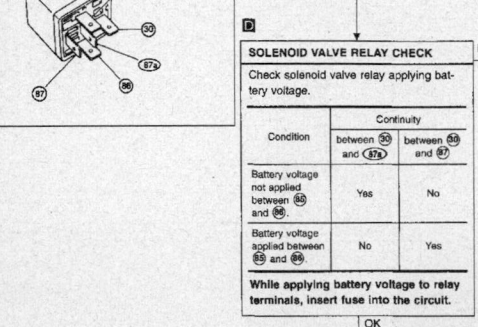

Condition	Continuity	
	between ㉟ and ㉘	between ㉟ and ㉗
Battery voltage not applied between ㉟ and ㉞	Yes	No
Battery voltage applied between ㉟ and ㉞	No	Yes

SOLENOID VALVE RELAY CHECK
Check solenoid valve relay applying battery voltage.

While applying battery voltage to relay terminals, insert fuse into the circuit.

↓ OK

Go to Diagnostic Procedure 5.

Fig. 175 Test 7: Warning Lamp Does (Part 2 of 2). 1997–99 Sentra &

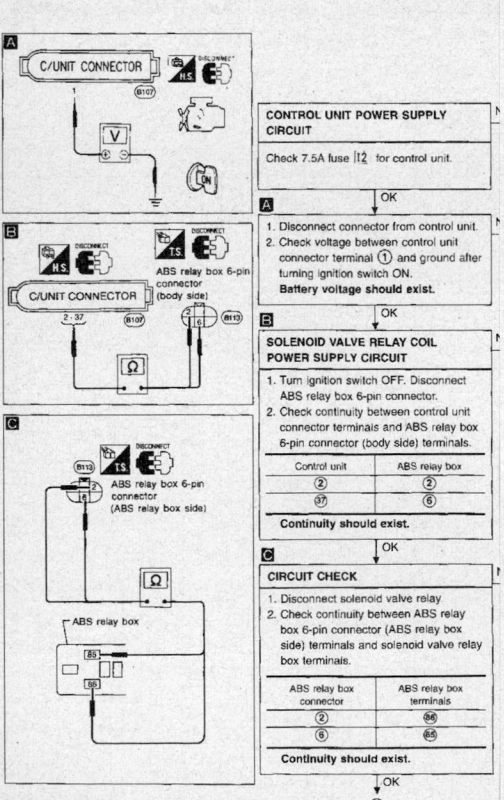

Fig. 176 Test 8: Warning Lamp Stays 3). 1997–99 Sentra & 200S

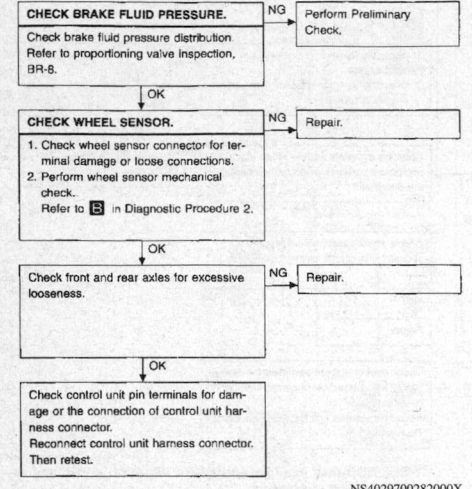

CHECK BRAKE FLUID PRESSURE.
Check brake fluid pressure distribution. Refer to proportioning valve inspection, BR-8. → NG → Perform Preliminary Check.

↓ OK

CHECK WHEEL SENSOR.
1. Check wheel sensor connector for terminal damage or loose connections.
2. Perform wheel sensor mechanical check. Refer to 𝐁 in Diagnostic Procedure 2. → NG → Repair.

↓ OK

Check front and rear axles for excessive looseness. → NG → Repair.

↓ OK

Check control unit pin terminals for damage or the connection of control unit harness connector. Reconnect control unit harness connector. Then retest.

NS4029700282000X

Fig. 181 Test 13: ABS Works Frequently. 1997–99 Sentra & 200SX

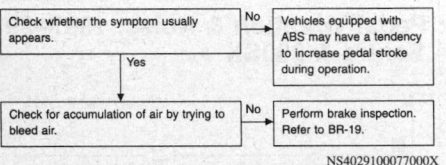

Check whether the symptom usually appears. → No → Vehicles equipped with ABS may have a tendency to increase pedal stroke during operation.

↓ Yes

Check for accumulation of air by trying to bleed air. → No → Perform brake inspection. Refer to BR-19.

NS4029100077000X

Fig. 184 Test 3: Brake Pedal Stroke Is Abnormally Large. Pickup

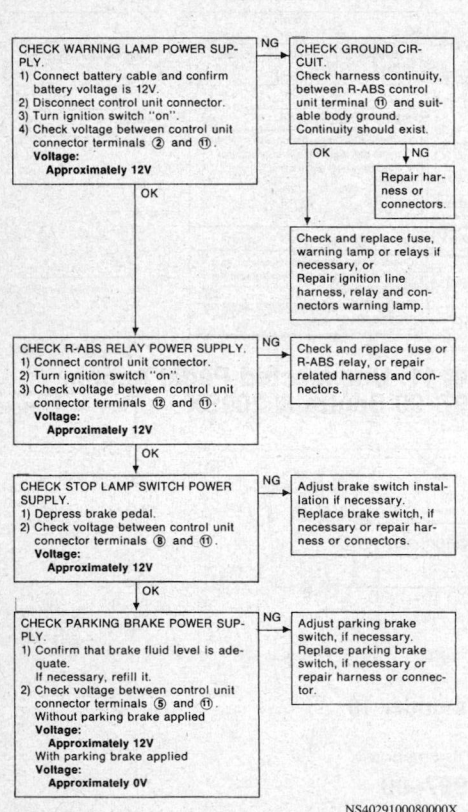

CHECK WARNING LAMP POWER SUPPLY.
1) Connect battery cable and confirm battery voltage is 12V.
2) Disconnect control unit connector.
3) Turn ignition switch "on".
4) Check voltage between control unit connector terminals ② and ⑪.
Voltage: Approximately 12V → NG → CHECK GROUND CIRCUIT. Check harness continuity between R-ABS control unit terminal ⑪ and suitable body ground. Continuity should exist.

OK ↓ NG → Repair harness or connectors.

Check and replace fuse, warning lamp or relays if necessary, or Repair ignition line harness, relay and connectors warning lamp.

CHECK R-ABS RELAY POWER SUPPLY.
1) Connect control unit connector.
2) Turn ignition switch "on".
3) Check voltage between control unit connector terminals ⑫ and ⑪.
Voltage: Approximately 12V → NG → Check and replace fuse or R-ABS related harness or connectors.

↓ OK

CHECK STOP LAMP SWITCH POWER SUPPLY.
1) Depress brake pedal.
2) Check voltage between control unit connector terminals ⑧ and ⑪.
Voltage: Approximately 12V → NG → Adjust brake switch installation if necessary. Replace brake switch, if necessary or repair harness or connectors.

↓ OK

CHECK PARKING BRAKE POWER SUPPLY.
1) Confirm that brake fluid level is adequate. If necessary, refill it.
2) Check voltage between control unit connector terminals ⑤ and ⑪.
Without parking brake applied Voltage: Approximately 12V
With parking brake applied Voltage: Approximately 0V → NG → Adjust parking brake switch, if necessary. Replace parking brake switch, if necessary or repair harness or connector.

NS4029100080000X

Fig. 187 Test 6: Main Power Supply & Ground circuit. Pickup

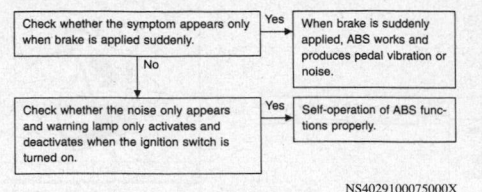

Check whether the symptom appears only when brake is applied suddenly. → Yes → When brake is suddenly applied, ABS works and produces pedal vibration or noise.

↓ No

Check whether the noise only appears and warning lamp only activates and deactivates when the ignition switch is turned on. → Yes → Self-operation of ABS functions properly.

NS4029100075000X

Fig. 182 Test 1: Pedal Vibration Or Noise. Pickup

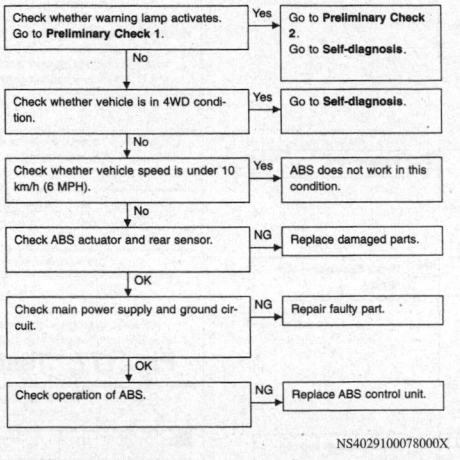

Check whether warning lamp activates. Go to Preliminary Check 1. → Yes → Go to Preliminary Check 2. Go to Self-diagnosis.

↓ No

Check whether vehicle is in 4WD condition. → Yes → Go to Self-diagnosis.

↓ No

Check whether vehicle speed is under 10 km/h (6 MPH). → Yes → ABS does not work in this condition.

↓ No

Check ABS actuator and rear sensor. → NG → Replace damaged parts.

↓ OK

Check main power supply and ground circuit. → NG → Repair faulty part.

↓ OK

Check operation of ABS. → NG → Replace ABS control unit.

NS4029100078000X

Fig. 185 Test 4: ABS Doesn't Work. Pickup

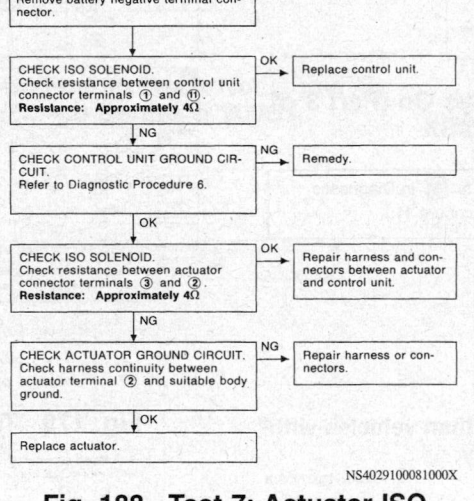

Remove battery negative terminal connector.

↓

CHECK ISO SOLENOID.
Check resistance between control unit connector terminals ① and ⑪. Resistance: Approximately 4Ω → OK → Replace control unit.

↓ NG

CHECK CONTROL UNIT GROUND CIRCUIT. Refer to Diagnostic Procedure 6. → NG → Remedy.

↓ OK

CHECK ISO SOLENOID.
Check resistance between actuator connector terminals ③ and ⑪. Resistance: Approximately 4Ω → OK → Repair harness and connectors between actuator and control unit.

↓ NG

CHECK ACTUATOR GROUND CIRCUIT. Check harness continuity between actuator terminal ② and suitable body ground. → NG → Repair harness or connectors.

↓ OK

Replace actuator.

NS4029100081000X

Fig. 188 Test 7: Actuator ISO Solenoid Short Circuit Or Open. Pickup

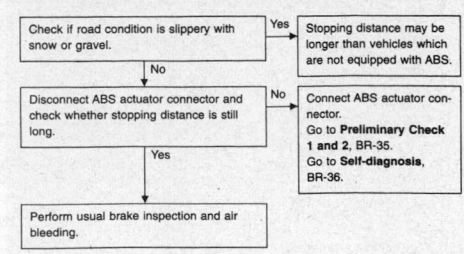

Check if road condition is slippery with snow or gravel. → Yes → Stopping distance may be longer than vehicles which are not equipped with ABS.

↓ No

Disconnect ABS actuator connector and check whether stopping distance is still long. → No → Connect ABS actuator connector. Go to Preliminary Check 1 and 2, BR-35. Go to Self-diagnosis, BR-36.

↓ Yes

Perform usual brake inspection and air bleeding.

NS4029100076000X

Fig. 183 Test 2: Long Stopping Distance. Pickup

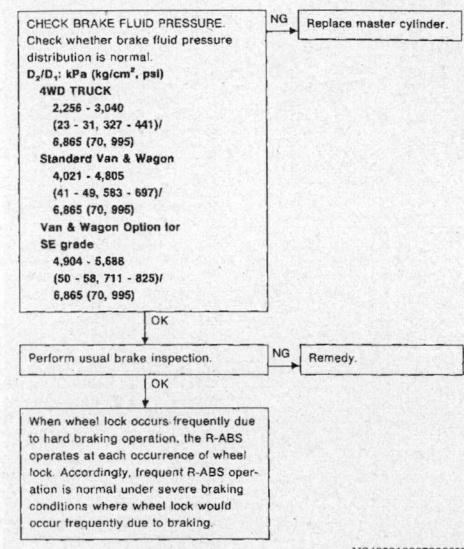

CHECK BRAKE FLUID PRESSURE.
Check whether brake fluid pressure distribution is normal.
D₂/D₁: kPa (kg/cm², psi)
4WD TRUCK
2,256 - 3,040 (23 - 31, 327 - 441)/ 6,865 (70, 995)
Standard Van & Wagon
4,021 - 4,805 (41 - 49, 583 - 697)/ 6,865 (70, 995)
Van & Wagon Option for SE grade
4,904 - 5,688 (50 - 58, 711 - 825)/ 6,865 (70, 995) → NG → Replace master cylinder.

↓ OK

Perform usual brake inspection. → NG → Remedy.

↓ OK

When wheel lock occurs frequently due to hard braking operation, the R-ABS operates at each occurrence of wheel lock. Accordingly, frequent R-ABS operation is normal under severe braking conditions where wheel lock would occur frequently due to braking.

NS4029100079000X

Fig. 186 Test 5: ABS Works Frequently. Pickup

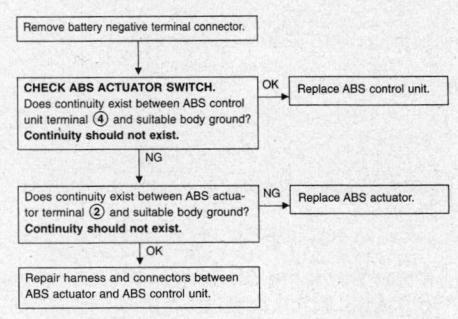

Remove battery negative terminal connector.

↓

CHECK ABS ACTUATOR SWITCH.
Does continuity exist between ABS control unit terminal ④ and suitable body ground? Continuity should not exist. → OK → Replace ABS control unit.

↓ NG

Does continuity exist between ABS actuator terminal ② and suitable body ground? Continuity should not exist. → NG → Replace ABS actuator.

↓ OK

Repair harness and connectors between ABS actuator and ABS control unit.

NS4029100082000A

Fig. 189 Test 8: Actuator ISO Solenoid Blocked. Pickup

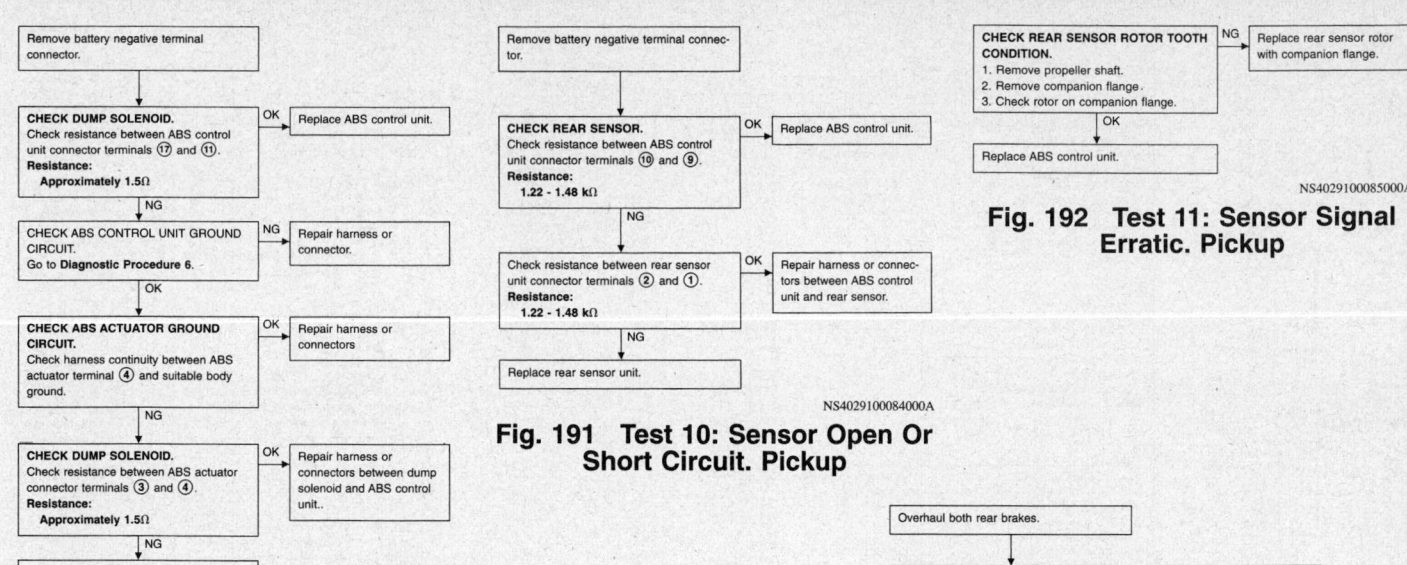

Fig. 192 Test 11: Sensor Signal
Erratic. Pickup

NS4029100085000A

Fig. 191 Test 10: Sensor Open Or
Short Circuit. Pickup

NS4029100084000A

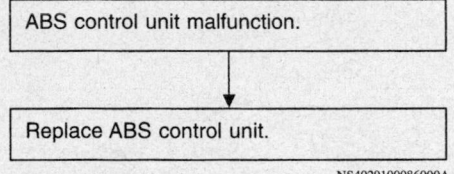

Fig. 190 Test 9: Actuator Dump
Solenoid Short Circuit. Pickup

NS4029100083000A

| ABS control unit malfunction. |
| Replace ABS control unit. |

NS4029100086000A

Fig. 193 Test 12: Control Unit.
Pickup

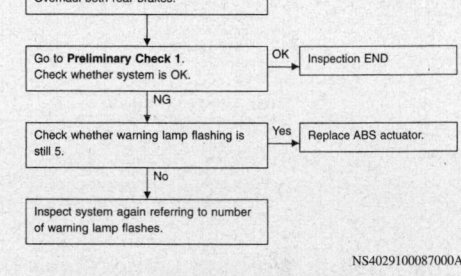

Fig. 194 Test 13: Other Problems.
Pickup

NS4029100087000A

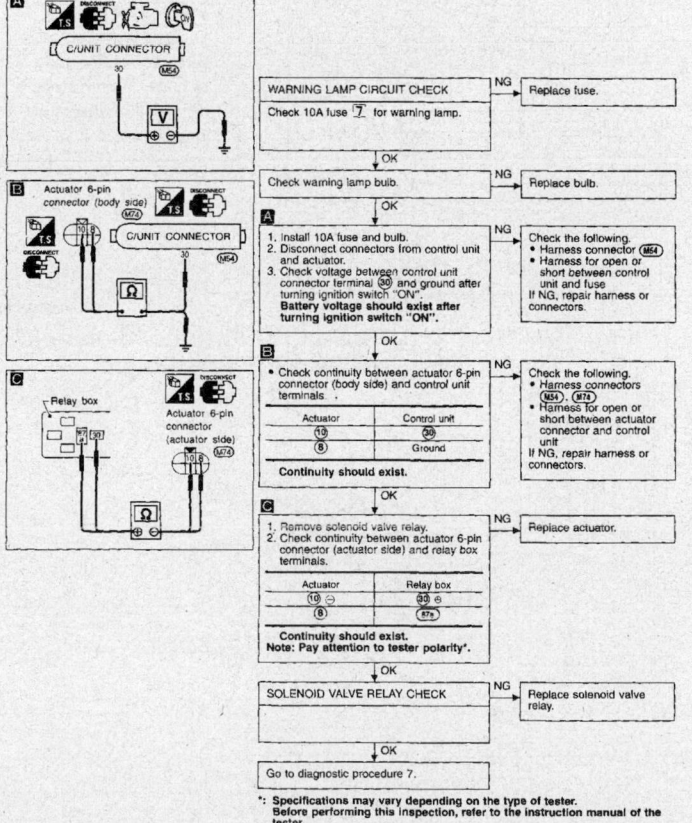

NS4029600221000X

*: Specifications may vary depending on the type of tester.
Before performing this inspection, refer to the instruction manual of the tester.

Fig. 195 Test 1: Warning Lamp Does Not Work
When Ignition Is On. 1996 Pathfinder

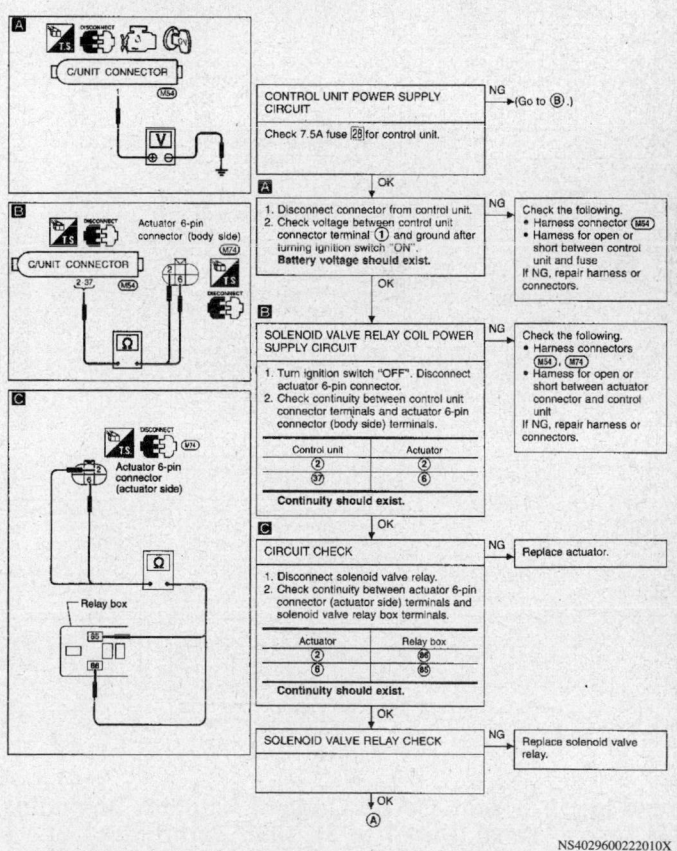

NS4029600222010X

Fig. 196 Test 2: Warning Lamp Stays On When
Ignition Switch Is On (Part 1 of 3). 1996 Pathfinder

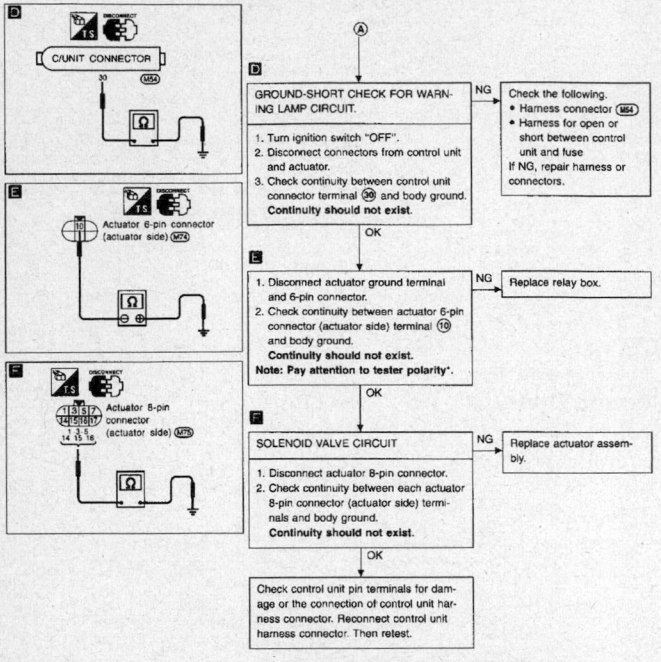

Fig. 196   Test 2: Warning Lamp Stays On When Ignition Switch Is On (Part 2 of 3). 1996 Pathfinder

NS4029600222020X

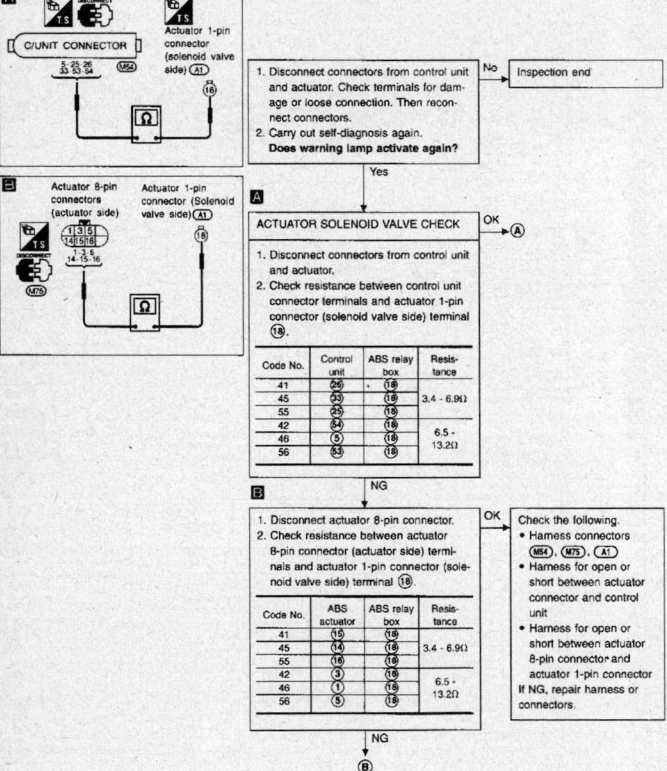

Fig. 197   Test 3: ABS Control Actuator Solenoid Valve (Part 1 of 3). 1996 Pathfinder

NS4029600223010X

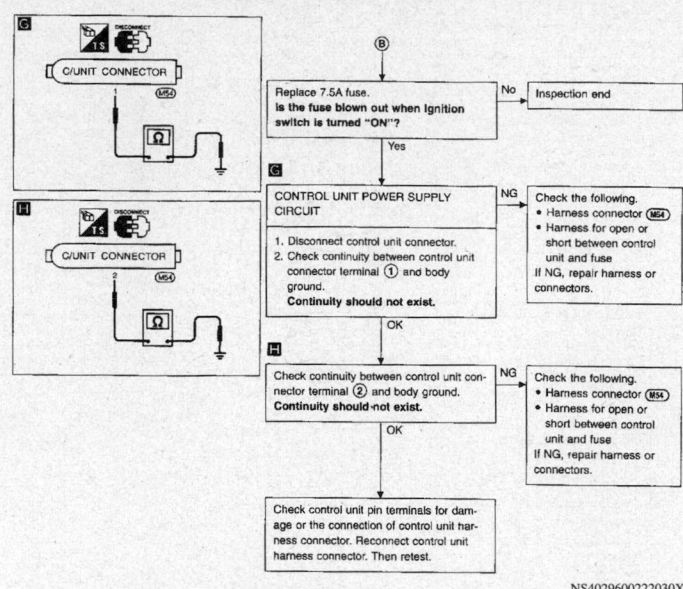

Fig. 196   Test 2: Warning Lamp Stays On When Ignition Switch Is On (Part 3 of 3). 1996 Pathfinder

NS4029600222030X

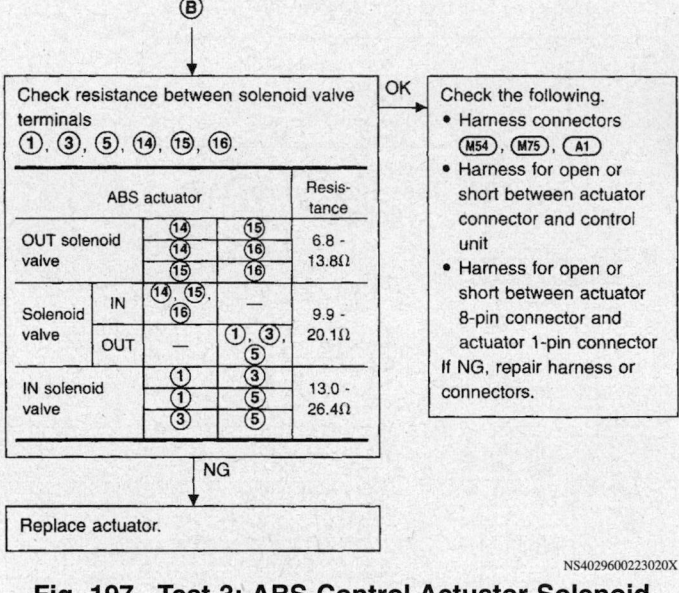

Fig. 197   Test 3: ABS Control Actuator Solenoid Valve (Part 2 of 3). 1996 Pathfinder

NS4029600223020X

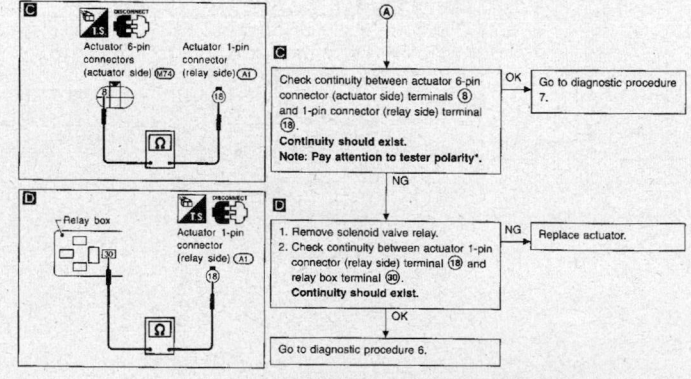

Fig. 197   Test 3: ABS Control Actuator Solenoid Valve (Part 3 of 3). 1996 Pathfinder

NS4029600223030X

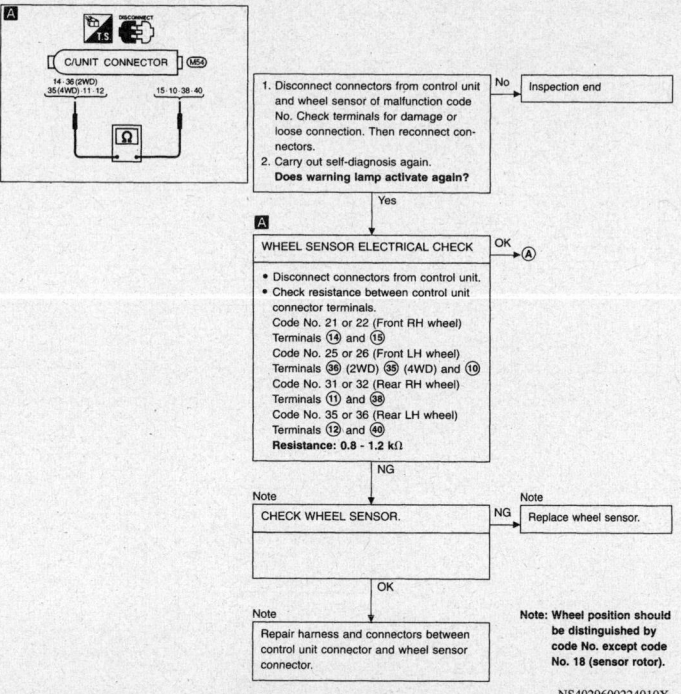

Ⓐ

1. Disconnect connectors from control unit and wheel sensor of malfunction code No. Check terminals for damage or loose connection. Then reconnect connectors.
2. Carry out self-diagnosis again. **Does warning lamp activate again?**

→ No → Inspection end

↓ Yes

Ⓐ

WHEEL SENSOR ELECTRICAL CHECK → OK → Ⓐ

- Disconnect connectors from control unit.
- Check resistance between control unit connector terminals.
  Code No. 21 or 22 (Front RH wheel)
  Terminals ⑭ and ⑮
  Code No. 25 or 26 (Front LH wheel)
  Terminals ㊱ (2WD) ㉟ (4WD) and ⑩
  Code No. 31 or 32 (Rear RH wheel)
  Terminals ⑪ and ㊳
  Code No. 35 or 36 (Rear LH wheel)
  Terminals ⑫ and ㊵
  Resistance: 0.8 - 1.2 kΩ

↓ NG

Note
CHECK WHEEL SENSOR. → NG → Note Replace wheel sensor.

↓ OK

Note
Repair harness and connectors between control unit connector and wheel sensor connector.

Note: Wheel position should be distinguished by code No. except code No. 18 (sensor rotor).

NS4029600224010X

Fig. 198   Test 4: Wheel Sensor Or Rotor (Part 1 of 2). 1996 Pathfinder

---

Ⓐ

Note
WHEEL SENSOR MECHANICAL CHECK → NG → Note Adjust tire pressure or replace tire(s).

Check for inflation pressure, wear and size of each tire.

↓ OK

Note
Check wheel bearing axial end play.

↓ OK

Note
Check sensor rotor for teeth damage. → NG → Note Replace sensor rotor.

↓ OK

Check control unit pin terminals for damage or the connection of control unit harness connector. Reconnect control unit harness connector. Then retest.

Note: Wheel position should be distinguished by code No. except code No. 18 (sensor rotor).

NS4029600224020X

Fig. 198   Test 4: Wheel Sensor Or Rotor (Part 2 of 2). 1996 Pathfinder

---

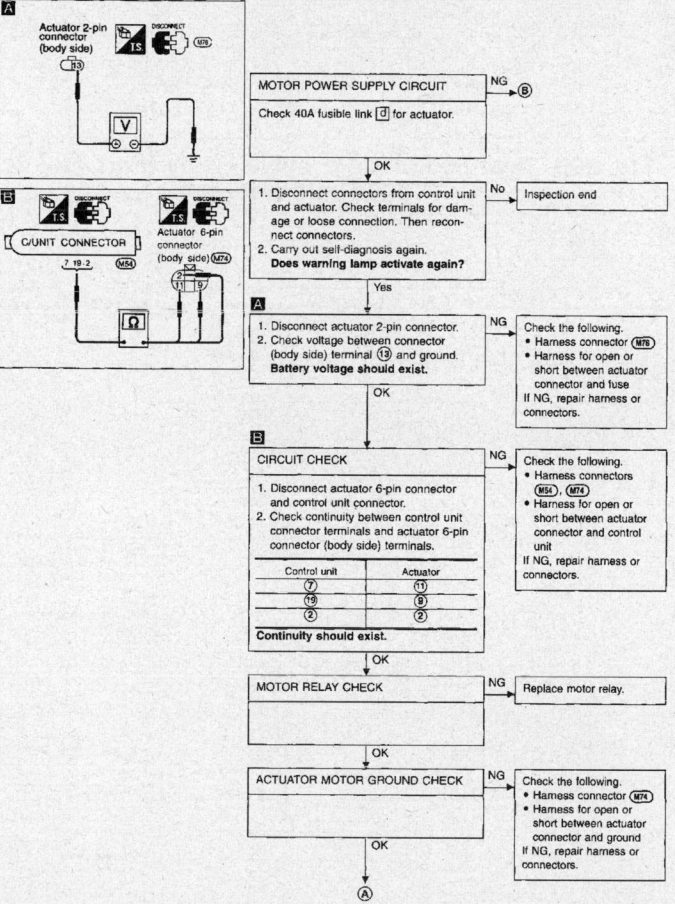

MOTOR POWER SUPPLY CIRCUIT → NG → Ⓑ

Check 40A fusible link ⓓ for actuator.

↓ OK

1. Disconnect connectors from control unit and actuator. Check terminals for damage or loose connection. Then reconnect connectors.
2. Carry out self-diagnosis again. **Does warning lamp activate again?**

→ No → Inspection end

↓ Yes

Ⓐ

1. Disconnect actuator 2-pin connector.
2. Check voltage between connector (body side) terminal ⑬ and ground. **Battery voltage should exist.**

→ NG → Check the following.
- Harness connector ⓜ76
- Harness for open or short between actuator connector and fuse
If NG, repair harness or connectors.

↓ OK

Ⓑ
CIRCUIT CHECK

1. Disconnect actuator 6-pin connector and control unit connector.
2. Check continuity between control unit connector terminals and actuator 6-pin connector (body side) terminals.

Control unit	Actuator
⑦	⑪
⑲	⑨
②	②

Continuity should exist.

→ NG → Check the following.
- Harness connectors ⓜ54, ⓜ74
- Harness for open or short between actuator connector and control unit
If NG, repair harness or connectors.

↓ OK

MOTOR RELAY CHECK → NG → Replace motor relay.

↓ OK

ACTUATOR MOTOR GROUND CHECK → NG → Check the following.
- Harness connector ⓜ74
- Harness for open or short between actuator connector and ground
If NG, repair harness or connectors.

↓ OK

Ⓐ

NS4029600225010X

Fig. 199   Test 5: Motor Relay Or Motor (Part 1 of 3). 1996 Pathfinder

---

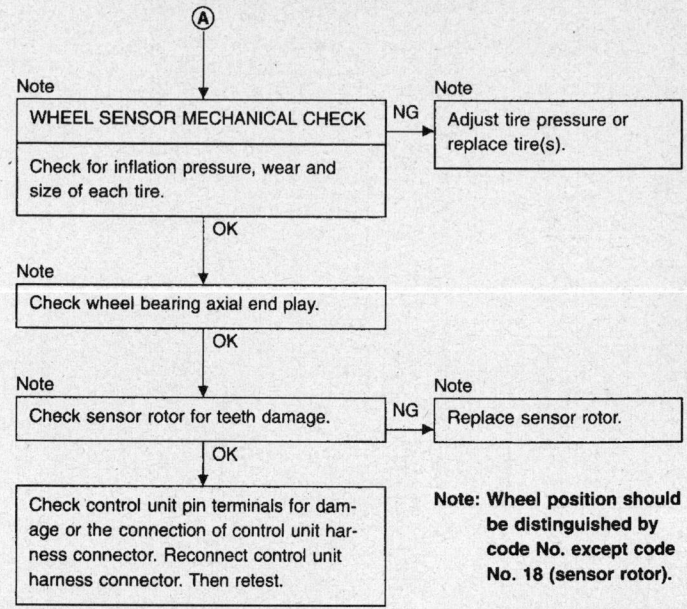

Ⓐ

Ⓒ
MOTOR RELAY CIRCUIT → NG → Replace relay box assembly.

1. Remove motor relay.
2. Check continuity between actuator connector (actuator side) terminals and relay connector terminals.

Actuator connector	Relay connector
②	㊱
⑪	㊵
⑨	㉚
⑬	㊲
Actuator motor positive terminal	㉚

Continuity should exist.

↓ OK

MOTOR CHECK → NG → Replace actuator assembly.

1. Connect actuator connectors.
2. Connect suitable wire between relay connector terminals ㉚ and ㊲. **Motor should operate. Do not connect wire for more than 5 seconds.**

↓ OK

Go to diagnostic procedure 7.

NS4029600225020X

Fig. 199   Test 5: Motor Relay Or Motor (Part 2 of 3). 1996 Pathfinder

---

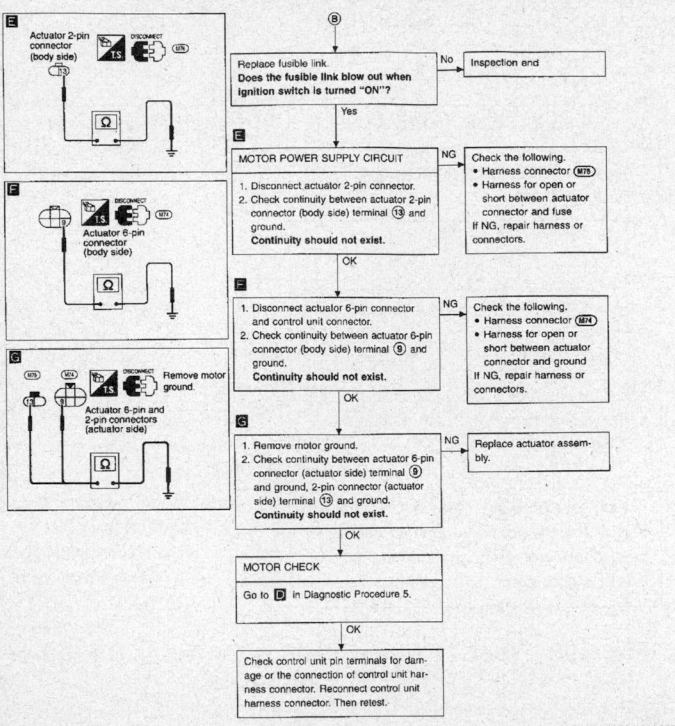

Actuator 2-pin connector (body side) 13

Actuator 6-pin connector (body side)

Actuator 6-pin and 2-pin connectors (actuator side) Remove motor ground.

Replace fusible link.
Does the fusible link blow out when ignition switch is turned "ON"?
No → Inspection end
Yes ↓

MOTOR POWER SUPPLY CIRCUIT
1. Disconnect actuator 2-pin connector.
2. Check continuity between actuator 2-pin connector (body side) terminal 13 and ground.
Continuity should not exist.
NG → Check the following.
• Harness connector (M76)
• Harness for open or short between actuator connector and fuse
If NG, repair harness or connectors.
OK ↓

1. Disconnect actuator 6-pin connector and control unit connector.
2. Check continuity between actuator 6-pin connector (body side) terminal 9 and ground.
Continuity should not exist.
NG → Check the following.
• Harness connector (M74)
• Harness for open or short between actuator connector and ground
If NG, repair harness or connectors.
OK ↓

1. Remove motor ground.
2. Check continuity between actuator 6-pin connector (actuator side) terminal 9 and ground, 2-pin connector (actuator side) terminal 13 and ground.
Continuity should not exist.
NG → Replace actuator assembly.
OK ↓

MOTOR CHECK
Go to D in Diagnostic Procedure 5.
OK ↓

Check control unit pin terminals for damage or the connection of control unit harness connector. Reconnect control unit harness connector. Then retest.

NS4029600225030X

Fig. 199   Test 5: Motor Relay Or Motor (Part 3 of 3). 1996 Pathfinder

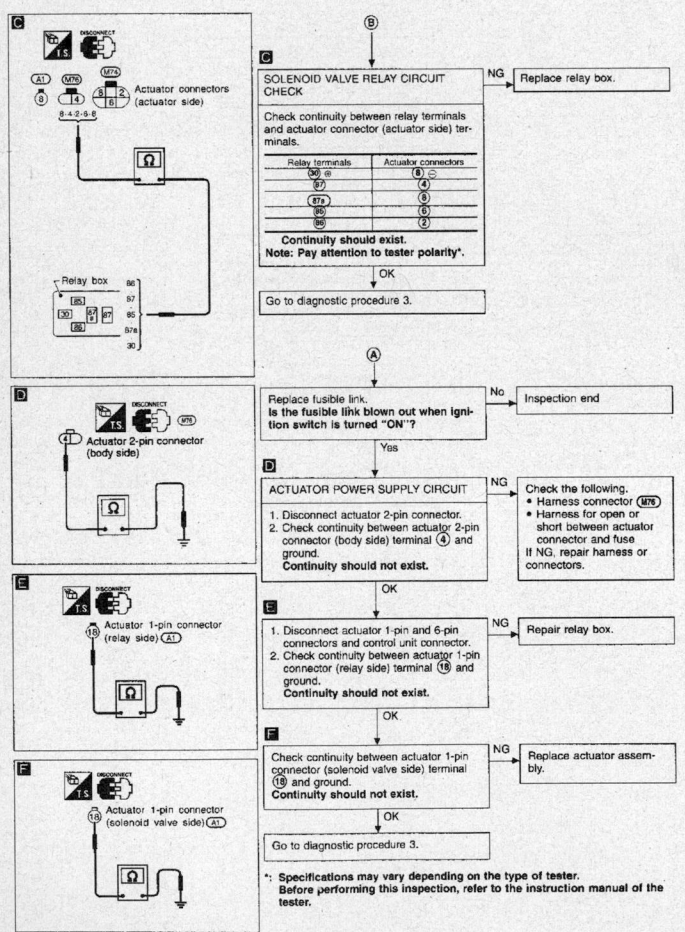

Actuator connectors (actuator side)

SOLENOID VALVE RELAY CIRCUIT CHECK
Check continuity between relay terminals and actuator connector (actuator side) terminals.
NG → Replace relay box.

Relay terminals	Actuator connectors
30	8
87	6
87a	5
86	6
85	2

Continuity should exist.
Note: Pay attention to tester polarity*.
OK ↓
Go to diagnostic procedure 3.

Relay box

Actuator 2-pin connector (body side)

Replace fusible link.
Is the fusible link blown out when ignition switch is turned "ON"?
No → Inspection end
Yes ↓

ACTUATOR POWER SUPPLY CIRCUIT
1. Disconnect actuator 2-pin connector.
2. Check continuity between actuator 2-pin connector (body side) terminal 4 and ground.
Continuity should not exist.
NG → Check the following.
• Harness connector (M76)
• Harness for open or short between actuator connector and fuse
If NG, repair harness or connectors.
OK ↓

Actuator 1-pin connector (relay side) A1

1. Disconnect actuator 1-pin and 6-pin connectors and control unit connector.
2. Check continuity between actuator 1-pin connector (relay side) terminal 18 and ground.
Continuity should not exist.
NG → Repair relay box.
OK ↓

Actuator 1-pin connector (solenoid valve side) A1

Check continuity between actuator 1-pin connector (solenoid valve side) terminal 18 and ground.
Continuity should not exist.
NG → Replace actuator assembly.
OK ↓
Go to diagnostic procedure 3.

*: Specifications may vary depending on the type of tester. Before performing this inspection, refer to the instruction manual of the tester.

NS4029600226020X

Fig. 200   Test 6: Solenoid Valve Relay (Part 2 of 2). 1996 Pathfinder

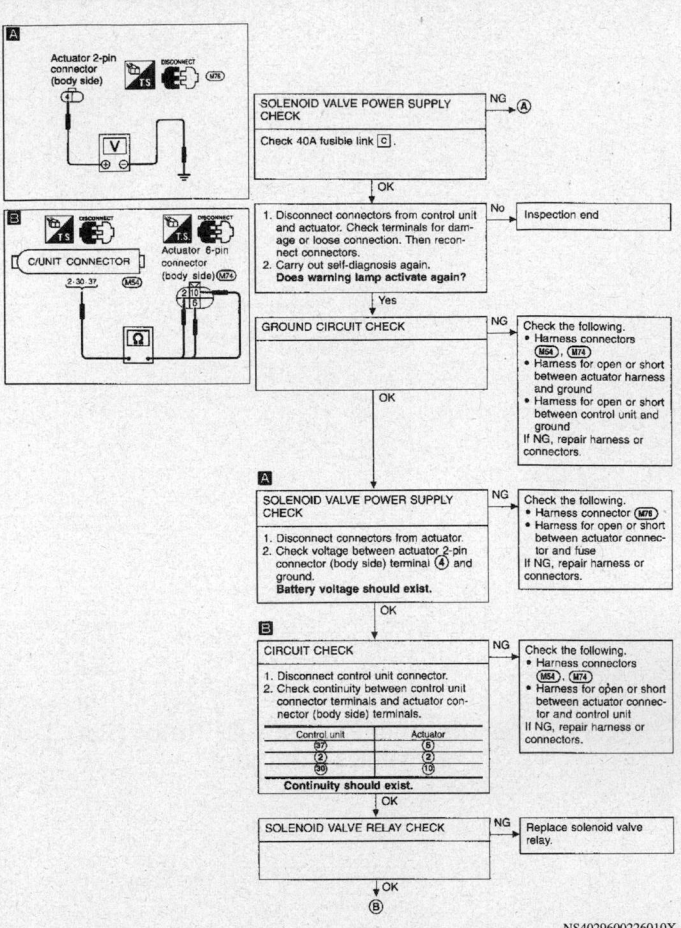

Actuator 2-pin connector (body side) 4

C/UNIT CONNECTOR 2-30·37 (M54)   **Actuator 6-pin connector (body side)** (M74)

SOLENOID VALVE POWER SUPPLY CHECK
Check 40A fusible link C.
NG → A

OK ↓

1. Disconnect connectors from control unit and actuator. Check terminals for damage or loose connection. Then reconnect connectors.
2. Carry out self-diagnosis again.
Does warning lamp activate again?
No → Inspection end
Yes ↓

GROUND CIRCUIT CHECK
NG → Check the following.
• Harness connectors (M54) (M74)
• Harness for open or short between actuator harness and ground
• Harness for open or short between control unit and ground
If NG, repair harness or connectors.
OK ↓

SOLENOID VALVE POWER SUPPLY CHECK
1. Disconnect connectors from actuator.
2. Check voltage between actuator 2-pin connector (body side) terminal 4 and ground.
Battery voltage should exist.
NG → Check the following.
• Harness connector (M76)
• Harness for open or short between actuator connector and fuse
If NG, repair harness or connectors.
OK ↓

CIRCUIT CHECK
1. Disconnect control unit connector.
2. Check continuity between control unit connector terminals and actuator connector (body side) terminals.

Control unit	Actuator
37	8
2	6
36	10

Continuity should exist.
NG → Check the following.
• Harness connectors (M54) (M74)
• Harness for open or short between actuator connector and control unit
If NG, repair harness or connectors.
OK ↓

SOLENOID VALVE RELAY CHECK
NG → Replace solenoid valve relay.
OK ↓
B

NS4029600226010X

Fig. 200   Test 6: Solenoid Valve Relay (Part 1 of 2). 1996 Pathfinder

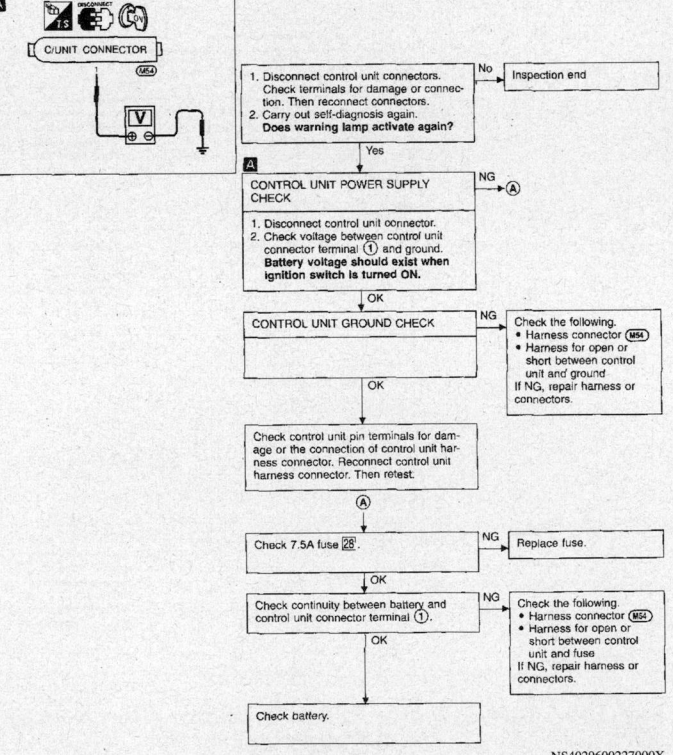

C/UNIT CONNECTOR (M54)

1. Disconnect control unit connectors. Check terminals for damage or connection. Then reconnect connectors.
2. Carry out self-diagnosis again.
Does warning lamp activate again?
No → Inspection end
Yes ↓

CONTROL UNIT POWER SUPPLY CHECK
NG → A
1. Disconnect control unit connector.
2. Check voltage between control unit connector terminal 1 and ground.
Battery voltage should exist when ignition switch is turned ON.
OK ↓

CONTROL UNIT GROUND CHECK
NG → Check the following.
• Harness connector (M54)
• Harness for open or short between control unit and ground
If NG, repair harness or connectors.
OK ↓

Check control unit pin terminals for damage or the connection of control unit harness connector. Reconnect control unit harness connector. Then retest.
A ↓

Check 7.5A fuse 28.
NG → Replace fuse.
OK ↓

Check continuity between battery and control unit connector terminal 1.
NG → Check the following.
• Harness connector (M54)
• Harness for open or short between control unit and fuse
If NG, repair harness or connectors.
OK ↓

Check battery.

NS4029600227000X

Fig. 201   Test 7: Power Supply Low Voltage. 1996 Pathfinder

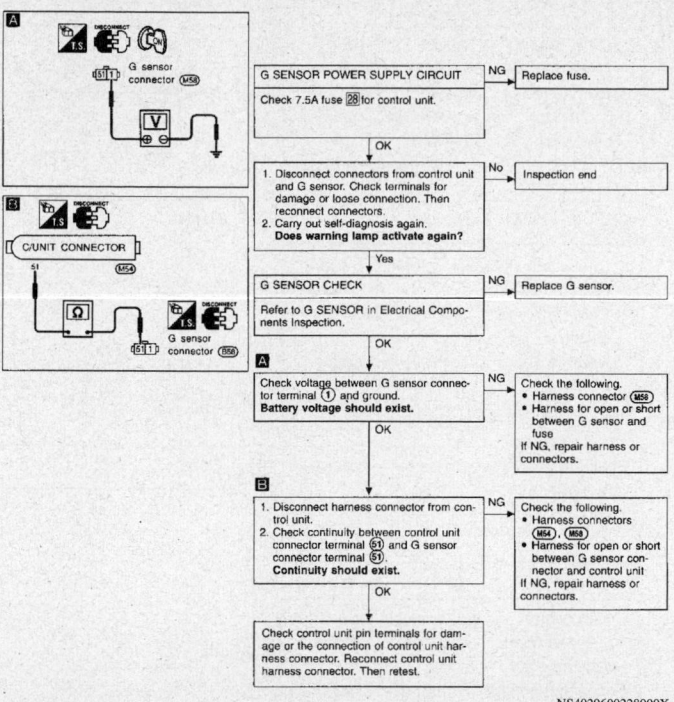

G SENSOR POWER SUPPLY CIRCUIT

Check 7.5A fuse 28 for control unit.
→ NG → Replace fuse.

↓ OK

1. Disconnect connectors from control unit and G sensor. Check terminals for damage or loose connection. Then reconnect connectors.
2. Carry out self-diagnosis again.
   Does warning lamp activate again?
→ No → Inspection end

↓ Yes

G SENSOR CHECK

Refer to G SENSOR in Electrical Components Inspection.
→ NG → Replace G sensor.

↓ OK

Check voltage between G sensor connector terminal ① and ground.
Battery voltage should exist.
→ NG → Check the following.
• Harness connector (M58)
• Harness for open or short between G sensor and fuse
If NG, repair harness or connectors.

↓ OK

1. Disconnect harness connector from control unit.
2. Check continuity between control unit connector terminal 51 and G sensor connector terminal 51.
   Continuity should exist.
→ NG → Check the following.
• Harness connectors (M54) (M58)
• Harness for open or short between G sensor connector and control unit
If NG, repair harness or connectors.

↓ OK

Check control unit pin terminals for damage or the connection of control unit harness connector. Reconnect control unit harness connector. Then retest.

NS4029600228000X

Fig. 202   Test 8: G Sensor. 1996 Pathfinder

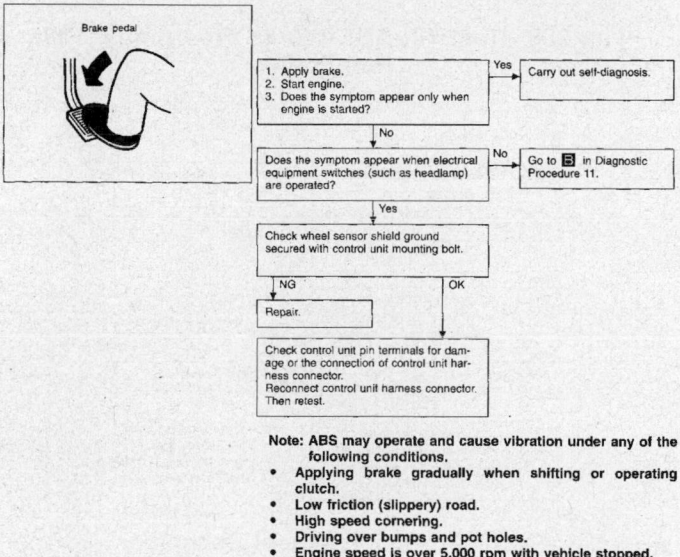

1. Apply brake.
2. Start engine.
3. Does the symptom appear only when engine is started?
→ Yes → Carry out self-diagnosis.

↓ No

Does the symptom appear when electrical equipment switches (such as headlamp) are operated?
→ No → Go to B in Diagnostic Procedure 11.

↓ Yes

Check wheel sensor shield ground secured with control unit mounting bolt.

NG ↓   ↓ OK

Repair.

Check control unit pin terminals for damage or the connection of control unit harness connector. Reconnect control unit harness connector. Then retest.

Note: ABS may operate and cause vibration under any of the following conditions.
• Applying brake gradually when shifting or operating clutch.
• Low friction (slippery) road.
• High speed cornering.
• Driving over bumps and pot holes.
• Engine speed is over 5,000 rpm with vehicle stopped.

NS4029600230000X

Fig. 204   Test 10: Pedal Vibration & Noise. 1996 Pathfinder

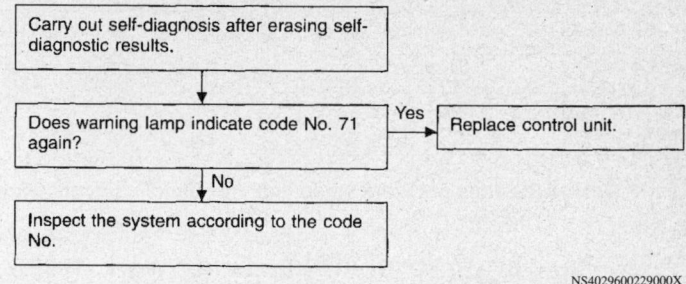

Carry out self-diagnosis after erasing self-diagnostic results.

↓

Does warning lamp indicate code No. 71 again?
→ Yes → Replace control unit.

↓ No

Inspect the system according to the code No.

NS4029600229000X

Fig. 203   Test 9: Control Unit. 1996 Pathfinder

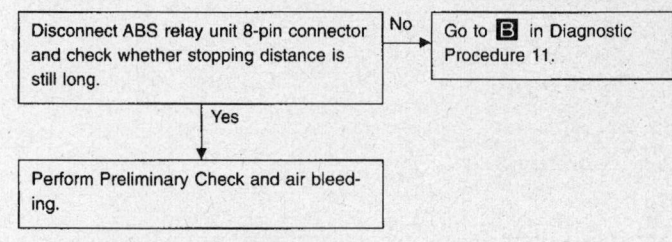

Disconnect ABS relay unit 8-pin connector and check whether stopping distance is still long.
→ No → Go to B in Diagnostic Procedure 11.

↓ Yes

Perform Preliminary Check and air bleeding.

Note: Stopping distance may be larger than vehicles without ABS when road condition is slippery.

NS4029600231000X

Fig. 205   Test 11: Long Stopping Distance. 1996 Pathfinder

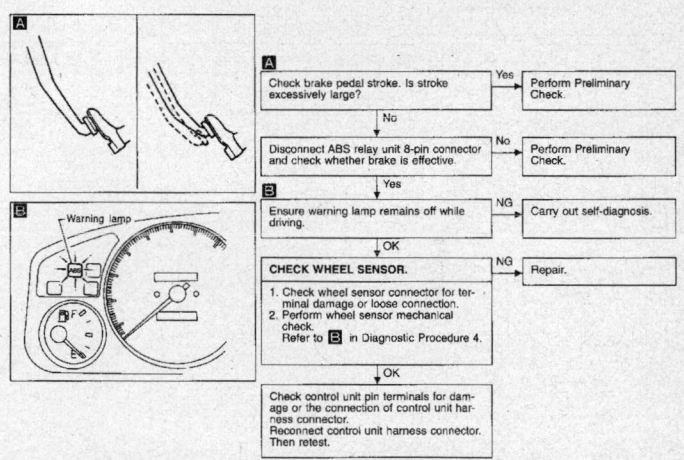

Check brake pedal stroke. Is stroke excessively large?
→ Yes → Perform Preliminary Check.

↓ No

Disconnect ABS relay unit 8-pin connector and check whether brake is effective.
→ No → Perform Preliminary Check.

↓ Yes

Ensure warning lamp remains off while driving.
→ NG → Carry out self-diagnosis.

↓ OK

CHECK WHEEL SENSOR.

1. Check wheel sensor connector for terminal damage or loose connection.
2. Perform wheel sensor mechanical check.
   Refer to B in Diagnostic Procedure 4.
→ NG → Repair.

↓ OK

Check control unit pin terminals for damage or the connection of control unit harness connector. Reconnect control unit harness connector. Then retest.

NS4029600232000X

Fig. 206   Test 12: Unexpected Pedal Action. 1996 Pathfinder

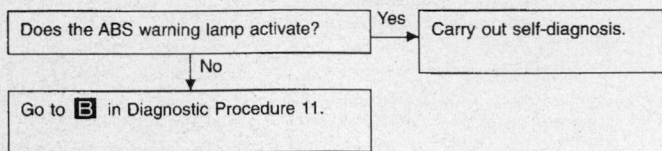

Does the ABS warning lamp activate? — Yes → Carry out self-diagnosis.

↓ No

Go to **B** in Diagnostic Procedure 11.

Note: ABS does not work when vehicle speed is under 10 km/h (6 MPH).

NS4029600233000X

Fig. 207 Test 13: ABS Does Not Work. 1996 Pathfinder

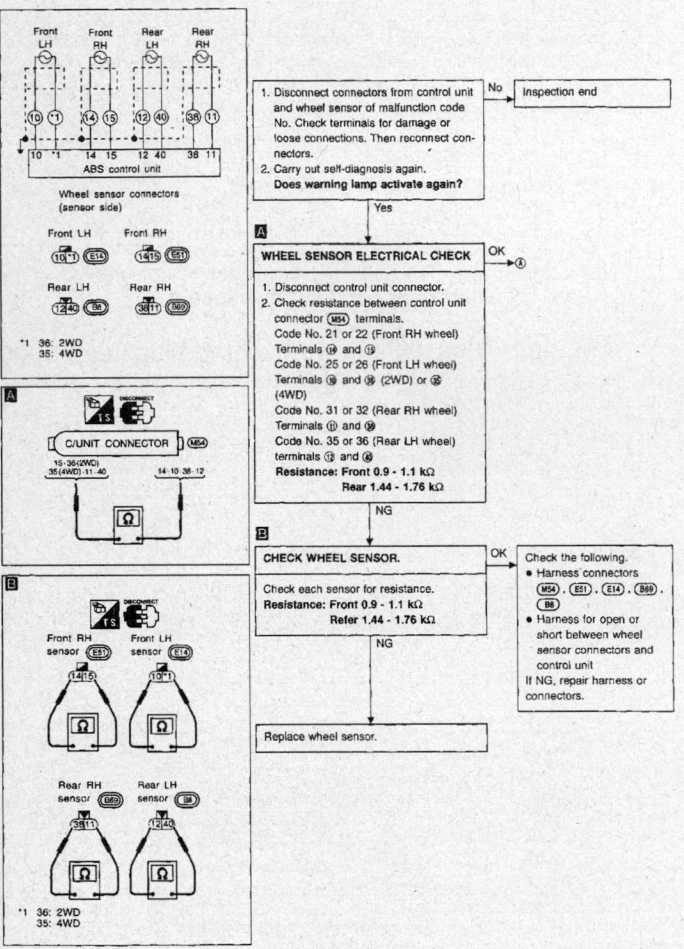

NS4029700284010X

Fig. 209 Test 1: Wheel Sensor or Rotor (Part 1 of 2). 1997–99 Pathfinder

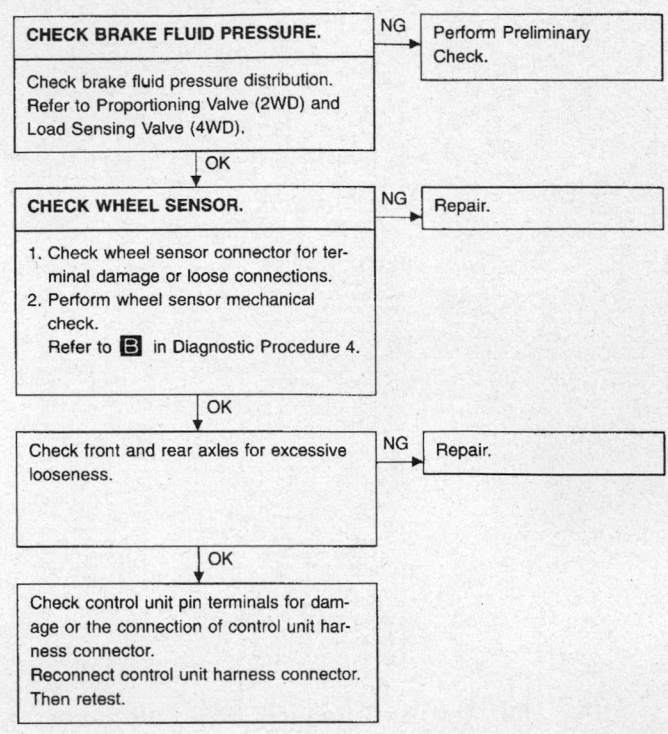

CHECK BRAKE FLUID PRESSURE. — NG → Perform Preliminary Check.

Check brake fluid pressure distribution. Refer to Proportioning Valve (2WD) and Load Sensing Valve (4WD).

↓ OK

CHECK WHEEL SENSOR. — NG → Repair.

1. Check wheel sensor connector for terminal damage or loose connections.
2. Perform wheel sensor mechanical check.
   Refer to **B** in Diagnostic Procedure 4.

↓ OK

Check front and rear axles for excessive looseness. — NG → Repair.

↓ OK

Check control unit pin terminals for damage or the connection of control unit harness connector.
Reconnect control unit harness connector. Then retest.

NS4029600234000X

Fig. 208 Test 14: ABS Works Frequently. 1996 Pathfinder

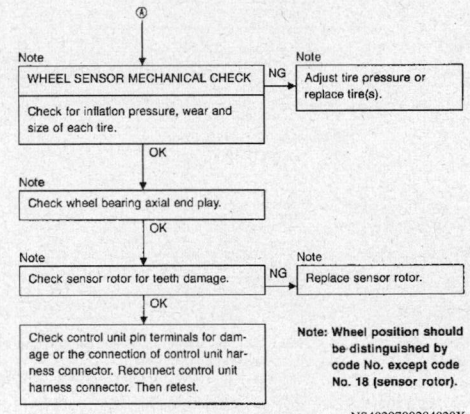

NS4029700284020X

Fig. 209 Test 1: Wheel Sensor or Rotor (Part 2 of 2). 1997–99 Pathfinder

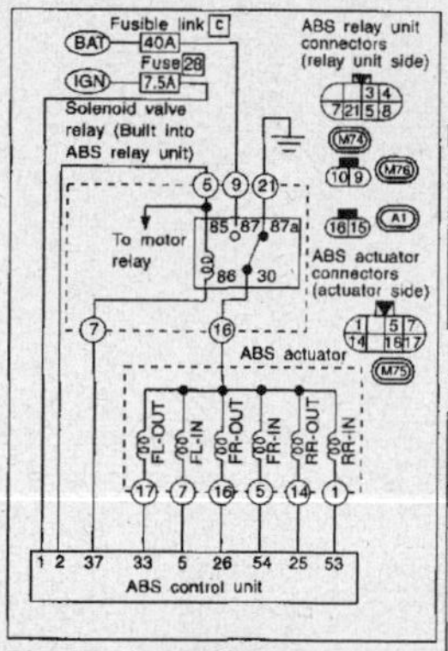

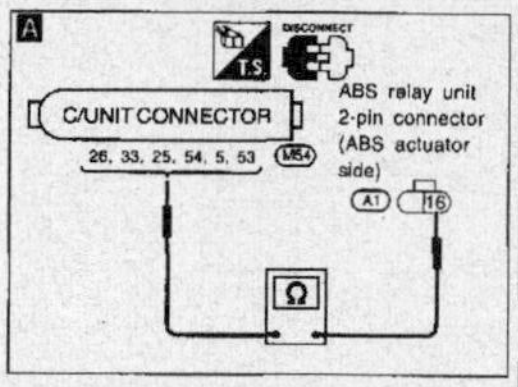

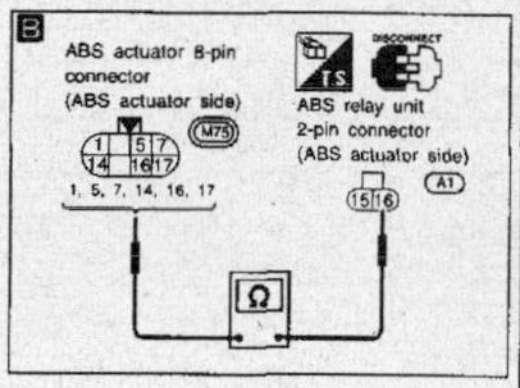

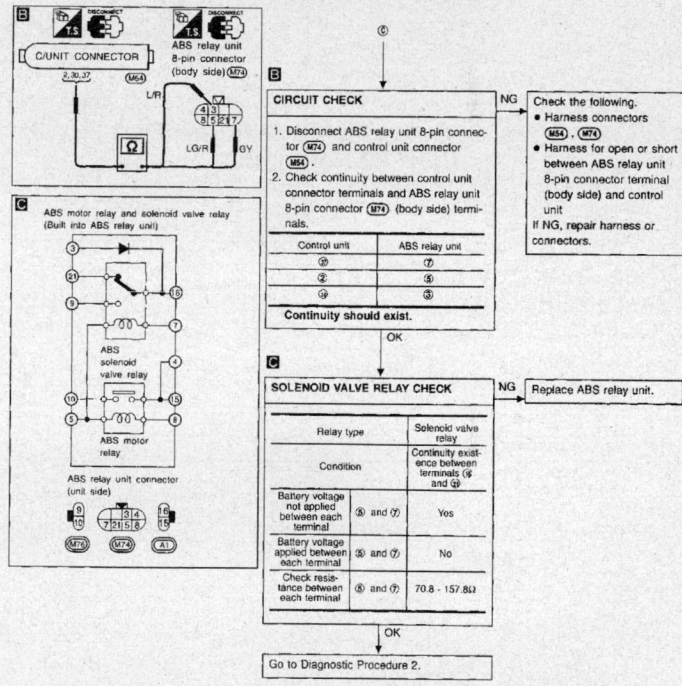

1. Disconnect connectors from control unit, ABS actuator and ABS relay unit. Check terminals for damage or loose connections. Then reconnect connectors.
2. Carry out self-diagnosis again.
Does warning lamp activate again?

No → Inspection end

Yes ↓

A

ABS ACTUATOR SOLENOID VALVE CHECK (OK → (B))

1. Disconnect connectors from control unit and ABS relay unit.
2. Check resistance between control unit connector terminals and ABS relay unit 2-pin connector (A1) (ABS actuator side) terminal.

Code No.	Control unit	ABS actuator	Resistance
41	(26)	(15)	3.1 - 6.2Ω
45	(33)	(16)	
55	(25)	(15)	
42	(54)	(16)	6.2 - 12.3Ω
46	(5)	(16)	
56	(53)	(16)	

NG ↓

B

1. Disconnect ABS actuator 8-pin connector.
2. Check resistance between ABS actuator 8-pin connector (M75) (ABS actuator side) terminals and ABS relay unit 2-pin connector (A1) (ABS actuator side) terminal.

Code No.	ABS actuator 8-pin	ABS relay unit 2-pin	Resistance
41	(16)	(16)	3.1 - 6.2Ω
45	(17)	(16)	
55	(14)	(16)	
42	(5)	(16)	6.2 - 12.3Ω
46	(7)	(16)	
56	(1)	(16)	

OK → Check the following.
- Harness connectors (M54), (M75), (A1)
- Harness for open or short between ABS relay unit connector and control unit
- Harness for open or short between ABS actuator 8-pin connector and ABS actuator 2-pin connector

If NG, repair harness or connectors.

NG ↓

(A)

NS4029700285010X

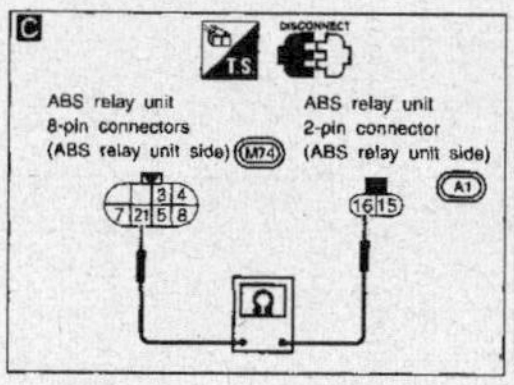

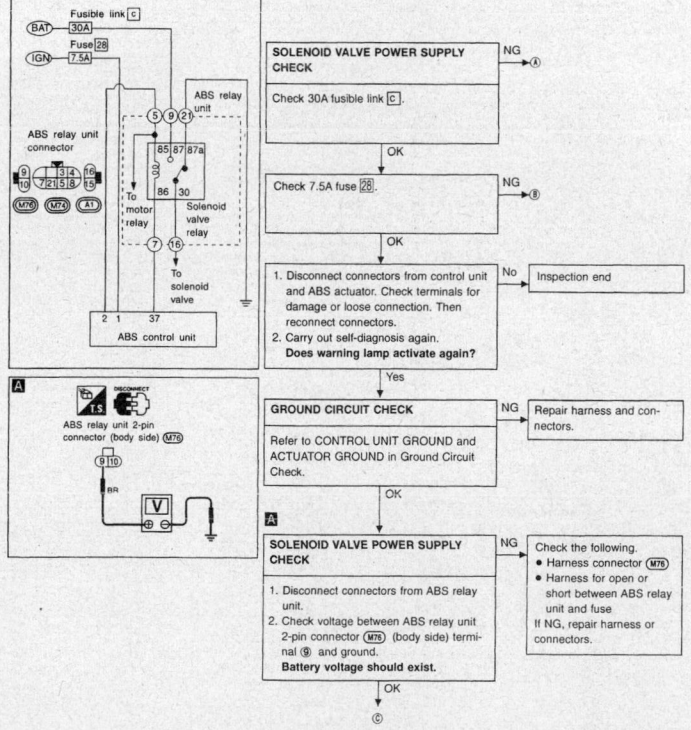

Fig. 210 Test 2: ABS Actuator Solenoid Valve (Part 1 of 2). 1997–99 Pathfinder

(A) ↓

Check resistance between solenoid valve terminals (1), (5), (7), (14), (16), (17).

ABS actuator			Resistance
OUT solenoid valve	(14)	(16)	6.2 - 12.4Ω
	(14)	(17)	
	(16)	(17)	
OUT and IN solenoid valve	(14), (16), (17)	(1), (5), (7)	9.3 - 18.5Ω
IN solenoid valve	(1)	(5)	12.4 - 24.6Ω
	(1)	(7)	
	(5)	(7)	

OK → Check the following.
- Harness connectors (M54), (M75), (A1)
- Harness for open or short between actuator connector and control unit
- Harness for open or short between relay unit 8-pin connector and relay unit 2-pin connector

If NG, repair harness or connectors.

NG ↓

Replace actuator.

(B) ↓

C

1. Disconnect ABS relay unit connectors.
2. Check continuity between ABS relay unit 2-pin connector (A1) (ABS relay unit side) terminal (16) and ABS relay unit 8-pin connector (M74) (ABS relay unit side) terminal (21).
Continuity should exist.

OK → Go to Diagnostic Procedure 3.

NG ↓

Replace ABS relay unit.

NS4029700285020X

Fig. 210 Test 2: ABS Actuator Solenoid Valve (Part 2 of 2). 1997–99 Pathfinder

SOLENOID VALVE POWER SUPPLY CHECK

Check 30A fusible link C.

NG → (A)

OK ↓

Check 7.5A fuse 28.

NG → (B)

OK ↓

1. Disconnect connectors from control unit and ABS actuator. Check terminals for damage or loose connection. Then reconnect connectors.
2. Carry out self-diagnosis again.
Does warning lamp activate again?

No → Inspection end

Yes ↓

GROUND CIRCUIT CHECK

Refer to CONTROL UNIT GROUND and ACTUATOR GROUND in Ground Circuit Check.

NG → Repair harness and connectors.

OK ↓

A

SOLENOID VALVE POWER SUPPLY CHECK

1. Disconnect connectors from ABS relay unit.
2. Check voltage between ABS relay unit 2-pin connector (M76) (body side) terminal (9) and ground.
Battery voltage should exist.

NG → Check the following.
- Harness connector (M76)
- Harness for open or short between ABS relay unit and fuse

If NG, repair harness or connectors.

OK ↓

(C)

NS4029700286010X

Fig. 211 Test 3: Solenoid Valve Relay (Part 1 of 3). 1997–99 Pathfinder

(C) ↓

B

CIRCUIT CHECK

1. Disconnect ABS relay unit 8-pin connector (M74) and control unit connector (M54).
2. Check continuity between control unit connector terminals and ABS relay unit 8-pin connector (M74) (body side) terminals.

Control unit	ABS relay unit
(37)	(7)
(2)	(5)
(30)	(3)

Continuity should exist.

NG → Check the following.
- Harness connectors (M54), (M74)
- Harness for open or short between ABS relay unit 8-pin connector terminal (body side) and control unit

If NG, repair harness or connectors.

OK ↓

C

SOLENOID VALVE RELAY CHECK

Relay type		Solenoid valve relay
Condition		Continuity existence between terminals (16) and (21)
Battery voltage not applied between each terminal	(5) and (7)	Yes
Battery voltage applied between each terminal	(5) and (7)	No
Check resistance between each terminal	(5) and (7)	70.8 - 157.8Ω

NG → Replace ABS relay unit.

OK ↓

Go to Diagnostic Procedure 2.

NS4029700286020X

Fig. 211 Test 3: Solenoid Valve Relay (Part 2 of 3). 1997–99 Pathfinder

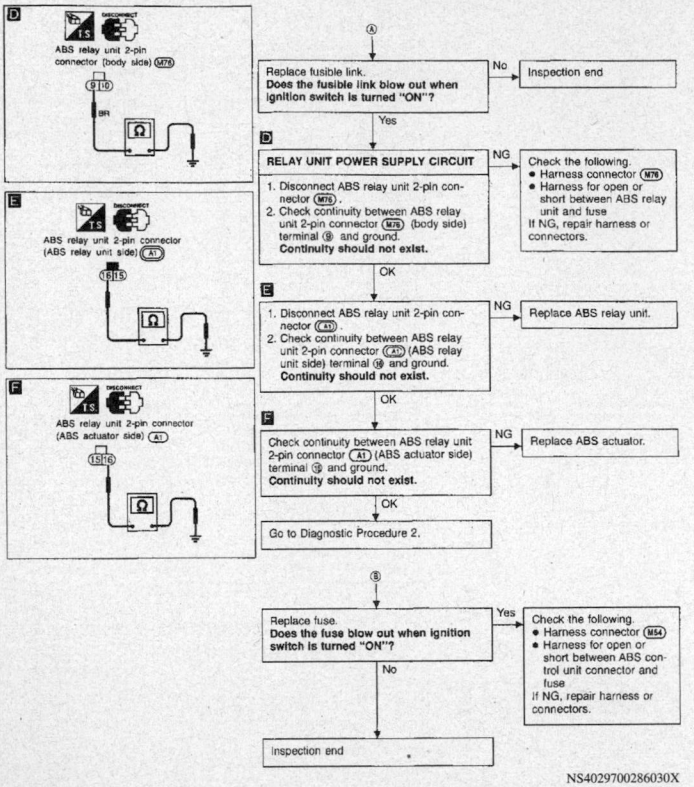

Fig. 211   Test 3: Solenoid Valve Relay (Part 3 of 3). 1997–99 Pathfinder

NS4029700286030X

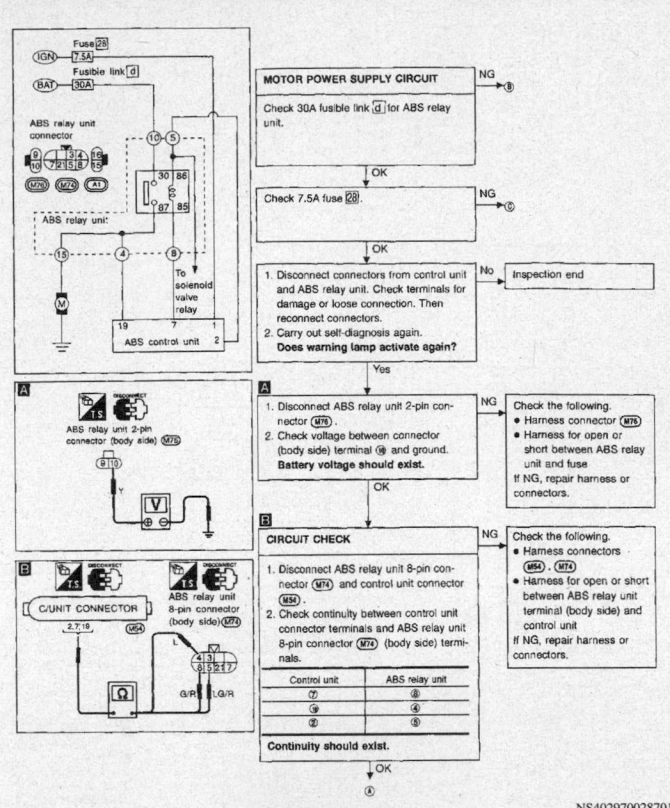

Fig. 212   Test 4: Motor Relay or Motor (Part 1 of 3). 1997–99 Pathfinder

NS4029700287010X

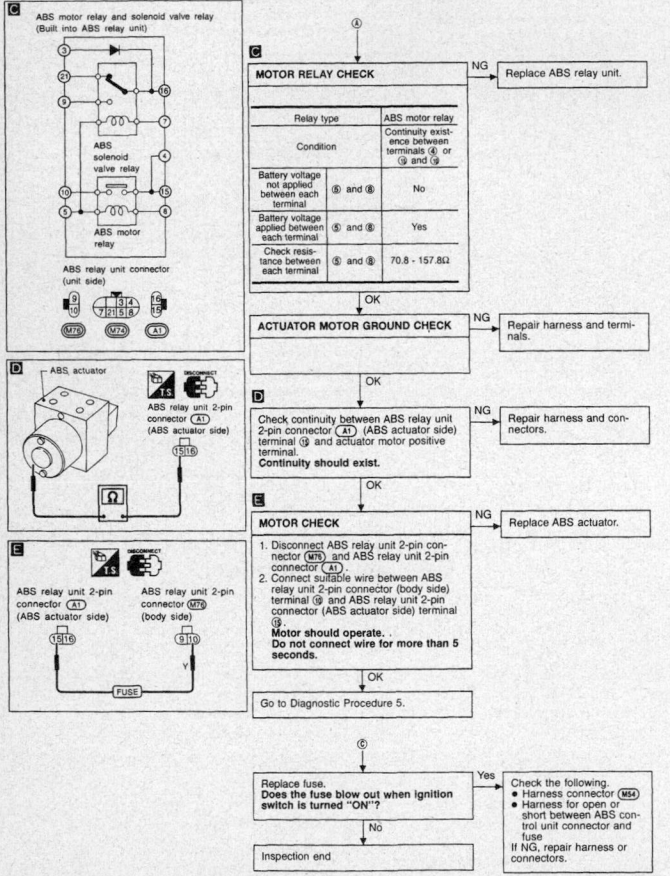

Fig. 212   Test 4: Motor Relay or Motor (Part 2 of 3). 1997–99 Pathfinder

NS4029700287020X

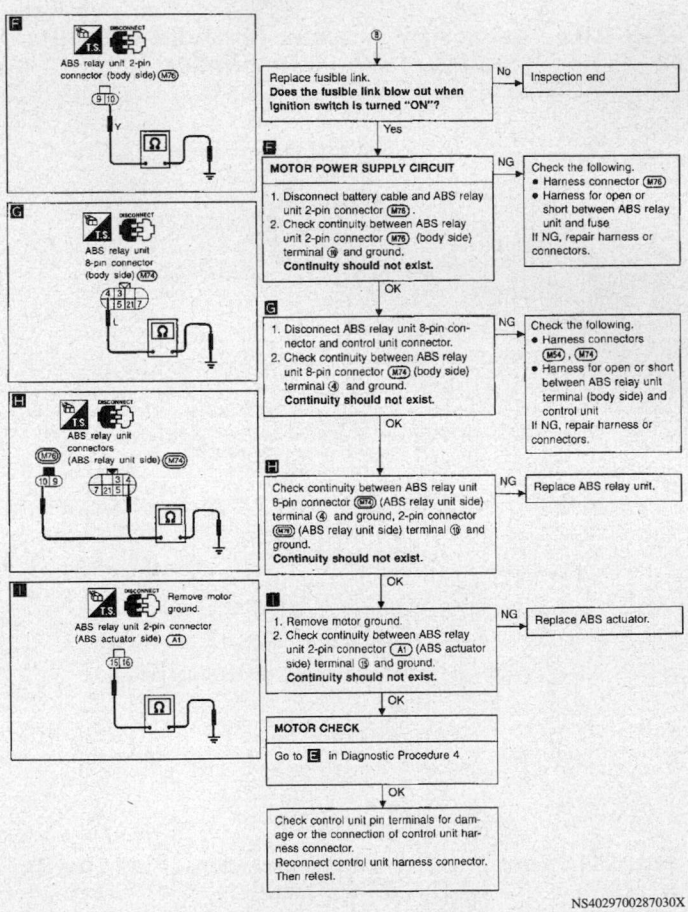

Fig. 212   Test 4: Motor Relay or Motor (Part 3 of 3). 1997–99 Pathfinder

NS4029700287030X

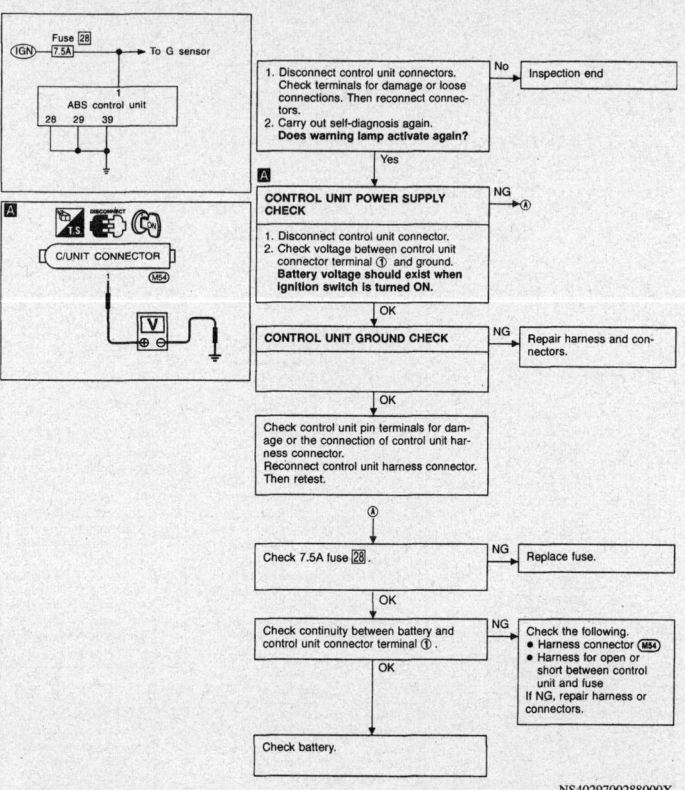

Fig. 213   Test 5: Low Voltage. 1997–99 Pathfinder

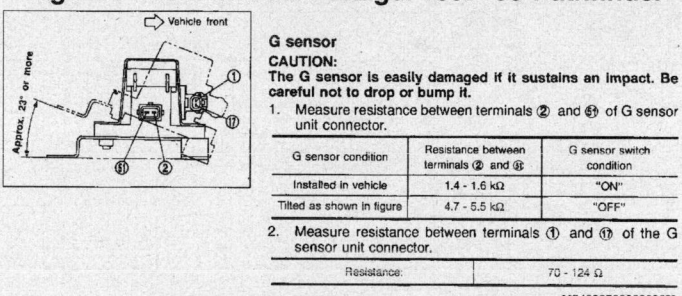

G sensor

CAUTION:
The G sensor is easily damaged if it sustains an impact. Be careful not to drop or bump it.

1. Measure resistance between terminals ② and ⑤ of G sensor unit connector.

G sensor condition	Resistance between terminals ② and ⑤	G sensor switch condition
Installed in vehicle	1.4 - 1.6 kΩ	"ON"
Tilted as shown in figure	4.7 - 5.5 kΩ	"OFF"

2. Measure resistance between terminals ① and ⑰ of the G sensor unit connector.

Resistance:	70 - 124 Ω

Fig. 214   Test 6: G Sensor (Part 2 of 2). 1997–99 Pathfinder

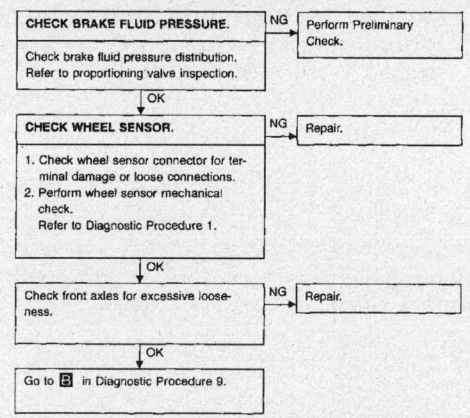

Fig. 216   Test 8: ABS Works Frequently. 1997–99 Pathfinder

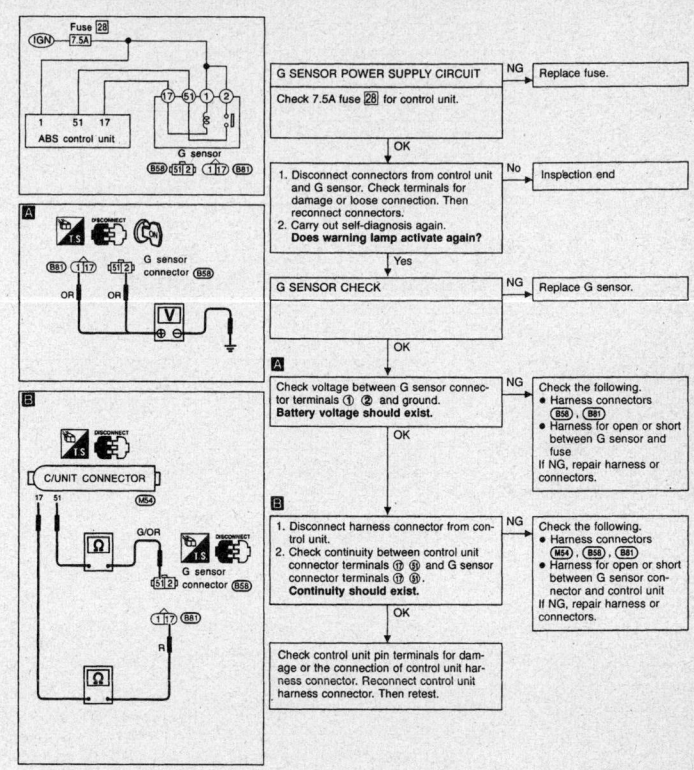

Fig. 214   Test 6: G Sensor (Part 1 of 2). 1997–99 Pathfinder

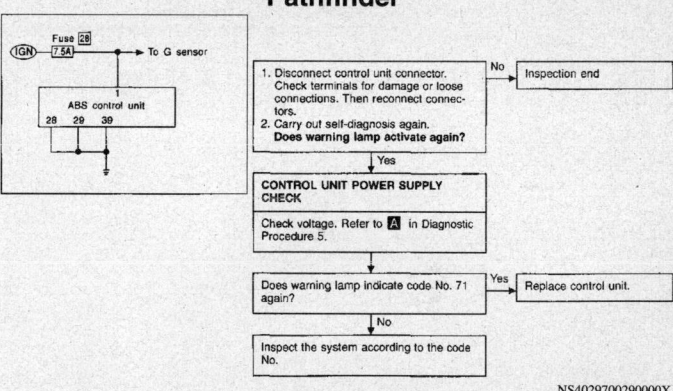

Fig. 215   Test 7: Control Unit. 1997–99 Pathfinder

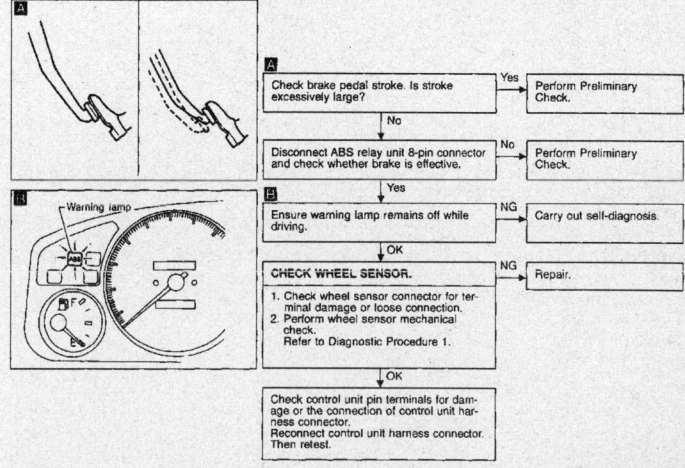

Fig. 217   Test 9: Unexpected Pedal Action. 1997–99 Pathfinder

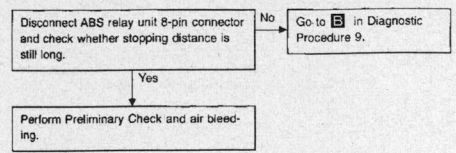

Disconnect ABS relay unit 8-pin connector and check whether stopping distance is still long. → No → Go to **B** in Diagnostic Procedure 9.

↓ Yes

Perform Preliminary Check and air bleeding.

Note: Stopping distance may be larger than vehicles without ABS when road condition is slippery.

NS4029700293000X

Fig. 218   Test 10: Long Stopping Distance. 1997–99 Pathfinder

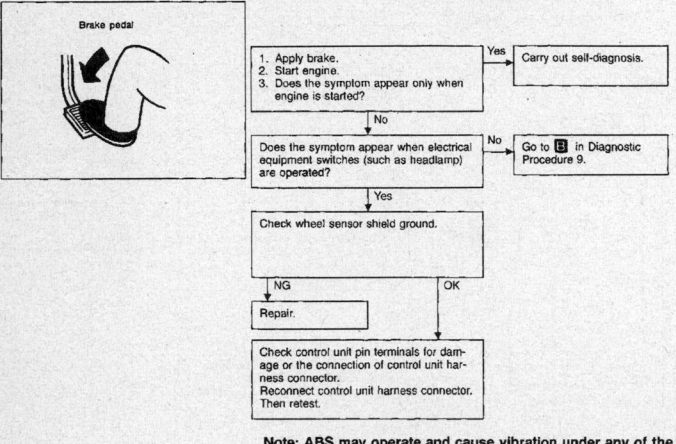

1. Apply brake.
2. Start engine.
3. Does the symptom appear only when engine is started? → Yes → Carry out self-diagnosis.

↓ No

Does the symptom appear when electrical equipment switches (such as headlamp) are operated? → No → Go to **B** in Diagnostic Procedure 9.

↓ Yes

Check wheel sensor shield ground.

NG ← → OK

Repair.

Check control unit pin terminals for damage or the connection of control unit harness connector.
Reconnect control unit harness connector.
Then retest.

Note: ABS may operate and cause vibration under any of the following conditions.
• Applying brake gradually when shifting or operating clutch.
• Low friction (slippery) road.
• High speed cornering.
• Driving over bumps and pot holes.
• Engine speed is over 5,000 rpm with vehicle stopped.

NS4029700295000X

Fig. 220   Test 12: Pedal Vibration & Noise. 1997–99 Pathfinder

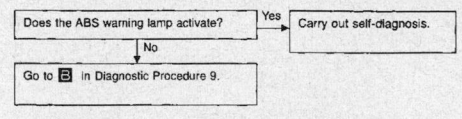

Does the ABS warning lamp activate? → Yes → Carry out self-diagnosis.

↓ No

Go to **B** in Diagnostic Procedure 9.

Note: ABS does not work when vehicle speed is under 10 km/h (6 MPH).

NS4029700294000X

Fig. 219   Test 11: ABS Does Not Work. 1997–99 Pathfinder

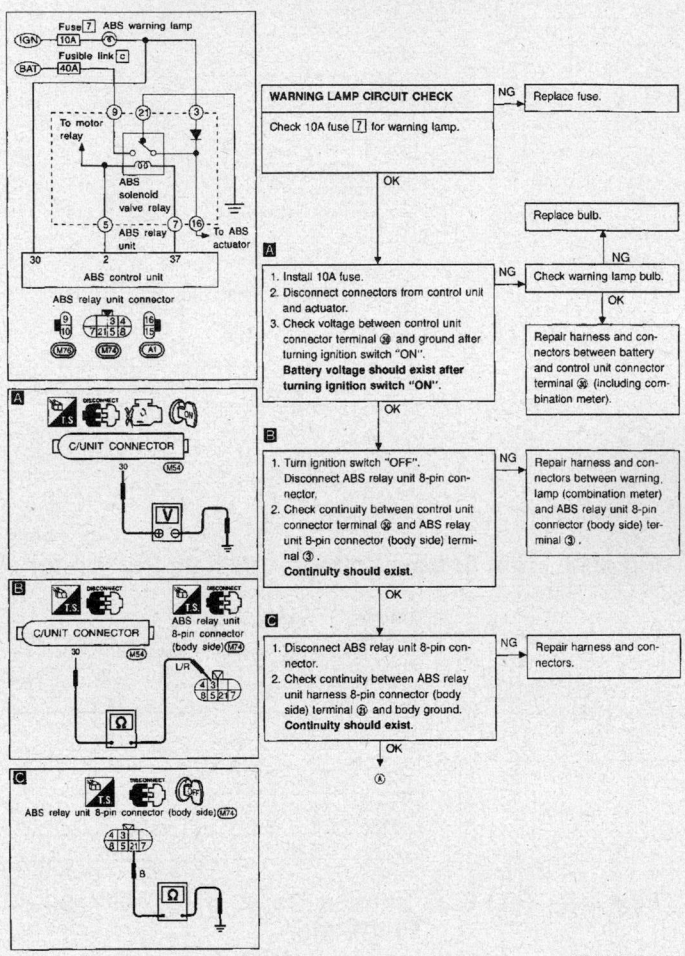

WARNING LAMP CIRCUIT CHECK

Check 10A fuse 7 for warning lamp. → NG → Replace fuse.

↓ OK

Replace bulb.

↑ NG

A
1. Install 10A fuse.
2. Disconnect connectors from control unit and actuator.
3. Check voltage between control unit connector terminal ③ and ground after turning ignition switch "ON".
Battery voltage should exist after turning ignition switch "ON". → NG → Check warning lamp bulb. → OK → Repair harness and connectors between battery and control unit connector terminal ③ (including combination meter).

↓ OK

B
1. Turn ignition switch "OFF".
Disconnect ABS relay unit 8-pin connector.
2. Check continuity between control unit connector terminal ③ and ABS relay unit 8-pin connector (body side) terminal ③.
Continuity should exist. → NG → Repair harness and connectors between warning lamp (combination meter) and ABS relay unit 8-pin connector (body side) terminal ③.

↓ OK

C
1. Disconnect ABS relay unit 8-pin connector.
2. Check continuity between ABS relay unit harness 8-pin connector (body side) terminal ⑤ and body ground.
Continuity should exist. → NG → Repair harness and connectors.

↓ OK

Ⓐ

NS4029700296010X

Fig. 221   Test 13: Warning Lamp Does Not Come On When Ignition Is Turned On (Part 1 of 2). 1997–99 Pathfinder

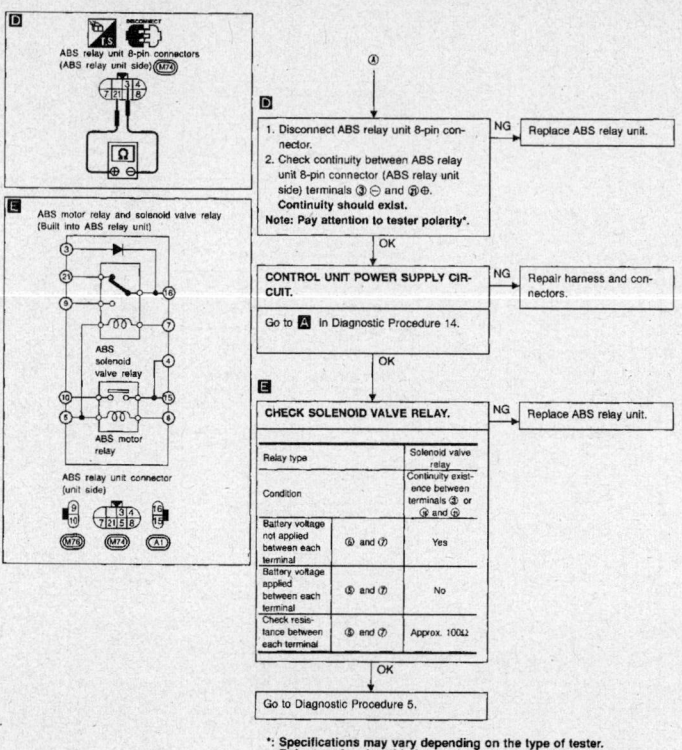

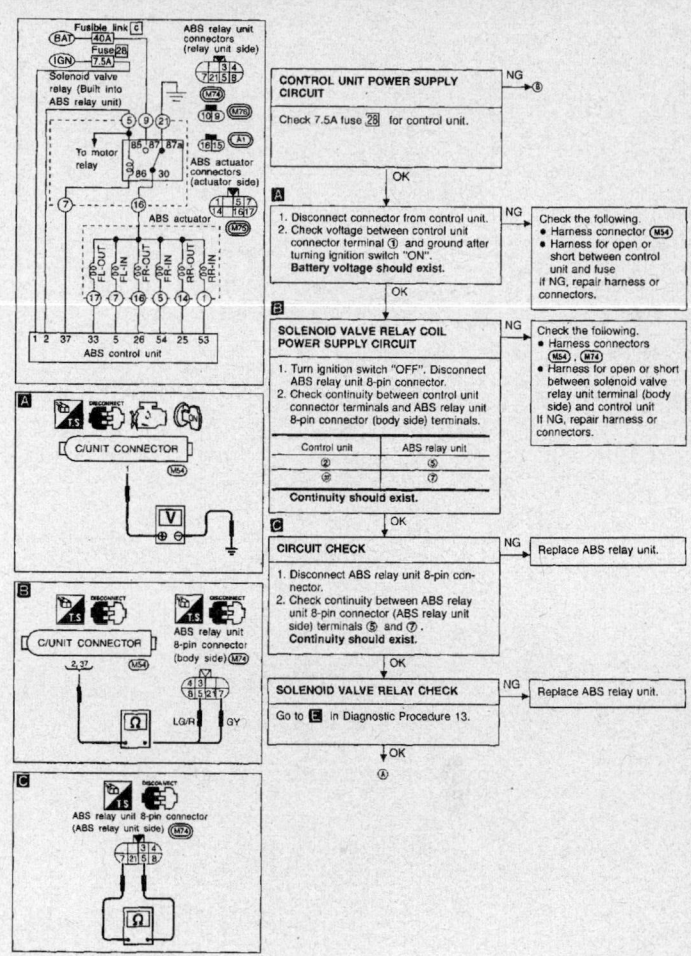

Fig. 221 Test 13: Warning Lamp Does Not Come On When Ignition Is Turned On (Part 2 of 2). 1997–99 Pathfinder

NS4029700296020X

Fig. 222 Test 14: Warning Lamp Stays On When Ignition Switch Is Turned On (Part 1 of 3). 1997–99 Pathfinder

NS4029700297010X

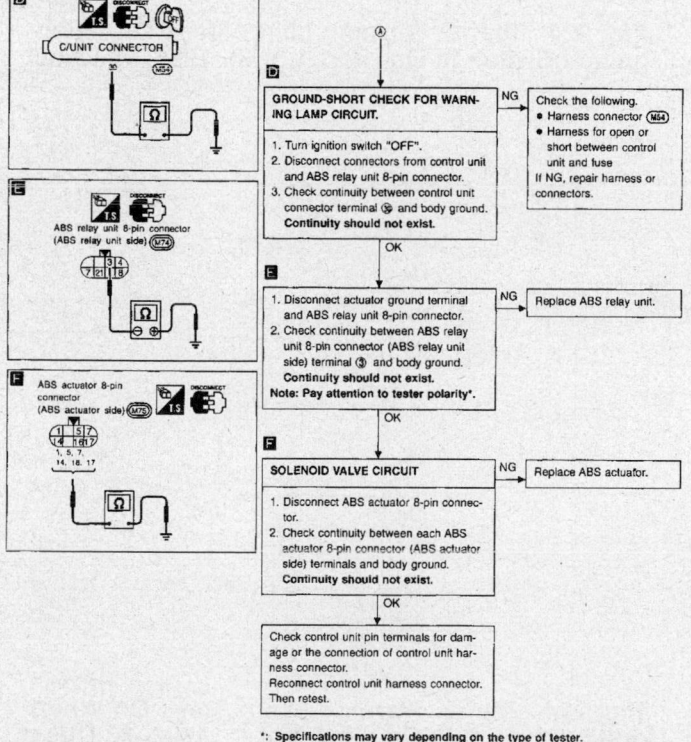

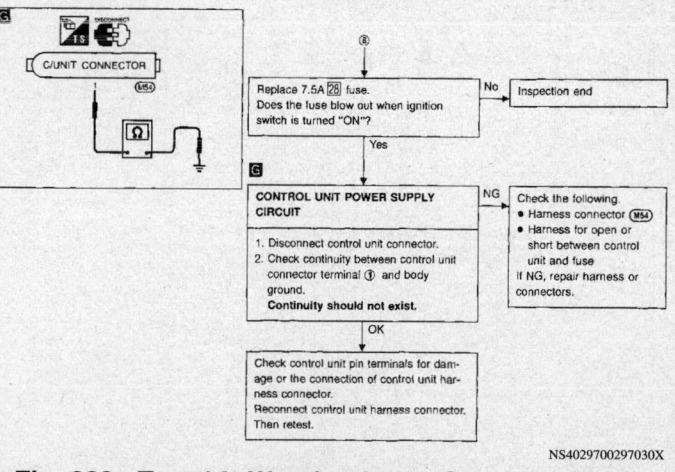

Fig. 222 Test 14: Warning Lamp Stays On When Ignition Switch Is Turned On (Part 3 of 3). 1997–99 Pathfinder

NS4029700297030X

NS4029700297020X

Fig. 222 Test 14: Warning Lamp Stays On When Ignition Switch Is Turned On (Part 2 of 3). 1997–99 Pathfinder

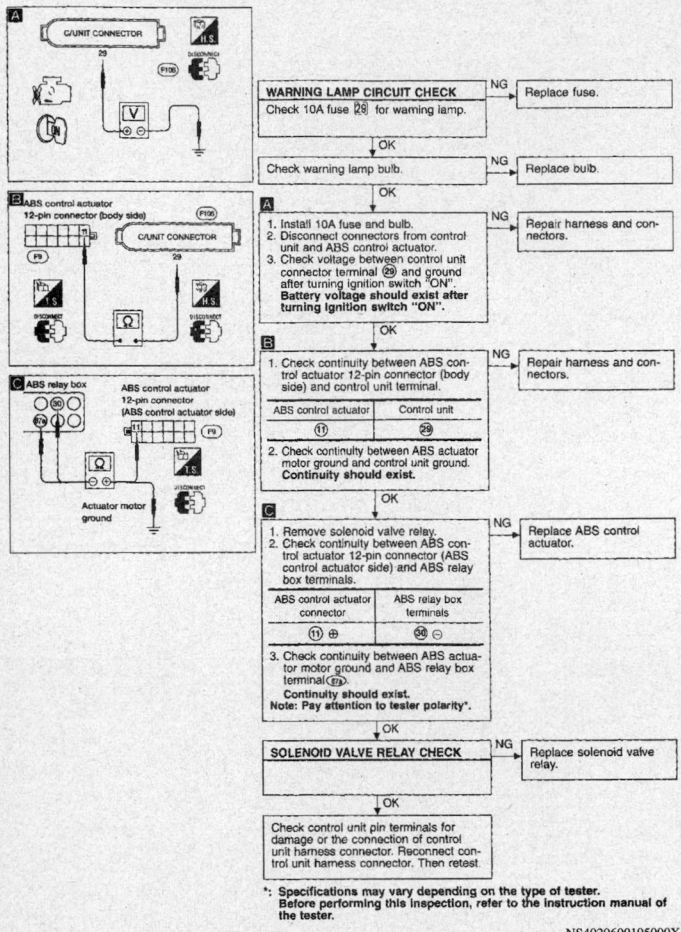

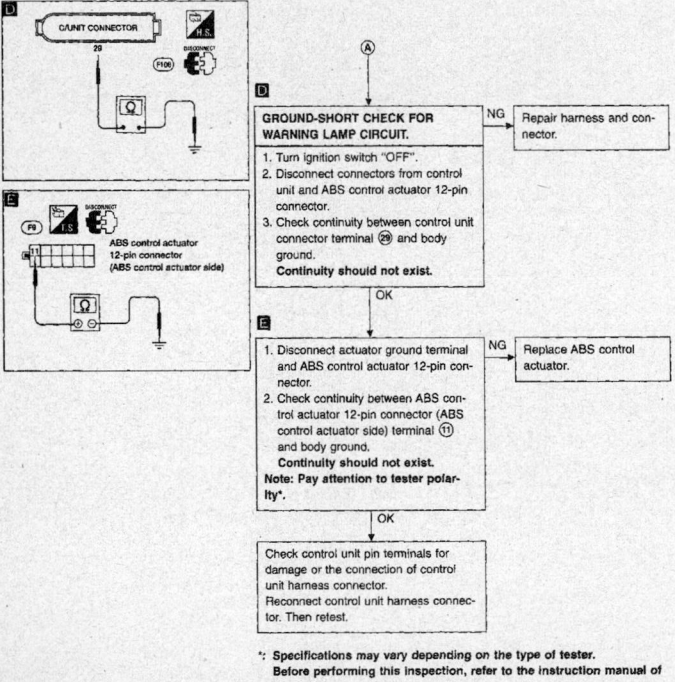

Fig. 223   Test 1: Warning Lamp Does Not Work When Ignition Is On. 1996–98 Quest

NS4029600195000X

NS4029600196020X

Fig. 224   Test 2: Warning Lamp Stays On When Ignition Switch Is On (Part 2 of 3). 1996–98 Quest

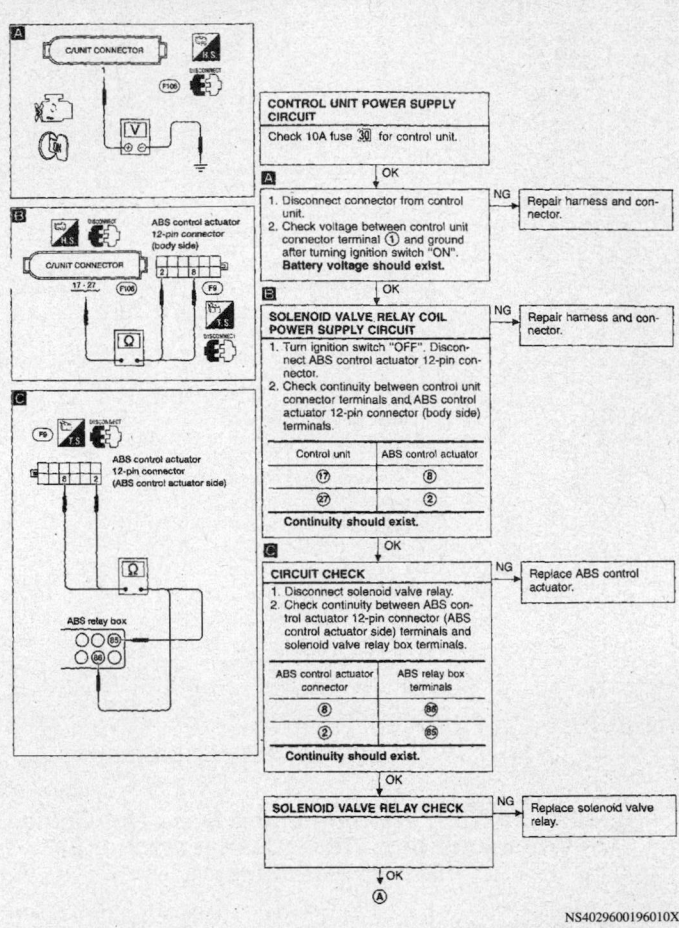

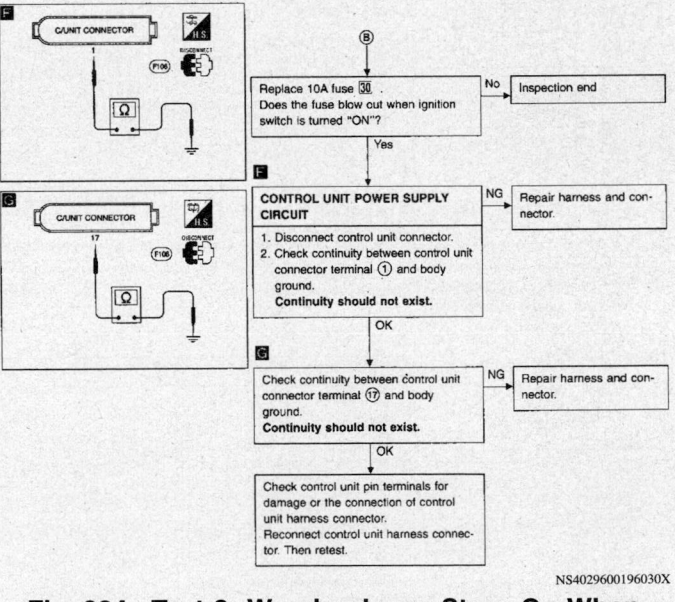

NS4029600196010X

Fig. 224   Test 2: Warning Lamp Stays On When Ignition Switch Is On (Part 1 of 3). 1996–98 Quest

NS4029600196030X

Fig. 224   Test 2: Warning Lamp Stays On When Ignition Switch Is On (Part 3 of 3). 1996–98 Quest

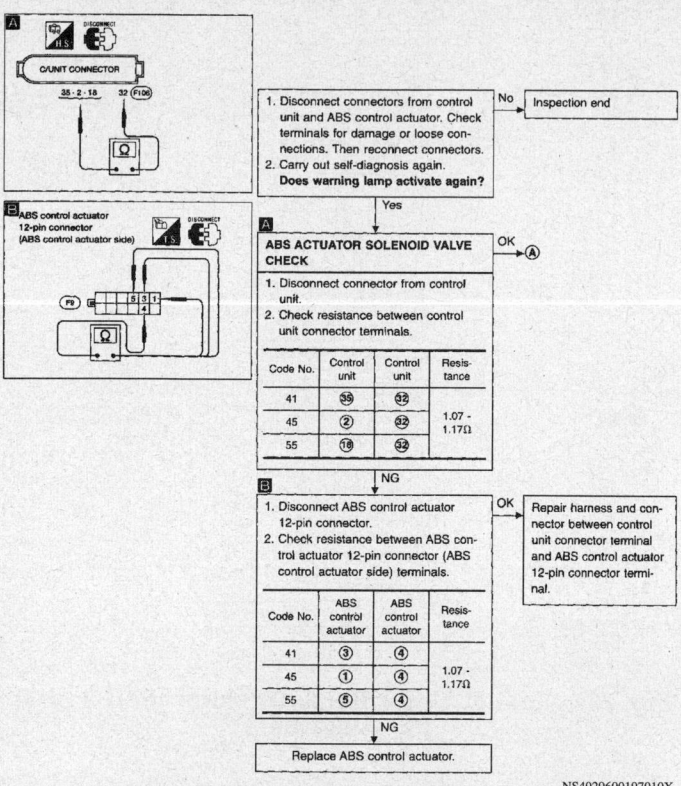

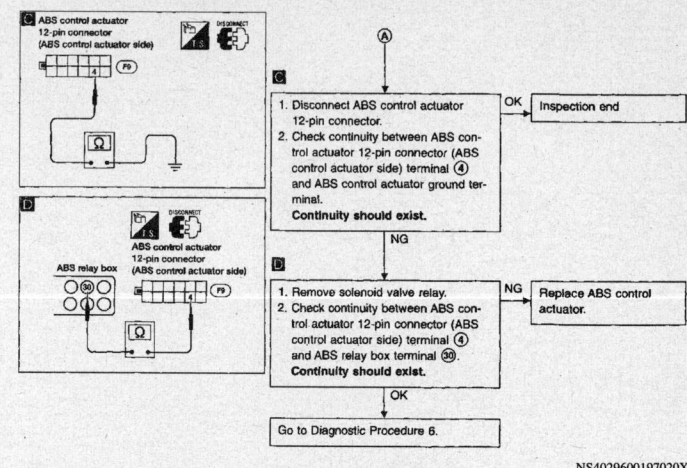

Fig. 225 Test 3: ABS Control Actuator Solenoid Valve (Part 2 of 2). 1996–98 Quest

NS4029600197020X

Fig. 225 Test 3: ABS Control Actuator Solenoid Valve (Part 1 of 2). 1996–98 Quest

NS4029600197010X

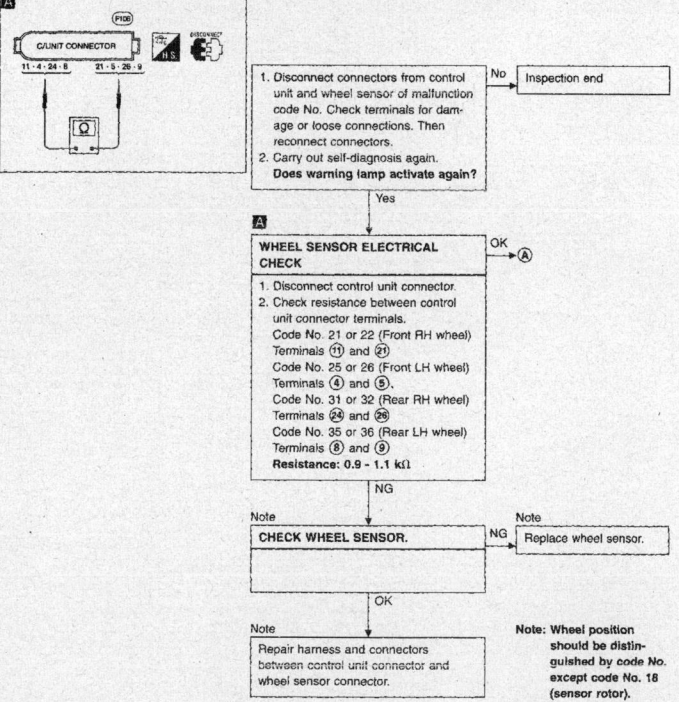

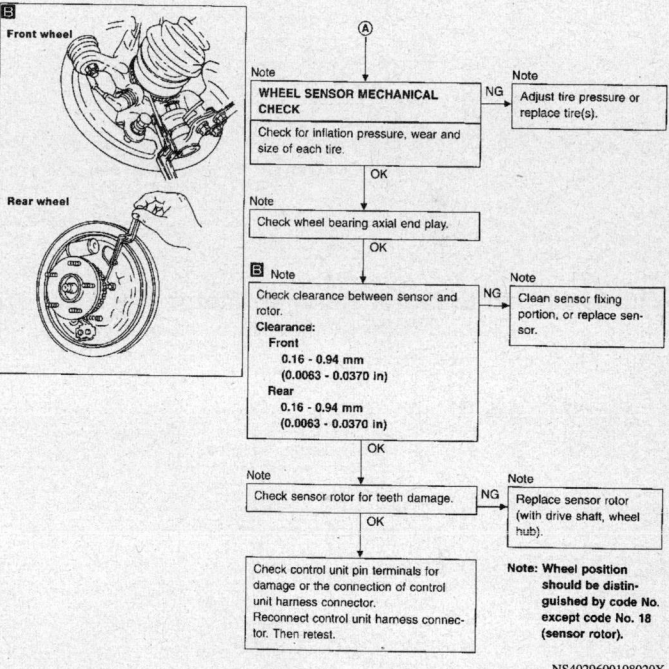

Fig. 226 Test 4: Wheel Sensor Or Rotor (Part 2 of 2). 1996–98 Quest

NS4029600198020X

NS4029600198010X

Fig. 226 Test 4: Wheel Sensor Or Rotor (Part 1 of 2). 1996–98 Quest

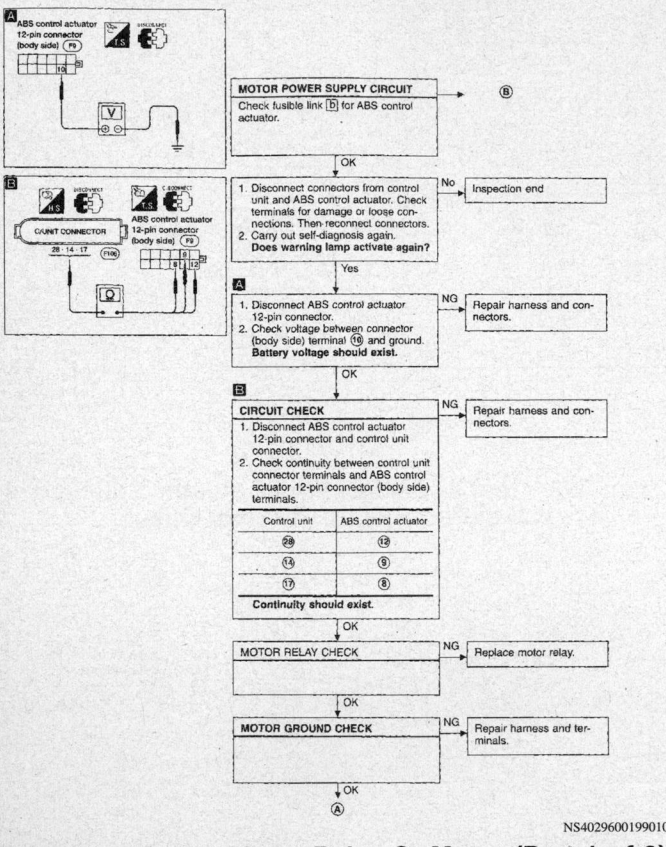

MOTOR POWER SUPPLY CIRCUIT
Check fusible link D for ABS control actuator. → B

OK ↓

1. Disconnect connectors from control unit and ABS control actuator. Check terminals for damage or loose connections. Then reconnect connectors.
2. Carry out self-diagnosis again.
Does warning lamp activate again? → No → Inspection end

Yes ↓ A

1. Disconnect ABS control actuator 12-pin connector.
2. Check voltage between connector (body side) terminal 10 and ground.
Battery voltage should exist. → NG → Repair harness and connectors.

OK ↓ B

CIRCUIT CHECK
1. Disconnect ABS control actuator 12-pin connector and control unit connector.
2. Check continuity between control unit connector terminals and ABS control actuator 12-pin connector (body side) terminals. → NG → Repair harness and connectors.

Control unit	ABS control actuator
28	12
14	9
17	8

Continuity should exist.

OK ↓

MOTOR RELAY CHECK → NG → Replace motor relay.

OK ↓

MOTOR GROUND CHECK → NG → Repair harness and terminals.

OK ↓ A

NS4029600199010X

**Fig. 227   Test 5: Motor Relay Or Motor (Part 1 of 3).
1996–98 Quest**

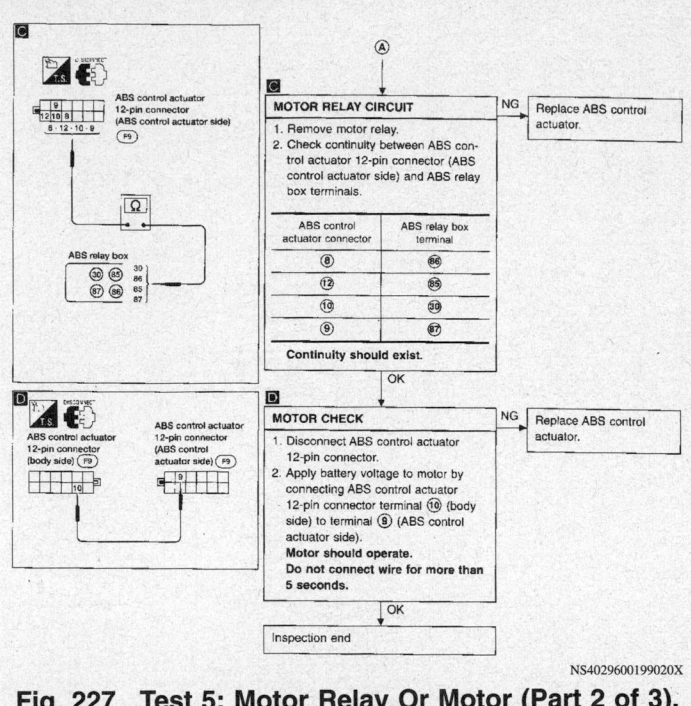

MOTOR RELAY CIRCUIT
1. Remove motor relay.
2. Check continuity between ABS control actuator 12-pin connector (ABS control actuator side) and ABS relay box terminals. → NG → Replace ABS control actuator.

ABS control actuator connector	ABS relay box terminal
8	86
12	85
10	30
9	87

Continuity should exist.

OK ↓

MOTOR CHECK
1. Disconnect ABS control actuator 12-pin connector.
2. Apply battery voltage to motor by connecting ABS control actuator 12-pin connector terminal 10 (body side) to terminal 9 (ABS control actuator side).
Motor should operate.
Do not connect wire for more than 5 seconds. → NG → Replace ABS control actuator.

OK ↓

Inspection end

NS4029600199020X

**Fig. 227   Test 5: Motor Relay Or Motor (Part 2 of 3).
1996–98 Quest**

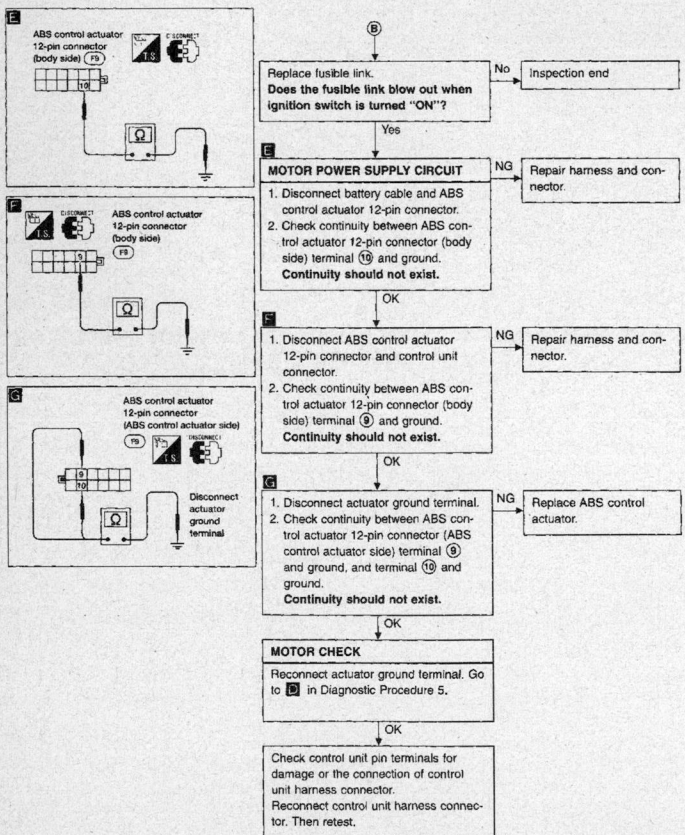

Replace fusible link.
Does the fusible link blow out when ignition switch is turned "ON"? → No → Inspection end

Yes ↓ E

MOTOR POWER SUPPLY CIRCUIT
1. Disconnect battery cable and ABS control actuator 12-pin connector.
2. Check continuity between ABS control actuator 12-pin connector (body side) terminal 10 and ground.
Continuity should not exist. → NG → Repair harness and connector.

OK ↓ F

1. Disconnect ABS control actuator 12-pin connector and control unit connector.
2. Check continuity between ABS control actuator 12-pin connector (body side) terminal 9 and ground.
Continuity should not exist. → NG → Repair harness and connector.

OK ↓ G

1. Disconnect actuator ground terminal.
2. Check continuity between ABS control actuator 12-pin connector (ABS control actuator side) terminal 9 and ground, and terminal 10 and ground.
Continuity should not exist. → NG → Replace ABS control actuator.

OK ↓

MOTOR CHECK
Reconnect actuator ground terminal. Go to D in Diagnostic Procedure 5.

OK ↓

Check control unit pin terminals for damage or the connection of control unit harness connector.
Reconnect control unit harness connector. Then retest.

NS4029600199030X

**Fig. 227   Test 5: Motor Relay Or Motor (Part 3 of 3).
1996–98 Quest**

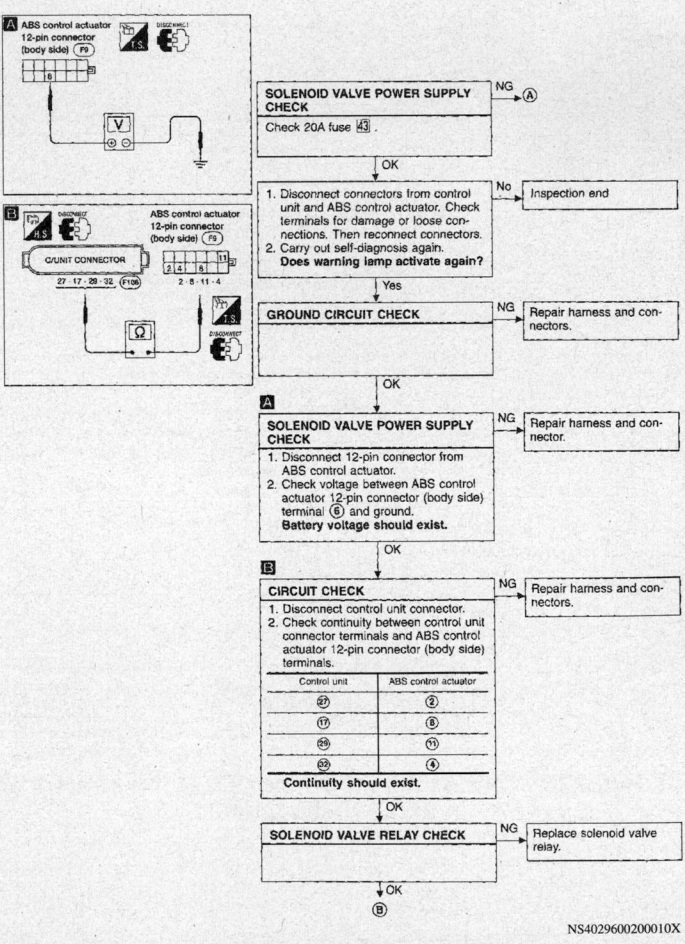

SOLENOID VALVE POWER SUPPLY CHECK
Check 20A fuse 43. → NG → A

OK ↓

1. Disconnect connectors from control unit and ABS control actuator. Check terminals for damage or loose connections. Then reconnect connectors.
2. Carry out self-diagnosis again.
Does warning lamp activate again? → No → Inspection end

Yes ↓

GROUND CIRCUIT CHECK → NG → Repair harness and connectors.

OK ↓ A

SOLENOID VALVE POWER SUPPLY CHECK
1. Disconnect 12-pin connector from ABS control actuator.
2. Check voltage between ABS control actuator 12-pin connector (body side) terminal 6 and ground.
Battery voltage should exist. → NG → Repair harness and connector.

OK ↓ B

CIRCUIT CHECK
1. Disconnect control unit connector.
2. Check continuity between control unit connector terminals and ABS control actuator 12-pin connector (body side) terminals. → NG → Repair harness and connectors.

Control unit	ABS control actuator
27	2
17	8
29	11
32	4

Continuity should exist.

OK ↓

SOLENOID VALVE RELAY CHECK → NG → Replace solenoid valve relay.

OK ↓ B

NS4029600200010X

**Fig. 228   Test 6: Solenoid Valve Relay (Part 1 of 2).
1996–98 Quest**

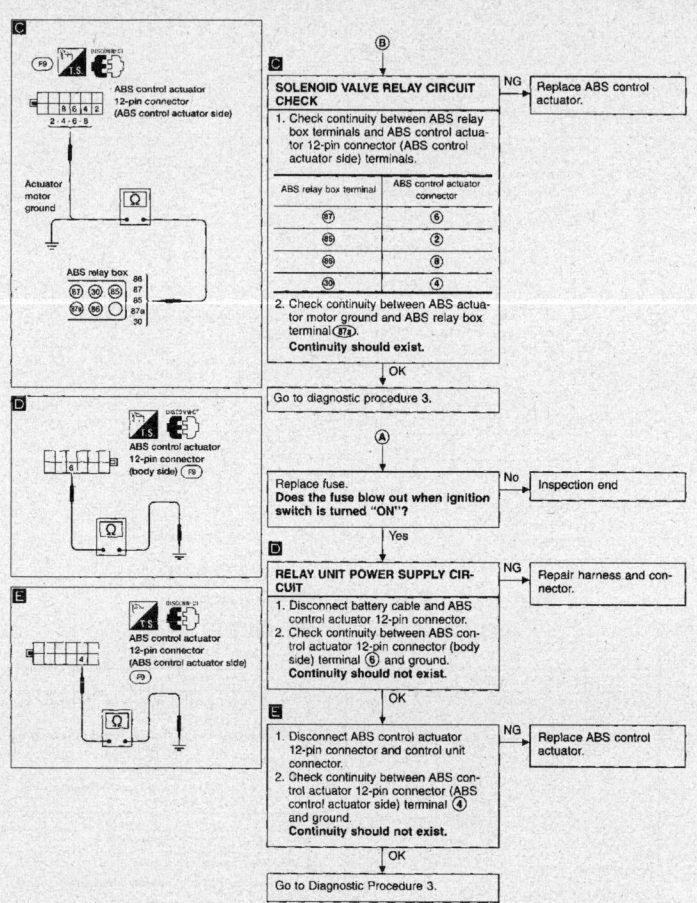

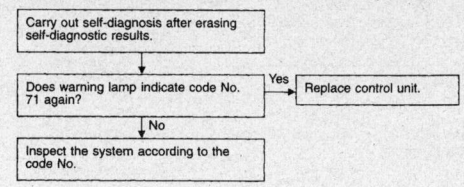

Fig. 228 Test 6: Solenoid Valve Relay (Part 2 of 2). 1996–98 Quest

Fig. 229 Test 7: Control Unit. 1996–98 Quest

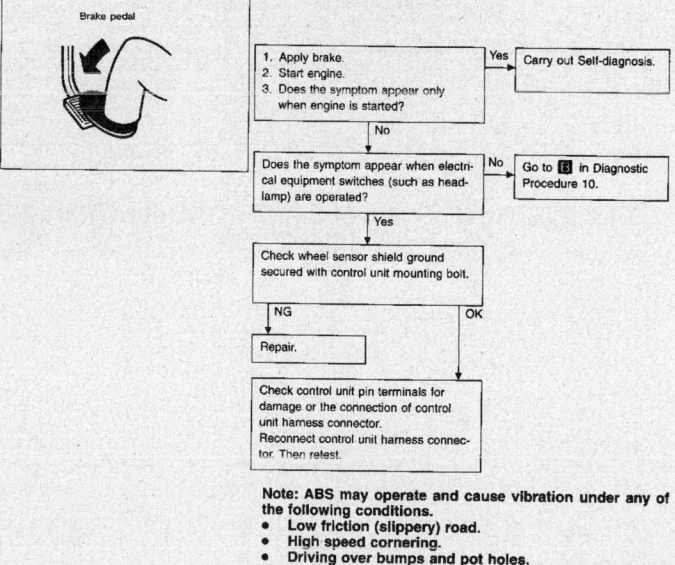

Note: ABS may operate and cause vibration under any of the following conditions.
- Low friction (slippery) road.
- High speed cornering.
- Driving over bumps and pot holes.
- Engine speed is over 5,000 rpm with vehicle stopped.

Fig. 230 Test 8: Pedal Vibration & Noise. 1996–98 Quest

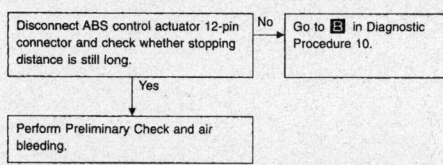

Note: Stopping distance may be longer than that of vehicles without ABS when road condition is slippery.

Fig. 231 Test 9: Long Stopping Distance. 1996–98 Quest

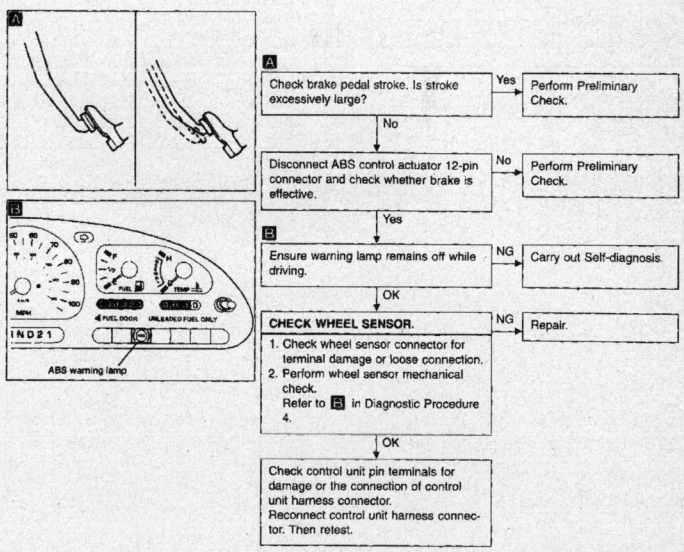

Fig. 232 Test 10: Unexpected Pedal Action. 1996–98 Quest

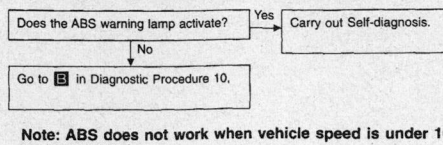

Does the ABS warning lamp activate? — Yes → Carry out Self-diagnosis.

↓ No

Go to **E** in Diagnostic Procedure 10.

Note: ABS does not work when vehicle speed is under 10 km/h (6 MPH).

NS4029600205000X

Fig. 233   Test 11: ABS Does Not Work. 1996–98 Quest

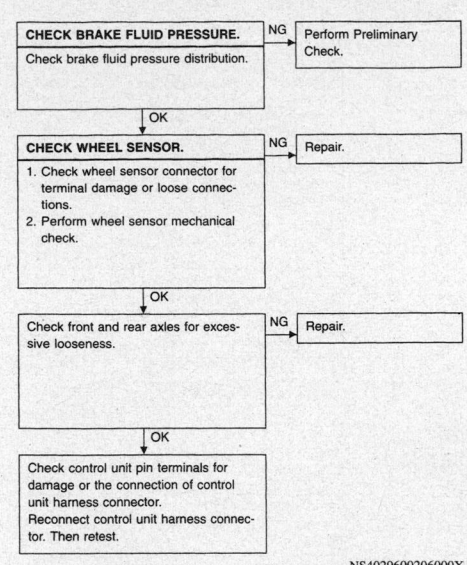

CHECK BRAKE FLUID PRESSURE. — NG → Perform Preliminary Check.

Check brake fluid pressure distribution.

↓ OK

CHECK WHEEL SENSOR. — NG → Repair.

1. Check wheel sensor connector for terminal damage or loose connections.
2. Perform wheel sensor mechanical check.

↓ OK

Check front and rear axles for excessive looseness. — NG → Repair.

↓ OK

Check control unit pin terminals for damage or the connection of control unit harness connector. Reconnect control unit harness connector. Then retest.

NS4029600206000X

Fig. 234   Test 12: ABS Works Frequently. 1996–98 Quest

Malfunction code No. 21, 22, 25, 26, 31, 32, 35, 36 or 18
NOTE:
Wheel position should be distinguished by code No. except code No. 18 (sensor rotor).

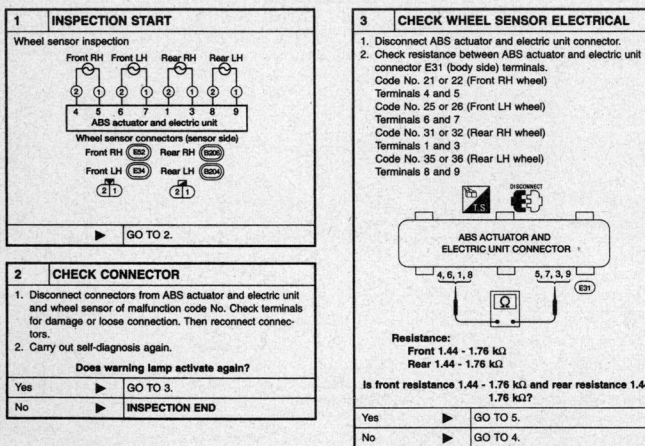

1 INSPECTION START

Wheel sensor inspection

Wheel sensor connectors (sensor side)

▶ GO TO 2.

2 CHECK CONNECTOR

1. Disconnect connectors from ABS actuator and electric unit and wheel sensor of malfunction code No. Check terminals for damage or loose connection. Then reconnect connectors.
2. Carry out self-diagnosis again.

Does warning lamp activate again?

| Yes | ▶ | GO TO 3. |
| No | ▶ | INSPECTION END |

3 CHECK WHEEL SENSOR ELECTRICAL

1. Disconnect ABS actuator and electric unit connector.
2. Check resistance between ABS actuator and electric unit connector E31 (body side) terminals.
   Code No. 21 or 22 (Front RH wheel)
   Terminals 4 and 5
   Code No. 25 or 26 (Front LH wheel)
   Terminals 6 and 7
   Code No. 31 or 32 (Rear RH wheel)
   Terminals 1 and 3
   Code No. 35 or 36 (Rear LH wheel)
   Terminals 8 and 9

ABS ACTUATOR AND ELECTRIC UNIT CONNECTOR

Resistance:
Front 1.44 - 1.76 kΩ
Rear 1.44 - 1.76 kΩ

Is front resistance 1.44 - 1.76 kΩ and rear resistance 1.44 - 1.76 kΩ?

| Yes | ▶ | GO TO 5. |
| No | ▶ | GO TO 4. |

NS4029900323010X

Fig. 235   Test 1: Wheel Sensor Or Rotor (Part 1 of 2). 1999 Quest

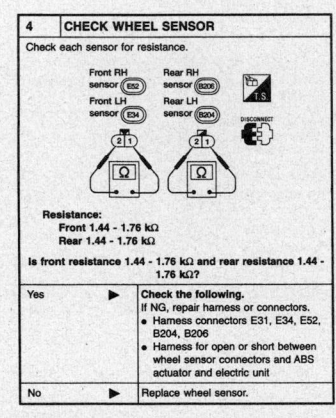

4 CHECK WHEEL SENSOR

Check each sensor for resistance.

Resistance:
Front 1.44 - 1.76 kΩ
Rear 1.44 - 1.76 kΩ

Is front resistance 1.44 - 1.76 kΩ and rear resistance 1.44 - 1.76 kΩ?

| Yes | ▶ | Check the following. If NG, repair harness or connectors. • Harness connectors E31, E34, E52, B204, B206 • Harness for open or short between wheel sensor connectors and ABS actuator and electric unit |
| No | ▶ | Replace wheel sensor. |

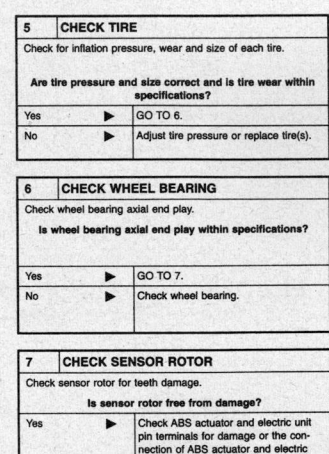

5 CHECK TIRE

Check for inflation pressure, wear and size of each tire.

Are tire pressure and size correct and is tire wear within specifications?

| Yes | ▶ | GO TO 6. |
| No | ▶ | Adjust tire pressure or replace tire(s). |

6 CHECK WHEEL BEARING

Check wheel bearing axial end play.

Is wheel bearing axial end play within specifications?

| Yes | ▶ | GO TO 7. |
| No | ▶ | Check wheel bearing. |

7 CHECK SENSOR ROTOR

Check sensor rotor for teeth damage.

Is sensor rotor free from damage?

| Yes | ▶ | Check ABS actuator and electric unit pin terminals for damage or the connection of ABS actuator and electric unit harness connector. Reconnect ABS actuator and electric unit harness connector. Then retest. |
| No | ▶ | Replace sensor rotor. |

NS4029900323020X

Fig. 235   Test 1: Wheel Sensor Or Rotor (Part 2 of 2). 1999 Quest

Malfunction code No. 41, 45, 51, 55, 42, 46, 52, 56, 63

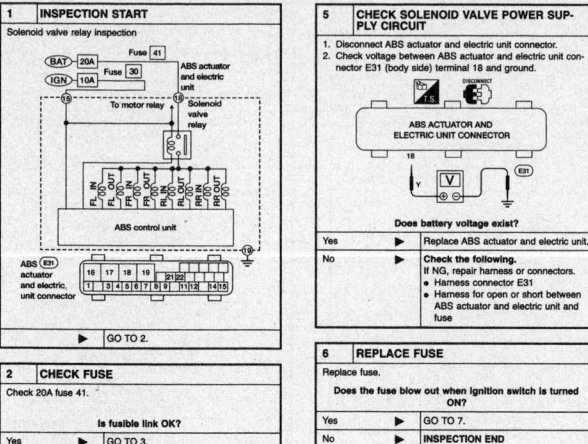

NS4029900324010X

Fig. 236 Test 2: ABS Actuator Solenoid Valve Or Relay (Part 1 of 2). 1999 Quest

7	CHECK SOLENOID VALVE RELAY POWER SUPPLY CIRCUIT FOR SHORT

1. Disconnect battery cable and ABS actuator and electric unit connector.
2. Check continuity between ABS actuator and electric unit connector E31 (body side) terminal 18 and ground.

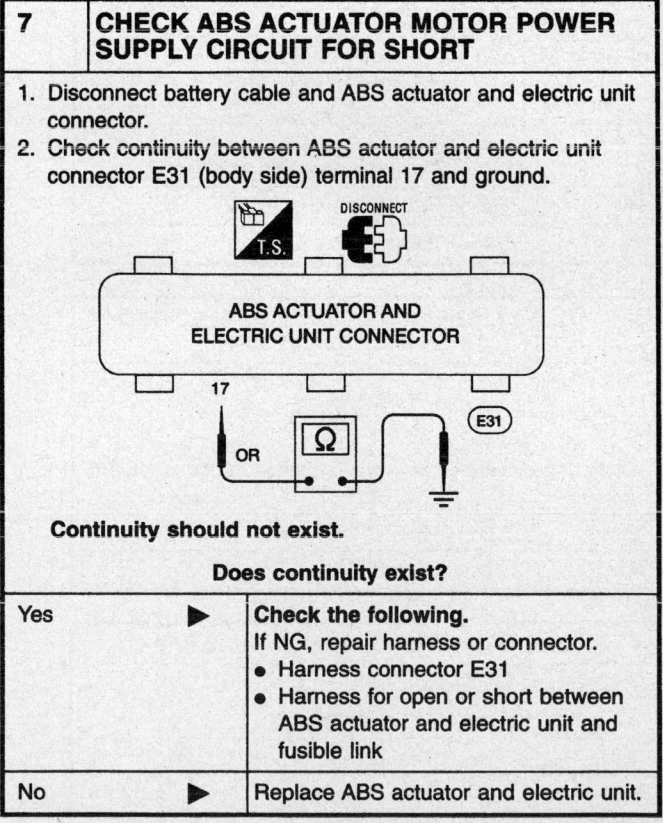

Continuity should not exist.

Does continuity exist?

Yes	▶	Check the following. If NG, repair harness or connector. • Harness connector E31 • Harness for open or short between ABS actuator and electric unit and fuse
No	▶	Replace ABS actuator and electric unit.

NS4029900324020X

Fig. 236 Test 2: ABS Actuator Solenoid Valve Or Relay (Part 2 of 2). 1999 Quest

---

Malfunction code No. 61

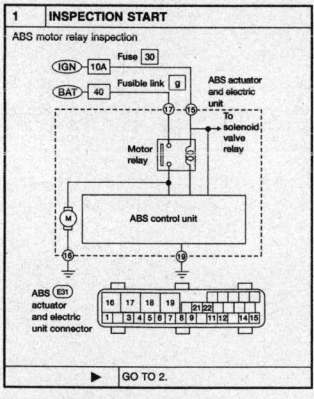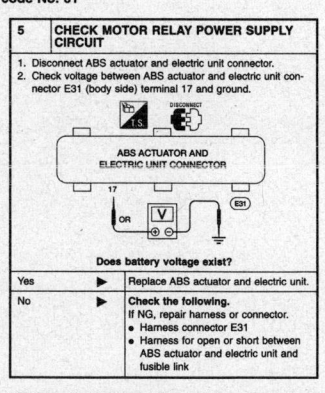

NS4029900325010X

Fig. 237 Test 3: Motor Relay Or Motor (Part 1 of 2). 1999 Quest

7	CHECK ABS ACTUATOR MOTOR POWER SUPPLY CIRCUIT FOR SHORT

1. Disconnect battery cable and ABS actuator and electric unit connector.
2. Check continuity between ABS actuator and electric unit connector E31 (body side) terminal 17 and ground.

Continuity should not exist.

Does continuity exist?

Yes	▶	Check the following. If NG, repair harness or connector. • Harness connector E31 • Harness for open or short between ABS actuator and electric unit and fusible link
No	▶	Replace ABS actuator and electric unit.

NS4029900325020X

Fig. 237 Test 3: Motor Relay Or Motor (Part 3 of 2). 1999 Quest

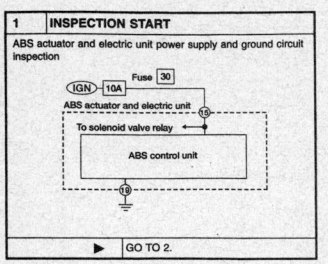

1	INSPECTION START
ABS actuator and electric unit power supply and ground circuit inspection	

2	CHECK FUSE
Check 10A fuse No. 30.	
Is fuse OK?	
Yes ▶	GO TO 3.
No ▶	GO TO 6.

3	CHECK CONNECTOR
1. Disconnect ABS actuator and electric unit connector. Check terminals for damage or loose connections. Then reconnect connector. 2. Carry out self-diagnosis again.	
Does warning lamp activate again?	
Yes ▶	GO TO 4.
No ▶	INSPECTION END

NS4029900326010X

Fig. 238   Test 4: Low Voltage (Part 1 of 2). 1999 Quest

1	INSPECTION START

ABS actuator and electric unit power supply and ground circuit inspection

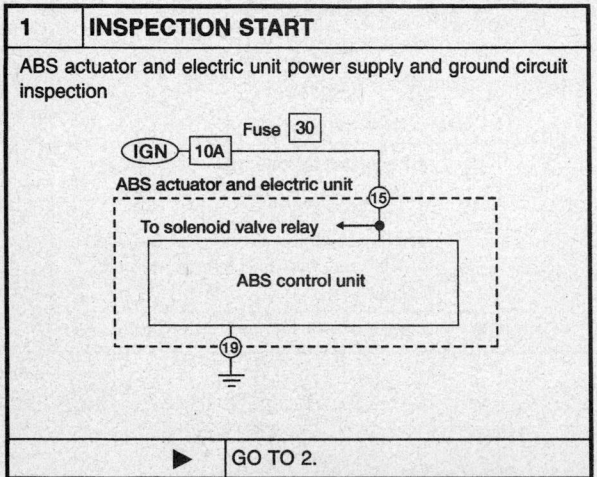

▶	GO TO 2.

2	CHECK CONNECTOR
1. Disconnect ABS actuator and electric unit connector. Check terminals for damage or loose connection. Then reconnect connector. 2. Carry out self-diagnosis again.	
Does warning lamp activate again?	
Yes ▶	GO TO 3.
No ▶	INSPECTION END

3	CHECK ABS ACTUATOR AND ELECTRIC UNIT POWER SUPPLY CIRCUIT
Check voltage.	
Does battery voltage exist when ignition switch is turned ON?	
Yes ▶	GO TO 4.
No ▶	Repair.

4	CHECK WARNING LAMP INDICATION
Does warning lamp indicate code No. 71 again?	
Yes or No	
Yes ▶	Replace ABS actuator and electric unit.
No ▶	Inspect the system according to the code No.

NS4029900327000X

Fig. 239   Test 5: Control Unit. 1999 Quest

4	CHECK ABS ACTUATOR AND ELECTRIC UNIT GROUND CIRCUIT
"ABS ACTUATOR AND ELECTRIC UNIT GROUND".	
Is ground circuit OK?	
Yes ▶	GO TO 5.
No ▶	Repair harness or connector.

5	CHECK ABS ACTUATOR AND ELECTRIC UNIT POWER SUPPLY CIRCUIT
1. Disconnect ABS actuator and electric unit connector. 2. Check voltage between ABS actuator and electric unit connector E31 (body side) terminal 15 and ground.	

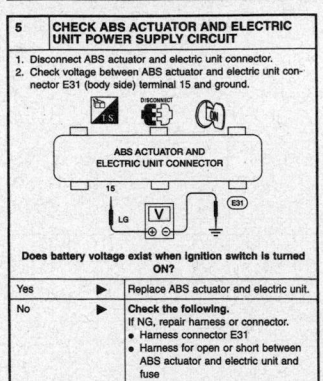

Does battery voltage exist when ignition switch is turned ON?	
Yes ▶	Replace ABS actuator and electric unit.
No ▶	Check the following. If NG, repair harness or connector. • Harness connector E31 • Harness for open or short between ABS actuator and electric unit and fuse

6	REPLACE FUSE
Replace fuse.	
Does the fuse blow out when ignition switch is turned ON?	
Yes ▶	GO TO 7.
No ▶	INSPECTION END

7	CHECK ABS ACTUATOR AND ELECTRIC UNIT POWER SUPPLY CIRCUIT FOR SHORT
1. Disconnect battery cable and ABS actuator and electric unit connector. 2. Check continuity between ABS actuator and electric unit connector E31 (body side) terminal 15 and ground.	

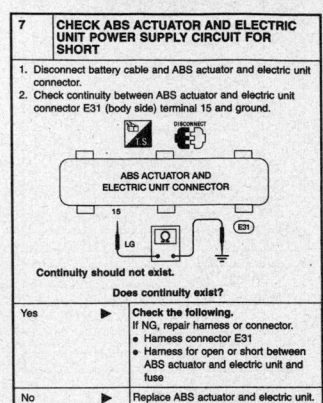

Continuity should not exist.

Does continuity exist?	
Yes ▶	Check the following. If NG, repair harness or connector. • Harness connector E31 • Harness for open or short between ABS actuator and electric unit and fuse
No ▶	Replace ABS actuator and electric unit.

NS4029900326020X

Fig. 238   Test 4: Low Voltage (Part 2 of 2). 1999 Quest

1	CHECK BRAKE FLUID PRESSURE
Check brake fluid pressure distribution.	
Is brake fluid pressure distribution normal?	
Yes ▶	GO TO 2.
No ▶	Repair. Then perform Preliminary Check.

2	CHECK WHEEL SENSOR
1. Check wheel sensor connector for terminal damage or loose connections. 2. Perform wheel sensor mechanical check.	
Is wheel sensor mechanism OK?	
Yes ▶	GO TO 3.
No ▶	Repair.

3	CHECK FRONT AXLE
Check front axles for excessive looseness.	
Is front axle installed properly?	
Yes ▶	Go to "3. CHECK WARNING LAMP INDICATION" in "2. Unexpected Pedal Action".
No ▶	Repair.

NS4029900328000X

Fig. 240   Test 6: ABS Works Frequently. 1999 Quest

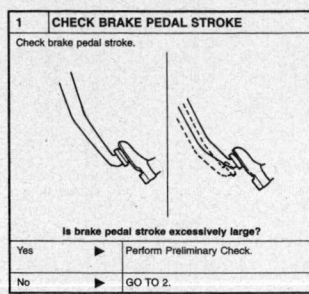

Fig. 241 Test 7: Unexpected Pedal Action. 1999 Quest

NS4029900329000X

1 CHECK BRAKE PEDAL STROKE

Check brake pedal stroke.

Is brake pedal stroke excessively large?

| Yes | ▶ | Perform Preliminary Check. |
| No | ▶ | GO TO 2. |

2 CHECK MECHANICAL BRAKE SYSTEM PERFORMANCE

Disconnect ABS actuator and electric unit connector and check whether brake is effective.

Does brake system function properly when brake pedal is depressed?

| Yes | ▶ | GO TO 3. |
| No | ▶ | Perform Preliminary Check. |

3 CHECK WARNING LAMP INDICATION

Ensure warning lamp remains off while driving.

ABS warning lamp

Is warning lamp turned off?

| Yes | ▶ | GO TO 4. |
| No | ▶ | Carry out self-diagnosis. |

4 CHECK WHEEL SENSOR

1. Check wheel sensor connector for terminal damage or loose connection.
2. Perform wheel sensor mechanical check.

Is wheel sensor mechanism OK?

| Yes | ▶ | Check ABS actuator and electric unit pin terminals for damage or the connection of ABS actuator and electric unit harness connector. Reconnect ABS actuator and electric unit harness connector. Then retest. |
| No | ▶ | Repair. |

Fig. 243 Test 9: ABS inoperative. 1999 Quest

NS4029900331000X

1 CHECK WARNING LAMP INDICATION

Does the ABS warning lamp activate?

Yes or No

| Yes | ▶ | Carry out self-diagnosis. |
| No | ▶ | CHECK WARNING LAMP INDICATION. |

NOTE:
ABS does not work when vehicle speed is under 10 km/h (6 MPH).

---

1 CHECK MECHANICAL BRAKE SYSTEM PERFORMANCE

Disconnect ABS actuator and electric unit connector and check whether stopping distance is still long.

Does brake system function properly when brake pedal is depressed?

| Yes | ▶ | Perform Preliminary Check and air bleeding (if necessary). |
| No | ▶ | CHECK WARNING LAMP INDICATION". |

NOTE:
Stopping distance may be longer for vehicles without ABS when road condition is slippery.

NS4029900330000X

Fig. 242 Test 8: Long Stopping Distance. 1999 Quest

1 INSPECTION START

Pedal vibration and noise inspection

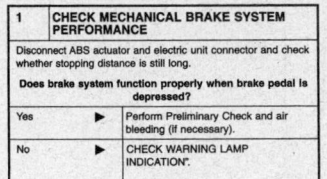

Brake pedal

| ▶ | GO TO 2. |

2 CHECK SYMPTOM

1. Apply brake.
2. Start engine.

Does the symptom appear only when engine is started?

| Yes | ▶ | Carry out self-diagnosis. |
| No | ▶ | CHECK WARNING LAMP INDICATION. |

NOTE:
ABS may operate and cause vibration under any of the following conditions.
- Applying brake gradually when shifting or operating clutch.
- Low friction (slippery) road.
- High speed cornering.
- Driving over bumps and pot holes.
- Engine speed is over 5,000 rpm with vehicle stopped.

NS4029900332000X

Fig. 244 Test 10: Pedal Vibration & Noise. 1999 Quest

---

1 INSPECTION START

Warning lamp circuit inspection

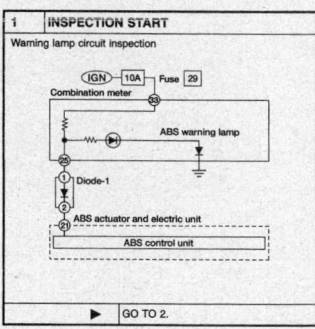

| ▶ | GO TO 2. |

2 CHECK FUSE

Check 10A fuse No. 29.

Is fuse OK?

| Yes | ▶ | GO TO 3. |
| No | ▶ | Replace fuse. |

3 CHECK WARNING LAMP ACTIVATE

Disconnect ABS actuator and electric unit connector.

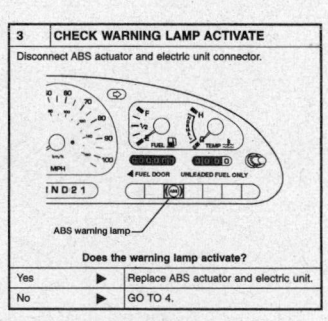

ABS warning lamp

Does the warning lamp activate?

| Yes | ▶ | Replace ABS actuator and electric unit. |
| No | ▶ | GO TO 4. |

4 CHECK HARNESS FOR SHORT

1. Disconnect ABS actuator and electric unit connector and combination meter connector M17.
2. Check continuity between ABS actuator and electric unit connector E31 (body side) terminal 21 and ground.

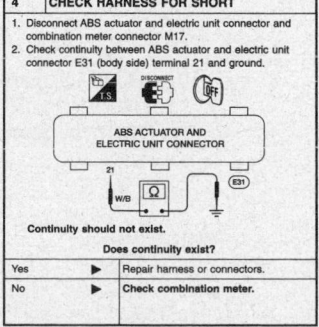

Continuity should not exist.

Does continuity exist?

| Yes | ▶ | Repair harness or connectors. |
| No | ▶ | Check combination meter. |

NS4029900333000X

Fig. 245 Test 11: Warning Lamp Does Not Illuminate w/Key On. 1999 Quest

---

1 INSPECTION START

ABS control unit inspection

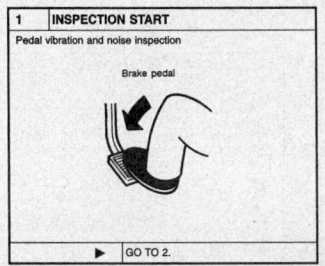

| ▶ | GO TO 2. |

2 CHECK FUSE

Check 10A fuse No. 30.

Is fuse OK?

| Yes | ▶ | GO TO 3. |
| No | ▶ | GO TO 10. |

3 CHECK HARNESS CONNECTOR

Check ABS actuator and electric unit pin terminals for damage or bad connection of ABS actuator and electric unit harness connector. Reconnect ABS actuator and electric unit harness connector. Then retest.

Does warning lamp stay on when ignition switch is turned ON?

| Yes | ▶ | GO TO 4. |
| No | ▶ | INSPECTION END |

4 CHECK ABS ACTUATOR AND ELECTRIC UNIT GROUND CIRCUIT

"ABS ACTUATOR AND ELECTRIC UNIT GROUND"

Is ground circuit OK?

| Yes | ▶ | GO TO 5. |
| No | ▶ | Repair harness or connector. |

5 CHECK ABS ACTUATOR AND ELECTRIC UNIT POWER SUPPLY CIRCUIT

1. Disconnect ABS actuator and electric unit connector.
2. Check voltage between ABS actuator and electric unit connector E31 (body side) terminal 15 and ground.

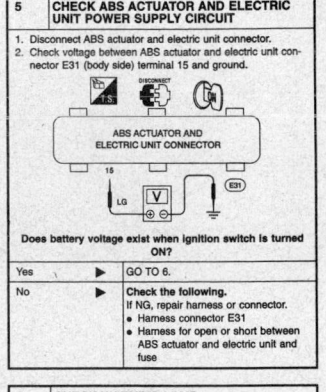

Does battery voltage exist when ignition switch is turned ON?

| Yes | ▶ | GO TO 6. |
| No | ▶ | Check the following. If NG, repair harness or connector. • Harness connector E31 • Harness for open or short between ABS actuator and electric unit and fuse |

6 CHECK WARNING LAMP

1. Disconnect ABS actuator and electric unit connector.
2. Connect suitable wire between ABS actuator and electric unit connector E31 (body side) terminal 21 and ground.

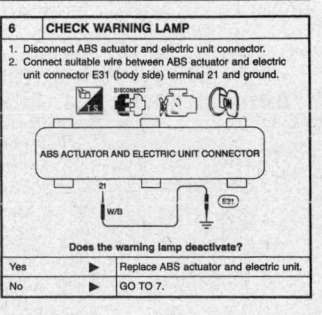

Does the warning lamp deactivate?

| Yes | ▶ | Replace ABS actuator and electric unit. |
| No | ▶ | GO TO 7. |

NS4029900334010X

Fig. 246 Test 12: Warning Lamp Remains Illuminated w/Key On (Part 1 of 2). 1999 Quest

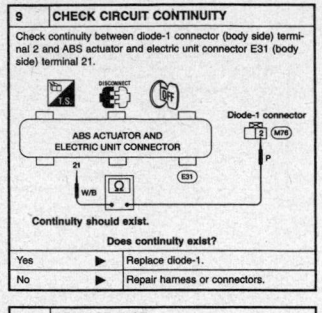

7 CHECK ABS WARNING LAMP CONTROL CIRCUIT FOR OPEN

1. Disconnect combination meter connector M17.
2. Check continuity between combination meter connector M17 (body side) terminal 25 and ABS actuator and electric unit connector E31 (body side) terminal 21.

NOTE:
Connect positive lead of multimeter to combination meter connector M17 (body side) terminal 25 and negative lead to ABS actuator and electric unit connector E31 (body side) terminal 21.

Continuity should exist.

Does continuity exist?

| Yes | ▶ | Check combination meter. |
| No | ▶ | GO TO 8. |

8 CHECK CIRCUIT CONTINUITY

1. Remove diode from diode-1 connector.
2. Check continuity between combination meter connector M17 (body side) terminal 25 and diode-1 connector (body side) terminal 1.

Continuity should exist.

Does continuity exist?

| Yes | ▶ | GO TO 9. |
| No | ▶ | Repair harness or connectors. |

9 CHECK CIRCUIT CONTINUITY

Check continuity between diode-1 connector (body side) terminal 2 and ABS actuator and electric unit connector E31 (body side) terminal 21.

Continuity should exist.

Does continuity exist?

| Yes | ▶ | Replace diode-1. |
| No | ▶ | Repair harness or connectors. |

10 REPLACE FUSE

Replace fuse.

Does the fuse blow out when ignition switch is turned ON?

| Yes | ▶ | GO TO 11. |
| No | ▶ | INSPECTION END |

11 CHECK ABS ACTUATOR AND ELECTRIC UNIT POWER SUPPLY CIRCUIT FOR SHORT

1. Disconnect battery cable and ABS actuator and electric unit connector.
2. Check continuity between ABS actuator and electric unit connector E31 (body side) terminal 15 and ground.

Continuity should not exist.

Does continuity exist?

| Yes | ▶ | Check the following. If NG, repair harness or connector. • Harness connector E31 • Harness for open or short between ABS actuator and electric unit and fuse |
| No | ▶ | Replace ABS actuator and electric unit. |

NS4029900334020X

Fig. 246   Test 12: Warning Lamp Remains Illuminated w/Key On (Part 2 of 2). 1999 Quest

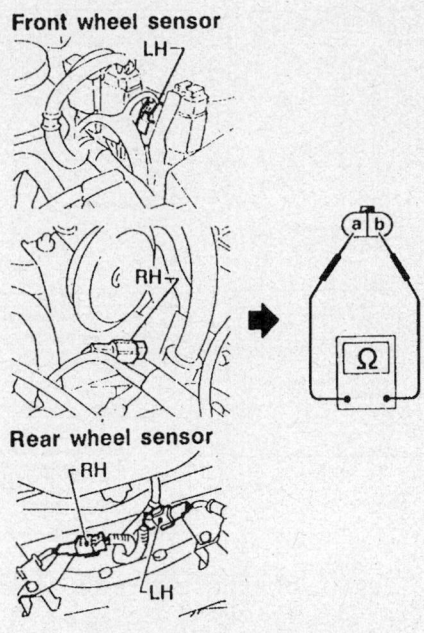

NS4029100110000X

Fig. 247   Wheel sensor inspection. Altima, Maxima, Sentra & 200SX

Condition	Continuity existence between terminals ③ and ④
Battery positive voltage not applied between terminals ① and ②.	No
Battery positive voltage applied between terminals ① and ②.	Yes

NS4029100112000X

Fig. 249   Actuator motor relay continuity check. Altima, Sentra & 200SX

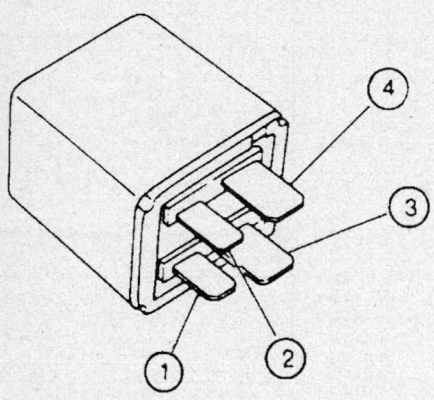

NS4029100111000X

Fig. 248   Actuator motor relay terminal locations. Altima, Sentra & 200SX

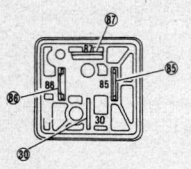

Condition	Continuity existence between terminals ㉚ and ㊸
Battery voltage not applied between terminals ㊇ and ㊈.	No
Battery voltage applied between terminals ㊇ and ㊈.	Yes

While applying battery voltage to relay terminals, insert fuse into the circuit.

NS4029500268000X

Fig. 250   Actuator motor relay. Maxima

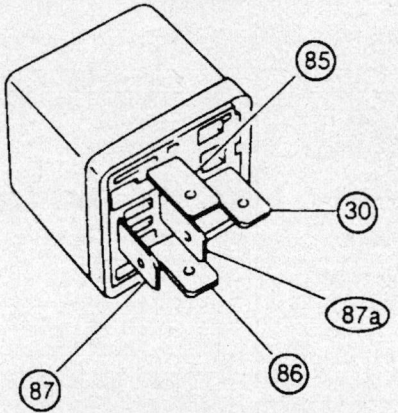

NS4029100113000X

Fig. 251   Solenoid valve relay terminal locations. Altima, Maxima, Sentra & 200SX

Condition	Continuity existence between terminals ㉚ and ㊸ₐ	Continuity existence between terminals ㉚ and ㊸
Battery positive voltage not applied between terminals ㊇ and ㊈.	Yes	No
Battery positive voltage applied between terminals ㊇ and ㊈.	No	Yes

NS4029100114000X

Fig. 252   Solenoid valve relay continuity check. Altima, Maxima, Sentra & 200SX

ANTI-LOCK BRAKES

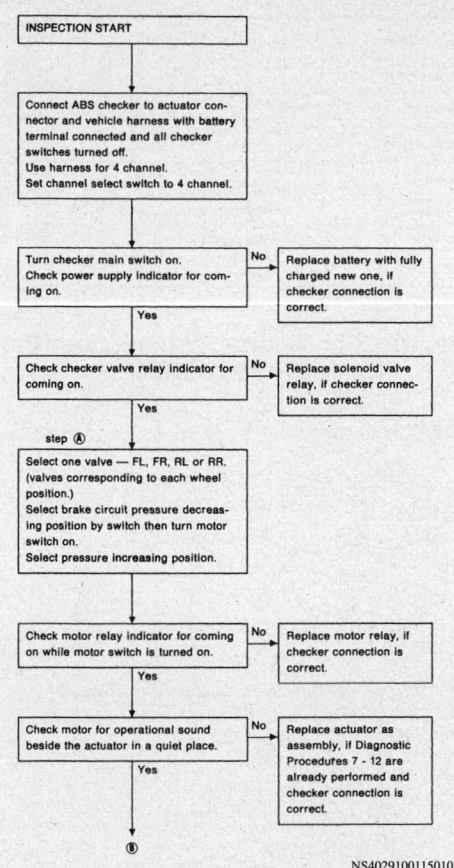

Fig. 253 **Electrical component inspection (Actuator, Part 1 of 2). 300ZX**

NS4029100115010X

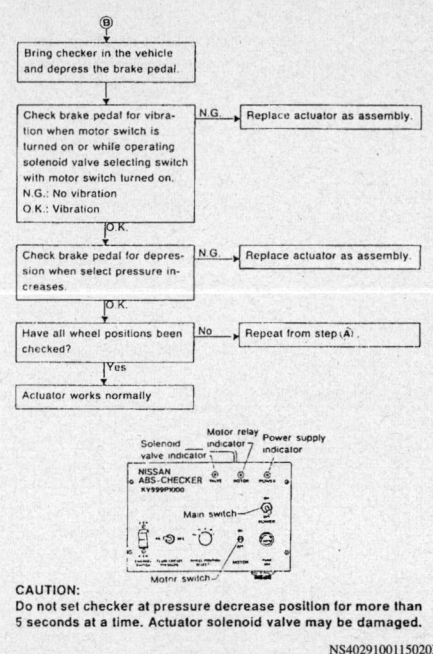

CAUTION:
Do not set checker at pressure decrease position for more than 5 seconds at a time. Actuator solenoid valve may be damaged.

NS4029100115020X

Fig. 253 **Electrical component inspection (Actuator, Part 2 of 2). 300ZX**

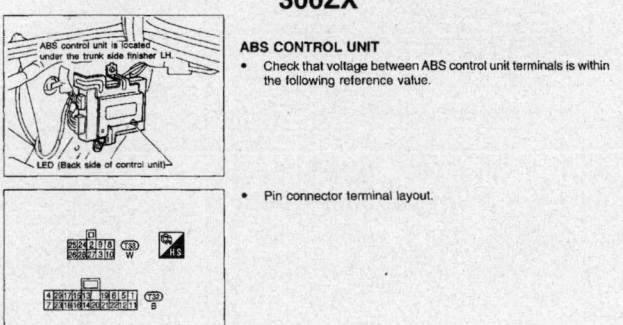

ABS CONTROL UNIT
- Check that voltage between ABS control unit terminals is within the following reference value.
- Pin connector terminal layout.

ABS control unit terminals and reference value

TERMINAL NO. +	TERMINAL NO. −	ITEM	CONDITION	DATA (Reference value)
1		Power source	Ignition switch "ON"	Battery voltage
4		Stop lamp switch signal	Brake pedal depressed	Approx. 12V
			Brake pedal released	Less than 2V
5		Motor monitor	ABS actuator motor operating (Perform "ACTIVE TEST" mode with CONSULT.)	Less than 2V
			ABS actuator motor not operating	Approx. 12V
6		Actuator monitor	ABS actuator relay operating (Engine is running.)	Less than 2V
			ABS actuator relay not operating (Ignition switch "ON")	Approx. 12V
7	Ground	Actuator monitor	ABS actuator relay operating (Engine is running.)	Approx. 12V
			ABS actuator relay not operating (Ignition switch "ON")	Approx. 0V
8		Front solenoid valve RH IN	ABS actuator operating (Perform "ACTIVE TEST" mode with CONSULT.)	Approx. 0V
9		Rear solenoid valve IN	Ignition switch turned "ON"	
10		Front solenoid valve LH IN	ABS actuator not operating (Engine is running with vehicle stopped.)	Approx. 12V
11		Motor monitor	ABS actuator motor operating (Perform "ACTIVE TEST" mode with CONSULT.)	Approx. 12V
			ABS actuator motor not operating	Approx. 0V
12		ABS warning lamp	ABS warning lamp "ON"	Approx. 0V
			ABS warning lamp "OFF"	Approx. 12V

NS4029700252010X

Fig. 254 **Electrical component inspection (Part 1 of 2). 1996 240SX**

TERMINAL NO. +	TERMINAL NO. −	ITEM	CONDITION	DATA (Reference value)
13	14	Front wheel sensor RH		
15	16	Rear wheel sensor	Wheel is rotating	Approx. 0.1 - 0.2V
17	18	Front wheel sensor LH		
23		Engine speed signal	Engine running at idle speed	Approx. 1.0V
			Engine running at 2,500 rpm	Approx. 3.1 - 3.3V
24		Front solenoid valve RH OUT	ABS actuator operating (Perform "ACTIVE TEST" mode with CONSULT.)	Approx. 0V
25	Ground	Rear solenoid valve OUT	Ignition switch "ON."	
26		Front solenoid valve LH OUT	ABS actuator not operating (Engine is running with vehicle stopped.)	Approx. 12V
29		Power source	—	Battery voltage

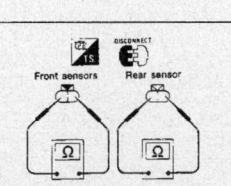

WHEEL SENSOR
Check resistance for each sensor.
Resistance: 0.6 - 3.3 kΩ

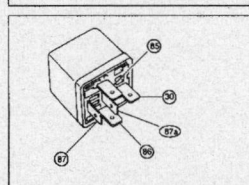

ACTUATOR MOTOR RELAY AND SOLENOID VALVE RELAY

Condition	Solenoid valve relay — Continuity existence between terminals ③⓪ and ⑧⑦ₐ	Actuator motor relay solenoid valve relay — Continuity existence between terminals ③⓪ and ⑧⑦
Battery voltage not applied between terminals ⑧⑤ and ⑧⑥	Yes	No
Battery voltage applied between terminals ⑧⑤ and ⑧⑥	No	Yes

NS4029700252020X

Fig. 254 **Electrical component inspection (Part 2 of 2). 1996 240SX**

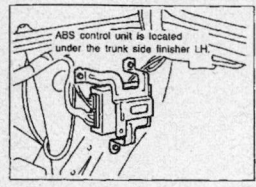

ABS control unit is located under the trunk side finisher LH.

INSPECTION OF ABS CONTROL UNIT

- Check that voltage between ABS control unit terminals is within the following reference value.

- Pin connector terminal layout.

ABS control unit inspection table

TERMINAL NO. +	TERMINAL NO. −	ITEM	CONDITION	DATA (Reference value)
10		Power source	Ignition switch "ON"	Battery voltage
6		Stop lamp switch signal	Brake pedal depressed	Approx. 12V
			Brake pedal released	Less than 2V
108		Motor relay	ABS actuator motor operating (Perform "ACTIVE TEST" mode with CONSULT.) Engine running	Less than 2V
			ABS actuator motor not operating	Approx. 12V
107		Solenoid valve relay	Solenoid valve relay operating (Engine is running.)	Less than 2V
			Solenoid valve relay not operating (Ignition switch "ON")	Approx. 12V
16	Ground	Actuator monitor	Solenoid valve relay operating (Engine is running.)	Approx. 12V
			Solenoid valve relay not operating (Ignition switch "ON")	Approx. 0V
101		Front solenoid valve RH IN	ABS actuator operating (Perform "ACTIVE TEST" mode with CONSULT.) Engine running	Approx. 0V
105		Rear solenoid valve IN		
103		Front solenoid valve LH IN	ABS actuator not operating (Engine is running with vehicle stopped.)	Approx. 12V
18		Motor monitor	ABS actuator motor operating (Perform "ACTIVE TEST" mode with CONSULT.) Engine running	Approx. 12V
			ABS actuator motor not operating	Approx. 0V
116		ABS warning lamp	ABS warning lamp "ON"	Approx. 0V
			ABS warning lamp "OFF"	Approx. 12V

NS4029700253010X

Fig. 255 Electrical component inspection (Part 1 of 2). 1997–98 240SX

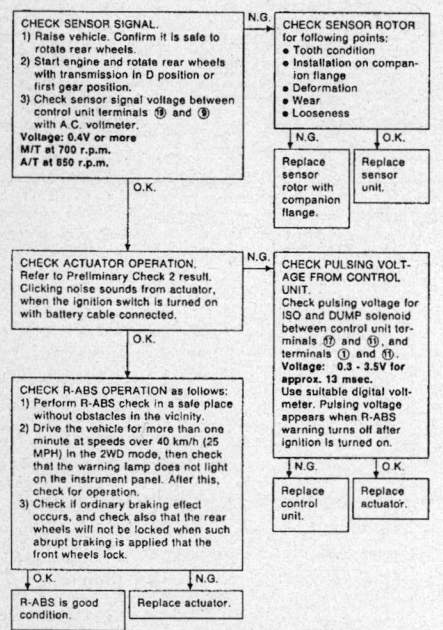

CHECK SENSOR SIGNAL.
1) Raise vehicle. Confirm it is safe to rotate rear wheels.
2) Start engine and rotate rear wheels with transmission in D position or first gear position.
3) Check sensor signal voltage between control unit terminals ⑱ and ⑨ with A.C. voltmeter.
Voltage: 0.4V or more
M/T at 700 r.p.m.
A/T at 850 r.p.m.

→ N.G. → CHECK SENSOR ROTOR for following points:
- Tooth condition
- Installation on companion flange
- Deformation
- Wear
- Looseness

→ N.G. → Replace sensor rotor with companion flange.

→ O.K. → Replace sensor unit.

O.K. ↓

CHECK ACTUATOR OPERATION.
Refer to Preliminary Check 2 result. Clicking noise sounds from actuator, when the ignition switch is turned on with battery cable connected.

→ N.G. → CHECK PULSING VOLTAGE FROM CONTROL UNIT.
Check pulsing voltage for ISO and DUMP solenoid between control unit terminals ⑰ and ⑲, and terminals ① and ⑪.
Voltage: 0.3 - 3.5V for approx. 13 msec.
Use suitable digital voltmeter. Pulsing voltage appears when R-ABS warning turns off after ignition is turned on.

→ N.G. → Replace control unit.

→ O.K. → Replace actuator.

O.K. ↓

CHECK R-ABS OPERATION as follows:
1) Perform R-ABS check in a safe place without obstacles in the vicinity.
2) Drive the vehicle for more than one minute at speeds over 40 km/h (25 MPH) in the 2WD mode, then check that the warning lamp does not light on the instrument panel. After this, check for operation.
3) Check if ordinary braking effect occurs, and check also that the rear wheels will not be locked when such abrupt braking is applied that the front wheels lock.

→ O.K. → R-ABS is good condition.

→ N.G. → Replace actuator.

NS4029100116000X

Fig. 256 Electrical component inspection (Sensor unit & actuator). Frontier, Pathfinder & Pickup

TERMINAL NO. +	TERMINAL NO. −	ITEM	CONDITION	DATA (Reference value)
2	12	Front wheel sensor RH	Wheel is rotating [Drive vehicle at 30 km/h (20 MPH).]	Approx. 0.1 - 0.2V / Approx. 200 Hz*1
4	14	Rear wheel sensor		Approx. 0.1 - 0.2V / Approx. 400 Hz*1
3	13	Front wheel sensor LH		Approx. 0.1 - 0.2V / Approx. 200 Hz*1
17		Engine speed signal	Engine running at idle speed	Approx. 1.0V
			Engine running at 2,000 rpm	Approx. 2.4V
109	Ground	Front solenoid valve RH OUT	ABS actuator operating (Perform "ACTIVE TEST" mode with CONSULT.)	Approx. 0V
113		Rear solenoid valve OUT	Engine running	
111		Front solenoid valve LH OUT	ABS actuator not operating (Engine is running with vehicle stopped.)	Approx. 12V

*1: Use oscilloscope checking, when pulse occurs.

NS4029700253020X

Fig. 255 Electrical component inspection (Part 2 of 2). 1997–98 240SX

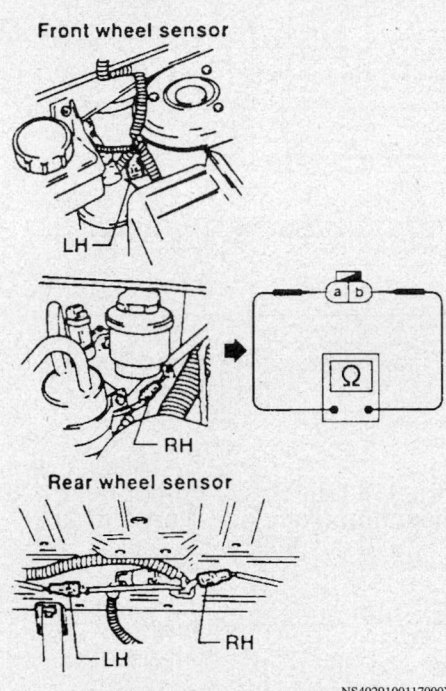

Front wheel sensor

LH

RH

Rear wheel sensor

LH

RH

NS4029100117000X

Fig. 257 Wheel sensor inspection. Quest

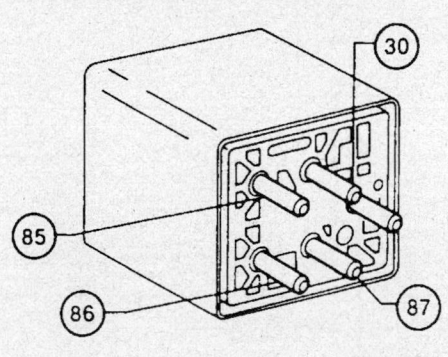

NS4029100118000X

Fig. 258 Actuator motor relay terminal locations. Quest

Condition	Continuity existence between terminals ⑳ and ㉘
Battery positive voltage not applied between terminals ㊄ and ㊅.	No
Battery positive voltage applied between terminals ㊄ and ㊅.	Yes

NS4029100119000X

Fig. 259 Actuator motor relay continuity check. Quest

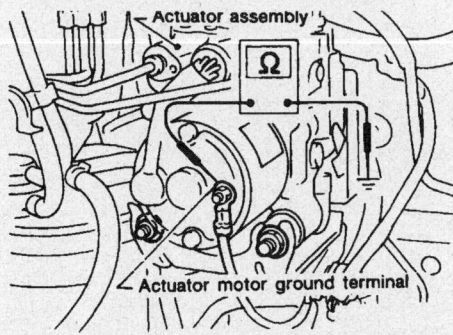

NS4029100122000A

Fig. 262 Actuator motor ground circuit check. Maxima

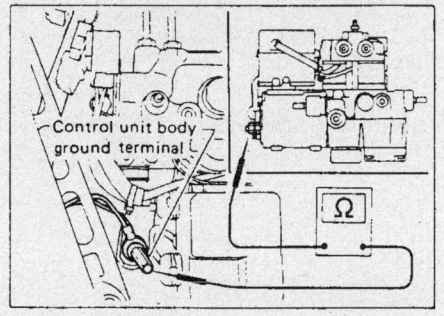

NS4029100125000X

Fig. 265 Actuator motor ground circuit check. 300ZX

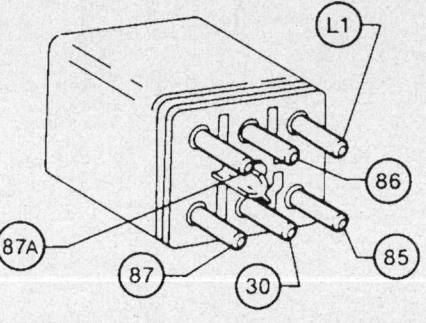

NS4029100120000X

Fig. 260 Solenoid valve relay terminal locations. Quest

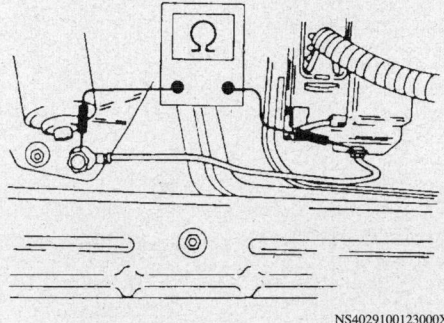

NS4029100123000X

Fig. 263 Actuator motor ground circuit check. Quest

Condition	Continuity existence between terminals ⑳ and ㉗ₐ	Continuity existence between terminals ⑳ and ㉗
Battery voltage not applied between terminals ㊄ and ㊅.	Yes	No
Battery voltage applied between terminals ㊄ and ㊅.	No	Yes

NS4029100121000X

Fig. 261 Solenoid valve relay continuity check. Quest

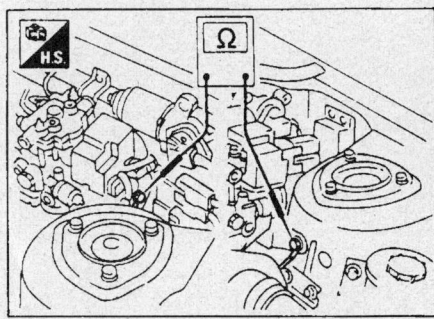

NS4029100124000X

Fig. 264 Actuator motor ground circuit check. 240SX

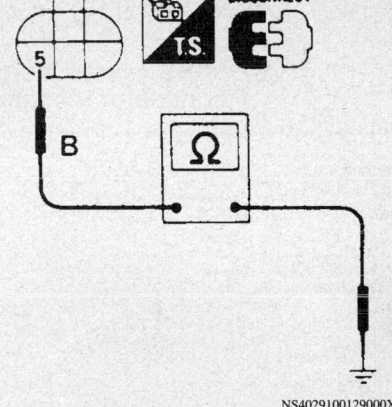

NS4029100129000X

Fig. 266 Relay box ground circuit check. Altima

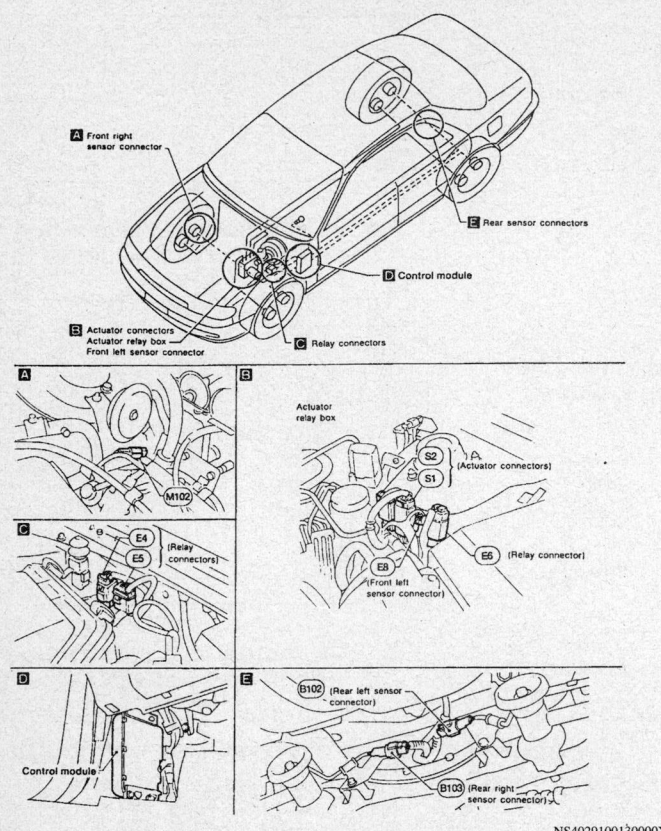

Fig. 267 ABS system component & harness connector locations. Altima

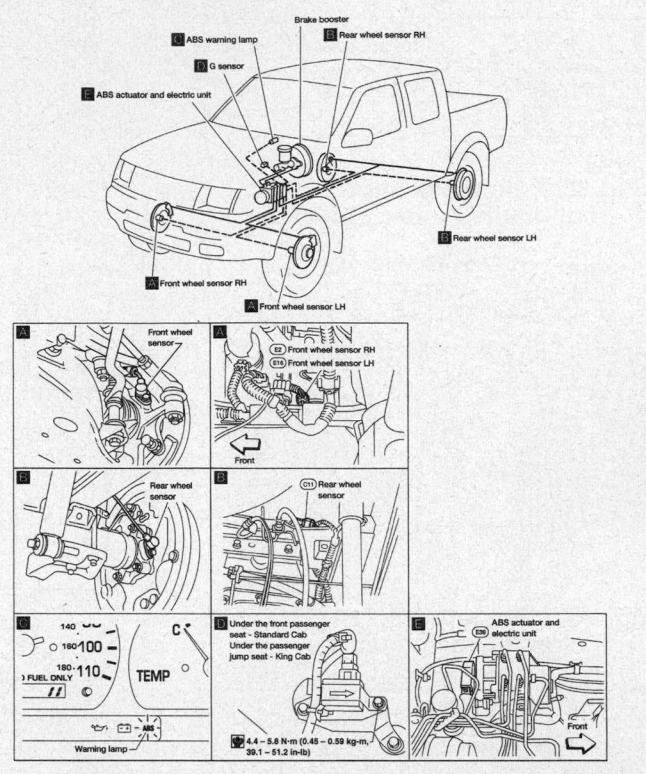

NS4029900360000X

Fig. 268 ABS system component & harness connector locations. Frontier

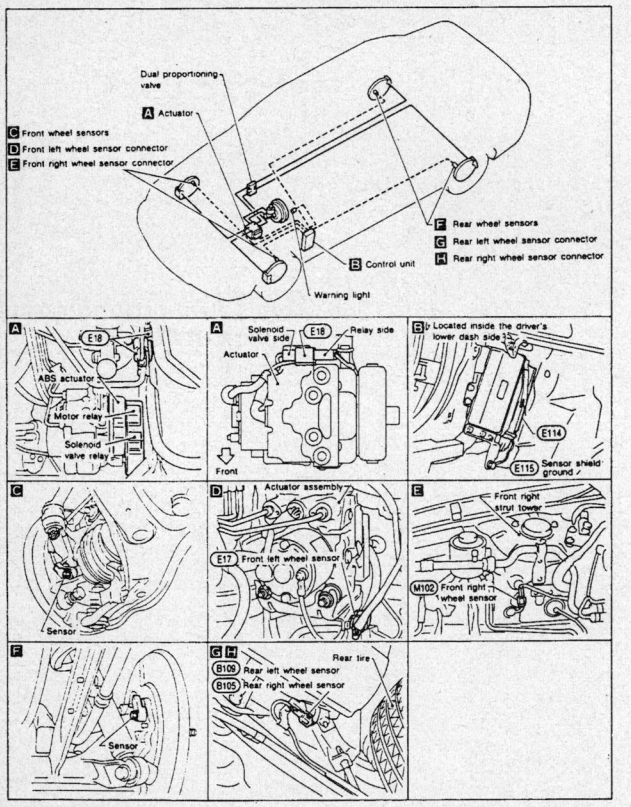

NS4029500187000X

Fig. 269 ABS system component & harness connector locations. Maxima

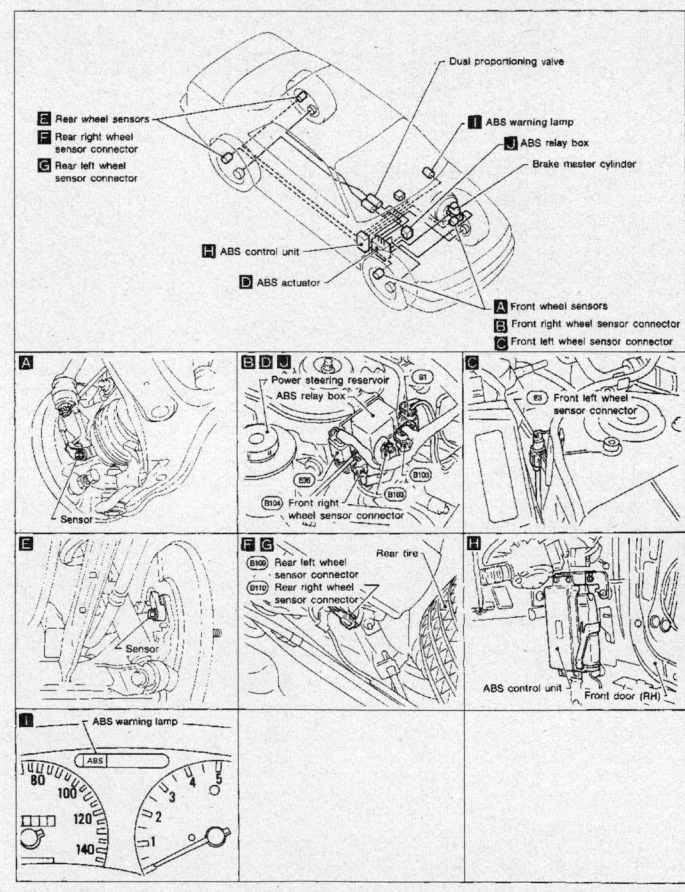

NS4029500188000X

Fig. 270 ABS system component & harness connector locations. Sentra & 200SX

ANTI-LOCK BRAKES

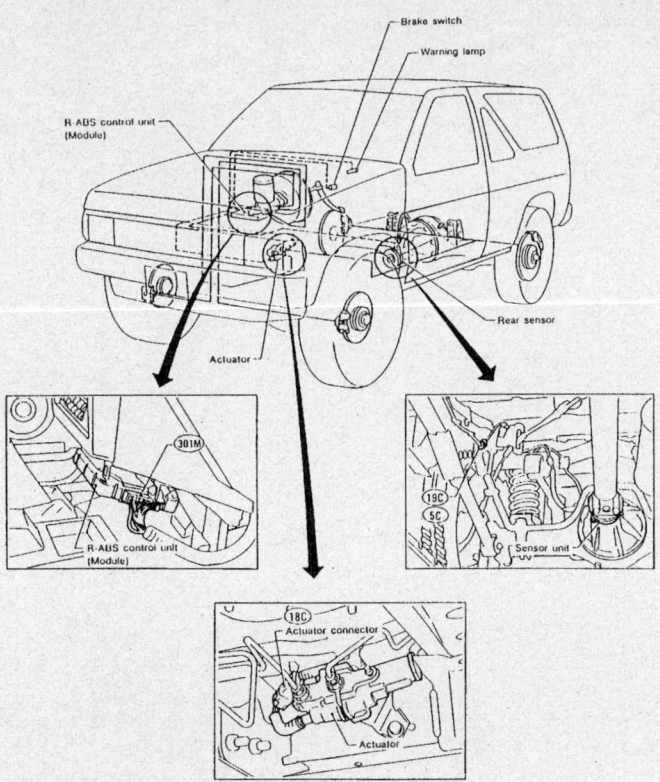

Fig. 271 ABS system component & harness connector locations. Pickup

NS4029100133000X

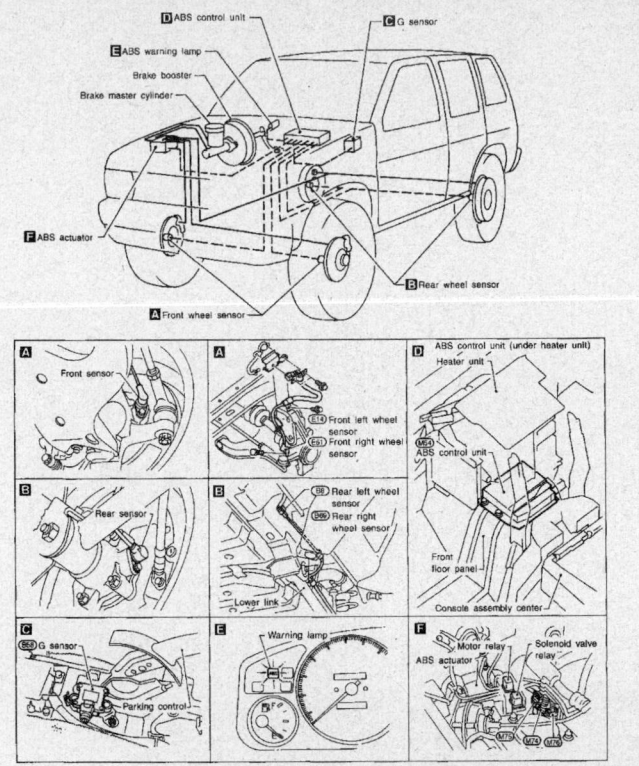

Fig. 272 ABS system component & harness connector locations. Pathfinder

NS4029600235000X

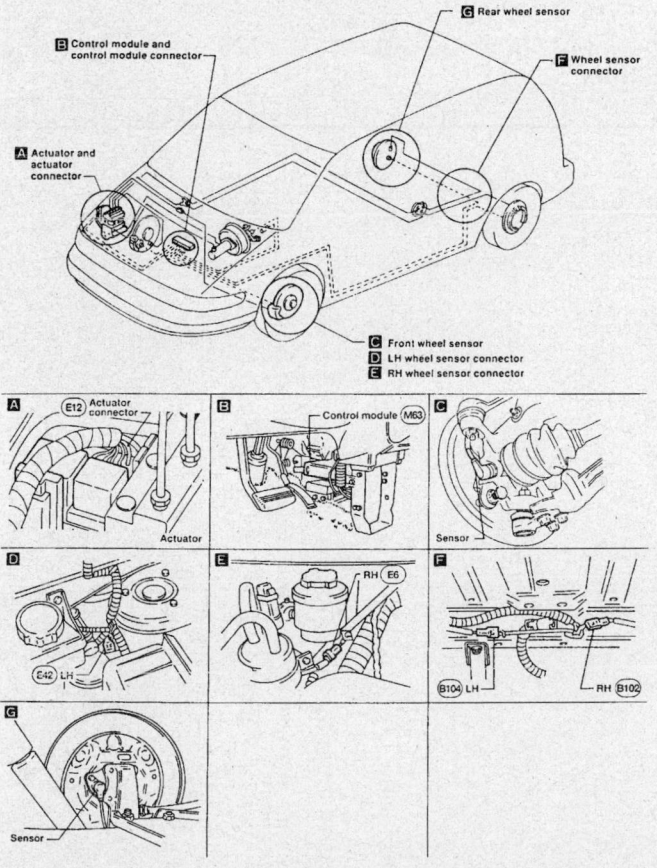

Fig. 273 ABS system component & harness connector locations. Quest

NS4029100134000X

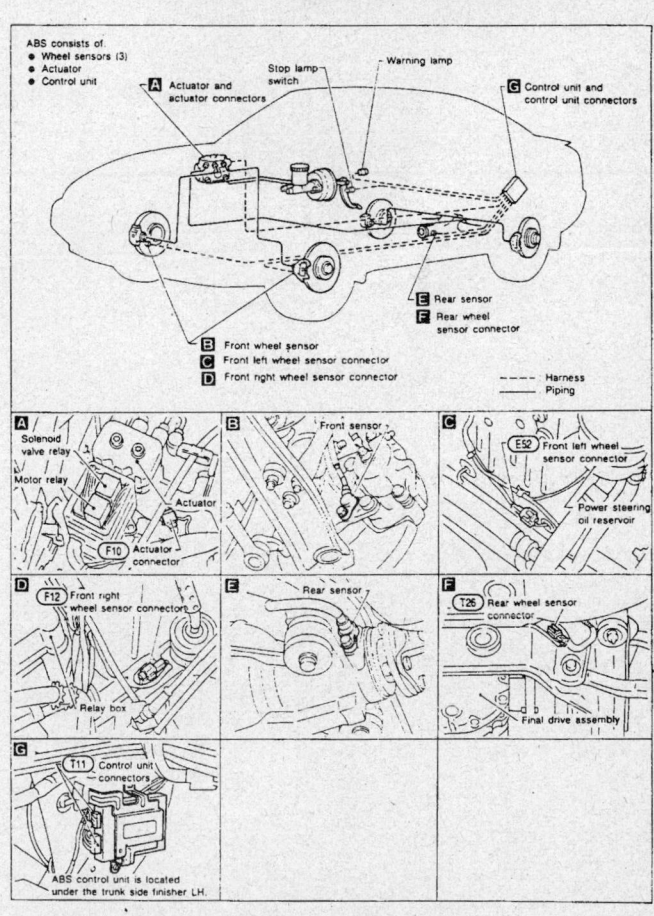

Fig. 274 ABS system component & harness connector locations. 240SX

NS4029500189000X

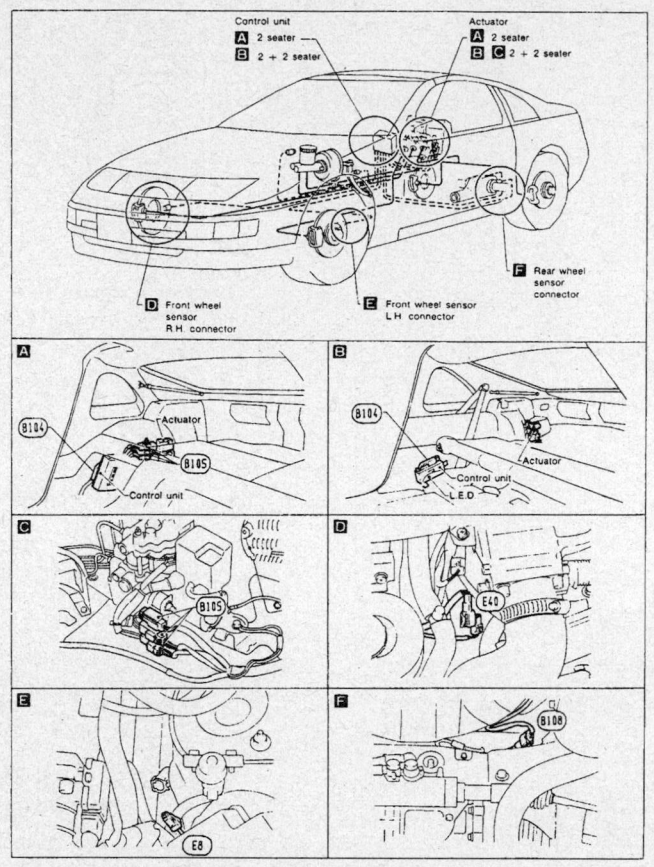

Fig. 275 ABS system component & harness connector locations. 300ZX

NS4029100137000X

Automatic Transmissions/ Transaxles

TABLE OF CONTENTS

Application Chart

Model/Year	Transaxle/ Transmission
1996	
Altima Less Limited Slip Differential	RE4F04A
Altima w/Limited Slip Differential	RE4F04V
Maxima Less Limited Slip Differential	RE4F04A
Maxima w/Limited Slip Differential	RE4F04V
Pathfinder	RE4R01A
Pickup	RL4R01A
Quest	RE4F04A
Sentra & 200SX Less Limited Slip Differential	RL4F03A
Sentra & 200SX w/Limited Slip Differential	RE4F03V
240SX	RE4R01A
300ZX Less Turbo	RE4R01A
300ZX Turbo	RE4R03A
1997	
Altima Less Limited Slip Differential	RE4F04A
Altima w/Limited Slip Differential	RE4F04V
Maxima Less Limited Slip Differential	RE4F04A
Maxima w/Limited Slip Differential	RE4F04V
Pathfinder	RE4R01A
Pickup	RE4R01A
Quest	RE4F04A
Sentra & 200SX Less Limited Slip Differential	RL4F03A
Sentra & 200SX w/Limited Slip Differential	RE4F03V
240SX	RE4R01A
1998	
Altima	RE4F04A
Frontier	RL4R01A
Maxima	RE4F04A
Pathfinder	RE4R01A
Quest	RE4F04A
Sentra w/1.6L Engine	RL4F03A
Sentra w/2.0L Engine	RE4F03A
200SX w/1.6L Engine	RL4F03A
200SX w/2.0L Engine	RE4F03A
240SX	RE4R01A
1999	
Altima	RE4F04A

Continued

Model/Year	Transaxle/ Transmission
1999	
Frontier w/2.4L Engine	RL4R01A
Frontier w/3.3L Engine	RE4R01A
Maxima	RE4F04A
Pathfinder	RE4R01A
Quest	RE4F04A
Sentra w/1.6L Engine	RL4F03A
Sentra w/2.0L Engine	RE4F03A

APPLICATION CHART

RE4R01A, RE4R03A & RL4R01A
Automatic Transmissions

NOTE: On Air Bag Equipped Models, Refer To "Air Bag System Precautions" Located In The Front Of This Manual For System Disarming & Arming Procedures.

INDEX

PRECAUTIONS

AIR BAG SYSTEMS

Refer to "Air Bag System Precautions" in the front of this manual for system disarming and arming procedures.

BATTERY GROUND CABLE

Prior to service, disconnect battery ground cable and isolate as required.

IDENTIFICATION

The transmission model number is located on a tag attached to the right side of the transmission case.

TROUBLESHOOTING

TRANSMISSION

Refer to **Figs. 1 and 2** when troubleshooting the transmission.

BRAKE TRANSMISSION SHIFT INTERLOCK

Pathfinder, Pickup & 240SX

Refer to **Fig. 3** when troubleshooting the brake transmission shift interlock.

300ZX

Refer to **Figs. 4 and 5** when troubleshooting the brake transmission shift interlock.

MAINTENANCE

FLUID CHECK

1. Ensure vehicle is at operating temperature, then park on a level surface and set parking brake.

2. Start engine, then move selector through each gear range ending in "P."
3. Check fluid with engine idling.
4. Fluid level should be within "HOT" range on dipstick.
5. Add fluid as necessary and recheck.

FLUID CHANGE

1. Raise and support vehicle, then remove oil pan to drain fluid.
2. Install oil pan using a new gasket, then fill transmission. **Use caution not to overfill transmission.**

ADJUSTMENTS

MANUAL LINKAGE

4WD Frontier, Pathfinder & Pickup

1. Place selector lever in Park range.
2. Loosen locknuts, **Fig. 6.**
3. Tighten turnbuckle until it aligns with inner cable, pulling selector lever toward reverse range side without pushing button.
4. Back off turnbuckle one turn and **torque** locknuts 36–48 inch lbs.
5. Move selector lever from Park range to 1 range. Ensure lever moves smoothly.

2WD Frontier, Pathfinder, Pickup, 240SX & 300ZX w/Floor Shift

1. Place selector lever in Park range.
2. Loosen locknuts, **Fig. 7.**
3. Tighten locknut X until it touches trunnion, pulling selector lever toward reverse range side without pushing button.
4. Back off locknut X one turn and **torque** locknut Y 8–11 ft. lbs.
5. Move selector lever from Park range to 1 range. Ensure lever moves smoothly.

2WD Frontier & Pickup w/Column Shift

1. Place selector lever in Park range.
2. Loosen locknuts, **Fig. 8.**
3. Tighten locknut A until it touches trunnion, pulling selector lever toward reverse range side without pushing button.
4. Back off locknut A two turns and **torque** locknut B to 8–11 ft. lbs.
5. Move selector lever from Park range to 1 range. Ensure lever moves smoothly.

INHIBITOR SWITCH

1. Remove manual control linkage or cable from manual shaft.
2. Place manual shaft in neutral.
3. Loosen switch attaching bolts.
4. Insert suitable aligning pin, into adjustment holes in inhibitor switch and manual shaft as near vertical as possible.
5. Install control linkage or cable, then tighten attaching bolts.

THROTTLE WIRE

RL4R01A Transmission

1. While pressing lock plate, **Fig. 9,** move adjusting tube in direction "T."
2. Return lock plate, then move throttle drum from P2 to P1 quickly.
3. Ensure throttle wire stroke "L" is within 1.5–1.65 inches between full throttle and idle.
4. **Adjust throttle wire stroke when throttle wire/accelerator wire is installed or after throttle body has been adjusted. Put marks on throttle wire to aid in measuring wire stroke.**

KICKDOWN SWITCH

1. Adjust accelerator cable as follows:
   a. Tighten adjusting nut, **Fig. 10,** until throttle drum starts to move, then

Symptom Chart

Numbers are arranged in order of probability.
Perform inspections starting with number one and work up. Circled numbers indicate that the transmission must be removed from the vehicle.

Column headers (ON vehicle): Fluid level · Control linkage · Inhibitor switch · Throttle position sensor (Adjustment) · Revolution sensor and speed sensor · Engine speed signal · Engine idling rpm · Line pressure · Control valve assembly · Shift solenoid valve A · Shift solenoid valve B · Line pressure solenoid valve · Torque converter clutch solenoid valve · Overrun clutch solenoid valve · Fluid temperature sensor · Accumulator N-D · Accumulator 1-2 · Accumulator 2-3 · Accumulator 3-4 (N-R) · Ignition switch and starter

Column headers (OFF vehicle): Torque converter · Oil pump · Reverse clutch · High clutch · Forward clutch · Forward one-way clutch · Overrun clutch · Low one-way clutch · Low & reverse brake · Brake band · Parking components

Part 1 of 3

Symptom	Probable causes (in order of probability; circled numbers = remove transmission)
Engine does not start in "N", "P" positions.	Control linkage 2, Inhibitor switch 3, Ignition switch and starter 1
Engine starts in position other than "N" and "P" positions.	Inhibitor switch 1, Ignition switch and starter 2
Transmission noise in "P" and "N" positions.	Fluid level 1, Throttle position sensor 3, Revolution sensor 4, Engine speed signal 5, Line pressure 2, Torque converter (6), Oil pump (7)
Vehicle moves when changing into "P" position or parking gear does not disengage when shifted out of "P" position.	Control linkage 1, Parking components (2)
Vehicle runs in "N" position.	Control linkage 1, Accumulator 2, Reverse clutch (4), High clutch (3), Forward clutch (5)
Vehicle will not run in "R" position (but runs in "D", "2" and "1" positions). Clutch slips. Very poor acceleration.	Control linkage 1, Line pressure 2, Control valve 4, Line pressure solenoid 3, Reverse clutch (5)(6)(7), Overrun clutch (8), Low & reverse brake (9)
Vehicle braked when shifting into "R" position.	Fluid level 1, Control linkage 2, Line pressure 3, Control valve 5, Line pressure solenoid 4, Reverse clutch (6)(8), Forward clutch (9), Low & reverse brake (7)
Sharp shock in shifting from "N" to "D" position.	Control linkage 2, Engine idling rpm 5, Line pressure 1, Control valve 3, Shift solenoid 7, Accumulator N-D 4, Accumulator 1-2 8, Forward clutch (9)
Vehicle will not run in "D" and "2" positions (but runs in "1" and "R" positions).	Control linkage 1, Parking components (2)
Vehicle will not run in "D", "1", "2" positions in "R" position). Clutch slips. Very poor acceleration.	Control linkage 1, Line pressure 2, Control valve 4, Line pressure solenoid 3, Forward clutch (6)(7)(8)(9), Low one-way clutch (10)
Clutches or brakes slip somewhat in starting.	Fluid level 1, Control linkage 2, Inhibitor switch 3, Line pressure 4, Control valve 6, Shift solenoid 5, Torque converter clutch solenoid 7, Accumulator 8, Forward clutch (13)(12)(10), Overrun clutch (9), Low & reverse brake (11)
Excessive creep.	Engine idling rpm 1
No creep at all.	Fluid level 1, Line pressure 2, Control valve 3, Torque converter (6)(5), High clutch (4)
Failure to change gear from "D1" to "D2".	Control linkage 2, Inhibitor switch 1, Throttle 5, Control valve 4, Shift solenoid 3, Brake band (6)
Failure to change gear from "D2" to "D3".	Control linkage 2, Inhibitor switch 1, Throttle 5, Control valve 4, Shift solenoid 3, High clutch (6), Overrun clutch (7)
Failure to change gear from "D3" to "D4".	Control linkage 2, Inhibitor switch 1, Throttle 3, Shift solenoid 5, Brake band (6)
Too high a gear change point from "D1" to "D2", from "D2" to "D3", from "D3" to "D4".	Inhibitor switch 1, Throttle 2, Control valve 3, Shift solenoid 4
Gear change directly from "D1" to "D3" occurs.	Control valve 2, Brake band (3)
Engine stops when shifting lever into "R", "D", "2" and "1".	Engine idling rpm 1, Line pressure 3, Control valve 2, Torque converter clutch solenoid (4)
Too sharp a shock in change from "D1" to "D2".	Inhibitor switch 1, Control valve 2, Shift solenoid 4, Accumulator 1-2 5, Accumulator 2-3 3, Brake band (6)
Too sharp a shock in change from "D2" to "D3".	Inhibitor switch 1, Control valve 2, Shift solenoid 4, Accumulator 2-3 3, High clutch (5), Overrun clutch (6)

Fig. 1 Transmission troubleshooting chart (Part 1 of 3). RE4R01A & RE4R03A transmissions

NS5029100519010A

Part 2 of 3

Symptom	Probable causes
Too sharp a shock in change from "D3" to "D4".	Inhibitor switch 1, Shift solenoid 2 4, Brake band (6), Overrun clutch (5)
Almost no shock or clutches slipping in change from "D1" to "D2".	Fluid level 1, Control valve 2, Shift solenoid 3 5, Accumulator 4, Brake band (6)
Almost no shock or slipping in change from "D2" to "D3".	Fluid level 1, Control valve 2, Shift solenoid 3 5, Accumulator 4, High clutch (6), Overrun clutch (7)
Almost no shock or slipping in change from "D3" to "D4".	Fluid level 1, Control valve 2, Shift solenoid 3 5, Accumulator 4, Brake band (6), Overrun clutch (7)
Vehicle braked by gear change from "D1" to "D2".	Control valve 1, High clutch (2)(4), Forward one-way clutch (5)(3)
Vehicle braked by gear change from "D2" to "D3".	Control valve 1, Brake band (2)
Vehicle braked by gear change from "D3" to "D4".	Control valve 1, High clutch (4), Brake band (3)(2)
Maximum speed not attained. Acceleration poor.	Fluid level 1, Control valve 2, Line pressure 5 3 4, (11)(10)(6)(7), (9)(8)
Failure to change gear from "D4" to "D3".	Inhibitor switch 1, Control valve 2, 6 4 5 3, Brake band (8), Overrun clutch (7)
Failure to change gear from "D3" to "D2" or from "D4" to "D2".	Inhibitor switch 1, Control valve 2, 5 3 4, High clutch (6)
Failure to change gear from "D2" to "D1" or from "D3" to "D1".	Inhibitor switch 1, Control valve 2, 5 3 4, Overrun clutch (7), Low & reverse brake (8)
Gear change shock felt during deceleration by releasing accelerator pedal.	Control valve 1, Shift solenoid 2 4, Overrun clutch (3)
Too high a change point from "D4" to "D3", from "D3" to "D2", from "D2" to "D1".	Inhibitor switch 1, Control valve 2
Kickdown does not operate when depressing pedal in "D4" within kickdown vehicle speed.	Inhibitor switch 1, Control valve 2, Shift solenoid 3 4
Kickdown operates or engine overruns when depressing pedal in "D4" beyond kickdown vehicle speed limit.	Inhibitor switch 2, Control valve 1, Shift solenoid 3 4
Races extremely fast or slips in changing from "D4" to "D3" when depressing pedal.	Control valve 1, Shift solenoid 2, High clutch (6)(7)
Races extremely fast or slips in changing from "D4" to "D2" when depressing pedal.	Control valve 1, Shift solenoid 2, 3 6 5, Brake band (8), Overrun clutch (7)
Races extremely fast or slips in changing from "D3" to "D2" when depressing pedal.	Control valve 1, Shift solenoid 2, 3 5 4, 6 7, (10)(9), Overrun clutch (8)
Races extremely fast or slips in changing from "D4" or "D3" to "D1" when depressing pedal.	Control valve 1, (6)(7)(8)
Vehicle will not run in any position.	Fluid level 1, Control linkage 2, (9)(5) (6), (8)(7)(10)
Transmission noise in "D", "2", "1" and "R" positions.	Control valve 1, (2)

Fig. 1 Transmission troubleshooting chart (Part 2 of 3). RE4R01A & RE4R03A transmissions

NS5029100519020A

Part 3 of 3

Symptom	Probable causes
Failure to change from "D3" to "2" when changing lever into "2" position.	Fluid level 7, Control linkage 1, Inhibitor switch 2, Control valve 6, Shift solenoid 5 4, 3, (9), Low & reverse brake (8)
Gear change from "22" to "23" in "2" position.	Control linkage 1
Engine brake does not operate in "1" position.	Fluid level 2, Inhibitor switch 1, Throttle 3, Revolution 4, Control valve 6, Shift solenoid 5, 7, Brake band (8), Low & reverse brake (9)
Gear change from "11" to "12" in "1" position.	Fluid level 2, Inhibitor switch 1
Does not change from "12" to "11" in "1" position.	Inhibitor switch 1, Control valve 2, 4 3, 5, (6), (7)
Large shock changing from "12" to "11" in "1" position.	Control valve 1, (2)
Transmission overheats.	Fluid level 1, Inhibitor switch 3, Control valve 2 4 6, 5, (14)(7)(8)(9)(11), 12, (13)(10)
ATF shoots out during operation. White smoke emitted from exhaust pipe during operation.	Fluid level 1, (2)(3)(5), (6), (7)(4)
Offensive smell at fluid charging pipe.	Fluid level 1, (2)(3)(4)(5)(7), (9)(6)
Torque converter is not locked up.	Inhibitor switch 3, Throttle 1, Revolution 2 4, Control valve 6 8, 7 5, (7)
Torque converter clutch piston slip.	Inhibitor switch 1, Control valve 2, 3 6, 5 4, (7)
Lock-up point is extremely high or low.	Inhibitor switch 1, Throttle 2, Control valve 4, 3
A/T does not shift to "D4" when driving with overdrive control switch "ON".	Inhibitor switch 2, Throttle 1, Revolution 3, Control valve 8 6 4, 5 7, (10), (9)
Engine is stopped at "R", "D", "2" and "1" positions.	Fluid level 1, Control valve 5 4 3, 2

Fig. 1 Transmission troubleshooting chart (Part 3 of 3). RE4R01A & RE4R03A transmissions

NS5029100519030A

back off 1 1/2–2 turns and secure with lock nut.

2. Adjust kickdown switch as follows:
   a. Adjust clearance "C", **Fig. 11,** between stopper rubber and end of kickdown switch thread while depressing accelerator pedal fully.
   b. Clearance "C," should be .012–.039 inch.

IN-VEHICLE REPAIRS

CONTROL VALVE ASSEMBLY & ACCUMULATORS

1. **On Frontier, Pathfinder and Pickup models,** remove front exhaust pipe.
2. **On all models,** raise and support vehicle, then remove oil pan and gasket and drain transmission fluid.
3. Remove fluid temperature sensor, if equipped or necessary.
4. Remove oil strainer, then valve body to case attaching bolts and disconnect harness electrical connector.
5. Remove solenoids and valves from valve body, if necessary.
6. Remove terminal cord assembly, if necessary.
7. Remove accumulator A, B, C and D, if necessary, using compressed air, **Fig.**

ROAD TEST SYMPTOM CHART

Numbers are arranged in order of probability.
Perform inspections starting with number one
and working up.
Circled numbers indicate that the transmission
must be removed from the vehicle.

☐ : Valve expected to be malfunctioning

NS5029100520010X

Fig. 2 Transmission troubleshooting chart (Part 1 of 4). RL4R01A transmission

NS5029100520020X

Fig. 2 Transmission troubleshooting chart (Part 2 of 4). RL4R01A transmission

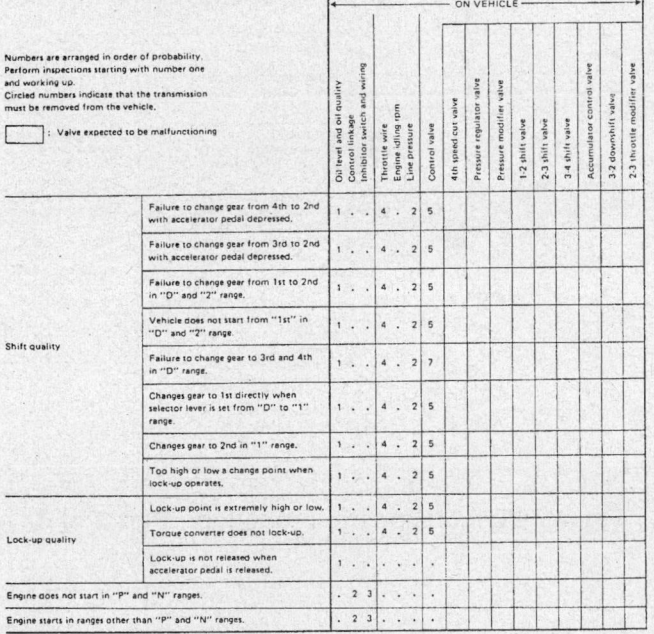

Numbers are arranged in order of probability.
Perform inspections starting with number one
and working up.
Circled numbers indicate that the transmission
must be removed from the vehicle.

☐ : Valve expected to be malfunctioning

NS5029100520030X

Fig. 2 Transmission troubleshooting chart (Part 3 of 4). RL4R01A transmission

NS5029100520040X

Fig. 2 Transmission troubleshooting chart (Part 4 of 4). RL4R01A transmission

SYMPTOM 1:
- Selector lever cannot be moved from "P" position with key in "ON" position and brake pedal applied.
- Selector lever can be moved from "P" position with key in "ON" position and brake pedal released.
- Selector lever can be moved from "P" position when key is removed from key cylinder.

SYMPTOM 2:
Ignition key cannot be removed when selector lever is set to "P" position. It can be removed when selector lever is set to any position except "P".

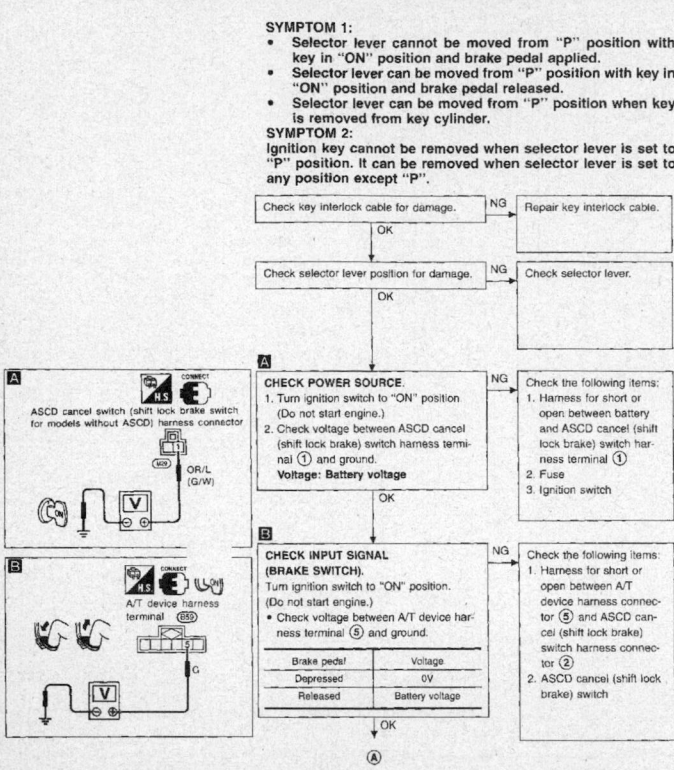

NS5029600585010X

Fig. 3 BTSI diagnostic procedure (Part 1 of 2). Pathfinder, Pickup & 240SX

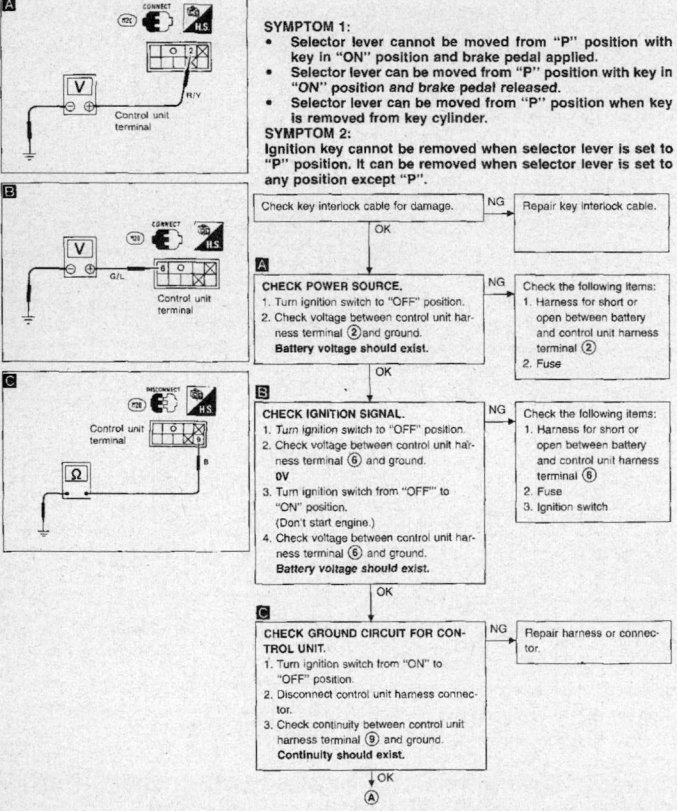

NS5029600588010X

Fig. 4 BTSI diagnostic procedure (Part 1 of 4). 300ZX

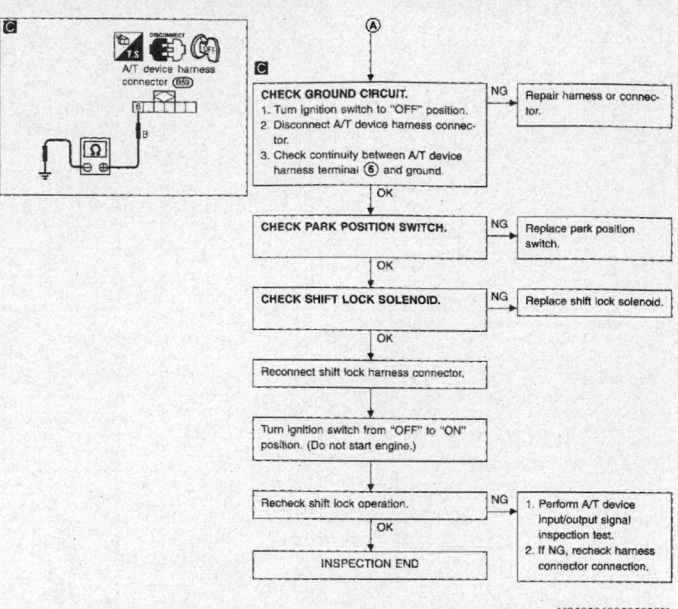

NS5029600585020X

Fig. 3 BTSI diagnostic procedure (Part 2 of 2). Pathfinder, Pickup & 240SX

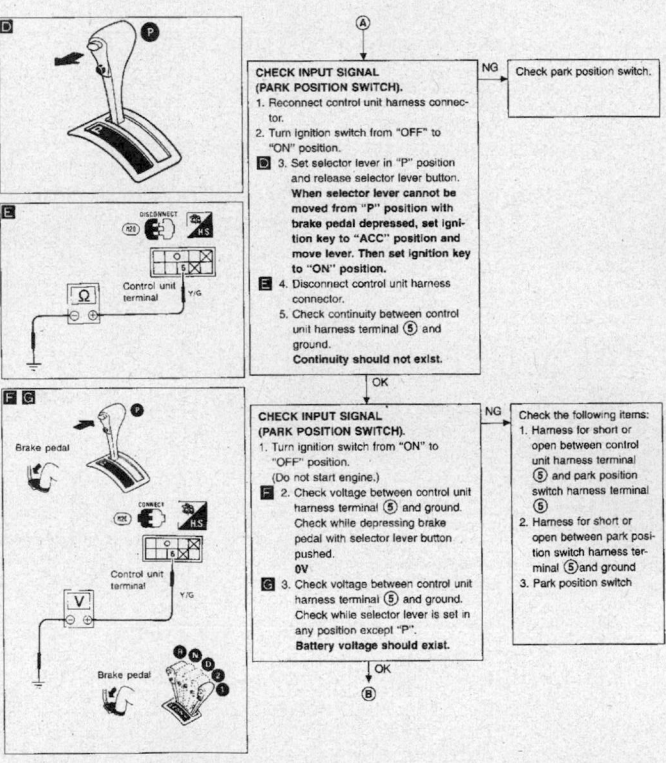

NS5029600588020X

Fig. 4 BTSI diagnostic procedure (Part 2 of 4). 300ZX

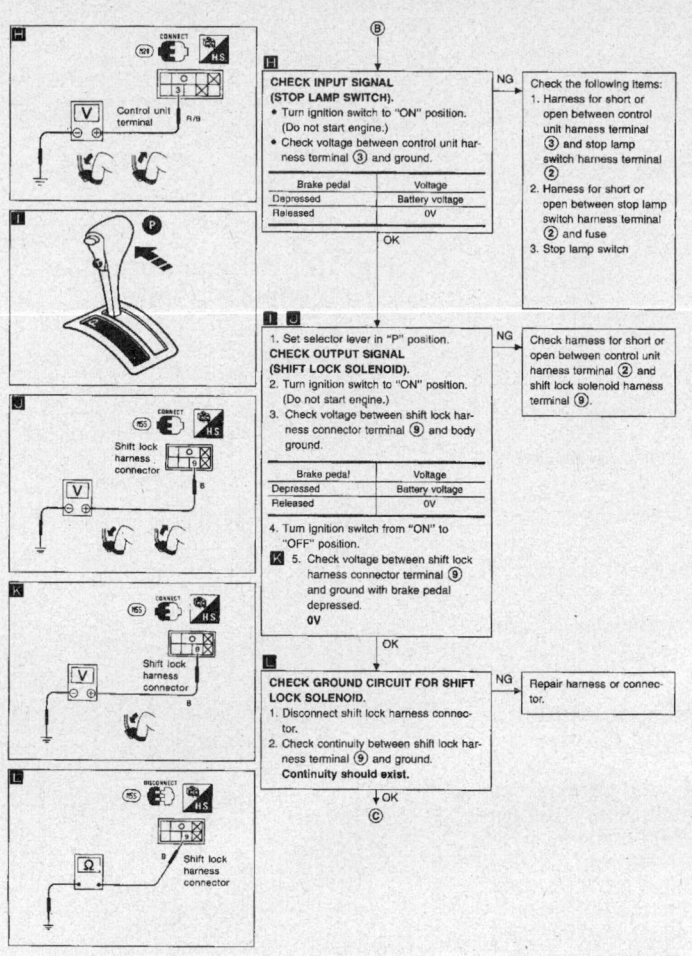

CHECK INPUT SIGNAL (STOP LAMP SWITCH).
- Turn ignition switch to "ON" position. (Do not start engine.)
- Check voltage between control unit harness terminal ③ and ground.

Brake pedal	Voltage
Depressed	Battery voltage
Released	0V

NG → Check the following items:
1. Harness for short or open between control unit harness terminal ③ and stop lamp switch harness terminal ②.
2. Harness for short or open between stop lamp switch harness terminal ② and fuse.
3. Stop lamp switch

OK ↓

1. Set selector lever in "P" position.
CHECK OUTPUT SIGNAL (SHIFT LOCK SOLENOID).
2. Turn ignition switch to "ON" position. (Do not start engine.)
3. Check voltage between shift lock harness connector terminal ⑨ and body ground.

Brake pedal	Voltage
Depressed	Battery voltage
Released	0V

4. Turn ignition switch from "ON" to "OFF" position.
5. Check voltage between shift lock harness connector terminal ⑨ and ground with brake pedal depressed.
0V

NG → Check harness for short or open between control unit harness terminal ② and shift lock solenoid harness terminal ⑨.

OK ↓

CHECK GROUND CIRCUIT FOR SHIFT LOCK SOLENOID.
1. Disconnect shift lock harness connector.
2. Check continuity between shift lock harness terminal ⑨ and ground.
Continuity should exist.

NG → Repair harness or connector.

OK ↓ Ⓒ

NS5029600588030X

Fig. 4 BTSI diagnostic procedure (Part 3 of 4). 300ZX

Ⓒ ↓

Check shift lock solenoid. — **NG** → Replace A/T shift lock control device assembly.

OK ↓

1. Reconnect shift lock harness connector.
2. Turn ignition switch from "OFF" to "ON" position.
3. Recheck shift lock operation.

NG →
1. Perform control unit input/output signal inspection test.
2. If NG, recheck harness connector connection.

OK ↓

INSPECTION END

NS5029600588040X

Fig. 4 BTSI diagnostic procedure (Part 4 of 4). 300ZX

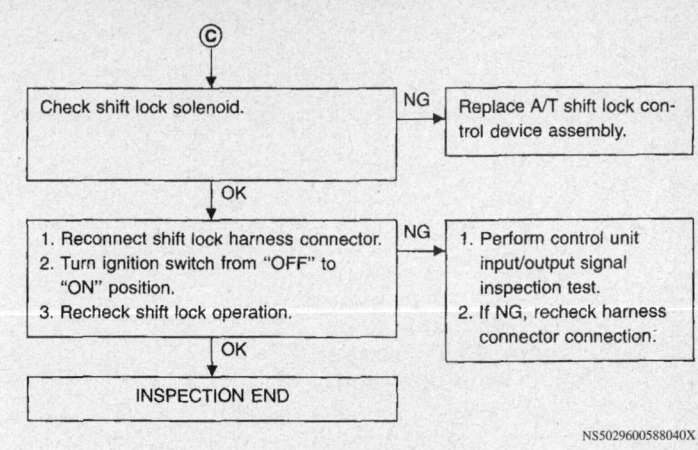

NS5028900140000X

Fig. 7 Manual linkage adjustment. 2WD Frontier, Pathfinder, Pickup, 240SX & 300ZX w/floor shift

Installation

1. Set key interlock cable to steering lock assembly and install lock plate.
2. Clamp cable to steering column and fix to control cable with band.
3. Set selector lever to P position.
4. Insert interlock rod into adjuster holder.
5. Install casing cap to bracket.
6. Move slider in order to fix adjuster holder to interlock rod.

REAR OIL SEAL

1. Raise and support vehicle, then disconnect driveshaft.
2. **On 4WD Frontier, Pathfinder and Pickup models,** remove transfer case. Refer to "4 Wheel Drive" section for transfer case removal.
3. **On all models,** use suitable tool to remove old seal.
4. Coat new seal with new transmission fluid and install.
5. Install driveshaft.

REVOLUTION SENSOR

1. Raise and support vehicle.
2. **On 300ZX models,** remove exhaust tube.
3. **On 4WD Frontier, Pathfinder, Pickup and 240SX models,** proceed as follows:
   a. Support transmission using suitable jack, then remove rear engine mounting crossmember.

Terminal No. ⊕	⊖	Item	Condition	Judgment standard
①		Shift lock signal	When selector lever is set in "P" position and brake pedal is depressed.	Battery voltage
			Except above	0V
②		Power source	Any condition	Battery voltage
③		Stop lamp switch	When brake pedal is depressed.	Battery voltage
			When brake pedal is released.	0V
⑤	⑨	Park position switch	• When the key is in key cylinder, selector lever is in "P" position, and selector lever button pushed. • When selector lever is set in any position except "P".	Battery voltage
			Except above	0V
⑥		Ignition signal		Battery voltage
			Except above	0V

NS5029600589000X

Fig. 5 Shift lock control unit inspection table. 300ZX

12. Cover each piston with a shop towel when removing.
8. Reverse procedure to install. **Always use new sealing parts.**

KEY INTERLOCK CABLE, REPLACE

Removal

1. Unlock slider from adjuster holder and remove rod from cable at shift selector.
2. Remove lock plate and cable from steering lock.

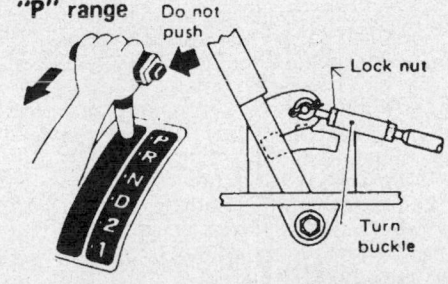

NS5028900139000X

Fig. 6 Manual linkage adjustment. 4WD Frontier, Pathfinder & Pickup

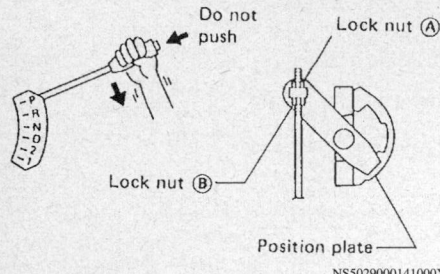

Fig. 8 Manual linkage adjustment. 2WD Frontier & Pickup w/column shift

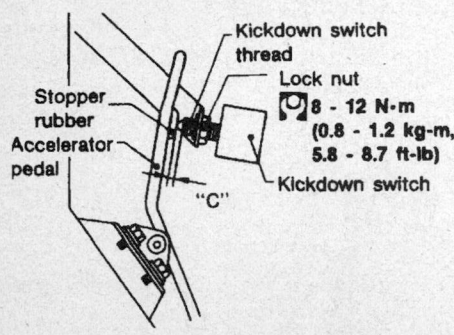

Fig. 11 Kickdown switch adjustment

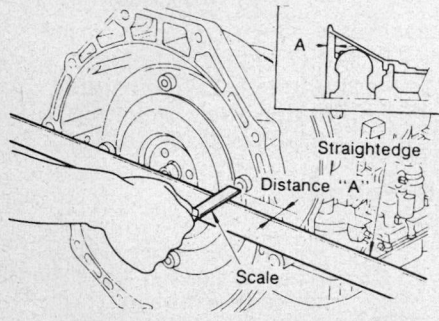

Fig. 13 Torque converter installation measurement. Frontier w/2.4L engine

b. Lower transmission as much as possible.
4. **On all models,** remove revolution sensor.
5. Reverse procedure to install.

PARKING COMPONENTS

1. **On 300ZX models,** remove exhaust tube.
2. **On all models,** remove driveshaft.
3. **On 4WD Frontier, Pathfinder and Pickup models,** remove transfer case. Refer to "4 Wheel Drive" section for transfer case removal.
4. **On 4WD Frontier, Pathfinder and Pickup models,** remove manual control linkage from adapter case.
5. **On 2WD Frontier, Pickup, 240SX and 300ZX models,** support transmission using a suitable jack, then remove rear engine mounting crossmember.
6. **On 4WD Frontier, Pathfinder and**

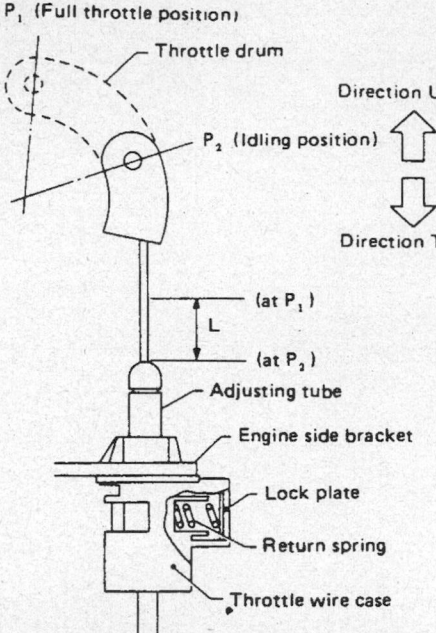

Fig. 9 Throttle wire adjustment. RL4R01A transmission

Pickup models, support transmission with a suitable jack, then remove adapter case from transmission.
7. **On 2WD Frontier, Pickup, 240SX and 300ZX models,** remove rear extension housing from transmission.
8. **On all models,** inspect parking components and replace as necessary.
9. Reverse procedure to install.

TRANSMISSION
REPLACE
FRONTIER
2.4L Engine

1. Raise and support vehicle.
2. Remove dipstick tube, then disconnect transmission cooler lines from transmission. Plug openings.
3. Mark propeller shaft flanges for assembly.
4. Remove mounting bolts and separate propeller shaft from final drive.
5. Remove propeller shaft. **Plug rear oil seal.**
6. Remove control cable from manual shaft.
7. Disconnect transmission and vehicle speed sensor harness connectors.
8. Disconnect throttle wire.
9. Remove starter motor.
10. Remove torque converter to drive plate mounting bolts.
11. Support transmission assembly with suitable jack. Secure to jack.
12. Remove rear mounting bracket from body and transmission assembly.
13. Remove bolts mounting transmission assembly to engine.
14. Remove transmission assembly by pulling backwards. slanting and lowering.

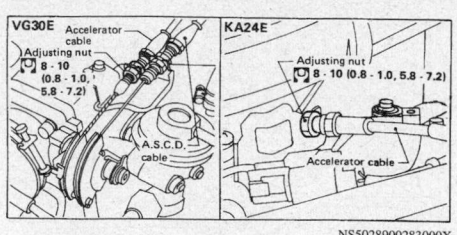

Fig. 10 Accelerator cable adjusting nut

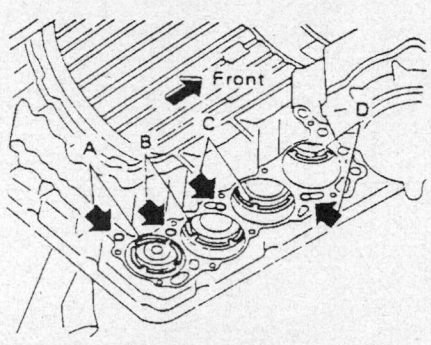

Fig. 12 Accumulator A, B, C & D removal

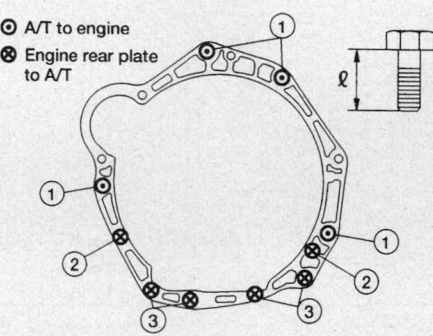

Fig. 14 Transmission attaching bolt specifications (Part 1 of 2). Frontier w/2.4L engine

15. Reverse procedure to install, noting the following:
    a. If drive plate runout is more than .0059 inch, replace drive plate and ring gear. **Do not allow magnetic materials to contact ring gear teeth.**
    b. When installing torque converter to transaxle, ensure distance A is more than 1.024 inch, **Fig. 13.**
    c. Tighten transaxle mounting bolts, **Fig. 14** to specifications.

3.3L Engine

1. Raise and support vehicle.
2. Remove front and rear exhaust pipes.
3. Remove dipstick tube, then disconnect transmission cooler lines from transmission. Plug openings.
4. Mark propeller shaft flanges for assembly.
5. Remove mounting bolts and separate

Bolt No.	Tightening torque ft-lb	Bolt length "ℓ" mm (in)
①	29 - 36	43 (1.69)
②	2.2 - 2.9	16 (0.63)
③	12 - 16	16 (0.63)

NS5029800755020X

Fig. 14 Transmission attaching bolt specifications (Part 2 of 2). Frontier w/2.4L engine

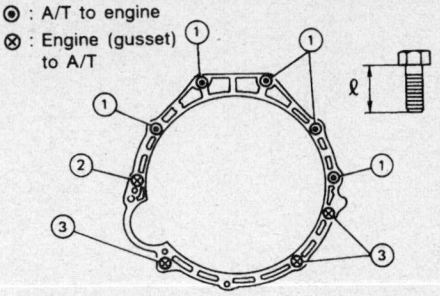

⊙ : A/T to engine
⊗ : Engine (gusset) to A/T

NS5019800756010X

Fig. 15 Transmission attaching bolt specifications (Part 1 of 2). Frontier w/3.3L engine

Bolt No.	Tightening torque ft-lb	Bolt length "ℓ" mm (in)
1	29 - 36	47.5 (1.870)
2	29 - 36	58.0 (2.283)
3	22 - 29	25.0 (0.984)
Gusset to engine	22 - 29	20.0 (0.787)

NS5019800756020X

Fig. 15 Transmission attaching bolt specifications (Part 2 of 2). Frontier w/3.3L engine

propeller shaft from final drive.
6. Remove propeller shaft. **Plug rear oil seal.**
7. Remove control linkage from transfer case.
8. Remove control cable from transmission manual shaft.
9. Disconnect transmission and vehicle speed sensor harness connectors.
10. Remove starter motor.
11. Remove gusset and rear plate cover mounting engine to transmission.
12. Remove torque converter to drive plate mounting bolts.
13. Support transmission assembly with suitable jack. Secure to jack.
14. Remove rear mounting bracket from body and transmission assembly.
15. Remove bolts mounting transmission assembly to engine.
16. Remove transmission and transfer case by lowering.
17. Reverse procedure to install, noting the following:
    a. If drive plate runout is more than .0059 inch, replace drive plate and ring gear. **Do not allow magnetic materials to contact ring gear teeth.**
    b. When installing torque converter to transaxle, ensure distance A is more than 1.024 inch, **Fig. 13.**
    c. Tighten transaxle mounting bolts, **Fig. 15** to specifications.

PATHFINDER & PICKUP

1. Raise and support vehicle.
2. Remove front exhaust pipe.
3. Remove dipstick tube, then disconnect transmission cooler lines from transmission and plug openings.
4. Remove propeller shaft(s) and insert plug into rear oil seal to prevent leakage.
5. **On 4WD models,** proceed as follows:
    a. Disconnect transfer control linkage from transfer case.
    b. Remove torsion bar adjusting nut, then slide back dust cover and remove snap ring from anchor arm.
    c. Remove torque arm attaching nuts, then slide torsion bar forward with torque arm attached and remove from vehicle.
    d. Remove second crossmember.
    e. Remove speedometer cable from transfer case, then disconnect control cable from transmission.
6. **On 2WD models,** remove speedome-

ter cable from transmission, then disconnect control linkage from selector lever.
7. **On all models,** disconnect transmission harness connectors, then remove starter motor.
8. Remove gusset attaching engine to transmission assembly, then the bolts attaching torque converter to driveplate.
9. Support transmission assembly with a suitable jack and secure to jack, then remove rear mounting bracket from body and transmission assembly.
10. Remove bolts attaching transmission assembly to engine.
11. **On 4WD models,** lower transmission assembly and remove from vehicle.
12. **On 2WD models,** slide transmission assembly backwards, slant and lower assembly, then remove from vehicle.
13. **On all models,** reverse procedure to install.

240SX

1. Raise and support vehicle.
2. Disconnect transmission harness connectors and clamps.
3. Remove dipstick tube, then disconnect transmission cooler line from right side of transmission and plug openings.
4. Disconnect control linkage from selector lever, then remove propeller shaft.
5. Remove heat shield from catalytic converter, then exhaust tube bracket and separate rear exhaust tube from converter.
6. Remove starter motor, then the gus-

sets and end plate.
7. Remove bolts attaching torque converter to driveplate.
8. Support transmission assembly with a suitable jack and secure to jack, then remove rear mounting bracket from body and transmission assembly.
9. Lower transmission as much as possible, then disconnect transmission cooler line from left side of transmission and plug opening.
10. Remove bolts attaching transmission assembly to engine, then lower assembly and remove from vehicle.
11. Reverse procedure to install.

300ZX

1. Raise and support vehicle.
2. Remove exhaust tube, then disconnect transmission harness connectors and clamps.
3. Remove dipstick tube, then disconnect transmission cooler lines from transmission and plug openings.
4. Disconnect control linkage from selector lever, then remove propeller shaft.
5. Remove starter motor if necessary, then the gusset attaching engine to transmission.
6. Remove bolts attaching torque converter to driveplate.
7. Support transmission assembly with a suitable jack and secure to jack, then remove rear mounting bracket from body and transmission assembly.
8. Remove bolts attaching transmission assembly to engine, then lower assembly and remove from vehicle.
9. Reverse procedure to install.

TIGHTENING SPECIFICATIONS

Year	Component	Torque/ Ft. Lbs.
1996–99	Control Valve Assembly To Transmission Case	60-80①
	Control Valve Lower Body To Upper Body	60-80①
	Detent Spring Manual Plate To Transmission	22–29
	Extension Housing To Transmission	14–18
	Inhibitor Switch	12–24①
	Line Pressure Solenoid	60-80①
	Oil Cooler Tube Bracket	48–72①
	Oil Pan To Transmission Housing	60-80①
	Oil Pump Cover To Oil Pump Housing	12–15
	Oil Strainer To Control Valve	60-80①
	Parking Actuator To Extension Housing	17–22
	Revolution Sensor To Extension Housing	48–60①
	Revolution Sensor To Transmission Case	48–60①
	Servo Assembly To Transmission Case	60-80①
	Three Unit Solenoid Assembly	60-80①
	Torque Converter Housing To Transmission	45–47
	Torque Converter To Driveplate	33–43

① — Inch lbs.

RE4F04A & RE4F04V Automatic Transaxles

NOTE: On Air Bag Equipped Models, Refer To "Air Bag System Precautions" Located In The Front Of This Manual For System Disarming & Arming Procedures.

INDEX

PRECAUTIONS

BATTERY GROUND CABLE

Prior to service, disconnect battery ground cable and isolate as required.

AIR BAG SYSTEMS

Refer to "Air Bag System Precautions" in the front of this manual for system disarming and arming procedures.

IDENTIFICATION

The transaxle is identified by a tag stamped into the transaxle case. Refer to **Fig. 1** for transaxle identification tag location.

TROUBLESHOOTING

TRANSAXLE

Refer to **Fig. 2** for transaxle troubleshooting.

BRAKE TRANSMISSION SHIFT INTERLOCK

Refer to **Fig. 3** when troubleshooting the brake transmission shift interlock.

MAINTENANCE

FLUID CHECK

Fluid level should be checked using "HOT" range on dipstick at fluid temperature of 151–171°F after vehicle has been driven approximately 15 minutes under normal driving conditions.
1. Check for fluid leakage.
2. Park vehicle on level surface and set parking brake.
3. Start engine, then move gear selector lever through all gear ranges, ending in Park.
4. Check fluid level with engine idling.
5. If fluid level is low, add Dexron II fluid to

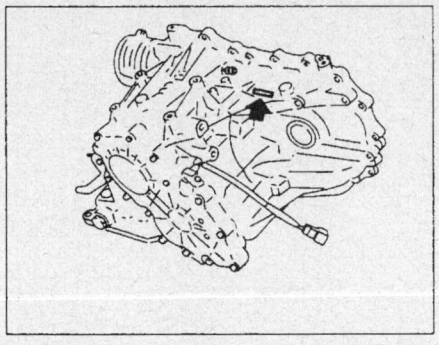

Fig. 1 Transaxle identification

Fig. 2 Transaxle troubleshooting chart (Part 2 of 3)

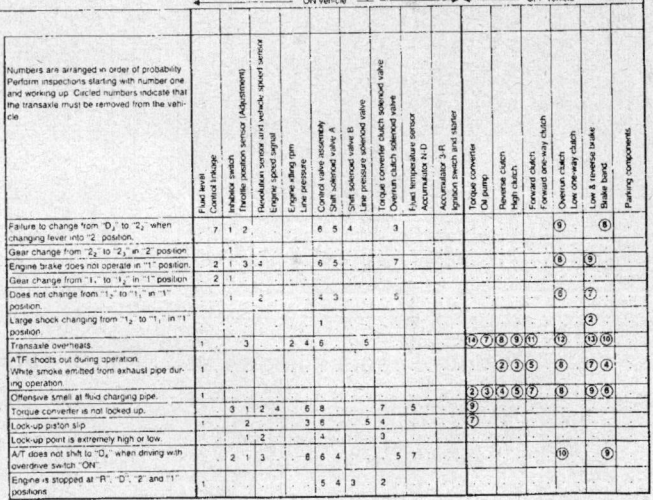

Fig. 2 Transaxle troubleshooting chart (Part 1 of 3)

Fig. 2 Transaxle troubleshooting chart (Part 3 of 3)

charging pipe. **Do not overfill transaxle fluid.**

ADJUSTMENTS

CONTROL CABLE

1. Place selector lever in Park.
2. Loosen locknuts.
3. Tighten locknut, **Fig. 4,** pulling selector lever toward Reverse side.
4. Move selector lever from Park to 1 range. Ensure selector lever moves smoothly.

INHIBITOR SWITCH

1. Remove control cable from manual shaft.
2. Set manual shaft in "N" position.
3. Loosen inhibitor switch fixing bolts.
4. Insert pin into adjustment holes in both inhibitor switch and manual shaft, as near vertical as possible, **Fig. 5.**

IN-VEHICLE REPAIRS

CONTROL VALVE ASSEMBLY & ACCUMULATOR, REPLACE

1. Drain fluid from transaxle, then remove oil and pan.
2. Disconnect transaxle solenoid harness electrical connector.
3. Remove stopper ring from transaxle solenoid harness terminal body.
4. Remove transaxle solenoid harness from transaxle case by pushing on terminal body.
5. Remove control valve assembly by removing fixed bolts, **Fig. 6. Do not drop manual valve, tube connector, tubes or 3-R accumulator return spring.**
6. Remove 3-R and N-D return springs by applying compressed air and holding each piston with a rag, if necessary.
7. Reverse procedure to install, noting the following:
   a. Set manual shaft in Neutral, then align manual plate with groove in manual valve.

SYMPTOM 1:
- Selector lever cannot be moved from "P" position with key in "ON" position and brake pedal applied.
- Selector lever can be moved from "P" position with key in "ON" position and brake pedal released.
- Selector lever can be moved from "P" position when key is removed from key cylinder.

SYMPTOM 2:
Ignition key cannot be removed when selector lever is set to "P" position. It can be removed when selector lever is set to any position except "P".

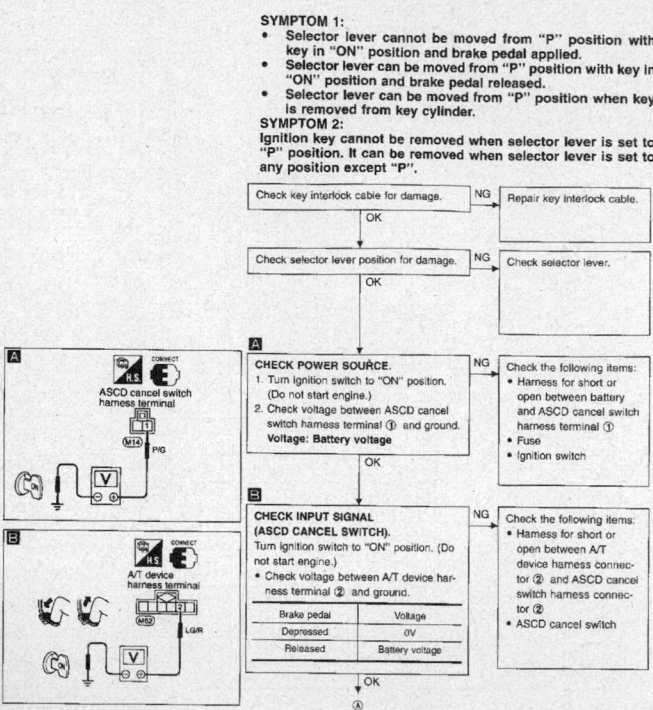

Fig. 3   BTSI diagnostic procedure (Part 1 of 2)

NS5029600586010X

Fig. 3   BTSI diagnostic procedure (Part 2 of 2)

NS5029600586020X

Unit: mm (in)

①	5 bolts	ℓ = 40 (1.57)
⊗	6 bolts	ℓ = 33 (1.30)
●	2 bolts	ℓ = 43.5 (1.713)

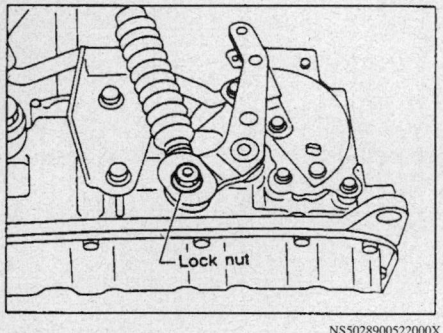

NS5028900522000X

Fig. 4   Control cable adjustment

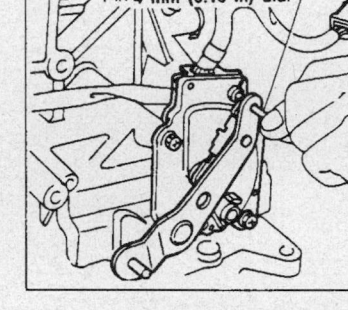

Pin 4 mm (0.16 in) dia.

NS5028900521000X

Fig. 5   Inhibitor switch adjustment

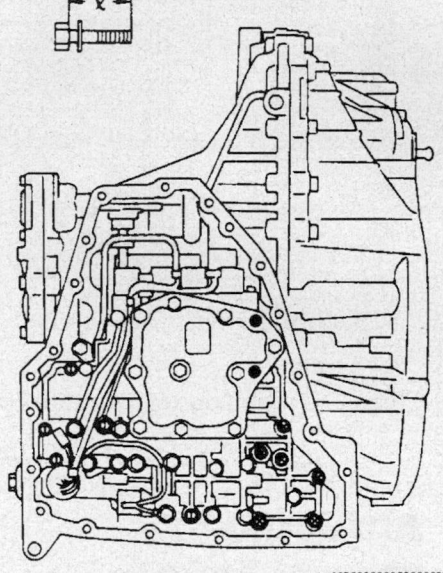

NS5028900520000X

Fig. 6   Control valve assembly bolt identification

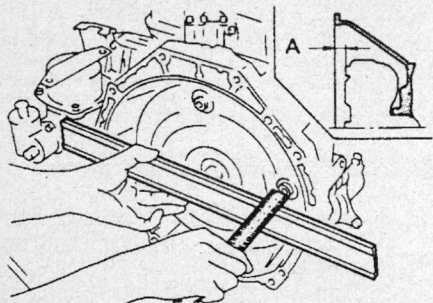

NS5029100544000X

Fig. 7   Torque converter clearance measurement. 1996–98

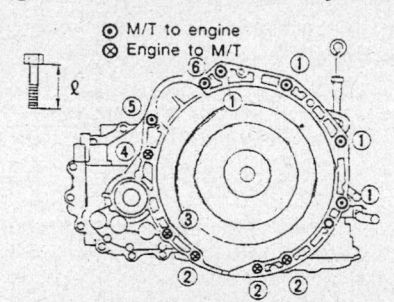

⊙ M/T to engine
⊗ Engine to M/T

Bolt No.	Tightening torque N·m (kg-m, ft-lb)	ℓ mm (in)
1	39 - 49 (4.0 - 5.0, 29 - 36)	45 (1.77)
2	30 - 36 (3.1 - 3.7, 22 - 27)	30 (1.18)
3	30 - 36 (3.1 - 3.7, 22 - 27)	40 (1.57)
4	74 - 83 (7.5 - 8.5, 54 - 61)	45 (1.77)
5	30 - 36 (3.1 - 3.7, 22 - 27)	80 (3.15)
6	30 - 36 (3.1 - 3.7, 22 - 27)	65 (2.56)

NS5029100545000X

Fig. 8   Transaxle to engine bolt location & tightening specifications. 1996–98 Altima

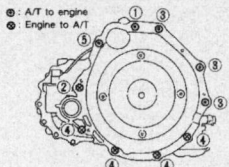

Bolt No.	Tightening torque N·m (kg-m, ft-lb)	mm (in)
1	70 - 79 (7.1 - 8.1, 51 - 59)	65 (2.56)
2	70 - 79 (7.1 - 8.1, 51 - 59)	52 (2.05)
3	70 - 79 (7.1 - 8.1, 51 - 59)	52 (2.05)
4	70 - 79 (7.1 - 8.1, 51 - 59)	40 (1.57)
5	70 - 79 (7.1 - 8.1, 51 - 59)	124 (4.88)

NS5029100546000A

Fig. 9   Transaxle to engine bolt location & tightening specifications. 1996–98 Maxima

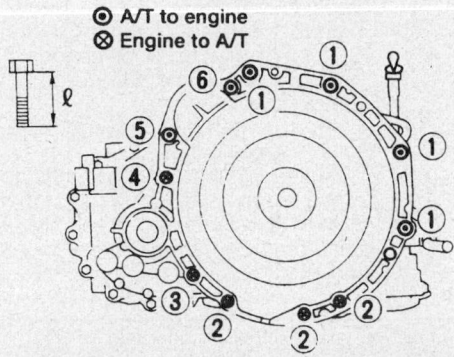

NS5029800733000X

Fig. 11   Transaxle attaching bolt specifications (Part 1 of 2). 1999 Altima, I30 & Maxima

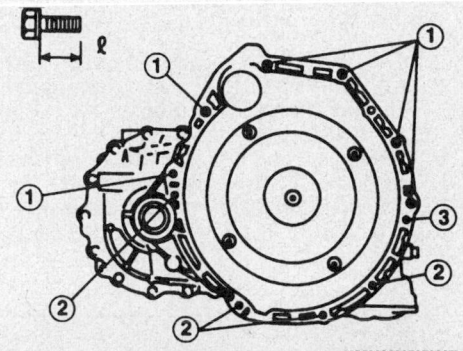

NS5029800737000X

Fig. 12   Transaxle attaching bolt specifications (Part 1 of 2). 1999 Quest

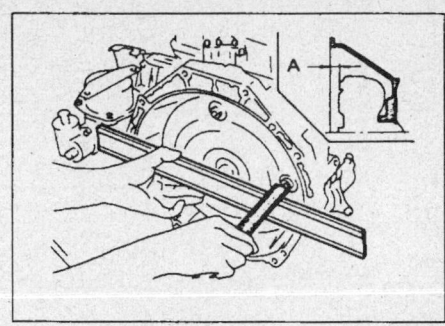

NS5028900523000X

Fig. 10   Torque converter installation measurement. 1999

Bolt No.	Tightening torque N·m (kg-m, ft-lb)	ℓ mm (in)
1	39 - 49 (4.0 - 5.0, 29 - 36)	45 (1.77)
2	30 - 36 (3.1 - 3.7, 22 - 27)	30 (1.18)
3	30 - 36 (3.1 - 3.7, 22 - 27)	40 (1.57)
4	74 - 83 (7.5 - 8.5, 54 - 61)	45 (1.77)
5	30 - 36 (3.1 - 3.7, 22 - 27)	80 (3.15)
6	30 - 36 (3.1 - 3.7, 22 - 27)	65 (2.56)

NS5029800734000X

Fig. 11   Transaxle attaching bolt specifications (Part 2 of 2). 1999 Altima, I30 & Maxima

3. Remove cotter pin and nut securing lower ball joint to knuckle.
4. Separate lower ball joint from knuckle.
5. Separate driveshaft from knuckle by tapping lightly (use a puller, if necessary). When removing driveshaft, cover boots to prevent damage.
6. Remove right driveshaft from transaxle.
7. Remove left driveshaft with a suitable puller tool. Use caution not to damage pinion mate shaft and side gear.
8. Remove bolts securing torque converter to driveplate by turning crankshaft.
9. When transaxle is disconnected, scribe matching marks on torque converter and driveplate to ease installation.
10. Reverse procedure to install, noting the following:
   a. When connecting torque converter to transaxle, measure distance "A" shown in **Fig. 7**. Correct distance on Altima and Maxima with VG30E engine is greater than .75 inch.
   b. Tighten transaxle securing bolts as shown in **Figs. 8 and 9**.
   c. Ensure fluid level is correct. Cycle selector lever through all positions and ensure correct operation.

1999

1. Remove battery and bracket.
2. Remove air cleaner and resonator.
3. Disconnect terminal cord assembly and park/neutral position switch wiring harnesses.
4. **On Quest models**, proceed as follows:
   a. Remove revolution sensor, ground and vehicle speed sensor connectors.
   b. Remove heated oxygen sensor.
   c. Remove exhaust manifolds.
5. **On all models**, remove crankshaft position sensor from assembly.

b. Following control valve installation, ensure selector lever can be moved to all positions.

KEY INTERLOCK CABLE, REPLACE

Removal

1. Unlock slider from adjuster holder and remove rod from cable at shift selector.
2. Remove lock plate and cable from steering lock.

Installation

1. Set key interlock cable to steering lock assembly and install lock plate.
2. Clamp cable to steering column and fix to control cable with band.

3. Set selector lever to P position.
4. Insert interlock rod into adjuster holder.
5. Install casing cap to bracket.
6. Move slider in order to fix adjuster holder to interlock rod.

TRANSAXLE

REPLACE

1996-98

1. Raise and support front of vehicle. Remove front wheels.
2. Remove wheel bearing locknut. **Do not allow brake hose to stretch or twist.**

Bolt No.	Tightening torque N·m (kg-m, ft-lb)	ℓ mm (in)
①	39 - 49 (4.0 - 5.0, 29 - 36)	60 (2.36)
②	30 - 40 (3.1 - 4.1, 22 - 30)	25 (0.98)
③*	30 - 40 (3.1 - 4.1, 22 - 30)	25 (0.98)

*: TORX bolt

NS5029800738000X

Fig. 12 Transaxle attaching bolt specifications (Part 2 of 2). 1999 Quest

6. Remove lefthand transaxle and body mounting bracket.
7. Disconnect control cable.
8. Raise and support vehicle.
9. Remove driveshafts as described under "Differential Side Oil Seal, Replace" in "In-Vehicle Service."
10. Disconnect oil cooler piping.
11. Remove starter motor.

12. Support engine with suitable jack under oil pan. **Do not place jack under oil pan drain plug.**
13. Remove center member.
14. Remove rear cover plate, then the torque converter mounting bolts.
15. Support transaxle with suitable jack.
16. Remove bolts mounting transaxle to engine.

17. Lower transaxle from vehicle.
18. Reverse procedure to install, noting the following:
    a. If drive plate runout is more than .0059 inch, replace drive plate and ring gear. **Do not allow magnetic materials to contact ring gear teeth.**
    b. When installing torque converter to transaxle, ensure distance A is more than .75 inch on Altima, Maxima and I30 models, or .55 inch on Quest models, **Fig. 10.**
    c. Tighten transaxle mounting bolts, **Figs. 11 and 12** to specifications.
    d. Tighten lefthand mounting bracket bolts to specifications.
    e. Tighten center member mounting bolts to specifications.
    f. Tighten rear plate cover bolts to specifications.
    g. Ensure fluid level is correct. Cycle selector lever through all positions and ensure correct operation.

TIGHTENING SPECIFICATIONS

Year	Component	Torque/ Ft. Lbs.
1996–99	Control Cable Locknut	23–31
	Control Valve Body To Transaxle Case	60–80②
	Converter Housing To Engine	①
	Detent Spring	66②
	Drain Plug	22–29
	Driveplate To Engine	105–112
	Driveplate To Torque Converter	33–43
	Governor Valve Body To Governor Shaft	48–60②
	Gusset To Converter Housing	12–15
	Inhibitor Switch To Transaxle Case	23–35②
	Oil Cooler Pipe To Transaxle Case	22–36
	Oil Strainer To Lower Valve Body	84–108②
	Oil Tube To Converter Housing	35–43②
	Revolution Sensor	43–60②
	Side Cover	20–22
	Speedometer Pinion	43–60②
	Transaxle Case To Converter Housing	32–35
	Transaxle Case To Front Cover	14–17

① — Refer to "Transaxle, Replace."

② — Inch lbs.

RE4F03A, RL4F03A & RE4F03V Automatic Transaxles

NOTE: On Air Bag Equipped Models, Refer To "Air Bag System Precautions" Located In The Front Of This Manual For System Disarming & Arming Procedures.

INDEX

PRECAUTIONS

BATTERY GROUND CABLE

Prior to service, disconnect battery ground cable and isolate as required.

AIR BAG SYSTEMS

Refer to "Air Bag System Precautions" in the front of this manual for system disarming and arming procedures.

IDENTIFICATION

The transaxle identification serial number is attached on the upper face of the transmission case.

TROUBLESHOOTING

TRANSAXLE

Refer to **Figs. 1 and 2,** when troubleshooting the transaxle.

BRAKE TRANSMISSION SHIFT INTERLOCK

Refer to **Figs. 3 through 4,** when troubleshooting the brake transmission shift interlock.

MAINTENANCE

FLUID CHECK

To check fluid, drive vehicle for at least 5 minutes to bring fluid to operating temperature (122–176°F). With vehicle on a level surface and engine idling in Park and parking brake applied, move gear selector through all gear positions and return to P position. Dipsticks may be marked with Hot and Cold ranges. Use cold range if fluid is between (86–120°F).

ROAD TEST SYMPTOM CHART
Numbers are arranged in order of probability.
Perform inspections starting with number one and work up.
Circled numbers indicate that the transaxle must be removed from the vehicle.
☐ : Valve expected to be malfunctioning

		ON VEHICLE														
		Oil level and oil quality	Control cable	Inhibitor switch and wiring	Throttle wire	Engine idling rpm	Line pressure	Control valve	Throttle valve & detent valve	Manual valve	Pressure regulator valve	3-4 shift valve	2-3 shift valve	1-2 shift valve	Overrun clutch control valve	Pressure modifier valve
Sharp shocks in shifting from "N" to "D" range		1	2		5	3	4	7								
Shift shocks	When shifting from 1st to 2nd or 2nd to 3rd	1	2		4		3	6								
	When shifting from 3rd to 4th	1	2		4		3	5								
	When shifting from D to 2 and 1 range. When O.D. switch is set from "ON" to "OFF"	1	2		4		3	5								
	When shifting from 2nd to 1st in "1" range	1	2		4		3	5								
Shift slippage when upshifting	When shifting from 1st to 2nd	1	2		4		3	5								
	When shifting from 2nd to 3rd	1	2		4		3	6								
	When shifting from 3rd to 4th	1	2		4		3	5								
Shift slippage with accelerator pedal depressed	When shifting from 4th to 2nd	1	2		5		3	6								
	When shifting from 4th to 3rd	1	2		4		3	6								
	When shifting from 4th to 1st and shifting from 3rd to 1st	1	2		5		3	6								
Poor power/acceleration	When vehicle starts	1	2		4		3	6								
	When upshifting	1	2		4		3	7								
No engine braking	When shifting from "D" to "2" and "1" range	1	2		4		3	5								
	When O.D. switch is set from "ON" to "OFF"	1	2		4		3	7								
	When shifting from 2nd to 1st in "1" range	1	2		4		3	5								
Shift quality	Too low a gear change point from 2nd to 3rd and from 3rd to 2nd	1			3		2	6								
	Too high a gear change point from 2nd to 3rd and from 3rd to 2nd	1			3		2	6								
	Too low a gear change point from 2nd to 1st in "1" range	1			3		2	6								
	Too high a gear change point from 2nd to 1st in "1" range	1			3		2	6								

NS5029100547010X

Fig. 1 Transaxle troubleshooting chart (Part 1 of 4). RL4F03A transaxle

Fig. 1 Transaxle troubleshooting chart (Part 2 of 4). RL4F03A transaxle

NS5029100547020X

Fig. 1 Transaxle troubleshooting chart (Part 4 of 4). RL4F03A transaxle

NS5029100547040X

Numbers are arranged in order of probability. Perform inspections starting with number one and work up. Circled numbers indicate that the transaxle must be removed from the vehicle.

☐ : Valve expected to be malfunctioning

Fig. 1 Transaxle troubleshooting chart (Part 3 of 4). RL4F03A transaxle

NS5029100547030X

Symptom Chart

Fig. 2 Transaxle troubleshooting chart (Part 1 of 3). RE4F03V transaxle

NS5028900328010X

Numbers are arranged in order of probability.
Perform inspections starting with number one and work up. Circled numbers indicate that the transaxle must be removed from the vehicle.

	ON vehicle																		OFF vehicle										
	Fluid level	Control cable	Inhibitor switch	Throttle position sensor (Adjustment)	Revolution sensor and vehicle speed sensor	Engine speed signal	Engine idling rpm	Line pressure	Control valve assembly	Shift solenoid valve A	Shift solenoid valve B	Line pressure solenoid valve	Torque converter clutch solenoid valve	Overrun clutch solenoid valve	Fluid temperature sensor	Accumulator N-D	Accumulator servo release	Ignition switch and starter	Torque converter	Oil pump	Reverse clutch	High clutch	Forward clutch	Forward one-way clutch	Overrun clutch	Low one-way clutch	Low & reverse brake	Brake band	Parking components
Too sharp a shock in change from "D₃" to "D₄".		.	1						2	3																		(3)	(4)
Almost no shock or clutches slipping in change from "D₁" to "D₂".	1	2						3	5				4															(6)	
Almost no shock or slipping in change from "D₂" to "D₃".	1	2						3	4													(8)						(6)	
Almost no shock or slipping in change from "D₃" to "D₄".	1	2						3	4													(3)						(6)	
Vehicle braked by gear change from "D₄" to "D₃".	1																					(3) (4)					(3) (3)		(2)
Vehicle braked by gear change from "D₃" to "D₂".	1																												(2)
Vehicle braked by gear change from "D₂" to "D₁".	1																					(4)			(3) (2)				
Maximum speed not attained. Acceleration poor.	1	2						5	3	4									(11) (14) (13) (7)							(9) (5)			
Failure to change gear from "D₃" to "D₄".	1	2		Note				6	4	5		3													(8)		(7)		
Failure to change gear from "D₂" to "D₃" or from "D₁" to "D₂".	1	2						5	3	4												(8)					(7)		
Failure to change gear from "D₁" to "D₂" or from "D₂" to "D₃".	1	2						5	3	4												(7)				(8)			
Gear change shock felt during deceleration by releasing accelerator pedal.		1					2	4				3																	
Too high a change point from "D₄" to "D₃", from "D₃" to "D₂", from "D₂" to "D₁".		1	2																										
Kickdown does not operate when depressing pedal in "D₄" within kickdown vehicle speed.		1	2						3	4																			
Kickdown operates or engine over-runs when depressing pedal in "D₄" beyond kickdown vehicle speed limit.		2	1						3	4																			
Races extremely fast or slips in changing from "D₄" to "D₃" when depressing pedal.	1		2					3	5															(6) (7)					
Races extremely fast or slips in changing from "D₄" to "D₂" when depressing pedal.	1		2					3	6	5		4												(8)				(7)	
Races extremely fast or slips in changing from "D₃" to "D₂" when depressing pedal.	1		2					3	5			4		6										(9) (7)				(8)	
Races extremely fast or slips in changing from "D₄" or "D₃" to "D₁" when depressing pedal.	1		2					3	4													(6) (7)			(8)				
Vehicle will not run in any position.	1	2						3						4				(3) (5)		(6)					(3) (5)		(3) (7) (9)	
Transaxle noise in "D", "2", "1" and "R" positions.	1																		(2)									

NS5028900328020X

Fig. 2 Transaxle troubleshooting chart (Part 2 of 3). RE4F03V transaxle

Numbers are arranged in order of probability.
Perform inspections starting with number one and work up. Circled numbers indicate that the transaxle must be removed from the vehicle.

	ON vehicle																		OFF vehicle										
	Fluid level	Control cable	Inhibitor switch	Throttle position sensor (Adjustment)	Revolution sensor and vehicle speed sensor	Engine speed signal	Engine idling rpm	Line pressure	Control valve assembly	Shift solenoid valve A	Shift solenoid valve B	Line pressure solenoid valve	Torque converter clutch solenoid valve	Overrun clutch solenoid valve	Fluid temperature sensor	Accumulator N-D	Accumulator servo release	Ignition switch and starter	Torque converter	Oil pump	Reverse clutch	High clutch	Forward clutch	Forward one-way clutch	Overrun clutch	Low one-way clutch	Low & reverse brake	Brake band	Parking components
Failure to change from "D₃" to "2" when changing lever into "2" position.	7	1	2			6	5		4			3																(9)	(8)
Gear change from "2₂" to "2₃" in "2" position.		1																											
Engine brake does not operate in "1" position.	2	1	3	4			6	5			7																	(8)	(9)
Gear change from "1₁" to "1₂" in "1" position.	2	1																											
Does not change from "1₂" to "1₁" in "1" position.						2	4	3																	(6)		(7)		
Large shock changing from "1₂" to "1₁" in "1" position.							1																				(2)		
Transaxle overheats.	1		3		2	4	6							(14) (7)		(8) (9)	(10) (11)		(12)	(13)	(15) (16)								
ATF shoots out during operation. White smoke emitted from exhaust pipe during operation.	1																	(2) (3) (5)		(6)		(1)							
Offensive smell at fluid charging pipe.	1																	(2) (3) (4) (5) (7)		(8)		(9)							
Torque converter is not locked up.		3	1	2	4		6	8			7		5					(9)											
Lock-up piston slip.		1		2			3	6			5	4						(7)											
Lock-up point is extremely high or low.		1		2			3	4																					
A/T does not shift to "D₄" when driving with overdrive switch "ON".		2	1	3			8	6	4			5	7												(10)				
Engine is stopped at "R", "D", "2" and "1" positions.	1						5	4	3	2																			

NS5028900328030X

Fig. 2 Transaxle troubleshooting chart (Part 3 of 3). RE4F03V transaxle

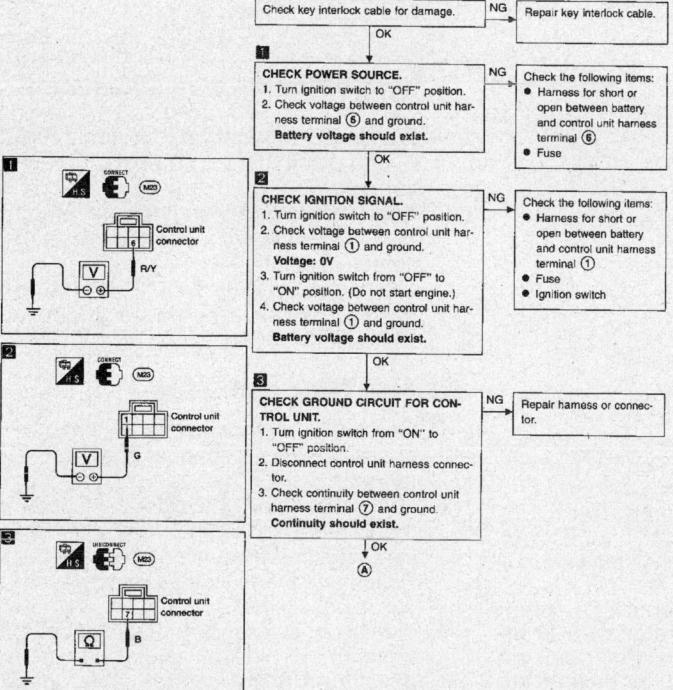

Check key interlock cable for damage. → NG → Repair key interlock cable.
OK ↓

1 CHECK POWER SOURCE.
1. Turn ignition switch to "OFF" position.
2. Check voltage between control unit harness terminal (6) and ground. Battery voltage should exist.
→ NG → Check the following items:
● Harness for short or open between battery and control unit harness terminal (6)
● Fuse
OK ↓

2 CHECK IGNITION SIGNAL.
1. Turn ignition switch to "OFF" position.
2. Check voltage between control unit harness terminal (1) and ground. Voltage: 0V
3. Turn ignition switch from "OFF" to "ON" position. (Do not start engine.)
4. Check voltage between control unit harness terminal (1) and ground. Battery voltage should exist.
→ NG → Check the following items:
● Harness for short or open between battery and control unit harness terminal (1)
● Fuse
● Ignition switch
OK ↓

3 CHECK GROUND CIRCUIT FOR CONTROL UNIT.
1. Turn ignition switch from "ON" to "OFF" position.
2. Disconnect control unit harness connector.
3. Check continuity between control unit harness terminal (7) and ground. Continuity should exist.
→ NG → Repair harness or connector.
OK ↓ (A)

NS5029600591010X

Fig. 3 BTSI diagnostic procedure (Part 1 of 4)

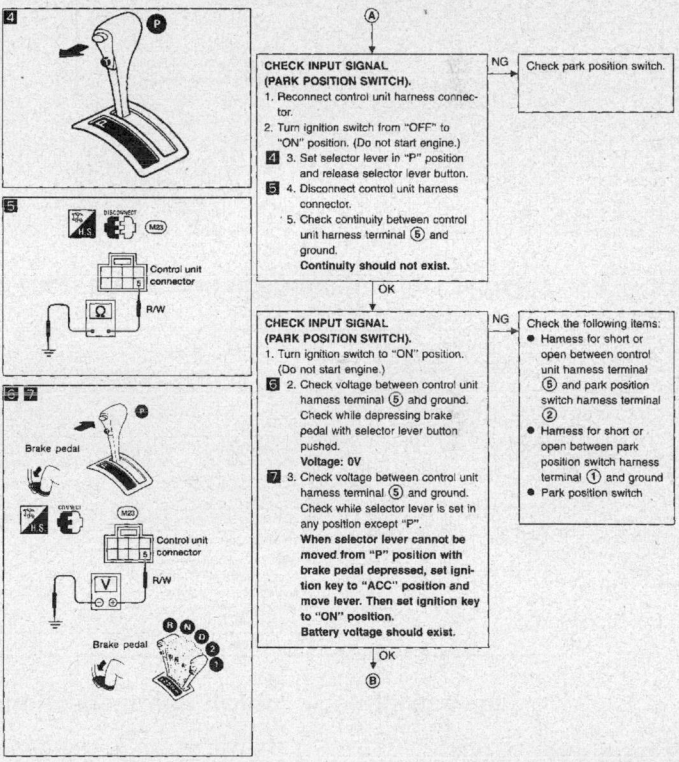

(A) ↓

4 CHECK INPUT SIGNAL (PARK POSITION SWITCH).
1. Reconnect control unit harness connector.
2. Turn ignition switch from "OFF" to "ON" position. (Do not start engine.)
3. Set selector lever in "P" position and release selector lever button.
4. Disconnect control unit harness connector.
5. Check continuity between control unit harness terminal (5) and ground. Continuity should not exist.
→ NG → Check park position switch.
OK ↓

CHECK INPUT SIGNAL (PARK POSITION SWITCH).
1. Turn ignition switch to "ON" position. (Do not start engine.)
2. Check voltage between control unit harness terminal (5) and ground. Check while depressing brake pedal with selector lever button pushed. Voltage: 0V
3. Check voltage between control unit harness terminal (5) and ground. Check while selector lever is set in any position except "P". When selector lever cannot be moved from "P" position with brake pedal depressed, set ignition key to "ACC" position and move lever. Then set ignition key to "ON" position. Battery voltage should exist.
→ NG → Check the following items:
● Harness for short or open between control unit harness terminal (5) and park position switch harness terminal (2)
● Harness for short or open between park position switch harness terminal (1) and ground
● Park position switch
OK ↓ (B)

NS5029600591020X

Fig. 3 BTSI diagnostic procedure (Part 2 of 4)

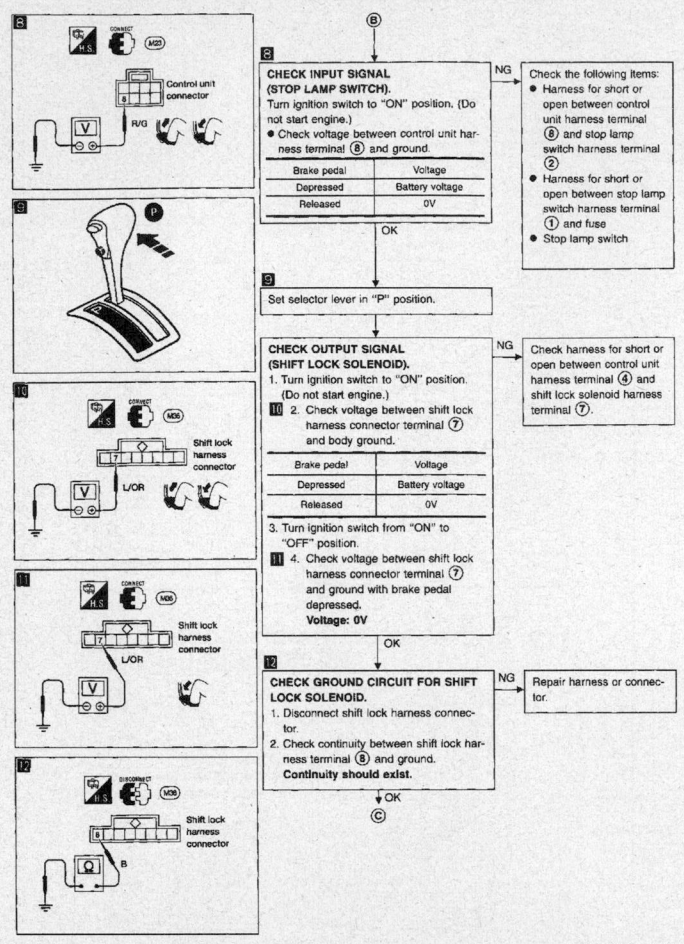

Fig. 3 BTSI diagnostic procedure (Part 3 of 4)

NS5029600591030X

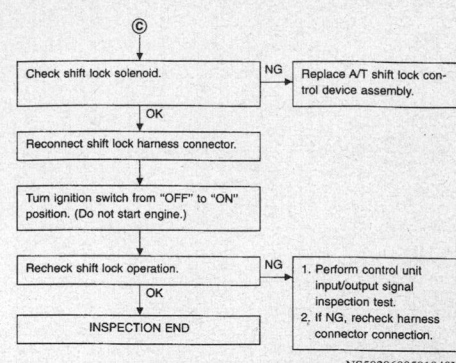

Fig. 3 BTSI diagnostic procedure
(Part 4 of 4)

NS5029600591040X

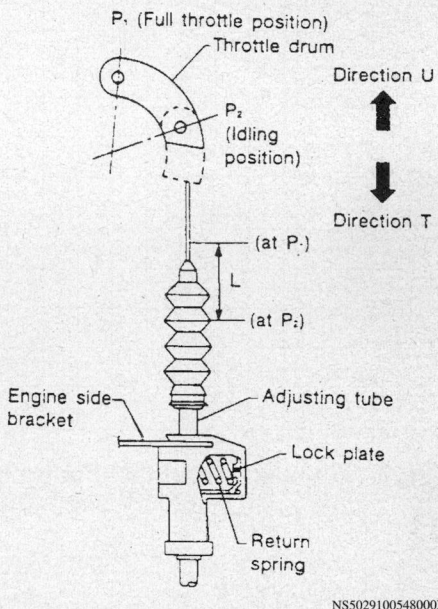

Fig. 5 Throttle wire adjustment

NS5029100548000X

Fig. 4 Shift lock control unit inspection table

Terminal No. ⊕	Terminal No. ⊖	Item	Condition	Judgement standard
1		Ignition signal	• Turn ignition switch to "ON" or "START" position.	Battery voltage
			• Except above	0V
6		Power source	• Any condition	Battery voltage
4		Shift lock signal	• Turn ignition switch to "ON" position • When selector lever is set in "P" position and brake pedal is depressed.	Battery voltage
			• Except above	0V
8	7	Stop lamp switch	• When brake pedal is depressed.	Battery voltage
			• When brake pedal is released.	0V
5		Park position switch	• When key is in key cylinder, selector lever is in "P" position, and selector lever button pushed. • When selector lever is set in any position except "P".	Battery voltage
			• Except above	0V

NS5029600592000X

FLUID CHANGE

1. Raise and support vehicle, then remove drain plug from transaxle oil pan to drain fluid.
2. After fluid has been drained, install drain plug and tighten to specifications.
3. **Fill transmission using caution not to overfill.**

ADJUSTMENTS

THROTTLE WIRE

1. Turn ignition switch to Off position.

2. While pressing lock plate, **Fig. 5,** move adjusting tube in direction "T," then return lock plate.
3. Move throttle drum from P2 to P1 quickly and ensure throttle wire stroke "L" is 1.079–1.236 inches between full throttle and idle.
4. **Adjust throttle wire stroke when throttle wire/accelerator wire is installed and adjusted. Put mark on throttle wire to aid in measuring wire stroke.**

CONTROL CABLE

1. Place selector lever in "P" position,

then loosen control cable locknut, **Fig. 6,** and place manual shaft in "P" position.
2. Adjust cable using long hole in control cable at transaxle end, **Fig. 6,** then tighten locknut.
3. Move selector lever from "P" to "1" and ensure selector lever moves smoothly without any sliding noise.

INHIBITOR SWITCH

1. Remove control cable end from manual shaft, then set manual shaft in "N" range.
2. Loosen inhibitor switch attaching bolts, then insert a .157 inch diameter pin into adjustment holes on both inhibitor switch and manual shaft as near vertical as possible.
3. Tighten inhibitor switch attaching bolts, then remove pin from adjusting hole.
4. Install and adjust control cable, then check continuity of inhibitor switch.

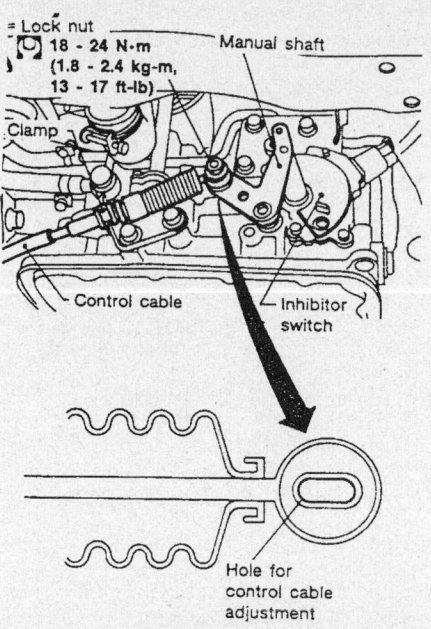

Fig. 6 Control cable adjustment

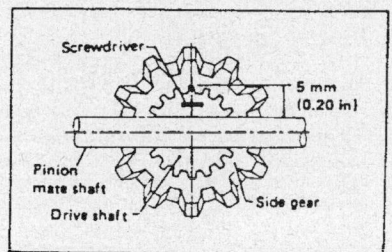

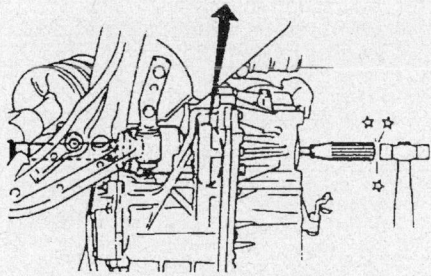

Fig. 9 Lefthand driveshaft removal

IN-VEHICLE REPAIRS

CONTROL VALVE ASSEMBLY & ACCUMULATOR

1. Raise and support vehicle, then remove drain plug from transaxle oil pan to drain fluid.
2. Remove oil pan and gasket.
3. Disconnect transaxle solenoid harness connector.
4. Remove stopper ring from solenoid harness terminal body, then the solenoid harness from transaxle case by pushing on terminal body.
5. Remove control valve assembly at-

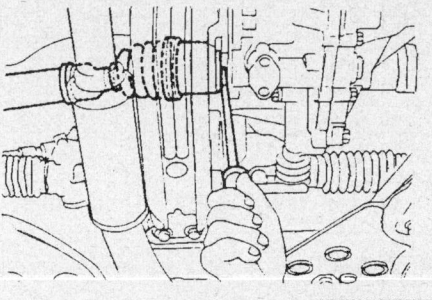

Fig. 7 Righthand driveshaft removal. Less support bearing

taching bolts, then the control valve assembly.
6. Remove 3-R and N-D accumulators by applying compressed air, if necessary. **Hold pistons with a rag when removing.**
7. Reverse procedure to install noting the following:
   a. Place manual shaft in Neutral, then align manual plate with groove in manual valve.
   b. After installation of control valve assembly, ensure selector lever can be moved to all positions.

DIFFERENTIAL SIDE OIL SEAL

1. Remove driveshafts as follows:
   a. Remove wheel bearing locknut, then the disc brake caliper and position aside.
   b. Remove tie-rod ball joint.
   c. Separate driveshaft from knuckle by lightly tapping it. If it is difficult to remove, use a suitable puller.
   d. Remove right driveshaft from transaxle by prying between transaxle case and inner CV housing with a suitable pry bar, **Figs. 7 and 8.**
   e. Remove left driveshaft from transaxle by driving shaft out from opposite side using a suitable tool, **Fig. 9. Use caution not to damage pinion mate shaft and side gear.**
2. Remove oil seals using seal puller tool No. ST33290001, or equivalent.
3. Apply ATF to oil seal surface, then install using drift tool No. KV31103000, or equivalent, for transaxle case side and tool No. ST35325000, or equivalent, for converter side.
4. Install oil seals so that dimension "A" and "B," **Fig. 10,** are within .217–.256 inch for dimension "A" and .020 inch or less for dimension "B."
5. Install driveshafts as follows:
   a. Set driveshaft installer tool No. KV38106700, or equivalent, along inner circumference of oil seal.
   b. Insert driveshaft into transaxle ensuring serrations are properly aligned, then remove tool.
   c. Push driveshaft, then press-fit circular clip on driveshaft into circular clip groove of side gear.
   d. Ensure shaft is properly meshed with side gear by attempting to pull flange out of slide joint.

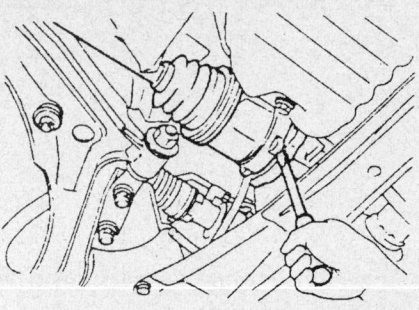

Fig. 8 Righthand driveshaft removal. With support bearing

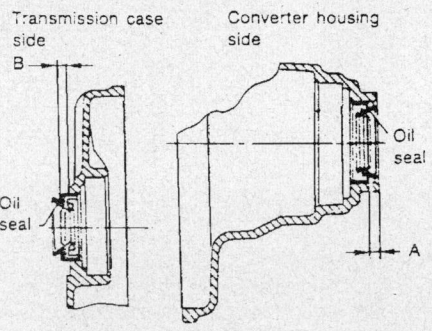

Fig. 10 Differential oil seal dimensions "A" & "B"

   e. Install driveshaft into knuckle.
   f. Install tie-rod ball joint, disc brake caliper and wheel bearing locknut and tighten as required.

GOVERNOR VALVE

1. Remove governor valve cap snap ring and spacer, then the cap and O-ring.
2. Remove governor valve assembly by pulling upwards.
3. Reverse procedures to install.

KEY INTERLOCK CABLE, REPLACE

Removal

1. Unlock slider from adjuster holder and remove rod from cable at shift selector.
2. Remove lock plate and cable from steering lock.

Installation

1. Set key interlock cable to steering lock assembly and install lock plate.
2. Clamp cable to steering column and fix to control cable with band.
3. Set selector lever to P position.
4. Insert interlock rod into adjuster holder.
5. Install casing cap to bracket.
6. Move slider in order to fix adjuster holder to interlock rod.

TRANSAXLE

REPLACE
1996–97

1. Remove battery and bracket, then the air duct.

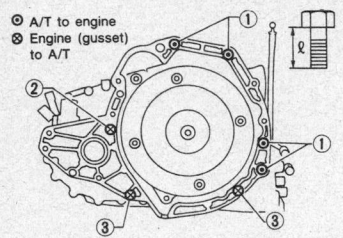

Bolt No.	Tightening torque N·m (kg-m, ft-lb)	Bolt length "ℓ" mm (in)
①	30 - 40 (3.1 - 4.1, 22 - 30)	50 (1.97)
②	30 - 40 (3.1 - 4.1, 22 - 30)	30 (1.18)
③	16 - 21 (1.6 - 2.1, 12 - 15)	25 (0.98)
Front gusset to engine	30 - 40 (3.1 - 4.1, 22 - 30)	20 (0.79)
Rear gusset to engine	16 - 21 (1.6 - 2.1, 12 - 15)	16 (0.63)

NS5029800703000X

Fig. 11 Transaxle mounting specifications. 1998–99 1.6L engine

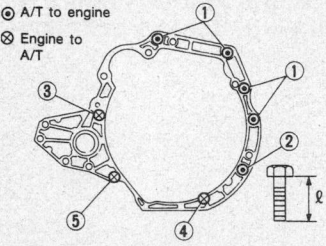

Bolt No.	Tightening torque N·m (kg-m, ft-lb)	Bolt length "ℓ" mm (in)
①	70 - 79 (7.1 - 8.1, 51 - 59)	55 (2.17)
②	70 - 79 (7.1 - 8.1, 51 - 59)	50 (1.97)
③	70 - 79 (7.1 - 8.1, 51 - 59)	65 (2.56)
④	16 - 21 (1.6 - 2.1, 12 - 15)	35 (1.38)
⑤	16 - 21 (1.6 - 2.1, 12 - 15)	45 (1.77)

NS5029800704000X

Fig. 12 Transaxle mounting specifications. 1998–99 2.0L engine

2. Disconnect transaxle solenoid and inhibitor switch harness connectors.
3. Disconnect throttle wire from engine compartment.
4. Raise and support vehicle, then drain ATF from transaxle.
5. Disconnect control cable from transaxle, then the oil cooler hoses.
6. Remove driveshafts, refer to "Differential Side Oil Seal" under "In-Vehicle Repairs."
7. Remove front exhaust tube, then the starter motor from the transaxle.
8. **On Sentra models equipped with SR20DE engine,** remove rear plate cover.
9. **On Sentra models equipped with GA16DE engine,** remove front gussets and rear engine plate.

10. **On all models,** remove bolts attaching torque converter to driveplate.
11. Place a suitable jack under oil pan to support engine.
12. Support transaxle with a suitable jack, then remove mountings from transaxle.
13. Remove bolts attaching engine to transaxle, then lower transaxle while supporting with a jack.

1998-99

1. Remove battery and bracket, then the air duct.
2. Disconnect transaxle solenoids, switches and sensors harness connectors.
3. Remove crankshaft position sensor.

4. **On models equipped with 1.6L engine,** disconnect throttle wire from engine.
5. **On all models,** raise and support vehicle, then drain transaxle fluid into suitable container.
6. Disconnect control cable from transaxle, then the oil cooler hoses.
7. Remove driveshafts as described under "Differential Side Oil Seal, Replace"
8. Remove intake manifold support bracket.
9. Remove starter motor from transaxle.
10. Remove upper transaxle to engine mounting bolts.
11. Support transaxle with suitable jack.
12. Remove center member.
13. Remove front and rear gussets, then the engine rear plate.
14. Remove torque converter mounting bolts.
15. Remove rear transaxle to engine bracket.
16. Support engine with suitable jack.
17. Remove rear transaxle mount.
18. Remove lower transaxle to engine mounting bolts.
19. Lower and remove transaxle.
20. Reverse procedure to install, noting the following:
    a. Ensure driveplate runout is less than .008 inch, approximately 4.53 inches from crankshaft center.
    b. **On models equipped with 1.6L engine,** ensure torque converter is more than .831 inch below housing.
    c. **On models equipped with 2.0L engine,** ensure torque converter is more than .626 inch below housing.
    d. Tighten transaxle mounting bolts according to **Figs. 11 and 12.**
    e. Adjust control cable.
    f. **On models equipped with 1.6L engine,** adjust throttle wire.

TIGHTENING SPECIFICATIONS

Year	Component	Torque/Ft. Lbs.
1996–99	Bearing Retainer To Transaxle Case	14–18
	Control Cable Securing Nut	72-96②
	Control Valve Body To Transaxle Case	60-84②
	Converter Housing To Engine	①
	Drain Plug	22–29
	Driveplate To Torque Converter	29–36
	Governor Shaft Securing Nut	36-60②
	Governor Valve Body To Governor Shaft	48-60②
	Gusset To Converter Housing	12–15
	Inhibitor Switch To Transaxle Case	12–24②
	Low & Reverse Brake Piston Retainer	60–84②
	Lower Valve Body To Upper Valve Body	60–84②
	Manual Shaft Locknut	23–31
	Oil Cooler Pipe To Transmission Case	22–36
	Oil Pan To Transaxle Case	48–60
	Oil Strainer To Lower Valve Body	84–108②
	Oil Tube To Converter Housing	48–60②
	Test Plug (Oil Pressure Inspection Hole)	48–84②
	Throttle Wire Securing Bolt	24–36②
	Transaxle Case To Converter Housing	14–17
	Transaxle Case To Front Cover	14–17

① — Bolts 1.97 inches or longer, 12 — 15 ft. lbs.; bolts 1.77 inches or smaller, 12–15 ft. lbs.
② — Inch lbs.

Front Wheel Drive Axles

INDEX

STEERING KNUCKLE SERVICE

ALTIMA & MAXIMA

Removal & Disassemble

1. Raise and support vehicle and remove wheel.
2. Unfasten brake caliper assembly, leaving brake line attached.
3. Separate driveshaft from steering knuckle by tapping on driveshaft.
4. Disconnect tie-rod from ball joint, then remove lower ball joint attaching nuts.
5. Remove steering knuckle-to-strut attaching bolts.
6. Remove wheel hub and steering knuckle, **Fig. 1,** as an assembly.
7. Separate wheel hub and steering knuckle using a suitable tool, **Fig. 2.**

Assemble & Installation

1. Install outer circlip into groove in steering knuckle, then press bearing outer race into knuckle.
2. Lubricate inner and outer bearing races with suitable grease.
3. Install inner circlip into groove in knuckle.
4. Install bearing inner races, then the outer grease seal.
5. Press hub into steering knuckle.
6. If driveshaft has not been removed from transaxle, adjust bearing preload as follows:
   a. Apply 5.5 tons pressure to bearing with a suitable press.
   b. Spin knuckle several times in each direction, then measure bearing preload using a suitable spring scale.
   c. Preload should measure .4–4.0 lbs. If reading is not within specifications, the wheel bearing must be replaced.
7. If driveshaft has been removed from transaxle, adjust bearing preload as follows:
   a. Position driveshaft in hub and **torque** wheel bearing locknut to 174–231 ft. lbs.
   b. Spin wheel hub several times in each direction, then measure preload using a suitable spring scale.
   c. Preload should measure 1.1–10.1 lbs. If reading is not within specifications, the wheel bearing must be replaced.
   d. Remove wheel bearing nut, then slide driveshaft out of hub.
8. Install inner grease seal into knuckle.
9. Install the assembly in reverse order of removal as outlined previously.

SENTRA & 200SX

Removal

1. Raise and support vehicle.
2. Remove wheel and tire assembly.
3. Remove wheel bearing locknut while depressing brake pedal.
4. Remove caliper.
5. Remove tie rod ball joint from knuckle.
6. Separate driveshaft from knuckle, **Fig. 3.**
7. Support arm assembly, then remove

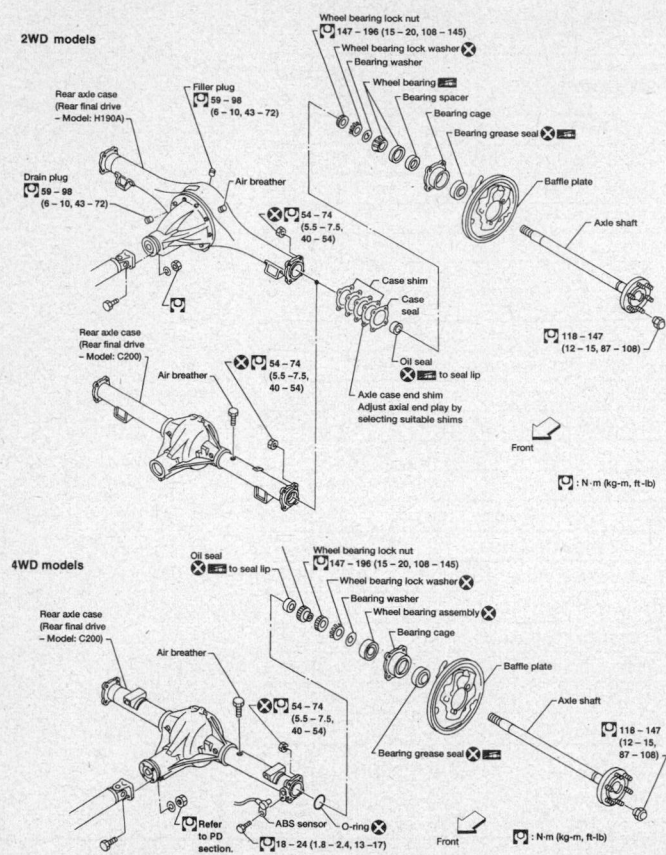

Fig. 1   Exploded view of wheel hub & steering knuckle assembly. Altima & Maxima

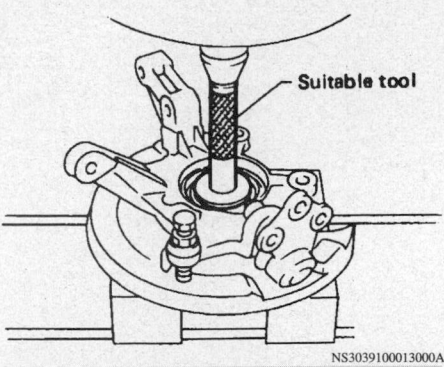

Fig. 2   Wheel hub removal. Altima & Maxima

lower strut adjusting bolts. **Make matching marks on strut and adjusting bolt.**

8. Remove lower ball joint to knuckle attaching nut.
9. Separate knuckle from lower ball joint stud, using a suitable tool.
10. Remove steering knuckle.

Disassemble

1. Remove outer hub inner race from knuckle.
2. Remove outside inner race from wheel hub.
3. Remove inner race from wheel bearing.
4. Remove snap ring.
5. Install inner race (inside) of removed wheel bearing, then remove wheel bearing assembly from knuckle.

Inspection

Inspect removed components for excessive wear and/or damage. Replace worn or damaged components as required.

Assemble

1. Press new wheel bearing assembly into knuckle working from outside of knuckle.
2. Install snap ring.
3. Coat seal lip with suitable grease.
4. Press hub into knuckle. **Do not ex-**

ceed 3.3 tons.

5. Check bearing preload as follows:
   a. Place press load onto wheel hub shaft (approximately 5 tons).
   b. Spin knuckle several times in both directions.
   c. Ensure wheels bearings operate smoothly.

Installation

Reverse removal procedure to install.

QUEST

Removal

1. Raise and support vehicle, then remove wheel.
2. Remove wheel bearing locknut.
3. Remove brake caliper assembly and brake rotor. Suspend caliper assembly with wire.
4. Using ball joint remover tool No. J25730-A, or equivalent, separate tie-rod ball joint from knuckle.
5. Remove lower strut mounting bolts and nuts, **Fig. 4.**
6. Remove lower ball joint cotter pin and retaining nut.
7. Strike knuckle with a hammer and pull down control arm to separate lower ball joint from knuckle.
8. Separate driveshaft from knuckle by lightly tapping driveshaft. If driveshaft

is hard to remove us a suitable puller. **Cover driveshaft boots with a shop towel to protect them during driveshaft removal.**

Disassemble

1. Using a hammer and suitable tool, drive wheel hub out of knuckle.
2. Using a suitable pressing tool, remove wheel bearing inner race from wheel hub.
3. Remove wheel bearing snap ring from knuckle.
4. Using a suitable pressing tool, press wheel bearing out of knuckle.

Assemble

1. Press new wheel bearing into knuckle. **Press only on outer race of wheel bearing.**
2. Install snap ring into groove of knuckle.
3. Install baffle plate and splash guard onto knuckle.
4. Press wheel hub into knuckle, holding wheel bearing inner race as shown in **Fig. 5.**
5. Spin knuckle several turns in both directions, ensure wheel bearings operate smoothly.

Installation

Reverse removal procedure, noting the following:

1. **Torque** lower strut mounting bolts and nuts to 94–108 ft. lbs.
2. **Torque** tie-rod ball joint nut to 22–29 ft. lbs.
3. Apply engine oil to threaded portion of driveshaft, then **torque** wheel bearing locknut to 174–231 ft. lbs.
4. Check wheel bearing endplay. Endplay should be .002 or less.
5. Ensure wheel bearing operates smoothly.

DRIVESHAFT

REPLACE

1. Raise and support vehicle, then remove wheel.
2. Unfasten brake caliper assembly, leaving brake line attached.
3. Remove tie-rod ball joint from knuckle, then separate driveshaft from steering knuckle by tapping on driveshaft.

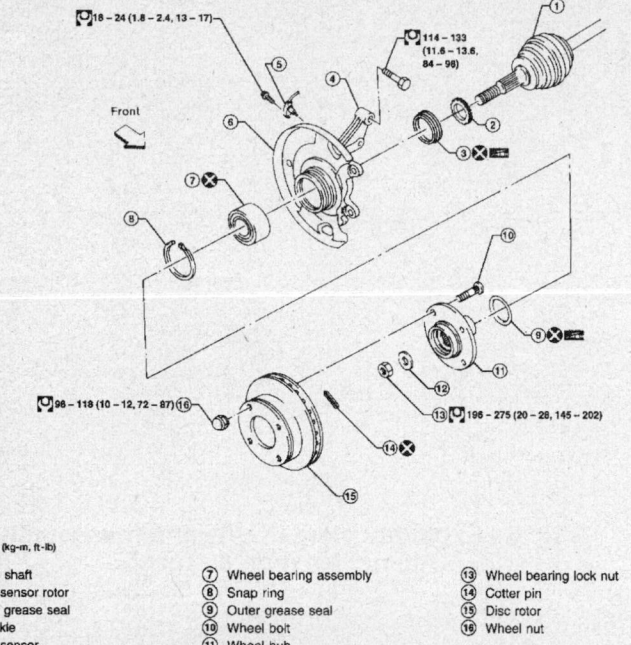

Fig. 3 Exploded view of wheel hub & steering knuckle assembly. Sentra & 200SX

: N·m (kg-m, ft-lb)

① Drive shaft	⑦ Wheel bearing assembly	⑬ Wheel bearing lock nut
② ABS sensor rotor	⑧ Snap ring	⑭ Cotter pin
③ Inner grease seal	⑨ Outer grease seal	⑮ Disc rotor
④ Knuckle	⑩ Wheel bolt	⑯ Wheel nut
⑤ ABS sensor	⑪ Wheel hub	
⑥ Baffle plate	⑫ Plain washer	

NS3039100014000A

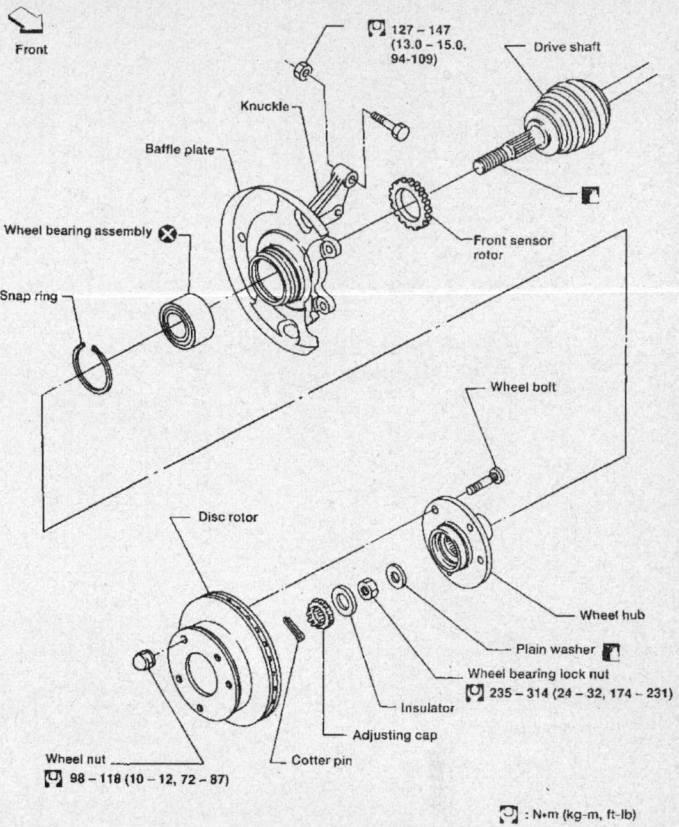

Fig. 4 Exploded view of wheel hub & steering knuckle assembly. Quest

: N·m (kg-m, ft-lb)

NS3039100015000A

When removing driveshafts, cover boots with cloth to prevent damage.
4. **On models equipped with automatic transaxle,** if replacing both driveshafts, remove righthand driveshaft before removing lefthand driveshaft.
5. **On all models,** use a large screwdriver to pry driveshaft out of transaxle.
6. Reverse procedure to install, noting the following:
   a. Install new oil seal in transaxle.
   b. Use oil seal protector tool Nos. KV38106800 and KV38106700, or equivalents, when inserting driveshaft into transaxle.
   c. After inserting driveshaft, press-fit circular clip into groove of transaxle side gear. **After installing clip, try to pull flange out of side joint by hand. If flange pulls out, circular clip is not properly installed into side gear.**

DRIVESHAFT SERVICE
DISASSEMBLY & INSPECTION

1. Remove boot bands from transaxle side of driveshaft, **Figs. 6 and 7.**
2. Place matching marks on slide joint housing and inner race, before separating joint assembly.
3. **On Sentra and 200SX models equipped with GA16DE engine,** proceed as follows:
   a. Place matching marks on spider assembly and driveshaft.
   b. Pry off snap ring, then remove spider assembly. **Do not disassemble spider assembly.**
   c. Cover driveshaft serration with tape

to prevent any damage to the boot during removal, remove boot from driveshaft.
4. **On models except Sentra and 200SX with GA16DE engine,** proceed as follows:
   a. Pry snap ring "A" with a screwdriver, then pull out slide joint housing.
   b. Place matching marks on inner race and driveshaft.
   c. Pry off snap ring "C," then remove ball cage, inner race and balls as a unit.
   d. Cover driveshaft serration with tape to prevent any damage to the boot during removal, remove boot from driveshaft.
5. **On all models,** place matching marks on driveshaft and joint assembly on wheel side of driveshaft.
6. Using a slide hammer, separate joint assembly from driveshaft. **Joint assembly cannot be disassembled.**
7. Remove boot bands, then the dust shield.
8. Using snap ring pliers, remove snap ring.
9. Press support bearing assembly out of driveshaft.
10. Press support bearing out of retainer.
11. Check boots for signs of fatigue, cracks or wear.
12. Check spider assembly for needle bearing and washer damage.
13. Check roller surfaces for scratches, wear or other damage.
14. Check serration for deformation.

15. Check slide joint housing for any damage.
16. Ensure support bearing rolls freely without noise, cracks, pitting or wear.

ASSEMBLY & INSTALLATION

ALTIMA, MAXIMA & QUEST

1. Assemble wheel side of driveshaft in the reverse order of disassembly, noting the following:
   a. When installing new large boot band, lock band in place using a suitable tool.
   b. **On Altima models,** pack boot on driveshaft with 3.53–4.23 ounces of suitable grease.
   c. **On Maxima models,** pack boot on driveshaft with 7.23–7.94 ounces of suitable grease.
   d. **On Quest models,** pack boot on driveshaft with 6.17–6.88 ounces of suitable grease.
   e. **On Altima models,** adjust boot of driveshaft so length L, **Fig. 8,** is 3.327–3.406 inches.
   f. **On Maxima models,** adjust boot of driveshaft so length L, **Fig. 8,** is 3.78–3.86 inches.
   g. **On Quest models,** adjust boot of driveshaft so length L, **Fig. 8,** is 3.406–3.484 inches.
2. **On all models,** install dynamic damper from transaxle side while holding it securely.

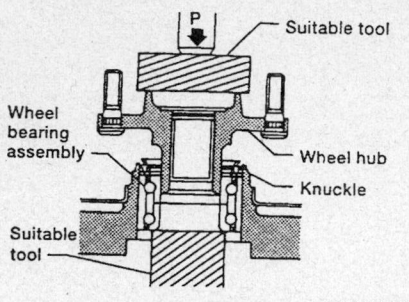

Fig. 5   Wheel hub installation in knuckle. Quest

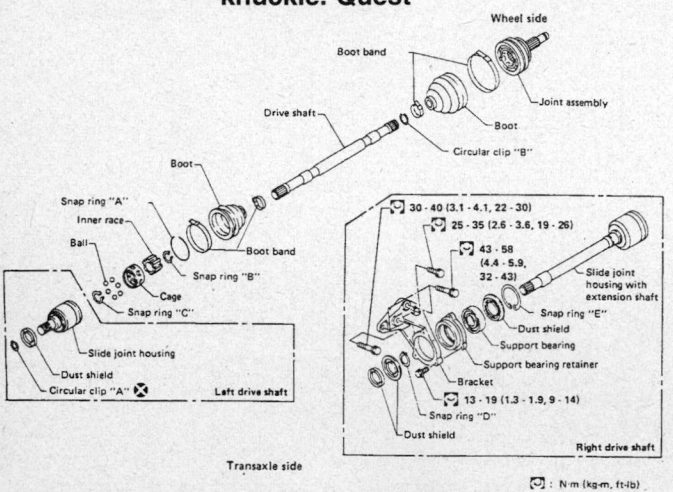

Fig. 7   Exploded view of driveshaft assembly. Sentra & 200SX

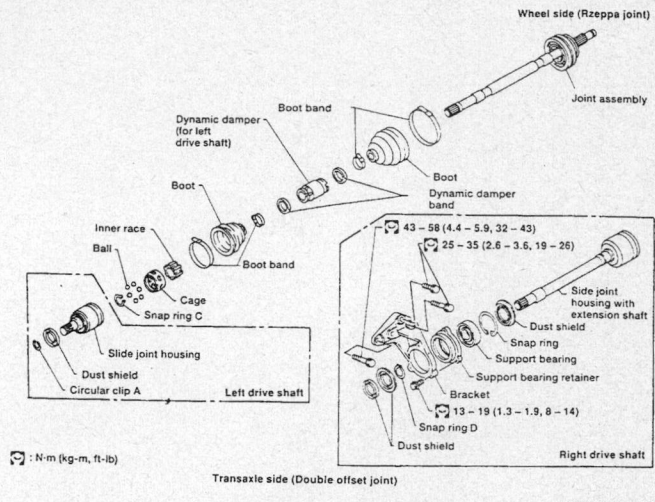

Fig. 6   Exploded view of driveshaft assembly. Altima, Maxima & Quest

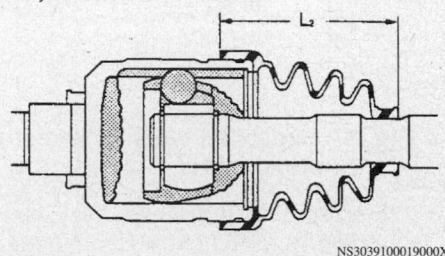

Fig. 8   Axle shaft boot installation

a. Pack boot with 5.47–6.17 ounces of suitable grease.
b. Set boot so that it does not swell and deform when its length is set at 3.78–3.86 inches, **Fig. 8.**
c. Ensure boot is properly installed on driveshaft groove, then lock new larger and smaller boot bands securely.

SR20DE Engine

1. Assemble transaxle side of driveshaft in reverse order of disassembly, noting the following:
   a. Pack boot with 4.94–5.64 ounces of suitable grease.
   b. Set boot so that it does not swell and deform when its length is set at 3.82–3.90 inches, **Fig. 8.**
   c. Ensure boot is properly installed on driveshaft groove, then lock new larger and smaller boot bands securely.
2. Assemble wheel side of driveshaft in reverse order of disassembly, noting the following:
   a. Pack boot with 3.70–4.41 ounces of suitable grease.
   b. Set boot so that it does not swell and deform when its length is set at 3.917–3.996 inches, **Fig. 8.**
   c. Ensure boot is properly installed on driveshaft groove, then lock new larger and smaller boot bands securely.

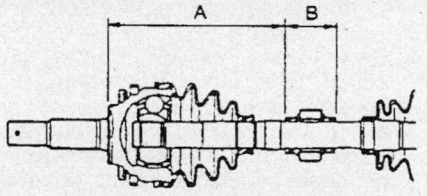

Fig. 9   Driveshaft length measurement. Altima, Maxima & Quest

3.99–4.07 inches.

SENTRA & 200SX

GA16DE Engine

1. Assemble transaxle side of driveshaft in reverse order of disassembly, noting the following:
   a. Pack boot with 7.94–8.29 ounces of suitable grease.
   b. Set boot so that it does not swell and deform when its length is set at 4.00–4.07 inches, **Fig. 8.**
   c. Ensure boot is properly installed on driveshaft groove, then lock new larger and smaller boot bands securely.
2. Assemble wheel side of driveshaft in reverse order of disassembly, noting the following:

3. Refer to **Fig. 9** for measurement locations, then adjust driveshaft length as follows:
   a. **On Altima models,** set length "A" on lefthand side driveshaft to 8.0 inches. Set length "A" on righthand side driveshaft to 7.31 inches. Set length "B" on lefthand side driveshaft to 2.76 inches. Set length "B" on righthand side driveshaft to 1.97 inches.
   b. **On Maxima models,** set length "A" to 8.43–8.82 inches. Set length "B" to 1.97 inches.
   c. **On Quest models,** set length "A" to 7.83–8.07 inches. Set length "B" to 2.76 inches.
4. **On all models,** assemble transaxle side of driveshaft in the reverse order of disassembly, noting the following:
   a. **On Altima models,** pack boot of driveshaft with 5.11–5.82 ounces of suitable grease.
   b. **On Maxima models,** pack boot of driveshaft with 5.64–6.35 ounces of suitable grease.
   c. **On Quest models,** pack boot of driveshaft with 7.41–8.11 ounces of suitable grease.
   d. **On Altima and Maxima models,** adjust boot on driveshaft so length L, **Fig. 8,** is 3.82–3.90 inches.
   e. **On Quest models,** adjust boot on driveshaft so length L, **Fig. 8,** is

All-Wheel Drive Systems

INDEX

DESCRIPTION

All wheel drive models equipped with the KA24E or VG33E engine use a TS82F driveshaft joint type. models equipped with the VG30E engine use a DS90 type drive-shaft joint.

ON VEHICLE SERVICE

OIL SEAL, REPLACE

Front Final Drive

1. Mark then remove front propeller shaft.
2. Loosen drive pinion nut using tool No. J34331, or equivalent.
3. Remove companion flange.
4. Remove front oil seal using a suitable oil seal remover.
5. Reverse procedure to install.

Shift Shaft Oil Seal

1. Mark then remove front propeller shaft.
2. Remove companion flange.
3. Remove transfer control lever from transfer outer shift lever, then the outer shift lever.
4. Remove shift shaft oil seal using a suit-able oil seal remover.
5. Reverse procedure to install.

DRIVESHAFT SERVICE

Refer to **Figs. 1 and 2** for driveshaft service.

DISASSEMBLE

TS82F

1. Remove plug seal from slide joint housing by lightly tapping around with suitable hammer.
2. Remove boot bands.
3. Put alignment marks in slide joint housing, then move boot and slide joint housing toward wheel side.
4. Put alignment marks on spider assem-bly and driveshaft.
5. Pry off snap ring, then remove spider assembly. **Do not disassemble spider assembly.**
6. Cover driveshaft serrations with suit-able tape then remove boot.

DS90

1. Remove boot bands.
2. Put alignment marks on slide joint housing and inner race, then separate joint assembly.
3. Pry off snap ring with screwdriver and pull out slide joint housing.

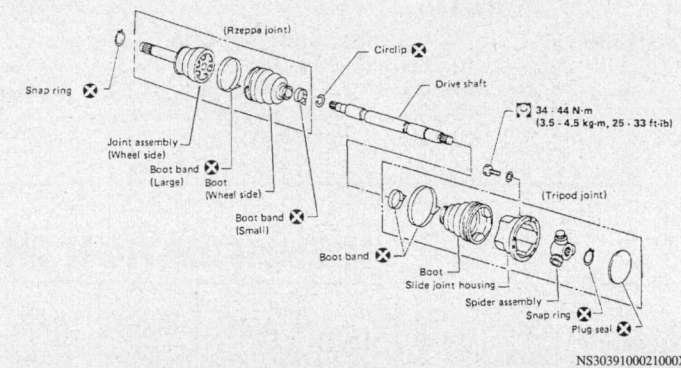

Fig. 1   Exploded view of front driveshaft. KA24E & VG33E engines

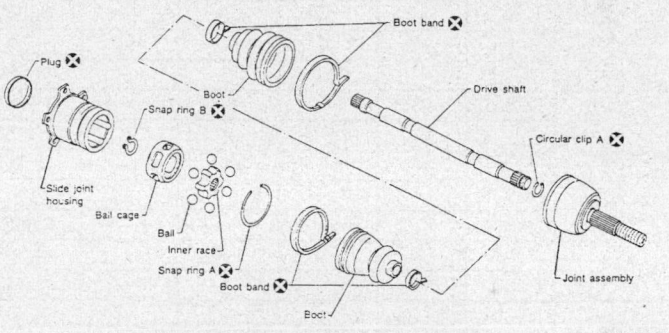

Fig. 2   Exploded view of front driveshaft. VG30E engine

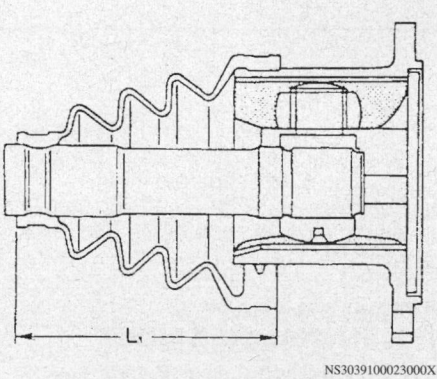

Fig. 3   Boot length

4. Put alignment marks on inner race and driveshaft.
5. Pry off snap ring, then remove ball cage, inner race and balls as a unit.
6. Cover driveshaft serrations with suit-able tape then remove boot.

ASSEMBLE

TS82F

1. Cover driveshaft serrations with suit-able tape then install boot, new small boot band and side joint housing on driveshaft.
2. Align mating marks then install spider assembly on driveshaft.
3. Install new snap ring.
4. Pack driveshaft boot and joint with 5.29–5.64 oz. of grease.
5. Install boot so that it does not swell and deform when its length is 4.02–4.09 inches, **Fig. 3.**
6. Lock new boot bands securely.
7. Install new plug seal to slide joint hous-ing by lightly tapping it.

DS90

1. Cover driveshaft serrations with suit-able tape then install boot and new small boot band on driveshaft.

2. Securely install ball cage, inner race and balls as a unit, ensuring alignment marks match.
3. Install new snap ring.
4. Pack driveshaft with 6.35–7.05 oz. of grease.
5. Align mating marks then install slide joint housing on driveshaft.
6. Install boot so that it does not swell and deform when its length is 3.66–3.74 inches, **Fig. 3.**
7. Lock new boot bands securely.

Drive Axles

INDEX

IDENTIFICATION CHART

Year	Model	Axle Code	2WD	4WD	Auto. Trans	Man. Trans.	Gear Ratio	Heavy Duty	Light Duty	Front Differential	Limited Slip	Engine
1996–99	Frontier & Pathfinder	H233B	X	—	X	—	4.363	—	—	—	—	VG33E
			—	X	X	—	4.363	—	—	—	X	VG33E
			—	X	X	—	4.636①	—	—	—	X	VG33E
		R200A	—	X	X	—	4.363	—	—	X	—	VG33E
			—	X	X	—	4.636①	—	—	X	—	VG33E
	Frontier & Pickup	C200A	X	—	—	X	3.900①	—	—	—	X	KA24E
		H190A	X	—	—	X	3.545②	—	—	—	X	KA24E
			X	—	X	—	4.111	—	—	—	X	KA24E
		H233B	—	—	—	—	4.625	—	—	—	X	KA24E
		R180A	—	X	—	—	4.625fd	—	—	—	—	KA24E
	240SX	R200	—	—	—	—	4.083	—	—	—	X	—
		R200V	—	—	—	—	4.083	—	—	—	—	—
	300ZX	R200V	—	—	—	—	4.083	—	—	—	—	—
		R230V	—	—	—	—	3.692	—	—	—	—	—

① — SE models. ② — Except SE models.

R180A DIFFERENTIAL

DISASSEMBLE

1. Remove extension tube and differential side shaft assembly, then remove differential side flange.
2. Remove side retainers, **Fig. 1.**
3. Remove differential case from carrier.
4. When replacing side bearing, extract bearing outer race from side retainer.
5. Loosen drive pinion nut, holding companion flange and pull off companion flange using a suitable puller.
6. Press drive pinion from carrier using a press. Remove drive pinion with rear bearing cone, bearing spacer and adjusting washers.
7. Remove oil seal.
8. Remove pinion bearing with pinion bearing spacer and front bearing cone.
9. Press rear bearing inner race from drive pinion.
10. Drive out front and rear bearing outer races and remove bearing.
11. Remove ring gear.
12. Place match marks on right and left hand side differential cases, then remove bolts and separate them.
13. Remove pinion mate shaft and the pinion mate gears, side gears and thrust washers.

EXTENSION SHAFT & DIFFERENTIAL SIDE SHAFT

1. Remove differential side shaft assembly from extension tube.
2. Cut rear axle bearing collar with cold chisel being careful not to damage differential side shaft, **Fig. 2.**
3. Reinstall differential side shaft into extension tube and secure with bolts. Remove rear axle bearing by drawing out differential side shaft from rear axle bearing with puller, **Fig. 3.**
4. Remove grease seal.

INSPECTION

Thoroughly clean all disassembled parts, and examine them to see that they are worn, damaged or otherwise faulty, and how they are affected. Repair or replace all faulty parts, whichever is necessary.

1. Check gear teeth for scoring, cracking or chipping, and ensure that tooth contact pattern indicates correct meshing depth. If any fault is evident, replace parts as required. **Drive pinion and drive gear are supplied as a set; therefore, should either part be damaged, replace as a set.**
2. Check pinion gear shaft, and pinion gear for scores and signs of wear, and replace as required. Follow the same procedure for side gear and their seats on differential case.
3. Inspect all bearing races and rollers for scoring, chipping or evidence of excessive wear.

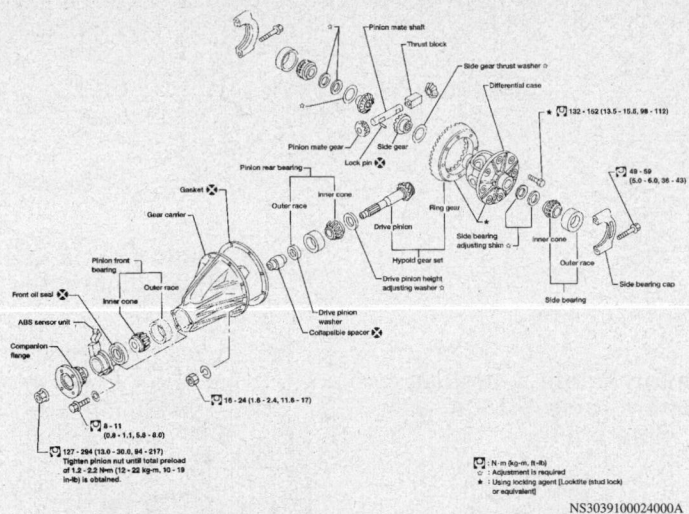

Fig. 1 Exploded view of differential carrier. R180A differential

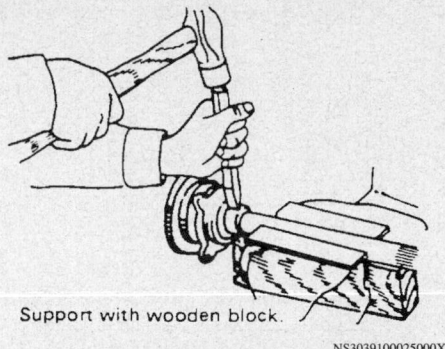

Fig. 2 Axle bearing collar removal. R180A differentials

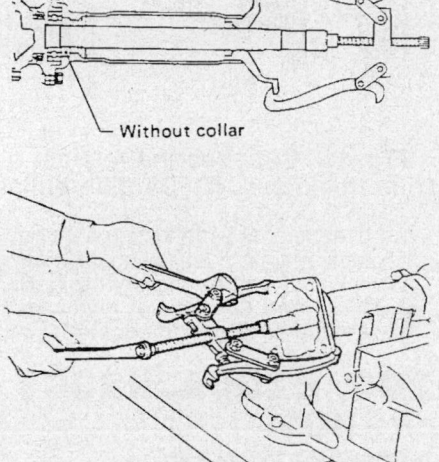

Fig. 3 Axle bearing removal. R180A differential

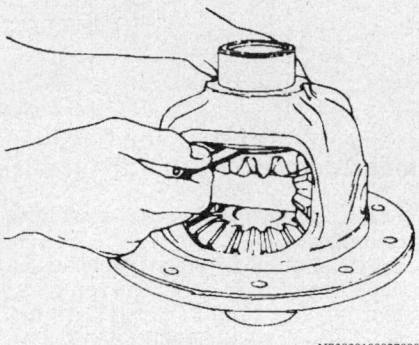

Fig. 4 Pinion to side gear backlash inspection. R180A differential

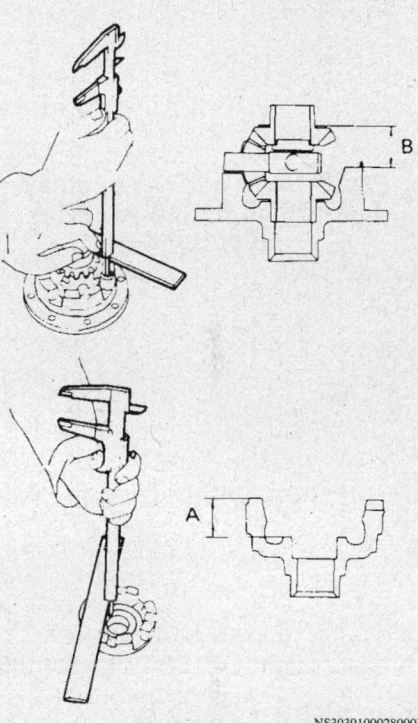

Fig. 5 Side gear thrust washer & differential case clearance inspection. R180A & R200A differentials

4. Inspect thrust washer faces. Small faults can be corrected with sandpaper. Inspect pinion mate-to-side gear backlash, **Fig. 4.** If clearance between side gear and thrust washer exceeds .0039–.0079 inch, replace thrust washers.
5. Inspect carrier and differential case for cracks or distortion. If either condition is evident, replace faulty parts.

ASSEMBLE

Reverse "Disassemble" procedure to assemble and note the following:

GEAR CASE ASSEMBLY

1. Measure clearance between side gear thrust washer and differential case at dimensions A and B, **Fig. 5,** then subtract value B from A. Clearance should be .0039–.0079 inch. If measurement does not fall within specifications,

clearance can be adjusted with a side gear thrust washer.
2. Apply gear oil to gear tooth surfaces and thrust surfaces and check if they turn properly.
3. Install left and right hand differential cases together.

EXTENSION TUBE & DIFFERENTIAL SIDE SHAFT

1. Measure extension tube at dimension A and dimension B, **Fig. 6,** then subtract value B from value A. Axle bearing endplay should be .0039 or less. If it is not, axle bearing endplay can be adjusted with bearing adjusting shims.
2. Using bearing driver tool No. J35764, or equivalent, install grease seal.
3. Install extension tube retainer, axle bearing and axle shaft bearing collar on differential side shaft.
4. Install differential side shaft assembly into extension tube.

DRIVE PINION PRELOAD ADJUSTMENT

Adjust preload of drive pinion with spacer and washer between front and rear bearing cones, regardless of thickness of pinion height adjusting washer.

This adjustment must be performed without oil seal inserted.

1. Press front and rear bearing outer races into gear carrier.
2. Insert pinion height adjusting washer of .1217 inch thickness and rear bearing cone into Dummy Shaft tool No. ST31212000, or equivalent, to make convenient to adjust pinion height, **Fig. 7.**
3. Install drive pinion bearing spacer, washer, front bearing cone, Drive Pinion Dummy Collar tool No. ST31214000, or equivalent, and companion flange on dummy shaft and tighten drive pinion nut using Stopper tool No. ST31852000, or equivalent, **Fig. 8.** Measure pinion bearing preload using Preload Gauge tool No. ST3127S000, or equivalent, and select washer and spacer that will provide required preload, **Fig. 9.**

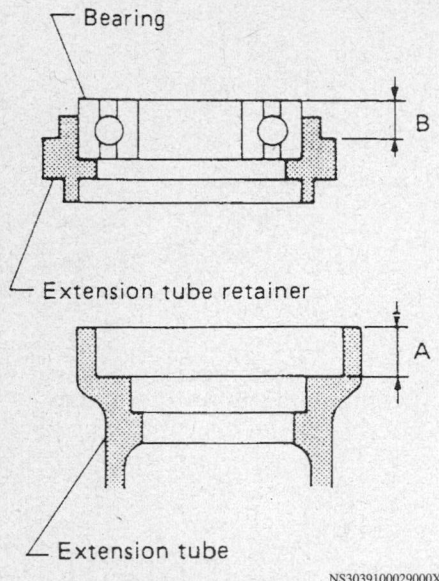

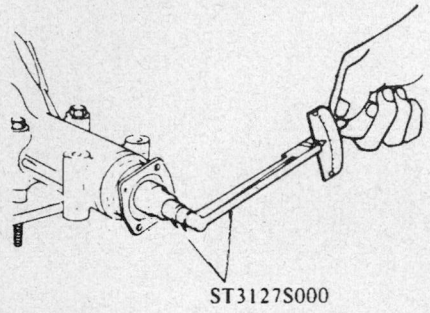

Fig. 6 Axle bearing endplay inspection. R180A & R200A differentials

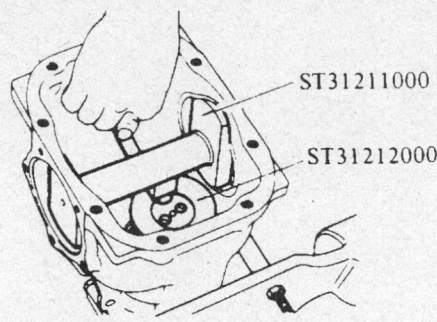

Fig. 7 Pinion height & preload adjustment tools. R180A differential

NS3039100030000X

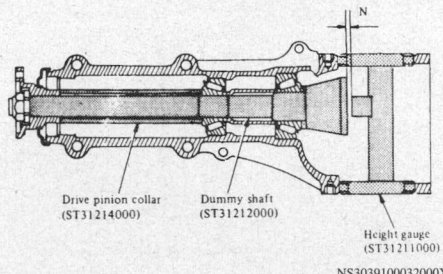

Fig. 10 Drive pinion height measurement. R180A differential

NS3039100032000X

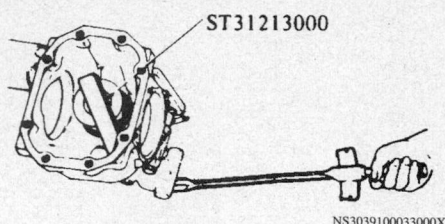

NS3039100033000X

Fig. 8 Pinion nut tightening. R180A differential

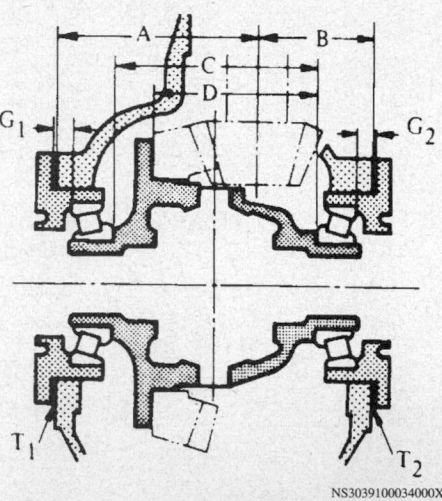

NS3039100034000X

Fig. 11 Side bearing retainer shim thickness. R180A differential

Pinion preload measurement figure:

NS3039100031000X

Fig. 9 Pinion preload measurement. R180A differential

DRIVE PINION HEIGHT ADJUSTMENT

Adjust pinion height with washer provided between rear bearing cone and back of pinion gear.

1. Install height gauge tool No. ST31211000, or equivalent, on carrier with dummy shaft mounted, **Fig. 10.**
2. Measure the clearance (N) between the tip end of height gauge and the end surface of dummy shaft, using a thickness gauge, **Fig. 10.**
3. The thickness of drive pinion height adjusting washer can be obtained from the following formula: T= WN-(H-D'-S) X 0.01 - 0.20 where T = required thickness of rear bearing adjusting washers in millimeters, W = thickness of washers temporarily inserted in millimeters, N = measured value with thickness gauge in millimeters, H = figure marked on the drive pinion head, D' = figure marked on the dummy shaft, S = figure marked on the height gauge and figures for H, D' and S are dimensional variations in a unit of 1/100mm against each standard measurement. **If values signifying H, D' and S are not**

given, **regard them as zero and compute.**
4. Install determined pinion height adjusting washer in drive pinion, and press rear bearing cone in, using base tool No. ST30901000, or equivalent.
5. Lubricate pinion front and rear bearings. Install drive pinion in gear carrier and the drive pinion bearing spacer and washer, front bearing cone and front bearing pilot spacer, pilot bearing and the front oil seal.
6. Install companion flange on drive pinion and **torque** nut to 123–145 ft. lbs.

SIDE BEARING RETAINER SHIMS

1. If the hypoid gear set, carrier, differential case, side bearing or side bearing retainer has been replaced with a new part, adjust the side bearing preload with adjusting shim. The required thickness of the right and left retainer shims can be obtained from the following formulas: T1= (ACG1-D) X 0.01 0.76-E; T2= (BDG2) X 0.01 0.76-F; where, T1 = required thickness of left side retainer shim in millimeters, **Fig. 11,** T2 = required thickness of right side retainer shim in millimeters, **Fig. 11,** A & B = figures marked on the gear carrier, **Fig. 12,** C & D = figures marked on the differential case, **Fig. 13,** E & F = differences in width of left or right side bearing against the standard width (20mm) in millimeters, **Fig. 14** (measure bearing width using master gauge KV38101900 and weight block ST32501000), G1 & G2 = figure marked on the left or right side retainer and figures for A, B, C, D, G1 and G2

are dimensional variations in a unit of 1/100mm against each standard measurement. **If values signifying A, B, C, D, G1 and G2 are not given, regard value as zero and compute.**

R200, R200A, R200V & R230V DIFFERENTIALS

DISASSEMBLE

1. **On R200A differential,** remove extension tube and differential side shaft assembly, then remove differential side flange.
2. **On R200, R200V and R230V differentials,** remove differential side flange, **Fig. 15.**
3. **On all models,** scribe marks between side bearing caps and carrier.
4. Remove side bearing cap bolts and the bearing caps.
5. Remove differential case assembly.
6. Loosen drive pinion nut, hold companion flange and pull companion flange.
7. Drive pinion from carrier. Take out drive pinion together with rear bearing inner race, bearing spacer and adjusting washer.
8. Remove oil seal.
9. Remove pilot bearing with pilot bearing spacer and front bearing inner race.
10. Remove side oil seal.
11. Press rear bearing inner race from drive pinion.
12. Drive out front and rear bearing outer races.

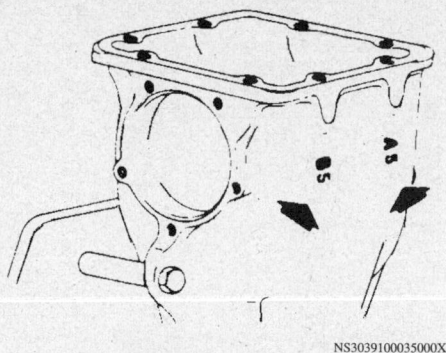

Fig. 12 Location of A & B values. R180A differential

NS3039100035000X

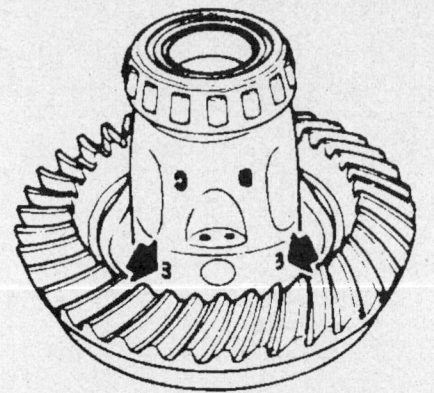

NS3039100036000X

Fig. 13 Location of C & D values. R180A differential

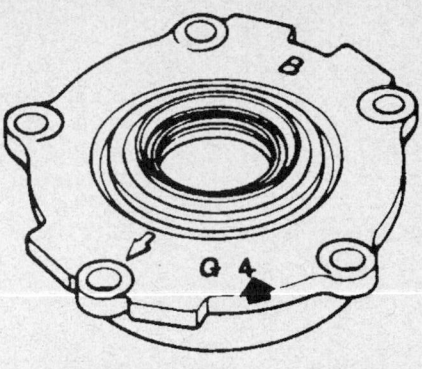

NS3039100037000X

Fig. 14 Location of G1 & G2 values. R180A differential

— Without collar

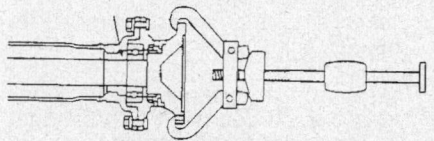

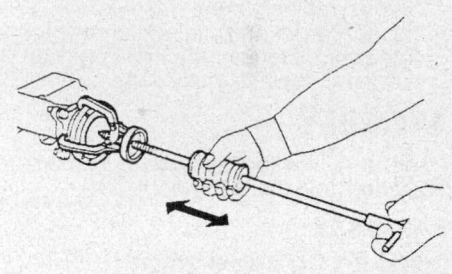

NS3039100039000X

Fig. 16 Axle bearing removal. R200A differential

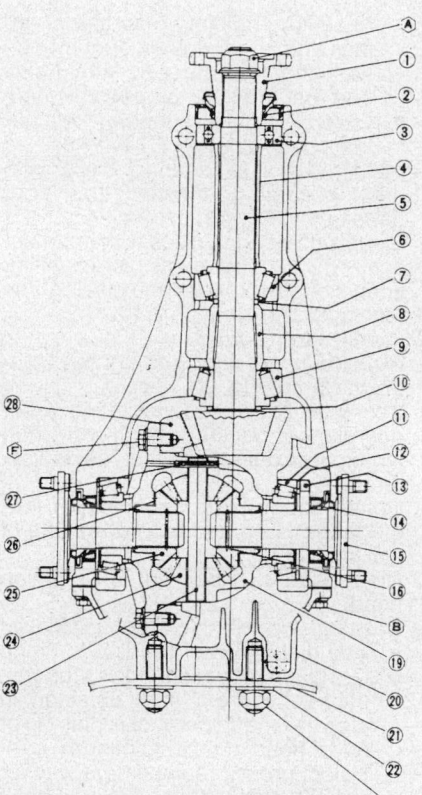

1 Companion flange
2 Front oil seal
   (Supply multi-purpose grease to oil seal lip when assembling)
3 Front pilot bearing
4 Front pilot bearing spacer
5 Drive pinion
6 Pinion front bearing
7 Pinion bearing adjusting washer
   (Adjust pinion bearing preload by selecting ⑦ and ⑧.)
8 Pinion bearing adjusting spacer
9 Pinion rear bearing
10 Pinion height adjusting washer
   (Adjust pinion height by selecting ⑩.)
11 Side bearing
12 Side bearing adjusting washer
   (Adjust side bearing preload and ring gear-to-drive pinion backlash by selecting ⑫.)
13 Side bearing spacer
14 Side oil seal
   (Supply multi-purpose grease to oil seal lip when assembling)
15 Side flange
16 Side flange circlip
17 Side bearing cap
18 Breather
   (Install with an arrow towards front.)
19 Differential case
20 Rear cover

21 Differential rear mounting member
22 Special washer
23 Pinion mate shaft
24 Pinion mate
25 Side gear
26 Thrust washer
   (Adjust the pinion mate-to-side gear backlash (or the clearance between the rear face of side gear and thrust washer) to 0.1 to 0.2 mm (0.039 to 0.0079 in) by ㉖.)
27 Lock pin
28 Ring gear

Tightening torque (T) of bolts and nuts   kg-m (ft-lb)
Ⓐ T : 19 to 22 (137 to 159)
Ⓑ T : 1.6 to 2.4 (12 to 17)
Ⓒ T : 9.0 to 10.0 (65 to 72)
Ⓓ T : 4.2 to 6.9 (30 to 50)
Ⓔ T : 7.5 to 9.5 (54 to 69)
Ⓕ T : 6.0 to 7.0 (43 to 51)

Using locking agent [Locktite (stud lock) or equivalent]

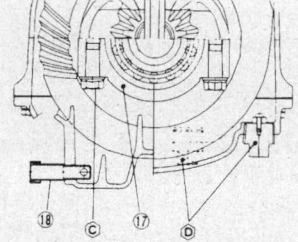

NS3039100038000X

Fig. 15 Cross-sectional view of differential carrier. R200, R200V & R230V differentials

DIFFERENTIAL SIDE SHAFT

R200A Differential

1. Cut rear axle bearing collar with cold chisel being careful not to damage differential side shaft, **Fig. 2.**
2. Reinstall differential side shaft into extension tube and secure with bolts. Remove rear axle bearing by drawing out differential side shaft from rear axle bearing with puller, **Fig. 16.**
3. Remove grease and oil seal.

R200 & R200A Differential Case

1. Remove bearing.
2. Remove ring gear.
3. Remove pinion mate shaft lockpin from ring gear side. **Lockpin is caulked at pin hole mouth on differential case.**
4. Remove pinion mate shaft and the pinion mate gears, side gears, thrust washers and thrust block, if equipped.

R200V & R230V Differential Case

1. Remove bearing.
2. Remove ring gear.
3. Place match marks on differential cases A and B.
4. Loosen screws and separate differential cases A and B.

INSPECTION

Thoroughly clean all disassembled parts, and examine them to see that they are worn, damaged or otherwise faulty, and how they are affected. Repair or replace all faulty parts, whichever is necessary.

1. Check gear teeth for scoring, cracking or chipping, and ensure that tooth contact pattern indicates correct meshing depth. If any fault is evident, replace parts as required. **Drive pinion and drive gear are supplied as a set; therefore, should either part be damaged, replace as a set.**
2. Check pinion gear shaft, and pinion gear for scores and signs of wear, and

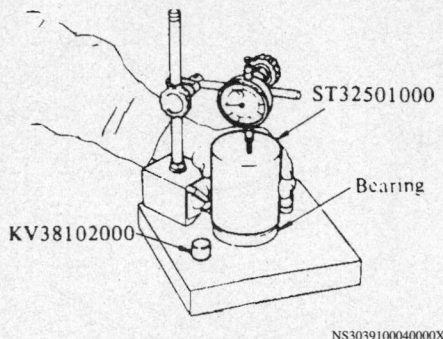

NS3039100040000X

Fig. 17 Bearing width measurement. R200, R200V & R230V differentials

replace as required. Follow the same procedure for side gear and their seats on differential case.

3. Inspect all bearing races and rollers for scoring, chipping or evidence of excessive wear.
4. Inspect thrust washer faces. Small faults can be corrected with sandpaper. Inspect pinion mate-to-side gear backlash. If clearance between side gear and thrust washer exceed specifications, replace thrust washers.
5. Inspect carrier and differential case for cracks or distortion. If either condition is evident, replace faulty parts.

ASSEMBLY

Reverse "Disassembly" procedure to assemble and note the following:

GEAR CASE

R200, R200V & R230V Differentials

1. **On R200 differential,** assemble pinion mates, side gears, thrust washers, and thrust block, if equipped, in differential case.
2. **On all models,** install pinion shaft to differential case.
3. Adjust side gear-to-pinion mate backlash or adjust the clearance between the rear face of side gear and thrust washer. Backlash or clearance should be .0039–.0079 inch, .0059 inch with tripod type driveshaft.
4. Lock pinion shaft lockpin.
5. Apply oil to gear tooth surfaces and thrust surfaces and check that they turn properly.
6. **On R200V and R230V differentials,** install differential case A to B.
7. **On all models,** place ring gear on differential case and apply a small amount of locking compound to the bolts, then install bolts.
8. **Torque** bolts to 51–58 ft. lbs.
9. Measure bearing width with a standard gauge (21.00mm thickness) and a weight block, about 5.5 lbs., prior to installation, **Fig. 17.**
10. Press side bearing inner race on differential case.

R200A Differential

1. Measure clearance between side gear

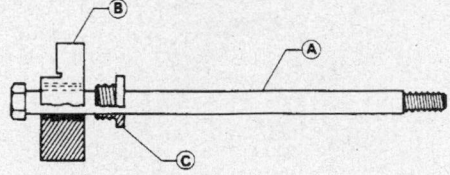

Tool number:
- Ⓐ Hex head long bolt (J25269-23)
- Ⓑ Gauge plate (J25269-1)
- Ⓒ Rear pinion bearing pilot (J25269-2)

NS3039100041000X

Fig. 18 Rear pinion bearing pilot & gauge plate installation on hex head long bolt. R200, R200V & R230V Differentials

thrust washer and differential case at dimensions A & B, **Fig. 5,** then subtract value B from A. Clearance should be .0039–.0079 inch. If measurement does not fall within specifications, clearance can be adjusted with a side gear thrust washer.

2. Apply gear oil to gear tooth surfaces and thrust surfaces and check if they turn properly.
3. Install left and right hand differential cases together.

DIFFERENTIAL SIDE SHAFT

R200A Differential

1. Measure extension tube at dimension A and dimension B, **Fig. 6,** then subtract value B from value A. Axle bearing endplay should be .0039 or less. If it is not, axle bearing endplay can be adjusted with bearing adjusting shims.
2. Using driver tool No. J26233, or equivalent, install grease seal.
3. Install extension tube retainer, axle bearing and axle shaft bearing collar on differential side shaft.

Drive Pinion Height & Preload, R200, R200V & R230V Differentials

1. Before adjusting pinion height and drive pinion bearing preload, set up each tool, rear pinion bearing and front pinion bearing as follows:
   a. Install rear pinion bearing pilot into gauge plate and slide over hex head long bolt, **Fig. 18.**
   b. Slide pinion rear bearing inner race, bearing preload adapter and pinion bearing adjusting spacer over hex head long bolt, **Fig. 19.**
   c. Install hex head long bolt assembly into gear carrier.
   d. Stand front bearing pilot support on workbench with appropriate side up and assemble front pinion bearing pilot, front pinion bearing inner race and lead preload washer, ensuring that all parts are seated, **Fig. 19.**
   e. Install assembly, **Fig. 20,** over hex

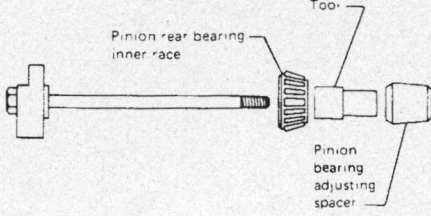

Tool number:
Bearing preload adapter (J25269-26)

NS3039100042000X

Fig. 19 Bearing preload adapter & pinion bearing adjusting spacer installation on hex head long bolt. R200, R200V & R230V Differentials

head long bolt into gear carrier. Install and finger tighten support nut, ensuring that all parts turn freely and that they are properly aligned.
   f. Carefully tighten support nut to obtain preload of 5.2–8.7 inch lbs.
2. Install two side bearing discs with arbor assembly, ensuring that arbor turns freely, **Fig. 21.**
3. Place side bearing discs with arbor assembly into differential carrier, lifting spring loaded plunger and placing it on face of gauge plate, **Fig. 22.**
4. Install bearing caps.
5. Install dial indicator and tighten holddown clamp, **Fig. 23.**
6. Zero dial indicator by rotating arbor and plunger back and forth while noting highest deflection, then set indicator at zero.
7. Rotate gauge plate until plunger falls off gauge plate and record reading of dial indicator.
8. Note head number on drive pinion head.
9. Calculate washer thickness as follows:
   a. Add dial indicator reading to 3mm.
   b. Using drive pinion head number, subtract it from sum obtained in step 9a if head number is plus (+) or add if head number is minus (-).
   c. Select proper replacement washer equal to total obtained in step 9b. If washer is not available in calculated thickness, use washer whose thickness is closest to calculated thickness.
10. To determine pinion bearing preload, disassemble pinion height/bearing preload tools and measure thickness of lead washer. This is correct size pinion bearing adjusting washer required.
11. If shims are not available in determined thickness, use shims so that total thickness is closest to calculated value. **Sometimes the correct dimension cannot be set with washers only. If this is the case, washers may be used in combination with drive pinion bearing adjusting spacers.**

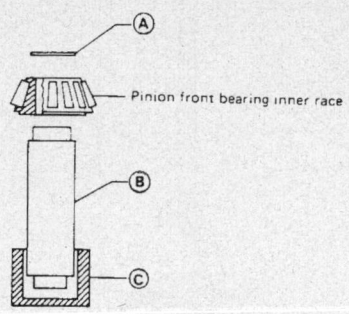

Tool number:
- Ⓐ Lead preload washer (J25269-25)
- Ⓑ Front pinion bearing pilot (J25269-3)
- Ⓒ Front bearing pilot support (J25269-29)

NS3039100043000X

Fig. 20 Front bearing pilot support assembly. R200, R200V & R230V Differentials

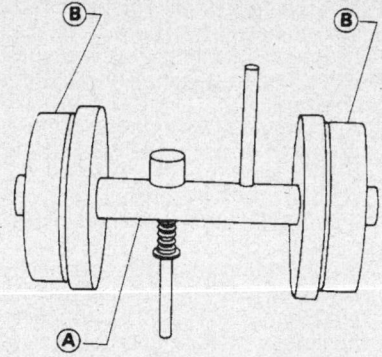

Tool number:
- Ⓐ Arbor assembly (J23597-1)
- Ⓑ Side bearing disc (J25269-4)

NS3039100044000X

Fig. 21 Arbor assembly w/side bearing discs. R200, R200V & R230V Differentials

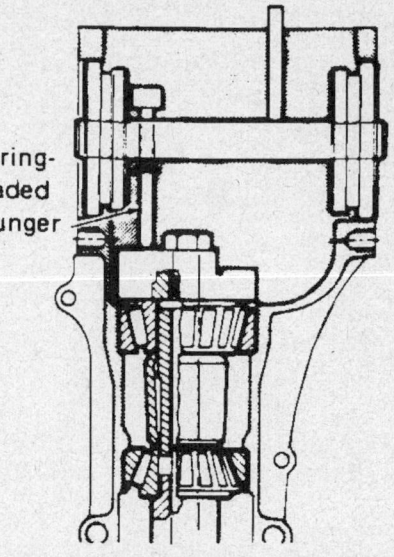

Spring-loaded plunger

NS3039100045000X

Fig. 22 Arbor assembly w/discs installation into differential carrier. R200, R200V & R230V Differentials

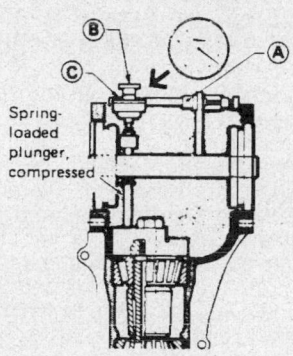

Spring-loaded plunger, compressed

Tool number:
- Ⓐ Hold down clamp (J8001-1)
- Ⓑ Dial indicator clamp (J8001-2)
- Ⓒ Dial indicator (J8001-6)

NS3039100046000X

Fig. 23 Dial indicator installation. R200, R200V & R230V Differentials

Side Bearing Washers, Except R200, R200V & R230V Differentials

1. If the hypoid gear set, carrier, differential case or side bearing has been replaced with new part, adjust the side bearing preload with adjusting washer. The required thicknesses of the left and right washers can be obtained from the following formulas: $T1 = (A-CD-H') \times 0.01$ 2.05; $T2 = (B-DH') \times 0.01$ 1.95; where $T1$ = required thickness of left side washer in millimeters, **Fig. 24**, $T2$ = required thickness of right side washer in millimeters, **Fig. 24**, A & B = figure marked on the gear carrier, **Fig. 25**, C & D = figure marked on the differential case, **Fig. 26**, E & F = differences in width of left or right side bearing against the standard width (21.00mm) and figures for A, B, C and

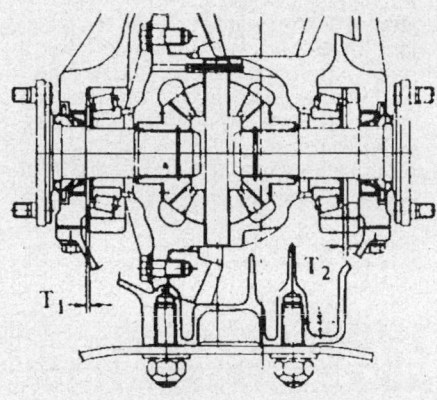

NS3039100047000X

Fig. 24 Side bearing washer thickness. Except R200, R200V & R230V Differentials

D are dimensional variations in a unit of $\frac{1}{100}$mm against each standard measurement. The decrease or increase in thickness of washers causes change in ring gear-to-pinion backlash. Before calculation, determine "G" value by measuring spacer thickness. If spacer is deformed or scratched, replace. **If values signifying A, B, C and D are not given, regard value as zero and compute.**

2. Install differential case assembly with side bearing outer races into carrier.
3. Insert left and right side bearing preload adjusting washers in place between side bearings and housing.
4. Drive in side bearing spacer between righthand washer and housing.
5. Align mark on bearing cap with that on carrier and install bearing cap on carrier. **Torque** bolts to 65–72 ft. lbs.
6. Measure ring gear-to-drive pinion backlash with a dial indicator and adjust to .0051–.0071 inch, **Fig. 27.** If below the specified value, replace left washer with a thinner one and right washer with a thicker one. If over, re-

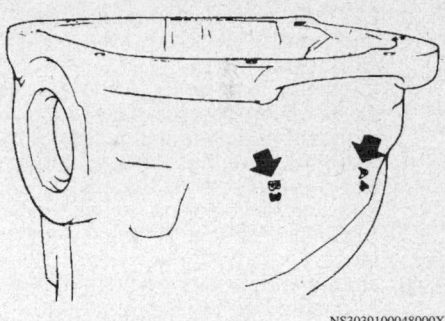

NS3039100048000X

Fig. 25 Location of A & B values. Except R200, R200V & R230V Differentials

place left washer with a thicker one and right washer with a thinner one. **To maintain correct preload at all times, do not change total thickness of washers.**

Side Bearing Washers, R200, R200V & R230V Differentials

1. The required thicknesses of the left and right adjusting washers can be obtained from the following formulas: $T1 = A - C D E - H$ 2.05mm; $T2 = B - D F G H$ 1.95mm; where $T1$ = required thickness of left side washer in millimeters, $T2$ = required thickness of right side washer in millimeters, A & B = figure marked on gear carrier, **Fig. 25**, C & D = figure marked on differential case, **Fig. 26**, E & F = side bearing measurements as determined in step 2, G = difference between 8.10mm and measured thickness of side spacer and H = figure marked on ring gear.
2. Calculate how far under standard thickness of 21mm the side bearings are using tool Nos. J25407-1,

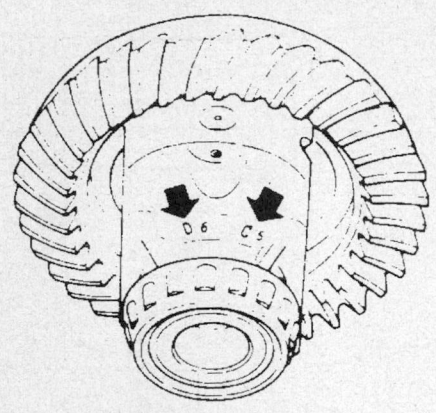

NS3039100049000X

Fig. 26 Location of C & D values. Except R200, R200V & R230V Differentials

J25407-2 and J25407-3, or equivalents, as follows:

a. Set weight block, 4 step gauge block and dial indicator on base plate.
b. Adjust dial indicator to zero.
c. Carefully slide 4 step gauge block and weight block out from under dial indicator.
d. Lubricate side bearing and place side bearing on base plate, ensuring that base plate has recess in it and that bearing will turn freely when positioned over recess.
e. Place weight block on side bearing.
f. Slide dial indicator onto weight block.
g. Rotate weight block several times to ensure bearing is properly seated.
h. Read dial indicator. Indicator should read .10–.30mm. **If needle fluctuates erratically, bearing is either dirty or faulty and should be cleaned or replaced as necessary.**
i. Measurement obtained for left side bearing is measurement E, step 1 and measurement obtained for right side bearing is measurement F.

3. Press in front and rear bearing outer races.
4. Install selected pinion height adjusting washer in drive pinion and press in rear bearing inner race.
5. Set drive pinion assembly in differential carrier and install drive pinion with suitable tool.
6. Apply suitable lubricant to cavity at sealing lips of oil seal, then install front oil seal.
7. Install companion flange and **torque** pinion nut to 137–159 ft. lbs.
8. Turn drive pinion in both directions several times, then measure pinion bearing preload. If preload is not 10–15.2 inch lbs., replace pinion bearing adjusting washer and spacer with a different thickness.
9. Install differential case assembly with side bearing outer races into gear carrier.

10. Insert selected left and right side bearing adjusting washers in place between side bearings and carrier.
11. Drive in side bearing spacer with suitable tool.
12. Align mark on bearing cap with that on gear carrier and install bearing cap on gear carrier.
13. Apply suitable lubricant to cavity at sealing lips of oil seal, then install side oil seal.
14. Measure ring gear to drive pinion backlash with a dial indicator. If backlash is less than .0051–.0071 inch, decrease thickness of right shim and increase thickness of left shim by same amount. If backlash exceeds .0051–.0071 inch, increase thickness of right shim and decrease thickness of left shim by same amount. **Never change the total amount of shims to prevent changing bearing preload.**
15. Check total preload, which should be 10.9–20.4 inch lbs. If preload is too great, add the same amount of shims to each side. If preload is too small, remove the same amount of shims from each side.
16. Recheck ring gear to drive pinion backlash and check runout of ring gear. If backlash varies excessively in different places, foreign matter may be trapped between ring gear and differential case.
17. If backlash varies greatly, hypoid gear set or differential case needs to be replaced.
18. Install rear cover with gasket.

H190A, C200A & H233B DIFFERENTIALS

DISASSEMBLE

1. Remove rear cover and scribe alignment marks between side bearing caps and carrier, then remove side bearing caps, side bearing adjuster, if equipped, and differential case.
2. Using suitable tools, remove drive pinion nut, companion flange and drive pinion.
3. Pry out oil seal, being careful not to scratch seal bore, then remove front pinion bearing inner race.
4. Drive out pinion bearing outer race.
5. Remove collapsible spacer and washer from drive pinion, as required.
6. Press out rear bearing inner race.

DIFFERENTIAL CASE

1. Using suitable tool, remove side bearing inner race.
2. Remove ring gear.
3. **On models equipped with two pinion type differential,** proceed as follows:
   a. Drive out pinion mate shaft lockpin from ring gear side.
   b. Remove pinion mate shaft, pinion mate gears, side gears and thrust washers, marking gears and thrust washers so that they can be installed in original position.

NS3039100050000X

Fig. 27 Ring & pinion backlash measurement. Except R200, R200V & R230V Differentials

4. **On models equipped with four pinion type differential,** proceed as follows:
   a. Scribe alignment marks on both lefthand and righthand differential case, then separate lefthand and righthand cases.
   b. Remove side thrust washers, side gear, thrust block if equipped, pinion mate thrust washer, pinion mate gear and pinion mate shaft.

INSPECTION

Thoroughly clean all disassembled parts, and examine them to see if they are worn, damaged or otherwise faulty, and how they are affected. Repair or replace all faulty parts, whichever is necessary.

1. Check gear teeth for scoring, cracking and chipping.
2. Check pinion gear shaft, and pinion gear for scores and wear, and replace as required. Follow the same procedure for side gear and their seats on differential case.
3. Inspect all bearing races and rollers for scoring, chipping or evidence of excessive wear.
4. Inspect thrust washer faces. Small faults can be corrected with sandpaper.
5. Inspect carrier and differential case for cracks or distortion. If either condition is evident, replace faulty parts.

ASSEMBLE

Reverse "Disassemble" procedure to assemble. Note the following procedures during assembly.

DIFFERENTIAL CASE ASSEMBLY
Two Pinion Type Differential

1. Assemble pinion mates, side gears, thrust washers, and thrust block, if

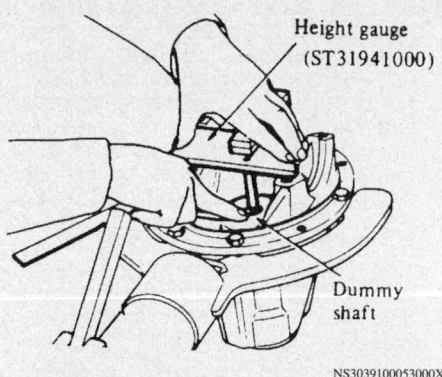

Fig. 28 Drive pinion marking

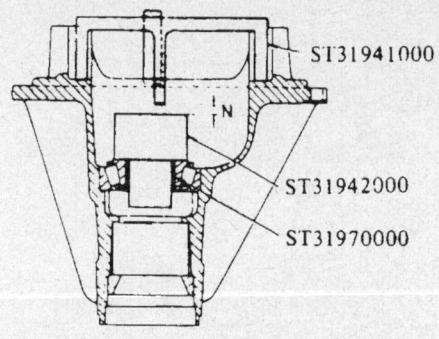

Fig. 29 Pinion height adjusting tools installation

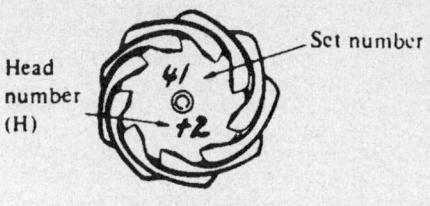

Fig. 30 Pinion height measurement

equipped, in differential case.

2. Install pinion shaft to differential case so that it meets lockpin holes.
3. Adjust pinion mate-to-side gear backlash or the clearance between the rear face of side gear and thrust washer to proper thickness by selecting side gear thrust washer.
4. Lock pinion shaft lockpin using a punch after it is secured into place.
5. Apply oil to gear tooth surfaces and thrust surfaces and check if they turn properly.
6. Apply suitable locking compound to ring gear attaching bolts, then place ring gear on differential case and install bolts and lock washers. **Torque** bolts to 58–72 ft. lbs. on models equipped with 10mm bolts and 98–112 ft. lbs. on models equipped with 12mm bolts, then bend up lock washers, if equipped.

Four Pinion Type Differential

1. Measure clearance between side gear thrust washer and differential case, **Fig. 5.** Clearance (A) and (B) should be .0039–.0079 inch.
2. If clearance is not as specified, adjust by installing correct side gear thrust washer.
3. Apply suitable gear oil to gear tooth surfaces and thrust surfaces, then install thrust washer, pinion mate shaft, pinion mate gear, pinion mate thrust washer, thrust block if equipped and side gear in differential case.
4. Assemble lefthand and righthand differential case, then the ring gear on differential case.
5. Apply suitable locking compound on ring gear attaching bolts, then install bolts. **Torque** attaching bolts in a criss-cross pattern to 58–69 ft. lbs. on H233B model axle, 51–58 ft. lbs. for 10mm bolts on C200A model axle and 98–112 ft. lbs. for 12mm bolts on C200A model axle.
6. Press side bearing inner race on differential case using suitable tools.

DRIVE PINION HEIGHT, H190A AXLE

Pathfinder

Adjust the pinion height with washer pro-

vided between rear bearing inner race and the back of pinion gear.

1. Press front and rear bearing outer races into gear carrier.
2. Install rear bearing on carrier and install dummy shaft and collar on rear bearing, and place height gauge on carrier, **Fig. 28.**
3. Measure the clearance (N) between the tip end of height gauge and the end surface of dummy shaft, using a thickness gauge, **Fig. 29.**
4. The thickness of drive pinion height adjusting washers can be obtained from the following formula: T = N-(H - D - S X 0.01) 2.18; where T = required thickness of rear bearing adjusting washers in millimeters, N = measured value with thickness gauge in millimeters, H = figure marked on the drive pinion head, **Fig. 30,** D = figure marked on the dummy shaft, S = figure marked on the height gauge and figures for H, D' and S are dimensional variations in a unit of $\frac{1}{100}$mm against each standard measurement. **If values signifying H, D' and S are not given, regard value as zero and compute.**
5. Install determined pinion height adjusting washer in drive pinion, and press rear bearing inner race in.

Frontier & Pickup

1. Ensure all parts are clean and that bearings are well lubricated.
2. Assemble pinion gear bearings into pinion preload shim selector tool No. J-34309, or equivalent, noting the following:
   a. Front pinion bearing — Ensure front pinion bearing is secured tightly against gauge anvil, then turn front pinion bearing pilot tool No. J-34309-5, or equivalent, to secure bearing in position.
   b. Rear pinion bearing — Rear pinion bearing pilot tool No. J-34309-15, or equivalent, is used to center rear pinion bearing only. Lock bearing to assembly with rear pinion bearing locking seat tool No. J-34309-4, or equivalent.
3. Position pinion preload shim selector tool No. J-34309-1, or equivalent, gauge screw assembly with pinion rear bearing inner cone installed into final drive housing.

4. Assemble front pinion bearing inner cone and gauge anvil tool No. J-34309-2, or equivalent, together with gauge screw tool No. J-34309-1, or equivalent, in final drive housing.
5. Ensure pinion height plate tool No. J-34309-16, or equivalent, will turn a full 360°, then hand tighten the two sections.
6. Turn assembly several times to seat bearings, then measure turning torque at end of gauge anvil. Turning **Torque** should be 9–11 inch lbs.
7. Place pinion height adapter tool No. J-34309-14, or equivalent, onto gauge plate and hand tighten. **Ensure all machined surfaces are clean.**
8. Install side bearing discs tool No. J-25269-18, or equivalent, and arbor into side bearing bores.
9. Install side bearing caps and cap attaching bolts. **Torque** attaching bolts to 36–43 ft. lbs.
10. Using a suitable feeler gauge, select standard pinion height adjusting washer thickness by measuring gap between pinion height adapter tool No. J-34309-14, or equivalent, and arbor.
11. Add or subtract head number on drive pinion head, **Fig. 30,** to measurement found in step 10 to determine the optimum pinion height adjusting washer thickness. **The head number on drive pinion head is in millimeters.**
12. Remove pinion preload selector tool No. J-34309, or equivalent, from final drive housing.

DRIVE PINION HEIGHT, C200A AXLE

Frontier

1. Ensure all parts are clean and that bearings are well lubricated.
2. Assemble pinion gear bearings into pinion preload shim selector tool No. J-34309, or equivalent, noting the following:
   a. Front pinion bearing — Ensure front pinion bearing is secured tightly against gauge anvil tool No. J-34309-2, or equivalent, then turn front pinion bearing pilot tool No. J-34309-5, or equivalent, to secure bearing in position.
   b. Rear pinion bearing — Rear pinion bearing pilot tool J-34309-15 or equivalent, is used to center rear pinion bearing only. Lock bearing to assembly with rear pinion bearing locking seat tool No. J-34309-4, or equivalent.
3. Position pinion preload shim selector

gauge screw assembly tool No. J-34309-1, or equivalent, with pinion rear bearing inner cone installed into final drive housing.

4. Assemble front pinion bearing inner cone and gauge anvil tool No. J-34309-2, or equivalent, together with gauge screw tool No. J-34309-1, or equivalent, in final drive housing.
5. Ensure pinion height plate tool No. J-34309-16, or equivalent, will turn a full 360°, then hand tighten the two sections.
6. Turn assembly several times to seat bearings, then measure turning torque at end of gauge anvil. Turning **torque** should be 9–11 inch lbs.
7. Place pinion height adapter tool No. J-34309-13, or equivalent, onto gauge plate and hand tighten. **Ensure all machined surfaces are clean.**
8. Install side bearing discs tool No. J-25269-4, or equivalent, and arbor into side bearing bores.
9. Install side bearing caps and cap attaching bolts. **Torque** attaching bolts to 65–72 ft. lbs.
10. Using a suitable gauges, select standard pinion height adjusting washer thickness by measuring gap between pinion height adapter tool No. J-34309-13, or equivalent, and arbor.
11. Add or subtract head number on drive pinion head, **Fig. 30,** to measurement found in step 10 to determine the optimum pinion height adjusting washer thickness. **The head number on drive pinion head is in millimeters.**
12. Remove pinion preload selector tool No. J-34309, or equivalent, from final drive housing.

DRIVE PINION HEIGHT & DRIVE PINION PRELOAD

1. Ensure all parts are clean and that bearings are well lubricated.
2. Assemble pinion gear bearings into pinion preload shim selector tool No. J-34309, or equivalent, noting the following:
   a. Front pinion bearing — Ensure front pinion bearing is secured tightly against gauge anvil tool No. J-34309-2, or equivalent, then turn front pinion bearing pilot tool No. J-34309-5,or equivalent, to secure bearing in position.
   b. Rear pinion bearing — Rear pinion bearing pilot tool No. J-34309-8, or equivalent, is used to center rear pinion bearing only. Lock bearing to assembly with rear pinion bearing locking seat tool No. J-34309-4, or equivalent.
3. Position pinion preload shim selector gauge screw assembly tool No. J-34309-1, or equivalent, with pinion rear bearing inner cone installed into final drive housing.
4. Assemble front pinion bearing inner cone and gauge anvil tool No. J-34309-2, or equivalent, together with gauge screw tool No. J-34309-1, or equivalent, in final drive housing.
5. Ensure pinion height plate tool No. J-34309-16, or equivalent, will turn a

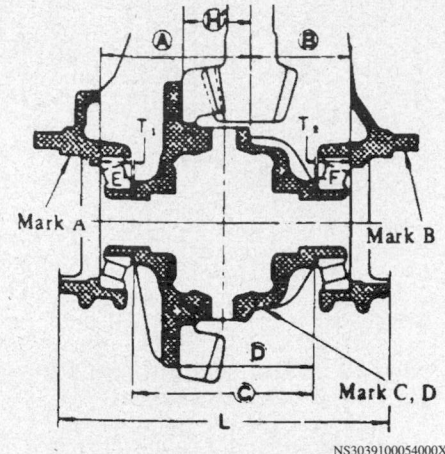

Fig. 31 Side bearing shim thickness. H190A axle

NS3039100054000X

full 360°, then hand tighten the two sections.
6. Turn assembly several times to seat bearings, then measure turning torque at end of gauge anvil. Turning **torque** should be 4–8 inch lbs.
7. Place pinion height adapter tool No. J-34309-12, or equivalent, onto gauge plate and hand tighten. **Ensure all machined surfaces are clean.**
8. Place solid pinion bearing adjusting spacer squarely into recessed portion of gauge anvil and rest its end on gauge screw tool No. J-34209-1, or equivalent.
9. Using a suitable feeler gauge, select correct thickness of pinion bearing preload adjusting washer. **The exact measurement obtained with feeler gauge is thickness of adjusting shim required.**
10. Install side bearing discs tool No. J-25269-18, or equivalent, and arbor into side bearing bores.
11. Install bearing caps and cap attaching bolts. **Torque** attaching bolts to 69–76 ft. lbs.
12. Using a suitable gauge, select standard pinion height adjusting washer thickness by measuring gap between pinion height adapter tool No. J-34309-12, or equivalent, and arbor.
13. Add or subtract head number on drive pinion head, **Fig. 30,** to measurement found in step 10 to determine the optimum pinion height adjusting washer thickness. **The head number on drive pinion head is in millimeters.**
14. Remove pinion preload selector tool No. J-34309, or equivalent, from final drive housing.

SIDE BEARING PRELOAD & FINAL ASSEMBLY
Except Pickup

1. If hypoid gear set, carrier, differential case or side bearing have been replaced with new ones, adjust the side bearing preload with adjusting shim. The required thickness of adjusting shim can be calculated by the following formulas: $T1 = (A - C D - H) \times 0.01$

$0.175\ E$; $T2 = (B - D H) \times 0.01\ 0.150\ F$; where $T1$ = required thickness of left side bearing adjusting shim in millimeters, **Fig. 31,** $T2$ = required thickness of right side bearing adjusting shim in millimeters, **Fig. 31,** A = figure marked on the left side bearing housing of gear carrier, B figure marked on the right side bearing of gear carrier, C & D = figure marked on the differential case, E & F: = differences in width of left or right side bearing against the standard width (20.00 mm) in millimeters, H = figure marked on the ring gear and figures for A, B, C, D and H are dimensional variations in a unit of $1/100$mm against each standard measurement. **If values signifying A, B, C, D and H are not given, regard value as zero and compute.**

2. Install determined side bearing adjusting shim on differential case, and press left and right side bearing inner races in.
3. Install differential case assembly into gear carrier, tapping with a rubber mallet.
4. Align mark on bearing cap with that on gear carrier, and install bearing cap on carrier. **Torque** bolts 36–43 ft. lbs. on all other models.
5. Measure ring gear-to-drive pinion backlash, **Fig. 32.** If backlash is too small, remove shims from left side and add them to right side. To reduce backlash, remove shims from right side and add them to left side.
6. At the same time, check side bearing preload. Bearing preload should be 10.4–17.4 inch lbs.

Pickup

1. Ensure all parts are clean and that bearings are well lubricated with suitable oil.
2. Remove carrier side bearing using a suitable puller, then reinstall all original side bearing adjusting shims on carrier side (away from ring gear).
3. Press on carrier side bearing using suitable tools.
4. Install carrier and bearings into final drive housing.
5. Install side bearing caps and cap attaching bolts. **Torque** attaching bolts to 36–43 ft. lbs. and tap on caps with suitable hammer to seat bearings.
6. Turn carrier several times to seat bearings, then measure carrier turning force with suitable spring scale. Turning force at ring gear bolt should be 8–9 lbs.
7. If turning force is not as specified, correct by adding to or subtracting from the total amount of shim thickness.
8. Press in front and rear bearing outer races, then install selected pinion height adjusting washer in drive pinion and press in rear bearing outer race.
9. Place pinion front bearing inner race in gear carrier.
10. Apply suitable lubricant to cavity at sealing lips of oil seal, then install front oil seal.
11. Install drive pinion washer, collapsible spacer and drive pinion in gear carrier.

12. Install companion flange and hold firmly, then insert pinion into companion flange.
13. Temporarily tighten pinion nut until there is no axial play. **Ensure threaded portion of drive pinion and pinion nut are free from oil or grease.**
14. Tighten pinion nut by degrees until preload is 10–14 inch lbs. **When checking preload, turn drive pinion several times in both directions to seat bearings.**
15. Install differential case assembly with side bearing outer races into gear carrier.
16. Align mark on bearing cap with mark on gear carrier and install bearing cap on gear carrier.
17. Measure ring gear to drive pinion backlash with dial indicator. If backlash is less than .0051–0071 inch, decrease thickness of left shim and increase thickness of right shim by same amount. If backlash exceeds .0051–.0071 inch, increase thickness of right shim and decrease thickness of left shim by same amount. **Never change the total amount of shims to prevent changing bearing preload.**
18. Check total preload, which should be 10–19 inch lbs. If preload is too great, remove same amount of shims from each side. If preload is too small, install same amount of shims on each side.
19. Recheck ring gear to drive pinion backlash and check runout of gear. If backlash varies excessively in different places, foreign matter may be trapped between ring gear and differential case.
20. If backlash varies greatly and ring gear runout is .0031 inch or less, the hypoid gear set or differential case needs to be replaced.

SIDE BEARING PRELOAD & FINAL ASSEMBLY, C200A AXLE
Pathfinder

1. Ensure all parts are clean and that bearings are well lubricated with suitable oil.
2. Install carrier and bearings into final drive housing.
3. Install side bearing spacer in position on ring gear end of carrier.
4. Install both of the original carrier side bearing preload shims on carrier end (opposite ring gear).
5. Install side bearing caps and cap attaching bolts. **Torque** attaching bolts to 65–72 ft. lbs. and tap on caps with suitable hammer to seat bearings.
6. Turn carrier several times to seat bearings, then measure carrier turning force with suitable spring scale. Turning force at ring gear bolt should be 8–9 lbs.
7. If turning force is not as specified, correct by adding to or subtracting from the total amount of shim thickness.

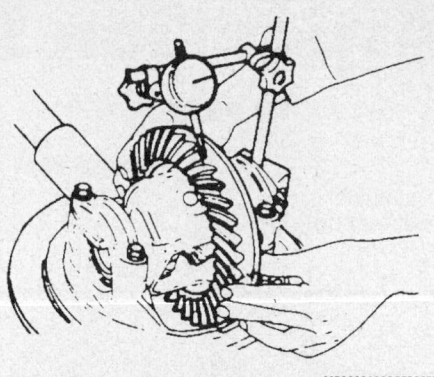

NS3039100055000X

Fig. 32 Ring & pinion backlash measurement. H190A axle

8. Press in front and rear bearing outer races, then install selected pinion height adjusting washer in drive pinion and press in rear bearing outer race.
9. Place pinion front bearing inner race in gear carrier.
10. Apply suitable lubricant to cavity at sealing lips of oil seal, then install front oil seal.
11. Install drive pinion spacer, drive pinion bearing and drive pinion in gear carrier.
12. Install companion flange into pinion using a suitable hammer.
13. **Torque** pinion nut 94 ft. lbs. **Ensure threaded portion of drive pinion and pinion nut are free from oil or grease.**
14. Tighten pinion nut by degrees until preload is 10–15 inch lbs. **When checking preload, turn drive pinion several times in both directions to seat bearings.**
15. Install differential case assembly with side bearing outer races into gear carrier.
16. Install right and left side bearing adjusting washers in position between side bearing and carrier, then drive in side bearing spacer using a suitable tool.
17. Align mark on bearing cap with mark on gear carrier and install bearing cap on gear carrier.
18. Measure ring gear to drive pinion backlash with dial indicator. If backlash is less than .0051–0071 inch, decrease thickness of left shim and increase thickness of right shim by same amount. If backlash exceeds .0051–.0071 inch, increase thickness of right shim and decrease thickness of left shim by same amount. **Never change the total amount of shims to prevent changing bearing preload.**
19. Check total preload, which should be 10–20 inch lbs. If preload is too great, remove same amount of shims from each side. If preload is too small, add same amount of shims to each side.
20. Recheck ring gear to drive pinion backlash and check runout of gear. If backlash varies excessively in different places, foreign matter may be trapped between ring gear and differential case.
21. If backlash varies greatly and ring gear runout is .0031 inch or less, the hypoid gear set or differential case needs to be replaced.

SIDE BEARING PRELOAD & FINAL ASSEMBLY, H233B AXLE

1. Press in front and rear bearing outer races, then install selected drive pinion adjusting washer in drive pinion and press in rear bearing outer race.
2. Place pinion front bearing inner race in gear carrier.
3. Apply suitable lubricant to cavity at sealing lips of oil seal, then install front oil seal.
4. Install drive pinion spacer, pinion bearing adjusting shim and drive pinion in gear carrier.
5. Install companion flange into drive pinion.
6. Temporarily **torque** pinion nut to 145–181 ft. lbs. **Ensure threaded portion of drive pinion and pinion nut are free from oil or grease.**
7. Measure pinion bearing preload. Preload should be 4–9 inch lbs. **When checking preload, turn drive pinion several times in both directions to seat bearings.**
8. Install differential case assembly with side bearing outer races into gear carrier.
9. Position side bearing adjusters on gear carrier with threads properly engaged, then lightly screw in adjusters.
10. Align mark on bearing cap with mark on gear carrier and install bearing cap on gear carrier. **Do not tighten cap attaching bolts at this point.**
11. Tighten both right and left side bearing adjusters alternately, then measure ring gear backlash with dial indicator. Backlash should be .0059–.0079 inch. If backlash is not as specified, adjust right and left side bearing adjusters by tightening them alternately until specified backlash is obtained.
12. Check total preload, which should be 9–17 inch lbs. If preload is not as specified, adjust right and left side bearing adjusters by tightening them alternately until specified preload is obtained.
13. **Torque** side bearing cap bolts to 69–76 ft. lbs., then place lock finger in position to prevent adjuster rotation during operation.
14. Recheck backlash and ring gear runout of gear. If backlash varies excessively in different places, foreign matter may be trapped between ring gear and differential case.
15. If backlash varies greatly and ring gear runout is .0031 inch or less, the hypoid gear set or differential case needs to be replaced.

Active Suspension Systems

INDEX

DESCRIPTION

This system, shown in **Figs. 1 and 2**, uses a shock absorber select switch, control unit, shock absorber sensors and control motors to control shock absorber valving. The system allows the driver to select the shock absorber valving that is suitable for various driving conditions.

TROUBLESHOOTING

300ZX

The shock absorber control unit has a self check function to determine whether the control unit is working properly. A malfunction is displayed by an L.E.D. which is located on select switch.

Refer to **Fig. 3** for system troubleshooting charts.

PATHFINDER

Terminal Inspection

1. Disconnect adjustable shock absorber connector.
2. Ensure continuity exists between terminal 3 of connector and body ground.
3. Measure voltage between terminals 2 and 3 then 1 and 3 of the connector and ensure voltage is as specified in **Fig. 4**.

Select Switch Inspection

Disconnect select switch connector, then connect an ohmmeter to switch and test for continuity as shown in **Fig. 5**.

Shock Absorber Inspection

Attach a suitable tool to shock absorber, then check for operating sound of the actuator when select switch is moved from one position to the other.

DIAGNOSIS & TESTING

300ZX

Refer to **Fig. 6** for diagnostic procedures.

PATHFINDER

Refer to **Fig. 7** for diagnostic procedures.

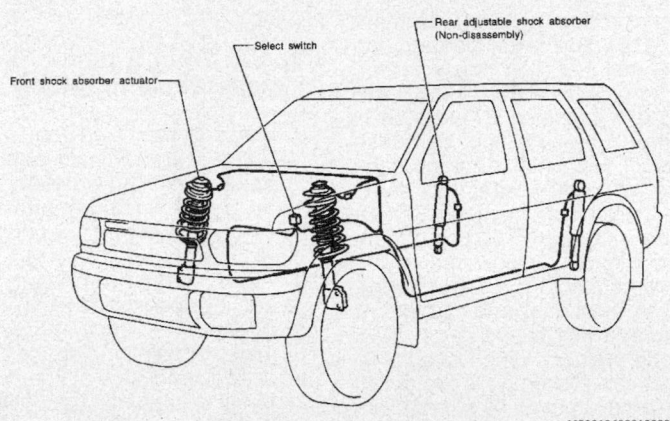

NS2019600010000X

Fig. 1 Adjustable shock absorber system components. Pathfinder

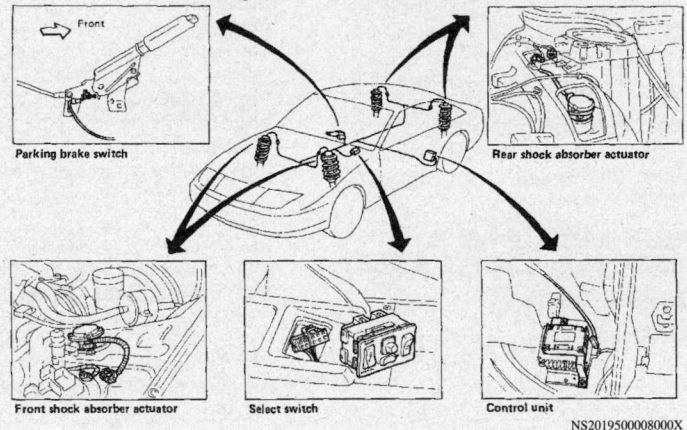

NS2019500008000X

Fig. 2 Adjustable shock absorber system components. 300ZX

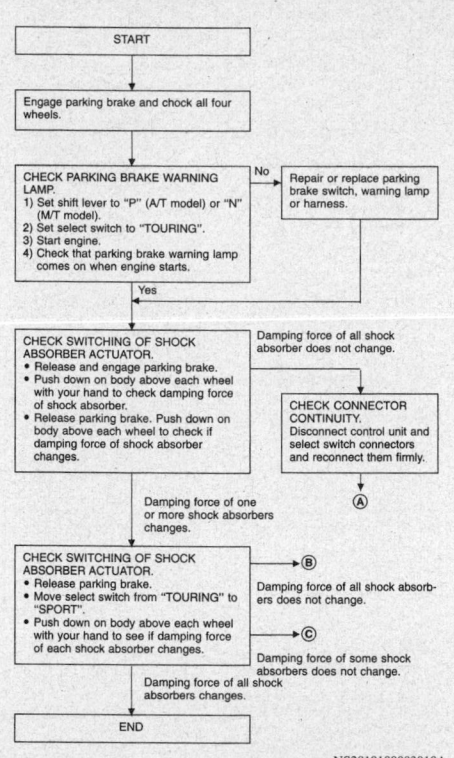

Part 1 flowchart (Fig. 3):

START

↓

Engage parking brake and chock all four wheels.

↓

CHECK PARKING BRAKE WARNING LAMP.
1) Set shift lever to "P" (A/T model) or "N" (M/T model).
2) Set select switch to "TOURING".
3) Start engine.
4) Check that parking brake warning lamp comes on when engine starts.

— No → Repair or replace parking brake switch, warning lamp or harness.

↓ Yes

CHECK SWITCHING OF SHOCK ABSORBER ACTUATOR.
• Release and engage parking brake.
• Push down on body above each wheel with your hand to check damping force of shock absorber.
• Release parking brake. Push down on body above each wheel to check if damping force of shock absorber changes.

— Damping force of all shock absorber does not change. → CHECK CONNECTOR CONTINUITY. Disconnect control unit and select switch connectors and reconnect them firmly. → (A)

↓ Damping force of one or more shock absorbers changes.

CHECK SWITCHING OF SHOCK ABSORBER ACTUATOR.
• Release parking brake.
• Move select switch from "TOURING" to "SPORT".
• Push down on body above each wheel with your hand to see if damping force of each shock absorber changes.

— Damping force of all shock absorbers does not change. → (B)
— Damping force of some shock absorbers does not change. → (C)

↓ Damping force of all shock absorbers changes.

END

NS2019100003010A

Fig. 3 Adjustable shock absorber system suspension troubleshooting charts (Part 1 of 3). 300ZX

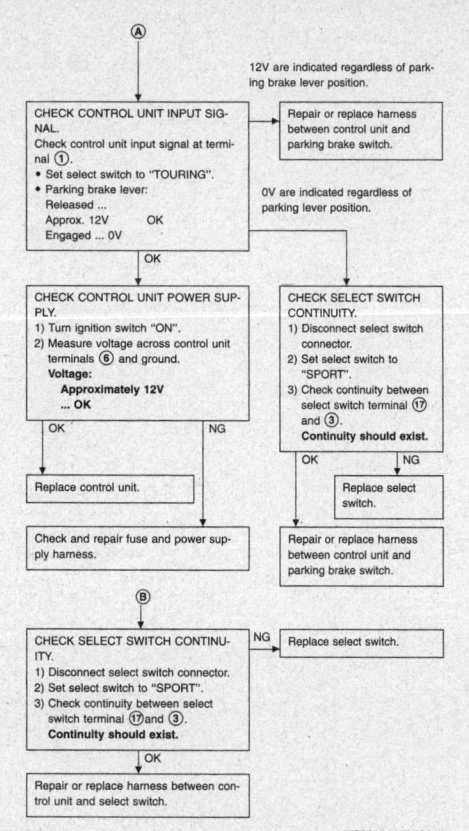

Part 2 flowchart (Fig. 3):

(A)

↓

CHECK CONTROL UNIT INPUT SIGNAL.
Check control unit input signal at terminal ①.
• Set select switch to "TOURING".
• Parking brake lever:
 Released ... Approx. 12V OK
 Engaged ... 0V OK

— 12V are indicated regardless of parking brake lever position. → Repair or replace harness between control unit and parking brake switch.
— 0V are indicated regardless of parking lever position.

↓ OK

CHECK CONTROL UNIT POWER SUPPLY.
1) Turn ignition switch "ON".
2) Measure voltage across control unit terminals ⑥ and ground.
Voltage: Approximately 12V ... OK

— OK → Replace control unit.
— NG → Check and repair fuse and power supply harness.

CHECK SELECT SWITCH CONTINUITY.
1) Disconnect select switch connector.
2) Set select switch to "SPORT".
3) Check continuity between select switch terminal ⑰ and ③.
Continuity should exist.

— OK → Repair or replace harness between control unit and parking brake switch.
— NG → Replace select switch.

(B)

↓

CHECK SELECT SWITCH CONTINUITY.
1) Disconnect select switch connector.
2) Set select switch to "SPORT".
3) Check continuity between select switch terminal ⑰ and ③.
Continuity should exist.

— NG → Replace select switch.

↓ OK

Repair or replace harness between control unit and select switch.

NS2019100003020A

Fig. 3 Adjustable shock absorber system suspension troubleshooting charts (Part 2 of 3). 300ZX

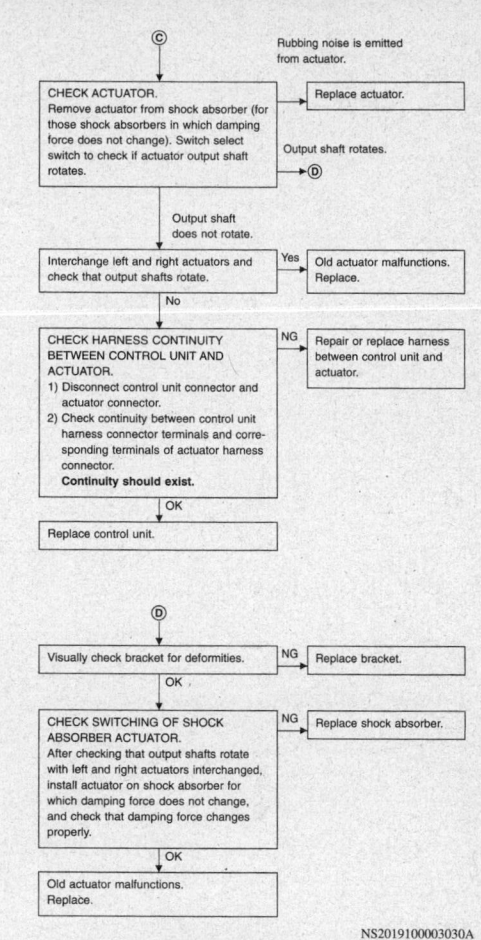

Part 3 flowchart (Fig. 3):

(C)

↓

CHECK ACTUATOR.
Remove actuator from shock absorber (for those shock absorbers in which damping force does not change). Switch select switch to check if actuator output shaft rotates.

— Rubbing noise is emitted from actuator. → Replace actuator.
— Output shaft rotates. → (D)

↓ Output shaft does not rotate.

Interchange left and right actuators and check that output shafts rotate.

— Yes → Old actuator malfunctions. Replace.

↓ No

CHECK HARNESS CONTINUITY BETWEEN CONTROL UNIT AND ACTUATOR.
1) Disconnect control unit connector and actuator connector.
2) Check continuity between control unit harness connector terminals and corresponding terminals of actuator harness connector.
Continuity should exist.

— NG → Repair or replace harness between control unit and actuator.

↓ OK

Replace control unit.

(D)

↓

Visually check bracket for deformities.

— NG → Replace bracket.

↓ OK

CHECK SWITCHING OF SHOCK ABSORBER ACTUATOR.
After checking that output shafts rotate with left and right actuators interchanged, install actuator on shock absorber for which damping force does not change, and check that damping force changes properly.

— NG → Replace shock absorber.

↓ OK

Old actuator malfunctions. Replace.

NS2019100003030A

Fig. 3 Adjustable shock absorber system suspension troubleshooting charts (Part 3 of 3). 300ZX

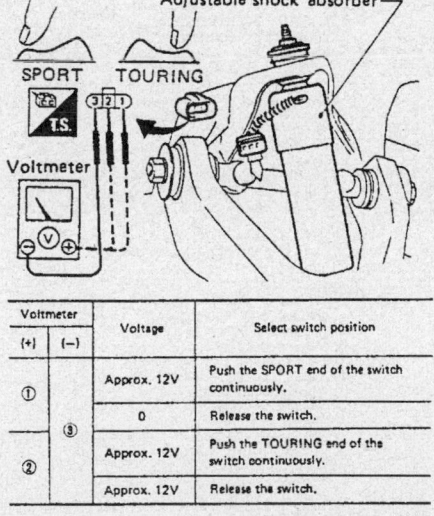

Voltmeter (+)	Voltmeter (−)	Voltage	Select switch position
①	③	Approx. 12V	Push the SPORT end of the switch continuously.
		0	Release the switch.
②		Approx. 12V	Push the TOURING end of the switch continuously.
		Approx. 12V	Release the switch.

NS2019100004000X

Fig. 4 Terminal inspection. Pathfinder

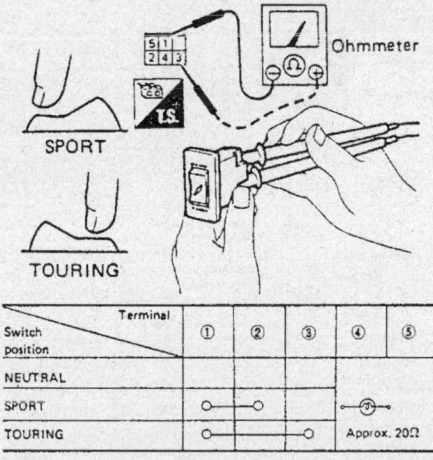

Switch position	Terminal ①	②	③	④	⑤
NEUTRAL					
SPORT	o—			—o	
TOURING	o—		—o	Approx. 20Ω	

NS2019100005000X

Fig. 5 Select switch inspection. Pathfinder

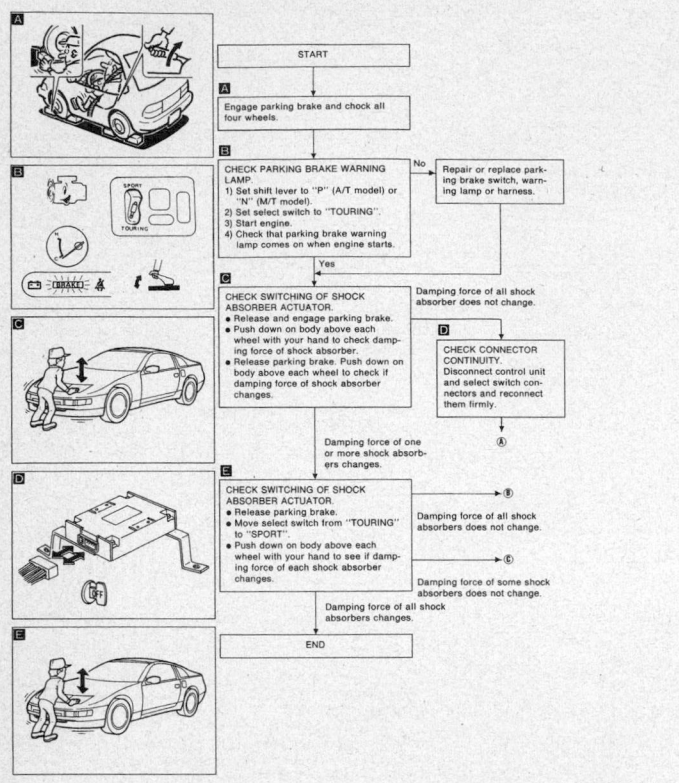

Fig. 6 Adjustable shock absorber system
diagnosis (Part 1 of 3). 300ZX

NS2019500009010X

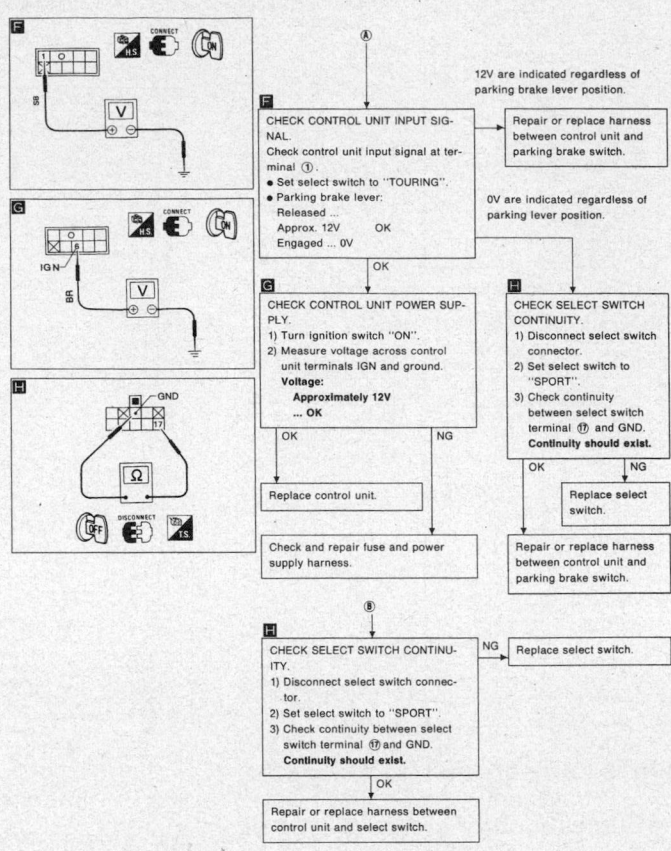

Fig. 6 Adjustable shock absorber system
diagnosis (Part 2 of 3). 300ZX

NS2019500009020X

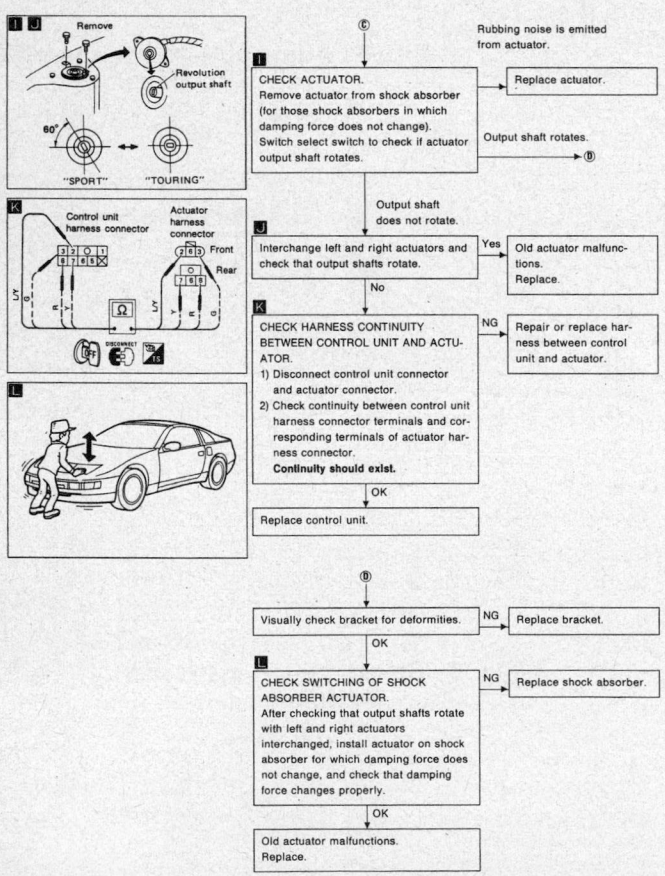

Fig. 6 Adjustable shock absorber system
diagnosis (Part 3 of 3). 300ZX

NS2019500009030X

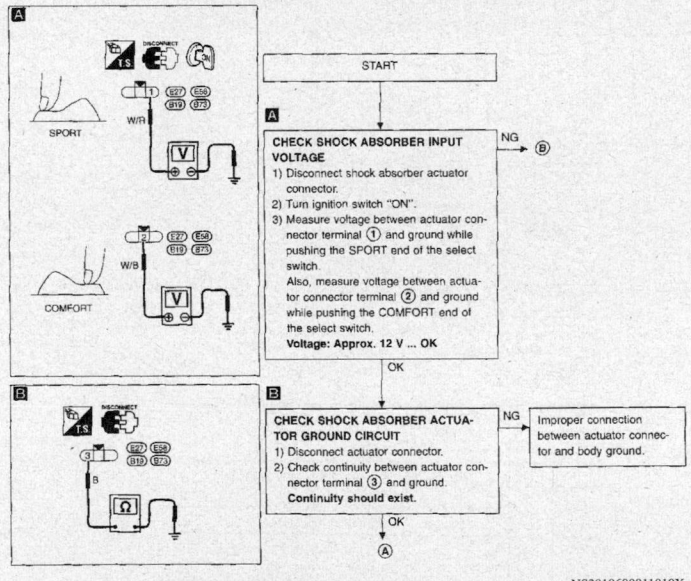

Fig. 7 Adjustable shock absorber system
diagnosis (Part 1 of 3). Pathfinder

NS2019600011010X

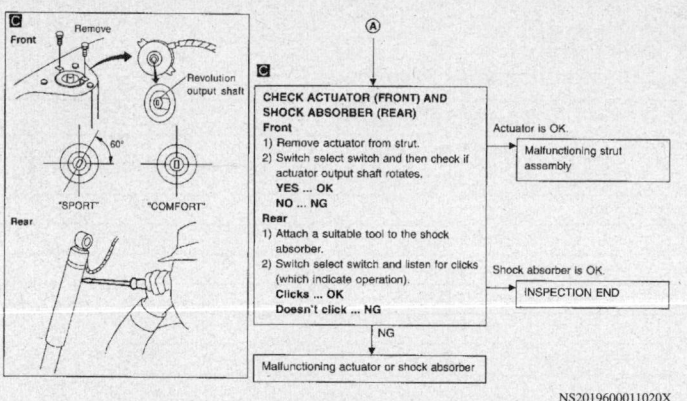

Fig. 7 Adjustable shock absorber system diagnosis (Part 2 of 3). Pathfinder

NS2019600011020X

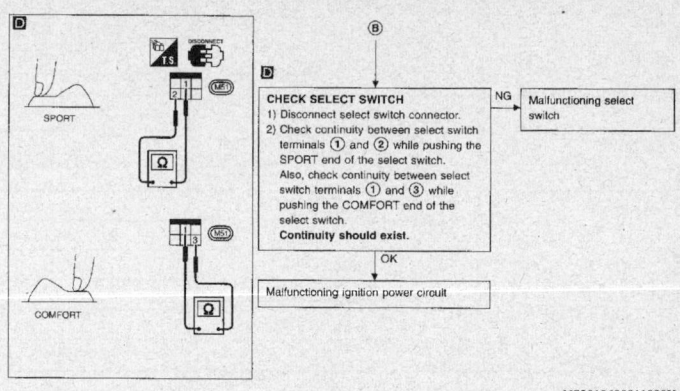

Fig. 7 Adjustable shock absorber system diagnosis (Part 3 of 3). Pathfinder

NS2019600011030X

Engine Rebuilding Specifications

INDEX

CYLINDER HEAD, VALVE GUIDE & VALVE SEATS

All Measurements Given In Inches, Unless Otherwise Specified.

Year	Engine	Cylinder Head Warpage Limit	Cylinder Head Overall Thickness②	Valve Guides Standard Inside Diameter	Stem to Guide Clearance Intake	Exhaust	Valve Seats Seat Width Intake	Exhaust
1996–99	GA16DE	.004	4.639–4.646	.2165–.2171	.0008–.0021	.0016–.0028	.042–.053	.042–.066
	SR20DE	.004	5.390–5.398	.2362–.2369	.0008–.0021	.0016–.0029	.055–.067	.067–.079
	KA24DE	.004	4.972–4.980	.2756–.2763	.0008–.0021	.0016–.0029	.058–.064	.071–.079
	VG30DE, VG30DETT	.004	5.433③	.2362–.2369	.0008–.0021	.0016–.0029	—	—
	VG30E, VG33E	.004	4.205–4.220	①	.0008–.0021	.0016–.0029	.069	.067
	VQ30DE	.004	4.972–4.980	.2362–.2369	.0008–.0029	.0016–.0029	.043–.052	.051–.060

① — Intake, .2756–.2763 inch; exhaust, .3150–.3154 inch.
② — Minimum thickness is overall thickness, less warpage limit, combined with amount of grinding of cylinder block gasket surface.
③ — To camshaft center.

VALVE SPRINGS
All Measurements Given In Inches, Unless Otherwise Specified.

Year	Engine	Valve Springs		
		Free Height	Assembled Tension Pounds @ Inches	Out of Square Limit
1996–99	GA16DE	①	②	③
	SR20DE	1.943	144.25 @ 1.181	.087
	KA24DE	1.756	123.37 @ 1.024	.075
	VG30DE, VG30DETT	1.697	120.60 @ 1.043	.071
	VG30E, VG33E	④	⑤	⑥
	VQ30DE	1.848	102.10 @ 1.085	.079

① — Intake, 2.071 inches; exhaust, 2.154 inches.
② — Intake 110 lbs. at 1.331 inches; exhaust, 122.6 lbs. at 1.346 inches.
③ — Intake, .091 inch; exhaust, .094 inch.
④ — Intake, 1.736 inches; exhaust, 2.016 inches.
⑤ — Intake 57.30 lbs. at .984 inches; exhaust, 117.70 lbs. at 1.181 inches.
⑥ — Intake, .075 inch; exhaust, .087 inch.

VALVES
All Measurements Given In Inches, Unless Otherwise Specified.

Year	Engine	Valves							
		Stem Diameter		Face Angle, Degrees	Margin		Clearance	
		Intake	Exhaust		Intake	Exhaust	Intake	Exhaust
1996–99	GA16DE	.2152–.2157	.2144–.2150	45½	.0350–.0430	.0350–.0430	.0080–.0190	.0120–.0230
	SR20DE	.2348–.2354	.2341–.2346	45½	.0430	.0510	0	0
	KA24DE	.2742–.2748	.2734–.2740	45½	.0374–.0492	.0453–.0571	0	0
	VG30DE, VG30DETT	.2348–.2354	.2341–.2346	45½	.0453–.0571	.0531–.0650	0	0
	VG33E	.2742–.2748	.3135–.3138	45½	.0453–.0571	.0531–.0650	0	0
	VQ30DE	.2348–.2354	.2341–.2346	45½	.0370–.0490	.0450–.0570	.0100–.0130	.0110–.0150

CAMSHAFT
All Measurements Given In Inches, Unless Otherwise Specified.

Year	Engine Model	Camshaft Journal Outer Diameter	Camshaft Bearing Clearance	Maximum Journal Run-Out	Camshaft Endplay	Lifter Bore Diameter	Lifter Outer Diameter	Lifter To Bore Clearance
1996–99	GA16DE	③	.0018–.0034	.0040	.0045–.0074	1.1811–1.1819	1.1795–1.1801	.0010–.0024
	SR20DE	1.0998–1.1006	.0018–.0034	.0040	.0022–.0055	.6693–.6701	.6685–.6690	.0003–.0016
	KA24DE	③	.0018–.0035	.0016	.0028–.0058	1.3386–1.3394	1.3370–1.3376	.0010–.0024
	VG30DE, VG30DETT	1.0998–1.1006	.0018–.0034	.0040	.0012–.0031	1.2205–1.2213	1.2187–1.2191	.0014–.0026
	VG30E, VG33E	①②	.0024–.0041	.0040	.0012–.0024	.6299–.6304	.6278–.6282	.0017–.0026
	VQ30DE	④	.0018–.0034	.0020	.0045–.0074	1.3780–1.3788	1.3764–1.3770	.0010–.0024

① — Journal 1, 1.8866–1.8874 inches; journals 2, 3 & 4, 1.8472–1.8480 inches; journal 5, 1.6701–1.6709 inches.
② — Both right & left side cams.
③ — 1996 models, journal 1, 1.0998–1.1006 inches; journals 2, 3 ,4 & 5, .9423–.9431 inches. 1997–99 models, journals 1 through 6, 1.0998–1.1006 inches.
④ — 1996 models, all journals .9226–.9234 inch: 1997–99 models, journal 1 1.0211–1.0218 inches, journals 2, 3, & 4 .9226–.9234 inch.

CRANKSHAFT, BEARINGS & RODS

All Measurements Given In Inches, Unless Otherwise Specified.

Engine Model	Crankshaft						Out Of Round ①	Taper①	Bearing Clearance		Connecting Rods	
	Standard Journal Diameter								Main Bearings	Connecting Rod Bearings	Piston Pin Bore Diameter	Side Clearance
	Main Bearing			Crank Pin								
	Grade 0	Grade 1	Grade 2	Grade 0	Grade 1	Grade 2						
GA16DE	1.9668–1.9671	1.9665–1.9668	1.9661–1.9665	1.5735–1.5738	1.5733–1.5735	1.5731–1.5733	.0002	.0001	.0007–.0017	.0004–.0014	.7480–.7485	.0079–.0185
SR20DE	2.1643–2.1646	2.1641–2.1643	2.1639–2.1641	1.8885–1.8887	1.8883–1.8885	1.8880–1.8883	.0002	.0002	.0002–.0009	.0008–.0018	.9835–.9843	.0079–.0138
KA24DE	2.3609–2.3612	1, 2.3606–2.3609	2.3603–2.3606	1.9672–1.9675	1.9670–1.9672	1.9668–1.9670	.0002	.0001	.0040	.0035	.8268–.8272	.0240
VG30DE, VG30DETT③	2.4790–2.4793	1, 2.4787–2.4790	2.4784–2.4787	1.9672–1.9675	1.9670–1.9672	1.9667–1.9670	.0002	.0002	.0011–.0022	.0011–.0019	.8661–.8666	.0079–.0138
VG30E, VG33E	2.4790–2.4793	2.4787–2.4790	2.4784–2.4787	1.9670–1.9675	1.9670–1.9675	1.9670–1.9675	.0002②	.0002②	.0011–.0022	.0006–.0021	.8261–.8265	.0079–.0138
VQ30DE	2.3610–2.3612	2.3607–2.3610	2.3605–2.3607	1.7704–1.7706	1.7702–1.7704	1.7699–1.7702	.0001	.0001	.0002–.0007	—	.8658–.8664	.0079–.0138

① — Maximum.   ② — Standard.   ③ — 300ZX.

PISTONS, PINS & RINGS

All Measurements Given In Inches, Unless Otherwise Specified.

Engine	Piston Diameter (Std.)			Piston to Cylinder Bore Clearance	Piston Pin Diameter	Piston Pin to Piston Clearance	Piston Ring End Gap			Piston Ring Side Clearance		
							Compression		Oil	Compression		Oil
	Grade 1	Grade 2	Grade 3				Top	2nd		Top	2nd	
GA16DE	2.9911–2.9915	2.9915–2.9919	2.9919–2.9923	.0006–.0014	.7476–.7481	.0002–.0007	.0079–.0138	.0146–.0205	.0079–.0236	.0016–.0031	.0012–.0028	—
SE20DE	3.3850–3.3854	3.3854–3.3858	3.3858–3.3862	.0004–.0012	.8657–.8662	.0002	.0079–.0118	.0138–.0197	.0390	.0018–.0031	.0012–.0036	.0390
KA24DE	3.5027–3.5031	3.5031–3.5035	3.5035–3.5039	.0008–.0016	.8263–.8267	.0002	.0110–.0205	.0177–.0272	.0079–.0272	.0016–.0031	.0012–.0028	—
VG30DE,	3.4242–3.4246	3.4246–3.4250	3.4250–3.4254	.0083–.0157	.8657–.8662	.0002	.0083–.0157	.0197–.0299	.0079–.0299	.0016–.0029	.0012–.0025	—
VG30DETT②	3.4242–3.4246	3.4246–3.4250	3.4250–3.4254	.0010–.0018	.8657–.8662	.0002	.0083–.0157	.0197–.0299	.0079–.0299	.0016–.0029	.0012–.0025	—
VG30E, VG33E	3.4238–3.4242①	3.4242–3.4246	3.4246–3.4250	.0010–.0018	.8256–.8261	.0002	.0083–.0173	.0071–.0173	.0079–.0299	.0016–.0029	.0012–.0025	.0006–.0075
VQ30DE	3.6606–3.6601	3.6610–3.6614	3.6614–3.6618	.0004–.0012	.8657–.8662	.0001–.0002	.0087–.0161	.0197–.0291	.0079–.0272	.0016–.0031	.0012–.0028	—

① — Grade No. 4, 3.4250–3.4254 inches; Grade No. 5, 3.4254–3.4258 inches.   ② — 300ZX.

CYLINDER BLOCK

All Measurements Given In Inches, Unless Otherwise Specified.

Year	Engine	Cylinder Bore Diameter (Std.)					Cylinder Bore Taper (Max.)	Cylinder Bore Out of Round (Max.)
		Grade No. 1 Inches	Grade No. 2 Inches	Grade No. 3 Inches	Grade No. 4 Inches	Grade No. 5 Inches		
1996–99	GA16DE	2.9921-2.9925	2.9935-2.9929	2.9929-2.9933	—	—	.0004	.0006
	SR20DE	3.3858-3.3862	3.3862-3.3866	3.3866-3.870	—	—	.0004	.0006
	KA24DE	3.5039-3.5043	3.5043-3.5047	3.5047-3.5051	3.5051-3.5055	3.5055-3.5059	.0004	.0006
	VG30DE, VG30DETT	3.4252-3.4256	3.4256-3.4260	3.4260-3.4264	3.4264-3.4268	3.4268-3.4272	.0006	.0006
	VG33E	3.6024-3.6027	3.6027-3.6031	3.6031-3.6035	—	—	.0006	.0006
	VQ30DE	3.6614-3.6618	3.6618-3.6622	3.6622-3.6626	—	—	.0004	.0006

OIL PUMP

All Measurements Given In Inches, Unless Otherwise Specified.

Year	Engine Model	Clearances				
		Body To Outer Gear	Inner Gear To Crescent	Outer Gear To Crescent	Housing To Inner Gear	Housing To Outer Gear
1996–99	GA16DE	.0043–.0079	.0085–.0129	.0083–.0126	.0020–.0035	.0020–.0043
	SE20DE	.0043–.0079	①	①	①	①
	KA24DE	.0043–.0079	①	①	①	①
	VG30DE, VG30DETT②	.0043–.0079	.0088–.0131	.0083–.0126	.0020–.0035	.0020–.0043
	VG30E, VG33E	.0043–.0079	.0047–.0091	.0083–.0126	.0020–.0035	.0020–.0043
	VQ30DE	.0045–.0102	.0071	.0020–.0035	.0012–.0075	.0018–.0036

① — Inner gear to outer gear tip clearance, .0016–.0071 inch; cover to inner gear clearance, .0020–.0035 inch; cover to outer gear clearance, .0020–.0043 inch; Inner gear to brazed portion clearance, .0018–.0036 inch.

② — 300ZX.

SUBARU
INDEX OF SERVICE OPERATIONS

Specifications

GENERAL ENGINE SPECIFICATIONS

Year	Engine, Liters	Fuel System	Bore x Stroke Inch (mm)	Compression Ratio	Max. H.P. @ RPM	Max. Torque @ RPM	Normal Oil Pressure
1996-97	1.8L	MPFI	3.46 x 2.95 (87.90 x 75)	9.5	110 @ 5600	110 @ 4400	①
	2.2L	MPFI	3.82 x 2.95 (97 x 75)	9.50	137 @ 5400	145 @ 4400	②
	2.5L	MPFI	3.92 x 3.11	9.70	165 @ 5600	162 @ 4000	—
	3.3L	MPFI	3.82 x 2.95 (97 x 75)	10.0	230 @ 5400	228 @ 4400	①
1998-99	2.2L	MPFI	3.82 X 2.95 (96.90 X 75)	10.0	142 @ 5600	149 @ 3600	①
	2.5L	MPFI	3.92 X 3.11 (99.50 X 79)	9.7	165 @ 5600	162 @ 4000	①

MPFI — Multi-Point Fuel Injection
① — Discharge performance I, 14 psi @ 600; Discharge performance II, 43 psi @ 5000.

② — Legacy discharge performance I, 14 psi @ 800; Legacy discharge performance II, 43 psi @ 5000.

Impreza discharge performance I, 14 psi @ 600; Impreza discharge performance II, 43 psi @ 5000.

TUNE UP SPECIFICATIONS

Year & Engine	Spark Plug Gap Inch	Ignition			Curb Idle Speed②		Fast Idle Speed②		Fuel Pressure, psi	Valve Lash, Inch	
		Firing Order①	Timing °BTDC	Timing Mark	Man. Trans.	Auto. Trans.	Man. Trans.	Auto. Trans.		Intake	Exhaust
1996-97											
1.8L	.041	A	20	B	700	700N	⑧	⑧	34–38⑥	⑤	⑤
2.2L	.041	A	⑦	B	700	700N	⑧	⑧	36	⑤	⑤
2.5L	.041	1-3-2-4	15	—	700	700N	—	—	36	—	—
3.3L	.041	④	20	C	—	610N	—	⑧	26–30③	⑤	⑤
1998-99											
2.2L	.041	1-3-2-4	⑦	—	700	700N	⑨	⑨	43.4	.008	.010
2.5L	.041	1-3-2-4	⑦	—	700	700N	⑨	⑨	43.4	.008	.010

BTDC — Before Top Dead Center
C — Cold
N — Neutral
① — Before disconnecting spark plug wires from distributor cap, determine location of number 1 wire in cap, as distributor position may have been altered from that shown.
② — When adjusting idle speed, set parking brake & chock drive wheels.
③ — Remove fuel pump connector, start engine & allow to stall, then crank

for five seconds & turn ignition switch to Off. Place shop towel under fuel filter, then install suitable fuel pressure gauge between fuel filter & hose. Install fuel pump connector, start engine & note fuel pressure at idle.
④ — Firing order 1-6-3-2-5-4.
⑤ — Equipped w/hydraulic valve lash adjusters.
⑥ — Remove fuel pump connector, start engine & allow to stall, then crank for five seconds & turn ignition

switch to Off. Place shop towel under fuel filter, then install suitable fuel pressure gauge between fuel filter & hose. Install fuel pump connector, start engine, disconnect pressure regulator vacuum hose from collector chamber & note fuel pressure at idle.
⑦ — Man. trans., 14 BTDC; auto. trans. 20 BTDC.
⑧ — Controlled by ECU.
⑨ — Controlled by PCM.

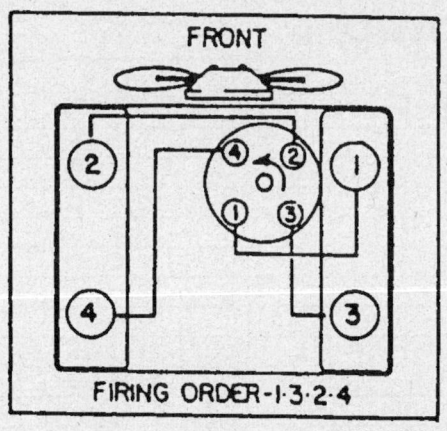

FIRING ORDER - 1·3·2·4

SB11393000002000X

Fig. A

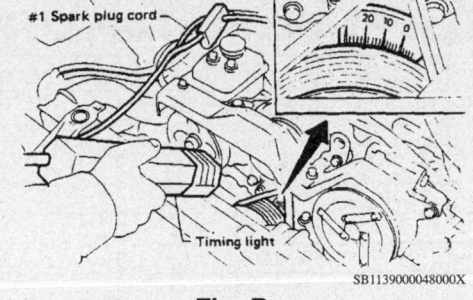

SB11390000048000X

Fig. B

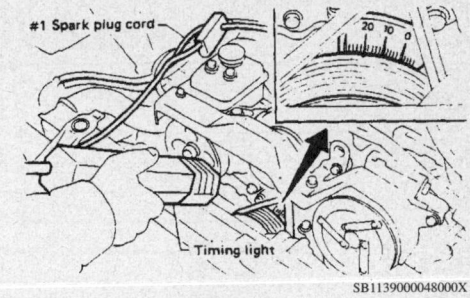

SB11390000048000X

Fig. C

FRONT WHEEL ALIGNMENT SPECIFICATIONS

Year	Model	Caster Angle, Degrees		Camber Angle, Degrees		Toe, Inch①	Ball Joint Inspection	
		Limits	Desired	Limits	Desired		Upper	Lower
1996–97	Impreza	+2 to +4	+3	−½ to +½	0	0	②	②
	Legacy	+2¹/₁₂ to +4¹/₁₂	+3¹/₁₂	−⁷/₁₂ to +⁵/₁₂	−¹/₁₂	0	②	②
	SVX	+4¹/₁₂ to +5⁷/₁₂	+4⁵/₆	−1⅙ to +⅓	−⁵/₁₂	0	②	②
1998	Forester	+2¹/₁₂ to +3⁷/₁₂	+2⅚	−¾ to +¼	−¼	0	②	②
	Impreza 2.2L	+2 to +4	+3	−½ to +½	0	0	②	②
	Impreza 2.5L	+2¹/₁₂ to +4½	+3¹/₁₂	−¾ to +¼	−¼	0	②	②
	Legacy	+2¹/₁₂ to +4¹/₁₂	+3¹/₁₂	−⁷/₁₂ to +⁵/₁₂	−¹/₁₂	0	②	②
1999	Forester	+1⁵/₁₆ to +3⅓	+2⁷/₁₂	−¾ to +¼	−¼	0	②	②
	Impreza 2.2L	+2 to +4	+3	−½ to +½	0	0	②	②
	Impreza 2.5L	+2¹/₁₂ to +4½	+3¹/₁₂	−¾ to +¼	−¼	0	②	②
	Legacy	+2¹/₁₂ to +4¹/₁₂	+3¹/₁₂	−⁷/₁₂ to +⁵/₁₂	−¹/₁₂	0	②	②

① — Toe-in (+); toe-out (-).

② — Refer to "Ball Joint Inspection" for procedure and specification.

REAR WHEEL ALIGNMENT SPECIFICATIONS

Year	Model	Camber Angle, Degrees Limits	Camber Angle, Degrees Desired	Toe, Inch①
1996–97	Impreza AWD	$-1\frac{2}{3}$ to $-\frac{1}{6}$	$-\frac{11}{12}$	−.12 to +.12
	Impreza FWD	$-1\frac{7}{12}$ to $-\frac{1}{12}$	$-\frac{5}{6}$	−.12 to +.12
	Legacy Sedan AWD	$-1\frac{3}{4}$ to $-\frac{1}{4}$	-1	−.12 to +.12
	Legacy Sedan FWD	$-1\frac{2}{3}$ to $-\frac{1}{6}$	$-\frac{11}{12}$	−.12 to +.12
	Legacy Wagon AWD	$-1\frac{2}{3}$ to $-\frac{1}{6}$	$-\frac{11}{12}$	−.12 to +.12
	Legacy Wagon FWD	$-1\frac{1}{2}$ to 0	$-\frac{3}{4}$	−.12 to +.12
	SVX	$-1\frac{5}{12}$ to $+\frac{1}{12}$	$-\frac{2}{3}$	−.12 to +.12
1998	Forester	$-1\frac{1}{3}$ to $+\frac{1}{6}$	$-\frac{7}{12}$	−.16 to −.04
	Impreza 2.2L	$-1\frac{2}{3}$ to $-\frac{1}{6}$	$-\frac{11}{12}$	−.12 to +.12
	Impreza 2.5L	$-1\frac{11}{12}$ to $-\frac{7}{12}$	$-1\frac{1}{6}$	−.12 to +.12
	Legacy Sedan AWD	$-1\frac{3}{4}$ to $-\frac{1}{4}$	-1	−.12 to +.12
	Legacy Sedan FWD	$-1\frac{2}{3}$ to $-\frac{1}{6}$	$-\frac{11}{12}$	−.12 to +.12
	Legacy Wagon AWD	$-1\frac{2}{3}$ to $-\frac{1}{6}$	$-\frac{11}{12}$	−.12 to +.12
	Legacy Wagon FWD	$-1\frac{1}{2}$ to 0	$-\frac{3}{4}$	−.12 to +.12
1999	Forester	-1 to $+\frac{1}{2}$	$-\frac{1}{4}$	+.04 to +.16
	Impreza 2.2L	$-1\frac{2}{3}$ to $-\frac{1}{6}$	$-\frac{11}{12}$	−.12 to +.12
	Impreza 2.5L	$-1\frac{11}{12}$ to $-\frac{7}{12}$	$-1\frac{1}{6}$	−.12 to +.12
	Legacy Sedan AWD	$-1\frac{3}{4}$ to $-\frac{1}{4}$	-1	−.12 to +.12
	Legacy Sedan FWD	$-1\frac{2}{3}$ to $-\frac{1}{6}$	$-\frac{11}{12}$	−.12 to + .12
	Legacy Wagon AWD	$-1\frac{2}{3}$ to $-\frac{1}{6}$	$-\frac{11}{12}$	−.12 to +.12
	Legacy Wagon FWD	$-1\frac{1}{2}$ to 0	$-\frac{3}{4}$	−.12 to +.12

FWD — Front Wheel Drive   4WD — Four Wheel Drive   ① — Toe-in (+); toe-out (-).

FLUID CAPACITIES & COOLING SYSTEM DATA

Year	Model	Cooling Capacity Qts. With Heater	Cooling Capacity Qts. With A/C	Radiator Cap Relief Pressure Lbs.	Thermo. Opening Temp. °F	Fuel Tank Gals.	Engine Oil Refill Qts.	Transmission Oil 4 Spd. Pts.	Transmission Oil 5 Spd. Pts.	Transmission Oil Auto. Trans. Qts.	Rear Axle Oil Pts.
1996-97	Impreza	6.3	6.3	13	173	13.2	⑤	—	7.4	⑧	—
	Legacy L, LS & LSi	6.3	6.3	13	173	15.9	①	—	②	7.5	—
	Legacy Outback	6.3	6.3	13	173	15.9	④	—	—	—	—
	Legacy 2.5 GT	6	6	13	173	15.9	4.7	—	—	—	—
	SVX	7.4	7.4	13	173	18.5	6.3	—	—	10	—

FLUID CAPACITIES & COOLING SYSTEM DATA—Continued

Year	Model	Cooling Capacity Qts.		Radiator Cap Relief Pressure Lbs.	Thermo. Opening Temp. °F	Fuel Tank Gals.	Engine Oil Refill Qts.	Transmission Oil			Rear Axle Oil Pts.
		With Heater	With A/C					4 Spd. Pts.	5 Spd. Pts.	Auto. Trans. Qts.	
1998	Forester	6.3	6.6	13	173	15.9	4.7	—	7.4	10⑦	1.6
	Impreza 2.2L	6.1	6.1	13	173	15.9	4.2	—	7.4	8.4⑦	1.4
	Impreza 2.5	6.3	6.3	13	173	15.9	4.7	—	7.4	10⑦	1.4
	Legacy 2.2L	6.1	6.1	13	173	15.9	4.2	—	7.4	8.4⑦	1.6
	Legacy 2.5L	6.3	6.3	13	173	15.9	4.7	—	7.4	10⑦	1.6
1999	Forester	③	③	16	173	15.9	5.3	—	7.4	9.8	1.6
	Impreza 2.2L	6.3	6.3	16	173	13.2	4.8	—	7.4	8.9	1.6
	Impreza 2.5L RS	6.3	6.3	16	173	13.2	5.3	—	7.4	8.9	1.6
	Legacy L	6.1	6.1	16	173	15.9	4.8	—	7.4	8.3	1.6
	Legacy SUS	6.3	6.3	16	173	15.9	5.3	—	—	7.5	1.6
	Legacy Wagon⑨	6.1	6.1	16	173	15.9	4.8	—	—	8.3	1.6
	Legacy Wagon⑥	6.3	6.3	16	173	15.9	5.3	—	7.4	8.3	1.6

4WD — Four wheel drive
① — Less LSi, 4.4 qts.; LSi models, 4.7 qts.
② — Less AWD, 7 pts.; w/AWD, 7.6 pts.
③ — M/T 6.3 qts.; A/T, 6.6 qts.
④ — 2.2L engine, 4.4 qts.; 2.5L engine, 4.7 qts.
⑤ — 1.8L engine, 4.2 qts.; 2.2L engine, 4.4 qts.
⑥ — Outback, Outback Ltd. & GT.
⑦ — Differential, 2.6 pts.
⑧ — Less AWD, 8.4 qts.; w/AWD, 8.75 qts.
⑨ — Brighton, "L" & Postal Delivery

LUBRICANT DATA

Year	Model	Lubricant Type					
		Transmission		Transfer Case	Rear Axle	Power Steering	Brake System
		Manual	Automatic				
1996–97	Impreza	80W-90 GL-5	Dexron IIE/III①	—	80W-90 GL-5	Dexron II/IIE	DOT 3 or 4
	Legacy	75W-90 GL-5	Dexron IIE/III①	—	75W-90 GL-5	Dexron II/IIE	DOT 3 or 4
	SVX	—	Dexron IIE/III①	—	75W-90 GL-5	Dexron II/IIE	DOT 3 or 4
1998	All	75W-90 GL-5	Dexron II/IIE/III①	—	80W-90 GL-5	Dexron II/IIE/III	DOT 3 or 4
1999	Forester	75W-90 GL-5	Dexron IIE/III①	—	80W-90 GL-5	Dexron IIE/III	DOT 3 or 4
	Impreza	75W-90 GL-5	Dexron IIE/III①	—	80W-90 GL-5	Dexron IIE/III	DOT 3 or 4
	Legacy	75W-90 GL-5	Dexron IIE/III①	—	80W-90 GL-5	Dexron II/IIE/III	DOT 3 or 4

① — Final drive, 80W-90 GL-5.

SUBARU

Electrical

NOTE: Refer To "Computer Relearn Procedures" Located In The Front Of This Manual For Computer Relearn Procedures.

NOTE: On Air Bag Equipped Models, Refer To "Air Bag System Precautions" Located In The Front Of This Manual For System Disarming & Arming Procedures.

INDEX

PRECAUTIONS

AIR BAG SYSTEMS

Refer to "Air Bag System Precautions" in the front of this manual for system disarming and arming procedures.

BATTERY GROUND CABLE

Prior to service, disconnect battery ground cable and isolate as required.

FUSE PANEL & FLASHER LOCATION

There are two fuse/relay panels. The engine compartment fuse/relay panel is located in the engine compartment, near the battery. The passenger compartment fuse/relay panel is located below the lefthand side of the instrument panel.

On Impreza models, the hazard and turn signal flasher is located behind the center of the instrument panel.

On SVX models, the hazard and turn signal flasher is located behind the lefthand side of the instrument panel, near the brake pedal bracket.

On Legacy models, the hazard and turn signal flasher is located below the lefthand side of the instrument panel, near the instrument panel wiring harness.

FUEL PUMP RELAY LOCATION

On SVX models, refer to **Fig. 1,** for fuel pump relay location.

On Impreza and Legacy models, refer to **Fig. 2,** for fuel pump relay location (2).

On Forester models, refer to **Fig. 3,** for fuel pump relay location.

RELAY CENTER LOCATION

Relays are located on both fuse/relay panels, refer to " Fuse Panel & Flasher Location" for relay center location.

STARTER
REPLACE

1. Disconnect solenoid wiring at starter.
2. Remove starter retaining bolts, then the starter from bellhousing.
3. Reverse procedure to install.

COIL PACK
REPLACE

1. Disconnect coil pack electrical connector, **Fig. 4.**

2. Disconnect spark plug wires from coil pack, noting wire position for installation.
3. Remove coil pack attaching bolts and remove coil pack.
4. Reverse procedure to install.

IGNITION SWITCH
REPLACE
FORESTER

1. Remove instrument panel lower cover.
2. Remove screws, then separate upper and lower column covers.
3. Remove knee protector and meter visor.
4. Disconnect ignition switch electrical connector.
5. Using a suitable drift and hammer, hit torn bolt heads to loosen and remove ignition switch.
6. Reverse procedure to install, noting the following:
   a. Tighten new ignition switch connecting bolts until heads twist off.

IMPREZA

1. Remove upper and lower steering column covers, then the knee protector.
2. Remove instrument cluster visor, then disconnect ignition switch electrical connectors.

Fig. 1   Fuel pump relay location. SVX

3. Using a drift or hammer, hit torn bolt head to loosen and remove ignition switch.
4. Reverse procedure to install. Tighten switch mounting bolts until heads twist off.

LEGACY

1. Remove upper and lower steering column covers.
2. Remove instrument panel lower cover.
3. Disconnect ignition switch electrical connector from main body harness.
4. Using a suitable hammer and punch hit the torn bolt head to loosen and remove ignition switch.
5. Reverse procedure to install. Tighten connecting bolt until head twist off.

NEUTRAL SAFETY SWITCH

REPLACE

EXCEPT 4-SPEED AUTOMATIC TRANSAXLE

1. Remove hand brake cover and center console.
2. Disconnect indicator light and neutral safety switch electrical connections.
3. Remove selector lever assembly retaining screws and lever assembly.
4. Remove safety switch retaining screws and switch from the selector lever assembly.
5. Reverse procedure to install.

4-SPEED AUTOMATIC TRANSAXLE

1. Detach cable from select lever.
2. Remove three inhibitor switch to transaxle retaining bolts.
3. Disconnect switch electrical connector and remove inhibitor switch.
4. Install new inhibitor switch and lightly install retaining bolts.
5. Adjust switch as follows:
   a. Ensure select lever is set in the N position.
   b. Insert stopper pin, tool No. 499267300, or equivalent, into the inhibitor switch lever and switch body.

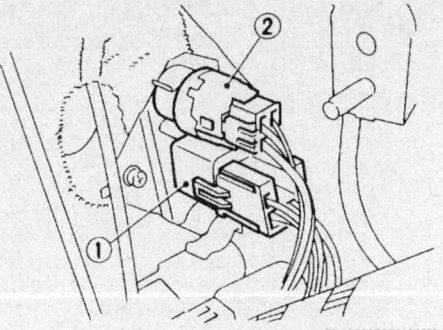

Fig. 2   Fuel pump relay location. Impreza & Legacy

   c. **Torque** retaining bolts to 36 inch lbs., then remove the stopper pin.
   d. Attach cable to select lever, then check for proper operation.

HEADLAMP SWITCH

REPLACE

Refer to "Combination Switch, Replace." for procedure.

STOP LIGHT SWITCH

REPLACE

Switch is located on bracket under dashboard, near top of brake pedal.
1. Remove locknut on pedal side of bracket.
2. Push switch through bracket and remove wiring connector.
3. Reverse procedure to install.

COMBINATION SWITCH

REPLACE

FORESTER

1. Remove instrument panel lower cover.
2. Remove screws, then the upper and lower column covers.
3. Remove switch attaching screws, then the switch.
4. Reverse procedure to install.

IMPREZA

1. Remove column lower cover, then disconnect air bag connectors located below steering column.
2. Disconnect combination switch electrical connectors.
3. Position front wheels in straight ahead position, then remove covers from both side of steering column.
4. Using T30 Torx bit, remove four Torx bolts located below steering wheel side covers.
5. Disconnect air bag and horn connectors on back side of air bag module. Remove air bag module and place it with pad side facing upward.
6. Using suitable puller, remove steering wheel.
7. Remove steering column cover.
8. Remove combination switch mounting bolts, then the switch.
9. Reverse procedure to install, noting the following:

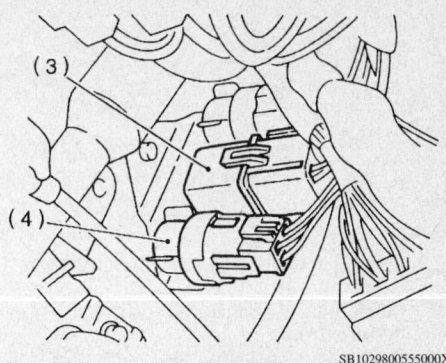

Fig. 3   Fuel pump relay location. Forester

   a. Before installing switch, ensure switch is off and front wheels are in straight ahead position.
   b. Align column cover and center roll connector as shown in **Fig. 5**.

LEGACY

1. Remove steering wheel as outlined under "Steering Wheel, Replace."
2. Remove upper and lower steering column covers.
3. Remove instrument panel lower cover.
4. Disconnect combination switch electrical connector from main body harness, then undo hold down band.
5. Remove switch.
6. Reverse procedure to install. Align center of roll connector, **Fig. 5**.

SVX

1. Remove air bag module as outlined under "Air Bag Systems" section of this chapter.
2. Raise and support vehicle, then remove front wheels.
3. Remove steering shaft universal joint, then the lower instrument panel trim panel.
4. Disconnect electrical connectors for ignition switch and combination switch.
5. Remove two steering shaft to instrument panel retaining bolts.
6. Pull steering shaft out from toe board.
7. Remove steering wheel as outlined under "Steering Wheel, Replace."
8. Remove steering column upper and lower covers, then two combination switch mounting bolts.
9. Remove combination switch.
10. Reverse procedure to install. Align center of roll connector, **Fig. 5**.

TURN SIGNAL SWITCH

REPLACE

Refer to "Combination Switch, Replace" for procedure.

STEERING WHEEL

REPLACE

1. Remove air bag module as outlined in the "Air Bag System" section.
2. Remove steering wheel trim pad.

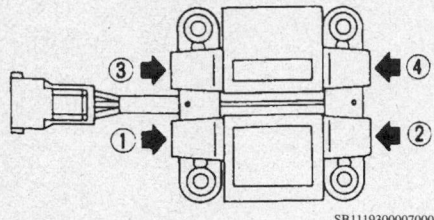

Fig. 4   Coil pack replacement

3. Mark steering wheel for reference during assembly.
4. Remove steering wheel retaining nut.
5. Using a suitable puller, separate steering wheel from steering shaft.
6. Reverse procedure to install.

INSTRUMENT CLUSTER
REPLACE
FORESTER

1. Move steering wheel to the lowest position.
2. Remove attaching screws from visor, then the visor.
3. Remove screws from combination meter, then pull meter out and disconnect electrical connector from back of meter assembly.
4. Remove instrument cluster.
5. Reverse procedure to install.

IMPREZA

1. Tilt steering wheel to lowest position, then remove instrument cluster visor.
2. Disconnect cluster electrical connector.
3. Remove cluster mounting screws, then slightly pull out cluster.
4. Disconnect connector and speedometer cable from back of cluster, then remove cluster.
5. Reverse procedure to install.

LEGACY

1. Tilt steering wheel down fully.
2. Remove screws from instrument cluster trim visor and pull out visor part way, then disconnect electrical connections and remove trim visor.
3. Remove screws from instrument cluster and pull out cluster part way, then disconnect electrical connections and remove Instrument cluster.
4. Reverse procedure to install.

SVX

1. Tilt steering wheel to lowest position, then retract steering wheel back.
2. Remove lower cover.
3. Push switch box assembly from rear side of switch, then disconnect connector and remove switch box assembly.
4. Remove visor, then disconnect clock connector.
5. Remove instrument cluster mounting screws, then the instrument cluster.
6. Reverse procedure to install.

RADIO
REPLACE
FORESTER

1. Remove front console, AT cover and center dash panel.
2. Remove attaching screws, then pull radio partially out from center console.
3. Disconnect electrical connectors and antenna lead from radio, then remove radio from vehicle.
4. Reverse procedure to install.

IMPREZA

1. As equipped, remove cup holder and ashtray.
2. Disconnect center instrument panel trim plate.
3. Remove radio mounting screws.
4. Disconnect electrical connectors and antenna lead, then remove radio.
5. Reverse procedure to install.

LEGACY

1. Remove hand brake cover and console cover.
2. Remove center panel mounting screws, then center panel.
3. Remove radio mounting screws, then radio.
4. Disconnect electrical connectors and antenna feeder cord.
5. Reverse procedure to install.

SVX

1. Tilt steering wheel to lowest position, then retract steering wheel back.
2. Remove lower cover.
3. Push switch box assembly from rear side of switch, then disconnect connector and remove switch box assembly.
4. Remove visor, then disconnect clock connector.
5. Remove center ventilation grille, then the auto A/C amplifier.
6. Remove radio inner panel, then the center panel.
7. Remove lefthand cowl panel. Roll carpet and disconnect antenna feeder cables.
8. Remove ashtray, then the radio mounting screws.
9. Close radio panel, slide radio outward and disconnect electrical connector.
10. Remove radio.
11. Reverse procedure to install.

WIPER MOTOR
REPLACE
FRONT

1. Remove weatherstrip and nets.
2. Disconnect wiper motor electrical connector.
3. Remove wiper motor attaching bolts.
4. Remove wiper motor link attaching nut, then separate link from motor.
5. Remove wiper motor from vehicle.
6. Reverse procedure to install.

REAR

1. Remove wiper arm from the shaft.

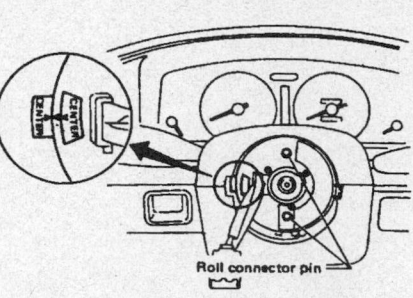

Fig. 5   Aligning tool connector. Impreza, Legacy & SVX

2. Remove cap and nut from wiper arm mounting.
3. Remove back door or rear gate inner trim.
4. Disconnect wiper motor electrical connections.
5. Disconnect washer hoses at joint, if equipped.
6. Remove wiper motor retaining bolts and the motor.
7. Reverse procedure to install.

WIPER SWITCH
REPLACE

Refer to "Combination Switch, Replace" for procedure.

WIPER TRANSMISSION
REPLACE
FORESTER

1. Remove wiper motor as outlined under "Wiper Motor, Replace."
2. Remove cowl cover.
3. Remove nut securing motor link on back side of motor.
4. Remove bolts securing sleeve unit.
5. Remove wiper link from service hole in front panel.
6. Reverse procedure to install.

IMPREZA & SVX

1. Remove wiper motor as outlined under "Wiper Motor, Replace."
2. Remove transaxle mounting bolts.
3. Remove wiper link from service hole in front panel.
4. Reverse procedure to install.

LEGACY

1. Remove wiper motor as outlined under "Wiper Motor, Replace."
2. Remove left side transaxle mounting nuts, then separate left and right wiper links at center joint. To separate links pry with standard screwdriver inserted into service hole in front panel.
3. Remove right side transaxle mounting nuts, right side transaxle mounting nuts.
4. Remove wiper links from service holes in front panel.
5. Reverse procedure to install. To assemble wiper links, push using grip of screwdriver.

BLOWER MOTOR
REPLACE
FORESTER
1. Remove glove box.
2. Disconnect blower motor harness connector.
3. Disconnect aspirator pipe, then remove blower motor assembly.
4. Reverse procedure to install.

IMPREZA & SVX
1. Remove glove compartment.
2. **On SVX models,** remove glove compartment support bracket.
3. **On all models,** disconnect blower motor electrical connector, then remove motor cool hose.
4. Remove motor mounting screws, then the motor assembly.
5. Reverse procedure to install.

LEGACY
1. Remove glove compartment.
2. Remove heater duct.
3. Disconnect intake door motor and blower motor electrical connectors.
4. Remove blower motor retaining bolts and the blower motor.

5. Reverse procedure to install.

HEATER CORE
REPLACE
1. Disconnect inlet and outlet heater hoses in engine compartment. Drain as much coolant as possible from heater unit and plug disconnected hoses.
2. Disconnect heater control and mode door cables, then vacuum hose from heater unit joint as equipped.
3. Remove instrument panel as outlined under "Dash Panel Service."
4. **On Impreza and Forester models,** remove steering column support beam.
5. **On all models,** remove evaporator as outlined under "Evaporator Core, Replace."
6. Remove heater unit.
7. Remove heater core from heater unit.
8. Reverse procedure to install, noting the following:
    a. **On Legacy models,** fitted length of heater hose to pipe is .79–.98 inch.
    b. **On Impreza and Forester models,** fitted length of heater hose to pipe is .99–1.18 inches.

c. **On SVX models,** fitted length of vacuum hose must exceed .31 inch.
d. **On all models, torque** heater unit attaching bolts to 4.0–6.9 ft. lbs.

EVAPORATOR CORE
REPLACE
1. Properly discharge A/C system.
2. Disconnect discharge and suction pipes and remove grommets from evaporator.
3. Remove undercover trim, if necessary.
4. Remove glove compartment, then the glove compartment support bracket, if necessary.
5. **On SVX models,** remove time control unit, then disconnect fan control amplifier harness.
6. **On all models,** disconnect electrical connector from evaporator.
7. Remove evaporator retaining bands or bolts, then the evaporator assembly.
8. Remove upper to lower evaporator case retaining bolts or clamps, then remove evaporator core from case.
9. Reverse procedure to install.

Engine

NOTE: Refer To "Computer Relearn Procedures" Located In The Front Of This Manual For Computer Relearn Procedures.

NOTE: On Air Bag Equipped Models, Refer To "Air Bag System Precautions" Located In The Front Of This Manual For System Disarming & Arming Procedures.

INDEX

PRECAUTIONS
AIR BAG SYSTEMS
Refer to "Air Bag System Precautions" in the front of this manual for system disarming and arming procedures.

FUEL SYSTEM PRESSURE RELIEF
1. Fold down rear seat back and remove floor mat, then remove access hole cover.

2. Disconnect fuel pump electrical connection.
3. Start engine and run until engine stalls.
4. After engine stalls crank engine for five more seconds, then place ignition switch in OFF position.

SUBARU

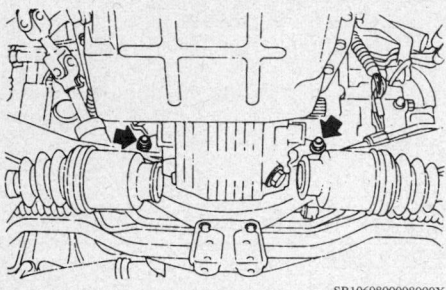

Fig. 1 Transmission to engine lower mounting nuts. Forester

5. Reconnect fuel pump electrical connector.

BATTERY GROUND CABLE

Prior to service, disconnect battery ground cable and isolate as required.

COMPRESSION PRESSURES

When checking compression pressures, ensure engine is at normal operating temperature and battery is completely charged. Remove all spark plugs and open throttle fully. Remove ignition coil harness, then install a suitable compression gauge. Crank engine and note compression gauge reading when gauge pointer is steady. Perform at least two measurements per cylinder to ensure compression readings are correct. The maximum compression difference between cylinders is 14 psi. Compression pressures should be 137–176 psi at 300 RPM.

ENGINE

REPLACE

FORESTER

1. Raise and support vehicle.
2. Release fuel pressure as outlined in "Precautions."
3. Disconnect battery cables and remove battery from vehicle.
4. Remove lower splash shield.
5. Drain engine coolant and oil into suitable containers.
6. Disconnect electrical connectors from main fan and sub fan motors.
7. Disconnect radiator outlet hose from thermostat cover.
8. Lower vehicle.
9. **On models equipped with automatic transmission,** remove radiator reservoir tank, then disconnect ATF cooler hoses from radiator.
10. **On all models,** remove v-belt covers, then disconnect inlet hose from radiator.
11. Remove radiator upper bracket, then the radiator.
12. Recover A/C refrigerant using a suitable A/C recovery station.
13. Disconnect connector from mass air flow sensor.

14. Remove air intake duct with air cleaner upper cover, then remove air cleaner element.
15. Remove chamber stay.
16. Loosen lock bolt and slider bolt and remove front side v-belt.
17. Remove power steering pump bracket and pump and place to one side.
18. Remove front and center exhaust pipe.
19. Remove nuts holding lower side of transmission to engine, **Fig. 1.**
20. Remove nuts from front rubber cushions to crossmember attaching studs, **Fig. 2.**
21. Lower vehicle and remove service hole plug.
22. Remove torque converter to drive plate attaching bolts.
23. Remove pitching stopper.
24. Disconnect fuel delivery hose, return hose and evaporative hose.
25. Support engine with a suitable lifting device.
26. Support transmission with a suitable jack.
27. Ensure all electrical connectors and hoses have been removed.
28. Remove upper attaching bolts from transmission.
29. Slightly raise engine, then raise transmission and move engine horizontally until mainshaft is withdrawn from clutch cover.
30. Lower engine and remove from vehicle.
31. Reverse procedure to install.

IMPREZA

1. Place vehicle on lift and open hood.
2. Relieve fuel system pressure as outlined under "Fuel System Pressure Relief" in this section.
3. Drain coolant.
4. Remove radiator assembly as follows:
   a. Disconnect radiator fan motor connector, then radiator hose from thermostat cover.
   b. **On models equipped with automatic transaxle,** disconnect transaxle cooler hoses from pipes.
   c. **On all models,** remove V-belt cover, then disconnect radiator inlet hose from radiator.
   d. Remove radiator upper bracket, then the radiator assembly.
5. Discharge A/C system, then disconnect A/C hoses from compressor.
6. Disconnect mass air flow sensor connector. Remove air intake duct with air cleaner upper cover, then air cleaner element.
7. Remove canister and bracket.
8. **On models equipped with A/C,** disconnect FICD solenoid valve and compressor connectors.
9. **On all models,** disconnect engine harness and oxygen sensor connectors.
10. Disconnect engine ground terminal and alternator connector and terminal.
11. Disconnect accelerator and cruise control cables.
12. **On models equipped with manual transaxle,** disconnect clutch release spring, clutch cable and hill holder cable. Disconnect hill holder on re-

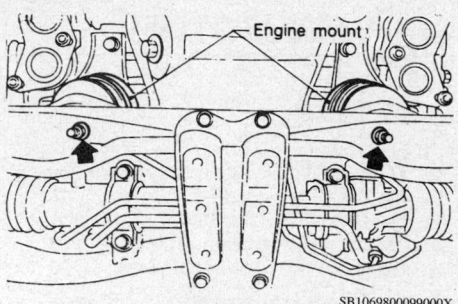

Fig. 2 Front rubber cushion attaching nuts. Forester

lease fork side and transfer it to PHV side.
13. **On all models,** disconnect cruise control and brake booster vacuum hoses, then the heater hoses.
14. Remove power steering pump from bracket. Position pump on right side wheel apron.
15. Raise and support vehicle, then remove front and center exhaust pipes.
16. Remove lower engine to transaxle mounting bolts, then the front cushion to front crossmember mounting nuts.
17. **On models equipped with automatic transaxle,** separate torque converter from driveplate as follows:
   a. Lower vehicle, then remove service hole plug.
   b. Remove torque converter to drive-plate bolts.
   c. Remove other bolt while rotating engine using crankshaft pulley wrench tool No. 499977000, or equivalent.
18. **On all models,** remove pitching stopper, then disconnect fuel and evaporation hoses.
19. Support engine with suitable lifting device and transaxle with jack.
20. Remove upper transaxle to engine mounting bolts.
21. Remove engine from vehicle as follows:
   a. Slightly raise engine, then the transaxle with jack.
   b. Move engine horizontally until mainshaft is withdrawn from clutch cover.
   c. Slowly move engine away from engine compartment.
22. Reverse procedure to install.

LEGACY

1. Relieve fuel system pressure as outlined under "Fuel System Pressure Relief."
2. Drain engine coolant into a suitable container.
3. Disconnect radiator fan electrical connection, then disconnect radiator outlet hose from thermostat cover.
4. **On models equipped with automatic transaxle,** disconnect ATF cooler hoses from pipes.
5. **On all models,** remove V-belt cover, then Disconnect radiator inlet hose from radiator.
6. Remove radiator upper bracket, then

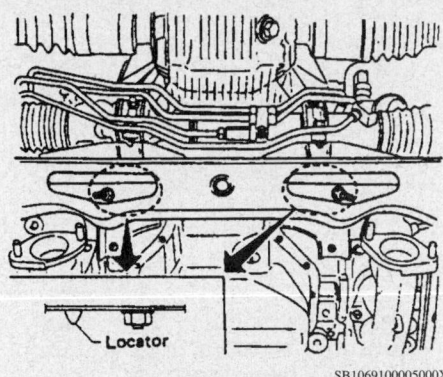

Fig. 3 Front rubber cushion installation. SVX

SB1069100005000X

Locator

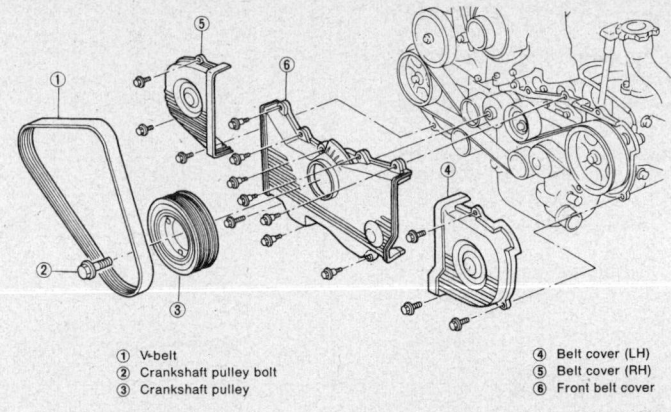

① V-belt
② Crankshaft pulley bolt
③ Crankshaft pulley

④ Belt cover (LH)
⑤ Belt cover (RH)
⑥ Front belt cover

SB1069700100000X

Fig. 4 Crankshaft pulley & belt cover replacement. 1.8L & 2.2L engines

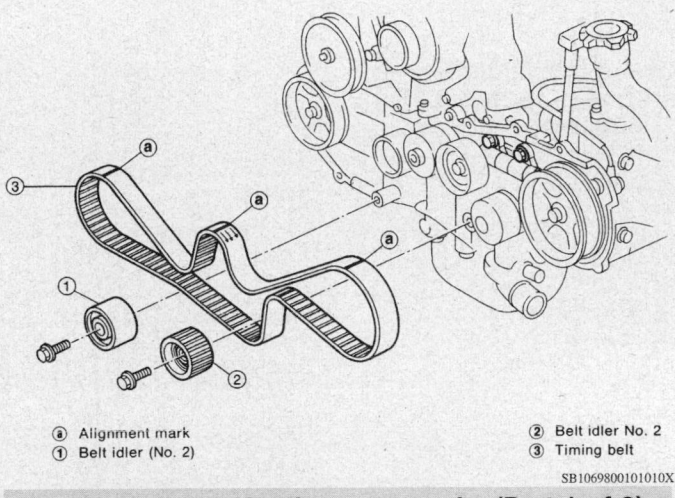

ⓐ Alignment mark
① Belt idler (No. 2)

② Belt idler No. 2
③ Timing belt

SB1069800101010X

Fig. 5 Timing belt alignment marks (Part 1 of 2). 1.8L & 2.2L engines

radiator assembly.

7. **On models equipped with A/C,** discharge and recover system refrigerant, then disconnect A/C pressure hoses from compressor.

8. **On all models,** disconnect mass air flow electrical connection, then remove air intake duct, air cleaner upper cover and air cleaner element.

9. Remove emissions canister and bracket.

10. Disconnect all cables, electrical connections and hoses. **Label all connections for installation reference.**

11. Loosen power steering pump lock bolt and slider bolt, then remove front side V-belt.

12. Remove power steering pipe with bracket from intake manifold.

13. Remove mounting bolts and power steering pump. Place pump on right side wheel apron.

14. Raise and support vehicle, then remove front exhaust pipe to engine mounting nuts.

15. Disconnect electrical connection from rear oxygen sensor then, separate center and rear exhaust pipes.

16. Remove center exhaust pipe mounting bolt from hanger bracket, then remove front and center exhaust pipe.

17. Remove lower transaxle to engine mounting nuts, then remove front cushion rubber to front crossmember nuts.

18. **On models equipped with automatic transaxle,** proceed as follows:
    a. Lower vehicle.
    b. Remove torque converter service hole plug.
    c. Remove torque converter to drive plate mounting bolts, then remove all other bolts from torque converter while rotating engine with crank pulley wrench tool No. 499977000, or equivalent.

19. **On all models,** remove engine pitching stopper, then disconnect fuel delivery hose, return hose and evaporation hose.

20. Support transaxle with suitable jack, then remove upper transaxle to engine mounting nuts.

21. Remove engine.

22. Reverse procedure to install.

SVX

1. Relieve fuel system pressure as outlined under " Fuel System Pressure Relief" in this section.

2. Raise and support vehicle.

3. Remove undercover, then drain cooling system.

4. Disconnect radiator hose from thermostat, then the transaxle lines from radiator.

5. Lower vehicle. Remove V belt cover, then disconnect radiator hose from water pipe.

6. Disconnect cooling fans electrical connectors, then remove radiator assembly.

7. Properly discharge A/C system.

8. Disconnect and plug discharge and suction hoses. **Ensure care is taken not to loose O-ring in low pressure hose.**

9. Remove collector cover, air intake boot, air cleaner upper cover and air filter.

10. Disconnect accelerator and cruise control cables.

11. Disconnect the following electrical connectors; engine harness, ignition coil, oxygen sensors, vehicle speed sensor 2, power steering, engine ground, alternator and A/C compressor.

12. Disconnect brakes booster, heater and power steering hoses.

13. Remove emission canister and bracket, then raise and support vehicle.

14. Remove oxygen sensor, then the front exhaust pipe and rear catalyst converter.

15. Disconnect transaxle cooler hose from pipe on transaxle.

16. Remove lower starter mounting nut, then the lower transaxle to engine nuts.

17. Remove front cushion rubber to front crossmember mounting nuts, then separate torque converter from driveplate.

18. Remove pitching stopper from bracket, then disconnect fuel hoses.

19. Support engine with suitable lifting device and transaxle with suitable stand.

20. Remove upper side transaxle to engine bolts.
21. Slightly raise engine and transaxle, then remove engine from vehicle.
22. Reverse procedure to install noting the following:
    a. When tightening front rubber cushion mounting bolts ensure they are positioned as shown in **Fig. 3.**
    b. Tighten bolts and nuts to specification.
    c. Refer to "Cooling System Bleed" for drain and refill procedure.

ENGINE SERVICE

1.8L & 2.2L ENGINES

Timing Belt, Tensioner & Idler

1. Remove v-belt and A/C belt tensioner.
2. Using crankshaft pulley wrench No. 499977000, or equivalent, hold crankshaft in position and remove crankshaft pulley bolt and pulley.
3. Remove left and right hand belt covers, then the front cover, **Fig. 4.**
4. If alignment marks on timing belt are faded or difficult to see, place new marks on timing belt before removal, **Fig. 5.**
5. Place white paint marks on belt in relation to sprocket marks, **Fig. 6.**
6. Loosen belt tensioner mounting bolts, **Fig. 7,** then remove belt idler.
7. Remove timing belt.
8. Reverse procedure to install, noting the following:
    a. Inspect timing belt teeth for cracks, breaks or wear and replace as necessary.
    b. Inspect timing belt tensioner for oil leakage, replace as necessary.
    c. Measure the extension rod of belt tensioner, **Fig. 8.**
    d. If measurement is not .606–.646 inch, replace tensioner.
    e. Inspect belt idler for smooth rotation, signs of abnormal wear or for grease leakage, replace if necessary
    f. Using a suitable press, push tensioner rod into tensioner and insert a .059 inch diameter pin into holes in tensioner to secure, **Fig. 9.**
    g. Compressing belt tensioner rod make take three minutes or more.
    h. Ensure belt rotation is correct during installation.
    i. With timing belt, tensioner and idler installed, loosen tensioner adjuster attaching bolts and move adjuster all the way to left. Tighten bolts.
    j. Ensure marks on timing belt and sprockets are aligned, then remove stopper pin from tensioner.

Valve Rocker Assembly

1. Disconnect PCV hose.
2. Remove valve cover.
3. Loosen valve rocker assembly bolt No. 1 as shown **Fig. 10. Do not remove bolt at this time.**
4. Remove remainder of valve rocker assembly bolts in numerical order as

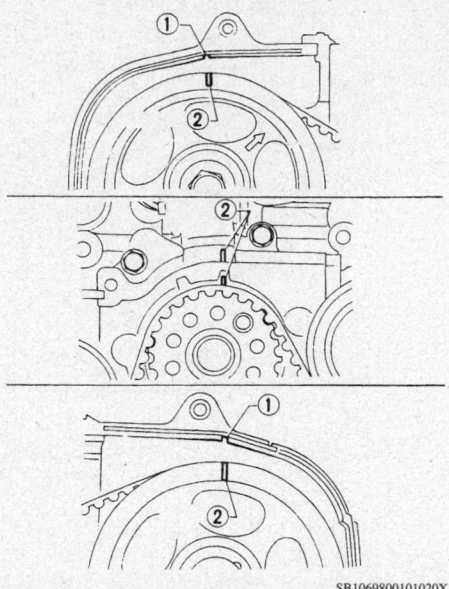

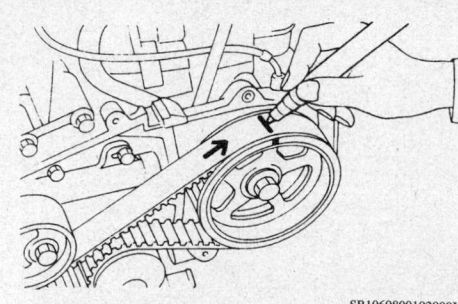

SB1069800102000X

Fig. 6   Sprocket to timing belt alignment marks. 1.8L & 2.2L engines.

SB1069800101020X

Fig. 5   Timing belt alignment marks (Part 2 of 2). 1.8L & 2.2L engines

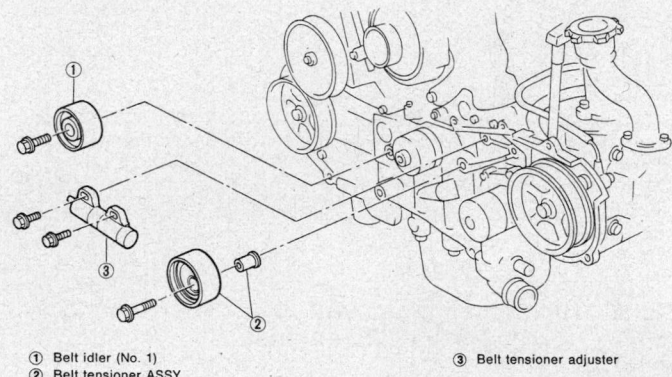

① Belt idler (No. 1)
② Belt tensioner ASSY
③ Belt tensioner adjuster

1) Remove belt idler (No. 1).
2) Remove belt tensioner assembly.
3) Remove belt tensioner adjuster.

SB1069800103000X

Fig. 7   Timing belt tensioner and idler. 1.8L & 2.2L engines.

shown **Fig. 10. Use caution not to gouge dowel pin.**
5. Remove bolt No. 1 and the rocker assembly. Position rocker arms with air vents facing upward.
6. Remove rocker shaft retaining bolts, rocker arms, springs and shaft supports from rocker shaft.
7. Position rocker arms with air vents facing upward.
8. Separate valve lash adjuster from valve rocker only if air bleeding or replacement is required. **Keep all parts in order of removal for proper installation.**
9. Bleed valve lash adjuster as follows:
    a. Submerge lash adjuster in a container of clean engine oil, then press check ball inward using a .08 inch diameter round bar.

b. While holding check ball inward, manually move plunger up and down at one second intervals until air bubbles disappear.
c. Release check ball and quickly push plunger in and lock it. Replace lash adjuster if plunger will not lock. **Allow valve lash adjuster to soak in engine oil until it is to be installed.**
10. Dip lash adjuster and rocker arm in clean engine oil and assemble them. **Fill rocker arm oil reservoir chamber with clean engine oil. Carefully install a new valve lash adjuster O-ring so as not to scratch it. Do not rotate lash adjuster during installation.**
11. Insert rocker shaft into rocker arms, springs and shaft supports in same

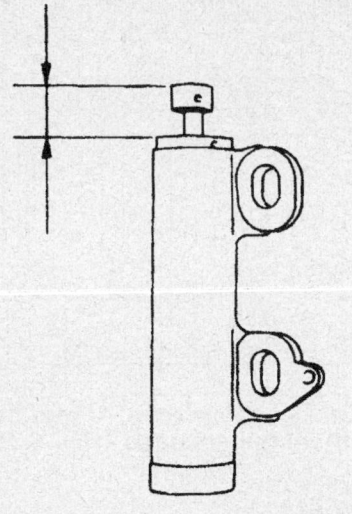

Fig. 8 Timing belt tensioner rod measurement. 1.8L & 2.2L engines

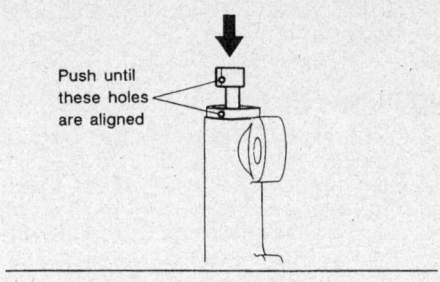

Push until these holes are aligned

Stopper pin

Fig. 9 Timing belt tensioner installation. 1.8L & 2.2L engines

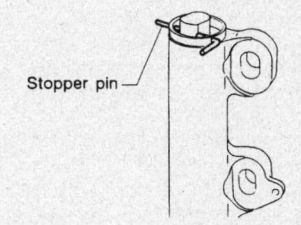

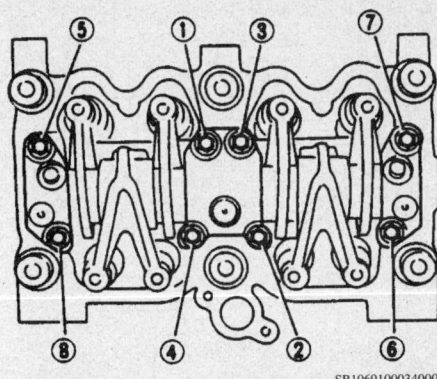

Fig. 10 Rocker assembly bolt loosening sequence. 1.8L & 2.2L engines

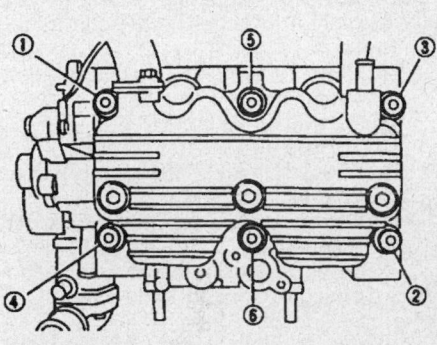

Fig. 12 Cylinder head bolt loosening sequence. 1.8L & 2.2L engines

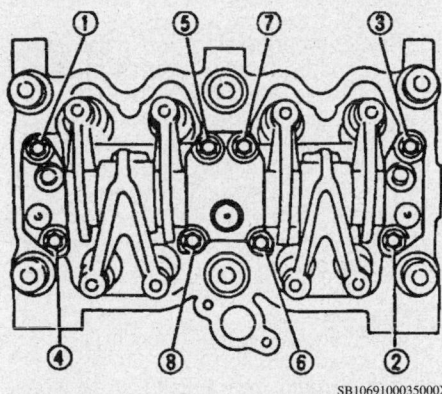

Fig. 11 Rocker assembly bolt tightening sequence. 1.8L & 2.2L engines

order as which they were removed. **Ensure cutout portion of rocker shaft faces oil holes in shaft supports.**
12. Align rocker shaft lock holes and install retaining bolts. Tighten bolts to specifications.
13. Install valve rocker assembly. Equally tighten rocker assembly bolts 1 through 4 as shown, **Fig. 11. Use caution not to gouge dowel pin.**
14. Tighten rocker assembly bolts 5 through 8, then bolts 1 through 4 to specifications as shown, **Fig. 11.**
15. Install rocker cover. Tighten bolts to specifications.
16. Install PCV valve.

Camshaft

1. Remove timing belt and related components as outlined previously in this section.
2. Remove valve rocker assembly as outlined previously in this section.
3. For lefthand camshaft, remove cam-angle sensor.
4. For lefthand camshaft, remove oil dipstick tube retaining bolt.

5. For either side, remove camshaft support and camshaft. Separate O-ring and oil seal from camshaft support.
6. Coat camshaft journals with clean engine oil, then install camshaft.
7. Install O-ring to camshaft support.
8. Install camshaft support and tighten to specifications.
9. Coat new oil seal lips with a suitable lubricant, then using oil seal guide tool No. 499597000, or equivalent, oil seal installer tool No. 499587100, or equivalent, and a hammer, install oil seal to camshaft support.
10. For lefthand camshaft, install oil dipstick tube retaining bolt.
11. For lefthand camshaft, install cam-angle sensor. Tighten to specifications.
12. Install valve rocker assembly, timing belt and related components as outlined previously in this section.

Cylinder Head

1. Remove drive belt, power steering pump, alternator and bracket.
2. Remove timing belt and related components as outlined previously in this section.
3. Remove valve rocker assembly as outlined previously in this section.
4. Remove camshaft as outlined previously in this section.
5. Disconnect spark plug wires, oil pressure switch electrical connector and blow-by hose.
6. Remove connector bracket retaining bolts, crank-angle and knock sensors.
7. Remove intake manifold and gasket.
8. Remove water pipe.
9. Separate cylinder head from cylinder block as follows:
   a. Loosen cylinder head retaining bolts No. 1 and 3 as shown, **Fig. 12. Do not remove bolts at this time.**
   b. Remove remainder of cylinder head retaining bolts in numerical

order as shown **Fig. 12.**
   c. Using a plastic hammer, tap on cylinder head while separating it from cylinder block.
   d. Remove bolts No. 1 and 3 with cylinder head and gasket.
10. Remove valves from cylinder head using valve spring remover tool No. 499718000, or equivalent. **Use caution not to damage oil seals. Keep all parts in order of removal for proper installation.**
11. For lefthand cylinder head, remove plug only if service is needed.
12. For lefthand cylinder head, install plug using oil seal installer tool No. 499587100, or equivalent.
13. For either cylinder head, install valves as follows:
   a. Coat valve stem with clean engine oil and insert valve into valve guide. **Use caution not to damage oil seal lip. Install all parts in same order as which they were removed.**
   b. Install valve spring with closed coil end facing cylinder head seat.
   c. Use valve spring remover tool No. 499718000, or equivalent, to compress valve spring and install retainer. Seat valve spring retainer by tapping it with a soft hammer.
14. Install camshaft and valve rocker assemblies as outlined previously in this section.
15. Install cylinder head with new gasket.

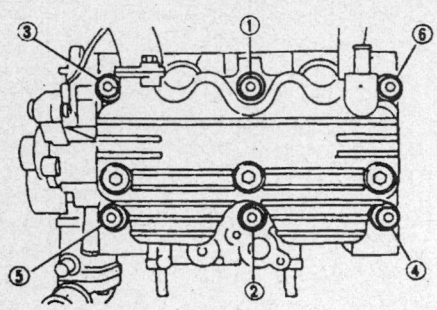

Fig. 13 Cylinder head bolt tightening sequence. 1.8L & 2.2L engines

16. **On models equipped with 2.2L engine,** using sequence shown in **Fig. 13,** tighten cylinder head bolts as follows:
    a. Coat bolt threads and washers with clean engine oil.
    b. **Torque** all six bolts to 22 ft. lbs.
    c. **Torque** all bolts to 51 ft. lbs.
    d. Loosen all bolts 180°, then loosen an additional 180°.
    e. **On models less turbocharger,** torque bolts 1 and 2 to 25 ft. lbs.
    f. **On models equipped with turbocharger,** torque bolts 1 and 2 to 27.1 ft. lbs.
    g. **On models less turbocharger,** torque bolts 3, 4, 5 and 6 to 11 ft. lbs.
    h. **On models equipped with turbocharger,** torque bolts 3, 4, 5 and 6–14 ft. lbs.
    i. **On all models,** tighten all bolts an additional 80°–90° in sequence. **Do not tighten bolts more than 90°.**
    j. Tighten all bolts an additional 80°–90° in sequence. **Ensure total retightening angle does not exceed 180°.**
17. **On models equipped with 1.8L engine,** using sequence shown in **Fig. 13,** tighten cylinder head bolts as follows:
    a. Coat bolt threads and washers with clean engine oil.
    b. **Torque** all cylinder head bolts to 22 ft. lbs., then again to 51 ft. lbs.
    c. Loosen all bolts 180°, then loosen an additional 180°.
    d. **Torque** bolts 1 and 2 to 25 ft. lbs.
    e. **Torque** bolts 3, 4, 5 and 6 to 11 ft. lbs.
    f. Tighten all bolts an additional 80–90.° **Do not tighten bolts more than 90.°**
    g. Tighten all bolts an additional 80°–90.° **Ensure total retightening angle does not exceed 180°.**
18. **On all models,** install timing belt and related components as outlined previously in this section.
19. Install water pipe.
20. Install intake manifold and gasket.
21. Install connector bracket retaining bolts, crank-angle and knock sensors.
22. Connect spark plug wires, oil pressure switch electrical connector and blow-by hose.

23. Install power steering pump, alternator and bracket.
24. Install drive belt.

Cylinder Block

1. Separate cylinder head from cylinder block.
2. Remove flywheel or driveplate housing cover.
3. Lock crankshaft using crankshaft stopper tool No. 498497100, or equivalent, then remove flywheel or driveplate.
4. Remove oil separator cover.
5. Remove water pump.
6. Remove oil pump retaining bolts, then using a flat blade screwdriver, separate oil pump from cylinder block. **Use caution not to scrape mating surfaces.**
7. Position cylinder block with No. 2 and 4 pistons facing upward.
8. Remove oil pan retaining bolts, then using oil pan cutter tool, or equivalent, separate oil pan from cylinder block. **Use caution not to scrape mating surfaces.**
9. Remove oil strainer stay, oil strainer, baffle plate and oil filter.
10. Remove pistons as follows:
    a. Remove service hole cover and plugs from both sides of crankcase.
    b. Rotate crankshaft until pistons for No. 1 and No. 2 cylinders are at BDC.
    c. Working through access holes, remove piston pin circlips for No. 1 and No. 2 pistons.
    d. Using piston pin remover tool No. 499097500, or equivalent, withdraw piston pins for No. 1 and No. 2 pistons.
    e. Repeat step 10 for cylinders 3 and 4 respectively.
11. Separate crankcase as follows:
    a. Remove crankcase half retaining bolts from No. 2 and 4 cylinder side of block.
    b. Loosen crankcase half retaining bolts from No. 1 and 3 cylinder side of block. Do not remove bolts at this time.
    c. Position crankcase so that cylinders No. 1 and 3 face upward.
    d. Remove retaining bolts and separate crankcase halves. **Use caution so connecting rod will not damage cylinder block.**
12. Remove rear oil seal.
13. Remove crankshaft and connecting rod assembly.
14. Remove crankshaft bearings from crankcase halves keeping them in order.
15. Mark and remove pistons from crankcase halves, then mate pistons with respective pins.
16. Remove connecting rod caps and rod bearings. **Keep all components in order to ensure proper assembly. Components that are to be reused should be installed in original position.**
17. Remove piston rings using a piston ring expander. Remove oil ring by hand.
18. Remove circlip.

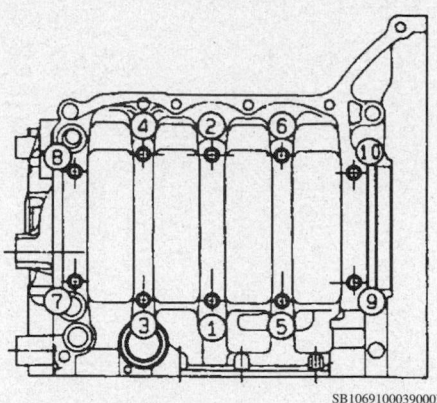

Fig. 14 Crankcase 10 mm bolt tightening sequence. 1.8L & 2.2L engines

19. Ensure all components are clean and free from foreign material and that oil passages are clear. Coat all friction surfaces with oil or suitable assembly lubricant.
20. Install connecting rods, proceed as follows:
    a. Seat connecting rod bearings in caps and rods, then coat bearing with clean engine oil.
    b. Ensure connecting rod and cap matching marks are aligned and install connecting rod assemblies with mark facing forward.
    c. Lubricate connecting rod bolt threads and ensure bolts are properly seated in cap and that caps are fully seated against connecting rods.
    d. Evenly tighten connecting rod nuts to specifications.
21. Install main bearings into crankcase halves, then coat bearing with clean engine oil.
22. Install crankshaft into lefthand crankcase.
23. Clean crankcase half mating surfaces with suitable solvent, then apply a thin bead of Three-Bond 1215, or equivalent sealant to one crankcase half. Ensure sealant does not enter oil or coolant passages.
24. Guide righthand crankcase half onto left case, then install and tighten retaining bolts as follows:
    a. **Torque** 10 mm bolts in sequence shown in **Fig. 14,** to 33–37 ft. lbs.
    b. Tighten 8 mm and 6 mm bolts in sequence shown in **Fig. 15.** Torque bolts 1 through 7 to 17–20 ft. lbs. and bolt 8 to 56.5 inch lbs.
25. Install piston rings onto pistons, positioning end gaps as shown, **Figs. 16 and 17.** After installation, bend pawl of upper oil ring rail upward and attach to hole in piston.
26. Install piston, proceed as follows:
    a. Prior to insertion, coat piston, pin guide and piston pin with clean engine oil.
    b. With No. 1 and 2 cylinders facing upward, turn crankshaft until No. 1 and 2 connecting rods are positioned at BDC.

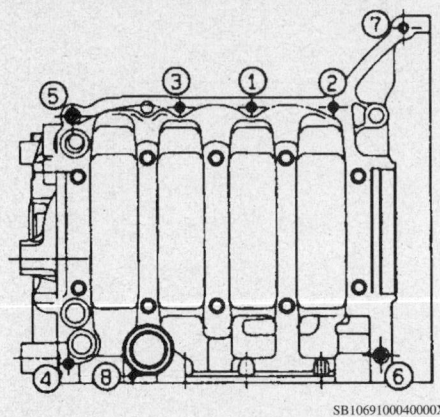

Fig. 15 Crankcase 8 mm & 6 mm bolt tightening sequence. 1.8L & 2.2L engines

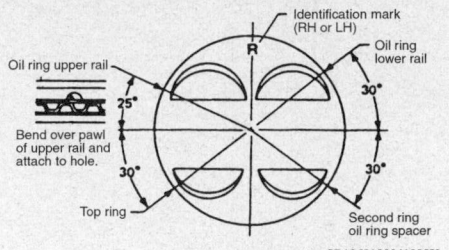

Fig. 16 Piston ring installation. 1.8L & 3.3L engines

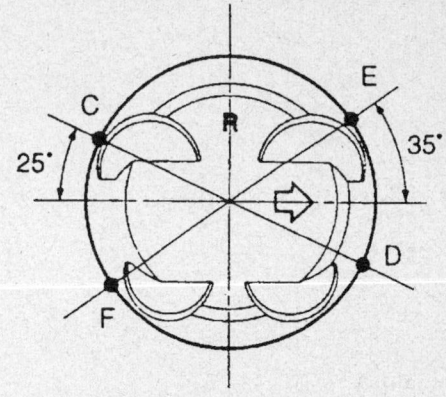

Fig. 17 Piston ring installation. 2.2L engine

Fig. 18 Timing belt guide. 2.5L engine w/manual transmission

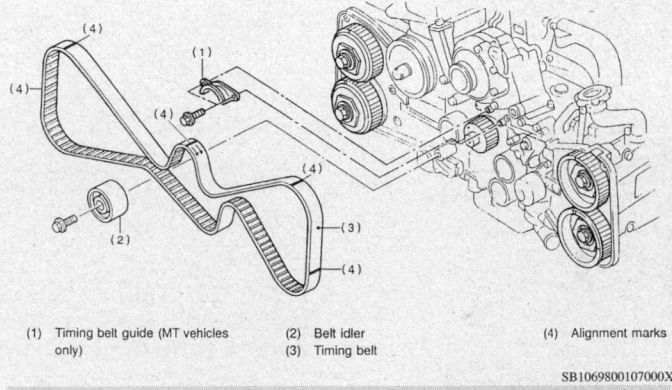

(1) Timing belt guide (MT vehicles only)
(2) Belt idler
(3) Timing belt
(4) Alignment marks

Fig. 19 Timing belt alignment marks. 2.5L engine

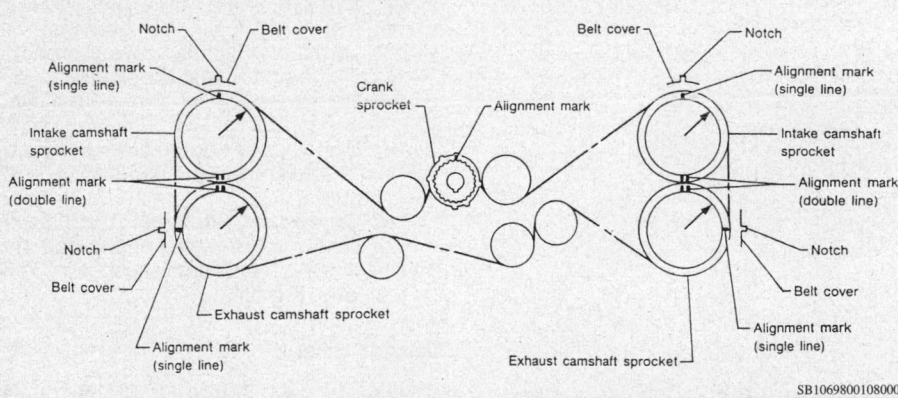

Fig. 20 Timing sprocket alignment marks. 2.5L engine

c. Insert piston into cylinder, align piston pin hole and connecting rod small end with pin guide tool No. 499017100, or equivalent, then install piston pin through access hole.

d. Install piston pin circlip.

e. Repeat step 26 for cylinders 3 and 4 respectively.

27. Apply Three-Bond 1105, or equivalent sealant, then install service access hole plugs and cover with new gaskets. Tighten plugs to specifications.

28. Coat outside surface of rear seal with engine oil and seal lip with grease, then install oil seal using a suitable tool.

29. Apply Three-Bond 1207C, or equivalent sealant, then install oil separator cover with new gasket and Tighten to specifications.

30. Install flywheel or driveplate and tighten bolts to specifications.

31. Apply Three-Bond 1215, or equivalent sealant to oil pump to cylinder block mating surface. Align flat surface of inner rotor with crankshaft and install oil pump assembly with new seal and O-ring. Tighten bolts to specifications.

32. Install water pump with new gasket. Tighten bolts to specifications.

33. Install baffle plate, oil strainer, stay and oil pan. Tighten bolts to specifications.

34. Install oil filter.

35. Install flywheel or driveplate housing cover.

36. Finalize installation by performing steps 14 through 22 of cylinder head service procedure.

2.5L ENGINE

Timing Belt, Tensioner & Idler

1. Remove v-belt cover, v-belt and A/C compressor drive belt tensioner.

2. Lock crankshaft into position using crankshaft pulley wrench tool No. 499977100, or equivalent, then remove pulley bolt and pulley.

3. Remove left, right and front belt covers.

4. **On models equipped with manual transmission,** remove timing belt guide, **Fig. 18.**

5. **On all models,** if alignment marks on timing belt are faded or difficult to see, put new marks on belt before removal, **Fig. 19.**

6. Align all sprockets and mark locations with white paint, **Fig. 20.**

7. Remove timing belt idler pulley, then the timing belt.

8. **Do not rotate engine after belt has been removed.**

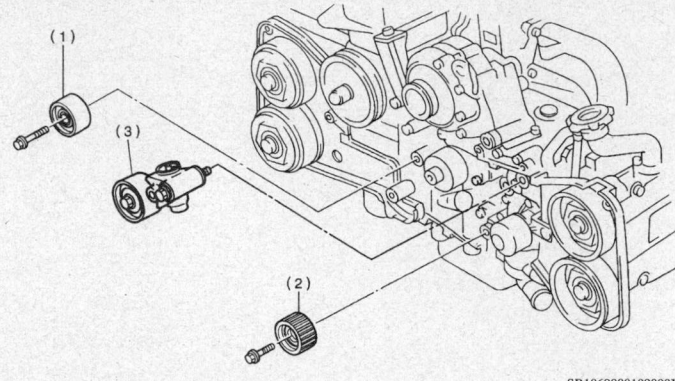

Fig. 21 Timing belt idler and tensioner. 2.5L engine

SB1069800109000X

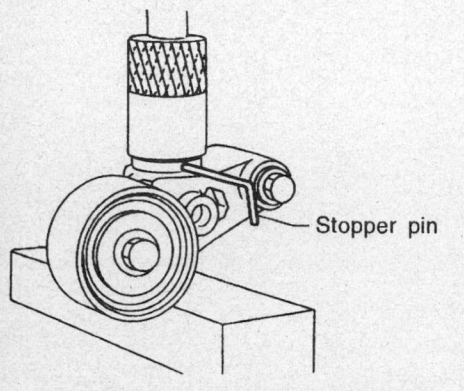

— Stopper pin

SB1069800111000X

Fig. 23 Timing belt tensioner installation. 2.5L engine

Fig. 24 Timing belt guide installation & adjustment. 2.5L engine w/manual transmission

SB1069800112000X

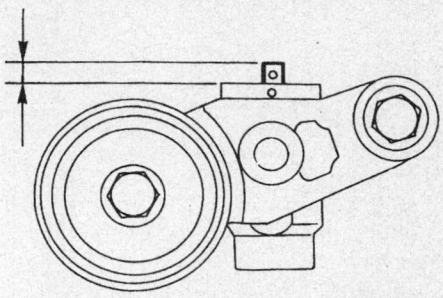

SB1069800110000X

Fig. 22 Timing belt tensioner rod measurement. 2.5L engine

9. Remove belt idler (1), belt idler No. 2 (2) and automatic belt tensioner (3), **Fig. 21.**
10. Reverse procedure to install, noting the following:
   a. Inspect timing belt for cracks, breaks or excessive wear, replace if necessary.
   b. Inspect tensioner for oil leaks or signs of excessive wear on rod ends, replace if necessary.
   c. Ensure adjuster rod does not move when a pressure of 66 lbs. is applied, replace if necessary.
   d. Measure extension of rod above tensioner body, **Fig. 22.**
   e. Replace if measurement is not .205–.244 inch.
   f. Using a suitable press, push tensioner rod into tensioner and insert a stopper pin to secure adjuster rod, **Fig. 23.**
   g. Install timing belt tensioner, idler and idler No. 2.
   h. Install timing belt ensuring all sprocket marks are properly aligned, then install belt idler.
   i. Remove stopper pin from timing belt tensioner.
   j. **On models equipped with manual transmission,** install timing belt guide.
   k. **On all models,** inspect and adjust clearance between timing belt and guide to a clearance of .019–.059 inch, **Fig. 24.**

Camshafts

Refer to **Fig. 25,** when removing the camshafts.
1. Remove timing belt and related components as outlined previously in this section.
2. Remove camshaft position sensor from left side camshaft.
3. Remove spark plug wires, then the rocker cover and gasket.
4. Loosen intake and exhaust camshaft cap bolts equally, a little at a time in alphabetical sequence, **Figs. 26 and 27,** then remove the camshaft caps and camshafts.
5. Note position of camshaft caps for installation reference.
6. Reverse procedure to install, noting the following:
   a. Apply clean engine oil to cylinder

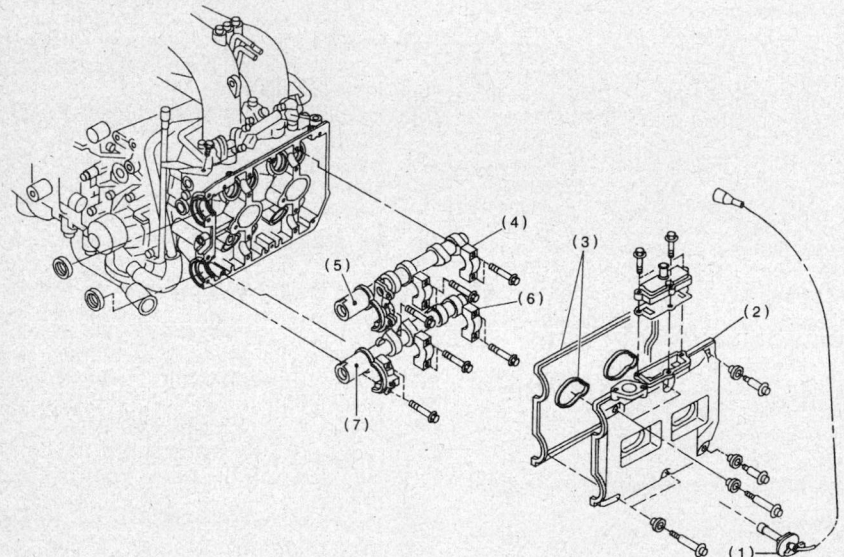

(1)	Spark plug cord	(4)	Intake camshaft cap (LH)	(7)	Exhaust camshaft (LH)
(2)	Rocker cover (LH)	(5)	Intake camshaft (LH)		
(3)	Rocker cover gasket (LH)	(6)	Exhaust camshaft cap (LH)		

SB1069800113000X

Fig. 25 Exploded view of camshafts. 2.5L engine

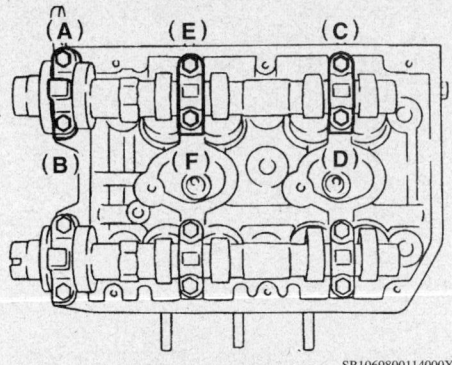

Fig. 26 Intake camshaft removal sequence. 2.5L engine

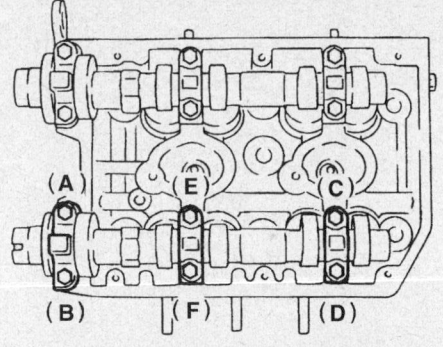

Fig. 27 Exhaust camshaft removal sequence. 2.5L engine

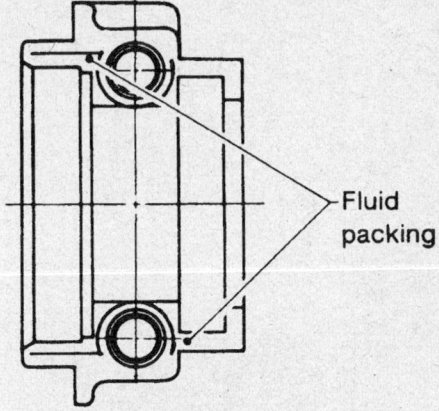

Fig. 28 Camshaft cap fluid packing. 2.5L engine

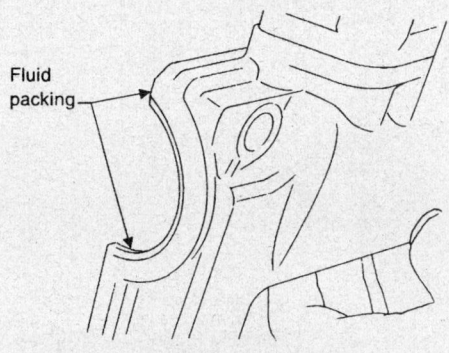

Fig. 29 Valve cover peripheral gasket fluid packing. 2.5L engine

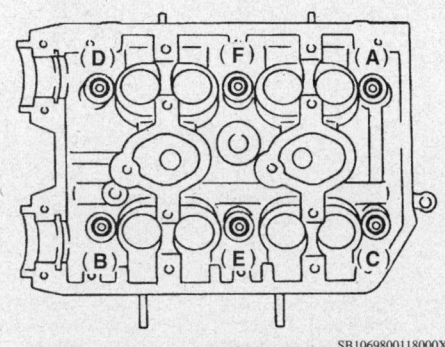

Fig. 30 Cylinder head bolt removal sequence. 2.5L engine

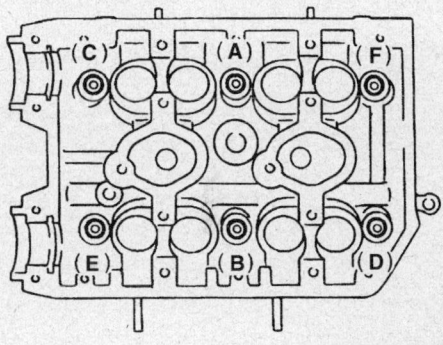

Fig. 31 Cylinder head tightening sequence. 2.5L engine

head at camshaft bearing locations before installing camshafts.
b. Apply fluid packing sparingly to cap mating surfaces, **Fig. 28.**
c. Gradually tighten caps in two stages in reverse sequence as removed.
d. Apply grease to new seal and install using oil seal guide tool No. 499597000, or equivalent and oil seal installer tool No. 499587100, or equivalent.
e. Apply fluid packing to valve cover peripheral gasket, **Fig. 29.**

Cylinder Head

1. Remove timing belt, cam sprockets and related components as outlined previously in this section.
2. Remove v-belt, alternator and A/C compressor and brackets.
3. Remove hoses and tubes from cylinder block.
4. Disconnect and remove connectors and brackets.
5. Remove intake manifold assembly and gasket.
6. Remove camshaft position sensor.
7. Remove rocker cover, camshafts and related parts.
8. Remove cylinder head bolts in alphabetical sequence, **Fig. 30.**
9. Leave bolts "A" and "D" partially threaded into cylinder head to prevent head from falling off.

10. While tapping cylinder head with plastic mallet, separate it from cylinder block.
11. Remove bolts "A" and "D" to remove cylinder head.
12. Remove cylinder head gasket.
13. Reverse procedure to install, noting the following:
a. Inspect cylinder head for warpage. If warpage exceeds specification, machine or replace cylinder head as necessary.
b. Install new cylinder head gasket and **torque** cylinder head bolts to 22 ft. lbs in alphabetical sequence, **Fig. 31.**
c. Then **torque** cylinder head bolts to 51 ft. lbs. in alphabetical order.
d. Back off all bolts by 180°, then back off 180° again.
e. **Torque** bolts "A" and "B" to 25 ft. lbs.
f. **Torque** bolts "C," "D," "E," and "F" to 11 ft. lbs.
g. Tighten all bolts an additional 80°–90° in alphabetical sequence.

Cylinder Block

1. Remove timing belt, camshaft sprockets and related parts as outlined previously.
2. Remove rocker cover, camshafts and related components.
3. Remove cylinder heads as described under "Engine Service."

4. Remove water pipe, **Fig. 32.**
5. **On models equipped with manual transmission,** remove clutch housing cover.
6. **On all models,** remove flywheel or drive plate.
7. Remove oil separator cover, water bypass pipes, water pump and oil pump from cylinder block, **Fig. 33.**
8. Remove oil pan using a suitable oil pan cutter tool.
9. Remove oil strainer stay, oil strainer, baffle plate and oil filter.
10. **On models equipped with automatic transmission,** remove oil cooler.
11. **On all models,** remove service hole cover and service hole plugs using a suitable hexagon wrench, **Fig. 34.**
12. Rotate crankshaft to bring No. 1 and No. 2 pistons to bottom dead center position, then remove piston circlip through service hole of No. 1 and No. 2 cylinders.
13. Draw out piston pin from No. 1 and No. 2 pistons using piston pin remover tool No. 499097700, or equivalent.
14. Repeat procedure for No. 3 and No. 4 pistons.
15. Mark pistons and pins for assembly reference.
16. Remove cylinder block attaching bolts on side of No. 2 and No. 4 cylinders.

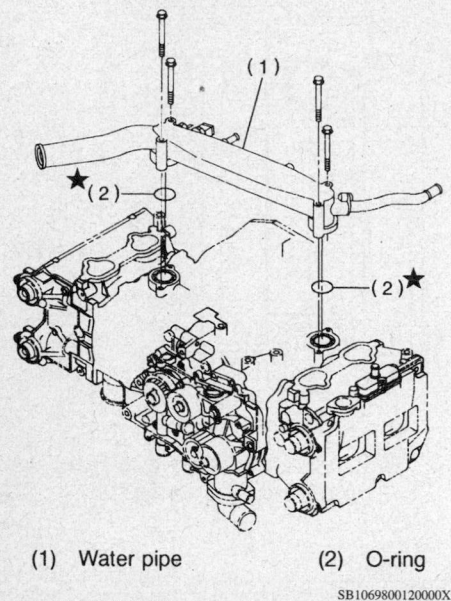

(1) Water pipe   (2) O-ring

SB1069800120000X

Fig. 32 Water pipe. 2.5L engine

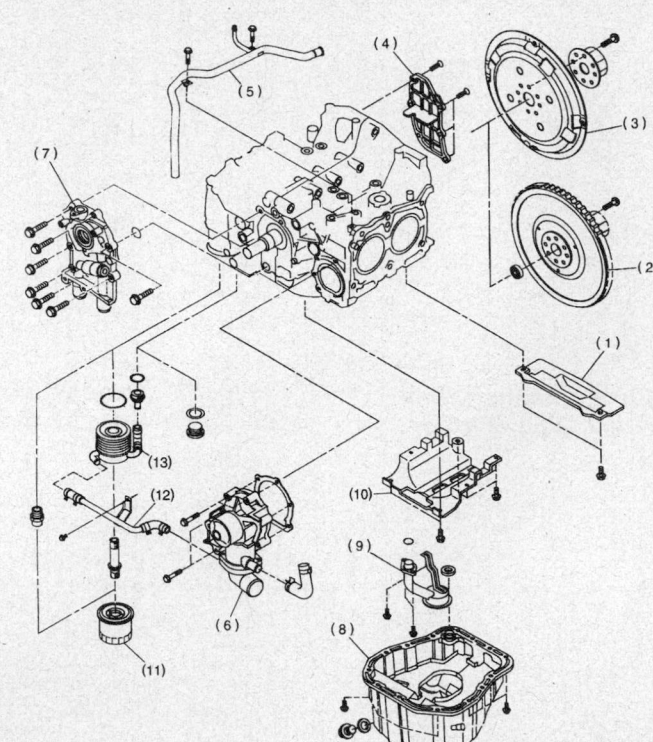

(1) Clutch housing cover (MT vehicles only)	(5) Water by-pass pipe	(10) Baffle plate
(2) Flywheel (MT vehicles only)	(6) Water pump	(11) Oil filter
(3) Drive plate (AT vehicles only)	(7) Oil pump	(12) Water by-pass pipe (AT vehicles only)
(4) Oil separator cover	(8) Oil pan	(13) Oil cooler (AT vehicles only)
	(9) Oil strainer	

SB1069800121000X

Fig. 33 Exploded view of water pump & oil pump. 2.5L engine

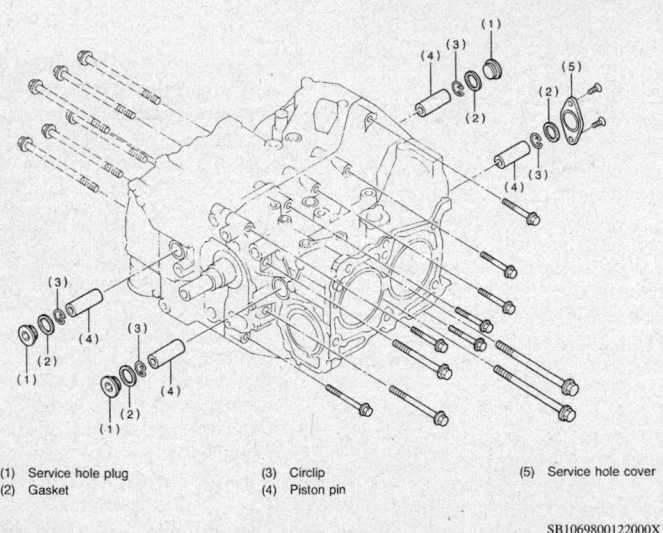

(1) Service hole plug	(3) Circlip	(5) Service hole cover
(2) Gasket	(4) Piston pin	

SB1069800122000X

Fig. 34 Piston pins & cylinder block. 2.5L engine

17. Back off attaching bolts on No. 1 and No. 3 cylinder side by two or three turns.
18. Set up cylinder block so No. 1 and No. 3 cylinders are on the upper side, then remove cylinder block connecting bolts, **Fig. 35.**
19. Separate left and right hand cylinder blocks, do not allow connecting rod to fall and damage cylinder block.
20. Remove rear oil seal, then the crankshaft and connecting rods.
21. Remove crankshaft bearings from cylinder block using a hammer handle.

22. Mark bearings for assembly reference.
23. Draw out each piston from cylinder block using wooden bar or hammer handle.
24. Mark pistons and cylinders for assembly reference.
25. Remove connecting rod cap and bearing, **Fig. 36,** then remove piston rings.
26. Mark rod caps, bearings and rings for assembly reference.
27. Remove circlip.
28. Reverse procedure to assemble, noting the following:
    a. Inspect cylinder block for warpage.
    b. Install connecting rod bearings, rods and pistons in their original locations.
    c. Ensure arrow on connecting rod cap faces front during installation.
    d. Install main bearings in their original locations, apply fluid packing to mating surfaces then install and temporarily tighten 10 mm cylinder block connecting bolts in alphabetical sequence, **Fig. 37.**
    e. **Torque** 10 mm cylinder block bolts to 33–39 ft. lbs.
    f. **Torque** 8 mm and 6 mm cylinder block bolts to 17–20 ft. lbs for bolts in locations "A"—"G" and to 60 inch lbs. for bolts in location " H."
    g. Install new gasket and apply fluid

SUBARU

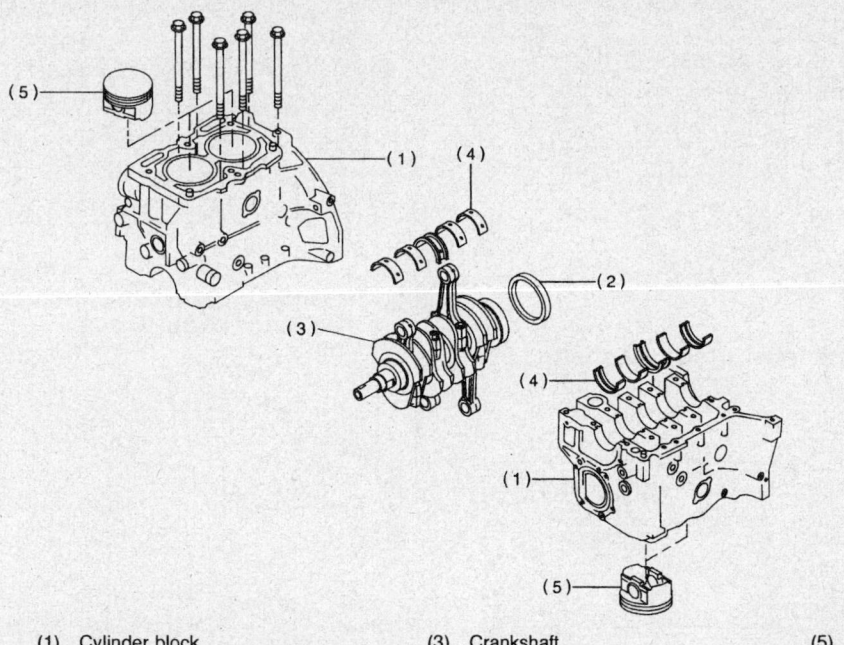

(1) Cylinder block
(2) Rear oil seal
(3) Crankshaft
(4) Crankshaft bearing
(5) Piston

SB1069800123000X

Fig. 35 Exploded view of cylinder block. 2.5L engine

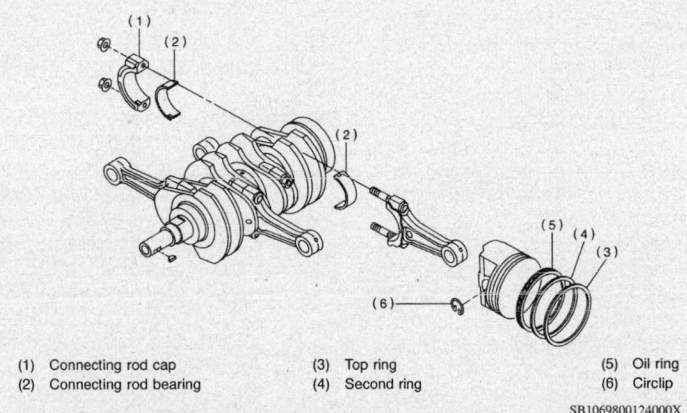

(1) Connecting rod cap
(2) Connecting rod bearing
(3) Top ring
(4) Second ring
(5) Oil ring
(6) Circlip

SB1069800124000X

Fig. 36 Exploded view of crankshaft & piston. 2.5L engine

packing to service hole plugs prior to installation.

3.3L ENGINE

Timing Belt, Tensioner & Idler

1. Remove drive belt, power steering pump, alternator and drive belt cover bracket.
2. Remove power steering pump bracket, A/C belt tensioner, A/C compressor and bracket.
3. Lock crankshaft using crankshaft pulley wrench tool No. 499977000, or equivalent, then remove pulley retaining bolt and pulley.
4. Remove lefthand, righthand and front belt covers.
5. Ensure timing belt rotation arrows and alignment marks are visible prior to belt removal. If original marks are

faded, new alignment marks can be made as follows:
   a. Align camshaft and crankshaft sprockets with notches in belt cover and cylinder block.
   b. Mark timing belt in relation to sprockets.
6. Loosen tensioner adjuster mounting bolts.
7. Remove belt idler, belt idler No. 2, timing belt, spacer, belt tensioner and tensioner adjuster.
8. Lock camshaft sprocket using camshaft sprocket wrench tool No. 499207100, or equivalent, then remove sprocket retaining bolt and sprocket.
9. Remove No. 2 lefthand and righthand belt covers.
10. Remove tensioner bracket.

11. Install tensioner bracket. Tighten bolts to specifications.
12. Install No. 2 righthand and lefthand belt covers.
13. Install crankshaft sprocket.
14. Install righthand, then the lefthand camshaft sprockets. Lock sprocket using tool No. 499207100, or equivalent, and tighten bolt to specifications. **Lefthand sprocket can be identified by a projection used to monitor cam-angle sensor.**
15. Vertically push tensioner adjuster rod into adjuster body using a suitable press, then completely insert stopper pin .059 inch diameter into tensioner adjuster to hold rod in place. **Do not allow press pressure to exceed 2205 lbs.**
16. Install tensioner adjuster. Ensure adjuster is positioned completely to the right and tighten retaining bolts.
17. Install belt tensioner. Tighten bolts to specifications.
18. Install belt idler. Tighten bolts to specifications.
19. Using sprocket wrench, turn sprockets to position alignment marks at the top.
20. Install timing belt. Position timing belt with rotation arrows facing in correct direction and sprocket and belt alignment marks properly aligned.
21. Install belt idler No. 2, then the belt idler. Tighten bolts to specifications.
22. Loosen tensioner adjuster retaining bolts, position adjuster completely to the left and tighten retaining bolts to specifications.
23. Ensure timing marks are properly aligned, then remove stopper pin from tension adjuster.
24. Install front, lefthand and righthand belt covers.
25. Install crankshaft pulley. Lock crankshaft using tool No. 499977000, or equivalent, and tighten pulley retaining bolt to specifications.
26. Install drive belt. Refer to "Belt Tension Data" for belt routing and tension data.
27. Install power steering pump bracket, A/C belt tensioner, A/C compressor and bracket.
28. Install drive belt, power steering pump, alternator and drive belt cover bracket.

Camshafts

1. Remove timing belt and related components as outlined previously in this section.
2. Disconnect cam angle sensor and ignition coil connectors.
3. Remove cam angle sensor and bracket, then fully loosen ignition coil mounting bolts.
4. Disconnect blow-by hose, then remove cylinder head cover and gasket.
5. Remove front camshaft cap, camshaft oil seal and plug.
6. Remove intake and exhaust camshafts as follows:
   a. **On lefthand side camshafts,** rotate intake camshaft (upper) and exhaust camshaft (lower) so notch at front end of each camshaft faces directly downward.

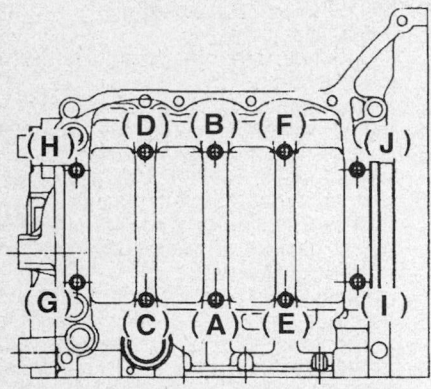

Fig. 37 Cylinder block bolt tightening sequence. 2.5L engine

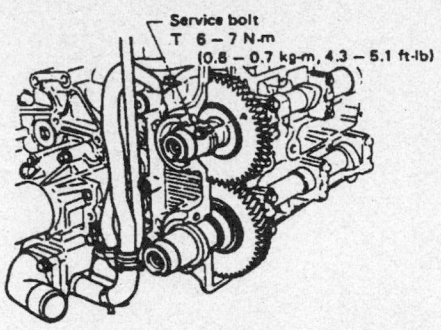

Fig. 38 Securing camshaft. 3.3L engine

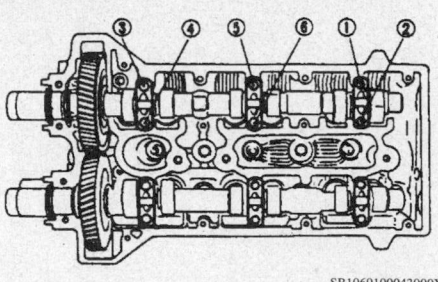

Fig. 39 Intake camshaft removal sequence. 3.3L engine

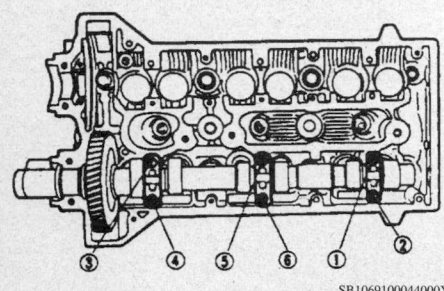

Fig. 40 Exhaust camshaft removal sequence. 3.3L engine

b. **On righthand side camshafts,** rotate intake camshaft (upper) and exhaust camshaft (lower) so notch at front end of each camshaft faces directly upward.

c. **On either side,** looking from rear side of camshaft gears, ensure match marks on gears are aligned.

d. Install .24 inch diameter bolt to sub-gear mounting bolt hole of intake camshaft gear to secure gear train, **Fig. 38.**

e. Loosen bolts on intake camshaft caps equally, a little at a time, in sequence shown in **Fig. 39.** Ensure as bolts are loosened, clearance between camshaft journal and cylinder head journal bearing increases evenly. If not, tighten bolts by reversing sequence in **Fig. 39,** and repeat this step.

f. Remove camshaft caps while holding intake camshaft, then remove camshaft. If intake camshaft is hard to remove, rotate exhaust camshaft counterclockwise.

g. Arrange caps in correct order. Caps must be installed in their original positions.

h. Loosen bolts on exhaust camshaft caps equally, a little at a time, in sequence shown in **Fig. 40.** Ensure as bolts are loosened, clearance between camshaft journal and cylinder head journal bearing increases evenly. If not, tighten bolts by reversing sequence in **Fig. 40,** and repeat this step.

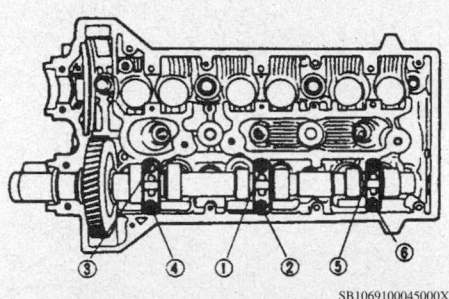

Fig. 41 Exhaust camshaft installation sequence. 3.3L engine

i. Remove camshaft caps while holding exhaust camshaft, then remove camshaft. Arrange caps in correct order. Caps must be installed in their original positions.

7. Remove hydraulic lash adjuster. Arrange adjusters in correct order. Adjusters must be installed in their original positions.

8. Service intake camshaft as follows:
   a. Using a rag, secure shaft portion of camshaft in vice, then remove bolt installed in sub-gear.
   b. Using camshaft gear wrench No. 49920-7200, or equivalent, turn sub-gear clockwise, then remove snap ring.
   c. Remove wave washer, sub-gear and gear spring.
   d. Reverse step 8 to assemble intake camshaft.

9. Install exhaust camshaft as follows:
   a. Install lash adjusters. Apply coat of clean engine oil to adjuster surface.
   b. Apply coat of clean engine oil to camshaft journals.
   c. Set exhaust camshaft on cylinder head with front end notch of camshaft facing directly downward.
   d. Attach camshaft caps in their original positions. Fully hand tighten cap bolts.
   e. Tighten cap bolts equally, a little at a time, in sequence shown in **Fig. 41,** to specifications. Ensure as bolts are tightened, clearance between camshaft journal and cylinder head journal bearing decreases evenly. If not, loosen bolts by reversing sequence in **Fig. 41,** and repeat this step.

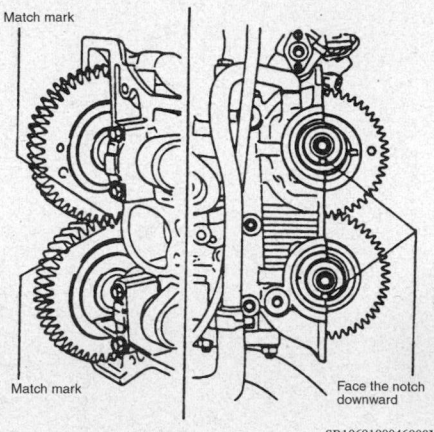

Fig. 42 Camshaft match mark alignment. 3.3L engine

10. Install intake camshaft as follows:
    a. Install lash adjusters. Apply coat of clean engine oil to adjuster surface.
    b. Apply coat of clean engine oil to camshaft journals.
    c. **On lefthand side camshafts,** align intake camshaft match mark with match mark of exhaust camshaft. Ensure notch on front end of camshafts are facing same direction (downward), **Fig. 42.**
    d. **On righthand side camshafts,** align intake camshaft match mark with match mark of exhaust camshaft. Ensure notch on front end of camshafts are facing same direction (upward), **Fig. 42.**
    e. **On either camshaft,** attach camshaft caps in their original positions. Fully hand tighten cap bolts. Ensure match marks on rear side of camshaft gears are aligned.
    f. Tighten cap bolts equally, a little at a time, in sequence shown in **Fig. 43,** to specifications. Ensure as bolts are tightened, clearance between camshaft journal and cylinder head journal bearing decreases evenly. If not, loosen bolts by reversing sequence in **Fig. 43,** and repeat this step.

11. Remove sub-gear securing bolt from intake camshaft gear.

12. Apply fluid packing for mating surface of front camshaft cover, then install camshaft cover.

13. Using oil seal guide No. 49959-7000

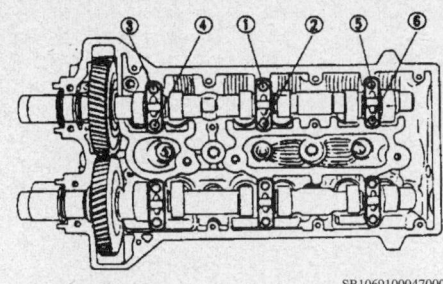

SB1069100047000X

Fig. 43 Intake camshaft installation sequence. 3.3L engine

and oil seal installer No. 49958-7300, or equivalents, lubricate and install new camshaft oil seal.

14. Using plug installer No. 49803-7100, or equivalent, install camshaft plug.
15. **On lefthand side camshafts,** install cylinder head cover. Apply soapy water over A and B shown in **Fig. 44.**
16. **On righthand side camshafts,** install cylinder head cover. Apply soapy water over A shown in **Fig. 44.**
17. **On either camshaft,** connect blow-by hose, then install ignition coils and cam angle sensor.

Cylinder Head

1. Remove timing belt and related components as outlined previously in this section.
2. Remove intake manifold as follows:
   a. Remove EGR valve, EGR pipe and backpressure transducer, then disconnect auxiliary air control valve connector.
   b. Disconnect blow-by, auxiliary air control valve and PCV hoses, then two water hoses from throttle body.
   c. Remove collector, then intake manifold assembly.
3. Remove exhaust manifold and gasket.
4. Remove cylinder head cover and camshafts as outlined previously in this section.
5. Remove dipstick, then heater pipe.
6. Separate cylinder head from cylinder block as follows:
   a. Remove cylinder head bolts in sequence shown in **Fig. 45. Leave bolts 5 and 8 engaged by four threads to prevent cylinder head from falling.** Cylinder head bolts come in two different lengths.
   b. Using plastic hammer, tap on cylinder head while separating it from cylinder block.
   c. Remove bolts 5 and 8 with cylinder head and gasket.
7. Remove hydraulic lash adjuster. Arrange adjusters in correct order. Adjusters must be installed in their original positions.
8. Using valve spring remover No. 49971-8000, or equivalent, compress valve spring, then remove spring retainer key.
9. Remove valves from cylinder head. **Use caution not to damage oil seals. Keep all parts in order of removal for proper installation.**
10. Install valve as follows:

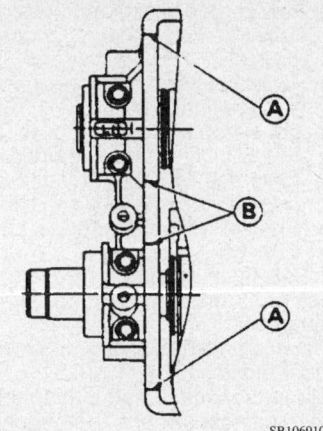

SB1069100048000X

Fig. 44 Cylinder head cover lube points. 3.3L engine

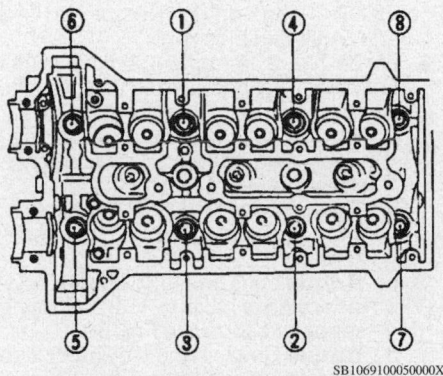

SB1069100050000X

Fig. 46 Cylinder head bolt tightening sequence. 3.3L engine

a. Coat valve stem with clean engine oil and insert valve into valve guide. **Use caution not to damage oil seal lip. Install all parts in same position as they were removed from.**
b. Install valve spring with closed coil end facing cylinder head seat.
c. Use valve spring remover tool No. 499718000, or equivalent, to compress valve spring and install retainer key. Seat valve spring retainer by tapping it with a soft hammer.
11. Apply coat of clean engine oil to hydraulic lash adjuster sliding surface, then install adjusters.
12. Install cylinder head with new gasket. Using sequence shown in **Fig. 46,** tighten cylinder head bolts as follows:
   a. Coat bolt threads and washers with clean engine oil.
   b. **Torque** all cylinder head bolts to 22 ft. lbs.
   c. **Torque** all bolts to 51 ft. lbs.
   d. Loosen all bolts 180°, then loosen an additional 180°.
   e. **Torque** all bolts to 20 ft. lbs.
   f. Tighten bolts 1, 2, 3 and 4, 80°–90° in sequence. **Do not tighten bolts more than 90°.**
   g. **Torque** bolts 5, 6, 7 and 8 in sequence to 33 ft. lbs.
   h. Tighten all bolts an additional 80°–90° in sequence. **Ensure total re-**

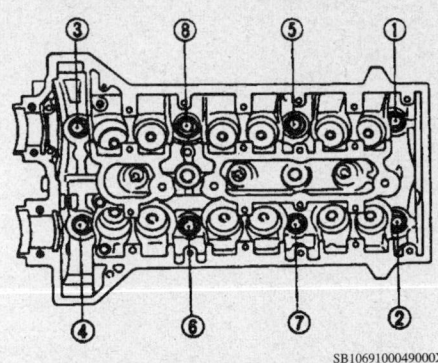

SB1069100049000X

Fig. 45 Cylinder head removal sequence. 3.3L engine

tightening angle (steps f and h) does not exceed 180°

13. Install camshafts, cylinder head covers and related parts.
14. Install exhaust manifold and gasket, then the collector and intake manifold assembly.
15. Connector blow-by, auxiliary air control valve and PCV hoses, then two water hoses from throttle body.
16. Install EGR valve, EGR pipe and backpressure transducer, then connect auxiliary air control valve connector.
17. Install timing belt and related components as outlined previously in this section.

Cylinder Block

1. Remove cylinder head and related components as outlined previously in this section.
2. Remove crank angle and knock sensors.
3. Lock crankshaft using crankshaft stopper tool No. 498497200, or equivalent, then remove driveplate.
4. Remove oil separator cover.
5. Remove water bypass pipe and pump.
6. Remove oil pump retaining bolts, then using a flat blade screwdriver, separate oil pump from cylinder block. **Use caution not to scrape mating surfaces.**
7. Position cylinder block with No. 2, 4 and 6 pistons facing upward.
8. Remove oil pan retaining bolts, then using oil pan cutter tool separate oil pan from cylinder block. **Use caution not to scrape mating surfaces.**
9. Remove oil strainer, baffle plate and oil filter.
10. Remove pistons as follows:
   a. Remove service hole cover and plugs from both sides of crankcase.
   b. Rotate crankshaft until pistons for No. 1 and No. 2 cylinders are at BDC.
   c. Working through access holes, remove piston pin circlips for No. 1 and No. 2 pistons.
   d. Using piston pin remover tool No. 499097500, or equivalent, withdraw piston pins for No. 1 and No. 2 pistons.
   e. Rotate crankshaft until pistons for No. 3 and No. 4 cylinders are at BDC, then remove piston circlip in

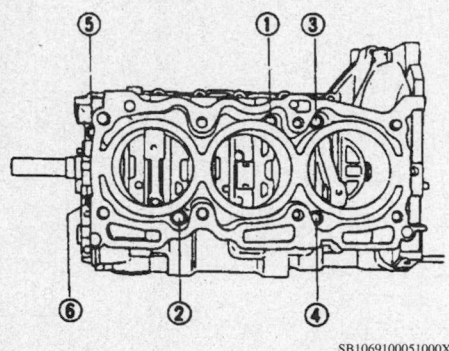

Fig. 47 Cylinder block tightening sequence (Nos. 2, 4 & 6 cylinder block side). 3.3L engine

same manner through service hole of No. 1 and No. 2 cylinders.

   f. Rotate crankshaft until pistons for No. 5 and No. 6 cylinder are at BDC, then remove piston circlip in same manner through service hole of No. 5 and No. 6 cylinders.

11. Separate crankcase as follows:

   a. Remove crankcase half retaining bolts from No. 1, 3 and 5 cylinder side of block.

   b. Loosen crankcase half retaining bolts from No. 2, 4 and 6 cylinder side of block. Do not remove bolts at this time.

   c. Position crankcase so that cylinders No. 2, 4 and 6 face upward.

   d. Remove retaining bolts and separate crankcase halves. **Use caution so connecting rod will not damage cylinder block.**

12. Remove rear oil seal.

13. Remove crankshaft and connecting rod assembly.

14. Remove crankshaft bearings from crankcase halves keeping them in order.

15. Mark and remove pistons from crankcase halves, then mate pistons with respective pins.

16. Remove connecting rod caps and rod bearings. **Keep all components in order to ensure proper assembly. Components that are to be reused should be installed in original position.**

17. Remove piston rings using a piston ring expander. Remove oil ring by hand.

18. Remove circlip.

19. Ensure all components are clean and free from foreign material and that oil passages are clear. Coat all friction surfaces with oil or suitable assembly lubricant.

20. Install connecting rods, proceed as follows:

   a. Seat connecting rod bearings in caps and rods, then coat bearing with clean engine oil.

   b. Ensure connecting rod and cap matching marks are aligned, then install connecting rod assemblies with mark facing forward.

   c. Lubricate connecting rod bolt threads and ensure bolts are prop-

erly seated in cap and that caps are fully seated against connecting rods.

   d. Evenly tighten connecting rod nuts to specifications.

21. Install piston ring, proceed as follows:

   a. Install oil ring spacer, upper rail and lower rail by hand, then the second ring and top ring with ring expander.

   b. Position ring end gaps as shown in **Fig. 16.**

22. Install main bearings into crankcase halves, then coat bearing with clean engine oil.

23. Install crankshaft on No. 1, 3 and 5 cylinder block half.

24. Clean crankcase half mating surfaces with suitable solvent, then apply a thin bead of Three-Bond 1215 sealant, or equivalent, to No. 1, 3 and 5 crankcase half. Ensure sealant does not enter oil or coolant passages.

25. Install O-rings on grooves of No. 1, 3 and 5 cylinder block.

26. Guide No. 2, 4 and 6 crankcase half onto No. 1, 3 and 5 case, then install and tighten retaining bolts as follows:

   a. **Torque** bolts on No. 2, 4 and 6 cylinder side of block in sequence shown in **Fig. 47**, to 11 ft. lbs.

   b. Tighten small bolt in crankcase, then position cylinder block horizontally.

   c. **Torque** bolts on No. 1, 3 and 5 cylinder side of block to 11 ft. lbs. using sequence shown in **Fig. 48.**

   d. **Torque** No. 2, 4 and 6 cylinder side of block a second time to 11 ft. lbs. using sequence shown in **Fig. 47.**

   e. Tighten bolts an additional 90°–110° on No. 2, 4 and 6 cylinder side of block in sequence shown in **Fig. 47.**

   f. Tighten bolts an additional 90°–110° on No. 1, 3 and 5 cylinder side of block in sequence shown in **Fig. 48.**

   g. Tighten other connecting bolts to specifications.

27. Using oil seal installer 499587200 and oil seal guide No. 499597100, or equivalents, install rear oil seal.

28. Install pistons, proceed as follows:

   a. Prior to insertion, coat piston, pin guide and piston pin with clean engine oil.

   b. With No. 1 and 2 cylinders facing upward, turn crankshaft until No. 3 and 4 connecting rods are positioned at BDC.

   c. Insert piston into cylinder, align piston pin hole and connecting rod small end with pin guide tool No. 499017100, or equivalent, then install piston pin through access hole.

   d. Install new piston pin circlip.

   e. Repeat step 28 for cylinders 1 and 2, then 5 and 6 respectively.

29. Apply Three-Bond 1105, or equivalent, sealant, then install service access hole plugs and cover with new gaskets.

30. Install baffle plate, oil strainer and O-ring.

31. Apply Three-Bond 1207F, or equivalent sealant, then install oil pan.

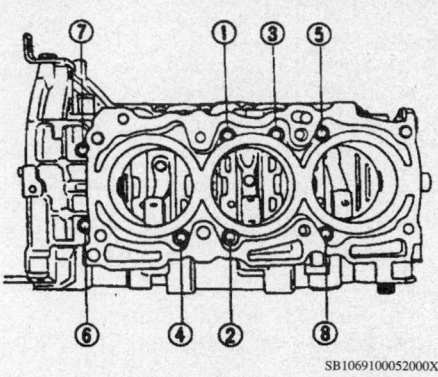

Fig. 48 Cylinder block tightening sequence (Nos. 1, 3 & 5 cylinder block side). 3.3L engine

32. Apply Three-Bond 1215B, or equivalent sealant, then install separator cover with new gasket.

33. Install driveplate.

34. Remove front oil seal, then install new seal using oil seal installer No. 499587100, or equivalent.

35. Apply Three-Bond 1215B, or equivalent sealant to oil pump to cylinder block mating surface. Align flat surface of inner rotor with crankshaft and install oil pump assembly with new seal and O-ring.

36. Install water pump with new gasket, water pipe and water bypass.

37. Install oil filter.

38. Apply coat of clean engine oil to hydraulic lash adjuster sliding surface, then install adjusters.

39. Install cylinder head with new gasket. Using sequence shown in **Fig. 45,** tighten cylinder head bolts as follows:

   a. Coat bolt threads and washers with clean engine oil.

   b. **Torque** all bolts in sequence to 22 ft. lbs.

   c. **Torque** all bolts in sequence to 51 ft. lbs.

   d. Back off all bolts 180°, then an additional 180°.

   e. **Torque** all bolts in sequence to 20 ft. lbs., then bolts 1, 2, 3 and 4, an additional 80°–90° in sequence. **Do not tighten bolts more than 90°. Then bolts 5, 6, 7 and 8 in sequence to 33 ft. lbs.**

   f. Tighten all bolts an additional 80°–90° in sequence. **Ensure total retightening angle does not exceed 180°.**

40. Install camshafts, cylinder head covers and related parts.

41. Install exhaust manifold and gasket, then the collector and intake manifold assembly.

42. Connector blow-by, auxiliary air control valve and PCV hoses, then two water hoses from throttle body.

43. Install EGR valve, EGR pipe and backpressure transducer, then connect auxiliary air control valve connector.

44. Install timing belt and related components as outlined previously in this section.

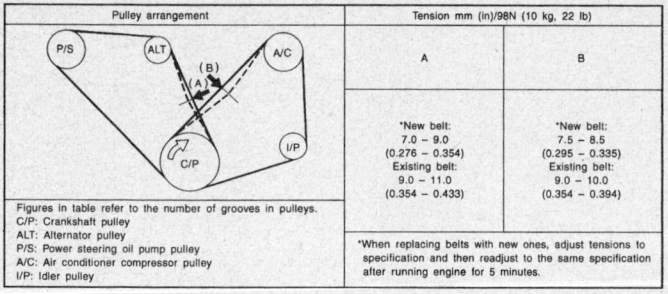

Pulley arrangement	Tension mm (in)/98N (10 kg, 22 lb)	
	A	B
	*New belt: 7.0 – 9.0 (0.276 – 0.354) Existing belt: 9.0 – 11.0 (0.354 – 0.433)	*New belt: 7.5 – 8.5 (0.295 – 0.335) Existing belt: 9.0 – 10.0 (0.354 – 0.394)

Figures in table refer to the number of grooves in pulleys.
C/P: Crankshaft pulley
ALT: Alternator pulley
P/S: Power steering oil pump pulley
A/C: Air conditioner compressor pulley
I/P: Idler pulley

*When replacing belts with new ones, adjust tensions to specification and then readjust to the same specification after running engine for 5 minutes.

SB1069100057000X

Fig. 49 Drive belt routing & tension data. Forester, Impreza & Legacy

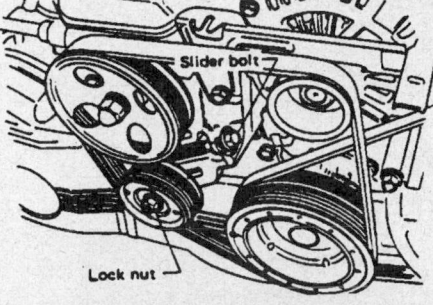

Pulley arrangement	Belt tension			
	Gauge		Belt tension [with 98 N (10 kg, 22 lb) force]	
	A	B	A	B
New belt	637 — 785 N (65 — 80 kg, 143 — 176 lb)	637 — 736 N (65 — 75 kg, 143 — 165 lb)	4.0 – 5.0 mm (0.157 – 0.197 in)	6.0 – 7.0 mm (0.236 – 0.276 in)
Existing belt	392 — 588 N (40 — 60 kg, 88 — 132 lb)	343 — 441 N (35 — 45 kg, 77 — 99 lb)	5.0 – 6.0 mm (0.197 – 0.236 in)	7.0 – 8.0 mm (0.276 – 0.315 in)

SB1069100059000X

Fig. 50 Drive belt routing & tension data. SVX

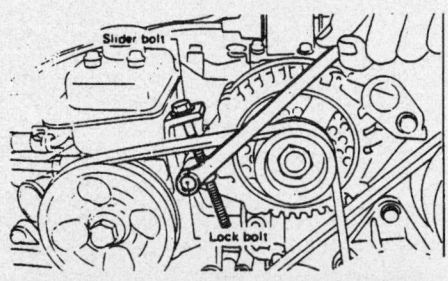

SB1069100062000X

Fig. 51 Upper soldier lock & slide bolt location. Forester, Impreza & Legacy

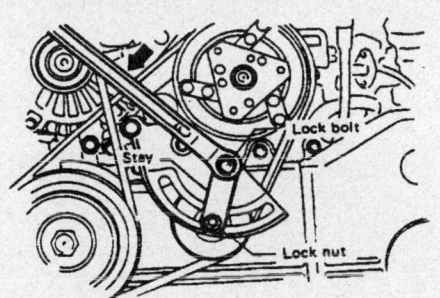

SB1069100063000X

Fig. 52 Lower soldier lock & slide bolt location. Forester, Impreza & Legacy

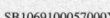

SB1069100064000X

Fig. 53 Front drive belt replacement. SVX

VALVE CLEARANCE SPECIFICATIONS

Equipped with hydraulic lifters, no adjustment required.

BELT TENSION DATA

Refer to **Figs. 49 and 50** for drive belt routing and tension data.

DRIVE BELT REPLACEMENT

FORESTER, IMPREZA & LEGACY

Where applicable, always replace drive belts in pairs.

Front Belt

1. Loosen upper soldier lock and slide bolts, **Fig. 51**.
2. Remove drive belt.
3. Install drive belt, then tighten upper soldier slide bolt, **Fig. 51**, until proper belt tension is achieved, **Fig. 49**.
4. Tighten upper soldier lock bolt, **Fig. 51**.
5. For new belt installation, readjust belt tension to specifications after running engine for five minutes.

Second Belt

1. Remove front drive belt as outlined previously.
2. Loosen lower soldier lock and slide bolts, **Fig. 51**.
3. Remove drive belt.
4. Install drive belt, then tighten lower sol-

SB1069100065000X

Fig. 54 Rear drive belt replacement. SVX

dier slide bolt, **Fig. 52**, until proper belt tension is achieved, **Fig. 49**.
5. Tighten lower soldier lock bolt, **Fig. 51**.
6. Install front drive belt as outlined previously.

SVX

Front Belt

1. Remove drive belt cover, then loosen locknut and slider bolt, **Fig. 53**.
2. Remove front drive belt.
3. Install drive belt. When proper belt tension is achieved, as specified in **Fig. 50**, tighten locknut.
4. For new belt installation, readjust belt tension to specifications after running engine for five minutes.
5. Install drive belt cover.

Rear Belt

1. Remove front drive belt as outlined previously.
2. Loosen locknut and bolt, **Fig. 54**.
3. Remove rear drive belt.

4. Install drive belt. When proper belt tension is achieved, as specified in **Fig. 50**, tighten lockbolt.
5. Install front drive belt as outlined previously.

COOLING SYSTEM BLEED

1. With engine cool, open radiator drain plug and drain coolant into a suitable container.
2. Remove radiator pressure cap. **Never open cap with engine hot.**
3. Remove and drain coolant reservoir.
4. If equipped, remove drain plug(s) from engine. When coolant is completely drained, install the plug(s).
5. Close radiator drain plug.
6. Install coolant reservoir.
7. **On models equipped with 1.8L and 2.2L engines,** remove air vent plug from radiator, **Fig. 55**.
8. **On all models,** slowly add coolant to radiator until fluid level reaches filler neck.
9. Slowly add coolant to reservoir until fluid level reaches Full mark.
10. Install radiator and reservoir caps.
11. Start and run engine at 2000–3000 RPM. When operating temperature is achieved, stop the engine.
12. With engine cool, remove radiator and reservoir caps. **Never open cap with engine hot.**
13. Add coolant as needed until fluid level is as specified in steps 8 and 9.
14. Install radiator and reservoir caps.
15. **On models equipped with 1.8L and 2.2L engine,** install air vent plug.

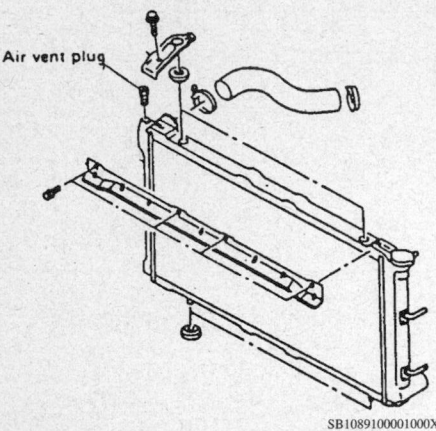

Fig. 55 Air vent plug location. 1.8L & 2.2L engine

THERMOSTAT
REPLACE

1. Remove thermostat housing mounting bolts, then the housing and gasket.
2. Remove thermostat.
3. Reverse procedure to install. **When installing thermostat, ensure jiggle pin is facing upward.**

WATER PUMP
REPLACE

1.8L & 2.2L ENGINES

1. Drain cooling system. Refer to "Cooling System Bleed."
2. Disconnect radiator outlet hose.
3. Remove radiator cooling fan motor assembly.
4. Remove drive belt(s). Refer to "Drive Belt Replacement."
5. Refer to "Engine Service" for removal of the timing belt, tensioner adjuster, lefthand camshaft pulley, lefthand rear timing belt cover and the tensioner bracket.
6. Disconnect heater and radiator hose from water pump.
7. Remove water pump retaining bolts, **Fig. 56,** then the pump.
8. Reverse procedure to install, noting the following:
   a. Tighten water pump mounting bolts in sequence, **Fig. 57.**
   b. Torque water pump mounting bolts to specification, **Fig. 56.**

2.5L ENGINE

1. Raise and support vehicle.
2. Remove splash shield.
3. Drain engine coolant into suitable container.
4. Disconnect electrical connectors from radiator main fan and sub fan motors.
5. Loosen lower attaching bolts for main fan and sub fan shrouds.
6. **On models equipped with automatic transmission,** remove water bypass pipe attaching bolt and water bypass hose.
7. **On all models,** disconnect radiator outlet hose and heater hose from water pump.

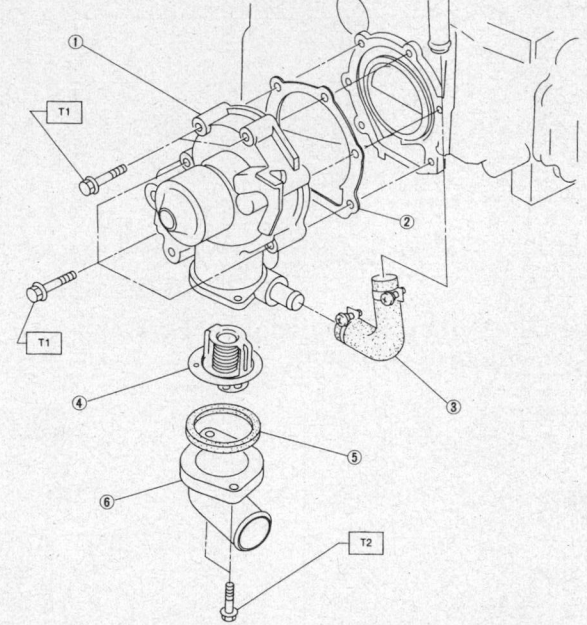

① Engine coolant pump ASSY
② Gasket
③ Heater hose
④ Thermostat
⑤ Gasket
⑥ Thermostat case

Tightening torque: N·m (kg-m, ft-lb)
T1: First 10 — 14 (1.0 — 1.4, 7 — 10)
    Second 10 — 14 (1.0 — 1.4, 7 — 10)
T2: 6 — 7 (0.6 — 0.7, 4.3 — 5.1)

SB1089500023000X

Fig. 56 Water pump replacement. 1.8L & 2.2L engines

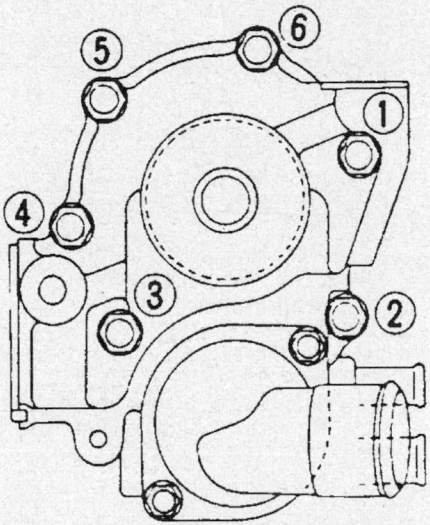

SB1089500024000X

Fig. 57 Water pump bolt tightening sequence. 1.8L, 2.2L & 2.5L engines

8. Lower vehicle and remove radiator main fan and sub fan assemblies.
9. Remove v-belts and timing belt.
10. Remove automatic timing belt tensioner and belt idler No. 2.
11. Remove camshaft position sensor.
12. Using camshaft sprocket wrench tool No. 499207300, or equivalent, remove left camshaft sprockets.
13. Remove tensioner bracket.
14. Remove left hand belt cover No. 2.
15. Remove water pump.
16. Reverse procedure to install, noting the following:
    a. Install new gasket.
    b. Install bolts and tighten in sequence, **Fig. 57,** in two steps to specification.

3.3L ENGINE

1. Drain cooling system.
2. Disconnect radiator outlet hose, then the radiator fan motor electrical connector.
3. Remove radiator bracket, then the radiator sub fan motor assembly.
4. Remove drive belts, then the timing belt.
5. Remove tensioner adjuster, then the cam angle sensor.
6. Remove left side camshaft pulley, then the left side rear timing belt cover.
7. Remove tensioner bracket, then disconnect radiator and heater hose from water pump.
8. Remove water pump.
9. Reverse procedure to install, tighten water pump bolts in sequence shown in **Fig. 58,** to specification.

RADIATOR
REPLACE

1. Remove battery from vehicle.
2. **On SVX models,** raise and support vehicle, then remove lower cover.
3. **On all models,** drain engine coolant.
4. Disconnect radiator outlet hoses, then

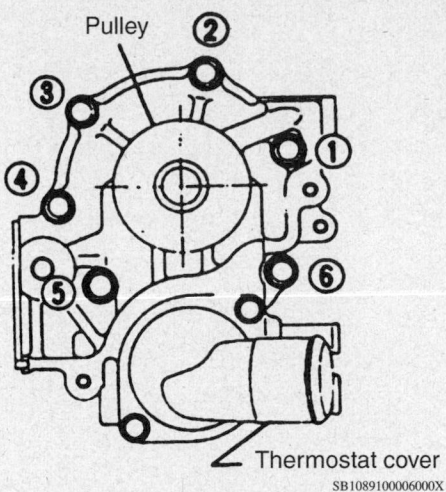

Fig. 58 Water pump replacement. 3.3L engine

ATF cooler hoses, **Figs. 59 through 62.**

5. **On SVX models,** lower vehicle.
6. **On all models,** remove drive belt cover, then disconnect inlet hoses.
7. **On SVX models,** remove reservoir tank and overflow hose.
8. **On all models,** disconnect electrical connections from radiator main fan and sub fan if equipped.
9. Remove radiator upper brackets.
10. **On Forester, Impreza and Legacy models,** place left upper radiator bracket between grille and body.
11. **On all models,** remove radiator assembly.
12. Reverse procedure to install. Refill and bleed cooling system as outlined under "Cooling System Bleed" in this section.

FUEL PUMP
REPLACE
FORESTER, IMPREZA & LEGACY

1. Relieve fuel system pressure as outlined under "Fuel System Pressure Relief" in this section.
2. Remove access hole lid, then disconnect fuel hoses.

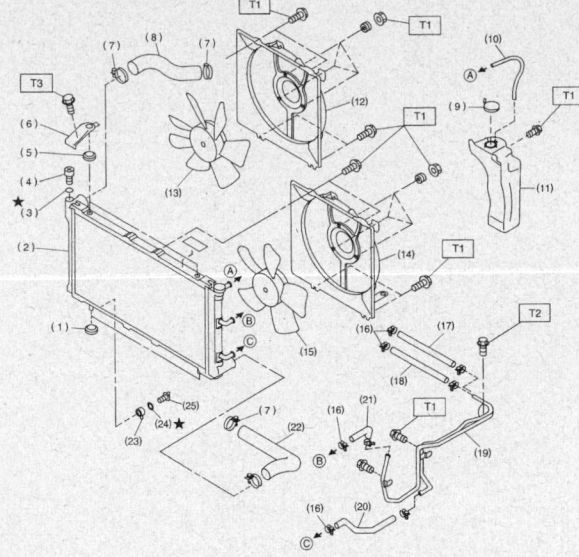

(1) Radiator lower cushion	(13) Radiator sub fan ASSY	(21) ATF inlet hose B (AT vehicles only)
(2) Radiator	(14) Main fan shroud	(22) Radiator outlet hose
(3) O-ring	(15) Radiator main fan ASSY	(23) Radiator drain pipe
(4) Air vent plug	(16) ATF hose clamp (AT vehicles only)	(24) Gasket
(5) Radiator upper cushion	(17) ATF inlet hose A (AT vehicles only)	(25) Radiator drain plug
(6) Radiator upper bracket	(18) ATF outlet hose A (AT vehicles only)	
(7) Clamp	(19) ATF pipe (AT vehicles only)	
(8) Radiator inlet hose	(20) ATF outlet hose B (AT vehicles only)	
(9) Engine coolant reservoir tank cap		
(10) Over flow hose		
(11) Engine coolant reservoir tank		
(12) Sub fan shroud		

Tightening torque: N·m (kg-m, ft-lb)
T1: 7.4±2.0 (0.75±0.20, 5.4±1.4)
T2: 12±3 (1.2±0.3, 8.7±2.2)
T3: 18±5 (1.8±0.5, 13.0±3.6)

SB1089800044000X

Fig. 59 Radiator replacement. Forester

3. Remove fuel pump mounting nuts, then the fuel pump.
4. Reverse procedure to install.

SVX

1. Relieve fuel system pressure as outlined under "Fuel System Pressure Relief" in this section.
2. Disconnect fuel hoses from top of fuel tank.
3. Remove fuel tank as follows:
   a. Raise and support vehicle, then remove rear exhaust pipe and muffler assembly.
   b. Separate rear axle shaft from differential, then remove propeller shaft and rear differential assembly.
   c. Remove rear sub frame, then separate fuel filler duct from pipe.
   d. Disconnect fuel hoses from pipes.
   e. Support fuel tank, then remove support bands.
   f. Remove fuel tank from vehicle.
4. Remove fuel pump in numbered sequence, **Fig. 63.**
5. Reverse procedure to install.

FUEL FILTER
REPLACE

1. Relieve fuel system pressure as outlined under "Fuel System Pressure Relief" in this section.
2. Disconnect hoses from fuel filter, **Fig. 64,** then remove filter from holder and vehicle.
3. Reverse procedure to install.

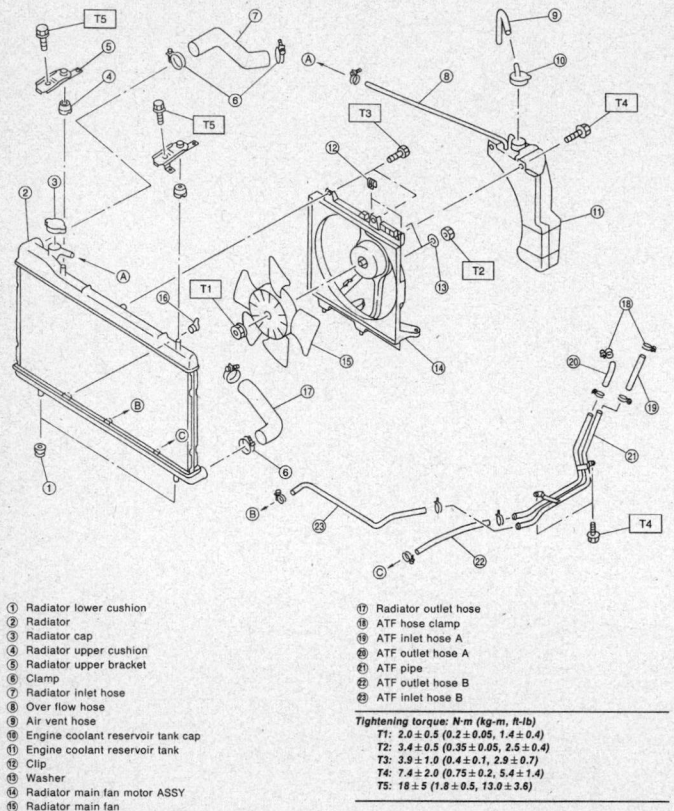

① Radiator lower cushion
② Radiator
③ Radiator cap
④ Radiator upper cushion
⑤ Radiator upper bracket
⑥ Clamp
⑦ Radiator inlet hose
⑧ Over flow hose
⑨ Air vent hose
⑩ Engine coolant reservoir tank cap
⑪ Engine coolant reservoir tank
⑫ Clip
⑬ Washer
⑭ Radiator main fan motor ASSY
⑮ Radiator main fan
⑯ Radiator drain plug

⑰ Radiator outlet hose
⑱ ATF hose clamp
⑲ ATF inlet hose A
⑳ ATF outlet hose A
㉑ ATF pipe
㉒ ATF outlet hose B
㉓ ATF inlet hose B

Tightening torque: N·m (kg-m, ft-lb)
T1: 2.0 ± 0.5 (0.2 ± 0.05, 1.4 ± 0.4)
T2: 3.4 ± 0.5 (0.35 ± 0.05, 2.5 ± 0.4)
T3: 3.9 ± 1.0 (0.4 ± 0.1, 2.9 ± 0.7)
T4: 7.4 ± 2.0 (0.75 ± 0.2, 5.4 ± 1.4)
T5: 18 ± 5 (1.8 ± 0.5, 13.0 ± 3.6)

SB1089500025000X

Fig. 60 Radiator replacement. Impreza

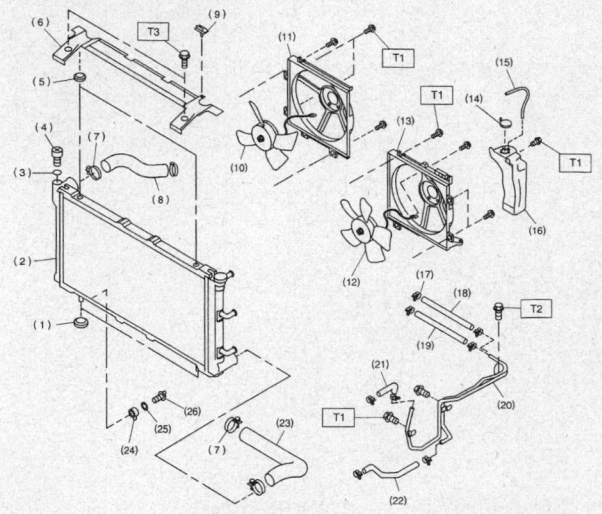

(1) Radiator lower cushion
(2) Radiator
(3) O-ring
(4) Air vent plug
(5) Radiator upper cushion
(6) Radiator upper bracket
(7) Clamp
(8) Radiator inlet hose
(9) Support
(10) Radiator sub fan ASSY
(11) Sub fan shroud
(12) Radiator main fan ASSY
(13) Main fan shroud

(14) Engine coolant reservoir tank cap
(15) Over flow hose
(16) Engine coolant reservoir tank
(17) ATF hose clamp (AT vehicles only)
(18) ATF inlet hose A (AT vehicles only)
(19) ATF outlet hose A (AT vehicles only)
(20) ATF pipe (AT vehicles only)
(21) ATF inlet hose B (AT vehicles only)

(22) ATF outlet hose B (AT vehicles only)
(23) Radiator outlet hose
(24) Radiator drain pipe
(25) Gasket
(26) Radiator drain plug

Tightening torque: N·m (kg-m, ft-lb)
T1: 7.4 ± 2.0 (0.75 ± 0.20, 5.4 ± 1.4)
T2: 12 ± 3 (1.2 ± 0.3, 8.7 ± 2.2)
T3: 18 ± 5 (1.8 ± 0.5, 13.0 ± 3.6)

SB1089500026000X

Fig. 61 Radiator replacement. Legacy

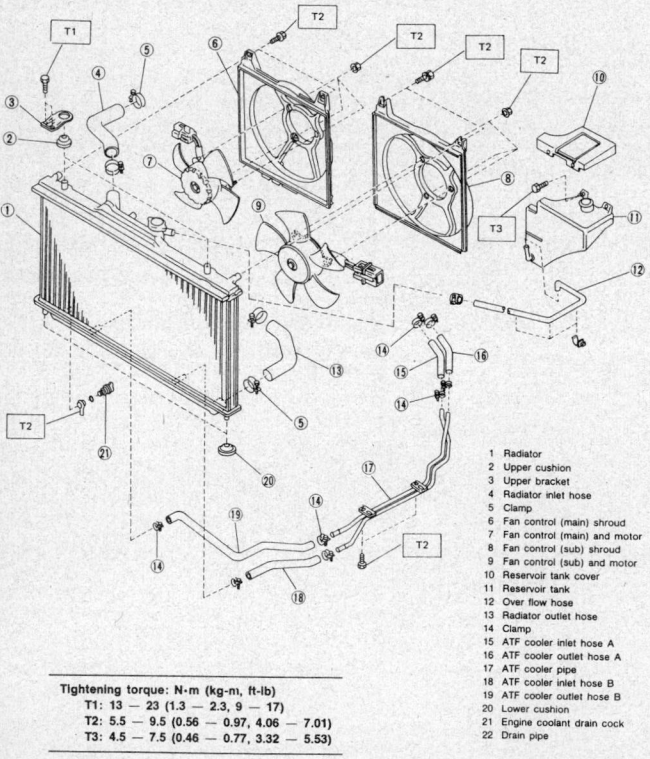

1 Radiator
2 Upper cushion
3 Upper bracket
4 Radiator inlet hose
5 Clamp
6 Fan control (main) shroud
7 Fan control (main) and motor
8 Fan control (sub) shroud
9 Fan control (sub) and motor
10 Reservoir tank cover
11 Reservoir tank
12 Over flow hose
13 Radiator outlet hose
14 Clamp
15 ATF cooler inlet hose A
16 ATF cooler outlet hose A
17 ATF cooler pipe
18 ATF cooler inlet hose B
19 ATF cooler outlet hose B
20 Lower cushion
21 Engine coolant drain cock
22 Drain pipe

Tightening torque: N·m (kg-m, ft-lb)
T1: 13 — 23 (1.3 — 2.3, 9 — 17)
T2: 5.5 — 9.5 (0.56 — 0.97, 4.06 — 7.01)
T3: 4.5 — 7.5 (0.46 — 0.77, 3.32 — 5.53)

SB1089500029000X

Fig. 62 Radiator replacement. SVX

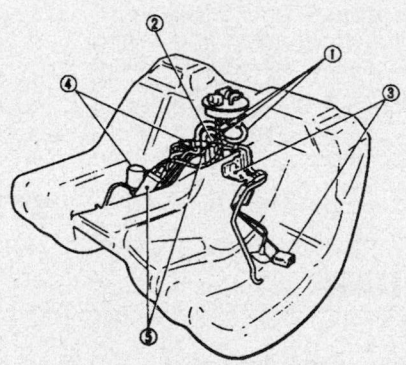

(1) Disconnect hoses and harness connector, and remove fuel tank cap.
(2) Remove bracket cover for installing each assembly bracket onto tank inner.
(3) Take out fuel meter unit LH.
(4) Take out fuel meter unit RH.
(5) Take out fuel pump ASSY.

SB1029100001000X

Fig. 63 Fuel pump replacement. SVX

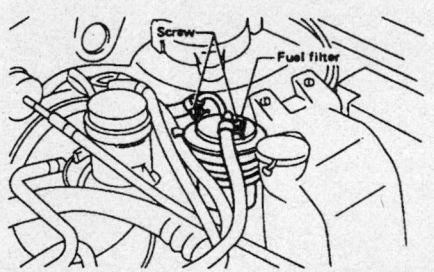

SB1029100004000X

Fig. 64 Fuel filter replacement

TIGHTENING SPECIFICATIONS

1.8L & 2.2L ENGINES

Year	Component	Torque/ Ft. Lbs.
1996–99	A/C Hoses	13–23
	Baffle Plate	43.2②
	Cam-Angle Sensor	43.2②
	Camshaft Sprockets	54–61
	Center Exhaust Pipe To Front Catalytic Converter	22–29
	Center Exhaust Pipe To Hanger Bracket	22–29
	Center Exhaust Pipe To Rear Exhaust Pipe	9–17
	Connecting Rod	32–34
	Crankcase Halves	①
	Crankshaft Pulley	66–79
	Cylinder Head	①
	Driveplate	51–55
	Engine Mount	40–61
	Engine To Transmission	34–40
	Flywheel	51–55
	Front Exhaust Pipe To Cylinder Head	18–25
	Front Exhaust Pipe To Front Catalytic Converter	19–26
	Lefthand Lower Camshaft Support	84②
	Lefthand Upper Camshaft Support	12
	Oil Pan	43②
	Oil Pump	56②
	Oil Separator Cover	56②
	Oil Strainer	84②
	Oil Strainer Stay	84②
	Pitching Stopper Rod To Body	35–49
	Pitching Stopper Rod To Engine Or Transmission	33–40
	Power Steering Pump	22–36
	Radiator	9–11
	Righthand Camshaft Support	12
	Rocker Arm Assembly	108②
	Rocker Cover	43②
	Rocker Shaft	43②
	Service Access Hole Cover	43②
	Service Access Hole Plugs	46–56
	Tensioner Bracket	17–20
	Timing Belt Covers	43②
	Timing Belt Idler	26–32
	Timing Belt Tensioner	26–32
	Timing Belt Tensioner Adjuster	17–20
	Torque Converter	17–20
	Water Pump	③

① — Refer to "Engine Service" for procedure & specifications.
② — Inch lbs.
③ — Refer to "Water Pump, Replace" for procedure & specifications.

2.5L ENGINE

Year	Component	Torque/Ft. Lbs.
1998-99	Baffle Plate	60③
	Camshaft Cap Bolts	13–16
	Camshaft Sprocket Bolts	54–62
	Connecting Rod Cap Nuts	32–34
	Coolant Reservoir Bolt	48–84③
	Crankshaft Pulley Bolt	123–137
	Cylinder Block Connecting Bolts (10 mm)	33–37
	Cylinder Block Connecting Bolts (6 & 8 mm)	②
	Drive Plate Bolts	51–55
	Flywheel Bolts	51–55
	Oil Pan Bolts	48③
	Oil Pump Bolts	60③
	Oil Separator Cover	60③
	Oil Strainer Bolts	84③
	Radiator Fan Shroud Bolts	48–84③
	Radiator Upper Bracket Bolt	9–17
	Rocker Cover Bolts	48③
	Service Hole Plug	46–56
	Service Hole Cover Screws	60③
	Tensioner Bracket Bolts	16–20
	Thermostat Case Bolts	48–60③
	Timing Belt Cover Bolts	36–48③
	Timing Belt Guide (MT)	84–96③
	Timing Belt Idler Pulley	16–20
	Timing Belt Tensioner	16–20
	Water Pipe Bolts	48–60③
	Water Pump Bolts	①

① — Tighten in two steps to 7–10 ft. lbs.
② — Refer to diagram in assembly procedure, bolts in position A-G, 16–20 ft. lbs.; bolts in position H, 5 ft. lbs.
③ — Inch lbs.

3.3L ENGINE

Year	Component	Torque/ Ft. Lbs.
1996–97	Baffle Plate	36–48②
	Camshaft Sprockets	80–94
	Connecting Rod Nut	32–34
	Crankshaft Pulley	108–123
	Cylinder Block	①
	Cylinder Head Bolt	①
	Cylinder Head Cover	48②
	Driveplate Reinforcement	51–55
	Exhaust Camshaft Cap	84–96②
	Front Camshaft Cap	96②
	Intake Camshaft Cap	84–96②
	Oil Filter	9–12
	Oil Level Gauge Guide	52–62②
	Oil Pan	40–48②
	Oil Pump	52–61②
	Oil Pump Cover	35–61②
	Oil Pump Relief Valve Plug	30–35
	Oil Separator Cover	52–61②
	Oil Strainer	84–96②
	Service Hole Cover	52–61②
	Service Hole Plug	46–56
	Thermostat Housing	52–61②
	Timing Belt Covers	48②
	Timing Belt Idler	26–32
	Timing Belt Tension Adjuster	17–20
	Timing Belt Tensioner	26–32
	Timing Belt Tensioner Bracket	17–20
	Water Pipe	7–10
	Water Pump	7–10

① — Refer to "Engine Service" for procedure & specifications.
② — Inch lbs.

NOTE: Refer To "Computer Relearn Procedures " Located In The Front Of This Manual For Computer Relearn Procedures.

INDEX

ADJUSTMENTS

HILL HOLDER

For Hill Holder adjustments, refer to the "Rear Axle & Suspension" section.

CLUTCH PEDAL

1. Remove clutch fork return spring.
2. Turn adjusting nut at fork end, **Fig. 1,** to obtain an endplay of .12–.16 inch. **When performing adjustment, use care not to twist clutch cable.**
3. Check to ensure clutch release lever full stroke measures .94–1.02 inches on Impreza or 1.004–1.063 inches on Legacy.

HYDRAULIC SYSTEM SERVICE

CLUTCH SYSTEM BLEED

Clutch pedal adjustment for hydraulic application type systems is completed by bleeding clutch system.
1. Install one end of vinyl tube into air bleeder of clutch damper. Place other end in suitable container.
2. Slowly depress and hold clutch pedal, then open bleeder for 1–2 seconds.
3. Close bleeder, then release clutch pedal. **Do not release clutch pedal with bleeder open.**
4. Repeat steps 2 and 3 until there are no air bubbles in vinyl tube. Tighten bleeder screw.
5. Repeat procedure using bleeder on operating cylinder.
6. Ensure no leaks are evident in system.

OPERATING CYLINDER, REPLACE

1. Disconnect and plug clutch pipe from operating cylinder.
2. Remove operating cylinder from transaxle.
3. Reverse procedure to install.

CLUTCH

REPLACE

1. Remove transaxle as outlined under "Transaxle, Replace."

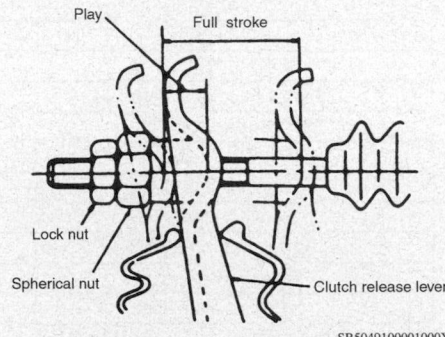

Fig. 1   Clutch pedal adjustments

SB5049100001000X

2. Remove six attaching bolts from pressure plate, then remove pressure plate and clutch disc.
3. When installing, apply light coat of grease to transaxle main driveshaft spline.
4. Install clutch disc guide into clutch disc. Then install on flywheel by inserting end of guide into needle bearing.
5. Remove clutch disc guide and reinstall transaxle.

TRANSAXLE

REPLACE

FORESTER

1. Raise and support hood.
2. Remove air intake duct and chamber.
3. Remove chamber stay.
4. Disconnect front and rear oxygen sensor connectors, transmission harness connector, transmission ground terminal, neutral position switch connector, back-up light connector and vehicle speed sensor connector.
5. Remove starter and pitching stopper.
6. **On models equipped with automatic transmission,** separate torque converter from drive plate, then remove ATF dipstick.
7. **On models equipped with manual transmission,** remove operating cylinder.
8. **On all models,** install engine support tool No. 927670000, or equivalent.
9. Remove upper right transmission to engine bolt.

10. Remove exhaust system.
11. Drain ATF into suitable container.
12. Disconnect ATF cooler hoses from pipes on transmission side, then remove ATF dipstick tube.
13. Remove propeller shaft.
14. **On models equipped with manual transmission,** remove gear shift rod and stay.
15. **On models equipped with automatic transmission,** remove shift selector cable from selector lever, then the bracket.
16. **On all models,** remove stabilizer bar clamp bolts.
17. Remove front drive shafts from transmission.
18. Remove lower transmission to engine mounting nuts.
19. Place suitable transmission jack under transmission.
20. Remove transmission rear crossmember, then the transmission.
21. Reverse procedure to install.

IMPREZA

1. Raise and support hood.
2. Remove manifold cover and air intake duct.
3. Disconnect oxygen sensor, transaxle harness and ground connectors.
4. Disconnect clutch release spring, clutch cable, hill holder and speedometer cable as equipped.
5. Remove starter, then the pitching stopper and bracket.
6. Remove transaxle oil level gauge, then the transaxle connector bracket.
7. Install engine support fixture tool No. 41099AA000, or equivalent, then remove right upper side of transaxle to engine bolts.
8. Remove exhaust system as follows:
   a. Raise and support vehicle.
   b. Remove front exhaust pipe, then center exhaust pipe.
   c. **On AWD models,** remove rear exhaust pipe.
9. **On AWD models,** remove propeller shaft as follows:
   a. Remove front cover of rear differential mount, then separate propeller shaft from rear differential.

b. Remove bolts holding center bearing onto body, then the propeller shaft.

10. **On all models,** remove gear shift rod and stay from transaxle.

11. Remove gear selector cable from selector lever and cable bracket.

12. Remove stabilizer clamp to crossmember bolts.

13. Remove front driveshaft from transaxle as follows:
   a. Remove and lower transverse link from housing.
   b. Remove spring pin and separate front driveshaft from each side of transaxle.

14. Remove lower side transaxle to engine nuts.

15. Place suitable transaxle jack stand under transaxle.

16. Remove transaxle rear crossmember.

17. Remove transaxle from vehicle. Move transaxle jack toward rear until mainshaft is withdrawn from clutch cover.

18. Reverse procedure to install, tighten all bolts/nuts to specifications.

LEGACY

1. Raise and support hood.

2. **On models less turbocharger,** remove manifold cover and air intake duct.

3. **On models equipped with turbocharger,** remove resonator chamber, then air inlet and outlet ducts, turbocharger cooling duct.

4. **On all models,** disconnect oxygen sensor, transaxle harness and ground connectors.

5. Disconnect neutral position switch, back-up lamp switch and vehicle speed sensor.

6. Disconnect clutch release spring, clutch cable, hill holder and speedometer cable as equipped.

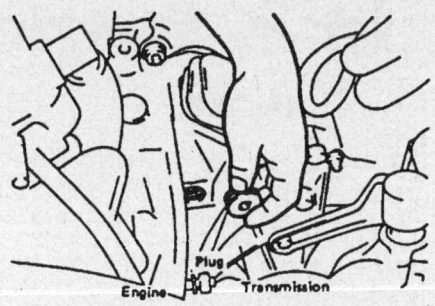

SB5038900003000X

Fig. 2 Plug removal. Legacy

7. Remove starter, then the pitching stopper and bracket.

8. **On models equipped with turbocharger,** remove clutch operating cylinder from transaxle case, then the plug, **Fig. 2.**

9. **On models equipped with turbocharger,** install a 6 mm bolt into bolt hole of release fork shaft, then drive out release fork shaft.

10. **On models equipped with turbocharger,** raise release fork to separate from release bearing tabs.

11. **On all models,** remove transaxle oil level gauge, then the transaxle connector bracket.

12. Install engine support fixture No. 41099AA000, or equivalent, then remove right upper side of transaxle to engine bolts.

13. Remove exhaust system as follows:
   a. **On models equipped with turbocharger,** separate center exhaust pipe from turbocharger.
   b. **On all models,** raise and support vehicle.
   c. **On models less turbocharger,** remove front exhaust pipe.

d. **On all models,** disconnect rear oxygen sensor, then remove center exhaust pipe.
   e. **On models equipped with turbocharger,** remove turbocharger lower cover, then center exhaust pipe.
   f. **On AWD models,** remove rear exhaust pipe.

14. **On AWD models,** remove propeller shaft as follows:
   a. Remove front cover of rear differential mount, then separate propeller shaft from rear differential.
   b. Remove bolts holding center bearing onto body, then the propeller shaft.

15. **On all models,** remove gear shift rod and stay from transaxle.

16. **On models equipped with turbocharger,** remove clutch damper from transaxle case.

17. **On all models,** remove stabilizer clamp to crossmember bolts.

18. Remove front driveshaft from transaxle as follows:
   a. Remove and lower transverse link from housing.
   b. Remove spring pin and separate front driveshaft from each side of transaxle.

19. Remove lower side transaxle to engine nuts.

20. Place suitable transaxle jack stand under transaxle.

21. Remove transaxle rear crossmember.

22. Remove transaxle from vehicle. Move transaxle jack toward rear until mainshaft is withdrawn from clutch cover.

23. Reverse procedure to install, noting the following:
   a. Ensure cutout portion of release fork shaft contacts spring pin.
   b. Tighten all bolts/nuts to specifications.

TIGHTENING SPECIFICATIONS

Year	Component	Torque/Ft. Lbs.
1996-99	Drive Plate	17–20
	Flywheel	51–56
	Operating Cylinder	25–30
	Pitching Stopper Rod To Transmission	33–40
	Pressure Plate	①
	Propeller Shaft	17–29
	Stabilizer Bar Clamps	17–20
	Starter Mounting Bolt	27–33
	Transmission To Engine	34–40

① — Refer to "Clutch, Replace" for procedure and specifications.

SUBARU

Rear Axle & Suspension

INDEX

HUB & BEARING

REPLACE

FORESTER, IMPREZA & LEGACY

1. Raise and support vehicle.
2. Remove rear wheel caps, then rear wheels. Loosen and retighten axle nut after removing wheels from vehicle.
3. **On FWD models,** using screwdriver, pry hub cap off.
4. **On all models,** unlock and remove axle nut, then return parking brake and loosen adjuster.
5. **On models equipped with disc brakes,** remove disc brake caliper and suspend caliper from strut, then remove disc rotor from hub. If rotor seizes on hub, drive off rotor by installing 8 mm bolt into hole in rotor.
6. **On models equipped with drum brakes,** proceed as follows:
   a. Remove brake drum from hub.
   b. If it is difficult to remove brake drum, then remove adjusting hole cover from back plate and turn adjusting screw until brake shoe separates from drum.
   c. If drum is difficult to remove, drive it out by installing 8 mm bolt into hole in brake drum.
7. **On all models,** disconnect parking brake cable end.
8. Remove lateral link assembly to rear housing attaching bolts. Discard self-locking nut.
9. Remove trailing link assembly to rear housing attaching bolts. Discard self-locking nut.
10. **On AWD models,** remove rear drive-shafts by disengaging bell joint from housing splines, then remove rear driveshaft assembly.
11. **On all models,** remove lower strut to rear housing mounting bolts, then separate strut from housing.
12. **On models equipped with anti-lock brakes,** remove rear ABS sensor from back plate.
13. **On all models,** remove rear housing (hub) from vehicle.
14. Reverse procedure to install.

SVX

1. Move select lever to Park position, then set parking brake.
2. Raise and support vehicle, then remove rear wheels. Loosen and retighten axle nut after removing wheels from vehicle.
3. Remove hub cap, then unlock and remove axle nut.
4. Return parking brake lever, then remove console box lid.
5. Loosen parking brake adjuster nut, then remove stabilizer link.
6. Remove ABS sensor and clamp, then disconnect parking brake cable clamp.
7. Disconnect brake hose from strut, then loosen caliper mounting bolts.
8. Disconnect trailing link and lateral link from housing.
9. Remove lower strut to housing mounting bolts, then the caliper assembly. Suspend caliper from strut.
10. Remove disc rotor from hub. If rotor seizes on hub, drive off rotor using 8 mm bolt into hole in rotor.
11. Remove parking brake lining, then disconnect cable from lining.
12. Remove parking brake cable clamp, then the cable from backing plate.
13. Separate strut from housing, then remove driveshaft from housing.
14. Remove rear housing (hub) mounting bolts, then the housing.
15. Reverse procedure to install.

REAR SUSPENSION

REPLACE

FORESTER & IMPREZA

Refer to **Figs. 1 and 2** when performing the following procedures.

TRAILING LINK

1. Raise and support vehicle.
2. Remove rear wheels.
3. Remove parking brake cable clamp and ABS sensor harness clamp from trailing link, if equipped.
4. Remove retaining bolts and the trailing link.
5. Reverse procedure to install. Refer to **Figs. 1 and 2** for tightening specifications.

LATERAL LINK

FWD Models

1. Raise and support vehicle, then remove rear exhaust pipe and muffler assembly.
2. Remove stabilizer from rear lateral link, then scribe alignment mark on adjusting bolt, adjusting wheel and crossmember.
3. Remove lateral links to housing mounting bolts.
4. Turn cap (lateral link) counterclockwise until it contacts stopper, then remove cap.
5. While holding adjusting bolt head with wrench, loosen self-locking nut.
6. On left lateral link, remove adjusting bolt, then front and rear lateral links.
7. On right lateral link, remove bolt securing crossmember to body, then adjusting bolt, front and rear lateral links.
8. Reverse procedure to install. Refer to **Fig. 1,** for tightening specifications.

AWD Models

1. Raise and support vehicle, then remove rear wheels.
2. Remove stabilizers, then ABS sensor harness from trailing link.
3. Loosen trailing link to housing retaining bolt, then remove double offset joint from differential.
4. Scribe alignment mark on adjusting bolt and crossmember.
5. Remove outer lateral link bolt on housing side.
6. Remove lateral links to crossmember mounting bolts, then remove lateral links.
7. Reverse procedure to install. Refer to **Fig. 2,** for tightening specifications.

CROSSMEMBER

FWD Models

1. Disconnect lateral links from housing.
2. Remove rear exhaust pipe and muffler assembly.
3. Remove heat shield cover.
4. Remove crossmember mounting bolts then the crossmember.
5. Reverse procedure to install. Refer to **Fig. 1,** for tightening specifications.

AWD Models

1. Raise and support vehicle, then remove rear wheels.
2. Remove rear exhaust pipe and muffler assembly.
3. Remove rear differential, then place transaxle jack under crossmember.
4. Remove crossmember mounting bolts, then the crossmember.
5. Scribe alignment mark on lateral link cam bolt and crossmember, then remove lateral links.
6. Reverse procedure to install. Refer to **Fig. 2,** for tightening specifications.

LEGACY

Refer to **Figs. 3 and 4** when performing the following procedures.

TRAILING LINK

1. Raise and support vehicle.
2. Remove rear wheels.
3. Remove parking brake cable clamp and ABS sensor harness clamp from trailing link, if equipped.
4. Remove retaining bolts and the trailing link.
5. Reverse procedure to install. Refer to **Figs. 3 and 4** for tightening specifications.

LATERAL LINK

FWD Models

1. Raise and support vehicle, then remove rear wheels.
2. Separate stabilizer link from lateral link.
3. Scribe an aligning mark on adjusting bolt, adjusting wheel and crossmember.
4. Remove bolts securing lateral links to housing.
5. Turn lateral link cap counterclockwise until it contacts stopper, then remove.
6. Loosen self locking nut while holding adjusting bolt with a suitable wrench. **Self locking nut must be loosened before turning adjusting nut.**
7. Remove left lateral links as follows:
   a. Remove adjusting bolt, then front and rear lateral links.
8. Remove right lateral links as follows:
   a. Support crossmember with suitable jackstand, then remove crossmember to vehicle body mounting bolts.
   b. Lower jackstand until adjusting bolt can be removed, then remove adjusting bolt, front and rear lateral links.
9. Reverse procedure to install.

AWD Models

1. Raise and support vehicle, remove rear wheels.
2. Separate stabilizer link from lateral link.
3. Remove parking brake cable clamp and ABS sensor harness clamp from trailing link, if equipped.
4. Loosen trailing link to body retaining bolt.
5. Remove trailing link to housing retaining bolt.
6. Remove axle shaft as outlined in the "Drive Axles" section.
7. Scribe an aligning mark on adjusting bolt, adjusting wheel and crossmember.
8. Loosen front lateral link retaining bolts.
9. Remove rear then front lateral links. **Self locking nut must be loosened before turning adjusting nut.**
10. Reverse procedure to install noting the following:
    a. Install Double Offset Joint (DOJ) with new spring pins.
    b. Refer to **Figs. 3 and 4** for tightening specifications.

CROSSMEMBER

FWD Models

1. Raise and support vehicle.
2. Remove rear wheels.
3. Disconnect lateral links from housing.
4. Remove exhaust pipe and muffler.
5. Remove four crossmember to body mounting bolts, then crossmember.
6. Reverse procedure to install, noting the following:
   a. Self-locking nut must be replaced.
   b. When tightening adjusting bolt, always tighten the nut and not the bolt.
   c. Tighten rubber bushings with vehicle on ground and at curb weight.
   d. Refer to **Figs. 3 and 4** for tightening specifications.

AWD Models

1. Raise and support vehicle.
2. Remove rear wheels.
3. Separate front exhaust pipe and rear exhaust pipe.
4. Remove exhaust pipe and muffler.
5. **On sedan models,** remove cross-member reinforcement lower.
6. **On all models,** remove rear differential.
7. Place a suitable transaxle jack under rear crossmember, then remove crossmember to body mounting bolts and crossmember.
8. Scribe an alignment mark on rear lateral link cam bolt and crossmember, then remove front and rear lateral links.
9. Reverse procedure to install, noting the following:
   a. Tighten rubber bushings with vehicle on ground and at curb weight.
   b. Adjust rear wheel alignment if necessary.
   c. Refer to **Figs. 3 and 4** for tightening specifications.

SVX

Refer to **Fig. 5** when performing the following procedures.

TRAILING LINK

1. Raise and support vehicle, then remove rear wheels.
2. Disconnect ABS sensor clamp, then

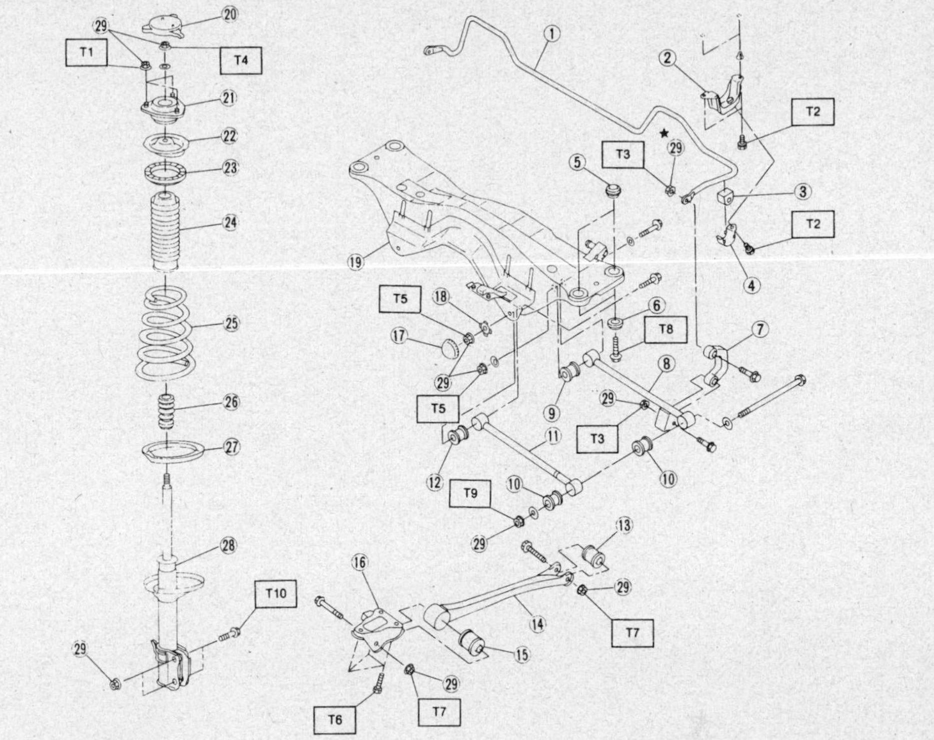

① Stabilizer
② Stabilizer bracket
③ Stabilizer bushing
④ Clamp
⑤ Floating bushing
⑥ Stopper
⑦ Stabilizer link
⑧ Rear lateral link
⑨ Bushing (C)
⑩ Bushing (A)
⑪ Front lateral link
⑫ Bushing (B)
⑬ Trailing link rear bushing
⑭ Trailing link
⑮ Trailing link front bushing
⑯ Trailing link bracket
⑰ Cap
⑱ Washer
⑲ Crossmember
⑳ Cap
㉑ Strut mount
㉒ Spring seat
㉓ Rubber seat upper
㉔ Dust cover
㉕ Coil spring
㉖ Helper
㉗ Rubber seat lower
㉘ Damper strut
㉙ Self-locking nut

Tightening torque: N·m (kg-m, ft-lb)
T1: 20 ± 6 (2.0 ± 0.6, 14.5 ± 4.3)
T2: 25 ± 7 (2.5 ± 0.7, 18.1 ± 5.1)
T3: 44 ± 6 (4.5 ± 0.6, 32.5 ± 4.3)
T4: 59 ± 10 (6.0 ± 1.0, 43 ± 7)
T5: 98 ± 15 (10.0 ± 1.5, 72 ± 11)
T6: 98 ± 20 (10.0 ± 2.0, 72 ± 14)
T7: 113 ± 15 (11.5 ± 1.5, 83 ± 11)
T8: 127 ± 20 (13.0 ± 2.0, 94 ± 14)
T9: 137 ± 20 (14.0 ± 2.0, 101 ± 14)
T10: 196^{+39}_{-10} $(20.0^{+4.0}_{-1.0},\ 145^{+29}_{-7})$

SB2039100013000X

Fig. 1 Exploded view of rear suspension assembly. FWD Impreza

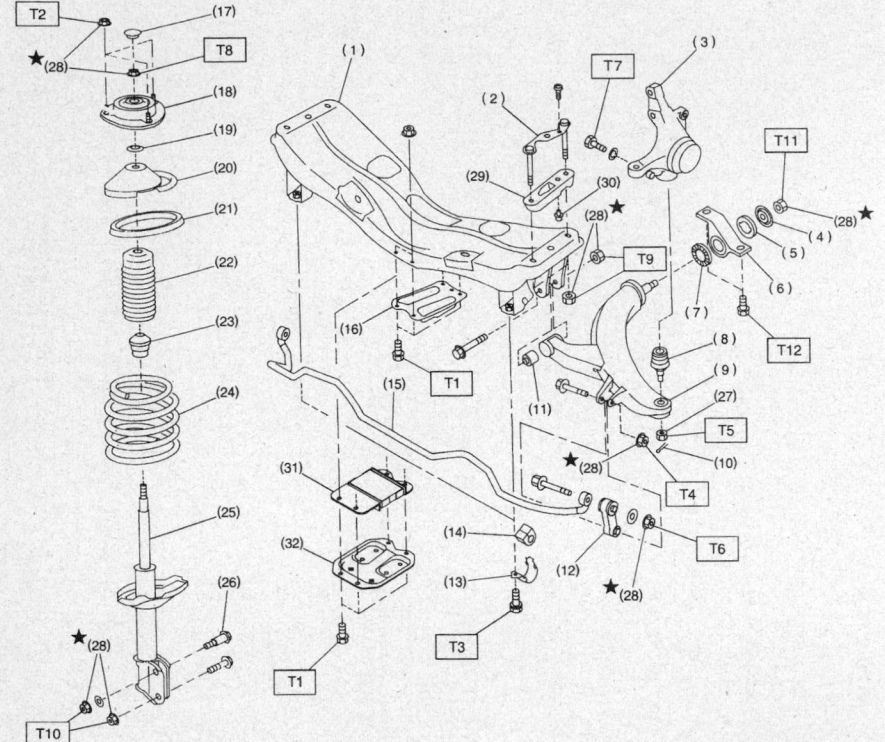

(1)	Front crossmember	(17)	Dust seal
(2)	Bolt ASSY	(18)	Strut mount
(3)	Housing	(19)	Spacer
(4)	Washer	(20)	Upper spring seat
(5)	Stopper rubber (Rear)	(21)	Rubber seat
(6)	Rear bushing	(22)	Dust cover
(7)	Stopper rubber (Front)	(23)	Helper
(8)	Ball joint	(24)	Coil spring
(9)	Transverse link	(25)	Damper strut
(10)	Cotter pin	(26)	Adjusting bolt
(11)	Front bushing	(27)	Castle nut
(12)	Stabilizer link	(28)	Self-locking nut
(13)	Clamp	(29)	Adapter front crossmember
(14)	Bushing	(30)	Clip
(15)	Stabilizer	(31)	Dynamic damper (MT model)
(16)	Jack-up plate (Except MT model)	(32)	Jack-up plate (MT model)

Tightening torque: N·m (kg-m, ft-lb)

T1: 18±5 (1.8±0.5, 13.0±3.6)
T2: 20±6 (2.0±0.6, 14.5±4.3)
T3: 25±4 (2.5±0.4, 18.1±2.9)
T4: 29±5 (3.0±0.5, 21.7±3.6)
T5: 39 (4, 29)
T6: 44±6 (4.5±0.6, 32.5±4.3)
T7: 49±10 (5.0±1.0, 36±7)
T8: 54±5 (5.5±0.5, 39.8±3.6)
T9: 98±15 (10.0±1.5, 72±11)
T10: 152±20 (15.5±2.0, 112±14)
T11: 186±10 (19.0±1.0, 137±7)
T12: 245±49 (25.0±5.0, 181±36)

SB2039100014000X

Fig. 2 Exploded view of rear suspension assembly. Forester & AWD Impreza

parking brake cable bracket.
3. Remove trailing link mounting screws, then the trailing link.
4. Reverse procedure to install, noting the following:
   a. When torquing trailing arm, ensure vehicle weight is on the suspension.
   b. Refer to **Fig. 5** for tightening specifications.

LATERAL LINK
1. Raise and support vehicle, then remove rear wheels.
2. Remove rear exhaust pipe, then the stabilizer link.
3. Remove parking brake cable, then the ABS sensor harness bracket.
4. Disconnect parking brake cable clamp.
5. Disconnect trailing link and lateral link from housing (hub).
6. Using driveshaft remover No. 28099PA100, or equivalent, separate

DOJ from differential. Use bolt on side bearing retainer as a support for tool.
7. Place mark on alignment adjustment bolt, then remove lateral link from sub frame.
8. Reverse procedure to install, noting the following:
   a. When torquing lateral link, ensure vehicle weight is on the suspension.
   b. Align alignment mark when installing adjustment bolt.
   c. Refer to **Fig. 5** for tightening specifications.

SUB FRAME
1. Raise and support vehicle, then remove rear wheels.
2. Position shift lever in Neutral position, then release parking brakes.
3. Remove rear exhaust pipe and muffler.
4. Remove propeller shaft as follows:
   a. Remove front exhaust cover, then propeller shaft to rear differential

mounting bolts.
   b. Remove bolts holding center bearing to body, then remove propeller shaft.
5. Remove rear differential as follows:
   a. Using driveshaft remover No. 28099PA100, or equivalent, separate DOJ from differential. Use bolt on side bearing retainer as a support for tool.
   b. Remove bracket to rear differential member mounting bolts, then support differential with suitable jack.
   c. Remove mounting bolts for bracket/rear differential to rear differential member.
   d. Remove self locking nuts which connect rear differential to rear sub frame.
   e. Slowly lower jack, move rear differential forward and remove bolts from rear sub frame.
   f. Remove rear differential assembly from body.
6. Remove fuel tank cover, then the differential member.
7. Remove stabilizers and brackets, then the trailing links.
8. Remove ABS sensor connector from backing plate and sub frame.
9. Place suitable jack under sub frame, then remove sub frame brackets. More than one person is needed to remove sub frame brackets.
10. Place alignment marks on adjustment bolt and sub frame.
11. Remove sub frame, then remove lateral links from frame.
12. Reverse procedure to install, noting the following:
   a. When torquing lateral link, ensure vehicle weight is on the suspension.
   b. Align alignment mark on sub frame and adjustment bolt.
   c. Refer to **Fig. 6** for tightening specifications.

STRUT
REPLACE
FORESTER & IMPREZA

Refer to **Figs. 1 and 2,** when performing the following procedure.
1. Depress brake pedal and secure it in that position using wooden block.
2. **On sedan models,** remove rear seat cushion and back rest.
3. **On wagon models,** remove rear speaker grille and service hole cap.
4. **On all models,** remove strut mount cap, then raise and support vehicle.
5. Remove rear wheels and brake hose clip.
6. **On models equipped with rear disc brakes,** remove union bolt from caliper.
7. **On models equipped with rear drum brakes,** disconnect brake hose from brake pipe on strut and brake pipe from drum brake.
8. **On all models,** remove lower and upper strut mounting bolts, then remove strut from vehicle.
9. Mount strut assembly in a suitable

spring compressor, then compress spring until tension is relieved from spring seats.

10. Remove strut rod self-locking nut using strut mount socket tool No. 9277600000, or equivalent, and a suitable wrench.

11. Remove upper strut mount, upper spring seat and upper rubber seat.

12. Slowly release spring tension, then remove coil spring, dust cover and helper spring.

13. Reverse procedure to install, noting the following:
   a. Mount coil spring with flat end towards top side and inclined end towards bottom side.
   b. Ensure upper spring seat is positioned with "Out " mark facing outward.
   c. Install strut rod with new locking nut.
   d. Refer to **Figs. 1 and 2** for tightening specifications.

LEGACY

Refer to **Figs. 3 and 4** when performing the following procedure.
1. **On sedan models,** remove rear seat cushion and back rest.
2. **On wagon models,** remove strut cap of rear quarter trim.
3. **On all models,** raise and support vehicle.
4. Remove rear wheels.
5. Disconnect brake hose from brake caliper.
6. **On models equipped with disc brakes,** remove union bolt from brake calliper.
7. **On models equipped with drum brakes,** disconnect brake hose from brake pipe strut, then disconnect brake hose from drum brake.
8. **On all models,** remove lower and upper strut mount retaining bolts, then the strut assembly.
9. Mount strut assembly in a suitable spring compressor. Ensure projections on compressor are seated on inner diameter of spring.
10. Compress spring until tension is relieved from spring seats.
11. Remove strut rod self-locking nut using a suitable socket wrench and strut mount socket tool No. 927760000, or equivalent.
12. Remove upper strut mount, upper spring seat and rubber seat from strut.
13. Slowly release spring tension, then remove coil spring, dust cover and helper from strut body.
14. Reverse procedure to install, noting the following:
   a. Mount coil spring with flat face toward lower spring seat.
   b. Use caution not to scratch piston rod.
   c. Install strut rod with new locking nut.
   d. Refer to **Figs. 3 and 4** for tightening specifications.
   e. Bleed brake hydraulic system.

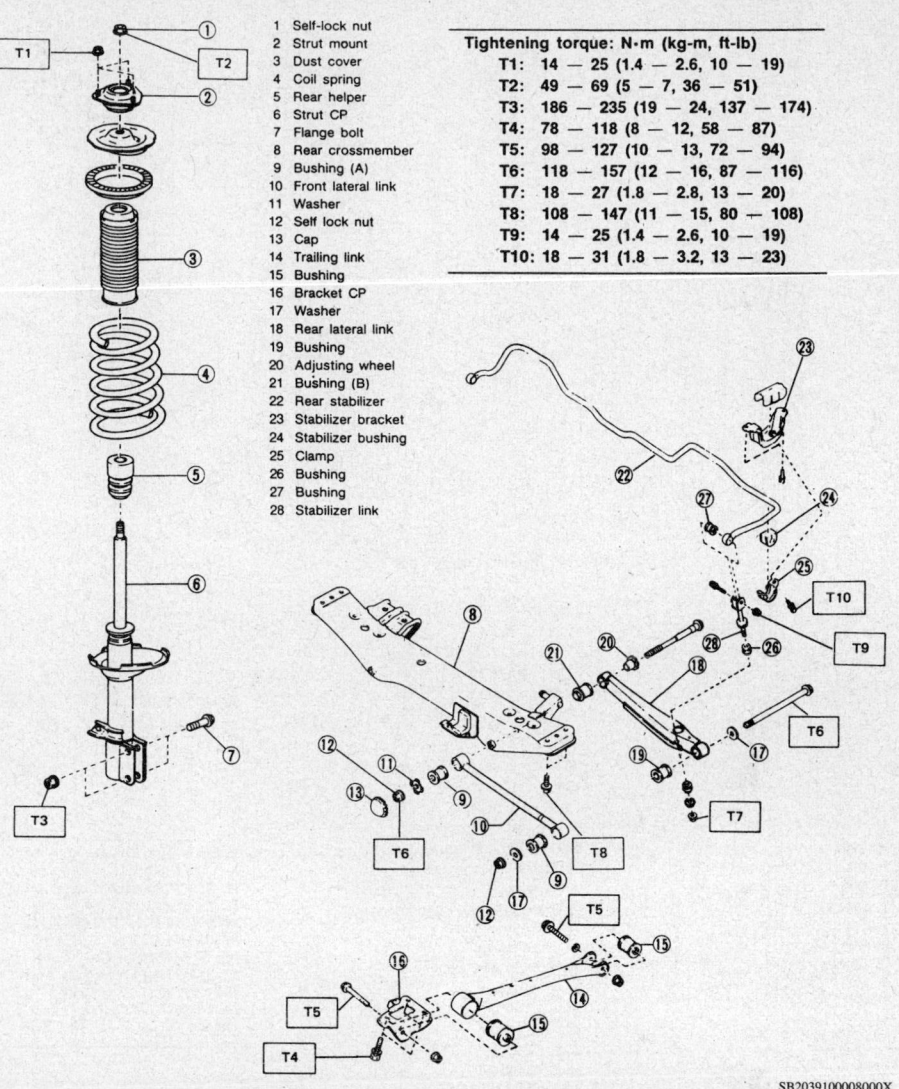

#	
1	Self-lock nut
2	Strut mount
3	Dust cover
4	Coil spring
5	Rear helper
6	Strut CP
7	Flange bolt
8	Rear crossmember
9	Bushing (A)
10	Front lateral link
11	Washer
12	Self lock nut
13	Cap
14	Trailing link
15	Bushing
16	Bracket CP
17	Washer
18	Rear lateral link
19	Bushing
20	Adjusting wheel
21	Bushing (B)
22	Rear stabilizer
23	Stabilizer bracket
24	Stabilizer bushing
25	Clamp
26	Bushing
27	Bushing
28	Stabilizer link

Tightening torque: N·m (kg-m, ft-lb)	
T1:	14 — 25 (1.4 — 2.6, 10 — 19)
T2:	49 — 69 (5 — 7, 36 — 51)
T3:	186 — 235 (19 — 24, 137 — 174)
T4:	78 — 118 (8 — 12, 58 — 87)
T5:	98 — 127 (10 — 13, 72 — 94)
T6:	118 — 157 (12 — 16, 87 — 116)
T7:	18 — 27 (1.8 — 2.8, 13 — 20)
T8:	108 — 147 (11 — 15, 80 — 108)
T9:	14 — 25 (1.4 — 2.6, 10 — 19)
T10:	18 — 31 (1.8 — 3.2, 13 — 23)

SB2039100008000X

Fig. 3 Exploded view of rear suspension assembly. FWD Legacy

SVX

Refer to **Fig. 5,** when performing the following procedure.
1. Raise and support vehicle, then remove rear wheels.
2. Remove rear quarter trim.
3. Separate brake hose from strut, then remove one lower strut mounting bolt.
4. Using suitable jack, support housing (hub), then remove upper strut mounting bolts.
5. Remove remaining lower mounting bolt, then the strut assembly from vehicle.
6. Mount strut assembly in a suitable spring compressor, then compress spring until tension is relieved from spring seats.
7. Remove strut rod self-locking nut using strut mount socket tool No. 20099PA000, or equivalent, and a suitable wrench.
8. Remove upper strut mount, upper spring seat and upper rubber seat.
9. Slowly release spring tension, then remove coil spring, dust cover, helper spring and lower rubber seat from strut body.
10. Reverse procedure to install, noting the following:
   a. Mount coil spring with flat face toward lower spring seat.
   b. Ensure helper and dust cover are aligned, **Fig. 7.**
   c. Ensure upper spring seat is positioned with "Out " mark facing outward.
   d. Install strut rod with new locking nut.
   e. Refer to **Fig. 5** for tightening specifications.

HILL HOLDER

The Hill holder is essentially a Pressure Hold Valve (PHV), **Fig. 8,** built into one brake circuit, that maintains hydraulic pressure in the brake circuit when the vehicle is facing uphill and the clutch pedal is depressed, **Fig. 9.**

The PHV lever, **Fig. 8,** is connected through a linkage to the clutch pedal and controlled by a camshaft which provides

SUBARU

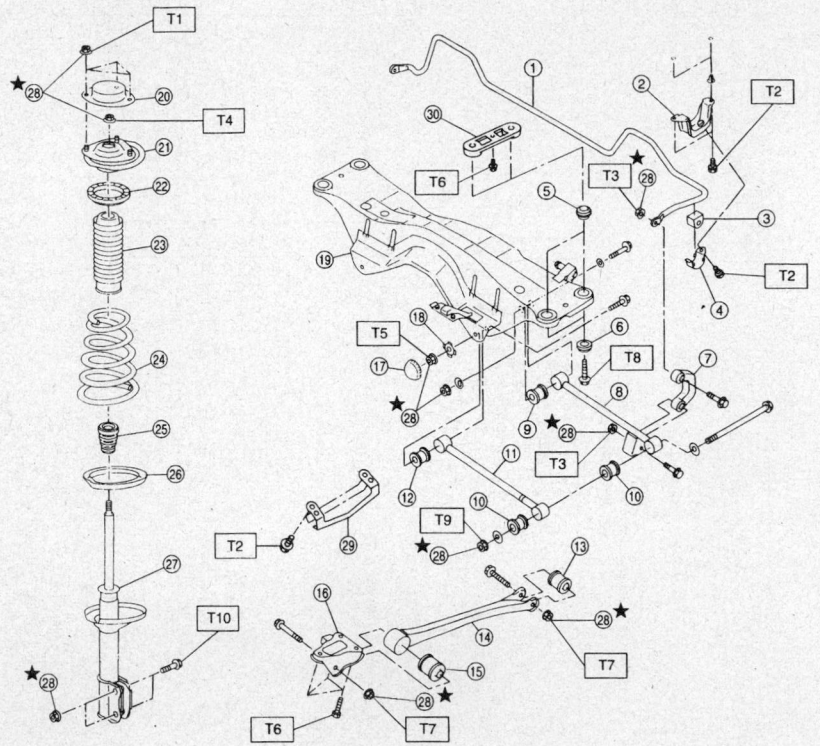

① Stabilizer
② Stabilizer bracket
③ Stabilizer bushing
④ Clamp
⑤ Floating bushing
⑥ Stopper
⑦ Stabilizer link
⑧ Rear lateral link
⑨ Bushing (C)
⑩ Bushing (A)
⑪ Front lateral link
⑫ Bushing (B)
⑬ Trailing link rear bushing
⑭ Trailing link
⑮ Trailing link front bushing

⑯ Trailing link bracket
⑰ Cap (Protection)
⑱ Washer
⑲ Rear crossmember
⑳ Strut mount cap
㉑ Strut mount
㉒ Rubber seat upper
㉓ Dust cover
㉔ Coil spring
㉕ Helper
㉖ Rubber seat lower
㉗ Damper strut
㉘ Self-locking nut
㉙ Crossmember reinforcement lower (Sedan model)
㉚ Adapter rear crossmember (OUTBACK model)

Tightening torque: N·m (kg-m, ft-lb)
T1: 20 ± 6 (2.0 ± 0.6, 14.5 ± 4.3)
T2: 25 ± 7 (2.5 ± 0.7, 18.1 ± 5.1)
T3: 44 ± 6 (4.5 ± 0.6, 32.5 ± 4.3)
T4: 59 ± 10 (6.0 ± 1.0, 43 ± 7)
T5: 98 ± 15 (10.0 ± 1.5, 72 ± 11)
T6: 98 ± 20 (10.0 ± 2.0, 72 ± 14)
T7: 113 ± 15 (11.5 ± 1.5, 83 ± 11)
T8: 127 ± 20 (13.0 ± 2.0, 94 ± 14)
T9: 137 ± 20 (14.0 ± 2.0, 101 ± 14)
T10: $196 ^{+39}_{-10}$ ($20.0 ^{+4.0}_{-1.0}$, $145 ^{+29}_{-7}$)

SB2039100009000X

Fig. 4 Exploded view of rear suspension assembly. AWD Legacy

the motion to the PHV driveshaft. The PHV driveshaft controls the clearance between the PHV inertia controlled ball and seal.

When the clutch pedal is depressed, the PHV driveshaft is pulled into the seal, allowing the ball free movement. If the vehicle is facing uphill, inertia will cause the ball to roll onto the seal, **Fig. 10**, thereby holding hydraulic pressure. When the clutch is released, **Fig. 11**, the driveshaft is forced into the ball chamber, unsealing the ball and releasing hydraulic pressure.

REMOVAL

1. Drain primary side of master cylinder.
2. Remove cable adjusting nut and clamp from clutch release bearing fork, then disconnect cable from engine bracket.
3. Remove cable from PHV.
4. Separate connector bracket from PHV, then remove brake lines using a suitable flare wrench.
5. Remove PHV bracket to frame retaining bolts and the PHV. **Do not allow**

any dirt to enter PHV.

INSPECTION

1. Inspect PHV cable boots and outer casing for damage, replace as necessary.
2. Inspect PHV cable inner core for corrosion and wear, replace as necessary.
3. Inspect PHV return spring for damage or corrosion.
4. Tilt PHV assembly and listen for ball rolling to ensure free operation.
5. Operate lever to ensure smooth operation. **Do not attempt to disassemble PHV. If unit is defective, it should be replaced.**

INSTALLATION

To install, reverse removal procedure, noting the following:
1. Apply lubricant to hooked portion of return spring, cable end of lever and cable end at clutch release bearing fork.
2. Bleed brakes after installation.

ADJUSTMENT

After replacing PHV cable or clutch cable, operate clutch pedal approximately 30 times to seat new parts prior to making any adjustments.
1. Ensure clutch is adjusted properly. Refer to "Clutch & Manual Transmission" section.
2. Road test vehicle to determine Hill holder performance on an uphill road of 3° inclination or more. If Hill holder is released late (engine tends to stall), loosen adjustment nut gradually, until smooth starting is obtained. If Hill holder releases early (vehicle rolls down incline), tighten adjustment nut until Hill holder releases late (engine tends to stall), then loosen adjustment nut gradually, until smooth starting is obtained.
3. Tighten to specifications.

STABILIZER BAR
REPLACE

1. Remove left and right stabilizer link to mount attaching nuts with washers and bushings.
2. Remove left and right stabilizer link to stabilizer attaching bolts, then separate links from stabilizer.
3. Remove left and right clamp to stabilizer attaching bolts, separate clamps from stabilizer, then remove stabilizer from vehicle.
4. Reverse procedure to install. Tighten to specifications.

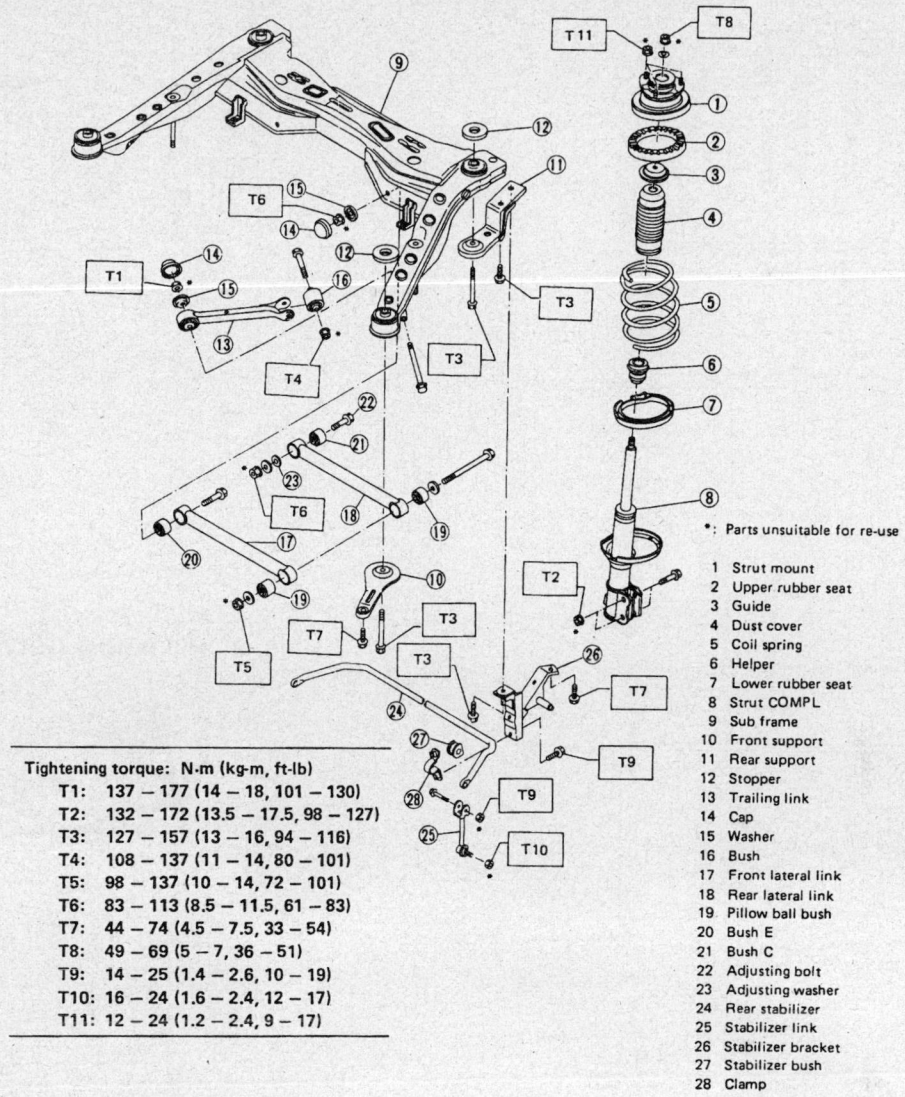

```
*: Parts unsuitable for re-use

 1  Strut mount
 2  Upper rubber seat
 3  Guide
 4  Dust cover
 5  Coil spring
 6  Helper
 7  Lower rubber seat
 8  Strut COMPL
 9  Sub frame
10  Front support
11  Rear support
12  Stopper
13  Trailing link
14  Cap
15  Washer
16  Bush
17  Front lateral link
18  Rear lateral link
19  Pillow ball bush
20  Bush E
21  Bush C
22  Adjusting bolt
23  Adjusting washer
24  Rear stabilizer
25  Stabilizer link
26  Stabilizer bracket
27  Stabilizer bush
28  Clamp
```

Tightening torque: N·m (kg-m, ft-lb)
T1: 137 — 177 (14 — 18, 101 — 130)
T2: 132 — 172 (13.5 — 17.5, 98 — 127)
T3: 127 — 157 (13 — 16, 94 — 116)
T4: 108 — 137 (11 — 14, 80 — 101)
T5: 98 — 137 (10 — 14, 72 — 101)
T6: 83 — 113 (8.5 — 11.5, 61 — 83)
T7: 44 — 74 (4.5 — 7.5, 33 — 54)
T8: 49 — 69 (5 — 7, 36 — 51)
T9: 14 — 25 (1.4 — 2.6, 10 — 19)
T10: 16 — 24 (1.6 — 2.4, 12 — 17)
T11: 12 — 24 (1.2 — 2.4, 9 — 17)

SB2039100010000X

Fig. 5 Exploded view of rear suspension. SVX

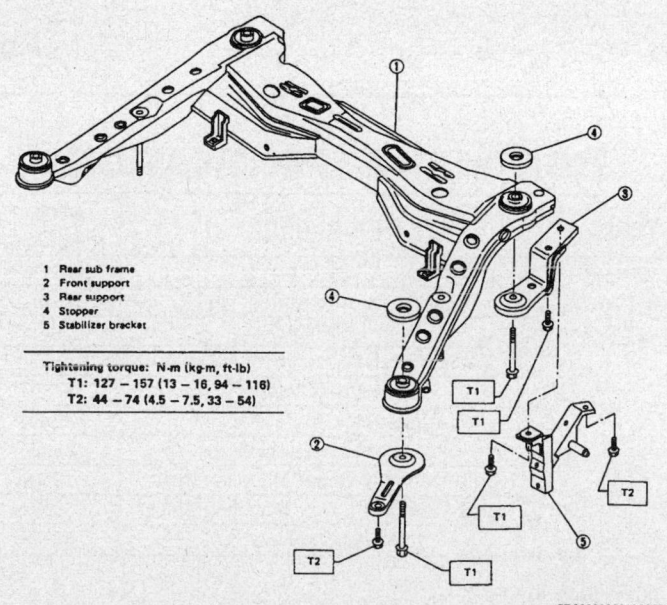

```
1  Rear sub frame
2  Front support
3  Rear support
4  Stopper
5  Stabilizer bracket
```

Tightening torque: N·m (kg-m, ft-lb)
T1: 127 — 157 (13 — 16, 94 — 116)
T2: 44 — 74 (4.5 — 7.5, 33 — 54)

SB2039100012000X

Fig. 6 Exploded view of sub frame. SVX

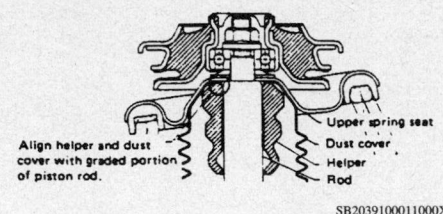

Fig. 7 Helper & dust cover alignment. SVX

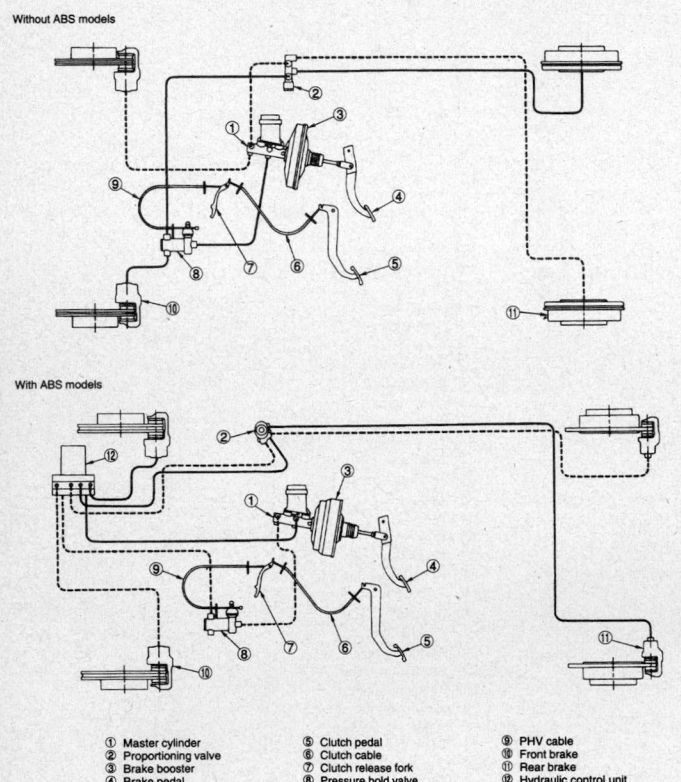

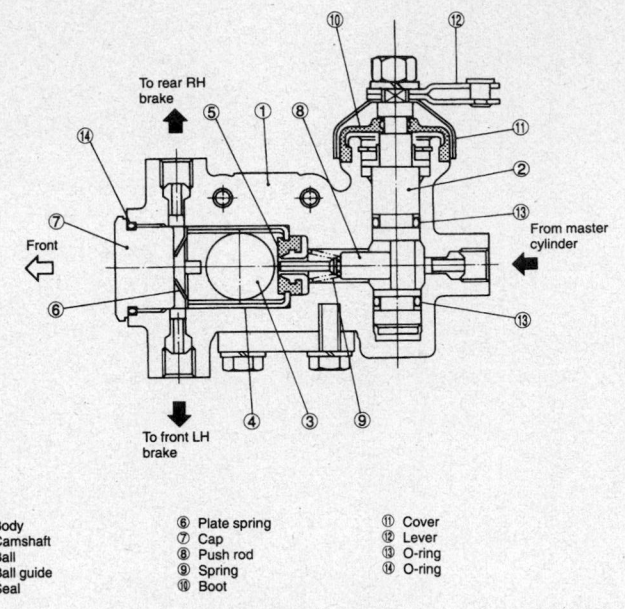

① Body	⑥ Plate spring	⑪ Cover
② Camshaft	⑦ Cap	⑫ Lever
③ Ball	⑧ Push rod	⑬ O-ring
④ Ball guide	⑨ Spring	⑭ O-ring
⑤ Seal	⑩ Boot	

SB2039100016000X

Fig. 8 Hill holder (PHV) valve

① Master cylinder	⑤ Clutch pedal	⑨ PHV cable
② Proportioning valve	⑥ Clutch cable	⑩ Front brake
③ Brake booster	⑦ Clutch release fork	⑪ Rear brake
④ Brake pedal	⑧ Pressure hold valve	⑫ Hydraulic control unit

SB2039100017000X

Fig. 9 Hill holder installation

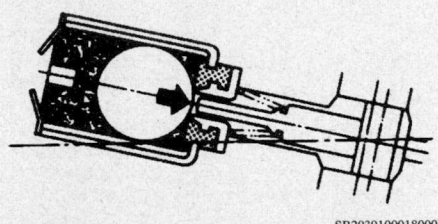

SB2039100018000X

Fig. 10 Hill holder activated

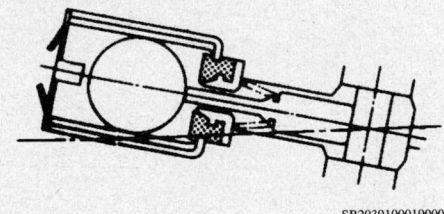

SB2039100019000X

Fig. 11 Hill holder deactivated

TIGHTENING SPECIFICATIONS

Year	Component	Torque/ Ft. Lbs.
1996–99	Axle Nut	123-152
	Hill Holder Adjustment Nut	22-39①
	Hub Nut	145
	Parking Brake Adjustment Locknut	40-65①
	Stabilizer Clamps	17-20
	Stabilizer Link To Lateral Link	29-37
	Stabilizer Link To Stabilizer	29-37
	Strut Assembly Upper Mounting Bolts	10-19
	Strut Assembly Lower Mounting Bolts	138-174
	Wheel Lug Nuts	58-72

① — Inch lbs.

Front Suspension & Steering

INDEX

WHEEL HUB & STEERING KNUCKLE

REPLACE

FORESTER, IMPREZA & LEGACY

Refer to **Fig. 1** when performing the following procedure.
1. Raise and support vehicle.
2. Remove front wheels, then unlock axle nut.
3. Using a suitable socket, remove axle nut. **Do not remove axle nut with wheel installed.**
4. Remove stabilizer link, then double off-set joint from transaxle spindle.
5. Remove driveshaft from knuckle. If it is difficult to remove, use remover tool No. 926470000 and plate tool No. 927140000, or equivalents.
6. Disconnect brake caliper from knuckle and secure to strut with wire.
7. Remove brake rotor from hub. If rotor is seized, install two 8 mm bolts in screw holes to remove.
8. Using a suitable puller, disconnect tie rod from knuckle.
9. **On models equipped with ABS,** remove ABS sensor assembly.
10. **On all models,** disconnect ball joint from knuckle.
11. Scribe alignment mark on camber adjustment bolt head, then remove knuckle to strut mounting bolts.
12. Remove knuckle assembly from vehicle.
13. Support knuckle using knuckle stand tool No. 927080000, or equivalent.
14. Using hub remover tool No. 927060000, or equivalent, press hub out of knuckle. If inner bearing race remains in hub, remove it with a suitable tool.
15. Remove disc cover from housing, then using standard screwdriver, remove outer and inner oil seals.
16. Remove snap ring.
17. Support hub using hub stand tool No. 927400000, or equivalent, then using bearing remover tool No. 927100000, or equivalent, press out inner race and bearing.
18. **On models equipped with ABS,** re-

move tone wheel, then reinstall tone wheel.
19. **On all models,** using hub stand and bearing remover, press new bearing into place. Always press outer race when installing bearing.
20. Install snap ring. Using hub stand and oil seal installer tool No. 927410000, or equivalent, press outer seal until it contacts bottom of housing and inner seal until it contacts circlip.
21. Install disc cover and **torque** bolts to 7–13 ft. lbs.
22. Install hub in hub stand. Using hub installer tool No. 927120000, or equivalent, press bearing into hub.
23. Assemble steering knuckle assembly to vehicle by reversing steps 1 through 14.

SVX

Refer to **Fig. 1** when performing the following procedure.
1. Raise and support vehicle, then remove front wheels.
2. Remove hub caps, then unlock axle nut.
3. Using a suitable socket, remove axle nut. **Do not remove axle nut with wheel installed.**
4. Remove ball joint retaining bolts, then disconnect ABS sensor from knuckle.
5. Disconnect brake hose clamp from strut, then scribe alignment mark on camber adjusting bolt and remove strut mounting nuts. **Do not remove strut bolts at this time.**
6. Disconnect brake caliper from knuckle and secure to strut with wire.
7. Remove driveshaft from knuckle. If it is difficult to remove, use remover tool No. 926470000 and plate tool No. 28099PA110, or equivalents.
8. Remove brake rotor from hub. If rotor is seized, install two 8 mm bolts in screw holes to remove.
9. Using a suitable puller, disconnect tie rod from knuckle, then remove knuckle and hub assembly.
10. Support knuckle and hub assembly using hub stand tool No. 28099PA080, or equivalent, then attach hub remover front tool No. 28099PA040, or equivalent, to knuckle and drive hub out of knuckle.
11. If inner bearing race remains in hub, re-

move using a suitable tool.
12. Remove brake backing plate from knuckle, then using a suitable screwdriver, remove inner and outer oil seals.
13. Remove snap ring, then support knuckle using housing stand front tool No. 28099PA010, or equivalent.
14. Using bearing installer front tool No. 28099PA000, or equivalent, press inner race to drive out bearing. **Do not remove outer race unless it is damaged.**
15. Using housing stand front tool No. 28099PA010 and bearing installer front tool No. 28099PA000, or equivalents, press outer race to install new bearing.
16. Install snap ring, then using oil seal installer front tool No. 28099PA030, or equivalent, press inner oil seal until it contacts circlip.
17. Using oil seal installer front tool No. 28099PA030, or equivalent, press outer oil seal until it contacts bottom of housing.
18. Install brake backing plate, attach hub assembly to hub stand, then using hub installer front, press hub assembly into knuckle.
19. Assemble steering knuckle assembly to vehicle by reversing steps 1 through 9.

BALL JOINT INSPECTION

1. Measure dimension "L," with 154 lbs. of download pressure placed on ball joint in the direction of "L," **Fig. 2.**
2. Measure dimension "L," with 154 lbs. of upload pressure placed on ball joint in the direction of "L," **Fig. 3.**
3. Calculate ball joint play using the following formula:
   a. $S = L2 - L1$.
   b. Ball joint play "S" equals .012 inch.
   c. Ball joint play should not exceed .012 inch.
   d. If ball joint play exceeds calculated figure, then replace with new ball joint.

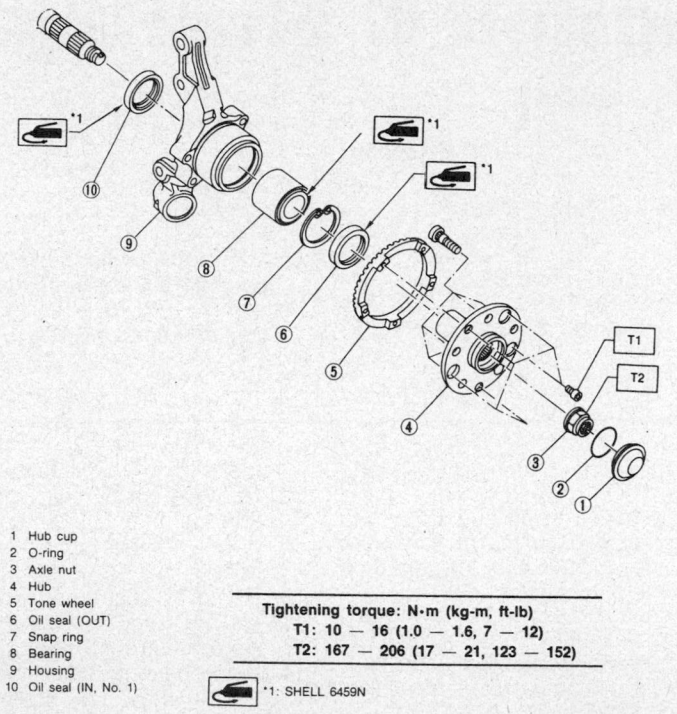

1 Hub cup
2 O-ring
3 Axle nut
4 Hub
5 Tone wheel
6 Oil seal (OUT)
7 Snap ring
8 Bearing
9 Housing
10 Oil seal (IN, No. 1)

Tightening torque: N·m (kg-m, ft-lb)
T1: 10 — 16 (1.0 — 1.6, 7 — 12)
T2: 167 — 206 (17 — 21, 123 — 152)

*1: SHELL 6459N

SB2049100002000X

Fig. 1   Exploded view of knuckle, hub & bearing

BALL JOINT

REPLACE

Refer to **Figs. 4 through 6** when performing the following procedure.
1. Raise and support vehicle.
2. Remove front wheels.
3. Remove cotter pin and castle nut from ball stud, then disconnect ball stud from transverse link.
4. Remove ball joint to housing retaining bolt and the ball joint.
5. Reverse procedure to install. Refer to **Figs. 4 through 6,** for tightening specifications.

STRUT

REPLACE

FORESTER & IMPREZA

Refer to **Fig. 4,** when performing the following procedure.
1. Raise and support vehicle, then remove front wheels.
2. Disconnect brake hose from caliper, then disconnect brake hose from strut.
3. Scribe alignment mark on camber adjusting bolt, then remove ABS sensor harness, if equipped.
4. Remove lower and upper strut mounting bolts, then the strut.
5. Compress coil spring using a suitable coil spring compressor, then remove self-locking nut using strut mount socket tool No. 927760000, or equivalent.
6. Remove strut mount, upper spring seat and upper rubber seat from strut assembly.
7. Remove coil spring, dust cover and helper spring.

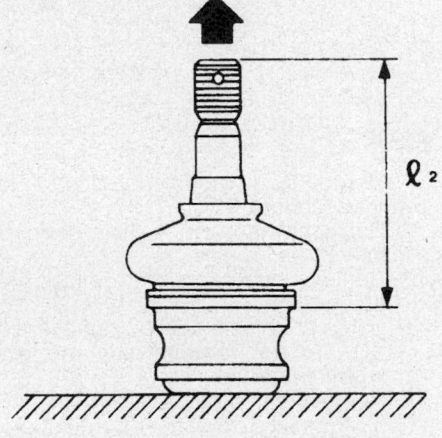

SB2029300016000X

Fig. 3   Ball joint play upload dimension measurement

8. Reverse procedure to install, noting the following:
   a. Mount coil spring with flat end towards top side and inclined end towards bottom side.
   b. Ensure upper spring seat is positioned with "Out" mark facing outward.
   c. Install strut rod with new locking nut.
   d. Refer to **Fig. 4** for tightening specifications.

LEGACY

Conventional Suspension

Refer to **Fig. 5,** when performing the following procedure.
1. Raise and support vehicle.

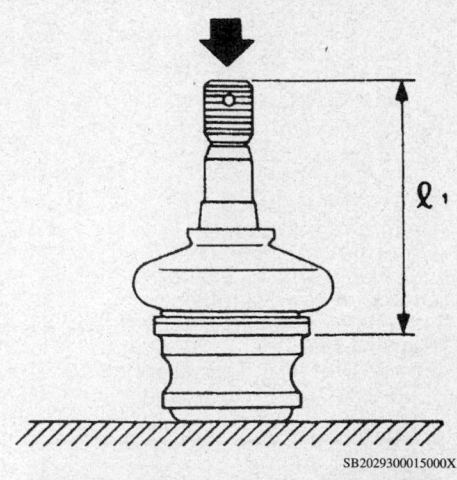

SB2029300015000X

Fig. 2   Ball joint play download dimension measurement

2. Remove front wheels.
3. Remove union bolts from caliper.
4. Disconnect brake hose from caliper.
5. Remove brake hose to strut bracket retaining clip, then separate brake hose from strut bracket.
6. Scribe an alignment mark on camber adjusting bolt.
7. **On models equipped with anti-lock brakes,** remove ABS sensor.
8. **On all models,** remove strut to body mounting bolts.
9. Remove strut assembly from vehicle.
10. Properly position strut assembly in spring compressor tool, then compress spring until it separates from upper seat.
11. Remove strut rod self-locking nut using socket tool No. 927760000, or equivalent.
12. Remove strut mount and associated parts.
13. Carefully release spring compressor tool.
14. Remove coil spring, then the strut from spring compressor tool.
15. Remove dust cover and helper from strut rod.
16. Reverse procedure to install, noting the following:
    a. Refer to **Fig. 5** for tightening specifications.
    b. Ensure hydraulic brake system is properly bled.
    c. Check and adjust wheel alignment as needed.

Pneumatic Suspension

Service on air spring strut assemblies is limited to replacement of the upper mount and the entire strut assembly. When performing the following procedure, refer to **Fig. 7.**
1. Ensure height control switch is turned Off and vehicle height is in "Normal" low position.
2. Raise and support vehicle.
3. Remove front wheels.
4. Disconnect brake hose from caliper.
5. Remove brake hose to strut bracket retaining clip, then separate brake hose from strut bracket.
6. **On models equipped with anti-lock**

brakes, remove ABS sensor.

7. **On Legacy models,** proceed as follows:
   a. Disconnect air line from solenoid valve.
   b. Disconnect solenoid valve electrical connector.
   c. Remove strut bracket to axle housing attaching bolts.

8. **On all models,** remove strut to shock tower retaining bolts and the strut assembly from vehicle.

9. Ensure all air has been discharged from air spring chamber, then remove strut mount retaining nut while holding strut shaft with spanner wrench tool No. 926510000, or equivalent. **Strut rod must be properly secured with spanner wrench to prevent damaging diaphragm.**

10. Reverse procedure to install noting the following:
    a. Refer to **Fig. 7,** for tightening specifications.
    b. Install air lines with new O-rings lightly lubricated with multi-purpose grease.
    c. Ensure hydraulic brake system is properly bled.
    d. Check and adjust wheel alignment as needed.

SVX

Refer to **Fig. 8,** when performing the following procedure.

1. Raise and support vehicle, then remove front wheels.

2. Remove stabilizer link, then disconnect ABS sensor clamp and brake hose clamp from strut.

3. Scribe an alignment mark on camber adjusting bolt and remove strut mounting nuts. **Do not remove strut bolts at this time.**

4. Support knuckle assembly with a suitable jack, then remove strut mount cap and three upper strut mounting nuts.

5. Remove bolts from lower strut mounting, then the strut assembly from vehicle.

6. Compress coil spring using a suitable coil spring compressor, then remove self-locking nut using strut mount socket tool No. 20099PA000, or equivalent.

7. Remove strut mount, upper spring seat and upper rubber seat from strut assembly.

8. Remove coil spring, dust cover, helper spring and lower rubber seat.

9. Install lower rubber seat to spring seat, then install coil spring so that its end face fits into spring seat, **Fig. 9.**

10. Install helper and dust cover to piston rod, ensure helper and dust cover are aligned with graded section of piston rod, **Fig. 10.**

11. Pull piston fully upward, then install rubber seat and spring seat, ensure upper spring seat is positioned with "OUT" mark facing outward.

12. Install strut mount to piston rod, then a new self-locking nut and temporarily tighten.

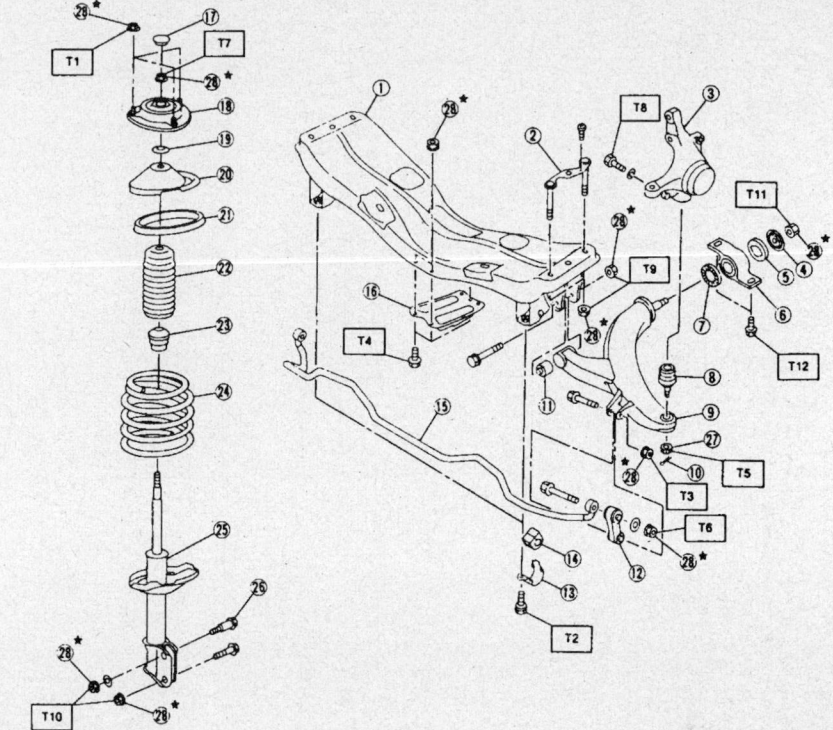

① Crossmember	⑮ Stabilizer
② Bolt ASSY	⑯ Jack-up plate
③ Housing	⑰ Dust seal
④ Washer	⑱ Strut mount
⑤ Stop rubber (Rear)	⑲ Spacer
⑥ Rear bushing	⑳ Upper spring seat
⑦ Stop rubber (Front)	㉑ Rubber seat
⑧ Ball joint	㉒ Dust cover
⑨ Transverse link	㉓ Helper
⑩ Cotter pin	㉔ Coil spring
⑪ Front bushing	㉕ Damper strut
⑫ Stabilizer link	㉖ Adjusting bolt
⑬ Clamp	㉗ Castle nut
⑭ Bushing	㉘ Self-locking nut

Tightening torque: N·m (kg-m, ft-lb)
T1: 20 ± 6 (2.0 ± 0.6, 14.5 ± 4.3)
T2: 25 ± 4 (2.5 ± 0.4, 18.1 ± 2.9)
T3: 29 ± 5 (3.0 ± 0.5, 21.7 ± 3.6)
T4: 32 ± 10 (3.3 ± 1.0, 24 ± 7)
T5: 39 (4, 29)
T6: 44 ± 6 (4.5 ± 0.6, 32.5 ± 4.3)
T7: 49 ⁺¹⁰ (5.0 ⁺¹·⁰ 36 ⁺⁷)
T8: 49 ± 10 (5.0 ± 1.0, 36 ± 7)
T9: 98 ± 15 (10.0 ± 1.5, 72 ± 11)
T10:152 ± 20 (15.5 ± 2.0, 112 ± 14)
T11:196 ± 25 (20.0 ± 2.5, 145 ± 18)
T12:245 ± 49 (25.0 ± 5.0, 181 ± 36)

SB2029100005000X

Fig. 4   Front suspension assembly. Forester & Impreza

13. Loosen coil spring carefully, then while fixing spring seat, tighten self-locking nut to specifications.

14. Assemble strut assembly to vehicle by reversing steps 1 through 5.

CONTROL ARM
REPLACE
LOWER
SVX

Refer to **Fig. 11** when performing the following procedure.

1. Raise and support vehicle, then remove front wheels.

2. Disconnect ball joint from steering knuckle, then remove rear support. **Do not remove rear support on both sides at once.**

3. Remove lower arm.

4. Reverse procedure to install, tightening bolts to specifications with vehicle weight on suspension.

STABILIZER BAR
REPLACE
IMPREZA & LEGACY

Refer to **Figs. 4 and 5** when performing the following procedure.

1. Raise and support vehicle.

2. Remove left and right stabilizer to transverse link retaining bolts. Separate plates from transverse link.

3. Remove left and right stabilizer clamp to crossmember retaining bolts. Separate clamps from stabilizer.

4. Remove jack-up plate and stabilizer.

5. Reverse procedure to install, noting the following:
   a. Ensure crossmember bushing is positioned in bent portion of shaft.
   b. Tighten retaining bolts with wheels on the ground and vehicle unloaded.
   c. Refer to **Figs.4 and 5** for tightening specifications.

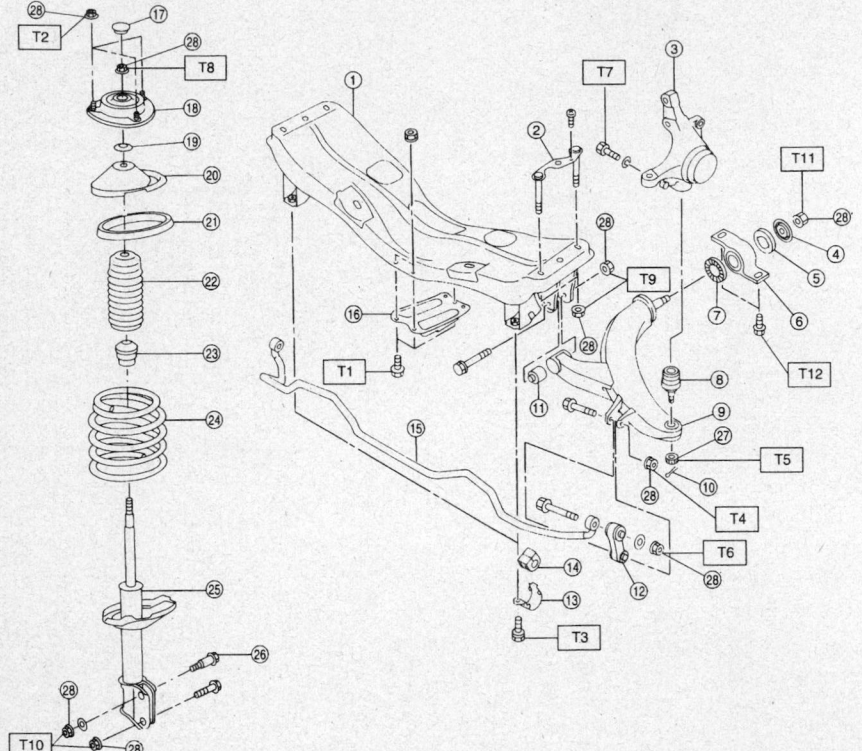

① Crossmember	⑮ Stabilizer
② Bolt ASSY	⑯ Jack-up plate
③ Housing	⑰ Dust seal
④ Washer	⑱ Strut mount
⑤ Stop rubber (Rear)	⑲ Spacer
⑥ Rear bushing	⑳ Upper spring seat
⑦ Stop rubber (Front)	㉑ Rubber seat
⑧ Ball joint	㉒ Dust cover
⑨ Transverse link	㉓ Helper
⑩ Cotter pin	㉔ Coil spring
⑪ Front bushing	㉕ Damper strut
⑫ Stabilizer link	㉖ Adjusting bolt
⑬ Clamp	㉗ Castle nut
⑭ Bushing	㉘ Self-locking nut

Tightening torque: N·m (kg-m, ft-lb)
T1: 18 ± 5 (1.8 ± 0.5, 13.0 ± 3.6)
T2: 20 ± 6 (2.0 ± 0.6, 14.5 ± 4.3)
T3: 25 ± 4 (2.5 ± 0.4, 18.1 ± 2.9)
T4: 29 ± 5 (3.0 ± 0.5, 21.7 ± 3.6)
T5: 39 (4, 29)
T6: 44 ± 6 (4.5 ± 0.6, 32.5 ± 4.3)
T7: 49 ± 10 (5.0 ± 1.0, 36 ± 7)
T8: 54 ± 5 (5.5 ± 0.5, 39.8 ± 3.6)
T9: 98 ± 15 (10.0 ± 1.5, 72 ± 11)
T10:152 ± 20 (15.5 ± 2.0, 112 ± 14)
T11:186 ± 10 (19.0 ± 1.0, 137 ± 7)
T12:245 ± 49 (25.0 ± 5.0, 181 ± 36)

SB2029100001000X

Fig. 5   Front suspension assembly. Legacy

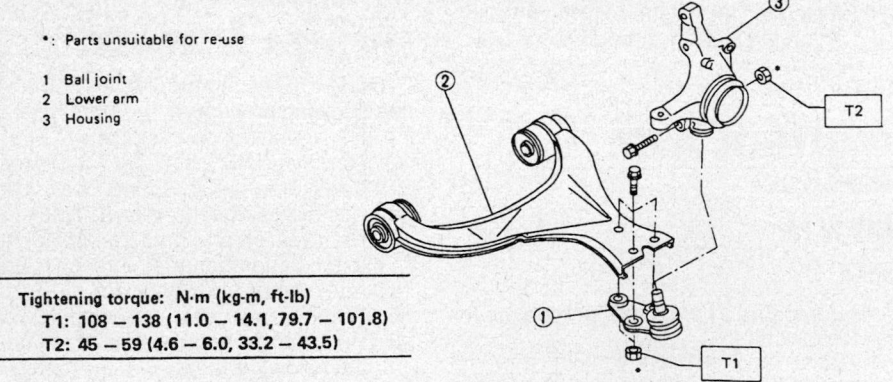

*: Parts unsuitable for re-use

1 Ball joint
2 Lower arm
3 Housing

Tightening torque: N·m (kg-m, ft-lb)
T1: 108 — 138 (11.0 — 14.1, 79.7 — 101.8)
T2: 45 — 59 (4.6 — 6.0, 33.2 — 43.5)

SB2029100006000X

Fig. 6   Ball joint replacement. SVX

SVX

Refer to **Fig. 12** when performing the following procedure.
1. Raise and support vehicle, then remove front wheels.
2. Remove stabilizer link, right ABS sensor clamp and right brake hose clamp.
3. Scribe an alignment mark on stabilizer and stabilizer lever, then remove both parts.
4. Remove stabilizer bushing, then the stabilizer from right side of vehicle.
5. Reverse procedure to install, aligning

paint mark on stabilizer bushing.

CROSSMEMBER
REPLACE
FORESTER, IMPREZA & LEGACY

Refer to **Figs. 4 and 5** when performing the following procedure.
1. Raise and support vehicle.
2. Remove stabilizer assembly as outlined under "Stabilizer Bar, Replace."
3. Disconnect tie rod ends from housing.
4. Remove front exhaust pipe.
5. Remove transverse link to crossmember retaining bolts.
6. Remove engine mount to crossmember retaining nuts.
7. Remove steering torque rod to pinion shaft self-locking nuts.
8. Using a suitable lift, raise engine approximately .39 inch.
9. Support crossmember with a suitable jack, then remove crossmember retaining nuts.
10. Lower crossmember from vehicle.
11. Reverse procedure to install. Refer to **Figs. 4 and 5** for tightening specifications.

POWER STEERING GEAR
REPLACE
FORESTER, IMPREZA & LEGACY
Removal

1. Raise and support vehicle.
2. Remove front wheels.
3. Remove front exhaust pipe assembly.
4. Disconnect tie rod ends from steering knuckles.
5. Remove jack-up plate and stabilizer bushing clamp from crossmember.
6. Disconnect fluid lines at center of steering gear. Connect extension tubing and discharge fluid by turning steering wheel from lock to lock.
7. Remove upper and lower universal joint to steering gear and intermediate shaft retaining bolts. Scribe matching marks between shaft, universal joint and steering gear, then disconnect joint from steering gear.
8. Disconnect fluid lines from upper then the lower side of steering gear control valve housing.
9. Remove steering gear clamp bolts, then the steering gear.

Installation

1. Position steering gear on crossmember, then install clamps and retaining bolts.
2. Connect fluid lines to lower port of valve housing and to center ports of gear. Connect upper line first.
3. Connect fluid lines to upper ports of valve housing. Connect lower line first.
4. Install steering shaft joint as follows:
   a. Align bolt hole on long end of yoke

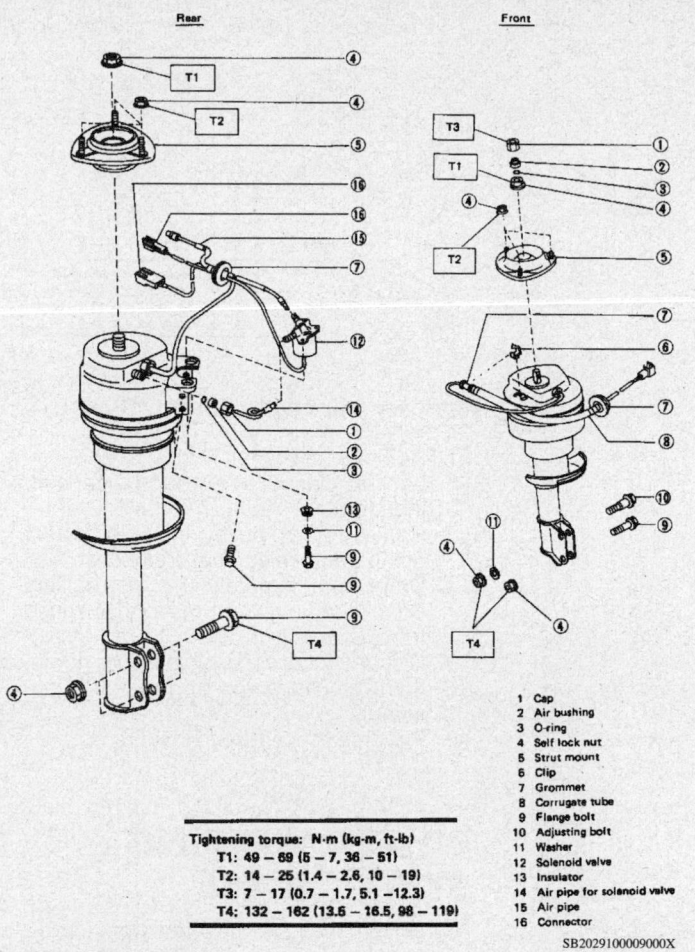

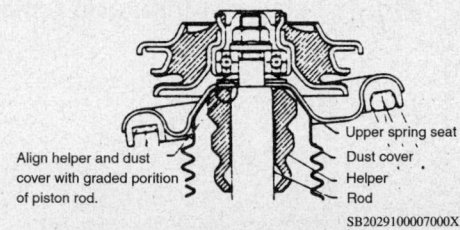

Fig. 8 Exploded view of strut assembly. SVX

Tightening torque: N·m (kg-m, ft-lb)		
T1: 34 – 48 (3.5 – 4.9, 25.1 – 35.4)		
T2: 49 – 59 (5.0 – 6.0, 36.1 – 43.5)		
T3: 132 - 172 (13.5 – 17.5, 97.4 – 126.9)		

SB2029100010000X

*: Parts unsuitable for re-use

1 Cap
2 Dust seal
3 Strut mount
4 Spacer
5 Upper spring seat
6 Upper rubber seat
7 Dust cover
8 Coil spring
9 Helper
10 Lower rubber seat
11 Strut COMPL
12 Adjusting bolt

Align helper and dust cover with graded portion of piston rod.

Upper spring seat
Dust cover
Helper
Rod

SB2029100007000X

Fig. 10 Helper & dust cover alignment. SVX

1 Cap
2 Air bushing
3 O-ring
4 Self lock nut
5 Strut mount
6 Clip
7 Grommet
8 Corrugate tube
9 Flange bolt
10 Adjusting bolt
11 Washer
12 Solenoid valve
13 Insulator
14 Air pipe for solenoid valve
15 Air pipe
16 Connector

SB2029100009000X

Tightening torque: N·m (kg-m, ft-lb)		
T1: 49 – 69 (5 – 7, 36 – 51)		
T2: 14 – 25 (1.4 – 2.6, 10 – 19)		
T3: 7 – 17 (0.7 – 1.7, 5.1 –12.3)		
T4: 132 – 162 (13.5 – 16.5, 98 – 119)		

Fig. 7 Pneumatic suspension components. Legacy

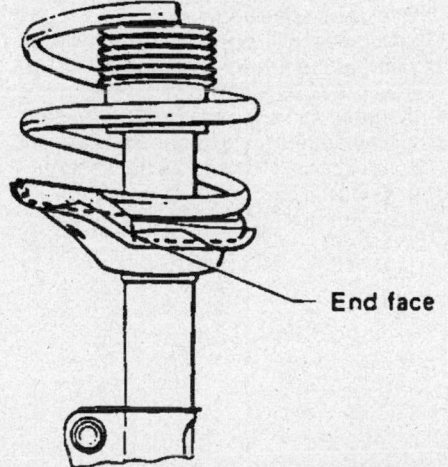

End face

SB2029100011000X

Fig. 9 Coil spring alignment. SVX

with notch in steering shaft and push joint onto shaft.

b. Align bolt hole in short end of yoke with notch in steering gear pinion shaft and engage yoke with pinion shaft.

c. Align matching marks made during removal.

d. Install universal yoke retaining bolts. Ensure both bolts are properly engaged in shaft notches, then

tighten bolts to specifications.
5. Reverse remaining procedure to complete installation. Tighten bolts and nuts to specifications.

SVX

Refer to **Fig. 13** when performing the following procedure.
1. Disconnect oxygen sensor and steering harness electrical connector, if equipped.
2. Raise and support vehicle, then the front wheels.
3. Remove undercover, then disconnect oxygen sensor harness from clip.
4. Remove collector cover and rear catalytic converter protector, then disconnect front exhaust pipe.
5. Using a suitable puller, disconnect tie rod ends from steering knuckles.
6. Remove spring pin securing transaxle spindle to inner CV joint, then remove inner CV joint from transaxle spindle and free from transaxle.
7. Disconnect pipe joint from upper hose, then drain fluid by rotating steering wheel left and right. Also disconnect other pipe and drain fluid.
8. Disconnect performance rod, then the lower arm ball joint from steering knuckle. Cover ball joint with a cloth to prevent damage.
9. Scribe alignment marks on upper and lower part of universal joint, then re-

move upper and lower universal joint bolts.
10. Remove universal joint in an upward direction, then the bolts securing gearbox to subframe and disconnect gearbox. **Do not turn steering wheel or misalignment of air bag system roll connector may occur.**
11. Turn gearbox assembly around so that control valve faces rear, then move gearbox assembly full right so that left tie rod end can be removed from subframe.
12. Remove gearbox assembly from vehicle.
13. Reverse procedure to install.

POWER STEERING PUMP
REPLACE
FORESTER, IMPREZA & LEGACY

1. Drain power steering fluid from reservoir.
2. Remove pulley belt cover bracket.
3. Loosen pump pulley nut, then remove alternator mounting bolts.
4. Loosen pulley belt(s), then remove pump pulley nut and pump pulley.
5. Disconnect and plug fluid lines from pump. Disconnect solid line first.
6. Remove three front pump mounting bolts, then the pump assembly.
7. Remove bracket mounting bolts, then the bracket.
8. Remove reservoir from pump.
9. Reverse procedure to install.

SVX

Refer to **Fig. 13** when performing the following procedure.

SUBARU

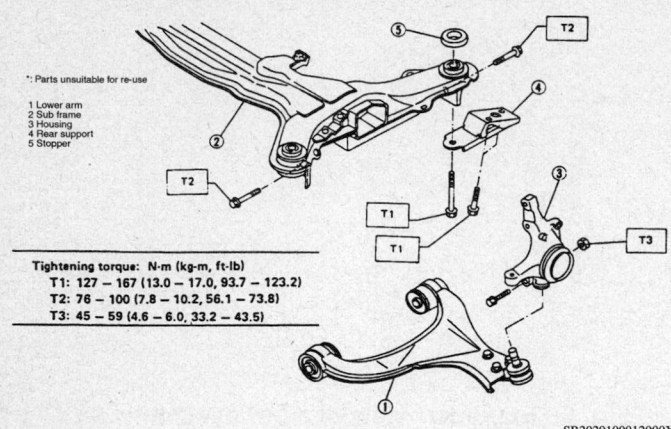

*: Parts unsuitable for re-use

1 Lower arm
2 Sub frame
3 Housing
4 Rear support
5 Stopper

Tightening torque: N·m (kg-m, ft-lb)
T1: 127 — 167 (13.0 — 17.0, 93.7 — 123.2)
T2: 76 — 100 (7.8 — 10.2, 56.1 — 73.8)
T3: 45 — 59 (4.6 — 6.0, 33.2 — 43.5)

SB2029100012000X

Fig. 11 Lower control arm replacement. SVX

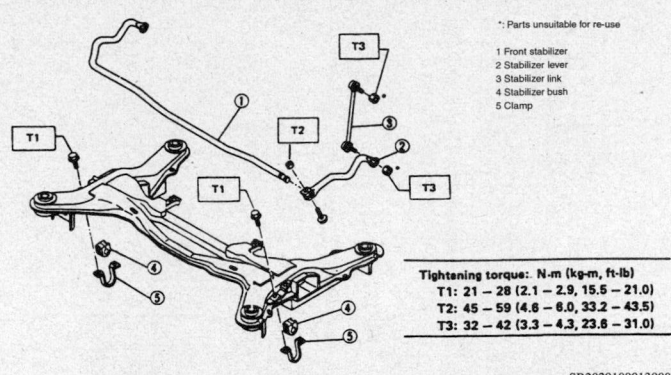

*: Parts unsuitable for re-use

1 Front stabilizer
2 Stabilizer lever
3 Stabilizer link
4 Stabilizer bush
5 Clamp

Tightening torque: N·m (kg-m, ft-lb)
T1: 21 — 28 (2.1 — 2.9, 15.5 — 21.0)
T2: 45 — 59 (4.6 — 6.0, 33.2 — 43.5)
T3: 32 — 42 (3.3 — 4.3, 23.6 — 31.0)

SB2029100013000X

Fig. 12 Stabilizer bar replacement. SVX

1. Remove belt cover.
2. Loosen idler pulley nuts and slider bolt, then remove V-belt.
3. Remove pump pulley, then disconnect pump switch electrical connector.
4. Drain approximately 0.3 qts. of fluid from reservoir, then disconnect hose from reservoir.
5. Disconnect pressure pipe from pump, then remove pump and reservoir assembly.
6. Reverse procedure to install.

POWER STEERING SYSTEM BLEED

1. Fill reservoir till 1.6 inches from top.
2. Start engine and turn steering wheel from lock to lock several times until bubbles stop appearing. Ensure fluid level is as specified.
3. If bubbles still appear, let vehicle sit with engine Off for one half hour. Repeat previous step.
4. If bubble still appear, check for a leaks in a power steering hoses and flare nut connections. Replace as necessary.

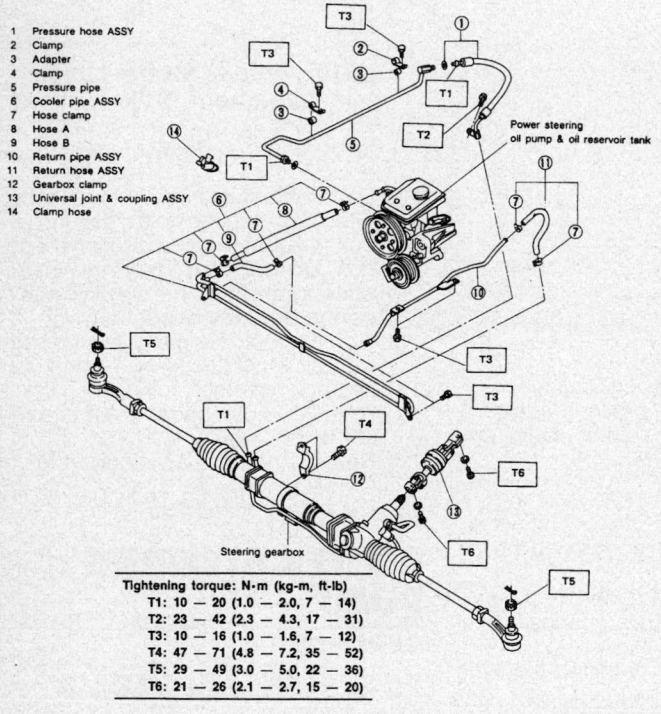

1 Pressure hose ASSY
2 Clamp
3 Adapter
4 Clamp
5 Pressure pipe
6 Cooler pipe ASSY
7 Hose clamp
8 Hose A
9 Hose B
10 Return pipe ASSY
11 Return hose ASSY
12 Gearbox clamp
13 Universal joint & coupling ASSY
14 Clamp hose

Power steering oil pump & oil reservoir tank

Steering gearbox

Tightening torque: N·m (kg-m, ft-lb)
T1: 10 — 20 (1.0 — 2.0, 7 — 14)
T2: 23 — 42 (2.3 — 4.3, 17 — 31)
T3: 10 — 16 (1.0 — 1.6, 7 — 12)
T4: 47 — 71 (4.8 — 7.2, 35 — 52)
T5: 29 — 49 (3.0 — 5.0, 22 — 36)
T6: 21 — 26 (2.1 — 2.7, 15 — 20)

SB6039100001000X

Fig. 13 Power steering gear & pump replacement. SVX

TIGHTENING SPECIFICATIONS

Year	Component	Torque/Ft. Lbs.
FORESTER, IMPREZA & LEGACY		
1996–99	Axle Nut	137
	Brake Caliper	36–51
	Caliper Mount Bracket	36–51
	Disc Brake Rotor Splash Shield	7–13
	Driveshaft Nut	137
	Engine Mount To Crossmember	14–24
	Hub Nut	137
	Power Steering Gear Retaining Clamps & Bolts	35–52
	Power Steering Line Fittings To Valve Housing Lower Ports	7–12
	Power Steering Line Fittings To Valve Housing Upper Ports	7–14
	Power Steering Pinion Shaft To Steering Torque Rod	10–14
	Speed Sensor	14–29
	Tie Rod End	18–22
	Universal Joint Pinch Bolt	17
	Universal Yoke	16–19
	Wheel Lug Nuts	58–72
SVX		
1996–97	ABS Tone Wheel To Hub	7–12
	Axle Nut	123–152
	Ball Joint To Knuckle	33–43
	Ball Joint To Lower Arm	79–101
	Driveshaft Nut	123–152
	Hub Nut	123–152
	Lower Arm To Crossmember	56–73
	Power Steering Gear To Crossmember	35–52
	Power Steering Pump Mounting Bolts	13–17
	Rear Support To Crossmember	93–123
	Stabilizer Clamp To Crossmember	15–21
	Stabilizer Lever To Stabilizer Bar	33–43
	Stabilizer Link Nuts	23–31
	Strut Assembly Nut	36–43
	Strut Assembly To Knuckle	97–126
	Strut Mount To Strut Tower	25–35
	Wheel Lug Nuts	72–86

Wheel Alignment

INDEX

PRELIMINARY INSPECTION

1. Check for proper tire pressure.
2. Inspect suspension components for damaged or broken pieces, replace as necessary.

FRONT WHEEL ALIGNMENT

CASTER

Caster angles are not adjustable. If caster is not within specifications, inspect suspension components for damage and repair as necessary, then recheck wheel alignment.

CAMBER

Adjust camber angles to specifications by rotating the strut mounting bolt, **Fig. 1.**

TOE-IN

1. Loosen both left and right tie rod locknuts.
2. Turn left and right tie rods an equal amount until toe-in is within specifications.
3. To increase toe-in, turn both tie rods counterclockwise an equal amount.

REAR WHEEL ALIGNMENT

CAMBER

Camber angles cannot be adjusted. If camber is not within specifications, inspect suspension components for damage and replace as necessary, then recheck wheel alignment.

TOE-IN

1. **On FWD models,** rotate bolt at lateral link, **Fig. 2,** clockwise while turning adjusting wheel counterclockwise to adjust toe-in. Rotate bolt counterclockwise while turning adjusting wheel clockwise to adjust toe-out.
2. **On SVX and AWD Impreza and Legacy models,** rotate bolt at lateral link, **Fig. 3,** clockwise to adjust toe-in. Ro-

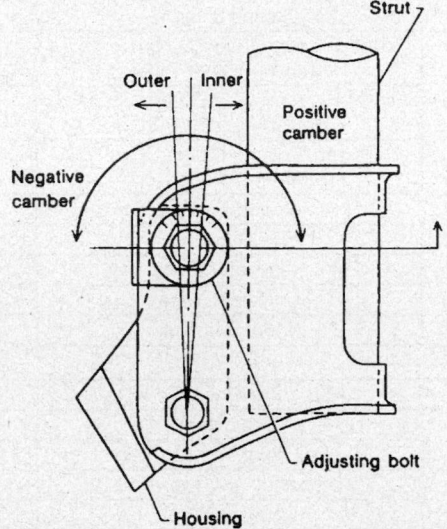

Fig. 1 Camber adjustment bolt location

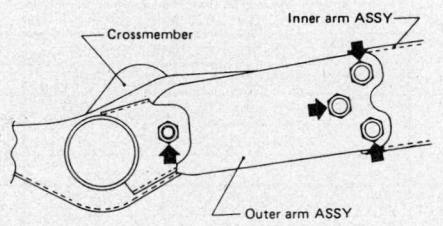

Fig. 3 Rear toe-in adjustment bolt location. SVX and AWD Impreza & Legacy

tate bolt counterclockwise to adjust toe-out.

3. **On Forester models,** loosen self locking nut on inner side of rear lateral link, **Fig. 4.**
   a. On left side of vehicle, when adjusting bolt is turned clockwise, toe is increased, when rotated counterclockwise, toe is decreased.
   b. On right side of vehicle, when adjusting bolt is turned clockwise, toe is decreased, when bolt is turned counterclockwise, toe is increased.

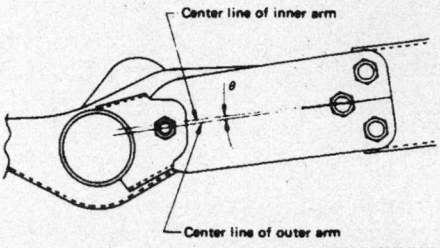

Fig. 2 Rear toe-in adjustment bolt location. FWD Impreza & Legacy

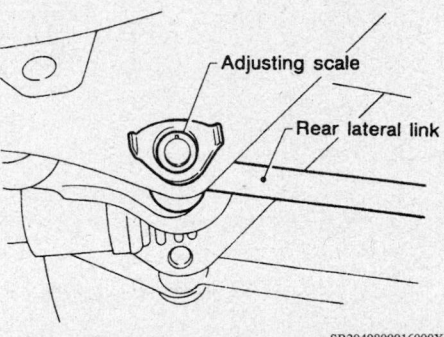

Fig. 4 Toe adjustment bolt. Forester

4. **On all models,** turn bolt to set rear toe adjustment at specified value, then **torque** self locking nut to 61–83 ft. lbs.

VEHICLE RIDE HEIGHT

1. Park vehicle on a level surface.
2. Ensure tires are properly inflated.
3. Take wheel arch height measurements, **Fig. 5.**
4. Refer to **Fig. 6.** If clearances are not as specified proceed as follows:
   a. **On models equipped with conventional suspension,** replace the respective coil springs.
   b. **On models equipped with pneumatic suspensions,** check for leaking air line or tank fittings, leaking or defective solenoid valves, defective control unit or height sensors. Repair as needed.

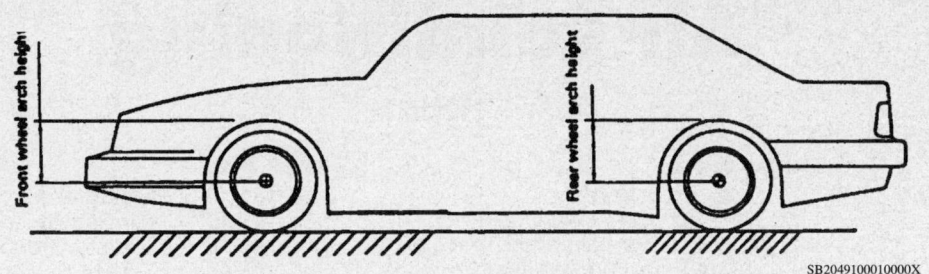

Fig. 5 Wheel arch height measurement

Model	Year	Body Style	Ride Height, Inch					
			Front			Rear		
			Minimum	Maximum	Preferred	Minimum	Maximum	Preferred
AWD MODELS								
Forester	1998–99	SUV	16.07	17.48	17.01	16.19	17.60	17.13
Impreza	1997–99	All	14.45	15.86	15.39	14.53	15.31	14.92
Legacy	1997–99	Sedan	14.22	15.63	15.16	13.39	15.00	14.53
		Wagon	14.22	15.63	15.16	13.98	15.39	14.92
SVX	1996–97	All	14.17	15.34	14.95	12.40	13.58	13.19
FWD MODELS								
Impreza	1996	All	14.45	15.86	15.39	14.49	15.27	14.88
Legacy	1996	Sedan	14.22	15.63	15.16	13.59	15.00	14.53
		Wagon	14.22	15.63	15.16	13.98	15.39	14.92

Fig. 6 Vehicle ride height specifications

SUBARU

Air Conditioning

INDEX

PRECAUTIONS

R134A SYSTEM

1. Do not use compressor oil that is not specifically designated for the R134a system.
2. The compressor oil used in R134a systems absorbs water very easily. When any system component is being removed, quickly install a blind plug to prevent contact with the outside air. **Ensure the service container for the compressor oil is tightly closed.**
3. Refrigerant boils at approximately -22°F (-30°C), it is cold enough to cause severe frostbite. Always wear goggles and gloves when working on an A/C system.
4. Never expose a container of R134a refrigerant to direct sunlight or to temperatures over 104°F (40°C). Exposure to this kind of heat could cause the pressure inside the container to increase to a dangerous level.
5. When R134a refrigerant is exposed to an open flame or hot metal it forms phosgene, a deadly gas. Never discharge R134a refrigerant directly into the atmosphere.

AIR BAG SYSTEMS

Refer to "Air Bag System Precautions" in the front of this manual for system disarming and arming procedures.

BATTERY GROUND CABLE

Prior to service, disconnect battery ground cable and isolate as required.

PERFORMANCE TEST

FORESTER, IMPREZA & SVX

Refer to **Figs. 1 through 4,** for system performance test.

LEGACY

The cooling performance of the air conditioner changes considerably with changes in surrounding conditions. To inspect for proper system operation, follow procedure outlined below:
1. Park vehicle indoors or in shade.
2. Open all windows and keep doors closed.

3. Connect manifold gauge set.
4. Set mode switch to A/C MAX position, then the air inlet control switch to CIRC.
5. Set temperature lever to COLD position.
6. Start engine and hold speed at 1500 RPM.
7. After air conditioner has been operating for 10 minutes, measure system pressures at high pressure (discharge side) and low pressure (suction) side.
8. Measure temperature of inlet air to blower and outlet air at dash panel grilles.
9. Measure temperature and humidity of ambient air approximately three feet in front of condenser.

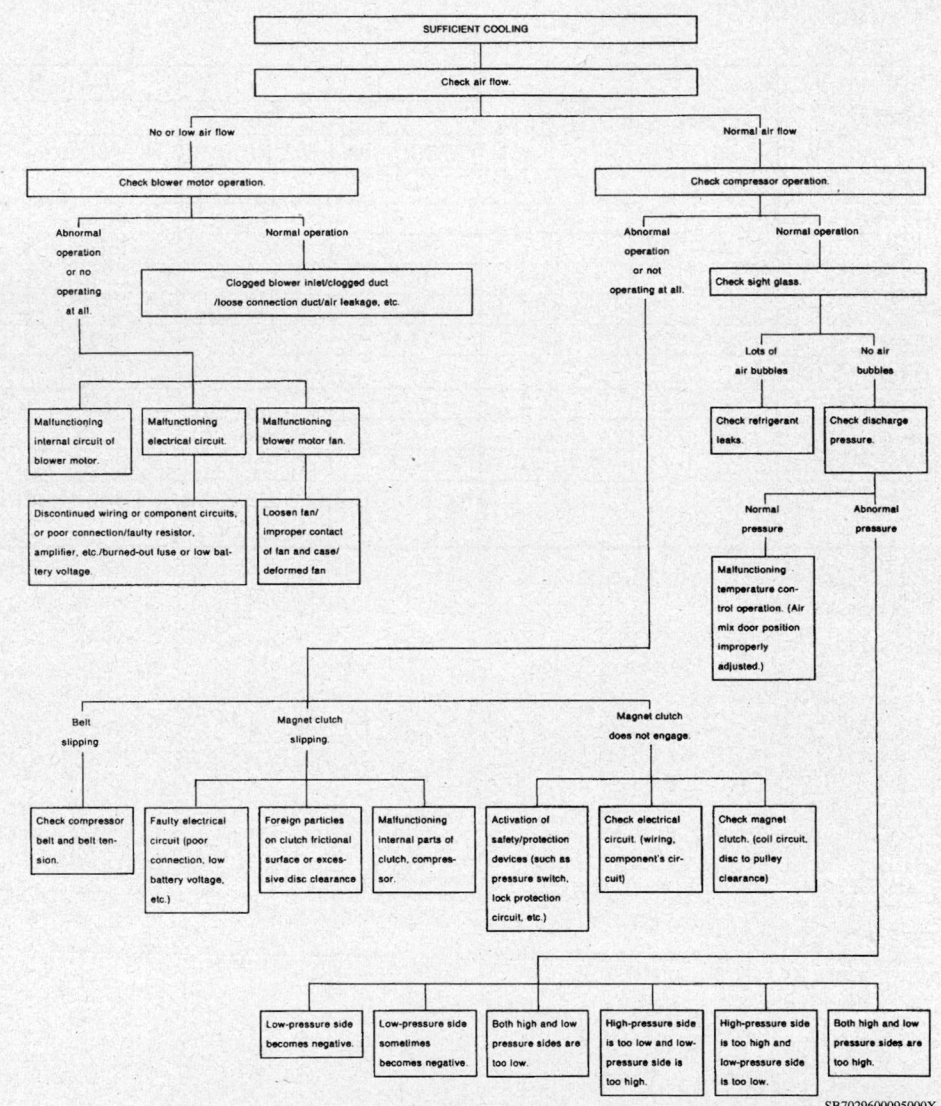

Fig. 1 A/C system diagnosis. Forester & Impreza

SB7029600095000X

Item to check / Amount of refrigerant	Adequate	Insufficient	Almost in refrigerant	Too much refrigerant
State in sight glass	CLEAR. Air bubbles sometimes appear when engine speed is increased or decreased. 	FOAMY or BUBBLY. Air bubbles always appear. 	FROSTY. Frost-like appears. 	NO FOAM. No air bubbles appear. 
Temperature of high and low pressure lines	High-pressure side is hot while low-pressure side is cold. (A big temperature difference between high and low-pressure side.)	High-pressure side is warm and low-pressure side is lightly cold. (Not so big temperature difference between high and low-pressure side.)	There is almost no temperature difference between high and low-pressure side.	High-pressure side is hot and low-pressure side is slightly warm. (Slight temperature difference between high and low pressure side.)
Pressure of system	Both pressure on high and low-pressure sides are normal.	Both pressure on high and low-pressure sides are slightly low.	High-pressure side is abnormally low.	Both pressure on high and low-pressure sides are abnormally high.

SB7029600096000X

Fig. 2   A/C system sight glass inspection. Forester & Impreza

Condition		Probable cause	Corrective action
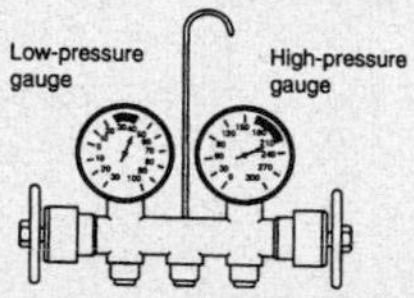 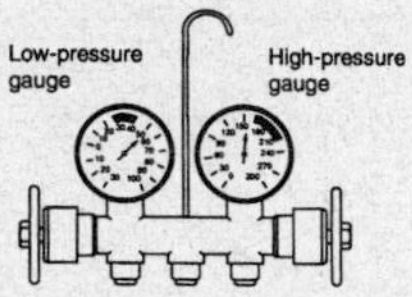	Insufficient cooling. Sweated suction line. No cooling. Sweating or frosted suction line.	Expansion valve allows too much refrigerant through evaporator. Faulty seal of O-ring in expansion valve.	Check valve for operation. If suction side does not show a pressure decrease, replace valve. 1. Discharge system. 2. Remove expansion valve and replace O-ring. 3. Evacuate and replace system.
AIR IN SYSTEM 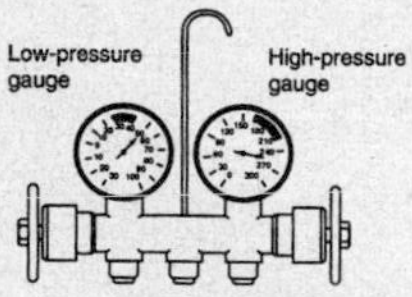	Insufficient cooling.	Air mixed with refrigerant in system.	1. Discharge system. 2. Replace receiver drier. 3. Evacuate and charge system.
MOISTURE IN SYSTEM 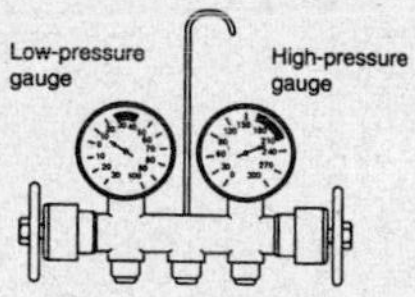	After operation for a while, pressure on suction side may show vacuum pressure reading. During this condition, discharge air will be warm. As warning of this, reading shows 39 kPa (0.4 kg/cm², 6 psi) vibration.	Drier is saturated with moisture. Moisture has frozen at expansion valve. Refrigerant flow is restricted.	1. Discharge system. 2. Replace receiver drier (twice if necessary). 3. Evacuate system completely (Repeat 30 minute evacuating three times.). 4. Recharge system.

SB7029300069020X

Fig. 3   Manifold gauge pressure readings (Part 2 of 3). Forester & Impreza

10. Compare test results with performance charts, **Figs. 5 and 6.**

OIL CHARGE
FORESTER & LEGACY

If compressor is replaced, drain oil from old compressor and measure, then drain new compressor. Refill new compressor with same amount that was drained from old compressor. Refill amount must be a minimum of 0.70 ounces.

When replacing other system components, add the following quantities of refrigerant oil: Evaporator, 3.90 ounces; Receiver Drier, 0.20 ounces; Condenser, 0.07 ounces; Hose, 0.03 ounces.

IMPREZA

If compressor is replaced, drain oil from old compressor and measure, then drain new compressor. Refill new compressor with same amount that was drained from old compressor. Refill amount must be a minimum of 3 ounces.

When replacing other system components, add the following quantities of refrig-

Condition		Probable cause	Corrective action
INSUFFICIENT REFRIGERANT CHARGE 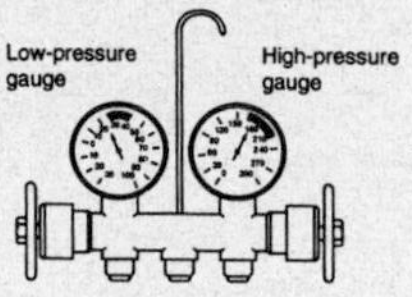	Insufficient cooling.	Refrigerant is small, or leaking a little.	1. Leak test. 2. Repair leak. 3. Charge system. Evacuate, as necessary, and recharge system.
ALMOST NO REFRIGERANT 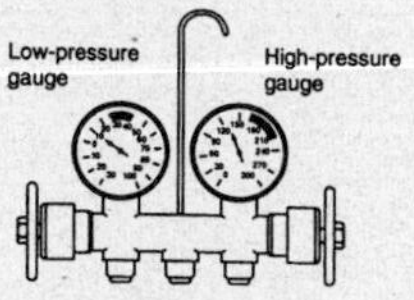	No cooling action.	Serious refrigerant leak.	Stop compressor immediately. 1. Leak test. 2. Discharge system. 3. Repair leak(s). 4. Replace receiver drier if necessary. 5. Check oil level. 6. Evacuate and recharge system.
FAULTY EXPANSION VALVE 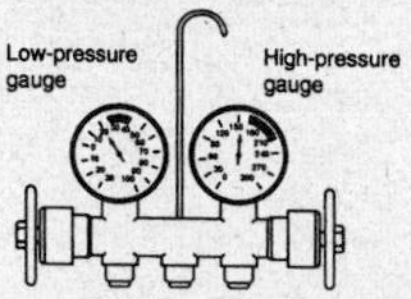	Slight cooling. Sweating or frosted expansion valve inlet.	Expansion valve restricts refrigerant flow. • Expansion valve is clogged. • Expansion valve is inoperative. • Valve stuck closed. Thermal bulb has lost charge.	If valve inlet reveals sweat or frost: 1. Discharge system. 2. Remove valve and clean it. Replace it if necessary. 3. Evacuate system. 4. Charge system. If valve does not operate: 1. Discharge system. 2. Replace valve. 3. Evacuate and charge system.

SB7029300069010X

Fig. 3   Manifold gauge pressure readings (Part 1 of 3). Forester & Impreza

erant oil: Evaporator, 2.8 ounces; Receiver Drier, 2 ounces; Condenser, 1.5 ounces;

Condition		Probable cause	Corrective action
FAULTY CONDENSER 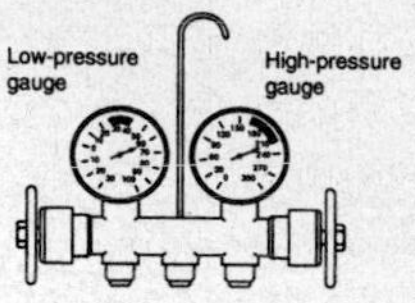	No cooling action. Engine may overheat. Suction line is very hot.	Condenser is often found not functioning well.	• Check condenser cooling fan. • Check condenser for dirt accumulation. • Check engine cooling system for overheat. • Check for refrigerant overcharge. If pressure remains high in spite of all above actions taken, remove and inspect the condenser for possible oil clogging.
HIGH-PRESSURE LINE BLOCKED 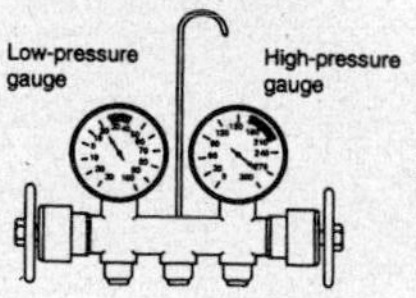	Insufficient cooling. Frosted high-pressure liquid line.	Drier clogged, or restriction in high-pressure line.	1. Discharge system. 2. Remove receiver drier or strainer and replace it. 3. Evacuate and charge system.
FAULTY COMPRESSOR 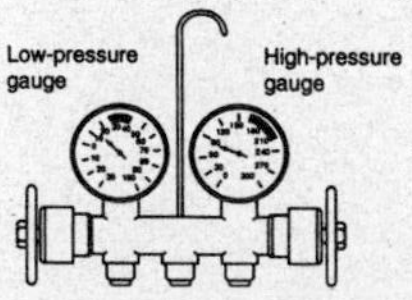	Insufficient cooling.	Internal problem in compressor, or damaged gasket and valve.	1. Discharge system. 2. Remove and check compressor. 3. Repair or replace compressor. 4. Check oil level. 5. Replace receiver drier. 6. Evacuate and charge system.

SB7029300069030X

Fig. 3   Manifold gauge pressure readings (Part 3 of 3). Forester & Impreza

Hose, 2 ounces.

SVX

Refer to oil charge table in **Fig. 7**, for oil replacement quantities when servicing the air conditioning system.

OIL LEVEL CHECK

No provision is made for checking oil

Gauge indication	Refrigerant cycle	Probable cause	Corrective action
Both high- and low-pressure sides are too high.	Pressure is reduced soon after water is splashed on condenser. No air bubbles appear in sight glass when pressure is reduced.	Excessive refrigerant charge in refrigeration cycle	Reduce refrigerant until specified pressure is obtained.
	Air suction by radiator or condenser fan is insufficient.	Insufficient condenser cooling performance 1) Condenser fin is clogged. 2) Improper rotation of radiator fan or condenser fan	• Clean condenser. • Check and repair cooling fan as necessary.
	• Low-pressure pipe is not cold. • When compressor is stopped, high-pressure value quickly drops by approximately 196 kPa (2 kg/cm², 28 psi). It will then decrease gradually thereafter.	Poor heat exchange in condenser (After compressor operation stops, high pressure decreases too slowly.) Air in refrigeration cycle	Evacuate repeatedly and recharge system.
	Engine tends to overheat.	Engine cooling systems malfunction.	Check and repair each engine cooling system.
	• Area near low-pressure pipe connection and service valves are considerably cold as compared with area near expansion valve outlet or evaporator. • Parts are sometimes covered with frost.	• Excessive liquid refrigerant on low-pressure side • Excessive refrigerant discharge flow • Expansion valve is open a little compared with the specification. 1) Improper thermal valve installation 2) Improper expansion valve adjustment	Replace expansion valve.
High-pressure side is too high and low-pressure side is too low.	Upper side of condenser and high-pressure side are hot, however, receiver drier is not so hot.	High-pressure hose or parts located between compressor and condenser are clogged or crushed.	• Check and repair or replace malfunctioning parts. • Check compressor oil for contamination.

SB7029200070010X

Fig. 4 Manifold gauge pressure readings (Part 1 of 3). SVX

Gauge indication	Refrigerant cycle	Probable cause	Corrective action
High-pressure side is too low and low-pressure side is too high.	High- and low-pressure sides become equal soon after compressor operation stops.	Compressor pressure operation is improper. Damaged inside packings for compressor	Replace compressor.
	No temperature differences between high and low-pressure sides	Compressor discharge capacity does not change. (Compressor stroke is set at maximum.)	Replace compressor.
Both high- and low-pressure sides are too low.	• There is a big temperature difference between receiver drier outlet and inlet. Outlet temperature is extremely low. • Receiver drier inlet and expansion valve are frosted.	Receiver drier inside is clogged a little.	• Replace receiver drier • Check compressor oil for contamination.
	• Temperature of expansion valve inlet is extremely low as compared with areas near receiver drier. • Expansion valve inlet may be frosted. • Temperature difference occurs somewhere in high-pressure side.	High-pressure pipe located between receiver drier and expansion valve is clogged.	• Check and repair malfunctioning parts. • Check compressor oil for contamination.
Both high and low-pressure sides are too low.	There is a big temperature difference between expansion valve inlet and outlet while the valve itself is frosted.	Expansion valve becomes closed a little compared with the specification. 1) Improper expansion valve adjustment 2) Malfunctioning thermal valve 3) Outlet and inlet may be clogged	• Remove foreign particles by using compressed air. • Check compressor oil for contamination.
	Area near low-pressure pipe connection and service valve are extremely cold as compared with area near expansion valve outlet and evaporator.	Low-pressure hose is clogged or crushed.	• Check and repair malfunctioning parts. • Check compressor oil for contamination.
	Air flow volume is not enough or low.	Evaporator is frozen. Compressor discharge capacity does not change. (Compressor stroke is set at maximum length.)	Replace compressor.

SB7029200070020X

Fig. 4 Manifold gauge pressure readings (Part 2 of 3). SVX

Gauge indication	Refrigerant cycle	Probable cause	Corrective action
Low-pressure side sometimes becomes negative.	• Air conditioning system does not function and does not cyclically cool the compartment air. • The system constantly function for a certain period of time after compressor is stopped and restarted.	Refrigerant does not discharge cyclically. Moisture is frozen at expansion valve outlet and inlet. Water is mixed in refrigeration cycle.	• Drain water from refrigerant cycle or replace refrigerant. • Replace receiver drier.
Low-pressure side becomes negative.	Receiver drier or front/rear side of expansion valve's pipe is frosted or dewed.	High-pressure side is closed and refrigerant does not flow. Expansion valve or receiver drier is frosted.	After the system is left at rest, start again in order to confirm whether or not problem is caused by water or foreign particles. • If the problem is due to water, drain water from refrigeration cycle or replace refrigerant. • If it is due to foreign particles, remove expansion valve and remove it with dry and compressed air. • If either oil the above method cannot correct the problem, replace expansion valve. • Replace receiver drier. • Check compressor oil for contamination.

SB7029200070030X

Fig. 4 Manifold gauge pressure readings (Part 3 of 3). SVX

level on these vehicles and oil is added according to component(s) being replaced. Refer to "Oil Charge."

BELT TENSION DATA

Refer to "Drive Belt Service" in "Engine" section.

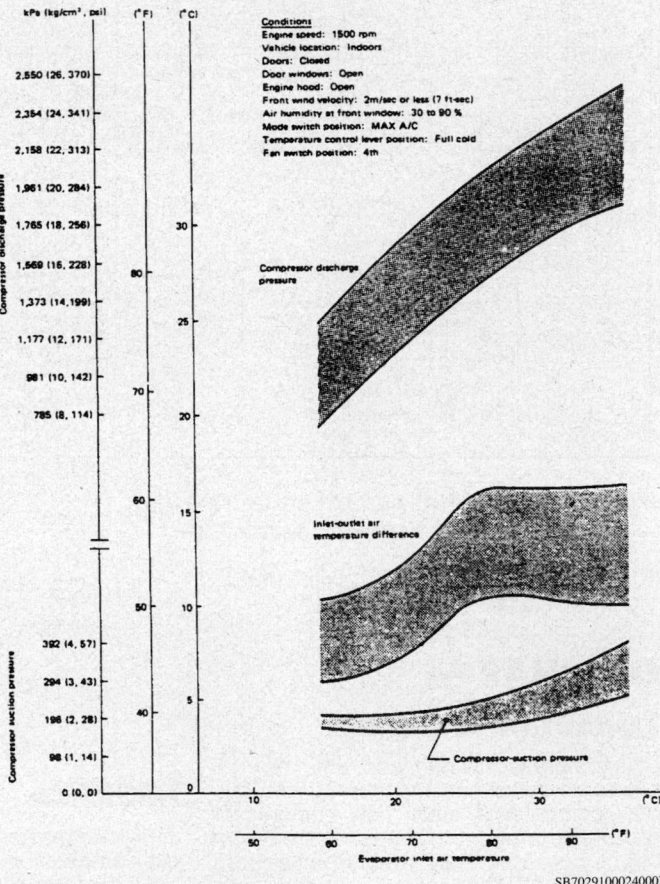

SB7029100024000X

Fig. 5 A/C system performance chart. Legacy w/Calsonic compressor

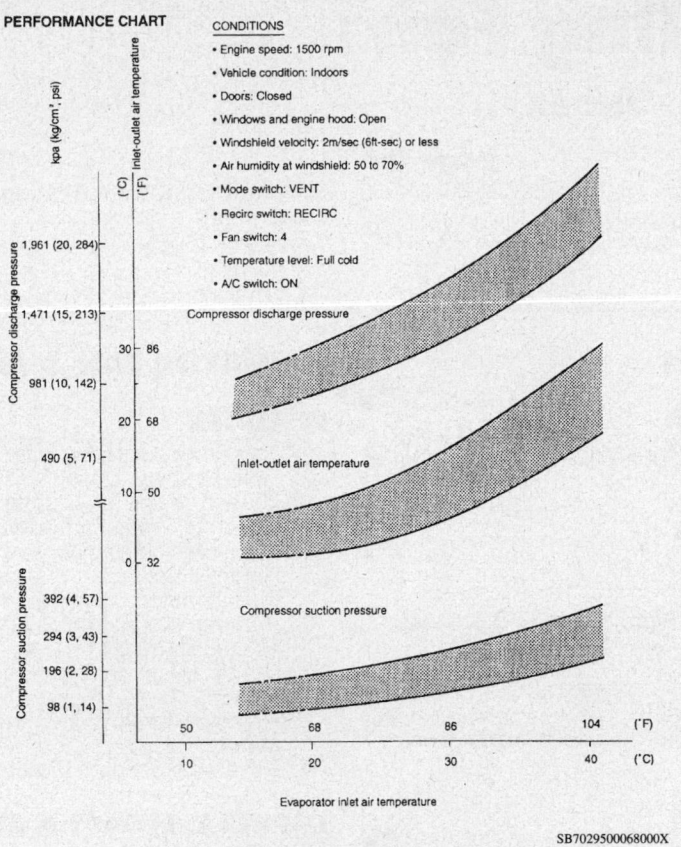

Fig. 6 A/C system performance chart. Legacy w/Zexel compressor

Unit: mℓ (US fl oz, Imp fl oz)

Item		Replenishment amount	Remarks
Compressor replacement		70 (2.4, 2.5)	Drain oil completely from new compressor and replenish compressor oil by amount indicated at left.
Evaporator replacement		70 (2.4, 2.5)	
Receiver dryer replacement		—	Replenishment is not necessary.
Condenser replacement	Oil does not appear to leak.	—	Replenishment is not necessary.
	Oil leaks from condenser in large quantities.	50 (1.7, 1.8)	
Flexible hose/pipe replacement	Oil does not appear to leak.	—	Replenishment is not necessary.
	Oil leaks in large quantities.	50 (1.7, 1.8)	
Refrigerant leaks	Oil does not appear to leak.	—	Replenishment is not necessary.
	Oil leaks in large quantities.	50 (1.7, 1.8)	
Every two years			

SB7029100031000X

Fig. 7 Oil charge table. SVX

A/C SPECIFICATIONS

Comprlessor Model	Refiringerrant Capacity, Lbs.	Refiringerrant Types	Refrigerant Oil			Compressor Clutch Air Gap, Inch	Charging Valve Locations	
			Viscosity	Total System Capacity, Ounces	Compressor Oil Level Check, Inches		High Press.	Low Press.
Forester	1.2-1.4	R134a	⑥	5.2	④	.012-.024	⑤	③
Impreza	1.3-1.5	R134a	②	—	④		⑤	③
Legacy	1.3-1.5	R134a	①	—	④	.012-.024	⑤	③
SVX	1.43	R134a	①	5.06	④	—	⑤	③

① — Type ZXL-100-PG, or equivalent.
② — Special Polyvalence Glycol (PAG) lubricant required.
③ — On low pressure line.

④ — Oil level inches cannot be checked.
⑤ — On high pressure line.

⑥ — Special Polyp Alkaline Glycol (PAG) ZXL200PG (DH-PR) retype compressor oil

Cooling Fans

INDEX

PRECAUTIONS

AIR BAG SYSTEMS

Refer to "Air Bag System Precautions" in the front of this manual for system disarming and arming procedures.

BATTERY GROUND CABLE

Prior to service, disconnect battery ground cable and isolate as required.

SYSTEM DIAGNOSIS & TESTING

MAIN FAN

FORESTER

Refer to **Fig. 1** for main fan diagnosis.

IMPREZA

1996

Refer to **Figs. 2 through 4** for main fan diagnosis.

1997

Refer to **Figs. 5 and 6** for main fan diagnosis.

1998-99

Refer to **Fig. 7** for main fan diagnosis.

LEGACY

1996

Refer to **Figs. 8 and 9** for radiator fan diagnosis.

1997

Refer to **Figs. 10 and 11** for radiator fan diagnosis.

1998-99

Refer to **Figs. 12 and 13** for radiator fan diagnosis.

SVX

Refer to **Figs. 14 through 16,** for radiator fan diagnosis.

SUB FAN

FORESTER

Refer to **Fig. 17** for sub fan diagnosis.

IMPREZA

1996

Refer to **Figs. 18 and 19** for sub fan diagnosis.

1997

Refer to **Fig. 20** for sub fan diagnosis.

1998-99

Refer to **Fig. 21** for sub fan diagnosis.

LEGACY

Refer to "Legacy" under "Main Fan" section for sub fan diagnosis.

SVX

Refer to "Main Fan" for condenser/sub fan diagnosis.

COMPONENT REPLACEMENT

CONDENSER FAN & MOTOR

1. Disconnect fan motor electrical connector.
2. **On Impreza models,** remove rightward radiator bracket, then condenser fan mounting bolts.
3. **On Legacy models,** loosen lower side condenser fan shroud mounting bolts, then remove upper side bolts.
4. **On Forester models,** remove condenser fan shroud bolts.
5. **On all models,** remove condenser fan assembly.
6. Reverse procedure to install.

RADIATOR FAN & MOTOR

FORESTER

1. Raise and support vehicle.
2. Remove lower splash shield.
3. Loosen lower fan shroud bolts, then disconnect radiator fan motor.
4. Lower vehicle and remove belts.
5. Remove upper fan shroud bolts then the fan motor assembly.
6. Remove clip that holds fan motor harness to shroud.
7. Cut tie straps that secure harness to shroud.
8. Remove three bolts, then the fan motor.
9. Reverse procedure to install.

IMPREZA, LEGACY & SVX

Removal

1. Disconnect fan motor electrical connector, then the harness from shroud, if necessary.
2. Remove shroud retaining bolts, then the shroud.
3. Remove fan motor mounting nuts, then separate motor from shroud.
4. Remove cooling fan mounting nuts, then separate cooling fan blades from fan motor.

Installation

1. Place cooling fan on fan motor, then install mounting nuts. Apply a suitable locking compound to mounting nuts then securely tighten.
2. Place fan motor on shroud and install mounting nuts. **Ensure fan does not contact shroud when installed.**
3. Assemble shroud to radiator.
4. Connect fan motor electrical connector, then secure wiring harness to shroud.

RADIATOR SUB FAN MOTOR

Refer to "Radiator Fan & Motor" for component replacement procedure.

DETECTING CONDITION:

Condition:
- Engine coolant temperature is above 95°C (203°F).
- Vehicle speed is below 19 km/h (12 MPH).

TROUBLE SYMPTOM:
- Radiator main fan does not rotate under the above conditions.

2A1 :	CHECK POWER SUPPLY TO MAIN FAN MOTOR.

CAUTION:
Be careful not to overheat engine during repair.
1) Turn ignition switch to OFF.
2) Disconnect connector from main fan motor.
3) Start the engine, and warm it up until engine coolant temperature increases over 95°C (203°F).
4) Stop the engine and turn ignition switch to ON.
5) Measure voltage between main fan motor connector and chassis ground.

Connector & terminal
(F17) No. 2 (+) — Chassis ground (–):

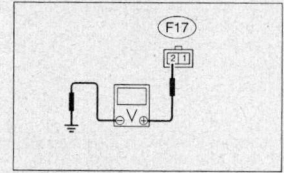

CHECK : **Is the voltage more than 10 V?**
YES : Go to step **2A2**.
NO : Go to step **2A5**.

SB1089800061010X

Fig. 1 Radiator main fan diagnosis (Part 1 of 5). Forester

2A2 :	CHECK GROUND CIRCUIT OF MAIN FAN MOTOR.

1) Turn ignition switch to OFF.
2) Measure resistance between main fan motor connector and chassis ground.

Connector & terminal
(F17) No. 1 — Chassis ground:

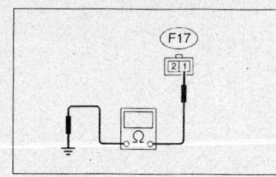

CHECK : **Is the resistance less than 5 Ω?**
YES : Go to step **2A3**.
NO : Repair open circuit in harness between main fan motor connector and chassis ground.

2A3 :	CHECK POOR CONTACT.

Check poor contact in main fan motor connector.

CHECK : **Is there poor contact in main fan motor connector?**
YES : Repair poor contact in main fan motor connector.
NO : Go to step **2A4**.

2A4 :	CHECK MAIN FAN MOTOR.

Connect battery positive (+) terminal to terminal No. 2, and negative (–) terminal to terminal No. 1 of main fan motor connector.

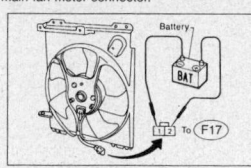

CHECK : **Does the main fan rotate?**
YES : Repair poor contact in main fan motor connector.
NO : Replace main fan motor with a new one.

2A5 :	CHECK POWER SUPPLY TO MAIN FAN RELAY.

1) Turn ignition switch to OFF.
2) Remove main fan relay from A/C relay holder.
3) Measure voltage between main fan relay terminal and chassis ground.

Connector & terminal
(F66) No. 26 (+) — Chassis ground (–):

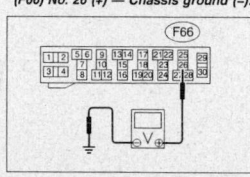

CHECK : **Is the voltage more than 10 V?**
YES : Go to step **2A6**.
NO : Go to step **2A7**.

2A6 :	CHECK POWER SUPPLY TO MAIN FAN RELAY.

1) Turn ignition switch to ON.
2) Measure voltage between main fan relay terminal and chassis ground.

Connector & terminal
(F66) No. 28 (+) — Chassis ground (–):

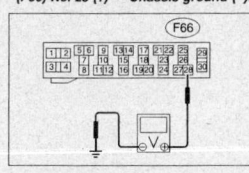

CHECK : **Is the voltage more than 10 V?**
YES : Go to step **2A16**.
NO : Go to step **2A12**.

2A7 :	CHECK 20 A FUSE.

1) Remove 20 A fuse from A/C relay holder.
2) Check condition of fuse.

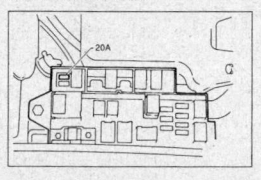

CHECK : **Is the fuse blown-out?**
YES : Replace fuse.
NO : Go to step **2A8**.

SB1089800061020X

Fig. 1 Radiator main fan diagnosis (Part 2 of 5). Forester

2A8 :	CHECK HARNESS CONNECTOR BETWEEN MAIN FUSE BOX AND A/C RELAY HOLDER 20 A FUSE.

1) Disconnect connector from main fuse box.
2) Disconnect connectors (F25) and (F26) from generator, and (F34) from SBF holder.
3) Measure resistance of harness connector between main fuse box connector and A/C relay holder 20 A fuse terminal.

Connector & terminal
(F35) No. 2 — (F27) No. 1:

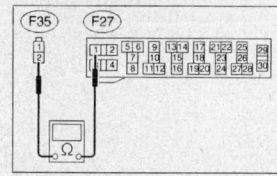

CHECK : **Is the resistance less than 1 Ω?**
YES : Go to step **2A9**.
NO : Repair open circuit in harness between main fuse box connector and 20 A fuse terminal.

2A9 :	CHECK POOR CONTACT.

Check poor contact in main fuse box connector.

CHECK : **Is there poor contact in main fuse box connector?**
YES : Repair poor contact in main fuse box connector.
NO : Go to step **2A10**.

2A10 :	CHECK POOR CONTACT.

Check poor contact in A/C relay holder 20 A fuse connector.

CHECK : **Is there poor contact in A/C relay holder 20 A fuse connector?**
YES : Repair poor contact in 20 A fuse
NO : Go to step **2A11**.

2A11 :	CHECK HARNESS CONNECTOR BETWEEN 20 A FUSE AND MAIN FAN RELAY IN A/C RELAY HOLDER.

Measure resistance of harness between 20 A fuse and main fan relay terminal.

Connector & terminal
(F27) No. 2 — (F66) No. 26:

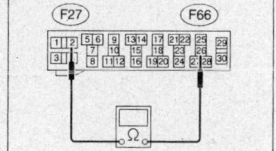

CHECK : **Is the resistance less than 1 Ω?**
YES : Repair poor contact in main fan relay connector.
NO : Repair open circuit in harness between 20 A fuse and main fan relay connector.

2A12 :	CHECK FUSE.

1) Turn ignition switch to OFF.
2) Remove fuse No. 18 from joint box.
3) Check condition of fuse.

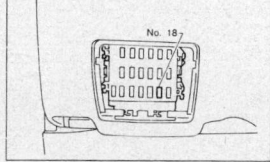

CHECK : **Is the fuse blown-out?**
YES : Replace fuse.
NO : Go to step **2A13**.

SB1089800061030X

Fig. 1 Radiator main fan diagnosis (Part 3 of 5). Forester

2A13 :	CHECK HARNESS CONNECTOR BETWEEN IGNITION SWITCH AND JOINT BOX.

1) Disconnect connector from ignition switch.
2) Separate connectors (F44) and (B61).
3) Disconnect connector (B159) from joint box.
4) Measure resistance of harness between ignition switch connector and joint box.

Connector & terminal
(B72) No. 4 — (B159) No. 8:

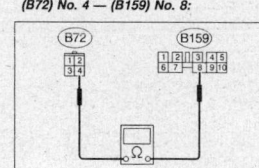

CHECK : **Is the resistance less than 1 Ω?**
YES : Go to step **2A14**.
NO : Repair harness and connector.

NOTE:
In this case, repair the following:
- Open circuit in harness between ignition switch connector and joint box.
- Poor contact in coupling connector (B61).

2A14 :	CHECK POOR CONTACT.

Check poor contact in ignition switch connector.

CHECK : **Is there poor contact in ignition switch connector?**
YES : Repair poor contact in ignition switch connector.
NO : Go to step **2A15**.

2A15 :	CHECK POOR CONTACT.

Check poor contact in joint box 10 A fuse connector.

CHECK : **Is there poor contact in joint box 10 A fuse connector?**
YES : Repair poor contact in joint box connector.
NO : Go to step **2A16**.

2A16 :	CHECK MAIN FAN RELAY.

1) Turn ignition switch to OFF.
2) Check continuity between main fan relay terminals.

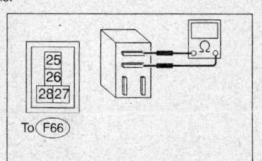

CHECK : **Does no continuity exist between terminals No. 25 and No. 26?**
YES : Go to step **2A17**.
NO : Replace main fan relay.

2A17 :	CHECK MAIN FAN RELAY.

1) Connect battery to terminals No. 27 and No. 28 of main fan relay.
2) Check continuity between main fan relay terminals.

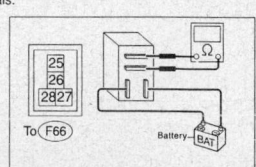

CHECK : **Does continuity exist between terminals No. 25 and No. 26?**
YES : Go to step **2A18**.
NO : Replace main fan relay.

SB1089800061040X

Fig. 1 Radiator main fan diagnosis (Part 4 of 5). Forester

SUBARU

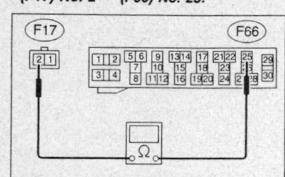

2A18 : CHECK HARNESS CONNECTOR BETWEEN MAIN FAN RELAY AND MAIN FAN MOTOR.

Measure resistance of harness between main fan motor connector and main fan relay terminal.

Connector & terminal
(F17) No. 2 — (F66) No. 25:

(CHECK) : *Is the resistance less than 1 Ω?*
(YES) : Go to step 2A19.
(NO) : Repair open circuit in harness between main fan motor and main fan relay connector.

2A19 : CHECK POOR CONTACT.

Check poor contact in main fan relay connector.

(CHECK) : *Is there poor contact in main fan relay connector?*
(YES) : Repair poor contact in main fan relay connector.
(NO) : Go to step 2A20.

2A20 : CHECK POOR CONTACT.

Check poor contact in main fan relay connector.

(CHECK) : *Is there poor contact in main fan motor connector?*
(YES) : Repair poor contact in main fan motor connector.
(NO) : Contact with SOA service.
NOTE:
Inspection by DTM is required, because probable cause is deterioration of multiple parts.

SB1089800061050X

Fig. 1   Radiator main fan diagnosis (Part 5 of 5). Forester

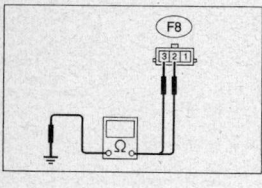

3) Measure resistance between main fan motor connector and body.
(CHECK) : **Connector & terminal**
(F8) No. 2 — Body/1 MΩ, or more
(F8) No. 3 — Body/1 MΩ, or more
(YES) : Go to next (CHECK)
(NO) : Repair short circuit between fuse & relay box and main fan motor connector.
(CHECK) : *Is there poor contact in fuse & relay box or main fan motor connector?*
(YES) : Repair poor contact in fuse & relay box or main fan motor connector.
(NO) : **Perform "On-Board Diagnostics II System" diagnostics procedure.**

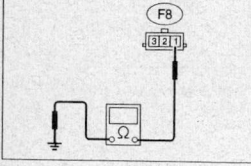

4 CHECK GROUND CIRCUIT OF MAIN FAN MOTOR.
1) Turn ignition switch to OFF.
2) Measure resistance between main fan motor connector and body.
(CHECK) : **Connector & terminal**
(F8) No. 1 — Body/5 Ω, or less
(YES) : Go to next (CHECK)
(NO) : Repair open circuit of harness between main fan motor connector and body.
(CHECK) : *Is there poor contact in main fan motor connector?*
(YES) : Repair poor contact in main fan motor connector.
(NO) : Go to step 5.

SB1089600045020X

Fig. 2   Radiator main fan motor power & ground circuit diagnosis (Part 2 of 3). 1996 Impreza

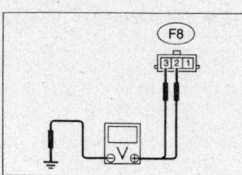

1 CHECK POWER SUPPLY TO MAIN FAN MOTOR.
CAUTION:
Be careful not to overheat engine during repair.
1) Turn ignition switch to OFF.
2) Disconnect connector from main fan motor.
3) Warm-up the engine until engine coolant temperature increases over 95°C (203°F).
4) Stop the engine and turn ignition switch to ON.
5) Measure voltage between main fan motor connector and body.
(CHECK) : **Connector & terminal**
(F8) No. 3 — Body/10 V, or more
(F8) No. 2 — Body/10 V, or more
(YES) : Go to step 4.
(NO) : Go to step 2.

2 CHECK FUSE.
1) Turn ignition switch to OFF.
2) Remove fuse No. 13 from fuse & relay box.
3) Check condition of fuse.
(CHECK) : *Does the fuse blown-out?*
(YES) : Replace fuse.
(NO) : Go to step 3.

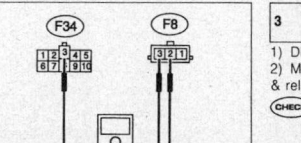

3 CHECK HARNESS CONNECTOR BETWEEN FUSE & RELAY BOX AND MAIN FAN MOTOR.
1) Disconnect connector from fuse & relay box.
2) Measure resistance of harness connector between fuse & relay box and main fan motor.
(CHECK) : **Connector & terminal**
(F34) No. 3 — (F8) No. 2/1 Ω, or less
(F34) No. 3 — (F8) No. 3/1 Ω, or less
(YES) : Go to next step.
(NO) : In this case, repair the following items:
● Open circuit of harness between fuse & relay box and main fan motor connector
● Open circuit of harness between fuse & relay box connector and coupling connector (F3)
● Open circuit of harness between coupling connector (F4) and main fan motor connector
● Poor contact in coupling connector (F3)

SB1089600045010X

Fig. 2   Radiator main fan motor power & ground circuit diagnosis (Part 1 of 3). 1996 Impreza

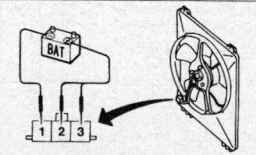

5 CHECK MAIN FAN MOTOR.
1) Turn ignition switch to OFF.
2) Disconnect connector from main fan motor.
(CHECK) : *Does the main fan rotate while connecting battery positive (+) terminal to terminals Nos. 2 and 3, and connecting battery negative (−) terminal to terminal No. 1 of main fan motor connector?*
(YES) : Repair poor contact in main fan motor connector.
(NO) : Replace main fan motor with a new one.

SB1089600045030X

Fig. 2   Radiator main fan motor power & ground circuit diagnosis (Part 3 of 3). 1996 Impreza

B: LO MODE OPERATION (WITH A/C MODEL)
CONDITION:
Condition (1) :
● Engine coolant temperature is below 89°C (192°F).
● A/C switch is turned ON.
● Vehicle speed is below 10 km/h (6 MPH).
Condition (2) :
● Engine coolant temperature is above 95°C (203°F).
● A/C switch is turned OFF.
● Vehicle speed is below 10 km/h (6 MPH).

TROUBLE SYMPTOM:
● Radiator main fan does not rotate at LO speed under conditions (1) and (2) above.

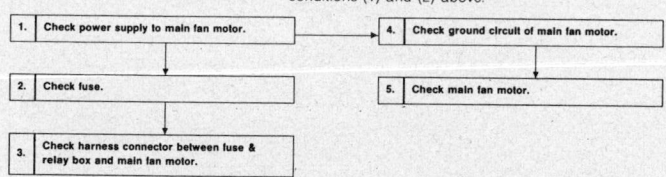

Fig. 3 **Radiator main fan motor Loo mode diagnosis (Part 1 of 4). 1996 Impreza**

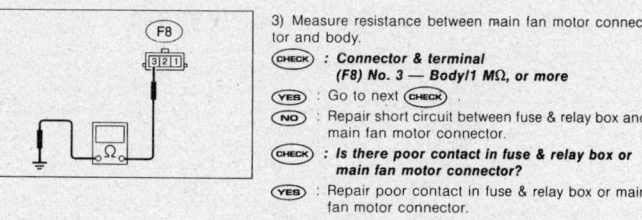

3) Measure resistance between main fan motor connector and body.
(CHECK) : *Connector & terminal*
(F8) No. 3 — Body/1 MΩ, or more
(YES) : Go to next **(CHECK)** .
(NO) : Repair short circuit between fuse & relay box and main fan motor connector.
(CHECK) : *Is there poor contact in fuse & relay box or main fan motor connector?*
(YES) : Repair poor contact in fuse & relay box or main fan motor connector.
(NO) : **Perform** "On-Board Diagnostics II System" diagnostics procedure.

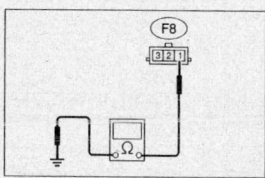

| 4 | **CHECK GROUND CIRCUIT OF MAIN FAN MOTOR.** |

1) Turn ignition switch to OFF.
2) Measure resistance between main fan motor connector and body.
(CHECK) : *Connector & terminal*
(F8) No. 1 — Body/5 Ω, or less
(YES) : Go to next **(CHECK)** .
(NO) : Repair open circuit of harness between main fan motor connector and body.
(CHECK) : *Is there poor contact in main fan motor connector?*
(YES) : Repair poor contact in main fan motor connector.
(NO) : Go to step 5.

SB1089600046030X

Fig. 3 **Radiator main fan motor Loo mode diagnosis (Part 3 of 4). 1996 Impreza**

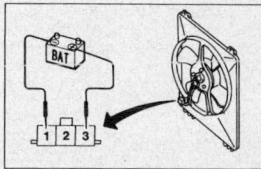

| 5 | **CHECK MAIN FAN MOTOR.** |

1) Turn ignition switch to OFF.
2) Disconnect connector from main fan motor.
(CHECK) : *Does the main fan rotate at LO speed while connecting battery positive (+) terminal to terminal No. 3, and connecting battery negative (–) terminal to terminal No. 1 of main fan motor connector?*
(YES) : Repair poor contact in main fan motor connector.
(NO) : Replace main fan motor with a new one.

SB1089600046040X

Fig. 3 **Radiator main fan motor Loo mode diagnosis (Part 4 of 4). 1996 Impreza**

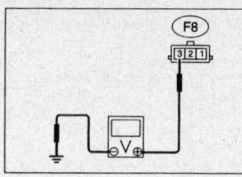

| 1 | **CHECK POWER SUPPLY TO MAIN FAN MOTOR.** |

CAUTION:
Be careful not to overheat engine during repair.
1) Turn ignition switch to OFF.
2) Disconnect connector from main fan motor.
3) Warm-up the engine until engine coolant temperature increases over 95°C (203°F).
4) Stop the engine and turn ignition switch to ON.
5) Turn A/C switch to OFF.
6) Measure voltage between main fan motor connector and body.
(CHECK) : *Connector & terminal*
(F8) No. 3 — Body/10 V, or more
(YES) : Go to step 4.
(NO) : Go to step 2.

| 2 | **CHECK FUSE.** |

1) Turn ignition switch to OFF.
2) Remove fuse No. 13 from fuse & relay box.
3) Check condition of fuse.
(CHECK) : *Is the fuse blown-out?*
(YES) : Replace fuse.
(NO) : Go to step 3.

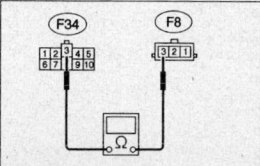

| 3 | **CHECK HARNESS CONNECTOR BETWEEN FUSE & RELAY BOX AND MAIN FAN MOTOR.** |

1) Disconnect connector from fuse & relay box.
2) Measure resistance of harness connector between fuse & relay box and main fan motor.
(CHECK) : *Connector & terminal*
(F34) No. 3 — (F8) No. 3/1 Ω, or less
(YES) : Go to next step.
(NO) : In this case, repair open circuit of harness between fuse & relay box and main fan motor connector.

SB1089600046020X

Fig. 3 **Radiator main fan motor Loo mode diagnosis (Part 2 of 4). 1996 Impreza**

C: HI MODE OPERATION (WITH A/C MODEL)
CONDITION:
Condition (1) :
● Engine coolant temperature is below 89°C (192°F).
● A/C switch is turned ON.
● Vehicle speed is over 20 km/h (12 MPH).
Condition (2) :
● Engine coolant temperature is above 95°C (203°F).
● A/C switch is turned OFF.
● Vehicle speed is over 20 km/h (12 MPH).
Condition (3) :
● Engine coolant temperature is above 95°C (203°F).
● A/C switch is turned ON.

TROUBLE SYMPTOM:
● Radiator main fan does not rotate at HI speed under conditions (1), (2) and (3) above.

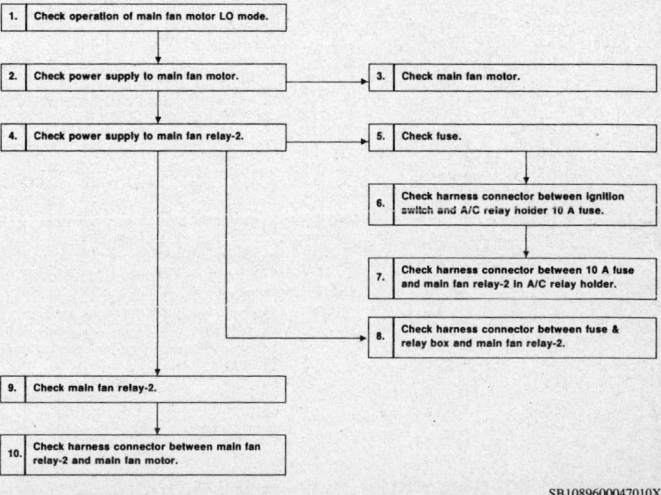

SB1089600047010X

Fig. 4 **Radiator main fan motor Hi mode diagnosis (Part 1 of 7). 1996 Impreza**

1 | CHECK OPERATION OF MAIN FAN MOTOR LO MODE.

CAUTION:
Be careful not to overheat engine during repair.
1) Warm-up the engine until engine coolant temperature increases over 95°C (203°F).
2) Stop the engine and turn ignition switch to ON.
3) Turn A/C switch to OFF.

(CHECK) : *Does the main fan operate at LO MODE?*
(YES) : Go to step 2.
(NO) : Go to LO MODE OPERATION diagnostics chart.

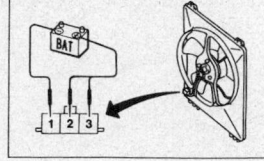

3 | CHECK MAIN FAN MOTOR.

1) Turn ignition switch to OFF.
2) Disconnect connector from main fan motor.

(CHECK) : *Does the main fan rotate at HI speed while connecting battery positive (+) terminal to terminals Nos. 2 and 3, and connecting battery negative (−) terminal to terminal No. 1 of main fan motor connector?*
(YES) : Repair poor contact in main fan motor connector.
(NO) : Replace main fan motor with a new one.

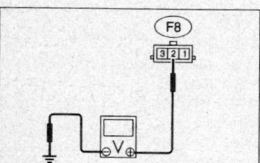

2 | CHECK POWER SUPPLY TO MAIN FAN MOTOR.

CAUTION:
Be careful not to overheat engine during repair.
1) Turn ignition switch to OFF.
2) Disconnect connector from main fan motor.
3) Warm-up the engine until engine coolant temperature increases over 95°C (203°F).
4) Stop the engine and turn ignition switch to ON.
5) Turn A/C switch to ON.
6) Measure voltage between main fan motor connector and body.

(CHECK) : *Connector & terminal*
(F8) No. 2 — Body/10 V, or more
(YES) : Go to step 3.
(NO) : Go to step 4.

SB1089600047020X

Fig. 4   Radiator main fan motor Hi mode diagnosis (Part 2 of 7). 1996 Impreza

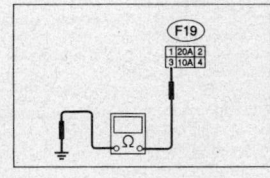

4 | CHECK POWER SUPPLY TO MAIN FAN RELAY-2.

1) Turn ignition switch to OFF.
2) Remove main fan relay-2 from A/C relay holder.
3) Turn ignition switch to ON.
4) Measure voltage between main fan relay-2 connector and body.

(CHECK) : *Connector & terminal*
(F21) No. 3 — Body/10 V, or more
(YES) : Go to next step.
(NO) : Go to step 5.

SB1089600047030X

Fig. 4   Radiator main fan motor Hi mode diagnosis (Part 3 of 7). 1996 Impreza

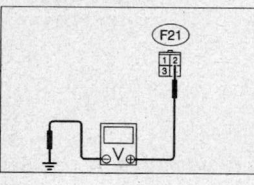

CAUTION:
Be careful not to overheat engine during repair.
5) Start and warm-up the engine until engine coolant temperature increases over 95°C (203°F).
6) Stop the engine and turn ignition switch to ON.
7) Turn A/C switch to ON.
8) Measure voltage between main fan relay-2 connector and body.

(CHECK) : *Connector & terminal (F21) No. 2 — Body/10 V, or more*
(YES) : Go to step 9.
(NO) : Go to step 8.

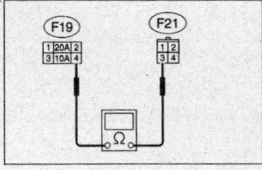

5) Measure resistance between A/C relay holder 10 A fuse connector and body.

(CHECK) : *Connector & terminal*
(F19) No. 3 — Body/1 MΩ, or more
(YES) : Go to next (CHECK)
(NO) : Repair short circuit between ignition switch and A/C relay holder 10 A fuse connector.

(CHECK) : *Is there poor contact in ignition switch or A/C relay holder 10 A fuse connector?*
(YES) : Repair poor contact in ignition switch or 10 A fuse connector.
(NO) : Go to step 7.

5 | CHECK FUSE.

1) Turn ignition switch to OFF.
2) Remove 10 A fuse from A/C relay holder.
3) Check condition of fuse.

(CHECK) : *Is the fuse blown-out?*
(YES) : Replace fuse.
(NO) : Go to step 6.

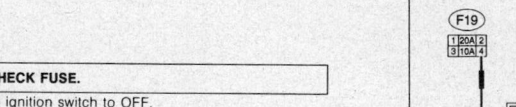

7 | CHECK HARNESS CONNECTOR BETWEEN 10 A FUSE AND MAIN FAN RELAY-2 IN A/C RELAY HOLDER.

1) Turn ignition switch to OFF.
2) Measure resistance of harness connector between 10 A fuse and main fan relay-2.

(CHECK) : *Connector & terminal*
(F19) No. 4 — (F21) No. 3/1 Ω, or less
(YES) : Go to next step.
(NO) : In this case, repair open circuit of harness between 10 A fuse and main fan relay-2 connector.

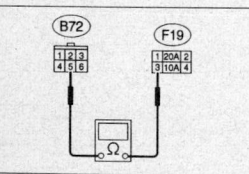

6 | CHECK HARNESS CONNECTOR BETWEEN IGNITION SWITCH AND A/C RELAY HOLDER 10 A FUSE.

1) Turn ignition switch to OFF.
2) Disconnect connector from ignition switch.
3) Disconnect connectors (F36) and (B35) from fuse & relay box.
4) Measure resistance of harness connector between ignition switch and A/C relay holder 10 A fuse.

(CHECK) : *Connector & terminal*
(B72) No. 5 — (F19) No. 3/1 Ω, or less
(YES) : Go to next step.
(NO) : In this case, repair the following items:
● Open circuit of harness between ignition switch connector and coupling connector (B49)
● Open circuit of harness between coupling connector (F30) and A/C relay holder 10 A fuse connector
● Poor contact in coupling connector (B49)

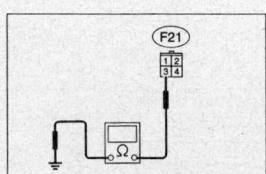

3) Measure resistance between main fan relay-2 connector and body.

(CHECK) : *Connector & terminal*
(F21) No. 3 — Body/1 MΩ, or more
(YES) : Repair poor contact in 10 A fuse or main fan relay-2 connector.
(NO) : Repair short circuit between 10 A fuse and main fan relay-2 connector.

SB1089600047050X

Fig. 4   Radiator main fan motor Hi mode diagnosis (Part 5 of 7). 1996 Impreza

SB1089600047040X

Fig. 4   Radiator main fan motor Hi mode diagnosis (Part 4 of 7). 1996 Impreza

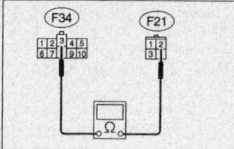

8　CHECK HARNESS CONNECTOR BETWEEN FUSE & RELAY BOX AND MAIN FAN RELAY-2.

1) Turn ignition switch to OFF.
2) Disconnect connector from fuse & relay box.
3) Measure resistance of harness connector between fuse & relay box and main fan relay-2.

(CHECK) : **Connector & terminal**
(F34) No. 3 — (F21) No. 2/1 Ω, or less

(YES) : Go to next step.

(NO) : In this case, repair open circuit of harness between fuse & relay box and main fan relay-2.

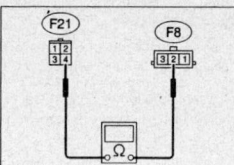

10　CHECK HARNESS CONNECTOR BETWEEN MAIN FAN RELAY-2 AND MAIN FAN MOTOR.

1) Turn ignition switch to OFF.
2) Measure resistance of harness connector between main fan relay-2 and main fan motor.

(CHECK) : **Connector & terminal**
(F21) No. 4 — (F8) No. 2/1 Ω, or less

(YES) : Go to next step.

(NO) : In this case, repair open circuit of harness between main fan relay-2 and main fan motor connector.

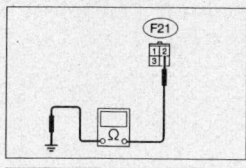

4) Measure resistance between main fan relay-2 connector and body.

(CHECK) : **Connector & terminal**
(F21) No. 2 — Body/1 MΩ, or more

(YES) : Repair poor contact in main fan relay-2 connector.

(NO) : Repair short circuit between fuse & relay box and main fan relay-2 connector.

9　CHECK MAIN FAN RELAY-2.

1) Turn ignition switch to OFF.
2) Remove main fan relay-2 from A/C relay holder.
3) Check continuity between main fan relay-2 terminals.

(CHECK) : ① Does continuity exist between terminals (2) and (4) while connecting battery to terminals (1) and (3)?
② Does no continuity exist between terminals (2) and (4) when battery is disconnected?

(YES) : Go to step 10.

(NO) : Replace main fan relay-2.

SB1089600047060X

Fig. 4　Radiator main fan motor Hi mode diagnosis (Part 6 of 7). 1996 Impreza

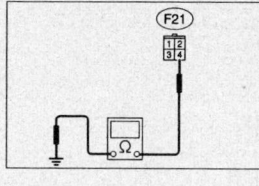

3) Measure resistance between main fan relay-2 connector and body.

(CHECK) : **Connector & terminal**
(F21) No. 4 — Body/1 MΩ, or more

(YES) : Go to next (CHECK) .

(NO) : Repair short circuit between main fan relay-2 and main fan motor connector.

(CHECK) : **Is there poor contact in main fan relay-2 or main fan motor connector?**

(YES) : Repair poor contact in main fan relay-2 or main fan motor connector.

(NO) : Perform "On-Board Diagnostics II System" diagnostics procedure.

SB1089600047070X

Fig. 4　Radiator main fan motor Hi mode diagnosis (Part 7 of 7). 1996 Impreza

DETECTING CONDITION:
● Engine coolant temperature is above 95°C (203°F).
TROUBLE SYMPTOM:
● Radiator main fan does not operate under the above condition.

1A1　CHECK POWER SUPPLY TO MAIN FAN MOTOR.

CAUTION:
Be careful not to overheat engine during repair.
1) Turn ignition switch to OFF.
2) Disconnect connector from main fan motor.
3) Warm-up the engine until engine coolant temperature increases over 95°C (203°F).
4) Stop the engine and turn ignition switch to ON.

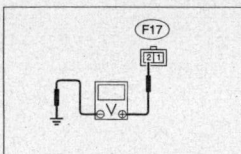

5) Measure voltage between main fan motor connector and chassis ground.
Connector & terminal
(F17) No. 2 (+) — Chassis ground (−):
(CHECK) : **Is the voltage more than 10 V?**
(YES) : Go to step 1A2.
(NO) : Go to step 1A5.

1A2　CHECK GROUND CIRCUIT OF MAIN FAN MOTOR.

1) Turn ignition switch to OFF.

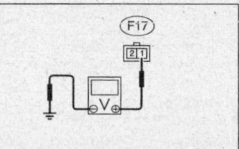

2) Measure resistance between main fan motor connector and chassis ground.
Connector & terminal
(F17) No. 1 — Chassis ground:
(CHECK) : **Is the resistance less than 5 Ω?**
(YES) : Go to step 1A3.
(NO) : Repair open circuit in harness between main fan motor connector and chassis ground.

SB1089600050010X

Fig. 5　Radiator main fan diagnosis (Part 1 of 4). 1997 Impreza less A/C

1A3　CHECK POOR CONTACT.

Check poor contact in main fan motor connector.

(CHECK) : **Is there poor contact in main fan motor connector?**

(YES) : Repair poor contact in main fan motor connector.

(NO) : Go to step 1A4.

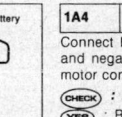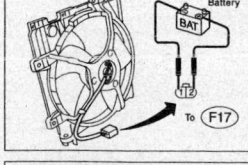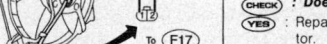

1A4　CHECK MAIN FAN MOTOR.

Connect battery positive (+) terminal to terminal No. 2 and negative (−) terminal to terminal No. 1 of main fan motor connector.

(CHECK) : **Does the main fan rotate?**

(YES) : Repair poor contact in main fan motor connector.

(NO) : Replace main fan motor with a new one.

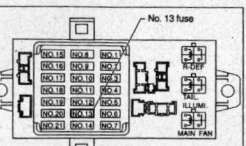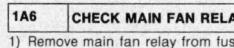

1A5　CHECK FUSE.

1) Turn ignition switch to OFF.
2) Remove fuse No. 13 from fuse and relay box.
3) Check condition of fuse.

(CHECK) : **Is the fuse blown-out?**

(YES) : Replace fuse.

(NO) : Go to step 1A6.

1A6　CHECK MAIN FAN RELAY.

1) Remove main fan relay from fuse and relay box.
2) Check continuity between main fan relay terminals.

(CHECK) : **Does no continuity exist between terminals No. 2 and No. 4?**

(YES) : Go to step 1A7.

(NO) : Replace main fan relay.

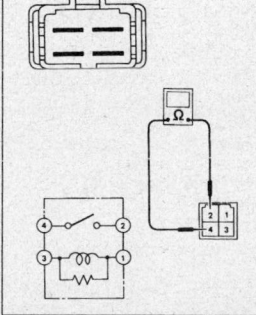

SB1089600050020X

Fig. 5　Radiator main fan diagnosis (Part 2 of 4). 1997 Impreza less A/C

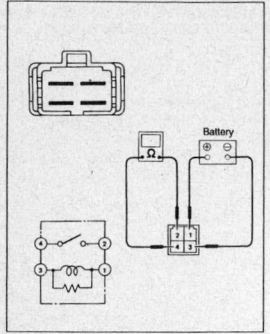

1A7	CHECK MAIN FAN RELAY.

1) Connect battery positive (+) terminal to terminal No. 1 of main fan relay, and negative (–) terminal to terminal No. 3.
2) Check continuity between main fan relay terminals.

CHECK : **Does continuity exist between terminals No. 2 and No. 4?**
YES : Go to step **1A8**.
NO : Replace main fan relay.

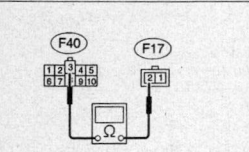

1A8	CHECK HARNESS CONNECTOR BETWEEN FUSE AND RELAY BOX AND MAIN FAN MOTOR.

1) Disconnect connector from fuse and relay box.
2) Measure resistance of harness connector between fuse and relay box and main fan motor.
Connector & terminal
(F40) No. 3 — (F17) No. 2:
CHECK : **Is the resistance less than 1 Ω?**
YES : Go to step **1A9**.
NO : Repair open circuit in harness between fuse and relay box and main fan motor connector.

1A9	CHECK POOR CONTACT.

Check poor contact in fuse and relay box connector.

CHECK : **Is there poor contact in fuse and relay box connector?**
YES : Repair poor contact in fuse and relay box connector.
NO : Go to step **1A10**.

SB1089600050030X

**Fig. 5   Radiator main fan diagnosis (Part 3 of 4).
1997 Impreza less A/C**

Condition (1):
● Engine coolant temperature is below 95°C (203°F).
● A/C switch is turned ON.
● Vehicle speed is below 19 km/h (12 MPH).
Condition (2):
● Engine coolant temperature is above 95°C (203°F).
● A/C switch is turned OFF.
● Vehicle speed is below 19 km/h (12 MPH).
TROUBLE SYMPTOM:
● Radiator main fan does not rotate under conditions (1) and (2) above.

1B1	CHECK POWER SUPPLY TO MAIN FAN MOTOR.

CAUTION:
Be careful not to overheat engine during repair.
1) Turn ignition switch to OFF.
2) Disconnect connector from main fan motor.
3) Warm-up the engine until engine coolant temperature increases over 95°C (203°F).
4) Stop the engine and turn ignition switch to ON.

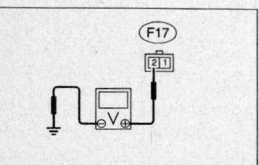

5) Measure voltage between main fan motor connector and chassis ground.
Connector & terminal
(F17) No. 2 (+) — Chassis ground (–):
CHECK : **Is the voltage more than 10 V?**
YES : Go to step **1B2**.
NO : Go to step **1B5**.

SB1089600051010X

**Fig. 6   Radiator main fan diagnosis (Part 1 of 4).
1997 Impreza with A/C**

1A10	CHECK POOR CONTACT.

Check poor contact in main fan motor connector.

CHECK : **Is there poor contact in main fan motor connector?**
YES : Repair poor contact in main fan motor connector.
NO : Probable cause is deterioration of multiple parts.

SB1089600050040X

**Fig. 5   Radiator main fan diagnosis (Part 4 of 4).
1997 Impreza less A/C**

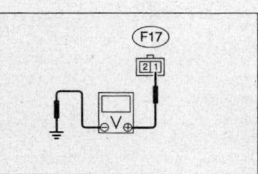

1B2	CHECK GROUND CIRCUIT OF MAIN FAN MOTOR.

1) Turn ignition switch to OFF.
2) Measure resistance between main fan motor connector and chassis ground.
Connector & terminal
(F17) No. 1 — Chassis ground:
CHECK : **Is the resistance less than 5 Ω?**
YES : Go to step **1B3**.
NO : Repair open circuit in harness between main fan motor connector and chassis ground.

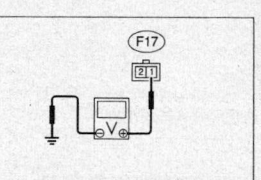

1B3	CHECK POOR CONTACT.

Check poor contact in main fan motor connector.

CHECK : **Is there poor contact in main fan motor connector?**
YES : Repair poor contact in main fan motor connector.
NO : Go to step **1B4**.

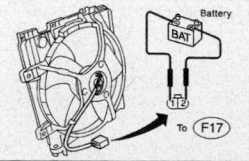

1B4	CHECK MAIN FAN MOTOR.

Connect battery positive (+) terminal to terminal No. 2, and negative (–) terminal to terminal No. 1 of main fan motor connector.
CHECK : **Does the main fan rotate?**
YES : Repair poor contact in main fan motor connector.
NO : Replace main fan motor with a new one.

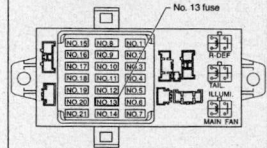

1B5	CHECK FUSE.

1) Turn ignition switch to OFF.
2) Remove fuse No. 13 from fuse and relay box.
3) Check condition of fuse.
CHECK : **Is the fuse blown-out?**
YES : Replace fuse.
NO : Go to step **1B6**.

SB1089600051020X

**Fig. 6   Radiator main fan diagnosis (Part 2 of 4).
1997 Impreza with A/C**

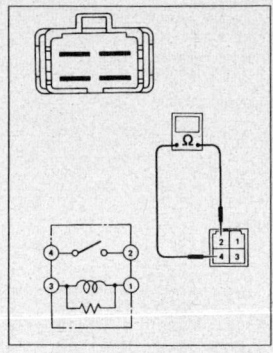

1B6 | **CHECK MAIN FAN RELAY.**

1) Remove main fan relay from fuse and relay box.
2) Check continuity between main fan relay terminals.

CHECK : **Does no continuity exist between terminals No. 2 and No. 4?**
YES : Go to step **1B7**.
NO : Replace main fan relay.

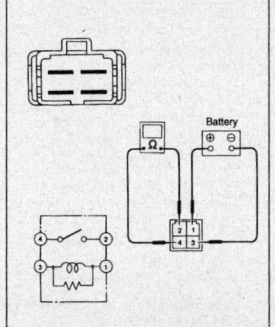

1B7 | **CHECK MAIN FAN RELAY.**

1) Connect battery to terminals No. 1 and No. 3 of main fan relay.
2) Check continuity between main fan relay terminals.

CHECK : **Does continuity exist between terminals No. 2 and No. 4?**
YES : Go to step **1B8**.
NO : Replace main fan relay.

SB1089600051030X

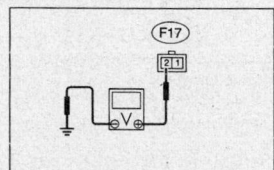

Fig. 6   Radiator main fan diagnosis (Part 3 of 4). 1997 Impreza with A/C

1B8 | **CHECK HARNESS CONNECTOR BETWEEN FUSE AND RELAY BOX AND MAIN FAN MOTOR.**

1) Disconnect connector from fuse and relay box.
2) Measure resistance of harness connector between fuse and relay box and main fan motor.

Connector & terminal
(F40) No. 3 — (F17) No. 2:
CHECK : *Is the resistance less than 1 Ω?*
YES : Go to step **1B9**.
NO : Repair open circuit in harness between fuse and relay box and main fan motor connector.

1B9 | **CHECK POOR CONTACT.**

Check poor contact in fuse and relay box connector.

CHECK : *Is there poor contact fuse and relay box connector?*
YES : Repair poor contact in fuse and relay box connector.
NO : Go to step **1B10**.

1B10 | **CHECK POOR CONTACT.**

Check poor contact in main fan motor connector.

CHECK : *Is there poor contact in main fan motor connector?*
YES : Repair poor contact in main fan motor connector.
NO : Probable cause is deterioration of multiple parts.

SB1089600051040X

Fig. 6   Radiator main fan diagnosis (Part 4 of 4). 1997 Impreza with A/C

DETECTING CONDITION:
● Engine coolant temperature is above 95°C (203°F).
● Vehicle speed is below 19 km/h (12 MPH).
TROUBLE SYMPTOM:
● Radiator main fan does not rotate under the above conditions.

2A1 | **CHECK POWER SUPPLY TO MAIN FAN MOTOR.**

CAUTION:
Be careful not to overheat engine during repair.

1) Turn ignition switch to OFF.
2) Disconnect connector from main fan motor.
3) Start the engine, and warm it up until engine coolant temperature increases over 95°C (203°F).
4) Stop the engine and turn ignition switch to ON.
5) Measure voltage between main fan motor connector and chassis ground.

Connector & terminal
(F17) No. 2 (+) — Chassis ground (−):

CHECK : *Is the voltage more than 10 V?*
YES : Go to step **2A2**.
NO : Go to step **2A5**.

2A2 | **CHECK GROUND CIRCUIT OF MAIN FAN MOTOR.**

1) Turn ignition switch to OFF.
2) Measure resistance between main fan motor connector and chassis ground.

Connector & terminal
(F17) No. 1 — Chassis ground:

CHECK : *Is the resistance less than 5 Ω?*
YES : Go to step **2A3**.
NO : Repair open circuit in harness between main fan motor connector and chassis ground.

2A3 | **CHECK POOR CONTACT.**

Check poor contact in main fan motor connector.

CHECK : *Is there poor contact in main fan motor connector?*
YES : Repair poor contact in main fan motor connector.
NO : Go to step **2A4**.

SB1089600053010X

Fig. 7   Radiator main fan diagnosis (Part 1 of 5). 1998-99 Impreza

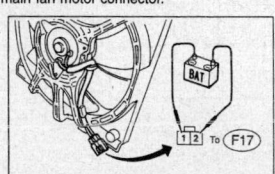

2A4 : | **CHECK MAIN FAN MOTOR.**

Connect battery positive (+) terminal to terminal No. 2, and negative (−) terminal to terminal No. 1 of main fan motor connector.

CHECK : *Does the main fan rotate?*
YES : Repair poor contact in main fan motor connector.
NO : Replace main fan motor with a new one.

2A5 | **CHECK POWER SUPPLY TO MAIN FAN RELAY.**

1) Turn ignition switch to OFF.
2) Remove main fan relay from A/C relay holder.
3) Measure voltage between main fan relay terminal and chassis ground.

Connector & terminal
(F66) No. 26 (+) — Chassis ground (−):

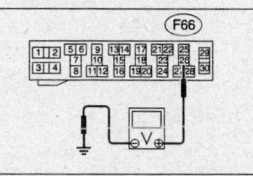

CHECK : *Is the voltage more than 10 V?*
YES : Go to step **2A6**.
NO : Go to step **2A7**.

2A6 : | **CHECK POWER SUPPLY TO MAIN FAN RELAY.**

1) Turn ignition switch to ON.
2) Measure voltage between main fan relay terminal and chassis ground.

Connector & terminal
(F66) No. 28 (+) — Chassis ground (−):

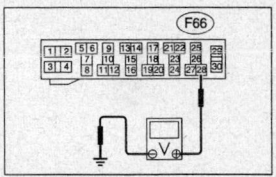

CHECK : *Is the voltage more than 10 V?*
YES : Go to step **2A16**.
NO : Go to step **2A12**.

2A7 : | **CHECK 20 A FUSE.**

1) Remove 20 A fuse from A/C relay holder.
2) Check condition of fuse.

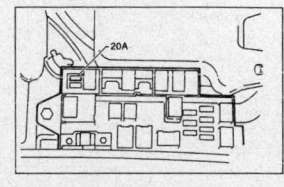

CHECK : *Is the fuse blown-out?*
YES : Replace fuse.
NO : Go to step **2A8**.

SB1089600053020X

Fig. 7   Radiator main fan diagnosis (Part 2 of 5). 1998-99 Impreza

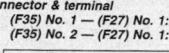

2A8 : CHECK HARNESS CONNECTOR BETWEEN MAIN FUSE BOX AND A/C RELAY HOLDER 20 A FUSE.

1) Disconnect connector from main fuse box.
2) Disconnect connectors (F25) and (F26) from generator, and (F34) from SBF holder.
3) Measure resistance of harness connector between main fuse box connector and A/C relay holder 20 A fuse terminals.

Connector & terminal
(F35) No. 1 — (F27) No. 1:
(F35) No. 2 — (F27) No. 1:

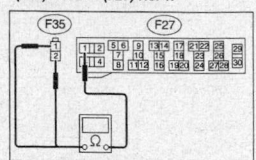

CHECK : *Is the resistance less than 1 Ω?*
YES : Go to step 2A9.
NO : Repair open circuit in harness between main fuse box connector and 20 A fuse terminal.

2A9 : CHECK POOR CONTACT.

Check poor contact in main fuse box connector.

CHECK : *Is there poor contact in main fuse box connector?*
YES : Repair poor contact in main fuse box connector.
NO : Go to step 2A10.

2A10 : CHECK POOR CONTACT.

Check poor contact in A/C relay holder 20 A fuse connector.

CHECK : *Is there poor contact in A/C relay holder 20 A fuse connector?*
YES : Repair poor contact in 20 A fuse.
NO : Go to step 2A11.

2A11 : CHECK HARNESS CONNECTOR BETWEEN 20 A FUSE AND MAIN FAN RELAY IN A/C RELAY HOLDER.

Measure resistance of harness between 20 A fuse and main fan relay terminal.

Connector & terminal
(F27) No. 2 — (F66) No. 26:

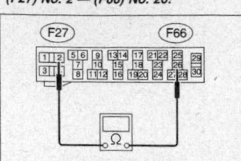

CHECK : *Is the resistance less than 1 Ω?*
YES : Repair poor contact in main fan relay connector.
NO : Repair open circuit in harness between 20 A fuse and main fan relay connector.

2A12 : CHECK FUSE.

1) Turn ignition switch to OFF.
2) Remove fuse No. 18 from joint box.
3) Check condition of fuse.

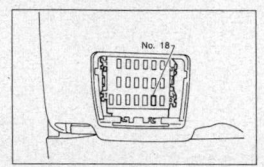

CHECK : *Is the fuse blown-out?*
YES : Replace fuse.
NO : Go to step 2A13.

SB1089600053030X

Fig. 7 Radiator main fan diagnosis (Part 3 of 5). 1998-99 Impreza

---

2A13 : CHECK HARNESS CONNECTOR BETWEEN IGNITION SWITCH AND JOINT BOX.

1) Disconnect connector from ignition switch.
2) Separate connectors (F44) and (B61).
3) Disconnect connector (B159) from joint box.
4) Measure resistance of harness between ignition switch connector and joint box.

Connector & terminal
(B72) No. 4 — (B159) No. 8:

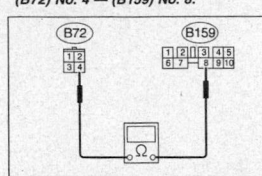

CHECK : *Is the resistance less than 1 Ω?*
YES : Go to step 2A14.
NO : Repair harness and connector.

NOTE:
In this case, repair the following:
● Open circuit in harness between ignition switch connector and joint box.
● Poor contact in coupling connector (B61).

2A14 : CHECK POOR CONTACT.

Check poor contact in ignition switch connector.

CHECK : *Is there poor contact in ignition switch connector?*
YES : Repair poor contact in ignition switch connector.
NO : Go to step 2A15.

2A15 : CHECK POOR CONTACT.

Check poor contact in joint box 10 A fuse connector.

CHECK : *Is there poor contact in joint box 10 A fuse connector?*
YES : Repair poor contact in joint box connector.
NO : Go to step 2A16.

2A16 : CHECK MAIN FAN RELAY.

1) Turn ignition switch to OFF.
2) Check continuity between main fan relay terminals.

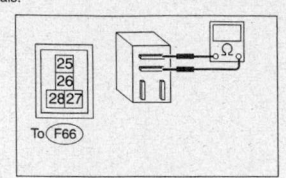

CHECK : *Does no continuity exist between terminals No. 25 and No. 26?*
YES : Go to step 2A17.
NO : Replace main fan relay.

2A17 : CHECK MAIN FAN RELAY.

1) Connect battery to terminals No. 27 and No. 28 of main fan relay.
2) Check continuity between main fan relay terminals.

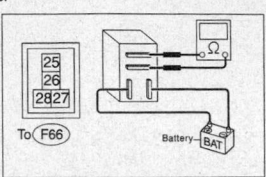

CHECK : *Does continuity exist between terminals No. 25 and No. 26?*
YES : Go to step 2A18.
NO : Replace main fan relay.

SB1089600053040X

Fig. 7 Radiator main fan diagnosis (Part 4 of 5). 1998-99 Impreza

---

2A18 : CHECK HARNESS CONNECTOR BETWEEN MAIN FAN RELAY AND MAIN FAN MOTOR.

Measure resistance of harness between main fan motor connector and main fan relay terminal.

Connector & terminal
(F17) No. 2 — (F66) No. 25:

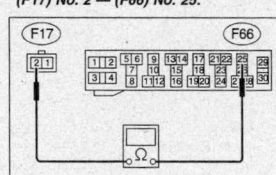

CHECK : *Is the resistance less than 1 Ω?*
YES : Go to step 2A19.
NO : Repair open circuit in harness between main fan motor and main fan relay connector.

2A19 : CHECK POOR CONTACT.

Check poor contact in main fan relay connector.

CHECK : *Is there poor contact in main fan relay connector?*
YES : Repair poor contact in main fan relay connector.
NO : Go to step 2A20.

2A20 : CHECK POOR CONTACT.

Check poor contact in main fan relay connector.

CHECK : *Is there poor contact in main fan motor connector?*
YES : Repair poor contact in main fan motor connector.
NO : Probable cause is deterioration of multiple parts.

SB1089600053050X

Fig. 7 Radiator main fan diagnosis (Part 5 of 5). 1998-99 Impreza

---

BI: DTC P1500 — RADIATOR FAN RELAY 1 CIRCUIT MALFUNCTION (FAN — 1) —

DTC DETECTING CONDITION:
● Two consecutive trips with fault

TROUBLE SYMPTOM:
● Radiator fan does not operate properly.
● Overheating

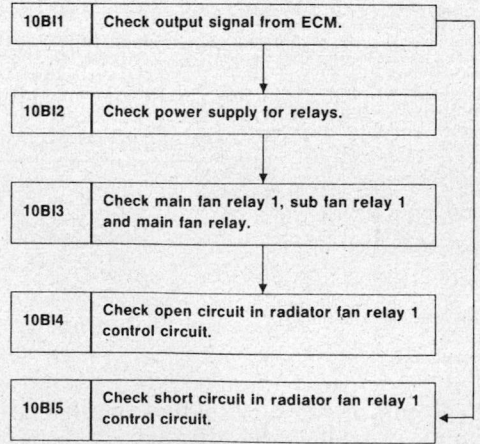

SB1089600055010X

Fig. 8 DTC P1500: Radiator Fan Circuit Malfunction (Part 1 of 6). 1996 Legacy

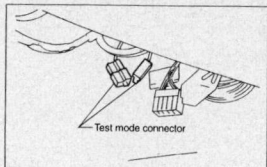

10BI1 | CHECK OUTPUT SIGNAL FROM ECM.

1) Turn ignition switch to OFF.
2) Connect test mode connector at the lower portion of instrument panel (on the driver's side), to the side of the center console box.
3) Turn ignition switch to ON.

Test mode connector

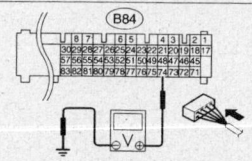

4) Measure voltage between ECM and chassis ground.
(CHECK) : **Connector & terminal (B84) No. 74 (+) — Chassis ground: Is the voltage more than 10 V?**
(YES) : Go to step **10BI5**.
(NO) : Go to step **10BI2**.

SB1089600055020X

Fig. 8   DTC P1500: Radiator Fan Circuit Malfunction (Part 2 of 6). 1996 Legacy

10BI2 | CHECK POWER SUPPLY FOR RELAYS.

Turn ignition switch to OFF.
(CHECK) : **Is the fuse in power supply circuit broken?**
(YES) : Replace the fuse.
(NO) : Go to step **10BI3**.

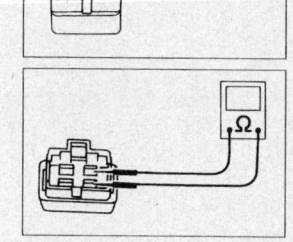

10BI3 | CHECK MAIN FAN RELAY 1, SUB FAN RELAY 1 AND MAIN FAN RELAY.

1) Remove main fan relay 1. (With A/C models only)
2) Measure resistance between main fan relay 1 terminals.
(CHECK) : **Terminal No. 1 — No. 3: Is the resistance between 87 and 107 Ω?**
(YES) : Go to next step 3).
(NO) : Replace main fan relay 1.

3) Remove sub fan relay 1. (With A/C models only)
Remove main fan relay. (Without A/C models only)
4) Measure resistance between sub fan relay 1 or main fan relay terminals.
(CHECK) : **Terminal No. 1 — No. 3: Is the resistance between 83 and 117 Ω?**
(YES) : Go to step **10BI4**.
(NO) : Replace sub fan relay 1.

SB1089600055030X

Fig. 8   DTC P1500: Radiator Fan Circuit Malfunction (Part 3 of 6). 1996 Legacy

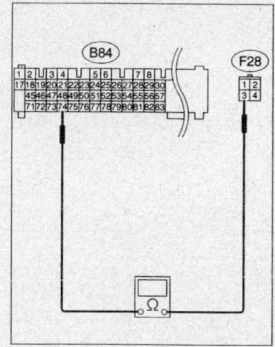

10BI4 | CHECK OPEN CIRCUIT IN RADIATOR FAN RELAY 1 CONTROL CIRCUIT.

1) Disconnect connector from ECM.
2) Disconnect connector from sub fan relay 1 or main fan relay.
3) Measure resistance of harness between ECM and main fan relay 1 connector.
NOTE:
With A/C models only.
(CHECK) : **Connector & terminal (B84) No. 74 — (F28) No. 3: Is the resistance less than 1 Ω?**
(YES) : Go to next (CHECK).
(NO) : Repair open circuit in harness between ECM and main fan relay 1 connector.
(CHECK) : **Is there poor contact in ECM or main fan relay 1 connector?**
(YES) : Repair poor contact in ECM or main fan relay 1 connector.
(NO) : Go to next step 4).

4) Measure resistance of harness between ECM and sub fan relay 1 (with A/C models) or main fan relay (without A/C models) connector.
(CHECK) : **Connector & terminal (B84) No. 74 — (F40) No. 4: Is the resistance less than 1 Ω?**
(YES) : Go to next (CHECK).
(NO) : Repair open circuit in harness between ECM and sub fan relay 1 (with A/C models) or main fan relay (without A/C models) connector.
(CHECK) : **Is there poor contact in ECM or sub fan relay 1 (with A/C models) and main fan relay (without A/C models) connector?**
(YES) : Repair poor contact in ECM or sub fan relay 1 (with A/C models) or main fan relay (without A/C models) connector.
(NO) : Go to next step 5) (with A/C models) or step 6) (without A/C models).

SB1089600055040X

Fig. 8   DTC P1500: Radiator Fan Circuit Malfunction (Part 4 of 6). 1996 Legacy

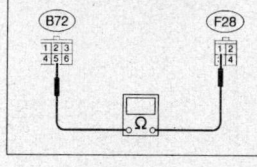

5) Measure resistance of harness between main fan relay 1 and ignition switch connector.
NOTE:
With A/C models only.
(CHECK) : **Connector & terminal (F28) No. 1 — (F72) No. 5: Is the resistance less than 1 Ω?**
(YES) : Go to next (CHECK).
(NO) : Repair open circuit in harness between main fan relay 1 and ignition switch connector.
(CHECK) : **Is there poor contact in main fan relay 1 or ignition switch connector?**
(YES) : Repair main fan relay 1 or ignition switch connector.
(NO) : Go to next step 6).

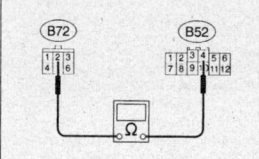

6) Measure resistance of harness between sub fan relay 1 (with A/C models) or main fan relay (without A/C models) and ignition switch connector.
(CHECK) : **Connector & terminal (B52) No. 4 — (F72) No. 2: Is the resistance less than 1 Ω?**
(YES) : Go to next (CHECK).
(NO) : Repair open circuit in harness between sub fan relay 1 (with A/C models) or main fan relay (without A/C models) and ignition switch connector.
(CHECK) : **Is there poor contact in sub fan relay 1 (with A/C models) or main fan relay (without A/C models) or ignition switch connector?**
(YES) : Repair poor contact in sub fan relay 1 (with A/C models) or main fan relay (without A/C models) or ignition switch connector.
(NO) : Replace ECM.

SB1089600055050X

Fig. 8   DTC P1500: Radiator Fan Circuit Malfunction (Part 5 of 6). 1996 Legacy

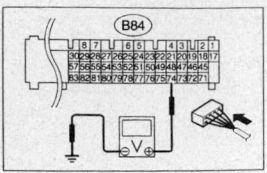

10BI5	CHECK SHORT CIRCUIT IN RADIATOR FAN RELAY 1 CONTROL CIRCUIT.

1) Turn ignition switch to OFF.
2) Remove main fan relay 1 and sub fan relay 1. (with A/C models)
   Remove main fan relay. (without A/C models)
3) Disconnect test mode connector.
4) Turn ignition switch to ON.
5) Measure voltage between ECM and chassis ground.

CHECK : **Connector & terminal**
(B84) No. 74 (+) — Chassis ground (–):
Is the voltage more than 10 V?

YES : Repair short circuit in radiator fan relay 1 control circuit and replace ECM.

NO : Go to next CHECK .

CHECK : **Is there poor contact in ECM connector?**

YES : Repair poor contact in ECM connector.

NO : Replace ECM.

SB1089600055060X

Fig. 8   DTC P1500: Radiator Fan Circuit Malfunction (Part 6 of 6). 1996 Legacy

CT: DTC P1500
— RADIATOR FAN RELAY 1 CIRCUIT LOW INPUT —

DTC DETECTING CONDITION:

● Two consecutive driving cycles with fault

TROUBLE SYMPTOM:

● Radiator fan does not operate properly.
● Overheating

SB1089700057010X

Fig. 10   DTC P1500: Radiator Fan Relay 1 Circuit Low Input (Part 1 of 6). 1997 Legacy

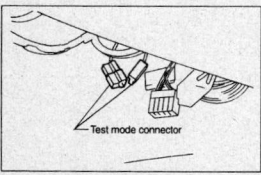

10CT1	CHECK OUTPUT SIGNAL FROM ECM.

1) Turn ignition switch to OFF.
2) Connect test mode connector at the lower portion of instrument panel (on the driver's side), to the side of the center console box.
3) Turn ignition switch to ON.

4) Measure voltage between ECM and chassis ground.

CHECK : **Connector & terminal**
(B84) No. 74 (+) — Chassis ground:
Does voltage change between 0 and 10 volts?

NOTE:
Radiator fan relay operation check can be executed using Subaru Select Monitor (Function mode: FD03).

YES : Repair poor contact in ECM connector.

NO : Go to step **10CT2.**

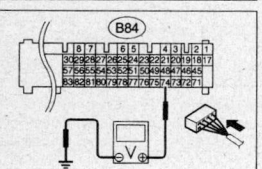

10CT2	CHECK GROUND SHORT CIRCUIT IN RADIATOR FAN RELAY 1 CONTROL CIRCUIT.

1) Turn ignition switch to OFF.
2) Disconnect connectors from ECM.
3) Measure resistance of harness between ECM connector and chassis ground.

CHECK : **Connector & terminal**
(B84) No. 74 — Chassis ground:
Is the resistance less than 10 Ω?

YES : Repair ground short circuit in radiator fan relay 1 control circuit.

NO : Go to step **10CT3.**

SB1089700057020X

Fig. 10   DTC P1500: Radiator Fan Relay 1 Circuit Low Input (Part 2 of 6). 1997 Legacy

BJ: DTC P1502
— RADIATOR FAN FUNCTION PROBLEM (FAN — F) —

DTC DETECTING CONDITION:

● Two consecutive trips with fault

TROUBLE SYMPTOM:

● Occurrence of noise
● Overheating

10BJ1	Check any other DTC (beside DTC P1502) on display.

NOTE:
If the vehicle, with the engine idling, is placed very close to a wall or another vehicle, preventing normal cooling function, the OBD system may detect malfunction.

10BJ1	CHECK ANY OTHER DTC (BESIDE DTC P1502) ON DISPLAY.

CHECK : **Is there any other DTC on display?**

YES : Inspect the relevant DTC

NO : Check engine cooling system.

SB1089600056000X

Fig. 9   DTC P1502: Radiator Fan Function Problem. 1996 Legacy

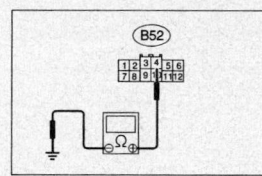

10CT3	CHECK POWER SUPPLY FOR RELAY.

1) Disconnect connector (B52) from fuse and relay box (F/B).
2) Turn ignition switch to ON.
3) Measure voltage between fuse and relay box (F/B) connector and chassis ground.

CHECK : **Connector & terminal**
(B52) No. 4 (+) — Chassis ground (–):
Is the voltage more than 10 V?

YES : Go to step **10CT4.**

NO : Repair open circuit in harness between ignition switch and fuse and relay box (F/B) connector.

10CT4	CHECK VEHICLE MODEL.

CHECK : **Is the vehicle equipped with A/C?**

YES : Go to step **10CT5.**

NO : Go to step **10CT6.**

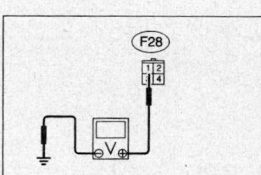

10CT5	CHECK POWER SUPPLY FOR MAIN FAN RELAY 1.

1) Turn ignition switch to OFF.
2) Connect connector (B52) to fuse and relay box (F/B).
3) Remove main fan relay 1.
4) Turn ignition switch to ON.
5) Measure voltage between main fan relay 1 connector and chassis ground.

CHECK : **Connector & terminal**
(F28) No. 1 (+) — Chassis ground (–):
Is the voltage more than 10 V?

YES : Go to step **10CT6.**

NO : Repair open circuit in harness between fuse and relay box (F/B) and main fan relay 1 connector.

SB1089700057030X

Fig. 10   DTC P1500: Radiator Fan Relay 1 Circuit Low Input (Part 3 of 6). 1997 Legacy

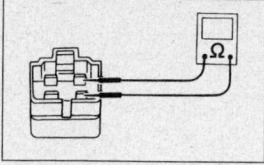

| 10CT6 | CHECK MAIN FAN RELAY 1, SUB FAN RELAY 1 AND MAIN FAN RELAY. |

1) Turn ignition switch to OFF.
2) Measure resistance between main fan relay 1 terminals. (With A/C models only)

(CHECK) : **Terminal**
No. 1 — No. 3:
Is the resistance between 87 and 107 Ω?

(YES) : Go to next step 3).

(NO) : Replace main fan relay 1.

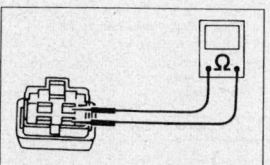

3) Remove sub fan relay 1. (With A/C models only)
Remove main fan relay. (Without A/C models only)
4) Measure resistance between sub fan relay 1 or main fan relay terminals.

(CHECK) : **Terminal**
No. 1 — No. 3:
Is the resistance between 83 and 117 Ω?

(YES) : Go to step **10CT7**.

(NO) : Replace sub fan relay 1.

SB1089700057040X

Fig. 10   DTC P1500: Radiator Fan Relay 1 Circuit Low Input (Part 4 of 6). 1997 Legacy

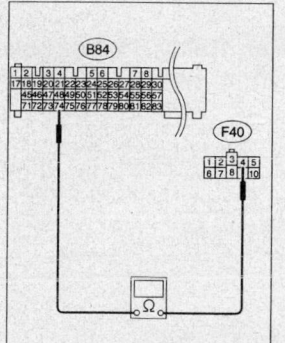

3) Measure resistance of harness between ECM and sub fan relay 1 (with A/C models) or main fan relay (without A/C models) connector.

(CHECK) : **Connector & terminal**
(B84) No. 74 — (F40) No. 4:
Is the resistance less than 1 Ω?

(YES) : Go to next (CHECK)

(NO) : Repair harness and connector.

NOTE:
In this case, repair the following:
● Open circuit in harness between ECM and sub fan relay 1 (with A/C models) or main fan relay (without A/C models) connector
● Poor contact in coupling connector (F45)
● Replace diode (A/C)

(CHECK) : **Is there poor contact in ECM or sub fan relay 1 (with A/C models) or main fan relay (without A/C models) connector?**

(YES) : Repair poor contact in ECM or sub fan relay 1 (with A/C models) or main fan relay (without A/C models) connector.

(NO) : probable cause is deterioration of multiple parts.

SB1089700057060X

Fig. 10   DTC P1500: Radiator Fan Relay 1 Circuit Low Input (Part 6 of 6). 1997 Legacy

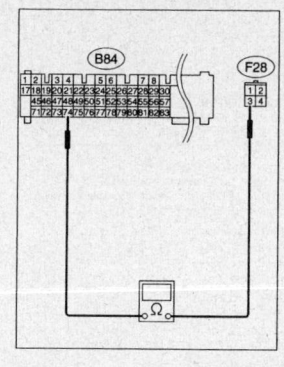

| 10CT7 | CHECK OPEN CIRCUIT IN RADIATOR FAN RELAY 1 CONTROL CIRCUIT. |

1) Disconnect connector (F40) from fuse and relay box (F/B).
2) Measure resistance of harness between ECM and main fan relay 1 connector.
NOTE:
With A/C models only.

(CHECK) : **Connector & terminal**
(B84) No. 74 — (F28) No. 3:
Is the resistance less than 1 Ω?

(YES) : Go to next (CHECK) .

(NO) : Repair harness and connector.
NOTE:
In this case, repair the following:
● Open circuit in harness between ECM and main fan relay 1 connector
● Poor contact in coupling connector (F45)

(CHECK) : **Is there poor contact in ECM or main fan relay 1 connector?**

(YES) : Repair poor contact in ECM or main fan relay 1 connector.

(NO) : Go to next step 3).

SB1089700057050X

Fig. 10   DTC P1500: Radiator Fan Relay 1 Circuit Low Input (Part 5 of 6). 1997 Legacy

CU: DTC P1502
— RADIATOR FAN FUNCTION PROBLEM —

DTC DETECTING CONDITION:
● Two consecutive driving cycles with fault

TROUBLE SYMPTOM:
● Occurrence of noise
● Overheating

NOTE:
If the vehicle, with the engine idling, is placed very close to a wall or another vehicle, preventing normal cooling function, the OBD system may detect malfunction.

| 10CU1 | CHECK ANY OTHER DTC (BESIDE DTC P1502) ON DISPLAY. |

(CHECK) : **Is there any other DTC on display?**

(YES) : Inspect the relevant DTC using "10. Diagnostics Chart with Trouble Code".

(NO) : Check engine cooling system.

SB1089700058000X

Fig. 11   DTC P1502: Radiator Fan Function Problem. 1997 Legacy

- **DTC DETECTING CONDITION:**
  - Two consecutive driving cycles with fault
- **TROUBLE SYMPTOM:**
  - Radiator fan does not operate properly.
  - Overheating

10BC1 : CHECK OUTPUT SIGNAL FROM ECM.

1) Turn ignition switch to OFF.
2) Connect test mode connector at the lower portion of instrument panel (on the driver's side), to the side of the center console box.

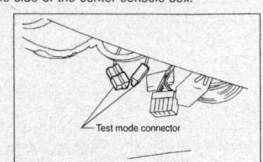

Test mode connector

3) Turn ignition switch to ON.
4) Measure voltage between ECM and chassis ground.

NOTE:
Radiator fan relay operation check can be executed using Subaru Select Monitor. For procedure, refer to "COMPULSORY VALVE OPERATION CHECK MODE".

Connector & terminal
(B84) No. 74 (+) — Chassis ground:

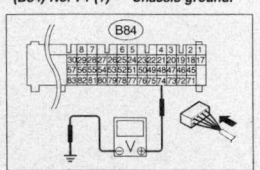

CHECK : *Does voltage change between 0 and 10 volts?*
YES : Repair poor contact in ECM connector.
NO : Go to step **10BC2**.

10BC2 : CHECK GROUND SHORT CIRCUIT IN RADIATOR FAN RELAY 1 CONTROL CIRCUIT.

1) Turn ignition switch to OFF.
2) Disconnect connectors from ECM.
3) Measure resistance of harness between ECM connector and chassis ground.

Connector & terminal
(B84) No. 74 — Chassis ground:

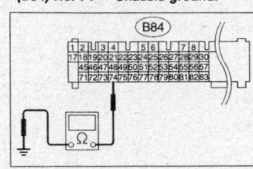

CHECK : *Is the resistance less than 10 Ω?*
YES : Repair ground short circuit in radiator fan relay 1 control circuit.
NO : Go to step **10BC3**.

SB1089800059010X

Fig. 12 DTC P0480: Cooling Fan Relay Circuit Low Input (Part 1 of 4). 1998-99 Legacy

10BC3 : CHECK POWER SUPPLY FOR RELAY.

1) Disconnect connector (B52) from fuse and relay box (F/B).
2) Turn ignition switch to ON.
3) Measure voltage between fuse and relay box (F/B) connector and chassis ground.

Connector & terminal
(B52) No. 4 (+) — Chassis ground (−):

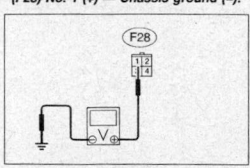

CHECK : *Is the voltage more than 10 V?*
YES : Go to step **10BC4**.
NO : Repair open circuit in harness between ignition switch and fuse and relay box (F/B) connector.

10BC4 : CHECK VEHICLE MODEL.

CHECK : *Is the vehicle equipped with A/C?*
YES : Go to step **10BC5**.
NO : Go to step **10BC8**.

10BC5 : CHECK POWER SUPPLY FOR MAIN FAN RELAY 1.

1) Turn ignition switch to OFF.
2) Connect connector (B52) to fuse and relay box (F/B).
3) Remove main fan relay 1.
4) Turn ignition switch to ON.
5) Measure voltage between main fan relay 1 connector and chassis ground.

Connector & terminal
(F28) No. 1 (+) — Chassis ground (−):

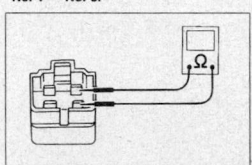

CHECK : *Is the voltage more than 10 V?*
YES : Go to step **10BC6**.
NO : Repair open circuit in harness between fuse and relay box (F/B) and main fan relay 1 connector.

10BC6 : CHECK MAIN FAN RELAY 1.

1) Turn ignition switch to OFF.
2) Measure resistance between main fan relay 1 terminals.

Terminal
No. 1 — No. 3:

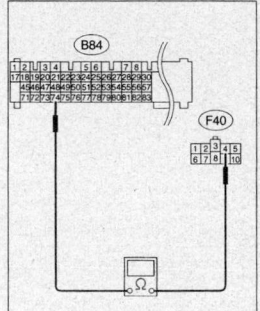

CHECK : *Is the resistance between 87 and 107 Ω?*
YES : Go to step **10BC7**.
NO : Replace main fan relay 1.

SB1089800059020X

Fig. 12 DTC P0480: Cooling Fan Relay Circuit Low Input (Part 2 of 4). 1998-99 Legacy

10BC7 : CHECK SUB FAN RELAY 1.

1) Remove sub fan relay 1.
2) Measure resistance between sub fan relay 1 or main fan relay terminals.

Terminal
No. 1 — No. 3:

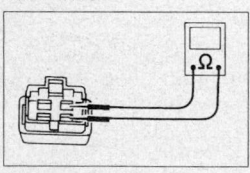

CHECK : *Is the resistance between 83 and 117 Ω?*
YES : Go to step **10BC9**.
NO : Replace sub fan relay 1.

10BC8 : CHECK MAIN FAN RELAY.

1) Remove main fan relay.
2) Measure resistance between sub fan relay 1 or main fan relay terminals.

Terminal
No. 1 — No. 3:

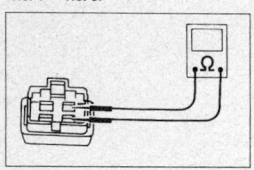

CHECK : *Is the resistance between 83 and 117 Ω?*
YES : Go to step **10BC13**.
NO : Replace main fan relay.

10BC9 : CHECK OPEN CIRCUIT IN RADIATOR FAN RELAY 1 CONTROL CIRCUIT.

1) Disconnect connector (F40) from fuse and relay box (F/B).
2) Measure resistance of harness between ECM and main fan relay 1 connector.

Connector & terminal
(B84) No. 74 — (F28) No. 3:

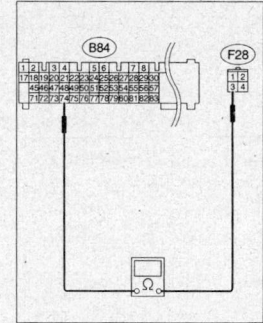

CHECK : *Is the resistance less than 1 Ω?*
YES : Go to step **10BC10**.
NO : Repair harness and connector.

NOTE:
In this case, repair the following:
- Open circuit in harness between ECM and main fan relay 1 connector
- Poor contact in coupling connector (F45)

10BC10 : CHECK POOR CONTACT.

Check poor contact in ECM or main fan relay 1 connector.

CHECK : *Is there poor contact in ECM or main fan relay 1 connector?*
YES : Repair poor contact in ECM or main fan relay 1 connector.
NO : Go to step **10BC11**.

SB1089800059030X

Fig. 12 DTC P0480: Cooling Fan Relay Circuit Low Input (Part 3 of 4). 1998-99 Legacy

10BC11 : CHECK OPEN CIRCUIT IN RADIATOR SUB FAN RELAY 1 CONTROL CIRCUIT.

Measure resistance of harness between ECM and sub fan relay 1 connector.

Connector & terminal
(B84) No. 74 — (F40) No. 4:

CHECK : *Is the resistance less than 1 Ω?*
YES : Go to step **10BC12**.
NO : Repair harness and connector.

NOTE:
In this case, repair the following:
- Open circuit in harness between ECM and sub fan relay 1 connector
- Poor contact in coupling connector (F45)
- Replace diode (A/C)

10BC12 : CHECK POOR CONTACT.

Check poor contact in ECM or sub fan relay 1 connector.

CHECK : *Is there poor contact in ECM or sub fan relay 1 connector?*
YES : Repair poor contact in ECM or sub fan relay 1 connector.
NO : probable cause is deterioration of multiple parts.

10BC13 : CHECK OPEN CIRCUIT IN RADIATOR MAIN FAN RELAY CONTROL CIRCUIT.

Measure resistance of harness between ECM and main fan relay connector.

Connector & terminal
(B84) No. 74 — (F40) No. 4:

CHECK : *Is the resistance less than 1 Ω?*
YES : Go to step **10BC14**.
NO : Repair harness and connector.

NOTE:
In this case, repair the following:
- Open circuit in harness between ECM and main fan relay connector
- Poor contact in coupling connector (F45)

10BC14 : CHECK POOR CONTACT.

Check poor contact in ECM or main fan relay connector.

CHECK : *Is there poor contact in ECM or main fan relay connector?*
YES : Repair poor contact in ECM or main fan relay connector.
NO : probable cause is deterioration of multiple parts.

SB1089800059040X

Fig. 12 DTC P0480: Cooling Fan Relay Circuit Low Input (Part 4 of 4). 1998-99 Legacy

COOLING FANS

- **DTC DETECTING CONDITION:**
  - Two consecutive driving cycles with fault
- **TROUBLE SYMPTOM:**
  - Occurrence of noise
  - Overheating

10BD1 : CHECK ANY OTHER DTC ON DISPLAY.

(CHECK) : *Is there any other DTC on display?*

(YES) : Inspect the relevant DTC using "10. Diagnostics Chart with Trouble Code for LHD   Vehicles".

(NO) : Check engine cooling system.

SB1089800060000X

Fig. 13 DTC P0483: Cooling Fan Function Problem. 1998-99 Legacy

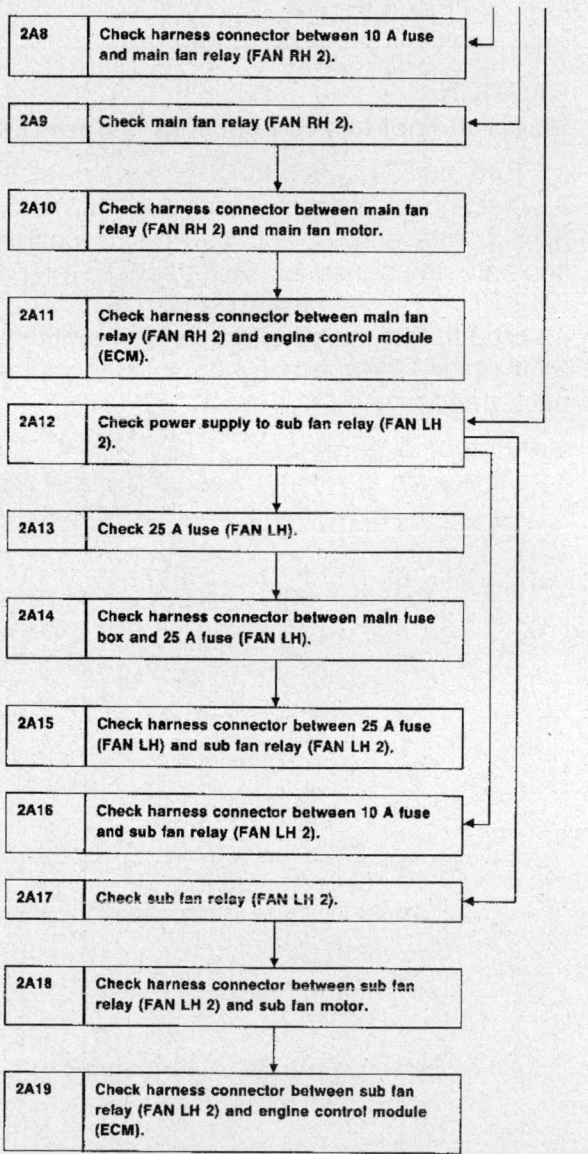

SB1089700041020X

Fig. 14 Radiator fan diagnosis, low mode, (Part 2 of 2). SVX

DEFECTING CONDITION

Condition (1):
- Engine coolant temperature is below 89°C (192°F).
- A/C switch is turned ON.
- Vehicle speed is less than 10 km/h (6 MPH).
- A/C intermediate pressure switch is turned OFF. [less than 1,275 ± 147 kPa (13.0 ± 1.5 kg/cm², 185 ± 21 psi).]

Condition (2):
- Engine coolant temperature is above 95°C (203°F).
- A/C switch is turned OFF.
- Vehicle speed is less than 10 km/h (6 MPH).

Condition (3):
- Engine coolant temperature is below 89°C (192°F).
- A/C switch is turned ON.
- Vehicle speed is more than 20 km/h (12 MPH).
- A/C intermediate pressure switch is turned OFF. [less than 1,275 ± 147 kPa (13.0 ± 1.5 kg/cm², 185 ± 21 psi).]

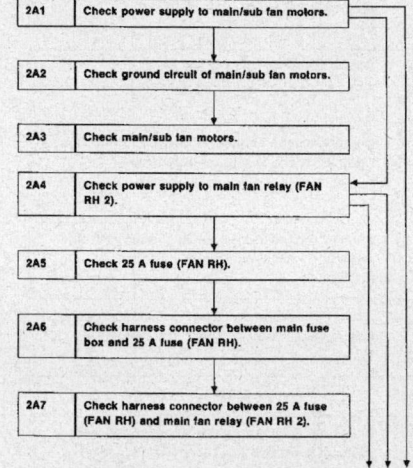

SB1089700041010X

Fig. 14 Radiator fan diagnosis, low mode, (Part 1 of 2). SVX

B: MEDIUM MODE OPERATION

DEFECTING CONDITION

Condition (1):
- Engine coolant temperature is below 89°C (192°F).
- A/C switch is turned ON.
- Vehicle speed is less than 10 km/h (6 MPH).
- A/C intermediate pressure switch is turned ON. [more than 1,569 ± 127 kPa (16.0 ± 1.3 kg/cm², 228 ± 18 psi).]

Condition (2):
- Engine coolant temperature is above 95°C (203°F).
- A/C switch is turned ON.
- Vehicle speed is less than 10 km/h (6 MPH).
- A/C intermediate pressure switch is turned OFF. [less than 1,275 ± 147 kPa (13.0 ± 1.5 kg/cm², 185 ± 21 psi).]

Condition (3):
- Engine coolant temperature is above 95°C (203°F).
- A/C switch is turned OFF.
- Vehicle speed is more than 20 km/h (12 MPH).

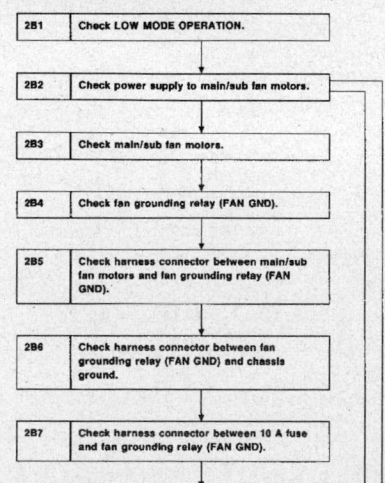

SB1089700042010X

Fig. 15 Radiator fan diagnosis medium mode, (Part 1 of 2). SVX

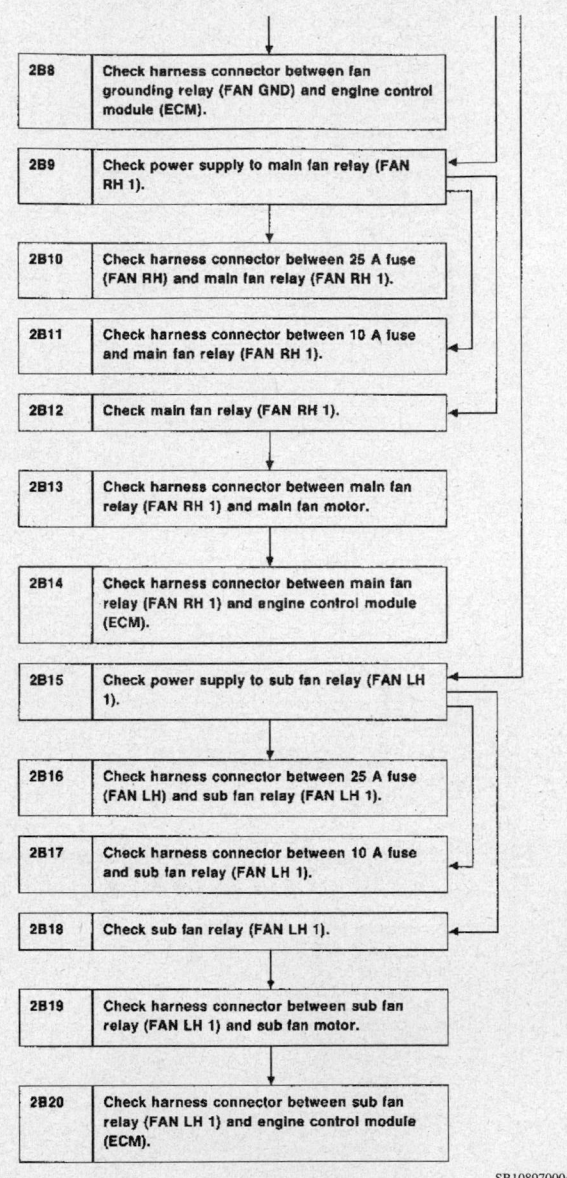

Fig. 15   Radiator fan diagnosis medium mode, (Part 2 of 2). SVX

C: HIGH MODE OPERATION

DEFECTING CONDITION

Condition (1):
- Engine coolant temperature is above 95°C (203°F).
- A/C switch is turned ON.
- Vehicle speed is less than 10 km/h (6 MPH).
- A/C intermediate pressure switch is turned ON. [more than 1,569 ± 127 kPa (16.0 ± 1.3 kg/cm², 228 ± 18 psi).]

Condition (2):
- Engine coolant temperature is below 89°C (192°F).
- A/C switch is turned ON.
- Vehicle speed is more than 20 km/h (12 MPH).
- A/C intermediate pressure switch is turned ON. [more than 1,569 ± 127 kPa (16.0 ± 1.3 kg/cm², 228 ± 18 psi).]

Condition (3):
- Engine coolant temperature is above 95°C (203°F).
- A/C switch is turned ON.
- Vehicle speed is more than 20 km/h (12 MPH).

2C1	Check LOW MODE/MEDIUM MODE OPERATIONS.

Fig. 16   Radiator fan diagnosis, high mode. SVX

DETECTING CONDITION:

Condition (1):
- Engine coolant temperature is below 95°C (203°F).
- A/C switch is turned ON.
- Vehicle speed is below 19 km/h (12 MPH).

Condition (2):
- Engine coolant temperature is above 100°C (212°F).
- A/C switch is turned OFF.
- Vehicle speed is below 19 km/h (12 MPH).

TROUBLE SYMPTOM:
- Radiator sub fan does not rotate under conditions (1) and (2) above.

3A1 :	CHECK POWER SUPPLY TO SUB FAN MOTOR.

CAUTION:
Be careful not to overheat engine during repair.

1) Turn ignition switch to OFF.
2) Disconnect connector from sub fan motor.
3) Start the engine, and warm it up until engine coolant temperature increases over 100°C (212°F).
4) Stop the engine and turn ignition switch to ON.
5) Measure voltage between sub fan motor connector and chassis ground.

Connector & terminal
(F16) No. 2 (+) — Chassis ground (–):

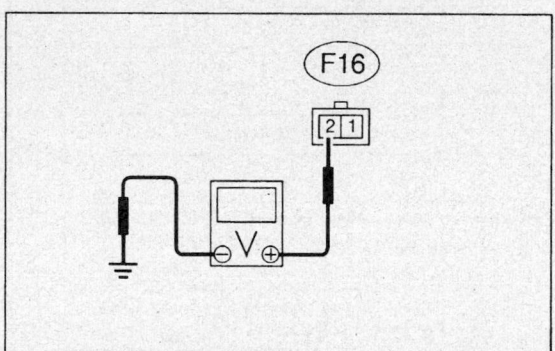

CHECK : *Is the voltage more than 10 V?*
YES : Go to step **3A2**.
NO : Go to step **3A5**.

Fig. 17   Radiator sub fan diagnosis (Part 1 of 5). Forester

3A2 : CHECK GROUND CIRCUIT OF SUB FAN MOTOR.

1) Turn ignition switch to OFF.
2) Measure resistance between sub fan motor connector and chassis ground.

Connector & terminal
(F16) No. 1 — Chassis ground:

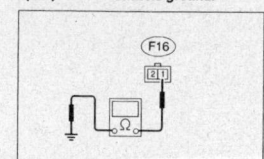

CHECK : **Is the resistance less than 5 Ω?**
YES : Go to step 3A3.
NO : Repair open circuit in harness between sub fan motor connector and chassis ground.

3A3 : CHECK POOR CONTACT.

Check poor contact in sub fan motor connector.

CHECK : **Is there poor contact in sub fan motor connector?**
YES : Repair poor contact in sub fan motor connector.
NO : Go to step 3A4.

3A4 : CHECK SUB FAN MOTOR.

Connect battery positive (+) terminal to terminal No. 2, and negative (–) terminal to terminal No. 1 of sub fan motor connector.

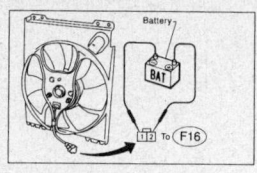

CHECK : **Does the sub fan rotate?**
YES : Repair poor contact in sub fan motor connector.
NO : Replace sub fan motor with a new one.

3A5 : CHECK POWER SUPPLY TO SUB FAN RELAY.

1) Turn ignition switch to OFF.
2) Remove sub fan relay from A/C relay holder.
3) Measure voltage between sub fan relay terminal and chassis ground.

Connector & terminal
(F28) No. 23 (+) — Chassis ground (–):

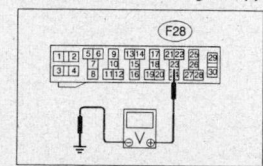

CHECK : **Is the voltage more than 10 V?**
YES : Go to step 3A6.
NO : Go to step 3A7.

SB1089800062020X

Fig. 17   Radiator sub fan diagnosis (Part 2 of 5). Forester

3A6 : CHECK POWER SUPPLY TO SUB FAN RELAY.

1) Turn ignition switch to ON.
2) Measure voltage between sub fan relay terminal and chassis ground.

Connector & terminal
(F28) No. 21 (+) — Chassis ground (–):

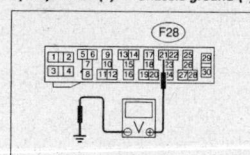

CHECK : **Is the voltage more than 10 V?**
YES : Go to step 3A16.
NO : Go to step 3A12.

3A7 : CHECK 20 A FUSE.

1) Remove 20 A fuse from A/C relay holder.
2) Check condition of fuse.

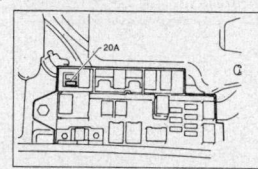

CHECK : **Is the fuse blown-out?**
YES : Replace fuse.
NO : Go to step 3A8.

3A8 : CHECK HARNESS CONNECTOR BETWEEN MAIN FUSE BOX AND A/C RELAY HOLDER 20 A FUSE.

1) Disconnect connector from main fuse box.
2) Disconnect connectors (F25) and (F26) from generator, and (F34) from SBF holder.
3) Measure resistance of harness connector between main fuse box connector and A/C relay holder 20 A fuse terminal.

Connector & terminal
(F35) No. 2 — (F27) No. 3:

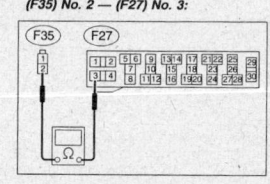

CHECK : **Is the resistance less than 1 Ω?**
YES : Go to step 3A9.
NO : Repair open circuit in harness between main fuse box connector and 20 A fuse terminal.

3A9 : CHECK POOR CONTACT.

Check poor contact in main fuse box connector.

CHECK : **Is there poor contact in main fuse box connector?**
YES : Repair poor contact in main fuse box connector.
NO : Go to step 3A10.

3A10 : CHECK POOR CONTACT.

Check poor contact in A/C relay holder 20 A fuse connector.

CHECK : **Is there poor contact in A/C relay holder 20 A fuse connector?**
YES : Repair poor contact in 20 A fuse
NO : Go to step 3A11.

SB1089800062030X

Fig. 17   Radiator sub fan diagnosis (Part 3 of 5). Forester

3A11 : CHECK HARNESS CONNECTOR BETWEEN 20 A FUSE AND SUB FAN RELAY IN A/C RELAY HOLDER.

Measure resistance of harness between 20 A fuse and sub fan relay terminal.

Connector & terminal
(F27) No. 4 — (F28) No. 23:

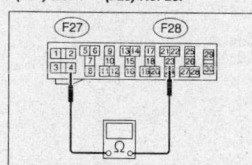

CHECK : **Is the resistance less than 1 Ω?**
YES : Repair poor contact in sub fan relay connector.
NO : Repair open circuit in harness between 20 A fuse and sub fan relay connector.

3A12 : CHECK FUSE.

1) Turn ignition switch to OFF.
2) Remove fuse No. 17 from joint box.
3) Check condition of fuse.

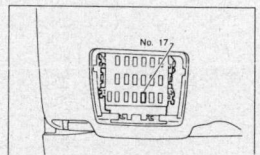

CHECK : **Is the fuse blown-out?**
YES : Replace fuse.
NO : Go to step 3A13.

3A13 : CHECK HARNESS CONNECTOR BETWEEN IGNITION SWITCH AND JOINT BOX.

1) Disconnect connector from ignition switch.
2) Separate connectors (F44) and (B61).
3) Disconnect connector (B159) from joint box.
4) Measure resistance of harness between ignition switch connector and joint box.

Connector & terminal
(B72) No. 4 — (B159) No. 8:

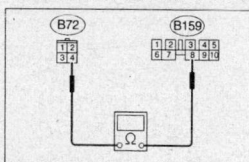

CHECK : **Is the resistance less than 1 Ω?**
YES : Go to step 3A14.
NO : Repair harness and connector.

NOTE:
In this case, repair the following:
● Open circuit in harness between ignition switch connector and joint box.
● Poor contact in coupling connector (B61).

3A14 : CHECK POOR CONTACT.

Check poor contact in ignition switch connector.

CHECK : **Is there poor contact in ignition switch connector?**
YES : Repair poor contact in ignition switch connector.
NO : Go to step 3A15.

3A15 : CHECK POOR CONTACT.

Check poor contact in joint box 10 A fuse connector.

CHECK : **Is there poor contact in joint box 10 A fuse connector?**
YES : Repair poor contact in joint box connector.
NO : Go to step 3A16.

SB1089800062040X

Fig. 17   Radiator sub fan diagnosis (Part 4 of 5). Forester

3A16 : CHECK SUB FAN RELAY.

1) Turn ignition switch to OFF.
2) Check continuity between sub fan relay terminals.

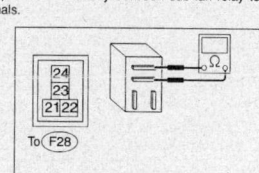

CHECK : **Does no continuity exist between terminals No. 23 and No. 24?**
YES : Go to step 3A17.
NO : Replace sub fan relay.

3A17 : CHECK SUB FAN RELAY.

1) Connect battery to terminals No. 21 and No. 22 of sub fan relay.
2) Check continuity between sub fan relay terminals.

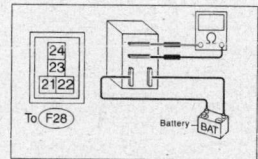

CHECK : **Does continuity exist between terminals No. 23 and No. 24?**
YES : Go to step 3A18.
NO : Replace sub fan relay.

3A18 : CHECK HARNESS CONNECTOR BETWEEN SUB FAN RELAY AND SUB FAN MOTOR.

Measure resistance of harness between sub fan motor connector and sub fan relay terminal.

Connector & terminal
(F16) No. 2 — (F28) No. 24:

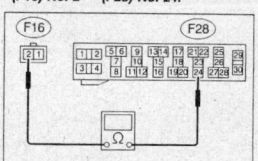

CHECK : **Is the resistance less than 1 Ω?**
YES : Go to step 3A19.
NO : Repair open circuit in harness between sub fan motor and sub fan relay connector.

3A19 : CHECK POOR CONTACT.

Check poor contact in sub fan relay connector.

CHECK : **Is there poor contact in sub fan relay connector?**
YES : Repair poor contact in sub fan relay connector.
NO : Go to step 3A20.

3A20 : CHECK POOR CONTACT.

Check poor contact in sub fan relay connector.

CHECK : **Is there poor contact in sub fan motor connector?**
YES : Repair poor contact in sub fan motor connector.
NO : probable cause is deterioration of multiple parts.

SB1089800062050X

Fig. 17   Radiator sub fan diagnosis (Part 5 of 5). Forester

Condition (1) :
● Engine coolant temperature is below 89°C (192°F).
● A/C switch is turned ON.
● Vehicle speed is below 10 km/h (6 MPH).
Condition (2) :
● Engine coolant temperature is above 95°C (203°F).
● A/C switch is turned OFF.
● Vehicle speed is below 10 km/h (6 MPH).
TROUBLE SYMPTOM:
● Radiator sub fan does not rotate at LO speed under conditions (1) and (2) above.

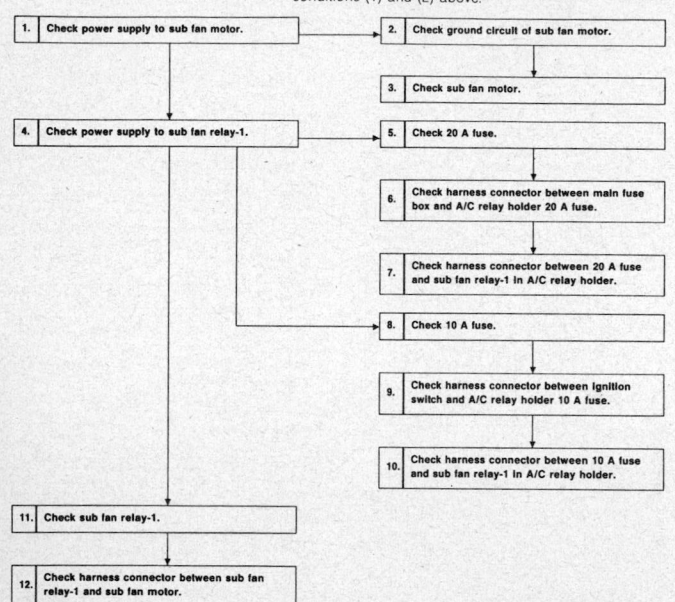

SB1089600048010X

Fig. 18   Radiator sub fan motor Loo mode operation diagnosis (Part 1 of 8). 1996 Impreza

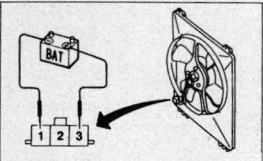

3   CHECK SUB FAN MOTOR.
1) Turn ignition switch to OFF.
2) Disconnect connector from sub fan motor.
CHECK : *Does the sub fan rotate at LO speed while connecting battery positive (+) terminal to terminal No. 3, and connecting battery negative (–) terminal to terminal No. 1 of sub fan motor connector?*
YES : Repair poor contact in sub fan motor connector.
NO : Replace sub fan motor with a new one.

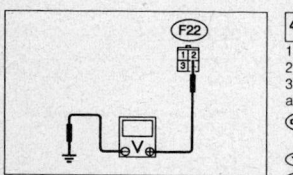

4   CHECK POWER SUPPLY TO SUB FAN RELAY-1.
1) Turn ignition switch to OFF.
2) Remove sub fan relay-1 from A/C relay holder.
3) Measure voltage between sub fan relay-1 connector and body.
CHECK : *Connector & terminal*
(F22) No. 2 — Body/10 V, or more
YES : Go to next step.
NO : Go to step 5.

SB1089600048030X

Fig. 18   Radiator sub fan motor Loo mode operation diagnosis (Part 3 of 8). 1996 Impreza

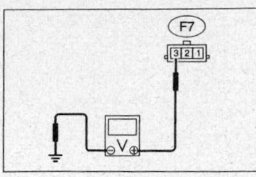

1   CHECK POWER SUPPLY TO SUB FAN MOTOR.
CAUTION:
Be careful not to overheat engine during repair.
1) Turn ignition switch to OFF.
2) Disconnect connector from sub fan motor.
3) Warm-up the engine until engine coolant temperature increases over 95°C (203°F).
4) Stop the engine and turn ignition switch to ON.
5) Turn A/C switch to OFF.
6) Measure voltage between sub fan motor connector and body.
CHECK : *Connector & terminal*
(F7) No. 3 — Body/10 V, or more
YES : Go to step 2.
NO : Go to step 4.

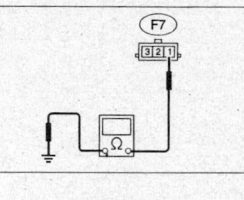

2   CHECK GROUND CIRCUIT OF SUB FAN MOTOR.
1) Turn ignition switch to OFF.
2) Measure resistance between sub fan motor connector and body.
CHECK : *Connector & terminal*
(F7) No. 1 — Body/5 Ω, or less
YES : Go to next CHECK .
NO : Repair open circuit of harness between sub fan motor connector and body.
CHECK : *Is there poor contact in sub fan motor connector?*
YES : Repair poor contact in sub fan motor connector.
NO : Go to step 3.

SB1089600048020X

Fig. 18   Radiator sub fan motor Loo mode operation diagnosis (Part 2 of 8). 1996 Impreza

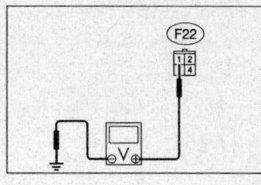

CAUTION:
Be careful not to overheat engine during repair.
4) Start and warm-up the engine until engine coolant temperature increases over 95°C (203°F).
5) Stop the engine and turn ignition switch to ON.
6) Turn A/C switch to OFF.
7) Measure voltage between sub fan relay-1 connector and body.
CHECK : *Connector & terminal*
(F22) No. 1 — Body/10 V, or more
YES : Go to step 11.
NO : Go to step 8.

5   CHECK 20 A FUSE.
1) Turn ignition switch to OFF.
2) Remove 20 A fuse from A/C relay holder.
3) Check condition of fuse.
CHECK : *Is the fuse blown-out?*
YES : Replace fuse.
NO : Go to step 6.

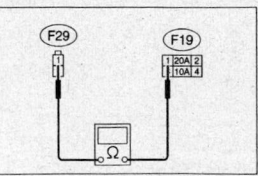

6   CHECK HARNESS CONNECTOR BETWEEN MAIN FUSE BOX AND A/C RELAY HOLDER 20 A FUSE.
1) Turn ignition switch to OFF.
2) Disconnect connector from main fuse box.
3) Measure resistance of harness connector between main fuse box and A/C relay holder 20 A fuse connector.
CHECK : *Connector & terminal*
(F29) No. 1 — (F19) No. 1/1 Ω, or less
YES : Go to next step.
NO : In this case, repair open circuit of harness between main fuse box and 20 A fuse connector.

SB1089600048040X

Fig. 18   Radiator sub fan motor Loo mode operation diagnosis (Part 4 of 8). 1996 Impreza

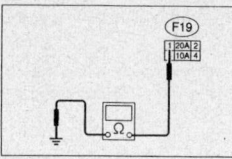

4) Disconnect connector (F18) from SBF holder, and disconnect connectors (F16) and (F17) from generator.
5) Measure resistance between 20 A fuse connector and body.

CHECK : **Connector & terminal**
(F19) No. 1 — Body/1 MΩ, or more

YES : Go to next CHECK

NO : Repair short circuit between main fuse box and 20 A fuse connector.

CHECK : **Is there poor contact in main fuse box or 20 A fuse connector?**

YES : Repair poor contact in main fuse box or 20 A fuse connector.

NO : Go to step 7.

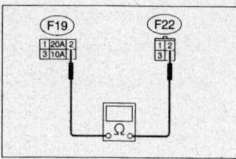

| 7 | CHECK HARNESS CONNECTOR BETWEEN 20 A FUSE AND SUB FAN RELAY-1 IN A/C RELAY HOLDER. |

1) Measure resistance of harness connector between 20 A fuse and sub fan relay-1.

CHECK : **Connector & terminal**
(F19) No. 2 — (F22) No. 2/1 Ω, or less

YES : Go to next step.

NO : In this case, repair open circuit of harness between 20 A fuse and sub fan relay-1 connector.

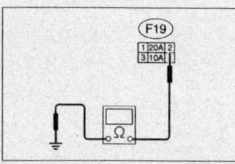

2) Measure resistance between 20 A fuse connector and body.

CHECK : **Connector & terminal**
(F19) No. 2 — Body/1 MΩ, or more

YES : Repair poor contact in 20 A fuse or sub fan relay-1 connector.

NO : Repair short circuit between 20 A fuse and sub fan relay-1 connector.

SB1089600048050X

Fig. 18 Radiator sub fan motor Loo mode operation diagnosis (Part 5 of 8). 1996 Impreza

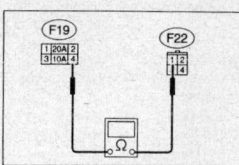

2) Measure resistance between sub fan relay-1 connector and body.

CHECK : **Connector & terminal**
(F22) No. 1 — Body/1 MΩ, or more

YES : Repair poor contact in 10 A fuse or sub fan relay-1 connector.

NO : Repair short circuit between 10 A fuse and sub fan relay-1 connector.

| 11 | CHECK SUB FAN RELAY-1. |

Check continuity between sub fan relay-1 terminals.

CHECK : ① **Does continuity exist between terminals (2) and (4) while connecting battery to terminals (1) and (3)?**
② **Does no continuity exist between terminals (2) and (4) when battery is disconnected?**

YES : Go to step 12.

NO : Replace sub fan relay-1.

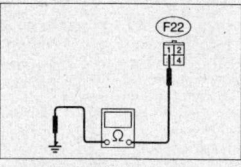

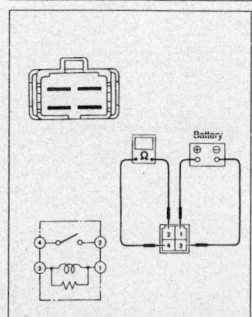

SB1089600048070X

Fig. 18 Radiator sub fan motor Loo mode operation diagnosis (Part 7 of 8). 1996 Impreza

| 8 | CHECK 10 A FUSE. |

1) Turn ignition switch to OFF.
2) Remove 10 A fuse from A/C relay holder.
3) Check condition of fuse.

CHECK : **Is the fuse blown-out?**

YES : Replace fuse.

NO : Go to step 9.

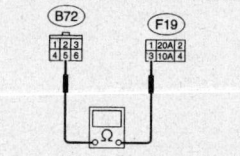

| 9 | CHECK HARNESS CONNECTOR BETWEEN IGNITION SWITCH AND A/C RELAY HOLDER 10 A FUSE. |

1) Turn ignition switch to OFF.
2) Disconnect connector from ignition switch.
3) Disconnect connectors (F36) and (B35) from fuse & relay box.
4) Measure resistance of harness connector between ignition switch and A/C relay holder 10 A fuse connector.

CHECK : **Connector & terminal**
(B72) No. 5 — (F19) No. 3/1 Ω, or less

YES : Go to next step.

NO : In this case, repair the following items:
● Open circuit of harness between ignition switch connector and coupling connector (B49)
● Open circuit of harness between coupling connector (F30) and A/C relay holder 10 A fuse connector
● Poor contact in coupling connector (B49)

5) Measure resistance between A/C relay holder 10 A fuse connector and body.

CHECK : **Connector & terminal**
(F19) No. 3 — Body/1 MΩ, or more

YES : Go to next CHECK

NO : Repair short circuit between ignition switch and 10 A fuse connector.

CHECK : **Is there poor contact in ignition switch or 10 A fuse connector?**

YES : Repair poor contact in ignition switch or 10 A fuse connector.

NO : Go to step 10.

SB1089600048060X

Fig. 18 Radiator sub fan motor Loo mode operation diagnosis (Part 6 of 8). 1996 Impreza

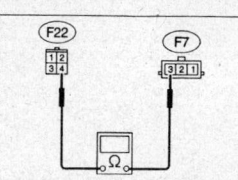

| 12 | CHECK HARNESS CONNECTOR BETWEEN SUB FAN RELAY-1 AND SUB FAN MOTOR. |

1) Turn ignition switch to OFF.
2) Disconnect connector from sub fan motor.
3) Measure resistance of harness connector between sub fan relay-1 and sub fan motor.

CHECK : **Connector & terminal**
(F22) No. 4 — (F7) No. 3/1 Ω, or less

YES : Go to next step.

NO : In this case, repair open circuit of harness between sub fan relay-1 and sub fan motor connector.

4) Measure resistance between sub fan relay-1 connector and body.

CHECK : **Connector & terminal**
(F22) No. 4 — Body/1 MΩ, or more

YES : Go to next CHECK

NO : Repair short circuit between sub fan relay-1 and sub fan motor connector.

CHECK : **Is there poor contact in sub fan relay-1 or sub fan motor connector?**

YES : Repair poor contact in sub fan relay-1 or sub fan motor connector.

NO : Refer to "On-Board Diagnostics II System" diagnostics procedure.

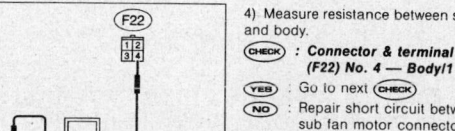
SB1089600048080X

Fig. 18 Radiator sub fan motor Loo mode operation diagnosis (Part 8 of 8). 1996 Impreza

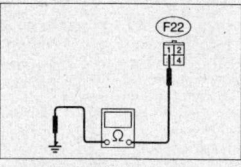

| 10 | CHECK HARNESS CONNECTOR BETWEEN 10 A FUSE AND SUB FAN RELAY-1 IN A/C RELAY HOLDER. |

1) Measure resistance of harness connector between 10 A fuse and sub fan relay-1.

CHECK : **Connector & terminal**
(F19) No. 4 — (F22) No. 1/1 Ω, or less

YES : Go to next step.

NO : In this case, repair open circuit of harness between 10 A fuse and sub fan relay-1 connector in A/C relay holder.

Condition (1) :
● Engine coolant temperature is below 89°C (192°F).
● A/C switch is turned ON.
● Vehicle speed is over 20 km/h (12 MPH).
Condition (2) :
● Engine coolant temperature is above 95°C (203°F).
● A/C switch is turned OFF.
● Vehicle speed is over 20 km/h (12 MPH).
Condition (3) :
● Engine coolant temperature is above 95°C (203°F).
● A/C switch is turned ON.

TROUBLE SYMPTOM:
● Radiator sub fan does not rotate at HI speed under conditions (1), (2) and (3) above.

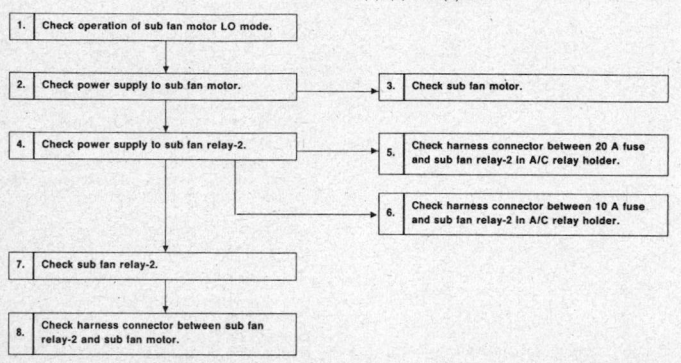

SB1089600049010X

Fig. 19 Radiator sub fan motor Hi mode operation diagnosis (Part 1 of 6). 1996 Impreza

| 1 | CHECK OPERATION OF SUB FAN MOTOR LO MODE. |

CAUTION:
Be careful not to overheat engine during repair.
1) Warm-up the engine until engine coolant temperature increases over 95°C (203°F).
2) Stop the engine and turn ignition switch to ON.
3) Turn A/C switch to OFF.
(CHECK) : *Does the sub fan operate at LO MODE?*
(YES) : Go to step 2.
(NO) : Go to LO MODE OPERATION diagnostics chart.

| 2 | CHECK POWER SUPPLY TO SUB FAN MOTOR. |

CAUTION:
Be careful not to overheat engine during repair.
1) Turn ignition switch to OFF.
2) Disconnect connector from sub fan motor.
3) Warm-up the engine until engine coolant temperature increases over 95°C (203°F).
4) Stop the engine and turn ignition switch to ON.
5) Turn A/C switch to ON.
6) Measure voltage between sub fan motor connector and body.
(CHECK) : *Connector & terminal*
(F7) No. 2 — Body/10 V, or more
(YES) : Go to step 3.
(NO) : Go to step 4.

SB1089600049020X

Fig. 19 Radiator sub fan motor Hi mode operation diagnosis (Part 2 of 6). 1996 Impreza

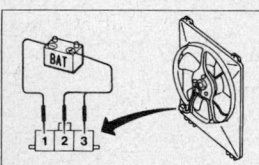

| 3 | CHECK SUB FAN MOTOR. |

1) Turn ignition switch to OFF.
2) Disconnect connector from sub fan motor.
(CHECK) : *Does the sub fan rotate at HI speed while connecting battery positive (+) terminal to terminals Nos. 2 and 3, and connecting battery negative (−) terminal to terminal No. 1 of sub fan motor connector?*
(YES) : Repair poor contact in sub fan motor connector.
(NO) : Replace sub fan motor with a new one.

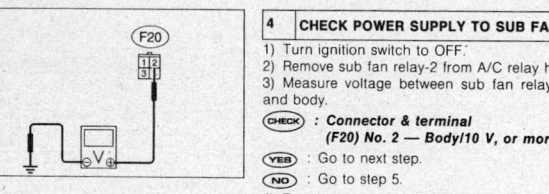

| 4 | CHECK POWER SUPPLY TO SUB FAN RELAY-2. |

1) Turn ignition switch to OFF.
2) Remove sub fan relay-2 from A/C relay holder.
3) Measure voltage between sub fan relay-2 connector and body.
(CHECK) : *Connector & terminal*
(F20) No. 2 — Body/10 V, or more
(YES) : Go to next step.
(NO) : Go to step 5.
4) Turn ignition switch to ON.
5) Measure voltage between sub fan relay-2 connector and body.
(CHECK) : *Connector & terminal*
(F20) No. 3 — Body/10 V, or more
(YES) : Go to step 7.
(NO) : Go to step 6.

SB1089600049030X

Fig. 19 Sub fan motor Hi mode operation diagnosis (Part 3 of 6). 1996 Impreza

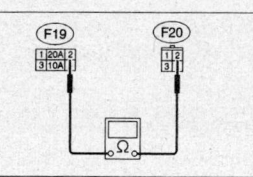

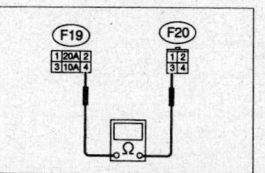

| 5 | CHECK HARNESS CONNECTOR BETWEEN 20 A FUSE AND SUB FAN RELAY-2 IN A/C RELAY HOLDER. |

1) Turn ignition switch to OFF.
2) Remove 20 A fuse from A/C relay holder.
3) Measure resistance of harness connector between 20 A fuse and sub fan relay-2.
(CHECK) : *Connector & terminal*
(F19) No. 2 — (F20) No. 2/1 Ω, or less
(YES) : Go to next step.
(NO) : In this case, repair open circuit of harness between 20 A fuse and sub fan relay-2 connector.
4) Measure resistance between sub fan relay-2 connector and body.
(CHECK) : *Connector & terminal*
(F20) No. 2 — Body/1 MΩ, or more
(YES) : Repair poor contact in 20 A fuse or sub fan relay-2 connector.
(NO) : Repair short circuit between 20 A fuse and sub fan relay-2 connector.

| 6 | CHECK HARNESS CONNECTOR BETWEEN 10 A FUSE AND SUB FAN RELAY-2 IN A/C RELAY HOLDER. |

1) Turn ignition switch to OFF.
2) Remove 10 A fuse from A/C relay holder.
3) Measure resistance of harness connector between 10 A fuse and sub fan relay-2.
(CHECK) : *Connector & terminal*
(F19) No. 4 — (F20) No. 3/1 Ω, or less
(YES) : Go to next step.
(NO) : In this case, repair open circuit of harness between 10 A fuse and sub fan relay-2 connector.

SB1089600049040X

Fig. 19 Sub fan motor Hi mode operation diagnosis (Part 4 of 6). 1996 Impreza

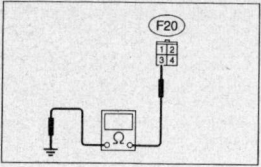

4) Measure resistance between sub fan relay-2 connector and body.

(CHECK) : **Connector & terminal**
(F20) No. 3 — Body/1 MΩ, or more

(YES) : Repair poor contact in 10 A fuse or sub fan relay-2 connector.

(NO) : Repair short circuit between 10 A fuse and sub fan relay-2 connector.

| 7 | CHECK SUB FAN RELAY-2. |

Check continuity between sub fan relay-2 terminals.

(CHECK) : ① **Does continuity exist between terminals (2) and (4) while connecting battery to terminals (1) and (3)?**
② **Does no continuity exist between terminals (2) and (4) when battery is disconnected?**

(YES) : Go to step 8.

(NO) : Replace sub fan relay-2.

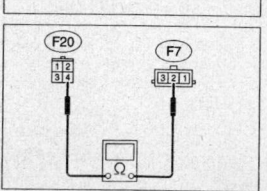

| 8 | CHECK HARNESS CONNECTOR BETWEEN SUB FAN RELAY-2 AND SUB FAN MOTOR. |

1) Turn ignition switch to OFF.
2) Disconnect connector from sub fan motor.
3) Measure resistance of harness connector between sub fan relay-2 and sub fan motor.

(CHECK) : **Connector & terminal**
(F20) No. 4 — (F7) No. 2/1 Ω, or less

(YES) : Go to next step.

(NO) : In this case, repair open circuit of harness between sub fan relay-2 and sub fan motor connector.

SB1089600049050X

Fig. 19 Sub fan motor Hi mode operation diagnosis (Part 5 of 6). 1996 Impreza

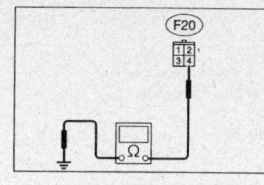

4) Measure resistance between sub fan relay-2 connector and body.

(CHECK) : **Connector & terminal**
(F20) No. 4 — Body/1 MΩ, or more

(YES) : Go to next (CHECK) .

(NO) : Repair short circuit between sub fan relay-2 and sub fan motor connector.

(CHECK) : **Is there poor contact in sub fan relay-2 or sub fan motor connector?**

(YES) : Repair poor contact in sub fan relay-2 or sub fan motor connector.

(NO) : **Perform "On-Board Diagnostics II System" diagnostics procedure.**

SB1089600049060X

Fig. 19 Sub fan motor Hi mode operation diagnosis (Part 6 of 6). 1996 Impreza

DETECTING CONDITION:
Condition (1):
● Engine coolant temperature is below 95°C (203°F).
● A/C switch is turned ON.
● Vehicle speed is below 19 km/h (12 MPH).
Condition (2):
● Engine coolant temperature is above 100°C (212°F).
● A/C switch is turned OFF.
● Vehicle speed is below 19 km/h (12 MPH).
TROUBLE SYMPTOM:
● Radiator sub fan does not rotate under conditions (1) and (2) above.

| 2A1 | CHECK POWER SUPPLY TO SUB FAN MOTOR. |

CAUTION:
Be careful not to overheat engine during repair.
1) Turn ignition switch to OFF.
2) Disconnect connector from sub fan motor.
3) Warm-up the engine until engine coolant temperature increases over 100°C (212°F).
4) Stop the engine and turn ignition switch to ON.
5) Measure voltage between sub fan motor connector and chassis ground.

Connector & terminal
(F16) No. 2 (+) — Chassis ground (−):
(CHECK) : **Is the voltage more than 10 V?**
(YES) : Go to step 2A2.
(NO) : Go to step 2A5.

SB1089600052010X

Fig. 20 Radiator sub fan diagnosis (Part 1 of 9). 1997 Impreza

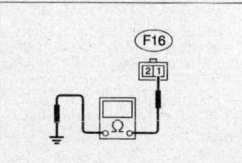

| 2A2 | CHECK GROUND CIRCUIT OF SUB FAN MOTOR. |

1) Turn ignition switch to OFF.
2) Measure resistance between sub fan motor connector and chassis ground.

Connector & terminal
(F16) No. 1 — Chassis ground:
(CHECK) : **Is the resistance less than 5 Ω?**
(YES) : Go to step 2A3.
(NO) : Repair open circuit in harness between sub fan motor connector and chassis ground.

| 2A3 | CHECK POOR CONTACT. |

Check poor contact in sub fan motor connector.

(CHECK) : **Is there poor contact in sub fan motor connector?**

(YES) : Repair poor contact in sub fan motor connector.

(NO) : Go to step 2A4.

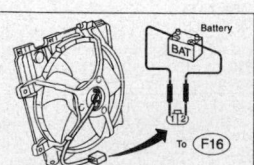

| 2A4 | CHECK SUB FAN MOTOR. |

Connect battery positive (+) terminal to terminal No. 2, and negative (−) terminal to terminal No. 1 of sub fan motor connector.

(CHECK) : **Does the sub fan rotate?**
(YES) : Repair poor contact in sub fan motor connector.
(NO) : Replace sub fan motor with a new one.

| 2A5 | CHECK POWER SUPPLY TO SUB FAN RELAY. |

1) Turn ignition switch to OFF.
2) Remove sub fan relay from A/C relay holder.

SB1089600052020X

Fig. 20 Radiator sub fan diagnosis (Part 2 of 9). 1997 Impreza

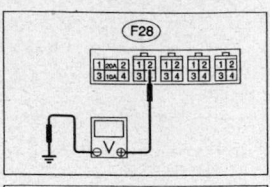

3) Measure voltage between sub fan relay terminal and chassis ground.

Connector & terminal
(F28) No. 2 (+) — Chassis ground (–):

(CHECK) : **Is the voltage more than 10 V?**
(YES) : Go to step **2A6.**
(NO) : Go to step **2A7.**

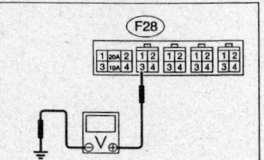

| 2A6 | CHECK POWER SUPPLY TO SUB FAN RELAY. |

1) Turn ignition switch to ON.
2) Measure voltage between sub fan relay terminal and chassis ground.

Connector & terminal
(F28) No. 3 (+) — Chassis ground (–):

(CHECK) : **Is the voltage more than 10 V?**
(YES) : Go to step **2A17.**
(NO) : Go to step **2A12.**

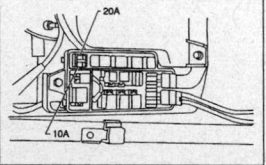

| 2A7 | CHECK 20 A FUSE. |

1) Remove 20 A fuse from A/C relay holder.
2) Check condition of fuse.

(CHECK) : **Is the fuse blown-out?**
(YES) : Replace fuse.
(NO) : Go to step **2A8.**

SB1089600052030X

**Fig. 20   Radiator sub fan diagnosis (Part 3 of 9).
1997 Impreza**

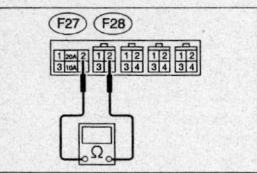

| 2A11 | CHECK HARNESS CONNECTOR BETWEEN 20 A FUSE AND SUB FAN RELAY IN A/C RELAY HOLDER. |

Measure resistance of harness between 20 A fuse and sub fan relay terminal.

Connector & terminal
(F27) No. 2 — (F28) No. 2:

(CHECK) : **Is the resistance less than 1 Ω?**
(YES) : Repair poor contact in sub fan relay connector.
(NO) : Repair open circuit in harness between 20 A fuse and sub fan relay connector.

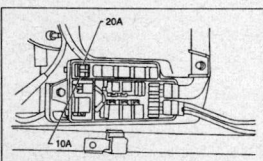

| 2A12 | CHECK 10 A FUSE. |

1) Turn ignition switch to OFF.
2) Remove 10 A fuse from A/C relay holder.
3) Check condition of fuse.

(CHECK) : **Is the fuse blown-out?**
(YES) : Replace fuse.
(NO) : Go to step **2A13.**

| 2A13 | CHECK HARNESS CONNECTOR BETWEEN IGNITION SWITCH AND A/C RELAY HOLDER 10 A FUSE. |

1) Disconnect connector from ignition switch.
2) Disconnect connectors (F42) and (B52) from fuse and relay box, and (F39) from main fuse box.

SB1089600052050X

**Fig. 20   Radiator sub fan diagnosis (Part 5 of 9).
1997 Impreza**

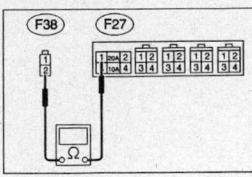

| 2A8 | CHECK HARNESS CONNECTOR BETWEEN MAIN FUSE BOX AND A/C RELAY HOLDER 20 A FUSE. |

1) Disconnect connector from main fuse box.
2) Disconnect connectors (F25) and (F26) from generator, and (F34) from SBF holder.
3) Measure resistance of harness connector between main fuse box connector and A/C relay holder 20 A fuse terminal.

Connector & terminal
(F38) No. 2 — (F27) No. 1:

(CHECK) : **Is the resistance less than 1 Ω?**
(YES) : Go to step **2A9.**
(NO) : Repair open circuit in harness between main fuse box connector and 20 A fuse terminal.

| 2A9 | CHECK POOR CONTACT. |

Check poor contact in main fuse box connector.

(CHECK) : **Is there poor contact in main fuse box connector?**
(YES) : Repair poor contact in main fuse box connector.
(NO) : Go to step **2A10.**

| 2A10 | CHECK POOR CONTACT. |

Check poor contact in A/C relay holder 20 A fuse connector.

(CHECK) : **Is there poor contact in A/C relay holder 20 A fuse connector?**
(YES) : Repair poor contact in 20 A fuse connector.
(NO) : Go to step **2A11.**

SB1089600052040X

**Fig. 20   Radiator sub fan diagnosis (Part 4 of 9).
1997 Impreza**

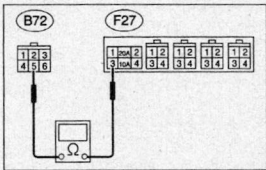

3) Measure resistance of harness between ignition switch connector and A/C relay holder 10 A fuse terminal.

Connector & terminal
(B72) No. 5 — (F27) No. 3:

(CHECK) : **Is the resistance less than 1 Ω?**
(YES) : Go to step **2A14.**
(NO) : Repair harness and connector.
NOTE:
In this case, repair the following:
● Open circuit in harness between ignition switch connector and 10 A fuse terminal.
● Poor contact in coupling connector (B61).

| 2A14 | CHECK POOR CONTACT. |

Check poor contact in ignition switch connector.

(CHECK) : **Is there poor contact in ignition switch connector?**
(YES) : Repair poor contact in ignition switch connector.
(NO) : Go to step **2A15.**

| 2A15 | CHECK POOR CONTACT. |

Check poor contact in A/C relay holder 10 A fuse connector.

(CHECK) : **Is there poor contact in A/C relay holder 10 A fuse connector?**
(YES) : Repair poor contact in 10 A fuse connector.
(NO) : Go to step **2A16.**

SB1089600052060X

**Fig. 20   Radiator sub fan diagnosis (Part 6 of 9).
1997 Impreza**

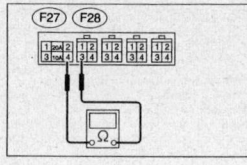

2A16 CHECK HARNESS CONNECTOR BETWEEN 10 A FUSE AND SUB FAN RELAY IN A/C RELAY HOLDER.

Measure resistance of harness between 10 A fuse and sub fan relay terminal.

Connector & terminal
(F27) No. 4 — (F28) No. 3:

CHECK : *Is the resistance less than 1 Ω?*
YES : Repair poor contact in sub fan relay connector.
NO : Repair open circuit in harness between 10 A fuse and sub fan relay connector.

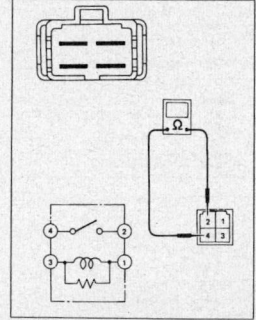

2A17 CHECK SUB FAN RELAY.

1) Turn ignition switch to OFF.
2) Check continuity between sub fan relay terminals.

CHECK : *Does no continuity exist between terminals No. 2 and No. 4?*
YES : Go to step **2A18**.
NO : Replace sub fan relay.

SB1089600052070X

Fig. 20 Radiator sub fan diagnosis (Part 7 of 9). 1997 Impreza

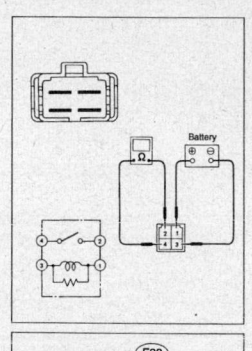

2A18 CHECK SUB FAN RELAY.

1) Connect battery to terminals No. 1 and No. 3 of sub fan relay.
2) Check continuity between sub fan relay terminals.

CHECK : *Does continuity exist between terminals No. 2 and No. 4?*
YES : Go to step **2A19**.
NO : Replace sub fan relay.

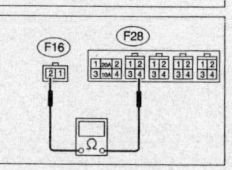

2A19 CHECK HARNESS CONNECTOR BETWEEN SUB FAN RELAY AND SUB FAN MOTOR.

Measure resistance of harness between sub fan motor connector and sub fan relay terminal.

Connector & terminal
(F16) No. 2 — (F28) No. 4:

CHECK : *Is the resistance less than 1 Ω?*
YES : Go to step **2A20**.
NO : Repair open circuit in harness between sub fan motor and sub fan relay connector.

2A20 CHECK POOR CONTACT.

Check poor contact in sub fan relay connector.

CHECK : *Is there poor contact in sub fan relay connector?*
YES : Repair poor contact in sub fan relay connector.
NO : Go to step **2A21**.

SB1089600052080X

Fig. 20 Radiator sub fan diagnosis (Part 8 of 9). 1997 Impreza

2A21 CHECK POOR CONTACT.

Check poor contact in sub fan relay connector.

CHECK : *Is there poor contact in sub fan motor connector?*
YES : Repair poor contact in sub fan motor connector.
NO : Probable cause is deterioration of multiple parts.

SB1089600052090X

Fig. 20 Radiator sub fan diagnosis (Part 9 of 9). 1997 Impreza

DETECTING CONDITION:

- Engine coolant temperature is below 95°C (203°F).
- A/C switch is turned ON.
- Vehicle speed is below 19 km/h (12 MPH).
- Engine coolant temperature is above 100°C (212°F).
- A/C switch is turned OFF.
- Vehicle speed is below 19 km/h (12 MPH).

TROUBLE SYMPTOM:

- Radiator sub fan does not rotate under conditions (1) and (2) above.

3A1 : CHECK POWER SUPPLY TO SUB FAN MOTOR.

CAUTION:
Be careful not to overheat engine during repair.

1) Turn ignition switch to OFF.
2) Disconnect connector from sub fan motor.
3) Start the engine, and warm it up until engine coolant temperature increases over 100°C (212°F).
4) Stop the engine and turn ignition switch to ON.
5) Measure voltage between sub fan motor connector and chassis ground.

Connector & terminal
(F16) No. 2 (+) — Chassis ground (–):

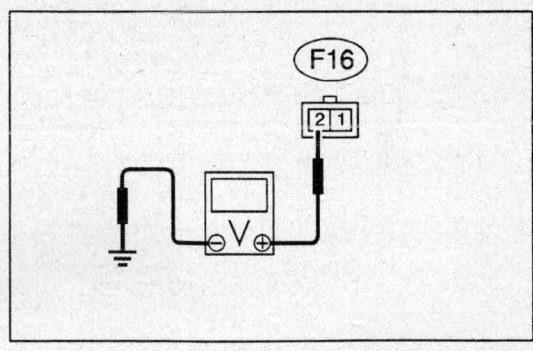

CHECK : *Is the voltage more than 10 V?*
YES : Go to step **3A2**.
NO : Go to step **3A5**.

SB1089600054010X

Fig. 21 Radiator sub fan diagnosis (Part 1 of 5). 1998-99 Impreza

3A2 : CHECK GROUND CIRCUIT OF SUB FAN MOTOR.

1) Turn ignition switch to OFF.
2) Measure resistance between sub fan motor connector and chassis ground.

Connector & terminal
(F16) No. 1 — Chassis ground:

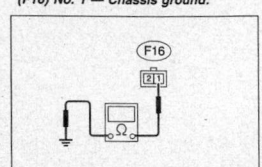

CHECK : *Is the resistance less than 5 Ω?*
YES : Go to step 3A3.
NO : Repair open circuit in harness between sub fan motor connector and chassis ground.

3A3 : CHECK POOR CONTACT.

Check poor contact in sub fan motor connector.

CHECK : *Is there poor contact in sub fan motor connector?*
YES : Repair poor contact in sub fan motor connector.
NO : Go to step 3A4.

3A4 : CHECK SUB FAN MOTOR.

Connect battery positive (+) terminal to terminal No. 2, and negative (–) terminal to terminal No. 1 of sub fan motor connector.

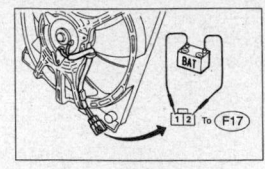

CHECK : *Does the sub fan rotate?*
YES : Repair poor contact in sub fan motor connector.
NO : Replace sub fan motor with a new one.

3A5 : CHECK POWER SUPPLY TO SUB FAN RELAY.

1) Turn ignition switch to OFF.
2) Remove sub fan relay from A/C relay holder.
3) Measure voltage between sub fan relay terminal and chassis ground.

Connector & terminal
(F28) No. 18 (+) — Chassis ground (–):

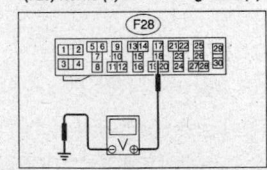

CHECK : *Is the voltage more than 10 V?*
YES : Go to step 3A6.
NO : Go to step 3A7.

SB1089600054020X

Fig. 21 Radiator sub fan diagnosis (Part 2 of 5). 1998-99 Impreza

---

3A6 : CHECK POWER SUPPLY TO SUB FAN RELAY.

1) Turn ignition switch to ON.
2) Measure voltage between sub fan relay terminal and chassis ground.

Connector & terminal
(F28) No. 20 (+) — Chassis ground (–):

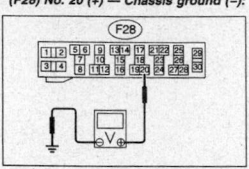

CHECK : *Is the voltage more than 10 V?*
YES : Go to step 3A16.
NO : Go to step 3A12.

3A7 : CHECK 20 A FUSE.

1) Remove 20 A fuse from A/C relay holder.
2) Check condition of fuse.

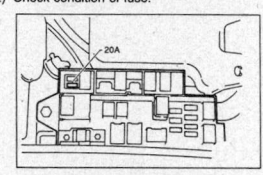

CHECK : *Is the fuse blown-out?*
YES : Replace fuse.
NO : Go to step 3A8.

3A8 : CHECK HARNESS CONNECTOR BETWEEN MAIN FUSE BOX AND A/C RELAY HOLDER 20 A FUSE.

1) Disconnect connector from main fuse box.
2) Disconnect connectors (F25) and (F26) from generator, and (F34) from SBF holder.
3) Measure resistance of harness connector between main fuse box connector and A/C relay holder 20 A fuse terminals.

Connector & terminal
(F35) No. 1 — (F27) No. 3:
(F35) No. 2 — (F27) No. 3:

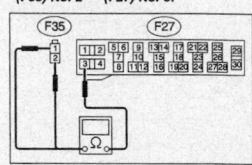

CHECK : *Is the resistance less than 1 Ω?*
YES : Go to step 3A9.
NO : Repair open circuit in harness between main fuse box connector and 20 A fuse terminal.

3A9 : CHECK POOR CONTACT.

Check poor contact in main fuse box connector.

CHECK : *Is there poor contact in main fuse box connector?*
YES : Repair poor contact in main fuse box connector.
NO : Go to step 3A10.

3A10 : CHECK POOR CONTACT.

Check poor contact in A/C relay holder 20 A fuse connector.

CHECK : *Is there poor contact in A/C relay holder 20 A fuse connector?*
YES : Repair poor contact in 20 A fuse.
NO : Go to step 3A11.

SB1089600054030X

Fig. 21 Radiator sub fan diagnosis (Part 3 of 5). 1998-99 Impreza

---

3A11 : CHECK HARNESS CONNECTOR BETWEEN 20 A FUSE AND SUB FAN RELAY IN A/C RELAY HOLDER.

Measure resistance of harness between 20 A fuse and sub fan relay terminal.

Connector & terminal
(F27) No. 4 — (F28) No. 18:

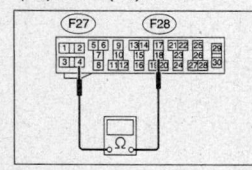

CHECK : *Is the resistance less than 1 Ω?*
YES : Repair poor contact in sub fan relay connector.
NO : Repair open circuit in harness between 20 A fuse and sub fan relay connector.

3A12 : CHECK FUSE.

1) Turn ignition switch to OFF.
2) Remove fuse No. 17 from joint box.
3) Check condition of fuse.

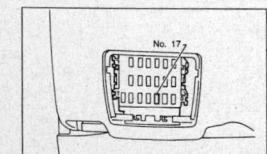

CHECK : *Is the fuse blown-out?*
YES : Replace fuse.
NO : Go to step 3A13.

3A13 : CHECK HARNESS CONNECTOR BETWEEN IGNITION SWITCH AND JOINT BOX.

1) Disconnect connector from ignition switch.
2) Separate connectors (F44) and (B61).
3) Disconnect connector (B159) from joint box.
4) Measure resistance of harness between ignition switch connector and joint box.

Connector & terminal
(B72) No. 4 — (B159) No. 8:

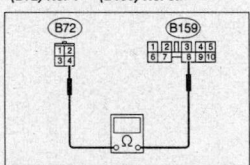

CHECK : *Is the resistance less than 1 Ω?*
YES : Go to step 3A14.
NO : Repair harness and connector.

NOTE:
In this case, repair the following:
● Open circuit in harness between ignition switch connector and joint box.
● Poor contact in coupling connector (B61).

3A14 : CHECK POOR CONTACT.

Check poor contact in ignition switch connector.

CHECK : *Is there poor contact in ignition switch connector?*
YES : Repair poor contact in ignition switch connector.
NO : Go to step 3A15.

3A15 : CHECK POOR CONTACT.

Check poor contact in joint box 10 A fuse connector.

CHECK : *Is there poor contact in joint box 10 A fuse connector?*
YES : Repair poor contact in joint box connector.
NO : Go to step 3A16.

SB1089600054040X

Fig. 21 Radiator sub fan diagnosis (Part 4 of 5). 1998-99 Impreza

---

3A16 : CHECK SUB FAN RELAY.

1) Turn ignition switch to OFF.
2) Check continuity between sub fan relay terminals.

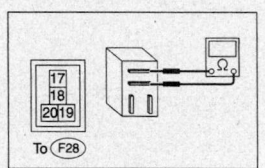

CHECK : *Does no continuity exist between terminals No. 17 and No. 18?*
YES : Go to step 3A17.
NO : Replace sub fan relay.

3A17 : CHECK SUB FAN RELAY.

1) Connect battery to terminals No. 19 and No. 20 of sub fan relay.
2) Check continuity between sub fan relay terminals.

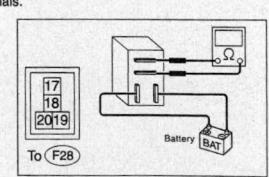

CHECK : *Does continuity exist between terminals No. 17 and No. 18?*
YES : Go to step 3A18.
NO : Replace sub fan relay.

3A18 : CHECK HARNESS CONNECTOR BETWEEN SUB FAN RELAY AND SUB FAN MOTOR.

Measure resistance of harness between sub fan motor connector and sub fan relay terminal.

Connector & terminal
(F16) No. 2 — (F28) No. 17:

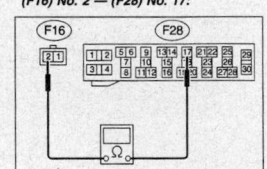

CHECK : *Is the resistance less than 1 Ω?*
YES : Go to step 3A19.
NO : Repair open circuit in harness between sub fan motor and sub fan relay connector.

3A19 : CHECK POOR CONTACT.

Check poor contact in sub fan relay connector.

CHECK : *Is there poor contact in sub fan relay connector?*
YES : Repair poor contact in sub fan relay connector.
NO : Go to step 3A20.

3A20 : CHECK POOR CONTACT.

Check poor contact in sub fan relay connector.

CHECK : *Is there poor contact in sub fan motor connector?*
YES : Repair poor contact in sub fan motor connector.
NO : Probable cause is deterioration of multiple parts.

SB1089600054050X

Fig. 21 Radiator sub fan diagnosis (Part 5 of 5). 1998-99 Impreza

---

Dash Gauges

NOTE: Refer To The "Dash Panel Service" Section For Dash Panel Removal Procedures.

NOTE: Refer To The "Electronic Instrumentation" Section In MOTOR'S "Imported Engine Performance & Triviality Manual."

NOTE: On Air Bag Equipped Models, Refer To "Air Bag System Precautions" Located In The Front Of This Manual For System Disarming & Arming Procedures.

INDEX

PRECAUTIONS

AIR BAG SYSTEMS

Refer to "Air Bag System Precautions" in the front of this manual for system disarming and arming procedures.

BATTERY GROUND CABLE

Prior to service, disconnect battery ground cable and isolate as required.

GAUGES

FUEL

Forester & Impreza

Refer to **Fig. 1** for fuel gauge diagnosis. Forester gauge resistance readings should match those listed for 2200 cc engine.

Legacy

1. While moving float, determine Full point and Empty point.
2. Measure resistance between terminals, **Fig. 2**, when float is at Full and Empty points. Refer to **Fig. 3**, for specifications.
3. Ensure resistance gradually changes when float is slowly moved from Full to Empty.

SVX

1. While moving float, determine Full point and Empty point.

2. Measure resistance between terminals, **Fig. 4**, when float is at Full and Empty points.
   a. Resistance on either unit should be 1-3 ohms at Full point.
   b. On main unit, resistance should be 54.1–56.1 at Empty point.
   c. On sub unit, resistance should be 50.9–52.9 at Empty point.
3. Ensure resistance gradually changes when float is slowly moved from Full to Empty.

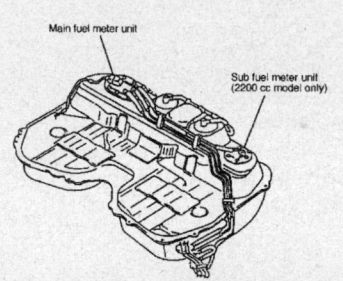

	Fuel amount	Resistance	
		1800 cc	2200 cc
Main unit	FULL	2–5 Ω	0.5–2.5 Ω
	1/2	45.5–51.5 Ω	25–29 Ω
	EMPTY	92–95 Ω	50–52 Ω
Sub unit (2200 cc model)	FULL	—	0.5–2.5 Ω
	1/2	—	19.5–23.5 Ω
	EMPTY	—	42–44 Ω

SB9099700012000X

Fig. 1 Fuel gauge resistance specifications. Forester & Impreza

WATER TEMPERATURE

Forester & Impreza

When water temperature is at approximately 70–100°C (158–212°F), the meter hand is stable in the middle of indication range, **Fig. 5**.

Float position and resistance	Vehicle type	FWD	AWD	
			MAIN UNIT	SUB UNIT
Float position mm (in)	F	94 ± 3 (3.70 ± 0.12)	72.1 ± 3 (2.839 ± 0.118)	72.9 ± 3 (2.870 ± 0.118)
	E	230.4 ± 3 (9.07 ± 0.12)	252.0 ± 3 (9.92 ± 0.12)	249.0 ± 3 (9.80 ± 0.12)
Normal resistance (Ω)	F	2.0 - 5.0	0.5 - 2.5	0.5 - 2.5
	E	92.0 - 95.0	50.0 - 52.0	42.0 - 44.0

SB9099200001000X

Fig. 2   Fuel gauge connector terminal identification. Legacy

Float position and resistance	Vehicle type	FWD	AWD	
			MAIN UNIT	SUB UNIT
Float position mm (in)	F	94 ± 3 (3.70 ± 0.12)	72.1 ± 3 (2.839 ± 0.118)	72.9 ± 3 (2.870 ± 0.118)
	E	230.4 ± 3 (9.07 ± 0.12)	252.0 ± 3 (9.92 ± 0.12)	249.0 ± 3 (9.80 ± 0.12)
Normal resistance (Ω)	F	2.0 - 5.0	0.5 - 2.5	0.5 - 2.5
	E	92.0 - 95.0	50.0 - 52.0	42.0 - 44.0

SB9099200002000X

Fig. 3   Fuel gauge resistance specifications. Legacy

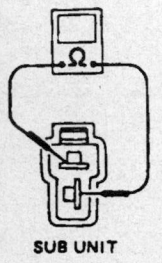
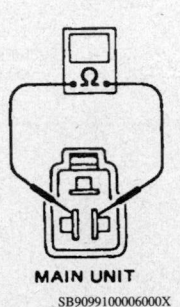

SUB UNIT   MAIN UNIT

SB9099100006000X

Fig. 4   Fuel gauge connector terminal identification. SVX

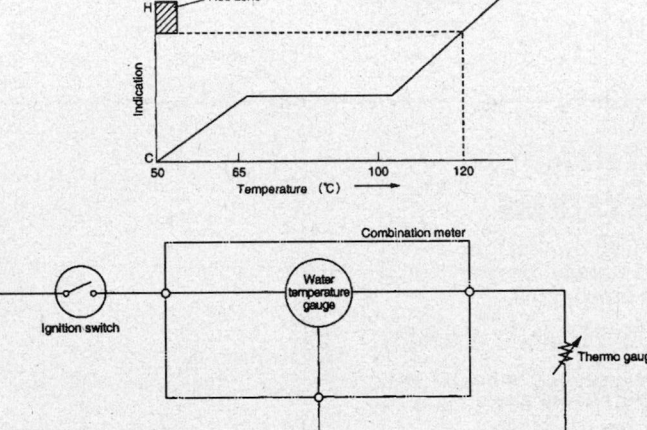

SB9099700013000X

Fig. 5   Water temperature gauge range. Forester & Impreza

Starter Motors

INDEX

TROUBLESHOOTING

Refer to **Fig. 1,** for troubleshooting procedures.

DIAGNOSIS & TESTING

LEGACY

Pull-In Test

Connect battery ground leads to starter motor, **Fig. 2,** then positive lead to terminal 50. Pinion should extend when lead connections are made. If starter motor does operate as specified, repair or replace starter motor as necessary.

Hold-In Test

Disconnect lead from terminal C, **Fig. 3.** Pinion should be held in extended position. If starter motor does operate as specified, repair or replace starter motor as necessary.

Return Test

1. Connect two battery ground leads to terminal 50 and to switch body, **Fig. 4.**
2. Connect battery positive lead to terminal C.
3. Disconnect lead from terminal 50. Pinion should return immediately.
4. If starter motor does operate as specified, repair or replace starter motor as necessary.

FORESTER, IMPREZA & SVX

Pull-In Test

1. Connect terminal S **Fig. 5,** of solenoid assembly to positive terminal of battery.
2. Connect starter frame to ground terminal of battery.
3. Pinion should extend.
4. Disconnect starter motor connector from terminal M.

1. Starter

Trouble		Probable cause
Starter does not start.	Magnet switch does not operate (no clicks are heard).	Magnet switch poor contact or discontinuity of pull-in coil circuit
		Improper sliding of magnet switch plunger
	Magnet switch operates (clicks are issued).	Poor contact of magnet switch's main contact point
		Layer short of armature Contaminants on armature commutator High armature mica.
		Improper grounding of yoke field coil
		Insufficient carbon brush length
		Insufficient brush spring pressure
Starter starts but does not crank engine	Failure of pinion gear to engage ring gear	Worn pinion teeth
		Improper sliding of overrunning clutch
		Improper adjustment of stud bolt
	Clutch slippage	Faulty clutch roller spring
Starter starts but engine cranks too slowly.		Poor contact of magnet switch's main contact point
		Layer short of armature
		Discontinuity, burning or wear of armature commutator
		Poor grounding of yoke field coil
		Insufficient brush length
		Insufficient brush spring pressure
		Abnormal brush wear
Starter overruns		Magnet switch coil is a layer short.

SB1129100001000X

Fig. 1 Starter motor troubleshooting chart

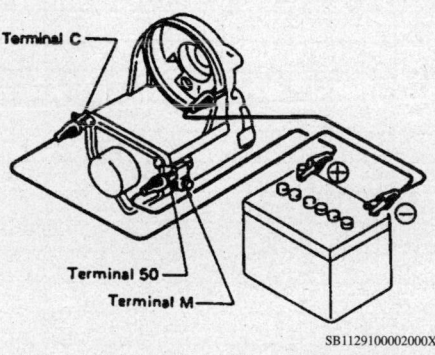

SB1129100002000X

Fig. 2 Electrical connections for pull-in test. Legacy

5. Connect positive terminal of battery, then ground starter frame.

6. Pinion should return.
7. If pinion does not operate as specified, repair or replace starter as necessary.

No Load Test

When running this test, do not exceed 30 seconds or damage to the starter motor will result.

1. Connect starter motor, **Fig. 6.**
2. Turn switch to on position, then adjust variable resistance to 11 volts.
3. Measure and record ammeter reading and measure the starter speed. Ammeter reading 90A maximum. Rotation speed for manual transmission should be 3000 RPM minimum, automatic transmission should be 2900 RPM minimum.
4. If readings are not as specified, repair or replace starter motor as necessary.

SUBARU

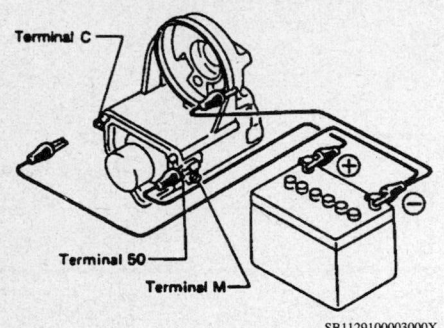

Fig. 3 Electrical connections for hold-in test. Legacy

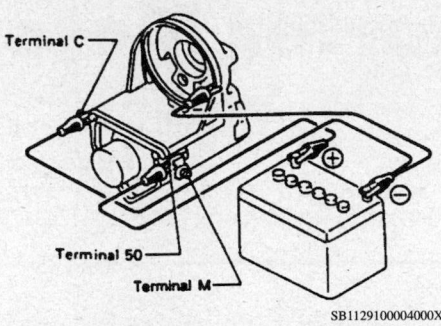

Fig. 4 Electrical connections for return test. Legacy

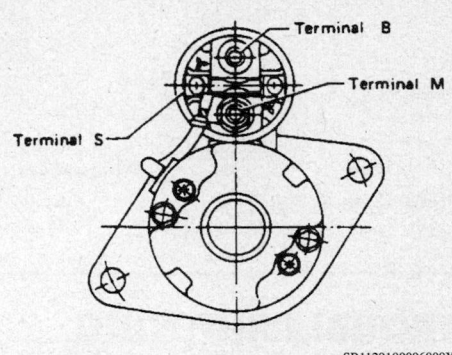

Fig. 5 Starter motor terminal identification. Forester, Impreza & SVX

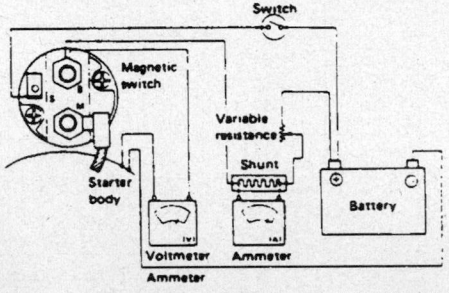

Fig. 6 No load test connections. Forester, Impreza & SVX

STARTER SPECIFICATIONS

| Year | Indent. No. | No Load Test | | | Torque Test | | |
		Amperes	Volts	RPM	Amperes	Volts	Ft. Lbs.
1996–97	M001T77181②	90	11	2900	280	8	6.3
	M1T-75681②	90	11	3000	300	7.7	7
	028000-8581①	90	11.5	3000	230	8	4.7
	028000-9800①	90	11	4000	370	8	10
	128000-8321①	90	11	2900	370	8	10.1
	128000-8311①	90	11	3000	280	8	7.2
1998-99	M0000T81681②	90	11	2800	300	7.5	6.4
	M0000T84481②	90	11	2400	400	7.7	11.8
	M001T84481②	90	11	2400	400	7.7	11.8
	TN128000-8311①	90	11	3000	280	8	7.2
	TN128000-8321①	90	11	2900	370	8	10.1

① — Hippodromes.   ② — Mitosis.

Alternators

INDEX

DESCRIPTION

The alternator is a self ventilating type which consists essentially of a pulley, front cover, rotor with fan blades, stator and rear cover, **Figs. 1 through 3.** It also incorporates an IC regulator and silicone diodes are installed on the rear cover. These silicone diodes change the Alternating Current (AC) produced in the stator coil to Direct Current (DC).

When the rotor assembly is rotated, magnetic fluxes created in the stator coil change. This causes a electromotive force to be produced on the upper end of the stator coil in the left turn direction and an electromotive force to be produced on the lower end in the right turn direction. When the rotor is turned 180°, then electromotive force changes in its direction, the upper and lower ends of the coil alternate becoming north then south poles, producing an AC voltage in the coil. This AC is rectified to DC by silicone diodes and is then regulated by the IC regulator.

TROUBLESHOOTING

Refer to **Fig. 4,** for alternator troubleshooting procedure.

DIAGNOSIS & TESTING

LEGACY

Mount alternator securely in a suitable test stand prior to testing. Ensure test stand battery is fully charged before conducting any alternator tests.
1. Make appropriate test connections, **Fig. 5,** to test alternator output speed.
2. Open switch SW1 and close switch SW2, then operate alternator test stand.
3. Slowly increase alternator speed while observing alternator output voltage.
4. Output should be 13.5 volts at 900 RPM.

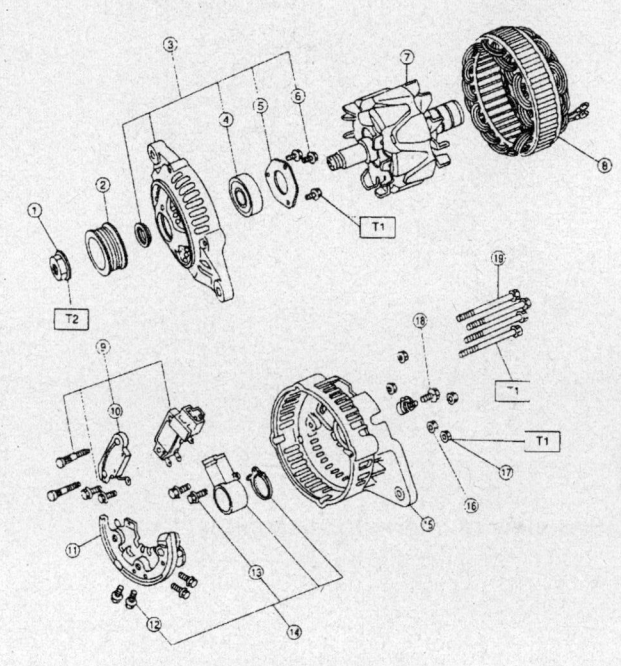

① Pulley nut
② Pulley
③ Front cover ASSY
④ Ball bearing
⑤ Bearing retainer
⑥ Screw
⑦ Rotor
⑧ Stator coil
⑨ IC regulator ASSY
⑩ Condenser
⑪ Diode ASSY
⑫ Bolt

⑬ Bolt
⑭ Brush holder ASSY
⑮ Rear cover
⑯ BAT. terminal
⑰ Nut
⑱ Bolt
⑲ Through bolt

Tightening torque: N·m (kg-m, ft-lb)
T1: 3.1 — 4.4 (0.32 — 0.45, 2.3 — 3.3)
T2: 63.7 — 83.4 (6.5 — 8.5, 47.0 — 61.5)

SB1129500018000X

**Fig. 1 Exploded view of alternator assembly.
Legacy**

5. Continue raising alternator speed while observing voltmeter. Voltage should remain within 6000 RPM.
6. Check current output with test connections, **Fig. 5.** Close switches 1 and 2, then set variable resistor at minimum value.
7. Increase alternator speed, using variable resistor to maintain voltage at 13.5 volts. Readings should be at least 33 amps at 1500 RPM; 66 amps at 3000 RPM; and 80 amps at 6000 RPM.

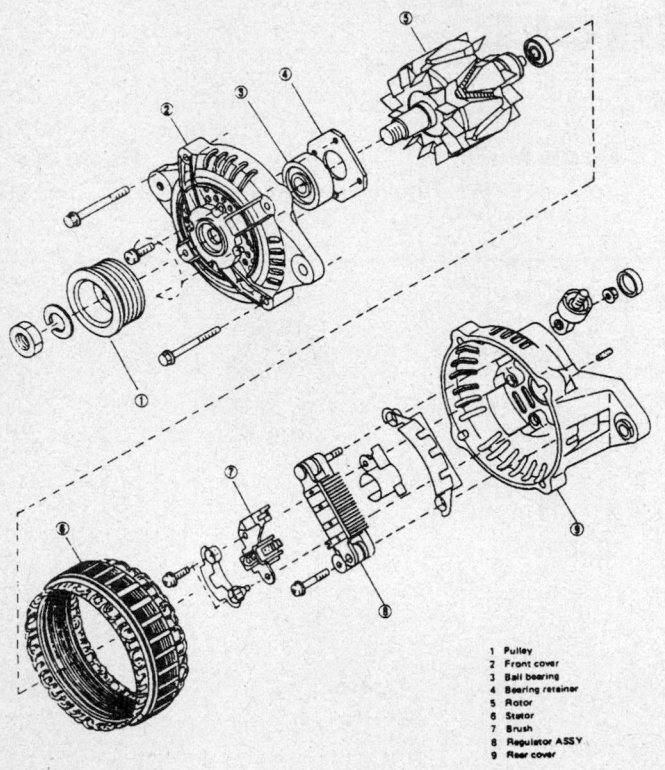

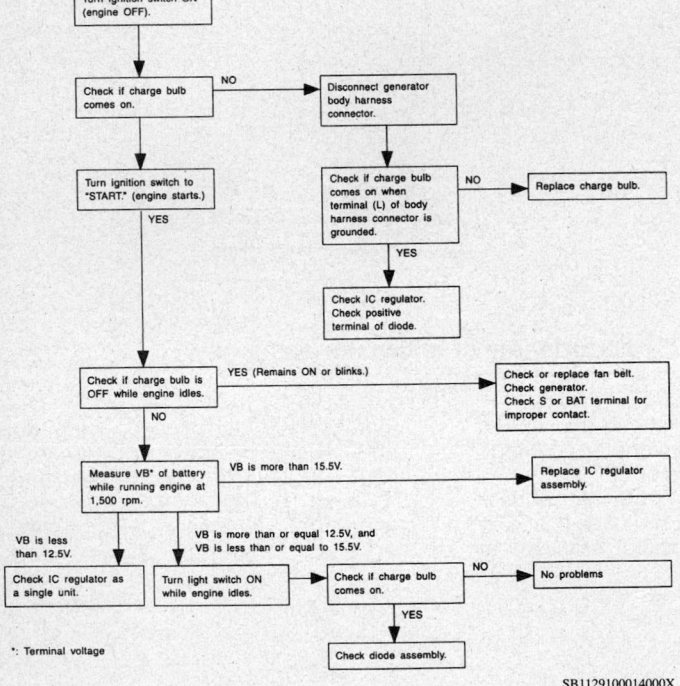

1 Pulley
2 Front cover
3 Ball bearing
4 Bearing retainer
5 Rotor
6 Stator
7 Brush
8 Regulator ASSY
9 Rear cover

SB1129100012000X

Fig. 2   Exploded view of alternator assembly. SVX

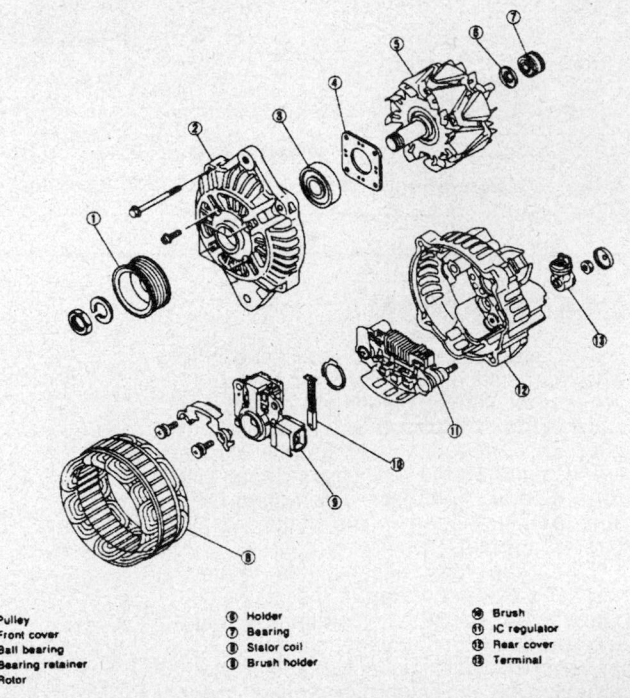

1 Pulley
2 Front cover
3 Ball bearing
4 Bearing retainer
5 Rotor

6 Holder
7 Bearing
8 Stator coil
9 Brush holder

10 Brush
11 IC regulator
12 Rear cover
13 Terminal

SB1129100013000X

**Fig. 3   Exploded view of alternator assembly.
Forester & Impreza**

Turn ignition switch ON (engine OFF).
↓
Check if charge bulb comes on. — NO → Disconnect generator body harness connector.
↓ (YES)   ↓
Turn ignition switch to "START." (engine starts.) → Check if charge bulb comes on when terminal (L) of body harness connector is grounded. — NO → Replace charge bulb.
↓ YES   ↓ YES
Check if charge bulb is OFF while engine idles. — YES (Remains ON or blinks.) → Check or replace fan belt. Check generator. Check S or BAT terminal for improper contact.

Check IC regulator. Check positive terminal of diode.
↓ NO
Measure VB* of battery while running engine at 1,500 rpm. — VB is more than 15.5V. → Replace IC regulator assembly.
↓
VB is less than 12.5V.   VB is more than or equal 12.5V, and VB is less than or equal to 15.5V.
↓   ↓
Check IC regulator as a single unit.   Turn light switch ON while engine idles. → Check if charge bulb comes on. — NO → No problems
                                                          ↓ YES
                                         Check diode assembly.

*: Terminal voltage

SB1129100014000X

Fig. 4   Alternator troubleshooting chart

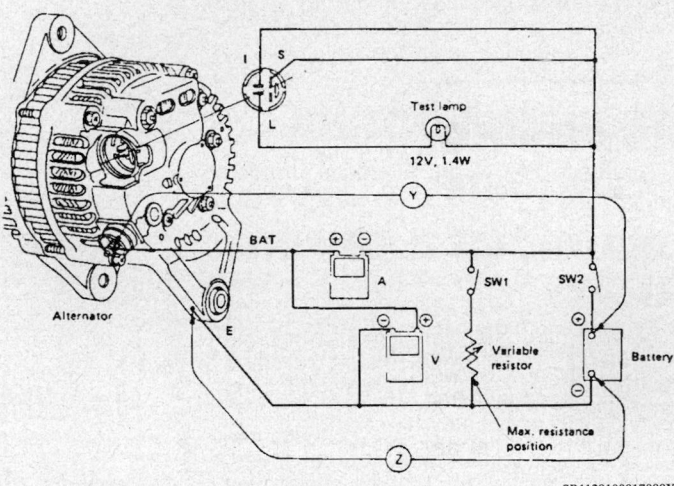

SB1129100017000X

**Fig. 5   Circuit for testing alternator voltage &
current output. Legacy**

ALTERNATOR SPECIFICATIONS

Year	Indent. No.	Current Rating		Integral Voltage Regulator	
		Amps @ 5000 RPM	Volts	Indent. No.	Voltage 68°F
1996–97	A2T39091	76	12	—	14.1-14.8
	A3TO8891	95	12	A866X21271	14.2-14.8
	LR160-137	60	12	TR1Z-56	14.2-14.8
	LR160-138	60	12	TR1Z-56	14.2-14.8
	LR185-701H	85	12	—	14.1-14.8
1998	A2TA7691	75	12	—	14.1-14.8
	LR185-701H	75	12	—	14.1-14.8
1999	A2TB2991	75	12	—	14.1-14.8
	LR185-701H	85	12	—	14.1-14.8

Speed Control Systems

INDEX

DESCRIPTION

SPEED CONTROL SYSTEM

The speed control system automatically controls vehicle speed without depressing the accelerator pedal. To achieve this, the speed sensor in the speedometer sends a feedback signal which is compared with the desired speed set in the computer memory. The difference between the sensor and memory speeds is transmitted to the solenoid valves which moves the actuator controlling the throttle and keeps the rate of speed constant.

SELF-DIAGNOSIS SYSTEM

The self-diagnosis function of the cruise control system uses an external select monitor. The self-diagnosis function operates in two categories; cruise cancel conditions diagnosis and real-time diagnosis, which are used depending on type of problems.

This system has built in memory, the select monitor must be connected before beginning diagnosis.

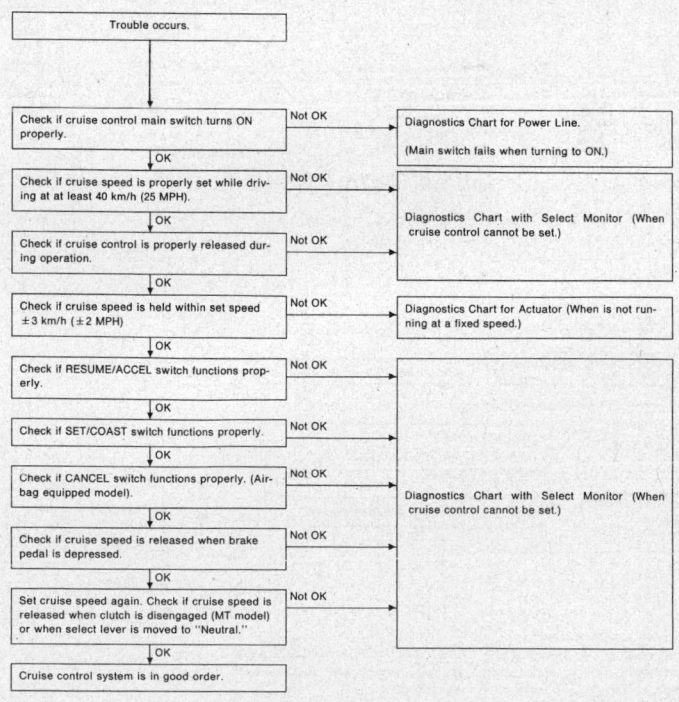

SB1109500022000X

**Fig. 1   Speed control basic troubleshooting chart.
1996–97 Impreza**

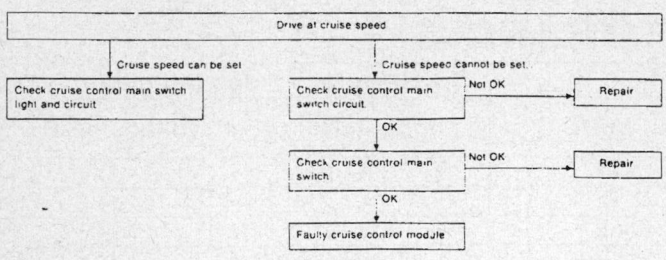

SB1109500023000X

Fig. 2 Speed control diagnostics chart for power line. 1996–97 Impreza

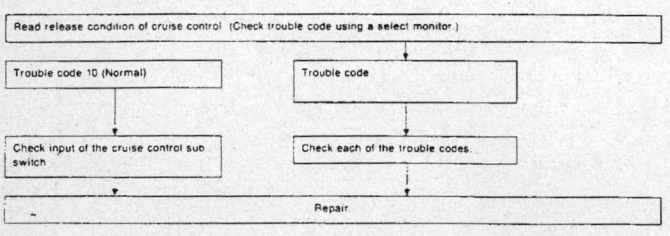

SB1109500025000X

Fig. 4 Speed control diagnostics chart w/select monitor. 1996–97 Impreza

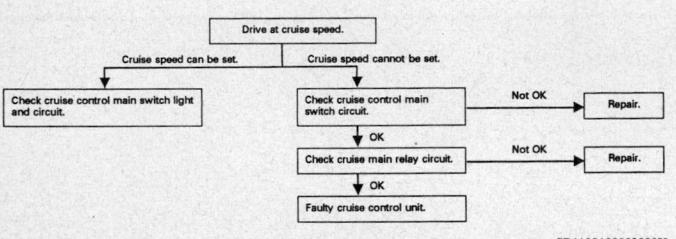

SB1109100003000X

Fig. 6 Speed control troubleshooting chart A. SVX

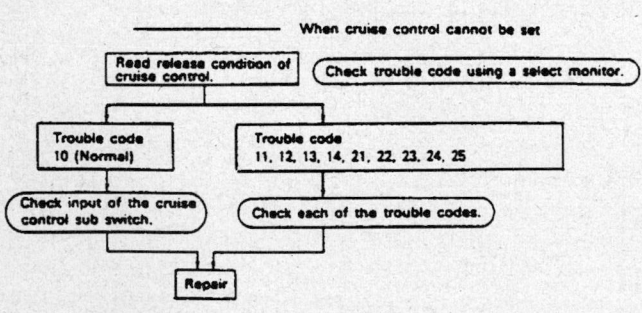

Check trouble code with a select monitor.
Check input of cruise control sub switch. (SET/COAST SW, RESUME/ACCEL SW)
Trouble code 11. Stop light switch, brake switch, inhibitor switch and clutch switch
Trouble code 12. Malfunction engine revolusion input signal
Trouble code 13. or 24. Failure in the speed sensor system
Trouble code 14. Simultaneous input signal of SET/SW and RESUME/SW
Trouble code 21. and 22. Malfunction in vacuum pump and vent valve
Trouble code 23. Malfunction in built-in relay of cruise control unit

SB1109100004000X

Fig. 7 Speed control troubleshooting chart B. SVX

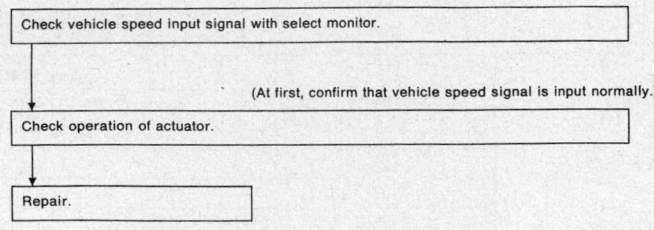

SB1109500024000X

Fig. 3 Speed control diagnostics chart for actuator. 1996–97 Impreza

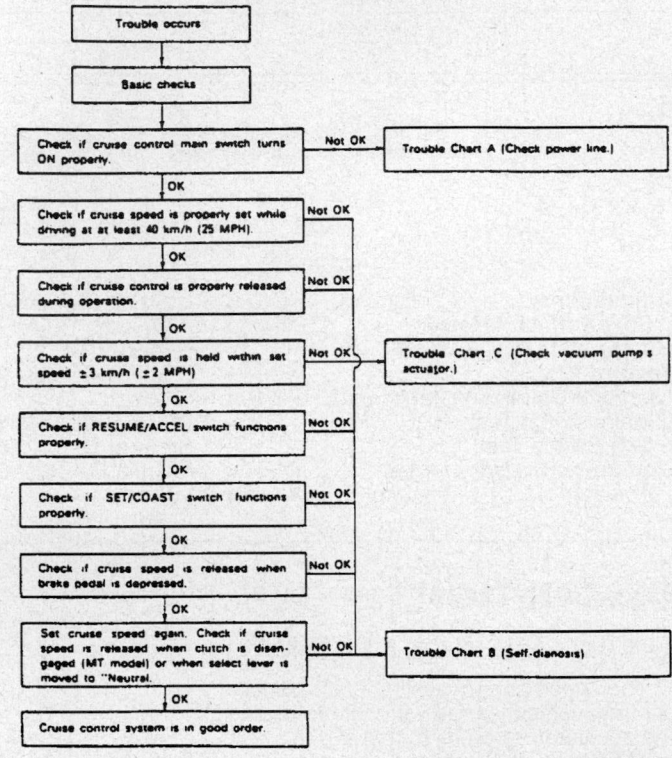

SB1109100002000X

Fig. 5 Speed control basic troubleshooting chart. SVX

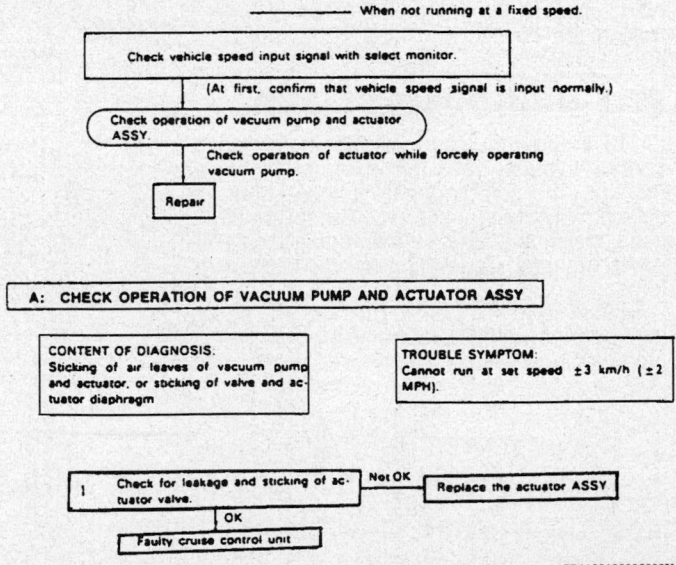

SB1109100005000X

Fig. 8 Speed control troubleshooting chart C. SVX

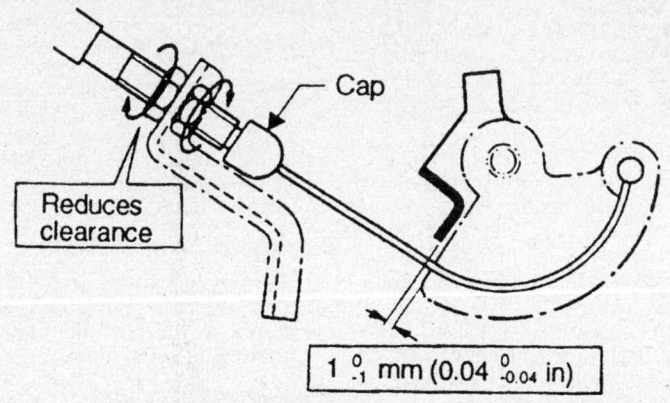

$$1 \, {}^{0}_{-1} \text{ mm } (0.04 \, {}^{0}_{-0.04} \text{ in})$$

SB1109100019000X

Fig. 9   Control cable adjustment. Impreza & Legacy

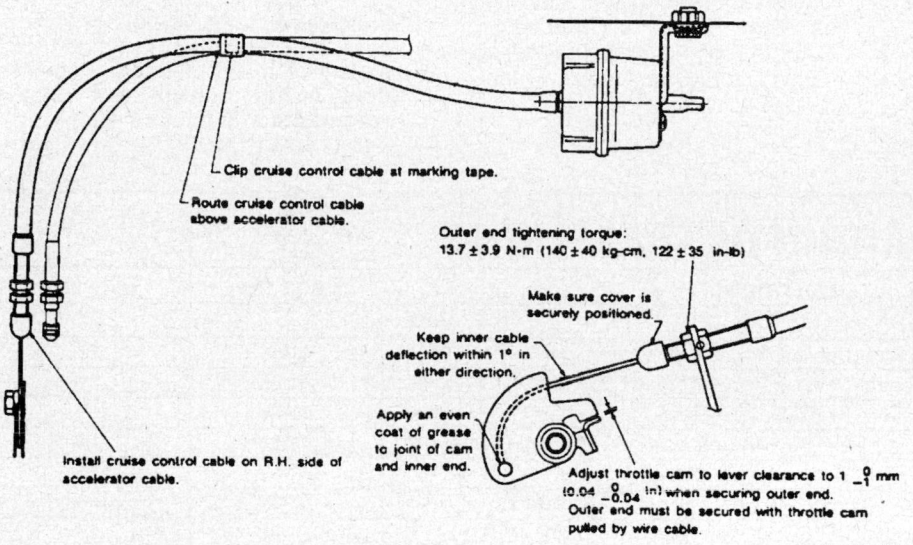

SB1109100021000X

Fig. 10   Control cable adjustment. SVX

Trouble code	Item	Contents of diagnosis
10	OK	Normal
11	Brake/switch, Stop light switch	Input signals from brake switch "OFF", stop light switch "ON" (Brake pedal is depressed.)
12	Clutch switch, N position	Input signals from clutch switch "OFF", inhibitor switch "N" (Clutch pedal is depressed, or select lever is set to "N".)
13	Speed limiter	Low-speed control limiter
14	Set switch and resume switch	Input signal from cancel switch "ON"
21	Vacuum valve	Faulty vacuum valve or valve drive system
22	Vent 2 valve	Faulty vent 2 valve or valve drive system
23	Vent 1 valve	Faulty vent 1 valve or valve drive system
24	Speed sensor	Faulty vehicle speed sensor
25	Control module	Faulty control module

SB1109500026000X

Fig. 11   Trouble code identification & description. Forester & Impreza

Cruise Cancel Conditions Diagnosis

This category of diagnosis requires actual vehicle driving in order to determine the problem (as when cruise speed is canceled during driving although no cruise cancel condition is entered).

Real-Time Diagnosis

This category is used to determine whether or not the input of output signal system is in good order, according to signal emitted from switches, sensors.

Vehicle cannot be driven at cruise speeds during this type of diagnosis.

Dummy signals are manually entered from the select monitor's keyboard to determine if certain system are operating satisfactory.

TROUBLESHOOTING
IMPREZA
1996-97

Refer to **Figs. 1 through 4** for troubleshooting procedures.

SVX

Refer to **Figs. 5 through 8** for troubleshooting procedures.

ADJUSTMENTS
SPEED CONTROL CABLE
Impreza & Legacy

Refer to **Fig. 9**, for control cable adjustment.

SVX

Refer to **Fig. 10**, for control cable adjustment.

SYSTEM DIAGNOSIS & TESTING
FORESTER

Refer to **Fig. 11** for trouble code identification and description.
Refer to **Figs. 12 through 22** for system diagnosis and testing.

IMPREZA
1996-97

Refer to **Fig. 11** for trouble code identification and description.
Refer to **Figs. 23 through 30** for system diagnosis and testing.

1998-99

Refer to "Forester" section for diagnosis and testing procedures.

LEGACY
1998

Refer to **Fig. 31** for trouble code identification and description.
Refer to **Figs. 32 through 41** for diagnosis and testing procedures.

SVX

Refer to **Fig. 42** for trouble code identification and description.
1. Connect select monitor to connector B35.
2. Turn ignition switch on, then turn cruise main switch to on position.
3. Turn select monitor on. All LED's will come on. Select monitor display will read, **Fig. 43**, after several seconds.
4. Press "/" three times. Select monitor display will read, **Fig. 44**.

5. Press "O." If cruise main switch is off, error 2 will appear. Turn cruise main switch on and repeat procedure.
6. Press "F," "B," "O" and "ENT" in that order and enter the desired designated code.

CRUISE CANCEL CONDITIONS

1. Connect select monitor.
2. Turn ignition and cruise main switch on and set select monitor in "FBO" mode.
3. Start engine and drive vehicle at least 25 mph with cruise speed set.
4. If cruise speed is canceled itself (without doing any cancel operations), a trouble code will appear on select monitor display.
5. Trouble code will be cleared by turning ignition or cruise main switch off.

REAL-TIME DIAGNOSIS

1. Inspect system switches as follows:
   a. Connect select monitor.
   b. Turn ignition switch and cruise main switch on.
   c. Set select monitor in "FAO" mode.
   d. Ensure normal indication is displayed when switches are operated, **Figs. 45 and 46.**
2. **On SVX models,** inspect output systems as follows:
   a. Connect select monitor.
   b. Turn ignition switch and cruise main switch on (engine off).
   c. Set transmission in Drive.
   d. Set select monitor in FB1 mode. The display will read, **Fig. 47,** until input OK is present.
   e. Press "O." Example, pressing " O" in Neutral shows "31 Motor" (which indicates a faulty motor) on display because power supply to vacuum pump motor is disconnected. When this is shown, set select lever to Drive and turn cruise main switch off. Then repeat test procedure. Refer to **Fig. 48,** for output system codes and **Fig. 49,** for select monitor display data.

ROAD TESTS

Acceleration Test

1. Turn main switch on.
2. Set vehicle at speed greater than 25 mph. Ensure vehicle accelerates with switch held in "Resume/Accede" position and optional speed is maintained with switch released.

Constant Speed Test

1. Turn main switch on.
2. Set switch to "Set/Coast" with vehicle speed over 25 mph. Ensure vehicle maintains set speed.

Deceleration Test

1. Turn main switch on.
2. Set vehicle at speed greater than 25 mph. Ensure vehicle decelerates with switch held in "Set/Coast" position and optional speed is maintained with switch released. **During deceleration, cruise control will release when speed reaches 19 mph.**

DIAGNOSTIC CHART INDEX

Test/Code	Description	Page No.	Fig. No.
FORESTER			
Test 2B	Cruise Control Cable & Vacuum Hose Diagnosis	41-86	12
Test 2C	Cruise Control Cable & Vacuum Hose Diagnosis	41-86	12
Test 2D	Actuator Testing	41-86	13
Test 2E	Power Supply Diagnosis	41-87	14
Test 7A	Basic Diagnostics	41-87	15
Test 7B	Check Indicator & Circuit In Cruise Control Main Switch	41-87	16
Test 7C	Cruise Control Main Switch	41-88	17
Test 8B	Brake Switch, Stop Light Switch	41-88	18
Test 8C	Clutch Switch, Inhibitor Switch	41-89	19
Test 8D	Vehicle Speed Sensor 2 System	41-90	20
Test 8E	Set/Coast Switch, Resume/Accede Switch, Cancel Switch	41-90	21
Test 8F	Vacuum Valve, Vent 2 Valve & Vent 1 Valve	41-92	22
Test 11	Brake Switch, Stop Light Switch	41-88	18
Test 12	Clutch Switch, Inhibitor Switch	41-89	19
Test 13	Vehicle Speed Sensor 2 System	41-90	20
Test 14	Set/Coast Switch, Resume/Accede Switch, Cancel Switch	41-90	21
Test 21	Vacuum Valve, Vent 2 Valve & Vent 1 Valve	41-92	22
Test 22	Vacuum Valve, Vent 2 Valve & Vent 1 Valve	41-92	22
Test 23	Vacuum Valve, Vent 2 Valve & Vent 1 Valve	41-92	22
Test 24	Vehicle Speed Sensor 2 System	41-90	20
1996-97 IMPREZA			
—	Check Indicator & Circuit In Cruise Control Main Switch Test	41-92	23
—	Cruise Control Main Switch Test	41-93	24
—	Set/Coast, Resume/Accede switch test	41-93	25
Code 11	Brake Switch/Stop Light Switch	41-94	26
Code 12	Clutch Switch, N Position	41-94	27
Code 13	Speed Limiter, Speed Sensor	41-94	28
Code 14	Set Switch/Resume Switch	41-95	29
Code 21	Vacuum Valve, Vent 1 Valve & Vent 2 Valve	41-95	30
Code 22	Vacuum Valve, Vent 1 Valve & Vent 2 Valve	41-95	30
Code 23	Vacuum Valve, Vent 1 Valve & Vent 2 Valve	41-95	30
Code 24	Speed Limiter, Speed Sensor	41-94	28

Continued

DIAGNOSTIC CHART INDEX—Continued

Test/Code	Description	Page No.	Fig. No.
1998-99 IMPREZA			
Test 2B	Cruise Control Cable & Vacuum Hose Diagnosis	41-86	12
Test 2C	Cruise Control Cable & Vacuum Hose Diagnosis	41-86	12
Test 2D	Actuator Testing	41-86	13
Test 2E	Power Supply Diagnosis	41-87	14
Test 7A	Basic Diagnostics	41-87	15
Test 7B	Check Indicator & Circuit In Cruise Control Main Switch	41-87	16
Test 7C	Cruise Control Main Switch	41-88	17
Test 8B	Brake Switch, Stop Light Switch	41-88	18
Test 8C	Clutch Switch, Inhibitor Switch	41-89	19
Test 8D	Vehicle Speed Sensor 2 System	41-90	20
Test 8E	Set/Coast Switch, Resume/Accede Switch, Cancel Switch	41-90	21
Test 8F	Vacuum Valve, Vent 2 Valve & Vent 1 Valve	41-92	22
Test 11	Brake Switch, Stop Light Switch	41-88	18
Test 12	Clutch Switch, Inhibitor Switch	41-89	19
Test 13	Vehicle Speed Sensor 2 System	41-90	20
Test 14	Set/Coast Switch, Resume/Accede Switch, Cancel Switch	41-90	21
Test 21	Vacuum Valve, Vent 2 Valve & Vent 1 Valve	41-92	22
Test 22	Vacuum Valve, Vent 2 Valve & Vent 1 Valve	41-92	22
Test 23	Vacuum Valve, Vent 2 Valve & Vent 1 Valve	41-92	22
Test 24	Vehicle Speed Sensor 2 System	41-90	20
1998 LEGACY			
—	Cruise Control Cable & Vacuum Hose Checks	41-85	32
—	Actuator Test	41-96	33
—	Vacuum Pump & Valve Diagnosis	41-96	34
—	Basic Diagnostic Procedure	41-97	36
—	Cruise Control Main Switch Inspection	41-98	37
—	Power Supply	41-97	35
Code 11	Brake Switch, Stop Light Switch, Clutch Switch (M/T), Inhibitor Switch (A/T)	41-99	38
Code 12	Vehicle Speed Sensor 2 System	41-100	39
Code 13	Vehicle Speed Sensor 2 System	41-100	39
Code 14	Set/Coast Switch, Resume/Accede Switch, Cancel Switch	41-101	40
Code 21	Vehicle Speed Sensor 2 System	41-100	39
Code 22	Set/Coast Switch, Resume/Accede Switch, Cancel Switch	41-101	40
Code 31	Vacuum Pump, Air Valve, Release Valve	41-102	41
Code 32	Vacuum Pump, Air Valve, Release Valve	41-102	41
Code 33	Vacuum Pump, Air Valve, Release Valve	41-102	41

B: CRUISE CONTROL CABLE

| 2B1 : | CHECK CRUISE CONTROL CABLE. |

Check cruise control cable installation.

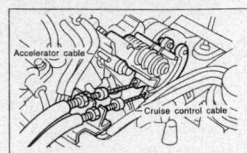

CHECK : **Is the cruise control cable securely installed to the left of the accelerator cable?**
YES : Go to step **2B2**.
NO : Install cruise control cable securely. Go to step **2B2**.

| 2B2 : | CHECK ACCELERATOR CABLE. |

Check function of accelerator cable.

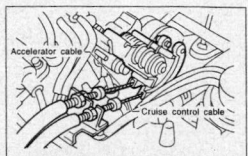

CHECK : **Does the accelerator cable throttle cam move when the cruise control throttle is moved by hand?**
YES : Repair accelerator cable throttle cam. Go to step **2B3**.
NO : Go to step **2B3**.

| 2B3 : | CHECK THROTTLE CAM. |

Check function of throttle cam.
CHECK : **Does the throttle cam move smoothly?**
YES : Go to step **2B4**.
NO : Repair throttle cam. Go to step **2B4**.

| 2B4 : | CHECK CABLE FREE PLAY. |

Ensure that throttle cam-to-lever clearance is within specifications.

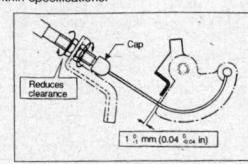

CHECK : **Is throttle cam-to-lever clearance between 0 and 1 mm (0 and 0.04 in)?**
YES : Go to step **2C1**.
NO : Adjust cable end by adjusting nuts. Go to step **2C1**.

NOTE:
Ensure that cap is positioned in groove.

C: VACUUM HOSE

| 2C1 : | CHECK VACUUM HOSE VISUALLY. |

Check vacuum hose (which connects actuator and intake manifold).

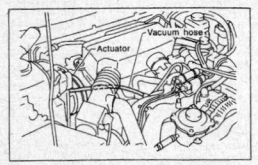

CHECK : **Is there disconnection or cracks in vacuum hose?**
YES : Replace vacuum hose. Go to step **2D1**.
NO : Go to step **2D1**.

SB1109800030000X

Fig. 12   Test 2B & 2C: Cruise Control Cable & Vacuum Hose Diagnosis. Forester & 1998–99 Impreza

| 2D4 : | MEASURE RESISTANCE OF VALVE. |

Measure resistance between terminals of actuator.
Terminals
No. 2 — No. 4:

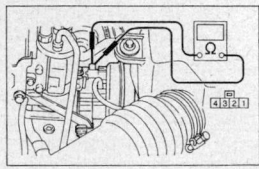

CHECK : **Is resistance less than 69 Ω?**
YES : Go to step **2D5**.
NO : Replace actuator.

| 2D5 : | CHECK FOR LEAKAGE AND STICKING OF VALVES. |

1) Disconnect connector from actuator.
2) Make sure that cruise control cable moves smoothly when connecting + (positive) battery cable to terminal No. 2 and – (negative) battery cable to terminals No. 1, 3 and 4 of actuator connector.

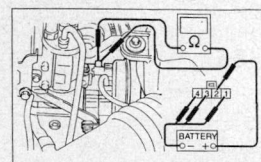

CHECK : **Does cruise control cable have a stroke of 35 mm (1.38 in) within 3 seconds?**
YES : Go to step **2D6**.
NO : Replace actuator. Go to step **2D6**.

| 2D6 : | CHECK FOR LEAKAGE AND STICKING OF VALVES. |

When the battery cable is disconnected from former condition make sure the cable returns to its original position smoothly.

CHECK : **Does cruise control cable get back to its original position within 1.5 seconds?**
YES : Go to step **2D7**.
NO : Replace actuator. Go to step **2D7**.

| 2D7 : | CHECK CABLE MOVEMENT. |

Connect + (positive) battery cable to terminal No. 2 and – (negative) battery cable to terminals No. 1, 3 and 4 of actuator connector.

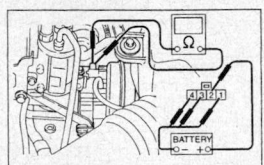

CHECK : **Does cruise control perform pull operation?**
YES : Go to step **2D8**.
NO : Replace actuator. Go to step **2D8**.

SB1109800031020X

Fig. 13   Test 2D: Actuator Testing (Part 2 of 3). Forester & 1998–99 Impreza

D: ACTUATOR

| 2D1 : | CHECK FUNCTION OF ACTUATOR. |

1) Disconnect vacuum hose from actuator.

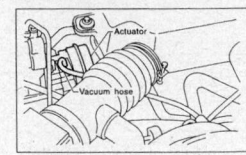

2) Connect vacuum pump.

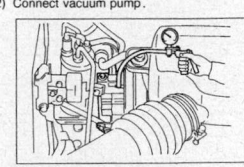

3) Make sure that cruise control cable moves smoothly and quickly when a vacuum pressure of 40.0 kPa (300 mmHg, 11.81 inHg) is applied to actuator.

CHECK : **Does cruise control cable have a stroke of 35 mm (1.38 in)?**
YES : Go to step **2D2**.
NO : Replace actuator. Go to step **2D2**.

NOTE:
● When vacuum pressure is released from condition 3) above, make sure the cable returns to its original position smoothly and quickly.
● After inspection, disconnect vacuum pump and connect vacuum hose.

| 2D2 : | MEASURE RESISTANCE OF VALVE. |

1) Disconnect connector from actuator.
2) Measure resistance between terminals of actuator.
Terminals
No. 2 — No. 3:

CHECK : **Is resistance less than 100 Ω?**
YES : Go to step **2D3**.
NO : Replace actuator.

| 2D3 : | MEASURE RESISTANCE OF VALVE. |

Measure resistance between terminals of actuator.
Terminals
No. 2 — No. 1:

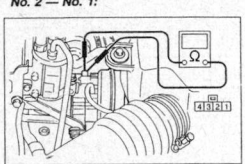

CHECK : **Is resistance less than 69 Ω?**
YES : Go to step **2D4**.
NO : Replace actuator.

SB1109800031010X

Fig. 13   Test 2D: Actuator Testing (Part 1 of 3). Forester & 1998–99 Impreza

| 2D8 : | CHECK CABLE MOVEMENT. |

Connect + (positive) battery cable to terminal No. 2 and – (negative) battery cable to terminals No. 1 and 4 of actuator connector.

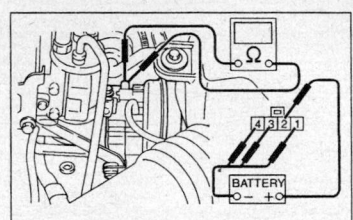

CHECK : **Does cruise control perform hold operation?**
YES : Go to step **2D9**.
NO : Replace actuator. Go to step **2D9**.

| 2D9 : | CHECK CABLE MOVEMENT. |

Connect + (positive) battery cable to terminal No. 2 and – (negative) battery cable to terminal No. 4 of actuator connector.

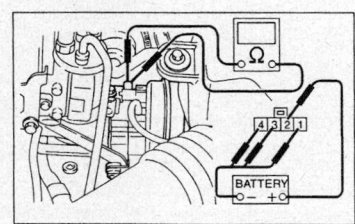

CHECK : **Does cruise control perform release operation?**
YES : Go to step **2E1**.
NO : Replace actuator. Go to step **2E1**.

SB1109800031030X

Fig. 13   Test 2D: Actuator Testing (Part 3 of 3). Forester & 1998–99 Impreza

E: POWER SUPPLY

> **2E1 : CHECK BATTERY.**

Measure battery specific gravity of electrolyte.

CHECK : *Is battery specific gravity more than 1.250?*

YES : Go to step **2E2**.

NO : Charge or replace battery. Go to step **2E2**.

> **2E2 : CHECK FUSES, CONNECTORS AND HARNESSES.**

Check the condition of the main and other fuses, and harnesses and connectors. Also check for proper grounding.

CHECK : *Is there anything unusual about the appearance of main fuse, fuse, harness, connector and grounding?*

YES : Repair or replace faulty parts. End of pre-inspection.

NO : End of pre-inspection.

SB1109800032000X

Fig. 14   Test 2E: Power Supply Diagnosis. Forester & 1998–99 Impreza

B: CHECK INDICATOR AND CIRCUIT IN CRUISE CONTROL MAIN SWITCH
DIAGNOSIS:
● Bulb failure or open harness of the indicator circuit in the cruise control main switch.
TROUBLE SYMPTOM:
● Cruise control can be set, normally indicator does not come on. (When main switch is pressed.)
WIRING DIAGRAM:

SB1109800034010X

Fig. 16   Test 7B: Check Indicator & Circuit In Cruise Control Main Switch (Part 1 of 2). Forester & 1998–99 Impreza

A: BASIC DIAGNOSTICS PROCEDURE

> **7A1 : DRIVE AT CRUISE SPEED.**

CHECK : *Can cruise speed be set?*

YES : Go to "CHECK INDICATOR AND CIRCUIT IN CRUISE CONTROL MAIN SWITCH".

NO : Go to "CHECK CRUISE CONTROL MAIN SWITCH".

SB1109800033000X

Fig. 15   Test 7A: Basic Diagnostics. Forester & 1998–99 Impreza

> **7B1 : CHECK CRUISE CONTROL MAIN SWITCH.**

1) Remove cruise control main switch.
2) Measure resistance between cruise control main switch terminals.

Terminals
No. 1 — No. 6:

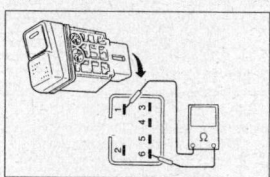

CHECK : *Is resistance between 10 and 80 Ω?*
YES : Go to step **7B2**.
NO : Replace switch illumination bulb.

> **7B2 : CHECK CIRCUIT BETWEEN CRUISE CONTROL MODULE AND CRUISE CONTROL MAIN SWITCH INDICATOR LIGHT.**

1) Turn the ignition switch to ON.
2) Turn cruise control main switch to ON.
3) Measure voltage between cruise control main switch connector and the chassis ground.

Connector & terminal
(B161) No. 1 (+) — Chassis ground (–):

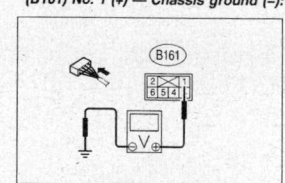

CHECK : *Is voltage more than 10 V?*
YES : Go to step **7B3**.
NO : Repair or replace wiring harness.

> **7B3 : CHECK CIRCUIT BETWEEN CRUISE CONTROL MODULE AND CRUISE CONTROL MAIN SWITCH INDICATOR LIGHT.**

1) Turn the ignition switch and cruise control main switch to OFF.
2) Remove the connector from the cruise control main switch.
3) Measure resistance of ground circuit between the cruise control main switch connector and chassis ground.

Connector & terminal
(B161) No. 6 (+) — Chassis ground (–):

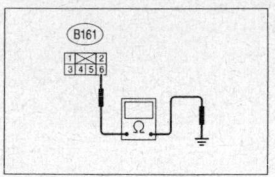

CHECK : *Is resistance less than 10 Ω?*
YES : Replace cruise control module.
NO : Repair or replace wiring harness.

SB1109800034020X

Fig. 16   Test 7B: Check Indicator & Circuit In Cruise Control Main Switch (Part 2 of 2). Forester & 1998–99 Impreza

C: CHECK CRUISE CONTROL MAIN SWITCH

DIAGNOSIS:
● Faulty cruise control main switch, or open harness.

TROUBLE SYMPTOM:
● Cruise control main switch is not turned ON and cruise control cannot be set.

NOTE:
When the main relay (built-in cruise control module) operates, the main switch circuit is in normal condition.
The main relay operation can be checked by hearing the operation sounds.
This operation sounds will be heard when ignition switch and cruise control main switch is turned to ON.

SB1109800035010X

Fig. 17   Test 7C: Cruise Control Main Switch (Part 1 of 3). Forester & 1998–99 Impreza

---

7C5 : CHECK CRUISE CONTROL MAIN SWITCH.

Measure resistance between cruise control main switch terminals.

Terminals
No. 3 — No. 5:

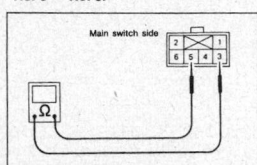

CHECK : **Is resistance less than 1 MΩ? (When switch is OFF.)**
YES : Go to step **7C6.**
NO : Replace cruise control main switch.

7C6 : CHECK HARNESS BETWEEN CRUISE CONTROL MAIN SWITCH CONNECTOR AND CHASSIS GROUND.

1) Connect connector.
2) Turn ignition switch to ON.
3) Turn cruise control main switch to ON.
4) Measure voltage between terminal of cruise control main switch and chassis ground.

Connector & terminal
(B161) No. 3 (+) — Chassis ground (–):

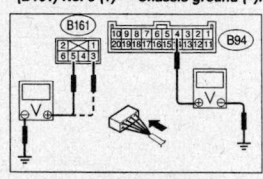

CHECK : **Is voltage more than 10 V?**
YES : Go to step **7C7.**
NO : Repair or replace wiring harness.

SB1109800035030X

Fig. 17   Test 7C: Cruise Control Main Switch (Part 3 of 3). Forester & 1998–99 Impreza

---

7C7 : CHECK HARNESS BETWEEN CRUISE CONTROL MAIN SWITCH CONNECTOR AND CHASSIS GROUND.

Measure voltage between terminal of cruise control main switch chassis ground.

Connector & terminal
(B161) No. 5 (+) — Chassis ground (–):

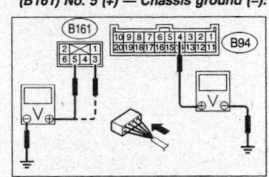

CHECK : **Is voltage more than 10 V?**
YES : Go to step **7C8.**
NO : Repair or replace wiring harness.

7C8 : CHECK HARNESS BETWEEN CRUISE CONTROL MODULE CONNECTOR AND CHASSIS GROUND.

Measure voltage between terminal of cruise control module and chassis ground.

Connector & terminal
(B94) No. 4 (+) — Chassis ground (–):

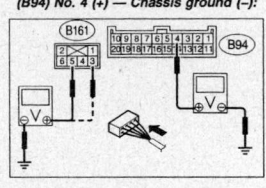

CHECK : **Is voltage more than 10 V?**
YES : Replace cruise control module.
NO : Repair or replace wiring harness.

NOTE:
Depress cruise control main switch with fingers while measuring voltage between (B161) No. 5 and chassis ground.

7C1 : CHECK FUSE.

Check fuse No. 18.

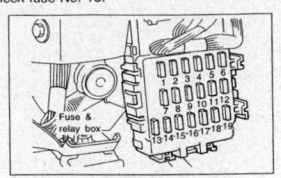

CHECK : **Is fuse No. 18 blown?**
YES : Replace fuse No. 18. Go to step **7C2.**
NO : Go to step **7C2.**

7C2 : CHECK POWER SUPPLY.

1) Turn ignition switch to ON.
2) Measure voltage between fuse & relay box connector and chassis ground.

Connector & terminal
(B152) No. 5 (+) — Chassis ground (–):

CHECK : **Is voltage more than 10 V?**
YES : Go to step **7C3.**
NO : Replace fuse No. 18. When fuse No. 18 is blown again, repair shorted parts of circuit.

7C3 : CHECK CRUISE CONTROL MAIN SWITCH.

1) Turn ignition switch to OFF.
2) Remove cruise control main switch and disconnect connector.
3) Turn ignition switch to ON.
4) Measure voltage between cruise control main switch connector and chassis ground.

Connector & terminal
(B161) No. 3 (+) — Chassis ground (–):

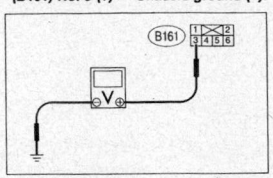

CHECK : **Is voltage more than 10 V?**
YES : Go to step **7C4.**
NO : Replace cruise control main switch.

7C4 : CHECK CRUISE CONTROL MAIN SWITCH.

Measure resistance between cruise control main switch terminals.

Terminals
No. 3 — No. 5:

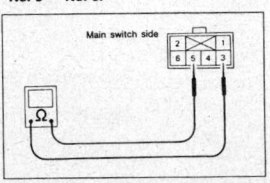

CHECK : **Is resistance less than 10 Ω? (When switch is ON.)**
YES : Go to step **7C5.**
NO : Replace cruise control main switch.

SB1109800035020X

Fig. 17   Test 7C: Cruise Control Main Switch (Part 2 of 3). Forester & 1998–99 Impreza

---

B: DIAGNOSTIC CODE 11 (BRAKE SWITCH, STOP LIGHT SWITCH)

DIAGNOSIS:
● Failure or disconnection of the stop light switch and brake switch.

TROUBLE SYMPTOM:
● Cruise control cannot be set.

WIRING DIAGRAM:

SB1109800036010X

Fig. 18   Test 8B, Code 11: Brake Switch, Stop Light Switch (Part 1 of 3). Forester & 1998–99 Impreza

8B1 : CHECK BRAKE SWITCH.

1) Turn ignition switch to ON.
2) Turn cruise control main switch to ON.
3) Apply parking brake securely.
4) Set select monitor in "Current Data Display & Save" mode.
5) Depress the brake pedal and check signals for proper operation.
   (1) The Stop Lamp Switch shown on the display turns from "OFF" to "ON".
   (2) The Brake Switch shown on the display turns from "OFF" to "ON".
6) Release the brake pedal.
7) Remove connector of stop and brake switch.
8) Check circuit between brake switch terminal.

Terminals
No. 1 — No. 4: (Brake switch)

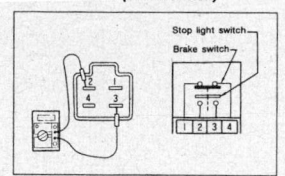

CHECK : *Is resistance less than 1 Ω? (When brake pedal is released.)*
YES : Go to step **8B2.**
NO : Replace brake and stop light switch.

8B2 : CHECK BRAKE SWITCH.

Check circuit between brake switch terminal.

Terminals
No. 1 — No. 4: (Brake switch)

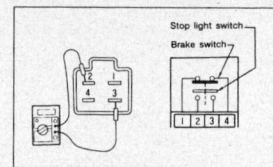

CHECK : *Is resistance more than 1 MΩ? (When brake pedal is depressed.)*
YES : Go to step **8B3.**
NO : Replace brake and stop light switch.

8B3 : CHECK STOP LIGHT SWITCH.

Check circuit between stop light switch terminal.

Terminals
No. 2 — No. 3: (Stop light switch)

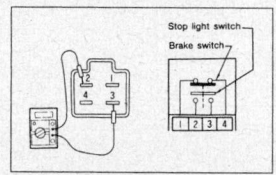

CHECK : *Is resistance more than 1 MΩ? (When brake pedal is released.)*
YES : Go to step **8B4.**
NO : Replace brake and stop light switch.

SB1109800036020X

Fig. 18 Test 8B, Code 11: Brake Switch, Stop Light Switch (Part 2 of 3). Forester & 1998–99 Impreza

---

8B4 : CHECK STOP LIGHT SWITCH.

Check circuit between stop light switch terminal.

Terminals
No. 2 — No. 3: (Stop light switch)

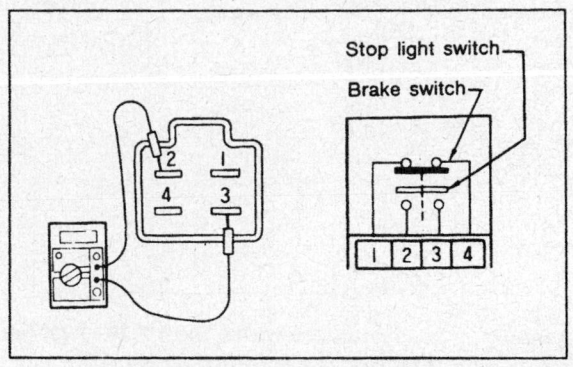

CHECK : *Is resistance less than 1 Ω? (When brake pedal is depressed.)*
YES : Replace cruise control module.
NO : Replace brake and stop light switch.

SB1109800036030X

Fig. 18 Test 8B, Code 11: Brake Switch, Stop Light Switch (Part 3 of 3). Forester & 1998–99 Impreza

---

C: DIAGNOSTIC CODE 12 (CLUTCH SWITCH, INHIBITOR SWITCH)

DIAGNOSIS:
• Failure or disconnection of the clutch switch. (MT)
• Failure or disconnection of the inhibitor switch. (AT)

TROUBLE SYMPTOM:
• Cruise control cannot be set.

SB1109800037010X

Fig. 19 Test 8C, Code 12: Clutch Switch, Inhibitor Switch (Part 1 of 3). Forester & 1998–99 Impreza

---

8C1 : CHECK CLUTCH SWITCH. (MT)

1) Turn ignition switch to ON.
2) Turn cruise control main switch to ON.
3) Apply parking brake securely.
4) Set select monitor in "Current Data Display & Save" mode.
5) Depress the clutch pedal and check signal for proper operation. (MT)
The Clutch/Inhibitor Switch shown on the display turns from "ON" to "OFF".
6) Disconnect connector of clutch switch.
7) Check continuity of the clutch switch.

Terminals
No. 1 — No. 2:

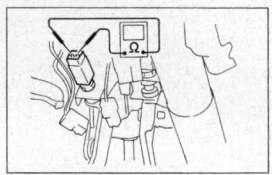

CHECK : *Is resistance less than 10 Ω? (When clutch pedal is released.)*
YES : Go to step **8C2.**
NO : Replace clutch switch.

8C2 : CHECK CLUTCH SWITCH. (MT)

Check continuity of the clutch switch.

Terminals
No. 1 — No. 2:

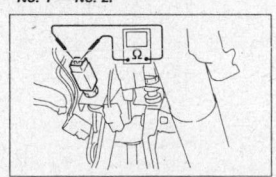

CHECK : *Is resistance more than 1 MΩ? (When clutch pedal is depressed.)*
YES : Replace cruise control module.
NO : Replace clutch switch.

8C3 : CHECK INHIBITOR SWITCH. (AT)

1) Turn ignition switch to ON.
2) Turn cruise control main switch to ON.
3) Apply parking brake securely.
4) Set select monitor in "Current Data Display & Save" mode.
5) Set the selector lever from P or N position to D position and check signal for proper operation. (AT)
The Clutch/Inhibitor Switch shown on the display turns from "ON" to "OFF".
6) Set the selector lever to P or N position.
7) Disconnect connector of inhibitor switch.
8) Check continuity of the inhibitor switch.

Terminals
No. 11 — No. 12:

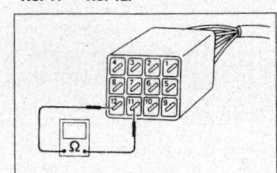

CHECK : *Is resistance less than 10 Ω? (When selector lever is in P or N.)*
YES : Go to step **8C4.**
NO : Replace inhibitor switch. Repair inhibitor switch wiring harness.

SB1109800037020X

Fig. 19 Test 8C, Code 12: Clutch Switch, Inhibitor Switch (Part 2 of 3). Forester & 1998–99 Impreza

---

SUBARU

8C4 : CHECK INHIBITOR SWITCH. (AT)

Check continuity of the inhibitor switch.

Terminals
No. 11 — No. 12:

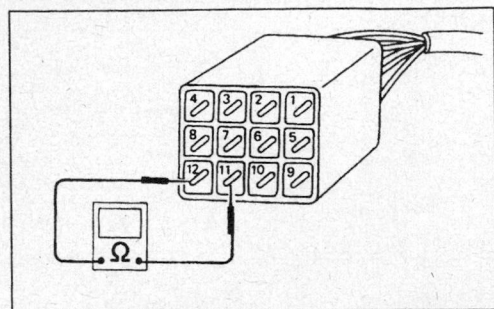

CHECK : *Is resistance more than 1 MΩ? (When selector lever is not in P or N.)*

YES : Replace cruise control module.

NO : Replace inhibitor switch. Repair inhibitor switch wiring harness.

SB1109800037030X

Fig. 19 Test 8C, Code 12: Clutch Switch, Inhibitor Switch (Part 3 of 3). Forester & 1998–99 Impreza

---

8D2 : CHECK INPUT SIGNAL FOR CRUISE CONTROL MODULE.

WARNING:
Be careful not to be caught up by the running wheels.

1) Set the vehicle on free roller, or lift-up the vehicle and support with safety stands.
2) Set oscilloscope to cruise control module connector terminals.
3) Start the engine.
4) Shift on the gear position, and keep the vehicle speed at constant.
5) Measure signal voltage.

Connector & terminal
(B94) No. 18 (+) — Chassis ground (–):

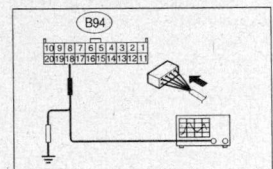

CHECK : *Is the voltage more than 2 V?*
YES : Replace cruise control module.
NO : Go to step 8D3.

NOTE:
● If the vehicle speed increases, the width of amplitude (W) decreases.

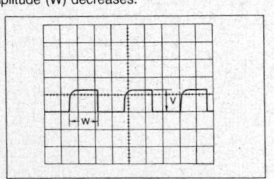

● If oscilloscope is not available, check input signal (vehicle speed signal) by using a select monitor. (Refer to the procedure as described below.)
● Using the select monitor:
1) Set the vehicle on free roller, or lift-up the vehicle and support with safety stands.
2) Turn ignition switch to OFF and set select monitor.

3) Turn ignition switch to ON.
4) Turn cruise control main switch to ON.
5) Set select monitor in "Current Data Display & Save" mode.
6) Drive the vehicle at speed greater than 40 km/h (25 MPH).
7) Check that vehicle speed indication on select monitor and speedometer are equal.
● When there is a disconnection or short circuit in the harness between the meter and the cruise control module, the indicated value will be 0 to 1.0 km/h (0 to 0.6 MPH).

8D3 : PERFORM A CIRCUIT TEST BETWEEN COMBINATION METER AND CRUISE CONTROL MODULE.

1) Turn ignition switch to OFF.
2) Remove combination meter.

3) Disconnect connector from cruise control module.
4) Measure resistance of harness connector between combination meter and cruise control module.

Connector & terminal
(i12) No. 11 — (B94) No. 18:

CHECK : *Is resistance less than 10 Ω?*
YES : Go to step 8D4.
NO : Repair or replace harness connector.

SB1109800038020X

Fig. 20 Test 8D, Codes 13 & 24: Vehicle Speed Sensor 2 System (Part 2 of 3). Forester & 1998–99 Impreza

---

D: DIAGNOSTIC CODE 13 AND 24 (VEHICLE SPEED SENSOR 2 SYSTEM)
DIAGNOSIS:
● Disconnection or short circuit of vehicle speed sensor 2 system.
TROUBLE SYMPTOM:
● Cruise control cannot be set. (Cancelled immediately.)
WIRING DIAGRAM:

8D1 : CHECK OPERATION OF SPEEDOMETER.

Make sure that speedometer indicates the vehicle speed by driving the vehicle.

CHECK : *Does speedometer indicate vehicle speed by driving vehicle?*
YES : Go to step 8D2.
NO : Repair combination meter circuit.

SB1109800038010X

Fig. 20 Test 8D, Codes 13 & 24: Vehicle Speed Sensor 2 System (Part 1 of 3). Forester & 1998–99 Impreza

---

8D4 : PERFORM A CIRCUIT TEST BETWEEN COMBINATION METER AND CRUISE CONTROL MODULE.

Measure resistance of harness connector between cruise control module and chassis ground to make sure that circuit does not short.

Connector & terminal
(B94) No. 18 (+) — Chassis ground (–):

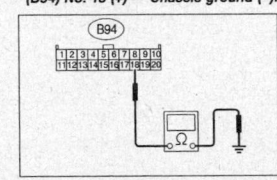

CHECK : *Is resistance more than 1 MΩ?*
YES : Go to step 8D5.
NO : Repair or replace harness connector.

8D5 : CHECK VEHICLE SPEED SENSOR 2.

1) Disconnect connector from vehicle speed sensor 2.
2) Measure resistance between terminals of vehicle speed sensor 2.

Terminals
No. 1 — No. 2:

CHECK : *Is resistance between 350 and 450 Ω?*
YES : Go to step 8D6.
NO : Replace vehicle speed sensor 2.

8D6 : CHECK VEHICLE SPEED SENSOR 2.

1) Set the vehicle on free roller, or lift-up the vehicle and support with safety stands.
WARNING:
Be careful not to be caught up by the running wheels.

2) Drive the vehicle at speed greater than 20 km/h (12 MPH).
3) Measure voltage between terminals of vehicle speed sensor 2.

NOTE:
Using an oscilloscope:
(1) Turn ignition switch to OFF.
(2) Set oscilloscope to vehicle speed sensor 2.
(3) Drive the vehicle at speed greater than 20 km/h (12 MPH).
(4) Measure signal voltage.

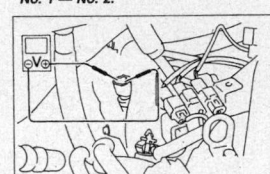

Terminals
No. 1 — No. 2:

SB1109800038030X

Fig. 20 Test 8D, Codes 13 & 24: Vehicle Speed Sensor 2 System (Part 3 of 3). Forester & 1998–99 Impreza

---

E: DIAGNOSTIC CODE 14 (SET/COAST SWITCH, RESUME/ACCEL SWITCH, CANCEL SWITCH)
DIAGNOSIS:
● Short circuit inside the SET SW and RESUME SW.
TROUBLE SYMPTOM:
● Cruise control cannot be set. (Cancelled immediately.)

SB1109800039010X

Fig. 21 Test 8E, Code 14: Set/Coast Switch, Resume/Accede Switch, Cancel Switch (Part 1 of 5). Forester & 1998–99 Impreza

8E1 : CHECK POWER SUPPLY.

1) Turn ignition switch to ON.
2) Turn cruise control main switch to ON.
3) Set select monitor in "Current Data Display & Save" mode.
4) Check signals for proper operation.
   (1) When pushing the SET/COAST switch: The SET/COAST switch shown on the display turns from "OFF" to "ON".
   (2) When pushing the RESUME/ACCEL switch: The RESUME/ACCEL switch shown on the display turns from "OFF" to "ON".
5) Turn ignition switch to OFF.
6) Disconnect connector from cruise control command switch.
7) Turn ignition switch to ON.
8) Measure voltage between cruise control command switch connector and chassis ground.

Terminals
   No. 1 (+) — Chassis ground (–):

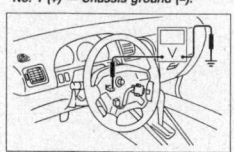

CHECK : Is voltage more than 10 V?
YES : Go to step 8E2.
NO : Repair or replace wiring harness between fuse & relay box and cruise control command switch.

8E2 : CHECK THE CRUISE CONTROL COMMAND SWITCH.

1) Turn ignition switch to OFF.
2) Connect connector of cruise control command switch.
3) Turn ignition switch to ON.
4) Measure voltage between cruise control command switch connector and chassis ground.

Terminals
   No. 2 (+) — Chassis ground (–):

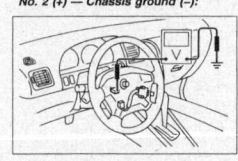

CHECK : Is voltage more than 10 V? (When SET/COAST switch is ON.)
YES : Go to step 8E3.
NO : Replace cruise control command switch.

8E3 : CHECK THE CRUISE CONTROL COMMAND SWITCH.

Measure voltage between cruise control command switch connector and chassis ground.

Terminals
   No. 3 (+) — Chassis ground (–):

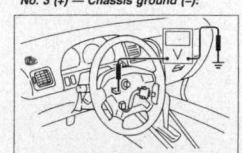

CHECK : Is voltage more than 10 V? (When RESUME/ACCEL switch is ON.)
YES : Go to step 8E4.
NO : Replace cruise control command switch.

SB1109800039020X

Fig. 21   Test 8E, Code 14: Set/Coast Switch, Resume/Accede Switch, Cancel Switch (Part 2 of 5). Forester & 1998–99 Impreza

8E4 : CHECK THE CRUISE CONTROL COMMAND SWITCH.

Measure voltage between cruise control command switch connector and chassis ground.

Terminals
   No. 2 (+) — Chassis ground (–):

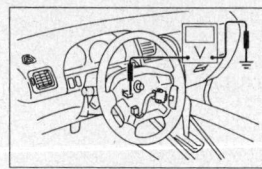

CHECK : Is voltage more than 10 V? (When CANCEL switch is ON.)
YES : Go to step 8E5.
NO : Replace cruise control command switch.

8E5 : CHECK THE CRUISE CONTROL COMMAND SWITCH.

Measure voltage between cruise control command switch connector and chassis ground.

Terminals
   No. 3 (+) — Chassis ground (–):

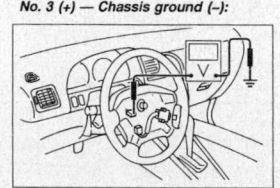

CHECK : Is voltage more than 10 V? (When CANCEL switch is ON.)
YES : Go to step 8E6.
NO : Replace cruise control command switch.

SB1109800039030X

Fig. 21   Test 8E, Code 14: Set/Coast Switch, Resume/Accede Switch, Cancel Switch (Part 3 of 5). Forester & 1998–99 Impreza

8E6 : CHECK THE CRUISE CONTROL COMMAND SWITCH.

1) Turn ignition switch to OFF.
2) Disconnect connector from cruise control command switch.
3) Measure resistance between terminals of cruise control command switch connector (switch side) to check the switch operation.

Terminals
   No. 1 — No. 2:

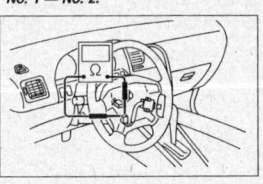

CHECK : Is resistance less than 10 Ω? (When SET/COAST switch is ON.)
YES : Go to step 8E7.
NO : Replace cruise control command switch.

8E7 : CHECK THE CRUISE CONTROL COMMAND SWITCH.

Measure resistance between terminals of cruise control command switch connector (switch side) to check the switch operation.

Terminals
   No. 1 — No. 2:

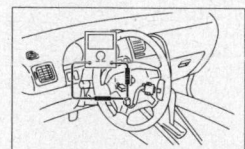

CHECK : Is resistance more than 1 MΩ? (When SET/COAST switch is OFF.)
YES : Go to step 8E8.
NO : Replace cruise control command switch.

8E8 : CHECK THE CRUISE CONTROL COMMAND SWITCH.

Measure resistance between terminals of cruise control command switch connector (switch side) to check the switch operation.

Terminals
   No. 1 — No. 3:

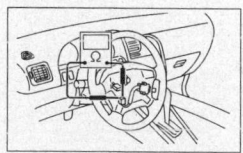

CHECK : Is resistance less than 10 Ω? (When RESUME/ACCEL switch is ON.)
YES : Go to step 8E9.
NO : Replace cruise control command switch.

8E9 : CHECK THE CRUISE CONTROL COMMAND SWITCH.

Measure resistance between terminals of cruise control command switch connector (switch side) to check the switch operation.

Terminals
   No. 1 — No. 3:

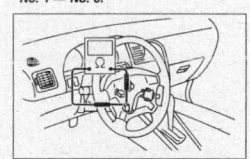

CHECK : Is resistance more than 1 MΩ? (When RESUME/ACCEL switch is OFF.)
YES : Go to step 8E10.
NO : Replace cruise control command switch.

8E10 : CHECK HARNESS CONNECTOR BETWEEN CRUISE CONTROL COMMAND SWITCH AND CRUISE CONTROL MODULE.

1) Disconnect connector from cruise control module.
2) Measure resistance of harness connector between cruise control command switch and cruise control module.

Connector & terminal
   No. 2 (command switch) — (B94) No. 6:

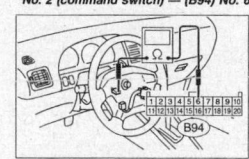

CHECK : Is resistance less than 10 Ω?
YES : Go to step 8E11.
NO : Repair or replace wiring harness.

SB1109800039040X

Fig. 21   Test 8E, Code 14: Set/Coast Switch, Resume/Accede Switch, Cancel Switch (Part 4 of 5). Forester & 1998–99 Impreza

8E11 : CHECK HARNESS CONNECTOR BETWEEN CRUISE CONTROL COMMAND SWITCH AND CRUISE CONTROL MODULE.

Measure resistance of harness connector between cruise control command switch and cruise control module.

Connector & terminal
   No. 3 (command switch) — (B94) No. 7:

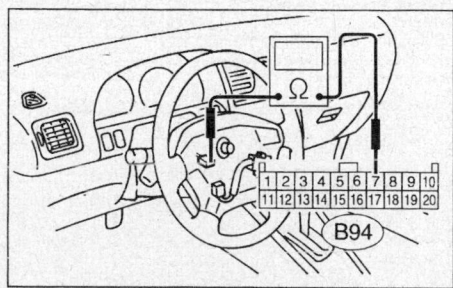

CHECK : Is resistance less than 10 Ω?
YES : Replace cruise control module.
NO : Repair or replace wiring harness.

SB1109800039050X

Fig. 21   Test 8E, Code 14: Set/Coast Switch, Resume/Accede Switch, Cancel Switch (Part 5 of 5). Forester & 1998–99 Impreza

F: DIAGNOSTIC CODE 21, 22 AND 23 (VACUUM VALVE, VENT 2 VALVE, VENT 1 VALVE)

DIAGNOSIS:
- Open or poor contact of vacuum valve, vent 2 valve and vent 1 valve.

TROUBLE SYMPTOM:
- Cruise control cannot be set. (Cancels immediately.)

SB1109800040010X

Fig. 22   Test 8F, Codes 21, 22 & 23: Vacuum Valve, Vent 2 Valve & Vent 1 Valve (Part 1 of 4). Forester & 1998–99 Impreza

---

8F4:	PERFORM A CIRCUIT TEST IN HARNESS BETWEEN ACTUATOR (VACUUM VALVE, VENT 2 VALVE AND VENT 1 VALVE) AND CRUISE CONTROL MODULE.

1) Disconnect connector from cruise control module.
2) Measure resistance of harness connector between cruise control module, vacuum valve, vent 2 valve and vent 1 valve.

Connector & terminal
(B7) No. 1 — (B94) No. 1:

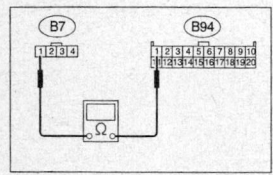

CHECK : *Is resistance less than 10 Ω?*
YES : Go to step 8F5.
NO : Repair or replace wiring harness between actuator and cruise control module.

8F5:	PERFORM A CIRCUIT TEST IN HARNESS BETWEEN ACTUATOR (VACUUM VALVE, VENT 2 VALVE AND VENT 1 VALVE) AND CRUISE CONTROL MODULE.

Measure resistance of harness connector between cruise control module, vacuum valve, vent 2 valve and vent 1 valve.

Connector & terminal
(B7) No. 2 — (B94) No. 8:

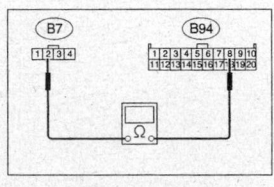

CHECK : *Is resistance less than 10 Ω?*
YES : Go to step 8F6.
NO : Repair or replace wiring harness between actuator and cruise control module.

SB1109800040030X

Fig. 22   Test 8F, Codes 21, 22 & 23: Vacuum Valve, Vent 2 Valve & Vent 1 Valve (Part 3 of 4). Forester & 1998–99 Impreza

---

8F1:	MEASURE RESISTANCE OF VACUUM VALVE, VENT 2 VALVE AND VENT 1 VALVE.

1) Disconnect connector from actuator.
2) Measure resistance of vacuum valve, vent 2 valve and vent 1 valve.

Terminals
No. 2 — No. 3:

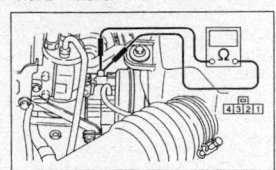

CHECK : *Is resistance less than 22 Ω?*
YES : Go to step 8F2.
NO : Replace actuator.

8F2:	MEASURE RESISTANCE OF VACUUM VALVE, VENT 2 VALVE AND VENT 1 VALVE.

Measure resistance of vacuum valve, vent 2 valve and vent 1 valve.

Terminals
No. 2 — No. 1:

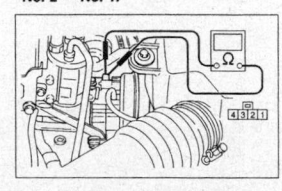

CHECK : *Is resistance less than 55 Ω?*
YES : Go to step 8F3.
NO : Replace actuator.

8F3:	MEASURE RESISTANCE OF VACUUM VALVE, VENT 2 VALVE AND VENT 1 VALVE.

Measure resistance of vacuum valve, vent 2 valve and vent 1 valve.

Terminals
No. 2 — No. 4:

CHECK : *Is resistance less than 55 Ω?*
YES : Go to step 8F4.
NO : Replace actuator.

SB1109800040020X

Fig. 22   Test 8F, Codes 21, 22 & 23: Vacuum Valve, Vent 2 Valve & Vent 1 Valve (Part 2 of 4). Forester & 1998–99 Impreza

---

8F6:	PERFORM A CIRCUIT TEST IN HARNESS BETWEEN ACTUATOR (VACUUM VALVE, VENT 2 VALVE AND VENT 1 VALVE) AND CRUISE CONTROL MODULE.

Measure resistance of harness connector between cruise control module, vacuum valve, vent 2 valve and vent 1 valve.

Connector & terminal
(B7) No. 3 — (B94) No. 11:

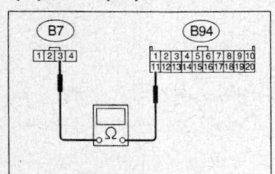

CHECK : *Is resistance less than 10 Ω?*
YES : Go to step 8F7.
NO : Repair or replace wiring harness between actuator and cruise control module.

8F7:	PERFORM A CIRCUIT TEST IN HARNESS BETWEEN ACTUATOR (VACUUM VALVE, VENT 2 VALVE AND VENT 1 VALVE) AND CRUISE CONTROL MODULE.

Measure resistance of harness connector between cruise control module, vacuum valve, vent 2 valve and vent 1 valve.

Connector & terminal
(B7) No. 4 — (B94) No. 2:

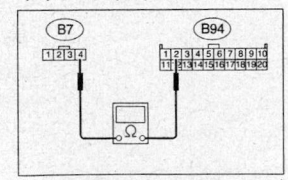

CHECK : *Is resistance less than 10 Ω?*
YES : Replace cruise control module.
NO : Repair or replace wiring harness between actuator and cruise control module.

SB1109800040040X

Fig. 22   Test 8F, Codes 21, 22 & 23: Vacuum Valve, Vent 2 Valve & Vent 1 Valve (Part 4 of 4). Forester & 1998–99 Impreza

---

A: CHECK INDICATOR AND CIRCUIT IN CRUISE CONTROL MAIN SWITCH

DIAGNOSIS:
- Bulb failure or open harness of the indicator circuit in the cruise control main switch.

TROUBLE SYMPTOM:
- Cruise control can be set, normally indicator does not come on. (When main switch is pressed.)

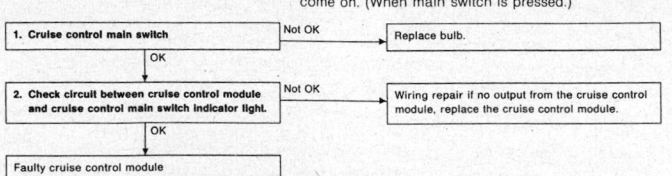

SB1109600041010X

Fig. 23   Check indicator & circuit in cruise control main switch test (Part 1 of 2). 1996-97 Impreza

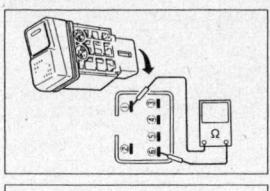

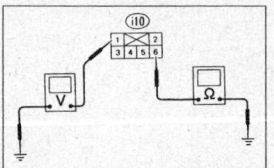

1. CRUISE CONTROL MAIN SWITCH

1) Remove cruise main switch.
Turn lower part of the housing upward to remove. If this cannot be done, insert a small screwdriver on the right hand side of the housing to remove the lock.
2) Measure resistance value between cruise control main switch terminals.

Terminal/Specified resistance:
No. 1 — No. 6/Approx. 120 Ω

2. CHECK CIRCUIT BETWEEN CRUISE CONTROL MODULE AND CRUISE CONTROL MAIN SWITCH INDICATOR LIGHT

1) Measure voltage between cruise control main switch and body. (Perform this measurement by turning ON the ignition switch and the cruise control main switch.)

Connector & terminal/Specified voltage:
(i10) No. 1 — Body/10 - 13 V

2) Remove the connector from the cruise control main switch.
3) Measure the resistance value between the cruise control main switch connector and the body.

Connector & terminal/Specified resistance:
(i10) No. 6 — Body/10 Ω, max.

SB1109600041020X

Fig. 23 Check indicator & circuit in cruise control main switch test (Part 2 of 2). 1996-97 Impreza

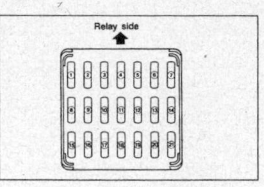

1. CHECK FUSE (NO. 18)

1) Check fuse.
Test circuit with a tester.
2) Checking voltage of the ignition power source
Turn ignition switch ON and measure the voltage between the fuse box connector and the body.

Connector & terminal/Specified voltage:
(B34) No. 4 — Body/10 - 13 V

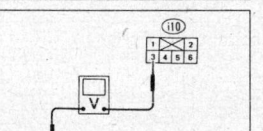

2. CHECK CRUISE CONTROL MAIN SWITCH

1) Remove cruise control main switch and disconnect connector.
Turn ignition switch ON and measure the voltage between cruise control main switch connector and body.

Connector & terminal/Specified voltage:
(i10) No. 3 — Body/10 - 13 V

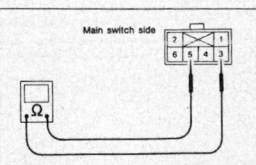

2) Check ON/OFF function of main switch
Measure resistance between main switch and terminal.

Terminal   /Specified resistance:
No. 3 — No. 5/10 Ω, max. (Switch ON)
1 MΩ, min. (Switch OFF)

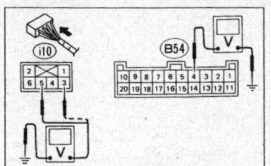

3. CHECK HARNESS BETWEEN CRUISE CONTROL MAIN SWITCH AND CRUISE CONTROL MODULE

1) Connect connector.
2) Turn ignition switch ON.
3) Turn cruise main switch ON.
4) Measure voltage between each of terminals and body.

Connector & terminal/Specified voltage:
(i10) No. 3 — Body/10 - 13 V
(i10) No. 5 — Body/10 - 13 V
(B54) No. 4 — Body/10 - 13 V

SB1109600042020X

Fig. 24 Cruise control main switch test (Part 2 of 2). 1996-97 Impreza

B: CHECK CRUISE CONTROL MAIN SWITCH

DIAGNOSIS:
● Faulty cruise control main switch, or open harness.

TROUBLE SYMPTOM:
● Cruise control main switch is not turned ON and cruise control cannot be set.

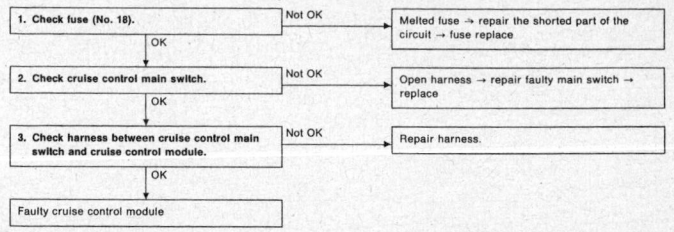

SB1109600042010X

Fig. 24 Cruise control main switch test (Part 1 of 2). 1996-97 Impreza

LED No.	Signal name	Display
1	—	—
2	—	—
3	SET/COAST switch	SE
4	RESUME/ACCEL switch	RE
5	—	—
6	—	—
7	—	—
8	—	—
9	—	—
10	—	—

ST	BR	SE	RE	IH
—	—	—	—	—
1	2	3	4	5
6	7	8	9	10

1. CHECK THE SIGNAL USING A SELECT MONITOR

● Measuring condition: Turn ON the ignition switch and cruise main switch.
● Operation of the function keys: FA0 ENT
When pushing the SET SW: LED No. 3 goes out — lights
When pushing the RESUME SW: LED No. 4 goes out — lights

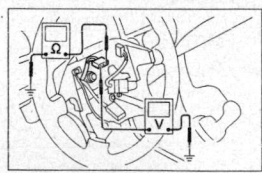

2. CHECK THE CRUISE SUB SWITCH

1) Separate connector from sub switch. (Use together with horn power supply.)
2) Check voltage between sub switch connector and body.

Terminals/Specified voltage:
No. 1 — Body/10 - 13 V

3) Check for harness short circuit between sub switch and cruise control module.

Terminals/Specified resistance:
No. 2 — Body/1 MΩ, min.
No. 3 — Body/1 MΩ, min.

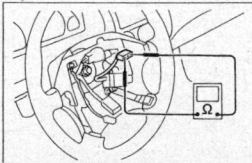

4) Check inner switch of the cruise control sub switch and check continuity at switch side connector.

Terminals:
No. 1 — 2 (SET/COAST SWITCH)
No. 1 — 3 (RESUME/ACCEL SWITCH)

Specified resistance:
10 Ω, max. (Switch ON)
1 MΩ, min. (Switch OFF)

SB1109600043000X

Fig. 25 Set/Coast, Resume/Accede switch test. 1996-97 Impreza

B: TROUBLE CODE 11
— BRAKE SW, STOP LIGHT SW —

DIAGNOSIS:
- Failure or disconnection of the stop light switch and brake switch.

TROUBLE SYMPTOM:
- Cruise control cannot be set.

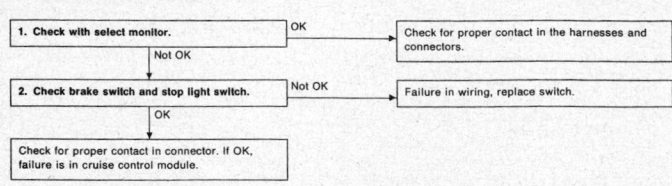

SB1109600044010X

Fig. 26 Code 11: Brake Switch/Stop Light Switch (Part 1 of 2). 1996-97 Impreza

C: TROUBLE CODE 12
— CLUTCH SWITCH, N POSITION —

DIAGNOSIS:
- Failure or disconnection of inhibitor switch
- Failure or disconnection of clutch switch

TROUBLE SYMPTOM:
- Cruise control cannot be set.

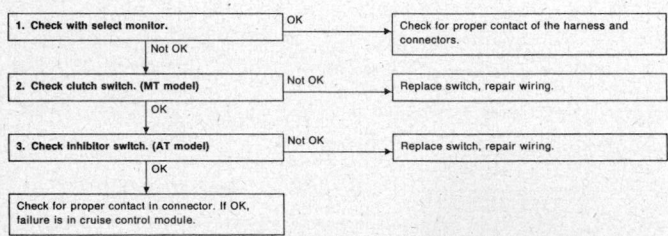

SB1109600045010X

Fig. 27 Code 12: Clutch Switch, N Position (Part 1 of 2). 1996-97 Impreza

LED No.	Signal name	Display
1	—	—
2	—	—
3	—	—
4	—	—
5	Clutch switch/inhibitor switch	IH
6	—	—
7	—	—
8	—	—
9	—	—
10	—	—

ST	BR	SE	RE	IH
—	—	—	—	—
1	2	3	4	5
6	7	8	9	10

1. CHECK WITH SELECT MONITOR
- Measurement condition: Turn ignition switch ON. Turn cruise main switch ON.
- Operation of function keys: FA0 ENT
1) When depressing clutch pedal; LED No. 5 goes out — lights.
2) When setting shift lever in N position; LED No. 5 goes out — lights.

2. CHECK CLUTCH SWITCH (MT MODEL)
1) Check items for the clutch switch. (Circuit test between terminals)
Terminals   /Specified resistance:
No. 1 — No. 2/10 Ω, max. (Without pedal depressing).
/1 MΩ, min. (Pedal depressing).

3. CHECK INHIBITOR SWITCH (AT MODEL)
1) When engine starts in the N position (the starter rotates), N position contact point of the inhibitor is normal.
2) Check the wiring harness.

SB1109600045020X

Fig. 27 Code 12: Clutch Switch, N Position (Part 2 of 2). 1996-97 Impreza

LED No.	Signal name	Display
1	Stop light switch	ST
2	Brake switch	BR
3	—	—
4	—	—
5	—	—
6	—	—
7	—	—
8	—	—
9	—	—
10	—	—

ST	BR	SE	RE	IH
—	—	—	—	—
1	2	3	4	5
6	7	8	9	10

1. CHECK WITH SELECT MONITOR
- Measurement condition: Turn ignition switch ON. Turn cruise main switch ON.
- Operation of the function keys: FA0 ENT
1) When depressing brake pedal (Set in the D range for AT, without depressing clutch pedal for MT)
Stop light switch: LED No. 1 goes out — lights.
Brake switch : LED No. 2 goes out — lights.

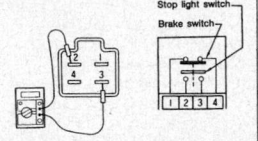

2. CHECK BRAKE SWITCH AND STOP LIGHT SWITCH
1) Remove connector of stop and brake switch.
2) Check circuit between each terminal.

Pedal operation	Brake switch between No. 1 — 4	Stop light switch between No. 2 — 3
Depressing the brake pedal.	Circuit failure	Circuit normal
Without depressing the brake pedal.	Circuit normal	Circuit failure

SB1109600044020X

Fig. 26 Code 11: Brake Switch/Stop Light Switch (Part 2 of 2). 1996-97 Impreza

D: TROUBLE CODE 13 AND 24
— SPEED LIMITER, SPEED SENSOR —

DIAGNOSIS:
- Disconnection or short circuit of speed sensor.

TROUBLE SYMPTOM:
- Cruise control cannot be set. (Cancelled immediately.)

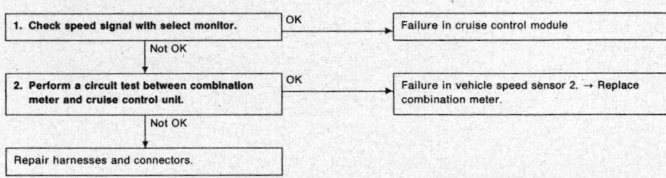

SB1109600046010X

Fig. 28 Codes 13 & 24: Speed Limiter, Speed Sensor (Part 1 of 2). 1996-97 Impreza

1. CHECK SPEED SIGNAL WITH SELECT MONITOR
- Driving condition: Running at speed greater than 40 km/h (25 MPH)
- Operation of the function keys: F02 ENT
NOTE:
- When there is a failure in the meter cable or the vehicle speed sensor 2, the indicated value of the meter will be incorrect.
- When there is a disconnection or short circuit in the harness between the meter and the cruise control module, the indicated value will be 0 — 1 km/h.

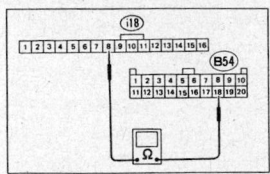

2. PERFORM A CIRCUIT TEST BETWEEN COMBINATION METER AND CRUISE CONTROL UNIT
1) Separate connectors from combination meter and cruise control module.
2) Perform a circuit test in the harnesses.
Connector & terminal/Specified resistance:
(i18) No. 8 — (B54) No. 18/10 Ω, max.

SB1109600046020X

Fig. 28 Codes 13 & 24: Speed Limiter, Speed Sensor (Part 2 of 2). 1996-97 Impreza

E: TROUBLE CODE 14
— SET SWITCH AND RESUME SWITCH
(CANCEL SW-ON) —

DIAGNOSIS:
● Short circuit inside the SET SW and RESUME SW.

TROUBLE SYMPTOM:
● Cruise control cannot be set. (Cancelled immediately.)

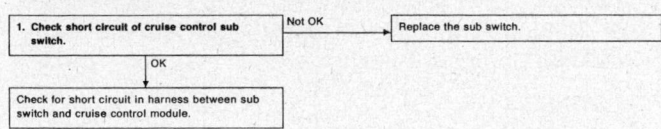

1. CHECK SHORT CIRCUIT OF CRUISE CONTROL SUB SWITCH

1) Separate connector of cruise control sub switch.
2) Measure resistance between each terminal of cruise control sub switch.

Terminal/Specified resistance:
  SET switch ON No. 1 — No. 2/10 Ω, max.
  RESUME switch ON No. 1 — No. 3/10 Ω, max.
  CANCEL switch ON No. 1 — No. 2/10 Ω, max.
                     No. 1 — No. 3/10 Ω, max.

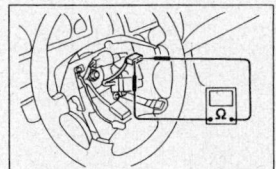

SB1109600047000X

Fig. 29   Code 14: Set Switch/Resume Switch. 1996-97 Impreza

Trouble code	Item	Contents of diagnosis
10	OK	Normal
11	BRAKE/ST/CL or N	● Input signals from brake switch "OFF", stop light switch "ON" (Brake pedal is in depressed condition.) ● Input signals from clutch switch "OFF", or inhibitor switch is in "N" position. [Clutch pedal is depressed (MT), or select lever is set to N position (AT).]
12	NOT SET SP	Out of cruise speed range
13	LOW SP LIM	Low-speed control limiter
14	CANCEL SW	Input signal from cancel switch
15	NO MEMORY	No memorized cruise speed
21	SP SENS NG	Faulty vehicle speed sensor 2
22	COM SW NG	Faulty SET/COAST switch or RESUME/ACCEL switch
23	RELAY NG	Faulty safety relay included in cruise control module
24	CPU RAM NG	Faulty CPU RAM included in cruise control module
31	MOTOR NG	Faulty vacuum motor or motor drive system
32	AIR VAL NG	Faulty air valve or valve drive system
33	REL VAL NG	Faulty release valve or valve drive system

SB1109500027000X

Fig. 31   Trouble code identification & description. Legacy

G: TROUBLE CODE 25
— CONTROL MODULE —

DIAGNOSIS:

● Faulty cruise control module.

TROUBLE SYMPTOM:

● Cruise control cannot be set.

Replace cruise control module.

SB1109600048000X

Fig. 30   Codes 21, 22 & 23: Vacuum Valve, Vent 1 Valve & Vent 2 Valve. 1996-97 Impreza

2B1 :   CHECK CRUISE CONTROL CABLE.

Check cruise control cable installation.

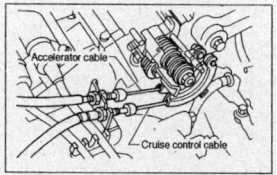

CHECK : **Is the cruise control cable securely installed to the left of the accelerator cable?**
YES : Go to step 2B2.
NO : Install cruise control cable securely. Go to step 2B2.

2B2 :   CHECK ACCELERATOR CABLE.

Check function of accelerator cable.

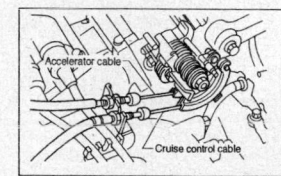

CHECK : **Does the accelerator cable throttle cam move when the cruise control throttle is moved by hand?**
YES : Repair accelerator cable throttle cam. Go to step 2B3.
NO : Go to step 2B3.

2B3 :   CHECK THROTTLE CAM.

Check function of throttle cam.
CHECK : **Does the throttle cam move smoothly?**
YES : Go to step 2B4.
NO : Repair throttle cam. Go to step 2B4.

2B4 :   CHECK CABLE FREE PLAY.

Ensure that throttle cam-to-lever clearance is within specifications.

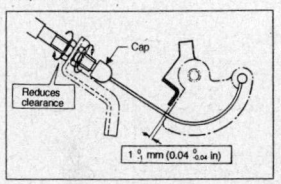

CHECK : **Is throttle cam-to-lever clearance between 0 and 1 mm (0 and 0.04 in)?**
YES : Go to step 2C1.
NO : Adjust cable end by adjusting nuts. Go to step 2C1.

NOTE:
Ensure that cap is positioned in groove.

C: VACUUM HOSE AND PIPE

2C1 :   CHECK VACUUM HOSE VISUALLY.

Check vacuum hose and pipe (which connect actuator and vacuum pump.)

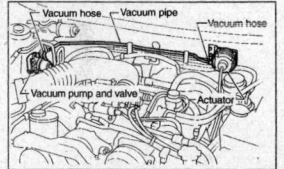

CHECK : **Is there disconnection or cracks in vacuum hose?**
YES : Replace vacuum hose. Go to step 2D1.
NO : Go to step 2D1.

SB1109800050000X

Fig. 32   Cruise control cable & vacuum hose checks. 1998 Legacy

2D1 : CHECK FUNCTION OF ACTUATOR.

1) Disconnect vacuum hose from actuator.

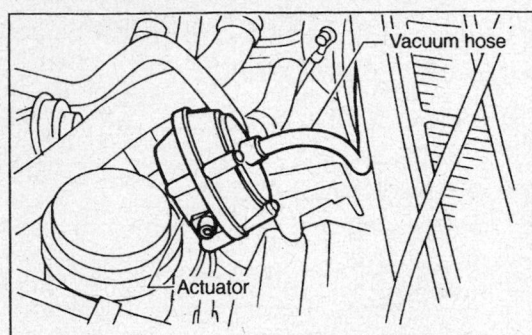

2) Connect vacuum pump as shown in figure.

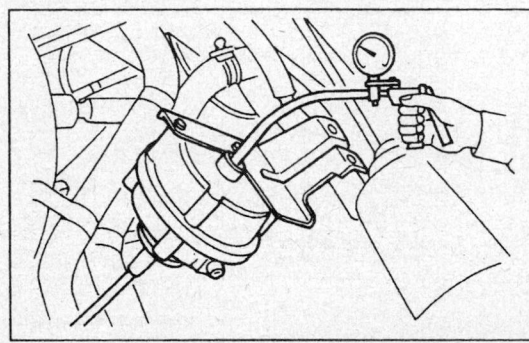

3) Make sure that cruise control cable moves smoothly and quickly when a vacuum pressure of 40.0 kPa (300 mmHg, 11.81 inHg) is applied to actuator.

CHECK : **Does cruise control cable have a stroke of 35 mm (1.38 in)?**

YES : Go to step **2E1**.

NO : Replace actuator. Go to step **2E1**.

NOTE:
● When vacuum pressure is released from condition 3) above, make sure the cable returns to its original position smoothly and quickly.
● After inspection, disconnect vacuum pump and connect vacuum hose.

SB1109800051000X

Fig. 33 Actuator test. 1998 Legacy

2E1 : MEASURE RESISTANCE OF VALVE.

1) Disconnect connector from vacuum pump and valve.
2) Measure resistance between terminals of vacuum pump and valve.

Terminals
    No. 2 — No. 3:

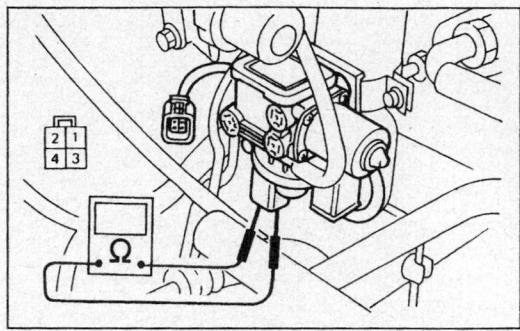

CHECK : **Is resistance less than 100 Ω?**

YES : Go to step **2E2**.

NO : Replace vacuum pump and valve.

2E2 : MEASURE RESISTANCE OF VALVE.

Measure resistance between terminals of vacuum pump and valve.

Terminals
    No. 2 — No. 1:

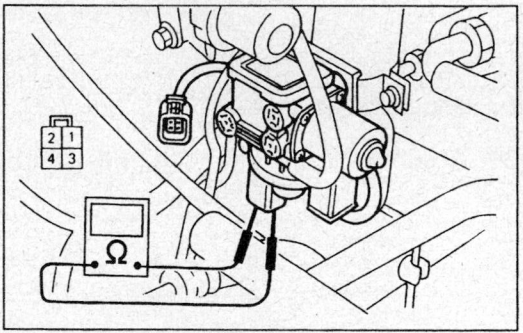

CHECK : **Is resistance less than 69 Ω?**

YES : Go to step **2E3**.

NO : Replace vacuum pump and valve.

SB1109800052010X

Fig. 34 Vacuum pump & valve diagnosis (Part 1 of 3). 1998 Legacy

2E3 : MEASURE RESISTANCE OF VALVE.

Measure resistance between terminals of vacuum pump and valve.

Terminals
No. 2 — No. 4:

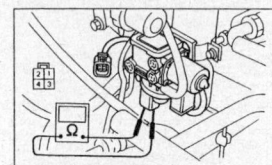

CHECK : **Is resistance less than 69 Ω?**
YES : Go to step **2E4.**
NO : Replace vacuum pump and valve.

2E4 : CHECK FOR LEAKAGE AND STICK-ING OF VALVES.

Make sure that cruise control cable moves smoothly when connecting + (positive) battery cable to terminal No. 2 and – (negative) battery cable to terminals No. 1, 3 and 4 of vacuum pump and valve connector.

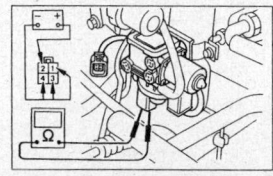

CHECK : **Does cruise control cable have a stroke of 35 mm (1.38 in) within 3 seconds?**
YES : Go to step **2E5.**
NO : Replace vacuum pump and valve. Go to step **2E5.**

SB1109800052020X

Fig. 34 Vacuum pump & valve diagnosis (Part 2 of 3). 1998 Legacy

7A1 : DRIVE AT CRUISE SPEED.

CHECK : **Can cruise speed be set?**
YES : Go to "CHECK INDICATOR AND CIR-CUIT IN CRUISE CONTROL MAIN SWITCH".
NO : Go to "CHECK CRUISE CONTROL MAIN SWITCH".

SB1109800053000X

Fig. 35 Power Supply. 1998 Legacy

2E5 : CHECK FOR LEAKAGE AND STICK-ING OF VALVES.

When the battery cable is disconnected from former condition make sure the cable returns to its original position smoothly.

CHECK : **Does cruise control cable get back to its original position within 1.5 seconds?**
YES : Go to step **2E6.**
NO : Replace vacuum pump and valve. Go to step **2E6.**

2E6 : CHECK CABLE MOVEMENT.

Connect + (positive) battery cable to terminal No. 2 and – (negative) battery cable to terminals No. 1, 3 and 4 of vacuum pump and valve connector.

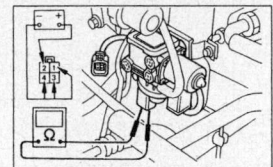

CHECK : **Does cruise control perform pull operation?**
YES : Go to step **2E7.**
NO : Replace vacuum pump and valve. Go to step **2E7.**

2E7 : CHECK CABLE MOVEMENT.

Connect + (positive) battery cable to terminal No. 2 and – (negative) battery cable to terminals No. 1 and 4 of vacuum pump and valve connector.

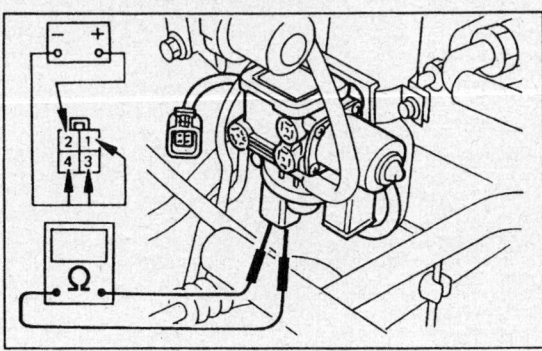

CHECK : **Does cruise control perform hold operation?**
YES : Go to step **2E8.**
NO : Replace vacuum pump and valve. Go to step **2E8.**

2E8 : CHECK CABLE MOVEMENT.

Connect + (positive) battery cable to terminal No. 2 and – (negative) battery cable to terminal No. 4 of vacuum pump and valve connector.

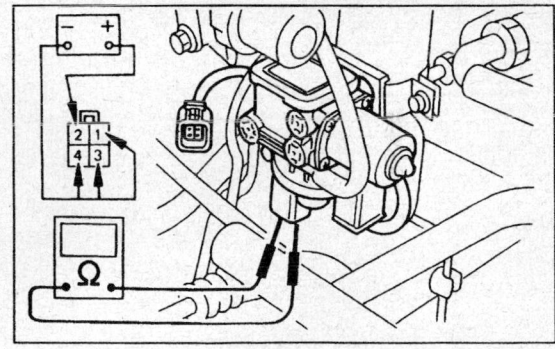

CHECK : **Does cruise control perform release operation?**
YES : Go to step **2F1.**
NO : Replace vacuum pump and valve. Go to step **2F1.**

SB1109800052030X

Fig. 34 Vacuum pump & valve diagnosis (Part 3 of 3). 1998 Legacy

DIAGNOSIS:
● Bulb failure or open harness of the indicator circuit in the cruise control main switch.
TROUBLE SYMPTOM:
● Cruise control can be set, normally indicator does not come on. (When main switch is pressed.)

SB1109800054010X

Fig. 36 Basic diagnostic procedure (Part 1 of 2). 1998 Legacy

SUBARU

7B1 : CHECK CRUISE CONTROL MAIN SWITCH.

1) Remove cruise control main switch.
2) Measure resistance between cruise control main switch terminals.

Terminals
  No. 1 — No. 6:

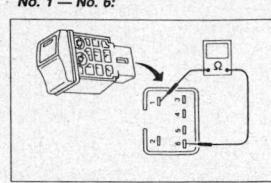

(CHECK) : *Is resistance between 10 and 80 Ω?*
(YES) : Go to step **7B2**.
(NO) : Replace switch illumination bulb.

7B2 : CHECK CIRCUIT BETWEEN CRUISE CONTROL MODULE AND CRUISE CONTROL MAIN SWITCH INDICATOR LIGHT.

1) Turn the ignition switch to ON.
2) Turn cruise control main switch to ON.
3) Measure voltage between cruise control main switch connector and the chassis ground.

Connector & terminal
  (i19) No. 1 (+) — Chassis ground (–):

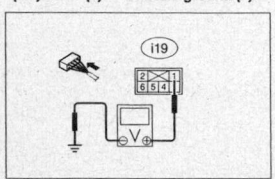

(CHECK) : *Is voltage more than 10 V?*
(YES) : Go to step **7B3**.
(NO) : Repair or replace wiring harness.

SB1109800054020X

Fig. 36 Basic diagnostic procedure (Part 2 of 2). 1998 Legacy

DIAGNOSIS:
● Faulty cruise control main switch, or open harness.
TROUBLE SYMPTOM:
● Cruise control main switch is not turned ON and cruise control cannot be set.
NOTE:
When the main relay (built-in cruise control module) operates, the main switch circuit is in normal condition.
The main relay operation can be checked by hearing the operation sounds.
This operation sounds will be heard when ignition switch and cruise control main switch is turned to ON.

SB1109800055010X

Fig. 37 Cruise control main switch inspection (Part 1 of 3). 1998 Legacy

7B3 : CHECK CIRCUIT BETWEEN CRUISE CONTROL MODULE AND CRUISE CONTROL MAIN SWITCH INDICATOR LIGHT.

1) Turn the ignition switch and cruise control main switch to OFF.
2) Remove the connector from the cruise control main switch.
3) Measure resistance of ground circuit between the cruise control main switch connector and chassis ground.

Connector & terminal
  (i19) No. 6 (+) — Chassis ground (–):

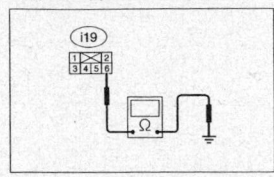

(CHECK) : *Is resistance less than 10 Ω?*
(YES) : Replace cruise control module.
(NO) : Repair or replace wiring harness.

7C1 : CHECK FUSE.

Check fuse No. 18.

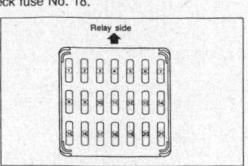

(CHECK) : *Is fuse No. 18 blown?*
(YES) : Replace fuse No. 18. Go to step **7C2**.
(NO) : Go to step **7C2**.

7C2 : CHECK POWER SUPPLY.

1) Turn ignition switch to ON.
2) Measure voltage between fuse & relay box connector and chassis ground.

Connector & terminal
  (B51) No. 4 (+) — Chassis ground (–):
(CHECK) : *Is voltage more than 10 V?*
(YES) : Go to step **7C3**.
(NO) : Replace fuse No. 18. When fuse No. 18 is blown again, repair shorted parts of circuit.

7C3 : CHECK CRUISE CONTROL MAIN SWITCH.

1) Turn ignition switch to OFF.
2) Remove cruise control main switch and disconnect connector.
3) Turn ignition switch to ON.
4) Measure voltage between cruise control main switch connector and chassis ground.

Connector & terminal
  (i19) No. 3 (+) — Chassis ground (–):

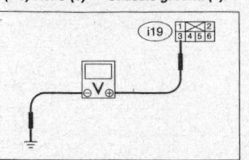

(CHECK) : *Is voltage more than 10 V?*
(YES) : Go to step **7C4**.
(NO) : Replace cruise control main switch.

7C4 : CHECK CRUISE CONTROL MAIN SWITCH.

Measure resistance between cruise control main switch terminals.

Terminals
  No. 3 — No. 5:

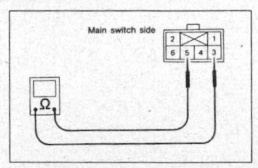

(CHECK) : *Is resistance less than 10 Ω? (When switch is ON.)*
(YES) : Go to step **7C5**.
(NO) : Replace cruise control main switch.

SB1109800055020X

Fig. 37 Cruise control main switch inspection (Part 2 of 3). 1998 Legacy

7C5 : CHECK CRUISE CONTROL MAIN SWITCH.

Measure resistance between cruise control main switch terminals.

Terminals
  No. 3 — No. 5:

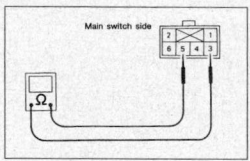

(CHECK) : *Is resistance more than 1 MΩ? (When switch is OFF.)*
(YES) : Go to step **7C6**.
(NO) : Replace cruise control main switch.

7C6 : CHECK HARNESS BETWEEN CRUISE CONTROL MAIN SWITCH CONNECTOR AND CHASSIS GROUND.

1) Connect connector.
2) Turn ignition switch to ON.
3) Turn cruise control main switch to ON.
4) Measure voltage between terminal of cruise control main switch and chassis ground.

Connector & terminal
  (i19) No. 3 (+) — Chassis ground (–):

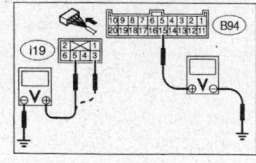

(CHECK) : *Is voltage more than 10 V?*
(YES) : Go to step **7C7**.
(NO) : Repair or replace wiring harness.

7C7 : CHECK HARNESS BETWEEN CRUISE CONTROL MAIN SWITCH CONNECTOR AND CHASSIS GROUND.

Measure voltage between terminal of cruise control main switch chassis ground.

Connector & terminal
  (i19) No. 5 (+) — Chassis ground (–):

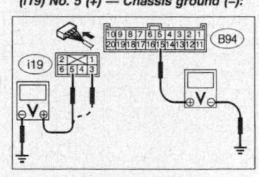

(CHECK) : *Is voltage more than 10 V?*
(YES) : Go to step **7C8**.
(NO) : Repair or replace wiring harness.

7C8 : CHECK HARNESS BETWEEN CRUISE CONTROL MODULE CONNECTOR AND CHASSIS GROUND.

Measure voltage between terminal of cruise control module and chassis ground.

Connector & terminal
  (B94) No. 15 (+) — Chassis ground (–):

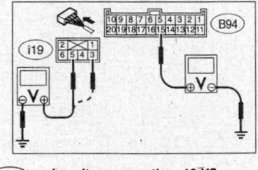

(CHECK) : *Is voltage more than 10 V?*
(YES) : Replace cruise control module.
(NO) : Repair or replace wiring harness.
NOTE:
Depress cruise control main switch with fingers while measuring voltage between (i19) No. 5 and chassis ground.

SB1109800055030X

Fig. 37 Cruise control main switch inspection (Part 3 of 3). 1998 Legacy

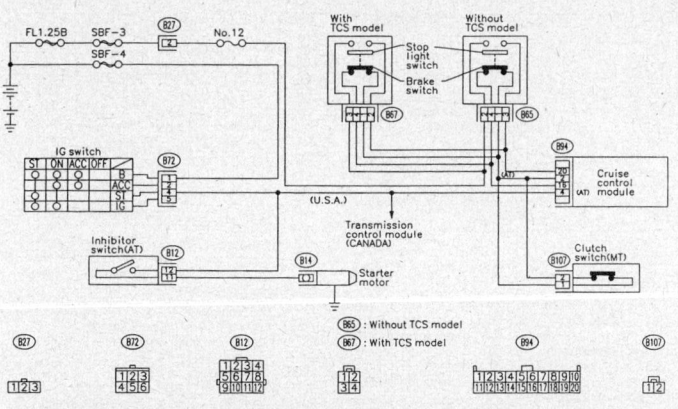

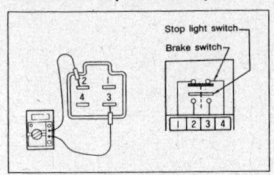

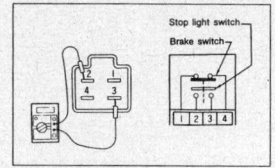

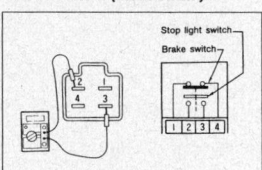

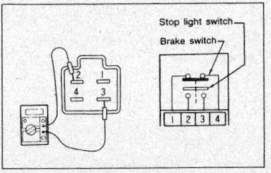

Fig. 38 Code 11: Brake Switch, Stop Light Switch, Clutch Switch (M/T), Inhibitor Switch (A/T), (Part 1 of 4). 1998 Legacy

---

8B1 : CHECK BRAKE SWITCH.

1) Turn ignition switch to ON.
2) Turn cruise control main switch to ON.
3) Apply parking brake securely.
4) Set select monitor in "Current Data Display & Save" mode.
5) Release the clutch pedal. (MT)
6) Depress the brake pedal and check signals for proper operation.
  (1) The Stop Lamp Switch shown on the display turns from "OFF" to "ON".
  (2) The Brake Switch shown on the display turns from "OFF" to "ON".
7) Release the brake pedal.
8) Remove connector of stop and brake switch.
9) Check circuit between brake switch terminal.

Terminals
  No. 1 — No. 4: (Brake switch)

CHECK : **Is resistance less than 1 Ω? (When brake pedal is released.)**
YES : Go to step **8B2**.
NO : Replace brake and stop light switch.

8B2 : CHECK BRAKE SWITCH.

Check circuit between brake switch terminal.
Terminals
  No. 1 — No. 4: (Brake switch)

CHECK : **Is resistance more than 1 MΩ? (When brake pedal is depressed.)**
YES : Go to step **8B3**.
NO : Replace brake and stop light switch.

8B3 : CHECK STOP LIGHT SWITCH.

Check circuit between stop light switch terminal.
Terminals
  No. 2 — No. 3: (Stop light switch)

CHECK : **Is resistance more than 1 MΩ? (When brake pedal is released.)**
YES : Go to step **8B4**.
NO : Replace brake and stop light switch.

Fig. 38 Code 11: Brake Switch, Stop Light Switch, Clutch Switch (M/T), Inhibitor Switch (A/T), (Part 2 of 4). 1998 Legacy

---

8B4 : CHECK STOP LIGHT SWITCH.

Check circuit between stop light switch terminal.
Terminals
  No. 2 — No. 3: (Stop light switch)

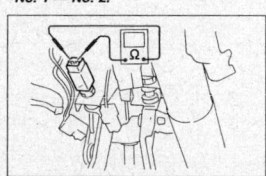

CHECK : **Is resistance less than 1 Ω? (When brake pedal is depressed.)**
YES : (MT) Go to step **8B5**. (AT) Go to step **8B7**.
NO : Replace brake and stop light switch.

8B5 : CHECK CLUTCH SWITCH. (MT)

1) Turn ignition switch to ON.
2) Turn cruise control main switch to ON.
3) Apply parking brake securely.
4) Set select monitor in "Current Data Display & Save" mode.
5) Depress the clutch pedal and check signal for proper operation.
The Clutch/Inhibitor Switch shown on the display turns from "ON" to "OFF".
6) Disconnect connector of clutch switch.
7) Check continuity of the clutch switch.

Terminals
  No. 1 — No. 2:

CHECK : **Is resistance less than 10 Ω? (When clutch pedal is released.)**
YES : Go to step **8B6**.
NO : Replace clutch switch.

8B6 : CHECK CLUTCH SWITCH. (MT)

Check continuity of the clutch switch.
Terminals
  No. 1 — No. 2:

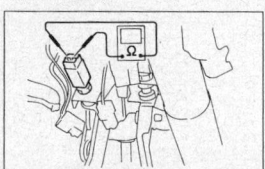

CHECK : **Is resistance more than 1 MΩ? (When clutch pedal is depressed.)**
YES : Replace cruise control module.
NO : Replace clutch switch.

Fig. 38 Code 11: Brake Switch, Stop Light Switch, Clutch Switch (M/T), Inhibitor Switch (A/T), (Part 3 of 4). 1998 Legacy

---

8B7 : CHECK INHIBITOR SWITCH. (AT)

1) Turn ignition switch to ON.
2) Turn cruise control main switch to ON.
3) Apply parking brake securely.
4) Set select monitor in "Current Data Display & Save" mode.
5) Set the selector lever from P or N position to D position and check signal for proper operation.
The Clutch/Inhibitor Switch shown on the display turns from "ON" to "OFF".
6) Set the selector lever to P or N position.
7) Disconnect connector of inhibitor switch.
8) Check continuity of the inhibitor switch.

Terminals
  No. 11 — No. 12:

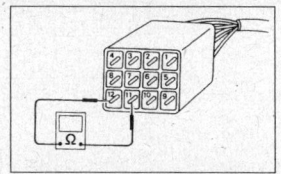

CHECK : **Is resistance less than 10 Ω? (When selector lever is in P or N.)**
YES : Go to step **8B8**.
NO : Replace inhibitor switch. Repair inhibitor switch wiring harness.

8B8 : CHECK INHIBITOR SWITCH. (AT)

Check continuity of the inhibitor switch.
Terminals
  No. 11 — No. 12:

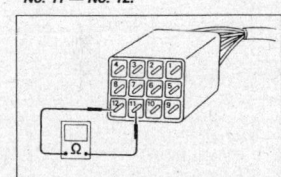

CHECK : **Is resistance more than 1 MΩ? (When selector lever is not in P or N.)**
YES : Replace cruise control module.
NO : Replace inhibitor switch. Repair inhibitor switch wiring harness.

Fig. 38 Code 11: Brake Switch, Stop Light Switch, Clutch Switch (M/T), Inhibitor Switch (A/T), (Part 4 of 4). 1998 Legacy

DIAGNOSIS:
- Disconnection or short circuit of vehicle speed sensor 2 system.

TROUBLE SYMPTOM:
- Cruise control cannot be set. (Cancelled immediately.)

SB1109800057010X

Fig. 39   Code 12, 13 & 21: Vehicle Speed Sensor 2 System (Part 1 of 4). 1998 Legacy

---

8C1 :   CHECK OPERATION OF SPEEDOMETER.

Make sure that speedometer indicates the vehicle speed by driving the vehicle.

CHECK : **Does speedometer indicate vehicle speed by driving vehicle?**
YES : Go to step **8C2**.
NO : Repair combination meter circuit.

8C2 :   CHECK INPUT SIGNAL FOR CRUISE CONTROL MODULE.

WARNING:
Be careful not to be caught up by the running wheels.

1) Set the vehicle on free roller, or lift-up the vehicle and support with safety stands.
2) Set oscilloscope to cruise control module connector terminals.
3) Start the engine.
4) Shift on the gear position, and keep the vehicle speed at constant.
5) Measure signal voltage.

Connector & terminal
(B94) No. 19 (+) — Chassis ground (–):

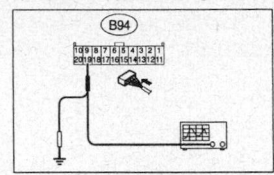

CHECK : **Is the voltage more than 2 V?**
YES : Replace cruise control module.
NO : Go to step **8C3**.

SB1109800057020X

Fig. 39   Code 12, 13 & 21: Vehicle Speed Sensor 2 System (Part 2 of 4). 1998 Legacy

---

NOTE:
- If the vehicle speed increases, the width of amplitude (W) decreases.

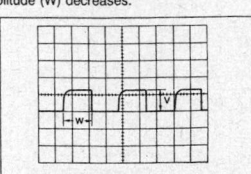

- If oscilloscope is not available, check input signal (vehicle speed signal) by using a select monitor. (Refer to the procedure as described below.)
- Using the select monitor:

1) Set the vehicle on free roller, or lift-up the vehicle and support with safety stands.
2) Turn ignition switch to OFF and set select monitor.
3) Turn ignition switch to ON.
4) Turn cruise control main switch to ON.
5) Set select monitor in "Current Data Display & Save" mode.
6) Drive the vehicle at speed greater than 40 km/h (25 MPH).
7) Check that vehicle speed indication on select monitor and speedometer are equal.
- When there is a disconnection or short circuit in the harness between the meter and the cruise control module, the indicated value will be 0 to 1.0 km/h (0 to 0.6 MPH).

8C3 :   PERFORM A CIRCUIT TEST BETWEEN COMBINATION METER AND CRUISE CONTROL MODULE.

1) Turn ignition switch to OFF.
2) Remove combination meter.

3) Disconnect connector from cruise control module.
4) Measure resistance of harness connector between combination meter and cruise control module.

Connector & terminal
(i10) No. 10 — (B94) No. 19:

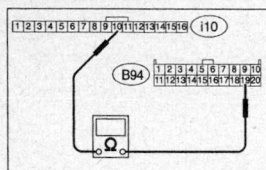

CHECK : **Is resistance less than 10 Ω?**
YES : Go to step **8C4**.
NO : Repair or replace harness connector.

8C4 :   PERFORM A CIRCUIT TEST BETWEEN COMBINATION METER AND CRUISE CONTROL MODULE.

Measure resistance of harness connector between cruise control module and chassis ground to make sure that circuit does not short.

Connector & terminal
(B94) No. 19 (+) — Chassis ground (–):

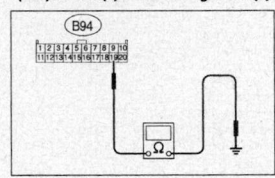

CHECK : **Is resistance more than 1 MΩ?**
YES : Go to step **8C5**.
NO : Repair or replace harness connector.

8C5 :   CHECK VEHICLE SPEED SENSOR 2.

1) Disconnect connector from vehicle speed sensor 2.
2) Measure resistance between terminals of vehicle speed sensor 2.

Terminals
No. 1 — No. 2:

CHECK : **Is resistance between 350 and 450 Ω?**
YES : Go to step **8C6**.
NO : Replace vehicle speed sensor 2.

SB1109800057030X

Fig. 39   Code 12, 13 & 21: Vehicle Speed Sensor 2 System (Part 3 of 4). 1998 Legacy

---

8C6 :   CHECK VEHICLE SPEED SENSOR 2.

1) Set the vehicle on free roller, or lift-up the vehicle and support with safety stands.

WARNING:
Be careful not to be caught up by the running wheels.

2) Drive the vehicle at speed greater than 20 km/h (12 MPH).
3) Measure voltage between terminals of vehicle speed sensor 2.

NOTE:
Using an oscilloscope:

(1) Turn ignition switch to OFF.
(2) Set oscilloscope to vehicle speed sensor 2.
(3) Drive the vehicle at speed greater than 20 km/h (12 MPH).
(4) Measure signal voltage.

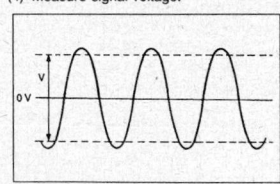

Terminals
No. 1 — No. 2:

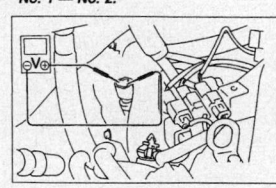

CHECK : **Is voltage more than 2 V (AC range)?**
YES : Repair or replace combination meter circuit.
NO : Replace vehicle speed sensor 2.

SB1109800057040X

Fig. 39   Code 12, 13 & 21: Vehicle Speed Sensor 2 System (Part 4 of 4). 1998 Legacy

---

DIAGNOSIS:
- Short circuit inside the SET/COAST SW and RESUME/ACCEL SW.

TROUBLE SYMPTOM:
- Cruise control cannot be set. (Cancelled immediately.)

SB1109800058010X

Fig. 40 Code 14 & 22: Set/Coast Switch, Resume/Accede Switch, Cancel Switch (Part 1 of 5). 1998 Legacy

---

8D1 : CHECK POWER SUPPLY.

1) Turn ignition switch to ON.
2) Turn cruise control main switch to ON.
3) Set select monitor in "Current Data Display & Save" mode.
4) Check signals for proper operation.
 (1) When pushing the SET/COAST switch:
 The SET/COAST switch shown on the display turns from "OFF" to "ON".
 (2) When pushing the RESUME/ACCEL switch:
 The RESUME/ACCEL switch shown on the display turns from "OFF" to "ON".
5) Turn ignition switch to OFF.
6) Disconnect connector from cruise control command switch.
7) Turn ignition switch to ON.
8) Measure voltage between cruise control command switch connector and chassis ground.

Terminals
(S1) No. 1 (+) — Chassis ground (–):

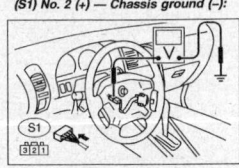

CHECK : *Is voltage more than 10 V?*
YES : Go to step 8D2.
NO : Repair or replace wiring harness between fuse & relay box and cruise control command switch.

8D2 : CHECK CRUISE CONTROL COMMAND SWITCH.

1) Turn ignition switch to OFF.
2) Connect connector of cruise control command switch.
3) Turn ignition switch to ON.
4) Measure voltage between cruise control command switch connector and chassis ground.

Terminals
(S1) No. 2 (+) — Chassis ground (–):

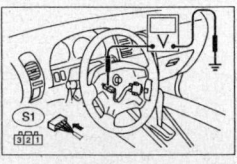

CHECK : *Is voltage more than 10 V? (When SET/COAST switch is ON.)*
YES : Go to step 8D3.
NO : Replace cruise control command switch.

8D3 : CHECK CRUISE CONTROL COMMAND SWITCH.

Measure voltage between cruise control command switch connector and chassis ground.

Terminals
(S1) No. 3 (+) — Chassis ground (–):

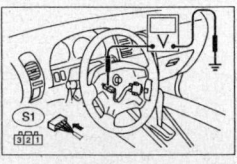

CHECK : *Is voltage more than 10 V? (When RESUME/ACCEL switch is ON.)*
YES : Go to step 8D4.
NO : Replace cruise control command switch.

SB1109800058020X

Fig. 40 Code 14 & 22: Set/Coast Switch, Resume/Accede Switch, Cancel Switch (Part 2 of 5). 1998 Legacy

---

8D4 : CHECK CRUISE CONTROL COMMAND SWITCH.

Measure voltage between cruise control command switch connector and chassis ground.

Terminals
(S1) No. 2 (+) — Chassis ground (–):

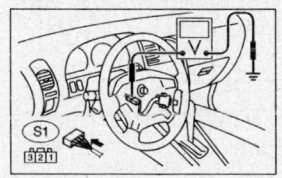

CHECK : *Is voltage more than 10 V? (When CANCEL switch is ON.)*
YES : Go to step 8D5.
NO : Replace cruise control command switch.

8D5 : CHECK CRUISE CONTROL COMMAND SWITCH.

Measure voltage between cruise control command switch connector and chassis ground.

Terminals
(S1) No. 3 (+) — Chassis ground (–):

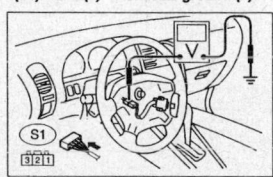

CHECK : *Is voltage more than 10 V? (When CANCEL switch is ON.)*
YES : Go to step 8D6.
NO : Replace cruise control command switch.

8D6 : CHECK CRUISE CONTROL COMMAND SWITCH.

1) Turn ignition switch to OFF.
2) Disconnect connector from cruise control command switch.
3) Measure resistance between terminals of cruise control command switch connector (switch side) to check the switch operation.

Terminals
No. 1 — No. 2:

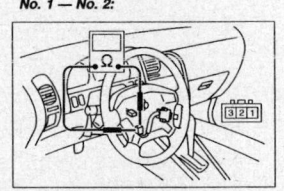

CHECK : *Is resistance less than 10 Ω? (When SET/COAST switch is ON.)*
YES : Go to step 8D7.
NO : Replace cruise control command switch.

SB1109800058030X

Fig. 40 Code 14 & 22: Set/Coast Switch, Resume/Accede Switch, Cancel Switch (Part 3 of 5). 1998 Legacy

---

8D7 : CHECK CRUISE CONTROL COMMAND SWITCH.

Measure resistance between terminals of cruise control command switch connector (switch side) to check the switch operation.

Terminals
No. 1 — No. 2:

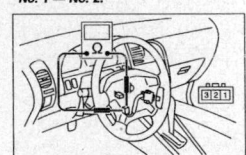

CHECK : *Is resistance more than 1 MΩ? (When SET/COAST switch is OFF.)*
YES : Go to step 8D8.
NO : Replace cruise control command switch.

8D8 : CHECK CRUISE CONTROL COMMAND SWITCH.

Measure resistance between terminals of cruise control command switch connector (switch side) to check the switch operation.

Terminals
No. 1 — No. 3:

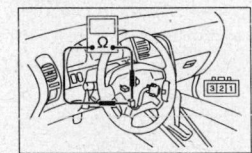

CHECK : *Is resistance less than 10 Ω? (When RESUME/ACCEL switch is ON.)*
YES : Go to step 8D9.
NO : Replace cruise control command switch.

8D9 : CHECK CRUISE CONTROL COMMAND SWITCH.

Measure resistance between terminals of cruise control command switch connector (switch side) to check the switch operation.

Terminals
No. 1 — No. 3:

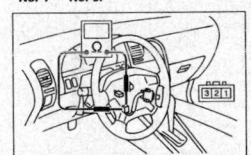

CHECK : *Is resistance more than 1 MΩ? (When RESUME/ACCEL switch is OFF.)*
YES : Go to step 8D10.
NO : Replace cruise control command switch.

8D10 : CHECK HARNESS CONNECTOR BETWEEN CRUISE CONTROL COMMAND SWITCH AND CRUISE CONTROL MODULE.

1) Disconnect connector from cruise control module.
2) Measure resistance of harness connector between cruise control command switch and cruise control module.

Connector & terminal
(S1) No. 2 — (B94) No. 10:

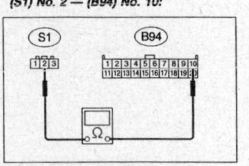

CHECK : *Is resistance less than 10 Ω?*
YES : Go to step 8D11.
NO : Repair or replace wiring harness.

SB1109800058040X

Fig. 40 Code 14 & 22: Set/Coast Switch, Resume/Accede Switch, Cancel Switch (Part 4 of 5). 1998 Legacy

---

8D11 : CHECK HARNESS CONNECTOR BETWEEN CRUISE CONTROL COMMAND SWITCH AND CRUISE CONTROL MODULE.

Measure resistance of harness connector between cruise control command switch and cruise control module.

Connector & terminal
(S1) No. 3 — (B94) No. 9:

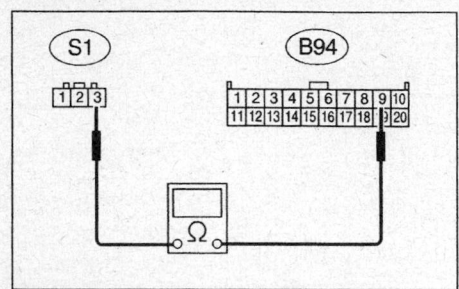

CHECK : **Is resistance less than 10 Ω?**
YES : Replace cruise control module.
NO : Repair or replace wiring harness.

SB1109800058050X

Fig. 40 Code 14 & 22: Set/Coast Switch, Resume/Accede Switch, Cancel Switch (Part 5 of 5). 1998 Legacy

---

8F1 : MEASURE RESISTANCE OF VACUUM PUMP MOTOR, AIR VALVE AND RELEASE VALVE.

1) Disconnect connector from vacuum pump and valve.
2) Measure resistance of vacuum pump motor, air valve and release valve.

Terminals
No. 2 — No. 3:

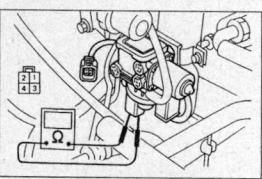

CHECK : **Is resistance approximately 46 Ω?**
YES : Go to step 8F2.
NO : Replace vacuum pump and valve.

8F2 : MEASURE RESISTANCE OF VACUUM PUMP MOTOR, AIR VALVE AND RELEASE VALVE.

Measure resistance of vacuum pump motor, air valve and release valve.

Terminals
No. 2 — No. 1:

CHECK : **Is resistance approximately 69 Ω?**
YES : Go to step 8F3.
NO : Replace vacuum pump and valve.

8F3 : MEASURE RESISTANCE OF VACUUM PUMP MOTOR, AIR VALVE AND RELEASE VALVE.

Measure resistance of vacuum pump motor, air valve and release valve.

Terminals
No. 2 — No. 4:

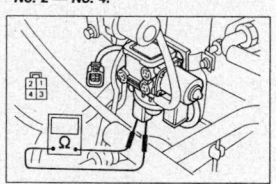

CHECK : **Is resistance approximately 69 Ω?**
YES : Go to step 8F4.
NO : Replace vacuum pump and valve.

8F4 : PERFORM A CIRCUIT TEST IN HARNESS BETWEEN VACUUM PUMP & VALVE AND CRUISE CONTROL MODULE.

1) Disconnect connector from cruise control module.
2) Measure resistance of harness connector between cruise control module, vacuum pump motor, air valve and release valve.

Connector & terminal
(B7) No. 1 — (B94) No. 5:

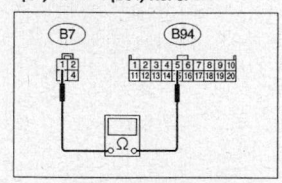

CHECK : **Is resistance less than 10 Ω?**
YES : Go to step 8F5.
NO : Repair or replace wiring harness between vacuum pump & valve and cruise control module.

SB1109800059020X

Fig. 41 Code 31, 32 & 33: Vacuum Pump, Air Valve, Release Valve (Part 2 of 4). 1998 Legacy

---

DIAGNOSIS:
● Open or poor contact of vacuum pump motor, air valve and release valve.
TROUBLE SYMPTOM:
● Cruise control cannot be set. (Cancels immediately.)
WIRING DIAGRAM:

SB1109800059010X

Fig. 41 Code 31, 32 & 33: Vacuum Pump, Air Valve, Release Valve (Part 1 of 4). 1998 Legacy

8F5 : PERFORM A CIRCUIT TEST IN HARNESS BETWEEN VACUUM PUMP & VALVE AND CRUISE CONTROL MODULE.

Measure resistance of harness connector between cruise control module, vacuum pump motor, air valve and release valve.

Connector & terminal
(B7) No. 2 — (B94) No. 14:

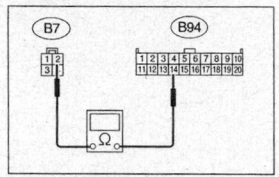

CHECK : **Is resistance less than 10 Ω?**
YES : Go to step 8F6.
NO : Repair or replace wiring harness between vacuum pump & valve and cruise control module.

8F6 : PERFORM A CIRCUIT TEST IN HARNESS BETWEEN VACUUM PUMP & VALVE AND CRUISE CONTROL MODULE.

Measure resistance of harness connector between cruise control module, vacuum pump motor, air valve and release valve.

Connector & terminal
(B7) No. 3 — (B94) No. 7:

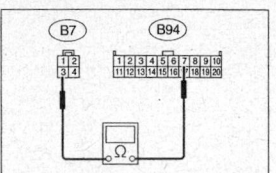

CHECK : **Is resistance less than 10 Ω?**
YES : Go to step 8F7.
NO : Repair or replace wiring harness between vacuum pump & valve and cruise control module.

SB1109800059030X

Fig. 41 Code 31, 32 & 33: Vacuum Pump, Air Valve, Release Valve (Part 3 of 4). 1998 Legacy

8F7 : PERFORM A CIRCUIT TEST IN HARNESS BETWEEN VACUUM PUMP & VALVE AND CRUISE CONTROL MODULE.

Measure resistance of harness connector between cruise control module, vacuum pump motor, air valve and release valve.

Connector & terminal
(B7) No. 4 — (B94) No. 13:

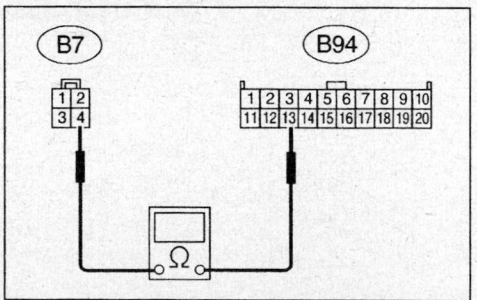

CHECK : **Is resistance less than 10 Ω?**
YES : Replace cruise control module.
NO : Repair or replace wiring harness between vacuum pump & valve and cruise control module.

SB1109800059040X

Fig. 41 Code 31, 32 & 33: Vacuum Pump, Air Valve, Release Valve (Part 4 of 4). 1998 Legacy

Function code indication		Item to measure		Contents of diagnosis
Code No.	Abbreviation	Trouble code	Abbreviation	
FB0	CANCEL	10	OK	Normal
		11	BR/ST/CL or N	Input signals from brake switch, stop lamp switch, inhibitor switch.
		12	E/G REV	Engine speed (rpm) limiter
		13	SPEED LIM	Low-speed control limiter
		14	SET+ RESUME	Simultaneous entry of two signals (Shorted circuit)
		21	MOTOR	Faulty motor or motor drive system
		22	VENT VALVE	Faulty vent valve and valve drive system
		23	C/U RELAY	Faulty relay built into cruise control unit
		24	SP SENSOR	Faulty vehicle speed sensor
		25	RESUME SW	Faulty resume switch

SB1109100011000X

Fig. 42 Trouble code identification & description. SVX

```
SELECT    SYSTEM
C / C : 0,    OTHERS : /
```
SB1109100010000X

Fig. 44 Select monitor display (button pressed). SVX

Function code indication		Item to measure	Content of items to be monitored
Code No.	Abbreviation		
FA0	ST	Stop light switch	LED No.1 comes on when switch is turned ON. (Brake pedal is depressed.)
	BR	Brake switch	LED No. 2 comes on when brake pedal is depressed.
	SE	SET/COAST switch	LED No. 3 comes on when switch is turned ON.
	RE	RESUME/ACCEL switch	LED No. 4 comes on when switch is turned ON.
	IH	Clutch switch/inhibitor switch	• LED No. 5 comes on when clutch pedal is depressed (MT model). • LED No. 5 comes on when select lever is set to "N" (AT model).

SB1109500028000X

Fig. 46 System switches test. Impreza & Legacy

Function code indication		Item to measure		Contents of diagnosis
Code No.	Abbreviation	Trouble code	Abbreviation	
FB1	OUTPUT	10	OK	Normal
		31	MOTOR	Open or shorted vacuum pump motor circuit/harness
		32	VENT VALVE	Open or shorted vent circuit/harness
		33	C/U RELAY	Deposited safety relay built into cruise control unit
		34	C/U VENT V	Faulty vent valve drive circuit of cruise control unit
		35	C/U MOTOR	Faulty vacuum pump motor drive circuit

SB1109100014000X

Fig. 48 Output system codes (Real-time diagnosis). SVX

```
SELECT    SYSTEM
EGI : 0,    OTHERS : /
```
SB1109100009000X

Fig. 43 Select monitor display (Power On). SVX

Function code indication		Item to measure	Content of items to be monitored
Code No.	Abbreviation		
FA0	1. SE	SET/COAST switch	LED 1 comes on when switch is turned ON.
	2. RE	RESUME/ACCEL switch	LED 2 comes on when switch is turned ON.
	4. ST	Stop light switch	LED 4 comes on when switch is turned ON (brake pedal is depressed)
	5. BR	Brake switch / inhibitor switch	• Brake switch [Set in the D range]. LED 5 comes on when brake pedal is depressed. • LED 5 comes on when select lever is set to "N".

SB1109100012000X

Fig. 45 System switches test. SVX

```
OUTPUT            ( F B I )
ready ?           Yes : 0
```
SB1109100013000X

Fig. 47 Select monitor display (O button pressed, Output systems). SVX

Indication of function code		Item to measure	Contents of items to be monitored
Code No.	Abbreviation		
F 00	CRUISE CONTROL	Cruise control unit identification	Reads ROM ID number of cruise control unit to display a possible communication state.
F 01	VSP (MPH)	Vehicle speed (MPH)	Displays vehicle speed data (in miles/h) determined by cruise control unit in relation to signal emitted from vehicle speed sensor on transmission.
F 02	VSP (km/h)	Vehicle speed (km/h)	Displays vehicle speed in km/h.
F 03	EREV (rpm)	Engine speed	Displays engine rpm determined by cruise speed control unit in relation to reference signal emitted from crank angle sensor.

SB1109100015000X

Fig. 49 Select monitor display data. SVX

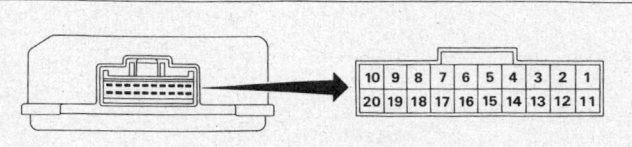

Content	Terminal No.	Measuring conditions and I/O signals (ignition switch ON and engine idling)
Vent valve	1	• Power supply is ON when vehicle is stopped. • ON-and-OFF (0 and 12 volts) operation is alternately repeated while cruise control is operating.
Safety valve	2	• Power supply is ON when vehicle is stopped. • ON-and-OFF (0 and 12 volts) operation is alternately repeated while cruise control is operating.
Ignition switch	3	• Battery voltage is present when switch is turned on.
Main switch	4	• When main switch is pressed, battery voltage is present. • When main switch is OFF, "0" volt is present.
Power Supply to vacuum valve, vent valve, safety valve and set Indicator	5	• When main switch is pressed, battery voltage is present.
SET/COAST switch	6	• When switch is turned ON, battery voltage is present. • When switch is turned OFF, "0" volt is present.
RESUME/ACCEL switch	7	• When switch is turned ON, battery voltage is present. • When switch is turned OFF, "0" volt is present.
Brake switch	8	Set select lever to any position other than "P" or "N" (AT model)/leave clutch released (MT model), with main switch ON. Then check that: • 0 volt is present when brake pedal is depressed. • Battery voltage is present when brake pedal is released, or • 0 volt is present when clutch pedal is depressed (MT model). • Battery voltage is present when clutch pedal is released (MT model). • 0 volt is present when select lever is set to "P" or "N" (AT model). • Battery voltage is present when select lever is in any position other than "P" or "N" (AT model).
Inhibitor switch Clutch switch	9	When switch is turned ON, "0" volt is present.
Vacuum valve	11	• Power supply is ON when vehicle is stopped. • ON-and-OFF (0 and 12 volts) operation is alternately repeated while cruise control is operating.
AT control (Set signal)	12	ECM emits a ground-level signal while driving vehicle at least 40 km/h (25 MPH) with SET switch ON.
GND	13	—
Select monitor (Output)	14	—
Select monitor (Input)	15	—
Vehicle speed sensor	18	• When all four wheels are raised off ground and any wheel is rotated manually, approximately 5 and 0 volt pulse signals are alternately sent to cruise control module.
Stop light switch	19	With ignition switch on or OFF: • Depress brake pedal to check that battery voltage is present. • "0" volt is present with brake pedal released.
GND	20	—

SB1109100018000X

Fig. 50 Control unit pin voltage test. Forester & Impreza

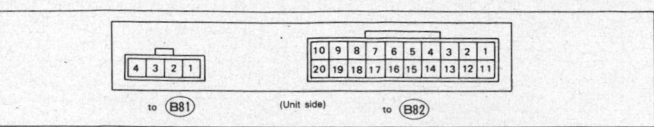

Content	Connector No.	Terminal No.	Measuring conditions and I/O signals (ignition switch ON and engine idling)
Main switch	(B81)	1	• When main switch is pressed, battery voltage is present; when it is released, approximately 6.5 volts are present. • When main switch is OFF, "0" volts are present.
Main relay (solenoid)		2	• When main switch is turned ON, indicator comes on and battery voltage is present. • When main switch is turned OFF, "0" volts are present.
Main relay (contacts)		4	↑
Engine speed (rpm) signal	(B82)	2	When engine starts, a pulse signal is entered (Observe using an oscilloscope.)
Vehicle speed sensor		7	When all four wheels are raised off ground and any wheel is rotated manually, approximately 5 and 0 volt pulse signals are alternately sent to cruise control unit.
Brake switch		15	Set select lever to any position other than "P" or "N" (AT model)/leave clutch released (MT model), with main switch ON. Then check that: • 0 volts are present when brake pedal is depressed. • Battery voltage is present when brake pedal is released, or • 0 volts are present when clutch pedal is depressed (MT model). • Battery voltage is present when clutch pedal is released (MT model). • 0 volts are present when select lever is set to "P" or "N" (AT model). • Battery voltage is present when select lever is in any position othern than "P" or "N" (AT model).
Stop light switch		20	With ignition switch ON or OFF: • Depress brake pedal to check that battery voltage is present. • "0" volts are present with brake pedal released.
SET/COAST switch		18	• When switch is turned ON, battery voltage is present. • When switch is turned OFF, "0" volts are present.
RESUME/ACCEL switch		19	↑
Set signal		11	ECU emits a ground-level signal while driving vehicle at least 40 km/h (25 MPH) with SET switch ON.
Power supply to vacuum motor, vent valve and safety valve		14	• "0" volts are present when vehicle is stopped. • Battery voltage is present while cruise control system is operating.
Vacuum motor output		8	• Power supply is ON when vehicle is stopped. • ON-and-OFF (0 and 12 volts) operation is alternately repeated while cruise control is operating.
Vent valve output		9	↑

Voltage at terminals (11, 14, 8 and 9) cannot be checked unless vehicle is driving at cruising speed.

SB1109500029000X

Fig. 51 Control unit pin voltage test. Legacy

COMPONENT DIAGNOSIS & TESTING

CONTROL UNIT PIN VOLTAGE TEST

Refer to **Figs. 50 through 52,** for pin voltage test.

MAIN SWITCH TEST

1. Turn ignition switch on.
2. Ensure main switch is not illuminated when in the off position.
3. Ensure main switch is illuminated when in the on position.
4. Leave main switch on.
5. Turn ignition switch off then on. Ensure main switch is not illuminated.

SUB SWITCH TEST

1. Ensure switch operation is proper in the "Set/Coast" and "Resume/Accede" positions.
2. Ensure switch returns to original position when released.

COMPONENT REPLACEMENT

VACUUM PUMP & VALVE

Forester, Legacy & Impreza

1. Disconnect vacuum pump electrical connector.
2. Disconnect vacuum hose from body side.
3. Remove vacuum pump retaining nuts.
4. **On Legacy models,** remove A/C receiver/drier bracket.
5. **On all models,** remove vacuum pump assembly.
6. Reverse procedure to install.

SVX

1. Remove battery.
2. Remove main fuse box mounting bolts, then position fuse box aside.
3. Disconnect vacuum pump wiring harness and hose.
4. Remove vacuum pump attaching bolts, then the pump.

5. Reverse procedure to install.

ACTUATOR

Forester

1. Remove air intake chamber, chamber stay and bands securing cruise control cable.
2. Remove cruise control cable end from throttle cam.
3. Disconnect cruise control vacuum hose from intake manifold.
4. Remove actuator attaching bolts, disconnect electrical connector from actuator, then remove actuator.
5. Reverse procedure to install.

CRUISE CONTROL MAIN SWITCH

Forester

1. Remove screws and clips from instrument panel lower cover, then the cover.
2. Disconnect electrical connector from switch, then remove switch by pushing it outward.
3. Reverse procedure to install.

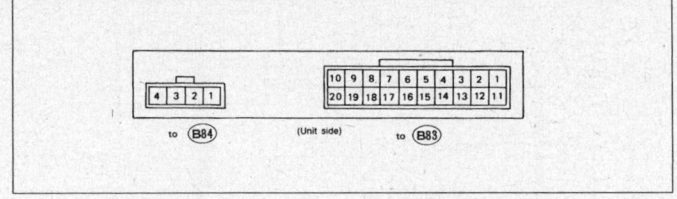

Content	Connector No.	Terminal No.	Measuring conditions and I/O signals (ignition switch ON and engine idling)
Main switch	B84	1	• When main switch is pressed, battery voltage is present; when it is released, approximately 6.5 volts are present. • When main switch is OFF, "0" volts are present.
Main relay (solenoid)		2	• When main switch is turned ON, indicator comes on and battery voltage is present. • When main switch is turned OFF, "0" volts are present.
Main relay (contacts)		4	↑
Engine speed (rpm) signal	B83	2	When engine starts, a pulse signal is entered (Observe using an oscilloscope.)
Vehicle speed sensor		7	When all four wheels are raised off ground and any wheel is rotated manually, approximately 5 and 0 volt pulse signals are alternately sent to cruise control unit.
Brake switch		15	Set select lever to any position other than "P" or "N", with main switch ON. Then check that: • 0 volts are present when brake pedal is depressed. • Battery voltage is present when brake pedal is released, or • 0 volts are present when select lever is set to "P" or "N". • Battery voltage is present when select lever is in any position other than "P" or "N".
Stop light switch		20	With ignition switch ON or OFF: • Depress brake pedal to check that battery voltage is present. • "0" volts are present with brake pedal released.
SET/COAST switch		18	• When switch is turned ON, battery voltage is present. • When switch is turned OFF, "0" volts are present.
RESUME/ACCEL switch		19	↑
Set signal		11	ECU emits a ground-level signal while driving vehicle at least 40 km/h (25 MPH) with SET switch ON.
Power supply to vacuum motor, vent valve and safety valve		14	• "0" volts are present when vehicle is stopped. • Battery voltage is present while cruise control system is operating.
Vacuum motor output		8	• Power supply is ON when vehicle is stopped. • ON-and-OFF (0 and 12 volts) operation is alternately repeated while cruise control is operating.
Vent valve output		9	↑

SB1109100017000X

Fig. 52 Control unit pin voltage test. SVX

Wiper Systems

INDEX

COMPONENT DIAGNOSIS & TESTING
FORESTER
WINDSHIELD WIPER SWITCH CONTINUITY TEST

Refer to **Fig. 1,** for connector pin identification and continuity tests.

WINDSHIELD WIPER MOTOR TEST

1. Connect battery and inspect wiper motor operation at low speed, **Fig. 2.**
2. Inspect wiper motor operation at high speed, **Fig. 3.**
3. Inspect wiper motor for proper stoppage. After operating motor at low speed, disconnect power and ensure motor stops, **Fig. 4.**
4. Reconnect battery and ensure wiper motor stops at "Auto Stop" after operating at low speed, **Fig. 5.**

REAR WIPER SWITCH CONTINUITY TEST

Fig. 6, for connector pin identification and continuity tests.

REAR WIPER MOTOR TEST

1. Connect battery to rear wiper motor and ensure proper operation of motor, **Fig. 7.**
2. After operating motor, disconnect power and inspect for proper stoppage, **Fig. 8.**
3. Reconnect battery and ensure wiper motor stops at "Auto Stop" after it has been operated, **Fig. 9.**

REAR WIPER RELAY TEST

Connect battery to terminal No. 1 and ground terminal No. 2, **Fig. 10.** Inspect for continuity between terminals, **Fig. 11.**

IMPREZA & LEGACY
WINDSHIELD WIPER SWITCH CONTINUITY TEST

Refer to **Fig. 12,** for connector pin identification and **Fig. 13,** for continuity test.

WINDSHIELD WIPER MOTOR TEST

Impreza

1. Inspect wiper motor low speed operation by connecting battery positive lead to terminal 2 of wiper motor connector and negative lead to terminal 4, **Fig. 14.**
2. Inspect wiper motor high speed operation by connecting battery positive lead to terminal 3 of wiper motor connector and negative lead to terminal 4, **Fig. 14.**
3. Inspect wiper motor for proper stoppage as follows:
   a. Connect battery positive lead to terminal 2 of wiper motor connector and negative lead to terminal 4, **Fig. 14.**
   b. After operating motor at low speed, disconnect positive lead from terminal 2.
   c. Reconnect battery positive lead to terminal 5 of wiper motor connector. Ensure wiper motor stops at auto stop after operating at low speed.

Legacy

1. Inspect wiper motor low speed operation by connecting battery positive lead to terminal 2 of wiper motor connector and negative lead to terminal 6, **Fig. 15.**

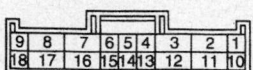

- **Wiper switch**

Terminal Switch position		16	7	17	8	INT1	INT2
OFF	OFF	o—o					
		×—		—×			
	MIST		o—	—o			
INT	OFF	o—o				o—	—o
		×—		—×			
	MIST		o—	—o		o—	—o
		×—		—×			
LO	OFF		o—	—o			
	MIST		o—	—o			
HI	OFF			o—	—o		
	MIST		o—	—o—o			

- **Washer switch**

Terminal Switch position	11	2
OFF		
ON	o——————o	

SB9029900022000X

Fig. 1   Wiper switch connector pin identification and continuity test. Forester

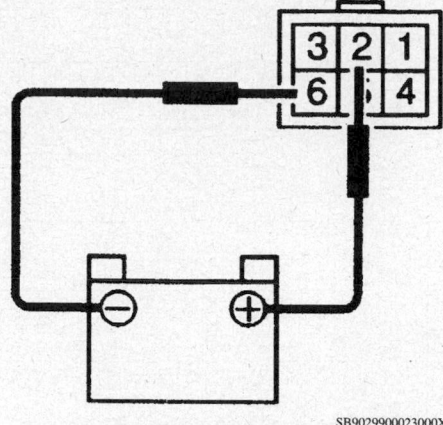

SB9029900023000X

Fig. 2   Wiper motor low speed operation. Forester

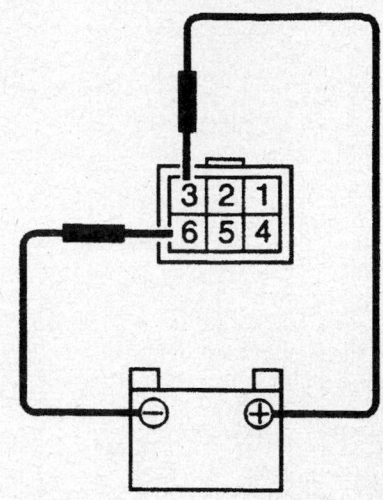

SB9029900024000X

Fig. 3   Wiper motor high speed operation. Forester

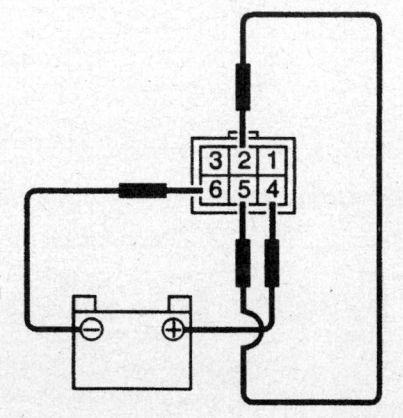

SB9029900026000X

Fig. 5   Wiper motor "Auto Stop" test. Forester.

Terminal Switch position	10	12	2
WASH	o——o		
OFF			
ON	o——o		
WASH	o——o——o		o

SB9029900027000X

Fig. 6   Rear wiper switch continuity test, less intermittent wiper. Forester

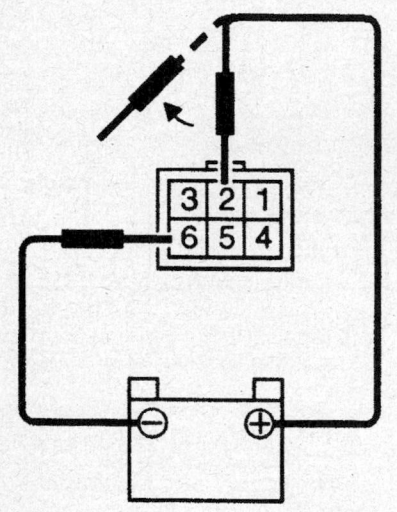

SB9029900025000X

Fig. 4   Wiper motor stop test. Forester

2. Inspect wiper motor high speed operation by connecting battery positive lead to terminal 3 of wiper motor connector and negative lead to terminal 6.
3. Inspect wiper motor for proper stoppage as follows:
   a. Connect battery positive lead to terminal 2 of wiper motor connector and negative lead to terminal 6.
   b. After operating motor at low speed, disconnect positive lead from terminal 2.
   c. Reconnect battery positive lead to terminal 4 of wiper motor connector, then connect a jumper lead between terminal 2 and 5. Ensure wiper motor stops at auto stop after operating at low speed.

REAR WIPER SWITCH CONTINUITY TEST

Refer to **Fig. 12,** for connector pin identification and **Figs. 16 and 17,** for continuity test.

REAR WIPER MOTOR TEST

1. Inspect wiper motor operation by connecting battery positive lead to terminal 2 of wiper motor connector and negative lead to terminal 3, **Fig. 18.**
2. Inspect wiper motor for proper stoppage as follows:
   a. After operating motor as outlined in step 1, disconnect positive lead from terminal 2.
   b. Reconnect battery positive lead to terminal 1 of wiper motor connector, then install a jumper wire between terminals 2 and 4. Ensure wiper motor stops at auto stop after it has been operated.

REAR WIPER RELAY CONTINUITY TEST

Refer to **Fig. 19,** for connector pin identification and **Fig. 20,** for continuity test.

SVX

WINDSHIELD WIPER SWITCH CONTINUITY TEST

Refer to **Fig. 21,** for connector pin identification and **Fig. 22,** for continuity test.

REAR WIPER SWITCH CONTINUITY TEST

Refer to **Fig. 21,** for connector pin identification and **Fig. 23,** for continuity test.

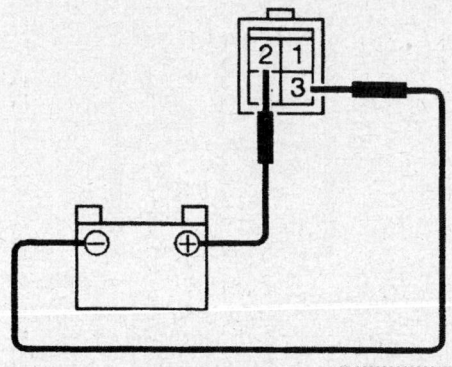

SB9029900028000X

Fig. 7   Rear wiper motor test. Forester

When current flows.	Between terminals No. 3 and No. 4	Continuity does not exist.
	Between terminals No. 3 and No. 5	Continuity exists.
When current does not flow.	Between terminals No. 3 and No. 4	Continuity exists.
	Between terminals No. 3 and No. 5	Continuity does not exist.
	Between terminals No. 1 and No. 2	Continuity exists.

SB9029900031000X

Fig. 10   Rear wiper relay continuity chart. Forester

Terminal (Wire color) Switch position		d-9 (Y)	d-8 (L)	d-6 (LY)	d-7 (LW)	INT1	INT2
OFF	OFF	o——o					
		x—		—x			
	MIST		o——o				
INT	OFF	o——o				o——o	
		x—		—x			
	MIST		o——o			o——o	
		x—		—x			
LO	OFF		o——o				
	MIST	o——o					
HI	OFF			o——o			
	MIST	o——o	o——o				

SB9029100009000X

Fig. 13   Windshield wiper switch continuity test. Impreza & Legacy

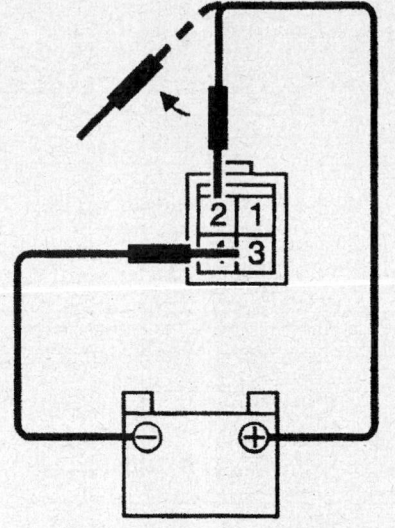

SB9029900029000X

Fig. 8   Rear wiper motor stoppage test. Forester

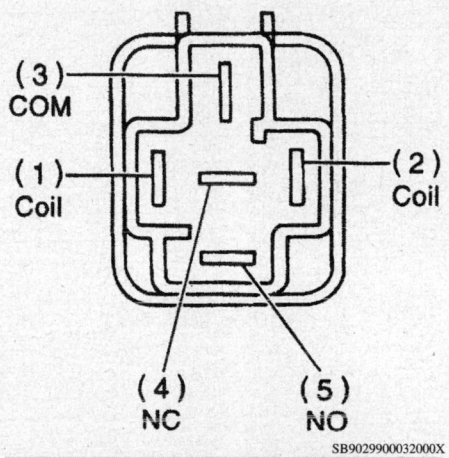

(3) COM

(1) Coil

(2) Coil

(4) NC

(5) NO

SB9029900032000X

Fig. 11   Rear wiper relay terminal location. Forester

SB9029100010000X

Fig. 14   Windshield wiper motor connector pin identification. Impreza

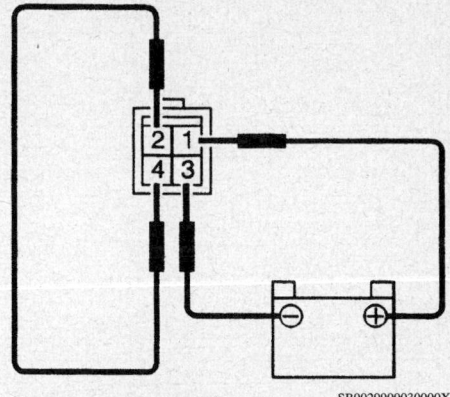

SB9029900030000X

Fig. 9   Rear wiper motor stoppage test. Forester

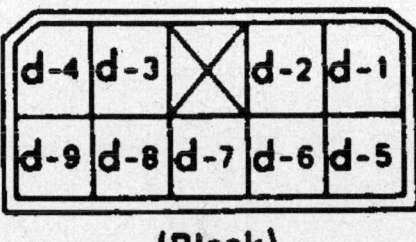

d-4	d-3	X	d-2	d-1
d-9	d-8	d-7	d-6	d-5

(Black)

SB9029100008000X

Fig. 12   Wiper switch connector pin identification. Impreza & Legacy

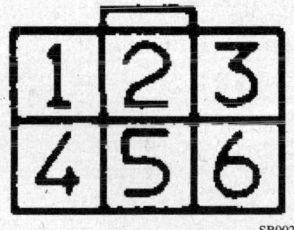

1	2	3
4	5	6

SB9029500020000X

Fig. 15   Windshield wiper motor connector pin identification. Legacy

SUBARU

WITHOUT INTERMITTENT REAR WIPER

Terminal (Wire color) / Switch position	d-2	d-1	d-3
WASH	○		○
OFF			
ON	○		○
WASH	○	○	○

WITH INTERMITTENT REAR WIPER

Terminal (Wire color) / Switch position	d-2	d-1	d-4	d-3
WASH	○	○		
OFF				
INT	○		○	
ON	○			○
WASH	○	○		○

SB9029100011000X

Fig. 16 Rear wiper switch continuity test. Impreza

Terminal (Wire color) / Switch position	d-2	d-1	d-3
WASH	○	○	○
OFF			
ON	○		○
WASH	○	○	○

SB9029500021000X

Fig. 17 Rear wiper switch continuity test

When current flows	Between terminals (3) and (5)	Continuity does not exist.
	Between terminals (3) and (4)	Continuity exists.
When current does not flow	Between terminals (3) and (5)	Continuity exists.
	Between terminals (3) and (4)	Continuity does not exist.
	Between terminals (1) and (2)	Continuity exists.

SB9029100014000X

Fig. 20 Rear wiper relay continuity test. Impreza & Legacy

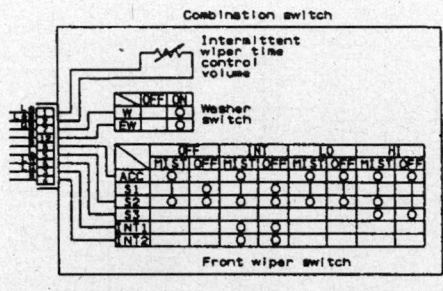

Fig. 22 Windshield wiper switch continuity test. SVX

SB9029100016000X

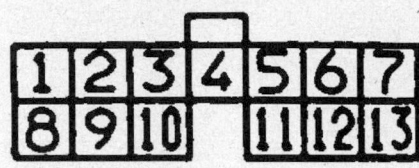

SB9029100012000X

Fig. 18 Rear wiper motor connector pin identification. Legacy

SB9029100015000X

Fig. 21 Wiper switch connector pin identification. SVX

Rear wiper & washer switch

	WASH	ON	INT	OFF	WASH	
	○	○			○	+ I R
	○				○	W R
	○				○	E W
			○			C I R

SB9029100017000X

Fig. 23 Rear wiper switch continuity test. SVX

Fig. 19 Rear wiper relay connector pin identification. Impreza & Legacy

SB9029100013000X

Air Bag System

NOTE: "Electrical Symbol & Wire Color Code Identification" Located In The Front Of This Manual May Be Used As An Aid When Using Wiring Circuits Found In This Section.

INDEX

AIR BAG SYSTEM DISARMING & ARMING

Disarming

1. Place ignition switch in the Off position.
2. **Wait 20 seconds before beginning repair procedures.**

Arming

1. Ensure no one is inside vehicle.
2. With ignition switch in the Off position, connect battery positive cable, then battery negative cable.
3. Wait at least 20 seconds, then turn ignition On and note air bag warning lamp operation, which should light for approximately eight seconds, then go off. If lamp remains illuminated or fails to light, refer to " Diagnosis and Testing."

DESCRIPTION & OPERATION

SYSTEM

FORESTER

The SRS airbag consists of an airbag control module, left and right sub sensors, electric sensor and safety sensor built into the control module, and the driver's and passenger's air bag modules.

A frontal impact causes the safety sensor, electric sensor and front sub sensor to input an impact signal to the CPU. The CPU judges whether the airbags should be inflated based on these signal values.

Input of a side impact signal that exceeds a preset value causes the airbag on the side that received the impact to inflate.

LEGACY & SVX

The SRS consists of a control unit, two front sensors, a safety sensor built into the

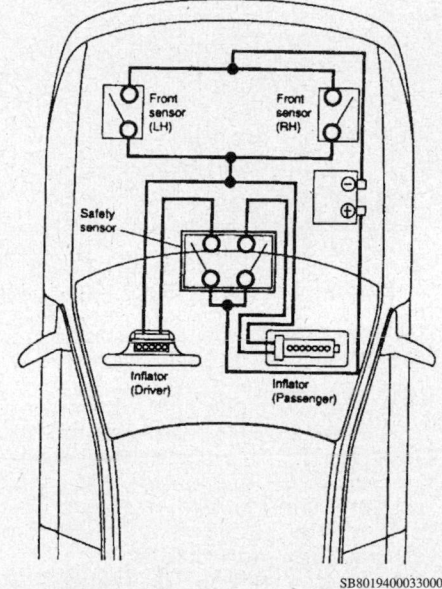

SB8019400033000X

Fig. 1 Supplemental Restraint System (SRS). Legacy & SVX

control unit and driver's and passenger's air bag modules, **Fig. 1**.

The front sensors are connected in parallel respectively. The front sensors and safety sensor are connected in series, so that the air bag will inflate if at least one front sensor and the safety sensor detect an impact at the same time.

IMPREZA

The SRS consists of a control unit, an electric sensor and a safety sensor which are built into the control unit and driver's and passenger's air bag modules, **Fig. 2**.

The electric sensor and safety sensor are connected in series, so that the air bag will inflate if the two sensors detect an impact at the same time.

SYSTEM COMPONENTS

FRONT SENSOR

Forester

One front sub sensor is installed on both left and right sides ahead of the front wheel apron wall. The front sub sensor is of the pendulum type, **Fig. 3**, if the front sensor receives a frontal impact exceeding a certain limit, the mass in the sensor revolves forward to turn the switch on.

Legacy & SVX

Front sensors are installed on either front wheel apron wall. If the roller type sensor receives a frontal impact exceeding a certain set limit, it rotates to turn the switch on, **Fig. 4**.

ELECTRIC SENSOR

Impreza

The electric sensor is built into the control unit. This sensor is of the semiconductor type and senses deceleration at collision by the change of electrical resistance and the impact sensing circuit, **Fig. 5**.

SAFETY SENSOR

Legacy & SVX

The safety sensor is built into the control unit. A dual pole rotary type safety sensor is used, **Fig. 6**.

Impreza

The safety sensor is built into the control unit. A piston type safety sensor is used, **Fig. 7**.

DRIVER'S AIR BAG MODULE

The air bag module is located at the center of the steering wheel and contains the air bag and inflator, **Fig. 8**. If a collision occurs, the inflator produces a large volume of nitrogen gas to rapidly inflate the air bag.

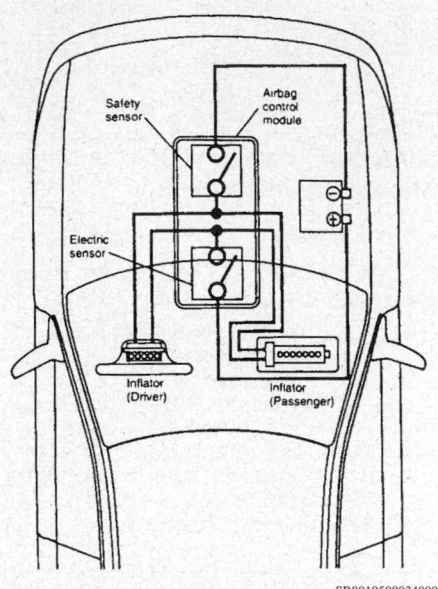

Fig. 2 Supplemental Restraint System (SRS). Impreza

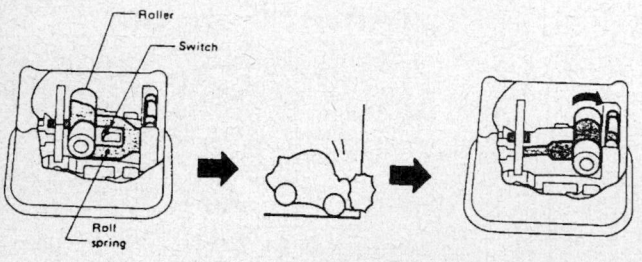

Fig. 4 Roller type sensor. Legacy & SVX

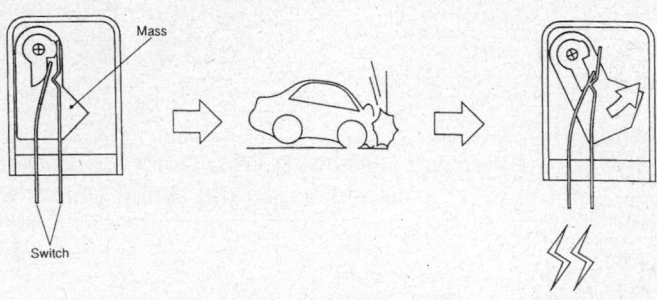

Fig. 3 Pendulum type sensor. Forester

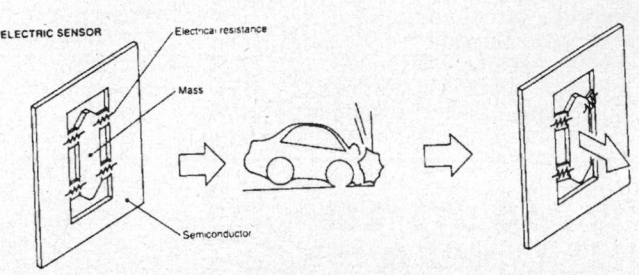

Fig. 5 Electric sensor. Impreza

PASSENGER'S AIR BAG MODULE

The air bag module is located on the passenger side of the instrument panel and contains the air bag and inflator, **Fig. 9.** If a collision occurs, the inflator, produces a large volume of nitrogen gas to rapidly inflate the air bag.

SIDE AIRBAG MODULE

The side airbag module is located at the outside of the front backrest, **Fig. 10.** It contains an airbag and an inflator. If a side collision occurs, the inflator produces a large volume of gas inflating the airbag in a very short period of time.

STEERING ROLL CONNECTOR

The steering roll connector is located between the steering column and steering wheel, **Fig. 11.** A flat cable stored in a spiral form transmits the control unit electrical signal to the steering wheel from the body harness.

AIR BAG CONNECTOR

The air bag control unit uses a connector with double lock and coupling error detection mechanisms. If coupling is incomplete, the air bag warning lamp will light.

1. To disconnect the air bag control unit connector, proceed as follows:

   a. Press wire one of the control unit, **Fig. 12,** until green lever two tilts upward. This unlocks the double lock. Pull off connector while pressing connector lock.
2. To connect the air bag control unit connector, proceed as follows:

   a. Insert connector until a click is heard, then push in green lever to apply the double lock.
3. To disconnect connector between harnesses, proceed as follows:

   a. Press lever one, **Fig. 13,** to pop green lever two out. This unlocks the double lock system. Separate the connector by pulling both sides while holding connector sections and pressing in lever one.
4. To connect the connector between harnesses, proceed as follows:

   a. Insert both connectors until a click is heard, then push in green lever until it clicks.

AIR BAG WARNING LAMP

The air bag warning lamp is located on the instrument cluster. It lights if a poor connection is present or if the air bag control unit detects an SRS problem or condition. When the SRS is functioning normally, the lamp will go off approximately eight seconds after the ignition is turned On.

WIRING HARNESS

The SRS wiring harness is entirely covered with a yellow protective conduit, and can easily be distinguished from harnesses of other systems.

PRECAUTIONS
AIR BAG SYSTEM

1. The electrical circuit necessary for SRS deployment is powered directly from the battery and backup power supply. To avoid unwanted deployment and possible personal injury, the SRS must be disarmed prior to performing service procedures. Refer to "Air Bag System Disarming & Arming."
2. When inspecting the SRS, use a digital circuit tester. **Using an analog circuit tester may cause unwanted deployment.**
3. Do not apply tester probe directly to any SRS connector terminal. Use a test harness when inspecting.
4. Do not inspect air bag module continuity with air bag removed from vehicle.
5. When storing a removed air bag module, place it parallel with floor with pad facing upward. Do not place module against a wall or place anything on the pad.
6. After removal, air bag module should be kept away from heat and light sources.
7. Use care not drop SRS components.
8. Do not subject SRS components to temperatures over 194°F.
9. Do not apply oil, grease or water to air bag unit.
10. Air bag module must not be disassembled.

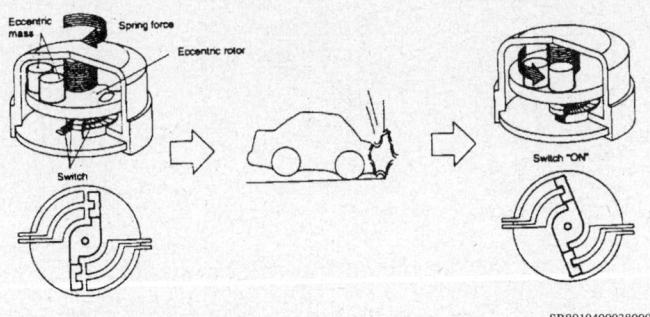

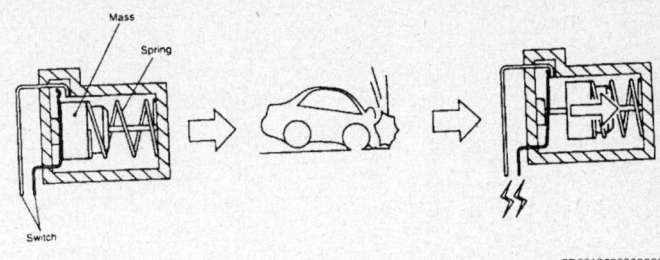

Fig. 7 Piston type safety sensor. Impreza

Fig. 6 Rotor type safety sensor. Legacy & SVX

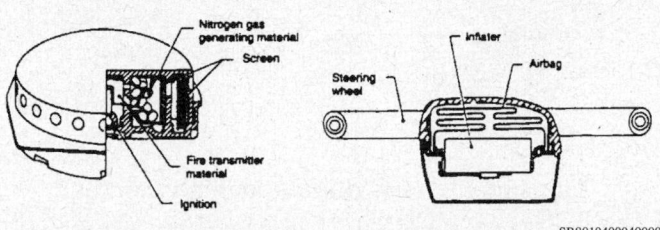

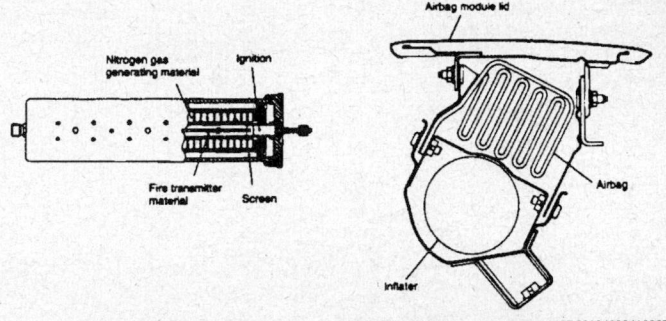

Fig. 8 Driver's air bag & inflator

Fig. 9 Passenger's air bag & inflator

11. Do not paint air bag to correct cosmetic flaws. It must be replaced.
12. If any damage or open circuits are found in SRS wiring harness, do not attempt to repair. Replace the defective harness.
13. Ensure grounding terminal is free from contamination before connecting SRS to ground.

BATTERY GROUND CABLE

Prior to service, disconnect battery ground cable and isolate as required.

SCHEDULED MAINTENANCE

The SRS must be inspected at 10 year intervals from the date the vehicle was manufactured. Inspect system for diagnostic trouble codes () and proper warning lamp operation. Refer to "Diagnosis & Testing. " Inspect air bag module for scratches and cracks and other damage. Inspect sensors, control unit and their mounting brackets for damage and proper mounting. Inspect system wiring harnesses and electrical connectors for damage, chafing and proper connection. Any components that shown signs of wear or damage should be replaced.

WIRING DIAGRAMS

Refer to **Figs. 14 through 28** for system wiring diagrams and connector locations.

WIRE HARNESS & CONNECTOR REPAIR

The SRS wiring harness is entirely covered with a yellow protective conduit, and can easily be distinguished from harnesses of other systems. Do not attempt to repair

SRS wiring harness or electrical connectors. Replace the harness if connectors or harness are found to be damaged or opened or if a designated DTC is output during self diagnosis.

COMPONENT LOCATIONS

Refer to **Figs. 29 through 32** for SRS component locations.

DIAGNOSIS & TESTING

Refer to **MOTOR's Air Bag Manual** for system diagnosis and testing.

COMPONENT SERVICE

The deployment electrical circuit is powered directly from the battery and backup power supply. To avoid unwanted deployment and possible personal injury, the SRS must be disarmed. Refer to " Air Bag System Disarming & Arming." Wait 20 seconds prior to starting any service.

DRIVER'S AIR BAG MODULE, REPLACE

1. Set front wheels in straight ahead position.
2. Disarm SRS as described under "Air Bag System Disarming & Arming."
3. Remove covers from both sides of steering wheel, if equipped, then using T30 Tore bit, remove Tore bolts.
4. Disconnect air bag and horn electrical connectors, then remove air bag unit, **Figs. 33 through 36.**
5. Reverse procedure to install, noting the following:
   a. Ensure ignition is turned Off.

b. Do not allow harness and connectors to interfere with other components.
c. Install new Tore bolts and tighten to specifications.
d. After completing installation, arm SRS as described under " Air Bag System Disarming & Arming."

PASSENGER'S AIR BAG MODULE, REPLACE

Forester

1. Disarm SRS as described under "Air Bag System Disarming & Arming."
2. Remove glove box.
3. Disconnect air bag connector, then remove seven bolts that secure passenger air bag.
4. Remove air bag from vehicle. Do not allow harness and connectors to interfere with other parts.
5. Reverse procedure to install.

Impreza

1. Disarm SRS as described under "Air Bag System Disarming & Arming."
2. Remove rear center console.
3. Pull cup holder upward.
4. Remove shift lever boot or cover from front center console.
5. Remove four front center console cover retaining screws, then the cover.
6. Remove four center console retaining bolts, then the center console.
7. Remove four radio attaching screws.
8. Pull radio assembly outward and disconnect electrical connectors and antenna lead.
9. Remove radio assembly.
10. Remove instrument panel driver side lower cover.
11. Disconnect seat belt timer electrical connector.

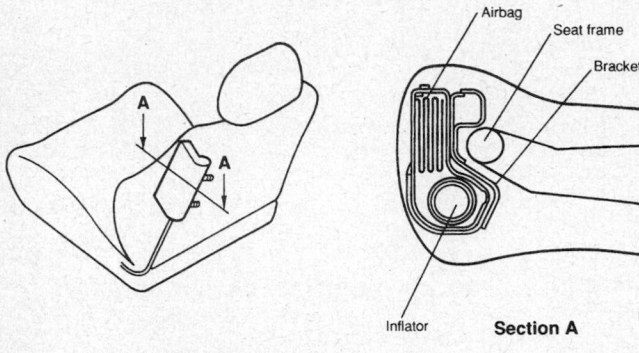

Fig. 10   Side airbag & inflator

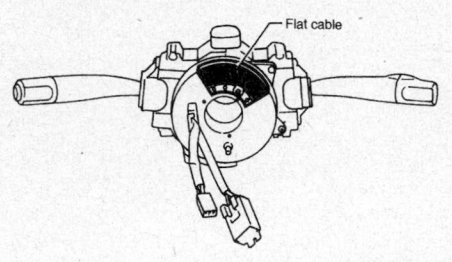

Fig. 11   Steering roll connector

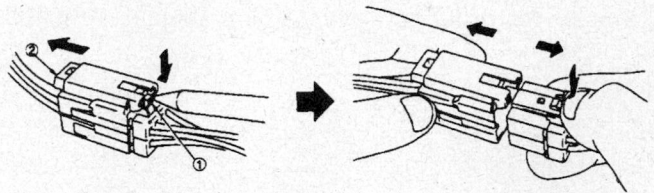

Fig. 13   Harness double lock connector

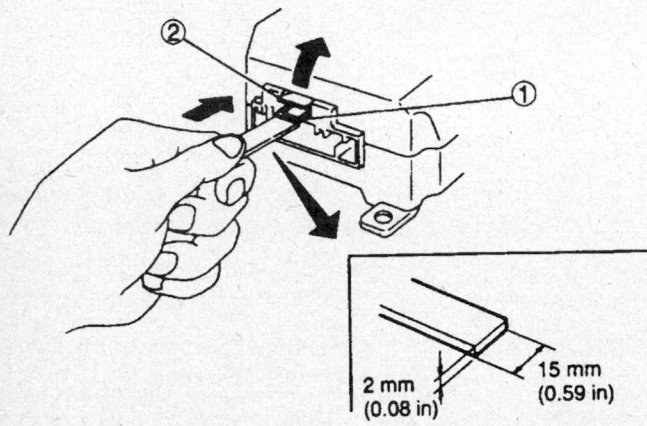

Fig. 12   Air bag control unit double lock connector

12. Remove glove compartment, then the pocket back panel.
13. Remove instrument panel console.
14. Remove steering column retaining bolts, then lower the steering column.
15. Remove retaining screw, then detach hood opening lever from instrument panel.
16. Place temperature switch in maximum cold position and mode switch to defrost position.
17. Disconnect temperature control and mode cables from links.
18. Disconnect instrument panel electrical connectors and tag them so they can be installed at proper locations.
19. Remove ten instrument panel attaching nuts and bolts, **Fig. 37**.
20. Remove front defroster grille, then remove two bolts.
21. Disconnect speedometer cable, then carefully remove instrument panel.
22. Disconnect passenger's air bag electrical connector.
23. Remove four air bag attaching bolts, then carefully remove air bag module, **Fig. 33**.
24. Reverse procedure to install, noting the following:
    a. Ensure ignition is turned Off.
    b. Do not allow harness and connectors to interfere with other components.
    c. Tighten air bag attaching bolts to torque listed in **Fig. 33**.
    d. After completing installation, arm SRS as described under " Air Bag System Disarming & Arming."

Legacy

1. Disarm SRS as described under "Air Bag System Disarming & Arming."
2. **On models equipped with manual transmission,** remove shift lever knob.
3. **On all models,** remove console cover and shift lever boot cover.
4. Remove console box.
5. Remove driver side instrument panel lower cover, then disconnect electrical connector.
6. Remove glove compartment.
7. Remove cover back panel from glove compartment opening.
8. Remove two steering column retaining screws, then lower the steering column.
9. Place temperature switch in maximum cold position.
10. Disconnect temperature control cable from link.
11. Remove bolt cover from each side of the instrument panel.
12. Remove rightward front sill cover, then disconnect air bag connector.
13. Disconnect instrument panel connectors and tag them so they can be installed at proper locations.

14. Remove instrument panel attaching bolts, **Fig. 38**.
15. Remove front defroster grille, then two instrument panel attaching bolts.
16. Disconnect speedometer cable, then carefully remove instrument panel.
17. Remove four passenger's air bag attaching bolts, then carefully remove air bag module, **Fig. 35**.
18. Reverse procedure to install, noting the following:
    a. Ensure ignition is turned Off.
    b. Do not allow harness and connectors to interfere with other components.
    c. Tighten air bag attaching bolts to torque listed in **Fig. 35**.
    d. After completing installation, arm SRS as described under " Air Bag System Disarming & Arming."

SVX

1. Disarm SRS as described under "Air Bag System Disarming & Arming."
2. Remove glove compartment.
3. Remove three bolts from steering support beam, **Fig. 39**.
4. Loosen nut retaining bracket to passenger's air bag module, **Fig. 36**.
5. Remove securing air bag module bracket to steering support beam, then the bracket.
6. Disconnect air bag electrical connector.
7. Remove four air bag retaining screws, then the module.
8. Reverse procedure to install, noting the following:
    a. Ensure ignition is turned Off.
    b. Do not allow harness and connectors to interfere with other components.
    c. Tighten air bag attaching bolts to torque listed in **Fig. 36**.
    d. After completing installation, arm SRS as described under " Air Bag System Disarming & Arming."

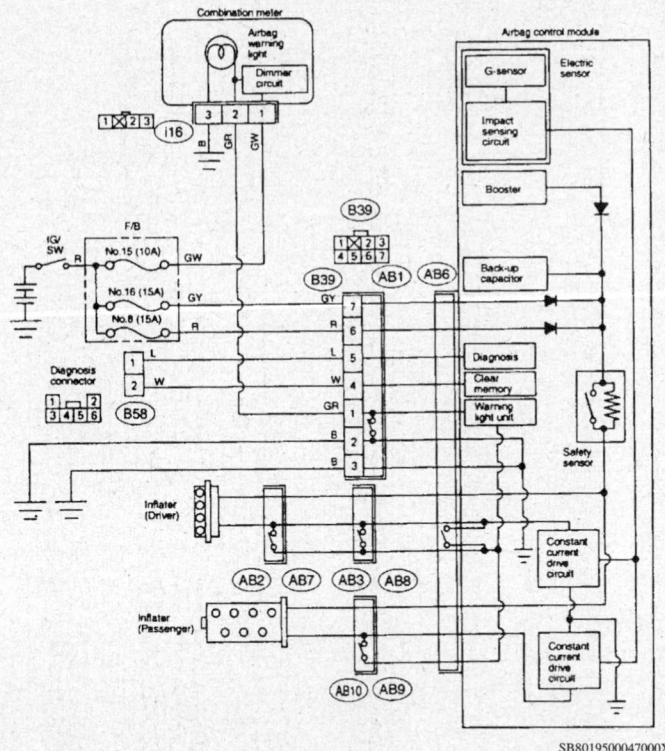

Fig. 14 SRS wiring diagram. 1996 Impreza

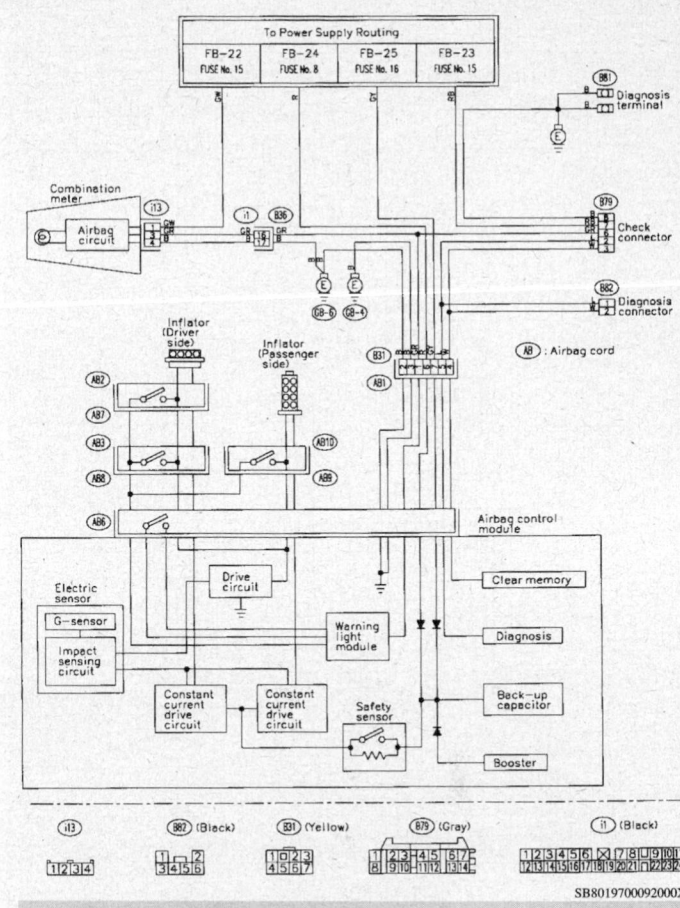

Fig. 15 SRS wiring diagram. 1997 Impreza

FRONT SENSOR, REPLACE

Legacy

1. Disarm SRS as described under "Air Bag System Disarming & Arming."
2. Remove lower instrument cover and cover panel, then disconnect air bag connectors AB3 and AB8 below steering column. **Do not connect these again until front sensors are securely installed.**
3. Remove front console box.
4. Disconnect two pin blue electrical connector (rightward side sensor) and two pin orange electrical connector (leftward side sensor) from air bag control unit.
5. Roll up floor mat and side sill cover, then remove front sensor harness from clip and protector.
6. Remove front wheels, then front mud shield.
7. Remove wiring harness clips securing front sensor harness.
8. Remove grommet, then the front sensor unit, **Fig. 35.**
9. Reverse procedure to install, noting the following:
   a. Tighten front sensor attaching nuts to specifications.
   b. After completing installation, arm SRS as described under "Air Bag System Disarming & Arming."

SVX

1. Disarm SRS as described under "Air Bag System Disarming & Arming."
2. Remove instrument panel lower cover and lower cover panel, then disconnect air bag electrical connector at harness spool. **Do not connect this connector again until front sensors are securely installed.**
3. Remove console panel and base on driver seat side.
4. Disconnect two pin blue electrical connector (rightward front sensor) and two pin orange electrical connector (leftward front sensor) from air bag control unit.
5. Roll up floor mat and remove side sill lower cover, then remove front sensor wiring harness from clip and protector.
6. Remove front wheels, then the front mud shield.
7. Remove wiring harness bracket, then pry off four clips securing front sensor harness.
8. Remove grommet, then the front sensor unit, **Fig. 36.**
9. Reverse procedure to install, noting the following:
   a. On models equipped with sunroof, route drain hose through grommet during grommet installation.
   b. Tighten front sensor attaching bolts to specifications.
   c. After completing installation, arm SRS as described under "Air Bag System Disarming & Arming."

MAIN HARNESS, REPLACE

Forester, Impreza & Legacy

1. Disarm SRS as described under "Air Bag System Disarming & Arming."
2. Remove lower cover and lower cover panel, then disconnect air bag connectors AB3 and AB8 below steering column. **Do not connect these connectors again until main harness is securely installed.**
3. Remove front console box.
4. Disconnect yellow connector from air bag control unit, then body harness connector from connector AB1.
5. Roll up floor mat and leftward side sill cover.
6. Remove main harness, **Fig. 35,** from clip and protector.
7. Reverse procedure to install. After completing installation, arm SRS as described under "Air Bag System Disarming & Arming."

SVX

1. Disarm SRS as described under "Air Bag System Disarming & Arming."
2. Remove lower cover and lower cover panel, then disconnect air bag connector at harness spool. **Do not connect this connector again until main harness is securely installed.**
3. Remove console panel and base on driver seat side.
4. Disconnect 12 pin yellow electrical connector from air bag control unit, then body harness connector B58 from connector AB1.
5. Roll up floor mat and remove leftward side sill lower cover.

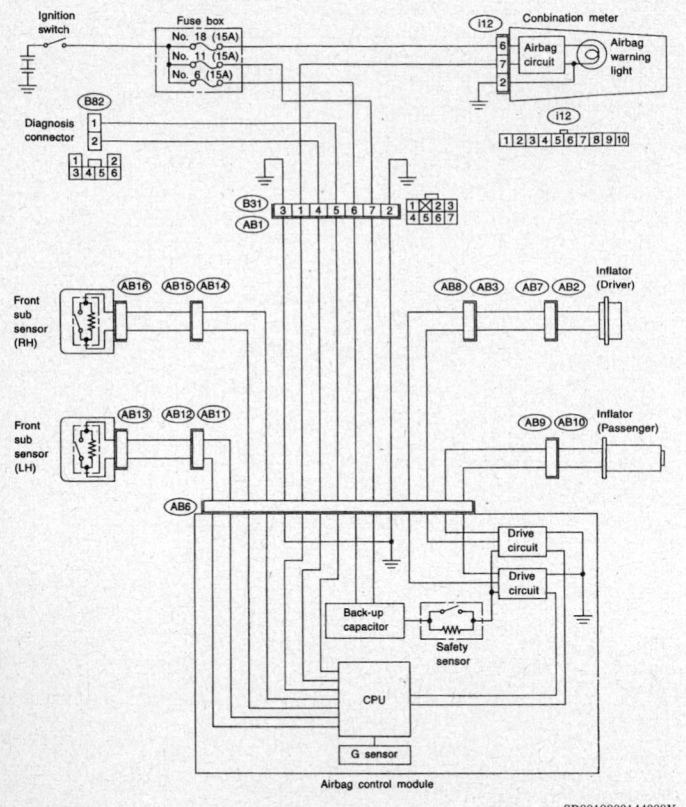

Fig. 16   SRS wiring diagram. 1998 Impreza

SB8019800144000X

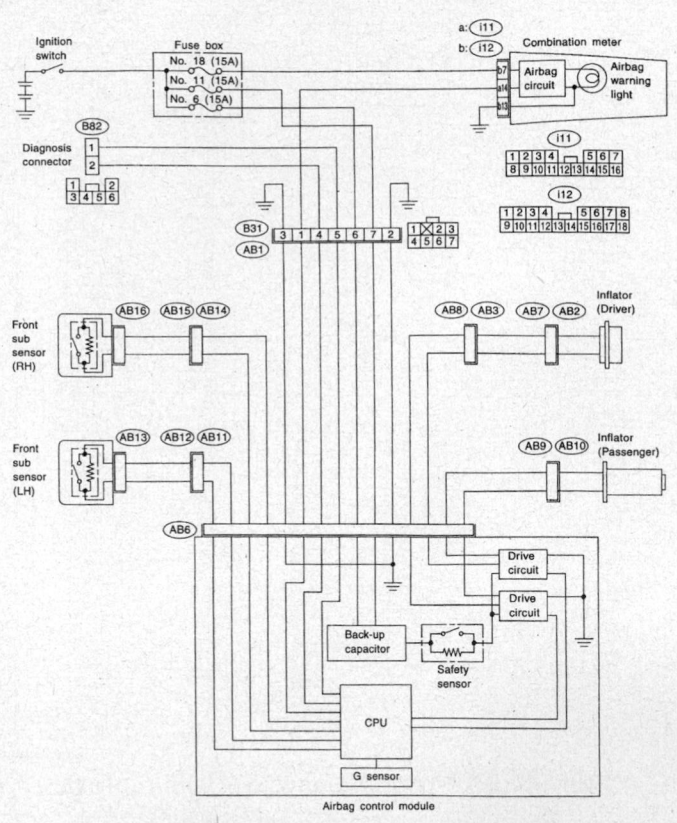

Fig. 17   SRS wiring diagram. 1999 Impreza

SB8019800145000X

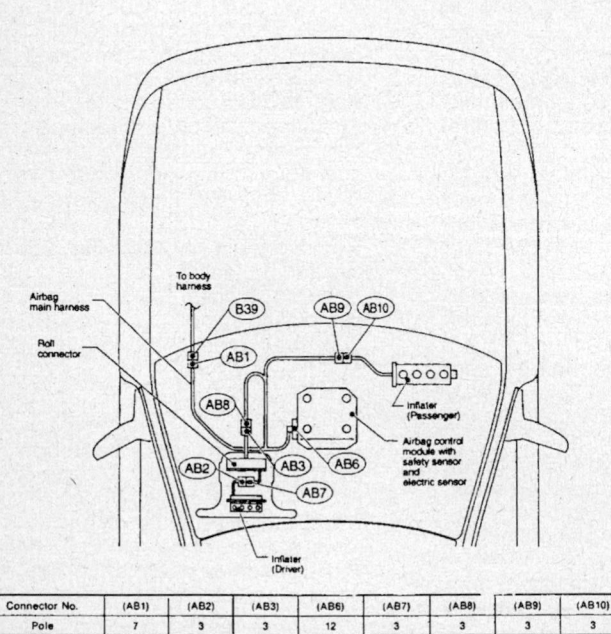

Connector No.	(AB1)	(AB2)	(AB3)	(AB6)	(AB7)	(AB8)	(AB9)	(AB10)
Pole	7	3	3	12	3	3	3	3
Color	Yellow	Yellow	Yellow	Yellow	Yellow	Yellow	Yellow	Yellow
Male/Female	Male	Female	Female	Female	Male	Male	Male	Female

SB8019500048000X

Fig. 18   SRS wiring harness connector locations. 1996 Impreza

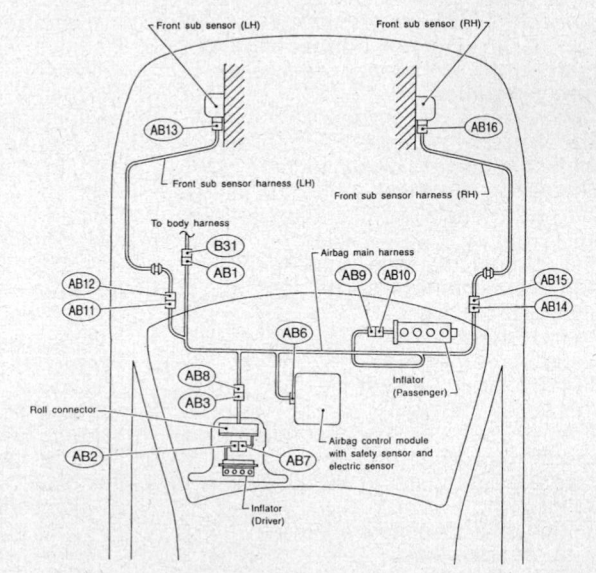

Connector No.	(AB1)	(AB2)	(AB3)	(AB6)	(AB7)	(AB8)	(AB9)
Pole	7	2	2	20	2	2	2
Color	Yellow	Yellow	Yellow	Yellow	Yellow	Yellow	Yellow
Male/Female	Male	Male	Male	Female	Female	Female	Female

Connector No.	(AB10)	(AB11)	(AB12)	(AB13)	(AB14)	(AB15)	(AB16)
Pole	2	2	2	2	2	2	2
Color	Yellow	Blue	Blue	Yellow	Blue	Blue	Yellow
Male/Female	Male	Female	Male	Female	Male	Male	Female

SB8019800146000X

Fig. 19   SRS component locations. 1998 Impreza

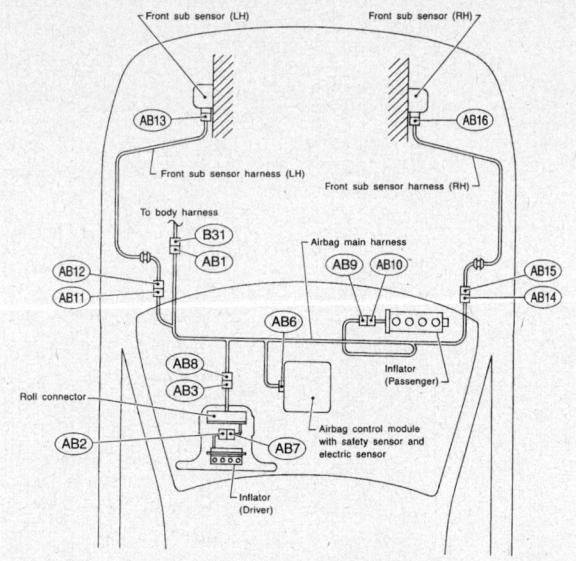

Connector No.	(AB1)	(AB2)	(AB3)	(AB6)	(AB7)	(AB8)	(AB9)
Pole	7	2	2	28	2	2	2
Color	Yellow	Yellow	Yellow	Yellow	Yellow	Yellow	Yellow
Male/Female	Male	Male	Male	Female	Female	Female	Female

Connector No.	(AB10)	(AB11)	(AB12)	(AB13)	(AB14)	(AB15)	(AB16)
Pole	2	2	2	2	2	2	2
Color	Yellow	Blue	Blue	Yellow	Blue	Blue	Yellow
Male/Female	Male	Female	Male	Female	Female	Male	Female

SB8019900139000X

Fig. 20   SRS component locations. 1999 Impreza

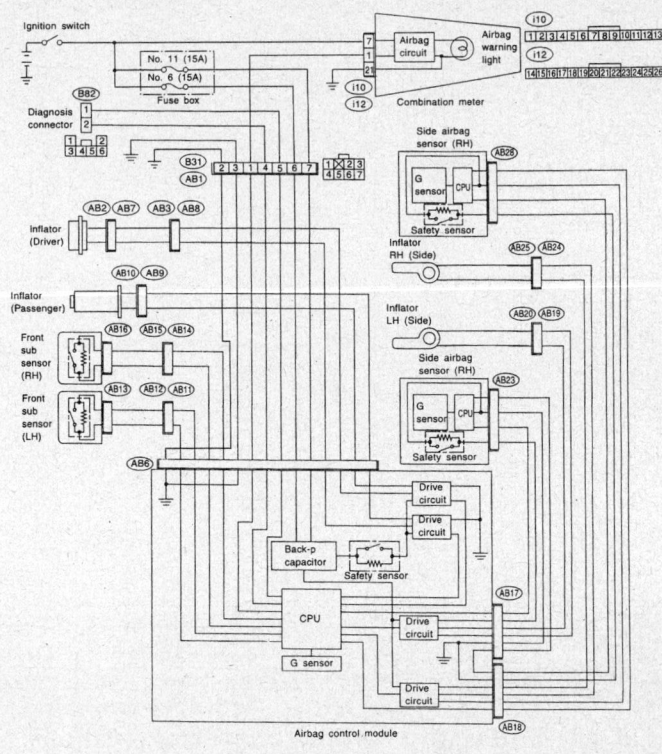

SB8019800147000X

Fig. 21   SRS wiring diagram. Forester

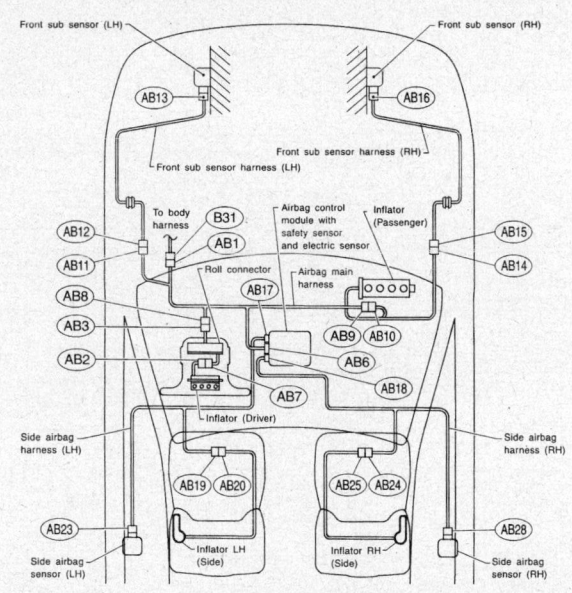

Connector No.	(AB1)	(AB2)	(AB3)	(AB6)	(AB7)	(AB8)	(AB9)	(AB10)	(AB11)	(AB12)	(AB13)
Pole	7	2	2	28	2	2	2	2	2	2	2
Color	Yellow	Yellow	Yellow	Yellow	Yellow	Yellow	Yellow	Yellow	Blue	Blue	Yellow
Male/Female	Male	Male	Male	Female	Female	Female	Female	Male	Female	Male	Female

Connector No.	(AB14)	(AB15)	(AB16)	(AB17)	(AB18)	(AB19)	(AB20)	(AB23)	(AB24)	(AB25)	(AB28)
Pole	2	2	2	12	12	2	2	4	2	2	4
Color	Blue	Blue	Yellow	Yellow	Yellow	Yellow	Yellow	Yellow	Yellow	Yellow	Yellow
Male/Female	Female	Male	Female	Female	Female	Female	Male	Female	Female	Male	Female

SB8019900131000X

Fig. 22   SRS wiring harness connector locations. Forester

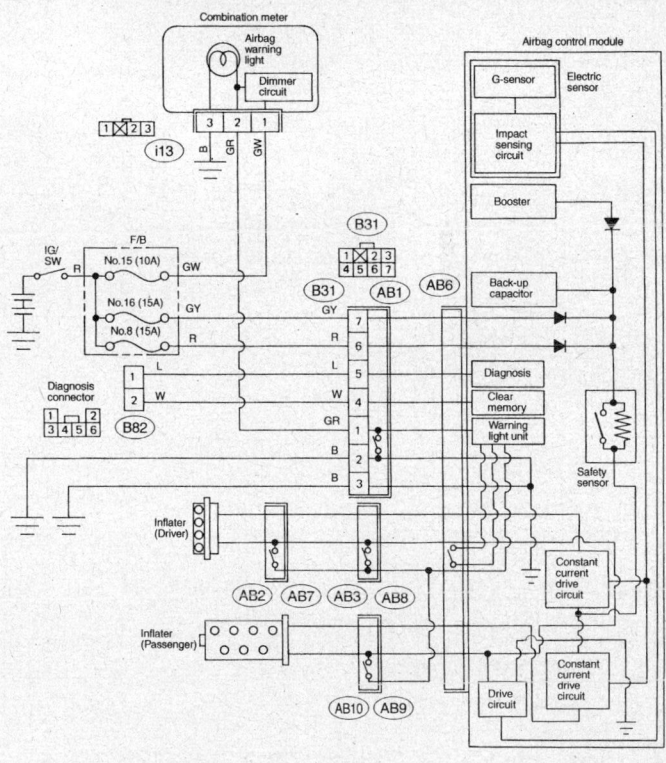

SB8019500051000X

Fig. 23   SRS wiring diagram. 1996 Legacy

SUBARU

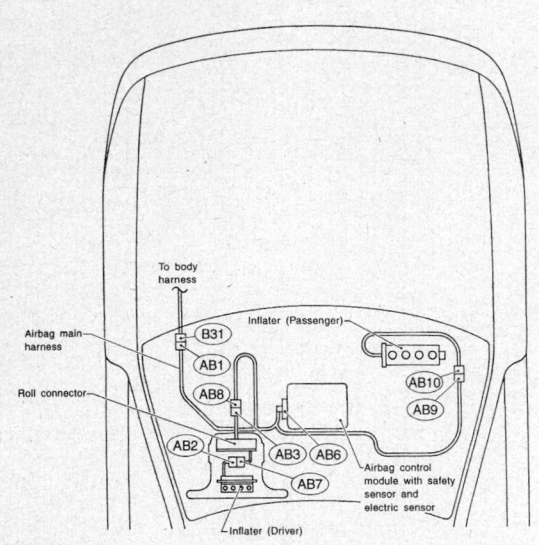

Connector No.	(AB1)	(AB2)	(AB3)	(AB6)	(AB7)	(AB8)	(AB9)	(AB10)
Pole	7	3	3	12	3	3	3	3
Color	Yellow	Yellow	Yellow	Yellow	Yellow	Yellow	Yellow	Yellow
Male/Female	Male	Female	Female	Female	Male	Male	Male	Female

SB8019500052000X

**Fig. 24   SRS wiring harness connector locations.
1996 Legacy**

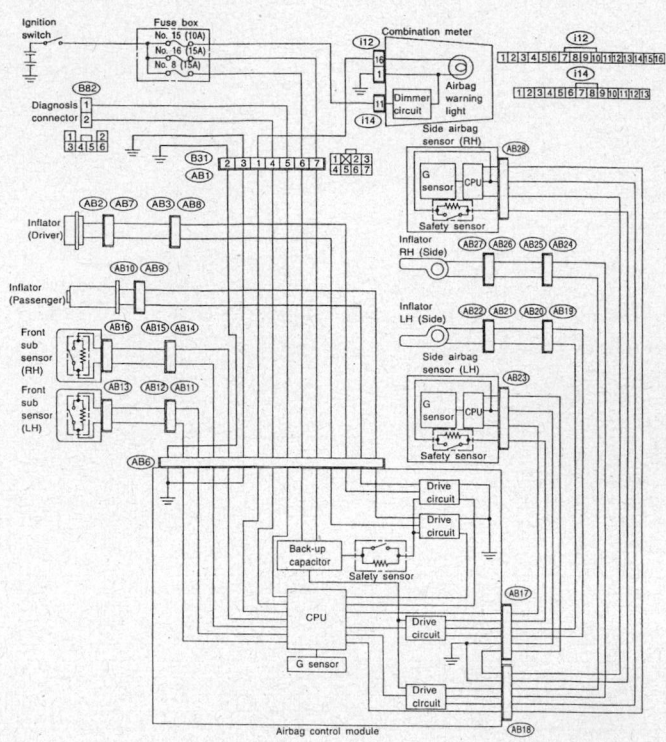

SB8019800148000X

Fig. 25   SRS wiring diagram. 1998 Legacy

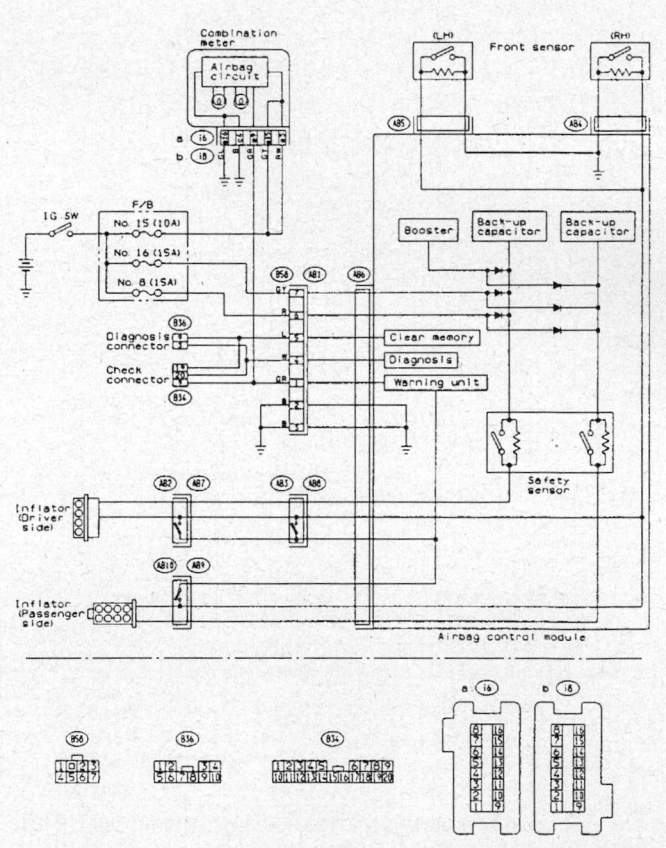

Connector No.	(AB1)	(AB2)	(AB3)	(AB6)	(AB7)	(AB8)	(AB9)	(AB10)	(AB11)
Pole	7	2	2	20	2	2	2	2	2
Color	Yellow	Yellow	Yellow	Yellow	Yellow	Yellow	Yellow	Yellow	Blue
Male/Female	Male	Male	Male	Female	Female	Female	Female	Male	Female

Connector No.	(AB12)	(AB13)	(AB14)	(AB15)	(AB16)	(AB17)	(AB18)	(AB19)	(AB20)
Pole	2	2	2	2	12	12	12	2	2
Color	Blue	Yellow	Blue	Blue	Yellow	Yellow	Yellow	Yellow	Yellow
Male/Female	Male	Female	Female	Male	Female	Female	Female	Female	Male

Connector No.	(AB21)	(AB22)	(AB23)	(AB24)	(AB25)	(AB26)	(AB27)	(AB28)	
Pole	2	2	4	2	2	2	2	4	
Color	Yellow	Yellow	Yellow	Yellow	Yellow	Yellow	Yellow	Yellow	
Male/Female	Female	Male	Female	Female	Male	Female	Male	Female	

SB8019800149000X

**Fig. 26   SRS wiring harness connector locations.
1998 Legacy**

SB8019400053000X

Fig. 27   SRS wiring diagram. SVX

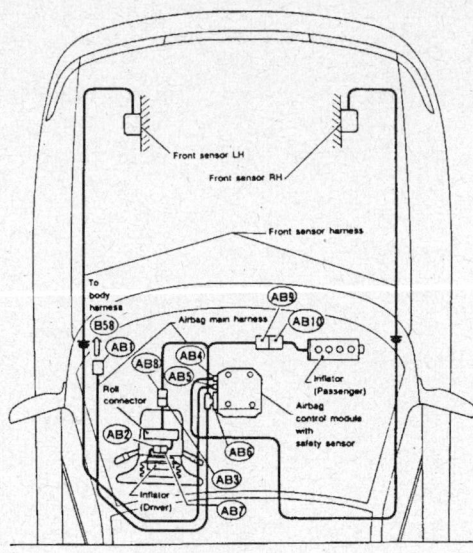

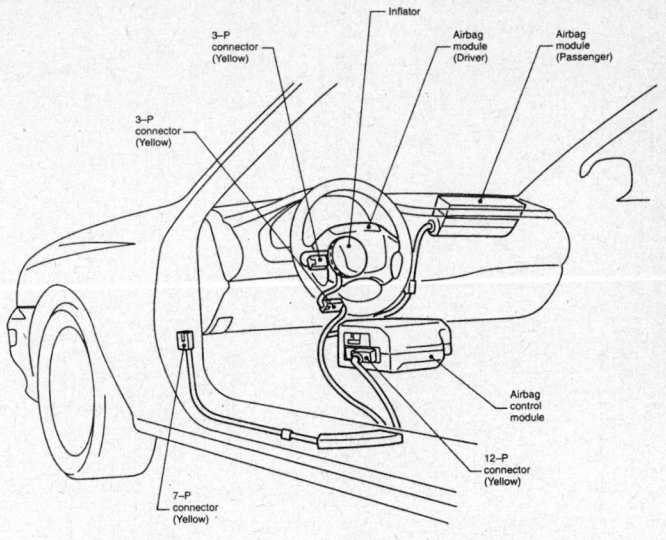

Fig. 29 SRS component locations. Impreza

Connector No.	(AB1)	(AB2)	(AB3)	(AB4)	(AB5)	(AB6)	(AB7)	(AB8)	(AB9)	(AB10)
Pole	7	3	3	2	2	12	3	3	3	3
Color	Yellow	Yellow	Yellow	Blue	Orange	Yellow	Yellow	Yellow	Yellow	Yellow
Male/Female	Male	Female	Female	Female	Female	Female	Male	Male	Male	Female

SB8019400054000X

Fig. 28 SRS wiring harness connector locations. SVX

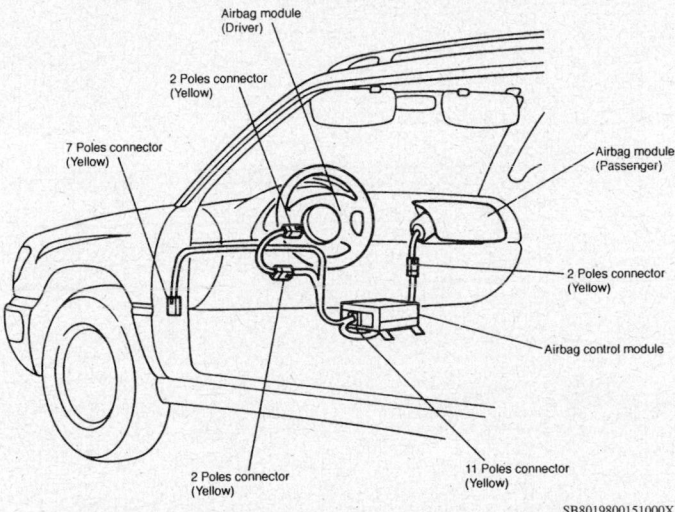

Fig. 30 SRS component locations. Forester

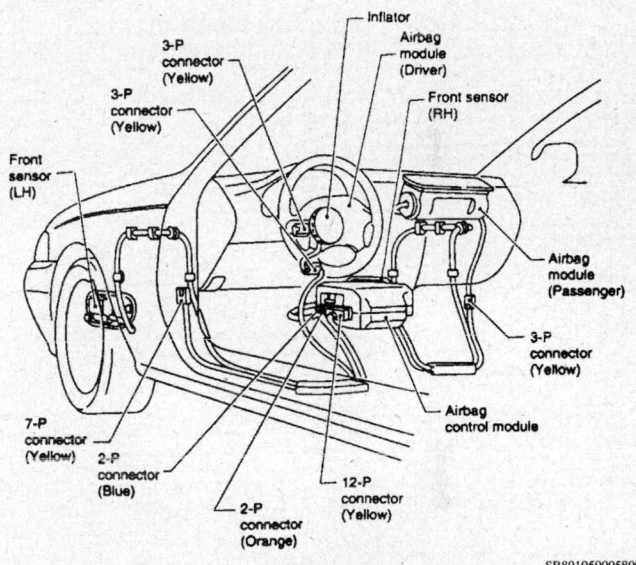

Fig. 31 SRS component locations. Legacy

6. Remove main harness, **Fig. 36,** from clip and protector.
7. Reverse procedure to install. After completing installation, arm SRS as described under "Air Bag System Disarming & Arming."

AIR BAG CONTROL UNIT, REPLACE

Forester

1. Disarm SRS as outlined in "Air Bag System Disarming & Arming."
2. Turn ignition switch to Off position.
3. Remove lower trim panel and disconnect air bag connectors at steering column.

4. Do not reconnect airbag connector until airbag control module is securely installed.
5. Remove instrument panel console.
6. Disconnect 11 pin connector from air bag control module.
7. Using a suitable T40 Tore bit, remove and discard Tore bolts in numerical order, **Fig. 40.**
8. Reverse procedure to install.

Impreza & Legacy

1. Disarm SRS as described under "Air Bag System Disarming & Arming."
2. Remove lower cover and lower cover panel, then disconnect air bag connectors AB3 and AB8 below steering column. **Do not connect these connectors again until air bag control unit is securely installed.**
3. Remove front console box.
4. Disconnect 12 pin yellow, two pin blue and two pin orange connectors from air bag control unit.
5. Using Tore bit, remove control unit bolts, then control unit, **Figs. 31 and 32.**
6. Reverse procedure to install, noting the following:
   a. Install new Tore bolts, then tighten to specifications.
   b. After completing installation, arm SRS as described under " Air Bag System Disarming & Arming."

SVX

1. Disarm SRS as described under "Air Bag System Disarming & Arming."
2. Remove lower cover and lower cover

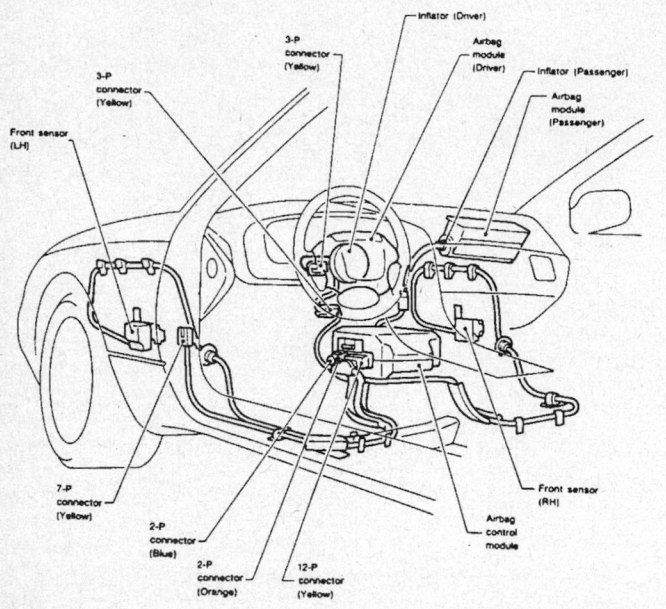

Fig. 32 SRS component locations. SVX

SB8019400059000X

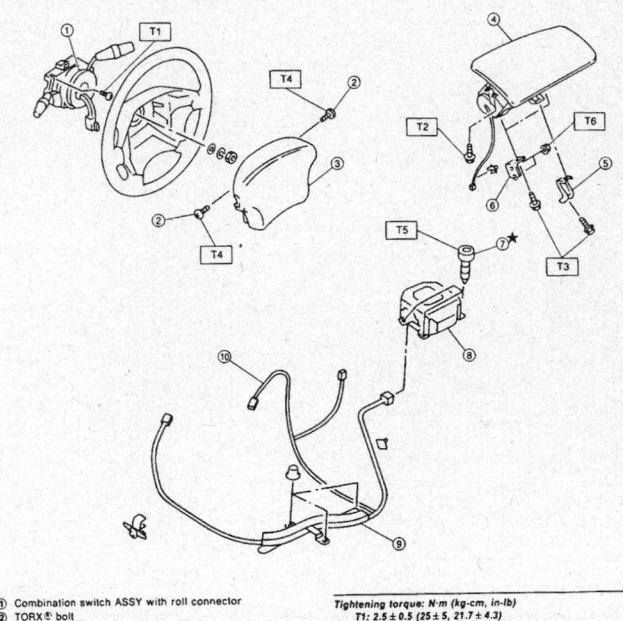

① Combination switch ASSY with roll connector
② TORX® bolt
③ Airbag module ASSY (Driver)
④ Airbag module ASSY (Passenger)
⑤ BRKT A
⑥ BRKT B
⑦ TORX® bolt
⑧ Airbag control module
⑨ Protector LH
⑩ Airbag main harness

Tightening torque: N·m (kgf-cm, in-lb)
T1: 2.5 ± 0.5 (25 ± 5, 21.7 ± 4.3)
T2: 4.4 ± 1.5 (45 ± 15, 39 ± 13)
T3: 7.4 ± 0.2 (75 ± 2, 65.1 ± 1.7)
T4: 9.8 ± 2.0 (100 ± 20, 87 ± 17)
T5: 9.81 ± 2.45 (100.0 ± 25.0, 86.8 ± 21.7)
T6: 17.7 ± 4.9 (180 ± 50, 156 ± 43)

SB8019500082000X

Fig. 33 SRS components. Impreza

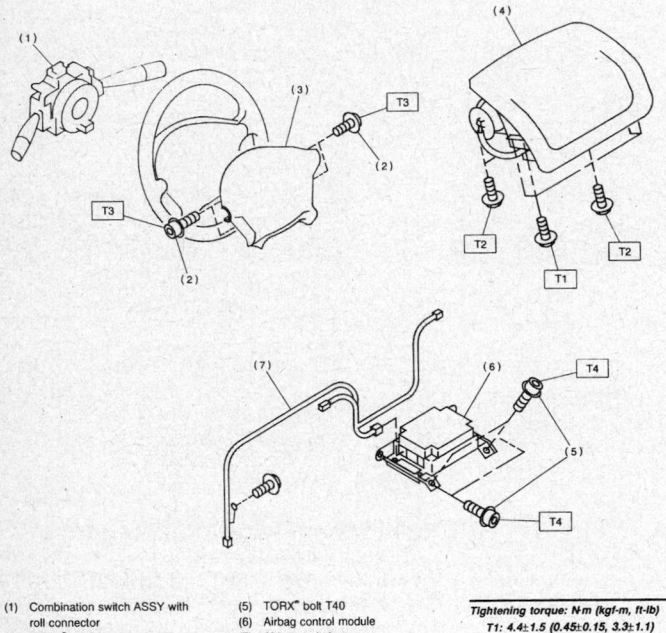

(1) Combination switch ASSY with roll connector
(2) TORX® bolt T30
(3) Airbag module ASSY (Driver)
(4) Airbag module ASSY (Passenger)
(5) TORX® bolt T40
(6) Airbag control module
(7) Airbag main harness

Tightening torque: N·m (kgf-m, ft-lb)
T1: 4.4 ± 1.5 (0.45 ± 0.15, 3.3 ± 1.1)
T2: 7.4 ± 2.0 (0.75 ± 0.2, 5.4 ± 1.4)
T3: 10 ± 2 (1.0 ± 0.2, 7.2 ± 1.4)
T4: 25 ± 2 (2.5 ± 0.2, 18.1 ± 1.4)

SB8019800152000X

Fig. 34 SRS components. Forester

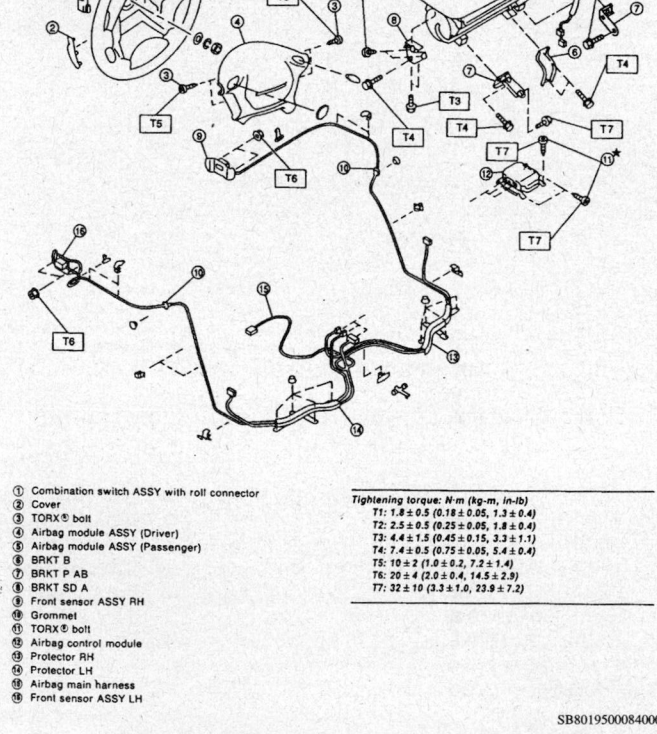

① Combination switch ASSY with roll connector
② Cover
③ TORX® bolt
④ Airbag module ASSY (Driver)
⑤ Airbag module ASSY (Passenger)
⑥ BRKT B
⑦ BRKT P AB
⑧ BRKT SD A
⑨ Front sensor ASSY RH
⑩ Grommet
⑪ TORX® bolt
⑫ Airbag control module
⑬ Protector RH
⑭ Protector LH
⑮ Airbag main harness
⑯ Front sensor ASSY LH

Tightening torque: N·m (kg-m, in-lb)
T1: 1.8 ± 0.5 (0.18 ± 0.05, 1.3 ± 0.4)
T2: 2.5 ± 0.5 (0.25 ± 0.05, 1.8 ± 0.4)
T3: 4.4 ± 1.5 (0.45 ± 0.15, 3.3 ± 1.1)
T4: 7.4 ± 0.5 (0.75 ± 0.05, 5.4 ± 0.4)
T5: 10 ± 2 (1.0 ± 0.2, 7.2 ± 1.4)
T6: 20 ± 4 (2.0 ± 0.4, 14.5 ± 2.9)
T7: 32 ± 10 (3.3 ± 1.0, 23.9 ± 7.2)

SB8019500084000X

Fig. 35 SRS components. Legacy

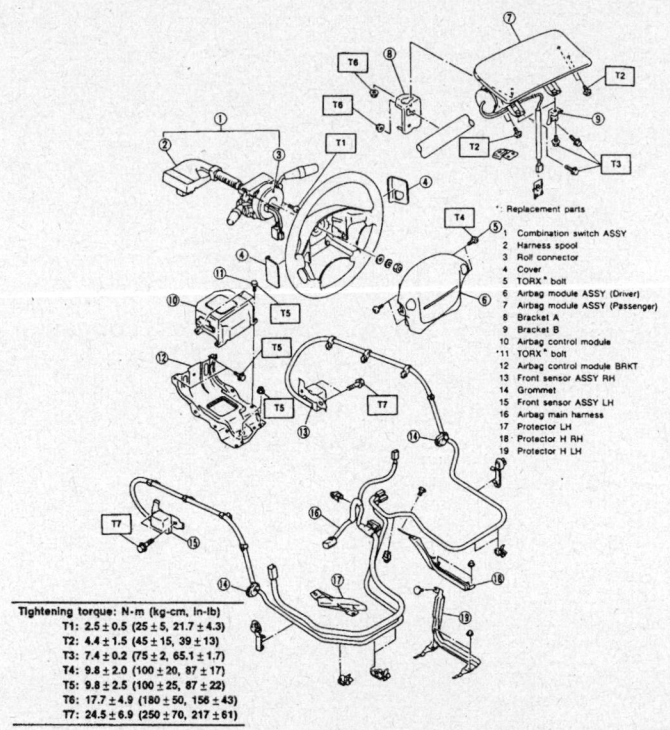

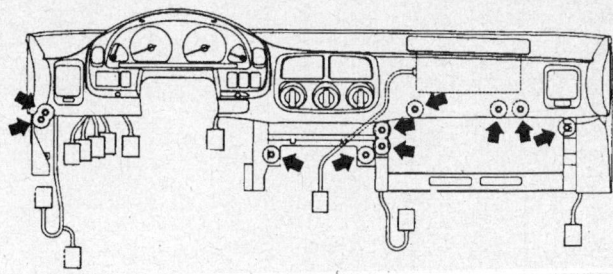

Fig. 37 Instrument panel attaching nut & bolt locations. Impreza

Tightening torque: N·m (kg-cm, in-lb)
T1: 2.5 ± 0.5 (25 ± 5, 21.7 ± 4.3)
T2: 4.4 ± 1.5 (45 ± 15, 39 ± 13)
T3: 7.4 ± 0.2 (75 ± 2, 65.1 ± 1.7)
T4: 9.8 ± 2.0 (100 ± 20, 87 ± 17)
T5: 9.8 ± 2.5 (100 ± 25, 87 ± 22)
T6: 17.7 ± 4.9 (180 ± 50, 156 ± 43)
T7: 24.5 ± 6.9 (250 ± 70, 217 ± 61)

*: Replacement parts
1 Combination switch ASSY
2 Harness spool
3 Roll connector
4 Cover
5 TORX* bolt
6 Airbag module ASSY (Driver)
7 Airbag module ASSY (Passenger)
7 Bracket A
8 Bracket B
10 Airbag control module
11 TORX bolt
12 Airbag control module BRKT
13 Front sensor ASSY RH
14 Grommet
15 Front sensor ASSY LH
16 Airbag main harness
17 Protector LH
18 Protector H RH
19 Protector H LH

Fig. 36 SRS components. SVX

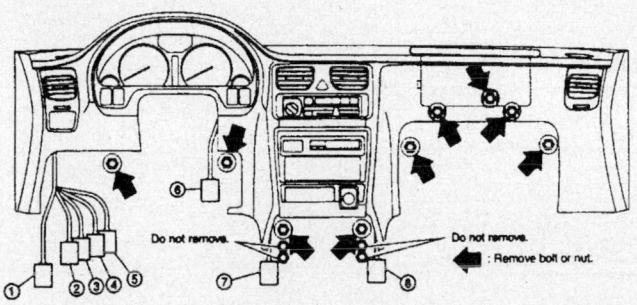

Do not remove. Do not remove.

◀ : Remove bolt or nut.

Fig. 38 Instrument panel attaching nut & bolt locations. Legacy

panel, then disconnect air bag connector at harness spool. **Do not connect this connector again until control unit is securely installed.**

3. Remove console panel and base on driver seat side, then the audio equipment.
4. Disconnect 12 pin yellow, two pin blue and two pin orange connectors from control unit.
5. Remove two nuts and bolts securing control unit bracket, then control unit and bracket as an assembly.
6. Using T30 Tore bit, remove control unit from bracket.
7. Reverse procedure to install, noting the following:
   a. Install new Tore bolts, then tighten to specifications.

   b. After completing installation, arm SRS as described under " Air Bag System Disarming & Arming."

COMBINATION SWITCH ASSEMBLY

1. Place front wheels in straight ahead position.
2. Disarm SRS as described under "Air Bag System Disarming & Arming."
3. Remove instrument panel lower cover from leftward side of instrument panel.
4. Disconnect air bag connector below steering column.
5. Disconnect combination switch connector from wiring harness.
6. Remove air bag module as described under "Air Bag Module, Replace."

7. Remove steering wheel retaining nut, then place alignment marks on wheel hub and shaft for use during installation.
8. Using a suitable fuller, remove wheel from shaft.
9. Remove steering column covers.
10. Remove combination switch attaching screws, then remove combination switch with roll connector, **Figs. 33 through 36.**
11. Reverse procedure to install, noting the following:
    a. Prior to installation, ensure front wheels are in straight ahead position and combination switch is in Off position.
    b. Tighten combination switch/roll connector attaching screws to specifications.
    c. After installing combination switch/roll connector, center the roll connector by turning connector pin clockwise until it stops. Turn pin approximately 2.65 turns counterclockwise, aligning marks, **Figs. 41 and 42.**
    d. After completing installation, arm SRS as described under " Air Bag System Disarming & Arming."

AIR BAG ASSEMBLY DISPOSAL

When handling a deployed air bag assembly, a face shield and rubber gloves should be worn. Vehicle interior and HVAC ducts should be vacuumed. If sinus or throat irritation is encountered during air bag removal, exit vehicle and breathe fresh air. If skin irritation is encountered, flush affected area with cool water. If sinus, throat, skin or any other type of irritation continues, consult a physician. Wash hands and rinse thoroughly with water after handling a deployed air bag assembly.

A deployed air bag should be removed as described under " Driver's Air Bag Module, Replace" or "Passenger's Air Bag Module, Replace." Place tape over air bag exhaust vents prior to removal. After unit has been removed, it should be placed in a heavy duty plastic bag, sealed securely, then placed with automotive scrap.

SUBARU

Fig. 39   Steering support beam nut removal. SVX

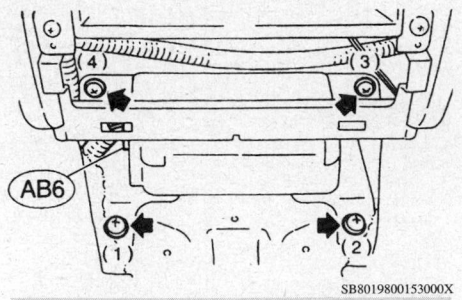

Fig. 40   Air bag control module bolt pattern. Forester

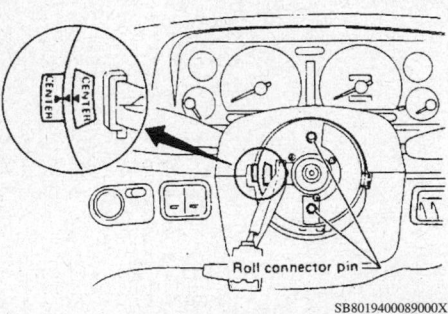

Fig. 41   Centering roll connector. Legacy & SVX

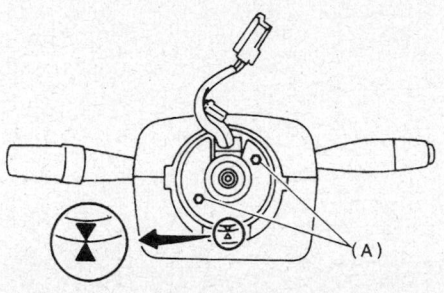

Fig. 42   Centering roll connector. Forester & Impreza

TIGHTENING SPECIFICATIONS

Year	Component	Torque/ Ft. Lbs.
FORESTER		
1998-99	Airbag Control Module	17-20
	Driver's Airbag Module	72-108②
	Passenger's Airbag Module	48-84②
IMPREZA & SVX		
1996-99	Air Bag Control Unit	84②
	Combination Switch w/Roll Connector	19②
	Driver Air Bag Module To Steering Wheel Screws	84②
	Front Sensor (SVX)	18
	Passenger Air Bag Module Bolts/Screws	①
	Passenger Air Bag Module Bracket Nuts (SVX)	13
	Steering Wheel Nut	25
LEGACY		
1996-99	Air Bag Control Unit	24②
	Combination Switch W/Roll Connector	19②
	Driver Air Bag Module To Steering Wheel Screws	12②
	Front Sensor	14
	Passenger Air Bag Module Bolts/Screws	①
	Steering Wheel Nut	25

① — Refer to "Passenger's Air Bag Module, Replace" procedure under "Component Service" section.

② — Inch lbs.

Dash Panel Service

NOTE: On Air Bag Equipped Models, Refer To "Air Bag System Precautions" Located In The Front Of This Manual For System Disarming & Arming Procedures.

NOTE: Refer To The "Dash Gauges" Section For Related Information.

INDEX

PRECAUTIONS
AIR BAG SYSTEMS

Refer to "Air Bag System Precautions" in the front of this manual for system disarming and arming procedures.

BATTERY GROUND CABLE

Prior to service, disconnect battery ground cable and isolate as required.

DASH PANEL
REPLACE
FORESTER

1. **On models equipped with manual transmission,** remove shift knob.
2. **On all models,** remove console cover and front cover, **Fig. 1.**
3. Remove console box, then remove lower cover and disconnect electrical connector.
4. Disconnect data link connector from lower cover.
5. Remove knee panel and glove box.
6. Remove center panel and disconnect connector.
7. Remove radio head assembly.
8. Remove two bolts and lower steering column.
9. Set temperature control switch to "FULL HOT," mode selector switch to "DEF" position and ricers switch to "FRESH" position.
10. Disconnect temperature control cable and mode control cable from heater unit then disconnect ricers control cable from intake unit.
11. Disconnect harness connectors, then remove attaching nuts and bolts, **Fig. 2.**
12. Remove front defroster grille and two bolts.
13. Remove instrument panel from vehicle.
14. Reverse procedure to install.

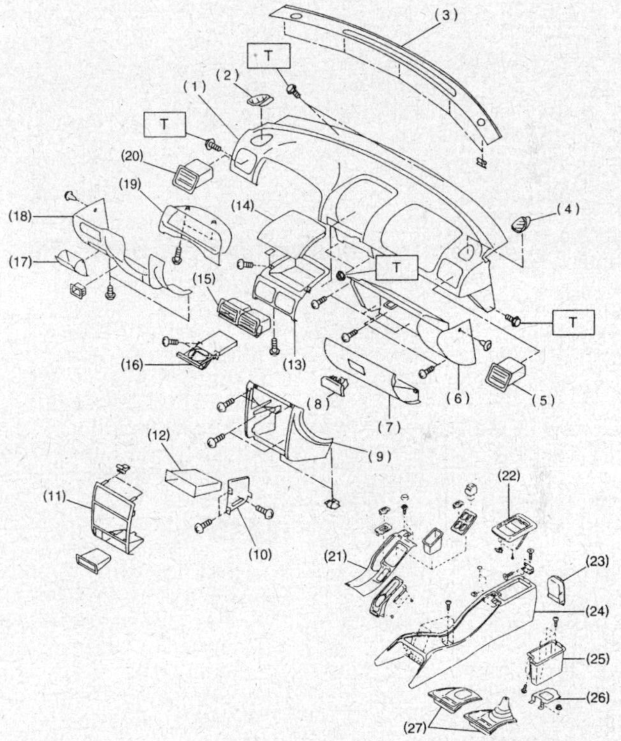

IMPREZA

1. Remove rear console box and cup holder, **Fig. 3.**

(1)	Pad & frame	(12)	Pocket	(23)	Rear cup holder
(2)	Grille side (D)	(13)	Panel center	(24)	Console box
(3)	Front def. grille	(14)	Center pocket lid	(25)	Console pocket
(4)	Grille side (P)	(15)	Grille center	(26)	Rear console BRKT
(5)	Grille vent (P)	(16)	Cup holder	(27)	Front cover
(6)	Glove box panel	(17)	Side pocket		
(7)	Glove box lid	(18)	Lower cover ASSY		
(8)	Knob	(19)	Meter visor		
(9)	Instrument panel center console	(20)	Grille vent (D)		
(10)	BRKT (Radio)	(21)	Console cover		
(11)	Center console cover	(22)	Console lid		

Tightening torque: N·m (kg-m, ft-lb)
T: 7±1 (0.7±0.1, 5.1±0.7)

SB9149800030000X

Fig. 1   Exploded view of instrument panel. Forester

2. **On models equipped with manual transmission,** turn over shift lever boot of front end.
3. **On models equipped with automat-** ic transmission, remove select lever cover.
4. **On all models,** remove center console and radio assembly.

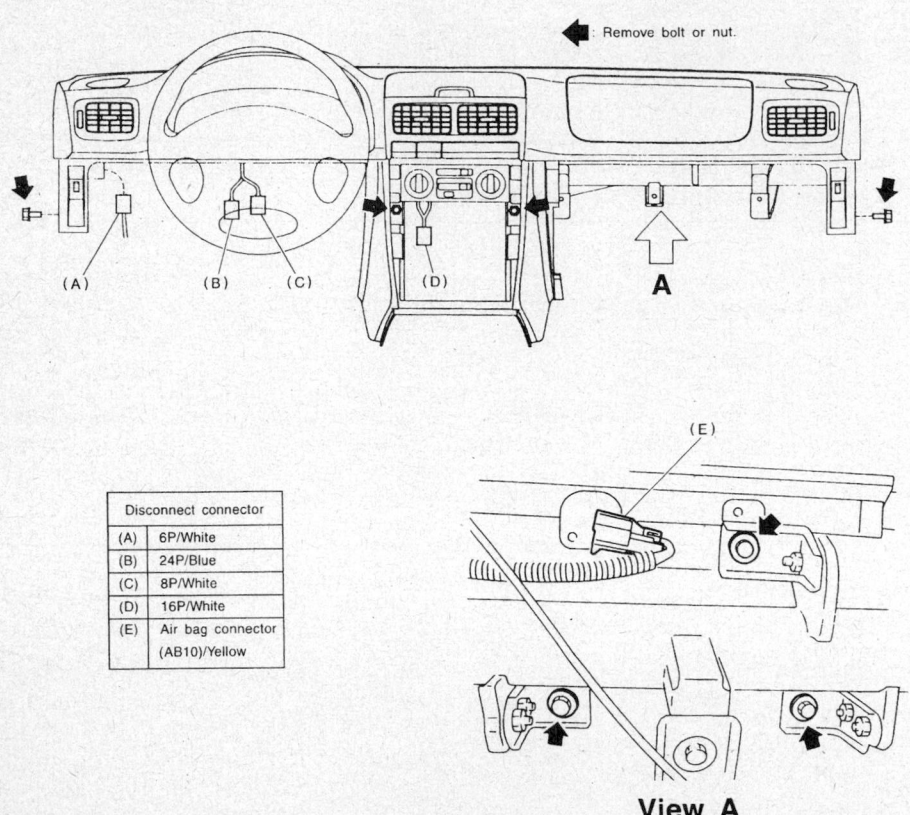

: Remove bolt or nut.

(A) (B) (C) (D) A

(E)

Disconnect connector	
(A)	6P/White
(B)	24P/Blue
(C)	8P/White
(D)	16P/White
(E)	Air bag connector (AB10)/Yellow

View A

SB9149800031000X

Fig. 2 Instrument panel attaching hardware. Forester

5. Remove lower cover, then disconnect seat belt timer connector.
6. Remove data link connector from lower cover.
7. Remove glove compartment, then pocket back panel.
8. Remove instrument panel console.
9. Remove two steering column mounting bolts, then lower steering column. Remove hood opener lever.
10. Set temperature control switch to full hot position, mode selector switch to defroster position and ricers switch to fresh position.
11. Disconnect temperature and mode control cables from heater unit, then ricers control cable from intake unit.
12. Disconnect harnesses and remove bolts/nuts, **Fig. 4.**
13. Remove front defroster grille and two bolts, **Fig. 5.**

14. Remove instrument panel assembly. Disconnect speedometer cable from back of instrument cluster.
15. Reverse procedure to install. When setting instrument panel into position, push three pins into grommets on body panel, **Fig. 6.**

LEGACY

Refer to **Fig. 7,** during removal and installation of the instrument panel.
1. Remove center console box.
2. Remove lower cover and disconnect connector.
3. Remove glove compartment, then remove glove compartment back panel.
4. Remove two bolts and lower steering column.
5. Set temperature control lever to MAX cold position, then disconnect temper-

ature control cable from heater module link.
6. Remove bolt cover and bolt from both side of instrument panel.
7. Remove front RH side sill cover, then disconnect air bag electrical connectors.
8. Disconnect all instrument panel electrical connections **Fig. 8. Mark connections for installation reference.**
9. Remove front defroster grille, then instrument panel mounting bolts and instrument panel.
10. Reverse procedure to install, noting the following:
    a. When setting instrument panel into position, push two pins into grommet on body panel.
    b. Set clips located at both inside ends of instrument panel onto body side.

SVX

1. Remove console box, then the front pillar upper trim panel, **Fig. 9.**
2. Remove radio ground wire, then the remote controlled rear view mirror switch.
3. Remove screw rivet located on lower side of lower cover.
4. Remove lower cover by removing six clips and three connectors.
5. Remove instrument panel lower cover, then disconnect air bag connector at harness spool.
6. Remove two screws from both left and right sides, **Fig. 10,** then lower steering column.
7. Remove caps from both ends of instrument panel, then remove bolts.
8. Remove two instrument panel switch assemblies by pressing forward, then disconnect switch connectors.
9. Remove visor, then disconnect clock connector.
10. Remove instrument cluster, then the meter visor, **Fig. 11,** and glove compartment.
11. Disconnect instrument and body harnesses, then the antenna lead.
12. Cover transmission select lever, then remove instrument panel by pulling forward.
13. Reverse procedure to install, noting the following:
    a. Push instrument panel into position by aligning five pins at end of instrument panel with grommets on body side.
    b. Set clips located at both inside end of instrument panel onto body side.

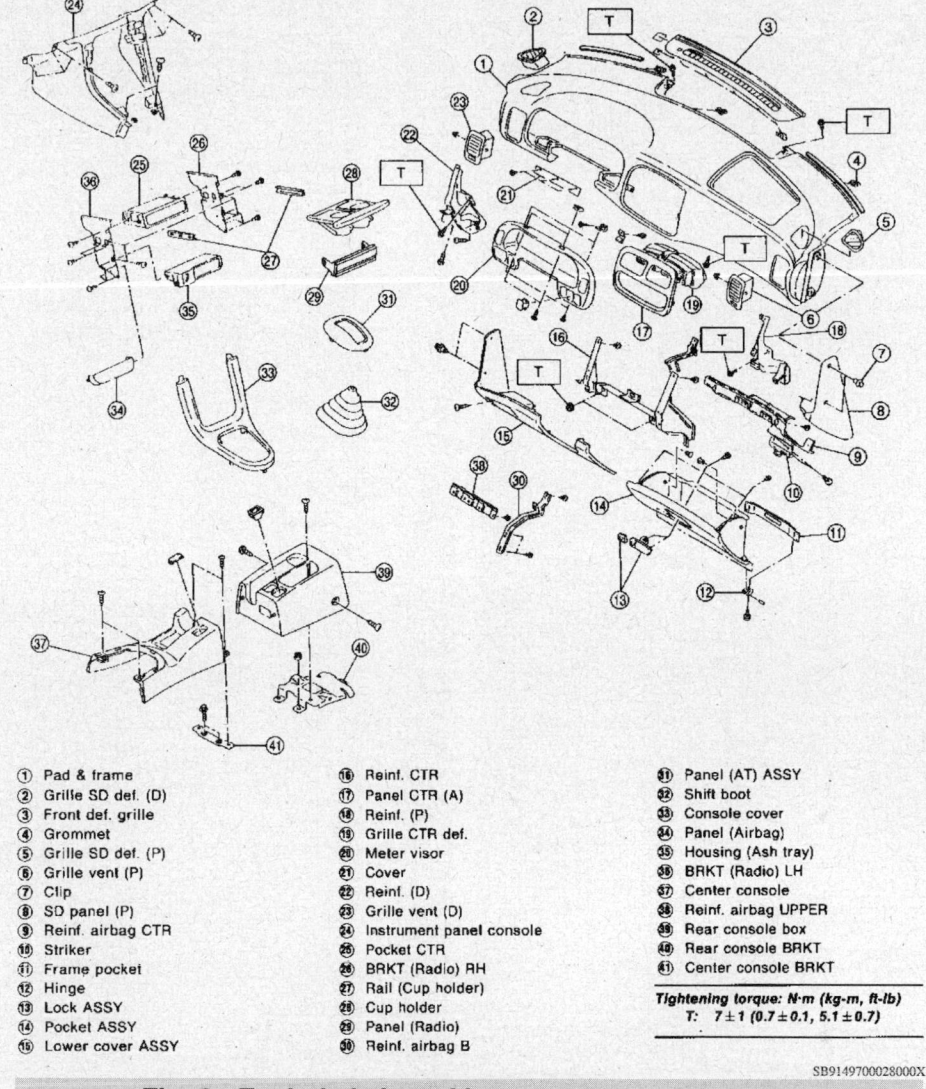

①	Pad & frame	⑯	Reinf. CTR	㉛	Panel (AT) ASSY
②	Grille SD def. (D)	⑰	Panel CTR (A)	㉜	Shift boot
③	Front def. grille	⑱	Reinf. (P)	㉝	Console cover
④	Grommet	⑲	Grille CTR def.	㉞	Panel (Airbag)
⑤	Grille SD def. (P)	⑳	Meter visor	㉟	Housing (Ash tray)
⑥	Grille vent (P)	㉑	Cover	㊱	BRKT (Radio) LH
⑦	Clip	㉒	Reinf. (D)	㊲	Center console
⑧	SD panel (P)	㉓	Grille vent (D)	㊳	Reinf. airbag UPPER
⑨	Reinf. airbag CTR	㉔	Instrument panel console	㊴	Rear console box
⑩	Striker	㉕	Pocket CTR	㊵	Rear console BRKT
⑪	Frame pocket	㉖	BRKT (Radio) RH	㊶	Center console BRKT
⑫	Hinge	㉗	Rail (Cup holder)		
⑬	Lock ASSY	㉘	Cup holder		
⑭	Pocket ASSY	㉙	Panel (Radio)		
⑮	Lower cover ASSY	㉚	Reinf. airbag B		

Tightening torque: N·m (kg-m, ft-lb)
T: 7 ± 1 (0.7 ± 0.1, 5.1 ± 0.7)

SB9149700028000X

Fig. 3   Exploded view of instrument panel. Impreza

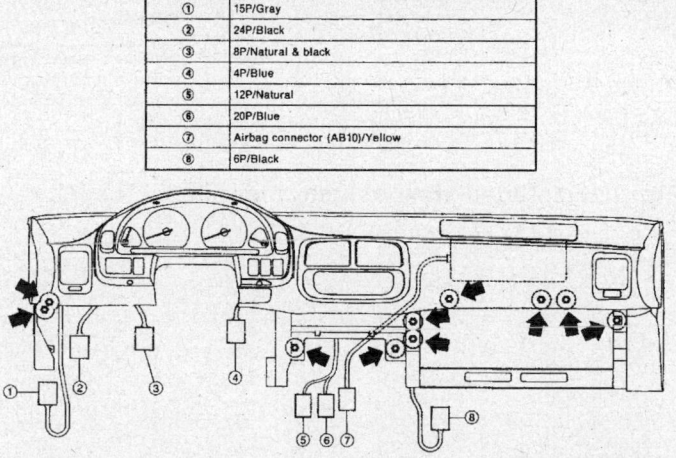

①	15P/Gray
②	24P/Black
③	8P/Natural & black
④	4P/Blue
⑤	12P/Natural
⑥	20P/Blue
⑦	Airbag connector (AB10)/Yellow
⑧	6P/Black

SB9149700029000X

**Fig. 4   Instrument panel mounting bolt locations.
Impreza**

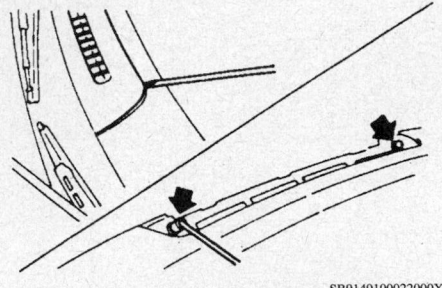

Fig. 5 Defroster grille & bolt removal. Impreza

SB9149100022000X

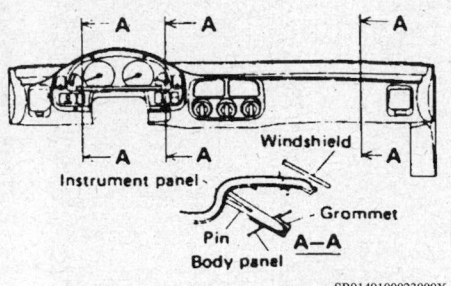

Fig. 6 Instrument panel installation. Impreza

SB9149100023000X

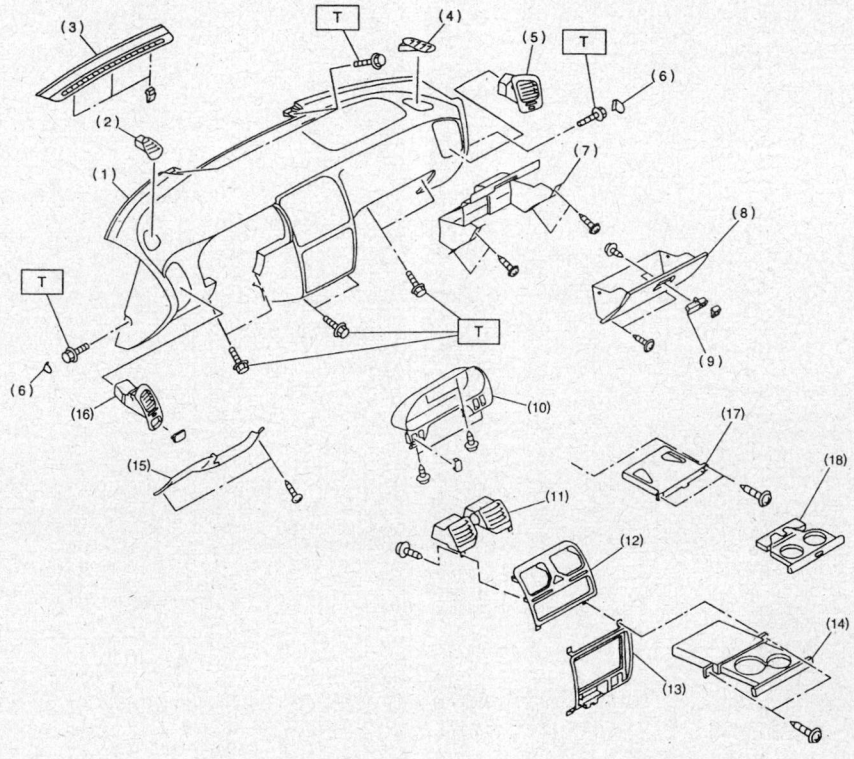

(1) Pad and frame	(9) Lock ASSY	(17) Cup holder BRKT
(2) Grille SD def. (D)	(10) Meter visor	(18) Cup holder
(3) Front def. grille	(11) Grille CTR vent.	
(4) Grille SD def. (P)	(12) Panel CTR upper	*Tightening torque: N·m (kg-m, ft-lb)*
(5) Grille vent (P)	(13) Panel CTR lower	*T: 7±1 (0.7±0.1, 5.1±0.7)*
(6) Cover	(14) Cup holder ASSY	
(7) Cover back panel	(15) Panel lower cover	
(8) Pocket ASSY	(16) Grille SD vent. (D)	

SB9149500024000X

Fig. 7 Exploded view of instrument panel. Legacy

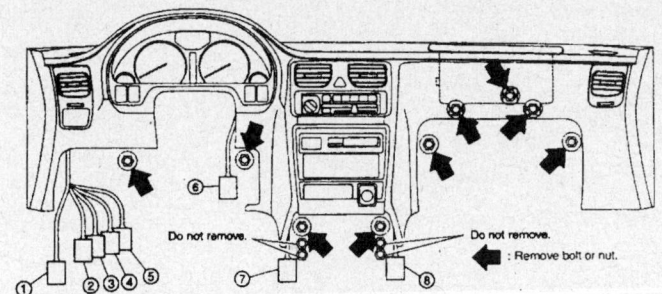

①	15P/Gray
②	22P/Brown
③	22P/White
④	20P/Blue
⑤	22P/Black
⑥	4P/Sky blue
⑦	1P/Black
⑧	1P/Black

SB9149500025000X

Fig. 8   Instrument panel electrical connector & bolt locations. Legacy

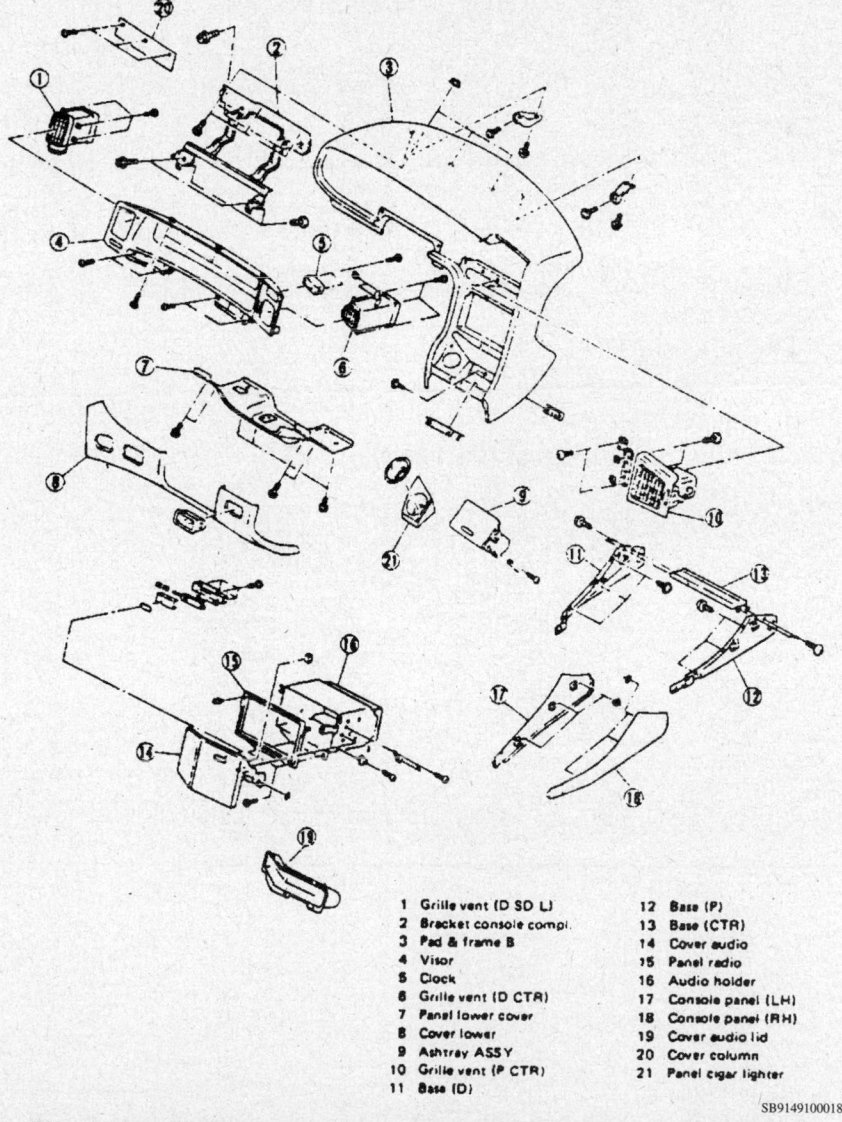

1	Grille vent (D SD L)	12	Base (P)
2	Bracket console compl.	13	Base (CTR)
3	Pad & frame B	14	Cover audio
4	Visor	15	Panel radio
5	Clock	16	Audio holder
6	Grille vent (D CTR)	17	Console panel (LH)
7	Panel lower cover	18	Console panel (RH)
8	Cover lower	19	Cover audio lid
9	Ashtray ASSY	20	Cover column
10	Grille vent (P CTR)	21	Panel cigar lighter
11	Base (D)		

SB9149100018010X

Fig. 9   Exploded view of instrument panel (Part 1 of 2). SVX

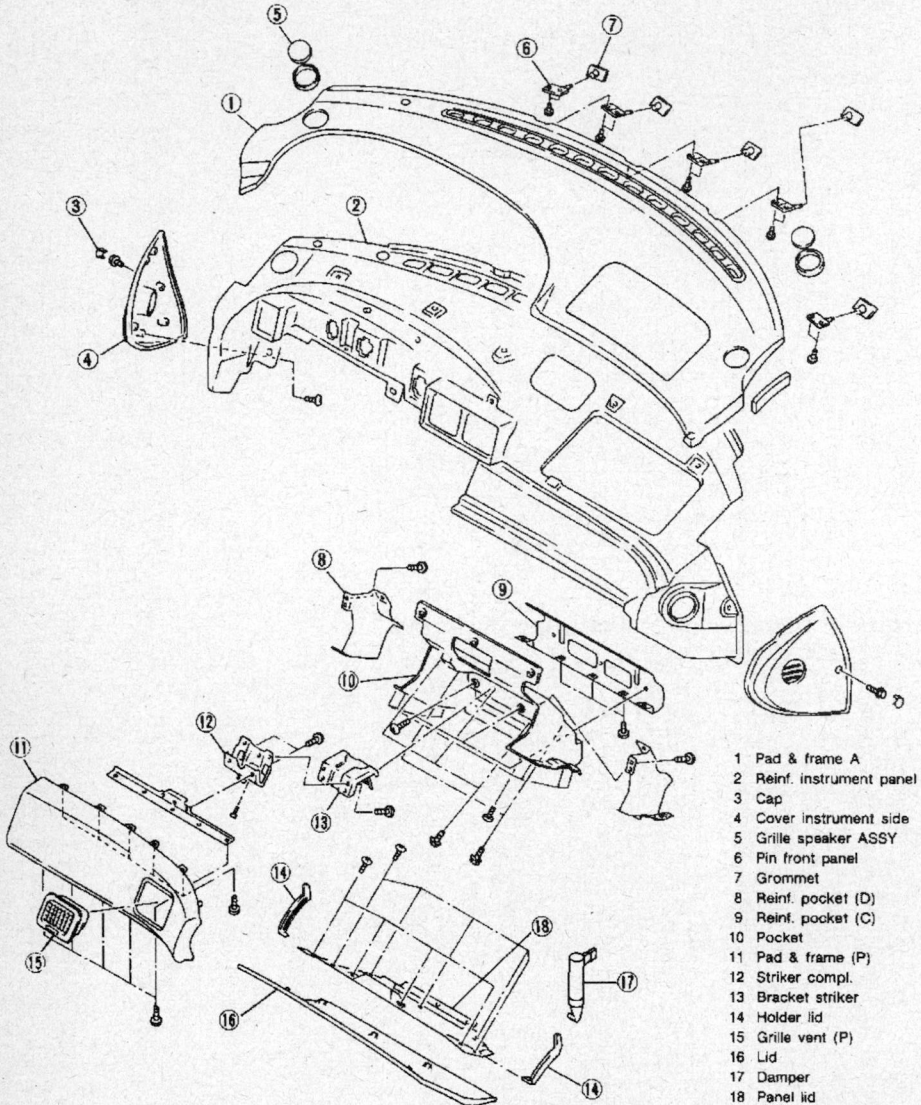

1 Pad & frame A
2 Reinf. instrument panel
3 Cap
4 Cover instrument side
5 Grille speaker ASSY
6 Pin front panel
7 Grommet
8 Reinf. pocket (D)
9 Reinf. pocket (C)
10 Pocket
11 Pad & frame (P)
12 Striker compl.
13 Bracket striker
14 Holder lid
15 Grille vent (P)
16 Lid
17 Damper
18 Panel lid

SB9149100018020A

Fig. 9 Exploded view of instrument panel (Part 2 of 2). SVX

SB9149100019000X

Fig. 10 Instrument panel lower screw removal. SVX

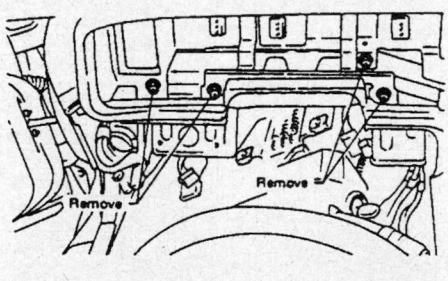

SB9149100020000X

Fig. 11 Meter visor removal. SVX

Steering Columns

41-127

NOTE: On Air Bag Equipped Models, Refer To " Air Bag System Precautions" Located In The Front Of This Manual For System Disarming & Arming Procedures.

INDEX

PRECAUTIONS

AIR BAG SYSTEMS

Refer to "Air Bag System Precautions" in the front of this manual for system disarming and arming procedures.

BATTERY GROUND CABLE

Prior to service, disconnect battery ground cable and isolate as required.

STEERING COLUMN SERVICE

Refer To **Figs. 1 through 4,** for steering column service.

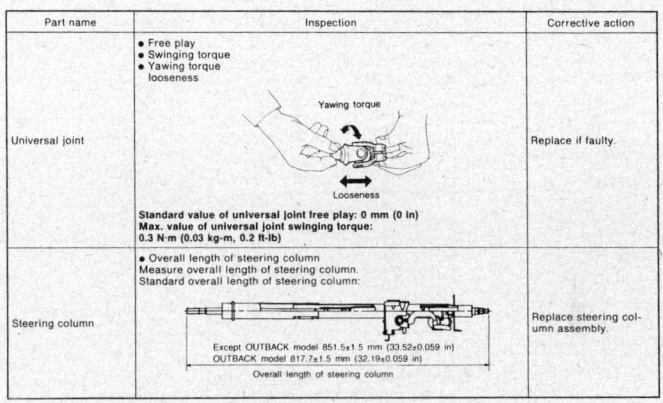

SB6049500011000X

Fig. 1 Exploded view of tilt steering column. Legacy

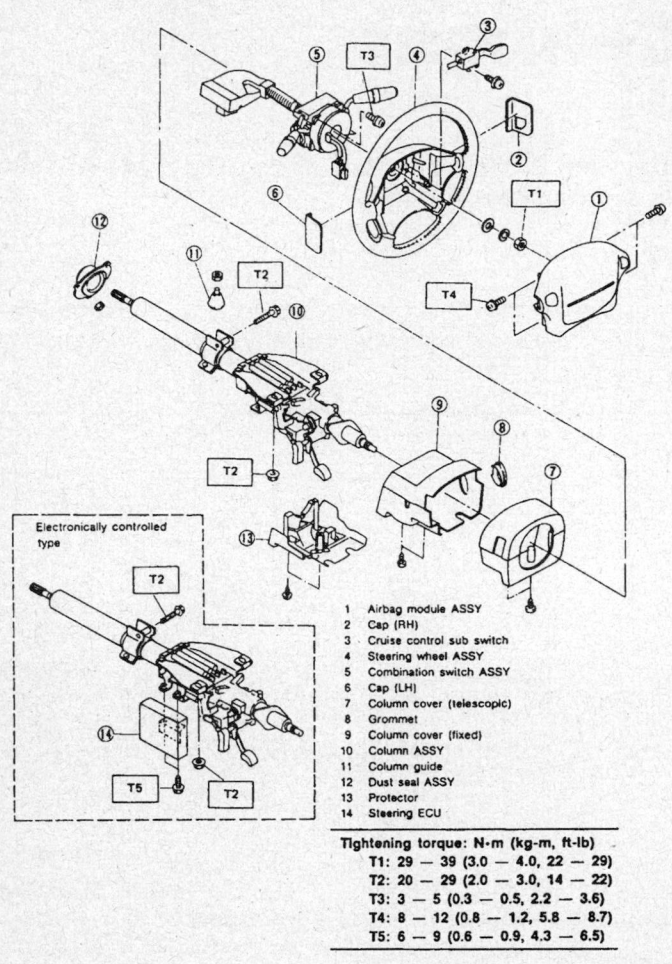

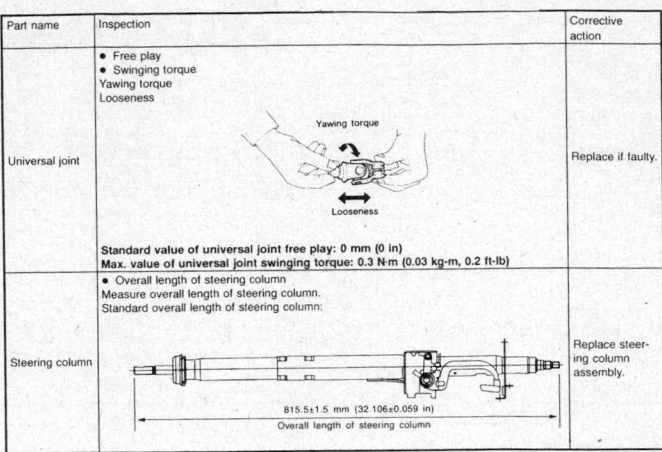

Fig. 3 Exploded view of steering column. Forester

Standard value of universal joint free play: 0 mm (0 in)
Max. value of universal joint swinging torque: 0.3 N·m (0.03 kg-m, 0.2 ft-lb)

Part name	Inspection	Corrective action
Universal joint	• Free play • Swinging torque Yawing torque Looseness	Replace if faulty.
Steering column	• Overall length of steering column Measure overall length of steering column. Standard overall length of steering column: 815.5±1.5 mm (32.106±0.059 in) Overall length of steering column	Replace steering column assembly.

SB6049800012000X

Electronically controlled type

1 Airbag module ASSY
2 Cap (RH)
3 Cruise control sub switch
4 Steering wheel ASSY
5 Combination switch ASSY
6 Cap (LH)
7 Column cover (telescopic)
8 Grommet
9 Column cover (fixed)
10 Column ASSY
11 Column guide
12 Dust seal ASSY
13 Protector
14 Steering ECU

Tightening torque: N·m (kg-m, ft-lb)
T1: 29 — 39 (3.0 — 4.0, 22 — 29)
T2: 20 — 29 (2.0 — 3.0, 14 — 22)
T3: 3 — 5 (0.3 — 0.5, 2.2 — 3.6)
T4: 8 — 12 (0.8 — 1.2, 5.8 — 8.7)
T5: 6 — 9 (0.6 — 0.9, 4.3 — 6.5)

SB6049100008000X

Fig. 2 Exploded view of tilt & telescopic steering column. SVX

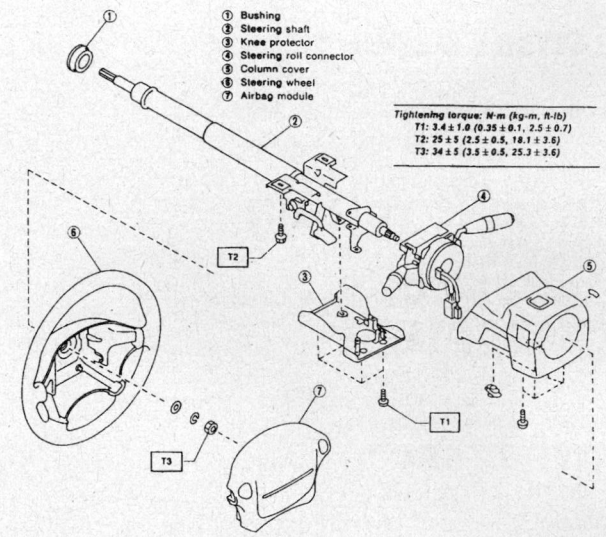

① Bushing
② Steering shaft
③ Knee protector
④ Steering roll connector
⑤ Column cover
⑥ Steering wheel
⑦ Airbag module

Tightening torque: N·m (kg-m, ft-lb)
T1: 3.4 ± 1.0 (0.35 ± 0.1, 2.5 ± 0.7)
T2: 25 ± 5 (2.5 ± 0.5, 18.1 ± 3.6)
T3: 34 ± 5 (3.5 ± 0.5, 25.3 ± 3.6)

SB6049100009000X

Fig. 4 Exploded view of tilt steering column. Impreza

Power Steering

INDEX

POWER STEERING PRESSURE SPECIFICATIONS

Year	Vehicle	Engine	Regular p.s.	Minimum Relief Pressure, p.s.	Maximum Relief Pressure, p.s.	Flow GPM @ RPM	Flow GPM @ RPM
1996–97	Impreza	1.8L	142	1067	1138	1.9 @ 1000	1.3 @ 3000
	Legacy	2.2L	142	1067	1138	1.9 @ 1000	1.3 @ 3000
	SVX①	3.3L	142	1109	1209	2.3 @ 1000	1.2 @ 3500
	SVX②	3.3L	142	1109	1209	2.4③	2.4③
1998–99	Forester	2.5L	142	1067	1138	1.9 @ 1000	1.3 @ 3000
	Impreza	All	142	1067	1138	1.9 @ 1000	1.3 @ 3000
	Legacy	All	142	1067	1138	1.9 @ 1000	1.3 @ 3000

① — Turbocharged engine. ② — Non Turbocharged engine. ③ — Engine speed sensing type.

PRECAUTIONS
AIR BAG SYSTEMS

Refer to "Air Bag System Precautions" in the front of this manual for system disarming and arming procedures.

BATTERY GROUND CABLE

Prior to service, disconnect battery ground cable and isolate as required.

DESCRIPTION

the power steering system is controlled by a belt driven vane style hydraulic pump. As the hydraulic oil is pressurized, it is controlled by the flow control valve which is located inside the oil pump assembly.

When the steering wheel is turned, the control valve connected to the pinion shaft activates to form an oil flow circuit corresponding to the rotational direction of the steering wheel helping reduce the effort required to operate the steering.

If the hydraulic system becomes inoperative, the steering shaft will be connected to the pinion shaft mechanically by means of the control valve. This allows the steering system to be operated as a manual steering system to maintain steering capabilities.

Maximum oil pressures are controlled by a hydraulic relief valve built into the flow control valve of the oil pump assembly.

TROUBLESHOOTING

Refer to **Figs. 1 and 2,** for basic troubleshooting procedures.

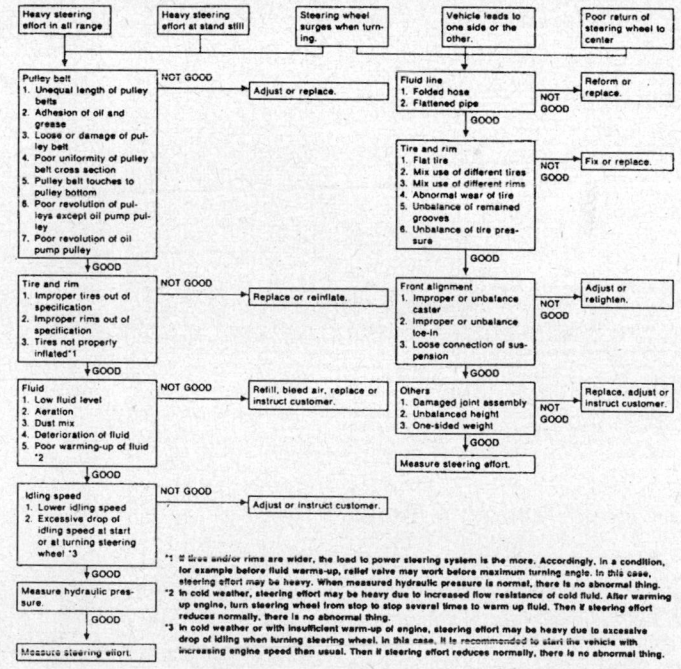

Fig. 1 Troubleshooting (steering condition)

DIAGNOSIS & TESTING
PRESSURE TESTS

Refer to "Power Steering Pressure Specifications" for test pressures.

Do not leave valve of pressure gauge closed or hold steering wheel at stop end for 5 seconds or more, as oil pump may be damaged.

1. Connect test equipment, **Fig. 3.**
2. Measure regular pressure at idling with valve open. If regular pressure is not as specified check the following:

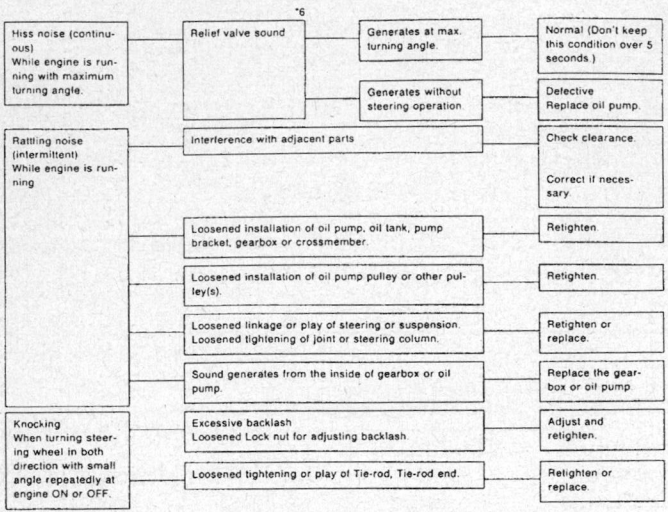

*6 Don't keep the relief valve operated over 5 sec. at any time or inner parts of the oil pump may be damaged due to rapid increase of fluid temperature.

SB6029100021010X

Fig. 2 Troubleshooting (noise & vibration, Part 1 of 3)

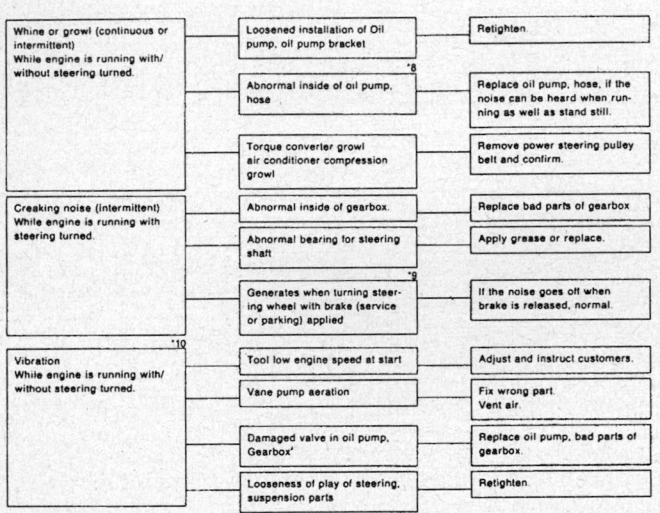

*8 Oil pump makes whine or growl noise slightly due to its mechanism. Even if the noise can be heard when steering wheel is turned at standstill there is no abnormal function in the system provided that the noise eliminates when the car is running.
*9 When stopping with service brake and/or parking brake applied, power steering can be operated easily due to its light steering effort. If doing so, the disk rotates slightly and makes creaking noise. The noise is generated by creaking between the disk and pads. If the noise goes off when the brake is released, there is no abnormal function in the system.
*10 There may be a little vibration around the steering devices when turning steering wheel at standstill, even though the component parts are properly adjusted and have no defects.
Hydraulic systems are likely to generate this kind of vibration as well as working noise and fluid noise because of combined conditions, i.e.,
Road surface and tire surface, Engine speed and turning speed of steering wheel, Fluid temperature and braking condition.
This phenomena does not indicate there is some abnormal function in the system.
The vibration can be known when steering wheel is turned repeatedly at various speeds from slow to rapid step by step with parking brake applied on concrete road and in "D" range for automatic transmission vehicle.

SB6029100021030X

Fig. 2 Troubleshooting (noise & vibration, Part 3 of 3)

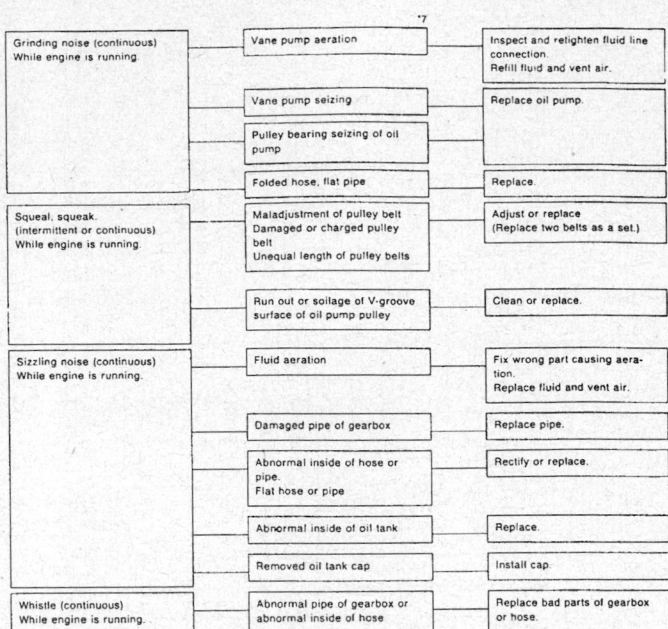

*7 Grinding noise may be heard immediately after the engine start in extremely cold condition. In this case, if the noise goes off during warm-up there is no abnormal function in the system. This is due to the fluid characteristic in extremely cold condition.

SB6029100021020X

Fig. 2 Troubleshooting (noise & vibration, Part 2 of 3)

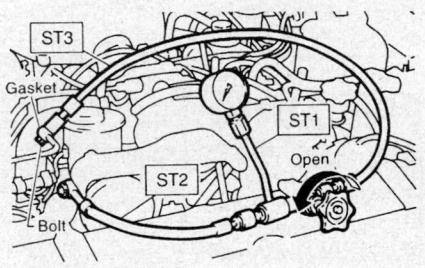

ST1	925711000	PRESSURE GAUGE
ST2	34099AC020	ADAPTER HOSE B
ST3	34099AC010	ADAPTER HOSE A

SB6029100022000X

Fig. 3 Pressure gauge connection

a. Flattened pipes or hoses.
b. Leakage of fluid lines.
c. Restricted fluid line.
3. Measure relief pressure at idling with valve closed. If relief pressure is not as specified check the following:
 a. Fluid leakage inside oil pump assembly.
 b. Excessive wear of vane pump mechanism.
 c. Incorrectly operating relief valve.
4. Measure working pressure of control valve at idling with valve opened, turning steering wheel from stop to stop. If

pressure is unsatisfactory, check operation of control valve.

STEERING EFFORT TESTS
FORESTER, IMPREZA & LEGACY

1. Measure steering effort in stand still with engine idling on concrete road. Steering effort should be 6.6 lbs. or less in both directions. If effort is not as specified, adjust backlash.
2. Measure steering effort in stand still with engine stalled on concrete road. Steering effort should be 66.2 ft. lbs. or

less in both directions.
3. If effort is not as specified, adjust backlash.
4. Remove joint assembly.
5. Measure steering wheel effort. Steering wheel effort should be .51 lbs. or less in both directions. Variation should be .24 lbs. or less.
6. Measure folding torque of joint assembly. Folding torque should be 1.23 lbs. or less for long yoke or 1.90 lbs. or less for short yoke. If folding torque is not as specified, replace joint assembly.
7. Inspect front wheels for unsteady revolution or rattling and brake for dragging.
8. Remove and inspect tie rod ends.
9. Measure rotating resistance of gearbox assembly. Rotating resistance should be 2.51 lbs. or less in straight ahead position and 3.55 ft. lbs. in all positions.

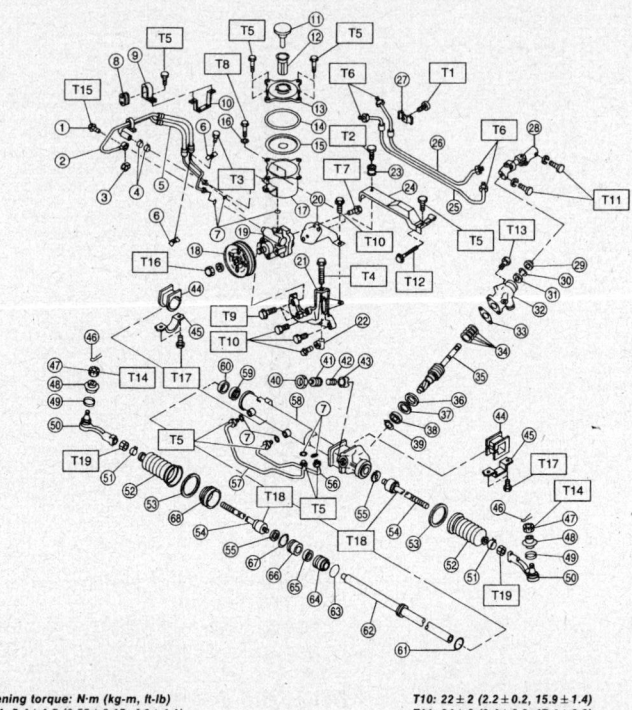

① Eye bolt	㉟ Pinion and valve ASSY
② Pipe C	㊱ Oil seal
③ Gasket	㊲ Back-up washer
④ Clip	㊳ Ball bearing
⑤ Pipe D	㊴ Snap ring
⑥ Clamp E	㊵ Lock nut
⑦ O-ring	㊶ Adjusting screw
⑧ Adapter	㊷ Spring
⑨ Clamp	㊸ Sleeve
⑩ Hose bracket	㊹ Adapter
⑪ Cap	㊺ Clamp
⑫ Strainer	㊻ Cotter pin
⑬ Shell upper	㊼ Castle nut
⑭ Rubber	㊽ Dust seal
⑮ Buffle	㊾ Clip
⑯ Seal washer	㊿ Tie-rod end
⑰ Shell lower	51 Small clip
⑱ Pulley	52 Boot
⑲ Oil pump	53 Large clip
⑳ Stiffener	54 Tie-rod
21 Bracket	55 Lock washer
22 Belt tension nut	56 Pipe B
23 Bush	57 Pipe A
24 Belt cover	58 Housing ASSY
25 Pipe E	59 Back-up washer
26 Pipe F	60 Oil seal
27 Clamp plate	61 Piston ring
28 Universal joint	62 Rack
29 Dust seal	63 O-ring
30 C-ring	64 Rack bushing
31 Oil seal	65 Oil seal
32 Valve housing	66 Rack stopper
33 Packing	67 Circlip
34 Seal ring	68 Spacer

SB6029800029020X

Fig. 4 Exploded view of power steering system (Part 2 of 2). Impreza

Tightening torque: N·m (kg-m, ft-lb)
T1: 5.4 ± 1.5 (0.55 ± 0.15, 4.0 ± 1.1)   T10: 22 ± 2 (2.2 ± 0.2, 15.9 ± 1.4)
T2: 6.4 ± 1.0 (0.65 ± 0.1, 4.7 ± 0.7)   T11: 34 ± 3 (2.4 ± 0.3, 17.4 ± 2.2)
T3: 7.4 ± 2.0 (0.75 ± 0.20, 5.4 ± 1.4)   T12: 25 ± 2 (2.5 ± 0.2, 18.1 ± 1.4)
T4: 8 ± 2 (0.8 ± 0.2, 5.8 ± 1.4)   T13: 25 ± 5 (2.5 ± 0.5, 18.1 ± 3.6)
T5: 13 ± 3 (1.3 ± 0.3, 9.4 ± 2.2)   T14: 27 ± 2 (2.75 ± 0.2, 19.9 ± 1.4)
T6: 15 ± 5 (1.5 ± 0.5, 10.8 ± 3.6)   T15: 39 ± 5 (4.0 ± 0.5, 28.9 ± 3.6)
T7: 15.7 ± 2.4 (1.60 ± 0.24, 11.6 ± 1.7) T16: 52 ± 10 (5.3 ± 1.0, 38 ± 7)
T8: 18 +5 −5 (1.8 +0.5 −0.5, 13.0 +3.6 −3.6) T17: 59 ± 12 (6.0 ± 1.2, 43 ± 9)
T9: 20.1 ± 2.5 (2.05 ± 0.25, 14.8 ± 1.8) T18: 78 ± 10 (8.0 ± 1.0, 58 ± 7)
                                          T19: 83 ± 5 (8.5 ± 0.5, 61.5 ± 3.6)

SB6029800029010X

Fig. 4 Exploded view of power steering system (Part 1 of 2). Impreza

10. Variation should not exceed 20 percent difference between clockwise and counterclockwise.
11. If rotating resistance is not as specified, adjust backlash.
12. Measure sliding resistance of gearbox assembly. Sliding resistance should be 68 lbs. Variation should not exceed 20 percent between left and right directions. If sliding resistance is not as specified, adjust backlash.

SVX

1. Measure steering effort in stand still with engine idling on concrete road. Steering effort should be as follows:
   a. **On engine RPM sensing type,** 6.8 lbs.
   b. **On vehicle speed sensing, electronically controlled type,** 5.1 lbs. or less in both directions.
   c. **On all models,** if effort is not as specified, adjust backlash.
2. Measure steering effort with vehicle stopped and engine off. Ensure wheels are off the ground during measurement. Steering effort should be 3.7 lbs. or less in both directions. If effort is not as specified, adjust backlash.
3. Remove joint assembly.
4. Measure steering wheel effort. Steering wheel effort should be .51 lbs. or less in both directions. Variation should be .24 lbs. or less.
5. Measure folding torque of joint assem-

bly. Folding torque should be 1.23 lbs. or less for long yoke or 1.90 lbs. or less for short yoke. If folding torque is not as specified, replace joint assembly.
6. Inspect front wheels for unsteady revolution or rattling and brake for dragging.
7. Remove and inspect tie rod ends.
8. Measure rotating resistance of gearbox assembly. Rotating resistance should be 2.36 lbs. or less in straight ahead position and in all positions 2.6 lbs. or less. Variation should not exceed 20 percent difference between clockwise and counterclockwise. If rotating resistance is not as specified, adjust backlash.
9. Measure sliding resistance of gearbox assembly. Sliding resistance should be 60 lbs. or less. Variation should not exceed 20 percent between left and right directions. If sliding resistance is not as specified, adjust backlash.

POWER STEERING SYSTEM SERVICE
POWER STEERING PUMP SERVICE
Disassemble

1. Place pump bracket (with pump installed) in soft jawed vise.
2. Disconnect oil pump switch electrical

connector, then remove oil pump switch, if equipped.
3. Remove valve assembly and spring.
4. Loosen rear body mounting bolts, then remove pump from bracket.
5. Place pump in soft jawed vise.
6. Remove rear body mounting bolts, rear body and gasket.
7. Remove cartridge assembly, pressure plate and pin from front body as a unit. Cartridge assembly consists of a rotor ten vanes and a cam.
8. Remove two types of Rings by hand.
9. Disassemble front body as follows:
   a. Pry off retaining ring from groove of front body at pulley location.
   b. Using a hand press, remove driveway (on cartridge side) and ball bearing out of driveway.
   c. Remove oil seal by attaching it to a hooked end plate placed in vise.

Assemble

1. Apply coat of lithium grease to oil seal, then using seal installer tool No. 926970000, or equivalent, hand press seal into front body.
2. Using guide tool No. 926980000, or equivalent, hand press drive bearing onto shaft.
3. Install retaining ring on oil seal.
4. Using guide tool No. 926980000, or equivalent, press shaft and bearing assembly into front body.
5. Lock driveway using retaining ring, then place front body in vise with pulley side facing down.
6. Position two Rings and pressure plate in front body.
7. Install cartridge as follows:

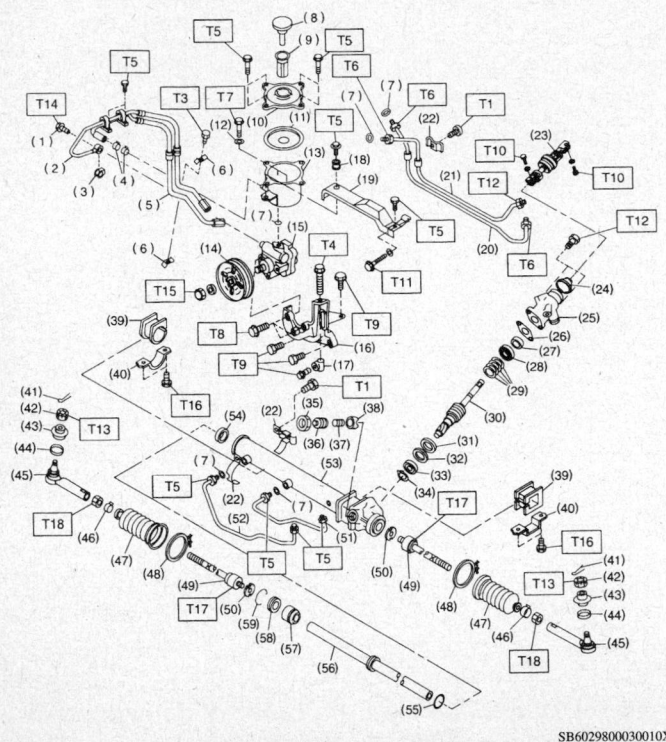

(1)	Eye bolt	(28)	Special bearing	(55)	Piston ring
(2)	Pipe C	(29)	Seal ring	(56)	Rack
(3)	Gasket	(30)	Pinion and valve ASSY	(57)	Rack bushing
(4)	Clip	(31)	Oil seal	(58)	Rack stopper
(5)	Pipe D	(32)	Back-up washer	(59)	Circlip
(6)	Clamp E	(33)	Ball bearing		
(7)	O-ring	(34)	Snap ring		
(8)	Cap	(35)	Lock nut		
(9)	Strainer	(36)	Adjusting screw		
(10)	Buffle	(37)	Spring		
(11)	Shell upper	(38)	Sleeve		
(12)	Seal washer	(39)	Adapter		
(13)	Shell lower	(40)	Clamp		
(14)	Pulley	(41)	Cotter pin		
(15)	Oil pump	(42)	Castle nut		
(16)	Bracket	(43)	Dust seal		
(17)	Belt tension nut	(44)	Clip		
(18)	Bush	(45)	Tie-rod end		
(19)	Belt cover	(46)	Band		
(20)	Pipe E	(47)	Boot		
(21)	Pipe F	(48)	Band		
(22)	Clamp plate	(49)	Tie-rod		
(23)	Universal joint	(50)	Lock washer		
(24)	Dust cover	(51)	Pipe B		
(25)	Valve housing	(52)	Pipe A		
(26)	Gasket	(53)	Housing ASSY		
(27)	Oil seal	(54)	Oil seal		

Tightening torque: N·m (kg-m, ft-lb)

T1: 6±1 (0.6±0.1, 4.3±0.7)
T2: 6.4±1.0 (0.65±0.1, 4.7±0.7)
T3: 7.4±2.0 (0.75±0.20, 5.4±1.4)
T4: 8±2 (0.8±0.2, 5.8±1.4)
T5: 13±3 (1.3±0.3, 9.4±2.2)
T6: 15±5 (1.5±0.5, 10.8±3.6)
T7: 18$^{-5}/_0$ (1.8$^{-0.5}/_0$, 13.0$^{-3.6}/_0$)
T8: 20.1±2.5 (2.05±0.25, 14.8±1.8)
T9: 22±2 (2.2±0.2, 15.9±1.4)
T10: 24±3 (2.4±0.3, 17.4±2.2)
T11: 25±2 (2.5±0.2, 18.1±1.4)
T12: 25±5 (2.5±0.5, 18.1±3.6)
T13: 27±2 (2.75±0.2, 19.9±1.4)
T14: 39±5 (4.0±0.5, 28.9±3.6)
T15: 52±10 (5.3±1.0, 38±7)
T16: 59±12 (6.0±1.2, 43±9)
T17: 78±10 (8.0±1.0, 58±7)
T18: 83±5 (8.5±0.5, 61.5±3.6)

SB6029800030020X

Fig. 5 Exploded view of power steering system (Part 2 of 2). Forester

SB6029800030010X

Fig. 5 Exploded view of power steering system (Part 1 of 2). Forester

a. Apply coat of automatic transmission fluid to vane. Refer to "Specifications" for proper fluid type.
b. Install cam, rotor and vane, then insert pin into holes in cam and pressure plate. Ensure vane is installed with "R" side facing cam.
8. Install rear body using new gasket, then hand tighten mounting bolts. Ensure pin hole of rear body aligns with pin in pump.
9. Remove pump from vise.
10. Place pump bracket in vise, then install pump on bracket.
11. **Torque** rear body mounting bolts in a crisscross pattern to 11–14 ft. lbs.
12. **Torque** rear body mounting bolts in a crisscross pattern to 22–29 ft. lbs.
13. Position spring and valve assembly in front body.
14. Install oil pump switch with Oaring, then connect electrical connector, if equipped.

POWER STEERING GEAR SERVICE

Forester, Impreza & Legacy

Refer to **Figs. 4 through 6** when performing the following procedure.
1. Place attachment tool No. 926200000, or equivalent, in suitable vise, then attach steering gear to tool.
2. Remove clip from boot, then push boot toward tie rod end.
3. Remove boot, big band and medium clips, then push rack fully into gearbox.
4. Straighten tie rod lock washer, using care not to strike rack.
5. Remove tie rod from rack.

6. Using spanner wrench tool No. 9262300000, or equivalent, loosen lockout, then remove adjusting screw.
7. Remove spring and sleeve, then remove dust seal of dust cover, if equipped.
8. Loosen two bolts securing valve assembly, then draw out input shaft and remove valve assembly.
9. Using pipe 1.73–1.81 inches ID and press, remove pinion and valve from valve housing.
10. Slide mounting rubber to expose slit.
11. Using wrench tool No. 926340000, or equivalent, rotate rack stopper in clockwise direction until end of circle comes out of stopper, then rotate rack in counterclockwise direction and pull out circle.
12. Pull rack assembly from cylinder side. Draw out rack bushing and rack stopper with rack assembly. Do not contact inner wall of cylinder.
13. Remove rack bushing and rack stopper from rack assembly.
14. Replace valve housing oil seal as follows:
    a. Using flathead screwdriver, pry off dust cover, then remove snap ring.
    b. Using flathead screwdriver, pry off oil seal.
    c. Using press and oil seal installer tool No. 926350000, or equivalent, press oil seal into valve housing.
    d. Install snap ring and dust seal.
15. Replace valve assembly low pressure seal as follows:
    a. Remove and discard snap ring.
    b. Press out and discard bearing and-backing washer using a 1.52–1.55

inches ID pipe as a support.
    c. Remove oil seal.
    d. Install pinion and valve into valve housing. Apply lubricant to outer diameter surface of input shaft and outer surface of valve body seal ring.
    e. Put installer tool No. 926360000 over pinion and insert oil seal, the press fit oil seal into housing using installer tool No. 926360000 and installer 926370000, or equivalents.
    f. Remove installer tool No. 926360000, then install backing washer.
    g. Using installer tool No. 926370000, or equivalent, press in ball bearing.
    h. Install snap ring.
16. Replace rack housing oil seal and back-up washer as follows:
    a. Using hammer and 1.02–1.06 inches diameter round rod, drive out oil seal and back-up washer from pinion housing side of rack.
    b. Using seal installer tool No. 926380000, or equivalent, press in oil seal.
17. Install rack housing in stand tool No. 926200000, or equivalent, then grease teeth of rack assembly. Do not block air passage with grease.
18. Install cover tool No. 926390001, or equivalent, over toothed portion of rack assembly. Ensure air passage is clear of grease.
19. Insert rack assembly into rack housing from cylinder side. Remove cover after it has passed completely through oil seal.
20. Install guide tool No. 926400000, or equivalent, over end of rack, then install rack bushing assembly.
21. Insert rack stopper into rack housing, then using wrench tool No. 926340000, or equivalent, wrap circle. Rotate wrench another 90°–180° after end of circle has been wrapped in.
22. Install rubber mounting onto rack housing.
23. Install valve assembly as follows:
    a. Apply grease to pinion gear and bearing of valve.

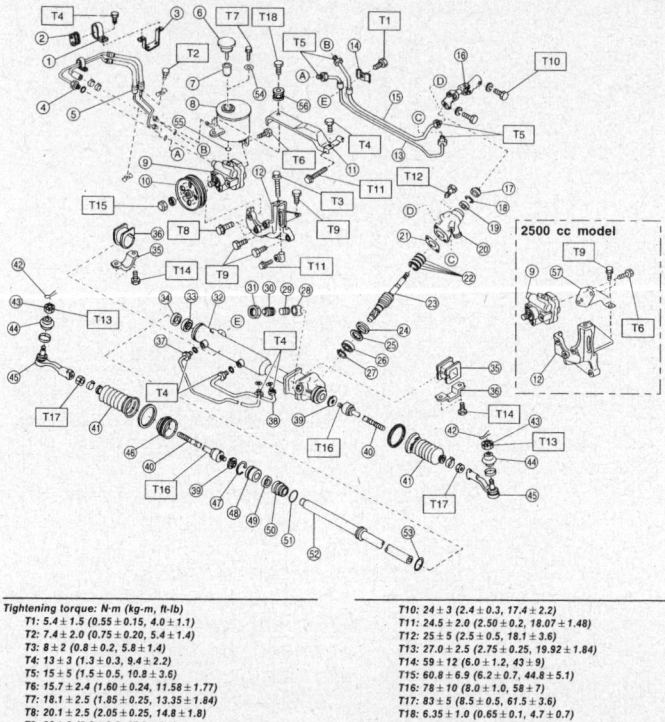

① Clamp		㉚ Adjusting screw
② Adapter		㉛ Lock nut
③ Hose bracket		㉜ Housing ASSY
④ Pipe C		㉝ Back-up washer
⑤ Pipe D		㉞ Oil seal
⑥ Cap		㉟ Adapter
⑦ Strainer		㊱ Clamp
⑧ Tank		㊲ Pipe A
⑨ Oil pump		㊳ Pipe B
⑩ Pulley		㊴ Lock washer
⑪ Belt cover		㊵ Tie-rod
⑫ Bracket		㊶ Boot
⑬ Pipe E		㊷ Cotter pin
⑭ Clamp plate		㊸ Castle nut
⑮ Pipe F		㊹ Dust seal
⑯ Universal joint		㊺ Tie-rod end
⑰ Dust seal		㊻ Spacer
⑱ C-ring		㊼ Circlip
⑲ Oil seal		㊽ Rack stopper
⑳ Valve housing		㊾ Oil seal
㉑ Packing		㊿ Rack bushing
㉒ Seal ring		51 O-ring
㉓ Pinion and valve ASSY		52 Rack
㉔ Oil seal		53 Piston ring
㉕ Back-up washer		54 Seal washer
㉖ Ball bearing		55 O-ring
㉗ Snap ring		56 Bush
㉘ Sleeve		57 Stay (2500 cc model only)
㉙ Spring		

SB6029800031020X

Fig. 6 Exploded view of power steering system (Part 2 of 2). Legacy

Tightening torque: N·m (kg-m, ft-lb)
T1: 5.4 ± 1.5 (0.55 ± 0.15, 4.0 ± 1.1)
T2: 7.4 ± 2.0 (0.75 ± 0.20, 5.4 ± 1.4)
T3: 8 ± 2 (0.8 ± 0.2, 5.8 ± 1.4)
T4: 13 ± 3 (1.3 ± 0.3, 9.4 ± 2.2)
T5: 15 ± 5 (1.5 ± 0.5, 10.8 ± 3.6)
T6: 15.7 ± 2.4 (1.60 ± 0.24, 11.58 ± 1.77)
T7: 18.1 ± 2.5 (1.85 ± 0.25, 13.35 ± 1.84)
T8: 20.1 ± 2.5 (2.05 ± 0.25, 14.8 ± 1.8)
T9: 22 ± 2 (2.2 ± 0.2, 15.9 ± 1.4)
T10: 24 ± 3 (2.4 ± 0.3, 17.4 ± 2.2)
T11: 24.5 ± 2.0 (2.50 ± 0.2, 18.07 ± 1.48)
T12: 25 ± 5 (2.5 ± 0.5, 18.1 ± 3.6)
T13: 27.0 ± 2.5 (2.75 ± 0.25, 19.92 ± 1.84)
T14: 59 ± 12 (6.0 ± 1.2, 43 ± 9)
T15: 60.8 ± 6.9 (6.2 ± 0.7, 44.8 ± 5.1)
T16: 78 ± 10 (8.0 ± 1.0, 58 ± 7)
T17: 83 ± 5 (8.5 ± 0.5, 61.5 ± 3.6)
T18: 6.35 ± 1.0 (0.65 ± 0.1, 4.7 ± 0.7)

SB6029800031010X

Fig. 6 Exploded view of power steering system (Part 1 of 2). Legacy

b. Center rack shaft to rack housing. If centered correctly, the distance from rack housing to end face of rack will be 2.99 inches.

c. With rack shaft teeth facing pinion side, insert packing and valve assembly in rack housing. When inserting valve assembly, face cutout portion of input shaft serration toward adjusting screw hole.

d. **Torque** bolts alternately to 14–22 ft. lbs.

24. Apply a suitable lubricant to sleeve insertion hole and dust seal or dust cover, if equipped.

25. Press fit dust seal into gearbox housing until distance between gearbox and dust seal is .08 inch or less.

26. Apply a suitable lubricant to sliding surface of sleeve and spring seat, then insert sleeve into pinion housing assembly.

27. Insert spring into sleeve screw, then pack screw with a suitable grease and install.

28. Install tie rods as follows:
a. Rotate input shaft until rack protrudes approximately 1.57 inches above end surface of gear.
b. Hold rack in this position, then tighten adjusting screw until it bottoms.
c. Install tie rods onto rack. Bend lock washer in two place.

29. Adjust rack and pinion backlash as follows:
a. **Torque** adjusting screw to 3.6 ft. lbs. to seat sleeve against rack, then loosen screw. Repeat this step twice.

b. **Torque** adjusting screw to 3.6 ft. lbs., then back off 30°
c. While holding adjusting screw in place, **torque** lockout to 22–36 ft. lbs.

30. Apply a suitable grease to groove of tie rod, then ensure boot is positioned without unusual inflation or deflation.

31. Install clips on boot, then assemble boot to gearbox while retaining gear flange. Fold back boot flange until large clip cannot be seen.

32. Install small boot end clip. Ensure boot end is positioned in groove on tie rod.

33. Screw in tie rod end lockout and tie rod end onto tie rod, then tighten lockout .59 inch from back of nut to threaded portion.

SVX

Refer to **Fig. 7,** when performing the following procedure.

1. Place attachment tool No. 926200000, or equivalent, in suitable vise, then attach steering gear to tool.
2. Disconnect pipes from steering body and control valve housing.
3. Remove tie rod end and lockout.
4. Pry off clip from small end of boot and slide it toward tie-rod end.
5. Remove lock wire from large end of boot, then cut and remove boot. Boot must be replace whenever it is removed.
6. Set rack so it protrudes about 1.57 inches, then straighten tie rod lock washer, using care not to strike rack.
7. Using wrench tool No. 34099PA100, or

equivalent, loosen lockout, then tighten adjusting screw until it bottoms.

8. Remove tie rod from rack, then the adjusting screw.
9. Remove spring and sleeve.
10. Remove two bolts securing valve assembly, then the valve housing assembly and valve assembly as a unit.
11. Remove snap ring from seal holder.
12. Push rack out of steering body while pushing it on valve side.
13. Remove high pressure seal as follows:
a. Push back-up ring and oil seal out by inserting seal remover tool No. 927580000, or equivalent, from valve side.
14. Remove oil seal and Oaring from holder assembly, then install new oil seal and Oaring.
15. Remove seal ring and Oaring from rack piston, then install new seal ring and Oaring.
16. Lubricate inner surface of seal ring sweater tool No. 34099PA000, or equivalent, and place tool over seal ring. Leave tool on seal ring for at least 10 minutes, until seal ring settles into place.
17. Assemble rack assembly as follows:
a. Place attachment tool No. 926200000, or equivalent, in suitable vise, then attach steering gear to tool.
b. Lubricate needle bearing.
c. Using tools, **Fig. 8,** install oil seal. Oil seal should be installed to near piston.
d. Install back-up ring to rack from gear side.
e. Apply grease to rack teeth grooves, sleeve's sliding portion and piston's sealing surface, then insert rack into cylinder side of steering body.
f. Lubricate and attach guide tool No. 34099PA020 to part of rack assembly which protrudes beyond cylinder side.
g. Lubricate inner surface of holder

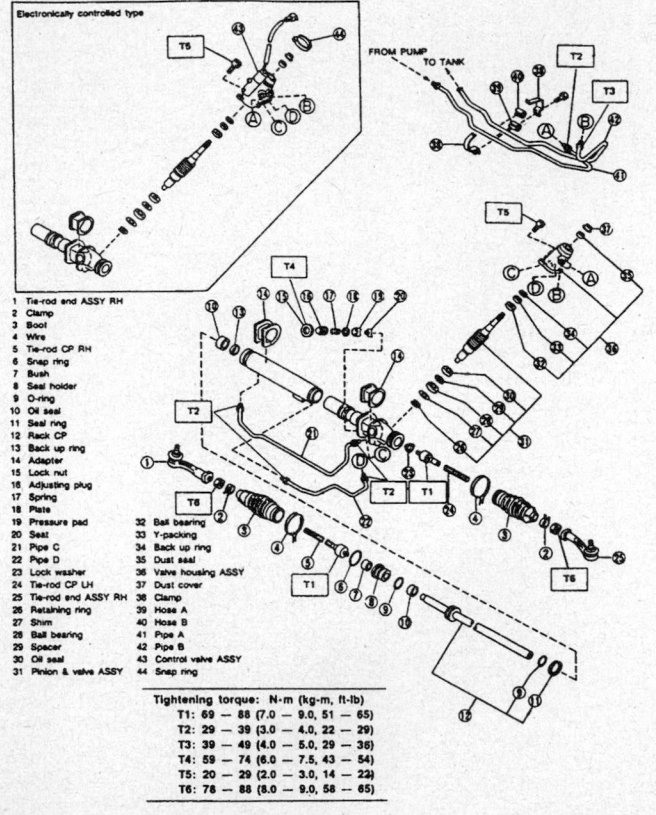

Fig. 7 Exploded view of power rack & pinion steering gear. SVX

1 Tie-rod end ASSY RH
2 Clamp
3 Boot
4 Wire
5 Tie-rod CP RH
6 Snap ring
7 Bush
8 Seal holder
9 O-ring
10 Oil seal
11 Seal ring
12 Rack CP
13 Back up ring
14 Adapter
15 Lock nut
16 Adjusting plug
17 Spring
18 Plate
19 Pressure pad
20 Seat
21 Pipe C
22 Pipe D
23 Lock washer
24 Tie-rod CP LH
25 Tie-rod end ASSY RH
26 Retaining ring
27 Shim
28 Ball bearing
29 Spacer
30 Oil seal
31 Pinion & valve ASSY
32 Ball bearing
33 Y-packing
34 Back up ring
35 Dust seal
36 Valve housing ASSY
37 Dust cover
38 Clamp
39 Hose A
40 Hose B
41 Pipe A
42 Pipe B
43 Control valve ASSY
44 Snap ring

Tightening torque: N·m (kg-m, ft-lb)		
T1: 69 – 88	(7.0 – 9.0,	51 – 65)
T2: 29 – 39	(3.0 – 4.0,	22 – 29)
T3: 39 – 49	(4.0 – 5.0,	29 – 36)
T4: 59 – 74	(6.0 – 7.5,	43 – 54)
T5: 20 – 29	(2.0 – 3.0,	14 – 22)
T6: 78 – 88	(8.0 – 9.0,	58 – 65)

SB6029100028000X

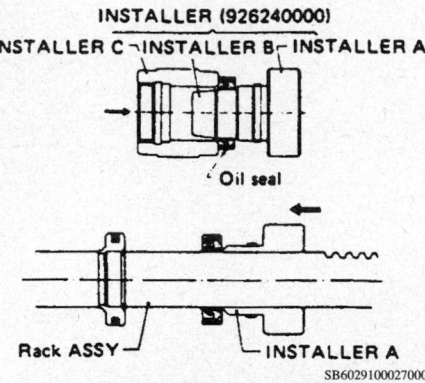

Fig. 8 Rack oil seal installation. SVX

SB6029100027000X

assembly and O-ring, then insert into rack assembly. Install snap ring to secure holder assembly.

h. Attach installer tool No. 926320000, or equivalent, to cylinder side of rack assembly, then drive back-up ring and oil seal into place on steering body. Push installer until its groove reaches end surface of holder assembly.

18. Install valve assembly as follows:

a. Attach shim(s) to stepped lip of steering body and pinion housing. Apply sealer (Fiji Bond C: No. 004403004) uniformly to lip side end surface of pinion housing. Use same number of shims as removed from steering body, valve housing and valve assembly.

b. Pull out rack assembly until it protrudes 2.99 inches beyond housing end face of pinion side.

c. Lubricate pinion gear teeth grooves and ball bearing.

d. Center rack shaft to rack housing. If centered correctly, the distance from rack housing to end face of rack will be 2.99 inches.

e. Position input shaft so that cutout section faces toward sleeve boss.

f. Push in valve assembly.

g. Center rack assembly as outlined in step d, then gradually **torque** socket bolts alternately 14–22 ft. lbs.

19. Apply a suitable lubricant to sliding surface of sleeve and spring seat, then insert sleeve into pinion housing assembly.

20. Insert spring into sleeve screw, then pack screw with a suitable grease and install.

21. Install tie rods as follows:

a. Rotate input shaft until rack protrudes approximately 1.57 inches above end surface of gear.

b. Hold rack in this position, then tighten adjusting screw until it bottoms.

c. Install tie rods onto rack.

22. Adjust rack and pinion backlash as follows:

a. **Torque** adjusting screw to 14 ft. lbs. to seat sleeve against rack, then loosen screw.

b. **Torque** adjusting screw to 3.6 ft. lbs., then loosen screw.

c. **Torque** adjusting screw to 3.6 ft. lbs., then back off 25°.

d. While holding adjusting screw in place, **torque** lockout to 43–54 ft. lbs.

23. Apply a suitable grease to groove of tie rod, then ensure boot is positioned without unusual inflation or deflation.

24. Wind two complete turns of lock wire on large end of boot, twist wire while pulling it upward with a force of 11 lbs. bend wire end along boot.

25. Install small boot end clip. Ensure boot end is positioned in groove on tie rod.

26. Screw in tie rod end lockout and tie rod end onto tie rod, then tighten lockout 1.00 inch from back of nut to threaded portion.

TIGHTENING SPECIFICATIONS

Model	Component	Torque/Ft. Lbs.
FORESTER, IMPREZA & LEGACY		
1996-99	Adjust Screw Lockout	22–36
	Inner Tie Rod To Rack	51–65
	Steering Rack Hydraulic Line Flare Nuts	7–12
	Steering Rack Retaining Clamp Bolts	35–52
	Steering Shaft Pinch Bolts	15–20
	Tie Rod End Lockout	51–65
	Tie Rod End To Steering Knuckle	18–22 ①
	Valve Housing To Rack	14–22
	Wheel Lug Nuts	58–72
SVX		
1996-97	Adjust Screw Lockout	43–54
	Hydraulic Line Flare Nuts (From Pump)	29–36
	Hydraulic Line Flare Nuts (Except From Pump)	22–29
	Inner Tie Rod To Rack	51–65
	Steering Shaft Pinch Bolts	15–20
	Steering Rack Retaining Clamp Bolts	35–52
	Tie Rod End Outer Lockout	58–65
	Tie Rod End To Steering Knuckle	22–36
	Valve Housing To Rack	14–22
	Wheel Lug Nuts	72–86

① — Castle nut may be tightened an additional 60° to align cotter pin.

Disc Brakes

INDEX

BRAKE PAD SERVICE

FRONT

1. Raise and support vehicle.
2. Remove front wheels.
3. **On Legacy Turbot and SVX models,** disconnect brake hose from strut.
4. **On all models,** remove caliper locking, then rotate caliper on guide pin, **Figs. 1 through 5.**
5. Remove brake pads from support.
6. Reverse procedure to install noting the following:
   a. **On 1996 Impreza models,** using wrench tool No. 925590000 and spacer tool No. 926440000, or equivalents, slowly rotate caliper piston until seated into caliper bore. **Ensure notch in piston face is aligned with tab on brake pad backing plate.**
   b. **On Legacy, SVX and 1997–99 Impreza models,** push piston into caliper body. When piston is difficult to insert, loosen the air bleeder, then push into place.
   c. **On all models,** refer to **Figs. 1 through 5,** for tightening values.
   d. After completing installation, depress brake pedal several times to seat brake pads against rotor. If pedal stroke is excessive, bleed hydraulic system as needed.

REAR

1. Raise and support vehicle.
2. Remove rear wheels.
3. Remove lower caliper retaining bolt, then pivot caliper upward, **Figs. 6 through 9.**
4. Remove brake pads and springs from support. **Note position of springs for proper installation.**
5. Reverse procedure to install noting the following:
   a. Press piston into caliper body using a suitable clamp.
   b. Refer to **Figs. 6 through 9,** for tightening values.
   c. After completing installation, depress brake pedal several times to seat brake pads against rotor. If pedal stroke is excessive, bleed hydraulic system as needed.

CALIPER SERVICE

REPLACEMENT

FRONT

1. Raise and support vehicle.
2. Remove front wheels.
3. Disconnect brake hose from caliper. Plug hose to prevent fluid leakage.
4. Remove caliper locking, rotate caliper on guide pin, then remove caliper, **Figs. 1 through 5.**
5. Reverse procedure to install noting the following:
   a. Refer to **Figs. 1 through 5,** for tightening values.
   b. After completing installation, bleed hydraulic system.

REAR

1. Raise and support vehicle.

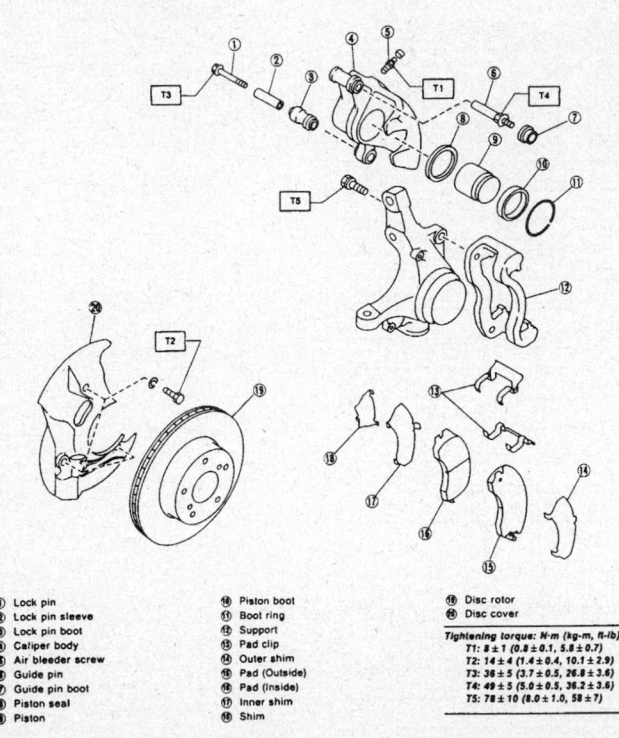

① Lock pin	⑨ Piston boot	⑱ Disc rotor
② Lock pin sleeve	⑩ Boot ring	⑲ Disc cover
③ Lock pin boot	⑪ Support	
④ Caliper body	⑫ Pad clip	
⑤ Air bleeder screw	⑬ Outer shim	
⑥ Guide pin	⑭ Pad (Outside)	
⑦ Guide pin boot	⑮ Pad (Inside)	
⑧ Piston seal	⑯ Inner shim	
⑨ Piston	⑰ Shim	

Tightening torque: N·m (kg-m, ft-lb)
T1: 8 ± 1 (0.8 ± 0.1, 5.8 ± 0.7)
T2: 14 ± 4 (1.4 ± 0.4, 10.1 ± 2.9)
T3: 36 ± 5 (3.7 ± 0.5, 26.8 ± 3.6)
T4: 49 ± 5 (5.0 ± 0.5, 36.2 ± 3.6)
T5: 78 ± 10 (8.0 ± 1.0, 58 ± 7)

SB4079100006000X

Fig. 1 Exploded view of front disc brake assembly. 1996 Impreza

① Caliper body	⑨ Support	
② Air bleeder screw	⑩ Pad clip	
③ Guide pin (Green)	⑪ Outer shim	
④ Pin boot	⑫ Inner shim	
⑤ Piston seal	⑬ Pad (Outside)	
⑥ Piston	⑭ Pad (Inside)	
⑦ Piston boot	⑮ Disc rotor	
⑧ Lock pin (Yellow)	⑯ Disc cover	

Tightening torque: N·m (kg-m, ft-lb)
T1: 8 ± 1 (0.8 ± 0.1, 5.8 ± 0.7)
T2: 18 ± 5 (1.8 ± 0.5, 13.0 ± 3.6)
T3: 37 ± 5 (3.8 ± 0.5, 27.5 ± 3.6)
T4: 78 ± 10 (8.0 ± 1.0, 58 ± 7)

SB4079700012000X

Fig. 2 Exploded view of front disc brake assembly. 1997 Impreza

2. Remove rear wheels.
3. Disconnect brake hose from caliper. Plug brake to prevent fluid leakage.
4. Remove caliper retaining bolts and the caliper, **Figs. 6 through 9.**
5. Reverse procedure to install noting the following:
   a. Refer to **Figs. 6 through 9,** for tightening values.
   b. After completing installation, bleed hydraulic system.

OVERHAUL

FRONT

Forester & Impreza

1. Remove caliper assembly as outlined.
2. Using a flathead screwdriver, remove boot ring from piston.
3. Place a wooden block between piston and caliper flange to prevent damage to caliper piston.
4. Gradually supply compressed air to caliper body to equally force pistons out of caliper.
5. Remove piston seal from caliper body, **Figs. 1 and 2,**

6. Remove locking sleeve and boot, then the guide pin boot from caliper body.
7. Reverse procedure to install, coating piston seal and inner surface of cylinder with brake fluid.

Legacy

1. Remove caliper as outlined.
2. Remove sleeve and the locking boot, **Fig. 4.**
3. Remove boot ring and piston boot.
4. Position a block of wood between piston bore and caliper ears, then remove piston from piston bore by gradually applying compressed air to brake fluid inlet port.
5. Remove piston seal. Use caution not to damage inner wall of cylinder.
6. Remove guide pin boot from caliper.
7. Reverse procedure to install.

SVX

1. Remove caliper assembly as outlined.
2. Place a wooden block between piston and caliper flange to prevent damage to caliper piston.
3. Gradually supply compressed air to

caliper body to equally force pistons out of caliper.
4. Remove piston boot and seal from caliper body, **Fig. 5.**
5. Remove locking sleeve and boot then guide pin boot from caliper body.
6. Reverse procedure to install, coating piston seal and inner surface of cylinder with brake fluid.

REAR

1. Remove caliper as outlined under "Caliper, Replace."
2. Position a block of wood between piston bore and caliper ears, then remove piston from piston bore by gradually applying compressed air to brake fluid inlet port, **Figs. 6 through 9.**
3. Remove piston boot and seal.
4. Reverse procedure to install.

HILL HOLDER SERVICE

Refer to "Rear Axle & Suspension" section in this chapter for Hill Holder service information.

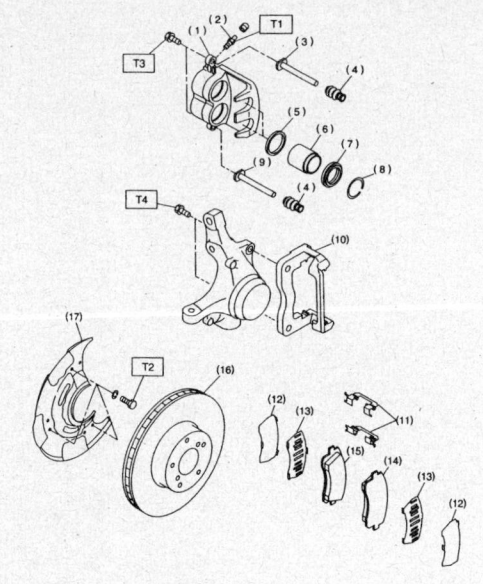

(1) Caliper body
(2) Air bleeder screw
(3) Guide pin (Green)
(4) Pin boot
(5) Piston seal
(6) Piston
(7) Piston boot
(8) Boot ring
(9) Lock pin (Yellow)
(10) Support
(11) Pad clip
(12) Outer shim
(13) Inner shim
(14) Pad (Outside)
(15) Pad (Inside)
(16) Disc rotor
(17) Disc cover

Tightening torque: N·m (kg-m, ft-lb)
T1: 8 ± 1 (0.8 ± 0.1, 5.8 ± 0.7)
T2: 18 ± 5 (1.8 ± 0.5, 13.0 ± 3.6)
T3: 37 ± 5 (3.8 ± 0.5, 27.5 ± 3.6)
T4: 78 ± 10 (8.0 ± 1.0, 58 ± 7)

SB4079800013000X

Fig. 3   Exploded view of front disc brake assembly. Forester & 1998-99 Impreza w/2.5L engine

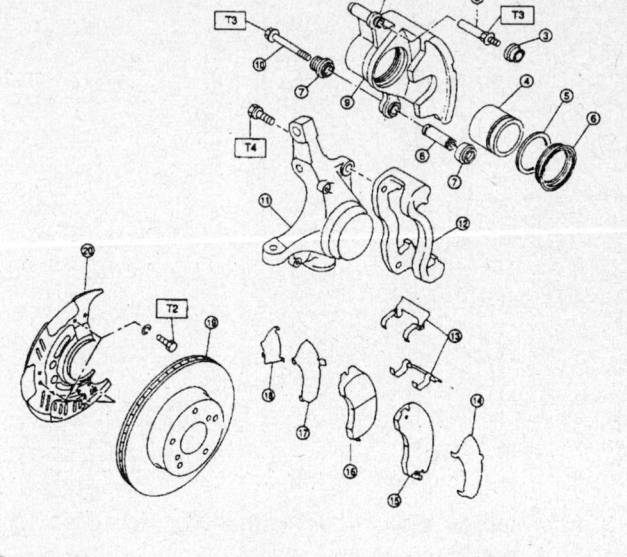

① Air bleeder screw
② Guide pin
③ Guide pin boot
④ Piston
⑤ Piston seal
⑥ Piston boot
⑦ Lock pin boot
⑧ Lock pin sleeve
⑨ Caliper body
⑩ Lock pin
⑪ Housing
⑫ Support
⑬ Pad clip
⑭ Outer shim
⑮ Outer pad
⑯ Inner pad
⑰ Inner shim
⑱ Shim
⑲ Disc rotor
⑳ Disc cover

Tightening torque: N·m (kg-m, ft-lb)
T1: 8 ± 1 (0.8 ± 0.1, 5.8 ± 0.7)
T2: 18 ± 5 (1.8 ± 0.5, 13.0 ± 3.6)
T3: 39 ± 5 (4 ± 0.5, 28.9 ± 3.6)
T4: 78 ± 10 (8.0 ± 1.0, 58 ± 7)

SB4079500010000X

Fig. 4   Exploded view of front disc brake assembly. Legacy

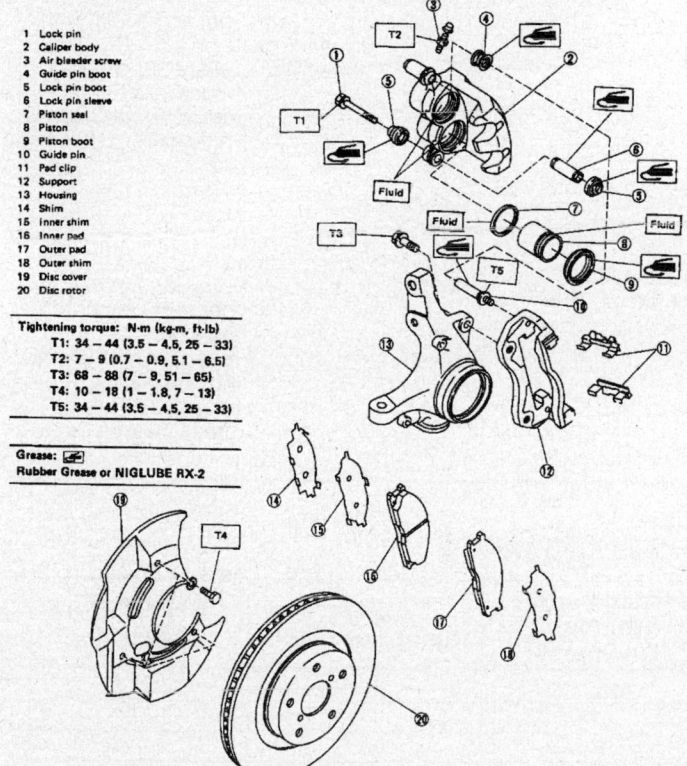

1 Lock pin
2 Caliper body
3 Air bleeder screw
4 Guide pin boot
5 Lock pin boot
6 Lock pin sleeve
7 Piston seal
8 Piston
9 Piston boot
10 Guide pin
11 Pad clip
12 Support
13 Housing
14 Shim
15 Inner shim
16 Inner pad
17 Outer pad
18 Outer shim
19 Disc cover
20 Disc rotor

Tightening torque: N·m (kg-m, ft-lb)
T1: 34 – 44 (3.5 – 4.5, 25 – 33)
T2: 7 – 9 (0.7 – 0.9, 5.1 – 6.5)
T3: 68 – 88 (7 – 9, 51 – 65)
T4: 10 – 18 (1 – 1.8, 7 – 13)
T5: 34 – 44 (3.5 – 4.5, 25 – 33)

Grease:
Rubber Grease or NIGLUBE RX-2

SB4079100005000X

Fig. 5   Exploded view of front disc brake assembly. SVX

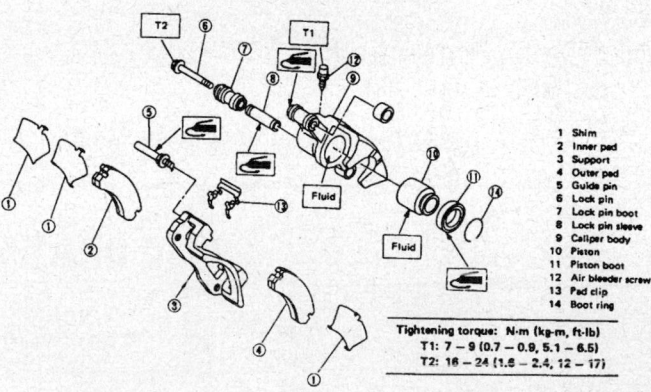

1 Shim
2 Inner pad
3 Support
4 Outer pad
5 Guide pin
6 Lock pin
7 Lock pin boot
8 Lock pin sleeve
9 Caliper body
10 Piston
11 Piston boot
12 Air bleeder screw
13 Pad clip
14 Boot ring

Tightening torque: N·m (kg-m, ft-lb)
T1: 7 – 9 (0.7 – 0.9, 5.1 – 6.5)
T2: 16 – 24 (1.6 – 2.4, 12 – 17)

SB4079100008000X

Fig. 6   Rear disc brake assembly. Impreza

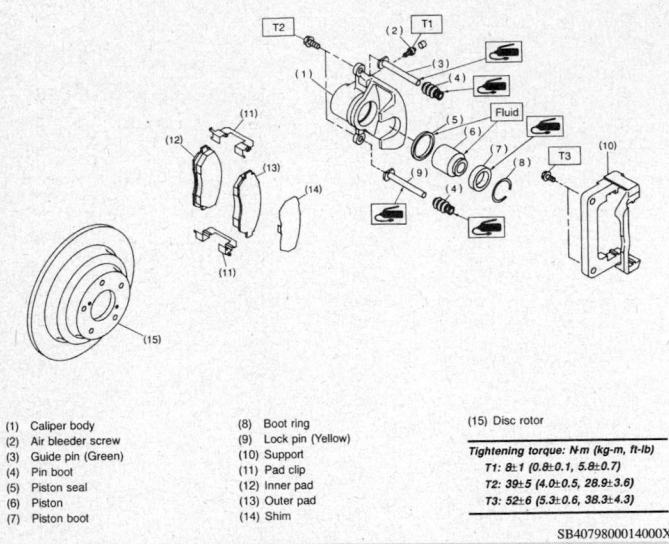

(1) Caliper body
(2) Air bleeder screw
(3) Guide pin (Green)
(4) Pin boot
(5) Piston seal
(6) Piston
(7) Piston boot

(8) Boot ring
(9) Lock pin (Yellow)
(10) Support
(11) Pad clip
(12) Inner pad
(13) Outer pad
(14) Shim

(15) Disc rotor

Tightening torque: N·m (kg-m, ft-lb)
T1: 8±1 (0.8±0.1, 5.8±0.7)
T2: 39±5 (4.0±0.5, 28.9±3.6)
T3: 52±6 (5.3±0.6, 38.3±4.3)

SB4079800014000X

Fig. 7 Rear disk brake assembly. Forester

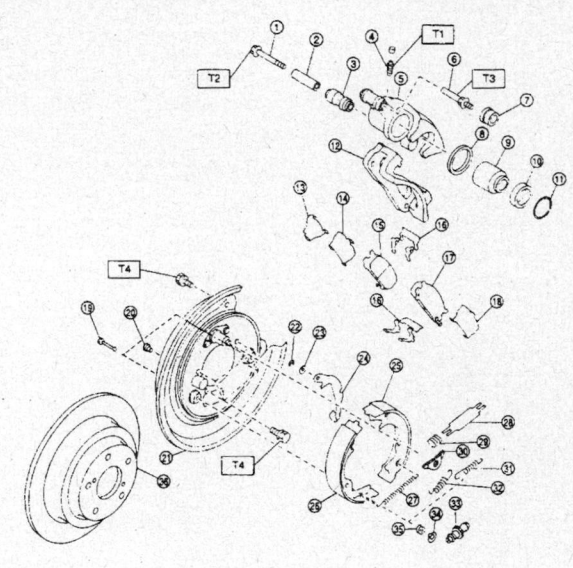

SB4079500011000X

① Lock pin
② Lock pin sleeve
③ Lock pin boot
④ Air bleeder screw
⑤ Caliper body
⑥ Guide pin
⑦ Guide pin boot
⑧ Piston seal
⑨ Piston
⑩ Piston boot
⑪ Boot ring
⑫ Support
⑬ Shim
⑭ Inner shim
⑮ Inner pad

⑯ Pad clip
⑰ Outer pad
⑱ Outer shim
⑲ Shoe hold-down pin
⑳ Cover
㉑ Back plate
㉒ Retainer
㉓ Spring washer
㉔ Parking brake lever
㉕ Parking brake shoe (Secondary)
㉖ Parking brake shoe (Primary)
㉗ Adjusting spring
㉘ Strut

㉙ Strut shoe spring
㉚ Shoe guide plate
㉛ Secondary shoe return spring
㉜ Primary shoe return spring
㉝ Adjuster
㉞ Shoe hold-down cup
㉟ Shoe hold-down spring
㉴ Disc rotor

Tightening torque: N·m (kg-m, ft-lb)
T1: 8 ± 1 (0.8 ± 0.1, 5.8 ± 0.7)
T2: 20 ± 4 (2.0 ± 0.4, 14.5 ± 2.9)
T3: 26 ± 5 (2.7 ± 0.5, 19.5 ± 3.6)
T4: 52 ± 6 (5.3 ± 0.6, 38.3 ± 4.3)

Fig. 8 Rear disc brake assembly. Legacy

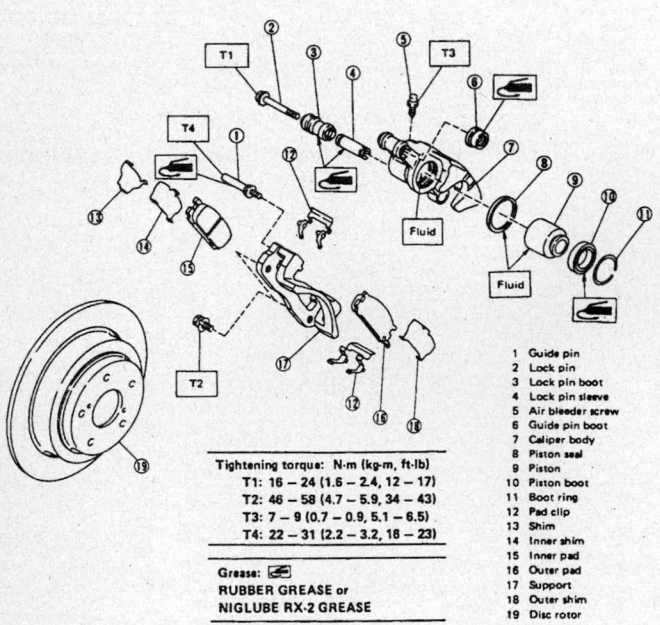

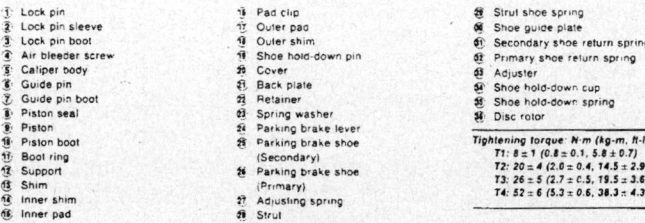

Tightening torque: N·m (kg-m, ft-lb)
T1: 16 – 24 (1.6 – 2.4, 12 – 17)
T2: 46 – 58 (4.7 – 5.9, 34 – 43)
T3: 7 – 9 (0.7 – 0.9, 5.1 – 6.5)
T4: 22 – 31 (2.2 – 3.2, 16 – 23)

Grease:
RUBBER GREASE or
NIGLUBE RX-2 GREASE

1 Guide pin
2 Lock pin
3 Lock pin boot
4 Lock pin sleeve
5 Air bleeder screw
6 Guide pin boot
7 Caliper body
8 Piston seal
9 Piston
10 Piston boot
11 Boot ring
12 Pad clip
13 Shim
14 Inner shim
15 Inner pad
16 Outer pad
17 Support
18 Outer shim
19 Disc rotor

SB4079100009000X

Fig. 9 Rear disc brake assembly. SVX

DISC BRAKE SPECIFICATIONS

Model	Year	Nominal Thickness	Minimum Refinish Thickness	Lateral Runabout (T.I.R.)	Caliper Bore Diva. (Inch)
FRONT					
Forester	1998–99	.945	.870	.0030	—
Impreza AWD	1996–99	.945	.870	.0030	—
Impreza L & L+ FWD	1996–99	.710	.630	.0030	—
Impreza LS FWD	1996–99	.945	.870	.0030	—
Legacy	1996–99	.945	.870	.0039	①
SVX	1996–97	1.100	1.020	.0039	
REAR					
Forester	1998–99	.394	.335	.0039	—

Continued

DISC BRAKE SPECIFICATIONS—Continued

Model	Year	Nominal Thickness	Minimum Refinish Thickness	Lateral Runabout (T.I.R.)	Caliper Bore Diva. (Inch)
REAR					
Impreza AWD	1996–99	.394	.335	.0039	—
Impreza LS FWD	1996–99	.390	.335	.0039	1.3752
Legacy	1996–99	.390	.335	.0039	②
SVX	1996–97	.390	.335	.0039	—

① — Nonjuror sedan & station wagon, 2.252 inches; Turbot sedan, .976 inch.

② — Nonjuror sedan & station wagon, 1.500 inches; Turbot sedan, 1.374 inches.

TIGHTENING SPECIFICATIONS

Year	Component	Torque/ Ft. Lbs.
FRONT		
1996-99	Air Bleeder Screw	60–72③
	Caliper Locking	25–30
	Caliper Support To Steering Knuckle	51–65
	Front Disc Cover	4–10
	Guide Pin	33–40
	Wheel Lug Nuts	58–72
REAR		
1996-99	Air Bleeder Screws	60–72③
	Caliper Body Retaining Bolts	①
	Caliper Support	34–43
	Guide Pin	16–23②
	Wheel Lug Nuts	58–72

① — Impreza & SVX; 16–23 ft. lbs., Legacy; 12–17 ft. lbs.

② — Legacy & SVX.

③ — Inch lbs.

Drum Brakes

INDEX

BRAKE SERVICE

FORESTER, IMPREZA & LEGACY

1. Raise and support vehicle, then remove rear wheels.
2. Remove brake drum. If difficult to remove brake drum, remove adjusting hole cover from back plate, then turn adjusting screw until shoe separate from drum.
3. Remove hold-down pin and cup.
4. Disconnect lower shoe return spring from shoes.
5. Remove shoes one by one from back plate with adjuster.
6. Reverse procedure to install. Refer to **Fig. 1,** for tightening specifications.

ADJUSTMENTS

PARKING BRAKE

Legacy

1. Pull parking brake lever three to five times. Mechanism should click six to seven times when a force of 55 lbs. is exerted on the lever.
2. If lever operation is not as specified, adjust lever stroke by turning adjuster nut, **Fig. 2.**
3. After adjustment procedure is complete, tighten adjuster lockout to specification.

Forester & Impreza

1. Pull parking brake lever with a force of approximately 44 lbs. Lever should click 7–8 notches.
2. If lever operation is not as specified, adjust lever stroke by turning adjuster

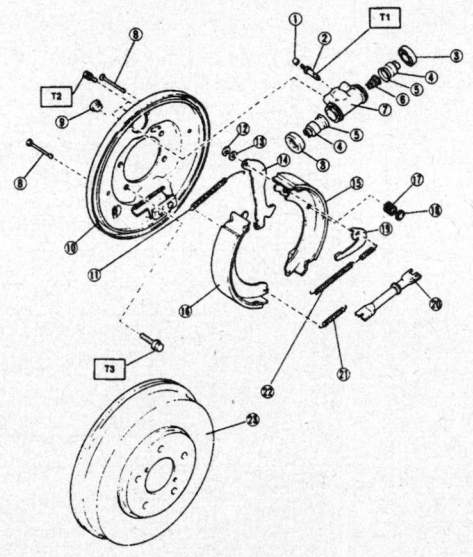

① Air bleeder cap	⑪ Upper shoe return spring	㉑ Lower shoe return spring
② Air bleeder screw	⑫ Retainer	㉒ Adjuster spring
③ Boot	⑬ Washer	㉓ Drum
④ Piston	⑭ Parking brake lever	
⑤ Cup	⑮ Brake shoe (Trailing)	**Tightening torque: N·m (kg-m, R-lb)**
⑥ Spring	⑯ Brake shoe (Leading)	T1: 8 ± 1 (0.8 ± 0.1, 5.8 ± 0.7)
⑦ Wheel cylinder body	⑰ Shoe hold down spring	T2: 10 ± 2 (1.0 ± 0.2, 7.2 ± 1.4)
⑧ Pin	⑱ Cup	T3: 52 ± 6 (5.3 ± 0.6, 38.3 ± 4.3)
⑨ Plug	⑲ Adjuster lever	
⑩ Back plate	⑳ Adjuster	

SB4089100003000X

Fig. 1 Exploded view of drum brake assembly. Forester, Impreza & Legacy

nut, **Fig. 2,** until parking brake lever stroke is set to specifications.
3. After adjustment procedure is complete, tighten adjuster lockout to specification.

DRUM BRAKE

On Impreza models, brake shoe clearances are automatically adjusted by pumping brake pedal several times as required.

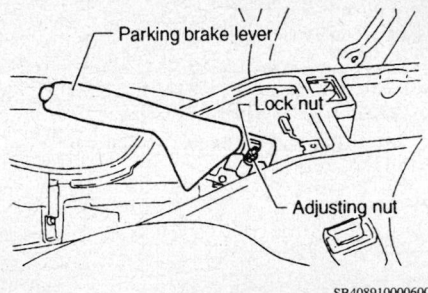

SB4089100006000X

Fig. 2 Parking brake adjustment. Forester & Impreza

DRUM BRAKE SPECIFICATIONS

Year	Model	Brake Drum Inside Dia. Inch	Maximum Refinish Dia. Inch
1996–99	Forester, Impreza & Legacy	9.0	9.079

TIGHTENING SPECIFICATIONS

Year	Component	Torque/Ft. Lbs.
FORESTER, IMPREZA & LEGACY		
1996–99	Air Bleeder Screw	60–72①
	Adjuster Nut	9–11
	Backing Plate Nuts	34–41
	Wheel Cylinder Nuts	72–108①
	Wheel Lug Nuts	58–72

① — Inch lbs.

Hydraulic Brake Systems

INDEX

DESCRIPTION

MASTER CYLINDER

The master cylinder is of the tandem type design and incorporates a fast fill valve in order to improve the feeling on braking. It has a dual design which consists of a primary and a secondary brake system. If one brake system becomes inoperative, the other line will provide braking action. The master cylinder is designed into a "pierce" form so that the rear section is inserted into the brake booster.

DUAL PROPORTIONING VALVE (DPV)

The dual proportioning valve is incorporated as a rear wheel hydraulic pressure control system for the diagonal braking configuration. During hard braking, the DPV prevents rear wheel locking by lowering the fluid pressure in the rear wheel cylinder lower than that of the in the front cylinder.

TROUBLESHOOTING

Refer to **Fig. 1,** when troubleshooting the hydraulic braking system.

COMPONENT REPLACEMENT

MASTER CYLINDER

1. Disconnect brake lines from master cylinder and plug the ends.
2. If applicable, disconnect fluid warning switch electrical connector.
3. Remove master cylinder retaining nuts and the master cylinder.
4. Reverse procedure to install.
5. Bleed hydraulic system after completing installation.

DUAL PROPORTIONING VALVE

Inspect brake line connections at DPV for fluid leakage. If leakage is found tighten lines or replace DPV.

1. Disconnect brake line flare nuts at all connections from DPV.
2. Remove retaining bolt, then DPV from vehicle. **Do not disassemble or adjust valve. The valve must be replaced as a unit.**
3. Reverse procedure to install, noting the following:
   a. **Torque** retaining bolt to 3–5 ft. lbs.
   b. **Torque** flare nuts to 11–14 ft. lbs.

COMPONENT SERVICE

MASTER CYLINDER

1. Remove master cylinder from vehicle.
2. **On 1996 models equipped with ABS,** remove secondary piston stopper screw with screwdriver, **Fig. 2.**
3. **On all models equipped with ABS,** remove cylinder pin, **Fig. 3.**
4. **On all models,** push piston inward, then remove snap ring.
5. Apply pressure to piston assembly while Inserting a small screwdriver into window of piston retainer and raise piston retainer latch, **Fig. 4.**
6. Remove primary and secondary piston assemblies. **Do not disassemble pistons. if disassembled, the spring settings will change.**
7. Inspect master cylinder inside diameter to piston clearance, Service limit is not to exceed 0.043 inch.
8. Clean all parts with clean brake fluid, **do not use part cleaning fluid or seals will swell.**
9. Coat master cylinder inner walls with clean brake fluid, then install secondary piston assembly from repair kit part No. 725771240.
10. Install primary piston, then press piston into bore approximately 0.39 inch.
11. Install piston stopper screw and gasket

Trouble and possible cause	Corrective action
1 Insufficient braking	
(1) Oil leakage from the hydraulic mechanism	Repair or replace (cup, piston, cylinder, pipe or hose)
(2) Entry of air into the hydraulic mechanism	Bleed
(3) Excessively wide shoe clearance	Adjust the clearance
(4) Wear, deteriorated surface material, adhering water or oil on the lining	Replace, grind or clean
(5) Improper operation of master cylinder, wheel cylinder, disc caliper, brake booster or check valve	Correct or replace
2 Unstable or uneven braking	
(1) Oil on the lining drum or rotor	Eliminate cause of oil leakage, clean, or replace
(2) Drum or rotor eccentricity	Correct or replace the drum or rotor
(3) Worn brake drum, or damage to the drum caused by sand	Correct by grinding, or replace
(4) Improper lining contact, deteriorated surface material, improper interior material, or wear	Correct by grinding, or replace
(5) Deformed backing plate	Correct or replace
(6) Improper tire inflation	Inflate to correct pressure
(7) Disordered wheel alignment	Adjust alignment
(8) Loosened backing plate or support installing bolts	Retighten
(9) Loosened rear wheel bearing	Retighten to normal tightening torque or replace
(10) Trouble in the hydraulic system	Replace the cylinder, brake pipe or hose
(11) Uneven effect of the hand brake	Check, adjust, or replace the rear brake and cable system
3 Excessive pedal stroke	
(1) Entry of air into the hydraulic mechanism	Bleed
(2) Excessive play in the master cylinder push rod	Adjust
(3) Oil leakage from the hydraulic mechanism	Repair or replace (cup, piston, cylinder, pipe or hose).
(4) Improperly adjusted shoe clearance	Adjust
(5) Improper lining contact or worn lining	Correct or replace
4 Brake dragging or improper brake return	
(1) Insufficient pedal play	Adjust play
(2) Improper master cylinder push rod return	Clean or replace the cylinder
(3) Clogged hydraulic system	Replace
(4) Improper return or adjustment of hand brake	Correct or adjust
(5) Weakened spring tension or breakage of shoe return spring	Replace the spring
(6) Excessively narrow shoe clearance	Adjust the clearance
(7) Improper wheel cylinder operation	Correct or replace

SB4099100001010X

Fig. 1 Hydraulic brake system troubleshooting chart (Part 1 of 2)

Trouble and possible cause	Corrective action
5 Brake noise (1) (creak sound)	
(1) Hardened or deteriorated lining	Replace the shoe ASSY or pad.
(2) Worn lining	Replace the shoe ASSY or pad.
(3) Loosened backing plate or support installing bolts	Retighten
(4) Loose rear wheel bearing	Retighten to normal tightening torque.
(5) Dirty drum or rotor	Clean the drum or rotor, or clean and replace the brake ASSY
6 Brake noise (2) (hissing sound)	
(1) Worn lining	Replace the shoe ASSY or pad.
(2) Improperly installed shoe or pad	Correct or replace the shoe ASSY or pad
(3) Loose or bent drum or rotor	Retighten or replace.
7 Brake noise (3) (click sound)	
In the case of the front brake	
(1) Excessively worn pad or support	Replace the pad or the support
In the case of the rear brake	
(1) Excessively worn shoe ridge	Replace the backing plate
(2) Excessively worn wheel cylinder piston	Replace the wheel cylinder ASSY
(3) Lack of oil on the shoe ridge surface anchor	Add more grease.

SB4099100001020X

Fig. 1 Hydraulic brake system troubleshooting chart (Part 2 of 2)

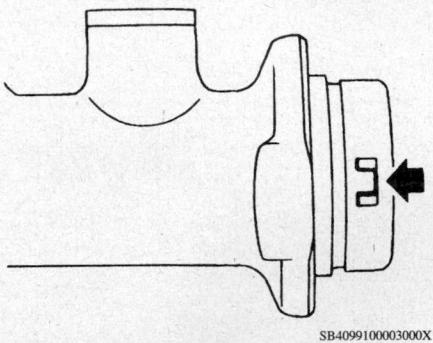

SB4099100003000X

Fig. 4 Removal of piston retainer

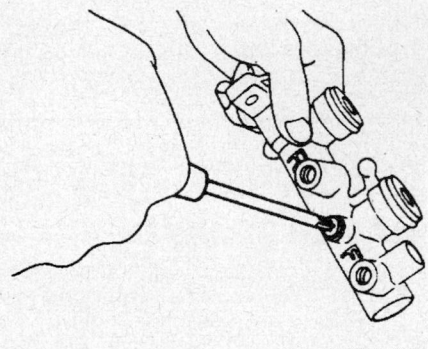

SB4099100002000X

Fig. 2 Secondary piston stopper screw location

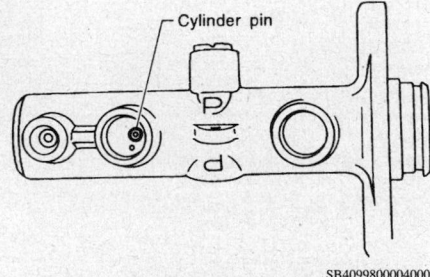

Cylinder pin

SB4099800004000X

Fig. 3 Cylinder pin location. Forester, Impreza & Legacy w/ABS

assembly, then **torque** to 5–6.5 ft. lbs.
12. Apply pressure to primary piston, then install snap ring.
13. Install retainer **Fig. 4.** Ensure retainer latch is securely engaged with master cylinder groove.
14. Install master cylinder in vehicle, then bleed brake system.

BRAKE SYSTEM BLEED

1. Ensure there are no fluid leaks from joints or connections.
2. When bleeding brakes, bleed brakes connected to the secondary chamber of the master cylinder, then bleed brakes connected to the primary chamber of the master cylinder.
3. Fit one end of vinyl tube into air bleeder and put the other end into a brake fluid container.
4. Slowly depress brake pedal and keep it depressed, then slowly open air bleeder to discharge air together with brake fluid. Keep brake bleeder open for approximately 1–2 seconds.
5. Close bleeder and slowly release brake pedal.
6. Repeat steps 4 and 5 until there are no more air bubbles in the vinyl tube.
7. Repeat steps 3, 4 and 5 at each wheel.

Power Brake Units

NOTE: On Models Equipped With Anti-Lock Brakes, Refer To "Anti-Lock Brakes" Section.

INDEX

DESCRIPTION

The brake booster is located inline between the master cylinder and the brake pedal. It serves to mechanically boost the force pushing the pistons of the master cylinder.

The brake booster consists of a power cylinder section and a power piston section. The power cylinder is made up of a front shell, rear shell and a diaphragm. The front and rear shells are connected with the diaphragm placed in between the two. The power cylinder chamber is closed to the atmosphere and the left and right chambers of the diaphragm are kept sealed.

The power piston is guided by a tube which slides along the rear shell. A pushrod, which is used to move the primary piston of the master cylinder, is attached to the left of the power piston. The right end of the pushrod closely contacts the rubber reaction disc built into the power piston.

The valve plunger is clinched by the operating pushrod and is pushed against the right wall of the power piston chamber by the valve return spring. The check valve maintains a constant level of vacuum pressure within the brake booster that utilizes the intake manifold vacuum pressure for power.

DIAGNOSIS & TESTING

Perform this procedure with the parking brakes applied.
1. Start engine, then stop after one or two minutes of running time.
2. Depress brake pedal several times with normal force.
3. If pedal travel decreases the more times the brake pedal is depressed, the brake booster and vacuum lines are functioning correctly.
4. If pedal travel does not decrease and remains firm, check brake booster vacuum hose and check valve for proper operation.
5. If vacuum hose and check valve are functioning properly, replace vacuum booster assembly.

POWER BRAKE UNIT SERVICE

BRAKE BOOSTER, REPLACE

Forester, Impreza & Legacy

1. Disconnect brake fluid level indicator connector, if equipped.
2. Remove master cylinder assembly.
3. Disconnect vacuum hose from brake booster.
4. Working from inside the passenger compartment, remove snap pin and operating rod clevis pin from brake pedal assembly.
5. Remove brake booster retaining nuts, then brake booster from vehicle.
6. Reverse procedure to install. **Torque** brake booster retaining nuts to 9–17 ft. lbs.

SVX

1. Raise and support vehicle and remove front stabilizer bar.
2. Drain approximately 1 quart of transmission fluid and loosen ATF level guide pipe bolts.
3. Remove cruise control actuator.
4. Disconnect positive terminal from starter motor.
5. Disconnect low-pressure AC pipe.
6. Disconnect vacuum hose from booster and remove master cylinder as outlined in "Hydraulic Brake System."
7. Remove snap pin, clevis pin and four brake booster to pedal bracket nuts, then the booster.
8. Reverse procedure to install.

OVERHAUL

The brake booster is not serviceable and must be replaced as an assembly.

Anti-Lock Brakes

TABLE OF CONTENTS

Forester

NOTE: On Air Bag Equipped Models, Refer To "Air Bag System Precautions" Located In The Front Of This Manual For System Disarming & Arming Procedures.

NOTE: Electrical Symbol & Wire Color Code Identification Located In The Front Of This Manual May Be Used As An Aid When Using Wiring Circuits Found In This Section.

INDEX

PRECAUTIONS

AIR BAG SYSTEMS

Refer to "Air Bag System Precautions" in the front of this manual for system disarming and arming procedures.

BATTERY GROUND CABLE

Prior to service, disconnect battery ground cable and isolate as required.

DESCRIPTION

The ABS 5.3i type incorporates a hydraulic control unit, ABS control module, valve relay and motor relay in one unit. The ABS system electronically controls brake fluid pressure to prevent wheel lockup during braking on slippery road surfaces.

If the ABS becomes inoperative, the fail safe system activate to ensure conventional brake system operation. A warning light illuminates to indicate the malfunction.

The front and rear wheels utilize a 4 sensor, 4 channel control design. The front wheels have an independent control design and the rear wheels have a select low control design.

TROUBLESHOOTING

Refer to **Fig. 1,** for troubleshooting procedures.

PRELIMINARY INSPECTION

1. Ensure battery voltage is 12 volts or more.
2. Ensure specific gravity of battery is 1.260.
3. Check condition of main and other fuses, harnesses and connector. Also check for proper grounding.
4. Check brake fluid level and for leakage.
5. Check for brake drag, brake pad and rotor condition.
6. Ensure tires are in good condition and at specified air pressure.

DIAGNOSIS & TESTING

ACCESSING DIAGNOSTIC TROUBLE CODES

Less Select Monitor

When on board diagnosis of the ABS control module detects a problem, the information (up to a maximum of three) will be stored in the EEP ROM as a diagnostic trouble code (DTC). When there are more than three, the most recent three will be stored. Stored codes will stay in memory until they are cleared.

1. Remove ABS diagnostic connector from side of driver's heater unit, **Fig. 2.**
2. Turn ignition switch to Off position.
3. Connect diagnosis connector terminal No. 6 to terminal No. 3.
4. Turn ignition switch to On position.
5. ABS warning light is set to the diagnostic mode and blinks to identify trouble codes.
6. After start code is displayed (11), trouble codes will be shown in order of last information first. Codes will repeat for a maximum of five minutes.
7. If there are no trouble codes in memory, code 11 will be the only code to appear.

With Select Monitor

Access the ABS system diagnostic trouble codes according to the tool manufacturers instructions.

Fig. 1 Troubleshooting chart

Symptom		Probable faulty units/parts
Vehicle instability during braking	Vehicle pulls to either side.	• ABSCM&H/U (solenoid valve) • ABS sensor • Brake (caliper & piston, pads) • Wheel alignment • Tire specifications, tire wear and air pressures • Incorrect wiring or piping connections • Road surface (uneven, camber)
	Vehicle spins.	• ABSCM&H/U (solenoid valve) • ABS sensor • Brake (pads) • Tire specifications, tire wear and air pressures • Incorrect wiring or piping connections
Poor braking	Long braking/stopping distance	• ABSCM&H/U (solenoid valve) • Brake (pads) • Air in brake line • Tire specifications, tire wear and air pressures • Incorrect wiring or piping connections
	Wheel locks.	• ABSCM&H/U (solenoid valve, motor) • ABS sensor • Incorrect wiring or piping connections
	Brake dragging	• ABSCM&H/U (solenoid valve) • ABS sensor • Master cylinder • Brake (caliper & piston) • Parking brake • Axle & wheels • Brake pedal play
	Long brake pedal stroke	• Air in brake line • Brake pedal play
	Vehicle pitching	• Suspension play or fatigue (reduced damping) • Incorrect wiring or piping connections • Road surface (uneven)
	Unstable or uneven braking	• ABSCM&H/U (solenoid valve) • ABS sensor • Brake (caliper & piston, pads) • Tire specifications, tire wear and air pressures • Incorrect wiring or piping connections • Road surface (uneven)
Vibration and/or noise (while driving on slippery roads)	Excessive pedal vibration	• Incorrect wiring or piping connections • Road surface (uneven)
	Noise from ABSCM&H/U	• ABSCM&H/U (mount bushing) • ABS sensor • Brake piping
	Noise from front of vehicle	• ABSCM & H/U (mount bushing) • ABS sensor • Master cylinder • Brake (caliper & piston, pads, rotor) • Brake piping • Brake booster & check valve • Suspension play or fatigue
	Noise from rear of vehicle	• ABS sensor • Brake (caliper & piston, pads, rotor) • Parking brake • Brake piping • Suspension play or fatigue

SB4029800191000X

Fig. 3 Diagnostic trouble code interpretation

Trouble code	Contents of diagnosis	
11	Start code • Trouble code is shown after start code. • Only start code is shown in normal condition.	
21	Abnormal ABS sensor (Open circuit or input voltage too high)	Front right ABS sensor
23		Front left ABS sensor
25		Rear right ABS sensor
27		Rear left ABS sensor
22	Abnormal ABS sensor (Abnormal ABS sensor signal)	Front right ABS sensor
24		Front left ABS sensor
26		Rear right ABS sensor
28		Rear left ABS sensor
29		Any one of four
31	Abnormal solenoid valve circuit(s) in ABS control module and hydraulic unit	Front right inlet valve
32		Front right outlet valve
33		Front left inlet valve
34		Front left outlet valve
35		Rear right inlet valve
36		Rear right outlet valve
37		Rear left inlet valve
38		Rear left outlet valve
41	Abnormal ABS control module	
42	Source voltage is abnormal.	
44	A combination of AT control abnormal	
51	Abnormal valve relay	
52	Abnormal motor and/or motor relay	
54	Abnormal stop light switch	
56	Abnormal G sensor output voltage	

SB4029800192000X

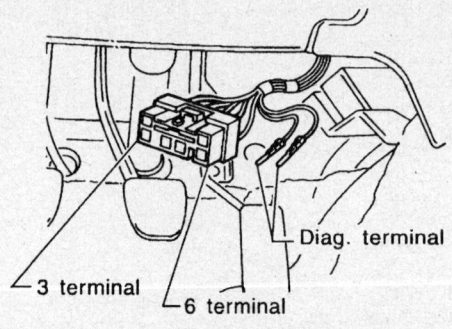

Fig. 2 Check connector terminal identification

SB4039800238000X

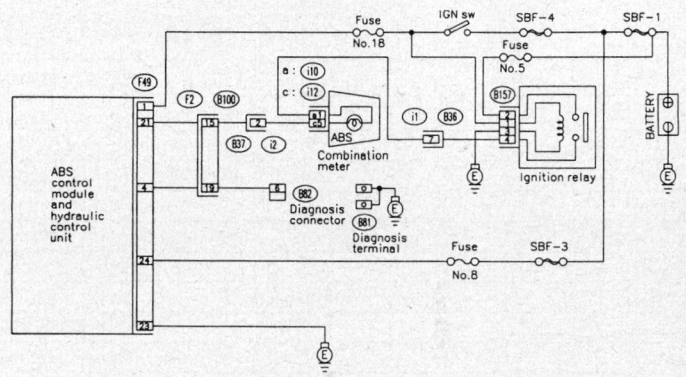

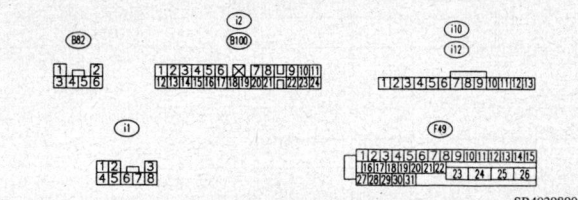

Fig. 4 ABS wiring diagram

SB4029800193000X

DIAGNOSTIC TROUBLE CODE INTERPRETATION

Refer to **Fig. 3,** for trouble code interpretation and identification.

WIRING DIAGRAM

Refer to **Fig. 4,** for ABS wiring diagram.

DIAGNOSTIC TESTS

Less Select Monitor

Refer to **Figs. 5 through 19,** for diagnostic tests.

With Select Monitor

Refer to **Figs. 20 through 41,** for diagnostic tests.

CLEARING DIAGNOSTIC TROUBLE CODES

1. Remove diagnosis connector from side of driver heater unit, **Fig. 42.**
2. Disconnect diagnosis connector terminal No. 6 from connector.
3. Connect and disconnect terminal 3 times within 12 seconds allowing at least a .2 second interval each time.
4. Ensure all codes are erased and that only code 11 (start code) remains in memory.

COMPONENT TESTING

Wheel Sensor

Remove wheel sensor as outlined under "Component Replacement." Measure resistance between terminals with a suitable volt ohm meter. resistance should be .8–1.2 Kohms. If sensor is not as specified, replace sensor.

G Sensor

1. Remove sensor as outlined in "Component Replcement."

2. Connect connector to G sensor and turn ignition switch to On position.
3. With sensor in horizontal position, **Fig. 44,** voltage should be 2.2–2.5 volts between terminal No. 2 and terminal No. 3, **Fig. 43.**
4. With sensor inclined forwards 90°, **Fig. 45,** voltage should measure 3.7–4.1 volts.
5. With sensor inclined backwards 90°, **Fig. 46,** voltage should measure .5–.9 volts.
6. If any voltage measurement is not as specified, replace G sensor.

Hydraulic Unit ABS Operation

1. Raise and support vehicle, then remove wheels.
2. Remove air bleeder screws from left and right front calipers.
3. Connect suitable pressure gauges to calipers and bleed air from gauges.
4. Start ABS sequence control as follows:
   a. Connect terminal No. 3 and terminal No. 6 of the diagnosis connector, **Fig. 42.**
   b. Set speed of all four wheels at 2 mph.
   c. Turn ignition switch to Off position.
   d. Within five seconds after ABS warning light goes out, depress brake pedal and hold it, turn ignition switch to On position and release pedal.
   e. Pedal must not be depressed when ignition switch is On, do not operate engine.
   f. After completion of ABS sequence, turn ignition switch to Off position.
5. When hydraulic unit begins to work, read values indicated on pressure gauges and compare with values specified, **Fig. 47.**
6. Repeat procedure for rear calipers, compare readings with **Fig. 47.**

DIAGNOSTIC CHART INDEX

Test	Description	Page No.	Fig. No.
LESS SELECT MONITOR			
Test A	ABS Warning Light Does Not Come On	41-148	5
Test B	ABS Warning Light Does Not Go Off	41-148	6
Test C	Trouble Code Does Not Appear	41-149	7
Code 21	Abnormal ABS Sensor, Open Circuit Or Input Voltage Too High	41-149	8
Code 22	Abnormal ABS Sensor Signal	41-151	9
Code 23	Abnormal ABS Sensor, Open Circuit Or Input Voltage Too High	41-149	8
Code 24	Abnormal ABS Sensor Signal	41-151	9
Code 25	Abnormal ABS Sensor, Open Circuit Or Input Voltage Too High	41-149	8
Code 26	Abnormal ABS Sensor Signal	41-151	9
Code 27	Abnormal ABS Sensor, Open Circuit Or Input Voltage Too High	41-149	8
Code 28	Abnormal ABS Sensor Signal	41-151	9
Code 29	Abnormal ABS Sensor Signal, Any One Of Four	41-152	10
Code 31	Abnormal Inlet Solenoid Valve Circuits In ABSCM & H/U	41-152	11
Code 32	Abnormal Outlet Solenoid Valve Circuits In ABSCM & H/U	41-153	12
Code 33	Abnormal Inlet Solenoid Valve Circuits In ABSCM & H/U	41-152	11
Code 34	Abnormal Outlet Solenoid Valve Circuits In ABSCM & H/U	41-153	12
Code 35	Abnormal Inlet Solenoid Valve Circuits In ABSCM & H/U	41-152	11
Code 36	Abnormal Outlet Solenoid Valve Circuits In ABSCM & H/U	41-153	12
Code 37	Abnormal Inlet Solenoid Valve Circuits In ABSCM & H/U	41-152	11
Code 38	Abnormal Outlet Solenoid Valve Circuits In ABSCM & H/U	41-153	12
Code 41	Abnormal ABS Control Module	41-153	13
Code 42	Source Voltage Is Abnormal	41-153	14
Code 44	A Combination Of AT Control Abnormal	41-154	15
Code 51	Abnormal Valve Relay	41-154	16
Code 52	Abnormal Motor And/Or Motor Relay	41-155	17
Code 54	Abnormal Stop Light Switch	41-155	18
Code 56	Abnormal G Sensor Output Voltage	41-156	19
WITH SELECT MONITOR			
Test C	Communication For Initializing Impossible	41-157	20
Test D	No Trouble Code	41-157	21
Code 21	Abnormal ABS Sensor, Open Or Short Circuit In ABS Sensor	41-158	22
Code 22	ABS Sensor Abnormal Signal	41-160	23
Code 23	Abnormal ABS Sensor, Open Or Short Circuit In ABS Sensor	41-158	22
Code 24	ABS Sensor Abnormal Signal	41-160	23
Code 25	Abnormal ABS Sensor, Open Or Short Circuit In ABS Sensor	41-158	22
Code 26	ABS Sensor Abnormal Signal	41-160	23
Code 27	Abnormal ABS Sensor, Open Or Short Circuit In ABS Sensor	41-158	22
Code 28	ABS Sensor Abnormal Signal	41-160	23
Code 29	Abnormal ABS Sensor Signal On Any One Of Four Sensors	41-162	24
Code 31	Inlet Solenoid Valve Malfunction	41-162	25
Code 32	Outlet Solenoid Valve Malfunction	41-162	26

Continued

Test	Description	Page No.	Fig. No.
WITH SELECT MONITOR			
Code 33	Inlet Solenoid Valve Malfunction	41-162	25
Code 34	Outlet Solenoid Valve Malfunction	41-162	26
Code 35	Inlet Solenoid Valve Malfunction	41-162	25
Code 36	Outlet Solenoid Valve Malfunction	41-162	26
Code 37	Inlet Solenoid Valve Malfunction	41-162	25
Code 38	Outlet Solenoid Valve Malfunction	41-162	26
Code 41	ABS Control Module Malfunction	41-163	27
Code 42	Power Supply Voltage Too Low	41-163	28
Code 42	Power Supply Voltage Too High	41-163	29
Code 44	ABS AT Control, Non Controlled	41-164	30
	ABS AT Control, Controlled	41-165	31
Code 51	Valve Relay Malfunction	41-165	32
	Valve Relay On Failure	41-166	33
Code 52	Open Circuit In Motor Relay Circuit	41-166	34
	Motor Relay On Failure	41-166	35
	Motor Malfunction	41-167	36
Code 54	Stop Light Switch Signal Circuit	41-168	37
Code 56	Open Or Short Circuit In G Sensor Circuit	41-168	38
	Battery Short In G Sensor Circuit	41-169	39
	Abnormal G Sensor High Output	41-170	40
	Detection Of G Sensor Stick	41-171	41

SUBARU

7A1 : CHECK IF OTHER WARNING LIGHTS TURN ON.

Turn ignition switch to ON (engine OFF).

CHECK : *Do other warning lights turn on?*
YES : Go to step **7A2**.
NO : Repair combination meter.

7A2 : CHECK ABS WARNING LIGHT BULB.

1) Turn ignition switch to OFF.
2) Remove combination meter.
3) Remove ABS warning light bulb from combination meter.

CHECK : *Is ABS warning light bulb OK?*
YES : Go to step **7A3**.
NO : Replace ABS warning light bulb.

7A3 : CHECK BATTERY SHORT OF ABS WARNING LIGHT HARNESS.

1) Disconnect connector (B100) from connector (F2).
2) Measure voltage between connector (B100) and chassis ground.

Connector & terminal
(B100) No. 15 (+) — Chassis ground (–):

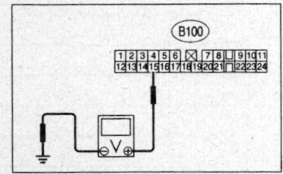

CHECK : *Is the voltage less than 3 V?*
YES : Go to step **7A4**.
NO : Repair warning light harness.

7A4 : CHECK BATTERY SHORT OF ABS WARNING LIGHT HARNESS.

1) Turn ignition switch to ON.
2) Measure voltage between connector (B100) and chassis ground.

Connector & terminal
(B100) No. 15 (+) — Chassis ground (–):

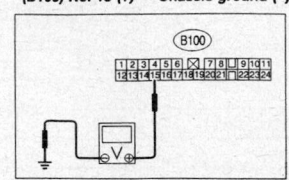

CHECK : *Is voltage less than 3 V?*
YES : Go to step **7A5**.
NO : Repair warning light harness.

7A5 : CHECK WIRING HARNESS.

1) Turn ignition switch to OFF.
2) Install ABS warning light bulb from combination meter.
3) Install combination meter.
4) Turn ignition switch to ON.
5) Measure voltage between connector (B100) and chassis ground.

Connector & terminal
(B100) No. 15 (+) — Chassis ground (–):

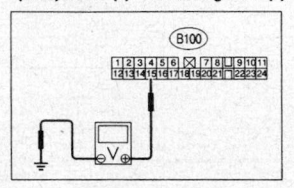

CHECK : *Is voltage between 10 V and 15 V?*
YES : Go to step **7A6**.
NO : Repair wiring harness.

SB4029800194010X

Fig. 5 Test A: ABS Warning Light Does Not Come On (Part 1 of 3). Less Select Monitor

---

7A10 : CHECK POOR CONTACT IN CONNECTORS.

Turn ignition switch to OFF.

CHECK : *Is there poor contact in connectors between combination meter and ABSCM&H/U?*

YES : Repair connector.
NO : Replace ABSCM&H/U.

SB4029800194030X

Fig. 5 Test A: ABS Warning Light Does Not Come On (Part 3 of 3). Less Select Monitor

---

7A6 : CHECK BATTERY SHORT OF ABS WARNING LIGHT HARNESS.

1) Turn ignition switch to OFF.
2) Measure voltage between connector (F2) and chassis ground.

Connector & terminal
(F2) No. 15 (+) — Chassis ground (–):

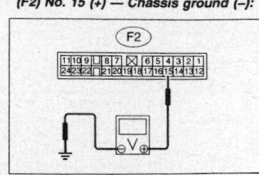

CHECK : *Is the voltage less than 3 V?*
YES : Go to step **7A7**.
NO : Repair wiring harness.

7A7 : CHECK BATTERY SHORT OF ABS WARNING LIGHT HARNESS.

1) Turn ignition switch to ON.
2) Measure voltage between connector (F2) and chassis ground.

Connector & terminal
(F2) No. 15 (+) — Chassis ground (–):

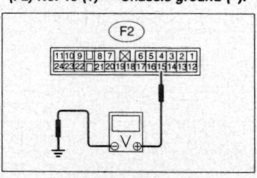

CHECK : *Is voltage less than 3 V?*
YES : Go to step **7A8**.
NO : Repair wiring harness.

7A8 : CHECK GROUND CIRCUIT OF ABSCM&H/U.

Measure resistance between ABSCM&H/U and chassis ground.

Connector & terminal
(F49) No. 23 — GND:

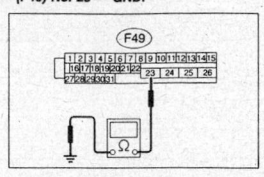

CHECK : *Is the resistance less than 0.5 Ω?*
YES : Go to step **7A9**.
NO : Repair ABSCM&H/U ground harness.

7A9 : CHECK WIRING HARNESS.

Measure resistance between connector (F2) and chassis ground.

Connector & terminal
(F2) No. 15 — Chassis ground:

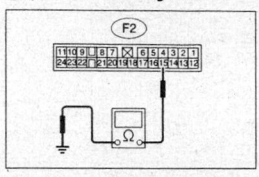

CHECK : *Is the resistance less than 0.5 Ω?*
YES : Go to step **7A10**.
NO : Repair harness/connector.

SB4029800194020X

Fig. 5 Test A: ABS Warning Light Does Not Come On (Part 2 of 3). Less Select Monitor

---

7B1 : CHECK INSTALLATION OF ABSCM&H/U CONNECTOR.

Turn ignition switch to OFF.

CHECK : *Is ABSCM&H/U connector inserted into ABSCM until the clamp locks onto it?*
YES : Go to step **7B2**.
NO : Insert ABSCM&H/U connector into ABSCM&H/U until the clamp locks onto it.

7B2 : CHECK DIAGNOSIS TERMINAL.

Measure resistance between diagnosis terminals (B81) and chassis ground.

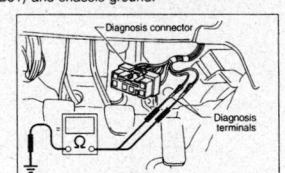

Terminals
Diagnosis terminal (A) — Chassis ground:
Diagnosis terminal (B) — Chassis ground:

CHECK : *Is the resistance less than 0.5 Ω?*
YES : Go to step **7B3**.
NO : Repair diagnosis terminal harness.

7B3 : CHECK DIAGNOSIS LINE.

1) Turn ignition switch to OFF.
2) Connect diagnosis terminal (B81) to diagnosis connector (B82) No. 6.
3) Disconnect connector from ABSCM&H/U.
4) Measure resistance between ABSCM&H/U connector and chassis ground.

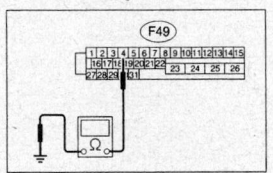

Connector & terminal
(F49) No. 4 — Chassis ground:

CHECK : *Is the resistance less than 0.5 Ω?*
YES : Go to step **7B4**.
NO : Repair harness connector between ABSCM&H/U and diagnosis connector.

7B4 : CHECK GENERATOR.

1) Start the engine.
2) Idle the engine.
3) Measure voltage between generator and chassis ground.

Terminal
Generator B terminal (+) — Chassis ground (–):

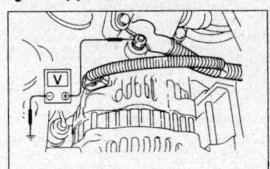

CHECK : *Is the voltage between 10 and 15 V?*
YES : Go to step **7B5**.
NO : Repair generator.

SB4029800195010X

Fig. 6 Test B: ABS Warning Light Does Not Go Off (Part 1 of 3). Less Select Monitor

7B5 : CHECK BATTERY TERMINAL.

Turn ignition switch to OFF.

CHECK : Is there poor contact at battery terminal?
YES : Repair battery terminal.
NO : Go to step 7B6.

7B6 : CHECK POWER SUPPLY OF ABSCM.

1) Disconnect connector from ABSCM&H/U.
2) Start engine.
3) Idle the engine.
4) Measure voltage between ABSCM&H/U connector and chassis ground.

Connector & terminal
(F49) No. 1 (+) — Chassis ground (–):

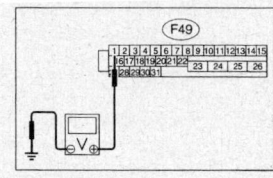

CHECK : Is the voltage between 10 and 15 V?
YES : Go to step 7B7.
NO : Repair ABSCM&H/U power supply circuit.

7B7 : CHECK WIRING HARNESS.

1) Disconnect connector (F2) from connector (B100).
2) Turn ignition switch to ON.

CHECK : Does the ABS warning light remain off?
YES : Go to step 7B8.
NO : Repair front wiring harness.

SB4029800195020X

Fig. 6   Test B: ABS Warning Light Does Not Go Off (Part 2 of 3). Less Select Monitor

---

7B8 : CHECK PROJECTION AT ABSCM&H/U.

1) Turn ignition switch to OFF.
2) Check for broken projection at the ABSCM&H/U terminal.

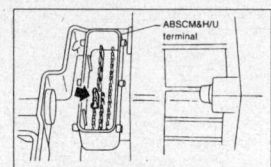

CHECK : Are the projection broken?
YES : Go to step 7B9.
NO : Replace ABSCM&H/U.

7B9 : CHECK ABSCM&H/U.

Measure resistance between ABSCM&H/U terminals.

Terminal
No. 21 — No. 23:

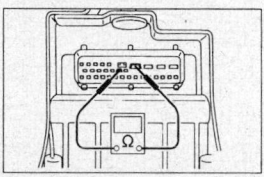

CHECK : Is the resistance more than 1 MΩ?
YES : Go to step 7B10.
NO : Replace ABSCM&H/U.

7B10 : CHECK WIRING HARNESS.

Measure resistance between connector (F2) and chassis ground.

Connector & terminal
(F2) No. 15 — Chassis ground:

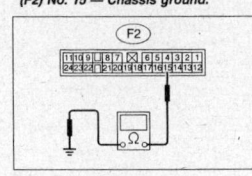

CHECK : Is the resistance less than 0.5 Ω?
YES : Go to step 7B11.
NO : Repair harness.

7B11 : CHECK WIRING HARNESS.

1) Connect connector to ABSCM&H/U.
2) Measure resistance between connector (F2) and chassis ground.

Connector & terminal
(F2) No. 15 — Chassis ground:

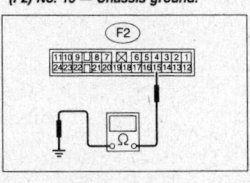

CHECK : Is the resistance more than 1 MΩ?
YES : Go to step 7B12.
NO : Repair harness.

7B12 : CHECK POOR CONTACT IN ABSCM&H/U CONNECTOR.

CHECK : Is there poor contact in ABSCM&H/U connector?
YES : Repair connector.
NO : Replace ABSCM&H/U.

SB4029800195030X

Fig. 6   Test B: ABS Warning Light Does Not Go Off (Part 3 of 3). Less Select Monitor

---

7C1 : CHECK DIAGNOSIS TERMINAL.

Measure resistance between diagnosis terminals (B81) and chassis ground.

Terminals
Diagnosis terminal (A) — Chassis ground:
Diagnosis terminal (B) — Chassis ground:

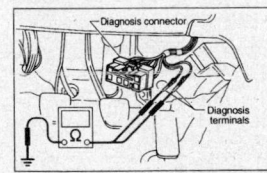

CHECK : Is the resistance less than 0.5 Ω?
YES : Go to step 7C2.
NO : Repair diagnosis terminal harness.

7C2 : CHECK DIAGNOSIS LINE.

1) Turn ignition switch to OFF.
2) Connect diagnosis terminal (B81) to diagnosis connector (B82) No. 6.
3) Disconnect connector from ABSCM&H/U.
4) Measure resistance between ABSCM&H/U connector and chassis ground.

Connector & terminal
(F49) No. 4 — Chassis ground:

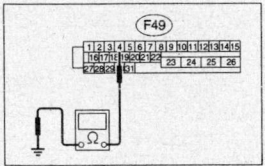

CHECK : Is the resistance less than 0.5 Ω?
YES : Go to step 7C3.
NO : Repair harness connector between ABSCM&H/U and diagnosis connector.

7C3 : CHECK POOR CONTACT IN ABSCM&H/U CONNECTOR.

CHECK : Is there poor contact in ABSCM&H/U connector?
YES : Repair connector.
NO : Replace ABSCM&H/U.

SB4029800196000X

Fig. 7   Test C: Trouble Code Does Not Appear. Less Select Monitor

---

8E1 : CHECK ABS SENSOR.

1) Turn ignition switch to OFF.
2) Disconnect connector from ABS sensor.
3) Measure resistance of ABS sensor connector terminals.

Terminal
Front RH No. 1 — No. 2:
Front LH No. 1 — No. 2:
Rear RH No. 1 — No. 2:
Rear LH No. 1 — No. 2:

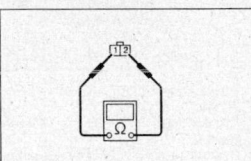

CHECK : Is the resistance between 0.8 and 1.2 kΩ?
YES : Go to step 8E2.
NO : Replace ABS sensor.

8E2 : CHECK BATTERY SHORT OF ABS SENSOR.

1) Disconnect connector from ABSCM&H/U.
2) Measure voltage between ABS sensor and chassis ground.

Terminal
Front RH No. 1 (+) — Chassis ground (–):
Front LH No. 1 (+) — Chassis ground (–):
Rear RH No. 1 (+) — Chassis ground (–):
Rear LH No. 1 (+) — Chassis ground (–):

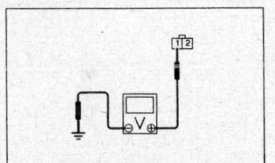

CHECK : Is the voltage less than 1 V?
YES : Go to step 8E3.
NO : Replace ABS sensor.

8E3 : CHECK BATTERY SHORT OF ABS SENSOR.

1) Turn ignition switch to ON.
2) Measure voltage between ABS sensor and chassis ground.

Terminal
Front RH No. 1 (+) — Chassis ground (–):
Front LH No. 1 (+) — Chassis ground (–):
Rear RH No. 1 (+) — Chassis ground (–):
Rear LH No. 1 (+) — Chassis ground (–):

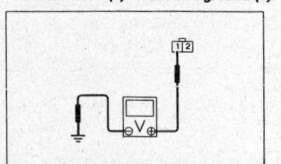

CHECK : Is the voltage less than 1 V?
YES : Go to step 8E4.
NO : Replace ABS sensor.

SB4029800197010X

Fig. 8   Codes 21, 23, 25 & 27: Abnormal ABS Sensor, Open Circuit Or Input Voltage Too High (Part 1 of 5). Less Select Monitor

8E4 : CHECK HARNESS/CONNECTOR BETWEEN ABSCM&H/U AND ABS SENSOR.

1) Turn ignition switch to OFF.
2) Connect connector to ABS sensor.
3) Measure resistance between ABSCM&H/U connector terminals.

Connector & terminal
Trouble code 21 / (F49) No. 11 — No. 12:
Trouble code 23 / (F49) No. 9 — No. 10:
Trouble code 25 / (F49) No. 14 — No. 15:
Trouble code 27 / (F49) No. 7 — No. 8:

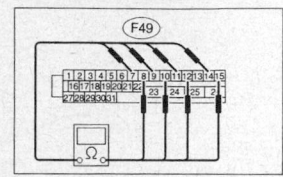

(CHECK) : **Is the resistance between 0.8 and 1.2 kΩ?**
(YES) : Go to step **8E5**.
(NO) : Repair harness/connector between ABSCM&H/U and ABS sensor.

8E5 : CHECK BATTERY SHORT OF HARNESS.

Measure voltage between ABSCM&H/U connector and chassis ground.

Connector & terminal
Trouble code 21 / (F49) No. 11 (+) — Chassis ground (–):
Trouble code 23 / (F49) No. 9 (+) — Chassis ground (–):
Trouble code 25 / (F49) No. 14 (+) — Chassis ground (–):
Trouble code 27 / (F49) No. 7 (+) — Chassis ground (–):

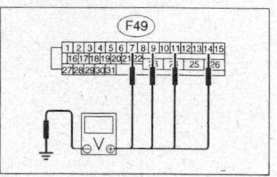

(CHECK) : **Is the voltage less than 1 V?**
(YES) : Go to step **8E6**.
(NO) : Repair harness between ABSCM&H/U and ABS sensor.

SB4029800197020X

Fig. 8 Codes 21, 23, 25 & 27: Abnormal ABS Sensor, Open Circuit Or Input Voltage Too High (Part 2 of 5). Less Select Monitor

---

8E6 : CHECK BATTERY SHORT OF HARNESS.

1) Turn ignition switch to ON.
2) Measure voltage between ABSCM&H/U connector and chassis ground.

Connector & terminal
Trouble code 21 / (F49) No. 11 (+) — Chassis ground (–):
Trouble code 23 / (F49) No. 9 (+) — Chassis ground (–):
Trouble code 25 / (F49) No. 14 (+) — Chassis ground (–):
Trouble code 27 / (F49) No. 7 (+) — Chassis ground (–):

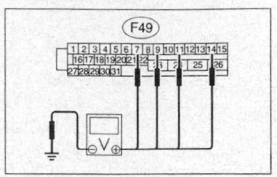

(CHECK) : **Is the voltage less than 1 V?**
(YES) : Go to step **8E7**.
(NO) : Repair harness between ABSCM&H/U and ABS sensor.

8E7 : CHECK INSTALLATION OF ABS SENSOR.

Tightening torque:
32±10 N·m (3.3±1.0 kg-m, 24±7 ft-lb)

(CHECK) : **Are the ABS sensor installation bolts tightened securely?**
(YES) : Go to step **8E8**.
(NO) : Tighten ABS sensor installation bolts securely.

8E8 : CHECK INSTALLATION OF TONE WHEEL.

Tightening torque:
13±3 N·m (1.3±0.3 kg-m, 9±2.2 ft-lb)

(CHECK) : **Are the tone wheel installation bolts tightened securely?**
(YES) : Go to step **8E9**.
(NO) : Tighten tone wheel installation bolts securely.

8E9 : CHECK ABS SENSOR GAP.

Measure tone wheel-to-pole piece gap over entire perimeter of the wheel.

Specifications	Front wheel	Rear wheel
	0.9 — 1.4 mm (0.035 — 0.055 in)	0.7 — 1.2 mm (0.028 — 0.047 in)

(CHECK) : **Is the gap within the specifications?**
(YES) : Go to step **8E10**.
(NO) : Adjust the gap.

NOTE:
Adjust the gap using spacers (Part No. 26755AA000). If spacers cannot correct the gap, replace worn sensor or worn tone wheel.

SB4029800197030X

Fig. 8 Codes 21, 23, 25 & 27: Abnormal ABS Sensor, Open Circuit Or Input Voltage Too High (Part 3 of 5). Less Select Monitor

---

8E10 : CHECK HUB RUNOUT.

Measure hub runout.

(CHECK) : **Is the runout less than 0.05 mm (0.0020 in)?**
(YES) : Go to step **8E11**.
(NO) : Repair hub.

8E11 : CHECK GROUND SHORT OF ABS SENSOR.

1) Turn ignition switch to ON.
2) Measure resistance between ABS sensor and chassis ground.

Terminal
Front RH No. 1 — Chassis ground:
Front LH No. 1 — Chassis ground:
Rear RH No. 1 — Chassis ground:
Rear LH No. 1 — Chassis ground:

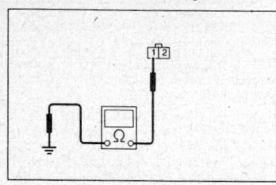

(CHECK) : **Is the resistance more than 1 MΩ?**
(YES) : Go to step **8E12**.
(NO) : Replace ABS sensor and ABSCM&H/U.

8E12 : CHECK GROUND SHORT OF HARNESS.

1) Turn ignition switch to OFF.
2) Connect connector to ABS sensor.
3) Measure resistance between ABSCM&H/U connector terminal and chassis ground.

Connector & terminal
Trouble code 21 / (F49) No. 11 — Chassis ground:
Trouble code 23 / (F49) No. 9 — Chassis ground:
Trouble code 25 / (F49) No. 14 — Chassis ground:
Trouble code 27 / (F49) No. 7 — Chassis ground:

(CHECK) : **Is the resistance more than 1 MΩ?**
(YES) : Go to step **8E13**.
(NO) : Repair harness between ABSCM&H/U and ABS sensor. Replace ABSCM&H/U.

8E13 : CHECK POOR CONTACT IN CONNECTORS.

(CHECK) : **Is there poor contact in connectors between ABSCM&H/U and ABS sensor?**
(YES) : Repair connector.
(NO) : Go to step **8E14**.

SB4029800197040X

Fig. 8 Codes 21, 23, 25 & 27: Abnormal ABS Sensor, Open Circuit Or Input Voltage Too High (Part 4 of 5). Less Select Monitor

---

8E14 : CHECK ABSCM&H/U.

1) Connect all connectors.
2) Erase the memory.
3) Perform inspection mode.
4) Read out the trouble code.

(CHECK) : **Is the same trouble code as in the current diagnosis still being output?**
(YES) : Replace ABSCM&H/U.
(NO) : Go to step **8E15**.

8E15 : CHECK ANY OTHER TROUBLE CODES APPEARANCE.

(CHECK) : **Are other trouble codes being output?**
(YES) : Proceed with the diagnosis corresponding to the trouble code.
(NO) : A temporary poor contact.

NOTE:
Check harness and connectors between ABSCM&H/U and ABS sensor.

SB4029800197050X

Fig. 8 Codes 21, 23, 25 & 27: Abnormal ABS Sensor, Open Circuit Or Input Voltage Too High (Part 5 of 5). Less Select Monitor

8I1 : CHECK INSTALLATION OF ABS SENSOR.

Tightening torque:
32±10 N·m (3.3±1.0 kg-m, 24±7 ft-lb)

CHECK : *Are the ABS sensor installation bolts tightened securely?*

YES : Go to step 8I2.

NO : Tighten ABS sensor installation bolts securely.

8I2 : CHECK INSTALLATION OF TONE WHEEL.

Tightening torque:
13±3 N·m (1.3±0.3 kg-m, 9±2.2 ft-lb)

CHECK : *Are the tone wheel installation bolts tightened securely?*

YES : Go to step 8I3.

NO : Tighten tone wheel installation bolts securely.

8I3 : CHECK ABS SENSOR GAP.

Measure tone wheel to pole piece gap over entire perimeter of the wheel.

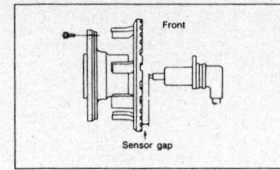

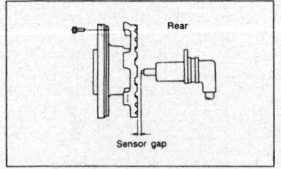

Specifications	Front wheel	Rear wheel
	0.9 — 1.4 mm (0.035 — 0.055 in)	0.7 — 1.2 mm (0.028 — 0.047 in)

CHECK : *Is the gap within the specifications?*

YES : Go to step 8I4.

NO : Adjust the gap.

NOTE:
Adjust the gap using spacer (Part No. 26755AA000). If spacers cannot correct the gap, replace worn sensor or worn tone wheel.

8I4 : CHECK OSCILLOSCOPE.

CHECK : *Is an oscilloscope available?*

YES : Go to step 8I5.

NO : Go to step 8I6.

SB4029800198010X

Fig. 9   Codes 22, 24, 26 & 28: Abnormal ABS Sensor Signal (Part 1 of 5). Less Select Monitor

---

8I5 : CHECK ABS SENSOR SIGNAL.

1) Raise all four wheels of ground.
2) Turn ignition switch OFF.
3) Connect the oscilloscope to the connector (B100).
4) Turn ignition switch ON.
5) Rotate wheels and measure voltage at specified frequency.

NOTE:
When this inspection is completed, the ABS control module sometimes stores the trouble code 29.

Connector & terminal
Trouble code 22 / (B100) No. 9 (+) — No. 22 (–):
Trouble code 24 / (B100) No. 11 (+) — No. 24 (–):
Trouble code 26 / (B100) No. 1 (+) — No. 12 (–):
Trouble code 28 / (B100) No. 3 (+) — No. 14 (–):
Specified voltage: 0.12 — 1 V (When it is 20 Hz.)

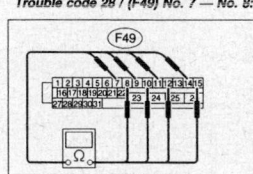

Standard output voltage: 0.12 – 1V
(When it is 20Hz.)

CHECK : *Is oscilloscope pattern smooth, as shown in figure?*

YES : Go to step 8I9.

NO : Go to step 8I6.

8I6 : CHECK CONTAMINATION OF ABS SENSOR OR TONE WHEEL.

Remove disc rotor or drum from hub in accordance with trouble code.

CHECK : *Is the ABS sensor pole piece or the tone wheel contaminated by dirt or other foreign matter?*

YES : Thoroughly remove dirt or other foreign matter.

NO : Go to step 8I7.

8I7 : CHECK DAMAGE OF ABS SENSOR OR TONE WHEEL.

CHECK : *Are there broken or damaged in the ABS sensor pole piece or the tone wheel?*

YES : Replace ABS sensor or tone wheel.

NO : Go to step 8I8.

8I8 : CHECK HUB RUNOUT.

Measure hub runout.

CHECK : *Is the runout less than 0.05 mm (0.0020 in)?*

YES : Go to step 8I9.

NO : Repair hub.

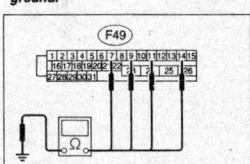

SB4029800198020X

Fig. 9   Codes 22, 24, 26 & 28: Abnormal ABS Sensor Signal (Part 2 of 5). Less Select Monitor

---

8I9 : CHECK RESISTANCE OF ABS SENSOR.

1) Turn ignition switch OFF.
2) Disconnect connector from ABS sensor.
3) Measure resistance between ABS sensor connector terminals.

Terminal
Front RH No. 1 — No. 2:
Front LH No. 1 — No. 2:
Rear RH No. 1 — No. 2:
Rear LH No. 1 — No. 2:

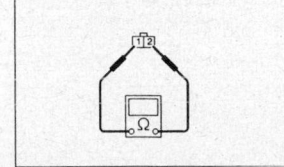

CHECK : *Is the resistance between 0.8 and 1.2 kΩ?*

YES : Go to step 8I10.

NO : Replace ABS sensor.

8I10 : CHECK GROUND SHORT OF ABS SENSOR.

Measure resistance between ABS sensor and chassis ground.

Terminal
Front RH No. 1 — Chassis ground:
Front LH No. 1 — Chassis ground:
Rear RH No. 1 — Chassis ground:
Rear LH No. 1 — Chassis ground:

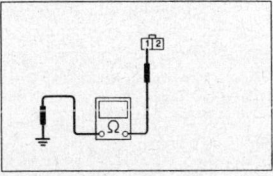

CHECK : *Is the resistance more than 1 MΩ?*

YES : Go to step 8I11.

NO : Replace ABS sensor.

SB4029800198030X

Fig. 9   Codes 22, 24, 26 & 28: Abnormal ABS Sensor Signal (Part 3 of 5). Less Select Monitor

---

8I11 : CHECK HARNESS/CONNECTOR BETWEEN ABSCM&H/U AND ABS SENSOR.

1) Connect connector to ABS sensor.
2) Disconnect connector from ABSCM&H/U.
3) Measure resistance at ABSCM&H/U connector terminals.

Connector & terminal
Trouble code 22 / (F49) No. 11 — No. 12:
Trouble code 24 / (F49) No. 9 — No. 10:
Trouble code 26 / (F49) No. 14 — No. 15:
Trouble code 28 / (F49) No. 7 — No. 9:

CHECK : *Is the resistance between 0.8 and 1.2 kΩ?*

YES : Go to step 8I12.

NO : Repair harness/connector between ABSCM&H/U and ABS sensor.

8I12 : CHECK GROUND SHORT OF HARNESS.

Measure resistance between ABSCM&H/U connector and chassis ground.

Connector & terminal
Trouble code 22 / (F49) No. 11 — Chassis ground:
Trouble code 24 / (F49) No. 9 — Chassis ground:
Trouble code 26 / (F49) No. 14 — Chassis ground:
Trouble code 28 / (F49) No. 7 — Chassis ground:

CHECK : *Is the resistance more than 1 MΩ?*

YES : Go to step 8I13.

NO : Repair harness/connector between ABSCM&H/U and ABS sensor.

8I13 : CHECK GROUND CIRCUIT OF ABSCM&H/U.

Measure resistance between ABSCM&H/U and chassis ground.

Connector & terminal
(F49) No. 23 — GND:

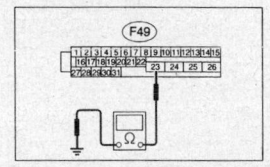

CHECK : *Is the resistance less than 0.5 Ω?*

YES : Go to step 8I14.

NO : Repair ABSCM&H/U ground harness.

SB4029800198040X

Fig. 9   Codes 22, 24, 26 & 28: Abnormal ABS Sensor Signal (Part 4 of 5). Less Select Monitor

---

8I14 : CHECK POOR CONTACT IN CONNECTORS.

CHECK : Is there poor contact in connectors between ABSCM&H/U and ABS sensor?

YES : Repair connector.

NO : Go to step 8I15.

8I15 : CHECK SOURCES OF SIGNAL NOISE.

CHECK : Is the car telephone or the wireless transmitter properly installed?

YES : Go to step 8I16.

NO : Properly install the car telephone or the wireless transmitter.

8I16 : CHECK SOURCES OF SIGNAL NOISE.

CHECK : Are noise sources (such as an antenna) installed near the sensor harness?

YES : Install the noise sources apart from the sensor harness.

NO : Go to step 8I17.

8I17 : CHECK SHIELD CIRCUIT.

1) Connect all connectors.
2) Measure resistance between shield connector and chassis ground.

Connector & terminal
Trouble code 22 / (B100) No. 23 — Chassis ground:
Trouble code 24 / (B100) No. 10 — Chassis ground:
Trouble code 26 / (B100) No. 2 — Chassis ground:
Trouble code 28 / (B100) No. 13 — Chassis ground:

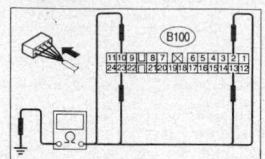

CHECK : Is the resistance less than 0.5 Ω?

YES : Go to step 8I18.

NO : Repair shield harness.

8I18 : CHECK ABSCM&H/U.

1) Connect all connectors.
2) Erase the memory.
3) Perform inspection mode.
4) Read out the trouble code.

CHECK : Is the same trouble code as in the current diagnosis still being output?

YES : Replace ABSCM&H/U.

NO : Go to step 8I19.

8I19 : CHECK ANY OTHER TROUBLE CODES APPEARANCE.

CHECK : Are other trouble codes being output?

YES : Proceed with the diagnosis corresponding to the trouble code.

NO : A temporary noise interference.

SB4029800198050X

Fig. 9 Codes 22, 24, 26 & 28: Abnormal ABS Sensor Signal (Part 5 of 5). Less Select Monitor

8J1 : CHECK IF THE WHEELS HAVE TURNED FREELY FOR A LONG TIME.

CHECK : Check if the wheels have been turned freely for more than one minute, such as when the vehicle is jacked-up, under full-lock cornering or when tire is not in contact with road surface.

YES : The ABS is normal. Erase the trouble code.

NOTE:
When the wheels turn freely for a long time, such as when the vehicle is towed or jacked-up, or when steering wheel is continuously turned all the way, this trouble code may sometimes occur.

NO : Go to step 8J2.

8J2 : CHECK TIRE SPECIFICATIONS.

CHECK : Are the tire specifications correct?

YES : Go to step 8J3.

NO : Replace tire.

8J3 : CHECK WEAR OF TIRE.

CHECK : Is the tire worn excessively?

YES : Replace tire.

NO : Go to step 8J4.

8J4 : CHECK TIRE PRESSURE.

CHECK : Is the tire pressure correct?

YES : Go to step 8J5.

NO : Adjust tire pressure.

8J5 : CHECK INSTALLATION OF ABS SENSOR.

Tightening torque:
32±10 N·m (3.3±1.0 kg-m, 24±7 ft-lb)

CHECK : Are the ABS sensor installation bolts tightened securely?

YES : Go to step 8J6.

NO : Tighten ABS sensor installation bolts securely.

8J6 : CHECK INSTALLATION OF TONE WHEEL.

Tightening torque:
13±3 N·m (1.3±0.3 kg-m, 9±2.2 ft-lb)

CHECK : Are the tone wheel installation bolts tightened securely?

YES : Go to step 8J7.

NO : Tighten tone wheel installation bolts securely.

8J7 : CHECK ABS SENSOR GAP.

Measure tone wheel to pole piece gap over entire perimeter of the wheel.

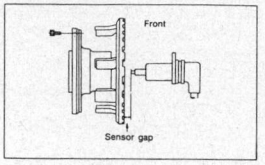
Front
Sensor gap

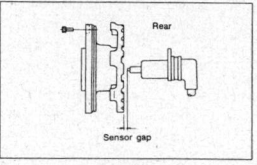
Rear
Sensor gap

Specifications	Front wheel	Rear wheel
	0.9 — 1.4 mm (0.035 — 0.055 in)	0.7 — 1.2 mm (0.028 — 0.047 in)

CHECK : Is the gap within the specifications?

YES : Go to step 8J8.

NO : Adjust the gap.

NOTE:
Adjust the gap using spacer (Part No. 26755AA000). If spacers cannot correct the gap, replace worn sensor or worn tone wheel.

SB4029800199010X

Fig. 10 Code 29: Abnormal ABS Sensor Signal, Any One Of Four (Part 1 of 2). Less Select Monitor

8J8 : CHECK OSCILLOSCOPE.

CHECK : Is an oscilloscope available?

YES : Go to step 8J9.

NO : Go to step 8J10.

8J9 : CHECK ABS SENSOR SIGNAL.

1) Raise all four wheels of ground.
2) Turn ignition switch OFF.
3) Connect the oscilloscope to the connector (B100).
4) Turn ignition switch ON.
5) Rotate wheels and measure voltage at specified frequency.

NOTE:
When this inspection is completed, the ABS control module sometimes stores the trouble code 29.

Connector & terminal
(B100) No. 9 (+) — No. 22 (−) (Front RH):
(B100) No. 11 (+) — No. 24 (−) (Front LH):
(B100) No. 1 (+) — No. 12 (−) (Rear RH):
(B100) No. 3 (+) — No. 14 (−) (Rear LH):
Specified voltage: 0.12 – 1 V (When it is 20 Hz.)

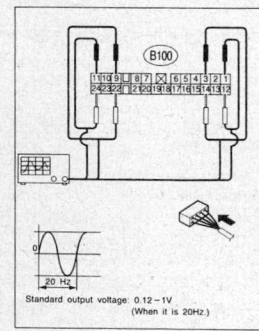

0
20 Hz
Standard output voltage: 0.12 — 1V
(When it is 20Hz.)

CHECK : Is oscilloscope pattern smooth, as shown in figure?

YES : Go to step 8J13.

NO : Go to step 8J10.

8J10 : CHECK CONTAMINATION OF ABS SENSOR OR TONE WHEEL.

Remove disc rotor from hub.

CHECK : Is the ABS sensor pole piece or the tone wheel contaminated by dirt or other foreign matter?

YES : Thoroughly remove dirt or other foreign matter.

NO : Go to step 8J11.

8J11 : CHECK DAMAGE OF ABS SENSOR OR TONE WHEEL.

CHECK : Are there broken or damaged teeth in the ABS sensor pole piece or the tone wheel?

YES : Replace ABS sensor or tone wheel.

NO : Go to step 8J12.

8J12 : CHECK HUB RUNOUT.

Measure hub runout.

CHECK : Is the runout less than 0.05 mm (0.0020 in)?

YES : Go to step 8J13.

NO : Repair hub.

8J13 : CHECK ABSCM&H/U.

1) Turn ignition switch to OFF.
2) Connect all connectors.
3) Erase the memory.
4) Perform inspection mode.
5) Read out the trouble code.

CHECK : Is the same trouble code as in the current diagnosis still being output?

YES : Replace ABSCM&H/U.

NO : Go to step 8J14.

8J14 : CHECK ANY OTHER TROUBLE CODES APPEARANCE.

CHECK : Are other trouble codes being output?

YES : Proceed with the diagnosis corresponding to the trouble code.

NO : A temporary poor contact.

SB4029800199020X

Fig. 10 Code 29: Abnormal ABS Sensor Signal, Any One Of Four (Part 2 of 2). Less Select Monitor

8N1 : CHECK INPUT VOLTAGE OF ABSCM&H/U.

1) Disconnect connector from ABSCM&H/U.
2) Run the engine at idle.
3) Measure voltage between ABSCM&H/U connector and chassis ground.

Connector & terminal
(F49) No. 1 (+) — Chassis ground (−):

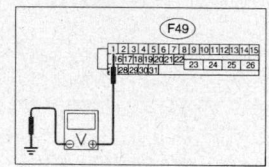
(F49)

CHECK : Is the voltage between 10 V and 15 V?

YES : Go to step 8N2.

NO : Repair harness connector between battery, ignition switch and ABSCM&H/U.

8N2 : CHECK GROUND CIRCUIT OF ABSCM&H/U.

1) Turn ignition switch to OFF.
2) Measure resistance between ABSCM&H/U connector and chassis ground.

Connector & terminal
(F49) No. 23 — Chassis ground:

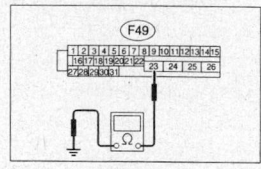
(F49)

CHECK : Is the resistance less than 0.5 Ω?

YES : Go to step 8N3.

NO : Repair ABSCM&H/U ground harness.

8N3 : CHECK POOR CONTACT IN CONNECTORS.

CHECK : Is there poor contact in connectors between generator, battery and ABSCM&H/U?

YES : Repair connector.

NO : Go to step 8N4.

8N4 : CHECK ABSCM&H/U.

1) Connect all connectors.
2) Erase the memory.
3) Perform inspection mode.
4) Read out the trouble code.

CHECK : Is the same trouble code as in the current diagnosis still being output?

YES : Replace ABSCM&H/U.

NO : Go to step 8N5.

8N5 : CHECK ANY OTHER TROUBLE CODES APPEARANCE.

CHECK : Are other trouble codes being output?

YES : Proceed with the diagnosis corresponding to the trouble code.

NO : A temporary poor contact.

SB4029800200000X

Fig. 11 Codes 31, 33, 35 & 37: Abnormal Inlet Solenoid Valve Circuits In ABSCM & H/U. Less Select Monitor

8R1 : CHECK INPUT VOLTAGE OF ABSCM&H/U.

1) Disconnect connector from ABSCM&H/U.
2) Run the engine at idle.
3) Measure voltage between ABSCM&H/U connector and chassis ground.

Connector & terminal
(F49) No. 1 (+) — Chassis ground (–):

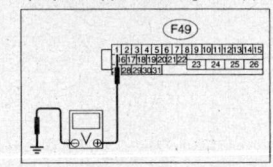

CHECK : *Is the voltage between 10 V and 15 V?*
YES : Go to step 8R2.
NO : Repair harness connector between battery, ignition switch and ABSCM&H/U.

8R2 : CHECK GROUND CIRCUIT OF ABSCM&H/U.

1) Turn ignition switch to OFF.
2) Measure resistance between ABSCM&H/U connector and chassis ground.

Connector & terminal
(F49) No. 23 — Chassis ground:

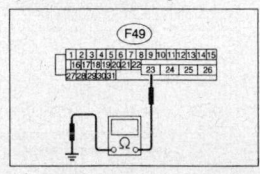

CHECK : *Is the resistance less than 0.5 Ω?*
YES : Go to step 8R3.
NO : Repair ABSCM&H/U ground harness.

SB4029800201000X

8R3 : CHECK POOR CONTACT IN CONNECTORS.

CHECK : *Is there poor contact in connectors between generator, battery and ABSCM&H/U?*
YES : Repair connector.
NO : Go to step 8R4.

8R4 : CHECK ABSCM&H/U.

1) Connect all connectors.
2) Erase the memory.
3) Perform inspection mode.
4) Read out the trouble code.

CHECK : *Is the same trouble code as in the current diagnosis still being output?*
YES : Replace ABSCM&H/U.
NO : Go to step 8R5.

8R5 : CHECK ANY OTHER TROUBLE CODES APPEARANCE.

CHECK : *Are other trouble codes being output?*
YES : Proceed with the diagnosis corresponding to the trouble code.
NO : A temporary poor contact.

Fig. 12   Code 32, 34, 36 & 38: Abnormal Outlet Solenoid Valve Circuits In ABSCM & H/U. Less Select Monitor

---

8S1 : CHECK GROUND CIRCUIT OF ABSCM&H/U.

1) Turn ignition switch to OFF.
2) Disconnect connector from ABSCM&H/U.
3) Measure resistance between ABSCM&H/U and chassis ground.

Connector & terminal
(F49) No. 23 — Chassis ground:

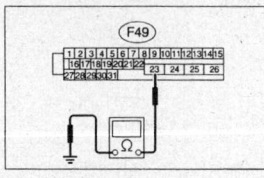

CHECK : *Is the resistance less than 0.5 Ω?*
YES : Go to step 8S2.
NO : Repair ABSCM&H/U ground harness.

8S2 : CHECK POOR CONTACT IN CONNECTORS.

CHECK : *Is there poor contact in connectors between battery, ignition switch and ABSCM&H/U?*
YES : Repair connector.
NO : Go to step 8S3.

8S3 : CHECK SOURCES OF SIGNAL NOISE.

CHECK : *Is the car telephone or the wireless transmitter properly installed?*
YES : Go to step 8S4.
NO : Properly install the car telephone or the wireless transmitter.

8S4 : CHECK SOURCES OF SIGNAL NOISE.

CHECK : *Are noise sources (such as an antenna) installed near the sensor harness?*
YES : Install the noise sources apart from the sensor harness.
NO : Go to step 8S5.

8S5 : CHECK ABSCM&H/U.

1) Connect all connectors.
2) Erase the memory.
3) Perform inspection mode.
4) Read out the trouble code.

CHECK : *Is the same trouble code as in the current diagnosis still being output?*
YES : Replace ABSCM&H/U.
NO : Go to step 8S6.

8S6 : CHECK ANY OTHER TROUBLE CODES APPEARANCE.

CHECK : *Are other trouble codes being output?*
YES : Proceed with the diagnosis corresponding to the trouble code.
NO : A temporary poor contact.

SB4029800202000X

Fig. 13   Code 41: Abnormal ABS Control Module. Less select Monitor

---

8T1 : CHECK GENERATOR.

1) Start engine.
2) Idling after warm-up.
3) Measure voltage between generator B terminal and chassis ground.

Terminal
Generator B terminal — Chassis ground:

CHECK : *Is the voltage between 10 V and 17 V?*
YES : Go to step 8T2.
NO : Repair generator.

8T2 : CHECK BATTERY TERMINAL.

Turn ignition switch to OFF.

CHECK : *Are the positive and negative battery terminals tightly clamped?*
YES : Go to step 8T3.
NO : Tighten the clamp of terminal.

8T3 : CHECK INPUT VOLTAGE OF ABSCM&H/U.

1) Disconnect connector from ABSCM&H/U.
2) Run the engine at idle.
3) Measure voltage between ABSCM&H/U connector and chassis ground.

Connector & terminal
(F49) No. 1 (+) — Chassis ground (–):

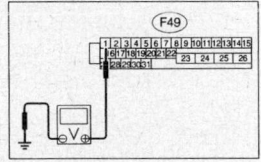

CHECK : *Is the voltage between 10 V and 17 V?*
YES : Go to step 8T4.
NO : Repair harness connector between battery, ignition switch and ABSCM&H/U.

8T4 : CHECK GROUND CIRCUIT OF ABSCM&H/U.

1) Turn ignition switch to OFF.
2) Measure resistance between ABSCM&H/U connector and chassis ground.

Connector & terminal
(F49) No. 23 — Chassis ground:

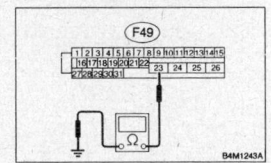

CHECK : *Is the resistance less than 0.5 Ω?*
YES : Go to step 8T5.
NO : Repair ABSCM&H/U ground harness.

SB4029800203010X

Fig. 14   Code 42: Source Voltage Is Abnormal (Part 1 of 2). Less Select Monitor

---

8T5 : CHECK POOR CONTACT IN CONNECTORS.

CHECK : *Is there poor contact in connectors between generator, battery and ABSCM&H/U?*
YES : Repair connector.
NO : Go to step 8T6.

8T6 : CHECK ABSCM&H/U.

1) Connect all connectors.
2) Erase the memory.
3) Perform inspection mode.
4) Read out the trouble code.

CHECK : *Is the same trouble code as in the current diagnosis still being output?*
YES : Replace ABSCM&H/U.
NO : Go to step 8T7.

8T7 : CHECK ANY OTHER TROUBLE CODES APPEARANCE.

CHECK : *Are other trouble codes being output?*
YES : Proceed with the diagnosis corresponding to the trouble code.
NO : A temporary poor contact.

SB4029800203020X

Fig. 14   Code 42: Source Voltage Is Abnormal (Part 2 of 2). Less Select Monitor

8U1 : CHECK SPECIFICATIONS OF THE ABSCM&H/U.

Check specifications of the mark to the ABSCM&H/U.

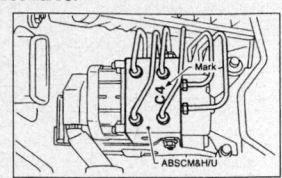

Mark	Model
C3	AWD AT
C4	AWD MT

CHECK : Is an ABSCM&H/U for AT model installed on a MT model?
YES : Replace ABSCM&H/U.
NO : Go to step 8U2.

8U2 : CHECK GROUND SHORT OF HARNESS.

1) Turn ignition switch to OFF.
2) Disconnect two connectors from TCM.
3) Disconnect connector from ABSCM&H/U.
4) Measure resistance between ABSCM&H/U connector and chassis ground.

Connector & terminal
(F49) No. 3 — Chassis ground:

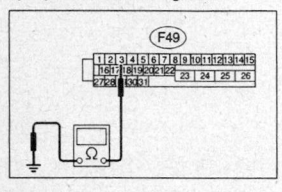

CHECK : Is the resistance more than 1 MΩ?
YES : Go to step 8U3.
NO : Repair harness between TCM and ABSCM&H/U.

SB4029800204010X

Fig. 15 Code 44: A Combination Of A/T Control Abnormal (Part 1 of 3). Less Select Monitor

8U10 : CHECK ANY OTHER TROUBLE CODES APPEARANCE.

CHECK : *Are other trouble codes being output?*

YES : Proceed with the diagnosis corresponding to the trouble code.

NO : A temporary poor contact.

SB4029800204030X

Fig. 15 Code 44: A Combination Of A/T Control Abnormal (Part 3 of 3). Less Select Monitor

8U3 : CHECK BATTERY SHORT OF HARNESS.

Measure voltage between ABSCM&H/U connector and chassis ground.

Connector & terminal
(F49) No. 3 (+) — Chassis ground (–):

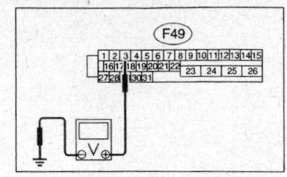

CHECK : Is the voltage less than 1 V?
YES : Go to step 8U4.
NO : Repair harness between TCM and ABSCM&H/U.

8U4 : CHECK BATTERY SHORT OF HARNESS.

1) Turn ignition switch to ON.
2) Measure voltage between ABSCM&H/U connector and chassis ground.

Connector & terminal
(F49) No. 3 (+) — Chassis ground (–):

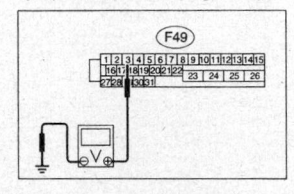

CHECK : Is the voltage less than 1 V?
YES : Go to step 8U5.
NO : Repair harness between TCM and ABSCM&H/U.

8U5 : CHECK TCM.

1) Turn ignition switch to OFF.
2) Connect all connectors to TCM.
3) Turn ignition switch to ON.
4) Measure voltage between TCM connector terminal and chassis ground.

Connector & terminal
(B56) No. 5 (+) — Chassis ground (–):

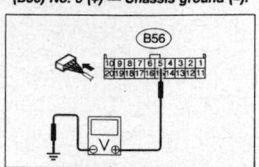

CHECK : Is the voltage between 10 V and 15 V?
YES : Go to step 8U7.
NO : Go to step 8U6.

8U6 : CHECK AT.

CHECK : Is the AT functioning normally?
YES : Replace TCM.
NO : Repair AT.

8U7 : CHECK OPEN CIRCUIT OF HARNESS.

Measure voltage between ABSCM&H/U connector and chassis ground.

Connector & terminal
(F49) No. 3 (+) — Chassis ground (–):
(F49) No. 31 (+) — Chassis ground (–):

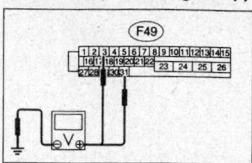

CHECK : Is the voltage between 10 V and 15 V?
YES : Go to step 8U8.
NO : Repair harness/connector between TCM and ABSCM&H/U.

8U8 : CHECK POOR CONTACT IN CONNECTORS.

CHECK : Is there poor contact in connectors between TCM and ABSCM&H/U?
YES : Repair connector.
NO : Go to step 8U9.

8U9 : CHECK ABSCM&H/U.

1) Turn ignition switch to OFF.
2) Connect all connectors.
3) Erase the memory.
4) Perform inspection mode.
5) Read out the trouble code.

CHECK : Is the same trouble code as in the current diagnosis still being output?
YES : Replace ABSCM&H/U.
NO : Go to step 8U10.

SB4029800204020X

Fig. 15 Code 44: A Combination Of A/T Control Abnormal (Part 2 of 3). Less Select Monitor

8V1 : CHECK INPUT VOLTAGE OF ABSCM&H/U.

1) Turn ignition switch to OFF.
2) Disconnect connector from ABSCM&H/U.
3) Run the engine at idle.
4) Measure voltage between ABSCM&H/U connector and chassis ground.

Connector & terminal
(F49) No. 1 (+) — Chassis ground (–):
(F49) No. 24 (+) — Chassis ground (–):

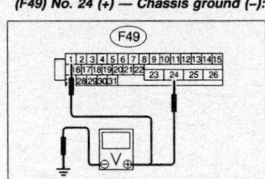

CHECK : Is the voltage between 10 V and 15 V?
YES : Go to step 8V2.
NO : Repair harness connector between battery and ABSCM&H/U.

8V2 : CHECK GROUND CIRCUIT OF ABSCM&H/U.

1) Turn ignition switch to OFF.
2) Measure resistance between ABSCM&H/U connector and chassis ground.

Connector & terminal
(F49) No. 23 — Chassis ground:

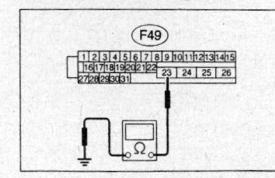

CHECK : Is the resistance less than 0.5 Ω?
YES : Go to step 8V3.
NO : Repair ABSCM&H/U ground harness.

8V3 : CHECK VALVE RELAY IN ABSCM&H/U.

Measure resistance between ABSCM&H/U and terminals.

Terminals
No. 23 (+) — No. 24 (–):

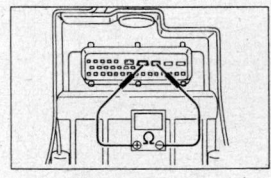

CHECK : Is the resistance more than 1 MΩ?
YES : Go to step 8V4.
NO : Replace ABSCM&H/U.

8V4 : CHECK POOR CONTACT IN CONNECTORS.

CHECK : Is there poor contact in connectors between generator, battery and ABSCM&H/U?
YES : Repair connector.
NO : Go to step 8V5.

8V5 : CHECK ABSCM&H/U.

1) Connect all connectors.
2) Erase the memory.
3) Perform inspection mode.
4) Read out the trouble code.

CHECK : Is the same trouble code as in the current diagnosis still being output?
YES : Replace ABSCM&H/U.
NO : Go to step 8V6.

SB4029800205010X

Fig. 16 Code 51: Abnormal Valve Relay (Part 1 of 2). Less Select Monitor

8V6 : CHECK ANY OTHER TROUBLE CODES APPEARANCE.

(CHECK) : *Are other trouble codes being output?*

(YES) : Proceed with the diagnosis corresponding to the trouble code.

(NO) : A temporary poor contact.

SB4029800205020X

Fig. 16 Code 51: Abnormal Valve Relay (Part 2 of 2). Less Select Monitor

---

8W5 : CHECK MOTOR OPERATION.

Operate the sequence control.

NOTE:
Use the diagnosis connector to operate the sequence control.

(CHECK) : *Can motor revolution noise (buzz) be heard when carrying out the sequence control?*

(YES) : Go to step **8W6**.

(NO) : Replace ABSCM&H/U.

8W6 : CHECK POOR CONTACT IN CONNECTORS.

Turn ignition switch to OFF.

(CHECK) : *Is there poor contact in connector between generator, battery and ABSCM&H/U?*

(YES) : Repair connector.

(NO) : Go to step **8W7**.

8W7 : CHECK ABSCM&H/U.

1) Connect all connectors.
2) Erase the memory.
3) Perform inspection mode.
4) Read out the trouble code.

(CHECK) : *Is the same trouble code as in the current diagnosis still being output?*

(YES) : Replace ABSCM&H/U.

(NO) : Go to step **8W8**.

8W8 : CHECK ANY OTHER TROUBLE CODES APPEARANCE.

(CHECK) : *Are other trouble codes being output?*

(YES) : Proceed with the diagnosis corresponding to the trouble code.

(NO) : A temporary poor contact.

SB4029800206020X

Fig. 17 Code 52: Abnormal Motor And/Or Motor Relay (Part 2 of 2). Less Select Monitor

---

8W1 : CHECK INPUT VOLTAGE OF ABSCM&H/U.

1) Turn ignition switch to OFF.
2) Disconnect connector from ABSCM&H/U.
3) Turn ignition switch to ON.
4) Measure voltage between ABSCM&H/U connector and chassis ground.

Connector & terminal
(F49) No. 25 (+) — Chassis ground (–):

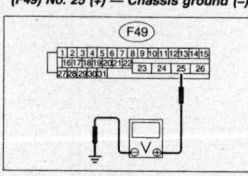

(CHECK) : *Is the voltage between 10 V and 15 V?*
(YES) : Go to step **8W2**.
(NO) : Repair harness/connector between battery and ABSCM&H/U and check fuse SBF-holder.

8W2 : CHECK GROUND CIRCUIT OF MOTOR.

1) Turn ignition switch to OFF.
2) Measure resistance between ABSCM&H/U connector and chassis ground.

Connector & terminal
(F49) No. 26 — Chassis ground:

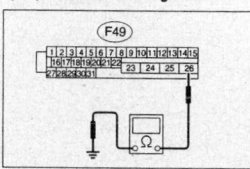

(CHECK) : *Is the resistance less than 0.5 Ω?*
(YES) : Go to step **8W3**.
(NO) : Repair ABSCM&H/U ground harness.

8W3 : CHECK INPUT VOLTAGE OF ABSCM&H/U.

1) Run the engine at idle.
2) Measure voltage between ABSCM&H/U connector and chassis ground.

Connector & terminal
(F49) No. 1 (+) — Chassis ground (–):

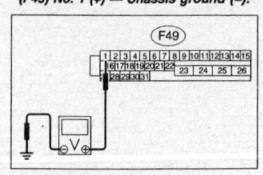

(CHECK) : *Is the voltage between 10 V and 15 V?*
(YES) : Go to step **8W4**.
(NO) : Repair harness connector between battery, ignition switch and ABSCM&H/U.

8W4 : CHECK GROUND CIRCUIT OF ABSCM&H/U.

1) Turn ignition switch to OFF.
2) Measure resistance between ABSCM&H/U connector and chassis ground.

Connector & terminal
(F49) No. 23 — Chassis ground:

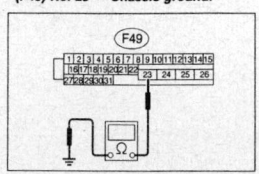

(CHECK) : *Is the resistance less than 0.5 Ω?*
(YES) : Go to step **8W5**.
(NO) : Repair ABSCM&H/U ground harness.

SB4029800206010X

Fig. 17 Code 52: Abnormal Motor And/Or Motor Relay (Part 1 of 2). Less Select Monitor

---

8X2 : CHECK OPEN CIRCUIT IN HARNESS.

1) Turn ignition switch to OFF.
2) Disconnect connector from ABSCM&H/U.
3) Depress brake pedal.
4) Measure voltage between ABSCM&H/U connector and chassis ground.

Connector & terminal
(F49) No. 2 (+) — Chassis ground (–):

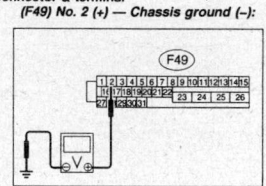

(CHECK) : *Is the voltage between 10 V and 15 V?*
(YES) : Go to step **8X3**.
(NO) : Repair harness between stop light switch and ABSCM&H/U.

8X3 : CHECK POOR CONTACT IN CONNECTORS.

(CHECK) : *Is there poor contact in connector between stop light switch and ABSCM&H/U?*

(YES) : Repair connector.
(NO) : Go to step **8X4**.

8X4 : CHECK ABSCM&H/U.

1) Connect all connectors.
2) Erase the memory.
3) Perform inspection mode.
4) Read out the trouble code.

(CHECK) : *Is the same trouble code as in the current diagnosis still being output?*

(YES) : Replace ABSCM&H/U.
(NO) : Go to step **8X5**.

8X5 : CHECK ANY OTHER TROUBLE CODES APPEARANCE.

(CHECK) : *Are other trouble codes being output?*

(YES) : Proceed with the diagnosis corresponding to the trouble code.

(NO) : A temporary poor contact.

SB4029800207000X

Fig. 18 Code 54: Abnormal Stop Light Switch. Less Select Monitor

8Y2 : CHECK SPECIFICATIONS OF ABSCM&H/U.

Check specifications of the mark to the ABSCM&H/U.

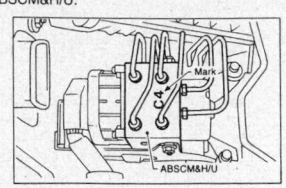

Mark	Model
C3	AWD AT
C4	AWD MT

CHECK : **Is an ABSCM for AWD model installed on a FWD model?**
YES : Replace ABSCM&H/U.
CAUTION:
Be sure to turn ignition switch to OFF when removing ABSCM&H/U.
NO : Go to step **8Y3**.

8Y3 : CHECK INPUT VOLTAGE OF G SENSOR.

1) Turn ignition switch to OFF.
2) Remove console box.
3) Disconnect G sensor from body. (Do not disconnect connector.)
4) Turn ignition switch to ON.
5) Measure voltage between G sensor connector terminals.

**Connector & terminal
(R70) No. 1 (+) — No. 3 (−):**

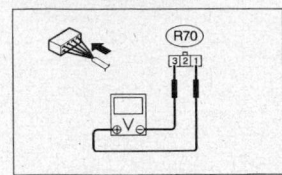

CHECK : **Is the voltage between 4.75 and 5.25 V?**
YES : Go to step **8Y4**.
NO : Repair harness/connector between G sensor and ABSCM&H/U.

SB4029800208010X

Fig. 19   Code 56: Abnormal G sensor Output Voltage (Part 1 of 4). Less Select Monitor

8Y4 : CHECK OPEN CIRCUIT IN G SENSOR OUTPUT HARNESS AND GROUND HARNESS.

1) Turn ignition switch to OFF.
2) Disconnect connector from ABSCM&H/U.
3) Measure resistance between ABSCM&H/U connector terminals.

**Connector & terminal
(F49) No. 30 — No. 28:**

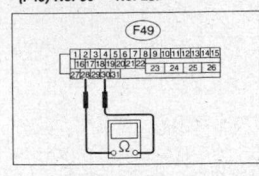

CHECK : **Is the resistance between 4.3 and 4.9 kΩ?**
YES : Go to step **8Y5**.
NO : Repair harness/connector between G sensor and ABSCM&H/U.

8Y5 : CHECK GROUND SHORT IN G SENSOR OUTPUT HARNESS.

1) Disconnect connector from G sensor.
2) Measure resistance between ABSCM&H/U connector and chassis ground.

**Connector & terminal
(F49) No. 6 — Chassis ground:**

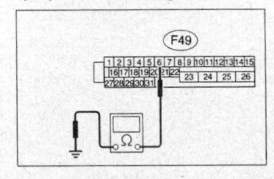

CHECK : **Is the resistance more than 1 MΩ?**
YES : Go to step **8Y6**.
NO : Repair harness between G sensor and ABSCM&H/U.

SB4029800208020X

Fig. 19   Code 56: Abnormal G sensor Output Voltage (Part 2 of 4). Less Select Monitor

8Y6 : CHECK BATTERY SHORT OF HARNESS.

Measure voltage between ABSCM&H/U connector and chassis ground.

**Connector & terminal
(F49) No. 6 (+) — Chassis ground (−):**

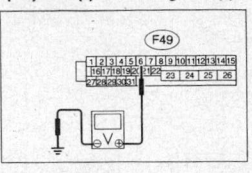

CHECK : **Is the voltage less than 1 V?**
YES : Go to step **8Y7**.
NO : Repair harness between G sensor and ABSCM&H/U.

8Y7 : CHECK BATTERY SHORT OF HARNESS.

1) Turn ignition switch to ON.
2) Measure voltage between ABSCM&H/U connector and chassis ground.

**Connector & terminal
(F49) No. 6 (+) — Chassis ground (−):**

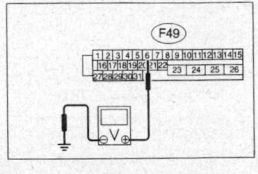

CHECK : **Is the voltage less than 1 V?**
YES : Go to step **8Y8**.
NO : Repair harness between G sensor and ABSCM&H/U.

8Y8 : CHECK GROUND SHORT OF HARNESS.

Measure resistance between ABSCM&H/U connector and chassis ground.

**Connector & terminal
(F49) No. 28 — Chassis ground:**

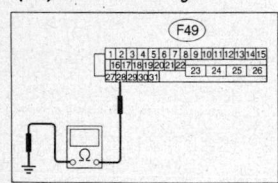

CHECK : **Is the resistance more than 1 MΩ?**
YES : Go to step **8Y9**.
NO : Repair harness between G sensor and ABSCM&H/U.
Replace ABSCM&H/U.

8Y9 : CHECK G SENSOR.

1) Turn ignition switch to OFF.
2) Remove G sensor from vehicle.
3) Connect connector to G sensor.
4) Connect connector to ABSCM&H/U.
5) Turn ignition switch to ON.
6) Measure voltage between G sensor connector terminals.

**Connector & terminal
(R70) No. 2 (+) — No. 3 (−):**

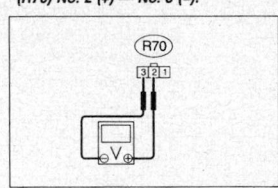

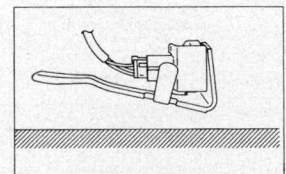

CHECK : **Is the voltage between 2.1 and 2.4 V when G sensor is horizontal?**
YES : Go to step **8Y10**.
NO : Replace G sensor.

SB4029800208030X

Fig. 19   Code 56: Abnormal G sensor Output Voltage (Part 3 of 4). Less Select Monitor

8Y10 : CHECK G SENSOR.

Measure voltage between G sensor connector terminals.

**Connector & terminal
(R70) No. 2 (+) — No. 3 (−):**

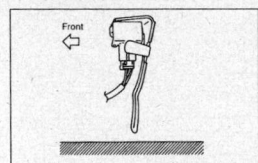

CHECK : **Is the voltage between 3.7 and 4.1 V when G sensor is inclined forwards to 90°?**
YES : Go to step **8Y11**.
NO : Replace G sensor.

8Y11 : CHECK G SENSOR.

Measure voltage between G sensor connector terminals.

**Connector & terminal
(R70) No. 2 (+) — No. 3 (−):**

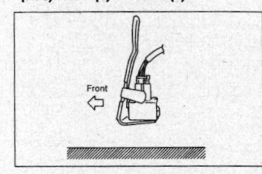

CHECK : **Is the voltage between 0.5 and 0.9 V when G sensor is inclined backwards to 90°?**
YES : Go to step **8Y12**.
NO : Replace G sensor.

8Y12 : CHECK POOR CONTACT IN CONNECTORS.

CHECK : **Is there poor contact in connector between ABSCM&H/U and G sensor?**
YES : Repair connector.
NO : Go to step **8Y13**.

8Y13 : CHECK ABSCM&H/U.

1) Connect all connectors.
2) Erase the memory.
3) Perform inspection mode.
4) Read out the trouble code.

CHECK : **Is the same trouble code as in the current diagnosis still being output?**
YES : Replace ABSCM&H/U.
NO : Go to step **8Y14**.

8Y14 : CHECK ANY OTHER TROUBLE CODES APPEARANCE.

CHECK : **Are other trouble codes being output?**
YES : Proceed with the diagnosis corresponding to the trouble code.
NO : A temporary poor contact.

SB4029800208040X

Fig. 19   Code 56: Abnormal G sensor Output Voltage (Part 4 of 4). Less Select Monitor

10C2 : CHECK GENERATOR.

1) Start the engine.
2) Idle the engine.
3) Measure voltage between generator and chassis ground.

Terminal
Generator B terminal (+) — Chassis ground (–):

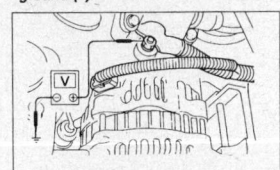

CHECK : **Is the voltage between 10 and 15 V?**
YES : Go to step **10C3**.
NO : Repair generator.

10C3 : CHECK BATTERY TERMINAL.

Turn ignition switch to OFF.

CHECK : **Is there poor contact at battery terminal?**
YES : Repair battery terminal.
NO : Go to step **10C4**.

10C4 : CHECK COMMUNICATION OF SELECT MONITOR.

Using the select monitor, check whether communication to other system (such as engine, AT, etc.) can be executed normally.

CHECK : **Are the name and year of the system displayed on the select monitor?**
YES : Go to step **10C5**.
NO : Repair select monitor communication cable and connector.

SB4029800209010X

10C5 : CHECK INSTALLATION OF ABSCM&H/U CONNECTOR.

Turn ignition switch to OFF.

CHECK : **Is ABSCM&H/U connector inserted into ABSCM&H/U until the clamp locks onto it?**
YES : Go to step **10C6**.
NO : Insert ABSCM&H/U connector into ABSCM&H/U until the clamp locks onto it.

10C6 : CHECK POWER SUPPLY OF ABSCM&H/U.

1) Disconnect connector from ABSCM&H/U.
2) Start engine.
3) Idle the engine.
4) Measure voltage between ABSCM&H/U connector and chassis ground.

Connector & terminal
(F49) No. 1 (+) — Chassis ground (–):

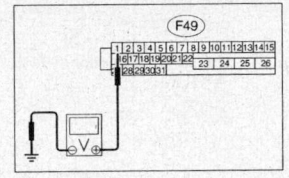

CHECK : **Is the voltage between 10 and 15 V?**
YES : Go to step **10C7**.
NO : Repair ABSCM&H/U power supply circuit.

10C7 : CHECK GROUND CIRCUIT OF ABSCM&H/U.

1) Turn ignition switch to OFF.
2) Measure resistance between ABSCM&H/U connector and chassis ground.

Connector & terminal
(F49) No. 23 — Chassis ground:

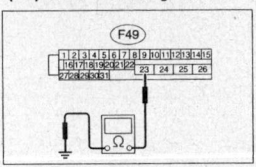

CHECK : **Is the resistance less than 0.5 Ω?**
YES : Repair harness/connector between ABSCM&H/U and select monitor.
NO : Go to step **10C8**.

10C8 : CHECK HARNESS/CONNECTOR BETWEEN ABSCM&H/U AND DATA LINK CONNECTOR.

1) Turn ignition switch OFF.
2) Measure resistance between ABSCM&H/U connector and data link connector.

Connector & terminal
(F49) No. 20 — (B40) No. 5:
(F49) No. 5 — (B40) No. 4:

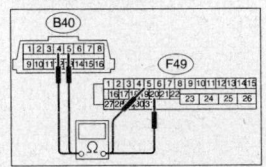

CHECK : **Is the resistance less than 0.5 Ω?**
YES : Repair harness and connector between ABSCM&H/U and data link connector.
NO : Go to step **10C9**.

SB4029800209020X

10C9 : CHECK POOR CONTACT IN CONNECTORS.

CHECK : **Is there poor contact in connectors between ABSCM&H/U and data link connector?**
YES : Repair connector.
NO : Replace ABSCM&H/U.

Fig. 20 Test C: Communication For Initializing Impossible (Part 1 of 2). With Select Monitor

Fig. 20 Test C: Communication For Initializing Impossible (Part 2 of 2). With Select Monitor

---

10D1 : CHECK WIRING HARNESS.

1) Turn ignition switch to OFF.
2) Disconnect connector (F2) from connector (B100).
3) Turn ignition switch to ON.

CHECK : **Does the ABS warning light remain off?**
YES : Go to step **10D2**.
NO : Repair front wiring harness.

10D2 : CHECK PROJECTION AT ABSCM&H/U.

1) Turn ignition switch to OFF.
2) Disconnect connector from ABSCM&H/U.
3) Check for broken projection at the ABSCM&H/U terminal.

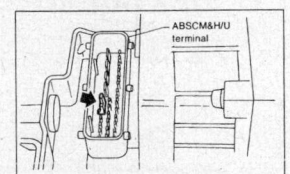

CHECK : **Are the projection broken?**
YES : Go to step **10D3**.
NO : Replace ABSCM&H/U.

10D3 : CHECK ABSCM&H/U.

Measure resistance between ABSCM&H/U terminals.

Terminals
No. 21 — No. 23:

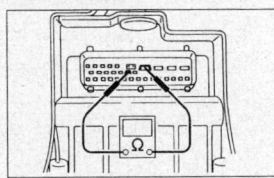

CHECK : **Is the resistance more than 1 MΩ?**
YES : Go to step **10D4**.
NO : Replace valve relay.

10D4 : CHECK WIRING HARNESS.

Measure resistance between connector (F2) and chassis ground.

Connector & terminal
(F2) No. 15 — Chassis ground:

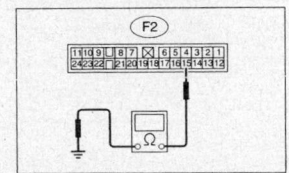

CHECK : **Is the resistance less than 0.5 Ω?**
YES : Go to step **10D5**.
NO : Repair harness.

SB4029800210010X

10D5 : CHECK WIRING HARNESS.

1) Connect connector to ABSCM&H/U.
2) Measure resistance between connector (F2) and chassis ground.

Connector & terminal
(F2) No. 15 — Chassis ground:

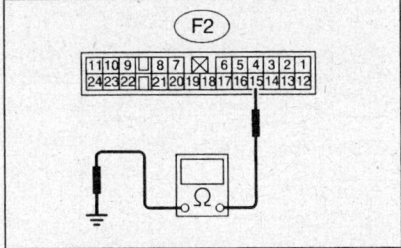

CHECK : **Is the resistance more than 1 MΩ?**
YES : Go to step **10D6**.
NO : Repair harness.

10D6 : CHECK POOR CONTACT IN ABSCM&H/U CONNECTOR.

CHECK : **Is there poor contact in ABSCM&H/U connector?**
YES : Repair connector.
NO : Replace ABSCM&H/U.

SB4029800210020X

Fig. 21 Test D: No Trouble Code (Part 1 of 2). With Select Monitor

Fig. 21 Test D: No Trouble Code (Part 2 of 2). With Select Monitor

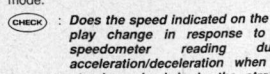

10H1 : CHECK OUTPUT OF ABS SENSOR USING SELECT MONITOR.

1) Select "Current data display & Save" on the select monitor.
2) Read the ABS sensor output corresponding to the faulty system in the select monitor data display mode.

CHECK : *Does the speed indicated on the display change in response to the speedometer reading during acceleration/deceleration when the steering wheel is in the straight-ahead position?*
YES : Go to step **10H2**.
NO : Go to step **10H9**.

10H2 : CHECK INSTALLATION OF ABS SENSOR.

Tightening torque:
32±10 N·m (3.3±1.0 kg-m, 24±7 ft-lb)

CHECK : *Are the ABS sensor installation bolts tightened securely?*
YES : Go to step **10H3**.
NO : Tighten ABS sensor installation bolts securely.

10H3 : CHECK INSTALLATION OF TONE WHEEL.

Tightening torque:
13±3 N·m (1.3±0.3 kg-m, 9±2.2 ft-lb)

CHECK : *Are the tone wheel installation bolts tightened securely?*
YES : Go to step **10H4**.
NO : Tighten tone wheel installation bolts securely.

10H4 : CHECK ABS SENSOR GAP.

Measure tone wheel-to-pole piece gap over entire perimeter of the wheel.

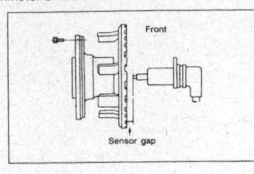
Front
Sensor gap

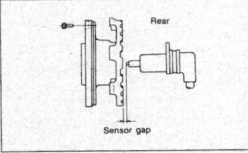
Rear
Sensor gap

	Front wheel	Rear wheel
Specifications	0.9 — 1.4 mm (0.035 — 0.055 in)	0.7 — 1.2 mm (0.028 — 0.047 in)

CHECK : *Is the gap within the specifications?*
YES : Go to step **10H5**.
NO : Adjust the gap.

NOTE:
Adjust the gap using spacers (Part No. 26755AA000). If spacers cannot correct the gap, replace worn sensor or worn tone wheel.

10H5 : CHECK HUB RUNOUT.

Measure hub runout.

CHECK : *Is the runout less than 0.05 mm (0.0020 in)?*
YES : Go to step **10H6**.
NO : Repair hub.

SB4029800211010X

10H6 : CHECK POOR CONTACT IN CONNECTORS.

Turn ignition switch to OFF.

CHECK : *Is there poor contact in connectors between ABSCM&H/U and ABS sensor?*
YES : Repair connector.
NO : Go to step **10H7**.

10H7 : CHECK ABSCM&H/U.

1) Connect all connectors.
2) Erase the memory.
3) Perform inspection mode.
4) Read out the trouble code.

CHECK : *Is the same trouble code as in the current diagnosis still being output?*
YES : Replace ABSCM&H/U.
NO : Go to step **10H8**.

10H8 : CHECK ANY OTHER TROUBLE CODES APPEARANCE.

CHECK : *Are other trouble codes being output?*
YES : Proceed with the diagnosis corresponding to the trouble code.
NO : A temporary poor contact.

NOTE:
Check harness and connectors between ABSCM&H/U and ABS sensor.

10H9 : CHECK ABS SENSOR.

1) Turn ignition switch to OFF.
2) Disconnect connector from ABS sensor.
3) Measure resistance of ABS sensor connector terminals.

Terminal
Front RH No. 1 — No. 2:
Front LH No. 1 — No. 2:
Rear RH No. 1 — No. 2:
Rear LH No. 1 — No. 2:

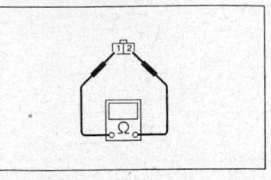

CHECK : *Is the resistance between 0.8 and 1.2 kΩ?*
YES : Go to step **10H10**.
NO : Replace ABS sensor.

SB4029800211020X

Fig. 22 Codes 21, 23, 25 & 27: Abnormal ABS Sensor, Open Or Short Circuit In ABS Sensor (Part 2 of 6). With Select Monitor

Fig. 22 Codes 21, 23, 25 & 27: Abnormal ABS Sensor, Open Or Short Circuit In ABS Sensor (Part 1 of 6). With Select Monitor

10H10 : CHECK BATTERY SHORT OF ABS SENSOR.

1) Disconnect connector from ABSCM&H/U.
2) Measure voltage between ABS sensor and chassis ground.

Terminal
Front RH No. 1 (+) — Chassis ground (–):
Front LH No. 1 (+) — Chassis ground (–):
Rear RH No. 1 (+) — Chassis ground (–):
Rear LH No. 1 (+) — Chassis ground (–):

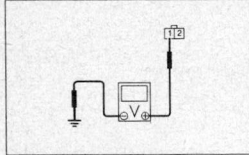

CHECK : *Is the voltage less than 1 V?*
YES : Go to step **10H11**.
NO : Replace ABS sensor.

10H11 : CHECK BATTERY SHORT OF ABS SENSOR.

1) Turn ignition switch to ON.
2) Measure voltage between ABS sensor and chassis ground.

Terminal
Front RH No. 1 (+) — Chassis ground (–):
Front LH No. 1 (+) — Chassis ground (–):
Rear RH No. 1 (+) — Chassis ground (–):
Rear LH No. 1 (+) — Chassis ground (–):

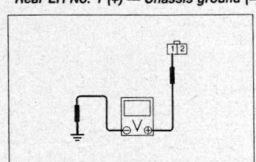

CHECK : *Is the voltage less than 1 V?*
YES : Go to step **10H12**.
NO : Replace ABS sensor.

SB4029800211030X

10H12 : CHECK HARNESS/CONNECTOR BETWEEN ABSCM&H/U AND ABS SENSOR.

1) Turn ignition switch to OFF.
2) Connect connector to ABS sensor.
3) Measure resistance between ABSCM&H/U connector terminals.

Connector & terminal
Trouble code 21 / (F49) No. 11 — No. 12:
Trouble code 23 / (F49) No. 9 — No. 10:
Trouble code 25 / (F49) No. 14 — No. 15:
Trouble code 27 / (F49) No. 7 — No. 8:

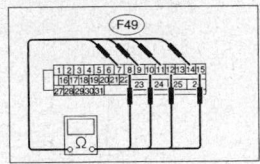
F49

CHECK : *Is the resistance between 0.8 and 1.2 kΩ?*
YES : Go to step **10H13**.
NO : Repair harness/connector between ABSCM&H/U and ABS sensor.

Fig. 22 Codes 21, 23, 25 & 27: Abnormal ABS Sensor, Open Or Short Circuit In ABS Sensor (Part 3 of 6). With Select Monitor

10H13 : CHECK BATTERY SHORT OF HARNESS.

Measure voltage between ABSCM&H/U connector and chassis ground.

Connector & terminal
Trouble code 21 / (F49) No. 11 (+) — Chassis ground (–):
Trouble code 23 / (F49) No. 9 (+) — Chassis ground (–):
Trouble code 25 / (F49) No. 14 (+) — Chassis ground (–):
Trouble code 27 / (F49) No. 7 (+) — Chassis ground (–):

F49

CHECK : *Is the voltage less than 1 V?*
YES : Go to step **10H14**.
NO : Repair harness between ABSCM&H/U and ABS sensor.

10H14 : CHECK BATTERY SHORT OF HARNESS.

1) Turn ignition switch to ON.
2) Measure voltage between ABSCM&H/U connector and chassis ground.

Connector & terminal
Trouble code 21 / (F49) No. 11 (+) — Chassis ground (–):
Trouble code 23 / (F49) No. 9 (+) — Chassis ground (–):
Trouble code 25 / (F49) No. 14 (+) — Chassis ground (–):
Trouble code 27 / (F49) No. 7 (+) — Chassis ground (–):

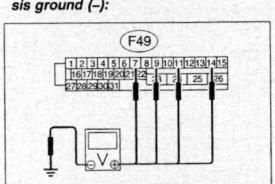
F49

CHECK : *Is the voltage less than 1 V?*
YES : Go to step **10H15**.
NO : Repair harness between ABSCM&H/U and ABS sensor.

10H15 : CHECK INSTALLATION OF ABS SENSOR.

Tightening torque:
32±10 N·m (3.3±1.0 kg-m, 24±7 ft-lb)

CHECK : *Are the ABS sensor installation bolts tightened securely?*
YES : Go to step **10H16**.
NO : Tighten ABS sensor installation bolts securely.

SB4029800211040X

Fig. 22 Codes 21, 23, 25 & 27: Abnormal ABS Sensor, Open Or Short Circuit In ABS Sensor (Part 4 of 6). With Select Monitor

10H16 : CHECK INSTALLATION OF TONE WHEEL.

Tightening torque:
13±3 N·m (1.3±0.3 kg-m, 9±2.2 ft-lb)

CHECK : *Are the tone wheel installation bolts tightened securely?*

YES : Go to step **10H17.**

NO : Tighten tone wheel installation bolts securely.

10H17 : CHECK ABS SENSOR GAP.

Measure tone wheel-to-pole piece gap over entire perimeter of the wheel.

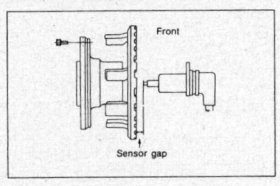

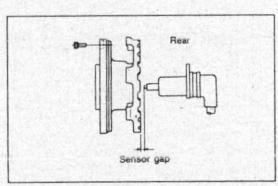

Specifications	Front wheel	Rear wheel
	0.9 — 1.4 mm (0.035 — 0.055 in)	0.7 — 1.2 mm (0.028 — 0.047 in)

CHECK : *Is the gap within the specificationss?*

YES : Go to step **10H18.**

NO : Adjust the gap.

NOTE:
Adjust the gap using spacers (Part No. 26755AA000). If spacers cannot correct the gap, replace worn sensor or worn tone wheel.

SB4029800211050X

10H18 : CHECK HUB RUNOUT.

Measure hub runout.

CHECK : *Is the runout less than 0.05 mm (0.0020 in)?*

YES : Go to step **10H19.**

NO : Repair hub.

10H19 : CHECK GROUND SHORT OF ABS SENSOR.

1) Turn ignition switch to ON.
2) Measure resistance between ABS sensor and chassis ground.

Terminal
Front RH No. 1 — Chassis ground:
Front LH No. 1 — Chassis ground:
Rear RH No. 1 — Chassis ground:
Rear LH No. 1 — Chassis ground:

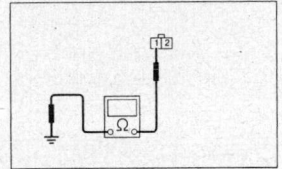

CHECK : *Is the resistance more than 1 MΩ?*

YES : Go to step **10H20.**

NO : Replace ABS sensor and ABSCM&H/U.

10H20 : CHECK GROUND SHORT OF HARNESS.

1) Turn ignition switch to OFF.
2) Connect connector to ABS sensor.
3) Measure resistance between ABSCM&H/U connector terminal and chassis ground.

Connector & terminal
Trouble code 21 / (F49) No. 11 — Chassis ground:
Trouble code 23 / (F49) No. 9 — Chassis ground:
Trouble code 25 / (F49) No. 14 — Chassis ground:
Trouble code 27 / (F49) No. 7 — Chassis ground:

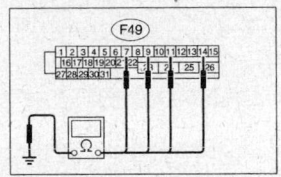

CHECK : *Is the resistance more than 1 MΩ?*

YES : Go to step **10H21.**

NO : Repair harness between ABSCM&H/U and ABS sensor.
And replace ABSCM&H/U.

10H21 : CHECK POOR CONTACT IN CONNECTORS.

CHECK : *Is there poor contact in connectors between ABSCM&H/U and ABS sensor?*

YES : Repair connector.

NO : Go to step **10H22.**

10H22 : CHECK ABSCM&H/U.

1) Connect all connectors.
2) Erase the memory.
3) Perform inspection mode.
4) Read out the trouble code.

CHECK : *Is the same trouble code as in the current diagnosis still being output?*

YES : Replace ABSCM&H/U.

NO : Go to step **10H23.**

10H23 : CHECK ANY OTHER TROUBLE CODES APPEARANCE.

CHECK : *Are other trouble codes being output?*

YES : Proceed with the diagnosis corresponding to the trouble code.

NO : A temporary poor contact.

NOTE:
Check harness and connectors between ABSCM&H/U and ABS sensor.

SB4029800211060X

Fig. 22   Codes 21, 23, 25 & 27: Abnormal ABS Sensor, Open Or Short Circuit In ABS Sensor (Part 6 of 6). With Select Monitor

Fig. 22   Codes 21, 23, 25 & 27: Abnormal ABS Sensor, Open Or Short Circuit In ABS Sensor (Part 5 of 6). With Select Monitor

10L1 : CHECK OUTPUT OF ABS SENSOR USING SELECT MONITOR.

1) Select "Current data display & Save" on the select monitor.
2) Read the ABS sensor output corresponding to the faulty system in the select monitor data display mode.

CHECK : *Does the speed indicated on the display change in response to the speedometer reading during acceleration/deceleration when the steering wheel is in the straight-ahead position?*

YES : Go to step **10L2**.
NO : Go to step **10L8**.

10L2 : CHECK POOR CONTACT IN CONNECTORS.

Turn ignition switch to OFF.

CHECK : *Is there poor contact in connectors between ABSCM&H/U and ABS sensor?*

YES : Repair connector.
NO : Go to step **10L3**.

10L3 : CHECK SOURCES OF SIGNAL NOISE.

CHECK : *Is the car telephone or the wireless transmitter properly installed?*

YES : Go to step **10L4**.
NO : Properly install the car telephone or the wireless transmitter.

10L4 : CHECK SOURCES OF SIGNAL NOISE.

CHECK : *Are noise sources (such as an antenna) installed near the sensor harness?*

YES : Install the noise sources apart from the sensor harness.
NO : Go to step **10L5**.

10L5 : CHECK SHIELD CIRCUIT.

1) Turn ignition switch to OFF.
2) Connect all connectors.
3) Measure resistance between shield connector and chassis ground.

Connector & terminal
    Trouble code 22 / (B100) No. 23 — Chassis ground:
    Trouble code 24 / (B100) No. 10 — Chassis ground:
    Trouble code 26 / (B100) No. 2 — Chassis ground:
    Trouble code 28 / (B100) No. 13 — Chassis ground:

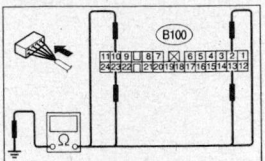

CHECK : *Is the resistance less than 0.5 Ω?*
YES : Go to step **10L6**.
NO : Repair shield harness.

10L6 : CHECK ABSCM&H/U.

1) Connect all connectors.
2) Erase the memory.
3) Perform inspection mode.
4) Read out the trouble code.

CHECK : *Is the same trouble code as in the current diagnosis still being output?*

YES : Replace ABSCM&H/U.
NO : Go to step **10L7**.

10L7 : CHECK ANY OTHER TROUBLE CODES APPEARANCE.

CHECK : *Are other trouble codes being output?*

YES : Proceed with the diagnosis corresponding to the trouble code.
NO : A temporary noise interference.

SB4029800212010X

Fig. 23 Codes 22, 24, 26 & 28: ABS Sensor Abnormal Signal (Part 1 of 6). With Select Monitor

10L8 : CHECK INSTALLATION OF ABS SENSOR.

Tightening torque:
    32±10 N·m (3.3±1.0 kg-m, 24±7 ft-lb)

CHECK : *Are the ABS sensor installation bolts tightened securely?*

YES : Go to step **10L9**.
NO : Tighten ABS sensor installation bolts securely.

10L9 : CHECK INSTALLATION OF TONE WHEEL.

Tightening torque:
    13±3 N·m (1.3±0.3 kg-m, 9±2.2 ft-lb)

CHECK : *Are the tone wheel installation bolts tightened securely?*

YES : Go to step **10L10**.
NO : Tighten tone wheel installation bolts securely.

10L10 : CHECK ABS SENSOR GAP.

Measure tone wheel to pole piece gap over entire perimeter of the wheel.

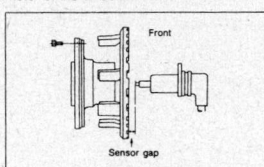

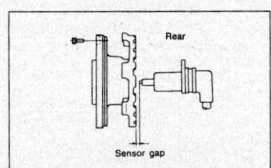

Specifications	Front wheel	Rear wheel
	0.9 — 1.4 mm (0.035 — 0.055 in)	0.7 — 1.2 mm (0.028 — 0.047 in)

CHECK : *Is the gap within the specifications?*
YES : Go to step **10L11**.
NO : Adjust the gap.

NOTE:
Adjust the gap using spacer (Part No. 26755AA000). If spacers cannot correct the gap, replace worn sensor or worn tone wheel.

10L11 : CHECK OSCILLOSCOPE.

CHECK : *Is an oscilloscope available?*
YES : Go to step **10L12**.
NO : Go to step **10L13**.

SB4029800212020X

Fig. 23 Codes 22, 24, 26 & 28: ABS Sensor Abnormal Signal (Part 2 of 6). With Select Monitor

10L12 : CHECK ABS SENSOR SIGNAL.

1) Raise all four wheels of ground.
2) Turn ignition switch OFF.
3) Connect the oscilloscope to the connector (B100) in accordance with trouble code.
4) Turn ignition switch ON.
5) Rotate wheels and measure voltage at specified frequency.

NOTE:
When this inspection is completed, the ABSCM&H/U sometimes stores the trouble code 29.

Connector & terminal
Trouble code 22 / (B100) No. 9 (+) — No. 22 (–):
Trouble code 24 / (B100) No. 11 (+) — No. 24 (–):
Trouble code 26 / (B100) No. 1 (+) — No. 12 (–):
Trouble code 28 / (B100) No. 3 (+) — No. 14 (–):
Specified voltage: 0.12 – 1 V (When it is 20 Hz.)

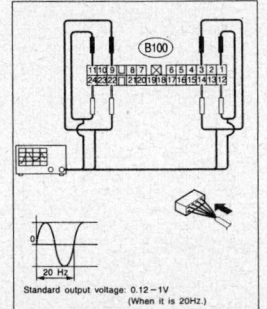

(CHECK) : Is oscilloscope pattern smooth, as shown in figure?
(YES) : Go to step 10L16.
(NO) : Go to step 10L13.

10L13 : CHECK CONTAMINATION OF ABS SENSOR OR TONE WHEEL.

Remove disc rotor or drum from hub in accordance with trouble code.

(CHECK) : Is the ABS sensor pole piece or the tone wheel contaminated by dirt or other foreign matter?
(YES) : Thoroughly remove dirt or other foreign matter.
(NO) : Go to step 10L14.

10L14 : CHECK DAMAGE OF ABS SENSOR OR TONE WHEEL.

(CHECK) : Are there broken or damaged in the ABS sensor pole piece or the tone wheel?
(YES) : Replace ABS sensor or tone wheel.
(NO) : Go to step 10L15.

10L15 : CHECK HUB RUNOUT.

Measure hub runout.

(CHECK) : Is the runout less than 0.05 mm (0.0020 in)?
(YES) : Go to step 10L16.
(NO) : Repair hub.

10L16 : CHECK RESISTANCE OF ABS SENSOR.

1) Turn ignition switch OFF.
2) Disconnect connector from ABS sensor.
3) Measure resistance between ABS sensor connector terminals.

Terminal
Front RH No. 1 — No. 2:
Front LH No. 1 — No. 2:
Rear RH No. 1 — No. 2:
Rear LH No. 1 — No. 2:

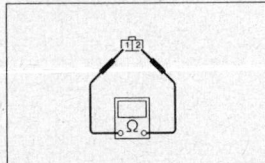

(CHECK) : Is the resistance between 0.8 and 1.2 kΩ?
(YES) : Go to step 10L17.
(NO) : Replace ABS sensor.

10L17 : CHECK GROUND SHORT OF ABS SENSOR.

Measure resistance between ABS sensor and chassis ground.

Terminal
Front RH No. 1 — Chassis ground:
Front LH No. 1 — Chassis ground:
Rear RH No. 1 — Chassis ground:
Rear LH No. 1 — Chassis ground:

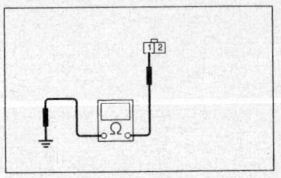

(CHECK) : Is the resistance more than 1 MΩ?
(YES) : Go to step 10L18.
(NO) : Replace ABS sensor.

SB4029800212040X

Fig. 23 Codes 22, 24, 26 & 28: ABS Sensor Abnormal Signal (Part 4 of 6). With Select Monitor

SB4029800212030X

Fig. 23 Codes 22, 24, 26 & 28: ABS Sensor Abnormal Signal (Part 3 of 6). With Select Monitor

10L18 : CHECK HARNESS/CONNECTOR BETWEEN ABSCM&H/U AND ABS SENSOR.

1) Connect connector to ABS sensor.
2) Disconnect connector from ABSCM&H/U.
3) Measure resistance at ABSCM&H/U connector terminals.

Connector & terminal
Trouble code 22 / (F49) No. 11 — No. 12:
Trouble code 24 / (F49) No. 9 — No. 10:
Trouble code 26 / (F49) No. 14 — No. 15:
Trouble code 28 / (F49) No. 7 — No. 8:

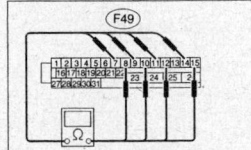

(CHECK) : Is the resistance between 0.8 and 1.2 kΩ?
(YES) : Go to step 10L19.
(NO) : Repair harness/connector between ABSCM&H/U and ABS sensor.

10L19 : CHECK GROUND SHORT OF HARNESS.

Measure resistance between ABSCM&H/U connector and chassis ground.

Connector & terminal
Trouble code 22 / (F49) No. 11 — Chassis ground:
Trouble code 24 / (F49) No. 9 — Chassis ground:
Trouble code 26 / (F49) No. 14 — Chassis ground:
Trouble code 28 / (F49) No. 7 — Chassis ground:

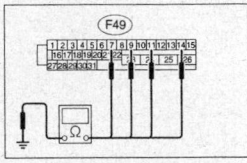

(CHECK) : Is the resistance more than 1 MΩ?
(YES) : Go to step 10L20.
(NO) : Repair harness/connector between ABSCM&H/U and ABS sensor.

10L20 : CHECK GROUND CIRCUIT OF ABSCM&H/U.

Measure resistance between ABSCM&H/U and chassis ground.

Connector & terminal
(F49) No. 23 — GND:

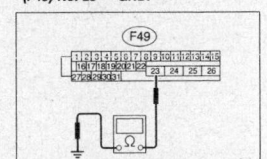

(CHECK) : Is the resistance less than 0.5 Ω?
(YES) : Go to step 10L21.
(NO) : Repair ABSCM&H/U ground harness.

10L21 : CHECK POOR CONTACT IN CONNECTORS.

(CHECK) : Is there poor contact in connectors between ABSCM&H/U and ABS sensor?
(YES) : Repair connector.
(NO) : Go to step 10L22.

10L22 : CHECK SOURCES OF SIGNAL NOISE.

(CHECK) : Is the car telephone or the wireless transmitter properly installed?
(YES) : Go to step 10L23.
(NO) : Properly install the car telephone or the wireless transmitter.

10L23 : CHECK SOURCES OF SIGNAL NOISE.

(CHECK) : Are noise sources (such as an antenna) installed near the sensor harness?
(YES) : Install the noise sources apart from the sensor harness.
(NO) : Go to step 10L24.

10L24 : CHECK SHIELD CIRCUIT.

1) Connect all connectors.
2) Measure resistance between shield connector and chassis ground.

Connector & terminal
Trouble code 22 / (B100) No. 23 — Chassis ground:
Trouble code 24 / (B100) No. 10 — Chassis ground:
Trouble code 26 / (B100) No. 2 — Chassis ground:
Trouble code 28 / (B100) No. 13 — Chassis ground:

(CHECK) : Is the resistance less than 0.5 Ω?
(YES) : Go to step 10L25.
(NO) : Repair shield harness.

10L25 : CHECK ABSCM&H/U.

1) Connect all connectors.
2) Erase the memory.
3) Perform inspection mode.
4) Read out the trouble code.

(CHECK) : Is the same trouble code as in the current diagnosis still being output?
(YES) : Replace ABSCM&H/U.
(NO) : Go to step 10L26.

10L26 : CHECK ANY OTHER TROUBLE CODES APPEARANCE.

(CHECK) : Are other trouble codes being output?
(YES) : Proceed with the diagnosis corresponding to the trouble code.
(NO) : A temporary noise interference.

SB4029800212060X

Fig. 23 Codes 22, 24, 26 & 28: ABS Sensor Abnormal Signal (Part 6 of 6). With Select Monitor

SB4029800212050X

Fig. 23 Codes 22, 24, 26 & 28: ABS Sensor Abnormal Signal (Part 5 of 6). With Select Monitor

10M1 : CHECK IF THE WHEELS HAVE TURNED FREELY FOR A LONG TIME.

CHECK : *Check if the wheels have been turned freely for more than one minute, such as when the vehicle is jacked-up, under full-lock cornering or when tire is not in contact with road surface.*

YES : The ABS is normal. Erase the trouble code.

NOTE:
When the wheels turn freely for a long time, such as when the vehicle is towed or jacked-up, or when steering wheel is continuously turned all the way, this trouble code may sometimes occur.

NO : Go to step 10M2.

10M2 : CHECK TIRE SPECIFICATIONS.

Turn ignition switch to OFF.

CHECK : *Are the tire specifications correct?*

YES : Go to step 10M3.

NO : Replace tire.

10M3 : CHECK WEAR OF TIRE.

CHECK : *Is the tire worn excessively?*

YES : Replace tire.

NO : Go to step 10M4.

10M4 : CHECK TIRE PRESSURE.

CHECK : *Is the tire pressure correct?*

YES : Go to step 10M5.

NO : Adjust tire pressure.

10M5 : CHECK INSTALLATION OF ABS SENSOR.

Tightening torque:
32±10 N·m (3.3±1.0 kg-m, 24±7 ft-lb)

CHECK : *Are the ABS sensor installation bolts tightened securely?*

YES : Go to step 10M6.

NO : Tighten ABS sensor installation bolts securely.

10M6 : CHECK INSTALLATION OF TONE WHEEL.

Tightening torque:
13±3 N·m (1.3±0.3 kg-m, 9±2.2 ft-lb)

CHECK : *Are the tone wheel installation bolts tightened securely?*

YES : Go to step 10M7.

NO : Tighten tone wheel installation bolts securely.

10M7 : CHECK ABS SENSOR GAP.

Measure tone wheel to pole piece gap over entire perimeter of the wheel.

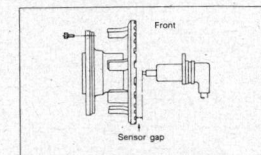

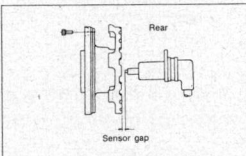

	Front wheel	Rear wheel
Specifications	0.9 — 1.4 mm (0.035 — 0.055 in)	0.7 — 1.2 mm (0.028 — 0.047 in)

CHECK : *Is the gap within the specifications?*

YES : Go to step 10M8.

NO : Adjust the gap.

NOTE:
Adjust the gap using spacer (Part No. 26755AA000). If spacers cannot correct the gap, replace worn sensor or worn tone wheel.

SB4029800213010X

10M8 : CHECK OSCILLOSCOPE.

CHECK : *Is an oscilloscope available?*

YES : Go to step 10M9.

NO : Go to step 10M10.

10M9 : CHECK ABS SENSOR SIGNAL.

1) Raise all four wheels of ground.
2) Turn ignition switch OFF.
3) Connect the oscilloscope to the connector (B100) in accordance with trouble code.
4) Turn ignition switch ON.
5) Rotate wheels and measure voltage at specified frequency.

NOTE:
When this inspection is completed, the ABSCM&H/U sometimes stores the trouble code 29.

Connector & terminal
(B100) No. 9 (+) — No. 22 (–) (Front RH):
(B100) No. 11 (+) — No. 24 (–) (Front LH):
(B100) No. 1 (+) — No. 12 (–) (Rear RH):
(B100) No. 3 (+) — No. 14 (–) (Rear LH):
Specified voltage: 0.12 — 1 V (When it is 20 Hz.)

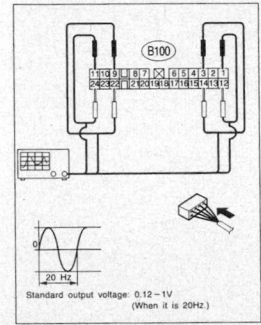

CHECK : *Is oscilloscope pattern smooth, as shown in figure?*

YES : Go to step 10M13.

NO : Go to step 10M10.

10M10 : CHECK CONTAMINATION OF ABS SENSOR OR TONE WHEEL.

Remove disc rotor from hub.

CHECK : *Is the ABS sensor pole piece or the tone wheel contaminated by dirt or other foreign matter?*

YES : Thoroughly remove dirt or other foreign matter.

NO : Go to step 10M11.

10M11 : CHECK DAMAGE OF ABS SENSOR OR TONE WHEEL.

CHECK : *Are there broken or damaged teeth in the ABS sensor pole piece or the tone wheel?*

YES : Replace ABS sensor or tone wheel.

NO : Go to step 10M12.

10M12 : CHECK HUB RUNOUT.

Measure hub runout.

CHECK : *Is the runout less than 0.05 mm (0.0020 in)?*

YES : Go to step 10M13.

NO : Repair hub.

10M13 : CHECK ABSCM&H/U.

1) Turn ignition switch to OFF.
2) Connect all connectors.
3) Erase the memory.
4) Perform inspection mode.
5) Read out the trouble code.

CHECK : *Is the same trouble code as in the current diagnosis still being output?*

YES : Replace ABSCM&H/U.

NO : Go to step 10M14.

10M14 : CHECK ANY OTHER TROUBLE CODES APPEARANCE.

CHECK : *Are other trouble codes being output?*

YES : Proceed with the diagnosis corresponding to the trouble code.

NO : A temporary poor contact.

SB4029800213020X

Fig. 24   Code 29: Abnormal ABS Sensor Signal On Any One Of Four Sensors (Part 1 of 2). With Select Monitor

Fig. 24   Code 29: Abnormal ABS Sensor Signal On Any One Of Four Sensors (Part 2 of 2). With Select Monitor

10Q1 : CHECK INPUT VOLTAGE OF ABSCM&H/U.

1) Turn ignition switch to OFF.
2) Disconnect connector from ABSCM&H/U.
3) Run the engine at idle.
4) Measure voltage between ABSCM&H/U connector and chassis ground.

Connector & terminal
(F49) No. 1 (+) — Chassis ground (–):

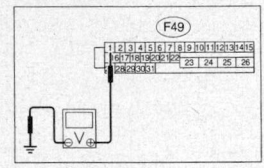

CHECK : *Is the voltage between 10 V and 15 V?*

YES : Go to step 10Q2.

NO : Repair harness connector between battery, ignition switch and ABSCM&H/U.

10Q2 : CHECK GROUND CIRCUIT OF ABSCM&H/U.

1) Turn ignition switch to OFF.
2) Measure resistance between ABSCM&H/U connector and chassis ground.

Connector & terminal
(F49) No. 23 — Chassis ground:

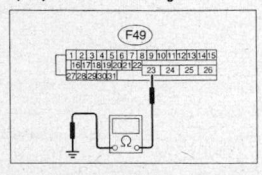

CHECK : *Is the resistance less than 0.5 Ω?*

YES : Go to step 10Q3.

NO : Repair ABSCM&H/U ground harness.

10Q3 : CHECK POOR CONTACT IN CONNECTORS.

CHECK : *Is there poor contact in connectors between generator, battery and ABSCM&H/U?*

YES : Repair connector.

NO : Go to step 10Q4.

10Q4 : CHECK ABSCM&H/U.

1) Connect all connectors.
2) Erase the memory.
3) Perform inspection mode.
4) Read out the trouble code.

CHECK : *Is the same trouble code as in the current diagnosis still being output?*

YES : Replace ABSCM&H/U.

NO : Go to step 10Q5.

10Q5 : CHECK ANY OTHER TROUBLE CODES APPEARANCE.

CHECK : *Are other trouble codes being output?*

YES : Proceed with the diagnosis corresponding to the trouble code.

NO : A temporary poor contact.

SB4029800214000X

Fig. 25   Codes 31, 33, 35 & 37: Inlet Solenoid Valve Malfunction. With Select monitor

10U1 : CHECK INPUT VOLTAGE OF ABSCM&H/U.

1) Turn ignition switch to OFF.
2) Disconnect connector from ABSCM&H/U.
3) Run the engine at idle.
4) Measure voltage between ABSCM&H/U connector and chassis ground.

Connector & terminal
(F49) No. 1 (+) — Chassis ground (–):

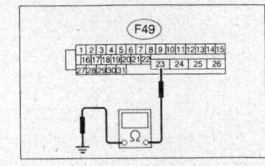

CHECK : *Is the voltage between 10 V and 15 V?*

YES : Go to step 10U2.

NO : Repair harness connector between battery, ignition switch and ABSCM&H/U.

10U2 : CHECK GROUND CIRCUIT OF ABSCM&H/U.

1) Turn ignition switch to OFF.
2) Measure resistance between ABSCM&H/U connector and chassis ground.

Connector & terminal
(F49) No. 23 — Chassis ground:

CHECK : *Is the resistance less than 0.5 Ω?*

YES : Go to step 10U3.

NO : Repair ABSCM&H/U ground harness.

10U3 : CHECK POOR CONTACT IN CONNECTORS.

CHECK : *Is there poor contact in connectors between generator, battery and ABSCM&H/U?*

YES : Repair connector.

NO : Go to step 10U4.

10U4 : CHECK ABSCM&H/U.

1) Connect all connectors.
2) Erase the memory.
3) Perform inspection mode.
4) Read out the trouble code.

CHECK : *Is the same trouble code as in the current diagnosis still being output?*

YES : Replace ABSCM&H/U.

NO : Go to step 10U5.

10U5 : CHECK ANY OTHER TROUBLE CODES APPEARANCE.

CHECK : *Are other trouble codes being output?*

YES : Proceed with the diagnosis corresponding to the trouble code.

NO : A temporary poor contact.

SB4029800215000X

Fig. 26   Codes 32, 34, 36 & 38: Outlet Solenoid Valve Malfunction. With Select Monitor

10V1 : CHECK GROUND CIRCUIT OF ABSCM&H/U.

1) Turn ignition switch to OFF.
2) Disconnect connector from ABSCM&H/U.
3) Measure resistance between ABSCM&H/U and chassis ground.

Connector & terminal
(F49) No. 23 — Chassis ground:

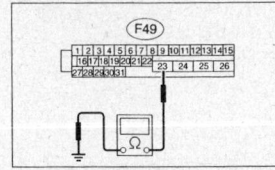

CHECK : *Is the resistance less than 0.5 Ω?*
YES : Go to step **10V2**.
NO : Repair ABSCM&H/U ground harness.

10V2 : CHECK POOR CONTACT IN CON-NECTORS.

CHECK : *Is there poor contact in connectors between battery, ignition switch and ABSCM&H/U?*
YES : Repair connector.
NO : Go to step **10V3**.

10V3 : CHECK SOURCES OF SIGNAL NOISE.

CHECK : *Is the car telephone or the wireless transmitter properly installed?*
YES : Go to step **10V4**.
NO : Properly install the car telephone or the wireless transmitter.

10V4 : CHECK SOURCES OF SIGNAL NOISE.

CHECK : *Are noise sources (such as an antenna) installed near the sensor harness?*
YES : Install the noise sources apart from the sensor harness.
NO : Go to step **10V5**.

10V5 : CHECK ABSCM&H/U.

1) Turn ignition switch to OFF.
2) Connect all connectors.
3) Erase the memory.
4) Perform inspection mode.
5) Read out the trouble code.

CHECK : *Is the same trouble code as in the current diagnosis still being output?*
YES : Replace ABSCM&H/U.
NO : Go to step **10V6**.

10V6 : CHECK ANY OTHER TROUBLE CODES APPEARANCE.

CHECK : *Are other trouble codes being output?*
YES : Proceed with the diagnosis corresponding to the trouble code.
NO : A temporary poor contact.

SB4029800216000X

Fig. 27 Code 41: ABS Control Module Malfunction. With Select Monitor

10W5 : CHECK POOR CONTACT IN CON-NECTORS.

CHECK : *Is there poor contact in connectors between generator, battery and ABSCM&H/U?*
YES : Repair connector.
NO : Go to step **10W6**.

10W6 : CHECK ABSCM&H/U.

1) Connect all connectors.
2) Erase the memory.
3) Perform inspection mode.
4) Read out the trouble code.

CHECK : *Is the same trouble code as in the current diagnosis still being output?*
YES : Replace ABSCM&H/U.
NO : Go to step **10W7**.

10W7 : CHECK ANY OTHER TROUBLE CODES APPEARANCE.

CHECK : *Are other trouble codes being output?*
YES : Proceed with the diagnosis corresponding to the trouble code.
NO : A temporary poor contact.

SB4029800217020X

Fig. 28 Code 42: Power Supply Voltage Too Low (Part 2 of 2). With Select Monitor

10W1 : CHECK GENERATOR.

1) Start engine.
2) Idling after warm-up.
3) Measure voltage between generator B terminal and chassis ground.

Terminal
Generator B terminal — Chassis ground:

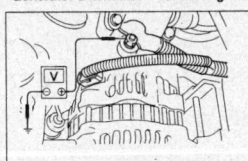

CHECK : *Is the voltage between 10 V and 15 V?*
YES : Go to step **10W2**.
NO : Repair generator.

10W2 : CHECK BATTERY TERMINAL.

Turn ignition switch to OFF.

CHECK : *Are the positive and negative battery terminals tightly clamped?*
YES : Go to step **10W3**.
NO : Tighten the clamp of terminal.

10W3 : CHECK INPUT VOLTAGE OF ABSCM&H/U.

1) Disconnect connector from ABSCM&H/U.
2) Run the engine at idle.
3) Measure voltage between ABSCM&H/U connector and chassis ground.

Connector & terminal
(F49) No. 1 (+) — Chassis ground (–):

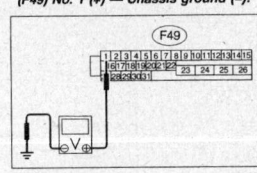

CHECK : *Is the voltage between 10 V and 15 V?*
YES : Go to step **10W4**.
NO : Repair harness connector between battery, ignition switch and ABSCM&H/U.

10W4 : CHECK GROUND CIRCUIT OF ABSCM&H/U.

1) Turn ignition switch to OFF.
2) Measure resistance between ABSCM&H/U connector and chassis ground.

Connector & terminal
(F49) No. 23 — Chassis ground:

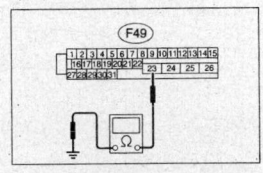

CHECK : *Is the resistance less than 0.5 Ω?*
YES : Go to step **10W5**.
NO : Repair ABSCM&H/U ground harness.

SB4029800217010X

Fig. 28 Code 42: Power Supply Voltage Too Low (Part 1 of 2). With Select Monitor

10X1 : CHECK GENERATOR.

1) Start engine.
2) Idling after warm-up.
3) Measure voltage between generator B terminal and chassis ground.

Terminal
Generator B terminal — Chassis ground:

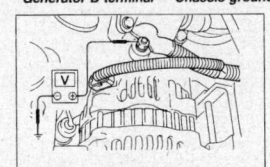

CHECK : *Is the voltage between 10 V and 17 V?*
YES : Go to step **10X2**.
NO : Repair generator.

10X2 : CHECK BATTERY TERMINAL.

Turn ignition switch to OFF.

CHECK : *Are the positive and negative battery terminals tightly clamped?*
YES : Go to step **10X3**.
NO : Tighten the clamp of terminal.

10X3 : CHECK INPUT VOLTAGE OF ABSCM&H/U.

1) Disconnect connector from ABSCM&H/U.
2) Run the engine at idle.
3) Measure voltage between ABSCM&H/U connector and chassis ground.

Connector & terminal
(F49) No. 1 (+) — Chassis ground (–):

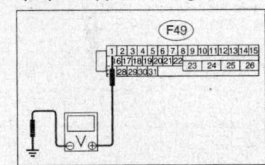

CHECK : *Is the voltage between 10 V and 17 V?*
YES : Go to step **10X4**.
NO : Repair harness connector between battery, ignition switch and ABSCM&H/U.

10X4 : CHECK GROUND CIRCUIT OF ABSCM&H/U.

1) Turn ignition switch to OFF.
2) Measure resistance between ABSCM&H/U connector and chassis ground.

Connector & terminal
(F49) No. 23 — Chassis ground:

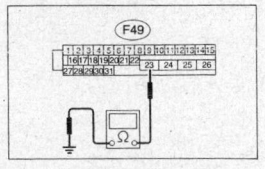

CHECK : *Is the resistance less than 0.5 Ω?*
YES : Go to step **10X5**.
NO : Repair ABSCM&H/U ground harness.

SB4029800218010X

Fig. 29 Code 42: Power Supply Voltage Too High (Part 1 of 2). With Select Monitor

10X5 : CHECK POOR CONTACT IN CONNECTORS.

CHECK : **Is there poor contact in connectors between generator, battery and ABSCM&H/U?**

YES : Repair connector.

NO : Go to step **10X6**.

10X6 : CHECK ABSCM&H/U.

1) Connect all connectors.
2) Erase the memory.
3) Perform inspection mode.
4) Read out the trouble code.

CHECK : **Is the same trouble code as in the current diagnosis still being output?**

YES : Replace ABSCM&H/U.

NO : Go to step **10X7**.

10X7 : CHECK ANY OTHER TROUBLE CODES APPEARANCE.

CHECK : **Are other trouble codes being output?**

YES : Proceed with the diagnosis corresponding to the trouble code.

NO : A temporary poor contact.

SB4029800218020X

Fig. 29   Code 42: Power Supply Voltage Too High (Part 2 of 2). With Select Monitor

10Y1 : CHECK SPECIFICATIONS OF THE ABSCM&H/U.

Check specifications of the mark to the ABSCM&H/U.

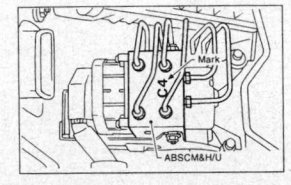

Mark	Model
C3	AWD AT
C4	AWD MT

CHECK : **Is an ABSCM&H/U for AT model installed on a MT model?**

YES : Replace ABSCM&H/U.

NO : Go to step **10Y2**.

10Y2 : CHECK GROUND SHORT OF HARNESS.

1) Turn ignition switch to OFF.
2) Disconnect two connectors from TCM.
3) Disconnect connector from ABSCM&H/U.
4) Measure resistance between ABSCM&H/U connector and chassis ground.

Connector & terminal
(F49) No. 3 — Chassis ground:

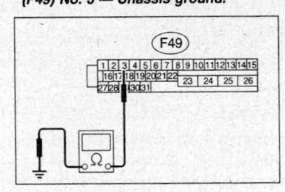

CHECK : **Is the resistance more than 1 MΩ?**

YES : Go to step **10Y3**.

NO : Repair harness between TCM and ABSCM&H/U.

10Y3 : CHECK TCM.

1) Connect all connectors to TCM.
2) Turn ignition switch to ON.
3) Measure voltage between TCM connector terminal and chassis ground.

Connector & terminal
(B55) No. 5 (+) — Chassis ground (–):

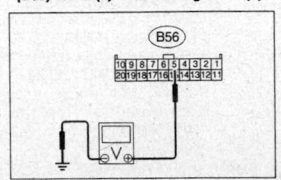

CHECK : **Is the voltage between 10 V and 15 V?**

YES : Go to step **10Y5**.

NO : Go to step **10Y4**.

10Y4 : CHECK AT.

CHECK : **Is the AT functioning normally?**

YES : Replace TCM.

NO : Repair AT.

SB4029800219010X

Fig. 30   Code 44: ABS A/T Control, Non Controlled (Part 1 of 2). With Select Monitor

10Y5 : CHECK OPEN CIRCUIT OF HARNESS.

Measure voltage between ABSCM&H/U connector and chassis ground.

Connector & terminal
(F49) No. 3 (+) — Chassis ground (–):
(F49) No. 31 (+) — Chassis ground (–):

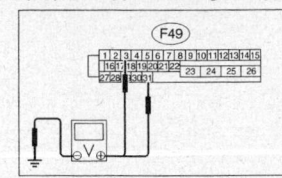

CHECK : Is the voltage more than 10 V?
YES : Go to step 10Y6.
NO : Repair harness/connector between AT control module and ABSCM&H/U.

10Y6 : CHECK POOR CONTACT IN CONNECTORS.

CHECK : Is there poor contact in connectors between AT control module and ABSCM&H/U?

YES : Repair connector.
NO : Go to step 10Y7.

10Y7 : CHECK ABSCM&H/U.

1) Connect all connectors.
2) Erase the memory.
3) Perform inspection mode.
4) Read out the trouble code.

CHECK : Is the same trouble code as in the current diagnosis still being output?
YES : Replace ABSCM&H/U.
NO : Go to step 10Y8.

10Y8 : CHECK ANY OTHER TROUBLE CODES APPEARANCE.

CHECK : Are other trouble codes being output?
YES : Proceed with the diagnosis corresponding to the trouble code.
NO : A temporary poor contact.

SB4029800219020X

Fig. 30 Code 44: ABS A/T Control, Non Controlled (Part 2 of 2). With Select Monitor

10Z6 : CHECK ANY OTHER TROUBLE CODES APPEARANCE.

CHECK : **Are other trouble codes being output?**

YES : Proceed with the diagnosis corresponding to the trouble code.

NO : A temporary poor contact.

SB4029800220020X

Fig. 31 Code 44: ABS A/T Control, Controlled (Part 2 of 2). With Select Monitor

10Z1 : CHECK BATTERY SHORT OF HARNESS.

1) Turn ignition switch to OFF.
2) Disconnect two connectors from AT control module.
3) Disconnect connector from ABSCM&H/U.
4) Measure voltage between ABSCM&H/U connector and chassis ground.

Connector & terminal
(F49) No. 3 (+) — Chassis ground (–):

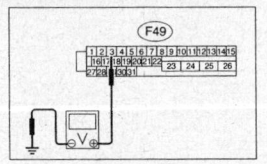

CHECK : Is the voltage less than 1 V?
YES : Go to step 10Z2.
NO : Repair harness between AT control module and ABSCM&H/U.

10Z2 : CHECK BATTERY SHORT OF HARNESS.

1) Turn ignition switch to ON.
2) Measure voltage between ABSCM&H/U connector and chassis ground.

Connector & terminal
(F49) No. 3 (+) — Chassis ground (–):

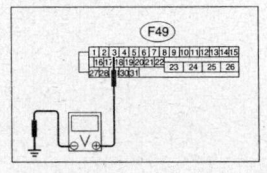

CHECK : Is the voltage less than 1 V?
YES : Go to step 10Z3.
NO : Repair harness between AT control module and ABSCM&H/U.

SB4029800220010X

Fig. 31 Code 44: ABS A/T Control, Controlled (Part 1 of 2). With Select Monitor

10Z3 : CHECK OPEN CIRCUIT OF HARNESS.

1) Turn ignition switch to OFF.
2) Connect all connectors to TCM.
3) Turn ignition switch to ON.
4) Measure voltage between ABSCM&H/U connector and chassis ground.

Connector & terminal
(F49) No. 3 (+) — Chassis ground (–):
(F49) No. 31 (+) — Chassis ground (–):

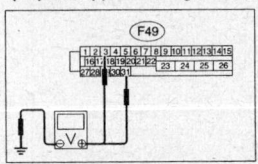

CHECK : Is the voltage between 10 V and 13 V?
YES : Go to step 10Z4.
NO : Repair harness/connector between TCM and ABSCM&H/U.

10Z4 : CHECK POOR CONTACT IN CONNECTORS.

Turn ignition switch to OFF.

CHECK : Is there poor contact in connectors between AT control module and ABSCM&H/U?

YES : Repair connector.
NO : Go to step 10Z5.

10Z5 : CHECK ABSCM&H/U.

1) Connect all connectors.
2) Erase the memory.
3) Perform inspection mode.
4) Read out the trouble code.

CHECK : Is the same trouble code as in the current diagnosis still being output?
YES : Replace ABSCM&H/U.
NO : Go to step 10Z6.

10AA1 : CHECK INPUT VOLTAGE OF ABSCM&H/U.

1) Turn ignition switch to OFF.
2) Disconnect connector from ABSCM&H/U.
3) Run the engine at idle.
4) Measure voltage between ABSCM&H/U connector and chassis ground.

Connector & terminal
(F49) No. 1 (+) — Chassis ground (–):
(F49) No. 24 (+) — Chassis ground (–):

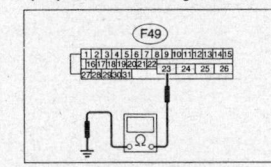

CHECK : Is the voltage between 10 V and 15 V?
YES : Go to step 10AA2.
NO : Repair harness connector between battery and ABSCM&H/U.

10AA2 : CHECK GROUND CIRCUIT OF ABSCM&H/U.

1) Turn ignition switch to OFF.
2) Measure resistance between ABSCM&H/U connector and chassis ground.

Connector & terminal
(F49) No. 23 — Chassis ground:

CHECK : Is the resistance less than 0.5 Ω?
YES : Go to step 10AA3.
NO : Repair ABSCM&H/U ground harness.

10AA3 : CHECK POOR CONTACT IN CONNECTORS.

CHECK : Is there poor contact in connectors between generator, battery and ABSCM&H/U?

YES : Repair connector.
NO : Go to step 10AA4.

10AA4 : CHECK ABSCM&H/U.

1) Connect all connectors.
2) Erase the memory.
3) Perform inspection mode.
4) Read out the trouble code.

CHECK : Is the same trouble code as in the current diagnosis still being output?
YES : Replace ABSCM&H/U.
NO : Go to step 10AA5.

10AA5 : CHECK ANY OTHER TROUBLE CODES APPEARANCE.

CHECK : Are other trouble codes being output?
YES : Proceed with the diagnosis corresponding to the trouble code.
NO : A temporary poor contact.

SB4029800221000X

Fig. 32 Code 51: Valve Relay Malfunction. With Select Monitor

10AB1 : CHECK VALVE RELAY IN ABSCM&H/U.

Measure resistance between ABSCM&H/U terminals.

Terminals
No. 23 (+) — No. 24 (–):

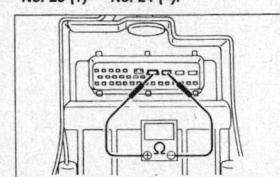

CHECK : *Is the resistance more than 1 MΩ?*
YES : Go to step **10AB2.**
NO : Replace ABSCM&H/U.

10AB2 : CHECK POOR CONTACT IN CONNECTORS.

CHECK : *Is there poor contact in connectors between generator, battery and ABSCM&H/U?*

YES : Repair connector.
NO : Go to step **10AB3.**

10AB3 : CHECK ABSCM&H/U.

1) Connect all connectors.
2) Erase the memory.
3) Perform inspection mode.
4) Read out the trouble code.

CHECK : *Is the same trouble code as in the current diagnosis still being output?*
YES : Replace ABSCM&H/U.
NO : Go to step **10AB4.**

SB4029800222000X

Fig. 33 Code 51: Valve Relay On Failure. With Select Monitor

10AB4 : CHECK ANY OTHER TROUBLE CODES APPEARANCE.

CHECK : *Are other trouble codes being output?*
YES : Proceed with the diagnosis corresponding to the trouble code.
NO : A temporary poor contact.

10AC1 : CHECK INPUT VOLTAGE OF ABSCM&H/U.

1) Turn ignition switch to OFF.
2) Disconnect connector from ABSCM&H/U.
3) Turn ignition switch to ON.
4) Measure voltage between ABSCM&H/U connector and chassis ground.

Connector & terminal
(F49) No. 25 (+) — Chassis ground (–):

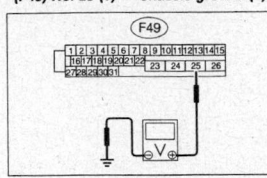

CHECK : *Is the voltage between 10 V and 13 V?*
YES : Go to step **10AC2.**
NO : Repair harness/connector between battery and ABSCM&H/U and check fuse SBF6.

10AC2 : CHECK GROUND CIRCUIT OF MOTOR.

1) Turn ignition switch to OFF.
2) Measure resistance between ABSCM&H/U connector and chassis ground.

Connector & terminal
(F49) No. 26 — Chassis ground:

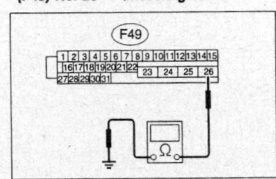

CHECK : *Is the resistance less than 0.5 Ω?*
YES : Go to step **10AC3.**
NO : Repair ABSCM&H/U ground harness.

10AC3 : CHECK MOTOR OPERATION.

Operate the sequence control.

NOTE:
Use the diagnosis connector to operate the sequence control.

CHECK : *Can motor revolution noise (buzz) be heard when carrying out the check sequence?*
YES : Go to step **10AC4.**
NO : Replace ABSCM&H/U.

10AC4 : CHECK POOR CONTACT IN CONNECTORS.

Turn ignition switch to OFF.

CHECK : *Is there poor contact in connector between hydraulic unit, relay box and ABSCM&H/U?*

YES : Repair connector.
NO : Go to step **10AC5.**

10AC5 : CHECK ABSCM&H/U.

1) Connect all connectors.
2) Erase the memory.
3) Perform inspection mode.
4) Read out the trouble code.

CHECK : *Is the same trouble code as in the current diagnosis still being output?*
YES : Replace ABSCM&H/U.
NO : Go to step **10AC6.**

10AC6 : CHECK ANY OTHER TROUBLE CODES APPEARANCE.

CHECK : *Are other trouble codes being output?*
YES : Proceed with the diagnosis corresponding to the trouble code.
NO : A temporary poor contact.

SB4029800223000X

Fig. 34 Code 52: Open Circuit In Motor Relay Circuit. With Select Monitor

10AD1 : CHECK MOTOR RELAY IN ABSCM&H/U.

Measure resistance between ABSCM&H/U terminals.

Terminals
No. 25 — No. 26:

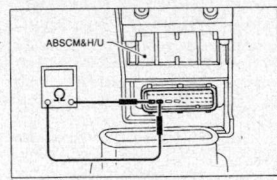

CHECK : *Is the resistance more than 1 MΩ?*
YES : Go to step **10AD2.**
NO : Replace ABSCM&H/U.

10AD2 : CHECK MOTOR OPERATION.

Operate the sequence control.

NOTE:
Use the diagnosis connector to operate the sequence control.

CHECK : *Can motor revolution noise (buzz) be heard when carrying out the sequence control?*
YES : Go to step **10AD3.**
NO : Replace ABSCM&H/U.

10AD3 : CHECK POOR CONTACT IN CONNECTORS.

Turn ignition switch to OFF.

CHECK : *Is there poor contact in connector between hydraulic unit, relay box and ABSCM&H/U?*

YES : Repair connector.
NO : Go to step **10AD4.**

10AD4 : CHECK ABSCM&H/U.

1) Connect all connectors.
2) Erase the memory.
3) Perform inspection mode.
4) Read out the trouble code.

CHECK : *Is the same trouble code as in the current diagnosis still being output?*
YES : Replace ABSCM&H/U.
NO : Go to step **10AD5.**

10AD5 : CHECK ANY OTHER TROUBLE CODES APPEARANCE.

CHECK : *Are other trouble codes being output?*
YES : Proceed with the diagnosis corresponding to the trouble code.
NO : A temporary poor contact.

SB4029800224000X

Fig. 35 Code 52: Motor Relay On Failure. With Select Monitor

SUBARU

10AE5 : CHECK MOTOR OPERATION.

Operate the sequence control.

NOTE:
Use the diagnosis connector to operate the
sequence control.

(CHECK) : ***Can motor revolution noise (buzz) be
heard when carrying out the
sequence control?***

(YES) : Go to step **10AE6.**

(NO) : Replace hydraulic unit.

**10AE6 : CHECK POOR CONTACT IN CON-
NECTORS.**

Turn ignition switch to OFF.

(CHECK) : ***Is there poor contact in connector
between generator, battery and
ABSCM&H/U?***

(YES) : Repair connector.

(NO) : Go to step **10AE7.**

10AE7 : CHECK ABSCM&H/U.

1) Connect all connectors.
2) Erase the memory.
3) Perform inspection mode.
4) Read out the trouble code.

(CHECK) : ***Is the same trouble code as in the
current diagnosis still being output?***

(YES) : Replace ABSCM&H/U.

(NO) : Go to step **10AE8.**

**10AE8 : CHECK ANY OTHER TROUBLE
CODES APPEARANCE.**

(CHECK) : ***Are other trouble codes being output?***

(YES) : Proceed with the diagnosis corresponding to the trouble code.

(NO) : A temporary poor contact.

SB4029800225020X

**Fig. 36   Code 52: Motor Malfunction (Part 2 of 2).
With Select Monitor**

**10AE1 : CHECK INPUT VOLTAGE OF
ABSCM&H/U.**

1) Turn ignition switch to OFF.
2) Disconnect connector from ABSCM&H/U.
3) Turn ignition switch to ON.
4) Measure voltage between ABSCM&H/U connector and chassis ground.
**Connector & terminal
(F49) No. 25 (+) — Chassis ground (–):**

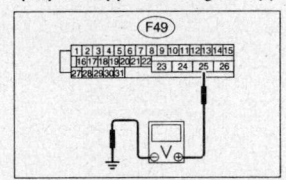

(CHECK) : ***Is the voltage between 10 V and 13 V?***
(YES) : Go to step **10AE2.**
(NO) : Repair harness/connector between bat-
tery and ABSCM&H/U and check fuse
SBF6.

**10AE2 : CHECK GROUND CIRCUIT OF
MOTOR.**

1) Turn ignition switch to OFF.
2) Measure resistance between ABSCM&H/U
connector and chassis ground.
**Connector & terminal
(F49) No. 26 — Chassis ground:**

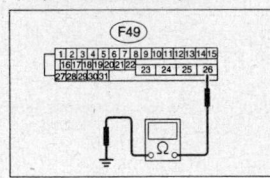

(CHECK) : ***Is the resistance less than 0.5 Ω?***
(YES) : Go to step **10AE3.**
(NO) : Repair ABSCM&H/U ground harness.

**10AE3 : CHECK INPUT VOLTAGE OF
ABSCM&H/U.**

1) Run the engine at idle.
2) Measure voltage between ABSCM&H/U connector and chassis ground.
**Connector & terminal
(F49) No. 1 (+) — Chassis ground (–):**

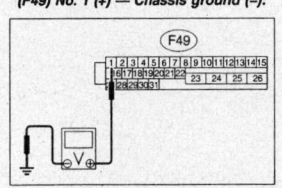

(CHECK) : ***Is the voltage between 10 V and 15 V?***
(YES) : Go to step **10AE4.**
(NO) : Repair harness connector between
battery, ignition switch and
ABSCM&H/U.

**10AE4 : CHECK GROUND CIRCUIT OF
ABSCM&H/U.**

1) Turn ignition switch to OFF.
2) Measure resistance between ABSCM&H/U
connector and chassis ground.
**Connector & terminal
(F49) No. 23 — Chassis ground:**

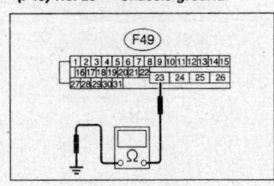

(CHECK) : ***Is the resistance less than 0.5 Ω?***
(YES) : Go to step **10AE5.**
(NO) : Repair ABSCM&H/U ground harness.

SB4029800225010X

**Fig. 36   Code 52: Motor Malfunction (Part 1 of 2).
With Select Monitor**

FORESTER

41-167

10AF1 : CHECK OUTPUT OF STOP LIGHT SWITCH USING SELECT MONITOR.

1) Select "Current data display & Save" on the select monitor.
2) Release the brake pedal.
3) Read the stop light switch output in the select monitor data display.

CHECK : *Is the reading indicated on monitor display less than 1.5 V?*
YES : Go to step **10AF2**.
NO : Go to step **10AF3**.

10AF2 : CHECK OUTPUT OF STOP LIGHT SWITCH USING SELECT MONITOR.

1) Depress the brake pedal.
2) Read the stop light switch output in the select monitor data display.

CHECK : *Is the reading indicated on monitor display between 10 V and 15 V?*
YES : Go to step **10AF5**.
NO : Go to step **10AF3**.

10AF3 : CHECK IF STOP LIGHTS COME ON.

Depress the brake pedal.

CHECK : *Do stop lights turn on?*
YES : Go to step **10AF4**.
NO : Repair stop lights circuit.

10AF4 : CHECK OPEN CIRCUIT IN HARNESS.

1) Turn ignition switch to OFF.
2) Disconnect connector from ABSCM&H/U.
3) Depress brake pedal.
4) Measure voltage between ABSCM&H/U connector and chassis ground.

Connector & terminal
(F49) No. 2 — Chassis ground:

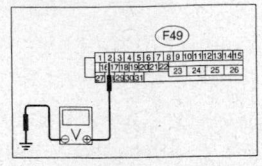

CHECK : *Is the voltage between 10 V and 15 V?*
YES : Go to step **10AF5**.
NO : Repair harness between stop light switch and ABSCM&H/U connector.

10AF5 : CHECK POOR CONTACT IN CONNECTORS.

CHECK : *Is there poor contact in connector between stop light switch and ABSCM&H/U?*
YES : Repair connector.
NO : Go to step **10AF6**.

10AF6 : CHECK ABSCM&H/U.

1) Connect all connectors.
2) Erase the memory.
3) Perform inspection mode.
4) Read out the trouble code.

CHECK : *Is the same trouble code as in the current diagnosis still being output?*
YES : Replace ABSCM&H/U.
NO : Go to step **10AF7**.

SB4029800226010X

10AF7 : CHECK ANY OTHER TROUBLE CODES APPEARANCE.

CHECK : *Are other trouble codes being output?*
YES : Proceed with the diagnosis corresponding to the trouble code.
NO : A temporary poor contact.

SB4029800226020X

Fig. 37 Code 54: Stop Light Switch Signal Circuit (Part 2 of 2). With Select Monitor

Fig. 37 Code 54: Stop Light Switch Signal Circuit (Part 1 of 2). With Select Monitor

---

10AG1 : CHECK SPECIFICATIONS OF ABSCM&H/U.

Check specifications of the mark to the ABSCM&H/U.

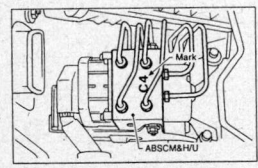

Mark	Model
C3	AWD AT
C4	AWD MT

CHECK : *Is an ABSCM for AWD model installed on a FWD model?*
YES : Replace ABSCM&H/U.

CAUTION:
Be sure to turn ignition switch to OFF when removing ABSCM&H/U.
NO : Go to step **10AG2**.

10AG2 : CHECK OUTPUT OF G SENSOR USING SELECT MONITOR.

1) Select "Current data display & Save" on the select monitor.
2) Read the G sensor output in select monitor data display.

CHECK : *Is the G sensor output on the monitor display between 2.1 and 2.5 V when the G sensor is in horizontal position?*
YES : Go to step **10AG3**.
NO : Go to step **10AG6**.

10AG3 : CHECK POOR CONTACT IN CONNECTORS.

CHECK : *Is there poor contact in connector between ABSCM&H/U and G sensor?*
YES : Repair connector.
NO : Go to step **10AG4**.

10AG4 : CHECK ABSCM&H/U.

1) Connect all connectors.
2) Erase the memory.
3) Perform inspection mode.
4) Read out the trouble code.

CHECK : *Is the same trouble code as in the current diagnosis still being output?*
YES : Replace ABSCM&H/U.
NO : Go to step **10AG5**.

10AG5 : CHECK ANY OTHER TROUBLE CODES APPEARANCE.

CHECK : *Are other trouble codes being output?*
YES : Proceed with the diagnosis corresponding to the trouble code.
NO : A temporary poor contact.

10AG6 : CHECK FREEZE FRAME DATA.

1) Select "Freeze frame data" on the select monitor.
2) Read front right wheel speed on the select monitor display.

CHECK : *Is the front right wheel speed on monitor display 0 km?*
YES : Go to step **10AG7**.
NO : Go to step **10AG15**.

10AG7 : CHECK FREEZE FRAME DATA.

Read front left wheel speed on the select monitor display.

CHECK : *Is the front left wheel speed on monitor display 0 km?*
YES : Go to step **10AG8**.
NO : Go to step **10AG15**.

10AG8 : CHECK FREEZE FRAME DATA.

Read rear right wheel speed on the select monitor display.

CHECK : *Is the rear right wheel speed on monitor display 0 km?*
YES : Go to step **10AG9**.
NO : Go to step **10AG15**.

SB4029800227010X

Fig. 38 Code 56: Open Or Short Circuit In G Sensor Circuit (Part 1 of 5). With Select Monitor

---

10AG9 : CHECK FREEZE FRAME DATA.

Read rear left wheel speed on the select monitor display.

CHECK : *Is the rear left wheel speed on monitor display 0 km?*
YES : Go to step **10AG10**.
NO : Go to step **10AG15**.

10AG10 : CHECK FREEZE FRAME DATA.

Read G sensor output on the select monitor display.

CHECK : *Is the G sensor output on monitor display more than 3.65 V?*
YES : Go to step **10AG11**.
NO : Go to step **10AG15**.

10AG11 : CHECK OPEN CIRCUIT IN G SENSOR OUTPUT HARNESS AND GROUND HARNESS.

1) Turn ignition switch to OFF.
2) Disconnect connector from ABSCM&H/U.
3) Measure resistance between ABSCM&H/U connector terminals.

Connector & terminal
(F49) No. 30 — No. 28:

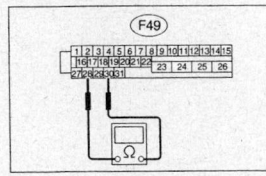

CHECK : *Is the resistance between 4.3 and 4.9 kΩ?*
YES : Go to step **10AG12**.
NO : Repair harness/connector between G sensor and ABSCM&H/U.

10AG12 : CHECK POOR CONTACT IN CONNECTORS.

CHECK : *Is there poor contact in connector between ABSCM&H/U and G sensor?*
YES : Repair connector.
NO : Go to step **10AG13**.

10AG13 : CHECK ABSCM&H/U.

1) Connect all connectors.
2) Erase the memory.
3) Perform inspection mode.
4) Read out the trouble code.

CHECK : *Is the same trouble code as in the current diagnosis still being output?*
YES : Replace ABSCM&H/U.
NO : Go to step **10AG14**.

10AG14 : CHECK ANY OTHER TROUBLE CODES APPEARANCE.

CHECK : *Are other trouble codes being output?*
YES : Proceed with the diagnosis corresponding to the trouble code.
NO : A temporary poor contact.

SB4029800227020X

Fig. 38 Code 56: Open Or Short Circuit In G Sensor Circuit (Part 2 of 5). With Select Monitor

10AG15 : CHECK INPUT VOLTAGE OF G SENSOR.

1) Turn ignition switch to OFF.
2) Remove console box.
3) Disconnect G sensor from body. (Do not disconnect connector.)
4) Turn ignition switch to ON.
5) Measure voltage between G sensor connector terminals.

Connector & terminal
(R70) No. 1 (+) — No. 3 (−):

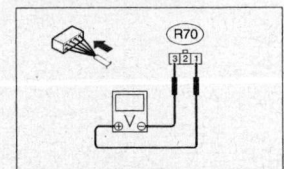

CHECK : **Is the voltage between 4.75 and 5.25 V?**
YES : Go to step **10AG16**.
NO : Repair harness/connector between G sensor and ABSCM&H/U.

10AG16 : CHECK OPEN CIRCUIT IN G SENSOR OUTPUT HARNESS AND GROUND HARNESS.

1) Turn ignition switch to OFF.
2) Disconnect connector from ABSCM&H/U.
3) Measure resistance between ABSCM&H/U connector terminals.

Connector & terminal
(F49) No. 30 — No. 28:

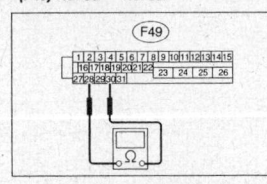

CHECK : **Is the resistance between 4.3 and 4.9 kΩ?**
YES : Go to step **10AG17**.
NO : Repair harness/connector between G sensor and ABSCM&H/U.

10AG17 : CHECK GROUND SHORT IN G SENSOR OUTPUT HARNESS.

1) Disconnect connector from G sensor.
2) Measure resistance between ABSCM&H/U connector and chassis ground.

Connector & terminal
(F49) No. 6 — Chassis ground:

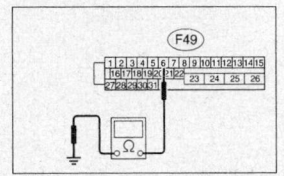

CHECK : **Is the resistance more than 1 MΩ?**
YES : Go to step **10AG18**.
NO : Repair harness between G sensor and ABSCM&H/U.

SB4029800227030X

Fig. 38 Code 56: Open Or Short Circuit In G Sensor Circuit (Part 3 of 5). With Select Monitor

10AG18 : CHECK G SENSOR.

1) Connect connector to G sensor.
2) Connect connector to ABSCM&H/U.
3) Turn ignition switch to ON.
4) Measure voltage between G sensor connector terminals.

Connector & terminal
(R70) No. 2 (+) — No. 3 (−):

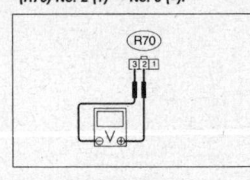

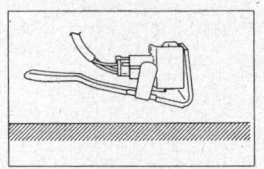

CHECK : **Is the voltage between 2.1 and 2.5 V when G sensor is horizontal?**
YES : Go to step **10AG19**.
NO : Replace G sensor.

10AG19 : CHECK G SENSOR.

Measure voltage between G sensor connector terminals.

Connector & terminal
(R70) No. 2 (+) — No. 3 (−):

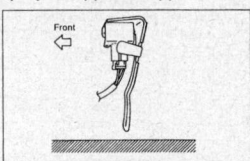

CHECK : **Is the voltage between 3.7 and 4.1 V when G sensor is inclined forwards to 90°?**
YES : Go to step **10AG20**.
NO : Replace G sensor.

10AG20 : CHECK G SENSOR.

Measure voltage between G sensor connector terminals.

Connector & terminal
(P11) No. 2 (+) — No. 3 (−):

CHECK : **Is the voltage between 0.5 and 0.9 V when G sensor is inclined backwards to 90°?**
YES : Go to step **10AG21**.
NO : Replace G sensor.

SB4029800227040X

Fig. 38 Code 56: Open Or Short Circuit In G Sensor Circuit (Part 4 of 5). With Select Monitor

10AG21 : CHECK POOR CONTACT IN CONNECTORS.

Turn ignition switch to OFF.

CHECK : **Is there poor contact in connector between ABSCM&H/U and G sensor?**

YES : Repair connector.
NO : Go to step **10AG22**.

10AG22 : CHECK ABSCM&H/U.

1) Connect all connectors.
2) Erase the memory.
3) Perform inspection mode.
4) Read out the trouble code.

CHECK : **Is the same trouble code as in the current diagnosis still being output?**
YES : Replace ABSCM&H/U.
NO : Go to step **10AG23**.

10AG23 : CHECK ANY OTHER TROUBLE CODES APPEARANCE.

CHECK : **Are other trouble codes being output?**
YES : Proceed with the diagnosis corresponding to the trouble code.
NO : A temporary poor contact.

SB4029800227050X

Fig. 38 Code 56: Open Or Short Circuit In G Sensor Circuit (Part 5 of 5). With Select Monitor

10AH2 : CHECK BATTERY SHORT OF HARNESS.

1) Turn ignition switch to OFF.
2) Remove console box.
3) Disconnect connector from G sensor.
4) Disconnect connector from ABSCM&H/U.
5) Measure voltage between ABSCM&H/U connector and chassis ground.

Connector & terminal
(F49) No. 6 (+) — Chassis ground (−):

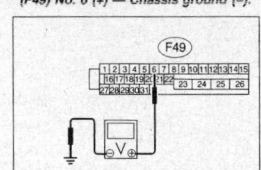

CHECK : **Is the voltage less than 1 V?**
YES : Go to step **10AH3**.
NO : Repair harness between G sensor and ABSCM&H/U.

10AH3 : CHECK BATTERY SHORT OF HARNESS.

1) Turn ignition switch to ON.
2) Measure voltage between ABSCM&H/U connector and chassis ground.

Connector & terminal
(F49) No. 6 (+) — Chassis ground (−):

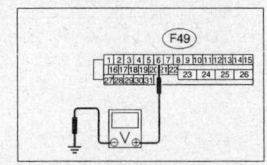

CHECK : **Is the voltage less than 1 V?**
YES : Go to step **10AH4**.
NO : Repair harness between G sensor and ABSCM&H/U.

10AH4 : CHECK ABSCM&H/U.

1) Turn ignition switch to OFF.
2) Connect all connectors.
3) Erase the memory.
4) Perform inspection mode.
5) Read out the trouble code.

CHECK : **Is the same trouble code as in the current diagnosis still being output?**
YES : Replace ABSCM&H/U.
NO : Go to step **10AH5**.

10AH5 : CHECK ANY OTHER TROUBLE CODES APPEARANCE.

CHECK : **Are other trouble codes being output?**
YES : Proceed with the diagnosis corresponding to the trouble code.
NO : A temporary poor contact.

SB4029800228000X

Fig. 39 Code 56: Battery Short In G Sensor Circuit. With Select Monitor

10AI3 :   CHECK ABSCM&H/U.

1) Connect all connectors.
2) Erase the memory.
3) Perform inspection mode.
4) Read out the trouble code.

(CHECK) : *Is the same trouble code as in the current diagnosis still being output?*
(YES) : Replace ABSCM&H/U.
(NO) : Go to step **10AI4**.

10AI4 :   CHECK ANY OTHER TROUBLE CODES APPEARANCE.

(CHECK) : *Are other trouble codes being output?*
(YES) : Proceed with the diagnosis corresponding to the trouble code.
(NO) : A temporary poor contact.

10AI5 :   CHECK OPEN CIRCUIT IN G SENSOR OUTPUT HARNESS AND GROUND HARNESS.

1) Turn ignition switch to OFF.
2) Disconnect connector from ABSCM&H/U.
3) Measure resistance between ABSCM&H/U connector terminals.

Connector & terminal
(F49) No. 30 — No. 28:

(CHECK) : *Is the resistance between 4.3 and 4.9 kΩ?*
(YES) : Go to step **10AI6**.
(NO) : Repair harness/connector between G sensor and ABSCM&H/U.

10AI6 :   CHECK GROUND SHORT OF HARNESS.

Measure resistance between ABSCM&H/U connector and chassis ground.

Connector & terminal
(F49) No. 28 — Chassis ground:

(CHECK) : *Is the resistance more than 1 MΩ?*
(YES) : Go to step **10AI7**.
(NO) : Repair harness between G sensor and ABSCM&H/U.
Replace ABSCM&H/U.

10AI7 :   CHECK G SENSOR.

1) Remove console box.
2) Remove G sensor from vehicle.
3) Connect connector to G sensor.
4) Connect connector to ABSCM&H/U.
5) Turn ignition switch to ON.
6) Measure voltage between G sensor connector terminals.

Connector & terminal
(P11) No. 2 (+) — No. 3 (–):

(CHECK) : *Is the voltage between 2.1 and 2.5 V when G sensor is horizontal?*
(YES) : Go to step **10AI8**.
(NO) : Replace G sensor.

10AI8 :   CHECK G SENSOR.

Measure voltage between G sensor connector terminals.

Connector & terminal
(R70) No. 2 (+) — No. 3 (–):

(CHECK) : *Is the voltage between 3.7 and 4.1 V when G sensor is inclined forwards to 90°?*
(YES) : Go to step **10AI9**.
(NO) : Replace G sensor.

10AI9 :   CHECK G SENSOR.

Measure voltage between G sensor connector terminals.

Connector & terminal
(R70) No. 2 (+) — No. 3 (–):

(CHECK) : *Is the voltage between 0.5 and 0.9 V when G sensor is inclined backwards to 90°?*
(YES) : Go to step **10AI10**.
(NO) : Replace G sensor.

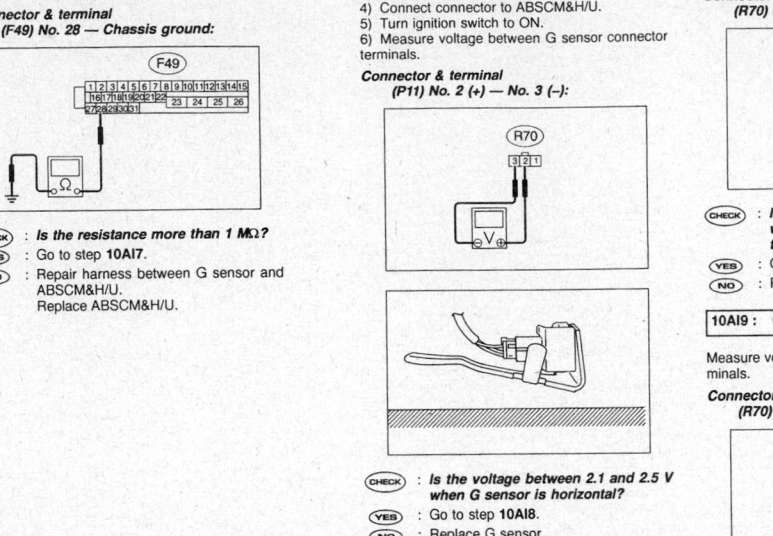

SB4029800229010X

Fig. 40   Code 56: Abnormal G Sensor High Output (Part 1 of 3). With Select Monitor

SB4029800229020X

Fig. 40   Code 56: Abnormal G Sensor High Output (Part 2 of 3). With Select Monitor

---

10AI10 :   CHECK ABSCM&H/U.

1) Turn ignition switch to OFF.
2) Connect all connectors.
3) Erase the memory.
4) Perform inspection mode.
5) Read out the trouble code.

(CHECK) : *Is the same trouble code as in the current diagnosis still being output?*
(YES) : Replace ABSCM&H/U.
(NO) : Go to step **10AI11**.

10AI11 :   CHECK ANY OTHER TROUBLE CODES APPEARANCE.

(CHECK) : *Are other trouble codes being output?*
(YES) : Proceed with the diagnosis corresponding to the trouble code.
(NO) : A temporary poor contact.

SB4029800229030X

Fig. 40   Code 56: Abnormal G Sensor High Output (Part 3 of 3). With Select Monitor

10AJ3 : CHECK OUTPUT OF G SENSOR USING SELECT MONITOR.

1) Turn ignition switch to OFF.
2) Remove console box.
3) Remove G sensor from vehicle. (Do not disconnect connector.)
4) Turn ignition switch to ON.
5) Select "Current data display & Save" on the select monitor.
6) Read the select monitor display.

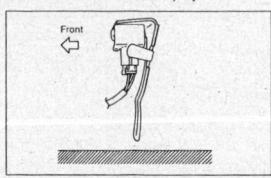

CHECK : **Is the G sensor output on the monitor display between 3.7 and 4.1 V when G sensor is inclined forwards to 90°?**

YES : Go to step **10AJ4**.
NO : Replace G sensor.

10AJ4 : CHECK OUTPUT OF G SENSOR USING SELECT MONITOR.

Read the select monitor display.

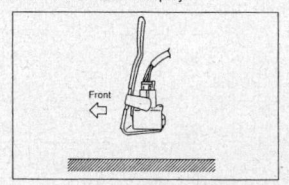

CHECK : **Is the G sensor output on the monitor display between 0.5 and 0.9 V when G sensor is inclined backwards to 90°?**

YES : Go to step **10AJ5**.
NO : Replace G sensor.

SB4029800230010X

Fig. 41 Code 56: Detection Of G Sensor Stick (Part 1 of 3). With Select Monitor

10AJ10 : CHECK G SENSOR.

Measure voltage between G sensor connector terminals.

Connector & terminal (P11) No. 2 (+) — No. 1 (–):

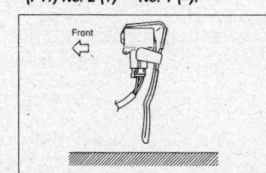

CHECK : **Is the voltage between 3.7 and 4.1 V when G sensor is inclined forwards to 90°?**

YES : Go to step **10AJ11**.
NO : Replace G sensor.

10AJ11 : CHECK G SENSOR.

Measure voltage between G sensor connector terminals.

Connector & terminal (P11) No. 2 (+) — No. 1 (–):

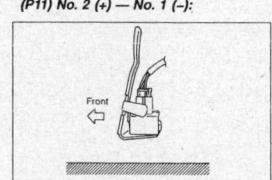

CHECK : **Is the voltage between 0.5 and 0.9 V when G sensor is inclined backwards to 90°?**

YES : Go to step **10AJ12**.
NO : Replace G sensor.

SB4029800230030X

Fig. 41 Code 56: Detection Of G Sensor Stick (Part 3 of 3). With Select Monitor

---

10AJ5 : CHECK POOR CONTACT IN CONNECTORS.

Turn ignition switch to OFF.

CHECK : **Is there poor contact in connector between ABSCM&H/U and G sensor?**

YES : Repair connector.
NO : Go to step **10AJ6**.

10AJ6 : CHECK ABSCM&H/U.

1) Connect all connectors.
2) Erase the memory.
3) Perform inspection mode.
4) Read out the trouble code.

CHECK : **Is the same trouble code as in the current diagnosis still being output?**

YES : Replace ABSCM&H/U.
NO : Go to step **10AJ7**.

10AJ7 : CHECK ANY OTHER TROUBLE CODES APPEARANCE.

CHECK : **Are other trouble codes being output?**

YES : Proceed with the diagnosis corresponding to the trouble code.
NO : A temporary poor contact.

10AJ12 : CHECK ABSCM&H/U.

1) Turn ignition switch to OFF.
2) Connect all connectors.
3) Erase the memory.
4) Perform inspection mode.
5) Read out the trouble code.

CHECK : **Is the same trouble code as in the current diagnosis still being output?**

YES : Replace ABSCM&H/U.
NO : Go to step **10AJ13**.

10AJ13 : CHECK ANY OTHER TROUBLE CODES APPEARANCE.

CHECK : **Are other trouble codes being output?**

YES : Proceed with the diagnosis corresponding to the trouble code.
NO : A temporary poor contact.

10AJ8 : CHECK OPEN CIRCUIT IN G SENSOR OUTPUT HARNESS AND GROUND HARNESS.

1) Turn ignition switch to OFF.
2) Disconnect connector from ABSCM&H/U.
3) Measure resistance between ABSCM&H/U connector terminals.

Connector & terminal (F49) No. 30 — No. 28:

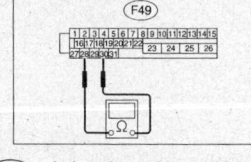

CHECK : **Is the resistance between 4.3 and 4.9 kΩ?**

YES : Go to step **10AJ9**.
NO : Repair harness/connector between G sensor and ABSCM&H/U.

10AJ9 : CHECK G SENSOR.

1) Remove console box.
2) Remove G sensor from vehicle.
3) Connect connector to G sensor.
4) Connect connector to ABSCM&H/U.
5) Turn ignition switch to ON.
6) Measure voltage between G sensor connector terminals.

Connector & terminal (P11) No. 2 (+) — No. 1 (–):

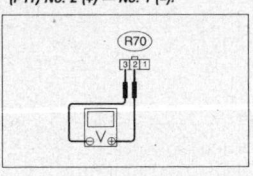

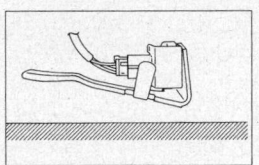

CHECK : **Is the voltage between 2.1 and 2.5 V when G sensor is horizontal?**

YES : Go to step **10AJ10**.
NO : Replace G sensor.

SB4029800230020X

Fig. 41 Code 56: Detection Of G Sensor Stick (Part 2 of 3). With Select Monitor

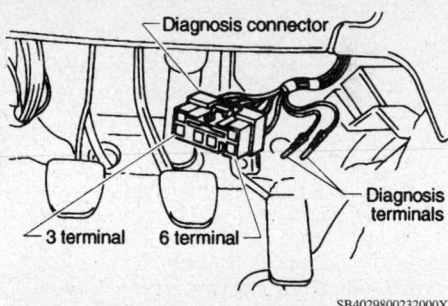

SB4029800232000X

Fig. 42 Diagnosis connector

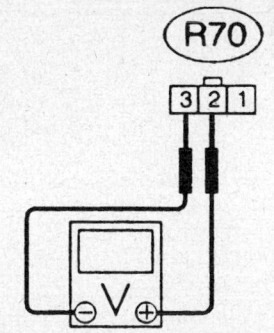

SB4029800233000X

Fig. 43 G sensor connector

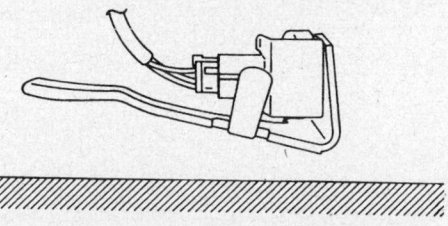

SB4029800234000X

Fig. 44 G sensor horizontal position

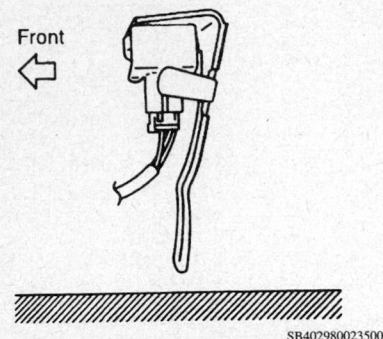

Front

SB4029800235000X

Fig. 45 G sensor inclined forwards 90°

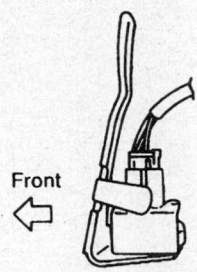

Front

SB4029800236000X

Fig. 46 G sensor inclined backwards 90°

	Front wheel	Rear wheel
Initial value	3,432 kPa (35 kg/cm², 498 psi)	3,432 kPa (35 kg/cm², 498 psi)
When decompressed	490 kPa (5 kg/cm², 71 psi) or less	490 kPa (5 kg/cm², 71 psi) or less
When compressed	3,432 kPa (35 kg/cm², 498 psi) or more	3,432 kPa (35 kg/cm², 498 psi) or more

SB4029800237000X

Fig. 47 ABS hydraulic pressure readings

SYSTEM SERVICE

Brake System Bleed

1. Start with wheels connecting to secondary chamber of master cylinder.
2. Inspect for leaks at joints and connections in brake system, repair as necessary.
3. Fit one end of a suitable vinyl hose over brake bleeder and place other end into a container filled with brake fluid.
4. Slowly depress brake pedal and keep depressed.
5. Open bleeder crew and release fluid for one to two seconds.
6. Close bleeder screw and release pedal.
7. Repeat steps until all air is discharged from system.

Component Replacement

ABS WHEEL SENSOR

Front

1. Disconnect ABS sensor connector located in engine compartment.
2. Remove bolts that secure sensor harness to strut and to body.
3. Remove bolts securing ABS sensor to housing, then the sensor.
4. Reverse procedure to install.

Rear

1. Remove rear seat and disconnect rear ABS sensor connector.
2. Remove rear sensor harness bracket from rear trailing link and bracket.
3. Remove rear ABS sensor from rear backing plate.
4. Reverse procedure to install.

ABS CONTROL MODULE & HYDRAULIC CONTROL UNIT

1. Remove air intake duct from engine to ease removal of ABSCM & H/U.
2. Use pressurized air to ensure no water or moisture exists around control unit.
3. Pull on lock of the ABSCM & H/U connector to remove it, then disconnect from ABSCM & H/U.
4. Unlock cable clip, then disconnect brake pipes from unit.
5. Do not allow brake fluid to come into contact with painted surfaces.
6. Remove mounting bolts, then the control unit.
7. ABSCM & H/U cannot be disassembled, do not attempt to loosen bolts and nuts.
8. Reverse procedure to install.

G SENSOR

1. Turn ignition switch to Off position.
2. Remove console cover.
3. Disconnect connector from G sensor, then remove sensor from vehicle.
4. Reverse procedure to install.

NOTE: On Air Bag Equipped Models, Refer To "Air Bag System Precautions" Located In The Front Of This Manual For System Disarming & Arming Procedures.

NOTE: Electrical Symbol & Wire Color Code Identification Located In The Front Of This Manual May Be Used As An Aid When Using Wiring Circuits Found In This Section.

INDEX

PRECAUTIONS
AIR BAG SYSTEMS

Refer to "Air Bag System Precautions" in the front of this manual for system disarming and arming procedures.

BATTERY GROUND CABLE

Prior to service, disconnect battery ground cable and isolate as required.

DESCRIPTION

The Anti-lock brake system (ABS) electrically controls brake fluid pressure to prevent wheel lock during braking on slippery road surfaces, improving steering stability and shortening the braking distance. If the ABS becomes inoperative, a fail-safe system activates to ensure conventional brake system operation.

The front and rear wheels utilize a four sensor, four channel control design. The front wheels have an independent design which controls fluid pressure to the left and right wheels. The rear wheels have a select low design, which provides the same pressure for the two rear wheels if either starts to lock.

The ABS consists of four tone wheels, four speed sensors, electronic control unit, a G sensor and a warning lamp. Refer to **Figs. 1 through 4,** for ABS component location and function.

TROUBLESHOOTING

Refer to **Figs. 5 through 10,** for ABS troubleshooting procedures. The ABS control unit receives and sends signals that control system functions. It is important that these input/output signals be consistent. Refer to **Fig. 11,** for control unit and sensor voltage and resistance specifications and **Fig. 12,** for input/output wiring circuit.

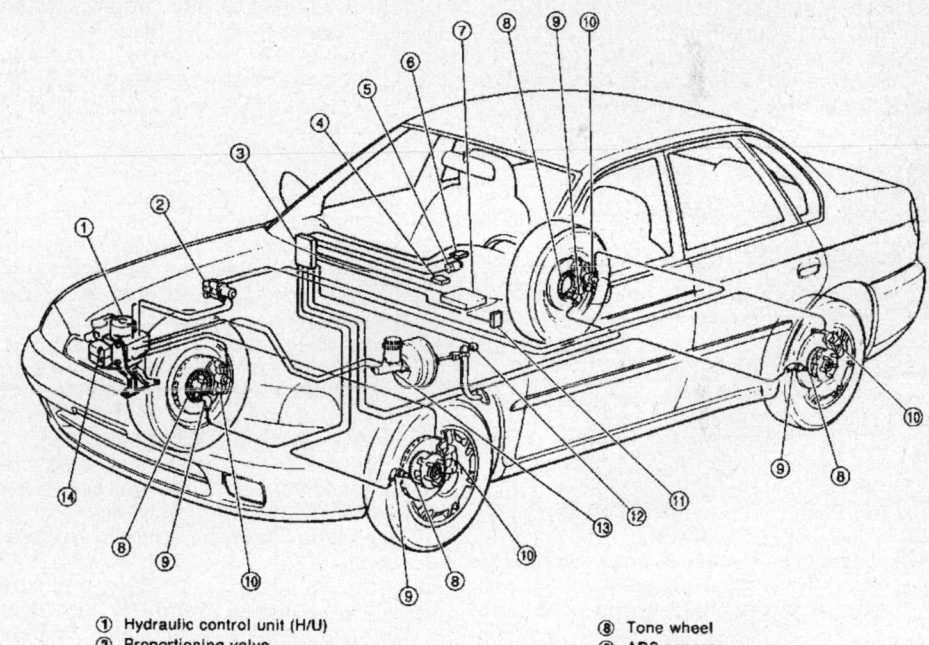

① Hydraulic control unit (H/U)
② Proportioning valve
③ ABS control module (ABSCM)
④ Diagnosis connector
⑤ ABS warning light
⑥ Data link connector (for Subaru select monitor)
⑦ Transmission control module (only AT vehicle)
⑧ Tone wheel
⑨ ABS sensor
⑩ Wheel cylinder
⑪ G sensor (only AWD vehicle)
⑫ Brake switch
⑬ Master cylinder
⑭ Relay box

SB4029100001000X

Fig. 1   ABS component locations

DIAGNOSIS & TESTING

System

Both warning light and LED remain on unless the ignition is turned off. Only one trouble code is displayed at a time. If multiple problems occur, only the first problem detected is displayed, that problem must be repaired first in order to check for further

trouble codes. If the LED does not activate even though the warning lamp is on, the power supply may be inoperative.

To perform self diagnosis, drive vehicle at a speed greater than 20 mph for at least one minute. If system is malfunctioning, a warning lamp on the dash panel will come on. Approximately ten seconds after the light comes on, an LED located on the ABS control unit displays a trouble code. This trouble code is determined by the number

Item	Function
Tone wheel	Attached to each wheel hub and rotates at the same speed as the hub.
Speed sensor	Emits a wheel speed signal during tone wheel rotation.
Electronic control unit	Receives wheel-speed signals from speed sensors and sends a control signal to hydraulic unit so that fluid pressure is optimally controlled.
Hydraulic control unit	Receives a control signal from electronic control unit and controls respective wheel cylinder fluid pressure.
G sensor (4WD manual transmission model)	Detects vehicle deceleration.
Warning lamp	Comes on when ABS becomes inoperative.

SB4029100002000X

Fig. 2 ABS components

of flashes the LED emits. To read codes, vehicle must remain running. Read LED codes, **Fig. 13.**

Refer to **Fig. 13,** for trouble code identification and **Fig. 14,** for ABS system wiring circuit.

DIAGNOSTIC TROUBLE CODE DIAGNOSIS

Diagnostic Trouble Code 0

1. Turn ignition switch to off position, then disconnect connector from ABS control unit.
2. Disassemble connector as follows:
   a. While pushing 1, disconnect connector, **Fig. 15.**
   b. Remove screw from portion 2, the move rubber boot 3 toward harness.
   c. Slide cover 4 in direction shown by arrow and remove.
3. Turn ignition switch to on position, then measure voltage between control unit connector terminal 1 and ground. Voltage should be 10-12 volts.
4. Start engine, then measure voltage between control unit connector terminal 15 and ground. Voltage should be 13.5 volts.
5. Turn ignition switch to off position, then connect connector to ABS control unit.
6. Turn ignition switch to on position, then measure voltage between control unit connector terminal 20 and ground. Voltage should be 0 volt.

Diagnostic Trouble Code 1-4

Turn ignition switch on, then ground check-connector terminals and check solenoid valve for operation. Each time solenoid activates, system circuit is interrupted. To check again, first turn ignition switch off then on.

1. If trouble code 1 is present, connect jumper wire between terminal 2 of check connector and ground. Listen for operation.
2. If trouble code 2 is present, connect jumper wire between terminal 11 of check connector and ground. Listen for operation.
3. If trouble code 3 is present, connect jumper wire between terminal 12 of check connector and ground. Listen for operation.
4. If trouble code 4 is present, connect jumper wire between terminal 3 of check connector and ground. Listen for operation.
5. Turn ignition switch to on position.
6. If trouble code 1 is present, measure voltage between control unit connector terminal 2 and ground. Voltage should be 0 volt with solenoid in operation.
7. If trouble code 2 is present, measure voltage between control unit connector terminal 35 and ground. Voltage should be 0 volt with solenoid in operation.
8. If trouble code 3 is present, measure voltage between control unit connector terminal 19 and ground. Voltage should be 0 volt with solenoid in operation.
9. If trouble code 4 is present, measure voltage between control unit connector terminal 18 and ground. Voltage should be 0 volt with solenoid in operation.

Diagnostic Trouble Codes 5 & 6

Use a digital circuit tester for this diagnostic procedure.

1. Disconnect connector from ABS control unit, then raise and support vehicle.
2. If trouble code 5 is present, measure voltage between ABS control unit connector terminals 4 and 5 on FWD Legacy models or terminals 4 and 22 on SVX and AWD Legacy models. Voltage should be 200-300 mVolts. At a creep speed on automatic transmission models.
3. If trouble code 6 is present, measure voltage between ABS control unit connector terminals 11 and 21. Voltage should be 200-300 mVolts. At a creep speed on automatic transmission models.
4. Disconnect ABS control unit connector.
5. If trouble code 5 is present, measure resistance between control unit connector terminal 5 on FWD Legacy models or terminal 22 on SVX and AWD Legacy models and ground. Resistance should be 1 Mohm minimum.
6. If trouble code 6 is present, measure resistance between control unit connector terminal 21 and ground. Resistance should be 1 Mohm minimum.
7. Disconnect sensor connector.
8. If trouble code 5 is present, measure resistance between lefthand sensor terminals. Resistance should be 800–1300 ohms.
9. If trouble code 6 is present, measure resistance between righthand sensor terminals. Resistance should be 800–1300 ohms.
10. Measure resistance between left or right sensor terminal 1 and ground. Resistance should be 1 Mohm minimum.

Diagnostic Trouble Codes 7 & 8

Use a digital circuit tester for this diagnostic procedure.

1. Disconnect connector from ABS control unit, then raise and support vehicle.
2. If trouble code 7 is present, measure voltage between ABS control unit connector terminals 24 and 26. Voltage should be 200-300 mVolts. At a creep speed on automatic transmission models.
3. If trouble code 8 is present, measure voltage between ABS control unit connector terminals 7 and 9. Voltage should be 200-300 mVolts. At a creep speed on automatic transmission models.
4. Disconnect ABS control unit connector.
5. If trouble code 7 is present, measure resistance between control unit connector terminal 26 and ground. Resistance should be 1 Mohm minimum.
6. If trouble code 8 is present, measure resistance between control unit connector terminal 9 and ground. Resistance should be 1 Mohm minimum.
7. Disconnect sensor connector.
8. If trouble code 7 is present, measure resistance between righthand sensor terminals. Resistance should be 800–1300 ohms.
9. If trouble code 8 is present, measure resistance between lefthand sensor terminals. Resistance should be 800–1300 ohms.
10. Measure resistance between left or right sensor terminal 1 and ground.

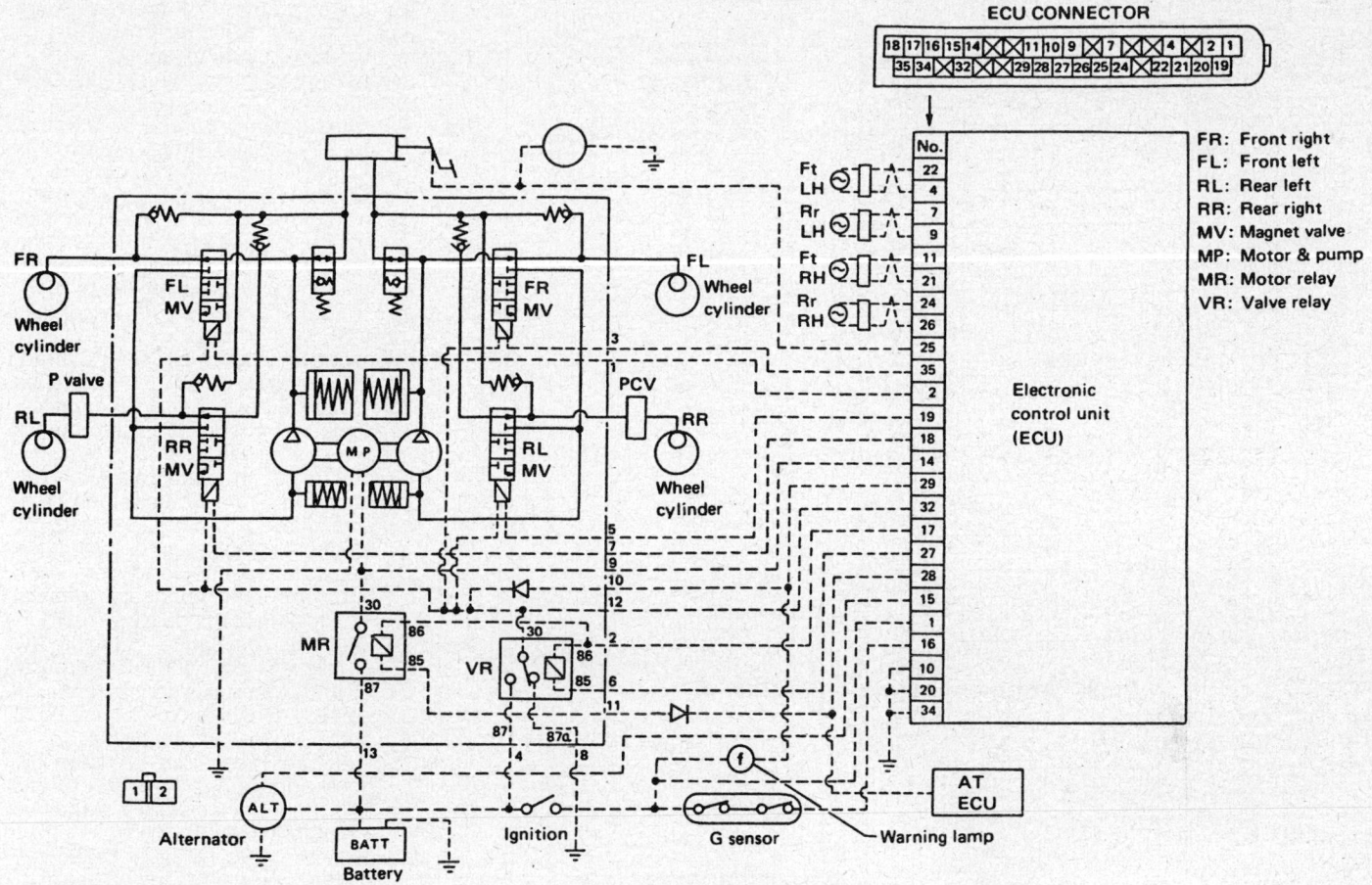

Fig. 3 ABS system diagram

SB40291000003000X

Fig. 4 Block diagram of ABS electronic circuits

SB4029100004000X

Fig. 4 Block diagram of ABS electronic circuits

Resistance should be 1 Mohm minimum.

Diagnostic Trouble Code 9

1. Turn ignition switch to off position, then disconnect ABS control unit connector.

2. Disassemble ABS control unit connector, then measure resistance between control unit connector terminals 17 and 28. Resistance should be 45-55 ohms.

3. Disconnect connectors from hydraulic unit.

4. Measure resistance between hydraulic unit connector F43 terminal 2 and connector R1 terminal 4. Resistance should be 1 Mohm minimum.

5. Remove motor relay, then attach tester probes, **Fig. 16.** Resistance should be 0 ohms when 12 volts are applied or 1 Mohms when no voltage is applied.

6. Disconnect connector from hydraulic unit.

7. Measure resistance between hydraulic unit terminals 5 and 6. Resistance should be 45-55 ohms.

   a. When resistance checks out unsatisfactory, check relay as a single unit. If resistance checks out satisfactory, replace hydraulic unit. If resistance checks out unsatisfactory, repair harness connector between ABS control unit and hydraulic unit.

8. Disconnect connectors from ABS control unit and hydraulic unit.

9. Measure resistance between hydraulic unit connector R1 terminal 5 and control unit connector terminal 28. Resistance should be 0 ohm.

10. Measure resistance between hydraulic unit connector R1 terminal 6 and control unit connector terminal 17. Resistance should be 0 ohm.

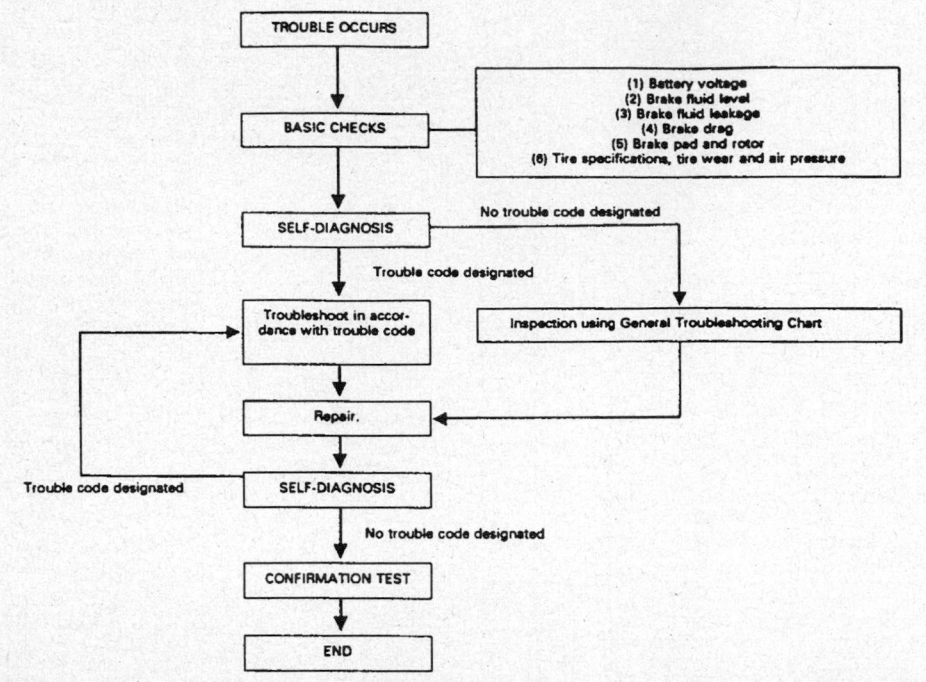

Fig. 5   Troubleshooting chart (basic)

SB4029100005000X

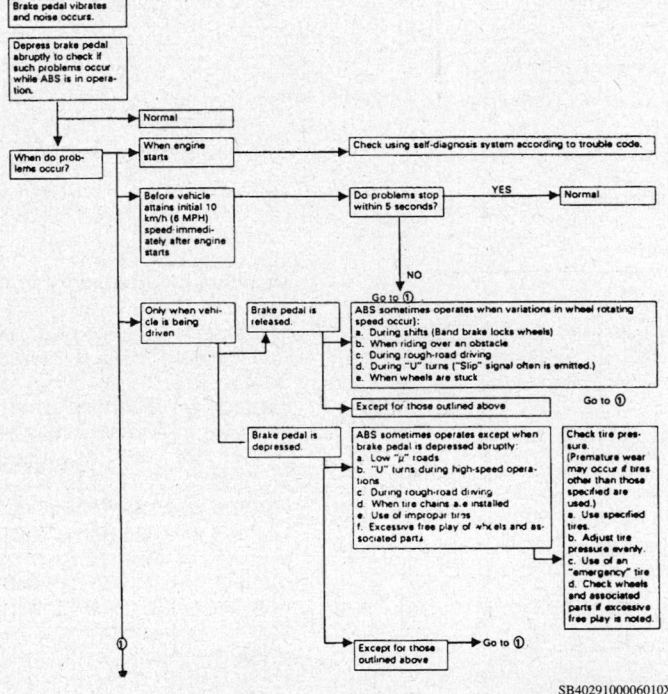

SB4029100006010X

Fig. 6   Troubleshooting chart A, Vibrating pedal & noise (Part 1 of 2)

11. Measure resistance between hydraulic unit connector R1 terminal 5 and ground. Resistance should be 1 Mohm minimum.
12. Measure resistance between hydraulic unit connector R1 terminal 7 and ground. Resistance should be 1 Mohm minimum.
13. Turn ignition switch to on position, then measure voltage between hydraulic unit connector F43 terminal 2 and ground. Voltage should be 10-12 volts.

Trouble Code 10

1. Turn ignition switch to off position, then disconnect ABS control unit connector.
2. Disassemble ABS control unit connector, then measure resistance between control unit connector terminals 17 and 27. Resistance should be 80-90 ohms.
3. Disconnect connectors from hydraulic unit.

4. Measure resistance between hydraulic unit connector F43 terminal 1 and connector R1 terminal 11. Resistance should be 1 Mohm minimum.
5. Remove valve relay, then attach tester probes, **Fig. 17.**
   a. With terminals 30 and 87 connected. Resistance should be 0 ohms when 12 volts are applied or 1 Mohms when no voltage is applied.
   b. With terminals 30 and 87a connected. Resistance should be 1 Mohm when 12 volts are applied or 0 ohms when no voltage is applied.
6. Disconnect connector from hydraulic unit.
7. Measure resistance between hydraulic unit terminals 6 and 12. Resistance should be 80-90 ohms. When resistance checks out unsatisfactory, check relay as a single unit.
8. Disconnect connectors from ABS control unit and hydraulic unit, then measure as follows:
   a. Measure resistance between hydraulic unit connector R1 terminal 6 and control unit connector terminal 17. Resistance should be 0 ohm.
   b. Measure resistance between hydraulic unit connector R1 terminal 12 and control unit connector terminal 27. Resistance should be 0 ohm.
   c. Measure resistance between hydraulic unit connector R1 terminal 6 and ground. Resistance should be 1 Mohm minimum.
   d. Measure resistance between hydraulic unit connector R1 terminal 12 and ground. Resistance should be 1 Mohm minimum.
   e. If the above resistances are satisfactory, replace hydraulic unit. If the above resistance are unsatisfactory, repair harness/connector between ABS control unit and hydraulic unit.
9. Turn ignition switch to on position, then measure voltage between hydraulic unit connector F43 terminal 1 and ground. Voltage should be 10-12 volts.

Diagnostic Trouble Code 16

1. To check power supply to ABS control unit, refer to " Trouble Code 0."
2. To check ABS sensor, refer to "Trouble Code 5 and 6" and "Trouble Code 7 and 8."

Component

SPEED SENSORS

1. Check pole piece of speed sensor for damage or foreign materials. Clean or replace as needed.
2. Measure resistance between speed sensor terminals. Refer to **Fig. 18,** for specifications. If resistance is not within specifications replace wheel sensor or adjust gap between sensor and tone wheel.
3. Check tone wheels teeth for cracks or dents. Replace if needed.
4. Clearances should be measured one at a time to ensure tone wheel and

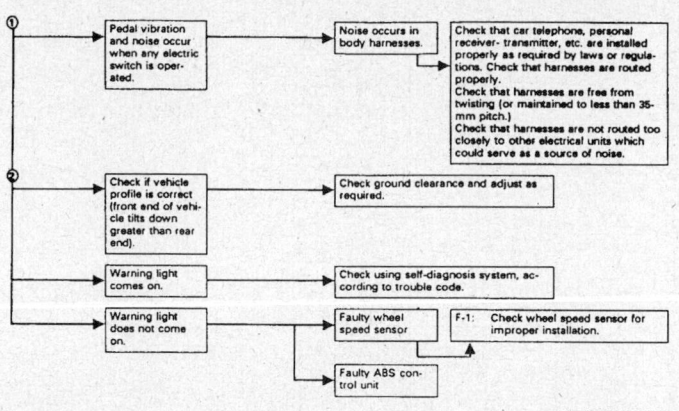

Fig. 6 Troubleshooting chart A, Vibrating pedal & noise (Part 2 of 2)

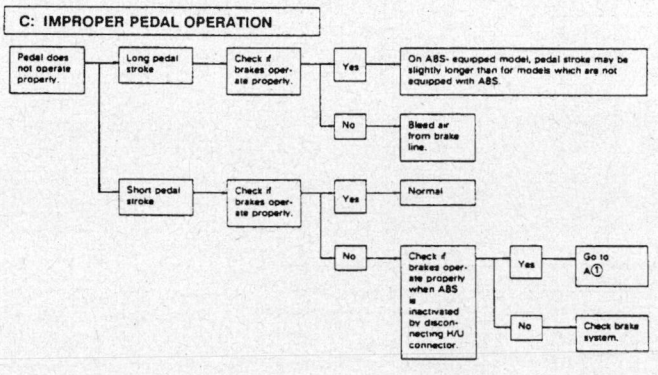

Fig. 8 Troubleshooting chart C (improper pedal operation)

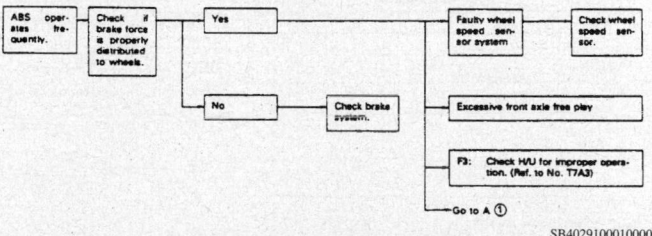

Fig. 10 Troubleshooting chart E (frequent ABS operation)

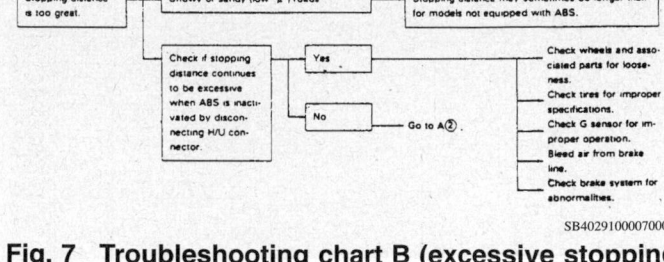

Fig. 7 Troubleshooting chart B (excessive stopping distance)

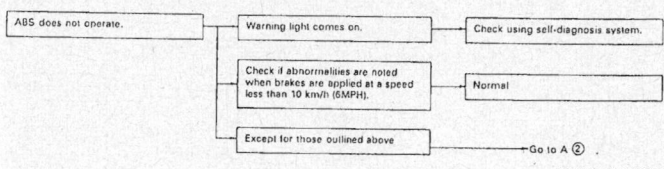

Fig. 9 Troubleshooting chart D (ABS inoperative)

Contents		Terminal No.	With engine idling	Input/output signals	
				Measured value	Measuring conditions
Wheel speed sensors	Left front wheel GND	22 4	0 V	200 ~ 300 mV	• No. 22 – No. 4 • Vehicle speed 2.75 km/h (1.7 MPH)
	Right front wheel GND	11 21	0 V	200 ~ 300 mV	• No. 11 – No. 21 • Vehicle speed 2.75 km/h (1.7 MPH)
	Left rear wheel GND	7 9	0 V	200 ~ 300 mV	• No. 7 – No. 9 • Vehicle speed 2.75 km/h (1.7 MPH)
	Right rear wheel GND	24 26	0 V	200 ~ 300 mV	• No. 24 – No. 26 • Vehicle speed 2.75 km/h (1.7 MPH)
G senor		16	13 ~ 14 V	0 V	
Stop light switch		25	0 V	13 ~ 14 V	When brake pedal is depressed.
Motor monitoring		14	0 V	13 ~ 14 V	When motor operates.
Valve power-supply monitoring		32	13 ~ 14 V	13 ~ 14 V	—
Hydraulic unit	Solenoid Left front wheel	2	13 ~ 14 V	0 V	When solenoid is energized to produce output.
	Right front wheel	35	13 ~ 14 V	0 V	
	Left rear wheel	18	13 ~ 14 V	0 V	
	Right rear wheel	19	13 ~ 14 V	0 V	
	Valve relay coil	27	0 V	0 V	—
	Motor relay coil	28	13 ~ 14 V	0 V	When motor operates to produce output
Warning light		29	70 mV	0 V	When warning activates to produce output or when valve relay is OFF
Power supply	Alternator	15	13 ~ 14 V	1.7 V	Ignition switch ON (Engine OFF)
	Battery	1	13 ~ 14 V	13 ~ 14 V	—
	Relay coil (valve, motor, etc)	17	13 ~ 14 V	13 ~ 14 V	—

Fig. 11 ABS control unit I/O signal

speed sensor are installed properly. Front clearance is .028–.039 inch and rear clearance is .020–.039 inch.

5. If clearance is narrow, adjust by using spacer part No. 26755AA000. If clearance is to wide check output voltage, replace speed sensor or tone wheel if output voltage is not within specifications. Refer to **Fig. 19.**

6. Output voltage can be checked by installing resistor and condenser, **Fig. 20,** then rotating wheel at 1.7 mph.

SYSTEM SERVICE

Brake System Bleed

Follow sequence in **Figs. 21 and 22. Torque** bleeder screws to 5–6.5 ft. lbs.

Component Replacement

FRONT SENSORS

1. Disconnect front speed sensor located in engine compartment, then remove bolts which secure harness to bracket. **Do not do damage pole piece located at tip of sensor during removal.**

2. Remove disc brake caliper and rotor from housing.

3. Remove front driveshaft, housing, then hub assembly.

4. Remove tone wheel while removing hub from housing and assembly. Refer to **Fig. 23.**

5. Reverse procedure to install, noting the following:
   a. Place a feeler gauge between speed sensors pole piece and tone wheels tooth face, on except SVX models, adjust clearance to .039–.059 inch. On SVX models, adjust clearance to .028–.039 inch.
   b. After clearance is obtained tighten speed sensor to housing.

REAR SENSORS

1. Remove rear seat, disconnect rear speed sensor and remove sensor harness bracket from rear trailing link.

2. Remove backing plate from speed sensor, then remove tone wheel from housing and hub assembly. **Do not damage pole piece of sensor and teeth of tone wheel during removal.**

3. Reverse procedures to install, noting the following:
   a. Place a feeler gauge between speed sensors pole piece and tone wheels tooth face, adjust clearance to .020–.039 inch.
   b. After clearance is obtained tighten

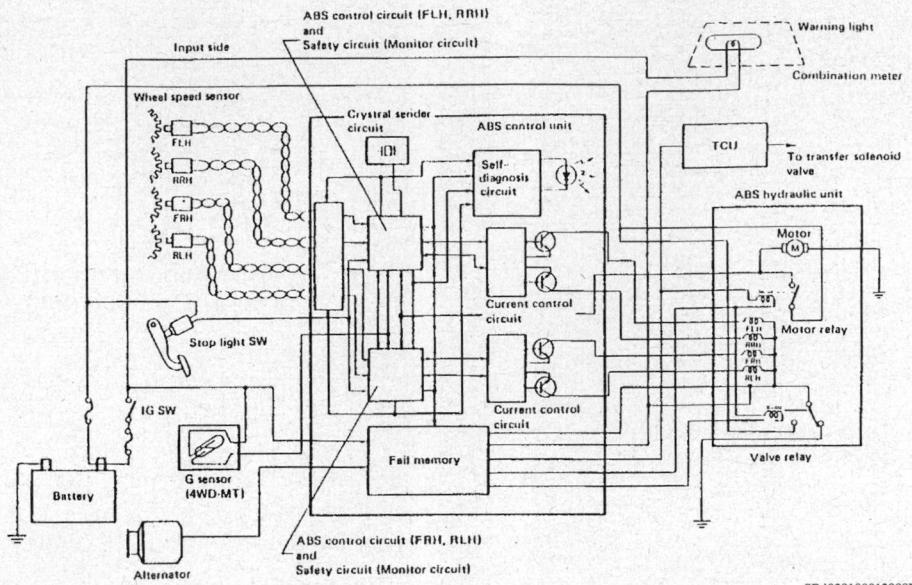

Fig. 12   I/O signal diagram

SB4029100012000X

Trouble code	Contents of diagnosis	
0 [LED OFF]	Improper power line voltage or faulty harness	
1	Broken or shorted solenoid valve circuit(s) in hydraulic unit	Left front wheel
2		Right front wheel
3		Right rear wheel
4		Left rear wheel
5	Faulty wheel speed sensor	Left front wheel
6		Right front wheel
7		Right rear wheel
8		Left rear wheel
9	Faulty motor and/or motor relay or broken or shorted harness circuit	
10	Faulty valve relay or broken or shorted harness circuit	
16	Faulty ABS control unit or G sensor or broken or shorted harness circuit	

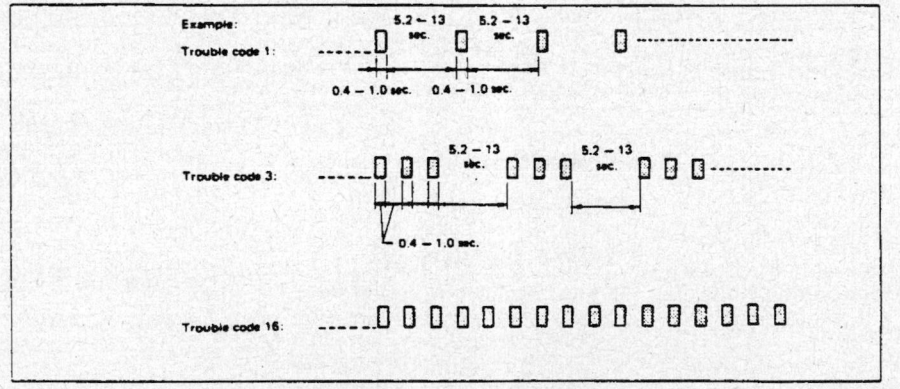

SB4029100013000X

Fig. 13   Diagnostic trouble code identification

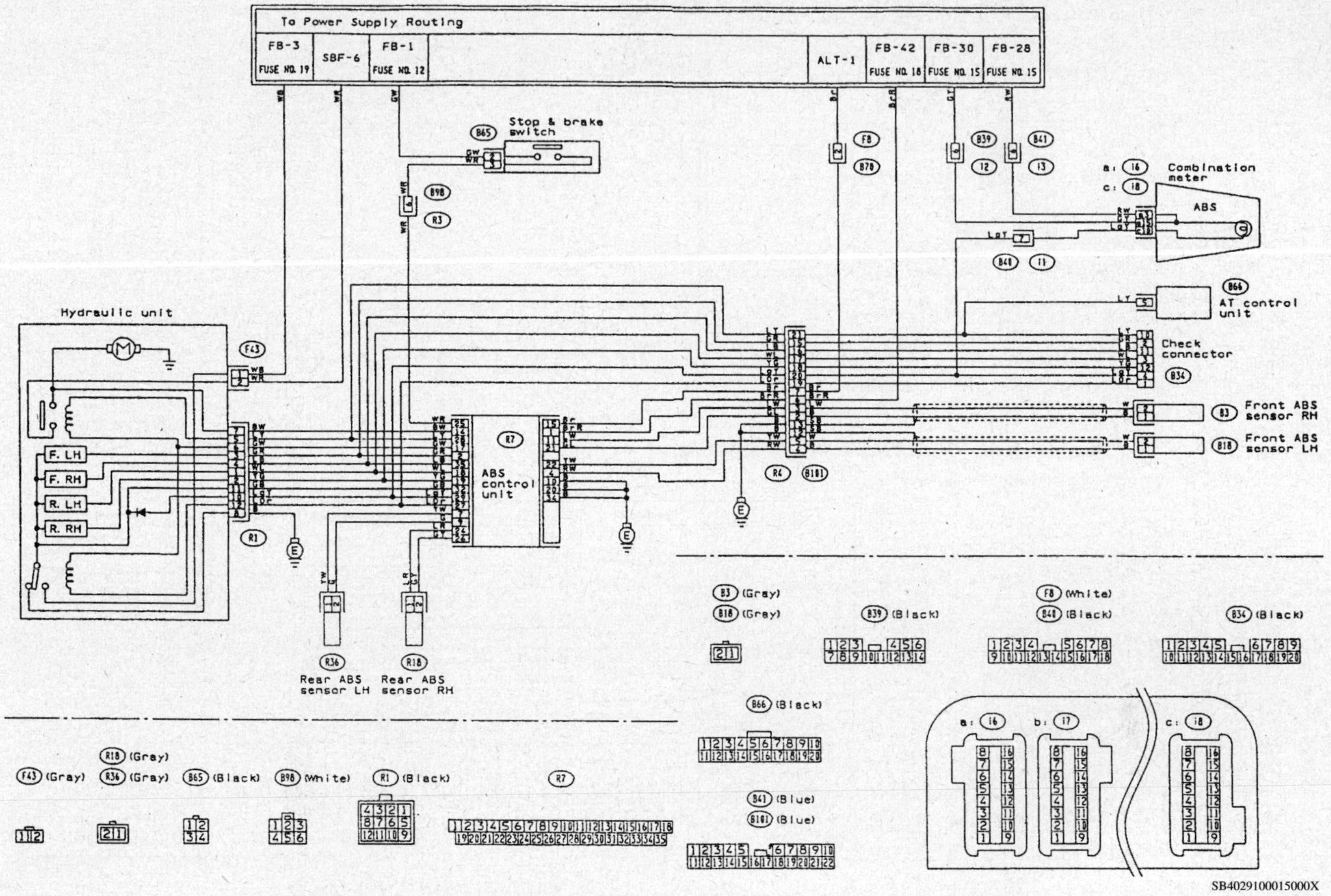

Fig. 14 Anti-Lock Brake System (ABS) wiring diagram. SVX

SB4029100015000X

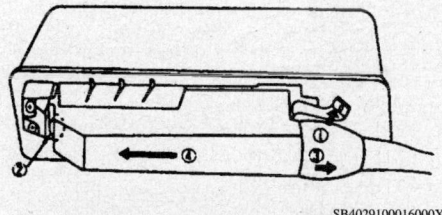

Fig. 15 ABS control unit connector disassemble

SB4029100016000X

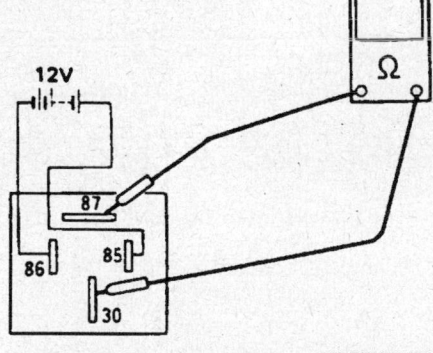

SB4029100017000X

Fig. 16 Motor relay inspection

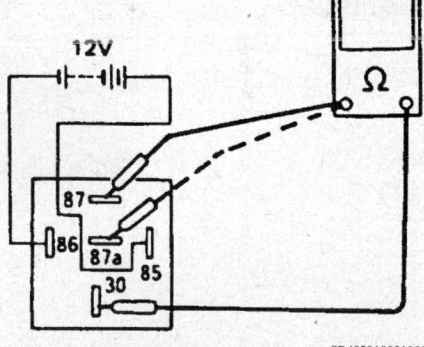

SB4029100018000X

Fig. 17 Valve relay inspection

ABS sensor	Model	Terminal No.	Standard
Front - LH	AWD AT AWD MT FWD	22 and 4 5 and 4	
Front - RH	ALL	11 and 21	1.0 ± 0.2 kΩ
Rear - LH	ALL	7 and 9	
Rear - RH	ALL	24 and 26	
Front - LH	AWD AT AWD MT FWD	22 and 10, 20, 34 5 and 4	
Front - RH	ALL	11 and 10, 20, 34	More than 1 × 10³ kΩ (Insulation resistance)
Rear - LH	ALL	7 and 10, 20, 34	
Rear - RH	ALL	24 and 10, 20, 34	

SB4029100019000X

Fig. 18 Speed sensor specification chart

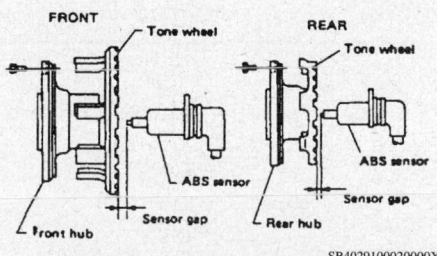

SB4029100020000X

Fig. 19 Tone wheel & hub clearance inspection

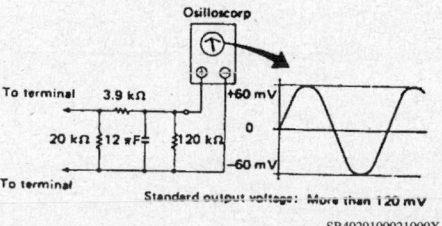

SB4029100021000X

Fig. 20 AV signal wiring diagram

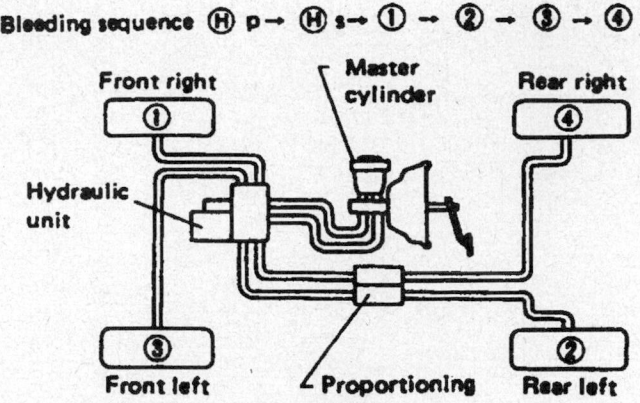

Bleeding sequence (H) p → (H) s → ① → ② → ③ → ④

Fig. 21 ABS unit bleeding sequence

SB4029100031000X

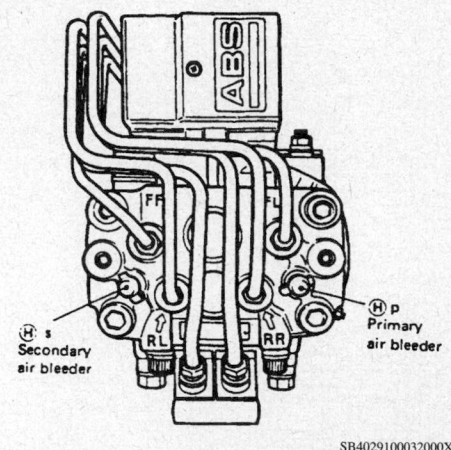

Fig. 22 ABS unit bleeding locations

SB4029100032000X

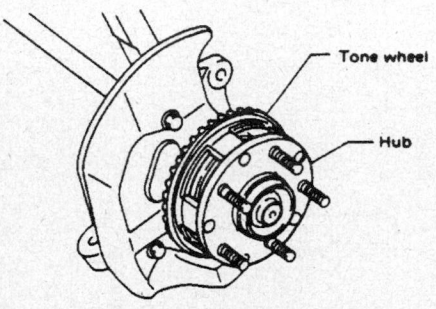

Fig. 23 Tone wheel & hub assembly

SB4029100022000X

	Condition	Terminal number	Standard	Diagram	Terminal location
Valve relay	Turning off electricity.	85 — 86	93 — 113 Ω		
		30 — 87a	0 Ω		
		30 — 87	∞		
	Turning on electricity between 85 and 86. (DC 12 V)	30 — 87a	∞Ω		
		30 — 87	0Ω		
			—		
Motor relay	Turning off electricity.	85 — 86	72 — 88 Ω		
		30 — 87	∞		
	Turning on electricity between 85 and 86. (DC 12 V)	30 — 87	0 Ω		

SB4029100027000X

Fig. 24 Hydraulic relay box specification chart. SVX

speed sensor to backing plate.

ABS HYDRAULIC UNIT

Replacement

1. Disconnect hydraulic unit electrical connector.
2. Disconnect air flow meter connector.
3. Remove upper and lower air cleaner cover.
4. Disconnect brake lines from unit.
5. Remove hydraulic unit noting the following:
   a. Hydraulic unit cannot be disassembled. Do not attempt to loosen nuts and bolts.
   b. Do not drop or bump hydraulic unit.
   c. Do not turn hydraulic unit upside down or place it on is side.
   d. Ensure care is taken to prevent foreign particles from getting into hydraulic unit.

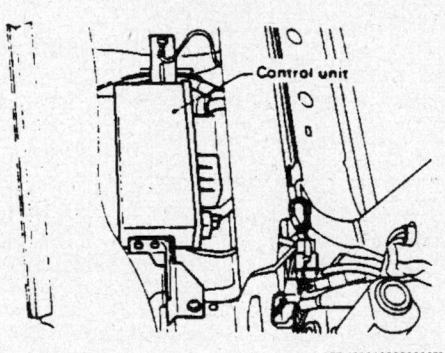

SB4029100028000X

Fig. 25 Electronic control unit

6. Reverse procedure to install. **Torque** hydraulic unit attaching bolts to 17–31 ft. lbs.

Inspection

1. Check bracket on vehicle, then all connectors.

2. Open hydraulic unit relay box and check for open or shorted circuits, **Fig. 24.**

ELECTRONIC CONTROL UNIT

1. Remove floor mat located under lower right side of front seat, then bolts that secure control unit, **Fig. 25.**
2. Remove screws that secure connector to unit, disconnect connector, then remove control unit.
3. Reverse procedure to install, checking that all connectors are connected properly.

NOTE: On Air Bag Equipped Models, Refer To "Air Bag System Precautions" Located In The Front Of This Manual For System Disarming & Arming Procedures.

NOTE: Electrical Symbol & Wire Color Code Identification Located In The Front Of This Manual May Be Used As An Aid When Using Wiring Circuits Found In This Section.

INDEX

PRECAUTIONS

AIR BAG SYSTEMS

Refer to "Air Bag System Precautions" in the front of this manual for system disarming and arming procedures.

BATTERY GROUND CABLE

Prior to service, disconnect battery ground cable and isolate as required.

DESCRIPTION

The Anti-lock brake system (ABS) electrically controls brake fluid pressure to prevent wheel lock during braking on slippery road surfaces, improving steering stability and shortening the braking distance. If the ABS becomes inoperative, a fail-safe system activates to ensure conventional brake system operation.

The ABS consists of four tone wheels, four speed sensors, electronic control unit, a G sensor and a warning lamp.

The electronic control unit has the capability of on-board diagnosis. The on-board diagnosis system is designed to detect problems after the vehicle has been driven at 6 mph or more for at least 20 seconds. If a problem is found, the ABS warning light will illuminate to inform the driver of the occurrence of a problem. When the warning light is on, the ABS system will be inactive and the normal braking function will work.

TROUBLESHOOTING

Refer to **Figs. 1 through 5,** for troubleshooting procedures.

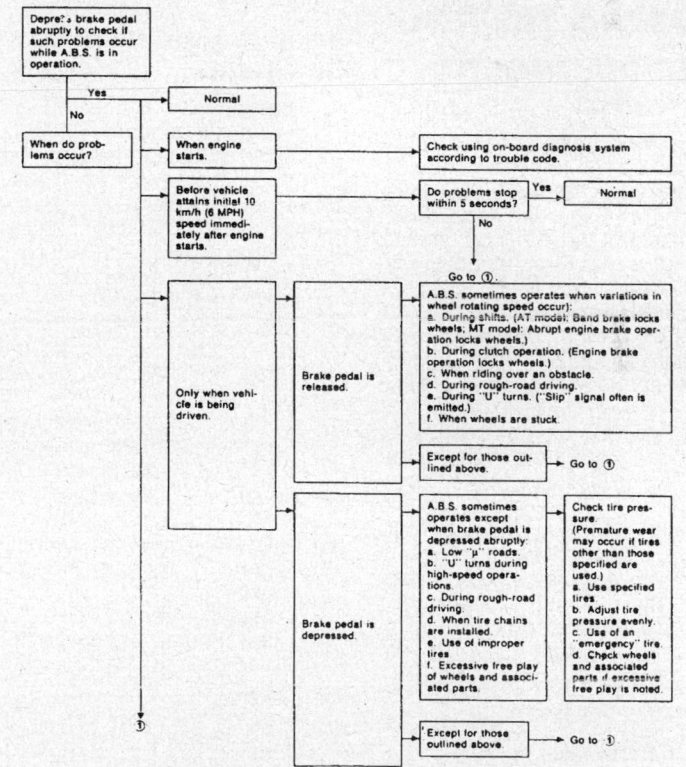

SB4029100033010X

Fig. 1 Troubleshooting chart (vibrating pedal & noise, Part 1 of 2)

PRELIMINARY INSPECTION

1. Ensure battery voltage is 12 volts or more.
2. Ensure specific gravity of battery is 1.260.
3. Check condition of main and other fuses, harnesses and connector. Also check for proper grounding.
4. Check brake fluid level and for leakage.
5. Check for brake drag, brake pad and rotor condition.
6. Ensure tires are in good condition and

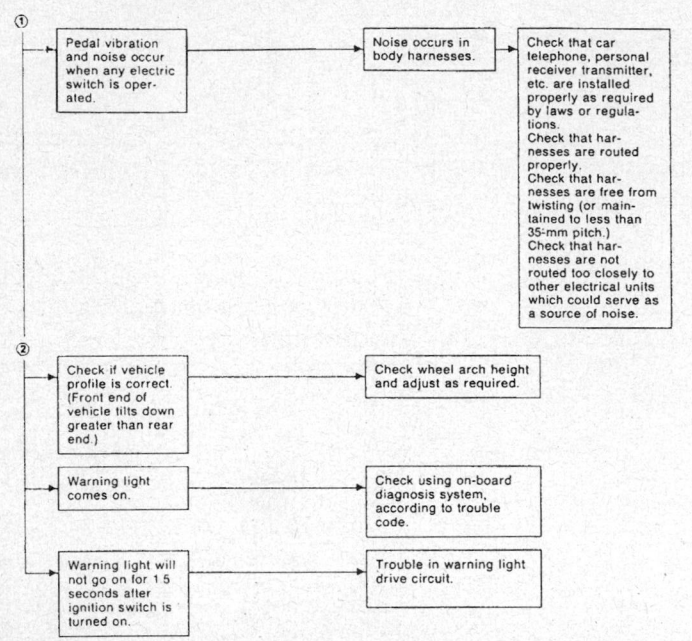

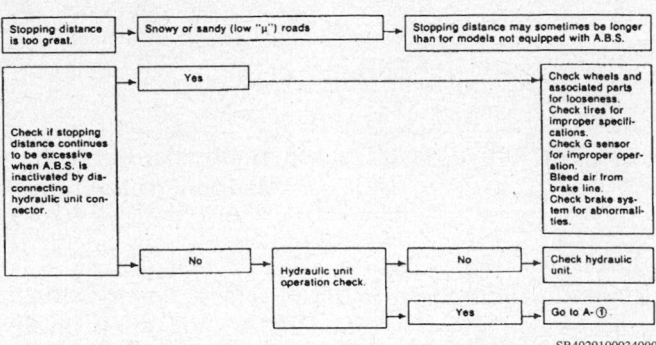

Fig. 2   Troubleshooting chart (excessive stopping distance)

Fig. 1   Troubleshooting chart (vibrating pedal & noise, Part 2 of 2)

at specified air pressure.

DIAGNOSIS & TESTING

ACCESSING DIAGNOSTIC TROUBLE CODES

When the control module detects a problem, the information (up to a maximum of three) will be stored in the EEPROM as a trouble code. When there are more than three, the most recent three will be stored. Stored codes will stay in memory until they are cleared.

1. Remove ABS check connector from under steering column, **Fig. 6.**
2. Turn ignition switch off, then ground ABS check connector terminal L, **Fig. 6.**
3. Turn ignition switch to on position. The ABS warning light is now in the diagnostic mode and blinks to identify trouble codes.
4. After start code (11) is shown, the trouble code(s) will be shown in order of the last information first. The code(s) will repeat for a maximum of 5 minutes. When there are no trouble codes in memory, only the start code (11) is shown.

DIAGNOSTIC TROUBLE CODE INTERPRETATION

Refer to **Fig. 7,** for trouble code interpretation and **Fig. 8,** for trouble code identification and description.

WIRING DIAGRAMS

Refer to wiring diagram, **Fig. 9,** when performing the following procedures.

DIAGNOSTIC PROCEDURE

Refer to **Fig. 10,** for proper diagnostic sequence.

DIAGNOSTIC TESTS

Warning Light Does Not Illuminate

1. Turn ignition switch to off position, then disconnect combination meter.
2. Check ABS warning light valve, then turn ignition switch to on position.
3. Measure voltage between combination meter connector i18 terminal 13. Voltage should be 10-12 volts.
4. Turn ignition switch off, then remove combination meter.
5. Disconnect connectors from ABS control module and hydraulic unit, then turn ignition switch to on position. Measure as follows:
   a. Measure voltage between control module connector terminal 29 and ground. Voltage should be 10-12 volts.
   b. Measure voltage between hydraulic unit connector terminal 10 and ground. Voltage should be 10-12 volts.
   c. Measure resistance between control module connector terminal 10 and ground. Resistance should be 0 ohms.
   d. Measure resistance between control module connector terminal 20 and ground. Resistance should be 0 ohms.
   e. Measure resistance between control module connector terminal 34 and ground. Resistance should be 0 ohms.
   f. Measure resistance between hydraulic unite connector terminal 8 and ground. Resistance should be 0 ohms.
6. Remove valve relay, then attach tester probes, **Fig. 11.**
   a. With terminals 30 and 87 connect-ed. Resistance should be 0 ohms when 12 volts are applied or 1 Mohm when no voltage is applied.
   b. With terminals 30 and 87a connect-ed. Resistance should be 1 Mohm when 12 volts are applied or 0 ohms when no voltage is applied.

Warning Light Remains On

1. Turn ignition switch to off position, then disconnect control module connector.
2. Turn ignition switch to on position, then measure voltage between control module connector terminal 29 and ground. Voltage should be 10-12 volts.
3. Turn ignition switch to on position, then measure voltage between control module connector terminal 1 and ground. Voltage should be 10-12 volts.
4. Measure resistance between control module connector terminal 10 and ground. Resistance should be 0 ohms.
5. Measure resistance between control module connector terminal 20 and ground. Resistance should be 0 ohms.
6. Measure resistance between control module connector terminal 34 and ground. Resistance should be 0 ohms.

Trouble Codes 21, 23, 25 & 27

1. Turn ignition switch to off position, then disconnect control module connector.
2. Measure resistance between control module connector terminals as follows:
   a. If trouble code 21 is present, measure between terminals 23 and 21. Resistance should be 800-1300 ohms.
   b. If trouble code 23 is present, measure between terminals 22 and 4 on AWD Impreza models or terminals 5 and 4 on FWD Impreza models. Resistance should be 800-1300 ohms.
   c. If trouble code 25 is present, measure between terminals 24 and 26. Resistance should be 800-1300 ohms.
   d. If trouble code 27 is present, measure between terminals 8 and 9. Resistance should be 800-1300 ohms.
3. Measure resistance between control module connector and ground as follows:

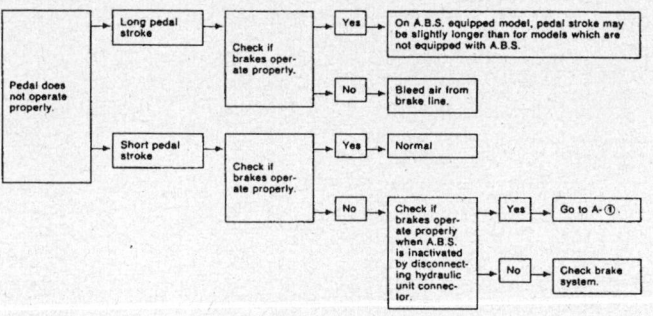

Fig. 3   Troubleshooting chart (improper pedal operation)

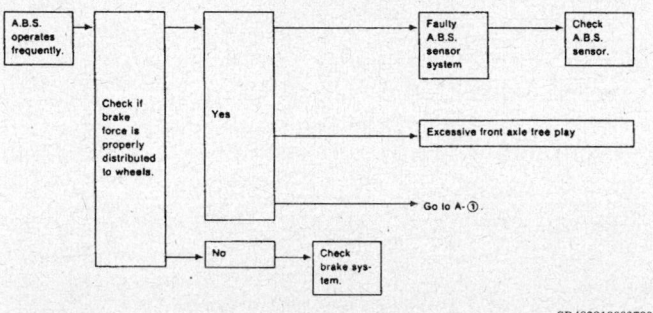

Fig. 5   Troubleshooting chart (frequent ABS operation)

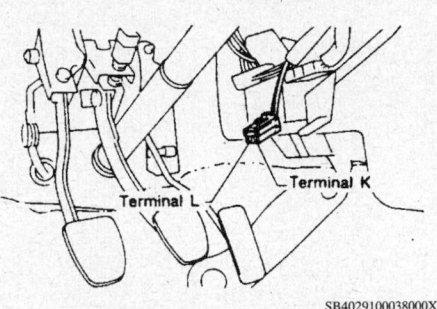

SB4029100036000X

Fig. 4   Troubleshooting chart (ABS inoperative)

SB4029100038000X

Fig. 6   Check connector terminal identification. Impreza

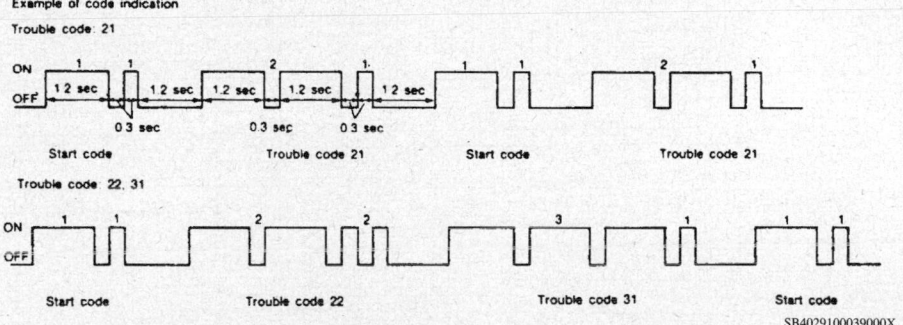

SB4029100039000X

Fig. 7   Diagnostic trouble code interpretation

a frequency of 10 Hz. Measure voltage as follows:
  a. If trouble code 21 is present, measure voltage between terminals 23 and 21. Voltage should be .12–1.0 volt at 10 Hz.
  b. If trouble code 23 is present, measure voltage between terminals 22 and 4 on AWD Impreza models or terminals 5 and 4 on FWD Impreza models. Voltage should be .12–1.0 volt at 10 Hz.
  c. If trouble code 25 is present, measure voltage between terminals 24 and 26. Voltage should be .12–1.0 volt at 10 Hz.
  d. If trouble code 27 is present, measure voltage between terminals 8 and 9. Voltage should be .12–1.0 volt at 10 Hz.
  e. When this inspection is completed, the control module could store trouble code 29.
11. Remove brake assembly to gain access to ABS sensor and tone wheel.
12. Check pole piece and tone wheel for accumulation of foreign particles. Clean as necessary.
13. Check tone wheel teeth for cracks or deformities. Replace as necessary.
14. **Torque** tone wheel to 7–12 ft. lbs.
15. Measure tone wheel to pole piece gap over entire perimeter of wheel. Gap for front wheel must be .035–.055 inch. Gap for rear wheel must be .028–.047 inch. If necessary, adjust gap using spacers part No. 26755AA000.
16. Check hub runout. Runout should be .0020 inch.
17. Turn ignition switch off, then disconnect ABS sensor connector.
18. Measure resistance between sensor terminals as follows:
  a. If trouble code 21 is present, measure between front righthand sensor terminals. Resistance should be 800-1300 ohms.

  a. If trouble code 21 is present, measure between terminals 23 and ground. Resistance should be 0 ohms.
  b. If trouble code 23 is present, measure between terminals 4 and ground. Resistance should be 0 ohms.
  c. If trouble code 25 is present, measure between terminals 24 and ground. Resistance should be 0 ohms.
  d. If trouble code 27 is present, measure between terminals 8 and ground. Resistance should be 0 ohms.
4. Turn ignition switch to on position.
5. Measure voltage between control module connector and ground as follows:
  a. If trouble code 21 is present, measure between terminals 23 and ground. Voltage should be 0 ohms.
  b. If trouble code 23 is present, measure between terminals 4 and ground. Voltage should be 0 ohms.
  c. If trouble code 25 is present, measure between terminals 24 and ground. Voltage should be 0 ohms.
  d. If trouble code 27 is present, measure between terminals 8 and ground. Voltage should be 0 ohms.
6. Turn ignition switch to off position, then raise and support vehicle.
7. Disconnect connector from control module, then remove connector cover as follows:
  a. Remove screw from portion 1, **Fig. 12,** then move rubber boot 2 back (toward harness).
  b. Slide cover 3 in direction, **Fig. 12,** and remove.
8. Connect connector back into control module, then connect an oscilloscope to the control module connector as outlined in step 10.
9. Turn ignition switch to on position.
10. Rotate wheels and measure voltage at

Trouble code	Contents of diagnosis	
NONE: A [Warning light OFF]	Trouble in warning light drive circuit (Warning light is not on for 1.5 seconds after ignition switch is on.)	
NONE: B [Warning light ON] or [Abnormal trouble code output]	Trouble in warning light drive circuit	
11	Start code: • Trouble code is shown after start code. • Only start code is shown in normal condition.	
21	Faulty A.B.S. sensor (Open circuit or input voltage excessive)	Front right-wheel sensor
23		Front left wheel sensor
25		Rear right wheel sensor
27		Rear left wheel sensor
22	Faulty A.B.S. sensor (When there is no open circuit or speed signal input.)	Front right wheel sensor
24		Front left wheel sensor
26		Rear right wheel sensor
28		Rear left wheel sensor
29	Faulty tone wheel, etc.	
31	Faulty solenoid valve circuit(s) in hydraulic unit	Front right wheel control
33		Front left wheel control
39		Rear wheels control
41	Faulty A.B.S. control module	
42	Source voltage is low.	
51	Faulty valve relay	
52	Faulty hydraulic motor and/or motor relay	
54	Faulty stop light circuit	
56	Use of improper A.B.S. control module specification, or faulty G sensor	

SB4029100040000X

Fig. 8   Trouble code description

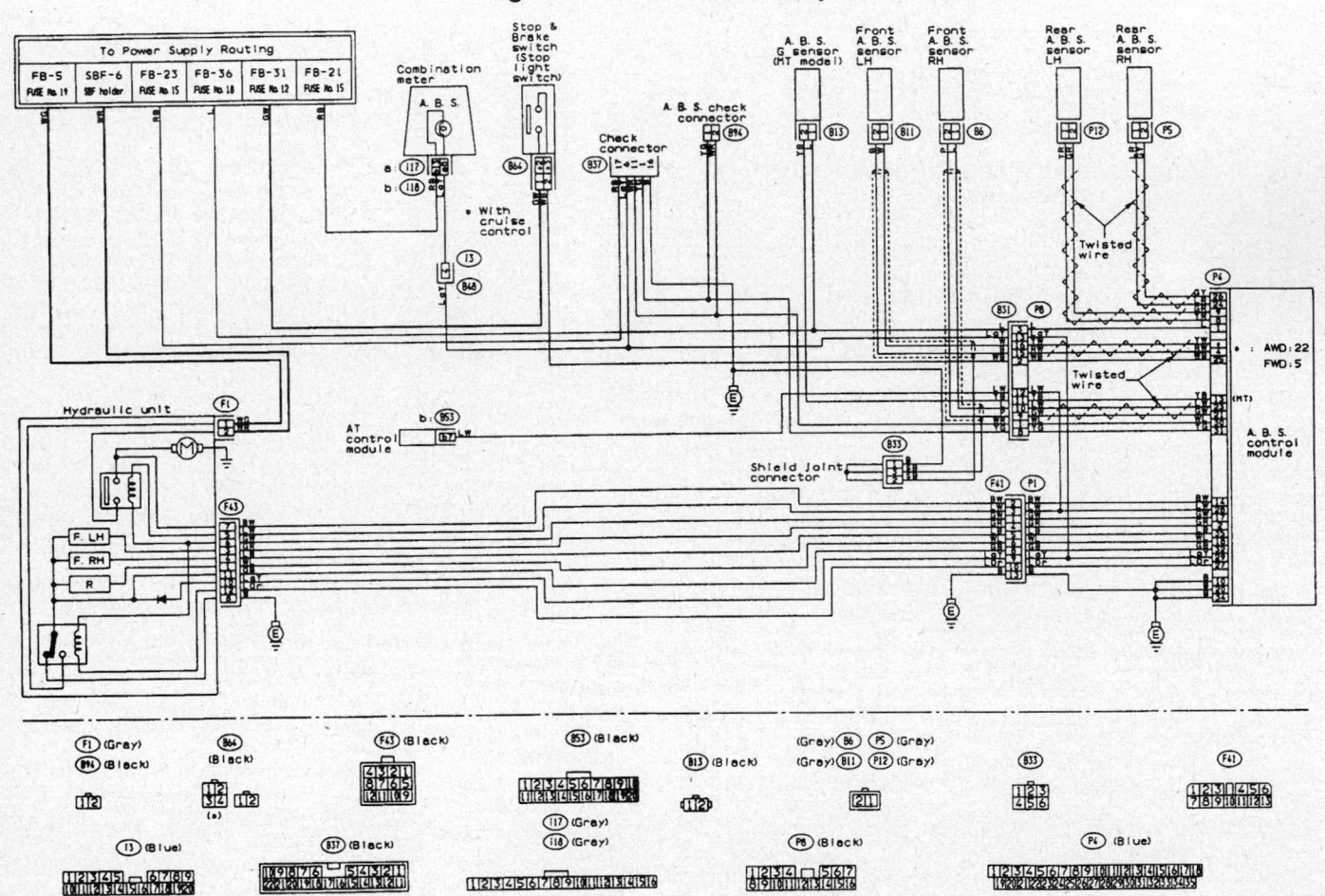

SB4029100042000X

Fig. 9   ABS system wiring diagram. Impreza

b. If trouble code 23 is present, measure between front lefthand sensor terminals. Resistance should be 800-1300 ohms.

c. If trouble code 25 is present, measure between rear righthand sensor terminals. Resistance should be 800-1300 ohms.

d. If trouble code 27 is present, measure between rear lefthand sensor terminals. Resistance should be 800-1300 ohms.

Trouble Codes 22, 24, 26 & 28

1. Turn ignition switch to off position, then raise and support vehicle.

2. Disconnect connector from control module, then remove connector cover as follows:

a. Remove screw from portion 1, **Fig. 12**, then move rubber boot 2 back (toward harness).

b. Slide cover 3 in direction, **Fig. 12**, and remove.

3. Connect connector back into control

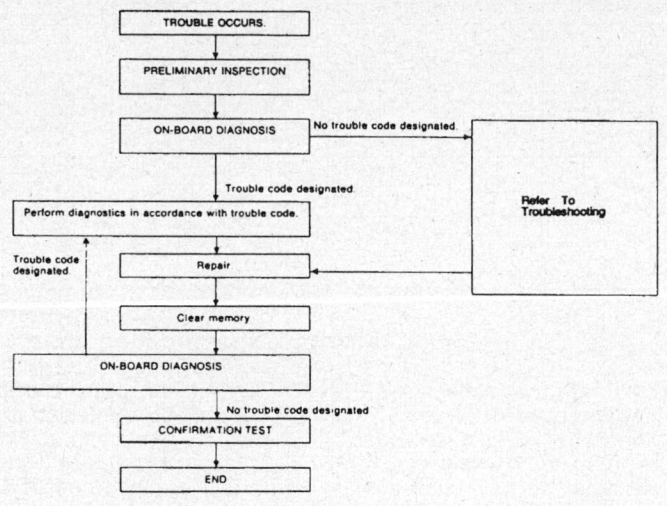

Fig. 10   Diagnostic sequence

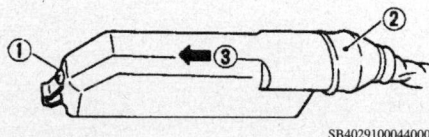

Fig. 12   Connector cover removal

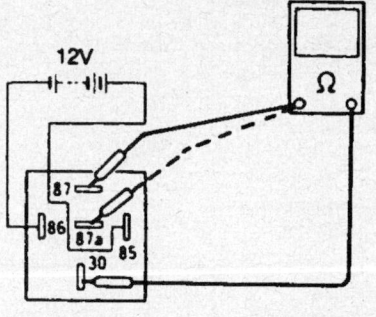

Fig. 11   Valve relay terminal identification

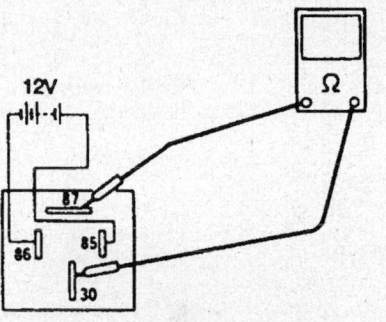

Fig. 13   Motor relay terminal identification

A.B.S. sensor	Model	Terminal No.	Standard
Front - LH	AWD AT	22 and 4	
	FWD AT	5 and 4	
Front - RH	ALL AT	23 and 21	1.0 ± 0.2 kΩ
Rear - LH	ALL AT	8 and 9	
Rear - RH	ALL AT	24 and 26	
Front - LH	AWD AT	22 and 10, 20, 34	
	FWD AT	5 and 10, 20, 34	More than 1 x 10³ kΩ (Insulation resistance)
Front - RH	ALL AT	23 and 10, 20, 34	
Rear - LH	ALL AT	8 and 10, 20, 34	
Rear - RH	ALL AT	24 and 10, 20, 34	

Fig. 14   Speed sensor specification chart

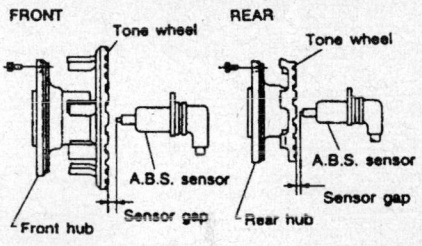

Fig. 15   Tone wheel & hub clearance measurement

module, then connect an oscilloscope to the control module connector as outlined in step 5.
4. Turn ignition switch to on position.
5. Rotate wheels and measure voltage at a frequency of 10 Hz. Measure voltage as follows:
   a. If trouble code 22 is present, measure voltage between terminals 23 and 21. Voltage should be .12–1.0 volt at 10 Hz.
   b. If trouble code 24 is present, measure voltage between terminals 22 and 4 on AWD Impreza models or terminals 5 and 4 on FWD Impreza models. Voltage should be .12–1.0 volt at 10 Hz.
   c. If trouble code 26 is present, measure voltage between terminals 24 and 26. Voltage should be .12–1.0 volt at 10 Hz.
   d. If trouble code 28 is present, measure voltage between terminals 8 and 9. Voltage should be .12–1.0 volt at 10 Hz.
   e. When this inspection is completed,

the control module could store trouble code 29.
6. Measure resistance between sensor terminals as follows:
   a. If trouble code 22 is present, measure between front righthand sensor terminals. Resistance should be 800-1300 ohms.
   b. If trouble code 24 is present, measure between front lefthand sensor terminals. Resistance should be 800-1300 ohms.
   c. If trouble code 26 is present, measure between rear righthand sensor terminals. Resistance should be 800-1300 ohms.
   d. If trouble code 28 is present, measure between rear lefthand sensor terminals. Resistance should be 800-1300 ohms.
7. Remove brake assembly to gain access to ABS sensor and tone wheel.
8. Check pole piece and tone wheel for accumulation of foreign particles. Clean as necessary.
9. Check tone wheel teeth for cracks or

deformities. Replace as necessary.
10. **Torque** tone wheel to 7–12 ft. lbs.
11. Measure tone wheel to pole piece gap over entire perimeter of wheel. Gap for front wheel must be .035–.055 inch. Gap for rear wheel must be .028–.047 inch. If necessary, adjust gap using spacers part No. 26755AA000.
12. Check hub runout. Runout should be .0020 inch.

Trouble Code 29

1. Turn ignition switch to off position, then raise and support vehicle.
2. Disconnect connector from control module, then remove connector cover as follows:
   a. Remove screw from portion 1, **Fig. 12,** then move rubber boot 2 back (toward harness).
   b. Slide cover 3 in direction, **Fig. 12,** and remove.
3. Connect connector back into control module, then connect an oscilloscope

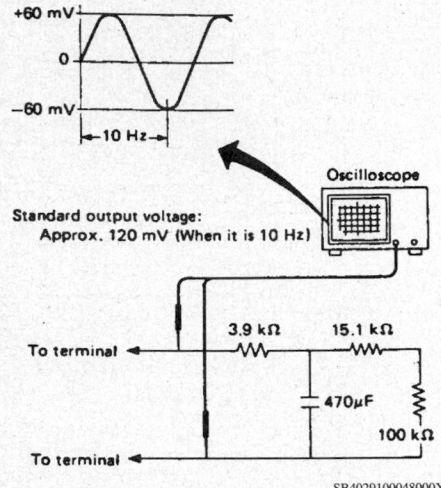

Standard output voltage:
Approx. 120 mV (When it is 10 Hz)

3.9 kΩ   15.1 kΩ

470μF

100 kΩ

To terminal

To terminal

SB4029100048000X

Fig. 16 Output voltage connection & specification

Condition		Terminal number	Standard	Diagram	Terminal location
Valve relay	Turning off electricity.	85 — 86	93 — 113 Ω		
		30 — 87a	0 Ω		
		30 — 87	∞		
	Turning on electricity between 85 and 86. (DC 12 V)	30 — 87a	∞		
		30 — 87	0 Ω		
Motor relay	Turning off electricity.	85 — 86	72 — 88 Ω		
		30 — 87	∞		
	Turning on electricity between 85 and 86. (DC 12 V)	30 — 87	0 Ω		

SB4029100049000X

Fig. 17 Hydraulic relay box specification chart

to the control module connector as outlined in step 5.

4. Turn ignition switch to on position.
5. Rotate wheels and measure voltage at a frequency of 10 Hz. Measure voltage as follows:
   a. If trouble code 21 is present, measure voltage between terminals 23 and 21. Voltage should be .12–1.0 volt at 10 Hz.
   b. If trouble code 23 is present, measure voltage between terminals 22 and 4 on AWD Impreza models or terminals 5 and 4 on FWD Impreza models. Voltage should be .12–1.0 volt at 10 Hz.
   c. If trouble code 25 is present, measure voltage between terminals 24 and 26. Voltage should be .12–1.0 volt at 10 Hz.
   d. If trouble code 27 is present, measure voltage between terminals 8 and 9. Voltage should be .12–1.0 volt at 10 Hz.
   e. When this inspection is completed, the control module could store trouble code 29.
6. Measure resistance between sensor terminals as follows:
   a. If trouble code 21 is present, measure between front righthand sensor terminals. Resistance should be 800-1300 ohms.
   b. If trouble code 23 is present, measure between front lefthand sensor terminals. Resistance should be 800-1300 ohms.
   c. If trouble code 25 is present, measure between rear righthand sensor terminals. Resistance should be 800-1300 ohms.
   d. If trouble code 27 is present, measure between rear lefthand sensor terminals. Resistance should be 800-1300 ohms.
7. Remove brake assembly to gain access to ABS sensor and tone wheel.
8. Check pole piece and tone wheel for accumulation of foreign particles. Clean as necessary.
9. Check tone wheel teeth for cracks or deformities. Replace as necessary.
10. **Torque** tone wheel to 7–12 ft. lbs.
11. Measure tone wheel to pole piece gap over entire perimeter of wheel. Gap for front wheel must be .035–.055 inch. Gap for rear wheel must be .028–.047 inch. If necessary, adjust gap using spacers part No. 26755AA000.
12. Check hub runout. Runout should be .0020 inch.

Trouble Codes 31, 33 & 39

1. Turn ignition switch to off position.
2. Disconnect connector from control module, then measure resistance between control module connector terminals as follows:
   a. If code 31 is present, measure between terminals 35 and 32. Resistance should be approximately 1 ohm.
   b. If code 33 is present, measure between terminals 2 and 32. Resistance should be approximately 1 ohm.
   c. If code 39 is present, measure between terminals 18 and 32. Resistance should be approximately 1 ohm.
3. Turn ignition switch to off position, then disconnect valve relay from hydraulic unit.
4. Turn ignition switch to on position, then measure voltage between control module connector terminals as follows:
   a. If code 31 is present, measure between terminals 35 and 20. Voltage should be 0 volts.
   b. If code 33 is present, measure between terminals 2 and 20. Voltage should be 0 volts.
   c. If code 39 is present, measure between terminals 18 and 20. Voltage should be 0 volts.
5. Turn ignition switch to off position, then disconnect hydraulic unit.
6. Turn ignition switch to on position, then measure voltage between control module connector terminals as follows:
   a. If code 31 is present, measure between terminals 35 and 20. Voltage should be 0 volts.
   b. If code 33 is present, measure between terminals 2 and 20. Voltage should be 0 volts.
   c. If code 39 is present, measure between terminals 18 and 20. Voltage should be 0 volts.

7. Turn ignition switch to off position, then disconnect connector from hydraulic unit.
8. Measure resistance between hydraulic unit terminals as follows:
   a. If code 31 is present, measure between terminals 4 and 11. Resistance should be approximately 1 ohm.
   b. If code 33 is present, measure between terminals 3 and 11. Resistance should be approximately 1 ohm.
   c. If code 39 is present, measure between terminals 1 and 11. Resistance should be approximately 1 ohm.

Trouble Code 41

Replace control module.

Trouble Code 42

1. Turn ignition switch to off position.
2. Disconnect connector from control module, then remove connector cover as follows:
   a. Remove screw from portion 1, **Fig. 12**, then move rubber boot 2 back (toward harness).
   b. Slide cover 3 in direction, **Fig. 12**, and remove.
3. Connect connector back into control module, then turn ignition switch to on position.
4. Measure input voltage between control module connector terminal 32 and ground. Voltage should be 9.2–12 volts.
5. Turn ignition switch to off position, then disconnect hydraulic unit connector.
6. Turn ignition switch to on position, then measure input voltage between hydraulic unit connector terminal 1 and ground. Voltage should be 10-12 volts.
7. Turn ignition switch to off position, then disconnect connectors from control module and hydraulic unit.
8. Measure resistance between control module connector terminal 32 and hydraulic unit connector terminal 1. Resistance should be 0 ohms.
9. Remove valve relay, then attach tester probes, **Fig. 11**.
   a. With terminals 30 and 87 connected. Resistance should be 0 ohms when 12 volts are applied or 1 Mohm when no voltage is applied.
   b. With terminals 30 and 87a connected. Resistance should be 1 Mohm

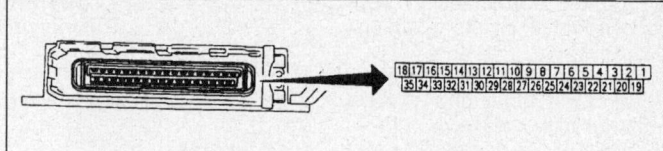

Contents		Terminal No.	Ignition switch ON, engine OFF	Input/output signals	
				Measured value	Measuring conditions
A.B.S. sensor	Front left wheel	FWD 5	0V	0.12 — 1V (When it is 10 Hz)	● No. 22 or No. 5 — No. 4
		AWD 22			
	GND	4			
	Front right wheel	23	0V	0.12 — 1V (When it is 10 Hz)	● No. 23 — No. 21
	GND	21			
	Rear left wheel	8	0V	0.12 — 1V (When it is 10 Hz)	● No. 8 — No. 9
	GND	9			
	Rear right wheel	24	0V	0.12 — 1V (When it is 10 Hz)	● No. 24 — No. 26
	GND	26			
G sensor (AWD MT model)		13	10 — 12V	0V	When slantting about 14° — 21.3° (0)
Check connector		30	—	—	—
		31	—	—	—
Stop light switch		25	0V	5 — 10V	When brake pedal is depressed.
Motor monitoring		14	0V	10 — 12V	When motor operates.
Valve power supply monitoring		32	10 — 12V	10 — 12V	—
Hydraulic unit	Solenoid Front left wheel	2	10 — 12V	0V	When solenoid is energized to produce output.
	Solenoid Front right wheel	35	10 — 12V	0V	
	Solenoid Rear wheel	18	10 — 12V	0V	
	Valve relay coil	27	0V	0V	—
	Motor relay coil	28	10 — 12V	0V	When motor operates to produce output.
Warning light		29	0V	10 — 12V	Ignition switch ON (Engine OFF)
Power supply	Battery	1	10 — 12V	10 — 12V	—
	Relay coil (valve, motor, etc.)	17	10 — 12V	10 — 12V	—
Grounding line		10	0V	0V	—
		20	0V	0V	—
		34	0V	0V	—

SB40291000050000X

Fig. 18 ABS control module pin voltage specifications

when 12 volts are applied or 0 ohms when no voltage is applied.

Trouble Code 51

1. Turn ignition switch to off position, then disconnect connector from control module.
2. Turn ignition switch to on position, then measure voltage between control module connector terminals 1 and 20. Voltage should be 10-12 volts.
3. Turn ignition switch to on position, then disconnect control module connector.
4. Remove connector cover, then connect connector back into control module.
5. Turn ignition switch to on position, then measure voltage between control module connector terminals 17 and 20. Voltage should be 10-12 volts.
6. Turn ignition switch to on position, then measure voltage between control module connector terminals 32 and 20. Voltage should be 10-12 volts.
7. Turn ignition switch to off position, then disconnect connectors from control module and hydraulic unit. Measure resistance as follows:
   a. Measure resistance between control module connector terminal 17 and hydraulic unit connector terminal 6. Resistance should be 0 ohms.
   b. Measure resistance between control module connector terminal 32 and hydraulic unit connector termi-

nal 11. Resistance should be 0 ohms.
   c. Measure resistance between control module connector terminal 27 and hydraulic unit connector terminal 12. Resistance should be 0 ohms.
8. Turn ignition switch to off position, then disconnect hydraulic unit connector.
9. Turn ignition switch to on position, then measure voltage between hydraulic unit connector terminal 1 and ground. Voltage should be 10-12 volts.
10. Remove valve relay, then attach tester probes, **Fig. 11.**
   a. With terminals 30 and 87 connected. Resistance should be 0 ohms when 12 volts are applied or 1 Mohm when no voltage is applied.
   b. With terminals 30 and 87a connected. Resistance should be 1 Mohm when 12 volts are applied or 0 ohms when no voltage is applied.

Trouble Code 52

1. Turn ignition switch to off position, then disconnect connector from control module.
2. Turn ignition switch to on position, then measure voltage between control module connector terminals 1 and 20. Voltage should be 10-12 volts.
3. Turn ignition switch to on position, then disconnect control module connector.
4. Remove connector cover, then connect connector back into control module.

5. Turn ignition switch to on position, then measure voltage between control module connector terminals 17 and 20. Voltage should be 10-12 volts.
6. Turn ignition switch to off position, then disconnect connectors from control module and hydraulic unit. Measure resistance as follows:
   a. Measure resistance between control module connector terminal 17 and hydraulic unit connector terminal 6. Resistance should be 0 ohms.
   b. Measure resistance between control module connector terminal 28 and hydraulic unit connector terminal 5. Resistance should be 0 ohms.
   c. Measure resistance between control module connector terminal 14 and hydraulic unit connector terminal 7. Resistance should be 0 ohms.
7. Turn ignition switch to off position, then disconnect hydraulic unit connector.
8. Measure voltage between hydraulic unit connector terminal 2 and ground. Voltage should be 10–12 volts.
9. Remove motor relay, then attach tester probes, **Fig. 13.** Resistance should be 0 ohms when 12 volts are applied or 1 Mohm when no voltage is applied.

Trouble Code 54

1. Turn ignition switch to off position, then disconnect control module connector.
2. Measure voltage between control module connector terminals 25 and 10. Voltage should be more than 4 volts when brake pedal is depressed.

Trouble Code 56

1. Position vehicle on a flat surface, then disconnect control module connector.
2. Remove cover from connector, then measure resistance between control module connector terminals 1 and 13. Resistance should be 550-670 ohms.
3. Disconnect G sensor connector, then measure resistance between G sensor terminals. Ensure sensor is horizontal during measurement. Resistance should be 550-670 ohms.
4. Turn ignition switch to on position, then connect G sensor.
5. Measure voltage between control module connector terminal 13 and ground. Voltage should be 10-12 volts.
6. Measure voltage between G sensor connector terminal 1 and ground. Voltage should be 10-12 volts.

CLEARING DIAGNOSTIC TROUBLE CODES

After completing necessary repairs, clear trouble code memory as follows:
1. After calling up a trouble code, disconnect ABS check connector terminal L from ground.
2. Repeat connecting and disconnecting terminal L from ground 3 times within approximately 12 seconds. Leave terminal L disconnected for at least ½ second each time.

SUBARU

COMPONENT TESTING

Speed Sensors

1. Check pole piece of speed sensor for damage or foreign materials. Clean or replace as needed.
2. Measure resistance between control module terminals. Refer to **Fig. 14,** for terminal identification and resistance specifications. If resistance is not within specifications replace wheel sensor or adjust gap between sensor and tone wheel.
3. Check tone wheels teeth for cracks or dents. Replace if needed.
4. Clearances, **Fig. 15,** (sensor gaps) should be measured one at a time to ensure tone wheel and speed sensor are installed properly. Clearances should be as follows:
   a. Front, .039–.059 inch.
   b. Rear, .031–.051 inch.
5. If clearance is narrow, adjust by using spacer part No. 26755AA000.
6. If clearance is wide, check outputted voltage as outlined in step 7. If outputted is not within specifications, replace sensor or tone wheel.
7. Output voltage can be checked by installing resistor and condenser, **Fig. 16,** then rotating wheel at 1.7 mph.

ABS Hydraulic Unit

1. Check bracket on vehicle, then all connectors.
2. Open hydraulic unit relay box and check for open or shorted circuits, **Fig. 17.**

ABS Control Module

Refer to **Fig. 18,** for control module input/output voltage signals.

G Sensor

1. Disconnect sensor connector and measure contact resistance between terminals as follows:
   a. With sensor on flat surface, resistance should be 550-670 ohms.
   b. Sensor should turn off from on (610 ohms to more than 100,000 ohms) when it is tilted in a range from 14–21.3°.

SYSTEM SERVICE

Brake System Bleed

Two technicians are required to bleed the brake system. Brake pedal operation must be very slow. Keep brake fluid reserve tank topped off to prevent entry of air into brake system during bleeding procedure. Check entire brake system for fluid leaks.

1. Start with brakes connected to secondary chamber of master cylinder first.
2. Fit one end of a vinyl tube onto air bleeder and place other end of tube into a container of brake fluid.
3. Slowly depress brake pedal and keep it depressed, then open air bleeder for 1–2 seconds.
4. Close air bleeder and slowly release brake pedal.
5. Repeat steps "3" and "4" until no more air comes out. **Allow 3–4 seconds between brake pedal operation.**
6. After bleeding brakes connected to secondary chamber of the master cylinder, repeat steps 2 through 5 on brakes connected to primary chamber of the master cylinder.
7. Fully depress brake pedal for 20 seconds and check entire system for leaks.
8. Turn ignition switch to off position.
9. With engine at idle, inspect brake pedal stroke as follows:
   a. Depress brake pedal with 110 lbs. of force, then measure distance between brake pedal and steering wheel.
   b. Release brake pedal, then measure distance between brake pedal and steering wheel again.
   c. The difference between both measurements should be 3.74 inches. **If measurement is not as specified it is possible that air is still in brake system.**
10. Turn ignition switch to off position, then top off brake fluid level.
11. Test drive vehicle at low speed and ensure proper brake operation.

Component Replacement

FRONT SENSOR

1. Disconnect sensor, located in engine compartment.
2. Remove sensor harness to bracket bolts, then sensor to housing bolts.
3. Remove brake caliper, brake rotor, driveshaft, knuckle and hub assemblies.
4. Remove tone wheel while removing hub from knuckle. Ensure teeth faces of tone wheel are not damaged during removal.
5. Reverse procedure to install, noting the following:
   a. Place a thickness gauge between sensor's pole piece and tone wheel's tooth face. After standard clearance is obtained over entire perimeter, **torque** sensor on housing to 17-31 ft. lbs.

REAR SENSOR

1. Remove rear seat and disconnect sensor connector.
2. Remove sensor harness bracket from trailing link, then sensor from rear back plate.
3. Remove rear tone wheel while removing hub from housing assembly. Ensure teeth faces of tone wheel are not damaged during removal.
4. Reverse procedure to install, noting the following:
   a. Place a thickness gauge between sensor's pole piece and tone wheel's tooth face. After standard clearance is obtained over entire perimeter, **torque** sensor on housing to 17-31 ft. lbs.

ABS HYDRAULIC UNIT

1. Remove canister from engine compartment, then disconnect lines from hydraulic unit and plug open ports to prevent foreign particles from entering unit.
2. Remove bolts which secure hydraulic unit to bracket, then remove unit from vehicle noting the following precautions:
   a. Hydraulic unit cannot be disassembled. Do not attempt to loosen nuts and bolts.
   b. Do not drop or bump hydraulic unit.
   c. Do not turn hydraulic unit upside down or place it on its side.
   d. Be careful to prevent foreign particles from getting into hydraulic unit.
3. Reverse procedure to install. **Torque** hydraulic unit attaching bolts to 17–31 ft. lbs.

ABS CONTROL MODULE

1. Remove floor mat located under lower right side of front seat.
2. Remove control module mounting screw, then slide out module.
3. Disconnect electrical connector from module.
4. Reverse procedure to install.

G SENSOR

1. Disconnect G sensor electrical connector.
2. Remove G sensor mounting bolt, then the sensor.
3. Reverse procedure to install. **Torque** sensor mounting bolt to 3–6.8 ft. lbs.

NOTE: On Air Bag Equipped Models, Refer To "Air Bag System Precautions" Located In The Front Of This Manual For System Disarming & Arming Procedures.

NOTE: Electrical Symbol & Wire Color Code Identification Located In The Front Of This Manual May Be Used As An Aid When Using Wiring Circuits Found In This Section.

INDEX

PRECAUTIONS

AIR BAG SYSTEMS

Refer to "Air Bag System Precautions" in the front of this manual for system disarming and arming procedures.

BATTERY GROUND CABLE

Prior to service, disconnect battery ground cable and isolate as required.

DESCRIPTION

The Anti-lock brake system (ABS) electrically controls brake fluid pressure to prevent wheel lock during braking on slippery road surfaces, improving steering stability and shortening the braking distance. If the ABS becomes inoperative, a fail-safe system activates to ensure conventional brake system operation.

The ABS consists of four tone wheels, four speed sensors, electronic control unit, a G sensor and a warning lamp.

The electronic control unit has the capability of on-board diagnosis. The on-board diagnosis system is designed to detect problems after the vehicle has been driven at 6 mph or more for at least 20 seconds. If a problem is found, the ABS warning light will illuminate to inform the driver of the occurrence of a problem. When the warning

Symptom		Probable faulty units/parts
Vehicle instability during braking	Vehicle pulls to either side.	• Hydraulic unit (solenoid valve) • ABS sensor • Brake (caliper & piston, pads) • Wheel alignment • Tire specifications, tire wear and air pressures • Incorrect wiring or piping connections • Road surface (uneven, camber)
	Vehicle spins.	• Hydraulic unit (solenoid valve) • ABS sensor • Brake (pads) • Tire specifications, tire wear and air pressures • Incorrect wiring or piping connections
Poor braking	Long braking/stopping distance	• Hydraulic unit (solenoid valve) • Brake (pads) • Air in brake line • Tire specifications, tire wear and air pressures • Incorrect wiring or piping connections
	Wheel locks.	• Hydraulic unit (solenoid valve, motor) • ABS sensor • Incorrect wiring or piping connections
	Brake dragging	• Hydraulic unit (solenoid valve) • ABS sensor • Master cylinder • Brake (caliper & piston) • Parking brake • Axle & wheels • Brake pedal play
	Long brake pedal stroke	• Air in brake line • Brake pedal play
	Vehicle pitching	• Suspension play or fatigue (reduced damping) • Incorrect wiring or piping connections • Road surface (uneven)
	Unstable or uneven braking	• Hydraulic unit (solenoid valve) • ABS sensor • Brake (caliper & piston, pads) • Tire specifications, tire wear and air pressures • Incorrect wiring or piping connections • Road surface (uneven)
Vibration and/or noise (while driving on slippery roads)	Excessive pedal vibration	• Incorrect wiring or piping connections • Road surface (uneven)
	Noise from hydraulic unit	• Hydraulic unit (mount bushing) • ABS sensor • Brake piping
	Noise from front of vehicle	• Hydraulic unit (mount bushing) • ABS sensor • Master cylinder • Brake (caliper & piston, pads, rotor) • Brake piping • Brake booster & check valve • Suspension play or fatigue
	Noise from rear of vehicle	• ABS sensor • Brake (caliper & piston, pads, rotor) • Parking brake • Brake piping • Suspension play or fatigue

SB4029700073000X

Fig. 1 Troubleshooting chart

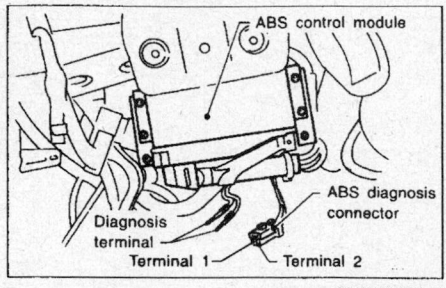

Fig. 2   Check connector terminal identification

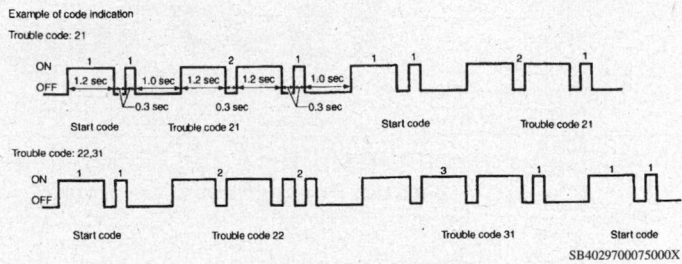

Fig. 3   Trouble code interpretation

light is on, the ABS system will be inactive and the normal braking function will work.

TROUBLESHOOTING

Refer to **Fig. 1** for troubleshooting procedures.

PRELIMINARY INSPECTION

1. Ensure battery voltage is 12 volts or more.
2. Ensure specific gravity of battery is 1.260.
3. Check condition of main and other fuses, harnesses and connector. Also check for proper grounding.
4. Check brake fluid level and for leakage.
5. Check for brake drag, brake pad and rotor condition.
6. Ensure tires are in good condition and at specified air pressure.

DIAGNOSIS & TESTING

ACCESSING DIAGNOSTIC TROUBLE CODES

Less Select Monitor

When the control module detects a problem, the information (up to a maximum of three) will be stored in the EEPROM as a trouble code. When there are more than three, the most recent three will be stored. Stored codes will stay in memory until they are cleared.
1. Remove ABS diagnosis connector from side of driver's heater unit, **Fig. 2.**

2. Turn ignition switch off, then connect ABS diagnosis connector terminal 2 to diagnosis terminal.
3. Turn ignition switch to on position. The ABS warning light is now in the diagnostic mode and blinks to identify trouble codes.
4. After start code (11) is shown, the trouble code(s) will be shown in order of the last information first. The code(s) will repeat for a maximum of 5 minutes. When there are no trouble codes in memory, only the start code (11) is shown.

With Select Monitor

Access ABS system diagnostic trouble codes according to tool manufactures instructions.

DIAGNOSTIC TROUBLE CODE INTERPRETATION

Refer to **Fig. 3,** for trouble code interpretation and **Fig. 4,** for trouble code identification and description.

WIRING DIAGRAM

Refer to wiring diagram, **Fig. 5,** when performing the following procedures.

DIAGNOSTIC TESTS

Less Select Monitor

Refer to diagnostic trouble code diagnosis, **Figs. 6 through 21,** when performing the following procedures.

With Select Monitor

Diagnose ABS system according to tool manufactures instructions.

CLEARING DIAGNOSTIC TROUBLE CODES

Less Select Monitor

After completing necessary repairs, clear trouble code memory as follows:
1. After calling up a trouble code, disconnect ABS diagnostic connector terminal 2 from diagnostic terminal.
2. Repeat connecting and disconnecting terminal 2 from diagnostic terminal 3 times within approximately 12 seconds. Leave terminal 2 disconnected for at least ½ second each time.
3. Ensure only start code 11 is shown after memory is cleared.

With Select Monitor

Erase ABS system diagnostic trouble codes according to tool manufactures instructions.

COMPONENT TESTING

Refer "1996 Impreza" for component testing.

SYSTEM SERVICE

Brake System Bleed

Refer "1996 Impreza" for brake system bleeding.

Component Replacement

Refer "1996 Impreza" for component replacement.

Trouble code	Contents of diagnosis	
11	Start code • Trouble code is shown after start code. • Only start code is shown in normal condition.	
21	Abnormal ABS sensor (Open circuit or input voltage too high)	Front right ABS sensor
23		Front left ABS sensor
25		Rear right ABS sensor
27		Rear left ABS sensor
22	Abnormal ABS sensor (Abnormal ABS sensor signal)	Front right ABS sensor
24		Front left ABS sensor
26		Rear right ABS sensor
28		Rear left ABS sensor
29		Any one of four
31	Abnormal solenoid valve circuit(s) in hydraulic unit	Front right inlet valve
32		Front right outlet valve
33		Front left inlet valve
34		Front left outlet valve
35		Rear right inlet valve
36		Rear right outlet valve
37		Rear left inlet valve
38		Rear left outlet valve
41	Abnormal ABS control module	
42	Source voltage is low.	
44	A combination of AT control abnormal	
46	Abnormal G sensor power supply voltage	
51	Abnormal valve relay	
52	Abnormal motor and/or motor relay	
54	Abnormal stop light switch	
56	Abnormal G sensor output voltage	

SB4029700076000X

Fig. 4 Trouble code description

SUBARU

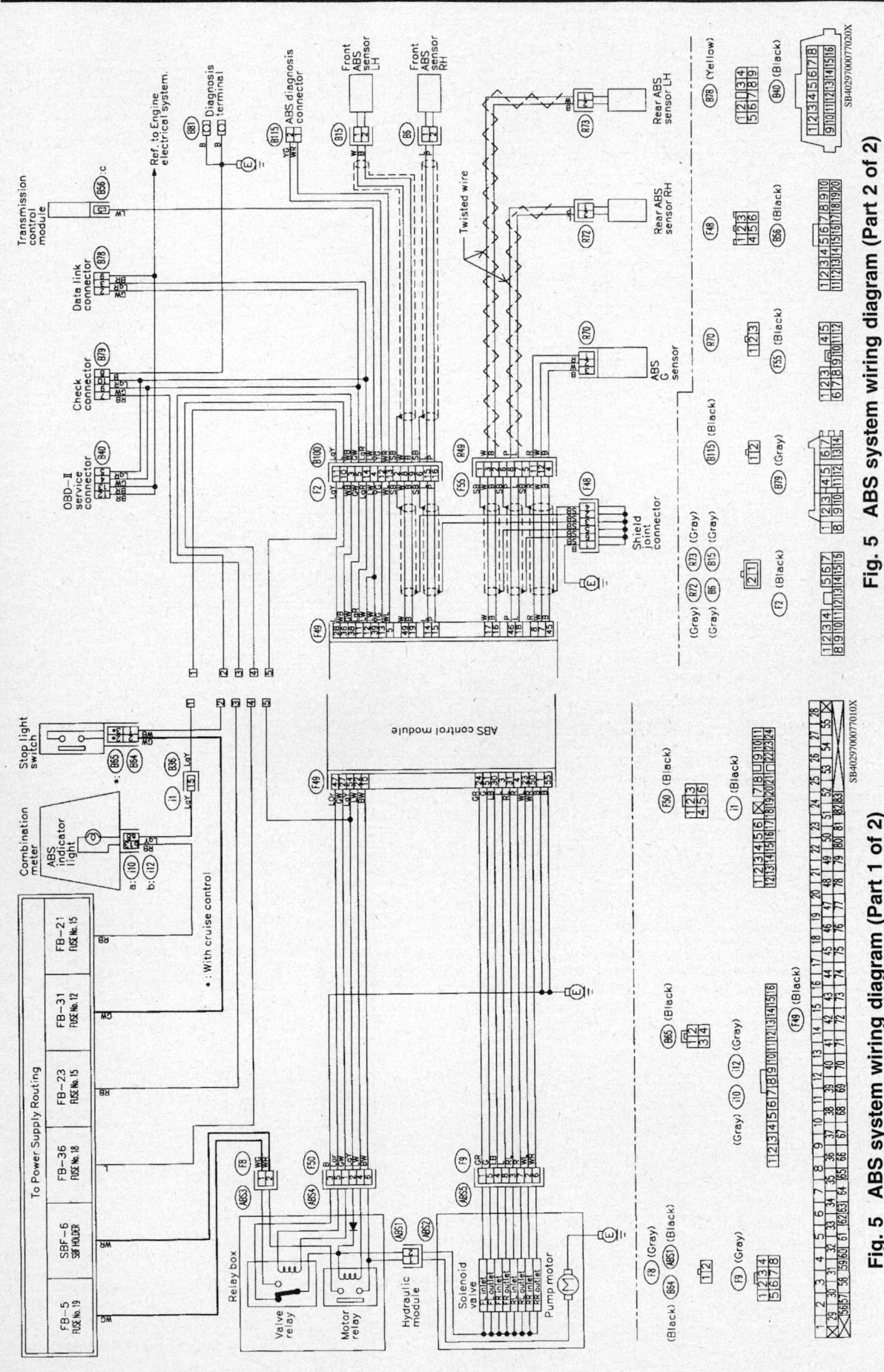

Fig. 5 ABS system wiring diagram (Part 2 of 2)

Fig. 5 ABS system wiring diagram (Part 1 of 2)

DIAGNOSTIC CHART INDEX

Test	Description	Page No.	Fig. No.
Test A	ABS Warning Light Does Not Come On	41-194	6
Test B	ABS Warning Light Does Not Go Off	41-194	7
Test C	Diagnostic Trouble Code Does Not Appear	41-195	8
Code 21	Abnormal ABS Sensor, Open Circuit Or Input Voltage Too High	41-196	9
Code 22	Abnormal ABS Sensor Signal, Irregular Signal Or Noise	41-197	10
Code 23	Abnormal ABS Sensor, Open Circuit Or Input Voltage Too High	41-196	9
Code 24	Abnormal ABS Sensor Signal, Irregular Signal Or Noise	41-197	10
Code 25	Abnormal ABS Sensor, Open Circuit Or Input Voltage Too High	41-196	9
Code 26	Abnormal ABS Sensor Signal, Irregular Signal Or Noise	41-197	10
Code 27	Abnormal ABS Sensor, Open Circuit Or Input Voltage Too High	41-196	9
Code 28	Abnormal ABS Sensor Signal, Irregular Signal Or Noise	41-197	10
Code 29	Abnormal ABS Sensor Signal, Any One Of Four	41-199	11
Code 31	Abnormal Inlet Solenoid Valve Circuit In Hydraulic Unit	41-200	12
Code 32	Abnormal Outlet Solenoid Valve Circuit In Hydraulic Unit	41-201	13
Code 33	Abnormal Inlet Solenoid Valve Circuit In Hydraulic Unit	41-200	12
Code 34	Abnormal Outlet Solenoid Valve Circuit In Hydraulic Unit	41-201	13
Code 35	Abnormal Inlet Solenoid Valve Circuit In Hydraulic Unit	41-200	12
Code 36	Abnormal Outlet Solenoid Valve Circuit In Hydraulic Unit	41-201	13
Code 37	Abnormal Inlet Solenoid Valve Circuit In Hydraulic Unit	41-200	12
Code 38	Abnormal Outlet Solenoid Valve Circuit In Hydraulic Unit	41-201	13
Code 41	Abnormal ABS Control Module	41-203	14
Code 42	Source Voltage Is Low	41-203	15
Code 44	A Combination Of AT Control Abnormal	41-204	16
Code 46	Abnormal G Sensor Power Supply Voltage	41-205	17
Code 51	Abnormal Valve Relay	41-205	18
Code 52	Abnormal Motor And/Or Motor Relay	41-209	19
Code 54	Abnormal Stop Light Switch	41-212	20
Code 56	Abnormal G Sensor Output Voltage	41-213	21

SUBARU

7A1	CHECK IF OTHER WARNING LIGHTS TURN ON.

Turn ignition switch to ON (engine OFF).

CHECK : **Do other warning lights turn on?**
YES : Go to step **7A2**.
NO : Repair combination meter.

7A2	CHECK ABS WARNING LIGHT BULB.

1) Turn ignition switch to OFF.
2) Remove combination meter.
3) Remove ABS warning light bulb from combination meter.

CHECK : **Is ABS warning light bulb OK?**
YES : Go to step **7A3**.
NO : Replace ABS warning light bulb.

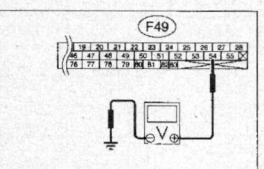

7A3	CHECK WIRING HARNESS.

1) Disconnect connector from ABSCM.
2) Disconnect connector (F50) from relay box.
3) Turn ignition switch to ON.
4) Measure voltage between connector (F49) and chassis ground.

Connector & terminal
(F49) No. 54 (+) — Chassis ground (−):

CHECK : **Is the voltage more than 10 V?**
YES : Go to step **7A4**.
NO : Repair broken wire in harness or connector.

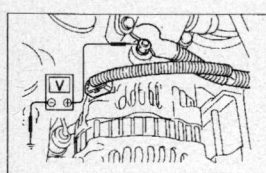

7A4	CHECK WIRING HARNESS.

1) Turn ignition switch to OFF.
2) Measure voltage between ABSCM connector (F49) and chassis ground.

Connector & terminal
(F49) No. 54 (+) — Chassis ground (−):

CHECK : **Is voltage less than 3 V?**
YES : Go to step **7A5**.
NO : Repair battery short of harness. .

SB4029700078010X

Fig. 6 Test A: ABS Warning Light Does Not Come On (Part 1 of 2). Less Select Monitor

7B1	CHECK INSTALLATION OF ABSCM CONNECTOR.

Turn ignition switch to OFF.

CHECK : **Is ABSCM connector inserted into ABSCM until the clamp locks onto it?**
YES : Go to step **7B2**.
NO : Insert ABSCM connector into ABSCM until the clamp locks onto it.

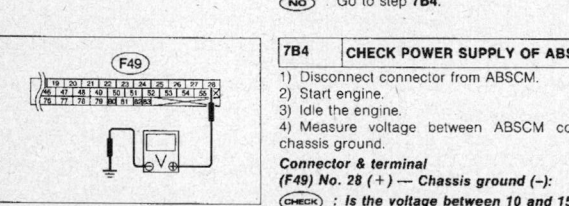

7B2	CHECK GENERATOR.

1) Start the engine.
2) Idle the engine.
3) Measure voltage between generator and chassis ground.

Terminal
Generator B terminal (+) — Chassis ground (−):

CHECK : **Is the voltage between 10 and 15 V?**
YES : Go to step **7B3**.
NO : Repair generator.

7B3	CHECK BATTERY TERMINAL.

Turn ignition switch to OFF.

CHECK : **Is there poor contact at battery terminal?**
YES : Repair battery terminal.
NO : Go to step **7B4**.

7B4	CHECK POWER SUPPLY OF ABSCM.

1) Disconnect connector from ABSCM.
2) Start engine.
3) Idle the engine.
4) Measure voltage between ABSCM connector and chassis ground.

Connector & terminal
(F49) No. 28 (+) — Chassis ground (−):

CHECK : **Is the voltage between 10 and 15 V?**
YES : Go to step **7B5**.
NO : Repair ABSCM power supply circuit.

SB4029700079010X

Fig. 7 Test B: ABS Warning Light Does Not Go Off (Part 1 of 5). Less Select Monitor

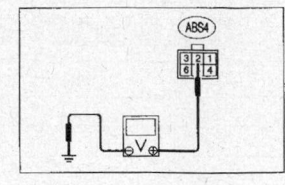

7A5	CHECK BATTERY SHORT OF RELAY BOX.

1) Disconnect connector from relay box.
2) Measure voltage between relay box and chassis ground.

Connector & terminal
(ABS4) No. 2 (+) — Chassis ground (−):

CHECK : **Is the voltage less than 1 V?**
YES : Go to step **7A6**.
NO : Replace relay box.

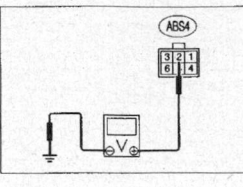

7A6	CHECK BATTERY SHORT OF RELAY BOX.

1) Turn ignition switch to ON.
2) Measure voltage between relay box and chassis ground.

Connector & terminal
(ABS4) No. 2 (+) — Chassis ground (−):

CHECK : **Is the voltage less than 1 V?**
YES : Go to step **7A7**.
NO : Replace relay box.

7A7	CHECK POOR CONTACT IN CONNECTORS.

Turn ignition switch to OFF.

CHECK : **Is there poor contact in connectors between combination meter and ABSCM?**
YES : Repair connector.
NO : Replace ABSCM.

SB4029700078020X

Fig. 6 Test A: ABS Warning Light Does Not Come On (Part 2 of 2). Less Select Monitor

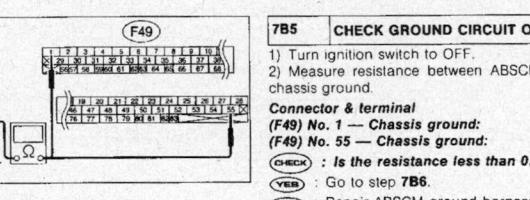

7B5	CHECK GROUND CIRCUIT OF ABSCM.

1) Turn ignition switch to OFF.
2) Measure resistance between ABSCM connector and chassis ground.

Connector & terminal
(F49) No. 1 — Chassis ground:
(F49) No. 55 — Chassis ground:

CHECK : **Is the resistance less than 0.5 Ω?**
YES : Go to step **7B6**.
NO : Repair ABSCM ground harness.

7B6	CHECK WIRING HARNESS.

1) Disconnect connector (F50) from relay box.
2) Turn ignition switch to ON.

CHECK : **Does the ABS warning light remain off?**
YES : Go to step **7B7**.
NO : Repair front wiring harness.

7B7	CHECK RELAY BOX.

1) Turn ignition switch to OFF.
2) Connect connector (F50) to relay box.
3) Remove valve relay from relay box.
4) Disconnect connector (ABS1) from hydraulic control unit.
5) Turn ignition switch to ON.

CHECK : **Does the ABS warning light remain off?**
YES : Go to step **7B8**.
NO : Repair relay box and check fuse.

SB4029700079020X

Fig. 7 Test B: ABS Warning Light Does Not Go Off (Part 2 of 5). Less Select Monitor

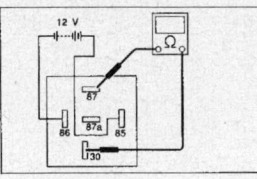

7B8 | **CHECK CONTACT POINT OF VALVE RELAY.**

1) Connect battery to valve relay terminals No. 85 and No. 86.
2) Measure resistance between valve relay terminals.

Terminals
No. 30 — No. 87:

CHECK : Is the resistance less than 0.5 Ω?
YES : Go to step **7B9**.
NO : Replace valve relay.

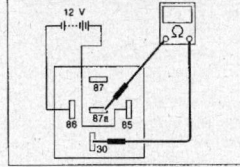

7B9 | **CHECK CONTACT POINT OF VALVE RELAY.**

Measure resistance between valve relay terminals.

Terminals
No. 30 — No. 87a:
Is the resistance more than 1 MΩ?

YES : Go to step **7B10**.
NO : Replace valve relay.

7B10 | **CHECK CONTACT POINT OF VALVE RELAY.**

1) Disconnect battery from valve relay terminals.
2) Measure resistance between valve relay terminals.

Terminals
No. 30 — No. 87:

CHECK : Is the resistance more than 1 MΩ?
YES : Go to step **7B11**.
NO : Replace valve relay.

7B11 | **CHECK CONTACT POINT OF VALVE RELAY.**

Measure resistance between valve relay terminals.

Terminals
No. 30 — No. 87a:

CHECK : Is the resistance less than 0.5 Ω?
YES : Go to step **7B12**.
NO : Replace valve relay.

SB4029700079030X

Fig. 7 Test B: ABS Warning Light Does Not Go Off (Part 3 of 5). Less Select Monitor

7B15 | **CHECK POOR CONTACT IN ABSCM CONNECTOR.**

CHECK : **Is there poor contact in ABSCM connector?**

YES : Repair connector.

NO : Replace ABSCM.

SB4029700079050X

Fig. 7 Test B: ABS Warning Light Does Not Go Off (Part 5 of 5). Less Select Monitor

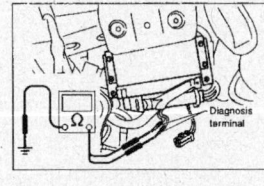

7B12 | **CHECK HYDRAULIC CONTROL UNIT.**

1) Turn ignition switch to OFF.
2) Connect connector (ABS1) to hydraulic control unit.
3) Turn ignition switch to ON.

CHECK : **Is the ABS warning light off?**
YES : Go to step **7B13**.
NO : Replace hydraulic control unit and check fuse No. 19.

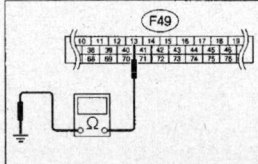

7B13 | **CHECK DIAGNOSIS TERMINAL.**

Measure resistance between diagnosis terminals (B81) and chassis ground.

Terminals
Diagnosis terminal (A) — Chassis ground:
Diagnosis terminal (B) — Chassis ground:

CHECK : **Is the resistance less than 1 Ω?**
YES : Go to step **7B14**.
NO : Repair diagnosis terminal harness.

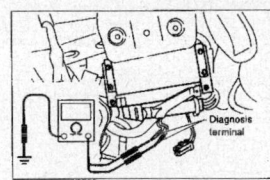

7B14 | **CHECK DIAGNOSIS LINE.**

1) Turn ignition switch to OFF.
2) Connect diagnosis terminal to ABS diagnosis connector (B115) No. 2.
3) Disconnect connector from ABSCM.
4) Measure resistance between ABSCM connector and chassis ground.

Connector & terminal
(F49) No. 13 — Chassis ground:

CHECK : **Is the resistance less than 1 Ω?**
YES : Go to step **7B15**.
NO : Repair harness connector between ABSCM and ABS diagnosis connector.

SB4029700079040X

Fig. 7 Test B: ABS Warning Light Does Not Go Off (Part 4 of 5). Less Select Monitor

7C1 | **CHECK DIAGNOSIS TERMINAL.**

Measure resistance between diagnosis terminals (B81) and chassis ground.

Terminals
Diagnosis terminal (A) — Chassis ground:
Diagnosis terminal (B) — Chassis ground:
CHECK : **Is the resistance less than 0.5 Ω?**
YES : Go to step **7C2**.
NO : Repair diagnosis terminal harness.

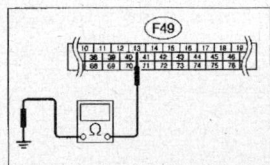

7C2 | **CHECK DIAGNOSIS LINE.**

1) Turn ignition switch to OFF.
2) Connect diagnosis terminal to ABS diagnosis connector (B115) No. 2.
3) Disconnect connector from ABSCM.
4) Measure resistance between ABSCM connector and chassis ground.

Connector & terminal
(F49) No. 13 — Chassis ground:

CHECK : **Is the resistance less than 0.5 Ω?**
YES : Go to step **7C3**.
NO : Repair harness connector between ABSCM and ABS diagnosis connector.

7C3 | **CHECK POOR CONTACT IN ABSCM CONNECTOR.**

CHECK : **Is there poor contact in ABSCM connector?**
YES : Repair connector.
NO : Replace ABSCM.

SB4029700080000X

Fig. 8 Test C: Diagnostic Trouble Code Does Not Appear. Less Select Monitor

SUBARU

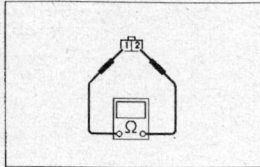

8E1 | CHECK ABS SENSOR.

1) Turn ignition switch to OFF.
2) Disconnect connector from ABS sensor.
3) Measure resistance of ABS sensor connector terminals.

Terminal
Front RH No. 1 — No. 2:
Front LH No. 1 — No. 2:
Rear RH No. 1 — No. 2:
Rear LH No. 1 — No. 2:

CHECK : *Is the resistance between 0.8 and 1.2 kΩ?*
YES : Go to step **8E2**.
NO : Replace ABS sensor.

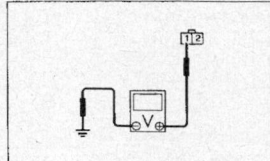

8E3 | CHECK BATTERY SHORT OF ABS SENSOR.

1) Turn ignition switch to ON.
2) Measure voltage between ABS sensor and chassis ground.

Terminal
Front RH No. 1 (+) — Chassis ground (–):
Front LH No. 1 (+) — Chassis ground (–):
Rear RH No. 1 (+) — Chassis ground (–):
Rear LH No. 1 (+) — Chassis ground (–):

CHECK : *Is the voltage less than 1 V?*
YES : Go to step **8E4**.
NO : Replace ABS sensor.

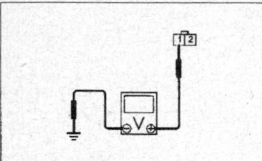

8E2 | CHECK BATTERY SHORT OF ABS SENSOR.

1) Disconnect connector from ABSCM.
2) Measure voltage between ABS sensor and chassis ground.

Terminal
Front RH No. 1 (+) — Chassis ground (–):
Front LH No. 1 (+) — Chassis ground (–):
Rear RH No. 1 (+) — Chassis ground (–):
Rear LH No. 1 (+) — Chassis ground (–):

CHECK : *Is the voltage less than 1 V?*
YES : Go to step **8E3**.
NO : Replace ABS sensor.

SB4029700081010X

Fig. 9   Codes 21, 23, 25 & 27: Abnormal ABS Sensor, Open Circuit Or Input Voltage Too High (Part 1 of 5). Less Select Monitor

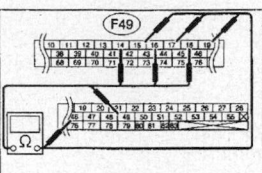

8E4 | CHECK HARNESS/CONNECTOR BETWEEN ABSCM AND ABS SENSOR.

1) Turn ignition switch to OFF.
2) Connect connector to ABS sensor.
3) Measure resistance between ABSCM connector terminals.

Connector & terminal
Trouble code 21 I (F49) No. 14 — No. 15:
Trouble code 23 I (F49) No. 49 — No. 19:
Trouble code 25 I (F49) No. 18 — No. 46:
Trouble code 27 I (F49) No. 16 — No. 17:

CHECK : *Is the resistance between 0.8 and 1.2 kΩ?*
YES : Go to step **8E5**.
NO : Repair harness/connector between ABSCM and ABS sensor.

SB4029700081020X

Fig. 9   Codes 21, 23, 25 & 27: Abnormal ABS Sensor, Open Circuit Or Input Voltage Too High (Part 2 of 5). Less Select Monitor

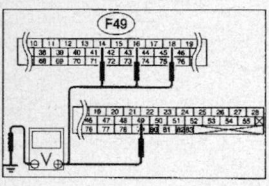

8E5 | CHECK BATTERY SHORT OF HARNESS.

Measure voltage between ABSCM connector and chassis ground.

Connector & terminal
Trouble code 21 I (F49) No. 14 (+) — Chassis ground (–):
Trouble code 23 I (F49) No. 49 (+) — Chassis ground (–):
Trouble code 25 I (F49) No. 18 (+) — Chassis ground (–):
Trouble code 27 I (F49) No. 16 (+) — Chassis ground (–):

CHECK : *Is the voltage less than 1 V?*
YES : Go to step **8E6**.
NO : Repair harness between ABSCM and ABS sensor.

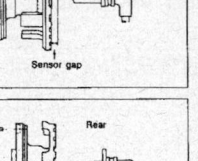

8E8 | CHECK INSTALLATION OF TONE WHEEL.

Tightening torque:
13 ± 3 N·m (1.3 ± 0.3 kg-m, 9 ± 2.2 ft-lb)

CHECK : *Are the tone wheel installation bolts tightened securely?*
YES : Go to step **8E9**.
NO : Tighten tone wheel installation bolts securely.

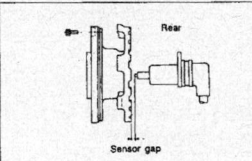

8E9 | CHECK ABS SENSOR GAP.

Measure tone wheel-to-pole piece gap over entire perimeter of the wheel.

CHECK : *Is the gap within the specifications shown in the following table?*

Specifications	Front wheel	Rear wheel
	0.9 — 1.4 mm (0.035 — 0.055 in)	0.7 — 1.2 mm (0.028 — 0.047 in)

YES : Go to step **8E10**.
NO : Adjust the gap.

NOTE:
Adjust the gap using spacers (Part No. 26755AA000). If spacers cannot correct the gap, replace worn sensor or worn tone wheel.

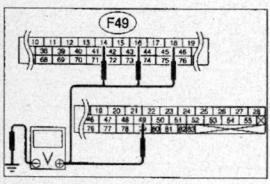

8E6 | CHECK BATTERY SHORT OF HARNESS.

1) Turn ignition switch to ON.
2) Measure voltage between ABSCM connector and chassis ground.

Connector & terminal
Trouble code 21 I (F49) No. 14 (+) — Chassis ground (–):
Trouble code 23 I (F49) No. 49 (+) — Chassis ground (–):
Trouble code 25 I (F49) No. 18 (+) — Chassis ground (–):
Trouble code 27 I (F49) No. 16 (+) — Chassis ground (–):

CHECK : *Is the voltage less than 1 V?*
YES : Go to step **8E7**.
NO : Repair harness between ABSCM and ABS sensor.

8E7 | CHECK INSTALLATION OF ABS SENSOR.

Tightening torque:
32 ± 10 N·m (3.3 ± 1.0 kg-m, 24 ± 7 ft-lb)

CHECK : *Are the ABS sensor installation bolts tightened securely?*
YES : Go to step **8E8**.
NO : Tighten ABS sensor installation bolts securely.

8E10 | CHECK HUB RUNOUT.

Measure hub runout.

CHECK : *Is the runout less than 0.05 mm (0.0020 in)?*
YES : Go to step **8E11**.
NO : Repair hub.

8E11 | CHECK POOR CONTACT IN CONNECTORS.

CHECK : *Is there poor contact in connectors between*
YES : Repair connector.
NO : Go to step **8E12**.

SB4029700081040X

Fig. 9   Codes 21, 23, 25 & 27: Abnormal ABS Sensor, Open Circuit Or Input Voltage Too High (Part 4 of 5). Less Select Monitor

SB4029700081030X

Fig. 9   Codes 21, 23, 25 & 27: Abnormal ABS Sensor, Open Circuit Or Input Voltage Too High (Part 3 of 5). Less Select Monitor

8E12 CHECK ABSCM.

1) Connect all connectors.
2) Erase the memory.
3) Perform inspection mode.
4) Read out the trouble code.

(CHECK) : **Is the same trouble code as in the current diagnosis still being output?**

(YES) : Replace ABSCM.

(NO) : Go to step **8E13**.

8E13 CHECK ANY OTHER TROUBLE CODES APPEARANCE.

(CHECK) : **Are other trouble codes being output?**

(YES) : Proceed with the diagnosis corresponding to the trouble code.

(NO) : A temporary poor contact.

NOTE:
Check harness and connectors between ABSCM and ABS sensor.

SB4029700081050X

Fig. 9 Codes 21, 23, 25 & 27: Abnormal ABS Sensor, Open Circuit Or Input Voltage Too High (Part 5 of 5). Less Select Monitor

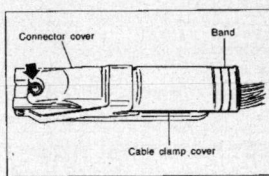

8I5 CHECK ABS SENSOR SIGNAL.

1) Raise all four wheels of ground.
2) Turn ignition switch OFF.
3) Disconnect connector from ABS control module.
4) Remove band.
5) Remove cable clamp cover.
6) Remove screws securing connector cover.

CAUTION:
Do not allow harness to catch on adjacent parts during installation.

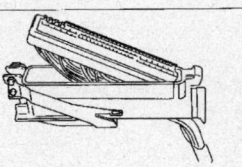

7) Remove connector cover.

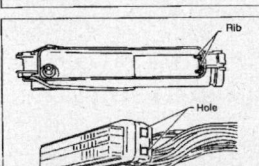

NOTE:
● To install, reverse above removal procedures.
● Align connector cover rib with connector hole before installation.

8) Connect connector to ABS control module.
9) Connect the oscilloscope to the ABS control module connector in accordance with trouble code.
10) Turn ignition switch ON.

SB4029700082020X

Fig. 10 Codes 22, 24, 26 & 28: Abnormal ABS Sensor Signal, Irregular Signal Or Noise (Part 2 of 7). Less Select Monitor

8I1 CHECK INSTALLATION OF ABS SENSOR.

Tightening torque:
32 ± 10 N·m (3.3 ± 1.0 kg-m, 24 ± 7 ft-lb)

(CHECK) : **Are the ABS sensor installation bolts tightened securely?**

(YES) : Go to step **8I2**.

(NO) : Tighten ABS sensor installation bolts securely.

8I2 CHECK INSTALLATION OF TONE WHEEL.

Tightening torque:
13 ± 3 N·m (1.3 ± 0.3 kg-m, 9 ± 2.2 ft-lb)

(CHECK) : **Are the tone wheel installation bolts tightened securely?**

(YES) : Go to step **8I3**.

(NO) : Tighten tone wheel installation bolts securely.

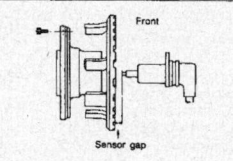

8I3 CHECK ABS SENSOR GAP.

Measure tone wheel to pole piece gap over entire perimeter of the wheel.

(CHECK) : **Is the gap within the specifications shown in the following table?**

Specifications	Front wheel	Rear wheel
	0.9 — 1.4 mm (0.035 — 0.055 in)	0.7 — 1.2 mm (0.028 — 0.047 in)

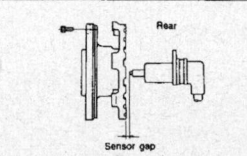

(YES) : Go to step **8I4**.

(NO) : Adjust the gap.

NOTE:
Adjust the gap using spacer (Part No. 26755AA000). If spacers cannot correct the gap, replace worn sensor or worn tone wheel.

8I4 CHECK OSCILLOSCOPE.

(CHECK) : **Is an oscilloscope available?**

(YES) : Go to step **8I5**.

(NO) : Go to step **8I6**.

SB4029700082010X

Fig. 10 Codes 22, 24, 26 & 28: Abnormal ABS Sensor Signal, Irregular Signal Or Noise (Part 1 of 7). Less Select Monitor

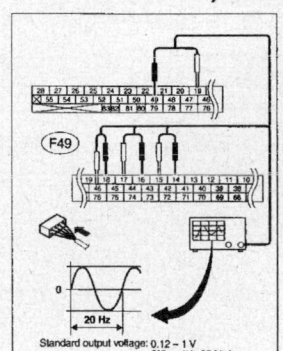

11) Rotate wheels and measure voltage at specified frequency.

NOTE:
When this inspection is completed, the ABS control module sometimes stores the trouble code 29.

Connector & terminal
Trouble code 22 I (F49) No. 14 (+) — No. 15 (−):
Trouble code 24 I (F49) No. 49 (+) — No. 19 (−):
Trouble code 26 I (F49) No. 18 (+) — No. 46 (−):
Trouble code 28 I (F49) No. 16 (+) — No. 17 (−):
Specified voltage: 0.12 — 1 V (When it is 20 Hz.)

(CHECK) : **Is oscilloscope pattern smooth, as shown in figure?**

(YES) : Go to step **8I9**.

(NO) : Go to step **8I6**.

8I6 CHECK CONTAMINATION OF ABS SENSOR OR TONE WHEEL.

Remove disc rotor or drum from hub in accordance with trouble code.

(CHECK) : **Is the ABS sensor pole piece or the tone wheel contaminated by dirt or other foreign matter?**

(YES) : Thoroughly remove dirt or other foreign matter.

(NO) : Go to step **8I7**.

8I7 CHECK DAMAGE OF ABS SENSOR OR TONE WHEEL.

(CHECK) : **Are there broken or damaged in the ABS sensor pole piece or the tone wheel?**

(YES) : Replace ABS sensor or tone wheel.

(NO) : Go to step **8I8**.

8I8 CHECK HUB RUNOUT.

Measure hub runout.

(CHECK) : **Is the runout less than 0.05 mm (0.0020 in)?**

(YES) : Go to step **8I9**.

(NO) : Repair hub.

SB4029700082030X

Fig. 10 Codes 22, 24, 26 & 28: Abnormal ABS Sensor Signal, Irregular Signal Or Noise (Part 3 of 7). Less Select Monitor

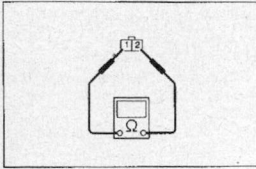

8I9 | CHECK RESISTANCE OF ABS SENSOR.

1) Turn ignition switch OFF.
2) Disconnect connector from ABS sensor.
3) Measure resistance between ABS sensor connector terminals.

Terminal
Front RH No. 1 — No. 2:
Front LH No. 1 — No. 2:
Rear RH No. 1 — No. 2:
Rear LH No. 1 — No. 2:

(CHECK) : Is the resistance between 0.8 and 1.2 kΩ?
(YES) : Go to step 8I10.
(NO) : Replace ABS sensor.

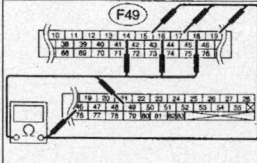

8I11 | CHECK HARNESS/CONNECTOR BETWEEN ABSCM AND ABS SENSOR.

1) Connect connector to ABS sensor.
2) Disconnect connector from ABS control module.
3) Measure resistance at ABSCM connector terminals.

Connector & terminal
Trouble code 22 I (F49) No. 14 — No. 15:
Trouble code 24 I (F49) No. 49 — No. 19:
Trouble code 26 I (F49) No. 18 — No. 46:
Trouble code 28 I (F49) No. 16 — No. 17:

(CHECK) : Is the resistance between 0.8 and 1.2 kΩ?
(YES) : Go to step 8I12.
(NO) : Repair harness/connector between ABSCM and ABS sensor.

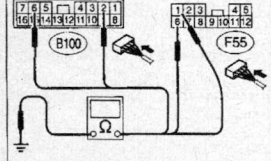

8I10 | CHECK GROUND SHORT OF ABS SENSOR.

Measure resistance between ABS sensor and chassis ground.

Terminal
Front RH No. 1 — Chassis ground:
Front LH No. 1 — Chassis ground:
Rear RH No. 1 — Chassis ground:
Rear LH No. 1 — Chassis ground:

(CHECK) : Is the resistance more than 1 MΩ?
(YES) : Go to step 8I11.
(NO) : Replace ABS sensor.

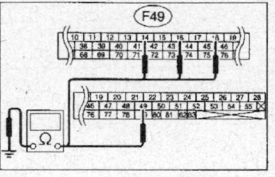

8I12 | CHECK GROUND SHORT OF HARNESS.

Measure resistance between ABSCM connector and chassis ground.

Connector & terminal
Trouble code 22 I (F49) No. 14 — Chassis ground:
Trouble code 24 I (F49) No. 49 — Chassis ground:
Trouble code 26 I (F49) No. 18 — Chassis ground:
Trouble code 28 I (F49) No. 16 — Chassis ground:

(CHECK) : Is the resistance more than 1 MΩ?
(YES) : Go to step 8I13.
(NO) : Repair harness/connector between ABSCM and ABS sensor.

SB4029700082040X

Fig. 10 Codes 22, 24, 26 & 28: Abnormal ABS Sensor Signal, Irregular Signal Or Noise (Part 4 of 7). Less Select Monitor

8I14 | CHECK POOR CONTACT IN CONNECTORS.

(CHECK) : Is there poor contact in connectors between ABSCM and ABS sensor?
(YES) : Repair connector.
(NO) : Go to step 8I15.

8I15 | CHECK SOURCES OF SIGNAL NOISE.

(CHECK) : Is the car telephone or the wireless transmitter properly installed?
(YES) : Go to step 8I16.
(NO) : Properly install the car telephone or the wireless transmitter.

8I16 | CHECK SOURCES OF SIGNAL NOISE.

(CHECK) : Are noise sources (such as an antenna) installed near the sensor harness?
(YES) : Install the noise sources apart from the sensor harness.
(NO) : Go to step 8I17.

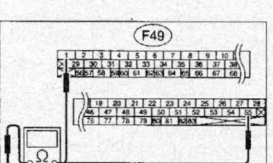

8I13 | CHECK GROUND CIRCUIT OF ABSCM.

Measure resistance between ABSCM and chassis ground.

Connector & terminal
(F49) No. 1 — GND:
(F49) No. 55 — GND:

(CHECK) : Is the resistance less than 0.5 Ω?
(YES) : Go to step 8I14.
(NO) : Repair ABSCM ground harness.

SB4029700082050X

Fig. 10 Codes 22, 24, 26 & 28: Abnormal ABS Sensor Signal, Irregular Signal Or Noise (Part 5 of 7). Less Select Monitor

8I18 | CHECK ABSCM.

1) Connect all connectors.
2) Erase the memory.
3) Perform inspection mode.
4) Read out the trouble code.

(CHECK) : Is the same trouble code as in the current diagnosis still being output?
(YES) : Replace ABSCM.
(NO) : Go to step 8I19.

8I19 | CHECK ANY OTHER TROUBLE CODES APPEARANCE.

(CHECK) : Are other trouble codes being output?
(YES) : Proceed with the diagnosis corresponding to the trouble code.
(NO) : A temporary noise interference.

SB4029700082070X

Fig. 10 Codes 22, 24, 26 & 28: Abnormal ABS Sensor Signal, Irregular Signal Or Noise (Part 7 of 7). Less Select Monitor

8I17 | CHECK SHIELD CIRCUIT.

1) Connect all connectors.
2) Measure resistance between shield connector and chassis ground.

Connector & terminal
Trouble code 22 I (B100) No. 6 — Chassis ground:
Trouble code 24 I (B100) No. 2 — Chassis ground:
Trouble code 26 I (F55) No. 6 — Chassis ground:
Trouble code 28 I (F55) No. 1 — Chassis ground:

(CHECK) : Is the resistance less than 0.5 Ω?
(YES) : Go to step 8I18.
(NO) : Repair shield harness.

SB4029700082060X

Fig. 10 Codes 22, 24, 26 & 28: Abnormal ABS Sensor Signal, Irregular Signal Or Noise (Part 6 of 7). Less Select Monitor

8J1	CHECK IF THE WHEELS HAVE TURNED FREELY FOR A LONG TIME.

(CHECK) : **Check if the wheels have been turned freely for more than one minute, such as when the vehicle is jacked-up, under full-lock cornering or when tire is not in contact with road surface.**

(YES) : The ABS is normal. Erase the trouble code.

NOTE:

When the wheels turn freely for a long time, such as when the vehicle is towed or jacked-up, or when steering wheel is continuously turned all the way, this trouble code may sometimes occur.

(NO) : Go to step **8J2**.

8J2	CHECK TIRE SPECIFICATIONS.

(CHECK) : **Are the tire specifications correct?**

(YES) : Go to step **8J3**.

(NO) : Replace tire.

8J3	CHECK WEAR OF TIRE.

(CHECK) : **Is the tire worn excessively?**

(YES) : Replace tire.

(NO) : Go to step **8J4**.

8J4	CHECK TIRE PRESSURE.

(CHECK) : **Is the tire pressure correct?**

(YES) : Go to step **8J5**.

(NO) : Adjust tire pressure.

8J5	CHECK INSTALLATION OF ABS SENSOR.

Tightening torque:
32 ± 10 N·m (3.3 ± 1.0 kg-m, 24 ± 7 ft-lb)

(CHECK) : **Are the ABS sensor installation bolts tightened securely?**

(YES) : Go to step **8J6**.

(NO) : Tighten ABS sensor installation bolts securely.

SB4029700083010X

Fig. 11   Code 29: Abnormal ABS Sensor Signal, Any One Of Four (Part 1 of 5). Less Select Monitor

8J6	CHECK INSTALLATION OF TONE WHEEL.

Tightening torque:
13 ± 3 N·m (1.3 ± 0.3 kg-m, 9 ± 2.2 ft-lb)

(CHECK) : Are the tone wheel installation bolts tightened securely?

(YES) : Go to step 8J7.

(NO) : Tighten tone wheel installation bolts securely.

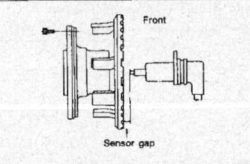

8J7	CHECK ABS SENSOR GAP.

Measure tone wheel to pole piece gap over entire perimeter of the wheel.

(CHECK) : **Is the gap within the specifications shown in the following table?**

Specifications	Front wheel	Rear wheel
	0.9 — 1.4 mm (0.035 — 0.055 in)	0.7 — 1.2 mm (0.028 — 0.047 in)

(YES) : Go to step 8J8.

(NO) : Adjust the gap.

NOTE:
Adjust the gap using spacer (Part No. 26755AA000). If spacers cannot correct the gap, replace worn sensor or worn tone wheel.

8J8	CHECK OSCILLOSCOPE.

(CHECK) : Is an oscilloscope available?

(YES) : Go to step 8J9.

(NO) : Go to step 8J10.

SB4029700083020X

Fig. 11   Code 29: Abnormal ABS Sensor Signal, Any One Of Four (Part 2 of 5). Less Select Monitor

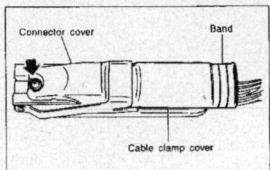

8J9	CHECK ABS SENSOR SIGNAL.

1) Raise all four wheels of ground.
2) Turn ignition switch OFF.
3) Disconnect connector from ABS control module.
4) Remove band.
5) Remove cable clamp cover.
6) Remove screws securing connector cover.

CAUTION:
Do not allow harness to catch on adjacent parts during installation.

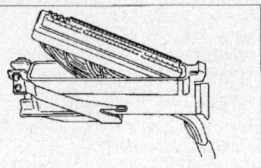

7) Remove connector cover.

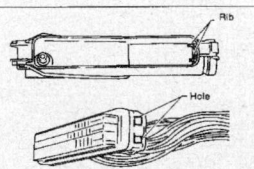

NOTE:
● To install, reverse above removal procedures.
● Align connector cover rib with connector hole before installation.

8) Connect connector to ABS control module.
9) Connect the oscilloscope to the ABS control module connector in accordance with trouble code.
10) Turn ignition switch ON.

SB4029700083030X

Fig. 11   Code 29: Abnormal ABS Sensor Signal, Any One Of Four (Part 3 of 5). Less Select Monitor

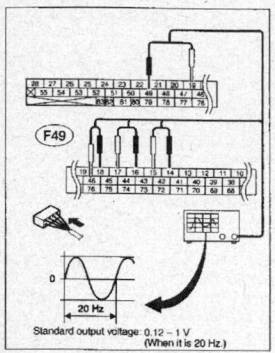

11) Rotate wheels and measure voltage at specified frequency.

NOTE:
When this inspection is completed, the ABS control module sometimes stores the trouble code 29.

Connector & terminal
(F49) No. 14 (+) — No. 15 (–) (Front RH):
(F49) No. 49 (+) — No. 19 (–) (Front LH):
(F49) No. 18 (+) — No. 46 (–) (Rear RH):
(F49) No. 16 (+) — No. 17 (–) (Rear LH):
Specified voltage: 0.12 – 1 V (When it is 20 Hz.)

(CHECK) : Is oscilloscope pattern smooth, as shown in figure?

(YES) : Go to step 8J13.

(NO) : Go to step 8J10.

8J10	CHECK CONTAMINATION OF ABS SENSOR OR TONE WHEEL.

Remove disc rotor from hub.

(CHECK) : Is the ABS sensor pole piece or the tone wheel contaminated by dirt or other foreign matter?

(YES) : Thoroughly remove dirt or other foreign matter.

(NO) : Go to step 8J11.

8J11	CHECK DAMAGE OF ABS SENSOR OR TONE WHEEL.

(CHECK) : Are there broken or damaged teeth in the ABS sensor pole piece or the tone wheel?

(YES) : Replace ABS sensor or tone wheel.

(NO) : Go to step 8J12.

8J12	CHECK HUB RUNOUT.

Measure hub runout.

(CHECK) : Is the runout less than 0.05 mm (0.0020 in)?

(YES) : Go to step 8J13.

(NO) : Repair hub.

8J13	CHECK ABSCM.

1) Turn ignition switch to OFF.
2) Connect all connectors.
3) Erase the memory.

SB4029700083040X

Fig. 11   Code 29: Abnormal ABS Sensor Signal, Any One Of Four (Part 4 of 5). Less Select Monitor

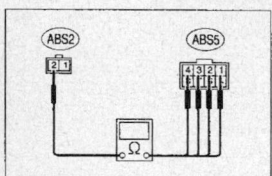

8N1	CHECK RESISTANCE OF SOLENOID VALVE.

1) Turn ignition switch to OFF.
2) Disconnect two connectors (ABS1, F9) from hydraulic unit.
3) Measure resistance between hydraulic unit connector terminals.

Connector & terminal
Trouble code 31 / (ABS5) No. 4 — (ABS2) No. 2:
Trouble code 33 / (ABS5) No. 1 — (ABS2) No. 2:
Trouble code 35 / (ABS5) No. 2 — (ABS2) No. 2:
Trouble code 37 / (ABS5) No. 3 — (ABS2) No. 2:

(CHECK) : Is the resistance between 7.8 and 9.2 Ω?

(YES) : Go to step 8N2.

(NO) : Replace hydraulic unit.

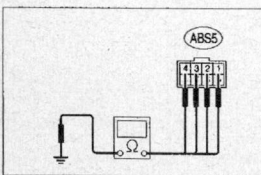

8N2	CHECK GROUND SHORT OF SOLENOID VALVE.

Measure resistance between hydraulic unit connector and chassis ground.

Connector & terminal
Trouble code 31 / (ABS5) No. 4 — Chassis ground:
Trouble code 33 / (ABS5) No. 1 — Chassis ground:
Trouble code 35 / (ABS5) No. 2 — Chassis ground:
Trouble code 37 / (ABS5) No. 3 — Chassis ground:

(CHECK) : Is the resistance more than 1 MΩ?

(YES) : Go to step 8N3.

(NO) : Replace hydraulic unit.

SB4029700084010X

Fig. 12   Codes 31, 33, 35 & 37: Abnormal Inlet Solenoid Valve Circuit In Hydraulic Unit (Part 1 of 5). Less Select Monitor

4) Perform inspection mode.
5) Read out the trouble code.

(CHECK) : Is the same trouble code as in the current diagnosis still being output?

(YES) : Replace ABSCM.

(NO) : Go to step 8J14.

8J14	CHECK ANY OTHER TROUBLE CODES APPEARANCE.

(CHECK) : Are other trouble codes being output?

(YES) : Proceed with the diagnosis corresponding to the trouble code.

(NO) : A temporary poor contact.

SB4029700083050X

Fig. 11   Code 29: Abnormal ABS Sensor Signal, Any One Of Four (Part 5 of 5). Less Select Monitor

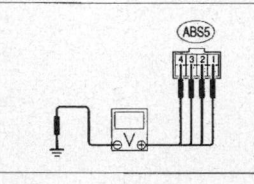

8N3	CHECK BATTERY SHORT OF SOLENOID VALVE.

1) Disconnect connector from ABSCM.
2) Measure voltage between hydraulic unit connector and chassis ground.

Connector & terminal
Trouble code 31 / (ABS5) No. 4 (+) — Chassis ground (–):
Trouble code 33 / (ABS5) No. 1 (+) — Chassis ground (–):
Trouble code 35 / (ABS5) No. 2 (+) — Chassis ground (–):
Trouble code 37 / (ABS5) No. 3 (+) — Chassis ground (–):

(CHECK) : Is the voltage less than 1 V?

(YES) : Go to step 8N4.

(NO) : Replace hydraulic unit.

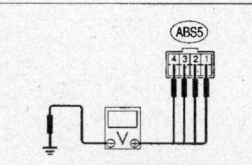

8N4	CHECK BATTERY SHORT OF SOLENOID VALVE.

1) Turn ignition switch to ON.
2) Measure voltage between hydraulic unit connector and chassis ground.

Connector & terminal
Trouble code 31 / (ABS5) No. 4 (+) — Chassis ground (–):
Trouble code 33 / (ABS5) No. 1 (+) — Chassis ground (–):
Trouble code 35 / (ABS5) No. 2 (+) — Chassis ground (–):
Trouble code 37 / (ABS5) No. 3 (+) — Chassis ground (–):

(CHECK) : Is the voltage less than 1 V?

(YES) : Go to step 8N5.

(NO) : Replace hydraulic unit.

SB4029700084020X

Fig. 12   Codes 31, 33, 35 & 37: Abnormal Inlet Solenoid Valve Circuit In Hydraulic Unit (Part 2 of 5). Less Select Monitor

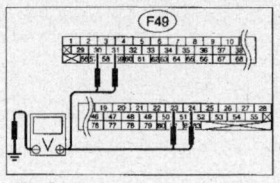

8N5 | **CHECK BATTERY SHORT OF HARNESS.**

1) Turn ignition switch to OFF.
2) Measure voltage between ABSCM connector and chassis ground.

Connector & terminal
Trouble code 31 / (F49) No. 30 (+) — Chassis ground (−):
Trouble code 33 / (F49) No. 24 (+) — Chassis ground (−):
Trouble code 35 / (F49) No. 23 (+) — Chassis ground (−):
Trouble code 37 / (F49) No. 31 (+) — Chassis ground (−):

(CHECK) : *Is the voltage less than 1 V?*
(YES) : Go to step **8N6**.
(NO) : Repair harness between ABSCM and hydraulic unit.

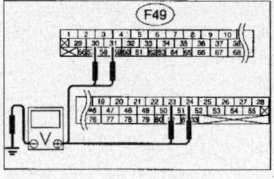

8N6 | **CHECK BATTERY SHORT OF HARNESS.**

1) Turn ignition switch to ON.
2) Measure voltage between ABSCM connector and chassis ground.

Connector & terminal
Trouble code 31 / (F49) No. 30 (+) — Chassis ground (−):
Trouble code 33 / (F49) No. 24 (+) — Chassis ground (−):
Trouble code 35 / (F49) No. 23 (+) — Chassis ground (−):
Trouble code 37 / (F49) No. 31 (+) — Chassis ground (−):

(CHECK) : *Is the voltage less than 1 V?*
(YES) : Go to step **8N7**.
(NO) : Repair harness between ABSCM and hydraulic unit.

SB4029700084030X

Fig. 12   Codes 31, 33, 35 & 37: Abnormal Inlet Solenoid Valve Circuit In Hydraulic Unit (Part 3 of 5). Less Select Monitor

8N10 | **CHECK ABSCM.**

1) Connect all connectors.
2) Erase the memory.
3) Perform inspection mode.
4) Read out the trouble code.

(CHECK) : *Is the same trouble code as in the current diagnosis still being output?*
(YES) : Replace ABSCM.
(NO) : Go to step **8N11**.

8N11 | **CHECK ANY OTHER TROUBLE CODES APPEARANCE.**

(CHECK) : *Are other trouble codes being output?*
(YES) : Proceed with the diagnosis corresponding to the trouble code.
(NO) : A temporary poor contact.

SB4029700084050X

Fig. 12   Codes 31, 33, 35 & 37: Abnormal Inlet Solenoid Valve Circuit In Hydraulic Unit (Part 5 of 5). Less Select Monitor

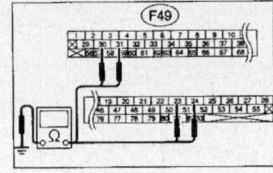

8N7 | **CHECK GROUND SHORT OF HARNESS.**

1) Turn ignition switch to OFF.
2) Measure resistance between ABSCM connector and chassis ground.

Connector & terminal
Trouble code 31 / (F49) No. 30 — Chassis ground:
Trouble code 33 / (F49) No. 24 — Chassis ground:
Trouble code 35 / (F49) No. 23 — Chassis ground:
Trouble code 37 / (F49) No. 31 — Chassis ground:

(CHECK) : *Is the resistance more than 1 MΩ?*
(YES) : Go to step **8N8**.
(NO) : Repair harness between ABSCM and hydraulic unit.

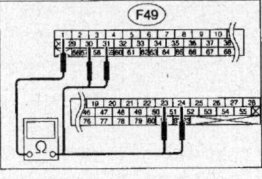

8N8 | **CHECK HARNESS/CONNECTOR BETWEEN ABSCM AND HYDRAULIC UNIT.**

1) Connect connector to hydraulic unit.
2) Measure resistance between ABSCM connector terminals.

Connector & terminal
Trouble code 31 / (F49) No. 30 — No. 1:
Trouble code 33 / (F49) No. 24 — No. 1:
Trouble code 35 / (F49) No. 23 — No. 1:
Trouble code 37 / (F49) No. 31 — No. 1:

(CHECK) : *Is the resistance between 8.3 and 9.7 Ω?*
(YES) : Go to step **8N9**.
(NO) : Repair harness/connector between ABSCM and hydraulic unit.

8N9 | **CHECK POOR CONTACT IN CONNECTORS.**

(CHECK) : *Is there poor contact in connectors between ABSCM and hydraulic unit?*
(YES) : Repair connector.
(NO) : Go to step **8N10**.

SB4029700084040X

Fig. 12   Codes 31, 33, 35 & 37: Abnormal Inlet Solenoid Valve Circuit In Hydraulic Unit (Part 4 of 5). Less Select Monitor

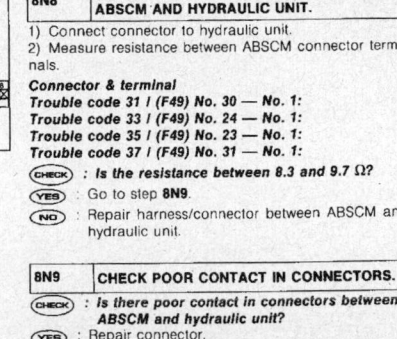

8R1 | **CHECK RESISTANCE OF SOLENOID VALVE.**

1) Turn ignition switch to OFF.
2) Disconnect two connectors (ABS1, F9) from hydraulic unit.
3) Measure resistance between hydraulic unit connector terminals.

Connector & terminal
Trouble code 32 / (ABS5) No. 8 — (ABS2) No. 2:
Trouble code 34 / (ABS5) No. 5 — (ABS2) No. 2:
Trouble code 36 / (ABS5) No. 6 — (ABS2) No. 2:
Trouble code 38 / (ABS5) No. 7 — (ABS2) No. 2:

(CHECK) : *is the resistance between 3.8 and 4.8 Ω?*
(YES) : Go to step **8R2**.
(NO) : Replace hydraulic unit.

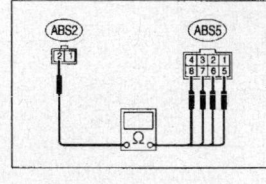

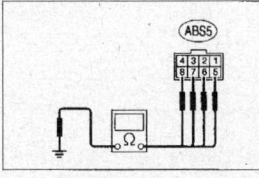

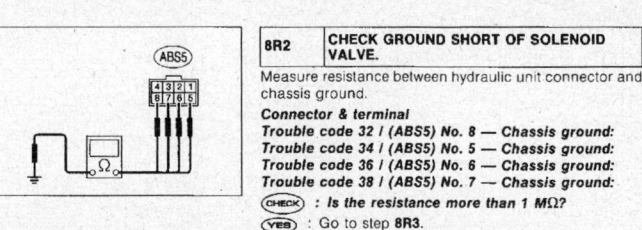

8R2 | **CHECK GROUND SHORT OF SOLENOID VALVE.**

Measure resistance between hydraulic unit connector and chassis ground.

Connector & terminal
Trouble code 32 / (ABS5) No. 8 — Chassis ground:
Trouble code 34 / (ABS5) No. 5 — Chassis ground:
Trouble code 36 / (ABS5) No. 6 — Chassis ground:
Trouble code 38 / (ABS5) No. 7 — Chassis ground:

(CHECK) : *Is the resistance more than 1 MΩ?*
(YES) : Go to step **8R3**.
(NO) : Replace hydraulic unit.

SB4029700085010X

Fig. 13   Codes 32, 34, 36 & 38: Abnormal Outlet Solenoid Valve Circuit In Hydraulic Unit (Part 1 of 5). Less Select Monitor

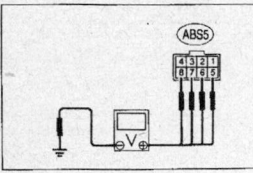

8R3 CHECK BATTERY SHORT OF SOLENOID VALVE.

1) Disconnect connector from ABSCM.
2) Measure voltage between hydraulic unit connector and chassis ground.

Connector & terminal
Trouble code 32 / (ABS5) No. 8 (+) — Chassis ground (−):
Trouble code 34 / (ABS5) No. 5 (+) — Chassis ground (−):
Trouble code 36 / (ABS5) No. 6 (+) — Chassis ground (−):
Trouble code 38 / (ABS5) No. 7 (+) — Chassis ground (−):

(CHECK) : Is the voltage less than 1 V?
(YES) : Go to step **8R4**.
(NO) : Replace hydraulic unit.

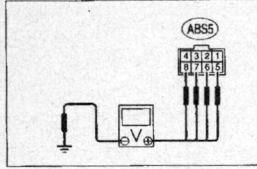

8R4 CHECK BATTERY SHORT OF SOLENOID VALVE.

1) Turn ignition switch to ON.
2) Measure voltage between hydraulic unit connector and chassis ground.

Connector & terminal
Trouble code 32 / (ABS5) No. 8 (+) — Chassis ground (−):
Trouble code 34 / (ABS5) No. 5 (+) — Chassis ground (−):
Trouble code 36 / (ABS5) No. 6 (+) — Chassis ground (−):
Trouble code 38 / (ABS5) No. 7 (+) — Chassis ground (−):

(CHECK) : Is the voltage less than 1 V?
(YES) : Go to step **8R5**.
(NO) : Replace hydraulic unit.

SB4029700085020X

Fig. 13 Codes 32, 34, 36 & 38: Abnormal Outlet Solenoid Valve Circuit In Hydraulic Unit (Part 2 of 5). Less Select Monitor

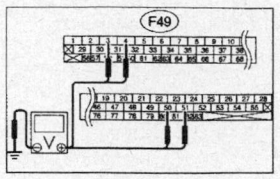

8R5 CHECK BATTERY SHORT OF HARNESS.

1) Turn ignition switch to OFF.
2) Measure voltage between ABSCM connector and chassis ground.

Connector & terminal
Trouble code 32 / (F49) No. 3 (+) — Chassis ground (−):
Trouble code 34 / (F49) No. 51 (+) — Chassis ground (−):
Trouble code 36 / (F49) No. 50 (+) — Chassis ground (−):
Trouble code 38 / (F49) No. 4 (+) — Chassis ground (−):

(CHECK) : Is the voltage less than 1 V?
(YES) : Go to step **8R6**.
(NO) : Repair harness between ABSCM and hydraulic unit.

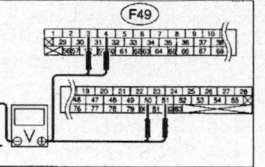

8R6 CHECK BATTERY SHORT OF HARNESS.

1) Turn ignition switch to ON.
2) Measure voltage between ABSCM connector and chassis ground.

Connector & terminal
Trouble code 32 / (F49) No. 3 (+) — Chassis ground (−):
Trouble code 34 / (F49) No. 51 (+) — Chassis ground (−):
Trouble code 36 / (F49) No. 50 (+) — Chassis ground (−):
Trouble code 38 / (F49) No. 4 (+) — Chassis ground (−):

(CHECK) : Is the voltage less than 1 V?
(YES) : Go to step **8R7**.
(NO) : Repair harness between ABSCM and hydraulic unit.

SB4029700085030X

Fig. 13 Codes 32, 34, 36 & 38: Abnormal Outlet Solenoid Valve Circuit In Hydraulic Unit (Part 3 of 5). Less Select Monitor

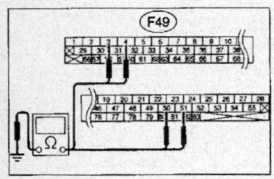

8R7 CHECK GROUND SHORT OF HARNESS.

1) Turn ignition switch to OFF.
2) Measure resistance between ABSCM connector and chassis ground.

Connector & terminal
Trouble code 32 / (F49) No. 3 — Chassis ground:
Trouble code 34 / (F49) No. 51 — Chassis ground:
Trouble code 36 / (F49) No. 50 — Chassis ground:
Trouble code 38 / (F49) No. 4 — Chassis ground:

(CHECK) : Is the resistance more than 1 MΩ?
(YES) : Go to step **8R8**.
(NO) : Repair harness between ABSCM and hydraulic unit.

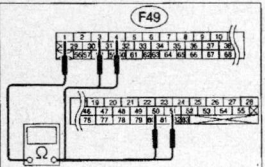

8R8 CHECK HARNESS/CONNECTOR BETWEEN ABSCM AND HYDRAULIC UNIT.

1) Connect connector to hydraulic unit.
2) Measure resistance between ABSCM connector terminals.

Connector & terminal
Trouble code 32 / (F49) No. 3 — No. 1:
Trouble code 34 / (F49) No. 51 — No. 1:
Trouble code 36 / (F49) No. 50 — No. 1:
Trouble code 38 / (F49) No. 4 — No. 1:

(CHECK) : Is the resistance between 4.3 and 5.3 Ω?
(YES) : Go to step **8R9**.
(NO) : Repair harness/connector between ABSCM and hydraulic unit.

8R9 CHECK POOR CONTACT IN CONNECTORS.

(CHECK) : Is there poor contact in connectors between ABSCM and hydraulic unit?
(YES) : Repair connector.
(NO) : Go to step **8R10**.

SB4029700085040X

Fig. 13 Codes 32, 34, 36 & 38: Abnormal Outlet Solenoid Valve Circuit In Hydraulic Unit (Part 4 of 5). Less Select Monitor

8R10 CHECK ABSCM.

1) Connect all connectors.
2) Erase the memory.
3) Perform inspection mode.
4) Read out the trouble code.

(CHECK) : **Is the same trouble code as in the current diagnosis still being output?**
(YES) : Replace ABSCM.
(NO) : Go to step **8R11**.

8R11 CHECK ANY OTHER TROUBLE CODES APPEARANCE.

(CHECK) : **Are other trouble codes being output?**
(YES) : Proceed with the diagnosis corresponding to the trouble code.
(NO) : A temporary poor contact.

SB4029700085050X

Fig. 13 Codes 32, 34, 36 & 38: Abnormal Outlet Solenoid Valve Circuit In Hydraulic Unit (Part 5 of 5). Less Select Monitor

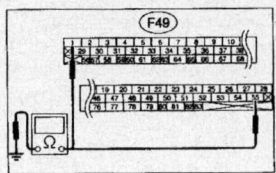

8S1	CHECK GROUND CIRCUIT OF ABSCM.

1) Turn ignition switch to OFF.
2) Disconnect connector from ABSCM.
3) Measure resistance between ABSCM and chassis ground.

Connector & terminal
(F49) No. 1 — Chassis ground:
(F49) No. 55 — Chassis ground:

(CHECK) : Is the resistance less than 0.5 Ω?
(YES) : Go to step **8S2**.
(NO) : Repair ABSCM ground harness.

8S2	CHECK POOR CONTACT IN CONNECTORS.

(CHECK) : Is there poor contact in connectors between battery, ignition switch and ABSCM?
(YES) : Repair connector.
(NO) : Go to step **8S3**.

8S3	CHECK SOURCES OF SIGNAL NOISE.

(CHECK) : Is the car telephone or the wireless transmitter properly installed?
(YES) : Go to step **8S4**.
(NO) : Properly install the car telephone or the wireless transmitter.

8S4	CHECK SOURCES OF SIGNAL NOISE.

(CHECK) : Are noise sources (such as an antenna) installed near the sensor harness?
(YES) : Install the noise sources apart from the sensor harness.
(NO) : Go to step **8S5**.

8S5	CHECK ABSCM.

1) Connect all connectors.
2) Erase the memory.
3) Perform inspection mode.
4) Read out the trouble code.

(CHECK) : Is the same trouble code as in the current diagnosis still being output?
(YES) : Replace ABSCM.
(NO) : Go to step **8S6**.

SB4029700086010X

Fig. 14 Code 41: Abnormal ABS Control Module (Part 1 of 2). Less Select Monitor

8S6	CHECK ANY OTHER TROUBLE CODES APPEARANCE.

(CHECK) : Are other trouble codes being output?
(YES) : Proceed with the diagnosis corresponding to the trouble code.
(NO) : A temporary poor contact.

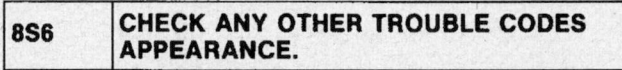

SB4029700086020X

Fig. 14 Code 41: Abnormal ABS Control Module (Part 2 of 2). Less Select Monitor

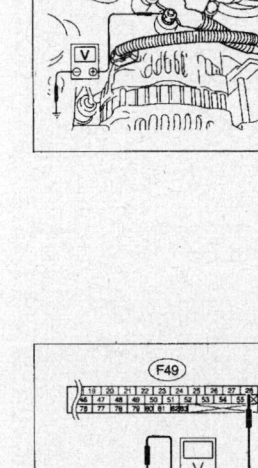

8T1	CHECK GENERATOR.

1) Start engine.
2) Idling after warm-up.
3) Measure voltage between generator B terminal and chassis ground.

Terminal
Generator B terminal — Chassis ground:

(CHECK) : Is the voltage between 10 V and 15 V?
(YES) : Go to step **8T2**.
(NO) : Repair generator.

8T2	CHECK BATTERY TERMINAL.

Turn ignition switch to OFF.

(CHECK) : Are the positive and negative battery terminals tightly clamped?
(YES) : Go to step **8T3**.
(NO) : Tighten the clamp of terminal.

8T3	CHECK INPUT VOLTAGE OF ABSCM.

1) Disconnect connector from ABSCM.
2) Run the engine at idle.
3) Measure voltage between ABSCM connector and chassis ground.

Connector & terminal
(F49) No. 28 (+) — Chassis ground (−):

(CHECK) : Is the voltage between 10 V and 15 V?
(YES) : Go to step **8T4**.
(NO) : Repair harness connector between battery, ignition switch and ABSCM.

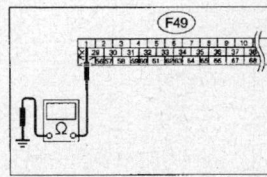

8T4	CHECK GROUND CIRCUIT OF ABSCM.

1) Turn ignition switch to OFF.
2) Measure resistance between ABSCM connector and chassis ground.

Connector & terminal
(F49) No. 1 — Chassis ground:

(CHECK) : Is the resistance less than 0.5 Ω?
(YES) : Go to step **8T5**.
(NO) : Repair ABSCM ground harness.

SB4029700087010X

Fig. 15 Code 42: Source Voltage Is Low (Part 1 of 2). Less Select Monitor

| 8T5 | CHECK POOR CONTACT IN CONNECTORS. |

CHECK : **Is there poor contact in connectors between generator, battery and ABSCM?**

YES : Repair connector.

NO : Go to step **8T6**.

| 8T6 | CHECK ABSCM. |

1) Connect all connectors.
2) Erase the memory.
3) Perform inspection mode.
4) Read out the trouble code.

CHECK : **Is the same trouble code as in the current diagnosis still being output?**

YES : Replace ABSCM.

NO : Go to step **8T7**.

| 8T7 | CHECK ANY OTHER TROUBLE CODES APPEARANCE. |

CHECK : **Are other trouble codes being output?**

YES : Proceed with the diagnosis corresponding to the trouble code.

NO : A temporary poor contact.

SB4029700087020X

Fig. 15 Code 42: Source Voltage Is Low (Part 2 of 2). Less Select Monitor

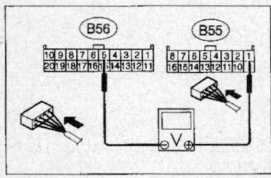

| 8U5 | CHECK TCM. |

1) Turn ignition switch to OFF.
2) Connect all connectors to TCM.
3) Turn ignition switch to ON.
4) Measure voltage between TCM connector terminals.

Connector & terminal
(B55) No. 1 (+) — (B56) No. 5 (–):

CHECK : **Is the voltage between 10 V and 13 V?**

YES : Go to step **8U7**.

NO : Go to step **8U6**.

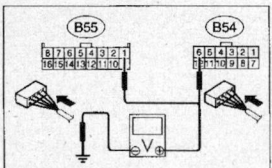

| 8U6 | CHECK TCM. |

Measure voltage between TCM connector and chassis ground.

Connector & terminal
(B54) No. 6 (+) — Chassis ground (–):
(B55) No. 1 (+) — Chassis ground (–):

CHECK : **Is the voltage between 10 V and 13 V?**

YES : Replace TCM.

NO : Repair harness/connector between battery, ignition switch and TCM.

SB4029700088020X

Fig. 16 Code 44: A Combination Of AT Control Abnormal (Part 2 of 3). Less Select Monitor

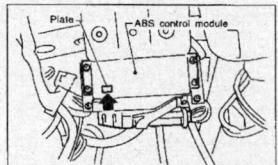

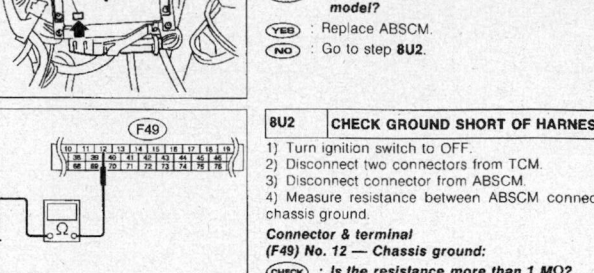

| 8U1 | CHECK SPECIFICATIONS OF THE ABSCM. |

Check specifications of the plate attached to the ABSCM.

CHECK : **Is an ABSCM for AT model installed on a MT model?**

YES : Replace ABSCM.

NO : Go to step **8U2**.

| 8U2 | CHECK GROUND SHORT OF HARNESS. |

1) Turn ignition switch to OFF.
2) Disconnect two connectors from TCM.
3) Disconnect connector from ABSCM.
4) Measure resistance between ABSCM connector and chassis ground.

Connector & terminal
(F49) No. 12 — Chassis ground:

CHECK : **Is the resistance more than 1 MΩ?**

YES : Go to step **8U3**.

NO : Repair harness between TCM and ABSCM.

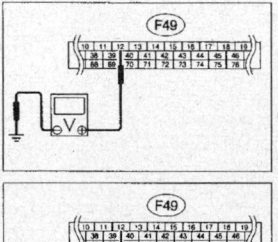

| 8U3 | CHECK BATTERY SHORT OF HARNESS. |

Measure voltage between ABSCM connector and chassis ground.

Connector & terminal
(F49) No. 12 (+) — Chassis ground (–):

CHECK : **Is the voltage less than 1 V?**

YES : Go to step **8U4**.

NO : Repair harness between TCM and ABSCM.

| 8U4 | CHECK BATTERY SHORT OF HARNESS. |

1) Turn ignition switch to ON.
2) Measure voltage between ABSCM connector and chassis ground.

Connector & terminal
(F49) No. 12 (+) — Chassis ground (–):

CHECK : **Is the voltage less than 1 V?**

YES : Go to step **8U5**.

NO : Repair harness between TCM and ABSCM.

SB4029700088010X

Fig. 16 Code 44: A Combination Of AT Control Abnormal (Part 1 of 3). Less Select Monitor

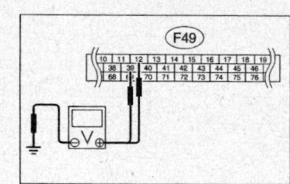

| 8U7 | CHECK OPEN CIRCUIT OF HARNESS. |

Measure voltage between ABSCM connector and chassis ground.

Connector & terminal
(F49) No. 12 (+) — Chassis ground (–):
(F49) No. 39 (+) — Chassis ground (–):

CHECK : **Is the voltage between 10 V and 13 V?**

YES : Go to step **8U8**.

NO : Repair harness/connector between TCM and ABSCM.

| 8U8 | CHECK POOR CONTACT IN CONNECTORS. |

CHECK : **Is there poor contact in connectors between TCM and ABSCM?**

YES : Repair connector.

NO : Go to step **8U9**.

| 8U9 | CHECK ABSCM. |

1) Turn ignition switch to OFF.
2) Connect all connectors.
3) Erase the memory.
4) Perform inspection mode.
5) Read out the trouble code.

CHECK : **Is the same trouble code as in the current diagnosis still being output?**

YES : Replace ABSCM.

NO : Go to step **8U10**.

| 8U10 | CHECK ANY OTHER TROUBLE CODES APPEARANCE. |

CHECK : **Are other trouble codes being output?**

YES : Proceed with the diagnosis corresponding to the trouble code.

NO : A temporary poor contact.

SB4029700088030X

Fig. 16 Code 44: A Combination Of AT Control Abnormal (Part 3 of 3). Less Select Monitor

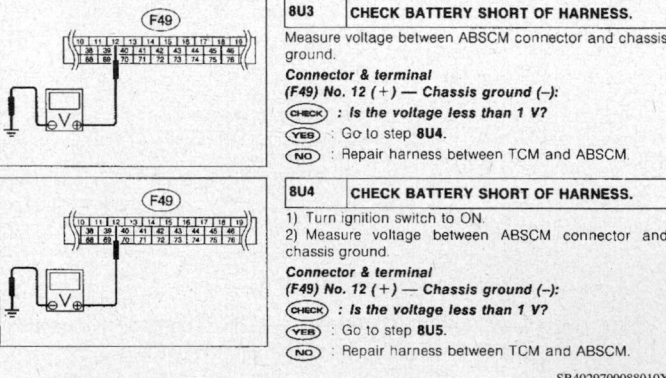

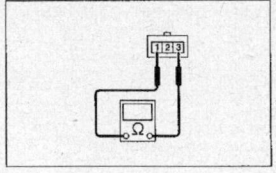

8V1	CHECK G SENSOR.

1) Turn ignition switch to OFF.
2) Remove console box.
3) Disconnect connector from G sensor.
4) Measure resistance of G sensor.

Terminal
No. 1 — No. 3:
(CHECK) : *Is the resistance between 42 and 58 kΩ?*
(YES) : Go to step **8V2**.
(NO) : Replace G sensor.

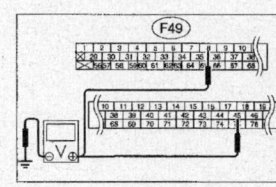

8V4	CHECK GROUND SHORT OF HARNESS.

Measure resistance between ABSCM connector and chassis ground.

Connector & terminal
(F49) No. 8 — Chassis ground:
(F49) No. 45 — Chassis ground:
(CHECK) : *Is the resistance more than 1 MΩ?*
(YES) : Go to step **8V5**.
(NO) : Repair harness between ABSCM and G sensor.

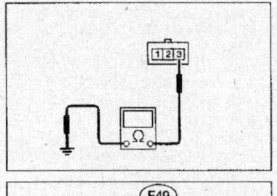

8V2	CHECK GROUND SHORT OF G SENSOR.

Measure resistance between G sensor and bracket.

Terminal
No. 3 — Bracket:
(CHECK) : *Is the resistance more than 1 MΩ?*
(YES) : Go to step **8V3**.
(NO) : Replace G sensor.

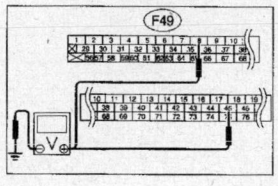

8V3	CHECK SHORT CIRCUIT IN HARNESS BETWEEN ABSCM AND G SENSOR.

1) Disconnect connector from ABSCM.
2) Measure resistance between ABSCM connector terminals.

Connector & terminal
(F49) No. 45 — No. 8:
(CHECK) : *Is the resistance more than 1 MΩ?*
(YES) : Go to step **8V4**.
(NO) : Repair harness between ABSCM and G sensor.

SB4029700089010X

Fig. 17 Code 46: Abnormal G Sensor Power Supply Voltage (Part 1 of 3). Less Select Monitor

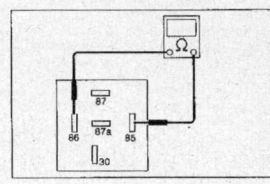

8V5	CHECK BATTERY SHORT OF HARNESS.

Measure voltage between ABSCM connector and chassis ground.

Connector & terminal
(F49) No. 8 (+) — Chassis ground (–):
(F49) No. 45 (+) — Chassis ground (–):
(CHECK) : *Is the voltage less than 1 V?*
(YES) : Go to step **8V6**.
(NO) : Repair harness between ABSCM and G sensor.

SB4029700089020X

Fig. 17 Code 46: Abnormal G Sensor Power Supply Voltage (Part 2 of 3). Less Select Monitor

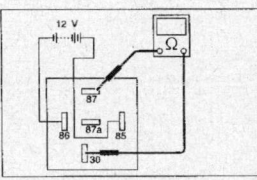

8W1	CHECK RESISTANCE OF VALVE RELAY.

1) Turn ignition switch to OFF.
2) Remove valve relay from relay box.
3) Measure resistance between valve relay terminals.

Terminals
No. 85 — No. 86:
(CHECK) : *Is the resistance between 93 and 113 Ω?*
(YES) : Go to step **8W2**.
(NO) : Replace valve relay.

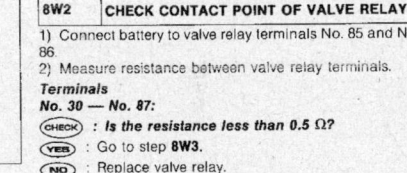

8V6	CHECK BATTERY SHORT OF HARNESS.

1) Turn ignition switch to ON.
2) Measure voltage between ABSCM and chassis ground.

Connector & terminal
(F49) No. 8 (+) — Chassis ground (–):
(F49) No. 45 (+) — Chassis ground (–):
(CHECK) : *Is the voltage less than 1 V?*
(YES) : Go to step **8V7**.
(NO) : Repair harness between ABSCM and chassis ground.

8V7	CHECK POOR CONTACT IN CONNECTORS.

(CHECK) : *Is there poor contact in connectors between ABSCM and G sensor?*
(YES) : Repair connector.
(NO) : Go to step **8V8**.

8V8	CHECK ABSCM.

1) Turn ignition switch to OFF.
2) Connect all connectors.
3) Erase the memory.
4) Perform inspection mode.
5) Read out the trouble code.
(CHECK) : *Is the same trouble code as in the current diagnosis still being output?*
(YES) : Replace ABSCM.
(NO) : Go to step **8V9**.

8V9	CHECK ANY OTHER TROUBLE CODES APPEARANCE.

(CHECK) : *Are other trouble codes being output?*
(YES) : Proceed with the diagnosis corresponding to the trouble code.
(NO) : A temporary poor contact.

SB4029700089030X

Fig. 17 Code 46: Abnormal G Sensor Power Supply Voltage (Part 3 of 3). Less Select Monitor

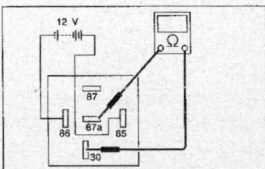

8W2	CHECK CONTACT POINT OF VALVE RELAY.

1) Connect battery to valve relay terminals No. 85 and No. 86.
2) Measure resistance between valve relay terminals.

Terminals
No. 30 — No. 87:
(CHECK) : *Is the resistance less than 0.5 Ω?*
(YES) : Go to step **8W3**.
(NO) : Replace valve relay.

8W3	CHECK CONTACT POINT OF VALVE RELAY.

Measure resistance between valve relay terminals.
Terminals
No. 30 — No. 87a:
Is the resistance more than 1 MΩ?
(YES) : Go to step **8W4**.
(NO) : Replace valve relay.

SB4029700090010X

Fig. 18 Code 51: Abnormal Valve Relay (Part 1 of 14). Less Select Monitor

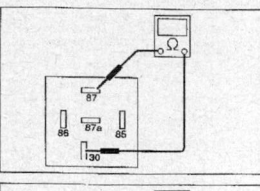

8W4	CHECK CONTACT POINT OF VALVE RELAY.

1) Disconnect battery from valve relay terminals.
2) Measure resistance between valve relay terminals.

Terminals
No. 30 — No. 87:

(CHECK) : Is the resistance more than 1 MΩ?
(YES) : Go to step 8W5.
(NO) : Replace valve relay.

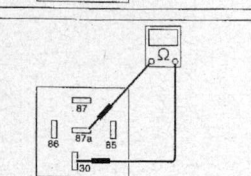

8W5	CHECK CONTACT POINT OF VALVE RELAY.

Measure resistance between valve relay terminals.

Terminals
No. 30 — No. 87a:

(CHECK) : Is the resistance less than 0.5 Ω?
(YES) : Go to step 8W6.
(NO) : Replace valve relay.

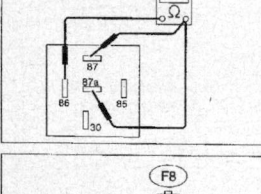

8W6	CHECK SHORT OF VALVE RELAY.

Measure resistance between valve relay terminals.

Terminals
No. 86 — No. 87:
No. 86 — No. 87a:

(CHECK) : Is the resistance more than 1 MΩ?
(YES) : Go to step 8W7.
(NO) : Replace valve relay.

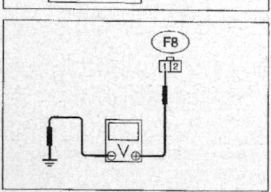

8W7	CHECK POWER SUPPLY FOR VALVE RELAY.

1) Disconnect connector (F8) from relay box.
2) Turn ignition switch to ON.
3) Measure voltage between relay box connector and chassis ground.

Connector & terminal
(F8) No. 1 (+) — Chassis ground (–):

(CHECK) : Is the voltage between 10 V and 13 V?
(YES) : Go to step 8W8.
(NO) : Repair harness between battery and relay box connector. Check fuse No. 19.

SB4029700090020X

Fig. 18   Code 51: Abnormal Valve Relay (Part 2 of 14). Less Select Monitor

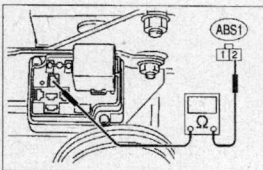

8W10	CHECK OPEN CIRCUIT IN CONTACT POINT CIRCUIT OF RELAY BOX.

1) Turn ignition switch to OFF.
2) Measure resistance between hydraulic unit connector and valve relay installing point.

Connector & terminal
(ABS1) No. 2 — Valve relay installing point No. 30:

(CHECK) : Is the resistance less than 0.5 Ω?
(YES) : Go to step 8W11.
(NO) : Replace relay box.

8W11	CHECK GROUND SHORT IN CONTACT POINT CIRCUIT OF RELAY BOX.

Measure resistance between hydraulic unit connector and chassis ground.

Connector & terminal
(ABS1) No. 2 — Chassis ground:

(CHECK) : Is the resistance more than 1 MΩ?
(YES) : Go to step 8W12.
(NO) : Replace relay box and check fuse SBF6.

8W12	CHECK BATTERY SHORT IN CONTACT POINT CIRCUIT OF RELAY BOX.

1) Disconnect connector from ABSCM.
2) Measure voltage between hydraulic unit connector and chassis ground.

Connector & terminal
(ABS1) No. 2 (+) — Chassis ground (–):

(CHECK) : Is the voltage less than 1 V?
(YES) : Go to step 8W13.
(NO) : Replace relay box. Check fuse No. 19 and SBF6.

SB4029700090040X

Fig. 18   Code 51: Abnormal Valve Relay (Part 4 of 14). Less Select Monitor

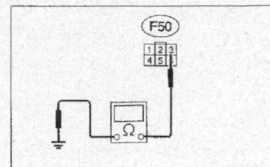

8W8	CHECK GROUND CIRCUIT OF RELAY BOX.

1) Turn ignition switch to OFF.
2) Disconnect connector (F50) from relay box.
3) Measure resistance between relay box connector and chassis ground.

Connector & terminal
(F50) No. 3 — Chassis ground:

(CHECK) : Is the resistance less than 0.5 Ω?
(YES) : Go to step 8W9.
(NO) : Repair relay box ground harness.

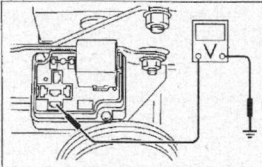

8W9	CHECK OPEN CIRCUIT AND GROUND SHORT IN POWER SUPPLY CIRCUIT OF RELAY BOX.

1) Disconnect connector (ABS1) from hydraulic unit.
2) Connect connector (F8) to relay box.
3) Turn ignition switch to ON.
4) Measure voltage of relay box.

Connector & terminal
Valve relay installing point No. 87 — Chassis ground:

(CHECK) : Is the voltage between 10 V and 13 V?
(YES) : Go to step 8W10.
(NO) : Replace relay box and check fuse No. 19.

SB4029700090030X

Fig. 18   Code 51: Abnormal Valve Relay (Part 3 of 14). Less Select Monitor

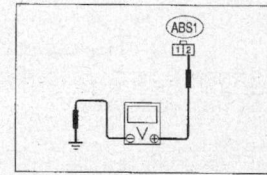

8W13	CHECK BATTERY SHORT IN CONTACT POINT CIRCUIT OF RELAY BOX.

1) Turn ignition switch to ON.
2) Measure voltage between hydraulic unit connector and chassis ground.

Connector & terminal
(ABS1) No. 2 (+) — Chassis ground (–):

(CHECK) : Is the voltage less than 1 V?
(YES) : Go to step 8W14.
(NO) : Replace relay box. Check fuse No. 19 and SBF6.

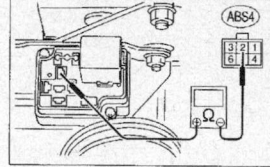

8W14	CHECK DIODE OF RELAY BOX.

1) Turn ignition switch to OFF.
2) Measure resistance between relay box connector and valve relay installing point.

Connector & terminal
Valve relay installing point No. 30 (+) — (ABS4) No. 2 (–):

(CHECK) : Is the resistance more than 1 MΩ?
(YES) : Go to step 8W15.
(NO) : Replace relay box.

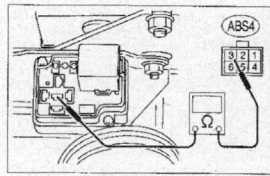

8W15	CHECK OPEN CIRCUIT IN GROUND CIRCUIT OF RELAY BOX.

Measure resistance between relay box connector and valve relay installing point.

Connector & terminal
(ABS4) No. 3 — Valve relay installing point No. 87a:

(CHECK) : Is the resistance less than 0.5 Ω?
(YES) : Go to step 8W16.
(NO) : Replace relay box.

SB4029700090050X

Fig. 18   Code 51: Abnormal Valve Relay (Part 5 of 14). Less Select Monitor

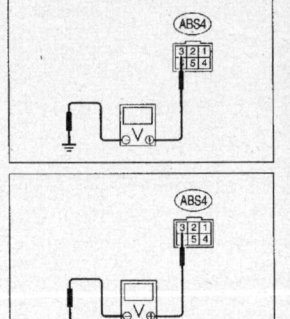

8W16 CHECK BATTERY SHORT IN GROUND CIRCUIT OF RELAY BOX.

Measure voltage between relay box connector and chassis ground.
Connector & terminal
(ABS4) No. 3 (+) — Chassis ground (–):
CHECK : *Is the voltage less than 1 V?*
YES : Go to step **8W17**.
NO : Replace relay box and check all fuses.

8W17 CHECK BATTERY SHORT IN GROUND CIRCUIT OF RELAY BOX.

1) Turn ignition switch to ON.
2). Measure voltage between relay box connector and chassis ground.
Connector & terminal
(ABS4) No. 3 (+) — Chassis ground (–):
CHECK : *Is the voltage less than 1 V?*
YES : Go to step **8W18**.
NO : Replace relay box and check all fuses.

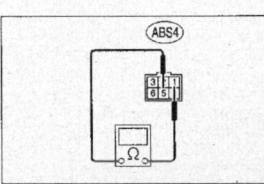

8W18 CHECK OPEN CIRCUIT IN CONTROL CIRCUIT OF RELAY BOX.

1) Turn ignition switch to OFF.
2) Install valve relay to relay box.
3) Measure resistance between relay box connector terminals.
Connector & terminal
(ABS4) No. 1 — No. 5:
CHECK : *Is the resistance between 93 and 113 Ω?*
YES : Go to step **8W19**.
NO : Replace relay box.

SB4029700090060X

Fig. 18 Code 51: Abnormal Valve Relay (Part 6 of 14). Less Select Monitor

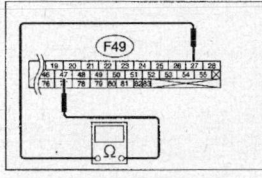

8W22 CHECK OPEN CIRCUIT IN CONTROL SYSTEM HARNESS OF VALVE RELAY.

1) Turn ignition switch to OFF.
2) Connect connector (F50) to relay box.
3) Measure resistance between ABSCM connector terminals.
Connector & terminal
(F49) No. 27 — No. 47:
CHECK : *Is the resistance between 93 and 113 Ω?*
YES : Go to step **8W23**.
NO : Repair harness between ABSCM and relay box. Check fuse No. 18.

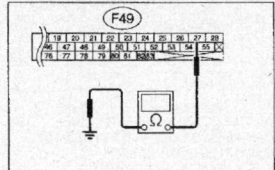

8W23 CHECK GROUND SHORT IN CONTROL SYSTEM HARNESS OF VALVE RELAY.

Measure resistance between ABSCM connector and chassis ground.
Connector & terminal
(F49) No. 27 — Chassis ground:
CHECK : *Is the resistance more than 1 MΩ?*
YES : Go to step **8W24**.
NO : Repair harness between ABSCM and relay box. Check fuse No. 18.

SB4029700090080X

Fig. 18 Code 51: Abnormal Valve Relay (Part 8 of 14). Less Select Monitor

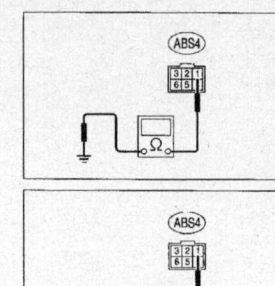

8W19 CHECK GROUND SHORT IN CONTROL CIRCUIT OF RELAY BOX.

Measure resistance between relay box connector and chassis ground.
Connector & terminal
(ABS4) No. 1 — Chassis ground:
CHECK : *Is the resistance more than 1 MΩ?*
YES : Go to step **8W20**.
NO : Replace relay box and check all fuses.

8W20 CHECK BATTERY SHORT IN CONTROL CIRCUIT OF RELAY BOX.

Measure voltage between relay box connector and chassis ground.
Connector & terminal
(ABS4) No. 1 (+) — Chassis ground (–):
CHECK : *Is the voltage less than 1 V?*
YES : Go to step **8W21**.
NO : Replace relay box. Check fuse No. 19 and SBF45A.

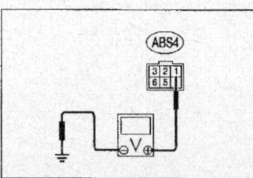

8W21 CHECK BATTERY SHORT IN CONTROL CIRCUIT OF RELAY BOX.

1) Turn ignition switch to ON.
2) Measure voltage between relay box connector and chassis ground.
Connector & terminal
(ABS4) No. 1 (+) — Chassis ground (–):
CHECK : *Is the voltage less than 1 V?*
YES : Go to step **8W22**.
NO : Replace relay box. Check fuse No. 19 and SBF45A.

SB4029700090070X

Fig. 18 Code 51: Abnormal Valve Relay (Part 7 of 14). Less Select Monitor

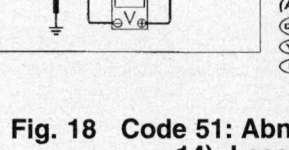

8W24 CHECK BATTERY SHORT IN CONTROL SYSTEM HARNESS OF VALVE RELAY.

Measure voltage between ABSCM connector and chassis ground.
Connector & terminal
(F49) No. 27 (+) — Chassis ground (–):
CHECK : *Is the voltage less than 1 V?*
YES : Go to step **8W25**.
NO : Repair harness between ABSCM and relay box and check all fuses.

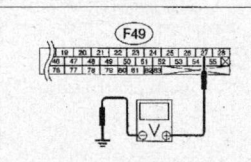

8W25 CHECK BATTERY SHORT IN CONTROL SYSTEM HARNESS OF VALVE RELAY.

1) Turn ignition switch to ON.
2) Measure voltage between ABSCM connector and chassis ground.
Connector & terminal
(F49) No. 27 (+) — Chassis ground (–):
CHECK : *Is the voltage less than 1 V?*
YES : Go to step **8W26**.
NO : Repair harness between ABSCM and relay box and check all fuses.

SB4029700090090X

Fig. 18 Code 51: Abnormal Valve Relay (Part 9 of 14). Less Select Monitor

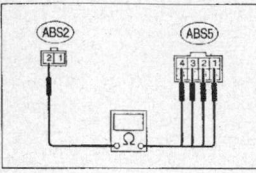

8W26 CHECK RESISTANCE OF INLET SOLENOID VALVE.

1) Turn ignition switch to OFF.
2) Disconnect connector from hydraulic unit.
3) Measure resistance between hydraulic unit connector terminals.

Connector & terminal
(ABS5) No. 4 — (ABS2) No. 2:
(ABS5) No. 1 — (ABS2) No. 2:
(ABS5) No. 2 — (ABS2) No. 2:
(ABS5) No. 3 — (ABS2) No. 2:

(CHECK) : *Is the resistance between 7.8 and 9.2 Ω?*
(YES) : Go to step **8W27**.
(NO) : Replace hydraulic unit.

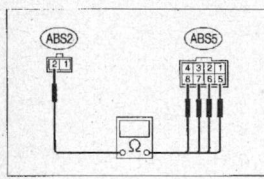

8W27 CHECK RESISTANCE OF OUTLET SOLENOID VALVE.

Measure resistance between hydraulic unit connector terminals.

Connector & terminal
(ABS5) No. 8 — (ABS2) No. 2:
(ABS5) No. 5 — (ABS2) No. 2:
(ABS5) No. 6 — (ABS2) No. 2:
(ABS5) No. 7 — (ABS2) No. 2:

(CHECK) : *Is the resistance between 3.8 and 4.8 Ω?*
(YES) : Go to step **8W28**.
(NO) : Replace hydraulic unit.

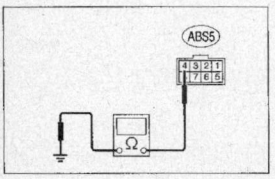

8W28 CHECK GROUND SHORT OF SOLENOID VALVE.

Measure resistance between hydraulic unit connector and chassis ground.

Connector & terminal
(ABS5) No. 4 — Chassis ground:

(CHECK) : *Is the resistance more than 1 MΩ?*
(YES) : Go to step **8W29**.
(NO) : Replace hydraulic unit and check all fuses.

SB4029700090100X

Fig. 18 Code 51: Abnormal Valve Relay (Part 10 of 14). Less Select Monitor

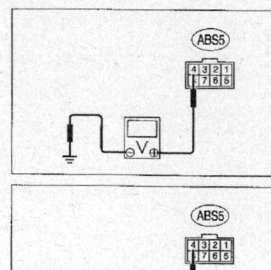

8W29 CHECK BATTERY SHORT OF SOLENOID VALVE.

Measure voltage between hydraulic unit connector and chassis ground.

Connector & terminal
(ABS5) No. 4 (+) — Chassis ground (–):

(CHECK) : *Is the voltage less than 1 V?*
(YES) : Go to step **8W30**.
(NO) : Replace hydraulic unit and check all fuses.

8W30 CHECK BATTERY SHORT OF SOLENOID VALVE.

1) Turn ignition switch to ON.
2) Measure voltage between hydraulic unit connector and chassis ground.

Connector & terminal
(ABS5) No. 4 (+) — Chassis ground (–):

(CHECK) : *Is the voltage less than 1 V?*
(YES) : Go to step **8W31**.
(NO) : Replace hydraulic unit and check all fuses.

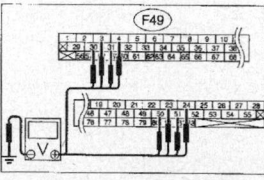

8W31 CHECK BATTERY SHORT OF HARNESS.

1) Turn ignition switch to OFF.
2) Disconnect connector from hydraulic unit.
3) Measure voltage between ABSCM connector and chassis ground.

Connector & terminal
(F49) No. 30 (+) — Chassis ground (–):
(F49) No. 24 (+) — Chassis ground (–):
(F49) No. 23 (+) — Chassis ground (–):
(F49) No. 31 (+) — Chassis ground (–):
(F49) No. 3 (+) — Chassis ground (–):
(F49) No. 51 (+) — Chassis ground (–):
(F49) No. 50 (+) — Chassis ground (–):
(F49) No. 4 (+) — Chassis ground (–):

(CHECK) : *Is the voltage less than 1 V?*
(YES) : Go to step **8W32**.
(NO) : Repair harness between hydraulic unit and ABSCM and check all fuses.

SB4029700090110X

Fig. 18 Code 51: Abnormal Valve Relay (Part 11 of 14). Less Select Monitor

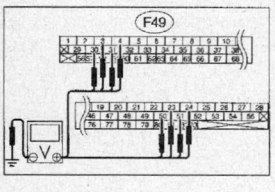

8W32 CHECK BATTERY SHORT OF HARNESS.

1) Turn ignition switch to ON.
2) Measure voltage between ABSCM connector and chassis ground.

Connector & terminal
(F49) No. 30 (+) — Chassis ground (–):
(F49) No. 24 (+) — Chassis ground (–):
(F49) No. 23 (+) — Chassis ground (–):
(F49) No. 31 (+) — Chassis ground (–):
(F49) No. 3 (+) — Chassis ground (–):
(F49) No. 51 (+) — Chassis ground (–):
(F49) No. 50 (+) — Chassis ground (–):
(F49) No. 4 (+) — Chassis ground (–):

(CHECK) : *Is the voltage less than 1 V?*
(YES) : Go to step **8W33**.
(NO) : Repair harness between hydraulic unit and ABSCM and check all fuses.

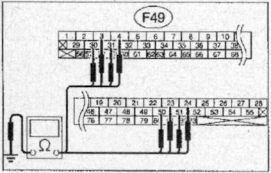

8W33 CHECK GROUND SHORT OF HARNESS.

1) Turn ignition switch to OFF.
2) Measure resistance between ABSCM connector and chassis ground.

Connector & terminal
(F49) No. 30 — Chassis ground:
(F49) No. 24 — Chassis ground:
(F49) No. 23 — Chassis ground:
(F49) No. 31 — Chassis ground:
(F49) No. 3 — Chassis ground:
(F49) No. 51 — Chassis ground:
(F49) No. 50 — Chassis ground:
(F49) No. 4 — Chassis ground:

(CHECK) : *Is the resistance more than 1 MΩ?*
(YES) : Go to step **8W34**.
(NO) : Repair harness between hydraulic unit and ABSCM.

SB4029700090120X

Fig. 18 Code 51: Abnormal Valve Relay (Part 12 of 14). Less Select Monitor

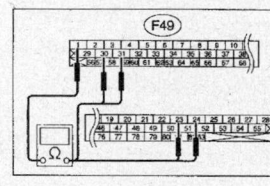

8W34 CHECK HARNESS/CONNECTOR BETWEEN ABSCM AND HYDRAULIC UNIT.

1) Connect connector to hydraulic unit.
2) Measure resistance between ABSCM connector terminals.

Connector & terminal
(F49) No. 30 — No. 1:
(F49) No. 24 — No. 1:
(F49) No. 23 — No. 1:
(F49) No. 31 — No. 1:

(CHECK) : *Is the resistance between 8.3 and 9.7 Ω?*
(YES) : Go to step **8W35**.
(NO) : Repair harness/connector between hydraulic unit and ABSCM.

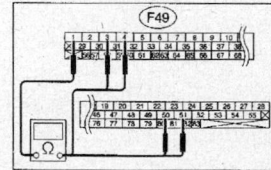

8W35 CHECK HARNESS/CONNECTOR BETWEEN ABSCM AND HYDRAULIC UNIT.

Measure resistance between ABSCM connector terminals.

Connector & terminal
(F49) No. 3 — No. 1:
(F49) No. 51 — No. 1:
(F49) No. 50 — No. 1:
(F49) No. 4 — No. 1:

(CHECK) : *Is the resistance between 4.3 and 5.3 Ω?*
(YES) : Go to step **8W36**.
(NO) : Repair harness/connector between hydraulic unit and ABSCM.

8W36 CHECK POOR CONTACT IN CONNECTORS.

(CHECK) : *Is there poor contact in connector between ABSCM and hydraulic unit?*

(YES) : Repair connector.
(NO) : Go to step **8W37**.

SB4029700090130X

Fig. 18 Code 51: Abnormal Valve Relay (Part 13 of 14). Less Select Monitor

8W37	CHECK ABSCM.

1) Connect all connectors.
2) Erase the memory.
3) Perform inspection mode.
4) Read out the trouble code.

(CHECK) : **Is the same trouble code as in the current diagnosis still being output?**

(YES) : Replace ABSCM.

(NO) : Go to step **8W38**.

8W38	CHECK ANY OTHER TROUBLE CODES APPEARANCE.

(CHECK) : **Are other trouble codes being output?**

(YES) : Proceed with the diagnosis corresponding to the trouble code.

(NO) : A temporary poor contact.

SB4029700090140X

Fig. 18 Code 51: Abnormal Valve Relay (Part 14 of 14). Less Select Monitor

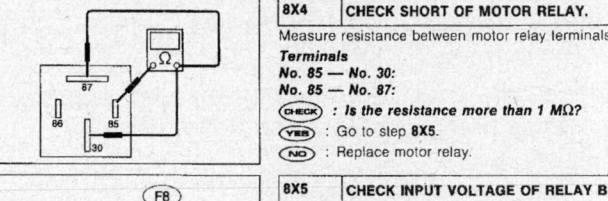

8X4	CHECK SHORT OF MOTOR RELAY.

Measure resistance between motor relay terminals.
Terminals
No. 85 — No. 30:
No. 85 — No. 87:
(CHECK) : **Is the resistance more than 1 MΩ?**
(YES) : Go to step **8X5**.
(NO) : Replace motor relay.

8X5	CHECK INPUT VOLTAGE OF RELAY BOX.

1) Disconnect connector (F8) from relay box.
2) Turn ignition switch to ON.
3) Measure voltage between relay box connector and chassis ground.
Connector & terminal
(F8) No. 2 (+) — Chassis ground (–):
(CHECK) : **Is the voltage between 10 V and 13 V?**
(YES) : Go to step **8X6**.
(NO) : Repair harness/connector between battery and relay box, and check fuse SBF6.

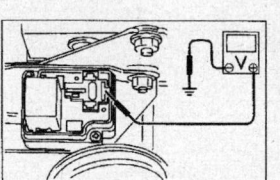

8X6	CHECK INPUT VOLTAGE OF MOTOR RELAY.

1) Turn ignition switch to OFF.
2) Connect connector (F8) to relay box.
3) Turn ignition switch to ON.
4) Measure voltage between relay box and chassis ground.
Connector & terminal
Relay installing point No. 87 (+) — Chassis ground (–):
(CHECK) : **Is the voltage between 10 V and 13 V?**
(YES) : Go to step **8X7**.
(NO) : Replace relay box, and check fuse SBF6.

SB4029700091020X

Fig. 19 Code 52: Abnormal Motor And/Or Motor Relay (Part 2 of 12). Less Select Monitor

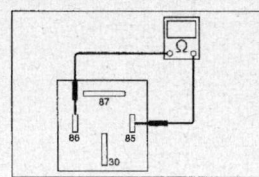

8X1	CHECK RESISTANCE OF MOTOR RELAY.

1) Turn ignition switch to OFF.
2) Remove motor relay from relay box.
3) Measure resistance between motor relay terminals.
Terminals
No. 85 — No. 86:
(CHECK) : **Is the resistance between 70 and 90 Ω?**
(YES) : Go to step **8X2**.
(NO) : Replace motor relay.

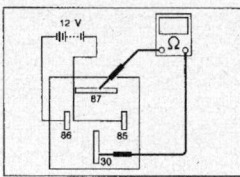

8X2	CHECK CONTACT POINT OF MOTOR RELAY.

1) Connect battery to motor relay terminals No. 85 and No. 86.
2) Measure resistance between motor relay terminals.
Terminals
No. 30 — No. 87:
(CHECK) : **Is the resistance less than 0.5 Ω?**
(YES) : Go to step **8X3**.
(NO) : Replace motor relay.

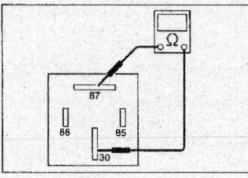

8X3	CHECK CONTACT POINT OF MOTOR RELAY.

1) Disconnect battery from motor relay terminals.
2) Measure resistance between motor relay terminals.
Terminals
No. 30 — No. 87:
(CHECK) : **Is the resistance more than 1 MΩ?**
(YES) : Go to step **8X4**.
(NO) : Replace motor relay.

SB4029700091010X

Fig. 19 Code 52: Abnormal Motor And/Or Motor Relay (Part 1 of 12). Less Select Monitor

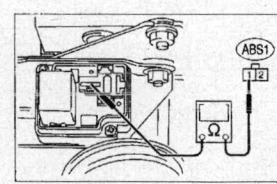

8X7	CHECK OPEN CIRCUIT IN CONTACT POINT CIRCUIT OF RELAY BOX.

1) Turn ignition switch to OFF.
2) Disconnect connector (ABS1) from hydraulic unit.
3) Measure resistance between hydraulic unit and motor relay installing portion.
Connector & terminal
(ABS1) No. 1 — Motor relay installing portion No. 30:
(CHECK) : **Is the resistance less than 0.5 Ω?**
(YES) : Go to step **8X8**.
(NO) : Replace relay box.

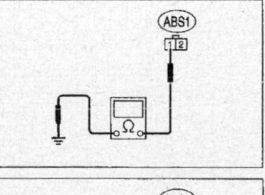

8X8	CHECK GROUND SHORT IN CONTACT POINT CIRCUIT OF RELAY BOX.

Measure resistance between hydraulic unit and chassis ground.
Connector & terminal
(ABS1) No. 1 — Chassis ground:
(CHECK) : **Is the resistance more than 1 MΩ?**
(YES) : Go to step **8X9**.
(NO) : Replace relay box. Check fuse No. 19.

8X9	CHECK BATTERY SHORT IN CONTACT POINT CIRCUIT OF RELAY BOX.

1) Disconnect connector from ABSCM.
2) Measure voltage between ABSCM connector and chassis ground.
Connector & terminal
(ABS1) No. 1 (+) — Chassis ground (–):
(CHECK) : **Is the voltage less than 1 V?**
(YES) : Go to step **8X10**.
(NO) : Replace relay box.

SB4029700091030X

Fig. 19 Code 52: Abnormal Motor And/Or Motor Relay (Part 3 of 12). Less Select Monitor

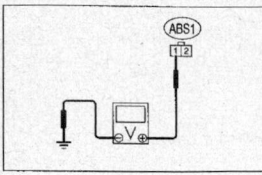

8X10 CHECK BATTERY SHORT IN CONTACT POINT CIRCUIT OF RELAY BOX.
1) Turn ignition switch to ON.
2) Measure voltage between ABSCM connector and chassis ground.
Connector & terminal
(ABS1) No. 1 (+) — Chassis ground (–):
CHECK : *Is the voltage less than 1 V?*
YES : Go to step **8X11**.
NO : Replace relay box.

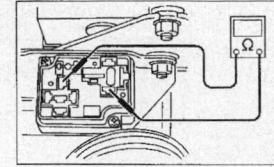

8X12 CHECK OPEN CIRCUIT IN CONTROL CIRCUIT OF RELAY BOX.
1) Remove valve relay from relay box.
2) Measure resistance between motor relay installing point and valve relay installing point.
Connector & terminal
Motor relay installing point No. 86 — Valve relay installing point No. 30:
CHECK : *Is the resistance less than 0.5 Ω?*
YES : Go to step **8X13**.
NO : Replace relay box.

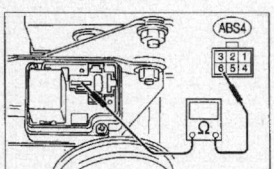

8X11 CHECK OPEN CIRCUIT IN MONITOR SYSTEM CIRCUIT OF RELAY BOX.
1) Turn ignition switch to OFF.
2) Disconnect connector (F50) from relay box.
3) Measure resistance between relay box connector and motor relay installing point.
Connector & terminal
(ABS4) No. 6 — Motor relay installing point No. 30:
CHECK : *Is the resistance less than 0.5 Ω?*
YES : Go to step **8X12**.
NO : Replace relay box.

SB4029700091040X

Fig. 19 Code 52: Abnormal Motor And/Or Motor Relay (Part 4 of 12). Less Select Monitor

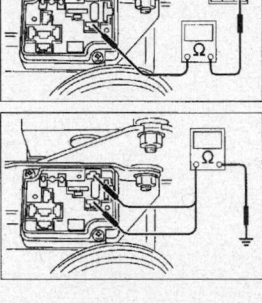

8X13 CHECK OPEN CIRCUIT IN CONTROL CIRCUIT OF RELAY BOX.
Measure resistance between motor relay installing point and relay box connector.
Connector & terminal
Motor relay installing point No. 86 — (ABS4) No. 4:
CHECK : *Is the resistance less than 0.5 Ω?*
YES : Go to step **8X14**.
NO : Replace relay box.

8X14 CHECK GROUND SHORT IN CONTROL CIRCUIT OF RELAY BOX.
Measure resistance between relay box and chassis ground.
Connector & terminal
Motor relay installing point No. 86 — Chassis ground:
Motor relay installing point No. 85 — Chassis ground:
CHECK : *Is the resistance more than 1 MΩ?*
YES : Go to step **8X15**.
NO : Replace relay box. Check fuse No. 19.

SB4029700091050X

Fig. 19 Code 52: Abnormal Motor And/Or Motor Relay (Part 5 of 12). Less Select Monitor

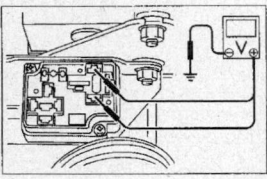

8X15 CHECK BATTERY SHORT IN CONTROL CIRCUIT OF RELAY BOX.
Measure voltage between motor relay installing point and chassis ground.
Connector & terminal
Motor relay installing point (+) No. 86 — Chassis ground (–):
Motor relay installing point (+) No. 85 — Chassis ground (–):
CHECK : *Is the voltage less than 1 V?*
YES : Go to step **8X16**.
NO : Replace relay box and check all fuses.

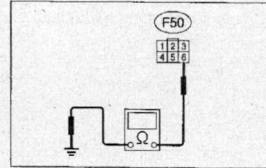

8X17 CHECK OPEN CIRCUIT IN MONITOR SYSTEM HARNESS.
1) Turn ignition switch to OFF.
2) Connect between terminals No. 10 and No. 1 of ABSCM connector (F49) with a lead wire.
3) Measure resistance between relay box connector and chassis ground.
Connector & terminal
(F50) No. 6 — Chassis ground:
CHECK : *Is the resistance less than 0.5 Ω?*
YES : Go to step **8X18**.
NO : Repair harness/connector between ABSCM and relay box.

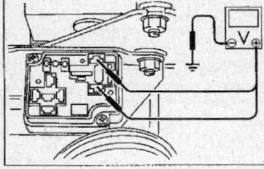

8X16 CHECK BATTERY SHORT IN CONTROL CIRCUIT OF RELAY BOX.
1) Turn ignition switch to ON.
2) Measure voltage between motor relay installing point and chassis ground.
Connector & terminal
Motor relay installing point (+) No. 86 — Chassis ground:
Motor relay installing point (+) No. 85 — Chassis ground:
CHECK : *Is the voltage less than 1 V?*
YES : Go to step **8X17**.
NO : Replace relay box and check all fuses.

SB4029700091060X

Fig. 19 Code 52: Abnormal Motor And/Or Motor Relay (Part 6 of 12). Less Select Monitor

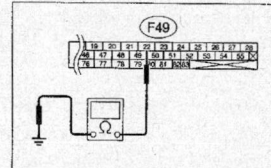

8X18 CHECK OPEN CIRCUIT IN RELAY CONTROL SYSTEM HARNESS.
1) Connect valve relay and motor relay to relay box.
2) Connect connector (F50) to relay box.
3) Connect connector to hydraulic unit.
4) Measure resistance between ABSCM connector and chassis ground.
Connector & terminal
(F49) No. 22 — Chassis ground:
CHECK : *Is the resistance between 70 and 90 Ω?*
YES : Go to step **8X19**.
NO : Repair harness/connector between ABSCM and relay box.

SB4029700091070X

Fig. 19 Code 52: Abnormal Motor And/Or Motor Relay (Part 7 of 12). Less Select Monitor

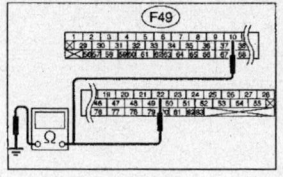

8X19 | **CHECK GROUND SHORT IN HARNESS BETWEEN RELAY BOX AND ABSCM.**

1) Disconnect connector (F50) from relay box.
2) Measure resistance between ABSCM connector and chassis ground.

Connector & terminal
(F49) No. 22 — Chassis ground:
(F49) No. 10 — Chassis ground:

(CHECK) : Is the resistance more than 1 MΩ?
(YES) : Go to step **8X20**.
(NO) : Repair harness between ABSCM and relay box. Check fuse No. 19 and SBF6.

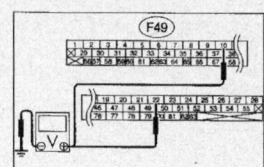

8X21 | **CHECK BATTERY SHORT IN HARNESS BETWEEN RELAY BOX AND ABSCM.**

1) Turn ignition switch to ON.
2) Measure voltage between ABSCM connector and chassis ground.

Connector & terminal
(F49) No. 22 (+) — Chassis ground (−):
(F49) No. 10 (+) — Chassis ground (−):

(CHECK) : Is the voltage less than 1 V?
(YES) : Go to step **8X22**.
(NO) : Repair harness between relay box and ABSCM. Check fuse SBF6.

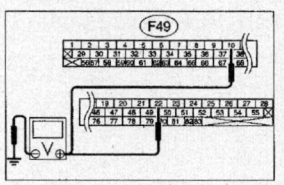

8X20 | **CHECK BATTERY SHORT IN HARNESS BETWEEN RELAY BOX AND ABSCM.**

Measure voltage between ABSCM connector and chassis ground.

Connector & terminal
(F49) No. 22 (+) — Chassis ground (−):
(F49) No. 10 (+) — Chassis ground (−):

(CHECK) : Is the voltage less than 1 V?
(YES) : Go to step **8X21**.
(NO) : Repair harness between relay box and ABSCM. Check fuse SBF6.

SB4029700091080X

Fig. 19   Code 52: Abnormal Motor And/Or Motor Relay (Part 8 of 12). Less Select Monitor

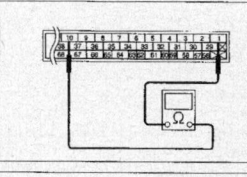
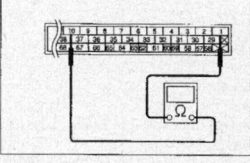

8X22 | **CHECK GROUND SHORT AT ABSCM MONITOR TERMINAL.**

1) Turn ignition switch to OFF.
2) Measure resistance between ABSCM terminals.

Terminal
No. 10 — No. 1:

(CHECK) : Is the resistance less than 0.5 Ω?
(YES) : Go to step **8X23**.
(NO) : Replace ABSCM.

8X23 | **CHECK BATTERY SHORT IN ABSCM CONNECTOR TERMINAL.**

1) Remove band.
2) Remove cable clamp cover.
3) Remove screws securing connector cover.

CAUTION:
Do not allow harness to catch on adjacent parts during installation.

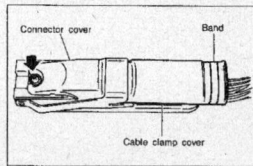
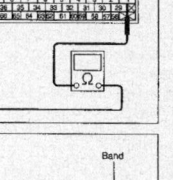
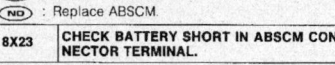

Connector cover   Band

Cable clamp cover

4) Remove connector cover.

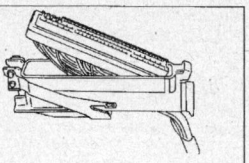

SB4029700091090X

Fig. 19   Code 52: Abnormal Motor And/Or Motor Relay (Part 9 of 12). Less Select Monitor

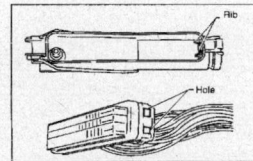

NOTE:
● To install, reverse above removal procedures.
● Align connector cover rib with connector hole before installation.

Rib

Hole

5) Connect all connectors.

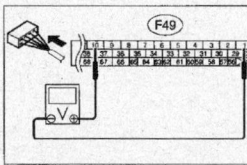

6) Measure voltage between ABSCM connector terminals.

Connector & terminal
(F49) No. 10 (+) — No. 1 (−):

(CHECK) : Is the voltage less than 2 V?
(YES) : Go to step **8X24**.
(NO) : Replace ABSCM.

8X24 | **CHECK BATTERY SHORT IN ABSCM CONNECTOR TERMINAL.**

1) Turn ignition switch to ON.
2) Measure voltage between ABSCM connector terminals.

Connector & terminal
(F49) No. 10 (+) — No. 1 (−):

(CHECK) : Is the voltage less than 2 V?
(YES) : Go to step **8X25**.
(NO) : Replace ABSCM.

8X25 | **CHECK CONDITION OF MOTOR GROUND.**

Tightening torque:
32 ± 10 N·m (3.3 ± 1.0 kg-m, 24 ± 7 ft-lb):

(CHECK) : Is the motor ground terminal tightly clamped?
(YES) : Go to step **8X26**.
(NO) : Tighten the clamp of motor ground terminal.

SB4029700091100X

Fig. 19   Code 52: Abnormal Motor And/Or Motor Relay (Part 10 of 12). Less Select Monitor

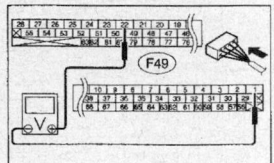

8X26 CHECK ABSCM MOTOR DRIVE TERMINAL.

1) Operate the check sequence.
2) Measure voltage between ABSCM connector terminals.

Connector & terminal
(F49) No. 22 (+) — No. 1 (–):

(CHECK) : *Does the voltage drop from between 10 V and 13 V to less than 1.5 V, and rise to between 10 V and 13 V again when carrying out the check sequence?*

(YES) : Go to step **8X27**.
(NO) : Replace ABSCM.

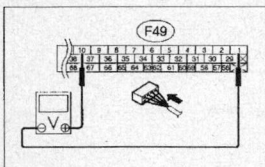

8X27 CHECK MOTOR OPERATION.

1) Operate the check sequence.
2) Measure voltage between ABSCM connector terminals.

Connector & terminal
(F49) No. 10 (+) — No. 1 (–):

(CHECK) : *Does the voltage raise from less than 1.5 V to between 10 V and 13 V, and return to less than 1.5 V again when carrying out the check sequence?*

(YES) : Go to step **8X28**.
(NO) : Replace hydraulic unit.

8X28 CHECK MOTOR OPERATION.

Operate the check sequence.

(CHECK) : *Can motor revolution noise (buzz) be heard when carrying out the check sequence?*

(YES) : Go to step **8X29**.
(NO) : Replace hydraulic unit.

8X29 CHECK POOR CONTACT IN CONNECTORS.

Turn ignition switch to OFF.

(CHECK) : *Is there poor contact in connector between hydraulic unit, relay box and ABSCM?*

(YES) : Repair connector.
(NO) : Go to step **8X30**.

SB4029700091110X

Fig. 19   Code 52: Abnormal Motor And/Or Motor Relay (Part 11 of 12). Less Select Monitor

---

8X30 CHECK ABSCM.

1) Connect all connectors.
2) Erase the memory.
3) Perform inspection mode.
4) Read out the trouble code.

(CHECK) : *Is the same trouble code as in the current diagnosis still being output?*

(YES) : Replace ABSCM.
(NO) : Go to step **8X31**.

8X31 CHECK ANY OTHER TROUBLE CODES APPEARANCE.

(CHECK) : *Are other trouble codes being output?*

(YES) : Proceed with the diagnosis corresponding to the trouble code.
(NO) : A temporary poor contact.

SB4029700091120X

Fig. 19   Code 52: Abnormal Motor And/Or Motor Relay (Part 12 of 12). Less Select Monitor

8Y1 CHECK STOP LIGHTS COME ON.

Depress the brake pedal.

(CHECK) : *Do stop lights come on?*

(YES) : Go to step **8Y2**.
(NO) : Repair stop lights circuit.

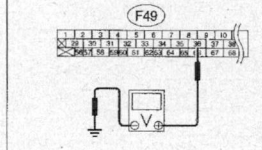

8Y2 CHECK OPEN CIRCUIT IN HARNESS.

1) Turn ignition switch to OFF.
2) Disconnect connector from ABSCM.
3) Depress brake pedal.
4) Measure voltage between ABSCM connector and chassis ground.

Connector & terminal
(F49) No. 36 — Chassis ground:

(CHECK) : *Is the voltage between 10 V and 13 V?*

(YES) : Go to step **8Y3**.
(NO) : Repair harness between stop light switch and ABSCM.

8Y3 CHECK POOR CONTACT IN CONNECTORS.

(CHECK) : *Is there poor contact in connector between stop light switch and ABSCM?*

(YES) : Repair connector.
(NO) : Go to step **8Y4**.

8Y4 CHECK ABSCM.

1) Connect all connectors.
2) Erase the memory.
3) Perform inspection mode.
4) Read out the trouble code.

(CHECK) : *Is the same trouble code as in the current diagnosis still being output?*

(YES) : Replace ABSCM.
(NO) : Go to step **8Y5**.

8Y5 CHECK ANY OTHER TROUBLE CODES APPEARANCE.

(CHECK) : *Are other trouble codes being output?*

(YES) : Proceed with the diagnosis corresponding to the trouble code.
(NO) : A temporary poor contact.

SB4029700092000X

Fig. 20   Code 54: Abnormal Stop light Switch. Less Select Monitor

8Z1	CHECK ALL FOUR WHEELS FOR FREE TURNING.

CHECK : *Have the wheels been turned freely such as when the vehicle is lifted up, or operated on a rolling road?*

YES : The ABS is normal. Erase the trouble code.

NO : Go to step **8Z2**.

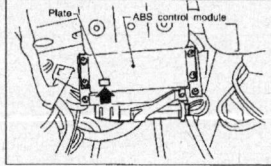

8Z2	CHECK SPECIFICATIONS OF ABSCM.

Check specifications of the plate attached to the ABSCM.

CHECK : *Is an ABSCM for 4WD model installed on a FWD model?*

CAUTION:
Be sure to turn ignition switch to OFF when removing ABSCM.

YES : Replace ABSCM.

NO : Go to step **8Z3**.

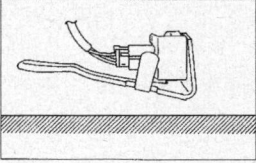

8Z3	CHECK INPUT VOLTAGE OF G SENSOR.

1) Turn ignition switch to OFF.
2) Remove console box.
3) Disconnect G sensor from body. (Do not disconnect connector.)
4) Turn ignition switch to ON.
5) Measure voltage between G sensor connector terminals.

Connector & terminal
(R70) No. 1 (+) — No. 3 (–):

CHECK : *Is the voltage between 4.75 and 5.25 V?*

YES : Go to step **8Z4**.

NO : Repair harness/connector between G sensor and ABSCM.

SB4029700093010X

Fig. 21 Code 56: Abnormal G Sensor Output Voltage (Part 1 of 4). Less Select Monitor

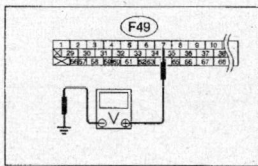

8Z7	CHECK BATTERY SHORT OF HARNESS.

1) Turn ignition switch to ON.
2) Measure voltage between ABSCM connector and chassis ground.

Connector & terminal
(F49) No. 7 (+) — Chassis ground (–):

CHECK : *Is the voltage less than 1 V?*

YES : Go to step **8Z8**.

NO : Repair harness between G sensor and ABSCM.

8Z8	CHECK G SENSOR.

1) Turn ignition switch to OFF.
2) Remove G sensor from vehicle.
3) Connect connector to G sensor.
4) Connect connector to ABSCM.
5) Turn ignition switch to ON.
6) Measure voltage between G sensor connector terminals.

Connector & terminal
(R70) No. 2 (+) — No. 1 (–):

CHECK : *Is the voltage between 2.1 and 2.4 V when G sensor is horizontal?*

YES : Go to step **8Z9**.

NO : Replace G sensor.

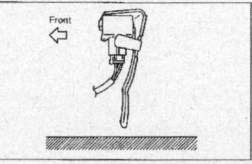

8Z9	CHECK G SENSOR.

Measure voltage between G sensor connector terminals.

Connector & terminal
(R70) No. 2 (+) — No. 1 (–):

CHECK : *Is the voltage between 3.7 and 4.1 V when G sensor is inclined forwards to 90°?*

YES : Go to step **8Z10**.

NO : Replace G sensor.

SB4029700093030X

Fig. 21 Code 56: Abnormal G Sensor Output Voltage (Part 3 of 4). Less Select Monitor

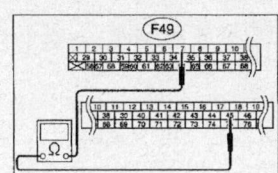

8Z4	CHECK OPEN CIRCUIT IN G SENSOR OUTPUT HARNESS AND GROUND HARNESS.

1) Turn ignition switch to OFF.
2) Disconnect connector from ABSCM.
3) Measure resistance between ABSCM connector terminals.

Connector & terminal
(F49) No. 7 — No. 45:

CHECK : *Is the resistance between 4.3 and 4.9 kΩ?*

YES : Go to step **8Z5**.

NO : Repair harness/connector between G sensor and ABSCM.

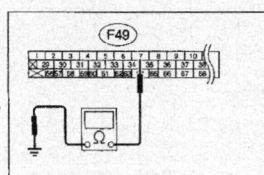

8Z5	CHECK GROUND SHORT IN G SENSOR OUTPUT HARNESS.

1) Disconnect connector from G sensor.
2) Measure resistance between ABSCM connector and chassis ground.

Connector & terminal
(F49) No. 7 — Chassis ground:

CHECK : *Is the resistance more than 1 MΩ?*

YES : Go to step **8Z6**.

NO : Repair harness between G sensor and ABSCM.

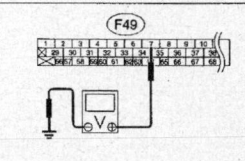

8Z6	CHECK BATTERY SHORT OF HARNESS.

Measure voltage between ABSCM connector and chassis ground.

Connector & terminal
(F49) No. 7 (+) — Chassis ground (–):

CHECK : *Is the voltage less than 1 V?*

YES : Go to step **8Z7**.

NO : Repair harness between G sensor and ABSCM.

SB4029700093020X

Fig. 21 Code 56: Abnormal G Sensor Output Voltage (Part 2 of 4). Less Select Monitor

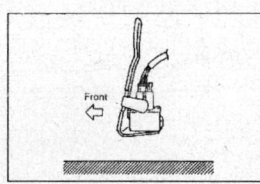

8Z10	CHECK G SENSOR.

Measure voltage between G sensor connector terminals.

Connector & terminal
(R70) No. 2 (+) — No. 1 (–):

CHECK : *Is the voltage between 0.5 and 0.9 V when G sensor is inclined backwards to 90°?*

YES : Go to step **8Z11**.

NO : Replace G sensor.

8Z11	CHECK POOR CONTACT IN CONNECTORS.

CHECK : *Is there poor contact in connector between ABSCM and G sensor?*

YES : Repair connector.

NO : Go to step **8Z12**.

8Z12	CHECK ABSCM.

1) Connect all connectors.
2) Erase the memory.
3) Perform inspection mode.
4) Read out the trouble code.

CHECK : *Is the same trouble code as in the current diagnosis still being output?*

YES : Replace ABSCM.

NO : Go to step **8Z13**.

8Z13	CHECK ANY OTHER TROUBLE CODES APPEARANCE.

CHECK : *Are other trouble codes being output?*

YES : Proceed with the diagnosis corresponding to the trouble code.

NO : A temporary poor contact.

SB4029700093040X

Fig. 21 Code 56: Abnormal G Sensor Output Voltage (Part 4 of 4). Less Select Monitor

SUBARU

1998–99 Impreza

NOTE: On Air Bag Equipped Models, Refer To "Air Bag System Precautions" Located In The Front Of This Manual For System Disarming & Arming Procedures.

NOTE: Electrical Symbol & Wire Color Code Identification Located In The Front Of This Manual May Be Used As An Aid When Using Wiring Circuits Found In This Section.

INDEX

PRECAUTIONS

AIR BAG SYSTEMS

Refer to "Air Bag System Precautions" in the front of this manual for system disarming and arming procedures.

BATTERY GROUND CABLE

Prior to service, disconnect battery ground cable and isolate as required.

DESCRIPTION

The Anti-lock brake system (ABS) electrically controls brake fluid pressure to prevent wheel lock during braking on slippery road surfaces, improving steering stability and shortening the braking distance. If the ABS becomes inoperative, a fail-safe system activates to ensure conventional brake system operation.

The ABS consists of four tone wheels, four speed sensors, electronic control unit, a G sensor and a warning lamp.

The electronic control unit has the capability of on-board diagnosis. The on-board diagnosis system is designed to detect problems after the vehicle has been driven at 6 mph or more for at least 20 seconds. If a problem is found, the ABS warning light will illuminate to inform the driver of the occurrence of a problem. When the warning light is on, the ABS system will be inactive and the normal braking function will work.

Refer to **Fig. 1,** for component location & description

TROUBLESHOOTING

Refer to **Fig. 2,** for troubleshooting procedures.

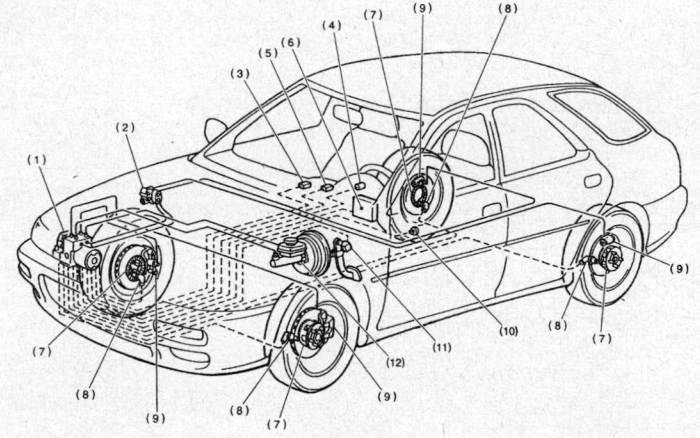

(1) ABS control module and hydraulic control unit (ABSCM&H/U)
(2) Proportioning valve
(3) Diagnosis connector
(4) ABS warning light
(5) Data link connector (for Subaru select monitor)
(6) Transmission control module (only AT vehicle)
(7) Tone wheel
(8) ABS sensor
(9) Wheel cylinder
(10) G sensor
(11) Brake switch
(12) Master cylinder

SB4029800149010X

Fig. 1   ABS component descriptions & locations (Part 1 of 2)

DIAGNOSIS & TESTING

PRELIMINARY INSPECTION

1. Ensure battery voltage is 12 volts or more and specific gravity is above 1.260.
2. Inspect brake fluid level and for brake fluid leakage.
3. Inspect brake drag.
4. Inspect brake pads and rotors.
5. Inspect tires for excessive wear and proper inflation.

ACCESSING DIAGNOSTIC TROUBLE CODES

Less Select Monitor

When on board diagnosis of the ABS control module detects a problem, the information (up to a maximum of three) will be stored in the EEP ROM as a diagnostic trouble code (DTC). When there are more than three, the most recent three will be stored. Stored codes will stay in memory until they are cleared.

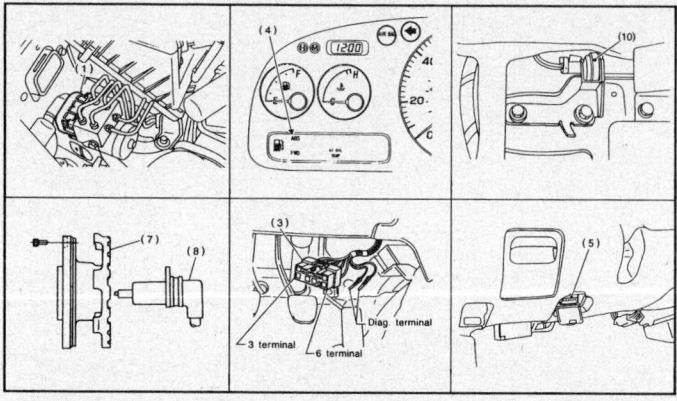

Fig. 1   ABS component descriptions & locations (Part 2 of 2)

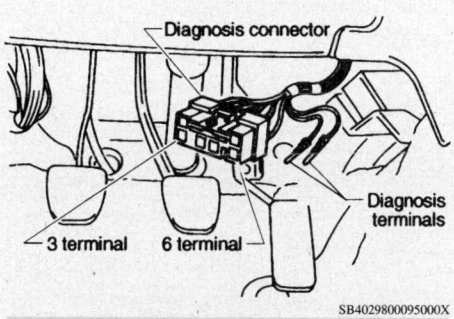

Fig. 3   Diagnostic connector

1. Remove ABS diagnostic connector from side of driver's heater unit, **Fig. 3.**
2. Turn ignition switch to Off position.
3. Connect diagnosis connector terminal No. 6 to terminal No. 3.
4. Turn ignition switch to On position.
5. ABS warning light is set to the diagnostic mode and blinks to identify trouble codes, **Fig. 4.**
6. After start code is displayed (11), trouble codes will be shown in order of last information first. Codes will repeat for a maximum of five minutes.
7. If there are no trouble codes in memory, code 11 will be the only code to appear.

With Select Monitor

Access the ABS system diagnostic trouble codes according to the tool manufacturers instructions.

DIAGNOSTIC TROUBLE CODE INTERPRETATION

Refer to **Fig. 5,** for trouble code interpretation.

WIRING DIAGRAM

Refer to **Fig. 6,** for ABS system wiring diagram.

DIAGNOSTIC TESTS

Less Select Monitor

Refer to **Figs. 7 through 25,** for diagnostic testing procedures.

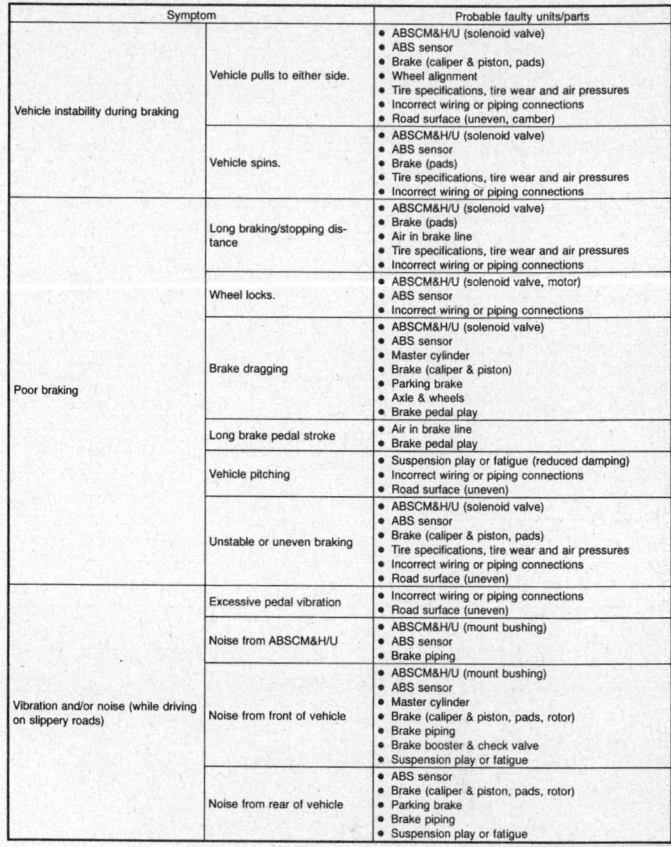

Fig. 2   ABS system troubleshooting

Symptom		Probable faulty units/parts
Vehicle instability during braking	Vehicle pulls to either side.	• ABSCM&H/U (solenoid valve) • ABS sensor • Brake (caliper & piston, pads) • Wheel alignment • Tire specifications, tire wear and air pressures • Incorrect wiring or piping connections • Road surface (uneven, camber)
	Vehicle spins.	• ABSCM&H/U (solenoid valve) • ABS sensor • Brake (pads) • Tire specifications, tire wear and air pressures • Incorrect wiring or piping connections
Poor braking	Long braking/stopping distance	• ABSCM&H/U (solenoid valve) • Brake (pads) • Air in brake line • Tire specifications, tire wear and air pressures • Incorrect wiring or piping connections
	Wheel locks.	• ABSCM&H/U (solenoid valve, motor) • ABS sensor • Incorrect wiring or piping connections
	Brake dragging	• ABSCM&H/U (solenoid valve) • ABS sensor • Master cylinder • Brake (caliper & piston) • Parking brake • Axle & wheels • Brake pedal play
	Long brake pedal stroke	• Air in brake line • Brake pedal play
	Vehicle pitching	• Suspension play or fatigue (reduced damping) • Incorrect wiring or piping connections • Road surface (uneven)
	Unstable or uneven braking	• ABSCM&H/U (solenoid valve) • ABS sensor • Brake (caliper & piston, pads) • Tire specifications, tire wear and air pressures • Incorrect wiring or piping connections • Road surface (uneven)
	Excessive pedal vibration	• Incorrect wiring or piping connections • Road surface (uneven)
Vibration and/or noise (while driving on slippery roads)	Noise from ABSCM&H/U	• ABSCM&H/U (mount bushing) • ABS sensor • Brake piping
	Noise from front of vehicle	• ABSCM&H/U (mount bushing) • ABS sensor • Master cylinder • Brake (caliper & piston, pads, rotor) • Brake piping • Brake booster & check valve • Suspension play or fatigue
	Noise from rear of vehicle	• ABS sensor • Brake (caliper & piston, pads, rotor) • Parking brake • Brake piping • Suspension play or fatigue

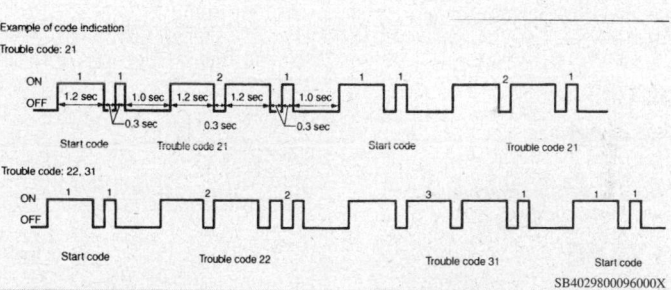

Fig. 4   Diagnostic trouble code blink interpretation

With Select Monitor

Refer to **Figs. 26 through 46,** for diagnostic testing procedures.

CLEARING DIAGNOSTIC TROUBLE CODES

Less Select Monitor

1. After calling up a trouble code, disconnect diagnosis connector terminal No. 6 from connector,
2. Connect and disconnect terminal three times within a 12 second span leaving terminal disconnected at least .2 seconds each time.
3. Ensure all codes are cleared and that code 11 (start code) is all that remains in memory.

With Select Monitor

Connect select monitor to data link connector and follow on screen prompts to erase diagnostic trouble codes.

SYSTEM SERVICE

Brake System Bleed

1. Start with wheels connecting to secondary chamber of master cylinder.
2. Inspect for leaks at joints and connection in brake system, repair as necessary.
3. Fit one end of a suitable vinyl hose over brake bleeder and place other

SUBARU

Trouble code	Contents of diagnosis	
11	Start code ● Trouble code is shown after start code. ● Only start code is shown in normal condition.	
21	Abnormal ABS sensor (Open circuit or input voltage too high)	Front right ABS sensor
23		Front left ABS sensor
25		Rear right ABS sensor
27		Rear left ABS sensor
22	Abnormal ABS sensor (Abnormal ABS sensor signal)	Front right ABS sensor
24		Front left ABS sensor
26		Rear right ABS sensor
28		Rear left ABS sensor
29		Any one of four
31	Abnormal solenoid valve circuit(s) in ABS control module and hydraulic unit	Front right inlet valve
32		Front right outlet valve
33		Front left inlet valve
34		Front left outlet valve
35		Rear right inlet valve
36		Rear right outlet valve
37		Rear left inlet valve
38		Rear left outlet valve
41	Abnormal ABS control module	
42	Source voltage is abnormal.	
44	A combination of AT control abnormal	
51	Abnormal valve relay	
52	Abnormal motor and/or motor relay	
54	Abnormal stop light switch	
56	Abnormal G sensor output voltage	

SB4029800147000X

Fig. 5   Diagnostic trouble code interpretation, less select monitor

end into a container filled with brake fluid.
4. Slowly depress brake pedal and keep depressed.
5. Open bleeder crew and release fluid for one to two seconds.
6. Close bleeder screw and release pedal.
7. Repeat steps until all air is discharged from system.

Component Replacement

ABS CONTROL MODULE & HYDRAULIC CONTROL UNIT, 5.3I TYPE

1. Remove air intake duct from engine to ease removal of control module and

hydraulic unit.
2. Use an air gun to dry the area around control unit.
3. Pull lock of the ABSCM&HU connector to remove it, then disconnect connector.
4. Unlock cable clip.
5. Disconnect brake pipes from ABSCM&HU, use care to ensure brake fluid does not come into contact with painted surfaces.

6. Remove ABSCM&HU from vehicle.
7. ABSCM&HU cannot be disassemble, do not attempt to loosen nuts and bolts.
8. Reverse procedure to install.

G SENSOR

1. Turn ignition switch to Off position.
2. Remove console cover.
3. Disconnect connector from G sensor, then remove sensor.
4. Reverse procedure to install.

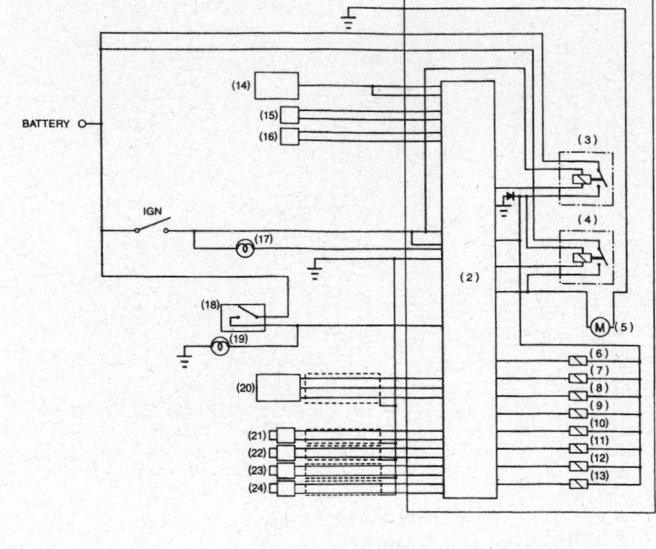

(1) ABS control module and hydraulic control unit (ABSCM&H/U)
(2) ABS control module area
(3) Valve relay
(4) Motor relay
(5) Motor
(6) Front left inlet solenoid valve
(7) Front left outlet solenoid valve
(8) Front right inlet solenoid valve
(9) Front right outlet solenoid valve
(10) Rear left inlet solenoid valve
(11) Rear left outlet solenoid valve
(12) Rear right inlet solenoid valve
(13) Rear right outlet solenoid valve
(14) Transmission control module (only AT model)
(15) Diagnosis connector
(16) Data link connector
(17) ABS warning light
(18) Stop light switch
(19) Stop light
(20) G sensor
(21) Front left ABS sensor
(22) Front right ABS sensor
(23) Rear left ABS sensor
(24) Rear right ABS sensor

SB4029800148000X

Fig. 6   ABS system wiring diagram

DIAGNOSTIC CHART INDEX

Test	Description	Page No.	Fig. No.
LESS SELECT MONITOR			
Test A	ABS Warning Light Does Not Come On (1998)	41-218	7
Test A	ABS Warning Light Does Not Come On (1999)	41-219	8
Test B	ABS Warning Light Does Not Go Off (1998)	41-220	9
Test B	ABS Warning Light Does Not Go Off (1999)	41-221	10
Test C	Trouble Code Does Not Appear	41-222	11
Code 21	Abnormal ABS Sensor, Open Circuit Or Input Voltage Too High	41-222	12
Code 22	Abnormal ABS Sensor, Abnormal ABS Sensor Signal	41-224	13
Code 23	Abnormal ABS Sensor, Open Circuit Or Input Voltage Too High	41-222	12
Code 24	Abnormal ABS Sensor, Abnormal ABS Sensor Signal	41-224	13
Code 25	Abnormal ABS Sensor, Open Circuit Or Input Voltage Too High	41-222	12
Code 26	Abnormal ABS Sensor, Abnormal ABS Sensor Signal	41-224	13

Continued

DIAGNOSTIC CHART INDEX—Continued

Test	Description	Page No.	Fig. No.
LESS SELECT MONITOR			
Code 27	Abnormal ABS Sensor, Open Circuit Or Input Voltage Too High	41-222	12
Code 28	Abnormal ABS Sensor, Abnormal ABS Sensor Signal	41-224	13
Code 29	ABS Sensor Signal, Any One Of Four	41-226	14
Code 31	Abnormal Inlet Solenoid Valve Circuits In ABSCM & H/U	41-227	15
Code 32	Abnormal Outlet Solenoid Valve Circuits In ABSCM & H/U	41-228	16
Code 33	Abnormal Inlet Solenoid Valve Circuits In ABSCM & H/U	41-227	15
Code 34	Abnormal Outlet Solenoid Valve Circuits In ABSCM & H/U	41-228	16
Code 35	Abnormal Inlet Solenoid Valve Circuits In ABSCM & H/U	41-227	15
Code 36	Abnormal Outlet Solenoid Valve Circuits In ABSCM & H/U	41-228	16
Code 37	Abnormal Inlet Solenoid Valve Circuits In ABSCM & H/U	41-227	15
Code 38	Abnormal Outlet Solenoid Valve Circuits In ABSCM & H/U	41-228	16
Code 41	Abnormal ABS Control Module	41-228	17
Code 42	Source Voltage Is Abnormal	41-229	18
Code 44	A Combination Of AT Control Abnormal (1998)	41-230	19
Code 44	A Combination Of AT Control Abnormal (1999)	41-231	20
Code 51	Abnormal Valve Relay	41-232	21
Code 52	Abnormal Motor And/Or Motor Relay	41-232	22
Code 54	Abnormal Stop Light Switch	41-233	23
Code 56	Abnormal G Sensor Output Voltage (1998)	41-233	24
Code 56	Abnormal G Sensor Output Voltage (1999)	41-235	25
WITH SELECT MONITOR			
Test D	No Trouble Code Appears On Select Monitor, ABS Warning Light Remains On	41-236	26
Code 21	Abnormal ABS Sensor, Open Or Short Circuit In ABS Sensor	41-237	27
Code 22	Abnormal ABS Sensor, ABS Sensor Abnormal Signal	41-239	28
Code 23	Abnormal ABS Sensor, Open Or Short Circuit In ABS Sensor	41-237	27
Code 24	Abnormal ABS Sensor, ABS Sensor Abnormal Signal	41-239	28
Code 25	Abnormal ABS Sensor, Open Or Short Circuit In ABS Sensor	41-237	27
Code 26	Abnormal ABS Sensor, ABS Sensor Abnormal Signal	41-239	28
Code 27	Abnormal ABS Sensor, Open Or Short Circuit In ABS Sensor	41-237	27
Code 28	Abnormal ABS Sensor, ABS Sensor Abnormal Signal	41-239	28
Code 29	Abnormal ABS Signal On Any One Of Four	41-240	29
Code 31	Inlet Solenoid Valve Malfunction	41-241	30
Code 32	Outlet Solenoid Valve Malfunction	41-242	31
Code 33	Inlet Solenoid Valve Malfunction	41-241	30
Code 34	Outlet Solenoid Valve Malfunction	41-242	31
Code 35	Inlet Solenoid Valve Malfunction	41-241	30
Code 36	Outlet Solenoid Valve Malfunction	41-242	31
Code 37	Inlet Solenoid Valve Malfunction	41-241	30
Code 38	Outlet Solenoid Valve Malfunction	41-242	31
Code 41	ABS Control & HCU Malfunction	41-242	32
Code 42	Power Supply Voltage Too Low	41-243	33
	Power Supply Voltage Too High	41-244	34
Code 44	ABS AT Control, Non Controlled	41-245	35
	ABS AT Control, Controlled	41-246	36
Code 51	Valve Relay Malfunction	41-246	37
	Valve Relay On Failure	41-247	38
Code 52	Open Circuit In Motor Relay Circuit	41-247	39
	Motor Relay On Failure	41-247	40
	Motor Malfunction	41-248	41
Code 54	Stop Light Switch Signal Circuit Malfunction	41-249	42
Code 56	Open Or Short Circuit In G Sensor Circuit	41-249	43
	Battery Short In G Sensor Circuit	41-251	44
	Abnormal G Sensor High Output	41-251	45
	Detection Of G sensor Stick	41-253	46

7A1 : CHECK IF OTHER WARNING LIGHTS TURN ON.

Turn ignition switch to ON (engine OFF).

- (CHECK) : *Do other warning lights turn on?*
- (YES) : Go to step **7A2**.
- (NO) : Repair combination meter.

7A2 : CHECK ABS WARNING LIGHT BULB.

1) Turn ignition switch to OFF.
2) Remove combination meter.
3) Remove ABS warning light bulb from combination meter.

- (CHECK) : *Is ABS warning light bulb OK?*
- (YES) : Go to step **7A3**.
- (NO) : Replace ABS warning light bulb.

7A3 : CHECK BATTERY SHORT OF ABS WARNING LIGHT HARNESS.

1) Disconnect connector (B100) from connector (F2).
2) Measure voltage between connector (B100) and chassis ground.

Connector & terminal
(B100) No. 8 (+) — Chassis ground (–):

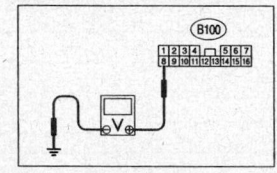

- (CHECK) : *Is the voltage less than 3 V?*
- (YES) : Go to step **7A4**.
- (NO) : Repair warning light harness.

7A4 : CHECK BATTERY SHORT OF ABS WARNING LIGHT HARNESS.

1) Turn ignition switch to ON.
2) Measure voltage between connector (B100) and chassis ground.

Connector & terminal
(B100) No. 8 (+) — Chassis ground (–):

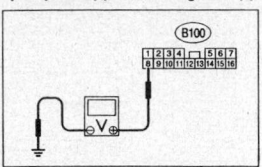

- (CHECK) : *Is voltage less than 3 V?*
- (YES) : Go to step **7A5**.
- (NO) : Repair warning light harness.

7A5 : CHECK WIRING HARNESS.

1) Turn ignition switch to OFF.
2) Install ABS warning light bulb from combination meter.
3) Install combination meter.
4) Turn ignition switch to ON.
5) Measure voltage between connector (B100) and chassis ground.

Connector & terminal
(B100) No. 8 (+) — Chassis ground (–):

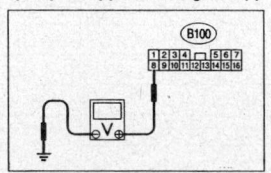

- (CHECK) : *Is voltage between 10 V and 15 V?*
- (YES) : Go to step **7A6**.
- (NO) : Repair wiring harness.

SB4029800150010X

Fig. 7   Test A: ABS Warning Light Does Not Come On (Part 1 of 3). 1998 Less Select monitor

7A6 : CHECK BATTERY SHORT OF ABS WARNING LIGHT HARNESS.

1) Turn ignition switch to OFF.
2) Measure voltage between connector (F2) and chassis ground.

Connector & terminal
(F2) No. 8 (+) — Chassis ground (–):

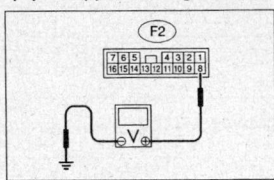

- (CHECK) : *Is the voltage less than 3 V?*
- (YES) : Go to step **7A7**.
- (NO) : Repair wiring harness.

7A7 : CHECK BATTERY SHORT OF ABS WARNING LIGHT HARNESS.

1) Turn ignition switch to ON.
2) Measure voltage between connector (F2) and chassis ground.

Connector & terminal
(F2) No. 8 (+) — Chassis ground (–):

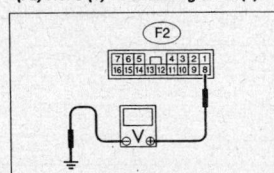

- (CHECK) : *Is voltage less than 3 V?*
- (YES) : Go to step **7A8**.
- (NO) : Repair wiring harness.

7A8 : CHECK GROUND CIRCUIT OF ABSCM&H/U.

Measure resistance between ABSCM&H/U and chassis ground.

Connector & terminal
(F49) No. 23 — GND:

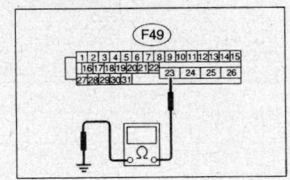

- (CHECK) : *Is the resistance less than 0.5 Ω?*
- (YES) : Go to step **7A9**.
- (NO) : Repair ABSCM&H/U ground harness.

7A9 : CHECK WIRING HARNESS.

Measure resistance between connector (F2) and chassis ground.

Connector & terminal
(F2) No. 8 — Chassis ground:

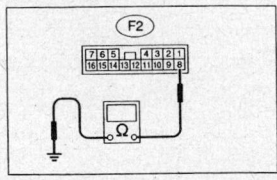

- (CHECK) : *Is the resistance less than 0.5 Ω?*
- (YES) : Go to step **7A10**.
- (NO) : Repair harness/connector.

SB4029800150020X

Fig. 7   Test A: ABS Warning Light Does Not Come On (Part 2 of 3). 1998 Less Select monitor

7A10 : CHECK POOR CONTACT IN CONNECTORS.

Turn ignition switch to OFF.

CHECK : **Is there poor contact in connectors between combination meter and ABSCM&H/U?**

YES : Repair connector.

NO : Replace ABSCM&H/U.

SB4029800150030X

Fig. 7 Test A: ABS Warning Light Does Not Come On (Part 3 of 3). 1998 Less Select monitor

---

7A6 : CHECK BATTERY SHORT OF ABS WARNING LIGHT HARNESS.

1) Turn ignition switch to OFF.
2) Measure voltage between connector (F2) and chassis ground.

Connector & terminal
(F2) No. 8 (+) — Chassis ground (–):

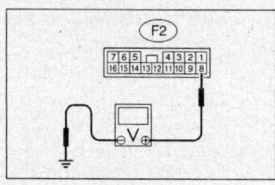

CHECK : **Is the voltage less than 3 V?**
YES : Go to step 7A7.
NO : Repair wiring harness.

7A7 : CHECK BATTERY SHORT OF ABS WARNING LIGHT HARNESS.

1) Turn ignition switch to ON.
2) Measure voltage between connector (F2) and chassis ground.

Connector & terminal
(F2) No. 8 (+) — Chassis ground (–):

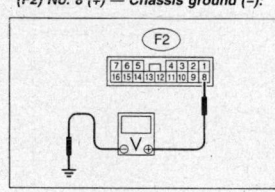

CHECK : **Is voltage less than 3 V?**
YES : Go to step 7A8.
NO : Repair wiring harness.

7A8 : CHECK GROUND CIRCUIT OF ABSCM&H/U.

Measure resistance between ABSCM&H/U and chassis ground.

Connector & terminal
(F49) No. 23 — GND:

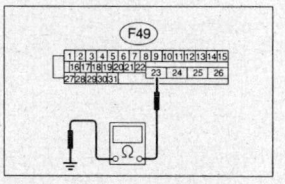

CHECK : **Is the resistance less than 0.5 Ω?**
YES : Go to step 7A9.
NO : Repair ABSCM&H/U ground harness.

7A9 : CHECK WIRING HARNESS.

Measure resistance between connector (F2) and chassis ground.

Connector & terminal
(F2) No. 8 — Chassis ground:

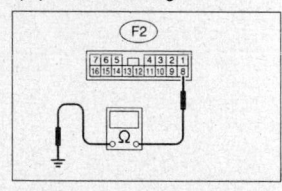

CHECK : **Is the resistance less than 0.5 Ω?**
YES : Go to step 7A10.
NO : Repair harness/connector.

SB4029800186020X

Fig. 8 Test A: ABS Warning Light Does Not Come On (Part 2 of 3). 1999 Less Select Monitor

---

7A1 : CHECK IF OTHER WARNING LIGHTS TURN ON.

Turn ignition switch to ON (engine OFF).

CHECK : **Do other warning lights turn on?**
YES : Go to step 7A2.
NO : Repair combination meter.

7A2 : CHECK ABS WARNING LIGHT BULB.

1) Turn ignition switch to OFF.
2) Remove combination meter.
3) Remove ABS warning light bulb from combination meter.

CHECK : **Is ABS warning light bulb OK?**
YES : Go to step 7A3.
NO : Replace ABS warning light bulb.

7A3 : CHECK BATTERY SHORT OF ABS WARNING LIGHT HARNESS.

1) Disconnect connector (B100) from connector (F2).
2) Measure voltage between connector (B100) and chassis ground.

Connector & terminal
(B100) No. 8 (+) — Chassis ground (–):

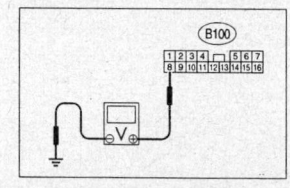

CHECK : **Is the voltage less than 3 V?**
YES : Go to step 7A4.
NO : Repair warning light harness.

7A4 : CHECK BATTERY SHORT OF ABS WARNING LIGHT HARNESS.

1) Turn ignition switch to ON.
2) Measure voltage between connector (B100) and chassis ground.

Connector & terminal
(B100) No. 8 (+) — Chassis ground (–):

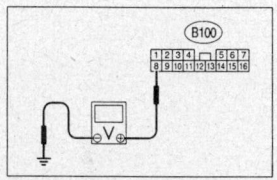

CHECK : **Is voltage less than 3 V?**
YES : Go to step 7A5.
NO : Repair warning light harness.

7A5 : CHECK WIRING HARNESS.

1) Turn ignition switch to OFF.
2) Install ABS warning light bulb from combination meter.
3) Install combination meter.
4) Turn ignition switch to ON.
5) Measure voltage between connector (B100) and chassis ground.

Connector & terminal
(B100) No. 8 (+) — Chassis ground (–):

CHECK : **Is voltage between 10 V and 15 V?**
YES : Go to step 7A6.
NO : Repair wiring harness.

SB4029800186010X

Fig. 8 Test A: ABS Warning Light Does Not Come On (Part 1 of 3). 1999 Less Select Monitor

---

7A10 : CHECK POOR CONTACT IN CONNECTORS.

Turn ignition switch to OFF.

CHECK : **Is there poor contact in connectors between combination meter and ABSCM&H/U?**

YES : Repair connector.

NO : Replace ABSCM&H/U.

SB4029800186030X

Fig. 8 Test A: ABS Warning Light Does Not Come On (Part 3 of 3). 1999 Less Select Monitor

7B1 : CHECK INSTALLATION OF ABSCM&H/U CONNECTOR.

Turn ignition switch to OFF.

CHECK : Is ABSCM&H/U connector inserted into ABSCM until the clamp locks onto it?

YES : Go to step 7B2.

NO : Insert ABSCM&H/U connector into ABSCM&H/U until the clamp locks onto it.

7B2 : CHECK DIAGNOSIS TERMINAL.

Measure resistance between diagnosis terminals (B81) and chassis ground.

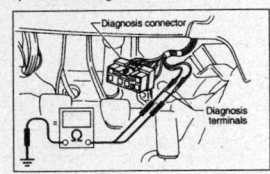

Terminals
Diagnosis terminal (A) — Chassis ground:
Diagnosis terminal (B) — Chassis ground:

CHECK : Is the resistance less than 0.5 Ω?

YES : Go to step 7B3.

NO : Repair diagnosis terminal harness.

7B3 : CHECK DIAGNOSIS LINE.

1) Turn ignition switch to OFF.
2) Connect diagnosis terminal (B81) to diagnosis connector (B82) No. 6.
3) Disconnect connector from ABSCM&H/U.
4) Measure resistance between ABSCM&H/U connector and chassis ground.

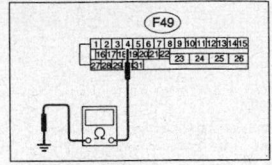

Connector & terminal
(F49) No. 4 — Chassis ground:

CHECK : Is the resistance less than 0.5 Ω?

YES : Go to step 7B4.

NO : Repair harness connector between ABSCM&H/U and diagnosis connector.

7B4 : CHECK GENERATOR.

1) Start the engine.
2) Idle the engine.
3) Measure voltage between generator and chassis ground.

Terminal
Generator B terminal (+) — Chassis ground (−):

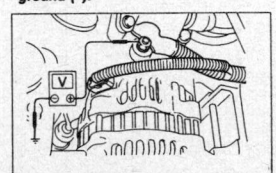

CHECK : Is the voltage between 10 and 15 V?

YES : Go to step 7B5.

NO : Repair generator.

SB4029800151010X

Fig. 9 Test B: ABS Warning Light Does Not Go Off (Part 1 of 3). 1998 Less Select Monitor

7B5 : CHECK BATTERY TERMINAL.

Turn ignition switch to OFF.

CHECK : Is there poor contact at battery terminal?

YES : Repair battery terminal.

NO : Go to step 7B6.

7B6 : CHECK POWER SUPPLY OF ABSCM.

1) Disconnect connector from ABSCM&H/U.
2) Start engine.
3) Idle the engine.
4) Measure voltage between ABSCM&H/U connector and chassis ground.

Connector & terminal
(F49) No. 1 (+) — Chassis ground (−):

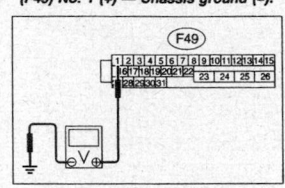

CHECK : Is the voltage between 10 and 15 V?

YES : Go to step 7B7.

NO : Repair ABSCM&H/U power supply circuit.

7B7 : CHECK WIRING HARNESS.

1) Disconnect connector (F2) from connector (B100).
2) Turn ignition switch to ON.

CHECK : Does the ABS warning light remain off?

YES : Go to step 7B8.

NO : Repair front wiring harness.

7B8 : CHECK PROJECTION AT ABSCM&H/U.

1) Turn ignition switch to OFF.
2) Check for broken projection at the ABSCM&H/U terminal.

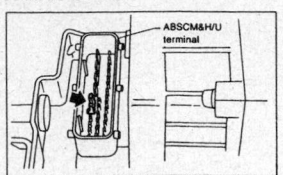

CHECK : Are the projection broken?

YES : Go to step 7B9.

NO : Replace ABSCM&H/U.

7B9 : CHECK ABSCM&H/U.

Measure resistance between ABSCM&H/U terminals.

Terminal
No. 21 — No. 23:

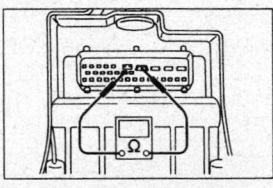

CHECK : Is the resistance more than 1 MΩ?

YES : Go to step 7B10.

NO : Replace ABSCM&H/U.

SB4029800151020X

Fig. 9 Test B: ABS Warning Light Does Not Go Off (Part 2 of 3). 1998 Less Select Monitor

7B10 : CHECK WIRING HARNESS.

Measure resistance between connector (F2) and chassis ground.

Connector & terminal
(F2) No. 8 — Chassis ground:

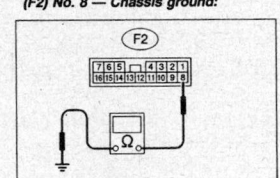

CHECK : Is the resistance less than 0.5 Ω?

YES : Go to step 7B11.

NO : Repair harness.

7B11 : CHECK WIRING HARNESS.

1) Connect connector to ABSCM&H/U.
2) Measure resistance between connector (F2) and chassis ground.

Connector & terminal
(F2) No. 8 — Chassis ground:

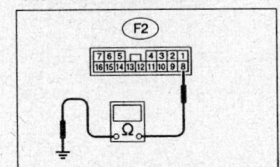

CHECK : Is the resistance more than 1 MΩ?

YES : Go to step 7B12.

NO : Repair harness.

7B12 : CHECK POOR CONTACT IN ABSCM&H/U CONNECTOR.

CHECK : Is there poor contact in ABSCM&H/U connector?

YES : Repair connector.

NO : Replace ABSCM&H/U.

SB4029800151030X

Fig. 9 Test B: ABS Warning Light Does Not Go Off (Part 3 of 3). 1998 Less Select Monitor

7B1 : CHECK INSTALLATION OF ABSCM&H/U CONNECTOR.

Turn ignition switch to OFF.

CHECK : **Is ABSCM&H/U connector inserted into ABSCM until the clamp locks onto it?**

YES : Go to step **7B2**.

NO : Insert ABSCM&H/U connector into ABSCM&H/U until the clamp locks onto it.

7B2 : CHECK DIAGNOSIS TERMINAL.

Measure resistance between diagnosis terminals (B81) and chassis ground.

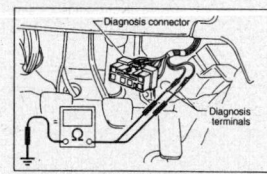

Terminals
Diagnosis terminal (A) — Chassis ground:
Diagnosis terminal (B) — Chassis ground:

CHECK : **Is the resistance less than 0.5 Ω?**

YES : Go to step **7B3**.

NO : Repair diagnosis terminal harness.

7B3 : CHECK DIAGNOSIS LINE.

1) Turn ignition switch to OFF.
2) Connect diagnosis terminal (B81) to diagnosis connector (B82) No. 6.
3) Disconnect connector from ABSCM.
4) Measure resistance between ABSCM&H/U connector and chassis ground.

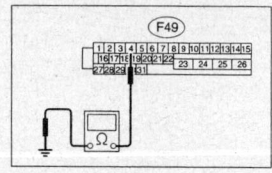

Connector & terminal
(F49) No. 4 — Chassis ground:

CHECK : **Is the resistance less than 0.5 Ω?**

YES : Go to step **7B4**.

NO : Repair harness connector between ABSCM&H/U and diagnosis connector.

7B4 : CHECK GENERATOR.

1) Start the engine.
2) Idle the engine.
3) Measure voltage between generator and chassis ground.

Terminal
Generator B terminal (+) — Chassis ground (–):

CHECK : **Is the voltage between 10 and 15 V?**

YES : Go to step **7B5**.

NO : Repair generator.

SB4029800187010X

Fig. 10   Test B: ABS Warning Light Does Not Go Off (Part 1 of 3). 1999 Less Select Monitor

---

7B5 : CHECK BATTERY TERMINAL.

Turn ignition switch to OFF.

CHECK : **Is there poor contact at battery terminal?**

YES : Repair battery terminal.

NO : Go to step **7B6**.

7B6 : CHECK POWER SUPPLY OF ABSCM.

1) Disconnect connector from ABSCM&H/U.
2) Start engine.
3) Idle the engine.
4) Measure voltage between ABSCM&H/U connector and chassis ground.

Connector & terminal
(F49) No. 1 (+) — Chassis ground (–):

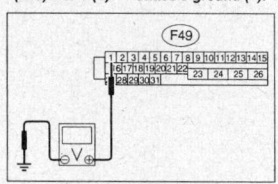

CHECK : **Is the voltage between 10 and 15 V?**

YES : Go to step **7B7**.

NO : Repair ABSCM&H/U power supply circuit.

7B7 : CHECK WIRING HARNESS.

1) Disconnect connector (F2) from connector (B100).
2) Turn ignition switch to ON.

CHECK : **Does the ABS warning light remain off?**

YES : Go to step **7B8**.

NO : Repair front wiring harness.

SB4029800187020X

Fig. 10   Test B: ABS Warning Light Does Not Go Off (Part 2 of 3). 1999 Less Select Monitor

---

7B8 : CHECK PROJECTION AT ABSCM&H/U.

1) Turn ignition switch to OFF.
2) Check for broken projection at the ABSCM&H/U terminal.

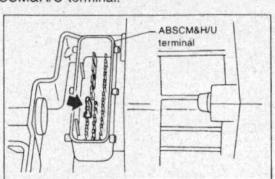

CHECK : **Are the projection broken?**

YES : Go to step **7B9**.

NO : Replace ABSCM&H/U.

7B9 : CHECK ABSCM&H/U.

Measure resistance between ABSCM&H/U terminals.

Terminal
No. 21 — No. 23:

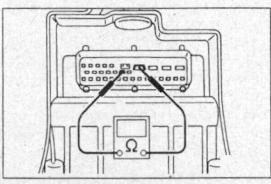

CHECK : **Is the resistance more than 1 MΩ?**

YES : Go to step **7B10**.

NO : Replace ABSCM&H/U.

7B10 : CHECK WIRING HARNESS.

Measure resistance between connector (F2) and chassis ground.

Connector & terminal
(F2) No. 8 — Chassis ground:

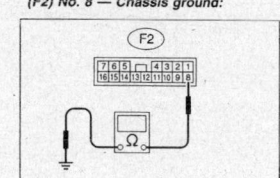

CHECK : **Is the resistance less than 0.5 Ω?**

YES : Go to step **7B11**.

NO : Repair harness.

7B11 : CHECK WIRING HARNESS.

1) Connect connector to ABSCM&H/U.
2) Measure resistance between connector (F2) and chassis ground.

Connector & terminal
(F2) No. 8 — Chassis ground:

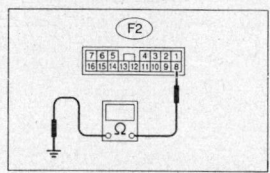

CHECK : **Is the resistance more than 1 MΩ?**

YES : Go to step **7B12**.

NO : Repair harness.

7B12 : CHECK POOR CONTACT IN ABSCM&H/U CONNECTOR.

CHECK : **Is there poor contact in ABSCM&H/U connector?**

YES : Repair connector.

NO : Replace ABSCM&H/U.

SB4029800187030X

Fig. 10   Test B: ABS Warning Light Does Not Go Off (Part 3 of 3). 1999 Less Select Monitor

7C1 : CHECK DIAGNOSIS TERMINAL.

Measure resistance between diagnosis terminals (B81) and chassis ground.

Terminals
Diagnosis terminal (A) — Chassis ground:
Diagnosis terminal (B) — Chassis ground:

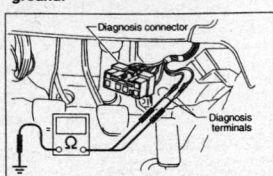

CHECK : *Is the resistance less than 0.5 Ω?*
YES : Go to step **7C2**.
NO : Repair diagnosis terminal harness.

7C2 : CHECK DIAGNOSIS LINE.

1) Turn ignition switch to OFF.
2) Connect diagnosis terminal (B81) to diagnosis connector (B82) No. 6.
3) Disconnect connector from ABSCM&H/U.
4) Measure resistance between ABSCM&H/U connector and chassis ground.

Connector & terminal
(F49) No. 4 — Chassis ground:

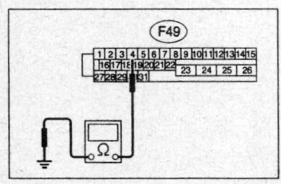

CHECK : *Is the resistance less than 0.5 Ω?*
YES : Go to step **7C3**.
NO : Repair harness connector between ABSCM&H/U and diagnosis connector.

SB4029800152000X

Fig. 11   Test C: Trouble Code Does Not Appear. 1998 Less Select Monitor

7C3 : CHECK POOR CONTACT IN ABSCM&H/U CONNECTOR.

CHECK : *Is there poor contact in ABSCM&H/U connector?*

YES : Repair connector.
NO : Replace ABSCM&H/U.

8E1 : CHECK ABS SENSOR.

1) Turn ignition switch to OFF.
2) Disconnect connector from ABS sensor.
3) Measure resistance of ABS sensor connector terminals.

Terminal
Front RH No. 1 — No. 2:
Front LH No. 1 — No. 2:
Rear RH No. 1 — No. 2:
Rear LH No. 1 — No. 2:

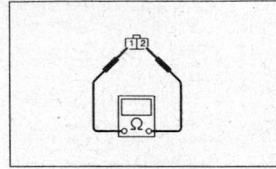

CHECK : *Is the resistance between 0.8 and 1.2 kΩ?*
YES : Go to step **8E2**.
NO : Replace ABS sensor.

8E2 : CHECK BATTERY SHORT OF ABS SENSOR.

1) Disconnect connector from ABSCM&H/U.
2) Measure voltage between ABS sensor and chassis ground.

Terminal
Front RH No. 1 (+) — Chassis ground (–):
Front LH No. 1 (+) — Chassis ground (–):
Rear RH No. 1 (+) — Chassis ground (–):
Rear LH No. 1 (+) — Chassis ground (–):

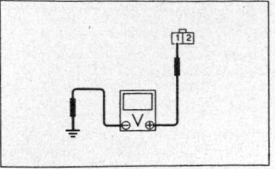

CHECK : *Is the voltage less than 1 V?*
YES : Go to step **8E3**.
NO : Replace ABS sensor.

8E3 : CHECK BATTERY SHORT OF ABS SENSOR.

1) Turn ignition switch to ON.
2) Measure voltage between ABS sensor and chassis ground.

Terminal
Front RH No. 1 (+) — Chassis ground (–):
Front LH No. 1 (+) — Chassis ground (–):
Rear RH No. 1 (+) — Chassis ground (–):
Rear LH No. 1 (+) — Chassis ground (–):

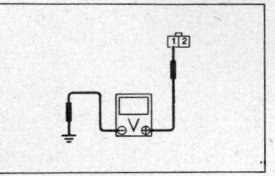

CHECK : *Is the voltage less than 1 V?*
YES : Go to step **8E4**.
NO : Replace ABS sensor.

SB4029800153010X

Fig. 12   Codes 21, 23, 25 & 27: Abnormal ABS Sensor, Open Circuit Or Input Voltage Too High (Part 1 of 5). Less Select Monitor

8E4 : CHECK HARNESS/CONNECTOR BETWEEN ABSCM&H/U AND ABS SENSOR.

1) Turn ignition switch to OFF.
2) Connect connector to ABS sensor.
3) Measure resistance between ABSCM&H/U connector terminals.

Connector & terminal
Trouble code 21 / (F49) No. 11 — No. 12:
Trouble code 23 / (F49) No. 9 — No. 10:
Trouble code 25 / (F49) No. 14 — No. 15:
Trouble code 27 / (F49) No. 7 — No. 8:

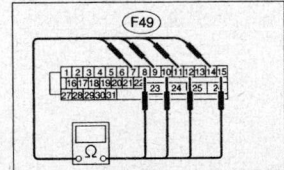

CHECK : *Is the resistance between 0.8 and 1.2 kΩ?*
YES : Go to step **8E5**.
NO : Repair harness/connector between ABSCM&H/U and ABS sensor.

8E5 : CHECK BATTERY SHORT OF HARNESS.

Measure voltage between ABSCM&H/U connector and chassis ground.

Connector & terminal
Trouble code 21 / (F49) No. 11 (+) — Chassis ground (–):
Trouble code 23 / (F49) No. 9 (+) — Chassis ground (–):
Trouble code 25 / (F49) No. 14 (+) — Chassis ground (–):
Trouble code 27 / (F49) No. 7 (+) — Chassis ground (–):

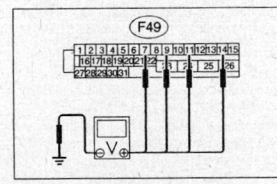

CHECK : *Is the voltage less than 1 V?*
YES : Go to step **8E6**.
NO : Repair harness between ABSCM&H/U and ABS sensor.

SB4029800153020X

Fig. 12   Codes 21, 23, 25 & 27: Abnormal ABS Sensor, Open Circuit Or Input Voltage Too High (Part 2 of 5). Less Select Monitor

8E6 : CHECK BATTERY SHORT OF HARNESS.

1) Turn ignition switch to ON.
2) Measure voltage between ABSCM&H/U connector and chassis ground.

Connector & terminal
  Trouble code 21 / (F49) No. 11 (+) — Chassis ground (–):
  Trouble code 23 / (F49) No. 9 (+) — Chassis ground (–):
  Trouble code 25 / (F49) No. 14 (+) — Chassis ground (–):
  Trouble code 27 / (F49) No. 7 (+) — Chassis ground (–):

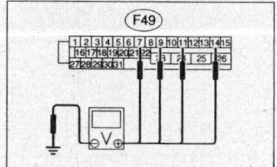

CHECK : **Is the voltage less than 1 V?**
YES : Go to step **8E7**.
NO : Repair harness between ABSCM&H/U and ABS sensor.

8E7 : CHECK INSTALLATION OF ABS SENSOR.

Tightening torque:
  32±10 N·m (3.3±1.0 kg-m, 24±7 ft-lb)

CHECK : **Are the ABS sensor installation bolts tightened securely?**
YES : Go to step **8E8**.
NO : Tighten ABS sensor installation bolts securely.

8E8 : CHECK INSTALLATION OF TONE WHEEL.

Tightening torque:
  13±3 N·m (1.3±0.3 kg-m, 9±2.2 ft-lb)

CHECK : **Are the tone wheel installation bolts tightened securely?**
YES : Go to step **8E9**.
NO : Tighten tone wheel installation bolts securely.

8E9 : CHECK ABS SENSOR GAP.

Measure tone wheel-to-pole piece gap over entire perimeter of the wheel.

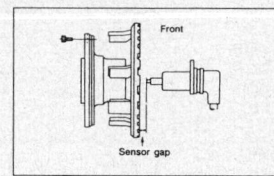

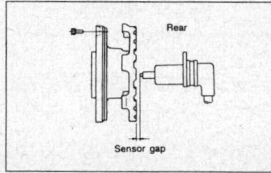

Specifications	Front wheel	Rear wheel
	0.9 — 1.4 mm (0.035 — 0.055 in)	0.7 — 1.2 mm (0.028 — 0.047 in)

CHECK : **Is the gap within the specifications?**
YES : Go to step **8E10**.
NO : Adjust the gap.

NOTE:
Adjust the gap using spacers (Part No. 26755AA000). If spacers cannot correct the gap, replace worn sensor or worn tone wheel.

SB4029800153030X

Fig. 12 Codes 21, 23, 25 & 27: Abnormal ABS Sensor, Open Circuit Or Input Voltage Too High (Part 3 of 5). Less Select Monitor

8E10 : CHECK HUB RUNOUT.

Measure hub runout.

CHECK : **Is the runout less than 0.05 mm (0.0020 in)?**
YES : Go to step **8E11**.
NO : Repair hub.

8E11 : CHECK GROUND SHORT OF ABS SENSOR.

1) Turn ignition switch to ON.
2) Measure resistance between ABS sensor and chassis ground.

Terminal
  Front RH No. 1 — Chassis ground:
  Front LH No. 1 — Chassis ground:
  Rear RH No. 1 — Chassis ground:
  Rear LH No. 1 — Chassis ground:

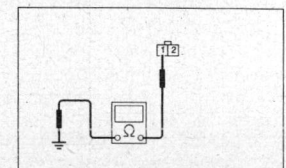

CHECK : **Is the resistance more than 1 MΩ?**
YES : Go to step **8E12**.
NO : Replace ABS sensor and ABSCM&H/U.

8E12 : CHECK GROUND SHORT OF HARNESS.

1) Turn ignition switch to OFF.
2) Connect connector to ABS sensor.
3) Measure resistance between ABSCM&H/U connector terminal and chassis ground.

Connector & terminal
  Trouble code 21 / (F49) No. 11 — Chassis ground:
  Trouble code 23 / (F49) No. 9 — Chassis ground:
  Trouble code 25 / (F49) No. 14 — Chassis ground:
  Trouble code 27 / (F49) No. 7 — Chassis ground:

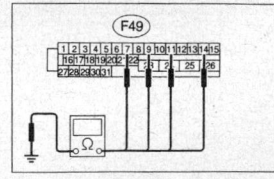

CHECK : **Is the resistance more than 1 MΩ?**
YES : Go to step **8E13**.
NO : Repair harness between ABSCM&H/U and ABS sensor.
Replace ABSCM&H/U.

8E13 : CHECK POOR CONTACT IN CONNECTORS.

CHECK : **Is there poor contact in connectors between ABSCM&H/U and ABS sensor?**
YES : Repair connector.
NO : Go to step **8E14**.

SB4029800153040X

Fig. 12 Codes 21, 23, 25 & 27: Abnormal ABS Sensor, Open Circuit Or Input Voltage Too High (Part 4 of 5). Less Select Monitor

---

8E14 : CHECK ABSCM&H/U.

1) Connect all connectors.
2) Erase the memory.
3) Perform inspection mode.
4) Read out the trouble code.

(CHECK) : *Is the same trouble code as in the current diagnosis still being output?*

(YES) : Replace ABSCM&H/U.

(NO) : Go to step **8E15**.

8E15 : CHECK ANY OTHER TROUBLE CODES APPEARANCE.

(CHECK) : *Are other trouble codes being output?*

(YES) : Proceed with the diagnosis corresponding to the trouble code.

(NO) : A temporary poor contact.

NOTE:
Check harness and connectors between ABSCM&H/U and ABS sensor.

SB4029800153050X

Fig. 12 Codes 21, 23, 25 & 27: Abnormal ABS Sensor, Open Circuit Or Input Voltage Too High (Part 5 of 5). Less Select Monitor

---

8I1 : CHECK INSTALLATION OF ABS SENSOR.

Tightening torque:
32±10 N·m (3.3±1.0 kg-m, 24±7 ft-lb)

(CHECK) : *Are the ABS sensor installation bolts tightened securely?*

(YES) : Go to step 8I2.

(NO) : Tighten ABS sensor installation bolts securely.

8I2 : CHECK INSTALLATION OF TONE WHEEL.

Tightening torque:
13±3 N·m (1.3±0.3 kg-m, 9±2.2 ft-lb)

(CHECK) : *Are the tone wheel installation bolts tightened securely?*

(YES) : Go to step 8I3.

(NO) : Tighten tone wheel installation bolts securely.

8I3 : CHECK ABS SENSOR GAP.

Measure tone wheel to pole piece gap over entire perimeter of the wheel.

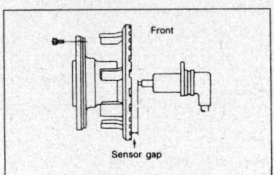

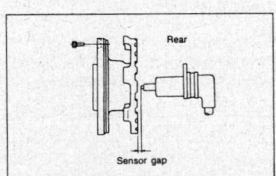

Specifications	Front wheel	Rear wheel
	0.9 — 1.4 mm (0.035 — 0.055 in)	0.7 — 1.2 mm (0.028 — 0.047 in)

(CHECK) : *Is the gap within the specifications?*

(YES) : Go to step 8I4.

(NO) : Adjust the gap.

NOTE:
Adjust the gap using spacer (Part No. 26755AA000). If spacers cannot correct the gap, replace worn sensor or worn tone wheel.

8I4 : CHECK OSCILLOSCOPE.

(CHECK) : *Is an oscilloscope available?*

(YES) : Go to step 8I5.

(NO) : Go to step 8I6.

SB4029800154010X

Fig. 13 Codes 22, 24, 26 & 28: Abnormal ABS Sensor, Abnormal ABS Sensor Signal (Part 1 of 5). Less Select Monitor

8I5 : CHECK ABS SENSOR SIGNAL.

1) Raise all four wheels of ground.
2) Turn ignition switch OFF.
3) Connect the oscilloscope to the connector.
4) Turn ignition switch ON.
5) Rotate wheels and measure voltage at specified frequency.

NOTE:
When this inspection is completed, the ABSCM&H/U sometimes stores the trouble code 29.

Connector & terminal
    Trouble code 22 / (B100) No. 5 (+) — No. 14 (–):
    Trouble code 24 / (B100) No. 7 (+) — No. 16 (–):
    Trouble code 26 / (F55) No. 6 (+) — No. 7 (–):
    Trouble code 28 / (F55) No. 1 (+) — No. 2 (–):

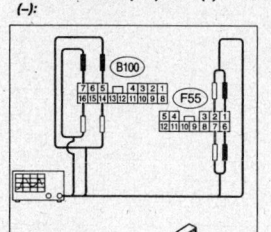

CHECK : Is oscilloscope pattern smooth, as shown in figure?
YES : Go to step 8I9.
NO : Go to step 8I6.

SB4029800154020X

Fig. 13   Codes 22, 24, 26 & 28: Abnormal ABS Sensor, Abnormal ABS Sensor Signal (Part 2 of 5). Less Select Monitor

8I6 : CHECK CONTAMINATION OF ABS SENSOR OR TONE WHEEL.

Remove disc rotor or drum from hub in accordance with trouble code.

CHECK : Is the ABS sensor pole piece or the tone wheel contaminated by dirt or other foreign matter?
YES : Thoroughly remove dirt or other foreign matter.
NO : Go to step 8I7.

8I7 : CHECK DAMAGE OF ABS SENSOR OR TONE WHEEL.

CHECK : Are there broken or damaged in the ABS sensor pole piece or the tone wheel?
YES : Replace ABS sensor or tone wheel.
NO : Go to step 8I8.

8I8 : CHECK HUB RUNOUT.

Measure hub runout.

CHECK : Is the runout less than 0.05 mm (0.0020 in)?
YES : Go to step 8I9.
NO : Repair hub.

8I9 : CHECK RESISTANCE OF ABS SENSOR.

1) Turn ignition switch OFF.
2) Disconnect connector from ABS sensor.
3) Measure resistance between ABS sensor connector terminals.

Terminal
    Front RH No. 1 — No. 2:
    Front LH No. 1 — No. 2:
    Rear RH No. 1 — No. 2:
    Rear LH No. 1 — No. 2:

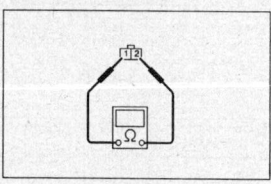

CHECK : Is the resistance between 0.8 and 1.2 kΩ?
YES : Go to step 8I10.
NO : Replace ABS sensor.

SB4029800154030X

Fig. 13   Codes 22, 24, 26 & 28: Abnormal ABS Sensor, Abnormal ABS Sensor Signal (Part 3 of 5). Less Select Monitor

8I10 : CHECK GROUND SHORT OF ABS SENSOR.

Measure resistance between ABS sensor and chassis ground.

Terminal
    Front RH No. 1 — Chassis ground:
    Front LH No. 1 — Chassis ground:
    Rear RH No. 1 — Chassis ground:
    Rear LH No. 1 — Chassis ground:

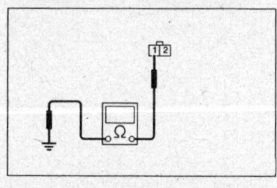

CHECK : Is the resistance more than 1 MΩ?
YES : Go to step 8I11.
NO : Replace ABS sensor.

8I11 : CHECK HARNESS/CONNECTOR BETWEEN ABSCM&H/U AND ABS SENSOR.

1) Connect connector to ABS sensor.
2) Disconnect connector from ABSCM&H/U.
3) Measure resistance at ABSCM&H/U connector terminals.

Connector & terminal
    Trouble code 22 / (F49) No. 11 — No. 12:
    Trouble code 24 / (F49) No. 9 — No. 10:
    Trouble code 26 / (F49) No. 14 — No. 15:
    Trouble code 28 / (F49) No. 7 — No. 8:

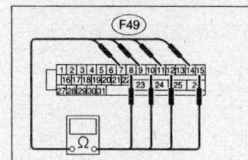

CHECK : Is the resistance between 0.8 and 1.2 kΩ?
YES : Go to step 8I12.
NO : Repair harness/connector between ABSCM&H/U and ABS sensor.

8I12 : CHECK GROUND SHORT OF HARNESS.

Measure resistance between ABSCM&H/U connector and chassis ground.

Connector & terminal
    Trouble code 22 / (F49) No. 11 — Chassis ground:
    Trouble code 24 / (F49) No. 9 — Chassis ground:
    Trouble code 26 / (F49) No. 14 — Chassis ground:
    Trouble code 28 / (F49) No. 7 — Chassis ground:

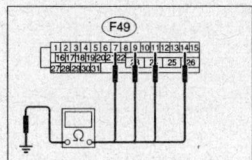

CHECK : Is the resistance more than 1 MΩ?
YES : Go to step 8I13.
NO : Repair harness/connector between ABSCM&H/U and ABS sensor.

8I13 : CHECK GROUND CIRCUIT OF ABSCM&H/U.

Measure resistance between ABSCM&H/U and chassis ground.

Connector & terminal
    (F49) No. 23 — GND:

CHECK : Is the resistance less than 0.5 Ω?
YES : Go to step 8I14.
NO : Repair ABSCM&H/U ground harness.

SB4029800154040X

Fig. 13   Codes 22, 24, 26 & 28: Abnormal ABS Sensor, Abnormal ABS Sensor Signal (Part 4 of 5). Less Select Monitor

8I14 : CHECK POOR CONTACT IN CONNECTORS.

CHECK : **Is there poor contact in connectors between ABSCM&H/U and ABS sensor?**

YES : Repair connector.

NO : Go to step 8I15.

8I15 : CHECK SOURCES OF SIGNAL NOISE.

CHECK : **Is the car telephone or the wireless transmitter properly installed?**

YES : Go to step 8I16.

NO : Properly install the car telephone or the wireless transmitter.

8I16 : CHECK SOURCES OF SIGNAL NOISE.

CHECK : **Are noise sources (such as an antenna) installed near the sensor harness?**

YES : Install the noise sources apart from the sensor harness.

NO : Go to step 8I17.

8I17 : CHECK SHIELD CIRCUIT.

1) Connect all connectors.
2) Measure resistance between shield connector and chassis ground.

Connector & terminal
Trouble code 22 / (B100) No. 15 — Chassis ground:
Trouble code 24 / (B100) No. 6 — Chassis ground:
Trouble code 26 / (F55) No. 8 — Chassis ground:
Trouble code 28 / (F55) No. 3 — Chassis ground:

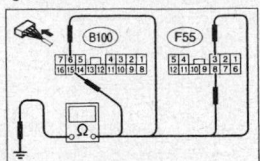

CHECK : **Is the resistance less than 0.5 Ω?**

YES : Go to step 8I18.

NO : Repair shield harness.

8I18 : CHECK ABSCM&H/U.

1) Connect all connectors.
2) Erase the memory.
3) Perform inspection mode.
4) Read out the trouble code.

CHECK : **Is the same trouble code as in the current diagnosis still being output?**

YES : Replace ABSCM&H/U.

NO : Go to step 8I19.

8I19 : CHECK ANY OTHER TROUBLE CODES APPEARANCE.

CHECK : **Are other trouble codes being output?**

YES : Proceed with the diagnosis corresponding to the trouble code.

NO : A temporary noise interference.

SB4029800154050X

Fig. 13   Codes 22, 24, 26 & 28: Abnormal ABS Sensor, Abnormal ABS Sensor Signal (Part 5 of 5). Less Select Monitor

8J1 : CHECK IF THE WHEELS HAVE TURNED FREELY FOR A LONG TIME.

CHECK : **Check if the wheels have been turned freely for more than one minute, such as when the vehicle is jacked-up, under full-lock cornering or when tire is not in contact with road surface.**

YES : The ABS is normal. Erase the trouble code.

NOTE:
When the wheels turn freely for a long time, such as when the vehicle is towed or jacked-up, or when steering wheel is continuously turned all the way, this trouble code may sometimes occur.

NO : Go to step 8J2.

8J2 : CHECK TIRE SPECIFICATIONS.

CHECK : **Are the tire specifications correct?**

YES : Go to step 8J3.

NO : Replace tire.

8J3 : CHECK WEAR OF TIRE.

CHECK : **Is the tire worn excessively?**

YES : Replace tire.

NO : Go to step 8J4.

8J4 : CHECK TIRE PRESSURE.

CHECK : **Is the tire pressure correct?**

YES : Go to step 8J5.

NO : Adjust tire pressure.

8J5 : CHECK INSTALLATION OF ABS SENSOR.

Tightening torque:
32±10 N·m (3.3±1.0 kg-m, 24±7 ft-lb)

CHECK : **Are the ABS sensor installation bolts tightened securely?**

YES : Go to step 8J6.

NO : Tighten ABS sensor installation bolts securely.

8J6 : CHECK INSTALLATION OF TONE WHEEL.

Tightening torque:
13±3 N·m (1.3±0.3 kg-m, 9±2.2 ft-lb)

CHECK : **Are the tone wheel installation bolts tightened securely?**

YES : Go to step 8J7.

NO : Tighten tone wheel installation bolts securely.

8J7 : CHECK ABS SENSOR GAP.

Measure tone wheel to pole piece gap over entire perimeter of the wheel.

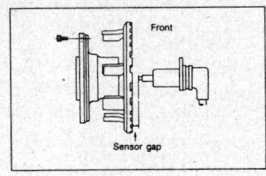

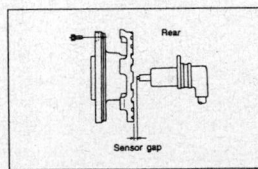

Specifications	Front wheel	Rear wheel
	0.9 — 1.4 mm (0.035 — 0.055 in)	0.7 — 1.2 mm (0.028 — 0.047 in)

CHECK : **Is the gap within the specifications?**

YES : Go to step 8J8.

NO : Adjust the gap.

NOTE:
Adjust the gap using spacer (Part No. 26755AA000). If spacers cannot correct the gap, replace worn sensor or worn tone wheel.

SB4029800155010X

Fig. 14   Code 29: ABS Sensor Signal, Any One Of Four (Part 1 of 2). Less Select Monitor

8J8 : CHECK OSCILLOSCOPE.

CHECK : *Is an oscilloscope available?*
YES : Go to step 8J9.
NO : Go to step 8J10.

8J9 : CHECK ABS SENSOR SIGNAL.

1) Raise all four wheels of ground.
2) Turn ignition switch OFF.
3) Connect the oscilloscope to the connector.
4) Turn ignition switch ON.
5) Rotate wheels and measure voltage at specified frequency.
NOTE:
When this inspection is completed, the ABSCM&H/U sometimes stores the trouble code 29.

Connector & terminal
(B100) No. 5 (+) — No. 14 (–) (Front RH):
(B100) No. 7 (+) — No. 16 (–) (Front LH):
(F55) No. 6 (+) — No. 7 (–) (Rear RH):
(F55) No. 1 (+) — No. 2 (–) (Rear LH):

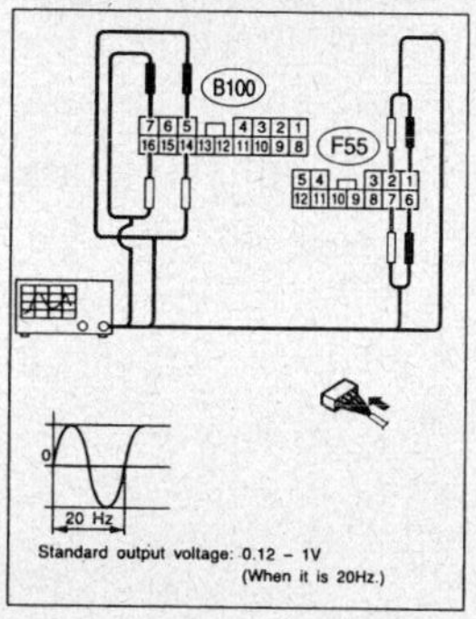

Standard output voltage: 0.12 – 1V
(When it is 20Hz.)

CHECK : *Is oscilloscope pattern smooth, as shown in figure?*
YES : Go to step 8J13.
NO : Go to step 8J10.

8J10 : CHECK CONTAMINATION OF ABS SENSOR OR TONE WHEEL.

Remove disc rotor from hub.

CHECK : *Is the ABS sensor pole piece or the tone wheel contaminated by dirt or other foreign matter?*
YES : Thoroughly remove dirt or other foreign matter.
NO : Go to step 8J11.

8J11 : CHECK DAMAGE OF ABS SENSOR OR TONE WHEEL.

CHECK : *Are there broken or damaged teeth in the ABS sensor pole piece or the tone wheel?*
YES : Replace ABS sensor or tone wheel.
NO : Go to step 8J12.

8J12 : CHECK HUB RUNOUT.

Measure hub runout.

CHECK : *Is the runout less than 0.05 mm (0.0020 in)?*
YES : Go to step 8J13.
NO : Repair hub.

8J13 : CHECK ABSCM&H/U.

1) Turn ignition switch to OFF.
2) Connect all connectors.
3) Erase the memory.
4) Perform inspection mode.
5) Read out the trouble code.

CHECK : *Is the same trouble code as in the current diagnosis still being output?*
YES : Replace ABSCM&H/U.
NO : Go to step 8J14.

8J14 : CHECK ANY OTHER TROUBLE CODES APPEARANCE.

CHECK : *Are other trouble codes being output?*
YES : Proceed with the diagnosis corresponding to the trouble code.
NO : A temporary poor contact.

SB4029800155020X

Fig. 14   Code 29: ABS Sensor Signal, Any One Of Four (Part 2 of 2). Less Select Monitor

8N1 : CHECK INPUT VOLTAGE OF ABSCM&H/U.

1) Disconnect connector from ABSCM&H/U.
2) Run the engine at idle.
3) Measure voltage between ABSCM&H/U connector and chassis ground.

Connector & terminal
(F49) No. 1 (+) — Chassis ground (–):

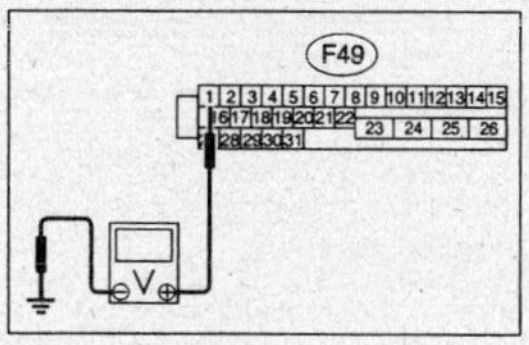

CHECK : *Is the voltage between 10 V and 15 V?*
YES : Go to step 8N2.
NO : Repair harness connector between battery, ignition switch and ABSCM&H/U.

8N2 : CHECK GROUND CIRCUIT OF ABSCM&H/U.

1) Turn ignition switch to OFF.
2) Measure resistance between ABSCM&H/U connector and chassis ground.

Connector & terminal
(F49) No. 23 — Chassis ground:

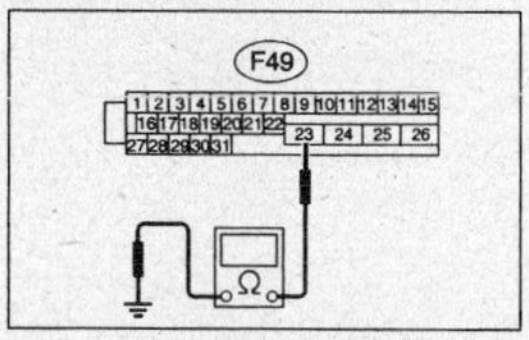

CHECK : *Is the resistance less than 0.5 Ω?*
YES : Go to step 8N3.
NO : Repair ABSCM&H/U ground harness.

8N3 : CHECK POOR CONTACT IN CONNECTORS.

CHECK : *Is there poor contact in connectors between generator, battery and ABSCM&H/U?*
YES : Repair connector.
NO : Go to step 8N4.

8N4 : CHECK ABSCM&H/U.

1) Connect all connectors.
2) Erase the memory.
3) Perform inspection mode.
4) Read out the trouble code.

CHECK : *Is the same trouble code as in the current diagnosis still being output?*
YES : Replace ABSCM&H/U.
NO : Go to step 8N5.

8N5 : CHECK ANY OTHER TROUBLE CODES APPEARANCE.

CHECK : *Are other trouble codes being output?*
YES : Proceed with the diagnosis corresponding to the trouble code.
NO : A temporary poor contact.

SB4029800156000X

Fig. 15   Codes 31, 33, 35 & 37: Abnormal Inlet Solenoid Valve Circuits In ABSCM & H/U. Less Select Monitor

8R1 : CHECK INPUT VOLTAGE OF ABSCM&H/U.

1) Disconnect connector from ABSCM&H/U.
2) Run the engine at idle.
3) Measure voltage between ABSCM&H/U connector and chassis ground.

Connector & terminal
    (F49) No. 1 (+) — Chassis ground (–):

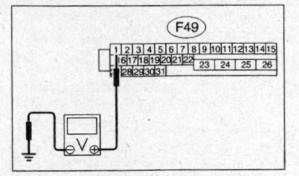

(CHECK) : *Is the voltage between 10 V and 15 V?*
(YES) : Go to step **8R2**.
(NO) : Repair harness connector between battery, ignition switch and ABSCM&H/U.

8R2 : CHECK GROUND CIRCUIT OF ABSCM&H/U.

1) Turn ignition switch to OFF.
2) Measure resistance between ABSCM&H/U connector and chassis ground.

Connector & terminal
    (F49) No. 23 — Chassis ground:

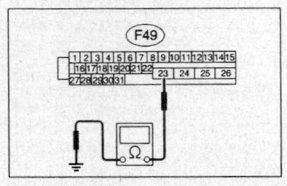

(CHECK) : *Is the resistance less than 0.5 Ω?*
(YES) : Go to step **8R3**.
(NO) : Repair ABSCM&H/U ground harness.

8R3 : CHECK POOR CONTACT IN CONNECTORS.

(CHECK) : *Is there poor contact in connectors between generator, battery and ABSCM&H/U?*
(YES) : Repair connector.
(NO) : Go to step **8R4**.

8R4 : CHECK ABSCM&H/U.

1) Connect all connectors.
2) Erase the memory.
3) Perform inspection mode.
4) Read out the trouble code.

(CHECK) : *Is the same trouble code as in the current diagnosis still being output?*
(YES) : Replace ABSCM&H/U.
(NO) : Go to step **8R5**.

8R5 : CHECK ANY OTHER TROUBLE CODES APPEARANCE.

(CHECK) : *Are other trouble codes being output?*
(YES) : Proceed with the diagnosis corresponding to the trouble code.
(NO) : A temporary poor contact.

SB4029800157000X

Fig. 16 Codes 32, 34, 36 & 38: Abnormal Outlet Solenoid Valve Circuits In ABSCM & H/U. Less Select Monitor

8S1 : CHECK GROUND CIRCUIT OF ABSCM&H/U.

1) Turn ignition switch to OFF.
2) Disconnect connector from ABSCM&H/U.
3) Measure resistance between ABSCM&H/U and chassis ground.

Connector & terminal
    (F49) No. 23 — Chassis ground:

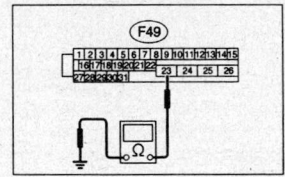

(CHECK) : *Is the resistance less than 0.5 Ω?*
(YES) : Go to step **8S2**.
(NO) : Repair ABSCM&H/U ground harness.

8S2 : CHECK POOR CONTACT IN CONNECTORS.

(CHECK) : *Is there poor contact in connectors between battery, ignition switch and ABSCM&H/U?*
(YES) : Repair connector.
(NO) : Go to step **8S3**.

8S3 : CHECK SOURCES OF SIGNAL NOISE.

(CHECK) : *Is the car telephone or the wireless transmitter properly installed?*
(YES) : Go to step **8S4**.
(NO) : Properly install the car telephone or the wireless transmitter.

8S4 : CHECK SOURCES OF SIGNAL NOISE.

(CHECK) : *Are noise sources (such as an antenna) installed near the sensor harness?*
(YES) : Install the noise sources apart from the sensor harness.
(NO) : Go to step **8S5**.

8S5 : CHECK ABSCM&H/U.

1) Connect all connectors.
2) Erase the memory.
3) Perform inspection mode.
4) Read out the trouble code.

(CHECK) : *Is the same trouble code as in the current diagnosis still being output?*
(YES) : Replace ABSCM&H/U.
(NO) : Go to step **8S6**.

8S6 : CHECK ANY OTHER TROUBLE CODES APPEARANCE.

(CHECK) : *Are other trouble codes being output?*
(YES) : Proceed with the diagnosis corresponding to the trouble code.
(NO) : A temporary poor contact.

SB4029800158000X

Fig. 17 Code 41: Abnormal ABS Control Module. Less Select Monitor

8T1 : CHECK GENERATOR.

1) Start engine.
2) Idling after warm-up.
3) Measure voltage between generator B terminal and chassis ground.

Terminal
Generator B terminal — Chassis ground:

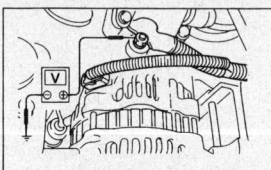

CHECK : *Is the voltage between 10 V and 17 V?*
YES : Go to step **8T2**.
NO : Repair generator.

8T2 : CHECK BATTERY TERMINAL.

Turn ignition switch to OFF.

CHECK : *Are the positive and negative battery terminals tightly clamped?*
YES : Go to step **8T3**.
NO : Tighten the clamp of terminal.

8T3 : CHECK INPUT VOLTAGE OF ABSCM&H/U.

1) Disconnect connector from ABSCM&H/U.
2) Run the engine at idle.
3) Measure voltage between ABSCM&H/U connector and chassis ground.

Connector & terminal
(F49) No. 1 (+) — Chassis ground (–):

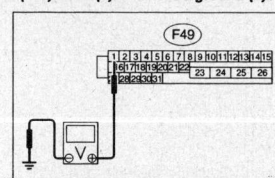

CHECK : *Is the voltage between 10 V and 17 V?*
YES : Go to step **8T4**.
NO : Repair harness connector between battery, ignition switch and ABSCM&H/U.

8T4 : CHECK GROUND CIRCUIT OF ABSCM&H/U.

1) Turn ignition switch to OFF.
2) Measure resistance between ABSCM&H/U connector and chassis ground.

Connector & terminal
(F49) No. 23 — Chassis ground:

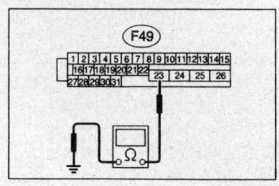

CHECK : *Is the resistance less than 0.5 Ω?*
YES : Go to step **8T5**.
NO : Repair ABSCM&H/U ground harness.

SB4029800159010X

Fig. 18 Code 42: Source Voltage Is Abnormal (Part 1 of 2). Less Select Monitor

8T5 : CHECK POOR CONTACT IN CON-NECTORS.

CHECK : *Is there poor contact in connectors between generator, battery and ABSCM&H/U?*

YES : Repair connector.
NO : Go to step **8T6**.

8T6 : CHECK ABSCM&H/U.

1) Connect all connectors.
2) Erase the memory.
3) Perform inspection mode.
4) Read out the trouble code.

CHECK : *Is the same trouble code as in the current diagnosis still being output?*
YES : Replace ABSCM&H/U.
NO : Go to step **8T7**.

8T7 : CHECK ANY OTHER TROUBLE CODES APPEARANCE.

CHECK : *Are other trouble codes being output?*
YES : Proceed with the diagnosis corresponding to the trouble code.
NO : A temporary poor contact.

SB4029800159020X

Fig. 18 Code 42: Source Voltage Is Abnormal (Part 2 of 2). Less Select Monitor

8U1 : CHECK SPECIFICATIONS OF THE ABSCM&H/U.

Check specifications of the mark to the ABSCM&H/U.

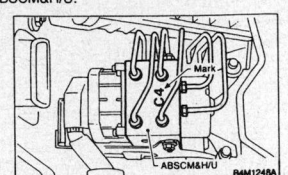

Mark	Model
C3	AWD AT
C4	AWD MT

CHECK : **Is an ABSCM&H/U for AT model installed on a MT model?**
YES : Replace ABSCM&H/U.
NO : Go to step **8U2.**

8U2 : CHECK GROUND SHORT OF HARNESS.

1) Turn ignition switch to OFF.
2) Disconnect two connectors from TCM.
3) Disconnect connector from ABSCM&H/U.
4) Measure resistance between ABSCM&H/U connector and chassis ground.

Connector & terminal
(F49) No. 3 — Chassis ground:

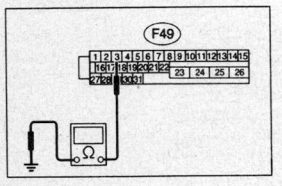

CHECK : **Is the resistance more than 1 MΩ?**
YES : Go to step **8U3.**
NO : Repair harness between TCM and ABSCM&H/U.

SB4029800160010X

Fig. 19 Code 44: A Combination Of A/T Control Abnormal (Part 1 of 3). 1998 Less Select Monitor

---

8U3 : CHECK BATTERY SHORT OF HARNESS.

Measure voltage between ABSCM&H/U connector and chassis ground.

Connector & terminal
(F49) No. 3 (+) — Chassis ground (–):

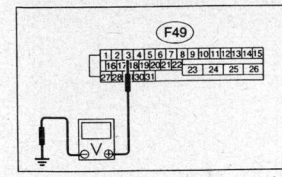

CHECK : **Is the voltage less than 1 V?**
YES : Go to step **8U4.**
NO : Repair harness between TCM and ABSCM&H/U.

8U4 : CHECK BATTERY SHORT OF HARNESS.

1) Turn ignition switch to ON.
2) Measure voltage between ABSCM&H/U connector and chassis ground.

Connector & terminal
(F49) No. 3 (+) — Chassis ground (–):

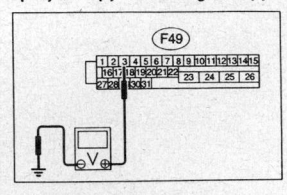

CHECK : **Is the voltage less than 1 V?**
YES : Go to step **8U5.**
NO : Repair harness between TCM and ABSCM&H/U.

SB4029800160010X

8U5 : CHECK TCM.

1) Turn ignition switch to OFF.
2) Connect all connectors to TCM.
3) Turn ignition switch to ON.
4) Measure voltage between TCM connector terminal and chassis ground.

Connector & terminal
(B56) No. 5 (+) — Chassis ground (–):

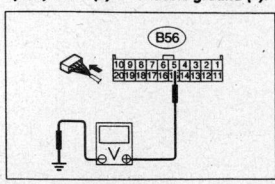

CHECK : **Is the voltage between 10 V and 15 V?**
YES : Go to step **8U7.**
NO : Go to step **8U6.**

8U6 : CHECK AT.

CHECK : **Is the AT functioning normally?**
YES : Replace TCM.
NO : Repair AT.

Fig. 19 Code 44: A Combination Of A/T Control Abnormal (Part 2 of 3). 1998 Less Select Monitor

---

8U7 : CHECK OPEN CIRCUIT OF HARNESS.

Measure voltage between ABSCM&H/U connector and chassis ground.

Connector & terminal
(F49) No. 3 (+) — Chassis ground (–):
(F49) No. 31 (+) — Chassis ground (–):

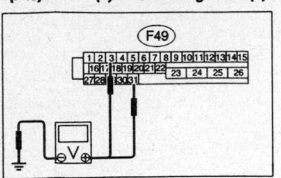

CHECK : **Is the voltage between 10 V and 15 V?**
YES : Go to step **8U8.**
NO : Repair harness/connector between TCM and ABSCM&H/U.

8U8 : CHECK POOR CONTACT IN CONNECTORS.

CHECK : **Is there poor contact in connectors between TCM and ABSCM&H/U?**
YES : Repair connector.
NO : Go to step **8U9.**

8U9 : CHECK ABSCM&H/U.

1) Turn ignition switch to OFF.
2) Connect all connectors.
3) Erase the memory.
4) Perform inspection mode.
5) Read out the trouble code.

CHECK : **Is the same trouble code as in the current diagnosis still being output?**
YES : Replace ABSCM&H/U.
NO : Go to step **8U10.**

SB4029800160020X

8U10 : CHECK ANY OTHER TROUBLE CODES APPEARANCE.

CHECK : **Are other trouble codes being output?**

YES : Proceed with the diagnosis corresponding to the trouble code.

NO : A temporary poor contact.

SB4029800160030X

Fig. 19 Code 44: A Combination Of A/T Control Abnormal (Part 3 of 3). 1998 Less Select Monitor

8U1 : CHECK SPECIFICATIONS OF THE ABSCM&H/U.

Check specifications of the mark to the ABSCM&H/U.

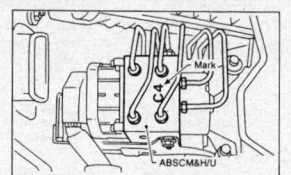

Mark	Model
C5	AWD AT
C6	AWD MT

CHECK : *Is an ABSCM&H/U for AT model installed on a MT model?*
YES : Replace ABSCM&H/U.
NO : Go to step **8U2**.

8U2 : CHECK GROUND SHORT OF HARNESS.

1) Turn ignition switch to OFF.
2) Disconnect two connectors from TCM.
3) Disconnect connector from ABSCM&H/U.
4) Measure resistance between ABSCM&H/U connector and chassis ground.

Connector & terminal
(F49) No. 3 — Chassis ground:

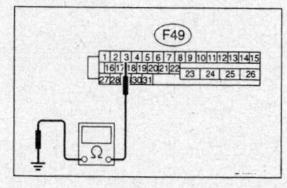

CHECK : *Is the resistance more than 1 MΩ?*
YES : Go to step **8U3**.
NO : Repair harness between TCM and ABSCM&H/U.

SB4029800188010X

Fig. 20   Code 44: A Combination Of A/T Control Abnormal (Part 1 of 3). 1999 Less Select Monitor

---

8U3 : CHECK BATTERY SHORT OF HARNESS.

Measure voltage between ABSCM&H/U connector and chassis ground.

Connector & terminal
(F49) No. 3 (+) — Chassis ground (–):

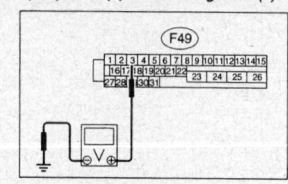

CHECK : *Is the voltage less than 1 V?*
YES : Go to step **8U4**.
NO : Repair harness between TCM and ABSCM&H/U.

8U4 : CHECK BATTERY SHORT OF HARNESS.

1) Turn ignition switch to ON.
2) Measure voltage between ABSCM&H/U connector and chassis ground.

Connector & terminal
(F49) No. 3 (+) — Chassis ground (–):

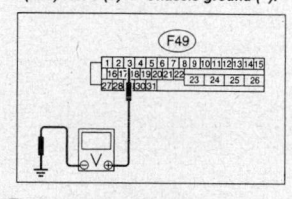

CHECK : *Is the voltage less than 1 V?*
YES : Go to step **8U5**.
NO : Repair harness between TCM and ABSCM&H/U.

8U5 : CHECK TCM.

1) Turn ignition switch to OFF.
2) Connect all connectors to TCM.
3) Turn ignition switch to ON.
4) Measure voltage between TCM connector terminal and chassis ground.

Connector & terminal
(B54) No. 19 (+) — Chassis ground (–):

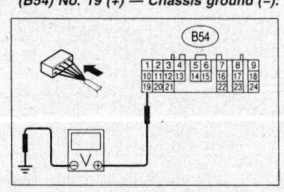

CHECK : *Is the voltage between 10 V and 15 V?*
YES : Go to step **8U7**.
NO : Go to step **8U6**.

8U6 : CHECK AT.

CHECK : *Is the AT functioning normally?*
YES : Replace TCM.
NO : Repair AT.

8U7 : CHECK OPEN CIRCUIT OF HARNESS.

Measure voltage between ABSCM&H/U connector and chassis ground.

Connector & terminal
(F49) No. 3 (+) — Chassis ground (–):
(F49) No. 31 (+) — Chassis ground (–):

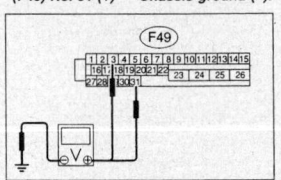

CHECK : *Is the voltage between 10 V and 15 V?*
YES : Go to step **8U8**.
NO : Repair harness/connector between TCM and ABSCM&H/U.

8U8 : CHECK POOR CONTACT IN CONNECTORS.

CHECK : *Is there poor contact in connectors between TCM and ABSCM&H/U?*
YES : Repair connector.
NO : Go to step **8U9**.

8U9 : CHECK ABSCM&H/U.

1) Turn ignition switch to OFF.
2) Connect all connectors.
3) Erase the memory.
4) Perform inspection mode.
5) Read out the trouble code.

CHECK : *Is the same trouble code as in the current diagnosis still being output?*
YES : Replace ABSCM&H/U.
NO : Go to step **8U10**.

SB4029800188020X

Fig. 20   Code 44: A Combination Of A/T Control Abnormal (Part 2 of 3). 1999 Less Select Monitor

---

8U10 :   CHECK ANY OTHER TROUBLE CODES APPEARANCE.

CHECK : *Are other trouble codes being output?*

YES : Proceed with the diagnosis corresponding to the trouble code.

NO : A temporary poor contact.

SB4029800188030X

Fig. 20   Code 44: A Combination Of A/T Control Abnormal (Part 3 of 3). 1999 Less Select Monitor

SUBARU

8V1 : CHECK INPUT VOLTAGE OF ABSCM&H/U.

1) Turn ignition switch to OFF.
2) Disconnect connector from ABSCM&H/U.
3) Run the engine at idle.
4) Measure voltage between ABSCM&H/U connector and chassis ground.

Connector & terminal
(F49) No. 1 (+) — Chassis ground (–):
(F49) No. 24 (+) — Chassis ground (–):

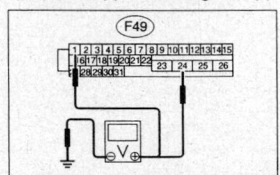

CHECK : **Is the voltage between 10 V and 15 V?**
YES : Go to step **8V2**.
NO : Repair harness connector between battery and ABSCM&H/U.

8V2 : CHECK GROUND CIRCUIT OF ABSCM&H/U.

1) Turn ignition switch to OFF.
2) Measure resistance between ABSCM&H/U connector and chassis ground.

Connector & terminal
(F49) No. 23 — Chassis ground:

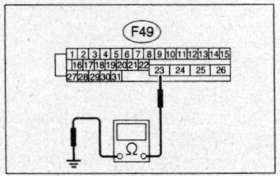

CHECK : **Is the resistance less than 0.5 Ω?**
YES : Go to step **8V3**.
NO : Repair ABSCM&H/U ground harness.

8V3 : CHECK VALVE RELAY IN ABSCM&H/U.

Measure resistance between ABSCM&H/U and terminals.

Terminals
No. 23 (+) — No. 24 (–):

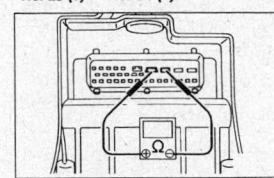

CHECK : **Is the resistance more than 1 MΩ?**
YES : Go to step **8V4**.
NO : Replace ABSCM&H/U.

8V4 : CHECK POOR CONTACT IN CONNECTORS.

CHECK : **Is there poor contact in connectors between generator, battery and ABSCM&H/U?**
YES : Repair connector.
NO : Go to step **8V5**.

8V5 : CHECK ABSCM&H/U.

1) Connect all connectors.
2) Erase the memory.
3) Perform inspection mode.
4) Read out the trouble code.

CHECK : **Is the same trouble code as in the current diagnosis still being output?**
YES : Replace ABSCM&H/U.
NO : Go to step **8V6**.

SB4029800161010X

Fig. 21   Code 51: Abnormal Valve Relay (Part 1 of 2). Less Select Monitor

---

8V6 :   CHECK ANY OTHER TROUBLE CODES APPEARANCE.

CHECK : **Are other trouble codes being output?**

YES : Proceed with the diagnosis corresponding to the trouble code.

NO : A temporary poor contact.

SB4029800161020X

Fig. 21   Code 51: Abnormal Valve Relay (Part 2 of 2). Less Select Monitor

8W1 : CHECK INPUT VOLTAGE OF ABSCM&H/U.

1) Turn ignition switch to OFF.
2) Disconnect connector from ABSCM&H/U.
3) Turn ignition switch to ON.
4) Measure voltage between ABSCM&H/U connector and chassis ground.

Connector & terminal
(F49) No. 25 (+) — Chassis ground (–):

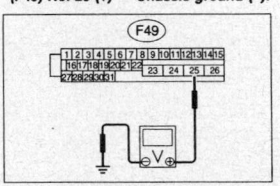

CHECK : **Is the voltage between 10 V and 15 V?**
YES : Go to step **8W2**.
NO : Repair harness/connector between battery and ABSCM&H/U and check fuse SBF-holder.

8W2 : CHECK GROUND CIRCUIT OF MOTOR.

1) Turn ignition switch to OFF.
2) Measure resistance between ABSCM&H/U connector and chassis ground.

Connector & terminal
(F49) No. 26 — Chassis ground:

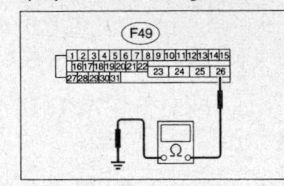

CHECK : **Is the resistance less than 0.5 Ω?**
YES : Go to step **8W3**.
NO : Repair ABSCM&H/U ground harness.

8W3 : CHECK INPUT VOLTAGE OF ABSCM&H/U.

1) Run the engine at idle.
2) Measure voltage between ABSCM&H/U connector and chassis ground.

Connector & terminal
(F49) No. 1 (+) — Chassis ground (–):

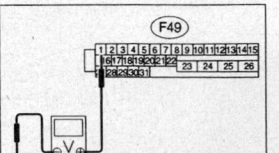

CHECK : **Is the voltage between 10 V and 15 V?**
YES : Go to step **8W4**.
NO : Repair harness connector between battery, ignition switch and ABSCM&H/U.

8W4 : CHECK GROUND CIRCUIT OF ABSCM&H/U.

1) Turn ignition switch to OFF.
2) Measure resistance between ABSCM&H/U connector and chassis ground.

Connector & terminal
(F49) No. 23 — Chassis ground:

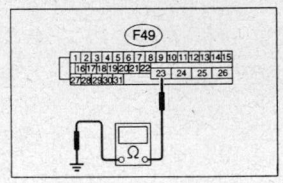

CHECK : **Is the resistance less than 0.5 Ω?**
YES : Go to step **8W5**.
NO : Repair ABSCM&H/U ground harness.

SB4029800162010X

Fig. 22   Code 52: Abnormal Motor And/Or Motor Relay (Part 1 of 2). Less Select Monitor

8W5 : CHECK MOTOR OPERATION.

Operate the sequence control.

NOTE:
Use the diagnosis connector to operate the sequence control.

CHECK : *Can motor revolution noise (buzz) be heard when carrying out the sequence control?*

YES : Go to step **8W6**.

NO : Replace ABSCM&H/U.

8W6 : CHECK POOR CONTACT IN CON-NECTORS.

Turn ignition switch to OFF.

CHECK : *Is there poor contact in connector between generator, battery and ABSCM&H/U?*

YES : Repair connector.

NO : Go to step **8W7**.

8W7 : CHECK ABSCM&H/U.

1) Connect all connectors.
2) Erase the memory.
3) Perform inspection mode.
4) Read out the trouble code.

CHECK : *Is the same trouble code as in the current diagnosis still being output?*

YES : Replace ABSCM&H/U.

NO : Go to step **8W8**.

8W8 : CHECK ANY OTHER TROUBLE CODES APPEARANCE.

CHECK : *Are other trouble codes being output?*

YES : Proceed with the diagnosis corresponding to the trouble code.

NO : A temporary poor contact.

SB4029800162020X

Fig. 22 Code 52: Abnormal Motor And/Or Motor Relay (Part 2 of 2). Less Select Monitor

---

| 8X1 : | CHECK STOP LIGHTS COME ON. |

Depress the brake pedal.

CHECK : *Do stop lights come on?*
YES : Go to step 8X2.
NO : Repair stop lights circuit.

| 8X2 : | CHECK OPEN CIRCUIT IN HARNESS. |

1) Turn ignition switch to OFF.
2) Disconnect connector from ABSCM&H/U.
3) Depress brake pedal.
4) Measure voltage between ABSCM&H/U connector and chassis ground.

Connector & terminal
(F49) No. 2 (+) — Chassis ground (–):

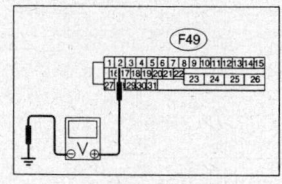

CHECK : *Is the voltage between 10 V and 15 V?*
YES : Go to step 8X3.
NO : Repair harness between stop light switch and ABSCM&H/U.

| 8X3 : | CHECK POOR CONTACT IN CON-NECTORS. |

CHECK : *Is there poor contact in connector between stop light switch and ABSCM&H/U?*

YES : Repair connector.
NO : Go to step 8X4.

SB4029800163000X

Fig. 23 Code 54: Abnormal Stop Light Switch. Less Select Monitor

---

| 8Y1 : | CHECK ALL FOUR WHEELS FOR FREE TURNING. |

CHECK : *Have the wheels been turned freely such as when the vehicle is lifted up, or operated on a rolling road?*
YES : The ABS is normal. Erase the trouble code.
NO : Go to step 8Y2.

| 8Y2 : | CHECK SPECIFICATIONS OF ABSCM&H/U. |

Check specifications of the mark to the ABSCM&H/U.

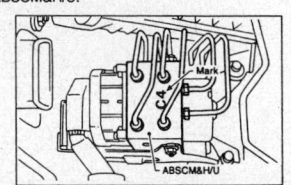

Mark	Model
C3	AWD AT
C4	AWD MT

CHECK : *Is an ABSCM for AWD model installed on a FWD model?*
YES : Replace ABSCM&H/U.

CAUTION:
Be sure to turn ignition switch to OFF when removing ABSCM&H/U.
NO : Go to step 8Y3.

| 8X4 : | CHECK ABSCM&H/U. |

1) Connect all connectors.
2) Erase the memory.
3) Perform inspection mode.
4) Read out the trouble code.

CHECK : *Is the same trouble code as in the current diagnosis still being output?*
YES : Replace ABSCM&H/U.
NO : Go to step 8X5.

| 8X5 : | CHECK ANY OTHER TROUBLE CODES APPEARANCE. |

CHECK : *Are other trouble codes being output?*
YES : Proceed with the diagnosis corresponding to the trouble code.
NO : A temporary poor contact.

| 8Y3 : | CHECK INPUT VOLTAGE OF G SEN-SOR. |

1) Turn ignition switch to OFF.
2) Remove console box.
3) Disconnect G sensor from body. (Do not disconnect connector.)
4) Turn ignition switch to ON.
5) Measure voltage between G sensor connector terminals.

Connector & terminal
(R70) No. 1 (+) — No. 3 (–):

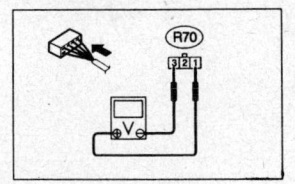

CHECK : *Is the voltage between 4.75 and 5.25 V?*
YES : Go to step 8Y4.
NO : Repair harness/connector between G sensor and ABSCM&H/U.

SB4029800164010X

Fig. 24 Code 56: Abnormal G Sensor Output Voltage (Part 1 of 4). 1998 Less Select Monitor

8Y4 : CHECK OPEN CIRCUIT IN G SENSOR OUTPUT HARNESS AND GROUND HARNESS.

1) Turn ignition switch to OFF.
2) Disconnect connector from ABSCM&H/U.
3) Measure resistance between ABSCM&H/U connector terminals.

Connector & terminal
(F49) No. 30 — No. 28:

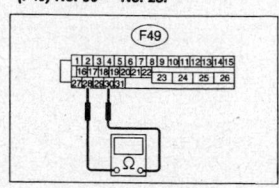

CHECK : *Is the resistance between 4.3 and 4.9 kΩ?*
YES : Go to step 8Y5.
NO : Repair harness/connector between G sensor and ABSCM&H/U.

8Y5 : CHECK GROUND SHORT IN G SENSOR OUTPUT HARNESS.

1) Disconnect connector from G sensor.
2) Measure resistance between ABSCM&H/U connector and chassis ground.

Connector & terminal
(F49) No. 6 — Chassis ground:

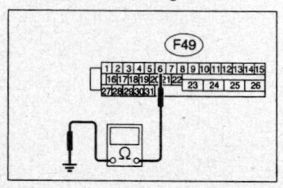

CHECK : *Is the resistance more than 1 MΩ?*
YES : Go to step 8Y6.
NO : Repair harness between G sensor and ABSCM&H/U.

8Y6 : CHECK BATTERY SHORT OF HARNESS.

Measure voltage between ABSCM&H/U connector and chassis ground.

Connector & terminal
(F49) No. 6 (+) — Chassis ground (–):

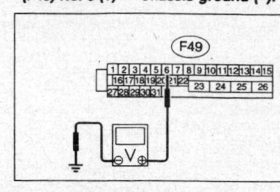

CHECK : *Is the voltage less than 1 V?*
YES : Go to step 8Y7.
NO : Repair harness between G sensor and ABSCM&H/U.

8Y7 : CHECK BATTERY SHORT OF HARNESS.

1) Turn ignition switch to ON.
2) Measure voltage between ABSCM&H/U connector and chassis ground.

Connector & terminal
(F49) No. 6 (+) — Chassis ground (–):

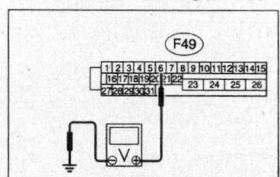

CHECK : *Is the voltage less than 1 V?*
YES : Go to step 8Y8.
NO : Repair harness between G sensor and ABSCM&H/U.

SB4029800164020X

Fig. 24 Code 56: Abnormal G Sensor Output Voltage (Part 2 of 4). 1998 Less Select Monitor

8Y8 : CHECK GROUND SHORT OF HARNESS.

Measure resistance between ABSCM&H/U connector and chassis ground.

Connector & terminal
(F49) No. 28 — Chassis ground:

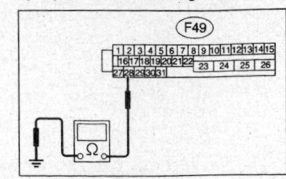

CHECK : *Is the resistance more than 1 MΩ?*
YES : Go to step 8Y9.
NO : Repair harness between G sensor and ABSCM&H/U.
Replace ABSCM&H/U.

8Y9 : CHECK G SENSOR.

1) Turn ignition switch to OFF.
2) Remove G sensor from vehicle.
3) Connect connector to G sensor.
4) Connect connector to ABSCM&H/U.
5) Turn ignition switch to ON.
6) Measure voltage between G sensor connector terminals.

Connector & terminal
(R70) No. 2 (+) — No. 3 (–):

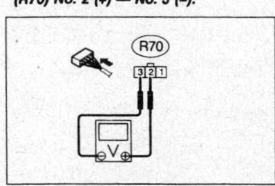

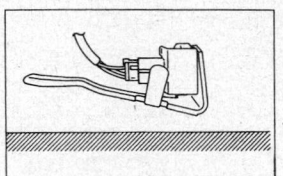

CHECK : *Is the voltage between 2.1 and 2.5 V when G sensor is horizontal?*
YES : Go to step 8Y10.
NO : Replace G sensor.

SB4029800164030X

Fig. 24 Code 56: Abnormal G Sensor Output Voltage (Part 3 of 4). 1998 Less Select Monitor

8Y10 : CHECK G SENSOR.

Measure voltage between G sensor connector terminals.

Connector & terminal
(R70) No. 2 (+) — No. 3 (–):

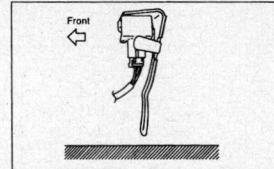

CHECK : *Is the voltage between 3.7 and 4.1 V when G sensor is inclined forwards to 90°?*
YES : Go to step 8Y11.
NO : Replace G sensor.

8Y11 : CHECK G SENSOR.

Measure voltage between G sensor connector terminals.

Connector & terminal
(R70) No. 2 (+) — No. 3 (–):

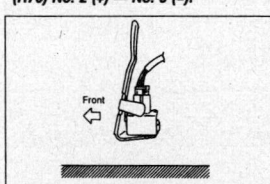

CHECK : *Is the voltage between 0.5 and 0.9 V when G sensor is inclined backwards to 90°?*
YES : Go to step 8Y12.
NO : Replace G sensor.

8Y12 : CHECK POOR CONTACT IN CONNECTORS.

CHECK : *Is there poor contact in connector between ABSCM&H/U and G sensor?*
YES : Repair connector.
NO : Go to step 8Y13.

8Y13 : CHECK ABSCM&H/U.

1) Connect all connectors.
2) Erase the memory.
3) Perform inspection mode.
4) Read out the trouble code.

CHECK : *Is the same trouble code as in the current diagnosis still being output?*
YES : Replace ABSCM&H/U.
NO : Go to step 8Y14.

8Y14 : CHECK ANY OTHER TROUBLE CODES APPEARANCE.

CHECK : *Are other trouble codes being output?*
YES : Proceed with the diagnosis corresponding to the trouble code.
NO : A temporary poor contact.

SB4029800164040X

Fig. 24 Code 56: Abnormal G Sensor Output Voltage (Part 4 of 4). 1998 Less Select Monitor

8Y1 : CHECK ALL FOUR WHEELS FOR FREE TURNING.

(CHECK) : *Have the wheels been turned freely such as when the vehicle is lifted up, or operated on a rolling road?*

(YES) : The ABS is normal. Erase the trouble code.

(NO) : Go to step **8Y2**.

8Y2 : CHECK SPECIFICATIONS OF ABSCM&H/U.

Check specifications of the mark to the ABSCM&H/U.

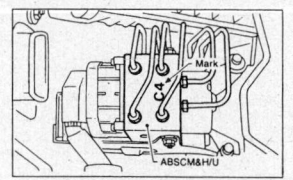

Mark	Model
C5	AWD AT
C6	AWD MT

(CHECK) : *Is an ABSCM for AWD model installed on a FWD model?*

(YES) : Replace ABSCM&H/U.

CAUTION:
Be sure to turn ignition switch to OFF when removing ABSCM&H/U.

(NO) : Go to step **8Y3**.

8Y3 : CHECK INPUT VOLTAGE OF G SENSOR.

1) Turn ignition switch to OFF.
2) Remove console box.
3) Disconnect G sensor from body. (Do not disconnect connector.)
4) Turn ignition switch to ON.
5) Measure voltage between G sensor connector terminals.

Connector & terminal
(R70) No. 1 (+) — No. 3 (−):

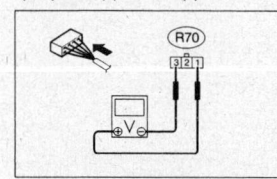

(CHECK) : *Is the voltage between 4.75 and 5.25 V?*

(YES) : Go to step **8Y4**.

(NO) : Repair harness/connector between G sensor and ABSCM&H/U.

SB4029800189010X

Fig. 25 Code 56: Abnormal G Sensor Output Voltage (Part 1 of 4). 1999 Less Select Monitor

8Y4 : CHECK OPEN CIRCUIT IN G SENSOR OUTPUT HARNESS AND GROUND HARNESS.

1) Turn ignition switch to OFF.
2) Disconnect connector from ABSCM&H/U.
3) Measure resistance between ABSCM&H/U connector terminals.

Connector & terminal
(F49) No. 30 — No. 28:

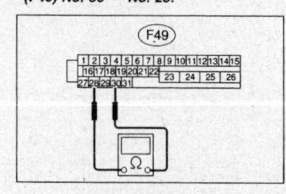

(CHECK) : *Is the resistance between 4.3 and 4.9 kΩ?*

(YES) : Go to step **8Y5**.

(NO) : Repair harness/connector between G sensor and ABSCM&H/U.

8Y5 : CHECK GROUND SHORT IN G SENSOR OUTPUT HARNESS.

1) Disconnect connector from G sensor.
2) Measure resistance between ABSCM&H/U connector and chassis ground.

Connector & terminal
(F49) No. 6 — Chassis ground:

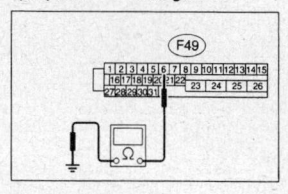

(CHECK) : *Is the resistance more than 1 MΩ?*

(YES) : Go to step **8Y6**.

(NO) : Repair harness between G sensor and ABSCM&H/U.

SB4029800189020X

Fig. 25 Code 56: Abnormal G Sensor Output Voltage (Part 2 of 4). 1999 Less Select Monitor

8Y6 : CHECK BATTERY SHORT OF HARNESS.

Measure voltage between ABSCM&H/U connector and chassis ground.

Connector & terminal
(F49) No. 6 (+) — Chassis ground (−):

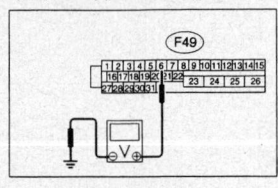

(CHECK) : *Is the voltage less than 1 V?*

(YES) : Go to step **8Y7**.

(NO) : Repair harness between G sensor and ABSCM&H/U.

8Y7 : CHECK BATTERY SHORT OF HARNESS.

1) Turn ignition switch to ON.
2) Measure voltage between ABSCM&H/U connector and chassis ground.

Connector & terminal
(F49) No. 6 (+) — Chassis ground (−):

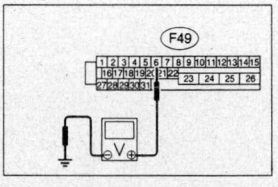

(CHECK) : *Is the voltage less than 1 V?*

(YES) : Go to step **8Y8**.

(NO) : Repair harness between G sensor and ABSCM&H/U.

8Y8 : CHECK GROUND SHORT OF HARNESS.

Measure resistance between ABSCM&H/U connector and chassis ground.

Connector & terminal
(F49) No. 28 — Chassis ground:

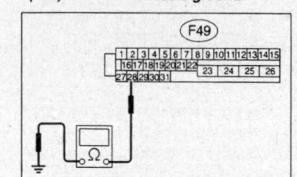

(CHECK) : *Is the resistance more than 1 MΩ?*

(YES) : Go to step **8Y9**.

(NO) : Repair harness between G sensor and ABSCM&H/U.
Replace ABSCM&H/U.

8Y9 : CHECK G SENSOR.

1) Turn ignition switch to OFF.
2) Remove G sensor from vehicle.
3) Connect connector to G sensor.
4) Connect connector to ABSCM&H/U.
5) Turn ignition switch to ON.
6) Measure voltage between G sensor connector terminals.

Connector & terminal
(R70) No. 2 (+) — No. 3 (−):

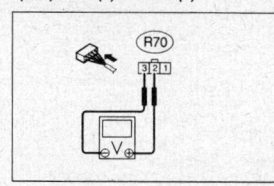

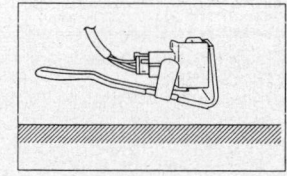

(CHECK) : *Is the voltage between 2.1 and 2.5 V when G sensor is horizontal?*

(YES) : Go to step **8Y10**.

(NO) : Replace G sensor.

SB4029800189030X

Fig. 25 Code 56: Abnormal G Sensor Output Voltage (Part 3 of 4). 1999 Less Select Monitor

SUBARU

8Y10 : CHECK G SENSOR.

Measure voltage between G sensor connector terminals.

Connector & terminal
(R70) No. 2 (+) — No. 3 (−):

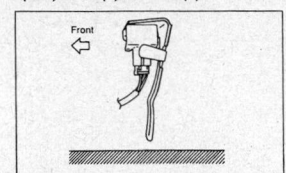

CHECK : **Is the voltage between 3.7 and 4.1 V when G sensor is inclined forwards to 90°?**
YES : Go to step **8Y11**.
NO : Replace G sensor.

8Y11 : CHECK G SENSOR.

Measure voltage between G sensor connector terminals.

Connector & terminal
(R70) No. 2 (+) — No. 3 (−):

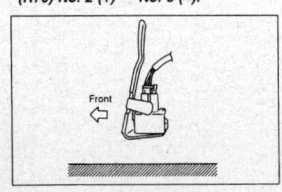

CHECK : **Is the voltage between 0.5 and 0.9 V when G sensor is inclined backwards to 90°?**
YES : Go to step **8Y12**.
NO : Replace G sensor.

8Y12 : CHECK POOR CONTACT IN CONNECTORS.

CHECK : **Is there poor contact in connector between ABSCM&H/U and G sensor?**
YES : Repair connector.
NO : Go to step **8Y13**.

8Y13 : CHECK ABSCM&H/U.

1) Connect all connectors.
2) Erase the memory.
3) Perform inspection mode.
4) Read out the trouble code.

CHECK : **Is the same trouble code as in the current diagnosis still being output?**
YES : Replace ABSCM&H/U.
NO : Go to step **8Y14**.

8Y14 : CHECK ANY OTHER TROUBLE CODES APPEARANCE.

CHECK : **Are other trouble codes being output?**
YES : Proceed with the diagnosis corresponding to the trouble code.
NO : A temporary poor contact.

SB4029800189040X

Fig. 25   Code 56: Abnormal G Sensor Output Voltage (Part 4 of 4). 1999 Less Select Monitor

10D1 : CHECK WIRING HARNESS.

1) Turn ignition switch to OFF.
2) Disconnect connector (F2) from connector (B100).
3) Turn ignition switch to ON.

CHECK : **Does the ABS warning light remain off?**
YES : Go to step **10D2**.
NO : Repair front wiring harness.

10D2 : CHECK PROJECTION AT ABSCM&H/U.

1) Turn ignition switch to OFF.
2) Disconnect connector from ABSCM&H/U.
3) Check for broken projection at the ABSCM&H/U terminal.

CHECK : **Are the projection broken?**
YES : Go to step **10D3**.
NO : Replace ABSCM&H/U.

10D3 : CHECK ABSCM&H/U.

Measure resistance between ABSCM&H/U terminals.

Terminals
No. 21 — No. 23:

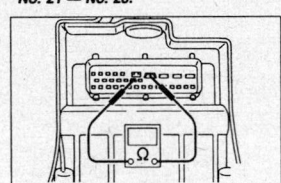

CHECK : **Is the resistance more than 1 MΩ?**
YES : Go to step **10D4**.
NO : Replace valve relay.

10D4 : CHECK WIRING HARNESS.

Measure resistance between connector (F2) and chassis ground.

Connector & terminal
(F2) No. 8 — Chassis ground:

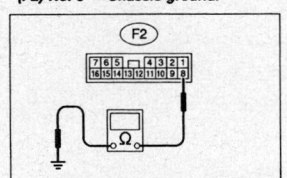

CHECK : **Is the resistance less than 0.5 Ω?**
YES : Go to step **10D5**.
NO : Repair harness.

SB4029800165010X

Fig. 26   Test D: No Trouble Code Appears On Select Monitor, ABS Warning Light Remains On (Part 1 of 2). With Select Monitor

10D5 : CHECK WIRING HARNESS.

1) Connect connector to ABSCM&H/U.
2) Measure resistance between connector (F2) and chassis ground.

Connector & terminal
(F2) No. 8 — Chassis ground:

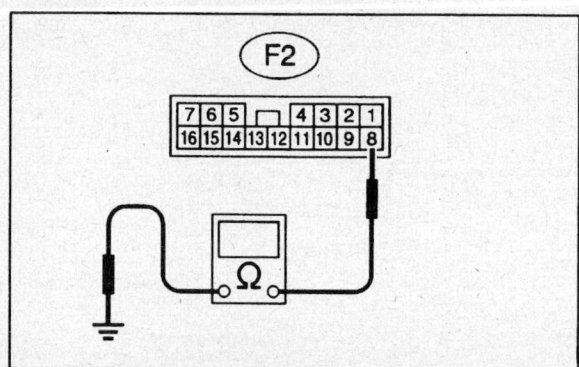

CHECK : *Is the resistance more than 1 MΩ?*

YES : Go to step **10D6**.

NO : Repair harness.

10D6 : CHECK POOR CONTACT IN ABSCM&H/U CONNECTOR.

CHECK : *Is there poor contact in ABSCM&H/U connector?*

YES : Repair connector.

NO : Replace ABSCM&H/U.

SB4029800165020X

Fig. 26   Test D: No Trouble Code Appears On Select Monitor, ABS Warning Light Remains On (Part 2 of 2). With Select Monitor

---

10H1 : CHECK OUTPUT OF ABS SENSOR USING SELECT MONITOR.

1) Select "Current data display & Save" on the select monitor.
2) Read the ABS sensor output corresponding to the faulty system in the select monitor data display mode.

CHECK : *Does the speed indicated on the display change in response to the speedometer reading during acceleration/deceleration when the steering wheel is in the straight-ahead position?*

YES : Go to step 10H2.

NO : Go to step 10H9.

10H2 : CHECK INSTALLATION OF ABS SENSOR.

Tightening torque:
32±10 N·m (3.3±1.0 kg-m, 24±7 ft-lb)

CHECK : *Are the ABS sensor installation bolts tightened securely?*

YES : Go to step 10H3.

NO : Tighten ABS sensor installation bolts securely.

10H3 : CHECK INSTALLATION OF TONE WHEEL.

Tightening torque:
13±3 N·m (1.3±0.3 kg-m, 9±2.2 ft-lb)

CHECK : *Are the tone wheel installation bolts tightened securely?*

YES : Go to step 10H4.

NO : Tighten tone wheel installation bolts securely.

10H4 : CHECK ABS SENSOR GAP.

Measure tone wheel-to-pole piece gap over entire perimeter of the wheel.

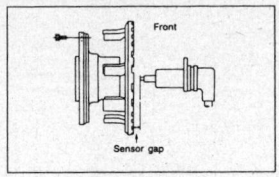

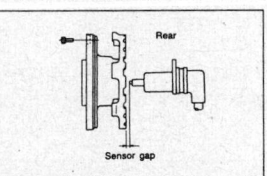

Specifications	Front wheel	Rear wheel
	0.9 — 1.4 mm (0.035 — 0.055 in)	0.7 — 1.2 mm (0.028 — 0.047 in)

CHECK : *Is the gap within the specifications?*

YES : Go to step 10H5.

NO : Adjust the gap.

NOTE:
Adjust the gap using spacers (Part No. 26755AA000). If spacers cannot correct the gap, replace worn sensor or worn tone wheel.

10H5 : CHECK HUB RUNOUT.

Measure hub runout.

CHECK : *Is the runout less than 0.05 mm (0.0020 in)?*

YES : Go to step 10H6.

NO : Repair hub.

SB4029800166040X

Fig. 27   Codes 21, 23, 25 & 27: Abnormal ABS Sensor, Open Or Short Circuit In ABS sensor (Part 1 of 6). With Select Monitor

---

10H6 : CHECK POOR CONTACT IN CONNECTORS.

Turn ignition switch to OFF.

CHECK : *Is there poor contact in connectors between ABSCM&H/U and ABS sensor?*

YES : Repair connector.

NO : Go to step 10H7.

10H7 : CHECK ABSCM&H/U.

1) Connect all connectors.
2) Erase the memory.
3) Perform inspection mode.
4) Read out the trouble code.

CHECK : *Is the same trouble code as in the current diagnosis still being output?*

YES : Replace ABSCM&H/U.

NO : Go to step 10H8.

10H8 : CHECK ANY OTHER TROUBLE CODES APPEARANCE.

CHECK : *Are other trouble codes being output?*

YES : Proceed with the diagnosis corresponding to the trouble code.

NO : A temporary poor contact.

NOTE:
Check harness and connectors between ABSCM&H/U and ABS sensor.

10H9 : CHECK ABS SENSOR.

1) Turn ignition switch to OFF.
2) Disconnect connector from ABS sensor.
3) Measure resistance of ABS sensor connector terminals.

Terminal
Front RH No. 1 — No. 2:
Front LH No. 1 — No. 2:
Rear RH No. 1 — No. 2:
Rear LH No. 1 — No. 2:

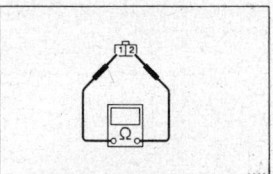

CHECK : *Is the resistance between 0.8 and 1.2 kΩ?*

YES : Go to step 10H10.

NO : Replace ABS sensor.

SB4029800166020X

Fig. 27   Codes 21, 23, 25 & 27: Abnormal ABS Sensor, Open Or Short Circuit In ABS sensor (Part 2 of 6). With Select Monitor

10H10 : CHECK BATTERY SHORT OF ABS SENSOR.

1) Disconnect connector from ABSCM&H/U.
2) Measure voltage between ABS sensor and chassis ground.

Terminal
Front RH No. 1 (+) — Chassis ground (–):
Front LH No. 1 (+) — Chassis ground (–):
Rear RH No. 1 (+) — Chassis ground (–):
Rear LH No. 1 (+) — Chassis ground (–):

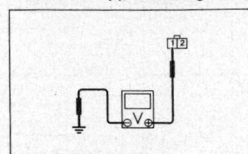

CHECK : *Is the voltage less than 1 V?*
YES : Go to step **10H11**.
NO : Replace ABS sensor.

10H11 : CHECK BATTERY SHORT OF ABS SENSOR.

1) Turn ignition switch to ON.
2) Measure voltage between ABS sensor and chassis ground.

Terminal
Front RH No. 1 (+) — Chassis ground (–):
Front LH No. 1 (+) — Chassis ground (–):
Rear RH No. 1 (+) — Chassis ground (–):
Rear LH No. 1 (+) — Chassis ground (–):

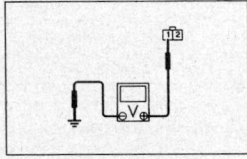

CHECK : *Is the voltage less than 1 V?*
YES : Go to step **10H12**.
NO : Replace ABS sensor.

SB4029800166030X

Fig. 27   Codes 21, 23, 25 & 27: Abnormal ABS Sensor, Open Or Short Circuit In ABS sensor (Part 3 of 6). With Select Monitor

10H12 : CHECK HARNESS/CONNECTOR BETWEEN ABSCM&H/U AND ABS SENSOR.

1) Turn ignition switch to OFF.
2) Connect connector to ABS sensor.
3) Measure resistance between ABSCM&H/U connector terminals.

Connector & terminal
Trouble code 21 / (F49) No. 11 — No. 12:
Trouble code 23 / (F49) No. 9 — No. 10:
Trouble code 25 / (F49) No. 14 — No. 15:
Trouble code 27 / (F49) No. 7 — No. 8:

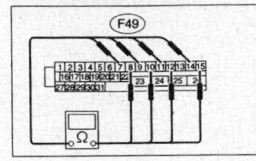

CHECK : *Is the resistance between 0.8 and 1.2 kΩ?*
YES : Go to step **10H13**.
NO : Repair harness/connector between ABSCM&H/U and ABS sensor.

10H13 : CHECK BATTERY SHORT OF HARNESS.

Measure voltage between ABSCM&H/U connector and chassis ground.

Connector & terminal
Trouble code 21 / (F49) No. 11 (+) — Chassis ground (–):
Trouble code 23 / (F49) No. 9 (+) — Chassis ground (–):
Trouble code 25 / (F49) No. 14 (+) — Chassis ground (–):
Trouble code 27 / (F49) No. 7 (+) — Chassis ground (–):

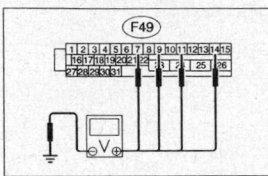

CHECK : *Is the voltage less than 1 V?*
YES : Go to step **10H14**.
NO : Repair harness between ABSCM&H/U and ABS sensor.

10H14 : CHECK BATTERY SHORT OF HARNESS.

1) Turn ignition switch to ON.
2) Measure voltage between ABSCM&H/U connector and chassis ground.

Connector & terminal
Trouble code 21 / (F49) No. 11 (+) — Chassis ground (–):
Trouble code 23 / (F49) No. 9 (+) — Chassis ground (–):
Trouble code 25 / (F49) No. 14 (+) — Chassis ground (–):
Trouble code 27 / (F49) No. 7 (+) — Chassis ground (–):

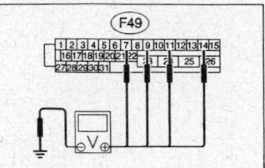

CHECK : *Is the voltage less than 1 V?*
YES : Go to step **10H15**.
NO : Repair harness between ABSCM&H/U and ABS sensor.

10H15 : CHECK INSTALLATION OF ABS SENSOR.

Tightening torque:
32±10 N·m (3.3±1.0 kg-m, 24±7 ft-lb)

CHECK : *Are the ABS sensor installation bolts tightened securely?*
YES : Go to step **10H16**.
NO : Tighten ABS sensor installation bolts securely.

SB4029800166040X

Fig. 27   Codes 21, 23, 25 & 27: Abnormal ABS Sensor, Open Or Short Circuit In ABS sensor (Part 4 of 6). With Select Monitor

10H16 : CHECK INSTALLATION OF TONE WHEEL.

Tightening torque:
13±3 N·m (1.3±0.3 kg-m, 9±2.2 ft-lb)

CHECK : *Are the tone wheel installation bolts tightened securely?*
YES : Go to step **10H17**.
NO : Tighten tone wheel installation bolts securely.

10H17 : CHECK ABS SENSOR GAP.

Measure tone wheel-to-pole piece gap over entire perimeter of the wheel.

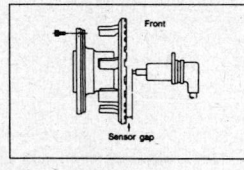

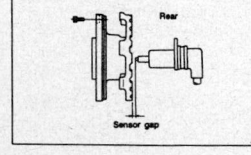

Specifications	Front wheel	Rear wheel
	0.9 — 1.4 mm (0.035 — 0.055 in)	0.7 — 1.2 mm (0.028 — 0.047 in)

CHECK : *Is the gap within the specificationss?*
YES : Go to step **10H18**.
NO : Adjust the gap.

NOTE:
Adjust the gap using spacers (Part No. 26755AA000). If spacers cannot correct the gap, replace worn sensor or worn tone wheel.

SB4029800166050X

Fig. 27   Codes 21, 23, 25 & 27: Abnormal ABS Sensor, Open Or Short Circuit In ABS sensor (Part 5 of 6). With Select Monitor

10H18 : CHECK HUB RUNOUT.

Measure hub runout.

CHECK : *Is the runout less than 0.05 mm (0.0020 in)?*
YES : Go to step **10H19**.
NO : Repair hub.

10H19 : CHECK GROUND SHORT OF ABS SENSOR.

1) Turn ignition switch to ON.
2) Measure resistance between ABS sensor and chassis ground.

Terminal
Front RH No. 1 — Chassis ground:
Front LH No. 1 — Chassis ground:
Rear RH No. 1 — Chassis ground:
Rear LH No. 1 — Chassis ground:

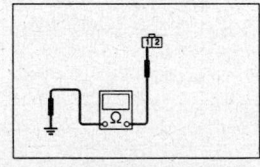

CHECK : *Is the resistance more than 1 MΩ?*
YES : Go to step **10H20**.
NO : Replace ABS sensor and ABSCM&H/U.

10H20 : CHECK GROUND SHORT OF HARNESS.

1) Turn ignition switch to OFF.
2) Connect connector to ABS sensor.
3) Measure resistance between ABSCM&H/U connector terminal and chassis ground.

Connector & terminal
Trouble code 21 / (F49) No. 11 — Chassis ground:
Trouble code 23 / (F49) No. 9 — Chassis ground:
Trouble code 25 / (F49) No. 14 — Chassis ground:
Trouble code 27 / (F49) No. 7 — Chassis ground:

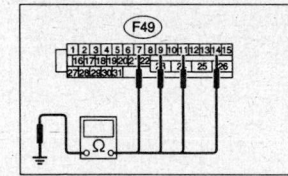

CHECK : *Is the resistance more than 1 MΩ?*
YES : Go to step **10H21**.
NO : Repair harness between ABSCM&H/U and ABS sensor. And replace ABSCM&H/U.

10H21 : CHECK POOR CONTACT IN CONNECTORS.

CHECK : *Is there poor contact in connectors between ABSCM&H/U and ABS sensor?*
YES : Repair connector.
NO : Go to step **10H22**.

10H22 : CHECK ABSCM&H/U.

1) Connect all connectors.
2) Erase the memory.
3) Perform inspection mode.
4) Read out the trouble code.

CHECK : *Is the same trouble code as in the current diagnosis still being output?*
YES : Replace ABSCM&H/U.
NO : Go to step **10H23**.

10H23 : CHECK ANY OTHER TROUBLE CODES APPEARANCE.

CHECK : *Are other trouble codes being output?*
YES : Proceed with the diagnosis corresponding to the trouble code.
NO : A temporary poor contact.

NOTE:
Check harness and connectors between ABSCM&H/U and ABS sensor.

SB4029800166060X

Fig. 27   Codes 21, 23, 25 & 27: Abnormal ABS Sensor, Open Or Short Circuit In ABS sensor (Part 6 of 6). With Select Monitor

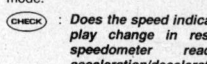
10L1 : CHECK OUTPUT OF ABS SENSOR USING SELECT MONITOR.

1) Select "Current data display & Save" on the select monitor.
2) Read the ABS sensor output corresponding to the faulty system in the select monitor data display mode.

CHECK : *Does the speed indicated on the display change in response to the speedometer reading during acceleration/deceleration when the steering wheel is in the straight-ahead position?*
YES : Go to step **10L2**.
NO : Go to step **10L8**.

10L2 : CHECK POOR CONTACT IN CONNECTORS.

Turn ignition switch to OFF.

CHECK : *Is there poor contact in connectors between ABSCM&H/U and ABS sensor?*
YES : Repair connector.
NO : Go to step **10L3**.

10L3 : CHECK SOURCES OF SIGNAL NOISE.

CHECK : *Is the car telephone or the wireless transmitter properly installed?*
YES : Go to step **10L4**.
NO : Properly install the car telephone or the wireless transmitter.

10L4 : CHECK SOURCES OF SIGNAL NOISE.

CHECK : *Are noise sources (such as an antenna) installed near the sensor harness?*
YES : Install the noise sources apart from the sensor harness.
NO : Go to step **10L5**.

10L5 : CHECK SHIELD CIRCUIT.

1) Turn ignition switch to OFF.
2) Connect all connectors.
3) Measure resistance between shield connector and chassis ground.

Connector & terminal
Trouble code 22 / (B100) No. 15 — Chassis ground:
Trouble code 24 / (B100) No. 6 — Chassis ground:
Trouble code 26 / (F55) No. 8 — Chassis ground:
Trouble code 28 / (F55) No. 3 — Chassis ground:

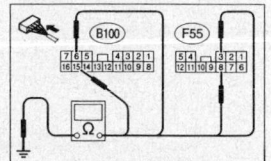

CHECK : *Is the resistance less than 0.5 Ω?*
YES : Go to step **10L6**.
NO : Repair shield harness.

10L6 : CHECK ABSCM&H/U.

1) Connect all connectors.
2) Erase the memory.
3) Perform inspection mode.
4) Read out the trouble code.

CHECK : *Is the same trouble code as in the current diagnosis still being output?*
YES : Replace ABSCM&H/U.
NO : Go to step **10L7**.

10L7 : CHECK ANY OTHER TROUBLE CODES APPEARANCE.

CHECK : *Are other trouble codes being output?*
YES : Proceed with the diagnosis corresponding to the trouble code.
NO : A temporary noise interference.

SB4029800167010X

Fig. 28 Codes 22, 24, 26 & 28: Abnormal ABS Sensor, ABS Sensor Abnormal Signal (Part 1 of 6). With Select Monitor

10L8 : CHECK INSTALLATION OF ABS SENSOR.

Tightening torque:
32±10 N·m (3.3±1.0 kg-m, 24±7 ft-lb)

CHECK : *Are the ABS sensor installation bolts tightened securely?*
YES : Go to step **10L9**.
NO : Tighten ABS sensor installation bolts securely.

10L9 : CHECK INSTALLATION OF TONE WHEEL.

Tightening torque:
13±3 N·m (1.3±0.3 kg-m, 9±2.2 ft-lb)

CHECK : *Are the tone wheel installation bolts tightened securely?*
YES : Go to step **10L10**.
NO : Tighten tone wheel installation bolts securely.

10L10 : CHECK ABS SENSOR GAP.

Measure tone wheel to pole piece gap over entire perimeter of the wheel.

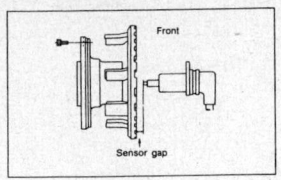

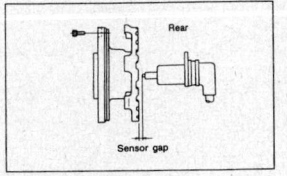

Specifications	Front wheel	Rear wheel
	0.9 — 1.4 mm (0.035 — 0.055 in)	0.7 — 1.2 mm (0.028 — 0.047 in)

CHECK : *Is the gap within the specifications?*
YES : Go to step **10L11**.
NO : Adjust the gap.

NOTE:
Adjust the gap using spacer (Part No. 26755AA000). If spacers cannot correct the gap, replace worn sensor or worn tone wheel.

10L11 : CHECK OSCILLOSCOPE.

CHECK : *Is an oscilloscope available?*
YES : Go to step **10L12**.
NO : Go to step **10L13**.

SB4029800167020X

Fig. 28 Codes 22, 24, 26 & 28: Abnormal ABS Sensor, ABS Sensor Abnormal Signal (Part 2 of 6). With Select Monitor

10L12 : CHECK ABS SENSOR SIGNAL.

1) Raise all four wheels of ground.
2) Turn ignition switch OFF.
3) Connect the oscilloscope to the connector.
4) Turn ignition switch ON.
5) Rotate wheels and measure voltage at specified frequency.

NOTE:
When this inspection is completed, the ABSCM&H/U sometimes stores the trouble code 29.

Connector & terminal
Trouble code 22 / (B100) No. 5 (+) — No. 14 (−):
Trouble code 24 / (B100) No. 7 (+) — No. 16 (−):
Trouble code 26 / (F55) No. 6 (+) — No. 7 (−):
Trouble code 28 / (F55) No. 1 (+) — No. 2 (−):

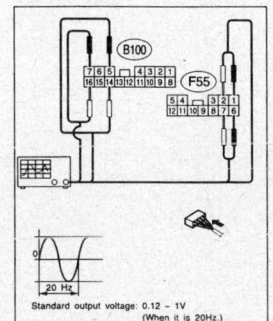

Standard output voltage: 0.12 – 1V
(When it is 20Hz.)

CHECK : *Is oscilloscope pattern smooth, as shown in figure?*
YES : Go to step **10L16**.
NO : Go to step **10L13**.

10L13 : CHECK CONTAMINATION OF ABS SENSOR OR TONE WHEEL.

Remove disc rotor or drum from hub in accordance with trouble code.

CHECK : *Is the ABS sensor pole piece or the tone wheel contaminated by dirt or other foreign matter?*
YES : Thoroughly remove dirt or other foreign matter.
NO : Go to step **10L14**.

10L14 : CHECK DAMAGE OF ABS SENSOR OR TONE WHEEL.

CHECK : *Are there broken or damaged in the ABS sensor pole piece or the tone wheel?*
YES : Replace ABS sensor or tone wheel.
NO : Go to step **10L15**.

10L15 : CHECK HUB RUNOUT.

Measure hub runout.

CHECK : *Is the runout less than 0.05 mm (0.0020 in)?*
YES : Go to step **10L16**.
NO : Repair hub.

SB4029800167030X

Fig. 28 Codes 22, 24, 26 & 28: Abnormal ABS Sensor, ABS Sensor Abnormal Signal (Part 3 of 6). With Select Monitor

10L16 : CHECK RESISTANCE OF ABS SENSOR.

1) Turn ignition switch OFF.
2) Disconnect connector from ABS sensor.
3) Measure resistance between ABS sensor connector terminals.

Terminal
Front RH No. 1 — No. 2:
Front LH No. 1 — No. 2:
Rear RH No. 1 — No. 2:
Rear LH No. 1 — No. 2:

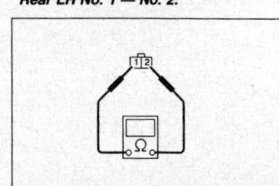

CHECK : *Is the resistance between 0.8 and 1.2 kΩ?*
YES : Go to step **10L17**.
NO : Replace ABS sensor.

10L17 : CHECK GROUND SHORT OF ABS SENSOR.

Measure resistance between ABS sensor and chassis ground.

Terminal
Front RH No. 1 — Chassis ground:
Front LH No. 1 — Chassis ground:
Rear RH No. 1 — Chassis ground:
Rear LH No. 1 — Chassis ground:

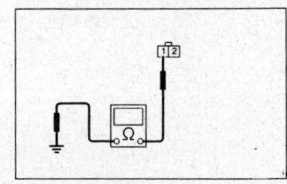

CHECK : *Is the resistance more than 1 MΩ?*
YES : Go to step **10L18**.
NO : Replace ABS sensor.

SB4029800167040X

Fig. 28 Codes 22, 24, 26 & 28: Abnormal ABS Sensor, ABS Sensor Abnormal Signal (Part 4 of 6). With Select Monitor

10L18 : CHECK HARNESS/CONNECTOR BETWEEN ABSCM&H/U AND ABS SENSOR.

1) Connect connector to ABS sensor.
2) Disconnect connector from ABSCM&H/U.
3) Measure resistance at ABSCM&H/U connector terminals.

Connector & terminal
Trouble code 22 / (F49) No. 11 — No. 12:
Trouble code 24 / (F49) No. 9 — No. 10:
Trouble code 26 / (F49) No. 14 — No. 15:
Trouble code 28 / (F49) No. 7 — No. 8:

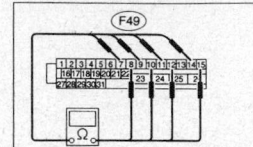

CHECK : **Is the resistance between 0.8 and 1.2 kΩ?**
YES : Go to step **10L19**.
NO : Repair harness/connector between ABSCM&H/U and ABS sensor.

10L19 : CHECK GROUND SHORT OF HARNESS.

Measure resistance between ABSCM&H/U connector and chassis ground.

Connector & terminal
Trouble code 22 / (F49) No. 11 — Chassis ground:
Trouble code 24 / (F49) No. 9 — Chassis ground:
Trouble code 26 / (F49) No. 14 — Chassis ground:
Trouble code 28 / (F49) No. 7 — Chassis ground:

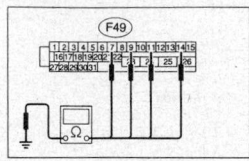

CHECK : **Is the resistance more than 1 MΩ?**
YES : Go to step **10L20**.
NO : Repair harness/connector between ABSCM&H/U and ABS sensor.

10L20 : CHECK GROUND CIRCUIT OF ABSCM&H/U.

Measure resistance between ABSCM&H/U and chassis ground.

Connector & terminal
(F49) No. 23 — GND:

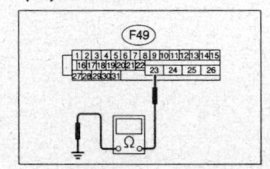

CHECK : **Is the resistance less than 0.5 Ω?**
YES : Go to step **10L21**.
NO : Repair ABSCM&H/U ground harness.

SB4029800167050X

10L21 : CHECK POOR CONTACT IN CONNECTORS.

CHECK : **Is there poor contact in connectors between ABSCM&H/U and ABS sensor?**
YES : Repair connector.
NO : Go to step **10L22**.

10L22 : CHECK SOURCES OF SIGNAL NOISE.

CHECK : **Is the car telephone or the wireless transmitter properly installed?**
YES : Go to step **10L23**.
NO : Properly install the car telephone or the wireless transmitter.

10L23 : CHECK SOURCES OF SIGNAL NOISE.

CHECK : **Are noise sources (such as an antenna) installed near the sensor harness?**
YES : Install the noise sources apart from the sensor harness.
NO : Go to step **10L24**.

10L24 : CHECK SHIELD CIRCUIT.

1) Connect all connectors.
2) Measure resistance between shield connector and chassis ground.

Connector & terminal
Trouble code 22 / (B100) No. 15 — Chassis ground:
Trouble code 24 / (B100) No. 6 — Chassis ground:
Trouble code 26 / (F55) No. 8 — Chassis ground:
Trouble code 28 / (F55) No. 3 — Chassis ground:

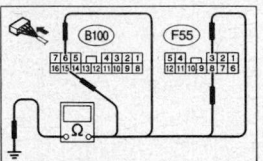

CHECK : **Is the resistance less than 0.5 Ω?**
YES : Go to step **10L25**.
NO : Repair shield harness.

10L25 : CHECK ABSCM&H/U.

1) Connect all connectors.
2) Erase the memory.
3) Perform inspection mode.
4) Read out the trouble code.

CHECK : **Is the same trouble code as in the current diagnosis still being output?**
YES : Replace ABSCM&H/U.
NO : Go to step **10L26**.

10L26 : CHECK ANY OTHER TROUBLE CODES APPEARANCE.

CHECK : **Are other trouble codes being output?**
YES : Proceed with the diagnosis corresponding to the trouble code.
NO : A temporary noise interference.

SB4029800167060X

Fig. 28   Codes 22, 24, 26 & 28: Abnormal ABS Sensor, ABS Sensor Abnormal Signal (Part 5 of 6). With Select Monitor

Fig. 28   Codes 22, 24, 26 & 28: Abnormal ABS Sensor, ABS Sensor Abnormal Signal (Part 6 of 6). With Select Monitor

10M1 : CHECK IF THE WHEELS HAVE TURNED FREELY FOR A LONG TIME.

CHECK : **Check if the wheels have been turned freely for more than one minute, such as when the vehicle is jacked-up, under full-lock cornering or when tire is not in contact with road surface.**
YES : The ABS is normal. Erase the trouble code.

NOTE:
When the wheels turn freely for a long time, such as when the vehicle is towed or jacked-up, or when steering wheel is continuously turned all the way, this trouble code may sometimes occur.

NO : Go to step **10M2**.

10M2 : CHECK TIRE SPECIFICATIONS.

Turn ignition switch to OFF.

CHECK : **Are the tire specifications correct?**
YES : Go to step **10M3**.
NO : Replace tire.

10M3 : CHECK WEAR OF TIRE.

CHECK : **Is the tire worn excessively?**
YES : Replace tire.
NO : Go to step **10M4**.

10M4 : CHECK TIRE PRESSURE.

CHECK : **Is the tire pressure correct?**
YES : Go to step **10M5**.
NO : Adjust tire pressure.

10M5 : CHECK INSTALLATION OF ABS SENSOR.

Tightening torque:
32±10 N·m (3.3±1.0 kg-m, 24±7 ft-lb)

CHECK : **Are the ABS sensor installation bolts tightened securely?**
YES : Go to step **10M6**.
NO : Tighten ABS sensor installation bolts securely.

10M6 : CHECK INSTALLATION OF TONE WHEEL.

Tightening torque:
13±3 N·m (1.3±0.3 kg-m, 9±2.2 ft-lb)

CHECK : **Are the tone wheel installation bolts tightened securely?**
YES : Go to step **10M7**.
NO : Tighten tone wheel installation bolts securely.

10M7 : CHECK ABS SENSOR GAP.

Measure tone wheel to pole piece gap over entire perimeter of the wheel.

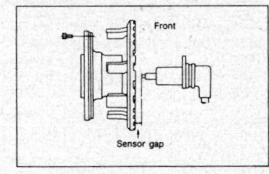

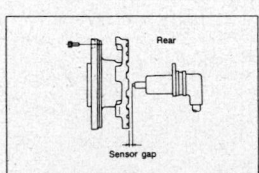

Specifications	Front wheel	Rear wheel
	0.9 — 1.4 mm (0.035 — 0.055 in)	0.7 — 1.2 mm (0.028 — 0.047 in)

CHECK : **Is the gap within the specifications?**
YES : Go to step **10M8**.
NO : Adjust the gap.

NOTE:
Adjust the gap using spacer (Part No. 26755AA000). If spacers cannot correct the gap, replace worn sensor or worn tone wheel.

SB4029800168010X

Fig. 29   Code 29: Abnormal ABS Signal On Any One Of Four (Part 1 of 2). With Select Monitor

10M8 : CHECK OSCILLOSCOPE.

CHECK : Is an oscilloscope available?
YES : Go to step **10M9**.
NO : Go to step **10M10**.

10M9 : CHECK ABS SENSOR SIGNAL.

1) Raise all four wheels of ground.
2) Turn ignition switch OFF.
3) Connect the oscilloscope to the connector.
4) Turn ignition switch ON.
5) Rotate wheels and measure voltage at specified frequency.

NOTE:
When this inspection is completed, the ABSCM&H/U sometimes stores the trouble code 29.

Connector & terminal
(B100) No. 5 (+) — No. 14 (–) (Front RH):
(B100) No. 7 (+) — No. 16 (–) (Front LH):
(F55) No. 6 (+) — No. 7 (–) (Rear RH):
(F55) No. 1 (+) — No. 2 (–) (Rear LH):

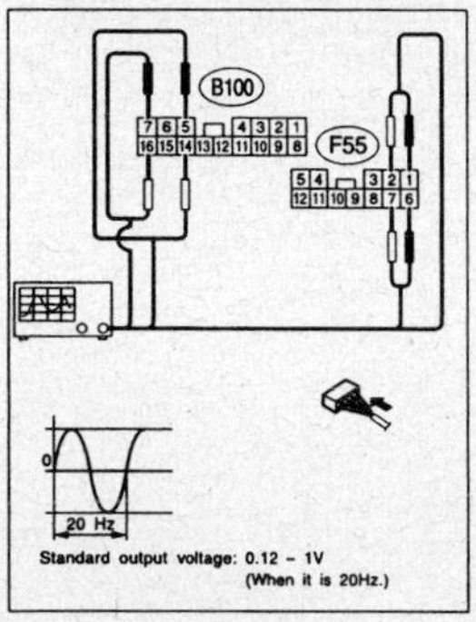

Standard output voltage: 0.12 – 1V
(When it is 20Hz.)

CHECK : Is oscilloscope pattern smooth, as shown in figure?
YES : Go to step **10M13**.
NO : Go to step **10M10**.

10M10 : CHECK CONTAMINATION OF ABS SENSOR OR TONE WHEEL.

Remove disc rotor from hub.

CHECK : Is the ABS sensor pole piece or the tone wheel contaminated by dirt or other foreign matter?
YES : Thoroughly remove dirt or other foreign matter.
NO : Go to step **10M11**.

10M11 : CHECK DAMAGE OF ABS SENSOR OR TONE WHEEL.

CHECK : Are there broken or damaged teeth in the ABS sensor pole piece or the tone wheel?
YES : Replace ABS sensor or tone wheel.
NO : Go to step **10M12**.

10M12 : CHECK HUB RUNOUT.

Measure hub runout.

CHECK : Is the runout less than 0.05 mm (0.0020 in)?
YES : Go to step **10M13**.
NO : Repair hub.

10M13 : CHECK ABSCM&H/U.

1) Turn ignition switch to OFF.
2) Connect all connectors.
3) Erase the memory.
4) Perform inspection mode.
5) Read out the trouble code.

CHECK : Is the same trouble code as in the current diagnosis still being output?
YES : Replace ABSCM&H/U.
NO : Go to step **10M14**.

10M14 : CHECK ANY OTHER TROUBLE CODES APPEARANCE.

CHECK : Are other trouble codes being output?
YES : Proceed with the diagnosis corresponding to the trouble code.
NO : A temporary poor contact.

SB4029800168020X

Fig. 29   Code 29: Abnormal ABS Signal On Any One Of Four (Part 2 of 2). With Select Monitor

10Q1 : CHECK INPUT VOLTAGE OF ABSCM&H/U.

1) Turn ignition switch to OFF.
2) Disconnect connector from ABSCM&H/U.
3) Run the engine at idle.
4) Measure voltage between ABSCM&H/U connector and chassis ground.

Connector & terminal
(F49) No. 1 (+) — Chassis ground (–):

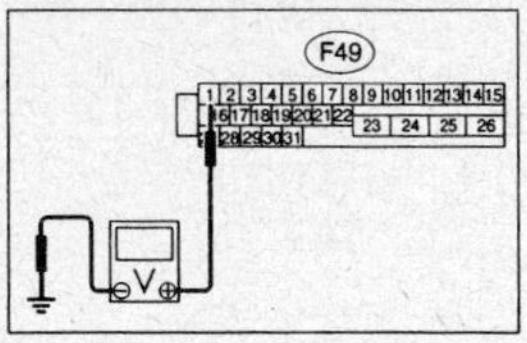

CHECK : Is the voltage between 10 V and 15 V?
YES : Go to step **10Q2**.
NO : Repair harness connector between battery, ignition switch and ABSCM&H/U.

10Q2 : CHECK GROUND CIRCUIT OF ABSCM&H/U.

1) Turn ignition switch to OFF.
2) Measure resistance between ABSCM&H/U connector and chassis ground.

Connector & terminal
(F49) No. 23 — Chassis ground:

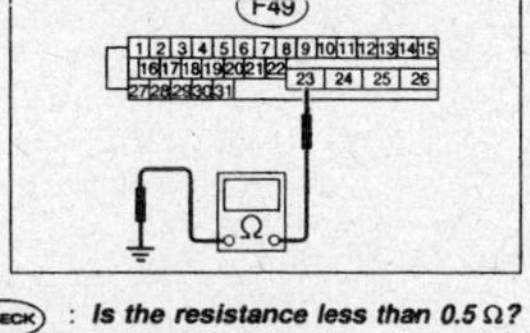

CHECK : Is the resistance less than 0.5 Ω?
YES : Go to step **10Q3**.
NO : Repair ABSCM&H/U ground harness.

10Q3 : CHECK POOR CONTACT IN CONNECTORS.

CHECK : Is there poor contact in connectors between generator, battery and ABSCM&H/U?
YES : Repair connector.
NO : Go to step **10Q4**.

10Q4 : CHECK ABSCM&H/U.

1) Connect all connectors.
2) Erase the memory.
3) Perform inspection mode.
4) Read out the trouble code.

CHECK : Is the same trouble code as in the current diagnosis still being output?
YES : Replace ABSCM&H/U.
NO : Go to step **10Q5**.

10Q5 : CHECK ANY OTHER TROUBLE CODES APPEARANCE.

CHECK : Are other trouble codes being output?
YES : Proceed with the diagnosis corresponding to the trouble code.
NO : A temporary poor contact.

SB4029800169000X

Fig. 30   Codes 31, 33, 35 & 37: Inlet Solenoid Valve Malfunction. With Select Monitor

10U1 : CHECK INPUT VOLTAGE OF ABSCM&H/U.

1) Turn ignition switch to OFF.
2) Disconnect connector from ABSCM&H/U.
3) Run the engine at idle.
4) Measure voltage between ABSCM&H/U connector and chassis ground.

Connector & terminal
(F49) No. 1 (+) — Chassis ground (−):

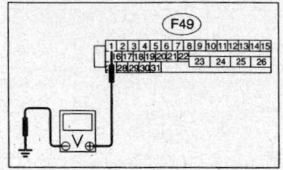

CHECK : *Is the voltage between 10 V and 15 V?*
YES : Go to step **10U2**.
NO : Repair harness connector between battery, ignition switch and ABSCM&H/U.

10U2 : CHECK GROUND CIRCUIT OF ABSCM&H/U.

1) Turn ignition switch to OFF.
2) Measure resistance between ABSCM&H/U connector and chassis ground.

Connector & terminal
(F49) No. 23 — Chassis ground:

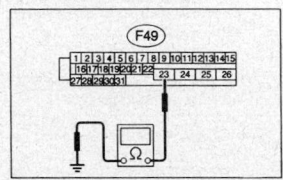

CHECK : *Is the resistance less than 0.5 Ω?*
YES : Go to step **10U3**.
NO : Repair ABSCM&H/U ground harness.

10U3 : CHECK POOR CONTACT IN CONNECTORS.

CHECK : *Is there poor contact in connectors between generator, battery and ABSCM&H/U?*
YES : Repair connector.
NO : Go to step **10U4**.

10U4 : CHECK ABSCM&H/U.

1) Connect all connectors.
2) Erase the memory.
3) Perform inspection mode.
4) Read out the trouble code.

CHECK : *Is the same trouble code as in the current diagnosis still being output?*
YES : Replace ABSCM&H/U.
NO : Go to step **10U5**.

10U5 : CHECK ANY OTHER TROUBLE CODES APPEARANCE.

CHECK : *Are other trouble codes being output?*
YES : Proceed with the diagnosis corresponding to the trouble code.
NO : A temporary poor contact.

SB4029800170000X

Fig. 31   Codes 32, 34, 36 & 38: Outlet Solenoid Valve Malfunction. With Select Monitor

10V1 : CHECK GROUND CIRCUIT OF ABSCM&H/U.

1) Turn ignition switch to OFF.
2) Disconnect connector from ABSCM&H/U.
3) Measure resistance between ABSCM&H/U and chassis ground.

Connector & terminal
(F49) No. 23 — Chassis ground:

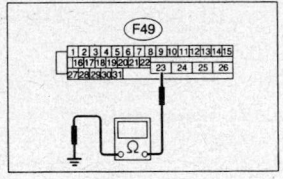

CHECK : *Is the resistance less than 0.5 Ω?*
YES : Go to step **10V2**.
NO : Repair ABSCM&H/U ground harness.

10V2 : CHECK POOR CONTACT IN CONNECTORS.

CHECK : *Is there poor contact in connectors between battery, ignition switch and ABSCM&H/U?*
YES : Repair connector.
NO : Go to step **10V3**.

10V3 : CHECK SOURCES OF SIGNAL NOISE.

CHECK : *Is the car telephone or the wireless transmitter properly installed?*
YES : Go to step **10V4**.
NO : Properly install the car telephone or the wireless transmitter.

10V4 : CHECK SOURCES OF SIGNAL NOISE.

CHECK : *Are noise sources (such as an antenna) installed near the sensor harness?*
YES : Install the noise sources apart from the sensor harness.
NO : Go to step **10V5**.

10V5 : CHECK ABSCM&H/U.

1) Turn ignition switch to OFF.
2) Connect all connectors.
3) Erase the memory.
4) Perform inspection mode.
5) Read out the trouble code.

CHECK : *Is the same trouble code as in the current diagnosis still being output?*
YES : Replace ABSCM&H/U.
NO : Go to step **10V6**.

10V6 : CHECK ANY OTHER TROUBLE CODES APPEARANCE.

CHECK : *Are other trouble codes being output?*
YES : Proceed with the diagnosis corresponding to the trouble code.
NO : A temporary poor contact.

SB4029800171000X

Fig. 32   Code 41: ABS Control & HCU Malfunction. With Select Monitor

10W1 : CHECK GENERATOR.

1) Start engine.
2) Idling after warm-up.
3) Measure voltage between generator B terminal and chassis ground.

Terminal
Generator B terminal — Chassis ground:

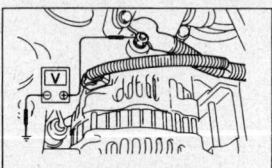

CHECK : *Is the voltage between 10 V and 15 V?*
YES : Go to step **10W2.**
NO : Repair generator.

10W2 : CHECK BATTERY TERMINAL.

Turn ignition switch to OFF.

CHECK : *Are the positive and negative battery terminals tightly clamped?*
YES : Go to step **10W3.**
NO : Tighten the clamp of terminal.

10W3 : CHECK INPUT VOLTAGE OF ABSCM&H/U.

1) Disconnect connector from ABSCM&H/U.
2) Run the engine at idle.
3) Measure voltage between ABSCM&H/U connector and chassis ground.

Connector & terminal
(F49) No. 1 (+) — Chassis ground (–):

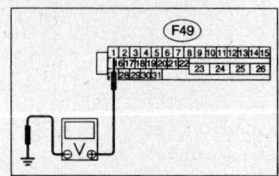

CHECK : *Is the voltage between 10 V and 15 V?*
YES : Go to step **10W4.**
NO : Repair harness connector between battery, ignition switch and ABSCM&H/U.

10W4 : CHECK GROUND CIRCUIT OF ABSCM&H/U.

1) Turn ignition switch to OFF.
2) Measure resistance between ABSCM&H/U connector and chassis ground.

Connector & terminal
(F49) No. 23 — Chassis ground:

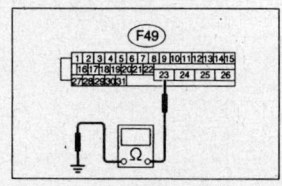

CHECK : *Is the resistance less than 0.5 Ω?*
YES : Go to step **10W5.**
NO : Repair ABSCM&H/U ground harness.

SB4029800172010X

Fig. 33 Code 42: Power Supply Voltage Too Low (Part 1 of 2). With Select Monitor

10W5 : CHECK POOR CONTACT IN CONNECTORS.

CHECK : *Is there poor contact in connectors between generator, battery and ABSCM&H/U?*
YES : Repair connector.
NO : Go to step **10W6.**

10W6 : CHECK ABSCM&H/U.

1) Connect all connectors.
2) Erase the memory.
3) Perform inspection mode.
4) Read out the trouble code.

CHECK : *Is the same trouble code as in the current diagnosis still being output?*
YES : Replace ABSCM&H/U.
NO : Go to step **10W7.**

10W7 : CHECK ANY OTHER TROUBLE CODES APPEARANCE.

CHECK : *Are other trouble codes being output?*
YES : Proceed with the diagnosis corresponding to the trouble code.
NO : A temporary poor contact.

SB4029800172020X

Fig. 33 Code 42: Power Supply Voltage Too Low (Part 2 of 2). With Select Monitor

10X1 : CHECK GENERATOR.

1) Start engine.
2) Idling after warm-up.
3) Measure voltage between generator B terminal and chassis ground.

Terminal
Generator B terminal — Chassis ground:

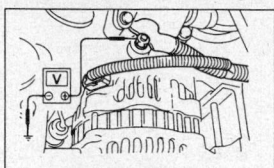

CHECK : *Is the voltage between 10 V and 17 V?*
YES : Go to step **10X2**.
NO : Repair generator.

10X2 : CHECK BATTERY TERMINAL.

Turn ignition switch to OFF.

CHECK : *Are the positive and negative battery terminals tightly clamped?*
YES : Go to step **10X3**.
NO : Tighten the clamp of terminal.

10X3 : CHECK INPUT VOLTAGE OF ABSCM&H/U.

1) Disconnect connector from ABSCM&H/U.
2) Run the engine at idle.
3) Measure voltage between ABSCM&H/U connector and chassis ground.

Connector & terminal
(F49) No. 1 (+) — Chassis ground (–):

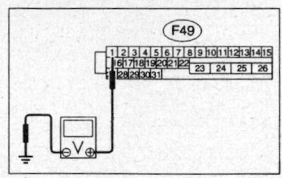

CHECK : *Is the voltage between 10 V and 17 V?*
YES : Go to step **10X4**.
NO : Repair harness connector between battery, ignition switch and ABSCM&H/U.

10X4 : CHECK GROUND CIRCUIT OF ABSCM&H/U.

1) Turn ignition switch to OFF.
2) Measure resistance between ABSCM&H/U connector and chassis ground.

Connector & terminal
(F49) No. 23 — Chassis ground:

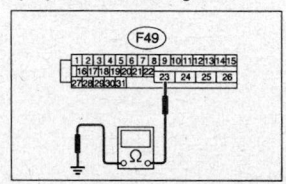

CHECK : *Is the resistance less than 0.5 Ω?*
YES : Go to step **10X5**.
NO : Repair ABSCM&H/U ground harness.

SB4029800173010X

Fig. 34   Code 42: Power Supply Voltage Too High (Part 1 of 2). With Select Monitor

10X5 : CHECK POOR CONTACT IN CONNECTORS.

CHECK : *Is there poor contact in connectors between generator, battery and ABSCM&H/U?*

YES : Repair connector.
NO : Go to step **10X6**.

10X6 : CHECK ABSCM&H/U.

1) Connect all connectors.
2) Erase the memory.
3) Perform inspection mode.
4) Read out the trouble code.

CHECK : *Is the same trouble code as in the current diagnosis still being output?*
YES : Replace ABSCM&H/U.
NO : Go to step **10X7**.

10X7 : CHECK ANY OTHER TROUBLE CODES APPEARANCE.

CHECK : *Are other trouble codes being output?*
YES : Proceed with the diagnosis corresponding to the trouble code.
NO : A temporary poor contact.

SB4029800173020X

Fig. 34   Code 42: Power Supply Voltage Too High (Part 2 of 2). With Select Monitor

10Y1 :	CHECK SPECIFICATIONS OF THE ABSCM&H/U.

Check specifications of the mark to the ABSCM&H/U.

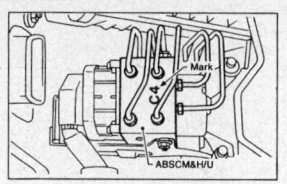

Mark	Model
C3	AWD AT
C4	AWD MT

CHECK : **Is an ABSCM&H/U for AT model installed on a MT model?**
YES : Replace ABSCM&H/U.
NO : Go to step **10Y2**.

10Y2 :	CHECK GROUND SHORT OF HAR-NESS.

1) Turn ignition switch to OFF.
2) Disconnect two connectors from TCM.
3) Disconnect connector from ABSCM&H/U.
4) Measure resistance between ABSCM&H/U connector and chassis ground.

Connector & terminal
(F49) No. 3 — Chassis ground:

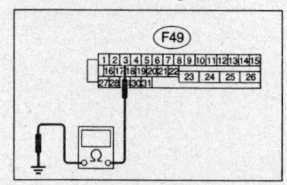

CHECK : **Is the resistance more than 1 MΩ?**
YES : Go to step **10Y3**.
NO : Repair harness between TCM and ABSCM&H/U.

10Y3 :	CHECK TCM.

1) Connect all connectors to TCM.
2) Turn ignition switch to ON.
3) Measure voltage between TCM connector terminal and chassis ground.

Connector & terminal
(B55) No. 5 (+) — Chassis ground (–):

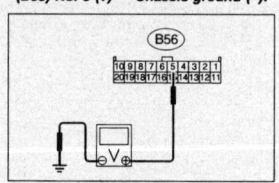

CHECK : **Is the voltage between 10 V and 15 V?**
YES : Go to step **10Y5**.
NO : Go to step **10Y4**.

10Y4 :	CHECK AT.

CHECK : **Is the AT functioning normally?**
YES : Replace TCM.
NO : Repair AT.

SB4029800174010X

Fig. 35   Code 44: ABS AT Control, Non Controlled (Part 1 of 2). With Select Monitor

10Y5 :	CHECK OPEN CIRCUIT OF HAR-NESS.

Measure voltage between ABSCM&H/U connector and chassis ground.
Connector & terminal
(F49) No. 3 (+) — Chassis ground (–):
(F49) No. 31 (+) — Chassis ground (–):

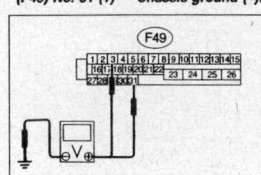

CHECK : **Is the voltage more than 10 V?**
YES : Go to step **10Y6**.
NO : Repair harness/connector between AT control module and ABSCM&H/U.

10Y6 :	CHECK POOR CONTACT IN CON-NECTORS.

CHECK : **Is there poor contact in connectors between AT control module and ABSCM&H/U?**
YES : Repair connector.
NO : Go to step **10Y7**.

10Y7 :	CHECK ABSCM&H/U.

1) Connect all connectors.
2) Erase the memory.
3) Perform inspection mode.
4) Read out the trouble code.

CHECK : **Is the same trouble code as in the current diagnosis still being output?**
YES : Replace ABSCM&H/U.
NO : Go to step **10Y8**.

10Y8 :	CHECK ANY OTHER TROUBLE CODES APPEARANCE.

CHECK : **Are other trouble codes being output?**
YES : Proceed with the diagnosis corresponding to the trouble code.
NO : A temporary poor contact.

SB4029800174020X

Fig. 35   Code 44: ABS AT Control, Non Controlled (Part 2 of 2). With Select Monitor

10Z1 : CHECK BATTERY SHORT OF HARNESS.

1) Turn ignition switch to OFF.
2) Disconnect two connectors from AT control module.
3) Disconnect connector from ABSCM&H/U.
4) Measure voltage between ABSCM&H/U connector and chassis ground.

Connector & terminal
(F49) No. 3 (+) — Chassis ground (–):

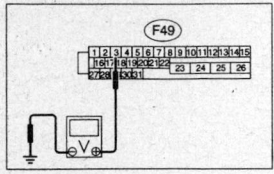

CHECK : *Is the voltage less than 1 V?*
YES : Go to step 10Z2.
NO : Repair harness between AT control module and ABSCM&H/U.

10Z2 : CHECK BATTERY SHORT OF HARNESS.

1) Turn ignition switch to ON.
2) Measure voltage between ABSCM&H/U connector and chassis ground.

Connector & terminal
(F49) No. 3 (+) — Chassis ground (–):

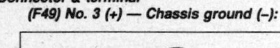
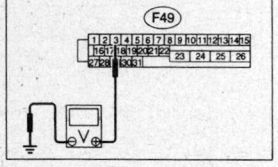

CHECK : *Is the voltage less than 1 V?*
YES : Go to step 10Z3.
NO : Repair harness between AT control module and ABSCM&H/U.

10Z3 : CHECK OPEN CIRCUIT OF HARNESS.

1) Turn ignition switch to OFF.
2) Connect all connectors to TCM.
3) Turn ignition switch to ON.
4) Measure voltage between ABSCM&H/U connector and chassis ground.

Connector & terminal
(F49) No. 3 (+) — Chassis ground (–):
(F49) No. 31 (+) — Chassis ground (–):

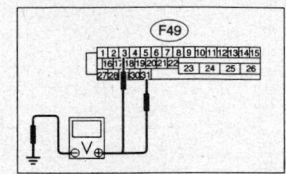

CHECK : *Is the voltage between 10 V and 13 V?*
YES : Go to step 10Z4.
NO : Repair harness/connector between TCM and ABSCM&H/U.

10Z4 : CHECK POOR CONTACT IN CONNECTORS.

Turn ignition switch to OFF.

CHECK : *Is there poor contact in connectors between AT control module and ABSCM&H/U?*
YES : Repair connector.
NO : Go to step 10Z5.

10Z5 : CHECK ABSCM&H/U.

1) Connect all connectors.
2) Erase the memory.
3) Perform inspection mode.
4) Read out the trouble code.

CHECK : *Is the same trouble code as in the current diagnosis still being output?*
YES : Replace ABSCM&H/U.
NO : Go to step 10Z6.

SB4029800175010X

Fig. 36 Code 44: ABS AT Control, Controlled (Part 1 of 2). With Select Monitor

---

10Z6 : CHECK ANY OTHER TROUBLE CODES APPEARANCE.

CHECK : *Are other trouble codes being output?*
YES : Proceed with the diagnosis corresponding to the trouble code.
NO : A temporary poor contact.

SB4029800175020X

Fig. 36 Code 44: ABS AT Control, Controlled (Part 2 of 2). With Select Monitor

---

10AA1 : CHECK INPUT VOLTAGE OF ABSCM&H/U.

1) Turn ignition switch to OFF.
2) Disconnect connector from ABSCM&H/U.
3) Run the engine at idle.
4) Measure voltage between ABSCM&H/U connector and chassis ground.

Connector & terminal
(F49) No. 1 (+) — Chassis ground (–):
(F49) No. 24 (+) — Chassis ground (–):

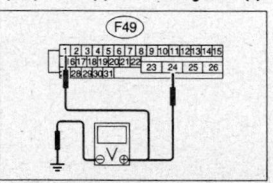

CHECK : *Is the voltage between 10 V and 15 V?*
YES : Go to step 10AA2.
NO : Repair harness connector between battery and ABSCM&H/U.

10AA2 : CHECK GROUND CIRCUIT OF ABSCM&H/U.

1) Turn ignition switch to OFF.
2) Measure resistance between ABSCM&H/U connector and chassis ground.

Connector & terminal
(F49) No. 23 — Chassis ground:

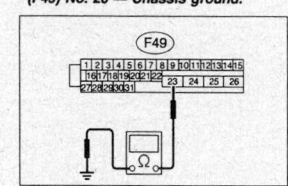

CHECK : *Is the resistance less than 0.5 Ω?*
YES : Go to step 10AA3.
NO : Repair ABSCM&H/U ground harness.

10AA3 : CHECK POOR CONTACT IN CONNECTORS.

CHECK : *Is there poor contact in connectors between generator, battery and ABSCM&H/U?*
YES : Repair connector.
NO : Go to step 10AA4.

10AA4 : CHECK ABSCM&H/U.

1) Connect all connectors.
2) Erase the memory.
3) Perform inspection mode.
4) Read out the trouble code.

CHECK : *Is the same trouble code as in the current diagnosis still being output?*
YES : Replace ABSCM&H/U.
NO : Go to step 10AA5.

10AA5 : CHECK ANY OTHER TROUBLE CODES APPEARANCE.

CHECK : *Are other trouble codes being output?*
YES : Proceed with the diagnosis corresponding to the trouble code.
NO : A temporary poor contact.

SB4029800176000X

Fig. 37 Code 51: Valve Relay Malfunction. With Select Monitor

10AB1 : CHECK VALVE RELAY IN ABSCM&H/U.

Measure resistance between ABSCM&H/U terminals.

Terminals
No. 23 (+) — No. 24 (–):

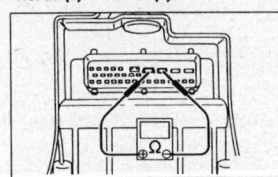

(CHECK) : *Is the resistance more than 1 MΩ?*
(YES) : Go to step **10AB2.**
(NO) : Replace ABSCM&H/U.

10AB2 : CHECK POOR CONTACT IN CONNECTORS.

(CHECK) : *Is there poor contact in connectors between generator, battery and ABSCM&H/U?*
(YES) : Repair connector.
(NO) : Go to step **10AB3.**

10AB3 : CHECK ABSCM&H/U.

1) Connect all connectors.
2) Erase the memory.
3) Perform inspection mode.
4) Read out the trouble code.

(CHECK) : *Is the same trouble code as in the current diagnosis still being output?*
(YES) : Replace ABSCM&H/U.
(NO) : Go to step **10AB4.**

10AB4 : CHECK ANY OTHER TROUBLE CODES APPEARANCE.

(CHECK) : *Are other trouble codes being output?*
(YES) : Proceed with the diagnosis corresponding to the trouble code.
(NO) : A temporary poor contact.

SB4029800177000X

Fig. 38 Code 51: Valve Relay On Failure. With Select Monitor

10AC1 : CHECK INPUT VOLTAGE OF ABSCM&H/U.

1) Turn ignition switch to OFF.
2) Disconnect connector from ABSCM&H/U.
3) Turn ignition switch to ON.
4) Measure voltage between ABSCM&H/U connector and chassis ground.

Connector & terminal
(F49) No. 25 (+) — Chassis ground (–):

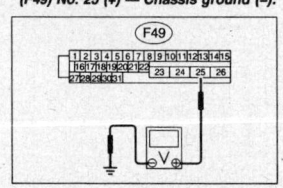

(CHECK) : *Is the voltage between 10 V and 13 V?*
(YES) : Go to step **10AC2.**
(NO) : Repair harness/connector between battery and ABSCM&H/U and check fuse SBF-holder.

10AC2 : CHECK GROUND CIRCUIT OF MOTOR.

1) Turn ignition switch to OFF.
2) Measure resistance between ABSCM&H/U connector and chassis ground.

Connector & terminal
(F49) No. 26 — Chassis ground:

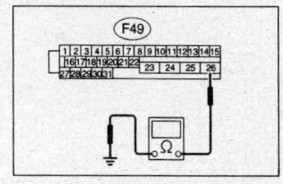

(CHECK) : *Is the resistance less than 0.5 Ω?*
(YES) : Go to step **10AC3.**
(NO) : Repair ABSCM&H/U ground harness.

10AC3 : CHECK MOTOR OPERATION.

Operate the sequence control.

NOTE:
Use the diagnosis connector to operate the sequence control.

(CHECK) : *Can motor revolution noise (buzz) be heard when carrying out the check sequence?*
(YES) : Go to step **10AC4.**
(NO) : Replace ABSCM&H/U.

10AC4 : CHECK POOR CONTACT IN CONNECTORS.

Turn ignition switch to OFF.

(CHECK) : *Is there poor contact in connector between hydraulic unit, relay box and ABSCM&H/U?*
(YES) : Repair connector.
(NO) : Go to step **10AC5.**

10AC5 : CHECK ABSCM&H/U.

1) Connect all connectors.
2) Erase the memory.
3) Perform inspection mode.
4) Read out the trouble code.

(CHECK) : *Is the same trouble code as in the current diagnosis still being output?*
(YES) : Replace ABSCM&H/U.
(NO) : Go to step **10AC6.**

10AC6 : CHECK ANY OTHER TROUBLE CODES APPEARANCE.

(CHECK) : *Are other trouble codes being output?*
(YES) : Proceed with the diagnosis corresponding to the trouble code.
(NO) : A temporary poor contact.

SB4029800178000X

Fig. 39 Code 52: Open Circuit In Motor Relay Circuit. With Select Monitor

10AD1 : CHECK MOTOR RELAY IN ABSCM&H/U.

Measure resistance between ABSCM&H/U terminals.

Terminals
No. 25 — No. 26:

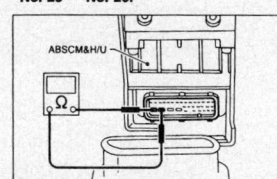

(CHECK) : *Is the resistance more than 1 MΩ?*
(YES) : Go to step **10AD2.**
(NO) : Replace ABSCM&H/U.

10AD2 : CHECK MOTOR OPERATION.

Operate the sequence control.

NOTE:
Use the diagnosis connector to operate the sequence control.

(CHECK) : *Can motor revolution noise (buzz) be heard when carrying out the sequence control?*
(YES) : Go to step **10AD3.**
(NO) : Replace ABSCM&H/U.

10AD3 : CHECK POOR CONTACT IN CONNECTORS.

Turn ignition switch to OFF.

(CHECK) : *Is there poor contact in connector between hydraulic unit, relay box and ABSCM&H/U?*
(YES) : Repair connector.
(NO) : Go to step **10AD4.**

10AD4 : CHECK ABSCM&H/U.

1) Connect all connectors.
2) Erase the memory.
3) Perform inspection mode.
4) Read out the trouble code.

(CHECK) : *Is the same trouble code as in the current diagnosis still being output?*
(YES) : Replace ABSCM&H/U.
(NO) : Go to step **10AD5.**

10AD5 : CHECK ANY OTHER TROUBLE CODES APPEARANCE.

(CHECK) : *Are other trouble codes being output?*
(YES) : Proceed with the diagnosis corresponding to the trouble code.
(NO) : A temporary poor contact.

SB4029800179000X

Fig. 40 Code 52: Motor Relay On Failure. With Select Monitor

10AE1 : CHECK INPUT VOLTAGE OF ABSCM&H/U.

1) Turn ignition switch to OFF.
2) Disconnect connector from ABSCM&H/U.
3) Turn ignition switch to ON.
4) Measure voltage between ABSCM&H/U connector and chassis ground.

Connector & terminal
(F49) No. 25 (+) — Chassis ground (–):

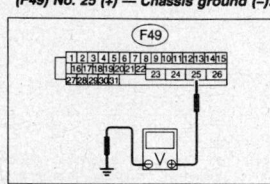

CHECK : *Is the voltage between 10 V and 13 V?*
YES : Go to step **10AE2**.
NO : Repair harness/connector between battery and ABSCM&H/U and check fuse SBF-holder.

10AE2 : CHECK GROUND CIRCUIT OF MOTOR.

1) Turn ignition switch to OFF.
2) Measure resistance between ABSCM&H/U connector and chassis ground.

Connector & terminal
(F49) No. 26 — Chassis ground:

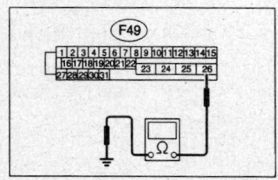

CHECK : *Is the resistance less than 0.5 Ω?*
YES : Go to step **10AE3**.
NO : Repair ABSCM&H/U ground harness.

10AE3 : CHECK INPUT VOLTAGE OF ABSCM&H/U.

1) Run the engine at idle.
2) Measure voltage between ABSCM&H/U connector and chassis ground.

Connector & terminal
(F49) No. 1 (+) — Chassis ground (–):

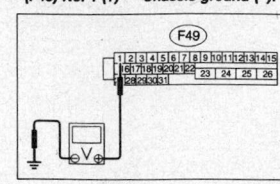

CHECK : *Is the voltage between 10 V and 15 V?*
YES : Go to step **10AE4**.
NO : Repair harness connector between battery, ignition switch and ABSCM&H/U.

10AE4 : CHECK GROUND CIRCUIT OF ABSCM&H/U.

1) Turn ignition switch to OFF.
2) Measure resistance between ABSCM&H/U connector and chassis ground.

Connector & terminal
(F49) No. 23 — Chassis ground:

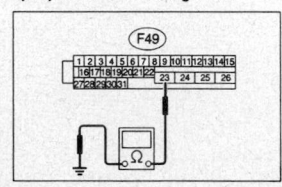

CHECK : *Is the resistance less than 0.5 Ω?*
YES : Go to step **10AE5**.
NO : Repair ABSCM&H/U ground harness.

SB4029800180010X

Fig. 41   Code 52: Motor Malfunction (Part 1 of 2). With Select Monitor

10AE5 : CHECK MOTOR OPERATION.

Operate the sequence control.

NOTE:
Use the diagnosis connector to operate the sequence control.

CHECK : *Can motor revolution noise (buzz) be heard when carrying out the sequence control?*
YES : Go to step **10AE6**.
NO : Replace hydraulic unit.

10AE6 : CHECK POOR CONTACT IN CONNECTORS.

Turn ignition switch to OFF.

CHECK : *Is there poor contact in connector between generator, battery and ABSCM&H/U?*

YES : Repair connector.
NO : Go to step **10AE7**.

10AE7 : CHECK ABSCM&H/U.

1) Connect all connectors.
2) Erase the memory.
3) Perform inspection mode.
4) Read out the trouble code.

CHECK : *Is the same trouble code as in the current diagnosis still being output?*
YES : Replace ABSCM&H/U.
NO : Go to step **10AE8**.

10AE8 : CHECK ANY OTHER TROUBLE CODES APPEARANCE.

CHECK : *Are other trouble codes being output?*
YES : Proceed with the diagnosis corresponding to the trouble code.
NO : A temporary poor contact.

SB4029800180020X

Fig. 41   Code 52: Motor Malfunction (Part 2 of 2). With Select Monitor

10AF1 : CHECK OUTPUT OF STOP LIGHT SWITCH USING SELECT MONITOR.

1) Select "Current data display & Save" on the select monitor.
2) Release the brake pedal.
3) Read the stop light switch output in the select monitor data display.

CHECK : *Is the reading indicated on monitor display less than 1.5 V?*
YES : Go to step **10AF2**.
NO : Go to step **10AF3**.

10AF2 : CHECK OUTPUT OF STOP LIGHT SWITCH USING SELECT MONITOR.

1) Depress the brake pedal.
2) Read the stop light switch output in the select monitor data display.

CHECK : *Is the reading indicated on monitor display between 10 V and 15 V?*
YES : Go to step **10AF5**.
NO : Go to step **10AF3**.

10AF3 : CHECK IF STOP LIGHTS COME ON.

Depress the brake pedal.

CHECK : *Do stop lights turn on?*
YES : Go to step **10AF4**.
NO : Repair stop lights circuit.

10AF4 : CHECK OPEN CIRCUIT IN HARNESS.

1) Turn ignition switch to OFF.
2) Disconnect connector from ABSCM&H/U.
3) Depress brake pedal.
4) Measure voltage between ABSCM&H/U connector and chassis ground.

Connector & terminal
(F49) No. 2 — Chassis ground:

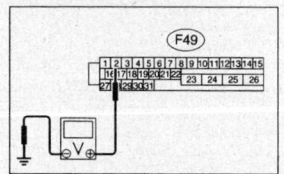

CHECK : *Is the voltage between 10 V and 15 V?*
YES : Go to step **10AF5**.
NO : Repair harness between stop light switch and ABSCM&H/U connector.

10AF5 : CHECK POOR CONTACT IN CONNECTORS.

CHECK : *Is there poor contact in connector between stop light switch and ABSCM&H/U?*
YES : Repair connector.
NO : Go to step **10AF6**.

10AF6 : CHECK ABSCM&H/U.

1) Connect all connectors.
2) Erase the memory.
3) Perform inspection mode.
4) Read out the trouble code.

CHECK : *Is the same trouble code as in the current diagnosis still being output?*
YES : Replace ABSCM&H/U.
NO : Go to step **10AF7**.

SB4029800181010X

Fig. 42 Code 54: Stop Light Switch Signal Circuit Malfunction (Part 1 of 2). With Select Monitor

10AF7 : CHECK ANY OTHER TROUBLE CODES APPEARANCE.

CHECK : *Are other trouble codes being output?*
YES : Proceed with the diagnosis corresponding to the trouble code.
NO : A temporary poor contact.

SB4029800181020X

Fig. 42 Code 54: Stop Light Switch Signal Circuit Malfunction (Part 2 of 2). With Select Monitor

10AG1 : CHECK SPECIFICATIONS OF ABSCM&H/U.

Check specifications of the mark to the ABSCM&H/U.

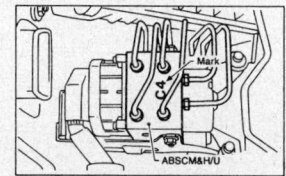

Mark	Model
C3	AWD AT
C4	AWD MT

CHECK : *Is an ABSCM for AWD model installed on a FWD model?*
YES : Replace ABSCM&H/U.

CAUTION:
Be sure to turn ignition switch to OFF when removing ABSCM&H/U.
NO : Go to step **10AG2**.

10AG2 : CHECK OUTPUT OF G SENSOR USING SELECT MONITOR.

1) Select "Current data display & Save" on the select monitor.
2) Read the G sensor output in select monitor data display.

CHECK : *Is the G sensor output on the monitor display between 2.1 and 2.5 V when the G sensor is in horizontal position?*
YES : Go to step **10AG3**.
NO : Go to step **10AG6**.

10AG3 : CHECK POOR CONTACT IN CONNECTORS.

CHECK : *Is there poor contact in connector between ABSCM&H/U and G sensor?*
YES : Repair connector.
NO : Go to step **10AG4**.

10AG4 : CHECK ABSCM&H/U.

1) Connect all connectors.
2) Erase the memory.
3) Perform inspection mode.
4) Read out the trouble code.

CHECK : *Is the same trouble code as in the current diagnosis still being output?*
YES : Replace ABSCM&H/U.
NO : Go to step **10AG5**.

10AG5 : CHECK ANY OTHER TROUBLE CODES APPEARANCE.

CHECK : *Are other trouble codes being output?*
YES : Proceed with the diagnosis corresponding to the trouble code.
NO : A temporary poor contact.

10AG6 : CHECK FREEZE FRAME DATA.

1) Select "Freeze frame data" on the select monitor.
2) Read front right wheel speed on the select monitor display.

CHECK : *Is the front right wheel speed on monitor display 0 km?*
YES : Go to step **10AG7**.
NO : Go to step **10AG15**.

10AG7 : CHECK FREEZE FRAME DATA.

Read front left wheel speed on the select monitor display.

CHECK : *Is the front left wheel speed on monitor display 0 km?*
YES : Go to step **10AG8**.
NO : Go to step **10AG15**.

10AG8 : CHECK FREEZE FRAME DATA.

Read rear right wheel speed on the select monitor display.

CHECK : *Is the rear right wheel speed on monitor display 0 km?*
YES : Go to step **10AG9**.
NO : Go to step **10AG15**.

SB4029800182010X

Fig. 43 Code 56: Open Or Short Circuit In G sensor Circuit (Part 1 of 5). With Select Monitor

SUBARU

10AG9 : CHECK FREEZE FRAME DATA.

Read rear left wheel speed on the select monitor display.

CHECK : *Is the rear left wheel speed on monitor display 0 km?*

YES : Go to step **10AG10**.
NO : Go to step **10AG15**.

10AG10 : CHECK FREEZE FRAME DATA.

Read G sensor output on the select monitor display.

CHECK : *Is the G sensor output on monitor display more than 3.65 V?*

YES : Go to step **10AG11**.
NO : Go to step **10AG15**.

10AG11 : CHECK OPEN CIRCUIT IN G SENSOR OUTPUT HARNESS AND GROUND HARNESS.

1) Turn ignition switch to OFF.
2) Disconnect connector from ABSCM&H/U.
3) Measure resistance between ABSCM&H/U connector terminals.

Connector & terminal
(F49) No. 30 — No. 28:

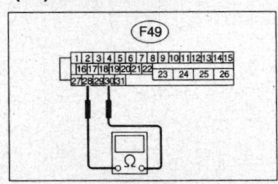

CHECK : *Is the resistance between 4.3 and 4.9 kΩ?*

YES : Go to step **10AG12**.
NO : Repair harness/connector between G sensor and ABSCM&H/U.

10AG12 : CHECK POOR CONTACT IN CONNECTORS.

CHECK : *Is there poor contact in connector between ABSCM&H/U and G sensor?*

YES : Repair connector.
NO : Go to step **10AG13**.

10AG13 : CHECK ABSCM&H/U.

1) Connect all connectors.
2) Erase the memory.
3) Perform inspection mode.
4) Read out the trouble code.

CHECK : *Is the same trouble code as in the current diagnosis still being output?*

YES : Replace ABSCM&H/U.
NO : Go to step **10AG14**.

10AG14 : CHECK ANY OTHER TROUBLE CODES APPEARANCE.

CHECK : *Are other trouble codes being output?*

YES : Proceed with the diagnosis corresponding to the trouble code.
NO : A temporary poor contact.

SB4029800182020X

Fig. 43   Code 56: Open Or Short Circuit In G sensor Circuit (Part 2 of 5). With Select Monitor

10AG15 : CHECK INPUT VOLTAGE OF G SENSOR.

1) Turn ignition switch to OFF.
2) Remove console box.
3) Disconnect G sensor from body. (Do not disconnect connector.)
4) Turn ignition switch to ON.
5) Measure voltage between G sensor connector terminals.

Connector & terminal
(R70) No. 1 (+) — No. 3 (–):

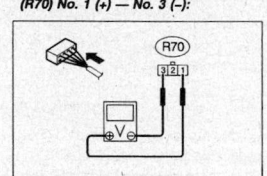

CHECK : *Is the voltage between 4.75 and 5.25 V?*

YES : Go to step **10AG16**.
NO : Repair harness/connector between G sensor and ABSCM&H/U.

10AG16 : CHECK OPEN CIRCUIT IN G SENSOR OUTPUT HARNESS AND GROUND HARNESS.

1) Turn ignition switch to OFF.
2) Disconnect connector from ABSCM&H/U.
3) Measure resistance between ABSCM&H/U connector terminals.

Connector & terminal
(F49) No. 30 — No. 28:

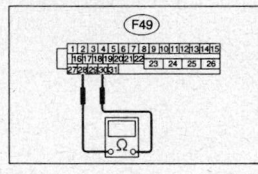

CHECK : *Is the resistance between 4.3 and 4.9 kΩ?*

YES : Go to step **10AG17**.
NO : Repair harness/connector between G sensor and ABSCM&H/U.

10AG17 : CHECK GROUND SHORT IN G SENSOR OUTPUT HARNESS.

1) Disconnect connector from G sensor.
2) Measure resistance between ABSCM&H/U connector and chassis ground.

Connector & terminal
(F49) No. 6 — Chassis ground:

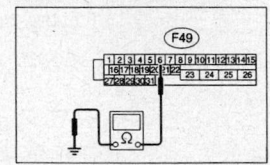

CHECK : *Is the resistance more than 1 MΩ?*

YES : Go to step **10AG18**.
NO : Repair harness between G sensor and ABSCM&H/U.

SB4029800182030X

Fig. 43   Code 56: Open Or Short Circuit In G sensor Circuit (Part 3 of 5). With Select Monitor

10AG18 : CHECK G SENSOR.

1) Connect connector to G sensor.
2) Connect connector to ABSCM&H/U.
3) Turn ignition switch to ON.
4) Measure voltage between G sensor connector terminals.

Connector & terminal
(R70) No. 2 (+) — No. 3 (–):

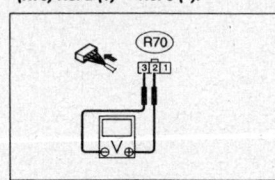

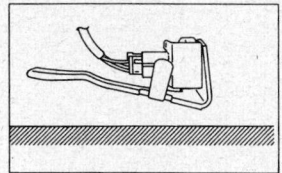

CHECK : **Is the voltage between 2.1 and 2.5 V when G sensor is horizontal?**
YES : Go to step **10AG19**.
NO : Replace G sensor.

10AG19 : CHECK G SENSOR.

Measure voltage between G sensor connector terminals.

Connector & terminal
(R70) No. 2 (+) — No. 3 (–):

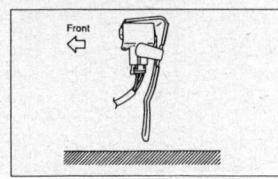

CHECK : **Is the voltage between 3.7 and 4.1 V when G sensor is inclined forwards to 90°?**
YES : Go to step **10AG20**.
NO : Replace G sensor.

10AG20 : CHECK G SENSOR.

Measure voltage between G sensor connector terminals.

Connector & terminal
(R70) No. 2 (+) — No. 3 (–):

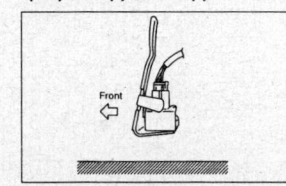

CHECK : **Is the voltage between 0.5 and 0.9 V when G sensor is inclined backwards to 90°?**
YES : Go to step **10AG21**.
NO : Replace G sensor.

SB4029800182040X

Fig. 43 Code 56: Open Or Short Circuit In G sensor Circuit (Part 4 of 5). With Select Monitor

---

10AH1 : CHECK OUTPUT OF G SENSOR USING SELECT MONITOR.

1) Select "Current data display & Save" on the select monitor.
2) Read G sensor output on the select monitor display.

CHECK : **Is the G sensor output on monitor display between 2.1 and 2.5 V when the G sensor is in horizontal position?**
YES : Replace ABSCM&H/U.
NO : Go to step **10AH2**.

10AH2 : CHECK BATTERY SHORT OF HARNESS.

1) Turn ignition switch to OFF.
2) Remove console box.
3) Disconnect connector from G sensor.
4) Disconnect connector from ABSCM&H/U.
5) Measure voltage between ABSCM&H/U connector and chassis ground.

Connector & terminal
(F49) No. 6 (+) — Chassis ground (–):

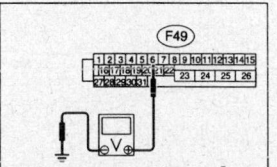

CHECK : **Is the voltage less than 1 V?**
YES : Go to step **10AH3**.
NO : Repair harness between G sensor and ABSCM&H/U.

10AH3 : CHECK BATTERY SHORT OF HARNESS.

1) Turn ignition switch to ON.
2) Measure voltage between ABSCM&H/U connector and chassis ground.

Connector & terminal
(F49) No. 6 (+) — Chassis ground (–):

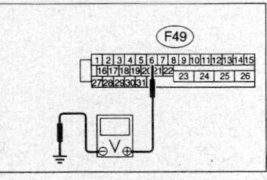

CHECK : **Is the voltage less than 1 V?**
YES : Go to step **10AH4**.
NO : Repair harness between G sensor and ABSCM&H/U.

10AH4 : CHECK ABSCM&H/U.

1) Turn ignition switch to OFF.
2) Connect all connectors.
3) Erase the memory.
4) Perform inspection mode.
5) Read out the trouble code.

CHECK : **Is the same trouble code as in the current diagnosis still being output?**
YES : Replace ABSCM&H/U.
NO : Go to step **10AH5**.

10AH5 : CHECK ANY OTHER TROUBLE CODES APPEARANCE.

CHECK : **Are other trouble codes being output?**
YES : Proceed with the diagnosis corresponding to the trouble code.
NO : A temporary poor contact.

SB4029800183000X

Fig. 44 Code 56: Battery Short In G Sensor Circuit. With Select Monitor

---

10AG21 : CHECK POOR CONTACT IN CONNECTORS.

Turn ignition switch to OFF.

CHECK : **Is there poor contact in connector between ABSCM&H/U and G sensor?**
YES : Repair connector.
NO : Go to step **10AG22**.

10AG22 : CHECK ABSCM&H/U.

1) Connect all connectors.
2) Erase the memory.
3) Perform inspection mode.
4) Read out the trouble code.

CHECK : **Is the same trouble code as in the current diagnosis still being output?**
YES : Replace ABSCM&H/U.
NO : Go to step **10AG23**.

10AG23 : CHECK ANY OTHER TROUBLE CODES APPEARANCE.

CHECK : **Are other trouble codes being output?**
YES : Proceed with the diagnosis corresponding to the trouble code.
NO : A temporary poor contact.

SB4029800182050X

Fig. 43 Code 56: Open Or Short Circuit In G sensor Circuit (Part 5 of 5). With Select Monitor

---

10AI1 : CHECK OUTPUT OF G SENSOR USING SELECT MONITOR.

1) Select "Current data display & Save" on the select monitor.
2) Read G sensor output on the select monitor display.

CHECK : **Is the G sensor output on monitor display 2.3±0.2 V when the G sensor is in horizontal position?**
YES : Go to step **10AI2**.
NO : Go to step **10AI6**.

10AI2 : CHECK POOR CONTACT IN CONNECTORS.

Turn ignition switch to OFF.

CHECK : **Is there poor contact in connector between ABSCM&H/U and G sensor?**
YES : Repair connector.
NO : Go to step **10AI3**.

10AI3 : CHECK ABSCM&H/U.

1) Connect all connectors.
2) Erase the memory.
3) Perform inspection mode.
4) Read out the trouble code.

CHECK : **Is the same trouble code as in the current diagnosis still being output?**
YES : Replace ABSCM&H/U.
NO : Go to step **10AI4**.

10AI4 : CHECK ANY OTHER TROUBLE CODES APPEARANCE.

CHECK : **Are other trouble codes being output?**
YES : Proceed with the diagnosis corresponding to the trouble code.
NO : A temporary poor contact.

10AI5 : CHECK OPEN CIRCUIT IN G SENSOR OUTPUT HARNESS AND GROUND HARNESS.

1) Turn ignition switch to OFF.
2) Disconnect connector from ABSCM&H/U.
3) Measure resistance between ABSCM&H/U connector terminals.

Connector & terminal
(F49) No. 30 — No. 28:

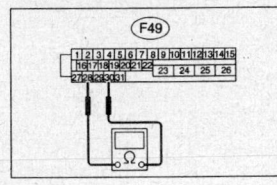

CHECK : **Is the resistance between 4.3 and 4.9 kΩ?**
YES : Go to step **10AI6**.
NO : Repair harness/connector between G sensor and ABSCM&H/U.

10AI6 : CHECK GROUND SHORT OF HARNESS.

Measure resistance between ABSCM&H/U connector and chassis ground.

Connector & terminal
(F49) No. 28 — Chassis ground:

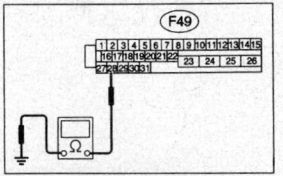

CHECK : **Is the resistance more than 1 MΩ?**
YES : Go to step **10AI7**.
NO : Repair harness between G sensor and ABSCM&H/U.
Replace ABSCM&H/U.

SB4029800184010X

Fig. 45 Code 56: Abnormal G Sensor High Output (Part 1 of 3). With Select Monitor

---

10AI7 : CHECK G SENSOR.

1) Remove console box.
2) Remove G sensor from vehicle.
3) Connect connector to G sensor.
4) Connect connector to ABSCM&H/U.
5) Turn ignition switch to ON.
6) Measure voltage between G sensor connector terminals.

Connector & terminal
(R70) No. 2 (+) — No. 3 (–):

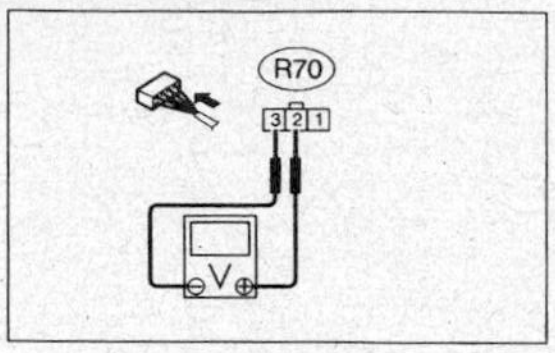

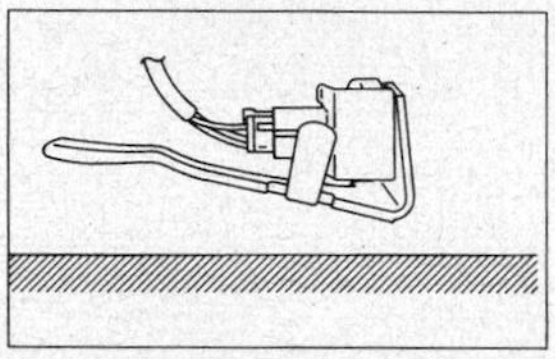

(CHECK) : *Is the voltage between 2.1 and 2.5 V when G sensor is horizontal?*
(YES) : Go to step **10AI8**.
(NO) : Replace G sensor.

10AI8 : CHECK G SENSOR.

Measure voltage between G sensor connector terminals.

Connector & terminal
(R70) No. 2 (+) — No. 3 (–):

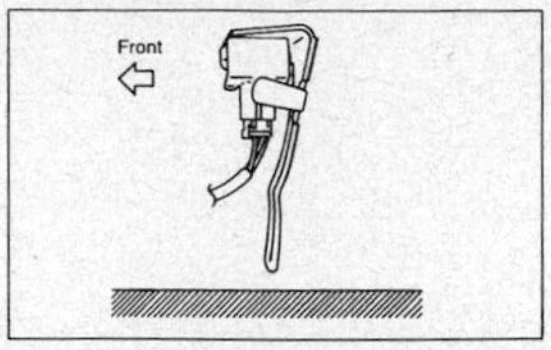

(CHECK) : *Is the voltage between 3.7 and 4.1 V when G sensor is inclined forwards to 90°?*
(YES) : Go to step **10AI9**.
(NO) : Replace G sensor.

10AI9 : CHECK G SENSOR.

Measure voltage between G sensor connector terminals.

Connector & terminal
(R70) No. 2 (+) — No. 3 (–):

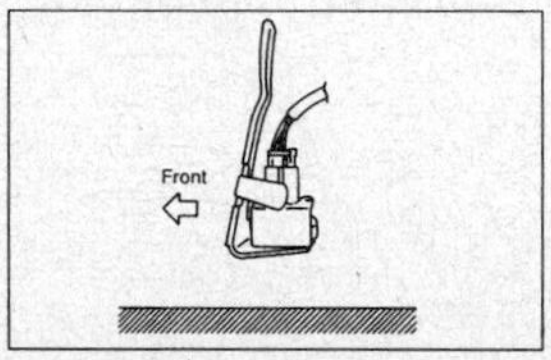

(CHECK) : *Is the voltage between 0.5 and 0.9 V when G sensor is inclined backwards to 90°?*
(YES) : Go to step **10AI10**.
(NO) : Replace G sensor.

SB4029800184020X

Fig. 45 Code 56: Abnormal G Sensor High Output (Part 2 of 3). With Select Monitor

10AI10 : CHECK ABSCM&H/U.

1) Turn ignition switch to OFF.
2) Connect all connectors.
3) Erase the memory.
4) Perform inspection mode.
5) Read out the trouble code.

(CHECK) : *Is the same trouble code as in the current diagnosis still being output?*
(YES) : Replace ABSCM&H/U.
(NO) : Go to step **10AI11**.

10AI11 : CHECK ANY OTHER TROUBLE CODES APPEARANCE.

(CHECK) : *Are other trouble codes being output?*
(YES) : Proceed with the diagnosis corresponding to the trouble code.
(NO) : A temporary poor contact.

SB4029800184030X

Fig. 45 Code 56: Abnormal G Sensor High Output (Part 3 of 3). With Select Monitor

10AJ1 :	CHECK ALL FOUR WHEELS FOR FREE TURNING.

CHECK : **Have the wheels been turned freely such as when the vehicle is lifted up, or operated on a rolling road?**

YES : The ABS is normal. Erase the trouble code.

NO : Go to step **10AJ2**.

10AJ2 :	CHECK OUTPUT OF G SENSOR USING SELECT MONITOR.

1) Select "Current data display & Save" on the select monitor.
2) Read the select monitor display.

CHECK : **Is the G sensor output on the monitor display between 2.1 and 2.5 V when the vehicle is in horizontal position?**

YES : Go to step **10AJ3**.

NO : Go to step **10AJ8**.

10AJ3 :	CHECK OUTPUT OF G SENSOR USING SELECT MONITOR.

1) Turn ignition switch to OFF.
2) Remove console box.
3) Remove G sensor from vehicle. (Do not disconnect connector.)
4) Turn ignition switch to ON.
5) Select "Current data display & Save" on the select monitor.
6) Read the select monitor display.

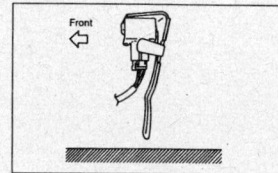

CHECK : **Is the G sensor output on the monitor display between 3.7 and 4.1 V when G sensor is inclined forwards to 90°?**

YES : Go to step **10AJ4**.

NO : Replace G sensor.

10AJ4 :	CHECK OUTPUT OF G SENSOR USING SELECT MONITOR.

Read the select monitor display.

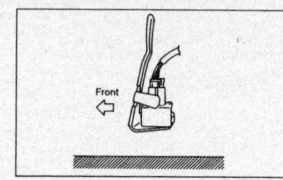

CHECK : **Is the G sensor output on the monitor display between 0.5 and 0.9 V when G sensor is inclined backwards to 90°?**

YES : Go to step **10AJ5**.

NO : Replace G sensor.

10AJ5 :	CHECK POOR CONTACT IN CONNECTORS.

Turn ignition switch to OFF.

CHECK : **Is there poor contact in connector between ABSCM&H/U and G sensor?**

YES : Repair connector.

NO : Go to step **10AJ6**.

10AJ6 :	CHECK ABSCM&H/U.

1) Connect all connectors.
2) Erase the memory.
3) Perform inspection mode.
4) Read out the trouble code.

CHECK : **Is the same trouble code as in the current diagnosis still being output?**

YES : Replace ABSCM&H/U.

NO : Go to step **10AJ7**.

10AJ7 :	CHECK ANY OTHER TROUBLE CODES APPEARANCE.

CHECK : **Are other trouble codes being output?**

YES : Proceed with the diagnosis corresponding to the trouble code.

NO : A temporary poor contact.

SB4029800185010X

Fig. 46   Code 56: Detection Of G Sensor Stick (Part 1 of 2). With Select Monitor

10AJ8 :	CHECK OPEN CIRCUIT IN G SENSOR OUTPUT HARNESS AND GROUND HARNESS.

1) Turn ignition switch to OFF.
2) Disconnect connector from ABSCM&H/U.
3) Measure resistance between ABSCM&H/U connector terminals.

Connector & terminal
(F49) No. 30 — No. 28:

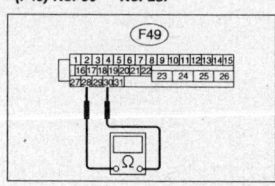

CHECK : **Is the resistance between 4.3 and 4.9 kΩ?**

YES : Go to step **10AJ9**.

NO : Repair harness/connector between G sensor and ABSCM&H/U.

10AJ9 :	CHECK G SENSOR.

1) Remove console box.
2) Remove G sensor from vehicle.
3) Connect connector to G sensor.
4) Connect connector to ABSCM&H/U.
5) Turn ignition switch to ON.
6) Measure voltage between G sensor connector terminals.

Connector & terminal
(R70) No. 2 (+) — No. 1 (–):

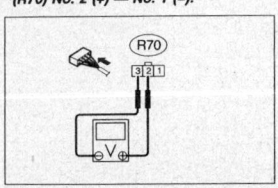

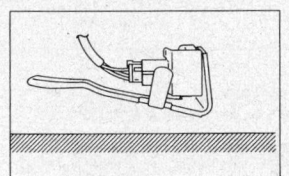

CHECK : **Is the voltage between 2.1 and 2.5 V when G sensor is horizontal?**

YES : Go to step **10AJ10**.

NO : Replace G sensor.

SB4029800185020X

Fig. 46   Code 56: Detection Of G sensor Stick (Part 2 of 2). With Select Monitor

SUBARU

1996-97 Legacy

INDEX

PRECAUTIONS

AIR BAG SYSTEMS

Refer to "Air Bag System Precautions" in the front of this manual for system disarming and arming procedures.

BATTERY GROUND CABLE

Prior to service, disconnect battery ground cable and isolate as required.

DESCRIPTION

The Anti-lock Brake System (ABS) electrically controls brake fluid pressure to prevent wheel lock during braking on slippery road surfaces, which improves directional steering stability as well as shortening the braking distance.

If ABS becomes inoperative, the fail-safe system activates to ensure it acts as a conventional brake system. The warning lamp also comes on to indicate that the ABS is malfunctioning.

The front and rear wheels utilize a four sensor, four channel control design. The front wheels have an independent control design, which independently controls fluid pressure to left and right front wheels. The rear wheels have a select low control design, which provides the same pressure control for the two rear wheels if either wheel starts to lock.

Refer to **Figs. 1 and 2** for system component location, description and operation.

TROUBLESHOOTING

Refer to **Figs. 3 and 4,** for troubleshooting procedures.

PRELIMINARY INSPECTION

1. Ensure battery voltage is 12 volts or more.
2. Ensure specific gravity of battery is 1.260.
3. Check condition of main and other fuses, harnesses and connector. Also check for proper grounding.
4. Check brake fluid level and for leakage.
5. Check for brake drag, brake pad and rotor condition.

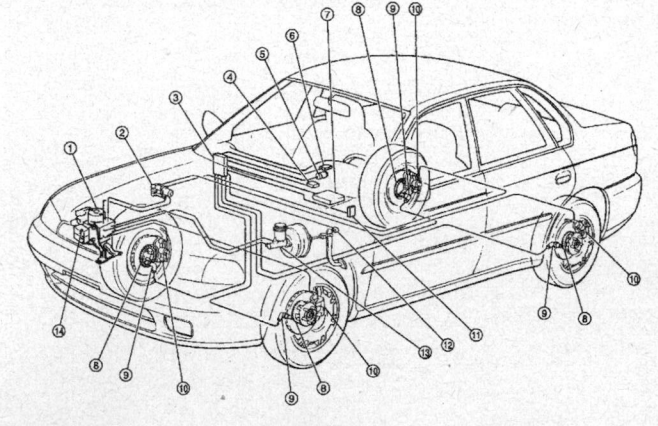

① Hydraulic control unit	⑥ Data link connector (for SUBARU select monitor)	⑨ ABS sensor
② Proportioning valve		⑩ Wheel cylinder
③ ABS control module	⑦ Transmission control module (only AT vehicle)	⑪ G sensor (only AWD vehicle)
④ Diagnosis connector		⑫ Brake switch
⑤ ABS warning light	⑧ Tone wheel	⑬ Master cylinder
		⑭ Relay box

SB4029600064000X

Fig. 1 ABS component locations

6. Ensure tires are in good condition and at specified air pressure.

INSPECTION MODE

The on board diagnosis system is designed to detect problems after the vehicle has been driven at 6 mph for more than 20 seconds. If a problem is found, the ABS warning lamp will illuminate to inform the drive of the occurrence of a problem. When the lamp is on the ABS system will be inactive and normal braking function will work. Problems will be stored in memory as trouble codes. Up to three codes can be stored in memory at one time.

DIAGNOSIS & TESTING

ACCESSING DIAGNOSTIC TROUBLE CODES

When the control module detects a problem, the information (up to a maximum of three) will be stored in the EEPROM as a trouble code. When there are more than three, the most recent three will be stored. Stored codes will stay in memory until they are cleared.

1. Remove ABS check connector from under side of drivers side heater unit, **Fig. 5.**

2. Turn ignition switch off, then ground ABS check connector terminal No. 6 to diagnosis terminal.
3. Turn ignition switch to the On position. ABS warning light is now in the diagnostic mode and will blink to identify trouble codes.
4. After start code (11) is shown, the trouble code(s) will be shown in order of the last information first. The code(s) will repeat for a maximum of 5 minutes. When there are no trouble codes in memory, only the start code (11) is shown.

DIAGNOSTIC TROUBLE CODE INTERPRETATION

Refer to **Fig. 6,** for trouble code interpretation and **Fig. 7,** for trouble code identification and description.

WIRING DIAGRAM

Refer to **Fig. 8** for wiring diagram.

CLEARING DIAGNOSTIC TROUBLE CODES

After completing necessary repairs, clear trouble code memory as follows:

1. After calling up a trouble code, disconnect ABS check connector terminal

Name	Function
ABS control module (ABSCM)	• Calculates and determine the conditions of the wheels and body from the wheel speeds and makes a proper decision suitable for the current situation to control the hydraulic unit. • In the ABS operation mode, the module outputs a cooperative control signal to the AT control module. (AT vehicles only) • Whenever the ignition switch is placed at ON, the module makes a self diagnosis. When anything wrong is detected, the module cuts off the system. • Communicates with the Subaru select monitor.
Hydraulic unit (H/U)	In the ABS operation mode, the H/U changes fluid passages to control the fluid pressure of the wheel cylinders in response to an instruction from the ABSCM. The H/U also constitutes the brake fluid passage from the master cylinder to the wheel cylinders together with pipings.
Wheel speed sensor (ABS sensor)	Detects the wheel speed in terms of a change in the magnetic flux density passing through the sensor, converts it into an electrical signal, and outputs the electrical signal to the ABSCM.
Tone wheel	Gives a change in the magnetic flux density by the teeth around the tone wheel to let the ABS sensor generate an electrical signal.
G sensor (AWD vehicle only)	Detects a change in G in the longitudinal direction of the vehicle and outputs it to the ABSCM in terms of a change in voltage.
Relay box	Accommodates the valve relay and motor relay.
Valve relay	Serves as a power switch for the solenoid valve and motor relay coil in response to an instruction from the ABSCM. The valve relay also constitutes one of the duplicated ABS warning light drive circuits.
Motor relay	Serves as a power switch for the pump motor in response to an instruction from the ABSCM.
Stop light switch	Transmits the information on whether the brake pedal is depressed or not to the ABSCM for use as a condition in determining ABS operation.
ABS warning light	Alerts the driver to an ABS fault. When the diagnosis connector and diagnosis terminal are connected, the light flashes to indicate a trouble codes in response to an instruction from the ABSCM.
AT control module (TCM) (AT vehicles only)	Provides shift controls (fixing the speed at 3rd or changing front and rear wheel transmission characteristics on AWD vehicle) in response to an instruction from the ABSCM.

SB4029600065000X

Fig. 2 ABS components

No. 6 from diagnosis terminal, **Fig. 5.**
2. Repeat connecting and disconnecting terminal No. 6 from diagnosis terminal three times within approximately 12 seconds. Leave terminal No. 6 disconnected for at least ½ second each time.

COMPONENT TESTING

Refer to **Fig. 9** when testing ABS component voltages.

SYSTEM SERVICE

Brake System Bleed

Two technicians are needed to bleed the brake system. Brake pedal operation must be very slow. Keep brake fluid reserve tank full to prevent air from entering the system during the bleeding procedure.
1. Connect ABS check connector diagnosis terminal to terminal No. 6. Connector is located beside driver side seat heater unit.
2. Start engine, then after ABS warning lamp goes out, depress brake pedal within 0.5 seconds.
3. Check entire brake system for fluid leaks.
4. Bleed air from right front caliper as follows:
   a. Fit one end of a vinyl tube onto air bleeder, place other end of tube into a container of brake fluid.
   b. Slowly depress brake pedal and keep it depressed, then open air bleeder for 1–2 seconds.
   c. Close air bleeder and slowly release brake pedal.
   d. Repeat steps "a" through "c" until no more air comes out. **Allow 3–4 seconds between brake pedal operations.**

5. Bleed air from right front caliper suction pipe as follows:
   a. Open air bleeder.
   b. Depress TCS off switch for 20 seconds or more. **Ensure no more air comes out from air bleeder.**
   c. Close air bleeder.
6. Repeat steps 4 and 5 for left front caliper and suction pipe.
7. Repeat step 4 for right rear caliper.
8. Repeat step 4 for left rear caliper.
9. Tighten air bleeders securely when bubbles are visible.
10. Operate front right outlet and rear left outlet valves to bleed air from hydraulic unit outlet circuit as follows:
    a. Press TCS OFF switch while depressing brake pedal.
    b. Ensure ABS warning lamp illuminates.
    c. Depress and release brake pedal 10 times or more while pressing TCS OFF switch.
    d. Repeat procedure until no more air escapes the reservoir tank.
11. Repeat step 10 for front left and rear right outlet valves.
12. Fully depress brake pedal for 20 seconds and ensure there are no leaks in brake system.
13. Turn ignition switch to off position and perform TCS sequence control.
14. With engine at idle, inspect brake pedal stroke as follows:
    a. Depress brake pedal with 110 lbs. of force, then measure distance between brake pedal and steering wheel.
    b. Release brake pedal, then measure distance between brake pedal and steering wheel again.

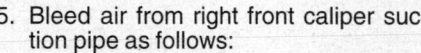

NOTE:
• To check harness for broken wires or short circuits, shake it while holding it or the connector.
• When ABS warning light illuminates, read and record trouble code indicated by ABS warning light.

SB4029600066000X

Fig. 3 Basic troubleshooting chart

c. The difference between both measurements should be 3.74 inches. **If measurement is not as specified it is possible that air is still in brake system.**
15. Turn ignition switch to off position, then top off brake fluid level.
16. Test drive vehicle at low speed and ensure proper brake operation.

Component Replacement

FRONT SENSOR

1. Disconnect sensor, located in engine compartment.
2. Remove sensor harness to bracket bolts, then the sensor to housing bolts.
3. Remove brake caliper, brake rotor, driveshaft, knuckle and hub assemblies.
4. Remove tone wheel while removing hub from knuckle. Ensure teeth faces of tone wheel are not damaged during removal.
5. Reverse procedure to install, noting the following:
   a. Place a thickness gauge between sensor's pole piece and tone wheel's tooth face.
   b. After standard clearance is obtained over entire perimeter, **torque** sensor to housing bolts to 17–31 ft. lbs.

REAR SENSOR

1. Remove rear seat and disconnect sensor connector.
2. Remove sensor harness bracket from

Symptom		Probable faulty units/parts
Vehicle instability during braking	Vehicle pulls to either side.	• Hydraulic unit (solenoid valve) • ABS sensor • Brake (caliper & piston, pads) • Wheel alignment • Tire specifications, tire wear and air pressures • Incorrect wiring or piping connections • Road surface (uneven, camber)
	Vehicle spins.	• Hydraulic unit (solenoid valve) • ABS sensor • Brake (pads) • Tire specifications, tire wear and air pressures • Incorrect wiring or piping connections
Poor braking	Long braking/stopping distance.	• Hydraulic unit (solenoid valve) • Brake (pads) • Air in brake line • Tire specifications, tire wear and air pressures • Incorrect wiring or piping connections
	Wheel locks.	• Hydraulic unit (solenoid valve, motor) • ABS sensor • Incorrect wiring or piping connections
	Brake dragging	• Hydraulic unit (solenoid valve) • ABS sensor • Master cylinder • Brake (caliper & piston) • Parking brake • Axle & wheels • Brake pedal play
	Long brake pedal stroke	• Air in brake line • Brake pedal play
	Vehicle pitching	• Suspension play or fatigue (reduced damping) • Incorrect wiring or piping connections • Road surface (uneven)
	Unstable or uneven braking	• Hydraulic unit (solenoid valve) • ABS sensor • Brake (caliper & piston, pads) • Tire specifications, tire wear and air pressures • Incorrect wiring or piping connections • Road surface (uneven)
Vibration and/or noise (while driving on slippery roads)	Excessive pedal vibration	• Incorrect wiring or piping connections • Road surface (uneven)
	Noise from hydraulic unit	• Hydraulic unit (mount bushing) • ABS sensor • Brake piping
	Noise from front of vehicle	• Hydraulic unit (mount bushing) • ABS sensor • Master cylinder • Brake (caliper & piston, pads, rotor) • Brake piping • Brake booster & check valve • Suspension play or fatigue
	Noise from rear of vehicle	• ABS sensor • Brake (caliper & piston, pads, rotor) • Parking brake • Brake piping • Suspension play or fatigue

SB4029600067000X

Fig. 4   General diagnostics chart

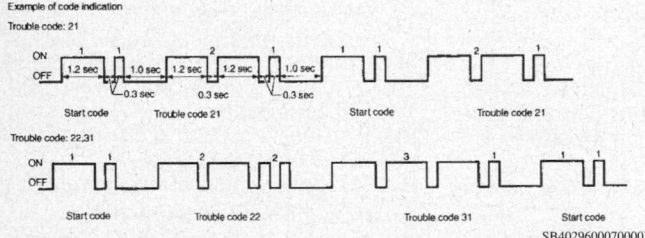

Example of code indication
Trouble code: 21

Trouble code: 22,31

SB4029600070000X

Fig. 6   Trouble code interpretation

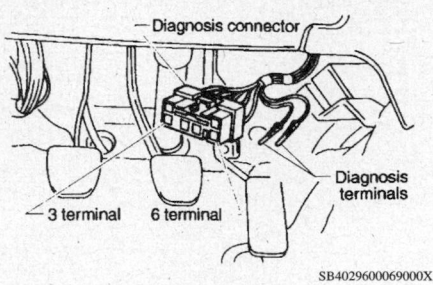

SB4029600069000X

Fig. 5   Check connector terminal identification

Trouble code	Contents of diagnosis	
11	Start code • Trouble code is shown after start code. • Only start code is shown in normal condition.	
21	Abnormal ABS sensor (Open circuit or input voltage too high)	Front right ABS sensor
23		Front left ABS sensor
25		Rear right ABS sensor
27		Rear left ABS sensor
22	Abnormal ABS sensor (Abnormal ABS sensor signal)	Front right ABS sensor
24		Front left ABS sensor
26		Rear right ABS sensor
28		Rear left ABS sensor
29		Any one of four
31	Abnormal solenoid valve circuit(s) in hydraulic unit	Front right inlet valve
32		Front right outlet valve
33		Front left inlet valve
34		Front left outlet valve
35		Rear right inlet valve
36		Rear right outlet valve
37		Rear left inlet valve
38		Rear left outlet valve
41	Abnormal ABS control module	
42	Source voltage is low.	
44	A combination of AT control abnormals	
46	Abnormal G sensor power supply voltage	
51	Abnormal valve relay	
52	Abnormal motor and/or motor relay	
54	Abnormal stop light switch	
56	Abnormal G sensor output voltage	

SB4029600071000X

Fig. 7   Trouble code description

trailing link, then the sensor from rear back plate.

3. Remove rear tone wheel while removing hub from housing assembly. Ensure teeth faces of tone wheel are not damaged during removal.

4. Reverse procedure to install, noting the following:
   a. Place a thickness gauge between sensor's pole piece and tone wheel's tooth face.
   b. After standard clearance is obtained over entire perimeter, **torque** sensor to housing bolts to 17-31 ft. lbs.

ABS HYDRAULIC UNIT

1. Remove air intake duct and canister from engine compartment.
2. Disconnect hydraulic unit electrical connector, then unlock cable clip.
3. Disconnect brake lines from hydraulic unit and plug open ports to prevent foreign particles from entering unit.
4. Remove hydraulic unit to bracket nuts and bolts, then the unit from the vehicle, noting the following precautions:
   a. Hydraulic unit cannot be disassem-

bled. Do not attempt to loosen nuts and bolts.
   b. Do not drop or bump hydraulic unit.
   c. Do not turn hydraulic unit upside down or place it on is side.
   d. Be careful to prevent foreign particles from getting into hydraulic unit.
5. Reverse procedure to install. **Torque** hydraulic unit attaching bolts to 17-31 ft. lbs.

ABS RELAY BOX

1. Remove air intake duct and canister from engine compartment
2. Disconnect connector from relay box.
3. Unlock cable clip.
4. Remove nuts which secure relay box to bracket, then the relay box and connector bracket from vehicle.
5. Reverse procedure to install.

ABS CONTROL MODULE

1. Turn ignition switch to off position.
2. Remove lower trim from front pillar.
3. Remove glove box and bracket.
4. Remove pocket back panel.
5. Remove bolt from bracket.
6. Remove bolt cover and bolt.

7. Remove control module upper mounting bolt.
8. Pull lower part of instrument panel rearward approximately two inches. **Do not pull panel more than 2.4 inches rearward or panel will be deformed.**
9. Remove instrument panel securing clips.
10. Remove control module lower mounting bolts.
11. While holding lower part of instrument panel rearward approximately two inches, remove control module.
12. Disconnect electrical connector from module.
13. Reverse procedure to install.

G SENSOR

1. Turn ignition switch to off position.
2. Remove console box.
3. Disconnect G sensor electrical connector.
4. Remove G sensor mounting bolt, then the sensor.
5. Reverse procedure to install. **Torque** sensor mounting bolt to 3-7 ft. lbs.

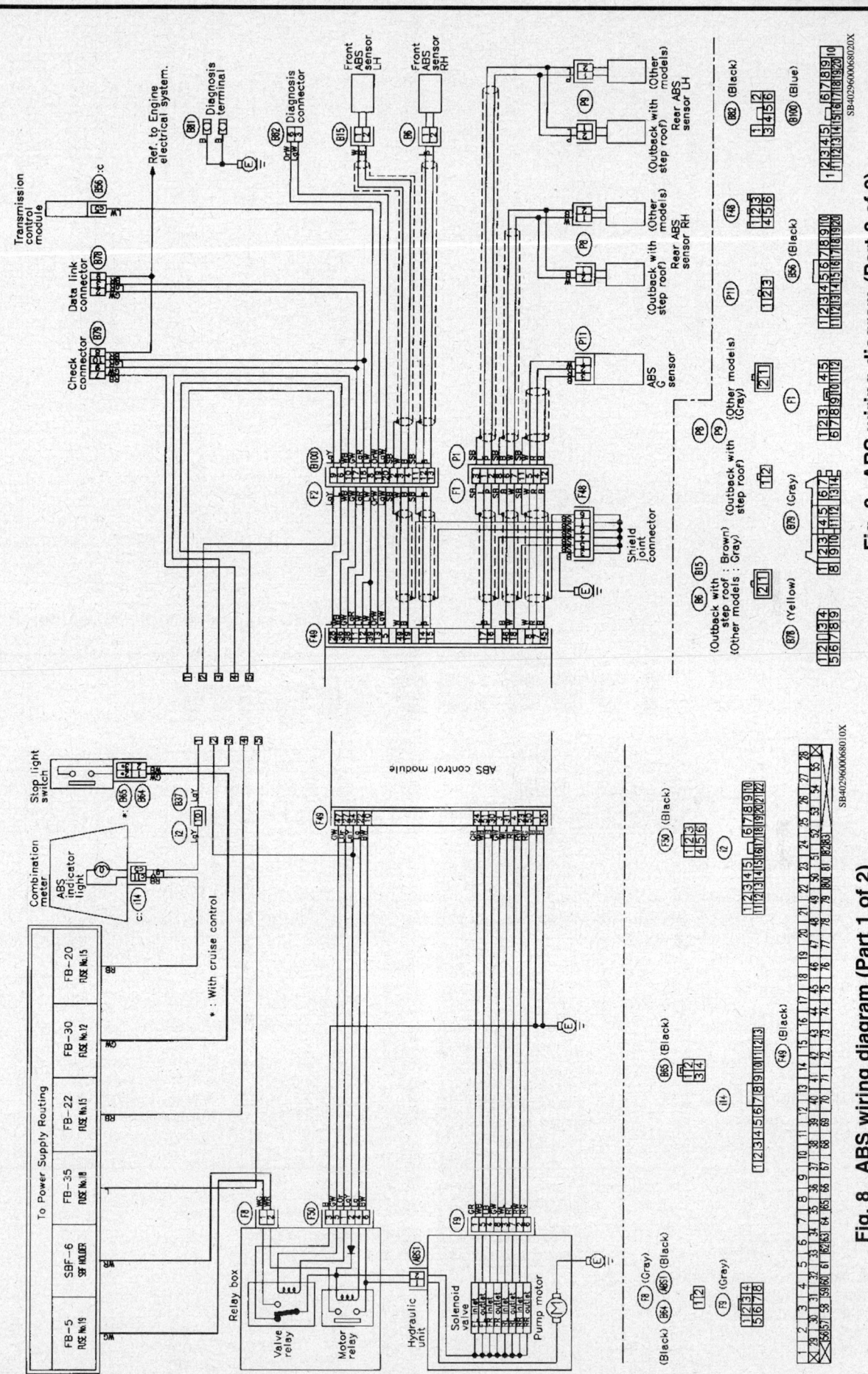

Fig. 8 ABS wiring diagram (Part 2 of 2)

Fig. 8 ABS wiring diagram (Part 1 of 2)

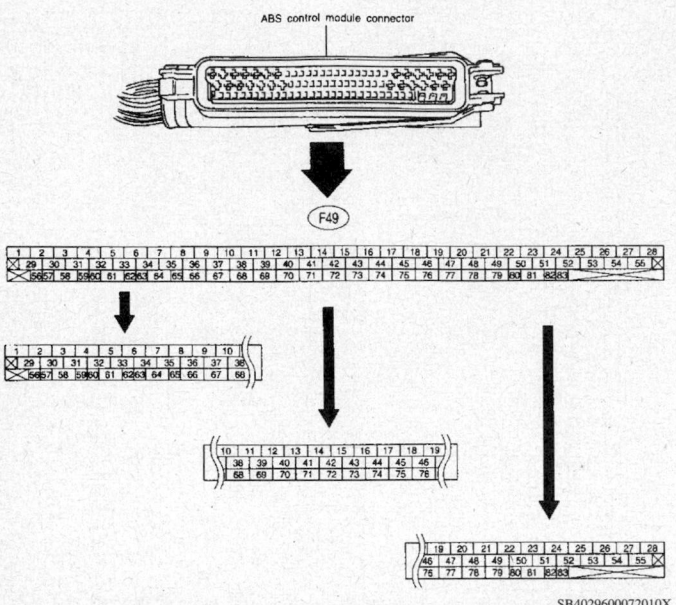

ABS control module connector

F49

SB4029600072010X

Fig. 9   ABS control module I/O signal (Part 1 of 2)

Contents			Terminal No.	Input/Output signal
				Measured value and measuring conditions
ABS sensor (Wheel speed sensor)	Front left wheel		49—19	0.12 — 1 V (When it is 20 Hz.)
	Front right wheel		14—15	
	Rear left wheel		16—17	
	Rear right wheel		18—46	
Hydraulic control unit	Solenoid valve	Front left outlet	51—1	10 — 13 V when the valve is OFF and less than 1.5 V when the valve is ON.
		Front right outlet	3—1	
		Rear left outlet	4—1	
		Rear right outlet	50—1	
		Front left inlet	24—1	
		Front right inlet	30—1	
		Rear left inlet	31—1	
		Rear right inlet	23—1	
Relay box	Valve relay power supply		27—1	10 — 13 V when ignition switch is ON.
	Valve relay coil		47—1	Less than 1.5 V when ignition switch is ON.
	Motor relay coil		22—1	More than 10 V when the ABS control does not operate still and less than 1.5 V when ABS operates.
	Motor monitoring		10—1	Less than 1.5 V when the ABS control does not operate still and more than 10 V when ABS operates.
G sensor (AWD model only)	power supply		8—45	4.75 — 5.25 V
	ground		45	—
	output		7—45	2.3 ± 0.2 V when vehicle is in horizontal position.
Stop light switch			36—1	Less than 1.5 V when the stop light is OFF and more than 4.5 V when the stop light is ON.
ABS warning light			54—1	Less than 1.5 V during 1.5 seconds when ignition switch is ON, and 10 — 14 V after 1.5 seconds.
AT ABS signal (AT model only)			12—1	Less than 1.5 V when the ABS control does not operate still and more than 5.5 V when ABS operates.
ABS operation signal monitor			39—1	Less than 1.5 V when the ABS control does not operate still and more than 5.5 V when ABS operates.
Select monitor	Data is received.		11—1	Less than 1.5 V when no data is received.
	Data is sent.		38—1	4.75 — 5.25 V when no data is sent.
Diagnosis connector	Terminal No. 3		5—1	10 — 14 V when ignition switch is ON.
	Terminal No. 6		13—1	10 — 14 V when ignition switch is ON.
Power supply			28—1	10 — 14 V when ignition switch is ON.
Grounding line			1	—
Grounding line			55	—

SB4029600072020X

Fig. 9   ABS control module I/O signal (Part 2 of 2)

1998-99 Legacy

NOTE: On Air Bag Equipped Models, Refer To "Air Bag System Precautions" Located In The Front Of This Manual For System Disarming & Arming Procedures.

NOTE: Electrical Symbol & Wire Color Code Identification Located In The Front Of This Manual May Be Used As An Aid When Using Wiring Circuits Found In This Section.

INDEX

PRECAUTIONS

AIR BAG SYSTEMS

Refer to "Air Bag System Precautions" in the front of this manual for system disarming and arming procedures.

BATTERY GROUND CABLE

Prior to service, disconnect battery ground cable and isolate as required.

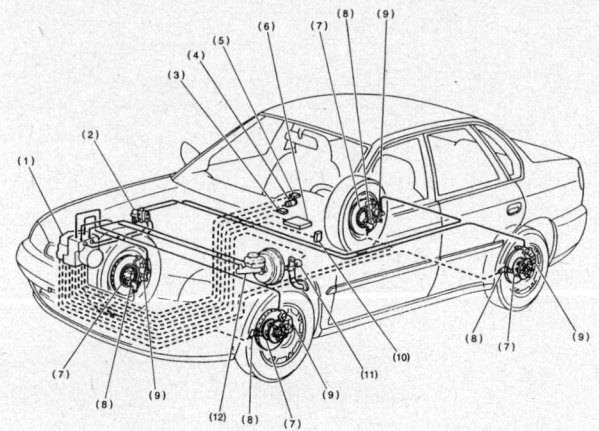

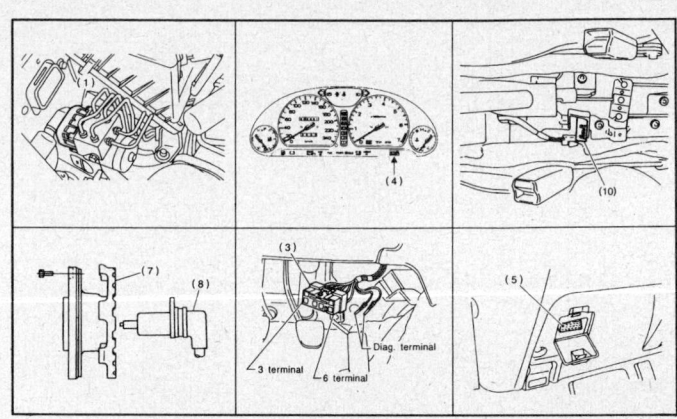

(1) ABS control module and hydraulic control unit (ABSCM&H/U)
(2) Proportioning valve
(3) Diagnosis connector
(4) ABS warning light
(5) Data link connector (for Subaru select monitor)
(6) Transmission control module (only AT vehicle)
(7) Tone wheel
(8) ABS sensor
(9) Wheel cylinder
(10) G sensor (only AWD vehicle)
(11) Brake switch
(12) Master cylinder

SB4029800143010X

Fig. 1   ABS component locations (Part 1 of 2)

SB4029800143020X

Fig. 1   ABS component locations (Part 2 of 2)

DESCRIPTION

The Anti-lock Brake System (ABS) electrically controls brake fluid pressure to prevent wheel lock during braking on slippery road surfaces, which improves directional steering stability as well as shortening the braking distance.

If ABS becomes inoperative, the fail-safe system activates to ensure it acts as a conventional brake system. The warning light also comes on to indicate that the ABS is malfunctioning.

Refer to **Fig. 1**, for component location & description

TROUBLESHOOTING

Refer to **Fig. 2**, for troubleshooting procedures.

DIAGNOSIS & TESTING
PRELIMINARY INSPECTION

1. Ensure battery voltage is 12 volts or more and specific gravity is above 1.260.
2. Inspect brake fluid level and for brake fluid leakage.
3. Inspect brake drag.
4. Inspect brake pads and rotors.
5. Inspect tires for excessive wear and proper inflation.

ACCESSING DIAGNOSTIC TROUBLE CODES

Less Select Monitor

When on board diagnosis of the ABS control module detects a problem, the information (up to a maximum of three) will be stored in the EEP ROM as a diagnostic trouble code (DTC). When there are more than three, the most recent three will be stored. Stored codes will stay in memory until they are cleared.

1. Remove ABS diagnostic connector from side of driver's heater unit, **Fig. 3**.
2. Turn ignition switch to Off position.
3. Connect diagnosis connector terminal No. 6 to terminal No. 3.
4. Turn ignition switch to On position.
5. ABS warning light is set to the diagnostic mode and blinks to identify trouble codes.
6. After start code is displayed (11), trouble codes will be shown in order of last information first. Codes will repeat for a maximum of five minutes.
7. If there are no trouble codes in memory, code 11 will be the only code to appear.

With Select Monitor

Access the ABS system diagnostic trouble codes according to the tool manufacturers instructions.

DIAGNOSTIC TROUBLE CODE INTERPRETATION

Refer to **Figs. 4 and 5**, for trouble code interpretation.

WIRING DIAGRAM

Refer to **Fig. 6**, for wiring diagram.

DIAGNOSTIC TESTS

Less Select Monitor

Refer to **Figs. 7 through 23**, when performing the following procedures.

With Select Monitor

Refer to **Figs. 24 through 48**, when performing the following procedures.

CLEARING DIAGNOSTIC TROUBLE CODES

Less Select Monitor

1. After calling up a trouble code, disconnect diagnosis connector terminal No.

6 from diagnosis terminal, **Fig. 3**.
2. Connect and disconnect terminal No. 6 three times within a 12 second span leaving terminal disconnected at least .2 second each time.
3. Upon completion, inspect to ensure only code 11 (start code) remains in memory.

With Select Monitor

Erase ABS DTC's according to tool manufacturers instructions.

COMPONENT TESTING

Refer to **Fig. 49**, when testing ABS component voltages.

SYSTEM SERVICE
Brake System Bleed

Two technicians are needed to bleed the brake system. Brake pedal operation must be very slow. Keep brake fluid reserve tank full to prevent air from entering the system during the bleeding procedure.

1. Connect ABS check connector diagnosis terminal to terminal No. 6. Connector is located beside driver side seat heater unit.
2. Start engine, then after ABS warning lamp goes out, depress brake pedal within 0.5 seconds.
3. Check entire brake system for fluid leaks.
4. Bleed air from right front caliper as follows:
   a. Fit one end of a vinyl tube onto air bleeder, place other end of tube into a container of brake fluid.
   b. Slowly depress brake pedal and keep it depressed, then open air bleeder for 1–2 seconds.
   c. Close air bleeder and slowly release brake pedal.
   d. Repeat steps "a" through "c" until no more air comes out. **Allow 3–4 seconds between brake pedal operations.**
5. Bleed air from right front caliper suction pipe as follows:
   a. Open air bleeder.

Symptom		Probable faulty units/parts
Vehicle instability during braking	Vehicle pulls to either side.	• ABSCM&H/U (solenoid valve) • ABS sensor • Brake (caliper & piston, pads) • Wheel alignment • Tire specifications, tire wear and air pressures • Incorrect wiring or piping connections • Road surface (uneven, camber)
	Vehicle spins.	• ABSCM&H/U (solenoid valve) • ABS sensor • Brake (pads) • Tire specifications, tire wear and air pressures • Incorrect wiring or piping connections
Poor braking	Long braking/stopping distance	• ABSCM&H/U (solenoid valve) • Brake (pads) • Air in brake line • Tire specifications, tire wear and air pressures • Incorrect wiring or piping connections
	Wheel locks.	• ABSCM&H/U (solenoid valve, motor) • ABS sensor • Incorrect wiring or piping connections
	Brake dragging	• ABSCM&H/U (solenoid valve) • ABS sensor • Master cylinder • Brake (caliper & piston) • Parking brake • Axle & wheels • Brake pedal play
	Long brake pedal stroke	• Air in brake line • Brake pedal play
	Vehicle pitching	• Suspension play or fatigue (reduced damping) • Incorrect wiring or piping connections • Road surface (uneven)
	Unstable or uneven braking	• ABSCM&H/U (solenoid valve) • ABS sensor • Brake (caliper & piston, pads) • Tire specifications, tire wear and air pressures • Incorrect wiring or piping connections • Road surface (uneven)
Vibration and/or noise (while driving on slippery roads)	Excessive pedal vibration	• Incorrect wiring or piping connections • Road surface (uneven)
	Noise from ABSCM&H/U	• ABSCM&H/U (mount bushing) • ABS sensor • Brake piping
	Noise from front of vehicle	• ABSCM&H/U (mount bushing) • ABS sensor • Master cylinder • Brake (caliper & piston, pads, rotor) • Brake piping • Brake booster & check valve • Suspension play or fatigue
	Noise from rear of vehicle	• ABS sensor • Brake (caliper & piston, pads, rotor) • Parking brake • Brake piping • Suspension play or fatigue

SB4029800139000X

Fig. 2 Troubleshooting chart

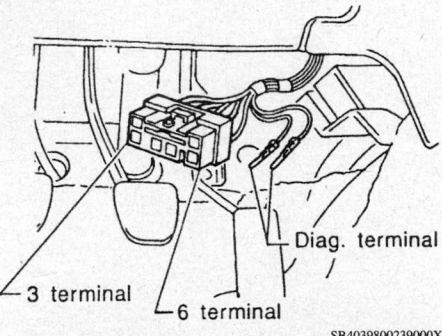

Diag. terminal

3 terminal   6 terminal

SB4039800239000X

Fig. 3 Check connector terminal identification. Less select monitor

b. Depress TCS off switch for 20 seconds or more. **Ensure no more air comes out from air bleeder.**
c. Close air bleeder.
6. Repeat steps 4 and 5 for left front caliper and suction pipe.
7. Repeat step 4 for right rear caliper.
8. Repeat step 4 for left rear caliper.
9. Tighten air bleeders securely when bubbles are visible.

10. Operate front right outlet and rear left outlet valves to bleed air from hydraulic unit outlet circuit as follows:
    a. Press TCS OFF switch while depressing brake pedal.
    b. Ensure ABS warning lamp illuminates.
    c. Depress and release brake pedal 10 times or more while pressing TCS OFF switch.

d. Repeat procedure until no more air escapes the reservoir tank.
11. Repeat step 10 for front left and rear right outlet valves.
12. Fully depress brake pedal for 20 seconds and ensure there are no leaks in brake system.
13. Turn ignition switch to off position and perform TCS sequence control.
14. With engine at idle, inspect brake pedal stroke as follows:
    a. Depress brake pedal with 110 lbs. of force, then measure distance between brake pedal and steering wheel.
    b. Release brake pedal, then measure distance between brake pedal and steering wheel again.
    c. The difference between both measurements should be 3.74 inches. **If measurement is not as specified it is possible that air is still in brake system.**
15. Turn ignition switch to off position, then top off brake fluid level.
16. Test drive vehicle at low speed and ensure proper brake operation.

Trouble code	Contents of diagnosis	
11	Start code ● Trouble code is shown after start code. ● Only start code is shown in normal condition.	
21	Abnormal ABS sensor (Open circuit or input voltage too high)	Front right ABS sensor
23		Front left ABS sensor
25		Rear right ABS sensor
27		Rear left ABS sensor
22	Abnormal ABS sensor (Abnormal ABS sensor signal)	Front right ABS sensor
24		Front left ABS sensor
26		Rear right ABS sensor
28		Rear left ABS sensor
29		Any one of four
31	Abnormal solenoid valve circuit(s) in ABS control module and hydraulic unit	Front right inlet valve
32		Front right outlet valve
33		Front left inlet valve
34		Front left outlet valve
35		Rear right inlet valve
36		Rear right outlet valve
37		Rear left inlet valve
38		Rear left outlet valve
41	Abnormal ABS control module	
42	Source voltage is abnormal.	
44	A combination of AT control abnormal	
51	Abnormal valve relay	
52	Abnormal motor and/or motor relay	
54	Abnormal stop light switch	
56	Abnormal G sensor output voltage	

SB4029800101000X

Fig. 4   Diagnostic trouble code interpretation. Less select monitor

Code	Display screen	Contents of diagnosis
—	Communication for initializing impossible	Select monitor communication failure
—	No trouble code	Although no trouble code appears on the select monitor display, the ABS warning light remains on.
21	Open or short circuit in front right ABS sensor circuit	Open or short circuit in front right ABS sensor circuit
22	Front right ABS sensor abnormal signal	Front right ABS sensor abnormal signal
23	Open or short circuit in front left ABS sensor circuit	Open or short circuit in front left ABS sensor circuit
24	Front left ABS sensor abnormal signal	Front left ABS sensor abnormal signal
25	Open or short circuit in rear right ABS sensor circuit	Open or short circuit in rear right ABS sensor circuit
26	Rear right ABS sensor abnormal signal	Rear right ABS sensor abnormal signal
27	Open or short circuit in rear left ABS sensor circuit	Open or short circuit in rear left ABS sensor circuit
28	Rear left ABS sensor abnormal signal	Rear left ABS sensor abnormal signal
29	Abnormal ABS sensor signal on any one of four sensor	Abnormal ABS sensor signal on any one of four
31	Front right inlet valve malfunction	Front right inlet valve malfunction
32	Front right outlet valve malfunction	Front right outlet valve malfunction
33	Front left inlet valve malfunction	Front left inlet valve malfunction
34	Front left outlet valve malfunction	Front left outlet valve malfunction
35	Rear right inlet valve malfunction	Rear right inlet valve malfunction
36	Rear right outlet valve malfunction	Rear right outlet valve malfunction
37	Rear left inlet valve malfunction	Rear left inlet valve malfunction
38	Rear left outlet valve malfunction	Rear left outlet valve malfunction
41	ABS control module malfunction	ABS control module and hydraulic control unit malfunction
42	Power supply voltage too low	Power supply voltage too low
42	Power supply voltage too high	Power supply voltage too high
44	ABS-AT control (Non Controlled)	ABS-AT control (Non Controlled)
44	ABS-AT control (Controlled)	ABS-AT control (Controlled)
51	Valve relay malfunction	Valve relay malfunction
51	Valve relay ON failure	Valve relay ON failure
52	Open circuit in motor relay circuit	Open circuit in motor relay circuit
52	Motor relay ON failure	Motor relay ON failure
52	Motor malfunction	Motor malfunction
54	Stop light switch signal circuit malfunction	Stop light switch signal circuit malfunction
56	Open or short circuit in G sensor circuit	Open or short circuit in G sensor circuit
56	Battery short in G sensor circuit	Battery short in G sensor circuit
56	Abnormal G sensor high μ output	Abnormal G sensor high μ output
56	Detection of G sensor stick	Detection of G sensor stick

NOTE:
High μ means high friction coefficient against road surface.

SB4029800097000X

Fig. 5   Diagnostic trouble code interpretation. With select monitor

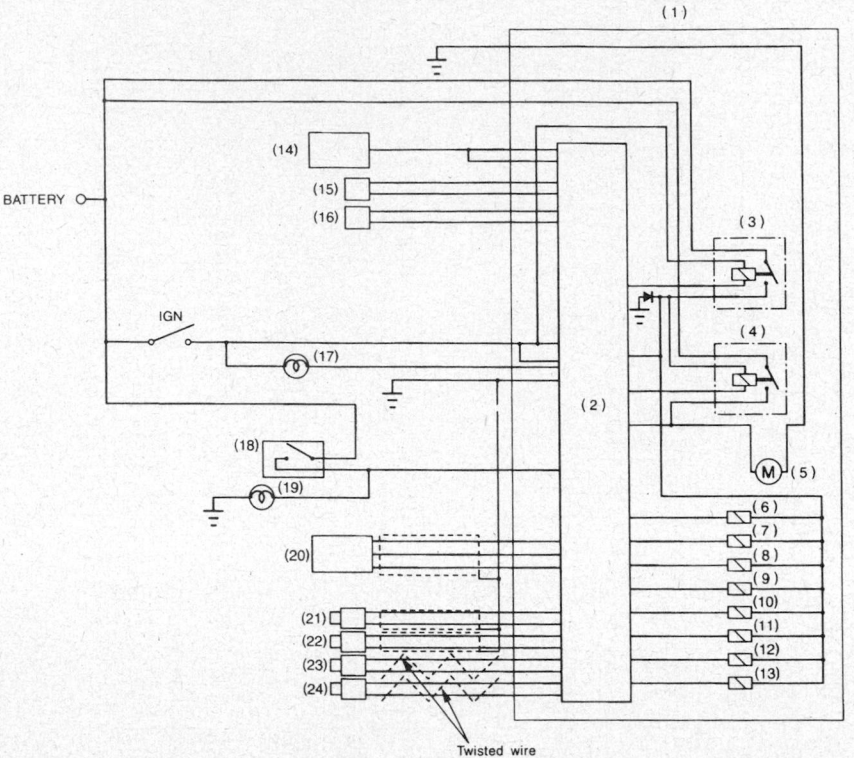

(1) ABS control module and hydrau-
    lic control unit (ABSCM&H/U)
(2) ABS control module area
(3) Valve relay
(4) Motor relay
(5) Motor
(6) Front left inlet solenoid valve
(7) Front left outlet solenoid valve
(8) Front right inlet solenoid valve

(9) Front right outlet solenoid valve
(10) Rear left inlet solenoid valve
(11) Rear left outlet solenoid valve
(12) Rear right inlet solenoid valve
(13) Rear right outlet solenoid valve
(14) Transmission control module
     (only AT model)
(15) Diagnosis connector
(16) Data link connector

(17) ABS warning light
(18) Stop light switch
(19) Stop light
(20) G sensor (only AWD model)
(21) Front left ABS sensor
(22) Front right ABS sensor
(23) Rear left ABS sensor
(24) Rear right ABS sensor

SB4029800144000X

Fig. 6 ABS wiring diagram

DIAGNOSTIC CHART INDEX

Test/Code	Description	Page No.	Fig. No.
LESS SELECT MONITOR			
Test A	ABS Warning Light Does Not Come On	41-264	7
Test B	ABS Warning Light Does Not Go Off	41-265	8
Test C	Trouble Code Does Not Appear	41-266	9
Code 21	Abnormal ABS Sensor, Open Circuit Or Input Voltage Too High	41-266	10
Code 22	Abnormal ABS Sensor, Abnormal ABS Sensor Signal	41-267	11
Code 23	Abnormal ABS Sensor, Open Circuit Or Input Voltage Too High	41-266	10
Code 24	Abnormal ABS Sensor, Abnormal ABS Sensor Signal	41-267	11
Code 25	Abnormal ABS Sensor, Open Circuit Or Input Voltage Too High	41-266	10
Code 26	Abnormal ABS Sensor, Abnormal ABS Sensor Signal	41-267	11
Code 27	Abnormal ABS Sensor, Open Circuit Or Input Voltage Too High	41-266	10
Code 28	Abnormal ABS Sensor, Abnormal ABS Sensor Signal	41-267	11
Code 29	Abnormal ABS Sensor Signal, Any One Of Four	41-270	12
Code 31	Abnormal Inlet Valve Circuit In ABSCM & H/U	41-271	13
Code 32	Abnormal Outlet Solenoid Valve Circuit In ABSCM & H/U	41-271	14
Code 33	Abnormal Inlet Valve Circuit In ABSCM & H/U	41-271	13
Code 34	Abnormal Outlet Solenoid Valve Circuit In ABSCM & H/U	41-271	14

Continued

1998–99 LEGACY

DIAGNOSTIC CHART INDEX—Continued

Test/Code	Description	Page No.	Fig. No.
LESS SELECT MONITOR			
Code 35	Abnormal Inlet Valve Circuit In ABSCM & H/U	41-271	13
Code 36	Abnormal Outlet Solenoid Valve Circuit In ABSCM & H/U	41-271	14
Code 37	Abnormal Inlet Valve Circuit In ABSCM & H/U	41-271	13
Code 38	Abnormal Outlet Solenoid Valve Circuit In ABSCM & H/U	41-271	14
Code 41	Abnormal ABS Control Module	41-272	15
Code 42	Source Voltage Is Abnormal	41-272	16
Code 44	A Combination Of AT Control Abnormal (1998)	41-273	17
Code 44	A combination Of AT Control Abnormal (1999))	41-274	18
Code 51	Abnormal Valve Relay	41-275	19
Code 52	Abnormal Motor And/Or Motor Relay	41-276	20
Code 54	Abnormal Stop Light Switch	41-277	21
Code 56	Abnormal G Sensor Output Voltage (1998)	41-277	22
Code 56	Abnormal G Sensor Output Voltage (1999)	41-278	23
WITH SELECT MONITOR			
Test C	Communication For Initializing Impossible	41-279	24
Test D	No Trouble Code	41-280	25
Code 21	Abnormal ABS Sensor, Open Or Short Circuit In ABS Sensor Circuit	41-281	26
Code 22	Abnormal ABS Sensor, ABS Sensor Abnormal Signal	41-283	27
Code 23	Abnormal ABS Sensor, Open Or Short Circuit In ABS Sensor Circuit	41-281	26
Code 24	Abnormal ABS Sensor, ABS Sensor Abnormal Signal	41-283	27
Code 25	Abnormal ABS Sensor, Open Or Short Circuit In ABS Sensor Circuit	41-281	26
Code 26	Abnormal ABS Sensor, ABS Sensor Abnormal Signal	41-283	27
Code 27	Abnormal ABS Sensor, Open Or Short Circuit In ABS Sensor Circuit	41-281	26
Code 28	Abnormal ABS Sensor, ABS Sensor Abnormal Signal	41-283	27
Code 29	Abnormal ABS Sensor Signal In Any One Of Four Sensor	41-286	28
Code 31	Inlet Solenoid Valve Malfunction	41-287	29
Code 32	Outlet Solenoid Valve Malfunction	41-287	30
Code 33	Inlet Solenoid Valve Malfunction	41-287	29
Code 34	Outlet Solenoid Valve Malfunction	41-287	30
Code 35	Inlet Solenoid Valve Malfunction	41-287	29
Code 36	Outlet Solenoid Valve Malfunction	41-287	30
Code 38	Outlet Solenoid Valve Malfunction	41-287	30
Code 41	ABS Control Module & Hydraulic Control Unit Malfunction	41-288	31
Code 42	Power Supply Voltage Too Low	41-288	32
	Power Supply Voltage Too High	41-289	33
Code 44	ABS AT Control, Non Controlled (1998)	41-290	34
	ABS AT Control, Controlled (1998)	41-291	35
	ABS AT Control, Non Controlled (1999)	41-292	36
	ABS AT Control, Controlled (1999)	41-293	37
Code 51	Valve Relay Malfunction	41-293	38
	Valve Relay On Failure	41-294	39
Code 52	Open Circuit In Motor Relay Circuit	41-294	40
	Motor Relay On Failure	41-294	41
	Motor Malfunction	41-295	42
Code 54	Stop Light Switch Signal Circuit Malfunction	41-296	43
Code 56	Open Or Short In G Sensor Circuit	41-296	44
	Battery Short In G Sensor Circuit	41-298	45
	Abnormal G Sensor High Output	41-298	46
	Detection Of G Sensor Stick	41-300	47
	Open Or Short Circuit In G Sensor Circuit	41-301	48

7A1 : CHECK IF OTHER WARNING LIGHTS TURN ON.

Turn ignition switch to ON (engine OFF).

CHECK : *Do other warning lights turn on?*
YES : Go to step 7A2.
NO : Repair combination meter.

7A2 : CHECK ABS WARNING LIGHT BULB.

1) Turn ignition switch to OFF.
2) Remove combination meter.
3) Remove ABS warning light bulb from combination meter.

CHECK : *Is ABS warning light bulb OK?*
YES : Go to step 7A3.
NO : Replace ABS warning light bulb.

7A3 : CHECK BATTERY SHORT OF ABS WARNING LIGHT HARNESS.

1) Disconnect connector (B100) from connector (F2).
2) Measure voltage between connector (B100) and chassis ground.

Connector & terminal
(B100) No. 9 (+) — Chassis ground (–):

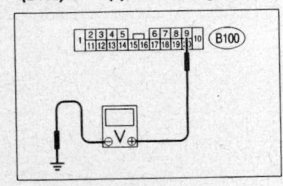

CHECK : *Is the voltage less than 3 V?*
YES : Go to step 7A4.
NO : Repair warning light harness.

7A4 : CHECK BATTERY SHORT OF ABS WARNING LIGHT HARNESS.

1) Turn ignition switch to ON.
2) Measure voltage between connector (B100) and chassis ground.

Connector & terminal
(B100) No. 9 (+) — Chassis ground (–):

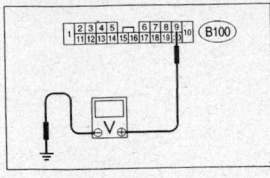

CHECK : *Is voltage less than 3 V?*
YES : Go to step 7A5.
NO : Repair warning light harness.

7A5 : CHECK WIRING HARNESS.

1) Turn ignition switch to OFF.
2) Install ABS warning light bulb from combination meter.
3) Install combination meter.
4) Turn ignition switch to ON.
5) Measure voltage between connector (B100) and chassis ground.

Connector & terminal
(B100) No. 9 (+) — Chassis ground (–):

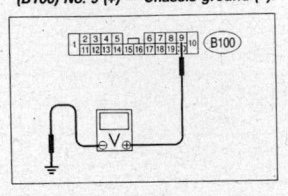

CHECK : *Is voltage between 10 V and 15 V?*
YES : Go to step 7A6.
NO : Repair wiring harness.

SB4029800098010X

Fig. 7   Test A: ABS Warning Light Does Not Come On (Part 1 of 3). Less Select Monitor

7A6 : CHECK BATTERY SHORT OF ABS WARNING LIGHT HARNESS.

1) Turn ignition switch to OFF.
2) Measure voltage between connector (F2) and chassis ground.

Connector & terminal
(F2) No. 9 (+) — Chassis ground (–):

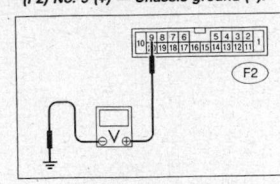

CHECK : *Is the voltage less than 3 V?*
YES : Go to step 7A7.
NO : Repair wiring harness.

7A7 : CHECK BATTERY SHORT OF ABS WARNING LIGHT HARNESS.

1) Turn ignition switch to ON.
2) Measure voltage between connector (F2) and chassis ground.

Connector & terminal
(F2) No. 9 (+) — Chassis ground (–):

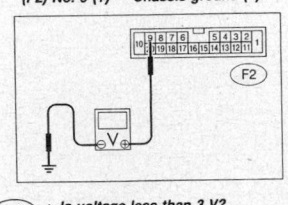

CHECK : *Is voltage less than 3 V?*
YES : Go to step 7A8.
NO : Repair wiring harness.

7A8 : CHECK GROUND CIRCUIT OF ABSCM&H/U.

Measure resistance between ABSCM&H/U and chassis ground.

Connector & terminal
(F49) No. 23 — GND:

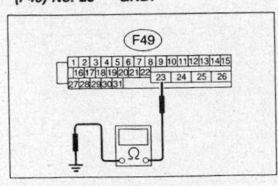

CHECK : *Is the resistance less than 0.5 Ω?*
YES : Go to step 7A9.
NO : Repair ABSCM&H/U ground harness.

7A9 : CHECK WIRING HARNESS.

Measure resistance between connector (F2) and chassis ground.

Connector & terminal
(F2) No. 9 — Chassis ground:

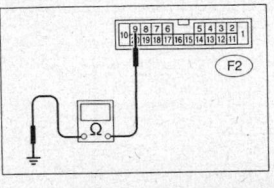

CHECK : *Is the resistance less than 0.5 Ω?*
YES : Go to step 7A10.
NO : Repair harness/connector.

SB4029800098020X

Fig. 7   Test A: ABS Warning Light Does Not Come On (Part 2 of 3). Less Select Monitor

7A10 :   CHECK POOR CONTACT IN CONNECTORS.

Turn ignition switch to OFF.

CHECK : *Is there poor contact in connectors between combination meter and ABSCM&H/U?*

YES : Repair connector.
NO : Replace ABSCM&H/U.

SB4029800098030X

Fig. 7   Test A: ABS Warning Light Does Not Come On (Part 3 of 3). Less Select Monitor

7B1 : CHECK INSTALLATION OF ABSCM&H/U CONNECTOR.

Turn ignition switch to OFF.

CHECK : *Is ABSCM&H/U connector inserted into ABSCM until the clamp locks onto it?*

YES : Go to step **7B2**.

NO : Insert ABSCM&H/U connector into ABSCM&H/U until the clamp locks onto it.

7B2 : CHECK DIAGNOSIS TERMINAL.

Measure resistance between diagnosis terminals (B81) and chassis ground.

Terminals
Diagnosis terminal (A) — Chassis ground:
Diagnosis terminal (B) — Chassis ground:

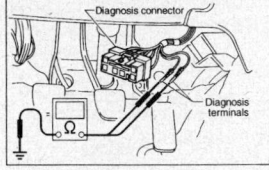

CHECK : *Is the resistance less than 0.5 Ω?*

YES : Go to step **7B3**.

NO : Repair diagnosis terminal harness.

7B3 : CHECK DIAGNOSIS LINE.

1) Turn ignition switch to OFF.
2) Connect diagnosis terminal (B81) to diagnosis connector (B82) No. 6.
3) Disconnect connector from ABSCM&H/U.
4) Measure resistance between ABSCM&H/U connector and chassis ground.

Connector & terminal
(F49) No. 4 — Chassis ground:

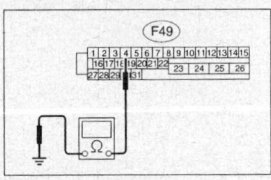

CHECK : *Is the resistance less than 0.5 Ω?*

YES : Go to step **7B4**.

NO : Repair harness connector between ABSCM&H/U and diagnosis connector.

7B4 : CHECK GENERATOR.

1) Start the engine.
2) Idle the engine.
3) Measure voltage between generator and chassis ground.

Terminal
Generator B terminal (+) — Chassis ground (−):

CHECK : *Is the voltage between 10 and 15 V?*

YES : Go to step **7B5**.

NO : Repair generator.

SB4029800099010X

Fig. 8 Test B: ABS Warning Light Does Not Go Off (Part 1 of 3). Less Select Monitor

7B5 : CHECK BATTERY TERMINAL.

Turn ignition switch to OFF.

CHECK : *Is there poor contact at battery terminal?*

YES : Repair battery terminal.

NO : Go to step **7B6**.

7B6 : CHECK POWER SUPPLY OF ABSCM.

1) Disconnect connector from ABSCM&H/U.
2) Start engine.
3) Idle the engine.
4) Measure voltage between ABSCM&H/U connector and chassis ground.

Connector & terminal
(F49) No. 1 (+) — Chassis ground (−):

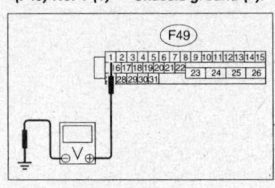

CHECK : *Is the voltage between 10 and 15 V?*

YES : Go to step **7B7**.

NO : Repair ABSCM&H/U power supply circuit.

7B7 : CHECK WIRING HARNESS.

1) Disconnect connector (F2) from connector (B100).
2) Turn ignition switch to ON.

CHECK : *Does the ABS warning light remain off?*

YES : Go to step **7B8**.

NO : Repair front wiring harness.

7B8 : CHECK PROJECTION AT ABSCM&H/U.

1) Turn ignition switch to OFF.
2) Check for broken projection at the ABSCM&H/U terminal.

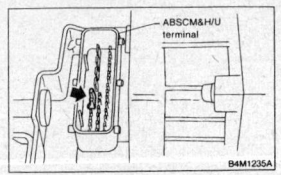

CHECK : *Are the projection broken?*

YES : Go to step **7B9**.

NO : Replace ABSCM&H/U.

7B9 : CHECK ABSCM&H/U.

Measure resistance between ABSCM&H/U terminals.

Terminal
No. 21 — No. 23:

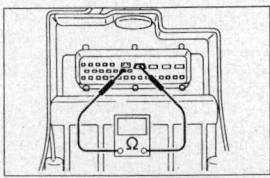

CHECK : *Is the resistance more than 1 MΩ?*

YES : Go to step **7B10**.

NO : Replace ABSCM&H/U.

SB4029800099020X

Fig. 8 Test B: ABS Warning Light Does Not Go Off (Part 2 of 3). Less Select Monitor

7B10 : CHECK WIRING HARNESS.

Measure resistance between connector (F2) and chassis ground.

Connector & terminal
(F2) No. 9 — Chassis ground:

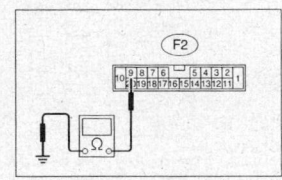

CHECK : *Is the resistance less than 0.5 Ω?*

YES : Go to step **7B11**.

NO : Repair harness.

7B11 : CHECK WIRING HARNESS.

1) Connect connector to ABSCM&H/U.
2) Measure resistance between connector (F2) and chassis ground.

Connector & terminal
(F2) No. 9 — Chassis ground:

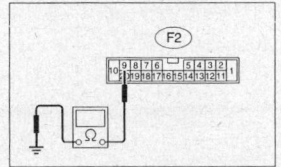

CHECK : *Is the resistance more than 1 MΩ?*

YES : Go to step **7B12**.

NO : Repair harness.

7B12 : CHECK POOR CONTACT IN ABSCM&H/U CONNECTOR.

CHECK : *Is there poor contact in ABSCM&H/U connector?*

YES : Repair connector.

NO : Replace ABSCM&H/U.

SB4029800099030X

Fig. 8 Test B: ABS Warning Light Does Not Go Off (Part 3 of 3). Less Select Monitor

7C1 : CHECK DIAGNOSIS TERMINAL.

Measure resistance between diagnosis terminals (B81) and chassis ground.

Terminals
Diagnosis terminal (A) — Chassis ground:
Diagnosis terminal (B) — Chassis ground:

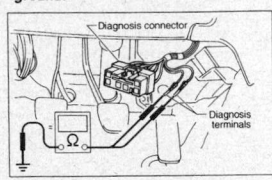

CHECK : *Is the resistance less than 0.5 Ω?*
YES : Go to step **7C2**.
NO : Repair diagnosis terminal harness.

7C2 : CHECK DIAGNOSIS LINE.

1) Turn ignition switch to OFF.
2) Connect diagnosis terminal (B81) to diagnosis connector (B82) No. 6.
3) Disconnect connector from ABSCM&H/U.
4) Measure resistance between ABSCM&H/U connector and chassis ground.

Connector & terminal
(F49) No. 4 — Chassis ground:

CHECK : *Is the resistance less than 0.5 Ω?*
YES : Go to step **7C3**.
NO : Repair harness connector between ABSCM&H/U and diagnosis connector.

SB4029800100000X

Fig. 9   Test C: Trouble Code Does Not Appear. Less Select Monitor

---

7C3 : CHECK POOR CONTACT IN ABSCM&H/U CONNECTOR.

CHECK : *Is there poor contact in ABSCM&H/U connector?*

YES : Repair connector.
NO : Replace ABSCM&H/U.

8E3 : CHECK BATTERY SHORT OF ABS SENSOR.

1) Turn ignition switch to ON.
2) Measure voltage between ABS sensor and chassis ground.

Terminal
Front RH No. 1 (+) — Chassis ground (–):
Front LH No. 1 (+) — Chassis ground (–):
Rear RH No. 1 (+) — Chassis ground (–):
Rear LH No. 1 (+) — Chassis ground (–):

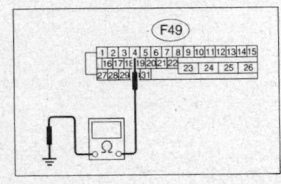

CHECK : *Is the voltage less than 1 V?*
YES : Go to step **8E4**.
NO : Replace ABS sensor.

SB4029800102020X

Fig. 10   Codes 21, 23, 25 & 27: Abnormal ABS Sensor, Open Circuit Or Input Voltage Too High (Part 2 of 5). Less Select Monitor

---

8E4 : CHECK HARNESS/CONNECTOR BETWEEN ABSCM&H/U AND ABS SENSOR.

1) Turn ignition switch to OFF.
2) Connect connector to ABS sensor.
3) Measure resistance between ABSCM&H/U connector terminals.

Connector & terminal
Trouble code 21 / (F49) No. 11 — No. 12:
Trouble code 23 / (F49) No. 9 — No. 10:
Trouble code 25 / (F49) No. 14 — No. 15:
Trouble code 27 / (F49) No. 7 — No. 8:

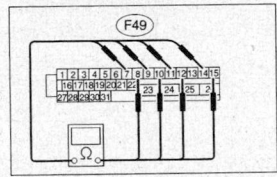

CHECK : *Is the resistance between 0.8 and 1.2 kΩ?*
YES : Go to step **8E5**.
NO : Repair harness/connector between ABSCM&H/U and ABS sensor.

8E1 : CHECK ABS SENSOR.

1) Turn ignition switch to OFF.
2) Disconnect connector from ABS sensor.
3) Measure resistance of ABS sensor connector terminals.

Terminal
Front RH No. 1 — No. 2:
Front LH No. 1 — No. 2:
Rear RH No. 1 — No. 2:
Rear LH No. 1 — No. 2:

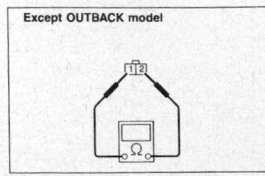

CHECK : *Is the resistance between 0.8 and 1.2 kΩ?*
YES : Go to step **8E2**.
NO : Replace ABS sensor.

8E2 : CHECK BATTERY SHORT OF ABS SENSOR.

1) Disconnect connector from ABSCM&H/U.
2) Measure voltage between ABS sensor and chassis ground.

Terminal
Front RH No. 1 (+) — Chassis ground (–):
Front LH No. 1 (+) — Chassis ground (–):
Rear RH No. 1 (+) — Chassis ground (–):
Rear LH No. 1 (+) — Chassis ground (–):

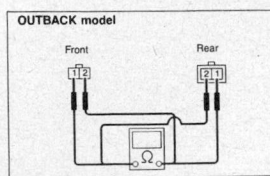

CHECK : *Is the voltage less than 1 V?*
YES : Go to step **8E3**.
NO : Replace ABS sensor.

SB4029800102010X

Fig. 10   Codes 21, 23, 25 & 27: Abnormal ABS Sensor, Open Circuit Or Input Voltage Too High (Part 1 of 5). Less Select Monitor

---

8E5 : CHECK BATTERY SHORT OF HARNESS.

Measure voltage between ABSCM&H/U connector and chassis ground.

Connector & terminal
Trouble code 21 / (F49) No. 11 (+) — Chassis ground (–):
Trouble code 23 / (F49) No. 9 (+) — Chassis ground (–):
Trouble code 25 / (F49) No. 14 (+) — Chassis ground (–):
Trouble code 27 / (F49) No. 7 (+) — Chassis ground (–):

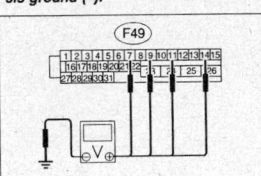

CHECK : *Is the voltage less than 1 V?*
YES : Go to step **8E6**.
NO : Repair harness between ABSCM&H/U and ABS sensor.

8E6 : CHECK BATTERY SHORT OF HARNESS.

1) Turn ignition switch to ON.
2) Measure voltage between ABSCM&H/U connector and chassis ground.

Connector & terminal
Trouble code 21 / (F49) No. 11 (+) — Chassis ground (–):
Trouble code 23 / (F49) No. 9 (+) — Chassis ground (–):
Trouble code 25 / (F49) No. 14 (+) — Chassis ground (–):
Trouble code 27 / (F49) No. 7 (+) — Chassis ground (–):

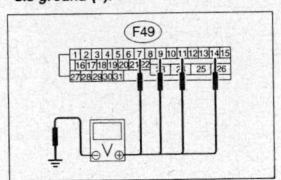

CHECK : *Is the voltage less than 1 V?*
YES : Go to step **8E7**.
NO : Repair harness between ABSCM&H/U and ABS sensor.

8E7 : CHECK INSTALLATION OF ABS SENSOR.

Tightening torque:
32±10 N·m (3.3±1.0 kg-m, 24±7 ft-lb)

CHECK : *Are the ABS sensor installation bolts tightened securely?*
YES : Go to step **8E8**.
NO : Tighten ABS sensor installation bolts securely.

SB4029800102030X

Fig. 10   Codes 21, 23, 25 & 27: Abnormal ABS Sensor, Open Circuit Or Input Voltage Too High (Part 3 of 5). Less Select Monitor

8E8 : CHECK INSTALLATION OF TONE WHEEL.

Tightening torque:
13±3 N·m (1.3±0.3 kg-m, 9±2.2 ft-lb)

CHECK : **Are the tone wheel installation bolts tightened securely?**
YES : Go to step **8E9.**
NO : Tighten tone wheel installation bolts securely.

8E9 : CHECK ABS SENSOR GAP.

Measure tone wheel-to-pole piece gap over entire perimeter of the wheel.

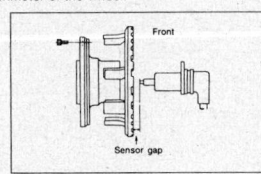
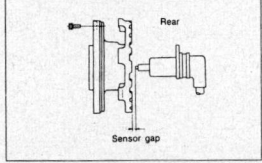

Specifications	Front wheel	Rear wheel
	0.9 – 1.4 mm (0.035 – 0.055 in)	0.7 – 1.2 mm (0.028 – 0.047 in)

CHECK : **Is the gap within the specifications?**
YES : Go to step **8E10.**
NO : Adjust the gap.

NOTE:
Adjust the gap using spacers (Part No. 26755AA000). If spacers cannot correct the gap, replace worn sensor or worn tone wheel.

8E10 : CHECK HUB RUNOUT.

Measure hub runout.

CHECK : **Is the runout less than 0.05 mm (0.0020 in)?**
YES : Go to step **8E11.**
NO : Repair hub.

8E11 : CHECK GROUND SHORT OF ABS SENSOR.

1) Turn ignition switch to ON.
2) Measure resistance between ABS sensor and chassis ground.

Terminal
Front RH No. 1 — Chassis ground:
Front LH No. 1 — Chassis ground:
Rear RH No. 1 — Chassis ground:
Rear LH No. 1 — Chassis ground:

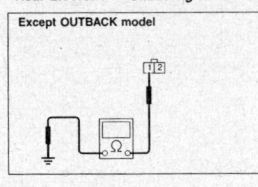
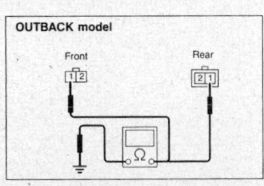

CHECK : **Is the resistance more than 1 MΩ?**
YES : Go to step **8E12.**
NO : Replace ABS sensor and ABSCM&H/U.

SB4029800102040X

Fig. 10 Codes 21, 23, 25 & 27: Abnormal ABS Sensor, Open Circuit Or Input Voltage Too High (Part 4 of 5). Less Select Monitor

---

8E12 : CHECK GROUND SHORT OF HARNESS.

1) Turn ignition switch to OFF.
2) Connect connector to ABS sensor.
3) Measure resistance between ABSCM&H/U connector terminal and chassis ground.

Connector & terminal
Trouble code 21 / (F49) No. 11 — Chassis ground:
Trouble code 23 / (F49) No. 9 — Chassis ground:
Trouble code 25 / (F49) No. 14 — Chassis ground:
Trouble code 27 / (F49) No. 7 — Chassis ground:

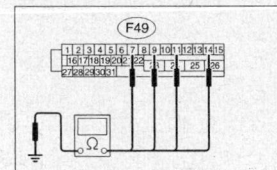

CHECK : **Is the resistance more than 1 MΩ?**
YES : Go to step **8E13.**
NO : Repair harness between ABSCM&H/U and ABS sensor. Replace ABSCM&H/U.

8E13 : CHECK POOR CONTACT IN CONNECTORS.

CHECK : **Is there poor contact in connectors between ABSCM&H/U and ABS sensor?**
YES : Repair connector.
NO : Go to step **8E14.**

8E14 : CHECK ABSCM&H/U.

1) Connect all connectors.
2) Erase the memory.
3) Perform inspection mode.
4) Read out the trouble code.

CHECK : **Is the same trouble code as in the current diagnosis still being output?**
YES : Replace ABSCM&H/U.
NO : Go to step **8E15.**

8E15 : CHECK ANY OTHER TROUBLE CODES APPEARANCE.

CHECK : **Are other trouble codes being output?**
YES : Proceed with the diagnosis corresponding to the trouble code.
NO : A temporary poor contact.

NOTE:
Check harness and connectors between ABSCM&H/U and ABS sensor.

SB4029800102050X

Fig. 10 Codes 21, 23, 25 & 27: Abnormal ABS Sensor, Open Circuit Or Input Voltage Too High (Part 5 of 5). Less Select Monitor

---

8I1 : CHECK INSTALLATION OF ABS SENSOR.

Tightening torque:
32±10 N·m (3.3±1.0 kg-m, 24±7 ft-lb)

CHECK : **Are the ABS sensor installation bolts tightened securely?**
YES : Go to step **8I2.**
NO : Tighten ABS sensor installation bolts securely.

8I2 : CHECK INSTALLATION OF TONE WHEEL.

Tightening torque:
13±3 N·m (1.3±0.3 kg-m, 9±2.2 ft-lb)

CHECK : **Are the tone wheel installation bolts tightened securely?**
YES : Go to step **8I3.**
NO : Tighten tone wheel installation bolts securely.

8I3 : CHECK ABS SENSOR GAP.

Measure tone wheel to pole piece gap over entire perimeter of the wheel.

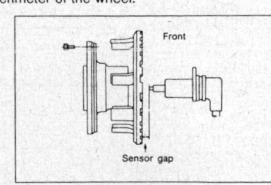
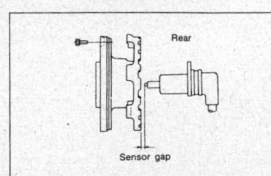

Specifications	Front wheel	Rear wheel
	0.9 – 1.4 mm (0.035 – 0.055 in)	0.7 – 1.2 mm (0.028 – 0.047 in)

CHECK : **Is the gap within the specifications?**
YES : Go to step **8I4.**
NO : Adjust the gap.

NOTE:
Adjust the gap using spacer (Part No. 26755AA000). If spacers cannot correct the gap, replace worn sensor or worn tone wheel.

8I4 : CHECK OSCILLOSCOPE.

CHECK : **Is an oscilloscope available?**
YES : Go to step **8I5.**
NO : Go to step **8I6.**

SB4029800103010X

Fig. 11 Codes 22, 24, 26 & 28: Abnormal ABS Sensor, Abnormal ABS Sensor Signal (Part 1 of 5). Less Select Monitor

---

8I5 : CHECK ABS SENSOR SIGNAL.

1) Raise all four wheels of ground.
2) Turn ignition switch OFF.
3) Connect the oscilloscope to the connector (B100) or connector (F1).
4) Turn ignition switch ON.
5) Rotate wheels and measure voltage at specified frequency.

NOTE:
When this inspection is completed, the ABS control module sometimes stores the trouble code 29.

Connector & terminal
Trouble code 22 / (B100) No. 12 (+) — No. 13 (–):
Trouble code 24 / (B100) No. 3 (+) — No. 4 (–):
Trouble code 26 / (F1) No. 5 (+) — No. 4 (–):
Trouble code 28 / (F1) No. 2 (+) — No. 1 (–):
Specified voltage: 0.12 — 1 V (When it is 20 Hz.)

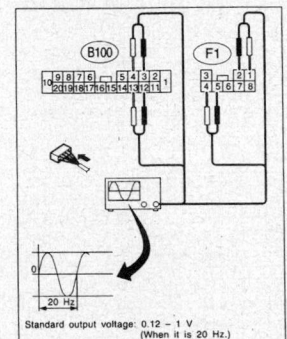

CHECK : *Is oscilloscope pattern smooth, as shown in figure?*
YES : Go to step 8I9.
NO : Go to step 8I6.

8I6 : CHECK CONTAMINATION OF ABS SENSOR OR TONE WHEEL.

Remove disc rotor or drum from hub in accordance with trouble code.

CHECK : *Is the ABS sensor pole piece or the tone wheel contaminated by dirt or other foreign matter?*
YES : Thoroughly remove dirt or other foreign matter.
NO : Go to step 8I7.

8I7 : CHECK DAMAGE OF ABS SENSOR OR TONE WHEEL.

CHECK : *Are there broken or damaged in the ABS sensor pole piece or the tone wheel?*
YES : Replace ABS sensor or tone wheel.
NO : Go to step 8I8.

8I8 : CHECK HUB RUNOUT.

Measure hub runout.

CHECK : *Is the runout less than 0.05 mm (0.0020 in)?*
YES : Go to step 8I9.
NO : Repair hub.

SB4029800103020X

Fig. 11   Codes 22, 24, 26 & 28: Abnormal ABS Sensor, Abnormal ABS Sensor Signal (Part 2 of 5). Less Select Monitor

8I9 : CHECK RESISTANCE OF ABS SENSOR.

1) Turn ignition switch OFF.
2) Disconnect connector from ABS sensor.
3) Measure resistance between ABS sensor connector terminals.

Terminal
Front RH No. 1 — No. 2:
Front LH No. 1 — No. 2:
Rear RH No. 1 — No. 2:
Rear LH No. 1 — No. 2:

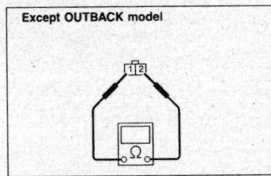
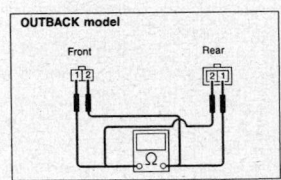

CHECK : *Is the resistance between 0.8 and 1.2 kΩ?*
YES : Go to step 8I10.
NO : Replace ABS sensor.

8I10 : CHECK GROUND SHORT OF ABS SENSOR.

Measure resistance between ABS sensor and chassis ground.

Terminal
Front RH No. 1 — Chassis ground:
Front LH No. 1 — Chassis ground:
Rear RH No. 1 — Chassis ground:
Rear LH No. 1 — Chassis ground:

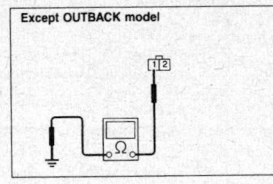
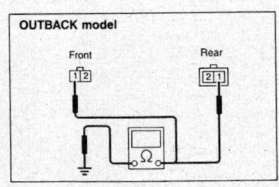

CHECK : *Is the resistance more than 1 MΩ?*
YES : Go to step 8I11.
NO : Replace ABS sensor.

SB4029800103030X

Fig. 11   Codes 22, 24, 26 & 28: Abnormal ABS Sensor, Abnormal ABS Sensor Signal (Part 3 of 5). Less Select Monitor

8I11 : CHECK HARNESS/CONNECTOR BETWEEN ABSCM&H/U AND ABS SENSOR.

1) Connect connector to ABS sensor.
2) Disconnect connector from ABSCM&H/U.
3) Measure resistance at ABSCM&H/U connector terminals.

Connector & terminal
Trouble code 22 / (F49) No. 11 — No. 12:
Trouble code 24 / (F49) No. 9 — No. 10:
Trouble code 26 / (F49) No. 14 — No. 15:
Trouble code 28 / (F49) No. 7 — No. 8:

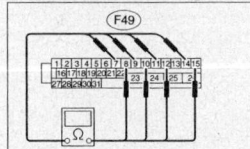

(CHECK) : *Is the resistance between 0.8 and 1.2 kΩ?*
(YES) : Go to step 8I12.
(NO) : Repair harness/connector between ABSCM&H/U and ABS sensor.

8I12 : CHECK GROUND SHORT OF HARNESS.

Measure resistance between ABSCM&H/U connector and chassis ground.

Connector & terminal
Trouble code 22 / (F49) No. 11 — Chassis ground:
Trouble code 24 / (F49) No. 9 — Chassis ground:
Trouble code 26 / (F49) No. 14 — Chassis ground:
Trouble code 28 / (F49) No. 7 — Chassis ground:

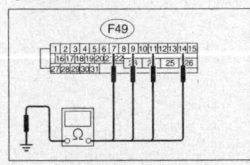

(CHECK) : *Is the resistance more than 1 MΩ?*
(YES) : Go to step 8I13.
(NO) : Repair harness/connector between ABSCM&H/U and ABS sensor.

8I13 : CHECK GROUND CIRCUIT OF ABSCM&H/U.

Measure resistance between ABSCM&H/U and chassis ground.

Connector & terminal
(F49) No. 23 — GND:

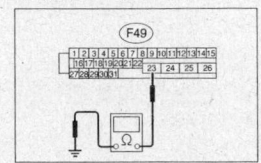

(CHECK) : *Is the resistance less than 0.5 Ω?*
(YES) : Go to step 8I14.
(NO) : Repair ABSCM&H/U ground harness.

SB4029800103040X

Fig. 11   Codes 22, 24, 26 & 28: Abnormal ABS Sensor, Abnormal ABS Sensor Signal (Part 4 of 5). Less Select Monitor

8I14 : CHECK POOR CONTACT IN CONNECTORS.

(CHECK) : *Is there poor contact in connectors between ABSCM&H/U and ABS sensor?*
(YES) : Repair connector.
(NO) : Go to step 8I15.

8I15 : CHECK SOURCES OF SIGNAL NOISE.

(CHECK) : *Is the car telephone or the wireless transmitter properly installed?*
(YES) : Go to step 8I16.
(NO) : Properly install the car telephone or the wireless transmitter.

8I16 : CHECK SOURCES OF SIGNAL NOISE.

(CHECK) : *Are noise sources (such as an antenna) installed near the sensor harness?*
(YES) : Install the noise sources apart from the sensor harness.
(NO) : Go to step 8I17.

8I17 : CHECK SHIELD CIRCUIT.

1) Connect all connectors.
2) Measure resistance between shield connector and chassis ground.

Connector & terminal
Trouble code 22 / (B100) No. 11 — Chassis ground:
Trouble code 24 / (B100) No. 2 — Chassis ground:
Trouble code 26 / Go to step 8I18.
Trouble code 28 / Go to step 8I18.

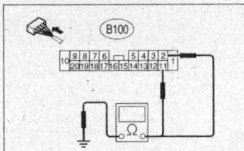

(CHECK) : *Is the resistance less than 0.5 Ω?*
(YES) : Go to step 8I18.
(NO) : Repair shield harness.

8I18 : CHECK ABSCM&H/U.

1) Connect all connectors.
2) Erase the memory.
3) Perform inspection mode.
4) Read out the trouble code.

(CHECK) : *Is the same trouble code as in the current diagnosis still being output?*
(YES) : Replace ABSCM&H/U.
(NO) : Go to step 8I19.

8I19 : CHECK ANY OTHER TROUBLE CODES APPEARANCE.

(CHECK) : *Are other trouble codes being output?*
(YES) : Proceed with the diagnosis corresponding to the trouble code.
(NO) : A temporary noise interference.

SB4029800103050X

Fig. 11   Codes 22, 24, 26 & 28: Abnormal ABS Sensor, Abnormal ABS Sensor Signal (Part 5 of 5). Less Select Monitor

8J1 : CHECK IF THE WHEELS HAVE TURNED FREELY FOR A LONG TIME.

(CHECK) : *Check if the wheels have been turned freely for more than one minute, such as when the vehicle is jacked-up, under full-lock cornering or when tire is not in contact with road surface.*

(YES) : The ABS is normal. Erase the trouble code.

NOTE:
When the wheels turn freely for a long time, such as when the vehicle is towed or jacked-up, or when steering wheel is continuously turned all the way, this trouble code may sometimes occur.

(NO) : Go to step 8J2.

8J2 : CHECK TIRE SPECIFICATIONS.

(CHECK) : *Are the tire specifications correct?*
(YES) : Go to step 8J3.
(NO) : Replace tire.

8J3 : CHECK WEAR OF TIRE.

(CHECK) : *Is the tire worn excessively?*
(YES) : Replace tire.
(NO) : Go to step 8J4.

8J4 : CHECK TIRE PRESSURE.

(CHECK) : *Is the tire pressure correct?*
(YES) : Go to step 8J5.
(NO) : Adjust tire pressure.

8J5 : CHECK INSTALLATION OF ABS SENSOR.

Tightening torque:
32±10 N·m (3.3±1.0 kg-m, 24±7 ft-lb)
(CHECK) : *Are the ABS sensor installation bolts tightened securely?*
(YES) : Go to step 8J6.
(NO) : Tighten ABS sensor installation bolts securely.

8J6 : CHECK INSTALLATION OF TONE WHEEL.

Tightening torque:
13±3 N·m (1.3±0.3 kg-m, 9±2.2 ft-lb)
(CHECK) : *Are the tone wheel installation bolts tightened securely?*
(YES) : Go to step 8J7.
(NO) : Tighten tone wheel installation bolts securely.

8J7 : CHECK ABS SENSOR GAP.

Measure tone wheel to pole piece gap over entire perimeter of the wheel.

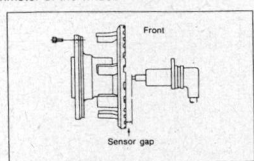

Front

Sensor gap

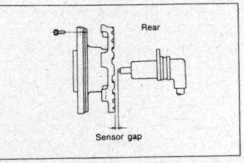

Rear

Sensor gap

Specifications	Front wheel	Rear wheel
	0.9 — 1.4 mm (0.035 — 0.055 in)	0.7 — 1.2 mm (0.028 — 0.047 in)

(CHECK) : *Is the gap within the specifications?*
(YES) : Go to step 8J8.
(NO) : Adjust the gap.

NOTE:
Adjust the gap using spacer (Part No. 26755AA000). If spacers cannot correct the gap, replace worn sensor or worn tone wheel.

SB4029800104010X

Fig. 12 Code 29: Abnormal ABS Sensor Signal, Any One Of Four (Part 1 of 2). Less Select Monitor

8J8 : CHECK OSCILLOSCOPE.

(CHECK) : *Is an oscilloscope available?*
(YES) : Go to step 8J9.
(NO) : Go to step 8J10.

8J9 : CHECK ABS SENSOR SIGNAL.

1) Raise all four wheels of ground.
2) Turn ignition switch OFF.
3) Connect the oscilloscope to the connector (B100) or connector (F1).
4) Turn ignition switch ON.
5) Rotate wheels and measure voltage at specified frequency.

NOTE:
When this inspection is completed, the ABS control module sometimes stores the trouble code 29.

Connector & terminal
(B100) No. 12 (+) — No. 13 (–) (Front RH):
(B100) No. 3 (+) — No. 4 (–) (Front LH):
(F1) No. 5 (+) — No. 4 (–) (Rear RH):
(F1) No. 2 (+) — No. 1 (–) (Rear LH):
Specified voltage: 0.12 — 1 V (When it is 20 Hz.)

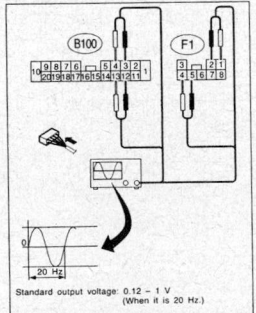

Standard output voltage: 0.12 – 1 V (When it is 20 Hz.)

(CHECK) : *Is oscilloscope pattern smooth, as shown in figure?*
(YES) : Go to step 8J13.
(NO) : Go to step 8J10.

8J10 : CHECK CONTAMINATION OF ABS SENSOR OR TONE WHEEL.

Remove disc rotor from hub.

(CHECK) : *Is the ABS sensor pole piece or the tone wheel contaminated by dirt or other foreign matter?*
(YES) : Thoroughly remove dirt or other foreign matter.
(NO) : Go to step 8J11.

8J11 : CHECK DAMAGE OF ABS SENSOR OR TONE WHEEL.

(CHECK) : *Are there broken or damaged teeth in the ABS sensor pole piece or the tone wheel?*
(YES) : Replace ABS sensor or tone wheel.
(NO) : Go to step 8J12.

8J12 : CHECK HUB RUNOUT.

Measure hub runout.
(CHECK) : *Is the runout less than 0.05 mm (0.0020 in)?*
(YES) : Go to step 8J13.
(NO) : Repair hub.

8J13 : CHECK ABSCM&H/U.

1) Turn ignition switch to OFF.
2) Connect all connectors.
3) Erase the memory.
4) Perform inspection mode.
5) Read out the trouble code.

(CHECK) : *Is the same trouble code as in the current diagnosis still being output?*
(YES) : Replace ABSCM&H/U.
(NO) : Go to step 8J14.

8J14 : CHECK ANY OTHER TROUBLE CODES APPEARANCE.

(CHECK) : *Are other trouble codes being output?*
(YES) : Proceed with the diagnosis corresponding to the trouble code.
(NO) : A temporary poor contact.

SB4029800104020X

Fig. 12 Code 29: Abnormal ABS Sensor Signal, Any One of Four (Part 2 of 2). Less Select Monitor

8N1 : CHECK INPUT VOLTAGE OF ABSCM&H/U.

1) Disconnect connector from ABSCM&H/U.
2) Run the engine at idle.
3) Measure voltage between ABSCM&H/U connector and chassis ground.

Connector & terminal
(F49) No. 1 (+) — Chassis ground (–):

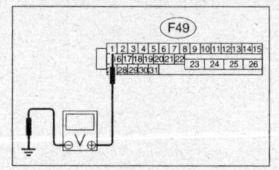

CHECK : **Is the voltage between 10 V and 15 V?**
YES : Go to step **8N2**.
NO : Repair harness connector between battery, ignition switch and ABSCM&H/U.

8N2 : CHECK GROUND CIRCUIT OF ABSCM&H/U.

1) Turn ignition switch to OFF.
2) Measure resistance between ABSCM&H/U connector and chassis ground.

Connector & terminal
(F49) No. 23 — Chassis ground:

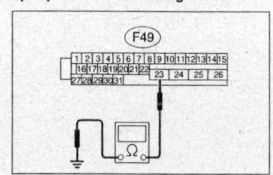

CHECK : **Is the resistance less than 0.5 Ω?**
YES : Go to step **8N3**.
NO : Repair ABSCM&H/U ground harness.

8N3 : CHECK POOR CONTACT IN CONNECTORS.

CHECK : **Is there poor contact in connectors between generator, battery and ABSCM&H/U?**
YES : Repair connector.
NO : Go to step **8N4**.

8N4 : CHECK ABSCM&H/U.

1) Connect all connectors.
2) Erase the memory.
3) Perform inspection mode.
4) Read out the trouble code.

CHECK : **Is the same trouble code as in the current diagnosis still being output?**
YES : Replace ABSCM&H/U.
NO : Go to step **8N5**.

8N5 : CHECK ANY OTHER TROUBLE CODES APPEARANCE.

CHECK : **Are other trouble codes being output?**
YES : Proceed with the diagnosis corresponding to the trouble code.
NO : A temporary poor contact.

SB4029800105000X

Fig. 13 Codes 31, 33, 35 & 37: Abnormal Inlet Valve Circuit In ABSCM & H/U. Less Select Monitor

8R1 : CHECK INPUT VOLTAGE OF ABSCM&H/U.

1) Disconnect connector from ABSCM&H/U.
2) Run the engine at idle.
3) Measure voltage between ABSCM&H/U connector and chassis ground.

Connector & terminal
(F49) No. 1 (+) — Chassis ground (–):

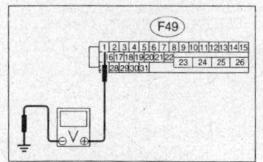

CHECK : **Is the voltage between 10 V and 15 V?**
YES : Go to step **8R2**.
NO : Repair harness connector between battery, ignition switch and ABSCM&H/U.

8R2 : CHECK GROUND CIRCUIT OF ABSCM&H/U.

1) Turn ignition switch to OFF.
2) Measure resistance between ABSCM&H/U connector and chassis ground.

Connector & terminal
(F49) No. 23 — Chassis ground:

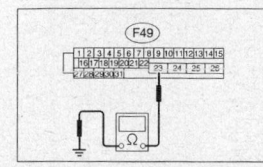

CHECK : **Is the resistance less than 0.5 Ω?**
YES : Go to step **8R3**.
NO : Repair ABSCM&H/U ground harness.

8R3 : CHECK POOR CONTACT IN CONNECTORS.

CHECK : **Is there poor contact in connectors between generator, battery and ABSCM&H/U?**
YES : Repair connector.
NO : Go to step **8R4**.

8R4 : CHECK ABSCM&H/U.

1) Connect all connectors.
2) Erase the memory.
3) Perform inspection mode.
4) Read out the trouble code.

CHECK : **Is the same trouble code as in the current diagnosis still being output?**
YES : Replace ABSCM&H/U.
NO : Go to step **8R5**.

8R5 : CHECK ANY OTHER TROUBLE CODES APPEARANCE.

CHECK : **Are other trouble codes being output?**
YES : Proceed with the diagnosis corresponding to the trouble code.
NO : A temporary poor contact.

SB4029800106000X

Fig. 14 Codes 32, 34, 36 & 38: Abnormal Outlet Solenoid Valve Circuit In ABSCM & H/U. Less Select Monitor

8S1 : CHECK GROUND CIRCUIT OF ABSCM&H/U.

1) Turn ignition switch to OFF.
2) Disconnect connector from ABSCM&H/U.
3) Measure resistance between ABSCM&H/U and chassis ground.

Connector & terminal
   (F49) No. 23 — Chassis ground:

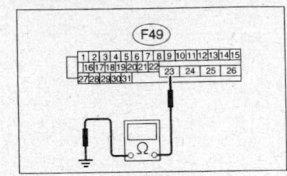

(CHECK) : **Is the resistance less than 0.5 Ω?**
(YES) : Go to step **8S2.**
(NO) : Repair ABSCM&H/U ground harness.

8S2 : CHECK POOR CONTACT IN CONNECTORS.

(CHECK) : **Is there poor contact in connectors between battery, ignition switch and ABSCM&H/U?**
(YES) : Repair connector.
(NO) : Go to step **8S3.**

8S3 : CHECK SOURCES OF SIGNAL NOISE.

(CHECK) : **Is the car telephone or the wireless transmitter properly installed?**
(YES) : Go to step **8S4.**
(NO) : Properly install the car telephone or the wireless transmitter.

8S4 : CHECK SOURCES OF SIGNAL NOISE.

(CHECK) : **Are noise sources (such as an antenna) installed near the sensor harness?**
(YES) : Install the noise sources apart from the sensor harness.
(NO) : Go to step **8S5.**

8S5 : CHECK ABSCM&H/U.

1) Connect all connectors.
2) Erase the memory.
3) Perform inspection mode.
4) Read out the trouble code.

(CHECK) : **Is the same trouble code as in the current diagnosis still being output?**
(YES) : Replace ABSCM&H/U.
(NO) : Go to step **8S6.**

8S6 : CHECK ANY OTHER TROUBLE CODES APPEARANCE.

(CHECK) : **Are other trouble codes being output?**
(YES) : Proceed with the diagnosis corresponding to the trouble code.
(NO) : A temporary poor contact.

SB4029800107000X

Fig. 15   Code 41: Abnormal ABS Control Module. Less Select Monitor

8T1 : CHECK GENERATOR.

1) Start engine.
2) Idling after warm-up.
3) Measure voltage between generator B terminal and chassis ground.

Terminal
   Generator B terminal — Chassis ground:

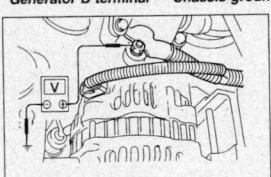

(CHECK) : **Is the voltage between 10 V and 17 V?**
(YES) : Go to step **8T2.**
(NO) : Repair generator.

8T2 : CHECK BATTERY TERMINAL.

Turn ignition switch to OFF.
(CHECK) : **Are the positive and negative battery terminals tightly clamped?**
(YES) : Go to step **8T3.**
(NO) : Tighten the clamp of terminal.

8T3 : CHECK INPUT VOLTAGE OF ABSCM&H/U.

1) Disconnect connector from ABSCM&H/U.
2) Run the engine at idle.
3) Measure voltage between ABSCM&H/U connector and chassis ground.

Connector & terminal
   (F49) No. 1 (+) — Chassis ground (−):

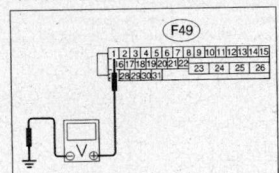

(CHECK) : **Is the voltage between 10 V and 17 V?**
(YES) : Go to step **8T4.**
(NO) : Repair harness connector between battery, ignition switch and ABSCM&H/U.

8T4 : CHECK GROUND CIRCUIT OF ABSCM&H/U.

1) Turn ignition switch to OFF.
2) Measure resistance between ABSCM&H/U connector and chassis ground.

Connector & terminal
   (F49) No. 23 — Chassis ground:

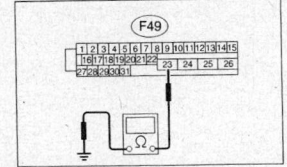

(CHECK) : **Is the resistance less than 0.5 Ω?**
(YES) : Go to step **8T5.**
(NO) : Repair ABSCM&H/U ground harness.

SB4029800108010X

Fig. 16   Code 42: Source Voltage Is Abnormal (Part 1 of 2). Less Select Monitor

**8T5 : CHECK POOR CONTACT IN CON-
NECTORS.**

CHECK : *Is there poor contact in connectors
between generator, battery and
ABSCM&H/U?*

YES : Repair connector.

NO : Go to step **8T6**.

8T6 : CHECK ABSCM&H/U.

1) Connect all connectors.
2) Erase the memory.
3) Perform inspection mode.
4) Read out the trouble code.

CHECK : *Is the same trouble code as in the
current diagnosis still being output?*

YES : Replace ABSCM&H/U.

NO : Go to step **8T7**.

**8T7 : CHECK ANY OTHER TROUBLE
CODES APPEARANCE.**

CHECK : *Are other trouble codes being output?*

YES : Proceed with the diagnosis corresponding to the trouble code.

NO : A temporary poor contact.

SB4029800108020X

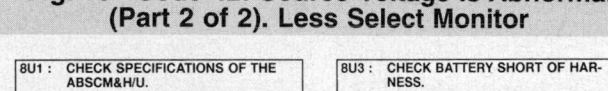

**Fig. 16 Code 42: Source Voltage Is Abnormal
(Part 2 of 2). Less Select Monitor**

**8U1 : CHECK SPECIFICATIONS OF THE
ABSCM&H/U.**

Check specifications of the mark to the
ABSCM&H/U.

Mark	Model
C1	FWD AT
C3	AWD AT
C4	AWD MT

CHECK : *Is an ABSCM&H/U for AT model
installed on a MT model?*

YES : Replace ABSCM&H/U.

NO : Go to step 8U2.

**8U2 : CHECK GROUND SHORT OF HAR-
NESS.**

1) Turn ignition switch to OFF.
2) Disconnect two connectors from TCM.
3) Disconnect connector from ABSCM&H/U.
4) Measure resistance between ABSCM&H/U
connector and chassis ground.

*Connector & terminal
(F49) No. 3 — Chassis ground:*

CHECK : *Is the resistance more than 1 MΩ?*

YES : Go to step 8U3.

NO : Repair harness between TCM and
ABSCM&H/U.

**8U3 : CHECK BATTERY SHORT OF HAR-
NESS.**

Measure voltage between ABSCM&H/U connector
and chassis ground.

*Connector & terminal
(F49) No. 3 (+) — Chassis ground (–):*

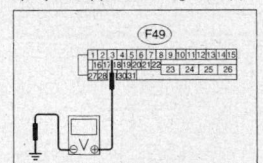

CHECK : *Is the voltage less than 1 V?*

YES : Go to step 8U4.

NO : Repair harness between TCM and
ABSCM&H/U.

**8U4 : CHECK BATTERY SHORT OF HAR-
NESS.**

1) Turn ignition switch to ON.
2) Measure voltage between ABSCM&H/U connector and chassis ground.

*Connector & terminal
(F49) No. 3 (+) — Chassis ground (–):*

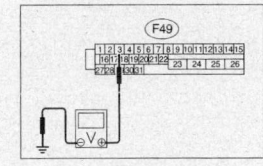

CHECK : *Is the voltage less than 1 V?*

YES : Go to step 8U5.

NO : Repair harness between TCM and
ABSCM&H/U.

SB4029800109010X

**Fig. 17 Code 44: A Combination Of AT Control
Abnormal (Part 1 of 3). 1998 Less Select Monitor**

8U5 : CHECK TCM.

1) Turn ignition switch to OFF.
2) Connect all connectors to TCM.
3) Turn ignition switch to ON.
4) Measure voltage between TCM connector terminal and chassis ground.

Connector & terminal
(B56) No. 5 (+) — Chassis ground (–):

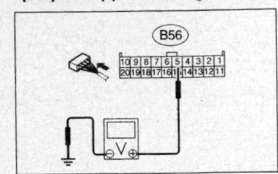

CHECK : *Is the voltage between 10 V and 15 V?*
YES : Go to step 8U7.
NO : Go to step 8U6.

8U6 : CHECK AT.

CHECK : *Is the AT functioning normally?*
YES : Replace TCM.
NO : Repair AT.

8U7 : CHECK OPEN CIRCUIT OF HARNESS.

Measure voltage between ABSCM&H/U connector and chassis ground.

Connector & terminal
(F49) No. 3 (+) — Chassis ground (–):
(F49) No. 31 (+) — Chassis ground (–):

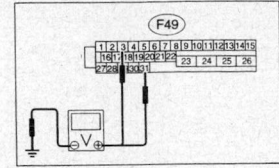

CHECK : *Is the voltage between 10 V and 15 V?*
YES : Go to step 8U8.
NO : Repair harness/connector between TCM and ABSCM&H/U.

8U8 : CHECK POOR CONTACT IN CONNECTORS.

CHECK : *Is there poor contact in connectors between TCM and ABSCM&H/U?*

YES : Repair connector.
NO : Go to step 8U9.

8U9 : CHECK ABSCM&H/U.

1) Turn ignition switch to OFF.
2) Connect all connectors.
3) Erase the memory.
4) Perform inspection mode.
5) Read out the trouble code.

CHECK : *Is the same trouble code as in the current diagnosis still being output?*
YES : Replace ABSCM&H/U.
NO : Go to step 8U10.

SB4029800109020X

Fig. 17 Code 44: A Combination Of AT Control Abnormal (Part 2 of 3). 1998 Less Select Monitor

8U10 : CHECK ANY OTHER TROUBLE CODES APPEARANCE.

CHECK : *Are other trouble codes being output?*

YES : Proceed with the diagnosis corresponding to the trouble code.

NO : A temporary poor contact.

SB4029800109030X

Fig. 17 Code 44: A Combination Of AT Control Abnormal (Part 3 of 3). 1998 Less Select Monitor

8U1 : CHECK SPECIFICATIONS OF THE ABSCM&H/U.

Check specifications of the mark to the ABSCM&H/U.

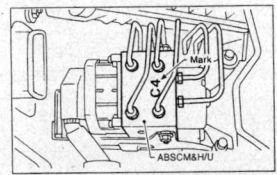

Mark	Model
C5	AWD AT
C6	AWD MT

CHECK : *Is an ABSCM&H/U for AT model installed on a MT model?*
YES : Replace ABSCM&H/U.
NO : Go to step 8U2.

8U2 : CHECK GROUND SHORT OF HARNESS.

1) Turn ignition switch to OFF.
2) Disconnect two connectors from TCM.
3) Disconnect connector from ABSCM&H/U.
4) Measure resistance between ABSCM&H/U connector and chassis ground.

Connector & terminal
(F49) No. 3 — Chassis ground:

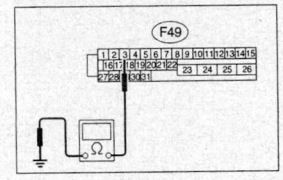

CHECK : *Is the resistance more than 1 MΩ?*
YES : Go to step 8U3.
NO : Repair harness between TCM and ABSCM&H/U.

8U3 : CHECK BATTERY SHORT OF HARNESS.

Measure voltage between ABSCM&H/U connector and chassis ground.

Connector & terminal
(F49) No. 3 (+) — Chassis ground (–):

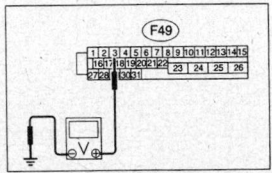

CHECK : *Is the voltage less than 1 V?*
YES : Go to step 8U4.
NO : Repair harness between TCM and ABSCM&H/U.

8U4 : CHECK BATTERY SHORT OF HARNESS.

1) Turn ignition switch to ON.
2) Measure voltage between ABSCM&H/U connector and chassis ground.

Connector & terminal
(F49) No. 3 (+) — Chassis ground (–):

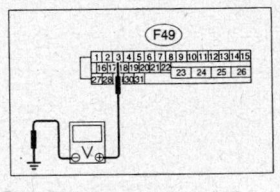

CHECK : *Is the voltage less than 1 V?*
YES : Go to step 8U5.
NO : Repair harness between TCM and ABSCM&H/U.

SB4029800114010X

Fig. 18 Code 44: A Combination Of AT Control Abnormal (Part 1 of 3). 1999 Less Select Monitor

8U5 : CHECK TCM.

1) Turn ignition switch to OFF.
2) Connect all connectors to TCM.
3) Turn ignition switch to ON.
4) Measure voltage between TCM connector terminal and chassis ground.

Connector & terminal
(B54) No. 19 (+) — Chassis ground (–):

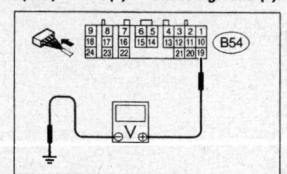

CHECK : *Is the voltage between 10 V and 15 V?*
YES : Go to step **8U7**.
NO : Go to step **8U6**.

8U6 : CHECK AT.

CHECK : *Is the AT functioning normally?*
YES : Replace TCM.

NO : Repair AT.

8U7 : CHECK OPEN CIRCUIT OF HARNESS.

Measure voltage between ABSCM&H/U connector and chassis ground.
Connector & terminal
(F49) No. 3 (+) — Chassis ground (–):
(F49) No. 31 (+) — Chassis ground (–):

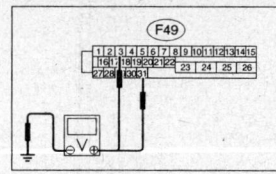

CHECK : *Is the voltage between 10 V and 15 V?*
YES : Go to step **8U8**.
NO : Repair harness/connector between TCM and ABSCM&H/U.

8U8 : CHECK POOR CONTACT IN CONNECTORS.

CHECK : *Is there poor contact in connectors between TCM and ABSCM&H/U?*

YES : Repair connector.
NO : Go to step **8U9**.

8U9 : CHECK ABSCM&H/U.

1) Turn ignition switch to OFF.
2) Connect all connectors.
3) Erase the memory.
4) Perform inspection mode.
5) Read out the trouble code.

CHECK : *Is the same trouble code as in the current diagnosis still being output?*
YES : Replace ABSCM&H/U.

NO : Go to step **8U10**.

SB4029800114020X

Fig. 18   Code 44: A Combination Of AT Control Abnormal (Part 2 of 3). 1999 Less Select Monitor

8U10 : CHECK ANY OTHER TROUBLE CODES APPEARANCE.

CHECK : *Are other trouble codes being output?*
YES : Proceed with the diagnosis corresponding to the trouble code.
NO : A temporary poor contact.

SB4029800114030X

Fig. 18   Code 44: A Combination Of AT Control Abnormal (Part 3 of 3). 1999 Less Select Monitor

8V1 : CHECK INPUT VOLTAGE OF ABSCM&H/U.

1) Turn ignition switch to OFF.
2) Disconnect connector from ABSCM&H/U.
3) Run the engine at idle.
4) Measure voltage between ABSCM&H/U connector and chassis ground.

Connector & terminal
(F49) No. 1 (+) — Chassis ground (–):
(F49) No. 24 (+) — Chassis ground (–):

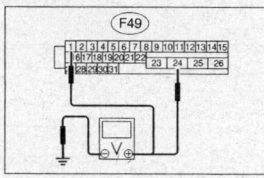

CHECK : *Is the voltage between 10 V and 15 V?*
YES : Go to step **8V2**.
NO : Repair harness connector between battery and ABSCM&H/U.

8V2 : CHECK GROUND CIRCUIT OF ABSCM&H/U.

1) Turn ignition switch to OFF.
2) Measure resistance between ABSCM&H/U connector and chassis ground.

Connector & terminal
(F49) No. 23 — Chassis ground:

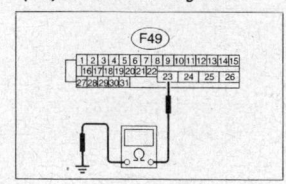

CHECK : *Is the resistance less than 0.5 Ω?*
YES : Go to step **8V3**.
NO : Repair ABSCM&H/U ground harness.

8V3 : CHECK VALVE RELAY IN ABSCM&H/U.

Measure resistance between ABSCM&H/U and terminals.
Terminals
No. 23 (+) — No. 24 (–):

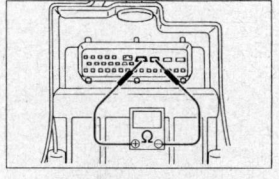

CHECK : *Is the resistance more than 1 MΩ?*
YES : Go to step **8V4**.
NO : Replace ABSCM&H/U.

8V4 : CHECK POOR CONTACT IN CONNECTORS.

CHECK : *Is there poor contact in connectors between generator, battery and ABSCM&H/U?*
YES : Repair connector.
NO : Go to step **8V5**.

8V5 : CHECK ABSCM&H/U.

1) Connect all connectors.
2) Erase the memory.
3) Perform inspection mode.
4) Read out the trouble code.

CHECK : *Is the same trouble code as in the current diagnosis still being output?*
YES : Replace ABSCM&H/U.
NO : Go to step **8V6**.

SB4029800110010X

Fig. 19   Code 51: Abnormal Valve Relay (Part 1 of 2). Less Select Monitor

8V6 :	CHECK ANY OTHER TROUBLE CODES APPEARANCE.

CHECK : **_Are other trouble codes being output?_**

YES : Proceed with the diagnosis corresponding to the trouble code.

NO : A temporary poor contact.

SB4029800110020X

Fig. 19 Code 51: Abnormal Valve Relay (Part 2 of 2). Less Select Monitor

8W1 :	CHECK INPUT VOLTAGE OF ABSCM&H/U.

1) Turn ignition switch to OFF.
2) Disconnect connector from ABSCM&H/U.
3) Turn ignition switch to ON.
4) Measure voltage between ABSCM&H/U connector and chassis ground.

**_Connector & terminal
(F49) No. 25 (+) — Chassis ground (–):_**

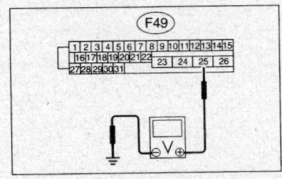

CHECK : **_Is the voltage between 10 V and 15 V?_**
YES : Go to step **8W2**.
NO : Repair harness/connector between battery and ABSCM&H/U and check fuse SBF-6.

8W2 :	CHECK GROUND CIRCUIT OF MOTOR.

1) Turn ignition switch to OFF.
2) Measure resistance between ABSCM&H/U connector and chassis ground.

**_Connector & terminal
(F49) No. 26 — Chassis ground:_**

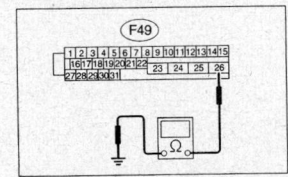

CHECK : **_Is the resistance less than 0.5 Ω?_**
YES : Go to step **8W3**.
NO : Repair ABSCM&H/U ground harness.

8W3 :	CHECK INPUT VOLTAGE OF ABSCM&H/U.

1) Run the engine at idle.
2) Measure voltage between ABSCM&H/U connector and chassis ground.

**_Connector & terminal
(F49) No. 1 (+) — Chassis ground (–):_**

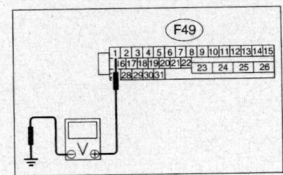

CHECK : **_Is the voltage between 10 V and 15 V?_**
YES : Go to step **8W4**.
NO : Repair harness connector between battery, ignition switch and ABSCM&H/U.

8W4 :	CHECK GROUND CIRCUIT OF ABSCM&H/U.

1) Turn ignition switch to OFF.
2) Measure resistance between ABSCM&H/U connector and chassis ground.

**_Connector & terminal
(F49) No. 23 — Chassis ground:_**

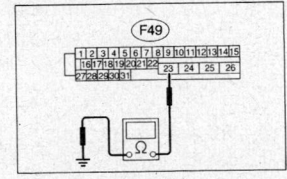

CHECK : **_Is the resistance less than 0.5 Ω?_**
YES : Go to step **8W5**.
NO : Repair ABSCM&H/U ground harness.

SB4029800111010X

Fig. 20 Code 52: Abnormal Motor And/Or Motor Relay (Part 1 of 2). Less Select Monitor

8W5 : CHECK MOTOR OPERATION.

Operate the sequence control.

NOTE:
Use the diagnosis connector to operate the sequence control.

CHECK : *Can motor revolution noise (buzz) be heard when carrying out the sequence control?*

YES : Go to step **8W6**.

NO : Replace ABSCM&H/U.

8W6 : CHECK POOR CONTACT IN CONNECTORS.

Turn ignition switch to OFF.

CHECK : *Is there poor contact in connector between generator, battery and ABSCM&H/U?*

YES : Repair connector.

NO : Go to step **8W7**.

8W7 : CHECK ABSCM&H/U.

1) Connect all connectors.
2) Erase the memory.
3) Perform inspection mode.
4) Read out the trouble code.

CHECK : *Is the same trouble code as in the current diagnosis still being output?*

YES : Replace ABSCM&H/U.

NO : Go to step **8W8**.

8W8 : CHECK ANY OTHER TROUBLE CODES APPEARANCE.

CHECK : *Are other trouble codes being output?*

YES : Proceed with the diagnosis corresponding to the trouble code.

NO : A temporary poor contact.

SB4029800111020X

Fig. 20   Code 52: Abnormal Motor And/Or Motor Relay (Part 2 of 2). Less Select Monitor

---

| 8X1 : | CHECK STOP LIGHTS COME ON. |

Depress the brake pedal.

CHECK : *Do stop lights come on?*

YES : Go to step **8X2**.

NO : Repair stop lights circuit.

| 8X2 : | CHECK OPEN CIRCUIT IN HARNESS. |

1) Turn ignition switch to OFF.
2) Disconnect connector from ABSCM&H/U.
3) Depress brake pedal.
4) Measure voltage between ABSCM&H/U connector and chassis ground.

Connector & terminal
(F49) No. 2 (+) — Chassis ground (–):

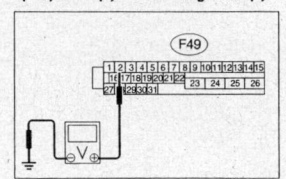

CHECK : *Is the voltage between 10 V and 15 V?*

YES : Go to step **8X3**.

NO : Repair harness between stop light switch and ABSCM&H/U.

| 8X3 : | CHECK POOR CONTACT IN CONNECTORS. |

CHECK : *Is there poor contact in connector between stop light switch and ABSCM&H/U?*

YES : Repair connector.

NO : Go to step **8X4**.

SB4029800112000X

Fig. 21   Code 54: Abnormal Stop Light Switch. Less Select Monitor

---

| 8X4 : | CHECK ABSCM&H/U. |

1) Connect all connectors.
2) Erase the memory.
3) Perform inspection mode.
4) Read out the trouble code.

CHECK : *Is the same trouble code as in the current diagnosis still being output?*

YES : Replace ABSCM&H/U.

NO : Go to step **8X5**.

| 8X5 : | CHECK ANY OTHER TROUBLE CODES APPEARANCE. |

CHECK : *Are other trouble codes being output?*

YES : Proceed with the diagnosis corresponding to the trouble code.

NO : A temporary poor contact.

| 8Y1 : | CHECK ALL FOUR WHEELS FOR FREE TURNING. |

CHECK : *Have the wheels been turned freely such as when the vehicle is lifted up, or operated on a rolling road?*

YES : The ABS is normal. Erase the trouble code.

NO : Go to step **8Y2**.

| 8Y2 : | CHECK SPECIFICATIONS OF ABSCM&H/U. |

Check specifications of the mark to the ABSCM&H/U.

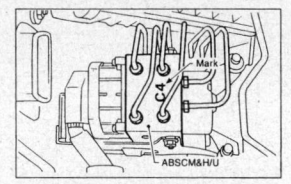

Mark	Model
C1	FWD AT
C3	AWD AT
C4	AWD MT

CHECK : *Is an ABSCM for AWD model installed on a FWD model?*

YES : Replace ABSCM&H/U.

CAUTION:
Be sure to turn ignition switch to OFF when removing ABSCM&H/U.

NO : Go to step **8Y3**.

| 8Y3 : | CHECK INPUT VOLTAGE OF G SENSOR. |

1) Turn ignition switch to OFF.
2) Remove console box.
3) Disconnect G sensor from body. (Do not disconnect connector.)
4) Turn ignition switch to ON.
5) Measure voltage between G sensor connector terminals.

Connector & terminal
(P11) No. 1 (+) — No. 3 (–):

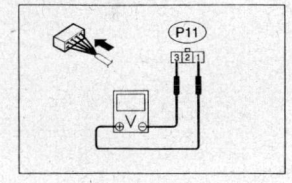

CHECK : *Is the voltage between 4.75 and 5.25 V?*

YES : Go to step **8Y4**.

NO : Repair harness/connector between G sensor and ABSCM&H/U.

SB4029800113010X

Fig. 22   Code 56: Abnormal G Sensor Output Voltage (Part 1 of 3). 1998 Less Select Monitor

---

8Y4 : CHECK OPEN CIRCUIT IN G SEN-SOR OUTPUT HARNESS AND GROUND HARNESS.

1) Turn ignition switch to OFF.
2) Disconnect connector from ABSCM&H/U.
3) Measure resistance between ABSCM&H/U connector terminals.

Connector & terminal
(F49) No. 30 — No. 28:

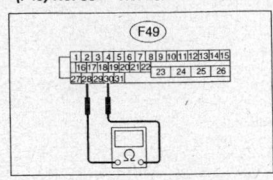

CHECK : *Is the resistance between 4.3 and 4.9 kΩ?*
YES : Go to step **8Y5**.
NO : Repair harness/connector between G sensor and ABSCM&H/U.

8Y5 : CHECK GROUND SHORT IN G SEN-SOR OUTPUT HARNESS.

1) Disconnect connector from G sensor.
2) Measure resistance between ABSCM&H/U connector and chassis ground.

Connector & terminal
(F49) No. 6 — Chassis ground:

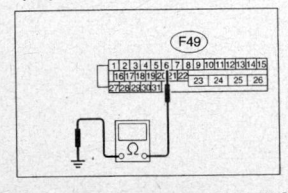

CHECK : *Is the resistance more than 1 MΩ?*
YES : Go to step **8Y6**.
NO : Repair harness between G sensor and ABSCM&H/U.

8Y6 : CHECK BATTERY SHORT OF HAR-NESS.

Measure voltage between ABSCM&H/U connector and chassis ground.

Connector & terminal
(F49) No. 6 (+) — Chassis ground (–):

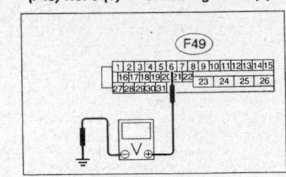

CHECK : *Is the voltage less than 1 V?*
YES : Go to step **8Y7**.
NO : Repair harness between G sensor and ABSCM&H/U.

8Y7 : CHECK BATTERY SHORT OF HAR-NESS.

1) Turn ignition switch to ON.
2) Measure voltage between ABSCM&H/U connector and chassis ground.

Connector & terminal
(F49) No. 6 (+) — Chassis ground (–):

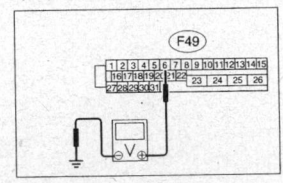

CHECK : *Is the voltage less than 1 V?*
YES : Go to step **8Y8**.
NO : Repair harness between G sensor and ABSCM&H/U.

SB4029800113020X

Fig. 22   Code 56: Abnormal G Sensor Output Voltage (Part 2 of 3). 1998 Less Select Monitor

8Y1 : CHECK ALL FOUR WHEELS FOR FREE TURNING.

CHECK : *Have the wheels been turned freely such as when the vehicle is lifted up, or operated on a rolling road?*
YES : The ABS is normal. Erase the trouble code.
NO : Go to step **8Y2**.

8Y2 : CHECK SPECIFICATIONS OF ABSCM&H/U.

Check specifications of the mark to the ABSCM&H/U.

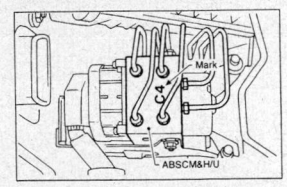

Mark	Model
C5	AWD AT
C6	AWD MT

CHECK : *Is an ABSCM for AWD model installed on a FWD model?*
YES : Replace ABSCM&H/U.

CAUTION:
Be sure to turn ignition switch to OFF when removing ABSCM&H/U.
NO : Go to step **8Y3**.

8Y3 : CHECK INPUT VOLTAGE OF G SEN-SOR.

1) Turn ignition switch to OFF.
2) Remove console box.
3) Disconnect G sensor from body. (Do not disconnect connector.)
4) Turn ignition switch to ON.
5) Measure voltage between G sensor connector terminals.

Connector & terminal
(P11) No. 1 (+) — No. 3 (–):

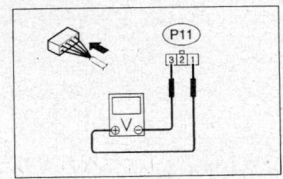

CHECK : *Is the voltage between 4.75 and 5.25 V?*
YES : Go to step **8Y4**.
NO : Repair harness/connector between G sensor and ABSCM&H/U.

SB4029800115010X

Fig. 23   Code 56: Abnormal G Sensor Output Voltage (Part 1 of 4). 1999 Less Select Monitor

8Y8 : CHECK GROUND SHORT OF HAR-NESS.

Measure resistance between ABSCM&H/U connector and chassis ground.

Connector & terminal
(F49) No. 28 — Chassis ground:

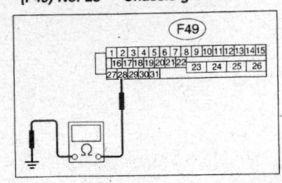

CHECK : *Is the resistance more than 1 MΩ?*
YES : Go to step **8Y9**.
NO : Repair harness between G sensor and ABSCM&H/U.
Replace ABSCM&H/U.

8Y9 : CHECK G SENSOR.

1) Turn ignition switch to OFF.
2) Remove G sensor from vehicle.
3) Connect connector to G sensor.
4) Connect connector to ABSCM&H/U.
5) Turn ignition switch to ON.
6) Measure voltage between G sensor connector terminals.

Connector & terminal
(P11) No. 2 (+) — No. 3 (–):

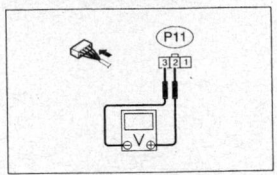

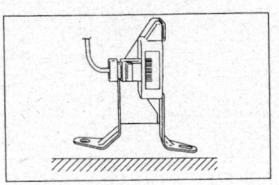

CHECK : *Is the voltage between 2.1 and 2.4 V when G sensor is horizontal?*
YES : Go to step **8Y10**.
NO : Replace G sensor.

SB4029800113030X

Fig. 22   Code 56: Abnormal G Sensor Output Voltage (Part 3 of 3). 1998 Less Select Monitor

8Y4 : CHECK OPEN CIRCUIT IN G SEN-SOR OUTPUT HARNESS AND GROUND HARNESS.

1) Turn ignition switch to OFF.
2) Disconnect connector from ABSCM&H/U.
3) Measure resistance between ABSCM&H/U connector terminals.

Connector & terminal
(F49) No. 30 — No. 28:

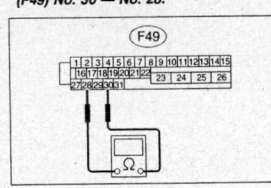

CHECK : *Is the resistance between 4.3 and 4.9 kΩ?*
YES : Go to step **8Y5**.
NO : Repair harness/connector between G sensor and ABSCM&H/U.

8Y5 : CHECK GROUND SHORT IN G SEN-SOR OUTPUT HARNESS.

1) Disconnect connector from G sensor.
2) Measure resistance between ABSCM&H/U connector and chassis ground.

Connector & terminal
(F49) No. 6 — Chassis ground:

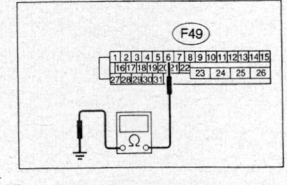

CHECK : *Is the resistance more than 1 MΩ?*
YES : Go to step **8Y6**.
NO : Repair harness between G sensor and ABSCM&H/U.

8Y6 : CHECK BATTERY SHORT OF HAR-NESS.

Measure voltage between ABSCM&H/U connector and chassis ground.

Connector & terminal
(F49) No. 6 (+) — Chassis ground (–):

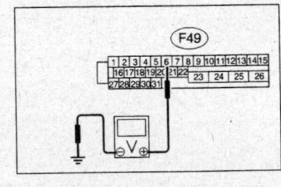

CHECK : *Is the voltage less than 1 V?*
YES : Go to step **8Y7**.
NO : Repair harness between G sensor and ABSCM&H/U.

8Y7 : CHECK BATTERY SHORT OF HAR-NESS.

1) Turn ignition switch to ON.
2) Measure voltage between ABSCM&H/U connector and chassis ground.

Connector & terminal
(F49) No. 6 (+) — Chassis ground (–):

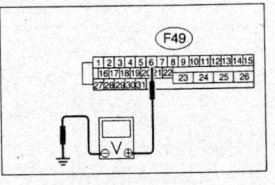

CHECK : *Is the voltage less than 1 V?*
YES : Go to step **8Y8**.
NO : Repair harness between G sensor and ABSCM&H/U.

SB4029800115020X

Fig. 23   Code 56: Abnormal G Sensor Output Voltage (Part 2 of 4). 1999 Less Select Monitor

8Y8 : CHECK GROUND SHORT OF HARNESS.

Measure resistance between ABSCM&H/U connector and chassis ground.

Connector & terminal
(F49) No. 28 — Chassis ground:

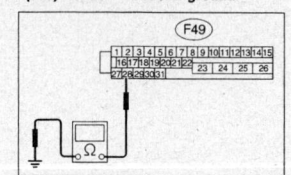

(CHECK) : **Is the resistance more than 1 MΩ?**
(YES) : Go to step **8Y9**.
(NO) : Repair harness between G sensor and ABSCM&H/U.
Replace ABSCM&H/U.

8Y9 : CHECK G SENSOR.

1) Turn ignition switch to OFF.
2) Remove G sensor from vehicle.
3) Connect connector to G sensor.
4) Connect connector to ABSCM&H/U.
5) Turn ignition switch to ON.
6) Measure voltage between G sensor connector terminals.

Connector & terminal
(P11) No. 2 (+) — No. 3 (–):

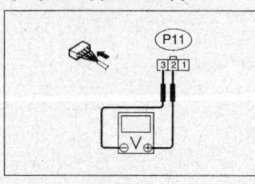

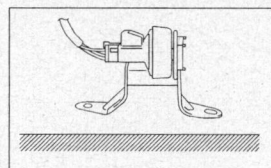

(CHECK) : **Is the voltage between 2.1 and 2.4 V when G sensor is horizontal?**
(YES) : Go to step **8Y10**.
(NO) : Replace G sensor.

SB4029800115030X

Fig. 23   Code 56: Abnormal G Sensor Output Voltage (Part 3 of 4). 1999 Less Select Monitor

8Y10 : CHECK G SENSOR.

Measure voltage between G sensor connector terminals.

Connector & terminal
(P11) No. 2 (+) — No. 3 (–):

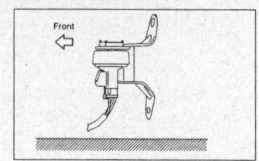

(CHECK) : **Is the voltage between 3.7 and 4.1 V when G sensor is inclined forwards to 90°?**
(YES) : Go to step **8Y11**.
(NO) : Replace G sensor.

8Y11 : CHECK G SENSOR.

Measure voltage between G sensor connector terminals.

Connector & terminal
(P11) No. 2 (+) — No. 3 (–):

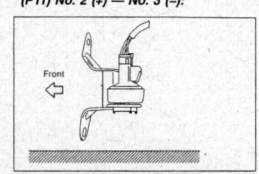

(CHECK) : **Is the voltage between 0.5 and 0.9 V when G sensor is inclined backwards to 90°?**
(YES) : Go to step **8Y12**.
(NO) : Replace G sensor.

8Y12 : CHECK POOR CONTACT IN CONNECTORS.

(CHECK) : **Is there poor contact in connector between ABSCM&H/U and G sensor?**
(YES) : Repair connector.
(NO) : Go to step **8Y13**.

8Y13 : CHECK ABSCM&H/U.

1) Connect all connectors.
2) Erase the memory.
3) Perform inspection mode.
4) Read out the trouble code.

(CHECK) : **Is the same trouble code as in the current diagnosis still being output?**
(YES) : Replace ABSCM&H/U.
(NO) : Go to step **8Y14**.

8Y14 : CHECK ANY OTHER TROUBLE CODES APPEARANCE.

(CHECK) : **Are other trouble codes being output?**
(YES) : Proceed with the diagnosis corresponding to the trouble code.
(NO) : A temporary poor contact.

SB4029800115040X

Fig. 23   Code 56: Abnormal G Sensor Output Voltage (Part 4 of 4). 1999 Less Select Monitor

10C1 : CHECK IGNITION SWITCH.

(CHECK) : **Is ignition switch ON?**
(YES) : Go to step **10C2**.
(NO) : Turn ignition switch ON, and select ABS/TCS mode using the select monitor.

10C2 : CHECK GENERATOR.

1) Start the engine.
2) Idle the engine.
3) Measure voltage between generator and chassis ground.

Terminal
Generator B terminal (+) — Chassis ground (–):

(CHECK) : **Is the voltage between 10 and 15 V?**
(YES) : Go to step **10C3**.
(NO) : Repair generator.

10C3 : CHECK BATTERY TERMINAL.

Turn ignition switch to OFF.
(CHECK) : **Is there poor contact at battery terminal?**
(YES) : Repair battery terminal.
(NO) : Go to step **10C4**.

10C4 : CHECK COMMUNICATION OF SELECT MONITOR.

Using the select monitor, check whether communication to other system (such as engine, AT, etc.) can be executed normally.

(CHECK) : **Are the name and year of the system displayed on the select monitor?**
(YES) : Go to step **10C5**.
(NO) : Repair select monitor communication cable and connector.

10C5 : CHECK INSTALLATION OF ABSCM&H/U CONNECTOR.

Turn ignition switch to OFF.

(CHECK) : **Is ABSCM&H/U connector inserted into ABSCM&H/U until the clamp locks onto it?**
(YES) : Go to step **10C6**.
(NO) : Insert ABSCM&H/U connector into ABSCM&H/U until the clamp locks onto it.

10C6 : CHECK POWER SUPPLY OF ABSCM&H/U.

1) Disconnect connector from ABSCM&H/U.
2) Start engine.
3) Idle the engine.
4) Measure voltage between ABSCM&H/U connector and chassis ground.

Connector & terminal
(F49) No. 1 (+) — Chassis ground (–):

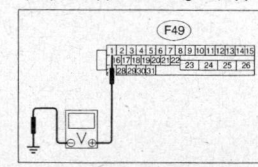

(CHECK) : **Is the voltage between 10 and 15 V?**
(YES) : Go to step **10C7**.
(NO) : Repair ABSCM&H/U power supply circuit.

SB4029800116010X

Fig. 24   Test C: Communication For Initializing Impossible (Part 1 of 2). With Select Monitor

10C7 : **CHECK GROUND CIRCUIT OF ABSCM&H/U.**

1) Turn ignition switch to OFF.
2) Measure resistance between ABSCM&H/U connector and chassis ground.

Connector & terminal
(F49) No. 23 — Chassis ground:

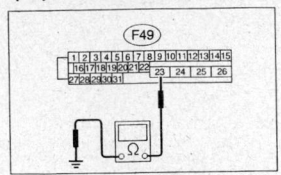

(CHECK) : **Is the resistance less than 0.5 Ω?**
(YES) : Repair harness/connector between ABSCM&H/U and select monitor.
(NO) : Go to step **10C8.**

10C8 : **CHECK HARNESS/CONNECTOR BETWEEN ABSCM&H/U AND DATA LINK CONNECTOR.**

1) Turn ignition switch OFF.
2) Measure resistance between ABSCM&H/U connector and data link connector.

Connector & terminal
(F49) No. 20 — (B40) No. 5:
(F49) No. 5 — (B40) No. 4:

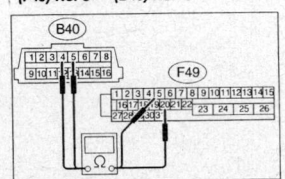

(CHECK) : **Is the resistance less than 0.5 Ω?**
(YES) : Repair harness and connector between ABSCM&H/U and data link connector.
(NO) : Go to step **10C9.**

10C9 : **CHECK POOR CONTACT IN CONNECTORS.**

(CHECK) : **Is there poor contact in connectors between ABSCM&H/U and data link connector?**
(YES) : Repair connector.
(NO) : Replace ABSCM&H/U.

SB4029800116020X

Fig. 24   Test C: Communication For Initializing Impossible (Part 2 of 2). With Select Monitor

10D1 : **CHECK WIRING HARNESS.**

1) Turn ignition switch to OFF.
2) Disconnect connector (F2) from connector (B100).
3) Turn ignition switch to ON.

(CHECK) : **Does the ABS warning light remain off?**
(YES) : Go to step **10D2.**
(NO) : Repair front wiring harness.

10D2 : **CHECK PROJECTION AT ABSCM&H/U.**

1) Turn ignition switch to OFF.
2) Disconnect connector from ABSCM&H/U.
3) Check for broken projection at the ABSCM&H/U terminal.

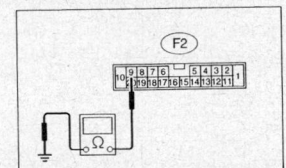

(CHECK) : **Are the projection broken?**
(YES) : Go to step **10D3.**
(NO) : Replace ABSCM&H/U.

10D3 : **CHECK ABSCM&H/U.**

Measure resistance between ABSCM&H/U terminals.

Terminals
No. 21 — No. 23:

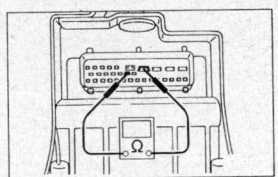

(CHECK) : **Is the resistance more than 1 MΩ?**
(YES) : Go to step **10D4.**
(NO) : Replace valve relay.

10D4 : **CHECK WIRING HARNESS.**

Measure resistance between connector (F2) and chassis ground.

Connector & terminal
(F2) No. 9 — Chassis ground:

(CHECK) : **Is the resistance less than 0.5 Ω?**
(YES) : Go to step **10D5.**
(NO) : Repair harness.

SB4029800117010X

Fig. 25   Test D: No Trouble Code (Part 1 of 2). With Select Monitor

10D5 : CHECK WIRING HARNESS.

1) Connect connector to ABSCM&H/U.
2) Measure resistance between connector (F2) and chassis ground.

Connector & terminal
(F2) No. 9 — Chassis ground:

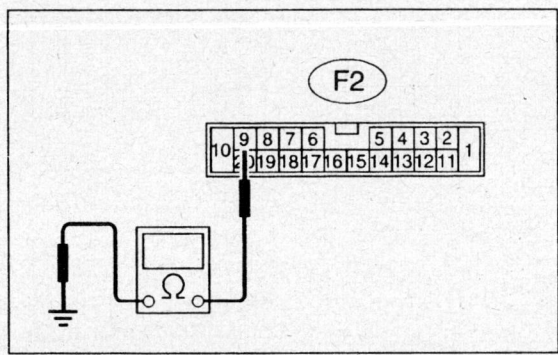

CHECK : **Is the resistance more than 1 MΩ?**
YES : Go to step **10D6**.
NO : Repair harness.

10D6 : CHECK POOR CONTACT IN ABSCM&H/U CONNECTOR.

CHECK : **Is there poor contact in ABSCM&H/U connector?**

YES : Repair connector.
NO : Replace ABSCM&H/U.

SB4029800117020X

Fig. 25 Test D: No Trouble Code (Part 2 of 2). With Select Monitor

---

10H1 : CHECK OUTPUT OF ABS SENSOR USING SELECT MONITOR.

1) Select "Current data display & Save" on the select monitor.
2) Read the ABS sensor output corresponding to the faulty system in the select monitor data display mode.

CHECK : **Does the speed indicated on the display change in response to the speedometer reading during acceleration/deceleration when the steering wheel is in the straight-ahead position?**
YES : Go to step 10H2.
NO : Go to step 10H9.

10H2 : CHECK INSTALLATION OF ABS SENSOR.

Tightening torque:
32±10 N·m (3.3±1.0 kg-m, 24±7 ft-lb)
CHECK : **Are the ABS sensor installation bolts tightened securely?**
YES : Go to step 10H3.
NO : Tighten ABS sensor installation bolts securely.

10H3 : CHECK INSTALLATION OF TONE WHEEL.

Tightening torque:
13±3 N·m (1.3±0.3 kg-m, 9±2.2 ft-lb)
CHECK : **Are the tone wheel installation bolts tightened securely?**
YES : Go to step 10H4.
NO : Tighten tone wheel installation bolts securely.

10H4 : CHECK ABS SENSOR GAP.

Measure tone wheel-to-pole piece gap over entire perimeter of the wheel.

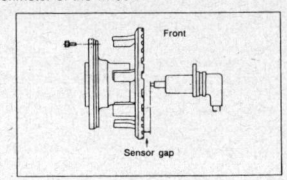

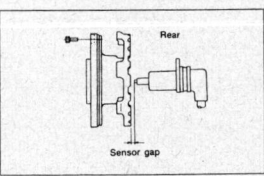

Specifications	Front wheel	Rear wheel
	0.9 — 1.4 mm (0.035 — 0.055 in)	0.7 — 1.2 mm (0.028 — 0.047 in)

CHECK : **Is the gap within the specifications?**
YES : Go to step 10H5.
NO : Adjust the gap.

NOTE:
Adjust the gap using spacers (Part No. 26755AA000). If spacers cannot correct the gap, replace worn sensor or worn tone wheel.

10H5 : CHECK HUB RUNOUT.

Measure hub runout.
CHECK : **Is the runout less than 0.05 mm (0.0020 in)?**
YES : Go to step 10H6.
NO : Repair hub.

SB4029800118010X

Fig. 26 Codes 21, 23, 25 & 27: Abnormal ABS Sensor, Open Or Short Circuit In ABS Sensor Circuit (Part 1 of 7). With Select Monitor

---

10H6 : CHECK POOR CONTACT IN CONNECTORS.

Turn ignition switch to OFF.
CHECK : **Is there poor contact in connectors between ABSCM&H/U and ABS sensor?**
YES : Repair connector.
NO : Go to step 10H7.

10H7 : CHECK ABSCM&H/U.

1) Connect all connectors.
2) Erase the memory.
3) Perform inspection mode.
4) Read out the trouble code.
CHECK : **Is the same trouble code as in the current diagnosis still being output?**
YES : Replace ABSCM&H/U.
NO : Go to step 10H8.

10H8 : CHECK ANY OTHER TROUBLE CODES APPEARANCE.

CHECK : **Are other trouble codes being output?**
YES : Proceed with the diagnosis corresponding to the trouble code.
NO : A temporary poor contact.
NOTE:
Check harness and connectors between ABSCM&H/U and ABS sensor.

10H9 : CHECK ABS SENSOR.

1) Turn ignition switch to OFF.
2) Disconnect connector from ABS sensor.
3) Measure resistance of ABS sensor connector terminals.

Terminal
Front RH No. 1 — No. 2:
Front LH No. 1 — No. 2:
Rear RH No. 1 — No. 2:
Rear LH No. 1 — No. 2:

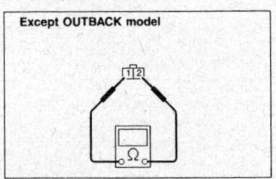

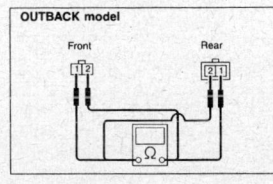

CHECK : **Is the resistance between 0.8 and 1.2 kΩ?**
YES : Go to step 10H10.
NO : Replace ABS sensor.

SB4029800118020X

Fig. 26 Codes 21, 23, 25 & 27: Abnormal ABS Sensor, Open Or Short Circuit In ABS Sensor Circuit (Part 2 of 7). With Select Monitor

10H10 : CHECK BATTERY SHORT OF ABS SENSOR.

1) Disconnect connector from ABSCM&H/U.
2) Measure voltage between ABS sensor and chassis ground.

Terminal
Front RH No. 1 (+) — Chassis ground (–):
Front LH No. 1 (+) — Chassis ground (–):
Rear RH No. 1 (+) — Chassis ground (–):
Rear LH No. 1 (+) — Chassis ground (–):

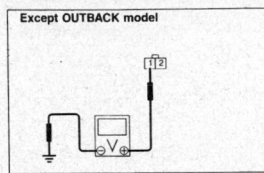

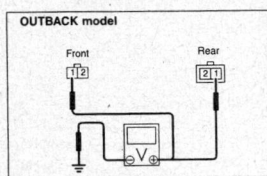

(CHECK) : *Is the voltage less than 1 V?*
(YES) : Go to step **10H11**.
(NO) : Replace ABS sensor.

10H11 : CHECK BATTERY SHORT OF ABS SENSOR.

1) Turn ignition switch to ON.
2) Measure voltage between ABS sensor and chassis ground.

Terminal
Front RH No. 1 (+) — Chassis ground (–):
Front LH No. 1 (+) — Chassis ground (–):
Rear RH No. 1 (+) — Chassis ground (–):
Rear LH No. 1 (+) — Chassis ground (–):

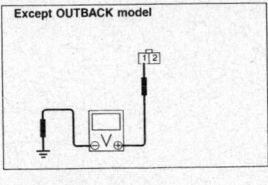

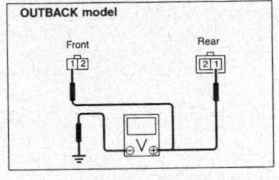

(CHECK) : *Is the voltage less than 1 V?*
(YES) : Go to step **10H12**.
(NO) : Replace ABS sensor.

SB4029800118030X

Fig. 26 Codes 21, 23, 25 & 27: Abnormal ABS Sensor, Open Or Short Circuit In ABS Sensor Circuit (Part 3 of 7). With Select Monitor

---

10H12 : CHECK HARNESS/CONNECTOR BETWEEN ABSCM&H/U AND ABS SENSOR.

1) Turn ignition switch to OFF.
2) Connect connector to ABS sensor.
3) Measure resistance between ABSCM&H/U connector terminals.

Connector & terminal
Trouble code 21 / (F49) No. 11 — No. 12:
Trouble code 23 / (F49) No. 9 — No. 10:
Trouble code 25 / (F49) No. 14 — No. 15:
Trouble code 27 / (F49) No. 7 — No. 8:

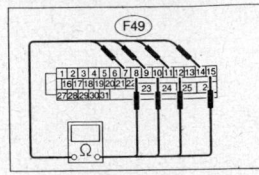

(CHECK) : *Is the resistance between 0.8 and 1.2 kΩ?*
(YES) : Go to step **10H13**.
(NO) : Repair harness/connector between ABSCM&H/U and ABS sensor.

10H13 : CHECK BATTERY SHORT OF HARNESS.

Measure voltage between ABSCM&H/U connector and chassis ground.

Connector & terminal
Trouble code 21 / (F49) No. 11 (+) — Chassis ground (–):
Trouble code 23 / (F49) No. 9 (+) — Chassis ground (–):
Trouble code 25 / (F49) No. 14 (+) — Chassis ground (–):
Trouble code 27 / (F49) No. 7 (+) — Chassis ground (–):

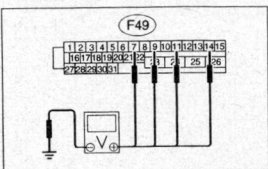

(CHECK) : *Is the voltage less than 1 V?*
(YES) : Go to step **10H14**.
(NO) : Repair harness between ABSCM&H/U and ABS sensor.

SB4029800118040X

Fig. 26 Codes 21, 23, 25 & 27: Abnormal ABS Sensor, Open Or Short Circuit In ABS Sensor Circuit (Part 4 of 7). With Select Monitor

---

10H14 : CHECK BATTERY SHORT OF HARNESS.

1) Turn ignition switch to ON.
2) Measure voltage between ABSCM&H/U connector and chassis ground.

Connector & terminal
Trouble code 21 / (F49) No. 11 (+) — Chassis ground (–):
Trouble code 23 / (F49) No. 9 (+) — Chassis ground (–):
Trouble code 25 / (F49) No. 14 (+) — Chassis ground (–):
Trouble code 27 / (F49) No. 7 (+) — Chassis ground (–):

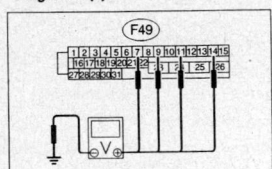

(CHECK) : *Is the voltage less than 1 V?*
(YES) : Go to step **10H15**.
(NO) : Repair harness between ABSCM&H/U and ABS sensor.

10H15 : CHECK INSTALLATION OF ABS SENSOR.

Tightening torque:
32±10 N·m (3.3±1.0 kg-m, 24±7 ft-lb)

(CHECK) : *Are the ABS sensor installation bolts tightened securely?*
(YES) : Go to step **10H16**.
(NO) : Tighten ABS sensor installation bolts securely.

10H16 : CHECK INSTALLATION OF TONE WHEEL.

Tightening torque:
13±3 N·m (1.3±0.3 kg-m, 9±2.2 ft-lb)

(CHECK) : *Are the tone wheel installation bolts tightened securely?*
(YES) : Go to step **10H17**.
(NO) : Tighten tone wheel installation bolts securely.

10H17 : CHECK ABS SENSOR GAP.

Measure tone wheel-to-pole piece gap over entire perimeter of the wheel.

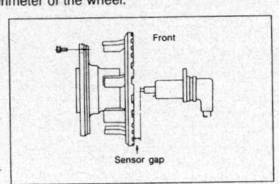

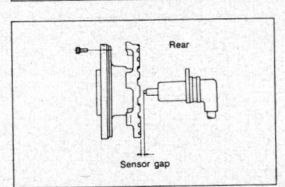

Specifications	Front wheel	Rear wheel
	0.9 – 1.4 mm (0.035 – 0.055 in)	0.7 – 1.2 mm (0.028 – 0.047 in)

(CHECK) : *Is the gap within the specifications?*
(YES) : Go to step **10H18**.
(NO) : Adjust the gap.

NOTE:
Adjust the gap using spacers (Part No. 26755AA000). If spacers cannot correct the gap, replace worn sensor or worn tone wheel.

SB4029800118050X

Fig. 26 Codes 21, 23, 25 & 27: Abnormal ABS Sensor, Open Or Short Circuit In ABS Sensor Circuit (Part 5 of 7). With Select Monitor

---

10H18 : CHECK HUB RUNOUT.

Measure hub runout.

(CHECK) : *Is the runout less than 0.05 mm (0.0020 in)?*
(YES) : Go to step **10H19**.
(NO) : Repair hub.

10H19 : CHECK GROUND SHORT OF ABS SENSOR.

1) Turn ignition switch to ON.
2) Measure resistance between ABS sensor and chassis ground.

Terminal
Front RH No. 1 — Chassis ground:
Front LH No. 1 — Chassis ground:
Rear RH No. 1 — Chassis ground:
Rear LH No. 1 — Chassis ground:

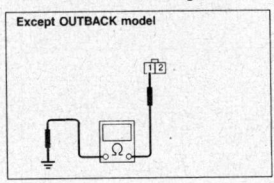

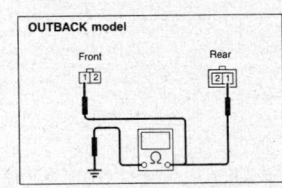

(CHECK) : *Is the resistance more than 1 MΩ?*
(YES) : Go to step **10H20**.
(NO) : Replace ABS sensor and ABSCM&H/U.

10H20 : CHECK GROUND SHORT OF HARNESS.

1) Turn ignition switch to OFF.
2) Connect connector to ABS sensor.
3) Measure resistance between ABSCM&H/U connector terminal and chassis ground.

Connector & terminal
Trouble code 21 / (F49) No. 11 — Chassis ground:
Trouble code 23 / (F49) No. 9 — Chassis ground:
Trouble code 25 / (F49) No. 14 — Chassis ground:
Trouble code 27 / (F49) No. 7 — Chassis ground:

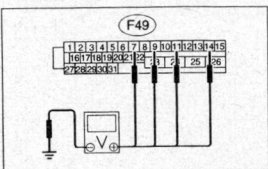

(CHECK) : *Is the resistance more than 1 MΩ?*
(YES) : Go to step **10H21**.
(NO) : Repair harness between ABSCM&H/U and ABS sensor. And replace ABSCM&H/U.

10H21 : CHECK POOR CONTACT IN CONNECTORS.

(CHECK) : *Is there poor contact in connectors between ABSCM&H/U and ABS sensor?*
(YES) : Repair connector.
(NO) : Go to step **10H22**.

SB4029800118060X

Fig. 26 Codes 21, 23, 25 & 27: Abnormal ABS Sensor, Open Or Short Circuit In ABS Sensor Circuit (Part 6 of 7). With Select Monitor

10H22 : CHECK ABSCM&H/U.

1) Connect all connectors.
2) Erase the memory.
3) Perform inspection mode.
4) Read out the trouble code.

(CHECK) : *Is the same trouble code as in the current diagnosis still being output?*

(YES) : Replace ABSCM&H/U.

(NO) : Go to step **10H23**.

10H23 : CHECK ANY OTHER TROUBLE CODES APPEARANCE.

(CHECK) : *Are other trouble codes being output?*

(YES) : Proceed with the diagnosis corresponding to the trouble code.

(NO) : A temporary poor contact.

NOTE:
Check harness and connectors between ABSCM&H/U and ABS sensor.

SB4029800118070X

Fig. 26 Codes 21, 23, 25 & 27: Abnormal ABS Sensor, Open Or Short Circuit In ABS Sensor Circuit (Part 7 of 7). With Select Monitor

---

10L1 : CHECK OUTPUT OF ABS SENSOR USING SELECT MONITOR.

1) Select "Current data display & Save" on the select monitor.
2) Read the ABS sensor output corresponding to the faulty system in the select monitor data display mode.

(CHECK) : *Does the speed indicated on the display change in response to the speedometer reading during acceleration/deceleration when the steering wheel is in the straight-ahead position?*

(YES) : Go to step **10L2**.

(NO) : Go to step **10L8**.

10L2 : CHECK POOR CONTACT IN CONNECTORS.

Turn ignition switch to OFF.

(CHECK) : *Is there poor contact in connectors between ABSCM&H/U and ABS sensor?*

(YES) : Repair connector.

(NO) : Go to step **10L3**.

10L3 : CHECK SOURCES OF SIGNAL NOISE.

(CHECK) : *Is the car telephone or the wireless transmitter properly installed?*

(YES) : Go to step **10L4**.

(NO) : Properly install the car telephone or the wireless transmitter.

10L4 : CHECK SOURCES OF SIGNAL NOISE.

(CHECK) : *Are noise sources (such as an antenna) installed near the sensor harness?*

(YES) : Install the noise sources apart from the sensor harness.

(NO) : Go to step **10L5**.

10L5 : CHECK SHIELD CIRCUIT.

1) Turn ignition switch to OFF.
2) Connect all connectors.
3) Measure resistance between shield connector and chassis ground.

Connector & terminal
Trouble code 22 / (B100) No. 11 — Chassis ground:
Trouble code 24 / (B100) No. 2 — Chassis ground:
Trouble code 26 / Go to step 10L6.
Trouble code 28 / Go to step 10L6.

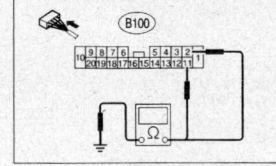

(CHECK) : *Is the resistance less than 0.5 Ω?*

(YES) : Go to step **10L6**.

(NO) : Repair shield harness.

10L6 : CHECK ABSCM&H/U.

1) Connect all connectors.
2) Erase the memory.
3) Perform inspection mode.
4) Read out the trouble code.

(CHECK) : *Is the same trouble code as in the current diagnosis still being output?*

(YES) : Replace ABSCM&H/U.

(NO) : Go to step **10L7**.

10L7 : CHECK ANY OTHER TROUBLE CODES APPEARANCE.

(CHECK) : *Are other trouble codes being output?*

(YES) : Proceed with the diagnosis corresponding to the trouble code.

(NO) : A temporary noise interference.

SB4029800119010X

Fig. 27 Codes 22, 24, 26 & 28: Abnormal ABS Sensor, ABS Sensor Abnormal Signal (Part 1 of 6). With Select Monitor

10L8 : CHECK INSTALLATION OF ABS SENSOR.

Tightening torque:
32±10 N·m (3.3±1.0 kg-m, 24±7 ft-lb)

(CHECK) : *Are the ABS sensor installation bolts tightened securely?*

(YES) : Go to step **10L9.**

(NO) : Tighten ABS sensor installation bolts securely.

10L9 : CHECK INSTALLATION OF TONE WHEEL.

Tightening torque:
13±3 N·m (1.3±0.3 kg-m, 9±2.2 ft-lb)

(CHECK) : *Are the tone wheel installation bolts tightened securely?*

(YES) : Go to step **10L10.**

(NO) : Tighten tone wheel installation bolts securely.

10L10 : CHECK ABS SENSOR GAP.

Measure tone wheel to pole piece gap over entire perimeter of the wheel.

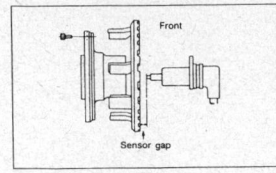

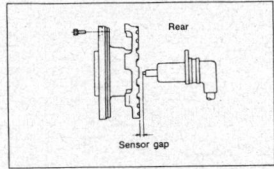

Specifications	Front wheel	Rear wheel
	0.9 — 1.4 mm (0.035 — 0.055 in)	0.7 — 1.2 mm (0.028 — 0.047 in)

(CHECK) : *Is the gap within the specifications?*

(YES) : Go to step **10L11.**

(NO) : Adjust the gap.

NOTE:
Adjust the gap using spacer (Part No. 26755AA000). If spacers cannot correct the gap, replace worn sensor or worn tone wheel.

10L11 : CHECK OSCILLOSCOPE.

(CHECK) : *Is an oscilloscope available?*

(YES) : Go to step **10L12.**

(NO) : Go to step **10L13.**

SB4029800119020X

Fig. 27   Codes 22, 24, 26 & 28: Abnormal ABS Sensor, ABS Sensor Abnormal Signal (Part 2 of 6). With Select Monitor

10L12 : CHECK ABS SENSOR SIGNAL.

1) Raise all four wheels of ground.
2) Turn ignition switch OFF.
3) Connect the oscilloscope to the connector (F1) or connector (B100) in accordance with trouble code.
4) Turn ignition switch ON.
5) Rotate wheels and measure voltage at specified frequency.

NOTE:
When this inspection is completed, the ABSCM&H/U sometimes stores the trouble code 29.

Connector & terminal
Trouble code 22 / (B100) No. 12 (+) — No. 13 (–):
Trouble code 24 / (B100) No. 3 (+) — No. 4 (–):
Trouble code 26 / (F1) No. 5 (+) — No. 4 (–):
Trouble code 28 / (F1) No. 2 (+) — No. 1 (–):
Specified voltage: 0.12 — 1 V (When it is 20 Hz.)

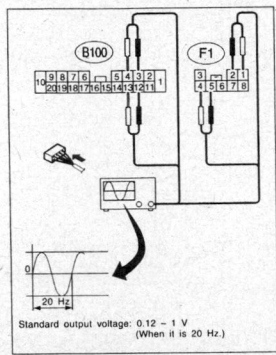

Standard output voltage: 0.12 – 1 V (When it is 20 Hz.)

(CHECK) : *Is oscilloscope pattern smooth, as shown in figure?*

(YES) : Go to step **10L16.**

(NO) : Go to step **10L13.**

SB4029800119030X

Fig. 27   Codes 22, 24, 26 & 28: Abnormal ABS Sensor, ABS Sensor Abnormal Signal (Part 3 of 6). With Select Monitor

10L13 : CHECK CONTAMINATION OF ABS SENSOR OR TONE WHEEL.

Remove disc rotor or drum from hub in accordance with trouble code.

(CHECK) : *Is the ABS sensor pole piece or the tone wheel contaminated by dirt or other foreign matter?*

(YES) : Thoroughly remove dirt or other foreign matter.

(NO) : Go to step **10L14.**

10L14 : CHECK DAMAGE OF ABS SENSOR OR TONE WHEEL.

(CHECK) : *Are there broken or damaged in the ABS sensor pole piece or the tone wheel?*

(YES) : Replace ABS sensor or tone wheel.

(NO) : Go to step **10L15.**

10L15 : CHECK HUB RUNOUT.

Measure hub runout.

(CHECK) : *Is the runout less than 0.05 mm (0.0020 in)?*

(YES) : Go to step **10L16.**

(NO) : Repair hub.

10L16 : CHECK RESISTANCE OF ABS SENSOR.

1) Turn ignition switch OFF.
2) Disconnect connector from ABS sensor.
3) Measure resistance between ABS sensor connector terminals.

Terminal
Front RH No. 1 — No. 2:
Front LH No. 1 — No. 2:
Rear RH No. 1 — No. 2:
Rear LH No. 1 — No. 2:

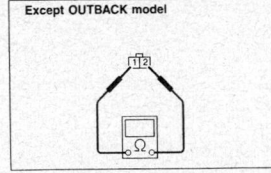

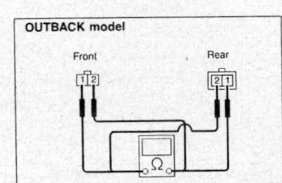

(CHECK) : *Is the resistance between 0.8 and 1.2 kΩ?*

(YES) : Go to step **10L17.**

(NO) : Replace ABS sensor.

10L17 : CHECK GROUND SHORT OF ABS SENSOR.

Measure resistance between ABS sensor and chassis ground.

Terminal
Front RH No. 1 — Chassis ground:
Front LH No. 1 — Chassis ground:
Rear RH No. 1 — Chassis ground:
Rear LH No. 1 — Chassis ground:

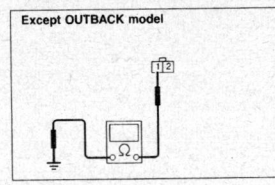

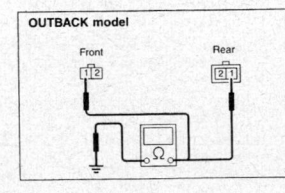

(CHECK) : *Is the resistance more than 1 MΩ?*

(YES) : Go to step **10L18.**

(NO) : Replace ABS sensor.

SB4029800119040X

Fig. 27   Codes 22, 24, 26 & 28: Abnormal ABS Sensor, ABS Sensor Abnormal Signal (Part 4 of 6). With Select Monitor

10L18 : CHECK HARNESS/CONNECTOR BETWEEN ABSCM&H/U AND ABS SENSOR.

1) Connect connector to ABS sensor.
2) Disconnect connector from ABSCM&H/U.
3) Measure resistance at ABSCM&H/U connector terminals.

Connector & terminal
Trouble code 22 / (F49) No. 11 — No. 12:
Trouble code 24 / (F49) No. 9 — No. 10:
Trouble code 26 / (F49) No. 14 — No. 15:
Trouble code 28 / (F49) No. 7 — No. 8:

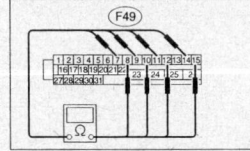

CHECK : *Is the resistance between 0.8 and 1.2 kΩ?*
YES : Go to step **10L19**.
NO : Repair harness/connector between ABSCM&H/U and ABS sensor.

10L19 : CHECK GROUND SHORT OF HARNESS.

Measure resistance between ABSCM&H/U connector and chassis ground.

Connector & terminal
Trouble code 22 / (F49) No. 11 — Chassis ground:
Trouble code 24 / (F49) No. 9 — Chassis ground:
Trouble code 26 / (F49) No. 14 — Chassis ground:
Trouble code 28 / (F49) No. 7 — Chassis ground:

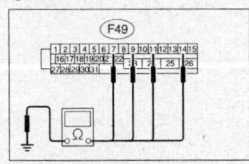

CHECK : *Is the resistance more than 1 MΩ?*
YES : Go to step **10L20**.
NO : Repair harness/connector between ABSCM&H/U and ABS sensor.

10L20 : CHECK GROUND CIRCUIT OF ABSCM&H/U.

Measure resistance between ABSCM&H/U and chassis ground.

Connector & terminal
(F49) No. 23 — GND:

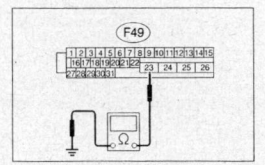

CHECK : *Is the resistance less than 0.5 Ω?*
YES : Go to step **10L21**.
NO : Repair ABSCM&H/U ground harness.

SB4029800119050X

Fig. 27   Codes 22, 24, 26 & 28: Abnormal ABS Sensor, ABS Sensor Abnormal Signal (Part 5 of 6). With Select Monitor

10L21 : CHECK POOR CONTACT IN CONNECTORS.

CHECK : *Is there poor contact in connectors between ABSCM&H/U and ABS sensor?*

YES : Repair connector.
NO : Go to step **10L22**.

10L22 : CHECK SOURCES OF SIGNAL NOISE.

CHECK : *Is the car telephone or the wireless transmitter properly installed?*
YES : Go to step **10L23**.
NO : Properly install the car telephone or the wireless transmitter.

10L23 : CHECK SOURCES OF SIGNAL NOISE.

CHECK : *Are noise sources (such as an antenna) installed near the sensor harness?*
YES : Install the noise sources apart from the sensor harness.
NO : Go to step **10L24**.

10L24 : CHECK SHIELD CIRCUIT.

1) Connect all connectors.
2) Measure resistance between shield connector and chassis ground.

Connector & terminal
Trouble code 22 / (B100) No. 11 — Chassis ground:
Trouble code 24 / (B100) No. 2 — Chassis ground:
Trouble code 26 / Go to step 10L25.
Trouble code 28 / Go to step 10L25.

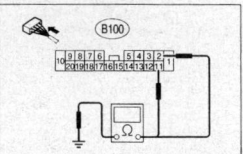

CHECK : *Is the resistance less than 0.5 Ω?*
YES : Go to step **10L25**.
NO : Repair shield harness.

10L25 : CHECK ABSCM&H/U.

1) Connect all connectors.
2) Erase the memory.
3) Perform inspection mode.
4) Read out the trouble code.

CHECK : *Is the same trouble code as in the current diagnosis still being output?*
YES : Replace ABSCM&H/U.
NO : Go to step **10L26**.

10L26 : CHECK ANY OTHER TROUBLE CODES APPEARANCE.

CHECK : *Are other trouble codes being output?*
YES : Proceed with the diagnosis corresponding to the trouble code.
NO : A temporary noise interference.

SB4029800119060X

Fig. 27   Codes 22, 24, 26 & 28: Abnormal ABS Sensor, ABS Sensor Abnormal Signal (Part 6 of 6). With Select Monitor

10M1 : CHECK IF THE WHEELS HAVE TURNED FREELY FOR A LONG TIME.

(CHECK) : *Check if the wheels have been turned freely for more than one minute, such as when the vehicle is jacked-up, under full-lock cornering or when tire is not in contact with road surface.*

(YES) : The ABS is normal. Erase the trouble code.

NOTE:
When the wheels turn freely for a long time, such as when the vehicle is towed or jacked-up, or when steering wheel is continuously turned all the way, this trouble code may sometimes occur.

(NO) : Go to step **10M2.**

10M2 : CHECK TIRE SPECIFICATIONS.

Turn ignition switch to OFF.

(CHECK) : *Are the tire specifications correct?*

(YES) : Go to step **10M3.**

(NO) : Replace tire.

10M3 : CHECK WEAR OF TIRE.

(CHECK) : *Is the tire worn excessively?*

(YES) : Replace tire.

(NO) : Go to step **10M4.**

10M4 : CHECK TIRE PRESSURE.

(CHECK) : *Is the tire pressure correct?*

(YES) : Go to step **10M5.**

(NO) : Adjust tire pressure.

10M5 : CHECK INSTALLATION OF ABS SENSOR.

Tightening torque:
32±10 N·m (3.3±1.0 kg-m, 24±7 ft-lb)

(CHECK) : *Are the ABS sensor installation bolts tightened securely?*

(YES) : Go to step **10M6.**

(NO) : Tighten ABS sensor installation bolts securely.

10M6 : CHECK INSTALLATION OF TONE WHEEL.

Tightening torque:
13±3 N·m (1.3±0.3 kg-m, 9±2.2 ft-lb)

(CHECK) : *Are the tone wheel installation bolts tightened securely?*

(YES) : Go to step **10M7.**

(NO) : Tighten tone wheel installation bolts securely.

10M7 : CHECK ABS SENSOR GAP.

Measure tone wheel to pole piece gap over entire perimeter of the wheel.

Specifications	Front wheel	Rear wheel
	0.9 — 1.4 mm (0.035 — 0.055 in)	0.7 — 1.2 mm (0.028 — 0.047 in)

(CHECK) : *Is the gap within the specifications?*

(YES) : Go to step **10M8.**

(NO) : Adjust the gap.

NOTE:
Adjust the gap using spacer (Part No. 26755AA000). If spacers cannot correct the gap, replace worn sensor or worn tone wheel.

SB4029800120010X

Fig. 28   Code 29: Abnormal ABS Sensor Signal In Any One Of Four Sensors (Part 1 of 2). With Select Monitor

10M8 : CHECK OSCILLOSCOPE.

(CHECK) : *Is an oscilloscope available?*

(YES) : Go to step **10M9.**

(NO) : Go to step **10M10.**

10M9 : CHECK ABS SENSOR SIGNAL.

1) Raise all four wheels of ground.
2) Turn ignition switch OFF.
3) Connect the oscilloscope to the connector (B100) or connector (F1).
4) Turn ignition switch ON.
5) Rotate wheels and measure voltage at specified frequency.

NOTE:
When this inspection is completed, the ABSCM&H/U sometimes stores the trouble code 29.

Connector & terminal
(B100) No. 12 (+) — No. 13 (–) (Front RH):
(B100) No. 3 (+) — No. 4 (–) (Front LH):
(B100) No. 5 (+) — No. 4 (–) (Rear RH):
(B100) No. 2 (+) — No. 1 (–) (Rear LH):
Specified voltage: 0.12 — 1 V (When it is 20 Hz.)

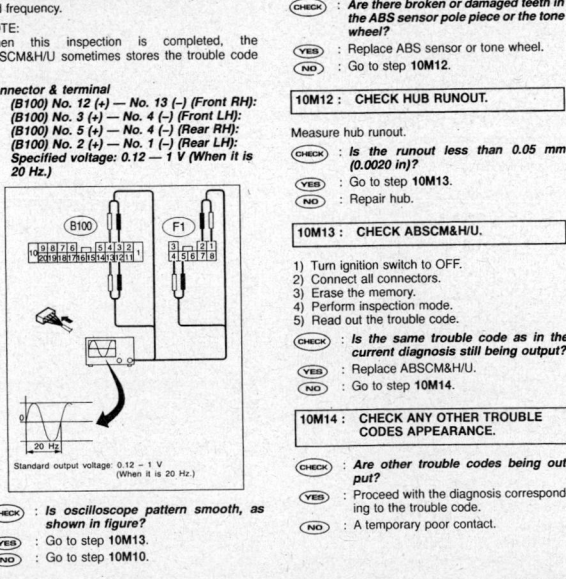

Standard output voltage: 0.12 – 1 V
(When it is 20 Hz.)

(CHECK) : *Is oscilloscope pattern smooth, as shown in figure?*

(YES) : Go to step **10M13.**

(NO) : Go to step **10M10.**

10M10 : CHECK CONTAMINATION OF ABS SENSOR OR TONE WHEEL.

Remove disc rotor from hub.

(CHECK) : *Is the ABS sensor pole piece or the tone wheel contaminated by dirt or other foreign matter?*

(YES) : Thoroughly remove dirt or other foreign matter.

(NO) : Go to step **10M11.**

10M11 : CHECK DAMAGE OF ABS SENSOR OR TONE WHEEL.

(CHECK) : *Are there broken or damaged teeth in the ABS sensor pole piece or the tone wheel?*

(YES) : Replace ABS sensor or tone wheel.

(NO) : Go to step **10M12.**

10M12 : CHECK HUB RUNOUT.

Measure hub runout.

(CHECK) : *Is the runout less than 0.05 mm (0.0020 in)?*

(YES) : Go to step **10M13.**

(NO) : Repair hub.

10M13 : CHECK ABSCM&H/U.

1) Turn ignition switch to OFF.
2) Connect all connectors.
3) Erase the memory.
4) Perform inspection mode.
5) Read out the trouble code.

(CHECK) : *Is the same trouble code as in the current diagnosis still being output?*

(YES) : Replace ABSCM&H/U.

(NO) : Go to step **10M14.**

10M14 : CHECK ANY OTHER TROUBLE CODES APPEARANCE.

(CHECK) : *Are other trouble codes being output?*

(YES) : Proceed with the diagnosis corresponding to the trouble code.

(NO) : A temporary poor contact.

SB4029800120020X

Fig. 28   Code 29: Abnormal ABS Sensor Signal In Any One of Four Sensors (Part 2 of 2). With Select Monitor

10Q1 : CHECK INPUT VOLTAGE OF ABSCM&H/U.

1) Turn ignition switch to OFF.
2) Disconnect connector from ABSCM&H/U.
3) Run the engine at idle.
4) Measure voltage between ABSCM&H/U connector and chassis ground.

Connector & terminal
(F49) No. 1 (+) — Chassis ground (–):

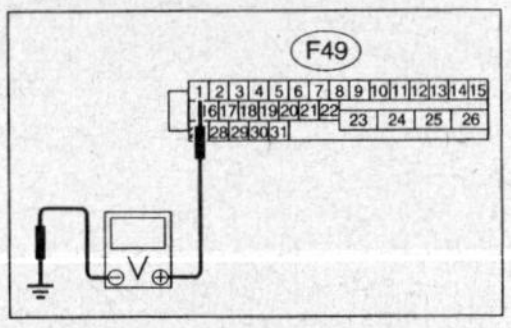

CHECK : *Is the voltage between 10 V and 15 V?*
YES : Go to step **10Q2**.
NO : Repair harness connector between battery, ignition switch and ABSCM&H/U.

10Q2 : CHECK GROUND CIRCUIT OF ABSCM&H/U.

1) Turn ignition switch to OFF.
2) Measure resistance between ABSCM&H/U connector and chassis ground.

Connector & terminal
(F49) No. 23 — Chassis ground:

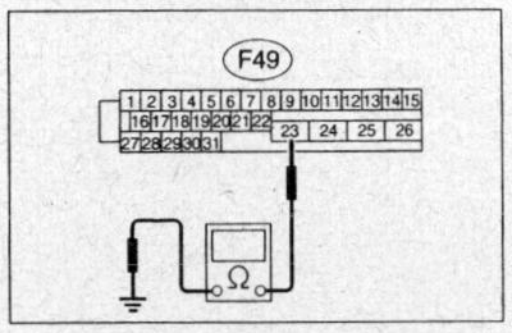

CHECK : *Is the resistance less than 0.5 Ω?*
YES : Go to step **10Q3**.
NO : Repair ABSCM&H/U ground harness.

10Q3 : CHECK POOR CONTACT IN CONNECTORS.

CHECK : *Is there poor contact in connectors between generator, battery and ABSCM&H/U?*
YES : Repair connector.
NO : Go to step **10Q4**.

10Q4 : CHECK ABSCM&H/U.

1) Connect all connectors.
2) Erase the memory.
3) Perform inspection mode.
4) Read out the trouble code.

CHECK : *Is the same trouble code as in the current diagnosis still being output?*
YES : Replace ABSCM&H/U.
NO : Go to step **10Q5**.

10Q5 : CHECK ANY OTHER TROUBLE CODES APPEARANCE.

CHECK : *Are other trouble codes being output?*
YES : Proceed with the diagnosis corresponding to the trouble code.
NO : A temporary poor contact.

SB4029800121000X

Fig. 29 Codes 31, 33, 35 & 37: Inlet Solenoid Valve Malfunction. With Select Monitor

10U1 : CHECK INPUT VOLTAGE OF ABSCM&H/U.

1) Turn ignition switch to OFF.
2) Disconnect connector from ABSCM&H/U.
3) Run the engine at idle.
4) Measure voltage between ABSCM&H/U connector and chassis ground.

Connector & terminal
(F49) No. 1 (+) — Chassis ground (–):

CHECK : *Is the voltage between 10 V and 15 V?*
YES : Go to step **10U2**.
NO : Repair harness connector between battery, ignition switch and ABSCM&H/U.

10U2 : CHECK GROUND CIRCUIT OF ABSCM&H/U.

1) Turn ignition switch to OFF.
2) Measure resistance between ABSCM&H/U connector and chassis ground.

Connector & terminal
(F49) No. 23 — Chassis ground:

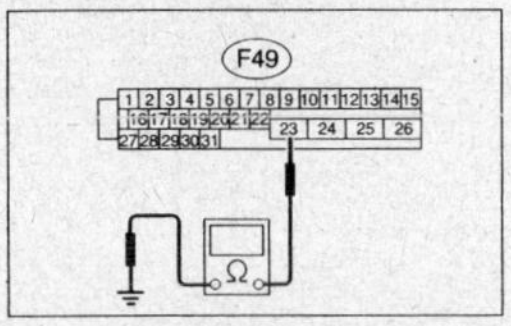

CHECK : *Is the resistance less than 0.5 Ω?*
YES : Go to step **10U3**.
NO : Repair ABSCM&H/U ground harness.

10U3 : CHECK POOR CONTACT IN CONNECTORS.

CHECK : *Is there poor contact in connectors between generator, battery and ABSCM&H/U?*
YES : Repair connector.
NO : Go to step **10U4**.

10U4 : CHECK ABSCM&H/U.

1) Connect all connectors.
2) Erase the memory.
3) Perform inspection mode.
4) Read out the trouble code.

CHECK : *Is the same trouble code as in the current diagnosis still being output?*
YES : Replace ABSCM&H/U.
NO : Go to step **10U5**.

10U5 : CHECK ANY OTHER TROUBLE CODES APPEARANCE.

CHECK : *Are other trouble codes being output?*
YES : Proceed with the diagnosis corresponding to the trouble code.
NO : A temporary poor contact.

SB4029800122000X

Fig. 30 Codes 32, 34, 36 & 38: Outlet Solenoid Valve Malfunction. With Select Monitor

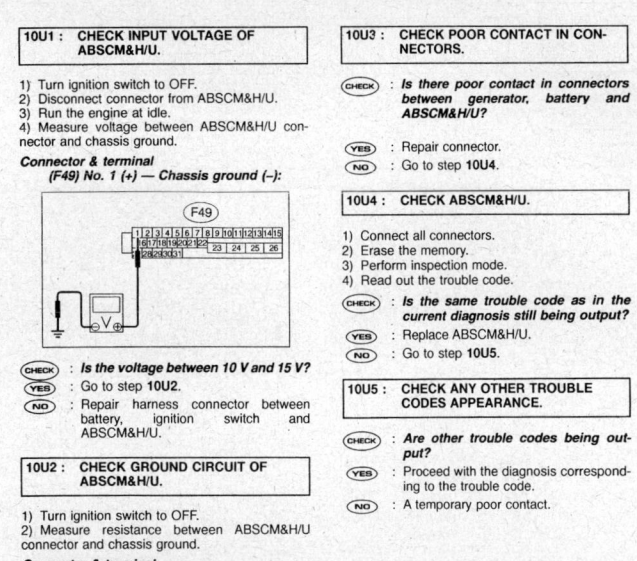

10V1 : CHECK GROUND CIRCUIT OF ABSCM&H/U.

1) Turn ignition switch to OFF.
2) Disconnect connector from ABSCM&H/U.
3) Measure resistance between ABSCM&H/U and chassis ground.

Connector & terminal
(F49) No. 23 — Chassis ground:

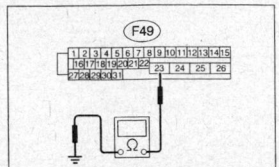

CHECK : *Is the resistance less than 0.5 Ω?*
YES : Go to step **10V2**.
NO : Repair ABSCM&H/U ground harness.

10V2 : CHECK POOR CONTACT IN CONNECTORS.

CHECK : *Is there poor contact in connectors between battery, ignition switch and ABSCM&H/U?*

YES : Repair connector.
NO : Go to step **10V3**.

10V3 : CHECK SOURCES OF SIGNAL NOISE.

CHECK : *Is the car telephone or the wireless transmitter properly installed?*
YES : Go to step **10V4**.
NO : Properly install the car telephone or the wireless transmitter.

10V4 : CHECK SOURCES OF SIGNAL NOISE.

CHECK : *Are noise sources (such as an antenna) installed near the sensor harness?*
YES : Install the noise sources apart from the sensor harness.
NO : Go to step **10V5**.

10V5 : CHECK ABSCM&H/U.

1) Turn ignition switch to OFF.
2) Connect all connectors.
3) Erase the memory.
4) Perform inspection mode.
5) Read out the trouble code.

CHECK : *Is the same trouble code as in the current diagnosis still being output?*
YES : Replace ABSCM&H/U.
NO : Go to step **10V6**.

10V6 : CHECK ANY OTHER TROUBLE CODES APPEARANCE.

CHECK : *Are other trouble codes being output?*
YES : Proceed with the diagnosis corresponding to the trouble code.
NO : A temporary poor contact.

SB4029800123000X

Fig. 31   Code 41: ABS Control Module & Hydraulic Control Unit Malfunction. With Select Monitor

10W1 : CHECK GENERATOR.

1) Start engine.
2) Idling after warm-up.
3) Measure voltage between generator B terminal and chassis ground.

Terminal
Generator B terminal — Chassis ground:

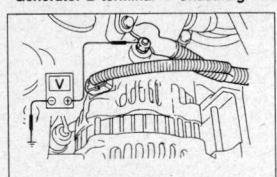

CHECK : *Is the voltage between 10 V and 15 V?*
YES : Go to step **10W2**.
NO : Repair generator.

10W2 : CHECK BATTERY TERMINAL.

Turn ignition switch to OFF.

CHECK : *Are the positive and negative battery terminals tightly clamped?*
YES : Go to step **10W3**.
NO : Tighten the clamp of terminal.

10W3 : CHECK INPUT VOLTAGE OF ABSCM&H/U.

1) Disconnect connector from ABSCM&H/U.
2) Run the engine at idle.
3) Measure voltage between ABSCM&H/U connector and chassis ground.

Connector & terminal
(F49) No. 1 (+) — Chassis ground (–):

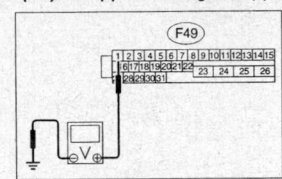

CHECK : *Is the voltage between 10 V and 15 V?*
YES : Go to step **10W4**.
NO : Repair harness connector between battery, ignition switch and ABSCM&H/U.

10W4 : CHECK GROUND CIRCUIT OF ABSCM&H/U.

1) Turn ignition switch to OFF.
2) Measure resistance between ABSCM&H/U connector and chassis ground.

Connector & terminal
(F49) No. 23 — Chassis ground:

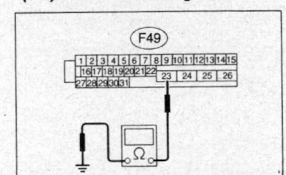

CHECK : *Is the resistance less than 0.5 Ω?*
YES : Go to step **10W5**.
NO : Repair ABSCM&H/U ground harness.

SB4029800124010X

Fig. 32   Code 42: Power Supply Voltage Too Low (Part 1 of 2). With Select Monitor

10W5 : CHECK POOR CONTACT IN CONNECTORS.

CHECK : *Is there poor contact in connectors between generator, battery and ABSCM&H/U?*

YES : Repair connector.

NO : Go to step **10W6**.

10W6 : CHECK ABSCM&H/U.

1) Connect all connectors.
2) Erase the memory.
3) Perform inspection mode.
4) Read out the trouble code.

CHECK : *Is the same trouble code as in the current diagnosis still being output?*

YES : Replace ABSCM&H/U.

NO : Go to step **10W7**.

10W7 : CHECK ANY OTHER TROUBLE CODES APPEARANCE.

CHECK : *Are other trouble codes being output?*

YES : Proceed with the diagnosis corresponding to the trouble code.

NO : A temporary poor contact.

SB4029800124020X

Fig. 32   Code 42: Power Supply Voltage Too Low (Part 2 of 2). With Select Monitor

---

10X1 : CHECK GENERATOR.

1) Start engine.
2) Idling after warm-up.
3) Measure voltage between generator B terminal and chassis ground.

Terminal
Generator B terminal — Chassis ground:

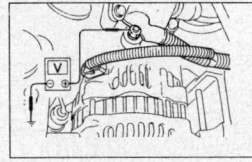

CHECK : *Is the voltage between 10 V and 17 V?*
YES : Go to step **10X2**.
NO : Repair generator.

10X2 : CHECK BATTERY TERMINAL.

Turn ignition switch to OFF.

CHECK : *Are the positive and negative battery terminals tightly clamped?*
YES : Go to step **10X3**.
NO : Tighten the clamp of terminal.

10X3 : CHECK INPUT VOLTAGE OF ABSCM&H/U.

1) Disconnect connector from ABSCM&H/U.
2) Run the engine at idle.
3) Measure voltage between ABSCM&H/U connector and chassis ground.

Connector & terminal
(F49) No. 1 (+) — Chassis ground (–):

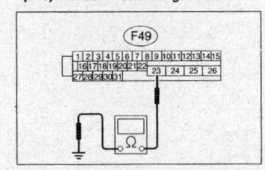

CHECK : *Is the voltage between 10 V and 17 V?*
YES : Go to step **10X4**.
NO : Repair harness connector between battery, ignition switch and ABSCM&H/U.

10X4 : CHECK GROUND CIRCUIT OF ABSCM&H/U.

1) Turn ignition switch to OFF.
2) Measure resistance between ABSCM&H/U connector and chassis ground.

Connector & terminal
(F49) No. 23 — Chassis ground:

CHECK : *Is the resistance less than 0.5 Ω?*
YES : Go to step **10X5**.
NO : Repair ABSCM&H/U ground harness.

SB4029800125010X

Fig. 33   Code 42: Power Supply Voltage Too High (Part 1 of 2). With Select Monitor

10X5 : CHECK POOR CONTACT IN CON-NECTORS.

(CHECK) : *Is there poor contact in connectors between generator, battery and ABSCM&H/U?*

(YES) : Repair connector.

(NO) : Go to step **10X6**.

10X6 : CHECK ABSCM&H/U.

1) Connect all connectors.
2) Erase the memory.
3) Perform inspection mode.
4) Read out the trouble code.

(CHECK) : *Is the same trouble code as in the current diagnosis still being output?*

(YES) : Replace ABSCM&H/U.

(NO) : Go to step **10X7**.

10X7 : CHECK ANY OTHER TROUBLE CODES APPEARANCE.

(CHECK) : *Are other trouble codes being output?*

(YES) : Proceed with the diagnosis corresponding to the trouble code.

(NO) : A temporary poor contact.

SB4029800125020X

Fig. 33   Code 42: Power Supply Voltage Too High (Part 2 of 2). With Select Monitor

10Y1 : CHECK SPECIFICATIONS OF THE ABSCM&H/U.

Check specifications of the mark to the ABSCM&H/U.

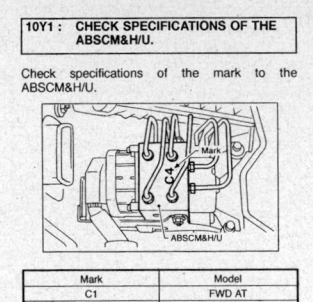

Mark	Model
C1	FWD AT
C3	AWD AT
C4	AWD MT

(CHECK) : *Is an ABSCM&H/U for AT model installed on a MT model?*

(YES) : Replace ABSCM&H/U.

(NO) : Go to step **10Y2**.

10Y2 : CHECK GROUND SHORT OF HARNESS.

1) Turn ignition switch to OFF.
2) Disconnect two connectors from TCM.
3) Disconnect connector from ABSCM&H/U.
4) Measure resistance between ABSCM&H/U connector and chassis ground.

Connector & terminal
(F49) No. 3 — Chassis ground:

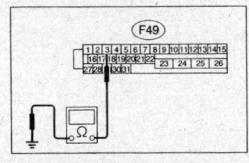

(CHECK) : *Is the resistance more than 1 MΩ?*

(YES) : Go to step **10Y3**.

(NO) : Repair harness between TCM and ABSCM&H/U.

10Y3 : CHECK TCM.

1) Connect all connectors to TCM.
2) Turn ignition switch to ON.
3) Measure voltage between TCM connector terminal and chassis ground.

Connector & terminal
(B56) No. 5 (+) — Chassis ground (–):

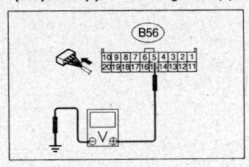

(CHECK) : *Is the voltage between 10 V and 15 V?*

(YES) : Go to step **10Y5**.

(NO) : Go to step **10Y4**.

10Y4 : CHECK AT.

(CHECK) : *Is the AT functioning normally?*

(YES) : Replace TCM.

(NO) : Repair AT.

SB4029800126010X

Fig. 34   Code 44: ABS AT Control, Non Controlled (Part 1 of 2). 1998 w/Select Monitor

10Y5 : CHECK OPEN CIRCUIT OF HARNESS.

Measure voltage between ABSCM&H/U connector and chassis ground.

Connector & terminal
(F49) No. 3 (+) — Chassis ground (–):
(F49) No. 31 (+) — Chassis ground (–):

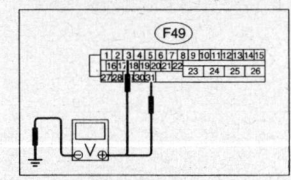

CHECK : *Is the voltage more than 10 V?*
YES : Go to step **10Y6**.
NO : Repair harness/connector between AT control module and ABSCM&H/U.

10Y6 : CHECK POOR CONTACT IN CONNECTORS.

CHECK : *Is there poor contact in connectors between AT control module and ABSCM&H/U?*

YES : Repair connector.
NO : Go to step **10Y7**.

10Y7 : CHECK ABSCM&H/U.

1) Connect all connectors.
2) Erase the memory.
3) Perform inspection mode.
4) Read out the trouble code.

CHECK : *Is the same trouble code as in the current diagnosis still being output?*
YES : Replace ABSCM&H/U.
NO : Go to step **10Y8**.

SB4029800126020X

Fig. 34   Code 44: ABS AT Control, Non Controlled (Part 2 of 2). 1998 w/Select Monitor

---

10Y8 : CHECK ANY OTHER TROUBLE CODES APPEARANCE.

CHECK : *Are other trouble codes being output?*
YES : Proceed with the diagnosis corresponding to the trouble code.
NO : A temporary poor contact.

10Z1 : CHECK BATTERY SHORT OF HARNESS.

1) Turn ignition switch to OFF.
2) Disconnect two connectors from AT control module.
3) Disconnect connector from ABSCM&H/U.
4) Measure voltage between ABSCM&H/U connector and chassis ground.

Connector & terminal
(F49) No. 3 (+) — Chassis ground (–):

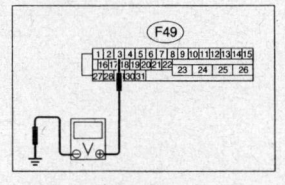

CHECK : *Is the voltage less than 1 V?*
YES : Go to step **10Z2**.
NO : Repair harness between AT control module and ABSCM&H/U.

10Z2 : CHECK BATTERY SHORT OF HARNESS.

1) Turn ignition switch to ON.
2) Measure voltage between ABSCM&H/U connector and chassis ground.

Connector & terminal
(F49) No. 3 (+) — Chassis ground (–):

CHECK : *Is the voltage less than 1 V?*
YES : Go to step **10Z3**.
NO : Repair harness between AT control module and ABSCM&H/U.

10Z3 : CHECK OPEN CIRCUIT OF HARNESS.

1) Turn ignition switch to OFF.
2) Connect all connectors to TCM.
3) Turn ignition switch to ON.
4) Measure voltage between ABSCM&H/U connector and chassis ground.

Connector & terminal
(F49) No. 3 (+) — Chassis ground (–):
(F49) No. 31 (+) — Chassis ground (–):

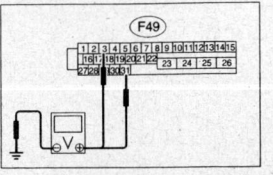

CHECK : *Is the voltage between 10 V and 13 V?*
YES : Go to step **10Z4**.
NO : Repair harness/connector between TCM and ABSCM&H/U.

10Z4 : CHECK POOR CONTACT IN CONNECTORS.

Turn ignition switch to OFF.

CHECK : *Is there poor contact in connectors between AT control module and ABSCM&H/U?*

YES : Repair connector.
NO : Go to step **10Z5**.

10Z5 : CHECK ABSCM&H/U.

1) Connect all connectors.
2) Erase the memory.
3) Perform inspection mode.
4) Read out the trouble code.

CHECK : *Is the same trouble code as in the current diagnosis still being output?*
YES : Replace ABSCM&H/U.
NO : Go to step **10Z6**.

SB4029800127010X

Fig. 35   Code 44: ABS AT Control, Controlled (Part 1 of 2). 1998 w/Select Monitor

---

10Z6 :   CHECK ANY OTHER TROUBLE CODES APPEARANCE.

CHECK : *Are other trouble codes being output?*
YES : Proceed with the diagnosis corresponding to the trouble code.
NO : A temporary poor contact.

SB4029800127020X

Fig. 35   Code 44: ABS AT Control, Controlled (Part 2 of 2). 1998 w/Select Monitor

10Y1 : CHECK SPECIFICATIONS OF THE ABSCM&H/U.

Check specifications of the mark to the ABSCM&H/U.

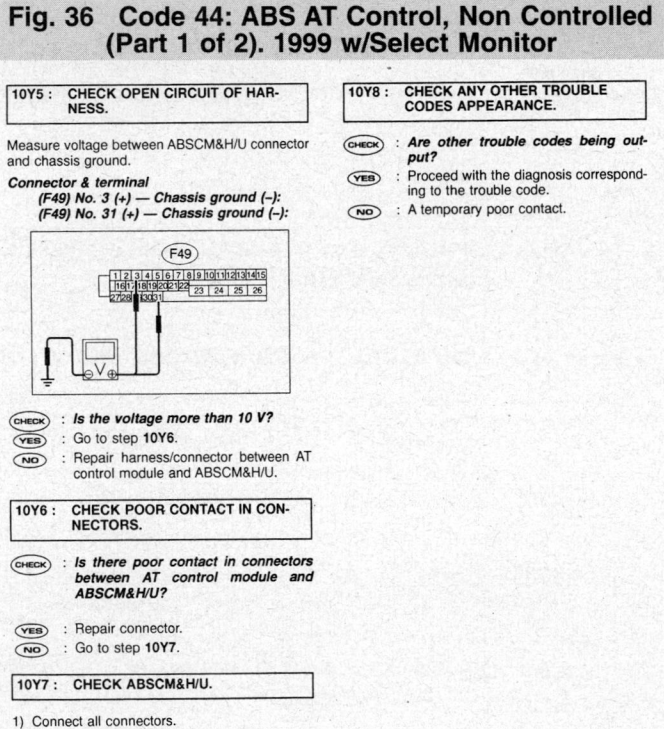

Mark	Model
C5	AWD AT
C6	AWD MT

CHECK : *Is an ABSCM&H/U for AT model installed on a MT model?*

YES : Replace ABSCM&H/U.

NO : Go to step **10Y2**.

10Y2 : CHECK GROUND SHORT OF HARNESS.

1) Turn ignition switch to OFF.
2) Disconnect two connectors from TCM.
3) Disconnect connector from ABSCM&H/U.
4) Measure resistance between ABSCM&H/U connector and chassis ground.

Connector & terminal
(F49) No. 3 — Chassis ground:

CHECK : *Is the resistance more than 1 MΩ?*
YES : Go to step **10Y3**.
NO : Repair harness between TCM and ABSCM&H/U.

10Y3 : CHECK TCM.

1) Connect all connectors to TCM.
2) Turn ignition switch to ON.
3) Measure voltage between TCM connector terminal and chassis ground.

Connector & terminal
(B54) No. 19 (+) — Chassis ground (–):

CHECK : *Is the voltage between 10 V and 15 V?*
YES : Go to step **10Y5**.
NO : Go to step **10Y4**.

10Y4 : CHECK AT.

CHECK : *Is the AT functioning normally?*
YES : Replace TCM.

NO : Repair AT.

SB4029800140010X

Fig. 36   Code 44: ABS AT Control, Non Controlled (Part 1 of 2). 1999 w/Select Monitor

10Y5 : CHECK OPEN CIRCUIT OF HARNESS.

Measure voltage between ABSCM&H/U connector and chassis ground.

Connector & terminal
(F49) No. 3 (+) — Chassis ground (–):
(F49) No. 31 (+) — Chassis ground (–):

CHECK : *Is the voltage more than 10 V?*
YES : Go to step **10Y6**.
NO : Repair harness/connector between AT control module and ABSCM&H/U.

10Y6 : CHECK POOR CONTACT IN CONNECTORS.

CHECK : *Is there poor contact in connectors between AT control module and ABSCM&H/U?*

YES : Repair connector.
NO : Go to step **10Y7**.

10Y7 : CHECK ABSCM&H/U.

1) Connect all connectors.
2) Erase the memory.
3) Perform inspection mode.
4) Read out the trouble code.

CHECK : *Is the same trouble code as in the current diagnosis still being output?*

YES : Replace ABSCM&H/U.

NO : Go to step **10Y8**.

10Y8 : CHECK ANY OTHER TROUBLE CODES APPEARANCE.

CHECK : *Are other trouble codes being output?*
YES : Proceed with the diagnosis corresponding to the trouble code.
NO : A temporary poor contact.

SB4029800140020X

Fig. 36   Code 44: ABS AT Control, Non Controlled (Part 2 of 2). 1999 w/Select Monitor

10Z1 : CHECK BATTERY SHORT OF HARNESS.

1) Turn ignition switch to OFF.
2) Disconnect two connectors from AT control module.
3) Disconnect connector from ABSCM&H/U.
4) Measure voltage between ABSCM&H/U connector and chassis ground.

Connector & terminal
(F49) No. 3 (+) — Chassis ground (–):

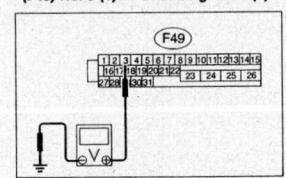

CHECK : *Is the voltage less than 1 V?*
YES : Go to step **10Z2**.
NO : Repair harness between AT control module and ABSCM&H/U.

10Z2 : CHECK BATTERY SHORT OF HARNESS.

1) Turn ignition switch to ON.
2) Measure voltage between ABSCM&H/U connector and chassis ground.

Connector & terminal
(F49) No. 3 (+) — Chassis ground (–):

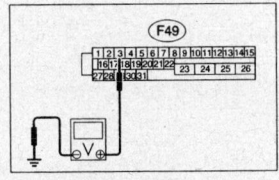

CHECK : *Is the voltage less than 1 V?*
YES : Go to step **10Z3**.
NO : Repair harness between AT control module and ABSCM&H/U.

10Z3 : CHECK OPEN CIRCUIT OF HARNESS.

1) Turn ignition switch to OFF.
2) Connect all connectors to TCM.
3) Turn ignition switch to ON.
4) Measure voltage between ABSCM&H/U connector and chassis ground.

Connector & terminal
(F49) No. 3 (+) — Chassis ground (–):
(F49) No. 31 (+) — Chassis ground (–):

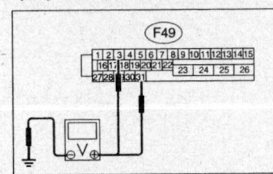

CHECK : *Is the voltage between 10 V and 13 V?*
YES : Go to step **10Z4**.
NO : Repair harness/connector between TCM and ABSCM&H/U.

10Z4 : CHECK POOR CONTACT IN CONNECTORS.

Turn ignition switch to OFF.

CHECK : *Is there poor contact in connectors between AT control module and ABSCM&H/U?*

YES : Repair connector.
NO : Go to step **10Z5**.

10Z5 : CHECK ABSCM&H/U.

1) Connect all connectors.
2) Erase the memory.
3) Perform inspection mode.
4) Read out the trouble code.

CHECK : *Is the same trouble code as in the current diagnosis still being output?*
YES : Replace ABSCM&H/U.
NO : Go to step **10Z6**.

SB4029800141010X

Fig. 37 Code 44: ABS AT Control, Controlled (Part 1 of 2). 1999 w/Select Monitor

---

10Z6 : CHECK ANY OTHER TROUBLE CODES APPEARANCE.

CHECK : *Are other trouble codes being output?*
YES : Proceed with the diagnosis corresponding to the trouble code.
NO : A temporary poor contact.

SB4029800141020X

Fig. 37 Code 44: ABS AT Control, Controlled (Part 2 of 2). 1999 w/Select Monitor

10AA1 : CHECK INPUT VOLTAGE OF ABSCM&H/U.

1) Turn ignition switch to OFF.
2) Disconnect connector from ABSCM&H/U.
3) Run the engine at idle.
4) Measure voltage between ABSCM&H/U connector and chassis ground.

Connector & terminal
(F49) No. 1 (+) — Chassis ground (–):
(F49) No. 24 (+) — Chassis ground (–):

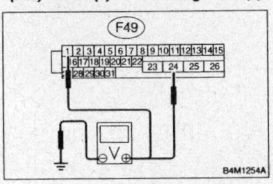

CHECK : *Is the voltage between 10 V and 15 V?*
YES : Go to step **10AA2**.
NO : Repair harness connector between battery and ABSCM&H/U.

10AA2 : CHECK GROUND CIRCUIT OF ABSCM&H/U.

1) Turn ignition switch to OFF.
2) Measure resistance between ABSCM&H/U connector and chassis ground.

Connector & terminal
(F49) No. 23 — Chassis ground:

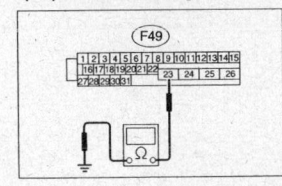

CHECK : *Is the resistance less than 0.5 Ω?*
YES : Go to step **10AA3**.
NO : Repair ABSCM&H/U ground harness.

10AA3 : CHECK POOR CONTACT IN CONNECTORS.

CHECK : *Is there poor contact in connectors between generator, battery and ABSCM&H/U?*
YES : Repair connector.
NO : Go to step **10AA4**.

10AA4 : CHECK ABSCM&H/U.

1) Connect all connectors.
2) Erase the memory.
3) Perform inspection mode.
4) Read out the trouble code.

CHECK : *Is the same trouble code as in the current diagnosis still being output?*
YES : Replace ABSCM&H/U.
NO : Go to step **10AA5**.

10AA5 : CHECK ANY OTHER TROUBLE CODES APPEARANCE.

CHECK : *Are other trouble codes being output?*
YES : Proceed with the diagnosis corresponding to the trouble code.
NO : A temporary poor contact.

SB4029800128000X

Fig. 38 Code 51: Valve Relay Malfunction. With Select Monitor

10AB1 : CHECK VALVE RELAY IN ABSCM&H/U.

Measure resistance between ABSCM&H/U terminals.

Terminals
No. 23 (+) — No. 24 (–):

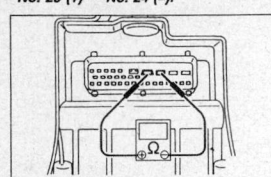

CHECK : **Is the resistance more than 1 MΩ?**
YES : Go to step **10AB2**.
NO : Replace ABSCM&H/U.

10AB2 : CHECK POOR CONTACT IN CONNECTORS.

CHECK : **Is there poor contact in connectors between generator, battery and ABSCM&H/U?**
YES : Repair connector.
NO : Go to step **10AB3**.

10AB3 : CHECK ABSCM&H/U.

1) Connect all connectors.
2) Erase the memory.
3) Perform inspection mode.
4) Read out the trouble code.

CHECK : **Is the same trouble code as in the current diagnosis still being output?**
YES : Replace ABSCM&H/U.
NO : Go to step **10AB4**.

10AB4 : CHECK ANY OTHER TROUBLE CODES APPEARANCE.

CHECK : **Are other trouble codes being output?**
YES : Proceed with the diagnosis corresponding to the trouble code.
NO : A temporary poor contact.

SB4029800129000X

Fig. 39 Code 51: Valve Relay On Failure. With Select Monitor

10AC1 : CHECK INPUT VOLTAGE OF ABSCM&H/U.

1) Turn ignition switch to OFF.
2) Disconnect connector from ABSCM&H/U.
3) Turn ignition switch to ON.
4) Measure voltage between ABSCM&H/U connector and chassis ground.

Connector & terminal
(F49) No. 25 (+) — Chassis ground (–):

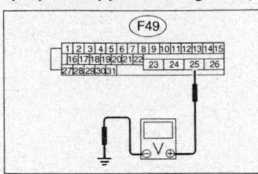

CHECK : **Is the voltage between 10 V and 13 V?**
YES : Go to step **10AC2**.
NO : Repair harness/connector between battery and ABSCM&H/U and check fuse SBF6.

10AC2 : CHECK GROUND CIRCUIT OF MOTOR.

1) Turn ignition switch to OFF.
2) Measure resistance between ABSCM&H/U connector and chassis ground.

Connector & terminal
(F49) No. 26 — Chassis ground:

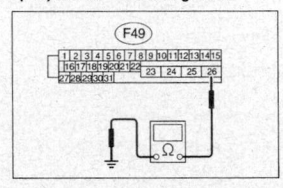

CHECK : **Is the resistance less than 0.5 Ω?**
YES : Go to step **10AC3**.
NO : Repair ABSCM&H/U ground harness.

10AC3 : CHECK MOTOR OPERATION.

Operate the sequence control.

NOTE:
Use the diagnosis connector to operate the sequence control.

CHECK : **Can motor revolution noise (buzz) be heard when carrying out the check sequence?**
YES : Go to step **10AC4**.
NO : Replace ABSCM&H/U.

10AC4 : CHECK POOR CONTACT IN CONNECTORS.

Turn ignition switch to OFF.

CHECK : **Is there poor contact in connector between hydraclic unit, relay box and ABSCM&H/U?**
YES : Repair connector.
NO : Go to step **10AC5**.

10AC5 : CHECK ABSCM&H/U.

1) Connect all connectors.
2) Erase the memory.
3) Perform inspection mode.
4) Read out the trouble code.

CHECK : **Is the same trouble code as in the current diagnosis still being output?**
YES : Replace ABSCM&H/U.
NO : Go to step **10AC6**.

10AC6 : CHECK ANY OTHER TROUBLE CODES APPEARANCE.

CHECK : **Are other trouble codes being output?**
YES : Proceed with the diagnosis corresponding to the trouble code.
NO : A temporary poor contact.

SB4029800130000X

Fig. 40 Code 52: Open Circuit In Motor Relay Circuit. With Select Monitor

10AD1 : CHECK MOTOR RELAY IN ABSCM&H/U.

Measure resistance between ABSCM&H/U terminals.

Terminals
No. 25 — No. 26:

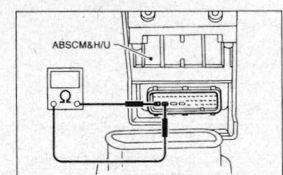

CHECK : **Is the resistance more than 1 MΩ?**
YES : Go to step **10AD2**.
NO : Replace ABSCM&H/U.

10AD2 : CHECK MOTOR OPERATION.

Operate the sequence control.

NOTE:
Use the diagnosis connector to operate the sequence control.

CHECK : **Can motor revolution noise (buzz) be heard when carrying out the sequence control?**
YES : Go to step **10AD3**.
NO : Replace ABSCM&H/U.

10AD3 : CHECK POOR CONTACT IN CONNECTORS.

Turn ignition switch to OFF.

CHECK : **Is there poor contact in connector between hydraulic unit, relay box and ABSCM&H/U?**
YES : Repair connector.
NO : Go to step **10AD4**.

10AD4 : CHECK ABSCM&H/U.

1) Connect all connectors.
2) Erase the memory.
3) Perform inspection mode.
4) Read out the trouble code.

CHECK : **Is the same trouble code as in the current diagnosis still being output?**
YES : Replace ABSCM&H/U.
NO : Go to step **10AD5**.

10AD5 : CHECK ANY OTHER TROUBLE CODES APPEARANCE.

CHECK : **Are other trouble codes being output?**
YES : Proceed with the diagnosis corresponding to the trouble code.
NO : A temporary poor contact.

SB4029800131000X

Fig. 41 Code 52: Motor Relay On Failure. With Select Monitor

10AE1 : CHECK INPUT VOLTAGE OF ABSCM&H/U.

1) Turn ignition switch to OFF.
2) Disconnect connector from ABSCM&H/U.
3) Turn ignition switch to ON.
4) Measure voltage between ABSCM&H/U connector and chassis ground.

Connector & terminal
(F49) No. 25 (+) — Chassis ground (–):

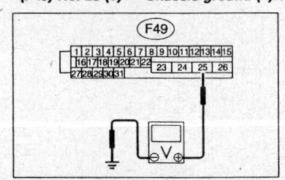

CHECK : **Is the voltage between 10 V and 13 V?**
YES : Go to step **10AE2.**
NO : Repair harness/connector between battery and ABSCM&H/U and check fuse SBF6.

10AE2 : CHECK GROUND CIRCUIT OF MOTOR.

1) Turn ignition switch to OFF.
2) Measure resistance between ABSCM&H/U connector and chassis ground.

Connector & terminal
(F49) No. 26 — Chassis ground:

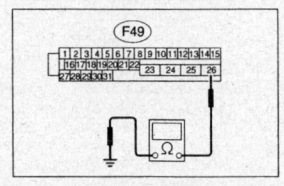

CHECK : **Is the resistance less than 0.5 Ω?**
YES : Go to step **10AE3.**
NO : Repair ABSCM&H/U ground harness.

10AE3 : CHECK INPUT VOLTAGE OF ABSCM&H/U.

1) Run the engine at idle.
2) Measure voltage between ABSCM&H/U connector and chassis ground.

Connector & terminal
(F49) No. 1 (+) — Chassis ground (–):

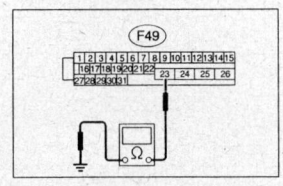

CHECK : **Is the voltage between 10 V and 15 V?**
YES : Go to step **10AE4.**
NO : Repair harness connector between battery, ignition switch and ABSCM&H/U.

10AE4 : CHECK GROUND CIRCUIT OF ABSCM&H/U.

1) Turn ignition switch to OFF.
2) Measure resistance between ABSCM&H/U connector and chassis ground.

Connector & terminal
(F49) No. 23 — Chassis ground:

CHECK : **Is the resistance less than 0.5 Ω?**
YES : Go to step **10AE5.**
NO : Repair ABSCM&H/U ground harness.

SB4029800132010X

Fig. 42 Code 52: Motor Malfunction (Part 1 of 2). With Select Monitor

---

10AE5 : CHECK MOTOR OPERATION.

Operate the sequence control.

NOTE:
Use the diagnosis connector to operate the sequence control.

CHECK : **Can motor revolution noise (buzz) be heard when carrying out the sequence control?**
YES : Go to step **10AE6.**
NO : Replace hydraulic unit.

10AE6 : CHECK POOR CONTACT IN CONNECTORS.

Turn ignition switch to OFF.

CHECK : **Is there poor contact in connector between generator, battery and ABSCM&H/U?**
YES : Repair connector.
NO : Go to step **10AE7.**

10AE7 : CHECK ABSCM&H/U.

1) Connect all connectors.
2) Erase the memory.
3) Perform inspection mode.
4) Read out the trouble code.

CHECK : **Is the same trouble code as in the current diagnosis still being output?**
YES : Replace ABSCM&H/U.
NO : Go to step **10AE8.**

10AE8 : CHECK ANY OTHER TROUBLE CODES APPEARANCE.

CHECK : **Are other trouble codes being output?**
YES : Proceed with the diagnosis corresponding to the trouble code.
NO : A temporary poor contact.

SB4029800132020X

Fig. 42 Code 52: Motor Malfunction (Part 2 of 2). With Select Monitor

10AF1 : CHECK OUTPUT OF STOP LIGHT SWITCH USING SELECT MONITOR.

1) Select "Current data display & Save" on the select monitor.
2) Release the brake pedal.
3) Read the stop light switch output in the select monitor data display.

(CHECK) : **Is the reading indicated on monitor display less than 1.5 V?**
(YES) : Go to step **10AF2**.
(NO) : Go to step **10AF3**.

10AF2 : CHECK OUTPUT OF STOP LIGHT SWITCH USING SELECT MONITOR.

1) Depress the brake pedal.
2) Read the stop light switch output in the select monitor data display.

(CHECK) : **Is the reading indicated on monitor display between 10 V and 15 V?**
(YES) : Go to step **10AF5**.
(NO) : Go to step **10AF3**.

10AF3 : CHECK IF STOP LIGHTS COME ON.

Depress the brake pedal.

(CHECK) : **Do stop lights turn on?**
(YES) : Go to step **10AF4**.
(NO) : Repair stop lights circuit.

10AF4 : CHECK OPEN CIRCUIT IN HARNESS.

1) Turn ignition switch to OFF.
2) Disconnect connector from ABSCM&H/U.
3) Depress brake pedal.
4) Measure voltage between ABSCM&H/U connector and chassis ground.

Connector & terminal
(F49) No. 2 — Chassis ground:

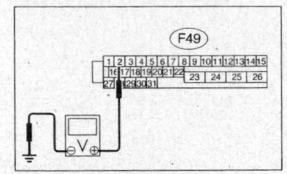

(CHECK) : **Is the voltage between 10 V and 15 V?**
(YES) : Go to step **10AF5**.
(NO) : Repair harness between stop light switch and ABSCM&H/U connector.

10AF5 : CHECK POOR CONTACT IN CONNECTORS.

(CHECK) : **Is there poor contact in connector between stop light switch and ABSCM&H/U?**
(YES) : Repair connector.
(NO) : Go to step **10AF6**.

10AF6 : CHECK ABSCM&H/U.

1) Connect all connectors.
2) Erase the memory.
3) Perform inspection mode.
4) Read out the trouble code.

(CHECK) : **Is the same trouble code as in the current diagnosis still being output?**
(YES) : Replace ABSCM&H/U.
(NO) : Go to step **10AF7**.

SB4029800133010X

Fig. 43   Code 54: Stop Light Switch Signal Circuit Malfunction (Part 1 of 2). With Select Monitor

10AF7 :   CHECK ANY OTHER TROUBLE CODES APPEARANCE.

(CHECK) : **Are other trouble codes being output?**
(YES) : Proceed with the diagnosis corresponding to the trouble code.
(NO) : A temporary poor contact.

SB4029800133020X

Fig. 43   Code 54: Stop Light Switch Signal Circuit Malfunction (Part 2 of 2). With Select Monitor

10AG1 : CHECK SPECIFICATIONS OF ABSCM&H/U.

Check specifications of the mark to the ABSCM&H/U.

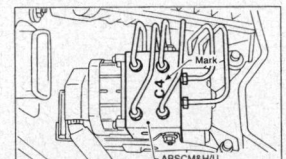

Mark	Model
C1	FWD AT
C3	AWD AT
C4	AWD MT

(CHECK) : **Is an ABSCM for AWD model installed on a FWD model?**
(YES) : Replace ABSCM&H/U.
CAUTION:
Be sure to turn ignition switch to OFF when removing ABSCM&H/U.
(NO) : Go to step **10AG2**.

10AG2 : CHECK OUTPUT OF G SENSOR USING SELECT MONITOR.

1) Select "Current data display & Save" on the select monitor.
2) Read the G sensor output in select monitor data display.

(CHECK) : **Is the G sensor output on the monitor display between 2.1 and 2.5 V when the G sensor is in horizontal position?**
(YES) : Go to step **10AG3**.
(NO) : Go to step **10AG6**.

10AG3 : CHECK POOR CONTACT IN CONNECTORS.

(CHECK) : **Is there poor contact in connector between ABSCM&H/U and G sensor?**
(YES) : Repair connector.
(NO) : Go to step **10AG4**.

10AG4 : CHECK ABSCM&H/U.

1) Connect all connectors.
2) Erase the memory.
3) Perform inspection mode.
4) Read out the trouble code.

(CHECK) : **Is the same trouble code as in the current diagnosis still being output?**
(YES) : Replace ABSCM&H/U.
(NO) : Go to step **10AG5**.

10AG5 : CHECK ANY OTHER TROUBLE CODES APPEARANCE.

(CHECK) : **Are other trouble codes being output?**
(YES) : Proceed with the diagnosis corresponding to the trouble code.
(NO) : A temporary poor contact.

10AG6 : CHECK FREEZE FRAME DATA.

1) Select "Freeze frame data" on the select monitor.
2) Read front right wheel speed on the select monitor display.

(CHECK) : **Is the front right wheel speed on monitor display 0 km?**
(YES) : Go to step **10AG7**.
(NO) : Go to step **10AG15**.

10AG7 : CHECK FREEZE FRAME DATA.

Read front left wheel speed on the select monitor display.

(CHECK) : **Is the front left wheel speed on monitor display 0 km?**
(YES) : Go to step **10AG8**.
(NO) : Go to step **10AG15**.

10AG8 : CHECK FREEZE FRAME DATA.

Read rear right wheel speed on the select monitor display.

(CHECK) : **Is the rear right wheel speed on monitor display 0 km?**
(YES) : Go to step **10AG9**.
(NO) : Go to step **10AG15**.

SB4029800134010X

Fig. 44   Code 56: Open Or Short In G Sensor Circuit (Part 1 of 5). 1998 w/Select Monitor

10AG9 : CHECK FREEZE FRAME DATA.

Read rear left wheel speed on the select monitor display.

(CHECK) : *Is the rear left wheel speed on monitor display 0 km?*

(YES) : Go to step **10AG10.**

(NO) : Go to step **10AG15.**

10AG10 : CHECK FREEZE FRAME DATA.

Read G sensor output on the select monitor display.

(CHECK) : *Is the G sensor output on monitor display more than 3.65 V?*

(YES) : Go to step **10AG11.**

(NO) : Go to step **10AG15.**

10AG11 : CHECK OPEN CIRCUIT IN G SENSOR OUTPUT HARNESS AND GROUND HARNESS.

1) Turn ignition switch to OFF.
2) Disconnect connector from ABSCM&H/U.
3) Measure resistance between ABSCM&H/U connector terminals.

Connector & terminal
(F49) No. 30 — No. 28:

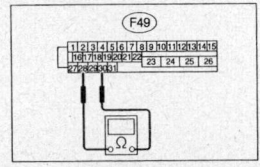

(CHECK) : *Is the resistance between 4.3 and 4.9 kΩ?*

(YES) : Go to step **10AG12.**

(NO) : Repair harness/connector between G sensor and ABSCM&H/U.

10AG12 : CHECK POOR CONTACT IN CONNECTORS.

(CHECK) : *Is there poor contact in connector between ABSCM&H/U and G sensor?*

(YES) : Repair connector.

(NO) : Go to step **10AG13.**

10AG13 : CHECK ABSCM&H/U.

1) Connect all connectors.
2) Erase the memory.
3) Perform inspection mode.
4) Read out the trouble code.

(CHECK) : *Is the same trouble code as in the current diagnosis still being output?*

(YES) : Replace ABSCM&H/U.

(NO) : Go to step **10AG14.**

10AG14 : CHECK ANY OTHER TROUBLE CODES APPEARANCE.

(CHECK) : *Are other trouble codes being output?*

(YES) : Proceed with the diagnosis corresponding to the trouble code.

(NO) : A temporary poor contact.

SB4029800134020X

Fig. 44   Code 56: Open Or Short In G Sensor Circuit (Part 2 of 5). 1998 w/Select Monitor

10AG15 : CHECK INPUT VOLTAGE OF G SENSOR.

1) Turn ignition switch to OFF.
2) Remove console box.
3) Disconnect G sensor from body. (Do not disconnect connector.)
4) Turn ignition switch to ON.
5) Measure voltage between G sensor connector terminals.

Connector & terminal
(P11) No. 1 (+) — No. 3 (–):

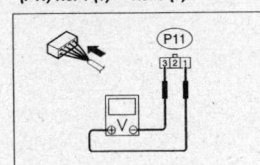

(CHECK) : *Is the voltage between 4.75 and 5.25 V?*

(YES) : Go to step **10AG16.**

(NO) : Repair harness/connector between G sensor and ABSCM&H/U.

10AG16 : CHECK OPEN CIRCUIT IN G SENSOR OUTPUT HARNESS AND GROUND HARNESS.

1) Turn ignition switch to OFF.
2) Disconnect connector from ABSCM&H/U.
3) Measure resistance between ABSCM&H/U connector terminals.

Connector & terminal
(F49) No. 30 — No. 28:

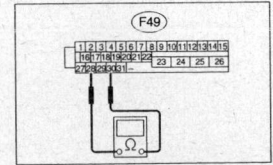

(CHECK) : *Is the resistance between 4.3 and 4.9 kΩ?*

(YES) : Go to step **10AG17.**

(NO) : Repair harness/connector between G sensor and ABSCM&H/U.

10AG17 : CHECK GROUND SHORT IN G SENSOR OUTPUT HARNESS.

1) Disconnect connector from G sensor.
2) Measure resistance between ABSCM&H/U connector and chassis ground.

Connector & terminal
(F49) No. 6 — Chassis ground:

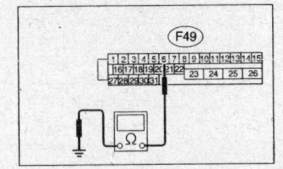

(CHECK) : *Is the resistance more than 1 MΩ?*

(YES) : Go to step **10AG18.**

(NO) : Repair harness between G sensor and ABSCM&H/U.

SB4029800134030X

Fig. 44   Code 56: Open Or Short In G Sensor Circuit (Part 3 of 5). 1998 w/Select Monitor

SUBARU

10AG18 : CHECK G SENSOR.

1) Connect connector to G sensor.
2) Connect connector to ABSCM&H/U.
3) Turn ignition switch to ON.
4) Measure voltage between G sensor connector terminals.

Connector & terminal
(P11) No. 2 (+) — No. 3 (–):

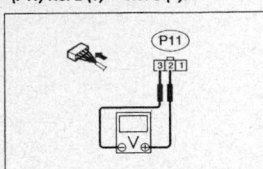

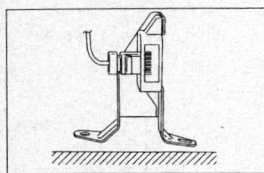

CHECK : Is the voltage between 2.1 and 2.5 V when G sensor is horizontal?
YES : Go to step 10AG19.
NO : Replace G sensor.

10AG19 : CHECK G SENSOR.

Measure voltage between G sensor connector terminals.

Connector & terminal
(P11) No. 2 (+) — No. 3 (–):

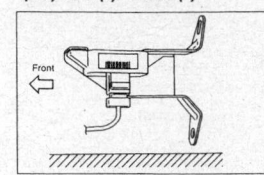

CHECK : Is the voltage between 3.7 and 4.1 V when G sensor is inclined forwards to 90°?
YES : Go to step 10AG20.
NO : Replace G sensor.

10AG20 : CHECK G SENSOR.

Measure voltage between G sensor connector terminals.

Connector & terminal
(P11) No. 2 (+) — No. 3 (–):

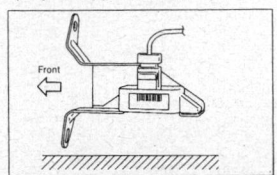

CHECK : Is the voltage between 0.5 and 0.9 V when G sensor is inclined backwards to 90°?
YES : Go to step 10AG21.
NO : Replace G sensor.

SB4029800134040X

Fig. 44 Code 56: Open Or Short In G Sensor Circuit (Part 4 of 5). 1998 w/Select Monitor

10AG21 : CHECK POOR CONTACT IN CONNECTORS.

Turn ignition switch to OFF.

CHECK : Is there poor contact in connector between ABSCM&H/U and G sensor?
YES : Repair connector.
NO : Go to step 10AG22.

10AG22 : CHECK ABSCM&H/U.

1) Connect all connectors.
2) Erase the memory.
3) Perform inspection mode.
4) Read out the trouble code.

CHECK : Is the same trouble code as in the current diagnosis still being output?
YES : Replace ABSCM&H/U.
NO : Go to step 10AG23.

10AG23 : CHECK ANY OTHER TROUBLE CODES APPEARANCE.

CHECK : Are other trouble codes being output?
YES : Proceed with the diagnosis corresponding to the trouble code.
NO : A temporary poor contact.

SB4029800134050X

Fig. 44 Code 56: Open Or Short In G Sensor Circuit (Part 5 of 5). 1998 w/Select Monitor

10AH1 : CHECK OUTPUT OF G SENSOR USING SELECT MONITOR.

1) Select "Current data display & Save" on the select monitor.
2) Read G sensor output on the select monitor display.

CHECK : Is the G sensor output on monitor display between 2.1 and 2.5 V when the G sensor is in horizontal position?
YES : Replace ABSCM&H/U.
NO : Go to step 10AH2.

10AH2 : CHECK BATTERY SHORT OF HARNESS.

1) Turn ignition switch to OFF.
2) Remove console box.
3) Disconnect connector from G sensor.
4) Disconnect connector from ABSCM&H/U.
5) Measure voltage between ABSCM&H/U connector and chassis ground.

Connector & terminal
(F49) No. 6 (+) — Chassis ground (–):

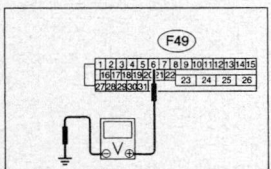

CHECK : Is the voltage less than 1 V?
YES : Go to step 10AH3.
NO : Repair harness between G sensor and ABSCM&H/U.

10AH3 : CHECK BATTERY SHORT OF HARNESS.

1) Turn ignition switch to ON.
2) Measure voltage between ABSCM&H/U connector and chassis ground.

Connector & terminal
(F49) No. 6 (+) — Chassis ground (–):

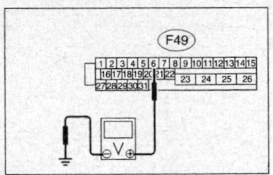

CHECK : Is the voltage less than 1 V?
YES : Go to step 10AH4.
NO : Repair harness between G sensor and ABSCM&H/U.

10AH4 : CHECK ABSCM&H/U.

1) Turn ignition switch to OFF.
2) Connect all connectors.
3) Erase the memory.
4) Perform inspection mode.
5) Read out the trouble code.

CHECK : Is the same trouble code as in the current diagnosis still being output?
YES : Replace ABSCM&H/U.
NO : Go to step 10AH5.

10AH5 : CHECK ANY OTHER TROUBLE CODES APPEARANCE.

CHECK : Are other trouble codes being output?
YES : Proceed with the diagnosis corresponding to the trouble code.
NO : A temporary poor contact.

SB4029800136000X

Fig. 45 Code 56: Battery Short In G Sensor Circuit. 1998 w/Select Monitor

10AI1 : CHECK OUTPUT OF G SENSOR USING SELECT MONITOR.

1) Select "Current data display & Save" on the select monitor.
2) Read G sensor output on the select monitor display.

CHECK : Is the G sensor output on monitor display 2.3±0.2 V when the G sensor is in horizontal position?
YES : Go to step 10AI2.
NO : Go to step 10AI6.

10AI2 : CHECK POOR CONTACT IN CONNECTORS.

Turn ignition switch to OFF.

CHECK : Is there poor contact in connector between ABSCM&H/U and G sensor? <Ref. to FOREWORD [T3C1].☆12>
YES : Repair connector.
NO : Go to step 10AI3.

10AI3 : CHECK ABSCM&H/U.

1) Connect all connectors.
2) Erase the memory.
3) Perform inspection mode.
4) Read out the trouble code.

CHECK : Is the same trouble code as in the current diagnosis still being output?
YES : Replace ABSCM&H/U.
NO : Go to step 10AI4.

10AI4 : CHECK ANY OTHER TROUBLE CODES APPEARANCE.

CHECK : Are other trouble codes being output?
YES : Proceed with the diagnosis corresponding to the trouble code.
NO : A temporary poor contact.

10AI5 : CHECK OPEN CIRCUIT IN G SENSOR OUTPUT HARNESS AND GROUND HARNESS.

1) Turn ignition switch to OFF.
2) Disconnect connector from ABSCM&H/U.
3) Measure resistance between ABSCM&H/U connector terminals.

Connector & terminal
(F49) No. 30 — No. 28:

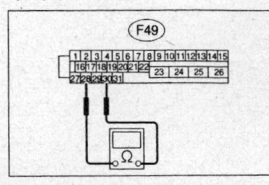

CHECK : Is the resistance between 4.3 and 4.9 kΩ?
YES : Go to step 10AI6.
NO : Repair harness/connector between G sensor and ABSCM&H/U.

10AI6 : CHECK GROUND SHORT OF HARNESS.

Measure resistance between ABSCM&H/U connector and chassis ground.

Connector & terminal
(F49) No. 28 — Chassis ground:

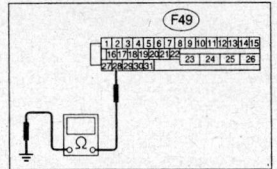

CHECK : Is the resistance more than 1 MΩ?
YES : Go to step 10AI7.
NO : Repair harness between G sensor and ABSCM&H/U.
Replace ABSCM&H/U.

SB4029800137010X

Fig. 46 Code 56: Abnormal G Sensor High Output (Part 1 of 3). 1998 w/Select Monitor

10AI7 : CHECK G SENSOR.

1) Remove console box.
2) Remove G sensor from vehicle.
3) Connect connector to G sensor.
4) Connect connector to ABSCM&H/U.
5) Turn ignition switch to ON.
6) Measure voltage between G sensor connector terminals.

Connector & terminal
  (P11) No. 2 (+) — No. 3 (–):

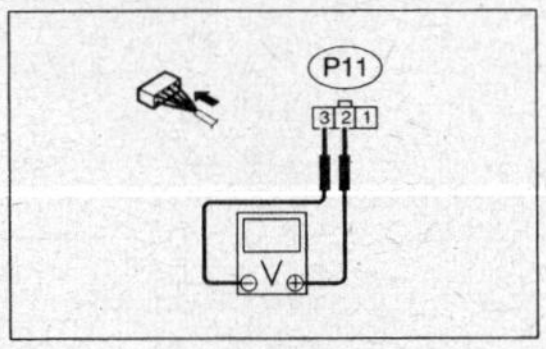

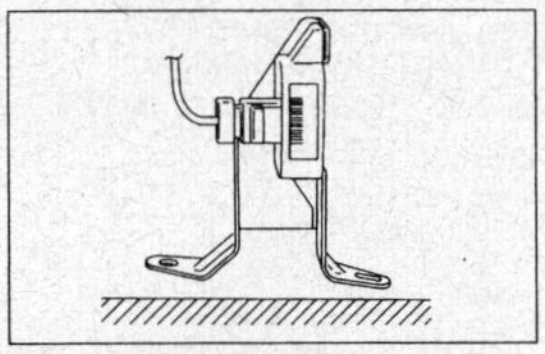

CHECK : *Is the voltage between 2.1 and 2.5 V when G sensor is horizontal?*
YES : Go to step **10AI8**.
NO : Replace G sensor.

10AI8 : CHECK G SENSOR.

Measure voltage between G sensor connector terminals.

Connector & terminal
  (P11) No. 2 (+) — No. 3 (–):

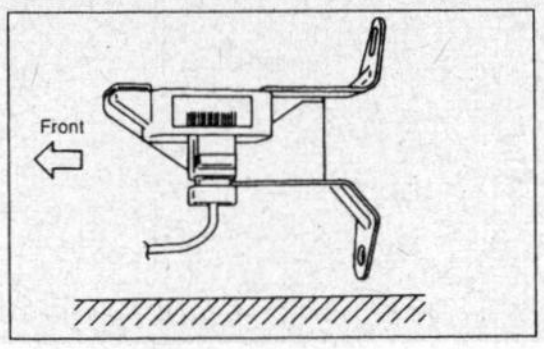

CHECK : *Is the voltage between 3.7 and 4.1 V when G sensor is inclined forwards to 90°?*
YES : Go to step **10AI9**.
NO : Replace G sensor.

10AI9 : CHECK G SENSOR.

Measure voltage between G sensor connector terminals.

Connector & terminal
  (P11) No. 2 (+) — No. 3 (–):

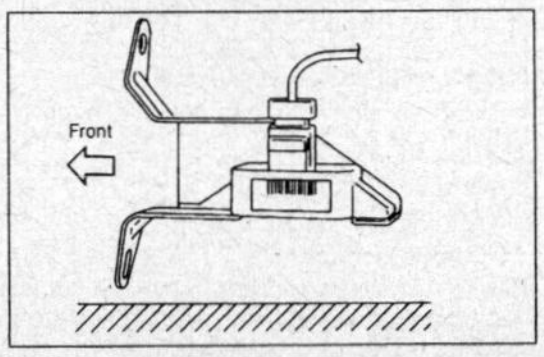

CHECK : *Is the voltage between 0.5 and 0.9 V when G sensor is inclined backwards to 90°?*
YES : Go to step **10AI10**.
NO : Replace G sensor.

SB4029800137020X

Fig. 46   Code 56: Abnormal G Sensor High Output (Part 2 of 3). 1998 w/Select Monitor

10AI10 :   CHECK ABSCM&H/U.

1) Turn ignition switch to OFF.
2) Connect all connectors.
3) Erase the memory.
4) Perform inspection mode.
5) Read out the trouble code.

CHECK : *Is the same trouble code as in the current diagnosis still being output?*

YES : Replace ABSCM&H/U.

NO : Go to step **10AI11**.

10AI11 :   CHECK ANY OTHER TROUBLE CODES APPEARANCE.

CHECK : *Are other trouble codes being output?*

YES : Proceed with the diagnosis corresponding to the trouble code.

NO : A temporary poor contact.

SB4029800137030X

Fig. 46   Code 56: Abnormal G Sensor High Output (Part 3 of 3). 1998 w/Select Monitor

10AJ1 : CHECK ALL FOUR WHEELS FOR FREE TURNING.

(CHECK) : *Have the wheels been turned freely such as when the vehicle is lifted up, or operated on a rolling road?*

(YES) : The ABS is normal. Erase the trouble code.

(NO) : Go to step **10AJ2**.

10AJ2 : CHECK OUTPUT OF G SENSOR USING SELECT MONITOR.

1) Select "Current data display & Save" on the select monitor.
2) Read the select monitor display.

(CHECK) : *Is the G sensor output on the monitor display between 2.1 and 2.5 V when the vehicle is in horizontal position?*

(YES) : Go to step **10AJ3**.

(NO) : Go to step **10AJ8**.

10AJ3 : CHECK OUTPUT OF G SENSOR USING SELECT MONITOR.

1) Turn ignition switch to OFF.
2) Remove console box.
3) Remove G sensor from vehicle. (Do not disconnect connector.)
4) Turn ignition switch to ON.
5) Select "Current data display & Save" on the select monitor.
6) Read the select monitor display.

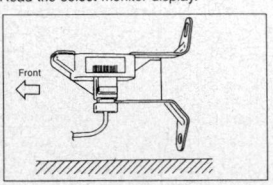

(CHECK) : *Is the G sensor output on the monitor display between 3.7 and 4.1 V when G sensor is inclined forwards to 90°?*

(YES) : Go to step **10AJ4**.

(NO) : Replace G sensor.

10AJ4 : CHECK OUTPUT OF G SENSOR USING SELECT MONITOR.

Read the select monitor display.

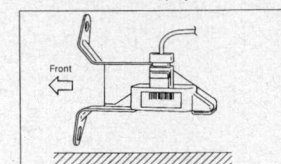

(CHECK) : *Is the G sensor output on the monitor display between 0.5 and 0.9 V when G sensor is inclined backwards to 90°?*

(YES) : Go to step **10AJ5**.

(NO) : Replace G sensor.

10AJ5 : CHECK POOR CONTACT IN CONNECTORS.

Turn ignition switch to OFF.

(CHECK) : *Is there poor contact in connector between ABSCM&H/U and G sensor?*

(YES) : Repair connector.

(NO) : Go to step **10AJ6**.

10AJ6 : CHECK ABSCM&H/U.

1) Connect all connectors.
2) Erase the memory.
3) Perform inspection mode.
4) Read out the trouble code.

(CHECK) : *Is the same trouble code as in the current diagnosis still being output?*

(YES) : Replace ABSCM&H/U.

(NO) : Go to step **10AJ7**.

10AJ7 : CHECK ANY OTHER TROUBLE CODES APPEARANCE.

(CHECK) : *Are other trouble codes being output?*

(YES) : Proceed with the diagnosis corresponding to the trouble code.

(NO) : A temporary poor contact.

SB4029800138010X

Fig. 47   Code 56: Detection Of G Sensor Stick (Part 1 of 3). 1998 w/Select Monitor

10AJ8 : CHECK OPEN CIRCUIT IN G SENSOR OUTPUT HARNESS AND GROUND HARNESS.

1) Turn ignition switch to OFF.
2) Disconnect connector from ABSCM&H/U.
3) Measure resistance between ABSCM&H/U connector terminals.

Connector & terminal
(F49) No. 30 — No. 28:

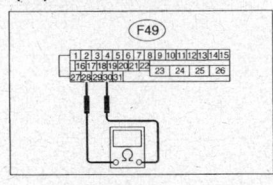

(CHECK) : *Is the resistance between 4.3 and 4.9 kΩ?*

(YES) : Go to step **10AJ9**.

(NO) : Repair harness/connector between G sensor and ABSCM&H/U.

10AJ9 : CHECK G SENSOR.

1) Remove console box.
2) Remove G sensor from vehicle.
3) Connect connector to G sensor.
4) Connect connector to ABSCM&H/U.
5) Turn ignition switch to ON.
6) Measure voltage between G sensor connector terminals.

Connector & terminal
(P11) No. 2 (+) — No. 1 (–):

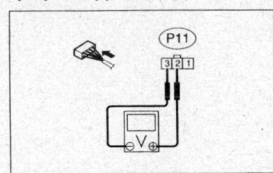

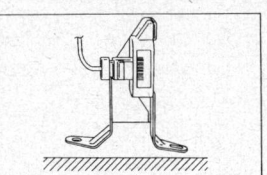

(CHECK) : *Is the voltage between 2.1 and 2.5 V when G sensor is horizontal?*

(YES) : Go to step **10AJ10**.

(NO) : Replace G sensor.

SB4029800138020X

Fig. 47   Code 56: Detection Of G Sensor Stick (Part 2 of 3). 1998 w/Select Monitor

10AJ10 : CHECK G SENSOR.

Measure voltage between G sensor connector terminals.

Connector & terminal
(P11) No. 2 (+) — No. 1 (–):

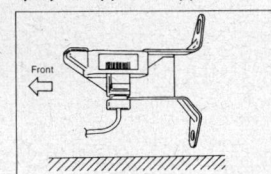

(CHECK) : *Is the voltage between 3.7 and 4.1 V when G sensor is inclined forwards to 90°?*

(YES) : Go to step **10AJ11**.

(NO) : Replace G sensor.

10AJ11 : CHECK G SENSOR.

Measure voltage between G sensor connector terminals.

Connector & terminal
(P11) No. 2 (+) — No. 1 (–):

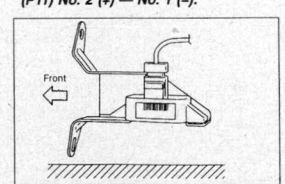

(CHECK) : *Is the voltage between 0.5 and 0.9 V when G sensor is inclined backwards to 90°?*

(YES) : Go to step **10AJ12**.

(NO) : Replace G sensor.

10AJ12 : CHECK ABSCM&H/U.

1) Turn ignition switch to OFF.
2) Connect all connectors.
3) Erase the memory.
4) Perform inspection mode.
5) Read out the trouble code.

(CHECK) : *Is the same trouble code as in the current diagnosis still being output?*

(YES) : Replace ABSCM&H/U.

(NO) : Go to step **10AJ13**.

10AJ13 : CHECK ANY OTHER TROUBLE CODES APPEARANCE.

(CHECK) : *Are other trouble codes being output?*

(YES) : Proceed with the diagnosis corresponding to the trouble code.

(NO) : A temporary poor contact.

SB4029800138030X

Fig. 47   Code 56: Detection Of G Sensor Stick (Part 3 of 3). 1998 w/Select Monitor

10AG1 : CHECK SPECIFICATIONS OF ABSCM&H/U.

Check specifications of the mark to the ABSCM&H/U.

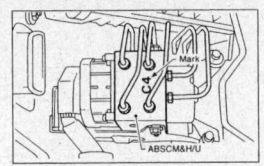

Mark	Model
C5	AWD AT
C6	AWD MT

CHECK : *Is an ABSCM for AWD model installed on a FWD model?*
YES : Replace ABSCM&H/U.

CAUTION:
Be sure to turn ignition switch to OFF when removing ABSCM&H/U.
NO : Go to step **10AG2**.

10AG2 : CHECK OUTPUT OF G SENSOR USING SELECT MONITOR.

1) Select "Current data display & Save" on the select monitor.
2) Read the G sensor output in select monitor data display.

CHECK : *Is the G sensor output on the monitor display between 2.1 and 2.5 V when the G sensor is in horizontal position?*
YES : Go to step **10AG3**.
NO : Go to step **10AG6**.

10AG3 : CHECK POOR CONTACT IN CONNECTORS.

CHECK : *Is there poor contact in connector between ABSCM&H/U and G sensor?*
YES : Repair connector.
NO : Go to step **10AG4**.

10AG4 : CHECK ABSCM&H/U.

1) Connect all connectors.
2) Erase the memory.
3) Perform inspection mode.
4) Read out the trouble code.

CHECK : *Is the same trouble code as in the current diagnosis still being output?*
YES : Replace ABSCM&H/U.
NO : Go to step **10AG5**.

10AG5 : CHECK ANY OTHER TROUBLE CODES APPEARANCE.

CHECK : *Are other trouble codes being output?*
YES : Proceed with the diagnosis corresponding to the trouble code.
NO : A temporary poor contact.

10AG6 : CHECK FREEZE FRAME DATA.

1) Select "Freeze frame data" on the select monitor.
2) Read front right wheel speed on the select monitor display.

CHECK : *Is the front right wheel speed on monitor display 0 km?*
YES : Go to step **10AG7**.
NO : Go to step **10AG15**.

10AG7 : CHECK FREEZE FRAME DATA.

Read front left wheel speed on the select monitor display.

CHECK : *Is the front left wheel speed on monitor display 0 km?*
YES : Go to step **10AG8**.
NO : Go to step **10AG15**.

10AG8 : CHECK FREEZE FRAME DATA.

Read rear right wheel speed on the select monitor display.

CHECK : *Is the rear right wheel speed on monitor display 0 km?*
YES : Go to step **10AG9**.
NO : Go to step **10AG15**.

SB4029800142010X

Fig. 48 Code 56: Open Or Short Circuit In G Sensor Circuit (Part 1 of 5). 1999 w/Select Monitor

10AG9 : CHECK FREEZE FRAME DATA.

Read rear left wheel speed on the select monitor display.

CHECK : *Is the rear left wheel speed on monitor display 0 km?*
YES : Go to step **10AG10**.
NO : Go to step **10AG15**.

10AG10 : CHECK FREEZE FRAME DATA.

Read G sensor output on the select monitor display.

CHECK : *Is the G sensor output on monitor display more than 3.65 V?*
YES : Go to step **10AG11**.
NO : Go to step **10AG15**.

10AG11 : CHECK OPEN CIRCUIT IN G SENSOR OUTPUT HARNESS AND GROUND HARNESS.

1) Turn ignition switch to OFF.
2) Disconnect connector from ABSCM&H/U.
3) Measure resistance between ABSCM&H/U connector terminals.

Connector & terminal
(F49) No. 30 — No. 26:

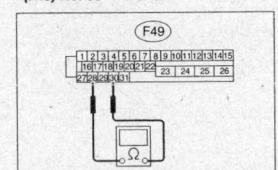

CHECK : *Is the resistance between 4.3 and 4.9 kΩ?*
YES : Go to step **10AG12**.
NO : Repair harness/connector between G sensor and ABSCM&H/U.

10AG12 : CHECK POOR CONTACT IN CONNECTORS.

CHECK : *Is there poor contact in connector between ABSCM&H/U and G sensor? <Ref. to FOREWORD [T3C1].☆14>*
YES : Repair connector.
NO : Go to step **10AG13**.

10AG13 : CHECK ABSCM&H/U.

1) Connect all connectors.
2) Erase the memory.
3) Perform inspection mode.
4) Read out the trouble code.

CHECK : *Is the same trouble code as in the current diagnosis still being output?*
YES : Replace ABSCM&H/U.
NO : Go to step **10AG14**.

10AG14 : CHECK ANY OTHER TROUBLE CODES APPEARANCE.

CHECK : *Are other trouble codes being output?*
YES : Proceed with the diagnosis corresponding to the trouble code.
NO : A temporary poor contact.

SB4029800142020X

Fig. 48 Code 56: Open Or Short Circuit In G Sensor Circuit (Part 2 of 5). 1999 w/Select Monitor

10AG15 : CHECK INPUT VOLTAGE OF G SENSOR.

1) Turn ignition switch to OFF.
2) Remove console box.
3) Disconnect G sensor from body. (Do not disconnect connector.)
4) Turn ignition switch to ON.
5) Measure voltage between G sensor connector terminals.

Connector & terminal
(P11) No. 1 (+) — No. 3 (–):

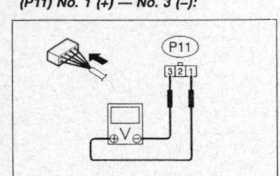

CHECK : **Is the voltage between 4.75 and 5.25 V?**
YES : Go to step **10AG16**.
NO : Repair harness/connector between G sensor and ABSCM&H/U.

10AG16 : CHECK OPEN CIRCUIT IN G SENSOR OUTPUT HARNESS AND GROUND HARNESS.

1) Turn ignition switch to OFF.
2) Disconnect connector from ABSCM&H/U.
3) Measure resistance between ABSCM&H/U connector terminals.

Connector & terminal
(F49) No. 30 — No. 28:

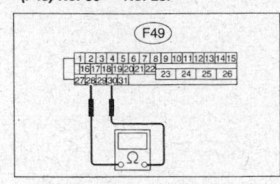

CHECK : **Is the resistance between 4.3 and 4.9 kΩ?**
YES : Go to step **10AG17**.
NO : Repair harness/connector between G sensor and ABSCM&H/U.

10AG17 : CHECK GROUND SHORT IN G SENSOR OUTPUT HARNESS.

1) Disconnect connector from G sensor.
2) Measure resistance between ABSCM&H/U connector and chassis ground.

Connector & terminal
(F49) No. 6 — Chassis ground:

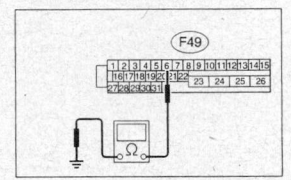

CHECK : **Is the resistance more than 1 MΩ?**
YES : Go to step **10AG18**.
NO : Repair harness between G sensor and ABSCM&H/U.

SB4029800142030X

10AG18 : CHECK G SENSOR.

1) Connect connector to G sensor.
2) Connect connector to ABSCM&H/U.
3) Turn ignition switch to ON.
4) Measure voltage between G sensor connector terminals.

Connector & terminal
(P11) No. 2 (+) — No. 3 (–):

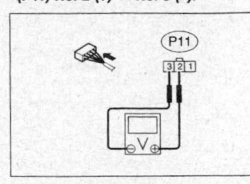

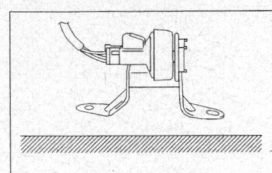

CHECK : **Is the voltage between 2.1 and 2.5 V when G sensor is horizontal?**
YES : Go to step **10AG19**.
NO : Replace G sensor.

10AG19 : CHECK G SENSOR.

Measure voltage between G sensor connector terminals.

Connector & terminal
(P11) No. 2 (+) — No. 3 (–):

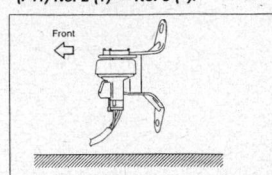

CHECK : **Is the voltage between 3.7 and 4.1 V when G sensor is inclined forwards to 90°?**
YES : Go to step **10AG20**.
NO : Replace G sensor.

10AG20 : CHECK G SENSOR.

Measure voltage between G sensor connector terminals.

Connector & terminal
(P11) No. 2 (+) — No. 3 (–):

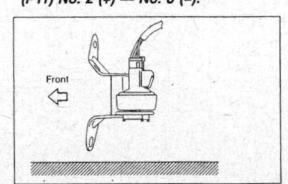

CHECK : **Is the voltage between 0.5 and 0.9 V when G sensor is inclined backwards to 90°?**
YES : Go to step **10AG21**.
NO : Replace G sensor.

SB4029800142040X

Fig. 48 Code 56: Open Or Short Circuit In G Sensor Circuit (Part 4 of 5). 1999 w/Select Monitor

---

Fig. 48 Code 56: Open Or Short Circuit In G Sensor Circuit (Part 3 of 5). 1999 w/Select Monitor

---

10AG21 : CHECK POOR CONTACT IN CONNECTORS.

Turn ignition switch to OFF.

CHECK : **Is there poor contact in connector between ABSCM&H/U and G sensor?**
YES : Repair connector.
NO : Go to step **10AG22**.

10AG22 : CHECK ABSCM&H/U.

1) Connect all connectors.
2) Erase the memory.
3) Perform inspection mode.
4) Read out the trouble code.

CHECK : **Is the same trouble code as in the current diagnosis still being output?**
YES : Replace ABSCM&H/U.
NO : Go to step **10AG23**.

10AG23 : CHECK ANY OTHER TROUBLE CODES APPEARANCE.

CHECK : **Are other trouble codes being output?**
YES : Proceed with the diagnosis corresponding to the trouble code.
NO : A temporary poor contact.

SB4029800142050X

Fig. 48 Code 56: Open Or Short Circuit In G Sensor Circuit (Part 5 of 5). 1999 w/Select Monitor

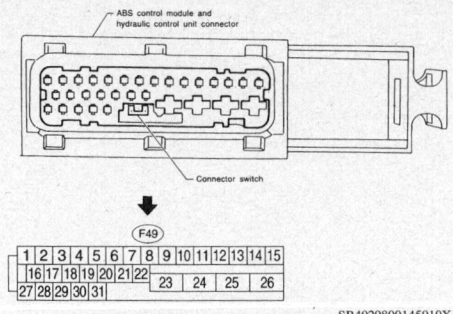

Fig. 49   ABS control module I/O references (Part 1 of 2)

	Contents		Terminal No. (+) — (−)	Input/Output signal Measured value and measuring conditions
ABS sensor*2 (Wheel speed sensor)	Front left wheel		9 — 10	0.12 — 1 V (When it is 20 Hz.)
	Front right wheel		11 — 12	
	Rear left wheel		7 — 8	
	Rear right wheel		14 — 15	
Valve relay power supply			24 — 23	10 — 15 V when ignition switch is ON.
Motor relay power supply			25 — 23	10 — 15 V when ignition switch is ON.
G sensor*2 (AWD model only)	power supply		30 — 28	4.75 — 5.25 V
	ground		28	—
	output		6 — 28	2.3±0.2 V when vehicle is in horizontal position.
Stop light switch*1			2 — 23	Less than 1.5 V when the stop light is OFF and, 10 — 15 V when the stop light is ON.
ABS warning light*2			21 — 23	Less than 1.5 V during 1.5 seconds when ignition switch is ON, and 10 — 15 V after 1.5 seconds.
AT ABS signal*2 (AT model only)			31 — 23	Less than 1.5 V when the ABS control does not operate still and more than 5.5 V when ABS operates.
ABS operation signal monitor*2			3 — 23	Less than 1.5 V when the ABS control does not operate still and more than 5.5 V when ABS operates.
Select monitor*2	Data is received.		20 — 23	Less than 1.5 V when no data is received.
	Data is sent.		5 — 23	4.75 — 5.25 V when no data is sent.
ABS diagnosis connector*2	Terminal No. 3		29 — 23	10 — 15 V when ignition switch is ON.
	Terminal No. 6		4 — 23	10 — 15 V when ignition switch is ON.
Power supply*1			1 — 23	10 — 15 V when ignition switch is ON.
Grounding line			23	—
Grounding line			26	—

*1: Measure the I/O signal voltage after removing the connector from the ABSCM&H/U terminal.
*2: Measure the I/O signal voltage at connector (F2) or (F1).

SB4029800145020X

Fig. 49   ABS control module I/O references (Part 2 of 2)

Automatic Transmissions

NOTE: On Air Bag Equipped Models, Refer To "Air Bag System Precautions" Located In The Front Of This Manual For System Disarming & Arming Procedures.

INDEX

PRECAUTIONS

AIR BAG SYSTEMS

Refer to "Air Bag System Precautions" in the front of this manual for system disarming and arming procedures.

BATTERY GROUND CABLE

Prior to service disconnect battery ground cable and isolate as required.

IDENTIFICATION

Refer to **Fig. 1,** for transmission identification number location.

DESCRIPTION

These transmissions are a 4 speed double row planetary gear type using a symmetric, 3 element single stage, 2 phase torque converter. This system uses a microcomputer for accurate control of the vehicle speed, engine brake and lock-up operations and gear shift timing. This system is also provided with an automatic drive pattern selecting function which selects between the "normal" and "power"drive patterns. The AWD models use an electronically controlled full-time version on the FWD transmission.

TROUBLESHOOTING

Problems in the electronic controlled automatic transmission may be caused by failure of the engine, the electronic control system, transmission components or by any combination of these. Troubleshooting should be started with simple and easy operations then proceeding to complicated and more difficult operations. When troubleshooting the transmission system, refer to **Fig. 2,** for the general troubleshooting chart.

MAINTENANCE

FLUID CHECK

1. With transmission fluid at operating temperature (140–176°F. Driving approximately 3–6 miles or 10 minute warm-up time), park vehicle on a level surface.
2. With engine idling, service and parking brake applied, move selector lever through all ranges and return to Park.
3. Allow engine to idle 1–2 minutes.
4. With engine idling, remove dipstick and check fluid level. Fluid level should be between the add and full marks.
5. Add ATF as necessary to bring level within limits.

FLUID CHANGE

Transmission fluid should be changed at 30 months or 30,000 mile intervals.

1. Remove transmission oil pan drain

SUBARU

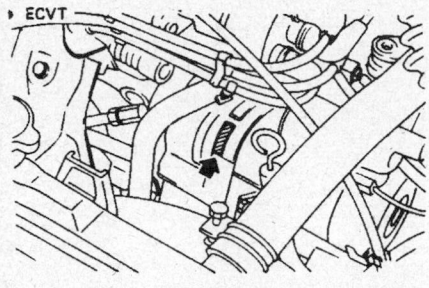

Fig. 1 Transmission identification

plug and allow fluid to drain.
2. Install drain plug with gasket and **torque** to 16.7–19.5 ft. lbs.
3. Check transmission fluid level as outlined under " Fluid Check."

ADJUSTMENTS

BRAKE BAND

If engine speed increases abruptly on 2–3 shift or if there is a delay of more than 1 second on a 3–2 kickdown, excessive clearance between reverse clutch drum and band may exist, adjusting screw should be rotated clockwise. If there is a braking action on 2–3 shift, excessive small brake band clearance may exist and adjusting screw should be rotated counterclockwise. Adjust brake band as follows:
1. Using socket tool No. 398603610, or equivalent, to hold adjusting screw in place, loosen locknut.
2. Loosen or tighten adjusting screw within ¾ turn, to properly adjust band, then **torque** to 19–21 ft. lbs.

If slipping occurs on a 2–3 shift, excessive small brake band clearance may exist. If transmission shifts directly from 1st to 3rd, excessive large brake band clearance may exist. Adjust brake band as follows:
1. Using socket 398603610, to hold adjusting screw in place, loosen locknut.
2. **Torque** adjusting screw to 6.5 ft. lbs., then back off adjusting screw 2 turns. **Torque** locknut to 19–21 ft. lbs.

INHIBITOR SWITCH

1. Disconnect cable end from select lever.
2. Disconnect inhibitor switch connector.
3. Check continuity in inhibitor switch circuits with select lever in each position, **Fig. 3.**
4. Ensure continuity does not exists in ignition circuit when select lever is in R, 3,2 and 1 position.
5. Ensure continuity exists at equal points when select lever is turned 1.5° in both directions from the N position. If not continuity exists in one direction but not in the other direction or if there is continuity at unequal points, adjust inhibitor switch as follows:
   a. Loosen three inhibitor switch mounting bolts.
   b. Shift select lever to N range.
   c. Insert stopper pin tool No. 499267300, or equivalent, as vertical as possible into holes in inhibitor switch lever and switch body, **Fig. 4.**
   d. **Torque** inhibitor screws to 2.2–2.9 ft. lbs.
   e. Repeat checks steps 1 through 5. Replace inhibitor switch if it is determined to be faulty.

TRANSMISSION

REPLACE

FORESTER

1. Open and support hood, then remove air intake duct and chamber.
2. Remove chamber stay, front and rear oxygen sensor connectors, transmission harness connector, transmission ground terminal and vehicle speed sensor No. 2.
3. Remove starter and pitching stopper.
4. Remove service hole plug, then remove torque converter to drive plate bolts.
5. Remove ATF oil dipstick.
6. Cover dipstick opening to prevent contamination of transmission fluid.
7. Remove upper right transmission to engine bolt.
8. Remove exhaust system.
9. Drain ATF into suitable container.
10. Disconnect ATF cooler hoses from pipes at transmission side and remove dipstick tube.
11. Remove front cover of rear differential, separate propeller shaft from rear differential and remove bolts holding center bearing to body.
12. Remove propeller shaft.
13. Disconnect shift selector cable from selector lever, then remove cable bracket from body.
14. Remove stabilizer clamp bolts, then the clamps.
15. Remove transverse link from housing, lower transverse link, then remove and discard spring pins from front drive shafts.
16. Remove shafts from each side of transmission.
17. Remove lower transmission to engine nuts, then place a suitable jack under transmission.
18. Remove transmission crossmember, then the transmission.
19. Reverse procedure to install.

IMPREZA & LEGACY

1. Raise and support hood.
2. **On models less turbocharger,** remove manifold cover and air intake duct.
3. **On models equipped with turbocharger,** remove resonator chamber, then air inlet and outlet ducts, turbocharger cooling duct.
4. **On all models,** disconnect oxygen sensor, transmission harness and ground connectors.
5. Disconnect speedometer cable.
6. Remove starter, then the pitching stopper and bracket.
7. Remove service hole plug from torque

Symptom	Problem parts
Starter does not rotate when select lever is in "P" or "N"; starter rotates when select lever is in "R", "D", "3" or "2".	1) Inhibitor switch 2) Select cable 3) Select lever 4) Starter motor and harness
Abnormal noise when select lever is in "P" or "N".	1) Strainer 2) Duty solenoid C 3) Oil pump 4) Drive plate 5) ATF level too high or too low
Hissing noise occurs during standing start.	1) Strainer 2) ATF level too high or too low
Noise occurs while driving in "D1".	1) Final gear 2) Planetary gear 3) Reduction gear 4) Differential gear oil level too high or too low
Noise occurs while driving in "D2".	1) Final gear 2) Low & reverse brake 3) Reduction gear 4) Differential gear oil level too high or too low
Noise occurs while driving in "D3".	1) Final gear 2) Low & reverse brake 3) Planetary gear 4) Reduction gear 5) Differential gear oil level too high or too low
Noise occurs while driving in "D4".	1) Final gear 2) Low & reverse brake 3) Planetary gear 4) Reduction gear 5) Differential gear oil level too high or too low
Engine stalls while shifting from one range to another.	1) Control valve 2) Lock-up damper 3) Engine performance 4) Input shaft
Vehicle moves when select lever is in "N".	1) Control module 2) Low clutch
Shock occurs when select lever is moved from "N" to "D".	1) Control module 2) Harness 3) Control valve 4) ATF deterioration 5) Dropping resistor
Excessive time lag occurs when select lever is moved from "N" to "D".	1) Control valve 2) Low clutch 3) Duty solenoid A 4) Seal ring 5) Front gasket transmission case
Shock occurs when select lever is moved from "N" to "R".	1) Control module 2) Harness 3) Control valve 4) ATF deterioration 5) Dropping resistor
Excessive time lag occurs when select lever is moved from "N" to "R".	1) Control valve 2) Low & reverse clutch 3) Reverse clutch 4) Duty solenoid A 5) Seal ring 6) Front gasket transmission case
Vehicle does not start in any shift range (engine stalls).	1) Parking brake mechanism 2) Planetary gear

Fig. 2 General troubleshooting chart (Part 1 of 5)

Symptom	Problem parts
Vehicle does not start in any shift range (engine revving up).	1) Strainer 2) Duty solenoid A 3) Control valve 4) Drive pinion 5) Hypoid gear 6) Axle shaft 7) Differential gear 8) Oil pump 9) Input shaft 10) Output shaft 11) Planetary gear 12) Drive plate 13) ATF level too low 14) Front gasket transmission case
Vehicle does not start in "R" range only (engine revving up).	1) Select cable 2) Select lever 3) Control valve 4) Low & reverse clutch 5) Reverse clutch
Vehicle does not start in "R" range only (engine stalls).	1) Low clutch 2) 2-4 brake 3) Planetary gear 4) Parking brake mechanism
Vehicle does not start in "D", "3" range only (engine revving up).	1) Low clutch 2) One-way clutch
Vehicle does not start in "D", "3" or "2" range only (engine revving up).	1) Low clutch
Vehicle does not start in "D", "3" or "2" range only (engine stalls).	1) Reverse clutch
Vehicle starts in "R" range only (engine revving up).	1) Control valve
Acceleration during standing starts is poor (high stall rpm).	1) Control valve 2) Low clutch 3) Reverse clutch 4) ATF level too low 5) Front gasket transmission case 6) Differential gear oil level too high or too low
Acceleration during standing starts is poor (low stall rpm).	1) Oil pump 2) Torque converter one-way clutch 3) Engine performance
Acceleration is poor when select lever is in "D", "3" or "2" range (normal stall rpm).	1) Control module 2) Control valve 3) High clutch 4) 2-4 brake 5) Planetary gear
Acceleration is poor when select lever is in "R" (normal stall rpm).	1) Control valve 2) High clutch 3) 2-4 brake 4) Planetary gear
No shift occurs from 1st to 2nd gear.	1) Control module 2) Vehicle speed sensor 1 (Rear) 3) Vehicle speed sensor 2 (Front) 4) Throttle position sensor 5) Shift solenoid 1 6) Control valve 7) 2-4 brake
No shift occurs from 2nd to 3rd gear.	1) Control module 2) Control valve 3) High clutch 4) Shift solenoid 2

SB5028900124020X

Fig. 2 General troubleshooting chart (Part 2 of 5)

Symptom	Problem parts
No shift occurs from 3rd to 4th gear.	1) Control module 2) Shift solenoid 1 3) ATF temperature sensor 4) Control valve 5) 2-4 brake
Engine brake is not effected when select lever is in "3" range.	1) Inhibitor switch 2) Control module 3) Throttle position sensor 4) Control valve
Engine brake is not effected when select lever is in "3" or "2" range.	1) Control valve
Engine brake is not effected when select lever is in "1" range.	1) Control valve 2) Low & reverse brake
Shift characteristics are erroneous.	1) Inhibitor switch 2) Control module 3) Vehicle speed sensor 1 (Front) 4) Vehicle speed sensor 2 (Rear) 5) Throttle position sensor 6) Control valve 7) Ground earth
No lock-up occurs.	1) Control module 2) Throttle position sensor 3) ATF temperature sensor 4) Control valve 5) Lock-up facing 6) Engine speed signal
Parking brake is not effected.	1) Select cable 2) Select lever 3) Parking mechanism
Shift lever cannot be moved or is hard to move from "P" range.	1) Control valve
ATF spurts out.	1) ATF level too high
Differential oil spurts out.	1) Differential gear oil too high
Differential oil level changes excessively.	1) Seal pipe 2) Double oil seal
Odor is produced from ATF supply pipe.	1) High clutch 2) 2-4 brake 3) Low & reverse clutch 4) Reverse clutch 5) Lock-up facing 6) ATF deterioration
Shock occurs from 1st to 2nd gear.	1) Control module 2) Throttle position sensor 3) Duty solenoid D 4) ATF temperature sensor 5) Duty solenoid A 6) Control valve 7) 2-4 brake 8) ATF deterioration 9) Engine performance 10) Dropping resistor 11) 2-4 brake timing solenoid
Slippage occurs from 1st to 2nd gear.	1) Control module 2) Throttle position sensor 3) Duty solenoid D 4) ATF temperature sensor 5) Duty solenoid A 6) Control valve 7) 2-4 brake 8) 2-4 brake timing solenoid 9) High clutch

SB5028900125030X

Fig. 2 General troubleshooting chart (Part 3 of 5)

converter cover.

8. Remove torque converter to drive plate attaching bolts. Do not drop bolts into torque converter.
9. While rotating engine, remove other bolts.
10. Remove front differential oil level gauge, then the transmission connector bracket.
11. Install engine support fixture tool No. 41099AA000, or equivalent, then remove right upper side of transmission to engine bolts.
12. Remove exhaust system as follows:
   a. **On models equipped with turbocharger,** separate center exhaust pipe from turbocharger.
   b. **On all models,** raise and support vehicle.
   c. **On models less turbocharger,** remove front exhaust pipe.
   d. **On models equipped with turbocharger,** remove turbocharger lower cover, then center exhaust pipe.
   e. **On AWD models,** remove rear exhaust pipe.
13. **On all models,** drain transmission fluid, then disconnect transmission lines from side of transmission.
14. **On AWD models,** remove propeller shaft as follows:
   a. Remove front cover of rear differential mount, then separate propeller

shaft from rear differential.
   b. Remove bolts holding center bearing onto body, then the propeller shaft.
15. **On all models,** remove gear selector cable from selector lever and cable bracket.
16. Remove stabilizer clamp to crossmember bolts.
17. Remove front driveshaft from transmission as follows:
   a. Remove and lower transverse link from housing.
   b. Remove spring pin and separate front driveshaft from each side of transmission.
18. Remove lower side transmission to engine nuts.
19. Place suitable transmission jack stand under transmission.
20. Remove transmission rear crossmember.
21. Remove transmission from vehicle. Move transmission and torque converter as a unit away from engine
22. Reverse procedure to install.

SVX

1. Position vehicle on hoist. Do not lift.
2. Disconnect hood damper, then open hood fully.
3. Remove throttle body cover.
4. Remove air intake boot, then engine hook under throttle body.

5. Remove pitching stopper and bracket. Disconnect transmission air vent hoses from bracket.
6. Disconnect the following electrical connectors:
   a. Transmission harness.
   b. Oxygen sensors.
   c. Vehicle speed sensor No. 2.
   d. Transmission ground.
7. Disconnect PCV hose, then blow-by hose from crankcase to collector.
8. Raise and support vehicle, then remove lower starter mounting bolts.
9. Lower vehicle, then disconnect power supply terminal and magnet coil connector.
10. Remove upper starter mounting bolts, then the starter.
11. Remove torque converter cover hole plug, then remove torque converter to drive plate attaching bolts. Separate torque converter from drive plate.
12. Install engine support fixture tool No. 927670000, or equivalent, then remove upper right side transmission to engine bolts.
13. Remove fluid level gauge from transmission and front differential, then raise and support vehicle.
14. Remove under cover, then oxygen sensor harness from clip.
15. remove front exhaust pipes and rear catalyst converter, then the front exhaust cover.
16. Remove propeller shaft to companion

Symptom	Problem parts
Shock occurs from 2nd to 3rd gear.	1) Control module 2) Throttle position sensor 3) Duty solenoid D 4) ATF temperature sensor 5) Duty solenoid A 6) Control valve 7) High clutch 8) 2-4 brake 9) ATF deterioration 10) Engine performance 11) 2-4 brake timing solenoid
Slippage occurs from 2nd to 3rd gear.	1) Control module 2) Throttle position sensor 3) Duty solenoid D 4) ATF temperature sensor 5) Duty solenoid A 6) Control valve 7) High clutch 8) 2-4 brake 9) 2-4 brake timing solenoid
Shock occurs from 3rd to 4th gear.	1) Control module 2) Throttle position sensor 3) Duty solenoid D 4) ATF temperature sensor 5) Duty solenoid A 6) Control valve 7) 2-4 brake timing solenoid 8) 2-4 brake 9) ATF deterioration 10) Engine performance 11) Low clutch timing solenoid 12) Low clutch
Slippage occurs from 3rd to 4th gear.	1) Control module 2) Throttle position sensor 3) Duty solenoid D 4) ATF temperature sensor 5) Duty solenoid A 6) Control valve 7) 2-4 brake 8) 2-4 brake timing solenoid
Shock occurs when select lever is moved from "3" to "2" range.	1) Control module 2) Throttle position sensor 3) ATF temperature sensor 4) Duty solenoid A 5) Control valve 6) Duty solenoid D 7) 2-4 brake 8) ATF deterioration 9) 2-4 brake timing solenoid
Shock occurs when select lever is moved from "D" to "1" range.	1) Control module 2) Throttle position sensor 3) ATF temperature sensor 4) Duty solenoid A 5) Control valve 6) ATF deterioration 7) Duty solenoid D 8) 2-4 brake timing solenoid 9) Low clutch timing solenoid

SB5028900125040X

Fig. 2 General troubleshooting chart (Part 4 of 5)

Symptom	Problem parts
Shock occurs when select lever is moved from "2" to "1" range.	1) Control module 2) Throttle position sensor 3) ATF temperature sensor 4) Duty solenoid A 5) Control valve 6) Low & reverse clutch 7) ATF deterioration 8) Duty solenoid D 9) 2-4 brake timing solenoid 10) Low clutch timing solenoid
Shock occurs when accelerator pedal is released at medium speeds.	1) Control module 2) Throttle position sensor 3) ATF temperature sensor 4) Duty solenoid A 5) Control valve 6) Lock-up damper 7) Engine performance 8) Duty solenoid D 9) 2-4 brake timing solenoid 10) Low clutch timing solenoid
Vibration occurs during straight-forward operation.	1) Control module 2) Duty solenoid B 3) Lock-up facing 4) Lock-up damper
Vibration occurs during turns (tight corner "braking" phenomenon).	1) Control module 2) Vehicle speed sensor 1 (Front) 3) Vehicle speed sensor 2 (Rear) 4) Throttle position sensor 5) ATF temperature sensor 6) Transfer clutch 7) Transfer valve 8) Duty solenoid C 9) ATF deterioration 10) Harness
Front wheel slippage occurs during standing starts.	1) Control module 2) Vehicle speed sensor 2 (Front) 3) FWD switch 4) Throttle position sensor 5) ATF temperature sensor 6) Control valve 7) Transfer clutch 8) Transfer valve 9) Transfer pipe 10) Duty solenoid C
Vehicle is not set in FWD mode.	1) Control module 2) FWD switch 3) Transfer clutch 4) Transfer valve 5) Duty solenoid C
Select lever is hard to move.	1) Select cable 2) Select lever 3) Detent spring 4) Manual plate
Select lever is too high to move (unreasonable resistance).	1) Detent spring 2) Manual plate
Select lever slips out of operation during acceleration or while driving on rough terrain.	1) Select cable 2) Select lever 3) Detent spring 4) Manual plate

SB5028900125050X

Fig. 2 General troubleshooting chart (Part 5 of 5)

Signal sent to TCM	Position	Pin No.
	P	4 — 3
	R	4 — 2
	N	4 — 1
	D	4 — 8
	3	4 — 7
	2	4 — 6
	1	4 — 5
Ignition circuit	P/N	12 — 11
Back-up light circuit	R	10 — 9

Inhibitor switch side connector

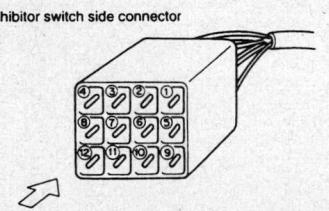

SB5028900170000X

Fig. 3 Inhibitor switch continuity inspection

flange attaching bolts, then the center bearing to body bolts. Remove propeller shaft from transmission.

17. Remove selector cable from selector lever assembly, then the selector cable bracket from body.
18. Remove performance rod.
19. Remove front axle from transmission as follows:
    a. Remove ball joint from knuckle arm of housing.
    b. Remove stabilizer link from bracket, then the brake hose and ABS sensor harness from start bracket.
    c. Remove spring pin holding axle shaft into front differential drive shaft.
    d. Remove axle shaft from transmission.
20. Disconnect transmission hoses from side of transmission, then remove lower side transmission to engine attaching bolts.
21. Place transmission jack under transmission, then remove rear crossmember to body bolts.
22. Remove transmission from vehicle. Move transmission and torque con-

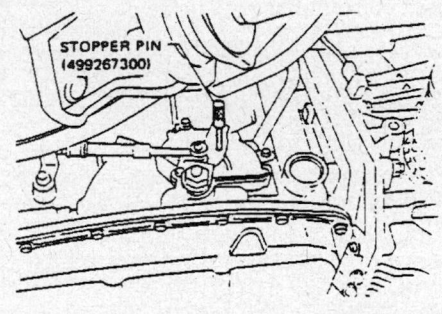

SB5028900171000X

Fig. 4 Inhibitor switch adjustment

verter as a unit away from engine
23. Reverse procedure to install.

SHIFT LOCK SYSTEM

Refer to **Figs. 5 through 8,** for shift lock system wiring diagrams and to **Fig. 9,** for diagnosis of the shift lock system.

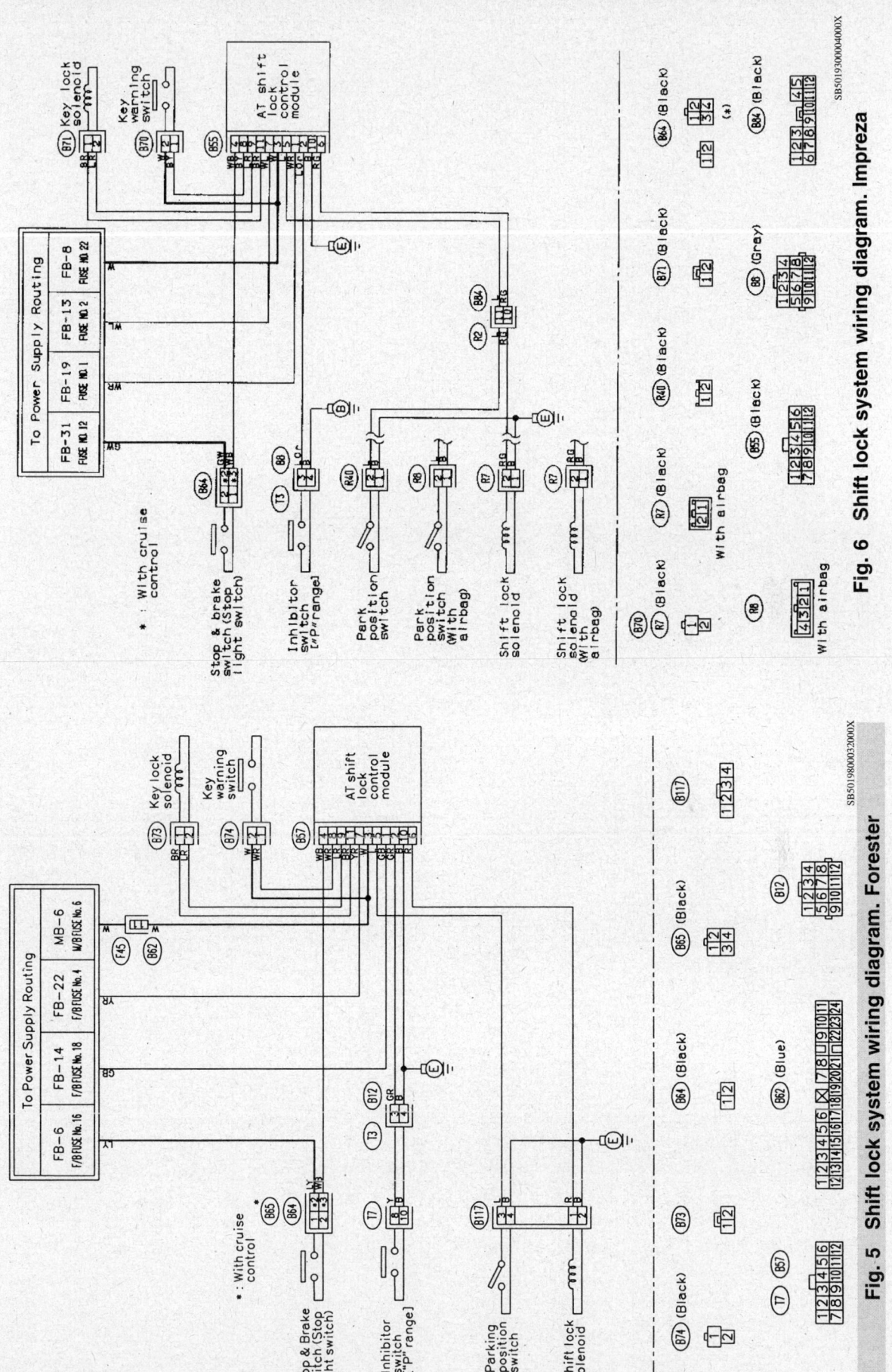

Fig. 6 Shift lock system wiring diagram. Impreza

Fig. 5 Shift lock system wiring diagram. Forester

SUBARU

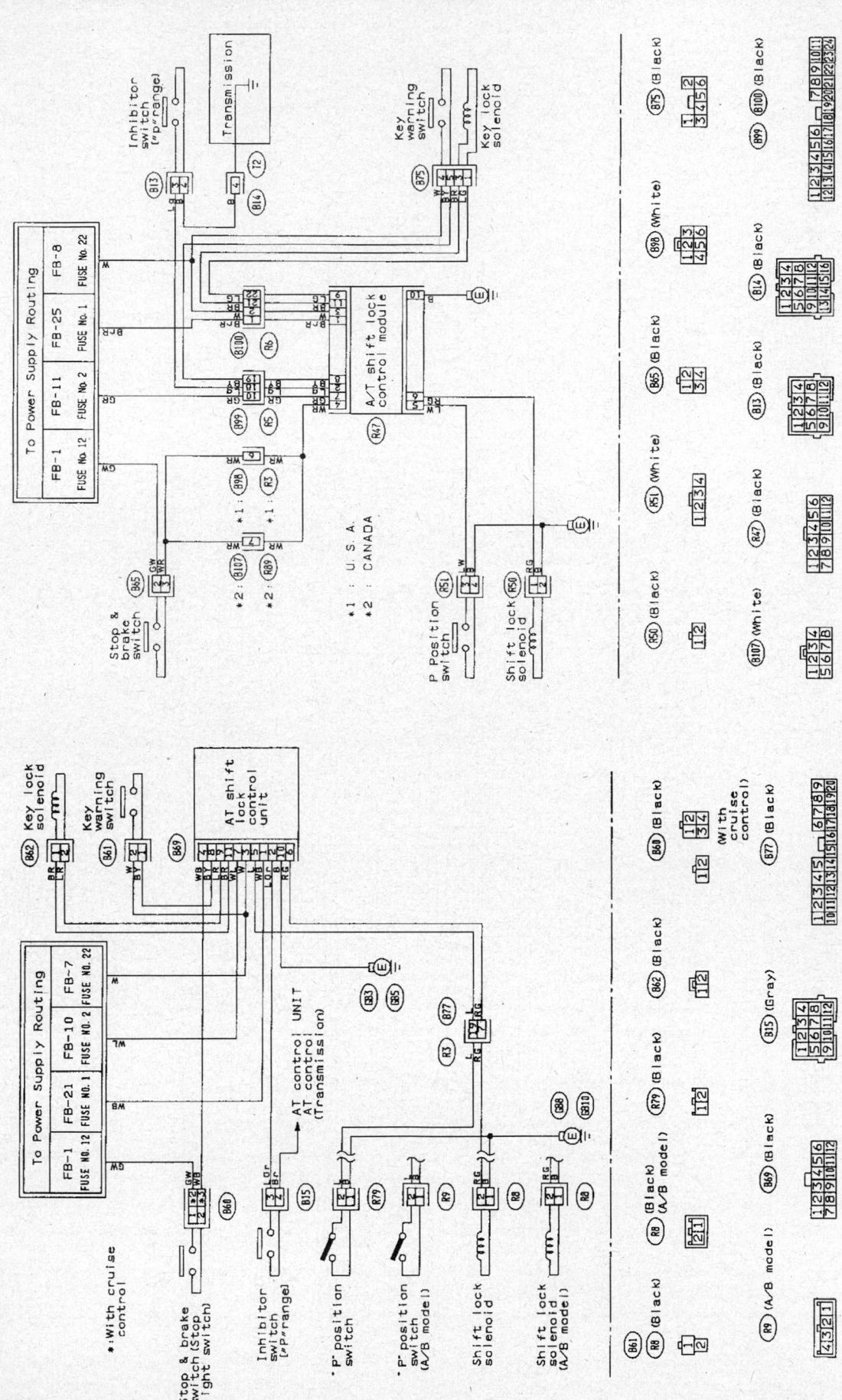

Fig. 8 Shift lock system wiring diagram. SVX

Fig. 7 Shift lock system wiring diagram. Legacy

SUBARU

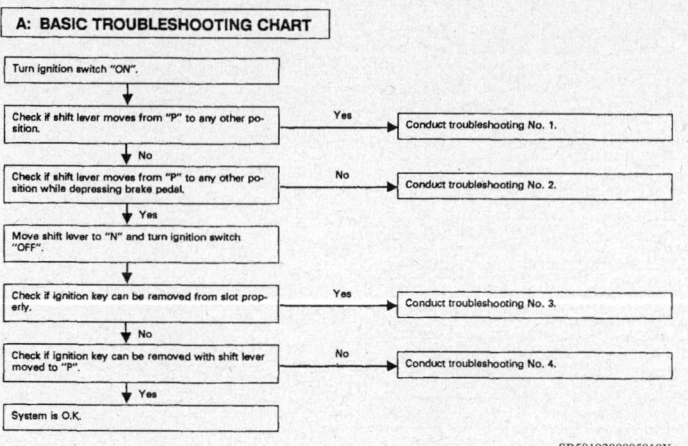

Fig. 9   Shift lock system diagnosis (Part 1 of 5)

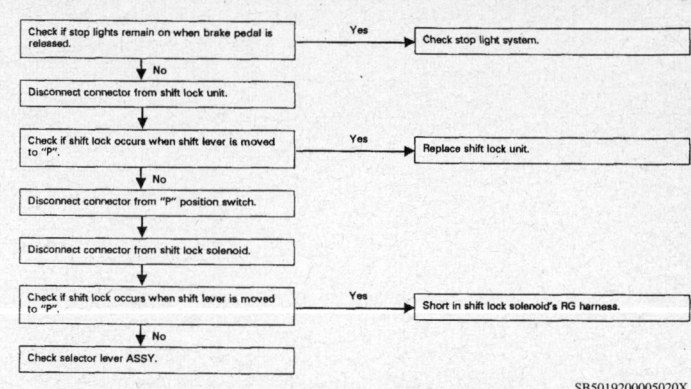

Fig. 9   Shift lock system diagnosis (Part 2 of 5)

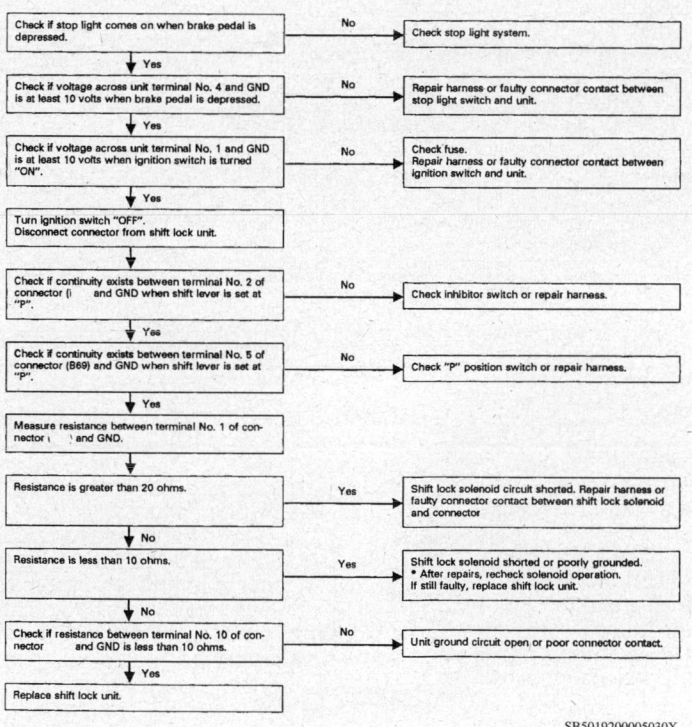

Fig. 9   Shift lock system diagnosis (Part 3 of 5)

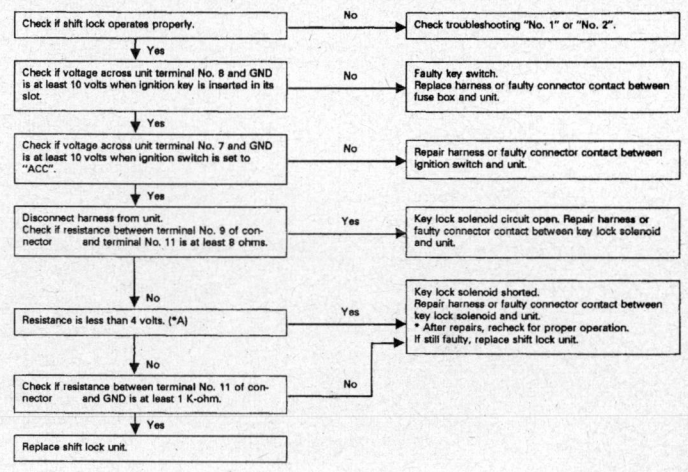

*A: When conducting operational checks of the key lock solenoid, do not apply 12 volts to solenoid for more than one second, since this may break solenoid circuit.

Fig. 9   Shift lock system diagnosis (Part 4 of 5)

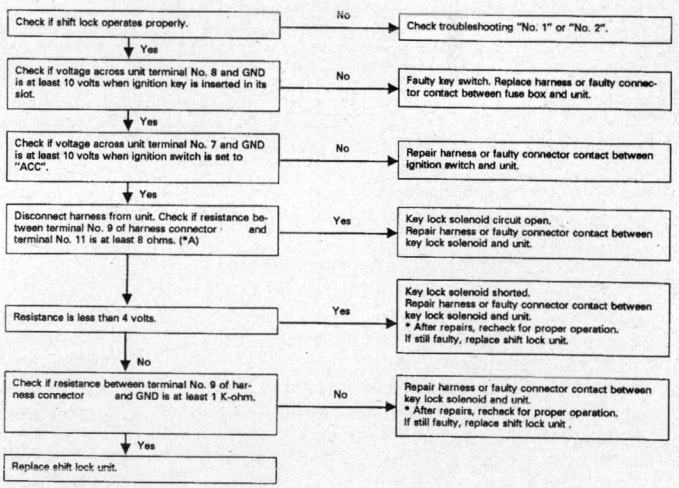

*A: When conducting operational checks of the key lock solenoid, do not apply 12 volts to solenoid for more than one second, since this may break solenoid circuit.

Fig. 9   Shift lock system diagnosis (Part 5 of 5)

TIGHTENING SPECIFICATIONS

Year	Component	Torque/Ft. Lbs.
1996-99	Ball Joint Pinch Bolt	33–42
	Center Bearing To Body	35–42
	Driveplate To Torque Converter	17–20
	Engine To Transmission (Lower Nuts)	34–40
	Engine To Transmission (Right Side Bolt)	34–40
	Exhaust Pipe To Cylinder Head	18–25
	Front Exhaust Pipe To Engine	19–23
	Performance Rod	33–42
	Pitching Stopper Bracket	27–31
	Pitching Stopper (Body Side)	35–39
	Pitching Stopper (Bracket Side)	25–40
	Propeller Shaft To Companion Flange	17–29
	Rear Crossmember To Body	40–61
	Rear Transmission Mount To Rear Crossmember	9–17
	Starter Motor	34–40
	Transverse Link To Front Crossmember	43–51
	Transverse Link To Stabilizer	14–22
	Wheel Lug Nuts	58–72

Front Wheel Drive Axles

INDEX

DRIVESHAFT

REPLACE

FORESTER, IMPREZA & LEGACY

1. Raise and support vehicle.
2. Remove front wheels.
3. Remove and discard axle nut.
4. Remove stabilizer and transverse link from crossmember.
5. Using a drift and hammer, remove and discard double offset joint spring pin, **Fig. 1.**
6. Remove double offset joint from transmission spindle.
7. Remove driveshaft assembly. If necessary, use puller tool No. 926470000, or equivalent.
8. Inspect all parts for wear, damage or corrosion and replace as necessary.
9. Reverse procedure to install noting the following:
   a. When replacing axle shaft, install new inner oil seal.
   b. Seat under cut free joint into hub using axle shaft installer tool No. 922431000 and extension tool No. 927130000, or equivalents.
   c. Install axle shaft to hub with new axle nut. Refer to **Fig. 1,** for tightening specifications.

SVX

1. Raise and support vehicle.
2. Remove tire and wheel assembly.
3. Depress brake pedal and remove axle nut.
4. Remove stabilizer link and disconnect anti-lock brake sensor harness and brake hose clamps from strut.
5. Scribe alignment marks on stabilizer and stabilizer lever. **If removing right-hand driveshaft,** loosen stabilizer clamp.
6. Remove spring pin at tripod joint, then CV joint from knuckle (remover and plate tool Nos. 92647000 and 28099PA110, or equivalent, may be required to separate joint and knuckle).
7. Reverse procedure to install.

DRIVESHAFT SERVICE

DISASSEMBLE

1. Remove axle shaft as described previously.
2. Straighten bent claw of large end of boot on double offset joint side of axle shaft, then loosen boot band.
3. Remove boot band on small end of double offset joint side in same manner, then slide boot away from joint.
4. Remove round circlip at neck of outer race on double offset joint side with screwdriver.
5. Remove outer race on double offset joint side from shaft assembly.
6. Remove balls and move cage to boot side, then turn cage by ½ pitch to track groove of inner race and remove snap ring, inner race, cage and boot. **The Constant Velocity Joint (CVJ) is not to be disassembled.**

INSPECTION

1. Check double offset joint and CV joint for seizure, corrosion, damage or excessive wear.
2. Check shaft for bending, twisting, damage and wear.
3. Check boot for wear, warping and cracking.

ASSEMBLE

1. Install boot on CV joint side and fill with 2–2.5 oz. of special constant velocity joint grease Molylex No. 2, or equivalent.
2. Position boot from double offset joint side at center of shaft, then insert cage of double offset joint with recess facing outward.
3. Install inner race of double offset joint onto shaft and secure with snap ring.

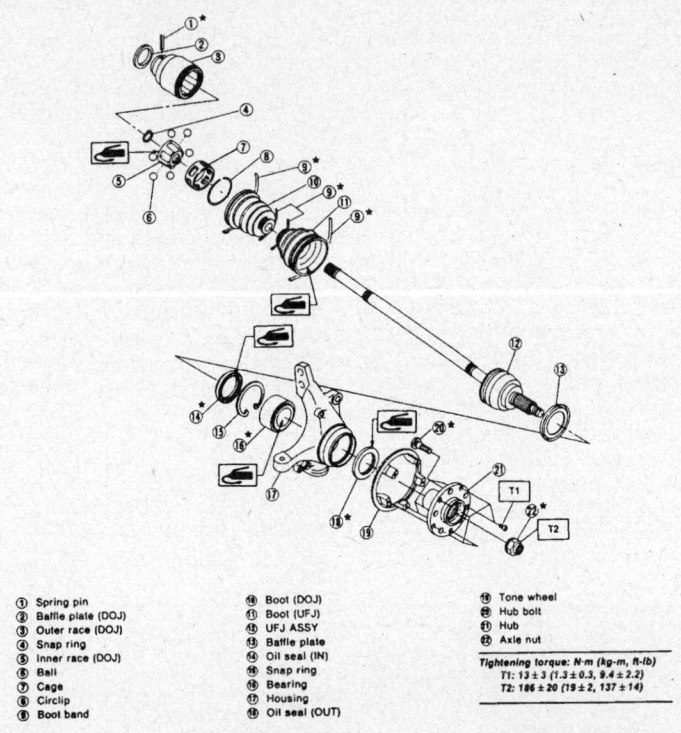

① Spring pin
② Baffle plate (DOJ)
③ Outer race (DOJ)
④ Snap ring
⑤ Inner race (DOJ)
⑥ Ball
⑦ Cage
⑧ Circlip
⑨ Boot band

⑩ Boot (DOJ)
⑪ Boot (UFJ)
⑫ UFJ ASSY
⑬ Baffle plate
⑭ Oil seal (IN)
⑮ Snap ring
⑯ Bearing
⑰ Housing
⑱ Oil seal (OUT)

⑲ Tone wheel
⑳ Hub bolt
㉑ Hub
㉒ Axle nut

Tightening torque: N·m (kg-m, ft-lb)
T1: 13 ± 3 (1.3 ± 0.3, 9.4 ± 2.2)
T2: 186 ± 20 (19 ± 2, 137 ± 14)

SB3039100003000X

Fig. 1 Exploded view of front drive axle. Forester, Impreza, Legacy (SVX similar)

4. Install cage, which was previously positioned, with protruding part aligned with track on inner race and then turn by ½ pitch. Apply .75–1 oz. of special grease to cage pocket and insert 6 balls into cage pocket, then fill interior of outer race with .75–1 oz. of special grease.
5. Align outer race track and ball positions, then fit outer race to inner race and cage.
6. Install circlip into groove on outer race of double offset joint, then pull shaft to ensure circlip is seated in groove.
7. Apply .75–1 oz. of grease to interior of double offset joint and shaft area, then fill boot with .75–1 oz. of grease and install. **When installing boot, position outer race of double offset joint at center of its travel.**
8. Install new boot bands using suitable tool and tighten until it cannot be moved by hand. **While tightening band, be sure there is enough air within boot.**
9. Tap on clip of band with suitable punch at end of tightening tool and cut off excess band at about .4 inch (10mm) from clip, then bend band over clip.
10. Fill CV joint boot and CV joint with special grease and install in same manner as double offset joint boot.

All-Wheel Drive Systems

INDEX

DESCRIPTION

The electronically controlled multi-plate transfer type AWD system consist of a transfer hydraulic pressure control unit incorporating a vehicle speed sensor, control unit and duty solenoid and a transfer clutch.

The control unit stores optimum transfer clutch torque data for a variety of driving conditions. When actual driving conditions are detected by the sensors, the control unit selects a duty ratio most suitable to the given condition from the memory. It then controls the operation of the transfer clutch by means of the hydraulic pressure which

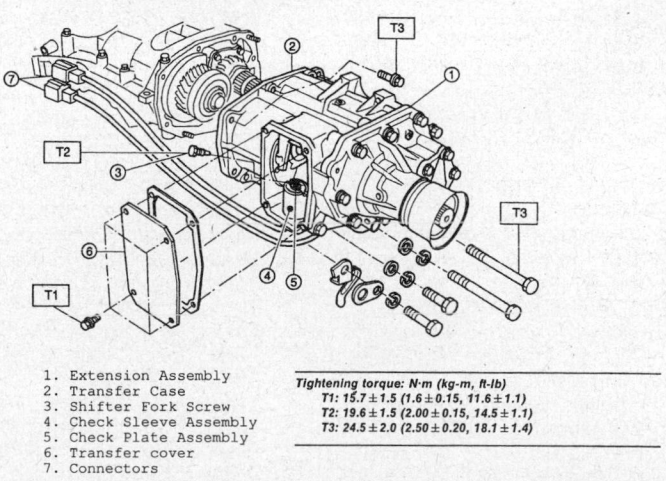

1. Extension Assembly
2. Transfer Case
3. Shifter Fork Screw
4. Check Sleeve Assembly
5. Check Plate Assembly
6. Transfer cover
7. Connectors

Tightening torque: N·m (kg-m, ft-lb)
T1: 15.7 ± 1.5 (1.6 ± 0.15, 11.6 ± 1.1)
T2: 19.6 ± 1.5 (2.00 ± 0.15, 14.5 ± 1.1)
T3: 24.5 ± 2.0 (2.50 ± 0.20, 18.1 ± 1.4)

SB3049100010000X

Fig. 1 Transfer case & extension assembly. Forester, Impreza & Legacy

SUBARU

controls the duty solenoid and provides optimum rear torque distribution.

Various sensors and the control unit also serve as gear shift control, lock-up control and hydraulic pressure control.

The AWD transfer system is housed in the extension case together with the bearing and rear drive shaft.

TRANSFER CASE

REPLACE

FORESTER, IMPREZA & LEGACY

Refer to **Fig. 1** when performing the following procedure.

Removal

1. Install transmission in a suitable holding stand.
2. Disconnect harness electrical connectors.
3. Remove transfer cover.
4. Remove shifter fork screw retaining the selector arm to shifter arm.
5. Remove transfer case and extension assembly.

Installation

1. Install transfer case and extension assembly.
2. Install selector arm to shifter arm and secure with shifter fork screw. **Ensure shifter arm is caught by pawl of rod and selector arm is engaged with reverse check sleeve assembly.**
3. Adjust neutral position as necessary by removing bolts holding reverse check sleeve assembly to case, move sleeve assembly outward and place adjustment shims between sleeve assembly and case to adjust clearance. When shim is removed, neutral position will move closer to reverse. When shim is added, neutral position will move closer to 1st gear. **Use caution not to break O-ring when replacing shim. Also, if shims cannot adjust clearance, replace accent shaft and repeat adjustment.**
4. Shift shifter arm to 5th and then to reverse to see if reverse check mechanism operates properly, then check to see if arm returns to neutral when released from reverse position. If arm does not return satisfactorily, replace reverse check plate.
5. Install transfer cover with gasket.
6. Connect harness electrical connectors.

SVX

Refer to "Transmission, Replace" for transfer case replacement

Drive Axles

INDEX

REAR AXLE SHAFT

REPLACE

FORESTER, IMPREZA & LEGACY

1. Raise and support vehicle.
2. Remove rear wheels. Loosen and retighten axle nut after removing wheels from vehicle.
3. Remove and discard axle nut, then return parking brake and loosen adjuster.
4. **On models equipped with disc brakes,** remove caliper support retaining bolts and the disc brake assembly. Suspend assembly from strut.
5. Remove disc brake rotor, then disconnect end of parking brake cable.
6. **On models equipped with drum brakes,** remove brake drum from hub. **If brake drum is difficult to remove drive it out by installing an 8 mm bolt into brake drum bolt hole.**
7. **On all models,** disconnect brake pipe from wheel cylinder, then disconnect end of parking brake cable.
8. Remove stabilizer clamp.
9. If equipped, remove speed sensor from backing plate.
10. Remove lateral link and trailing link-to-housing retaining bolts.
11. Using a drift and hammer, remove Double Offset Joint spring pin.
12. Remove double offset joint from differential spindle.
13. Remove driveshaft assembly. If necessary, use puller tool No. 926470000, or equivalent.
14. Inspect all parts for wear damage or corrosion and replace as necessary.
15. Reverse procedure to install noting the following:
    a. Seat bell joint into hub using axle shaft installer tool No. 922431000 and extension tool No. 927130000, or equivalents.
    b. Install axle shaft to hub with new axle nut.

SVX

1. Move select lever to Park position, then set parking brake.
2. Raise and support vehicle, then remove rear wheels. Loosen and retighten axle nut after removing wheels from vehicle.
3. Move shift lever to Neutral position, then the parking brake lever forward.
4. Disconnect rear exhaust pipe, then remove stabilizer link.
5. Remove ABS clamps, then the parking brake cable bracket.
6. Disconnect parking brake cable clamp, then the brake hose from strut.
7. Disconnect trailing link and lateral link from housing.
8. Using driveshaft remover tool No. 28099PA100, or equivalent, remove double offset joint from rear differential. Use bolt on side bearing retainer as supporting point for remover.
9. Remove axle nut and driveshaft. If driveshaft is hard to remove, use remover tool No. 926470000 and plate tool No. 28099PA110, or equivalents.
10. Reverse procedure to install, noting the following:
    a. Seat bell joint into hub using axle shaft installer tool No. 922431000 and adapter tool No. 927390000, or equivalents.
    b. Install axle shaft to hub with new axle nut.
    c. Using side oil seal protector tool No. 28099PA090, or equivalent, install double offset joint.

REAR AXLE SHAFT SERVICE

Refer to "Front Axle Shaft Service" in the "Front Wheel Drive Axle" section for disassemble and assembly procedures of the Double Offset Joint.

DIFFERENTIAL SERVICE

MAINTENANCE

Fluid Check

Remove differential filler plug and check to ensure gear oil level is at bottom of filler plug hole.

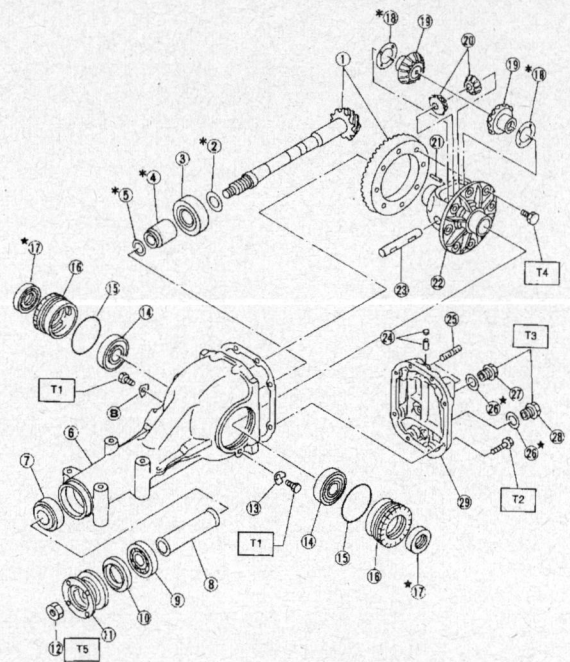

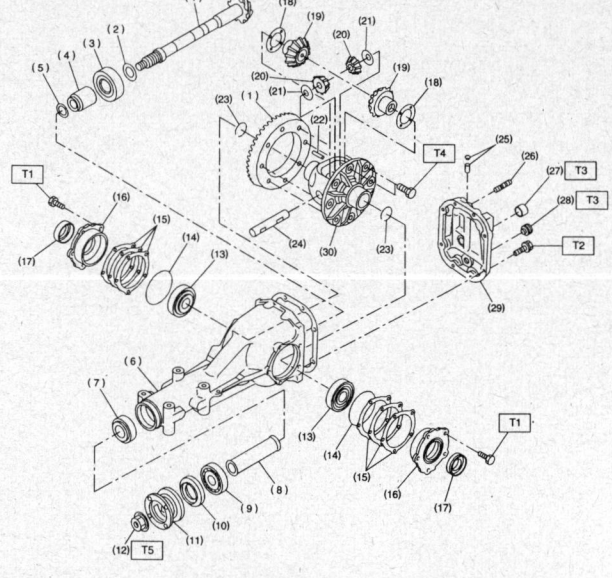

(1) Pinion crown gear set	(18) Side gear
(2) Pinion height adjusting shim	(20) Pinion mate gear
(3) Rear bearing	(21) Pinion shaft lock pin
(4) Bearing preload adjusting spacer	(22) Differential case
(5) Bearing preload adjusting washer	(23) Pinion mate shaft
(6) Differential carrier	(24) Air breather cap
(7) Front bearing	(25) Stud bolt
(8) Collar	(26) Gasket
(9) Pilot bearing	(27) Oil filler plug
(10) Front oil seal	(28) Oil drain plug
(11) Companion flange	(29) Rear cover
(12) Self-locking nut	
(13) Lock plate	
(14) Side bearing	
(15) O-ring	
(16) Axle shaft holder	
(17) Side oil seal	
(18) Side gear thrust washer	

Tightening torque: N·m (kg-m, ft-lb)
T1: 22 — 27 (2.2 — 2.8, 16 — 20)
T2: 23 — 26 (2.3 — 2.7, 17 — 20)
T3: 30 — 38 (3.1 — 3.9, 22 — 28)
T4: 57 — 67 (5.8 — 6.8, 42 — 49)
T5: 167 — 196 (17.0 — 20.0, 123 — 145)

SB3039100005000X

Fig. 1 Exploded view of drive axle assembly. Legacy AWD models

(1) Pinion crown gear set	(14) O-ring	(28) Oil drain plug
(2) Pinion height adjusting washer	(15) Side bearing retainer shim	(29) Rear cover
(3) Rear bearing	(16) Side bearing retainer	(30) Differential case
(4) Bearing preload adjusting spacer	(17) Side oil seal	
(5) Bearing preload adjusting washer	(18) Side gear thrust washer	
(6) Differential carrier	(19) Side gear	
(7) Front bearing	(20) Pinion mate gear	
(8) Spacer	(21) Pinion mate gear washer	
(9) Pilot bearing	(22) Pinion shaft lock pin	
(10) Front oil seal	(23) Circlip	
(11) Companion flange	(24) Pinion mate shaft	
(12) Self-locking nut	(25) Air breather cap	
(13) Side bearing	(26) Stud bolt	
	(27) Oil filler plug	

Tightening torque: N·m (kg-m, ft-lb)
T1: 10.3±1.5 (1.05±0.15, 7.6±1.1)
T2: 29.4±4.9 (3.00±0.50, 21.7±3.6)
T3: 44.1±3.9 (4.50±0.40, 32.5±2.9)
T4: 103.0±9.8 (10.50±1.00, 75.9±7.2)
T5: 181.4±14.7 (18.50±1.50, 133.8±10.8)

SB3039800020000X

Fig. 2 Exploded view of drive axle assembly. Forester & Impreza

Fluid Change

Differential gear oil should be changed at intervals of 30 months or 30,000 miles.

1. Remove differential drain plug and allow gear oil to drain.
2. Install differential drain plug with gasket. **Torque** plug to 18 ft. lbs.
3. Remove differential filler plug and add gear oil to oil level is at bottom of differential filler plug hole, then install filler plug. Refer to "Lubricant Data" for lubricant type.
4. Do not mix brands or weights of oil.

DISASSEMBLE

1. Place attachment tool No. 398217700, or equivalent, in a suitable vise, then attach drive axle assembly to tool.
2. Remove plug, then drain differential gear oil.
3. Loosen attaching bolts, then remove spindles, using a suitable tool.
4. Mark position of left and right side retainers to facilitate installation, then attach tool No. 398457700, or equivalent, to differential case and remove retainers using a suitable puller, **Figs. 1 and 2.**
5. Remove differential carrier. Ensure teeth do not contact case. **When replacing side bearing, pull bearing cup from side bearing retainer.**
6. Remove bearing cone from differential carrier, using puller tool No. 399527700, or equivalent.
7. Remove drive gear by straightening lock plates and removing retaining bolts.
8. Drive out pinion shaft lockpin using a suitable punch. **Lockpin is staked to the differential case, do not drive out before unstaking.**
9. Remove pinion shaft, pinion gears, side gears and thrust washers. **On models equipped with limited slip differential, replacement differential case components, Fig. 3, are not available, therefore disassemble is not recommended.**
10. Hold companion flange using tool No. 398427700, or equivalent, then remove drive pinion nut.
11. Remove companion flange using a suitable puller.
12. Using a suitable drift, press end of pinion shaft and remove with bearing inner race, spacer and washer.
13. Press rear bearing inner race from drive pinion by supporting inner race with tool No. 398517700, or equivalent.
14. Remove oil seal from differential carrier.
15. Remove pilot bearing with front bearing inner race using a suitable drift.
16. When replacing pinion bearings, tap front bearing outer race and rear bearing outer race using a brass drift.

ASSEMBLE

1. Reverse procedure to assemble, **Figs. 1 and 2.**
   a. Apply gear oil when installing bearings and thrust washers.
   b. Ensure left and righthand races of bearings are installed in correct positions.
2. Adjust pinion bearing preload as follows:
   a. Adjust pinion bearing preload with a spacer and washer between front and rear bearings. The adjustment must be carried out without the oil seal.
   b. Press front and rear bearing outer races into differential carrier using a suitable drift.
   c. Insert dummy pinion shaft tool No. 398507702 with pinion height adjusting washer and rear bearing inner race into carrier.
   d. Install preload adjusting spacer and washer, front bearing inner race, dummy collar tool No. 398507703

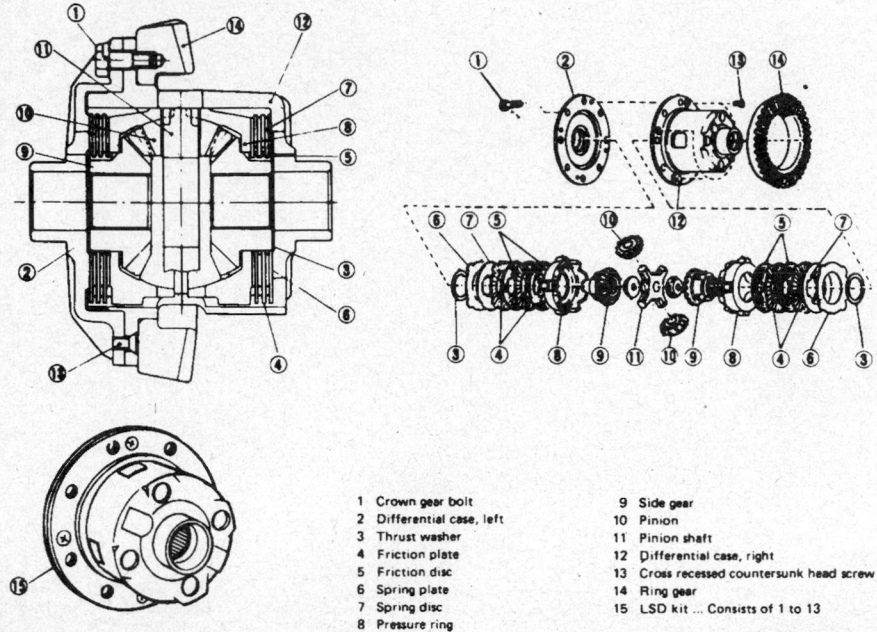

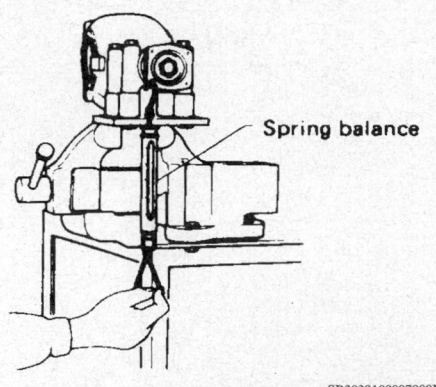

Fig. 4   Pinion bearing preload inspection

Part No.	Length In In. (mm)
383695201	2.213 (56.2)
383695202	2.220 (56.4)
383695203	2.228 (56.6)
383695204	2.236 (56.8)
383695205	2.244 (57.0)
383695206	2.252 (57.2)

SB3039100008000X

Fig. 5   Pinion bearing preload adjustment spacer identification chart

1	Crown gear bolt
2	Differential case, left
3	Thrust washer
4	Friction plate
5	Friction disc
6	Spring plate
7	Spring disc
8	Pressure ring
9	Side gear
10	Pinion
11	Pinion shaft
12	Differential case, right
13	Cross recessed countersunk head screw
14	Ring gear
15	LSD kit ... Consists of 1 to 13

SB3039100006000X

Fig. 3   Exploded view of limited slip differential case assembly. AWD models

and companion flange.

e. Rotate drive pinion by hand to seat bearings and tighten pinion nut while measuring preload, **Fig. 4.** Select the adjusting washer and spacer so that specified preload is obtained when nut is **torqued** to 123–145 ft. lbs., **Figs. 5 and 6.**

3. Adjust drive pinion height as follows:

a. Adjust pinion height with a washer installed between rear bearing inner race and back of pinion gear.

b. Install dummy shaft, collar and gauge, tool set No. 398501600, or equivalent, and apply specified preload on bearings, **Fig. 7.**

c. Measure clearance between end of gauge and end surface of dummy shaft by using a feeler gauge.

d. Obtain thickness of pinion height adjusting washer, **Fig. 8,** to be installed from the following formula: $T = To + N - (H \times .01) - .20$mm when T = thickness of pinion height adjusting washer in mm, To = thickness of washer temporarily inserted in mm, N = reading of thickness gauge in mm and H = figure marked on drive piston head.

e. Install selected pinion height washer on drive pinion and press rear bearing inner race into position using tool No. 398177700, or equivalent.

f. Insert drive pinion into gear carrier, installed previously, selected preload adjusting spacer, washer, oil seal, companion flange and tighten with pinion nut. **Torque** pinion nut to 123–145 ft. lbs.

4. Assemble differential case as follows:

a. Install side gears and pinion gears with thrust washers and pinion shaft into differential case. **Apply**

gear oil on both sides of thrust washers and side gears before installing.

b. Measure clearance between differential case and back of side gear.

c. Adjust clearance as specified by selecting the side gear thrust washer. Side gear back clearance should be .004–.008 inch, **Fig. 9.**

d. Check condition of rotation after applying oil to gear tooth surfaces and thrust surfaces.

e. After driving in pinion shaft lockpin, stake both sides of hole to prevent pin from falling out.

f. Install drive gear on differential case. **Torque** attaching bolts to 51–58 ft. lbs., then lock washer. **Tighten diagonally while tapping bolt heads.**

5. Measure width of side bearing as follows:

a. Before installing side bearings, measure bearing width by using a weight block of about 5.5 lbs., **Fig. 10.** Standard bearing width is .787 inch.

b. Press side bearing inner race onto differential case using a suitable drift and tool No. 398497701 included in puller set No. 399527700, or equivalents, **Fig. 11.**

6. Adjust side gear preload as follows:

a. The gear backlash and side gear preload can be determined by side retainer shim thickness.

b. When replacing differential carrier, differential case, side bearing and side retainer, **Fig. 12,** obtain left and right retainer shim thicknesses, **Fig. 13,** by the following formula: $T1$ (left) = $(A + C + G - D - E + H) \times .01 + .76$mm; $T2$ (right) = $(B + D + G - F - H) \times .01 + .76$mm. when $T1$ & $T2$ = thickness of left and right side retainer adjusting shims in mm, A & B = figure mark on differential carrier, C & D = figure mark on differential case, E & F = difference of width of left and right side bearings from standard width 20mm expressed in a unit of $1/100$mm, G = figure marked on side retainer and H = figure marked on drive gear. **If figure is not marked, regard as zero.**

c. Use several shims to obtain calculated thickness.

d. Reverse disassemble procedure to install differential case to differential carrier.

e. Install selected shim and O-ring on side retainer, then install retainer on carrier with arrow on retainer facing, **Fig. 14. Torque** to 7–9 ft. lbs.

f. Measure drive gear to drive pinion backlash. Backlash should be .004–.008 inch. If reading is not within limits, correct by decreasing shim thickness on one side and increasing shim thickness on the other side by the same amount. Total shim thickness must be the same to maintain proper preload.

g. At the same time measure rotating resistance of drive pinion. Compare with resistance when differential case was not installed, if the increase in resistance is not within

Part No.	Thickness In In. (mm)
383705200	.1020 (2.59)
383715200	.1012 (2.57)
383725200	.1004 (2.55)
383735200	.0996 (2.53)
383745200	.0988 (2.51)
383755200	.0980 (2.49)
383765200	.0972 (2.47)
383775200	.0965 (2.45)
383785200	.0957 (2.43)
383795200	.0949 (2.41)
383805200	.0941 (2.39)
383815200	.0933 (2.37)
383825200	.0925 (2.35)
383835200	.0917 (2.33)
383845200	.0909 (2.31)

SB3039100009000X

Fig. 6 Pinion bearing preload adjustment washer identification chart

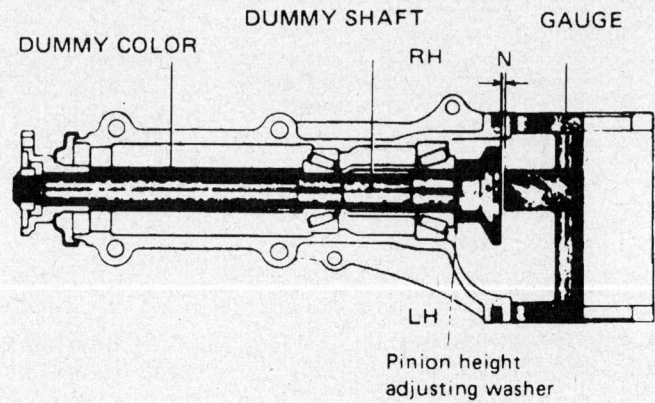

SB3039100010000X

Fig. 7 Installation position of tools for adjusting drive pinion height

Part No.	Thickness In In. (mm)
383495200	.1217 (3.09)
383505200	.1228 (3.12)
383515200	.1240 (3.15)
383525200	.1252 (3.18)
383535200	.1264 (3.21)
383545200	.1276 (3.24)
383555200	.1287 (3.27)
383565200	.1299 (3.30)
383575200	.1311 (3.33)
383585200	.1323 (3.36)
383595200	.1335 (3.39)
383605200	.1346 (3.42)
383615200	.1358 (3.45)
383625200	.1370 (3.48)
383635200	.1382 (3.51)
383645200	.1394 (3.54)
383655200	.1406 (3.57)
383665200	.1417 (3.60)
383675200	.1429 (3.63)
383685200	.1441 (3.66)

SB3039100011000X

Fig. 8 Pinion height adjustment washer identification chart

.07–.43 ft. lbs., readjust side retainer shim.

h. Recheck backlash between drive gear and pinion after readjusting shims, **Fig. 15.**

i. Check drive gear runout and pinion and drive gear rotation for smoothness, **Fig. 16.**

7. Check and adjust tooth contact of drive gear, proceed as follows:

a. Apply red lead to both sides of three of four drive gear teeth.

b. Check the contact pattern after rotating drive gear several times. **Ensure red lead is completely removed after inspection.**

8. Using a suitable drift install oil seal and rear cover. **Apply chassis grease to seal lips before installation.**

9. After installation in vehicle, fill differential as described under "Maintenance." **Torque** differential assembly nut to 51–58 ft. lbs., propeller shaft flange yoke to companion flange to 13–18 ft. lbs. and spindle retaining bolt to 23.1–27 ft. lbs.

Part No.	Thickness In In. (mm)
383445201	.0295-.0315 (.75-.80)
383445202	.0315-.0335 (.80-.85)
383445203	.0335-.0354 (.85-.90)

SB3039100012000X

Fig. 9 Side gear thrust washer identification chart

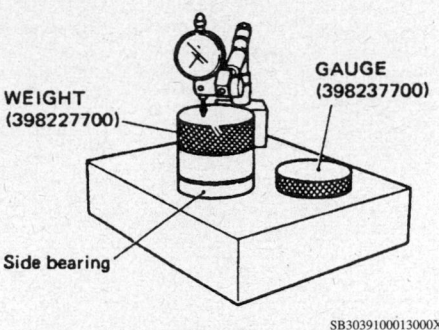

SB3039100013000X

Fig. 10 Side bearing width measurement

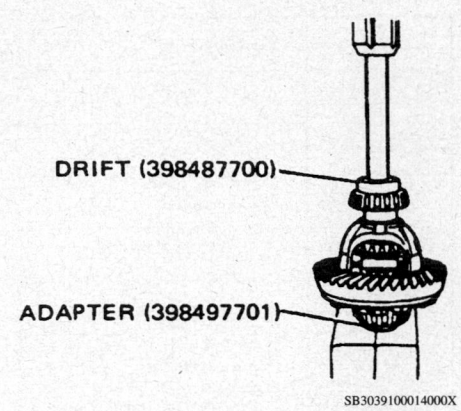

SB3039100014000X

Fig. 11 Side bearing Installation

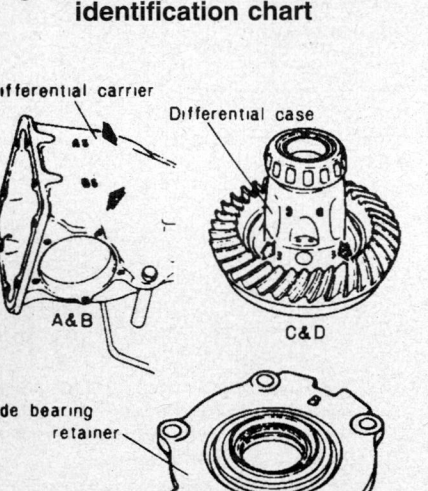

SB3039100015000X

Fig. 12 Differential markings positions

Part No.	Thickness In In. (mm)
383475201	.0079 (.20)
383475202	.0098 (.25)
383475203	.0118 (.30)
383475204	.0158 (.40)
383475205	.0197 (.50)

SB3039100016000X

Fig. 13 Side retainer adjustment shim identification chart

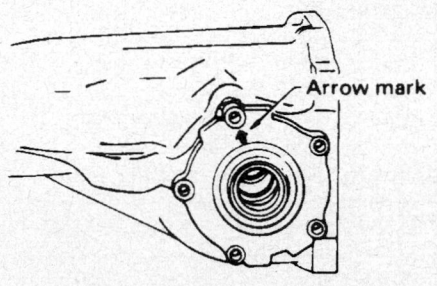

SB3039100017000X

Fig. 14 Side bearing retainer position

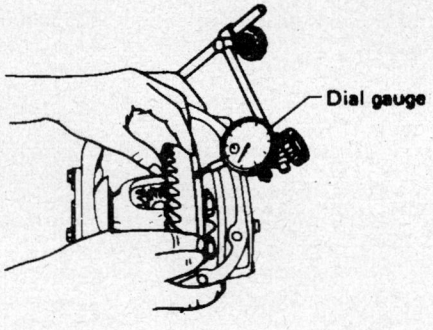

SB3039100019000X

Fig. 16 Runout measurement

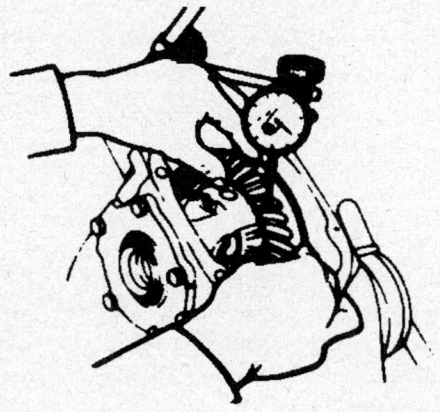

SB3039100018000X

Fig. 15 Backlash measurement

REAR AXLE IDENTIFICATION

Year	Model	Axle ID①	Gear Ratio
MANUAL TRANSMISSION			
1996–99	Forester	—	4.11
	Impreza	37/9	4.11
	Legacy	37/9	4.11
	SVX	39/11	3.50
AUTOMATIC TRANSMISSION			
1996–99	Forester	—	4.44
	Impreza	39/10	4.11
	Legacy	39/10	3.90
	SVX	39/11	3.50

① — Number of gear teeth.

SUBARU

Engine Rebuilding Specifications

INDEX

CYLINDER HEAD, VALVE GUIDE & VALVE SEATS

All measurements given in inches, unless otherwise specified.

Year	Engine, Liter	Cylinder Head			Valve Guides				Valve Seats		
		Warp-age Limit	Grind-ing Limit	Stand-ard Height	Stand-ard Inside Dia-meter	Protru-sion Above Head	Stem To Guide Clearance		Seat Angle Degrees	Seat Width	
							Intake	Exhaust		Intake	Exhaust
1996–99	1.8L	.0020	.0040	3.870	.2362-.2367	.6890-.7090	.0014-.0024	.0016-.0026	45	.028-.055	.055-.071
	2.2L	.0020	.0040	3.870	.2362-.2367	.689-.709	.0014-.0024	.0016-.0026	45	.020-.055	.055-.071
	2.5L	.0020	.012	5.02	.2362-.2368	.472-.488	.0014-.0024	.0016-.0026	45	.039-.067	.059-.087
	3.3L	.0020	.0118	5.020	.2362-.2367	.3350	.0012-.0022	.0016-.0026	45	.039-.067	.059-.087

VALVE SPRINGS

All measurements given in inches, unless otherwise specified.

Year	Engine, Liter	Free Length	Seated Pressure Pounds @ Inches	Compressed Pressure Pounds @ Inches	Out Of Square Limit
1996–99	1.8L	1.8173	42.8–49.4 lbs. @ 1.457	90.2–103.9 lbs. @ 1.150	.079
	2.2L	1.7342	39.2–45.0 lbs. @ 1.147	91.1–103.0 lbs. @ 1.110	.075
	2.5L	1.8913	32.9-37.7 lbs. @ 1.654	102.3-117.7 lbs. @ 1.315	.083
	3.3L	①	②	③	④

① — Inner, 1.374 inches; outer, 1.433 inches.
② — Inner, 13.2–15 lbs. @ 1.083 inches; outer, 28–32 lbs. @ 1.140 inches.
③ — Inner, 33.1–37.9 lbs. @ .772 inch; outer, 69.5–80 lbs. @ .831 inch.
④ — Inner, .059 inch; outer, .063 inch.

VALVES

All measurements given in inches, unless otherwise specified.

Year	Engine, Liter	Stem Diameter		Overall Length		Face Angle Degrees	Margin		Valve Clearance	
		Intake	Exhaust	Intake	Exhaust		Intake	Exhaust	Intake	Exhaust
1996–99	1.8L	.2343-.2348	.2341-.2346	3.9760	3.9840	45	.039	.047	①	①
	2.2L	.2343-.2348	.2341-.2346	3.9760	3.9840	45	.039	.047	①	①
	2.5L	.2343-.2348	.2343-.2348	4.1690	4.1810	45	—	—	①	①
	3.3L	.2344-.2350	.2341-.2346	3.5433	3.5768	45	.031	.039	①	①

① — Equipped w/hydraulic valve lash adjusters.

CAMSHAFT

All measurements given in inches, unless otherwise specified.

Year	Engine, Liter	Camshaft Journal Diameter	Bend Limit	Camshaft Bearing Clearance	Thrust Clearance	Cam Lobe Height	Valve Lash Adjuster		
							O.D.	Cylinder Head Adjuster Hole I.D.	Adjuster To Hole Clearance
1996–99	1.8L	①	.0010	.0022-.0035	.0012-.0102	1.2742-1.2781	②	—	—
	2.2L	①	.0010	.0022-.0035	.0012-.0102	③	②	—	—
	2.5L	⑦	.0008	.0015-.0028	.0016-.0031	⑧	1.2976-1.2982	1.2990-1.2998	.0007-.0022
	3.3L	④	.0008	.0015-.0028	⑤	⑥	1.2978-1.2982	1.2996-1.3004	.0011-.0031

① — Front, 1.2573–1.2579 inches; center, 1.4738–1.4744 inches; rear, 1.4935–1.4941 inches.

② — Valve rocker clearance between arm & shaft, .0008–.0021 inch.

③ — Intake, 1.2596–1.2635 inches; exhaust, 1.2844–1.2883 inches.

④ — No. 1, 1.2577–1.2584 inches; Nos. 2, 3 & 4, 1.1002–1.1009 inches.

⑤ — Intake, .0012–.0035 inch; exhaust, .0008–.0031 inch.

⑥ — Intake, 1.5374–1.5413 inches; exhaust, 1.5689–1.5728 inches.

⑦ — Front, 1.2577–1.2584 inches; center, 1.1002–1.1009 inches; rear, 1.1002–1.1009 inches.

⑧ — Intake, 1.6614–1.6654 inches; exhaust, 1.6732–1.6772 inches.

CRANKSHAFT, BEARINGS & RODS

All measurements given in inches, unless otherwise specified.

Year	Engine, Liter	Crankshaft				Bearing Clearance			Connecting Rods	
		Standard Diameter		Out Of Round, All	Taper, All	Main Bearings	Connecting Rod Bearings	Thrust Bearing Clearance	Pin Bore Diameter	Side Clearance
		Main Bearing	Crank Pin							
1996–99	1.8L	2.3616-2.3625	2.0466-2.0472	.0012	—	.0004-.0012	.0006-.0018	.0012-.0045	—	.0028-.0130
	2.2L	2.3616-2.3625	2.0466-2.0472	.0012	—	.0004-.0012	.0006-.0018	.0012-.0045	—	.0028-.0130
	2.5L	2.3619-2.3625	1.8891-1.8898	.0008	—	②	.0004-.0015	.0012-.0045	—	.0028-.0130
	3.3L	2.3619-2.3625	2.0466-2.0472	.0012	.0028	①	.0008-.0018	.0012-.0045	—	.0028-.0130

① — No. 1-3-7, .0002–.0014 inch; No. 2-4-6, .0005–.0015 inch; No. 5, .0005–.0013 inch.

② — Nos. 1 & 5, .0001–.0012 inch; Nos. 2, 3 & 4, .0004–.0013 inch.

PISTONS, PINS & RINGS

All measurements given in inches, unless otherwise specified.

Year	Engine, Liter	Piston Std. Diameter	Piston Clearance	Piston Pin Diameter	Piston Pin To Piston Clearance	Piston Ring End Gap		Piston Ring Side Clearance	
						Comp.	Oil	Comp.	Oil
1996–99	1.8L	①	.0004–.0012	—	.0002–.0004	.0079–.0138	.0079–.0276	②	—
	2.2L	③	.0004–.0012	—	.0002–.0004	.0079–.0138	.0079–.0276	②	—
	2.5L	⑥	.0004–.0012	—	.0002–.0004	⑦	.0079–.0236	⑧	—
	3.3L	③	.0004–.0012	—	.0002–.0003	④	.0079–.0236	⑤	—

① — Grade size symbol A, 3.4600–3.4604 inches; symbol B, 3.4596–3.4600 inches; symbol C, 3.4592–3.4596 inches.

② — Top ring, .0016–.0031 inch; second ring, .0012–.0028 inch.

③ — Grade size symbol A, 3.8144–3.8148 inches; symbol B, 3.8140–3.8144 inches; symbol C, 3.8136–3.8140 inches.

④ — Top ring, .0079–.0118 inch; 2nd ring, .0146–.0205 inch.

⑤ — Top ring, .0016–.0035 inch; 2nd ring, .0012–.0028 inch.

⑥ — Grade A, 3.9167–3.9171 inches; grade B, , 3.9163–3.9167 inches.

⑦ — Top ring, .0079–.0138 inch; second ring, .0146–.0205 inch.

⑧ — Top ring, .0016–.0031 inch; second ring, .0012–.0028 inch.

CYLINDER BLOCK

All measurements given in inches, unless otherwise specified.

Year	Engine, Liter	Bore Diameter			Cylinder Bore Taper Max.	Cylinder Bore Out Of Round Max.
		Symbol A	Symbol B	Symbol C		
1996–99	1.8L	3.4608–3.4612	3.4604–3.4608	3.4600–3.4604	.0020	.0020
	2.2L	3.8151–3.8155	3.8148–3.8151	3.8144–3.8148	.0020	.0020
	2.5L	3.9175-3.9179	3.9171-3.9175	—	.0020	.0020
	3.3L	3.8151–3.8155	3.8148–3.8151	3.8144–3.8148	.0020	.0020

OIL PUMP

All measurements given in inches, unless otherwise specified.

| Year | Engine Liter | Rotor | | | | Height Of Oil Pump Case Protrusion, Inch | Side Clearance Between Rotor & Crankcase, Inch | Case Clearance Between Rotor & Crankcase, Inch | Relief Valve Spring, Inch |
		Inner Rotor O.D.	Outer Rotor O.D.	Height	Housing Depth				
1996–99	1.8L	—	3.07	—	—	—	.0008-.0028	.0039-.0069	—
	2.2L	—	3.07	—	—	—	.0008-.0028	.0039-.0069	—
	2.5L	—	3.07	.39	—	—	.0008-.0028	.0039-.0069	—
	3.3L	—	3.07	—	—	—	.0008-.0028	.0039-.0069	①

① — Free length, 2.902 inches; installed length, 2.154 inches; load when installed, 20.9 lbs.

GENERAL INFORMATION

Manual Information Locator, Inside Rear Cover

GENERAL INFORMATION

Specifications

GENERAL ENGINE SPECIFICATIONS

Year	Engine, Liter	Fuel System	Bore & Stroke Inch (mm)	Compression Ratio	Maximum Brake HP @ RPM	Maximum Torque Ft. Lbs. @ RPM	Normal Oil Pressure, psi @ 4000 RPM
1996-99	1.3L	TBI	2.91 X 2.97 (74 X 75.5)	9.5	70 @ 5500	74 @ 3000	47-61
	1.6L	MPI	2.95 X 3.54 (75 X 90)	9.5	95 @ 5600	98 @ 4000	47–61
	1.8L	MPI	3.31 X 3.27 (84 X 83)	9.8	120 @ 6500	114 @ 3500	55-67
	2.5L	MPI	3.31 X 2.95	9.5	155 @ 6500	160 @ 4000	55-67

TUNE UP SPECIFICATIONS

Year & Engine	Spark Plug Gap Inch	Ignition Timing — Firing Order Fig.②	Ignition Timing — Timing ° BTDC	Ignition Timing — Timing Mark	Curb Idle Speed③ — Man. Trans.	Curb Idle Speed③ — Auto. Trans.	Fast Idle Speed	Fuel Pressure psi	Valve Lash⑨ — Intake	Valve Lash⑨ — Exhaust
1996–99 ESTEEM										
1.6L	.029	1-3-4-2	5①	D	700-800	750-850	⑦	38-44	.0050-.0070	.0070-.0080
1996–98 SIDEKICK										
1.6L	.029	1-3-4-2	5⑤	B	750-850	800-1050	⑦	36-42	.0070-.0080	.0070-.0080
1.8L	.029	1-3-4-2	5④	C	800/1000	800-1000	⑦	34–39	⑧	⑧
1996–99 SWIFT										
1.3L	.041	1-3-4-2	5⑥	A	700-950	800-950	⑦	34-40	.0090-.0110	.0102-.0118
1996–98 X-90										
1.6L	.029	1-3-4-2	5⑤	B	800-1000	800-1000	⑦	34-39	.0070-.0080	.0070-.0080
1999 GRAND VITARA										
2.5L	.041	1-6-5-4-3-2	5	-	800/1000	800/1000	⑦	34–39	⑧	⑧

BTDC — Before Top Dead Center

① — Connect jumper wire between terminals D & E of diagnostic connector No. 1. The diagnostic connector is located on the lefthand side of the engine compartment, in the engine compartment relay box.

② — Before disconnecting spark plug wires from distributor cap, determine location of number 1 wire in cap, as distributor position may have been altered from that shown.

③ — Highest idle speeds listed are with idle-up actuator energized. When adjusting idle speed, set parking brake & chock drive wheels.

④ — Remove cap from monitor coupler & connect jumper wire between terminals 3 & 4 of connector. The monitor coupler is located on the lefthand side of the engine compartment.

⑤ — Remove cap from monitor coupler & connect jumper wire between terminals D & E of connector. The monitor coupler is located in the engine compartment, next to the battery.

⑥ — Remove cap from monitor coupler & connect jumper wire between terminals C & D of connector. The monitor coupler is located in the engine compartment, next to the ignition coil.

⑦ — Controlled by idle air control valve.

⑧ — Equipped with hydraulic lash adjusters, no adjustment is necessary.

⑨ — Measure valve lash with engine at operation temperature.

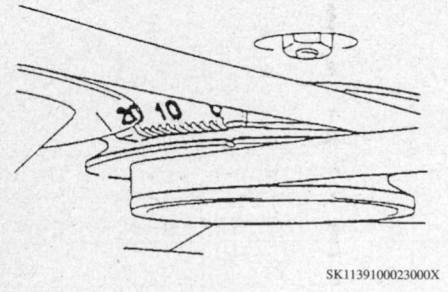

Fig. A

SK1139100023000X

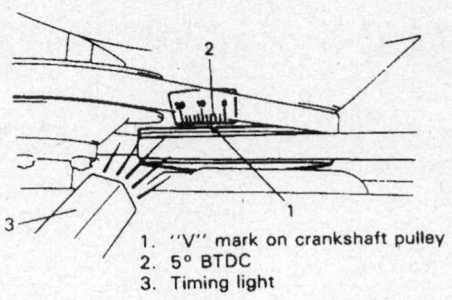

1. "V" mark on crankshaft pulley
2. 5° BTDC
3. Timing light

SK1139400061000X

Fig. B

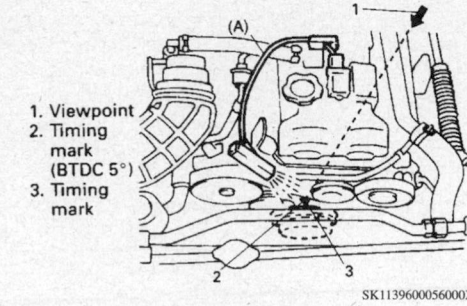

1. Viewpoint
2. Timing mark (BTDC 5°)
3. Timing mark

SK1139600056000X

Fig. C

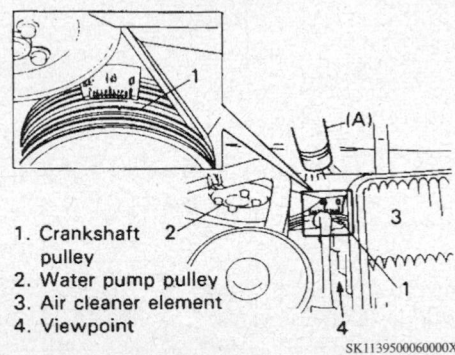

1. Crankshaft pulley
2. Water pump pulley
3. Air cleaner element
4. Viewpoint

SK1139500060000X

Fig. D

FRONT WHEEL ALIGNMENT SPECIFICATIONS

Year	Model	Caster Angle, Degrees		Camber Angles, Degrees		Toe, Inch①	Kingpin Inclination, Degrees		Ball Joint Wear
		Limits	Desired	Limits	Desired		Limits	Desired	
1996–99	Grand Vitara	+1⅔ to 3⅔	+2⅔	- 1 to + 1	0	-.080 to + .080	—	—	②
	Sidekick	+½ to +2½	+1½	−½ to +1½	+½	+.080 to +.240	—	—	②
	Swift	+1 to +5	+3	−1 to +1	0	−.079 to +.079	9¹¹⁄₁₂ to 15¹¹⁄₁₂	12¹¹⁄₁₂	②
	Esteem	+1 to +5	+3	-1 to +1	0	−.079 to +.079	9⁷⁄₁₂ to 15⁷⁄₁₂	12⁷⁄₁₂	②
	X-90	+½ to +2½	+1½	-½ to +1½	+½	+.080 to +.240	—	—	②

① — Toe-in (+); toe-out (-).

② — Refer to "Ball Joint Inspection" in "Front Suspension & Steering" section.

REAR WHEEL ALIGNMENT SPECIFICATIONS

Year	Model	Toe, Inch①
1996–99	Swift	0 to +.158
	Esteem	-.079 to +.079

① — Toe-in (+); toe-out (-).

FLUID CAPACITIES & COOLING SYSTEM DATA

| Year | Model | Coolant System Capacity Qts. | Radiator Cap Relief Pressure psi | Thermo. Open Temp. °F | Fuel Tank Gals. | Engine Oil Qts.① | Transmission | | Differ-ential |
							Man. Trans. Pts.	Auto. Trans. Refill Qts.②	
1996–99	Esteem	4.8	12.8	190	13.5	3.3	5	5.7	—
	Grand Vitara	8.5	12.8	190	17.4	5.2	5.8	7.5	—
	Sidekick	5.5	12.8	179	14.5	4.4	③	⑤	④
	Sidekick Sport	6.9	12.8	179	18.5	5.3	③	6.5	④
	Swift	4.9	12.8	190	10.6	3.5	5	5.2	—
	Swift GT	4.9	12.8	179	10.6	3.5	4.7	5.4	—
	X-90	5.3	12.8	190	14.5	4.3	③	⑤	④

① — Includes filter.
② — Approximate, make final check with dipstick.

③ — 2WD, 4 pts.; 4WD, transmission, 3.2 pts., transfer, 3.6 pts.
④ — Front, 2.1 pts.; rear, 4.6 pts.

⑤ — 2.6 qts. for pan removal; 7.3 qts. for overhaul.

LUBRICANT DATA

| Year | Lubricant Type | | | | | |
| | Transmission | | Transfer Case | Rear Axle | Power Steering | Brake System |
	Manual	Automatic				
1996–99	75W-90	Dexron III	75W-90	75W-90	Dexron III	DOT 3

Electrical

NOTE: On Air Bag Equipped Models, Refer To "Air Bag System Precautions" Located In The Front Of This Manual For System Disarming & Arming Procedures.

INDEX

PRECAUTIONS

AIR BAG SYSTEMS

Refer to "Air Bag System Precautions" in the front of this manual for system disarming and arming procedures.

BATTERY GROUND CABLE

Prior to service, disconnect battery ground cable and isolate as required.

SUZUKI

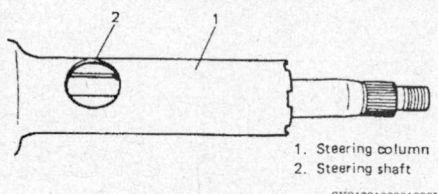

Fig. 1 Ignition lock/switch installation

SK9129100001000X

FUEL PUMP RELAY LOCATION

ESTEEM

The fuel pump relay is located in the relay box on the lefthand side of the engine compartment.

GRAND VITARA

The fuel pump relay is located below the instrument panel on the lefthand side next to the fuse box.

SWIFT

The fuel pump relay is located on the lefthand side of the engine compartment.

SIDEKICK & X-90

The fuel pump relay is located behind the center of the instrument panel, on the heater unit.

FUSE PANEL & FLASHER LOCATION

The fuse panel and flasher are located under the lefthand side of the instrument panel.

STARTER
REPLACE

1. Disconnect solenoid electrical connector and battery cable from starter terminals.
2. Remove two starter motor attaching bolts, then the starter.
3. Reverse procedure to install.

DISTRIBUTOR
REPLACE
SIDEKICK & X-90 w/1.6L ENGINE

1. Disconnect distributor electrical connector.
2. Remove distributor cap, then turn crankshaft clockwise until rotor is positioned at No. 1 terminal of cap.
3. Remove distributor flange bolt, then the distributor assembly.
4. Apply engine oil to distributor O-ring, then align punch mark on gear with "V" mark on housing.
5. Insert distributor into case ensuring center of distributor flange coincides with flange bolt hole provided in gear

case. When inserting distributor completely, rotor should be in one o'clock position.
6. Install distributor cap, then connect distributor electrical connector.

SWIFT

1. Disconnect vacuum hose.
2. Disconnect electrical connectors, then remove distributor cap.
3. Remove hold-down bolts, then the distributor.
4. Reverse procedure to install, noting the following:
   a. Fit dogs of distributor coupling into slots of camshaft.
   b. If dogs cannot be fit into slots, turn distributor shaft 180°.

ESTEEM

1. Disconnect electrical connectors, then remove distributor cap.
2. Remove flange bolts, then the distributor.
3. Reverse procedure to install, noting the following:
   a. Fit dogs of distributor coupling into slots of camshaft.
   b. If dogs cannot be fit into slots, turn distributor shaft 180°.
   c. Check and adjust ignition timing.

IGNITION COIL
REPLACE

1. Remove ignition coil cover.
2. Remove ignition coil retaining bolt, then the coil from the spark plug.
3. Reverse procedure to install.

IGNITION LOCK
REPLACE

Refer to "Ignition Switch, Replace" for replacement procedure.

IGNITION SWITCH
REPLACE

1. Remove steering wheel as outlined under "Steering Wheel, Replace."
2. Remove combination switch as outlined under "Combination Switch, Replace."
3. Remove steering column from vehicle as follows:
   a. Disconnect all electrical connectors from steering column.
   b. **On Swift models,** remove steering shaft joint cover.
   c. **On all models,** disconnect steering joint by removing joint bolt.
   d. Remove steering column mounting bolts.
   e. **On Swift models with automatic transaxle,** remove back drive cable from column assembly.
   f. **On all models,** remove steering column from vehicle.
4. Using center punch, remove steering lock/switch mounting bolts. Use care not to damage aluminum part of steering lock/switch body.
5. Turn ignition key to ACC or ON posi-

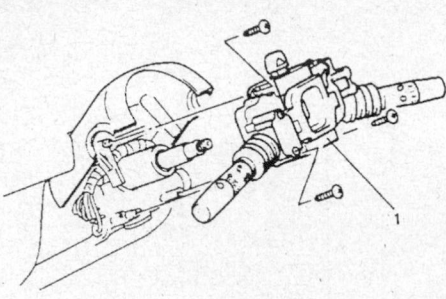

1. Combination switch

SK9049100001000X

Fig. 2 Combination switch replacement

tion, then remove lock/switch assembly from steering column.
6. Install ignition lock/switch to steering column as follows:
   a. Position oblong hole of steering shaft in center of hole in column, **Fig. 1.**
   b. Turn ignition key to ACC or ON position, then install lock/switch assembly onto column.
   c. Turn ignition key to LOCK position, then remove key.
   d. Align hub on lock/switch with oblong hole of steering shaft. Ensure steering shaft is locked.
   e. Tighten bolts until heads of bolts twist off.
   f. Using ignition key, ensure smooth operation of steering shaft.
7. Reverse steps 1 through 3 to complete assembly.

COMBINATION SWITCH
REPLACE

1. Remove steering wheel as outlined under "Steering Wheel, Replace."
2. Remove steering column covers.
3. Disconnect lead wire at coupler from combination switch.
4. Remove combination switch attaching bolts, then the switch **Fig. 2.**
5. Reverse procedure to install.

STEERING WHEEL
REPLACE

1. Disarm and remove air bag module from steering wheel as outlined in "Air Bag System."
2. Remove steering wheel shaft nut.
3. Scribe alignment marks on steering wheel and shaft for installation reference.
4. Remove steering wheel with suitable puller.
5. Reverse procedure to install, noting the following:
   a. Align marks on shaft and steering wheel.
   b. **Torque** shaft nut to 25 ft. lbs.

INSTRUMENT CLUSTER
REPLACE
EXCEPT GRAND VITARA

1. Remove steering wheel trim panels.

1. Blower motor unit
2. Blower motor resistor
3. Control relay
4. Blower fan
5. Motor assembly

SK7029600044000X

Fig. 3   Exploded view of blower motor assembly. Esteem

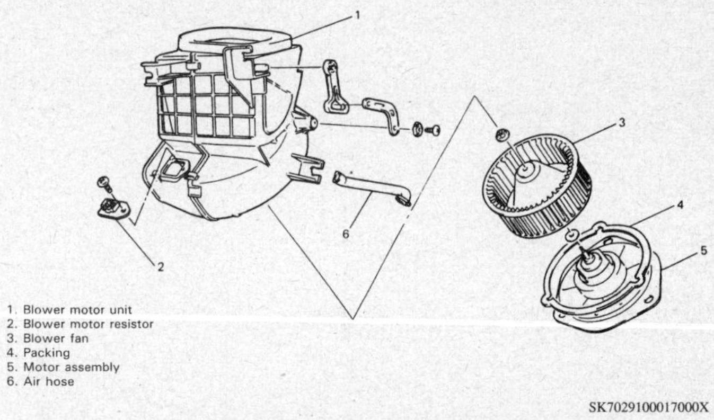

1. Blower motor unit
2. Blower motor resistor
3. Blower fan
4. Packing
5. Motor assembly
6. Air hose

SK7029100017000X

Fig. 4   Exploded view of blower motor assembly. Sidekick, Swift & X-90

2. Lower steering column.
3. Remove instrument panel cluster bezel attaching screws and bezel.
4. Disconnect speedometer cable and wire harness electrical connector, then remove instrument cluster.
5. Reverse procedure to install.

GRAND VITARA

1. Remove column hole cover.
2. Remove instrument cluster trim panel.
3. Remove screws attaching cluster to dash panel, then disconnect couplers from cluster.
4. Remove cluster from dash panel.
5. Reverse procedure to install.

WIPER MOTOR

REPLACE

FRONT

1. Disconnect linkage assembly from wiper motor shaft.
2. Disconnect electrical connectors from wiper motor.
3. Remove wiper motor attaching bolts, then the wiper motor.

REAR

1. Remove wiper blade and arm assembly.
2. Remove access panel on back door.
3. Disconnect linkage assembly from wiper motor shaft.
4. Disconnect electrical connectors from wiper motor.
5. Remove wiper motor attaching bolts, then the wiper motor.

BLOWER MOTOR

REPLACE

ESTEEM

1. Disarm and remove air bag modules as outlined under "Precautions."
2. Remove glove compartment and holder stay.
3. Remove engine control module (ECM) and instrument panel lower member.
4. Disconnect all electrical connectors from blower motor.

5. Disconnect fresh air control cable from blower motor case.
6. Remove blower motor attaching bolts, then the blower motor, **Fig. 3.**
7. Reverse procedure to install.

GRAND VITARA

1. Remove ECM with bracket from blower motor unit.
2. Disconnect harness clamps from dash panel.
3. Remove three blower motor attaching screws, then disconnect electrical connector.
4. Remove blower motor.
5. Reverse procedure to install.

SIDEKICK, SWIFT & X-90

1. Disarm and remove air bag module from steering wheel as outlined under "Precautions."
2. Remove glove compartment and holder stay.
3. Disconnect all electrical connectors from blower motor.
4. Disconnect fresh air control cable from blower motor case.
5. Remove blower motor attaching bolts, then the blower motor **Fig. 4.**
6. Reverse procedure to install.

HEATER CORE

REPLACE

ESTEEM

Refer to "Blower Motor, Replace," for heater core replacement procedure.

GRAND VITARA

1. Drain engine coolant into suitable container, then disconnect heater hoses from heater core.
2. Remove instrument panel as outlined in "Dash Panel" section.
3. **On models equipped with A/C,** remove cooling unit as outlined under "Evaporator, Replace."
4. **On all models,** disconnect rear duct from heater unit.
5. Disconnect mode actuator lead wires at coupler.

6. **On models equipped with A/C,** remove A/C control unit.
7. **On all models,** remove SDM.
8. Remove heater unit.
9. Remove heater core pipe clamps and grommet.
10. Remove heater core from unit.
11. Reverse procedure to install.

SIDEKICK & X-90

1. Drain radiator into suitable container and disconnect water hoses from heater core.
2. Remove instrument panel assembly as outlined under "Dash Panel Service."
3. Remove heater case attaching bolts.
4. Remove heater core from heater unit, **Fig. 5.**
5. Reverse procedure to install.

SWIFT

1. Drain radiator into suitable container and disconnect water hoses from heater core.
2. Disconnect all wires and cables from heater and blower units.
3. Remove steering wheel and steering column as outlined under "Ignition Switch & Lock Assembly, Replace."
4. Disconnect speedometer cable, then remove speedometer assembly.
5. Remove both front speaker garnishes and center cover.
6. Remove instrument panel member mounting bolts.
7. Remove instrument panel and panel member as an assembly.
8. Remove heater unit, **Fig. 6.**
9. Remove heater unit clips and screws, then separate heater unit.
10. Remove heater core from heater unit.
11. Reverse procedure to install.

EVAPORATOR CORE

REPLACE

ESTEEM

1. Remove air bag module from steering wheel as outlined under "Air Bag System."
2. Recover refrigerant from A/C system. **Care should be taken to avoid excess compressor oil discharge with refrigerant.**

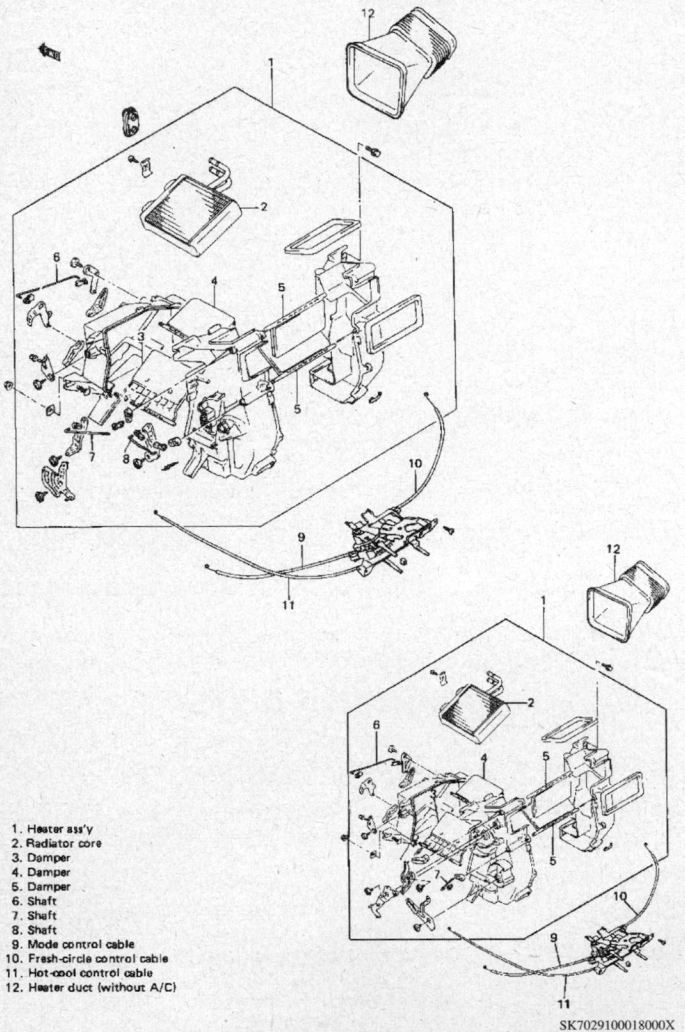

1. Heater ass'y
2. Radiator core
3. Damper
4. Damper
5. Damper
6. Shaft
7. Shaft
8. Shaft
9. Mode control cable
10. Fresh-circle control cable
11. Hot-cool control cable
12. Heater duct (without A/C)

SK7029100018000X

Fig. 5 Exploded view of heater unit. Sidekick & X-90

1. Heater case
2. Damper
3. Heater core
4. Heater case
5. Control lever
6. Control shaft

SK7029100019000X

Fig. 6 Exploded view of heater unit. Swift

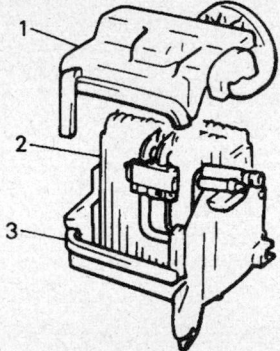

1. Upper case
2. Evaporator
3. Lower case

SK7029600045000X

Fig. 7 Evaporator case separation. Esteem

3. Remove blower motor unit as outlined in "Blower Motor, Replace".
4. Disconnect A/C amplifier and thermistor wire connectors.
5. Disconnect compressor suction hose and receiver/dryer outlet hose from cooling unit fittings. **Cap all opened fittings to prevent moisture from entering A/C system.**
6. Remove evaporator case, then the evaporator unit.
7. Remove case clamps, then separate evaporator case halves, **Fig. 7.**
8. Remove evaporator core attaching screws, then the evaporator core.
9. Reverse procedure to install.

GRAND VITARA

1. Recover refrigerant from A/C system. **Care should be taken to avoid excess compressor oil discharge with refrigerant.**
2. Disconnect compressor suction pipe and receiver/dryer outlet pipe from cooling unit.
3. Remove blower motor as outlined under "Blower Motor, Replace."
4. Disconnect thermistor wire coupler.
5. Remove evaporator with case.
6. Separate evaporator case halves, then remove evaporator.
7. Reverse procedure to install.

SIDEKICK, SWIFT & X-90

1. Disarm and remove air bag modules as outlined under " Precautions."
2. Recover refrigerant from A/C system. **Care should be taken to avoid excess compressor oil discharge with refrigerant.**
3. Remove all electrical connectors and fresh air control cable from blower motor.
4. Remove glove compartment, blower motor and heater to evaporator connecting band.
5. **On Swift models,** disconnect A/C amplifier connector.
6. **On all models,** disconnect thermistor wire connector.
7. Disconnect compressor suction hose and receiver/dryer outlet hose from cooling unit fittings. **Cap all opened fittings to prevent moisture from entering A/C system.**
8. Remove evaporator case attaching bracket, then the evaporator unit.
9. Remove case clamps, then separate evaporator case halves, **Fig. 8.**
10. Remove evaporator core attaching screws, then the evaporator core.
11. Reverse procedure to install.

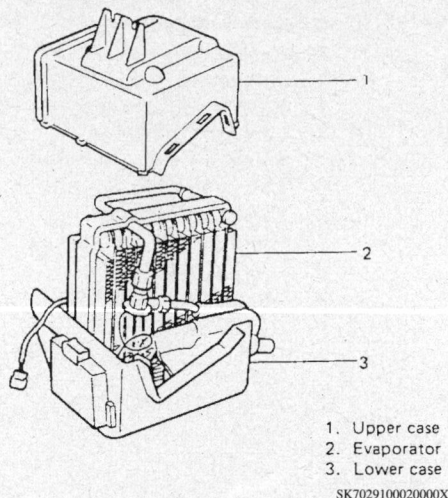

1. Upper case
2. Evaporator
3. Lower case

SK7029100020000X

Fig. 8 Evaporator case separation. Sidekick, X-90 & Swift

1.3L Engine

NOTE: On Air Bag Equipped Models, Refer To "Air Bag System Precautions" Located In The Front Of This Manual For System Disarming & Arming Procedures.

INDEX

PRECAUTIONS

AIR BAG SYSTEMS

Refer to "Air Bag System Precautions" in the front of this manual for system disarming and arming procedures.

FUEL SYSTEM PRESSURE RELIEF

1. Place manual transaxle models in Neutral or automatic transaxle models in Park, then set parking brake and block drive wheels.
2. Remove main fuse box cover and engine cooling water reservoir.
3. Detach main fuse box from body and disconnect coupler from fuel pump relay, **Fig. 1.**
4. Remove fuel filler cap to release fuel vapor pressure in tank, then install cap.
5. Start and run engine until it stalls. Repeat cranking engine three times for three seconds each time to dissipate fuel pressure in fuel lines.

BATTERY GROUND CABLE

Prior to service, disconnect battery ground cable and isolate as required.

COMPRESSION PRESSURE

Standard compression pressure is 199 psi with a minimum of 154 psi. Maximum allowable difference between cylinders is 14.2 psi.

ENGINE

REPLACE

1. Relieve fuel system pressure as outlined under " Precautions."

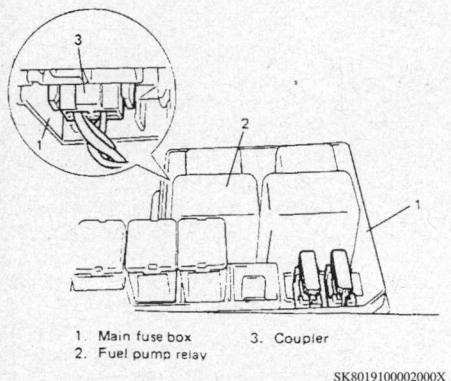

1. Main fuse box
2. Fuel pump relay
3. Coupler

SK8019100002000X

Fig. 1 Fuel pump relay coupler location

2. Remove battery and tray, then the engine hood.
3. Drain coolant system into appropriate container.
4. Remove air cleaner assembly with Air Flow Meter (AFM) outlet hose.
5. Remove radiator cooling fan, then the battery ground cable from transaxle.
6. Disconnect following electrical wires:
   a. **On models equipped with automatic transaxles,** disconnect direct clutch and second brake connectors.
   b. Disconnect shift switch and speed sensor connectors.
   c. **On models equipped with manual transaxles,** disconnect back-up light switch connector.
   d. **On all models,** disconnect noise filter ground wire, then the Idle Speed Control (ISC) valve connector.
   e. Disconnect high tension cable from ignition coil, then the distributor Crank Angle Sensor (CAS) connector.
   f. **On models equipped with California emissions,** disconnect Recirculated Exhaust Gas Temperature Sensor (REGTS) and Exhaust Gas Recirculation Vacuum Switching Valve (EGR VSV) connectors.
   g. **On all models,** disconnect Water Temperature Sensor (WTS) and oxygen sensor connectors.
   h. Disconnect canister purge VSV connector, then the ground wire from intake manifold.
   i. Disconnect Throttle Position Sensor (TPS) and fuel injector connectors.
   j. Disconnect all electrical wires from alternator and starter.
   k. Disconnect oil pressure gauge connector.
   l. Ensure all wires are free of clamps on engine.
7. Disconnect following cables:
   a. Disconnect accelerator cable from throttle lever and bracket.
   b. **On models equipped with manual transaxle,** disconnect clutch cable.
   c. **On models equipped with automatic transaxle,** disconnect gear

1. Rear torque rod
2. Rear torque rod bracket
3. Torque rod stiffener
4. Left mounting body bracket
5. Left mounting
6. Left mounting bracket
7. Right mounting bracket
8. Right mounting
9. Rear mounting bracket
10. Rear mounting
11. Rear mounting body No. 1 bracket
12. Rear mounting body No. 2 bracket

Tightening torque
(A) 50 – 60 N·m
5.0 – 6.0 kg-m
36.5 – 43.0 lb-ft

(B) 40 – 50 N·m
4.0 – 5.0 kg-m
29.0 – 36.0 lb-ft

(C) 18 – 28 N·m
1.8 – 2.8 kg-m
13.5 – 20.0 lb-ft

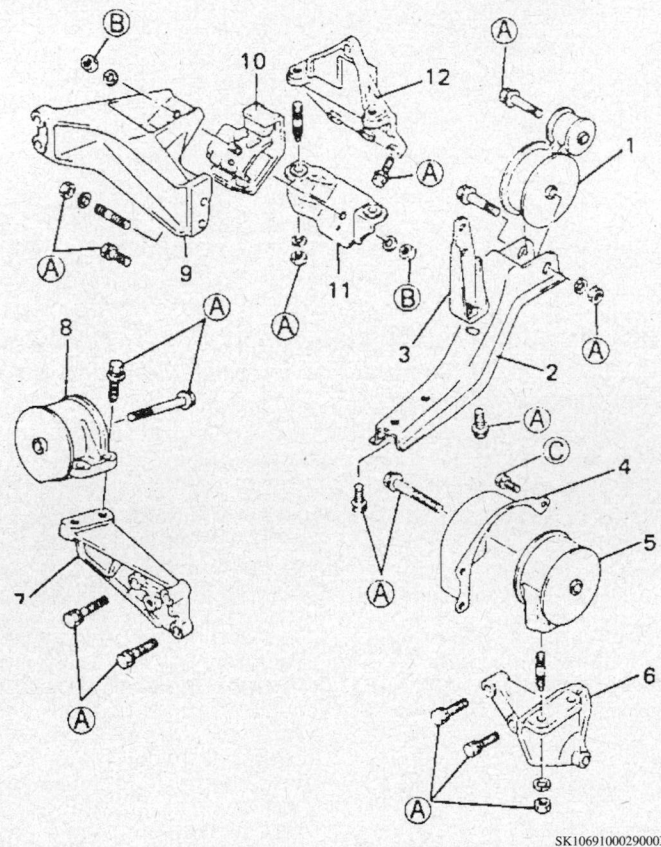

SK1069100029000X

Fig. 2 Exploded view of engine mounting. Automatic transaxle

select and oil pressure control cables.
   d. **On all models,** disconnect speed meter cable from transaxle.
8. Disconnect brake booster and canister purge hoses.
9. **On models equipped with California emissions,** disconnect A/C VSV hose.
10. **On all models,** disconnect fuel feed and return hoses.
11. Disconnect heater inlet and outlet hoses, then remove charcoal canister from body.
12. Raise and support vehicle, then remove exhaust pipe from manifold.
13. **On models equipped with manual transaxle,** remove gear shift control shaft and extension rod.
14. **On all models,** drain engine and tran-

saxle oil into appropriate container.
15. Remove lefthand driveshaft joint from differential gear of transaxle. Remove righthand driveshaft joint from center bearing support.
16. **On models equipped with automatic transaxle,** remove rear torque rod bracket from transaxle case.
17. **On all models,** lower vehicle, then install engine lifting device.
18. **On models equipped with manual transaxle,** remove rear mounting from body. On automatic transaxle, remove rear mounting nut, **Figs. 2 and 3.**
19. **On all models,** remove lefthand side engine mounting bracket bolts and mounting bolt.
20. Remove righthand side engine mounting from bracket.

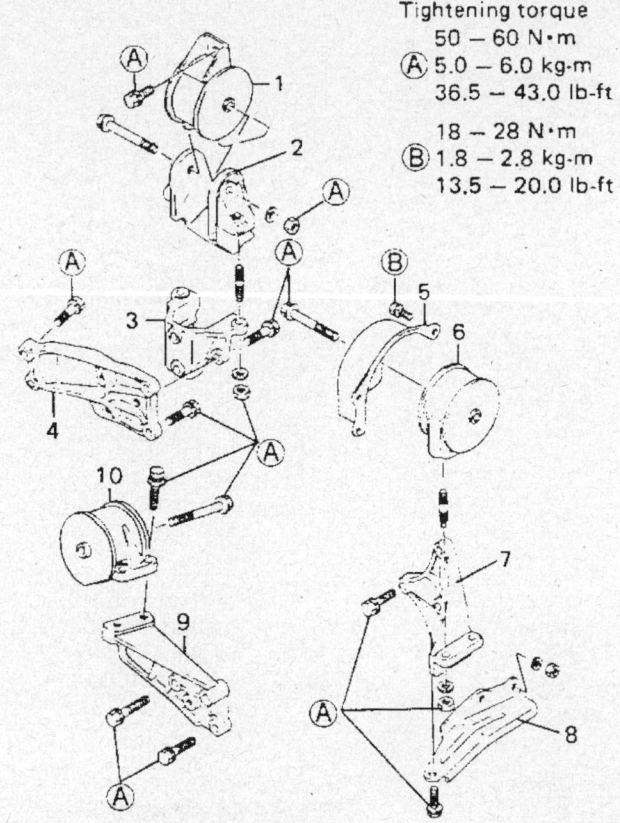

Tightening torque
50 — 60 N·m
Ⓐ 5.0 — 6.0 kg·m
36.5 — 43.0 lb-ft

18 — 28 N·m
Ⓑ 1.8 — 2.8 kg·m
13.5 — 20.0 lb-ft

1. Rear mounting	5. Left mounting body bracket
2. Rear mounting No. 2 bracket	6. Left mounting
3. Rear mounting No. 1 bracket	7. Left mounting bracket
	8. Stiffener
4. Rear mounting bracket	9. Right mounting bracket
	10. Right mounting

SK1069100030000X

Fig. 3   Exploded view of engine mounting. Manual transaxle

21. **Ensure all hoses, electric wires and cable are disconnected from engine and transaxle.**
22. Remove engine and transaxle from vehicle.
23. Remove torque convertor housing lower plate.
24. Remove driveplate bolts. Use flat head screwdriver to lock driveplate and driveplate gear.
25. Remove engine to transaxle attaching bolts, then separate engine from transaxle.
26. Reverse procedure to install, tighten all bolts and nuts to specification.

INTAKE MANIFOLD
REPLACE

1. Drain coolant system into appropriate container.
2. Remove air cleaner.
3. Disconnect the following electrical connectors:

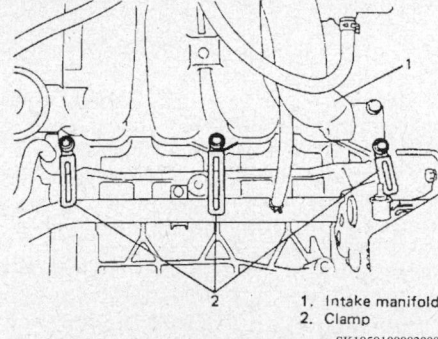

1. Intake manifold
2. Clamp

SK1059100002000X

Fig. 5   Intake manifold clamps replacement

a. ISC solenoid valve and radiator cooling fan thermo switch.
b. **On models equipped with California emissions,** EGR vacuum switching valve.

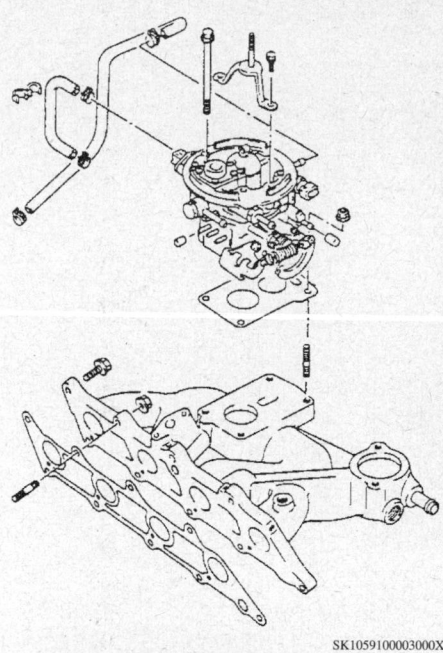

SK1059100003000X

Fig. 4   Throttle body & intake manifold replacement

   c. **On all models,** TPS, then the ground wires from intake manifold.
   d. Water temperature sensor and gauge, then the fuel injector.
4. Disconnect the following hoses:
   a. Vacuum advance from distributor, then the PCV.
   b. Power steering and brake booster from intake manifold.
   c. **On models equipped with California emissions,** EGR modulator and EGR VSV.
   d. **On all models,** canister purge from intake manifold and pipe.
   e. Fuel feed and return from throttle body.
5. Remove accelerator cable from throttle body.
6. Remove cooling water hoses from intake manifold and throttle body.
7. Remove intake manifold with throttle body from cylinder head, **Fig. 4.**
8. Reverse procedure to install, noting the following:
   a. Use new gasket on intake manifold to cylinder head.
   b. Install clamps on manifold, **Fig. 5.**
   c. Tighten bolts and nuts to specification.

EXHAUST MANIFOLD
REPLACE

1. Disconnect oxygen sensor coupler, then release sensor wire from clamps.
2. Remove exhaust manifold cover and manifold stiffener bolt.
3. Remove exhaust pipe from manifold.
4. Remove exhaust manifold and gasket from cylinder head, **Fig. 6.**
5. Reverse procedure to install, noting the following:

SUZUKI

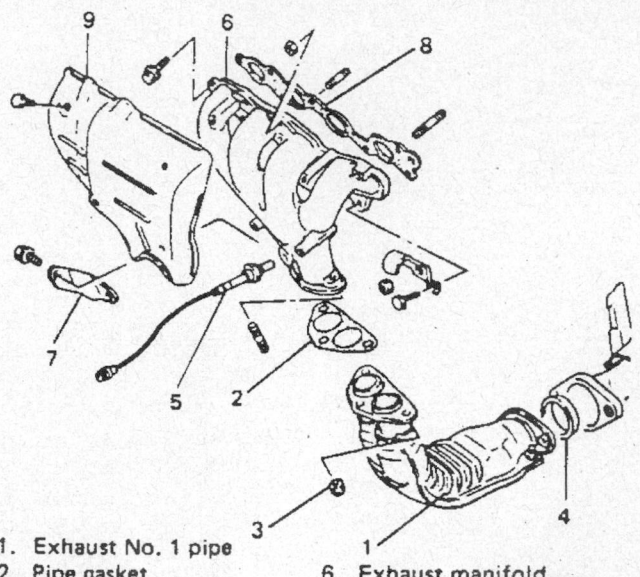

1. Exhaust No. 1 pipe
2. Pipe gasket
3. Pipe nut
4. Pipe seal
5. Oxygen sensor
6. Exhaust manifold
7. Exhaust manifold stiffener
8. Exhaust manifold gasket
9. Exhaust manifold cover

SK1079100001000X

Fig. 6 Exploded view of exhaust manifold

a. Inspect gasket for deterioration or damage, replace as necessary.
b. Tighten bolts and nuts to specification.

CYLINDER HEAD
REPLACE
REMOVAL

1. Relieve fuel system pressure as outlined under "Precautions."
2. Drain coolant system into appropriate container.
3. Remove air cleaner assembly with AFM outlet hose.
4. Disconnect the following electrical connectors:
   a. Idle Speed Control (ISC) valve.
   b. High tension cord from distributor, then the distributor Crank Angle Sensor (CAS).
   c. **On models equipped with California emissions,** Recirculated Exhaust Gas Temperature Sensor (REGTS) and Exhaust Gas Recirculation Vacuum Switching Valve (EGR VSV).
   d. **On all models,** Water Temperature Sensor (WTS) and oxygen sensor.
   e. Canister purge VSV, then the ground from intake manifold.
   f. Throttle Position Sensor (TPS) and fuel injector.
   g. Water Temperature Gauge (WTG) and radiator fan thermo switch.
   h. Ensure all wires are free of clamps on engine.
5. Disconnect vacuum hoses from brake booster and canister purge.
6. Remove accelerator cable from throttle lever and bracket.
7. Remove radiator hose from thermostat

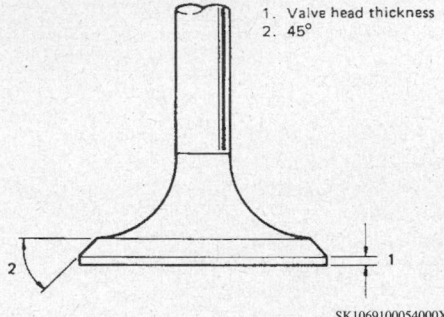

1. Valve head thickness
2. 45°

SK1069100054000X

Fig. 8 Valve head thickness measurement

housing, heater hose from cylinder head and throttle body hose from throttle body.
8. Remove fuel feed and return hoses from delivery pipe.
9. Remove timing belt as outlined under "Timing Belt, Replace."
10. Remove alternator adjusting arm stiffener, then the intake manifold bracket.
11. Remove cylinder head cover.
12. Using 18 mm hexagon socket, remove cylinder head bolts.
13. Remove cylinder head, intake manifold, exhaust manifold, distributor, fuel delivery pipe and injectors as an assembly. **Do not place assembly on flat surface as one valve is in the open position.**

DISASSEMBLE

1. Remove intake manifold with throttle body, exhaust manifold and distributor from cylinder head.
2. Remove rocker arm shafts, rocker arms, springs and camshaft as outlined under "Camshaft, Replace."
3. Using valve lifter tools, No. 09916-

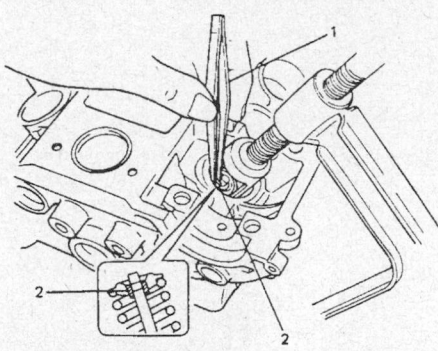

1. Special tool (Forceps 09916-84510)
2. Valve cotters

SK1069100053000X

Fig. 7 Valve cotters replacement

14510 and No. 09916-48210 or equivalent, compress valve springs, then using forceps remove valve cotters, **Fig. 7.**
4. Release tool and remove spring retainer and valve spring.
5. Remove valve from cylinder head.
6. Remove valve stem seal from valve guide, then the valve spring seat.
7. Using valve guide remover tool, No. 09916-46010 or equivalent, drive valve guide out from combustion chamber side to valve spring side.

INSPECTION
Valve Guides

Using micrometer and bore gauge, take diameter readings on valve stems and guides to check stem to guide clearance. Take reading at more than one place along length of each stem and guide.

If clearance exceeds 0.0027 inch for intake stems or 0.0035 inch for exhaust stems, replace valve and valve guide.

Valves

1. Remove all carbon from valves.
2. Inspect each valve for wear, burn or distortion, replace as necessary.
3. Measure thickness of valve head, **Fig. 8.** If measured thickness exceeds 0.023 inch for intake valves or 0.027 inch for exhaust valves, replace valve.
4. Inspect valve stem end face for pitting and wear. If pitting or wear of stem end face is present, valve stem may be resurfaced, providing that its length will not be reduced to less than 0.14 inch. If length becomes less that specified, valve must be replaced **Fig. 9.**
5. Using dial gauge, check each valve for radial runout, **Fig. 10.** If measure runout exceeds 0.003 inch, replace valve.
6. Inspect seating contact width on each valve as follows:
   a. Apply a uniform coat of red-lead paste to valve seat.
   b. Tap each seat to valve head. Valve lapping tool must be used.
   c. Pattern produced on seating face of each valve must be a continuous ring without any break, width of pattern must be within 0.0512–0.0590 inch, **Fig. 11.** Any valve seat not

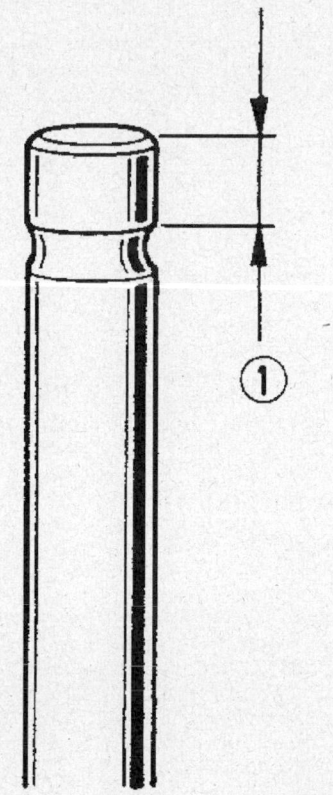

Fig. 9   Valve stem end face measurement

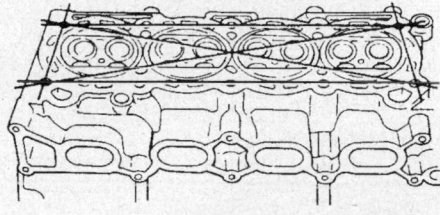

Fig. 12   Cylinder head distortion measurement

producing uniform contact or showing seating contact that is off the specified width must be repaired.

Cylinder Head

1. Inspect cylinder head for cracks in intake and exhaust ports, combustion chambers and head surface.
2. Using straightedge and thickness gauge, check gasket surface at six locations, **Fig. 12**. If distortion limit of 0.002 inch is exceeded, correct gasket surface with a surface plate and abrasive paper. If abrasive paper fails to reduce thickness gauge readings to within specification, replace cylinder head.
3. Inspect manifold seating faces in same manner as step two. If distortion limit of 0.004 inch is exceeded, correct in same manner as step two. If thickness gauge readings are not within specification, replace cylinder head.

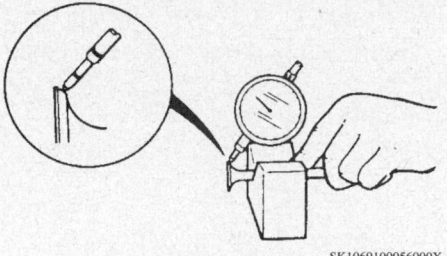

Fig. 10   Valve radial runout measurement

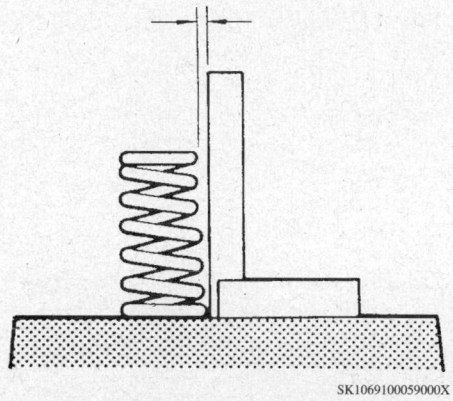

Fig. 13   Valve spring squareness measurement

Valve Springs

1. Ensure valve spring free length and preload are within specification.
2. Using square and surface plate, check each spring for squareness, **Fig. 13**. Springs that exceed 0.079 inch out of square must be replaced.

ASSEMBLE

1. Ream guide holes using 12 mm reamer to remove burrs.
2. Heat cylinder head uniformly to a temperature of 176–212°F, then drive new oversize valve guide into hole using tools, **Fig. 14**. Drive new valve guide until valve guide installer contact cylinder head. Ensure valve guide protrudes 0.55 inch from cylinder head.
3. Ream valve guide bore using 7 mm reamer. Clean bore after reaming.
4. Install valve spring seat on cylinder head.
5. Lubricate and install new valve stem seal to valve guide, **Fig. 15**. Install seal to guide by pushing tool by hand.
6. Lubricate and install valves, then valve spring and spring retainer. Each valve spring has top end (large pitch end) and bottom end (small pitch end). Small pitch end must be facing bottom (spring seat side), **Fig. 16**.
7. Compress valve spring and fit two valve cotters into groove provided on valve stem.
8. Install intake manifold with throttle body, exhaust manifold and delivery pipe with injectors to cylinder head.

INSTALLATION

1. Install new head gasket with TOP mark

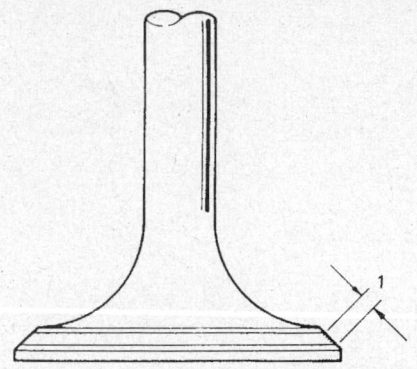

1. Valve seat contact width

Fig. 11   Valve seating contact width measurement

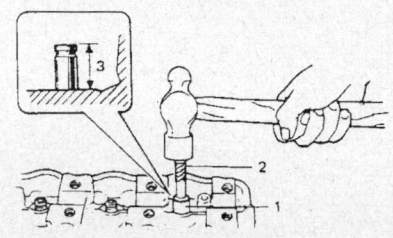

1. Special tool (Valve guide installer attachment 09917-88210)
2. Special tool (Valve guide installer handle 09916-57321)
3. Valve guide protrusion (14mm)

Fig. 14   Valve guide replacement

on gasket on top and facing crankshaft pulley side.
2. Install cylinder head, then using sequence shown in **Fig. 17**, **torque** cylinder head bolts in two or three steps to 48–54 ft. lbs.
3. Install rocker arm shafts, rocker arms, springs and camshaft as outlined under "Camshaft, Replace."
4. Install cylinder head cover, then the timing belt inside covers. Ensure rubber seal is installed between water pump and cylinder head, **Fig. 18**.
5. Install distributor to cylinder head.
6. Adjust valve lash as outlined under "Valve Adjustment."
7. Reverse procedure to install.

VALVE LIFTERS

Replace valve lifters as outlined under "Cylinder Head, Replace."

VALVE CLEARANCE SPECIFICATIONS

Refer to "Tune Up Specifications" for proper valve clearance.

VALVE ADJUSTMENT

1. Remove cylinder head cover.
2. Raise and support vehicle, then remove right side fender apron extension.
3. Using 17 mm socket, turn crankshaft

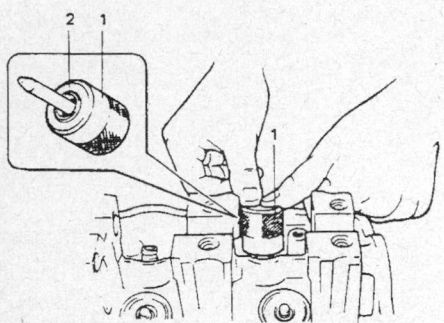

1. Special tool (Valve stem seal installer 09917-98210)
2. Valve stem seal

SK1069100063000X

Fig. 15 Valve stem seal replacement

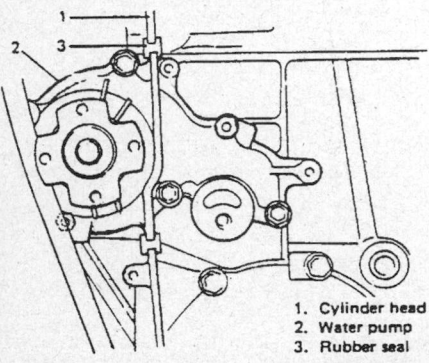

1. Cylinder head
2. Water pump
3. Rubber seal

SK1069100066000X

Fig. 18 Water pump rubber seal Installation

pulley clockwise until " V" mark on pulley aligns with "0" mark on timing belt cover.
4. Remove distributor cap, then check if rotor is positioned, **Fig. 19**. If rotor is out of place, turn crankshaft clockwise one full turn.
5. Check valve lash at valves 1, 2, 5 and 7, **Fig. 20**.
6. Using a suitable feeler gauge, measure clearance at gap (A), **Fig. 21**.
7. If clearance is not as specified, adjust by turning adjusting screw until correct clearance is obtained, **Fig. 21**.
8. After adjustment, tighten screw locknut to specification while holding adjusting screw with screwdriver.
9. Rotate crankshaft one full turn.
10. Check valve lash at valves 3, 4, 6 and 8 in same manner.
11. Install valve cover and distributor cap. Tighten bolts to specification.
12. Install air cleaner assembly.

ROCKER ARMS

For rocker arm replacement procedure, refer to "Camshaft, Replace," found in this section.

ROCKER ARMS

REPLACE

For rocker arm shaft replacement procedure, refer to " Camshaft, Replace," found in this section.

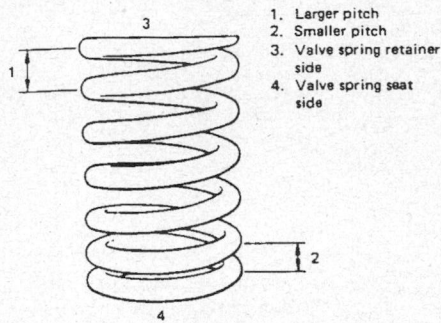

1. Larger pitch
2. Smaller pitch
3. Valve spring retainer side
4. Valve spring seat side

SK1069100064000X

Fig. 16 Valve spring replacement

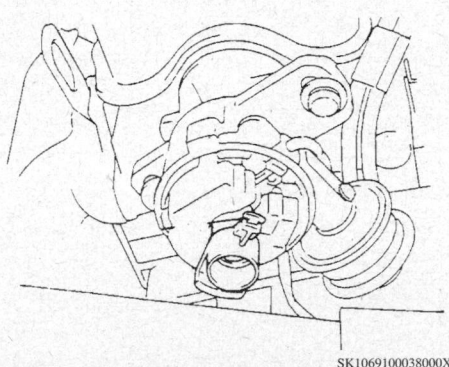

SK1069100038000X

Fig. 19 Rotor position inspection

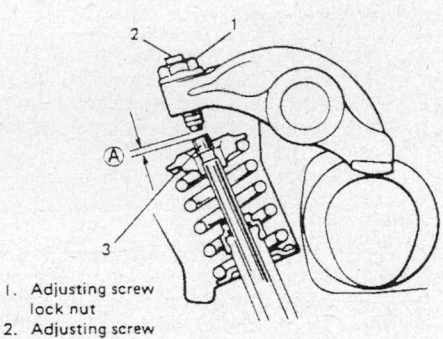

1. Adjusting screw lock nut
2. Adjusting screw
3. Valve stem

SK1069100040000X

Fig. 21 Valve lash measurement

TIMING BELT

REPLACE

REMOVAL

1. Raise and support vehicle.
2. Remove right side fender apron extension. Do not push center pin in too far as it may fall into fender.
3. Remove alternator/water pump belt and water pump pulley.
4. Remove crankshaft pulley as follows:
a. Lock crankshaft to loosen crankshaft timing belt pulley bolt and crankshaft pulley bolts, **Figs. 22 and 23**. If engine is in vehicle, it is necessary to remove crankshaft timing belt pulley bolt. If engine is removed from vehicle, crankshaft timing belt pulley bolt need not be removed.
b. Using 17 mm socket remove crank-

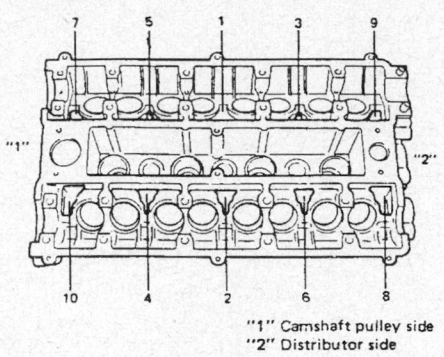

"1" Camshaft pulley side
"2" Distributor side

SK1069100065000X

Fig. 17 Cylinder head tightening sequence

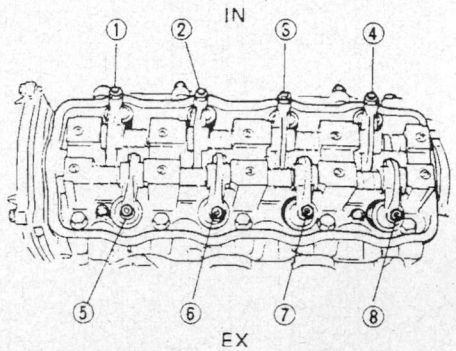

SK1069100039000X

Fig. 20 Valve identification

shaft pulley bolts and timing belt pulley bolt.
5. Remove timing outside cover.
6. Loosen tensioner bolt and stud, then push tensioner plate fully upward and remove timing belt from pulleys.

INSPECTION

1. Inspect timing belt for wear or cracks, replace as necessary.
2. Ensure tensioner rotates smoothly.

INSTALLATION

1. Install tensioner plate on tensioner. Lug of tensioner plate must fit in hole of tensioner.
2. Install tensioner assembly. Finger tighten tensioner bolt only at this time. Plate movement in upward direction should cause tensioner to move in same direction. If not, repeat step one.
3. Remove cylinder head cover, then completely loosen all Valve adjusting screws and locknuts on intake and exhaust rocker arms.
4. Turn camshaft pulley clockwise until timing mark on pulley aligns with "V" mark on belt inside cover, **Fig. 24**.
5. Turn crankshaft timing belt pulley bolt clockwise until punch mark on pulley aligns with arrow mark on oil pump case, **Fig. 24**.
6. Install timing belt on pulleys with drive side of belt free from any slack and with tensioner plate pushed up by finger. **Match arrow mark on timing belt with rotating direction of crankshaft (clockwise). In this position, No. 4 piston is at top dead center (TDC) of**

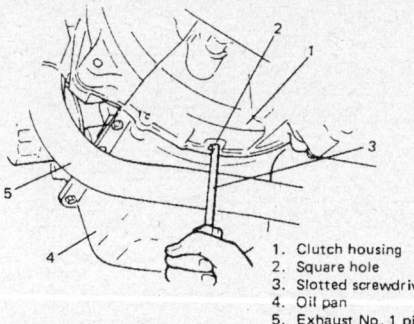

1. Clutch housing
2. Square hole
3. Slotted screwdriver
4. Oil pan
5. Exhaust No. 1 pipe

SK1069100031000X

Fig. 22 Crankshaft position lock. Manual transaxle

compression stroke.

7. Turn crankshaft two rotations clockwise after installing belt to take up slack of belt. Ensure marks on all pulleys are aligned.
8. Tighten tensioner stud, then the tensioner bolt.
9. Ensure seal is between water pump and oil pump case, then install timing belt outside cover.
10. Remove crankshaft timing belts pulley bolt, then install crankshaft pulley. Tighten bolts to specification.
11. Adjust valves as outlined under "Valve Adjustment."
12. Install water pump pulley and drive belt.
13. Install cylinder head cover, then the air cleaner assembly.
14. Install right side fender apron extension.

CAMSHAFT
REPLACE
REMOVAL

1. Remove cylinder head cover.
2. Remove distributor from cylinder head.
3. Loosen all valve adjusting screw locknuts, then turn adjusting screws back completely.
4. Remove rocker arm shaft screws, then pull out both rocker arm shafts.
5. Remove rocker arms and springs.
6. Remove timing belt as outlined under "Timing Belt, Replace."
7. Insert rod into hole of camshaft, then remove camshaft pulley bolt.
8. Remove distributor case and camshaft from cylinder head.

INSPECTION
Rocker Arm & Shaft

1. Using a suitable micrometer and a bore gauge, measure rocker shaft diameter and rocker arm inside diameter. Note readings.
2. Rocker shaft diameter should be 0.628–0.629 inch. If diameter is not as specified, replace shaft.
3. Rocker arm inside diameter should be 0.629–0.630 inch. If diameter is not as specified, replace arm.
4. Take readings obtained in steps 2 and

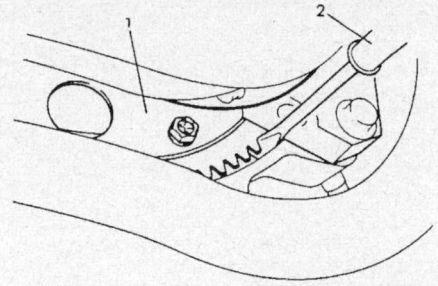

1. Drive plate
2. Slotted screwdriver

SK1069100032000X

Fig. 23 Crankshaft position lock. Automatic transaxle

3 and the difference between the two readings is arm to shaft clearance. Arm to shaft clearance should be 0.0005–0.0017 inch. If clearance is not as specified, replace shaft or arm as necessary.
5. Using "V" blocks and a suitable dial indicator, check runout of rocker arm shaft. Runout should not exceed 0.004 inch.

Camshaft Lobe Height & Runout

1. Using a micrometer, measure cam lobe height. If measured height is below 1.4975 inches for intake or exhaust cam, replace camshaft.
2. Using dial gauge, measure camshaft runout. If measured runout exceeds 0.0039 inch, replace camshaft.

Camshaft Journal Wear

1. Measure journal diameter at four places on each journal to specification, **Fig. 25**.
2. Using bore gauge, measure journal bores in cylinder head. Journal bore diameter should be as specified, **Fig. 25**.
3. Subtract journal diameter measurement from journal bore measurement to determine journal clearance. Journal clearance should not exceed 0.0059 inch.
4. If journal clearance exceeds specification, replace camshaft and/or cylinder head.

INSTALLATION

Reverse removal procedure to install, noting the following:
1. Install camshaft to cylinder head from transaxle case side.
2. Install rocker arm shafts as specified, **Fig. 26**.
3. Adjust valve lash as outlined under "Valve Adjustment."

PISTON & ROD ASSEMBLY

Before replacing the piston and connecting rods, remove carbon from top of cylinder bore. When installing first and second rings, direct marked side of each ring to-

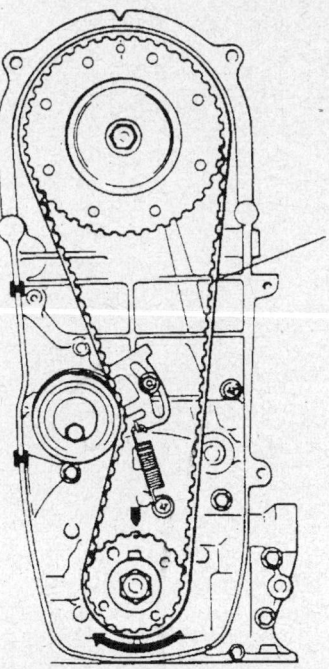

Direction of crankshaft

1. Drive side of belt

SK1069100037000X

Fig. 24 Timing belt pulley alignment

ward top of piston, **Fig. 27**. The compression ring gap should be staggered and not inline with the oil ring gap, **Fig. 28**.

Each piston top is stamped with a No. 1 or 2, depending on its outer diameter. A No. 1 stamped piston, outer diameter should be 2.9126–2.9130 inches and a No. 2 stamped piston, outer diameter should be 2.9122–2.9126 inches.

When installing piston and connecting rod assemblies, ensure number on piston top matches cylinder number stamped in block, **Fig. 29,** and arrows on top of pistons are facing front of engine, crankshaft pulley side, **Fig. 30**.

Pistons are available in standard sizes and oversizes of 0.0098 inch and 0.0196 inch.

MAIN & ROD BEARINGS

MAIN BEARINGS

Two types of main bearings are available, standard and 0.0098 inch (0.25 mm) undersize. Each have five kinds of bearings differing in tolerance. Each main bearing cap is stamped with a number and an arrow. When installing bearing cap, arrow must point toward crankshaft pulley side, **Fig. 31**. Check main bearing clearance as follows:
1. Clean bearings and crankshaft main journals using a suitable solvent.
2. Place a piece of gaging plastic the full width of the bearing (parallel to crankshaft) on journal, avoiding oil passage hole.
3. Install bearing cap and tighten cap

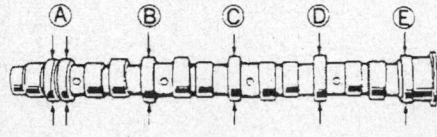

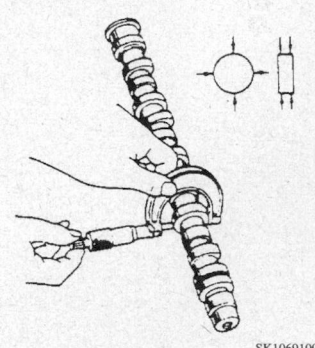

	Camshaft journal dia.	Journal bore dia.
A	44.125 – 44.150 mm (1.7372 – 1.7381 in.)	44.200 – 44.216 mm (1.7402 – 1.7407 in.)
B	44.325 – 44.350 mm (1.7451 – 1.7460 in.)	44.400 – 44.416 mm (1.7480 – 1.7486 in.)
C	44.525 – 44.550 mm (1.7530 – 1.7539 in.)	44.600 – 44.616 mm (1.7560 – 1.7565 in.)
D	44.725 – 44.750 mm (1.7609 – 1.7618 in.)	44.800 – 44.816 mm (1.7638 – 1.7644 in.)
E	44.925 – 44.950 mm (1.7687 – 1.7697 in.)	45.000 – 45.016 mm (1.7716 – 1.7723 in.)

SK1069100051000X

Fig. 25 Camshaft journal measurement specification (Part 2 of 2)

SK1069100050000X

Fig. 25 Camshaft journal measurement specification (Part 1 of 2)

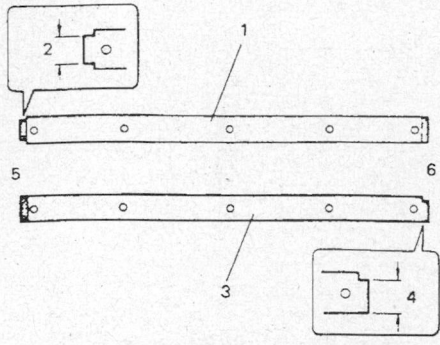

1. Intake rocker arm shaft
2. 14mm (0.55 in)
3. Exhaust rocker arm shaft
4. 15mm (0.59 in)
5. Camshaft pulley side
6. Distributor side

SK1069100052000X

Fig. 26 Rocker arm shaft replacement

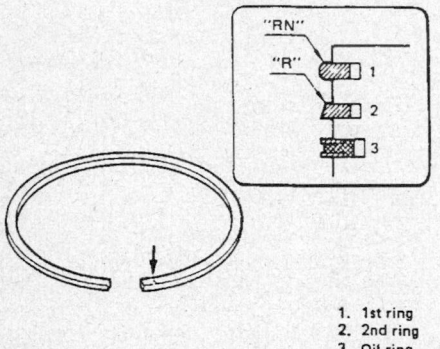

1. 1st ring
2. 2nd ring
3. Oil ring

SK1069100067000X

Fig. 27 Piston ring replacement

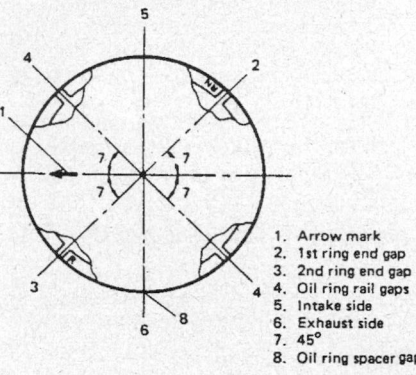

1. Arrow mark
2. 1st ring end gap
3. 2nd ring end gap
4. Oil ring rail gaps
5. Intake side
6. Exhaust side
7. 45°
8. Oil ring spacer gap

SK1069100068000X

Fig. 28 Piston ring end gap locations

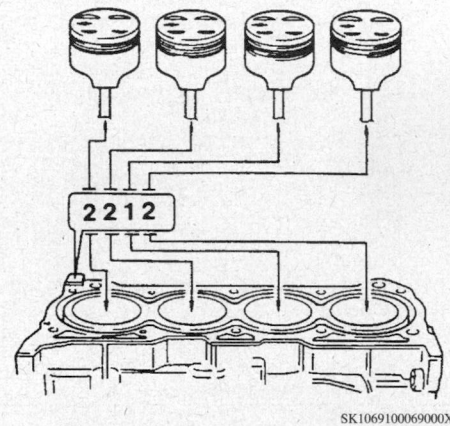

SK1069100069000X

Fig. 29 Piston to cylinder Installation position

bolts to specification. **Do not rotate crankshaft while gaging plastic is installed.**

4. Remove bearing cap. Using scale on gaging plastic envelope, measure gaging plastic width at widest point, **Fig. 32.**
5. If clearance exceeds 0.0023 inch, replace bearing. Always replace both upper and lower inserts as a unit. **A new standard bearing may produce proper clearance, if not, it will be necessary to regrind crankshaft journal for use of 0.0098 inch undersize bearing. After selecting appropriate bearing, recheck clearance.**

Standard Bearing Selection

If bearing is in poor condition or bearing clearance is out of specification, select a new standard bearing according to the following procedure.

1. Using a suitable micrometer, measure journal diameter.
2. Crank webs of No. 2 and No. 3 cylinder has five stamped numbers, **Fig. 33.** The numbers represent the following journal diameters:
   a. No. 1 - 1.7714–1.7716 inches.

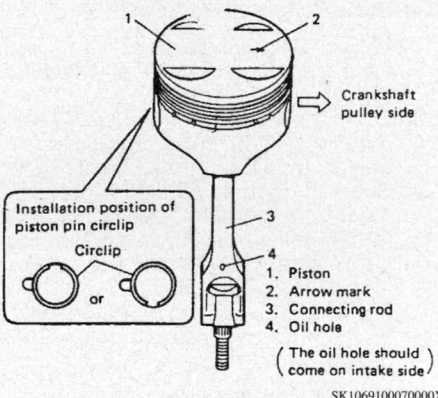

1. Piston
2. Arrow mark
3. Connecting rod
4. Oil hole

(The oil hole should come on intake side)

SK1069100070000X

Fig. 30 Piston Installation

b. No. 2 - 1.7712–1.7714 inches.
c. No. 3 - 1.7710–1.7712 inches.
3. The first, second, third, fourth and fifth stamped numbers on the crank web, indicate journal diameters at bearing caps 1, 2, 3, 4 and 5 respectively. For example, the first No. 3 indicates that journal diameter at bearing No. 1 is within 1.7710–1.7712 inches and second No. 1 indicates that journal diameter at bearing cap No. 2 is within 1.7714–1.7716 inches.
4. Using a suitable micrometer, check bearing cap bore without bearing. There are five letters stamped on mating surface of cylinder block, **Fig. 34.** These letters represent cap bore diam-

eters as follows:
a. "A" - 1.9292–1.9294 inches.
b. "B" - 1.9294–1.9296 inches.
c. "C" - 1.9296–1.9298 inches.
5. The first, second, third, fourth and fifth (left to right) stamped letters indicate cap bore diameter of bearing caps 1, 2, 3, 4 and 5 respectively, **Fig. 34.** For example, the "B" indicates that cap bore diameter of bearing cap No. 1 is within 1.9294–1.9296 inches and the fifth letter "A" indicates that cap bore diameter of cap No. 5 is within 1.9292–1.9294 inches.
6. There are five types of standard bearings differing in thickness. Each bearing has a painted identification color on its side. Each color indicates thickness at center of bearing as follows:
a. Green - 0.0786–0.0787 inch.
b. Black - 0.0787–0.0788 inch.
c. Colorless (no paint) - 0.0788–0.0789 inch.
d. Yellow - 0.0789–0.0790 inch.
e. Blue - 0.0790–0.0791 inch.
7. From the number stamped on crank web, **Fig. 33,** and the letters stamped on surface of cylinder block, **Fig. 34,** determine new standard bearing to be

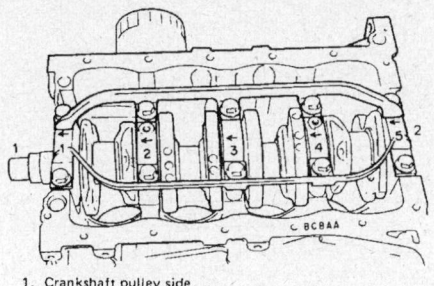

1. Crankshaft pulley side
2. Flywheel side

SK1069100072000X

Fig. 31 Main bearing caps Installation

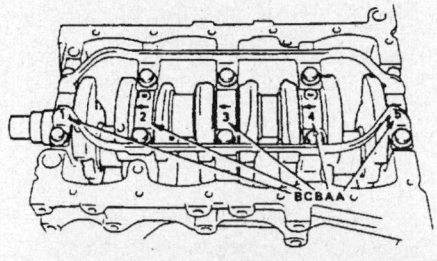

SK1069100076000X

Fig. 34 Cap bore diameter selection

installed to journal, by referring to table, **Fig. 35.** For example, if number stamped on crank web is 3 and letter stamped on cylinder block is B, install new standard bearing with a yellow painted identification mark.

8. Using gaging plastic, check bearing clearance with new standard bearing selected. If clearance exceeds limits, use next thicker bearing and recheck clearance.
9. If replacing crankshaft or cylinder block, select new standard bearings by numbers stamped on new crankshaft or letters stamped on cylinder surface.

Undersize Bearing Selection

1. The 0.0098 inch undersize bearing is available in five different thicknesses. To distinguish them, each bearing has a painted identification color on its side. Each color indicates thickness at center of bearing as follows:
   a. Green and red - 0.0835–0.0836 inch.
   b. Black and red - 0.0836–0.0837 inch.
   c. Red - 0.0837–0.0838 inch.
   d. Yellow and red - 0.0838–0.0839 inch.
   e. Blue and red - 0.0839–0.0840 inch.
2. If crankshaft has to be re-ground to undersize, grind journal and select undersize bearing to be used as follows:
   a. Grind journal to obtain a finished diameter a 1.7612–1.7618 inches.
   b. Using a suitable micrometer, measure re-ground journal diameter. Measurement should be made in two directions perpendicular to each other in order to check for out of round condition.
   c. From journal diameter measured

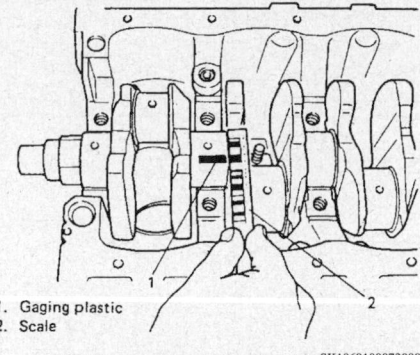

1. Gaging plastic
2. Scale

SK1069100073000X

Fig. 32 Main bearing clearance measurement

above and letters stamped on cylinder block, select appropriate undersize bearing to be installed referring to **Fig. 36.**
d. Check bearing clearance with undersize bearing selected.

CONNECTING ROD BEARING

Two types of rod bearings are available, standard and a 0.0098 inch undersize bearing. To distinguish them, the undersize bearing has the stamped number US025 on its back and the standard size bearing has no markings. Check rod bearing clearance as follows:

1. Clean bearings and crankshaft pin using a suitable solvent.
2. Place a piece of gaging plastic the full width of the crankpin as contacted by bearing (parallel to crankshaft), avoiding oil passage hole.
3. Install rod bearing cap and tighten cap bolts to specification. Ensure arrow mark on cap is pointed toward crankshaft pulley. **Do not rotate crankshaft while gaging plastic is installed.**
4. Remove rod bearing cap. Using scale on gaging plastic envelope, measure gaging plastic width at widest point, **Fig. 37.**
5. If clearance exceeds 0.0031 inch, use a new standard size bearing and remeasure clearance.
6. If clearance cannot be brought within specification using new standard size bearing, regrind crankpin to undersize and use 0.0098 inch undersize bearing.

OIL PUMP
REPLACE
REMOVAL

1. Raise and support vehicle.
2. Drain engine oil into appropriate container.
3. Remove water pump belt, pulley, alternator and bracket.
4. Remove timing belt as outlined under " Timing Belt , Replace."
5. Remove engine oil level gauge and its guide bolt.
6. Remove crankshaft timing belt pulley and timing belt guide.

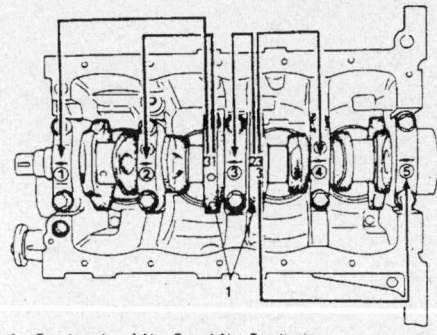

1. Crank webs of No. 2 and No. 3 cylinders

SK1069100075000X

Fig. 33 Crankshaft journal diameters selection

		Numeral stamped on crank web (Journal diameter)		
		1	2	3
Alphabet stamped on mating surface	A	Green	Black	Colorless
	B	Black	Colorless	Yellow
	C	Colorless	Yellow	Blue

New standard bearing to be installed.

SK1069100077000X

Fig. 35 Standard bearing chart

7. Remove oil pan and oil pump strainer.
8. Remove oil pump attaching bolts, then the oil pump.

INSTALLATION

1. Install two oil pump pins and new oil pump gasket to cylinder block.
2. Install oil pump to crankshaft, using tool shown, **Fig. 38.**
3. Install oil pump attaching bolts, **Fig. 39,** tighten bolts to specification. Ensure oil seal lip is not upturned, then remove tool.
4. Install rubber seal between oil pump and water pump, **Fig. 40.**
5. If edge of pump gasket bulges out, cut bulge off with sharp knife. Gasket edge must be smooth and flush with end faces of pump case and cylinder block.
6. Install timing belt guide, key and crankshaft timing belt pulley, **Fig. 41.** Timing belt guide must be installed with concave side facing oil pump.
7. Install timing belt as outlined under "Timing Belt, Replace."

OIL PUMP SERVICE
DISASSEMBLE

1. Remove oil level gauge guide from pump.
2. Remove rotor plate, then the inner and outer rotors.

INSPECTION

1. Inspect oil seal lip for damage, replace as necessary.
2. Inspect inner and outer rotors, rotor plate and oil pump case for excessive wear or damage.
3. Using thickness gauge, measure radial clearance between outer rotor and

Alphabets stamped on mating surface of cylinder block		Measured journal diameter		
		44.744 — 44.750 mm (1.7616 — 1.7618 in.)	44.738 — 44.744 mm (1.7614 — 1.7616 in.)	44.732 — 44.738 mm (1.7612 — 1.7614 in.)
	A	Green & Red	Black & Red	Red only
	B	Black & Red	Red only	Yellow & Red
	C	Red only	Yellow & Red	Blue & Red

Undersize beraing to be installed.

SK1069100078000X

Fig. 36   Undersize bearing chart

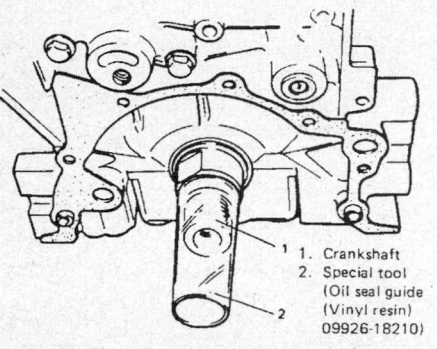

1. Crankshaft
2. Special tool (Oil seal guide (Vinyl resin) 09926-18210)

SK1099100003000X

Fig. 38   Oil pump replacement

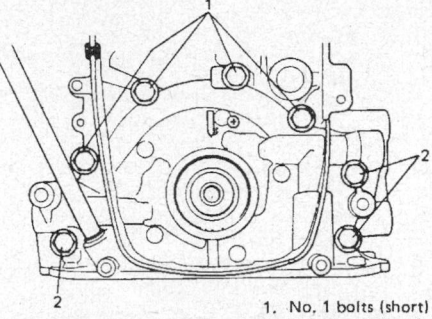

1. No. 1 bolts (short)
2. No. 2 bolts (long)

SK1099100004000X

Fig. 39   Oil pump bolt location

5. Install guide seal to pump case, then the oil level gauge guide.

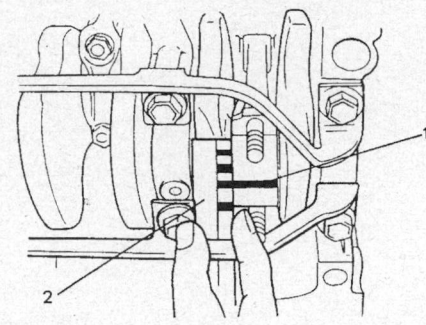

1. Gaging plastic
2. Scale

SK1069100071000X

Fig. 37   Rod bearing clearance measurement

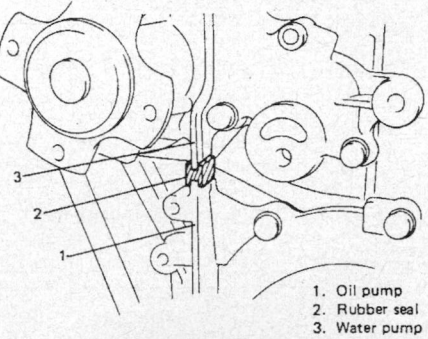

1. Oil pump
2. Rubber seal
3. Water pump

SK1099100005000X

Fig. 40   Water pump rubber seal replacement

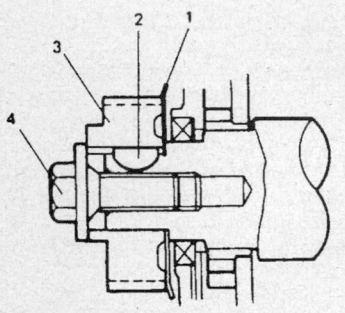

1. Timing belt guide
2. Key
3. Crankshaft timing belt pulley
4. Pulley bolt

SK1099100006000X

Fig. 41   Guide, key & pulley replacement

case, **Fig. 42.** If clearance exceeds 0.0122 inch, replace outer rotor or case.
4. Using straightedge and thickness gauge, measure side clearance, **Fig. 43.** Clearance should not exceed 0.0059 inch.

ASSEMBLE

1. Clean and dry all disassembled parts.
2. Apply thin coat of engine oil to inner and outer rotors, oil seal lip portion and inside surfaces of oil pump case and plate.
3. Install inner and outer rotors to case.
4. Install rotor plate. Tighten screws securely. **Ensure gears turn smoothly by hand.**

BELT TENSION DATA

Belt	Belt Deflection Inch①
A/C	.20-.25
A/C & Power Steering	.31-.39
Alternator & Water Pump	②

① — With 22 lbs. pressure applied.
② — New, .20–.27; used, .24–.31.

COOLING SYSTEM BLEED

This engine does not require a specific bleed procedure. After filling coolant system, run engine to operating temperature with radiator/pressure cap off. Air will then be automatically bled through cap opening.

THERMOSTAT
REPLACE

1. Drain coolant system into appropriate container, then remove thermostat cap from intake manifold.
2. Remove thermostat.
3. Install thermostat, ensuring air breather valve is positioned to front side of engine.

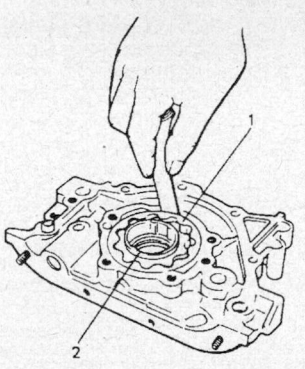

1. Outer rotor
2. Inner rotor

SK1099100001000X

Fig. 42   Oil pump gear radial clearance measurement

4. Install gasket and thermostat cap to intake manifold, then fill and bleed coolant system.

WATER PUMP
REPLACE

1. Drain coolant system into appropriate container.

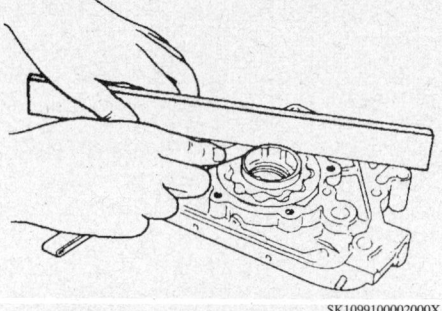

Fig. 43 Oil pump gear side clearance measurement

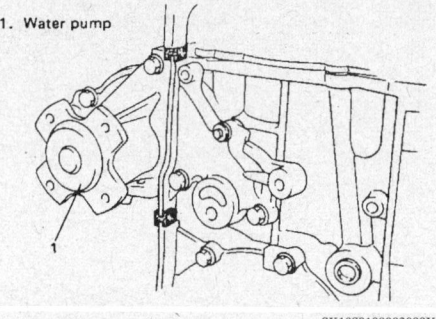

1. Water pump

SK1089100003000X

Fig. 44 Water pump replacement

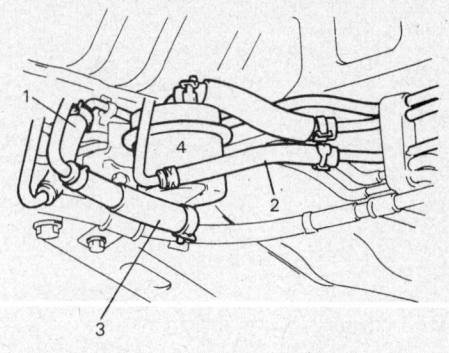

1. Return hose
2. Vapor hose
3. Feed hose
4. Fuel filter

SK1029100005000X

Fig. 45 Fuel filter replacement

SK1099100002000X

2. Remove timing belt as outlined under "Timing Belt, Replace."
3. Remove water pump assembly, **Fig. 44.**
4. Reverse procedure to install, noting the following:
   a. Use new gasket for water pump to cylinder block.
   b. Tighten all bolts to specification.
   c. Install rubber seal between water pump and oil pump and another between water pump and cylinder head, **Fig. 44.**

RADIATOR

REPLACE

1. Drain cooling system.
2. Disconnect cooling fan electrical connector.
3. Disconnect radiator inlet and outlet hoses and reservoir tank hose.

4. **On models equipped with automatic transaxle,** disconnect transaxle cooler lines at radiator.
5. **On all models,** remove radiator and cooling fan motor.
6. Reverse procedure to install

FUEL PUMP

REPLACE

1. Relieve fuel system pressure as outlined under " Precautions."
2. Remove rear seat cushion.
3. Disconnect fuel level gauge and fuel pump lead wire couplers, then detach wire tape.
4. Raise and support vehicle.
5. Disconnect fuel filler hose from tank, then breather hose from filler neck.
6. Drain fuel into appropriate container, then remove fuel hoses from pipes.
7. Remove fuel tank from vehicle.

8. Remove fuel pump and level gauge from fuel tank.
9. Reverse procedure to install.

FUEL FILTER

REPLACE

The fuel filter is located in front of the fuel tank and filters the fuel sent under pressure from the fuel pump. The fuel filter cannot be disassembled, it must replaced as an assembly, **Fig. 45.**

TIGHTENING SPECIFICATIONS

Year	Component	Torque/Ft. Lbs.
1996–99	Camshaft Timing Belt Pulley Bolt	41-46
	Connecting Rod Bearing Cap Nut	25
	Crankshaft Main Bering Cap Bolt	37-41
	Crankshaft Pulley Bolts	108②
	Crankshaft Timing Belt Pulley Bolt	94
	Cylinder Head Bolt	①
	Cylinder Head Cover Bolt	36②
	Exhaust Manifold Bolt	14-20
	Flywheel Bolt	49-52
	Intake Manifold Bolt	14-20
	Oil Drain Plug	22-28
	Oil Pan Bolt/Nut	96②
	Oil Pressure Switch	10
	Oil Pump Case Bolt	96②
	Oil Pump Rotor Plate Screw	72-108②
	Oil Pump Strainer Bolt	96②
	Timing Belt Cover Bolt	96②
	Timing Belt Tensioner Bolt	18-21
	Timing Belt Tensioner Stud	96②
	Valve Adjustment Screw Locknut	12

① — Refer to "Cylinder Head, Replace" for tightening procedure.
② — Inch lbs.

1.6L Engine

NOTE: On Air Bag Equipped Models, Refer To "Air Bag System Precautions" Located In The Front Of This Manual For System Disarming & Arming Procedures.

INDEX

PRECAUTIONS

AIR BAG SYSTEMS

Refer to "Air Bag System Precautions" in the front of this manual for system disarming and arming procedures.

FUEL SYSTEM PRESSURE RELIEF

1. **On models equipped with manual transaxle or transmission,** place shifter in Neutral.
2. **On models equipped with automatic transaxle or transmission,** place shifter in the Park position, then set parking brake and block drive wheels.
3. **On all models,** disconnect fuel pump relay, **Fig. 1.**
4. Remove fuel filler cap to release fuel vapor pressure in tank, then install cap.
5. Start and run engine until it stalls. Repeat cranking engine three times for three seconds each time to dissipate fuel pressure in fuel lines.

BATTERY GROUND CABLE

Prior to service, disconnect battery ground cable and isolate as required.

COMPRESSION PRESSURE

Standard compression pressure is 199 psi with a minimum of 170 psi. Maximum allowable difference between cylinders is 14.2 psi.

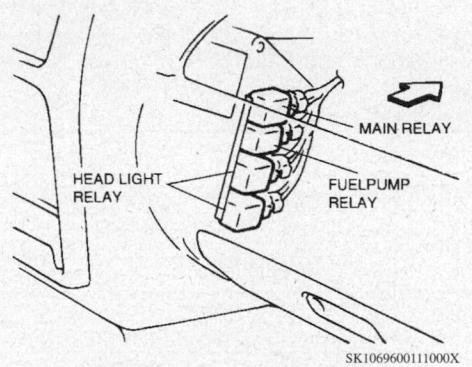

Fig. 1   Fuel pump relay

ENGINE MOUNT
REPLACE
ESTEEM

Refer to **Fig. 2** for engine mount replacement.

SIDEKICK & X-90
Lefthand Mount

1. Remove radiator shroud.
2. Raise and support vehicle.
3. Remove skid pan from under vehicle, then the exhaust pipe to bracket nut.
4. Remove engine mount to engine bolts, **Fig. 3.**
5. Lower vehicle and support engine.
6. Remove exhaust bracket bolts and bracket, then the engine mount to frame bracket bolts.
7. Raise engine slightly and remove engine mount assembly.

8. Remove mount from mount to frame bracket.
9. Reverse procedure to install.

Righthand Mount

1. Remove radiator shroud.
2. Raise and support vehicle.
3. Remove skid pan from under vehicle, then lower and support engine.
4. Disconnect electrical connections from starter.
5. Remove engine mount to frame bracket bolts, **Fig. 3.**
6. Remove engine mount to engine bracket bolts.
7. Raise engine slightly and remove engine mount assembly.
8. Remove mount from mount to frame bracket.
9. Reverse procedure to install.

ENGINE
REPLACE
ESTEEM

1. Relieve fuel system pressure as outlined under " Precautions."
2. Disconnect winshield washer hose, then remove engine hood.
3. Drain cooling system, then remove radiator and cooling fan as outlined under "Radiator, Replace."
4. Remove air cleaner inlet hose, then the air cleaner case.
5. Disconnect accelerator cable from throttle body.
6. **On models equipped with manual transaxle,** disconnect clutch cable from transaxle.

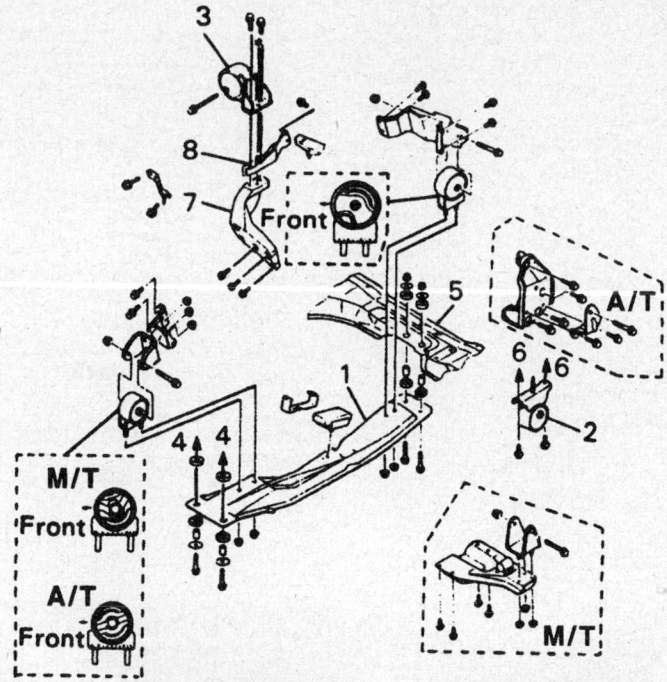

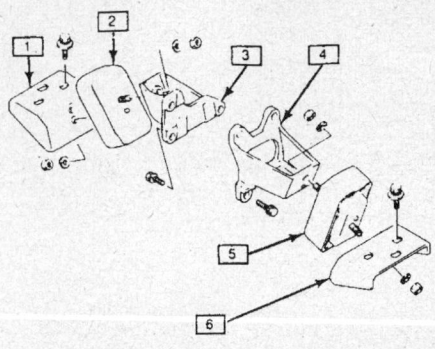

1	CHASSIS SIDE MOUNTING BRACKET (LEFT SIDE)
2	MOUNTING (LEFT SIDE)
3	ENGINE SIDE MOUNTING BRACKET (LEFT SIDE)
4	ENGINE SIDE MOUNTING BRACKET (RIGHT SIDE)
5	MOUNTING (RIGHT SIDE)
6	CHASSIS SIDE MOUNTING BRACKET (RIGHT SIDE)

SK1069100080000X

Fig. 3 Engine mounts. Sidekick & X-90

1. Mounting member
2. Left mounting
3. Right mounting
4. To front member
5. Suspension frame
6. To body
7. Right mounting bracket
8. Right mounting bracket stiffener

SK1069500150000X

Fig. 2 Engine mounts. Esteem

7. **On models equipped with automatic transaxle,** disconnect gear select cable from transaxle.
8. **On all models,** disconnect brake booster vacuum hose from intake manifold.
9. Disconnect canister purge hose from EVAP canister purge valve, then the MAP sensor hose from intake surge tank.
10. Disconnect all engine electrical connectors. Mark connectors for installation reference.
11. Disconnect fuel feed hose, feed pipe and return hose from fuel pressure regulator.
12. Disconnect heater hoses, then remove right and left engine covers.
13. Remove front exhaust pipe.
14. **On models equipped with manual transaxle,** remove gear shift control shaft from transaxle, then the extension rod.
15. **On all models,** drain engine oil and transaxle fluid.
16. Remove drive shaft joints from differential gear as outlined in "Front Wheel Drive" section.
17. Remove A/C compressor from brakcet and position aside.
18. Disconnect power steering hose from pump. Plug hose and pump port.
19. Install a suitable engine lifting device.
20. Remove mounting member from front member and suspension frame.
21. Remove lefthand engine mount from body.
22. Remove righthand engine mount, mount bracket and stiffener.
23. Ensure all electrical connectors and vacuum hoses are disconnected, then lower engine and transaxle assembly from the vehicle.
24. Reverse procedure to install.

SIDEKICK & X-90

1. Relieve fuel system pressure as outlined under " Precautions."
2. Mark hood for reference and remove hood.
3. Drain coolant system into appropriate container, then remove radiator fan and fan shroud.
4. Remove air intake pipe with hoses, then disconnect accelerator cable and transmission throttle cable from throttle body, if equipped.
5. Remove intake manifold stiffener, then electrical harnesses from clamps.
6. Remove starter motor, then disconnect electrical connectors, ground wires and hoses as necessary.
7. Loosen bolts securing engine to transmission, then raise and support vehicle.
8. Drain engine oil into appropriate container, then disconnect fuel feed and return hoses from pipes.
9. Remove righthand transmission stiffener and transmission fluid hose clamp bolt, if equipped.
10. Remove exhaust pipes, lefthand transmission stiffener, then the clutch or torque converter housing lower plate.
11. **On models equipped with automatic transmission,** remove torque converter bolts, using gear stopper tool, No. 09927-56010 or equivalent, to secure flywheel.
12. **On models equipped with power steering,** disconnect power steering pump with hoses attached and position aside.
13. **On models equipped with A/C,** disconnect A/C compressor with bracket attached and position aside.
14. **On all models,** remove nuts securing engine to transmission, then lower vehicle and support transmission with a suitable jack. **Do not lift or support automatic transmission by oil pan.**
15. Install a suitable lifting device, then remove right and left engine mounting bracket bolts.
16. Remove engine assembly from chassis and transmission by sliding towards front, then carefully hoisting from vehicle.
17. Reverse procedure to install, noting the following:
    a. Tighten nuts and bolts to specification.
    b. Adjust water pump, power steering pump and A/C compressor drive belt tension.
    c. Adjust accelerator and transmission throttle cable play.
    d. Ensure there are no fuel, water or exhaust gas leakages.

INTAKE MANIFOLD
REPLACE

1. Relieve fuel system pressure as outlined under " Precautions."
2. Drain coolant system.
3. Remove air intake pipe, then disconnect accelerator cable and transmission throttle cable from throttle body, **Fig. 4.**

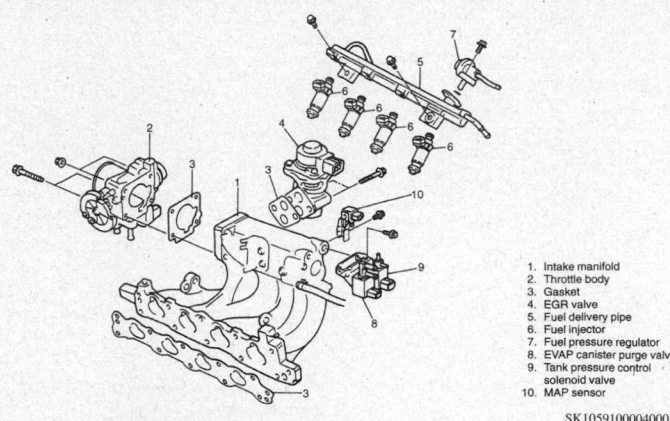

1. Intake manifold
2. Throttle body
3. Gasket
4. EGR valve
5. Fuel delivery pipe
6. Fuel injector
7. Fuel pressure regulator
8. EVAP canister purge valve
9. Tank pressure control solenoid valve
10. MAP sensor

SK1059100004000X

Fig. 4 Exploded view of throttle body & intake manifold. 16 valve engine

4. Disconnect electrical connectors, ground wires and hoses as necessary.
5. Disconnect fuel feed hose joint, using a back-up wrench while loosening flare nut, then remove fuel return hose from pipe.
6. Remove alternator adjustment arm stiffener, intake manifold stiffener, Nos. 1 and 2 stiffener with EGR modulator.
7. Remove intake manifold with surge tank and throttle body from cylinder head.
8. Reverse procedure to install, noting the following:
   a. Adjust accelerator and transmission throttle cable play.
   b. Ensure there are no fuel, water or exhaust gas leakages.

EXHAUST MANIFOLD
REPLACE

1. Remove air intake pipe with bracket and air cleaner outlet hose.
2. Disconnect oxygen sensor electrical connector, then remove manifold stiffener.
3. Remove manifold upper cover, then the exhaust pipe from manifold.
4. Remove manifold mounting bolts and nut, then the manifold.
5. Reverse procedure to install.

CYLINDER HEAD
REPLACE

1. Relieve fuel system pressure as outlined under " Precautions."
2. Drain coolant system into appropriate container, then remove intake manifold stiffener.
3. Disconnect electrical connectors, ground wires, vacuum hoses and coolant hoses as necessary.
4. Disconnect fuel feed and return lines, then remove throttle cover.
5. Disconnect accelerator cable and transmission throttle cable from throttle body, if equipped.
6. Remove air intake pipe and pipe bracket, then the cylinder head cover.
7. Loosen all valve lash adjusting screws fully, then remove timing belt as outlined under "Timing Belt, Replace."

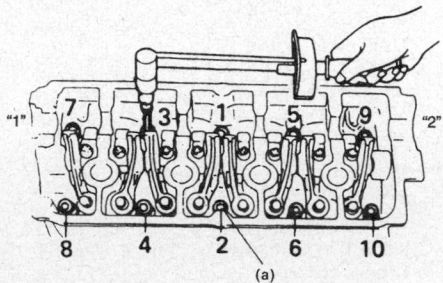

(a)

"1": Camshaft pulley side
"2": Ignition coil side

SK1069100084000X

Fig. 6 Cylinder head bolt tightening sequence. 16 valve engine

8. Disconnect exhaust pipe from manifold, then remove exhaust manifold stiffener.
9. Loosen cylinder head bolts in order, **Fig. 5,** using a 8 mm hexagon wrench bit tool, No. 09900-00415 and hexagon wrench socket tool, No. 09900-00411 or equivalent.
10. Remove components that may interfere with removal, then the cylinder head with intake and exhaust manifolds and distributor using a suitable lifting device.
11. Reverse procedure to install, noting the following:
    a. Install new cylinder head gasket with side marked TOP facing upward toward the crankshaft pulley side.
    b. Ensure oil jet (venturi plug) is installed and not plugged.
    c. Apply engine oil to cylinder head bolts, then using sequence shown in **Fig. 6, torque** bolts in three steps; first step to 25 ft. lbs., second step to 40 ft. lbs., third step to 48–51 ft. lbs.
    d. Adjust accessory belt tensions, valve clearance, accelerator cable and transmission throttle cable play and ignition timing.
    e. Ensure there are no fuel, coolant or exhaust leaks.

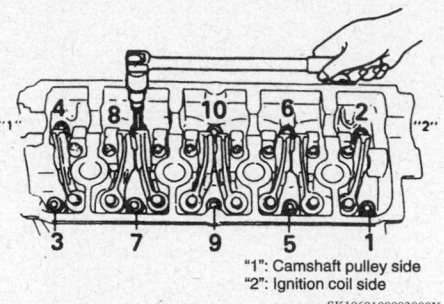

"1": Camshaft pulley side
"2": Ignition coil side

SK1069100083000X

Fig. 5 Cylinder head bolt loosening sequence. 16 valve engine

VALVE CLEARANCE SPECIFICATIONS

Valve clearance for intake and exhaust valves should be 0.0031–0.0047 inch (cold) or 0.0047–0.0063 inch (hot).

VALVE ADJUSTMENT

1. Remove cylinder head cover.
2. Rotate crankshaft clockwise using a 17 mm socket until " V" mark on pulley aligns with "0" calibration on timing belt cover.
3. Remove distributor cap and check rotor position. If rotor is pointing to No. 1 cylinder on distributor cap, check valve lash at valves 1, 2, 5 and 7, **Fig. 7.** If rotor is pointing to No. 4 cylinder on distributor cap, check valve lash at valves 3, 4, 6 and 8, **Fig. 7.**
4. If valve lash is out of specification, adjust as necessary. Use tappet adjuster wrench tool, No. 09917-18210, or equivalent, for 16 valve engines.
5. Install cylinder head cover.

ROCKER ARMS
REPLACE
REMOVAL

1. Remove front grille, **Fig. 8.**
2. Remove hood lock from front upper member, then disconnect horn electrical connector and remove front upper member from body, **Fig. 9.**
3. Drain coolant system into appropriate container.
4. **On Sidekick and X-90 models,** proceed as follows:
   a. **On models equipped with automatic transmission,** place a drain pan under radiator and disconnect transmission hoses from radiator.
   b. **On all models,** remove cooling fan/clutch and radiator shroud, then disconnect reservoir tank and hoses from radiator.
   c. Remove radiator.
5. **On all models** remove timing belt as outlined under "Timing Belt,, Replace."
6. Remove camshaft timing belt pulley using camshaft pulley holder tool, No. 09917-68220, or equivalent, then remove cylinder head cover.
7. Remove distributor as outlined in the

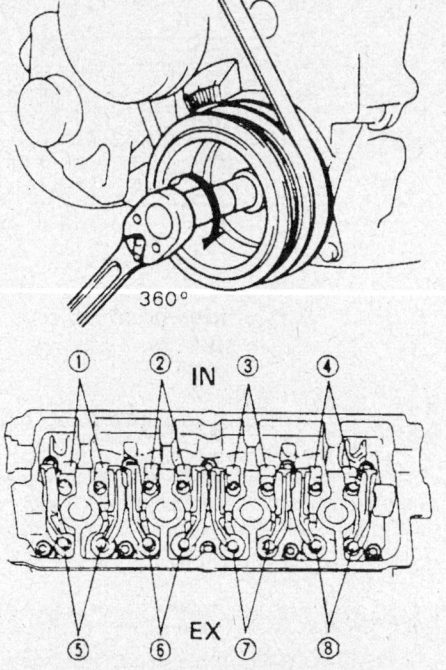

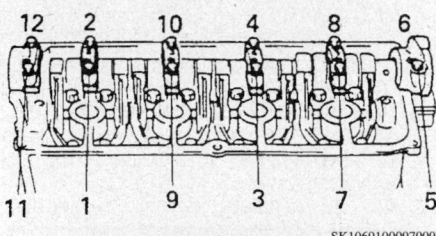

Fig. 7 Valve identification

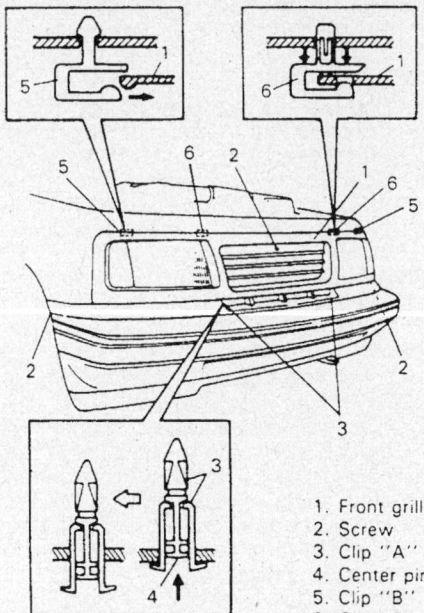

Fig. 8 Front grille replacement

1. Front grille
2. Screw
3. Clip "A"
4. Center pin
5. Clip "B"
6. Clip "C"

SK1069100095000X

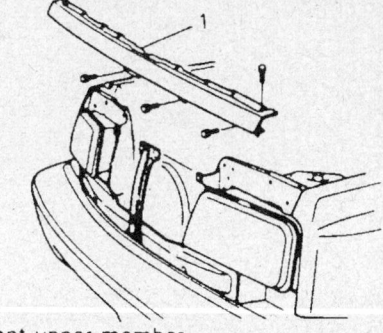

1. Front upper member

SK1069100096000X

Fig. 9 Front upper member replacement

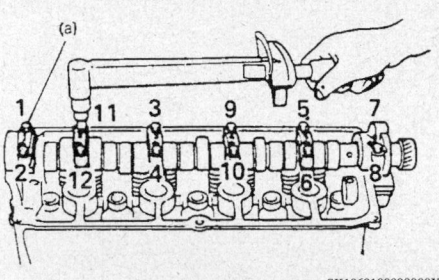

SK1069100098000X

Fig. 11 Camshaft housing bolt tightening sequence

Fig. 10 Camshaft housing bolt loosening sequence

"Electrical" section, then the distributor case from cylinder head. **Place a rag or container under case to catch oil after removal of case.**

8. Loosen all valve lash adjusting screws all the way to allow rocker arms to move freely.
9. Loosen camshaft housing bolts in sequence, **Fig. 10,** then remove camshaft housing and camshaft.
10. Remove rocker arm shaft plug and timing belt inner cover, then the intake rocker arm with clip from rocker arm shaft.
11. Remove rocker arm shaft bolts, then push off rocker arm shaft end to distributor side and remove O-ring from shaft.
12. Remove exhaust rocker arms and wave washer by pulling rocker arm shaft to front side.

INSPECTION

1. Inspect rocker arm cam face and adjusting screw tip for excessive wear. Replace if necessary.
2. Using "V" blocks and a dial gauge, check rocker arm shaft runout. If runout exceeds 0.008 inch, replace rocker arm shaft.
3. Check rocker arm to rocker arm shaft

clearance using a micrometer and bore gauge. Measure rocker arm inner diameter (ID) and rocker arm shaft outer diameter (OD), difference between two readings is arm to shaft clearance. Rocker arm ID should be 0.629–0.630 inch, rocker arm shaft OD should be 0.6287–0.6293 inch and arm to shaft clearance should be 0.0001–0.0014 inch with a limit of 0.0035 inch. If limit is exceeded, replace shaft or arm as necessary.
4. Check camshaft wear using a micrometer. Height of intake lobes should be 1.4551–1.4557 inches with a limit of 1.4512 inches, exhaust lobes should be 1.4328–1.4334 inches with a limit of 1.4289 inches. If measured height is below limit, replace camshaft.
5. Using "V" blocks and a dial gauge, check camshaft runout. If runout exceeds 0.0039 inch, replace camshaft.
6. Inspect camshaft journals and camshaft housings for pitting, scratches, wear or damage. Do not replace cylinder head without replacing housing.
7. Check camshaft journal clearance using a suitable gauging plastic as follows:
   a. Clean camshaft housings and journals, then install camshaft on cylinder head.
   b. Place pieces of gauging plastic the full width of camshaft journal onto camshaft journals parallel to camshaft.
   c. Install camshaft housings, then using sequence shown in **Fig. 11,** **torque** bolts in two or three steps to 7–9 ft. lbs. **Do not rotate camshaft while gauging plastic is installed.**
   d. Loosen camshaft housings bolts in sequence, **Fig. 10,** then remove housings and using scale on gauging plastic envelope, measure

gauging plastic width at its widest point. Journal clearance should be 0.0016–0.0032 inch with a limit of 0.0047 inch.
8. If camshaft journal clearances exceed limit, measure journal housing bores and outer diameter of camshaft journals. Camshaft journal bore diameter should be 1.1024–1.1031 inches and camshaft journal OD should be 1.1000–1.1008 inches. Replace camshaft or cylinder head assembly, whichever difference from specification is greater.

INSTALLATION

1. Apply engine oil to rocker arm shaft and rocker arms, then install rocker arm shaft, exhaust side rocker arms and wave washer.
2. Install rocker arm shaft O-ring, then set rocker arm shaft so that cut part faces down and is parallel with head cover mating surface.
3. Install rocker arm shaft bolts and tighten to specification.
4. Fill arm pivot holding portions of rocker arm shaft with small amounts of engine oil, then install intake rocker arms with clips to rocker arm shaft.
5. Apply engine oil to lobes and journals on camshaft and journals on cylinder head, install camshaft to cylinder head.
6. Apply engine oil to camshaft housings journal surfaces and Suzuki bond No. 1215 sealant No. 99000-31110 or equivalent, to surface of No. 6 camshaft housing which will mate with cylinder head.
7. Apply engine oil to housing bolts, then

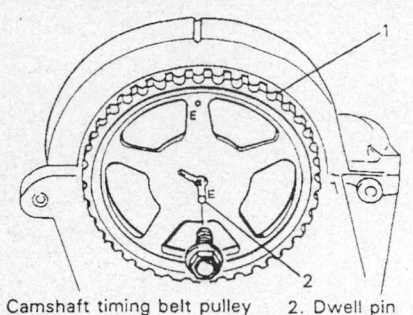

1. Camshaft timing belt pulley   2. Dwell pin

SK1069100099000X

Fig. 12 Camshaft pulley to camshaft position, slot "E"

using sequence shown in **Fig. 11, torque** bolts in three or four steps to 7–9 ft. lbs.

8. Apply engine oil to camshaft oil seal lip, then press-fit oil seal until it becomes flush with housing surface.
9. Install rocker arm shaft plug and timing belt inner cover, then tighten rocker arm shaft plug to specification.
10. Install camshaft timing belt pulley to camshaft while fitting pin on camshaft into slot at "E" mark, **Fig. 12.**
11. Tighten camshaft timing belt pulley bolt to specification using camshaft pulley holder tool, No. 09917-68220 or equivalent.
12. Install timing belt as outlined under "Timing Belt,, Replace."
13. Apply Suzuki bond No. 1215 sealant, No. 99000-31110 or equivalent, to part "A," **Fig. 13,** then install distributor case to cylinder head and tighten to specification.
14. Install distributor assembly as outlined in the " Electrical" section.
15. Adjust valve clearance as outlined under "Valve Adjustment, " then install cylinder head cover and air intake pipe.
16. Install radiator and fill coolant system.
17. Install hood lock to front upper member, connect horn electrical connector, then install front upper member to body.
18. Remove clip "C," **Fig. 8,** from front grille and install to body, then install front grille.
19. Ensure there are no water or oil leaks.
20. Adjust ignition timing.

VALVE & VALVE SPRINGS
REPLACE
DISASSEMBLE

1. Remove cylinder head assembly as outlined under " Cylinder Head, Replace," then the distributor gear case, intake manifold with throttle body and exhaust manifold from cylinder head.
2. Remove rocker arms, rocker arm shaft and camshaft as outlined under "Rocker Arms, Replace" and "Camshaft, Replace."
3. Compress valve springs using valve lifter tool, No. 09916-14510 and valve

lifter attachment tool, No. 09916-14910 or equivalent, then remove valve cotters using forceps tool, No. 09916-84510 or equivalent.
4. Remove valve lifter and valve lifter attachment, then spring retainers and valve springs.
5. Remove valves from cylinder head. **Prior to removing valves from head, ensure there are no burrs on valve stems.**
6. Remove valve stem oil seals from valve guides, then the spring seats.
7. Drive valve guides out from combustion chamber side to valve spring side using valve guide remover tool, No. 09916-44910 or equivalent.
8. Place disassembled components in order so they can be installed in their original positions. **Do not reuse valve stem seals or valve guides.**
9. Inspect all components for wear, burn, distortion and proper clearances and replace as necessary.

ASSEMBLE

1. Ream valve guide bores using 11 mm reamer tool, No. 09916-38210 and reamer handle tool, No. 09916-34541 or equivalent, to remove burrs and true bores.
2. Heat cylinder head uniformly to a temperature of 176–212°F so head will not be distorted, then drive new valve guides into bores using valve guide installer handle tool, No. 09916-58210 and valve guide installer attachment tool, No. 09916-56011 or equivalent. Drive valve guides in until valve guide installer contacts cylinder head. After Installation, ensure guides protrude by 0.045 inch from cylinder head.
3. Ream valve guides using 5.5 mm reamer tool, No. 09916-34550 and reamer handle tool, No. 09916-34541 or equivalent, then install valve seats to cylinder head.
4. Apply engine oil to new stem seals and spindle of valve stem seal installer tool, No. 09917-98221 or equivalent, fit oil seal to spindle. Install seals to valve guides by hand, using valve guide installer handle tool, No. 09916-58210 or equivalent.
5. Apply engine oil to valve stem seals, valve stems and valve guides, then install valves into guides.
6. Install valve springs and spring retainers.
7. Compress valve springs using valve lifter tool, No. 09916-14510 and valve lifter attachment tool, No. 09916-14910 or equivalent, then fit two valve cotters into groove in valve stems using forceps tool, No. 09916-84510 or equivalent.
8. Install rocker arms, rocker arm shaft and camshaft as outlined under "Camshaft, Replace."
9. Install distributor gear case, intake manifold with throttle body and exhaust manifold to cylinder head, then the cylinder head assembly as outlined under "Cylinder Head, Replace."

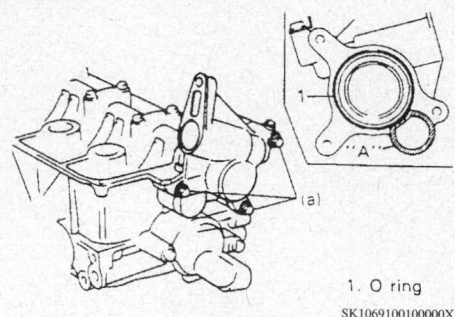

1. O ring

SK1069100100000X

Fig. 13 Sealant application part "A"

TIMING BELT
REPLACE

With the timing belt removed, avoid turning the camshaft or crankshaft. If movement is required, exercise extreme caution to avoid valve damage caused by piston contact.

REMOVAL

1. Remove power steering or A/C compressor belt, if equipped.
2. **On Sidekick and X-90 models,** remove fan shroud, radiator cooling fan, water pump drive belt and water pump pulley. **If it is difficult to remove fan shroud, drain coolant into appropriate container, then disconnect radiator inlet hose from radiator.**
3. **On Esteem models,** remove water pump drive belt and water pump pulley.
4. **On all models,** remove crankshaft pulley, then the timing belt outer cover.
5. Turn crankshaft to align timing marks, **Fig. 14,** then remove timing belt tensioner, tensioner plate, tensioner spring and timing belt, **Fig. 15.** Do not rotate camshaft or crankshaft more than 90° clockwise or counterclockwise after timing belt is removed or damage to pistons or valves may result.

INSTALLATION

1. Install tensioner plate to tensioner, inserting lug of tensioner plate into hole in tensioner.
2. Install tensioner and tensioner plate, then hand tighten tensioner bolt.
3. Ensure timing mark on camshaft timing belt pulley is aligned with "V" mark on cylinder head cover and punch mark on crankshaft timing belt pulley is aligned with arrow mark on oil pump case. **Do not rotate camshaft or crankshaft more than 90° clockwise or counterclockwise while timing belt is removed or damage to pistons or valves may result.**
4. With timing marks aligned and tensioner pushed upwards, install timing belt on two pulleys so that drive side of belt is free of slack. **When installing belt, match arrow mark on belt with rotational direction of crankshaft.**
5. Install tensioner spring, **Fig. 16,** then hand tighten tensioner stud.

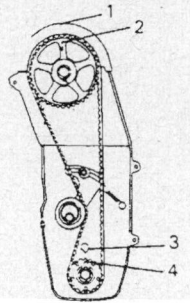

1. "V" mark on cylinder head cover
2. Timing mark by "E" on camshaft timing belt pulley
3. Arrow mark on oil pump case
4. Punch mark on crankshaft timing belt pulley

SK1069100087000X

Fig. 14 Timing belt pulley mark location. 16 valve engine

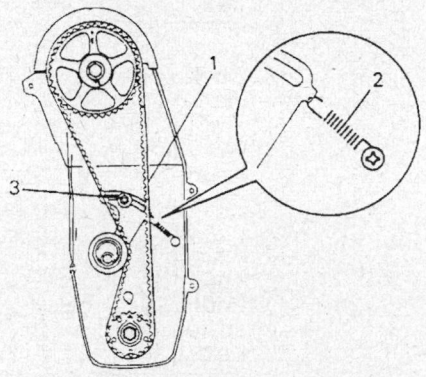

1. Drive side of belt
2. Tensioner spring
3. Tensioner stud

SK1069100089000X

Fig. 16 Timing belt tensioner spring replacement. 16 valve engine

6. Take up slack of timing belt by turning crankshaft two rotations clockwise. Tighten tensioner stud, then the tensioner bolt to specification and ensure timing marks are properly aligned.
7. Install timing belt outer cover, ensuring seal is between water pump and oil pump case.
8. Install crankshaft pulley, tighten bolts to specification.
9. Install radiator fan shroud, water pump pulley, cooling fan and water pump drive belt.
10. Install power steering or A/C compressor belts, if equipped.
11. Ensure all nuts and bolts are tightened to specification.

CAMSHAFT
REPLACE

Refer to "Rocker Arms, Replace" for camshaft replacement.

PISTON & ROD ASSEMBLY

Each standard size piston has a No. 1 or No. 2 stamped on it representing outer diameter. There are also numbers stamped

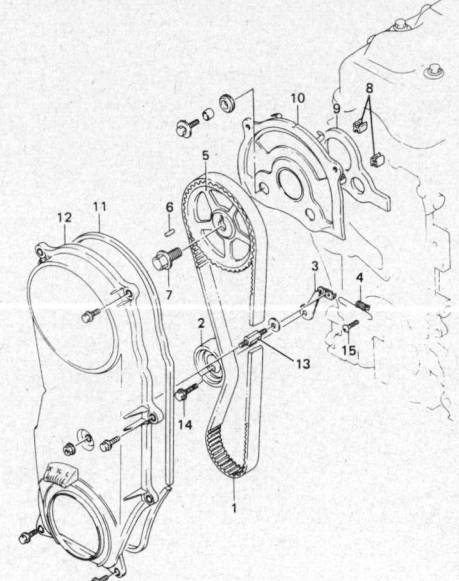

1. Timing belt
2. Tensioner
3. Tensioner plate
4. Tensioner spring
5. Camshaft timing pulley
6. Pin
7. Pulley bolt
8. Seal
9. Inside cover seal
10. Inside cover
11. Outside cover seal
12. Outside cover
13. Tensioner stud
14. Tensioner bolt
15. Tensioner spring bolt

SK1069100088000X

Fig. 15 Timing belt & tensioner. 16 valve engine

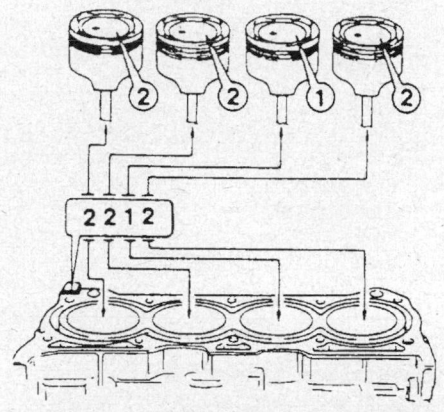

SK1069100104000X

Fig. 17 Piston & cylinder bore identification

on cylinder block machined surface representing inner diameters of cylinders, **Fig. 17**. Stamped numbers on pistons and stamped numbers on cylinder block should correspond.

Before replacing the piston and connecting rods, decarbonize the top of the cylinder bore. When installing first and second rings, marked side of each ring should be toward top of piston, **Fig. 18**. The compression ring gap should be staggered and not inline with the oil ring gap, **Fig. 19**. Install piston, **Fig. 20**.

MAIN & ROD BEARINGS

Select new standard size main bearings as follows:
1. Crank webs of No. 2 and No. 3 cylinders have 5 stamped numbers on them, **Fig. 21**. These numbers represent journal diameters at bearing caps 1, 2, 3, 4 and 5 respectively. These

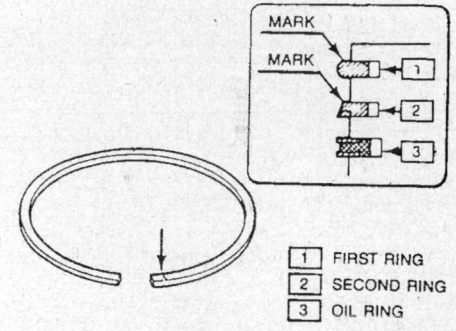

1 FIRST RING
2 SECOND RING
3 OIL RING

SK1069100105000X

Fig. 18 Piston ring replacement

numbers, 1, 2 and 3, represent the following diameters: No. 1, 2.0470–2.0472 inches; No. 2, 2.0468–2.0470 inches and No. 3, 2.0465–2.0468 inches.
2. Mating surface of cylinder block has 5 letters stamped on it, **Fig. 21**. These letters represent main bearing cap bore diameters at bearing caps 1, 2, 3, 4 and 5 respectively. These letters, A, B and C, represent the following diameters: A, 2.2047–2.2050 inches; B, 2.2050–2.2052 inches and C, 2.2052–2.2054 inches.
3. There are 5 standard bearing thicknesses, distinguished by paint marks as follows: green, 0.0786–0.0787 inch; black, 0.0787–0.0788 inch; colorless, 0.0788–0.0789 inch; yellow, 0.0789–0.0790 inch and blue, 0.0790–0.0791 inch.
4. Using numbers stamped on No. 2 and No. 3 crank webs and letters stamped on mating surface of cylinder block, determine new bearing to be installed using chart shown, **Fig. 22**.

Main bearings also come in 0.25 mm undersize, available in five thicknesses distinguished by paint marks as follows: green

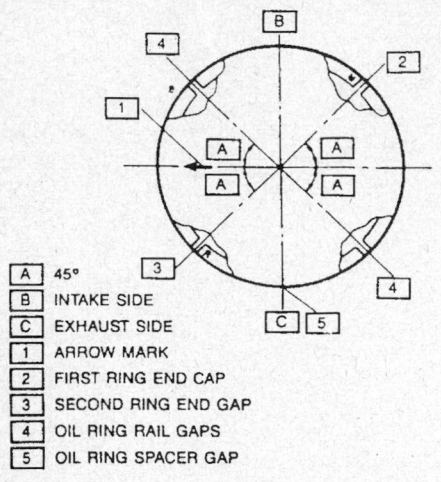

A	45°
B	INTAKE SIDE
C	EXHAUST SIDE
1	ARROW MARK
2	FIRST RING END CAP
3	SECOND RING END GAP
4	OIL RING RAIL GAPS
5	OIL RING SPACER GAP

SK1069100106000X

Fig. 19 Piston ring end gap position

1	PISTON
2	ARROW MARK
3	CONNECTING ROD
4	OIL HOLE (THE OIL HOLE SHOULD BE ON INTAKE SIDE)

SK1069100107000X

Fig. 20 Piston replacement

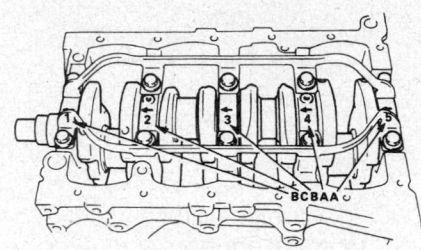

1. Crank webs of No. 2 and No. 3 cylinders

SK1069100108000X

Fig. 21 Crank web numbers & main bearing cap bore letters locations

		Numeral stamped on crank web (Journal diameter)		
		1	2	3
Alphabet stamped on mating surface (Bearing cap bore dia.)	A	Green	Black	Colorless
	B	Black	Colorless	Yellow
	C	Colorless	Yellow	Blue
		New standard bearing to be installed.		

SK1069100109000X

Fig. 22 Standard size main bearing selection chart

		Measured journal diameter		
		51.744–51.750 mm (2.0371–2.0373 in.)	51.738–51.744 mm (2.0369–2.0371 in.)	51.732–51.738 mm (2.0367–2.0369 in.)
Alphabets stamped on mating surface of cylinder block	A	Green & Red	Black & Red	Red only
	B	Black & Red	Red only	Yellow & Red
	C	Red only	Yellow & Red	Blue & Red
		Undersize bearing to be installed		

SK1069100110000X

Fig. 23 Undersize main bearing selection chart

and red, 0.0835–0.0836 inch; black and red, 0.0836–0.0837 inch; red, 0.0837–0.0838 inch; yellow and red, 0.0838–0.0839 inch and blue and red, 0.0939–0.0840 inch.

When necessary to install undersize bearings, regrind journal to 2.0367–2.0373 inches diameter, measure re-ground journal diameter in two perpendicular directions, then using journal diameter measured and letters stamped on cylinder block, select the proper bearing using the chart shown, **Fig. 23.**

Two kinds of rod bearings are available, standard and a 0.0098 inch undersize bearing. To distinguish them, the undersize bearing has the stamped number "US025" on its backside.

CRANKSHAFT REAR OIL SEAL

REPLACE

ESTEEM

1. Remove transaxle.
2. **On models equipped with manual transaxle,** remove clutch cover and clutch disc.
3. **On all models,** remove driveplate or flywheel.
4. Using a suitable seal puller, remove rear main oil seal from cylinder block.
5. Reverse procedure to install.

SIDEKICK & X-90

1. Remove transmission and transfer case.
2. **On models equipped with manual transmission,** remove clutch cover and clutch disc.
3. **On all models,** remove flywheel.
4. Remove rear main oil seal using a universal seal puller.
5. Reverse procedure to install.

OIL PAN

REPLACE

ESTEEM

1. Raise and support vehicle.
2. Drain engine oil, then remove engine under covers.
3. Remove front exhaust pipe, then the transalxe stiffener.
4. Using a suitable jack or lifting device, support engine and transaxle assembly.
5. Remove crossmember, then the oil pan.
6. Reverse procedure to install.

SIDEKICK & X-90

1. Raise and support vehicle.
2. Remove front differential assembly from chassis. Refer to "Drive Axles" for removal procedure.
3. Drain engine oil into appropriate container.
4. Remove clutch or torque converter housing lower plate.
5. Remove oil pan.
6. Reverse procedure to install.

OIL PUMP

REPLACE

1. Remove timing belt and tensioner as outlined under "Timing Belt, Replace."
2. Remove alternator and mounting brackets, then the power steering pump bracket or A/C compressor bracket, if equipped.
3. Lock crankshaft using gear stopper tool, No. 09927-56010 or equivalent, on flywheel, then remove crankshaft timing belt pulley.
4. Remove oil pan as outlined under "Oil Pan, Replace."
5. Remove oil pump mounting bolts, then the oil pump.
6. Inspect oil pump as follows:
   a. Inspect oil lip seal for wear or damage.
   b. Inspect oil pump outer and inner gears, gear plates and oil pump housing for excessive wear or damage.

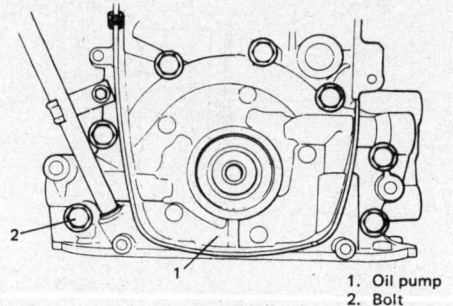

1. Oil pump
2. Bolt

SK1099100007000X

Fig. 24 Oil pump bolt location

c. Using thickness gauge, check radial clearance between outer rotor and case. Radial clearance should be 0.0122 inch. If clearance exceeds specifications, replace outer rotor or case.
d. Using straightedge, check side clearance of oil pump. Side clearance should be 0.0059 inch.
7. Reverse procedure to install, noting the following:
a. Use oil seal guide tool, No. J34853 or equivalent, during Installation.
b. Install bolts, **Fig. 24**.
c. Install rubber seals between oil pump and water pump.

BELT TENSION DATA

Belt	Belt Deflection Inch①
A/C	②
Alternator & Water Pump	.24–.31

① — With 22 lbs. pressure applied.
② — On Sidekick and X-90 models, .24–.36; on Esteem models, .30–.40.

COOLING SYSTEM BLEED

This engine does not require a specific bleed procedure. After filling coolant system, run engine to operating temperature with radiator/pressure cap off. Air will then be automatically bled through cap opening.

THERMOSTAT
REPLACE

1. Drain coolant system into appropriate container, then remove thermostat cap from intake manifold.
2. Remove thermostat.
3. Install thermostat, ensuring air breather valve is positioned to front side of engine.
4. Install gasket and thermostat cap to intake manifold, then fill and bleed coolant system.

WATER PUMP
REPLACE

1. Drain coolant system into appropriate container.

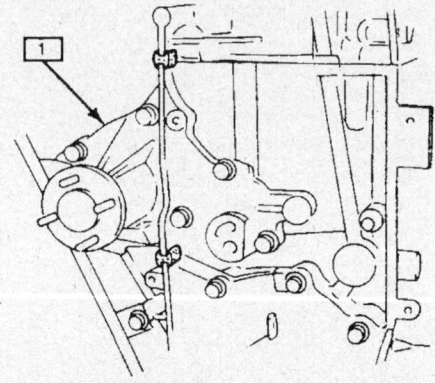

1 WATER PUMP

SK1089100004000X

Fig. 25 Water pump front cover seal replacement

2. Remove timing belt and tensioner as outlined under "Timing Belt, Replace."
3. Remove seal between oil pump and water pump, then the dipstick tube with dipstick.
4. Remove alternator adjusting arm, then the water pump.
5. Reverse procedure to install, using new gasket and rubber seals, **Fig. 25**.

RADIATOR
REPLACE
ESTEEM

1. Drain cooling system, then disconnect cooling fan motor electrical connector.
2. Remove front grill assembly.
3. Disconnect inlet, outlet and reservoir tank hoses from radiator.
4. **On models equipped with automatic transaxle,** place a suitable container under transaxle fluid line to radiator connections, then disconnect fluid lines from radiator.
5. **On all models,** remove radiator and cooling fan assembly.
6. Reverse procedure to install.

SIDEKICK & X-90

1. Drain cooling system.
2. Disconnect cooling fan electrical connector.
3. **On models equipped with automatic transmission,** disconnect transmission cooler lines at radiator.
4. **On all models,** remove cooling fan clutch and radiator shroud.
5. Disconnect radiator inlet and outlet hoses and reservoir tank hose.
6. Remove radiator.
7. Reverse procedure to install.

FUEL PUMP
REPLACE
ESTEEM

1. Relieve fuel system pressure as outlined under "Precautions."
2. Remove rear seat cushion, rear right

1. Fuel filter
2. Outlet pipe
3. Inlet pipe
4. Wrenches

SK1029100003000X

Fig. 26 Fuel filter removal. Sidekick & X-90

seat back, right side sill cuff, right front partition trim and right rear door opening trim.
3. Disconnect fuel pump and fuel level gauge wire at coupler.
4. Raise and support vehicle, then remove exhaust muffler.
5. Disconnect fuel filler and breather hoses from filler neck.
6. Using a suitable hand operated pump, drain fuel tank through fuel tank filler.
7. Disconnect fuel lines from tank.
8. Remove fuel tank from vehicle, then the fuel pump from tank.
9. Reverse procedure to install.

SIDEKICK & X-90

1. Relieve fuel system pressure as outlined under "Precautions."
2. Remove rear bumper cover.
3. Disconnect level gauge and fuel pump lead wire couplers.
4. Remove fuel tank filler hose and inlet valve, then drain fuel tank into appropriate container.
5. Remove fuel filter inlet pipe from filter, then the vapor and return hoses.
6. Remove tank protector, then the fuel tank.
7. Remove fuel pump from fuel tank.
8. Reverse procedure to install.

FUEL FILTER
REPLACE
ESTEEM

1. Relieve fuel system pressure as outlined under "Precautions."
2. Place suitable container under fuel filter at rear center of engine compartment.
3. Disconnect inlet and outlet hoses from fuel filter.
4. Remove fuel filter and bracket from dash panel.
5. Remove fuel filter from bracket.

SUZUKI

6. Reverse procedure to install.

SIDEKICK & X-90

1. Relieve fuel system pressure as outlined under "Precautions."
2. Raise vehicle and support vehicle.
3. Disconnect inlet and outlet pipes from fuel filter using two wrenches, **Fig. 26.**
4. Remove fuel filter from chassis frame.
5. Reverse procedure to install, noting the following:
   a. Ensure gasket surfaces are free from damage.
   b. Ensure inlet and outlet pipes come into recess, **Fig. 27.**
   c. **Torque** union bolts to 22–28.5 lb. ft.
   d. Ensure there are no fuel leaks at each connection.

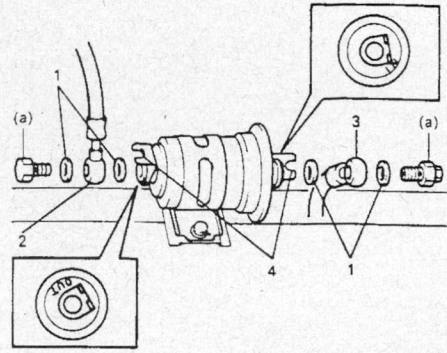

1. Gasket
2. Outlet pipe
3. Inlet pipe
4. Recess

SK1029100004000X

Fig. 27   Fuel filter Installation

TIGHTENING SPECIFICATIONS

Year	Component	Torque/Ft. Lbs.
1996–99	Camshaft Housing Bolts	④
	Camshaft Timing Pulley Bolt	41–46
	Connecting Rod Bearing Cap Nut	24–27
	Cooling Fan Nut	84–108⑤
	Crankshaft Main Bearing Cap Bolt	37–41
	Crankshaft Pulley Bolts	11–13
	Crankshaft Timing Belt Pulley Bolt	94
	Cylinder Head Bolts	③
	Cylinder Head Cover Bolt	84–108⑤
	Cylinder Head Venturi Plug	36–48⑤
	Driveplate②	55–58
	Engine Mounting Chassis Side Bracket Bolt	29–43
	Engine Mounting Engine Side Bracket Bolt	29–43
	Engine Mounting Nut	29–36
	Exhaust Manifold Nut & Bolt	14–20
	Exhaust Manifold Stiffener Nut	29–43
	Exhaust Pipe Nut & Bolts	29–43
	Flywheel Bolt①	55–58
	Fuel Feed Pipe Flare Nut	29–36
	Intake Manifold Nuts & Bolts	14–20
	Intake Manifold Stiffener Bolts	29–43
	Oil Pan Drain Plug	22–29
	Oil Pan Nuts & Bolts	84–108⑤
	Oil Pressure Switch	9–11
	Oil Pump Case Bolts	84–108⑤
	Oil Pump Rotor Plate Screw	84–108⑤
	Oil Pump Stay Bolt	84–108⑤
	Oil Pump Strainer Bolt	84–108⑤
	Rocker Arm Shaft Bolts	84–108⑤
	Rocker Arm Shaft Plug	22–25
	Thermostat Case Bolts	8–12
	Throttle Body Bolt	14–20
	Timing Belt Cover Nuts & Bolts	84–108⑤
	Timing Belt Tensioner Bolt	16–20

Continued

TIGHTENING SPECIFICATIONS—Continued

Year	Component	Torque/Ft. Lbs.
1996–99	Timing Belt Tensioner Stud	84–108⑤
	Torque Converter Bolts	44–51
	Transmission Stiffener Bolts	29–43
	Transmission To Engine Bolts	51–72
	Valve Adjusting Screw Locknut	96–108⑤
	Water Pump Bolt	96–108⑤

① — Manual transmission.
② — Automatic transmission.
③ — Refer to "Cylinder Head, Replace" for tightening procedure.
④ — Refer to "Rocker Arms, Replace" for tightening procedure.
⑤ — Inch lbs.

1.8L Engine

NOTE: On Air Bag Equipped Models, Refer To "Air Bag System Precautions" Located In The Front Of This Manual For System Disarming & Arming Procedures.

INDEX

PRECAUTIONS

AIR BAG SYSTEMS

Refer to "Air Bag System Precautions" in the front of this manual for system disarming and arming procedures.

FUEL SYSTEM PRESSURE RELIEF

1. Place manual transmission models in Neutral or automatic transmission models in Park, then set parking brake and block drive wheels.
2. Disconnect fuel pump relay, **Fig. 1.**
3. Remove fuel filler cap to release fuel vapor pressure in tank, then install cap.
4. Start and run engine until it stalls. Repeat cranking engine three times for three seconds each time to dissipate fuel pressure in fuel lines.

BATTERY GROUND CABLE

Prior to service, disconnect battery ground cable and isolate as required.

COMPRESSION PRESSURE

Standard compression pressure is 199 psi with a minimum of 170 psi. Maximum allowable difference between cylinders is 14.2 psi.

ENGINE
REPLACE

1. Relieve fuel system pressure as outlined under " Precautions."
2. Mark hood for reference and remove hood.
3. Drain engine oil and coolant.
4. Remove radiator fan, fan shroud and cooling fan.
5. Disconnect accelerator cable.
6. **On models equipped with automatic transmission,** disconnect throttle cable.
7. **On all models,** remove strut tower bar.
8. Remove air intake pipe with hoses, then disconnect accelerator cable and transmission throttle cable from throttle body.
9. Remove electrical harness connectors.
10. Remove fuel feed and return lines.
11. Remove heater hoses from heater core.
12. Remove EVAP canister hose and brake booster vacuum hose.
13. Remove MAP sensor hose.
14. **On models equipped with power steering,** disconnect power steering pump with hoses attached and position aside.
15. **On models equipped with A/C,** disconnect A/C compressor with bracket attached and position aside.
16. **On all models,** raise and support vehicle.
17. Remove transfer case as outlined in "Transfer Case " section.
18. Remove exhaust pipe.
19. Remove righthand transmission stiffener and transmission fluid hose clamp bolt, if equipped.
20. Remove clutch housing lower plate.
21. **On models equipped with automatic transmission,** remove torque converter bolts.

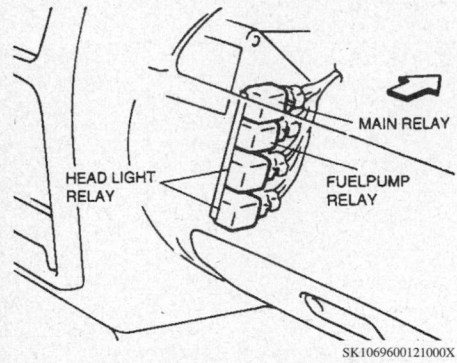

Fig. 1   Fuel pump relay

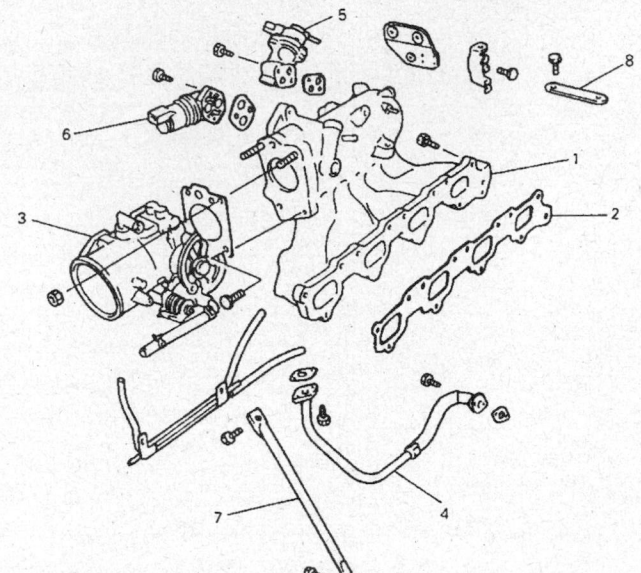

1. Intake manifold
2. Intake manifold gasket
3. Throttle body
4. EGR pipe
5. EGR valve
6. IAC valve
7. Intake manifold front stiffener
8. Intake manifold rear stiffener

Fig. 2   Exploded view of throttle body & intake manifold

22. **On all models,** lower vehicle and re-move starter motor.
23. Raise and support vehicle, then support transmission using a suitable jack.
24. Loosen bolts securing engine to transmission.
25. Install a suitable lifting device, then remove right and left engine mounting bracket bolts.
26. Remove engine assembly from chassis and transmission by sliding towards front, then carefully hoisting from vehicle.
27. Reverse procedure to install, noting the following:
    a. Tighten nuts and bolts to specification.
    b. Adjust water pump, power steering pump and A/C compressor drive belt tension.
    c. Adjust accelerator and transmission throttle cable play.

INTAKE MANIFOLD
REPLACE

1. Relieve fuel system pressure as outlined under " Precautions."
2. Drain engine coolant.
3. Remove strut tower bar and air temperature sensor.
4. Remove air cleaner upper case and outlet hose as a unit.
5. Remove throttle cover, then disconnect accelerator cable.
6. **On models equipped with automatic transmission,** disconnect throttle cable.
7. **On all models,** disconnect the following electrical connectors:
    a. Exhaust gas recirculation (EGR) valve.
    b. Idle air control (IAC) valve.
    c. Throttle position (TP) sensor.
    d. Manifold absolute pressure (MAP) sensor.
    e. Evaporative emissions (EVAP) solenoid purge valve.
    f. Ground terminal from intake manifold.
8. Disconnect hoses as necessary.
9. Remove throttle body, **Fig. 2.**
10. Remove intake manifold front and rear stiffeners.
11. Disconnect water pipe from intake manifold.
12. Remove intake manifold and gasket from cylinder head.

13. Reverse procedure to install, noting the following:
    a. Install new intake manifold gasket.
    b. Tighten to specifications.
    c. Adjust accelerator and transmission throttle cable play.
    d. Ensure there are no fuel, water or exhaust gas leakages.

EXHAUST MANIFOLD
REPLACE

1. Remove strut tower bar.
2. Disconnect heated oxygen sensor electrical connector, then remove manifold upper cover.
3. Remove manifold stiffener, then the exhaust pipe from manifold.
4. Remove manifold mounting bolts and nut, then the manifold and gasket.
5. Reverse procedure to install.

CYLINDER HEAD
REPLACE

1. Relieve fuel system pressure as outlined under " Precautions"
2. Drain engine oil and coolant, then remove strut tower bar.
3. Remove air cleaner outlet hose.
4. Disconnect accelerator cable.
5. **On models equipped with automatic transmission,** disconnect throttle cable.
6. **On all models,** remove 1st timing chain as outlined in "Timing Chain, Replace".
7. Disconnect the following electrical connectors:
    a. Exhaust gas recirculation (EGR) valve.
    b. Idle air control (IAC) valve.
    c. Throttle position (TP) sensor.
    d. Manifold absolute pressure (MAP) sensor.
    e. Evaporative emissions (EVAP) solenoid purge valve.

f. Heated oxygen sensor (H2OS).
g. Coolant temperature switch.
h. Engine coolant temperature (ECT) sensor.
i. Injector wire harness.
j. Ground terminal from intake manifold.
8. Disconnect hoses and lines, as necessary.
9. Remove intake manifold front stiffener.
10. Disconnect water pipe from intake manifold.
11. Remove exhaust pipe and exhaust manifold stiffener.
12. Loosen cylinder head bolts in sequence, **Fig. 3.** Remove M6 bolt.
13. Using a suitable lifting device, remove cylinder head with intake and exhaust manifolds.
14. Reverse procedure to install. Apply engine oil to cylinder head bolts, then using sequence shown in **Fig. 4,** tighten bolts as follows:
    a. **Torque** bolts to 39 ft. lbs.
    b. **Torque** bolts to 61 ft. lbs.
    c. Loosen bolts completely using sequence shown in **Fig. 3.**
    d. **Torque** bolts to 76 ft. lbs.
    e. **Torque** M6 bolt to 8 ft. lbs. after securing head bolts.

VALVE CLEARANCE SPECIFICATIONS

The 1.8L engine is equipped with hydraulic lash adjusters and valve clearance is not adjustable.

TIMING CHAIN
REPLACE

1. Drain engine oil and engine coolant.
2. Remove oil pan as outlined in "Oil Pan, Replace. " Remove oil strainer, **Fig. 5.**
3. Remove cylinder head cover.
4. Remove water bypass and bypass hose No. 2, **Fig. 6.**

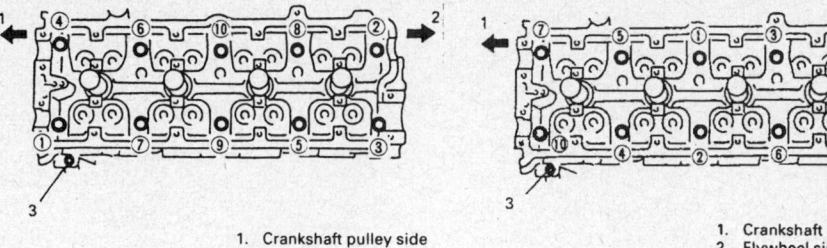

1. Crankshaft pulley side
2. Flywheel side
3. Bolt (M6)

SK1069600112000X

Fig. 3 Cylinder head bolt loosening sequence

1. Crankshaft pulley side
2. Flywheel side
3. Bolt (M6)

SK1069600113000X

Fig. 4 Cylinder head bolt tightening sequence

CAMSHAFT
REPLACE

1. Drain engine oil and coolant.
2. Remove oil pan as outlined in "Oil Pan, Replace."
3. Remove cylinder head cover.
4. Remove timing chain cover, No. 2 timing chain and chain tensioner as outlined in "Timing Chain, Replace".
5. Remove camshaft position sensor (CMP), **Fig. 12**.
6. Rotate crankshaft to position key as shown, **Fig. 13**.
7. Loosen, then remove camshaft housing bolts in sequence, **Fig. 14**. Note and mark location of camshaft housings.
8. Remove camshafts.
9. Reverse procedure to install, noting the following:
   a. Match key on crankshaft to timing mark, **Fig. 15**.
   b. Apply engine oil to lobes and journals.
   c. Align marks on cylinder head and camshafts, **Fig. 16**.
   d. Replace camshaft housings in original positions.
   e. Using sequence shown in **Fig. 17** tighten camshaft housing bolts to specification.
   f. Tighten all nuts and bolts to specification.

PISTON & ROD ASSEMBLY

Each standard size piston has a No. 1 or No. 2 stamped on it representing outer diameter. There are also red or blue colors painted on cylinder block surface representing inner diameters of cylinders **Fig. 18**. Stamped numbers on pistons and painted colors on cylinder block should correspond, **Fig. 19**.

OIL PAN
REPLACE

1. Raise and support vehicle.
2. Remove oil level gauge.
3. Remove front differential assembly from chassis. Refer to "Drive Axles" for removal procedure.
4. Remove tie rod, center link and idler arm.
5. Drain engine oil.
6. Remove oil pan and lower pan to crossmember bolts.
7. Insert wrench into oil pan and remove oil strainer bolts.
8. Remove oil pan.
9. Reverse procedure to install, noting the following:
   a. Clean mating surface of oil pan and crankcase.
   b. Apply sealant No. 99000–31150 or equivalent, to mating surface of oil pan.
   c. Tighten to specification.

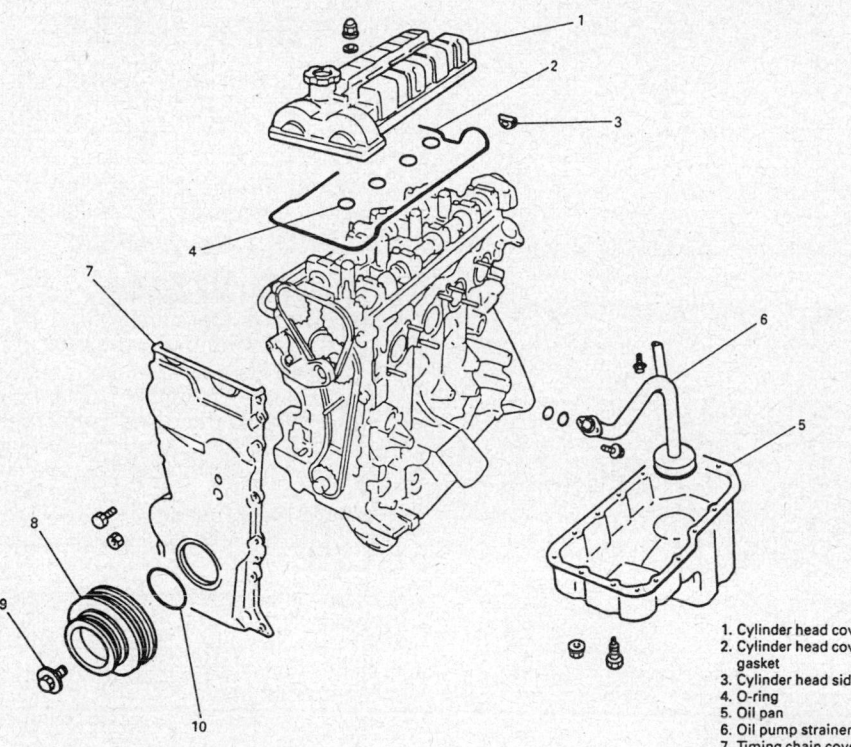

1. Cylinder head cover
2. Cylinder head cover gasket
3. Cylinder head side seal
4. O-ring
5. Oil pan
6. Oil pump strainer
7. Timing chain cover
8. Crankshaft pulley
9. Crankshaft pulley bolt
10. Oil seal

SK1069600114000X

Fig. 5 Timing chain cover removal

5. Remove cooling fan, fan pulley and fan belt.
6. Turn drive belt tensioner center bolt in a clockwise direction and remove alternator belt.
7. Remove water pump pulley, belt tensioner and idler pulley.
8. Disconnect radiator outlet hose from thermostat housing.
9. Remove A/C compressor from bracket and position aside.
10. Remove crankshaft pulley using puller tool No. 09044036011 and attachment No. 09926–58010 or equivalents.
11. Remove timing case cover.
12. Rotate crankshaft until key on crankshaft points straight up, arrow mark on idler sprocket points straight up and marks on sprockets match with marks on cylinder head, **Fig. 7**.
13. Remove timing chain tensioner No. 2 by turning intake camshaft counter-clockwise a little while pushing back pad, **Fig. 8**.
14. Remove camshaft sprockets and timing chain.
15. Remove timing chain guide No. 1, then adjuster No. 1 and tensioner, **Fig. 9**.
16. Remove idler sprocket and 1st timing chain. Remove crankshaft timing sprocket, if necessary.
17. Reverse procedure to install, noting the following:
   a. Install No. 1 timing chain by aligning dark blue plate of chain with match mark on idler sprocket, **Fig. 10**, then ensure yellow plate chain aligns with match mark on crankshaft timing sprocket, **Fig. 11**.
   b. Apply sealant No. 99000–31150 or equivalent, to timing case cover.
   c. Tighten to specification.

1. Water bypass pipe
2. Water bypass hose No.2
3. Cooling fan pulley
4. Water pump pulley
5. Generator belt tensioner

SK1069600115000X

Fig. 6 Water bypass & bypass hose No. 2 removal

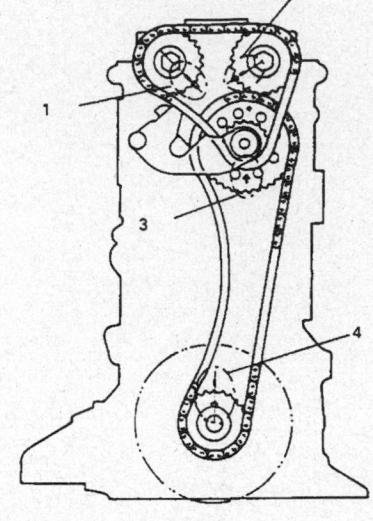

1. Timing marks of intake camshaft timing sprocket
2. Timing marks of exhaust camshaft timing sprocket
3. Arrow mark on idler sprocket
4. Timing marks of crankshaft timing sprocket

SK1069600116000X

Fig. 7 Timing chain marks

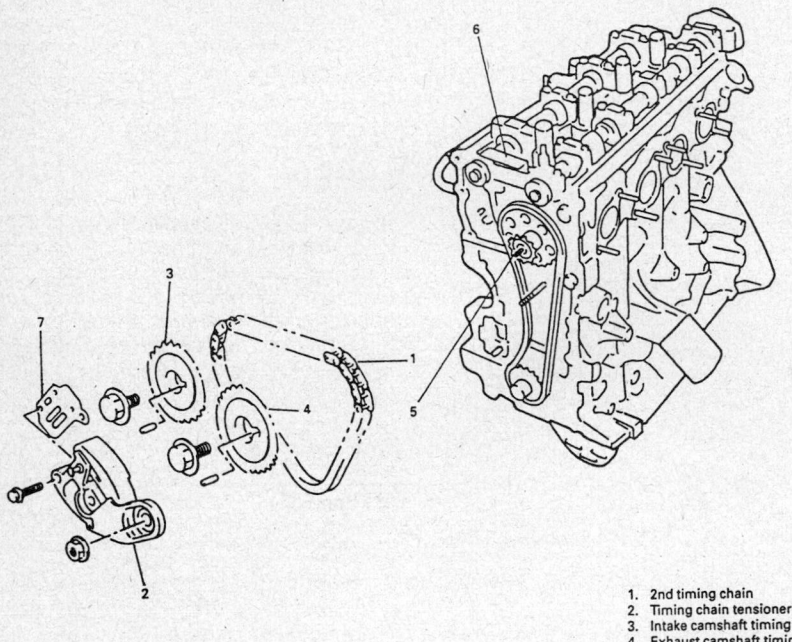

1. 2nd timing chain
2. Timing chain tensioner adjuster No.2
3. Intake camshaft timing sprocket
4. Exhaust camshaft timing sprocket
5. Idler sprocket
6. Timing chain guide No.2
7. Tensioner adjuster No.2 gasket

SK1069600117000X

Fig. 8 Timing chain tensioner adjuster No. 2 removal

OIL PUMP
REPLACE

1. Remove oil pan as outlined under "Oil Pan, Replace."
2. Remove oil pump sprocket cover.
3. Remove oil pump mounting bolts, then the oil pump.
4. Inspect oil pump as follows:
   a. Inspect oil lip seal for wear or damage.
   b. Inspect pump outer and inner rotors, pump housing and relief valve for excessive wear or damage.
   c. Measure free length of relief spring. Free length should be 2.5 inches.
   d. Using thickness gauge, check radial clearance between outer rotor and case. Radial clearance should be 0.0059 inch. If clearance exceeds specifications, replace outer rotor or case.
   e. Using straightedge, check oil pump side clearance. Side clearance should be 0.0043 inch.
5. Reverse procedure to install. Tighten to specifications.

BELT TENSION DATA

Year	Belt Deflection Inch①	
	New	Used
1996-99	.16–.20	.20-.27

① — With 22 lbs. pressure applied between fan pulley & crankshaft pulley.

COOLING SYSTEM BLEED

This engine does not require a specific bleed procedure. After filling coolant system, run engine to operating temperature with radiator/pressure cap off. Air will then be automatically bled through cap opening.

THERMOSTAT
REPLACE

1. Drain coolant system into appropriate container.
2. Remove radiator outlet hose at thermostat housing, then the housing.
3. Remove thermostat.
4. Reverse procedure to install noting the following:
   a. Ensure air breather valve is positioned to front side of engine.
   b. Fill and bleed coolant system.

RADIATOR
REPLACE

Refer to "1.6L Engine" for radiator replacement.

FUEL PUMP
REPLACE

Refer to "1.6L Engine" for fuel pump replacement.

FUEL FILTER
REPLACE

Refer to "1.6L Engine," for fuel filter replacement.

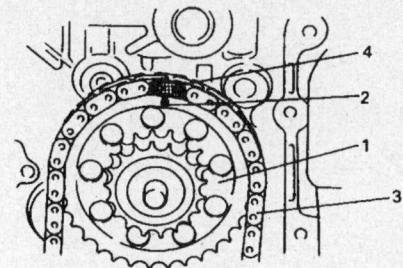

1. Idler sprocket
2. Match mark on idler sprocket
3. 1st timing chain
4. Dark blue plate

SK1069600119000X

Fig. 10 Idler sprocket & No. 1 timing chain blue plate alignment

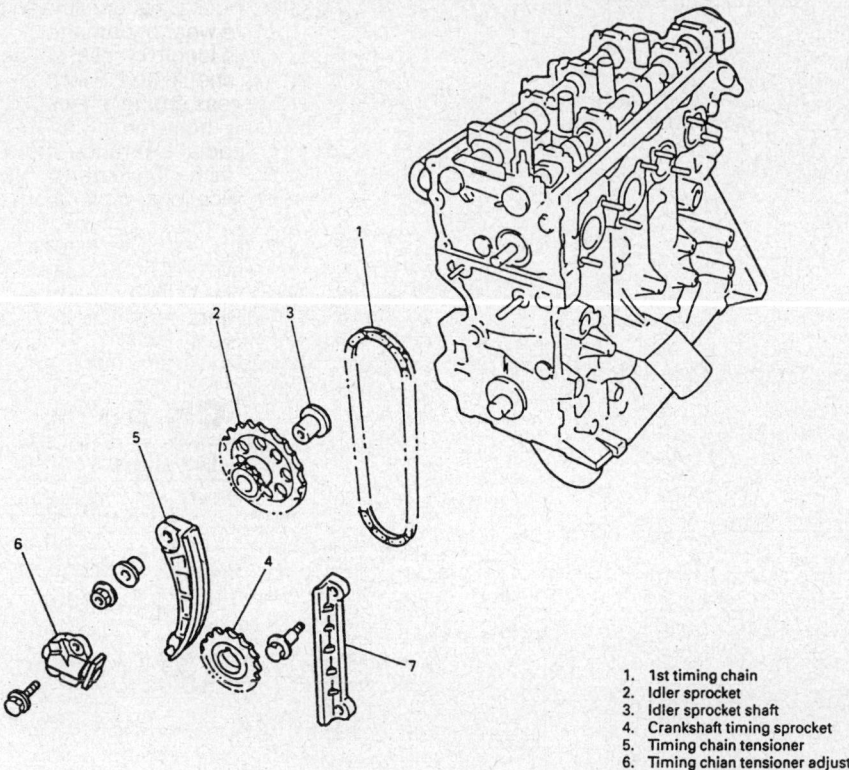

1. 1st timing chain
2. Idler sprocket
3. Idler sprocket shaft
4. Crankshaft timing sprocket
5. Timing chain tensioner
6. Timing chian tensioner adjuster No.1
7. Timing chain guide No.1

SK1069600118000X

Fig. 9 No. 1 timing chain removal

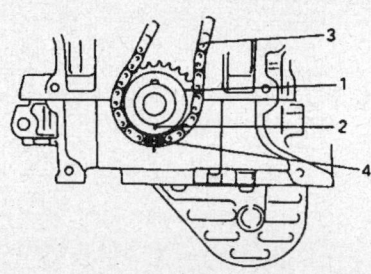

1. Crankshaft timing sprocket
2. Match mark
3. 1st timing chain
4. Yellow plate

SK1069600120000X

Fig. 11 Crankshaft sprocket & No. 1 timing chain yellow plate alignment

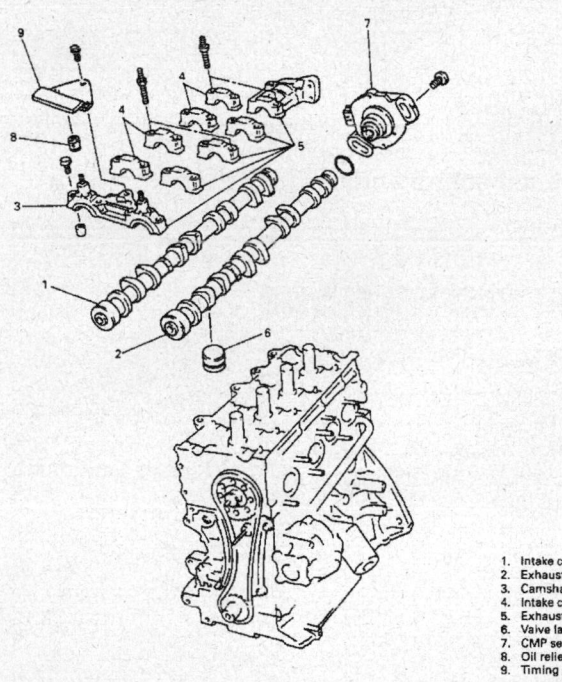

1. Intake camshaft
2. Exhaust camshaft
3. Camshaft housing
4. Intake camshaft housing
5. Exhaust camshaft housing
6. Valve lash adjuster
7. CMP sensor
8. Oil relief valve
9. Timing chain guide No.2

SK1069600122000X

Fig. 12 Exploded view of camshaft components

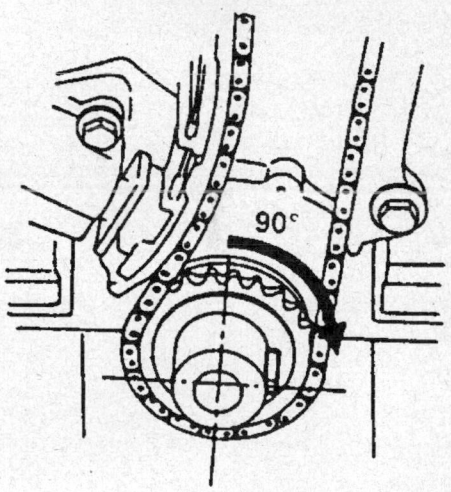

SK1069600123000X

Fig. 13 Crankshaft key position for camshaft removal

SUZUKI

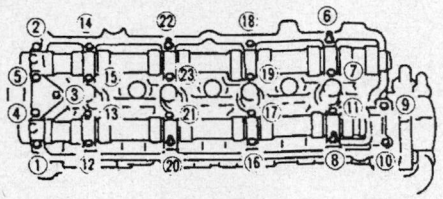

Fig. 14 Camshaft bolt removal sequence

SK1069600124000X

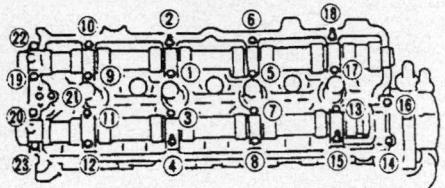

Fig. 17 Camshaft bolt tightening sequence

SK1069600127000X

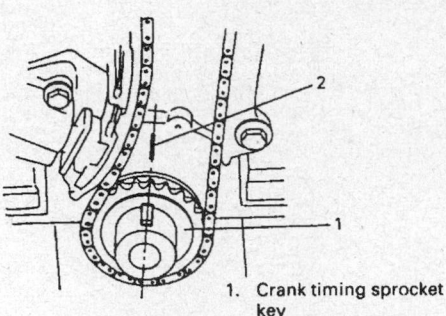

1. Crank timing sprocket key
2. Timing mark

SK1069600125000X

Fig. 15 Crankshaft key alignment

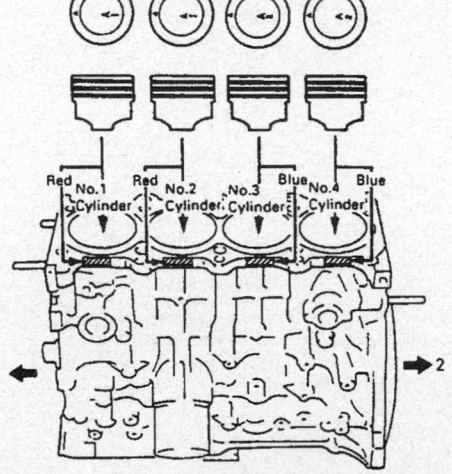

1. Crankshaft pulley side
2. Flywheel side

SK1069600128000X

Fig. 18 Piston & cylinder diagram

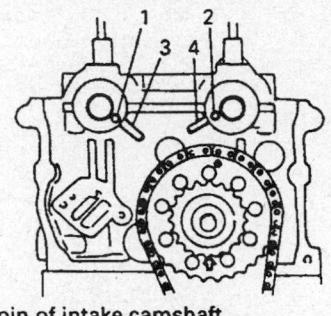

1. Knock pin of intake camshaft
2. Knock pin of exhaust camshaft
3. Match mark of intake camshaft
4. Match mark of exhaust camshaft

SK1069600126000X

Fig. 16 Camshafts & cylinder head alignment

	Piston	Cylinder		Piston-to-cylinder clearance
Number at the top (mark)	Outer diameter	Mark	Bore diameter	
1	83.98 – 83.99 mm (3.3063 – 3.3066 in.)	Red	84.01 – 84.02 mm (3.3075 – 3.3078 in.)	0.02 – 0.04 mm (0.0008 – 0.0015 in.)
2	83.97 – 83.98 mm (3.3059 – 3.3062 in.)	Blue	84.00 – 84.01 mm (3.3071 – 3.3074 in.)	0.02 – 0.04 mm (0.0008 – 0.0015 in.)

SK1069600129000X

Fig. 19 Piston & cylinder chart

TIGHTENING SPECIFICATIONS

Year	Component	Torque/Ft. Lbs.
1996–99	A/C Compressor Bracket	40
	Alternator Belt Tensioner	18
	Alternator Idler Pulley	33
	Bypass Pipe	17
	Camshaft Housing Bolts	96②
	Camshaft Timing Pulley Bolt	44
	Connecting Rod Bearing Cap Nut	33
	Crankshaft Pulley Bolt	108
	Cylinder Head Bolts	①
	Cylinder Head Cover Bolt	96②
	Engine Mounting Bracket Bolt	37
	Engine Mounting Engine Side Bracket Bolt	37
	Engine Mounting Nut	37
	Exhaust Manifold Nut & Bolt	17
	Exhaust Manifold Stiffener	37
	Exhaust Pipe	37
	Flywheel Bolt	51

Continued

1.8L ENGINE

TIGHTENING
SPECIFICATIONS—Continued

Year	Component	Torque/Ft. Lbs.
1996–99	Intake Manifold Front Stiffener	36
	Intake Manifold Nut & Bolt	17
	Intake Manifold Rear Stiffener	18
	Oil Drain Plug	26
	Oil Pan Bolt	96②
	Oil Pump Case Bolt	108②
	Oil Pump Mounting	15
	Oil Pump Relief Valve Retainer	21
	Oil Pump Sprocket Cover	96②
	Oil Pump Strainer Bracket Bolt	96②
	Oil Pump Strainer Bolts	96②
	Spark Plugs	18
	Strut Tower Bar	65
	Throttle Body Bolt	114②
	Timing Chain Cover Bolt	96②
	Timing Chain Guide No. 1	96②
	Timing Chain Tensioner No. 1	19
	Timing Chain Tensioner Adjuster No. 1	96②
	Timing Chain No. 2 Tensioner Bolt	96②
	Timing Chain No. 2 Tensioner Stud	33
	Torque Converter Bolt	47
	Transmission To Engine	58
	Transmission Stiffener	37
	Water Pump Bolt	18

① — Refer to "Cylinder Head, Replace" for tightening procedure.

② — Inch lbs.

SUZUKI

2.5L Engine

NOTE: On Air Bag Equipped Models, Refer To "Air Bag System Precautions" Located In The Front Of This Manual For System Disarming & Arming Procedures.

INDEX

PRECAUTIONS

AIR BAG SYSTEMS

Refer to "Air Bag System Precautions" in the front of this manual for system disarming and arming procedures.

BATTERY GROUND CABLE

Prior to service, disconnect battery ground cable and isolate as required.

FUEL SYSTEM PRESSURE RELIEF

1. Place manual transmission models in Neutral or automatic transmission models in Park, then set parking brake and block drive wheels.
2. Disconnect fuel pump relay.
3. Remove fuel filler cap to release fuel vapor pressure in tank, then install cap.
4. Start and run engine until it stalls. Repeat cranking engine three times for three seconds each time to dissipate fuel pressure in fuel lines.

COMPRESSION PRESSURE

Standard compression pressure is 228 psi with a minimum of 185 psi. Maximum allowable difference between cylinders is 14.2 psi.

ENGINE

REPLACE

1. Relieve fuel pressure as outlined under "Precautions."
2. Remove hood, then drain engine oil and coolant into suitable containers.
3. Remove radiator, fan shroud, cooling fan and radiator reservoir.
4. Remove accelerator and throttle cables from throttle body.
5. Remove strut tower bar and surge tank cover.
6. Disconnect IAT sensor electrical connector, then remove air cleaner upper case, intake air hose, intake air pipe and surge tank pipe as an assembly.
7. Remove oil level and transmission fluid gauge guides.
8. Remove ignition coil covers.
9. Disconnect electrical connectors from all sensors, fuel injectors and ignition coils.
10. Disconnect heater hoses, vacuum lines and EVAP canister hoses.
11. Remove IAC and EVAP canister purge valves.
12. Disconnect fuel feed and return lines.
13. Remove EVAP canister.
14. Remove power steering pump assembly.
15. Remove A/C compressor assembly.
16. Remove steering shaft lower assembly.
17. Raise and support vehicle, then remove front differential housing with differential.
18. Remove front exhaust pipe, then exhaust manifold stiffener from transmission.
19. Remove transmission fluid hose clamps from engine mounting bracket.
20. Remove clutch housing lower plate.
21. Remove torque converter bolts.
22. Remove starter motor, then lower vehicle.
23. Support transmission, then remove mounting bolts and nuts securing transmission to engine.
24. Install suitable lifting device on engine.
25. Disconnect engine side mounting brackets.
26. Ensure all hoses, cables and wiring is disconnected from engine.
27. Lift engine, then remove from chassis by sliding toward front, then out of vehicle.
28. Reverse procedure to install.

INTAKE MANIFOLD

REPLACE

1. Relieve fuel pressure as outlined under "Precautions."
2. Drain engine coolant into suitable containers.
3. Remove accelerator and throttle cables from throttle body.
4. Remove strut tower bar and surge tank cover.
5. Disconnect IAT sensor electrical connector, then remove air cleaner upper case, intake air hose, intake air pipe and surge tank pipe as an assembly.
6. Disconnect hoses from throttle body.
7. Disconnect injector harness connector.
8. Disconnect brake booster hose from intake manifold.
9. Disconnect TP, MAF and IAC electrical connectors.
10. Disconnect ground terminal from intake collector.
11. Remove clamp bracket from intake collector.
12. Disconnect electrical connectors from sensors attached to intake manifold.
13. Disconnect PCV hose and breather hoses from valve cover.
14. Disconnect EVAP purge valve hoses.
15. Disconnect fuel feed and return lines.
16. Remove throttle body and intake collector from intake manifold.
17. Remove eight intake manifold bolts and four nuts.
18. Remove intake manifold.
19. Reverse procedure to install. Tighten bolts and nuts to specifications.

EXHAUST MANIFOLD

REPLACE

1. Remove air cleaner upper case and intake air hose.
2. Disconnect O_2 sensor connectors.
3. Remove oil level gauge guide.
4. Disconnect EGR pipe from manifold.
5. Remove exhaust manifold covers.
6. Raise and support vehicle.
7. **On models equipped with 4WD,** reference mark, then remove front propeller shaft.
8. **On all models,** remove front exhaust pipe.

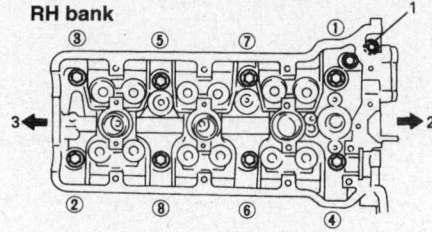

RH bank

LH bank

1. Hex hole bolt
2. Timing chain side
3. Flywheel side

SK1069900152000X

Fig. 1   Cylinder head bolt loosening sequence

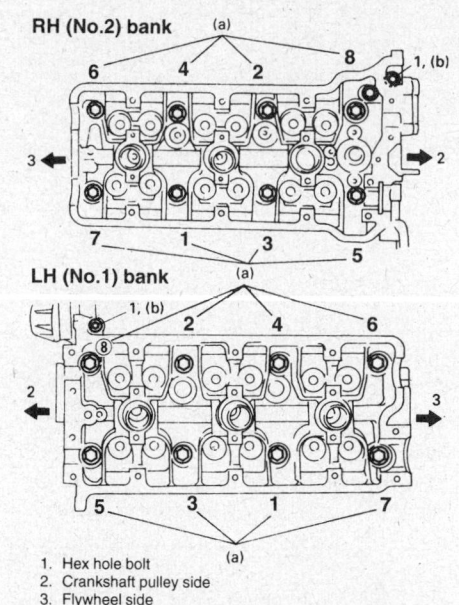

RH (No.2) bank

LH (No.1) bank

1. Hex hole bolt
2. Crankshaft pulley side
3. Flywheel side

SK1139900076000X

Fig. 2   Cylinder head bolt tightening sequence

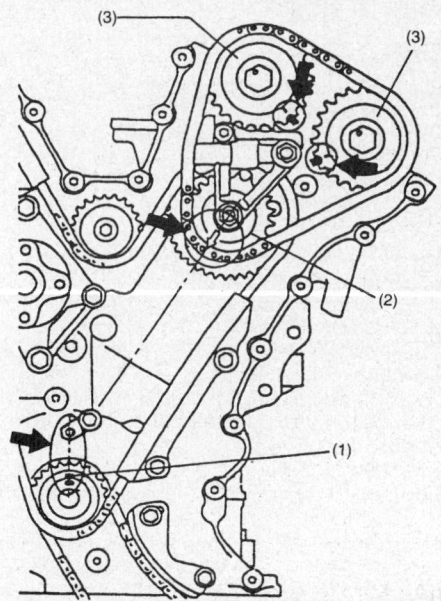

SK1139900083000X

Fig. 3   Timing mark alignment

9. Disconnect exhaust manifold stiffener from transmission.
10. Remove exhaust manifolds and gaskets from engine.
11. Reverse procedure to install.

CYLINDER HEAD
REPLACE

1. Relieve fuel pressure as outlined under "Precautions."
2. Drain engine oil and coolant into suitable containers.
3. Remove intake manifold as outlined under "Intake Manifold, Replace."
4. Remove exhaust manifold as outlined under "Exhaust Manifold, Replace."
5. Remove timing chains as outlined under "Timing Chain, Replace."
6. Remove water outlet cap.
7. Remove valve covers.
8. Loosen cylinder head bolts in sequence shown, **Fig. 1.**
9. Remove cylinder head.
10. Reverse procedure to install, noting the following:
    a. Apply clean engine oil to threads of bolts.
    b. **Torque** (A) bolts to 39 ft. lbs. using sequence shown, **Fig. 2.**
    c. **Torque** (A) bolts in order again to 61 ft. lbs.
    d. Loosen bolts in reverse order of tightening.
    e. **Torque** (A) bolts in sequence to 39 ft. lbs.
    f. **Torque** (A) bolts to 76 ft. lbs.
    g. **Torque** (B) bolt to 8 ft. lbs.

VALVE CLEARANCE SPECIFICATIONS

The 2.5L engine is equipped with hydraulic lash adjusters and valve clearance is not adjustable.

TIMING CHAIN
REPLACE

1. Drain engine oil and coolant into suitable containers.
2. Remove intake manifold as outlined under "Intake Manifold, Replace."
3. Remove valve covers.
4. Remove cooling fan, clutch and water pump pulley.
5. Remove radiator and thermostat cap.
6. Remove power steering and A/C drive belts.
7. Remove power steering pump and bracket.
8. Raise and support vehicle, then remove oil pan as outlined under "Oil Pan, Replace."
9. Using camshaft pulley holder tool No. 09917–68221, or equivalent, lock crankshaft pulley and remove bolt.
10. Using suitable puller, remove crankshaft pulley.
11. Remove CKP sensor as required.
12. Remove timing chain cover.
13. Rotate crankshaft to align timing marks as shown, **Fig. 3.**
14. Remove No. 3 timing chain adjuster, **Fig. 4.**
15. Using suitable wrench, hold camshaft at hexagonal area and remove sprocket bolts.
16. Remove camshaft sprockets, then left bank timing chain.
17. Remove timing chain guide Nos. 1 and 2, **Fig. 5.**
18. Remove No. 1 timing chain adjuster, **Fig. 5.**
19. Remove No. 1 idler sprocket and timing chain.
20. Remove No. 2 idler sprocket and sprocket shaft.
21. Remove timing chain tensioner.
22. Using suitable wrench, hold camshaft at hexagonal area and remove sprocket bolt.
23. Remove timing chain camshaft and crankshaft sprockets.
24. Remove timing chain guide No. 3, **Fig. 6.**
25. Remove camshaft housing bolts in order shown, **Fig. 7.**
26. Remove camshafts and chain as an assembly.
27. Remove No. 2 tensioner adjuster, **Fig. 6.**
28. Reverse procedure to install, noting the following:
    a. **Torque** camshaft housing bolts in sequence shown, **Fig. 8,** to 9 ft. lbs.
    b. Refer to **Fig. 9** for sprocket timing alignment marks.

CAMSHAFT
REPLACE

1. To remove right camshafts, remove timing chain as outlined under "Timing Chain, Replace."
2. Remove CMP sensor.
3. Loosen left camshaft housing bolts in sequence shown, **Fig. 10.**
4. Remove camshafts.
5. Reverse procedure to install. **Torque** left camshaft housing bolts in sequence shown, **Fig. 11,** to 9 ft. lbs.

PISTON & ROD ASSEMBLY

Each standard size piston has a No. 1 or No. 2 stamped on it representing outer diameter. There is also a No. 1 or No. 2 stamped on the cylinder block surface representing inner diameters of cylinders. Stamped numbers on pistons and cylinder block should correspond.

OIL PAN
REPLACE

1. Remove oil level gauge guide, then raise and support vehicle.
2. Remove front wheel and tire assemblies.
3. Remove power steering gear assembly as outlined under "Power Steering Gear, Replace."
4. **On models equipped with 4WD,** remove front differential housing.
5. **On all models,** drain engine oil into suitable container.
6. Remove lower oil pan from upper oil pan.
7. Remove oil strainer bracket.
8. Detach radiator outlet pipe from upper oil pan.
9. Remove upper oil pan bolts.
10. Lower oil pan and allow to rest on strainer and crossmember.
11. Remove oil strainer through opening between oil pan and lower crankcase.
12. Remove oil pan.
13. Reverse procedure to install. **Torque** (B) bolts to 8 ft. lbs. and (C) bolts to 20 ft. lbs., **Fig. 12.**

1. LH bank 2nd timing chain
2. Timing chain tensioner adjuster No.3
3. LH bank intake camshaft sprocket
4. LH bank exhaust camshaft sprocket
5. Camshaft sprocket bolt
6. Timing chain guide No.4
7. Timing chain guide No.5
8. Idler sprocket No.2

SK1139900084000X

Fig. 4   Left bank timing chain components

OIL PUMP
REPLACE

1. Drain engine oil and coolant into suitable containers.
2. Remove timing cover as outlined under "Timing Chain, Replace."
3. Remove oil pan as outlined under "Oil Pan, Replace."
4. Loosen oil pump chain guide bolts.
5. Remove oil pump from crankcase.
6. Reverse procedure to install.

BELT TENSION DATA

Year	Belt Deflection Inch①	
	New	Used
1999	.16–.35	.16–.35

① — With 22 lbs. pressure applied between fan pulley & crankshaft pulley.

COOLING SYSTEM BLEED

This engine does not require a specific bleed procedure. After filling coolant system, run engine to operating temperature with radiator/pressure cap off. Air will then be automatically bled through cap opening.

THERMOSTAT
REPLACE

1. Drain coolant into suitable container.
2. Disconnect radiator inlet hose.
3. Remove fan shroud with cooling fan.
4. Remove thermostat cap.
5. Remove thermostat.
6. Reverse procedure to install.

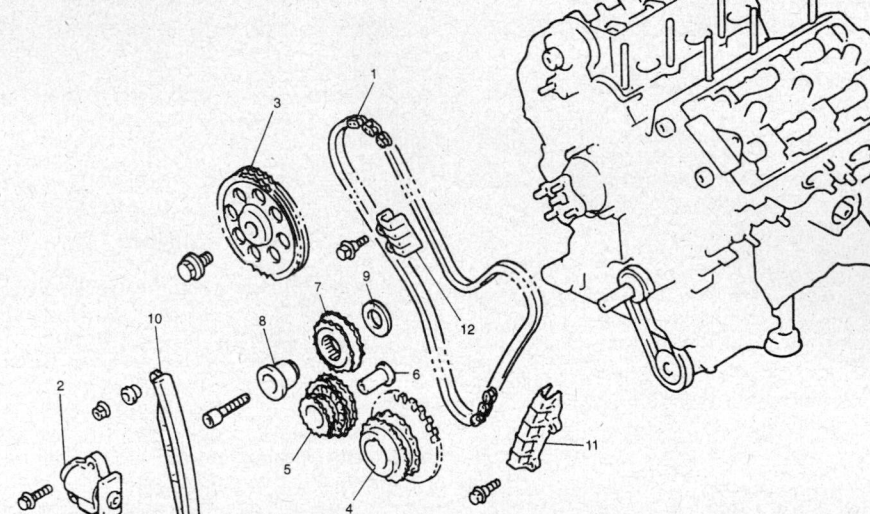

1. 1st timing chain
2. Timing chain tensioner adjuster No.1
3. RH bank 1st timing chain intake camshaft sprocket
4. 1st timing chain crankshaft sprocket
5. Idler sprocket No.2
6. Shaft
7. Idler sprocket No.1
8. Shaft
9. Washer
10. Timing chain tensioner
11. Timing chain guide No.1
12. Timing chain guide No.2

SK1139900085000X

Fig. 5   Right bank No. 1 timing chain components

RADIATOR
REPLACE

1. Drain coolant into suitable container.
2. Disconnect automatic transmission cooler lines.
3. Loosen cooling fan/clutch mounting nuts.
4. Disconnect radiator inlet hose.
5. Remove power steering oil tank stay bolts from radiator support.
6. Remove radiator shroud securing clips.
7. Remove cooling fan clutch and shroud.

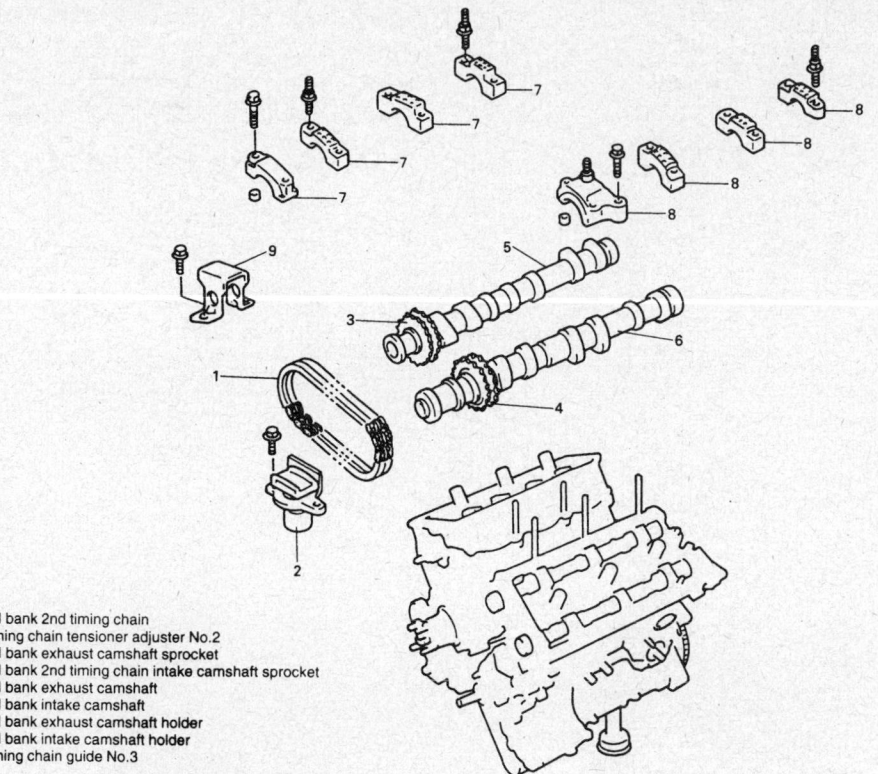

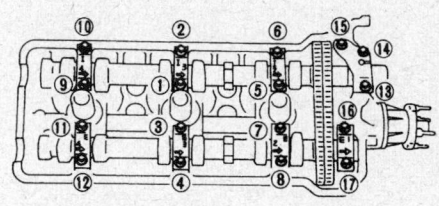

Fig. 7 Camshaft bolt loosening sequence

SK1139900087000X

Fig. 8 Camshaft bolt tightening sequence

SK1139900088000X

1. RH bank 2nd timing chain
2. Timing chain tensioner adjuster No.2
3. RH bank exhaust camshaft sprocket
4. RH bank 2nd timing chain intake camshaft sprocket
5. RH bank exhaust camshaft
6. RH bank intake camshaft
7. RH bank exhaust camshaft holder
8. RH bank intake camshaft holder
9. Timing chain guide No.3

SK1139900086000X

Fig. 6 Right bank No. 2 timing chain components

8. Disconnect remaining hoses from radiator.
9. Remove radiator.
10. Reverse procedure to install.

FUEL PUMP

REPLACE

1. Remove fuel tank.
2. Remove fuel pump assembly from tank.
3. Reverse procedure to install.

FUEL FILTER

REPLACE

1. Relieve fuel pressure as outlined under "Precautions."
2. Raise and support vehicle.
3. Disconnect inlet and outlet hoses from filter.
4. Remove filter from frame of vehicle.
5. Reverse procedure to install.

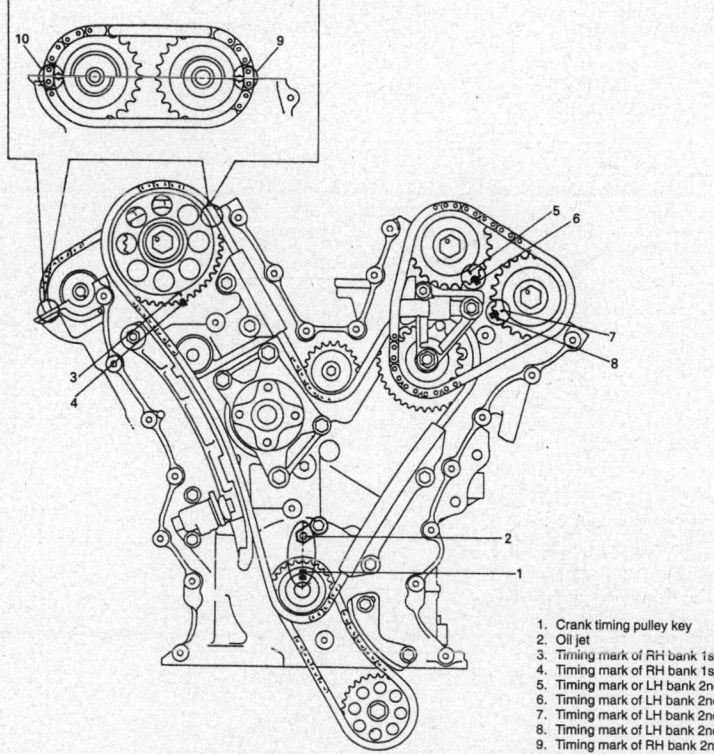

1. Crank timing pulley key
2. Oil jet
3. Timing mark of RH bank 1st timing chain sprocket
4. Timing mark of RH bank 1st timing chain
5. Timing mark or LH bank 2nd timing chain intake sprocket
6. Timing mark of LH bank 2nd timing chain
7. Timing mark of LH bank 2nd timing chain exhaust sprocket
8. Timing mark of LH bank 2nd timing chain
9. Timing mark of RH bank 2nd timing chain intake sprocket
10. Timing mark of RH bank 2nd timing chain exhaust sprocket

SK1139900089010X

Fig. 9 Timing chain alignment marks (Part 1 of 2)

SUZUKI

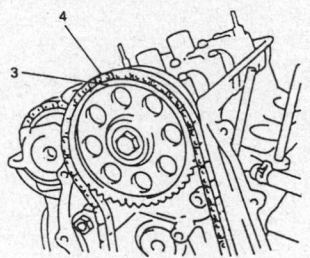

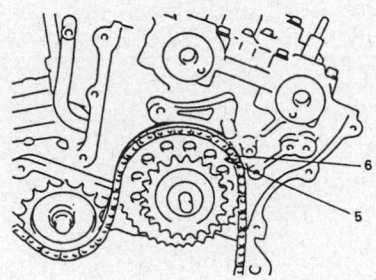

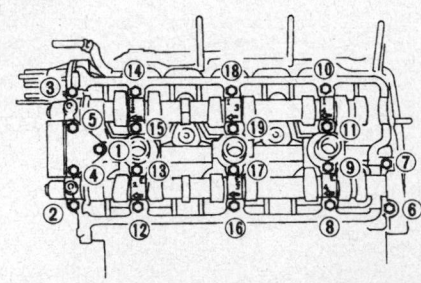

3. Match mark of RH bank 1st timing chain sprocket
4. Silver plate (LH) of 1st timing chain

5. Match mark of idler sprocket No.2
6. Silver plate (RH) of 1st timing chain

SK1069900153000X

Fig. 10 Left camshaft loosening sequence. 2.5L engine

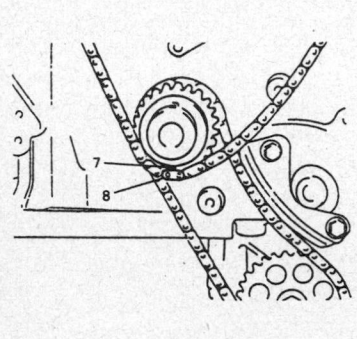

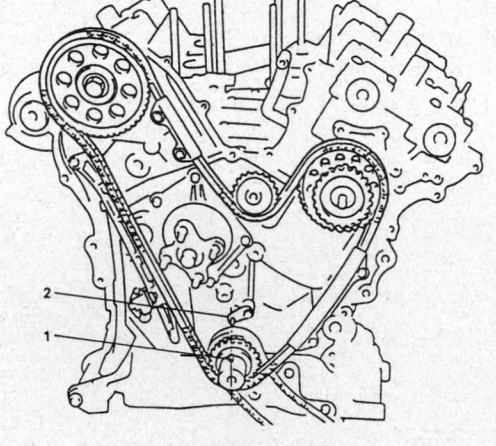

7. Match mark of crankshaft timing sprocket
8. Gold or Yellow plate of 1st timing chain

1. Crank timing pulley key
2. Oil jet

SK1139900089020X

Fig. 9 Timing chain alignment marks (Part 2 of 2)

LH bank

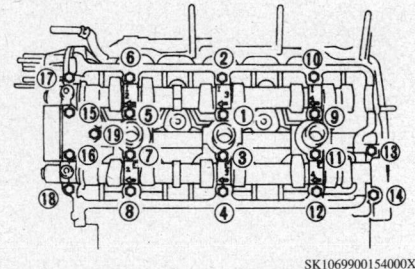

SK1069900154000X

Fig. 11 Left camshaft tightening sequence

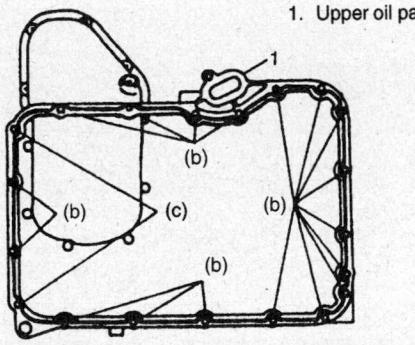

1. Upper oil pan

SK1069900155000X

Fig. 12 Oil pan bolt tightening locations

TIGHTENING SPECIFICATIONS

Year	Component	Torque/Ft. Lbs.
1999	Camshaft Housing	②
	CKP Sensor	60④
	Connecting Rod Bearing Cap Nut	33
	Cylinder Head	①
	Cylinder Head Cover	96④
	Engine Mounting Bracket Bolt	37
	Engine Mounting Engine Side Bracket Bolt	37
	Engine Mounting Nut	37
	Exhaust Manifold	22
	Exhaust Manifold Stiffener	37
	Intake Manifold	17
	Oil Drain Plug	26
	Oil Pan Lower Bolt	96④
	Oil Pan Upper Bolt	③
	Oil Pump Case	108④
	Oil Pump Mounting	20
	Oil Pump Strainer	96④
	Spark Plugs	18
	Throttle Body	108④
	Timing Chain Cover	96④
	Timing Chain Guide No. 1	96④
	Timing Chain Tensioner No. 1	19
	Timing Chain Tensioner Adjuster No. 1	96④
	Timing Chain No. 2 Tensioner Bolt	96④
	Timing Chain No. 2 Tensioner Stud	33
	Transmission To Engine	58
	Water Pump	18

① — Refer to "Cylinder Head, Replace" for tightening procedure.

② — Refer to "Camshaft, Replace" for tightening procedure.

③ — Refer to "Oil Pan, Replace" for tightening procedure.

④ — Inch lbs.

Clutch & Manual Transmission

INDEX

ADJUSTMENTS

CLUTCH PEDAL HEIGHT

1. Loosen clutch cable locknut and turn adjusting nut as necessary until clutch pedal height is as follows:
   a. **On Sidekick and X-90 models,** clutch pedal should be 5 mm higher than brake pedal, **Fig. 1.**
   b. **On Swift models,** clutch pedal should be 8 mm higher than brake pedal, **Fig. 2.**
   c. **On Esteem models,** clutch pedal height (dimension A) should be 15 mm higher than brake pedal, **Fig. 3.**
   d. **On Grand Vitara models,** clutch pedal height (dimension A) should be 20 mm higher than brake pedal, **Fig. 4.**
2. **On all models,** Tighten locknut after adjustment is completed.

CLUTCH PEDAL FREE TRAVEL

1. Depress clutch pedal until resistance is felt, then measure distance traveled, **Fig. 5.** Free travel should measure as follows:
   a. **On Grand Vitara, Sidekick and X-90 models,** clutch pedal free travel should be 0.6–1.1 inches.
   b. **On Esteem and Swift models,** clutch pedal free travel should be 0.6–0.8 inch.
2. **On all models,** if clutch pedal free travel is not within specification, adjust free travel as follows:
   a. **On Sidekick and X-90 models,** turn joint nut as necessary, **Fig. 6.** Ensure cable outer nuts are tightened to specification.
   b. **On Esteem and Swift models,** turn joint nut as necessary, **Fig. 7.**
3. **On all models,** after adjustment check clutch function with engine running.

CLUTCH

REPLACE

1. **On front wheel drive models,** remove transaxle from vehicle as outlined under "Transaxle, Replace."
2. **On rear wheel drive models,** remove transmission from vehicle as outlined under "Transmission, Replace."
3. **On all models,** loosen pressure plate attaching bolts one turn at a time, then remove bolts, pressure plate and clutch disc.

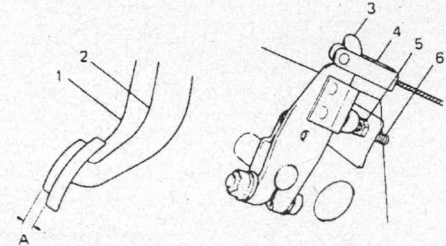

1. Clutch pedal
2. Brake pedal
3. Clutch pedal shaft arm
4. Clutch cable assembly
5. Lock nut
6. Adjust bolt
A: Height difference 5 mm/0.2 in.

SK5049100009000X

Fig. 1 Clutch pedal height adjustment. Sidekick & X-90

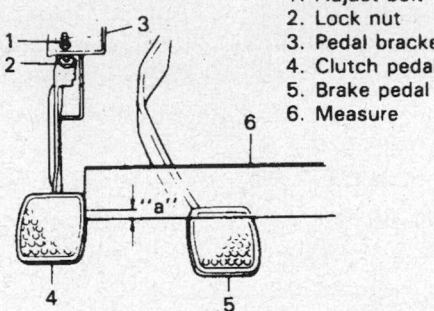

1. Adjust bolt
2. Lock nut
3. Pedal bracket
4. Clutch pedal
5. Brake pedal
6. Measure

SK5049500015000X

Fig. 3 Clutch pedal height adjustment. Esteem

4. Install new clutch disc and pressure plate assembly. Tighten attaching bolts one turn at a time while ensuring disc and plate are properly aligned.
5. Install transaxle or transmission and adjust clutch as outlined under "Clutch Pedal, Adjustments."

TRANSMISSION

REPLACE

GRAND VITARA

1. Remove transmission shift control lever and transfer shift control knob.
2. Remove breather hose from clamp at rear of cylinder head.
3. Remove starter motor.
4. Remove transmission mounting bolts.
5. Drain oil from transmission and transfer into suitable container.

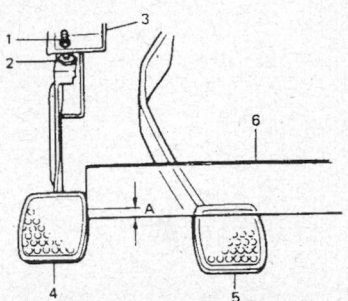

1. Clutch pedal
2. Brake pedal
6.
A: Height difference 8 mm/0.3 in.

1. Adjust bolt
2. Lock nut
3. Pedal bracket
4. Clutch pedal
5. Brake pedal
6. Measure

SK5049100010000X

Fig. 2 Clutch pedal height adjustment. Swift

6. Reference mark, then remove propeller shaft.
7. Remove clutch cylinder from transmission.
8. Remove clutch housing lower plate.
9. Disconnect 4WD, speed sensor and back up lamp electrical connectors.
10. Support transmission and transfer using suitable transmission jack.
11. Remove rear engine mounting member.
12. Move transmission and transfer assembly rearward, then lower.
13. Remove wiring harness and breather hose.
14. Seperate gear shift lever case and transfer assembly from transmission.
15. Reverse procedure to install.

SIDEKICK & X-90

1. Remove console box attaching screws, then the console box and bracket.
2. Lift up boot cover and boot No. 2.
3. Remove boot clamp, then boot No. 1 from transmission shift lever case.
4. Press down on shift control case cover and turn counterclockwise, then remove shift control lever.
5. **On 4WD models,** remove transfer case shift control lever knob.
6. **On 2WD models,** remove extension case.
7. **On all models,** disconnect transmission breather hose from rear of cylinder head.
8. Remove wiring harness clamp from rear end of intake manifold.
9. Remove starter motor, then the transmission to engine attaching bolts.

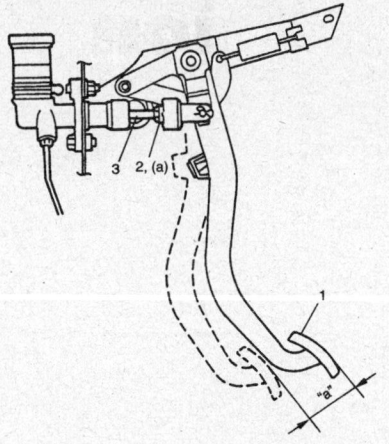

1. Clutch pedal
2. Clevis lock nut
3. Push rod

SK5049900037000X

Fig. 4 Clutch pedal height adjustment. Grand Vitara

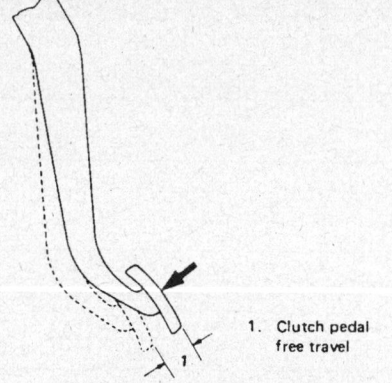

1. Clutch pedal free travel

SK5049100011000X

Fig. 5 Clutch pedal free travel measurement

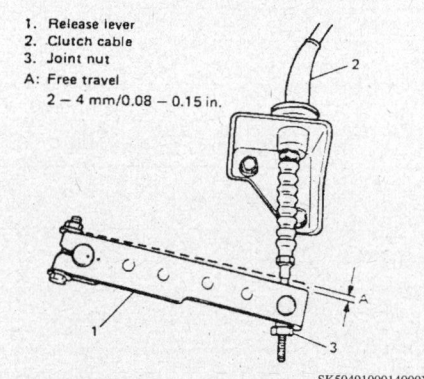

1. Release lever
2. Clutch cable
3. Joint nut
A: Free travel
   2 – 4 mm/0.08 – 0.15 in.

SK5049100014000X

Fig. 7 Clutch pedal free travel adjustment. Esteem & Swift

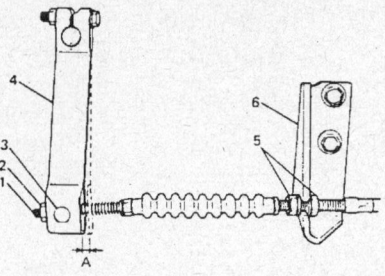

1. Inner cable
2. Joint nut
3. Joint pin
   (Apply grease)
4. Clutch release arm
5. Cable outer nut
6. Bracket
A: Free travel of release arm
   0.5 – 1.5 mm/0.02 – 0.06 in.

SK5049100013000X

Fig. 6 Clutch pedal free travel adjustment. Sidekick & X-90

10. Drain oil from transmission and transfer case into appropriate container.
11. Remove front and rear propeller shafts.
12. Disconnect clutch cable from transmission housing.
13. Remove clutch housing lower plate, then the exhaust center pipe.
14. Remove nuts retaining speedometer cable and disengage cable to transfer case.
15. Install a suitable jack under transmission and transfer case.
16. Remove engine rear mounting crossmember attaching bolts, then the crossmember.
17. Move transmission rearward and lower from vehicle.
18. Remove transmission wiring harness from transmission.
19. **On 4WD models,** remove gear shift lever case and transfer case from transmission assembly.
20. **On 2WD models,** remove gear shift lever case and extension case from transmission assembly.
21. **On all models,** reverse procedure to install.

TRANSAXLE
REPLACE
ESTEEM

1. Remove clutch cable joint nut, joint pin from cable, then cable from bracket.
2. Disconnect wiring harness clamps and connectors.
3. Remove starter and starter plate.
4. Remove exhaust manifold cover and loosen nuts on exhaust No. 1 pipe.
5. Raise and support vehicle.
6. Drain transmission oil.
7. Remove left side engine cover and exhaust No. 1 pipe.
8. Remove gear shift control shaft bolt and nut, then detach control shaft from

gear shift shaft.
9. Remove extension rod nut, then the rod and washers.
10. Remove clutch housing lower plate and disconnect stabilizer joint from suspension arm.
11. Remove ball stud from right and left knuckles, then disconnect each suspension arm.
12. Using suitable large screwdrivers, pry away shaft joints at differential side to access and remove snap ring for lefthand drive shaft.
13. Remove center bearing support bolts and pull out center drive shaft from differential gear.
14. Remove transaxle stiffener.
15. Support transaxle using suitable jack.
16. Remove transaxle to engine bolt and nut.
17. Remove engine rear mounting bracket bolts.
18. Lower vehicle and remove No. 1 lefthand engine mounting bracket.
19. Remove any remaining parts connected to transaxle.
20. Remove transmission while disconnecting input shaft from clutch disc, then lower transaxle out of vehicle.
21. Reverse procedure to install. Tighten to specifications.

SWIFT

1. Remove battery and tray.
2. Remove clutch cable joint nut, joint pin

from cable and cable from bracket.
3. Disconnect wiring harness clamps and couplers.
4. Remove speedometer cable from case, then disconnect radiator outlet pipe from transmission side cover.
5. Remove transmission upper attaching bolts, then the starter motor.
6. Raise and support vehicle, then drain transmission oil into appropriate container.
7. Remove lefthand side fender apron extension, then the exhaust pipe from manifold.
8. Disconnect control shaft from gear shift shaft, then remove extension rod with washers.
9. Remove clutch housing lower plate, then disconnect lower suspension (control) arm from steering knuckle.
10. Disconnect lefthand side driveshaft joint from differential gear of transmission.
11. Remove center bearing support bolts and pull out center driveshaft from differential gear.
12. Remove transmission stiffener, then the transmission to engine attaching bolt.
13. Remove engine rear mounting bracket and bolts.
14. Lower vehicle as necessary and support engine and transmission with suitable jacks.
15. Remove engine mounting lefthand bracket and stiffener, then remove any parts still attached to transmission.
16. Pull transmission rearward to disconnect input shaft from clutch disc.
17. Lower and remove transmission from vehicle.
18. Reverse procedure to install, noting the following:
    a. Apply Suzuki No. 1215 sealant or equivalent, to threads of engine rear mounting bracket upper bolt.
    b. Push in lefthand side driveshaft joint fully. Ensure snap ring of shaft engages with differential gear.
    c. Apply grease to gear shift control shaft bushing. Do not lubricate extension rod bushing.
    d. Adjust clutch cable as outlined under "Clutch Pedal, Adjustments."

TIGHTENING SPECIFICATIONS

ESTEEM

Year	Component	Torque/Ft. Lbs.
1996–99	Ball Stud Bolt	44
	Center Bearing Support	37
	Drain Plug	16
	Engine Mounting LH Bracket Bolt	37
	Engine Rear Mounting Bracket Bolt	37
	Exhaust Pipe	37
	Extension Rod Nut	24
	Gear Shift Control Shaft	13
	Stabilizer Bar Link	21
	Speedometer Gear to Case Bolt	48①
	Transmission Case Bolt	65
	Transmission Case Lower Stiffener	37

① — Inch lbs.

GRAND VITARA

Year	Component	Torque/Ft. Lbs.
1999	Transmission Drain Plug	33
	Transmission Case Bolt	62
	Rear Member Mount	37
	Propeller Shaft	37
	Transmission Case Nut	62
	Rear Engine Mounting Bolts	37
	Control Lever Boot Cover	48①
	Transfer Drain Plug	17

① — Inch lbs.

SIDEKICK & X-90

Year	Component	Torque/Ft. Lbs.
1996–99	Cable Outer Bolt	48①
	Clutch Cable Outer Nut	11-14
	Clutch Cover Bolt	14-20
	Clutch Start Switch Locknut	108①
	Drain Plug	14-20
	Engine Rear Mounting Bolt/Nut	29-43
	Flywheel Bolt	56
	Release Arm Bolt	14-20
	Transfer Case To Transmission	14-20
	Transmission To Engine Bolt/Nut	51-72
	Universal Joint Flange Bolt	37-43

① — Inch lbs.

SWIFT

Year	Component	Torque/Ft. Lbs.
1996–99	Cable Bracket Bolt	14-20
	Clutch Cable Outer Bolt	48①
	Clutch Cover Bolt	14-20
	Drain Plug	14-16
	Engine Mounting LH Bracket Bolt	29-43
	Engine Mounting LH Bracket Nut	37-43
	Engine Rear Mounting Bracket Bolt	29-43
	Extension Rod Nut	19-28
	Extension Rod Stud Bolt	11-14
	Flywheel Bolt	42-47
	Gear Shift Housing to Boot Cover	48①
	Release Arm Bolt	8-11
	Speedometer Gear to Case Bolt	48①
	Transmission Case Bolt	11-15

① — Inch lbs.

Rear Axle & Suspension

INDEX

HUB & BEARING
REPLACE
ESTEEM

1. Raise and support vehicle.
2. Remove brake drum and spindle cap.
3. Remove spindle nut and washer, then pull off wheel hub using puller tools No. 09943–17912 and No. 09942–15510, or equivalents.
4. Wheel bearing and hub form a solid unit. If wheel bearing is defective, replace hub as an assembly.
5. Reverse procedure to install, noting the following:
   a. Apply sealant No. 99000–31090 or equivalent, to mating surfaces of brake back plate and knuckle.
   b. Install new spindle nut.
   c. Tighten to specification.

GRAND VITARA, SIDEKICK & X-90

1. Drain differential gear oil into appropriate container.
2. Raise and support vehicle.
3. Remove wheel and brake drum, then the rear wheel bearing retainer nuts from axle housing.
4. **On models equipped with ABS,** remove wheel speed sensor.
5. **On all models,** if there is no clearance between rear wheel bearing retainer and parking shoe, loosen parking cable adjusting nut and pull down brake shoe hold pin stopper plate.
6. Using axle shaft tool No. J37781 and puller tool No. J2619-01 or equivalents, remove axle shaft.
7. **On models equipped with ABS,** grind a flat spot on one area of sensor ring, then remove using chisel.
8. **On all models,** remove retainer ring from axle shaft using a grinder to flatten two parts of bearing retainer ring.
9. With a chisel remove retainer ring, then using a suitable press remove bearing from axle shaft.
10. Reverse procedure to install. Apply Suzuki Bond No. 1215 or equivalent, to mating surface of bearing retainer to brake backing plate. Tighten to specification.

SWIFT

1. Remove brake drum.
2. Remove wheel bearings from brake drum.

3. Reverse procedure to install, noting the following:
   a. Install both bearings with sealed side outward.
   b. Fill 40 percent of bearing cavity with bearing lubricant.

STRUT
REPLACE
SWIFT

1. Raise and support vehicle, then remove rear wheels.
2. Using suitable jack, support rear axle housing to prevent it from lowering.
3. Remove strut support nuts, then push strut fully downward to compress strut.
4. Remove strut lower mount bolt.
5. Lower jack slightly to facilitate strut removal.
6. Remove strut from knuckle by pulling it upward, **Fig. 1.** If strut is hard to remove, open slit of knuckle using wedge.
7. Reverse procedure to install, noting the following:
   a. Align projection of strut with slit of knuckle. Push strut into knuckle

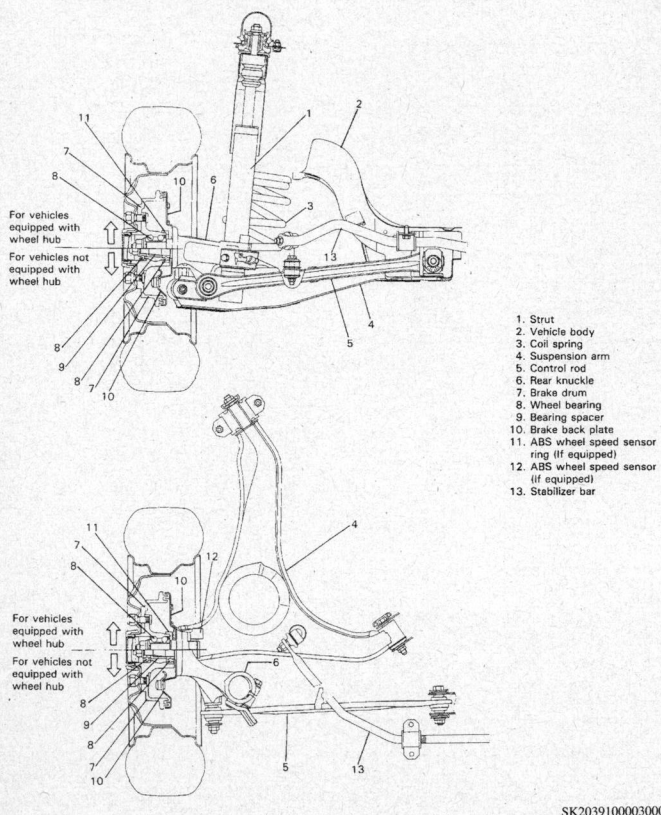

For vehicles equipped with wheel hub

For vehicles not equipped with wheel hub

For vehicles equipped with wheel hub

For vehicles not equipped with wheel hub

1. Strut
2. Vehicle body
3. Coil spring
4. Suspension arm
5. Control rod
6. Rear knuckle
7. Brake drum
8. Wheel bearing
9. Bearing spacer
10. Brake back plate
11. ABS wheel speed sensor ring (If equipped)
12. ABS wheel speed sensor (if equipped)
13. Stabilizer bar

SK2039100003000X

Fig. 1 Sectional views of rear suspension. Swift

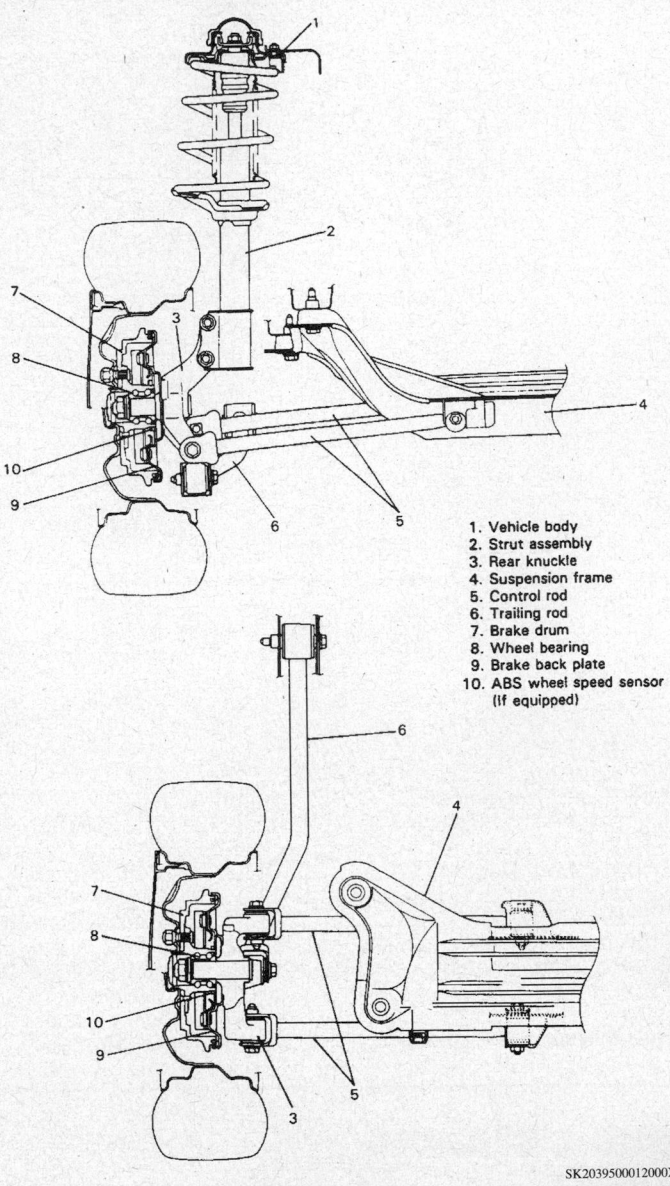

1. Vehicle body
2. Strut assembly
3. Rear knuckle
4. Suspension frame
5. Control rod
6. Trailing rod
7. Brake drum
8. Wheel bearing
9. Brake back plate
10. ABS wheel speed sensor (If equipped)

SK2039500012000X

Fig. 2 Cross-sectional view of rear suspension. Esteem

until upper end of knuckle contacts projection of strut.
  b. Tighten all bolts and nuts to specification.

ESTEEM

1. Raise and support vehicle, allowing rear suspension to hang free.
2. Remove rear wheel.
3. Remove E-ring securing brake hose.
4. Disconnect brake pipe from wheel cylinder and install bleeder plug cap to prevent fluid loss.
5. Remove strut bracket bolts and nuts, then the brake hose from strut.
6. Remove strut, **Fig. 2.**
7. Reverse procedure to install, noting the following:
  a. Tighten all bolts and nuts to specification.
  b. Bleed and test brake system.

SHOCK ABSORBER
REPLACE
GRAND VITARA, SIDEKICK & X-90

1. Raise and support vehicle.
2. Using suitable jack, support rear axle housing to prevent it from lowering.
3. Remove upper and lower attaching bolt, **Fig. 3,** then remove shock absorber.
4. Reverse procedure to install.

COIL SPRING
REPLACE
GRAND VITARA, SIDEKICK & X-90

1. Raise and support vehicle, then remove rear wheels.
2. Using suitable jack, support rear axle housing.
3. Disconnect parking brake cable hangers from trailing rod and chassis body.
4. Remove shock absorber lower mounting bolt, **Fig. 3.**
5. **On models equipped with ABS,** remove wheel speed sensor clamps from upper rod and axle housing.
6. **On Grand Vitara models,** remove E ring for brake line from crossmember, then disconnect breather hose from axle housing.
7. **On all models,** lower rear axle housing gradually until coil spring can be re-

moved. Remove coil spring.
8. Reverse procedure to install.

SWIFT

Refer to "Control Arm, Replace" for coil spring replacement.

CONTROL ARM
REPLACE
GRAND VITARA
Upper

1. Raise and support vehicle, then remove rear wheel and tire assembly.
2. **On models equipped with ABS,** disconnect wheel speed sensor harness clamp from arm.
3. **On all models,** remove upper control arm.
4. Reverse procedure to install.

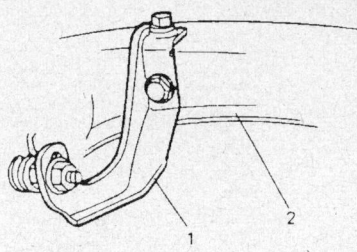

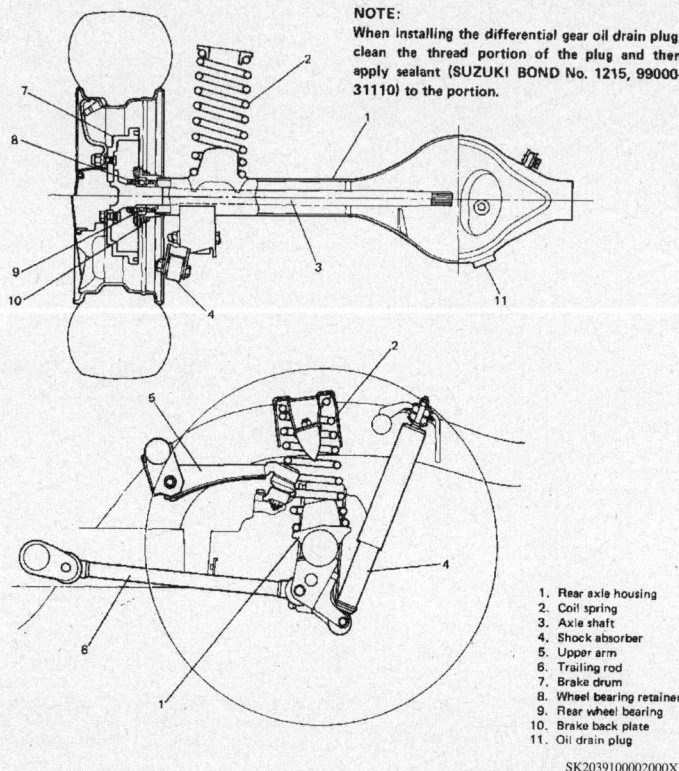

NOTE:
When installing the differential gear oil drain plug, clean the thread portion of the plug and then apply sealant (SUZUKI BOND No. 1215, 99000-31110) to the portion.

1. Rear axle housing
2. Coil spring
3. Axle shaft
4. Shock absorber
5. Upper arm
6. Trailing rod
7. Brake drum
8. Wheel bearing retainer
9. Rear wheel bearing
10. Brake back plate
11. Oil drain plug

SK2039100002000X

Fig. 3 Cross-sectional views of rear suspension & axle assembly. Grand Vitara, Sidekick & X-90

1. Bracket
2. Upper arm

SK2039100007000X

Fig. 4 Upper arm bracket replacement. Sidekick & X-90

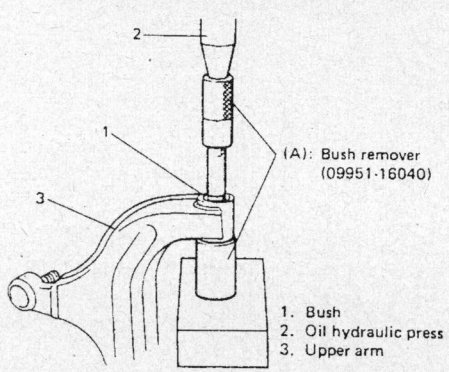

(A): Bush remover (09951-16040)

1. Bush
2. Oil hydraulic press
3. Upper arm

SK2039100009000X

Fig. 6 Upper arm bushing replacement. Sidekick & X-90

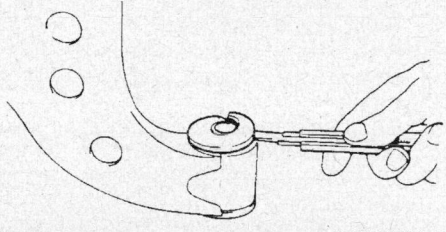

SK2039100008000X

Fig. 5 Upper arm bushing flange removal. Sidekick & X-90

Lower

1. Raise and support vehicle, then remove rear wheel and tire assembly.
2. Support rear axle housing using suitable jack.
3. Remove front mounting bolt, then rear mounting bolt.
4. Remove lower control arm.
5. Reverse procedure to install.

SIDEKICK & X-90

Upper

1. Raise and support vehicle.
2. Remove bracket from upper arm, **Fig. 4.**
3. Using suitable jack, support axle housing.
4. Remove upper arm ball joint bracket from differential carrier.
5. Remove upper arm front bolts, then the upper arm.
6. Remove cotter pin from castle nut of ball joint stud, then the castle nut.
7. Using suitable bearing puller, remove bracket from ball joint stud.

8. Remove ball joint boot set ring and boot.
9. To replace upper arm front bushing, cut off rubber flange, **Fig. 5,** then using tools, **Fig. 6,** press out bushing.
10. Reverse procedure to install.

SWIFT

1. Raise and support vehicle, then remove rear wheels.
2. Confirm rear toe setting, **Fig. 9.**
3. Remove control rod inside bolt and outside nut.
4. Disconnect stabilizer bar from control arm, then loosen rear mount nut of control arm.
5. Loosen front nut of control arm, then disconnect parking brake cable clamp from control arm.
6. Place suitable jack under control arm, then remove lower mount nut of knuckle.
7. Separate lower mount of knuckle from control arm by pulling brake assembly to outside of vehicle.
8. Lower jack gradually and remove coil spring.
9. Remove control arm front bracket attaching bolts, then the control arm.
10. Reverse procedure to install, noting the following:
    a. Install control arm with slit "A" facing outside of body. Ensure bushing is installed properly in regard to its vertical direction, **Fig. 7.**
    b. Tighten all bolts and nuts to specification.
    c. Set rear toe adjustment.

STEERING KNUCKLE
REPLACE
ESTEEM

1. Disconnect and plug brake hose to wheel cylinder.
2. **On models equipped with ABS,** remove wheel speed sensor.
3. **On all models,** remove brake backing plate from knuckle.
4. Loosen control rod outer bolts, trailing rod rear bolt and strut bracket nuts.
5. Disconnect control rods from knuckle.
6. Disconnect trailing rod from knuckle, then remove knuckle from strut, **Fig. 8.**
7. Reverse procedure to install, noting the following:
    a. Apply sealant No. 99000–31090 or equivalent, to mating surfaces of brake back plate and knuckle.
    b. Install new spindle nut.
    c. Tighten to specification.
    d. Bleed brake system.

SWIFT

1. Raise and support vehicle, then remove rear wheels.
2. Remove rear brake drum.
3. Disconnect brake line from wheel cylinder.
4. Remove brake backing plate from knuckle.
5. Support suspension arm with suitable jack.
6. Confirm rear toe setting, **Fig. 9.** Remove nut and washer from inside of control arm.
7. Remove control arm outside nut from knuckle stud bolt.

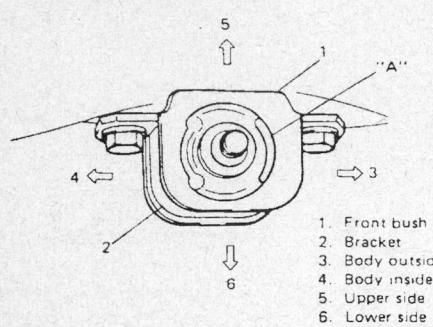

Fig. 7   Control arm bushing replacement. Swift

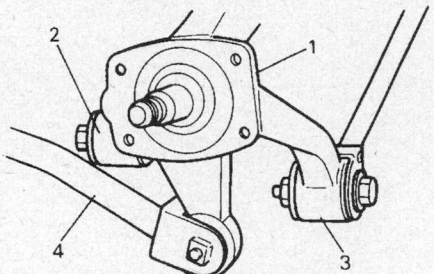

1. Knuckle
2. No.1 control rod
3. No.2 control rod
4. Trailing rod

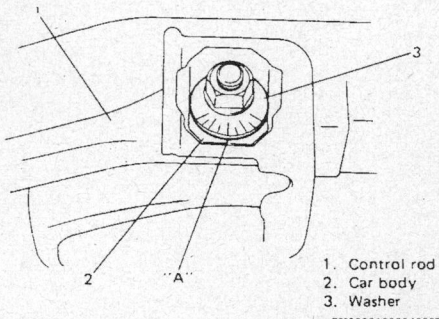

1. Control rod
2. Car body
3. Washer

Fig. 9   Rear toe measurement. Swift

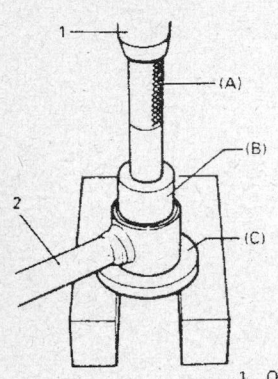

Special Tool
(A): 09924-74510
(B): 09951-16030
(C): 09951-26010

1. Oil hydraulic press
2. Trailing rod

Fig. 10   Trailing arm bushing replacement. Sidekick & X-90

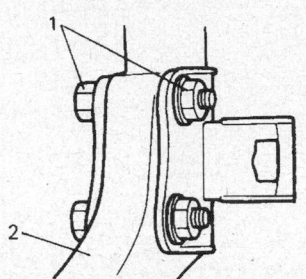

1. Strut bracket bolt & nut
2. Knuckle

Fig. 8   Rear suspension components. Esteem

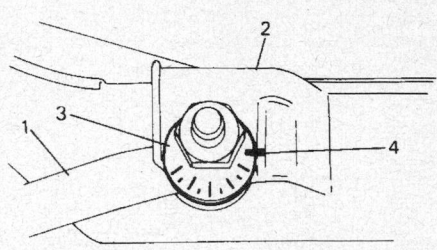

1. No.2 control rod
2. Suspension frame
3. Washer
4. Match marks

Fig. 11   Toe adjustment. Esteem

8. Remove strut and knuckle lower mounting bolts.
9. Disconnect knuckle from suspension arm, then remove knuckle from strut.
10. Reverse procedure to install.

TRAILING ROD
REPLACE
ESTEEM

1. Raise and support vehicle, then disconnect parking brake cable hanger from trailing rod, **Fig. 2.**
2. Remove trailing rod rear mounting bolts, then the trailing arm.
3. Reverse procedure to install.

SIDEKICK & X-90

1. Raise and support vehicle, then disconnect parking brake cable hanger from trailing rod.
2. Using suitable jack, support rear axle housing.
3. Remove trailing rod rear mounting bolts, then the trailing arm.

4. Remove trailing rod bushings using press and tools, **Fig. 10.**
5. Reverse procedure to install.

CONTROL ROD
REPLACE
ESTEEM

1. Raise and support vehicle.
2. **On models equipped with ABS,** remove ABS speed sensor pipe from No. 2 control arm.
3. **On all models,** place match marks on washer and frame for adjustment reference, **Fig. 11.**
4. Remove suspension frame cap.
5. Remove No. 2 control rod from frame and knuckle.
6. Remove No. 1 control rod from frame and knuckle.
7. Reverse procedure to install, noting the following:
   a. Install No. 1 control rod with welded nut toward rear, **Fig. 12.**
   b. Insert inner and outer bolts from vehicle front and tighten temporarily by hand.
   c. Install No. 2 control rod with welded nut toward front.
   d. Insert No. 2 control rod bolt from vehicle front and outer bolt from rear. Tighten finger tight.
   e. Set rear toe adjustment.
   f. Tighten all bolts and nuts to specifications.

SWIFT

1. Raise and support vehicle.
2. Disconnect brake flexible hose from control rod. Confirm rear toe setting, **Fig. 9.**
3. Remove control rod outside and inside nuts, then the control rod.
4. Reverse procedure to install, noting the following:
   a. Install control rod inside bolt with cam facing downward.
   b. Tighten all bolts and nuts to specification.
   c. Set rear toe adjustment as confirmed before removal.

STABILIZER BAR
REPLACE
SWIFT

1. Raise and support vehicle.
2. Remove stabilizer bar left and right end nuts.
3. Remove stabilizer bar brackets, then the stabilizer bar.
4. Reverse procedure to install, noting the following:
   a. Ensure paint on stabilizer bar aligns with mounting bushing.
   b. Tighten bolts and nuts to specification.

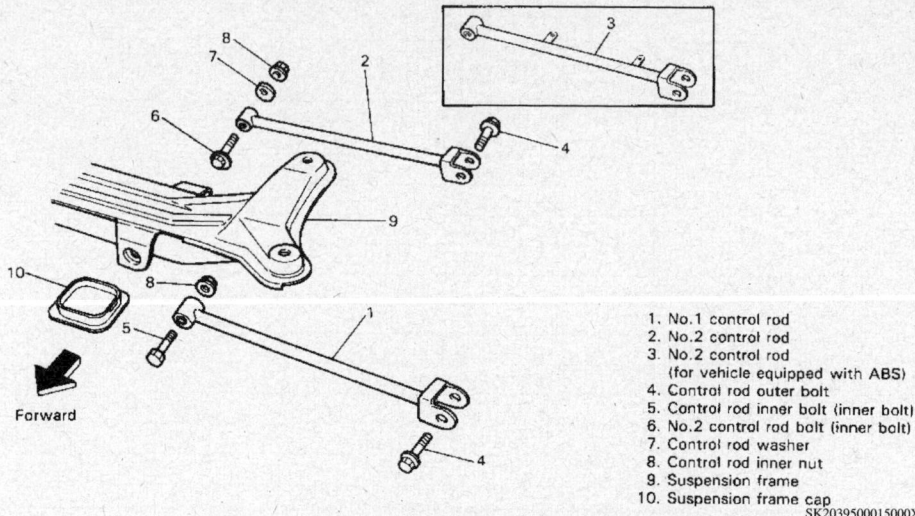

1. No.1 control rod
2. No.2 control rod
3. No.2 control rod
   (for vehicle equipped with ABS)
4. Control rod outer bolt
5. Control rod inner bolt (inner bolt)
6. No.2 control rod bolt (inner bolt)
7. Control rod washer
8. Control rod inner nut
9. Suspension frame
10. Suspension frame cap

SK2039500015000X

Fig. 12   Control rods assembly. Esteem

TIGHTENING SPECIFICATIONS

ESTEEM

Year	Component	Torque/Ft. Lbs.
1996–99	Axle Nut	127
	Brake Backing Plate Bolts	17
	Brake Line To Brake Backing Plate	12
	Control Rod Bolts	65
	Hub Nut	127
	Rear Spindle Nut	127
	Strut Bracket	65
	Strut Lower Mount Bolt	65
	Strut Upper Nut	40
	Strut Upper Mount Nut	21
	Suspension Frame Bolt	65
	Trailing Rod Bolts	65
	Wheel Lug Nut	62
	Wheel Speed Sensor Bolt	17

GRAND VITARA

Year	Component	Torque/Ft. Lbs.
1999	Bearing Retainer Nut	17
	Lower Control Arm	65
	Shock Absorber Lock Nut	21
	Shock Absorber Lower Nut	62
	Upper control Arm	65
	Wheel Lug Nut	69

SUZUKI

SIDEKICK & X-90

Year	Component	Torque/Ft. Lbs.
1996–99	Ball Joint Bracket to Carrier Bracket Bolts	29-43
	Ball Joint Castle Nut	33-50
	Bearing Retainer Nut	14-20
	Brake Drum Nut	37-57
	Brake Line Flare Nuts	11–15
	Carrier Bolts	14–20
	Propeller Shaft Nuts	29-43
	Shaft Bearing Nuts	14-20
	Shock Absorber Nuts	58-72
	Trailing Rod Nuts	58-72
	Upper Arm Front Nut	58-72
	Wheel Lug Nut	37–58

SWIFT

Year	Component	Torque/Ft. Lbs.
1996–99	Brake Caliper Carrier Bolt	29-43
	Brake Caliper Mount Bolt	29-43
	Brake Disc Dust Cover Bolt	29-43
	Brake Drum Backing Plate	14-20
	Control Rod Nut	51-65
	Knuckle Arm Lower Mount Nut	29-43
	Rear Spindle Nut (Disc Brake)	108-144
	Rear Spindle Nut (Drum Brake)	58-86
	Strut Lower Mount Bolt	36-50
	Strut Support Nut	20-27
	Strut Upper Nut	29-43
	Suspension Arm Front Nut	36-50
	Suspension Arm Mounting Bracket Bolt	25-39
	Suspension Arm Rear Nut	29-43
	Wheel Lug Nut	36-50

Transfer Case

INDEX

TRANSFER CASE

REPLACE

1. Remove distributor assembly, then install a suitable block of wood to prevent engine from hanging down when rear crossmember is removed.
2. Remove console assembly, then the transmission and transfer case shift levers.
3. Raise and support vehicle.
4. Drain transfer case into appropriate container.
5. Remove front and rear propeller shafts.
6. Remove exhaust center pipe, then disconnect speedometer cable or speed sensor connector.
7. Support transmission using suitable jack, then remove rear crossmember.
8. Lower transmission slowly and check that wood block acts as a stopper for the engine.
9. Remove transmission jack, then lower vehicle.
10. Remove gear shift lever case attaching bolts.
11. Remove breather hose.
12. Remove gear shift lever case, then the transfer case center bolt.
13. Raise and support vehicle.
14. Remove transfer case mounting attaching bolts.
15. Support transfer case using suitable jack.
16. Disconnect 4WD switch electrical connector.
17. Remove front case attaching bolts.
18. Slide transfer case rearward and remove.
19. Reverse procedure to install.

Front Suspension & Steering

NOTE: For Front Axle Service Procedures Not Covered In This Section, Refer To The "Front Wheel Drive Axles" Section.

INDEX

PRECAUTIONS

AIR BAG SYSTEMS

Refer to "Air Bag System Precautions" in the front of this manual for system disarming and arming procedures.

BATTERY GROUND CABLE

Prior to service, disconnect battery ground cable and isolate as required.

WHEEL BEARING

ADJUST

The cassette type double taper roller bearing is so designed as to provide proper preload as long as it is tightened to specified torque.

HUB & BEARING

REPLACE

ESTEEM

1. Raise and support vehicle, then remove front wheels.

SUZUKI

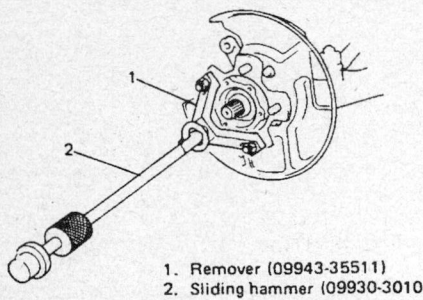

1. Remover (09943-35511)
2. Sliding hammer (09930-30102)

SK2049100001000X

Fig. 1 Wheel hub replacement. Sidekick & X-90

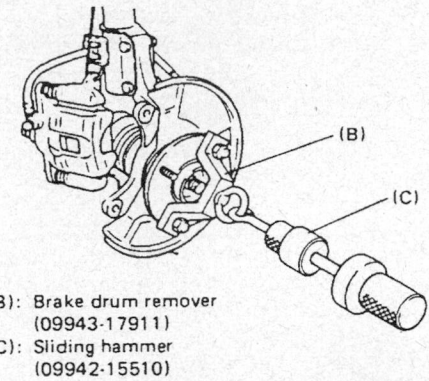

(B): Brake drum remover (09943-17911)
(C): Sliding hammer (09942-15510)

SK2049100002000X

Fig. 2 Wheel hub replacement. Swift

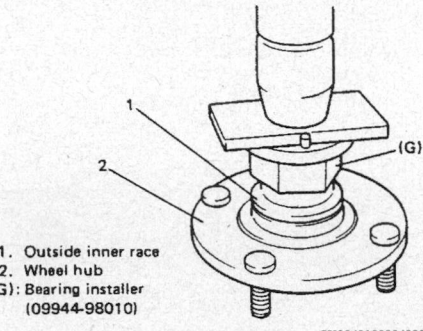

1. Outside inner race
2. Wheel hub
(G): Bearing installer (09944-98010)

SK2049100004000X

Fig. 4 Outside inner race replacement. Swift

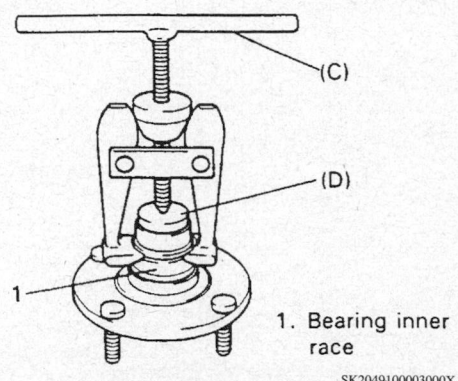

1. Bearing inner race

SK2049100003000X

Fig. 3 Wheel bearing inner race replacement. Swift

2. Remove driveshaft nut while depressing brake pedal.
3. Remove caliper carrier and caliper. Position caliper aside to prevent bending or twisting of brake hose.
4. Remove brake disc screws, then the disc using by two 8 mm bolts screwed into disc face.
5. Remove wheel hub using puller tools No. 09943–17912 and 09942–15510 or equivalents.
6. Remove hub studs, then the wheel bearing inner race using tools No. 09913–65810 and No. 09913–85230 or equivalents.
7. Reverse procedure to install, noting the following:
   a. Install outside inner race, using suitable shop press.
   b. Apply Suzuki grease, No. 99000-25010 or equivalent, to outside bearing, outside inner race and oil seal lip.
   c. Install and secure new driveshaft nut.
   d. Tighten all bolts and nuts to specification.

GRAND VITARA

1. Raise and support vehicle, then remove wheel and tire assembly.
2. Remove axle shaft drive flange or hub cap.
3. **On models equipped with ABS,** remove wheel speed sensor from knuckle and harness clamp from strut.
4. **On all models,** remove caliper bolt, then suspend caliper.
5. Remove brake disc.
6. Remove front wheel bearing lock washer by loosening four screws.
7. Remove front wheel bearing lock nut using special tool No. 09951–16050, or equivalent.
8. Remove front wheel bearing washer.
9. Remove wheel hub complete with bearings and oil seals. If hub cannot be removed by hand, remove using puller No. 09943–35511 and handle No. 09942–15510, or equivalent.
10. **On models equipped with ABS,** remove sensor rotor.
11. **On all models,** remove oil seals, then bearing circlip.
12. Using hydraulic press, remove bearing race.
13. Remove hub bolts from hub.
14. Reverse procedure to install.

SIDEKICK & X-90
Removal

1. Raise vehicle and remove wheel.
2. Remove locking hub assembly.
3. Remove brake caliper assembly, then suspend out of way.
4. Remove brake disc, then the bearing lock plate retaining screws and lock plate.
5. Using bearing tool, No. J37763 or equivalent, remove wheel bearing locknut and washer.
6. Remove entire wheel hub assembly. If assembly cannot be removed by hand use tools, **Fig. 1,** to remove.
7. Remove wheel bearing oil seal, then the bearing circlip.
8. Remove bearing outer race using bearing installer handle tool, No. J8092 and front wheel hub bearing remover tool, No. J37772 or equivalent, by tapping out with hammer.

Installation

1. Using bearing installer handle tool, No. J8092 and front wheel hub bearing installer tool, No. J37777 or equivalent, press fit bearing outer race until firmly seated in wheel hub.
2. Pack bearing with Suzuki Super Grease, No. 99000-25010 or equivalent.
3. Install bearing circlip, then the bearing oil seal using front wheel hub and bearing oil seal installer tool, No. J37774 or equivalent.

4. Fill oil seal recess and cover oil seal lip with Suzuki Super Grease No. 99000-25010 or equivalent.
5. Install wheel hub assembly onto front wheel spindle, then the spindle thrust washer.
6. Using wheel bearing tightening tool, No. J37763 or equivalent, install wheel bearing nut, then tighten to specification.
7. Install brake disc and caliper assembly, then tighten caliper bolt to specification.
8. Install wheel, then the locking hub assembly.

SWIFT

1. Raise and support vehicle, then remove front wheels.
2. Remove driveshaft nut while depressing brake pedal.
3. Remove caliper carrier bolts, then the carrier with caliper.
4. Remove brake disc screws, then the disc using 8 mm bolts.
5. Remove wheel hub using tools, **Fig. 2.**
6. Remove hub studs, then the wheel bearing inner race using tools, **Fig. 3.**
7. Reverse procedure to install, noting the following:
   a. Install outside inner race, **Fig. 4.**
   b. Apply Suzuki grease, No. 99000-25010 or equivalent, to outside bearing, outside inner race and oil seal lip.
   c. Tighten all bolts and nuts to specification.
   d. Install driveshaft nut, after tightening nut to specification, secure nut with suitable calking compound.

BALL JOINT INSPECTION

1. Raise and support vehicle.
2. Grasp tire at top and bottom.
3. Shake tire in a side to side motion and check for any ball joint movement. Replace ball joint if there is any movement.
4. Check ball stud and ball joint dust cover for damage. Replace ball joint if any damage is present.

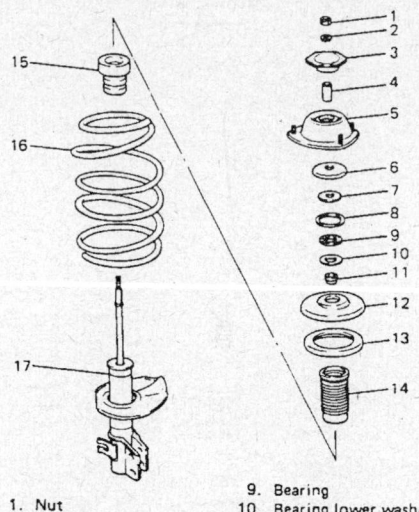

1. Nut
2. Washer
3. Stopper
4. Inner spacer
5. Support comp.
6. Bearing seat
7. Bearing upper washer
8. Bearing seal
9. Bearing
10. Bearing lower washer
11. Bearing spacer
12. Coil spring upper seat
13. Coil spring seat
14. Strut cover
15. Bump stopper
16. Coil spring
17. Strut

SK2029100002000X

Fig. 5 Exploded view of strut assembly. Swift

BALL JOINT
REPLACE
ESTEEM & SWIFT

Ball joint and suspension arm cannot be separated, refer to "Suspension Arm, Replace" for ball joint replacement.

GRAND VITARA, SIDEKICK & X-90

Refer to "Suspension Arm, Replace" for ball joint replacement.

COIL SPRING
REPLACE

1. Raise and support vehicle. Remove wheels.
2. Remove locking hub, then the front axle shaft circlip and washer.
3. Remove brake caliper assembly, then suspend out of way.
4. **On models equipped with ABS,** remove harness clamp bolt and sensor from knuckle.
5. **On all models,** remove brake disc, then the stabilizer ball joint.
6. Using tie rod end remover tool, No. J21687-02 or equivalent, remove tie rod end.
7. Using a suitable jack, support the suspension arm, then remove the lower strut bracket from the suspension arm.
8. Remove ball stud castle nut from ball stud.
9. Lower jack, then remove steering knuckle and wheel hub assembly.
10. Remove coil spring.
11. Reverse procedure to install.

STRUT
REPLACE
ESTEEM

1. Raise and support vehicle.
2. Remove wheels, allowing front suspension to hang free.
3. Remove brake hose from strut bracket.
4. **On models equipped with ABS,** remove ABS wheel speed sensor
5. **On all models,** remove lower strut bracket retaining bolts.
6. Supporting strut, then remove upper strut retaining bolts and strut.
7. Reverse procedure to install. Tighten to specification.

GRAND VITARA

1. Remove strut tower bar.
2. Raise and support vehicle, then remove wheel and tire assembly.
3. Remove brake hose from strut.
4. **On models equipped with ABS,** remove speed sensor harness clamp bolt.
5. **On all models,** remove strut bracket bolts, then support lower arm with suitable jack.
6. Remove strut support nuts while supporting strut by hand.
7. Remove strut from vehicle.
8. Reverse procedure to install.

SIDEKICK & X-90

1. Raise and support vehicle. Remove wheels.
2. Remove brake line from strut damper bracket.
3. Remove lower strut bracket retaining bolts.
4. Supporting the strut, remove the upper strut retaining bolts, then the strut.
5. Reverse procedure to install.

SWIFT

1. Raise and support vehicle. Allow front suspension to hang free.
2. Remove wheels, then disconnect brake hose clip from strut bracket.
3. Remove strut lower attaching bolts, then the upper support nuts.
4. Remove strut from vehicle.

COIL SPRING & STRUT SERVICE
SWIFT
Disassemble

1. Using spring compressor, compress spring until tension is released from upper spring seat. Tension is released when strut turns lightly with spring held stationary.
2. Remove strut nut, then disassemble strut, **Fig. 5.**

Assemble

1. Spring should be compressed to a length of nine inches (230 mm).

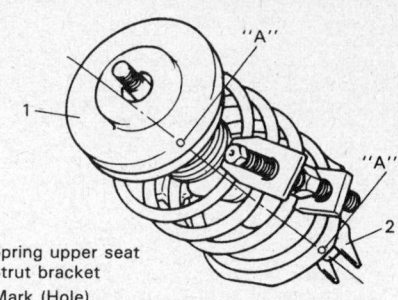

1. Spring upper seat
2. Strut bracket
A: Mark (Hole)

SK2029100003000X

Fig. 6 Spring upper seat alignment. Swift

2. Mate spring end with stepped part of lower spring seat.
3. Assemble strut in reverse numbered sequence, **Fig. 5,** noting the following:
   a. Align spring upper seat with strut bracket, **Fig. 6.**
   b. Tighten bolts and nuts to specification.
4. Reverse procedure to install.

STEERING KNUCKLE
REPLACE
GRAND VITARA

1. Raise and support vehicle, then remove wheel and tire assembly.
2. **On 4WD models,** remove axle shaft drive flange, circlip and spindle washer.
3. **On 2WD models,** remove front hub cap.
4. **On all models,** remove wheel hub as outlined under "Hub & Bearing, Replace."
5. Using suitable jack, support lower arm, then disconnect tie rod end from knuckle using tie rod remover.
6. Remove ball stud nut, then the strut bracket bolts from strut bracket.
7. Remove steering knuckle from ball stud using suitable puller.
8. While lowering jack, remove knuckle and wheel spindle assembly.
9. Remove oil seal, dust cover and wheel spindle from steering knuckle.
10. Reverse procedure to install, noting the following:
    a. Coat mating surface of wheel spindle and steering knuckle with Suzuki Bond No. 1215 or equivalent.
    b. Fill in spindle recess and knuckle seal recess with Suzuki lithium grease No. 99000-25010 or equivalent.
    c. Drive in knuckle oil seal until its end contacts stepped surface of knuckle using tools, **Fig. 7.**

SIDEKICK & X-90

1. Raise and support vehicle. Remove wheel.
2. Remove wheel hub as outlined under "Hub & Bearing, Replace."
3. Using suitable jack, support lower arm, then disconnect tie rod end from knuckle using tie rod remover.

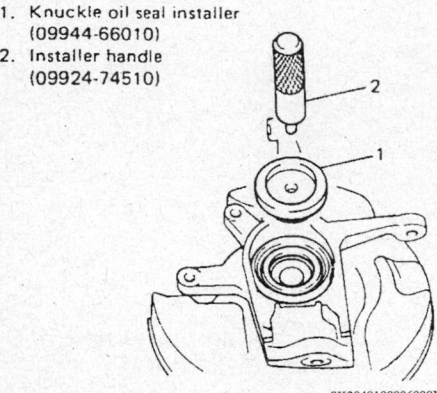

1. Knuckle oil seal installer
   (09944-66010)
2. Installer handle
   (09924-74510)

SK2049100006000X

Fig. 7 Steering knuckle oil seal replacement. Sidekick & X-90

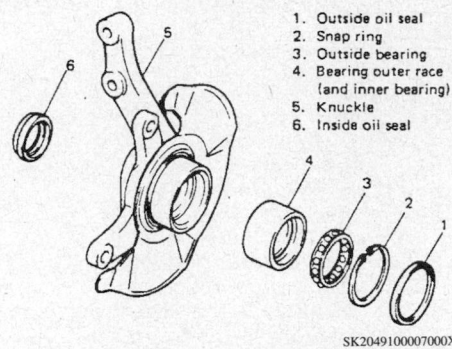

1. Outside oil seal
2. Snap ring
3. Outside bearing
4. Bearing outer race
   (and inner bearing)
5. Knuckle
6. Inside oil seal

SK20491000007000X

Fig. 8 Exploded view of steering knuckle & bearing. Swift

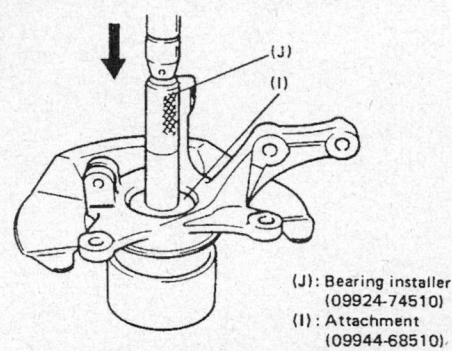

(J): Bearing installer
(09924-74510)
(I): Attachment
(09944-68510)

SK2049100008000X

Fig. 9 Bearing outer race/inner bearing removal. Swift

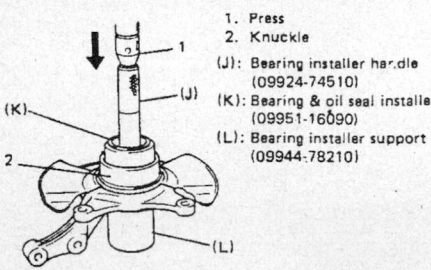

1. Press
2. Knuckle
(J): Bearing installer handle
   (09924-74510)
(K): Bearing & oil seal installer
   (09951-16090)
(L): Bearing installer support
   (09944-78210)

SK2049100009000X

Fig. 10 Bearing outer race/inner bearing installation. Swift

(J): Bearing installer handle
   (09924-74510)
(K): Bearing & oil seal installer
   (09944-66010)
(L): Bearing installer support
   (09944-78210)

SK2049100010000X

Fig. 11 Outer oil seal replacement. Swift

Assemble

Once bearing outer race is removed, bearing set (outer race, bearings and inner races) should be replaced.
1. Press fit bearing outer race/inner bearing using tools, **Fig. 10.**
2. Lubricate and install bearing outer race, bearings and oil seals.
3. Drive in inside oil seal until flush with stopped surface of knuckle.
4. Drive in outside oil seal until its end contacts snap ring using tools, **Fig. 11.**

Installation

1. Reverse removal procedure to install.

STABILIZER BAR
REPLACE
ESTEEM

1. Raise and support vehicle.
2. Remove stabilizer link nuts, washers and cushions, **Fig. 12.**
3. Remove stabilizer mount brackets, then the stabilizer bar.
4. Reverse procedure to install, noting the following:
   a. Ensure paint on stabilizer bar aligns with mount bushings for correct side to side installation.
   b. Tighten all bolts and nuts to specification.

GRAND VITARA

1. Raise and support vehicle, then remove stabilizer bar mount bracket bolts.
2. Remove stabilizer ball joint nuts, washers and bushings.
3. Remove stabilizer bar with ball joints attached.
4. Remove ball joints from stabilizer bar.
5. Reverse procedure to install.

SIDEKICK, X-90 & SWIFT

1. Raise and support vehicle.
2. Disconnect stabilizer ball joint from front suspension arms, **Figs. 13 and 14.**
3. Remove stabilizer bar mount bushing bracket bolts, then the stabilizer bar.
4. Reverse procedure to install, noting the following:
   a. Ensure paint on stabilizer bar aligns

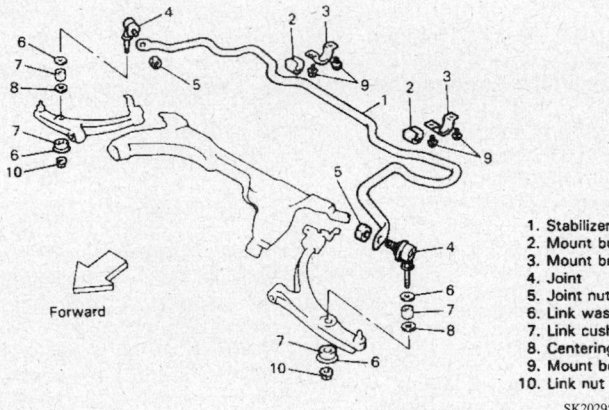

1. Stabilizer bar
2. Mount bush
3. Mount bracket
4. Joint
5. Joint nut
6. Link washer
7. Link cushion
8. Centering washer
9. Mount bolt
10. Link nut

Forward

SK2029500011000X

Fig. 12 Stabilizer bar replacement. Esteem

4. Remove ball stud nut, then the strut bracket bolts from strut bracket.
5. Remove steering knuckle from ball stud by tapping with hammer.
6. While lowering jack, remove knuckle and wheel spindle assembly.
7. Remove oil seal, dust cover and wheel spindle from steering knuckle.
8. Reverse procedure to install, noting the following:
   a. Coat mating surface of wheel spindle and steering knuckle with Suzuki Bond No. 1215 or equivalent.
   b. Fill in spindle recess and knuckle seal recess with Suzuki lithium grease No. 99000-25010 or equivalent.
   c. Drive in knuckle oil seal until its end contacts stepped surface of knuckle using tools, **Fig. 7.**

SWIFT
Removal

1. Raise and support vehicle.
2. Remove wheel hub as outlined under "Wheel Hub & Bearing, Replace."
3. Disconnect tie rod end from knuckle using tie rod remover.
4. Remove strut bracket bolts from strut bracket, then the ball stud bolt.
5. Remove knuckle.

Disassemble

1. Remove outside oil seal, snap ring, outside bearing, inside oil seal and inside bearing, **Fig. 8.**
2. Remove bearing outer race/inner bearing using press and tools, **Fig. 9.**

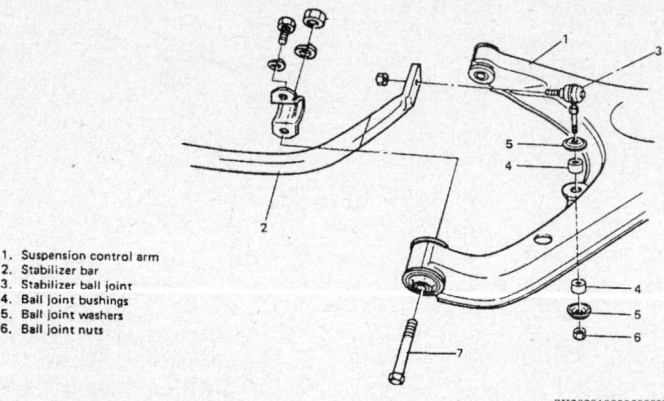

1. Suspension control arm
2. Stabilizer bar
3. Stabilizer ball joint
4. Ball joint bushings
5. Ball joint washers
6. Ball joint nuts

SK2029100005000X

Fig. 13 Stabilizer bar replacement. Sidekick & X-90

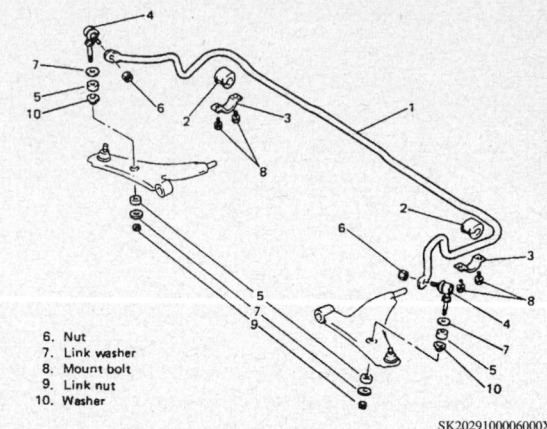

1. Stabilizer bar   6. Nut
2. Mount bush   7. Link washer
3. Mount braket   8. Mount bolt
4. Joint   9. Link nut
5. Link cushion   10. Washer

SK2029100006000X

Fig. 14 Stabilizer bar replacement. Swift

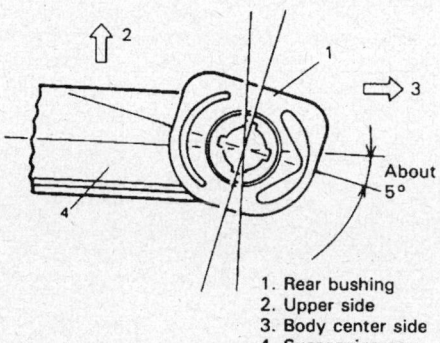

About 5°

1. Rear bushing
2. Upper side
3. Body center side
4. Suspension arm

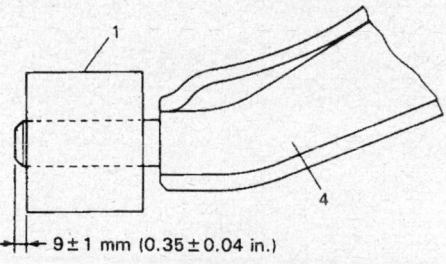

9 ± 1 mm (0.35 ± 0.04 in.)

SK2029500012000X

Fig. 15 Suspension arm rear bushing replacement. Esteem

with mount bushings for correct side to side Installation.
b. Tighten all bolts and nuts to specification.

SUSPENSION ARM
REPLACE
ESTEEM
Removal

1. Raise and support vehicle, then remove stabilizer links.
2. Remove ball stud bolt, then the suspension arm bracket bolts.
3. Remove rear bracket and suspension arm.
4. Using press, remove rear bushing.
5. Cut off flange of front bushing, then remove bushing using press.

Installation

1. Install front bushing using press. When installed, bushing should protrude equally on both sides.

2. Install rear bushing to suspension arm as follows:
a. Push in rear bushing in direction and angle, **Fig. 15,** then drive into position.
3. Install suspension arm and suspension arm bracket.
4. Install ball stud to knuckle, then the suspension arm rear bracket.
5. Install stabilizer links.
6. Tighten all bolts and nuts to specification.
7. Install wheels, then lower vehicle.
8. Check toe setting.

GRAND VITARA

1. Remove coil spring as outlined under "Coil Spring, Replace."
2. Remove control arm bolts and nuts.
3. Remove control arm.
4. Remove front bushing using special tool Nos. 09951–16060, 09924–74510 and 09951–46020, or equivalent and hydraulic press.
5. Remove rear bushing using special tool Nos. 09951–46020, 09913–80112 and 09925–58210, or equivalent and hydraulic press.
6. Reverse procedure to install, noting the following:
a. Install front bushing using special tool Nos. 09951–16060 and 09913–85210, or equivalent and hydraulic press.
b. Install rear bushing using special tool Nos. 09925–58210 and 09913–85210, or equivalent and hydraulic press.
c. Reverse remainder of procedure to install.

SIDEKICK & X-90
Removal

1. Remove coil spring as outlined under "Coil Spring, Replace."
2. Remove lower arm bracket bolts, then the lower arm.
3. Remove ball joint assembly attaching bolts, then the ball joint.
4. Cut off 5 mm of bushing flange, then using press and tools, **Fig. 16,** remove front bushing.
5. Cut off bushing flange, then using press and bushing remover set, tool No. 09951–16040, or equivalent, re-

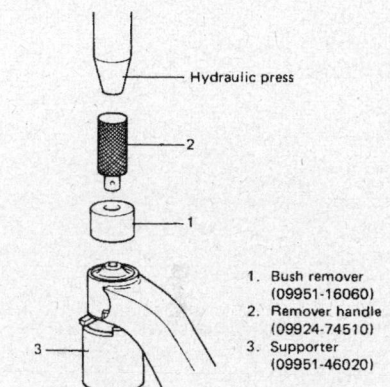

Hydraulic press

1. Bush remover (09951-16060)
2. Remover handle (09924-74510)
3. Supporter (09951-46020)

SK2029100007000X

Fig. 16 Suspension control arm front bushing replacement. Sidekick & X-90

move rear bushing.

Installation

1. Press fit front bushing until its flange contacts housing edge of lower arm. Set bushing in arm aligning hollow areas, **Fig. 17.**
2. Press fit rear bushing ensuring lower arm housing is held between its flanges.
3. Install ball joint to lower arm. Tighten bolts to specification.
4. Install lower arm to chassis.
5. Refer to "Coil Spring, Replace" to complete installation procedure.

SWIFT
Removal

1. Raise and support vehicle, then remove stabilizer links.
2. Remove ball stud bolt, then the suspension arm bracket bolts.
3. Remove rear bracket and suspension arm.
4. Using press, remove rear bushing.
5. Cut off flange of front bushing, then remove bushing using press.

Installation

1. Install front bushing using press. When installed, bushing should protrude equally on both sides.

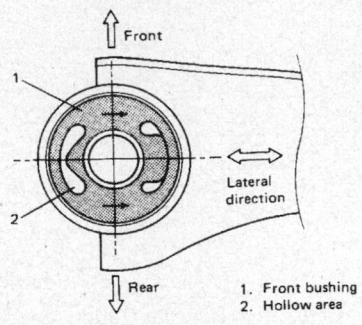

Fig. 17 Suspension control arm front bushing alignment. Sidekick & X-90

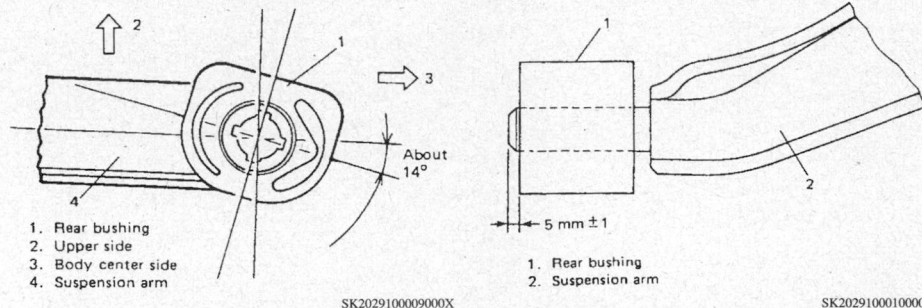

1. Rear bushing
2. Upper side
3. Body center side
4. Suspension arm

Fig. 18 Suspension arm rear bushing. Swift

About 14°

5 mm ±1

1. Rear bushing
2. Suspension arm

Fig. 19 Suspension arm rear bushing replacement. Swift

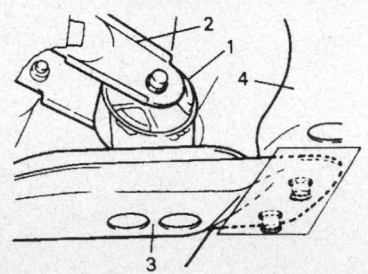

1. Engine rear mounting
2. Mounting bracket
3. Mounting member
4. Suspension frame

Fig. 20 Engine rear mounting & bracket removal. Esteem

2. Install rear bushing to suspension arm as follows:
   a. Push in rear bushing in direction and angle shown in **Fig. 18,** then drive into position, **Fig. 19.**
3. Install suspension arm and suspension arm bracket.
4. Install ball stud to knuckle, then the suspension arm rear bracket.
5. Install stabilizer links.
6. Tighten all bolts and nuts to specification.
7. Install wheels, then lower vehicle.
8. Check toe setting and adjust as required.

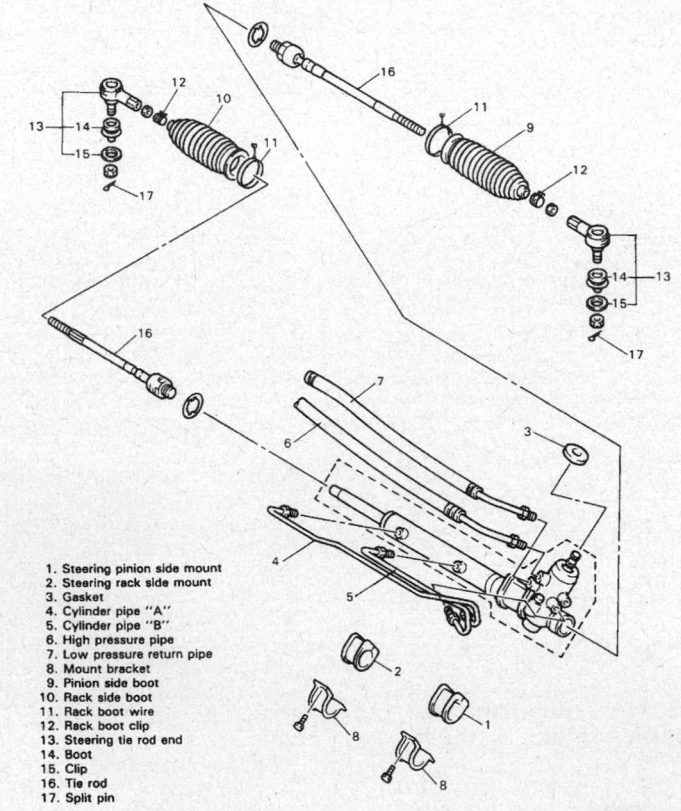

1. Steering pinion side mount
2. Steering rack side mount
3. Gasket
4. Cylinder pipe "A"
5. Cylinder pipe "B"
6. High pressure pipe
7. Low pressure return pipe
8. Mount bracket
9. Pinion side boot
10. Rack side boot
11. Rack boot wire
12. Rack boot clip
13. Steering tie rod end
14. Boot
15. Clip
16. Tie rod
17. Split pin

Fig. 21 Power steering box components. Esteem

POWER STEERING GEAR

REPLACE

ESTEEM

1. Drain oil from power steering fluid reservoir.
2. Loosen, but do not remove steering shaft upper joint bolt.
3. Remove lower joint bolt.
4. With wheels in straight-ahead position, separate pinion and lower joint.
5. Raise and support vehicle, then remove front wheels.
6. Remove castle nut from steering knuckle.
7. Using tie rod removal tool No. 09913–65210 or equivalent, remove tie rod end from knuckle.
8. **On models equipped with manual transmission,** disconnect gear shift control shaft and extension rod form transmission.
9. **On all models,** remove engine rear mounting and bracket, **Fig. 20.**
10. Detach mounting member from suspension frame.
11. Remove cylinder pipes "A" and " B" from steering gear box, **Fig. 21.**
12. Disconnect high and low pressure pipes from steering box.
13. Remove steering gear box.
14. Reverse procedure to install.

GRAND VITARA

The power steering gear is serviced as an assembly only.
1. Remove fluid from tank using large syringe, or equivalent.
2. Disconnect high pressure pipe from steering gear box by removing union bolt.
3. Disconnect low pressure hose from steering gear box.
4. Remove steering lower shaft assembly.
5. Raise and support vehicle, then remove front wheel and tire assemblies.
6. Disconnect tie rod ends from knuckles.
7. Remove steering gear box mounting bolts.
8. Remove steering gear box from vehicle.
9. Reverse procedure to install.

SIDEKICK & X-90

1. Disconnect coolant reservoir tank from radiator.
2. Remove steering lower shaft attaching bolt, then the center link end from pitman arm.
3. Disconnect pressure hose from gearbox and return hose from oil tank.
4. Remove three steering gearbox attaching bolts.

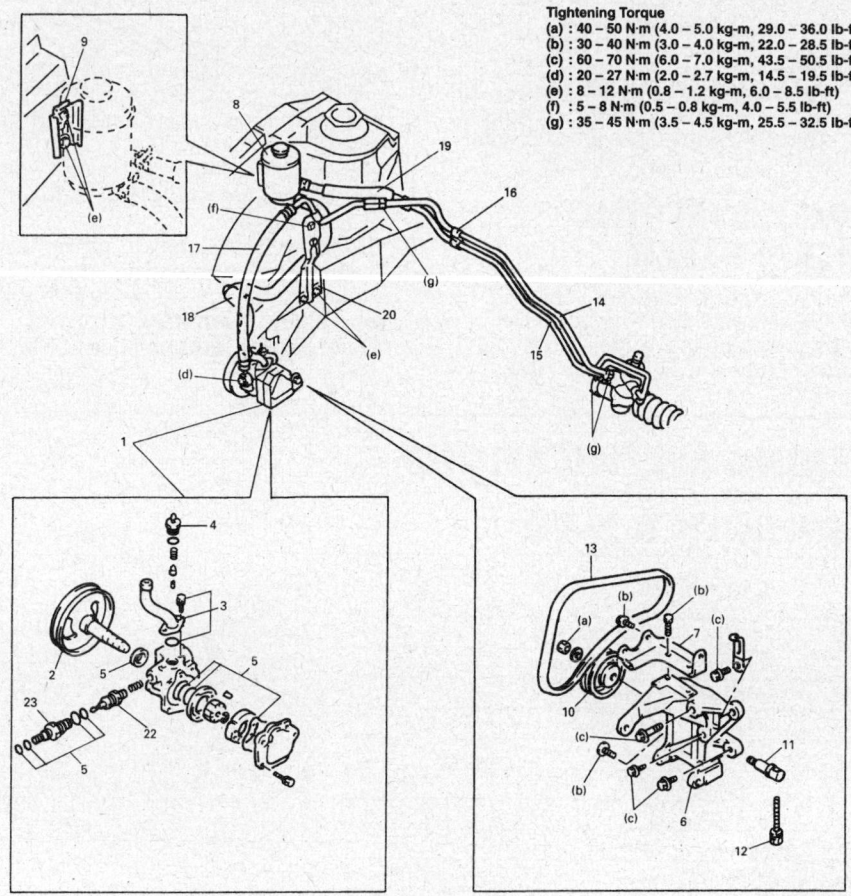

Tightening Torque
(a) : 40 – 50 N·m (4.0 – 5.0 kg-m, 29.0 – 36.0 lb-ft)
(b) : 30 – 40 N·m (3.0 – 4.0 kg-m, 22.0 – 28.5 lb-ft)
(c) : 60 – 70 N·m (6.0 – 7.0 kg-m, 43.5 – 50.5 lb-ft)
(d) : 20 – 27 N·m (2.0 – 2.7 kg-m, 14.5 – 19.5 lb-ft)
(e) : 8 – 12 N·m (0.8 – 1.2 kg-m, 6.0 – 8.5 lb-ft)
(f) : 5 – 8 N·m (0.5 – 0.8 kg-m, 4.0 – 5.5 lb-ft)
(g) : 35 – 45 N·m (3.5 – 4.5 kg-m, 25.5 – 32.5 lb-ft)

1. Power steering pump assembly	9. Fluid (oil) tank bracket	18. Low pressure hose No.1
2. Pulley	10. Belt tension pulley	19. Low pressure hose No.2
3. Connector set	11. Belt tension pulley bolt	20. Hose stay
4. Power steering pressure switch	12. Belt tension bolt	21. Blank
(Terminal set)	13. Power steering belt	22. Relief valve
5. Seal set	14. High pressure pipe	23. Connector
6. Compressor bracket	15. Low pressure pipe	
7. Pump bracket	16. Pipe clamp	
8. Power steering fluid (oil) tank	17. High pressure hose	

SK6029500008000X

Fig. 22 Power steering pump replacement. Esteem & Swift

5. Disconnect steering lower shaft joint, then remove steering gearbox.
6. Remove pitman arm from gearbox.
7. Reverse procedure to install.

SWIFT

1. Loosen steering shaft upper joint bolt, but do not remove, then remove lower joint bolt and separate pinion and lower joint.
2. Raise and support vehicle, then remove front wheels.
3. Disconnect tie rods from steering knuckles using tie rod end remover tool, No. 09913-65210 or equivalent, then remove exhaust pipe.
4. **On models equipped with automatic transmission,** remove rear engine torque rod and torque rod bracket.
5. **On models equipped with manual transmission,** disconnect transmission side of gear shift control shaft and extension rod.

6. **On all models,** disconnect piping from steering gearbox.
7. Remove steering gearbox mounting bolts and steering gearbox.
8. Reverse procedure to install.

POWER STEERING PUMP

REPLACE

ESTEEM & SWIFT

1. Remove engine right side undercover, then loosen belt tension pulley to remove power steering belt, **Fig. 22.**
2. Disconnect high pressure hose and suction hose from pump.
3. Disconnect pressure switch lead harness.
4. **On models equipped with A/C,** remove compressor and position aside.
5. **On all models,** remove power steering pump and bracket.

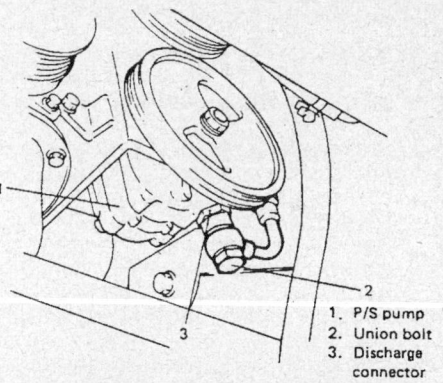

1. P/S pump
2. Union bolt
3. Discharge connector

SK6039100001000X

Fig. 23 Discharge connector location. Sidekick & X-90

6. Reverse procedure to install. Tighten to specification.

GRAND VITARA

1. Remove suction hose from pump.
2. Remove oil tank with suction hose.
3. Remove union bolt, then disconnect high pressure pipe from pump.
4. Disconnect pressure switch electrical connector.
5. Remove power steering belt.
6. Remove power steering pump mounting bolts.
7. Remove power steering pump.
8. Reverse procedure to install.

SIDEKICK & X-90

Before removing joints at inlet and outlet ports clean fitting thoroughly.
1. Disconnect water reservoir tank from radiator.
2. **On models equipped with A/C,** loosen A/C compressor adjusting bolt and pivot bolts.
3. **On models less A/C,** loosen power steering pump adjusting and mounting bolts.
4. Remove power steering belt.
5. Remove union bolt. Hold discharge connector with wrench to prevent fluid from draining, **Fig. 23.**
6. Disconnect pump suction hose from oil tank, then the pump pressure switch lead wire at switch terminal.
7. Remove engine oil filter, then the pump adjusting and mounting bolts.
8. Remove power steering pump. **Plug ports to prevent any foreign matter from entering.**
9. Reverse procedure to install.

MANUAL STEERING GEAR

REPLACE

SIDEKICK & X-90

1. Remove steering lower shaft attaching bolt, then the center link end from pitman arm.
2. Remove three steering gearbox attaching bolts.
3. Disconnect steering lower shaft joint, then remove steering gearbox.

4. Reverse procedure to install.

SWIFT

1. Slide drivers seat back as far as possible.
2. Remove front part of drivers floor mat, then the steering shaft joint cover.
3. Loosen steering shaft upper joint bolt but do not remove.
4. Remove steering shaft lower joint bolt, then disconnect lower joint from pinion.
5. Raise and support vehicle, remove front wheels.
6. Disconnect tie rods ends from knuckles using tie rod remover.

7. Remove steering gear case mounting bolts, case bracket and steering gear.
8. Reverse procedure to install, noting the following:
   a. Ensure steering wheel and brake discs are in straight ahead position.
   b. Tighten lower steering shaft joint bolt first, then the upper bolt.

POWER STEERING SYSTEM BLEED

1. Raise and support front of vehicle.
2. Fill oil tank with fluid to specified level, then turn steering wheel left or right three or four times.

3. After running engine at idling speed for three to five seconds, stop engine and add fluid to meet specification.
4. With engine stopped, turn steering wheel to right and left as far as possible, then repeat a few times and add fluid to specified level.
5. With engine idling, repeat stop-to-stop turn of steering wheel until all foam in oil tank is gone.
6. **Bleed air completely. If air remains in fluid, power steering pump may make humming noise or steering wheel may feel heavy.**
7. Ensure fluid is filled to specified level.

TIGHTENING SPECIFICATIONS

SIDEKICK & X-90

Year	Component	Torque/Ft. Lbs.
1996–99	A/C Compressor Adjustment Bolt	18-22
	A/C Compressor Pivot Bolt	18-22
	Ball Joint Bolt	51-75
	Ball Joint Stud Castle Nut	33-50
	Bump Stopper	29-43
	Caliper Bolt	51-75
	Center Link Castle Nut	22-50
	Control Arm Front Nut	51-75
	Control Arm Rear Nut	65-101
	Locking Hub Bolt	15-22
	Locking Hub Cover Bolt	72-96①
	Power Steering Gearbox Union Bolt	22-28
	Power Steering Pump Adjustment Bolt	15-21
	Power Steering Pump Mounting Bolt	15-21
	Power Steering Pump Union Bolt	37-50
	Stabilizer Bar Ball Joint Nut	29-43
	Steering Gearbox Bolt	51-72
	Steering Lower Shaft Bolt	15-21
	Strut Bracket Nut	58-75
	Strut Nut	50-75
	Strut Support Nut	15-22
	Tie Rod End Castle Nut	22-39
	Wheel Bearing Locknut	89-140
	Wheel Lug Nut	37-58

① — Inch lbs.

GRAND VITARA

Year	Component	Torque/Ft. Lbs.
1999	Pump Bracket Bolt	33
	Power Steering Gear	40
	Steering Shaft Nut	24
	Tie Rod End Lock Nut	47
	Tie Rod End Nut	35
	Wheel Lug Nut	69

SWIFT

Year	Component	Torque/Ft. Lbs.
1996–99	Axle Nut	109-144①
	Ball Stud Nut	37-50
	Bracket Nut	72-108
	Driveshaft Nut	109-144①
	Hub Nut	109-144①
	Stabilizer Bracket Bolt	14-20
	Stabilizer Joint Nut	29-43
	Stabilizer Link Nut	14-20
	Steering Gear Case Bolt	15-21
	Steering Shaft Joint Bolt	15-21
	Strut Bracket Nut	50-65
	Strut Nut	29-43
	Strut Support Nut	16-23
	Suspension Arm Bracket Bolt	61-72
	Suspension Arm Rear Bracket Bolt	22-39
	Tie Rod End Castle Nut	22-39
	Tie Rod End Locknut	25-39
	Wheel Lug Nut	37-50

①–After tightening to specification, secure nut with a suitable calking compound.

ESTEEM

Year	Component	Torque/Ft. Lbs.
1996–99	ABS Wheel Speed Sensor	17
	Axle Nut	127
	Ball Stud Nut	44
	Brake Disc Mount	48①
	Caliper Carrier Bolt	62
	Driveshaft Nut	127
	Hub Nut	127
	Power Steering Cylinder Pipes A & B	15
	Power Steering Gear Mounting Brackets	40
	Power Steering High & Low Pressure Pipes	24
	Power Steering Pump Mounting Bracket	48
	Stabilizer Bracket Bolt	17
	Stabilizer Joint Nut	37
	Stabilizer Link Nut	21
	Steering Knuckle Castle Nut	26-40
	Steering Shaft Joint Bolt	19
	Strut Bracket Nut	65
	Strut Nut	40
	Strut Support Nut	21
	Suspension Arm Front Bushing Bolt	65
	Suspension Arm Rear Bracket Bolt	27
	Tie Rod End Castle Nut	33
	Wheel Lug Nut	62

① — Inch lbs.

SUZUKI

Wheel Alignment

INDEX

PRELIMINARY INSPECTION

Steering and vibration complaints are not always the result of improper alignment. An additional item to be checked is the possibility of tire lead. Lead is the deviation of the vehicle from a straight path on a level road without hand pressure on the steering wheel.

Before making any adjustment affecting toe setting, the following checks and inspections should be made to ensure correctness of alignment readings and adjustments.

1. Check all tires for proper inflation pressures and approximately same tread wear.
2. Check suspension parts for excessive looseness, replace as needed.
3. Check runout of wheels and tires.
4. Check vehicle ride height; if out of limits and a correction is to be made, it must be made before adjusting toe.
5. Consideration must be given to excess loads, such as tool boxes. If this excess load is normally carried in vehicle, it should remain in vehicle during alignment checks.
6. Vehicle must be on a level surface both front and rear and side to side.

FRONT WHEEL ALIGNMENT

ADJUSMENT

CAMBER & CASTER

Camber and caster are preset and cannot be adjusted. If camber or caster are not within specifications, check suspension and frame for damaged parts.

TOE-IN

Toe-In is adjusted by changing tie rod length.

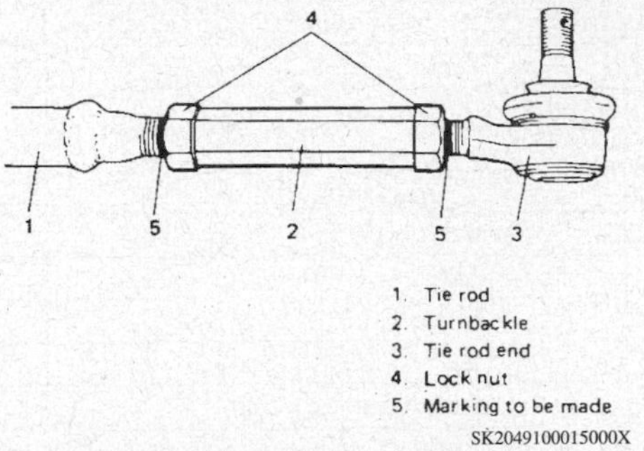

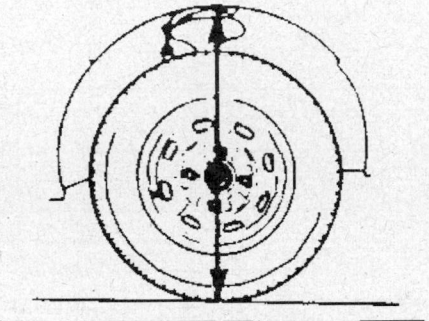

1. Tie rod
2. Turnbackle
3. Tie rod end
4. Lock nut
5. Marking to be made

SK2049100015000X

Fig. 1 Toe-in adjustment

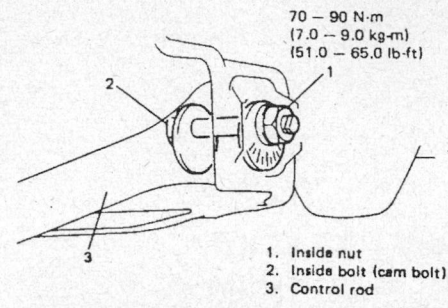

70 — 90 N·m
(7.0 — 9.0 kg-m)
(51.0 — 65.0 lb-ft)

1. Inside nut
2. Inside bolt (cam bolt)
3. Control rod

SK2049100016000X

Fig. 2 Rear toe adjustment. Swift & Esteem

SK2049100017000X

Fig. 3 Ride height measurement

1. Loosen right and left tie rod end locknuts, **Fig. 1.**
2. Rotate turnbuckle and adjust toe-in to specification. **Ensure rack boots do not twist during this procedure.**
3. Thread lengths, **Fig. 1,** should be equal lengths. **Torque** locknuts to 51–72 ft. lbs.

REAR WHEEL ALIGNMENT

ADJUSTMENT

CAMBER & CASTER

Camber and caster are preset and cannot be adjusted. If camber or caster are not within specifications, check suspension and frame for damaged parts.

TOE-IN

Swift & Esteem

1. Loosen right and left control rod inside nuts, **Fig. 2.**
2. Adjust toe to specification by turning right and left control rod inside bolts by the same amount.
3. After adjustment, **torque** right and left inside nuts to 51–65 ft. lbs., while holding cam bolt with another wrench to prevent it from turning.

VEHICLE RIDE HEIGHT

Right to left ride height difference should be within .6 inch (15 mm) with curb weight, **Fig. 3.**

Air Conditioning

NOTE: On Air Bag Equipped Models, Refer To "Air Bag System Precautions" Located In The Front Of This Manual For System Disarming & Arming Procedures.

INDEX

PRECAUTIONS

AIR BAG SYSTEMS

Refer to "Air Bag System Precautions" in the front of this manual for system disarming and arming procedures.

BATTERY GROUND CABLE

Prior to service, disconnect battery ground cable and isolate as required.

PERFORMANCE TEST

1. Connect manifold gauge set to high and low sides of system at compressor service valves, **Figs. 1 and 2.**
2. Start engine and allow to run at approximately 2000 RPM, then activate air conditioner.
3. Set blower switch to HI position and temperature lever to COOL position.
4. Open all windows and doors, then position dry bulb thermometer in cool air outlet and psychrometer (combination dry/wet bulb thermometer) near to evaporator inlet.
5. Check that high pressure gauge reading is between 200–220 psi. **If high pressure gauge reading is above specified range, pour water on condenser until specified range is reached. If gauge reading is below specified range, cover condenser front surface area.**
6. Ensure dry bulb portion of psychrometer is 77–95°F, then operate system until all gauges and thermometers have stabilized.
7. Compare temperatures of dry and wet bulb portions of psychrometer, then determine relative humidity using graph, **Fig. 3.** Record reading.
8. Measure the difference in dry bulb temperatures at cool air outlet and evaporator inlet. Record reading.
9. Using information gathered in steps 8 and 9, determine if system is operating properly by using graph, **Fig. 4.** Intersection of the two points should be within the diagonal lines as shown.

OIL CHARGE

When replacing compressor, drain 1.4

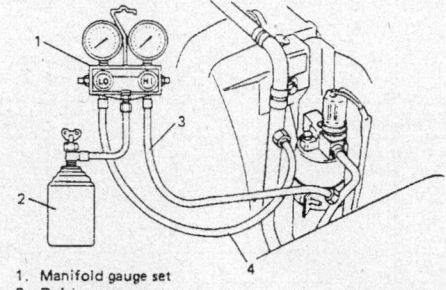

1. Manifold gauge set
2. Refrigerant can
3. High pressure side (Delivery side hose)
4. Low pressure side (Suction side hose)

SK7029100021000X

Fig. 1 Manifold gauge set connections. Grand Vitara, Sidekick & X-90

ounces from replacement compressor prior to installation. When replacing other components, add the following amounts of oil to system: Condenser, 1 ounce; Receiver/Drier, .33 ounce.

OIL LEVEL CHECK

No provision is made for checking oil level on these vehicles and oil is added according to component(s) being replaced. Refer to "Oil Charge" as outlined.

BELT TENSION DATA

When checking drive belt deflection, apply 22 lbs. of pressure between compressor clutch pulley and crankshaft pulley.

SWIFT

Adjust belt until deflection is within .30–.40 inch.

GRAND VITARA

Adjust belt until deflection is within .16–.35 inch.

ESTEEM

Adjust belt until deflection is within .30–.40 inch.

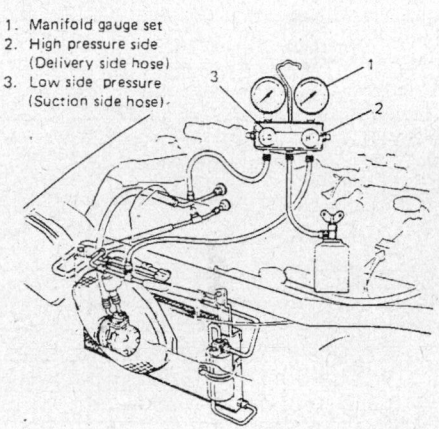

1. Manifold gauge set
2. High pressure side (Delivery side hose)
3. Low side pressure (Suction side hose)

SK7029100022000X

Fig. 2 Manifold gauge set connections. Esteem & Swift

SIDEKICK & X-90 w/1.6L ENGINE

Adjust belt until deflection is within .24–.35 inch.

SIDEKICK w/1.8L ENGINE

A tensioner controls the belt tension on this engine.

REFRIGERANT RECOVERY PROCEDURE

The use of refrigerant recovery and recycling stations allows the recovery and reuse of refrigerant after contaminants and moisture have been removed.

When using a recovery or recycling station, follow the manufacturer's operating instructions, noting the following:

1. **Use extreme caution and observe all safety and service precautions related to use of refrigerants.**
2. Connect refrigerant recycling station hoses to vehicle A/C service ports and recovery station inlet fitting. Hoses should have shutoff devices or check valve within 12 inches of hose ends to

SUZUKI

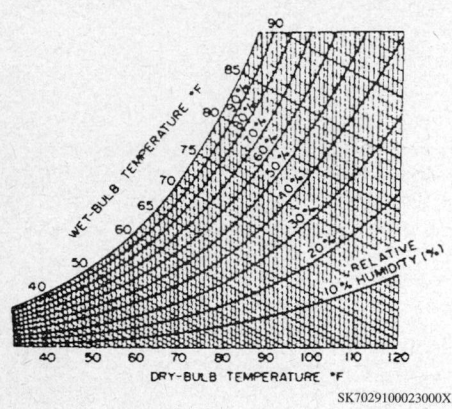

Fig. 3 Relative humidity graph

minimize introduction of air into recycling station and to minimize amount of

refrigerant release when hoses are disconnected.

3. Turn recycling station ON to start recovery process. Allow recycling station to pump refrigerant from A/C system until station pressure gauge indicates vacuum.
4. After vehicle A/C system has been evacuated, close station inlet valve, if equipped.
5. Turn station OFF. On some stations the pump will automatically be turned Off by a low pressure switch.
6. Allow vehicle A/C system to remain closed for approximately two minutes. Observe vacuum level indicated on gauge. If pressure does not rise, disconnect recycling station hoses.
7. If system pressure rises, repeat steps 3 through 6 until vacuum level remains stable for two minutes.

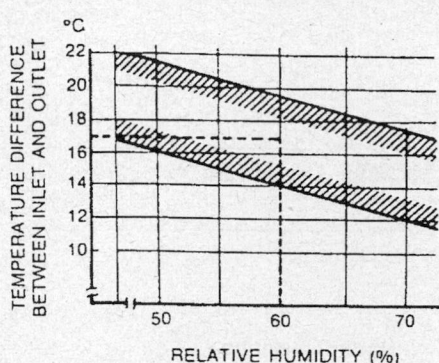

Fig. 4 Temperature humidity chart

8. Service A/C system as necessary, then evacuate and recharge A/C system.

A/C SPECIFICATIONS

Year	Model	Refrigerant		Refrigerant Oil			Compressor Clutch Air Gap, Inches
		Capacity, Lbs.	Type	Viscosity	Total System Capacity, Ounces	Compressor Oil Level Check, Inches	
1996–99	Esteem	1.4	R-134a	②	5	①	.012–.020
	Grand Vitara	1.1–1.4	R-134a	②	5	①	.012–.024
	Sidekick	1.4	R-134a	②	③	①	④
	Swift	1.1	R-134a	②	2.7	①	.016–.028
	X-90	1.4	R-134a	②	③	①	④

① — Oil level cannot be checked. Refer to "Oil Charge" for compressor oil level adjustment.

② — Use only the proper compressor oil designated for use with R-134a.

③ — Nippondenso compressor, 3.3 oz.; Sanden compressor, 3.0 oz.

④ — Nippondenso compressor, .016–.028; Sanden compressor, .014–.025

Cooling Fans

NOTE: On Air Bag Equipped Models, Refer To "Air Bag System Precautions" Located In The Front Of This Manual For System Disarming & Arming Procedures.

INDEX

PRECAUTIONS

AIR BAG SYSTEMS

Refer to "Air Bag System Precautions" in the front of this manual for system disarming and arming procedures.

BATTERY GROUND CABLE

Prior to service, disconnect battery ground cable and isolate as required.

SYSTEM DIAGNOSIS & TESTING

COOLANT FAN

Refer to **Fig. 1,** for proper procedures.

A/C CONDENSER FAN

Refer to **Fig. 2,** for proper procedures.

COMPONENT SERVICE

FAN THERMO SWITCH

Replacement

1. Drain coolant system into appropriate container.
2. Disconnect thermo switch connector from thermo switch.
3. Remove thermo switch from thermostat case.
4. Reverse procedure to install.

Inspection

1. Immerse switch in water up to suitable level, then connect suitable ohmmeter.
2. Heat water gradually, noting if there is no continuity (switch Off) when water temperature is under 190°F and continuity (switch On) when temperature is above 199°F.

	TEST	RESULT	ACTION
A1.	Start and run engine. Make certain that engine coolant temperature is below 93° C (199° F).	RADIATOR FAN MOTOR operates.	GO TO A2.
		RADIATOR FAN MOTOR does not operate.	GO TO A3.
A2.	Disconnect RADIATOR FAN SWITCH connector.	RADIATOR FAN MOTOR continues to operate.	Repair short to voltage in BLU wire between RADIATOR FAN SWITCH and RADIATOR FAN MOTOR.
		RADIATOR FAN MOTOR stops running.	Replace RADIATOR FAN SWITCH.
A3.	Run engine until engine coolant temperature is above 98° C (208° F).	RADIATOR FAN MOTOR operates.	All systems diagnosed in this cell are functioning normally.
		RADIATOR FAN MOTOR does not operate.	GO TO A4.
A4.	Disconnect RADIATOR FAN SWITCH connector. Connect a fused jumper between RADIATOR FAN SWITCH connector cavities 1 and 2.	RADIATOR FAN operates.	Replace RADIATOR FAN SWITCH.
		RADIATOR FAN does not operate.	GO TO A5.
A5.	Turn ignition switch to "OFF." Backprobe RADIATOR FAN MOTOR connector with a digital multimeter from cavity 1 to chassis ground. Measure resistance.	More than 0.3 ohms.	Repair BLK ground wire between RADIATOR FAN MOTOR and G101.
		Less than 0.3 ohms.	GO TO A6.
A6.	Backprobe RADIATOR FAN MOTOR connector with a test lamp from cavity 2 to chassis ground.	Test lamp lights.	Replace RADIATOR FAN MOTOR.
		Test lamp does not light.	GO TO A7.
A7.	Connect a test lamp from RADIATOR FAN SWITCH connector cavity 1 to chassis ground.	Test lamp lights.	Repair open in BLU wire between RADIATOR FAN SWITCH and RADIATOR FAN MOTOR.
		Test lamp does not light.	Repair open in BLK/WHT wire between RADIATOR FAN SWITCH and JUNCTION BLOCK.

SK1089100005000X

Fig. 1   Coolant fan diagnostic chart. Swift

3. If not within specifications, replace fan thermo switch.

WATER TEMPERATURE SWITCH

Replacement

1. Disconnect thermo switch connector from thermo switch.
2. Remove switch from vehicle.
3. Reverse procedure to install.

Inspection

1. Immerse switch in silicon oil or glycerin up to level shown, **Fig. 3,** then connect suitable ohmmeter.
2. **On Sidekick models,** check for continuity (switch open) with temperature of liquid above 235°F.
3. **On Swift models,** check for continuity (switch open) with temperature of liquid above 226°F.
4. **On all models,** if continuity is not within specification, replace water temperature switch.

COMPRESSOR/COOLING FAN RELAY

Replacement

1. Disconnect relay connector from relay.
2. Remove relay from vehicle.
3. Reverse procedure to install.

Inspection

1. Using suitable ohmmeter, connect to relay as shown, **Fig. 4.**
2. If open continuity is found between terminals 3 and 4, replace relay.

	TEST	RESULT	ACTION
B1.	Turn ignition switch to "ON." Press A/C switch.	A/C CONDENSER FAN operates.	All systems diagnosed in this cell are functioning normally.
		A/C CONDENSER FAN does not operate.	GO TO B2.
B2.	Backprobe A/C CONDENSER FAN connector with a test lamp from cavity 2 to chassis ground.	Test lamp lights.	GO TO B3.
		Test lamp does not light.	GO TO B4.
B3.	Disconnect A/C CONDENSER FAN connector. Connect a digital multimeter from cavity 1 to chassis ground. Measure resistance.	More than 0.3 ohms.	Repair BLK ground wire between A/C CONDENSER FAN and G104.
		Less than 0.3 ohms.	Replace A/C CONDENSER FAN.
B4.	Backprobe A/C CONDENSER FAN RELAY connector with a test lamp from cavity 4 to chassis ground.	Test lamp lights.	Repair open in BLU/BLK wire between A/C CONDENSER FAN and A/C CONDENSER FAN RELAY.
		Test lamp does not light.	GO TO B5.
B5.	Backprobe A/C CONDENSER FAN RELAY connector with a test lamp from cavity 2 to chassis ground.	Test lamp does not light.	GO TO B6.
		Test lamp lights.	GO TO B7.
B6.	Backprobe A/C CLUTCH RELAY connector with a test lamp from cavity 2 to chassis ground.	Test lamp lights.	Repair open in RED wire between A/C CLUTCH RELAY and A/C CONDENSER FAN RELAY.
		Test lamp does not light.	Repair open in RED wire between A/C CLUTCH RELAY and FUSIBLE LINK BOX.
B7.	Backprobe A/C CONDENSER FAN RELAY connector with a test lamp from cavity 1 to chassis ground.	Test lamp lights.	GO TO B8.
		Test lamp does not light.	GO TO B9.
B8.	Disconnect A/C CONDENSER FAN RELAY connector. Connect a digital multimeter from cavity 3 to chassis ground. Measure resistance.	More than 0.3 ohms.	Repair BLK ground wire between A/C CONDENSER FAN RELAY and G104.
		Less than 0.3 ohms.	Replace A/C CONDENSER FAN RELAY.
B9.	Backprobe A/C CLUTCH RELAY connector with a test lamp from cavity 4 to chassis ground.	Test lamp lights.	Repair open in BLK/WHT wire between A/C CLUTCH RELAY and A/C CONDENSER FAN RELAY.
		Test lamp does not light.	GO TO B10.
B10.	Backprobe A/C CLUTCH RELAY connector with a test lamp from cavity 1 to chassis ground.	Test lamp lights.	GO TO B11.
		Test lamp does not light.	GO TO B13.
B11.	Disconnect A/C AMPLIFIER connector. Connect a jumper from A/C AMPLIFIER connector cavity 7 to chassis ground. Backprobe A/C CLUTCH RELAY with a test lamp from cavity 4 to chassis ground.	Test lamp does not light.	GO TO B12.
		Test lamp lights.	A/C AMPLIFIER diagnosis.
B12.	Remove jumper. Disconnect A/C CLUTCH RELAY connector. Connect a digital multimeter from A/C CLUTCH RELAY connector cavity 3 to A/C AMPLIFIER connector cavity 7. Measure resistance.	More than 0.3 ohms.	Repair open in PNK wire between A/C CLUTCH RELAY and A/C AMPLIFIER.
		Less than 0.3 ohms.	Replace A/C CLUTCH RELAY.
B13.	Backprobe DUAL PRESSURE SWITCH connector with a test lamp from cavity 1 to chassis ground.	Test lamp lights.	Repair open in YEL wire between DUAL PRESSURE SWITCH and A/C CLUTCH RELAY.
		Test lamp does not light.	GO TO B14.
B14.	Backprobe DUAL PRESSURE SWITCH connector with a test lamp from cavity 2 to chassis ground.	Test lamp lights.	Replace DUAL PRESSURE SWITCH.
		Test lamp does not light.	GO TO B15.
B15.	Backprobe connector C111 with a test lamp from cavity 3 to chassis ground.	Test lamp lights.	Repair open in LT GRN wire between connector C111 and DUAL PRESSURE SWITCH.
		Test lamp does not light.	Repair open in BLK/WHT wire between connector C111 and JUNCTION BLOCK.

SK1089100006000X

Fig. 2   A/C condenser fan diagnostic chart. Swift

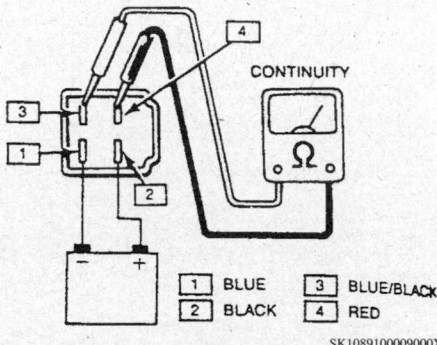

1	WATER TEMP. SWITCH
2	SILICON OIL OR GLYCERIN

SK1089100008000X

Fig. 3   Water temperature switch inspection

1	BLUE	3	BLUE/BLACK
2	BLACK	4	RED

SK1089100009000X

Fig. 4   Compressor/cooling fan relay inspection

Dash Gauges

NOTE: On Air Bag Equipped Models, Refer To "Air Bag System Precautions" Located In The Front Of This Manual For System Disarming & Arming Procedures.

NOTE: Refer To The "Dash Panel Service" Section For Dash Panel Removal Procedures.

NOTE: Electrical Symbol & Wire Color Code Identification Located In The Front Of This Manual May Be Used As An Aid When Using Wiring Circuits Found In This Section.

INDEX

PRECAUTIONS

AIR BAG SYSTEMS

Refer to "Air Bag System Precautions" in the front of this manual for system disarming and arming procedures.

BATTERY GROUND CABLE

Prior to service, disconnect battery ground cable and isolate as required.

GAUGES

COOLANT TEMPERATURE

This temperature indicating system consists of a sending unit, located on the cylinder head and an electrical temperature gauge. As engine temperature increases or decreases, the resistance of the sending unit changes, in turn controlling current flow through the gauge. When engine temperature is low sending unit resistance is high, current flow through the gauge is restricted and the gauge pointer remains against the stop or moves very little. As engine temperature increases sending unit resistance decreases and current flow through the gauge increases, resulting in increased pointer movement.

FUEL GAUGES

The fuel gauge system consists of a sending unit and an electric fuel gauge. The sending unit is a variable resistor that is controlled by a float. Corresponding to actual fuel level, the float will rise or fall. When the ignition is turned to the On position, voltage is applied to the gauge, completing the gauge ground circuit through the sending unit.

Trouble	Possible cause	Correction
Fuel level meter shows no operation.	Meter fuse blown	Replace fuse to check for short.
	Fuel meter faulty	Check meter.
	Fuel level gauge unit faulty	Check gauge unit.
	Wiring or grounding faulty	Repair.
Coolant (Water) temp. meter shows no operation.	Meter fuse blown	Replace fuse to check for short.
	Coolant (Water) temp. meter faulty	Check meter.
	Coolant (Water) temp. gauge unit faulty	Check gauge unit.
	Wiring or grounding faulty	Repair.
Oil pressure light shows no lighting.	Light fuse blown	Replace fuse to check for short.
	Bulb burnt out	Replace bulb.
	Oil pressure switch faulty	Check switch.
	Wiring or grounding faulty	Repair.

SK9099100002000X

Fig. 1   Troubleshooting chart

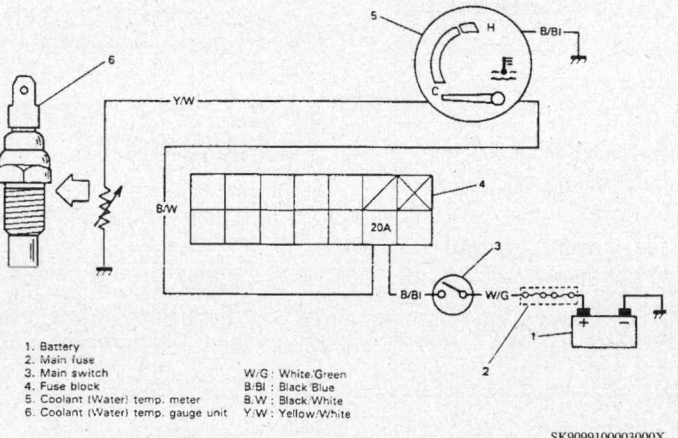

1. Battery
2. Main fuse
3. Main switch
4. Fuse block
5. Coolant (Water) temp. meter
6. Coolant (Water) temp. gauge unit

W/G : White/Green
B/Bl : Black/Blue
B/W : Black/White
Y/W : Yellow/White

SK9099100003000X

Fig. 2   Coolant temperature meter & gauge unit wiring

OIL PRESSURE LIGHT

This oil pressure indicating system incorporates an oil pressure switch installed in the cylinder block and oil pressure light in

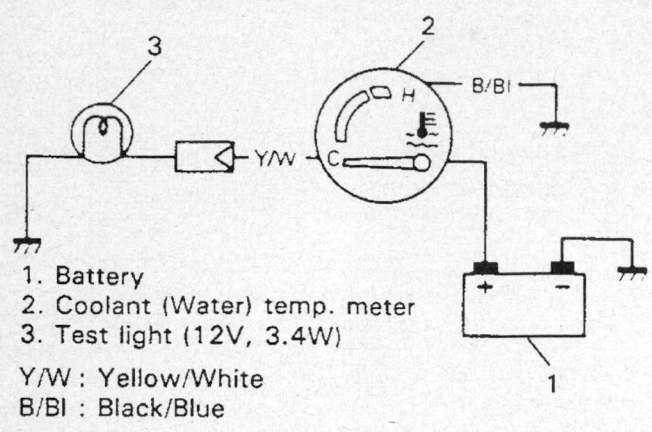

1. Battery
2. Coolant (Water) temp. meter
3. Test light (12V, 3.4W)

Y/W : Yellow/White
B/Bl : Black/Blue

SK9099100004000X

Fig. 3   Coolant temperature meter inspection

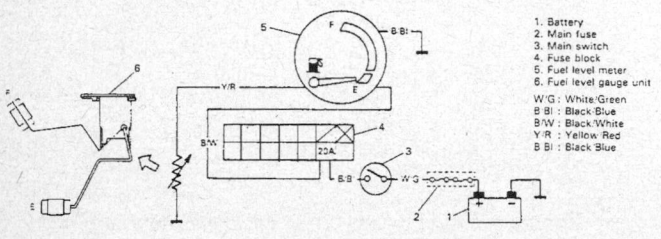

1. Battery
2. Main fuse
3. Main switch
4. Fuse block
5. Fuel level meter
6. Fuel level gauge unit

W/G : White/Green
B/Bl : Black/Blue
B/W : Black/White
Y/R : Yellow/Red
B/Bl : Black/Blue

SK9099100006000X

Fig. 5   Fuel level meter & gauge unit wiring

Position	Resistance
E	120 ± 8 Ω
F	5 ± 2 Ω
1/2	32.5 ± 4 Ω

SK9099100008000X

Fig. 7   Gauge unit float position-to-resistance chart

Temperature	Resistance
50°C (122°F)	189.4 – 259.6 Ω
115°C (239°F)	24.2 – 28.1 Ω

SK9099500014000X

Fig. 4   Gauge unit temperature resistance chart

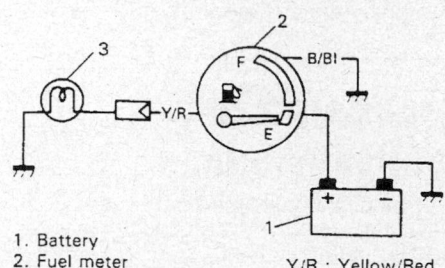

1. Battery
2. Fuel meter
3. Test light (12V, 3.4W)

Y/R : Yellow/Red
B/Bl : Black/Blue

SK9099100007000X

Fig. 6   Fuel level meter inspection

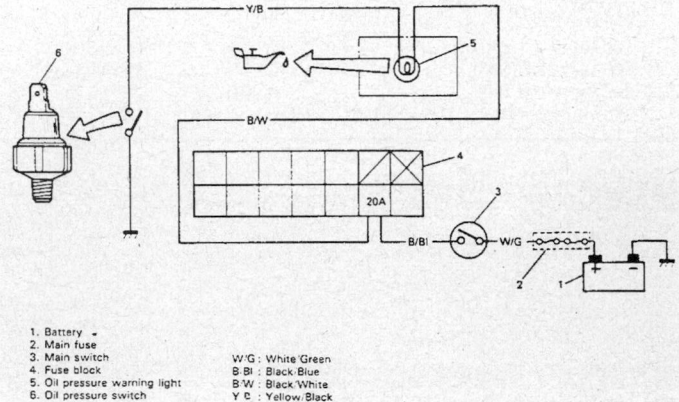

1. Battery
2. Main fuse
3. Main switch
4. Fuse block
5. Oil pressure warning light
6. Oil pressure switch

W/G : White/Green
B/Bl : Black/Blue
B/W : Black/White
Y/B : Yellow/Black

SK9099100009000X

Fig. 8   Oil pressure light wiring

the combination meter. When the engine is started the oil pressure acts upon the switch in such a way that it turns the switch "OFF."

TROUBLESHOOTING

Refer to troubleshooting chart, **Fig. 1**.

DIAGNOSIS & TESTING

COOLANT (WATER) TEMPERATURE METER & GAUGE UNIT

1. Disconnect Yellow/White lead wire going to gauge unit installed on intake manifold, **Fig. 2**.
2. Using a 12 volt (3.4 W) bulb, ground wire as shown, **Fig. 3**.

3. Turn ignition On. Ensure bulb is lighted with meter pointer wavering several seconds after.
4. If meter is faulty, replace as necessary.
5. After warming up gauge unit, ensure resistance decreases with the increase of temperature as shown, **Fig. 4**

FUEL LEVEL METER & GAUGE UNIT

1. Remove rear seat, then disconnect Yellow/Red lead wire going to gauge unit, **Fig. 5**.
2. Using a 12 volt (3.4 W) bulb, ground lead wire as shown, **Fig. 6**.
3. Turn ignition switch On. Ensure bulb is lighted with meter pointer wavering

several seconds after.
4. If meter is faulty, replace as necessary.
5. Using an ohmmeter, ensure resistance of level gauge unit changes with a change of float position, **Fig. 7**.

OIL PRESSURE LIGHT

1. Using a suitable ohmmeter, disconnect Yellow/Black and Black/White lead wires from oil pressure switch. Measure switch continuity, **Fig. 8**.
2. With engine running, there should be no continuity.
3. With engine stopped, there should be continuity.

Starter Motors

DESCRIPTION

CONVENTIONAL TYPE

A conventional type starter uses four individually wound magnets to produce a strong magnetic field, which in turn forces the armature to turn against these fields. Because these magnetic fields are constantly opposing themselves, the starter engages until power is lost to the plunger. This starter is used on the Suzuki vehicles, **Figs. 1 through 4.**

TROUBLESHOOTING

Refer to **Fig. 5,** for troubleshooting charts.

DIAGNOSIS & TESTING

PERFORMANCE TEST

Each test must be performed within 3–5 seconds to avoid damage to coil from burning.

Pull-In Test

1. Disconnect field coil from terminal "M."
2. Connect test leads as shown, **Fig. 6.**
3. Ensure pinion (overrunning clutch) jumps out.

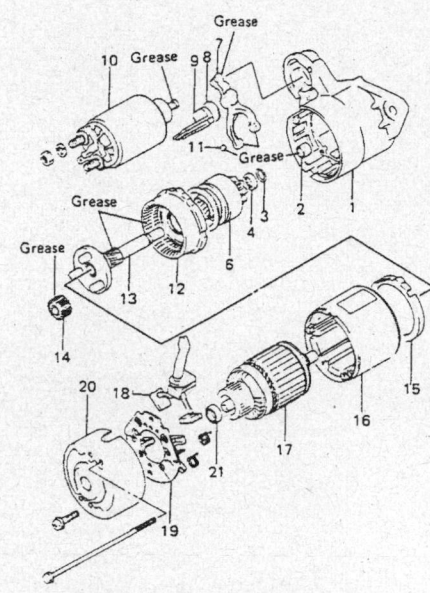

1. Front housing
2. Bush
3. Ring
4. Stop ring
5. Pinion gear
6. Over-running clutch
7. Lever
8. Plate
9. Seal rubber
10. Magnetic switch
11. Ball
12. Internal gear
13. Gear shaft ass'y
14. Idle gear
15. Packing
16. Yoke
17. Armature
18. Brush
19. Brush holder
20. Rear bracket
21. Bearing
22. Spring washer

SK1129100002000X

Fig. 1 Exploded view of starter motor. Sidekick & X-90

4. If pinion is not as specified, replace magnetic switch.

Hold-In Test

1. Perform "Pull-In Test," then disconnect negative lead from terminal "M," **Fig. 7.**
2. Ensure pinion remains outside. If pinion retracts, replace magnetic switch.

Pinion Return Test

1. Perform "Hold-In Test," then disconnect negative lead from body, **Fig. 8.**
2. Ensure pinion retracts quickly. If pinion remains out, replace magnetic switch.

No-Load Performance Test

1. Connect test leads as shown, **Fig. 9.**
2. Ensure pinion moves out and motor runs without stopping.
3. Measure ammeter current. Refer to "Starter Motor Specifications" for correct specification.

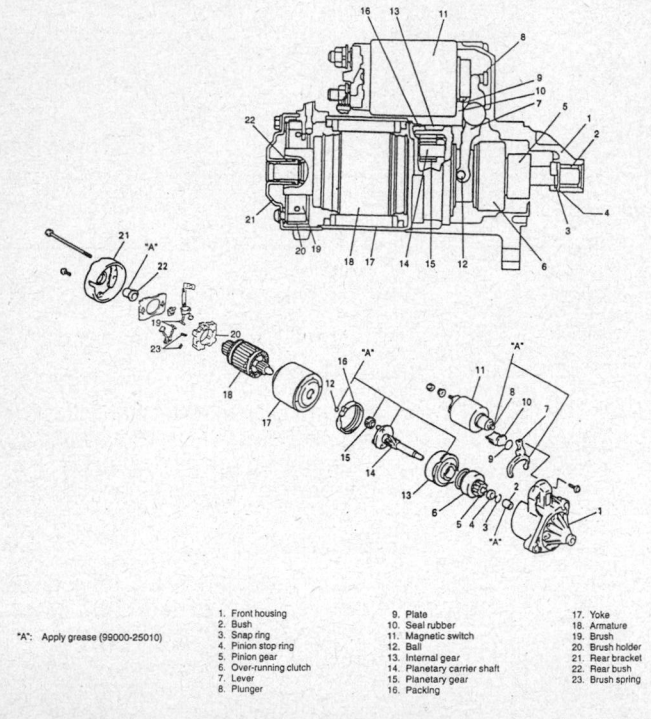

"A": Apply grease (99000-25010)

1. Front housing	9. Plate	17. Yoke
2. Bush	10. Seal rubber	18. Armature
3. Snap ring	11. Magnetic switch	19. Brush
4. Pinion gear	12. Ball	20. Brush holder
5. Pinion gear	13. Internal gear	21. Rear bracket
6. Over-running clutch	14. Planetary carrier shaft	22. Rear bush
7. Lever	15. Planetary gear	23. Brush spring
8. Plunger	16. Packing	

SK1129900016000X

Fig. 2   Exploded view of starter motor. Grand Vitara

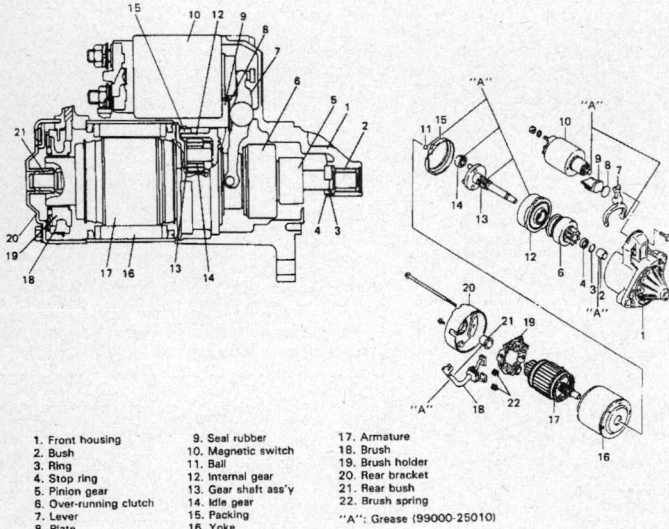

1. Front housing	9. Seal rubber	17. Armature
2. Bush	10. Magnetic switch	18. Brush
3. Ring	11. Ball	19. Brush holder
4. Stop ring	12. Internal gear	20. Rear bracket
5. Pinion gear	13. Gear shaft ass'y	21. Rear bush
6. Over-running clutch	14. Idle gear	22. Brush spring
7. Lever	15. Packing	"A": Grease (99000-25010)
8. Plate	16. Yoke	

SK1129500015000X

Fig. 4   Exploded view of starter motor. Esteem & Swift w/automatic transaxle

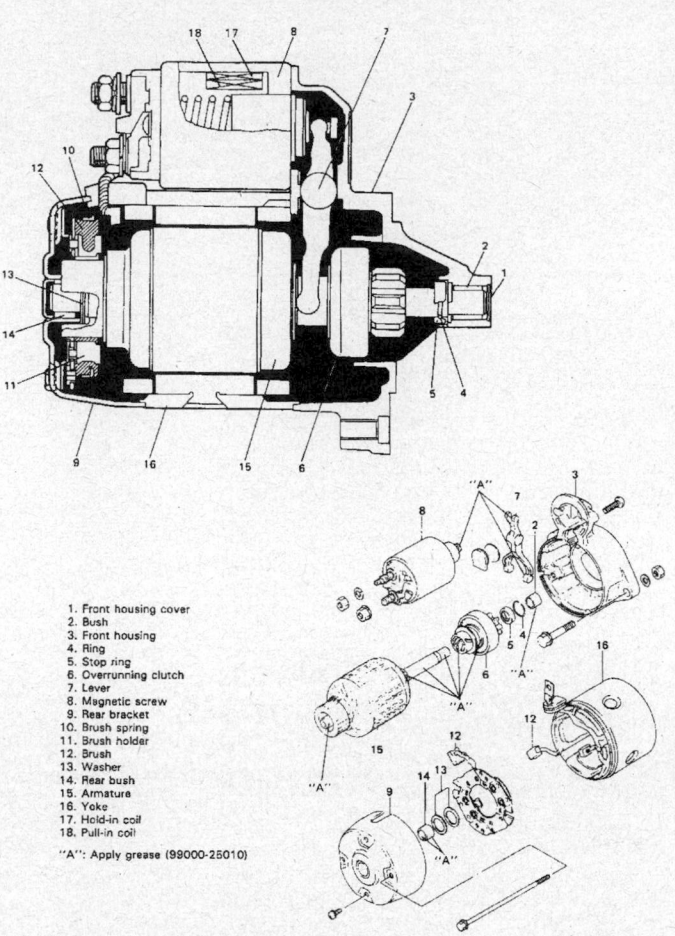

1. Front housing cover
2. Bush
3. Front housing
4. Ring
5. Stop ring
6. Overrunning clutch
7. Lever
8. Magnetic switch
9. Rear bracket
10. Brush spring
11. Brush holder
12. Brush
13. Washer
14. Rear bush
15. Armature
16. Yoke
17. Hold-in coil
18. Pull-in coil

"A": Apply grease (99000-25010)

SK1129500014000X

Fig. 3   Exploded view of starter motor. Swift w/manual transaxle

Condition	Possible Cause	Correction
Motor not running	No operating sound of magnetic switch	
	1. Clutch pedal is not depressed fully or clutch start switch is not adjusted (M/T)	Depress clutch pedal or adjust clutch start switch
	2. Shift lever switch is not in P or N, or not adjusted (A/T)	Shift in P or N, or adjust switch
	3. Battery run down	Recharge battery
	4. Battery voltage too low due to battery deterioration	Replace battery
	5. Poor contact in battery terminal connection	Retighten or replace
	6. Loose grounding cable connection	Retighten
	7. Fuse set loose or blown off	Tighten or replace
	8. Poor contacting action of ignition switch	Replace
	9. Lead wire coupler loose in place	Retighten
	10. Open-circuit between ignition switch and magnetic switch	Repair
	11. Open-circuit in pull-in coil	Replace magnetic switch
	12. Poor sliding of plunger	Replace
Motor not running	Operating sound of magnetic switch heard	
	1. Battery run down	Recharge battery
	2. Battery voltage too low due to battery deterioration	Replace battery
	3. Loose battery cable connections	Retighten
	4. Burnt main contact point, or poor contacting action of magnetic switch	Replace magnetic switch
	5. Brushes are seating poorly or worn down	Repair or replace
	6. Weakened brush spring	Replace
	7. Burnt commutator	Replace
	8. Poor grounding of field coil	Repair
	9. Layer short-circuit of armature	Replace
	10. Crankshaft rotation obstructed	Repair

SK1129100005010X

Fig. 5   Troubleshooting chart (Part 1 of 2)

Condition	Possible Cause	Correction
Starting motor running but too slow (small torque)	If battery and wiring are satisfactory, inspect starting motor	
	1. Insufficient contact of magnetic switch main contacts	Replace
	2. Layer short-circuit of armature	Replace
	3. Disconnected, burnt or worn commutator	Repair or replace
	4. Poor grounding of field coil	Repair
	5. Worn brushes	Replace
	6. Weakened brush springs	Replace spring
	7. Burnt or abnormally worn end bushings	Replace
Starting motor running, but not cranking engine	1. Worn pinion tip	Replace over-running clutch
	2. Poor sliding of over-running clutch	Replace
	3. Over-running clutch slipping	Replace
	4. Worn teeth of ring gear	Replace flywheel
	5. Shock absorber slipping (Reduction type)	Replace
Noise	1. Abnormally worn bush	Replace
	2. Worn pinion or worn teeth of ring gear	Replace pinion or flywheel
	3. Poor sliding of pinion (failure in return movement)	Repair or replace
Starting motor does not stop running	1. Fused contact points of magnetic switch	Replace
	2. Short-circuit between turns of magnetic switch coil (layer short-circuit)	Replace
	3. Failure of returning action in ignition switch	Replace

SK1129100005020X

Fig. 5   Troubleshooting chart (Part 2 of 2)

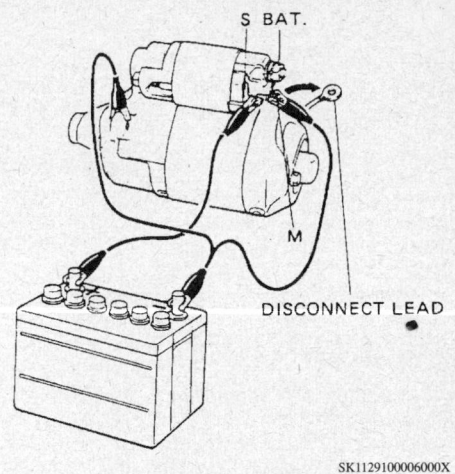

SK1129100006000X

Fig. 6   Pull-in test lead connections

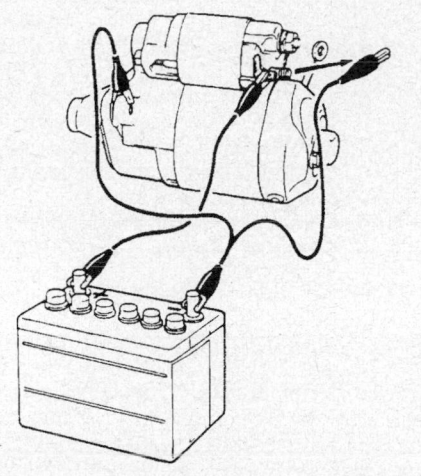

SK1129100007000X

Fig. 7   Hold-in test lead connections

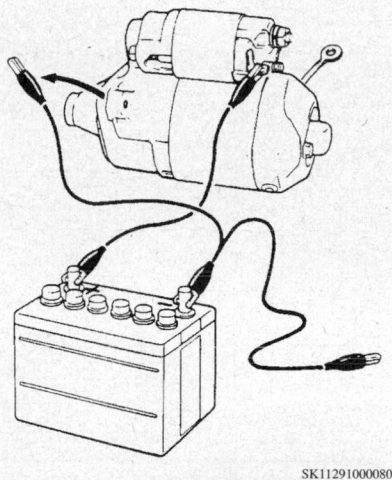

SK1129100008000X

Fig. 8   Pinion return test lead connections

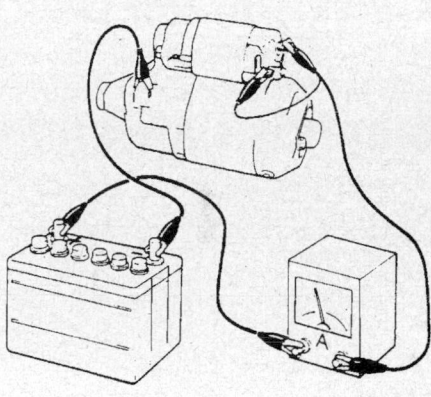

SK1129100009000X

Fig. 9   No-load performance test lead connections

STARTER SPECIFICATIONS

Year	Model	Volts	Output, kW	Direction of Rotation	Brush Length, Inch	No. of Pinion Teeth	No Load Test		
							Amps	Volts	RPM②
1996–99	Esteem	12	①	CW	⑧	8	90	11	3000
	Grand Vitara	12	①	CW	.44	8	90	11	3000
	Sidekick & X-90	12	⑨	CW	.69	9	90	11	3000
	Swift	12	④	CW	⑤	8	⑥	⑦	③

① — Automatic transaxle, 1.4; manual transaxle, 1.2.
② — Minimum.
③ — Automatic transaxle 3000–4000 RPM; manual transaxle 6600 RPM.
④ — Automatic transaxle, 1.2 kW; manual transaxle, .9 kW.
⑤ — Automatic transaxle, .69 inch; manual transaxle, .67 inch.
⑥ — Automatic transaxle, 50–75 amps; manual transaxle, 60 amps.
⑦ — Automatic transaxle, 11 volts; manual transaxle, 11.5 volts.
⑧ — Automatic transaxle, .65 inch; manual transaxle, .69 inch.
⑨ — Automatic transmission, 1.4; manual transmission, 1.2.

SUZUKI

Alternators

DESCRIPTION

The alternator is a small, high RPM, high performance type with an IC regulator incorporated. The IC regulator uses integrated circuits which control the voltage produced by the alternator.

TROUBLESHOOTING

FAULTY INDICATOR LAMP OPERATION

Refer to **Fig. 1,** for troubleshooting chart.

DIAGNOSIS & TESTING

When testing alternator, note the following:
1. Do not reverse polarities of IG and L terminals.
2. Do not short IG and L terminals. Always connect these terminals through a lamp.
3. Do not connect any current load between L and E terminals.

UNDERCHARGED BATTERY

1. Ensure undercharged condition has not been caused by accessories left on for extended periods.
2. Check drive belt for proper tension.
3. Inspect wiring for defects. Ensure all connections are clean and tight, including slip connectors at alternator and bulkhead. Also, check battery cable connections at battery, starter and ignition ground cable.
4. Connect a suitable voltmeter and ammeter as shown, **Fig. 2.** Connect voltmeter between alternator B terminal and ground. Connect ammeter between alternator B terminal and battery positive terminal.
5. Perform no-load check as follows:
   a. Increase engine speed from idle to 2000 RPM and note readings. Voltage readings will vary with regulator case temperature.
   b. **On Esteem models,** if voltage is higher than 14.4 volts at 68°F, check brush ground. If brush ground is satisfactory, replace IC regulator.

Symptom	Possible cause	Correction
Charge light does not light with ignition ON and engine off	• Fuse blown • Light burned out • Wiring connection loose • IC regulator faulty	Check fuse Replace light Tighten loose connections Replace IC regulator
Charge light does not go out with engine running (battery requires frequent recharging)	• Drive belt loose or worn • Battery cables loose, corroded or worn • IC regulator or alternator faulty • Wiring faulty	Adjust or replace drive belt Repair or replace cables Check charging system Repair wiring

SK1129100010000X

Fig. 1   Indicator lamp troubleshooting chart

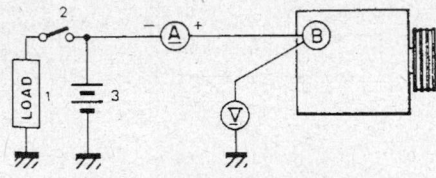

1. Load
2. Load switch
3. Battery

A: DC ammeter 100A range
V: DC voltmeter 20V range
B: Generator output terminal

SK1129100011000X

Fig. 2   Alternator output inspection

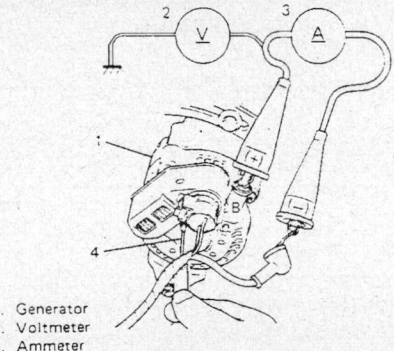

1. Generator
2. Voltmeter
3. Ammeter
4. Small screwdriver to ground F (NEVER contact it with magnetic switch terminal of starting motor)

SK1129100013000X

Fig. 3   Grounding terminal F. Swift

c. **On Grand Vitara, Sidekick and X–90 models,** if voltage is higher than 15 volts at 68°F, check brush ground. If brush ground is satisfactory, replace IC regulator.
d. **On Swift models,** if voltage is higher than 14.8 volts at 77°F, replace IC regulator.
e. **On Swift models,** if voltage is below 14.2 volts, check IC regulator and alternator by measuring voltage at B terminal while grounding F terminal, **Fig. 3.** If voltage is above 14.8 volts, replace IC regulator.
f. **On Esteem models,** if voltage is below 13.6 volts, perform load check.
g. **On Grand Vitara, Sidekick and X–90 models,** if voltage is below 14.4 volts, perform load check.
h. **On Swift models,** if voltage is below 14.2 volts, perform load check.
6. Perform load check as follows:
   a. Run engine at 2000 RPM, switch on headlights and heater blower motor.
   b. Current should be at least 20 amps, if less than 20 amps, alternator is defective.

OVERCHARGED BATTERY

If an overcharging condition exists, such as spewing of electrolyte, check field windings for grounds and shorts. If defective, replace rotor and test regulator using a suitable tester.

ALTERNATOR SPECIFICATIONS

Year	Model	Current Rating		Voltage Regulator	
		Amps	Volts	Voltage	RPM
1996–99	Esteem	70	12	13.6–14.4	—
	Grand Vitara	85	12	13.6–14.4	—
	Sidekick	55	12	14.4–15.0	—
	Swift	55	12	14.4–15.0	—
	X-90	55	12	14.4–15.0	—

Speed Control Systems

NOTE: On Air Bag Equipped Models, Refer To " Air Bag System Precautions" Located In The Front Of This Manual For System Disarming & Arming Procedures.

NOTE: Electrical Symbol & Wire Color Code Identification Located In The Front Of This Manual May Be Used As An Aid When Using Wiring Circuits Found In This Section.

INDEX

DESCRIPTION

This cruise control system is a device which maintains a preset vehicle speed during high speed vehicle operation. The system will maintain any desired constant speed between 25–75 mph without depressing the accelerator pedal. Other cruise control system functions include: SET COAST and ACCEL RESUME switches, to change vehicle speed without using accelerator pedal.
CANCEL switch, to end cruise control operation.
ACCEL RESUME switch, to resume speed stored in memory automatically after cruise control is cancelled.

The main components of the cruise control system are vehicle speed sensor, control unit, actuator, SET COAST switch, ACCEL RESUME switch and CANCEL switch, **Figs. 1 through 3.**

PRECAUTIONS

AIR BAG SYSTEMS

Refer to "Air Bag System Precautions" in the front of this manual for system disarming and arming procedures.

BATTERY GROUND CABLE

Prior to service, disconnect battery ground cable and isolate as required.

TROUBLESHOOTING

PRELIMINARY CHECKS

When performing preliminary checks refer to function test, **Fig. 4**

ADJUSTMENTS

ACTUATOR CABLE

1. Remove actuator cover, loosen lock nuts.
2. Adjust cable to obtain .04–.08 inch play, **Fig. 5,** with actuator lever fully closed.
3. **Torque** locknuts to 4 ft. lbs.

BRAKE LIGHT SWITCH

1. Start engine.
2. Depress brake pedal a few times.
3. Apply approximately 66 lbs. of pressure to brake pedal and hold, then measure pedal height. Pedal height should be greater than 5.12 inches.
4. Adjust brake light switch as required.

SHIFT SELECTOR SWITCH

1. Shift select lever to "N" range.
2. Ensure engine starts in "N" and " P" ranges but does not start in "D," "2," "L" or " R" range.
3. Check back-up lamps light in "R" range.

SYSTEM DIAGNOSIS & TESTING

EXCEPT GRAND VITARA

When performing system diagnosis and testing refer to wiring diagrams, **Figs. 6 through 8** and control unit electrical connector terminal identification diagram, **Fig. 9.**

Indicator Light Circuit

1. With ignition switch in the On position, check voltage between terminal 17 of control unit connector and ground, **Fig. 9.**
2. Circuit is good if within 10–14 volts.
3. If not test lead wires, connectors, fuses, if good replace indicator light bulb.

Shift Switch Circuit

1. Check resistance between terminal 14 of control unit electrical connector and ground, **Fig. 9,** with shift lever set in "P" or " N" range and main switch On.
2. If continuity exist, then shift switch is in good condition.
3. If not check lead wires, grounds and electrical connectors.
4. If these items are in good condition, then check shift switch for continuity,

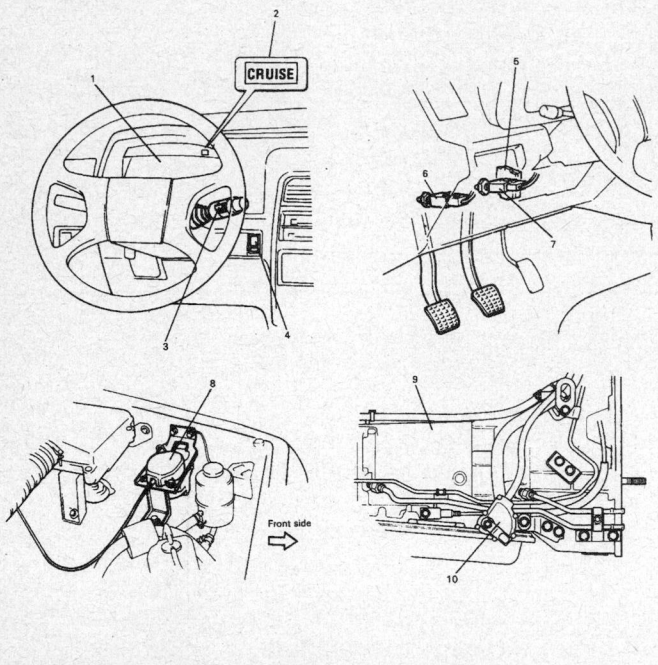

Fig. 1 Cruise control system components. Manual transaxle & transmission

1. Vehicle speed sensor (Reed switch within combination meter)
2. Indicator light
3. SET COAST/ACCEL RESUME/ CANCEL switch
4. Cruise main switch
5. Cruise control unit (right side of steering column)
6. Clutch pedal position switch (For M/T vehicle)
7. Stop light switch
8. Cruise control actuator
9. Automatic transmission
10. Shift switch (For A/T vehicle)

SK1109300001000X

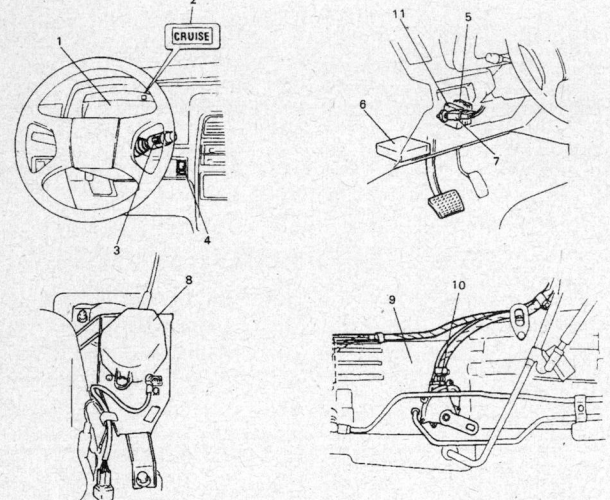

Fig. 3 Cruise control components. Automatic transaxle & transmission

1. Vehicle speed sensor (Reed switch within combination meter)
2. Indicator light
3. SET COAST/ACCEL RESUME/ CANCEL switch
4. Cruise main switch
5. Cruise control unit (right side of steering column)
6. Engine control module (ECM)
7. Brake light switch
8. Cruise control actuator
9. Automatic transmission
10. Shift switch
11. Transmission control module (TCM)

SK1109400003000X

refer to "Component Diagnosis & Testing" as outlined in this section.

Set Coast/Accel/Resume/ Cancel Switch Circuit

1. Check continuity between the following terminals:
   a. With "ACCEL/RESUME" switch in the On position, terminal 12 of control unit electrical connector and ground, **Fig. 9**.

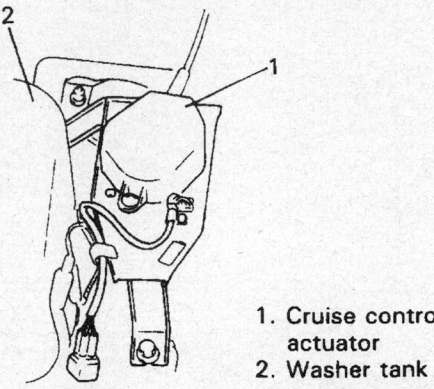

1. Cruise control actuator
2. Washer tank

SK1109300002000X

Fig. 2 Cruise control actuator. Manual transaxle & transmission

Condition	Inspection item number
Vehicle speed can be set but indicator light fails to light.	1, 12
Vehicle speed cannot be set even when SET COAST switch is pressed.	3, 4, 5, 6, 7, 8, 9, 12
Vehicle speed is unstable.	2, 8, 9, 10, 11, 12
Difference (± α km/h) between actual vehicle speed during constant cruising and preset one is large.	2, 10, 11, 12
Acceleration or deceleration by using ACCEL RESUME/SET COAST switches is not attained.	3, 12
Cruise control is not cancelled even when CANCEL switch is turned ON.	3, 12
ACCEL RESUME switch fails to resume preset vehicle speed after cruise control is cancelled.	3, 12
Cruise control is not cancelled even when shift lever is shifted to N range during constant cruising.	4, 12
Cruise control is not cancelled even when brake pedal is depressed during constant cruising.	7, 12
Automatic transmission is not shifted to O/D gear or is not occured lock-up.	10, 11, 12

SK1109400019010X

Fig. 4 Cruise control function test (Part 1 of 2)

	Inspection item
1	Indicator light circuit
2	Actuator cable play
3	SET COAST/ACCEL RESUME/CANCEL switch circuit
4	Shift switch circuit
5	Vehicle speed sensor circuit
6	Cruise main switch circuit
7	Stop light switch circuit
8	Actuator circuit
9	Brake switch circuit
10	Coolant temp. switch signal circuit
11	Throttle valve opening signal circuit
12	Cruise control unit and its circuit

SK1109400019020X

Fig. 4 Cruise control function test (Part 2 of 2)

b. Turn rear left tire slowly with right rear tire locked.
c. Check ohmmeter for deflection between infinity and omega, 2–3 pulses for each tire revolution.
2. If continuity occurs as outlined above, then speed sensor circuit is good.
3. If not test wires and electrical connectors. If they are good test speed sensor, refer to "Component Diagnosis & Testing" as outlined in this section.

Cruise Main Switch Circuit

1. With cruise and main switch in the On position, check voltage between terminal 16 of control unit electrical connector and ground **Fig. 9**.
2. If within 10–14 volts, then switch circuit is good.
3. If not check wires, grounds and electrical connectors.

2. If no continuity exist, then check wires and electrical connectors. If circuit is good, then test switch, refer to "Component Diagnosis & Testing" as outlined in this section.

Vehicle Speed Sensor Circuit

1. Check continuity between terminal 11 of control unit electrical connector and ground, **Fig. 9**, while proceeding as follows:
   a. Raise and support rear of vehicle.

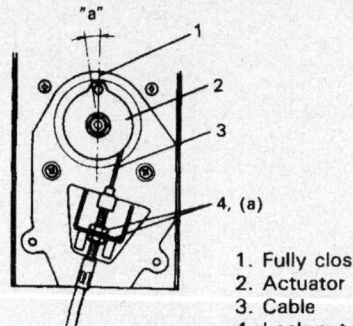

1. Fully closed position
2. Actuator lever
3. Cable
4. Lock nut

SK1109400005000X

Fig. 5   Actuator cable adjustment

4. If good, check cruise main switch, refer to "Component Diagnosis & Testing" as outlined in this section.

Brake Light Switch Circuit

1. With brake pedal depressed check voltage between terminal 4 of control unit electrical connector.
2. If within 10–14 volts, brake light switch circuit is good.
3. If not check wires, connectors and fuses.
4. If good, then check brake light switch, refer to "Component Diagnosis & Testing" as outlined in this section.

Actuator Circuit

1. Check resistance between terminal 3 and 7 of control unit electrical connector, **Fig. 9.**
2. If with 15 ohms plus or minus 3 ohms, then actuator circuit is good.
3. If not check wires and electrical connectors.
4. If good, then check actuator, refer "Component Diagnosis & Testing" as outlined in this section.

Brake Switch Circuit

1. Check continuity between terminals 3 and 15 of control unit electrical connector, **Fig. 9.**
2. If continuity exist then the circuit is good.
3. If not check wires and connectors of each relate circuit.
4. If good, then check brake switch, refer "Component Diagnosis & Testing" as outlined in this section.

Coolant Temperature Switch Circuit

1. With ignition switch in the On position, check voltage between terminal 10 and ground, **Fig. 9.**
2. With engine temperature below 77°F voltage should read 0–1 volt.
3. With engine temperature above 86°F voltage should read 10–14 volt.

Throttle Valve Opening Circuit

1. Check voltage between terminal 2 and body ground, **Fig. 9.**
2. If duty signal appears, **Fig. 10,** then throttle valve opening signal is good.
3. If not then check wires, fuses, electrical connectors and ECM.

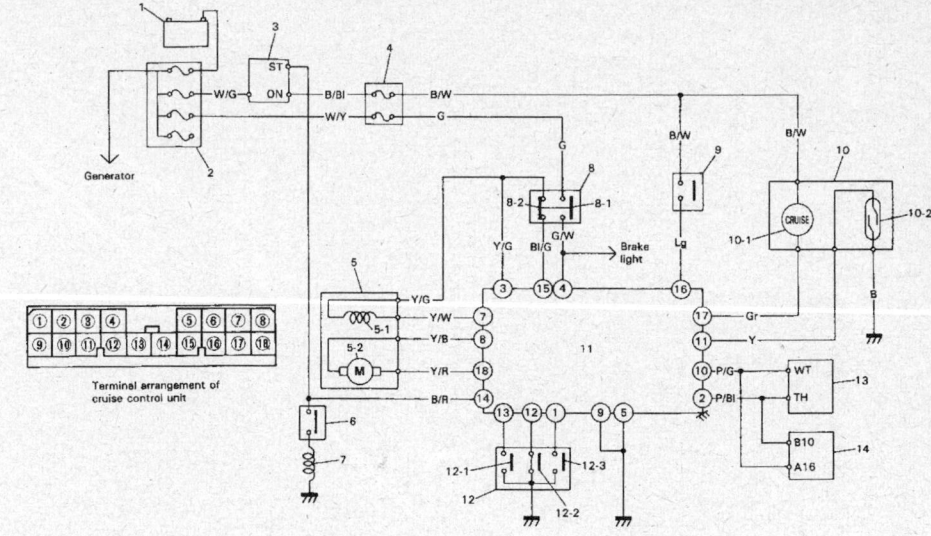

1. Battery
2. Main fuse
3. Ignition switch
4. Circuit fuse
5. Cruise control actuator
5-1. Actuator clutch
5-2. Actuator motor
6. A/T shift switch
7. Starting motor relay
8. Brake (light) switch
8-1. Brake light switch
8-2. Brake switch
9. Cruise main switch
10. Combination meter
10-1. "CRUISE" indicator light
10-2. Speed sensor
11. Cruise control unit
12. Combination switch
12-1. SET COAST switch
12-2. ACCEL RESUME switch
12-3. CANCEL switch
13. Transmission control module (TCM)
14. Engine control module (ECM)

SK1109400007000X

Fig. 6   Cruise control system wiring diagram. Swift

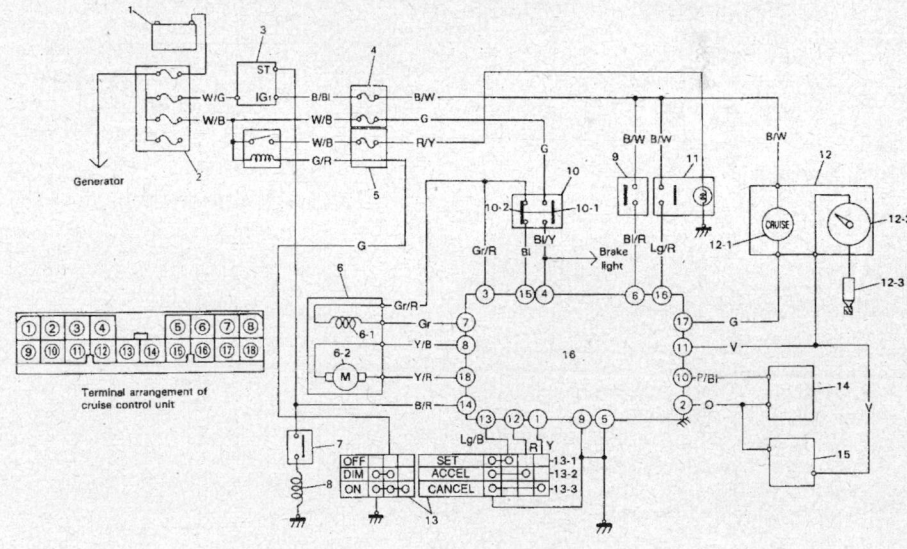

1. Battery
2. Main fuse
3. Ignition switch
4. Junction/fuse block
5. Relay box
6. Cruise control actuator
6-1. Actuator clutch
6-2. Actuator motor
7. A/T shift switch
8. Starting motor relay
9. Auto cruise clutch pedal position switch
10. Brake (light) switch
10-1. Brake light switch
10-2. Brake switch
11. Cruise main switch
12. Combination meter
12-1. "CRUISE" indicator light
12-2. Speedometer
12-3. Vehicle speed sensor (VSS)
13. Combination switch
13-1. SET COAST switch
13-2. ACCEL RESUME switch
13-3. CANCEL switch
14. Transmission control module (TCM)
15. Engine control module (ECM)
16. Cruise control unit

SK1109500026000X

Fig. 7   Cruise control system wiring diagram. Esteem

Cruise Control Unit Circuit

1. Disconnect cruise control unit connector from control unit, then perform voltage test, **Fig. 11,** and resistance test, **Fig. 12.**
2. If all items within system are in good condition and cruise control system fails to operate properly, then replace control unit.

GRAND VITARA

When performing system diagnosis and testing refer to wiring diagram, **Fig. 13,** and control unit electrical connector terminal identification diagram, **Fig. 14.**

Refer to **Figs. 15 through 24** for system diagnosis procedures.

COMPONENT DIAGNOSIS & TESTING
EXCEPT GRAND VITARA
Indicator Light

1. With ignition switch in the On position,

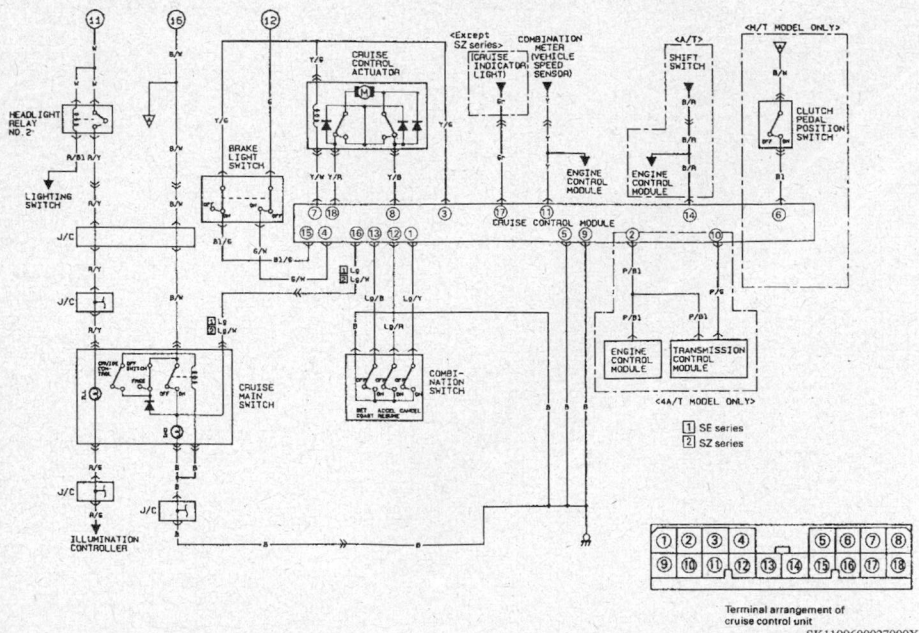

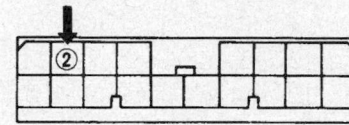

Viewed from wire harness side

Fig. 8 Cruise control system wiring diagram. Sidekick & X-90

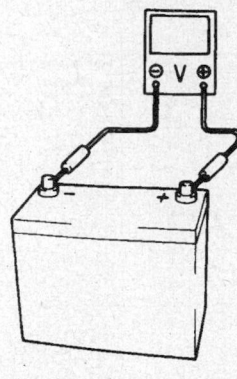

Viewed from wire harness side

Fig. 9 Control unit electrical connector terminal identification. Except Grand Vitara

check voltage between terminal 17 of control unit connector and ground, **Fig. 9.**

2. Circuit is good if within 10–14 volts.
3. If not test lead wires, connectors, fuses, if good replace indicator light bulb.

Shift Switch

Refer to "Automatic Transaxle & Transmissions" for shift switch replacement procedure.

Vehicle Speed Sensor

1. Remove combination meter from instrument panel.
2. Check continuity between speed sensor and ground, **Fig. 25.**
3. Four pulses should occur within one complete revolution of flat on speedometer cable.
4. If not good replace speed sensor.

Cruise Main Switch

1. Connect 12 volts battery positive power to terminal 3 of cruise main switch and negative to terminal 5, **Fig. 26.**
2. Connect positive terminal of circuit tester to terminal 1 and negative to terminal 5.
3. Turn cruise switch, circuit tester should read 10–14 volts.
4. Push switch Off, voltage should read 0–1 volt.
5. If not replace cruise main switch.

Brake Light Switch

1. Disconnect brake light switch electrical connector, then remove switch from pedal bracket.
2. Using an ohmmeter check switch for continuity, **Fig. 27,** if defective then replace switch.
3. After installing brake switch, refer to

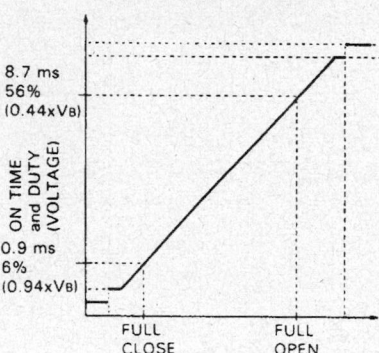

SIGNAL CHARACTERISTIC

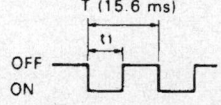

Fig. 10 Throttle valve opening signal circuit test

"Adjustments " for adjustment procedure.

Actuator

1. With engine in the Off position, pull wiring harness terminals from connector, **Fig. 28,** by unlocking terminal lock in connector.

2. Disconnect cruise control actuator electrical connector.
3. Check for continuity between terminals 1 and 3, **Fig. 28.**
4. Resistance of clutch coil should read 15 ohms plus or minus 3 ohms.
5. Connect terminals 2 and 3 to battery positive and terminals 1 and 4 to ground, **Fig. 29.**
6. Ensure motor pulls cable actuating lever to the fully open position.
7. Disconnect probe from terminal 3 ensuring cable returns quickly, allowing actuator lever to return to the fully closed position.
8. Connect battery positive to terminal 3 and battery ground to terminal 1.
9. Ensure clutch operation maintains actuator cable position at this time.
10. With actuator lever pulled by hand to its fully open position, **Fig. 30,** connect terminal 3 and 4 to battery positive and terminals 1 and 2 to battery ground.
11. Ensure cable is released by motor and actuator lever returns to fully closed position.
12. If any of the preceding test failed, replace actuator.
13. Ensure terminals are properly secured in connector.

Set Coast/Accel Resume/ Cancel Switch

1. Remove turn signal/dimmer switch assembly.
2. Using a suitable circuit tester, check continuity between terminals, **Fig. 31,** at each switch position, **Fig. 32.**
3. If check result is not good then replace turn signal/dimmer switch assembly.

GRAND VITARA

Refer to **Figs. 33 through 36** for component diagnosis and testing.

Fig. 11 voltage inspection table:

TERMINAL	CIRCUIT	CONDITION	NORMAL VOLTAGE
①	CANCEL switch	Ignition switch ON, CANCEL switch OFF	10—14 V
		Ignition switch ON, CANCEL switch ON	0 V
②	Throttle valve opening signal from ECM	Ignition switch ON. Voltage varies as specified at graph in previous page while throttle valve is opened gradually.	
③	Brake switch	Ignition switch and cruise main switch ON, and brake pedal released	About 9 V
		Ignition switch and cruise main switch ON, and brake pedal depressed	0—1 V
④	Brake light switch	Brake pedal released	0—1 V
		Brake pedal depressed	10—14 V
⑤	Ground	—	—
⑦	Actuator clutch	Ignition switch and cruise main switch ON, and brake pedal released	About 9 V
⑧	Actuator motor	Ignition and cruise main switch ON	10—14 V
⑨	Ground	—	—
⑩	Coolant temp. switch signal	Ignition switch ON Engine coolant temp. is below 25°C (77°F)	0—1 V
		Ignition switch ON Engine coolant temp. is above 30°C (86°F)	10—14 V
⑪	Vehicle speed sensor	Igniton switch and cruise main switch ON. Hoist rear end of vehicle. Turn rear left tire slowly with rear right tire locked	Indicator deflection repeated between 0—1 V and 3—5 V
⑫	ACCEL RESUME switch	Ignition and cruise main switch ON ACCEL RESUME switch OFF	10—14 V
		Ignition and cruise main switch ON ACCEL RESUME switch ON	0—1 V
⑬	SET COAST switch	Ignition and cruise main switch ON SET COAST switch OFF	10—14 V
		Ignition and cruise main switch ON SET COAST switch ON	0—1 V
⑭	Shift switch	Ignition and cruise main switch ON Selector lever in "P" or "N" range	0—1 V
		Ignition and cruise main switch ON Selector lever in "R", "D", "2" or "L" range	10—14 V
⑮	Actuator clutch power supply	Ignition switch ON Cruise main switch ON	About 9 V
⑯	Cruise main switch	Ignition and cruise main switch ON	10—14 V
		Ignition switch ON. Cruise main switch OFF	0—1 V
⑰	CRUISE indicator light	Ignition switch ON	10—14 V
⑱	Actuator motor	Ignition and cruise main switch ON	10—14 V

SK1109400017000X

Fig. 11   Cruise control unit voltage inspection

Fig. 12 resistance inspection table:

TERMINALS	CIRCUIT	CONDITION	NORMAL RESISTANCE
①—Body ground	CANCEL switch	CANCEL switch OFF	No continuity
		CANCEL switch ON	Continuity
③—⑦	Actuator clutch		12—18Ω
③—⑮	Brake switch	Brake pedal released	Continuity
		Brake pedal depressed	No continuity
⑤—Body ground	Ground	—	Continuity
⑨—Body ground	Ground	—	Continuity
⑪—Body ground	Vehicle speed sensor	Hoist rear end of vehicle. Turn rear left tire slowly with rear right tire locked	Ohmmeter indicator deflect between continuity and ∞
⑫—Body ground	ACCEL RESUME switch	ACCEL RESUME switch OFF	No continuity
		ACCEL RESUME switch ON	Continuity
⑬—Body ground	SET COAST switch	SET COAST switch OFF	No continuity
		SET COAST switch ON	Continuity
⑭—Body ground	Shift switch	Selector lever in "P" or "N" range	Continuity
		Selector lever in "R", "D", "2" or "L" range	No continuity

SK1109400018000X

Fig. 12   Cruise control unit resistance inspection

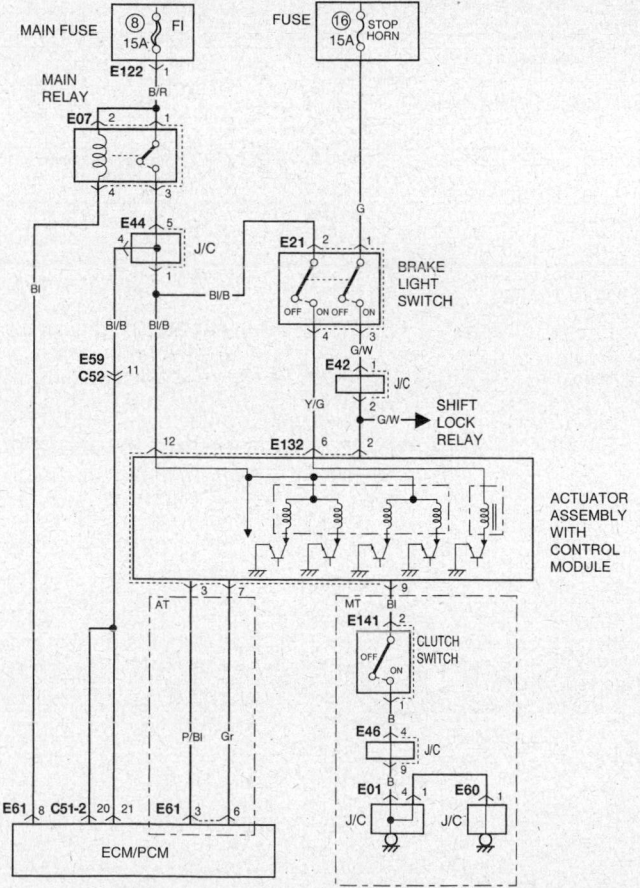

SK1109900028010X

Fig. 13   Cruise control system wiring diagram (Part 1 of 2). Grand Vitara

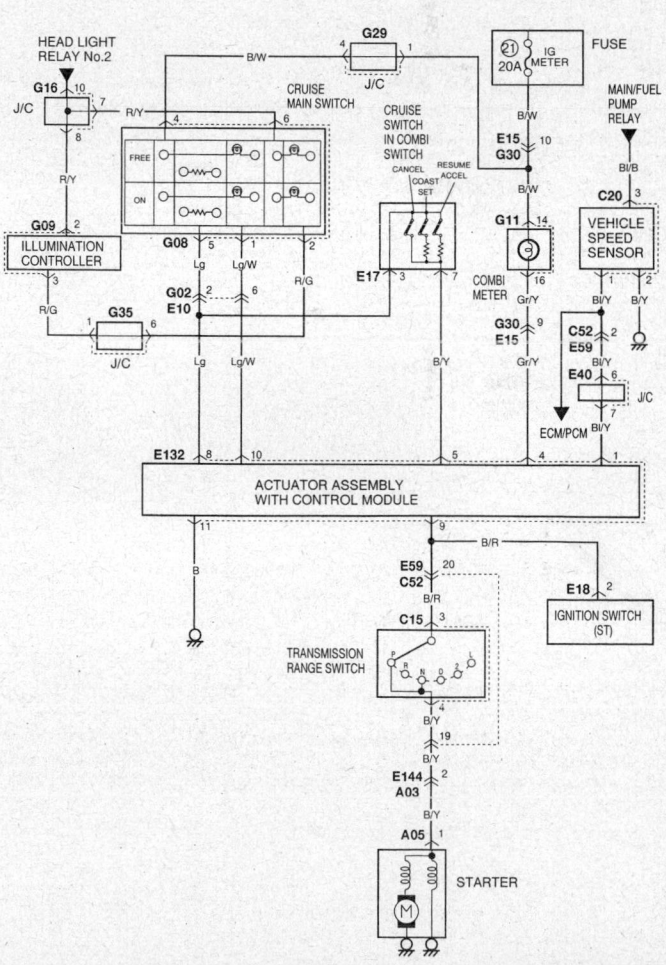

SK1109900028020X

Fig. 13   Cruise control system wiring diagram (Part 2 of 2). Grand Vitara

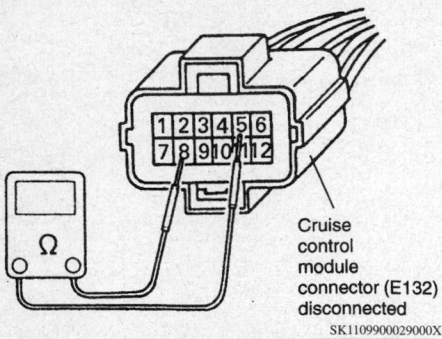

Cruise control module connector (E132) disconnected

SK1109900029000X

Fig. 14 Control unit electrical connector terminal identification. Grand Vitara

STEP	ACTION	YES	NO
1	Check Circuit for Short. 1) Disconnect connector from cruise control module with ignition switch OFF. 2) Turn ignition switch ON. Does cruise main switch indicator lamp turn ON?	"Lg/W" circuit is shorted to ground.	Go to Step 2.
2	Check Circuit for Open 1) Check for proper connection to cruise control module at terminal E132-10. 2) If OK, connect terminal E132-10 to ground. Does indicator lamp turn ON at ignition switch ON?	Lamp circuit is OK.	Go to Step 3.
3	Lamp Bulb Check 1) Remove cruise main switch from instrument panel. 2) Remove lamp bulb and check it. Is bulb in good condition?	"B/W" or "Lg/W" circuit is open.	Replace bulb.

Figure for Step 2.

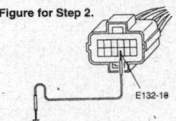

E132-10

SK1109900030000X

Fig. 15 Main switch indicator lamp circuit inspection. Grand Vitara

STEP	ACTION	YES	NO
1	Check Circuit for Short. 1) Disconnect connector from cruise control module with ignition switch OFF. 2) Turn ignition switch ON. Does "CRUISE" indicator lamp turn ON?	"Gr/Y" circuit is shorted to ground.	Go to Step 2.
2	Check Circuit for Open. 1) Check for proper connection to cruise control module at terminal E132-4. 2) If OK, connect terminal E132-4 to ground. Does indicator lamp turn ON at ignition switch ON?	Lamp circuit is OK.	Go to Step 3.
3	Lamp Bulb Check 1) Remove combination meter from instrument panel. 2) Remove lamp bulb and check it. Is bulb in good condition?	"B/W" or "Gr/Y" circuit is open.	Replace bulb.

Figure for Step 2.

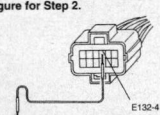

E132-4

SK1109900031000X

Fig. 16 Cruise indicator lamp circuit inspection. Grand Vitara

STEP	ACTION	YES	NO

1	Switch Circuit Check
	1) Disconnect connector from cruise control module with ignition switch OFF.
	2) Check for proper connection to cruise control module at terminal E132-8.
	3) If OK, check resistance between terminal E132-8 and E132-5 under each condition below.
	  All switches OFF : Infinity
	  COAST/SET switch rotated (ON) : 200 – 240Ω
	  RESUME/ACCEL switch rotated (ON) : 820 – 1000Ω
	  CANCEL switch pressed (ON) : About 0Ω
	4) Turn ignition switch ON and check voltage between terminal E132-8 and ground under each condition below.
	  Cruise main switch released (OFF) : 0V
	  Cruise main switch pressed (ON) : 10 – 14V
	Are check results in above steps 3) and 4) satisfactory?
		Switch circuit is OK.	Go to Step 2.

2	Cruise Main Switch Check 1) Check cruise main switch for operation. Is switch in good condition?	Go to step 3.	Replace.
3	COAST/SET, RESUME/ACCEL and CANCEL Switches Check 1) Check COAST/SET, RESUME/ACCEL and CANCEL switches for operation. Are all switches in good condition?	"B/Y" or "Lg" circuit is open or short.	Replace.

Figure for Step 1.

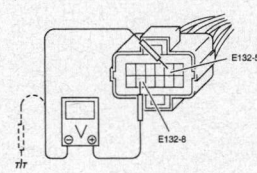 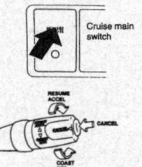

E132-5

E132-8

Cruise main switch

RESUME ACCEL CANCEL

COAST SET

SK1109900032000X

Fig. 17 Multi-function switch circuit inspection. Grand Vitara

STEP	ACTION	YES	NO
1	Vehicle Speed Sensor Circuit Check 1) Disconnect connector from cruise control module with ignition switch OFF. 2) Check for proper connection to cruise control module at terminal E132-1. 3) If OK, check for continuity between terminals E132-1 and E59-2, terminals C52-2 and C20-1. Is check result satisfactory?	VSS circuit is OK.	"L/Y" circuit is open.

Figure for Step 1.

E132-1

E59-2

C20-1

C52-2

SK1109900033000X

Fig. 18 VSS circuit inspection. Grand Vitara

STEP	ACTION	YES	NO
1	Stop Lamp Switch (With Pedal Position Switch) Circuits Check 1)Disconnect connector from cruise control module with ignition switch OFF. 2)Check for proper connection to cruise control module at terminals E132-2 and E132-6. 3)If OK, turn ignition switch ON. 4)Check Voltage between each terminal and ground under each condition below. <table><tr><td>CONDITION \ TERMINAL</td><td>E132-2</td><td>E132-6</td></tr><tr><td>Brake pedal released</td><td>0 V</td><td>10 – 14 V</td></tr><tr><td>Brake pedal depressed</td><td>10 – 14 V</td><td>0 V</td></tr></table> Is check result satisfactory?	Stop lamp switch (with pedal position switch) circuits are OK.	Go to Step 2.
2	Stop Lamp Switch Position Check 1)Check stop lamp switch for installation position. Is check result satisfactory?	Go to Step 3.	Adjust.
3	Stop Lamp Switch (With Pedal Position Switch) Check 1)Disconnect connector from stop lamp switch. 2)Check for proper connection to stop lamp switch at all terminals. 3)If OK, check stop lamp and pedal position switches for operation. Is this switch in good condition?	"Y/G" or "G/W" circuit is open or short.	Replace.

Figure for Step 1.

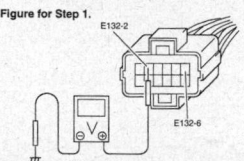

SK1109900034000X

Fig. 19 Stop lamp switch circuit inspection. Grand Vitara

STEP	ACTION	YES	NO
1	Clutch Pedal Position Switch Circuit Check 1)Disconnect connector from cruise control module with ignition switch OFF. 2)Check for proper connection to cruise control module at terminal E132-9. 3)If OK, check for resistance between terminal E132-9 and ground under each condition below. Clutch pedal released : Infinity Clutch pedal depressed : Continuity Is check result satisfactory?	Clutch pedal position switch circuit is OK.	Go to Step 2.
2	Clutch Pedal Position Switch Position Check 1)Check clutch pedal position switch for installation position. Is check result satisfactory?	Go to Step 3.	Adjust.
3	Clutch Pedal Position Switch Check 1)Disconnect connector from clutch pedal position switch. 2)Check for proper connection to clutch pedal position switch at all terminals. 3)If OK, check clutch pedal position switch for operation. is this switch in good condition?	"Bl" or "B" circuit is open or short.	Replace.

Figure for Step 1.

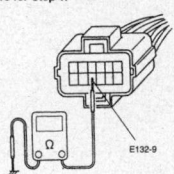

SK1109900036000X

Fig. 21 Clutch pedal position switch circuit inspection. Grand Vitara

STEP	ACTION	YES	NO
1	Overdrive off Command Signal Circuit Check 1)Disconnect connector from cruise control module with ignition switch OFF. 2)Check for proper connection to cruise control module at terminal E132-3. 3)If OK, turn ignition switch ON. 4)Check voltage between terminal E132-3 and ground. Is it 10–14 V?	This signal circuit is OK.	Check "P/Bl" wire for open and short. If OK, substitute a known-good PCM and recheck.

Figure for Step 1.

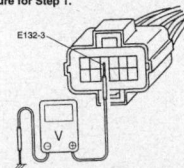

SK1109900038000X

Fig. 23 Overdrive & TCC Off command signal circuit inspection. Grand Vitara

STEP	ACTION	YES	NO
1	Transmission Range Switch Circuit Check 1)Disconnect connector from cruise control module with ignition switch OFF. 2)Check for proper connection to cruise control module at terminal E132-9. 3)If OK, connect ohmmeter between terminal E132-9 and ground. 4)Check for continuity under each condition below. Selector lever at "P" or "N" range : Continuity "R", "D", "2" or "L" range : Infinity Is check result satisfactory?	Transmission range switch circuit is OK.	Go to Step 2.
2	Transmission Range Switch Check 1)Disconnect transmission range switch connector. 2)Check for proper connection to transmission range switch at disconnected connector terminals. 3)If OK, check transmission range switch for operation. Is check result satisfactory?	"B/R" or "B/Y" circuit is open or short.	Adjust or replace.

Figure for Step 1.

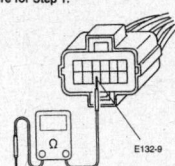

SK1109900035000X

Fig. 20 Transmission range switch circuit inspection. Grand Vitara

STEP	ACTION	YES	NO
1	Powertrain Control Module (PCM) Diagnostic Trouble Code Check 1)Check PCM for DTC. Is there a DTC related to throttle position sensor?	Check and repair TP sensor.	Go to Step 2.
2	Throttle Valve Opening Signal Circuit Check 1)Turn ignition switch ON. 2)Check voltage between terminal E61-6 of PCM connector connected and ground. Does voltage vary linearly according to throttle opening?	Throttle valve opening signal circuit is OK.	Go to Step 3.
3	Supply Voltage Check 1)Disconnect connector from PCM with ignition switch OFF. 2)Check for proper connection to PCM at terminal E61-6. 3)If OK, connect "Bl" wire terminal of main relay to ground with service wire. 4)Turn ignition switch ON. 5)Check voltage between terminal E61-6 of PCM connector and ground. Is it 10–14 V?	Check TP sensor and circuits. If OK, substitute a known-good PCM and recheck.	Check "Gr" wire for open and short. If OK, proceed to cruise control module power and ground circuits check.

Figure for Step 2.

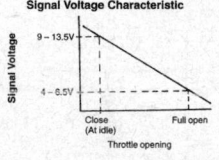

SK1109900037000X

Fig. 22 Throttle vale opening signal circuit inspection. Grand Vitara

STEP	ACTION	YES	NO
1	Power and Ground Circuits Check 1)Disconnect connector from cruise control module with ignition switch OFF. 2)Check for proper connection to cruise control module at terminals E132-12 and E132-11. 3)If OK, turn ignition switch ON. 4)Check voltage between terminals E132-12 and E132-11. Does voltmeter indicate 10–14 V?	Power and ground circuits are OK.	"Bl/B" or "B" circuit is open.

Figure for Step 1.

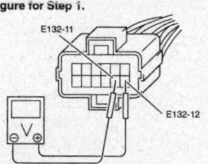

SK1109900039000X

Fig. 24 Cruise control module power & ground circuit inspection. Grand Vitara

For vehicle produced in Canada

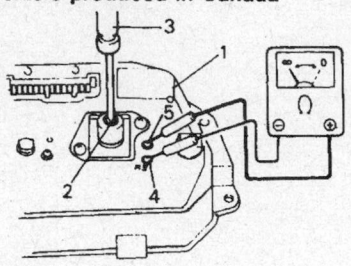

For vehicle produced in Japan

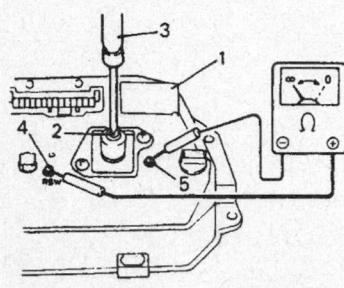

1. Combination meter
2. Speedometer cable joint
3. Screwdriver
4. "VSS" screw
5. "GND" screw

SK1109400011000X

Fig. 25   Vehicle speed sensor

Viewed from coupler side

SK1109300013010X

Fig. 28   Cruise control actuator connector terminal identification (Part 1 of 2)

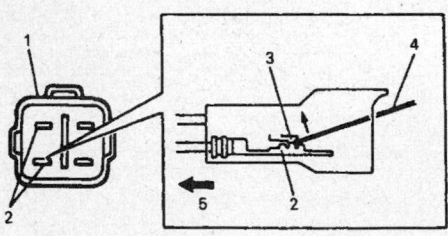

1. Coupler
2. Actuator terminals
3. Terminal lock
4. Thin wire
5. Pull out while unlocking

SK1109300013020X

Fig. 28   Cruise control actuator connector terminal identification (Part 2 of 2)

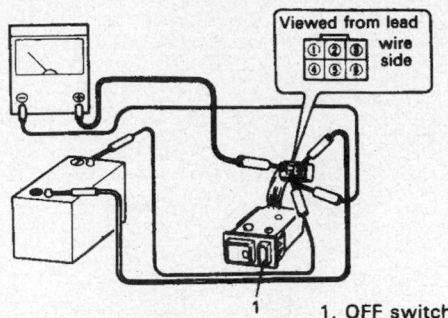

1. OFF switch

SK1109300012000X

Fig. 26   Cruise main switch voltage test

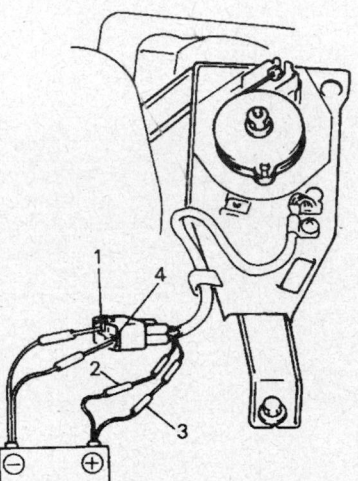

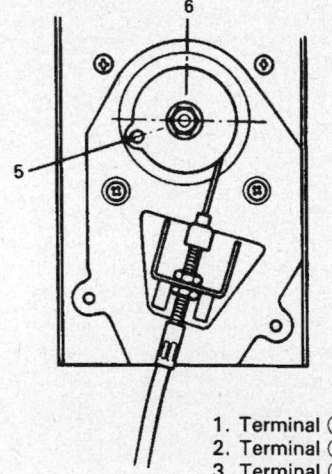

1. Terminal ①
2. Terminal ②
3. Terminal ③
4. Terminal ④
5. Fully open position
6. Fully closed position

SK1109300014000X

Fig. 29   Actuator terminals 1, 2, 3 & 4 location

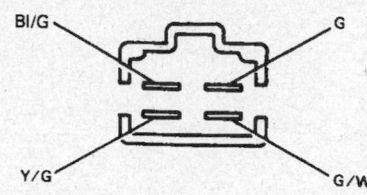

Brake light switch

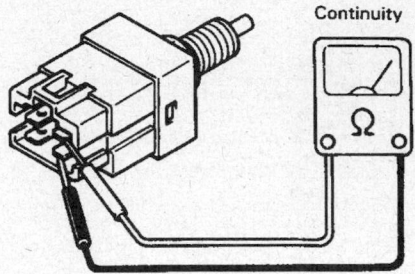

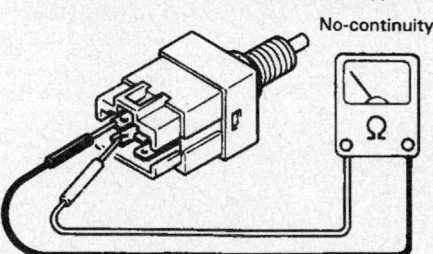

Brake switch

SK1049400002000X

Fig. 27   Brake light switch test

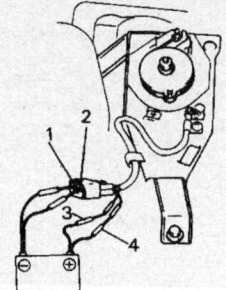

Viewed from coupler side

Terminal	③	①	②	④
OFF				
SET COAST (ON)	○—————○			
ACCEL RESUME (ON)	○		○	
CANCEL (ON)	○			○

SK1109300021000X

Fig. 32 Set coast, Accel resume & cancel switch position inspection

SK1109300020000X

Fig. 31 Set coast, Accel resume & cancel switch continuity inspection

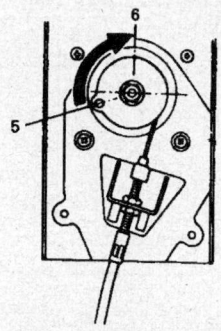

1. Terminal ①
2. Terminal ②
3. Terminal ③
4. Terminal ④
5. Fully open position
6. Fully closed position

SK1109300015000X

Fig. 30 Cruise control actuator fully closed position

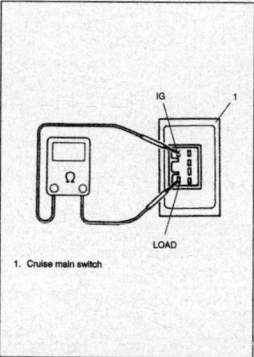

Inspection
1) Disconnect battery negative cable from battery.
2) Disconnect connector from cruise main switch.
3) Remove cruise main switch from instrument panel.
4) Check for resistance between "IG" and "LOAD" terminals.

Switch button released : Infinity
Switch button pressed : About 3.9 kΩ

If check result is not satisfactory, replace.
5) Install cruise main switch to instrument panel and connect connector securely.

1. Cruise main switch

SK1109900040000X

Fig. 33 Cruise control main switch inspection. Grand Vitara

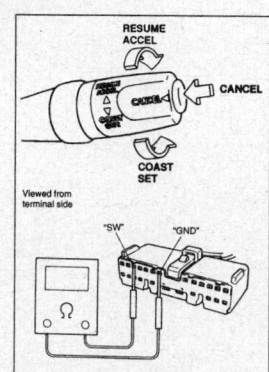

CAUTION:
Never disassemble combination switch assembly. Disassembly will spoil its original functions.

Inspection
1) Disable air bag system.
2) Disconnect connector of COAST/SET, RESUME/ACCEL and CANCEL switches.
3) Check for resistance between "SW" and "GND" terminals of disconnected switch connector under each condition below.

All switches released (OFF) : Infinity
CANCEL switch pressed (ON) : About 0 Ω
COAST/SET switch rotated (ON) : 200–240 Ω
RESUME/ACCEL switch rotated (ON) : 820–1000 Ω

If check result is not satisfactory, replace combination switch assembly.

SK1109900041000X

Fig. 34 Multi-function switch inspection. Grand Vitara

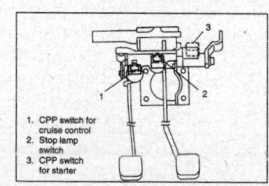

Removal
1) Disconnect CPP switch connector with ignition switch OFF.
2) Remove CPP switch from pedal bracket.

1. CPP switch for cruise control
2. Stop lamp switch
3. CPP switch for starter

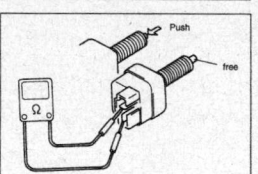

Inspection
Check for resistance between terminals under each condition below.

When switch shaft is free : Continuity
When switch shaft is pushed : No continuity

If check result is not satisfactory, replace.

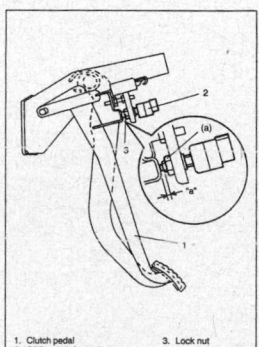

Installation and Adjustment
1) Install CPP switch to pedal bracket.
2) With clutch pedal released, adjust switch position so that clearance between end of thread and clutch pedal bracket is within specification.

Clearance "a" : 1.5–2.0 mm (0.06–0.08 in)

3) Tighten lock nut to specified torque.

Tightening Torque
(a): 7.5 N·m (0.75 kg-m, 5.5 lb-ft)

4) Connect connector to CPP switch securely.

1. Clutch pedal
2. CPP switch for cruise control
3. Lock nut

SK1109900043000X

Fig. 36 Clutch pedal position switch inspection. Grand Vitara

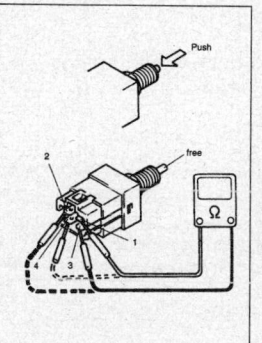

1) Disconnect negative cable from battery.
2) Disconnect stop lamp switch connector and remove stop lamp switch from pedal bracket.
3) Check switch (two contacts) for resistance under each of following each conditions.

CONDITION TERMINALS	FREE	PUSH
Between terminals "1" and "3" (Contact for stop lamp)	Continuity	No continuity
Between terminals "2" and "4" (Contact for brake pedal position)	No continuity	Continuity

If check result is not satisfactory, replace stop lamp switch.
4) Install stop lamp switch and adjust its position.

SK1109900042000X

Fig. 35 Stop lamp switch inspection. Grand Vitara

SUZUKI

Wiper Systems

NOTE: On Air Bag Equipped Models, Refer To "Air Bag System Precautions" Located In The Front Of This Manual For System Disarming & Arming Procedures.

NOTE: Wire Color Code Identification & Symbol Identification Located In The Front Of This Manual May Be Used As An Aid When Using Wiring Circuits Found In This Section.

INDEX

PRECAUTIONS

AIR BAG SYSTEMS

Refer to "Air Bag System Precautions" in the front of this manual for system disarming and arming procedures.

BATTERY GROUND CABLE

Prior to service, disconnect battery ground cable and isolate as required.

TROUBLESHOOTING

Refer to **Fig. 1** for troubleshooting procedures.

SYSTEM DIAGNOSIS & TESTING

GRAND VITARA

FRONT

Refer to **Fig. 2** for wiring diagram, and to **Fig. 3** for switch diagnosis and testing.

REAR

Refer to for **Fig. 4** wiring diagram, and to **Fig. 5** for switch diagnosis and testing.

SIDEKICK, SWIFT & X-90

FRONT

Refer to wiring diagrams, **Figs. 6 and 7,** during diagnosis and testing procedures.

Wiper/Washer Switch Test

Refer to **Figs. 8 and 9,** while using a circuit tester to measure switch for terminal to terminal continuity.

No-Load Run Test

1. Perform low-speed test as follows:
   a. Connect battery positive terminal to blue terminal on motor and battery negative terminal to black lead wire on motor.

Trouble	Possible cause	Correction
Wiper malfunctions or does not return to original position.	• Wiper fuse blown	Replace blown fuse to check for short.
	• Wiper motor faulty	Check motor.
	• Wiper control switch faulty	Check switch.
	• Wiring or grounding faulty	Repair.
Washer malfunctions.	• Washer hose or nozzle clogged	Repair.
	• Washer motor faulty	Check motor.
	• Wiper control switch faulty	Check switch.
	• Wiring faulty	Repair.

SK9029100001000X

Fig. 1 Troubleshooting chart

b. If motor rotates at 45–55 RPM, motor is operating properly.
c. If not, motor is defective, replace motor.
2. Perform high-speed test as follows:
   a. Connect battery positive terminal to blue/red terminal on motor and battery negative terminal to black lead wire on motor.
   b. If motor rotates at 68–78 RPM, motor is operating properly. If not, replace motor.

Automatic Stop Action Test

1. Connect battery positive terminal to yellow/blue terminal of motor on Sidekick or yellow/black terminal of motor on Swift and battery negative terminal to black lead wire on motor, then connect a jumper between blue/white and blue terminals of motor.
2. Motor output shaft should come to a halt at a certain angular position, corresponding to starting position of wiper blade.
3. Stop motor a number of times and ensure motor stops in same position each time.

Brush & Commutator Test

1. Using a circuit tester, measure continuity between blue terminal and black lead wire.
2. If continuity is poor, check brush to commutator contact area.

3. If contact area is fouled, use a cloth dampened with gasoline to clean area.
4. If contact area is coarse or burnt, use a suitable sandpaper to smooth it.

Intermittent Wiper Relay Test

1. Disconnect wiper and washer switch electrical connector, then turn wiper switch to INT position.
2. Connect battery positive terminal to yellow/white terminal on Sidekick or yellow/blue terminal on Swift and battery negative terminal to black terminal.
3. If an operating sound is emitted, relay is operating properly.

REAR

Refer to wiring diagrams, **Fig. 10,** during diagnosis and testing procedures.

Wiper/Washer Switch Test

Refer to **Fig. 11,** while using a circuit tester to measure switch for terminal to terminal continuity.

No-Load Run Test

1. Connect battery positive terminal to orange terminal on motor and battery negative terminal to black lead wire on motor.
2. If motor rotates at 38–46 RPM, motor is operating properly. If not, replace motor.

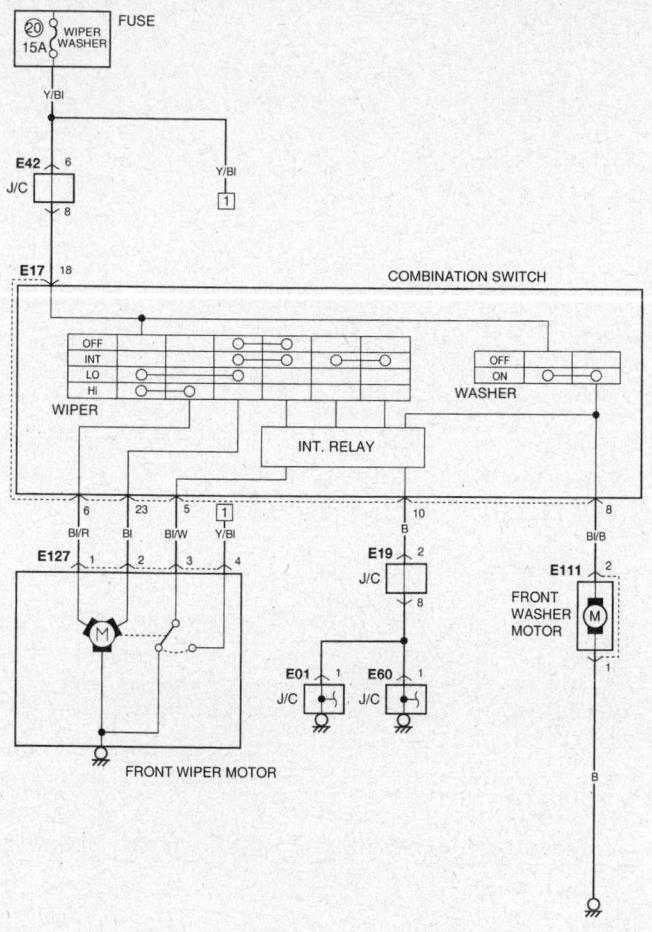

Fig. 2 Front wiper system wiring diagram. Grand Vitara

SK9029900016000X

1) Disconnect negative cable at battery.
2) Disconnect combination switch lead wire coupler.
3) Use a circuit tester to check the continuity at each switch position. If any continuity is not obtained, replace switch.

Fig. 3 Front wiper switch inspection. Grand Vitara

SK9029900014000X

Automatic Stop Action Test

1. Connect battery positive terminal to yellow/blue terminal of motor and battery negative terminal to black lead wire on motor, then connect a jumper between orange and blue/green terminals of motor.
2. Motor output shaft should come to a halt at a certain angular position, corresponding to starting position of wiper blade.
3. Stop motor a number of times and ensure motor stops in same position each time.

Brush & Commutator Test

1. Using a circuit tester, measure continuity between orange terminal and black lead wire.
2. If continuity is poor, check brush to commutator contact area.
3. If contact area is fouled, use a cloth dampened with gasoline to clean area.
4. If contact area is coarse or burnt, use a suitable sandpaper to smooth it.

ESTEEM

WIPER/WASHER SWITCH TEST

Refer to **Fig. 12** while using a circuit tester to measure switch for terminal to terminal continuity.

AUTOMATIC STOP ACTION TEST

1. Connect battery positive terminal to No. 3 terminal of motor and battery negative terminal to black lead wire on motor, then connect a jumper between No. 1 and No. 4 terminals of motor, **Fig. 13.**
2. Motor output shaft should come to a halt at a certain angular position, corresponding to starting position of wiper blade.
3. Stop motor a number of times and ensure motor stops in same position each time.

WIPER MOTOR SPEED TEST

1. Connect battery positive terminal to No. 1 terminal of motor and battery negative terminal to black lead wire on motor, **Fig. 14.** Ensure motor rotates at low speed of 47–57 RPM.
2. Connect battery positive terminal to No. 2 terminal of motor and battery negative terminal to black lead wire on motor. Ensure motor rotates at high speed of 70–84 RPM.

SUZUKI

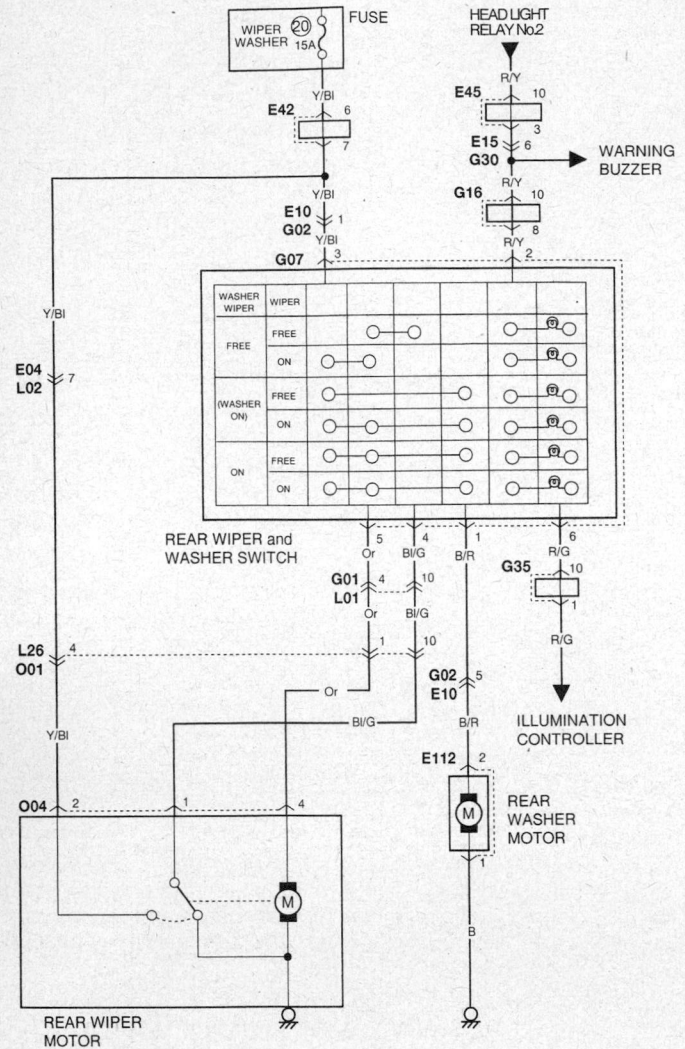

Fig. 4 Rear wiper system wiring diagram. Grand Vitara

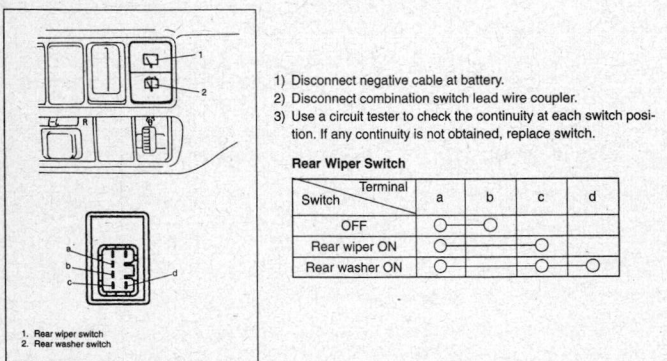

Fig. 5 Rear wiper switch inspection. Grand Vitara

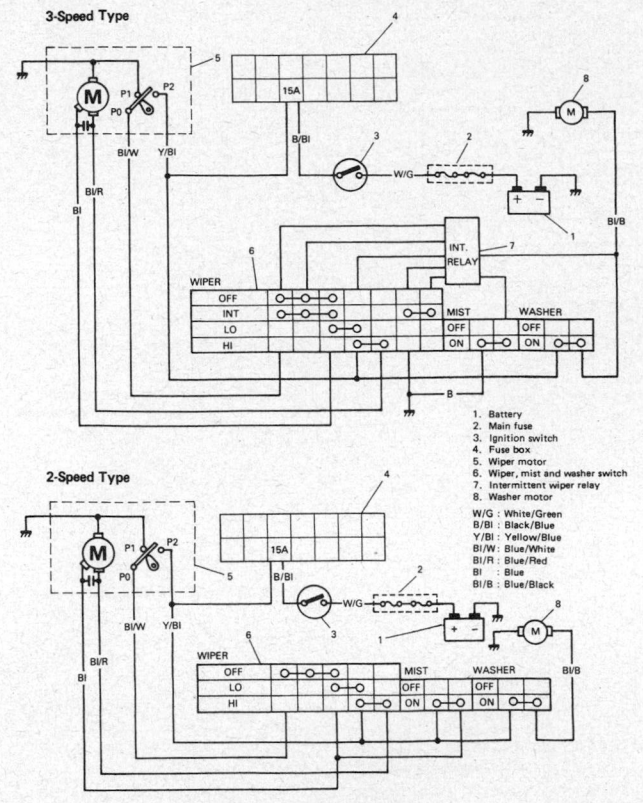

Fig. 6 Front wiper/washer system wiring. Sidekick & X-90

1. Battery
2. Main fuse
3. Ignition switch
4. Fuse box
5. Wiper motor
6. Wiper, mist and washer switch
7. Intermittent wiper relay
8. Washer motor

W/G : White/Green
B/Bl : Black/Blue
Y/Bl : Yellow/Blue
Bl/W : Blue/White
Bl/R : Blue/Red
Bl : Blue
Bl/B : Blue/Black

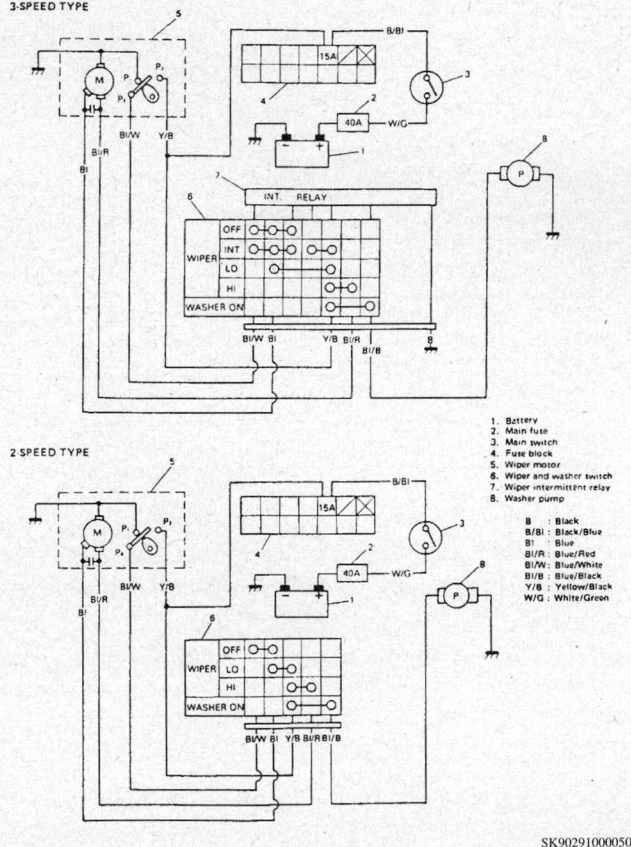

Fig. 7 Front wiper/washer system wiring. Swift

1. Battery
2. Main fuse
3. Main switch
4. Fuse block
5. Wiper motor
6. Wiper and washer switch
7. Wiper intermittent relay
8. Washer pump

B : Black
B/Bl : Black/Blue
Bl : Blue
Bl/R : Blue/Red
Bl/W : Blue/White
Bl/B : Blue/Black
Y/B : Yellow/Black
W/G : White/Green

SUZUKI

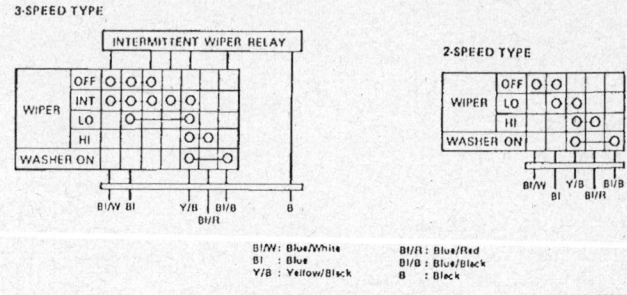

3-SPEED TYPE															
	WIPER SWITCH					MIST SWITCH		WASHER SWITCH							
WIRE COLOR / SWITCH POSITION	Bl/W	TO INT. RELAY	Bl	Y/Bl	Bl/R	B	TO INT. RELAY	Bl	TO INT. RELAY	Y/Bl	Bl/B				
OFF	o—o	o—o								o—o					
INT	o					o—o				o—o					
LO			o—o				o—o								
HI				o—o											
2 SPEED TYPE								Bl	Y/Bl						
OFF										o—o					
LO			o												
HI			o—o												

Bl/W : Blue/White
Y/Bl : Yellow/Blue
B : Black
Bl : Blue
Bl R : Blue/Red

SK9029100006000X

Fig. 8 Front wiper/washer switch continuity check. Sidekick & X-90

Fig. 9 Front wiper/washer switch continuity check. Swift

Bl/W: Blue/White   Bl/R: Blue/Red
Bl : Blue   Bl/B: Blue/Black
Y/B : Yellow/Black   B : Black

SK9029100007000X

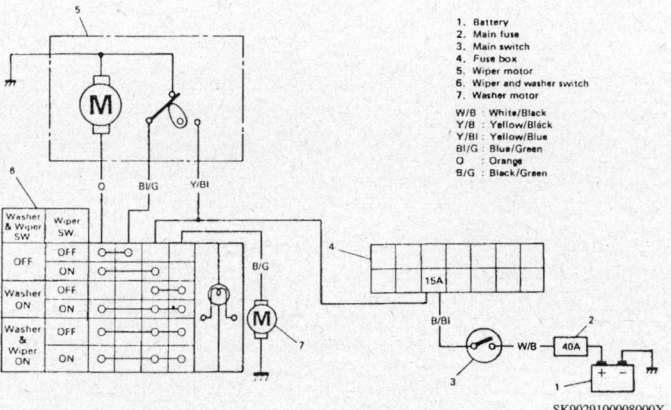

1. Battery
2. Main fuse
3. Main switch
4. Fuse box
5. Wiper motor
6. Wiper and washer switch
7. Washer motor

W/B : White/Black
Y/B : Yellow/Black
Y/Bl : Yellow/Blue
Bl/G : Blue/Green
O : Orange
B/G : Black/Green

SK9029100008000X

Fig. 10 Rear wiper/washer system wiring. Sidekick & Swift

REAR WIPER & WASHER SWITCH CONTINUITY			
O			B/G
R/Y	Y/Bl	R/G	Bl/G

B/G : Black/Green   R/G : Red/Green
Y/Bl : Yellow/Blue   R/Y : Red/Yellow
O : Orange   Bl/G : Blue/Green

CONTINUITY BETWEEN TERMINALS		
Switch Position		Terminal-to-Terminal Continuity
Washer & Wiper	Wiper	
OFF	OFF	Bl/G — O
	ON	Y/Bl — O
WASHER ON	OFF	B/G — Y/Bl
	ON	B/G — Y/Bl — O
WASHER & WIPER ON	OFF	B/G — Y/Bl
	ON	B/G — Y/Bl — O

R/G, an illumination light lead wire of lighting switch, produces constant R/G — R/Y continuity.

SK9029100009000X

Fig. 11 Rear wiper/washer switch continuity check. Sidekick & Swift

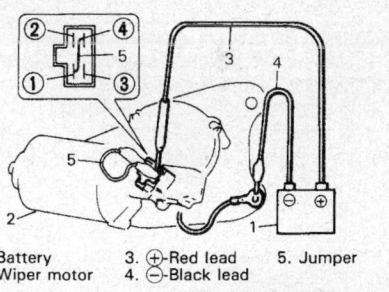

1. Battery   3. (+)-Red lead   5. Jumper
2. Wiper motor   4. (−)-Black lead

SK9029500012000X

Fig. 13 Automatic stop action test. Esteem

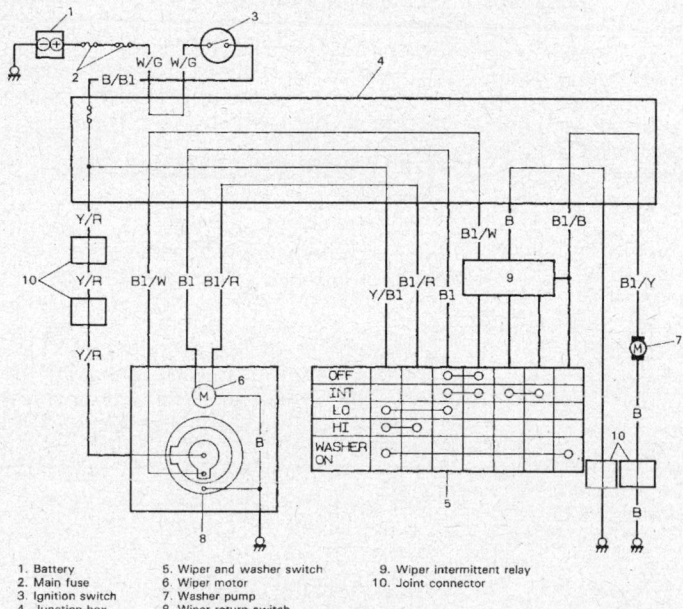

1. Battery   5. Wiper and washer switch   9. Wiper intermittent relay
2. Main fuse   6. Wiper motor   10. Joint connector
3. Ignition switch   7. Washer pump
4. Junction box   8. Wiper return switch

SK9029500011000X

Fig. 12 Wiper/washer switch test. Esteem

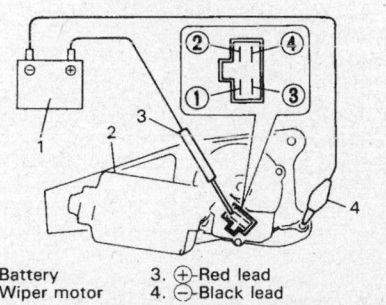

1. Battery   3. (+)-Red lead
2. Wiper motor   4. (−)-Black lead

SK9029500013000X

Fig. 14 Wiper motor speed test. Esteem

Air Bag System

INDEX

AIR BAG SYSTEM DISARMING & ARMING

Disarming

1. Ensure front wheels are pointed straight ahead, then turn ignition switch to Lock position.
2. Remove IGN and CIG & RADIO fuse from junction block No. 1.
3. Remove Connector Position Assurance (CPA) and disconnect lower steering column (yellow two-cavity) connector at base of steering column.
4. Remove CPA and disconnect yellow 2-way connector from passenger inflator module.
5. **On models with passenger air bag,** open glove box door and gently pry off passenger inflator module connector retainer.

Arming

1. Turn ignition switch to Lock position.
2. **On models with passenger air bag,** connect passenger inflator module 2-way connector and secure with CPA.
3. **On all models,** connect lower steering column yellow two-cavity connector and secure with CPA.
4. Install IGN and CIG & RADIO fuses.
5. Turn ignition switch to ACC or On positions and verify that the air bag indicator illuminates steady for approximately six seconds and then turns off.

DESCRIPTION & OPERATION

The Supplemental Restraint System (SRS) offers driver and front passenger protection in addition to seat belts by deploying steering wheel and instrument panel air bags if the vehicle is in a frontal collision of sufficient force up to 30° off vehicle centerline.

System components include: Sensing and Diagnostic Module (SDM), driver's and passenger's air bag modules, contact coil assembly, SRS wiring harness and air bag warning lamp and on Swift models, forward discriminating sensor.

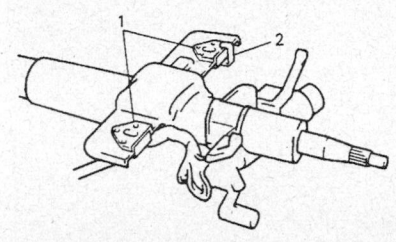

1. Capsules
2. Ripping plate

SK8019400033000X

Fig. 1 Steering column capsule & ripping plate inspection

SYSTEM COMPONENTS

SENSING & DIAGNOSTIC MODULE (SDM)

The SDM sensing device converts vehicle velocity changes into electrical signals. These signals are processed and compared to memory values. If a signal exceeds the specified value stored, an additional signal processing is performed and compared to the memory value. When two of the generated signals exceed the stored value or when one of the generated signals exceeds the stored value and the forward discriminating sensor closes, current is supplied to deploy the air bag modules.

The SDM also monitors SRS components and stores Diagnostic Trouble Codes (DTCs) if a system condition is encountered. Once a DTC has been stored, the SDM will light the air bag warning lamp.

AIR BAG MODULE

Driver's

Located in the steering wheel, the driver's air bag module consists of an inflatable bag and inflator (a canister of gas generating material and initiating device). Current passing from the SDM through the initiator ignites the inflator material, producing a gas that rapidly inflates the bag.

Passenger's

Located in the instrument panel, the passenger's air bag module consists of an inflatable bag, an inflator (a canister of gas and initiating device) and a pressure sens-

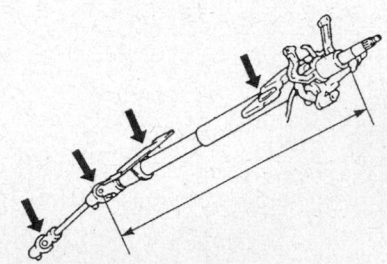

SK8019400034000X

Fig. 2 Steering column inspection

ing device. Current passing from the SDM through the initiator generates pressure, depressing a plunger and releasing the stored gas that rapidly inflates the bag. The pressure sensing devices ensures there is adequate pressure to inflate the bag.

CONTACT COIL

Combined with the combination switch assembly on the steering column, the contact coil assembly has two deployment loop coils and a horn circuit coil. This allows steering wheel rotation while maintaining continuous deployment loop contact.

FORWARD DISCRIMINATING SENSOR

Located in the front of the vehicle, the forward discriminating sensor consists of a sensing element, open switch contacts and diagnostic resistor. If there is a severe vehicle velocity change warranting air bag deployment, the sensing element closes the contacts. Connected in parallel with the switch, the diagnostic resistor will causes a voltage drop in conjunction with the SDM resistors, allowing the SDM to monitor the forward discriminating sensor and associated circuitry.

PRECAUTIONS

AIR BAG SYSTEM

1. To avoid unwanted deployment and possible personal injury, always disarm the Supplemental Restraint System (SRS) prior to performing service

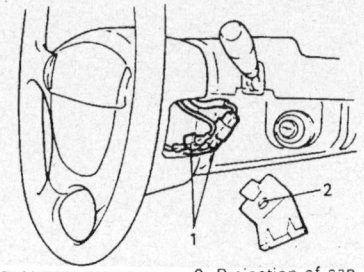

1. Horn connectors   2. Projection of cap

SK8019400035000X

Fig. 3   Steering wheel cap removal & horn disconnection

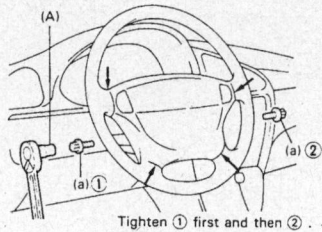

Tighten ① first and then ② .

SK8019400036000X

Fig. 4   Driver air bag module replacement

specified, when troubleshooting the SRS. Do not use any non-powered probe type testers.

5. Use digital multi-meter with a maximum test current of 10 mA or less at the minimum range of resistance measurement, only.
6. Do not attempt to measure air bag module resistance.
7. Discriminating sensor must always be installed with arrow mark facing vehicle front.
8. Inspect sensors for cracks, deformities or rust prior to installation and replace as necessary.
9. When handling or storing an air bag module, always position it with pad side facing upward.
10. Carry air bag module with pad facing away from body.
11. Keep air bag assembly free of oil, grease, detergents and water.
12. Do not expose air bag assembly to temperatures that exceed 200° F.
13. Do not use air bag system components from another vehicle. Always install new replacement components.
14. Inspect all components prior to installation. Do not install any that appear to have been improperly handled or stored or that show any signs of damage.
15. When performing service procedures, do not expose sensors, wiring or other air bag system components to heat guns, welding or spray guns.
16. Do not modify steering wheel, instrument panel or any SRS component, as system performance may be hampered.
17. Do not paint air bag module to correct cosmetic flaws. It must be replaced.
18. If SRS and another vehicle system are both in need of repair, service SRS prior to any other system.
19. Always follow caution/warning label instructions on labels attached to SRS components.
20. Do not dispose of undeployed air bag modules. Modules must be deployed before being scraped.
21. Immediately after deployment, air bag modules are very hot. Wait at least 30 minutes before handling deployed modules.
22. Do not strike or jar SDM. Do not apply power to SRS when SDM is not rigidly attached to vehicle with all mounting bracket fasteners carefully tightened to specifications.

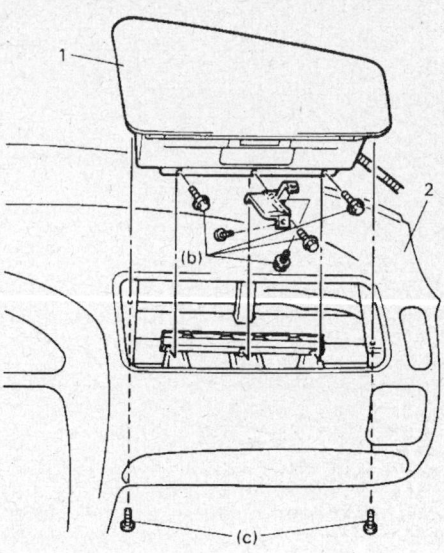

1. Passenger air bag (inflator) module
2. Instrument panel

SK8019500109000X

Fig. 5   Passenger air bag module replacement. Esteem

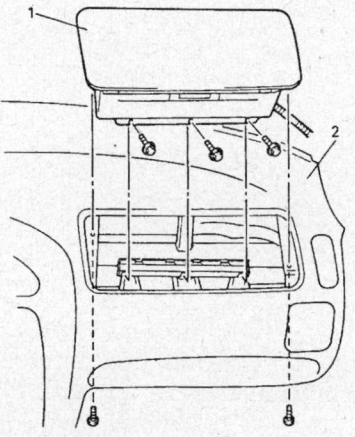

1. Passenger air bag (inflator) module
2. Instrument panel

SK8019400037000X

Fig. 6   Passenger air bag module replacement. Swift

procedures. Refer to "Air Bag System Disarming & Arming." The Sensing and Diagnostic Module (SDM) can maintain sufficient deployment voltage for up to 10 seconds after ignition has been turned Off, air bag fuse removed or battery disconnected. Performing service before the minimum 10 second lapse may cause unwanted deployment and possible injury.

2. When handling a deployed air bag assembly, a face shield and rubber gloves should be worn. Vehicle interior and HVAC ducts should be vacuumed. If sinus or throat irritation is encountered during air bag removal, exit vehicle and breathe fresh air. If skin irritation is encountered, flush affected area with cool water. If any type of irritation continues, consult a physician. Wash hands and rinse thoroughly with water after handling a deployed air bag assembly.
3. A deployed air bag unit should be placed in a heavy duty plastic bag, sealed securely, then placed with automotive scrap.
4. **Do not use electrical test equipment such as battery or A/C powered voltmeters, Ohmmeters or any type of electrical equipment other than**

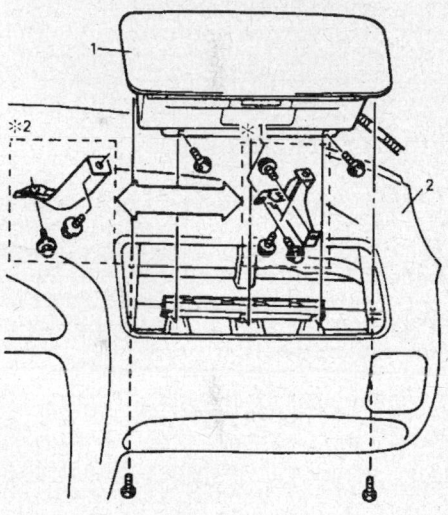

※1: SE series
※2: SZ series

1. Passenger air bag (inflator) module
2. Instrument panel

SK8019600050000X

Fig. 7   Passenger air bag module replacement. Sidekick & X-90

23. Do not apply power to SRS unless all components are connected or diagnostic chart specifies.
24. When using electric welding equipment, disarm SRS as outlined under "Air Bag System Disarming & Arming."

BATTERY GROUND CABLE

Prior to service, disconnect battery ground cable and isolate as required.

DIAGNOSIS & TESTING

Refer to MOTOR'S "Air Bag Manual" for diagnosis and testing.

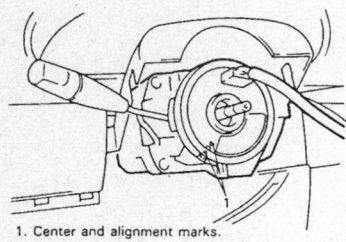

1. Center and alignment marks.

SK8019400038000X

Fig. 8 Contact coil unit centering

COLLISION INSPECTION

On vehicles which have experienced an SRS deployment, certain air bag components must be replaced. To determine which components require replacement, refer to the "General Information" section located at the front of MOTORS "Air Bag Manual."

All system components should be inspected for dents, cracks, exposure to excessive heat and other damage, even if deployment did not take place. To ensure proper SRS operation, the vehicle structure must be returned to its original configuration. When repairing the vehicle, the SRS must be disarmed as outlined under "Air Bag System Disarming & Arming." Also, when performing service procedures, do not expose components or wiring to heat guns, welding or spray guns. To ensure proper system operation on a vehicle involved in a collision, perform procedures as outlined under "Diagnosis and Testing."

The following components should be inspected whether air bag deployment has occurred or not:

1. Inspect steering column and steering shaft joints for damage as follows:
   a. Ensure the two capsules are securely attached to steering column bracket. Also inspect ripping plate (2), **Fig. 1**, for cracks. Inspect components for looseness and other damage. Replace column if any damage is discovered.
   b. Measure steering column assembly length, **Fig. 2**. Replace column if length is less than 20.79 inches on models except Grand Vitara, or 35.24 inches for Grand Vitara.
   c. Inspect steering shaft joints for looseness, cracks and other damage and replace as necessary.
   d. Inspect steering shaft for smoothness of rotation. If, rotation is not smooth, replace steering column.
   e. Ensure steering column and shaft are not bent or cracked or they must be replaced.
2. Inspect driver's air bag module and steering wheel as follows:
   a. If air bag has not deployment, inspect module trim cover for cracks and other damage. Also inspect air bag module for proper mounting to steering wheel. Replace air bag module or steering wheel if needed.

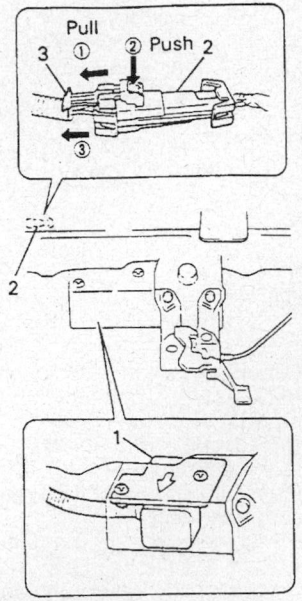

1. Forward (discriminating) sensor
2. Sensor connector
3. Connector Position Assurance (CPA)

SK8019400039000X

Fig. 9 Forward sensor unit replacement

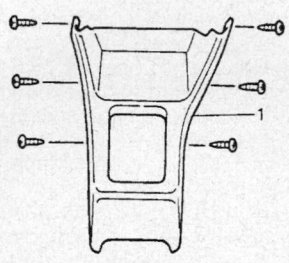

1. Center console

SK8019400040000X

Fig. 11 Center console replacement. Swift

   b. Inspect steering wheel for cracks and damage, then replace as necessary.
   c. Inspect wiring harness for proper connection and damage or replace harness in case of damage.
3. Inspect passenger's air bag and instrument panel, knee bolster and reinforcement as follows:
   a. If air bag has not deployed, inspect module trim cover for cracks, dents and other damage. Replace air bag module as necessary. Also inspect air bag module for proper mounting to instrument panel.
   b. Inspect instrument panel, knee bolster and reinforcement for distortion, cracking, bending and other damage. Repair or replace faulty components.
   c. Inspect wiring harness for proper connection and damage. If damage is present, replace wiring harness.

DRIVER SIDE

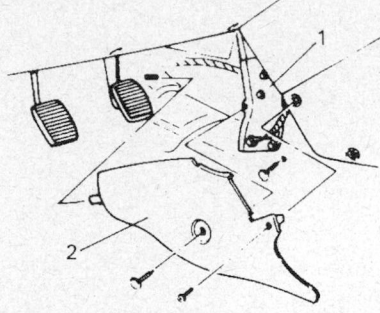

PASSENGER SIDE

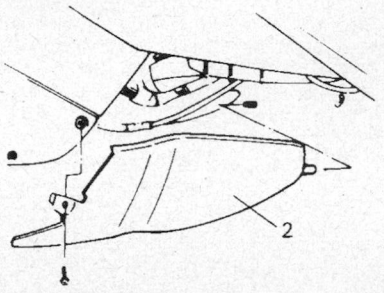

1. Steering support member lower brace
2. Console box extension

SK8019500110000X

Fig. 10 Console box extension & steering support brace removal. Esteem

4. Inspect forward sensor and mounting bracket as follows:
   a. If forward sensor is in area of accident damage (an area which is bent, crushed or damaged), it should be replaced.
   b. Sensor wiring harness and connectors should be inspected for chafing and interference with other components.
   c. Inspect sensor mounting bracket for damage or rust and replace as necessary.
   d. To ensure proper forward sensor operation, the vehicle structure must be returned to its original configuration.
5. Inspect SDM and mounting bracket as follows:
   a. If SDM is in area of accident damage (an area which is bent, crushed or damaged), it should be replaced.
   b. SDM wiring harness and connectors should be inspected for chafing and interference with other components. Also inspect SDM connector and terminals for tightness.
   c. Inspect SDM and mounting bracket for dents, cracks and other damage, then replace if necessary.
   d. To ensure proper SDM operation, the vehicle structure must be returned to its original configuration.
6. Inspect contact coil and combination switch as follows:
   a. Inspect contact coil and combination switch case for damage and replace if damage is found.

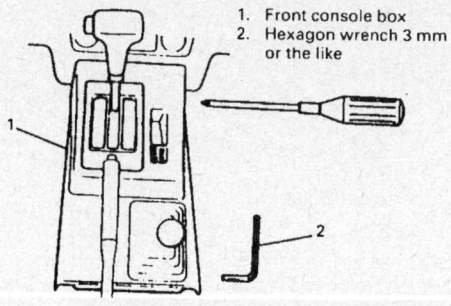

1. Front console box
2. Hexagon wrench 3 mm or the like

SK8019600051000X

Fig. 12   Rear & front console box replacement. Sidekick & X-90

b. Inspect wiring harness and connectors for damage and tightness.
7. Inspect air bag system wiring harness as follows:
   a. Inspect harness and connectors for damage, tightness and proper routing.
   b. Inspect harness for proper mounting to harness clamps.
   c. Inspect harness grommets for proper installation and proper routing through grommets.
   d. Wiring harness and connectors should be inspected for chafing and interference with other components.
   e. Inspect wiring harness for heat damage.
   f. If wiring harness is found to be faulty, it should be replaced.
8. Inspect seat belts and mountings for damage, then repair or replace as needed.

COMPONENT SERVICE

When servicing the vehicle, the SRS should be disarmed as outlined under "Air Bag System Disarming & Arming." Also, when performing service procedures, do not expose components or wiring to heat guns, welding or spray guns.

AIR BAG MODULE, REPLACE

DRIVER

Removal

1. Disarm SRS as outlined under "Air Bag System Disarming & Arming."
2. Remove cap from righthand side of steering wheel, then disconnect horn connector, **Fig. 3.**
3. Using suitable Torx wrench and socket, remove bolts attaching air bag unit to steering wheel, **Fig. 4.**
4. Tilt air bag module forward and disconnect electrical connector, then remove module. Handle with cover facing away from body.

Installation

1. Position air bag module to steering wheel, then connect electrical connector. **Ensure connector properly engages module, wiring is properly routed and not caught between module and wheel. Support air bag**

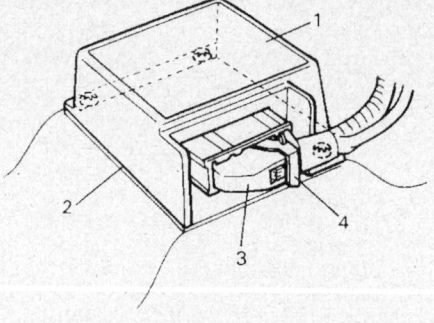

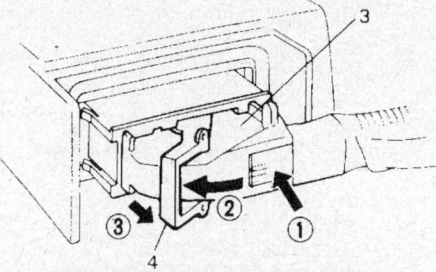

1 2 : Release locking of lock lever
3 : After unlocked disconnect connector

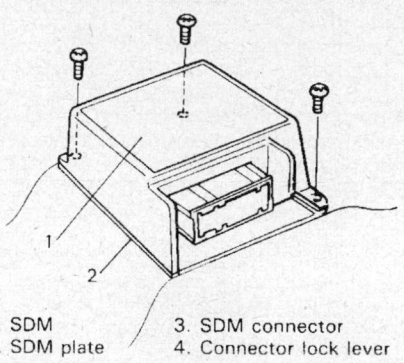

1. SDM
2. SDM plate
3. SDM connector
4. Connector lock lever

SK8019500108000X

Fig. 13   SDM replacement. Esteem

in position: Do not allow it to hang from wiring or connector.
2. Install attaching bolts and tighten to specifications: lefthand bolt first, then righthand bolt. Ensure clearance between air bag module and steering wheel is uniform
3. Connect horn connector and secure connector to cap projection, then install cap to steering wheel lower cover.
4. Arm SRS as outlined under "Air Bag System Disarming & Arming."

PASSENGER

1. Disarm SRS as outlined under "Air Bag System Disarming & Arming."
2. Remove passenger's air bag module attaching screws, then air bag module, **Figs. 5 through 7.**
3. Reverse procedure to install, tighten attaching screws to specifications and arm SRS as outlined under "Air Bag System Disarming & Arming."

CONTACT COIL, REPLACE

REMOVAL

1. Disarm SRS as outlined under "Air Bag

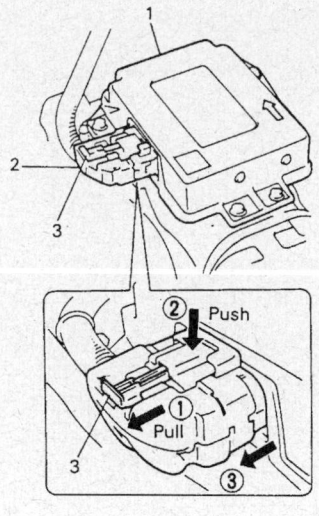

1. SDM
2. SDM connector
3. Connector Position Assurance (CPA)

SK8019400041000X

Fig. 14   SDM electrical connector removal. Swift

System Disarming & Arming."
2. Place front wheels in straight–ahead position, then turn ignition to Lock and remove key.
3. Remove driver's air bag module as outlined under " Air Bag Module, Replace."
4. Remove steering wheel retaining nut.
5. Place alignment marks on wheel hub and steering shaft for assembly reference.
6. Using suitable steering wheel puller, remove wheel from column shaft.
7. Remove steering column hole cover and knee protector, then steering column upper and lower covers. If upper cover is difficult to remove, loosen steering shaft upper joint bolt, then steering column mounting bolts.
8. Loosen contact coil and combination switch assembly wiring harness clamps and bands, then disconnect connectors.
9. Remove contact coil and combination switch attaching screws, then remove coil and switch assembly. **Contact coil is part of the combination switch. Do not attempt to remove coil from switch.**

INSTALLATION

1. Ensure front wheels are in straight–ahead position and ignition is turned to Lock.
2. Slowly rotate contact coil counterclockwise with light force until it stops. Rotate in a clockwise direction approximately two and one half turns, aligning

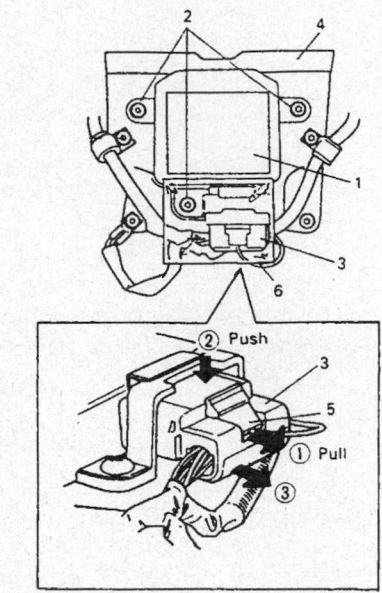

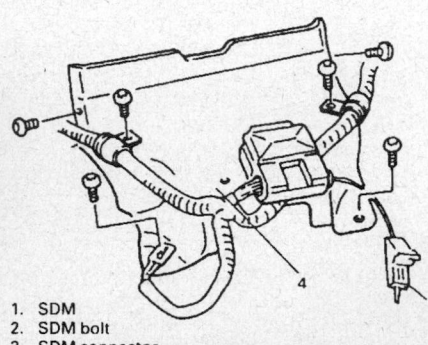

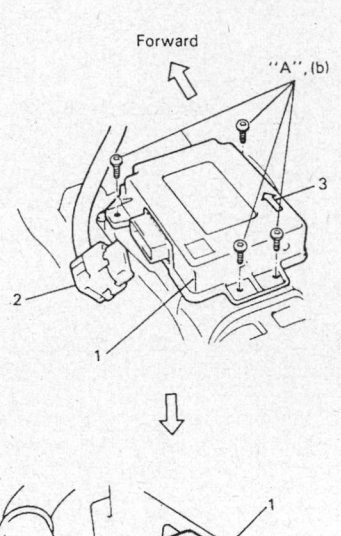

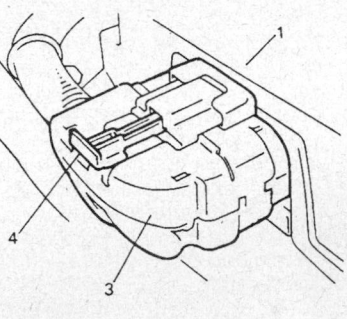

3. Remove sensor attaching screws, then sensor.
4. Reverse procedure to install, noting following:
   a. Apply thread locking compound No. 99000-32050 or equivalent, to screw threads prior to installing sensor.
   b. When installing forward sensor, ensure arrow stamped on sensor faces toward vehicle front.
   c. Tighten attaching screws to specifications.
   d. Ensure sensor connector is properly installed and connector position assurance (CAP) is properly engaged.
   e. Arm SRS as outlined under "Air Bag System Disarming & Arming."

SENSING & DIAGNOSTIC MODULE (SDM), REPLACE

Use care not to strike or jar SDM. Improper handling could result in improper SRS operation. Never connect SRS power source when the SDM is not rigidly attached to vehicle with all mounting bracket fasteners carefully tightened to specifications.
1. Disarm air bag as outlined under "Air Bag System Disarming & Arming."
2. **On Esteem models,** remove console box extensions from right and left sides of console, then the steering support member lower brace, **Fig. 10.**
3. **On Swift models,** remove center console attaching screws, then the center console, **Fig. 11.**
4. **On Grand Vitara, Sidekick and X-90 models,** remove rear and front console boxes, **Fig. 12.**
5. **On Grand Vitara models,** remove center trim panel, radio, clock, tuner pocket and radio opening cover.
6. **On all models,** disconnect SDM electrical connector, **Figs. 13 through 15.**
7. Remove SDM attaching screws, then the SDM, **Fig. 16.**
8. Reverse procedure to install, noting following:
   a. Position SDM to mounting with arrow facing toward the front of the vehicle.
   b. Apply suitable thread lock cement and tighten attaching screws to specifications.
   c. Ensure SDM electrical connector properly engages, then push lock tab down. Also ensure wiring is properly routed.
   d. Arm SRS as outlined under "Air Bag System Disarming & Arming."

AIR BAG MODULE DISPOSAL

When handling a deployed air bag assembly, safety glasses and rubber gloves should be worn. Vehicle interior and HVAC ducts should be vacuumed. If sinus or throat irritation is encountered during air bag removal, exit vehicle and breathe fresh air. If skin irritation is encountered, flush affected area with cool water. If sinus, throat, skin or any other type of irritation continues, consult a

1. SDM
2. SDM connector
3. Arrow
4. CPA

Fig. 16   SDM replacement. Swift

physician. Wash hands and rinse thoroughly with water after handling a deployed air bag assembly.

A deployed air bag unit should be removed as outlined under "Air Bag Module, Replace." After unit has been removed, it should be placed in a heavy duty plastic bag and sealed securely, then placed with automotive scrap.

All undeployed air bag units must be deployed prior to disposal.

OUTSIDE VEHICLE DEPLOYMENT

1. Disarm SRS as outlined under "Air Bag System Disarming & Arming."
2. Remove air bag module(s) as outlined under "Air Bag Module, Replace."
3. Connect special air bag deployment harness tool No. 09932-75030 or equivalent. Plug harness leads together.
4. If deploying a driver's air bag module, place air bag with cover side upward, in a clear, well ventilated outdoor location free of flammable objects. Area should be clear for at least six feet in all directions.
5. If deploying a passengers air bag module, proceed as follows:
   a. Install air bag to special deployment adapter tool No. 09932-75040 or equivalent, with cover side facing upward, **Fig. 17.**
   b. Position air bag and adapter on ground. This area should be clear

1. SDM
2. SDM bolt
3. SDM connector
4. SDM bracket
5. Connector Position Assurance (CPA)
6. SDM cover

Fig. 15   SDM replacement. Sidekick & X-90

the centering marks, **Fig. 8.** New coil assemblies are locked in center position by a pin.
3. Position contact coil assembly and combination switch to steering column, then install attaching screws and connect all except yellow electrical connectors. On new coil assemblies, remove centering pin.
4. Install steering column upper and lower covers, then hole cover and knee protector.
5. Align steering wheel hub and shaft marks made during disassemble. Install wheel and tighten retaining nut to specifications.
6. Install driver's air bag module as outlined under "Air Bag Module, Replace."
7. Arm SRS as outlined under "Air Bag System Disarming & Arming."

FORWARD SENSOR, REPLACE

1. Disarm SRS as outlined under "Air Bag System Disarming & Arming."
2. Disconnect forward sensor electrical connector, **Fig. 9.**

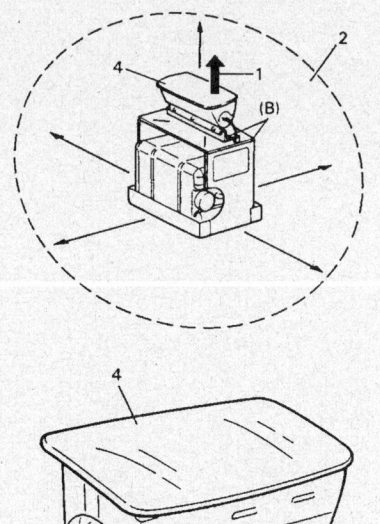

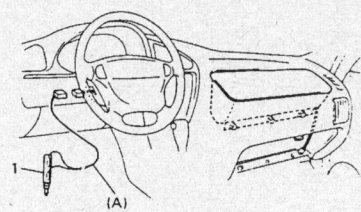

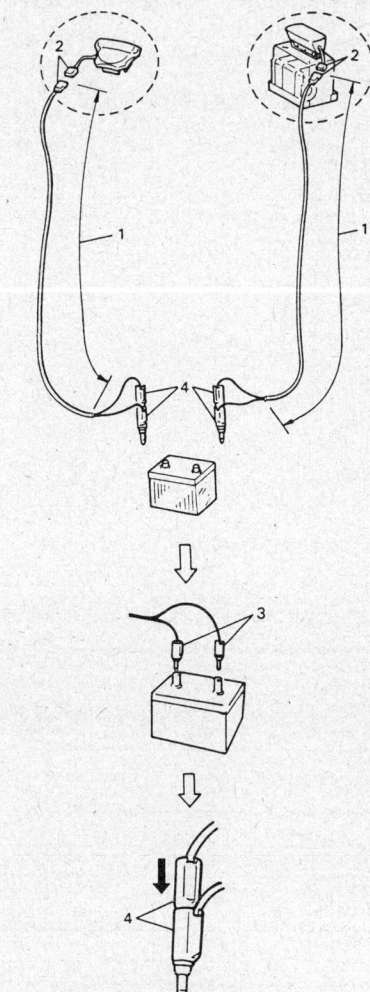

1. Short deployment harness leads

SK8019400045000X

Fig. 19 Connecting deployment harness to driver's air bag connector

2. Remove all objects from seats and instrument panel, then open vehicle windows.
3. If deploying driver's air bag module, remove cap from lefthand side of steering wheel and disconnect electrical connector.
4. If deploying passenger's air bag module, open glove compartment, push inward on lefthand and righthand side stoppers and remove compartment, then disconnect electrical connector.
5. Ensure air bag modules are firmly mounted to vehicle.
6. Connect special air bag deployment harness tool No. 09932-75030 or equivalent and plug harness leads together.
7. Stretch deployment harness from air bag module out full length, approximately 33 ft.
8. Position a fully charged 12 volt battery near end of harness opposite air bag module. **Do not connect battery to deployment harness at this time.**
9. Connect deployment harness to air bag module electrical connector, **Fig. 19.**
10. Cover windshield and front window openings with drop cloth, then ensure no people, animals or objects are in area of vehicle.
11. Separate two deployment harness plug leads.
12. Deploy air bag module by contacting one plug lead to battery positive terminal and other lead to negative terminal, **Fig. 20.**
13. **When deploying air bag, ensure area is clear.** No poisonous gas is produced upon deployment. However, do not inhale gas since it could irritate throat and can cause choking.
14. Allow at least 30 minutes after deployment for air bag components to cool.
15. Do not attempt to disassemble air bags: they cannot be used again.
16. If air bags did not deploy, consult Suzuki for disposal procedures.

---

1. Trim cover must face up
2. 185 cm (6 feet) of clearance
3. Mounting attachment
4. Bag opening side

SK8019400043000X

Fig. 17 Mounting passenger's air bag unit to deployment adapter

and well ventilated for at least six feet in all directions and free of people, animals and any flammable objects.

c. Fill deployment adapter plastic reservoir with water.
d. Ensure air bag unit is securely mounted to adapter.
6. Stretch deployment harness from module out to its full length, approximately 33 ft.
7. Position a fully charged 12 volt battery near end of harness opposite air bag unit. **Do not connect battery to deployment harness at this time.**
8. Connect deployment harness to air bag module electrical connector.
9. Ensure no people, animals or objects are in area of air bag unit.
10. Contact one plug lead to battery positive terminal and other lead to negative terminal, then air bag module should deploy, **Fig. 18.** Module will jump approximately one foot into air.
11. No poisonous gas is produced upon

---

1. Stretch deployment harness to full length 10 m (33 ft).
2. Connect connectors.
3. Connect one banana plug to positive terminal of 12V vehicle battery and then the other to negative terminal to immediately deploy.
4. Short the two deployment harness leads.

SK8019400044000X

Fig. 18 Air bag unit deployment outside vehicle

deployment. However, do not inhale gas since it could irritate throat and can cause choking.
12. Allow at least 30 minutes after deployment for air bag components to cool.
13. Do not attempt to disassemble air bag: it cannot be used again.
14. If air bag did not deploy, consult Suzuki for disposal procedures.

IN-VEHICLE DEPLOYMENT

Before scrapping a vehicle equipped with air bag(s), air bag module(s) must be deployed.
1. Turn ignition to Lock position.

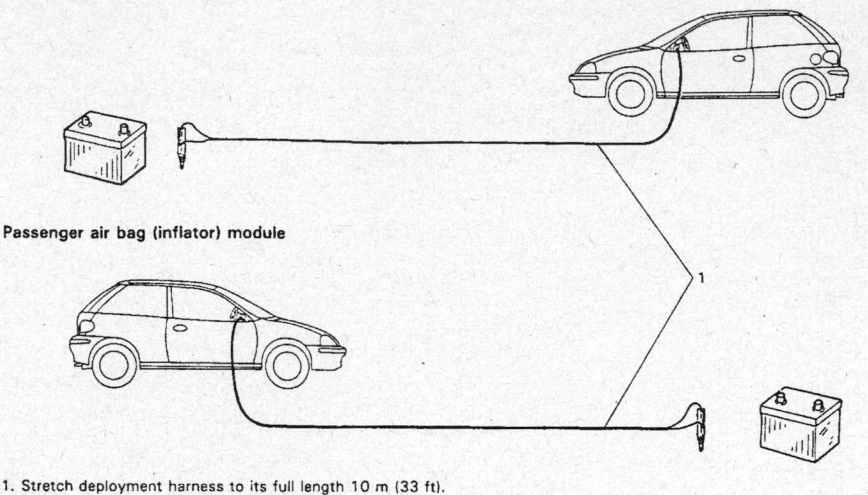

Driver air bag (inflator) module

Passenger air bag (inflator) module

1

1. Stretch deployment harness to its full length 10 m (33 ft).

SK8019400046000X

Fig. 20 In-vehicle air bag module deployment

TIGHTENING SPECIFICATIONS

Component	Torque/Ft. Lbs.
SWIFT	
Air Bag Module Mounting Bolts, Driver's	13.5–20①
Air Bag Module Mounting Lower Bolts, Passenger's	36–60②
Air Bag Module Mounting Upper Bolts, Passenger's	13.5–19.5
Forward Sensor Attaching Screws	36–60②
SDM Bolts	36–60②
Steering Wheel Nut	18.5–28.5
GRAND VITARA	
Air Bag Module Mounting Bolts, Driver's	17①
Air Bag Module Mounting Lower Bolts, Passenger's	48②
Air Bag Module Mounting Upper Bolts, Passenger's	16.5
SDM Bolts	60②
SIDEKICK & X-90	
Air Bag Module Mounting Bolts, Driver's	17①
Air Bag Module Mounting Lower Bolts, Passenger's	48②
Air Bag Module Mounting Upper Bolts, Passenger's	16.5
SDM Bolts	48②
Steering Wheel Nut	23.5

① — Tighten lefthand first, then righthand.

② — Inch lbs.

Dash Panel Service

NOTE: On Air Bag Equipped Models, Refer To " Air Bag System Precautions" Located In The Front Of This Manual For System Disarming & Arming Procedures.

NOTE: Refer To "Dash Gauges" Section For Related Information.

INDEX

PRECAUTIONS

AIR BAG SYSTEMS

Refer to "Air Bag System Precautions" in the front of this manual for system disarming and arming procedures.

BATTERY GROUND CABLE

Prior to service, disconnect battery ground cable and isolate as required.

DASH PANEL

REPLACE

GRAND VITARA

1. Remove console box, glove box and column hole cover.
2. Disconnect electrical connectors and cables from heater unit and blower motor assembly.
3. Remove steering column as outlined under "Steering Column, Replace."
4. Disconnect speedometer connector, then remove.
5. Disconnect SDM electrical connector and air bag ground terminal.
6. Remove hood release.
7. Disconnect remaining electrical connectors.
8. Remove instrument panel retaining screws and bolt, **Fig. 1.**
9. Remove instrument panel from vehicle.
10. Reverse procedure to install.

SIDEKICK & X-90

1. Remove two screws from front of console, then two back lockpins from rear of console.
2. Holding shifter boot inward, remove housing and console.
3. Remove steering column covers.
4. Remove four attaching screws from instrument cluster front shroud, then the shroud.
5. Remove instrument cluster attaching screws and pull cluster rearward.

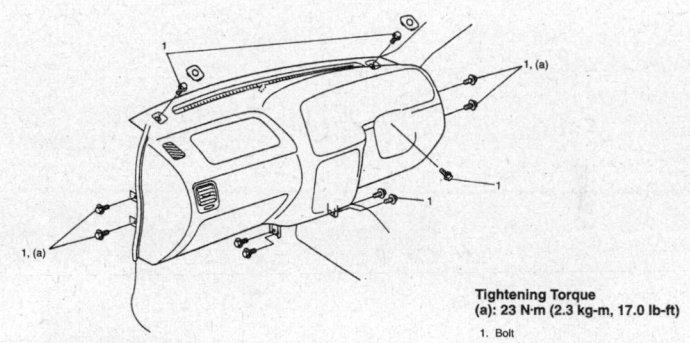

Tightening Torque
(a): 23 N·m (2.3 kg-m, 17.0 lb-ft)
1. Bolt

SK9149900003000X

Fig. 1 Instrument panel replacement. Grand Vitara

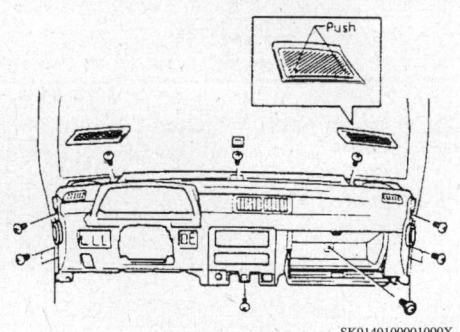

SK9149100001000X

Fig. 2 Instrument panel mounting bolts. Swift

6. Remove speedometer, then disconnect cluster wiring harness and remove cluster.
7. Remove three inspection screw covers, then the three upper housing attaching bolts.
8. Remove three lower housing attaching bolts located on the driver's side of the instrument panel.
9. Remove center support dash mount.
10. Open glove compartment and remove two glove compartment lockpins, then lift glove compartment out of the instrument panel.
11. Remove three instrument panel attaching screws from lower RH side of the instrument panel.
12. Remove handle bar from RH side of the instrument panel.
13. Remove hood release lever attaching bolt.
14. Disconnect center mounting bracket from the radio and ashtray.
15. Disconnect dash panel wiring harness and remove instrument panel.
16. Reverse procedure to install.

SWIFT

1. Remove console box.
2. Disconnect all wires and cables from heater and blower units.
3. Remove steering wheel, steering column and steering joint upper bolt.
4. Disconnect speedometer cable, then remove speedometer assembly.
5. Remove both front speaker garnishes and center cover.
6. Remove instrument panel member mounting bolts, **Fig. 2.**
7. Remove instrument panel and panel member as an assembly.
8. Reverse procedure to install.

ESTEEM

1. Remove console box and front extension.
2. Disconnect all wires and cables from heater and blower units.

3. Remove steering wheel, steering column and steering joint upper bolt.
4. Remove engine control module (ECM).
5. Remove engine hood opener.
6. Remove front pillar trim on both sides.
7. Remove all electrical connectors to dash panel.
8. Remove body ground at center of floor.
9. Remove instrument panel mounting bolts, **Fig. 3,** then instrument panel.
10. Reverse procedure to install.

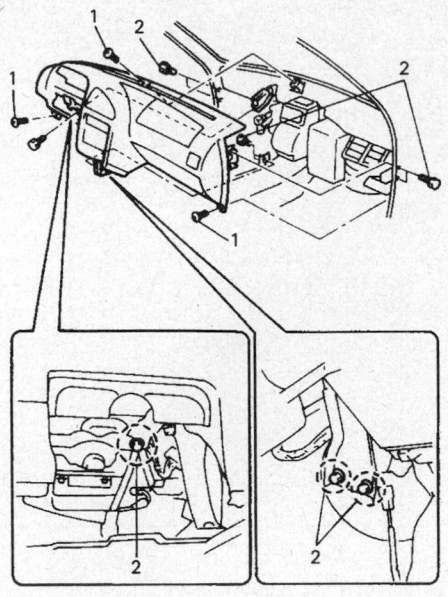

1. Mounting screw
2. Mounting bolt

SK9149500002000X

Fig. 3 Instrument panel mounting bolts. Esteem

Steering Columns

NOTE: On Air Bag Equipped Models, Refer To "Air Bag System Precautions" Located In The Front Of This Manual For System Disarming & Arming Procedures.

INDEX

PRECAUTIONS
AIR BAG SYSTEMS

Refer to "Air Bag System Precautions" in the front of this manual for system disarming and arming procedures.

SERVICE

It is important that only the specified screws, bolts and nuts be used during the mandatory assembling sequence and torqued to specifications to ensure proper breakaway action of column under impact. Avoid using excessively long bolts as they may prevent a portion of the steering column from collapsing under impact.

When removing or installing, steering wheel, ignition switch or lock, turn signal switch, adjusting transaxle or transmission linkage or installing and adjusting neutral start or back-up light switch, refer to appropriate car chapter.

If a shift tube shows a sheared plastic injection, a new shift tube must be installed. If a steering shaft shows a sheared plastic, but it is not bent, it can be repaired by using a Service Steering Shaft Repair Kit part number 7810077. The kit contains instructions and dimensions for all steering columns. On some models, the attaching brackets will shear under impact and must also be replaced.

STEERING COLUMN DAMAGE

When the steering column is removed from the vehicle, it is extremely susceptible to damage. Dropping the steering column assembly on its end could collapse the steering shaft assembly or loosen plastic injections that keep the steering column assembly rigid. Leaning on the steering column assembly could cause the jacket to bend or deform. Any of these conditions could impair the steering column assembly's collapsible design. If the steering wheel must be removed, use only the specified steering wheel puller and steering wheel puller bolts. Never hammer on the end of the shaft.

BATTERY GROUND CABLE

Prior to service, disconnect battery ground cable and isolate as required.

STEERING COLUMN
REPLACE
GRAND VITARA

1. Position front wheel straight ahead, then lock ignition switch and remove key.

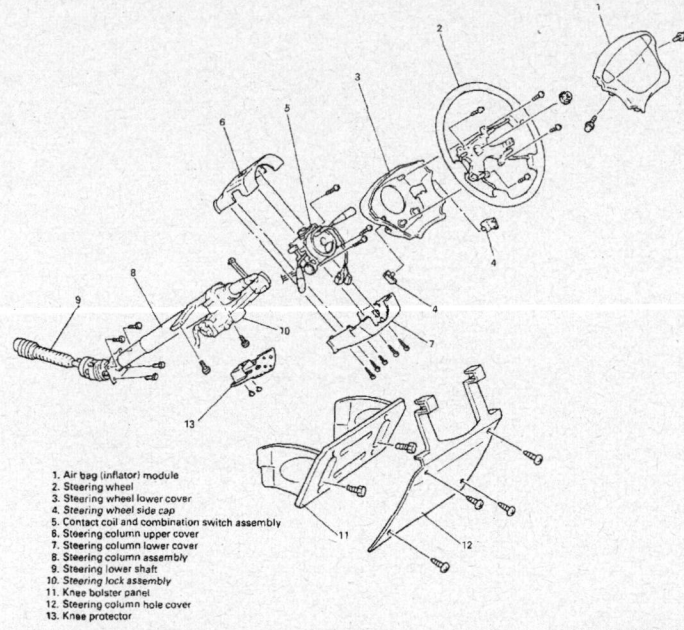

1. Air bag (inflator) module
2. Steering wheel
3. Steering wheel lower cover
4. Steering wheel side cap
5. Contact coil and combination switch assembly
6. Steering column upper cover
7. Steering column lower cover
8. Steering column assembly
9. Steering lower shaft
10. Steering lock assembly
11. Knee bolster panel
12. Steering column hole cover
13. Knee protector

SK6049600005000X

Fig. 1 Exploded view of steering column. Sidekick & X-90

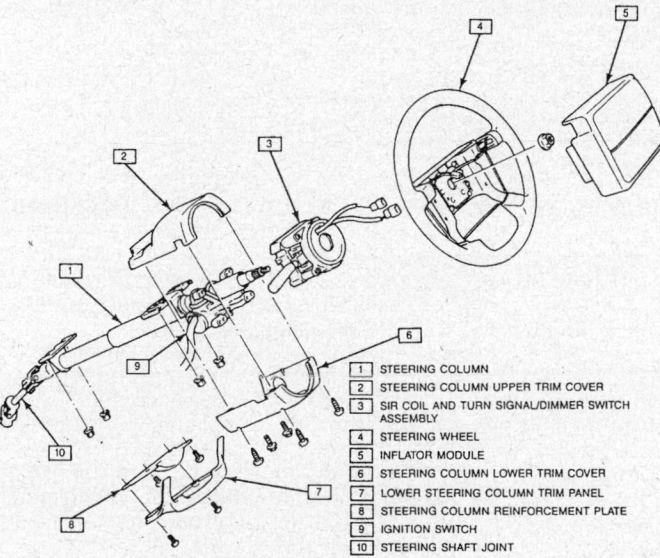

1	STEERING COLUMN
2	STEERING COLUMN UPPER TRIM COVER
3	SIR COIL AND TURN SIGNAL/DIMMER SWITCH ASSEMBLY
4	STEERING WHEEL
5	INFLATOR MODULE
6	STEERING COLUMN LOWER TRIM COVER
7	LOWER STEERING COLUMN TRIM PANEL
8	STEERING COLUMN REINFORCEMENT PLATE
9	IGNITION SWITCH
10	STEERING SHAFT JOINT

GC6049100063000X

Fig. 3 Exploded view of steering column. Swift

2. Remove steering column hole cover, then disconnect electrical connectors from column.
3. Reference shaft joint and shaft, then remove bolt from shaft side of shaft joint.
4. Loosen shaft bolt on lower side, then move shaft joint to shaft lower side.
5. Remove 6 steering column mounting bolts.
6. Remove shift key interlock cable, then remove steering column from vehicle.

SIDEKICK & X-90

1. Remove steering wheel and contact coil, **Fig. 1.**
2. Remove hole cover and knee bolster panel.
3. Disconnect electrical connectors for ignition switch, contact coil and combination switch.
4. Disconnect steering joint bolt and steering column bolts.
5. **On models with automatic transmission,** disconnect shift interlock cable from ignition switch assembly and clamp.
6. **On all models,** remove steering column assembly.
7. Reverse procedure to install, noting the following:
   a. **Torque** interlock cable screw to 19 inch lbs.
   b. **Torque** steering column lower mounting nuts, then upper mounting nuts to 17 ft. lbs.
   c. **Torque** steering shaft upper joint to 18 ft. lbs.

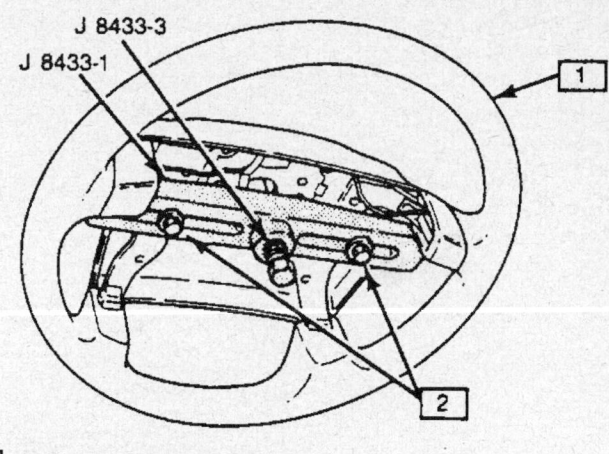

| 1 | STEERING WHEEL |
| 2 | TWO 1/4 X 2-INCH THROUGH BOLTS AND NUTS |

GC6049100062000X

Fig. 2 Steering wheel removal. Swift

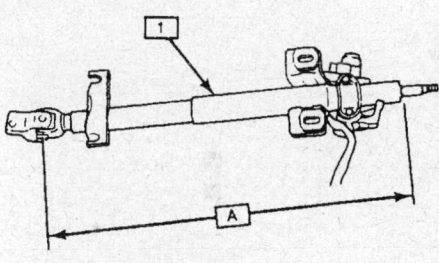

| A | 532.5 mm (20.96 INCHES) |
| 1 | STEERING COLUMN |

GC6049100064000X

Fig. 4 Steering column measurement. Swift

SWIFT

Wheels must be in a straight forward position and the key must be in the Lock position when removing or installing column to ensure proper alignment of components during installation.

Care must be taken when handling column with a live inflator module. Never point bag deploy surface toward you and never stand column on steering wheel. Accidental deployment in these positions may cause injury. Always face bag deploy surface toward open space to allow for unrestricted expansion.

1. Remove steering wheel as follows:
   a. Remove four screw from rear of steering wheel, then remove inflator module from steering wheel.
   b. Remove steering attaching nut.
   c. Attach wheel puller tool Nos. J 8433-1 and J 8433-3 or equivalents, **Fig. 2,** then remove steering wheel.
2. Remove steering shaft trim panel.
3. Remove lower column steering trim panel attaching screws, then trim panel.
4. Remove lower column reinforcement plate attaching screws, then plate.

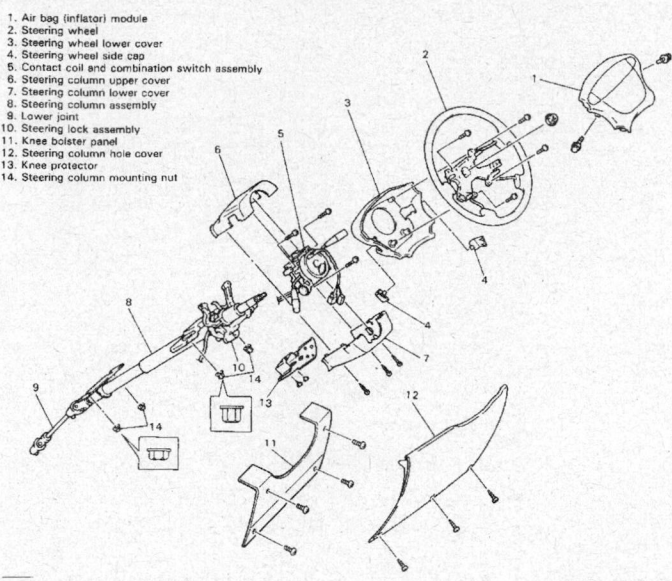

1. Air bag (inflator) module
2. Steering wheel
3. Steering wheel lower cover
4. Steering wheel side cap
5. Contact coil and combination switch assembly
6. Steering column upper cover
7. Steering column lower cover
8. Steering column assembly
9. Lower joint
10. Steering lock assembly
11. Knee bolster panel
12. Steering column hole cover
13. Knee protector
14. Steering column mounting nut

SK6049500004000X

Fig. 5 Exploded view of steering column. Esteem

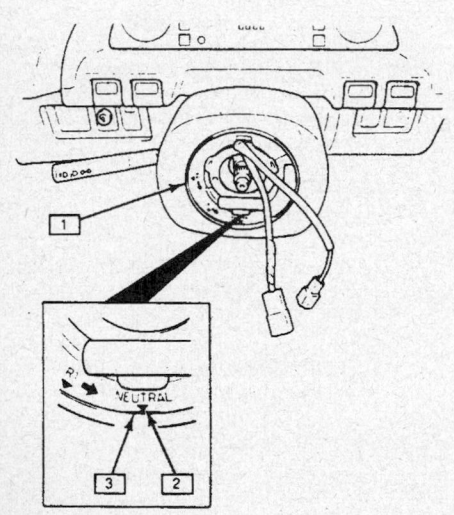

1	SIR COIL
2	NEUTRAL MARK
3	ALIGNMENT MARK

GC6049100123000X

Fig. 7 SIR coil position inspection. Swift

5. Disconnect steering column electrical connectors.
6. **On models with automatic transaxle,** remove transaxle shift interlock cable from ignition switch.
7. **On all models,** remove column to steering shaft joint pinch bolt, **Fig. 3.**
8. Remove two upper and lower column attaching bolts, then column.
9. Measure column as shown in **Fig. 4.** If measurement is less than 20.96 inches, replace column.
10. Reverse procedure to install, noting the following:

a. **Torque** upper and lower steering column attaching bolts to 124 inch lbs.
b. **Torque** steering column to steering shaft pinch bolt to 18 ft. lbs.

ESTEEM

1. Remove steering wheel, contact coil and combination switch, **Fig. 5.**
2. Remove hole cover and knee bolster panel.
3. Remove steering column harness from column.
4. Disconnect electrical connectors
5. Remove steering joint upper cover, then upper joint bolt.
6. Remove steering column mounting nuts.
7. **On models with automatic transaxle,** disconnect shift interlock cable from ignition switch with switch positioned at ACC. After disconnecting, turn lock switch to LOCK position.
8. **On all models,** remove steering column.
9. Reverse procedure to install, noting the following:

a. **Torque** steering column upper mounting nuts, then lower mounting nuts to 10.5 ft. lbs.
b. **Torque** steering shaft upper joint to 18 ft. lbs.

STEERING COLUMN SERVICE

SIR COIL & TURN SIGNAL & DIMMER SWITCH

Remove steering wheel as outlined in "Steering Column, Replace" in this section.
1. Remove six screws retaining upper and lower steering column covers, then remove column covers.
2. Remove two electrical connectors from fuse box, one from the SIR harness and one from the main wiring harness, **Fig. 6.**

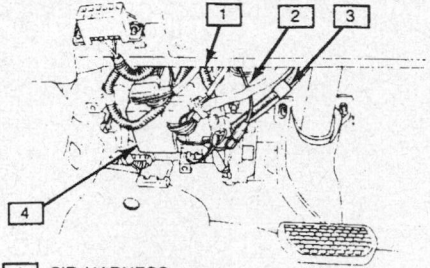

1	SIR HARNESS
2	MAIN WIRE HARNESS (HORN)
3	SIR COIL AND TURN SIGNAL/DIMMER SWITCH HARNESS
4	FUSE BLOCK

GC6049100122000X

Fig. 6 Electrical connector locations. Swift

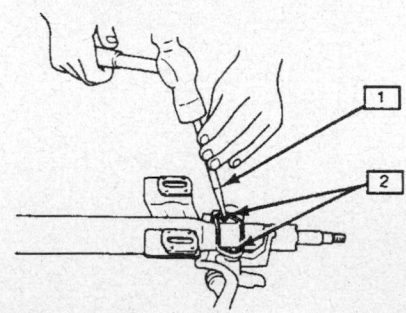

| 1 | CENTER PUNCH |
| 2 | STEERING COLUMN LOCK BOLTS |

GC6049100124000X

Fig. 8 Steering column lock bolts removal. Swift

3. Remove SIR coil and turn signal/dimmer switch attaching screws, then switch assembly.
4. Reverse procedure to install, noting the following:

a. Ensure SIR coil is centered. If not position wheels of vehicle in the straightforward position.
b. Check position of SIR coil, **Fig. 7.**
c. If Neutral mark is at the alignment mark the coil is centered and no adjustment is necessary.
d. If R1 mark is close to the alignment mark coil is one rotation off to the right from its center state and needs to be adjusted on turn counterclockwise. The R2 mark indicates that the coil is two rotations off.
e. If L1 mark is close to the alignment mark coil is one rotation off to the left from its center state and needs to be adjusted on turn clockwise. The L2 mark indicates that the coil is two rotations off.
f. To adjust remove SIR coil, hold coil lead at its base and turn in the direction specified in steps d and e. Then replace SIR coil.

STEERING COLUMN LOCK

Remove steering wheel as outlined in "Steering Column, Replace" in this section.
1. Remove ignition switch attaching screw, then switch.

2. Remove ignition key warning switch attaching screws, then switch.
3. Loosen and remove two steering column lock retaining bolts using a center punch, **Fig. 8. When using center punch do not damage aluminum parts of lock assembly.**
4. Turn ignition key to On or ACC position, then remove lock assembly from steering column.
5. Reverse procedure to install.

Manual Steering Gears

INDEX

SIDEKICK & X-90

OIL LEVEL CHECK

Oil surface level should be as shown, **Fig. 1.** If not, add suitable lubricant as necessary.

WORM SHAFT ADJUSTMENT

The steering gear is provided with an adjustment bolt, **Fig. 2,** which provides preload to selector shaft. If necessary, adjust as follows:
1. Check worm shaft to ensure it is free from thrust play.
2. Position pitman arm so it is parallel with worm shaft as shown, **Fig. 3. With pitman arm in this position, front wheels should be in a straight forward position.**
3. Using torque wrench, measure worm shaft starting torque, **Fig. 2.** Starting torque should be .4–.7 ft. lbs.
4. If torque is not as specified, adjust adjusting bolt until torque is as specified.
5. If worm shaft starting torque is within specifications, check worm shaft operating torque in its entire operating range (turning worm shaft all the way to the right and left).
6. Worm shaft operating torque should be under .9 ft. lbs. for Sidekick. If torque is not as specified, readjust worm shaft starting torque in a straight forward position using adjusting bolt, **Fig. 2,** then recheck worm shaft operating torque.
7. If specification is not as specified after readjustment, replace steering gear.

SWIFT

For the following procedures remove steering gear case from vehicle as outlined under "Steering Gear, Replace" in the "Front Suspension & Steering" section of this chapter.

STEERING RACK PLUNGER, REPLACE

Remove rack plunger in numbered sequence, **Fig. 4.**

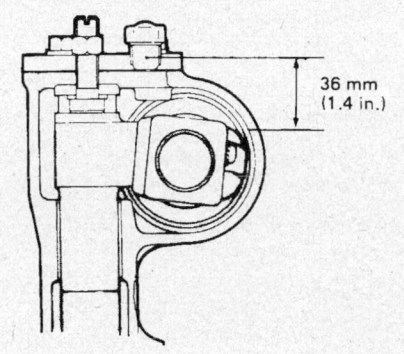

36 mm (1.4 in.)

SK6039100002000X

Fig. 1   Oil level check

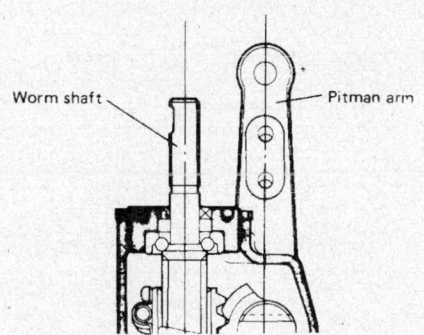

Worm shaft — Pitman arm

SK6039100005000X

Fig. 3   Pitman arm installation

Reverse numbered sequence to install, noting the following:
1. Apply grease lightly to sliding part of plunger against rack.
2. After tightening rack damper screw to tightest point, turn back by 0–90° and check for rotation torque of pinion, **Fig. 5.** Pinion torque should be .58–.94 ft. lbs.

STEERING PINION, REPLACE

1. Remove rack plunger as outlined under "Steering Rack Plunger, Replace."
2. Remove gear case packing, then bearing plug using 43 mm socket.
3. To separate pinion from housing, tap as shown, **Fig. 6,** with plastic hammer.

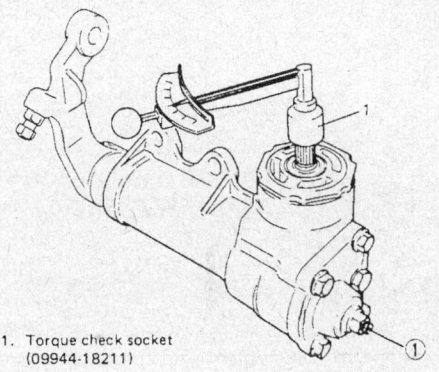

1. Torque check socket (09944-18211)

SK6039100004000X

Fig. 2   Steering gear adjustment bolt

4. Remove pinion assembly.
5. Reverse procedure to install, torquing pinion bearing plug to specification.

STEERING RACK, REPLACE

1. Move both boots toward tie rod ends, then remove tie rods from steering rack.
2. Remove steering pinion as outlined under "Steering Pinion, Replace."
3. Remove rack from case as shown, **Fig. 7.**
4. Reverse procedure to install, noting the following:
   a. Apply grease to entire teeth surface of rack.
   b. Ensure rack side mount is positioned as shown, **Fig. 8.**

PINION BEARING, REPLACE

1. Remove steering rack as outlined under "Steering Rack, Replace."
2. Remove pinion bearing from case using slide hammer and bearing remover tool No. 09921-20200 or equivalent.
3. Reverse procedure to install, noting the following:
   a. Apply grease to rollers of pinion bearing.
   b. Press fit pinion bearing into gear case using bearing installer tool No. 09943-88211 or equivalent.

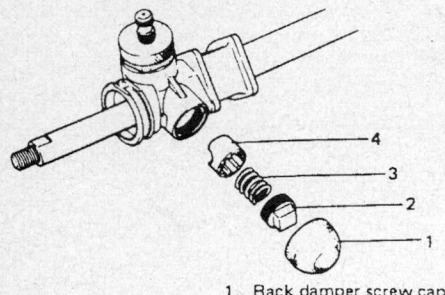

1. Rack damper screw cap
2. Rack damper screw
3. Rack plunger spring
4. Rack plunger

SK6039100007000X

Fig. 4 Rack plunger replacement. Swift

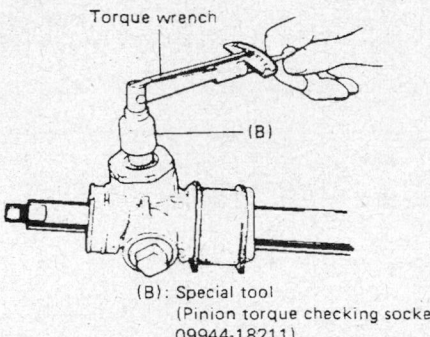

(B): Special tool
(Pinion torque checking socket 09944-18211)

SK6039100008000X

Fig. 5 Rotation torque of pinion inspection. Swift

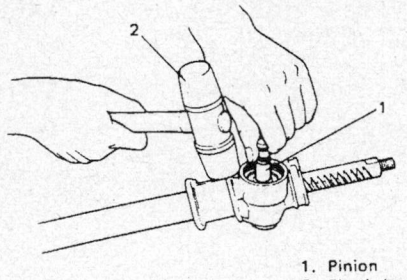

1. Pinion
2. Plastic hammer

SK6039100009000X

Fig. 6 Steering pinion removal. Swift

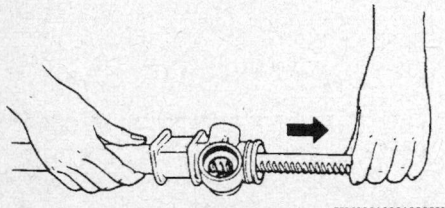

SK6039100010000X

Fig. 7 Steering rack removal. Swift

RACK BUSHING, REPLACE

1. Remove steering rack as outlined under "Steering Rack, Replace."
2. Remove snap ring, then bushing from housing using bushing remover tool No. 09944-48210 or equivalent.
3. Reverse procedure to install, noting the following:
   a. Apply grease to entire inner surface of bushing.
   b. Press fit bushing as shown, **Fig. 9.**

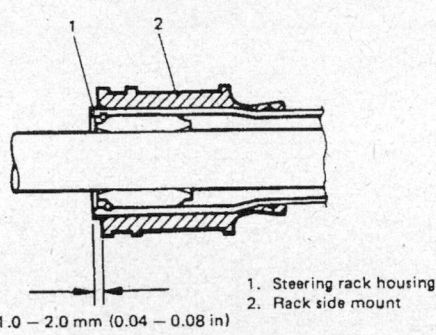

1.0 – 2.0 mm (0.04 – 0.08 in)

1. Steering rack housing
2. Rack side mount

SK6039100011000X

Fig. 8 Rack side mount installation. Swift

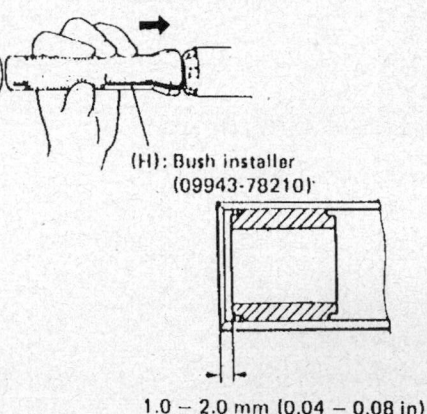

(H): Bush installer (09943-78210)

1.0 – 2.0 mm (0.04 – 0.08 in)

SK6039100012000X

Fig. 9 Rack bushing installation. Swift

TIGHTENING SPECIFICATIONS

Year	Component	Torque/Ft. Lbs.
SIDEKICK & X-90		
1996–99	Center Link Castle Nut	22–50
	Idler Arm Nut	50–57
	Pitman Arm Nut	101–129
	Steering Gear Bolt	50–72
	Steering Shaft Joint Bolt	14–22
	Tie Rod End Castle Nut	22–39
	Tie Rod End Locknut	36–58
SWIFT		
1996–99	Steering Gear Case Bolt	15–22
	Steering Pinion Bearing Plug	58–80
	Steering Shaft Joint Bolt	15–22
	Tie Rod End Castle Nut	22–39
	Tie Rod End Locknut	26–39

Power Steering

NOTE: On Air Bag Equipped Models, Refer To "Air Bag System Precautions" Located In The Front Of This Manual For System Disarming & Arming Procedures.

INDEX

POWER STEERING PRESSURE SPECIFICATIONS

Year	Model	Hydraulic Pressure, psi	Backpressure, psi	Relief Pressure, psi
1996–99	Sidekick & X-90	1000	142	850–1140
	Grand Vitara	1066	142	1024–1138
	Swift	711	142	640–924
	Esteem	1137	142	1109–1208

PRECAUTIONS

AIR BAG SYSTEMS

Refer to "Air Bag System Precautions" in the front of this manual for system disarming and arming procedures.

BATTERY GROUND CABLE

Prior to service, disconnect battery ground cable and isolate as required.

TROUBLESHOOTING

Refer to **Fig. 1** for troubleshooting procedures.

DIAGNOSIS & TESTING

STEERING WHEEL PLAY

With engine Off, move steering wheel lightly in both directions without turning wheels and measure distance along its circumference. Distance measured should be less than 1.2 inch.

STEERING FORCE

1. Place vehicle on a level surface and set steering wheel to straight ahead position.
2. Ensure tire pressure is proper, then start engine and warm power steering fluid to 122–140°F.
3. With engine idling, measure steering force using a spring balancer hooked to steering wheel, **Fig. 2.**
4. Steering force should be less than 11 lbs. on Sidekick and X-90 and less than 8.8 lbs. on Esteem and Swift.

POWER STEERING BELT TENSION

1. Ensure belt is free of damage and fits properly in pulley groove.
2. Check belt deflection at midway point between power steering pulley and crankshaft pulley using about 22 lbs. of force.
3. Belt deflection should be .16–.35 inch on Grand Vitara, .24–.35 inch on Sidekick, X-90 and Esteem and .31–.39 inch on Swift.

IDLE UP SYSTEM

With A/C turned Off, if equipped, turn steering wheel and ensure engine idling speed is not slowed down even when load is applied by power steering pump.

HYDRAULIC PRESSURE IN CIRCUIT

1. **On Sidekick and X-90 models,** thoroughly clean hose connections, then disconnect pressure hose from pump and connect oil pressure gauge tool No. 09915-77410 and attachment hose set tool No. 09915-77420 or equivalents, as shown, **Fig. 3. When connecting gauge, route hose so that it does not contact power steering belt or hinder movement of center link.**
2. **On Esteem, Grand Vitara and Swift models,** thoroughly clean hose connections, then disconnect pressure hose and connect oil pressure gauge tool No. 09915-77410 or equivalent, between high pressure hose and high pressure pipe as shown, **Fig. 4.**

3. **On all models,** fill power steering fluid reservoir and bleed system of air, refer to "Air Bleeding" procedure as outlined.
4. With engine idling, turn steering wheel to right and left stops to warm fluid in reservoir to 122–140°F. **Do not hold steering against stop for longer than 10 seconds or damage to components may occur.**
5. With wheels straight forward and engine running at idle, check backpressure on gauge, pressure should be lower than 142 psi. If pressure is higher than 142 psi, check control valve and pipes for obstruction.
6. **On Sidekick and X-90 models,** increase engine speed to 1500 RPM minimum, then close gauge valve gradually while observing pressure increase and record relief pressure, which should be 850–1140 psi. If pressure is higher than 1140 psi, relief valve may have malfunctioned, replace power steering pump. If lower than 850 psi, power steering pump may have failed or relief valve spring setting is incorrect, replace power steering pump. **Do not close gauge valve for longer than 10 seconds or damage to components may occur.**
7. **On Grand Vitara, Swift and Esteem models,** increase engine speed to 1500 RPM minimum, then close gauge valve gradually while observing pressure increase and record relief pressure, which should be 640–924 psi. If pressure is higher than 924 psi, relief valve may have malfunctioned, replace steering gear components. If pressure is lower than 640 psi, power

Condition	Possible Cause	Correction
Steering wheel feels heavy (at low speed)	1. Fluid deteriorated, low viscosity, different type of fluid mixed	Replace fluid.
	2. Pipes or hoses deformed, air entering through joint	Replace defective part.
	3. Insufficient air purging from P/S circuit	Purge air.
	4. P/S belt worn, lacking in tension	Adjust belt tension or replace belt as necessary.
	5. Tire inflation pressure excessively low	Inflate tire.
	6. Front end alignment maladjusted	Check and adjust front end alignment.
	7. Steering wheel installed improperly (twisted)	Install steering wheel correctly.
	8. Bind in tie rod or tie rod end ball joint	Replace defective part.
	9. P/S pump hydraulic pressure fails to increase	Replace P/S pump.
	10. P/S pump hydraulic pressure increases but slowly	Replace P/S pump.
	NOTE: Make sure to warm up engine fully before measuring hydraulic pressure from pump.	
Steering wheel feels heavy momentarily when turning it to the left (right)	1. Air drawn in due to insufficient amount of fluid	Add fluid and purge air.
	2. Slipping P/S belt	Adjust belt tension or replace belt as necessary.
	3. Refer to check items 9 and 10 in above section	
No idle-up	1. P/S pump pressure switch defective	Replace P/S pump.
Poor recovery from turns	NOTE: To check steering wheel for recovery, with car running at 22 mile/h (35 km/h), turn it 90° and let it free. It should return more than 60°.	
	1. Deformed pipes or hoses	Replace defective part.
	2. Steering column installed improperly	Install steering column correctly.
	3. Front end alignment maladjusted	Check and adjust front end alignment.
	4. Ball joints binding	Replace defective part.
	5. Refer to items 9 and 10 in above section	

SK6029100001010X

Fig. 1 Troubleshooting chart (Part 1 of 2)

Condition	Possible Cause	Correction
Vehicle pulls to one side during straight driving	1. Low or uneven tire inflation pressure	Inflate tires to proper pressure or adjust right & left tires inflation pressure.
	2. Front end alignment maladjusted	Check and adjust front end alignment.
	3. Malfunction of control valve in gear box	Replace gear box.
	4. Refer to check items 9 and 10 in previous page	
Steering wheel play is large and vehicle wanders	1. Loose steering shaft nut	Retighten.
	2. Loose linkage or joints	Retighten.
	3. Loose gear box fastening bolt	Retighten.
	4. Front wheel bearing worn	Replace wheel bearing.
Oil leakage	1. Loose joints of (hydraulic pressure) pipes and hoses	Retighten.
	2. Deformed or damaged pipes or hoses	Replace defective part.
Abnormal noise	NOTE: Some sound may be heard through steering column when turning steering wheel with vehicle at a stop but it is not an abnormal noise but operating sound of valve in gear box.	
	1. Air drawn in due to insufficient amount of fluid	Add fluid and purge air.
	2. Air mixed into fluid from pipes or hoses	Replace pipes or hoses.
	3. Slipping (loose) P/S belt	Adjust belt tension.
	4. Worn P/S belt	Replace belt.
	5. Loose gear box fastening bolt	Retighten bolts.
	6. Loose pitman arm nut	Retighten nut.
	7. Loose linkage or joints	Retighten.
	8. Pipes or hoses in contact with part of vehicle body	Install pipes and hoses correctly.
	9. Vanes of P/S pump defective	Replace pump.
	10. Malfunction of control valve in gear box	Replace gear box.
	11. Bearing of P/S pump shaft defective	Replace pump.

SK6029100001020X

Fig. 1 Troubleshooting chart (Part 2 of 2)

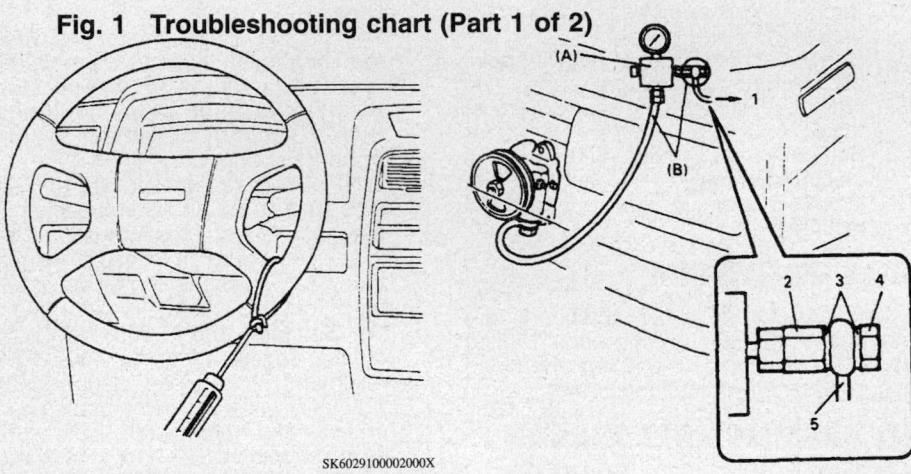

SK6029100002000X

Fig. 2 Steering force inspection

1. To gear box
2. Attachment
3. Washer
4. Union bolt
5. Pressure hose

SK6029100003000X

Fig. 3 Oil pressure gauge installation. Sidekick & X-90

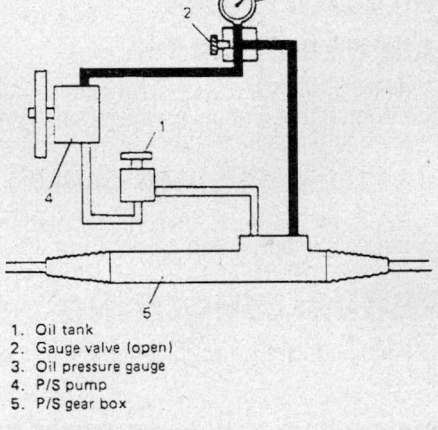

1. Oil tank
2. Gauge valve (open)
3. Oil pressure gauge
4. P/S pump
5. P/S gear box

SK6029100004000X

Fig. 4 Oil pressure gauge installation. Swift

steering pump may have failed or relief valve spring setting is incorrect, replace power steering pump. **Do not close gauge valve for longer than 10 seconds or damage to components may occur.**

8. **On Sidekick and X-90 models,** open gauge valve fully and increase engine speed to 1500 RPM minimum, then turn steering wheel left or right stop and record relief pressure reading, pressure should be 850–1140 psi. If pressure is lower than 850 psi, steering gear may have failed, replace steering gear. **Do not hold steering against stop for longer than 10 sec-**

onds **or damage to components may occur.**

9. **On Esteem and Swift models,** open gauge valve fully and increase engine speed to 1500 RPM minimum, then turn steering wheel left or right stop and record relief pressure reading, pressure should be 640–924 psi. If pressure is lower than 640 psi, steering gear may have failed, replace

steering gear. **Do not hold steering against stop for longer than 10 seconds or damage to components may occur.**

POWER STEERING SYSTEM SERVICE

AIR BLEEDING

1. Raise and support front of vehicle.
2. Fill oil tank with fluid to specified level, then turn steering wheel left or right three or four times.
3. After running engine at idling speed for three to five seconds, stop engine and add fluid to meet specification.
4. With engine stopped, turn steering

1. Pulley
2. Shaft
3. Pressure switch
4. P/S pump body
5. Flow control valve ass'y (built in relief valve)
6. Cam ring
7. Rotor
8. Vane
9. Cover

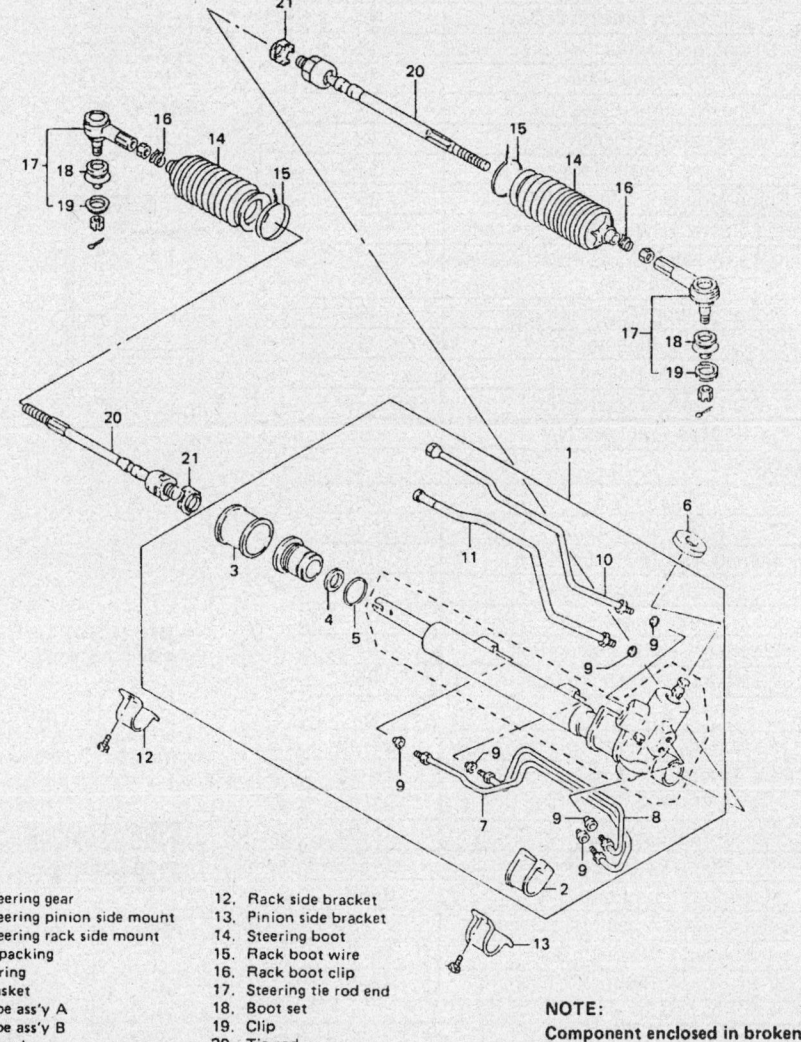

SK6029100005000X

Fig. 5 Exploded view of power steering pump

1. Steering gear
2. Steering pinion side mount
3. Steering rack side mount
4. U-packing
5. O-ring
6. Gasket
7. Pipe ass'y A
8. Pipe ass'y B
9. Ferrule
10. Pressure pipe
11. Return pipe

12. Rack side bracket
13. Pinion side bracket
14. Steering boot
15. Rack boot wire
16. Rack boot clip
17. Steering tie rod end
18. Boot set
19. Clip
20. Tie rod
21. Tie rod lock washer

NOTE:
Component enclosed in broken line cannot be disassembled.

SK6029100006000X

Fig. 6 Exploded view of power steering gear. Swift

wheel to right and left as far as possible, then repeat a few times and add fluid to specified level.

5. With engine idling, repeat stop-to-stop turn of steering wheel until all foam in oil tank is gone.

6. **Bleed air completely. If air remains in fluid, power steering pump may make humming noise or steering wheel may feel heavy.**

7. Ensure fluid is filled to specified level.

POWER STEERING PUMP OVERHAUL

1. Remove power steering pump as outlined under "Power Steering Pump, Replace" in "Front Suspension & Steering" section.
2. Using transfer flange lock holder tool No. 09930-40113 or equivalent, remove pump pulley.
3. Remove suction connector bolts, then the pressure switch and flow control assembly, **Fig. 5**.
4. Remove pump cover bolts, then the cam ring.
5. Remove snap ring and pull out rotor. When pulling rotor out of shaft, be careful not to lose vanes.
6. Remove shaft and oil seal.
7. Reverse procedure to install, ensuring rotor is installed to shaft with splined part chamfered side facing cover.

STEERING GEAR OVERHAUL

Esteem, Sidekick & X-90

The power steering gear on these models cannot be serviced.

Swift

Refer to **Fig. 6** when servicing steering gear.

1. Remove steering gear as outlined under "Power Steering Gear, Replace" in "Front Suspension & Steering" section.
2. Move boot to expose section of tie rod and steering gear, then remove tie rod with tie rod end as shown, **Fig. 7**.
3. Using ring nut wrench tool No. 09917-23610, or equivalent, remove adjustment cover, then the O-ring and or U-packing.
4. Reverse procedure to assemble, noting the following:
   a. Apply Suzuki super grease to O-ring and U-packing of adjustment cover and install in groove of adjustment cover.
   b. Tighten adjustment cover and tie rod to specification.
   c. Use new tie rod lockwasher and caulk after installation.

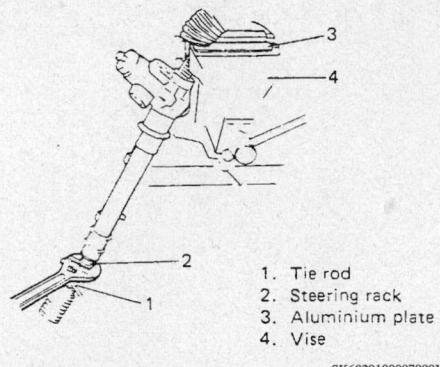

1. Tie rod
2. Steering rack
3. Aluminium plate
4. Vise

SK6029100007000X

Fig. 7 Tie rod end removal. Swift

TIGHTENING SPECIFICATIONS

Year	Component	Torque/Ft. Lbs.
ESTEEM		
1996–99	Belt Tension Pulley Nut	33
	Compressor Bracket Bolt	47
	Discharge Connector Bolts	43
	Pipe Clamp Bolt	8
	Pipe To Pump Flare Nut	32
	Pressure Switch	13
	Pump Cover Bolts	17
	Pump Mounting Bracket Bolts	25
	Steering Gear Cylinder Pipe Flare Nuts	14
	Steering Gear High & Low Pressure Pipe Flare Nuts	24
	Steering Gear Mounting Bolts	40
	Suction Connector Bolt	8
	Tie Rod Ball Nut	65
	Tie Rod End Castle Nut	25.5–39.5
	Tie Rod End Lock Nut	32.5
SIDEKICK & X-90		
1996–99	Castle Nut	36
	Lower Shaft Bolt	18
	Pitman Arm To Sector Shaft	101
	Pump Adjusting Bolt	18
	Pump Union Bolt	43
	Steering Gear Mounting Bolt	61
	Steering Gear Union Bolt	25
SWIFT		
1996–99	Discharge Connector Bolts	29–43
	Pipe Assembly A & B Flare Nut	15–21
	Pressure Pipe Flare Nut	22–28
	Pressure Switch	19–21
	Pump Cover Bolts	14–15
	Return Pipe Flare Nut	29–36
	Steering Gear Adjustment Cover	29–36
	Suction Connector Bolt	5–7
	Tie Rod	44–57

Disc Brakes

INDEX

BRAKE PAD SERVICE

FRONT

1. Raise and support vehicle, then remove wheels.
2. Remove caliper pin bolts, **Figs. 1 through 4.**
3. Remove caliper from caliper carrier. Hang removed caliper with wire hook to prevent damage to brake hose.
4. Remove brake pads.
5. Reverse procedure to install.

REAR

1. Raise and support vehicle, then remove wheels.
2. Remove caliper pin bolts, then release parking brake lever.
3. Remove caliper from caliper carrier. Hang removed caliper with wire hook to prevent damage to brake hose.
4. Remove brake pads.
5. Reverse procedure to install, noting the following:
   a. Using tool No. 09945-16030 or equivalent, **Fig. 5,** turn caliper piston clockwise to obtain clearance between disc and pad.
   b. Depress brake pedal five times to obtain proper disc to pad clearance.

ROTOR

REPLACE

1. Raise and support vehicle, then remove wheels.
2. Remove caliper as outlined under "Caliper Service." **During removal, be careful not to damage brake flexible hose or depress brake pedal.**
3. **On Swift models,** remove brake disc screws.
4. **On all models,** remove rotor by using two 8 mm bolts, **Fig. 6.**
5. Reverse procedure to install.

CALIPER SERVICE

REMOVAL

Front

1. Remove approximately ⅔ of brake fluid from master cylinder.
2. Raise and support vehicle.
3. Mark relationship between front wheel and axle, then remove wheel and tire assembly.

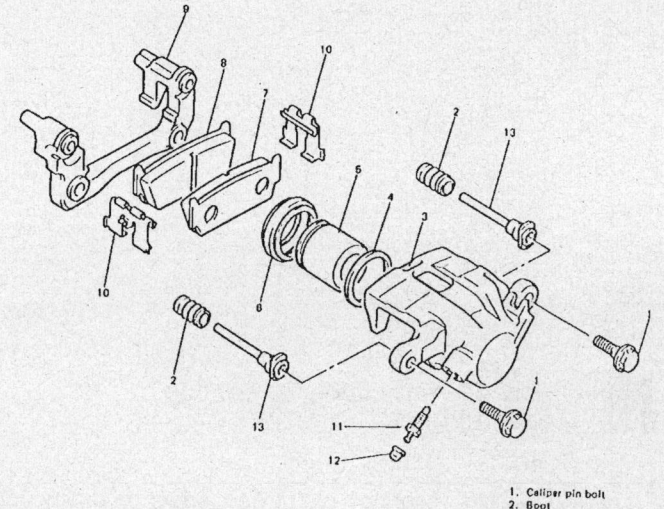

1. Caliper pin bolt
2. Boot
3. Disc brake caliper (Disc brake cylinder)
4. Piston seal
5. Disc brake piston
6. Cylinder boot
7. Disc brake inner pad
8. Disc brake outer pad
9. Brake caliper carrier
10. Pad spring
11. Bleeder plug
12. Bleeder plug cap
13. Caliper pin

SK4079100004000X

Fig. 1 Exploded view of front caliper assembly. Sidekick & X-90

4. Remove inlet fitting attaching bolt, copper washer and inlet fitting from caliper housing. Plug opening in inlet fitting to prevent fluid loss and contamination. **Do not crimp brake hose, as this may damage internal structure of hose. If only shoe and lining assemblies are to be replaced, do not disconnect brake line fitting from caliper.**
5. Remove caliper slide pins and the caliper.
6. Remove shoe and lining assembly.
7. Remove bracket attaching bolts and the bracket.
8. Remove slide pin boot from bracket.

Rear

1. Raise and support vehicle, then remove wheels.
2. Remove brake hose mounting bolt from caliper. Drain brake fluid into appropriate container.
3. Release parking brake lever and remove caliper pin bolts.
4. Remove caliper from carrier, then the parking brake cable retaining clip.

5. Disconnect parking brake cable from camshaft lever on caliper, then remove cover.

DISASSEMBLE

Front

1. Drain brake fluid from caliper.
2. Use clean shop towels to pad interior of caliper assembly, then remove piston by directing compressed air into caliper brake hose inlet hole, **Fig. 7. Use just enough air pressure to ease piston out of bore. Do not place fingers in front of piston for any reason when applying compressed air. This could result in serious personal injury.**
3. Remove dust boot from piston.
4. Using a small piece of wood or plastic, remove piston seal from bore. **Do not use a metal tool of any kind to remove seal as it may damage bore.**
5. Remove bleeder valve.
6. Inspect piston for scoring, nicks, corrosion and wear and replace as needed.
7. Inspect caliper housing and seal

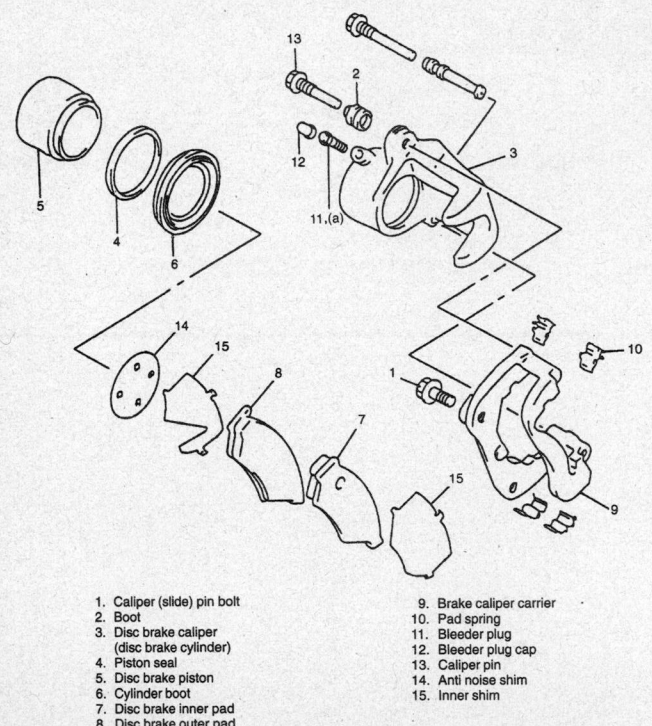

1. Caliper (slide) pin bolt
2. Boot
3. Disc brake caliper (disc brake cylinder)
4. Piston seal
5. Disc brake piston
6. Cylinder boot
7. Disc brake inner pad
8. Disc brake outer pad
9. Brake caliper carrier
10. Pad spring
11. Bleeder plug
12. Bleeder plug cap
13. Caliper pin
14. Anti noise shim
15. Inner shim

SK4079900018000X

Fig. 2   Exploded view of front caliper assembly. Grand Vitara

1. Caliper bolt
2. Boot
3. Cylinder slide bush
4. Bleeder plug cap
5. Bleeder plug
6. Disc brake caliper (Disc brake cylinder)
7. Piston seal
8. Disc brake piston
9. Cylinder boot
10. Set ring (boot ring)
11. Disc brake inner pad
12. Disc brake outer pad
13. Brake caliper carrier
14. Carrier bolt
15. Pad support plate No.1
16. Pad support plate No.2
17. Anti-noise shim
18. Pad wear plate (wear indicator)

SK4079500017000X

Fig. 3   Exploded view of front caliper assembly. Esteem

groove for corrosion, nicks, scoring and excessive wear and use crocus cloth to polish away corrosion from housing bore. Replace caliper housing if corrosion in and around seal groove will not clean up with crocus cloth.
8. Clean all parts with denatured alcohol. Dry with unlubricated compressed air. Blow out all passages in housing and bleeder valve.

Rear

1. Clean caliper with brake fluid, then remove piston and boot by turning piston counterclockwise with piston installer tool No. 09945-16030 or equivalent.
2. Remove piston seal. **Be careful not to damage inside (bore side) of cylinder.**
3. Using snap ring pliers (closing type) tool No. 09945-16010 or equivalent, remove snap ring.
4. Remove spring seat No. 2, coil spring and seat No. 1.
5. Using snap ring pliers, remove key plate snap ring, then the key plate, pushrod and rod.
6. Remove return spring, **Fig. 8,** then the lever, camshaft and camshaft boot.

ASSEMBLE
Front

1. Apply suitable grease to piston seal and cylinder wall, then install the seal. Check to ensure piston seal is not twisted.
2. Apply suitable grease to sliding portion of piston and install dust boot.

3. Insert edge of dust boot into boot groove, then slowly force piston fully into cylinder.
4. Install bleeder valve.

Rear

1. Position camshaft bearing as shown, **Fig. 9.**
2. Determine camshaft position in the cylinder as shown, **Fig. 10.**
3. Assemble rod, seal ring and key plate onto pushrod, then install as an assembly. Ensure pin A of key plate fits into hole B in cylinder when installing, **Fig. 11.**
4. Turn camshaft while pressing screw part of pushrod by hand. Ensure pushrod moves about .039 inch (1 mm) up and down, **Fig. 12.**
5. After installation of seat No. 1, coil spring and spring seat No. 2, tighten with spring installer tool No. 09945-16040, or equivalent, **Fig. 13,** until spring seat No. 2 lightly contacts snap ring fixing key plate. Install snap ring and remove tool.
6. Install camshaft lever nut.

INSTALLATION
Front

1. Apply suitable grease to inner face of slide pin boot.
2. Install slide pin boot to bracket.
3. Install bracket and attaching bolts.
4. Install shoe and lining assembly, ensure wear indicators are located on trailing edge of shoe assemblies during forward wheel rotation.

5. Install caliper assembly to bracket. Tighten attaching bolts to specifications.
6. Attach hose to caliper.
7. Install wheel and tire assembly, then lower vehicle.
8. Fill master cylinder to proper level and bleed brakes. **Before moving vehicle, pump brake pedal several times to be sure it is firm. Do not move vehicle until a firm pedal is obtained.**

Rear

1. Install cover, then connect parking brake cable to camshaft lever on caliper.
2. Install parking brake cable retaining clip, then the caliper onto carrier.
3. Install caliper pin bolts, then adjust parking brake cable as outlined under "Parking Brake Service."
4. Install brake hose mounting bolt into caliper.
5. Fill master cylinder to proper level and bleed brakes. **Before moving vehicle, pump brake pedal several times to be sure it is firm. Do not move vehicle until a firm pedal is obtained.**

PARKING BRAKE SERVICE
ADJUSTMENT
Swift

Parking brake lever should be adjusted so lever comes up 4–9 notches with 44 lbs. of pull applied, **Fig. 14.**

Adjust travel by loosening self locking nut, **Fig. 15.**

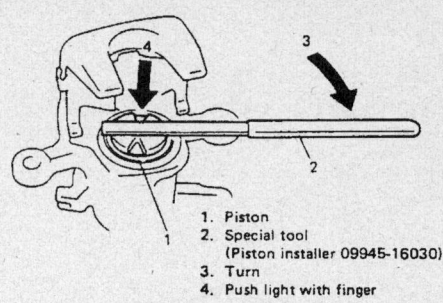

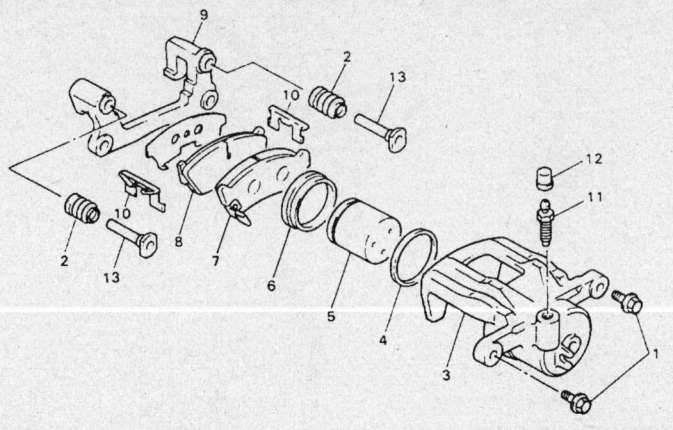

1. Caliper pin bolt
2. Boot
3. Disc brake caliper (Disc brake cylinder)
4. Piston seal
5. Disc brake piston
6. Cylinder boot
7. Disc brake inner pad
8. Disc brake outer pad
9. Brake caliper carrier
10. Pad spring
11. Bleeder plug
12. Bleeder plug cap
13. Caliper pin

SK4079100005000X

1. Piston
2. Special tool (Piston installer 09945-16030)
3. Turn
4. Push light with finger

SK4079100007000X

Fig. 5   Rear caliper piston adjustment. Swift

Fig. 4   Exploded view of front caliper assembly. Swift

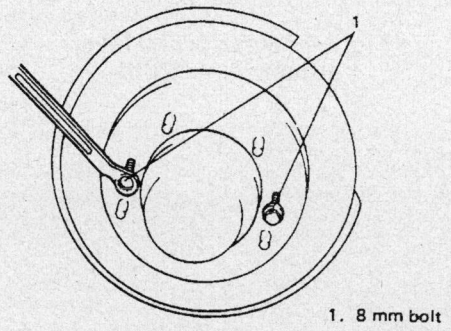

1. 8 mm bolt

SK4079100006000X

Fig. 6   Brake rotor removal

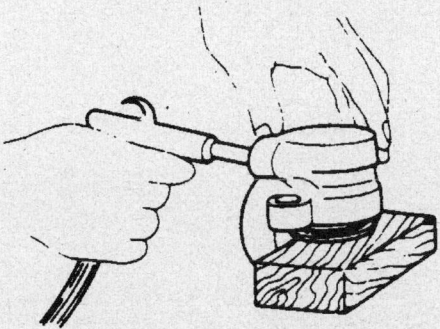

GC4079100034000X

Fig. 7   Caliper piston removal

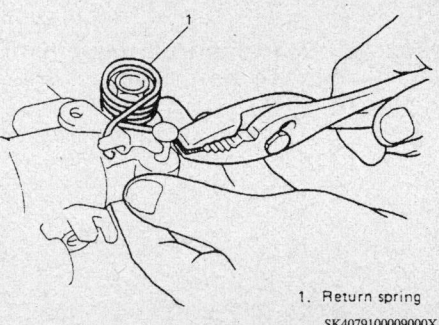

1. Return spring

SK4079100009000X

Fig. 8   Rear return spring removal. Swift

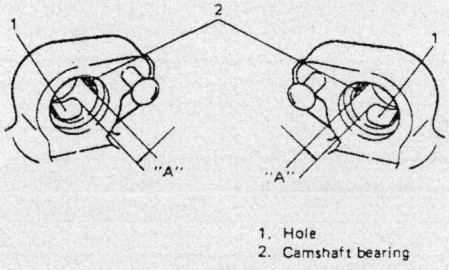

1. Hole
2. Camshaft bearing
"A": 8 mm (0.31 in.)

SK4079100010000X

Fig. 9   Rear camshaft bearing installation. Swift

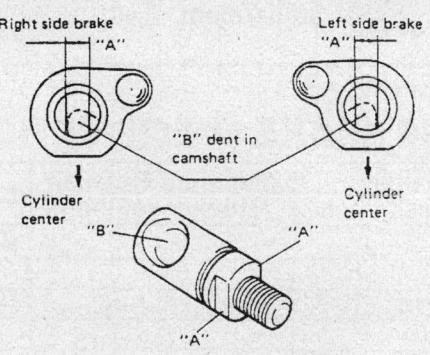

Right side brake   Left side brake
"A"   "A"

"B" dent in camshaft

Cylinder center   Cylinder center

SK4079100011000X

Fig. 10   Rear camshaft installation. Swift

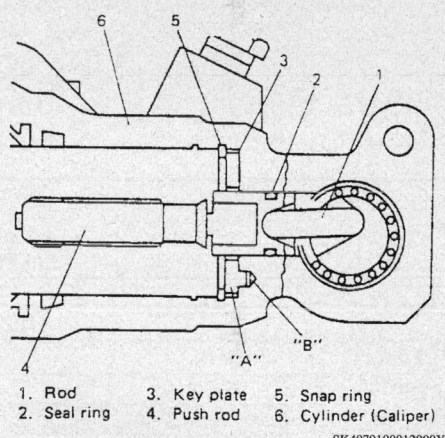

1. Rod   3. Key plate   5. Snap ring
2. Seal ring   4. Push rod   6. Cylinder (Caliper)

SK4079100012000X

Fig. 11   Rear pushrod assembly installation. Swift

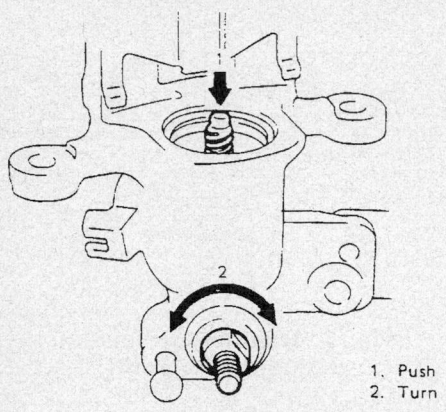

Fig. 12   Rear pushrod movement inspection. Swift

SK4079100013000X

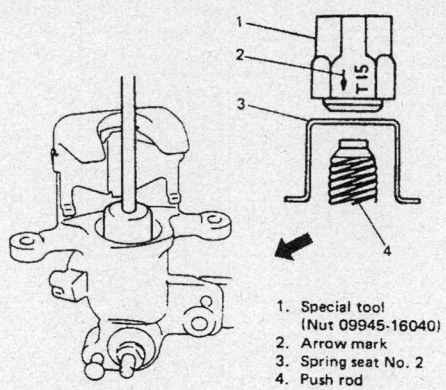

1. Special tool (Nut 09945-16040)
2. Arrow mark
3. Spring seat No. 2
4. Push rod

SK4079100014000X

Fig. 13   Rear coil spring assembly adjustment. Swift

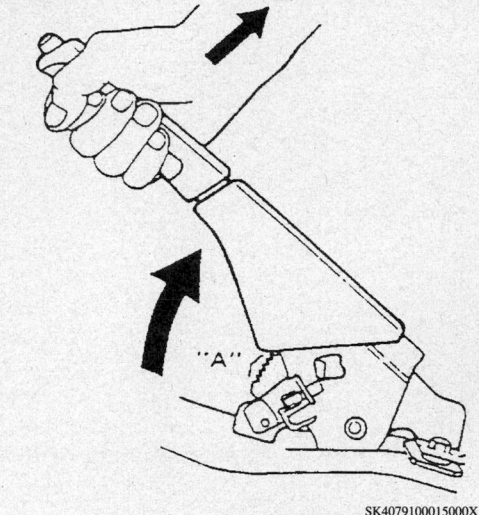

SK4079100015000X

Fig. 14   Rear brake lever adjustment. Swift

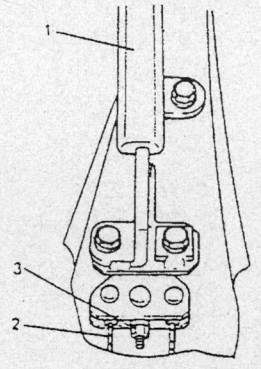

1. Parking brake lever
2. Brake cable
3. Self locking nut

SK4079100016000X

Fig. 15   Rear parking brake lever adjustment. Swift

DISC BRAKE SPECIFICATIONS

Year	Model	Nominal Thickness, Inch	Minimum Refinish Thickness, Inch	Lateral Runout (TIR)	Caliper Bore Diameter, Inch
FRONT					
1996–99	Esteem	0.590	0.240	0.0039	—
	Grand Vitara	.866	.787	.0060	—
	Sidekick	①	②	.0060	1.894
	Swift	.730	.650	.0039	—
	X-90	①	②	.0060	1.894
REAR					
1996–97	Swift	.394	.315	.0039	—

① — 2-door models, .394 inch; 4-door models, .670 inch.

② — 2-door models, .315 inch; 4-door models, .590 inch.

TIGHTENING SPECIFICATIONS

Year	Component	Torque/ Ft. Lbs.
ESTEEM		
1996–99	Brake Pipe Flare Nut	11
	Caliper Carrier Bolts	61
	Caliper Pin Bolt	19
	Flexible Hose Bolt	17
	Wheel Lug Nuts	69
GRAND VITARA		
1999	Brake Pipe Flare Nut	11
	Caliper Pin Bolt	23
	Flexible Hose Bolt	17
	Wheel Lug Nut	65
SIDEKICK & X-90		
1996–99	Bleeder Screw	7
	Brake Hose Bolt	17
	Brake Pipe Flare Nut	11
	Caliper Carrier Bolt	61
	Caliper Guide Pin	19
	Master Cylinder Nut	9
	Wheel Lug Nut	69
SWIFT		
1996–99	Caliper Carrier Bolts	29–43
	Caliper Hose	15–18
	Caliper Mounting Bolts	16–23
	Front Drive Shaft Nut	109–146
	Wheel Lug Nuts	37–58

Drum Brakes

INDEX

BRAKE SERVICE

BRAKE DRUM, REPLACE

Grand Vitara, Sidekick & X-90

1. Engage parking brake, then raise and support vehicle.
2. Remove wheels and brake drum nuts, then release parking brake lever.
3. Loosen parking brake cable locking nut, then lift rear part of brake lever cover to access brake cable.
4. Remove brake drum by fitting two 8 mm bolts into holes on drum and extracting drum off wheel hub.
5. Reverse procedure to install, noting the following:
   a. Tighten drum nuts to specification.
   b. Depress brake pedal five times to obtain proper drum to shoe clearance.
   c. Adjust parking brake cable as outlined under "Parking Brake, Adjust."

Swift

1. Raise and support vehicle, then remove wheel and spindle cap.
2. **On sedan models,** remove drum screws.
3. **On all models,** unstake and remove spindle nut and washer, then release parking brake lever.
4. Remove parking brake lever cover, then loosen parking brake cable locking nut.
5. To increase clearance between shoe and drum, proceed as follows:
   a. Remove backing plate plug.
   b. Insert screwdriver into plug hole till its tip contacts shoe hold-down spring, then push hold-down spring as shown, **Fig. 1.**
6. Using slide hammer and drum remover tools, pull off brake drum.
7. Reverse procedure to install, noting the following:
   a. Before installing drum, maximize brake shoe to drum clearance by pushing down on ratchet using a screwdriver.
   b. Put brake shoe hold-down spring back to its original position, **Fig. 2.**
   c. Tighten spindle nut to specification. Caulk spindle nut after tightening.
   d. Depress brake pedal five times to obtain proper drum to shoe clearance.
   e. Adjust parking brake cable as outlined under "Parking Brake, Adjust."

Esteem

1. Raise and support vehicle, then remove wheel.
2. Remove drum screws.
3. Release parking brake lever.
4. Remove parking brake lever cover, then loosen parking brake cable locking nut.
5. To increase clearance between shoe and drum, proceed as follows:

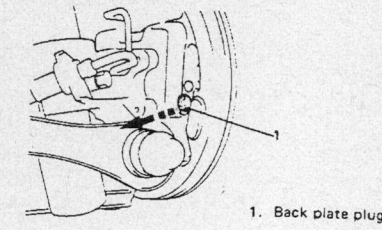

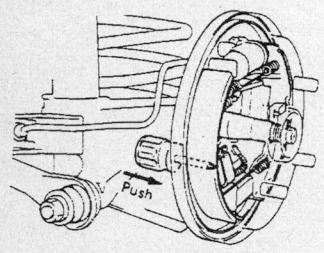

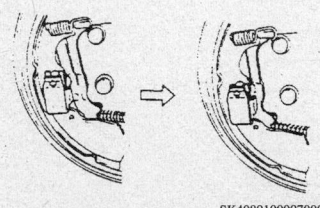

SK4089100007000X

Fig. 1 Brake shoe clearance adjustment. Esteem & Swift

a. Remove backing plate plug.
b. Insert screwdriver into plug hole till its tip contacts shoe hold-down spring, then push hold-down spring as shown, **Fig. 1.**
6. Remove brake drum by fitting two 8 mm bolts into holes on drum and extracting drum off wheel hub.
7. Reverse procedure to install, noting the following:
   a. Before installing drum, maximize brake shoe to drum clearance by pushing down on ratchet using a screwdriver.
   b. Put brake shoe hold-down spring back to its original position, **Fig. 2.**
   c. Tighten spindle nut to specification.
   d. Depress brake pedal five times to obtain proper drum to shoe clearance.
   e. Adjust parking brake cable as outlined under "Parking Brake, Adjust."

BRAKE SHOE, REPLACE
Sidekick & X-90

Refer to **Figs. 3** and **Fig. 4** during replacement procedure.

1. Remove drum as outlined under "Brake Drum, Replace."
2. Remove shoe hold-down springs, then disconnect parking brake cable from parking brake shoe lever.
3. Remove brake shoe assembly.
4. Remove brake strut rod and spring from brake shoes.
5. Remove parking brake shoe lever from shoe rim.
6. Reverse procedure to install.

Esteem & Swift

Refer to **Fig. 5,** during replacement procedure.
1. Remove drum as outlined under "Brake Drum, Replace."
2. Remove shoe hold-down springs, then disconnect parking brake cable from parking brake shoe lever.
3. Remove brake shoe assembly.
4. Remove brake strut rod and spring from brake shoes.
5. Remove parking brake shoe lever from shoe rim.
6. Reverse procedure to install.

WHEEL CYLINDER, REPLACE

Grand Vitara, Sidekick & X-90

1. Remove drum as outlined under "Brake Drum, Replace."
2. Remove brake shoes as outlined under "Brake Shoe, Replace."
3. Loosen brake pipe flare nut. **Fluid should not leak out of pipe or cylinder.**
4. Remove wheel cylinder mounting bolts, then disconnect brake pipe from wheel cylinder.
5. Reverse procedure to install, noting the following:
   a. Apply water tight sealant to wheel cylinder and backing plate mating surface.
   b. Tighten wheel cylinder mounting bolts and brake pipe flare nut to specification.
   c. Bleed brake system.

Esteem & Swift

1. Remove drum as outlined under "Brake Drum, Replace."

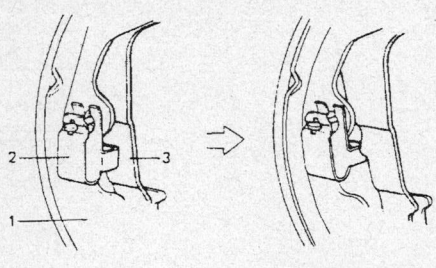

1. Brake shoe
2. Shoe hold down spring
3. Parking brake shoe lever

SK4089100008000X

Fig. 2 Hold-down spring location. Esteem & Swift

2. Remove brake shoes as outlined under "Brake Shoe, Replace."
3. Loosen brake pipe flare nut. **Fluid should not leak out of pipe or cylinder.**
4. Remove wheel cylinder mounting bolts, then disconnect brake pipe from wheel cylinder.
5. Reverse procedure to install, noting the following:
   a. Tighten wheel cylinder mounting bolts and brake pipe to specification.
   b. Bleed brake system.

ADJUSTMENTS
PARKING BRAKE

1. Parking brake lever should be adjusted as follows:
   a. **On Esteem models,** 3–5 notches.
   b. **On Grand Vitara, Sidekick and X-90 models,** 6–8 notches.
   c. **On Swift models,** 4–9 notches.
2. **On all models,** lever should be adjusted with 44 lbs. of pull applied, **Fig. 6.**
3. Adjust travel by loosening self locking nut, **Fig. 7.**

SERVICE BRAKE

These brakes are self-adjusting, but do require adjustment for proper drum to shoe clearance when brake shoe has been replaced or brake drum has been removed.

Adjustment is automatically accomplished by depressing brake pedal 5 times with approximately 66 lbs. force on brake pedal.

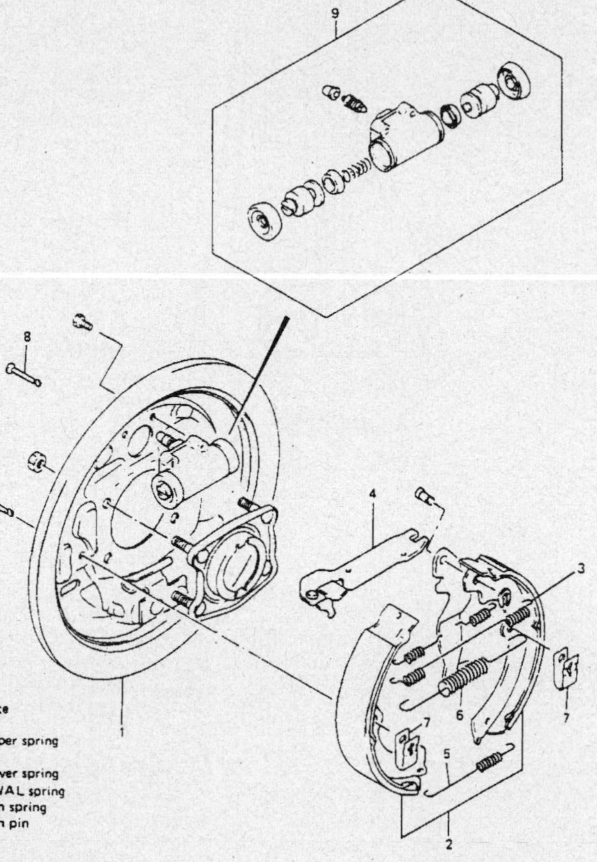

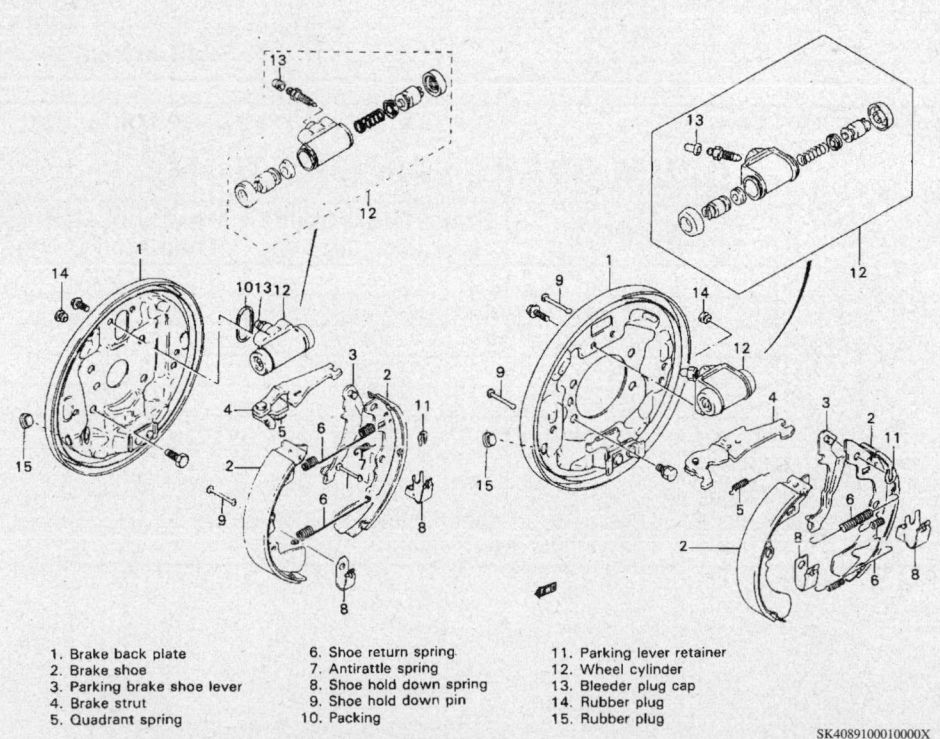

1. Brake back plate
2. Brake shoe
3. Shoe return upper spring
4. Brake strut rod
5. Shoe return lower spring
6. Shoe return RWAL spring
7. Shoe hold down spring
8. Shoe hold down pin
9. Wheel cylinder

SK4089100009000X

Fig. 3 Exploded view of brake assembly. Sidekick & X-90

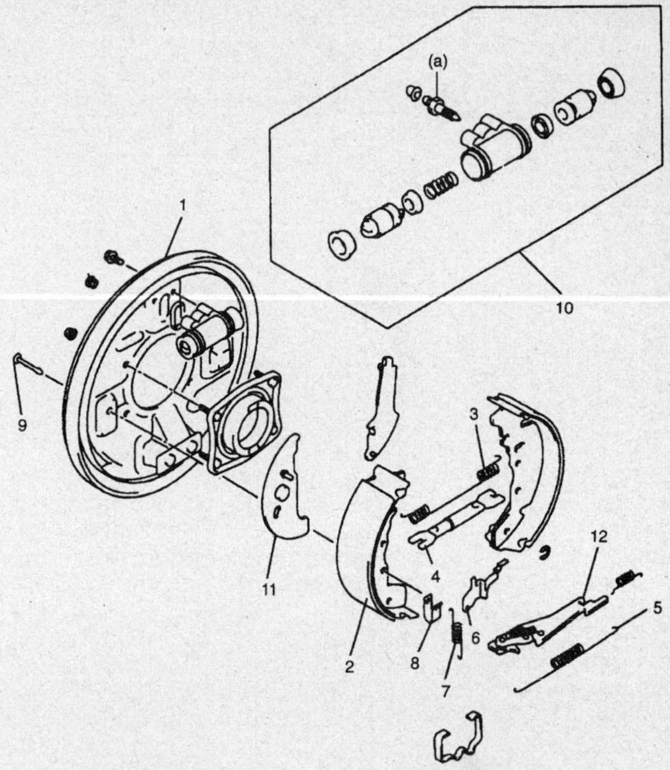

1. Brake back plate
2. Brake shoe
3. Shoe return upper spring
4. Adjuster
5. Shoe return lower spring
6. Adjuster lever
7. Adjuster spring
8. Shoe hold down spring
9. Shoe hold down pin
10. Wheel cylinder
11. Link
12. Brake strut

SK4089900014000X

Fig. 4 Exploded view of brake assembly. Grand Vitara

1. Brake back plate
2. Brake shoe
3. Parking brake shoe lever
4. Brake strut
5. Quadrant spring
6. Shoe return spring
7. Antirattle spring
8. Shoe hold down spring
9. Shoe hold down pin
10. Packing
11. Parking lever retainer
12. Wheel cylinder
13. Bleeder plug cap
14. Rubber plug
15. Rubber plug

SK4089100010000X

Fig. 5 Exploded view of brake assembly. Esteem & Swift

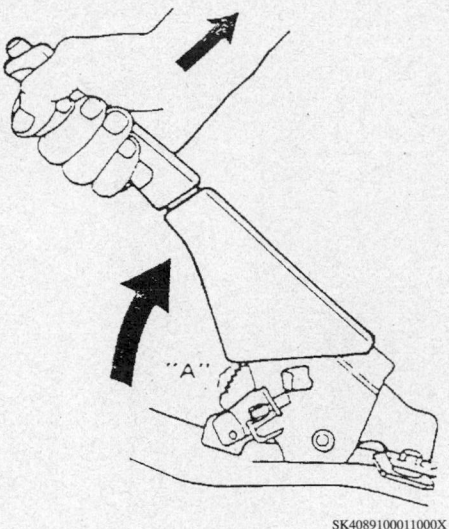

Fig. 6 Parking brake lever
         adjustment

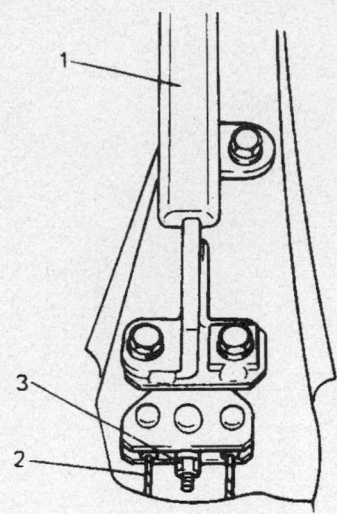

1. Parking brake lever
2. Brake cable
3. Self locking nut

SK4089100013000X

Fig. 7 Parking brake lever
         adjustment. Esteem, Sidekick,
         Swift & X-90

DRUM BRAKE SPECIFICATIONS

Year	Model	Brake Drum Inside Diameter, Inches	Maximum Refinish Diameter, Inches
1996–99	Esteem	7.87	7.95
	Grand Vitara	8.66	8.74
	Sidekick	③	④
	Swift①	7.09	7.16
	Swift②	7.87	7.95
	X-90	8.66	8.74

① — Hatchback model.
② — Sedan model.
③ — 2-door models, 8.66 inches; 4-door models, 10.00 inches.
④ — 2-door models, 8.74 inches; 4-door models, 10.07 inches.

TIGHTENING SPECIFICATIONS

Year	Component	Torque/Ft. Lbs.
GRAND VITARA, SIDEKICK & X-90		
1996–99	Backing Plate Nut	17
	Bleeder Screw	7–9
	Booster Nut	9.5
	Brake Pipe Flare Nut	11.5
	Brake Hose Bolt (Samurai)	15–28
	Brake Hose Bolt (Sidekick & X-90)	15–18
	Brake Pedal Shaft Nut	14–20
	Master Cylinder Nut	9.5
	Rear Drum Nut	37–57
	Wheel Cylinder Mounting Bolt	9–12
	Wheel Lug Nut	69
SWIFT		
1996–97	Backing Plate Mounting Bolt (Drum)	14-20
	Bleeder Screw	6–7
	Booster Nut	9–11
	Brake Hose Bolt	15–18
	Brake Pedal Shaft Nut	14–20
	Front Driveshaft Nut	109–144
	Master Cylinder Bolt	9–11
	Rear Spindle Nut	109–144
	Wheel Cylinder Mounting Bolt	8–9
ESTEEM		
1996–97	Backing Plate Mounting Bolt (Drum)	17
	Bleeder Screw	6
	Booster Nut	9.5
	Brake Hose Bolt	17
	Brake Pedal Shaft Nut	17
	Master Cylinder Nut	9.5
	Wheel Cylinder Mounting Bolt	9
	Wheel Lug Nut	61.5

DRUM BRAKES

SUZUKI

Hydraulic Brake Systems

INDEX

DESCRIPTION

When the brake pedal is depressed, a vacuum builds up in the booster which amplifies the pedal force, pressing on the piston in the master cylinder. The piston raises the hydraulic pressure in the cylinder. This hydraulic pressure is then applied to each respective brake caliper and wheel cylinder and acts to press the brake pads and shoes against the rotating discs and drums. The resulting friction converts the rotational energy to thermal energy, stopping the vehicle.

TROUBLESHOOTING

LOW BRAKING FORCE

1. Fluid leakage from brake lines and/or hoses.
2. Air in brake system.
3. Malfunctioning wheel cylinder and/or caliper assembly.

BRAKE PULL

1. Malfunctioning wheel cylinder and/or caliper assembly.
2. Loose calipers.
3. Restricted brake line or hose.

EXCESSIVE PEDAL TRAVEL

1. Partial brake system failure.
2. Insufficient fluid in master cylinder reservoirs.
3. Air in system.

DRAGGING BRAKES

1. Master cylinder pistons not returning correctly.
2. Restricted brake line or hose.
3. Wheel cylinder or caliper piston sticking.

BRAKE WARNING LIGHT ON OR FLASHING, AFTER ENGINE START

1. Insufficient fluid in master cylinder reservoirs.
2. Fluid leakage from brake lines and/or hoses.

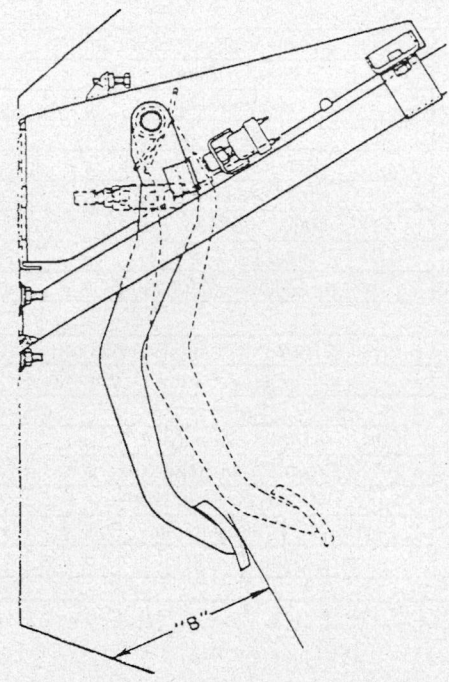

SK40991000006000X

Fig. 1 Pedal arm to wall clearance measurement

BRAKE WARNING LIGHT ON, w/BRAKE PEDAL APPLIED

1. Insufficient fluid in master cylinder reservoirs.
2. Fluid leakage from brake lines and/or hoses.

DIAGNOSIS & TESTING

ROAD TEST

Brakes should be tested on dry, clean, smooth and reasonable level roadway which is not crowned. Road test brakes by making brake applications with both light and heavy pedal forces at various speeds to determine if car stops evenly and effectively.

Also road test vehicle to see if it pulls to one side without brake application. If it does, check tire pressure, front end alignment and front suspension attachments for looseness.

BRAKE FLUID LEAKAGE INSPECTION

Check master cylinder fluid levels. While a slight drop in reservoir level does result from normal lining wear, an abnormally low level indicates a leak in the system. In such a case, check the entire brake system for leakage. If even a slight evidence of leakage is noted, the cause should be corrected or defective parts should be replaced.

SUBSTANDARD OR CONTAMINATED BRAKE FLUID

Improper brake fluid, mineral oil or water in the fluid may cause the brake fluid to boil or the rubber components in the hydraulic system to deteriorate.

If deterioration of rubber is evident, disassemble all hydraulic parts and wash with alcohol. Dry these parts with compressed air before assemble to keep alcohol out of the system. Replace all rubber parts in the system, including hoses. Also, when working on the brake mechanisms, check for fluid on linings. If excessive fluid is found, replace pads/shoes.

If master cylinder piston seals are satisfactory, check for leakage or excessive heat conditions. If condition is not found, drain fluid, flush with brake fluid, refill and bleed system.

The system must be flushed if there is any doubt as to the grade of fluid in the system or if fluid has been used which contained parts that have been subjected to contaminated fluid.

ADJUSTMENTS

BRAKE PEDAL HEIGHT

The brake pedal should be at the same height as clutch pedal. Ensure distance between brake booster mounting surface (with gasket) and pushrod clevis pin hole is as follows:

1. **On Grand Vitara models,** 7.60–7.99 inches (193–203 mm)

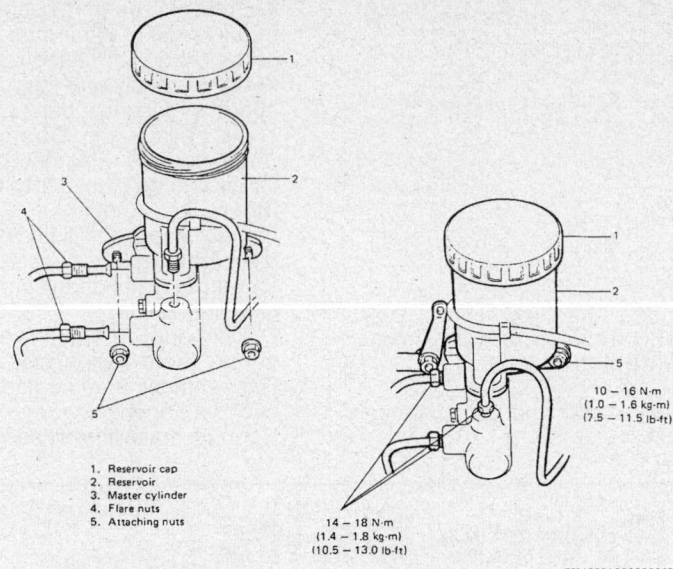

Fig. 1

1. Reservoir cap
2. Reservoir
3. Master cylinder
4. Flare nuts
5. Attaching nuts

10 – 16 N·m
(1.0 – 1.6 kg·m)
(7.5 – 11.5 lb-ft)

14 – 18 N·m
(1.4 – 1.8 kg·m)
(10.5 – 13.0 lb-ft)

SK4099100003000X

Fig. 2   Reservoir connector screw location

2. **On Sidekick and X-90 models,** 6.60–6.64 inches (167.6–168.6 mm).
3. **On Esteem and Swift models,** 4.51–4.54 inches (114.5–115.5 mm).

BRAKE PEDAL TRAVEL INSPECTION

1. Start engine, then depress brake pedal a few times.
2. Apply approximately 66 lbs. load to brake pedal and measure pedal arm to wall clearance, "B," **Fig. 1.**
3. Clearance should not exceed the following:
   a. **On Sidekick and X-90 models,** 3.15 inches (80 mm).
   b. **On Esteem models,** 3.54 inches (90 mm).
   c. **On Swift models,** 2.36 inches (60 mm).
4. **On all models,** possible causes for a low pedal are:
   a. Worn rear brake shoes.
   b. Brake lines need bleeding.
   c. Booster pushrod out of alignment.
   d. Rear brake shoes malfunctioning.

COMPONENT REPLACEMENT

MASTER CYLINDER

1. Clean any dirt from around reservoir cap. Remove cap, then drain brake fluid into appropriate container.
2. Remove reservoir connector screw, **Fig. 2,** then the reservoir.
3. Disconnect brake lines from master cylinder. **Do not allow brake fluid to get on painted surfaces.**
4. Remove master cylinder attaching bolts, then the master cylinder.
5. Adjust clearance of booster piston rod to master cylinder piston as follows:
   a. Push piston rod several times to ensure reaction disc is in place.
   b. Measure with gasket in place on

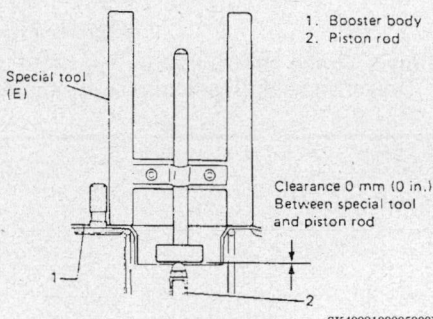

Special tool
(E)

1. Booster body
2. Piston rod

Clearance 0 mm (0 in.)
Between special tool
and piston rod

SK4099100005000X

Fig. 4   Piston rod length adjustment

master cylinder and booster at atmospheric pressure.
   c. Set measuring tool No. 09950-98210 or equivalent, on master cylinder and push pin until it contacts piston, **Fig. 3.**
   d. Turn tool upside down and place on booster, **Fig. 4.** Adjust booster piston rod length until rod end contacts piston head.
6. When adjusted, if negative pressure is applied to booster with engine at idle, piston to piston rod clearance should be as follows:
   a. **On Sidekick and X-90 models less ABS,** .010–.020 inch (.25–.50 mm)
   b. **On Sidekick and X-90 models with ABS,** .006–.014 inch (.14–.35 mm)
   c. **On Swift models,** .004–.013 inch (.10–.35 mm)
   d. **On Esteem models less ABS,** .010–.020 inch (.25–.50 mm)
   e. **On Esteem models with ABS,** 0 inch (0 mm)
7. **On all models,** install reservoir on master cylinder, then the reservoir connector screw.
8. Install master cylinder on studs, then the mounting nuts.
9. Connect hydraulic lines.

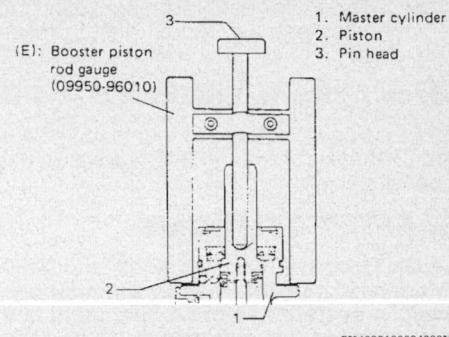

(E): Booster piston rod gauge (09950-96010)

1. Master cylinder
2. Piston
3. Pin head

SK4099100004000X

Fig. 3   Piston installation

10. Fill reservoir with brake fluid.
11. Check brake pedal height and pedal travel as outlined under "Adjustments."

COMPONENT SERVICE

MASTER CYLINDER OVERHAUL

1. Remove master cylinder as outlined under "Master Cylinder, Replace."
2. Remove circlip, then the primary piston.
3. Remove piston stopper bolt, then using compressed air, remove secondary piston. Blow compressed air into hole where stopper bolt was removed.
4. Reverse procedure to assemble.

BRAKE SYSTEM BLEED

Brake fluid is extremely damaging to paint. If fluid should accidentally touch painted surface, immediately wipe fluid from paint and clean painted surface.

SYSTEM BLEED

Esteem & Swift

The hydraulic lines of the brake system are based on a diagonal split system. When a brake line or hose is disconnected, bleeding operation must be performed at both ends of the line disconnected.

1. Fill master cylinder reservoir. Reservoir should be kept at least half full during bleeding operation.
2. Remove bleeder plug cap, then attach vinyl tube to bleeder plug of component to be bled. Insert other end of tube into suitable container.
3. Depress brake pedal several times, then while holding pedal depressed, loosen bleeder plug ½ turn.
4. When fluid pressure in cylinder is almost depleted, retighten bleeder plug.
5. Repeat steps 3 and 4, until there are no more air bubbles in hydraulic line.
6. When bubbles stop, depress and hold brake pedal, then tighten bleeder plug.
7. Attach bleeder cap.
8. After completing bleeding operation, apply fluid pressure to hydraulic system and check for leakage.
9. Fill master cylinder reservoir up to specified level.

SUZUKI

10. Check brake pedal for sponginess. If pedal is spongy, repeat entire procedure.

Grand Vitara, Sidekick & X-90

Bleeding is required at four places; both front wheels, pressure limit valve and left rear wheel cylinder, **Fig. 5.**

MASTER CYLINDER

On Grand Vitara, Sidekick and X-90 models, when the master cylinder hydraulic system has been opened in any way, the master cylinder must be bled before system bleeding can be done.

1. Fill master cylinder reservoir with brake fluid. Wait for at least 1 minute before proceeding.

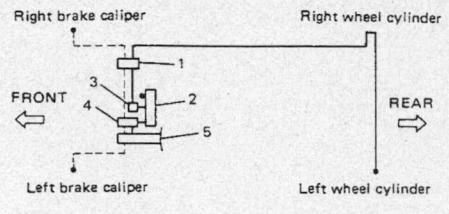

1. 4-way joint
2. Pressure limit valve
3. 2-way joint
4. P & Differential valve
5. Master cylinder
   : air bleeding point

SK4099100002000X

Fig. 5   Brake system bleed points. Sidekick & X-90

2. Disconnect brake line from primary (rear brakes) side.

3. With discharge port opened, depress brake pedal gradually. With discharge port closed with finger, release brake pedal gradually and keep it closed for about 5 seconds before depressing brake pedal again. **Do not lift finger off port while releasing brake pedal as air will be drawn into master cylinder.**

4. Repeat step 3 until liquid comes out of discharge port. Repeat step 3 at least four more times, then connect primary side brake pipe.

5. Disconnect two brake lines from secondary (front brakes) side.

6. Repeat steps 3 and 4 keeping fingers over both open ports.

7. Connect brake lines to secondary side.

Power Brake Units

INDEX

DESCRIPTION

When the brake pedal is depressed, a vacuum builds up in the booster which amplifies the pedal force, pressing on the piston in the master cylinder. The piston raises the hydraulic pressure in the cylinder. This hydraulic pressure is then applied to each respective brake cylinder and acts to press the brake pads and shoes against the rotating rotor discs and rotors. The resulting friction converts the rotational energy to thermal energy, stopping the vehicle.

POWER BRAKE UNIT SERVICE

POWER BRAKE UNIT, REPLACE

1. Remove master cylinder from booster as outlined under " Master Cylinder, Replace," in the "Hydraulic Brakes " section.
2. Disconnect pushrod clevis from brake pedal arm.
3. Disconnect vacuum hose from booster.
4. Remove booster attaching nuts, then the booster assembly.
5. Reverse procedure to install, then ensure brake pedal height and pedal travel is correct as outlined under "Brake Pedal Height, Adjust," and "Brake Pedal Travel Check" in the "Hydraulic Brakes" section.

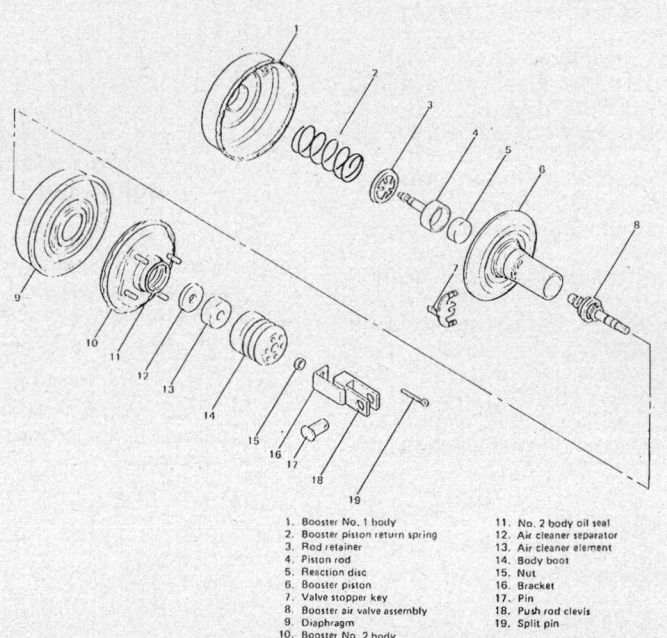

1. Booster No. 1 body
2. Booster piston return spring
3. Rod retainer
4. Piston rod
5. Reaction disc
6. Booster piston
7. Valve stopper key
8. Booster air valve assembly
9. Diaphragm
10. Booster No. 2 body
11. No. 2 body oil seal
12. Air cleaner separator
13. Air cleaner element
14. Body boot
15. Nut
16. Bracket
17. Pin
18. Push rod clevis
19. Split pin

SK4039100003000X

Fig. 1   Exploded view of booster assembly. Swift

BRAKE BOOSTER OVERHAUL

Swift

Refer to **Fig.1,** when performing this procedure.

1. Remove piston rod from booster, then the pushrod clevis and nut.
2. Set booster in booster overhaul set, No. 09950-88210 or equivalent, **Fig. 2.**
3. Tighten tool bolt clockwise until No. 1 body projecting part and No. 2 body depressed part fit each other, **Fig. 3.** Mark both body parts.

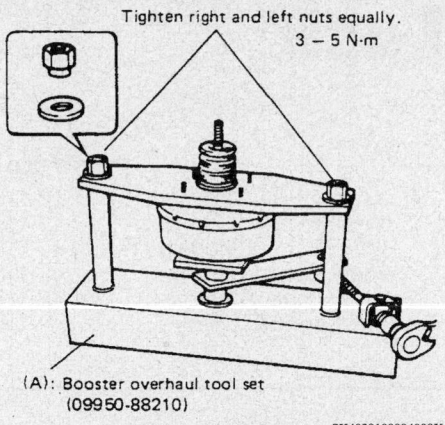

Fig. 2 Positioning booster in booster overhaul set. Swift

(A): Booster overhaul tool set (09950-88210)

SK4039100004000X

Tighten right and left nuts equally. 3 – 5 N·m

4. Remove booster from tool, then separate No. 1 and No. 2 bodies. **Hold both bodies carefully to prevent either** body from jumping off by spring force.

5. Remove piston return spring.

6. From No. 2 body, remove boot, air cleaner elements and air cleaner separator.

7. While compressing air valve spring, remove valve stopper key, then the booster air valve assembly. **Air valve assembly cannot be disassembled.**

8. **On Swift models,** remove diaphragm from booster piston.

9. **On all models,** remove reaction disc from booster piston.

10. **On Swift models,** using oil seal replacers, No. 09951-16020 and No. 09951-18210 or equivalent, remove oil seal from No. 2 body.

11. **On all models,** reverse procedure to assemble. Ensure brake pedal height and pedal travel are correct as outlined under "Brake Pedal Height, Adjust," and "Brake Pedal Travel Check" in the "Hydraulic Brakes" section.

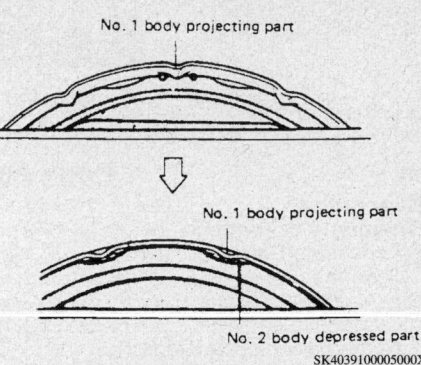

SK4039100005000X

Fig. 3 Booster body depression alignment. Swift

Esteem, Grand Vitara, Sidekick & X-90

The booster unit is not serviceable and should be replaced as a unit.

Anti-Lock Brakes

NOTE: Wire Code Identification & Symbol Identification Located In The Front Of This Manual May Be Used As An Aid When Using Wiring Circuits Found In This Section.

NOTE: On Air Bag Equipped Models, Refer To "Air Bag System Precautions" Located In The Front Of This Manual For System Disarming & Arming Procedures.

TABLE OF CONTENTS

Rear Wheel Anti-Lock

INDEX

PRECAUTIONS

AIR BAG SYSTEMS

Refer to "Air Bag System Precautions" in the front of this manual for system disarming and arming procedures.

BATTERY GROUND CABLE

Prior to service, disconnect battery ground cable and isolate as required.

DESCRIPTION

On Sidekick models, the Rear Wheel Anti-Lock (RWAL) system is controlled by the rear hydraulic brake line pressure which is regulated by a pressure limit valve. The pressure limit valve is located under the master cylinder and consists of two valves. One is a dump valve which releases pressure into an accumulator and the other is an isolation valve which holds rear brake pressure. The valve is controlled by a microcomputer which is a part of the RWAL control module. The RWAL control module is installed near the fuse box located under the LH side of the instrument panel.

The RWAL control module operates by receiving signals from the speed sensor in the rear differential and the stop light switch. It is designed to make the pressure limit valve (dump/isolation valve) operate when the brake pedal is depressed for hard braking.

The RWAL control module conducts system check and self-check at engine start and during normal driving. The main components are monitored and when any faulty condition is detected, the RWAL operation is stopped and the brake fluid warning light illuminates.

TROUBLESHOOTING

Refer to **Fig. 1,** for troubleshooting flow charts, **Fig. 2,** for wiring diagram and **Fig. 3,** for connector pin identification.

DIAGNOSIS & TESTING

ACCESSING DIAGNOSTIC TROUBLE CODES

Release parking brake. Momentarily jump terminal 5 of monitor coupler to terminal 3, **Fig. 4.** Connect jumper for longer than 2 seconds. Brake warning light should start flashing.

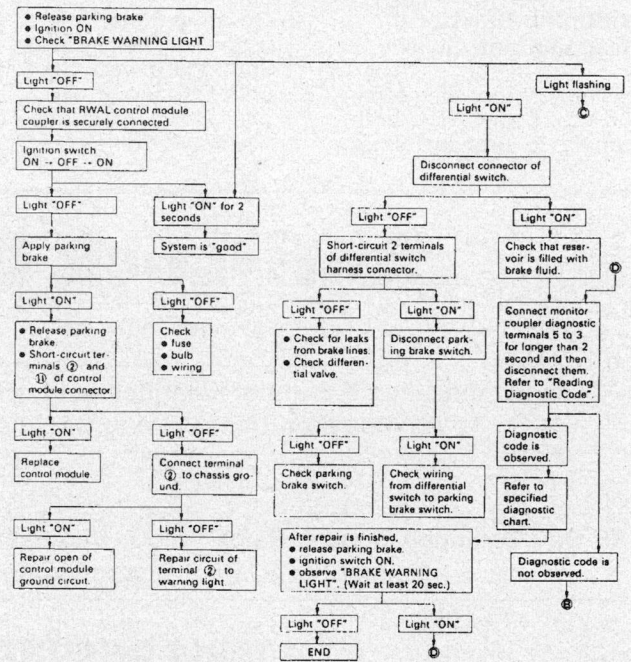

Fig. 1   Troubleshooting chart (Part 1 of 3)

SK4029100001010X

DIAGNOSTIC TROUBLE CODE INTERPRETATION

Each code consists of short flashes and a final long flash. Flashing is repeated until ignition key is turned Off.

If engine is turned Off before code is read, the code will be lost. There may be cases where the code will reappear when the engine is restarted. But in other cases it may be necessary to drive the vehicle to reproduce the same problem.

Even when more than one system fault exists, only the smallest diagnostic code is flashed out.

Refer to **Fig. 5,** for diagnostic code table.

DIAGNOSTIC TESTS

Refer to **Figs. 6 through 16,** for diagnostic code charts.

COMPONENT TESTING

RWAL System Electric Circuit Check

The electrical circuit of the RWAL system

can be checked by measuring voltage of the RWAL control module connector terminals. **RWAL control module cannot be checked by itself. It is strictly prohibited to connect voltmeter or ohmmeter to RWAL control module with harness connector disconnected from it.**

Battery must be fully charged to perform this test as terminal voltage will be directly affected by battery voltage.

1. Remove RWAL control module from body.
2. Connect RWAL control module harness coupler to RWAL ECM.
3. Ensure voltage at each terminal of coupler connection is as specified, **Fig. 17.**

Wheel Speed Sensor

1. Raise and support vehicle, then remove sensor cover.
2. Disconnect coupler.
3. Using an ohmmeter, measure resistance between sensor terminals and between terminal and sensor body.
   a. Resistance between terminals

:

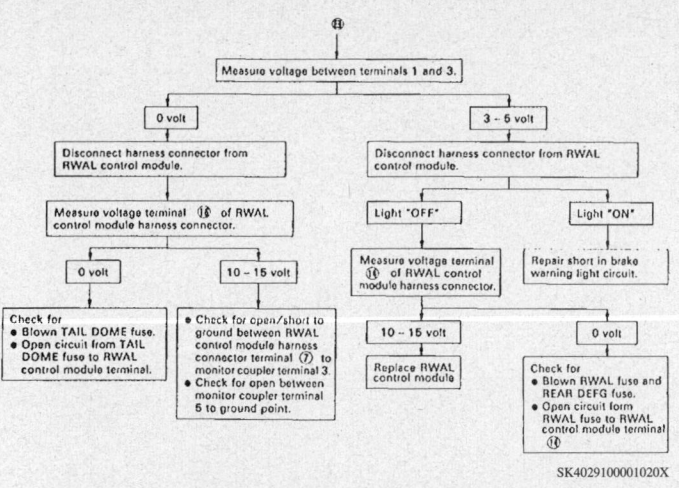

Fig. 1 Troubleshooting chart (Part 2 of 3)

SK4029100001020X

SK4029100001030X

Fig. 1 Troubleshooting chart (Part 3 of 3)

should be 1282.5–1567.5 ohms at 77°F.

b. Resistance between terminal and sensor body should be 100,000 ohms.

4. Replace wheel sensor if resistance is not as specified.

4WD Switch

1. Turn ignition switch Off, then raise and support vehicle.
2. Disconnect 4WD switch connector, then connect ohmmeter to connector terminals.
3. Ensure 4WD switch turns On at only 4WD (4H and 4L) position.
4. Replace 4WD switch if not as specified.

Stop Light Switch

1. Disconnect coupler from stop light switch.
2. Connect ohmmeter to switch terminals, then check for continuity, **Fig. 18.**
3. With brake pedal released no continuity should exist.
4. With brake pedal applied continuity should exist.
5. Replace switch if not as specified.

RWAL Relay

1. Remove monitor coupler bracket.
2. Disconnect yellow coupler from RWAL relay, then remove RWAL relay from its bracket.
3. Measure resistance between terminals A and B, then terminals C and D, **Fig. 19.**
4. Resistance between terminals A and B should be infinity.
5. Resistance between terminals C and D should be 90–110 ohms.
6. If resistance is as specified, proceed to step 7. If resistance is not as specified, replace relay.
7. Measure continuity between terminals A and B when battery is connected to terminals C and D, **Fig. 20.**
8. Replace relay if not as specified.

Pressure Limit (Isolation/Dump) Valve

The pressure limit valve is not serviceable. It must be replaced as an assembly if test results are not satisfactory.

1. Turn ignition switch Off, then disconnect coupler from pressure limit valve.
2. Measure resistance between terminals as shown, **Figs. 21 and 22.**
3. Resistance should be as shown, **Fig. 21.**
4. If resistance is not as specified, replace valve.

SYSTEM SERVICE

SERVICE PRECAUTIONS

Before performing any repairs on the ABS system, note the following precautions:

1. If any welding work is to be done on the vehicle using and arc welder, the EBCM and hydraulic modulator connectors should be disconnected.
2. Hydraulic modulator and EBCM connectors should never be disconnected when the ignition switch is on.
3. Do not use a fast charger to charge battery when battery is connected. Always disconnect battery from system before using a fast charger. **Never disconnect battery from system with engine running.**
4. Always note routing, position and mounting of electrical components, wiring and connectors of the ABS system.
5. Many components of the ABS system are non-serviceable and must be replaced as assemblies. **Do not disassemble any component which is designated non-serviceable.**
6. After any component of the ABS system has been replaced it will be necessary to check the system. Refer to "Diagnosis & Testing."

Brake System Bleed

Bleed brakes as outlined in "Hydraulic Brake System."

Component Replacement

RWAL CONTROL MODULE

1. Remove left side radio speaker from instrument panel.
2. Remove engine ECM with cover, bracket and fuse box from steering column holder.
3. Disconnect coupler from RWAL control module, then remove RWAL control module from dash panel.
4. Reverse procedure to install.

WHEEL SPEED SENSOR

1. Turn ignition switch Off, then remove sensor cover.
2. Disconnect coupler from sensor, then remove sensor from differential carrier.
3. Reverse procedure to install, noting the following:
   a. Check O-ring for damage, replace as necessary.
   b. Ensure sensor tooth is free from any metal particles.
   c. Coat O-ring with thin film of differential oil.

4WD SWITCH

1. Turn ignition switch Off, then raise and support vehicle.
2. Unclamp 4WD switch wiring, then disconnect switch coupler.
3. Lower vehicle, then remove boot cover of transfer gear shift lever from floor panel.
4. Remove 4WD switch.
5. Reverse procedure to install.

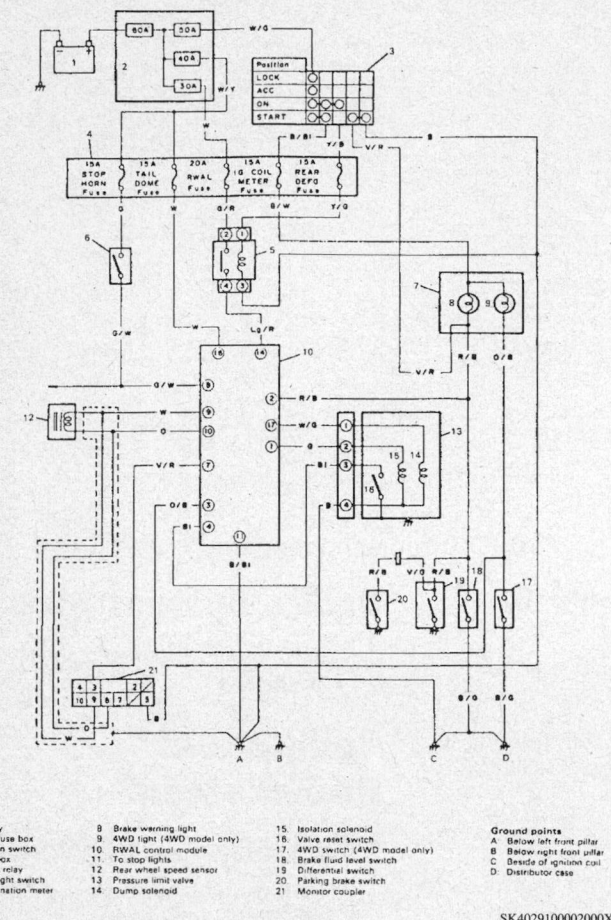

Fig. 2   RWAL wiring diagram

1. Battery
2. Main fuse box
3. Ignition switch
4. Fuse box
5. RWAL relay
6. Stop light switch
7. Combination meter
8. Brake warning light
9. 4WD light (4WD model only)
10. RWAL control module
11. To stop lights
12. Rear wheel speed sensor
13. Pressure limit valve
14. Dump solenoid
15. Isolation solenoid
16. Valve reset switch
17. 4WD switch (4WD model only)
18. Brake fluid level switch
19. Differential switch
20. Parking brake switch
21. Monitor coupler

Ground points
A. Below left front pillar
B. Below right front pillar
C. Beside of ignition coil
D. Distributor case

SK4029100002000X

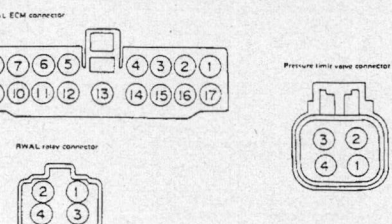

Fig. 3   Connector pin identification

SK4029100003000X

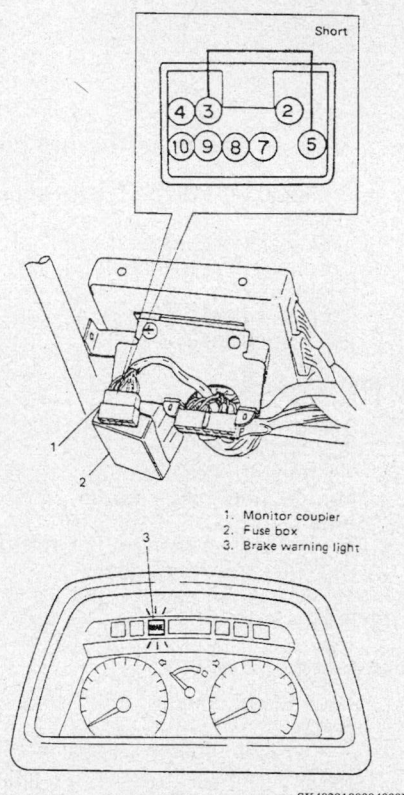

1. Monitor coupler
2. Fuse box
3. Brake warning light

SK4029100004000X

Fig. 4   Accessing diagnostic trouble code

DIAGNOSTIC CHART INDEX

Code	Description	Page No.	Fig. No.
—	Diagnostic Code Table	42-117	5
Code 2	Open Isolation Solenoid Circuit	42-117	6
Code 3	Open Dump Solenoid Circuit	42-117	7
Code 4	Valve Rest Switch Closed	42-117	8
Code 5	System Dumps Too Many Times	42-118	9
Code 6	Rear Speed Sensor Signal Change Rapidly	42-118	10
Code 7	Shorted Isolation Solenoid Circuit	42-119	11
Code 8	Shorted Dump Solenoid Circuit	42-119	12
Code 9	Open Rear Wheel Speed Circuit	42-119	13
Code 10	Stop Light Switch Remains On	42-119	14
Code 11	Shorted Rear Wheel Speed Sensor Circuit	42-120	15
Code 13	RWAL ECM Malfunction	42-120	16

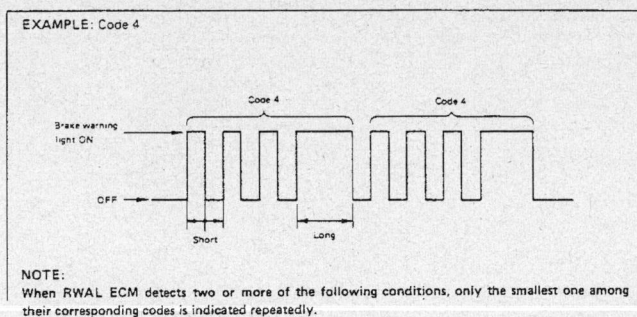

NOTE:
When RWAL ECM detects two or more of the following conditions, only the smallest one among their corresponding codes is indicated repeatedly.

DIAGNOSTIC CODE NO.	CONDITION	ACTION TO TAKE
2	Open isolation solenoid circuit	
3	Open dump solenoid circuit	
4	Valve reset switch closed	
5	System dumps too many times (Condition occurs when brake is applied during driving.)	Diagnose according to diagnosis procedure for each code.
6	Rear wheel speed sensor signal changed rapidly (Condition only occurs while driving.)	
7	Shorted isolation solenoid circuit	
8	Shorted dump solenoid circuit	
9	Open rear wheel speed sensor circuit	
10	Stop light switch remains ON	
11	Shorted rear wheel speed sensor circuit	
13	RWAL ECM malfunction	

SK4029100005000X

Fig. 5 Diagnostic trouble code table

DIAGNOSTIC CODE 2
Open isolation solenoid circuit

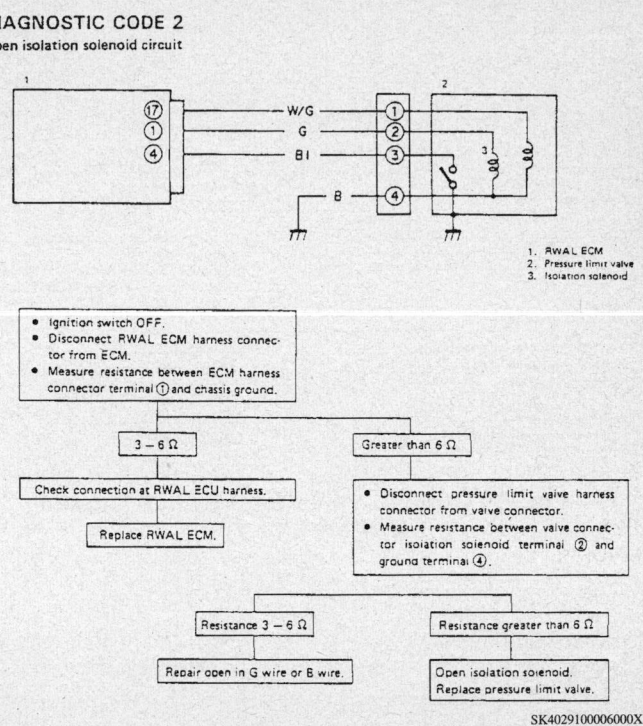

SK4029100006000X

Fig. 6 Code 2: Open Isolation Solenoid Circuit

DIAGNOSTIC CODE 3
Open dump solenoid circuit

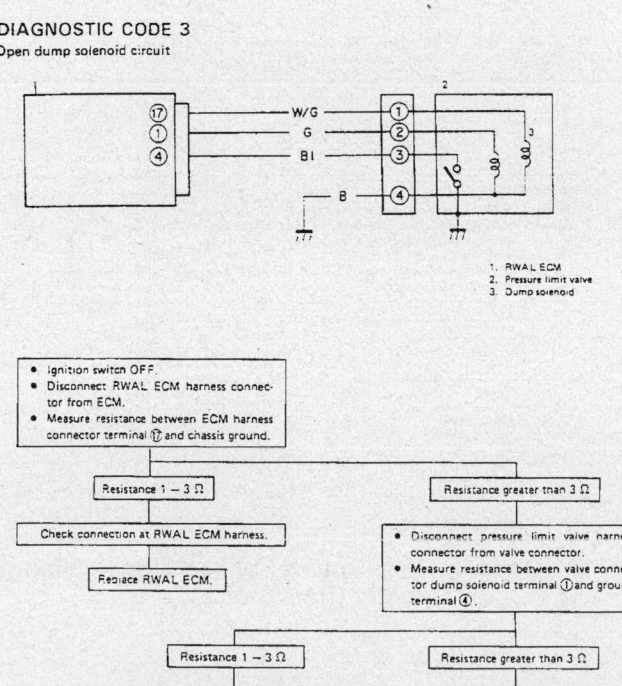

SK4029100007000X

Fig. 7 Code 3: Open Dump Solenoid Circuit

DIAGNOSTIC CODE 4
Valve reset switch closed

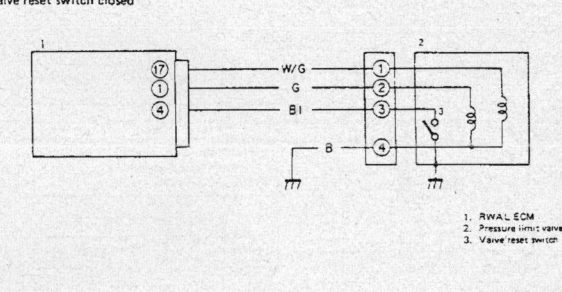

NOTE:
This code remains in memory as long as +12V battery power is supplied to RWAL ECM. Therefore, to erase this code, disconnect negative cable from battery for at least 5 seconds.

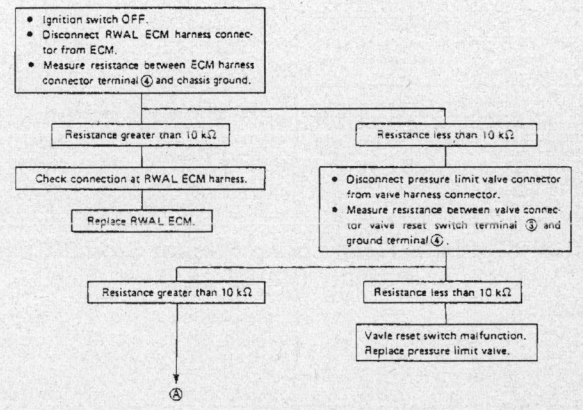

SK4029100008010X

Fig. 8 Code 4: Valve Rest Switch Closed
(Part 1 of 2)

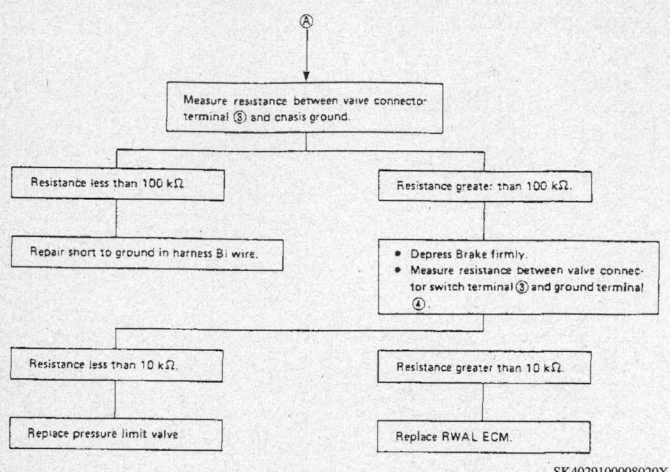

Fig. 8   Code 4: Valve Rest Switch Closed
(Part 2 of 2)

SK4029100008020X

DIAGNOSTIC CODE 6

Rear wheel speed sensor signal changed rapidly. This condition is detected only while driving at higher than 35 mph.

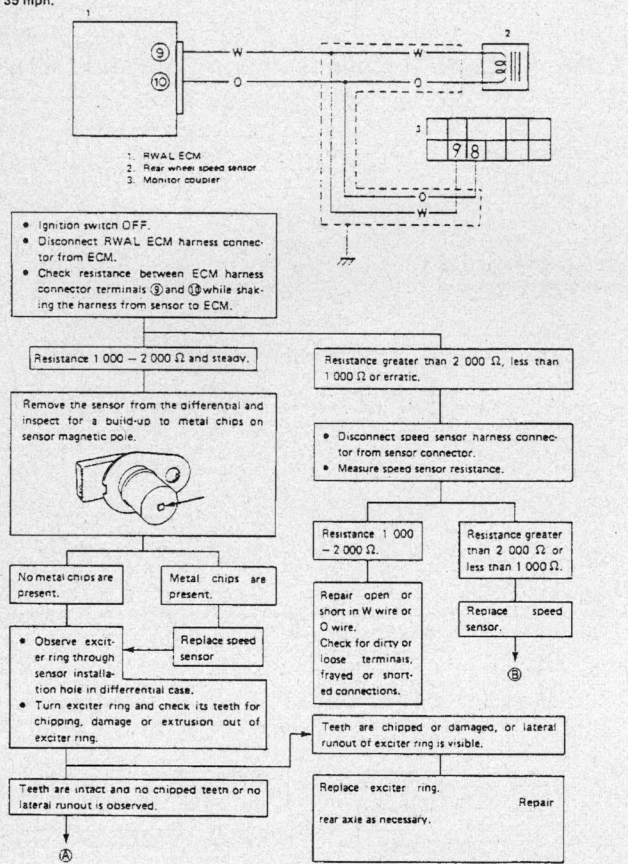

Fig. 10   Code 6: Rear Speed Sensor Signal Change Rapidly (Part 1 of 2)

SK4029100010010X

DIAGNOSTIC CODE 5

System dumps too many times. It is possible that this condition arises only when brake is applied during driving.

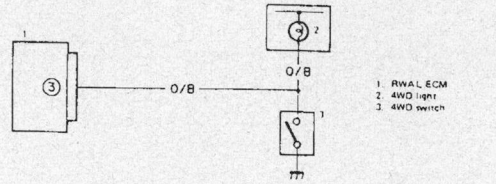

1. RWAL ECM
2. 4WD light
3. 4WD switch

NOTE:

This code remains in memory as long as +12V battery power is supplied to RWAL ECM. Therefore, to erase this code, disconnect negative cable from battery for at least 5 seconds.

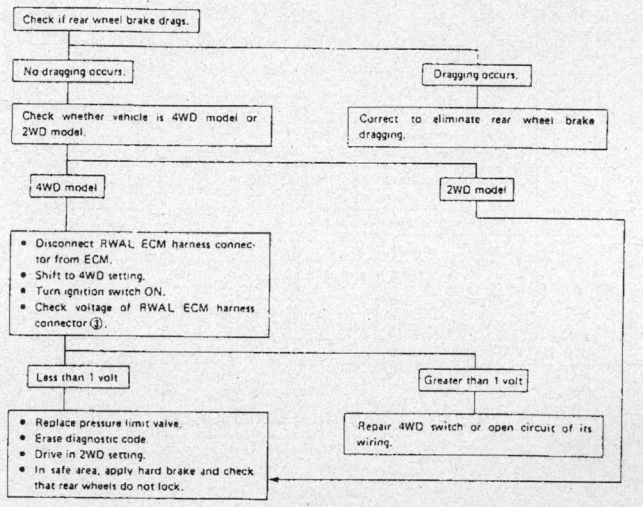

Fig. 9   Code 5: System Dumps Too Many Times

SK4029100009000X

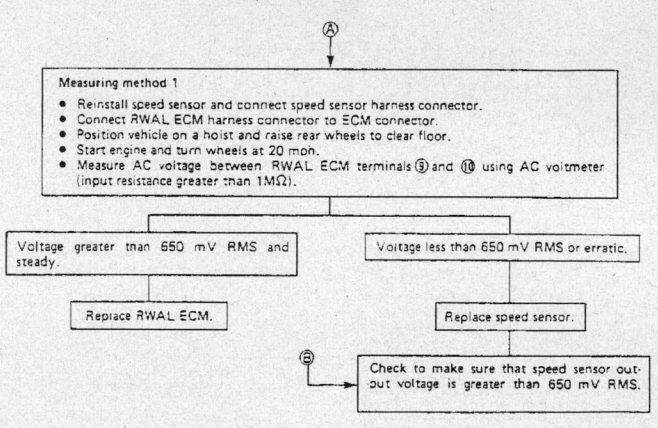

Fig. 10   Code 6: Rear Speed Sensor Signal Change Rapidly (Part 2 of 2)

SK4029100010020X

DIAGNOSTIC CODE 7
Shorted isolation solenoid circuit

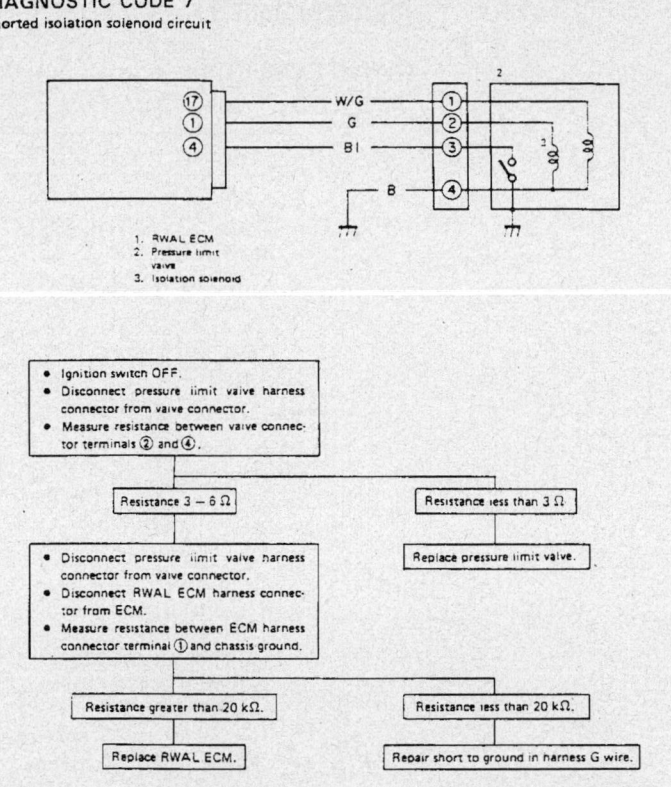

1. RWAL ECM
2. Pressure limit valve
3. Isolation solenoid

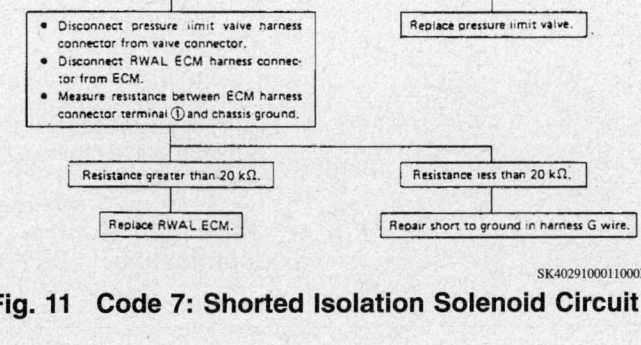

SK4029100011000X

Fig. 11   Code 7: Shorted Isolation Solenoid Circuit

DIAGNOSTIC CODE 8
Shorted dump solenoid circuit

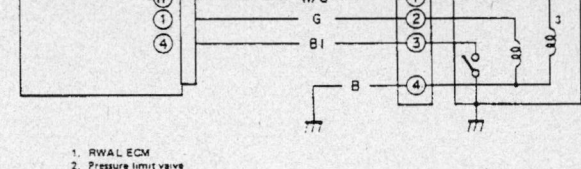

1. RWAL ECM
2. Pressure limit valve
3. Dump valve

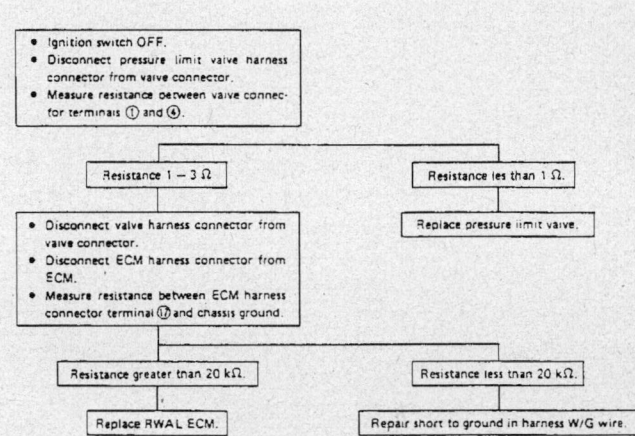

SK4029100012000X

Fig. 12   Code 8: Shorted Dump Solenoid Circuit

DIAGNOSTIC CODE 9
Open rear wheel speed sensor circuit

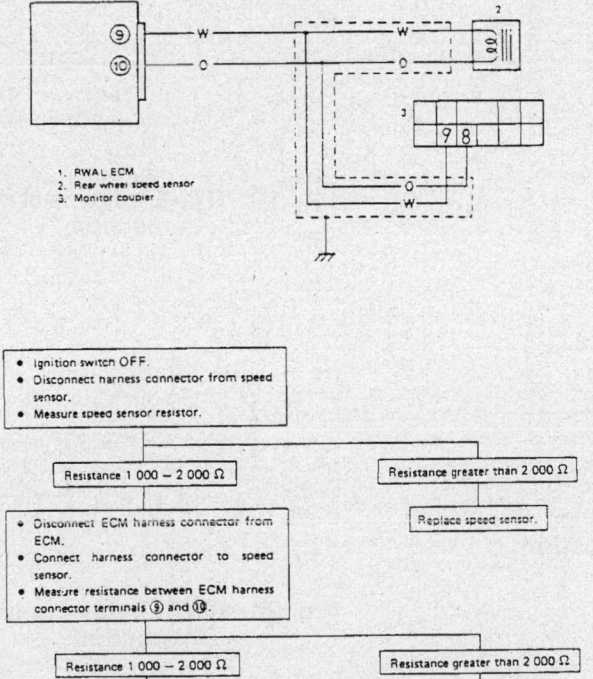

1. RWAL ECM
2. Rear wheel speed sensor
3. Monitor coupler

SK4029100013000X

Fig. 13   Code 9: Open Rear Wheel Speed Circuit

DIAGNOSTIC CODE 10
Stop light switch remains ON. This condition is detected only while driving at higher than 37.5 mph.

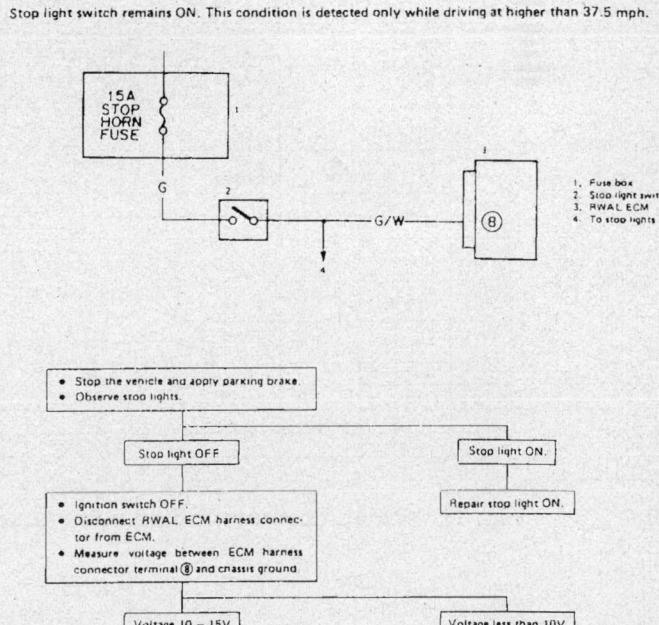

1. Fuse box
2. Stop light switch
3. RWAL ECM
4. To stop lights

SK4029100014000X

Fig. 14   Code 10: Stop Light Switch Remains On

DIAGNOSTIC CODE 11
Shorted rear wheel speed sensor circuit

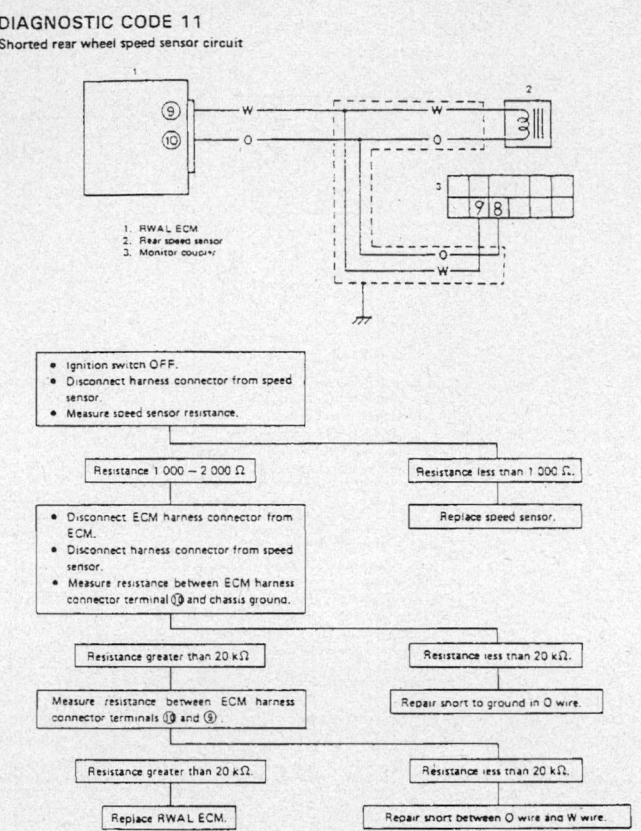

1. RWAL ECM
2. Rear speed sensor
3. Monitor coupler

- Ignition switch OFF.
- Disconnect harness connector from speed sensor.
- Measure speed sensor resistance.

| Resistance 1 000 – 2 000 Ω | Resistance less than 1 000 Ω. |

| Resistance less than 1 000 Ω. | Replace speed sensor. |

- Disconnect ECM harness connector from ECM.
- Disconnect harness connector from speed sensor.
- Measure resistance between ECM harness connector terminal ⑩ and chassis ground.

| Resistance greater than 20 kΩ | Resistance less than 20 kΩ. |

| Resistance less than 20 kΩ. | Repair short to ground in O wire. |

| Measure resistance between ECM harness connector terminals ⑩ and ⑨ |

| Resistance greater than 20 kΩ | Resistance less than 20 kΩ. |

| Replace RWAL ECM. | Repair short between O wire and W wire. |

SK4029100015000X

Fig. 15 Code 11: Shorted Rear Wheel Speed Sensor Circuit

TER-MINAL	CIRCUIT	NORMAL VOLTAGE	CONDITION
①	Isolation solenoid	0V (10 – 15V)	During normal driving (When hard brake is applied during driving)
②	Brake warning light	10 – 15V / 0 – 3V	When brake warning light is OFF / When brake warning light is ON
③	4WD signal	10 – 15V / 0 – 0.5V	In 2WD setting / In 4WD setting
④	Valve reset switch	4 – 5V (0 – 0.5V)	During normal driving (When hard brake is applied during driving)
⑤	———		
⑥	———		
⑦	Diagnostic test terminal	3 – 5V / 0 – 0.5V	When diagnostic test terminal is open / When diagnostic test terminal is grounded
⑧	Stop light switch	0 – 0.5V / 10 – 15V	When no brake is applied / When brake is applied
⑨ – ⑩	Rear wheel speed sensor	About 3.5V (AC)	When driving at about 20 mph
⑪	ECM ground	0V	Normal condition
⑭	Power source (ignition)	10 – 15V	When ignition switch is ON
⑮	Power source (battery)	10 – 15V	Normal condition
⑰	Dump solenoid	0V	During normal driving

SK4029100017000X

Fig. 17 RWAL control module voltage specification

DIAGNOSTIC CODE 13

RWAL ECM malfunction

| Replace RWAL ECM. |

SK4029100016000X

Fig. 16 Code 13: RWAL ECM Malfunction

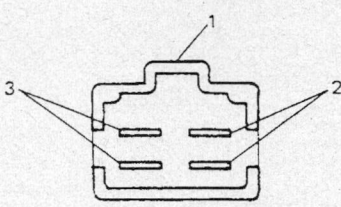

1. Stop light switch (Brake pedal switch)
2. Stop light switch terminals
3. Switch terminals for A/T lock-up system

SK4029100018000X

Fig. 18 Stop light terminal identification

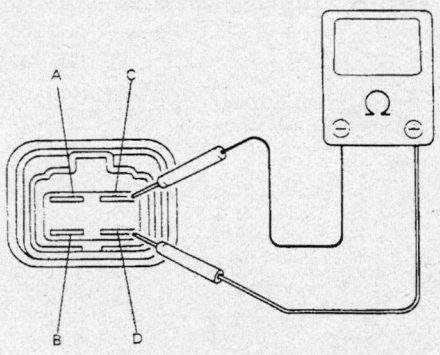

SK4029100019000X

Fig. 19 RWAL relay resistance inspection

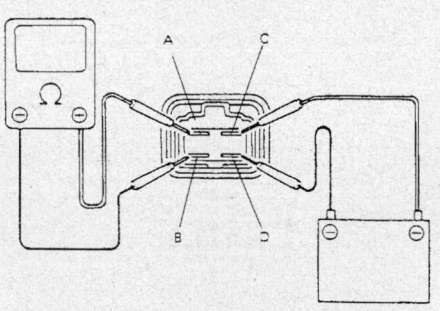

SK4029100020000X

Fig. 20 RWAL relay continuity inspection

	TERMINALS	RESISTANCE at 20°C (68°F)
ISOLATION VALVE SOLENOID	ISO — GND	3 — 6 ohms
DUMP VALVE SOLENOID	DUMP — GND	1 — 3 ohms
BRAKE RESET SWITCH	RESET — VALVE BODY	∞ (infinity)

SK4029100021000X

Fig. 21 Pressure limit valve resistance specification

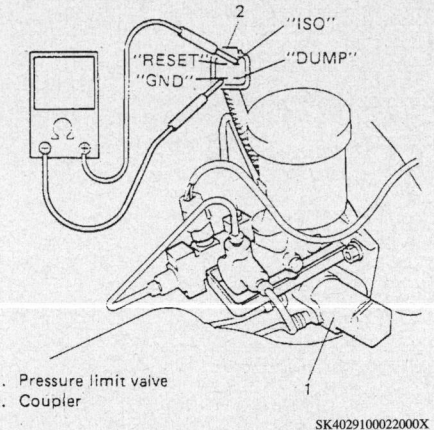

1. Pressure limit valve
2. Coupler

SK4029100022000X

Fig. 22 Pressure limit valve terminal identification

ABS-VI Anti-Lock

NOTE: Electrical Symbol & Wire Color Code Identification Located In The Front Of This Manual May Be Used As An Aid When Using Wiring Circuits Found In This Section.

NOTE: On Air Bag Equipped Models, Refer To "Air Bag System Precautions" Located In The Front Of This Manual For System Disarming & Arming Procedures.

INDEX

PRECAUTIONS

AIR BAG SYSTEMS

Refer to "Air Bag System Precautions" in the front of this manual for system disarming and arming procedures.

BATTERY GROUND CABLE

Prior to service, disconnect battery ground cable and isolate as required.

TROUBLESHOOTING

Refer to "Diagnosis & Testing" for troubleshooting procedures.

DIAGNOSIS & TESTING

Accessing Diagnostic Trouble Codes

The Diagnostic Trouble Codes (DTC) can be accessed by connecting a Tech 1 bi-directional scan tool equipped with ABS-Air Bag cartridge tool No. 09932–65020, or equivalents, to the Data Link Connector (DLC). The DLC is located under the left-hand side of the instrument panel, left of the steering column. Each input and output to the system can be monitored by the scan tool, monitoring inputs and outputs allows for fault confirmation and repair verification. The "Scan" tool can also be used to manually control components and perform functional tests. Refer to **Fig. 1** for "Scan" tool functions.

Wiring Circuits

Refer to **Figs. 2 through 6** for system wiring diagrams and connectors.

SUZUKI

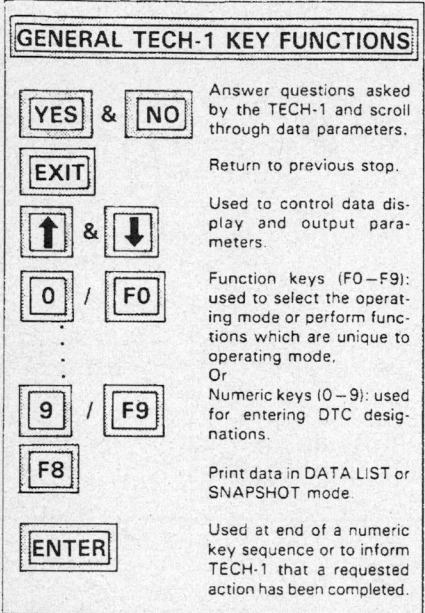

GENERAL TECH-1 KEY FUNCTIONS

YES & NO	Answer questions asked by the TECH-1 and scroll through data parameters.
EXIT	Return to previous stop.
↑ & ↓	Used to control data display and output parameters.
0 / F0 ⋮ 9 / F9	Function keys (F0–F9): used to select the operating mode or perform functions which are unique to operating mode. Or Numeric keys (0–9): used for entering DTC designations.
F8	Print data in DATA LIST or SNAPSHOT mode.
ENTER	Used at end of a numeric key sequence or to inform TECH-1 that a requested action has been completed.

SK4029500027000X

Fig. 1   Tech 1 scan tool key function

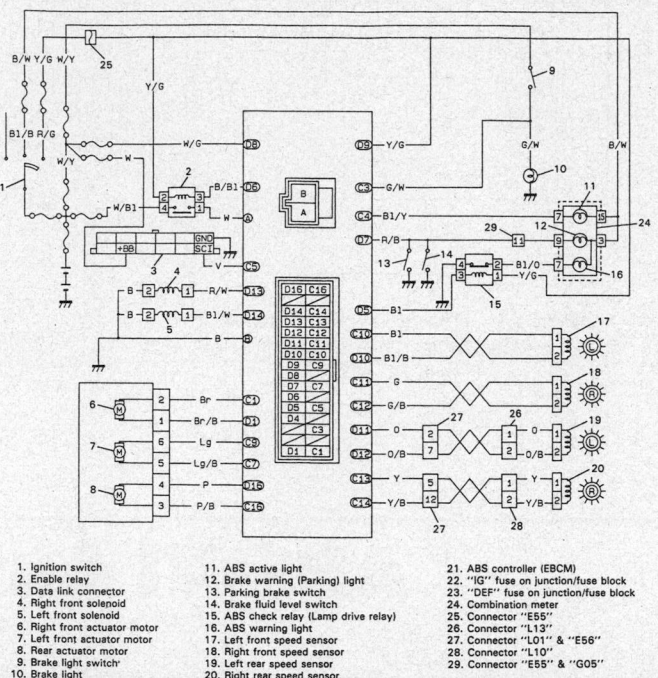

1. Ignition switch
2. Enable relay
3. Data link connector
4. Right front solenoid
5. Left front solenoid
6. Right front actuator motor
7. Left front actuator motor
8. Rear actuator motor
9. Brake light switch
10. Brake light

11. ABS active light
12. Brake warning (Parking) light
13. Parking brake switch
14. Brake fluid level switch
15. ABS check relay (Lamp drive relay)
16. ABS warning light
17. Left front speed sensor
18. Right front speed sensor
19. Left rear speed sensor
20. Right rear speed sensor

21. ABS controller (EBCM)
22. "IG" fuse on junction/fuse block
23. "DEF" fuse on junction/fuse block
24. Combination meter
25. Connector "E55"
26. Connector "L13"
27. Connector "L01" & "E56"
28. Connector "L10"
29. Connector "E55" & "G05"

SK4029500028000X

Fig. 2   ABS-VI system wiring circuit. Swift

Diagnostic Trouble Code Interpretation

Refer to "Diagnostic Chart Index" for diagnostic trouble code interpretation and identification.

Diagnostic Tests

Refer to, **Figs. 8 through 61** for diagnostic test procedures.

Clearing Diagnostic Trouble Codes

1. Select scan tool function F2 for "Trouble Codes-DTC."
2. After DTC have been reviewed, Tech-1 will prompt, "Clear Codes," with question mark, press "Yes," and DTCs will be cleared.

SYSTEM SERVICE

Brake System Bleed

Bleed brakes as outlined in "Hydraulic Brake System."

Component Replacement

ENABLE RELAY

1. Remove enable relay cover, **Fig. 62.**
2. Disconnect relay from electrical connector.
3. Reverse procedure to install.

ABS LAMP DRIVER MODULE

1. Remove fasteners on lower sound insulator panel under steering column.
2. Disconnect lamp driver module from instrument panel harness on left side near parking brake.
3. Reverse procedure to install.

ABS HYDRAULIC MODULATOR SOLENOID ASSEMBLY

1. Disconnect solenoid electrical connector. Remove Torx head bolts, then the solenoid assembly.
2. Reverse procedure to install, **torque** ABS modulator assembly Torx head bolts, "A" to 3 ft. lbs. and "B" to 3.5 ft. lbs., **Fig. 63.**

ELECTRONIC BRAKE CONTROL MODULE (EBCM)

1. Remove fasteners on lower sound insulator panel under steering column.
2. Remove EBCM, to dash panel attaching screws, **Fig. 64.**
3. Disconnect EBCM electrical connectors, then remove EBCM, **Fig. 65.**
4. Reverse procedure to install.

FRONT WHEEL SPEED SENSOR

1. Raise and support vehicle, then remove wheel and tire assembly.
2. Disconnect wheel sensor connector.
3. Remove speed sensor from steering knuckle.
4. Reverse procedure to install, noting the following:
   a. Check O-ring for damage replace as required.
   b. Install front wheel speed sensor to steering knuckle, **torque** sensor bolt 6–8 ft. lbs.

REAR WHEEL SPEED SENSOR

1. Raise and support vehicle.
2. Remove rear wheel and tire assembly.
3. Disconnect sensor electrical connector, remove sensor assembly from backing plate.
4. Reverse procedure to install, **torque**-sensor assembly attaching bolt to 6–8 ft. lbs.

ABS HYDRAULIC MODULATOR & MASTER CYLINDER ASSEMBLY

To avoid injury, due to the retained load on the modulator assembly. Use the TECH 1 scan or suitable equivalent to perform the "Gear Tension Relief Sequence" outlined under "Component Testing" before removing the brake control and motor assembly.

1. Disconnect two solenoid electrical connectors, **Fig. 66.**
2. Disconnect fluid level sensor connector, then the 6-pin and 3-pin motor pack electrical connectors.
3. Drain brake fluid from master cylinder
4. Place a shop cloth between brake pipe connections and the top of the motor pack assembly, then disconnect brake pipes from the assembly. **Plug open lines to prevent fluid loss and contamination.**
5. Remove two ABS hydraulic modulator assembly attaching nuts.
6. Remove modulator assembly from vehicle.
7. To separate hydraulic modulator from

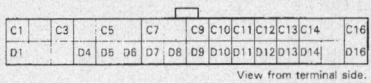

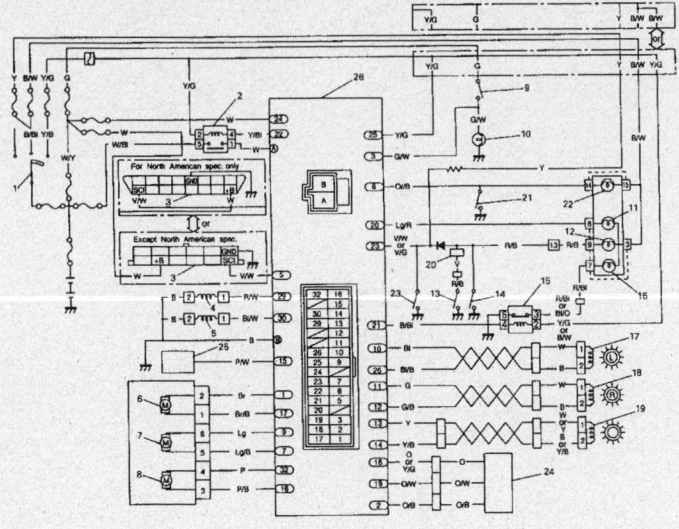

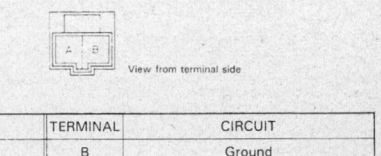
View from terminal side.

TERMINAL	CIRCUIT	TERMINAL	CIRCUIT
C1	Right front motor high	D1	Right front motor low
C3	Stop light switch (Brake switch terminal)		
		D4	ABS active light
C5	Serial data	D5	ABS warning light relay
		D6	Enable relay
C7	Left front motor low	D7	Brake warning light
		D8	Backup power supply
C9	Left front motor high	D9	Ignition power supply
C10	Left front wheel speed sensor (high)	D10	Left front wheel speed sensor (low)
C11	Right front wheel speed sensor (high)	D11	Left rear wheel speed sensor (high)
C12	Right front wheel speed sensor (low)	D12	Left rear wheel speed sensor (low)
C13	Right rear wheel speed sensor (high)	D13	Right front solenoid
C14	Right rear wheel speed sensor (low)	D14	Left front solenoid
C16	Rear motor low	D16	Rear motor high

SK4029500029000X

Fig. 4   EBCM 32 way electrical connector. Swift

View from terminal side

TERMINAL	CIRCUIT	TERMINAL	CIRCUIT
A	Battery power supply	B	Ground

SK4029500030000X

Fig. 6   EBCM 2 way electrical connector

1. Ignition switch
2. Enable relay
3. Data link connector
4. Right front solenoid
5. Left front solenoid
6. Right front actuator motor
7. Left front actuator motor
8. Rear actuator motor
9. Stop light switch
10. Stop light
11. ABS active light (If equipped)
12. Brake warning (Parking) light
13. Parking brake switch
14. Brake fluid level switch
15. ABS check relay (Lamp drive relay)
16. ABS warning light
17. Left front wheel speed sensor
18. Right front wheel speed sensor
19. Rear wheel speed sensor
20. DRL controller (For North American spec. only)
21. 4WD switch
22. 4WD indicator light
23. Differential switch
24. G sensor
25. ECM
26. EBCM

SK4029600094000X

Fig. 3   ABS-VI system wiring circuit. Sidekick & X-90

View from terminal side.

TERMINAL	CIRCUIT	TERMINAL	CIRCUIT
1	Right front motor high	17	Right front motor low
2	G sensor	18	G sensor
3	Stop light switch (Brake switch terminal)	19	G sensor
		20	ABS active light
		21	ABS warning light relay
5	Serial data	22	Enable relay
6	4WD switch	23	Brake warning light
7	Left front motor low	24	Backup power supply
		25	Ignition power supply
9	Left front motor high	26	Left front wheel speed sensor (low)
10	Left front wheel speed sensor (high)		
11	Right front wheel speed sensor (high)		
12	Right front wheel speed sensor (low)	29	Right front solenoid
13	Rear wheel speed sensor (high)	30	Left front solenoid
14	Rear wheel speed sensor (low)		
15	Engine control module (ECM)	32	Rear motor high
16	Rear motor low		

SK4029600095000X

Fig. 5   EBCM 32 way electrical connector. Sidekick & X-90

master cylinder, proceed as follows:

a. Remove six Torx head screws that attach gear the gear cover.

b. Remove four Torx head screws that attach the motor pack assembly.

c. Remove two modulator assembly to master cylinder through bolts, then separate master cylinder from modulator assembly.

d. Remove two transfer tubes with O-rings from master cylinder or modulator assembly.

e. Remove through bolt O-rings from master cylinder and modulator assemblies.

f. If modulator assembly is to be replaced, ensure gears are installed in the same position as they were removed. Refer to "ABS Hydraulic Modulator Gears" in "Component Replacement" section.

8. Reverse procedure to assemble and install, noting the following:

a. If master cylinder and hydraulic modulator were separated, use new transfer tube assemblies and new O-rings.

b. **Torque** modulator assembly to master cylinder through bolts to 12 ft. lbs.

c. **Torque** modulator assembly to vacuum booster nuts to 20 ft. lbs.

d. Bleed hydraulic system as outlined in "ABS System Bleeding."

e. **Torque** modulator assembly, **Fig. 67,** mounting nuts to 6–8 ft. lbs.

f. **Torque** hydraulic brake pipe fittings to 11–13 ft. lbs.

g. Bleed hydraulic system as outlined in "ABS System Bleeding."

ABS HYDRAULIC MODULATOR GEARS

Do not attempt to repair defective motor packs or modulator assemblies. Modulator drive gear replacement is the only service that can be performed on these assemblies. The modulator drive gears are under spring load and will turn during disassemble. After removing hydraulic modulator drive gear cover, do not place fingers into the gear set.

1. Remove ABS hydraulic modulator assembly as outlined under "Component Replacement."

2. Remove six Torx head screws attaching gear cover.

3. Remove four motor pack to modulator assembly Torx head screws, then separate motor pack assembly from hydraulic modulator assembly. **Use care not to drop or damage motor pack assembly. If motor pack assembly is dropped or damaged during handling, it must be replaced.**

4. Turn modulator gear to position piston in the center of its travel.

5. Place a screwdriver through the holes in gears into recessed hole in the modulator base. **Do not allow gear to turn while removing retaining nut.**

6. Remove three modulator drive gear to modulator driveshaft retaining nuts, then the gears from modulator.

7. Reverse procedure to install, noting the following:

    a. **Do not allow gears to turn when tightening retaining nuts.**

    b. **Torque** retaining nuts to 75 inch lbs.

    c. Rotate each modulator gear counterclockwise until movement stops, before positioning motor pack assembly onto hydraulic modulator.

    d. **Torque** motor pack assembly to hydraulic modulator assembly Torx head screws to 40 inch lbs.

    e. **Torque** gear cover Torx screws to 27 inch lbs.

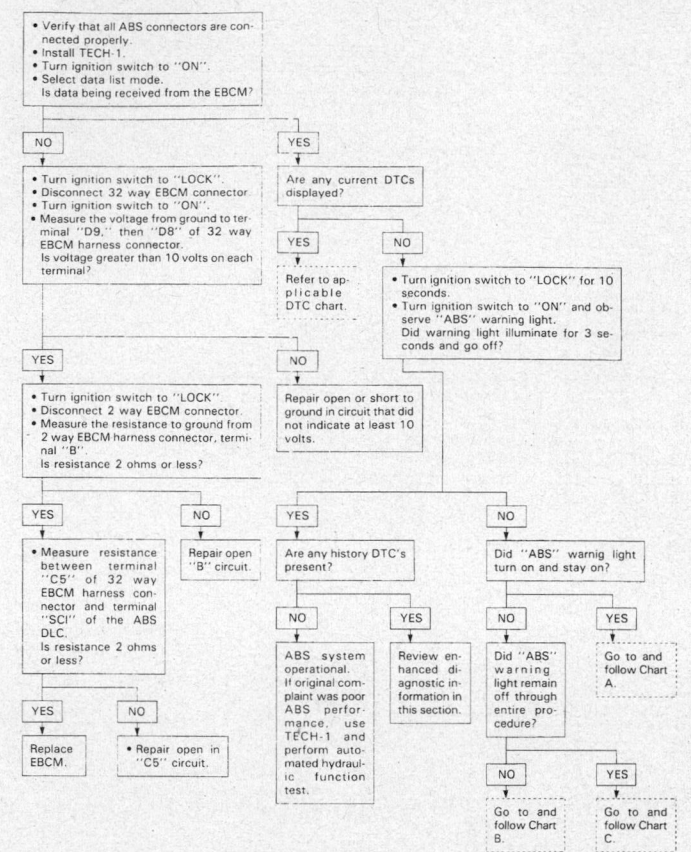

SK4029500031000X

Fig. 7 Diagnostic circuit check

DIAGNOSTIC CHART INDEX

Test	Description	Page No.	Fig. No.
Test A	ABS (Amber) Warning Light ON Constantly, No DTCs Stored	42-126	8
Test B	ABS (Amber) Warning Light ON Intermittently, No DTCs Stored	42-126	9
Test C	ABS (Amber) Warning Light OFF Constantly, No DTCs Stored	42-126	10
Test D	Tech-1 Displays Undefined DTCs	42-126	11
Code 14	ABS Enable Relay Contact Circuit Open	42-127	12
Code 15	ABS Enable Relay Circuit Shorted To Battery Or Always Closed	42-128	13
Code 16	ABS Enable Relay Coil Circuit Open	42-128	14
Code 17	ABS Enable Relay Coil Circuit Shorted To Ground	42-128	15
Code 18	ABS Enable Relay Coil Shorted To Battery	42-128	16
Code 21	Left Front Wheel Speed, Zero Or Unreasonable	42-129	17
Code 22	Right Front Wheel Speed, Zero Or Unreasonable	42-129	18
Code 23	Left Rear Wheel Speed, Zero Or Unreasonable	42-130	19
Code 24	Right Rear Wheel Speed, Zero Or Unreasonable	42-131	20
Code 25	Left Front Excessive Wheel Speed Variation	42-131	21
Code 26	Right Front Excessive Wheel Speed Variation	42-132	22
Code 27	Left Rear Excessive Wheel Speed Variation	42-133	23
Code 28	Right Rear Excessive Wheel Speed Variation	42-133	24
Code 36	Low System Voltage	42-134	25
Code 37	High System Voltage	42-134	26
Code 38	Left Front ESB Will Not Hold Motor	42-134	27
Code 41	Right Front ESB Will Not Hold Motor	42-135	28
Code 42	Rear ESB Will Not Hold Motor	42-135	29
Code 44	Left Front Channel Will Not Move	42-135	30

Continued

DIAGNOSTIC CHART INDEX—Continued

Test	Description	Page No.	Fig. No.
Code 45	Right Front Channel Will Not Move	42-135	31
Code 46	Rear Channel Will Not Move	42-136	32
Code 47	Left Front Motor Free Spins	42-136	33
Code 48	Right Front Motor Free Spins	42-136	34
Code 51	Rear Motor Free Spins	42-137	35
Code 52	Left Front Channel In Release Too Long	42-137	36
Code 53	Right Front Channel In Release Too Long	42-138	37
Code 54	Rear Channel In Release Too Long	42-138	38
Code 55	EBCM Malfunction	42-138	39
Code 56	Left Front Motor Circuit Open	42-139	40
Code 57	Left Front Motor Circuit Shorted To Ground	42-139	41
Code 58	Left Front Motor Circuit Shorted To Battery	42-139	42
Code 61	Right Front Motor Circuit Open	42-139	43
Code 62	Right Front Motor Circuit Shorted To Ground	42-140	44
Code 63	Right Front Motor Circuit Shorted To Battery	42-140	45
Code 64	Rear Motor Circuit Open	42-140	46
Code 65	Rear Motor Circuit Shorted To Ground	42-140	47
Code 66	Rear Motor Circuit Shorted To Battery	42-141	48
Code 76	Left Front Solenoid Circuit Open Or Shorted To Battery	42-141	49
Code 77	Left Front Solenoid Circuit Shorted To Ground	42-141	50
Code 78	Right Front Solenoid Circuit Open Or Shorted To Battery	42-141	51
Code 81	Right Front Solenoid Circuit Shorted To Ground	42-142	52
Code 82	Calibration Malfunction	42-142	53
Code 86	EBCM Turned On Red Brake Warning Light	42-142	54
Code 87	Brake Warning Light Circuit Open	42-142	55
Code 88	Brake Warning Light Circuit Shorted To Battery	42-142	56
Code 91	Open Brake Switch During Deceleration	42-143	57
Code 92	Open Brake Switch When ABS Was Required	42-143	58
Code 93	Code 91 Or 92 Set In Current Or Previous Ignition Cycle	42-143	59
Code 94	Brake Switch Contacts Always Closed	42-143	60
Code 95	Brake Switch Circuit Open	42-144	61

SUZUKI

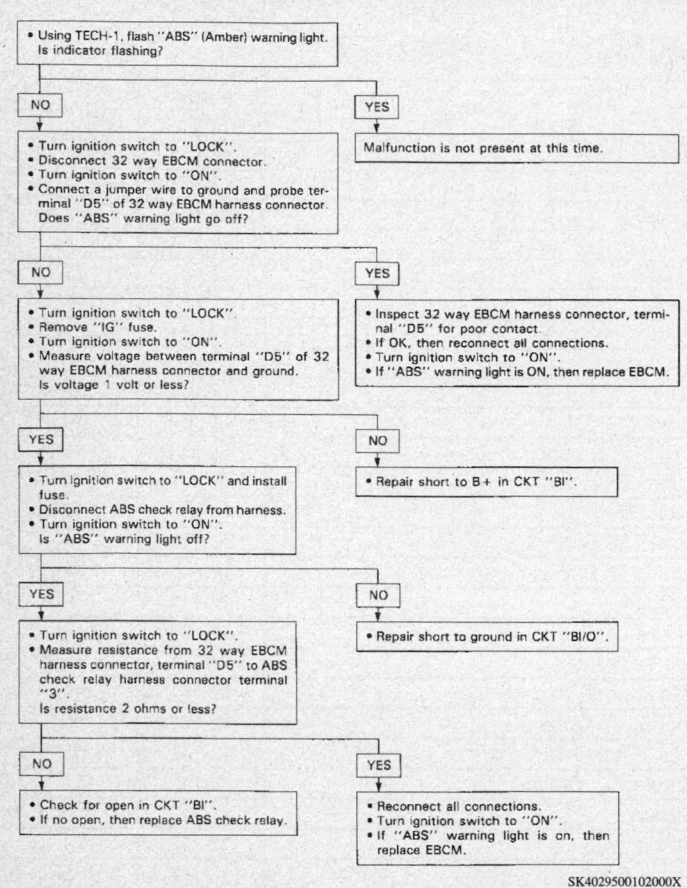

Fig. 8   Test A: ABS (Amber) Warning Light ON Constantly, No DTCs Stored

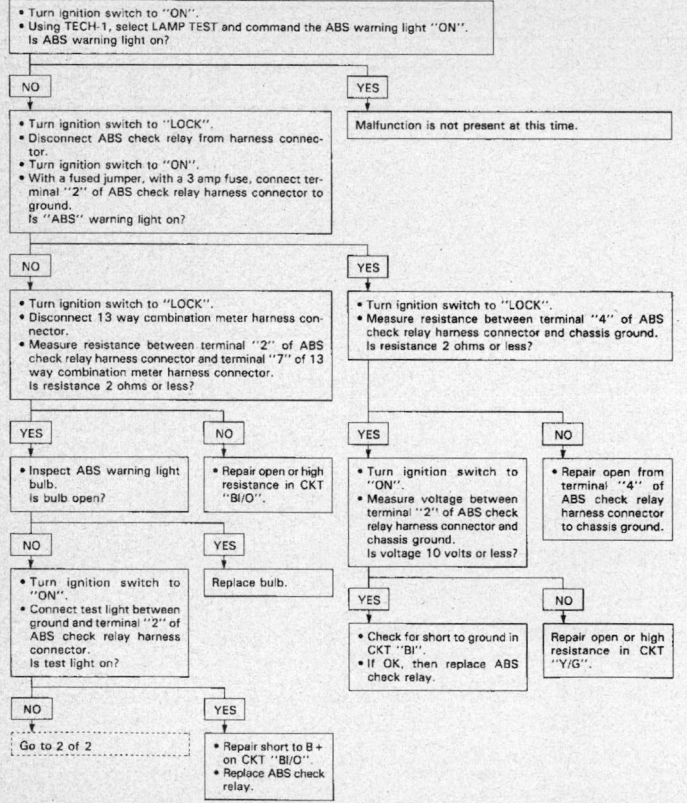

Fig. 10   Test C: ABS (Amber) Warning Light OFF Constantly, No DTCs Stored (Part 1 of 2)

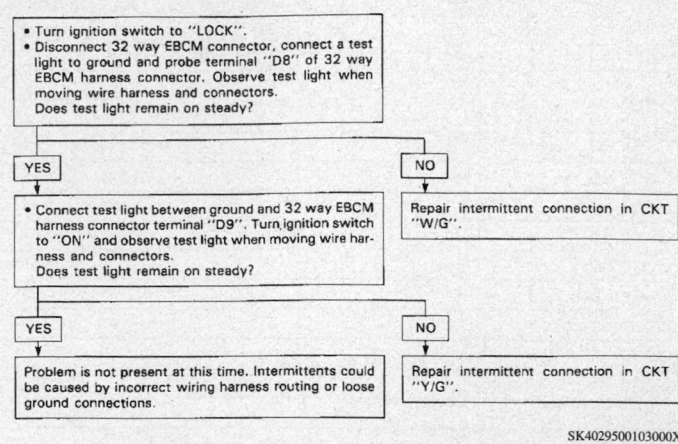

Fig. 9   Test B: ABS (Amber) Warning Light ON Intermittently, No DTCs Stored

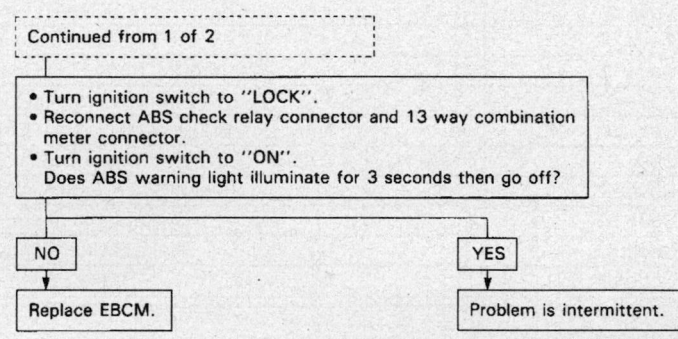

Fig. 10   Test C: ABS (Amber) Warning Light OFF Constantly, No DTCs Stored (Part 2 of 2)

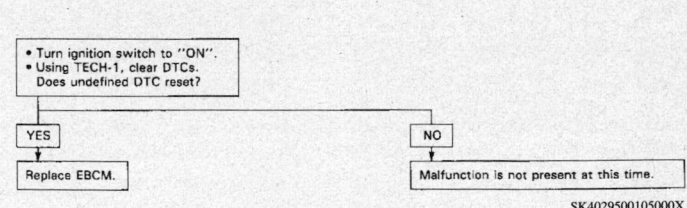

Fig. 11   Test D: Tech-1 Displays Undefined DTCs

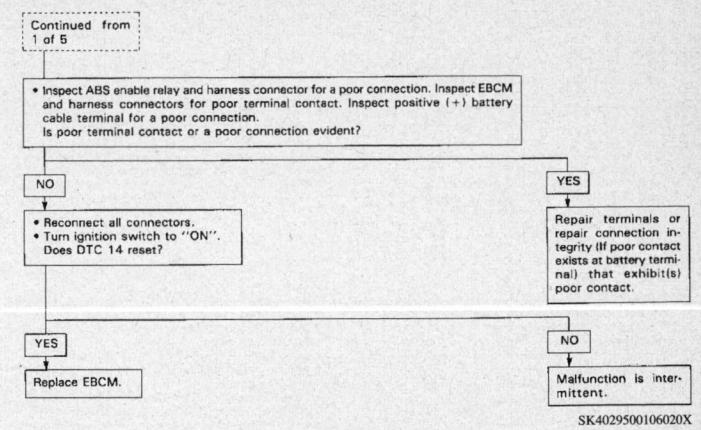

Fig. 12   Code 14: ABS Enable Relay Contact Circuit
Open (Part 2 of 5)

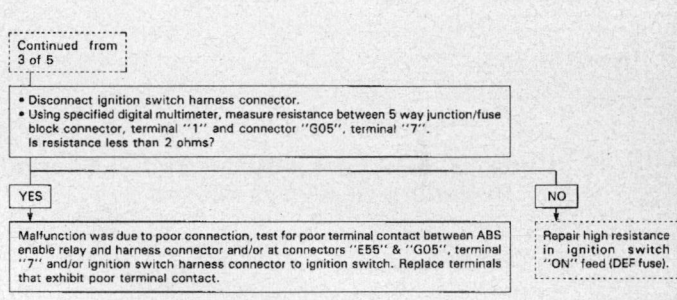

Fig. 12   Code 14: ABS Enable Relay Contact Circuit
Open (Part 4 of 5)

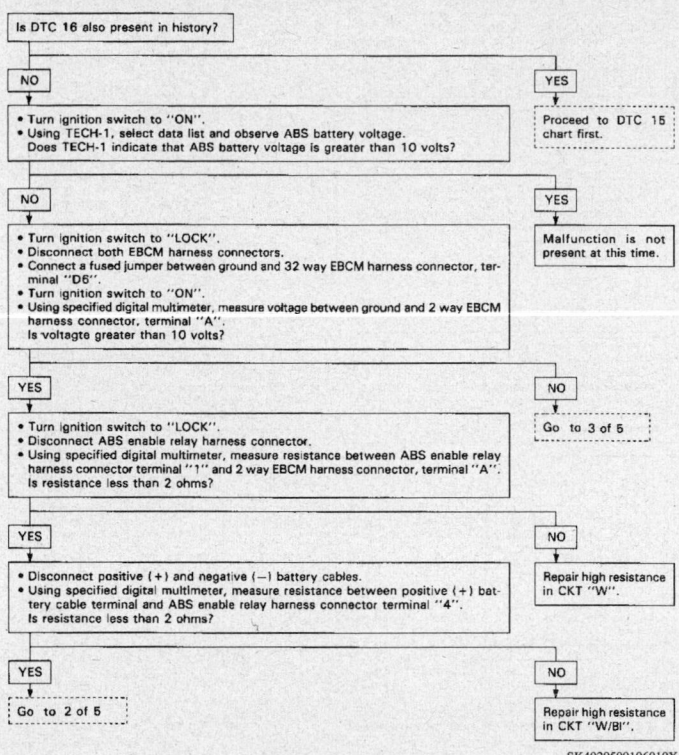

Fig. 12   Code 14: ABS Enable Relay Contact Circuit
Open (Part 1 of 5)

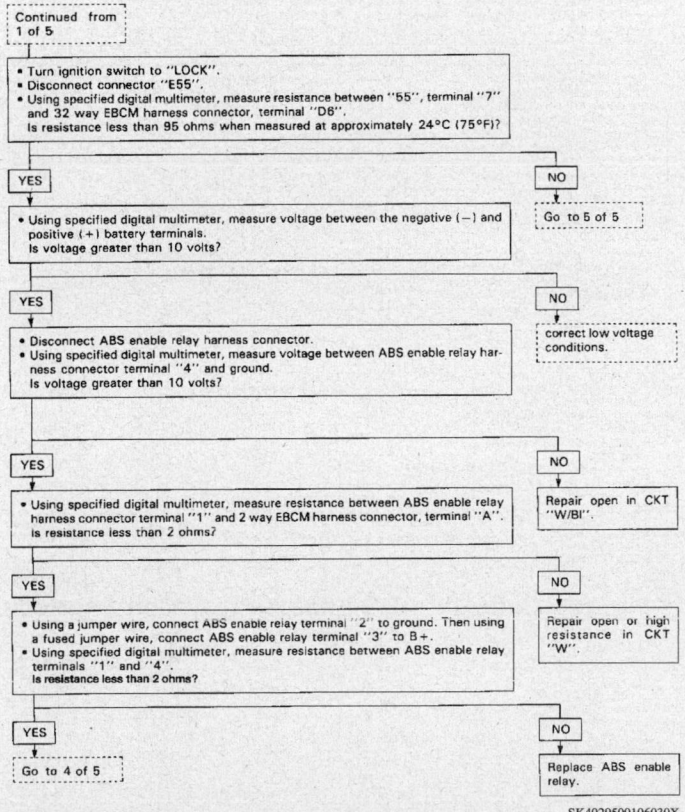

Fig. 12   Code 14: ABS Enable Relay Contact Circuit
Open (Part 3 of 5)

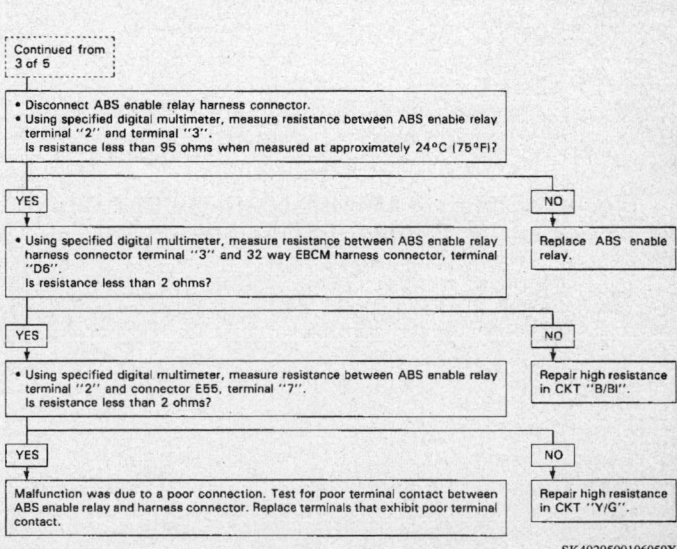

Fig. 12   Code 14: ABS Enable Relay Contact Circuit
Open (Part 5 of 5)

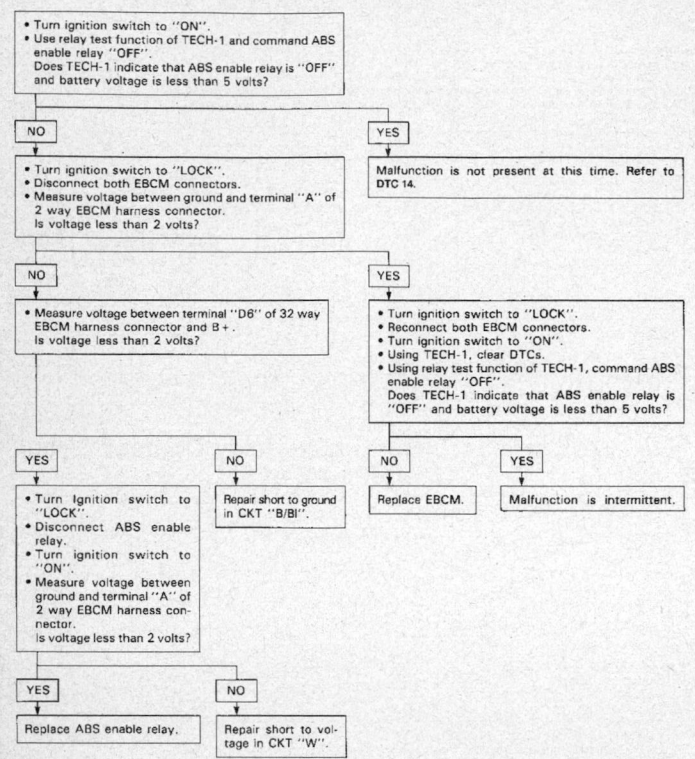

Fig. 13   Code 15: ABS Enable Relay Circuit Shorted
To Battery Or Always Closed

SK4029500107000X

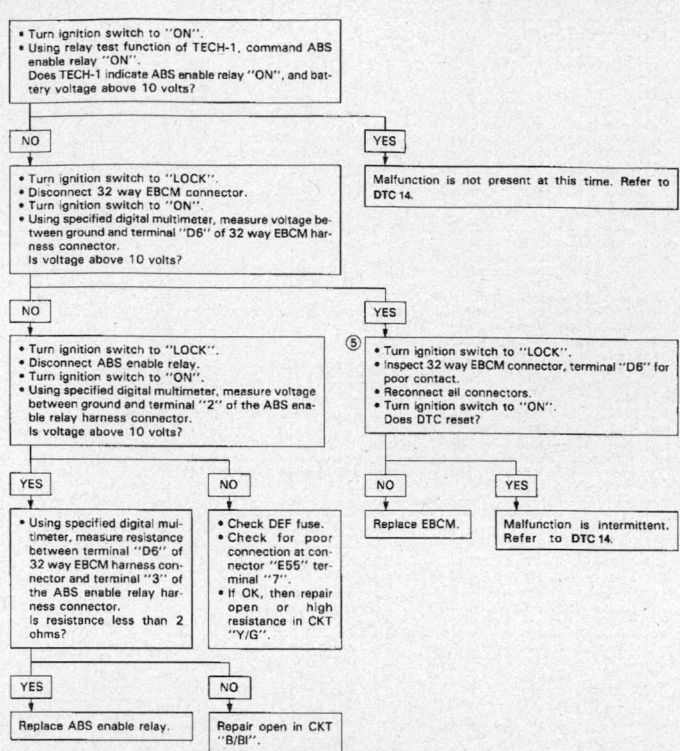

Fig. 14   Code 16: ABS Enable Relay Coil Circuit
Open

SK4029500108000X

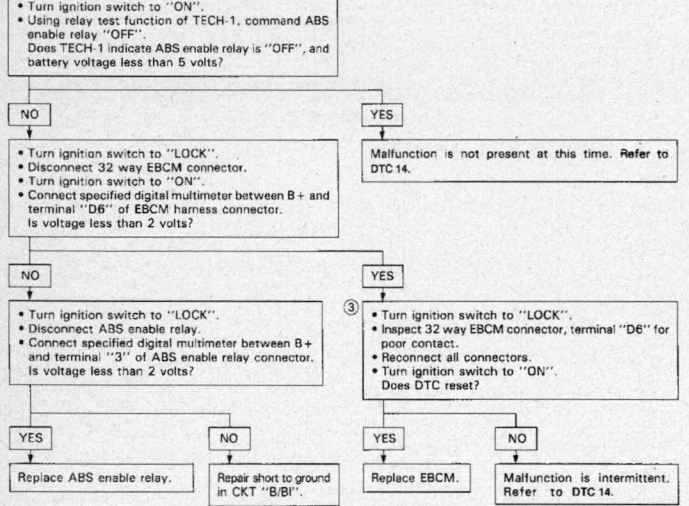

Fig. 15   Code 17: ABS Enable Relay Coil Circuit
Shorted To Ground

SK4029500109000X

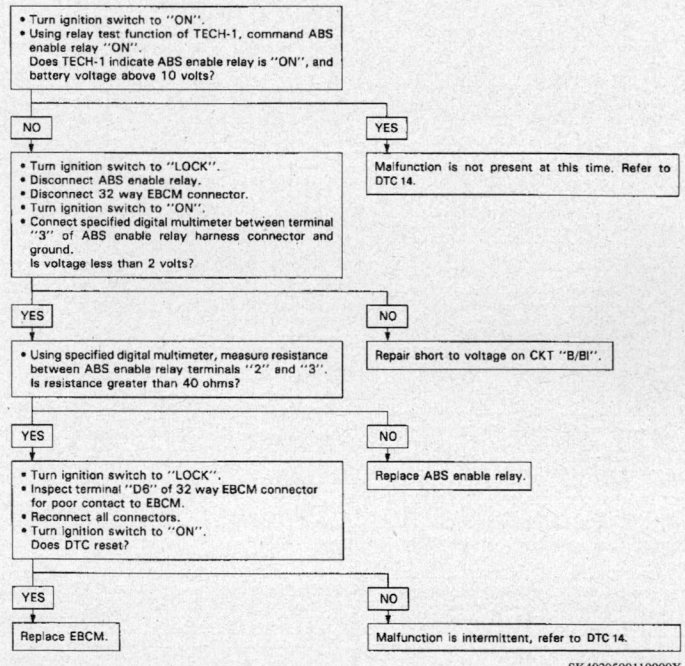

Fig. 16   Code 18: ABS Enable Relay Coil Shorted
To Battery

SK4029500110000X

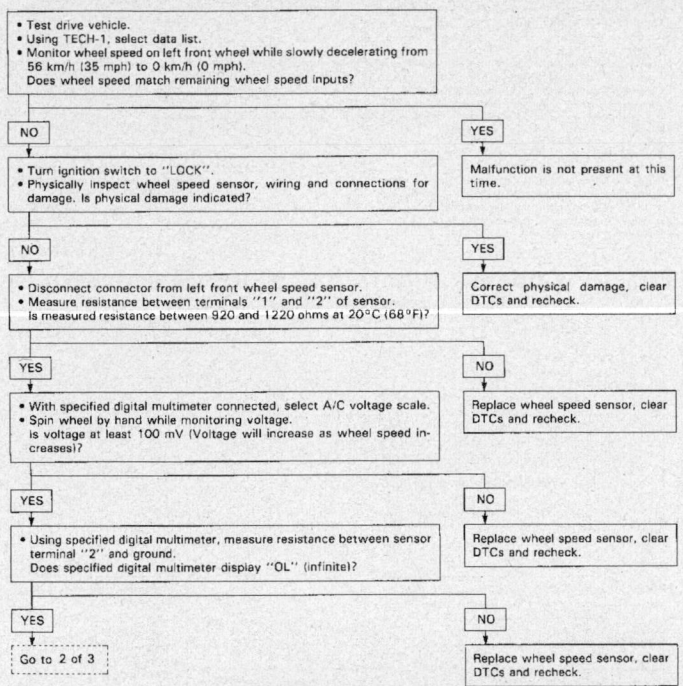

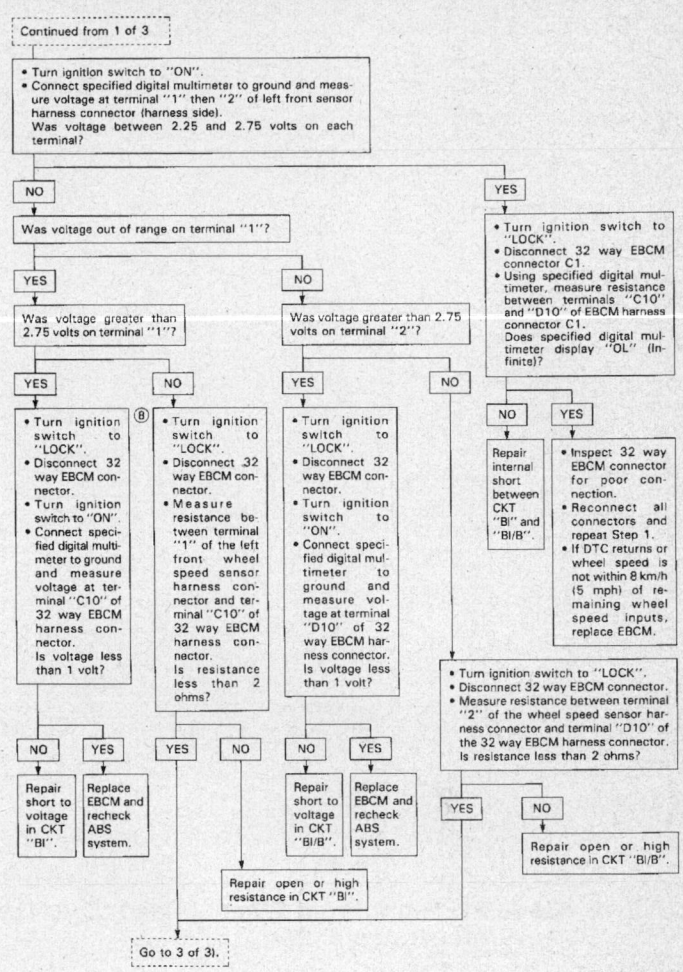

Fig. 17   Code 21: Left Front Wheel Speed, Zero Or Unreasonable (Part 1 of 3)

SK4029500111010X

Fig. 17   Code 21: Left Front Wheel Speed, Zero Or Unreasonable (Part 2 of 3)

SK4029500111020X

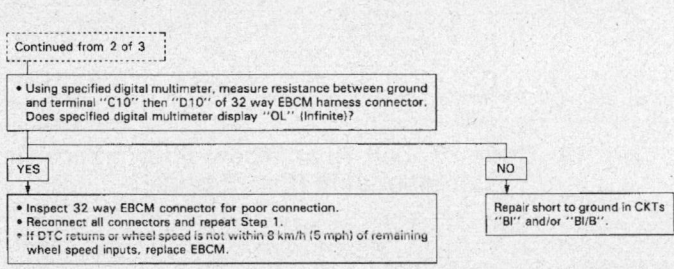

Fig. 17   Code 21: Left Front Wheel Speed, Zero Or Unreasonable (Part 3 of 3)

SK4029500111030X

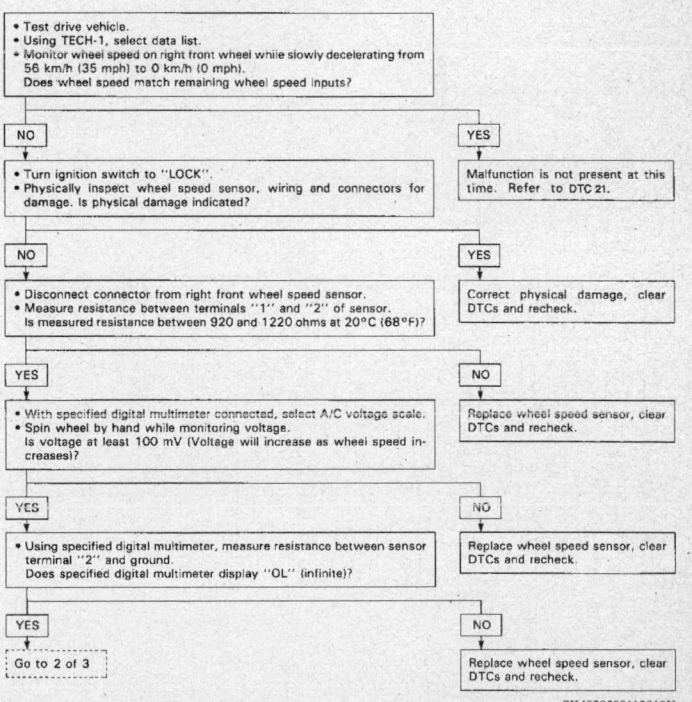

Fig. 18   Code 22: Right Front Wheel Speed, Zero Or Unreasonable (Part 1 of 3)

SK4029500112010X

ABS-VI ANTI-LOCK   42-129

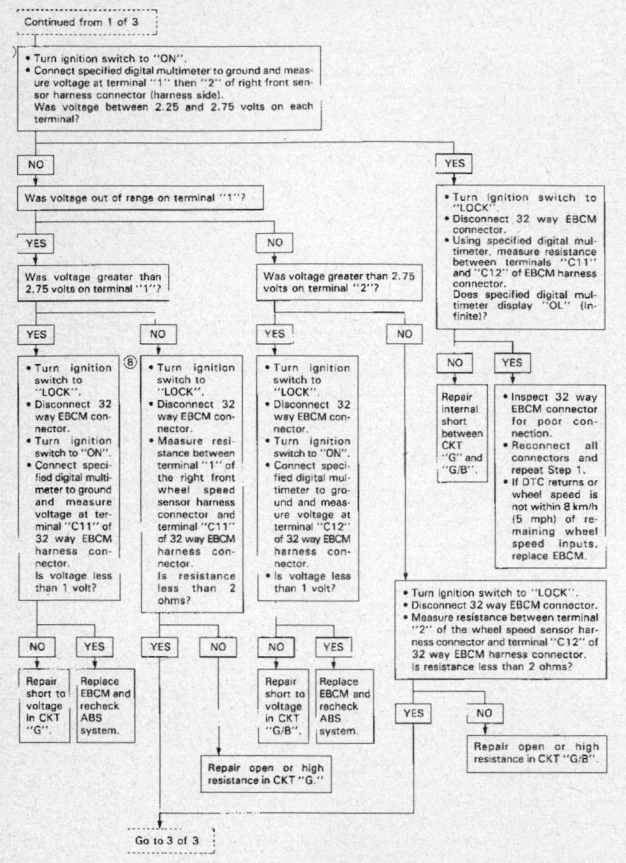

Fig. 18   Code 22: Right Front Wheel Speed, Zero Or
Unreasonable (Part 2 of 3)

SK4029500112020X

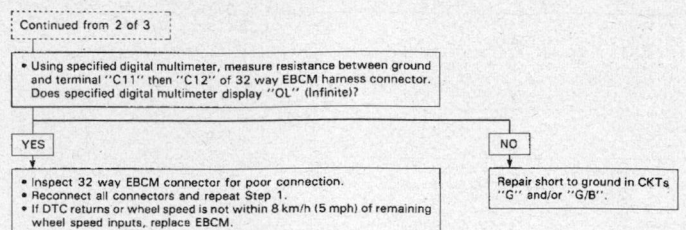

Fig. 18   Code 22: Right Front Wheel Speed, Zero Or
Unreasonable (Part 3 of 3)

SK4029500112030X

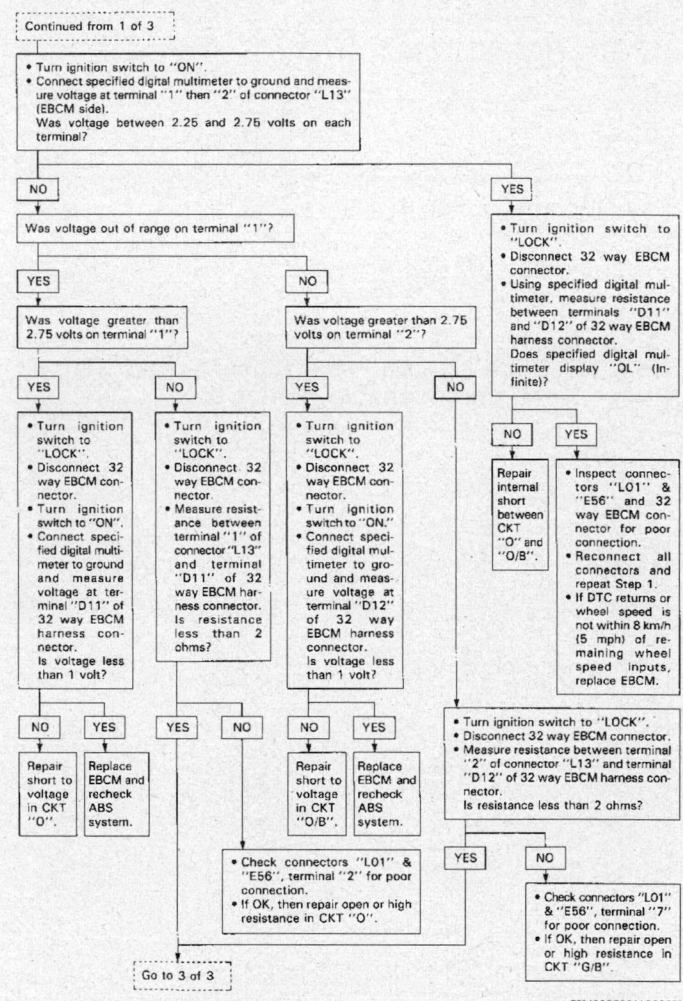

Fig. 19   Code 23: Left Rear Wheel Speed, Zero Or
Unreasonable (Part 2 of 3)

SK4029500113020X

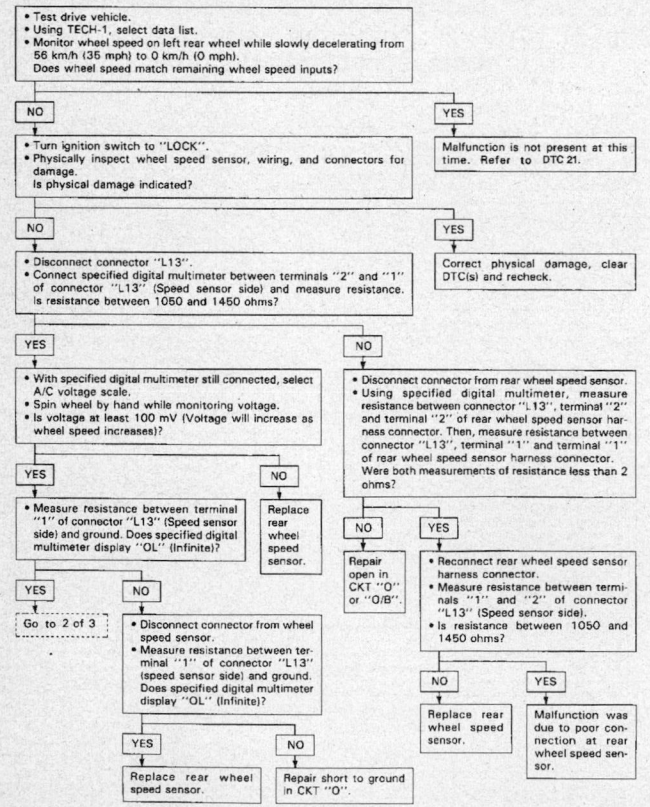

Fig. 19   Code 23: Left Rear Wheel Speed, Zero Or
Unreasonable (Part 1 of 3)

SK4029500113010X

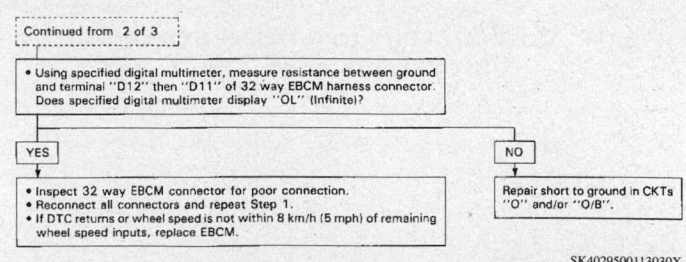

Fig. 19   Code 23: Left Rear Wheel Speed, Zero Or
Unreasonable (Part 3 of 3)

SK4029500113030X

ABS-VI ANTI-LOCK

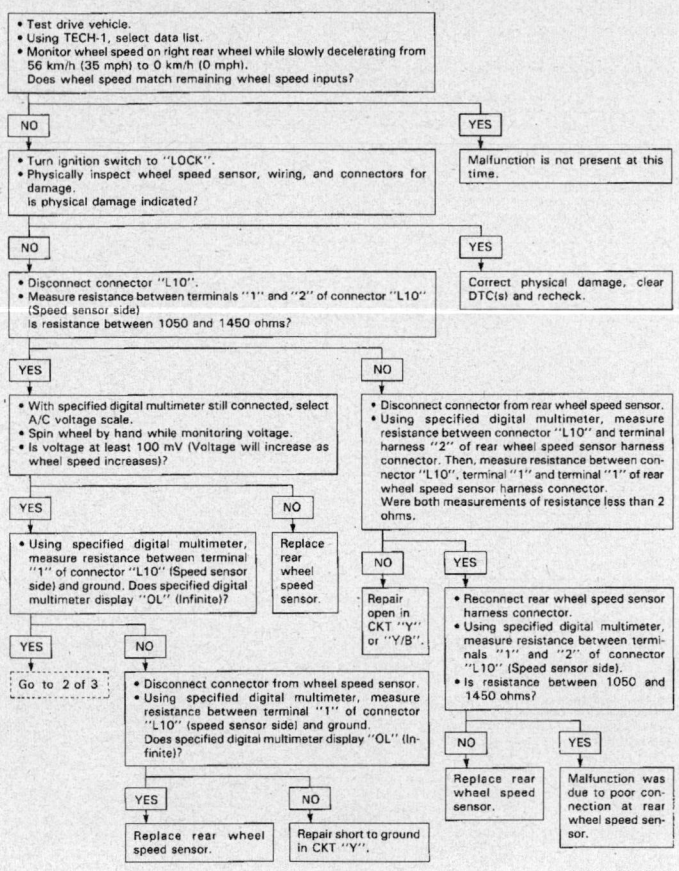

Fig. 20 Code 24: Right Rear Wheel Speed, Zero Or Unreasonable (Part 1 of 3)

SK4029500114010X

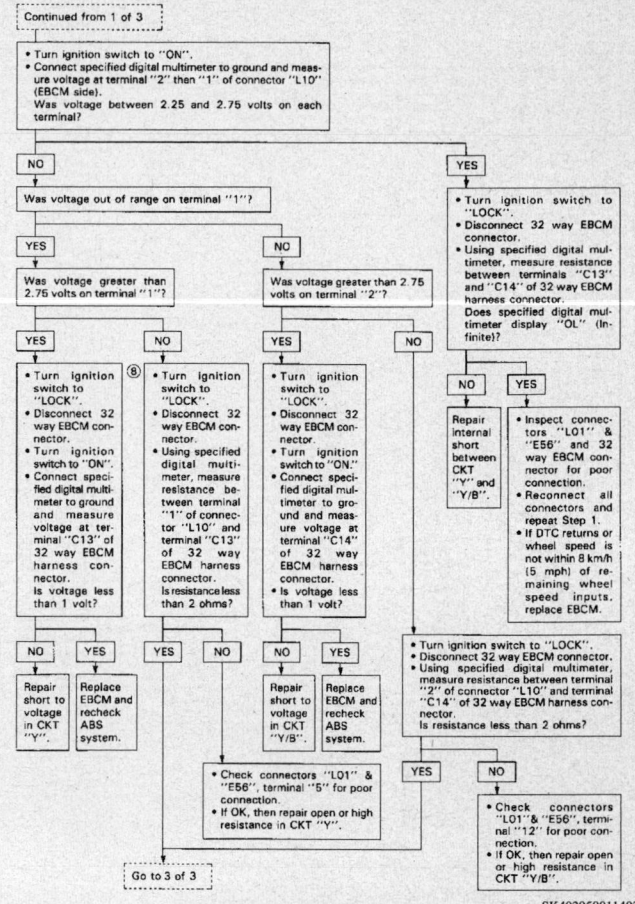

Fig. 20 Code 24: Right Rear Wheel Speed, Zero Or Unreasonable (Part 2 of 3)

SK4029500114020X

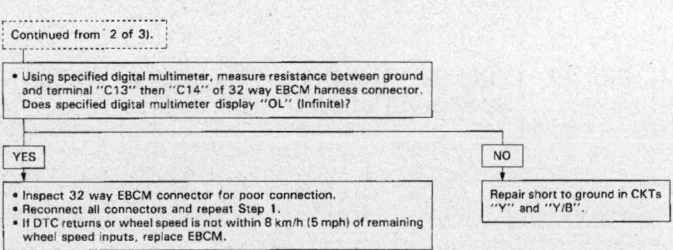

Fig. 20 Code 24: Right Rear Wheel Speed, Zero Or Unreasonable (Part 3 of 3)

SK4029500114030X

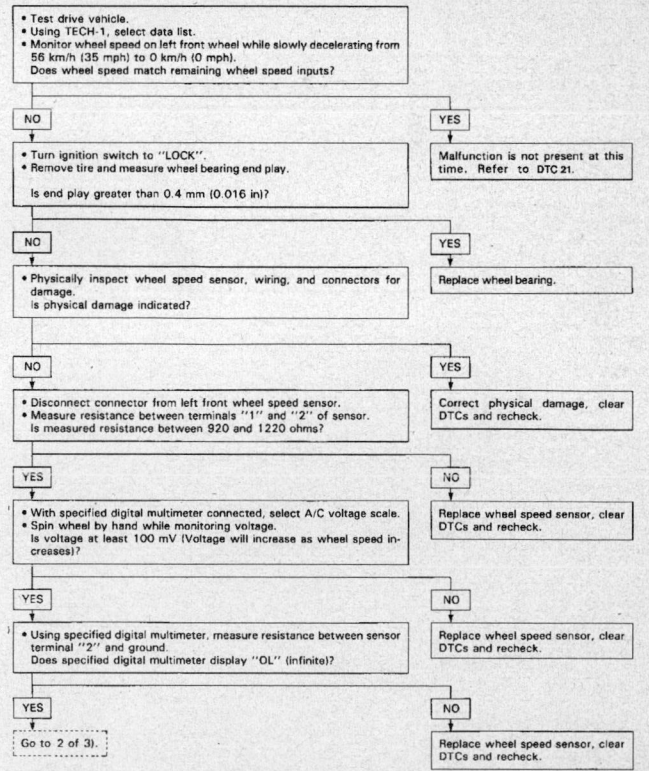

Fig. 21 Code 25: Left Front Excessive Wheel Speed Variation (Part 1 of 3)

SK4029500115010X

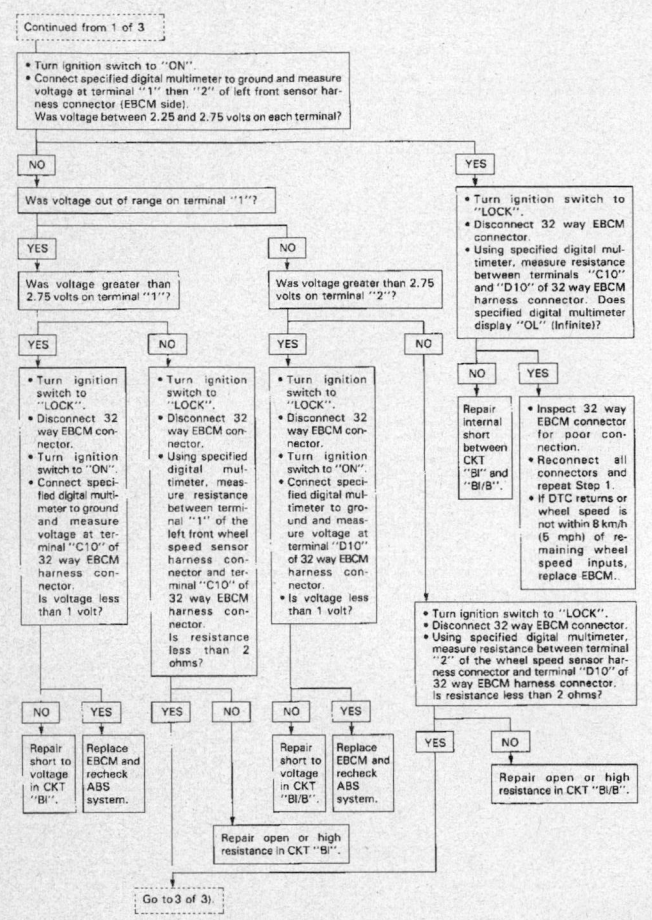

Fig. 21 Code 25: Left Front Excessive Wheel Speed Variation (Part 2 of 3)

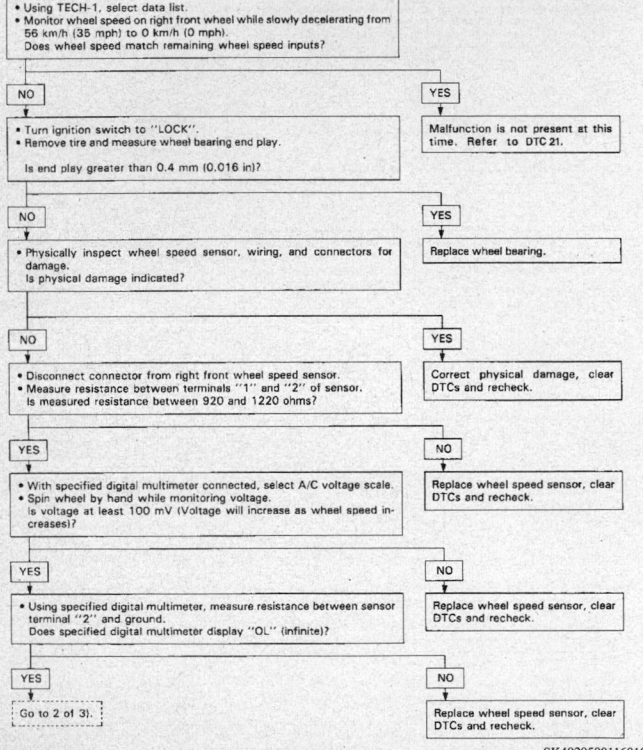

Fig. 22 Code 26: Right Front Excessive Wheel Speed Variation (Part 1 of 3)

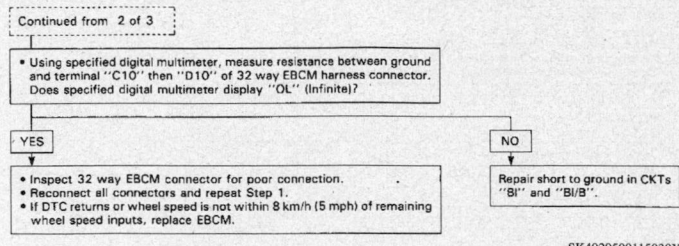

Fig. 21 Code 25: Left Front Excessive Wheel Speed Variation (Part 3 of 3)

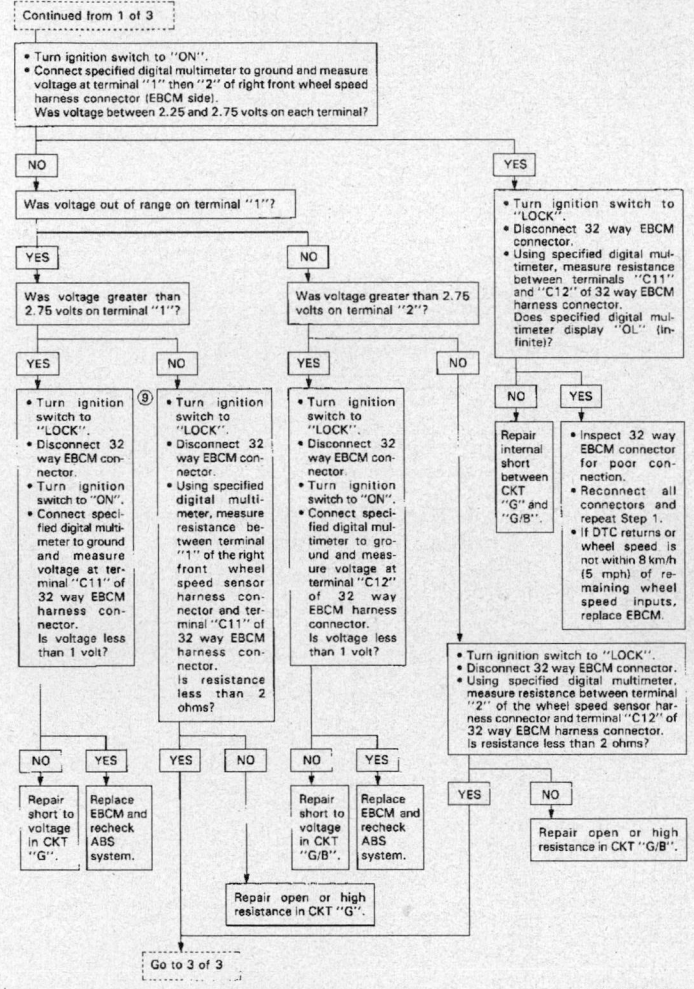

Fig. 22 Code 26: Right Front Excessive Wheel Speed Variation (Part 2 of 3)

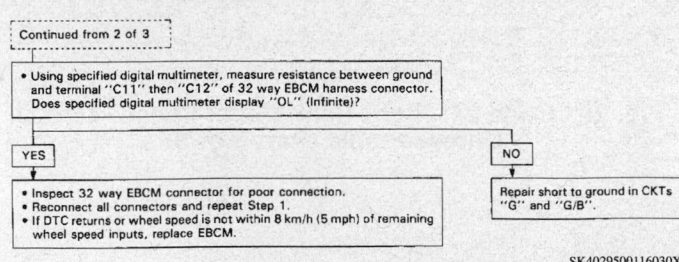

Fig. 22 Code 26: Right Front Excessive Wheel Speed Variation (Part 3 of 3)

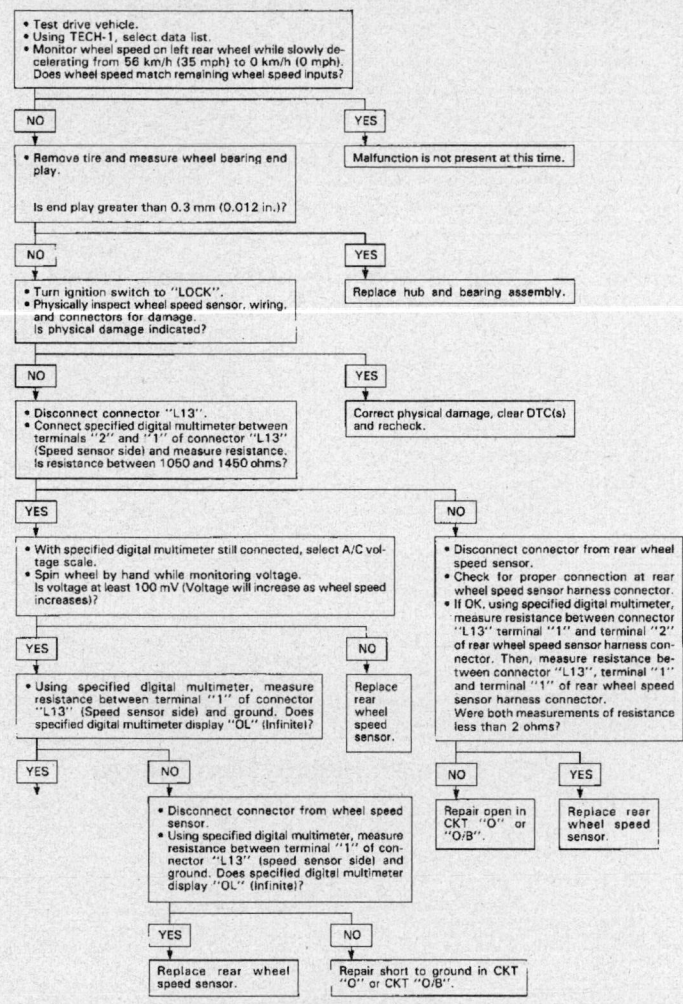

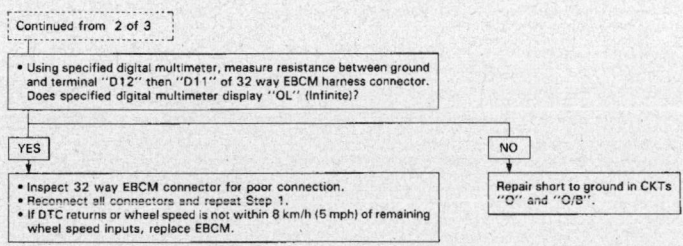

Fig. 23 Code 27: Left Rear Excessive Wheel Speed Variation (Part 1 of 3)

Fig. 23 Code 27: Left Rear Excessive Wheel Speed Variation (Part 3 of 3)

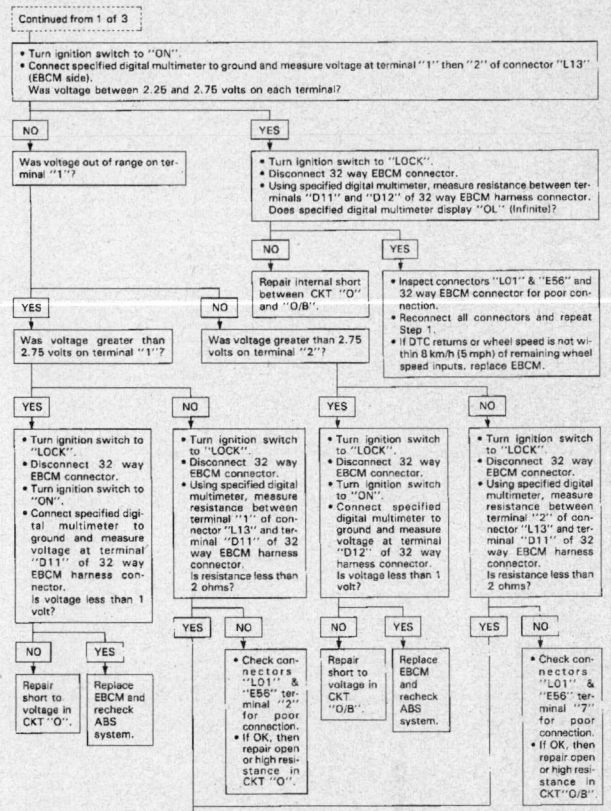

Fig. 23 Code 27: Left Rear Excessive Wheel Speed Variation (Part 2 of 3)

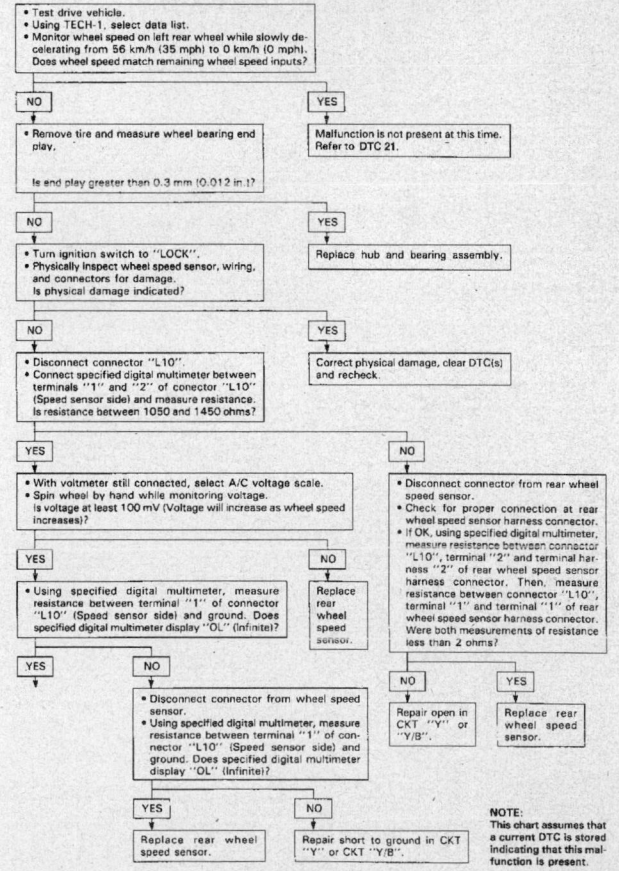

Fig. 24 Code 28: Right Rear Excessive Wheel Speed Variation (Part 1 of 3)

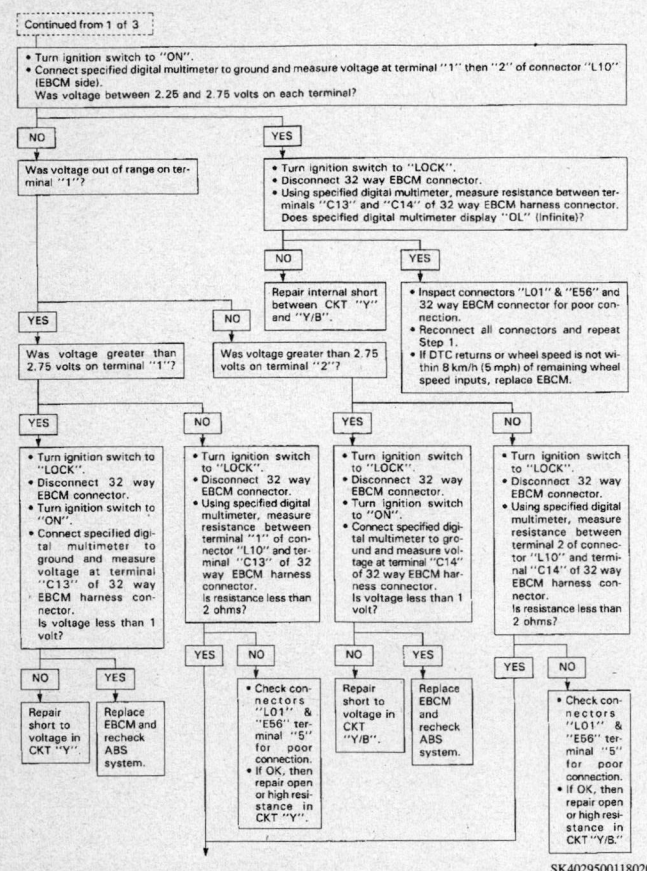

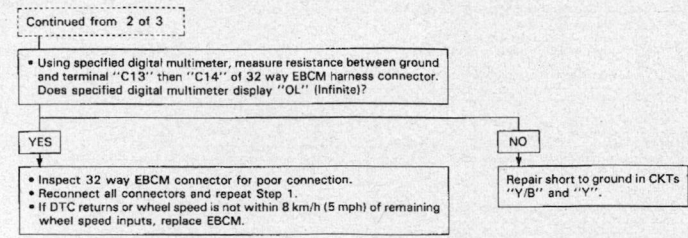

Fig. 24   Code 28: Right Rear Excessive Wheel Speed Variation (Part 3 of 3)

SK4029500118030X

Fig. 24   Code 28: Right Rear Excessive Wheel Speed Variation (Part 2 of 3)

SK4029500118020X

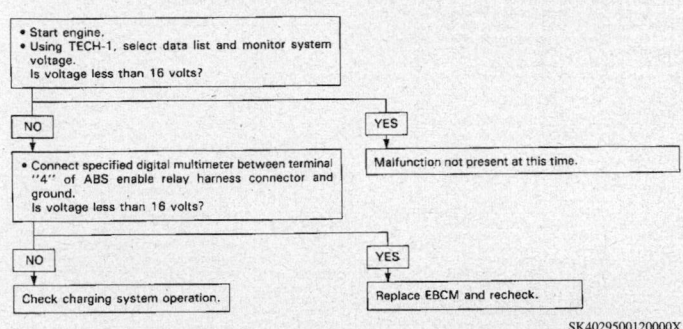

Fig. 26   Code 37: High System Voltage

SK4029500120000X

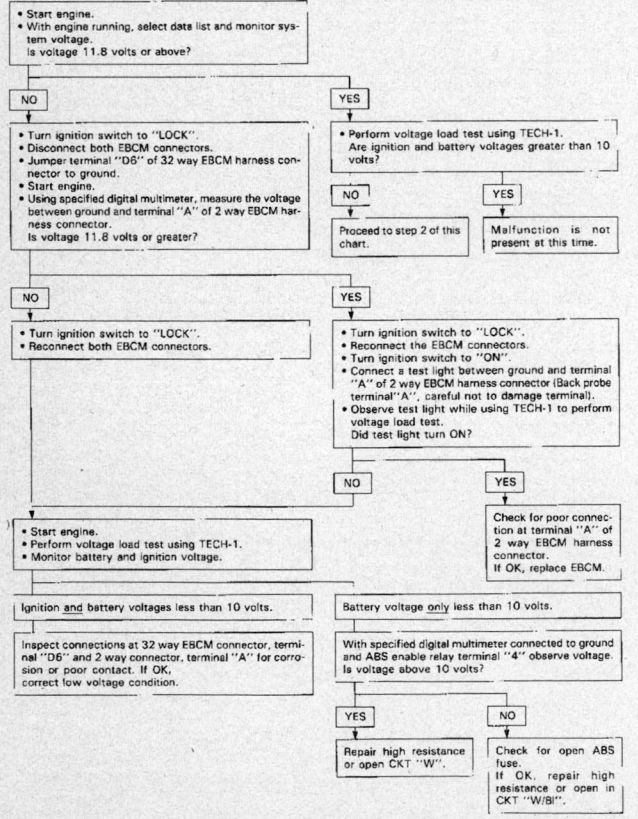

Fig. 25   Code 36: Low System Voltage

SK4029500119000X

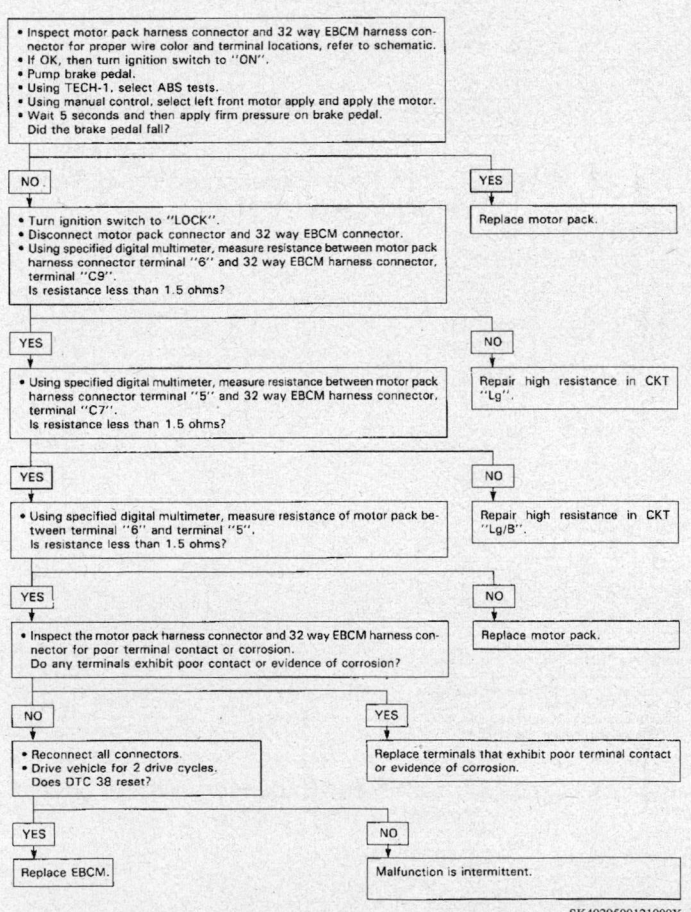

Fig. 27   Code 38: Left Front ESB Will Not Hold Motor

SK4029500121000X

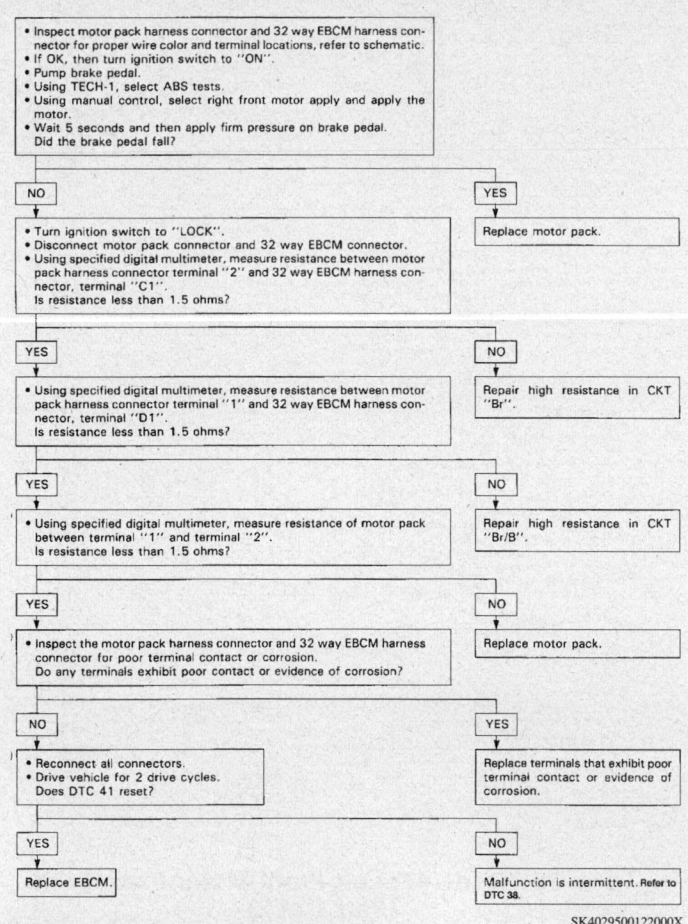

Fig. 28 Code 41: Right Front ESB Will Not Hold Motor

SK4029500122000X

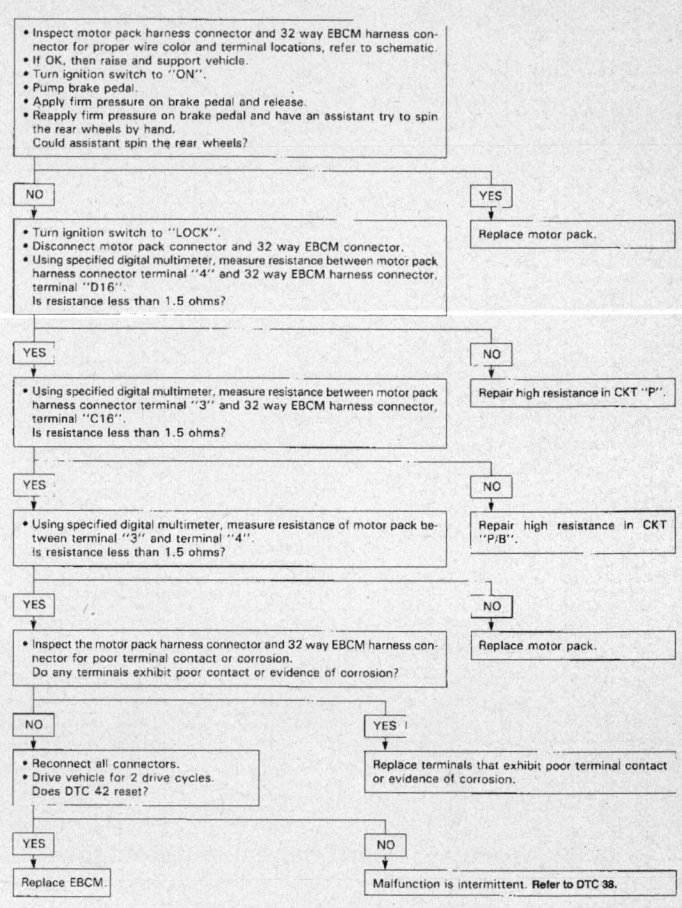

Fig. 29 Code 42: Rear ESB Will Not Hold Motor

SK4029500123000X

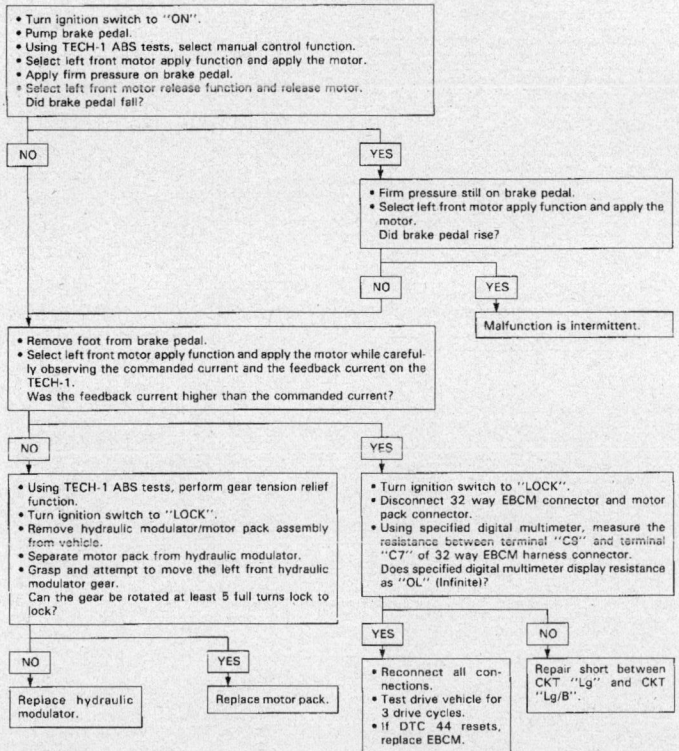

Fig. 30 Code 44: Left Front Channel Will Not Move

SK4029500124000X

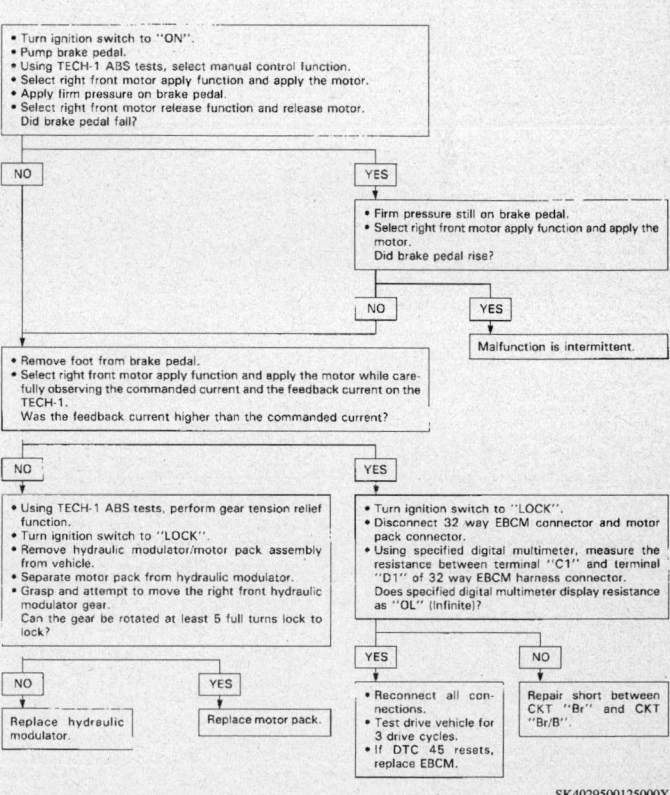

Fig. 31 Code 45: Right Front Channel Will Not Move

SK4029500125000X

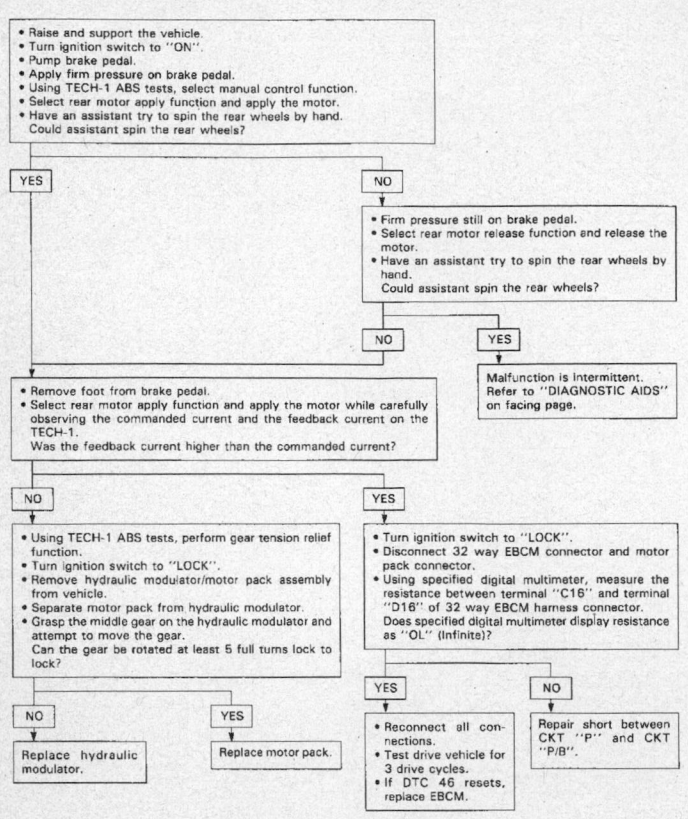

Fig. 32   Code 46: Rear Channel Will Not Move

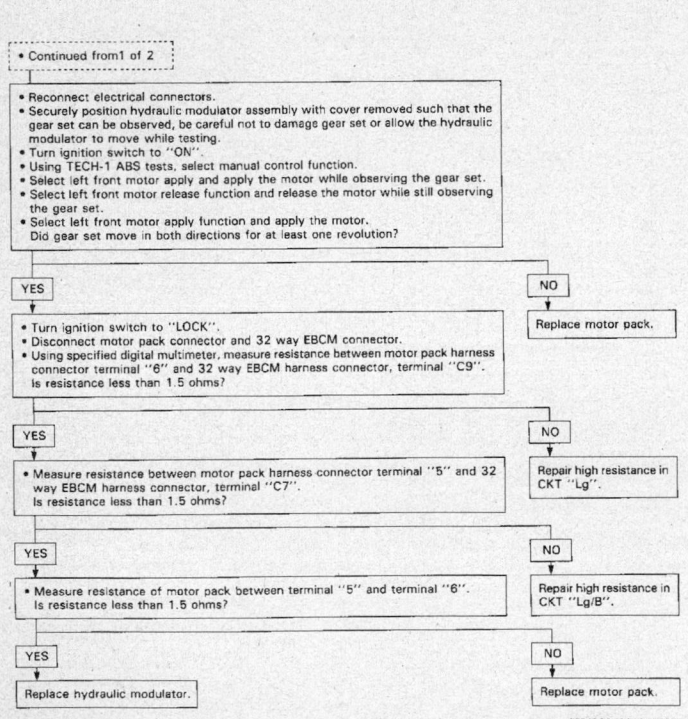

Fig. 33   Code 47: Left Front Motor Free Spins
(Part 2 of 2)

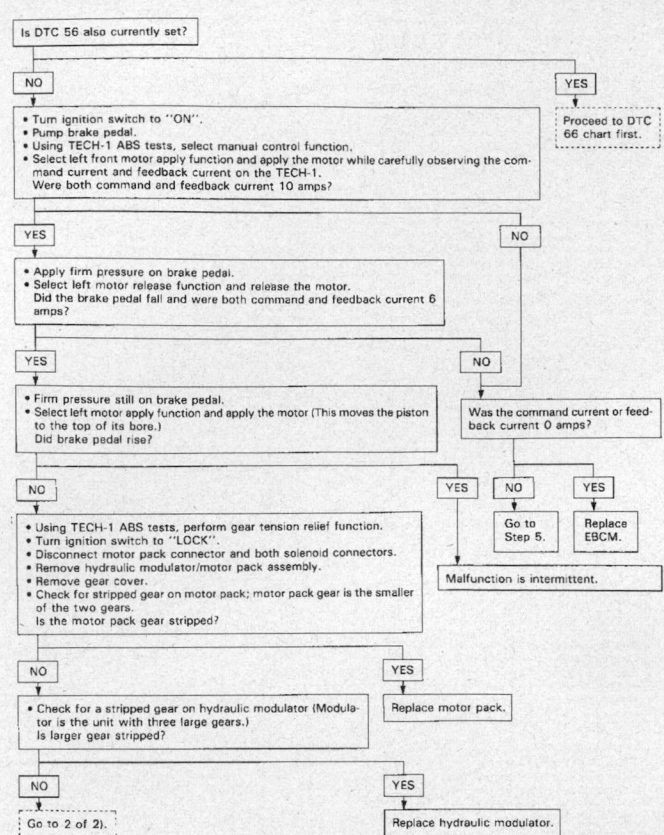

Fig. 33   Code 47: Left Front Motor Free Spins
(Part 1 of 2)

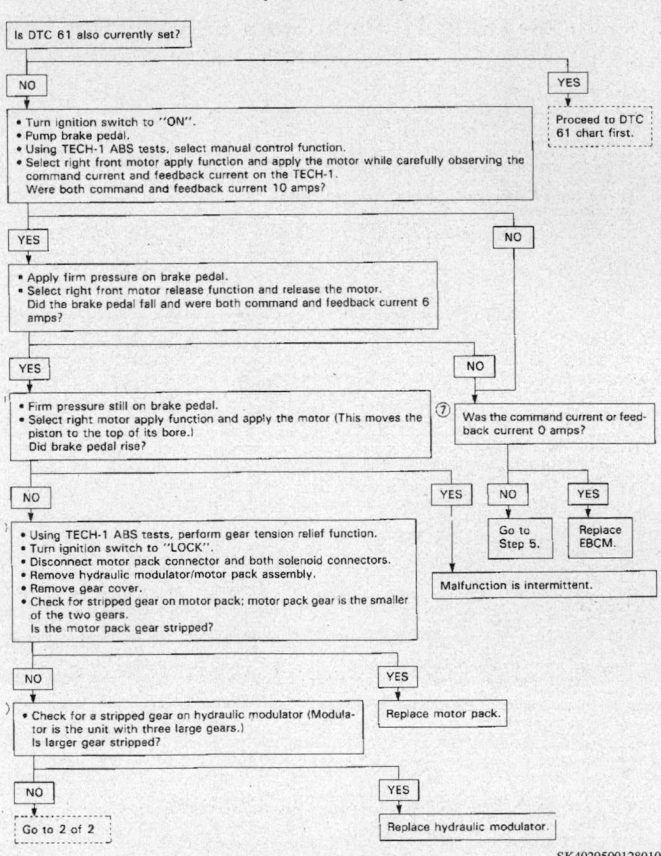

Fig. 34   Code 48: Right Front Motor Free Spins
(Part 1 of 2)

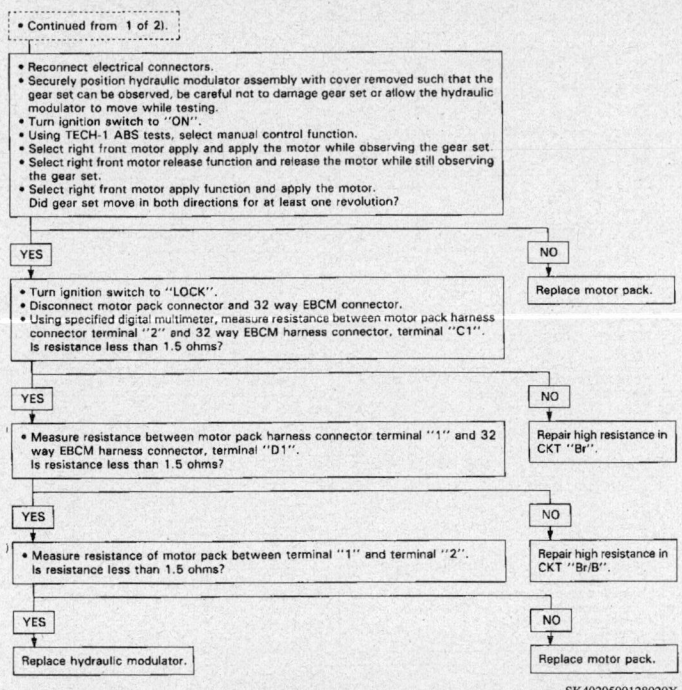

Fig. 34   Code 48: Right Front Motor Free Spins
(Part 2 of 2)

SK4029500128020X

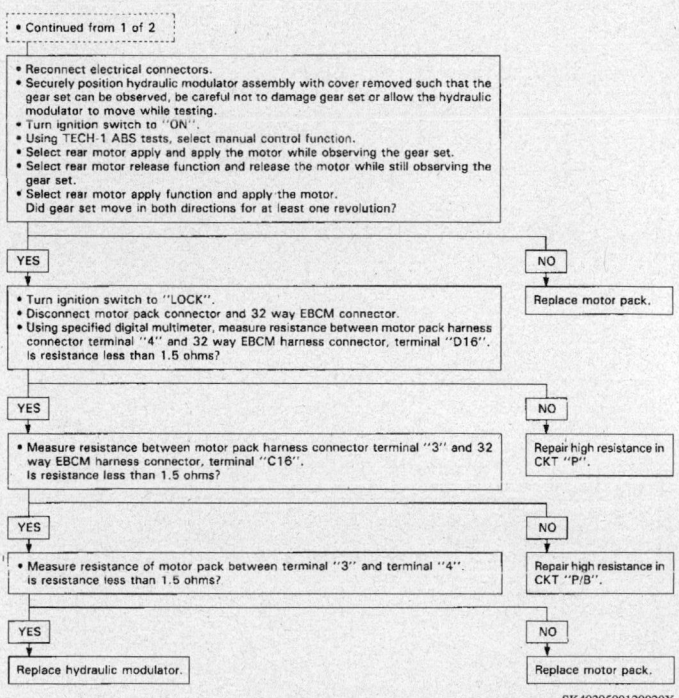

Fig. 35   Code 51: Rear Motor Free Spins
(Part 2 of 2)

SK4029500129020X

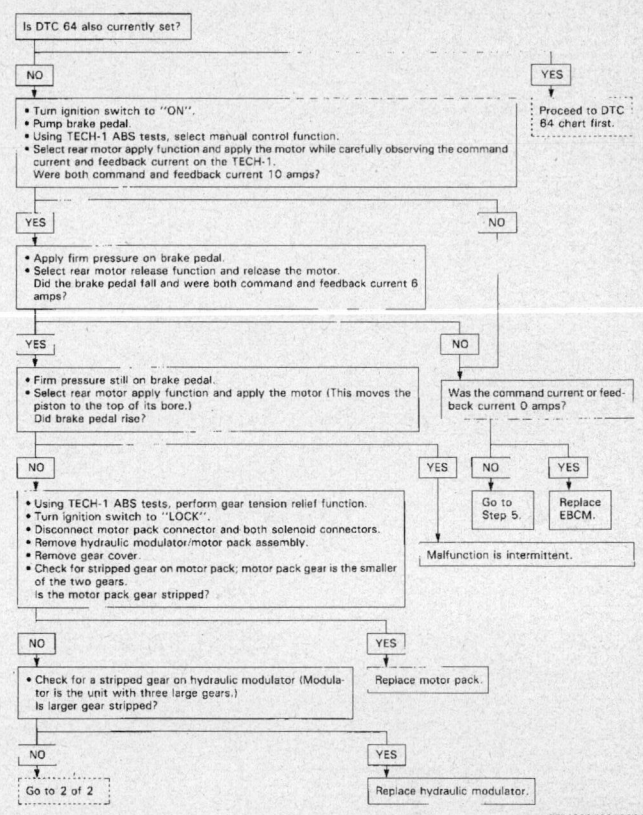

Fig. 35   Code 51: Rear Motor Free Spins
(Part 1 of 2)

SK4029500129010X

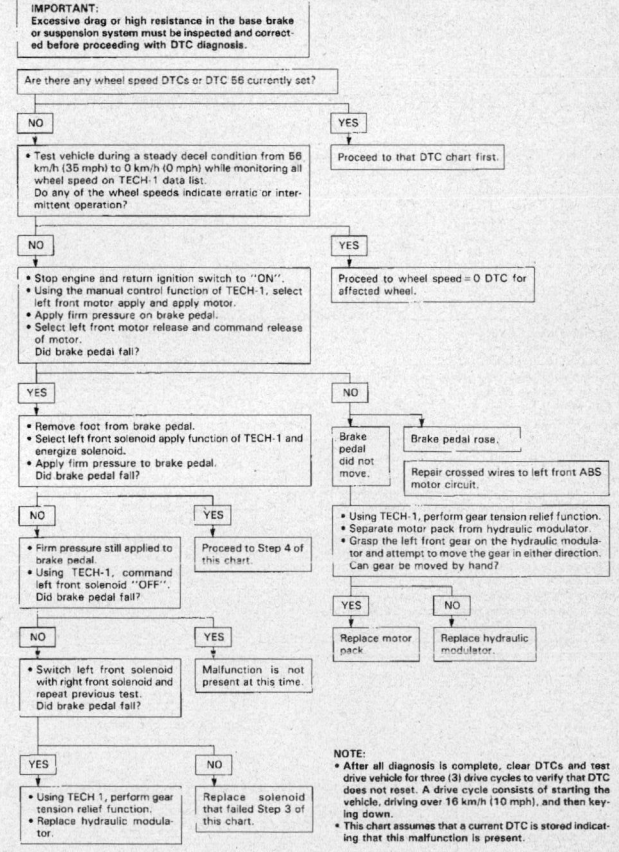

Fig. 36   Code 52: Left Front Channel In Release Too
Long

SK4029500130000X

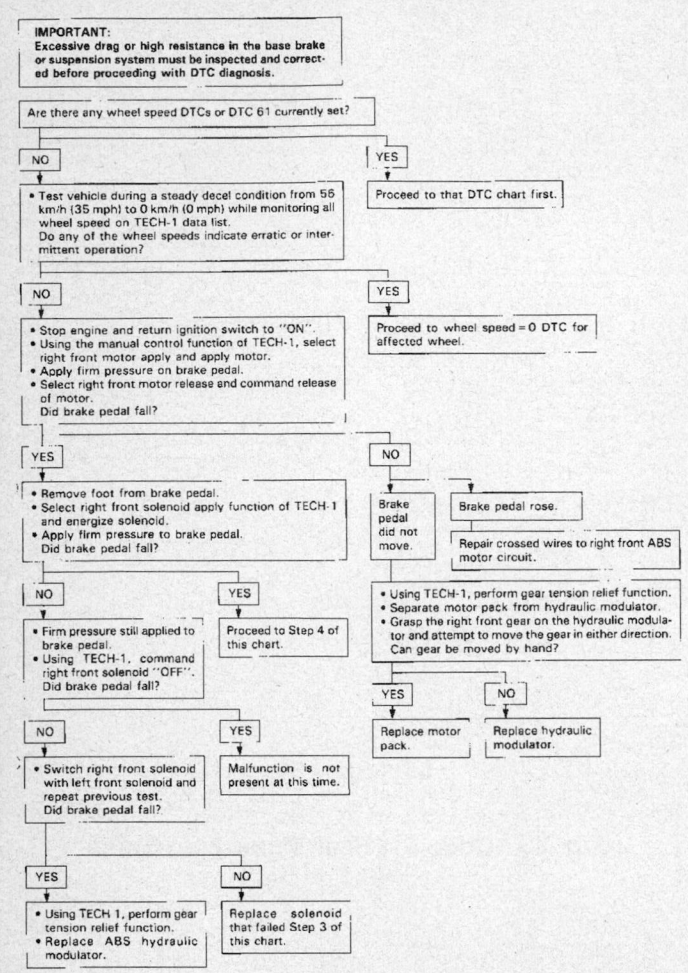

IMPORTANT:
Excessive drag or high resistance in the base brake or suspension system must be inspected and corrected before proceeding with DTC diagnosis.

Are there any wheel speed DTCs or DTC 61 currently set?

NO
• Test vehicle during a steady decel condition from 56 km/h (35 mph) to 0 km/h (0 mph) while monitoring all wheel speed on TECH-1 data list.
Do any of the wheel speeds indicate erratic or intermittent operation?

YES
Proceed to that DTC chart first.

NO
• Stop engine and return ignition switch to "ON".
• Using the manual control function of TECH-1, select right front motor apply and apply motor.
• Apply firm pressure on brake pedal.
• Select right front motor release and command release of motor.
Did brake pedal fall?

YES
Proceed to wheel speed = 0 DTC for affected wheel.

YES
• Remove foot from brake pedal.
• Select right front solenoid apply function of TECH-1 and energize solenoid.
• Apply firm pressure to brake pedal.
Did brake pedal fall?

NO
Brake pedal did not move.

Brake pedal rose.

Repair crossed wires to right front ABS motor circuit.

NO
• Firm pressure still applied to brake pedal.
• Using TECH-1, command right front solenoid "OFF".
Did brake pedal fall?

YES
Proceed to Step 4 of this chart.

• Using TECH-1, perform gear tension relief function.
• Separate motor pack from hydraulic modulator.
• Grasp the right front gear on the hydraulic modulator and attempt to move the gear in either direction.
Can gear be moved by hand?

NO
• Switch right front solenoid with left front solenoid and repeat previous test.
Did brake pedal fall?

YES
Malfunction is not present at this time.

YES
Replace motor pack.

NO
Replace hydraulic modulator.

YES
• Using TECH-1, perform gear tension relief function.
• Replace ABS hydraulic modulator.

NO
Replace solenoid that failed Step 3 of this chart.

SK4029500131000X

Fig. 37   Code 53: Right Front Channel In Release Too Long

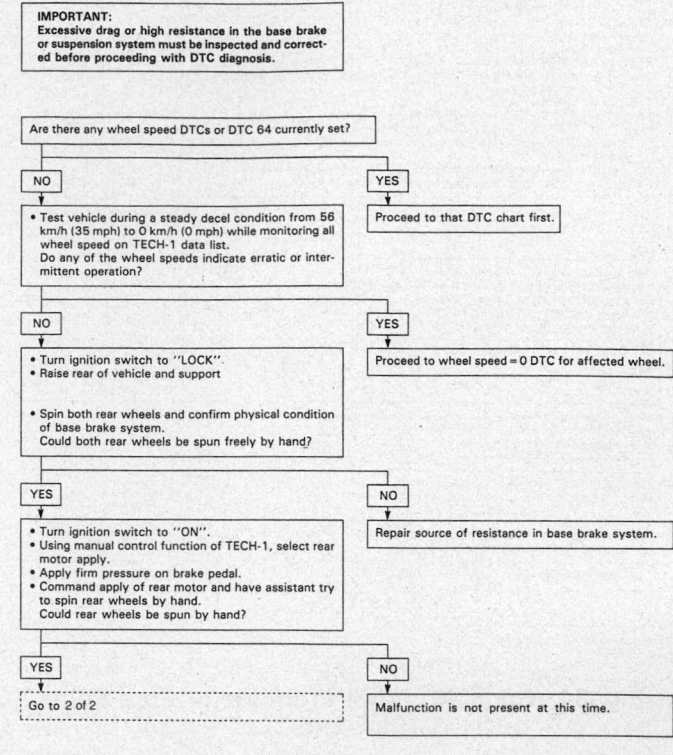

IMPORTANT:
Excessive drag or high resistance in the base brake or suspension system must be inspected and corrected before proceeding with DTC diagnosis.

Are there any wheel speed DTCs or DTC 64 currently set?

NO
• Test vehicle during a steady decel condition from 56 km/h (35 mph) to 0 km/h (0 mph) while monitoring all wheel speed on TECH-1 data list.
Do any of the wheel speeds indicate erratic or intermittent operation?

YES
Proceed to that DTC chart first.

NO
• Turn ignition switch to "LOCK".
• Raise rear of vehicle and support

• Spin both rear wheels and confirm physical condition of base brake system.
Could both rear wheels be spun freely by hand?

YES
Proceed to wheel speed = 0 DTC for affected wheel.

YES
• Turn ignition switch to "ON".
• Using manual control function of TECH-1, select rear motor apply.
• Apply firm pressure on brake pedal.
• Command apply of rear motor and have assistant try to spin rear wheels by hand.
Could rear wheels be spun by hand?

NO
Repair source of resistance in base brake system.

YES
Go to 2 of 2

NO
Malfunction is not present at this time.

SK4029500132010X

Fig. 38   Code 54: Rear Channel In Release Too Long (Part 1 of 2)

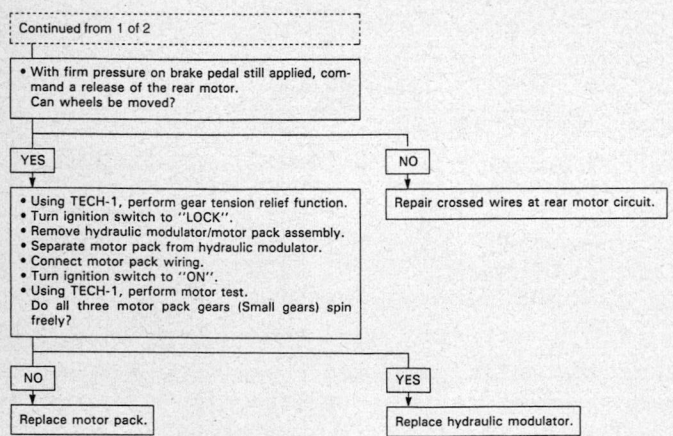

Continued from 1 of 2

• With firm pressure on brake pedal still applied, command a release of the rear motor.
Can wheels be moved?

YES
• Using TECH-1, perform gear tension relief function.
• Turn ignition switch to "LOCK".
• Remove hydraulic modulator/motor pack assembly.
• Separate motor pack from hydraulic modulator.
• Connect motor pack wiring.
• Turn ignition switch to "ON".
• Using TECH-1, perform motor test.
Do all three motor pack gears (Small gears) spin freely?

NO
Repair crossed wires at rear motor circuit.

NO
Replace motor pack.

YES
Replace hydraulic modulator.

SK4029500132020X

Fig. 38   Code 54: Rear Channel In Release Too Long (Part 2 of 2)

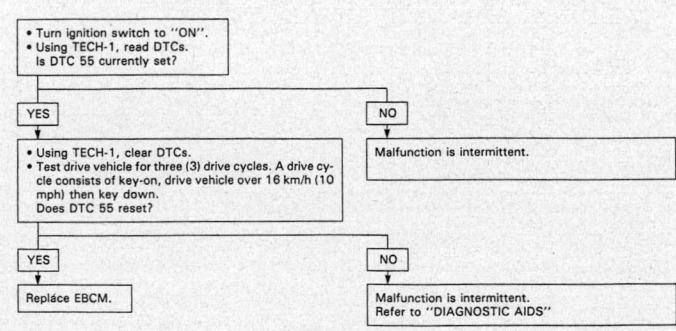

• Turn ignition switch to "ON".
• Using TECH-1, read DTCs.
Is DTC 55 currently set?

YES
• Using TECH-1, clear DTCs.
• Test drive vehicle for three (3) drive cycles. A drive cycle consists of key-on, drive vehicle over 16 km/h (10 mph) then key down.
Does DTC 55 reset?

NO
Malfunction is intermittent.

YES
Replace EBCM.

NO
Malfunction is intermittent.
Refer to "DIAGNOSTIC AIDS"

SK4029500133000X

Fig. 39   Code 55: EBCM Malfunction

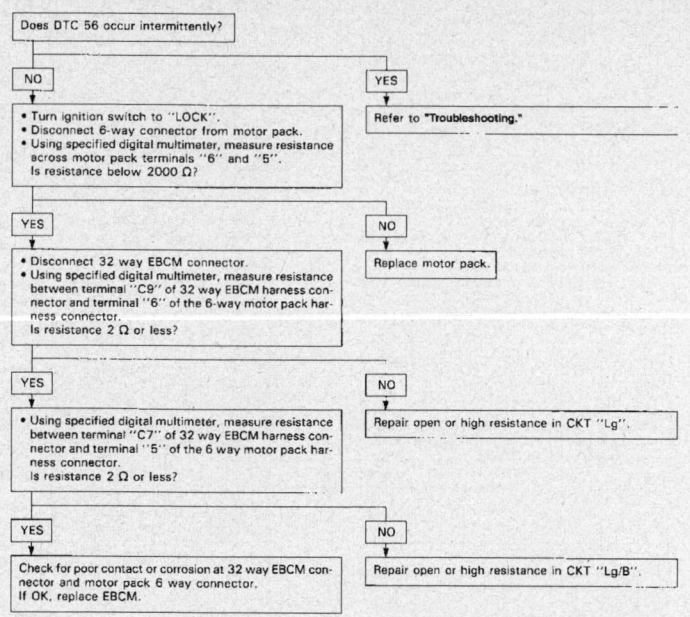

SK4029500134000X

Fig. 40   Code 56: Left Front Motor Circuit Open

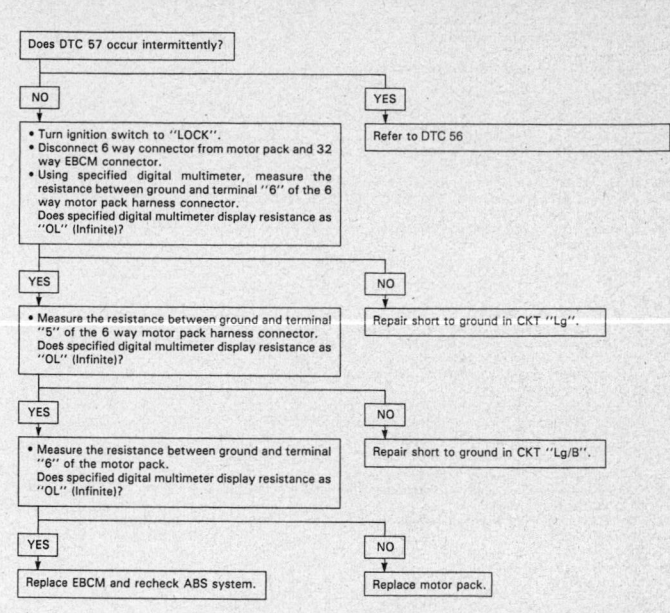

SK4029500135000X

Fig. 41   Code 57: Left Front Motor Circuit Shorted To Ground

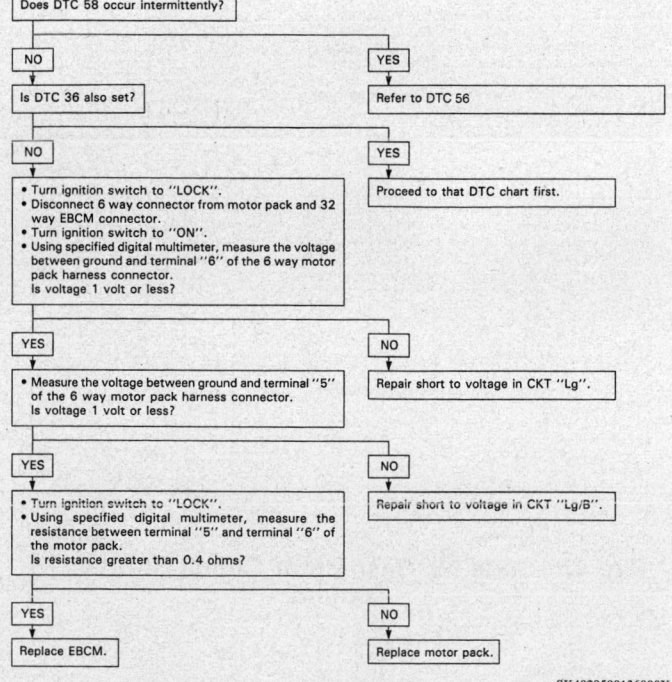

SK4029500136000X

Fig. 42   Code 58: Left Front Motor Circuit Shorted To Battery

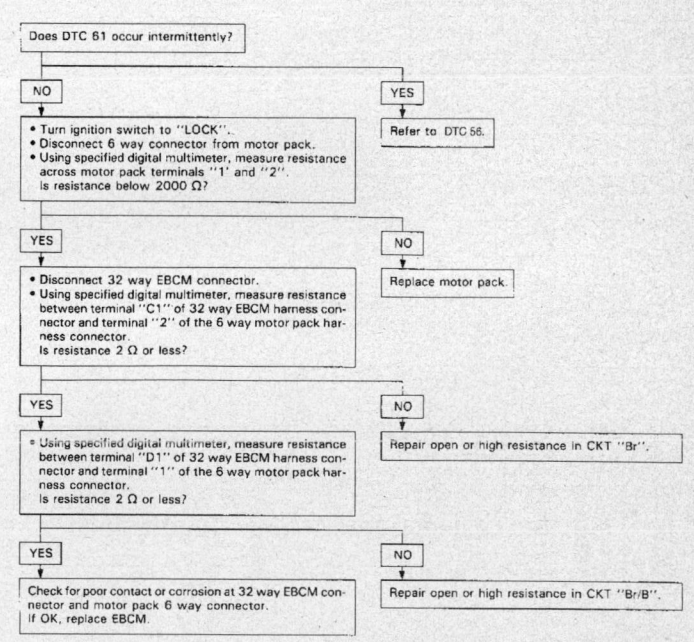

SK4029500137000X

Fig. 43   Code 61: Right Front Motor Circuit Open

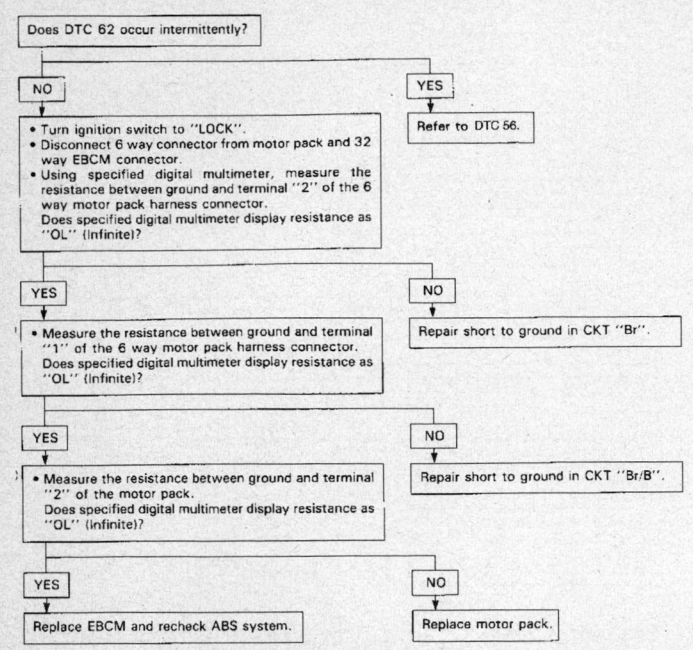

Fig. 44   Code 62: Right Front Motor Circuit Shorted To Ground

SK4029500138000X

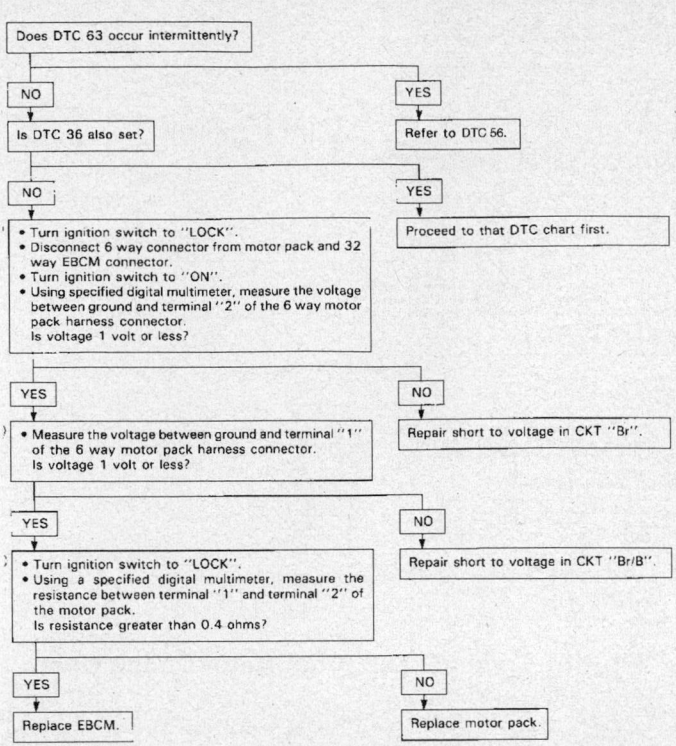

Fig. 45   Code 63: Right Front Motor Circuit Shorted To Battery

SK4029500139000X

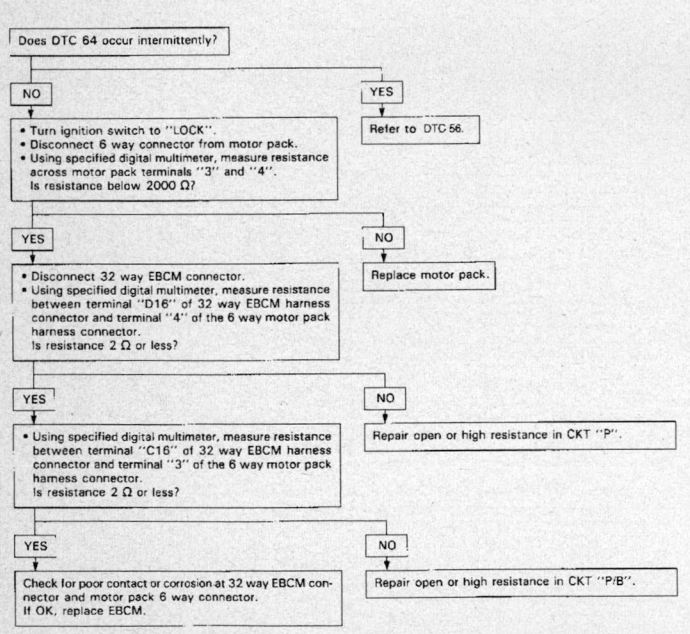

Fig. 46   Code 64: Rear Motor Circuit Open

SK4029500140000X

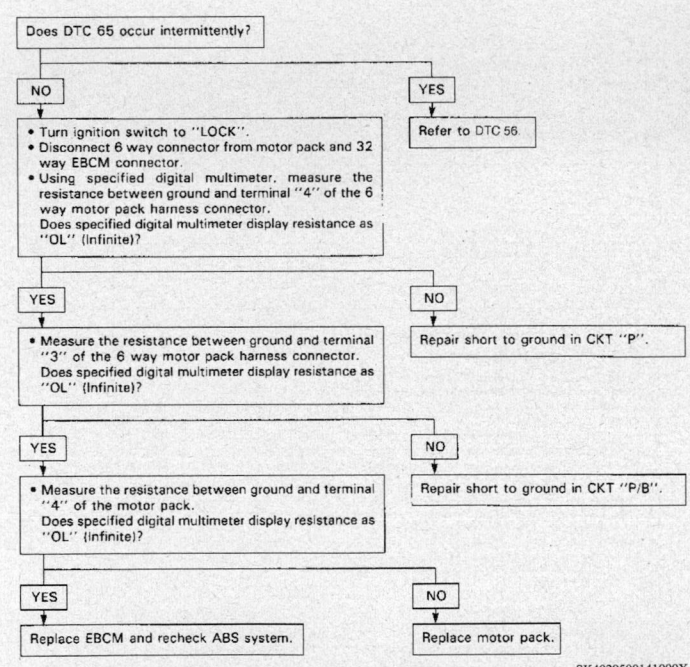

Fig. 47   Code 65: Rear Motor Circuit Shorted To Ground

SK4029500141000X

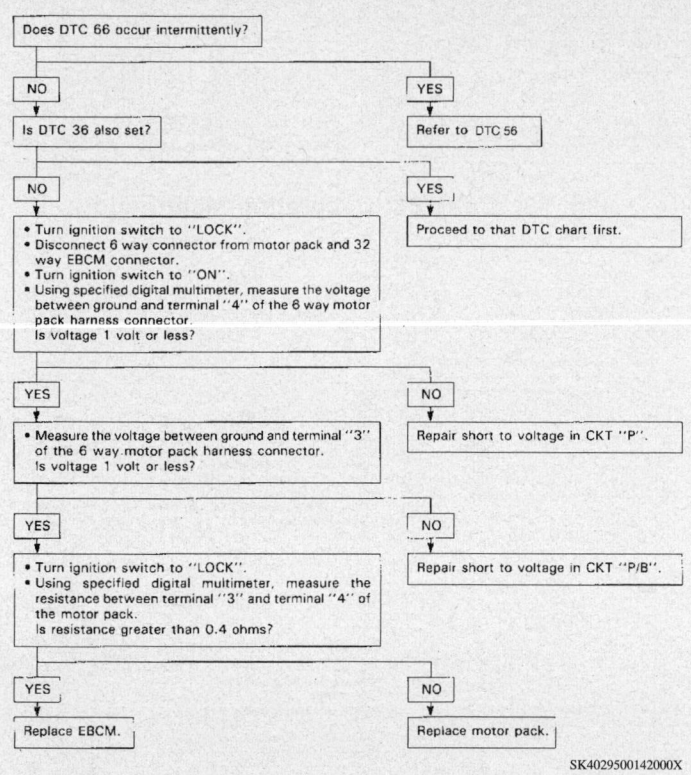

Fig. 48 Code 66: Rear Motor Circuit Shorted To Battery

SK4029500142000X

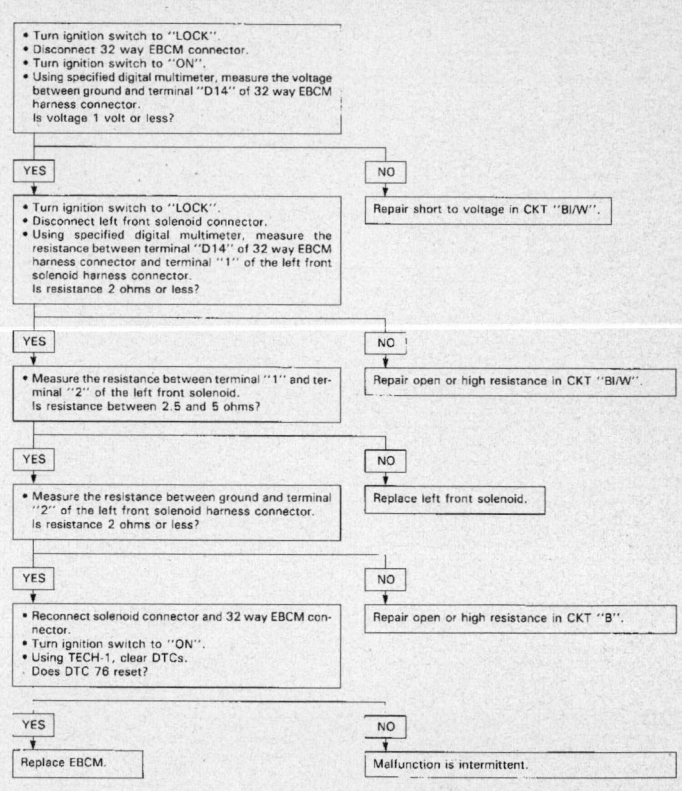

Fig. 49 Code 76: Left Front Solenoid Circuit Open Or Shorted To Battery

SK4029500143000X

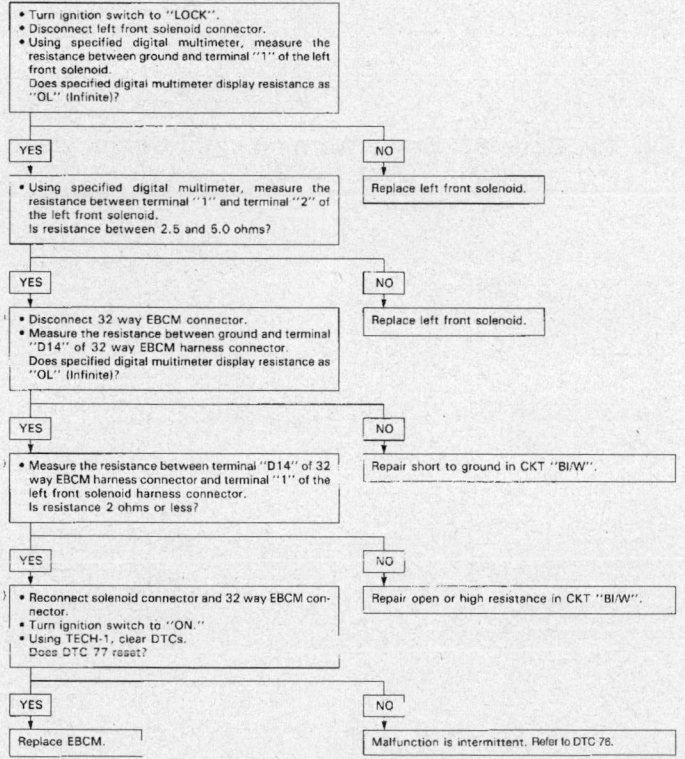

Fig. 50 Code 77: Left Front Solenoid Circuit Shorted To Ground

SK4029500144000X

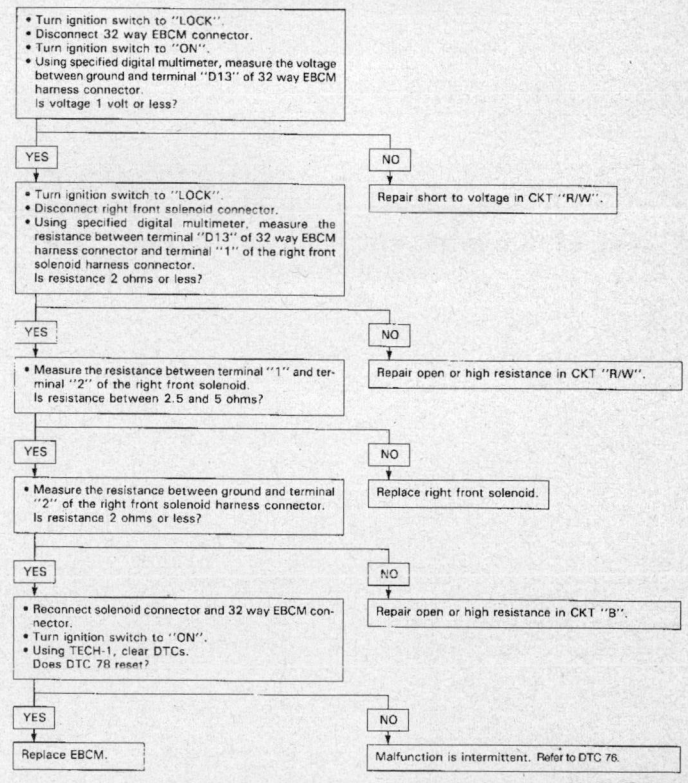

Fig. 51 Code 78: Right Front Solenoid Circuit Open Or Shorted To Battery

SK4029500145000X

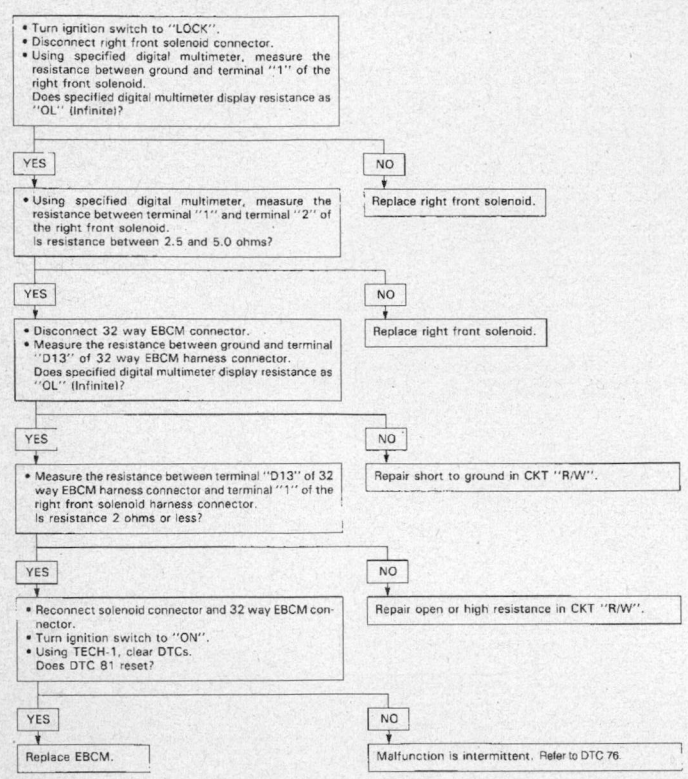

Fig. 52 Code 81: Right Front Solenoid Circuit Shorted To Ground

SK4029500146000X

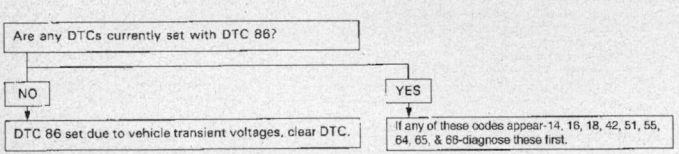

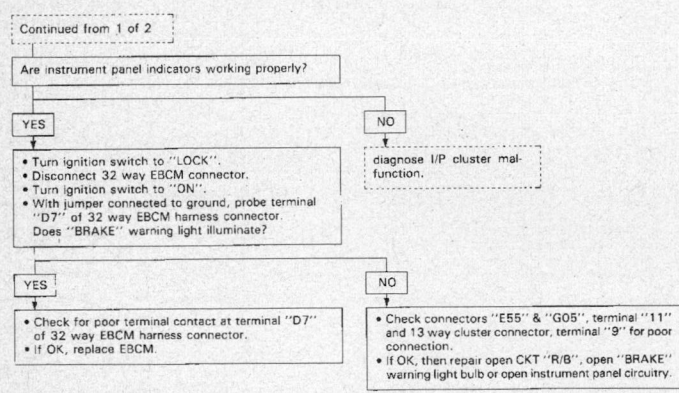

Fig. 54 Code 86: EBCM Turned On Red Brake Warning Light

SK4029500148000X

Fig. 55 Code 87: Brake Warning Light Circuit Open (Part 2 of 2)

SK4029500149020X

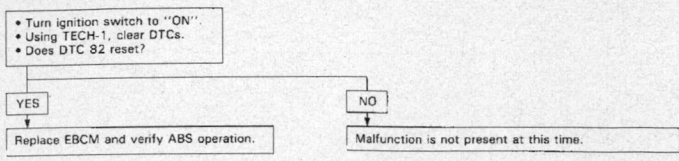

Fig. 53 Code 82: Calibration Malfunction

SK4029500147000X

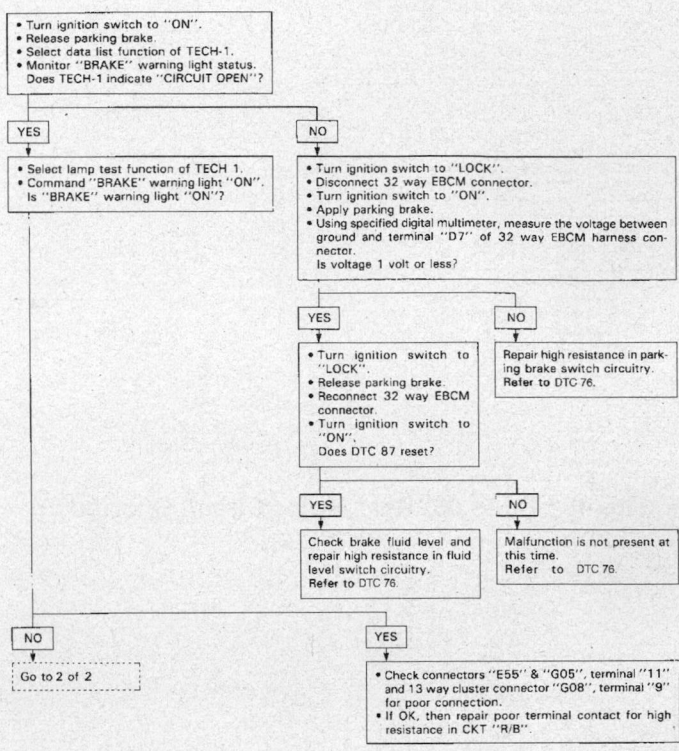

Fig. 55 Code 87: Brake Warning Light Circuit Open (Part 1 of 2)

SK4029500149010X

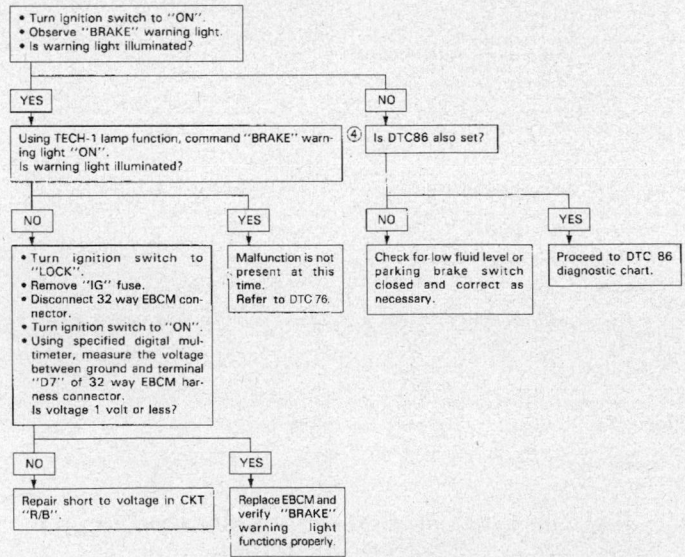

Fig. 56 Code 88: Brake Warning Light Circuit Shorted To Battery

SK4029500150000X

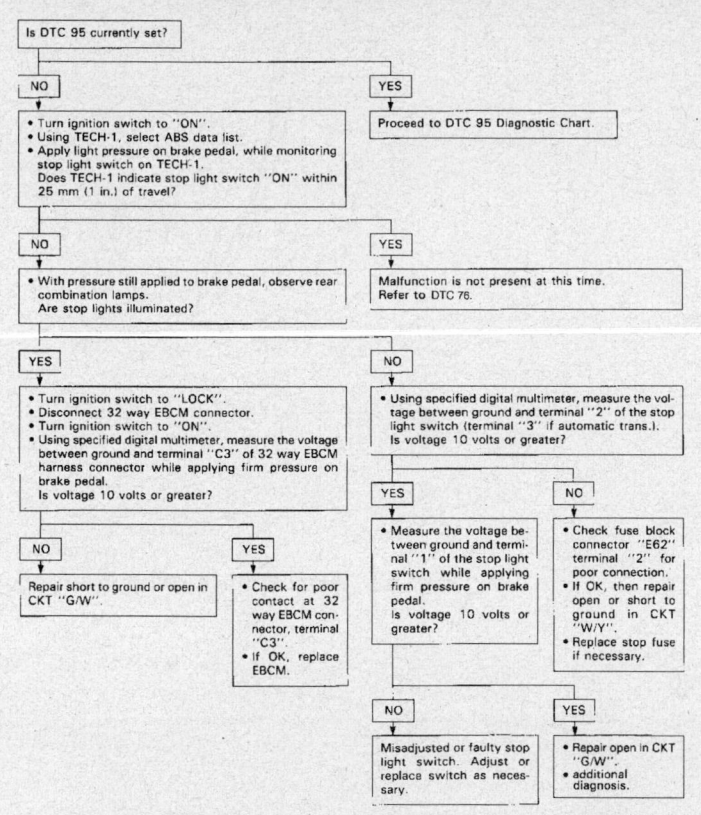

Fig. 57 Code 91: Open Brake Switch During Deceleration

SK4029500151000X

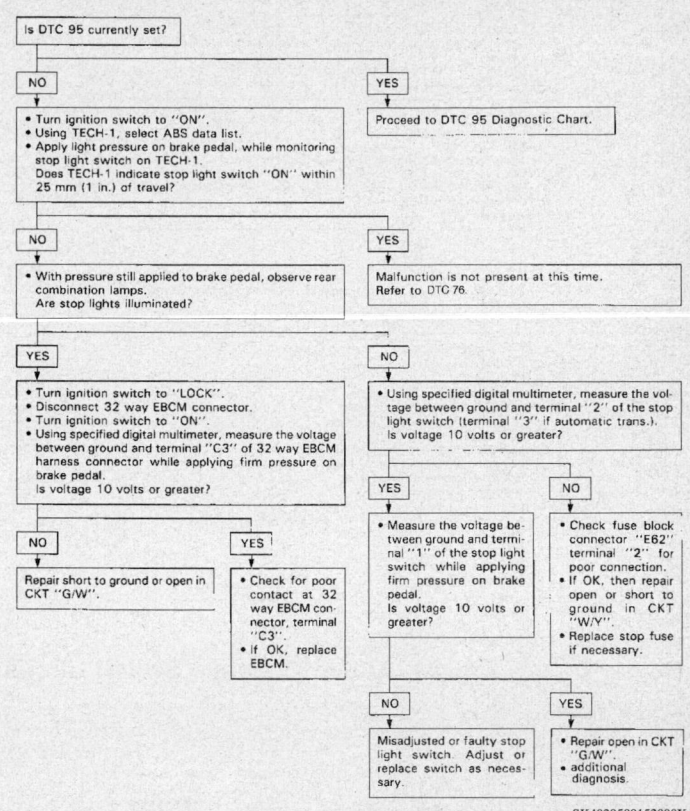

Fig. 58 Code 92: Open Brake Switch When ABS Was Required

SK4029500152000X

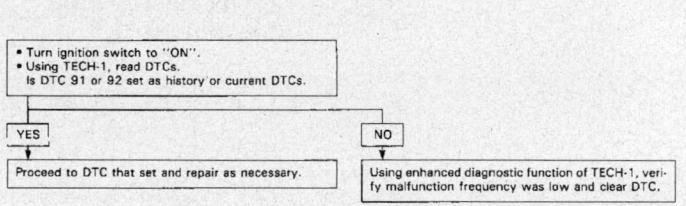

Fig. 59 Code 93: Code 91 Or 92 Set In Current Or Previous Ignition Cycle

SK4029500153000X

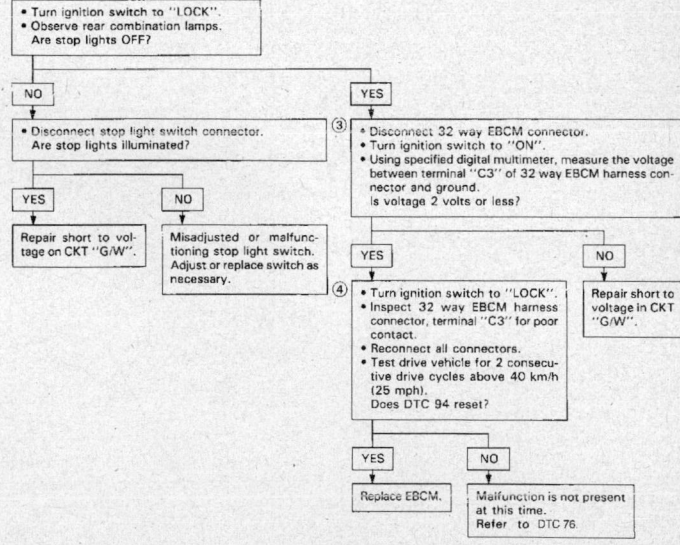

SK4029500154000X

Fig. 60 Code 94: Brake Switch Contacts Always Closed

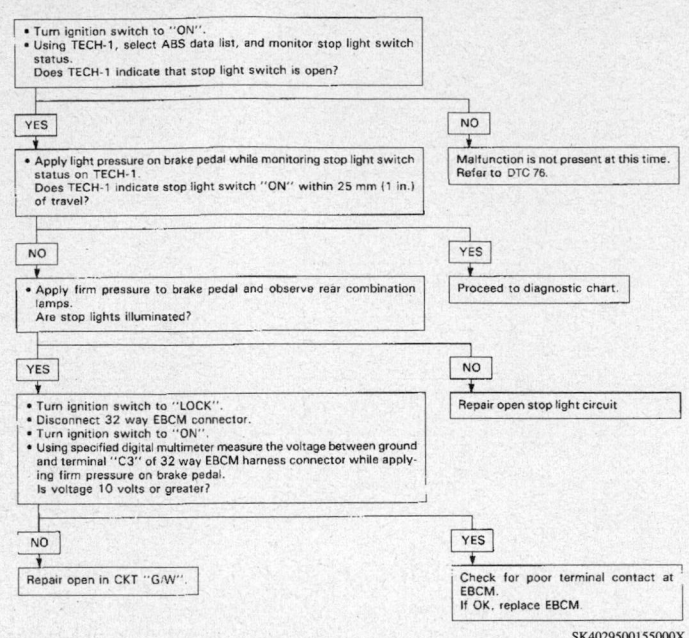

Fig. 61   Code 95: Brake Switch Circuit Open

SK4029500155000X

1. ABS enable relay

SK4029500087000X

Fig. 62   ABS enable relay location

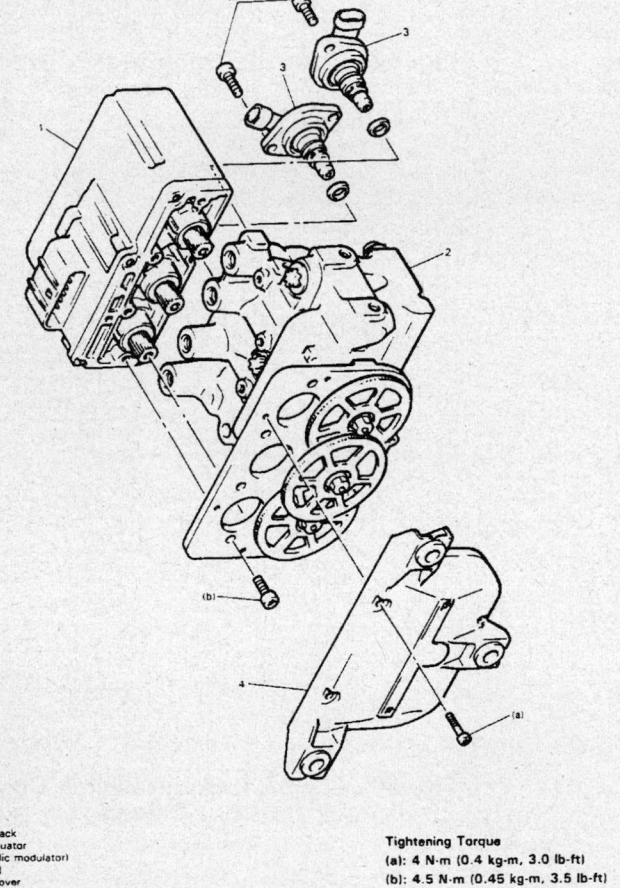

1. Motor pack
2. ABS actuator (Hydraulic modulator)
3. Solenoid
4. Under cover

Tightening Torque
(a): 4 N·m (0.4 kg-m, 3.0 lb-ft)
(b): 4.5 N·m (0.45 kg-m, 3.5 lb-ft)

SK4029500088000X

Fig. 63   Exploded view of ABS modulator assembly

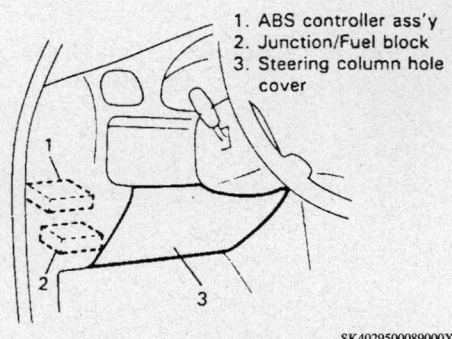

1. ABS controller ass'y
2. Junction/Fuel block
3. Steering column hole cover

SK4029500089000X

Fig. 64   Lower dash panel replacement

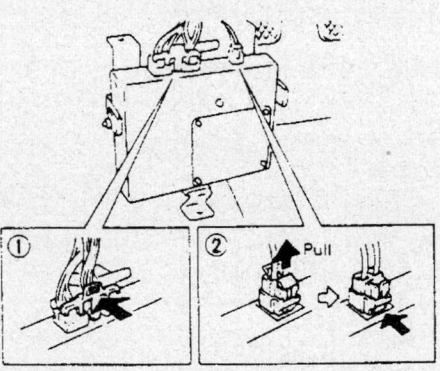

SK4029500090000X

Fig. 65   ABS electronic brake control module replacement

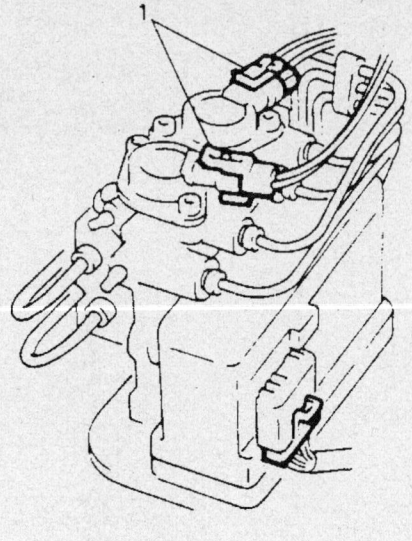

1. Solenoid couplers

SK4029500091000X

Fig. 66 ABS solenoid electrical connector location

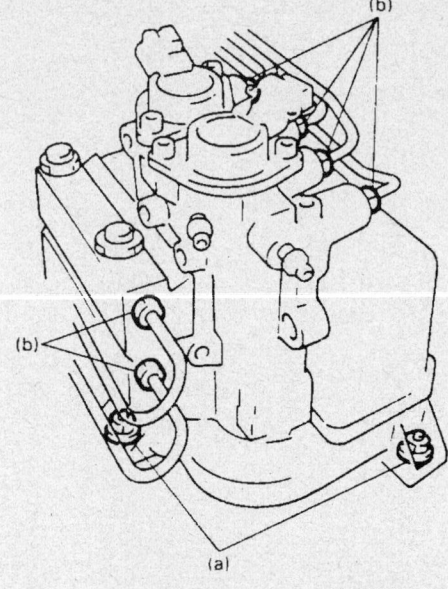

SK4029500092000X

Fig. 67 ABS modulator assembly replacement

Esteem

INDEX

PRECAUTIONS
AIR BAG SYSTEMS

Refer to "Air Bag System Precautions" in the front of this manual for system disarming and arming procedures.

BATTERY GROUND CABLE

Prior to service, disconnect battery ground cable and isolate as required.

DESCRIPTION

The ABS controls the fluid pressure applied to the wheel cylinder of each brake from the master cylinder so that each wheel is not locked even when hard braking is applied. This ABS is a 4–wheel type which control the fluid pressure applied to the wheel cylinder of each of the four brakes to prevent each wheel from getting locked. Refer to **Fig. 1** for component description and location.

TROUBLESHOOTING

Refer to "Diagnosis & Testing" for troubleshooting procedures.

DIAGNOSIS & TESTING

Accessing Diagnostic Trouble Codes

USING ANALOG VOLTMETER AND/OR WARNING LAMP

1. Using jumper wire connect diagnostic

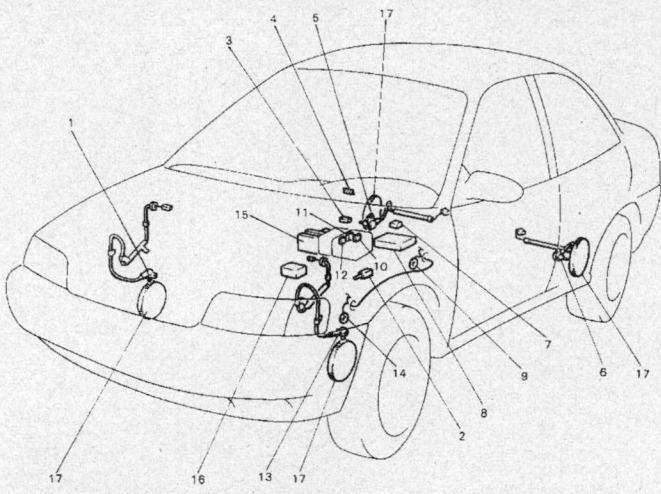

Fig. 1   ABS system components

1. Wheel speed sensor (Right-front)
2. Stop lamp switch
3. Data link connector
4. "ABS" warning lamp
5. Wheel speed sensor (Right-rear)
6. Wheel speed sensor (Left-rear)
7. Diode
8. ABS control module
9. Ground for ABS control module
10. ABS fail-safe relay (Solenoid valve relay)
11. DIAG-2 connector
12. ABS pump motor relay
13. Wheel speed sensor (Left-front)
14. Ground for ABS pump motor
15. ABS hydraulic unit
16. G sensor (4WD vehicle only)
17. Wheel speed sensor rotor (ring)

SK4029600201000X

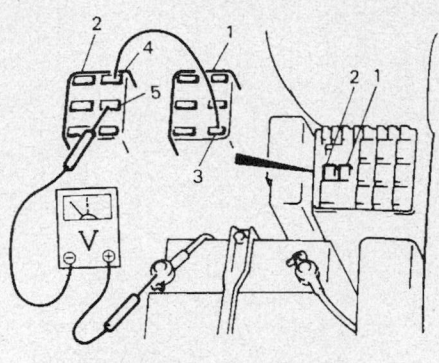

1. DIAG-1 connector
2. DIAG-2 connector
3. Ground terminal
4. Diag. switch terminal
5. Diag. output terminal

SK4029500156000X

Fig. 2   DIAG-2 connector

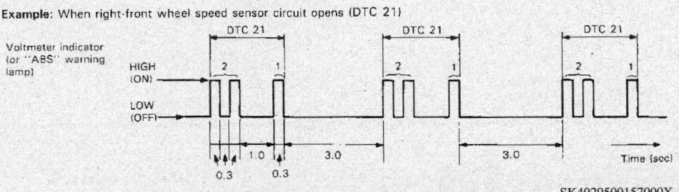

Example: When right-front wheel speed sensor circuit opens (DTC 21)

Fig. 3   flash code interpretation

SK4029500157000X

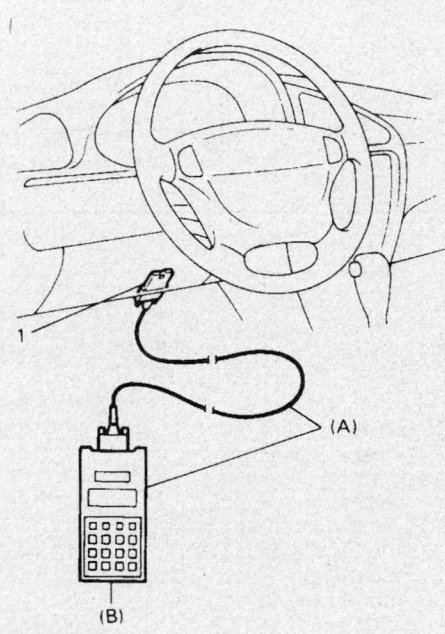

1. Data link connector (DLC)

SK4029500158000X

Fig. 4   Data link connector location

DTC 12 is displayed.

switch terminal of DIAG-2 connector to ground, **Fig. 2.**

2. Connect positive probe of analog voltmeter to positive terminal of battery and negative probe to diagnostic output terminal of DIAG-2 connector.
3. Turn ignition to On position.
4. Read deflection of voltmeter indicator which represents diagnostic trouble codes, **Fig. 3.** When more than two diagnostic trouble codes are stored in memory, deflection for each code is repeated three times starting with the smallest code number in increasing order.
5. After completing check, turn ignition to Off position and disconnect jumper wire from DIAG-2 connector.

USING TECH-1 SCAN TOOL

1. After setting cartridge for ABS to Tech-1, connect Tech-1 to data link connector, **Fig. 4.**
2. Turn ignition switch to On position.
3. Read diagnostic trouble codes according to instruction displayed on Tech-1. Refer to tool manufactures instructions for further details.
4. After completing check, turn ignition switch to Off position and disconnect Tech-1 from DLC.

Diagnostic Trouble Code Interpretation

Refer to **Fig. 5** for diagnostic trouble code interpretation.

Wiring Diagrams

Refer to **Fig. 6** for anti-lock brake system wiring diagram.

Diagnostic Tests

Refer to **Figs. 7 through 18** for diagnostic trouble code diagnosis.

Clearing Diagnostic Trouble Codes

1. Turn ignition switch to Off position.
2. Using jumper wire, connect diagnostic switch terminal of DIAG-2 connector to diagnostic output terminal.
3. Turn ignition switch to On position for at least 10 seconds.
4. Turn ignition switch to Off position and disconnect jumper wire from DIAG-2 connector.
5. Perform "Accessing Diagnostic Trouble Codes" and confirm that normal

SYSTEM SERVICE

Brake System Bleed

Brake fluid is extremely damaging to paint. If fluid should accidentally touch painted surface, immediately wipe fluid from paint and clean painted surface.

The hydraulic lines of the brake system are based on a diagonal split system. When

a brake line or hose is disconnected, bleeding operation must be performed at both ends of the line disconnected.

1. Fill master cylinder reservoir. Reservoir should be kept at least half full during bleeding operation.
2. Remove bleeder plug cap, then attach vinyl tube to bleeder plug of component to be bled. Insert other end of tube into suitable container.
3. Depress brake pedal several times, then while holding pedal depressed, loosen bleeder plug ½ turn.
4. When fluid pressure in cylinder is almost depleted, retighten bleeder plug.
5. Repeat steps 3 and 4, until there are no more air bubbles in hydraulic line.
6. When bubbles stop, depress and hold brake pedal, then tighten bleeder plug.
7. Attach bleeder cap.
8. After completing bleeding operation, apply fluid pressure to hydraulic system and check for leakage.
9. Fill master cylinder reservoir up to specified level.
10. Check brake pedal for sponginess. If pedal is spongy, repeat entire procedure.

Component Replacement

CONTROL MODULE

1. Remove steering column hole cover and knee bolster panel from instrument panel.
2. Disconnect ABS control module electrical connectors.
3. Remove two ABS control module attaching bolts and module.
4. Reverse procedure to install.

FRONT WHEEL SPEED SENSOR

1. Raise and support vehicle.
2. Disconnect wheel speed sensor electrical connectors.
3. Push out grommet of harness from inner fender to outside of vehicle.
4. Remove harness clamp bolts and front wheel speed sensor from knuckle

DTC	VOLTMETER INDICATION (or "ABS" warning lamp flashing pattern)	DIAGNOSTIC AREA
15		G sensor (if equipped) or ABS control module
18		Wheel speed sensor and/or rotor or hydraulic unit
21		Right-front
25		Left-front
31		Right-rear
35		Left-rear
22		Right-front
26		Left-front
32		Right-rear
36		Left-rear
41		Right-front
45		Left-front
51		Right-rear
55		Left-rear
57		Solenoid and pump motor power circuit
61		ABS pump motor (in hydraulic unit) circuit
63		ABS fail-safe relay circuit
71		ABS control module
12		Normal

Wheel speed sensor circuit and rotor (grouping DTC 22, 26, 32, 36)
Solenoid (in hydraulic unit) circuit (grouping DTC 41, 45, 51, 55)

SK4029500159000X

Fig. 5 Diagnostic trouble code interpretation

5. Reverse procedure to install. **Torque** attaching bolts to 17 ft. lbs.

REAR WHEEL SPEED SENSOR

1. Raise and support vehicle.
2. Disconnect wheel speed sensor electrical connectors and remove connector and harness from suspension frame.
3. Remove harness clamp bolts and rear wheel speed sensor from knuckle

4. Reverse procedure to install. **Torque** attaching bolts to 17 ft. lbs.

G SENSOR

1. Turn ignition to Off position.
2. Remove console box extensions.
3. Disconnect electrical connector from sensor.
4. Remove sensor and bracket from floor.
5. Reverse procedure to install.

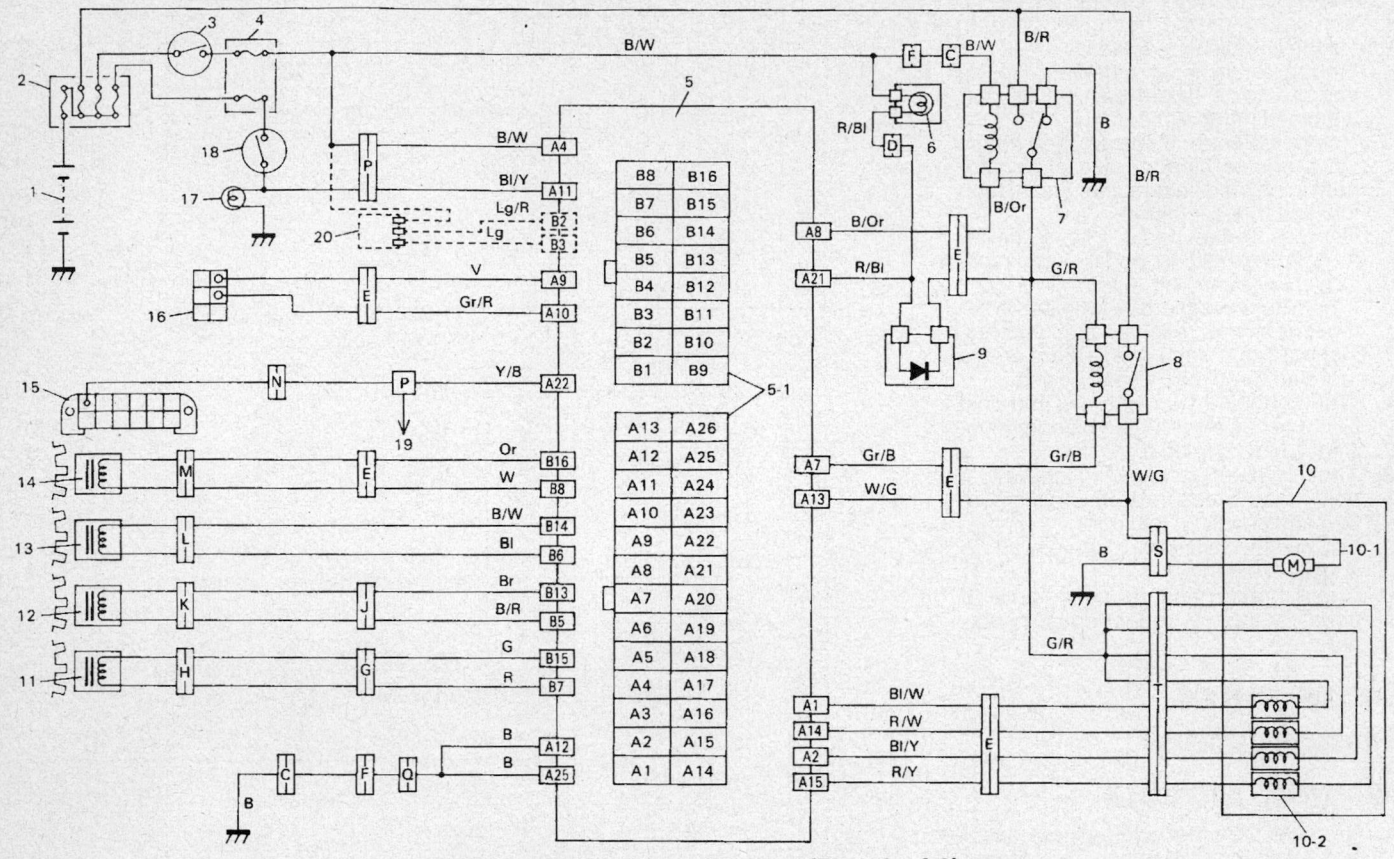

Fig. 6   ABS wiring diagram (Part 1 of 2)

1. Battery
2. Main fuses
3. Ignition switch
4. Circuit fuses
5. ABS control module
5-1. Terminal arrangement
    for ABS control module
6. "ABS" warning lamp
7. ABS fail-safe relay
   (Solenoid valve relay)
8. ABS pump motor relay
9. Diode
10. ABS hydraulic unit
10-1. Pump motor
10-2. Solenoid valves
11. Right-rear wheel speed sensor
12. Left-rear wheel speed sensor
13. Right-front wheel speed sensor
14. Left-front wheel speed sensor
15. Data link connector
16. Diagnosis-2 connector
    (DIAG-2)
17. Stop lamp
18. Stop lamp switch
19. To ECM, TCM and SDM
    (if equipped)
20. G sensor (if equipped)

A ~ P: Connector

Wire color
B   : Black
B/Or : Black/Orange
B/R : Black/Red
B/W : Black/White
Bl   : Blue
Bl/Y : Blue/Yellow
Bl/W : Blue/White
Br   : Brown
G   : Green
G/R : Green/Red
Gr   : Gray
Gr/B : Gray/Black
Gr/R : Gray/Red
Or   : Orange
R   : Red
R/Bl : Red/Blue
R/W : Red/White
R/Y : Red/Yellow
V   : Violet
W   : White

TERMINAL	CIRCUIT	TERMINAL	CIRCUIT
A1	Left-front solenoid valve	A23	—
A2	Left-rear solenoid valve	A24	—
A3		A25	Ground
A4	Ignition switch	A26	—
A5			
A6	—	B1	—
A7	ABS pump motor relay	B2	G sensor signal (if equipped)
A8	ABS fail-safe relay	B3	G sensor ground (if equipped)
A9	Diagnosis switch terminal	B4	—
A10	Diagnosis output terminal	B5	Left-rear wheel speed sensor (−)
A11	Stop lamp switch	B6	Right-front wheel speed sensor (−)
A12	Ground	B7	Right-rear wheel speed sensor (−)
A13	Motor voltage monitor	B8	Left-front wheel speed sensor (−)
A14	Right-front solenoid valve	B9	
A15	Right-rear solenoid valve	B10	—
A16	—	B11	
A17	—	B12	
A18	—	B13	Left-rear wheel speed sensor (+)
A19	—	B14	Right-front wheel speed sensor (+)
A20	—	B15	Right-rear wheel speed sensor (+)
A21	"ABS" warning lamp	B16	Left-front wheel speed sensor (+)
A22	Data link connector		

Fig. 6   ABS wiring diagram (Part 2 of 2)

SK4029500160020X

DIAGNOSTIC CHART INDEX

Code	Description	Page No.	Fig. No.
Chart A	ABS Warning Lamp Circuit Check, Lamp Does Not Come On At Ignition Switch On	42-150	7
Chart B	ABS Warning Lamp Circuit Check, Lamp Comes On Steady	42-150	8
Chart C	ABS Warning Lamp Circuit Check, Lamp Flashes Continuously While Ignition Switch Is On	42-150	9
Chart D	DTC Is Not Outputted From Diagnostic Output Terminal, Even With Diagnostic Switch Terminal Connected To Ground	42-151	10
Code 15	G Sensor Circuit On 4WD Vehicle Or ABS Control Module On 2WD Vehicle	42-151	11
Code 18	Wheel Speed Sensor/Rotor Or ABS Hydraulic Unit	42-152	12
Cod 21	Wheel Speed Sensor Circuits	42-152	13
Cod 22	Wheel Speed Sensor Circuits	42-152	13
Cod 25	Wheel Speed Sensor Circuits	42-152	13
Cod 26	Wheel Speed Sensor Circuits	42-152	13
Cod 31	Wheel Speed Sensor Circuits	42-152	13
Cod 32	Wheel Speed Sensor Circuits	42-152	13
Cod 35	Wheel Speed Sensor Circuits	42-152	13
Cod 36	Wheel Speed Sensor Circuits	42-152	13
Cod 41	Solenoid Circuits	42-153	14
Cod 45	Solenoid Circuits	42-153	14
Cod 51	Solenoid Circuits	42-153	14
Cod 55	Solenoid Circuits	42-153	14
Code 57	Solenoid & Pump Motor Power Source Circuit	42-153	15
Code 61	ABS Pump Motor Circuit	42-154	16
Code 63	ABS Fail-Safe Relay Circuit	42-154	17
Code 71	ABS Control Module	42-155	18

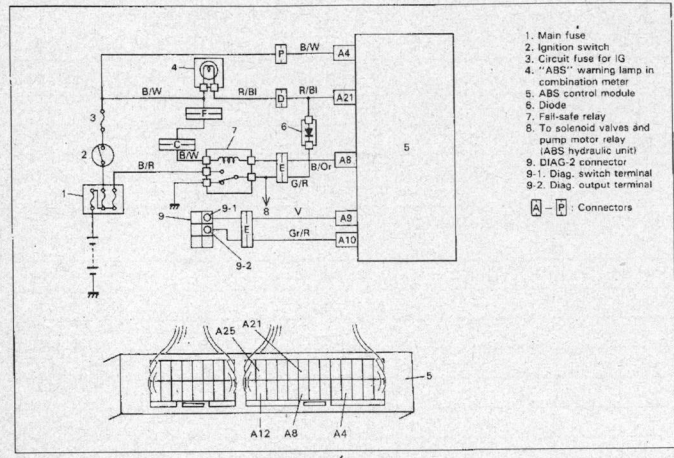

CIRCUIT DESCRIPTION

Operation (ON/OFF) of the "ABS" warning lamp is controlled by the ABS control module and the fail-safe relay. When the ignition switch is turned ON, the ABS control module switches the contact point of the fail-safe relay from the lamp circuit side (relay OFF) to the hydraulic unit circuit side (relay ON). (Immediately after the ignition switch was turned ON, however, the relay is switched from OFF in the order of ON→OFF→ON as the initial check of the fail-safe relay.)

If the Antilock brake system is in good condition, the ABS control module turns the "ABS" warning lamp ON at the ignition switch ON, keeps it ON for 2 seconds only and then turns it OFF. If an abnormality in the system is detected, the lamp is turned ON by both ABS control module and fail-safe relay. Also, it is turned ON by the fail-safe relay when the connector of the ABS control module was disconnected.

When the lamp drive circuit A21 of the ABS control module becomes open, the lamp flashes twice and turns OFF as the initial check of the relay.

The lamp is turned ON when the ABS control module is in the mode to clear the diagnostic trouble code (the diag. switch terminal and the diag. output terminal are connected or when the "V" circuit and "Gr/R" circuit are shorted).

SK4029500161010X

Fig. 7   Chart A: ABS Warning Lamp Circuit Check, Lamp Does Not Come On At Ignition Switch On (Part 1 of 2)

INSPECTION

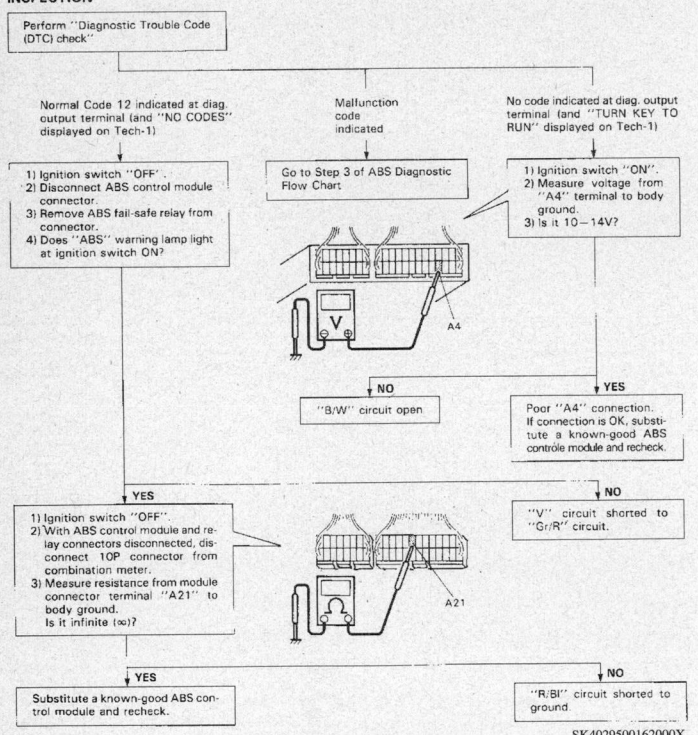

SK4029500162000X

Fig. 8   Chart B: ABS Warning Lamp Circuit Check, Lamp Comes On Steady

INSPECTION

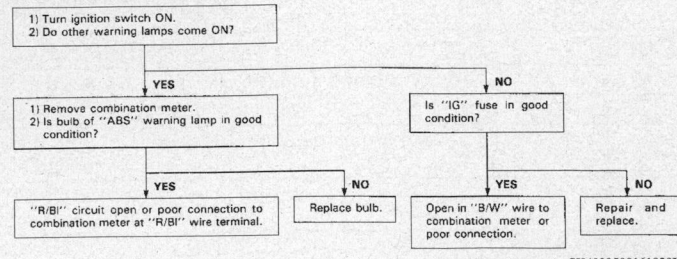

SK4029500161020X

Fig. 7   Chart A: ABS Warning Lamp Circuit Check, Lamp Does Not Come On At Ignition Switch On (Part 2 of 2)

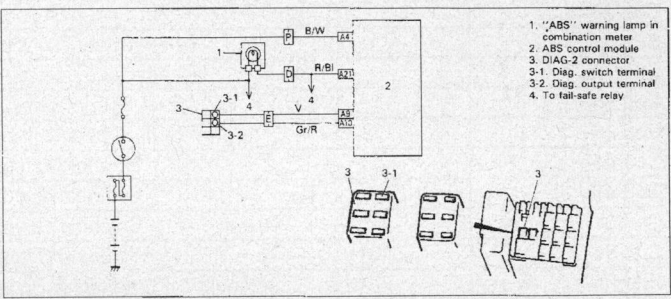

CIRCUIT DESCRIPTION

When the diag. switch terminal is shorted or connected to the ground with the ignition switch ON, the diag. trouble code (DTC) is indicated by flashing of the "ABS" warning lamp only in following cases.
- Normal DTC (12) is indicated if no malfunction DTC is detected in the ABS.
- A history malfunction DTC is indicated by flashing of the lamp if a current malfunction DTC is not detected at that point although a history malfunction DTC is stored in memory.

INSPECTION

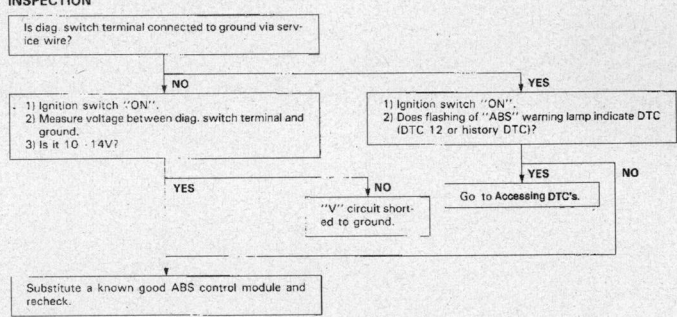

SK4029500163000X

Fig. 9   Chart C: ABS Warning Lamp Circuit Check, Lamp Flashes Continuously While Ignition Switch Is On

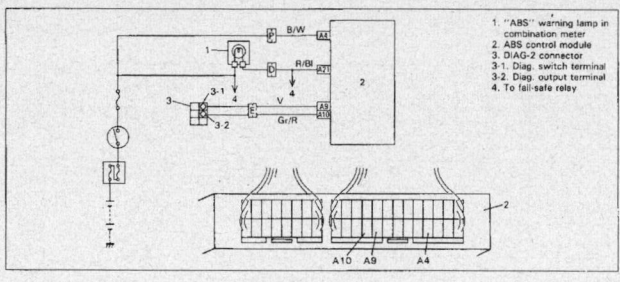

CIRCUIT DESCRIPTION

When the diag. switch terminal is connected to the ground with the ignition switch turned ON, the ABS control module outputs a diagnostic trouble code (DTC, voltage change signal) from the diag. output terminal. Connecting or shorting the diag. switch terminal and the output terminal will set the mode to clear DTC.

INSPECTION

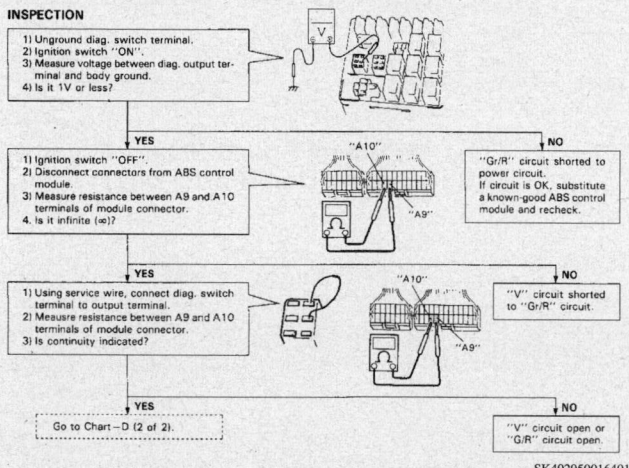

Fig. 10 Chart D: DTC Is Not Outputted From Diagnostic Output Terminal, Even With Diagnostic Switch Terminal Connected To Ground (Part 1 of 2)

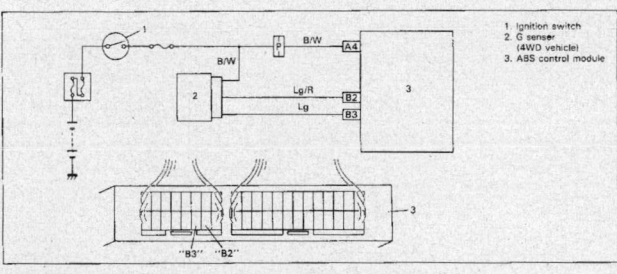

DESCRIPTION

2WD Vehicle

2WD vehicle is not equipped with a G sensor. When an ABS control module for 4WD vehicle is installed to the 2WD vehicle, this DTC is set as G sensor signal is not inputted.

4WD Vehicle

While a 4WD vehicle is at stop or running, if the potential difference between the sensor signal terminal "B2" and the sensor ground terminal "B3" is not within the specified voltage value, or if the signal voltage while at a stop does not vary from that while running, this DTC is set.

Therefore, this DTC may be set when a 4WD vehicle is lifted up and its wheel(s) is turned. In such case, clear the DTC and check again.

INSPECTION

2WD Vehicle— | Change with ABS control module for 2WD vehicle and recheck.

4WD Vehicle

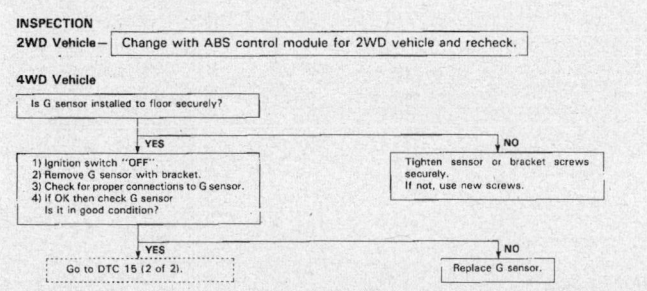

Fig. 11 Code 15: G Sensor Circuit On 4WD Vehicle Or ABS Control Module On 2WD Vehicle (Part 1 of 2)

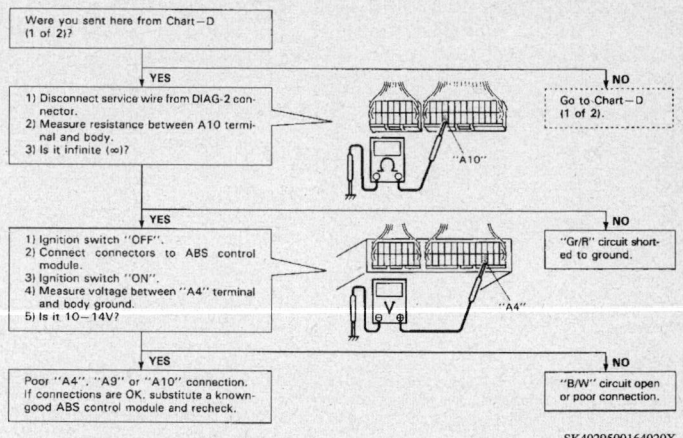

SK4029500164020X

Fig. 10 Chart D: DTC Is Not Outputted From Diagnostic Output Terminal, Even With Diagnostic Switch Terminal Connected To Ground (Part 2 of 2)

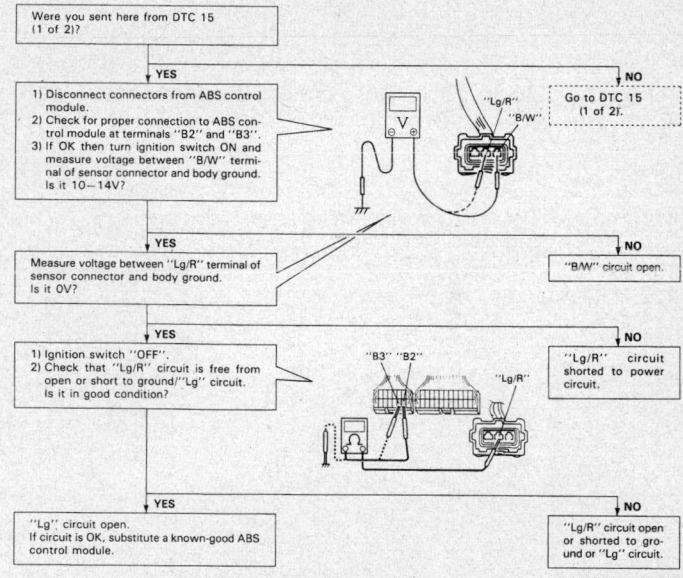

SK4029500165020X

Fig. 11 Code 15: G Sensor Circuit On 4WD Vehicle Or ABS Control Module On 2WD Vehicle (Part 2 of 2)

SUZUKI

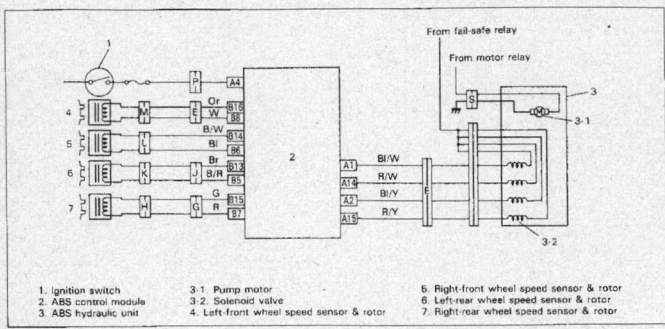

1. Ignition switch
2. ABS control module
3. ABS hydraulic unit
4. Left-front wheel speed sensor & rotor

3-1. Pump motor
3-2. Solenoid valve

5. Right-front wheel speed sensor & rotor
6. Left-rear wheel speed sensor & rotor
7. Right-rear wheel speed sensor & rotor

DESCRIPTION

When no other malfunction DTC is detected and ABS control is performed for longer than approx. 1 minute continuously (high and low voltage repetition was detected for longer than approx. 1 minute continuously at the solenoid monitor terminal "A1", "A14", "A2" or "A15") this DTC will be set.

INSPECTION

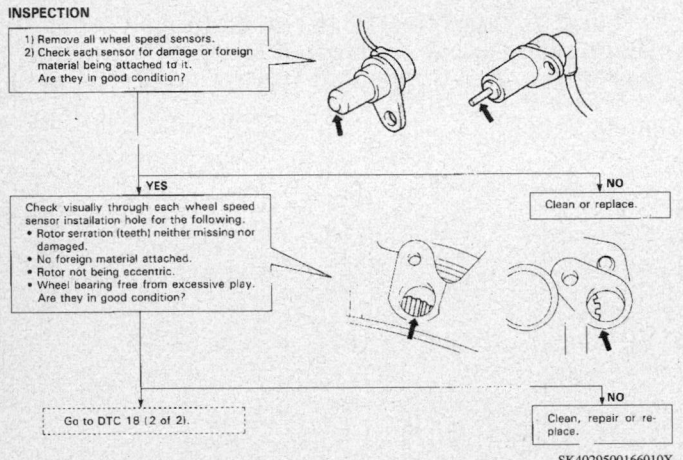

SK4029500166010X

Fig. 12 Code 18: Wheel Speed Sensor/Rotor Or ABS Hydraulic Unit (Part 1 of 2)

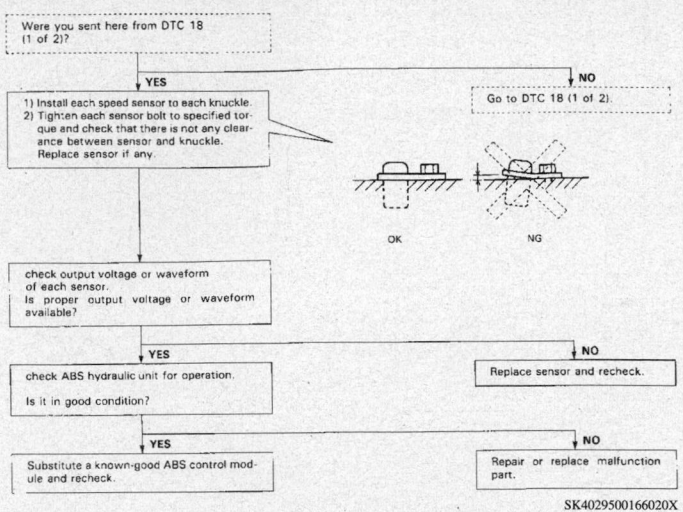

SK4029500166020X

Fig. 12 Code 18: Wheel Speed Sensor/Rotor Or ABS Hydraulic Unit (Part 2 of 2)

DTC 21, 22—RIGHT-FRONT WHEEL SPEED SENSOR CIRCUIT
25, 26—LEFT-FRONT WHEEL SPEED SENSOR CIRCUIT
31, 32—RIGHT-REAR WHEEL SPEED SENSOR CIRCUIT
35, 36—LEFT-REAR WHEEL SPEED SENSOR CIRCUIT

1. Ignition switch
2. ABS control module
3. Left-front wheel speed sensor
4. Right-front wheel speed sensor
5. Left-rear wheel speed sensor
6. Right-rear wheel speed sensor

DISCRIPTION

The ABS control module monitors the voltage at the positive (+) terminal of each sensor while the ignition switch is ON. When the voltage is not within the specified range, an applicable DTC will be set. Also, when no sensor signal is inputted at starting or while running, an applicable DTC will be set.

NOTE:

When the vehicle was operated in any of the following ways, one of these DTC's may be set even when the sensor is in good condition. If such possibility is suspected, repair the trouble (dragging of brake, etc.) of the vehicle, clear DTC once and then after performing the driving test as described in Step 4 of "ABS DIAG. FLOW CHART", check whether or not any abnormality exists.
—The vehicle was driven with parking brake pulled.
—The vehicle was driven with brake dragging.
—Wheel spin occurred while driving.
—Wheel(s) was turned while the vehicle was jacked up.
—The vehicle was stuck.

SK4029500167010X

Fig. 13 Code 21, 22, 25, 26, 31, 32, 35 & 36: Wheel Speed Sensor Circuits (Part 1 of 3)

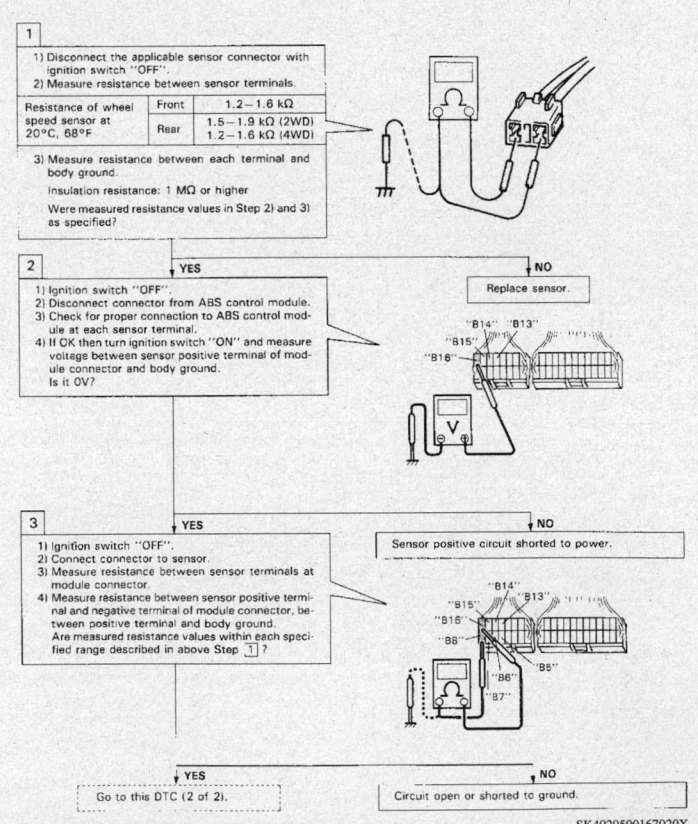

SK4029500167020X

Fig. 13 Code 21, 22, 25, 26, 31, 32, 35 & 36: Wheel Speed Sensor Circuits (Part 2 of 3)

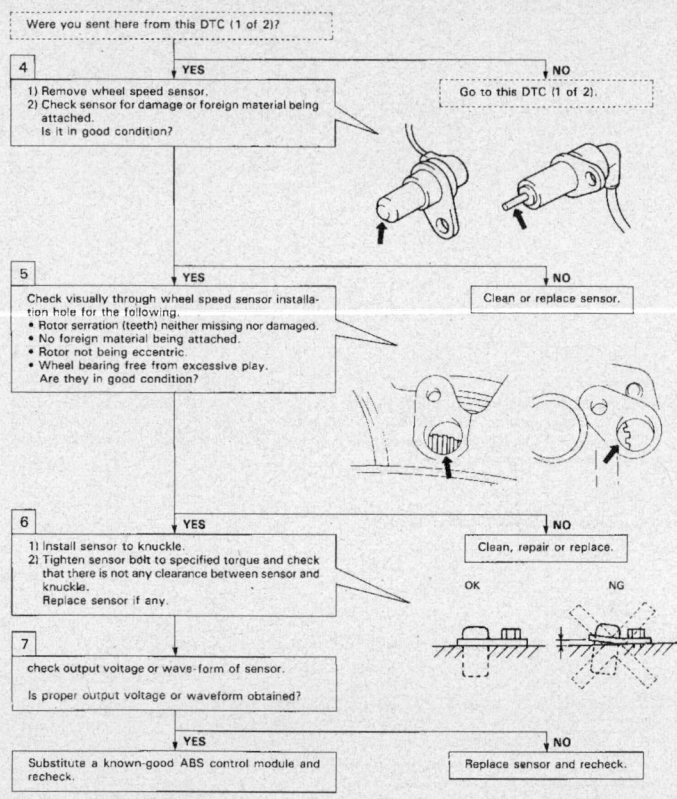

Were you sent here from this DTC (1 of 2)?

4
1) Remove wheel speed sensor.
2) Check sensor for damage or foreign material being attached.
Is it in good condition?

→ NO → Go to this DTC (1 of 2).

5
Check visually through wheel speed sensor installation hole for the following.
• Rotor serration (teeth) neither missing nor damaged.
• No foreign material being attached.
• Rotor not being eccentric.
• Wheel bearing free from excessive play.
Are they in good condition?

→ NO → Clean or replace sensor.

6
1) Install sensor to knuckle.
2) Tighten sensor bolt to specified torque and check that there is not any clearance between sensor and knuckle.
Replace sensor if any.

→ NO → Clean, repair or replace.

OK   NG

7
check output voltage or wave-form of sensor.
Is proper output voltage or waveform obtained?

→ NO → Replace sensor and recheck.

Substitute a known-good ABS control module and recheck.

SK4029500167030X

Fig. 13 Code 21, 22, 25, 26, 31, 32, 35 & 36: Wheel Speed Sensor Circuits (Part 3 of 3)

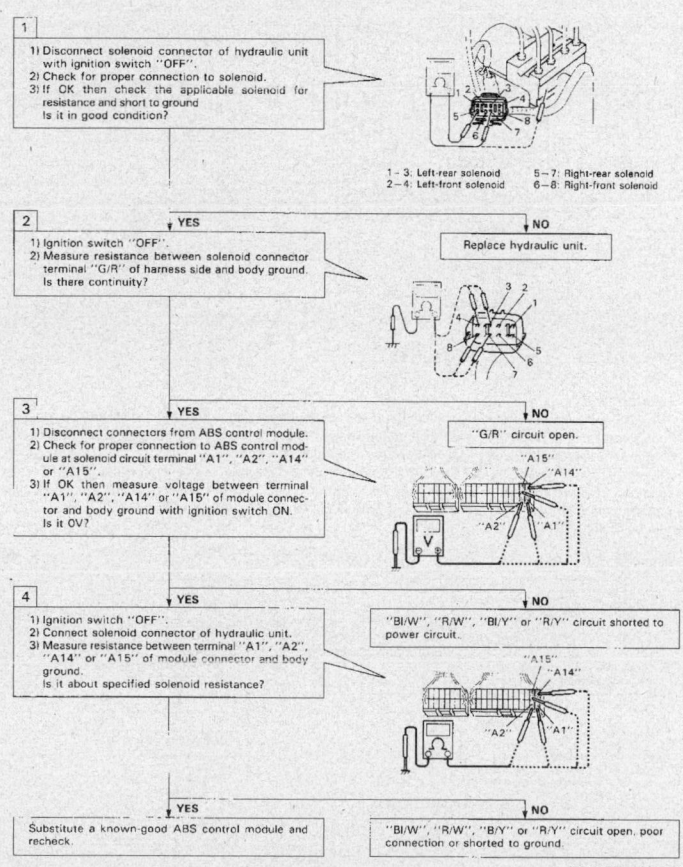

1
1) Disconnect solenoid connector of hydraulic unit with ignition switch "OFF".
2) Check for proper connection to solenoid.
3) If OK then check the applicable solenoid for resistance and short to ground
Is it in good condition?

1 – 3: Left-rear solenoid   5 – 7: Right-rear solenoid
2 – 4: Left-front solenoid   6 – 8: Right-front solenoid

2
1) Ignition switch "OFF".
2) Measure resistance between solenoid connector terminal "G/R" of harness side and body ground.
Is there continuity?

→ YES → Replace hydraulic unit.

3
1) Disconnect connectors from ABS control module.
2) Check for proper connection to ABS control module at solenoid circuit terminal "A1", "A2", "A14" or "A15".
3) If OK then measure voltage between terminal "A1", "A2", "A14" or "A15" of module connector and body ground with ignition switch ON.
Is it 0V?

→ NO → "G/R" circuit open.

4
1) Ignition switch "OFF".
2) Connect solenoid connector of hydraulic unit.
3) Measure resistance between terminal "A1", "A2", "A14" or "A15" of module connector and body ground.
Is it about specified solenoid resistance?

→ NO → "Bl/W", "R/W", "Bl/Y" or "R/Y" circuit shorted to power circuit.

→ NO → "Bl/W", "R/W", "B/Y" or "R/Y" circuit open, poor connection or shorted to ground.

Substitute a known-good ABS control module and recheck.

SK4029500168020X

Fig. 14 Code 41, 45, 51 & 55: Solenoid Circuits (Part 2 of 2)

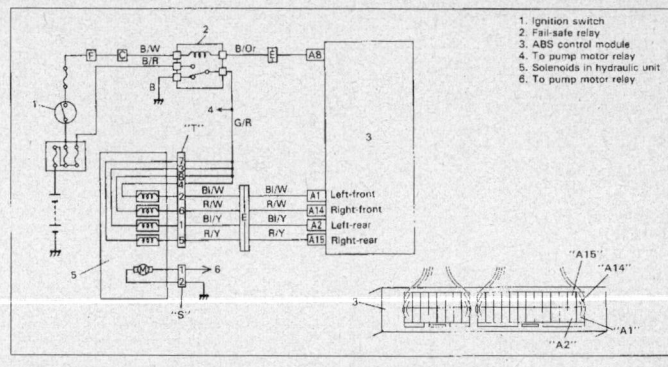

1. Ignition switch
2. Fail-safe relay
3. ABS control module
4. To pump motor relay
5. Solenoids in hydraulic unit
6. To pump motor relay

DESCRIPTION

The ABS control module monitors the voltage of each terminal ("A1", "A14", "A2" and "A15") of the solenoid circuit constantly with the ignition switch turned ON. It sets this DTC when the terminal voltage does not become low/high for the ON/OFF command from the module to the solenoid or the voltage difference between solenoid circuit terminals exceeds the specified value with the solenoid turned OFF.

INSPECTION

Check in each step of the flow chart as described below.

Step 1 — Check resistance of the solenoid and short-circuit to the ground in the hydraulic unit.
Step 2 — Check that the circuit between the solenoid and fail-safe relay is open.
Step 3 — Check that the circuit between the solenoid and ABS control module is shorted to the power.
Step 4 — Check that the circuit between the solenoid and ABS control module is open and shorted to the ground.

SK4029500168010X

Fig. 14 Code 41, 45, 51 & 55: Solenoid Circuits (Part 1 of 2)

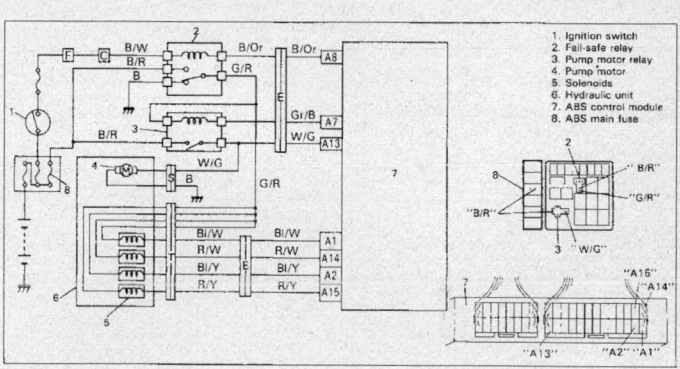

1. Ignition switch
2. Fail-safe relay
3. Pump motor relay
4. Pump motor
5. Solenoids
6. Hydraulic unit
7. ABS control module
8. ABS main fuse

DESCRIPTION

The ABS control module monitors the voltage at each terminal ("A1", "A14", "A2" and "A15") of the solenoid circuit constantly with the ignition switch turned ON as well as the voltage at the monitor terminal "A13" of the pump motor circuit. When all four solenoid terminal voltages are below the specified value or the voltage at the motor monitor terminal became below the specified value while the pump motor is operating, this DTC will be set. As soon as the voltage rises to the specified level, the set DTC will be cleared.

INSPECTION

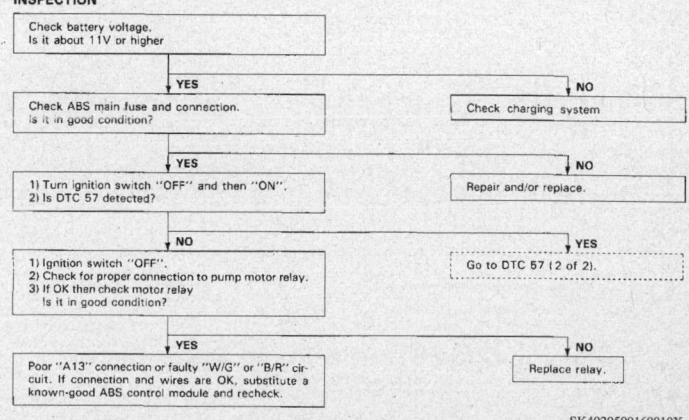

Check battery voltage.
Is it about 11V or higher?

→ NO → Check charging system

Check ABS main fuse and connection.
Is it in good condition?

→ NO → Repair and/or replace.

1) Turn ignition switch "OFF" and then "ON".
2) Is DTC 57 detected?

→ YES → Go to DTC 57 (2 of 2).

1) Ignition switch "OFF".
2) Check for proper connection to pump motor relay.
3) If OK then check motor relay
Is it in good condition?

→ NO → Replace relay.

Poor "A13" connection or faulty "W/G" or "B/R" circuit. If connection and wires are OK, substitute a known-good ABS control module and recheck.

SK4029500169010X

Fig. 15 Code 57: Solenoid & Pump Motor Power Source Circuit (Part 1 of 2)

Were you sent here from DTC 57 (1 of 2)?

YES ↓   **NO** → Go to DTC 57 (1 of 2).

1) Ignition switch "ON".
2) Measure voltage between ABS control module connector terminal "A1", "A2", "A14" and "A15" and body ground.
   Is it about 9V or less at all 4 terminals?

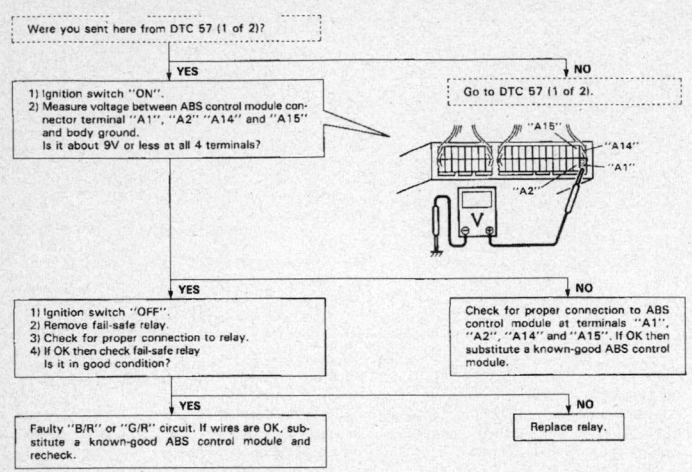

"A15"
"A14"
"A1"
"A2"

YES ↓   **NO** → Check for proper connection to ABS control module at terminals "A1", "A2", "A14" and "A15". If OK then substitute a known-good ABS control module.

1) Ignition switch "OFF".
2) Remove fail-safe relay.
3) Check for proper connection to relay.
4) If OK then check fail-safe relay
   Is it in good condition?

YES ↓   **NO** → Replace relay.

Faulty "B/R" or "G/R" circuit. If wires are OK, substitute a known-good ABS control module and recheck.

SK4029500169020X

Fig. 15   Code 57: Solenoid & Pump Motor Power Source Circuit (Part 2 of 2)

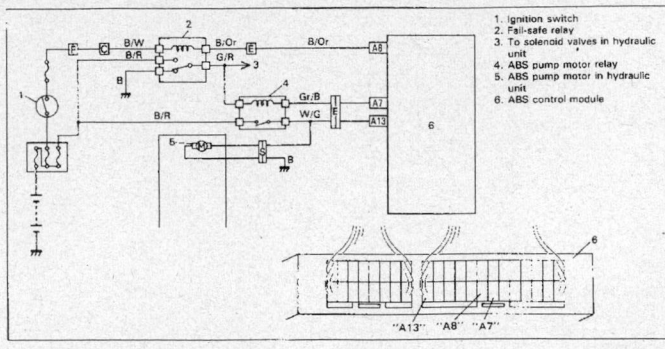

1. Ignition switch
2. Fail-safe relay
3. To solenoid valves in hydraulic unit
4. ABS pump motor relay
5. ABS pump motor in hydraulic unit
6. ABS control module

"A13" "A8" "A7"

DESCRIPTION

The ABS control module monitors the voltage at the monitor terminal "A13" of the pump motor circuit constantly with the ignition switch turned ON. It sets this DTC when the voltage at the monitor terminal "A13" does not become high/low according to ON/OFF commands to the motor relay of the module (does not follow these commands).

INSPECTION

Does (or Did) pump motor remain running at ignition switch "ON" or "OFF"?

YES ↓   **NO** → Go to DTC 61 (2 of 2).

Check pump motor relay
Is it in good condition?

YES ↓   **NO** → Replace relay.

1) Ignition switch "OFF".
2) Install motor relay.
3) Disconnect ABS control module connector and turn ignition switch ON.
   Does motor run then?

YES ↓   **NO** → Substitute a known-good ABS control module and recheck.

"W/G" circuit shorted to power circuit

SK4029500170010X

Fig. 16   Code 61: ABS Pump Motor Circuit (Part 1 of 2)

Were you sent here from DTC 61 (1 of 2)?

YES ↓   **NO** → Go to DTC 61 (1 of 2).

1) Ignition switch "OFF".
2) Check for proper connection to motor relay.
3) If OK then check motor relay
   Is it in good condition?

YES ↓   **NO** → Replace motor relay.

1) Check for proper connection to pump motor.
2) If OK then check pump motor
   Is it in good condition?

YES ↓   **NO** → Replace pump motor.

1) Disconnect ABS control module connectors.
2) Check for proper connection to module at terminals "A7" and "A13".
3) If OK then check "Gr/B" and "G/R" circuit for open and short to ground.
   Is it in good condition?

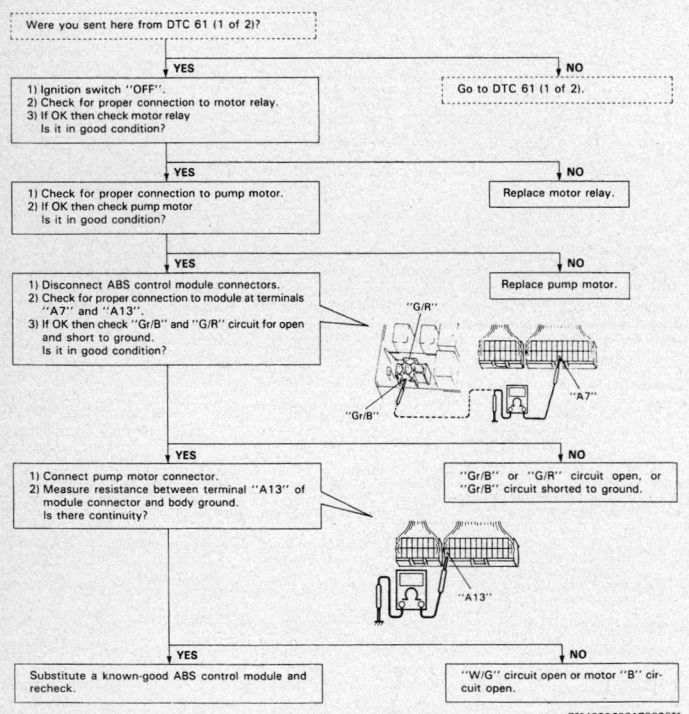

"G/R"
"Gr/B"
"A7"

YES ↓   **NO** → "Gr/B" or "G/R" circuit open, or "Gr/B" circuit shorted to ground.

1) Connect pump motor connector.
2) Measure resistance between terminal "A13" of module connector and body ground.
   Is there continuity?

"A13"

YES ↓   **NO** → "W/G" circuit open or motor "B" circuit open.

Substitute a known-good ABS control module and recheck.

SK4029500170020X

Fig. 16   Code 61: ABS Pump Motor Circuit (Part 2 of 2)

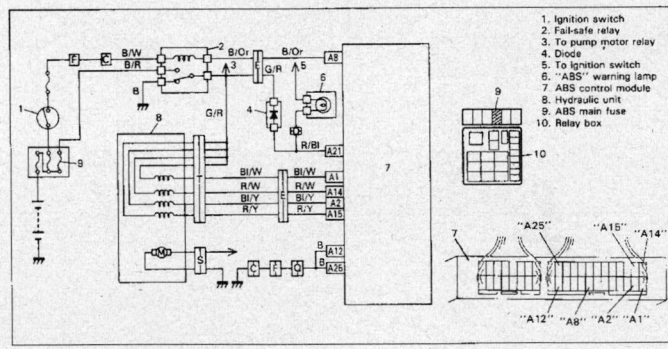

1. Ignition switch
2. Fail-safe relay
3. To pump motor relay
4. Diode
5. To Ignition switch
6. "ABS" warning lamp
7. ABS control module
8. Hydraulic unit
9. ABS main fuse
10. Relay box

"A25" "A15" "A14"
"A12" "A8" "A2" "A1"

DESCRIPTION

The ABS control module monitors the voltage at each terminal ("A1", "A14", "A2" and "A15") of the solenoid circuit constantly with the ignition switch turned ON. Also, immediately after the ignition switch is turned "ON", perform an initial check as follows.
Switch the fail-safe relay in the order of ON→OFF→ON and check if the voltage at 4 solenoid circuit terminals changes to High→Low→High. If anything faulty is found in the initial check and when the voltage at all solenoid circuit terminals is low with the ignition switch turned ON and ABS not operated, this DTC will be set.

INSPECTION

Check battery voltage.
Is it about 11V or higher?

YES ↓   **NO** → Check charging system

Check ABS main fuse and connection.
Is it in good condition?

YES ↓   **NO** → Repair and then replace.

1) Ignition switch "OFF".
2) Remove fail-safe relay.
3) Check for proper connection to fail-safe relay.
4) If OK then check fail-safe relay
   Is it in good condition?

YES ↓   **NO** → Replace relay.

Go to DTC 63 (2 of 2).

SK4029500171010X

Fig. 17   Code 63: ABS Fail-Safe Relay Circuit (Part 1 of 2)

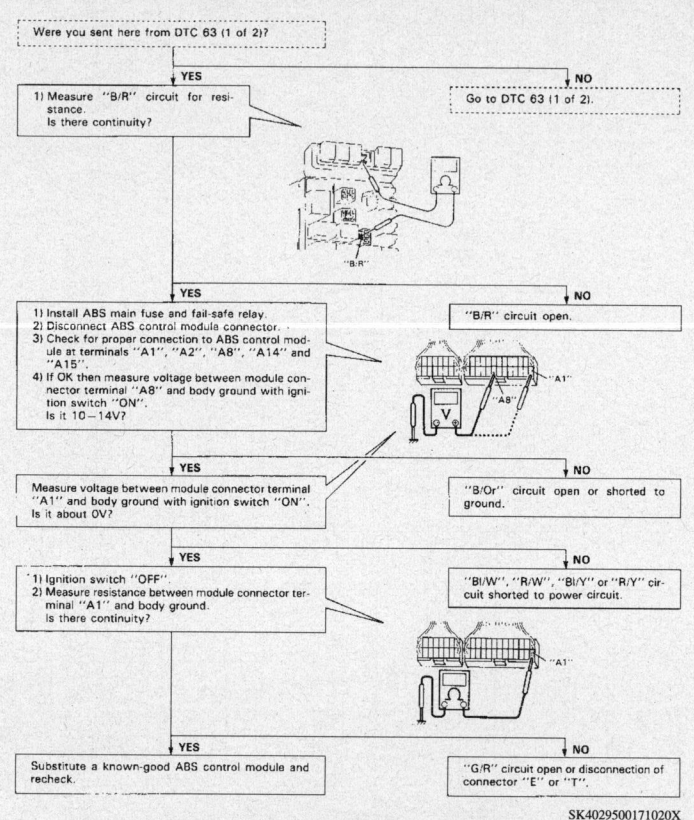

YES → 1) Measure "B/R" circuit for resistance.
Is there continuity?

NO → Go to DTC 63 (1 of 2).

YES → 1) Install ABS main fuse and fail-safe relay.
2) Disconnect ABS control module connector.
3) Check for proper connection to ABS control module at terminals "A1", "A2", "A8", "A14" and "A15".
4) If OK then measure voltage between module connector terminal "A8" and body ground with ignition switch "ON".
Is it 10—14V?

NO → "B/R" circuit open.

YES → Measure voltage between module connector terminal "A1" and body ground with ignition switch "ON".
Is it about 0V?

NO → "B/Or" circuit open or shorted to ground.

YES → 1) Ignition switch "OFF".
2) Measure resistance between module connector terminal "A1" and body ground.
Is there continuity?

NO → "Bl/W", "R/W", "Bl/Y" or "R/Y" circuit shorted to power circuit.

YES → Substitute a known-good ABS control module and recheck.

NO → "G/R" circuit open or disconnection of connector "E" or "T".

SK4029500171020X

Fig. 17 Code 63: ABS Fail-Safe Relay Circuit (Part 2 of 2)

DESCRIPTION

This DTC will be set when an internal fault is detected in the ABS control module and when an ABS control module for 2WD vehicle is installed in the 4WD vehicle by mistake as well.

INSPECTION

1) Ignition switch "OFF".
2) Disconnect connectors from ABS control module.
3) Check for proper connection to ABS control module at all terminals.
Are they in good condition?

YES → Substitute a known-good ABS control module and recheck.

NO → Repair or replace.

SK4029500172000X

Fig. 18 Code 71: ABS Control Module

Grand Vitara

NOTE: Electrical Symbol & Wire Color Code Identification Located In The Front Of This Manual May Be Used As An Aid When Using Wiring Circuits Found In This Section.

NOTE: On Air Bag Equipped Models, Refer To "Air Bag System Precautions" Located In The Front Of This Manual For System Disarming & Arming Procedures.

INDEX

PRECAUTIONS

AIR BAG SYSTEMS

Refer to "Air Bag System Precautions" in the front of this manual for system disarming and arming procedures.

BATTERY GROUND CABLE

Prior to service, disconnect battery ground cable and isolate as required.

SUZUKI

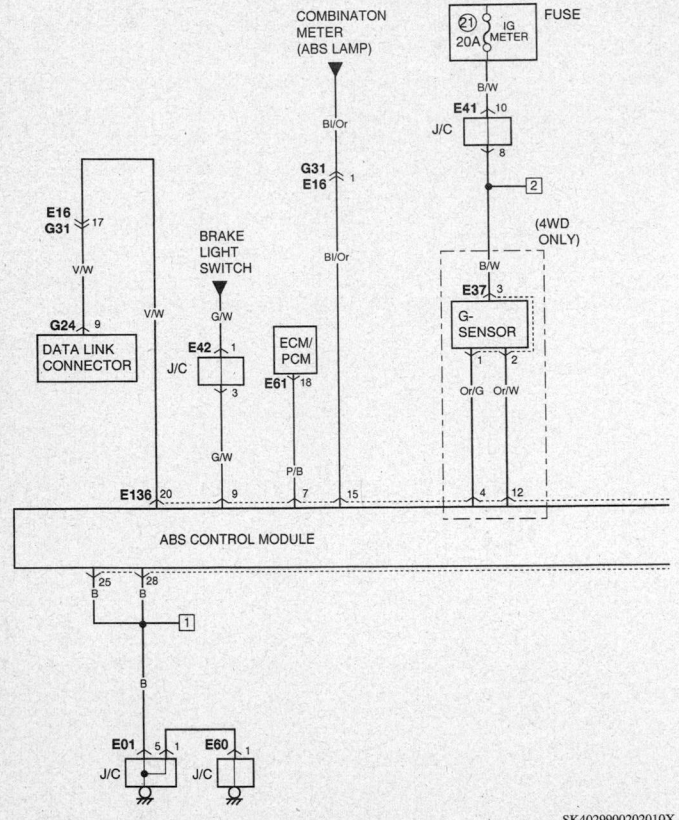

Fig. 1 ABS system wiring circuit (Part 1 of 2). Grand Vitara

SK4029900202010X

Fig. 1 ABS system wiring circuit (Part 2 of 2). Grand Vitara

SK4029900202020X

TROUBLESHOOTING

Refer to "Diagnosis & Testing" for troubleshooting procedures.

DIAGNOSIS & TESTING

Accessing Diagnostic Trouble Codes

The Diagnostic Trouble Codes (DTC) can be accessed by connecting a Tech 1 bi-directional scan tool equipped with ABS-Air Bag cartridge tool No. 09932–65020, or equivalents, to the Data Link Connector (DLC). The DLC is located under the left-hand side of the instrument panel, left of the steering column. Each input and output to the system can be monitored by the scan tool, monitoring inputs and outputs allows for fault confirmation and repair verification. The "Scan" tool can also be used to manually control components and perform functional tests. Refer to **Fig. 1** for "Scan" tool functions.

Wiring Circuit

Refer to **Fig. 1** for system wiring diagram.

Diagnostic Trouble Code Interpretation

Refer to "Diagnostic Chart Index" for diagnostic trouble code interpretation and identification.

Diagnostic Tests

Refer to **Figs. 2 through 13** for diagnostic test procedures.

Clearing Diagnostic Trouble Codes

1. Select scan tool function F2 for "Trouble Codes-DTC."
2. After DTC have been reviewed, Tech-1 will prompt, "Clear Codes," with question mark, press "Yes," and DTCs will be cleared.

SYSTEM SERVICE

Brake System Bleed

Bleed brakes as outlined in "Hydraulic Brake System."

Component Replacement

FRONT WHEEL SPEED SENSOR

1. Raise and support vehicle, then remove wheel and tire assembly.
2. Disconnect wheel sensor connector.
3. Remove speed sensor from steering knuckle.
4. Reverse procedure to install, noting the following:
   a. Check O-ring for damage replace as required.
   b. Install front wheel speed sensor to

steering knuckle, **torque** sensor bolt 6–8 ft. lbs.

REAR WHEEL SPEED SENSOR

1. Raise and support vehicle.
2. Remove rear wheel and tire assembly.
3. Disconnect sensor electrical connector, remove sensor assembly from backing plate.

4. Reverse procedure to install, **torque**-sensor assembly attaching bolt to 6–8 ft. lbs.

ABS ELECTRONIC CONTROL UNIT

Refer to "ABS Hydraulic Control Unit" for procedures.

ABS HYDRAULIC CONTROL UNIT

1. Remove brake lines from ABS hydraulic control module.
2. Disconnect electrical connector from ABS control module.
3. Remove 3 nuts, then lift hydraulic control unit off of bracket.
4. Reverse procedure to install.
5. Bleed system as outlined under "Brake System, Bleed."

DIAGNOSTIC CHART INDEX

Code	Description	Page No.	Fig. No.
Table A	ABS Lamp Does Not Illuminate w/Key On	42-157	2
Table B	ABS Lamp Remains Illuminated	42-157	3
Table C	ABS Lamp Flashes Continuously w/Key On	42-158	4
Table D	No DTC Output w/Diagnostic Switch Terminal Grounded	42-158	5
Code 15	G Sensor Circuit	42-158	6
Code 18	Wheel Speed Sensor, Rotor Or Hydraulic Unit	42-158	7
Code 21	Speed Sensor Circuit	42-159	8
Code 22	Speed Sensor Circuit	42-159	8
Code 25	Speed Sensor Circuit	42-159	8
Code 26	Speed Sensor Circuit	42-159	8
Code 31	Speed Sensor Circuit	42-159	8
Code 32	Speed Sensor Circuit	42-159	8
Code 35	Speed Sensor Circuit	42-159	8
Code 36	Speed Sensor Circuit	42-159	8
Code 41	Solenoid Circuit	42-159	9
Code 45	Solenoid Circuit	42-159	9
Code 46	Solenoid Circuit	42-159	9
Code 57	Solenoid & Pump Motor Power Supply	42-159	10
Code 61	ABS Pump Motor Circuit	42-159	11
Code 63	ABS Fail Safe Relay Circuit	42-159	12
Code 71	ABS Control Module	42-159	13

STEP	ACTION	YES	NO
1	1) Turn ignition switch ON. Do other warning lamp come ON?	Go to step 2.	Go to step 3.
2	1) Remove combination meter. Is bulb of ABS warning lamp in good condition?	"Bl/O" circuit open or poor connection to combination meter at "Bl/O" terminal.	Replace bulb.
3	Is IG fuse in good condition?	Open in "B/W" wire to combination meter or poor connection.	Repair and replace.

SK4029900203000X

Fig. 2   Table A: ABS Lamp Does Not Illuminate w/Key On

STEP	ACTION	YES	NO
1	Perform diagnostic trouble code check. Is there any DTC (including code No.12, NO CODES on tech-1) exists?	Go to step 2.	Go to step 4.
2	Is it malfunction DTC (other than code No.12) exists at step 1?	Go to step 7 of ABS diagnostic flow table in this section.	Go to step 3.
3	1) Ignition switch OFF. 2) Disconnect ABS hydraulic unit/control module connector. Does ABS warning lamp light at ignition switch ON?	Poor ABS hydraulic unit/control module connector terminal(s) "A25", "A17" and/or "A10" connection.	"P" circuit shorted to ground.
4	1) Disconnect ABS hydraulic unit/control module connector. 2) Check for proper connection to ABS hydraulic unit/control module connector at terminals "A17," "A25" and "A10". 3) If OK then ignition switch "ON" and measure voltage at terminal A25 of connector. Is it 10 – 14 V?	Go to step 5.	"B/W" circuit open.
5	1) Ignition switch OFF. 2) With ABS control module connector disconnected, disconnect 16p connector from combination meter. 3) Measure resistance from connector terminal "A17" to body ground. Is it infinity?	Go to step 6.	"Bl/O" wire shorted to ground.
6	1) Measure resistance from connector terminal "A10" to body ground. Is continuity indicated?	Substitute a known-good ABS hydraulic unit control module assembly and recheck.	"B" circuit open.

SK4029900204000X

Fig. 3   Table B: ABS Lamp Remains Illuminated

STEP	ACTION	YES	NO
1	Is diag. switch terminal connected to ground via service wire?	Go to step 3.	Go to step 2.
2	1) Ignition switch ON. 2) Measure voltage between diag. switch terminal and ground. Is it 10 – 14 V?	Substitute a known-good ABS hydraulic unit/control module assembly and recheck.	"P" wire circuit shorted to ground.
3	1) Ignition switch ON. 2) Does flashing of ABS warning lamp indicate DTC (DTC 12 or history DTC)?	Go to step 7 of ABS diagnostic flow table in this section.	Substitute a known-good ABS hydraulic unit/control module assembly and recheck.

SK4029900205000X

Fig. 4   Table C: ABS Lamp Flashes Continuously w/Key On

STEP	ACTION	YES	NO
1	Is it shorted diag. switch terminal and ground terminal by service wire properly?	Go to step 2.	Connect service wire securely.
2	1) Disconnect service wire. 2) Disconnect ABS hydraulic unit/control module connector. 3) Measure resistance between diag. switch terminal and connector terminal "A8". Is it infinite (∞)?	"P" circuit open.	Go to step 3.
3	1) Measure resistance between ground terminal of monitor connector and body ground. Is continuity indicated?	Go to step 4.	"B" circuit open or poor connection.
4	1) Check for proper connection to ABS hydraulic unit/control module at terminal "A8" and "A10". 2) If OK, then check "ABS" warning lamp circuit referring to TABLE A, B and C. Is it in good condition?	Substitute a known-good ABS hydraulic with/control module assembly and recheck.	Repair "ABS" warning lamp circuit.

SK4029900206000X

Fig. 5   Table D: No DTC Output w/Diagnostic Switch Terminal Grounded

STEP	ACTION	YES	NO
1	Is G sensor installed floor securely?	Go to step 2.	Tighten sensor or bracket screw securely. If not, using new screw.
2	1) Ignition switch OFF. 2) Remove G sensor with bracket. 3) Check for proper connection to G sensor. 4) If OK then check G sensor referring to item INSPECTION of G sensor. 5) Is it in good condition?	Go to step 3.	Replace G sensor.
3	1) Disconnect connectors from ABS hydraulic unit/control module assembly (See Fig. A) and G sensor. 2) Check for proper connection to ABS control module at terminals A14 and A4. 3) If OK, then turn ignition switch ON and measure voltage between B/W terminal of sensor connector and body ground. Is it 10 – 14 V?	Go to step 4.	"B/W" circuit open.
4	Measure voltage between "O/W" terminal of sensor connector and body ground. Is it 0 V?	Go to step 5.	"O/W" circuit shorted to power circuit.
5	1) Ignition switch OFF. 2) Check that "O/W" circuit is free from open or short to ground and "O/G" circuit. Is it in good condition? (See Fig. B)	"O/G" circuit open. If circuit is OK, substitute a known-good ABS hydraulic unit/control module assembly.	"O/W" circuit open or shorted to ground or "O/G" circuit.

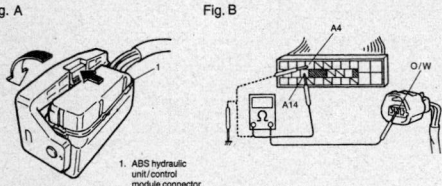

Fig. A   Fig. B

1. ABS hydraulic unit/control module connector

SK4029900207000X

Fig. 6   Code 15: G Sensor Circuit

STEP	ACTION	YES	NO
1	1) Remove all speed sensors. 2) Check each sensor for damage or foreign material being attached to it. Are they in good condition? See Fig. A	Go to step 2.	Clean or replace.
2	Check visually all wheel speed sensor installation hole for the following. • Rotor serration (teeth) neither missing nor damaged. • No foreign material attached. • Rotor not being eccentric. • Wheel bearing free from excessive play. Are they in good condition? See Fig. B	Go to step 3.	Clean repair or replace.
3	1) Install each speed sensor to each knuckle and/or axle housing. 2) Tighten each sensor bolt to specified torque. Is there any clearance between sensor and knuckle or axle housing? See Fig. C	Replace sensor.	Go to step 4.
4	Check output voltage or waveform of each sensor. Is proper output voltage or waveform available?	Go to step 5.	Replace sensor and recheck.
5	Check ABS hydraulic unit. Is it in good condition?	Substitute a known-good ABS hydraulic unit/control module assembly and recheck.	Replace ABS, hydraulic unit/control module assembly.

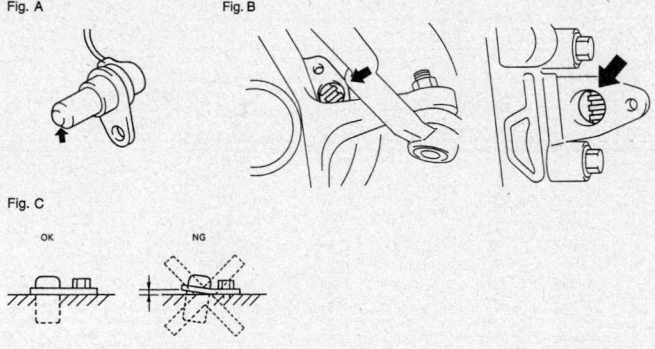

Fig. A   Fig. B

Fig. C

OK   NG

SK4029900208000X

Fig. 7   Code 18: Wheel Speed Sensor, Rotor Or Hydraulic Unit

STEP	ACTION	YES	NO
1	1) Disconnect the applicable sensor connector with ignition switch OFF. 2) Measure resistance between sensor terminals. 　Resistance of wheel speed sensor: 1.2 – 1.6 kΩ 　(at 20°C, 68°F) 3) Measure resistance between each terminal and body ground. 　Insulation resistance: 1MΩ or higher Were measured resistance values in step 2) and 3) as specified? (See Fig. A)	Go to step 2.	Replace sensor.
2	1) Ignition switch OFF. 2) Disconnect connector from ABS hydraulic unit/control module assembly. (See Fig. B) 3) Check for proper connection to ABS hydraulic unit/control module assembly at each sensor terminal. 4) If OK then, turn ignition switch ON and measure voltage between sensor positive terminal of module connector and body ground. Is it 0V?	Go to step 3.	Sensor positive circuit shorted to power.
3	1) Ignition switch OFF. 2) Connect connector to sensor. 3) Measure resistance between sensor terminals at module connector. 4) Measure resistance between sensor positive terminal and negative terminal of module connector, between positive terminal and body ground. Are measured resistance values within each specified range described in above step 1?	Go to step 4.	Circuit open or shorted to ground.
4	1) Remove wheel speed sensor. 2) Check sensor for damage or foreign material being attached. Is it in good condition? (See Fig. C)	Go to step 5.	Clean or replace sensor.
5	Check visually through wheel speed sensor installation hole for following. ● Rotor serration (teeth) neither missing or damaged. ● No foreign material being attached. ● Rotor not being eccentric. ● Wheel bearing free from excessive play. Are they in good condition? (See Fig. D)	Go to step 6.	Clean, repair or replace.
6	1) Install sensor to knuckle or axle housing. 2) Tighten sensor bolt to specified torque and check that there is not any clearance between sensor and knuckle or axle housing. (See Fig. E) 　Replace sensor if any. Referring to item OUTPUT VOLTAGE INSPECTION of FRONT WHEEL SPEED SENSOR, check output voltage or waveform of sensor. Is proper output voltage or waveform obtained?	Substitute a known-good ABS hydraulic unit/control module assembly and recheck.	Replace sensor and recheck.

SK4029900209010X

Fig. 8　Codes 21, 22, 25, 26, 31, 32, 35 & 36: Speed Sensor Circuit (Part 1 of 2)

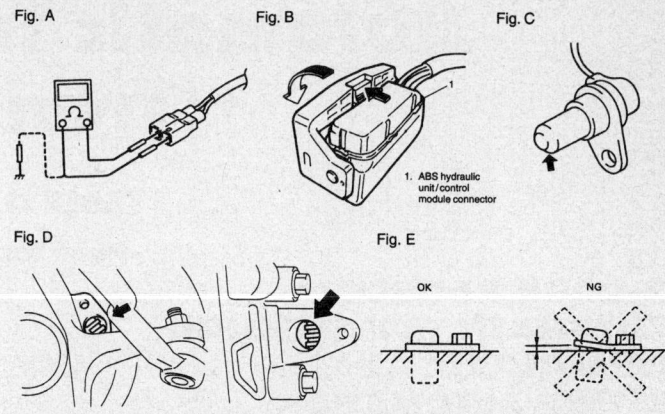

SK4029900209020X

Fig. 8　Codes 21, 22, 25, 26, 31, 32, 35 & 36: Speed Sensor Circuit (Part 2 of 2)

STEP	ACTION	YES	NO
1	Check battery voltage. Is it about 11 V or higher?	Go to step 2.	Check charging system referring to "CHARGING SYSTEM" section.
2	Check ABS main fuse and connection. Is it in good condition?	Go to step 3.	Repair and/or replace fuse.
3	1) Ignition switch OFF. 2) Disconnect ABS hydraulic unit/control module connector. 3) Check proper connection to ABS hydraulic unit/control module connector at terminal A27. 4) If OK, then measure voltage between connector terminal A27 and body ground. Is it 10 – 14 V?	Substitute a known-good ABS hydraulic unit/control module assembly and recheck.	"W/Bl" circuit open.

SK4029900211000X

Fig. 10　Code 57: Solenoid & Pump Motor Power Supply

STEP	ACTION	YES	NO
1	1) Check solenoid and solenoid referring to item "ABS HYDRAULIC UNIT OPERATION CHECK" in this section. Is it in good condition?	Check terminals "A11" and "A27" connection. If connections OK, substitute a known-good ABS hydraulic unit/control module assembly and recheck.	Go to step 2.
2	1) Ignition switch "OFF". 2) Disconnect ABS hydraulic unit/control module connector. 3) Check for proper connection to ABS hydraulic unit/control module connector at terminal "A11". 4) If OK, then measure voltage between terminal "A11" of module connector and body ground. Is it 10 – 14 V?	Substitute a known-good ABS hydraulic unit/control module assembly and recheck.	"W/Bl" circuit open.

SK4029900210000X

Fig. 9　Codes 41, 45 & 46: Solenoid Circuit

STEP	ACTION	YES	NO
1	1) Check pump motor referring to item "ABS HYDRAULIC UNIT OPERATION CHECK" in this section. Is it in good condition?	Check terminals "A11" and "A27" connection. If connections OK, substitute a known-good ABS hydraulic unit/control module assembly and recheck.	Go to step 2.
2	1) Ignition switch OFF. 2) Disconnect ABS hydraulic unit/control module connector. 3) Check for proper connection to ABS hydraulic unit/control module connector at terminal "A27". 4) If OK, then measure voltage between terminal "A27" of module connector and body ground. Is it 10 – 14V?	Go to step 3.	"W/Bl" circuit open.
3	Measure resistance between connector terminal "A28" of ABS hydraulic unit/control module assembly. Is it infinite (∞)?	"B" circuit open.	Substitute a known-good ABS hydraulic unit/control module and recheck.

SK4029900212000X

Fig. 11　Code 61: ABS Pump Motor Circuit

STEP	ACTION	YES	NO
1	Check battery voltage. Is it about 11 V or higher?	Go to step 2.	Check charging system referring to "CHARGING SYSTEM" section.
2	Check ABS main fuse and connection. Is it in good condition?	Go to step 3.	Repair and/or replace fuse.
3	1) Ignition switch OFF. 2) Disconnect ABS hydraulic unit/control module connector. 3) Check proper connection to ABS hydraulic unit/control module at terminal "A11". 4) If OK, then measure voltage between connector terminal A11, and body ground. Is it 10 – 14 V?	Substitute a known-good ABS hydraulic unit/control module assembly and recheck.	"W/Bl" circuit open or short to ground.

SK4029900213000X

Fig. 12　Code 63: ABS Fail Safe Relay Circuit

STEP	ACTION	YES	NO
1	1) Ignition switch OFF. 2) Disconnect connectors from ABS control module. 3) Check for proper connection to ABS control module at all terminals. Are they in good condition?	Substitute a known-good ABS control module and recheck.	Repair or replace.

SK4029900214000X

Fig. 13　Code 71: ABS Control Module

Automatic Transmissions/ Transaxles

TABLE OF CONTENTS

2-Door Sidekick Automatic Transmission (THM 3L30)

NOTE: On Air Bag Equipped Models, Refer To "Air Bag System Precautions" Located In The Front Of This Manual For System Disarming & Arming Procedures.

INDEX

PRECAUTIONS

AIR BAG SYSTEMS

Refer to "Air Bag System Precautions" in the front of this manual for system disarming and arming procedures.

FUEL SYSTEM PRESSURE RELEASE

1. Disconnect fuel pump harness connector at the fuel tank rear side. **Cover fuel pipe line with rag after relieving pressure as certain pressure may still remain.**
2. Start engine and let idle until engine stops by itself, then turn ignition switch to Off. **Failure to relieve fuel system pressure prior to disconnecting fuel system components may cause fire or personal injury.**
3. Connect fuel pump harness connector.
4. After repairs have been completed, connect positive battery terminal to fuel pump drive terminal and the negative terminal to the chassis. Ensure fuel pump operates at this time.

BATTERY GROUND CABLE

Prior to service, disconnect battery ground cable and isolate as required.

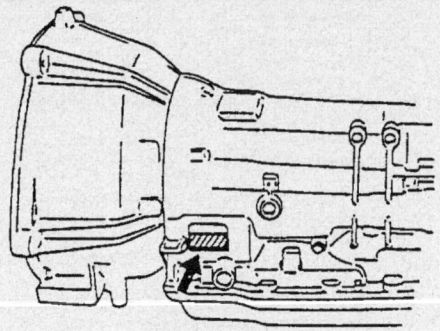

Fig. 1 Transmission identification

IDENTIFICATION

Refer to **Fig. 1,** for proper transmission identification.

DESCRIPTION

The THM 3L30 transmission is a fully automatic unit which can provide three forward speeds and reverse. The units primary components include a four-element hydraulic torque converter and a compound planetary gear set, **Fig. 2.**

Three multiple disc clutches, a roller clutch and a band provide the friction elements required to obtain the desired function of the compound planetary gear set.

Oil pressure and shift points of the transmission are controlled by a vacuum modulator that senses engine torque as a relation to engine vacuum.

TROUBLESHOOTING

Before start of troubleshooting, perform the following preliminary checking procedure:
1. Check and correct fluid level.
2. Road test vehicle to verify transmission problem using all selective ranges, noting discrepancies.
3. If engine performance indicates that engine tune-up is required, this should be performed before road testing is completed or transmission correction is attempted. Poor engine performance can result in transmission problems.
4. Check kickdown cable adjustment.
5. Check and correct vacuum lines and fittings.
6. Check and correct select cable.
7. Perform oil pressure test.
8. Isolate unit or circuit involved in malfunction.

For troubleshooting of this transmission refer to **Fig. 3.**

MAINTENANCE

FLUID CHECK

To check fluid, drive vehicle for at least 15 minutes to bring fluid to operating temperature (200°F). With vehicle on a level surface and engine idling in Park and parking brake applied, move the selector lever through each gear range. Check the level on the dipstick, it should be at the "Full Hot" mark. To bring the fluid level from the ADD mark to the FULL HOT mark requires one pint of fluid. If vehicle cannot be driven sufficiently to bring fluid to operating temperature, the level on the dipstick should be between the two dimples on the dipstick with fluid temperature at 70°F.

If additional fluid is required, use only Dexron II automatic transmission fluid.

When adding fluid, do not overfill, as foaming and loss of fluid through the vent may occur as the fluid heats up. Also, if fluid level is too low, complete loss of drive may occur especially when cold, which can cause transmission failure. The oil should be drained, the oil pan removed, the screen cleaned and fresh fluid added every 100,000 miles. For vehicles subjected to more severe use such as heavy city traffic especially in hot weather, prolonged periods of idling or towing, this maintenance should be performed every 15,000 miles.

FLUID CHANGE

1. Raise and support vehicle.
2. Remove lower propeller shaft universal joint flange and position aside to the right.
3. Place suitable container under oil pan, then remove oil pan attaching bolts except for the three rear bolts.
4. Loosen three rear oil pan bolts, then drain fluid from front side of oil pan.
5. Remove three remaining attaching bolts, then the oil pan and gasket.
6. Check the strainer screen and clean or

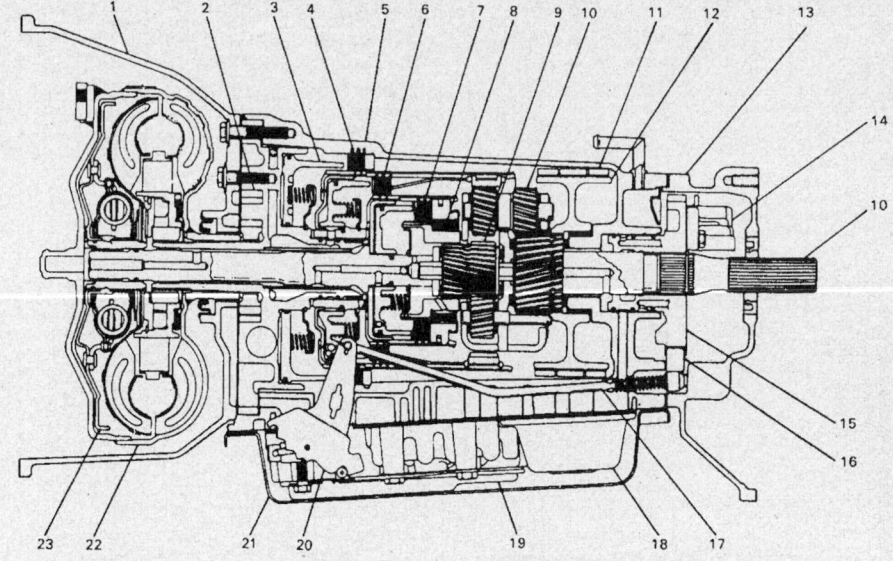

1. Torque converter housing	7. 3rd clutch	12. Planetary rear sun gear	18. Servo piston cover
2. Oil pump	8. Sprag assembly	13. Adapter case	19. Valve body assembly
3. Reverse clutch piston	(one-way clutch)	14. Governor assembly	20. Select shaft inner lever
4. Reverse clutch plate	9. Planetary input sun gear	15. Governor hub	21. Oil pan
5. Transmission case	10. Planetary gear carrier	16. Parking lock pawl	22. Torque converter
6. 2nd clutch	11. Low brake band	17. Parking lock actuator	23. Torque converter clutch

Fig. 2 Cross-sectional view of THM 3L30 transmission

replace as necessary.
7. Install oil pan and new gasket. Tighten oil pan attaching bolts to specifications.
8. Connect propeller shaft to differential flange. Tighten bolts to specification.
9. Lower vehicle and add proper amount of Dexron II or equivalent.

ADJUSTMENTS

SELECT CABLE

1. Shift selector to Neutral position.
2. Move manual select lever to Low position, which is the lowest position of switch, then set cable to cable bracket with E-ring.
3. While installing cable end through manual select lever, shift manual select lever back to Neutral position and fix position by tightening adjusting nut and locknut, **Fig. 4. Cable adjustment must be made so there is no clearance between lever and adjust nut.** Tighten locknut to specification.
4. Ensure proper operation of all ranges.

BRAKE INTERLOCK CABLE

1. Shift select lever to P range, then turn key to lock position.
2. Pull manual release knob and hold, then shift select lever to R range. Ensure inner cable is not bent, then loosen locknuts and pull cable out in F direction **Fig. 5,** until free of slack.
3. Secure cable with nuts A and B.

KICKDOWN CABLE

1. Ensure accelerator cable play is within .04–.06 inch (10–15 mm). If needed adjust cable.

	Condition	Possible cause	Correction
CONCERNS TRANSMISSION FLUID	Low fluid level.	• Fluid coming out of oil filler tube.	Adjust fluid level.
		• External fluid leak.	Repair leak.
		• Failed vacuum modulator.	Replace modulator.
	Fluid coming out of oil filler tube.	• Fluid level too high.	Adjust level.
		• Coolant in transmission fluid.	Replace radiator.
		• Breather hose pinched.	Correct piping.
		• Leak in oil pump suction circuit.	Overhaul.
	External fluid leaks in the area of torque converter housing.	• Leaking torque converter.	Replace torque converter.
		• Converter housing oil seal.	Replace oil seal.
		• Converter housing to case seal.	Replace seal.
		• Loose fastening bolts.	Tighten bolts.
	External fluid leaks in the area of transmission case and transfer adapter case.	• Manual select shaft seal.	Replace oil seal.
		• Adapter case seal.	Replace oil seal.
		• Oil pan gasket.	Replace gasket.
		• Adapter case gasket.	Replace gasket.
		• Vacuum modulator O ring.	Replace O ring.
		• Cooler line fittings.	Tighten fastenings.
		• Oil filler tube O ring.	Replace O ring.
		• Kick-down cable O ring.	Replace cable.
		• Line pressure gauge connection.	Tighten plug.
		• Electrical connector O ring.	Replace O ring.
	Low fluid pressure.	• Low fluid level.	Adjust fluid level.
		• Clogged oil pump screen.	Wash screen.
		• Leak in oil pump suction circuit.	Overhaul.
		• Leak in oil pressure circuit.	Overhaul.
		• Pressure regulator valve malfunction.	Overhaul oil pump.
		• Sealing ball (plug) in valve body dropped out.	Replace valve body.
	High fluid pressure.	• Modulator vacuum line leaky or interrupted.	Repair line.
		• Failed vacuum modulator.	Replace modulator.
		• Leak in any part of engine or accessory vacuum system.	Repair leak.
		• Pressure regulator valve malfunction.	Overhaul oil pump.
	Excessive smoke coming from exhaust.	Failed vacuum modulator.	Replace modulator.

TH5028900638010X

Fig. 3 Troubleshooting chart (Part 1 of 5)

	Condition	Possible cause	Correction
CONCERNS CONVERTER	No converter clutch applied.	• 12 volts not being supplied to transmission.	
		• Ground inside of transmission.	Tighten bolt.
		• Defective connector, wiring harness, or solenoid.	Repair or replace.
		• Defective pressure switch.	Replace switch.
		• Sticking converter clutch control valve.	Overhaul oil pump.
		• Solenoid O ring cut or leaking.	Replace solenoid.
		• Oil pump wear plate ro gasket mispositioned or damaged.	Repair or replace.
		• High or uneven bolt torque on converter housing to oil pump bolts.	Adjust torque.
		• Cut O ring on turbine shaft.	Replace converter.
	No converter clutch release or shudder.	• Sticking converter clutch control valve.	Overhaul oil pump.
		• Restricted converter clutch apply passage.	Overhaul.
		• Low fluid or pressure.	
		• Engine not tuned properly.	
		• Cut O ring on turbine shaft.	Replace converter.
STARTING	No starting in any drive range.	• Low fluid level.	
		• Clogged oil pump screen.	Wash screen.
		• Manual valve link or manual select shaft inner lever disconnected.	Repair linkage.
		• Input shaft broken.	Replace shaft.
		• Pressure regulator valve stuck in open position.	Overhaul oil pump.
		• Failed oil pump.	Replace oil pump.
	No starting in any drive range for a time. Driving possible only after repeatedly moving select lever to and fro.	Manual valve position does not coincide with valve body channels:	
		• Manual select shaft spring pin dropped out.	Install spring pin.
		• Manual valve link bent.	Replace link.
		• Manual select shaft nut loose.	Tighten nut.
	No starting after select lever from P to D, 2 or L (inadequate engine acceleration).	• Parking pawl does not disengage.	Repair or replace.
	Sudden starting only after increase of engine r/m.	• Servo piston jamming.	Repair or replace.
		• Low fluid level.	
		• Oil pump defective.	Replace oil pump.
		• Oil pump screen missing.	Replace screen ass'y.
		• Sealing ball (plug) in valve body dropped out.	Replace valve body.

TH5028900638020X

Fig. 3 Troubleshooting chart (Part 2 of 5)

2. Loosen kickdown cable locknut and adjusting nut, **Fig. 6.**
3. With accelerator pedal depressed fully and kickdown cable pulled in A direction, **Fig. 6,** adjust locknut to bracket clearance to 0–.039 inch (0–1 mm) by turning locknut. **When adjusting clearance, ensure adjusting nut does not contact bracket.**
4. Release accelerator pedal and adjust locknut to bracket clearance to 0–.039 inch (0–1 mm) by tightening adjusting nut. Use care to keep locknut in place.
5. When turning adjusting nut, position nut as shown, **Fig. 7.** When adjusting nut position is determined, fit adjusting nut to bracket as shown, **Fig. 7.**
6. Tighten locknut securely.

IN-VEHICLE REPAIRS

SPEEDOMETER DRIVEN GEAR, REPLACE

1. Remove bolt securing driven gear housing retainer, then the retainer.
2. Pull speedometer driven gear from housing.
3. Install speedometer driven gear into housing, then the retainer into slot of driven gear housing.
4. Install retainer attaching bolt.

REAR EXTENSION OIL SEAL, REPLACE

1. Remove propeller shaft.
2. Remove oil seal using suitable tool.
3. Lubricate new seal lip with transmission fluid and install seal into extension housing with seal installation tool No. J-21426, or equivalent.
4. Install propeller shaft.

VACUUM MODULATOR, REPLACE

1. Disconnect vacuum hose from modulator stem.
2. Using wrench tool No. 09920-36020/J-23100, or equivalent, remove modulator assembly from transmission.
3. Reverse procedure to install using new O-ring seal. Tighten modulator to specification.
4. Check and adjust fluid level.

SELECT CABLE, REPLACE

1. Remove console box. Push in center pin first, then remove rear clips.
2. Remove four bolts and raise manual selector assembly.
3. Remove cable clip, washer and outer cable E-ring, then disconnect cable from selector.
4. Raise and support vehicle.
5. Remove locknut from cable end at transmission.
6. Pull down manual select lever and disconnect cable and lever.
7. Remove cable and E-ring.
8. Reverse procedure to install.

BRAKE INTERLOCK CABLE, REPLACE

1. Remove meter hood and steering cover.
2. Remove back drive cable clamp screw, then disconnect cable eye end.
3. Remove console box, then disconnect cable by loosening locknut and cable end clip in manual selector assembly.
4. Reverse procedure to install.

KICKDOWN CABLE, REPLACE

1. Pushing cable toward "A," remove plastic joint at end of cable, **Fig. 8.**
2. Loosen nut at bracket and disconnect cable, then remove cable bracket.
3. Pull cable out, then apply screwdriver at flange " A" and disconnect inner cable end connected to valve, **Fig. 9.**
4. Reverse procedure to install.

TRANSMISSION

REPLACE

1. Relieve fuel system pressure as outlined under " Precautions."
2. Remove the following components from engine compartment:

Fig. 3 Troubleshooting chart (Part 3 of 5)

	Condition	Possible cause	Correction
STARTING	Heavy jerking when starting.	• Low fluid pressure. • Wrong modulator valve. • Pressure regulator valve stuck. • Sealing ball (plug) in valve body dropped out.	Overhaul. Overhaul oil pump. Repalce valve body.
	No starting in D or 2 range, but in L and R range.	• Input sprag installed backwards. • Input sprag failure.	Correct direction. Replace sprag.
	No starting in D or 2 and L (proper driving in R).	• Low band worn, does not grip. • Servo piston jamming. • Excessive leak in servo piston. • Parking pawl does not disengage.	Replace band. Repair or replace. Replace ring. Repair or replace.
	No starting in R range (proper driving in all other ranges).	• Reverse clutch failure.	Replace damaged parts.
	Drive in select lever position N.	• Inadequate select cable. • Planetary gear carrier broken. • Improper adjustment of low band.	Adjust cable. Replace planetary gear. Adjust servo piston.
GEAR CHANGE	No 1 – 2 upshift in D and 2 (transmission remains in 1st gear at all speeds).	• Governor valves stuck. • 1 – 2 shift valve stuck in 1st gear position. • Seal rings (oil pump hub) leaky. • Large leak in governor pressure circuit. • Governor oil screen clogged.	Overhaul governor. Overhaul valve body. Replace seal rings. Overhaul governor. Wash screen.
	No 2 – 3 upshift in D (transmission remains in 2nd gear at all speeds).	• 2 – 3 shift valve stuck. • Large leak in governor pressure circuit.	Overhaul valve body. Overhaul governor.
	Upshifts in D and 2 only at full throttle.	• Failed vacuum modulator. • Modulator vacuum line leaky or interrupted. • Leak in any part of engine or accessory vacuum system. • Kick-down valve or cable stuck.	Replace modulator. Repair line. Repair leak. Replace cable or overhaul.
	Upshifts in D and 2 only at part throttle.	• Kick-down pressure regulator valve stuck. • Kick-down cable broken or misadjusted.	Overhaul. Adjust or replace cable.
	Driving only in 1st gear of D and 2 range (transmission blocks in 2nd gear and R).	• 1st and R control valve stuck in 1st or R position.	Overhaul valve body.

TH5028900638030X

Fig. 3 Troubleshooting chart (Part 4 of 5)

	Condition	Possible cause	Correction
GEAR CHANGE	No part throttle 3 – 2 downshift at low vehicle speeds.	• 3 – 2 downshift control valve stuck.	Overhaul valve body.
	No forced downshift.	• Kick-down cable broken or improperly adjusted. • Kick-down pressure regulator valve stuck.	Adjust or replace cable. Overhaul.
	After full throttle upshifting, transmission shifts immediately into lower gear upon easing off accelerator pedal.	• Kick-down valve stuck in open position. • Kick-down cable stuck. • Modulator vacuum line interrupted.	Overhaul. Replace cable. Repair line.
	At higher speeds, transmission shifts into lower gear.	• Manual select shaft spring pin dropped out. • Loose connection of manual valve link. • Pressure loss at governor.	Install spring pin. Repair connection. Repair governor.
	Hard disengagement of select lever from P position.	• Steel guide bushing of parking lock actuator missing. • Manual select shaft stuck.	Replace adapter case. Overhaul.
SHIFTS	Slipping 1 – 2 upshifts (engine flares).	• Low fluid pressure. • Sealing ball (plug) in valve body dropped out. • Second clutch piston seals leaking. • Second clutch piston check ball stuck open. • Second clutch piston cranked or broken. • Second clutch plates worn. • Seal rings of oil pump hub leaky.	Replace valve body. Replace seals. Wash or replace piston. Replace piston. Replace plates. Replace seal rings.
	Slipping 2 – 3 upshifts (engine flares).	• Low fluid pressure. • Low band adjustment loose. • Third clutch piston seals leaking. • Third clutch piston check ball stuck open. • Third clutch piston cracked or broken. • Wear of input shaft bushing. • Sealing ball (plug) in valve body dropped out.	Adjust servo piston. Replace seals. Wash or replace piston. Replace piston. Replace oil pump. Replace valve body.
	Abrupt 1 – 2 upshift.	• High fluid pressure. • 1 – 2 accumulator valve stuck. • Spring cushion of second clutch broken.	Overhaul valve body. Replace cushion plate.

TH5028900638040X

a. Wiring harness couplers, breather hose clamp, kickdown cable, vacuum hose, transmission to engine bolts and starter.
3. Raise and support vehicle.
4. Drain transfer oil into appropriate container.
5. Remove front and rear propeller shafts.
6. Release select cable by removing nut from end of cable and E-ring from bracket.
7. Remove select cable bracket, then disconnect oil cooler hoses from pipes.
8. Remove torque converter housing lower plate.
9. Holding driveplate stationary using gear stopper tool No. 09927-56010, or equivalent, remove plate attaching bolts.
10. Remove exhaust center pipe, then engine to transmission nuts.
11. Remove meter cable end nut and disconnect cable.
12. Support transmission using suitable jack, then remove rear mounting member bolts and member.
13. Remove transmission and transfer case from vehicle.
14. Remove transfer case attaching bolts, then separate transfer from transmission.
15. Remove torque converter from transmission.
16. Reverse procedure to install. Tighten to specifications.

	Condition	Possible cause	Correction
SHIFTS	Abrupt 2 — 3 upshift.	• High fluid pressure. • Incorrect low band adjustment.	Adjust servo piston.
	Abrupt 3 — 2 detent downshift at high speed.	• High speed downshift valve stuck open. • Low band adjustment.	Overhaul valve body. Adjust servo piston.
	Abrupt 3 — 2 coast downshift.	• Low speed downshift timing valve stuck open.	Overhaul valve body.
	Flare on high speed forced downshift.	• Low fluid pressure. • Low band adjustment loose.	Adjust servo piston.
	Flare on low speed forced downshift.	• Low fluid pressure. • Low band adjustment loose. • High speed downshift timing valve stuck in closed position. • One-way clutch does not lock on 3 — 1 down shifting.	Adjust servo piston. Overhaul valve body. Replace sprag.
ENGINE BRAKING	No engine braking in L range.	• Select cable improperly adjusted. • Manual low control valve stuck.	Adjust cable. Overhaul valve body.
	No engine braking in 2 range.	• Select cable improperly adjusted.	Adjust cable.
	No park.	• Select cable improperly adjusted. • Parking lock actuator spring, parking pawl or governor hub malfunctioning.	Adjust cable. Repair or replace.
NOISES	Excessive noises in all drive ranges.	• Too much backlash between sun gear and planetary gears. • Lock plate on planetary carrier loose. • Thrust bearing defective. • Bearing bushings worn and excessive transmission axial play. • Converter housing bolt loose and contacting converter.	Replace gears. Replace planetary gear. Replace bearing. Replace transmission case. Tighten bolts.
	Screeching noise when starting.	• Torque converter failure.	Replace converter.
	Short vibrating, hissing noise shortly before 1 — 2 upshift.	• Spring cushion of reverse clutch wearing into transmission case.	Replace transmission case.
	Buzzing noise.	• Clogged oil pump screen.	Wash screen.
ABRASIVE	Excessive amount of iron dust (can be picked up by magnet) in oil pan.	• Oil pump, governor hub or second clutch hub.	Wash or replace.
	Excessive amount of aluminum dust (cannot be picked up by magnet) in oil pan.	• Thrust face in case, rear bore of case or torque converter inside.	Wash or replace.

TH5028900638050X

Fig. 3   Troubleshooting chart (Part 5 of 5)

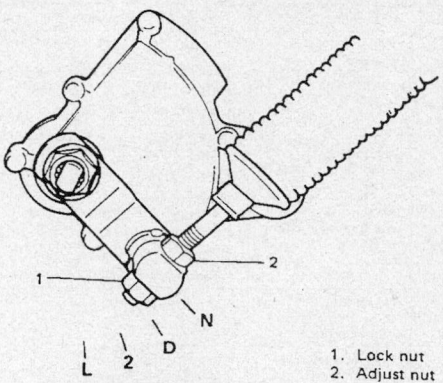

1. Lock nut
2. Adjust nut

TH5029100009000X

Fig. 4   Select cable adjustment

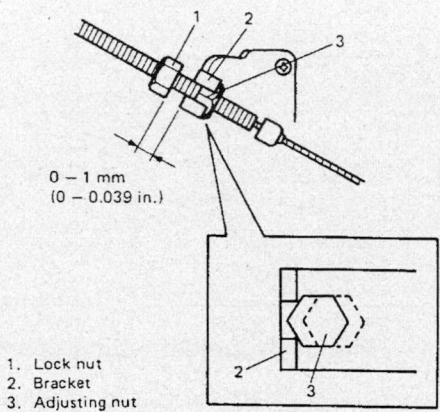

0 — 1 mm
(0 — 0.039 in.)

1. Lock nut
2. Bracket
3. Adjusting nut

TH5029100012000X

Fig. 7   Kickdown cable nut adjustment

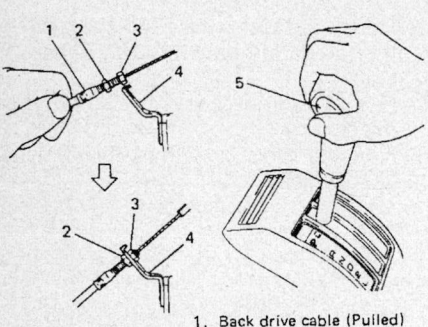

1. Back drive cable (Pulled)
2. Lock nut
3. Adjust nut
4. Bracket
5. Push button (Depressed fully)

TH5029100010000X

Fig. 5   Backdrive cable adjustment

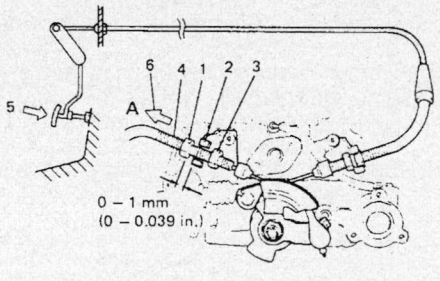

0 — 1 mm
(0 — 0.039 in.)

1. Lock nut   4. Kick-down cable
2. Bracket   5. Depress accelerator pedal fully
3. Adjusting nut   6. Pull kick-down cable

TH5029100011000X

Fig. 6   Kickdown cable adjustment

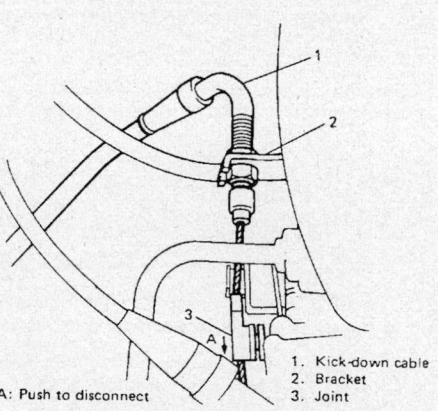

A: Push to disconnect

1. Kick-down cable
2. Bracket
3. Joint

TH5029100013000X

Fig. 8   Kickdown cable plastic joint removal

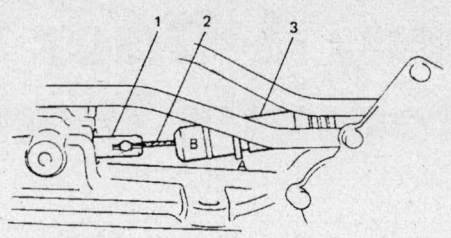

1. Kick-down valve
2. Inner cable
3. Kick-down cable
A: Apply screwdriver to remove
B: Apply grease

*Copyrighted Material Reprinted with Permission from
Hydra-Matic Div., GM Corp.*

TH5029100014000X

Fig. 9   Kickdown cable removal

TIGHTENING SPECIFICATIONS

Year	Component	Torque/Ft. Lbs.
1996–99	Driveplate Bolt	54.5–57.5
	Driveplate To Converter Bolt	40
	Engine Rear Mounting Bolt/Nut	36
	Kick-Down Cable Bracket Bolt	8
	Oil Cooler Hose Clamp	12①
	Oil Pan Bolt	9
	Propeller Shaft To Differential	37
	Select Cable Bracket Bolt	17
	Select Cable Locknut	5
	Select Lever Shaft Nut	14
	Selector Assembly To Floor Bolt	13
	Transfer To Transmission Bolt	17
	Transmission Case Plug	11–13
	Transmission To Engine Bolt/Nut	62
	U-Joint Flange Bolt	40
	Vacuum Modulator	38

① — Inch lbs.

Grand Vitara, 4-Door Sidekick & X-90 Automatic Transmission

NOTE: On Air Bag Equipped Models, Refer To " Air Bag System Precautions" Located In The Front Of This Manual For System Disarming & Arming Procedures.

INDEX

PRECAUTIONS

AIR BAG SYSTEMS

Refer to "Air Bag System Precautions" in the front of this manual for system disarming and arming procedures.

BATTERY GROUND CABLE

Prior to service, disconnect battery ground cable and isolate as required.

FUEL SYSTEM PRESSURE RELEASE

1. Disconnect fuel pump harness connector at the fuel tank rear side. **Cover fuel pipe line with rag after relieving pressure as certain pressure may still remain.**
2. Start engine and let idle until engine stops by itself, then turn ignition switch to Off. **Failure to relieve fuel system pressure prior to disconnecting fuel system components may cause fire or personal injury.**
3. Connect fuel pump harness connector.
4. After repairs have been completed, connect positive battery terminal to fuel pump drive terminal and the negative terminal to the chassis. Ensure fuel pump operates at this time.

IDENTIFICATION

Refer to **Fig. 1,** for transmission identification.

DESCRIPTION

This unit is a fully automatic, electronically controlled, transmission which can provide four forward speeds and reverse. The units primary components include a three-element hydraulic torque converter and a compound planetary gear set.

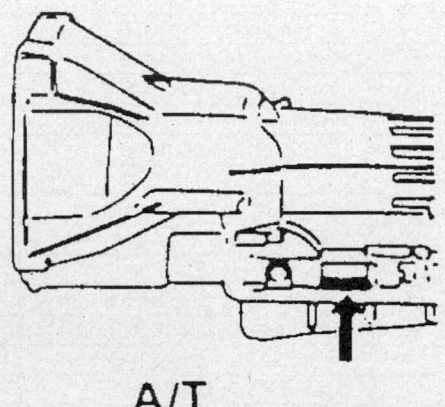

A/T

SK5029100001000X

Fig. 1 Transmission identification

TROUBLESHOOTING

Refer to **Figs. 2 through 6** when troubleshooting this transmission.

MAINTENANCE

FLUID CHECK

1. Drive vehicle for approximately 15 minutes to bring fluid up to normal operating temperature.
2. With vehicle on level surface, apply parking brake and block drive wheels.
3. With selector lever in Park position, start engine, then move selector lever through each range and return to Park.
4. Remove dipstick and check fluid level.
5. Fluid level should be between HOT marks on dipstick.
6. Add fluid as required to bring fluid to specified level. When adding fluid use only Dexron II type transmission fluid or equivalent.

FLUID CHANGE

Under normal driving conditions, trans-

mission fluid should be changed every 100,000 miles. To service, proceed as follows:

1. Raise and support vehicle.
2. With engine cool, remove drain plug and drain fluid from oil pan.
3. Install drain plug and tighten to specification.
4. Lower vehicle and fill transmission with Dexron II or equivalent.
5. Check fluid as outlined under "Fluid Level Check."

ADJUSTMENTS

THROTTLE CABLE

Ensure distance "A" in **Fig. 7,** is .031–.059 inch. Adjust as necessary.

SELECT CABLE

1. Loosen cable end nut, then shift select lever and manual shift lever to Neutral position, **Fig. 8.** Ensure nut and cable joint sufficient clearance. If select cable has been removed, push cable in direction as shown, **Fig. 8.**
2. Hand tighten nut "A," **Fig. 9,** until it contacts manual select cable joint, then tighten nut "B" with wrench.
3. Confirm proper operation of select cable.

SHIFT SWITCH

1. Shift select lever to Neutral position.
2. Align groove in switch with match marks on shaft.
3. Ensure engine only starts in Neutral and Park ranges and back-up lamps illuminate in Reverse range.

TRANSMISSION

REPLACE

GRAND VITARA

1. Remove front console box and shift boot.

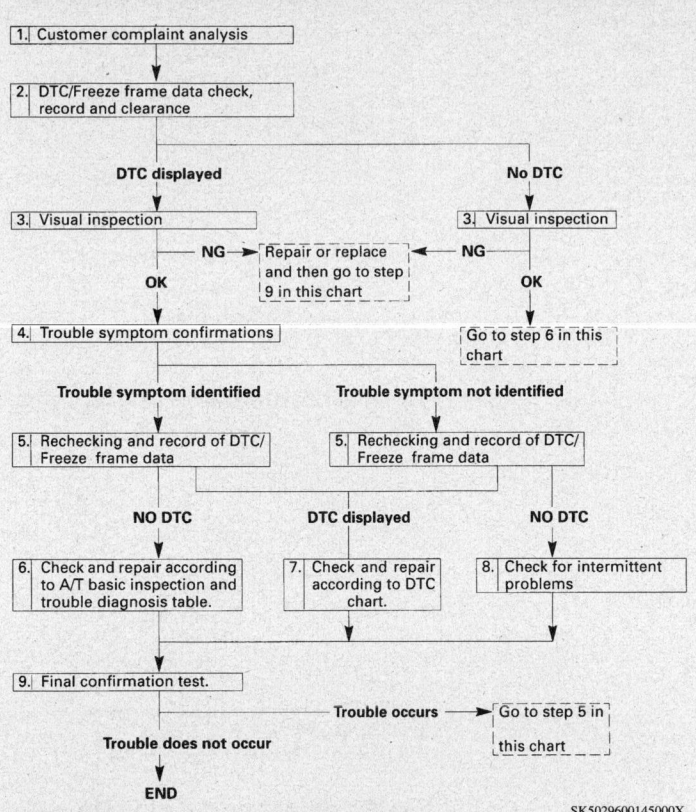

Fig. 2   Transmission troubleshooting chart

SK5029600145000X

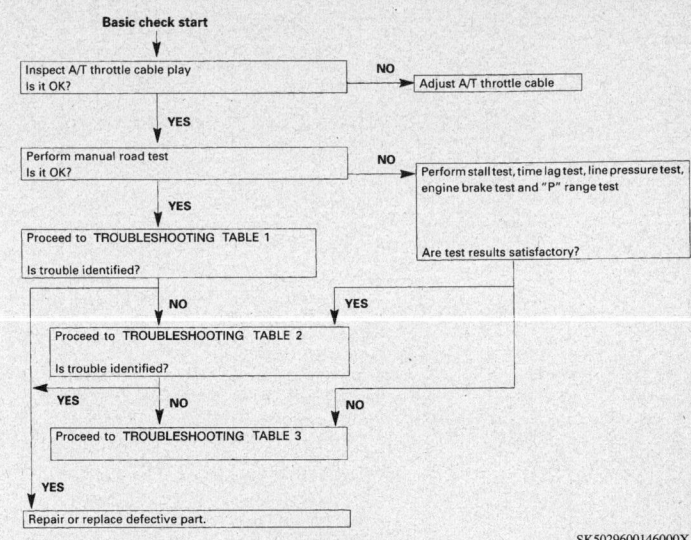

Fig. 3   Transmission basic check

SK5029600146000X

Condition	Possible Cause	Correction
TCC does not operate	• Brake light switch circuit faulty • Cruise Control signal circuit faulty	DIAGNOSTIC FLOW CHART A1
Gear does not change to 4th	• Cruise Control signal circuit faulty	DIAGNOSTIC FLOW CHART A2

SK5029600147000X

Fig. 4   Troubleshooting diagnosis table 1

	Condition	Possible Cause	Correction
Gear shift	Poor 3–4 shift, excessive slippage	• 3–4 shift valve sticking	Replace.
		• Shift solenoid valve–B sticking	Replace.
	Excessive shock on 1–2 shift	• Regulator valve sticking	Replace.
		• Faulty accumulator, second brake piston	Replace.
	Excessive shock on 2–3 shift	• Regulator valve sticking	Replace.
		• Faulty accumulator, direct clutch piston	Replace.
	Excessive shock on 3–4 shift	• Regulator valve sticking	Replace.
	Non operate lock–up system	• TCC (Lock-up) control valve sticking	Replace.
		• Solenoid valve No.2 (TCC solenoid valve) sticking	Replace.

SK5029600148020X

**Fig. 5   Troubleshooting diagnosis table 2
(Part 2 of 2)**

	Condition	Possible Cause	Correction
Transmission fluid	Low fluid pressure	• Clogged oil pump strainer	Wash strainer.
		• Malfunction of pressure regulator valve	Overhaul valve body.
	High fluid pressure	• Pressure regulator valve	Overhaul valve body.
Running condition	Unable to run in all range	• Regulator valve stick	Replace.
		• Clogged oil strainer	Wash strainer.
		• Seized or broken planetary gear	Repair or replace
		• Faulty manual valve	Replace.
Running condition	Poor 1st speed running or excessive slippage in "D" or "2"	• Faulty 1–2 shift valve	Replace.
Gear shift	Poor 1–2 shift, excessive slippage	• Regulator valve sticking	Replace.
		• 1–2 shift valve sticking	Replace.
		• Shift solenoid valve–B sticking	Replace.
		• Intermediate coast modulator valve sticking	Replace.
	Poor 2–3 shift, excessive slippage	• 2–3 shift valve sticking	Replace.
		• Shift solenoid valve–A sticking	Replace.
	Poor start or surging in "D" range	• Regulator valve sticking	Replace.

SK5029600148010X

**Fig. 5   Troubleshooting diagnosis table 2
(Part 1 of 2)**

	Condition	Possible Cause	Correction
Transmission fluid	Low fluid pressure	• Leakage from oil pressure circuit	Overhaul.
Running condition	Unable to run in all range	• Wear in oil pump	Replace.
		• Seizure in oil pump	Replace.
		• Fluid pressure leakage to over drive clutch due to wear of oil pump bushing	Replace.
		• Faulty in torque converter	Replace.

SK5029600149010X

**Fig. 6   Troubleshooting diagnosis table 3
(Part 1 of 2)**

	Condition	Possible Cause	Correction
Running condition	Poor 1st speed running or excessive slippage in "D" or "2"	• Fluid pressure leakage from forward clutch due to wear or breakage of O/D case seal ring	Replace.
		• Overdrive clutch slipping	Replace.
	Unable to run or excessive slippage in "L" range	• Fluid pressure leakage of forward clutch due to wear or breakage of O/D case seal ring	Replace.
		• Reverse brake disc slipping	Replace.
		• Broken brake piston O-ring	Replace.
	Unable to run or excessive slippage in "R" range	• Fluid pressure leakage to direct clutch due to wear or breakage of center support seal ring	Replace.
		• Worn direct clutch	Replace.
Gear shift	Poor 1–2 shift, excessive slippage	• Fluid pressure leakage to overdrive clutch due to wear or breakage of O/D case seal ring	Replace.
		• Faulty second brake	Replace.
		• Broken O-ring of second brake piston	Replace.
		• Faulty second coast brake (in "2" range)	Replace.
	Poor 2–3 shift, excessive slippage	• Fluid pressure leakage to overdrive clutch due to wear or breakage of O/D case seal ring	Replace.
		• Worn direct clutch bushing	Replace.
		• Direct clutch slipping	Replace.
		• Foreign material caught in direct clutch piston check ball	Replace.
	Poor start or surging in "D" range	• Fluid pressure leakage of forward clutch due to wear or breakage of O/D case seal ring	Replace.
		• Malfunction of forward clutch	Replace.
	Poor 3–4 shift, excessive slippage	• Faulty overdrive brake	Replace.
		• Faulty overdrive clutch	Replace.
	Poor start or juddering in "R" range	• Fluid pressure leakage of direct clutch due to wear or breakage of oil center support seal ring	Replace.
		• Worn direct clutch	Replace.
	Excessive shock on 1–2 shift	• Faulty one-way clutch	Replace.
	Non operate lock-up system	• Faulty torque converter	Replace.
Abnormal noise	Abnormal noise in "P" or "N" range	• Worn oil pump	Replace.

SK5029600149020X

Fig. 6 Troubleshooting diagnosis table 3 (Part 2 of 2)

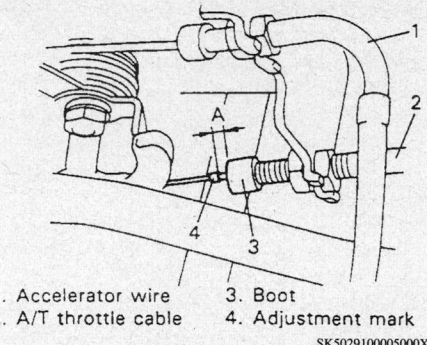

1. Accelerator wire   3. Boot
2. A/T throttle cable   4. Adjustment mark

SK5029100005000X

Fig. 7 Throttle cable adjustment

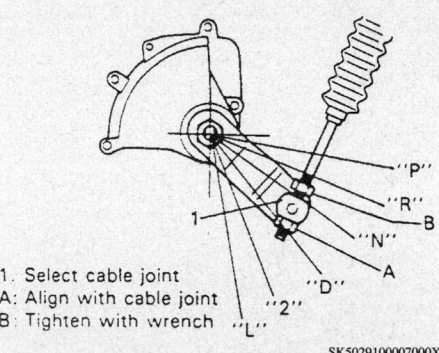

1. Select cable joint
A: Align with cable joint
B: Tighten with wrench

SK5029100007000X

Fig. 9 Select cable adjustment

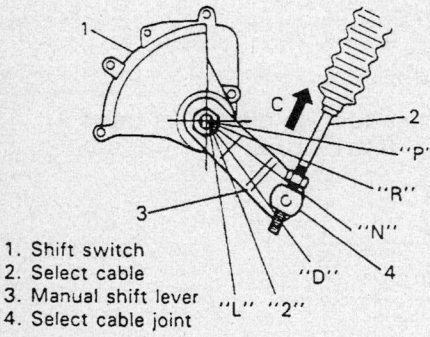

1. Shift switch
2. Select cable
3. Manual shift lever
4. Select cable joint

SK5029100006000X

Fig. 8 Shift switch range locations

2. Remove boot from transfer case gear shift lever, if equipped.
3. Rotate shift control lever counterclockwise to remove.
4. Remove battery, dip stick and oil filler tube.
5. Disconnect A/T throttle cable from throttle cam and bracket.
6. Disconnect wiring harness connectors.
7. Remove starter motor.
8. Remove engine to transmission mounting bolts.
9. Drain transfer oil into suitable container.
10. Raise and support vehicle, then refer-

ence mark and remove propeller shafts.
11. Remove select cable bracket.
12. Remove front exhaust pipe.
13. Disconnect oil cooler hoses from pipes.
14. Remove right case stiffener.
15. Remove torque converter housing lower plate.
16. Remove torque converter mount bolts.
17. Remove remaining engine to transmission nuts.
18. Disconnect speed sensor, then support transmission using suitable jack.
19. Remove rear member.
20. Move assembly rearward, then lower from vehicle.
21. Separate transfer case and transmission as required.
22. Reverse procedure to install.

SIDEKICK & X-90

1. Relieve fuel system pressure as outlined under "Precautions."
2. Remove clips at rear of console box, then the console box mounting screws at front and retaining clips at rear and console box.
3. Remove shift lever boot cover, then the No. 2 boot.
4. Remove transfer gear shift lever boot clamp, then the transfer gear shift boot.
5. To remove shift control lever, push

down gear shift control case cover with fingers and turn it counterclockwise.
6. To remove transfer shift control lever, push down gear shift control case cover with fingers and turn it counterclockwise.
7. Remove battery, dipstick and oil filler tube.
8. Disconnect A/T throttle cable from throttle cam and bracket.
9. Disconnect wiring harness couplers, then remove starter. Do not disconnect starter wiring harness.
10. Remove upper transmission to engine bolts. Right side bolt is longer.
11. Drain transfer oil into appropriate container. If transmission is to be overhauled, drain transmission fluid into appropriate container.
12. Place match marks on joint flanges and propeller shafts, then remove both propeller shafts.
13. Remove nut from end of select cable and E-ring from bracket. Position cable aside.
14. Remove select cable bracket, then remove front exhaust pipes.
15. Remove case left stiffener, then disconnect oil cooler hoses from pipes. Plug all open fittings.
16. On right stiffener, remove bolt "A" and loosen bolt "B," Fig. 10.
17. Install driveplate holding tool, part No. 09927-56010 or equivalent, then remove torque converter mounting bolts.
18. Remove lower engine to transmission nuts, then disconnect speedometer cable.
19. Install suitable transmission jack, then remove rear mounting member, torque

stopper member and torque stopper bushing.

20. Remove transmission, transfer case and torque converter as an assembly. **Keep transmission/transfer assembly horizontal. If assembly is tilted, torque converter may fall off causing personal injury.**

21. Remove wiring harness and breather hoses.

22. Remove transfer case mounting bolts, then separate transfer case from transmission.

23. Reverse procedure to install. Tighten to specifications.

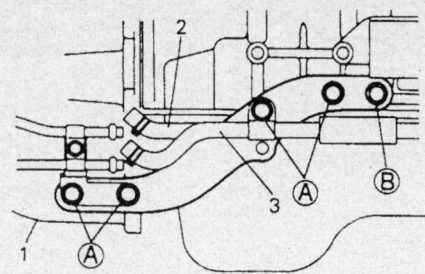

1. Converter housing
2. Outlet hose
3. Inlet hose

SK5029100008000X

Fig. 10 Case right stiffener mounting bolts

TIGHTENING SPECIFICATIONS

Year	Component	Torque/ Ft. Lbs.
1996–99	Case Stiffener Bolts	29–43
	Drain Plug	14–20
	Driveplate To Converter Bolts	44–50
	Engine Rear Mounting Bolts	29–43
	Engine Rear Mounting Bracket Bolts	29–43
	Engine Rear Mounting Member Bolts	29–43
	Engine To Transmission Nuts	51–72
	Exhaust Pipe Bracket Bolts	29–43
	Exhaust Pipe To Manifold Nuts	37–51
	Muffler To Exhaust Bolts	29–43
	Oil Filler Tube Bolts	14–20
	Select Cable Bracket Bolts	14–20
	Torque Converter Bolts	44–51
	Torque Stopper Bolts	29–43
	Universal Joint Flange Nuts & Bolts	37–43

① — Inch lbs.

SUZUKI
Swift Automatic Transaxle

NOTE: On Air Bag Equipped Models, Refer To " Air Bag System Precautions" Located In The Front Of This Manual For System Disarming & Arming Procedures.

PRECAUTIONS
AIR BAG SYSTEMS

Refer to "Air Bag System Precautions" in the front of this manual for system disarming and arming procedures.

BATTERY GROUND CABLE

Prior to service, disconnect battery ground cable and isolate as required.

FUEL SYSTEM PRESSURE RELEASE

1. Disconnect fuel pump harness connector at the fuel tank rear side. **Cover fuel pipe line with rag after relieving pressure as certain pressure may still remain.**
2. Start engine and let idle until engine stops by itself, then turn ignition switch to Off. **Failure to relieve fuel system pressure prior to disconnecting fuel system components may cause fire or personal injury.**
3. Connect fuel pump harness connector.
4. After repairs have been completed, connect positive battery terminal to fuel pump drive terminal and the negative terminal to the chassis. Ensure fuel pump operates at this time.

IDENTIFICATION

Refer to **Fig. 1,** for proper transaxle identification.

DESCRIPTION

This automatic transaxle is an electronically controlled three speed automatic transaxle, utilizing a hydraulic torque converter, countershaft and differential.

The transaxle uses two planetary gears, two disc clutches, one band brake, one disc brake and one one-way clutch.

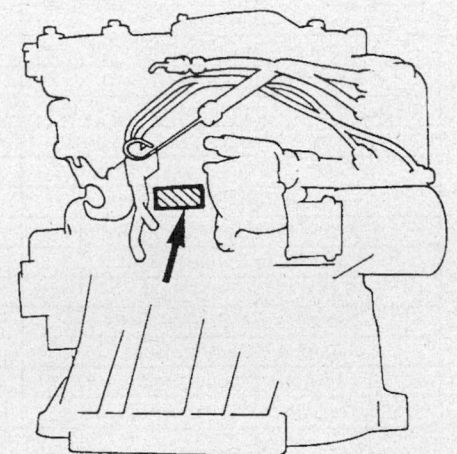

SK5029100009000X

Fig. 1 Transaxle identification

TROUBLESHOOTING

Refer to **Figs. 2 through 6** when troubleshooting transaxle.

MAINTENANCE
FLUID CHECK

1. Drive vehicle for approximately 15 minutes to bring fluid up to normal operating temperature.
2. With vehicle on level surface, apply parking brake and block drive wheels.
3. With selector lever in Park position, start engine, then move selector lever through each range and return to Park.
4. Remove dipstick and check fluid level.
5. Fluid level should be between HOT marks on dipstick.
6. Add fluid as required to bring fluid to specified level. When adding fluid use only Dexron II type transaxle fluid or equivalent.

FLUID CHANGE

Under normal driving conditions, fluid level should be changed and oil strainer cleaned every 100,000 miles. To service, proceed as follows:

1. Raise and support front of vehicle.
2. Remove drain plug and drain fluid from oil pan into appropriate container.
3. Remove oil pan attaching bolts and the oil pan.
4. Remove oil strainer-to-valve body attaching bolts, then the oil strainer.
5. Clean strainer and oil pan in suitable solvent. Engine magnet in oil pan is positioned directly below oil strainer.
6. Install oil strainer and attaching bolts. Tighten to specification.
7. Install oil pan using new gasket. Tighten to specification. **Two of the oil pan attaching bolts have crossed grooves on the bolt head. When installing these two bolts, coat threads with suitable sealant and install in positions shown, Fig. 7.**
8. Lower vehicle and refill oil pan with approximately 1.5 quarts of Dexron II type transaxle fluid or equivalent.
9. Check fluid level as previously described and adjust as necessary.

ADJUSTMENTS
INTERLOCK CABLE

1. Loosen cable nuts "A" and " B" as shown, **Fig. 8.**
2. Shift selector lever to Park position.
3. While pulling outer cable as far as possible in direction of arrow "C," **Fig. 8,** align nut "B" with bracket and tighten locknut "A." When outer cable is pulled in " C" direction, release shaft spring in steering lock should be depressed fully.
4. After adjustment is complete, ensure the following:
   a. With selector lever in Park position, ensure ignition key can be turned from "ACC" to "LOCK" position and removed from ignition switch.
   b. Ensure ignition key cannot be

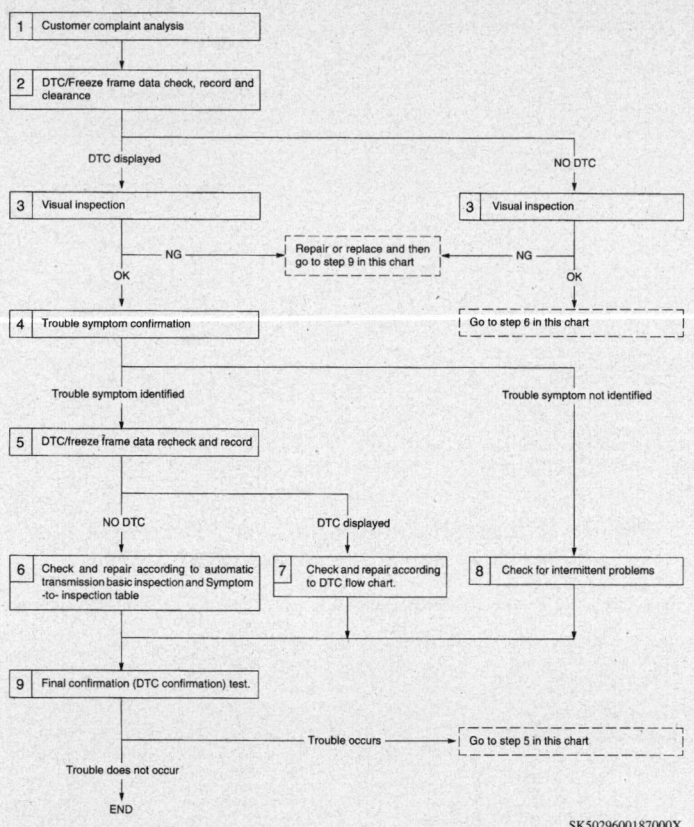

Fig. 2 Transaxle diagnostic flow chart

SK5029600187000X

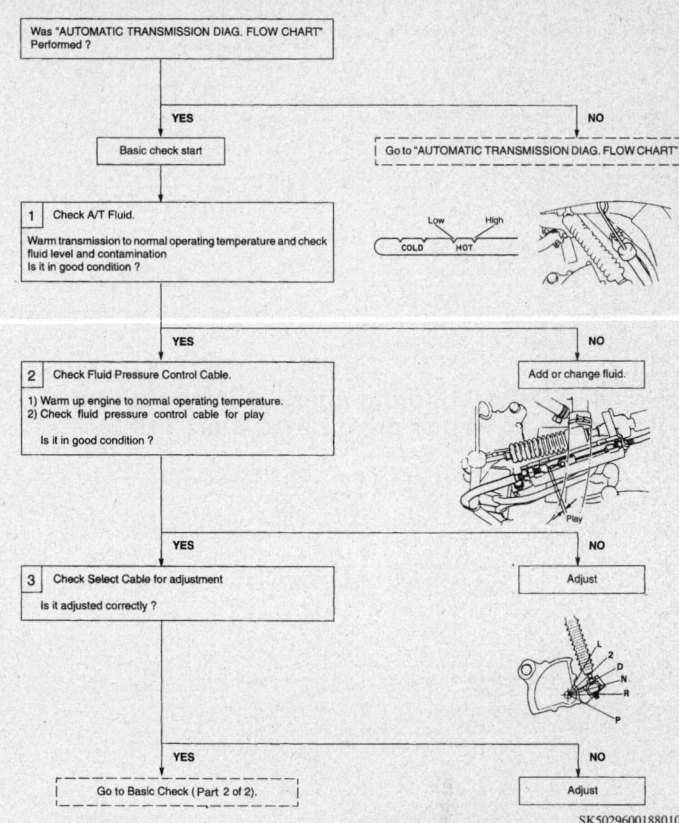

Fig. 3 Transaxle basic check (Part 1 of 2)

SK5029600188010X

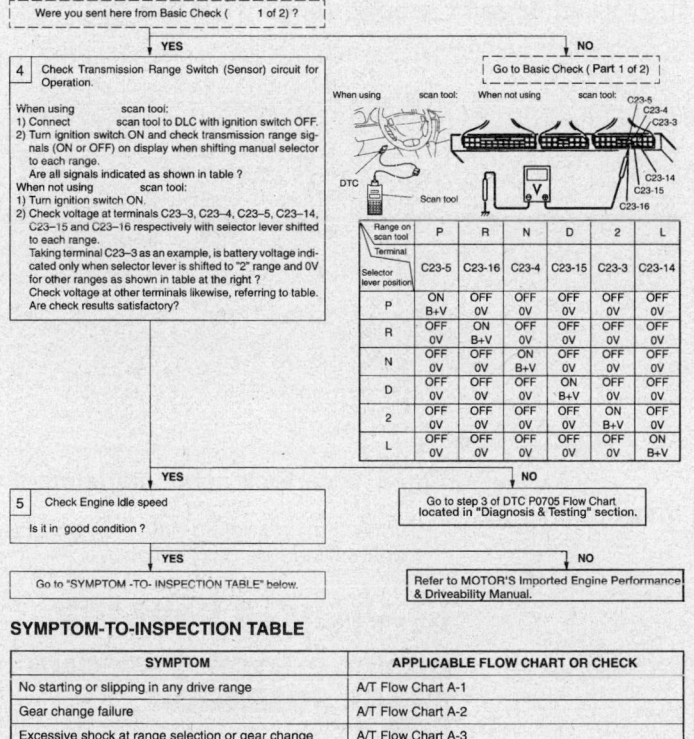

SYMPTOM-TO-INSPECTION TABLE

SYMPTOM	APPLICABLE FLOW CHART OR CHECK
No starting or slipping in any drive range	A/T Flow Chart A-1
Gear change failure	A/T Flow Chart A-2
Excessive shock at range selection or gear change	A/T Flow Chart A-3
Engine brake fails to operate	Engine Brake Check
Gear shift failure in "D" or "2" range	A/T Flow Chart B-1
Gear is shifted to 2nd or 3rd in "L" range	A/T Flow Chart B-2
Vehicle does not move backward in "R" range	

SK5029600188020X

Fig. 3 Transaxle basic check (Part 2 of 2)

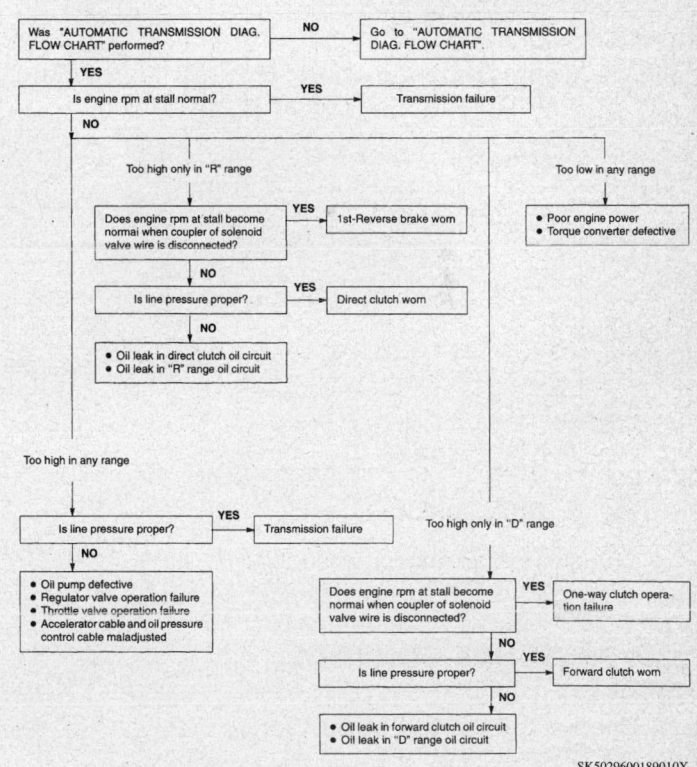

SK5029600189010X

Fig. 4 Troubleshooting chart "A:" No starting or slipping in any drive range (Part 1 of 3)

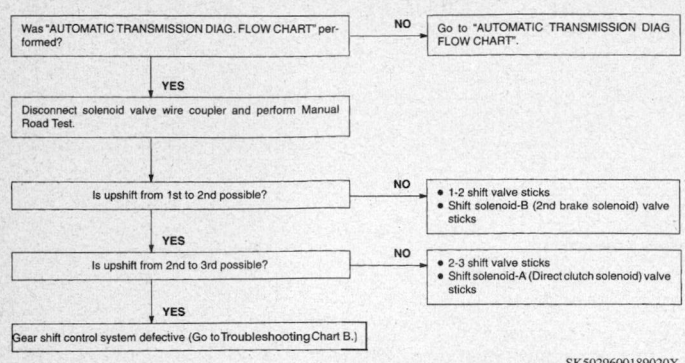

Fig. 4 Troubleshooting chart "A:" No starting or slipping in any drive range (Part 2 of 3)

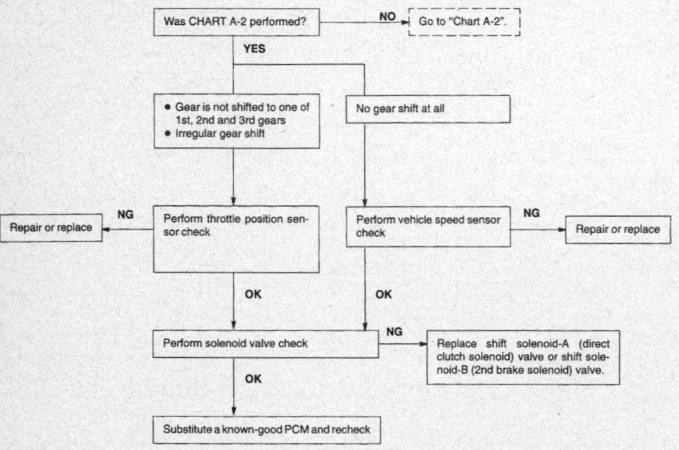

Fig. 5 Troubleshooting chart "B:" Gear shift failure in drive or second range (Part 1 of 2)

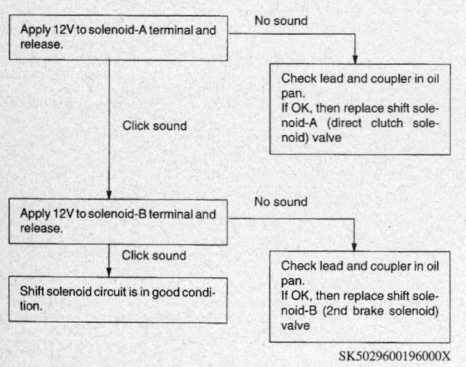

Fig. 6 Shift solenoid check

turned to Lock position when selector lever is in any other range than Park.

OIL PRESSURE CONTROL CABLE

1. Check and, if necessary, adjust accelerator cable.
2. Start engine and allow to reach normal operating temperature.
3. Remove control cable cover and ensure boot to inner cable stopper clearance is 0–.020 inch as shown, **Fig. 9.**
4. If clearance is not as specified, loosen, then tighten adjusting nuts "A" until specified clearance is obtained. If clearance is still not within specifica-

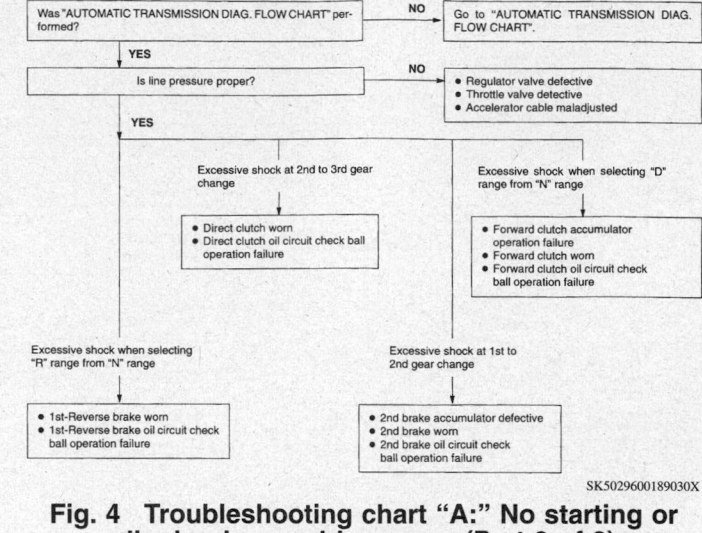

Fig. 4 Troubleshooting chart "A:" No starting or slipping in any drive range (Part 3 of 3)

Gear shift to 2nd may occur when selector lever is shifted from D or 2 to L, but this is normal.

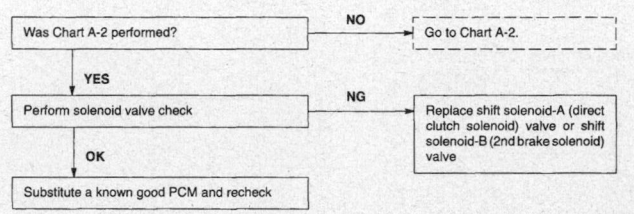

Fig. 5 Troubleshooting chart "B:" Gear shift failure in drive or second range (Part 2 of 2)

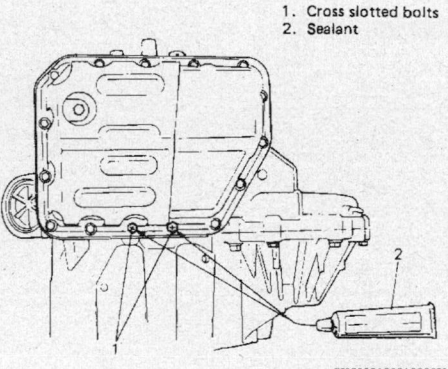

1. Cross slotted bolts
2. Sealant

Fig. 7 Oil pan installation

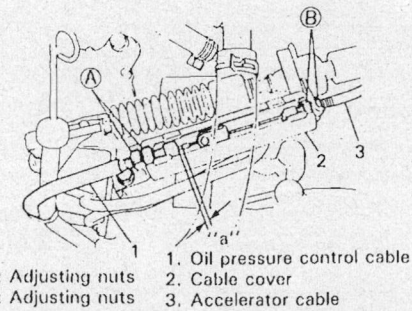

Ⓐ : Adjusting nuts
Ⓑ : Adjusting nuts

1. Oil pressure control cable
2. Cable cover
3. Accelerator cable

Fig. 9 Oil pressure control cable adjustment

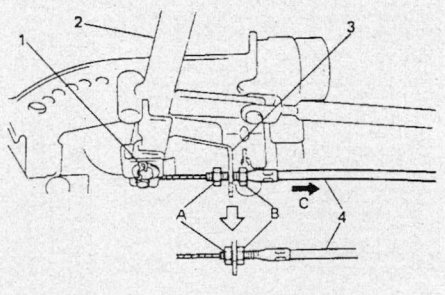

1. Clip
2. Selector lever (P position)
3. Bracket
4. Back drive cable

A: Lock nut
B: Adjust nut
C: Pull for adjusting

Fig. 8 Interlock cable adjustment

tions, turn adjusting nuts " B" and repeat procedure outlined above.

IN-VEHICLE REPAIRS

DIRECT CLUTCH & SECOND BRAKE SOLENOIDS, REPLACE

1. Drain transaxle fluid into appropriate container and remove oil pan.
2. Disconnect electrical connectors from direct clutch and second brake solenoids, then remove solenoids, **Fig. 10.**
3. Remove solenoid wire harness with grommet from upper side.
4. Reverse procedure to install.

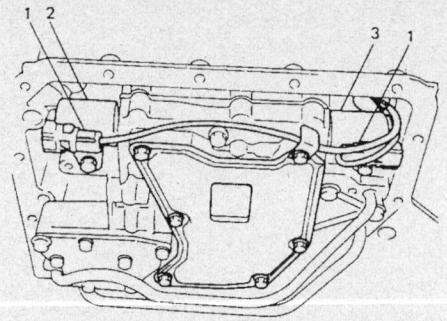

1. Coupler
2. 2nd brake solenoid
3. Direct clutch solenoid

SK5029100016000X

Fig. 10   Direct clutch & second brake solenoid replacement

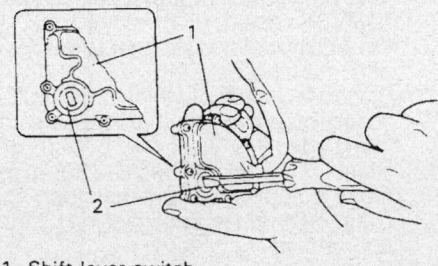

1. Shift lever switch
2. Shift lever switch joint

SK5029100019000X

Fig. 13   Shift lever switch installation

OIL PRESSURE CONTROL CABLE, REPLACE

1. Remove cable cover, then disconnect oil pressure control cable from accelerator cable.
2. Drain transaxle fluid into appropriate container and remove oil pan.
3. Disconnect oil pressure control cable from throttle valve cam, then remove cable from transaxle case, **Fig. 11.**
4. Reverse procedure to install.

TRANSAXLE SELECTOR LEVER, REPLACE

1. Remove selector lever knob, then the console assembly.
2. Remove selector indicator assembly, then disconnect cable from selector lever.
3. Disconnect interlock cable and the shift lock solenoid electrical connector.
4. Raise and support vehicle.
5. Remove housing attaching nuts, then the housing seat and housing with selector lever.
6. Reverse procedure to install.

TRANSAXLE SELECTOR CABLE, REPLACE

Removal

1. Remove console assembly, then the selector indicator assembly.
2. Disconnect selector cable from selector lever, floor and transaxle.
3. Raise and support vehicle.

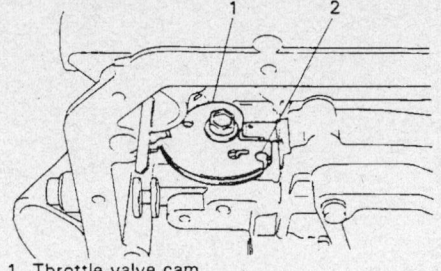

1. Throttle valve cam
2. Oil pressure control cable end

SK5029100017000X

Fig. 11   Oil pressure control cable replacement

4. Remove selector cable from front panel.

Installation

1. Raise and support vehicle.
2. Position selector cable in front panel, then lower vehicle.
3. Apply suitable grease to selector cable pin, then connect cable to lever.
4. Install selector indicator, then the console assembly.
5. Connect cable to bracket on transaxle, then slide cable into manual select joint hole and position manual shift lever in Neutral range.
6. Turn nut "A," **Fig. 12,** by hand until it contacts manual select cable joint, then tighten nut "B" with wrench.
7. After tightening cable nuts, check the following:
   a. With selector lever in Park position, vehicle cannot move when pushed.
   b. With selector lever in Neutral position, vehicle cannot be driven.
   c. With selector in Drive, Second or Low ranges, vehicle can be driven.
   d. With selector lever in Reverse range, vehicle can be backed up.

SHIFT LEVER SWITCH, REPLACE

Removal

1. Disconnect electrical connectors from shift lever switch.
2. Remove shift lever switch from manual shift shaft.

Installation

1. Shift manual shift lever to Manual range.
2. Using a suitable screwdriver, turn shift lever switch to the position as shown, **Fig. 13,** and ensure a click is heard from joint at this position.
3. Install switch to manual shift shaft, then move the shaft in direction of arrow, **Fig. 14,** until a click is heard. Stop at this position and tighten to specification.
4. Connect electrical connectors to switch, then install clamp.
5. Apply parking brake and block wheels, then check the following:
   a. With selector lever in Park position and ignition switch On, ensure starter motor operates.
   b. With selector lever in Neutral posi-

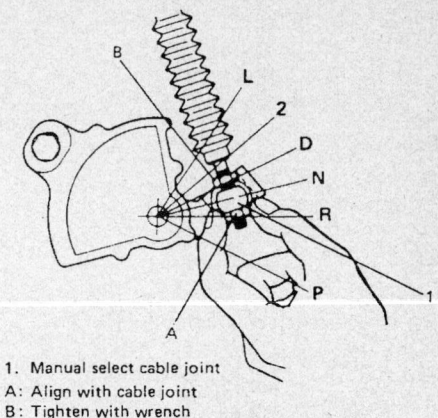

1. Manual select cable joint
A: Align with cable joint
B: Tighten with wrench

SK5029100018000X

Fig. 12   Transaxle selector cable installation

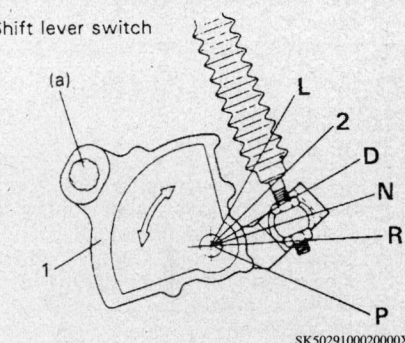

1. Shift lever switch

SK5029100020000X

Fig. 14   Shift lever switch adjustment

tion and ignition switch On, ensure starter motor operates.
   c. After moving selector lever from Neutral to Low position, then back to Neutral position, ensure starter motor operates with ignition switch On.
   d. With selector lever in Park position and ignition switch On, ensure starter motor operates.
   e. In any range other than Park or Neutral positions, ensure starter motor cannot be operated.
   f. With selector lever in Reverse position and ignition switch On, (engine not running), ensure back-up lamps light.

INTERLOCK CABLE, REPLACE

1. Remove steering column cover and column hole cover.
2. Remove interlock cable clamp screw, located at steering lock.
3. Push in release shaft "A" fully, then disconnect cable end. **Do not remove release shaft E-ring.**
4. Remove console box and parking brake lever cover.
5. Remove cable by loosening nut and removing clip in manual selector.
6. Reverse procedure to install.

SPEED SENSOR, REPLACE

1. Disconnect wiring harness clamp, then the speed sensor coupler.

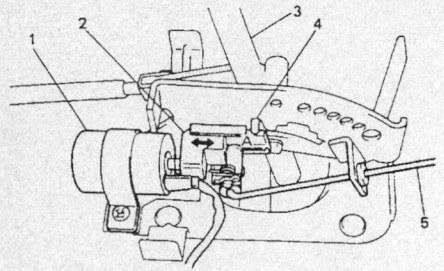

1. Back drive solenoid assembly
2. Lock plate
3. Selector lever (in P)
4. Detent pin
5. Manual release rod
A: Apply grease

SK5029100021000X

Fig. 15 Shift lock solenoid replacement

2. Remove speed sensor bolt.
3. Remove sensor by gripping sensor body.
4. Reverse procedure to install.

SHIFT LOCK SOLENOID, REPLACE

1. Shift selector lever to Low position, then remove console box, parking brake lever cover, shift control lever cover and select indicator.
2. Remove shift lock solenoid attaching screw, then the solenoid, **Fig. 15.**
3. Reverse procedure to install, noting the following:
   a. Ensure detent pin is locked at Park position by lock plate.
   b. Ensure lock plate is pulled in when ignition key is turned On.

TRANSAXLE
REPLACE

The engine and transaxle must be removed as an assembly.
1. Relieve fuel system pressure as outlined under " Precautions."
2. Remove battery and tray, then the engine hood.
3. Drain coolant system into appropriate container.
4. Remove air cleaner assembly with Air Flow Meter (AFM) outlet hose.
5. Remove radiator cooling fan, then the battery ground cable from transaxle.
6. Disconnect the following electrical wires:
   a. Disconnect direct clutch and second brake connectors.
   b. Disconnect shift switch and speed sensor connectors.
   c. Disconnect noise filter ground wire, then the Idle Speed Control (ISC) valve connector.
   d. Disconnect high tension cable from ignition coil, then the Distributor Crank Angle Sensor (CAS) connector.
   e. **On California models,** disconnect

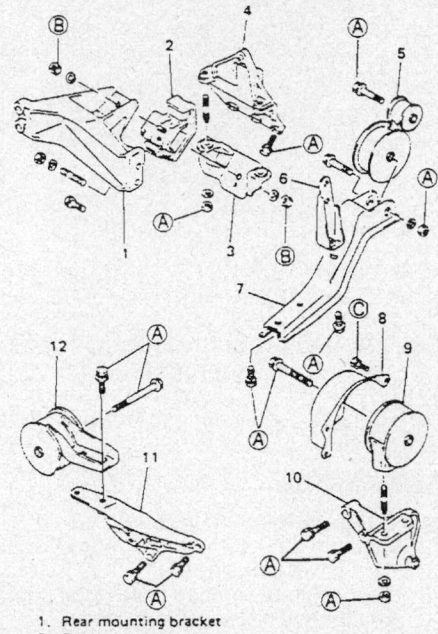

1. Rear mounting bracket
2. Rear mounting
3. Rear mounting body No. 1 bracket
4. Rear mounting body No. 2 bracket
5. Rear torque rod
6. Rear torque rod stiffener
7. Rear torque rod bracket
8. Left mounting body bracket
9. Left mounting
10. Left mounting bracket
11. Right mounting bracket
12. Right mounting

Tightening torque
50 — 60 N·m
Ⓐ 5.0 — 6.0 kg-m
36.5 — 43.0 lb-ft

40 — 50 N·m
Ⓑ 4.0 — 5.0 kg-m
29.0 — 36.0 lb-ft

18 — 28 N·m
Ⓒ 1.8 — 2.8 kg-m
13.5 — 20.0 lb-ft

SK5029100022000X

Fig. 16 Engine mounting

the Recirculated Exhaust Gas Temperature Sensor (REGTS) and the Exhaust Gas Recirculation Vacuum Switching Valve (EGR VSV) connectors.
   f. **On all models,** disconnect the Water Temperature Sensor (WTS) and oxygen sensor connectors.
   g. Disconnect canister purge VSV connector, then the ground wire from intake manifold.
   h. Disconnect Throttle Position Sensor (TPS) and fuel injector connectors.
   i. Disconnect all electrical wires from alternator and starter.
   j. Disconnect oil pressure gauge connector.
   k. Ensure all wires are free of clamps on engine.
7. Disconnect the following cables:
   a. Disconnect accelerator cable from throttle lever and bracket.
   b. Disconnect gear select and oil pressure control cables.
   c. Disconnect speedometer cable from transaxle.
8. Disconnect brake booster and canister purge hoses.

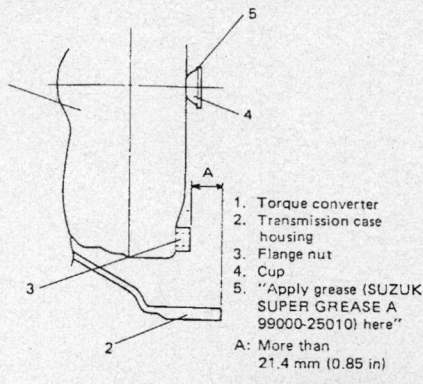

1. Torque converter
2. Transmission case housing
3. Flange nut
4. Cup
5. "Apply grease (SUZUKI SUPER GREASE A 99000-25010) here"

A: More than 21.4 mm (0.85 in)

SK5029100023000X

Fig. 17 Torque converter installation

9. **On California models,** disconnect A/C VSV hose.
10. **On all models,** disconnect fuel feed and return hoses.
11. Disconnect heater inlet and outlet hoses, then remove charcoal canister from body.
12. Raise and support vehicle, then remove exhaust pipe from manifold.
13. Drain engine and transmission oil into appropriate container.
14. Remove LH side driveshaft joint from differential gear of transaxle. Remove RH side driveshaft joint from center bearing support.
15. Remove rear torque rod bracket from transaxle case.
16. Lower vehicle, then install engine lifting device.
17. Remove rear mounting nut, **Fig. 16.**
18. Remove left side engine mounting bracket bolts and mounting bolt.
19. Remove right side engine mounting from bracket.
20. **Ensure all hoses, electric wires and cable are disconnected from engine and transaxle.**
21. Remove engine and transaxle from vehicle.
22. Remove torque convertor housing lower plate.
23. Remove driveplate bolts. Use flat head screwdriver to lock driveplate and driveplate gear.
24. Remove starter motor, then the transaxle stiffener.
25. Remove engine to transaxle attaching bolts, then separate engine from transaxle.
26. Reverse procedure to install, noting the following:
   a. Apply grease around cup at center of torque converter, **Fig. 17.**
   b. Measure distance "A," **Fig. 17.** This distance should exceed .85 inch. If distance is less than specified, the torque converter is improperly installed.
   c. Tighten to specification.

TIGHTENING SPECIFICATIONS

Year	Component	Torque/ Ft. Lbs.
1996–99	Drain Plug	14–17
	Driveplate To Converter Bolt	13–14
	Engine Rear Mounting Bolt	36–43
	Oil Cooler Hose Clamp	12①
	Oil Pan Bolt	36–48①
	Oil Strainer Bolt	48①
	Selector Housing Nut	8–12
	Selector Lever Shaft Nut	13–16
	Shift Lever Switch Bolt	10–17
	Shift Solenoid Bolt	6–7
	Speed Sensor Bolt	6–7
	Transmission Case Plug	5–7
	Transmission To Engine Bolt/Nut	29–43

① — Inch lbs.

Esteem Automatic Transaxle

NOTE: On Air Bag Equipped Models, Refer To " Air Bag System Precautions" Located In The Front Of This Manual For System Disarming & Arming Procedures.

INDEX

PRECAUTIONS

AIR BAG SYSTEMS

Refer to "Air Bag System Precautions" in the front of this manual for system disarming and arming procedures.

BATTERY GROUND CABLE

Prior to service, disconnect battery ground cable and isolate as required.

IDENTIFICATION

Refer to **Fig. 1,** for location of transaxle identification plate.

DESCRIPTION

This is a four speed with overdrive fully automatic electronically controlled transaxle, providing four forward gears, the fourth gear being overdrive and reverse **Fig. 2. The torque converter is a three element, one step and two phase type and is equipped with an electronically controlled lock-up mechanism. The gear shift device consists of two sets of planetary gear units, 4 disc type clutches, a** disc type brake, a band type brake and two one-way clutches. The gear select lever has an overdrive cut switch which allows shift-up to the overdrive mode and shift-down from the overdrive mode.

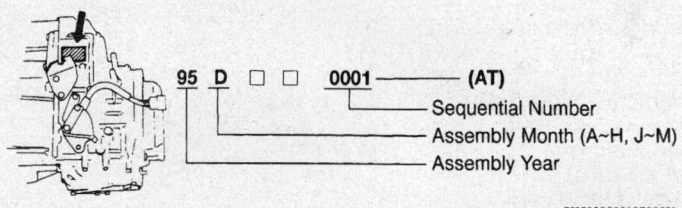

Fig. 1 Transaxle identification

TROUBLESHOOTING

Refer to **Figs. 3 and 4** for diagnostic flow chart and basic check, then to **Figs. 5 through 7** for symptom troubleshooting charts.

MAINTENANCE

FLUID CHECK

1. Park vehicle on level ground, then apply parking brake and block wheels.
2. Start engine and allow to reach normal operating temperature, then move gear selector through all gear positions.
3. Place gear selector in Park, then check fluid level.
4. If fluid level is low, add a suitable ATF. Refer to " Lubricant Data Charts" for fluid capacity and type.

FLUID CHANGE

1. Raise and support vehicle.
2. Remove drain plug and drain transaxle fluid.
3. Remove transaxle oil pan and gasket, then the fluid filter screen and gasket.

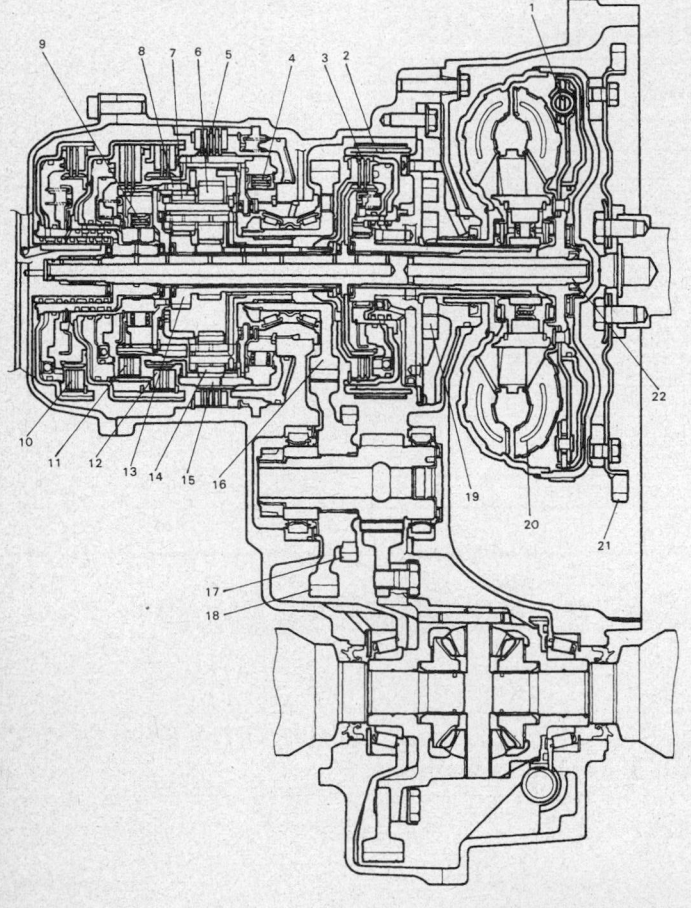

Fig. 2 Cross sectional view of transaxle

1. Torque converter clutch (TCC)
2. 2nd and 4th brake band
3. Reverse clutch
4. One way clutch No.1
5. 1st and reverse brake
6. Front large planetary pinion
7. Rear planetary pinion
8. Rear planetary ring gear
9. One way clutch No.0
10. Forward clutch
11. Coast clutch
12. Overdrive clutch
13. Planetary sun gear
14. Front small planetary pinion
15. Front planetary ring gear
16. Counter drive gear
17. Parking lock gear
18. Counter driven gear
19. Oil pump
20. Torque convertor
21. Drive plate
22. Input shaft

SK5029500198000X

4. Reverse procedure to install, noting the following:
   a. Add suitable ATF. Refer to "Lubricant Data Charts" for fluid capacity and type.
   b. Start engine and move gear selector through all gear positions, then place gear selector in Park.
   c. Recheck fluid level and add fluid if necessary.

ADJUSTMENTS

SELECT CABLE

1. Place shift lever and manual lever to Neutral position.
2. If select cable has been moved, push in direction " C" until cable bottoms out

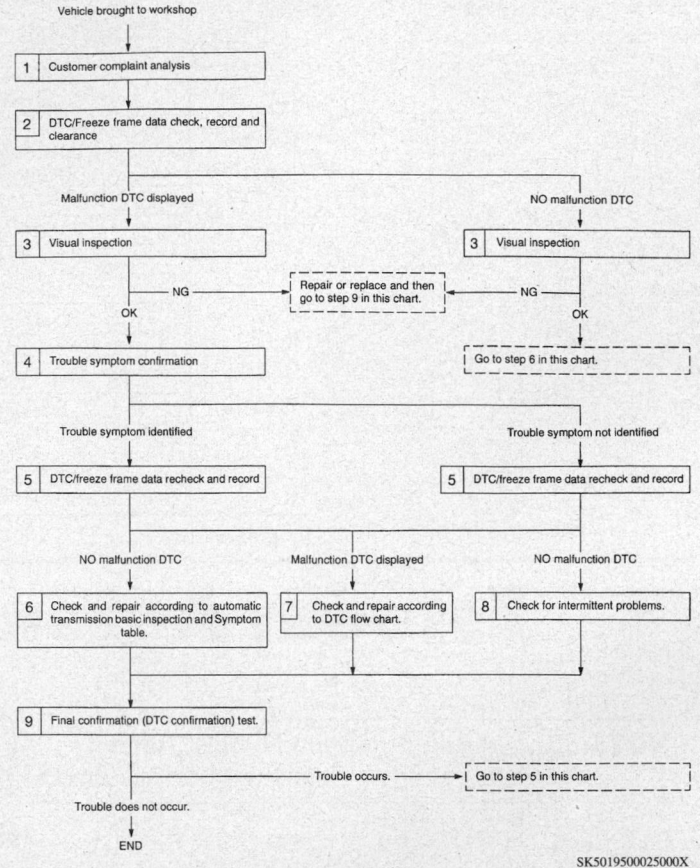

Fig. 3 Diagnostic flow chart

SK5019500025000X

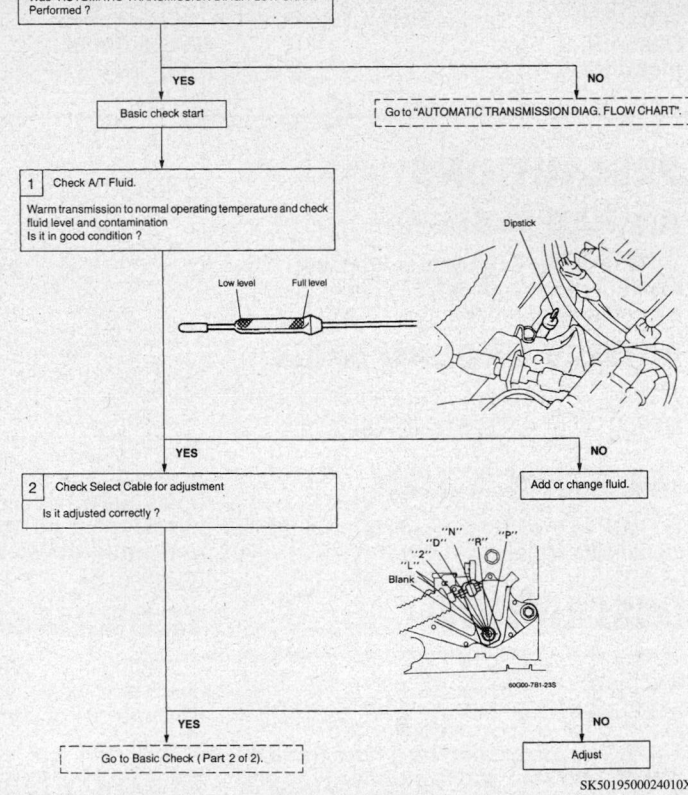

Fig. 4 Basic check (Part 1 of 2)

SK5019500024010X

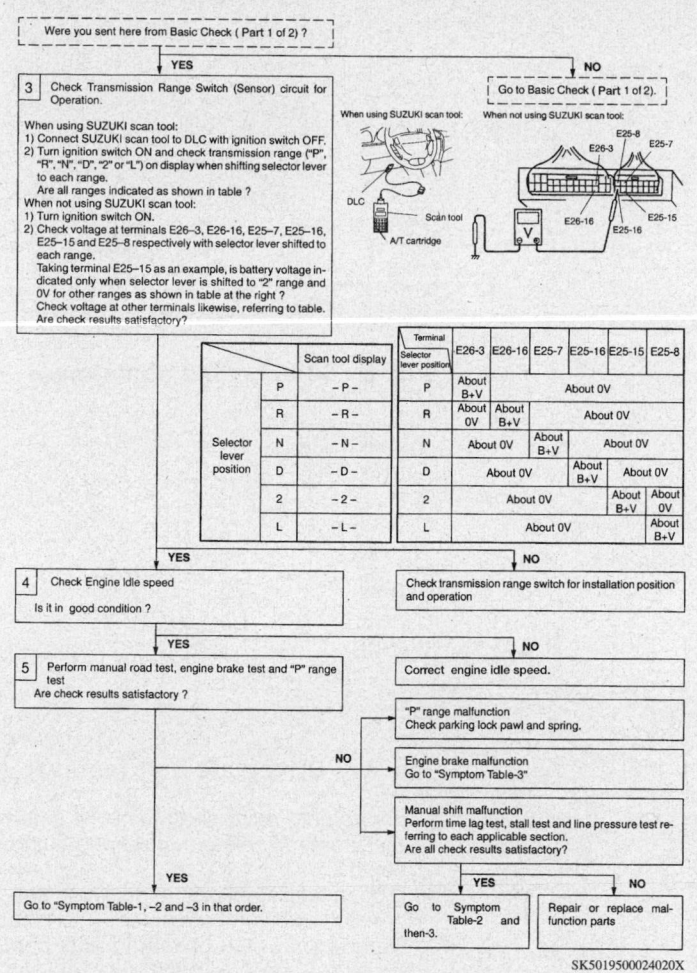

Were you sent here from Basic Check (Part 1 of 2)?

- **YES** →
- **NO** → Go to Basic Check (Part 1 of 2).

3 Check Transmission Range Switch (Sensor) circuit for Operation.

When using SUZUKI scan tool:
1) Connect SUZUKI scan tool to DLC with ignition switch OFF.
2) Turn ignition switch ON and check transmission range ("P", "R", "N", "D", "2" or "L") on display when shifting selector lever to each range.
Are all ranges indicated as shown in table?

When not using SUZUKI scan tool:
1) Turn ignition switch ON.
2) Check voltage at terminals E26-3, E26-16, E25-7, E25-16, E25-15 and E25-8 respectively with selector lever shifted to each range.
Taking terminal E25-15 as an example, is battery voltage indicated only when selector lever is shifted to "2" range and 0V for other ranges as shown in table at the right?
Check voltage at other terminals likewise, referring to table.
Are check results satisfactory?

Selector lever position	Scan tool display	Terminal selector lever position	E26-3	E26-16	E25-7	E25-16	E25-15	E25-8
P	– P –	P	About B+V	About 0V				
R	– R –	R	About 0V	About B+V	About 0V			
N	– N –	N	About 0V		About B+V	About 0V		
D	– D –	D	About 0V			About B+V	About 0V	
2	– 2 –	2	About 0V				About B+V	About 0V
L	– L –	L	About 0V					About B+V

- **YES** →
- **NO** → Check transmission range switch for installation position and operation

4 Check Engine Idle speed. Is it in good condition?

- **YES** →
- **NO** → Correct engine idle speed.

5 Perform manual road test, engine brake test and "P" range test. Are check results satisfactory?

- **NO** →
  - "P" range malfunction. Check parking lock pawl and spring.
  - Engine brake malfunction. Go to "Symptom Table-3".
  - Manual shift malfunction. Perform time lag test, stall test and line pressure test referring to each applicable section. Are all check results satisfactory?
    - **YES** → Go to Symptom Table-2 and then-3.
    - **NO** → Repair or replace malfunction parts.
- **YES** → Go to "Symptom Table-1, -2 and -3 in that order."

SK5019500024020X

Fig. 4   Basic check (Part 2 of 2)

and then verify select lever is in Neutral position, **Fig. 8.**

3. Turn nut "A" until contact with manual select cable joint is made then tighten nut "B," **Fig. 8.** Ensure cable nut and joint have sufficient clearance.
4. Verify select cable operation after adjustment is made.

TRANSMISSION RANGE SWITCH

1. Disconnect transmission range switch.
2. Using an ohmmeter, ensure continuity exists as shown in **Fig. 9.**
3. If continuity check fails, proceed with steps 4–8.
4. Place manual lever to Neutral position.
5. Using a suitable ohmmeter, check for continuity between pins 7 and 9 of range switch connector, **Fig. 10.**
6. Rotate range switch until ohmmeter indicates continuity, then **torque** bolts to 14 ft. lbs.
7. Connect transmission range switch.
8. Ensure engine starts only in Neutral and Park positions and ensure backup lamps are on when in Reverse.

TRANSAXLE

REPLACE

1. Relieve fuel system pressure as outlined under " Precautions."

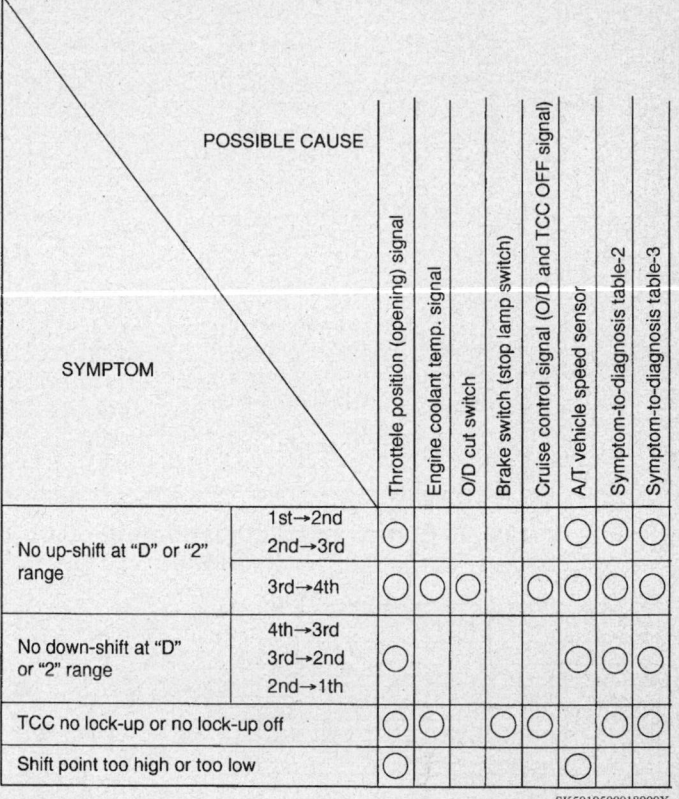

Fig. 5   Symptom troubleshooting chart (Electrical Circuit)

SYMPTOM		Throttle position (opening) signal	Engine coolant temp. signal	O/D cut switch	Brake switch (stop lamp switch)	Cruise control signal (O/D and TCC OFF signal)	A/T vehicle speed sensor	Symptom-to-diagnosis table-2	Symptom-to-diagnosis table-3
No up-shift at "D" or "2" range	1st→2nd	○					○	○	○
	2nd→3rd								
	3rd→4th	○	○	○			○	○	○
No down-shift at "D" or "2" range	4th→3rd						○	○	○
	3rd→2nd								
	2nd→1th								
TCC no lock-up or no lock-up off		○	○		○	○			
Shift point too high or too low		○						○	

SK5019500018000X

Fig. 6   Symptom troubleshooting chart (Valve Mechanism)

	Condition	Possible cause	Correction
	Vehicle does not move at any range.	• Manual valve faulty • Primary regulator valve faulty	Clean or replace. Clean or replace.
No gear change	1st↔2nd	• 1–2 shift valve faulty	Clean or replace.
	2nd↔3rd	• 2–3 shift valve faulty	Clean or replace.
	3rd↔4th	• 3–4 shift valve faulty	Clean or replace.
Harsh engagement	P, N↔R	• Reverse clutch accumulator faulty	Clean or replace.
	N→D	• Forward clutch accumulator faulty • 2nd and 4th brake accumulator faulty • 2nd and 4th brake modulator valve faulty • 2nd and 4th brake modulator control valve faulty	Clean or replace. Clean or replace. Clean or replace.
	1st→2nd at D or 2 range	• 2nd and 4th brake accumulator faulty • 2nd and 4th brake modulator valve faulty • 2nd and 4th brake modulator control valve faulty	Clean or replace.
	2nd→3rd at D range	• Overdrive clutch accumulator faulty • 2–3 timing valve faulty	Clean or replace. Clean or replace.
	3rd→4th at D range	• 2nd and 4th brake accumulator faulty • 2nd and 4th brake modulator valve faulty • 2nd and 4th brake modulator control valve faulty	Clean or replace.
	All gear changes	• Throttle pressure control valve faulty • Primary regulator valve faulty • Accumulator control valve faulty	Clean or replace. Clean or replace. Clean or replace.
	TCC no lock-up	• TCC modulator valve faulty • TCC control valve faulty • TCC control solenoid faulty • Secondary regulator valve faulty	Clean or replace. Clean or replace. Clean or replace. Clean or replace.
	TCC no lock-up off	• TCC control solenoid faulty • TCC control valve faulty	Clean or replace. Clean or replace..
	Excessive slip (low line pressure)	• Throttle pressure control solenoid circuit or valve faulty • Primary regulator valve faulty	Check solenoid duty. If OK, clean or replace. Clean or replace.

SK5019500019000X

	Condition	Possible Cause	Correction
Vehicle does not move at	1st, 2nd, 3rd and 4th gears	• Forward clutch faulty	Repair or replace.
	Reverse gear	• Reverse clutch faulty	Repair or replace.
	3rd and 4th gears	• Overdrive clutch faulty	Repair or replace.
	2nd and 4th gears	• 2nd/4th brake faulty	Repair or replace.
	Reverse gear	• 1st/Reverse brake faulty	Repair or replace.
	1st (D or 2) gear	• One-way clutch No.1 faulty	Repair or replace.
	any forward and reverse gear	• Parking lock pawl faulty	Repair or replace.
	TCC no lock-up or no lock-up off, shock when lock-up or engine stalls when starting off and stopping	• Torque converter clutch	Inspect and replace as necessary.
No up-shift	1st→2nd	• 2nd/4th brake faulty	Repair or replace.
	2nd→3rd	• Overdrive clutch faulty	Repair or replace.
	3rd→4th	• 2nd/4th brake faulty	Repair or replace.
No engine braking	2nd or 3rd gear	• Coast clutch faulty • 2nd/4th brake faulty	Repair or replace.
	1 st gear in L range	• 1st/Reverse brake faulty	Repair or replace.

SK5019500020000X

Fig. 7 Symptom troubleshooting chart (Clutch & Brake)

Terminal No. Switch position	1	2	3	4	5	6	7	8	9
P					○—○		○—○		
R			○—○						
N				○—○			○—○		
D		○—○							○
2		○—○							○
L	○—○								○

SK5029500228000X

Fig. 9 Transmission range switch continuity check

2. Disconnect transaxle ground cable.
3. Disconnect electrical connectors from transaxle.
4. Remove gear select cable from transaxle.
5. Drain cooling system and remove water intake pipe.
6. Remove upper transaxle to engine bolts.
7. Remove starter motor and plate.
8. Remove exhaust manifold cover, then manifold to pipe No. 1 nuts.
9. Properly support engine and remove or disconnect any components necessary to remove transaxle.
10. Raise and support vehicle while still supporting engine.
11. Drain transaxle fluid.
12. Remove engine under covers.
13. Disconnect oil cooler hoses.
14. Remove mounting member, exhaust pipe and stiffener.
15. Remove transaxle housing lower plate.
16. While holding driveplate with suitable large screwdriver, remove driveplate bolts, **Fig. 11.**
17. Using two suitable large screwdrivers,

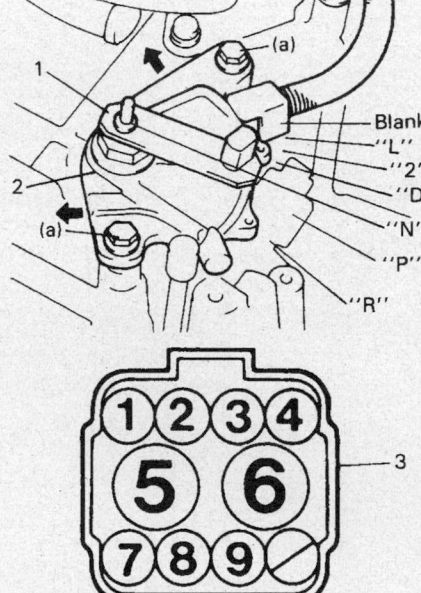

1. Manual shift lever
2. Transmission range switch
3. Transmission range switch coupler

SK5029500227000X

Fig. 10 Transmission range switch adjustment

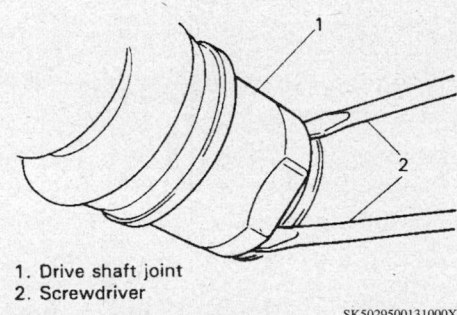

1. Drive shaft joint
2. Screwdriver

SK5029500131000X

Fig. 12 Snap ring fitting removal

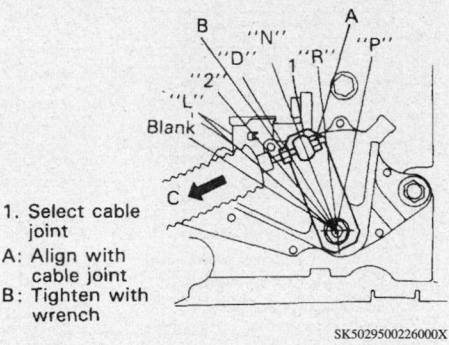

1. Select cable joint
A: Align with cable joint
B: Tighten with wrench

SK5029500226000X

Fig. 8 Select cable adjustment

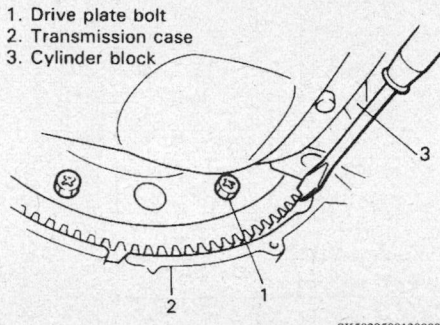

1. Drive plate bolt
2. Transmission case
3. Cylinder block

SK5029500130000X

Fig. 11 Driveplate bolt removal

pry against drive shaft joints at differential side to release snap ring fitting, **Fig. 12.**
18. Disconnect stabilizer joints from suspension arms on both sides
19. Remove ball stud bolts and nuts from knuckles and detach suspension arms, then pull out both drive shaft joints from differential.
20. Remove engine rear mounting and bracket.
21. Remove lower engine to transaxle bolt and nut. Ensure transmission is still suitably supported.
22. Remove bolts from lefthand engine mounting.
23. Remove transmission and torque converter from engine compartment.
24. Reverse procedure to install, noting the following:
    a. Ensure each drive shaft joint is fully seated and snap ring is in place.
    b. Adjust select cable.
    c. Tighten to specification.

TIGHTENING SPECIFICATIONS

Year	Component	Torque/ Ft. Lbs.
1996–99	Drain Plug	29
	Driveplate Bolts	14
	Engine Mounting Nuts	33
	Engine Mounting Member Bolts & Nuts	40
	Exhaust Manifold To Pipes	36
	Oil Cooler Hose Clamp	12①
	Oil Pump Bolts	9
	Shift Lever Switch Bolt	5
	Stabilizer Link Nuts	20
	Steering Knuckle Ball Stud	43
	Transmission Case Bolt	22
	Transmission Rear Cover Bolts	18
	Transmission To Engine Bolt/Nut	65

① — Inch lbs.

Front Wheel Drive Axles

INDEX

DRIVESHAFT

REPLACE

Sidekick & X-90

REMOVAL

1. Raise and support vehicle, then drain transaxle oil into appropriate container.
2. Remove locking hub, then the driveshaft circlip.
3. Remove stabilizer ball joint nut, then the tie rod castle nut.
4. Remove caliper bolt, then the caliper from disc.
5. Remove knuckle ball joint stud nut, then support lower arm with suitable jack.
6. Remove strut bracket bolts.
7. Remove knuckle and wheel hub assembly, by lowering jack.
8. On right driveshaft, detach snap ring fitted on spline of differential side joint from differential side gear, pull inboard joint using a tire lever, **Fig. 1.** Remove driveshaft from differential assembly.
9. On left driveshaft, disconnect driveshaft bolts, then remove driveshaft from differential assembly.

INSTALLATION

Reverse removal procedure to install.

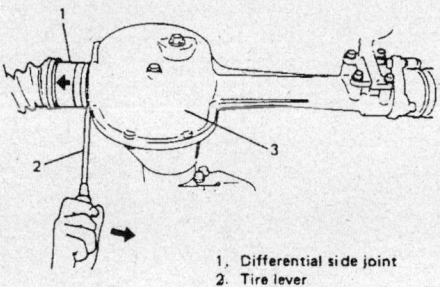

1. Differential side joint
2. Tire lever
3. Front differential assembly

SK3039100003000X

Fig. 1 Snap ring from differential side gear removal. Sidekick & X-90

Esteem & Swift

DOUBLE OFFSET JOINT (DOJ) TYPE

This type of front driveshaft is used for manual transaxle models.

REMOVAL

LH Shaft

1. Remove caulking and driveshaft nut and washer.
2. Drain transmission oil into appropriate container.
3. Using large size screwdrivers, pull out

driveshaft joint. This will release snap ring fitting of joint spline at differential side, **Fig. 2.**
4. Disconnect stabilizer joint from suspension arm.
5. Remove ball stud bolt and nut, then separate suspension arm from knuckle.
6. Remove driveshaft assembly.

RH Shaft

1. Remove caulking and driveshaft nut and washer.
2. Using plastic hammer, drive out driveshaft joint. This will release snap ring fitting of joint spline at center shaft, **Fig. 3.**
3. Disconnect stabilizer joint from suspension arm.
4. Remove ball stud bolt and nut, then separate suspension arm from knuckle.
5. Remove driveshaft assembly.
6. Drain transmission oil into appropriate container.
7. Loosen center bearing support bolts, then remove center shaft from differential side gear.

INSTALLATION

Reverse removal procedure to install LH and RH driveshafts, noting the following:
1. Install wheel side joint to steering

knuckle first and DOJ to differential side.

TRIPOD JOINT TYPE

This type of front driveshaft is used for automatic transmission models. Refer to "Double Offset Joint (DOJ) Type" for service procedures.

DRIVESHAFT SERVICE

Sidekick & X-90

DISASSEMBLE

Only the double off-set joints are serviceable, **Fig. 4. Do not disassemble wheel side joint or ball joint of differential side joint, Fig. 5. If any problem exists, replace these joints as an assembly.**
1. Remove boot band from differential side joint.
2. Remove circlip, then the housing of differential side joint.
3. Remove circlip (snap ring), then the ball joint, **Fig. 6.**
4. Remove inside and outside boots from shaft.

ASSEMBLE

1. Apply joint grease, supplied in repair kit, to wheel side joint.
2. Fit wheel side boot on shaft. Fill inside of boot with joint grease, then install boot bands.
3. Fit differential side boot on shaft. Apply joint grease, supplied in repair kit, to differential side joint.
4. Install differential side ball joint on shaft. Position flush side of joint to wheel side joint. Fit snap ring in groove of shaft.
5. Fill inside of differential side boot with joint grease, then install housing.
6. Attach boot to housing using boot band. When clamping boot band, bend its end in reverse direction against driveshaft rotating direction.

Esteem & Swift

DOUBLE OFFSET JOINT (DOJ) TYPE

DISASSEMBLE
Driveshaft

Do not disassemble wheel side joint. If any problem is found, replace as an assembly.
1. Remove boot band of differential side joint.
2. Slide boot toward center of shaft. Remove snap ring from outer race, then take shaft out of outer race, **Fig. 7.**
3. Using snap ring pliers, remove circlip (snap ring) used to attach bearing cage.
4. Remove bearing cage and boot from shaft.

Center Shaft & Bearing Support

1. Remove right side oil seal from center

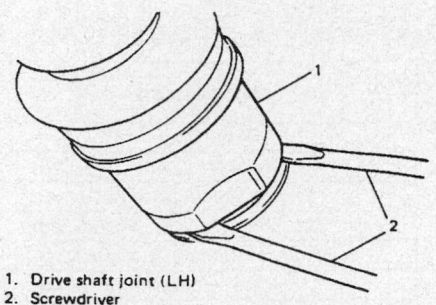
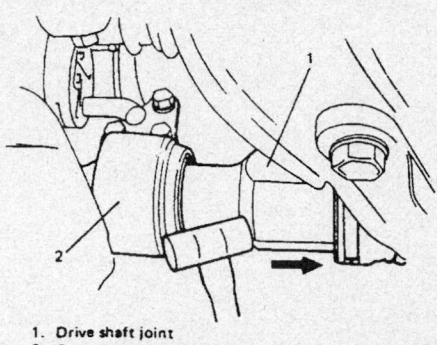

1. Drive shaft joint (LH)
2. Screwdriver

SK3039100008000X

Fig. 2 Snap ring from differential removal. Esteem & Swift

1. Drive shaft joint
2. Center bearing support

SK3039100009000X

Fig. 3 Driveshaft from center bearing support removal. Esteem & Swift

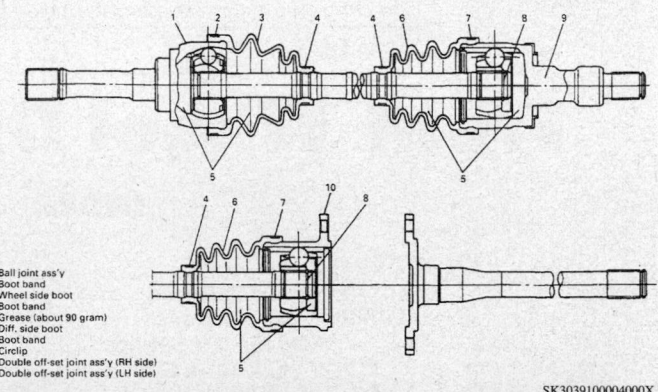

1. Ball joint ass'y
2. Boot band
3. Wheel side boot
4. Boot band
5. Grease (about 90 gram)
6. Diff. side boot
7. Boot band
8. Circlip
9. Double off-set joint ass'y (RH side)
10. Double off-set joint ass'y (LH side)

SK3039100004000X

Fig. 4 Cross-sectional view of driveshaft assembly. Sidekick & X-90

1. Drive shaft oil seal
2. Double off-set joint (DOJ)
3. Joint circlip
4. DOJ boot
5. Ball joint boot
6. Ball joint assembly (RH side)
7. Drive shaft assembly (LH side)
8. Left drive shaft
9. Drive shaft bearing circlip
10. Drive shaft bearing

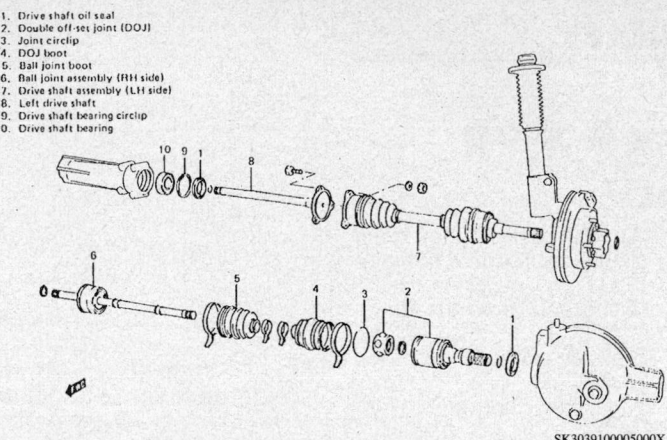

SK3039100005000X

Fig. 5 Exploded view of front axle assembly. Sidekick & X-90

bearing support, then circlip.
2. Using press, draw out center shaft from center bearing.
3. Remove left side oil seal from center bearing support.
4. Remove bearing support circlip.
5. Remove center bearing from center bearing support.

ASSEMBLE
Driveshaft

1. Install boot onto driveshaft until small diameter side fits into shaft groove. At-

tach boot band.
2. Install bearing cage. Smaller outside diameter should be installed to shaft end, **Fig. 8.**
3. Using snap ring pliers, install circlip (snap ring).
4. Apply grease, supplied in repair kit, to entire surface of bearing cage.
5. Insert bearing cage into outer race, then attach snap ring into groove of outer race. Ensure opening of snap ring is not in alignment with a ball (bearing).

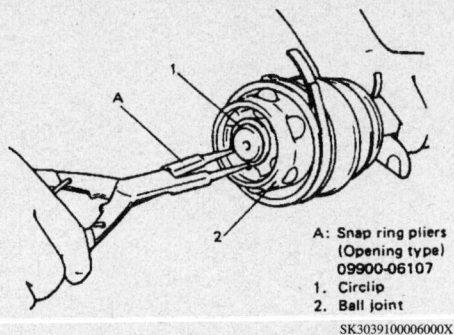

A: Snap ring pliers
(Opening type)
09900-06107
1. Circlip
2. Ball joint

SK3039100006000X

Fig. 6   Circlip from ball joint removal. Sidekick & X-90

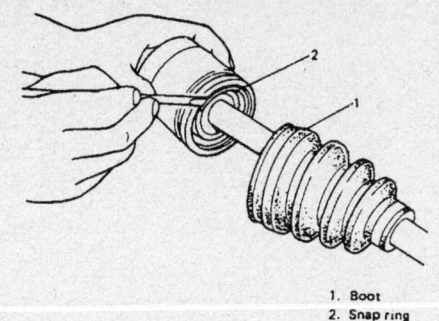

1. Boot
2. Snap ring

SK3039100010000X

Fig. 7   Snap ring from outer race removal. Esteem & Swift

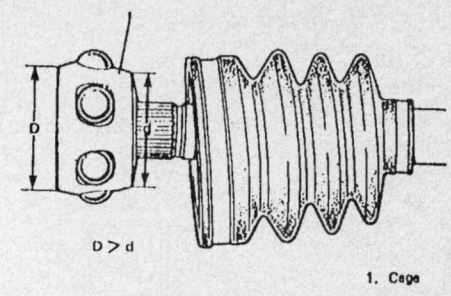

D > d

1. Cage

SK3039100011000X

Fig. 8   Bearing cage installation. Esteem & Swift w/double offset joint type driveshaft.

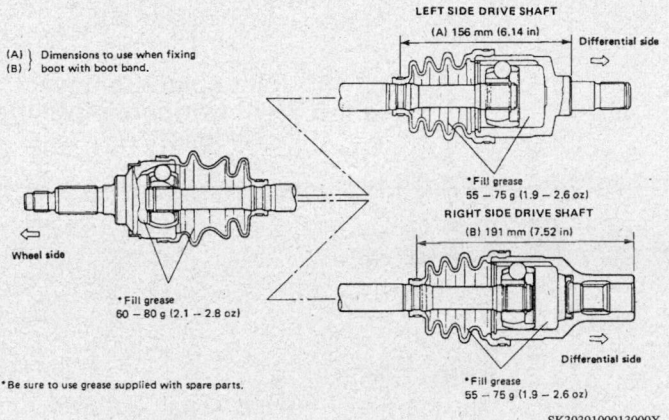

(A) | Dimensions to use when fixing
(B) | boot with boot band.

LEFT SIDE DRIVE SHAFT
(A) 156 mm (6.14 in)   Differential side

*Fill grease
55 – 75 g (1.9 – 2.6 oz)

RIGHT SIDE DRIVE SHAFT
(B) 191 mm (7.52 in)

Wheel side

*Fill grease
60 – 80 g (2.1 – 2.8 oz)

Differential side

*Fill grease
55 – 75 g (1.9 – 2.6 oz)

*Be sure to use grease supplied with spare parts.

SK3039100013000X

Fig. 9   Boot length measurement. Swift

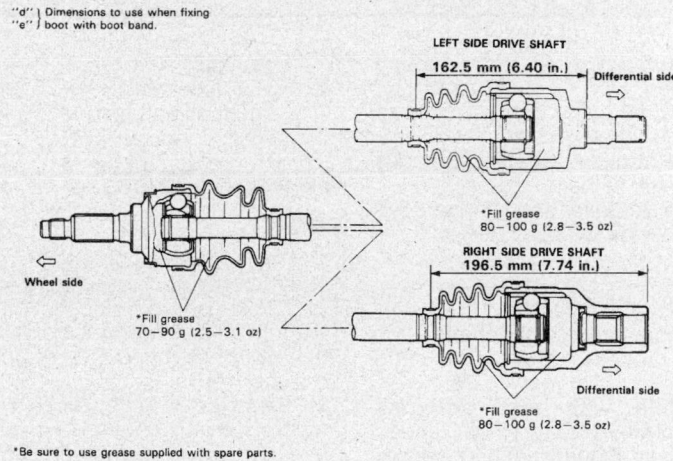

"d" | Dimensions to use when fixing
"e" | boot with boot band.

LEFT SIDE DRIVE SHAFT
162.5 mm (6.40 in.)   Differential side

*Fill grease
80 – 100 g (2.8 – 3.5 oz)

RIGHT SIDE DRIVE SHAFT
196.5 mm (7.74 in.)

Wheel side

*Fill grease
70 – 90 g (2.5 – 3.1 oz)

Differential side

*Fill grease
80 – 100 g (2.8 – 3.5 oz)

*Be sure to use grease supplied with spare parts.

SK3039500045000X

Fig. 10   Boot length measurement. Esteem

6. Apply grease to inside of outer race, then install boot to outer race. Insert screwdriver into boot on outer race side, allowing air to enter boot.
7. When attaching boot to outer race with boot band, ensure measurements are as shown, **Figs. 9 and 10.**

Center Shaft & Bearing Support

Assemble in reverse order of disassemble, noting the following:

1. Ensure circlip securely fits in groove in center bearing support.
2. Ensure left side oil seal is in proper direction, **Fig. 11.**
3. After press-fitting center shaft from left side oil side, ensure circlip securely fits in groove in shaft.
4. Ensure right side oil seal is in proper direction, **Fig. 12.**

TRIPOD JOINT TYPE

DISASSEMBLE

1. Remove tripod joint boot band, then

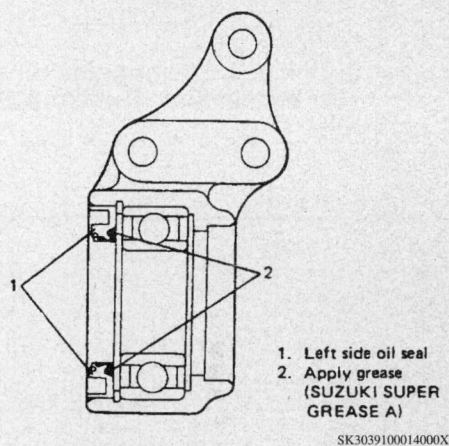

1. Left side oil seal
2. Apply grease
(SUZUKI SUPER GREASE A)

SK3039100014000X

Fig. 11   Left side oil seal installation. Esteem & Swift

the tripod joint housing.
2. Using snap ring pliers, remove circlip (snap ring), then pull out spider from shaft, **Fig. 13.**
3. Remove boot band, then pull out differential side boot from shaft.
4. Remove band of dynamic damper, then pull out damper through shaft.
5. Remove boot band of wheel side joint boot, then pull out boot through shaft.

ASSEMBLE

1. Apply black grease supplied in repair kit to wheel side joint.
2. Install wheel side boot on shaft, fill boot with grease and fasten boot with bands.
3. Install dynamic damper on shaft, then the differential side boot on shaft.
4. Apply yellow grease supplied in repair kit to tripod joint.
5. Install tripod joint spider on shaft, positioning chamfered spline inward (wheel side), then fasten with circlip (snap ring).
6. Fill differential side boot with grease, then install housing.
7. Attach boot band. Bend each boot band against forward rotation of driveshaft.

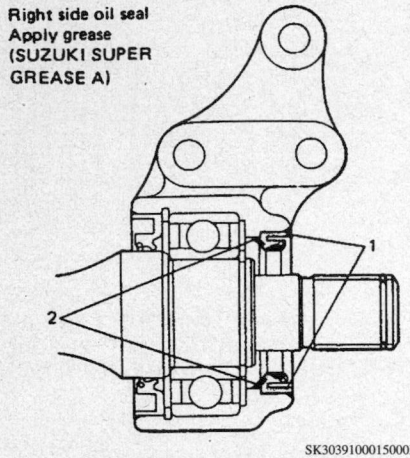

1. Right side oil seal
2. Apply grease (SUZUKI SUPER GREASE A)

SK3039100015000X

Fig. 12 Right side oil seal installation. Esteem & Swift

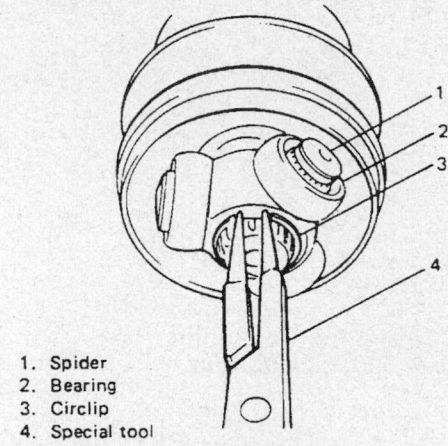

1. Spider
2. Bearing
3. Circlip
4. Special tool
Snap ring pliers 09900-06107)

SK3039100016000X

Fig. 13 Joint spider removal. Esteem & Swift w/tripod joint type driveshaft

Drive Axles

INDEX

DESCRIPTION

On Grand Vitara, Sidekick and X-90 models, the differential assemblies installed to the front and rear axles use a hypoid bevel pinion and gear. The rear differential is set in an axle housing while the front differential is set in an aluminum housing mounted under the chassis frame. The reduction ratio for manual transmission equipped vehicles is different from automatic transmission equipped vehicles, **Figs. 1 and 2.**

DIFFERENTIAL

REPLACE

SIDEKICK & X-90

FRONT

1. Raise and support vehicle, then drain oil.
2. Disconnect breather hose.
3. Disconnect and support propeller shaft.
4. Remove left mounting bracket bolts and driveshaft flange bolts, **Fig. 3.**
5. Support differential and remove bolts from crossmember and right end of housing.
6. Disconnect RH side driveshaft joint and remove housing assembly using suitable pry bars.

7. Reverse procedure to install, noting the following:
   a. **Torque** mounting bracket bolts to 37 ft. lbs.
   b. **Torque** front driveshaft flange bolts to 36.5–43 ft. lbs.
   c. **Torque** propeller shaft flange bolts to 36.5–43 ft. lbs.

REAR

1. Raise and support vehicle.
2. Remove right and left axle shafts.
3. Remove propeller shaft bolts and shaft.
4. **On models with rear anti-lock brakes,** remove rear wheel speed sensor cover, then disconnect sensor electrical connector.
5. **On all models,** support axle assembly and remove upper arm mounting bolts and lower axle. **Rear shock absorbers must remain installed during this process. Without them, axle may fall and cause personal injury.**
6. Remove differential fastening nuts and the differential.
7. Reverse procedure to install, noting the following:
   a. Clean all mating surfaces and apply Suzuki bond sealant, No. 1215.
   b. **Torque** rear differential carrier nuts to 36.5–43 ft. lbs.
   c. **Torque** upper arm bolts to 29–43 ft. lbs.
   d. **Torque** propeller shaft flange bolts

to 36.5–43 ft. lbs.
   e. Fill axle with SAE 75W-90 hypoid gear oil and **torque** fill plug to 32 ft. lbs.

GRAND VITARA

FRONT

1. Raise and support vehicle, then drain differential oil into suitable container.
2. Disconnect air and breather hoses from differential housing.
3. Reference mark, then remove propeller shaft.
4. Remove 3 bolts for left mounting bracket and 3 bolts for driveshaft.
5. Remove 2 bolts from crossmember.
6. Support differential using suitable jack, then remove mounting bolts on right end of housing.
7. Using 2 large screwdrivers as levers, pull out side driveshaft from differential.
8. Remove differential housing from vehicle.

REAR

1. Raise and support vehicle, then drain differential oil into suitable container.
2. Remove rear brake drums and axle shafts.
3. Reference mark and remove propeller shaft.
4. Remove 8 nuts securing differential to housing.

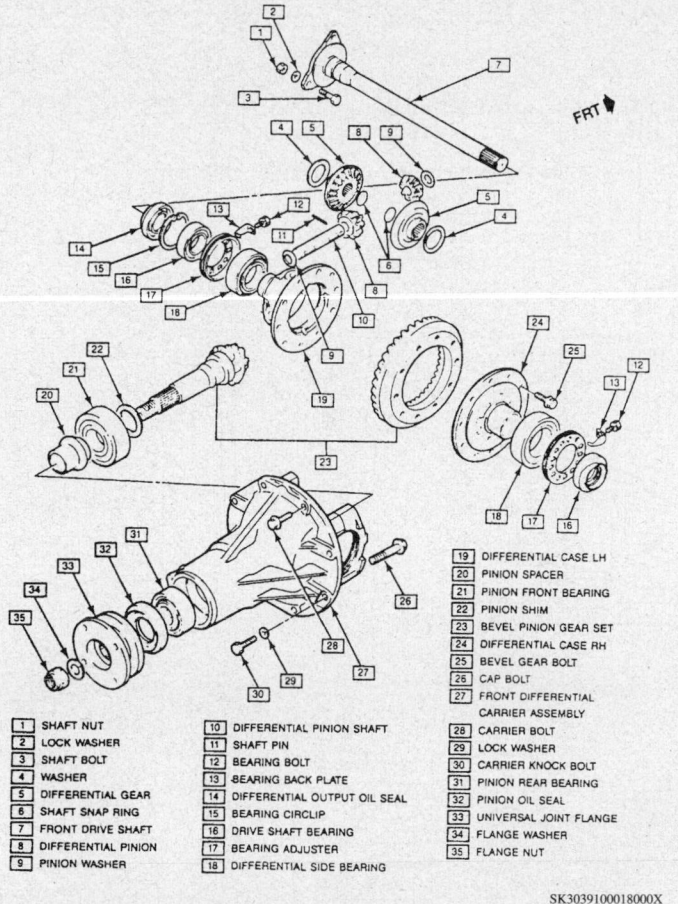

Fig. 1 Exploded view of front differential. Sidekick & X-90

1	SHAFT NUT
2	LOCK WASHER
3	SHAFT BOLT
4	WASHER
5	DIFFERENTIAL GEAR
6	SHAFT SNAP RING
7	FRONT DRIVE SHAFT
8	DIFFERENTIAL PINION
9	PINION WASHER
10	DIFFERENTIAL PINION SHAFT
11	SHAFT PIN
12	BEARING BOLT
13	BEARING BACK PLATE
14	DIFFERENTIAL OUTPUT OIL SEAL
15	BEARING CIRCLIP
16	DRIVE SHAFT BEARING
17	BEARING ADJUSTER
18	DIFFERENTIAL SIDE BEARING
19	DIFFERENTIAL CASE LH
20	PINION SPACER
21	PINION FRONT BEARING
22	PINION SHIM
23	BEVEL PINION GEAR SET
24	DIFFERENTIAL CASE RH
25	BEVEL GEAR BOLT
26	CAP BOLT
27	FRONT DIFFERENTIAL CARRIER ASSEMBLY
28	CARRIER BOLT
29	LOCK WASHER
30	CARRIER KNOCK BOLT
31	PINION REAR BEARING
32	PINION OIL SEAL
33	UNIVERSAL JOINT FLANGE
34	FLANGE WASHER
35	FLANGE NUT

SK3039100018000X

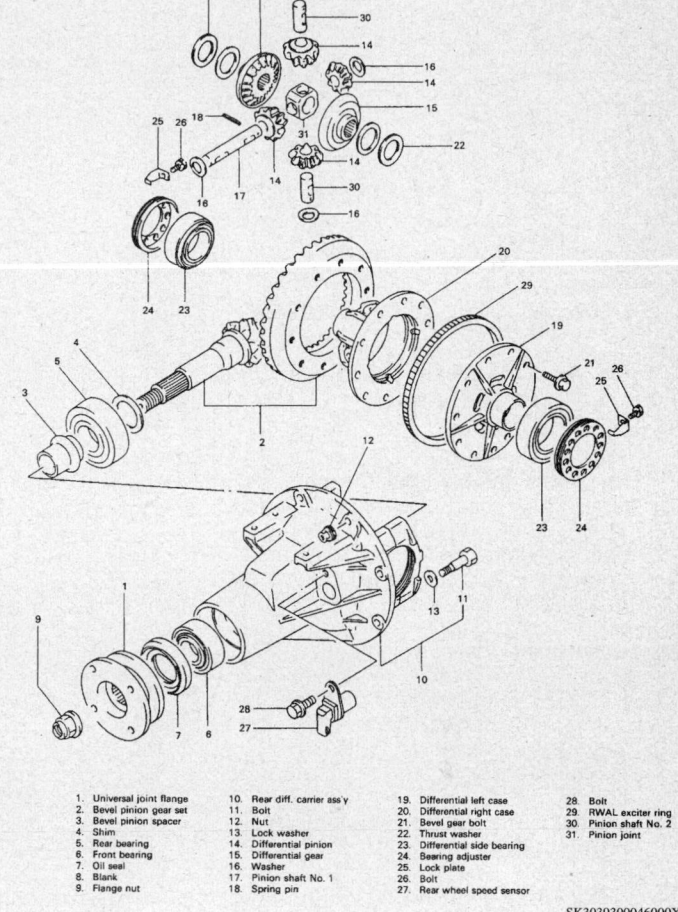

1.	Universal joint flange	10.	Rear diff. carrier ass'y
2.	Bevel pinion gear set	11.	Bolt
3.	Bevel pinion spacer	12.	Nut
4.	Shim	13.	Lock washer
5.	Rear bearing	14.	Differential pinion
6.	Front bearing	15.	Differential gear
7.	Oil seal	16.	Washer
8.	Blank	17.	Pinion shaft No. 1
9.	Flange nut	18.	Spring pin

19.	Differential left case	28.	Bolt
20.	Differential right case	29.	RWAL exciter ring
21.	Bevel gear bolt	30.	Pinion shaft No. 2
22.	Thrust washer	31.	Pinion joint
23.	Differential side bearing		
24.	Bearing adjuster		
25.	Lock plate		
26.	Bolt		
27.	Rear wheel speed sensor		

SK3039300046000X

Fig. 2 Exploded view of rear differential. Sidekick & X-90

5. Remove differential from vehicle.
6. Reverse procedure to install. **Torque** differential nuts to 40 ft. lbs.

DIFFERENTIAL SERVICE
GRAND VITARA
FRONT
Disassemble

1. Remove drive shaft using plastic hammer.
2. Remove 8 bolts securing carrier to housing.
3. Remove carrier.
4. Set special tool No. 09944–76010, or equivalent into suitable vise and place carrier on special tool.
5. Reference mark differential side bearing caps.
6. Remove inner hose and actuator bracket bolt.
7. Remove differential side bearing caps and bolts.
8. Remove bearing adjusters, outer races and drive bevel gear with differential case.
9. Rotate assembly with special tool 90°, then secure in vise.
10. Remove air inlet union.
11. Hold universal joint flange using special tool No. 09922–66020, or equivalent, then remove flange nut.

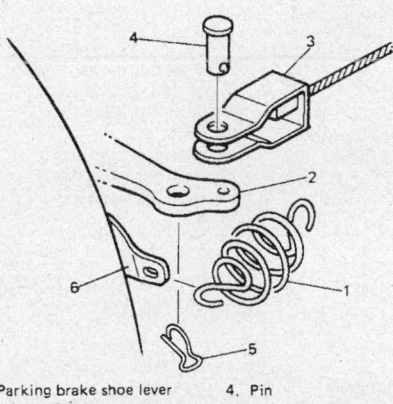

1.	Parking brake shoe lever return spring
2.	Parking brake shoe lever
3.	Parking brake cable joint
4.	Pin
5.	Clip
6.	Brake back plate

SK3039100021000X

Fig. 3 Mounting bracket removal. Sidekick & X-90

12. Reference mark drive bevel pinion and companion flange.
13. Using puller No. 09913–65135, or equivalent, remove companion flange from pinion.
14. Using puller No. 09913–85230, or equivalent, remove differential side bearings.
15. Secure carrier into suitable vise using differential left side. Remove axle hub, side gears and shims from differential left case.
16. Using bearing puller and hydraulic press, remove bevel pinion front bearing.
17. Using suitable brass drift, remove bevel pinion bearing outer races.

Assemble

1. Install differential gears, free axle hub and washers to left case, then attach left case to right case.
2. Install bevel gear on differential case and **torque** bolts to 62 ft. lbs. Use thread lock sealant.
3. Install side bearing using installer No. 09944–66020, or equivalent and hydraulic press.
4. Install actuator to differential case as shown, **Fig. 4**.
5. Install side bearing using installer No. 09944–66020, or equivalent and hydraulic press onto other side of differential case.
6. Install bevel pinion dummy No.09926–78311, or equivalent with bearings.
7. Tighten flange nut until a bearing preload of 8–15 inch lbs. is recorded.
8. Set dial indicator to mounting dummy and zero indicator to surface plate.
9. Place mounting dummy and indicator

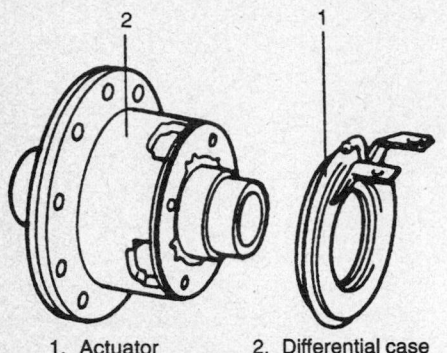

1. Actuator 2. Differential case

SK3019900001000X

Fig. 4 Actuator installation. Grand Vitara

on pinion dummy and measure between 0 position and extended dial gauge measuring tip.

10. Obtain shim thickness by adding measurement E to measurement C, minus measurement printed on pinion, **Fig. 5.**

11. Select shim closest to on needed , **Fig. 6.**

12. With new pinion spacer inserted, install rear bearing to differential.

13. Using seal installer No. 09951–18210, or equivalent and plastic hammer, install oil seal.

14. Tighten flange nut gradually until bearing preload of 8–15 inch lbs. is obtained.

15. Install air inlet union with thread sealant.

16. Place bearing outer races on bearings, then install case assembly in carrier.

17. Install side bearing adjusters.

18. Insert 2 side bearing cap bolts 2 or 3 threads, then press down bearing cap by hand.

19. Install actuator bracket to bearing cap.

20. Tighten both bearing adjusters at same time to obtain backlash of .005–.007 inch.

21. Measure pinion preload with spring balance or torque wrench. When preload of bevel pinion is 5.73 lbs., composite preload of both pinion bearings and side bearings should be between 6.17 and 7.05 lbs., **Fig. 7.**

22. Check gear tooth contact as follows:
    a. Clean tooth surface of 10 bevel gears.
    b. Paint with gear marking compound evenly.
    c. Turn gear to bring painted part in mesh with bevel pinion, then rotate back and forth several times.
    d. Bring painted part up and check contact pattern, **Fig. 8.**

23. Stake flange nut using suitable punch and hammer.

24. Apply sealant to housing side evenly.

25. Position and install carrier bolts as shown, **Fig. 9.**

26. **Torque** bolts to 17 ft. lbs.

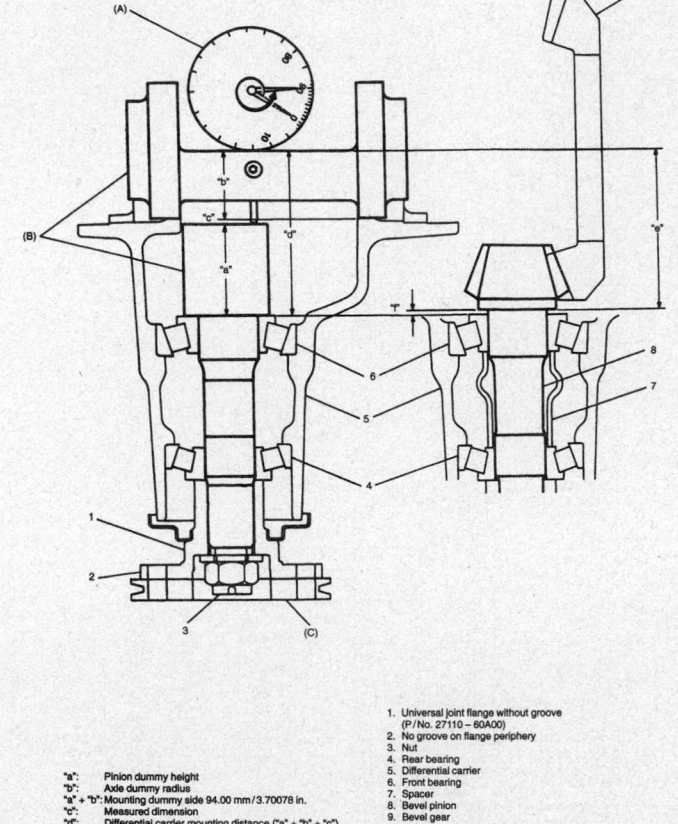

"a":	Pinion dummy height
"b":	Axle dummy radius
"a" + "b":	Mounting dummy side 94.00 mm / 3.70078 in.
"c":	Measured dimension
"d":	Differential carrier mounting distance ("a" + "b" + "c")
"e":	Bevel pinion mounting distance (Marked in shaft in mm)
"f":	Shim size for mounting distance adjustment ("d" – "e")

1. Universal joint flange without groove (P/No. 27110 – 60A00)
2. No groove on flange periphery
3. Nut
4. Rear bearing
5. Differential carrier
6. Front bearing
7. Spacer
8. Bevel pinion
9. Bevel gear

Special Tool
(A): 09900-20606
(B): 09926-78311
(C): 09922-75222

SK3019900002000X

Fig. 5 Front pinion shim measurement. Grand Vitara

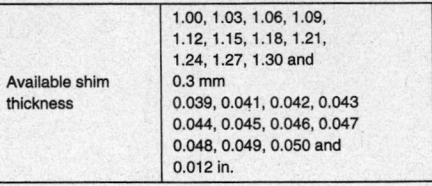

| Available shim thickness | 1.00, 1.03, 1.06, 1.09, 1.12, 1.15, 1.18, 1.21, 1.24, 1.27, 1.30 and 0.3 mm |
| | 0.039, 0.041, 0.042, 0.043 0.044, 0.045, 0.046, 0.047 0.048, 0.049, 0.050 and 0.012 in. |

SK3019900003000X

Fig. 6 Front shim selection chart. Grand Vitara

REAR

Disassemble

1. Secure differential assembly, then reference mark side bearing caps.
2. Remove differential side bearing lock plates and bearing caps.
3. Remove bearing adjusters, outer races and bevel gear with case.
4. Remove drive bevel gear, pinion gear and shaft.
5. Using special tool Nos. 09913–85230 and 09913–61510, or equivalent, remove side bearings.
6. Hold universal joint flange using special tool No. 09922–66020, or equivalent, then remove flange nut.
7. Reference mark drive bevel pinion and companion flange.
8. Using puller No. 09913–65135, or equivalent, remove companion flange from pinion.
9. Remove bevel pinion with rear bearing, shim and spacer from carrier.
10. Using bearing puller and hydraulic press, remove bevel pinion rear bearing.
11. Using hammer and suitable brass drift, remove front, then rear bearing outer race and oil seal.

Assemble

1. Using special tool Nos. 09924–74510, 09926–68310 and 09913–75510, or equivalent and hydraulic press, install pinion bearing outer races.
2. **On models equipped with automatic transmission**, proceed as follows:

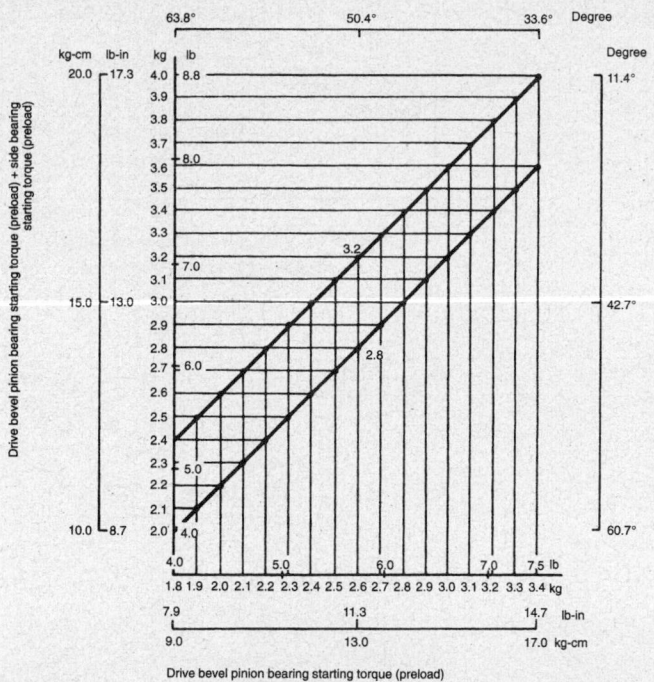

Fig. 7 Preload reference chart. Grand Vitara

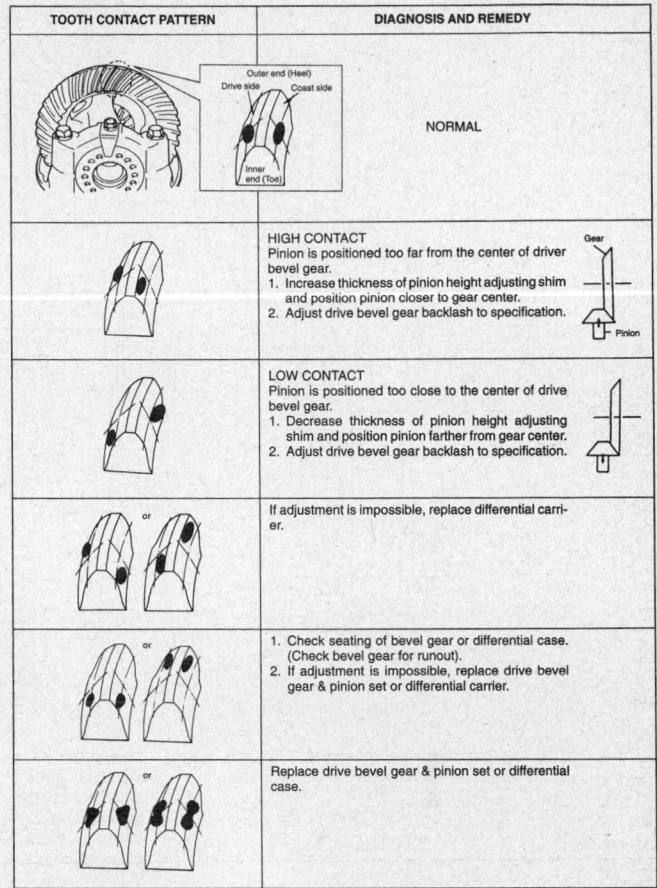

TOOTH CONTACT PATTERN	DIAGNOSIS AND REMEDY
Outer end (Heel), Drive side, Coast side, Inner end (Toe)	NORMAL
	HIGH CONTACT Pinion is positioned too far from the center of driver bevel gear. 1. Increase thickness of pinion height adjusting shim and position pinion closer to gear center. 2. Adjust drive bevel gear backlash to specification.
	LOW CONTACT Pinion is positioned too close to the center of drive bevel gear. 1. Decrease thickness of pinion height adjusting shim and position pinion farther from gear center. 2. Adjust drive bevel gear backlash to specification.
or	If adjustment is impossible, replace differential carrier.
or	1. Check seating of bevel gear or differential case. (Check bevel gear for runout). 2. If adjustment is impossible, replace drive bevel gear & pinion set or differential carrier.
or	Replace drive bevel gear & pinion set or differential case.

Fig. 8 Gear tooth contact pattern. Grand Vitara

a. Apply oil to and install side gear, pinions, pinion shaft, thrust washer and spring washer into right case.
b. Check pinion gear for smooth rotation.
c. Align pinion shaft hole position with differential case, then drive 3 spring pins flush with end surface of case.
d. Place bevel gear on differential case and **torque** bolts to 62 ft. lbs.
e. Install special tool No. 09928–06010–002, or equivalent, and check preload.
f. Side gear preload should be 1.8 ft. lbs.

3. **On models equipped with manual transmission,** proceed as follows:
   a. Apply oil to and install side gear, pinions, pinion shaft, thrust washer and spring washer into right case.
   b. Check pinion gear for smooth rotation.
   c. Install differential right case and **torque** bolts to 30 ft. lbs.
   d. Place bevel gear on differential case and **torque** bolts to 62 ft. lbs.
   e. Install special tool No. 09928–06010–002 or equivalent, and check preload.
   f. Side gear preload should be 1.8 ft. lbs.
4. **On all models,** install side bearing using installer No. 09944–66020, or equivalent and hydraulic press.
5. Install side bearing using installer No. 09944–66020, or equivalent and hydraulic press onto other side of differential case.
6. Set dial indicator to mounting dummy and zero indicator to surface plate.
7. Place mounting dummy and indicator

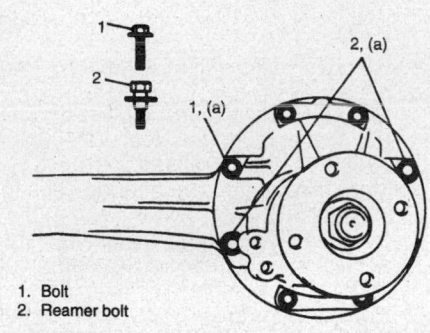

1. Bolt
2. Reamer bolt

Fig. 9 Carrier bolt installation. Grand Vitara

on pinion dummy and measure between 0 position and extended dial gauge measuring tip.
8. Obtain shim thickness by adding measurement F to measurement C, minus measurement printed on pinion, **Fig. 10.**
9. Select shim closest to on needed , **Fig. 11.**
10. With new pinion spacer inserted, install rear bearing to differential.
11. Using seal installer No. 09951–18210, or equivalent and plastic hammer, install oil seal.

12. Tighten flange nut gradually until bearing preload of 8–15 inch lbs. is obtained.
13. Place bearing outer races on bearings, then install case assembly in carrier.
14. Install side bearing adjusters.
15. Insert 2 side bearing cap bolts 2 or 3 threads, then press down bearing cap by hand.
16. Install actuator bracket to bearing cap.
17. Tighten both bearing adjusters at same time to obtain backlash of .005–.007 inch.
18. Measure pinion preload with spring balance or torque wrench. When preload of bevel pinion is 5.73 lbs., composite preload of both pinion bearings and side bearings should be between 6.17 and 7.05 lbs., **Fig. 7.**
19. Check gear tooth contact as follows:
    a. Clean tooth surface of 10 bevel gears.
    b. Paint with gear marking compound evenly.
    c. Turn gear to bring painted part in mesh with bevel pinion, then rotate back and forth several times.
    d. Bring painted part up and check contact pattern,**Fig. 8.**
20. Stake flange nut using suitable punch and hammer.
21. Apply sealant to housing side evenly.

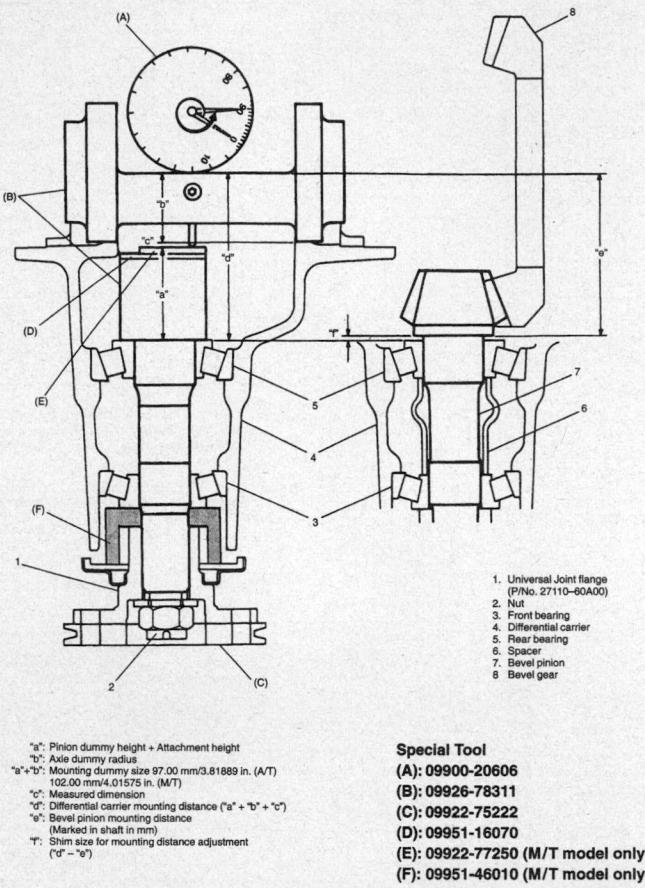

"a": Pinion dummy height + Attachment height
"b": Axle dummy radius
"a"+"b": Mounting dummy size 97.00 mm/3.81889 in. (A/T)
102.00 mm/4.01575 in. (M/T)
"c": Measured dimension
"d": Differential carrier mounting distance ("a" + "b" + "c")
"e": Bevel pinion mounting distance
(Marked in shaft in mm)
"f": Shim size for mounting distance adjustment
("d" – "e")

1. Universal Joint flange
(P/No. 27110–60A00)
2. Nut
3. Front bearing
4. Differential carrier
5. Rear bearing
6. Spacer
7. Bevel pinion
8. Bevel gear

Special Tool
(A): 09900-20606
(B): 09926-78311
(C): 09922-75222
(D): 09951-16070
(E): 09922-77250 (M/T model only)
(F): 09951-46010 (M/T model only)

SK3019900007000X

Fig. 10   Rear pinion shim measurement. Grand Vitara

Available shim thickness	1.00, 1.03, 1.06, 1.09, 1.12, 1.15, 1.18, 1.21, 1.24, 1.27, 1.30 and 0.3 mm 0.039, 0.041, 0.042, 0.043 0.044, 0.045, 0.046, 0.047 0.048, 0.049, 0.050 and 0.012 in.

SK3019900008000X

Fig. 11   Rear shim selection chart. Grand Vitara

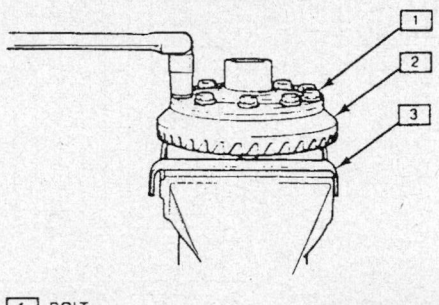

1 BOLT
2 DRIVE BEVEL GEAR
3 ALUMINUM PLATE

SK3039100035000X

Fig. 13   Bevel gear removal. Sidekick & X-90

and pinion must be replaced as a set.

Assemble

1. Assemble bevel pinion bearing outer races using bearing installer tool Nos. J8092, J37759 and J37758 or equivalents.
2. Assemble differential side gear and side pinion with pinion shaft.
3. Mount dial indicator to top surface of side gear. Move lower end of side gear up and down, noting movement of indicator, **Fig. 14.**
4. Install a .043 inch thrust washer and ensure a .005–.014 inch side gear thrust play is obtained.
5. Drive spring pin in until it is flush with the differential case surface.
6. Install bevel gear to differential case and **torque** bolts to 70 ft. lbs.
7. Mount dial indicator tool to back of side gear, **Fig. 15.**
8. Install a .043 inch thrust washer and side thrust gear installation tool No. J35138 or equivalent, onto differential side gear.
9. Move tool up and down in a straight forward manner and ensure a side gear thrust play of .005–.014 inch is obtained.
10. Install side bearings using bearing installation tool No. J8092 and J24433 or equivalents. **Be sure to use side bearing removal tool No. J8107-4 or equivalent, to protect the lower bearing.**
11. Install depth gauge setting tool No. J21777 or equivalent, while holding bearing in position, **Fig. 16.** Use low

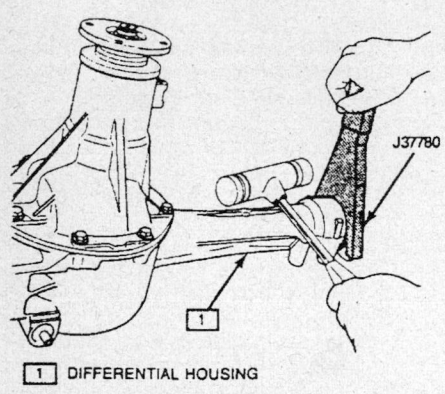

1 DIFFERENTIAL HOUSING

J37780

SK3039100034000X

Fig. 12   Axle shaft removal. Sidekick & X-90

22. position and install carrier bolts.
23. **Torque** bolts to 40 ft. lbs.

SIDEKICK & X-90

FRONT

Disassemble

1. Remove front RH driveshaft using suitable plastic hammer and axle removal tool No. J37780 or equivalent, **Fig. 12.**

2. Remove differential assembly from housing.
3. Mount differential assembly, using differential holding tool Nos. J37769 and J3289-01 or equivalents.
4. Mark differential side bearing caps for installation.
5. Remove side bearing lock plate, caps, adjusters, outer races and bevel pinion and gear assembly.
6. Rotate differential assembly using flange holding tool No. J8614-01 or equivalent.
7. Remove universal joint flange nut, bevel pinion, flange and oil seal using seal removal tool Nos. J8614-01 and J26941 or equivalents.
8. Remove differential side bearing using bearing removal tool Nos. J22888 and J8107-4 or equivalents.
9. Remove bevel gear attaching bolts, then the gear, **Fig. 13. When mounting differential in a vise, use aluminum plates to avoid damage.**
10. Drive out spring pin. Disassemble differential side gears, pinions, washers and shaft in differential case.
11. Press out bevel pinion gear using side bearing remover tool No. J22912-01 or equivalent.
12. Drive out bevel pinion bearing outer race using suitable tools. **Bevel gear**

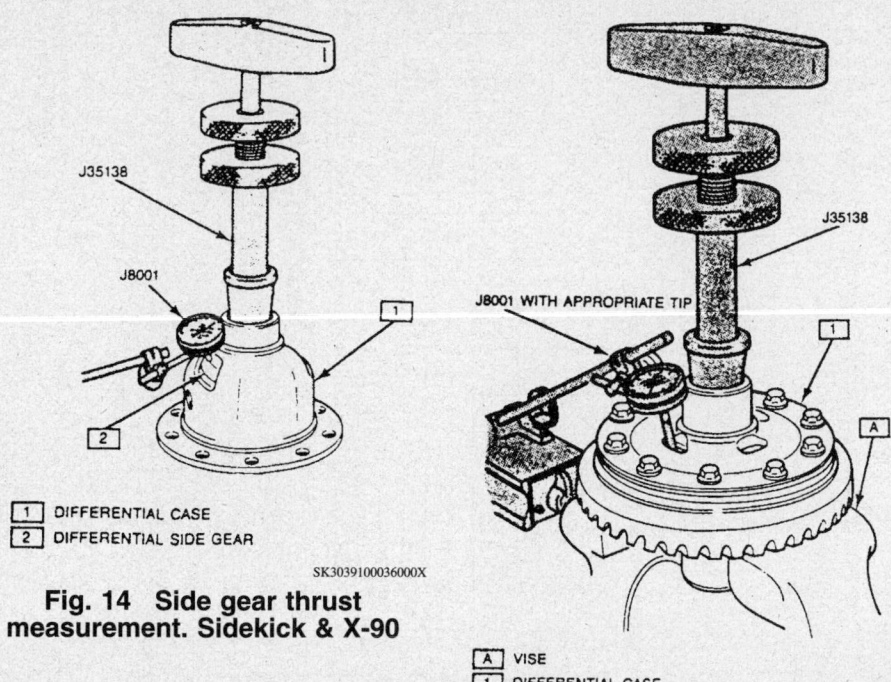

Fig. 14 Side gear thrust measurement. Sidekick & X-90

1 DIFFERENTIAL CASE
2 DIFFERENTIAL SIDE GEAR

SK3039100036000X

A VISE
1 DIFFERENTIAL CASE

SK3039100037000X

Fig. 15 Bearing preload adjustment. Sidekick & X-90

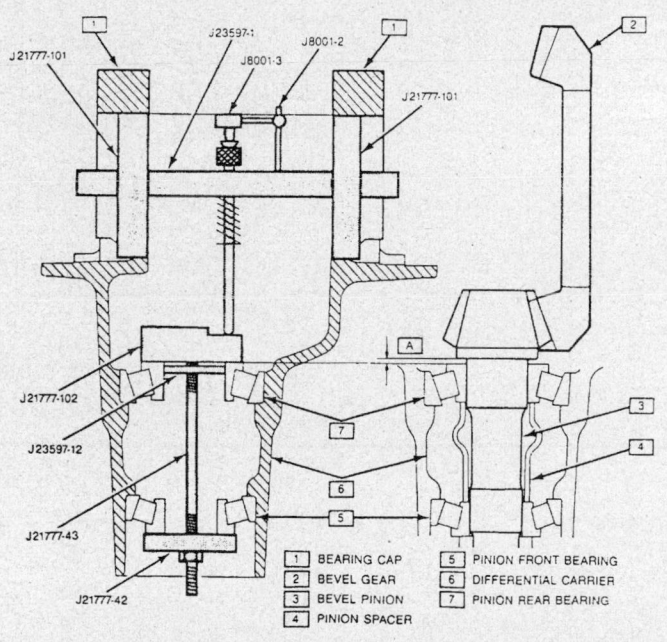

1 BEARING CAP
2 BEVEL GEAR
3 BEVEL PINION
4 PINION SPACER
5 PINION FRONT BEARING
6 DIFFERENTIAL CARRIER
7 PINION REAR BEARING

SK3039100038000X

Fig. 16 Bevel pinion mounting distance. Sidekick & X-90

step on the gauge plate.

12. **Torque** tool nut to 19 inch lbs. and rotate gauge plate several times to seat bearings.

13. **Torque** tool nut to 19 inch lbs. or until gauge plate rotates smoothly with torque wrench.

14. Install pinion setting gauge tool No. J23597 or equivalent and assemble the gauge shaft in the carrier so that the dial indicator rod is centered on the gauging area of the gauge block.

15. Install side bearing caps and **torque** bolts to 63 ft. lbs.

16. Adjust dial indicator until a zero reading is obtained.

17. Adjust the position of gauge shaft mounting post so contact button touches the indicator pad.

18. Push the dial indicator downward into the gauge plate until the needle rotates ¾ of a turn then tighten in this position.

19. Slowly rotate the gauge shaft back and forth. At the point of greatest deflection, reset the dial indicator to zero. Repeat and ensure zero reading.

20. Rotate the gauge shaft until the dial indicator rod no longer touches the gauge plate.

21. Read movement on the dial indicator. Total movement on the dial indicator indicates thickness of shim required.

22. Assemble pinion rear bearing, pinion shim and bevel pinion assembly.

23. Install front bearing to differential carrier with new spacer inserted.

24. Install oil seal into differential carrier until seal is flush with carrier end. Apply grease to lip of seal.

25. Install pinion washer and nut. Hold pinion flange and rotate pinion to seat bearing. Tighten pinion flange nut until endplay is taken up. **Preload specification is reached when endplay is no longer detectable. No further tightening should be attempted until preload has been checked.**

26. Using an inch lb. torque wrench, adjust bearing preload **torque** to 11 inch lbs.

27. Install bevel gear and differential case assembly, side bearing outer races, bearing adjusters and bearing caps, noting alignment mark.

28. **Torque** bearing caps bolts to 63 ft. lbs.

29. Turn bearing adjuster to push side bearing lightly so that outer races are in contact with inner races, **Fig. 17.**

30. Measure preload of pinion with an inch lb. torque wrench.

31. Adjust side bearing until gear backlash and bearing preload are within specification, **Fig. 18.**

32. Install bearing lock plates.

33. Clean mating surfaces of housing and carrier and apply Suzuki Bond No. 1215 (part No. 99000-31110).

34. Position differential assembly in housing with two reamer bolts, then install six bolts, **torquing** to 17 ft. lbs.

REAR

Use front differential procedure with the exception of the following:

1. **On models with rear anti-lock brakes,** an exciter ring is attached to the left case. To remove exciter ring, tap along ring rim evenly with copper hammer. To install exciter ring, press fit ring as shown, **Fig. 19.** Ensure end face of left case is flush with or higher than end face of exciter ring.

2. **On all models,** rear differential side bearing installation requires the use of bearing installer tool No. J37758 or equivalent, in place of tool No. J24433 or equivalent.

3. Rear differential is a four pinion type. After installing pinions, align pinion shaft hole position with differential case and drive in three spring pins until they are flush with the end surface of case, **Fig. 20.**

4. Use the high step on pinion setting gauge tool No. J21777-102 or equivalent gauge plate when setting pinion depth in rear differential, **Fig. 16.**

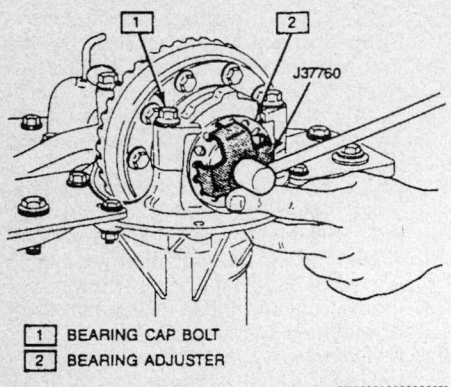

1 BEARING CAP BOLT
2 BEARING ADJUSTER

SK3039100039000X

**Fig. 17   Side bearing adjustment.
Sidekick & X-90**

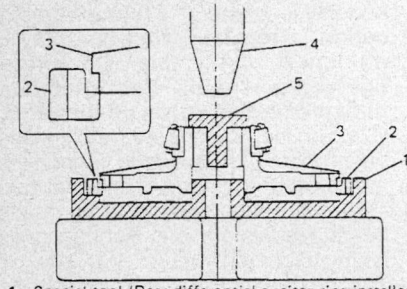

1. Special tool (Rear differential exciter ring installer 09928-26010)
2. Exciter ring
3. Differential left case
4. Press
5. Special tool (Bearing installer jig 09913-85230-002)

SK3039100041000X

**Fig. 19   Exciter ring installation.
Sidekick & X-90 w/rear anti-lock
brakes**

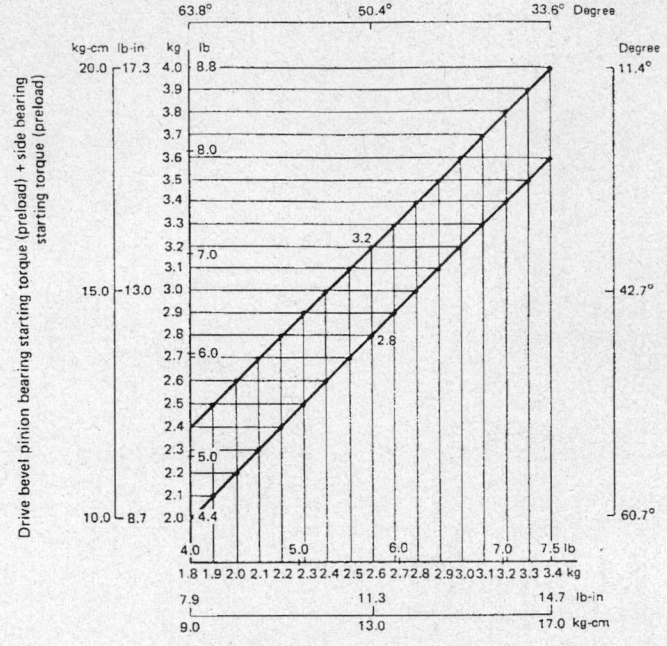

SK3039100040000X

Fig. 18   Combination of preloads. Sidekick & X-90

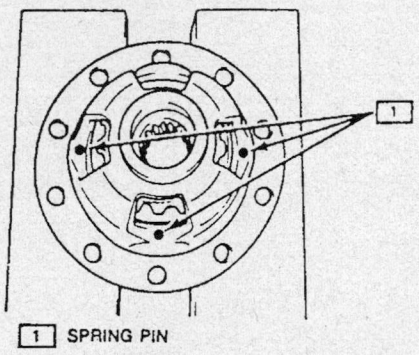

1 SPRING PIN

SK3039100042000X

**Fig. 20   Spring pins installation.
Sidekick & X-90**

Engine Rebuilding Specifications

INDEX

CYLINDER HEAD, VALVE GUIDE & VALVE SEATS

Year	Engine Liter	Cylinder Head Warpage Limit	Valve Guides				Valve Seats		
			Inner Diameter	Stem To Guide Clearance		Seat Angle, Degrees	Seat Width		
				Intake	Exhaust		Intake	Exhaust	
1996–99	1.3L	.002	.2756–.2761	.0008–.0019	.0014–.0025	45	.0512–.0590	.0512–.0590	
	1.6L	.002	.2166–.2170	.0008–.0018	.0018–.0028	45	.0433–.0512	.0433–.0512	
	1.8L	.002	.2362–.2366	.0008–.0018	.0018–.0028	45	.0433–.0512	.0433–.0512	
	2.5L	.002	.2362–.2367	.0008–.0018	.0018–.0028	45	.0433–.0512	.0433–.0512	

VALVE SPRINGS

Year	Engine Liter	Free Length	Installed Height	Seated Pressure Pounds @ Inches	Comp. Pressure Pounds @ Inches	Out Of Square Limit
1996–99	1.3L	1.8937	—	54.7–64.3 @ 1.63	50.2 @ 1.63	.079
	1.6L	1.4043	—	23.6–27.5 @ 1.24	20.5 @ 1.24	.079
	1.8L	1.6339	—	49.2–56.7 @ 1.28	46.7 @ 1.28	.079
	2.5L	①	—	—	—	②

① — Inner: 1.3780 inches. Outer: 1.5441 inches.

② — Inner: .063 inch. Outer: .070 inch.

VALVES

Year	Engine Liter	Valves							
		Stem Diameter		Face Angle, Degrees	Min. Margin Intake/ Exhaust	Clearance			
		Intake	Exhaust			Intake		Exhaust	
						Cold	Hot	Cold	Hot
1996–99	1.3L	.2742–.2748	.2737–.2742	45	.023–.027	.0051–.0067	.009–.011	.0063–.0079	.0102–.0118
	1.6L	.2152–.2157	.2142–.2148	45	.024–.027	.0031–.0047	.0047–.0063	.0031–.0047	.0047–.0063
	1.8L	.2348–.2354	.2239–.2344	45	—	—	—	—	—
	2.5L	.2348–.2354	.2362–.2367	45	—	—	—	—	—

CAMSHAFT

Year	Engine Liter	Camshaft Journal Diameter	Maximum Journal Runout	Camshaft Journal Clearance
1996–99	1.3L	①	.0039	.0020–.0036
	1.6L	1.1000–1.1008	.0039	.0016–.0032
	1.8L	②	.0039	.0008–.0029
	2.5L	1.0236–1.0249	.0039	—

① — Starting from front of cam, measure No. 1 journal, 1.7372–1.7381 inches, No. 2 journal, 1.7451–1.7460 inches, No. 3 journal, 1.7530–1.7539 inches, No. 4 journal, 1.7609–1.7618 inches & No. 5 journal, 1.7687–1.7697 inches.
② — Journal No. 1, 1.0220–1.0228; journal No. 2 & 3, 1.1795–1.1803.

CRANKSHAFT, BEARINGS & RODS

Year & Model	Engine Liter	Crankshaft				Bearing Clearance			Connecting Rods	
		Main Bearing Journal Diameter	Connecting Rod Journal Diameter	Max. Out Of Round All	Max. Taper All	Main Bearings	Connecting Rod Bearings	Crankshaft Endplay	Pin Bore Diameter	Side Clearance
1996–99	1.3L	③	1.6529–1.6535	.0004	.0004	.0008–.0016	.0008–.0019	.0044–.0122	.6680–.6684	.0039–.0078
	1.6L	②	1.7316–1.7322	.0004	.0004	.0008–.0016	.0008–.0019	.0044–.0122	.7482–.7486	.0039–.0078
	1.8L	①	1.9678–1.9685	.0004	.0004	.0010–.0018	.0018–.0024	.0039–.0138	.8269–.8272	.0099–.0150
	2.5L	—	—	.0004	.0004	.0016–.0022	.0099–.0157			—

① — Journal stamped No. 1, 2.2832–2.2834 inches; journal stamped No. 2, 2.2830–2.2832 inches; journal stamped No. 3, 2.2828–2.2829 inches.
② — Journal stamped No. 1, 2.0470–2.0472 inches; journal stamped No. 2, 2.0468–2.0470 inches; journal stamped No. 3, 2.0465–2.0468 inches; refer to text for identification.
③ — The counter weights of No. 1 cylinder have four stamped numbers, they indicate the journal diameters at bearing caps respectively. No. 1, 1.7714–17716 inch; No. 2, 1.7712–1.7714 inch & No. 3, 1.7710–1.7712 inch

PISTONS, PINS & RINGS

Year	Engine Liter	Piston Dia.	Piston Clearance	Piston Pin Diameter	Piston Ring End Gap			Piston Ring Side Clearance	
					Top	Second	Oil	Top	Second
1996–99	1.3L	①	.0008–.0015	.6691–.6693	.0079–.0118	.0079–.0118	.0079–.0275	.0012–.0027	.0008–.0023
	1.6L	2.9516–2.9523	.0008–.0015	.7479–.7480	.0079–.0137	.0079–.0137	.0079–.0275	.0012–.0027	.0008–.0023
	1.8L	3.3059–3.3066	.0008–.0015	.8267–.8270	.0079–.0137	.0138–.0196	.0079–.0275	.0008–.0015	.0008–.0015

① — Piston stamped No. 1, 2.9126–2.9130 inches; piston stamped No. 2, 2.9122–2.9126 inches; refer to text for identification.

② — Piston stamped No. 1, 2.9520–2.9524 inches; piston stamped No. 2, 2.9516–2.9520 inches; refer to text for identification.

CYLINDER BLOCK

Year	Engine Liter	Cylinder Bore Diameter (Std.)	Cylinder Bore Taper Max.	Cylinder Bore Out Of Round Max.
1996–99	1.3L	①	.0039	.0039
	1.6L	2.9586	.0039	.0039
	1.8L	3.3090	.004	.004
	2.5L	3.3075	.004	.004

① — Cylinder stamped No. 1, 2.9138–2.9142 inches; cylinder stamped No. 2, 2.9134–2.9138 inches; refer to text for identification.

② — Cylinder stamped No. 1, 2.9531–2.9535 inches; cylinder stamped No. 2, 2.9528–2.531 inches; refer to text for identification.

OIL PUMP

Year	Engine Liter	Side Clearance	Gear To Body Clearance
1996–99	1.3L	.0059	.0122
	1.6L	.0059	.0122
	1.8L	.0043	.0059
	2.5L	.0043	.0059

TOYOTA AVALON, CAMRY & CAMRY SOLARA

INDEX OF SERVICE OPERATIONS

Specifications

GENERAL ENGINE SPECIFICATIONS

Year	Model	Engine, Liter	Fuel System	Bore & Stroke	Compression Ratio	Maximum Brake H.P. @ RPM	Maximum Torque Ft. Lbs. @ RPM	Normal Oil Pressure, psi
1996	Avalon	3.0L	Fuel Inj.	3.44 x 3.27	10.5	192 @ 5200	210 @ 4400	②
	Camry	2.2L	Fuel Inj.	3.43 x 3.58	9.5	125 @ 5400	145 @ 4400	①
		3.0L	Fuel Inj.	3.44 x 3.27	10.5	188 @ 5200	203 @ 4400	②
1997–98	Avalon	3.0L	Fuel Inj.	3.44 x 3.27	10.5	200 @ 5200	214 @ 4400	②
	Camry	2.2L	Fuel Inj.	3.43 x 3.58	9.5	133 @ 5200	147 @ 4400	①
		3.0L	Fuel Inj.	3.44 x 3.27	10.5	194 @ 5200	209 @ 4400	②
1999	Avalon	3.0L	Fuel Inj.	3.44 x 3.27	10.5	200 @ 5200	214 @ 4400	②
	Camry	2.2L	Fuel Inj.	3.43 x 3.58	9.5	133 @ 5200	147 @ 4400	①
		3.0L	Fuel Inj.	3.44 x 3.27	10.5	194 @ 5200	209 @ 4400	②
	Camry Solara	2.2L	Fuel Inj.	3.43 x 3.27	9.5	135 @ 5200	147 @ 4400	①
		3.0L	Fuel Inj.	3.44 x 3.27	10.5	200 @ 5200	214 @ 4400	②

① — At idle, 4.3 psi or more; at 3000 RPM, 36–71 psi.

② — At idle, 4.3 psi or more; at 3000 RPM, 43–78 psi.

TUNE UP SPECIFICATIONS

Year, Model & Engine	Spark Plug Gap Inch	Firing Order Fig.②	Timing BTDC④	Timing Mark Fig.	Curb Idle Speed① Man. Trans.	Curb Idle Speed① Auto. Trans.	Fuel Pump Pressure, psi	Valve Clearance, Inch Int.	Valve Clearance, Inch Exh.
1996–99									
Avalon 3.0L	.043	③	10	C	.700	700N	44-50	.006–.010	.010–.014
Camry 2.2L	.043	⑤	10	A	750	750N	44-50	.007–.011	.011–.015
Camry 3.0L	.043	③	10	B	700	700N	44-50	.006–.010	.010–.014
Camry Solara 2.2L	.043	⑤	10	A	750	750N	44-50	.007–.011	.011–.015
Camry Solara 3.0L	.043	③	10	B	.700	700N	44-50	.006–.010	.010–.014

N — Neutral
BTDC — Before Top Dead Center
① — Controlled by idle air control valve.
② — Before disconnecting spark plug wires from distributor cap, deter-mine location of number 1 wire in cap, as distributor position may have been altered from that shown.
③ — Firing order, 1-2-3-4-5-6.
④ — With jumper wire connected between check connector (DLC1) terminals TE1 & E1.
⑤ — No. 1 cylinder located at front of engine, cylinder numbering 1-2-3-4; firing order 1-3-4-2.

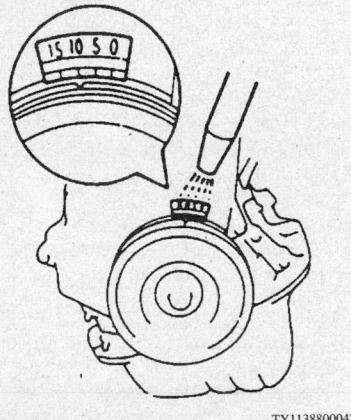

Fig. A

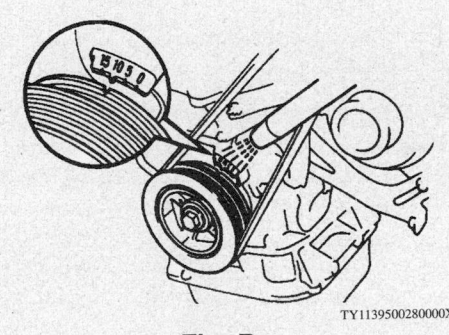

Fig. B

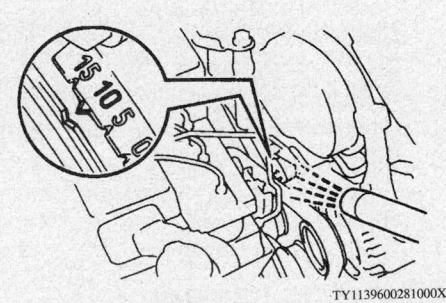

Fig. C

FRONT WHEEL ALIGNMENT SPECIFICATIONS

| Year | Model | Caster Angle, Degrees | | Camber Angle, Degrees | | Toe, Inch③ | Toe-Out on Turns, Deg. | | Steering Axis Inclination, Deg. | Ball Joint Wear |
		Limits	Desired	Limits	Desired		Inner Wheel	Outer Wheel		
1996	Avalon	+⁷/₁₂ to +1¹¹/₁₂	+1⅙	−1⅓ to +⅙	−⁷/₁₂	−.08 to +.08	36	31¼	13¹/₁₂	④
	Camry	+⁷/₁₂ to +1¹¹/₁₂	+1⅙	−1⅓ to +⅙	−⁷/₁₂	−.08 to +.08	②	①	13¹/₁₂	④
1997–98	Avalon	+1¹³/₃₀ to +2¹⁴/₁₅	+2¹¹/₁₆	−1⅓ to +²/₁₅	−³⁷/₆₀	−.08 to +.08	35¾	31⁵/₁₂	13¹/₁₅	④
	Camry	+1⁵/₁₂ to +2¹¹/₁₂	+2⅙	−1⅓ to +⅙	−⁷/₁₂	−.08 to +.08	⑤	⑥	13¹/₁₅	④
1999	Avalon	+1¹³/₃₀ to +2¹⁴/₁₅	+2¹¹/₁₆	−1⅓ to +²/₁₅	−³⁷/₆₀	−.08 to +.08	35¾	31⁵/₁₂	13¹/₁₅	④
	Camry	+1⁵/₁₂ to +2¹¹/₁₂	+2⅙	−1⅓ to +⅙	−⁷/₁₂	−.08 to +.08	⑤	⑥	13¹/₁₅	④
	Camry Solara	+1⁵/₁₂ to +2¹¹/₁₂	+2⅙	−1⅓ to +⅙	−⁷/₁₂	−.08 to +.08	⑤	⑥	13¹/₁₅	④

① — With P195/70R14 tires, 32⅙; w/P205/65R15 tires, 31⅓.
② — With P195/70R14 tires, 37⅓; w/P205/65R15 tires, 36.
③ — Toe-in (+); toe-out (-).
④ — Refer to "Ball Joint Inspection" under "Front Suspension & Steering."
⑤ — With P195/70R14 tires, 37⅕; w/P205/65R15 tires, 35¾.
⑥ — With P195/70R14 tires, 32⅓; w/P205/65R15 tires, 31⁵/₁₂.

REAR WHEEL ALIGNMENT SPECIFICATIONS

| Year | Model | Camber Angle, Degrees | | Toe, Inch① |
		Limits	Desired	
1996	Avalon	-1½ to 0	-¾	+.08 to +.24
	Camry ②	-1⅙ to +⅓	-⁷/₁₂	+.08 to +.24
	Camry ③	-1 to +½	-¼	+.08 to +.24
1997	Avalon	-1½ to 0	-¾	+.08 to +.24
	Camry	-1½ to 0	-¾	+.08 to +.24
1998	Avalon	-1³¹/₆₀ to -¹/₆₀	-²³/₃₀	+.8 to +.24
	Camry	-1½ to 0	-¾	+.08 to +.24
1999	Avalon	-1³¹/₆₀ to -¹/₆₀	-²³/₃₀	+.8 to +.24
	Camry	-1½ to 0	-¾	+.08 to +.24
	Camry Solara	-1½ to 0	-¾	+.08 to +.24

① — Toe-in (+); toe-out (-).
② — Coupe & sedan.
③ — Wagon.

FLUID CAPACITIES & COOLING SYSTEM DATA

| Year | Model & Engine | Cooling Capacity Qts. | Radiator Cap Relief Pressure, Lbs. | Thermo. Opening Temp. °F | Fuel Tank Gals. | Engine Oil Refill Qts.② | Transaxle Oil | | Differential Oil Pts. |
							Man. Trans. Pts.	Auto. Trans. Qts.①	
1996	Avalon	9.8	14	180	18.5	5.0	—	7.1	1.8
	Camry 2.2L	6.7	13	180	18.5	3.8	5.4	5.9	3.4
	Camry 3.0L	9.8	14	180	18.5	5.0	—	7.1	1.8
1997–98	Avalon	9.4	14	180	18.5	5.0	—	7.1	1.8
	Camry 2.2L	7.3	13	180	18.5	3.8	3.8	5.9	3.4
	Camry 3.0L	9.7	14	180	18.5	5.0	5.0	7.1	1.8

Continued

FLUID CAPACITIES & COOLING SYSTEM DATA—Continued

Year	Model & Engine	Cooling Capacity Qts.	Radiator Cap Relief Pressure, Lbs.	Thermo. Opening Temp. °F	Fuel Tank Gals.	Engine Oil Refill Qts.②	Transaxle Oil		Differential Oil Pts.
							Man. Trans. Pts.	Auto. Trans. Qts.①	
1999	Avalon	9.4	14	180	18.5	5.0	—	7.1	1.8
	Camry 2.2L	7.3	13	180	18.5	3.8	3.8	5.9	3.4
	Camry 3.0L	9.7	14	180	18.5	5.0	5.0	7.1	1.8
	Camry Solara 2.2	7.3	13	180	18.5	3.8	3.8	5.9	3.4
	Camry Solara 3.0	9.7	14	180	18.5	5.0	5.0	7.1	1.8

① — Approximate, make final check w/dipstick.

② — With filter change.

LUBRICANT DATA

Year	Model	Lubricant Type				
		Transmission		Rear Axle	Power Steering	Brake System
		Manual	Automatic			
1996–99	All	75W-90 GL-5	Dexron II/IIE/III	—	Dexron II/IIE/III	DOT 3

Electrical

NOTE: On Air Bag Equipped Models, Refer To "Air Bag System Precautions" Located In The Front Of This Manual For System Disarming & Arming Procedures.

INDEX

PRECAUTIONS

AIR BAG SYSTEMS

Refer to "Air Bag System Precautions" in the front of this manual for system disarming and arming procedures.

AUDIO CODED ANTI-THEFT SYSTEM

Some models are equipped with an audio coded anti-theft system that will disable the radio when battery power is removed from the radio. The system can be identified by the "ANTI-THEFT SYSTEM" on the cassette tape lid. Obtain the three digit code from the customer for input before disconnecting battery power to the audio unit. Reset system after service as follows:

1. Obtain three digit code from customer.
2. Depress No. 1 (PROG) button while depressing righthand side of TUNE SEEK button, - - - will appear in tape operation display.
3. Enter code as follows:
   a. To enter first digit, press No. 1 (PROG) button a sufficient number of times, starting with zero, to enter digit (if first digit of code is five press button six times).
   b. To enter second digit, press No. 2 (APS) button a sufficient number of times, starting with zero, to enter digit.
   c. To enter third digit press, No. 3 (RPT) button a sufficient number of times, starting with zero, to enter digit.
4. If three dashes (- - -) appear in tape operation display during input of digits, restart procedure from beginning.
5. When code digits are correctly input and displayed, press and hold SCAN button until SEC appears in tape operation display.
6. When SEC disappears from display audio unit should be operative.
7. If unit is not operative or Err is displayed, repeat procedure. **Attempting to input code more than nine times may permanently disable audio unit.**

BATTERY GROUND CABLE

Prior to service, disconnect battery ground cable and isolate as required.

FUSE PANEL & FLASHER LOCATION

AVALON

The main fuse/relay panel is located under the lower lefthand end of the instrument panel. The engine compartment fuse/relay panel is located on the lefthand front corner of the engine compartment. The flasher unit is located behind the instrument cluster.

CAMRY & CAMRY SOLARA

The passenger compartment fuse block is located behind the driver side kick panel. The engine compartment fuse/relay panel is located behind the battery. The turn signal/hazard flasher is located behind the lefthand side of the instrument panel, left of the steering column.

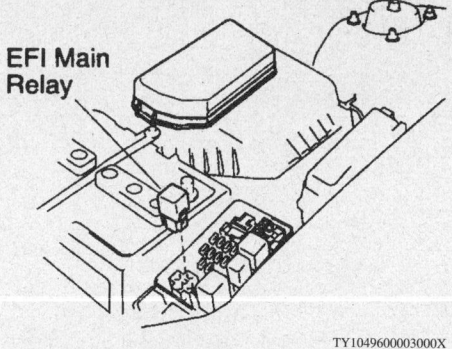

EFI Main Relay

TY1049600003000X

Fig. 1 Fuel pump relay location

FUEL PUMP RELAY LOCATION

The fuel pump relay is located in the engine compartment relay box, **Fig. 1.**

RELAY CENTER LOCATION

AVALON

The main relay/fuse panel is located under the lower lefthand end of the instrument panel. The engine compartment relay/fuse panel is located on the front lefthand corner of the engine compartment. The relay/fusible link panel is located on the lefthand side of the engine compartment, next to the air filter box. Relay block No. 8 (A/C clutch and radiator fans) is located on the lefthand side of the engine compartment, on the shock tower.

CAMRY & CAMRY SOLARA

There are three relay centers. One is located below the righthand side of the instrument panel, another behind the upper center of the instrument cluster and the third is on the righthand side of the engine compartment.

STARTER
REPLACE
AVALON

1. **On models equipped with coded audio anti-theft systems,** refer to "Precautions" for code procedures.
2. **On all models,** remove battery and tray.
3. **On models equipped with cruise control,** remove cruise control actuator as follows:
   a. Remove bolt, clip and actuator cover.
   b. Disconnect actuator connector and clamp.
   c. Remove three bolts, and disconnect actuator with bracket.
4. **On all models,** disconnect starter connector and starter to battery cable.
5. Remove attaching bolts, then the starter.
6. Reverse procedure to install, noting the following:

a. **Torque** starter mounting bolts to 29 ft. lbs.
b. Reset audio anti-theft system, if necessary, as outlined under "Precautions."

CAMRY & CAMRY SOLARA

1. **On models equipped with coded audio anti-theft systems,** refer to "Precautions" for code procedures.
2. **On models equipped with cruise control,** remove battery and cruise control actuator.
3. **On all models,** disconnect electrical connectors from starter motor.
4. Remove starter motor attaching bolts, heat shield (if equipped), then the starter motor.
5. Reverse procedure to install.

ALTERNATOR
REPLACE
2.2L ENGINE
With A/C

1. Disconnect wire routing clamps and wiring connectors from alternator.
2. Loosen adjuster lock bolt, pivot bolt and adjusting bolt, then remove drive belt.
3. Remove adjuster lock bolt, pivot bolt and adjusting bolt, then the alternator.
4. Reverse procedure to install, noting the following:
   a. Tension drive belt as outlined under "Belt Tension Data" in the "5S-FE 2.2L Engine" section.
   b. **Torque** pivot bolt to 38 ft. lbs.
   c. **Torque** adjustment lock bolt to 13 ft. lbs.

Less A/C

1. Disconnect wire routing clamps and wiring connectors from alternator.
2. Loosen pivot bolt and adjusting bolt, then remove drive belt.
3. Remove pivot bolt and adjusting bolt, then the alternator.
4. Reverse procedure to install, noting the following:
   a. Tension drive belt as outlined under "5S-FE 2.2L Engine."
   b. **Torque** pivot bolt to 38 ft. lbs.
   c. **Torque** adjustment lock bolt to 13 ft. lbs.

3.0L ENGINE

1. Loosen alternator pivot bolt, adjusting lock bolt, and adjusting bolt, then remove drive belt, **Fig. 2.**
2. Disconnect alternator connector.
3. Disconnect alternator to battery cable.
4. Disconnect wire harness from clip.
5. Remove pivot bolt, plate washer, adjusting lock bolt and alternator.
6. Reverse procedure to install, noting the following:
   a. Tension drive belt as outlined under "Belt Tension Data" in the "1MZ-FE Engine" section.
   b. **Torque** pivot bolt to 41 ft. lbs.
   c. **Torque** adjustment lock bolt to 13 ft. lbs.

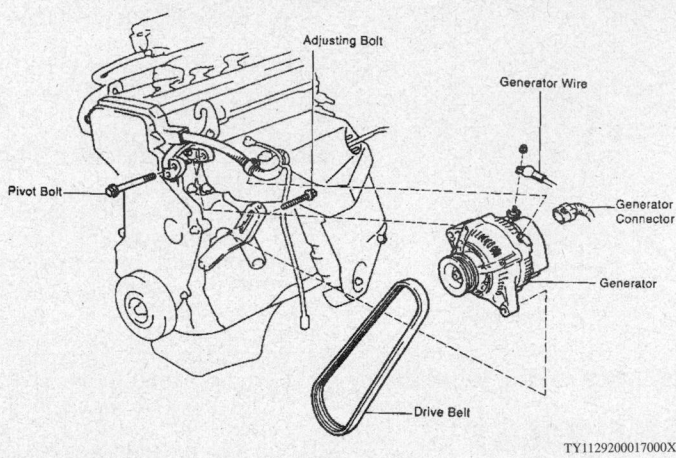

Fig. 2 Alternator removal. 3.0L engine

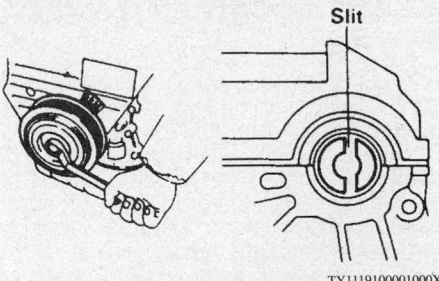

TY1119100001000X

Fig. 3 Setting No. 1 cylinder to TDC. 2.2L engine

DISTRIBUTOR
REPLACE
2.2L ENGINE

1. **On models equipped with coded audio anti-theft systems,** refer to "Precautions" for code procedures.
2. **On all models,** disconnect accelerator linkage from throttle linkage, then remove air cleaner cover, resonator and hose.
3. Disconnect electrical connectors, then mark and remove spark plug wires.
4. Remove distributor bolts, then distributor and O-ring.
5. Reverse procedure to install, noting the following:
   a. Set No. 1 cylinder to TDC by turning crankshaft clockwise. Position slit of camshaft, **Fig. 3.**
   b. Install new O-ring, then align cutout of coupling with mark on housing.
   c. Insert distributor, aligning center of flange with bolt hole on cylinder head, then tighten hold-down bolts.
   d. Reverse remaining installation procedure, then adjust ignition timing.
   e. **Torque** hold-down bolt to 14 ft. lbs.
   f. Reset audio anti-theft system, if necessary, as outlined under "Precautions."

COIL PACK
REPLACE
3.0L ENGINE

1. **On models equipped with coded audio anti-theft systems,** refer to "Precautions" for code procedures.
2. **On all models,** disconnect high-tension cords from ignition coils.
3. Disconnect ignition coil connectors and remove ignition coils from lefthand cylinder head.
4. Reverse procedure to install.

2.2L ENGINE

1. Drain engine coolant into a suitable container, then remove air cleaner cap.
2. Disconnect accelerator cable from throttle body.

3. **On models equipped with automatic transaxle,** disconnect throttle cable from throttle body.
4. **On all models,** disconnect throttle position sensor and IAC valve connectors.
5. Disconnect vacuum hoses from throttle body, then remove attaching bolts.
6. Remove throttle body from intake manifold and set aside
7. Disconnect high tension cords from ignition coils, then the electrical connectors.
8. Disconnect wire clamp from manifold stay.
9. Remove retaining bolts, then the ignition coils and manifold stay.
10. Remove attaching bolts, then the coils from manifold stay.
11. Reverse procedure to install noting the following:
    a. **Torque** ignition coil bolts to 87 inch lbs.
    b. **Torque** manifold stay 12mm head bolts to 15 ft. lbs.
    c. **Torque** manifold stay 14mm head bolts to 31 ft. lbs.

IGNITION LOCK
REPLACE

1. **On models equipped with coded audio anti-theft systems,** refer to "Precautions" for code procedures.
2. **On all models,** remove upper and lower steering column covers.
3. Place ignition lock in ACC position.
4. Using a suitable thin rod or screwdriver, press down on lockpin through hole in lock body, **Fig. 4.**
5. Place new ignition lock in ACC position, then slide into lock body.
6. Ensure lockpin is engaged and lock turns freely.
7. Reset audio anti-theft system, if necessary, as outlined under "Precautions."

IGNITION SWITCH
REPLACE
AVALON

1. **On models equipped with coded**

audio anti-theft systems, refer to "Precautions" for code procedures.
2. **On all models,** remove upper and lower steering column covers.
3. Place ignition switch in OFF position, then disconnect ignition switch connector.
4. Remove four retaining screws and ignition switch. If necessary, remove lower steering column.
5. Reverse procedure to install. Reset audio anti-theft system, if necessary, as outlined under "Precautions."

CAMRY & CAMRY SOLARA

1. **On models equipped with coded audio anti-theft systems,** refer to "Precautions" for code procedures.
2. **On all models,** remove steering wheel, and if equipped, upper and lower steering column covers.
3. Disconnect electrical connectors from ignition switch.
4. Turn ignition key to ACC position and remove ignition key cylinder.
5. Remove screw and ignition switch.
6. Reverse procedure to install. Reset audio anti-theft system, if necessary, as outlined under "Precautions."

NEUTRAL SAFETY SWITCH
REPLACE
REMOVAL

1. Disconnect electrical connector from neutral safety switch.
2. Disconnect shift control cable.
3. Remove shift control lever retaining nut, then remove lever, **Fig. 5.**
4. Straighten shaft nut locktab, then remove shaft nut.
5. Remove retaining bolts, then neutral safety switch.

INSTALLATION

1. Place switch onto shaft, then install retaining bolts hand tight.
2. Install shaft nut and locktab washer, tighten nut and stake locktab.
3. Install shift arm and nut.
4. Adjust switch as outlined under "Adjustment."

ADJUSTMENT

1. Disconnect shift control cable from

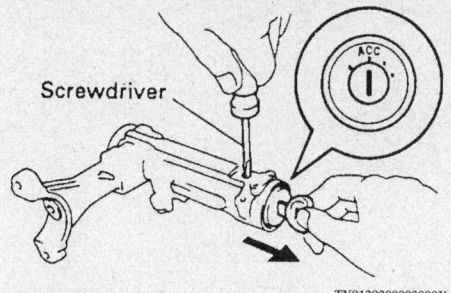

Fig. 4 Ignition lock removal

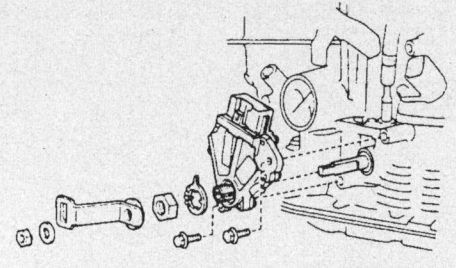

Fig. 5 Neutral safety switch removal

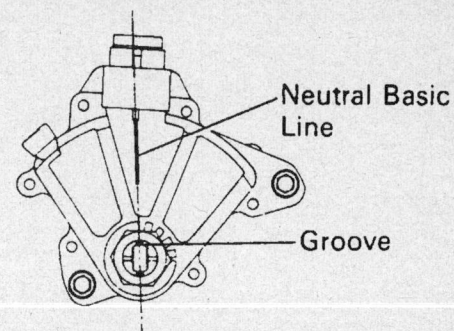

Fig. 6 Neutral start switch adjustment. Camry & Camry Solara

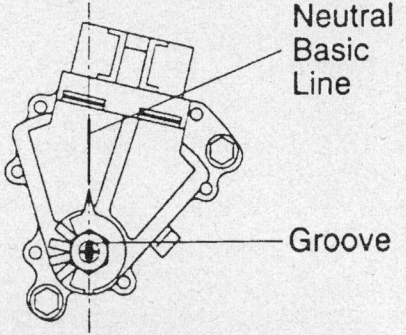

Fig. 7 Neutral start switch adjustment. Avalon

shift lever, then loosen neutral safety switch bracket bolt.
2. Position transmission shift lever into Neutral.
3. Align switch shaft groove with neutral base line, then tighten switch bracket bolt, **Figs. 6 and 7.**
4. Connect electrical connector to switch.

HEADLAMP SWITCH
REPLACE
AVALON

1. **On models equipped with coded audio anti-theft systems,** refer to "Precautions" for code procedures.
2. **On all models,** remove upper and lower steering column covers.
3. Disconnect headlamp switch electrical connector.
4. Remove retaining screws and switch, **Fig. 8.**
5. Reverse procedure to install, reset audio anti-theft system, if necessary, as outlined under "Precautions."

CAMRY & CAMRY SOLARA

Refer to "Combination Switch, Replace."

STOP LIGHT SWITCH
REPLACE
AVALON

1. Remove panel from lower lefthand side of instrument panel.
2. Disconnect stop lamp switch connector.
3. Loosen jam nut, then unscrew switch from pedal bracket.
4. Reverse procedure to install. Adjust switch by threading switch in or out of bracket, then tighten locknut.

CAMRY & CAMRY SOLARA

1. Remove brake pedal tension spring.
2. Disconnect switch wire connector.
3. Remove switch mounting nut, then slide switch from mounting bracket.
4. Reverse procedure to install.

COMBINATION SWITCH
REPLACE
CAMRY & CAMRY SOLARA

1. **On models equipped with coded audio anti-theft systems,** refer to "Precautions" for code procedures.

2. **On all models,** remove steering wheel as outlined under "Steering Wheel, Replace."
3. Remove steering column upper and lower covers.
4. Remove combination switch, **Fig. 9.**
5. Reverse procedure to install. Reset audio anti-theft system, if necessary, as outlined under "Precautions."

TURN SIGNAL SWITCH
REPLACE
AVALON

1. **On models equipped with coded audio anti-theft systems,** refer to "Precautions" for code procedures.
2. **On all models,** remove upper and lower steering column covers.
3. Disconnect turn signal switch electrical connector.
4. Remove retaining screws, then remove switch, **Fig. 8.**
5. Reverse procedure to install. Reset audio anti-theft system, if necessary, as outlined under "Precautions."

CAMRY & CAMRY SOLARA

Refer to "Combination Switch, Replace" for procedure.

STEERING WHEEL
REPLACE

During the following procedures do not store air bag pad face down. If air bag module is dropped, dented or otherwise damaged, replace with a new part. It is recommended that only new parts be used for replacement.

Ensure ignition switch is in OFF position during air bag module removal. Disconnecting the module with switch in ON or ACC position will cause an error code to be stored in air bag system ECU.
1. Place front wheels in a straight ahead position.
2. Remove blind hole plugs on back of steering wheel to access Torx mounting screws.
3. Using a suitable driver, back out Torx screws evenly. They are retained in pad by a cage, **Fig. 10.**
4. Without pulling on or placing a strain on connector wire, disconnect lead from pad.
5. Remove retaining nut, then place match marks on steering wheel and column shaft.
6. Install steering wheel puller tool No. 09950–50011 (09951–05010, 09952–05010, 09953–05020, 09954–05020) or equivalent, and press wheel from shaft. **Do not strike shaft or puller.**
7. Reverse procedure to install, noting the following:
   a. Turn spiral cable fully clockwise until it reaches stop, then turn back clockwise three turns and align red marks, **Fig. 11.**
   b. **Torque** steering wheel nut to 26 ft. lbs.
   c. **Torque** torx steering wheel pad retaining screws to 7 ft. lbs.

INSTRUMENT CLUSTER
REPLACE
AVALON

1. **On models equipped with coded audio anti-theft systems,** refer to "Precautions" for code procedures.
2. **On all models,** remove steering wheel as outlined under "Steering Wheel, Replace."
3. Remove upper and lower steering column cover.
4. Remove trim panels around instrument cluster, **Fig. 12,** then remove instrument cluster.
5. Reverse procedure to install. Reset audio anti-theft system, if necessary, as outlined under "Precautions."

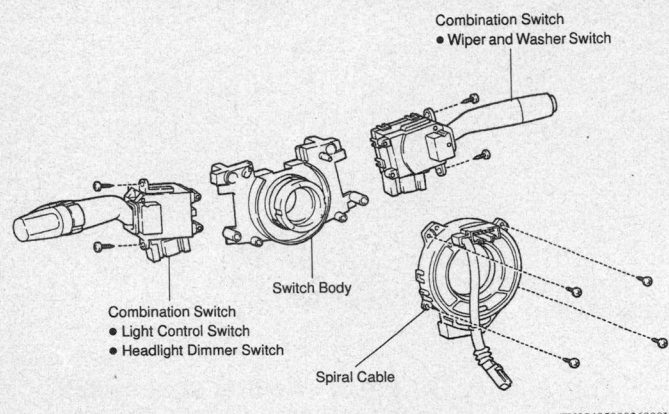

Fig. 8 Light control & wiper switch. Avalon

CAMRY & CAMRY SOLARA

1. **On models equipped with coded audio anti-theft systems,** refer to "Precautions" for code procedures.
2. **On all models,** pull front door inside scuff plate to remove.
3. Pull front door opening cover rearward to remove.
4. Remove hood lock release lever attaching screws, then pull rearward to remove.
5. Remove cowl side trim panel clip, then pull rearward to remove.
6. Remove steering wheel as outlined under "Steering Wheel, Replace."
7. Remove steering column cover.
8. Remove console upper panel.
9. Remove two rear console box attaching bolts and screws, then remove box.
10. Depress coin box sides, then pull box rearward to remove.
11. Remove coin box bezel attaching screws, then the coin box bezel.
12. Remove four instrument panel lower pad attaching bolts and screw, then the lower pad.
13. Disconnect combination switch electrical connectors.
14. Remove combination switch attaching screws, then the switch.
15. Pull undercover No. 2 rearward to remove.
16. Remove instrument panel lower panel attaching screws, then pull panel rearward to remove.
17. Remove front console box clips, then the two attaching screws and box.
18. Remove glove compartment attaching screws, then the glove compartment.
19. Using suitable taped screwdriver, remove center cluster finish panel.
20. Remove four cluster finish panel attaching screws.
21. Using suitable taped screwdriver, remove cluster finish panel and disconnect electrical connectors.
22. Remove four instrument cluster attaching screws, pull cluster rearward, disconnect electrical connectors, then remove cluster.
23. Reverse procedure to instal. Reset audio anti-theft system, if necessary, as outlined under "Precautions."

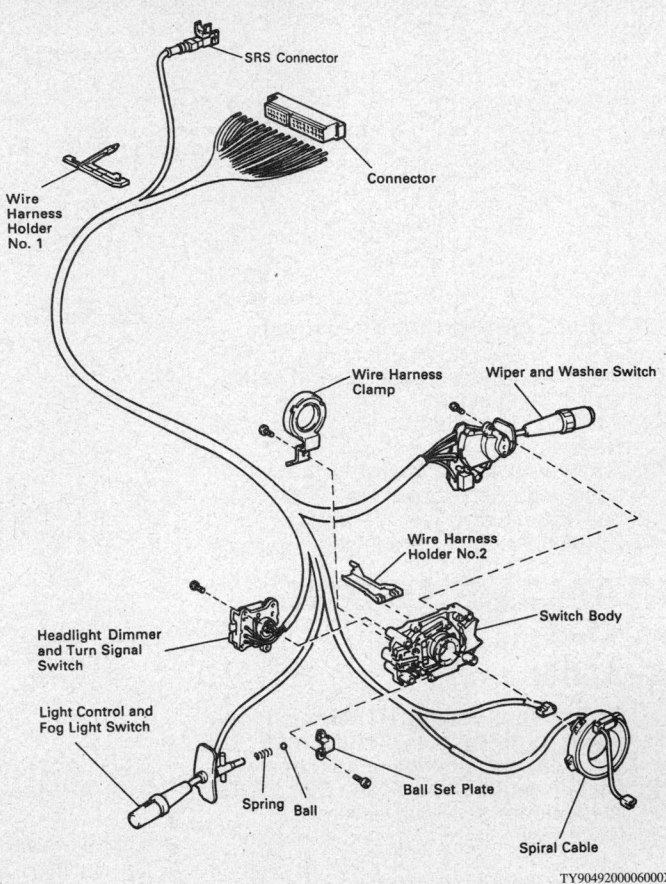

Fig. 9 Combination switch assembly. Camry & Camry Solara

RADIO
REPLACE

1. **On models equipped with coded audio anti-theft systems,** refer to "Precautions" for code procedures.
2. **On all models,** remove center upper trim panel.
3. Remove retaining screws. Slide out and disconnect electrical connectors and antenna lead from audio unit.
4. Reverse procedure to install, reset audio anti-theft system, if necessary, as outlined under "Precautions."

WIPER MOTOR
REPLACE
AVALON

1. **On models equipped with coded audio anti-theft systems,** refer to "Precautions" for code procedures.
2. **On all models,** remove wiper arms, **Fig. 13.**
3. Carefully lift weather strip away from cowl trim.
4. Remove clips, then slide cowl louvers forward.
5. Disconnect wiper linkage from wiper motor
6. Remove wiper motor mounting bolts, then the wiper motor.
7. Reverse procedure to install. Reset

audio anti-theft system, if necessary, as outlined under "Precautions."

CAMRY & CAMRY SOLARA

Front

1. **On models equipped with coded audio anti-theft systems,** refer to "Precautions" for code procedures.
2. **On all models,** disconnect wiper motor wire connector, then remove wiper motor service cover, if equipped.
3. Remove wiper motor attaching bolts.
4. Using a screwdriver, disconnect wiper link from wiper motor and remove wiper motor.
5. Reverse procedure to install. Reset audio anti-theft system, if necessary, as outlined under "Precautions."

Rear

1. **On models equipped with coded audio anti-theft systems,** refer to "Precautions" for code procedures.
2. **On all models,** remove wiper arm and rear door trim cover.
3. Disconnect wiper motor wire connector.
4. Remove wiper motor bracket attaching bolt, then the wiper motor and bracket.
5. Reverse procedure to install. Reset audio anti-theft system, if necessary, as outlined under "Precautions."

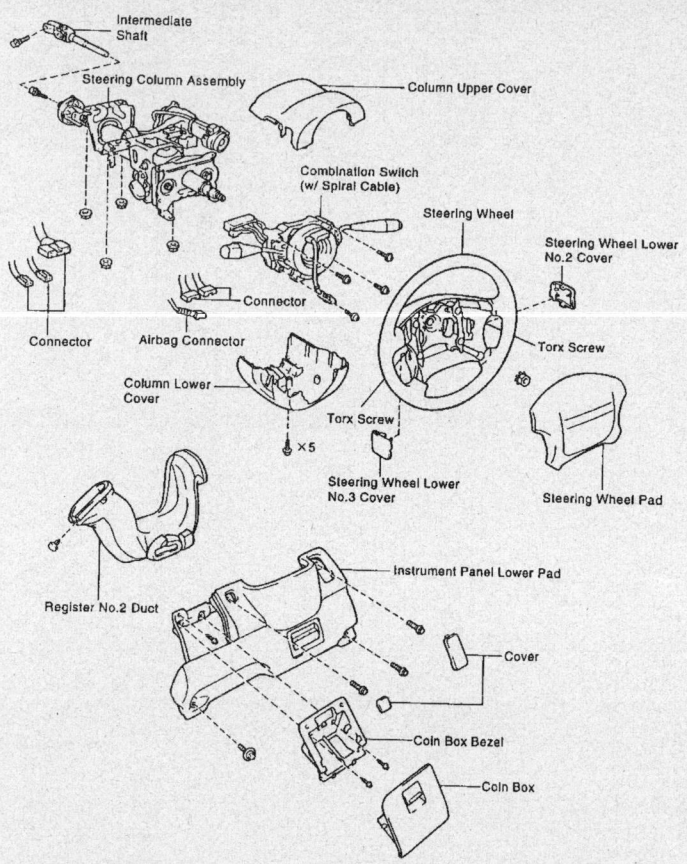

Fig. 10 Steering wheel replacement

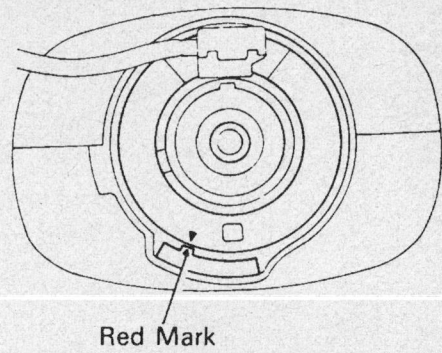

Red Mark

TY6049300001000X

Fig. 11 Spiral cable installation alignment

WIPER SWITCH

REPLACE

AVALON

1. **On models equipped with coded audio anti-theft systems,** refer to "Precautions" for code procedures.
2. **On all models,** remove upper and lower steering column covers.
3. Disconnect wiper switch electrical connector.
4. Remove retaining screws, then the switch, **Fig. 8.**
5. Reverse procedure to install. Reset audio anti-theft system, if necessary, as outlined under "Precautions."

CAMRY & CAMRY SOLARA

Refer to "Combination Switch, Replace" for procedure.

BLOWER MOTOR

REPLACE

1. **On models equipped with coded audio anti-theft systems,** refer to "Precautions" for code procedures.
2. **On all models,** remove instrument panel lower panel and undercover No. 2.
3. Disconnect connector bracket electrical connector.
4. Remove blower motor attaching screws, then the blower motor.
5. Reverse procedure to install. Reset

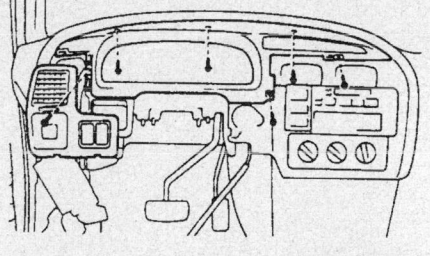

TY9099500093000X

Fig. 12 Instrument cluster replacement. Avalon

audio anti-theft system, if necessary, as outlined under "Precautions."

HEATER CORE

REPLACE

AVALON

1. Drain engine coolant.
2. Remove instrument panel as outlined under "Dash Panel Service."
3. Remove water valve control cable guide, **Fig. 14.**
4. Remove three heater core clamps.
5. Pull heater core to the left and remove from vehicle
6. Reverse procedure to install.

CAMRY & CAMRY SOLARA

1996

1. **On models equipped with coded**

audio anti-theft systems, refer to "Precautions" for code procedures.
2. **On all models,** recover A/C refrigerant as outlined under "Air Conditioning" and drain coolant.
3. Disconnect water inlet control cable from water valve.
4. Disconnect water hoses from heater core pipes.
5. Remove instrument panel and reinforcements as outlined under "Dash Panel Service."
6. Remove blower unit, as follows:
   a. Disconnect ECU electrical connector, then remove ECU and bracket.
   b. Disconnect connector bracket electrical connector, then remove connector bracket.
   c. Disconnect blower unit electrical connector.
   d. Disconnect air inlet damper control cable.
   e. Remove three blower unit attaching screws and nut, then the blower unit.
7. Disconnect and cap liquid and suction tube from block joint, **Fig. 15.**
8. Remove heater protector attaching clips, then the protector.
9. Remove three heater core attaching screws and clamps.
10. Disconnect and cap heater pipes, then remove heater core.
11. Reverse procedure to install. Reset audio anti-theft system, if necessary, as outlined under "Precautions."

1997-99

1. **On models equipped with coded audio anti-theft systems,** refer to "Precautions" for code procedures.
2. **On all models,** drain engine coolant into a suitable container, then recover A/C refrigerant as outlined in "Air Conditioning" section.
3. Disconnect water hoses from A/C unit, then remove No. 1 lower instrument panel.
4. Remove lefthand instrument lower panel.
5. Release claws pull out heater protector, then remove 3 screws and plates.
6. Disconnect and cap heater pipes, then remove heater core.
7. Reverse procedure to install. Reset audio anti-theft systems, if necessary,

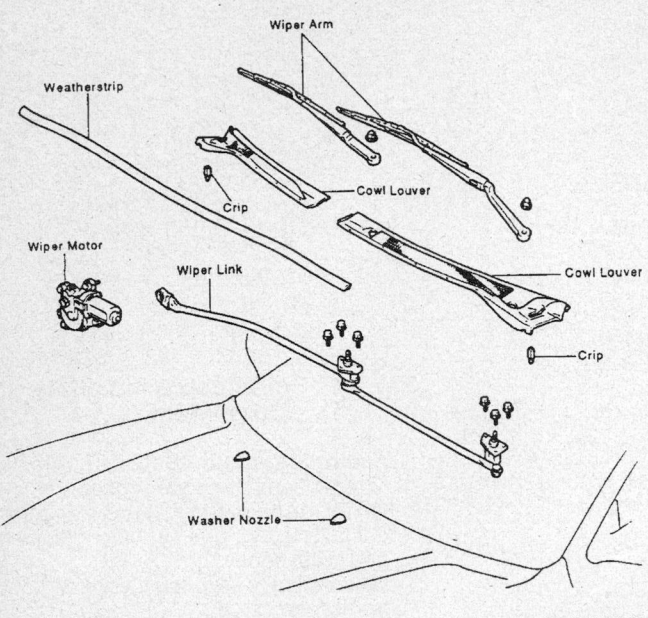

Fig. 13   Wiper motor replacement. Avalon

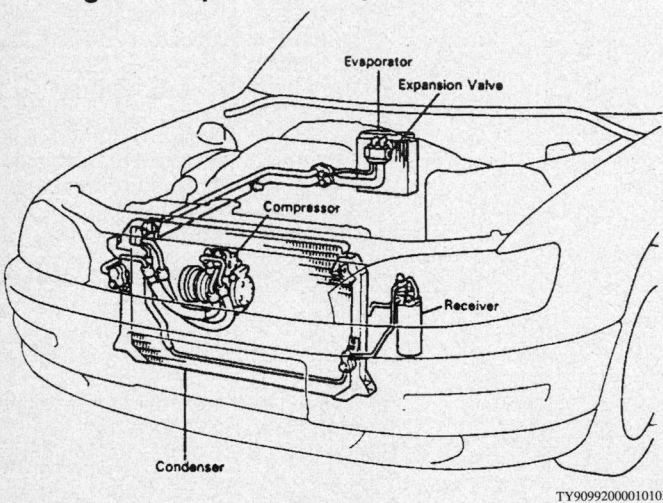

Fig. 15   A/C system components (Part 1 of 2). 1996 Camry

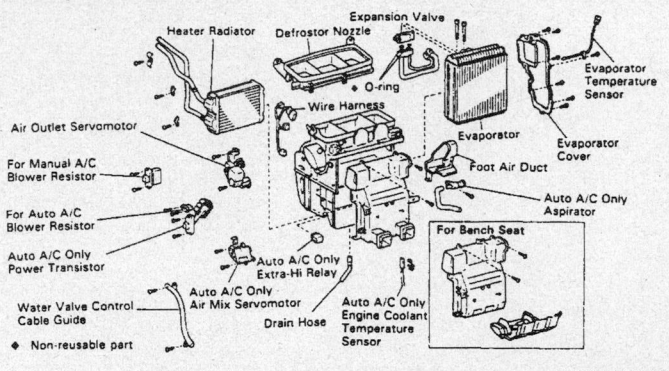

Fig. 14   Exploded view of HVAC unit. Avalon

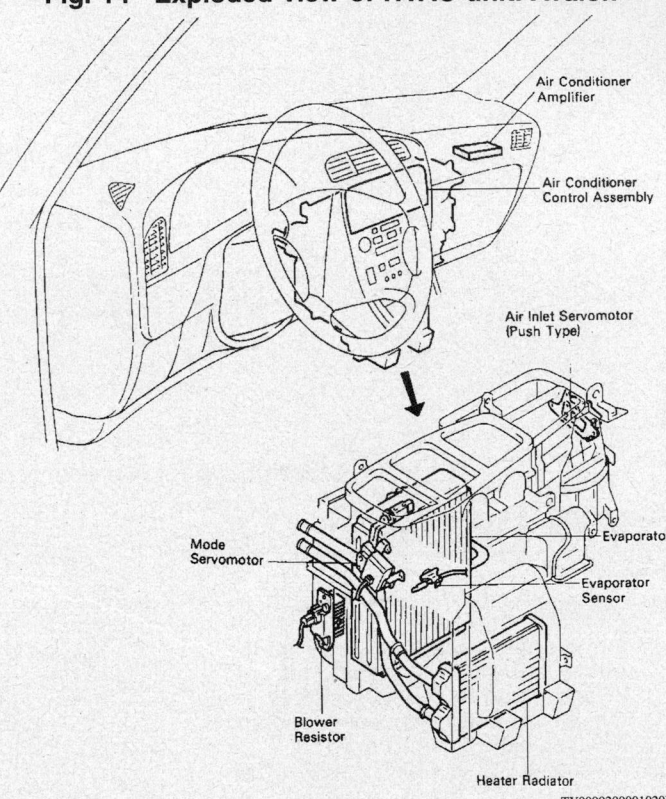

Fig. 15   A/C system components (Part 2 of 2). 1996 Camry

as outlined under "Precautions"

EVAPORATOR CORE
REPLACE
AVALON

1. **On models equipped with coded audio anti-theft systems,** refer to "Precautions" for code procedures.
2. **On all models,** remove glove compartment, then the righthand instrument panel undercover.
3. Remove ECM, ECU and bracket.
4. Remove blower and housing unit, **Fig. 16.**
5. Discharge and recover A/C system refrigerant.
6. Disconnect liquid tube and suction tube.
7. Remove thermister from evaporator.
8. Remove evaporator cover, **Fig. 14.**
9. Pull out evaporator.

10. Reverse procedure to install, noting the following:
    a. Evacuate and recharge system and check for leaks.
    b. If evaporator is replaced, add 1.4 oz. of suitable refrigerant oil to evaporator.
    c. Reset audio anti-theft system, if necessary, as outlined under "Precautions."

CAMRY & SOLARA

1. **On models equipped with coded audio anti-theft systems,** refer to "Precautions" for code procedures.
2. **On all models,** recover refrigerant as outlined in "Air Conditioning" section.
3. Remove blower unit, as follows:
    a. Remove glove compartment.
    b. Disconnect ECU electrical connector, then remove ECU and bracket.

c. Disconnect connector bracket electrical connector, then remove connector bracket.
d. Disconnect blower unit electrical connector.
e. Disconnect air inlet damper control cable.
f. Remove three blower unit attaching screws and nut, then the blower unit.
4. Disconnect and cap evaporator liquid and suction tubes.
5. Remove evaporator cover.
6. Remove evaporator assembly, then separate evaporator and expansion tube.
7. Reverse procedure to install. Reset audio anti-theft system, if necessary, as outlined under "Precautions."

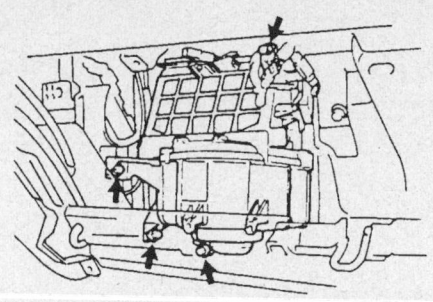

TY7029500251000X

Fig. 16 Blower & housing unit removal. Avalon

5S-FE 2.2L Engine

NOTE: On Air Bag Equipped Models, Refer To "Air Bag System Precautions" Located In The Front Of This Manual For System Disarming & Arming Procedures.

NOTE: For Procedures Not Found In This Section, Refer to Toyota Celica & Supra "5S-FE 2.2L Engine" Section.

INDEX

PRECAUTIONS

AIR BAG SYSTEMS

Refer to "Air Bag System Precautions" in the front of this manual for system disarming and arming procedures.

AUDIO CODED ANTI-THEFT SYSTEM

Some models are equipped with an audio coded anti-theft system that will disable the radio when the battery cable is disconnected. The system can be identified by the words "ANTI-THEFT SYSTEM" on the cassette tape lid. Obtain three digit customer code for input. Reset system after service as follows:

1. Obtain three digit audio anti-theft code.
2. Depress 1 (PROG) button while depressing righthand side of TUNE SEEK button, - - - will appear in tape operation display.
3. To enter first digit, depress 1 (PROG) button repeatedly until number of times depressed equals first digit beginning with zero (depress 1 button six times if first digit is five).
4. To enter second digit, depress 2 (APS) button repeatedly until the number of times depressed equals the second digit beginning with zero.
5. To enter third digit, depress 3 (RPT) button repeatedly until the number of times depressed equals the third digit beginning with zero.
6. If - - - is displayed during code input, repeat procedure.
7. When code appears in display, depress and hold SCAN button until SEC appears.
8. When SEC disappears audio system should be operative.
9. If Err is displayed, repeat procedure. **Attempting to input code more than nine times may permanently disable audio system.**

BATTERY GROUND CABLE

Prior to service, disconnect battery ground cable and isolate as required.

COMPRESSION PRESSURE

1. Start engine and warm to normal operating temperature.
2. Disconnect distributor electrical connector.
3. Disconnect spark plug wires.

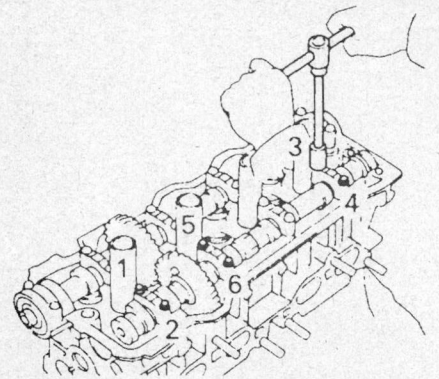

Fig. 1 Exhaust camshaft bearing cap bolt loosening sequence

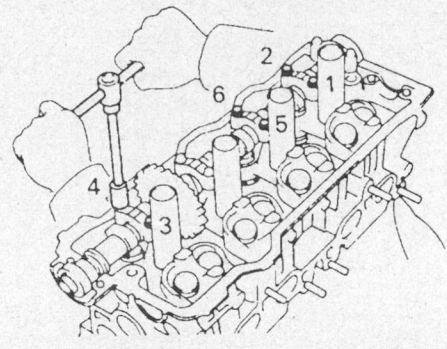

Fig. 2 Intake camshaft bearing cap bolt loosening sequence

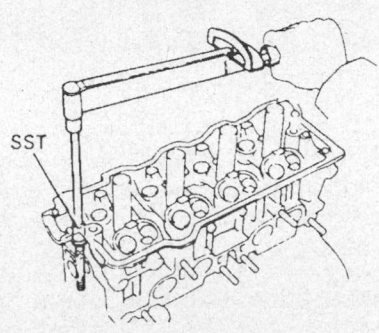

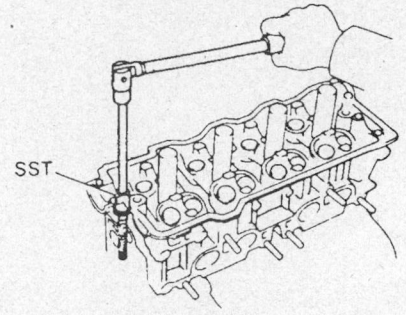

Fig. 3 Cylinder head bolt loosening sequence

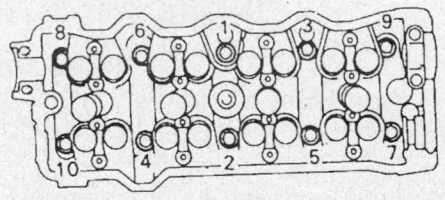

Fig. 4 Cylinder head bolt tightening sequence (Step 1)

4. Insert compression gauge into spark plug hole.
5. Fully open throttle.
6. While cranking engine, measure compression pressure.
7. Compression pressure should be 142–178 psi.
8. Maximum pressure difference between cylinders should not exceed 14 psi.

ENGINE
REPLACE
1996

1. **On models equipped with coded audio anti-theft systems,** refer to "Precautions" for code procedures.
2. **On all models,** remove battery and tray.
3. Scribe hood installation alignment marks, then remove hood.
4. Remove engine undercover.
5. Drain engine coolant and oil into suitable containers.
6. Disconnect accelerator cable from throttle body.
7. **On models equipped with automatic transaxle,** disconnect throttle cable from throttle body.
8. **On all models,** disconnect air intake temperature sensor electrical connector.
9. Disconnect cruise control actuator cable from clamp on resonator and air cleaner.
10. Loosen air cleaner hose clamp bolt, then remove air cleaner cap clips.
11. Disconnect air cleaner hose from throttle body, then remove air cleaner cap with resonator and hose assembly.
12. Remove air cleaner case attaching bolts, then remove cleaner case.
13. **On models equipped with cruise control,** remove cruise control actuator.
14. **On all models,** disconnect ground strap from battery carrier.
15. Remove radiator as outlined under "Radiator Replace," then disconnect coolant reservoir hose.
16. Disconnect washer tank electrical connector and hose, then remove washer tank assembly.

17. Disconnect engine relay box electrical connectors, then remove relay box.
18. Disconnect the following:
    a. Two connectors on lefthand fender apron.
    b. Igniter connector.
    c. Noise filter connector.
    d. Check connector.
    e. A/C magnet switch connector.
    f. Vacuum sensor connector.
    g. Back-up lamp connector.
    h. Righthand fender apron ground strap.
    i. Speed sensor connector.
19. Disconnect heater hoses.
20. Place suitable container below fuel return hose, then disconnect hose.
21. Place suitable container below fuel inlet hose, then disconnect hose.
22. **On models equipped with manual transaxle,** remove starter, then clutch release cylinder. **Do not disconnect clutch release cylinder tube.**
23. **On all models,** disconnect transaxle control cables.
24. Disconnect vacuum sensor hose and brake booster vacuum hose from air intake chamber, then charcoal canister vacuum hose.

25. Remove instrument panel undercover, lower instrument panel, glove compartment door and glove compartment.
26. Disconnect two engine ECU electrical connectors, then the four cowl wiring electrical connectors.
27. In engine compartment, remove engine wire harness attaching nuts, then pull harness from cowl.
28. **On models equipped with A/C,** disconnect A/C compressor electrical connector, remove A/C belt and compressor attaching bolts, then position A/C compressor assembly aside. **Do not disconnect compressor tubes.**
29. **On all models,** disconnect front exhaust pipe, then remove driveshafts.
30. **On models equipped with power steering,** disconnect power steering pump electrical connector, remove belt and pump attaching bolts, then position power steering pump assembly aside. **Do not disconnect pump hoses.**
31. **On all models,** remove lefthand engine mount attaching bolts, then disconnect mount.
32. Remove righthand rear engine mount hole plugs, then remove attaching nuts and disconnect mount.
33. Remove righthand front engine mount attaching bolts, then disconnect mount.
34. Install suitable engine lifting equipment.
35. Remove engine moving control rod.
36. Remove engine and transaxle assembly.
37. **On models equipped with automatic transaxle,** remove starter assembly.
38. **On all models,** separate engine and transaxle.
39. Remove No. 2 righthand engine mount bracket.
40. Remove front righthand engine mount.
41. Remove rear righthand engine mount.

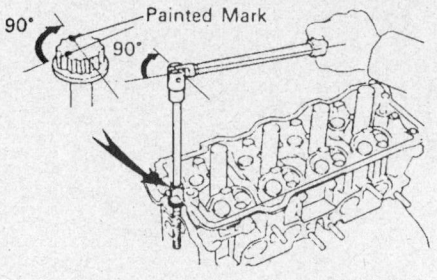

Fig. 5   Cylinder head bolt tightening sequence (Step 2)

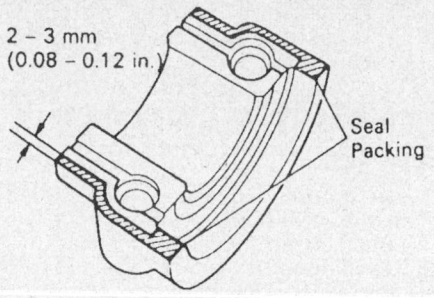

Fig. 6   No. 1 bearing cap seal packing

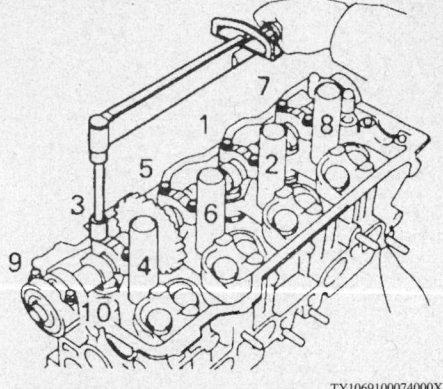

Fig. 7   Intake camshaft bearing cap bolt tightening sequence

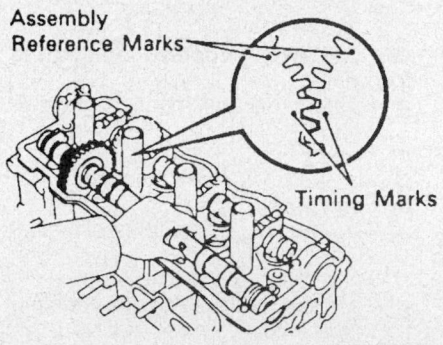

Fig. 8   Camshaft gear timing mark location

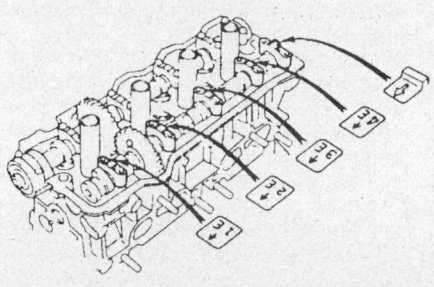

Fig. 9   Exhaust bearing cap location

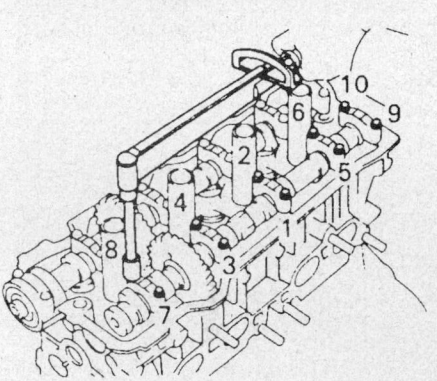

Fig. 10   Exhaust camshaft bearing cap bolt tightening sequence

42. Reverse procedure to install, noting the following:
   a. Tighten attaching nuts and bolts to specifications.
   b. Reset audio anti-theft system, if necessary, as outlined under "Precautions."

CAMRY SOLARA & 1997-99 CAMRY

1. **On models equipped with coded audio anti-theft systems,** refer to "Precautions" for code procedures
2. **On all models,** remove hood and front fender apron seals.
3. Drain engine coolant and oil into suitable containers.
4. **On Camry Solara models,** remove center front suspension upper brace.
5. **On all models,** disconnect accelerator cable.
6. Disconnect IAT sensor connector, then the VSV connector for EVAP.
7. Disconnect PCV hose from cylinder head cover, then EVAP hose from throttle body.
8. Disconnect EVAP hose from VSV, then remove air cleaner cap from air cleaner case.
9. Remove air cleaner hose from throttle body, then the cap and hose assembly.
10. Remove air filter, then the air cleaner case.
11. Remove cruise control actuator, then the battery and tray.
12. Remove radiator as outlined under "Radiator Replace."
13. Remove front exhaust pipe as follows:
   a. Remove bolts holding support stay to support bracket, then the support bracket to front frame.
   b. Remove bolts and nuts holding front exhaust pipe to center exhaust pipe, then the front exhaust pipe to exhaust manifold.
   c. Remove front exhaust pipe, gasket and support bracket.
14. Disconnect alternator wire, then the connector and wire clamp from alternator.
15. Disconnect starter cable, then the connector.
16. Disconnect DLC1 from bracket, then engine wire clamp from bracket on righthand fender apron.
17. Disconnect MAP sensor connector and wire clamp from bracket.
18. Disconnect ground strap connectors from lefthand and righthand fender aprons.
19. Disconnect engine wire protector clamp from battery bracket.
20. Disconnect engine wire from clamp on fuel filter.
21. Disconnect ground cable from transaxle, then the brake booster vacuum hose from intake manifold.
22. Disconnect heater hose from water outlet, then heater hose from water bypass pipe.
23. Disconnect fuel inlet hose from fuel filter, then the MAP sensor vacuum hose from gas filter on intake manifold.
24. Remove under cover, then disconnect 3 ECM connectors.
25. Disconnect 3 cowl wire connectors from connectors on bracket.
26. Remove grommet from cowl panel, then pull out cowl wire.
27. Disconnect drive shaft, then the transaxle control cable(s) from transaxle.
28. **On models equipped with manual transaxle,** remove starter, then disconnect clutch release cylinder and

tube from transaxle.
29. **On all models,** disconnect electrical connector from A/C compressor, then remove the drive belt.
30. Remove A/C compressor from engine, then remove cylinder head insulator.
31. Disconnect power steering pump pressure switch connector, then loosen bolts and remove drive belt.
32. Remove power steering pump from engine.
33. Remove bolts attaching transaxle to lefthand engine mounting insulator.
34. Remove nuts attaching rear engine mounting bracket to front frame.
35. Remove bolts attaching front engine mounting insulator to front frame.
36. Attach engine chain hoist to engine hangers. **Do not attempt to hang engine by hooking chain to any other part.**
37. Remove engine moving control rod, then lift engine and transaxle carefully out of vehicle. **Ensure that engine is clear of all wiring, hoses and cables.**
38. Place engine and transaxle onto a suitable stand, then remove front engine mounting insulator.
39. Remove rear engine mounting insulator, then the No. 2 righthand engine mounting bracket.
40. **On models equipped with automatic transaxle,** disconnect throttle cable from throttle body, then remove starter.

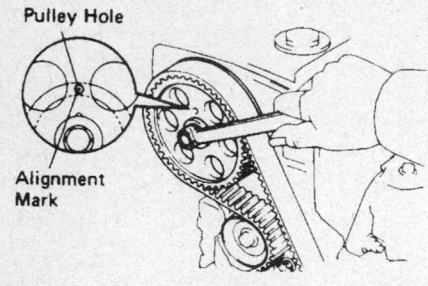

Fig. 11 Camshaft sprocket alignment

41. **On all models,** disconnect VSS connector and back-up switch connector.
42. **On models equipped with automatic transaxle,** disconnect PNP switch connector, then the two solenoid connectors.
43. **On all models,** remove No. 1 exhaust manifold stay, then the No. 2 exhaust manifold stay and lefthand stiffner plate.
44. Remove intake manifold stay, then the righthand stiffner plate
45. Remove exhaust pipe bracket, then the oil pan insulator and No. 2 rear end plate.
46. **On models equipped with automatic transaxle,** remove torque converter clutch bolts.
47. **On all models,** remove transaxle from engine.
48. **On models equipped with manual transaxle,** remove clutch cover and flywheel.
49. **On all models,** remove drive plate and No.1 rear end plate.
50. Reverse procedure to install noting the following:
    a. Tighten attaching nuts and bolts to specifications.
    b. Reset audio anti-theft systems, if necessary, as outlined under "Precautions"

INTAKE MANIFOLD
REPLACE

1. **On models equipped with coded audio anti-theft systems,** refer to "Precautions" for code procedures.
2. **On models equipped with automatic transmission,** remove throttle cable bracket from cylinder head cover.
3. **On all models,** remove accelerator and actuator cable bracket from cylinder head cover.
4. Disconnect all electrical connectors, hoses, cables, fuel lines and electrical equipment that will interfere with removal of intake manifold.
5. Remove air tube, and if equipped, power steering air hoses.
6. Remove manifold stay.
7. Remove intake manifold attaching bolts, then the intake manifold and gasket.
8. Reverse procedure to install, noting the following:
    a. Tighten to specifications.

---

b. Reset audio anti-theft system, if necessary, as outlined under "Precautions."

EXHAUST MANIFOLD
REPLACE

1. **On models equipped with coded audio anti-theft systems,** refer to "Precautions" for code procedures.
2. **On all models,** remove exhaust pipe from exhaust manifold.
3. Disconnect all electrical connectors, hoses, cables, fuel lines and electrical equipment that will interfere with removal of exhaust manifold.
4. Remove lower insulators, and if necessary, catalytic converter.
5. Remove exhaust manifold attaching bolts, then exhaust manifold and gasket.
6. Reverse procedure to install, noting the following:
    a. Tighten fasteners to specifications.
    b. Reset audio anti-theft system, if necessary, as outlined under "Precautions."

CYLINDER HEAD
REPLACE
REMOVAL

1. **On models equipped with coded audio anti-theft systems,** refer to "Precautions" for code procedures.
2. **On models equipped with automatic transmission,** disconnect throttle cable from throttle body.
3. **On all models,** drain coolant into a suitable container.
4. Disconnect accelerator cable from throttle body.
5. Disconnect the following:
    a. Air intake connector.
    b. Cruise control actuator cable from clamp on resonator and air cleaner cap.
    c. Loosen air cleaner hose clamp bolt, then disconnect four air cleaner cap clips.
    d. Air cleaner hose from throttle body. Remove air cleaner cap together with resonator and air cleaner hose.
6. Remove alternator drive belt, then disconnect alternator connector and wire. Remove alternator.
7. Remove distributor as outlined under "Distributor, Replace."
8. Disconnect front exhaust pipe.
9. **On Federal models,** disconnect oxygen sensor connector, then remove six bolts and manifold upper heat insulator.
10. **On California models,** disconnect main and sub-oxygen sensor connectors, then remove six bolts and manifold upper heat insulator.
11. **On all models,** remove bolt, nut and manifold No. 1 stay.
12. Remove bolt, nut and manifold stay.
13. **On Federal models,** remove six nuts and exhaust manifold, then four bolts and lower heat insulator.

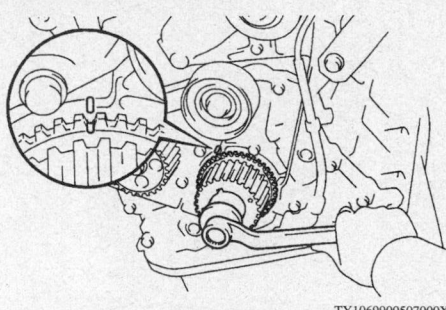

Fig. 12 Crankshaft timing pulley & oil pump body alignment marks

14. **On California models,** remove the following parts:
    a. Six nuts, exhaust manifold and catalytic converter.
    b. Three bolts.
    c. Manifold lower heat insulator.
    d. Eight bolts.
    e. Two catalytic converter heat insulators
    f. Three bolts and two nuts.
    g. Exhaust manifold, gasket, retainer and cushion.
    h. Catalytic converter.
15. **On all models,** disconnect oil pressure switch connector and engine wire (for oxygen sensor(s)) from engine hanger.
16. Disconnect following connectors:
    a. Water temperature sender gauge connector.
    b. Water temperature sensor connector.
17. Disconnect following hoses from water outlet:
    a. Upper radiator hose.
    b. Water bypass pipe hose.
    c. Heater water hose.
    d. ISC water bypass hose.
    e. Two EVAP BVSV vacuum hoses.
18. Remove two bolts, gasket and water outlet.
19. Disconnect following hoses from water bypass pipe:
    a. ISC water bypass hose.
    b. Heater water hose.
    c. **On models equipped with oil cooler,** two oil cooler water bypass hoses.
20. **On all models,** remove two bolts, two nuts, water bypass pipe, gasket and O-ring.
21. Disconnect following connectors from throttle body:
    a. Throttle position sensor connector.
    b. ISC valve connector.
22. Disconnect following hoses from top end of throttle body:
    a. PCV hose.
    b. Two vacuum hoses from EGR vacuum modulator.
    c. Vacuum hose from EVAP VSV.
23. Remove four throttle body mounting bolts.
24. Disconnect following hoses from bottom end of throttle body:
    a. Water bypass hose from water outlet.

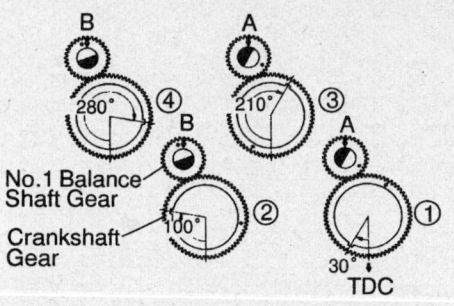

Fig. 13   Crankshaft gear & No.1 balance shaft gear measurement

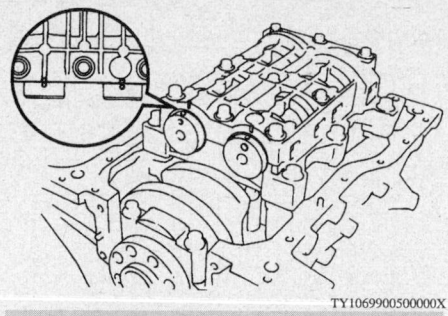

Fig. 14   Balance shafts & No. 2 housing alignment marks

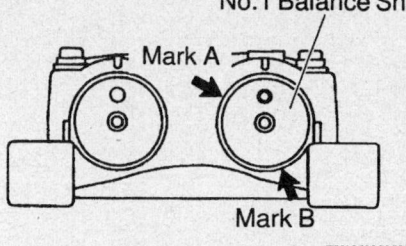

Fig. 15   No. 1 balance shaft alignment marks

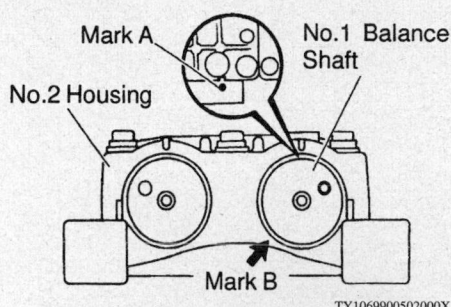

Fig. 16   No. 2 balance shaft housing No. 1 balance shaft alignment marks

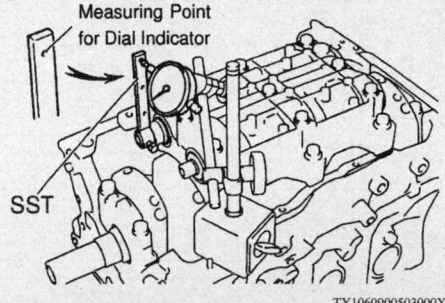

Fig. 17   Balance shaft & crankshaft gear backlash measurement

b. Water bypass hose from water bypass pipe.
c. Air hose from air tube.

25. **On California models,** disconnect and remove the following EGR system components:
   a. EGR gas temperature sensor connector.
   b. Remove two vacuum hoses from EGR VSV and vacuum hose from charcoal canister.
   c. Disconnect vacuum hose clamp, then loosen union nut of EGR pipe.
   d. Remove two bolts, EGR valve, vacuum modulator, vacuum hoses assembly and gasket.

26. **On all models,** disconnect vacuum sensor hose and brake booster hose from intake chamber and vacuum sensing hose.

27. **On models equipped with A/C,** disconnect A/C magnetic clutch VSV connector, then the air hose from A/C VSV.

28. **On all models,** disconnect two air hoses from air pump.

29. Remove three air pump bolts, wire clamp and air tube.

30. Disconnect engine wire ground strap from intake manifold.

31. Disconnect knock sensor and EGR VSV connectors.

32. Remove intake manifold as follows:
   a. Remove four bolts, No. 1 air intake chamber and manifold stays.
   b. **On California models,** remove wire bracket.
   c. **On all models,** remove six bolts, two nuts, intake manifold and gasket.

d. Disconnect two wire clamps from wire bracket on intake manifold.

33. Remove delivery pipe and injectors as follows:
   a. Disconnect injector connectors.
   b. Loosen pulsation damper, then disconnect fuel inlet hose.
   c. Disconnect fuel return hose.
   d. Remove two bolts and delivery pipe together with four injectors. **Do not drop injectors when removing delivery pipe.**
   e. Remove four insulators and two spacers from cylinder head.
   f. Pull out four injectors from delivery pipe.
   g. Remove O-ring and grommet from each injector.

34. Remove camshaft timing pulley as outlined under "Timing Belt, Replace."

35. Remove No. 1 idler pulley and tension spring.

36. Remove No. 3 timing belt cover. **Support timing belt so that meshing of crankshaft timing pulley and timing belt does not shift. Do not allow dust, oil or water to come in contact with timing belt.**

37. Remove engine hangers, alternator bracket and oil pressure switch.

38. Remove cylinder head cover and gasket. Arrange grommets in correct order so they can be installed in original position.

39. Remove high-tension cord, clamp and PCV valve.

40. Remove camshafts. **Since clearance of camshafts is small, camshaft must be level when removed. If camshaft is not kept level, shaft thrust may crack or damage camshaft.**

41. Remove exhaust camshaft as follows:
   a. Set knock pin of intake camshaft at 10–45° BTDC of camshaft angle. The above angle allows No. 2 and No. 4 cylinder cam lobes of exhaust camshaft to push their valve lifters evenly.
   b. Secure exhaust camshaft sub-gear to drive gear with a service bolt. Recommended service bolt is .63–.79 inch (16–20 mm) long and has a .2362 inch (6 mm) thread diameter and a .0393 inch (1 mm) thread pitch. When removing camshaft, ensure torsional spring force of sub-gear has been eliminated by

above operation.
   c. Remove two bolts and bearing cap.
   d. Uniformly loosen and remove six bolts on No. 1, No. 2 and No. 4 bearing caps in several passes in sequence shown, **Fig. 1.** Remove No. 1, No. 2 and No. 4 bearing caps.
   e. Alternately loosen and remove two bolts on No. 3 bearing cap. As the two No. 3 bearing cap bolts are loosened. Ensure camshaft is lifted out evenly. If camshaft is not being lifted out evenly, retighten two No. 3 bearing cap bolts, then reverse order of Steps e through a and reset knock pin of intake camshaft 10–45° BTDC and repeat Steps b through e.
   f. Remove No. 3 bearing cap and exhaust camshaft.

42. Remove intake camshaft as follows:
   a. Set knock pin of intake camshaft at 80–115° BTDC of camshaft angle. The above angle allows No. 1 and No. 3 cylinder cam lobes of intake camshaft to push their valve lifters evenly.
   b. Remove two bolts, front bearing cap and oil seal.
   c. Uniformly loosen and remove six bolts on No. 1, No. 3 and No. 4 bearing caps in several passes in sequence shown, **Fig. 2.** Do not remove No. 2 bearing cap bolts at this time. Remove No. 1, No. 3 and No. 4 bearing caps.
   d. Alternately loosen and remove two bolts on No. 2 bearing cap. As two

Adjusting Spacer Selection Chart (Off–Vehicle)

Measured backlash mm (in.)	01	02	03	04	05	06	07	08	09	10	11	12	13	14	15	16	17	18	19	20	21	22	23	24	25	26	27	28	29	30	31	32	33	34	35	36	37	38	39	40
0.000–0.004 (0.0000–0.0002)	03	03	05	05	07	07	09	09	11	11	13	13	15	15	17	17	19	19	21	21	23	23	25	25	27	27	29	29	31	31	33	33	35	35	37	37	39	39		
0.005–0.040 (0.0002–0.0016)																																								
0.041–0.046 (0.0016–0.0018)		01	01	01	01	01	03	03	05	05	07	07	09	09	11	11	13	13	15	15	17	17	19	19	21	21	23	23	25	25	27	27	29	29	31	31	33	33	35	35
0.047–0.053 (0.0019–0.0021)			01	01	01	01	01	03	03	05	05	07	07	09	09	11	11	13	13	15	15	17	17	19	19	21	21	23	23	25	25	27	27	29	29	31	31	33	33	35
0.054–0.060 (0.0021–0.0024)				01	01	01	01	01	03	03	05	05	07	07	09	09	11	11	13	13	15	15	17	17	19	19	21	21	23	23	25	25	27	27	29	29	31	31	33	33
0.061–0.067 (0.0024–0.0026)					01	01	01	01	01	03	03	05	05	07	07	09	09	11	11	13	13	15	15	17	17	19	19	21	21	23	23	25	25	27	27	29	29	31	31	33
0.068–0.074 (0.0027–0.0029)						01	01	01	01	01	03	03	05	05	07	07	09	09	11	11	13	13	15	15	17	17	19	19	21	21	23	23	25	25	27	27	29	29	31	31
0.075–0.081 (0.0030–0.0032)							01	01	01	01	01	03	03	05	05	07	07	09	09	11	11	13	13	15	15	17	17	19	19	21	21	23	23	25	25	27	27	29	29	31
0.082–0.088 (0.0032–0.0035)								01	01	01	01	01	03	03	05	05	07	07	09	09	11	11	13	13	15	15	17	17	19	19	21	21	23	23	25	25	27	27	29	29
0.089–0.095 (0.0035–0.0037)									01	01	01	01	01	03	03	05	05	07	07	09	09	11	11	13	13	15	15	17	17	19	19	21	21	23	23	25	25	27	27	29
0.096–0.102 (0.0038–0.0040)										01	01	01	01	01	03	03	05	05	07	07	09	09	11	11	13	13	15	15	17	17	19	19	21	21	23	23	25	25	27	27
0.103–0.109 (0.0041–0.0043)											01	01	01	01	01	03	03	05	05	07	07	09	09	11	11	13	13	15	15	17	17	19	19	21	21	23	23	25	25	27
0.110–0.116 (0.0043–0.0046)												01	01	01	01	01	03	03	05	05	07	07	09	09	11	11	13	13	15	15	17	17	19	19	21	21	23	23	25	25
0.117–0.123 (0.0046–0.0048)													01	01	01	01	01	03	03	05	05	07	07	09	09	11	11	13	13	15	15	17	17	19	19	21	21	23	23	25
0.124–0.130 (0.0049–0.0051)														01	01	01	01	01	03	03	05	05	07	07	09	09	11	11	13	13	15	15	17	17	19	19	21	21	23	23
0.131–0.137 (0.0052–0.0054)															01	01	01	01	01	03	03	05	05	07	07	09	09	11	11	13	13	15	15	17	17	19	19	21	21	23
0.138–0.144 (0.0054–0.0057)																01	01	01	01	01	03	03	05	05	07	07	09	09	11	11	13	13	15	15	17	17	19	19	21	21
0.145–0.151 (0.0057–0.0059)																	01	01	01	01	01	03	03	05	05	07	07	09	09	11	11	13	13	15	15	17	17	19	19	21
0.152–0.158 (0.0060–0.0062)																		01	01	01	01	01	03	03	05	05	07	07	09	09	11	11	13	13	15	15	17	17	19	19
0.159–0.165 (0.0063–0.0065)																			01	01	01	01	01	03	03	05	05	07	07	09	09	11	11	13	13	15	15	17	17	19
0.166–0.172 (0.0065–0.0068)																				01	01	01	01	01	03	03	05	05	07	07	09	09	11	11	13	13	15	15	17	17
0.173–0.179 (0.0068–0.0070)																					01	01	01	01	01	03	03	05	05	07	07	09	09	11	11	13	13	15	15	17
0.180–0.186 (0.0071–0.0073)																						01	01	01	01	01	03	03	05	05	07	07	09	09	11	11	13	13	15	15
0.187–0.193 (0.0074–0.0076)																							01	01	01	01	01	03	03	05	05	07	07	09	09	11	11	13	13	15
0.194–0.200 (0.0076–0.0079)																								01	01	01	01	01	03	03	05	05	07	07	09	09	11	11	13	13
0.201–0.207 (0.0080–0.0081)																									01	01	01	01	01	03	03	05	05	07	07	09	09	11	11	13
0.208–0.214 (0.0082–0.0084)																										01	01	01	01	01	03	03	05	05	07	07	09	09	11	11
0.215–0.221 (0.0085–0.0087)																											01	01	01	01	01	03	03	05	05	07	07	09	09	11
0.222–0.228 (0.0087–0.0090)																												01	01	01	01	01	03	03	05	05	07	07	09	09
0.229–0.235 (0.0090–0.0093)																													01	01	01	01	01	03	03	05	05	07	07	09
0.236–0.242 (0.0093–0.0095)																														01	01	01	01	01	03	03	05	05	07	07
0.243–0.249 (0.0096–0.0098)																															01	01	01	01	01	03	03	05	05	07
0.250–0.256 (0.0098–0.0101)																																01	01	01	01	01	03	03	05	05
0.257–0.263 (0.0101–0.0104)																																	01	01	01	01	01	03	03	05
0.264–0.270 (0.0104–0.0106)																																		01	01	01	01	01	03	03
0.271–0.277 (0.0107–0.0109)																																			01	01	01	01	01	03
0.278–0.284 (0.0109–0.0112)																																				01	01	01	01	01
0.285–0.291 (0.0112–0.0115)																																					01	01	01	01
0.292–0.298 (0.0115–0.0117)																																						01	01	01
0.299–0.305 (0.0118–0.0120)																																							01	01
0.306–0.313 (0.0120–0.0123)																																								01

Standard backlash (at punch mark A):
0.005 – 0.40 mm (0.0002 – 0.0016 in.)

EXAMPLE: The No.26 spacers are installed, and the measured backlash is 0.120 mm (0.0047 in.). Replace the No. 26 spacers with new No.11 spacers.

New spacer thickness   mm (in.)

No.	Thickness	No.	Thickness	No.	Thickness	No.	Thickness
01	1.74 (0.0685)	11	1.84 (0.0724)	21	1.94 (0.0764)	31	2.04 (0.0803)
03	1.76 (0.0693)	13	1.86 (0.0732)	23	1.96 (0.0772)	33	2.06 (0.0811)
05	1.78 (0.0701)	15	1.88 (0.0740)	25	1.98 (0.0780)	35	2.08 (0.0819)
07	1.80 (0.0709)	17	1.90 (0.0748)	27	2.00 (0.0787)	37	2.10 (0.0827)
09	1.82 (0.0717)	19	1.92 (0.0756)	29	2.02 (0.0975)	39	2.12 (0.0835)

TY1069900504000X

Fig. 18 Spacer selection chart

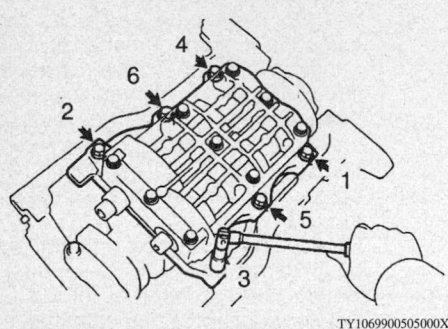

TY1069900505000X

Fig. 19 Engine balancer loosening sequence

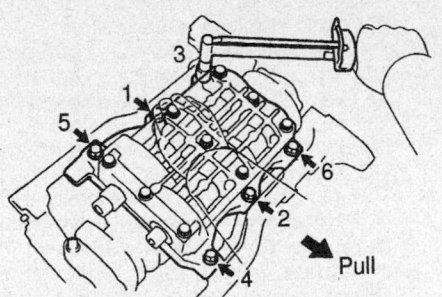

TY1069900506000X

Fig. 20 Engine balancer tightening sequence

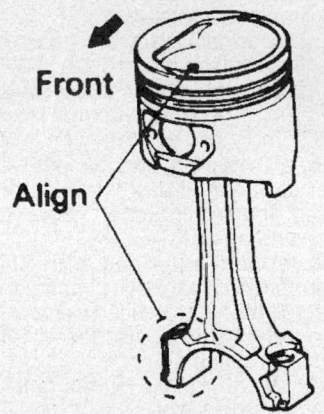

TY1069100079000X

Fig. 21 Piston & connecting rod assembly

No. 2 bearing cap bolts are loosened, ensure camshaft is lifted out evenly after breaking adhesion on front bearing cap. If camshaft is not being lifted out evenly, retighten two No. 2 bearing cap bolts, then reverse order of Steps d through a and reset knock pin of intake camshaft 80–115° BTDC and repeat Steps b through d.

e. Remove No. 2 bearing cap and exhaust camshaft.

43. Disassemble exhaust camshaft as follows:

a. Mount hexagon wrench portion of camshaft in a suitable vise. **Do not damage camshaft.**

b. Insert a service bolt into service hole of camshaft sub-gear, then using a screwdriver, turn sub-gear clockwise and remove service bolt.

Do not damage camshaft.

c. Using snap ring pliers, remove snap ring.

d. Remove wave washer, camshaft sub-gear and camshaft gear spring.

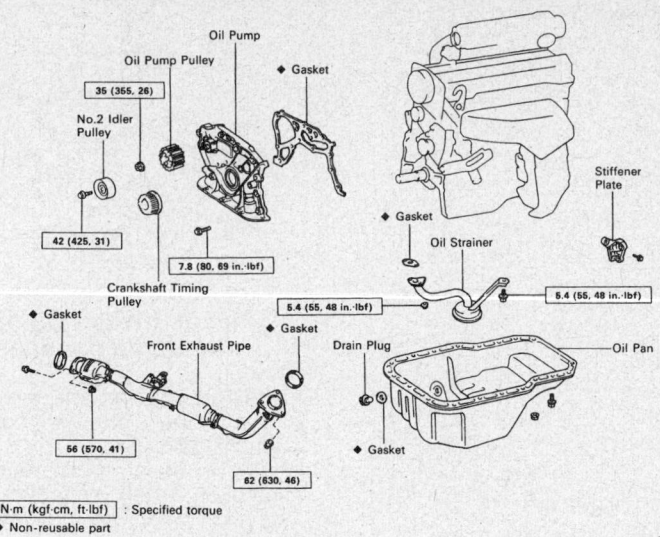

Fig. 22 Oil pump & components

N·m (kgf·cm, ft·lbf) : Specified torque
◆ Non-reusable part

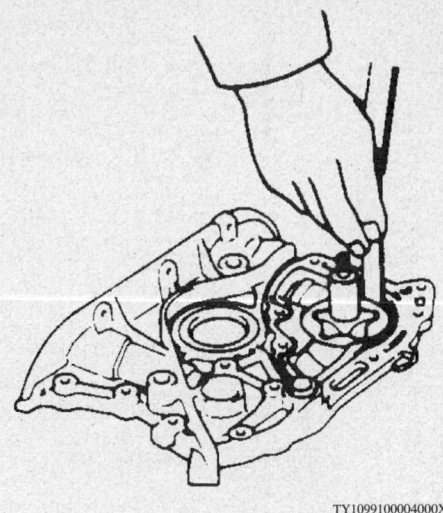

Fig. 23 Oil pump rotor body clearance inspection

44. Remove cylinder head as follows:
 a. Using a 12–point 12 mm socket, tool No. 09011-38121, or equivalent, uniformly loosen and remove cylinder head bolts in several passes as shown, **Fig. 3. Cylinder head warpage or cracking may occur from removing bolts in incorrect order.**
 b. Lift cylinder head from dowels on cylinder block and place cylinder head on wooden blocks on a bench.

INSTALLATION

1. Install new gasket on engine block, then place cylinder head on cylinder block.
2. Coat cylinder head bolt threads and under bolt head with clean engine oil, then install cylinder head bolts.
3. Using a 12–point 12 mm socket, tool No. 09011-38121, or equivalent, uniformly tighten cylinder head bolts in several passes as shown, **Fig. 4. Torque** bolts to 36 ft. lbs.
4. Mark front of cylinder head bolt with paint, then retighten bolts 90° in numerical order shown in **Fig. 4.** Ensure painted mark is 90° to front, **Fig. 5.**
5. Screw threads of spark plug tube coated with adhesive into cylinder head. Using spark plug tube nut and 30 mm socket wrench, tighten spark plug tubes to 29 ft. lbs.
6. Assemble exhaust camshaft as follows:
 a. Mount hexagon wrench head portion of camshaft in a suitable vise.
 b. Install camshaft gear spring, camshaft sub-gear and wave washer. Align pins on gears with spring ends.
 c. Using snap ring pliers, install snap ring.
 d. Insert a service bolt into service hole of camshaft sub-gear, then using a screwdriver, align holes of

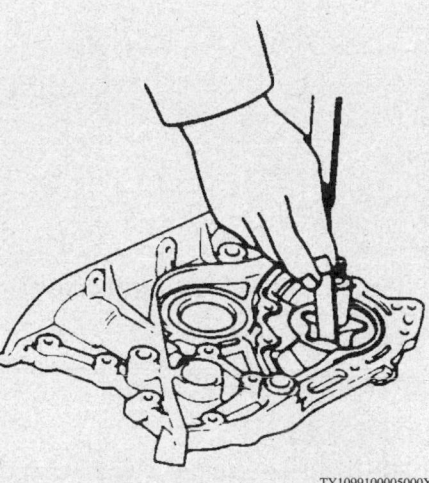

Fig. 24 Oil pump rotor body clearance inspection

camshaft main and sub-gear by turning camshaft sub-gear clockwise and install a service bolt.
7. Install intake camshaft as follows:
 a. **Since clearance of camshafts is small, camshaft must be level when installed. If camshaft is not kept level, shaft thrust may crack or damage camshaft.**
 b. Apply multi-purpose grease to thrust portion of camshaft.
 c. Place camshaft at 80–115° BTDC of camshaft angle on cylinder head. This angle allows No. 1 and No. 3 cylinder cam lobes of intake camshaft to push their valve lifters evenly.
 d. Apply seal packing to No. 1 bearing cap as shown in **Fig. 6.** Install bearing caps in their proper locations.
 e. Apply a thin coat of clean engine oil on threads and under bolt head of bearing cap bolts. Install and uniformly **torque** bolts to 14 ft. lbs. in several passes, **Fig. 7.**

 f. Apply suitable grease to new oil seal lip, then using crankshaft front oil seal replacer tool No. 09223-46011, or equivalent, tap in seal.
8. Install exhaust camshaft as follows:
 a. Set knock pin of intake camshaft to 10–45° BTDC of camshaft angle. This angle allows No. 2 and No. 4 cylinder cam lobes of exhaust camshaft to push their valve lifters evenly.
 b. Apply suitable grease to thrust portions of camshaft. Engage exhaust camshaft gear to intake camshaft gear by matching timing marks on each gear.
 c. Roll down exhaust camshaft onto bearing journals while engaging gears with each other. **There are also assembly reference marks on each gear as shown in Fig. 8. Do not use these marks.**
 d. Turn intake camshaft clockwise or counterclockwise little by little until exhaust camshaft sits in bearing journals evenly without rocking camshaft on bearing journals. **It is very important to place camshaft in bearing journals evenly while tightening bearing caps as shown in Fig. 9.**
 e. Install bearing caps in their proper locations.
 f. Apply a light coat of clean engine oil on threads and under bolt head of bearing cap bolts. Install and uniformly **torque** ten bearing cap bolts to 14 ft. lbs. in several passes as shown in **Fig. 10.**
 g. Remove service bolt.
9. Reverse removal steps 1 through 42 to complete installation. After installation is complete, adjust valves. Refer to "Valve Adjustment" for procedure.
10. Check and adjust ignition timing and toe-in as necessary.
11. Reset audio anti-theft system, if necessary, as outlined under "Precautions."

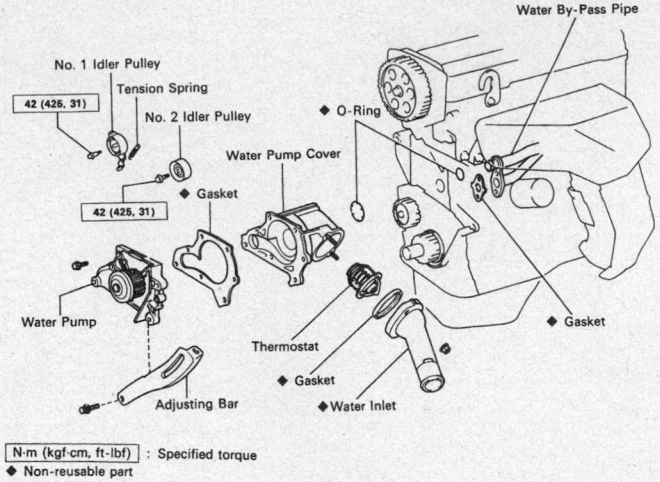

Fig. 25 Water pump removal

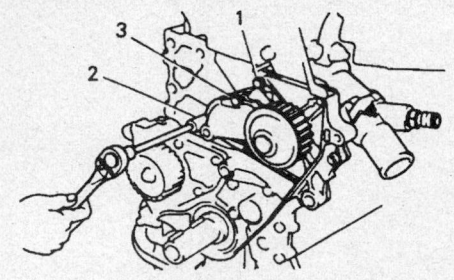

Fig. 26 Water pump bolt tightening sequence

VALVE CLEARANCE SPECIFICATIONS

Valve clearance of .007–.011 inch intake and .011–.015 inch exhaust should be indicated.

VALVE ADJUSTMENT

Valve adjustment is accomplished by installing shims to achieve the proper valve clearance. Shims are available in .0020 inch (.050 mm) increments.

1. Crank engine until No. 1 cylinder is at TDC compression stroke and adjust the following valves to specifications: intake Nos. 1 and 2, exhaust Nos. 1 and 3.
2. Rotate engine one complete revolution clockwise and adjust the following valves to specifications: intake Nos. 3 and 4, exhaust Nos. 2 and 4.

VALVE GUIDES

1. Using a suitable tool and hammer, strike valve guide bushing to break it off at cylinder head casting.
2. Heat cylinder head to 176–212°F (80–100°C).
3. Using suitable valve guide removal tool, tap out bushing.
4. Install snap ring on new valve guide, then install new valve guide using tool as outlined above and driving in from reverse side of removal.
5. Ream new valve guide, if necessary.

HYDRAULIC LIFTERS

REPLACE

Inspect lifters for excessive wear and/or damage. Replace worn or damaged valve lifters as required. Lubricate hydraulic valve lifter before installation.

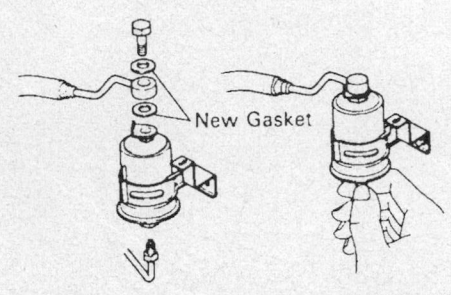

Fig. 27 Fuel filter replacement

TIMING BELT
REPLACE
REMOVAL

1. **On models equipped with coded audio anti-theft systems,** refer to "Precautions" for code procedures.
2. **On all models,** remove right front wheel and undercover.
3. Remove cruise control actuator and bracket (if equipped).
4. Remove accessory drive belts, then alternator and alternator bracket.
5. Using suitable jack, raise engine slightly. **Position block of wood between jack and engine to prevent damage.**
6. Remove right side engine mount through bolt, then the mount.
7. Remove spark plugs, then upper timing belt cover and gasket.
8. Rotate crankshaft pulley until pulley groove is aligned with "0" indication on timing marks, then ensure camshaft sprocket hole is aligned with bearing cap No. 1 alignment mark, **Fig. 11. If camshaft sprocket is not aligned properly, engine is not set at TDC compression. Rotate crankshaft an additional 360° and recheck.**
9. If timing belt is to be reused, draw arrow on belt to indicate direction of rotation and make reference marks between timing belt and camshaft sprocket.
10. Loosen spring loaded idler pulley at-

taching bolt, then pry pulley as far to the left as possible. Temporarily tighten attaching bolt.
11. Remove timing belt from camshaft sprocket, then remove camshaft sprocket attaching bolt, washer and sprocket.
12. Remove crankshaft pulley attaching bolt, then using suitable puller, remove crankshaft pulley.
13. Remove lower timing belt cover and gasket.
14. If timing belt is to be reused, make reference marks between timing belt and crankshaft sprocket, then remove belt and belt guide.
15. Remove spring loaded idler pulley attaching bolt, then the pulley and tension spring.
16. Remove fixed idler pulley attaching bolt, then the idler pulley.
17. Pry off crankshaft sprocket with two screwdrivers.
18. While holding oil pump sprocket with suitable tool, remove oil pump nut and sprocket.

INSTALLATION

1. Install oil pump sprocket. Tighten attaching nut to specification.
2. Install crankshaft sprocket, then the fixed idler pulley. Tighten idler pulley attaching bolt to specification.
3. Install spring loaded idler pulley and loosely install attaching bolt. Install spring, then pry pulley as far to the left as possible and tighten attaching bolt.
4. Temporarily install timing belt on crankshaft sprocket, oil pump sprocket, fixed idler pulley and water pump sprocket. Align timing marks of crankshaft timing pulley and oil pump body as in **Fig. 12.**
5. If belt is being reused, install in proper direction and align reference mark on crankshaft sprocket made during removal procedures. **The engine should be cold during belt installation.**
6. Install timing belt guide, cup side up on crankshaft sprocket, then the lower timing cover.
7. Install crankshaft pulley. Tighten attaching bolt to specification. Ensure crankshaft pulley groove is still aligned with "0" timing mark, indicating No. 1 cylinder is at TDC of compression stroke.
8. Install camshaft sprocket, washer and attaching bolt. Tighten attaching bolt to

specification. Rotate camshaft by turning sprocket attaching bolt to align bearing cap mark and camshaft sprocket, **Fig. 11.**

9. Install timing belt on camshaft sprocket. If timing belt is being reused, align reference marks made during removal procedures.
10. Ensure belt has tension between crankshaft sprocket, water pump sprocket and camshaft sprocket.
11. Loosen spring loaded idler pulley attaching bolt just enough to allow pulley to move by itself under spring tension. Allow pulley to take up belt tension.
12. Rotate crankshaft clockwise two complete revolutions, from TDC compression stroke to TDC compression stroke, then tighten spring loaded idler pulley to specification. **Ensure timing belt has tension between water pump sprocket and camshaft sprocket.**
13. Install upper timing belt cover and spark plugs.
14. Install right side engine mount, then lower engine.
15. Install alternator bracket, alternator and accessory drive belts.
16. Install cruise control actuator and bracket.
17. Install engine undercover and right front wheel, then battery ground cable.
18. Reset audio anti-theft system, if necessary, as outlined under "Precautions."

CAMSHAFT

REPLACE

Refer to "Cylinder Head, Replace" for camshaft removal procedures.

BALANCE SHAFT

REPLACE

REMOVAL

1. Remove engine and place on a stand, as outlined under "Engine Replace."
2. Remove timing belt and pulleys as outlined under "Timing Belt Replace."
3. Remove cylinder head as outlined under "Cylinder Head Replace."
4. Remove oil dipstick, then remove oil pan and oil pump as outlined under "Oil Pump Replace."
5. Remove power steering pump bracket, then the knock sensor and oil filter.
6. Remove water pump and water bypass pipe as outlined under "Water Pump, Replace."
7. Remove oil cooler, then the rear oil seal retainer.
8. Using suitable tool measure thrust clearance of No. 1 and No. 2 balance shafts of engine balancer. Standard thrust clearance should be .0024–.0043 inch, and maximum clearance should be .11–.0043 inch. If clearance is greater than maximum, replace balance shaft housings and bearings. If necessary, replace balance shaft.
9. Check and adjust backlash of crankshaft gear and No. 1 balance shaft

gear. Backlash between crankshaft gear and No. 1 balance shaft gear varies with rotation of balance shaft and deviation of crankshaft gear. Accordingly, it is necessary to measure backlash at 4 points shown in **Fig. 13.**

10. Turn crankshaft 2 or 3 revolutions to settle crankshaft gear and No. 1 balance shaft gear. When No. 1 piston is at TDC, ensure that punch marks of balance shafts are aligned with grooves of No. 2 housing as shown in, **Fig. 14.**
11. Ensure that punch marks "A" and " B" are at positions on No. 1 balance shaft as shown in, **Fig. 15.**
12. First turn crankshaft clockwise, align groove of No. 2 balance shaft housing with alignment mark "A" of No. 1 balance shaft as shown in **Fig. 16.**
13. Set measuring tool No. 09224–74010 and a dial indicator as shown in **Fig. 17. Ensure that needle of dial indicator is perpendicular to tool and that it is placed in middle of 3rd indention.**
14. Lightly rotate No.1 balance shaft by hand and measure backlash. To prevent excessive backlash due to thrust clearance, measure backlash while pressing on rear of No. 1 balance shaft. Standard backlash at punch mark " A" .0002–.0016 inch, **Do not turn No. 1 balance shaft strongly.**
15. Remove dial indicator, then rotate crankshaft clockwise to align groove of No. 2 housing with punch mark "B" as in **Fig. 16.**
16. Set tool and dial indicator, then measure backlash. Standard backlash at punch mark "B": .0002–.0024 inch.
17. Remove dial indicator, then rotate crankshaft clockwise again to align groove of No. 2 housing with punch mark "A."
18. Set dial indicator , then measure backlash. Standard backlash at punch mark "A": .0002–.0016 inch.
19. Remove dial indicator, then rotate crankshaft clockwise again and align groove of No. 2 housing with punch mark "B."
20. Set dial indicator , then measure backlash. Standard backlash at punch mark "B": .0002–.0024 inch.
21. Remove dial indicator. If even one of 4 points measured exceeds backlash specification, adjust backlash with new spacers.
22. **Use same size spacers for both left and right sides.**
23. Varying spacer thickness by .0008 inch will change backlash by about .0006 inch.
24. If backlash is greater than permitted maximum, select a thinner shim and if less than specification select a thicker shim, **Fig. 18.**
25. Uniformly loosen bolts and remove engine balancer in sequence as shown in, **Fig. 19.**

INSTALLATION

1. Rotate crankshaft and set No. 1 cylinder to TDC, then set balance shafts so that punch marks of balance shafts are

aligned with grooves of No. 2 housing as in, **Fig. 14.**
2. Clean installation surface of spacer, then place spacer on cylinder block.
3. Place engine balancer on cylinder block, then ensure that punch marks on balancer shafts are aligned with grooves of No. 2 housing.
4. While pulling center of engine balancer in direction of arrow, uniformly tighten bolts in sequence as shown in, **Fig. 20.**
5. Ensure that punch marks of balance shafts are aligned with grooves of No. 2 housing.
6. Check and adjust backlash of crankshaft gear and No. 1 balance shaft gear as in, "Removal Section."
7. Reverse procedure to install. Tighten all bolts and nuts to specifications.

PISTON & ROD ASSEMBLY

Only standard pistons are available, if piston bore is not within specifications, replace piston and/or cylinder block. When assembling piston onto connecting rod, ensure mark on top of piston and mark on connecting rod are on same side, **Fig. 21.** When installing piston and connecting rod assembly, ensure mark on top of piston is facing toward front of engine.

MAIN & ROD BEARINGS

Only standard bearings are available. If crankshaft journals or crankpins are worn or scored, the crankshaft must be replaced.

OIL PAN

REPLACE

1. **On models equipped with coded audio anti-theft systems,** refer to "Precautions" for code procedures.
2. **On all models,** remove engine hood.
3. Raise and support vehicle.
4. Remove engine undercovers, then drain engine oil.
5. Disconnect exhaust pipe from catalytic converter.
6. Remove suspension lower crossmember, then the engine mount center member.
7. Remove stiffener plate, then the oil dipstick.
8. Remove oil pan attaching bolts, then the oil pan. **Use caution not to damage oil pan flange.**
9. Remove two attaching bolts, nuts, oil pan baffle plate, then the oil strainer with gasket, **Fig. 22.**
10. Attach a suitable hoist to engine, then lift and suspend engine with hoist.
11. Remove timing belt and pulleys. Refer to "Timing Belt, Replace" for procedure.
12. Remove oil pump attaching bolts, then the oil pump.
13. Reverse procedure to install, noting the following:
    a. Use new gaskets and O-ring seals as applicable.

b. Tighten fasteners to specifications.

c. Reset audio anti-theft system, if necessary, as outlined under "Precautions."

OIL PUMP
REPLACE

Refer to "Oil Pan, Replace" for procedure.

OIL PUMP SERVICE

1. Using a suitable feeler gauge, measure clearance between driven rotor and pump case, **Fig. 23.**
2. Clearance should be .0039–.0067 inch. If feeler gauge clearance obtained exceeds .0079 inch, replace oil pump rotor set and/or pump case.
3. Using a feeler gauge, measure clearance between both rotor tips, **Fig. 24.** Clearance should be .0016–.0067 inch. If feeler gauge clearance obtained exceeds .0079 inch, replace oil pump rotor set.

BELT TENSION DATA

Belt tension is as follows using a belt tension gauge. A new belt is considered used after five minutes of use.

Belt	New, Lbs.	Used, Lbs.
Alternator Less A/C	100–150	75–115
Alternator w/A/C	170–180	120–140
Power Steer.	100–150	60–100

COOLING SYSTEM BLEED

These engines do not require a specified bleed procedure. After filling cooling system, run engine to operating temperature with radiator/pressure cap off. Air will then be automatically bled through cap opening.

THERMOSTAT
REPLACE

1. **On models equipped with coded audio anti-theft systems,** refer to "Precautions" for code procedures.

2. **On all models,** drain coolant into a suitable container.
3. Disconnect radiator from water inlet housing.
4. Remove water inlet housing attaching nuts from water pump, then remove inlet housing.
5. Remove thermostat and gasket.
6. Reverse procedure to install. Reset audio anti-theft system, if necessary, as outlined under "Precautions."

WATER PUMP
REPLACE

1. **On models equipped with coded audio anti-theft systems,** refer to "Precautions" for code procedures.
2. **On all models,** drain engine coolant, then disconnect lower radiator hose from coolant inlet housing and coolant temperature switch connector.
3. Remove timing belt and sprockets. Refer to "Timing Belt, Replace" for procedure.
4. Remove alternator belt adjusting bar.
5. Remove water bypass tubes to water pump cover attaching bolts, then the three water pump attaching bolts, **Fig. 25.**
6. Remove water pump and pump cover as an assembly, then remove two O-rings and gasket.
7. Remove water pump to water pump cover attaching bolts, then remove water pump.
8. Reverse procedure to install, noting the following:
   a. Tighten water pump bolts to specifications in sequence shown, **Fig. 26.**
   b. Reset audio anti-theft system, if necessary, as outlined under "Precautions."

RADIATOR
REPLACE

1. **On models equipped with coded audio anti-theft systems,** refer to "Precautions" for code procedures.
2. **On all models,** raise and support vehicle.
3. Drain coolant from engine and radiator into a suitable container.

4. Remove cruise control actuator cover.
5. Disconnect upper radiator and coolant reservoir hoses from radiator.
6. Disconnect lower radiator hose at engine, then transaxle oil cooler extension lines.
7. Disconnect electric cooling fan and temperature sensor connectors, then cruise control cable from holder on fan shroud.
8. Remove upper radiator mounts, then lift out radiator and cooling fans as a unit.
9. Remove transaxle cooler extension lines and lower radiator hose from radiator.
10. Remove securing bolts, then the electric cooling fans and shrouds.
11. Remove lower radiator mounts.
12. Reverse procedure to install. Reset audio anti-theft system, if necessary, as outlined under "Precautions."

FUEL PUMP
REPLACE

1. **On models equipped with coded audio anti-theft systems,** refer to "Precautions" for code procedures.
2. **On all models,** remove rear seat cushion.
3. Disconnect fuel pump connector, then remove five screws and service hole cover.
4. Remove fuel pump lead wire, then disconnect fuel line from fuel pump bracket. **Remove fuel filter cap to prevent fuel from flowing out.**
5. Remove fuel pump bracket assembly, gasket and pull pump out.
6. Reverse procedure to install. Reset audio anti-theft system, if necessary, as outlined under "Precautions."

FUEL FILTER
REPLACE

Refer to **Fig. 27** for replacement procedure.

TIGHTENING SPECIFICATIONS

Year	Component	Torque, Ft. Lbs.
1996–99	A/C Compressor	20
	Alternator Bracket To Cylinder Head	31
	Camshaft Timing Pulley To Camshaft	40
	Catalytic Converter To Exhaust Manifold	22
	Cylinder Head Bolts To Cylinder Block	①
	Cylinder Head Cover To Cylinder Head	33
	Engine Moving Control Rod	47
	Engine Balancer To Cylinder Block	36
	Exhaust Manifold To Cylinder Head	36
	Front Engine Mount	59
	Front Engine Mount Bracket	57
	Front Exhaust Pipe	46
	Front Exhaust Pipe To Exhaust Manifold	46
	Front Exhaust Pipe To Main Catalytic Converter	46
	Fuel Inlet Hose	22
	Intake Manifold To Cylinder Head	14
	LH Engine Mount	47
	Manifold Stay	31
	No. 2 Engine Mount Bracket	38
	No. 2 Idler Pulley To Cylinder Block	31
	Oil Pan Bolts	48②
	Oil Pump Bolts	84②
	Oil Pump Pulley To Oil Pump Driveshaft	20
	Oil Strainer	48②
	Power Steering Pump	31
	Rear Engine Mount	48
	Rear Engine Mount Bracket	47
	Spark Plug Tube To Cylinder Head	29
	Stiffener Plate	27
	Throttle Body To Cylinder Head	13
	Water Pump Bolts	84②

① — Refer to "Cylinder Head, Replace" for tightening procedure.

② — Inch lbs.

NOTE: On Air Bag Equipped Models, Refer To "Air Bag System Precautions" Located In The Front Of This Manual For System Disarming & Arming Procedures.

INDEX

PRECAUTIONS

AIR BAG SYSTEMS

Refer to "Air Bag System Precautions" in the front of this manual for system disarming and arming procedures.

AUDIO CODED ANTI-THEFT SYSTEM

Some models are equipped with an audio coded anti-theft system that will disable the radio when battery power is removed from the radio. The system can be identified by the words "ANTI-THEFT SYSTEM" on the cassette tape lid. Obtain the code from the customer for input before disconnecting battery power to the audio unit. Reset system after service as follows:
1. Obtain three digit code from customer.
2. Depress No. 1 (PROG) button while depressing righthand side of TUNE SEEK button, - - - will appear in tape operation display.
3. Enter code as follows:
   a. To enter first digit press No. 1 (PROG) button a sufficient number of times, starting with zero, to enter digit (if first digit of code is five press button six times).
   b. To enter second digit press No. 2 (APS) button a sufficient number of times, starting with zero, to enter digit.
   c. To enter third digit press No. 3 (RPT) button a sufficient number of times, starting with zero, to enter digit.
4. If three dashes (- - -) appear in tape operation display during input of digits, restart procedure from beginning.
5. When code digits are correctly input and displayed, press and hold SCAN button until SEC appears in tape operation display.
6. When SEC disappears from display audio unit should be operative.

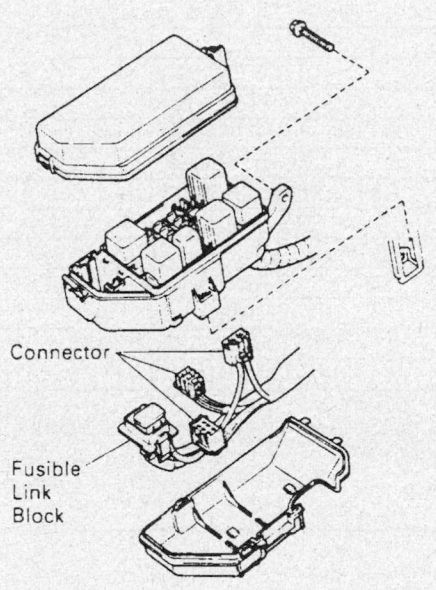

Connector

Fusible Link Block

TY1069500326000X

Fig. 1 Relay box removal. Avalon

7. If unit is not operative or Err is displayed, repeat procedure. **Attempting to input code more than nine times may permanently disable audio unit.**

BATTERY GROUND CABLE

Prior to service, disconnect battery ground cable and isolate as required.

COMPRESSION PRESSURE

1. Start and run engine until it reaches normal operating temperature.
2. Remove ignition coils as outlined under "Coil Pack, Replace."
3. Remove spark plugs.
4. Insert compression gauge into spark plug hole.
5. Fully open throttle.
6. While cranking engine, measure compression pressure.
7. Compression pressure should be 145–218 psi.
8. Maximum allowable difference between cylinders is 15 psi.

ENGINE

REPLACE

AVALON

1. **On models equipped with coded audio anti-theft systems,** refer to "Precautions" for code procedures.
2. **On all models,** remove battery, battery tray and hood.
3. Remove engine undercover, then remove engine fender apron seals.
4. Drain engine coolant and engine oil into suitable containers.
5. Disconnect accelerator cable.
6. Remove air cleaner cap assembly and air cleaner case.
7. Remove cruise control actuator.
8. Remove radiator as outlined under "Radiator Replace."
9. Remove front exhaust pipe and catalytic converter as an assembly.
10. Disconnect engine wire harness from engine compartment relay box as follows:
    a. Remove bolt, and disconnect relay box from bracket, **Fig. 1.**
    b. Remove upper and lower covers.
    c. Disconnect three connectors and fusible link block from relay box.
11. Disconnect the following connectors, cables, clamps and hoses:
    a. Windshield wiper motor connector.
    b. Two igniter connectors and one noise filter connector on lefthand fender apron.

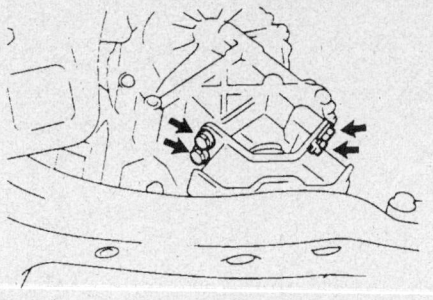

Fig. 2 Transaxle mount. Avalon

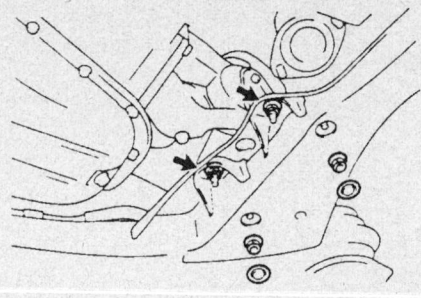

Fig. 3 Rear engine mount. Avalon

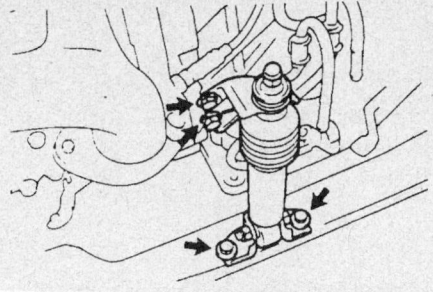

Fig. 4 Engine mount absorber removal. Avalon

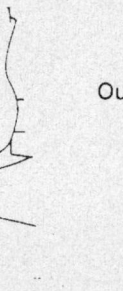

Fig. 5 Front engine mount. Avalon

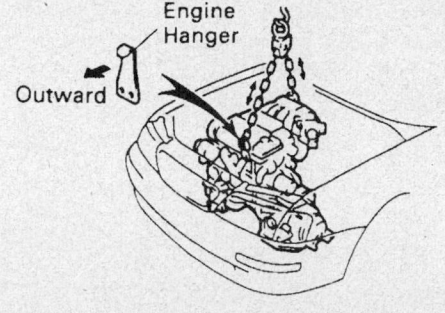

Fig. 6 Engine hanger installation. Avalon

Fig. 7 Righthand engine mount stay removal. Avalon

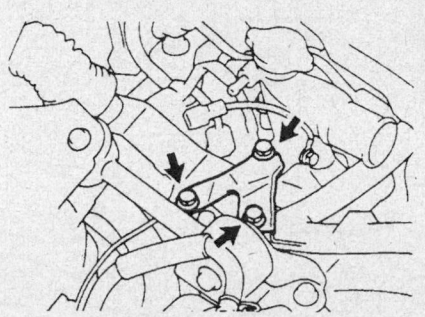

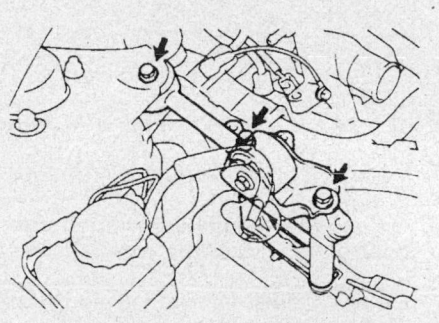

Fig. 8 Movement control rod & No. 2 righthand engine mount removal. Avalon

c. Ground strap connectors from lefthand and righthand fender apron.
d. Engine compartment main wire harness connectors on lefthand fender apron.
e. Ground cable from battery to body bracket.
f. Engine wire protector clamp from battery to body bracket.
g. Engine wiring clamps from fuel filter and bracket on righthand fender apron.
h. Brake booster vacuum hose from air intake chamber.
i. Radiator and heater hoses.
j. Fuel hoses from fuel filter and return pipe.
k. **On California models,** EVAP hose from pipe on emission control valve set.
l. **Except California models,** EVAP hose from charcoal canister.
m. **On all models,** two vacuum hoses from vacuum tank for ACIS.
12. Disconnect engine wire harness connectors from ECM under dash as follows.
   a. Remove under dash cover.
   b. Disconnect three ECM connectors and three cowl wire connectors.
   c. Disconnect grommet from cowl panel, then pull engine wire harness through cowl.
13. Remove driveshafts as outlined in "Drive Axles" section.
14. Without discharging system, disconnect A/C compressor from engine and secure aside.
15. Disconnect transaxle control cable from transaxle.
16. Without disconnecting hoses, remove power steering pump from engine and

secure aside.
17. Remove four bolts holding transaxle to mounting insulator, **Fig. 2.**
18. Remove two hole plugs in subframe, then disconnect rear engine mounting bracket from subframe, **Fig. 3.**
19. Remove engine mounting absorber, **Fig. 4.**
20. Disconnect front engine mounting by removing three bolts holding mounting insulator to subframe, **Fig. 5.**
21. Attach a suitable engine lifting device to engine as follows:
   a. Install No. 2 engine hanger, tool No. 12282–20020, or equivalent, with two bolts tool No. 91642–80825 to engine. Ensure correct location, **Fig. 6. Torque** bolts to 14 ft. lbs.
   b. Attach engine lifting device to engine hangers. **Do not attempt to lift engine by hooking chain to any other part.**
22. Remove three bolts and ground strap,

then the righthand engine mounting stay, **Fig. 7.**
23. Remove three bolts, then remove engine control rod and No. 2 righthand engine mounting bracket, **Fig. 8.**
24. Remove engine and transaxle assembly from vehicle. Ensure sufficient clearance for transaxle Park/Neutral position switch during removal.
25. Place engine and transaxle assembly onto a suitable stand.
26. Remove four bolts and front engine mounting insulator from engine.
27. Remove four bolts, then the rear engine mounting insulator and bracket assembly.
28. Separate transaxle from engine as follows:
   a. Disconnect throttle cable from throttle body, then remove starter.
   b. Disconnect engine wire harness from transaxle.
   c. Remove two bolts and flywheel housing cover.
   d. Turn crankshaft pulley bolt to gain access to all six torque converter bolts.
   e. Hold crankshaft pulley bolt with a wrench, and remove bolts.
   f. Remove lefthand and righthand exhaust manifold stays.
   g. Remove transaxle to engine bolts and ground strap.
   h. Remove transaxle together with torque converter from engine.
   i. Remove eight bolts, rear plate, drive plate and front spacer.
29. Reverse procedure to install, noting the following:
   a. Use suitable thread Loctite on

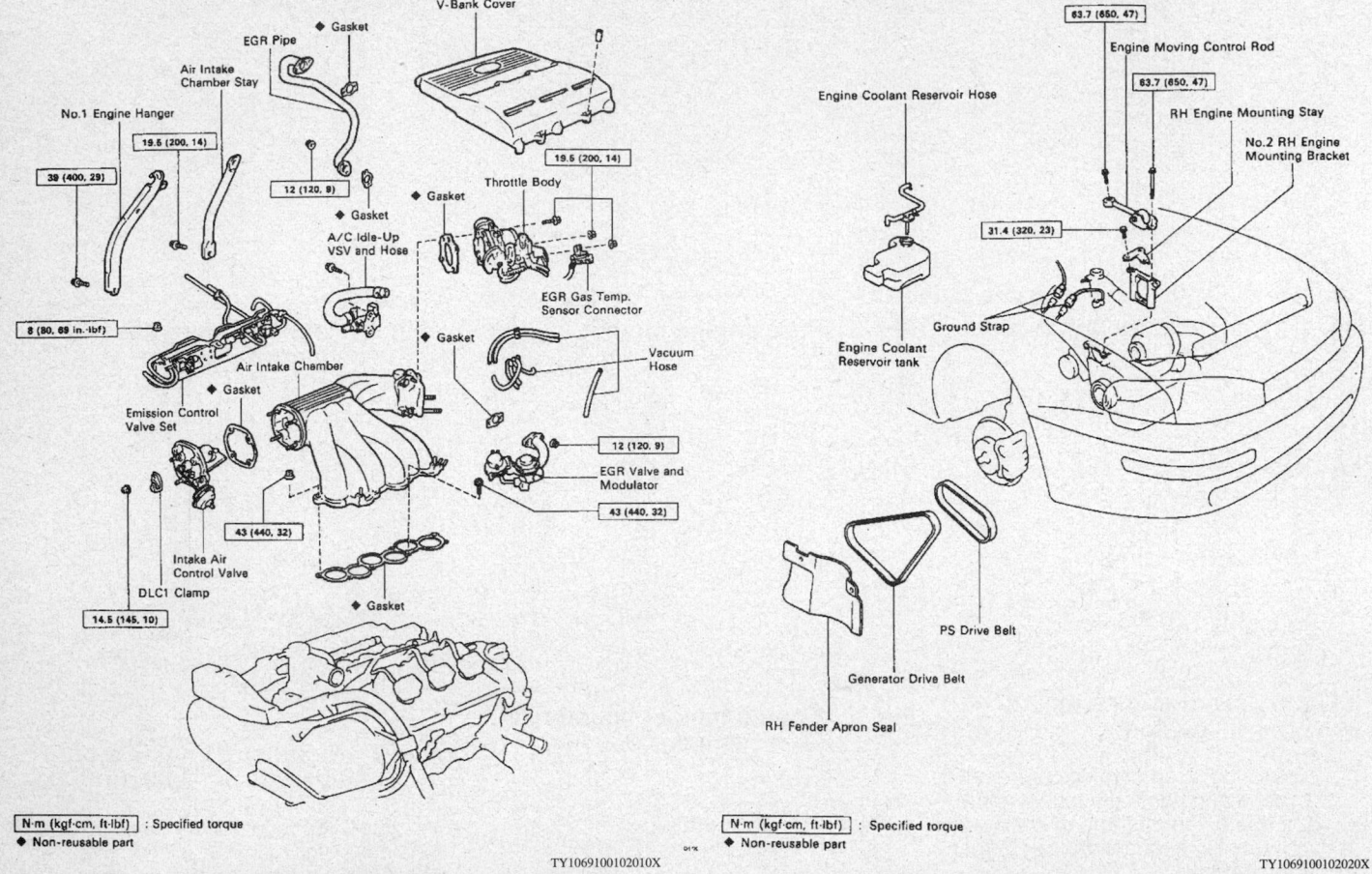

N·m (kgf·cm, ft·lbf) : Specified torque
◆ Non-reusable part

TY1069100102010X

Fig. 9   Cylinder head replacement (Part 1 of 5)

N·m (kgf·cm, ft·lbf) : Specified torque
◆ Non-reusable part

TY1069100102020X

Fig. 9   Cylinder head replacement (Part 2 of 5)

torque converter drive plate and torque converter mounting bolts.
  b. Tighten bolts to specifications.
  c. Use caution during engine installation not to damage PNP switch.
  d. Use new gaskets and manifold nuts when installing exhaust pipe.
  e. Reset audio anti-theft system, if necessary, as outlined under "Precautions."

CAMRY & CAMRY SOLARA

1. **On models equipped with coded audio anti-theft systems,** refer to "Precautions" for code procedures.
2. **On all models,** remove battery and tray, then the hood.
3. Raise and support vehicle, then drain engine oil and coolant into a suitable container.
4. Disconnect accelerator and throttle cables.
5. Remove air cleaner cap, volume air flow meter and air cleaner hose, as follows:
  a. Disconnect volume air flow meter connector, wire clamp and accelerator cable clamp.
  b. Disconnect PCV hose and loosen air cleaner hose clamp bolt.
  c. Disconnect four air cleaner cap clips, then remove air cleaner cap and volume air flow meter together with air cleaner hose.
  d. Remove air cleaner element and

three bolts, then the air cleaner case.
6. **On models equipped with cruise control,** remove cruise control actuator.
7. **On all models,** remove radiator, then disconnect engine wiring as follows:
  a. Two bolts to engine relay box.
  b. Five connectors from relay box.
  c. Two igniter connectors and noise filter connector.
  d. Connector from lefthand fender apron and two ground straps.
8. Disconnect engine attaching vacuum hoses and heater hoses.
9. Place suitable container below fuel lines, then disconnect lines.
10. Disconnect transaxle control cable from transaxle.
11. Disconnect passenger compartment engine control wiring electrical connectors as follows:
  a. Three ECM connectors.
  b. Five cowl connectors.
  c. Cooling fan ECU connector.
  d. Wire clamp, then remove two nuts and pull engine wire from cowl panel.
12. Remove A/C compressor leaving pressure hoses connected. Position compressor and hoses aside.
13. Remove front exhaust pipe.
14. Remove both drive axles, then the power steering pressure tube.

15. Disconnect hydraulic cooling fan pressure hose.
16. Remove power steering pump, do not disconnect hoses and position aside.
17. Remove four left engine mount attaching bolts, then disconnect mount.
18. Remove two right rear engine mount hole plugs, then the four bolts and mount.
19. Remove four engine mounting shock absorber attaching bolts.
20. Remove three front right engine mount attaching bolts, then the mount.
21. Install suitable engine lifting equipment, then remove coolant reservoir tank.
22. Disconnect all ground straps, then remove No. 1 righthand engine mount three attaching bolts and mount.
23. Remove engine moving control rod and No. 2 right engine mount.
24. Remove engine and transaxle assembly, then the starter.
25. Separate engine/transaxle assembly.
26. Reverse procedure to install. Reset audio anti-theft system, if necessary, as outlined under "Precautions."

INTAKE MANIFOLD
REPLACE

Refer to "Cylinder Head, Replace" for procedure.

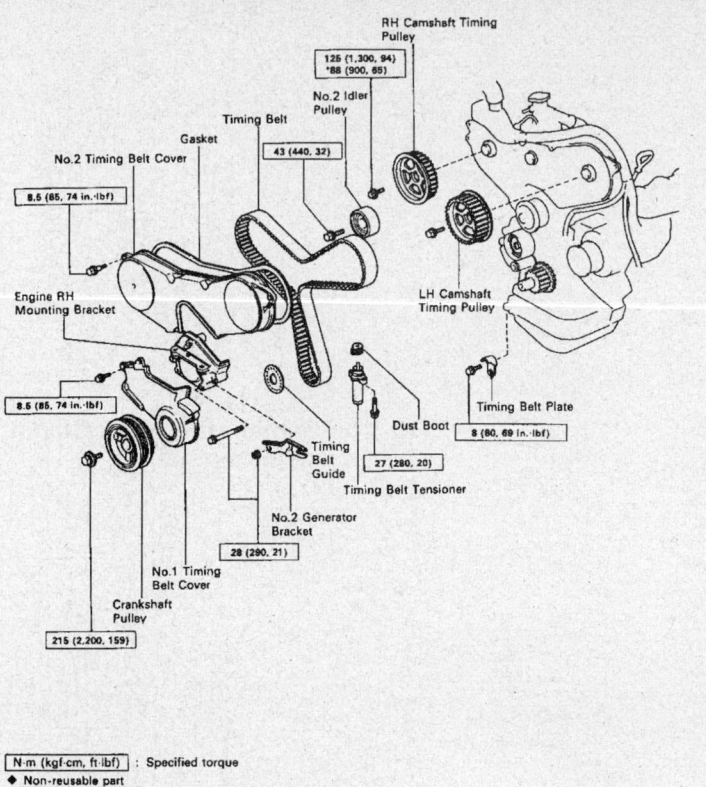

TY1069100102030X

Fig. 9   Cylinder head replacement (Part 3 of 5)

EXHAUST MANIFOLD
REPLACE

Refer to "Cylinder Head, Replace" for procedure.

CYLINDER HEAD
REPLACE

1. **On models equipped with coded audio anti-theft systems,** refer to "Precautions" for code procedures.
2. **On all models,** remove battery tray and cruise control module.
3. Raise and support vehicle, drain coolant, then remove air cleaner case, volume air flow meter and air cleaner hose, **Fig. 9.**
4. Disconnect ground straps and remove righthand engine mount.
5. Disconnect radiator and heater hoses.
6. Disconnect fuel lines, then the hydraulic motor pressure hose.
7. Remove valve cover, then the emission control valve set as follows:
   a. Disconnect vacuum hoses from fuel pressure control vacuum switching valve (VSV), fuel pressure regulator, cylinder head from rear plate, intake air control valve VSV, EGR vacuum modulator and EGR valve.
   b. Disconnect air control valve, fuel pressure and EGR VSV connectors.
   c. Remove two nuts, then emission control valve set.
8. Remove air intake chamber as follows:
   a. Remove all vacuum hoses, then

data link connector No. 1 and No. 2 ground straps.
   b. Remove hydraulic motor pressure hose from air intake chamber, then the ground strap.
   c. Disconnect righthand oxygen sensor connector clamp from power steering pressure tube, then the tube.
   d. Disconnect power steering air hoses.
9. Remove No. 1 engine hanger, then the air chamber stay.
10. Remove EGR pipe, then disconnect the following connectors:
   a. Throttle position sensor.
   b. IAC valve.
   c. EGR gas temperature sensor.
   d. A/C idle-up valve.
   e. Camshaft position sensor.
11. Disconnect all vacuum, two water bypass and air assist hoses.
12. Remove air intake chamber and gasket.
13. Remove intake air control valve from air intake chamber.
14. Remove A/C idle-up VSV from air intake chamber.
15. Remove throttle body from air intake chamber.
16. Disconnect EGR valve and vacuum modulator from air intake chamber, then engine wire from engine lefthand

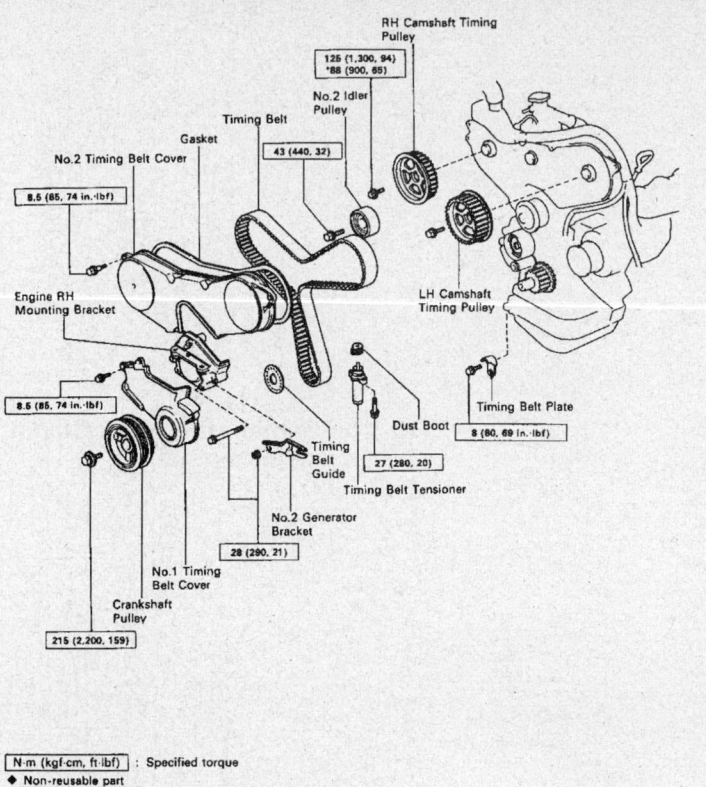

TY1069100102040X

Fig. 9   Cylinder head replacement (Part 4 of 5)

side as follows:
   a. Three injector connectors.
   b. Three ignition coil connectors.
17. Disconnect wiring from timing belt cover, engine rear and righthand rear side, then remove ignition coils and spark plugs.
18. Remove front exhaust pipe then the timing belts following procedure outlined under "Timing Belt, Replace."
19. Remove camshaft timing pulleys and No. 2 idler pulley.
20. Remove No. 3 timing belt cover, then the cylinder head rear plate.
21. Remove water inlet pipe and air assist and vacuum hoses.
22. Remove intake manifold deliver pipes and injectors, then the fuel pressure regulator from lefthand delivery pipe.
23. Remove thermal vacuum valve (TVV) from intake manifold.
24. Remove fuel pulsation damper and No. 1 and No. 2 fuel pipes.
25. Remove delivery pipes and injectors, than the water outlet.
26. Remove engine hangers, then the lefthand exhaust manifold.
27. Remove oil dipstick and tube, then the power steering bracket.
28. Remove EGR pipe, then the righthand exhaust manifold.
29. Remove valve covers, then the camshafts as follows:

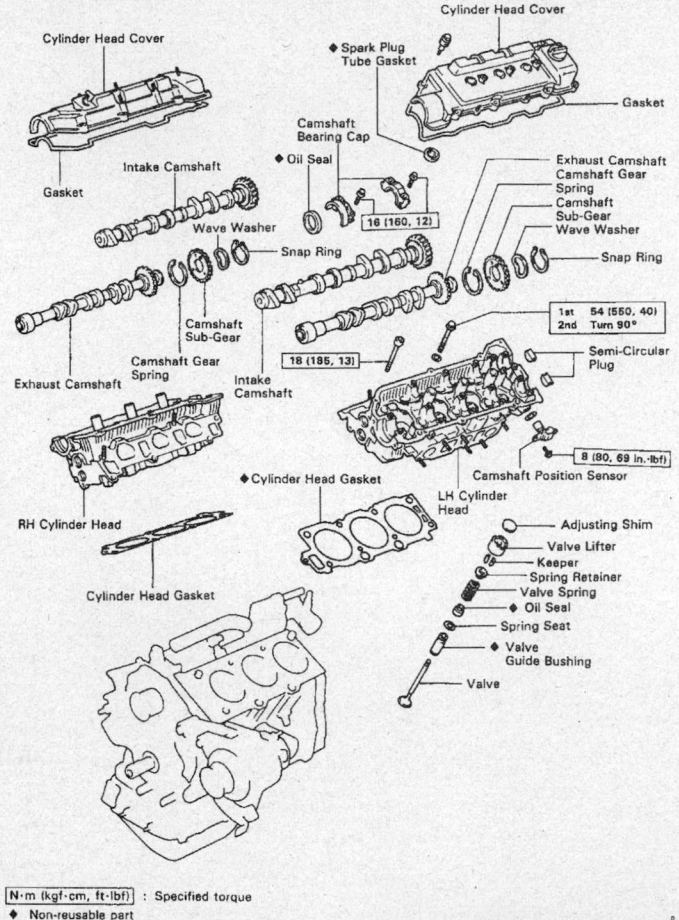

N·m (kgf·cm, ft·lbf) : Specified torque
◆ Non-reusable part

TY1069100102050X

Fig. 9   Cylinder head replacement (Part 5 of 5)

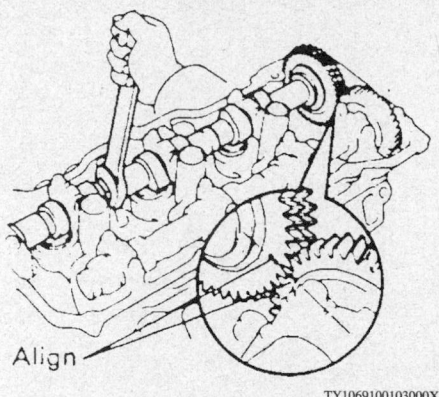

TY1069100103000X

Fig. 10   Camshaft drive & driven gear alignment

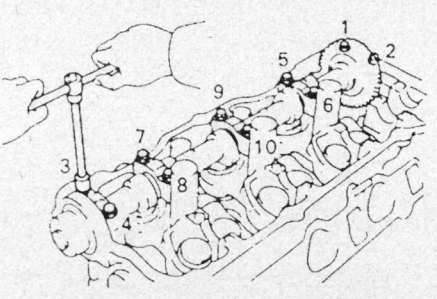

TY1069100105000X

Fig. 13   Righthand cylinder head exhaust camshaft bearing cap bolt loosening sequence

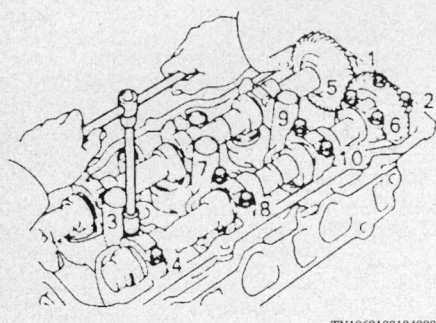

TY1069100104000X

Fig. 11   Righthand cylinder head intake camshaft bearing cap bolt loosening sequence. 1996–97

a. **Camshaft thrust clearance is small. To remove, hold camshaft level and pull upward.**
b. Remove righthand cylinder head intake camshaft. Align timing marks on camshaft drive and driven gears by turning camshaft with a suitable wrench, **Fig. 10.**
c. Install suitable bolt to secure exhaust camshaft sub-gear to driven gear.
d. Uniformly loosen and remove ten bearing cap attaching bolts in several passes, in sequence shown, **Figs. 11 and 12,** then the five bear-

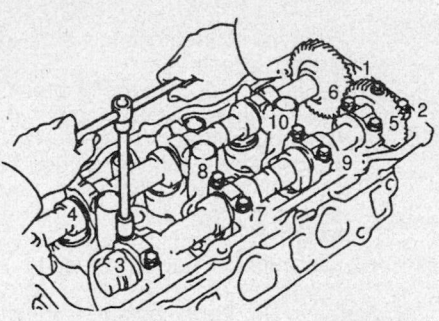

TY1069900496000X

Fig. 12   Righthand cylinder head intake camshaft bearing cap bolt loosening sequence. 1998-99

ing caps and intake camshaft assembly.
e. Remove righthand cylinder head exhaust camshaft.
f. Using sequence shown in **Fig. 13,** remove ten bearing cap bolts in several passes.
g. Remove five bearing caps, oil seal and exhaust camshaft.
h. Align lefthand cylinder head camshaft drive and driven gears by turning camshaft, **Fig. 10.**
i. Install suitable bolt to secure left-hand cylinder head exhaust cam-

shaft sub-gear to driven gear.
j. Uniformly loosen and remove ten lefthand cylinder head intake camshaft bearing cap attaching bolts in several passes, then remove five bearing caps and intake camshaft, **Fig. 14.**
k. Using sequence shown in **Fig. 15,** remove ten bearing cap attaching bolts in several passes.
l. Remove five bearing caps, oil seal and exhaust camshaft assembly. Arrange bearing caps in correct order.
30. Remove cylinder head assemblies as follows:
a. Using a suitable tool, remove two 8 mm recessed cylinder head bolts.
b. Using sequence shown in **Fig. 16,** loosen and remove cylinder head attaching bolts in several passes,
c. Lift cylinder head(s) from cylinder block dowels and position cylinder head on suitable work area. If cylinder head is difficult to remove, use suitable wedge to separate cylinder head from block. **Do not damage cylinder head to engine block mating surface.**
31. Reverse procedure to install, noting the following:
a. Place cylinder head(s) onto block. Place a new cylinder head gasket in position on block as shown in **Fig. 17.**
b. Apply a light coat of clean engine oil onto bolt threads and under bolt

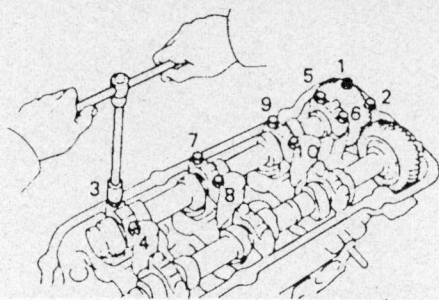

Fig. 14 Lefthand cylinder head intake camshaft bearing cap bolt loosening sequence

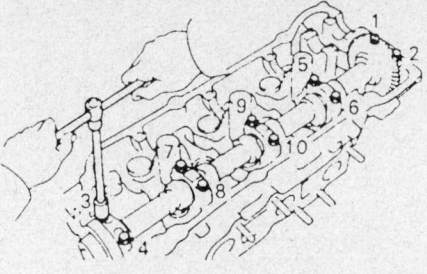

Fig. 15 Lefthand cylinder head exhaust camshaft bearing cap bolt loosening sequence. 1MZ-FE

— 12 Pointed Head Bolt

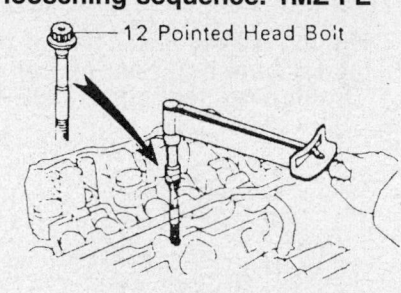

Front ◄—

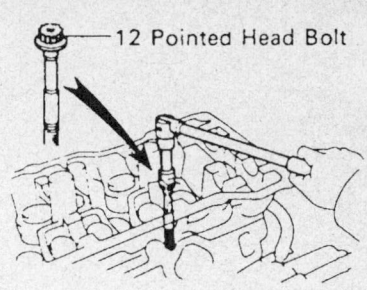

Fig. 16 Cylinder head bolt loosening sequence

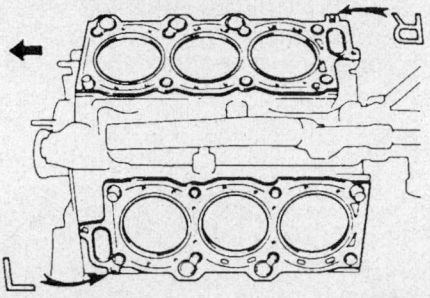

Fig. 17 Cylinder head gasket identification

heads, then install 12–sided cylinder head attaching bolts.

c. Using sequence shown in **Fig. 18** **torque** bolts in several passes to 40 ft. lbs.

d. Place a dab of paint or scribe a mark on front of each bolt head, then tighten bolts in correct sequence an additional 90.°

e. Ensure that paint mark is now at a 90° angle to front.

f. Install two recessed head bolts and **torque** to 13 ft. lbs.

32. Install camshaft assemblies as follows:

a. To install exhaust camshaft of righthand cylinder head, apply new engine oil to thrust portion and journal of camshaft.

b. Place exhaust camshaft at a 90° angle of timing mark, then apply suitable grease to oil seal lip.

c. Install oil seal to camshaft, then apply seal packing part No. 08826-00080, or equivalent, to No. 1 bearing cap.

d. Install five bearing caps in their proper locations, **Fig. 19**.

e. Apply light coat of engine oil on threads and under heads of bearing cap bolts, then install uniformly, tighten ten bearing caps bolts in several passes to specification as shown in **Fig. 20**.

33. To install intake camshaft of righthand cylinder head, proceed as follows:

a. Apply new engine oil to thrust portion and journal of camshaft.

b. Place intake camshaft at a 90° angle of timing mark.

c. Install five bearing caps in their

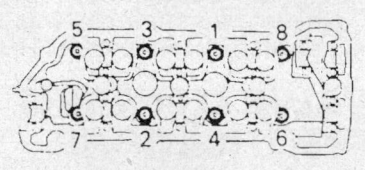

Front ◄—

Fig. 18 Cylinder head bolt tightening sequence

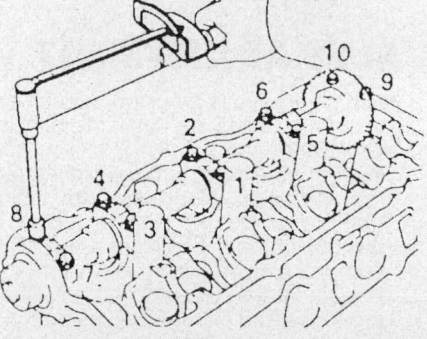

Fig. 20 Righthand cylinder head exhaust camshaft bearing cap bolt tightening sequence

proper locations, **Fig. 21**.

d. Apply light coat of engine oil on threads and under heads of bearing cap bolts, then install and tighten ten bearing caps bolts in several passes to specification as shown in **Figs. 22 and 23**.

e. Remove service bolt.

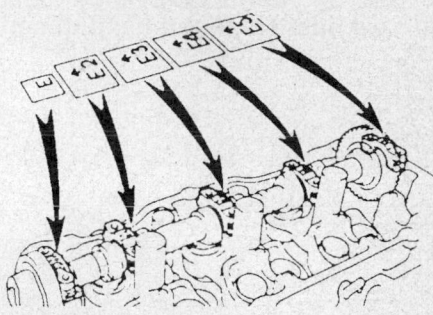

Fig. 19 Righthand cylinder head exhaust camshaft bearing cap locations

34. To install lefthand cylinder head exhaust camshaft, proceed as follows:

a. Apply suitable grease to thrust portion of camshaft, then to new oil seal.

b. Apply seal packing material part No. 08826-00080, or equivalent, to bearing No. 1, then install five bearing caps in their proper locations, **Fig. 24**.

c. Apply light coat of engine oil on threads and under heads of bearing cap bolts, then install and tighten ten bearing caps bolts in several passes to specification, **Figs. 25 and 26**.

35. To install lefthand cylinder head intake camshaft, proceed as follows:

a. Apply suitable grease to thrust portion of camshaft, then to new oil seal.

b. Align timing marks of camshaft drive and driven gears, **Fig. 10**.

c. Place intake camshaft on cylinder

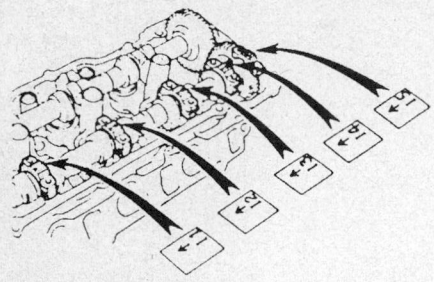

Fig. 21 Righthand cylinder head intake camshaft bearing cap locations

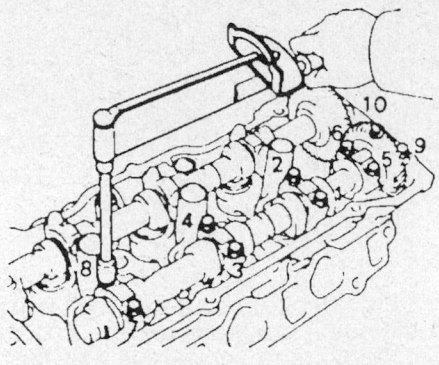

Fig. 22 Righthand cylinder head intake camshaft bearing cap bolt tightening sequence. 1996–97

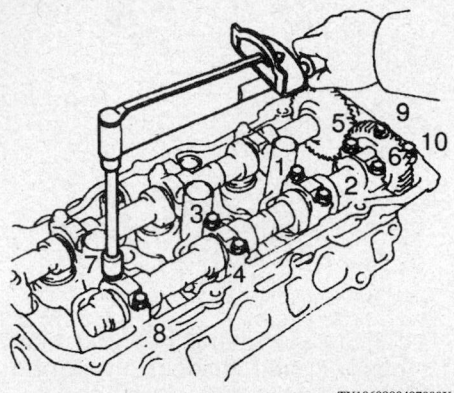

Fig. 23 Righthand cylinder head intake camshaft bearing cap bolt tightening sequence. 1998–99

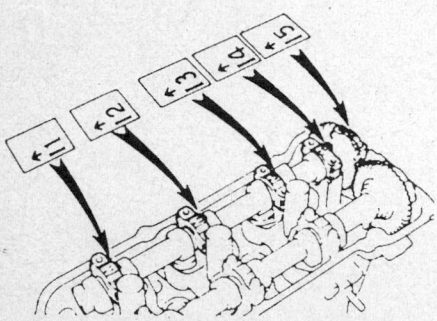

Fig. 24 Lefthand cylinder head exhaust camshaft bearing cap locations

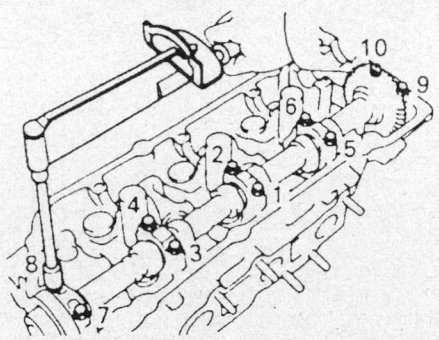

Fig. 25 Lefthand cylinder head exhaust camshaft bearing cap bolt tightening sequence. 1996–97

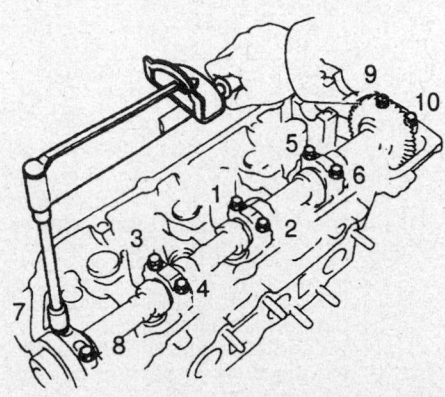

Fig. 26 Lefthand cylinder head exhaust camshaft bearing cap bolt tightening sequence. 1998-99

Fig. 27 Lefthand cylinder head intake camshaft bearing cap locations

VALVE CLEARANCE SPECIFICATIONS

Valve clearance on cold engines should be .006–.010 inch, intake and .010–.014 inch exhaust.

VALVE ADJUSTMENT

Valve clearance is adjusted through the use of shims. Shims are available in increments of .0020 inch.

1. With engine cold, turn crankshaft pulley and align its groove with timing mark "0" of No. 1 timing belt cover. In this position No. 1 cylinder is at TDC of compression stroke.
2. Ensure intake valves on No. 1 cylinder are loose and exhaust valves on No. 1 cylinder are tight. If not turn crankshaft one complete revolution (360°) and align the timing marks.
3. Using a feeler gauge, measure clearance between valve lifter and camshaft. Record valve clearance measurements that are not to specification.
4. With engine set to No. 1 cylinder at

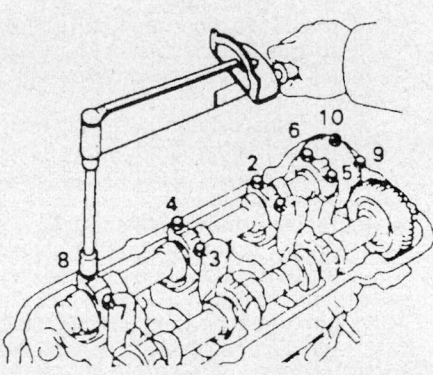

Fig. 28 Lefthand cylinder head intake camshaft bearing cap bolt tightening sequence

TDC compression stroke, check the following valves:
a. Both intake valves on righthand intake camshaft No. 1 cylinder.

head, then install five bearing caps in proper locations, **Fig. 27.**
d. Apply light coat of engine oil on threads and under heads of bearing cap bolts, then install and tighten ten bearing caps bolts in several passes to specification, **Fig. 28.**
e. Remove service bolt.
36. Reverse remaining procedure to install, noting the following:
a. Tighten fasteners to specifications.
b. Adjust valves following procedure outlined under " Valve Adjustment."
c. Reset audio anti-theft system, if necessary, as outlined under "Precautions."

mm (in.)

Shim No.	Thickness	Shim No.	Thickness
1	2.50 (0.0984)	10	2.95 (0.1161)
2	2.55 (0.1004)	11	3.00 (0.1181)
3	2.60 (0.1024)	12	3.05 (0.1201)
4	2.65 (0.1043)	13	3.10 (0.1220)
5	2.70 (0.1063)	14	3.15 (0.1240)
6	2.75 (0.1083)	15	3.20 (0.1260)
7	2.80 (0.1102)	16	3.25 (0.1280)
8	2.85 (0.1122)	17	3.30 (0.1299)
9	2.90 (0.1142)		

TY1069100137000X

Fig. 29 Valve clearance shim chart

   b. Both exhaust valves on lefthand exhaust camshaft No. 2 cylinder.
   c. Both exhaust valves on righthand exhaust camshaft No. 3 cylinder.
   d. Both intake valves on lefthand intake camshaft No. 6 cylinder.
5. Turn crankshaft ⅔ of a revolution (240°) and check the following valves:
   a. Both intake valves on lefthand intake camshaft No. 2 cylinder.
   b. Both intake valves on righthand intake camshaft No. 3 cylinder.
   c. Both exhaust valves on lefthand exhaust camshaft No. 4 cylinder.
   d. Both exhaust valves on righthand exhaust camshaft No. 5 cylinder.
6. Turn crankshaft another ⅔ of a revolution (240°) and check the following valve:
   a. Both exhaust valves on righthand exhaust camshaft No. 1 cylinder.
   b. Both intake valves on lefthand intake camshaft No. 4 cylinder.
   c. Both intake valves on righthand intake camshaft No. 5 cylinder.
   d. Both exhaust valves on lefthand exhaust camshaft No. 6 cylinder.
7. Turn crankshaft so that cam lobe for valve that is to be adjusted faces up, then using suitable tools, depress valve lifter between camshaft and valve lifter. **Before depressing valve lifter, position notch toward spark plug.**
8. Remove adjusting shim with suitable small screwdriver and magnetic finger.
9. Determine replacement shim size as follows:
   a. Using suitable micrometer, measure thickness of removed shim.
   b. New shim thickness should equal measured valve clearance less clearance specification plus thickness of used shim.
   c. Select new shim with thickness as close as possible to value calculated in step b, **Fig. 29.**
10. Install new shim, then recheck valve clearance.

VALVE GUIDES

1. Using a suitable tool and hammer, strike valve guide bushing to break it off at cylinder head casting.
2. Heat cylinder head to 176–212°F.

3. Using suitable valve guide removal tool, tap out bushing.
4. Install snap ring on new valve guide, then install new valve guide using tool as outlined above and driving in from reverse side of removal.
5. Ream new valve guide, if necessary. Refer to "Valve Specifications" for stem clearances.

HYDRAULIC LIFTERS
REPLACE

   Check lifters for excessive wear and/or damage. Replace worn or damaged valve lifters as required. Lubricate hydraulic valve lifter before installation.

TIMING BELT
REPLACE
REMOVAL

1. **On models equipped with coded audio anti-theft systems,** refer to "Precautions" for code procedures.
2. **On all models,** disconnect coolant reservoir hose.
3. Remove coolant reservoir tank.
4. Remove alternator drive belt.
5. Remove righthand front wheel and fender apron seal.
6. Remove power steering drive belt and disconnect ground straps.
7. Remove righthand engine mount stay.
8. Remove engine movement control rod and No. 2 righthand engine mount bracket.
9. Loosen alternator pivot bolt, then remove alternator No. 2 bracket.
10. Using crankshaft pulley bolt tool Nos. 09213-54015 and 09330-00021, or equivalents, remove crankshaft pulley bolt.
11. Using crankshaft pulley puller tool Nos. 09950–50011 (09951–05010, 09952–05010, 09953–05010, 09953–05020, 09954–05020) or equivalent, remove crankshaft pulley.
12. Remove No. 1 timing belt cover.
13. Remove engine wiring to No. 3 timing belt cover attaching bolt, then disconnect engine wiring from clamp.
14. Remove No. 2 timing belt cover.
15. Remove righthand engine mount bracket.
16. Remove timing belt guide.
17. If original timing belt will be used, ensure there are four alignment (installation) marks on timing belt by turning crankshaft pulley. The four marks should be as follows; R-CAM (indicating righthand camshaft), L-CAM (indicating lefthand camshaft), CR (indicating crankshaft) and dots across timing belt located between idler pulley and crankshaft sprocket. If original timing marks have disappeared, place new installation marks before removing timing belt, **Fig. 30.**
18. Place No. 1 cylinder at TDC of compression stroke by turning crankshaft pulley and aligning pulley groove (v notch) with No. 1 timing belt cover timing mark "0." Ensure timing marks on

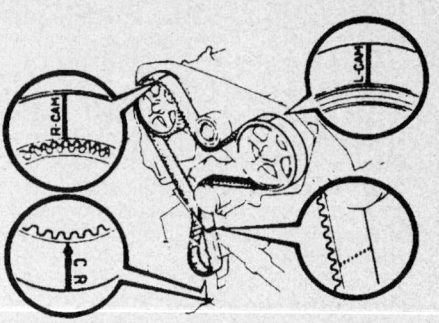

TY1069100138000X

Fig. 30 Sprocket & timing belt installation alignment

camshaft timing sprockets and No. 3 timing belt cover are properly aligned. If not, turn crankshaft sprocket 360° (one complete revolution) and align marks.
19. Remove timing belt tensioner.
20. Remove timing belt from camshaft timing sprocket as follows:
   a. If installation marks have disappeared, before removing timing belt, place new installation marks on timing belt to match timing marks on camshaft timing sprockets.
   b. Loosen tension between lefthand and righthand camshaft timing sprockets by slightly turning righthand camshaft timing sprocket clockwise.
   c. Remove timing belt from camshaft timing sprocket.
   d. If installation marks have disappeared, after removing timing belt from camshaft sprockets, place a new installation mark on timing belt to match end of No. 1 timing belt cover.
21. Remove sprockets, No. 2 idler pulley and crankshaft pulley. When crankshaft pulley bolt is loosened, position of timing mark on crankshaft pulley and installation mark may slip. Check and align marks as necessary.
22. Remove No. 1 timing belt cover and timing belt guide.
23. Remove timing belt. If installation marks have disappeared, place new installation marks on timing belt to match drilled mark on crankshaft timing sprocket.

INSTALLATION

1. Install crankshaft timing sprocket and No. 1 idler pulley, if removed. Tighten idler pulley attaching bolt to specification.
2. With engine cold, temporarily install timing belt. Remove any oil or water from crankshaft timing sprocket, No. 1 idler and water pump pulley. Align installation mark on timing belt with drilled mark on crankshaft timing sprocket.
3. Install timing belt onto crankshaft timing sprocket, No. 1 idler and water pump pulley.
4. Install timing belt guide.
5. Install No. 1 timing belt cover.

6. Install crankshaft pulley and tighten attaching bolt to specification.
7. Install No. 2 idler pulley and tighten attaching bolt to specification.
8. Install lefthand camshaft timing sprocket, slide sprocket with flange side facing outward. Align knock pin hole on camshaft with knock pin groove on timing sprocket and install knock pin. Tighten attaching bolt to specification.
9. To correctly obtain crankshaft positioning, proceed as follows:
   a. Place No. 1 cylinder at TDC of compression stroke.
   b. To accomplish this, turn crankshaft pulley and align groove on pulley with "0" mark on No. 1 timing cover.
10. To correctly obtain righthand camshaft timing sprocket position, proceed as follows:
    a. Turn camshaft and align knock pin hole on camshaft with timing mark on No. 3 timing belt cover.
    b. In this position, righthand camshaft is correctly aligned.
11. To correctly obtain lefthand camshaft timing sprocket position, proceed as follows:
    a. Turn camshaft timing sprocket and align timing marks on camshaft timing sprocket and No. 3 timing belt cover.
    b. In this position, lefthand camshaft is correctly aligned.
12. Install timing belt onto lefthand camshaft timing sprocket. Ensure installation mark on timing belt matches end of No. 1 timing belt cover. If installation marks do not align properly, shift meshing of timing belt and crankshaft timing sprocket until they align. Do not over shift timing belt meshing.
13. Remove any water, oil or dirt from lefthand camshaft timing sprocket.
14. Using a suitable tool, slightly turn lefthand camshaft timing sprocket clockwise. Align installation mark on timing belt with timing mark on camshaft timing sprocket and hang timing belt on lefthand camshaft timing sprocket. Using a suitable tool, align timing marks on lefthand camshaft sprocket and No. 3 timing belt cover. Ensure timing belt has tension between crankshaft timing sprocket and lefthand camshaft sprocket.
15. Install righthand camshaft timing sprocket and timing belt on sprocket. Remove any water, oil or dirt from righthand camshaft sprocket and No. 2 idler pulley. Hang timing belt on righthand camshaft timing sprocket. Align timing marks on righthand camshaft timing sprocket and No. 3 timing belt cover. Slide righthand camshaft timing sprocket onto camshaft assembly. Using a suitable tool, align knock pin hole on camshaft with knock pin groove on sprocket, then install pin.
16. Using a suitable tool, install and tighten attaching bolt to specification.
17. Correctly set timing belt tensioner as follows:
    a. Place a plate washer between tensioner and a press tool block.

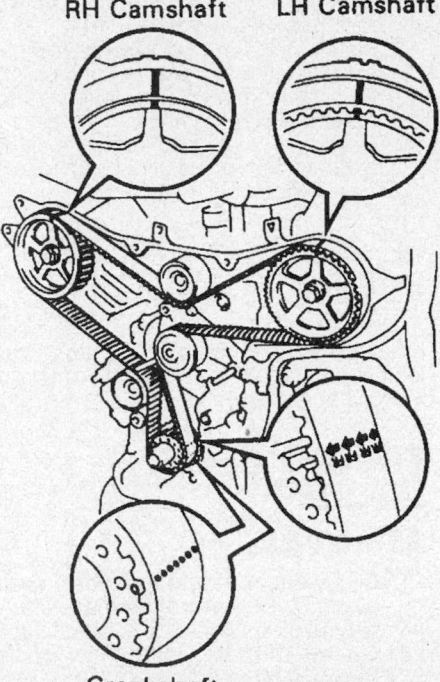

RH Camshaft   LH Camshaft

Crankshaft

TY1069100139000X

Fig. 31   Timing mark inspection

b. Using a suitable press, slowly apply press force (approximately 220 lbs., more may be needed) to pushrod.
c. Align holes on pushrod and housing, then pass a .049 inch (1.27 mm) hexagon wrench through alignment holes to keep setting position of pushrod. Release press force.
18. Install timing belt tensioner. Tighten attaching bolts to specification.
19. Remove wrench installed in step 17c.
20. Check valve timing as follows:
    a. Turn crankshaft pulley two complete revolutions from TDC to TDC. Turn crankshaft clockwise.
    b. Ensure each pulley/sprocket aligns with timing marks, **Fig. 31**.
    c. If timing marks do not align, remove timing belt and correctly install it.
21. Reverse removal procedure to complete installation. Reset audio anti-theft system, if necessary, as outlined under "Precautions."

CAMSHAFT
REPLACE

Refer to "Cylinder Head, Replace" for camshaft removal procedures.

PISTON & ROD ASSEMBLY

Pistons are available in standard and oversizes of .020 inch (.50 mm). When assembling piston onto connecting rod, ensure mark on top of piston and mark on connecting rod are on same side, **Fig. 32**.

When installing piston and connecting rod assembly, ensure mark on top of piston is facing toward front of engine.

MAIN & ROD BEARINGS

Main and connecting rod bearings are available in standard and undersizes of .010 inch (.25 mm).

OIL PAN
REPLACE

1. **On models equipped with coded audio anti-theft systems,** refer to "Precautions" for code procedures.
2. **On all models,** drain engine oil into a suitable container, then remove oil dipstick.
3. Remove timing belt and pulleys as outlined under " Timing Belt, Replace."
4. Disconnect crankshaft position sensor electrical connector, engine wiring from clamp and alternator electrical connector.
5. Remove alternator wire attaching nut and disconnect, then the engine wire from three clamps.
6. Remove six No. 3 timing belt cover attaching bolts, then the cover.
7. Remove alternator and crankshaft position sensor.
8. Remove four oil hole cover plates.
9. Remove A/C compressor drive belt. Disconnect electrical connector. Remove compressor, do not disconnect hoses, then position assembly aside.
10. Remove A/C compressor housing bracket.
11. Remove front exhaust pipe and bracket.
12. Remove flywheel housing undercover.
13. Remove two No. 1 oil pan to transaxle attaching bolts.
14. Remove No. 2 oil pan attaching bolt, then using suitable blade between No. 1 and No. 2 oil pans, cut off sealer and remove No. 2 oil pan.
15. Remove oil strainer.
16. Remove remaining No. 1 oil pan attaching bolts, then using suitable screwdriver pry downward on oil pan to remove.
17. Remove oil baffle plate, then the oil pump with O-ring.
18. Reverse procedure to install. Reset audio anti-theft system, if necessary, as outlined under "Precautions."

OIL PUMP
REPLACE

Refer to "Oil Pan, Replace" for procedure.

OIL PUMP SERVICE

1. Remove driven and drive rotor, then the relief valve.
2. Inspect relief valve. Replace if worn or damaged.
3. Using a suitable feeler gauge, measure clearance between driven rotor and pump body. Clearance obtained

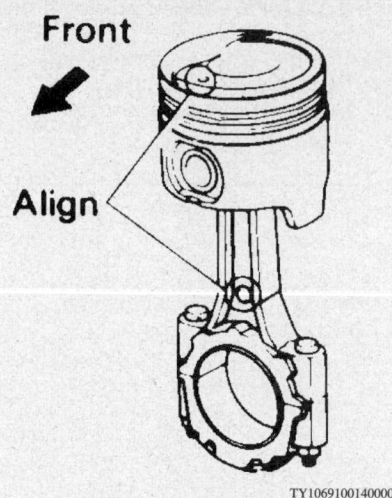

Fig. 32 Piston & connecting rod assembly

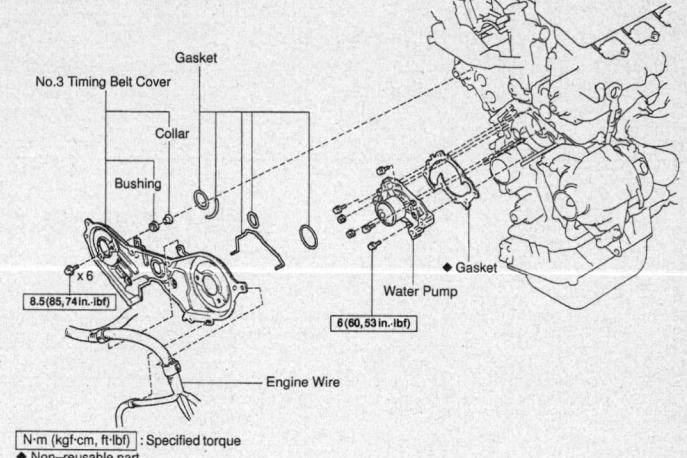

Fig. 33 Water pump assembly

should be .0039–.0069 inch and should not exceed .0118 inch. If not, replace oil pump rotor set and/or pump body.

4. Using a feeler gauge, measure clearance between both rotor tips. Clearance obtained should be .0043–.0094 inch and should not exceed .0138 inch. If not, replace oil pump rotor set.

5. Using a suitable feeler gauge and a flat block, measure side clearance by placing flat block (square edge) across pump body and measuring (using feeler gauge) between flat edge and top of rotor assembly. Clearance obtained should be .0012–.0035 inch and should not exceed .0059 inch. If not, replace oil pump rotor set and/or pump body assembly.

BELT TENSION DATA

Belt tension is as follows using a belt tension gauge. A new belt is considered used after five minutes of use.

Belt	New Lbs.	Used Lbs.
Alternator	170–180	95–135
Power Steer.	150–185	95–135

COOLING SYSTEM BLEED

1. Remove radiator cap, then drain coolant from engine and radiator drain cocks into a suitable container. Engine drain cocks are located at front center and rear right of cylinder block.
2. Close drain cocks and tighten to specification.
3. To release air from system, loosen union bolt of water outlet five revolutions.
4. Slowly refill system with coolant, then tighten union bolt to specification.
5. Install radiator cap, then start engine and check for leaks.
6. Check coolant level and fill as necessary.

THERMOSTAT
REPLACE

1. **On models equipped with coded audio anti-theft systems,** refer to "Precautions" for code procedures.
2. **On all models,** drain engine coolant into a suitable container.
3. Remove air cleaner cap, volume air flow meter and air cleaner hose, as follows:
   a. Disconnect volume air flow meter electrical connector and wire clamp.
   b. Disconnect accelerator cable clamp and PCV hose.
   c. Loosen air cleaner hose clamp bolt.
   d. Disconnect four air cleaner air cap clips.
   e. Remove air cleaner cap, volume air meter and air cleaner hose as an assembly.
4. Disconnect heater hose and hydraulic motor pressure hose.
5. Remove two water inlet to cylinder head engine wiring attaching nuts, then disconnect wiring.
6. Disconnect engine coolant temperature sensor (ECT) electrical connector.
7. Remove water inlet pipe and O-ring.
8. Remove water inlet, then the thermostat and gasket.
9. Reverse procedure to install. Reset audio anti-theft system, if necessary, as outlined under "Precautions."

WATER PUMP
REPLACE

1. **On models equipped with coded audio anti-theft systems,** refer to "Precautions" for code procedures.
2. **On all models,** drain engine coolant into a suitable container.
3. Remove time belt and pulleys as outlined under "Timing, Belt, Replace."
4. Remove No. 2 idler pulley, **Fig. 33.**
5. Disconnect engine wiring from No. 3 timing belt cover, then remove cover.
6. Remove water pump attaching bolts, then the water pump.

7. Reverse procedure to install. Reset audio anti-theft system, if necessary, as outlined under "Precautions."

RADIATOR
REPLACE

1. **On models equipped with coded audio anti-theft systems,** refer to "Precautions" for code procedures.
2. **On all models,** raise and support vehicle.
3. Drain coolant from engine and radiator into a suitable container.
4. Remove battery and tray, then disconnect cruise control actuator and mounting from body.
5. Disconnect upper radiator and coolant reservoir hoses from radiator.
6. Disconnect lower radiator hose at engine, then transaxle oil cooler extension lines.
7. Disconnect electric cooling fan connectors, then cruise control cable from holder on fan shroud.
8. Remove upper radiator mounts, then lift out radiator and cooling fans as a unit.
9. Remove transaxle cooler extension lines and lower radiator from radiator.
10. Remove electric cooling fans and shrouds.
11. Remove lower radiator mounts.
12. Reverse procedure to install. Reset audio anti-theft system, if necessary, as outlined under "Precautions."

FUEL PUMP
REPLACE

1. **On models equipped with coded audio anti-theft systems,** refer to "Precautions" for code procedures.
2. **On all models,** remove rear seat cushion, then floor service hole cover.
3. Remove fuel pump lead wire.
4. Using suitable tool, disconnect fuel pipe and hose from fuel pump bracket.
5. Remove fuel pump bracket and gasket from fuel tank.

6. Remove fuel pump from fuel pump bracket.
7. Reverse procedure to install. Reset audio anti-theft system, if necessary, as outlined under "Precautions."

FUEL FILTER
REPLACE

1. Remove fuel pump as outlined under "Fuel Pump Replace."
2. Remove fuel sender gauge. **Ensure** that arm of sender gauge should not bend.
3. Remove screw, then pull out filter and remove O-ring from filter.
4. Reverse procedure to install.

TIGHTENING SPECIFICATIONS

Year	Component	Torque, Ft. Lbs.
1996–99	A/C Compressor To Alternator Bracket	18
	A/C Compressor To Cylinder Block	18
	Air Intake Chamber Stay To Air Intake Chamber	14
	Air Intake Chamber Stay To Cylinder Head	14
	Air Intake Chamber To Intake Manifold	32
	Camshaft Bearing Cap To Cylinder Head	12
	Camshaft Timing Pulley	⑤
	Connecting Rod Cap	④
	Coolant Drain Cock To Cylinder Block	29
	Crankshaft Position Sensor	72①
	Crankshaft Pulley	159
	Cylinder Head	②
	Cylinder Head Cover	72①
	Delivery Pipe To Intake Chamber	84①
	Drain Hose Clamp To Cylinder Block	14
	Driveplate	61
	EGR Pipe To Right hand Exhaust Manifold	108①
	Emission Control Valve Set To Air Intake Chamber	72①
	Engine Mounting Absorber To Transaxle	35
	Engine Moving Control Rod To No. 2 RH Engine Mount Bracket	47
	Engine RH Mount Bracket To Cylinder Block	21
	Exhaust Manifold	36
	Flywheel	61
	Front Exhaust Pipe To Exhaust Manifold	46
	Front RH Engine Mount To Cylinder Block	47
	Front RH Engine Mount To Front Suspension Member	59
	Fuel Inlet Hose To Fuel Filter	22
	Fuel Pipe To Fuel Pump Bracket	22
	Fuel Pump Bracket To Fuel Tank	35①
	Hydraulic Pressure Pipe To Air Intake Chamber	14
	Intake Manifold	11
	Knock Sensor	29
	LH Engine Mount To Transaxle	47
	Main Bearing Caps	③
	No. 1 Idler Pulley To Oil Pump	25
	No. 1 Oil Pan To Cylinder Block	14
	No. 1 Oil Pan To Oil Pump	72①
	No. 1 Oil Pan To Rear Oil Seal Retainer	72①
	No. 2 Oil Pan To No. 1 Oil Pan	72①
	No. 2 Idler Pulley	32
	No. 3 Timing Belt Cover	84①
	Oil Drain Plug	27
	Oil Hole Cover Plate	72①

Continued

1MZ-FE 3.0L ENGINE

TIGHTENING
SPECIFICATIONS—Continued

Year	Component	Torque, Ft. Lbs.
1996–99	Oil Pan Baffle Plate	72①
	Oil Pressure Switch	108①
	Oil Pump (10 mm Bolt)	72①
	Oil Pump (12 mm Bolt)	14
	Oil Strainer	72①
	Power Steering Pump	31
	Power Steering Pump Bracket	32
	Rear End Plate To Cylinder Block	72①
	Rear Oil Seal Retainer	72①
	RH Engine Mount Stay To Intake Manifold	21
	RH Engine Mount Stay To No. 2 RH Engine Mount Bracket	21
	RH Rear Engine Mount To Cylinder Block	57
	RH Rear Engine Mount To Front Suspension Member	59
	Spark Plug	13
	Throttle Body	14
	Timing Belt Tensioner	20
	Water Bypass Pipe To Cylinder Block	74
	Water Inlet To Housing	72①
	Water Pump	72①

① — Inch lbs.

② — Refer to "Cylinder Head, Replace" for tightening procedure.

③ — First torque to 45 ft. lbs., then tighten an additional 90.°

④ — First torque to 18 ft. lbs., then tighten an additional 90.°

⑤ — With tool No. 09960-10010 (09962-01000), or equivalent, to 65 ft. lbs.; less tool No. 09960-10010 (09962-01000), or equivalent, to 94 ft. lbs.

NOTE: On Air Bag Equipped Models, Refer To "Air Bag System Precautions" Located In The Front Of This Manual For System Disarming & Arming Procedures.

INDEX

PRECAUTIONS
AIR BAG SYSTEMS

Refer to "Air Bag System Precautions" in the front of this manual for system disarming and arming procedures.

AUDIO CODED ANTI-THEFT SYSTEM

Some models are with an audio coded anti-theft system that will disable the radio when the battery cable is disconnected. The system can be identified by the words "ANTI-THEFT SYSTEM" on the cassette tape lid. Obtain three digit customer code for input. Reset system after service as follows:

1. Obtain three digit audio anti-theft code.
2. Depress 1 (PROG) while depressing righthand side of TUNE SEEK button, - - - will appear in tape operation display.
3. To enter the first digit, depress 1 (PROG) button repeatedly until the number of times depressed equals the first digit beginning with zero (depress the 1 button six times if the first digit is five).
4. To enter second digit, depress 2 (APS) button repeatedly until the number of times depressed equals the second digit beginning with zero.
5. To enter third digit, depress 3 (RPT) button repeatedly until the number of times depressed equals the third digit beginning with zero.
6. If - - - is displayed during code input, repeat procedure.
7. When code appears in display, depress and hold SCAN button until SEC appears.
8. When SEC disappears audio system should be operative.
9. If Err is displayed, repeat procedure. **Attempting to input code more than nine times may permanently disable audio system.**

ADJUSTMENTS
CLUTCH PEDAL HEIGHT

1. Measure clutch pedal height as shown, **Fig. 1.**

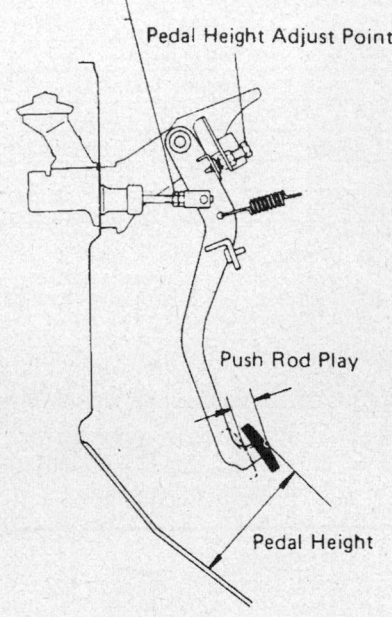

Push Rod Play and Freeplay Adjust Point

Pedal Height Adjust Point

Push Rod Play

Pedal Height

TY5049100013000X

Fig. 1   Clutch pedal height

2. Clutch pedal height should be 6.33–6.72 inches.
3. If clutch pedal height is not as specified, remove lower instrument panel finish panel and air duct.
4. Loosen clutch pedal locknut, then rotate stopper bolt until specified height is achieved.
5. Tighten locknut.
6. Check clutch pedal freeplay by depressing clutch pedal until resistance is felt. Freeplay should be .197–.591 inch. Pushrod play at top of pedal should be .039–.197 inch.
7. If necessary to adjust freeplay, loosen locknut and rotate pushrod until freeplay is as specified.
8. Tighten locknut.
9. Ensure clutch pedal height and freeplay are as specified, then reinstall air duct and finish panel.

HYDRAULIC SYSTEM SERVICE
CLUTCH SLAVE CYLINDER, REPLACE

1. **On models equipped with coded audio anti-theft systems,** refer to "Precautions" for code procedures.
2. **On all models,** remove fluid using syringe, then disconnect clutch line tube.
3. Remove clevis pin and clip with spring washer.
4. Remove clutch slave cylinder.
5. Reverse procedure to install, noting the following:
   a. Tighten fasteners to specifications.
   b. Bleed and adjust system as outlined under "Clutch System Bleed" and "Adjustments."
   c. Reset audio anti-theft system, if necessary, as outlined under "Precautions."

CLUTCH RELEASE CYLINDER, REPLACE

1. **On models equipped with coded audio anti-theft systems,** refer to "Precautions" for code procedures.
2. **On all models,** using suitable tool, disconnect clutch line tube. Use suitable container to catch fluid.
3. Remove release cylinder attaching bolts, then remove cylinder.
4. Reverse procedure to install. Tighten attaching bolts to specifications, then bleed clutch system as outlined under "Clutch System Bleed."

CLUTCH SYSTEM BLEED

If any service is performed on the clutch system or air is suspected in the clutch lines, bleed the system as follows:

1. Fill clutch reservoir with suitable brake fluid. **Do not allow fluid to come in contact with painted surfaces.**
2. Check reservoir frequently, add fluid as required.
3. Connect vinyl tube to bleeder plug, then insert other tube end in half full container of brake fluid.

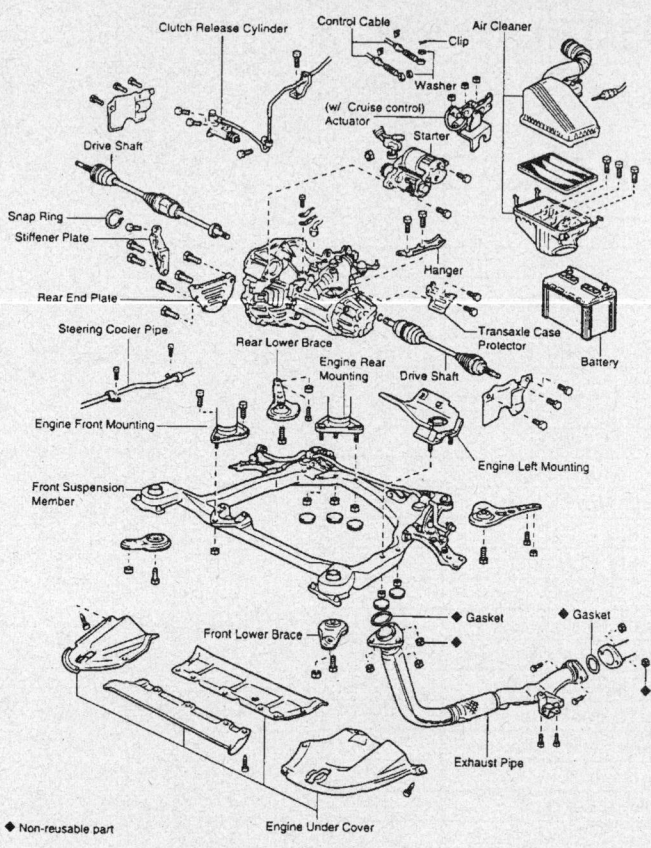

Fig. 2 Transaxle replacement

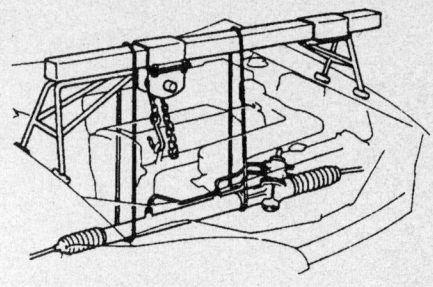

TY5039200206000X

Fig. 3 Engine & steering gear support

4. Slowly pump clutch pedal several times.
5. While depressing pedal, loosen bleeder plug until fluid runs out. Close bleeder plug.
6. Repeat procedure until air bubbles are not evident in the fluid. **Do not reuse the fluid that was bled.**

CLUTCH

REPLACE

1. **On models equipped with coded audio anti-theft systems,** refer to "Precautions" for code procedures.
2. **On all models,** remove transaxle assembly as outlined under "Transaxle, Replace."
3. Place installation alignment marks on clutch cover and flywheel.
4. Loosen each set bolt one turn at a time until spring tension is released.
5. Remove clutch cover attaching bolts, then remove cover and disc.
6. Remove release bearing, fork and boot.
7. Using suitable calipers, measure clutch disc rivet head depth. Minimum rivet depth should be .012 inch. If not as indicated, replace clutch disc.
8. Using suitable dial indicator, measure

flywheel runout. Maximum runout should be .004 inch. If not as indicated, replace flywheel.
9. Measure clutch disc runout. Maximum runout is .031 inch. If not as indicated, replace disc.
10. Reverse procedure to install, noting the following:
    a. Using suitable tool, install clutch disc.
    b. Match clutch cover and flywheel alignment marks, then **torque** cover bolts to 14 ft. lbs. one turn at a time in a criss-cross pattern. Ensure clutch disc and pressure plate remain aligned.
    c. Reset audio anti-theft system, if necessary, as outlined under "Precautions."

TRANSAXLE

REPLACE

1. **On models equipped with coded audio anti-theft systems,** refer to "Precautions" for code procedures.
2. **On all models,** remove air cleaner assembly with air hose, **Fig. 2.**
3. Remove cruise control actuator cover, disconnect electrical connector and dismount actuator assembly.

4. Remove clutch release cylinder and tube clamp.
5. Disconnect starter electrical connector, then remove starter.
6. Disconnect back-up lamp switch electrical connector.
7. Disconnect wire harness clamp, then remove ground cables.
8. Disconnect shifter control cables.
9. Remove three upper transaxle attaching bolts, then disconnect vehicle speed sensor electrical connector.
10. Install suitable engine support fixture to engine, then tie steering gear to support fixture using a suitable material, **Fig. 3.**
11. Remove front wheel and tire assembly.
12. Raise and support vehicle, then remove engine undercovers and side covers.
13. Drain transaxle oil, then remove driveshafts.
14. Remove stabilizer bar bracket, then the steering gear housing to front suspension member (subframe) attaching bolt.
15. Remove exhaust pipe.
16. Remove engine to transaxle stiffener plate.
17. Disconnect front and rear engine mount from suspension member.
18. Using suitable jack stand and wood block, raise engine and transaxle slightly.
19. Remove lefthand engine mount.
20. Disconnect steering cooler pipe from suspension member.
21. Remove fender liner setscrews and front suspension member.
22. Support transaxle assembly using suitable jack stand, then remove transaxle to engine attaching bolts and transaxle assembly.
23. Reverse procedure to install, noting the following:
    a. Tighten attaching nuts and bolts to specifications.
    b. Check front alignment.
    c. Reset audio anti-theft system, if necessary, as outlined under "Precautions."

TIGHTENING SPECIFICATIONS

Year	Component	Torque, Ft. Lbs.
E53 TRANSAXLE		
1996–99	Axle Hub Nut	217
	Back-Up Light Switch	30
	Bleeder Plug	84①
	Clutch Accumulator	14
	Clutch Cover	14
	Clutch Line Union	11
	Clutch Release Cylinder To Transaxle	108①
	Drain Plug	36
	Driveshaft Center Bearing Lock Bolt	24
	Driveshaft To Pinion Shaft	48
	Engine Absorber Lock Bolt	35
	Engine Mount To Suspension Member	59
	Filler Plug	36
	Front Exhaust Pipe To Converter	32
	Front Exhaust Pipe To Manifold	46
	Front Lower Brace To Body	27
	Front Suspension Member To Body	134
	Rear Lower Brace To Body (Bolt)	24
	Rear Lower Brace To Body (Nut)	27
	Selecting Bellcrank Lock Bolt	14
	Shift Lever Lock Bolt	36
	Shift & Select Lever Lock Bolt	14
	Speed Sensor Lock Bolt	72①
	Stabilizer Bar Bracket	14
	Steering Gear Housing To Suspension Member	134
	Stiffener Plate To Engine	13
	Stiffener Plate To Transaxle	27
	Transaxle To Engine (10 mm Bolt)	34
	Transaxle To Engine (12 mm Bolt)	47
	Transaxle To Starter	29
S51 TRANSAXLE		
1996–97	Axle Hub Nut	137
	Back-Up Lamp Switch	33
	Clutch Release Cylinder To Housing	108①
	Clutch Release Bearing Retainer	60①
	Control Shaft Cover	27
	Drain Plug	36
	Driveshaft Center Bearing Lock Bolt	24
	Engine Mount To Sub Frame	59
	Filler Plug	36
	Front Exhaust Pipe To Center Pipe	32
	Front Exhaust Pipe To Converter	46
	Input Shaft Oil Receiver	60①
	Output Shaft Front Bearing Lock Plate	13
	Reverse Shift Arm Bracket	13
	Side Bearing Retainer	13
	Starter To Clutch Housing	29
	Stiffener Plate To Clutch Housing	27
	Straight Screw Plug (Reverse Restrict Pin)	108①
	Straight Screw Plug (Shift Fork Shaft)	108①
	Sub Frame To Body	134
	Transaxle Case	22
	Transaxle Case Protector	13

Continued

TIGHTENING
SPECIFICATIONS—Continued

Year	Component	Torque, Ft. Lbs.
S51 TRANSAXLE		
1996–97	Transaxle To Engine (8 mm)	96①
	Transaxle To Engine (10 mm)	34
	Transaxle To Engine (12 mm)	47
	Transaxle To Starter	29

① — Inch lbs.

Rear Axle & Suspension

NOTE: On Air Bag Equipped Models, Refer To "Air Bag System Precautions" Located In The Front Of This Manual For System Disarming & Arming Procedures.

INDEX

PRECAUTIONS
AIR BAG SYSTEMS

Refer to "Air Bag System Precautions" in the front of this manual for system disarming and arming procedures.

AUDIO CODED ANTI-THEFT SYSTEM

Some models are with an audio coded anti-theft system that will disable the radio when the battery cable is disconnected. The system can be identified by the words "ANTI-THEFT SYSTEM" on the cassette tape lid. Obtain three digit customer code for input. Reset system after service as follows:

1. Obtain three digit audio anti-theft code.
2. Depress 1 (PROG) while depressing righthand side of TUNE SEEK button, - - - will appear in tape operation display.
3. To enter the first digit, depress 1 (PROG) button repeatedly until the number of times depressed equals the first digit beginning with zero (depress the 1 button six times if the first digit if five).
4. To enter second digit, depress 2 (APS) button repeatedly until the number of times depressed equals the second digit beginning with zero.
5. To enter third digit, depress 3 (RPT) button repeatedly until the number of times depressed equals the third digit beginning with zero.
6. If - - - is displayed during code input, repeat procedure.
7. When code appears in display, de-

press and hold SCAN button until SEC appears.
8. When SEC disappears audio system should be operative.
9. If Err is displayed, repeat procedure. **Attempting to input code more than nine times may permanently disable audio system.**

BATTERY GROUND CABLE

Prior to service, disconnect battery ground cable and isolate as required.

HUB & BEARING
REPLACE

1. **On models equipped with drum brakes,** remove brake drum, **Fig. 1.**
2. **On models equipped with disc brakes,** remove brake caliper and position aside using suitable wire, then remove brake rotor.
3. **On all models,** using suitable dial indicator, measure bearing play in axial direction. Maximum of .0020 inch should be indicated. If not as indicated, replace bearing.
4. Using suitable dial indicator, measure deviation at surface of axle hub outside hub bolt. Maximum of .0028 inch should be indicated. If not as indicated, replace axle shaft and bearing.
5. Remove four rear axle hub attaching bolts, then the axle hub and O-ring.
6. **On models equipped with anti-lock brakes,** do not disassemble rear axle shaft and bearing.
7. **On models less anti-lock brakes,**

using suitable hammer and chisel, unstake and remove locknut.
8. **On all models,** using suitable tool, remove axle shaft from axle hub.
9. Remove bearing inner race (outside).
10. Reverse procedure to install.

REAR AXLE CARRIER
REPLACE

1. Remove rear axle hub as outlined under "Hub & Bearing, Replace."
2. Remove brake hose from shock absorber.
3. Remove backing plate from rear axle carrier and position aside using suitable wire.
4. **On models equipped with anti-lock brakes,** remove ABS speed sensor from axle carrier and disconnect Load Sensing Proportioning Valve (LSPV) spring from lower arm.
5. **On all models,** loosen but do not remove three axle carrier attaching nuts, **Fig. 2.**
6. Disconnect strut rod from axle carrier.
7. Remove axle carrier three attaching nuts and bolts, then remove axle carrier.
8. Reverse procedure to install.

COIL SPRING
REPLACE

1. Remove rear seat, then package tray trim.
2. Raise and support vehicle, then remove rear wheels.

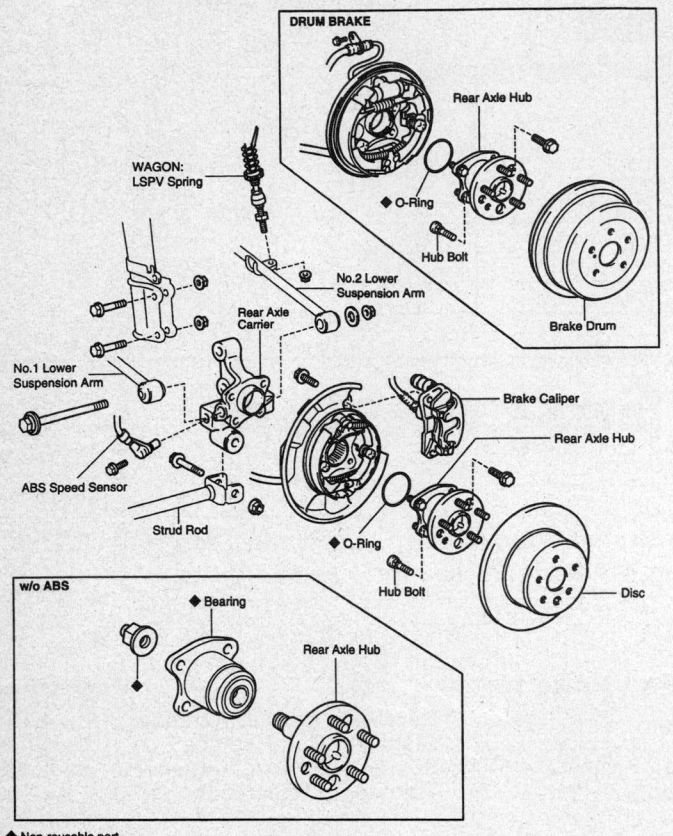

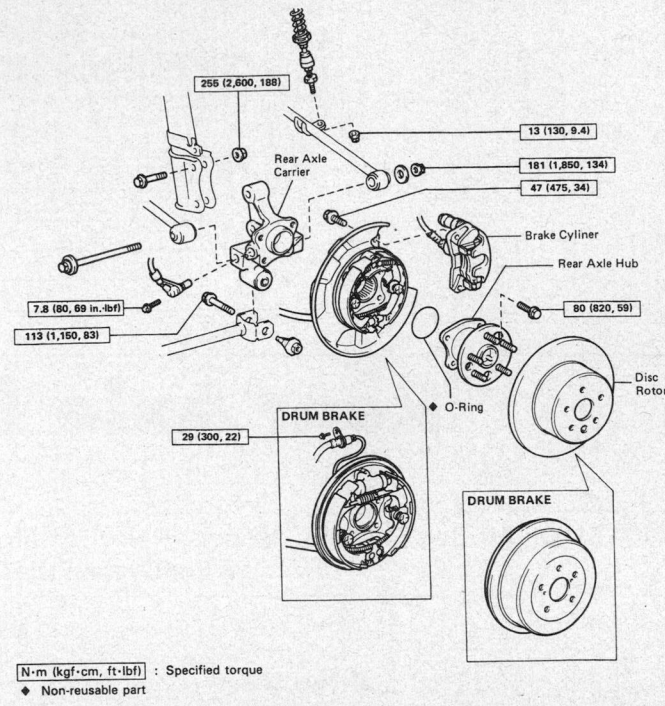

Fig. 2 Rear axle carrier replacement

| N·m (kgf·cm, ft·lbf) | : Specified torque |

◆ Non-reusable part

Fig. 1 Rear axle hub replacement

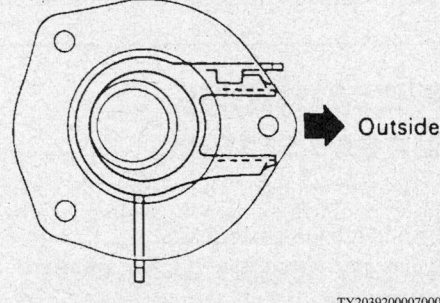

Fig. 5 Upper support position

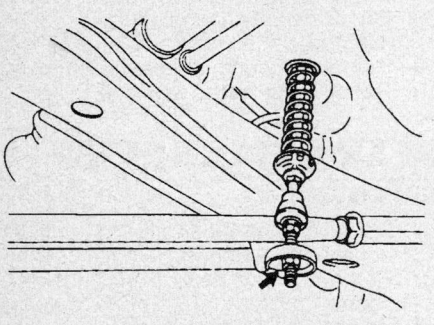

Fig. 3 Load Sensing Proportioning Valve (LSPV) spring removal

3. **On models equipped with ABS,** proceed as follows:
   a. Disconnect Load Sensing Proportioning Valve (LSPV) spring from lower arm, **Fig. 3.**
   b. Disconnect ABS speed sensor wire, then brake hose from shock absorber.
4. **On all models,** disconnect stabilizer bar link from shock absorber.
5. Support rear axle carrier with a suitable jack, loosen two lower shock attaching nuts, then remove three upper support attaching nuts.
6. Lower rear axle carrier, remove two lower attaching bolts, then remove shock absorber from vehicle.
7. Remove cap, attach spring compress tool No. 09727-30021, or equivalent,

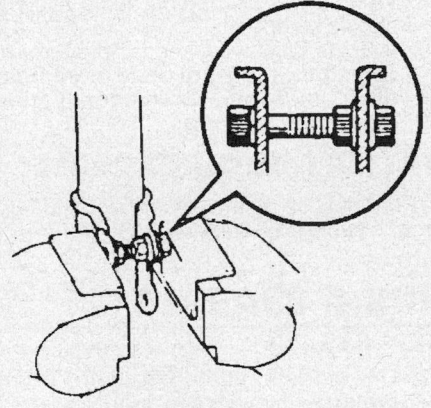

Fig. 4 Shock absorber installation

then compress spring.
8. Install a bolt and two nuts to bracket at lower portion of shock absorber, then place in vice, **Fig. 4.**
9. Using spring compress tool to hold upper support, remove shock absorber attaching nut, then the coil spring.
10. Reverse procedure to install, noting the following:
    a. When replacing upper support, use a new attaching nut.
    b. Rotate upper support and set in direction as shown in **Fig. 5.**
    c. Tighten all nuts and bolts to specifications.

STABILIZER BAR
REPLACE
1. Raise and support rear of vehicle, then remove rear wheels.
2. Remove bolts securing stabilizer bar to link brackets and bushings.
3. Remove bolts securing stabilizer bar to frame, then remove stabilizer bar.
4. Reverse procedure to install. Tighten to specifications.

SUSPENSION ARM
REPLACE
Refer to "Lower Suspension Arm & Strut Rod, Replace" for procedure.

LOWER SUSPENSION ARM & STRUT ROD
REPLACE
1. Raise and support vehicle, then remove rear wheels.

2. Remove two strut rod attaching nuts and bolts, then the strut rod, **Fig. 6.**
3. **On models equipped with ABS,** disconnect Load Sensing Proportioning Valve (LSPV) spring from lower arm, **Fig. 3.**
4. **On all models,** remove No. 2 lower suspension arm attaching nuts, then suspension arm.
5. Remove stabilizer bar bushing retainer, then exhaust center and tail pipe.
6. Support suspension member with a suitable jack. Remove six nuts, then left and right suspension member lower stopper.
7. Lower suspension member. Remove No. 1 lower suspension arm attaching bolts, then suspension arm.
8. Reverse procedure to install. Tighten nuts and bolts to specifications.

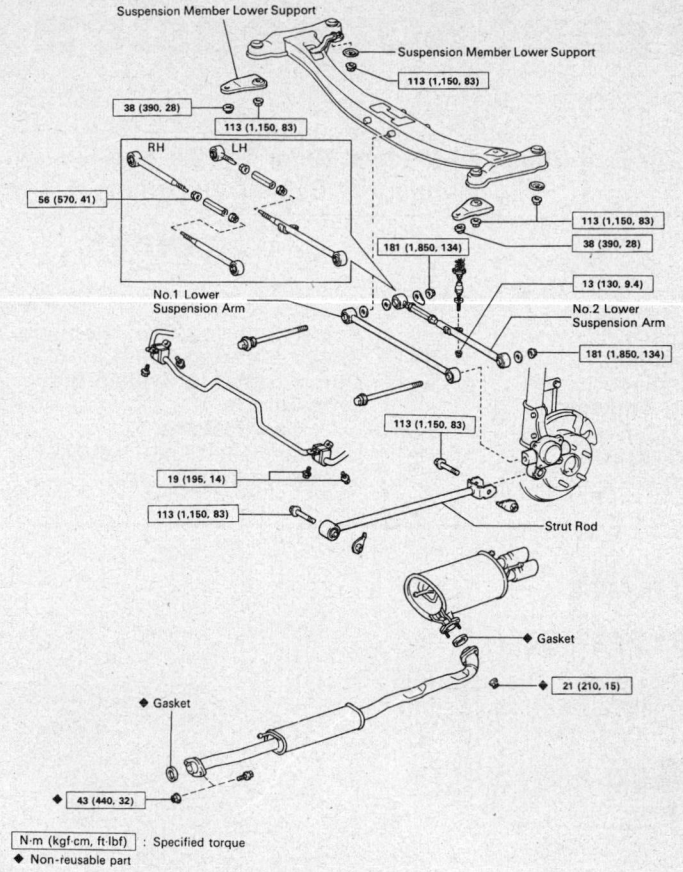

TY2039200009000X

Fig. 6 Rear suspension

TIGHTENING SPECIFICATIONS

Year	Component	Torque, Ft. Lbs.
1996–99	ABS Speed Sensor Bolt	72①
	Axle Bearing Locknut	90
	Axle Bearing Set Bolt	90
	Axle Carrier To Shock Absorber	188
	Lower Suspension Arm To Suspension Member	134
	Lower Suspension Arm To Rear Axle Carrier	134
	Load Sensing Proportioning Valve (LSPV) Spring To Lower Suspension Arm	108①
	Stabilizer Bar Bushing Retainer	14
	Stabilizer Bar Link Set Nut	47
	Suspension Member To Body (14 mm)	28
	Suspension Member To Body (17 mm)	83
	Suspension Upper Support To Body	29
	Suspension Upper Support To Piston Rod	36
	Wheel Lug Nuts	76

① — Inch lbs.

REAR AXLE & SUSPENSION

Front Suspension & Steering

NOTE: On Air Bag Equipped Models, Refer To "Air Bag System Precautions" Located In The Front Of This Manual For System Disarming & Arming Procedures.

INDEX

PRECAUTIONS

AIR BAG SYSTEMS

Refer to "Air Bag System Precautions" in the front of this manual for system disarming and arming procedures.

AUDIO CODED ANTI-THEFT SYSTEM

Some models are with an audio coded anti-theft system that will disable the radio when the battery cable is disconnected. The system can be identified by the word "ANTI-THEFT SYSTEM" on the cassette tape lid. Obtain three digit customer code for input. Reset system after service as follows:

1. Obtain three digit audio anti-theft code.
2. Depress 1 (PROG) while depressing righthand side of TUNE SEEK button, - - - will appear in tape operation display.
3. To enter first digit, depress 1 (PROG) button repeatedly until number of times depressed equals first digit beginning with zero (depress 1 button six times if first digit is five).
4. To enter second digit, depress 2 (APS) button repeatedly until number of times depressed equals the second digit beginning with zero.
5. To enter third digit, depress 3 (RPT) button repeatedly until number of times depressed equals third digit beginning with zero.
6. If - - - is displayed during code input, repeat procedure.
7. When code appears in display, depress and hold SCAN button until SEC appears.
8. When SEC disappears audio system should be operative.
9. If Err is displayed, repeat procedure. **Attempting to input code more than nine times may permanently disable audio system.**

BATTERY GROUND CABLE

Prior to service, disconnect battery ground cable and isolate as required.

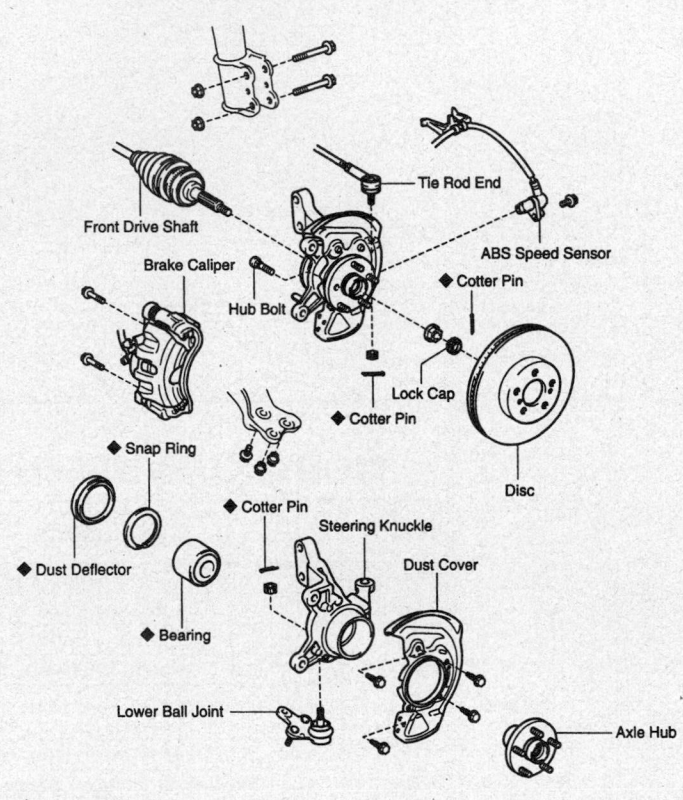

Fig. 1 Exploded view of knuckle, hub & bearing

Labels: Tie Rod End, ABS Speed Sensor, Cotter Pin, Front Drive Shaft, Brake Caliper, Hub Bolt, Lock Cap, Cotter Pin, Snap Ring, Cotter Pin, Steering Knuckle, Disc, Dust Cover, Dust Deflector, Bearing, Lower Ball Joint, Axle Hub

◆ Non-reusable part

TY2049200013000X

WHEEL BEARING

ADJUST

These models incorporate lubed for life, sealed front wheel bearings with no provision for adjustment.

HUB & STEERING KNUCKLE

REPLACE

1. Raise and support vehicle, then remove front wheels.
2. Remove brake caliper and support with wire, then the rotor, **Fig. 1.**
3. Place a dial indicator near center of axle hub and check backlash in bearing shaft direction, **Fig. 2.** If backlash is greater than .002 inch, replace bearing.
4. Place a dial indicator at surface of axle hub outside hub bolt and check hub runout, **Fig. 3.** If runout is greater than .002 inch, replace axle hub.
5. Install rotor and brake caliper, then remove driveshaft locknut while applying brakes.
6. Remove brake caliper and support

with wire. Remove rotor.

7. Remove ABS speed sensor from steering knuckle, then loosen nuts on lower side of shock absorber. **Do not remove bolts at this time.**
8. Disconnect tie rod end from steering knuckle using tie rod end separator tool No. 09610–20012 or equivalent.
9. Remove lower ball joint from lower suspension arm.
10. Remove bolts on lower side of shock absorber, then the steering knuckle and hub.
11. Using a suitable screwdriver, remove dust deflector.
12. Remove lower ball joint using ball joint puller tool No. 09628-62011, or equivalent, then the hub using rear axle shaft puller tool No. 09520-00031, or equivalent.
13. Remove inner race hub using bearing remover tool No. 09950-00020, or equivalent, and a suitable press.
14. Remove dust cover, then the bearing snap ring from steering knuckle.
15. Place inner race on outside of bearing, then using countershaft bearing replacer tool No. 09310-35010, or equivalent, and a hammer, remove bearing.
16. Reverse procedure to install, noting the following:
    a. Press new bearing into steering knuckle using steering knuckle oil seal replacer tool No. 09608-32010, or equivalent.
    b. Press hub into steering knuckle using countershaft bearing replacer tool No. 09310-35010 and steering knuckle oil seal replacer tool No. 09608-32010, or equivalents.
    c. Install a new dust deflector using transmission and transfer bearing replacer tool No. 09316-60010, or equivalent, and a hammer. **Align holes for ABS speed sensor in dust deflector and steering knuckle.**

BALL JOINT INSPECTION

1. Remove ball joint as outlined under "Ball Joint, Replace."
2. Move ball joint stud back and forth five times, then install nut.
3. Using torque wrench, turn nut continuously one turn every 2–4 seconds and take torque reading on fifth turn.
4. If torque reading is not 9–29 inch lbs., replace ball joint.

BALL JOINT
REPLACE

1. Raise and support vehicle, then remove front wheels.
2. Remove steering knuckle and hub as outlined under " Hub & Steering Knuckle, Replace."
3. Using a suitable screwdriver, remove driveshaft dust deflector from steering knuckle.
4. Remove lower ball joint using ball joint puller tool No. 09628-62011, or equivalent.

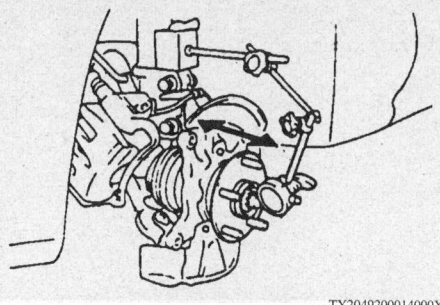
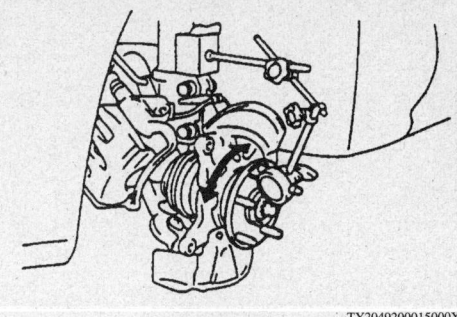

TY2049200014000X TY2049200015000X

Fig. 2 Bearing backlash measurement **Fig. 3 Hub runout measurement**

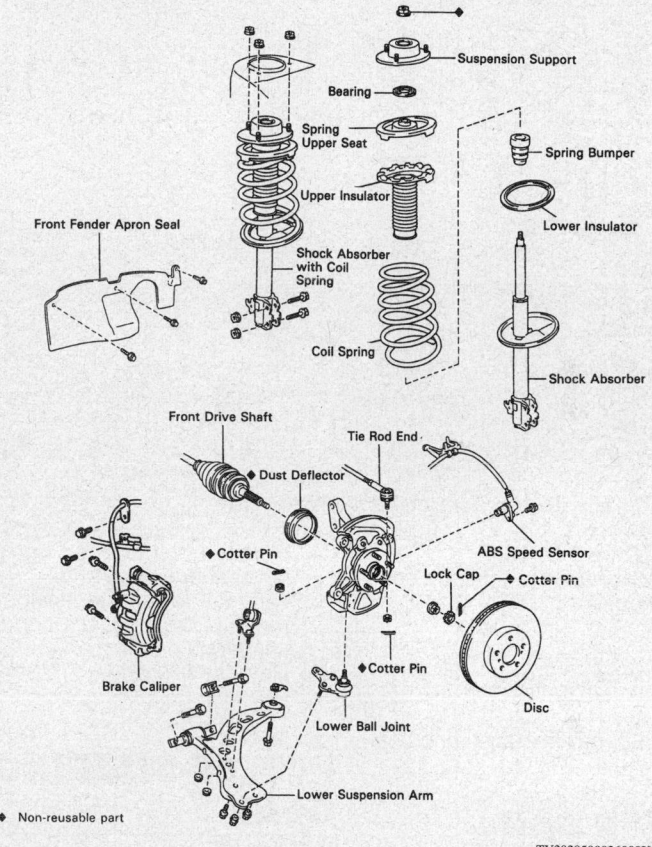

TY2029500026000X

Fig. 4 Exploded view of strut assembly

5. Inspect ball joint as outlined under "Ball Joint Inspection."
6. Reverse procedure to install, noting the following:
    a. Install a new dust deflector using transmission and transfer bearing replacer tool No. 09316-60010, or equivalent.

COIL SPRING
REPLACE

1. Raise and support vehicle, then remove front wheels.
2. Disconnect brake hose and anti-lock brake system speed sensor wire from shock absorber.
3. Remove lower strut attaching nuts and bolts, **Fig. 4.**
4. Remove three nuts holding top of suspension support.

5. Remove strut from body. **Cover driveshaft boot to prevent damage during removal.**
6. Using coil spring compressor tool No. 09727-00045, 09727-30020, or equivalent, compress coil spring.
7. Install a bolt and two nuts to lower portion of strut shell and secure in vise.
8. Using spring seat holding tool No. 09729-22031, or equivalent, remove nut, suspension upper support, upper insulator, coil spring, spring bumper and lower insulator. **Do not disassemble spring lower seat.**
9. Reverse procedure to install, noting the following:
    a. Fit lower end of coil spring into gap of lower seat.
    b. Prior to installation of nut, rotate upper support until lowest bolt on support is aligned with projection

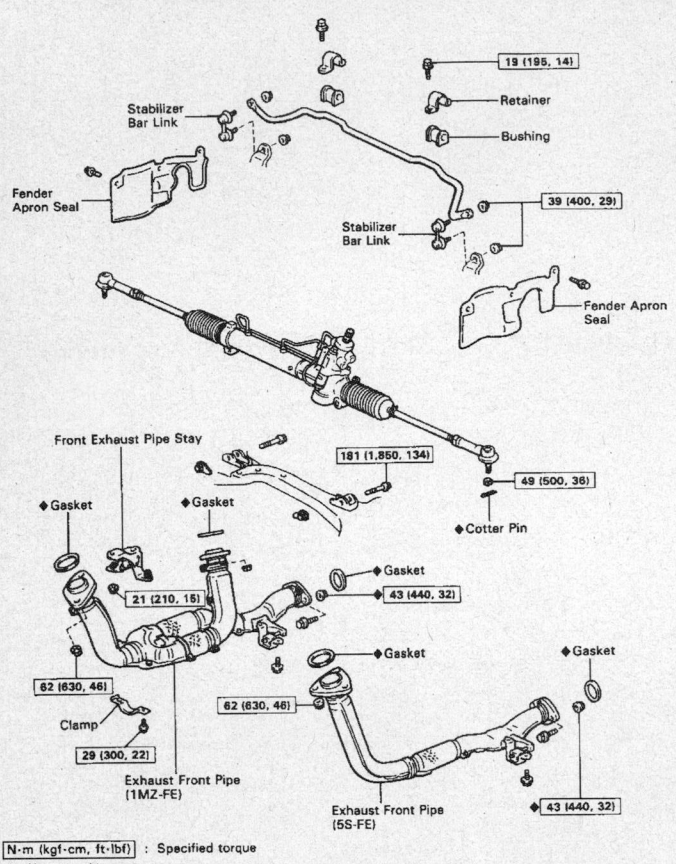

N·m (kgf·cm, ft·lbf) : Specified torque
◆ Non-reusable part

TY2029200008000X

Fig. 5 Exploded view of stabilizer bar

N·m (kgf·cm, ft·lbf) : Specified torque
◆ Non-reusable part

TY2029200006000X

Fig. 6 Exploded view of lower suspension arm

part of spring lower seat.
c. Tighten all attaching nuts and bolts to specifications.

STRUT
REPLACE

Refer to "Coil Spring, Replace" for procedure.

STABILIZER BAR
REPLACE

1. Raise and support vehicle, then remove front wheels.
2. Remove left and right stabilizer bar links.
3. Remove left and right brackets and bushings, **Fig. 5.**
4. Remove stabilizer bar from lefthand side, **Ensure not to damage pressure feed tube.**
5. Reverse procedure to install.

SUSPENSION ARM
REPLACE
LOWER

1. Raise and support vehicle, then remove front wheels.
2. Disconnect lower suspension arm from lower ball joint.
3. Remove two bolts on front side of lower suspension arm, **Fig. 6.**

4. Remove bolt and nut on rear side of lower suspension arm.
5. Remove lower suspension arm, then remove bushing stopper from lower suspension arm shaft.
6. Reverse procedure to install.

POWER STEERING GEAR
REPLACE

1. Place front wheels facing straight ahead.
2. Using tie rod end removal tool No. 09610–20012 or equivalent, disconnect lefthand and righthand tie rod ends.
3. Place matchmarks on intermediate shaft and control valve shaft, then disconnect intermediate shaft.
4. Remove attaching nut, then the clamp plate.
5. Using a disconnect tool No. 09631–22020 or equivalent, disconnect pressure feed and return tubes.
6. Remove attaching bolts and disconnect stabilizer bar, **Do not remove stabilizer bar.**
7. Remove No. 1 fuel tube protector.
8. Remove power steering gear attaching bolts and nuts.
9. Lift up on stabilizer bar, then remove power steering gear from left side of vehicle, **Fig. 7.**

10. Reverse procedure to install, tighten attaching bolts and nuts to specifications.

POWER STEERING PUMP
REPLACE

Refer to **Figs. 8 and 9** when replacing power steering pump, noting the following:
1. Disconnect and connect pressure line using power steering hose nut wrench set tool No. 09631-22020, or equivalent.
2. Bleed power steering system after installation.

POWER STEERING SYSTEM BLEED

1. Ensure fluid in reservoir tank is at proper level.
2. With engine speed below 1000 RPM, turn steering wheel from stop to stop three or four times, keeping at full stop position for two to three seconds. Ensure fluid is not foamy or cloudy.
3. Measure fluid lever with engine running then stop engine and measure fluid level again, **Fig. 10.** Maximum rise of fluid is .20 inch.
4. If a problem is found, proceed as follows:
   a. Disconnect return hose from reservoir tank and drain fluid.
   b. Fill reservoir tank with fresh fluid.

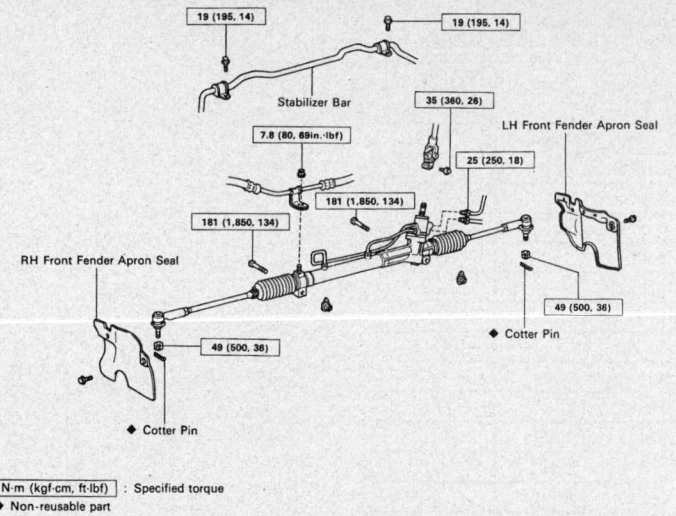

N·m (kgf·cm, ft·lbf) : Specified torque
◆ Non-reusable part

TY6039200005000X

Fig. 7   Steering gear removal

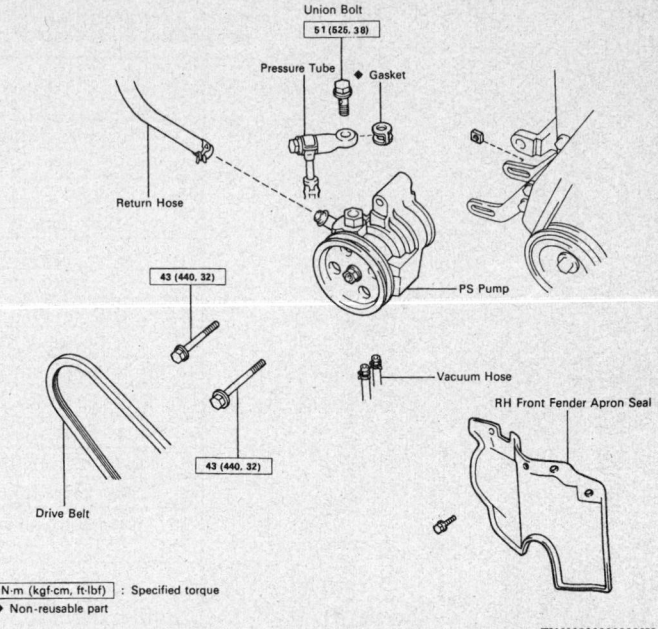

N·m (kgf·cm, ft·lbf) : Specified torque
◆ Non-reusable part

TY6039200008000X

Fig. 8   Power steering pump removal. Camry & Camry Solara w/5S-FE engine

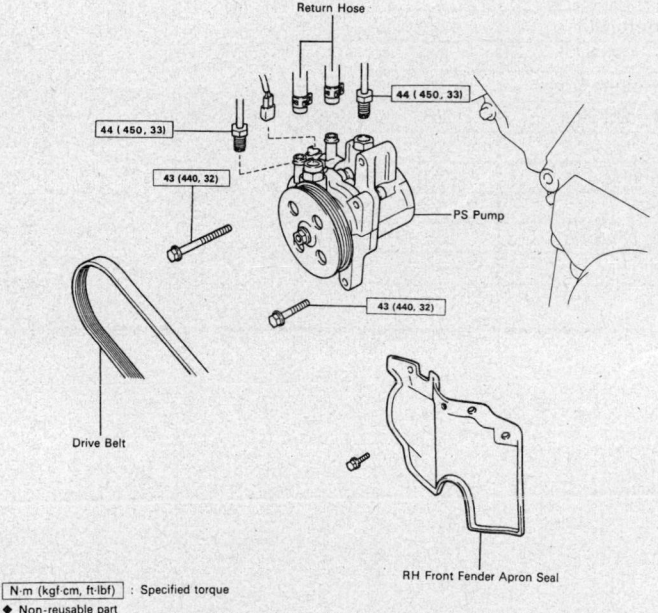

N·m (kgf·cm, ft·lbf) : Specified torque
◆ Non-reusable part

TY6039200009000X

Fig. 9   Power steering pump removal. Avalon, Camry & Camry Solara w/1MZ-FE engine

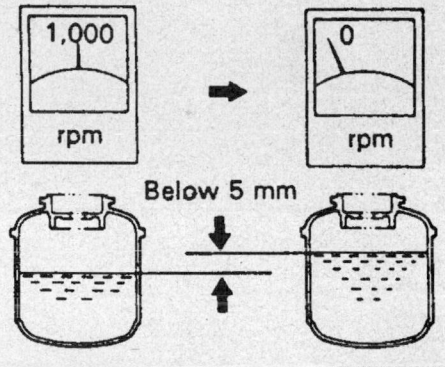

TY6039100011000X

Fig. 10   Power steering system bleed

Ensure some fluid remains in reservoir tank.

d. Repeat steps b and c four or five times until there is no more air in fluid.

e. Connect return hose and correct fluid level.

c. With return hose placed into a suitable container, start engine and run at 1000 RPM. **After one or two** seconds, fluid will begin to discharge from return hose. Stop engine immediately at this time.

TIGHTENING SPECIFICATIONS

Year	Component	Torque, Ft. Lbs.
1996-99	ABS Speed Sensor To Steering Knuckle	72①
	ABS Speed Sensor Wire To Strut Bolt	48①
	Ball Joint To Lower Suspension Arm	94
	Ball Joint To Steering Knuckle	90
	Brake Caliper Bolts	79
	Brake Hose To Strut Bolt	22
	Driveshaft To Axle Hub Locknut	217
	Dust Cover To Steering Knuckle	72①
	Front Exhaust Pipe To Converter Nuts	32
	Front Exhaust Pipe To Manifold Nuts	46
	Lower Suspension Arm Mounting Bolts	152
	Power Steering Pump Mounting Bolts	32
	Power Steering Pump Pressure Tubes	33
	Stabilizer Bar End Bracket To Lower Suspension Arm	41
	Stabilizer Bar Link Nuts	47
	Stabilizer Bar Retainer Bracket Bolts	14
	Steering Rack Line Clamp Nut	72①
	Steering Rack Mounting Bolts	134
	Steering Rack Pressure & Return Tubes	18
	Steering Rack Universal Joint Bolt	26
	Strut Nut	36
	Strut To Steering Knuckle	156
	Strut To Strut Tower	59
	Tie Rod End To Steering Knuckle	36
	Wheel Lug Nut	76

① — Inch lbs.

Wheel Alignment

INDEX

PRELIMINARY INSPECTION

1. Check tires for wear and proper inflation.
2. Check wheel runout, .039 (1 mm) inch should be indicated.
3. Check front wheel bearings, front suspension, steering linkage and ball joints for wear or looseness.
4. Ensure front shock absorbers are functioning properly.

FRONT WHEEL ALIGNMENT

CASTER & CAMBER

Camry

Camber and caster are not adjustable. If camber and caster angle are not within specifications, check for worn or damaged suspension parts and replace as necessary.

TOE-IN

1. Remove clamps from steering gear boots.
2. Loosen tie rod end locknuts.
3. Turn left and right tie rod ends an equal amount to adjust toe-in.
4. Ensure length of both tie rods are equal following adjustment.
5. Following adjustment, install steering gear boot clamps and **torque** tie rod locknuts to 54 ft. lbs.

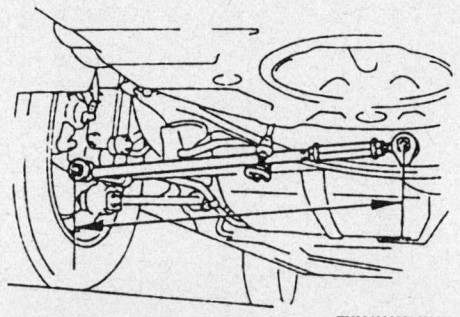

TY2049300016000X

Fig. 1 Rear toe-in adjustment. Camry

REAR WHEEL ALIGNMENT

CAMBER

Camber angle is preset and not adjustable. If camber angle is not to specification, inspect and/or replace suspension components as required.

TOE-IN

Camry

1. Measure length of left and right No. 2 lower suspension arms, **Fig. 1.**
2. Adjust length of lower suspension arms if difference in length is greater than .04 inch.
3. Loosen locknuts and turn left and right adjusting tubes an equal distance to adjust toe-in.
4. One turn of adjusting tube will adjust

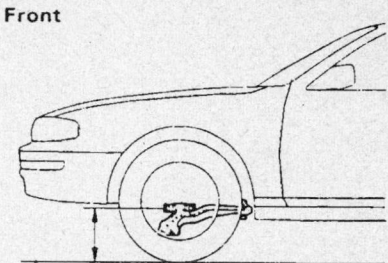

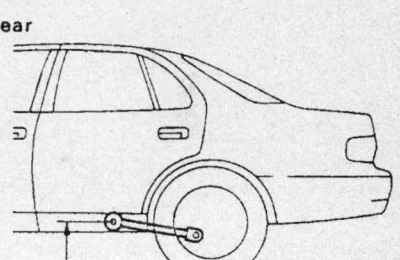

TY2049200018000X

Fig. 2 Vehicle ride height measurement

toe-in approximately .264 inch.
5. Following adjustment, **torque** locknuts to 41 ft. lbs.

VEHICLE RIDE HEIGHT

Refer to **Figs. 2 through 4** for ride height measurements and trim height specifications.

Tire size	Front	Rear
P195/70R14	210 mm (8.27 in.)	262 mm (10.31 in.)
P205/65R15	213 mm (8.39 in.)	267 mm (10.51 in.)

TY2049300022000X

Fig. 3   Vehicle ride height specifications. Avalon & Camry sedan/coupe

Tire size	Front
P195/70R14	210 mm (8.27 in.)
P205/65R15	214 mm (8.43 in.)
Rear	
P195/70R14	272 mm (10.71 in.)
P205/65R15	277 mm (10.91 in.)

TY2049400051000X

Fig. 4   Vehicle ride height specifications. Camry wagon

TOYOTA CELICA
INDEX OF SERVICE OPERATIONS

Specifications

GENERAL ENGINE SPECIFICATIONS

Year	Engine	Fuel System	Bore & Stroke	Compression Ratio	Maximum Brake H.P. @ RPM	Maximum Torque Ft. Lbs. @ RPM	Normal Oil Pressure, psi @ RPM
1996–97	1.8L 7A-FE	Fuel Inj.	3.19 x 3.37	9.5	105 @ 5200	117 @ 2800	36–71 @ 3000
	2.2L 5S-FE	Fuel Inj.	3.43 x 3.58	9.5	130 @ 5400	145 @ 4400	36–71 @ 3000
1998–99	2.2L 5S-FE	Fuel Inj.	3.43 x 3.58	9.5	130 @ 5400	145 @ 4400	36–71 @ 3000

TUNE UP SPECIFICATIONS

The following specifications are published from the latest information available. This data should be used only in the absence of a decal affixed in the engine compartment.

When checking ignition timing, it may be necessary to disconnect certain hoses and/or electrical connectors. Refer to vehicle emission control label for specific instructions.

Before disconnecting spark plug wires from distributor cap, determine location of No. 1 wire in cap, as distributor position may have been altered from that shown.

Year	Engine	Spark Plug Gap, Inch	Ignition Timing			Curb Idle Speed, RPM		Fuel Pump Pressure, psi	Valve Clearance, Inch	
			Firing Order	Timing, °BTDC	Timing Mark Fig.	Man. Trans.	Auto. Trans.		Int.	Exh.
1996	1.8L 7A-FE	.031	1-3-4-2	10②	B	700	700N	38–44	.006–.010	.010–.014
	2.2L 5S-FE	.043	1-3-4-2	10①	B	750	750N	38–44	.007–.011	.011–.015
1997	1.8L 7A-FE	.031	1-3-4-2	10②	B	700	700N	38–44	.006–.010	.010–.014
	2.2L 5S-FE	.043	1-3-4-2	10②	B	750	750N	38–44	.007–.011	.011–.015
1998–99	2.2L 5S-FE	.043	1-3-4-2	8–12①	B	700	700N	38–44	.007–.011	.011–.015

BTDC — Before Top Dead Center
N — Neutral

① — With check connector terminals T & E shorted.

② — With terminals TE1 & E1 connected of DLC1.

TY1139100111000X

Fig. A

FRONT WHEEL ALIGNMENT SPECIFICATIONS

The specifications listed below are for unloaded vehicles.

| Year | Engine | Caster Angle, Degrees | | Camber Angle, Degrees | | Toe-In, Inch | Toe-Out On Turns, Deg. | | Ball Joint Wear |
		Limits	Desired	Limits	Desired		Outer Wheel	Inner Wheel	
1996	1.8L	+1⅓ to +2⅚	+2 1/12	-1½ to 0	-¾	+.06 to +.22	30 11/15	36 9/10	①
	2.2L	+1 11/30 to +2 13/15	+2 7/60	-1⅗ to -1/10	-51/60	+.06 to +.22	30 19/30	36 11/15	①
1997	1.8L	+1⅓ to +2⅚	+2 1/12	-1 31/60 to -1/60	-23/30	-.08 to +.08	30 11/15	36 9/10	①
	2.2L	+1 11/30 to +2 13/15	+2 7/60	-1 3/10 to -1/10	-51/60	-.08 to +.08	30 11/15	36 9/10	①
1998–99	2.2L	+1⅓ to +2⅚	+2 1/12	-1 31/60 to -1/60	-23/30	-.08 to +.08	30 11/15	36 9/10	①

① — Refer to "Ball Joint Inspection" under "Front Suspension & Steering."

REAR WHEEL ALIGNMENT SPECIFICATIONS

The specifications listed below are for unloaded vehicles.

| Year | Engine | Camber Angle, Degrees | | Toe-In, Inch |
		Limits	Desired	
1996	1.8L	-2 1/60 to -29/60	-1 14/15	+.06 to +.22
	2.2L	-1 11/12 to -½	-1⅙	+.06 to +.22
1997	1.8L	-2 to -½	-1 4/15	+.06 to +.22
	2.2L	-1 11/12 to -½	-1⅙	+.06 to +.22
1998–99	2.2L	-2 to -½	-1⅙	+.06 to +.22

FLUID CAPACITIES & COOLING SYSTEM DATA

| Year | Engine | Cooling Capacity, Qts. | | Radiator Cap Relief Pressure, Lbs. | Thermo. Opening Temp., °F | Fuel Tank, Gals. | Engine Oil Refill, Qts.① | Transmission/Transaxle Oil | | | Axle Oil, Pints |
		Less A/C	With A/C					4 Speed, Pints	5 Speed, Pints	Auto. Trans., Qts.	
1996	1.8L	②	②	13	180	15.9	4.0	—	5.4	8	—
	2.2L	③	③	13	180	15.9	4.0	—	5.4	5.9	3.4
1997	1.8L	④	④	10.7	180	15.9	3.9	—	4	8	3.4
	2.2L	③	③	10.7	180	15.9	4.1	—	5.4	5.9	—
1998–99	2.2L	7.3	7.3	13	180	15.9	3.8	—	4.6	5.9	3.4

① — With oil filter change. ③ — Man. trans., 7.1; auto. trans., 7.5. ④ — 7A-FE engine.
② — Man. trans., 8.6; auto. trans., 7.

LUBRICANT DATA

| Year | Model | Lubricant Type | | | | |
| | | Transaxle | | Rear Axle | Power Steering | Brake System |
		Manual	Automatic			
1996	Celica	75W-90 GL-3/4/5	Dexron II/IIE/III	—	Dexron II/IIE/III	DOT 3
1997–99	Celica	75W-90 GL-4/5	Dexron II/IIE/III	—	Dexron II/IIE/III	DOT 3

Electrical

NOTE: On Air Bag Equipped Models, Refer To "Air Bag System Precautions" Located In The Front Of This Manual For System Disarming & Arming Procedures.

INDEX

PRECAUTIONS
AIR BAG SYSTEMS

Refer to "Air Bag System Precautions" in the front of this manual for system disarming and arming procedures.

BATTERY GROUND CABLE

Prior to service, disconnect battery ground cable and isolate as required.

AUDIO CODED ANTI-THEFT SYSTEM

Some models are equipped with an audio coded anti-theft system that will disable the radio when the battery cable is disconnected. The system can be identified by the "ANTI-THEFT SYSTEM" on the cassette tape lid. Obtain 3 digit customer code for input. Reset system after service as follows:
1. Obtain 3 digit audio anti-theft code.
2. Depress 1 (PROG) while depressing righthand side of TUNE SEEK button, - - - will appear in tape operation display.
3. To enter the first digit, depress 1 (PROG) button repeatedly until the number of times depressed equals the first digit beginning with zero (depress the 1 button six times if the first digit if five).
4. To enter second digit, depress 2 (APS) button repeatedly until the number of times depressed equals the second digit beginning with zero.
5. To enter third digit, depress 3 (RPT) button repeatedly until the number of times depressed equals the second digit beginning with zero.
6. If - - - is displayed during code input, repeat procedure.
7. When code appears in display, depress and hold SCAN button until SEC appears.

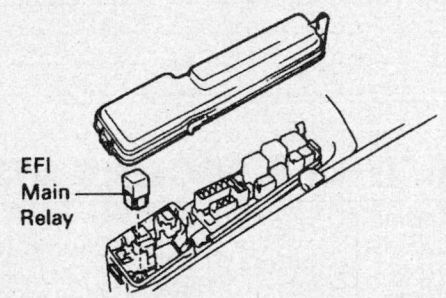

Fig. 1 Fuel pump relay

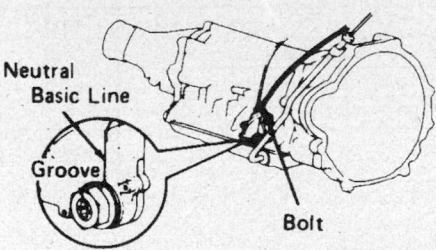

Fig. 2 Neutral safety switch adjustment

8. When SEC disappears audio system should be operative.
9. If Err is displayed, repeat procedure. **Attempting to input code more than nine times may permanently disable audio system.**

FUSE PANEL & FLASHER LOCATION

There are three fuse blocks; the first is located on the left front kick panel, the second is on the right front kick panel and the third is next to the battery. On models equipped with ABS brakes, an additional fuse block is located in the engine compartment. The turn signal/hazard flasher is on the left front kick panel fuse block.

FUEL PUMP RELAY LOCATION

The fuel pump relay is located in the engine compartment relay center, **Fig. 1**

RELAY CENTER LOCATION

The relay center is located at the left-hand front of the engine compartment on the fender apron.

STARTER
REPLACE
5S-FE ENGINE

1. Obtain audio anti-theft code, if equipped, as outlined in "Precautions."
2. Remove air cleaner case assembly as follows:
   a. Disconnect air intake temperature sensor connector.
   b. Disconnect four air cleaner cap clips.
   c. Disconnect air cleaner hose from throttle body and remove air cleaner cap and filter element.
   d. Remove three air cleaner case retaining bolts, then the case.
3. Remove engine compartment relay box as follows:
   a. Remove two relay box retaining nuts and disconnect relay box from the battery.
   b. Remove lower cover from relay box.
   c. Disconnect fusible link cassette

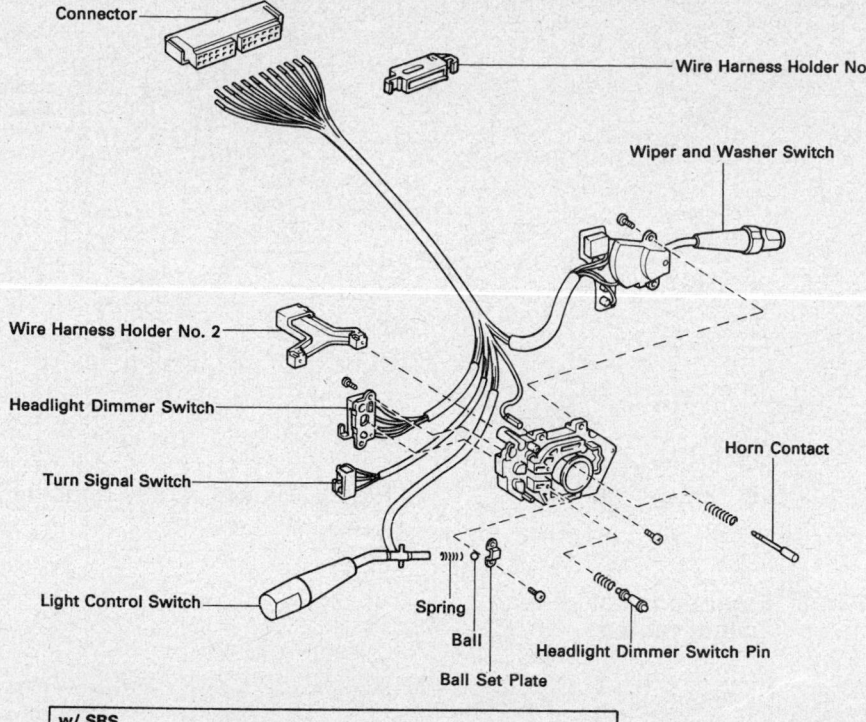

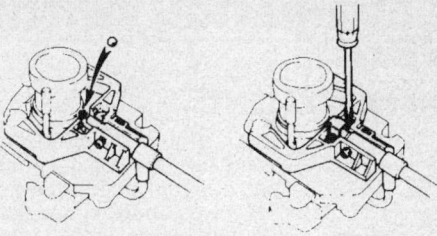

Fig. 4 Positioning ball onto spring

Fig. 3 Exploded view of combination switch

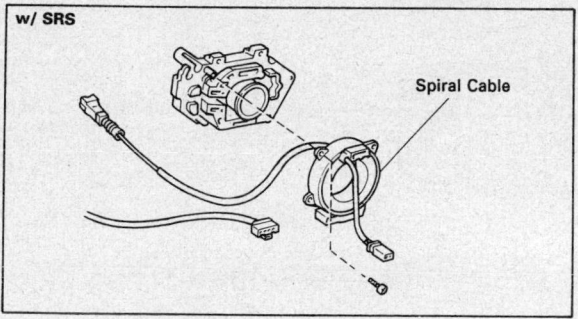

5. Remove distributor attaching bolts, then remove.
6. Reverse to install. Reset audio coded anti-theft, if equipped, as outlined in "Precautions."

IGNITION LOCK
REPLACE

1. Obtain audio anti-theft code, if equipped, as outlined in "Precautions."
2. Turn ignition switch to ACC position.
3. Insert a small diameter rod into hole located on side of lock cylinder, then while holding down pin, remove lock cylinder.
4. Reverse procedure to install. Ensure lock cylinder is in ACC position.
5. Reset audio coded anti-theft, if equipped, as outlined in "Precautions."

IGNITION SWITCH
REPLACE

1. Obtain audio anti-theft code, if equipped, as outlined in "Precautions."
2. Remove steering wheel as outlined under "Steering Wheel, Replace."
3. Disconnect electrical connectors from ignition switch.
4. Turn ignition key to ACC position and remove ignition key cylinder.
5. Remove screw and ignition switch.
6. Reverse procedure to install. Reset audio coded anti-theft, if equipped, as outlined in "Precautions."

NEUTRAL SAFETY SWITCH
REPLACE

1. Raise and support vehicle.
2. Loosen neutral safety switch bracket bolt.
3. Position transmission shift lever into Neutral.
4. Align switch shaft groove with neutral base line, **Fig. 2,** then retighten switch bracket bolt.
5. Connect electrical connector to switch.

STOP LIGHT SWITCH
REPLACE

1. Remove brake pedal tension spring.
2. Disconnect switch wire connector.
3. Remove switch mounting nut, then slide switch from mounting bracket.
4. Reverse procedure to install.

---

and two connectors of the engine wire from relay box.
4. **On models equipped with cruise control,** disconnect cruise control actuator connector, then remove four actuator retaining bolts and remove actuator.
5. **On all models,** disconnect starter electrical connector and starter wire.
6. Remove two starter retaining bolts, then the starter.
7. Reverse procedure to install, **torque** starter retaining bolts to 29 ft. lbs.
8. Reset audio coded anti-theft, if equipped, as outlined in "Precautions."

7A-FE ENGINE

1. Obtain audio anti-theft code, if equipped, as outlined under "Precautions."
2. Remove air cleaner assembly, then disconnect the following:
   a. IAT sensor connector.

b. Accelerator cable and cruise control actuator cable.
   c. Vacuum hose from throttle body at air cleaner assembly hose.
3. Disconnect engine wire clamp from transaxle.
4. Remove starter motor attaching bolts and the starter motor.
5. Reverse procedure to install.

DISTRIBUTOR
REPLACE

1. Obtain audio anti-theft code, if equipped, as outlined in "Precautions."
2. **On models equipped with 5S-FE engines,** remove air cleaner hose.
3. **On all models,** disconnect distributor electrical connector.
4. Disconnect spark plug wires from plugs and ignition coil.

COMBINATION SWITCH
REPLACE
REPLACEMENT

1. Obtain audio anti-theft code, if equipped, as outlined in "Precautions."
2. Pull wheel pad out from steering wheel and disconnect air bag connector. **When removing wheel pad, take care not to pull air bag wire harness. When storing wheel pad, keep upper surface of the pad facing upward. Never disassemble wheel pad.**
3. Remove horn button screws and horn button.
4. Scribe alignment marks on steering wheel and steering shaft.
5. Remove steering wheel nut.
6. Using a steering wheel puller, remove steering wheel.
7. Remove steering column upper and lower covers.
8. Remove combination switch.
9. Reverse procedure to install. Reset audio coded anti-theft, if equipped, as outlined in "Precautions."

SERVICE

Headlight & Dimmer Switch

1. Obtain audio anti-theft code, if equipped, as outlined in "Precautions."
2. Pull wheel pad out from steering wheel and disconnect air bag connector. **When removing wheel pad, take care not to pull air bag wire harness. When storing wheel pad, keep upper surface of the pad facing upward. Never disassemble wheel pad.**
3. Remove steering wheel, then upper and lower steering column covers.
4. Disconnect combination switch connector, then using a small screwdriver, disengage headlight and dimmer switch wiring from combination switch connector. **Note position of wires.**
5. **On models equipped with cruise control, removal of slip ring may be necessary.** Remove screws, headlight and dimmer switch, then ball and spring assembly, **Fig. 3.**
6. **On all models,** install headlight and dimmer switch onto combination switch.
7. Insert spring into headlight and dimmer lever, than install lever and screw onto combination switch.
8. Position ball on the spring, **Fig. 4,** and place headlight and dimmer switch lever into HI position. Install screws and clamp, **Fig. 4.**
9. Ensure switch operates smoothly in each position.
10. Install electrical terminals into combination switch connector in the same position as they were removed.
11. Install combination switch connector, then the steering column upper and lower covers and steering wheel.
12. Connect battery ground cable. Reset audio coded anti-theft, if equipped, as outlined in "Precautions."

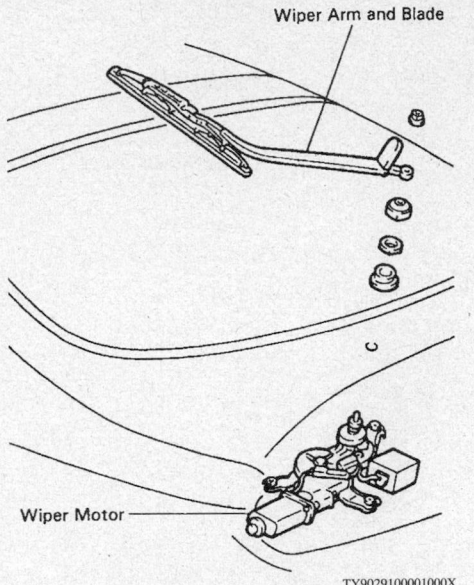

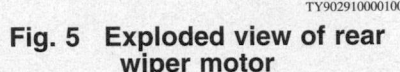

Fig. 5   Exploded view of rear wiper motor

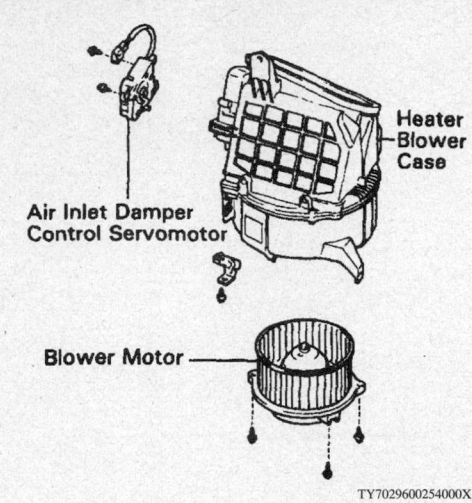

Fig. 6   Blower motor removal

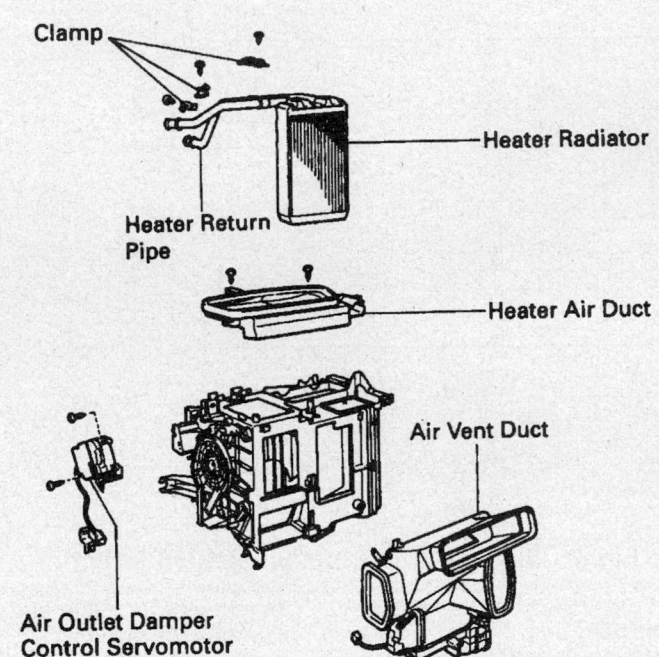

Fig. 7   Heater core removal

Hazard & Turn Signal Switch

1. Obtain audio anti-theft code, if equipped, as outlined in "Precautions."
2. Pull wheel pad out from steering wheel and disconnect air bag connector. **When removing wheel pad, take care not to pull air bag wire harness. When storing wheel pad, keep upper surface of the pad facing upward. Never disassemble wheel pad.**
3. Remove steering wheel, then the upper and lower steering column covers.
4. Disconnect hazard and turn signal switch connector, then using a small screwdriver, disengage hazard and turn signal switch wiring from combination switch connector. **Note position of wires.**
5. Remove screws, clamp, hazard and turn signal switch assembly from combination switch.
6. Reverse procedure to install. Reset audio coded anti-theft, if equipped, as outlined in "Precautions."

Windshield Wiper/Washer Switch

1. Obtain audio anti-theft code, if equipped, as outlined in "Precautions."
2. Pull wheel pad out from steering wheel

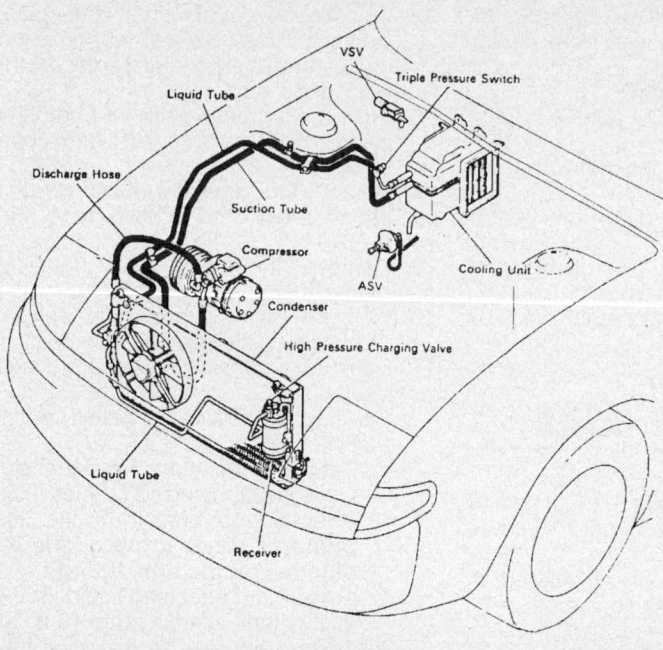

Fig. 8   A/C system components

TY7029100001000X

Fig. 9   Cooling unit

TY7029100002000X

and disconnect air bag connector. **When removing wheel pad, take care not to pull air bag wire harness. When storing wheel pad, keep upper surface of the pad facing upward. Never disassemble wheel pad.**

3. Remove steering wheel, then upper and lower steering column covers.
4. Remove steering wheel and upper and lower steering column covers.
5. Disconnect wire terminal from horn contact.
6. Disconnect windshield wiper/washer switch connector, then using a small screwdriver, disengage windshield wiper/washer switch wiring from combination switch connector. **Note position of wires.**
7. Remove screw, clamp and windshield wiper/washer switch assembly.
8. Reverse procedure to install. Reset audio coded anti-theft, if equipped, as outlined in "Precautions."

STEERING WHEEL
REPLACE

1. Obtain audio anti-theft code, if equipped, as outlined in "Precautions."
2. Position front wheels facing straight ahead.
3. Pull wheel pad out from steering wheel and disconnect air bag connector. **When removing wheel pad, take care not to pull air bag wire harness. When storing wheel pad, keep upper surface facing upward. Never disassemble wheel pad.**
4. Remove steering wheel pad.
5. Place alignment marks on steering wheel and mainshaft for assembly reference.
6. Remove nut attaching steering wheel to steering shaft.

7. Using a suitable puller, remove steering wheel.
8. Reverse procedure to install. Reset audio coded anti-theft, if equipped, as outlined in "Precautions."

INSTRUMENT CLUSTER
REPLACE

1. Obtain audio anti-theft code, if equipped, as outlined under "Precautions."
2. Pull wheel pad out from steering wheel and disconnect air bag connector. **When removing wheel pad, take care not to pull air bag wire harness. When storing wheel pad, keep upper surface of the pad facing upward. Never disassemble wheel pad.**
3. Remove steering wheel, then upper and lower steering column covers.
4. Remove engine hood release lever from lower part of instrument panel.
5. Remove scuff plate, then the six left side I/P lower finish panel attaching screws, then remove finish panels.
6. Using a screwdriver, remove screw caps from lower instrument cluster finish panel.
7. Remove five instrument cluster finish panel attaching screws, then the panel.
8. Remove four combination meter attaching screws.
9. Disconnect electrical connectors from rear of combination meter and remove meter.
10. Remove speedometer cable by pushing on pawls on right and left sides of the meter bracket.
11. Reverse to install. Reset audio coded anti-theft, if equipped, as outlined under "Precautions."

RADIO
REPLACE

1. Obtain audio anti-theft code, if equipped, as outlined under "Precautions."
2. Pull wheel pad out from steering wheel and disconnect air bag connector. **When removing wheel pad, take care not to pull air bag wire harness. When storing wheel pad, keep upper surface of the pad facing upward. Never disassemble wheel pad.**
3. Remove steering wheel, then upper and lower steering column covers.
4. Remove console upper panel, then using a screwdriver remove four console cap screws.
5. Remove four screws and two bolts that attach console box to floor.
6. Disconnect all electrical connectors, then remove console box.
7. Remove two center cluster finish panel attaching screws, then using a screwdriver remove center cluster finish panel and disconnect electrical connector.
8. Remove four radio attaching screws, then disconnect antenna lead, speaker and electrical connectors and remove radio.
9. Reverse to install. Reset audio coded anti-theft, if equipped, as outlined under "Precautions."

WIPER MOTOR
REPLACE

FRONT

1. Disconnect wiper motor wire connector, then remove wiper motor service cover, if equipped.
2. Remove wiper motor attaching bolts.
3. Using a screwdriver disconnect wiper link from wiper motor and remove wiper motor.
4. Reverse procedure to install.

REAR

1. Remove wiper arm and rear door trim cover.
2. Disconnect wiper motor wire connector.
3. Remove wiper motor bracket attaching bolts and wiper motor and bracket, **Fig. 5.**

WIPER SWITCH
REPLACE

Refer to "Combination Switch, Replace" procedure.

BLOWER MOTOR
REPLACE

1. Remove cooling unit as outlined under "Evaporator Core, Replace."
2. Disconnect blower motor connector.
3. Disconnect electrical connector from air inlet damper control servomotor.
4. Remove wire harness.
5. Remove blower unit retaining nuts and the blower unit.
6. Remove wire harness clamp from blower unit.
7. Remove three blower motor screws and pull blower motor with fan from bottom of blower unit, **Fig. 6.**
8. Reverse procedure to install.

HEATER CORE
REPLACE

1. Remove cooling unit as outlined under "Evaporator Core, Replace."

2. Drain engine coolant from radiator.
3. Disconnect water hoses from heater unit.
4. Remove pipe grommets.
5. Disconnect heater unit connector and remove wire harness.
6. Remove four retaining nuts and the heater unit, **Fig. 7.**
7. Remove heater air duct from heater unit.
8. Remove heater core pipe clamps and pull out heater core with return pipe.
9. Reverse procedure to install.

EVAPORATOR CORE
REPLACE

1. Obtain audio anti-theft code, if equipped, as outlined under "Precautions."
2. Discharge and recover A/C refrigerant, then disconnect suction tube from cooling unit outlet fitting.
3. Disconnect liquid tube from cooling unit inlet fitting **Fig. 8,** then cap open fittings immediately to keep moisture from entering the system.
4. Remove grommets from inlet and outlet fittings.
5. Remove glove box and reinforcement, then disconnect electrical connectors.
6. Remove three nuts and four bolts that attach the cooling unit to the instrument panel and cowl.
7. With cooling unit removed from vehicle, disconnect connectors from upper case unit.
8. Remove four clips and four screws that attach upper case to lower case, **Fig. 9.**
9. Remove thermistor and thermistor holder, then the lower case.
10. Remove packing and heat sensing tube from suction and liquid tubes.
11. Remove expansion valve from evaporator.
12. Reverse procedure to install, noting the following:
    a. **Torque** bolt attaching expansion valve, suction and liquid lines tubes to evaporator core to 48 inch lbs. **Ensure O-rings are properly positioned on the tube fittings.**
    b. **Torque** nut attaching liquid tube to cooling unit inlet fitting to 10 ft. lbs.
    c. **Torque** nut attaching suction tube to cooling unit outlet fitting to 24 ft. lbs.
    d. Add specified amount of compressor oil to compressor before recharging system as outlined under "Air Conditioning."
    e. Reset audio coded anti-theft, if equipped, as outlined under "Precautions."

7A-FE 1.8L Engine

NOTE: For Procedures Not Found In This Section, Refer To Toyota Corolla Engine Section.

NOTE: On Air Bag Equipped Models, Refer To "Air Bag System Precautions" Located In The Front Of This Manual For System Disarming & Arming Procedures.

INDEX

PRECAUTIONS

AIR BAG SYSTEMS

Refer to "Air Bag System Precautions" in the front of this manual for system disarming and arming procedures.

BATTERY GROUND CABLE

Prior to service, disconnect battery ground cable and isolate as required.

AUDIO CODED ANTI-THEFT SYSTEM

Some models are equipped with an audio coded anti-theft system that will disable the radio when the battery cable is disconnected. The system can be identified by the "ANTI-THEFT SYSTEM" on the cassette tape lid. Obtain 3 digit customer code for input. Reset system after service as follows:

1. Obtain 3 digit audio anti-theft code.
2. Depress 1 (PROG) while depressing righthand side of TUNE SEEK button, - - - will appear in tape operation display.
3. To enter the first digit, depress 1 (PROG) button repeatedly until the number of times depressed equals the first digit beginning with zero (depress the 1 button six times if the first digit if five).
4. To enter second digit, depress 2 (APS) button repeatedly until the number of times depressed equals the second digit beginning with zero.
5. To enter third digit, depress 3 (RPT) button repeatedly until the number of times depressed equals the second digit beginning with zero.
6. If - - - is displayed during code input, repeat procedure.
7. When code appears in display, depress and hold SCAN button until SEC appears.
8. When SEC disappears audio system should be operative.
9. If Err is displayed, repeat procedure. **Attempting to input code more than nine times may permanently disable audio system.**

COMPRESSION PRESSURE

1. Start engine and warm to normal operating temperature.
2. Remove charge air cooler.

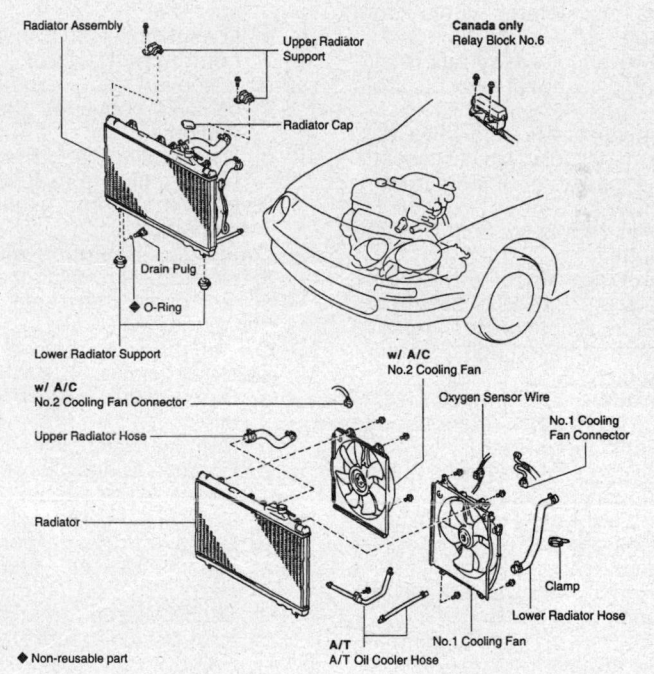

Fig. 1 Radiator replace.

3. Disconnect solenoid resistor connector.
4. Disconnect cold start injector connector.
5. Disconnect distributor connectors.
6. Remove spark plugs.
7. Insert compression pressure gauge into spark plug hole.
8. Fully open throttle.
9. Measure compression pressure while cranking engine.
10. Standard compression pressure is 191 psi or more. Minimum pressure should be 142 psi.

11. Compression pressure difference between cylinders should not exceed 14 psi.

ENGINE
REPLACE

1. Obtain audio anti-theft code, if equipped, as outlined in "Precautions."
2. Remove hood and engine undercover.
3. Drain engine coolant, then engine oil.
4. Remove air cleaner assembly as follows:
   a. Disconnect intake air temperature sensor electrical connector.
   b. Disconnect accelerator cable from bracket on air cleaner cap.
   c. Disconnect four air cleaner cap clips, then air hose from air pipe.
   d. Disconnect air cleaner hose from throttle body, then remove air cleaner cap and element.
   e. Remove three air cleaner case retaining bolts, then the case.
5. Disconnect accelerator cable from throttle body.
6. Remove two engine relay box retaining nuts and disconnect relay box from battery.
7. Remove lower cover from relay box, then disconnect fusible link cassette and two connectors of engine wire from relay box.
8. Remove A/C relay box from bracket, then the battery.
9. **On models equipped with cruise control,** disconnect cruise control actuator electrical connector, remove four actuator attaching bolts, actuator and bracket.
10. **On all models,** disconnect electric cooling fan connector, then remove upper radiator support seal.
11. Disconnect coolant reservoir hose, then remaining radiator hoses.
12. **On models equipped with automatic transmission,** disconnect oil cooler hoses from the radiator.
13. **On all models,** remove two radiator upper support retaining bolts.
14. Lift radiator out of engine compartment, then remove radiator reservoir tank.
15. Disconnect wires and connectors from check connector, igniter connector and vacuum sensor connector.
16. Disconnect ground strap from left fender apron.
17. Disconnect engine wire clamp from wire bracket, then remove bracket retaining bolts and bracket.
18. Disconnect noise filter.
19. Disconnect two vacuum hoses from charcoal canister, then remove canister retaining bolts and canister.
20. Disconnect heater hose from water inlet.
21. Disconnect speedometer cable from transaxle.
22. Disconnect fuel hoses, catching any leaking fluid in a container.
23. Remove three clutch release cylinder retaining bolts, then the clutch release cylinder from the transaxle.
24. Disconnect transaxle control cables from transaxle.
25. Disconnect the following vacuum hoses:
   a. Vacuum sensor hose from gas filter on air intake chamber.
   b. Brake booster hose from air intake chamber.
   c. Three A/C hoses from air switching valve (ASV) on air intake chamber.
   d. A/C hose from air pipe.
26. Remove engine wire clamp from wire bracket on right fender apron, then disconnect two cowl wire connectors.
27. Disconnect electrical connectors.
28. Remove two engine wire to cowl panel attaching nuts, then pull wire from panel.
29. Raise and support vehicle.
30. Remove lower crossmember attaching bolts and nuts, then the crossmember.
31. Remove front exhaust pipe as follows:
   a. Disconnect oxygen sensor connector.
   b. Loosen bolt, then disconnect clamp from support bracket.
   c. Remove front exhaust pipe-to-catalytic converter attaching bolts and nuts.
   d. Disconnect support hook on front exhaust pipe from support bracket, then remove front exhaust pipe and gaskets.
32. **On models equipped with automatic transmission,** disconnect transaxle control cable from engine mounting center member.
33. **On all models,** remove front driveshafts as follows:
   a. Remove tire and wheel assemblies.
   b. Remove cotter pin and locknut cap.
   c. Remove bearing locknut while depressing brake pedal.
   d. Drain oil from transaxle.
   e. Remove brake caliper from steering knuckle and suspend it with wire.
   f. Scribe reference marks on hub and rotor disc, then remove rotor disc.
   g. Remove cotter pin and tie rod end nut from steering knuckle, then using tie rod end removal tool No. 09628-62011, or equivalent, separate tie rod end from steering knuckle.
   h. Remove bolt and two nuts attaching lower arm to steering knuckle, then disconnect lower arm from steering knuckle.
   i. Using puller tool No. 09950-20017, or equivalent, disconnect left side driveshaft from steering knuckle. **Cover driveshaft boot shaft with cloth to prevent damage.**
   j. Using a hammer and hub nut wrench, remove left side driveshaft from transaxle. **Ensure care is taken to not damage dust cover. Cover hub nut wrench with cloth to prevent damage to transaxle body.**
   k. Use a hammer and brass bar to tap out right side driveshaft.
34. Disconnect heater hose from water inlet pipe.
35. **On models equipped with A/C,** proceed as follows:
   a. Disconnect A/C compressor connector, then remove drive belt.
   b. Remove four A/C compressor retaining bolts, pull compressor away from mounting.
   c. Using wire, suspend compressor from radiator support.
36. **On all models,** remove power steering pump drive belt.
37. Remove two power steering pump attaching bolts, then use a wire to suspend pump from cowl.
38. Remove eight engine mounting center member attaching bolts, then the center member.
39. Remove front engine mounting through bolt and mounting insulator.
40. Remove two mounting bracket attaching bolts and bracket.
41. Remove rear engine mounting through bolt and mounting insulator.
42. Remove three mounting bracket attaching bolts and bracket.
43. Remove connector from ground wire on righthand fender apron.
44. Remove three right side engine mounting stay attaching bolts and mounting stay.
45. Remove two left side engine mounting stay attaching bolts and mounting stay.
46. Remove ground strap from transaxle.
47. Attach an engine chain hoist, or equivalent, to engine hangers.
48. Remove through bolt and three lefthand mounting insulator attaching bolts, then the insulator.
49. Remove three lefthand mounting bracket attaching bolts.
50. Remove through bolt and two righthand mounting insulator attaching bolts, then the insulator.
51. Lift engine slowly and carefully out of vehicle. **Ensure to not hit power steering gear housing or neutral start switch.**
52. Reverse procedure to install. Reset audio coded anti-theft, if equipped, as outlined in "Precautions."

RADIATOR
REPLACE

1. Drain coolant.
2. Disconnect radiator hoses, **Fig. 1.**
3. Disconnect coolant reservoir hose.
4. Disconnect No. 1 cooling fan connector.
5. **On models equipped with A/C,** disconnect No. 2 cooling fan connector.
6. **On models equipped with automatic transmission,** disconnect transmission oil cooler hoses.
7. **On all models,** remove upper radiator support seal.
8. Reverse procedure to install.

TIGHTENING SPECIFICATIONS

Year	Component	Torque, Ft. Lbs.
1996–97	A/C Compressor To A/C Compressor Bracket	18
	Bearing Cap Bolts	①
	Camshaft Timing Pulley	43
	Center & Rear Mount To Member	38
	Connecting Rod Cap	22③
	Crankshaft Bearing Cap	44
	Crankshaft Pulley	87
	Cylinder Head	①
	Driveplate (A/T)	47
	Engine Coolant Drain Plug	25
	Engine Mount Member	45
	Exhaust Manifold To Cylinder Head	25
	Exhaust Pipe-To-Manifold	46
	Flywheel (M/T)	58
	Front Mount to Member	35
	Fuel Evaporation Vent Tube	16②
	Fuel Inlet Hose To Fuel Filter	22
	Fuel Inlet Pipe To Tank	30②
	Fuel Pump To Tank	30②
	Fuel Sender Gauge	30②
	Fuel Tank Drain Plug	9
	Fuel Tank Straps	29
	Idler Pulley	27
	Insulator To Body Bracket Through Bolt	64
	Insulator To Engine Mount Bracket (Bolt)	29
	Insulator To Engine Mount Bracket (Nut)	38
	Intake Manifold To Cylinder Head	29
	LH Mounting Insulator To Bracket (Bolt)	47
	LH Mounting Insulator To Bracket (Nut)	38
	LH Mount Insulator To Transaxle Case	35
	LH Mount Stay	15
	LH Mount Through Bolt	64
	Oil Cooler Pipe	25
	Oil Dipstick Guide	82②
	Oil Pan	43②
	Oil Pump	12
	Oil Strainer	82②
	Power Steering Pump Bracket	29
	Radiator Support	9
	RH Mounting Insulator To Bracket Bolt	47
	RH Mounting Insulator To Bracket Nut	38
	RH Mount Stay	31
	RH Mount Through Bolt	64
	Spark Plug	13
	Thermostat Water Inlet	82②
	Water Pump	11

① — Refer to "Cylinder Head, Replace" in Toyota Corolla "Engine" section, for tightening procedure.

② — Inch lbs.

③ — Plus an additional 90.°

5S-FE 2.2L Engine

NOTE: On Air Bag Equipped Models, Refer To "Air Bag System Precautions" Located In The Front Of This Manual For System Disarming & Arming Procedures.

INDEX

PRECAUTIONS

AIR BAG SYSTEMS

Refer to "Air Bag System Precautions" in the front of this manual for system disarming and arming procedures.

BATTERY GROUND CABLE

Prior to service, disconnect battery ground cable and isolate as required.

AUDIO CODED ANTI-THEFT SYSTEM

Some models are equipped with an audio coded anti-theft system that will disable the radio when the battery cable is disconnected. The system can be identified by the "ANTI-THEFT SYSTEM" on the cassette tape lid. Obtain 3 digit customer code for input. Reset system after service as follows:

1. Obtain 3 digit audio anti-theft code.
2. Depress 1 (PROG) while depressing righthand side of TUNE SEEK button, - - - will appear in tape operation display.
3. To enter the first digit, depress 1 (PROG) button repeatedly until the number of times depressed equals the first digit beginning with zero (depress the 1 button six times if the first digit if five).
4. To enter second digit, depress 2 (APS) button repeatedly until the number of times depressed equals the second digit beginning with zero.
5. To enter third digit, depress 3 (RPT) button repeatedly until the number of times depressed equals the second digit beginning with zero.
6. If - - - is displayed during code input, repeat procedure.
7. When code appears in display, depress and hold SCAN button until SEC appears.
8. When SEC disappears audio system should be operative.
9. If Err is displayed, repeat procedure.

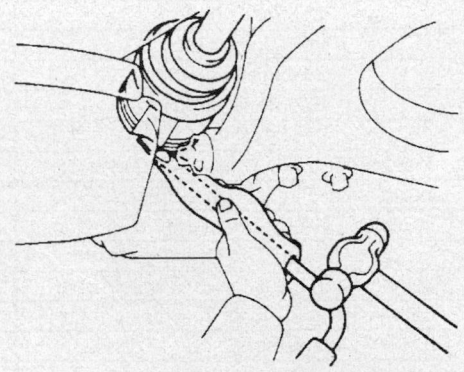

Fig. 1   Left side driveshaft removal

TY1069100012000X

Attempting to input code more than nine times may permanently disable audio system.

COMPRESSION PRESSURE

1. Start engine and warm to normal operating temperature.
2. Disconnect distributor connectors.
3. Remove spark plugs.
4. Insert compression pressure gauge into spark plug hole.
5. Fully open throttle.
6. Measure compression pressure while cranking engine.
7. Standard compression pressure is 178 psi or more. Minimum pressure should be 142 psi.
8. Compression pressure difference between cylinders should not exceed 14 psi.

ENGINE

REPLACE

1. Obtain audio anti-theft code, if equipped, as outlined in "Precautions."
2. Remove hood and engine undercover.
3. Drain engine coolant, then engine oil.
4. Remove air cleaner assembly as follows:
   a. Disconnect intake air temperature sensor electrical connector.
   b. Disconnect accelerator cable from bracket on air cleaner cap.
   c. Disconnect four air cleaner cap clips, then air hose from air pipe.
   d. Disconnect air cleaner hose from throttle body, then remove air cleaner cap and element.
   e. Remove three air cleaner case retaining bolts, then the case.
5. Disconnect accelerator cable from throttle body.
6. Remove two engine relay box retaining nuts and disconnect relay box from battery.
7. Remove lower cover from relay box, then disconnect fusible link cassette and two connectors of engine wire from relay box.
8. Remove A/C relay box from bracket, then the battery.
9. **On models equipped with cruise control,** disconnect cruise control actuator electrical connector, remove four actuator attaching bolts, actuator and bracket.
10. **On all models,** disconnect electric cooling fan connector, then remove upper radiator support seal.
11. Disconnect coolant reservoir hose, then remaining radiator hoses.
12. **On models equipped with automatic transmission,** disconnect oil cooler hoses from the radiator.
13. **On all models,** remove two radiator upper support retaining bolts.
14. Lift radiator out of engine compartment, then remove radiator reservoir tank.
15. Remove two wiper arms, then outside lower windshield molding.
16. Remove two bolts and four nuts that attach upper suspension mounting

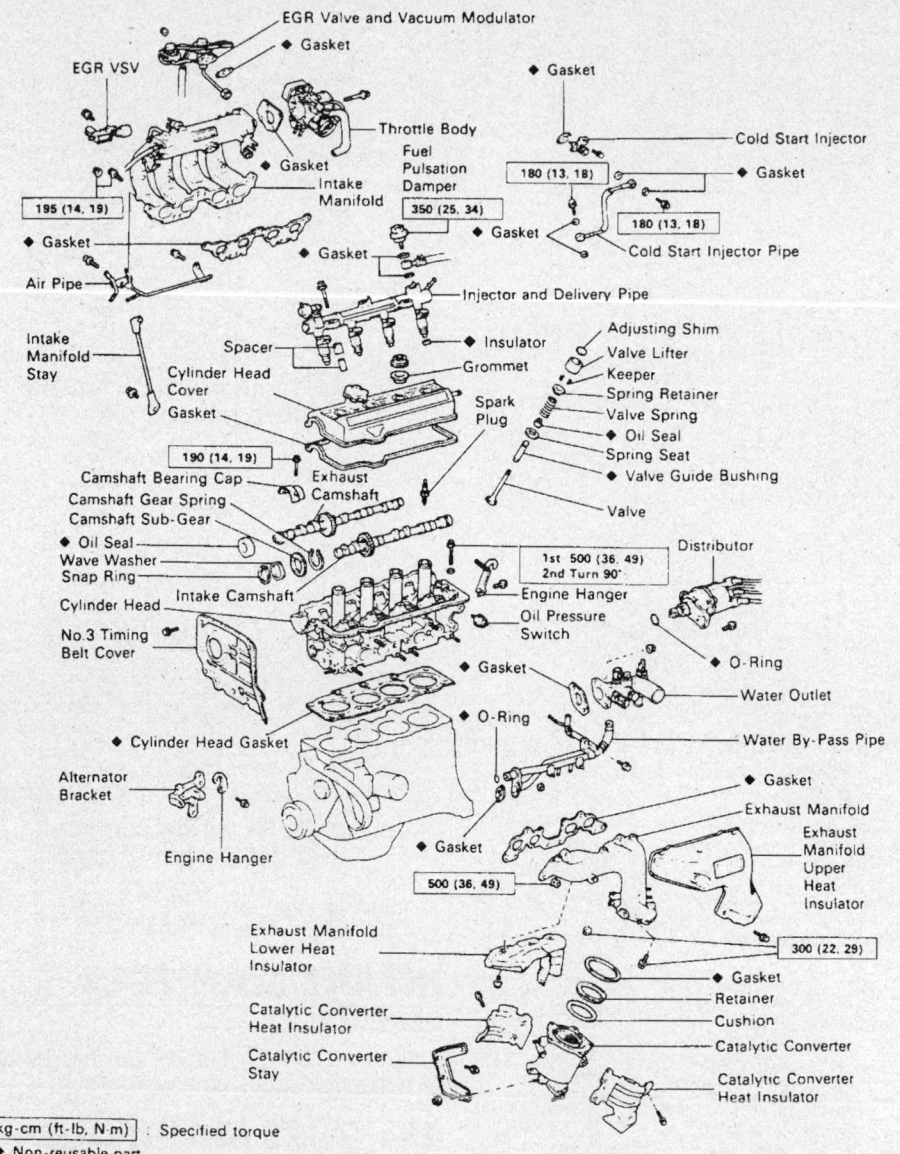

Fig. 2 Cylinder head components

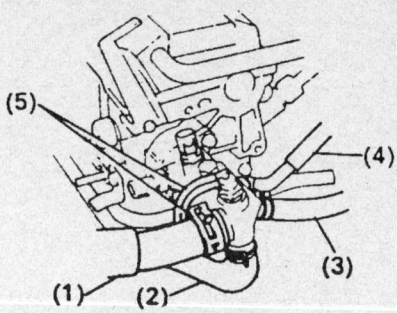

- (1) Upper radiator hose
- (2) Water by-pass pipe hose
- (3) Heater water hose
- (4) ISC water by-pass hose
- (5) Two EVAP BVSV vacuum hoses

TY1069100014000X

Fig. 3 Cooling system & vacuum hoses

34. Raise and support vehicle.
35. Remove lower crossmember attaching bolts and nuts, then the crossmember.
36. Remove front exhaust pipe as follows:
    a. Disconnect oxygen sensor connector.
    b. Loosen bolt, then disconnect clamp from support bracket.
    c. Remove front exhaust pipe-to-catalytic converter attaching bolts and nuts.
    d. Disconnect support hook on front exhaust pipe from support bracket, then remove front exhaust pipe and gaskets.
37. **On models equipped with automatic transmission,** disconnect transaxle control cable from engine mounting center member.
38. **On all models,** remove front driveshafts as follows:
    a. Remove tire and wheel assemblies.
    b. Remove cotter pin and locknut cap.
    c. Remove bearing locknut while depressing brake pedal.
    d. Drain oil from transaxle.
    e. Remove brake caliper from steering knuckle and suspend it with wire.
    f. Scribe reference marks on hub and rotor disc, then remove rotor disc.
    g. Remove cotter pin and tie rod end nut from steering knuckle, then using tie rod end removal tool No. 09628-62011, or equivalent, separate tie rod end from steering knuckle.
    h. Remove bolt and two nuts attaching lower arm to steering knuckle, then disconnect lower arm from steering knuckle.
    i. Using puller tool No. 09950-20017, or equivalent, disconnect left side driveshaft from steering knuckle. **Cover driveshaft boot shaft with cloth to prevent it from damage.**
    j. Using a hammer and hub nut wrench or an equivalent, remove

brace to cowl and strut towers.
17. Remove upper suspension mounting brace.
18. Disconnect ignition coil connector and high-tension cord.
19. Remove two ignition coil attaching bolts and ignition coil.
20. Disconnect wires and connectors from check connector, igniter connector and vacuum sensor connector.
21. Disconnect ground strap from left fender apron.
22. Disconnect engine wire clamp from wire bracket, then remove bracket retaining bolts and bracket.
23. Disconnect noise filter.
24. Disconnect two vacuum hoses from charcoal canister, then remove canister retaining bolts and canister.
25. Disconnect heater hose from water inlet.
26. Disconnect speedometer cable from transaxle.
27. Disconnect fuel hoses, catching any

leaking fluid in a container.
28. Remove three clutch release cylinder retaining bolts, then the clutch release cylinder from the transaxle.
29. Disconnect transaxle control cables from transaxle.
30. Disconnect the following vacuum hoses:
    a. Vacuum sensor hose from gas filter on air intake chamber.
    b. Brake booster hose from air intake chamber.
    c. Three A/C hoses from air switching valve (ASV) on air intake chamber.
    d. A/C hose from air pipe.
31. Remove engine wire clamp from wire bracket on right fender apron, then disconnect two cowl wire connectors.
32. Disconnect ECU, A/C amplifier, cowl wire and O/D diode electrical connectors.
33. Remove two engine wire to cowl panel attaching nuts, then pull wire from panel.

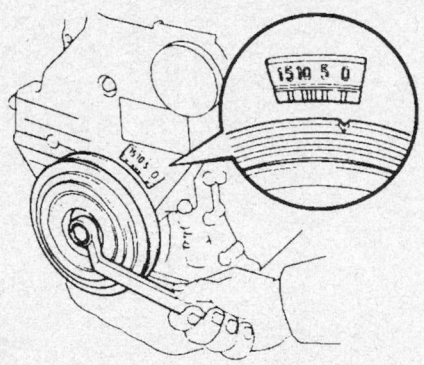

TY1069100015000X

Fig. 4 Crankshaft pulley & timing mark alignment

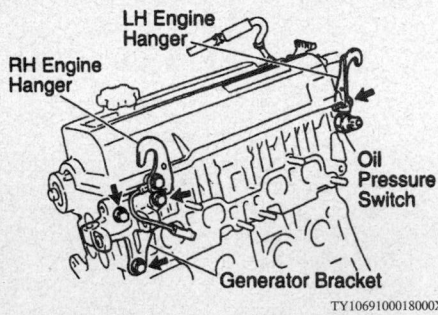

TY1069100018000X

Fig. 7 Engine hanger removal & disconnecting ground strap

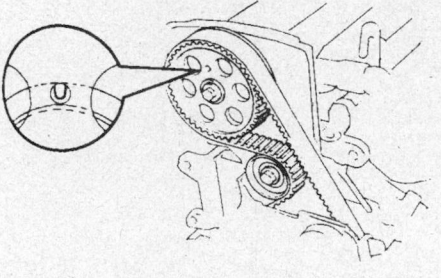

TY1069100016000X

Fig. 5 Bearing cap mark alignment

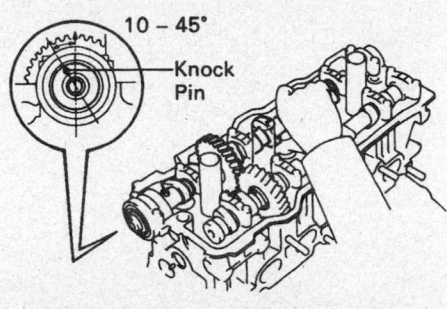

TY1069100019000X

Fig. 8 Setting knock pin of intake camshaft to 10–45° BTDC

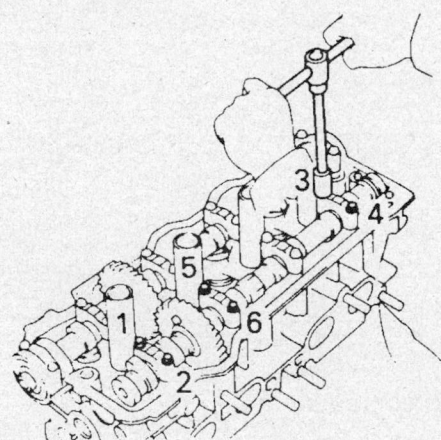

TY1069100021000X

Fig. 10 Exhaust camshaft bearing cap bolt loosening sequence

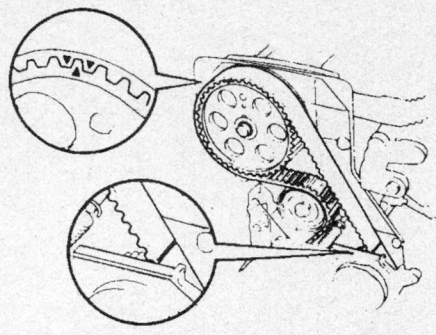

TY1069100017000X

Fig. 6 Timing belt & camshaft pulley matchmarks

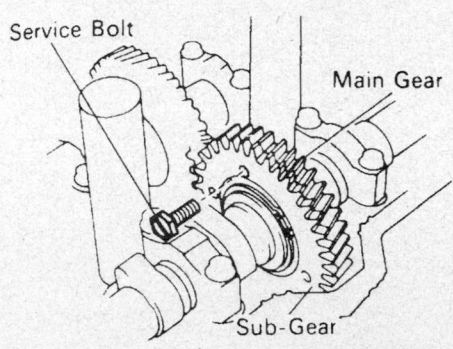

TY1069100020000X

Fig. 9 Securing camshaft sub-gear to drive gear

---

left side driveshaft from transaxle, **Fig. 1. Ensure care is taken not to damage dust cover. Cover hub nut wrench with cloth so transaxle body is not damaged.**

    k. Remove two bolts of center bearing bracket and pull out right side driveshaft together with center bearing case and center driveshaft.

39. Disconnect heater hose from water inlet pipe.
40. **On models equipped with A/C,** proceed as follows:
    a. Disconnect A/C compressor connector, then remove drive belt.
    b. Remove four A/C compressor retaining bolts, pull compressor away from mounting.
    c. Using wire, suspend compressor from radiator support.
41. **On all models,** remove power steering pump drive belt.
42. Remove two power steering pump attaching bolts, then use a wire to suspend pump to cowl.
43. Remove eight engine mounting center member attaching bolts, then the center member.
44. Remove front engine mounting through bolt and mounting insulator.
45. Remove two mounting bracket attaching bolts and bracket.
46. Remove rear engine mounting through bolt and mounting insulator.
47. Remove three mounting bracket attaching bolts and bracket.
48. Remove connector from ground wire on righthand fender apron.
49. Remove three right side engine

mounting stay attaching bolts and mounting stay.
50. Remove two left side engine mounting stay attaching bolts and mounting stay.
51. Remove ground strap from transaxle.
52. Attach an engine chain hoist, or equivalent, to engine hangers.
53. Remove through bolt and three left-hand mounting insulator attaching bolts, then the insulator.
54. Remove three lefthand mounting bracket attaching bolts.
55. Remove through bolt and two right-hand mounting insulator attaching bolts, then the insulator.
56. Lift engine slowly and carefully out of vehicle. **Be careful not to hit power steering gear housing or neutral start switch.**
57. Reverse procedure to install. Reset

audio coded anti-theft, if equipped, as outlined in "Precautions."

INTAKE MANIFOLD
REPLACE

Refer to "Cylinder Head, Replace," for intake manifold replacement procedure.

EXHAUST MANIFOLD
REPLACE

Refer to "Cylinder Head, Replace," for exhaust manifold replacement.

CYLINDER HEAD
REPLACE

1. Obtain audio anti-theft code, if equipped, then drain engine coolant.
2. **On models equipped with automatic transaxle,** disconnect throttle cable from throttle body.
3. **On all models,** disconnect accelerator cable from throttle body.
4. **On models equipped with cruise control,** disconnect cruise control actuator electrical connector, remove four actuator attaching bolts, actuator and bracket.
5. **On all models,** remove air cleaner assembly as follows:
    a. Disconnect intake air temperature sensor electrical connector.
    b. Disconnect accelerator cable from bracket on air cleaner cap.
    c. Disconnect four air cleaner cap clips, then air hose from air pipe.

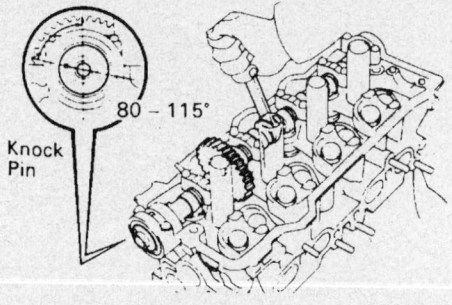

Fig. 11 Setting knock pin of intake camshaft to 80–115° BTDC

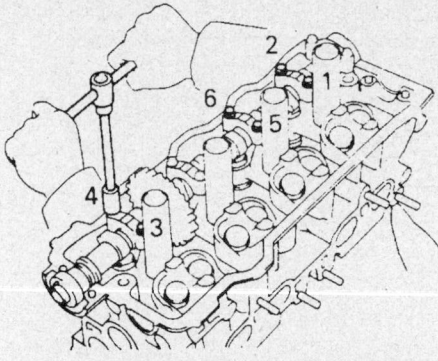

Fig. 12 Intake camshaft bearing cap bolt loosening sequence

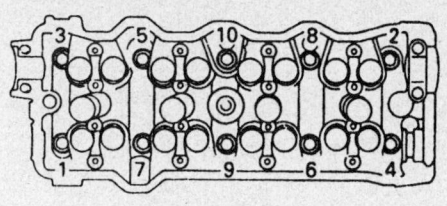

Fig. 13 Cylinder head bolt loosening sequence

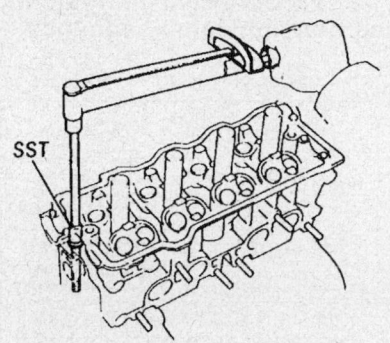

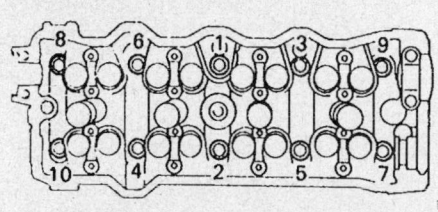

Fig. 14 Cylinder head bolt tightening sequence

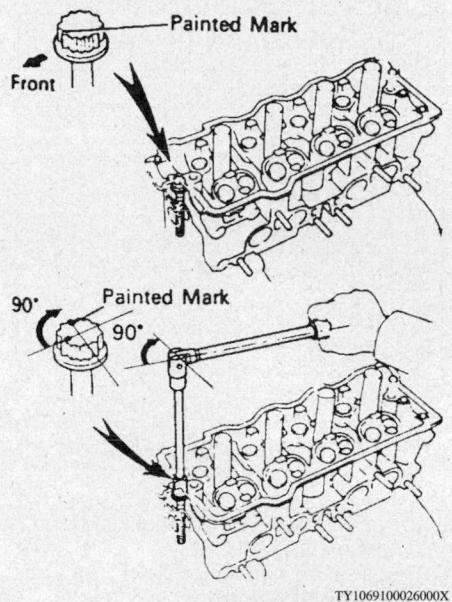

Fig. 15 Cylinder head bolt marking

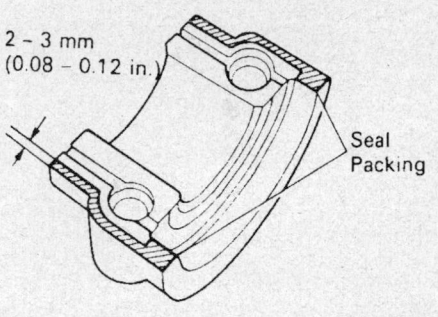

Fig. 16 Bearing cap packing

d. Disconnect air cleaner hose from throttle body, then remove air cleaner cap and element.
e. Remove three air cleaner case retaining bolts, then the case.
6. Remove alternator, then A/C compressor without disconnecting A/C lines.
7. Disconnect distributor electrical connector, then using a screwdriver separate high tension cord from ignition coil.
8. Disconnect spark plug wires from spark plugs, then remove distributor.
9. Remove engine undercovers.
10. Raise and support vehicle.
11. Remove lower crossmember attaching bolts and nuts, then the crossmember.
12. Remove front exhaust pipe as follows:
   a. Disconnect oxygen sensor connector.
   b. Loosen bolt, then disconnect clamp from support bracket.
   c. Remove front exhaust pipe-to-catalytic converter attaching bolts and nuts.
   d. Disconnect support hook on front exhaust pipe from support bracket, then remove front exhaust pipe and gaskets.
13. **On California models,** disconnect

sub-oxygen sensor connector.
14. **On all models,** disconnect main oxygen sensor connector and lower vehicle.
15. Remove six manifold upper heat insulator attaching bolts and insulator.
16. Remove two bolts and nuts from catalytic converter stay.
17. Remove six exhaust manifold retaining nuts, then exhaust manifold and catalytic converter assembly.
18. Separate exhaust manifold and catalytic converter assembly as shown in **Fig. 2.**
19. Disconnect water temperature sender gauge connector, water temperature sensor connector and cold start injector time switch connector.
20. Disconnect cooling system hoses and vacuum hoses shown in **Fig. 3.**
21. Remove two water outlet attaching bolts, water outlet and gasket.
22. Remove two water bypass pipe attaching bolts and nuts, water bypass pipe and gasket.
23. Remove O-ring from water bypass hose.
24. Disconnect throttle position sensor

electrical connector and idle speed control valve connector.
25. Disconnect PCV hose, vacuum modulator vacuum hoses and vacuum switching valve vacuum hoses from throttle body.
26. Remove four throttle body attaching bolts, throttle body and gasket.
27. Remove two cold start injector pipe union bolts, four injector gaskets and injector pipe. **When removing union bolts, place a shop towel under injector pipe and slowly loosen union bolt.**
28. Remove two cold start injector bolts, cold start injector and gasket.
29. **On California models,** disconnect EGR gas temperature sensor connector.
30. **On all models,** remove vacuum hoses from EGR vacuum switching valve and vacuum hose from charcoal canister.
31. Loosen union nut from EGR pipe, then two EGR attaching bolts, EGR valve, vacuum modulator, vacuum hoses assembly and gasket.
32. Disconnect vacuum sensor hose and brake booster hoses from air intake chamber.
33. Disconnect two A/C vacuum hoses from air switching valve on air intake chamber.

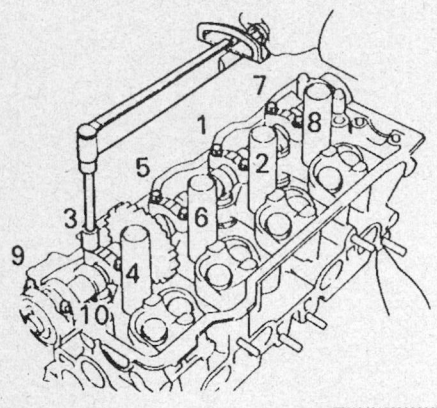

Fig. 17 Intake camshaft bearing cap bolt tightening sequence

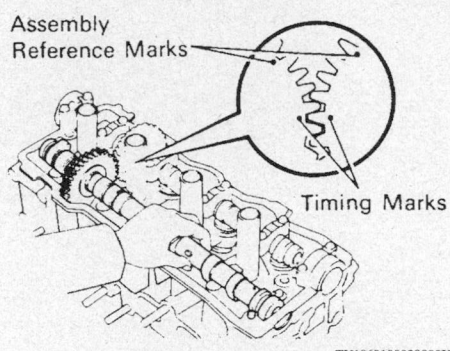

Fig. 18 Intake & exhaust gear timing mark alignment

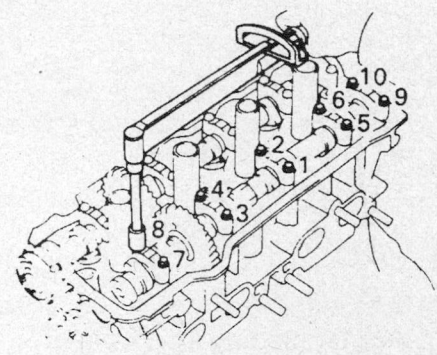

Fig. 19 Exhaust camshaft bearing cap bolt tightening sequence

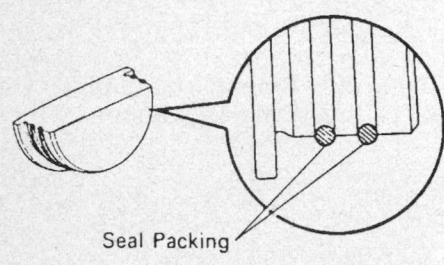

Fig. 20 Semi-circular plugs to cylinder head installation

Shim No.	Thickness	Shim No.	Thickness
1	2.500 (0.0984)	10	2.950 (0.1161)
2	2.550 (0.1004)	11	3.000 (0.1181)
3	2.600 (0.1024)	12	3.050 (0.1201)
4	2.650 (0.1043)	13	3.100 (0.1220)
5	2.700 (0.1063)	14	3.150 (0.1240)
6	2.750 (0.1083)	15	3.200 (0.1260)
7	2.800 (0.1102)	16	3.250 (0.1280)
8	2.850 (0.1122)	17	3.300 (0.1299)
9	2.900 (0.1142)		

New shim thickness   mm (in.)

Fig. 21 Intake valve shim size chart

Shim No.	Thickness	Shim No.	Thickness
1	2.500 (0.0984)	10	2.950 (0.1161)
2	2.550 (0.1004)	11	3.000 (0.1181)
3	2.600 (0.1024)	12	3.050 (0.1201)
4	2.650 (0.1043)	13	3.100 (0.1220)
5	2.700 (0.1063)	14	3.150 (0.1240)
6	2.750 (0.1083)	15	3.200 (0.1260)
7	2.800 (0.1102)	16	3.250 (0.1280)
8	2.850 (0.1122)	17	3.300 (0.1299)
9	2.900 (0.1142)		

New shim thickness   mm (in.)

Fig. 22 Exhaust valve shim size chart

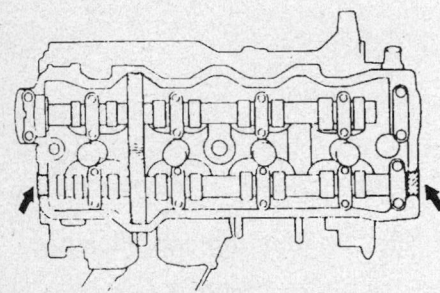

34. Disconnect air hose from intake manifold, air hose from A/C air switching valve and two air hoses from power steering pump.
35. Disconnect engine wire clamp, then remove two bolts wire bracket and air tube.
36. Disconnect engine wire ground strap from intake manifold, then remove EGR vacuum switching valve.
37. Disconnect two wire clamps from wire brackets on top of intake manifold.
38. Disconnect wire clip from accelerator bracket, then remove two intake manifold stay attaching bolts and stay.
39. Loosen pulsation damper and two bolts holding delivery pipe to cylinder head.
40. Remove pulsation damper and disconnect fuel inlet hose from delivery pipe.
41. Remove two bolts and delivery pipe together with four injectors. **Be careful not to drop injectors, when removing delivery pipe.**
42. Remove right front wheel assembly, then the power steering drive belt.
43. Slightly raise engine assembly enough to remove weight from right side engine mounting assembly.
44. Disconnect connector from ground wire on right side fender apron.
45. Remove righthand engine mounting stay and disconnect power steering reservoir tank from bracket.
46. Remove right side engine mounting insulator through bolt, two nuts and insulator.
47. Lower engine, then remove three right side engine mounting bracket attaching bolts and bracket.
48. Remove spark plugs.
49. Disconnect engine wire from alternator bracket and adjusting bar.
50. Remove five timing belt cover attaching bolts, cover and two gaskets.
51. Turn crankshaft pulley and align its groove with timing mark " 0 " of the No. 1 timing belt cover, **Fig. 4.**
52. Check that hole of camshaft timing pulley is aligned with timing mark of bearing cap, **Fig. 5.** If not turn crankshaft 360.°
53. Scribe matchmarks on timing belt and camshaft timing pulley to match end of No. 1 timing belt cover as shown in **Fig. 6.**
54. Remove timing belt from camshaft pulley.
55. Using torque wrench adapter tool No. 09249-63010 and driveshaft holding tool No. 09278-54012, or equivalents, remove camshaft pulley bolt, plate washer and pulley.
56. Remove No. 1 idler pulley and tension spring.
57. Remove four No. 3 timing belt cover attaching bolts and cover. **Support timing belt, so meshing of crankshaft timing pulley and timing belt does not shift. Be careful not to drop anything inside timing belt cover. Do not let belt come in contact with oil, water or dust.**
58. Remove engine hangers attaching bolts, engine hangers and ground strap, **Fig. 7.**
59. Remove three alternator bracket attaching bolts, bracket and oil pressure switch.
60. Remove cylinder head cover attaching nuts, grommets, cover and gasket. **Arrange grommets in correct order, so that they can be installed in their original position. This eliminates any possibility of oil leakage when original gaskets are used.**
61. **Before removing camshafts note that thrust clearance of the camshaft is small and camshaft must be kept level while it is being removed. If camshaft is not kept level, the portion of the cylinder head receiving the shaft thrust may crack or be damaged, causing camshaft to seize or break.**
62. Remove exhaust camshaft as follows:

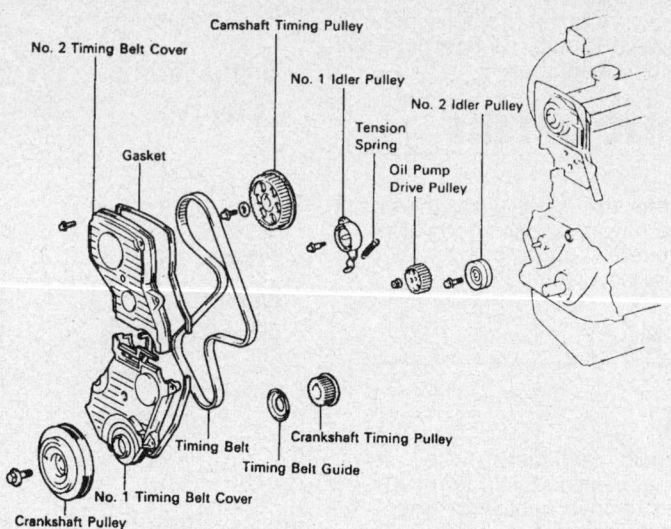

Fig. 23   Timing belt components

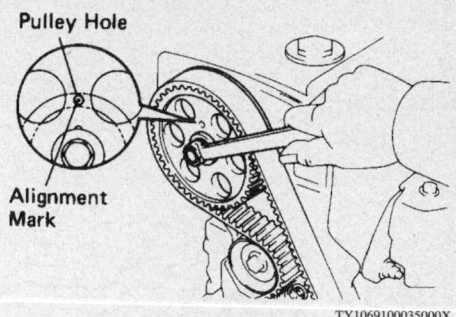

Fig. 24   Camshaft sprocket alignment

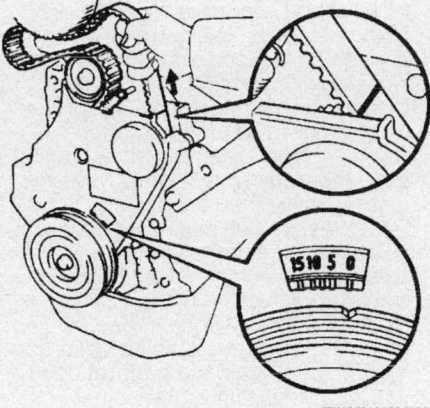

Fig. 25   Timing belt alignment inspection

a. Set knock pin of intake camshaft at 10–45° BTDC of camshaft angle, **Fig. 8.** This angle allows No. 2 and No. 4 cylinder lobes of the exhaust camshaft to push their valve lifters evenly.

b. Using a 6mm bolt, secure camshaft sub-gear to drive gear as shown in **Fig. 9.** This will remove torsional spring force of sub-gear.

c. Remove two rear bearing cap retaining bolts and bearing cap.

d. Uniformly loosen and remove six bolts on No. 1, No. 2 and No. 4 bearing caps with several passes and in sequence shown in **Fig. 10. Do not remove No. 3 bearing cap bolts at this time.**

e. Remove No. 1, No. 2 and No. 4 bearing caps.

f. Alternately loosen and remove No. 3 bearing cap retaining bolts. When removing No. 3 bearing cap bolts, ensure camshaft is being lifted out straight and level. If camshaft is not lifted out straight and level, retighten No. 3 bearing cap bolts. Then reverse order of above steps from step (e) to step (a) and reset knock pin of intake camshaft at 10–45° BTDC, then repeat steps from (b) to (e) once again. **Do not pry on or attempt to force camshaft with a tool or other object.**

g. Remove No. 3 bearing cap and remove camshaft.

63. Remove intake camshaft as follows:
    a. Set knock pin of intake camshaft at 80–115° BTDC of camshaft angle as shown in **Fig. 11.** This angle allows No. 1 and No. 3 cylinder cam lobes of the intake camshaft to push their lifters evenly.
    b. Remove two front bearing cap and oil seal retaining bolts, then the front bearing cap and oil seal.
    c. Uniformly loosen and remove bolts on No. 1, No. 3 and No. 4 bearing caps in several passes and sequence shown in **Fig. 12.**
    d. Alternately loosen and remove No.

2 bearing cap retaining bolts. When removing No. 3 bearing cap bolts, ensure camshaft is being lifted out straight and level. If camshaft is not lifted out straight and level, retighten No. 3 bearing cap bolts. Then reverse order of above steps from step (c) to step (a) and reset knock pin of intake camshaft at 80–115° BTDC, then repeat steps from (b) and (c) once again. **Do not pry on or attempt to force camshaft with a tool or other object.**

e. Remove No. 2 bearing cap and camshaft.

64. Uniformly loosen and remove ten cylinder head retaining bolts in sequence shown in **Fig. 13. Head warpage or cracking could result from removing bolts in the incorrect order.**

65. Lift cylinder head from dowels on the cylinder block.

66. Reverse procedure to install, noting the following:
    a. When placing a new gasket in position on cylinder block, ensure direction is correct.
    b. Apply a light coat of engine oil to threads of cylinder head bolts. Install and uniformly **torque** cylinder

head bolts to 36 ft. lbs. in several passes in sequence shown in **Fig. 14.**

c. Mark cylinder head bolt with paint as shown in **Fig. 15.** Retighten cylinder head bolts an additional 90.° Ensure painted mark is now at a 90° angle to the front.

d. Install spark plug tubes and tighten to specifications.

e. Apply multi-purpose grease to thrust portion of intake camshaft and place camshaft at 80–115° BTDC of camshaft angle on cylinder head.

f. Apply seal packing to No. 1 bearing cap as shown in **Fig. 16,** then install bearing caps in their proper locations. Apply a light coat of engine oil to bearing cap retaining bolts and **torque** to 14 ft. lbs. in several passes in sequence shown in **Fig. 17.**

g. Apply multi-purpose grease to new oil seal lip, then using seal installation tool No. 09223-46011, or equivalent, tap in oil seal.

h. Set knock pin of intake camshaft at 10–45° BTDC of camshaft angle.

i. Apply multi-purpose grease to thrust portion of exhaust camshaft, then engage exhaust camshaft gear to intake camshaft gear by matching timing marks on each gear as shown in **Fig. 18.** Roll down exhaust camshaft onto bearing journals while engaging gears with each other.

j. Turn intake camshaft clockwise or counterclockwise a little at a time until exhaust camshaft sits in bearing journals evenly without rocking camshaft on bearing journals. **It is very important to replace camshaft in bearing journals evenly while tightening bearing caps.**

k. Install bearing caps in their proper position, then apply a light coat of engine oil to bearing cap retaining bolts. Install and uniformly **torque** ten bearing cap bolts to 14 ft. lbs. in several passes, in sequence shown in **Fig. 19.**

l. Remove service bolt holding subgear and main gear, then check valve clearance adjust clearance if necessary.

m. Apply seal packing to semi-circular plugs and install them into cylinder head as shown in **Fig. 20.**

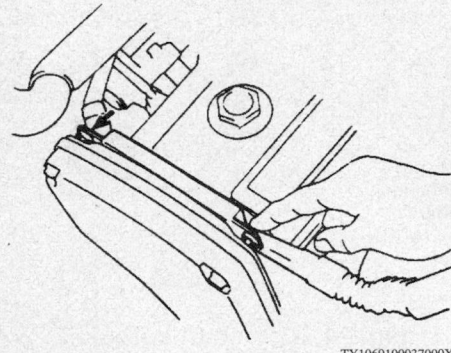

Fig. 26 Engine wire to No. 2 timing belt cover installation

n. Reset audio coded anti-theft, if equipped, as outlined in " Precautions."

VALVE CLEARANCE SPECIFICATIONS

Year	Stem-To-Guide Clearance	
	Intake	Exhaust
1996–99	.007–.011	.011–.015

VALVE ADJUSTMENT

Valve adjustment is accomplished by installing the proper thickness shim to achieve proper valve clearance. Shims are available in .0020 inch (.050 mm) increments, **Figs. 21 and 22.**

1. With engine cold, place No. 1 cylinder at TDC of compression stroke by turning the crankshaft pulley and aligning its groove with the timing mark "0" of the timing pointer.
2. Ensure valves on No. 1 cylinder are loose and valve on No. 4 cylinder are tight. If not turn crankshaft 360° (one complete revolution) and align timing marks.
3. With engine in this position check clearance of the following valves:
   a. No. 1 intake and exhaust valves.
   b. No. 2 intake valves.
   c. No. 3 exhaust valves.
4. Turn crankshaft pulley 360° (one complete revolution) and align timing marks as outlined previously and check the following valves:
   a. No. 2 exhaust valves.
   b. No. 3 intake valves.
   c. No. 4 intake and exhaust valves.

VALVE GUIDES

1. Using a suitable tool and hammer, strike valve guide bushing to break it off at cylinder head casting.
2. Heat cylinder head to 176–212°F (80–100°C).
3. Using suitable valve guide removal tool, tap out bushing.
4. Install snap ring on new valve guide, then install new valve guide using tool as above and driving in from the reverse side of removal.

5. Ream new valve guide, if necessary. Refer to "Valve Clearance Specifications" for stem clearances.

HYDRAULIC LIFTERS
REPLACE

Check lifters for excessive wear and/or damage. Replace worn or damaged valve lifters as required. Lubricate hydraulic valve lifter before installation.

TIMING BELT
REPLACE
REMOVAL

1. Obtain audio anti-theft code, if equipped, as outlined in " Precautions," then remove right front wheel and engine undercover.
2. Remove cruise control actuator and bracket (if equipped).
3. Remove accessory drive belts, then alternator and alternator bracket.
4. Using suitable jack, raise engine enough to remove weight from right side engine mounting.
5. Disconnect connector from ground wire on right side fender apron.
6. Remove right side engine mounting stay, then disconnect power steering reservoir tank from bracket.
7. Remove right side engine mounting insulator through bolt, two mounting insulator attaching nuts and the insulator.
8. Remove three right side engine mounting bracket attaching bolts and mount, lower jack and perform operation with engine fully down.
9. Remove spark plugs, then disconnect engine wire from alternator bracket and adjusting bar.
10. Remove No. 2 timing belt cover and two gaskets, **Fig. 23.**
11. Rotate crankshaft pulley until pulley groove is aligned with " 0" indication on timing marks, then ensure camshaft sprocket hole is aligned bearing cap No. 1 alignment mark, **Fig. 24. If camshaft sprocket is not aligned properly, engine is not set at TDC compression. Rotate crankshaft an additional 360° and recheck.**
12. If timing belt is to be reused, draw arrow on belt to indicate direction of rotation and make reference marks between timing belt and camshaft sprocket.
13. Loosen spring loaded idler pulley attaching bolt, then pry pulley as far to the left as possible. Temporarily tighten attaching bolt.
14. Remove timing belt from camshaft sprocket, then remove camshaft sprocket attaching bolt, washer and sprocket.
15. Remove crankshaft pulley attaching bolt, if timing belt is to be reused, proceed as follows:
   a. After loosening crankshaft pulley bolt, check that timing belt match mark aligns with end of No. 1 timing belt cover when crankshaft pulley

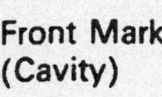
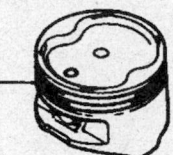

Front Mark (Cavity)

Front Mark (Protrusion)

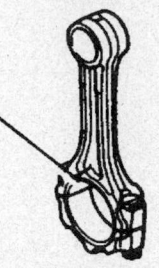

Fig. 27 Piston & connecting rod assembly

groove is aligned with timing mark "0" of No. 1 timing belt cover as shown in **Fig. 25.** If match mark aligns, proceed to step 16. If match mark does not align, proceed to step b.
   b. If match mark is out of alignment on clockwise side, align match mark by pulling timing belt up on washer pump pulley side while turning crankshaft pulley counterclockwise.
   c. After aligning match mark, hold timing belt and turn crankshaft pulley clockwise. Align its groove with timing mark "0"of No. 1 timing belt cove.
   d. If match mark is out of alignment on counterclockwise side, align match mark by pulling timing belt up on No. 1 idler pulley side while turning crankshaft pulley clockwise.
   e. After aligning match mark, hold timing belt and turn crankshaft pulley counterclockwise. Align its groove with timing mark "0" of No. 1 timing cover.
16. Using puller tool No. 09213-60017, or equivalent, remove crankshaft pulley, when reusing timing belt remove pulley without turning it.
17. Remove No. 1 timing belt cover, gasket timing belt guide.
18. If timing belt is to be reused, draw a direction arrow on the timing belt and make reference marks between timing belt and crankshaft timing pulley, then remove belt.
19. Remove No. 1 idler pulley attaching bolt, then pulley and tension spring.
20. Remove No. 2 idler pulley attaching bolt, then the idler pulley.
21. Pry off crankshaft timing pulley with two screwdrivers.
22. While holding oil pump sprocket with suitable tool, remove oil pump nut and sprocket.

INSTALLATION

1. Install oil pump pulley. Tighten attaching nut to specification.

2. Install crankshaft timing pulley, aligning timing pulley set key with key groove of the pulley. Slide pulley on, facing flange side inward.
3. Install No. 2 idler pulley. Tighten idler pulley attaching bolt to specification. Ensure pulley moves smoothly.
4. Install spring loaded No. 1 idler pulley and loosely install attaching bolt. Install spring, then pry pulley as far to left as possible and tighten attaching bolt. Ensure pulley moves smoothly.
5. Temporarily install timing belt as follows:
   a. Using crankshaft pulley bolt, turn crankshaft pulley and position key groove of the pulley upward.
   b. Remove any oil or water on the crankshaft, oil pump, water pump, No. 1 and No. 2 idler pulleys.
   c. Install timing belt onto crankshaft pulley, oil pump pulley, No. 1 idler pulley, water pump pulley and No. 2 idler pulley. If belt is being reused, install in proper direction and align reference mark on crankshaft pulley made during removal procedures. **The engine should be cold during belt installation.**
6. Install timing belt guide, cup side outward.
7. Install No. 1 timing belt cover.
8. Install crankshaft pulley. Tighten attaching bolt to specification. Ensure crankshaft pulley groove is still aligned with " 0" timing mark, indicating No. 1 cylinder is at TDC of compression stroke.
9. Install camshaft timing pulley, washer and attaching bolt. Tighten attaching bolt to specification. Rotate camshaft by turning sprocket attaching bolt to align bearing cap mark and camshaft timing pulley, **Fig. 24.**
10. Install timing belt on camshaft timing pulley. If timing belt is being reused, align reference marks made during removal procedures.
11. Ensure belt has tension between crankshaft timing pulley and camshaft timing pulley.
12. Loosen No. 1 idler pulley attaching bolt ½ turn, rotate crankshaft clockwise two complete revolutions, from TDC compression stroke to TDC compression stroke, check that each pulley aligns with timing marks. If timing marks do not align, remove timing belt and reinstall. Tighten No. 1 idler pulley to specification.
13. Install No. 2 timing belt cover and install two clamps of engine wire to each bolt, **Fig. 26.**
14. Install engine wire to alternator bracket and adjusting bar.
15. Install spark plugs, then the right side engine mounting bracket.
16. Install right side engine mounting insulator, then power steering reservoir to bracket.
17. Install right side engine mounting stay, then connect ground connector to ground wire on right fender apron.
18. Install power steering belt, pivot bolt and adjusting bolt.
19. Install alternator, then the cruise con-

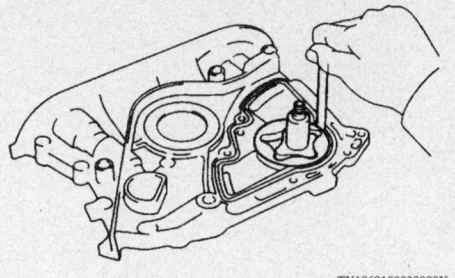
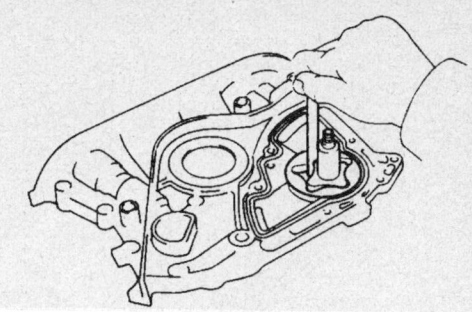

TY1069100039000X

Fig. 28 Side clearance inspection

TY1069100040000X

Fig. 29 Rotor tip clearance inspection

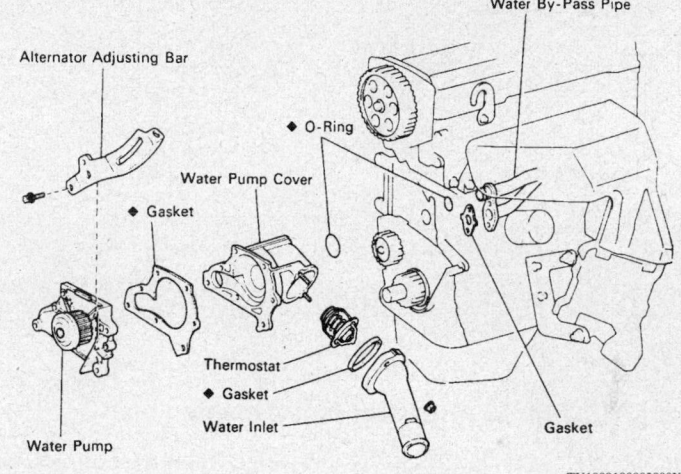

TY1089100002000X

Fig. 30 Water pump removal

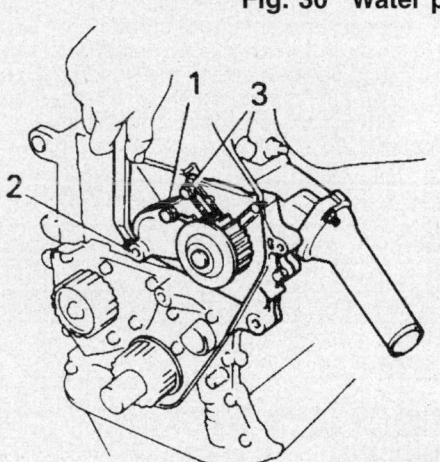

TY1089100003000X

Fig. 31 Water pump bolt removal sequence

trol actuator and bracket.
20. Install engine undercover and right front wheel, then battery ground cable.

CAMSHAFT
REPLACE

Refer to "Cylinder Head, Replace" for camshaft removal procedures.

PISTON & ROD ASSEMBLY

If piston bore is not within specifications,

replace piston and/or cylinder block. When assembling piston onto connecting rod, ensure mark on top of piston and mark on connecting rod are on same side, **Fig. 27.** When installing piston and connecting rod assembly, ensure mark on top of piston is facing toward front of engine.

MAIN & ROD BEARINGS

Undersize bearings are not available. If crankshaft journals or crankpins are worn or scored, the crankshaft must be replaced.

OIL PAN
REPLACE

1. Obtain audio anti-theft code, if equipped, as outlined under " Precautions."
2. Remove hood and engine undercovers, then drain engine oil.
3. Remove suspension lower crossmember attaching nuts and bolts, then the crossmember.
4. Remove front exhaust pipe as outlined in "Engine, Replace."
5. Remove eight engine center member attaching bolts, then center member.
6. Remove two stiffener plate attaching bolts and plate.
7. Remove oil dipstick, oil pan attaching nuts and bolts.
8. Insert blade of tool No. 09032-00100,

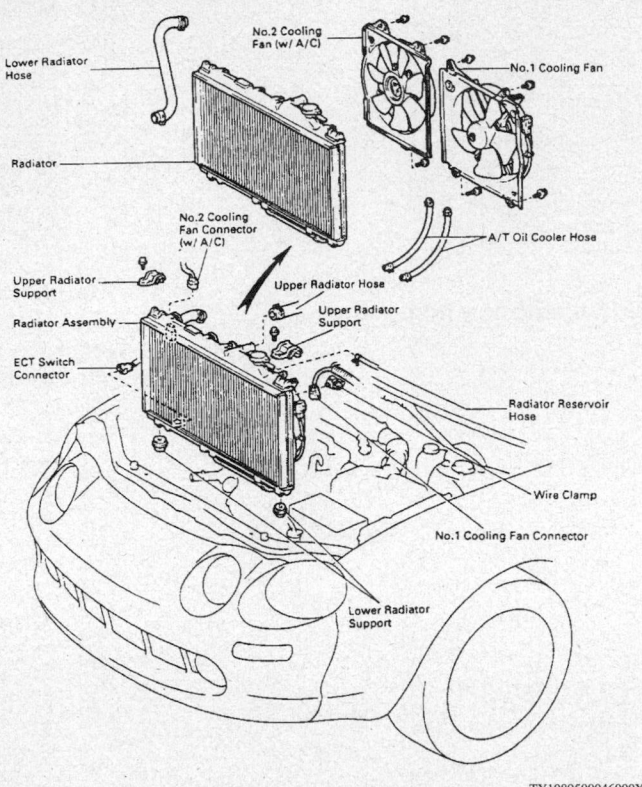

Fig. 32 Radiator replacement

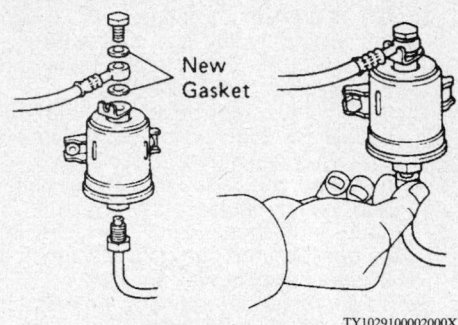

Fig. 33 Fuel filter replacement

or equivalent, between cylinder block and oil pan, cut off applied sealer and remove oil pan.

9. Remove oil strainer and baffle plate attaching nuts and bolts, oil strainer, baffle plate and gasket.

10. Suspend engine with engine chain hoist, then remove timing belt, No. 2 idler pulley, crankshaft timing pulley and oil pump pulley as outlined in "Timing Belt, Replace."

11. Remove 12 oil pump attaching bolts, then using a plastic faced hammer remove oil pump by gently tapping on oil pump body.

12. Reverse procedure to install. Reset audio coded anti-theft, if equipped, as outlined under "Precautions."

OIL PUMP
REPLACE

Refer to "Oil Pan, Replace" for procedure.

OIL PUMP SERVICE

1. Using snap ring pliers, remove snap ring from oil pump body.
2. Remove retainer, spring and relief valve.
3. Remove two pump body cover bolts, pump body cover, O-ring, drive and driven gears.
4. Coat relief valve with engine oil and check that it falls smoothly into valve hole by its own weight. If it does not, replace valve and if necessary replace oil pump assembly.
5. Using a feeler gauge, measure clear-

ance between driven rotor and body, **Fig. 28**. If clearance is greater than .0079 inch, replace rotors as a set. If necessary replace oil pump.

6. Using a feeler gauge, measure clearance between drive and driven rotors, **Fig. 29**. If tip clearance is greater than .0079 inch, replace rotors as a set.

BELT TENSION DATA

Belt	New, Lbs.	Used, Lbs.
Alt. Less A/C	100–150	75–115
Alt. w/A/C	170–180	120–140
Power Steering	100–150	60–100

COOLING SYSTEM BLEED

These engines do not require a specified bleed procedure. After filling cooling system, run engine to operating temperature with radiator/pressure cap off. Air will then be automatically bled through cap opening.

THERMOSTAT
REPLACE

1. Obtain audio anti-theft code, if equipped, as outlined in "Precautions."
2. Drain engine coolant into suitable container.
3. Remove lower radiator hose, then water inlet and thermostat.
4. Reverse procedure to install. Ensure

jiggle valve is aligned with upper side of inlet stud bolt.

WATER PUMP
REPLACE

1. Obtain audio anti-theft code, if equipped, as outlined in "Precautions," then drain engine coolant.
2. Disconnect lower radiator hose from water inlet.
3. Remove timing belt as outlined in "Timing Belt, Replace."
4. Remove idler pulleys and alternator belt adjusting bar.
5. Remove two water pump to water bypass pipe attaching nuts, **Fig. 30**.
6. Remove three water pump attaching bolts in sequence shown in **Fig. 31**.
7. Pull out water pump and water pump cover, then remove gasket and two O-rings from water pump and water bypass pipe.
8. Separate water pump and water pump cover, then remove water inlet and thermostat from water pump cover.
9. Reverse procedure to install.

RADIATOR
REPLACE

1. Drain coolant.
2. Disconnect No. 1 cooling fan connector, **Fig. 32**.
3. **On models equipped with A/C,** disconnect No. 2 cooling fan connector.
4. **On all models,** disconnect engine coolant temperature switch connector.
5. Disconnect coolant reservoir hose.
6. Disconnect radiator hoses.
7. **On models equipped with automatic transmission,** disconnect transmission oil cooler hoses.
8. **On all models,** remove upper radiator support, then radiator.
9. Reverse procedure to install.

FUEL PUMP
REPLACE

1. Obtain audio anti-theft code, if equipped, as outlined in "Precautions," then drain fuel from tank.
2. Remove fuel tank, then the fuel pump bracket from tank.
3. Remove fuel pump from fuel pump bracket.
4. Remove filter from pump.
5. Reverse procedure to install.

FUEL FILTER
REPLACE

Refer to **Fig. 33** for replacement procedure.

TIGHTENING SPECIFICATIONS

Year	Component	Torque, Ft. Lbs.
1996–99	A/C Compressor	20
	Alternator Bracket	③
	Bearing Cap Bolts	①
	Camshaft Timing Pulley	27
	Center Engine Mount	38
	Center Engine Mount Insulator	54
	Crankshaft Pulley	80
	Cylinder Head	①
	Cylinder Head Cover	④
	Driveplate	61
	EGR Valve Bolt	9
	EGR Valve Union Nut	43
	Engine Hanger	18
	Exhaust Manifold	31
	Exhaust Pipe To Catalytic Converter	46
	Exhaust Pipe To Center Exhaust	32
	Flywheel	65
	Front Engine Mount Bracket	⑤
	Front Engine Mount Through Bolt	64
	Fuel Hose Union Bolts	22
	Idler Pulley	31
	Intake Manifold	14
	LH Engine Mount Bracket	⑥
	LH Engine Mount Nut	⑥
	LH Engine Mount Stay	15
	LH Engine Mount Through Bolt	64
	Lower Suspension Crossmember	116
	Main Bearing Cap	43
	No. 3 Timing Belt Cover	69②
	Oil Pump Pulley	21
	Power Steering Pump Adjusting Bolt	29
	Power Steering Pump Bracket	32
	Rear End Plate	82②
	Rear Engine Mount Bracket	57
	Rear Engine Mount Through Bolt	64
	Rear Oil Seal Retainer	82②
	RH Engine Mount Bracket	38
	RH Engine Mount Stay	54
	Spark Plugs	13
	Spark Plug Tubes	29
	Suspension Upper Brace Bolt	15
	Suspension Upper Brace Nut	47
	Water Bypass Pipe	82②
	Water Outlet	11

① — Refer to "Cylinder Head, Replace" for tightening procedure.
② — Inch lbs.
③ — 1996–97, 31 ft. lbs.; 1989–99 40 ft. lbs.
④ — 1996–97, 17 ft. lbs.; 1989–99 33 ft. lbs.
⑤ — 1996–97, 57 ft. lbs.; 1989–99 65 ft. lbs.
⑥ — 1996–97, 38 ft. lbs.; 1989–99 47 ft. lbs.

Clutch & Manual Transaxle

NOTE: On Air Bag Equipped Models, Refer To "Air Bag System Precautions" Located In The Front Of This Manual For System Disarming & Arming Procedures.

INDEX

PRECAUTIONS

AIR BAG SYSTEMS

Refer to "Air Bag System Precautions" in the front of this manual for system disarming and arming procedures.

BATTERY GROUND CABLE

Prior to service, disconnect battery ground cable and isolate as required.

AUDIO CODED ANTI-THEFT SYSTEM

Some models are equipped with an audio coded anti-theft system that will disable the radio when the battery cable is disconnected. The system can be identified by the "ANTI-THEFT SYSTEM" on the cassette tape lid. Obtain 3 digit customer code for input. Reset system after service as follows:

1. Obtain 3 digit audio anti-theft code.
2. Depress 1 (PROG) while depressing righthand side of TUNE SEEK button, - - - will appear in tape operation display.
3. To enter the first digit, depress 1 (PROG) button repeatedly until the number of times depressed equals the first digit beginning with zero (depress the 1 button six times if the first digit if five).
4. To enter second digit, depress 2 (APS) button repeatedly until the number of times depressed equals the second digit beginning with zero.
5. To enter third digit, depress 3 (RPT) button repeatedly until the number of times depressed equals the second digit beginning with zero.
6. If - - - is displayed during code input, repeat procedure.
7. When code appears in display, depress and hold SCAN button until SEC appears.
8. When SEC disappears audio system should be operative.
9. If Err is displayed, repeat procedure. **Attempting to input code more than nine times may permanently disable audio system.**

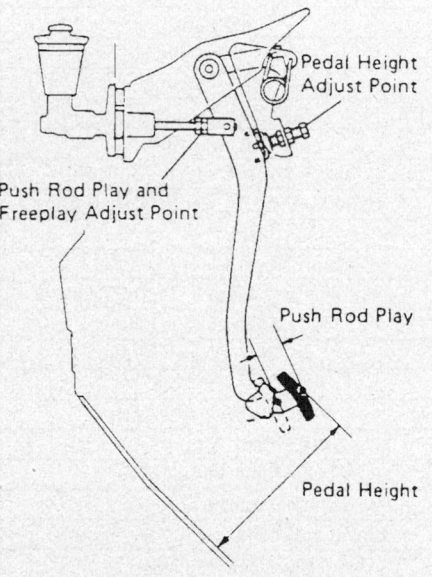

Fig. 1 Clutch pedal adjustment

TY5049100012000X

ADJUSTMENTS

CLUTCH PEDAL HEIGHT

1. Check clutch pedal height, **Fig. 1.**
2. Clutch pedal height should be 6.41–6.80 inches.
3. If clutch pedal height is not as specified, loosen locknut and turn adjusting bolt until specified clutch pedal height is obtained, then tighten adjusting bolt locknut.
4. Clutch freeplay should be .197–.591 inch.
5. If clutch pedal freeplay is not as specified, loosen locknut and turn pushrod adjusting screw until specified pedal freeplay is obtained.

6. Tighten locknut, then recheck clutch pedal height.

HYDRAULIC SYSTEM SERVICE

CLUTCH SYSTEM BLEED

If any service is performed on the clutch system or air is suspected in the clutch lines, bleed the system.
1. Fill clutch reservoir with suitable brake fluid. **Do not allow fluid to come in contact with painted surfaces.**
2. Check reservoir frequently, add fluid as required.
3. Connect vinyl tube to bleeder plug, then insert other tube end in half full container of brake fluid.
4. Slowly pump clutch pedal several times.
5. While depressing, pedal, loosen bleeder plug until fluid runs out, then close bleeder plug.
6. Repeat procedure until air bubbles are evident in the fluid. **Do not reuse the fluid that was bled.**

CLUTCH SLAVE CYLINDER, REPLACE

1. Remove clutch slave cylinder hose or tube.
2. Remove slave cylinder.
3. Reverse procedure to install. Tighten bolts to specifications.
4. Bleed clutch system.

CLUTCH

REPLACE

1. Remove transaxle assembly as outlined under "Transaxle, Replace."
2. Place installation alignment on clutch cover and flywheel.
3. Loosen each set bolt one turn at a time until spring tension is released.
4. Remove clutch cover attaching bolts, then cover and disc.
5. Remove release bearing, fork and boot.

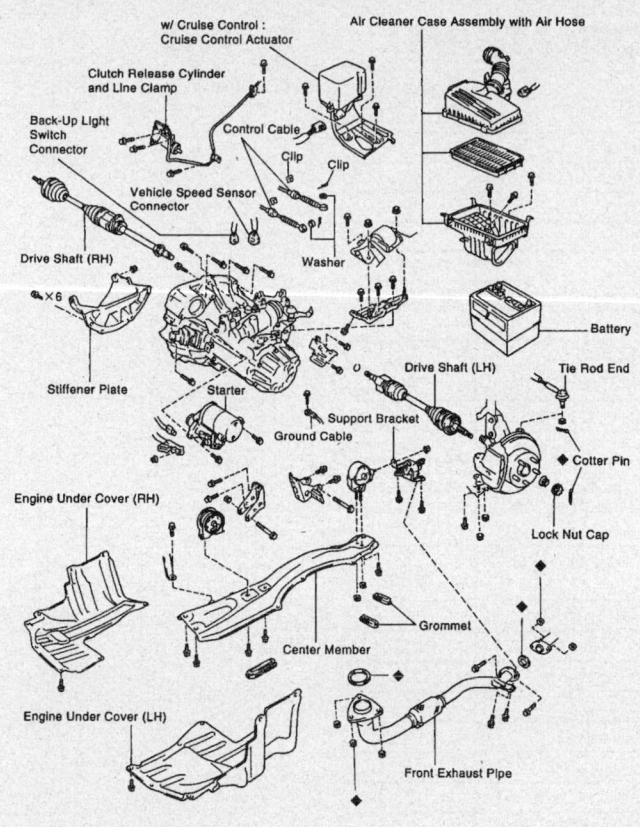

w/ Cruise Control : Cruise Control Actuator
Air Cleaner Case Assembly with Air Hose
Clutch Release Cylinder and Line Clamp
Back-Up Light Switch Connector
Control Cable
Clip
Clip
Vehicle Speed Sensor Connector
Washer
Drive Shaft (RH)
×6
Battery
Drive Shaft (LH)
Tie Rod End
Stiffener Plate
Starter
Support Bracket
Ground Cable
Cotter Pin
Engine Under Cover (RH)
Lock Nut Cap
Grommet
Center Member
Engine Under Cover (LH)
Front Exhaust Pipe

◆ Non-reusable part

TY5039600207000X

Fig. 2   Transaxle replacement. S54 transaxle

Vehicle Speed Sensor Connector
Air Cleaner Case Assembly with Air Hose
Back-Up Light Switch Connector
Engine Wires Clamp
Starter
Control Cable
RH Drive Shaft
Clip
Washer
Clutch Release Cylinder and Line
Engine Rear Mounting Insulator
Engine Front Mounting Bracket
Engine Rear Mounting Bracket
Engine Front Mounting Insulator
LH Drive Shaft
Ground Cable
Center Crossmember
Tie Rod End
Grommet
Cotter Pin
Exhaust Front Pipe Support Bracket
Grommet
Gasket
Lock Nut Cap
◆ Gasket
RH Engine Under Cover
Exhaust Front Pipe
Oxygen Sensor Connector
LH Engine Under Cover

◆ Non-reusable part

TY5039600208000X

Fig. 3   Transaxle replacement. C52 transaxle

6. Using suitable calipers, measure clutch disc rivet head depth. Minimum rivet depth should be .012 inch. If not as indicated, replace clutch disc.
7. Using suitable dial indicator, measure flywheel runout. Maximum runout should be .004 inch. If not as indicated, replace flywheel.
8. Measure clutch disc runout, maximum runout is .031 inch. If not as indicated, replace disc.
9. Using suitable calipers, measure diaphragm spring depth and width. Depth should be .024 inch and width should be .197 inch. If not as indicated, replace clutch cover.
10. Reverse to install, noting the following:
   a. Using clutch guide tool No. 09301–17010 or 093201–20020, or equivalent, install clutch disc.
   b. Match clutch cover and flywheel alignment marks, then tighten cover bolts to specifications, one turn at a time in a criss-cross pattern, ensuring clutch disc and pressure plate remain aligned.
   c. Using suitable dial indicator, check

diaphragm spring tip alignment, .020 inch is maximum allowable out of alignment.

TRANSAXLE
REPLACE

Refer to **Figs. 2 and 3** when replacing transaxle.
1. Obtain audio anti-theft code, if equipped, as outlined in "Precautions."
2. Drain engine coolant, oil and transaxle fluid.
3. Remove battery.
4. Remove air cleaner case assembly and air hose.
5. Remove cruise control actuator, if equipped.
6. Disconnect starter connector and remove starter.
7. Remove clutch release cylinder and line clamp.
8. Disconnect transaxle ground cable.
9. Disconnect back-up lamp switch and VSS connector.
10. Disconnect control cable from transaxle.

11. Remove three upper side transaxle mounting bolts.
12. Remove engine upper side left mounting bolt and nut.
13. Install engine support fixture over engine compartment.
14. Remove front wheel.
15. Raise and support vehicle, then remove engine under cover.
16. Remove lefthand and righthand side driveshafts.
17. Remove front exhaust pipe and pipe support bracket.
18. Remove engine front mounting insulator and bracket.
19. Remove engine rear mounting insulator and bracket.
20. Remove engine left lower mounting bolt.
21. Remove center member and stiffener plate.
22. Remove transaxle mounting bolts.
23. Lower engine left side and remove transaxle from engine.
24. Reverse procedure to install. Tighten to specifications.

TIGHTENING SPECIFICATIONS

Year	Component	Torque, Ft. Lbs.
1996–99	Back-Up Lamp Switch	30
	Center Member To Engine Mounting	47
	Clutch Bleeder Plug	6
	Clutch Cover To Flywheel	14
	Clutch Line Union	11
	Clutch Master Cylinder To Body	27
	Clutch Release Cylinder To Body	9
	Clutch Release Fork Support	27
	Control Shaft Cover To Transmission Case	14
	Control Shift Lever Retainer To Plate	9
	Drain Plug	29
	Filler Plug	29
	Front Bearing Retainer To Transmission Case	8
	LH Engine Mounting Stay To LH Engine Mounting	15
	LH Engine Mounting Stay To Transaxle	15
	LH Engine Mounting To Bracket	35
	LH Engine Mounting To Transaxle	38
	Lock Ball Assembly	29
	Mounting Insulator To Bracket	64
	Oil Receiver To Transaxle Case	13
	Oil Receiver To Transmission Case	8
	Output Shaft Front Bearing Lock Plate Bolt	8
	Rear Bearing Retainer To Transmission Case	14
	Reverse Idler Gear Shaft Lock Bolt	22
	Reverse Restrict Pin Holder	14
	Reverse Shift Arm Bracket To Transaxle Case	13
	Ring Gear To Differential Case	71
	Selecting Spring Cover To Control Shift Lever Retainer	43①
	Shift Select Lever Shaft Lock Bolt	22
	Shift Fork To Fork Shaft	12
	Speedometer Shaft Sleeve Lock Plate Bolt	8
	Straight Screw Plug	18
	Transaxle Case To Transmission Case	22
	Transaxle To Engine (10 mm Bolt)	47
	Transaxle To Engine (12 mm Bolt)	47
	Transaxle To Front Engine Mounting	57
	Transaxle To Rear End Plate (8 mm Bolt)	8
	Transaxle To Rear End Plate (10 mm Bolt)	17
	Transaxle To Rear Engine Mounting	57
	Transaxle To Starter	29
	Transmission Case Cover To Transmission Case	13
	Transmission Case Protector To Transmission Case	9
	5th Driven Gear Locknut	87

① — Inch lbs.

Rear Axle & Suspension

INDEX

HUB & BEARING
REPLACE

1. Remove brake drum or rotor and check bearing axial play. Play should not exceed .002 inch.
2. Remove speed sensor.
3. **On models equipped with drum brakes,** disconnect brake line from wheel cylinder, **Fig. 1.**
4. **On all models,** remove 4 bolts holding axle hub to axle carrier and remove axle hub and rear brake assembly.
5. Remove O-ring.
6. Remove strut rod from axle carrier, then remove No. 1 and 2 suspension arms, then remove axle carrier to shock absorber attaching bolts.
7. Place hub in suitable vise. Using hammer and chisel, loosen stake part of nut and remove nut.
8. Using axle shaft remover tool No. 09550-20017, or equivalent, push axle shaft off axle hub.
9. Remove oil seal, then inside portion of bearing inner race.
10. Using puller tool No. 09950-10010, or equivalent, pull outside portion of bearing inner race from axle shaft.
11. To replace wheel bearing, place old inner race (outside) on bearing, then using bearing remover tool Nos. 09552-10010 and 09555-10010, or equivalent, press out bearing.
12. Apply MP grease around bearing outer race and replacer pipe tool No. 09550-10012, or equivalent, press new bearing into axle hub.
13. Using countershaft bearing replacer tool No. 09310-35010, or equivalent, drive new oil seal into axle hub.
14. Apply MP grease to oil seal lip.
15. Place inside portion of bearing inner race on bearing.
16. Using installer tool Nos. 09636-20010 and 09228-22020, or equivalents, press inner race with axle hub onto axle shaft.
17. Tighten axle hub nut to specification.
18. Place new O-ring on axle carrier.
19. Install axle hub and rear brake assembly with four bolts. Tighten bolts to specifications.
20. **On models equipped with drum brakes,** connect brake line to wheel cylinder, then install brake drum and bleed brakes.
21. **On models equipped with disc brakes,** install rotor and caliper assembly.
22. **On models equipped with ABS,** install speed sensor.

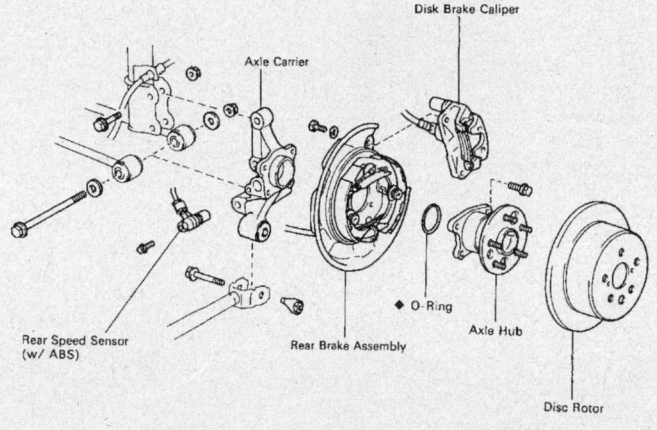

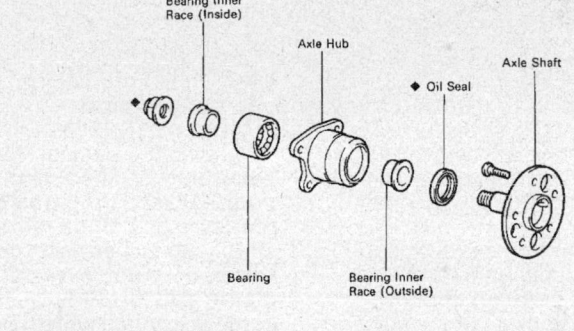

Fig. 1 Exploded view of rear wheel bearing

STRUT ROD
REPLACE

1. Raise and support rear of vehicle.
2. Remove nut and bolt securing strut rod to axle carrier, **Fig. 2.**
3. Remove nut and bolt securing strut rod to body, then remove strut rod.
4. Reverse procedure to install. Prior to tightening attaching nuts and bolts, lower vehicle to ground and bounce vehicle up and down several times to stabilize suspension, then tighten attaching nuts and bolts to specification with vehicle weight on suspension.

SHOCK ABSORBER
REPLACE

Refer to "Coil Spring, Replace" for shock absorber replacement procedures.

COIL SPRING
REPLACE

1. **On coupe models,** remove rear speaker board.
2. **On hatchback models,** remove rear speaker grill.
3. **On models equipped with ABS,** disconnect speed sensor electrical connector from shock absorber.
4. **On all models,** disconnect brake hose from wheel cylinder or caliper, then disconnect brake hose from shock absorber.
5. Working inside vehicle, loosen nut securing suspension support to shock absorber, **Fig. 2. Do not remove nut at this time.**
6. Disconnect stabilizer bar from shock absorber.
7. Remove bolts securing shock absorber to axle carrier, then disconnect shock absorber from carrier.

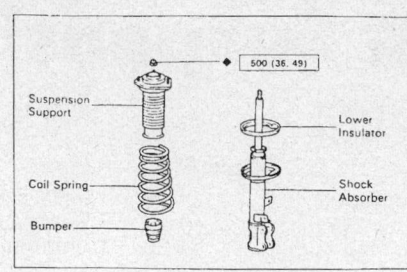

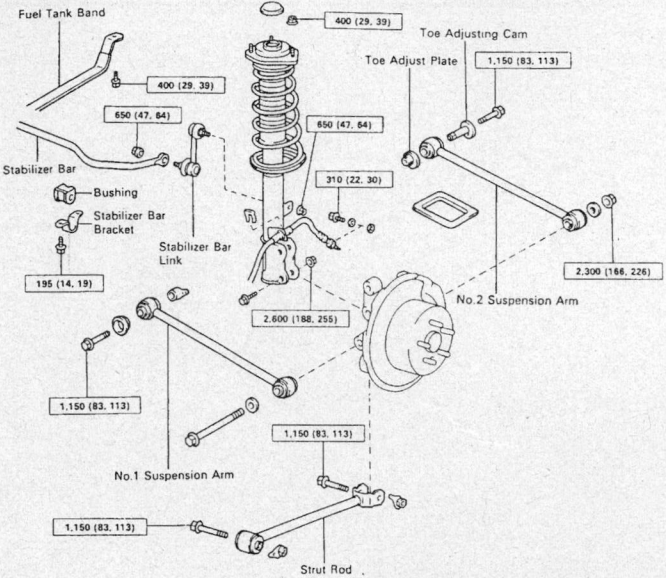

Fig. 2 Exploded view of rear suspension

TY2039100001000X

STABILIZER BAR
REPLACE

1. Raise and support rear of vehicle, then remove rear wheels.
2. Disconnect bolts securing stabilizer bar to axle housing, **Fig. 2.**
3. Disconnect bolts securing stabilizer bar to frame, then remove stabilizer bar.
4. Reverse procedure to install.

SUSPENSION ARM
REPLACE
REMOVAL

1. Raise and support vehicle.
2. Remove Nos. 1 and 2 suspension arm-to-steering knuckle attaching nut and bolt, **Fig. 2.**
3. Scribe reference marks on adjusting cam, then remove No. 2 suspension arm-to-crossmember attaching nut and bolt. Remove suspension arm.
4. Remove No. 1 suspension arm attaching nut, plate and bolt, then remove suspension arm.

INSTALLATION

1. Install serrated bushing side of No. 1 suspension arm in crossmember, then install bolt, plate and nut. Do not tighten at this time. **Suspension arms are marked with "L" of " R" for installation identification.**
2. Install serrated bushing side of No. 2 suspension arm in crossmember, then install cam, bolt and nut, but do not tighten. Align cam reference marks made during removal. **Ensure side of suspension arm with spot of white paint is facing outward.**
3. Connect Nos. 1 and 2 suspension arms on steering knuckle, then install attaching bolt and nut. Do not tighten at this time.
4. Lower vehicle to ground, then bounce vehicle up and down several times to stabilize suspension.
5. With vehicle weight on suspension, tighten attaching nuts and bolts to specifications.

8. Working inside vehicle, remove nuts securing suspension support to vehicle body, then remove shock absorber, **Fig. 2.**
9. Install a bolt and two nuts in shock absorber lower mounting bracket and clamp unit in a suitable vise using lower mounting bracket as clamping surface.
10. Using a suitable spring compressor, compress coil spring.
11. Remove nut securing suspension support to shock absorber, then remove suspension support, coil spring, insulator and spring bumper, **Fig. 2. Shock absorber is filled with colorless, odorless and non-poisonous high pressure gas. Upon removal, handle shock absorber with care. Do not score or scratch exposed part of piston rod or allow paint or oil to come in contact with it. Do not rotate piston rod and cylinder assembly with shock absorber fully extended. When discarding shock absorber, drill a small hole in bottom of cylinder to relieve pressure.**
12. Reverse procedure to install.

TIGHTENING SPECIFICATIONS

Year	Component	Torque, Ft. Lbs.
1996–99	ABS Speed Sensor To Steering Knuckle (w/ABS)	6
	Ball Joint To Lower Arm	94
	Ball Joint To Steering Knuckle	93
	Center Bearing Case To Center Bearing Bracket	47
	Disc Brake Caliper To Steering Knuckle	79
	Front Disc Brake Hose Union Bolt	22
	Front Exhaust Pipe Support To Body	14
	Front Exhaust Pipe To Rear Exhaust Pipe	32
	Hub Bearing Locknut	137
	Lower Arm Damper Plate Bolt	48
	Lower Arm Front Setting Nut	156
	Lower Arm Rear Bracket To Body	72
	Lower Arm Rear Nut	101
	Piston Rod To Suspension Support	34
	Shock Absorber To Steering Knuckle	224
	Stabilizer Bar To Lower Arm	26
	Stabilizer Bracket To Body	13
	Suspension Arm Shaft To Body	112
	Suspension Crossmember To Body	112
	Suspension Support To Body	59
	Tie Rod End Locknut	41
	Tie Rod End To Steering Knuckle	36
	Wheel Lug Nut	76

Front Suspension & Steering

NOTE: On Air Bag Equipped Models, Refer To "Air Bag System Precautions" Located In The Front Of This Manual For System Disarming & Arming Procedures.

INDEX

PRECAUTIONS

AIR BAG SYSTEMS

Refer to "Air Bag System Precautions" in the front of this manual for system disarming and arming procedures.

BATTERY GROUND CABLE

Prior to service, disconnect battery ground cable and isolate as required.

HUB & BEARING

REPLACE

1. Raise and support front of vehicle, then remove tire and wheel assembly.
2. Remove cotter pin and bearing locknut cap.
3. With brake pedal depressed, remove bearing locknut, **Fig. 1.**
4. Remove brake caliper from steering knuckle and suspend out of way.
5. Remove disc rotor, then ensure bearing play in axial direction does not exceed .002 inch.
6. **On models equipped with ABS,** remove speed sensor from steering knuckle.
7. **On all models,** remove cotter pin and nut, then, using suitable puller, disconnect tie rod end from steering knuckle.
8. Remove steering knuckle-to-strut lower bracket attaching nuts and bolts.
9. Disconnect steering knuckle from lower suspension arm.
10. Using plastic hammer, tap axle shaft to loosen it while removing steering knuckle and axle hub. Using puller tool No. 09950-20017, or equivalent, remove hub from axle shaft. **Cover driveshaft boot with cloth to prevent damage.**
11. Remove ball joint from steering knuckle.
12. Remove steering knuckle inner seal.
13. Using suitable pliers, remove axle hub snap ring.
14. Remove bolts securing disc brake dust cover to steering knuckle.
15. Using suitable puller, remove hub from

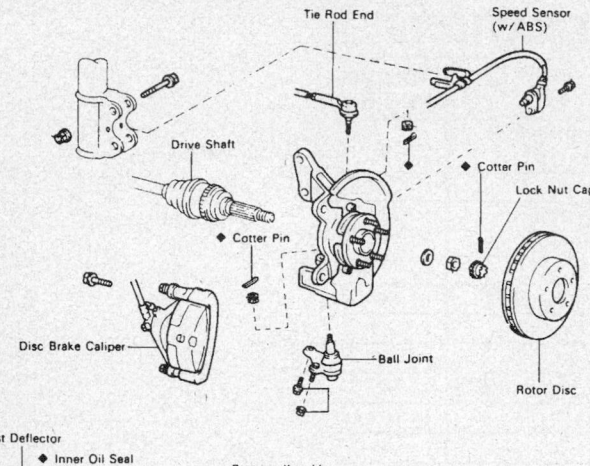

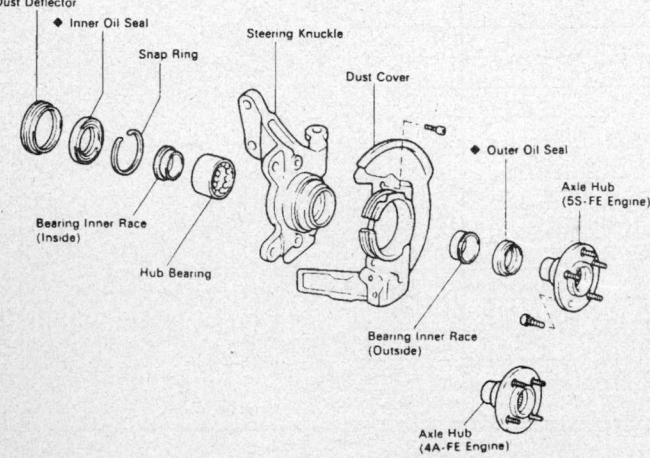

Fig. 1   Exploded view of axle hub & steering knuckle

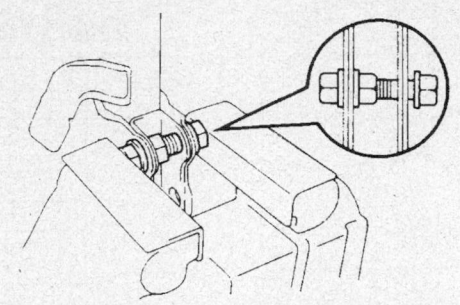

Fig. 2   Setting strut assembly into vise

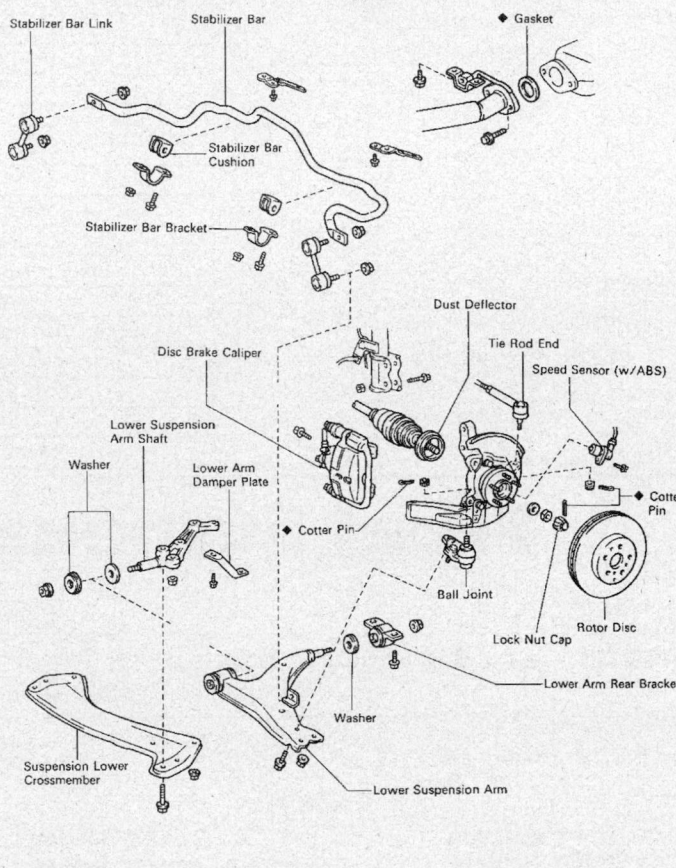

◆ Non-reusable part

Fig. 3   Exploded view of front suspension

steering knuckle.

16. Remove inside bearing inner race from bearing.
17. Using suitable puller, remove outside inner race from axle hub.
18. Using suitable screwdriver, remove oil seal from steering knuckle.
19. Place an outside bearing inner race on bearing and, using suitable tool and hammer, drive out bearing. **Always replace the bearing as an assembly.**
20. Using suitable tool, press new bearing into steering knuckle.
21. Rotate and insert the side lip of a new outer oil seal into seal tool No. 09608-32010, or equivalent, then, using seal installer tool No. 09710-14012, or equivalent, drive oil seal into steering knuckle.
22. Apply suitable grease to oil seal lip.
23. Install disc brake dust cover.
24. Apply suitable grease to oil seal and bearing, then, using suitable tool, press hub into steering knuckle.
25. Install hub snap ring in steering knuckle.
26. Using suitable tool, drive a new oil seal and dust deflector (if equipped) into steering knuckle surface, then apply suitable grease to oil seal lip and axle shaft.
27. If removed, install ball joint.
28. Reverse procedure to install, tighten two strut to steering knuckle attaching

nuts and bolts, steering knuckle to lower suspension arm attaching bolts, tie rod end attaching nut and bearing locknut to specifications.

BALL JOINT INSPECTION

1. Raise front of vehicle and place a 7–8 inch block under one tire.
2. Lower vehicle until the front springs are about half loaded. Place stands under vehicle.
3. Ensure front wheels are in a straight forward position, then chock front wheels.
4. Using suitable lever, move lower control arm up and down and check ball

joint for excessive play. If any ball joint play is observed, replace ball joint.
5. Repeat procedure for opposite ball joint.

COIL SPRING
REPLACE

1. Remove union bolt and two washers, then disconnect brake hose from disc caliper.
2. Drain brake fluid into a suitable container, then remove clip from brake hose and separate brake hose from bracket.
3. Remove speed sensor wire harness clamp bracket bolt and disconnect wire harness clamp.

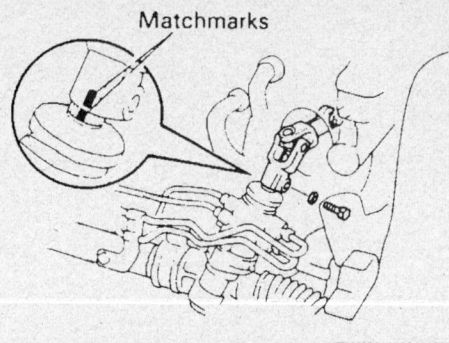

Fig. 4 Universal joint & control valve shaft matchmarks

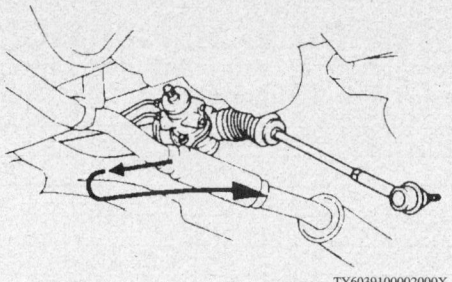

Fig. 5 Steering gear removal

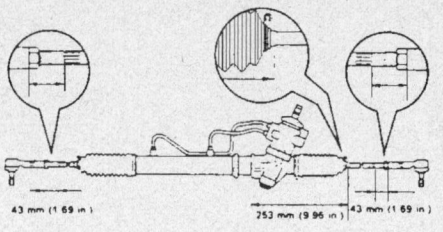

Fig. 6 Steering gear installation dimensions

4. Remove lower strut assembly-to-steering knuckle attaching bolts.
5. Remove three nuts holding top of strut assembly to body, then remove strut assembly. **Cover driveshaft boot with cloth to avoid damage.**
6. Install a bolt and two nuts to assembly bracket as shown in **Fig. 2,** then secure assembly in a vise.
7. Compress coil spring, using spring compression tool No. 09727-30020, or equivalent, then retain seat with tool No. 09729-22031, or equivalent, and remove suspension support nut.
8. Remove suspension support, spring seat, spring, insulators and bumper.
9. Reverse procedure to install, noting the following:
   a. When installing upper spring seat, face the "OUT" mark of the seat towards outside of vehicle.
   b. Tighten three strut assembly-to-body nuts and two strut assembly-to-steering knuckle bolts to specifications.
   c. Pack suspension support bearing with suitable multi-purpose grease before installing dust cover.
   d. Tighten brake caliper bolts to specification.

STRUT
REPLACE

Refer to "Coil Spring, Replace" for procedure.

CONTROL ARM
REPLACE
LOWER

1. Raise and support vehicle, then re-

move wheel and tire assembly.
2. Remove steering knuckle to lower suspension arm attaching bolt and two nuts, **Fig. 3.**
3. Remove attaching nut, then disconnect stabilizer link from lower suspension arm.
4. Remove lower suspension arm, except lefthand arm on models equipped with automatic transaxle, as follows:
   a. Remove lower suspension arm front setting nut and washer.
   b. Remove lower suspension arm rear bracket bolts, then the lower suspension arm.
   c. Remove four attaching bolts and two nuts, then the suspension lower crossmember.
   d. Remove attaching bolt and nut, then the lower suspension arm shaft.
5. Remove lefthand lower suspension arm on models equipped with automatic transaxle as follows:
   a. Remove lower suspension arm front setting nut and washer.
   b. Remove four attaching bolts and two nuts, then the lower crossmember.
   c. Remove attaching bolt and nut, then the lower suspension arm and lower arm shaft.
6. Reverse procedure to install. Tighten attaching nuts and bolts to specifications.

STEERING KNUCKLE
REPLACE

Refer to "Hub & Bearing, Replace" for steering knuckle replacement procedure.

POWER STEERING GEAR
REPLACE

1. Position front wheels facing straight ahead, then using seat belt of the driver's seat, fix steering wheel so that it will not turn.
2. Scribe matchmarks on universal joint and control valve shaft as shown in **Fig. 4.**
3. Loosen bolt on upper side of universal joint, then remove bolt on lower side and disconnect universal joint.
4. Remove cotter pin and nut at tie rod end, then using pressing tool No. 09611-22012, or equivalent, disconnect tie rod end from knuckle arm.
5. Using line removal tool No. 09631-22020, or equivalent, disconnect pressure and return lines from gear housing.
6. Slide gear housing to the right side of the vehicle, then pull gear housing out through lefthand lower side of vehicle body, **Fig. 5. Do not damage pressure tubes.**
7. Reverse procedure to install, noting the following:
   a. Set gear housing so that it matches dimensions shown in **Fig. 6,** with gear housing at center point.
   b. Align matchmarks on universal joint and control valve shaft.
   c. Check steering wheel center point and toe-in.

TIGHTENING SPECIFICATIONS

Year	Component	Torque, Ft. Lbs.
1996–99	Axle Carrier To Backing Plate	53
	Axle Hub To Axle Carrier	59
	Axle Shaft To Axle Hub	90
	Brake Tube Flare Nut	11
	Differential To Support Member (Rear Side)	108
	Differential To Support Member (Upper Side)	70
	Drain Plug	36
	Driveshaft To Side Gear Shaft	51
	Filler Plug	29
	Fuel Tank Band To Body	29
	No. 1 & No. 2 Suspension Arm To Axle Carrier	166
	Parking Brake Cable To Backing Plate	6
	Propeller Shaft To Companion Flange	54
	Rear Crossmember To Body	53
	Rear Disc Brake Caliper To Axle Carrier	34
	Rear Disc Brake Hose Union Bolt	22
	Rear Driveshaft To Axle Hub	137
	Rear Shock Absorber To Body	29
	Rear Shock Absorber To Holding Nut	36
	Rear Shock Absorber To Rear Axle Carrier	188
	Rear Shock Absorber To Stabilizer Bar Link	47
	Rear Speed Sensor To Axle Carrier	14
	Stabilizer Bar Bracket To Body	14
	Stabilizer Bar Link To Stabilizer Bar	47
	Strut Rod To Axle Carrier	83
	Strut Rod To Body	83
	Suspension Arm To Axle Carrier	90
	Suspension Arm To Body	83
	Wheel Lug Nut	76

Wheel Alignment

INDEX

PRELIMINARY INSPECTION

Prior to checking and resetting front wheel alignment, check wheel runout with a dial indicator. Wheel runout should not exceed .039 inch (1.0 mm).

Inspect the following prior to adjusting wheel alignment.

1. Check tires for wear and proper inflation pressure.
2. Check front wheel bearings, front suspension, steering linkage and ball joints for wear or looseness.
3. Ensure front shock absorbers are functioning properly.

FRONT WHEEL ALIGNMENT

CASTER & CAMBER

Caster is not adjustable. If caster is not within specifications, check for worn or damaged suspension parts and replace are required.

1. Remove front wheels.
2. Remove two nuts from lower side of shock absorber.
3. Coat threads of nuts with engine oil and temporarily install.
4. Adjust camber by pushing or pulling lower side of shock absorber in direction in which camber adjustment is required, **Fig. 1.**
5. Tighten nuts, then check camber.
6. If camber is not within specifications, estimate how much additional camber adjustment is required and select camber adjusting bolt from, **Figs. 2 and 3.**
7. Install selected bolts and adjust camber by pushing or pulling lower side of shock absorber in direction in which camber adjustment is required.
8. **Torque** nuts to 113 ft. lbs.

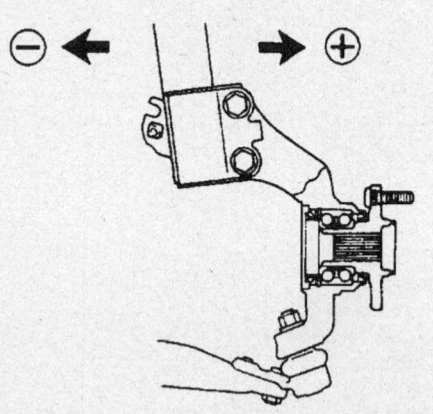

TY2049600055000X

Fig. 1 Front camber adjustment

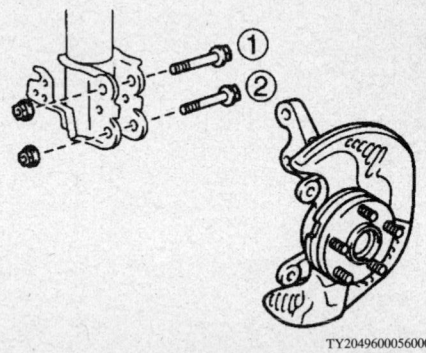

TY2049600056000X

Fig. 2 Front camber adjustment bolts

Bolt	Set Bolt	Adjusting Bolt		
	Original	OD=13.9 mm	OD=13.3 mm	OD=12.4 mm
	11	•11	•11	•11
		1 Dot	2 Dots	3 Dots
Adjusting Value	① ②	① ②	① ②	① ②
15'	●	●		
30'	●		●	
45'	●			●
1°00'		●		●
1°15'			●	●
1°30'				● ●

TY2049600057000X

Fig. 3 Front camber adjust bolt selection chart

TOE-IN

Measure length of tie rod end on each side and adjust to be equal. Adjust toe-in by turning tubes equal amounts. Clamp adjusting tubes after aligning clamps with tube slots. Lock tie rod ends so that inner and outer ends are at right angles to each other.

REAR WHEEL ALIGNMENT

CAMBER

Measure camber angle with suitable wheel alignment gauge and adjust to specifications. If reading is not within specification, check for worn or damaged bushings, bent or damaged rear suspension components and replace as required.

TOE-IN

1. Measure length of lefthand and righthand No. 2 lower suspension arms.
2. If the difference between lefthand and righthand suspension arm length is greater than .04 inch, adjust toe-in by turning adjusting tubes, **Fig. 4.** One turn of each adjusting tube will adjust toe-in about .36 inch.
3. **Torque** lock nuts to 55 ft. lbs.

VEHICLE RIDE HEIGHT

Refer to **Figs. 5 and 6,** for trim height and specifications.

LH

RH

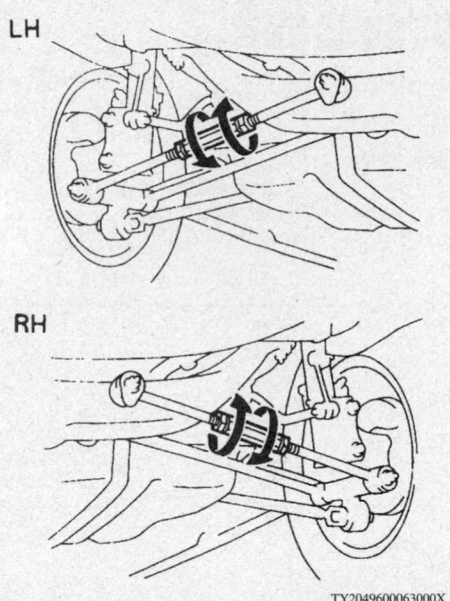

TY2049600063000X

Fig. 4   Rear toe-in adjustment

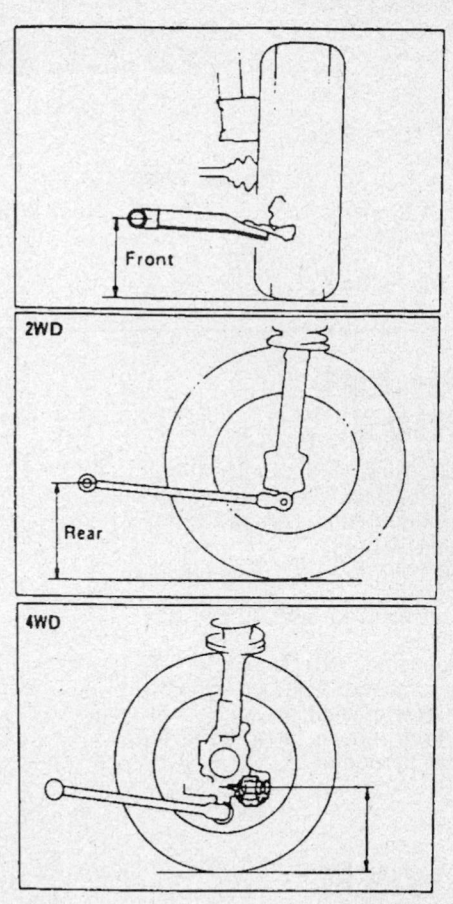

Front

2WD

Rear

4WD

TY20491000005000X

Fig. 5   Ride height measurement

Tire size	Front mm (in.)	Rear mm (in.)
P185/70R14	187.6 (7.39)	255.8 (10.07)
P205/55R15	182.6 (7.19)	250.0 (9.84)

TY2049600054000X

Fig. 6   Ride height specifications

Specifications

GENERAL ENGINE SPECIFICATIONS

Year	Engine	Fuel System	Bore & Stroke, Inches	Compression Ratio	Maximum Brake H.P. @ RPM	Maximum Torque Ft. Lbs. @ RPM	Normal Oil Pressure, psi
1996	1.6L 4A-FE	SFI	3.19 x 3.03	9.5	②	100 @ 4800	①
	1.8L 7A-FE	SFI	3.19 x 3.37	9.5	105 @ 5800	117 @ 2800	①
1997	1.6L 4A-FE	SFI	3.19 x 3.03	9.5	100 @ 5600	105 @ 4400	①
	1.8L 7A-FE	SFI	3.19 x 3.37	9.5	105 @ 5200	117 @ 2800	①
1998–99	1.8L 1ZZ-FE	EFI	79.0 x 91.5	10.0	120 @ 5600	122 @ 4400	③

① — At idle, 43 psi or more; @ 3000 RPM, 36–71 psi.

② — California, 100 @ 5800; Federal, 105 @ 5800.

③ — At idle, 43 psi or more; @ 3000 RPM, 48–78 psi.

TUNE UP SPECIFICATIONS

The following specifications are published from the latest information available. This data should be used only in the absence of a decal affixed in the engine compartment.

When checking ignition timing, it may be necessary to disconnect certain hoses and/or electrical connectors. Refer to vehicle emission control label for specific instructions.

Before disconnecting spark plug wires from distributor cap, determine location of No. 1 wire in cap, as distributor position may have been altered from that shown.

Year	Engine	Spark Plug Gap, Inch	Firing Order	Timing, ° BTDC②	Timing Mark, Fig.	Curb Idle Speed, RPM① Man. Trans.	Curb Idle Speed, RPM① Auto. Trans.	Fuel Pump Pressure, psi	Valve Clearance, Inch Int.	Valve Clearance, Inch Exh.
1996–97	1.6L 4A-FE	.031	1-3-4-2	10	A	700N	700N	38–44	.006–.010	.010–.014
	1.8L 7A-FE	.031	1-3-4-2	10	A	700N	700N	38–44	.006–.010	.010–.014
1998–99	1.8L 1ZZ-FE	.043	1-3-4-2	10	B	700	700N	44-50	.006–.010	.010–.014

BTDC — Before Top Dead Center
N — Neutral

① — Controlled by idle air controller.

② — With check terminal TE1 & E1 connected.

TY1139100115000X

Fig. A

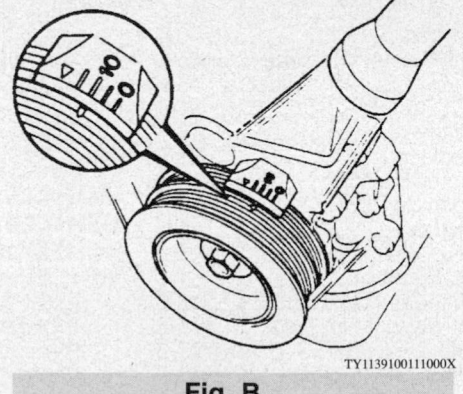

TY1139100111000X

Fig. B

FRONT WHEEL ALIGNMENT SPECIFICATIONS

The specifications listed below are for unloaded vehicles

Year	Model	Caster Angle, Degrees		Camber Angle, Degrees		Toe-In, Inch	Toe-Out on Turns, Deg.		Steering Axis Inclination, Deg.	Ball Joint Wear
		Limits	Desired	Limits	Desired		Outer Wheel	Inner Wheel		
1996–97	All	$+7/12$ to $+21/12$	$+1\frac{1}{3}$	$-11/12$ to $+7/12$	$-\frac{1}{6}$	.04	39	33	$+12\frac{2}{3}$	①
1998–99	All	$+3/10$ to $+21/15$	$+1\frac{1}{3}$	$-14/15$ to $+17/30$	$-11/16$	$-.04$ to $+.12$	39	33	$+12\frac{2}{3}$	①

① — Refer to "Ball Joint Inspection" under "Front Suspension & Steering."

REAR WHEEL ALIGNMENT SPECIFICATIONS

The specifications listed below are for unloaded vehicles

Year	Camber Angle, Degrees		Toe-In, Inch
	Limits	Desired	
1996–99	$-1\frac{2}{3}$ to $-\frac{1}{6}$	$-11/12$	+.08 to .24

FLUID CAPACITIES & COOLING SYSTEM DATA

Year	Engine	Coolant Capacity, Qts.		Radiator Cap Relief Pressure, Lbs.	Thermo. Opening Temp., °F	Fuel Tank, Gals.	Engine Oil Refill, Qts.①	Transmission/ Transaxle Oil		Axle Oil, Pints
		Auto Trans.	Man. Trans.					Manual Trans, Pints	Auto. Trans. Qts.	
1996	1.6L 4A-FE	③	②	13	180	13.2	3.2	5.2	5.8	2.2
	1.8L 7A-FE	⑤	④	13	180	13.2	3.9	5.2	8	—
1997	1.6L 4A-FE	6.2	6.3	13	180	13.2	3.2	5.2	5.8	2.2
	1.8L 7A-FE	6.4	6.6	13	180	13.2	3.9	4	8	—
1998–99	1.8L 1ZZ-FE	6	6	13	169	13.2	3.9	4	⑥	3

① — With filter change.
② — With Nippondenso radiator, 5.6 qts.; with Harrison radiator, 6.3 qts.; with Toyota radiator, 5.5 qts.
③ — With Nippondenso & Harrison radiators, 6.2 qts.; with Toyota radiator, 5.5 qts.
④ — With Nippondenso radiator, 5.8 qts.; with Harrison radiator, 6.6 qts.
⑤ — With Nippondenso radiator, 6.6 qts.; with Harrison radiator, 6.4 qts.
⑥ — Models w/A131L transaxle, 5.8 qts.; w/A245E transaxle, 8 qts.

LUBRICANT DATA

Year	Lubricant Type					
	Transaxle		Transfer Case	Rear Axle	Power Steering	Brake System
	Manual	Automatic				
1996–99	75W-90 GL4/5	Dexron II/IIE/III	—	—	Dexron II/IIE/III	DOT 3

Electrical

NOTE: On Air Bag Equipped Models, Refer To "Air Bag System Precautions" Located In The Front Of This Manual For System Disarming & Arming Procedures.

NOTE: Refer To "Computer Relearn Procedures" Located In The Front Of This Manual For Computer Relearn Procedures.

INDEX

PRECAUTIONS

AIR BAG SYSTEM

Refer to "Air Bag System Precautions" in the front of this manual for system disarming and arming procedures.

BATTERY GROUND CABLE

Prior to service, disconnect battery ground cable and isolate as required.

AUDIO CODED ANTI-THEFT SYSTEM

Some models are equipped with an audio coded anti-theft system that will disable the radio when the battery cable is disconnected. The system can be identified by the words "ANTI-THEFT SYSTEM" on the cassette tape lid. Obtain three digit customer code for input. Reset system after service as follows:

1. Obtain three digit audio anti-theft code.
2. Depress 1 (PROG) while depressing righthand side of TUNE SEEK button, - - will appear in tape operation display.
3. To enter first digit, depress 1 (PROG) button repeatedly until the number of times depressed equals the first digit beginning with zero (depress the 1 button six times if the first digit is five).
4. To enter second digit, depress 2 (APS) button repeatedly until the number of times depressed equals the second digit beginning with zero.
5. To enter third digit, depress 3 (RPT) button repeatedly until the number of times depressed equals the third digit

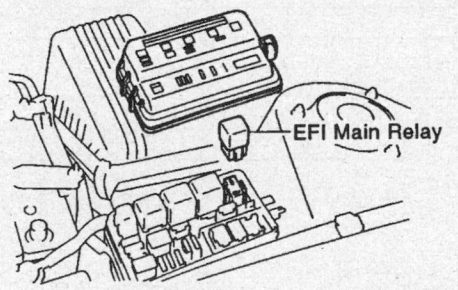

Fig. 1 Fuel pump relay location

beginning with zero.
6. If - - - is displayed during code input, repeat procedure.
7. When code appears in display, depress and hold SCAN button until SEC appears.
8. When SEC disappears audio system should be operative.
9. If Err is displayed, repeat procedure. **Attempting to input code more than nine times may permanently disable audio system.**

FUSE PANEL & FLASHER LOCATION

There are two fuse blocks; the first is on the left front kick panel and the second is behind the battery. The turn signal/hazard flasher is under the dash, left of the steering column.

FUEL PUMP RELAY LOCATION

The fuel pump relay is located in the engine compartment relay center, on the left-hand side of the engine compartment, **Fig. 1.**

RELAY CENTER LOCATION

Refer to **Figs. 2 and 3** for relay center location.

STARTER

REPLACE

1996-97

1. **On models with audio coded anti-theft system,** obtain three digit anti-theft code.
2. **On all models,** remove air cleaner assembly.
3. Disconnect electrical connectors from starter motor.
4. Remove starter motor attaching bolts, heat shield (if equipped), then the starter motor.
5. Reverse procedure to install. Reset audio anti-theft system, if equipped, as outlined under "Precautions."

1998-99

1. Remove battery and then the tray.

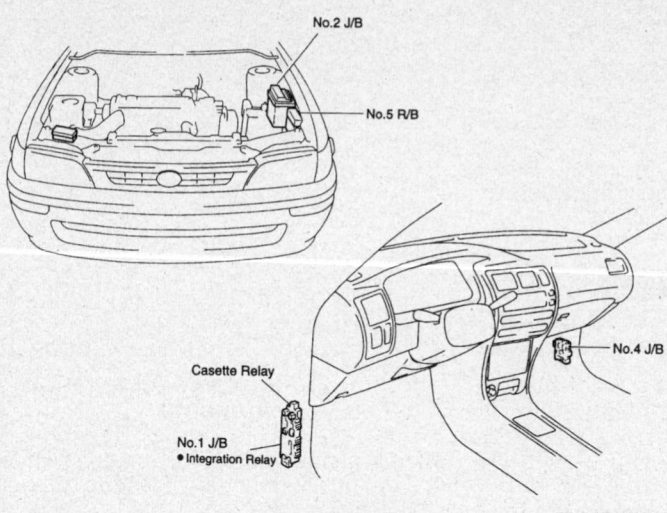

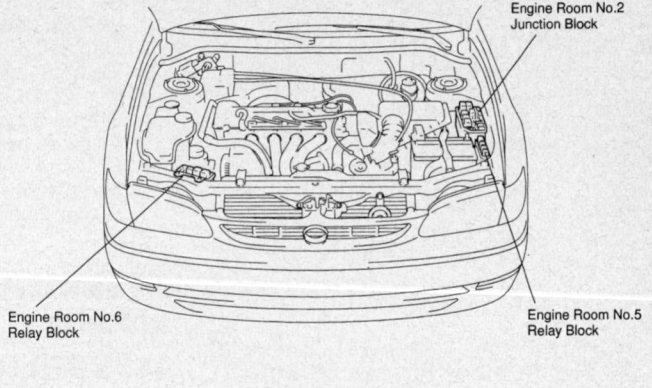

Fig. 2   Relay center location. 1996–97

TY1049900009000X

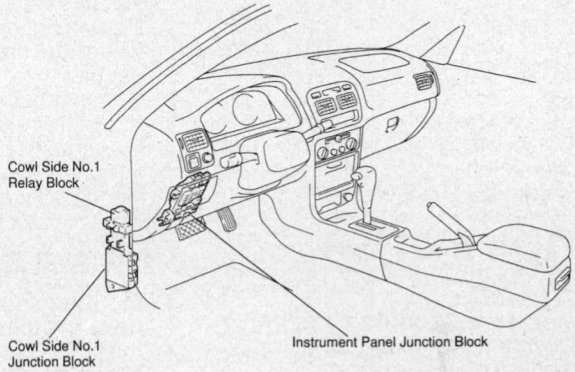

Fig. 3   Relay center location. 1998–99

TY1049900010000X

2. Disconnect engine coolant reservoir hose from radiator.
3. Remove reservoir attaching bolts, then the reservoir.
4. Remove righthand engine under cover, then the wire clamp.
5. Disconnect electrical connectors from starter motor.
6. Remove starter motor attaching bolts, then the starter motor.
7. Reverse procedure to install. **Torque** bolts to 29 ft. lbs.

ALTERNATOR
REPLACE
1996–97

1. **On models with audio coded anti-theft system,** obtain three digit anti-theft code.
2. **On all models,** loosen alternator pivot and adjusting bolt and remove drive belt.
3. Disconnect electrical connectors.
4. Remove wiring harness from two clips.
5. Remove pivot bolt, nut and adjusting lock bolt.
6. Remove alternator from bracket.
7. Reverse procedure to install. **Torque** adjusting bolt to 14 ft. lbs. and pivot bolt to 45 ft. lbs.

1998–99

1. Release tensioner (clockwise) and remove drive belt.
2. Remove dust cap and nut, then the wire harness.
3. Disconnect electrical connectors from alternator.
4. Remove attaching bolts, then the alternator.
5. Reverse procedure to install. **Torque** 14mm bolts to 18 ft. lbs. and 17mm bolts to 40 ft. lbs.

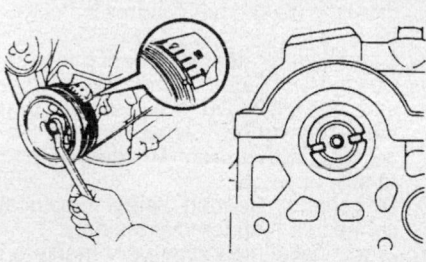

TY1119100003000X

Fig. 4   Setting No. 1 cylinder to TDC

DISTRIBUTOR
REPLACE

1. **On models with audio coded anti-theft system,** obtain three digit anti-theft code.
2. **On all models,** disconnect electrical connectors, then mark and remove spark plug wires.
3. Remove distributor bolts, then distributor and O-ring.
4. Reverse procedure to install, noting the following:
   a. Set No. 1 cylinder to TDC by turning crankshaft clockwise. Position slit of camshaft on righthand head, **Fig. 4.**

b. Install new O-ring, then align cutout of coupling with mark on housing.
c. Install distributor aligning center of flange with bolt hole on cylinder head.
d. Adjust ignition timing. **Torque** hold-down bolt to 15 ft. lbs.
e. Reset audio anti-theft system, if equipped, as outlined under "Precautions."

COIL PACK
REPLACE

1. Disconnect high tension cords from ignition coils.
2. Disconnect electrical connectors from ignition coils.
3. Remove attaching bolts and nuts, then the ignition coils.
4. Reverse procedure to install. **Torque** attaching bolts and nuts to 7 ft. lbs.

IGNITION LOCK
REPLACE

1. **On models with audio coded anti-theft system,** obtain three digit anti-theft code.
2. **On all models,** turn ignition switch to ACC position.

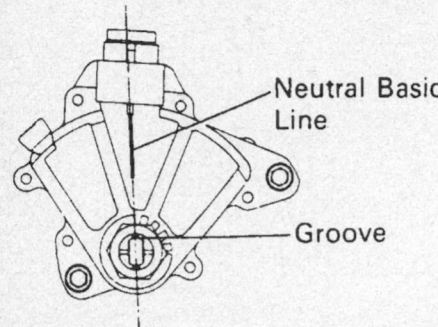

Fig. 5 Neutral start switch adjustment

TY9049100004000X

3. Insert a small diameter rod into hole located on side of lock cylinder, then while holding down pin, remove lock cylinder.
4. Reverse procedure to install. Ensure lock cylinder is in ACC position. Reset audio anti-theft system, if equipped, as outlined under "Precautions."

IGNITION SWITCH
REPLACE

1. **On models with audio coded anti-theft system,** obtain three digit anti-theft code.
2. **On all models,** remove steering wheel, upper and lower covers.
3. Disconnect electrical connectors from ignition switch.
4. Turn ignition key to ACC position and remove ignition key cylinder.
5. Remove screw and ignition switch.
6. Reverse procedure to install. Reset audio anti-theft system, if equipped, as outlined under "Precautions."

NEUTRAL SAFETY SWITCH
ADJUST

1. Raise and support vehicle.
2. Disconnect shift control cable from shift lever, then loosen neutral safety switch bracket bolt.
3. Position transmission shift lever into Neutral.
4. Align switch shaft groove with neutral base line, then retighten switch bracket bolt, **Fig. 5.**
5. Connect electrical connector to switch.

STOP LIGHT SWITCH
REPLACE

1. Remove brake pedal tension spring.
2. Disconnect switch wire connector.
3. Remove switch mounting nut, then slide switch from mounting bracket.
4. Reverse procedure to install.

COMBINATION SWITCH
REPLACE

1. **On models with audio coded anti-theft system,** obtain three digit anti-theft code.

2. **On all models,** remove steering wheel as outlined under "Steering Wheel, Replace."
3. Remove steering column upper and lower covers.
4. Remove combination switch with spiral cable assembly.
5. Reverse procedure to install. Reset audio anti-theft system, if equipped, as outlined under "Precautions."

STEERING WHEEL
REPLACE
LESS AIR BAG

1. Remove trim cover from center of steering wheel.
2. Place alignment marks on steering wheel and mainshaft for assembly reference.
3. Remove nut attaching steering wheel to steering shaft.
4. Using a suitable puller, remove steering wheel. On some models, a steering wheel puller may not be necessary.
5. Reverse procedure to install.

WITH AIR BAG

1. **On models with audio coded anti-theft system,** obtain three digit anti-theft code.
2. **On all models,** position front wheels straight ahead.
3. Remove No. 2 and 3 steering wheel pad covers, then loosen steering wheel pad Torx screws until screw circumference groove catches on screw case.
4. Carefully pull steering wheel pad rearward, then disconnect air bag electrical connector. **Do not pull air bag wiring harness. Store air bag assembly with upper surface of pad facing upward.**
5. Disconnect steering wheel electrical connector, then remove set nut.
6. Place installation alignment marks on steering wheel and main shaft.
7. Using suitable steering wheel puller, remove steering wheel.
8. Reverse procedure to install, noting the following:
   a. If spiral cable was removed, ensure front wheels are straight ahead, the turn spiral cable counterclockwise by hand until becomes harder to turn cable, then rotate cable clockwise three turn to align red mark, **Fig. 6.**
   b. **Torque** steering wheel attaching bolt to 26 ft. lbs.
   c. **Torque** steering wheel pad attaching Torx screws to 78 inch lbs.
   d. Reset audio anti-theft system, if equipped, as outlined under "Precautions."

INSTRUMENT CLUSTER
REPLACE

1. **On models with audio coded anti-theft system,** obtain three digit anti-theft code.

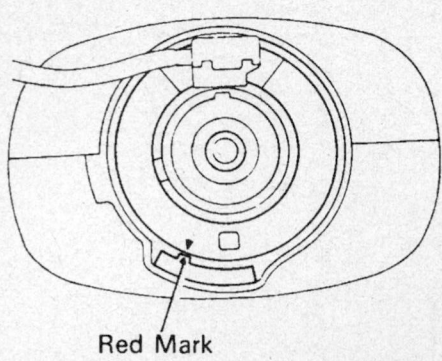

Fig. 6 Spiral cable installation alignment

TY6049300001000X

2. **On all models,** remove steering wheel as outlined under "Steering Wheel, Replace."
3. Remove following parts:
   a. Steering column cover.
   b. Shifting hole bezel.
   c. Rear console box.
   d. Engine hood release lever.
   e. Lower finish panel.
   f. Combination switch.
   g. Lower panel.
4. Remove center cluster lower finish panel, then disconnect connector.
5. Remove center cluster finish panel and combination meter.
6. Remove following parts:
   a. Lower center finish panel.
   b. Cluster finish panel subassembly.
   c. Heater to register duct No. 2.
   d. Side defroster nozzle No. 2.
7. Disconnect connectors, then remove five bolts, then two bolts and junction block Nos. 1 and 4.
8. Remove instrument panel.
9. Reverse procedure to install. Reset audio anti-theft system, if equipped, as outlined under "Precautions."

RADIO
REPLACE

1. **On models with audio coded anti-theft system,** obtain three digit anti-theft code.
2. **On all models,** remove instrument panel center finish panel.
3. Remove radio attaching screws, then pull rearward.
4. Disconnect electrical connectors and antenna lead, then remove radio.
5. Reverse procedure to install. Reset audio anti-theft system, if equipped, as outlined under "Precautions."

WIPER MOTOR
REPLACE
FRONT

1. **On models with audio coded anti-theft system,** obtain three digit anti-theft code.
2. **On all models,** remove wiper arms, then the hood to cowl top seal.
3. Remove cowl louver, then the wiper motor attaching bolts.

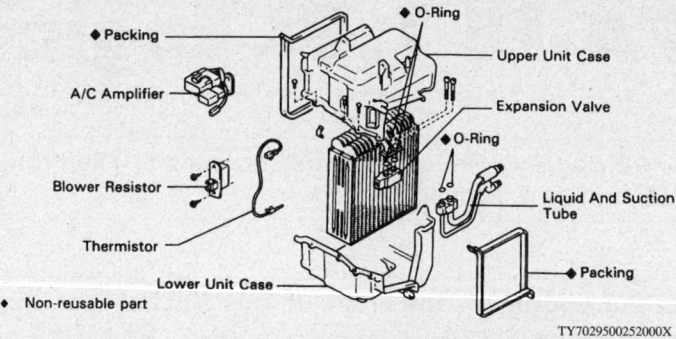

◆ Packing
Upper Unit Case
◆ O-Ring
A/C Amplifier
Expansion Valve
◆ O-Ring
Blower Resistor
Liquid And Suction Tube
Thermistor
Lower Unit Case
◆ Packing
◆ Non-reusable part

TY7029500252000X

Fig. 7 Exploded view of cooling unit

4. Disconnect electrical connector, then remove wiper motor.
5. Reverse procedure to install noting the following:
   a. **Torque** wiper motor bolts to 48 inch lbs.
   b. **Torque** wiper arms nuts to 15 ft. lbs.
   c. Reset audio anti-theft system, if equipped, as outlined under "Precautions."

REAR

1. Remove wiper arm and rear door trim cover.
2. Disconnect wiper motor wire connector.
3. Remove wiper motor bracket attaching bolts and wiper motor and bracket.
4. Reverse procedure to install.

WIPER SWITCH

REPLACE

Refer to "Combination Switch, Replace" procedure.

BLOWER MOTOR

REPLACE

1. **On models with audio coded anti-theft system,** obtain three digit anti-theft code.
2. **On all models,** remove glove compartment assembly, then disconnect blower motor electrical connector.
3. Remove blower motor attaching screws, then the blower motor.
4. Reverse procedure to install.

HEATER CORE

REPLACE

1. Remove cooling unit as described under "Evaporator Core, Replace."
2. Drain engine coolant from radiator.
3. Disconnect water hoses from heater core pipes.
4. Remove pipe grommets.
5. Remove instrument panel as described under "Dash Panel Service."
6. Remove instrument panel reinforcement No. 1 brace.

7. Remove instrument panel reinforcement No. 2 brace.
8. Remove duct heater to register No. 3.
9. Remove front defroster nozzle.
10. Remove heater unit.
11. Reverse procedure to install.

EVAPORATOR CORE

REPLACE

1. **On models with audio coded anti-theft system,** obtain three digit anti-theft code.
2. **On all models,** discharge system refrigerant as outlined in "Air Conditioning" section, then disconnect refrigerant lines at cooling unit, capping all openings.
3. Remove front door scuff plate.
4. Remove glove compartment.
5. Disconnect blower resistor connector, **Fig. 7.**
6. Disconnect A/C amplifier connector.
7. Remove cooling unit and A/C amplifier.
8. Disconnect A/C harness from thermistor.
9. Remove thermistor connector from upper case.
10. Separate upper and lower evaporator case.
11. Remove evaporator core from cooling unit.
12. Remove blower motor resistor from upper case.
13. Remove thermistor from evaporator.
14. Remove expansion valve, liquid and suction tube from evaporator.
15. Reverse procedure to install, then evacuate and recharge system and check for leaks. If evaporator is replaced, add 1.4–1.7 oz. of new refrigerant oil to compressor. Reset audio anti-theft system, if equipped, as outlined under "Precautions."

NOTE: On Air Bag Equipped Models, Refer To "Air Bag System Precautions" Located In The Front Of This Manual For System Disarming & Arming Procedures.

NOTE: Refer To "Computer Relearn Procedures" Located In The Front Of This Manual For Computer Relearn Procedures.

INDEX

PRECAUTIONS

AIR BAG SYSTEMS

Refer to "Air Bag System Precautions" in the front of this manual for system disarming and arming procedures.

BATTERY GROUND CABLE

Prior to service, disconnect battery ground cable and isolate as required.

AUDIO CODED ANTI-THEFT SYSTEM

Some models are equipped with an audio coded anti-theft system that will disable the radio when the battery cable is disconnected. The system can be identified by the words "ANTI-THEFT SYSTEM" on the cassette tape lid. Obtain three digit customer code for input. Reset system after service as follows:

1. Obtain three digit audio anti-theft code.
2. Depress 1 (PROG) while depressing righthand side of TUNE SEEK button, - - - will appear in tape operation display.
3. To enter the first digit, depress 1 (PROG) button repeatedly until the number of times depressed equals the first digit beginning with zero (depress the 1 button six times if the first digit is five).
4. To enter second digit, depress 2 (APS) button repeatedly until the number of times depressed equals the second digit beginning with zero.
5. To enter third digit, depress 3 (RPT) button repeatedly until the number of times depressed equals the third digit beginning with zero.
6. If - - - is displayed during code input, repeat procedure.
7. When code appears in display, depress and hold SCAN button until SEC appears.
8. When SEC disappears audio system should be operative.
9. If Err is displayed, repeat procedure. **Attempting to input code more than nine times may permanently disable audio system.**

COMPRESSION PRESSURE

1. Start engine and warm to normal operating temperature, then turn engine off.
2. Disconnect distributor connectors.
3. Disconnect spark plug wires.
4. Remove spark plugs.
5. Insert compression gauge into spark plug hole.
6. Fully open throttle.
7. While cranking engine, measure compression pressure.
8. Compression pressure should be 142–191 psi or more. Maximum difference between each cylinder is 14 psi.

ENGINE

REPLACE

1. **On models with audio coded anti-theft system,** obtain three digit anti-theft code.
2. **On all models,** remove engine hood and undercover, air cleaner hose and air cleaner assembly.
3. Drain engine and transmission oil, then disconnect two oil cooler hoses.
4. Drain coolant from radiator, then remove two heater hoses.
5. Disconnect coolant reservoir hose, then remove coolant reservoir.
6. Remove radiator attaching bolts, then the radiator and cooling fan as an assembly.
7. Disconnect throttle cables from carburetor, then all necessary electrical connectors.
8. Disconnect brake booster, power steering, MAP hose from gas filter, A/C actuator connector and A/C and EBCV vacuum hoses.
9. **On models equipped with cruise control,** remove cruise control actuator.
10. **On all models,** disconnect engine wire as follows:
    a. Remove lefthand front door scuff plate, lower finish panel and righthand front door scuff plate.
    b. Remove lower panel with glove compartment door.
    c. Remove radio, center cluster finish panel and rear console box.
    d. **On models equipped with manual transaxle,** remove shift lever knob.
    e. **On models equipped with automatic transaxle,** remove shifting hole bezel.
    f. **On all models,** remove finish lower center panel and floor carpet bracket.
    g. Disconnect three ECM connectors and cowl wire connector.
    h. Pull out engine wire from cowl panel.
11. Remove charcoal canister.
12. Disconnect heater water hoses.
13. Disconnect fuel hoses from fuel pump.
14. **On models with power steering,** remove power steering pump and bracket and position aside. **Do not**

disconnect power steering pump hoses.

15. **On models equipped with A/C,** remove A/C compressor and bracket and position aside. **Do not disconnect refrigerant lines.**

16. **On all models,** disconnect speedometer cable from transaxle.

17. **On models equipped with manual transaxle,** remove clutch release cylinder from transaxle and position aside. **Do not disconnect fluid line from release cylinder.**

18. **On all models,** disconnect transmission shifter control cables.

19. Raise and support vehicle.

20. Disconnect exhaust pipe from exhaust manifold.

21. Disconnect driveshafts from transaxle.

22. Disconnect front, center and rear mounting from center member.

23. Remove engine mounting member, then lower vehicle and install suitable engine lifting equipment.

24. Remove three mounting stay bolts, then righthand mounting.

25. Remove two mounting stay bolts, then remove lefthand mounting.

26. Remove engine and transaxle assembly. **Ensure care is taken as not to damage power steering pump or throttle position sensor during removal.**

27. Place engine in suitable work stand, then disconnect back-up lamp and neutral safety switch electrical connectors.

28. Remove rear end plate.

29. **On models equipped with automatic transaxle,** remove six torque convertor mounting bolts.

30. **On all models,** remove starter, then transaxle from engine.

31. Reverse procedure to install. Tighten attaching nuts and bolts to specifications. Reset audio anti-theft system, if equipped, as outlined under "Precautions."

INTAKE MANIFOLD
REPLACE

1. **On models with audio coded anti-theft system,** obtain three digit anti-theft code.

2. **On all models,** remove air cleaner assembly.

3. Disconnect all electrical connectors, hoses, cables, fuel lines and electrical equipment that will interfere with removal of and intake manifold. Ensure following are removed:
   a. Ground strap.
   b. ISC valve connector.
   c. Cold start injector connector.
   d. Throttle position sensor connector.
   e. If equipped, EGR VSV and gas temperature sensor connectors.
   f. Vacuum sensor connector.
   g. Disconnect wire clamp from vacuum pipe and remove engine wire from manifold.
   h. Vacuum sensor hose from gas filter.
   i. Fuel return hose from air pipe.

4. Remove manifold stay, then water by-pass hose from air pipe.

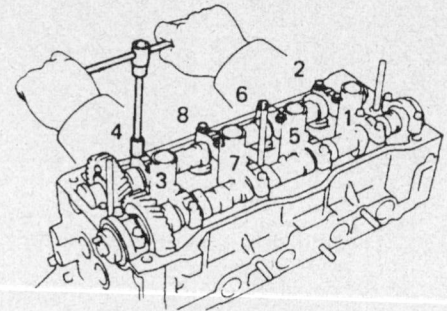

TY1069100085000X

Fig. 1 Intake camshaft bearing cap bolt removal

5. Remove intake retaining bolts, ground strap, intake manifold and gasket.

6. Reverse procedure to install. Tighten to specifications. Reset audio anti-theft system, if equipped, as outlined under "Precautions."

EXHAUST MANIFOLD
REPLACE

1. **On models with audio coded anti-theft system,** obtain three digit anti-theft code.

2. **On all models,** remove exhaust pipe from exhaust manifold.

3. Disconnect all electrical connectors, hoses, cables, fuel lines and electrical equipment that will interfere with removal of exhaust manifold.

4. Remove manifold stay, then insulator.

5. Remove exhaust manifold attaching bolts, then exhaust manifold, insulators and gasket.

CYLINDER HEAD
REPLACE

1. **On models with audio coded anti-theft system,** obtain three digit anti-theft code.

2. **On all models,** remove undercover, then drain engine coolant and engine oil.

3. Disconnect exhaust pipe from exhaust manifold.

4. Remove air cleaner assembly.

5. Remove distributor and alternator.

6. Disconnect accelerator cable and throttle cable, if equipped.

7. Remove cruise control actuator cable.

8. Disconnect all necessary electrical connectors.

9. Disconnect necessary vacuum lines.

10. Disconnect radiator hoses from engine.

11. Disconnect heater hoses, then remove water outlet.

12. Remove exhaust manifold upper shield, then the manifold.

13. Disconnect hoses from water inlet housing and remove housing.

14. **On models with 4A-FE engine,** remove fuel delivery pipe with fuel injectors as an assembly.

15. **On models with 7A-FE engine,** remove engine hanger nut, then engine hanger.

16. **On models with 7A-FE engine,** disconnect following hoses and connectors:
   a. Ground strap connector and MAP connector.
   b. A/C pressure switch.
   c. Engine wire from righthand fender apron.
   d. MAP sensor hose from gas filter.
   e. Brake booster vacuum hose.
   f. **On models equipped with A/C,** A/C vacuum hose from actuator, then A/C actuator connector.
   g. **On models equipped with power steering,** air hose from air pipe.

17. **On all models,** disconnect engine wire clamp, then remove intake manifold stay and air pipe.

18. Remove cold start injector pipe.

19. Remove EGR vacuum modulator.

20. Disconnect PCV and water hoses from intake manifold, then remove the manifold.

21. **On models equipped with 7A-FE engine,** remove righthand engine mounting insulator.

22. **On models equipped with 4A-FE engine,** remove water pump pulley, then the drive belt.

23. **On all models,** remove power steering pump stay if equipped, then the spark plugs.

24. Remove cylinder head cover and gasket.

25. Remove No. 3 and No. 2 timing belt covers.

26. If timing belt is to be replaced, refer to "Timing Belt, Replace" for procedure. If timing belt is to be reused, proceed as follows:
   a. Turn crankshaft pulley and align groove with "0" mark on the No. 1 timing belt cover. **Ensure all valve lifters on the No. 1 cylinder are loose. If not, turn crankshaft pulley one complete revolution.**
   b. Place alignment marks on the camshaft timing pulley and belt.
   c. Loosen idler pulley bolt, then push idler pulley as far left as possible and temporarily tighten it.
   d. Remove timing belt from camshaft timing pulleys. **Support timing belt so meshing of crankshaft timing pulley and timing belt does not shift.**
   e. Remove camshaft timing pulley.

27. **On models with 7A-FE engine,** remove engine hanger, alternator bracket, oil dipstick guide and dipstick and water inlet No. 2.

28. **On all models,** measure camshaft thrust clearance. If clearance is greater than .0043 inch, replace camshaft and/or cylinder head.

29. Loosen No. 1 intake and exhaust bearing cap bolts gradually, then remove bearing caps.

30. Secure intake camshaft sub-gear to main gear, using a suitable 6 mm bolt.

31. Loosen bearing cap bolts gradually in sequence shown in **Figs. 1 and 2,** then remove the bearing caps.

32. Remove intake and exhaust camshafts. **Do not pry on camshafts or cylinder head.**

TY1069100086000X

Fig. 2 Exhaust camshaft bearing cap bolt removal

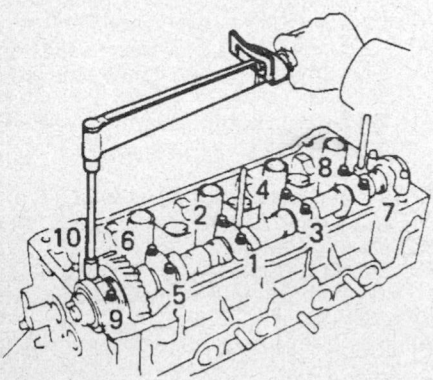

TY1069100090000X

Fig. 5 Exhaust camshaft bearing cap bolt tightening sequence

33. Remove semi-circular plugs.
34. Loosen and remove cylinder head attaching bolts gradually in sequence shown in **Fig. 3. Head warpage or cracking could result from removing cylinder head bolts in incorrect order.**
35. Remove cylinder head.
36. Reverse procedure to install. Noting the following:
    a. Cylinder head bolts are in lengths of 3.54 inches (90 mm) and 4.25 inches (108 mm). Install bolts labeled "A" in righthand side and bolts labeled "B" in exhaust manifold side, **Fig. 4.**
    b. Using sequence shown in **Fig. 4, torque** cylinder head attaching bolts in several passes to 22 ft. lbs. Mark front of cylinder head bolts with paint. Tighten bolts an additional 90° in sequence, then another 90° in sequence.
    c. **Torque** bearing cap attaching bolts gradually in three steps in sequence, **Figs. 5 and 6,** to 9 ft. lbs.
    d. Reset audio anti-theft system, if equipped, as outlined under "Precautions."

VALVE CLEARANCE SPECIFICATIONS

Clearance should be .006–.010 inch on intake valves and .010–.014 inch on exhaust valves.

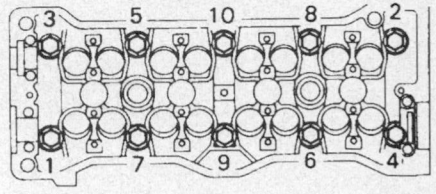

TY1069100087000X

Fig. 3 Cylinder head bolt removal sequence

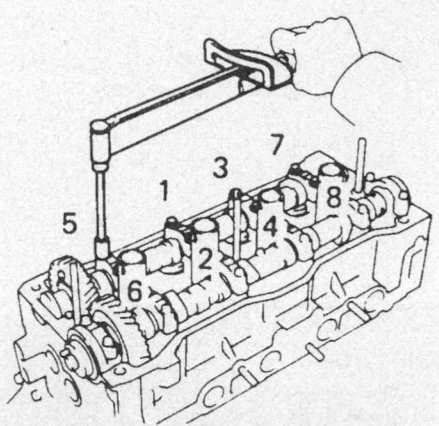

TY1069100091000X

Fig. 6 Intake camshaft bearing cap bolt tightening sequence

VALVE ADJUSTMENT

Valve adjustment is accomplished by installing shims to achieve the proper valve clearance. Shims are available in .0020 inch (.050 mm) increments, **Fig. 7.**
1. With No. 1 piston at TDC on compression stroke, adjust following valves to specification: No. 1 intake and exhaust, No. 2 intake and No. 3 exhaust.
2. Turn crankshaft in normal direction of rotation one full revolution (360°) and adjust following cylinders valves to specification: No. 2 exhaust, No. 3 intake and No. 4 intake and exhaust.

VALVE GUIDES

1. Using a suitable tool and hammer, strike valve guide bushing to break it off at cylinder head casting.
2. Heat cylinder head to 176–212°F (80–100°C).
3. Using suitable valve guide removal tool, tap out bushing.
4. Install snap ring on new valve guide, then install new valve guide using tool as described above, drive in from opposite side of removal.
5. Ream new valve guide, if necessary. Refer to "Valve Specifications" for stem clearances.

HYDRAULIC LIFTERS
REPLACE

Check lifters for excessive wear and/or damage. Replace worn or damaged valve lifters as required. Lubricate hydraulic valve lifter before installation.

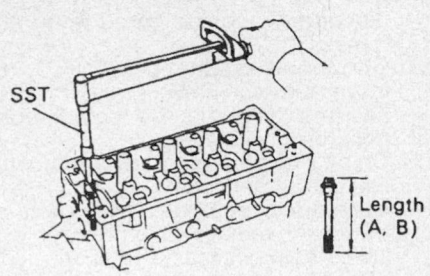

Fig. 4 Cylinder head bolt tightening sequence

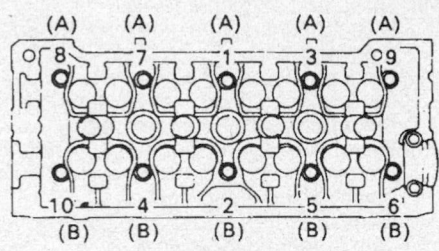

Shim No.	Thickness	Shim No.	Thickness
1	2.55 (0.1004)	9	2.95 (0.1161)
2	2.60 (0.1024)	10	3.00 (0.1181)
3	2.65 (0.1043)	11	3.05 (0.1201)
4	2.70 (0.1063)	12	3.10 (0.1220)
5	2.75 (0.1083)	13	3.15 (0.1240)
6	2.80 (0.1102)	14	3.20 (0.1260)
7	2.85 (0.1122)	15	3.25 (0.1280)
8	2.90 (0.1142)	16	3.30 (0.1299)

New shim thickness mm (in.)

HINT: New shims have the thickness in millimeters imprinted on the face.

TY1069300093000X

Fig. 7 Valve adjustment shim chart

TIMING BELT
REPLACE
REMOVAL

1. **On models with audio coded anti-theft system,** obtain three digit anti-theft code.
2. **On all models,** remove right front wheel, then right side undercover.
3. Remove washer tank.
4. **On models equipped with cruise control,** remove cruise control actuator.
5. **On all models,** loosen water pump pulley bolts and remove drive belt.
6. **On models equipped with A/C,** remove A/C compressor drive belt, then the A/C compressor and bracket and position aside.
7. **On models equipped with power steering,** remove power steering pump drive belt.
8. **On all models,** disconnect alternator connector and wire, oil pressure switch

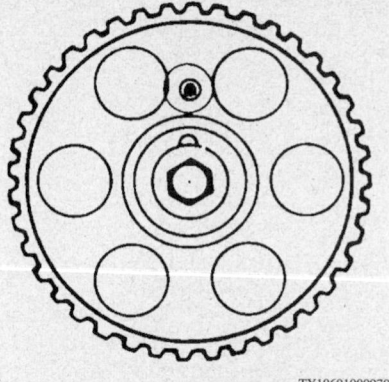

Fig. 8 Camshaft sprocket alignment

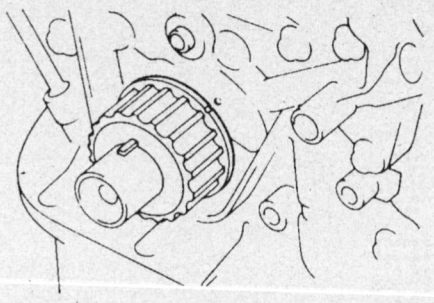

Fig. 9 Crankshaft sprocket alignment

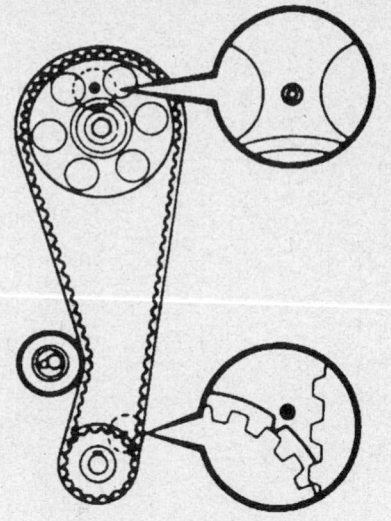

Fig. 10 Timing belt alignment inspection. 4A-FE engine

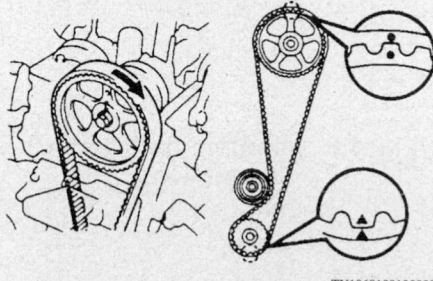

Fig. 11 Timing belt alignment inspection. 7A-FE engine

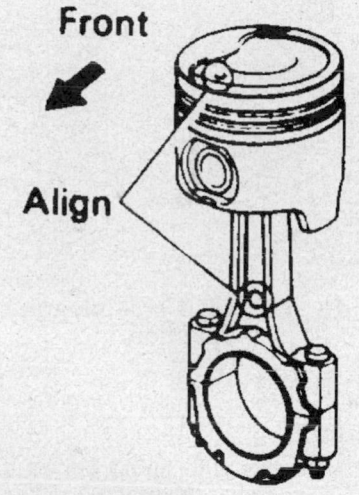

Fig. 12 Piston & connecting rod assembly

connector and equipped with A/C, compressor connector. Remove bolt(s) with engine wire cover and disconnect engine wire from cylinder head.

9. Remove spark plugs, cylinder head cover and gasket.
10. Set cylinder No. 1 to TDC of compression stroke by rotating crankshaft pulley as necessary to align pulley groove with "0"timing mark. Ensure valve lifters on No. 1 cylinder are loose. If not rotate crankshaft pulley one complete revolution.
11. Remove righthand mounting insulator, then the water pump pulley.
12. Remove crankshaft pulley using a suitable puller.
13. Remove timing belt covers, then the timing belt guide from crankshaft.
14. Remove timing belt and idler pulley. **If belt is to be reused, place reference marks on belt and pulleys, then place a mark on belt noting direction of rotation.**
15. Remove crankshaft timing pulley.
16. Remove camshaft timing pulley.
17. Inspect idler pulley for smooth operation.
18. Measure tension spring free length, free length should be 1.512 inches (38.4 mm).
19. Check tension spring, tension should be 8.4 lbs. at 1.976 inches.

INSTALLATION

1. Install camshaft timing pulley, then tighten attaching bolt to specification.

2. Align hole in camshaft pulley with mark on bearing cap, **Fig. 8.**
3. Install crankshaft timing pulley, then align timing marks as shown in **Fig. 9.**
4. Install timing belt idler pulley, then the tension spring. Position idler pulley as far left as it will go and temporarily tighten bolt.
5. Install timing belt. If old belt is used, align marks made during disassembly an install belt in proper direction of rotation.
6. Loosen idler pulley mounting bolt and allow idler pulley to tension belt, then rotate crankshaft clockwise two revolutions.
7. Check timing marks to ensure proper alignment as shown in **Figs. 10 and 11.**
8. Tighten idler pulley mounting bolt to specification.
9. Check timing belt deflection. Deflection should be .020–.024 inch (5–6 mm) at 4.4 lbs.
10. Install timing belt guide on crankshaft. **Cup side of guide should face outward.**
11. Install timing belt covers.
12. Install crankshaft pulley, then pulley attaching bolt and tighten to specification.
13. Install water pump pulley temporarily.
14. Install righthand engine mount insulator.
15. Install righthand mounting stay.
16. Install cylinder head cover and gasket.
17. Install spark plugs.
18. Install power steering drive belt.
19. Install A/C compressor and bracket, then the drive belt.
20. Install alternator drive belt. Adjust drive belts to specifications as outlined under "Belt Tension Data."
21. Tighten water pump pulley bolts, then install air cleaner assembly.
22. Install righthand undercover, then the right front wheel.
23. Reset audio anti-theft system, if equipped, as outlined under "Precautions."

CAMSHAFT

REPLACE

Refer to "Cylinder Head, Replace" for camshaft removal procedure.

PISTON & ROD ASSEMBLY

Pistons are available in standard and oversize of .050 inch. If piston bore is not within specifications, replace piston and/or cylinder block. When assembling piston onto connecting rod, ensure mark on top of piston and mark on connecting rod are on same side, **Fig. 12.** When installing piston and connecting rod assembly, ensure mark on top of piston is facing toward front of engine.

MAIN & ROD BEARINGS

Main and connecting rod bearings are available in standard and undersizes of .010 inch (.25mm).

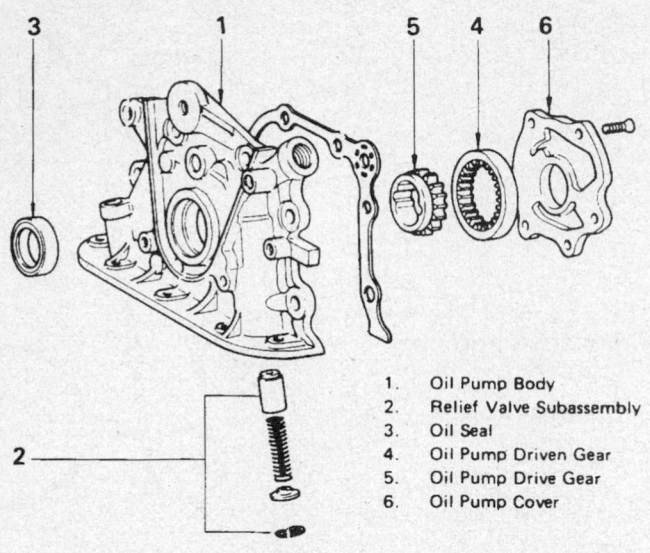

1. Oil Pump Body
2. Relief Valve Subassembly
3. Oil Seal
4. Oil Pump Driven Gear
5. Oil Pump Drive Gear
6. Oil Pump Cover

TY10991000006000X

Fig. 13   Exploded view of oil pump

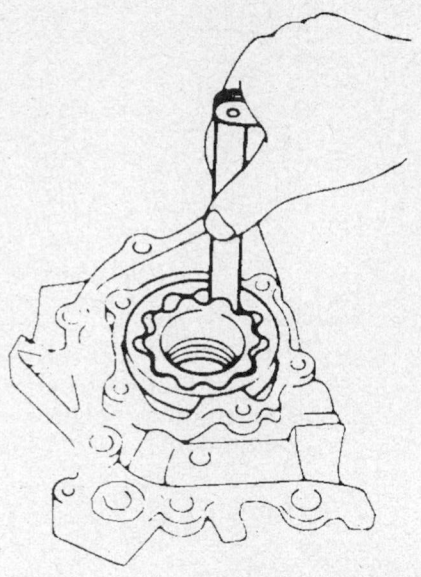

TY10991000007000X

Fig. 14   Oil pump tip clearance inspection

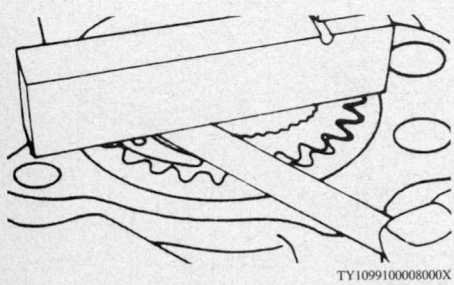

TY10991000008000X

Fig. 15   Oil pump side clearance inspection

OIL PAN
REPLACE

1. **On models with audio coded anti-theft system,** obtain three digit anti-theft code.
2. **On all models,** scribe hood installation alignment marks, then remove hood and engine undercovers.
3. Drain engine oil.
4. Remove timing belt as outlined.
5. Remove oil dipstick and dipstick guide.
6. Remove front exhaust pipe.
7. Remove center mount and stiffening plate.
8. Disconnect oil cooler hose and union from oil pan.
9. Remove oil pan attaching nuts and bolts, then remove pan.
10. Remove oil strainer.
11. Remove oil baffle plate.
12. Remove oil pump attaching bolts, then oil pump.
13. Reverse procedure to install. Reset audio anti-theft system, if equipped, as outlined under "Precautions."

OIL PUMP
REPLACE

Refer to "Oil Pan, Replace" for procedure.

OIL PUMP SERVICE

1. Remove oil pump cover, drive gear and driven gear, **Fig. 13.**
2. Remove oil seal and relief valve subassembly.
3. Check contact surfaces of oil seal and drive gear for damage and wear.
4. Using suitable feeler gauge, measure clearance between rotor tips, **Fig. 14.** If clearance is greater than .0138 inch (.35 mm), replace rotor set.
5. Measure side clearance between rotor and cover, **Fig. 15.** If clearance exceeds .0039 inch (.10 mm), replace rotor or pump body as necessary.
6. Measure body clearance between driven rotor and pump body, **Fig. 16.** If clearance is greater than .0079 inch (.20 mm), replace rotor or pump body as necessary.

BELT TENSION DATA

Belt tension is as follows using a belt tension gauge. A new belt is considered used after five minutes of use.

Engine	Belt	New, Lbs.	Used, Lbs.
4A-FE	Air Cond.	140–180	80–120
	Alternator	140–180	110–150
	Power Steer.	100–150	60–100
7A-FE	Air Cond.	140–180	80–120
	Alternator	170–180	95–135
	Power Steer.	100–150	60–100

COOLING SYSTEM BLEED

These engines do not require a specified bleed procedure. After filling cooling system, run engine to operating temperature with radiator/pressure cap off. Air will then be automatically bled through cap opening.

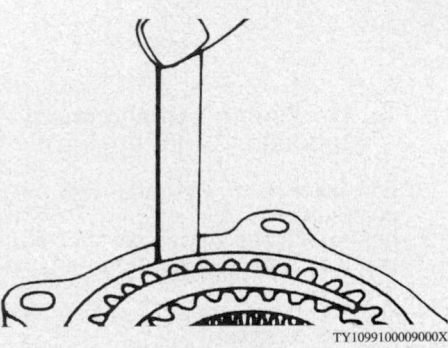

TY10991000009000X

Fig. 16   Oil pump body clearance inspection

THERMOSTAT
REPLACE

1. **On models with audio coded anti-theft system,** obtain three digit anti-theft code.
2. **On all models,** drain engine coolant.
3. Disconnect ECT switch connector.
4. Remove water inlet housing attaching nuts, then remove water housing.
5. Remove thermostat and gasket.
6. Reverse procedure to install. Reset audio anti-theft system, if equipped, as outlined under "Precautions."

WATER PUMP
REPLACE

1. **On models with audio coded anti-theft system,** obtain three digit anti-theft code.
2. **On all models,** drain coolant.
3. Remove righthand engine mount.
4. Remove No. 2 and 3 timing belt covers.
5. **On models equipped with power steering,** remove front mount hole cover, remove mount attaching nut and through bolt, then remove mount.

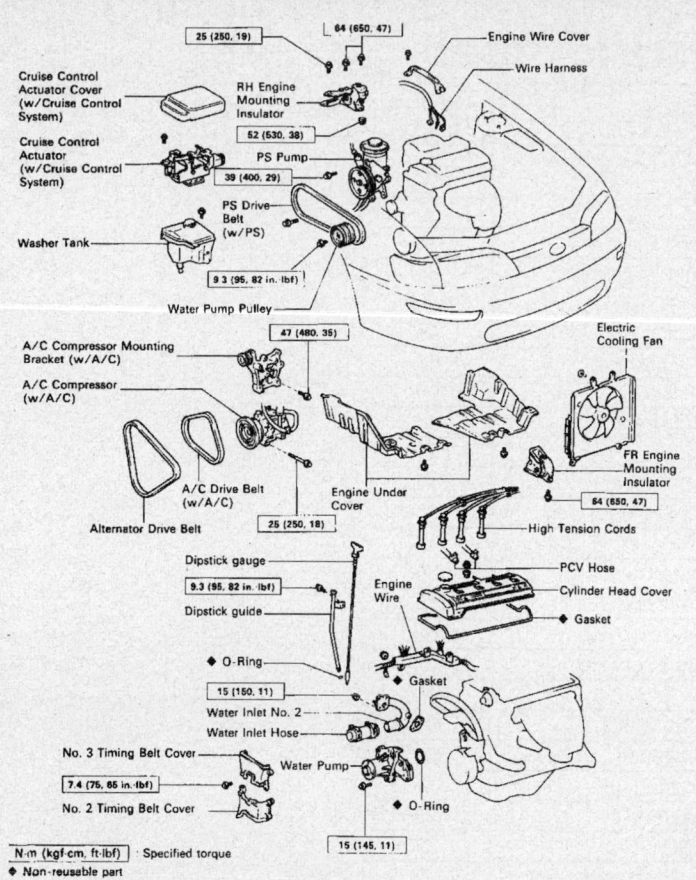

Cruise Control
Actuator Cover
(w/Cruise Control
System)

Cruise Control
Actuator
(w/Cruise Control
System)

25 (250, 19)

64 (650, 47)

Engine Wire Cover

Wire Harness

RH Engine
Mounting
Insulator

52 (530, 38)

PS Pump

39 (400, 29)

PS Drive
Belt
(w/PS)

Washer Tank

9 3 (95, 82 in·lbf)

Water Pump Pulley

47 (480, 35)

A/C Compressor Mounting
Bracket (w/A/C)

A/C Compressor
(w/A/C)

A/C Drive Belt
(w/A/C)

Alternator Drive Belt

25 (250, 18)

Engine Under
Cover

Electric
Cooling Fan

FR Engine
Mounting
Insulator

64 (650, 47)

High Tension Cords

Dipstick gauge

9.3 (95, 82 in·lbf)

Dipstick guide

Engine
Wire

PCV Hose

Cylinder Head Cover

◆ Gasket

◆ O-Ring

◆ Gasket

15 (150, 11)

Water Inlet No. 2

Water Inlet Hose

No. 3 Timing Belt Cover

7.4 (75, 65 in·lbf)

Water Pump

No. 2 Timing Belt Cover

◆ O-Ring

15 (145, 11)

N·m (kgf·cm, ft·lbf) : Specified torque
◆ Non-reusable part

TY1089300008000X

Fig. 17 Water pump removal

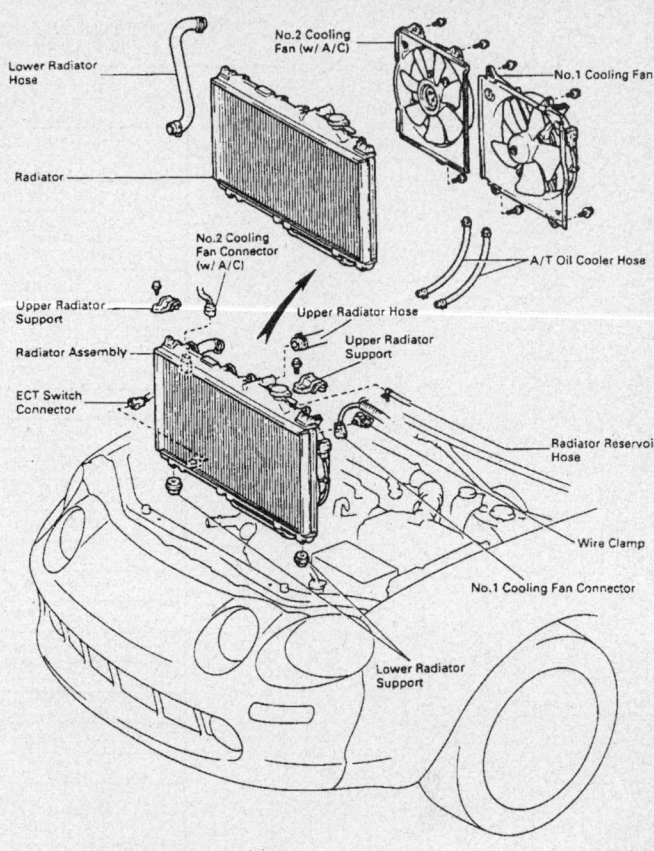

Lower Radiator
Hose

No.2 Cooling
Fan (w/ A/C)

No.1 Cooling Fan

Radiator

No.2 Cooling
Fan Connector
(w/ A/C)

A/T Oil Cooler Hose

Upper Radiator
Support

Radiator Assembly

ECT Switch
Connector

Upper Radiator Hose

Upper Radiator
Support

Radiator Reservoir
Hose

Wire Clamp

No.1 Cooling Fan Connector

Lower Radiator
Support

TY1089500046000X

Fig. 18 Radiator replacement

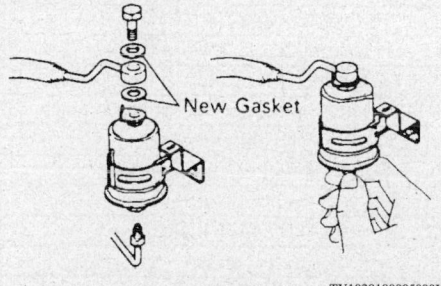

New Gasket

TY1029100005000X

Fig. 19 Fuel filter replacement

6. **On models equipped with power steering,** remove electric cooling fan.
7. **On all models,** disconnect engine wire.
8. Disconnect water inlet and water by-pass hoses from inlet pipe, **Fig. 17.**
9. Disconnect heater water hose from inlet pipe.
10. Remove water inlet pipe attaching nuts and clamp bolts, then remove inlet pipe and O-ring.
11. Remove water pump and water pump pulley. **Do not get coolant on timing belt.**
12. Reverse procedure to install. Reset audio anti-theft system, if equipped, as outlined under "Precautions."

RADIATOR

REPLACE

1. **On models with audio coded anti-theft system,** obtain three digit anti-theft code.
2. **On all models,** drain engine coolant.
3. Disconnect cooling fan electrical connector, **Fig. 18.**

4. Disconnect radiator hoses.
5. Disconnect coolant reservoir hose.
6. **On models equipped with automatic transaxle,** disconnect oil cooler hoses.
7. **On all models,** remove radiator supports, radiator and electric cooling fan.
8. Remove electric cooling fan from radiator.
9. Reverse procedure to install.

FUEL PUMP

REPLACE

1. **On models with audio coded anti-theft system,** obtain three digit anti-theft code.
2. **On all models,** remove rear seat cushion.
3. Disconnect fuel pump connector, then remove five screws and service hole cover.
4. Remove fuel pump lead wire, then disconnect fuel line from fuel pump bracket. **Remove fuel filter cap to prevent fuel from flowing out.**
5. Remove fuel pump bracket assembly, gasket and pull pump out.
6. Reverse procedure to install. Reset audio anti-theft system, if equipped, as outlined under "Precautions."

FUEL FILTER

REPLACE

Refer to **Fig. 19** for replacement procedure.

TIGHTENING SPECIFICATIONS

Year	Component	Torque, Ft. Lbs.
1996–97	A/C Compressor To A/C Compressor Bracket	18
	Bearing Cap Bolts	①
	Camshaft Timing Pulley	43
	Center & Rear Mount To Member	38
	Connecting Rod Cap	22③
	Crankshaft Bearing Cap	44
	Crankshaft Pulley	87
	Cylinder Head	①
	Driveplate (Auto. Trans.)	47
	Engine Coolant Drain Plug	25
	Engine Mount Member	45
	Exhaust Manifold To Cylinder Head	25
	Exhaust Pipe-To-Manifold	46
	Flywheel (Manual Trans.)	58
	Front Mount to Member	35
	Fuel Evaporation Vent Tube	16②
	Fuel Inlet Hose To Fuel Filter	22
	Fuel Inlet Pipe To Tank	30②
	Fuel Pump To Tank	30②
	Fuel Sender Gauge	30②
	Fuel Tank Drain Plug	9
	Fuel Tank Straps	29
	Idler Pulley	27
	Insulator To Body Bracket Through Bolt	64
	Insulator To Engine Mount Bracket Bolt	29
	Insulator To Engine Mount Bracket Nut	38
	Intake Manifold To Cylinder Head	29
	LH Mounting Insulator To Bracket Bolt	47
	LH Mounting Insulator To Bracket Nut	38
	LH Mount Insulator To Transaxle Case	35
	LH Mount Stay	15
	LH Mount Through Bolt	64
	Oil Cooler Pipe	25
	Oil Dipstick Guide	7
	Oil Pan	43②
	Oil Pump	16③
	Oil Strainer	7
	Power Steering Pump Bracket	29
	RH Mounting Insulator To Bracket Bolt	47
	RH Mounting Insulator To Bracket Nut	38
	RH Mount Stay	31
	RH Mount Through Bolt	64
	Spark Plug	13
	Thermostat Water Inlet	7
	Water Pump	11

① — Refer to "Cylinder Head, Replace" for tightening procedure.
② — Inch lbs.
③ — Tighten an additional 90°.

1ZZ-FE 1.8L Engine

NOTE: On Air Bag Equipped Models, Refer To "Air Bag System Precautions" Located In The Front Of This Manual For System Disarming & Arming Procedures.

NOTE: Refer To "Computer Relearn Procedures" Located In The Front Of This Manual For Computer Relearn Procedures.

INDEX

PRECAUTIONS

AIR BAG SYSTEMS

Refer to "Air Bag System Precautions" in the front of this manual for system disarming and arming procedures.

BATTERY GROUND CABLE

Prior to service, disconnect battery ground cable and isolate as required.

COMPRESSION PRESSURE

1. Start engine and warm to normal operating temperature, then turn engine off.
2. Disconnect distributor connectors.
3. Disconnect spark plug wires.
4. Remove spark plugs.
5. Insert compression gauge into spark plug hole.
6. Fully open throttle.
7. While cranking engine, measure compression pressure.
8. Compression pressure should be 145–218 psi or more. Maximum difference between each cylinder is 15 psi.

ENGINE

REPLACE

1. Remove battery and tray, then the engine hood.
2. Remove engine undercovers, then drain engine coolant into a suitable container.
3. Drain engine and transaxle oil into a suitable container, then disconnect accelerator cable.
4. Remove washer tank.

5. **On models equipped with cruise control,** disconnect cruise control actuator as follows:
   a. Disconnect actuator connector, then the wire clamp from actuator bracket.
   b. Remove actuator from body attaching bolts.
6. **On all models,** remove air cleaner cap as follows:
   a. Disconnect IAT sensor connector, then the EVAP vapor hose.
   b. Remove clamps, then the air cleaner cap from air cleaner case.
   c. Loosen air cleaner hose clamp, disconnect air cleaner hose from throttle body, then remove cap and hose.
7. Remove air filter, then disconnect engine wire from clamp on air cleaner case.
8. Remove VSV bracket and air cleaner case attaching bolts, then the air cleaner case.
9. Remove fuel tube clamp, then disconnect fuse tube from fuel pipe on vehicle side.
10. Disconnect heater hose from water by-pass.
11. Disconnect brake booster vacuum hose, then the heater hose from water hose union on cylinder head.
12. Disconnect DLC1, then the VSV connector for EVAP.
13. Release tensioner and remove drive belt.
14. Remove alternator as outlined under "Alternator, Replace"
15. Remove radiator as outlined under "Radiator, Replace."
16. **On models equipped with A/C,** disconnect A/C compressor electrical

connector. Using a suitable torx socket (T40) remove compressor attaching bolts, then the compressor.
17. **On models equipped with manual transaxle,** remove attaching bolt from bracket. Remove tube, then the clutch release cylinder from transaxle.
18. **On all models,** disconnect transaxle control cable(s).
19. Remove two engine relay box retaining nuts and disconnect relay box then the three connectors.
20. Remove clamps, disconnect negative cable, then the positive cable from engine wire.
21. Remove attaching bolt, then disconnect ground cable from transaxle.
22. Remove lower center finish panel.
23. Remove attaching bolts, then disconnect ECM and three connectors.
24. Disconnect cowl wire connectors from bracket, then the heated oxygen sensor connector.
25. Pull out engine wire from cabin.
26. Disconnect power steering oil pressure switch connector.
27. Using a holding tool Nos. 09960–10010, 09962–01000 and 09963–01000, or equivalents, remove power steering pulley bolt and pulley.
28. Remove power steering pump and reposition aside.
29. Remove bolt and pipe clamp, then disconnect center exhaust pipe from front exhaust pipe.
30. Remove front exhaust pipe and gaskets from exhaust manifold.
31. Disconnect driveshafts from transaxle then the driveshaft heat insulator.
32. Remove front mounting insulator to mounting bracket attaching through bolt and nut.

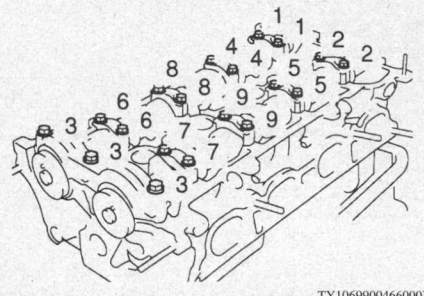

Fig. 1 Camshaft bearing cap removal

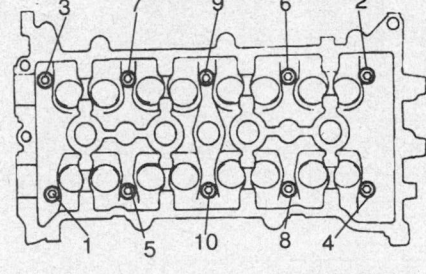

Fig. 2 Cylinder head bolt removal sequence

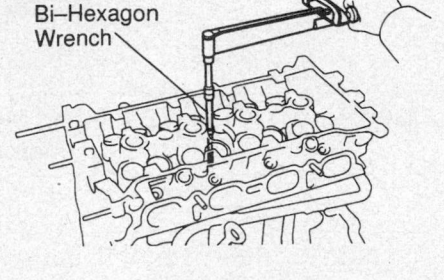

Fig. 3 cylinder head tightening sequence

33. Remove attaching bolts, then the front engine mounting bracket.
34. Remove through bolt attaching rear mounting insulator to mounting bracket.
35. Remove attaching bolts, then the rear engine mounting bracket.
36. Disconnect PVC hose from cylinder head, then the wire harness protector cover.
37. Install engine hangers tool Nos. 12281–20021 for front, 12281–15040, or equivalent, for rear.
38. Install bolt No. 91512–B1016, or equivalent, then tighten to specifications.
39. Attach engine sling device to engine hangers. **Do not attempt to hang engine by hooking engine to any other part.**
40. **On models equipped with manual transaxle,** Remove attaching bolts, then the lefthand mounting stay.
41. **On all models,** remove through bolt and nut attaching lefthand mounting insulator to mounting bracket.
42. Remove attaching bolts, then the lefthand mounting insulator.
43. Disconnect ground strap from body.
44. Remove righthand mounting bracket from engine mounting insulator bolt and nuts.
45. Remove bolt attaching A/C piping clamp to righthand engine mounting insulator then the insulator.
46. Lift engine and transaxle, slowly and carefully out of vehicle. **Ensure engine is clear of power steering gear, all wiring, hoses and cable.**
47. Place engine in a suitable work stand, then disconnect back-up lamp and neutral safety switch electrical connectors.
48. Remove rear endplate.
49. **On models equipped with automatic transaxle,** remove torque converter mounting bolts.
50. **On all models,** remove starter, then separate transaxle from engine.
51. Reverse procedure to install. Tighten attaching nuts and bolts to specifications.

INTAKE MANIFOLD
REPLACE

Refer to "Cylinder Head, Replace" for intake manifold replacement procedure.

EXHAUST MANIFOLD
REPLACE

Refer to "Cylinder Head, Replace" for exhaust manifold replacement procedure.

CYLINDER HEAD
REPLACE

1. Drain engine coolant into a suitable container.
2. Release drive belt tensioner, then remove.
3. Remove alternator as outlined in "Alternator, Replace."
4. Remove air cleaner cap as follows:
   a. Disconnect IAT sensor connector, then the EVAP vapor hose.
   b. Remove clamps, then the air cleaner cap from air cleaner case.
   c. Loosen hose clamp, disconnect air cleaner hose from throttle body, then remove cap and cleaner hose.
5. **On models equipped with automatic transaxle,** disconnect throttle cable.
6. **On all models,** disconnect accelerator cable.
7. Remove oxygen sensor and gasket.
8. Remove front exhaust pipe to exhaust manifold attaching bolts and springs, then the gasket.
9. Remove exhaust manifold stay attaching bolts.
10. Remove heat insulator from dash panel.
11. Remove upper heat insulator.
12. Remove exhaust manifold and gasket.
13. Remove lower heat insulator from exhaust manifold.
14. Remove coil pack as outlined in "Coil Pack, Replace."
15. Remove spark plugs, then the PCV hoses.
16. Disconnect throttle body position sensor, MAP sensor, then the IAC valve connectors.
17. Disconnect two water bypass hose hoses.
18. Remove throttle body and gasket from intake manifold.
19. Remove wire harness protector cover.
20. Remove fuel pipe clamp, then disconnect fuel tube connector from fuel pipe.
21. Disconnect electrical connectors from injectors.
22. Remove delivery pipe together with injectors and fuel pipe.

23. Remove spacers from cylinder head.
24. Disconnect ECT sensor, then the camshaft position sensor connectors.
25. Disconnect two ground wires from cylinder head.
26. Disconnect engine wire protector from brackets on intake manifold.
27. Disconnect EVAP, then brake booster vacuum hoses.
28. Remove bolt, then nut and hose clamp.
29. Remove intake manifold stay.
30. Remove intake manifold retaining bolts and nuts.
31. Remove brackets, then the intake manifold and gasket.
32. Remove engine hanger, then the camshaft position and ECT sensors.
33. Remove PCV valve, then the grommet and oil filler cap
34. Remove timing chain as outlined in "Timing Chain, Replace."
35. Hold hexagonal head wrench portion of camshaft with a wrench, then remove bolts and timing sprockets.
36. Loosen bearing cap bolts gradually in sequence **Fig. 1,** then remove bearing caps.
37. Remove intake and exhaust camshafts. **Do not pry on camshaft or cylinder head.**
38. Disconnect upper radiator hose, then the heater hose from water hose union.
39. Loosen and remove cylinder head retaining bolts gradually in sequence, **Fig. 2. Head warpage or cracking could result from removing cylinder head bolts in an incorrect order.**
40. Remove bolt securing water bypass to cylinder head.
41. Lift cylinder head from dowels on the cylinder block.
42. Reverse procedure to install noting the following:
   a. Place cylinder head quietly in order not to damage gasket.

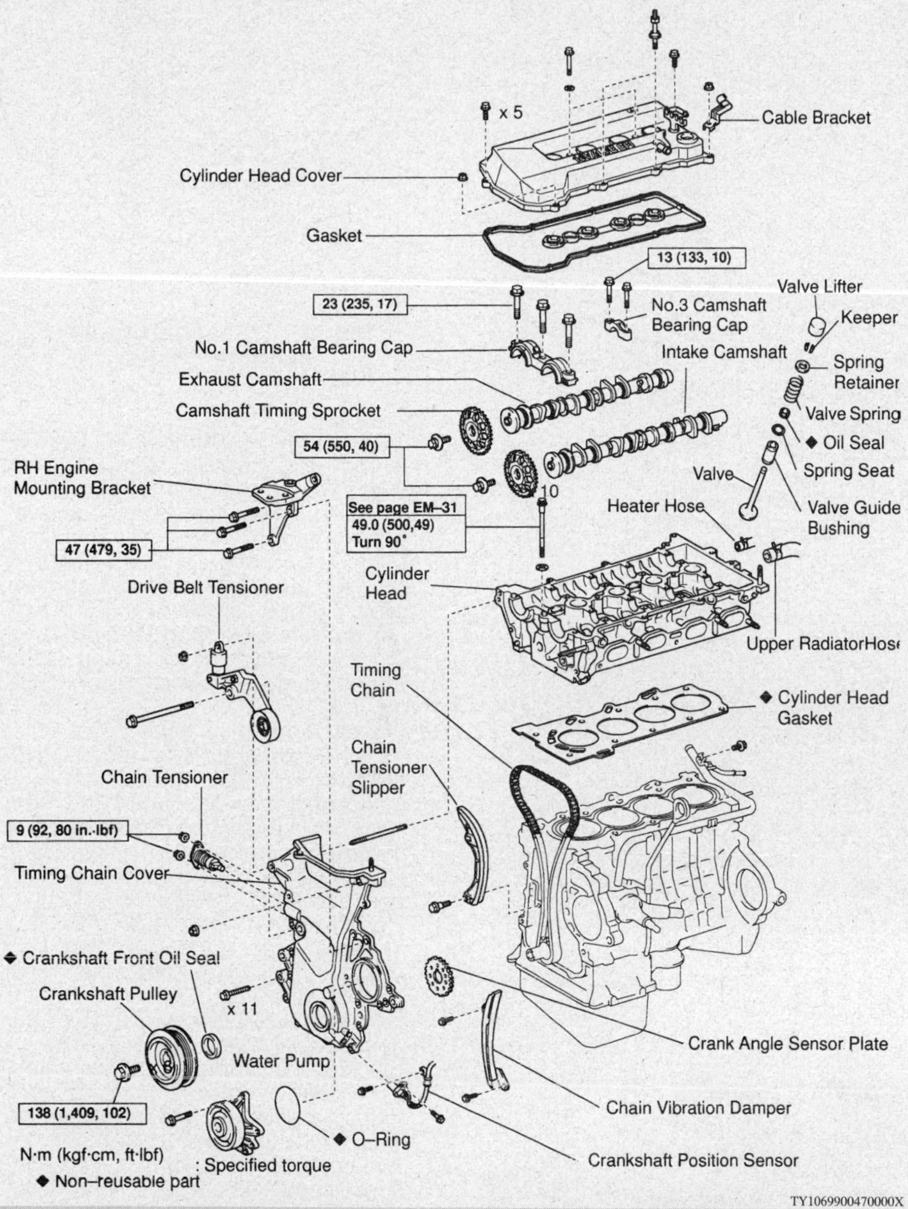

Cylinder Head Cover

Cable Bracket

Gasket

13 (133, 10)

23 (235, 17)

Valve Lifter

No.3 Camshaft Bearing Cap

Keeper

No.1 Camshaft Bearing Cap

Intake Camshaft

Spring Retainer

Exhaust Camshaft

Camshaft Timing Sprocket

Valve Spring

54 (550, 40)

◆ Oil Seal

RH Engine Mounting Bracket

Valve

Spring Seat

See page EM–31
49.0 (500, 49)
Turn 90°

Heater Hose

Valve Guide Bushing

47 (479, 35)

Cylinder Head

Drive Belt Tensioner

Timing Chain

Upper RadiatorHose

Chain Tensioner Slipper

◆ Cylinder Head Gasket

Chain Tensioner

9 (92, 80 in.-lbf)

Timing Chain Cover

Crank Angle Sensor Plate

◆ Crankshaft Front Oil Seal

Crankshaft Pulley

Water Pump

Chain Vibration Damper

138 (1,409, 102)

Crankshaft Position Sensor

N·m (kgf·cm, ft·lbf)
: Specified torque
◆ Non–reusable part

TY1069900470000X

Fig. 4 Camshaft Nos. 1 & 3 bearing cap identification

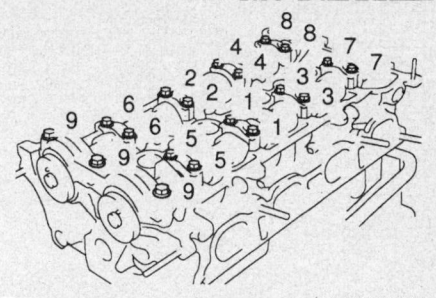

TY1069900469000X

Fig. 5 Camshaft bearing cap tightening sequence

	New lifter thickness		mm (in.)		
Lifter No.	Thickness	Lifter No.	Thickness	Lifter No.	Thickness
06	5.060 (0.1992)	30	5.300 (0.2087)	54	5.540 (0.2181)
08	5.080 (0.2000)	32	5.320 (0.2094)	56	5.560 (0.2189)
10	5.100 (0.2008)	34	5.340 (0.2102)	58	5.580 (0.2197)
12	5.120 (0.2016)	36	5.360 (0.2110)	60	5.600 (0.2205)
14	5.140 (0.2024)	38	5.380 (0.2118)	62	5.620 (0.2213)
16	5.160 (0.2031)	40	5.400 (0.2126)	64	5.640 (0.2220)
18	5.180 (0.2039)	42	5.420 (0.2134)	66	5.660 (0.2228)
20	5.200 (0.2047)	44	5.440 (0.2142)	68	5.680 (0.2236)
22	5.220 (0.2055)	46	5.460 (0.2150)	70	5.700 (0.2244)
24	5.240 (0.2063)	48	5.480 (0.2157)	72	5.720 (0.2252)
26	5.260 (0.2071)	50	5.500 (0.2165)	74	5.740 (0.2260)
28	5.280 (0.2079)	52	5.520 (0.2173)		

TY1069900472000X

Fig. 7 Exhaust valve shim size chart

VALVE ADJUSTMENT

Valve adjustment is accomplished by installing shims to achieve the proper valve clearance. Shims are available in .0020 inch (.050 mm) increments, **Figs. 6 and 7.**
1. With No. 1 piston at TDC on compression stroke , adjust following valves to specification: No. 1 intake and exhaust, No. 2 intake and No. 3 exhaust.
2. Turn crankshaft in normal direction or rotation one full revolution (360°) and adjust following cylinder valves to specification: No. 2 exhaust, No.3 intake and No. 4 intake and exhaust.

VALVE GUIDES

1. Using a suitable tool and hammer, strike valve guide bushing to break it off at cylinder head casting.
2. Heat cylinder head to 176–212°F (80–100°C).
3. Using a suitable valve guide removal tool, tap out bushings
4. Install snap ring on new valve guide, then install new valve guide using tool as described above, drive in from opposite side of removal.
5. Ream new valve guide, if necessary. Refer to "Valve Cleearance Specifications" for stem clearance

	New lifter thickness		mm (in.)		
Lifter No.	Thickness	Lifter No.	Thickness	Lifter No.	Thickness
06	5.060 (0.1992)	30	5.300 (0.2087)	54	5.540 (0.2181)
08	5.080 (0.2000)	32	5.320 (0.2094)	56	5.560 (0.2189)
10	5.100 (0.2008)	34	5.340 (0.2102)	58	5.580 (0.2197)
12	5.120 (0.2016)	36	5.360 (0.2110)	60	5.600 (0.2205)
14	5.140 (0.2024)	38	5.380 (0.2118)	62	5.620 (0.2213)
16	5.160 (0.2031)	40	5.400 (0.2126)	64	5.640 (0.2220)
18	5.180 (0.2039)	42	5.420 (0.2134)	66	5.660 (0.2228)
20	5.200 (0.2047)	44	5.440 (0.2142)	68	5.680 (0.2236)
22	5.220 (0.2055)	46	5.460 (0.2150)	70	5.700 (0.2244)
24	5.240 (0.2063)	48	5.480 (0.2157)	72	5.720 (0.2252)
26	5.260 (0.2071)	50	5.500 (0.2165)	74	5.740 (0.2260)
28	5.280 (0.2079)	52	5.520 (0.2173)		

TY1069900471000X

Fig. 6 Intake valve shim size chart

b. Apply a light coat of engine oil to threads of cylinder head bolts.
c. Using sequence **Fig. 3, torque** cylinder head attaching bolts in several passes to 36 ft. lbs. Mark front of cylinder head bolts with paint. Tighten bolts an additional 90° in sequence, then tighten bolts an additional 90° in sequence.
d. **Torque** No. 1 camshaft bearing cap to 17 ft. lbs. and No. 3 camshaft bearing caps to 10 ft. lbs., **Fig. 4** in sequence **Fig. 5.**

VALVE CLEARANCE SPECIFICATIONS

Clearance should be .006–.010 inch on intake valves and .010–.014 inch on exhaust valves.

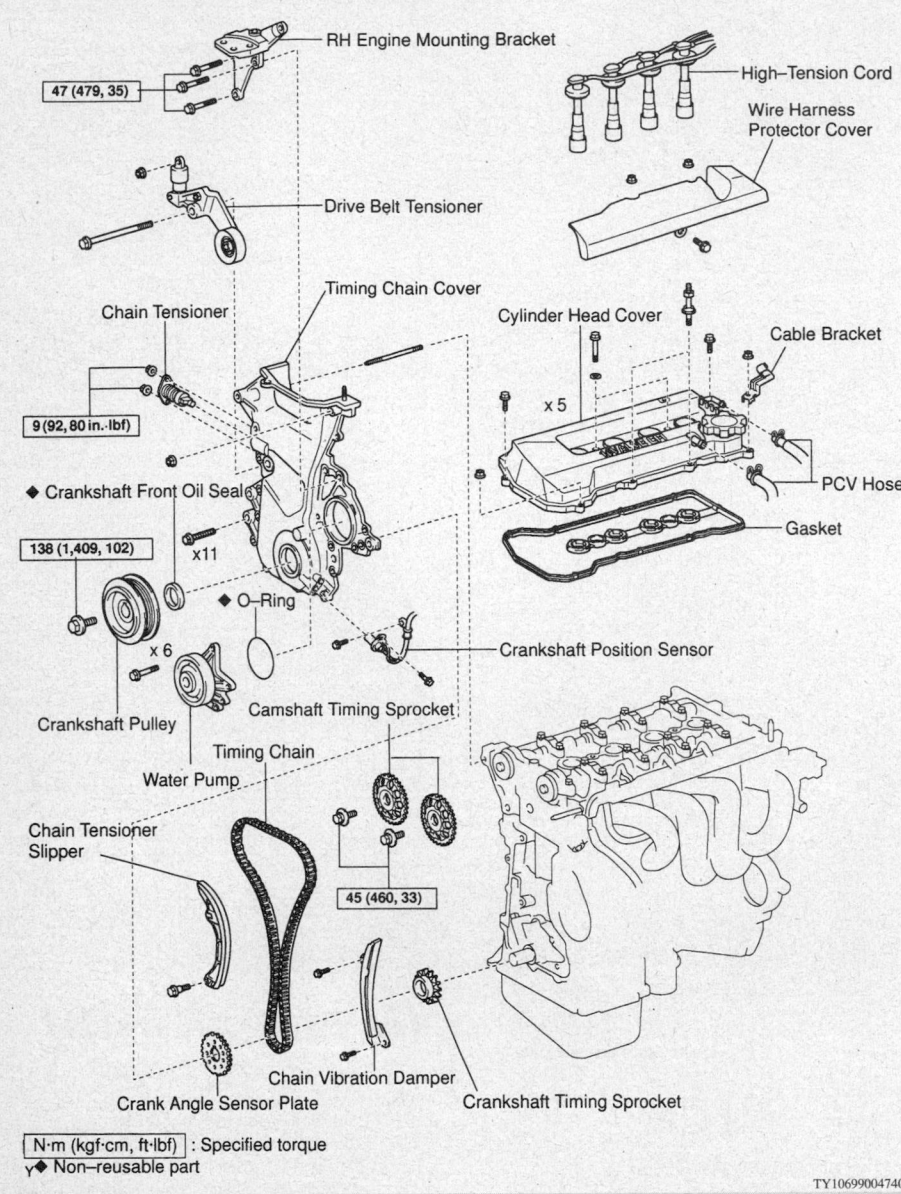

RH Engine Mounting Bracket

47 (479, 35)

Drive Belt Tensioner

High–Tension Cord

Wire Harness Protector Cover

Timing Chain Cover

Chain Tensioner

Cylinder Head Cover

Cable Bracket

9 (92, 80 in.·lbf)

x 5

◆ Crankshaft Front Oil Seal

PCV Hose

138 (1,409, 102)   x11

Gasket

◆ O–Ring

x 6

Crankshaft Position Sensor

Crankshaft Pulley

Camshaft Timing Sprocket

Timing Chain

Water Pump

Chain Tensioner Slipper

45 (460, 33)

Crank Angle Sensor Plate

Chain Vibration Damper

Crankshaft Timing Sprocket

N·m (kgf·cm, ft·lbf) : Specified torque
γ◆ Non–reusable part

TY1069900474000X

Fig. 8 Exploded view of timing components

HYDRAULIC LIFTERS
REPLACE

Check lifters for excessive wear and/or damage. Replace worn or damaged valve lifters as required. Lubricate hydraulic valve lifter before installation.

TIMING CHAIN
REPLACE
REMOVAL

1. Drain engine coolant into a suitable container, then remove washer tank.
2. Remove righthand front wheel, then righthand engine under cover.
3. Release tensioner and remove drive belt, **Fig. 8**
4. Remove alternator as outlined under "Alternator, Replace."

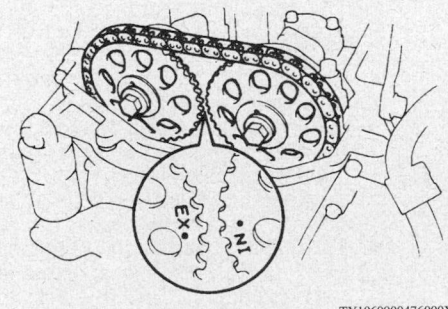

TY1069900476000X

Fig. 10 Camshaft sprocket alignment

5. Disconnect power steering oil pressure switch connector.
6. Using a holding tool Nos.09960–

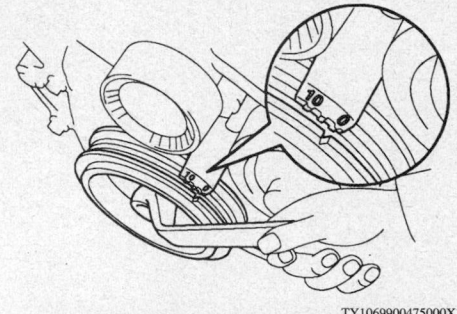

TY1069900475000X

Fig. 9 Crankshaft pulley alignment mark

10010, 09962–01000 and 09963–01000, or equivalent, remove power steering pulley bolt and pulley.
7. Remove power steering pump and reposition aside.
8. Place jack under engine. **Place a wooden block between jack and engine.**
9. **On models equipped with A/C,** remove bolt attaching A/C piping clamp to righthand engine mounting insulator.
10. **On all models,** remove bolts, nuts, then the righthand engine mounting insulator.
11. Disconnect high-tension cords from clamp on cylinder head cover, then the cords from spark plugs.
12. Disconnect two PCV hoses from cylinder head cover.
13. Remove attaching nuts, then the bolt and wire harness protector cover.
14. Remove attaching bolts, then seal washers and nuts.
15. Remove cable bracket, then the cylinder head cover and gasket
16. Set No.1 cylinder to TDC of compression stroke by rotating crankshaft pulley as necessary to align pulley groove with "0" timing mark, **Fig. 9.**
17. Ensure that point mark of camshaft timing sprockets are in straight line on timing chain cover surface, **Fig. 10.**
18. Using crankshaft pulley holder tool Nos. 09213–70010, 09330–00021, or equivalents, remove pulley bolt.
19. Using crankshaft remover tool Nos. 09950–50011, 09951–05010, 09952–05010, 09953–05020 and 09954–05020, or equivalents, remove crankshaft pulley.
20. Remove crankshaft position sensor, then the drive belt tensioner.
21. Remove righthand engine mounting bracket.
22. Remove chain tensioner, then the water pump.
23. Remove timing chain cover retaining bolts, then the nuts.
24. Using a torx wrench socket (E8) or equivalent, remove stud bolt.
25. Remove timing chain cover by prying portions between cylinder head and cylinder block.**Ensure not to damage the contact surface of timing chain**

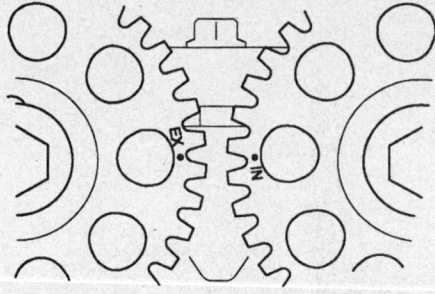

Fig. 11 Camshaft sprocket alignment marks

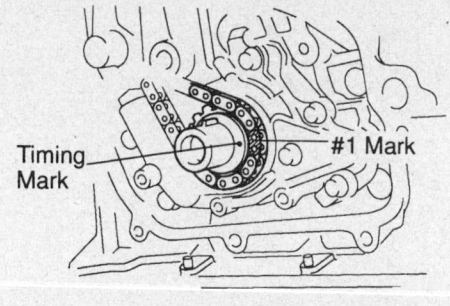

Fig. 12 Timing chain & crankshaft sprocket alignment marks

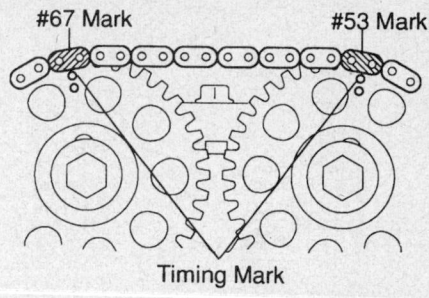

Fig. 13 Timing chain & camshaft timing sprocket alignment marks

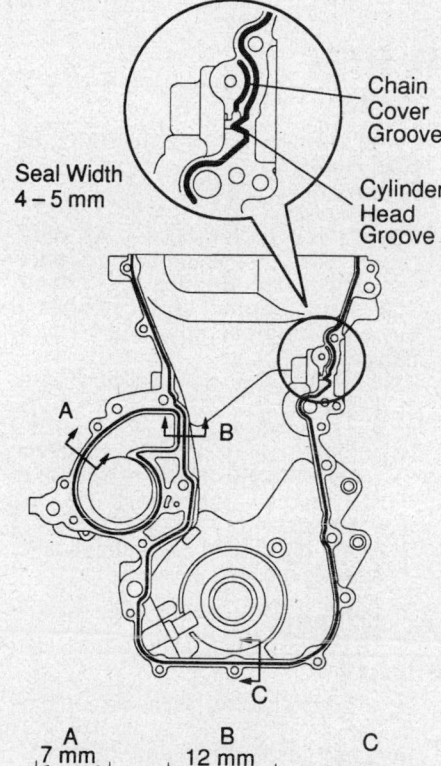

Fig. 14 Timing chain cover sealant application

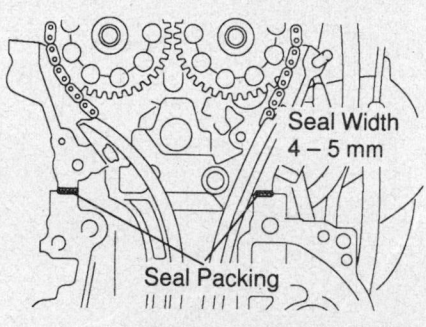

Fig. 15 Timing chain cover sealant packing locations

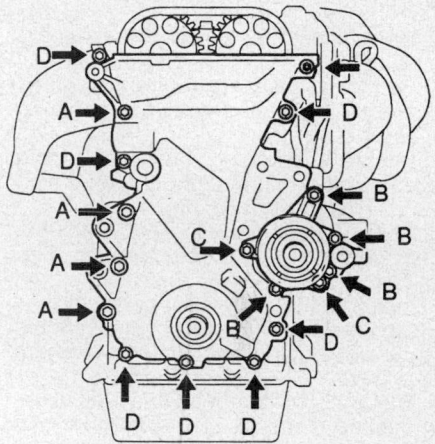

Fig. 16 Timing chain cover, O-ring & water pump tightening chart

3. Using a crankshaft pulley bolt, turn crankshaft and set key facing upward.
4. Install chain vibration damper, then tighten to specification.
5. Using installation tool No. 09223–22010 or equivalent, install timing chain on crankshaft timing sprocket with No. 1 mark link aligned with mark on crankshaft timing sprocket, **Fig. 12.**
6. Install timing chain on camshaft timing sprocket with No. 53 and No. 67 mark links aligned with timing marks on camshaft timing sprockets, **Fig. 13.**
7. Install chain tensioner slipper, then tighten to specification, **do not turn crankshaft.**
8. Install crank angle sensor plate, with "F" mark facing forward.
9. Apply sealant part No. 08826–00100, or equivalent, to timing chain cover, **Fig. 14.** Install a nozzle that has been cut to a 4–5 mm (.16–.02 inch) opening.
10. Apply sealant part No. 08826–00080, or equivalent, to two locations, **Fig. 15.** Install a nozzle that has been cut to a 4–5 mm (.16–.02 inch) opening.
11. Install timing chain cover, O-ring and water pump. Tighten bolts as follows:
    a. **Torque** 10mm "C" bolts to 80 inch lbs.
    b. **Torque** 10mm "A" bolts to 10 inch lbs.
    c. **Torque** remaining 10mm bolts to 8 ft. lbs.
    d. **Torque** 12mm bolts to 14 ft. lbs., as shown in **Fig. 16.**

12. Using a torx wrench socket or equivalent, install stud bolt and tighten to specification.
13. Apply sealant part No. 08826–00080, or equivalent, to threads of bolts, then install righthand engine mounting bracket and tighten to specification.
14. Install drive belt tensioner then tighten to specification.
15. Install crankshaft position sensor, then tighten to specification.
16. Align crankshaft pulley set key with key groove of pulley and slide on pulley.
17. Using holding tool Nos. 09213–70010 and 09330–00021, or equivalent, install pulley bolt and tighten to specification.
18. Install chain tensioner as follows:
    a. Release ratchet pawl, fully push in plunger and apply hook to pin so that plunger cannot spring out.
    b. Insert O-ring by hand until it reaches to chamfering position, then install nut temporaly.
    c. By tightening nut insert chain tensioner to installation position, then tighten nuts to specification.
19. Rotate crankshaft clockwise and disconnect plunger knock pin from hook,

cover, cylinder head and cylinder block.
26. Remove crank angle sensor plate, then the chain tensioner slipper.
27. Remove timing chain and crankshaft timing sprocket.
28. Remove chain vibration damper, then the camshaft timing sprockets.

INSTALLATION

1. Install camshaft timing sprockets then tighten to specification.
2. Align point marks of camshaft timing sprockets, **Fig. 11.**

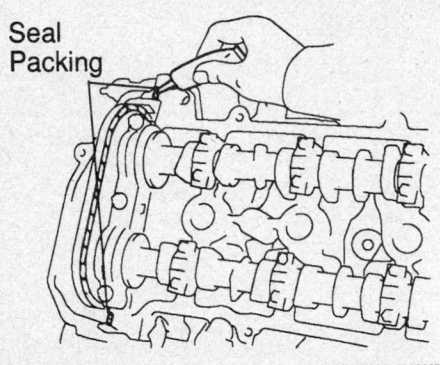

Seal Packing

Fig. 17 Cylinder head cover sealant application

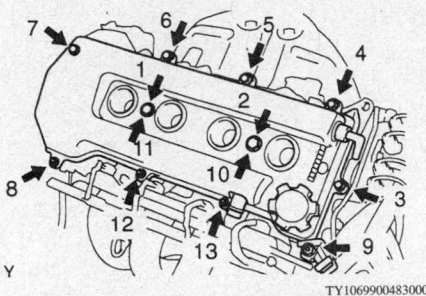

Fig. 18 Cylinder head cover tightening sequence

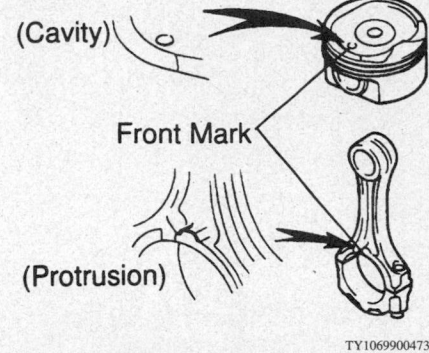

(Cavity)

Front Mark

(Protrusion)

Fig. 19 Piston & connecting rod assembly

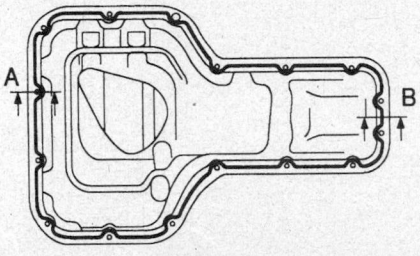

Seal Width 4 – 5 mm

6 mm

A   B

Fig. 20 Oil pan sealant application

then ensure that slipper is pushed by plunger.

20. Rotate crankshaft pulley and align its groove with timing mark " 0" of timing chain cover.
21. Ensure that point marks of timing sprocket are in straight line on timing chain cover surface, **Fig. 10.**
22. Apply sealant part No. 08826–00080, or equivalent, to proper location, **Fig. 17.**
23. Install gasket to cylinder head cover.
24. Install cylinder head cover, then the cable bracket with bolts, sea washers and nuts.
25. Uniformly tighten bolts and nuts in sequence, **Fig. 18.** Then **torque** with washers to 8 ft. lbs., less washers to 80 inch lbs.
26. Install wire harness protector cover, then the PCV hoses to cylinder head cover.
27. Connect high-tension cords to spark plugs, then to clamp on cylinder head cover.
28. Install righthand engine mounting insulator. Tighten bolts and nuts as follows:
    a. **Torque** "A" bolts to 47 ft. lbs.
    b. **Torque** "B" bolts to 19 ft. lbs.
    c. **Torque** nuts to 38 ft. lbs.
29. **On model equipped with A/C,** install bolt attaching A/C piping clamp to righthand engine mounting insulator.
30. **On all models,** install power steering pump and tighten to specification.
31. Using a holding tool Nos. 09960–10010, 09962–01000 and 09963–01000, or equivalent, install power steering pulley nut and tighten to specification.
32. Connect power steering switch electrical connector.
33. Install alternator as outlined under "Alternator, Replace."
34. Release tensioner and install drive belt, then the righthand engine under-cover.
35. Install righthand front wheel, then the washer tank.
36. Refill engine with coolant, then start engine and check for coolant leaks.

CAMSHAFT
REPLACE

Refer to "Cylinder Head, Replace" for camshaft removal procedure.

PISTON & ROD ASSEMBLY

If piston bore is not within specifications, replace piston and/or cylinder block. When assembling piston onto connecting rod, ensure mark on top of piston and mark on connecting rod are on the same side, **Fig. 19.**

MAIN & ROD BEARINGS

Undersized bearings are not available. If crankshaft journals or crankpins are worn or scored, the crankshaft must be replaced.

OIL PAN
REPLACE

1. Remove engine as outlined under "Engine, Replace"
2. Remove attaching bolts and nuts.
3. Insert a cutting blade tool No. 09032–00100, or equivalent, cut between bearing cap sub-assembly and oil pan.
4. Remove oil pan. **Ensure not to damage oil pan contact surface of bearing cap sub-assembly and oil pan flange.**
5. Reverse procedure to install noting the following:
    a. Apply sealant part No. 08826–00080, or equivalent, to locations shown, **Fig. 20.** Install a nozzle that has been cut to a 4–5mm (.16–.20 inch) opening.
    b. Uniformly tighten bolts and nuts to specifications.

OIL PUMP
REPLACE

1. Drain engine oil into a suitable container.
2. Remove timing chain and crankshaft timing sprocket as outlined under "Timing Chain, Replace."
3. Remove attaching bolts, then the oil pump.
4. Reverse procedure to install, then tighten to specification and check for leaks.

OIL PUMP SERVICE

1. Remove plug, then the spring and relief valve, **Fig. 21.**
2. Remove pump body cover, then the drive and driven rotors.
3. Inspect oil jet for damage or clogging.
4. Using suitable feeler gauge and precision straight edge, measure rotor side clearance, **Fig. 22.** If clearance is greater than .0059 inch (.15mm), replace rotor set or oil pump if necessary.
5. Using suitable feeler gauge, measure clearance between rotor tips, **Fig. 23.**

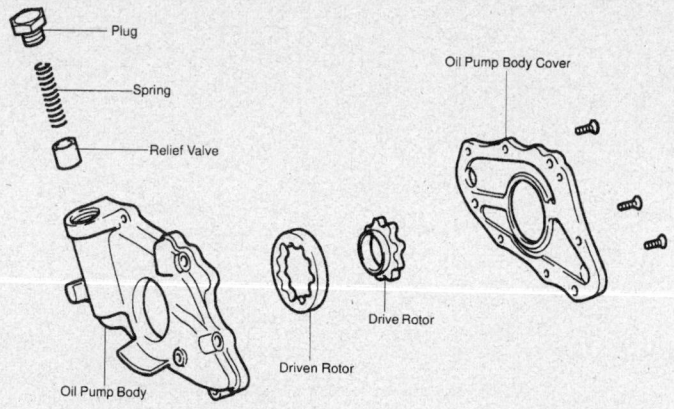

Fig. 21 Exploded view of oil pump

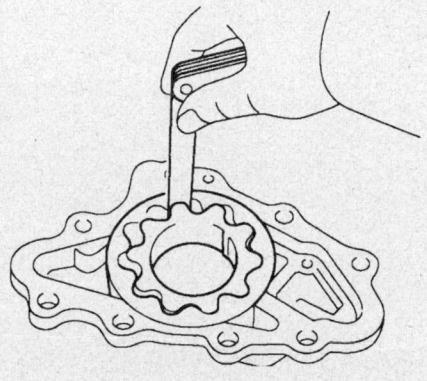

Fig. 23 Oil pump tip clearance inspection

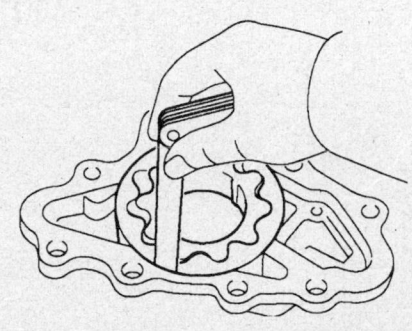

Fig. 24 Oil pump body clearance inspection

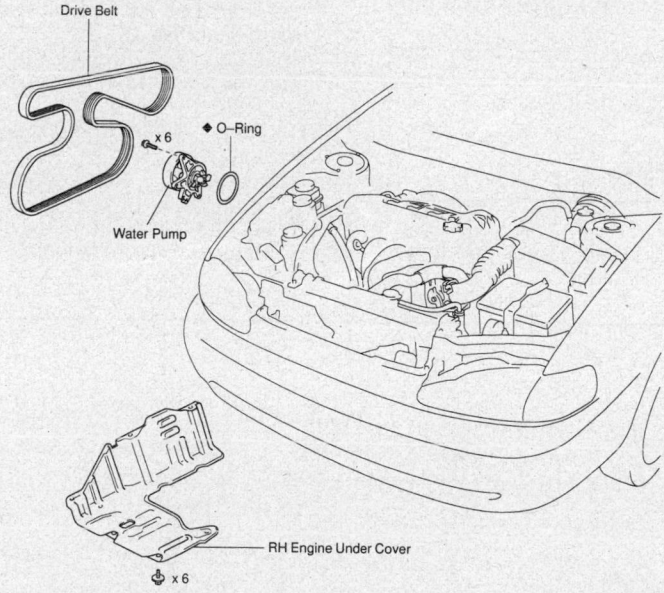

Fig. 25 Exploded view of water pump components

If clearance is greater than .0138 inch (.35mm), replace rotor set.
6. Using suitable feeler gauge, measure between driven rotor and body, **Fig.**

24. If clearance is greater than .0118 inch (.30mm), replace rotor set or oil pump if necessary.

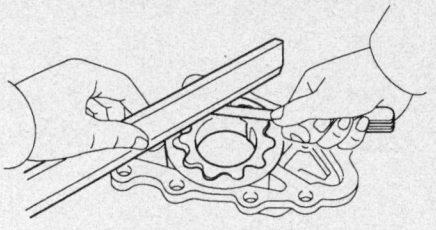

Fig. 22 Oil pump side clearance inspection

BELT TENSION DATA

Engine is equipped with automatic tensioner and can not be adjusted.

COOLING SYSTEM BLEED

This engine does not require a specified bleed procedure. After filling cooling system, run engine to operating temperature with radiator/pressure cap off. Air will then be automatically bled through cap opening.

THERMOSTAT
REPLACE

1. Drain engine coolant into a suitable container.
2. Release tensioner and remove drive belt.
3. Remove alternator as outlined in, "Alternator, Replace."
4. Disconnect ECT switch connector, then remove water inlet from cylinder block.
5. Remove thermostat and gasket.
6. Reverse procedure to install.

WATER PUMP
REPLACE

1. Remove righthand engine undercover, then drain engine coolant into a suitable container.
2. Release tensioner and remove drive belt.
3. Remove attaching bolts, then the water pump and O-ring, **Fig. 25.**
4. Reverse procedure to install. **Do not remove righthand engine mounting bracket and alternator when water pump alone is replaced.**

RADIATOR
REPLACE

1. Drain engine coolant, then remove engine under covers.
2. Disconnect Nos. 1 and 2 electric cooling fan connectors, **Fig. 26.**
3. Disconnect radiator hoses.
4. disconnect coolant reservoir hose.
5. **On models equipped with automatic transaxle,** disconnect oil cooler hoses.

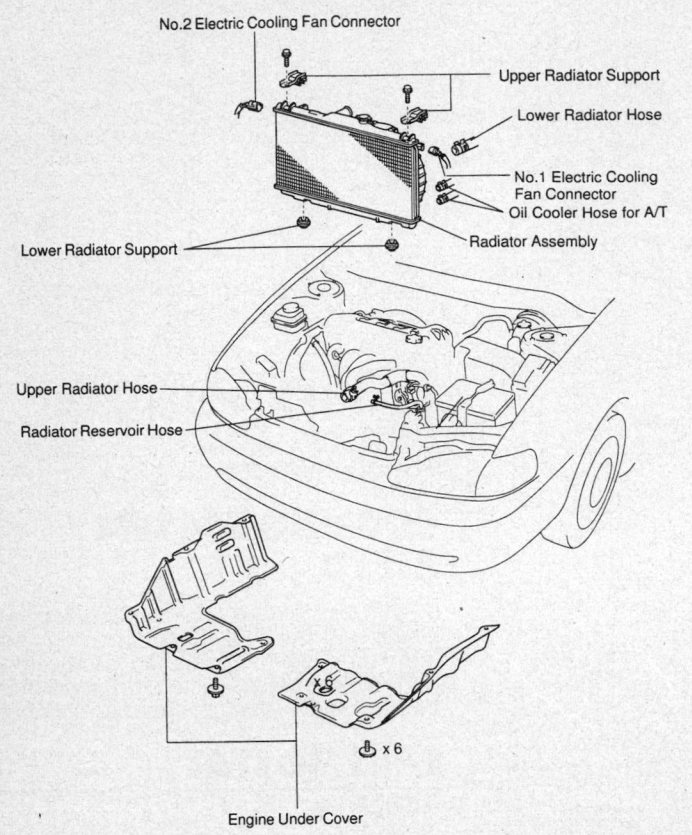

Fig. 26 Radiator replacement

TY1069900490000X

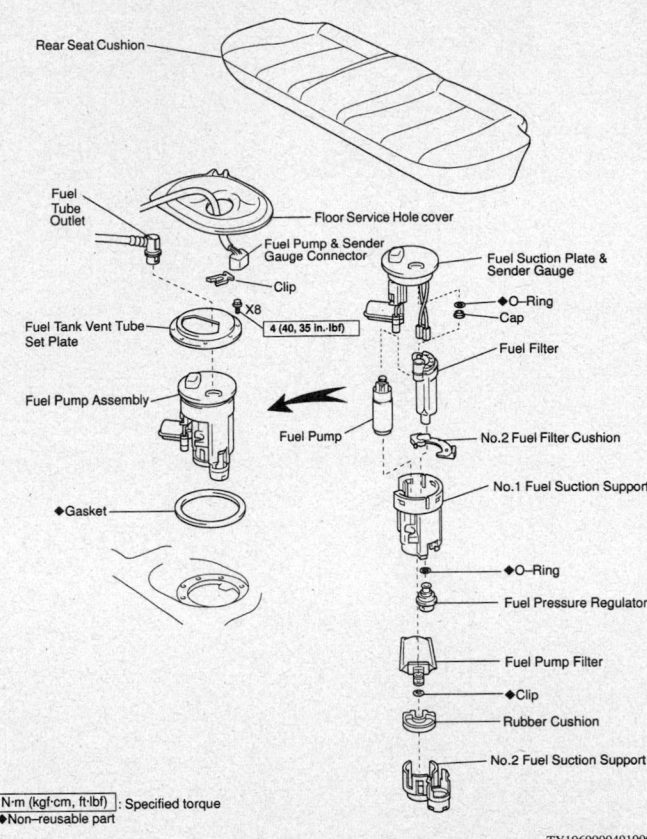

Fig. 27 Exploded view of fuel pump assembly

TY1069900491000X

6. **On all models,** remove radiator supports, radiator and cooling fan.
7. Remove electric cooling fan from radiator.
8. Reverse procedure to install.

FUEL PUMP
REPLACE

1. Remove rear seat cushion, then the floor carpet.
2. Remove floor service hole cover, then disconnect electrical connector from fuel pump.

3. Remove clip, then disconnect fuel tube from fuel pump.
4. Remove bolts and fuel tank vent tube set plate.
5. Pull out fuel pump, then remove gasket.
6. Reverse procedure to install.

FUEL FILTER
REPLACE

1. Remove fuel pump as outlined under "Fuel Pump, Replace."

2. Using a small screwdriver, remove No. 2 fuel suction support.
3. Pull out fuel pressure regulator from fuel filter, then remove clip and pull out pump filter, **Fig. 27.**
4. Remove No. 1 fuel suction support, then the No. 2 fuel filter cushion from fuel filter.
5. Remove fuel filter and pump from fuel suction plate.
6. Disconnect fuel pump connector from fuel pump.
7. Pull out fuel pump from fuel filter.
8. Reverse procedure to install.

TIGHTENING SPECIFICATIONS

Year	Component	Torque, Ft. Lbs.
1998-99	A/C Compressor To A/C Compressor Bracket	18
	Camshaft Position Sensor	80④
	Camshaft Timing Pulley	40
	Chain Vibration Damper	8
	Chain Tensioner Slipper	14
	Chain Tensioner	80④
	Connecting Rod Cap	15②
	Clutch Release Cylinder	9
	Crankshaft Bearing Cap	①
	Crankshaft Position Sensor	80④
	Crankshaft Pulley	102
	Cylinder Head	36②
	Cylinder Head Cover Bolts	③
	Drive Belt Tensioner Bolt	51
	Drive Belt Tensioner Nut	21
	Drive Plate (Auto. Trans.)	61
	Drive Shaft Heat Insulator	13
	Engine Coolant Drain Plug	9
	Engine Hanger To Cylinder Head	28
	Exhaust Manifold Heat Insulator	9
	Exhaust Manifold To Cylinder Head	27
	Exhaust Manifold Stay To Cylinder Block	37
	Exhaust Manifold Stay To Exhaust Manifold	37
	Front Engine Mounting Bracket To Mounting Insulator	64
	Front Engine Mounting Bracket To Transaxle	57
	Front Exhaust Pipe To Center Exhaust Pipe	24
	Front Exhaust Pipe To Manifold	46
	Flywheel	36②
	Heated Oxygen Sensor	14
	Intake Manifold To Cylinder Head	14
	Intake Manifold Stay To Cylinder Block	14
	Intake Manifold Stay To Cylinder Head	14
	Ignition Coil	80④
	Knock Sensor	29
	LH Engine Mounting Insulator To Body	48
	LH Engine Mounting Insulator To Mounting Bracket	64
	LH Engine Mounting Stay To Mounting Insulator	15
	LH Engine Mounting Stay To Transaxle	15
	No. 1 Camshaft Bearing Cap	17
	No. 2 Camshaft Bearing Cap	10
	Oil Filter Union To Cylinder Block	21
	Oil Pan Drain Plug	27
	Oil Pan To Cylinder Block	80④
	Oil Strainer To Cylinder Block	80④
	Power Steering Pump	27
	Power Steering Pump Pulley	32
	RH Engine Mounting Bracket To Timing Chain Cover	35
	RH Engine Mounting Insulator to Bracket Bolt	47
	RH Engine Mounting Insulator To Bracket Nut	38
	RH Engine Mounting Insulator To Fender Apron	19

TIGHTENING
SPECIFICATIONS—Continued

Year	Component	Torque, Ft. Lbs.
1998-99	Rear Engine Mounting Bracket To Mounting Insulator	64
	Rear Engine Mounting Bracket To Transaxle	51
	Timing Chain Cover To Cylinder Block	⑥
	Timing Chain Cover to Cylinder Head	⑤
	Water Bypass Pipe To Cylinder Block	80④
	Water Pump To Cylinder Block	8
	Water Pump To Timing Chain Cover	⑥

① — Tighten 12 point bolts in 4 steps as follows; first step, 16 ft. lbs.; second step, 32 ft. lbs.; third step, tighten an additional 45°; fourth step, tighten an additional 45°. Torque hexagon head bolts to 14 ft. lbs. using several passes. If any bolt will not reach torque specification, replace.

② — Tighten an additional 90°.

③ — With washer, 80 inch lbs.; without washer, 8 ft. lbs.

④ — Inch lbs.

⑤ — 10mm "A" bolts, to 10 ft. lbs.; 10mm head bolts, 8 ft. lbs.; stud bolt, 84 inch lbs.

⑥ — 10mm bolts, 8 ft. lbs.; 12mm bolts, 14 ft. lbs.

Clutch & Manual Transaxle

NOTE: On Air Bag Equipped Models, Refer To "Air Bag System Precautions" Located In The Front Of This Manual For System Disarming & Arming Procedures.

NOTE: Refer To "Computer Relearn Procedures" Located In The Front Of This Manual For Computer Relearn Procedures.

INDEX

PRECAUTIONS
AIR BAG SYSTEMS

Refer to "Air Bag System Precautions" in the front of this manual for system disarming and arming procedures.

AUDIO CODED ANTI-THEFT SYSTEM

Some models are equipped with an audio coded anti-theft system that will disable the radio when the battery cable is disconnected. The system can be identified by the words "ANTI-THEFT SYSTEM" on the cassette tape lid. Obtain three digit customer code for input. Reset system after service as follows:

1. Obtain three digit audio anti-theft code.
2. Depress 1 (PROG) while depressing righthand side of TUNE SEEK button, - - - will appear in tape operation display.
3. To enter the first digit, depress 1 (PROG) button repeatedly until the number of times depressed equals the first digit beginning with zero (depress the 1 button six times if the first digit is five).
4. To enter second digit, depress 2 (APS) button repeatedly until the number of times depressed equals the second digit beginning with zero.
5. To enter third digit, depress 3 (RPT) button repeatedly until the number of times depressed equals the third digit beginning with zero.
6. If - - - is displayed during code input, repeat procedure.
7. When code appears in display, depress and hold SCAN button until SEC appears.
8. When SEC disappears audio system should be operative.
9. If Err is displayed, repeat procedure. **Attempting to input code more than nine times may permanently disable audio system.**

BATTERY GROUND CABLE

Prior to service, disconnect battery ground cable and isolate as required.

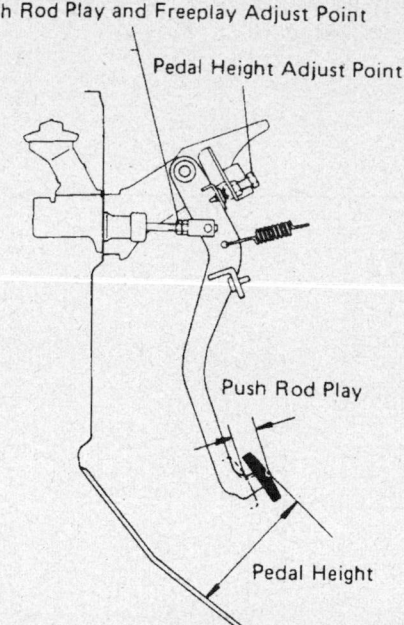

Push Rod Play and Freeplay Adjust Point

Pedal Height Adjust Point

Push Rod Play

Pedal Height

TY5049100013000X

Fig. 1 Clutch pedal height adjustment

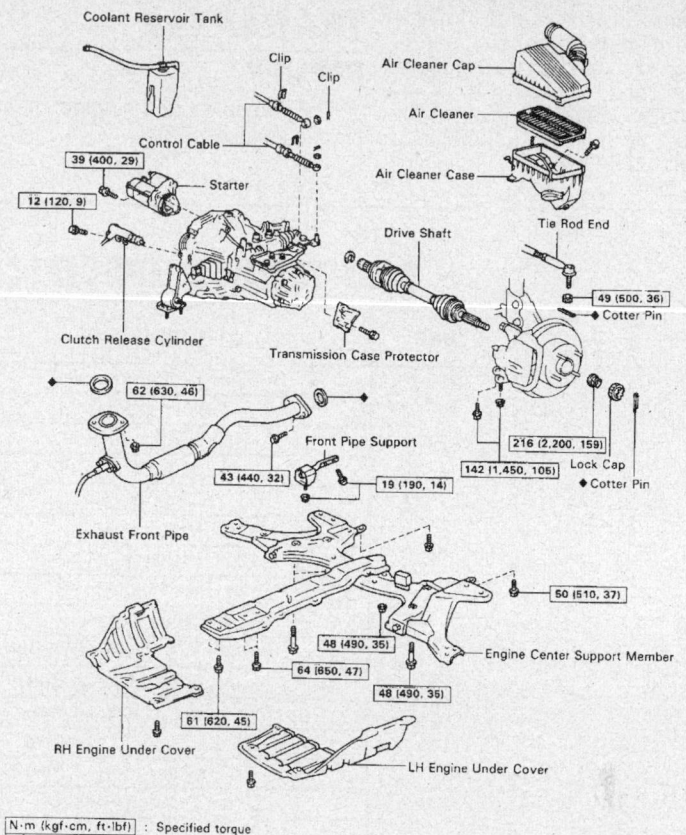

Coolant Reservoir Tank

Clip

Clip

Air Cleaner Cap

Air Cleaner

Air Cleaner Case

Control Cable

39 (400, 29)

12 (120, 9)

Starter

Drive Shaft

Tie Rod End

49 (500, 36)
Cotter Pin

Clutch Release Cylinder

Transmission Case Protector

62 (630, 46)

Front Pipe Support

216 (2,200, 159)

Lock Cap

43 (440, 32)

142 (1,450, 105)

Cotter Pin

19 (190, 14)

Exhaust Front Pipe

50 (510, 37)

48 (490, 35)

Engine Center Support Member

64 (650, 47)

48 (490, 35)

61 (620, 45)

RH Engine Under Cover

LH Engine Under Cover

N·m (kgf·cm, ft·lbf) : Specified torque
◆ Non-reusable part

TY5039300189000X

Fig. 2 Transaxle replacement

ADJUSTMENTS

CLUTCH PEDAL HEIGHT

1. Measure clutch pedal height as shown, **Fig. 1.**
2. Clutch pedal height should be 5.50–6.00 inches.
3. If clutch pedal height is not as specified, remove lower instrument panel finish panel and air duct.
4. Loosen clutch pedal locknut, then rotate stopper bolt until specified height is achieved.
5. Tighten locknut.
6. Check clutch pedal freeplay by depressing clutch pedal until resistance is felt. Freeplay should be .039–.197 inch. pushrod play at top of pedal should be .197–.591 inch.
7. If necessary to adjust freeplay, loosen locknut and rotate pushrod until freeplay is as specified.
8. Tighten locknut.
9. Ensure clutch pedal height and freeplay are as specified, then reinstall air duct and finish panel.

HYDRAULIC SYSTEM SERVICE

CLUTCH SLAVE CYLINDER, REPLACE

1. **On models with audio coded anti-theft system,** obtain three digit anti-theft code.
2. **On all models,** remove brake booster.
3. Remove clutch tube from clutch hose.
4. Remove clip, clevis pin and return spring.
5. Remove clutch slave cylinder, then if necessary clutch tube from cylinder.
6. Reverse procedure to install. Tighten

to specifications, then bleed and adjust system. Reset audio anti-theft system, if equipped, as outlined under "Precautions."

CLUTCH RELEASE CYLINDER, REPLACE

1. **On models with audio coded anti-theft system,** obtain three digit anti-theft code.
2. **On all models,** using suitable tool, disconnect clutch line tube, using suitable container to catch fluid.
3. Remove release cylinder attaching bolts, then remove cylinder.
4. Reverse procedure to install. Tighten attaching bolts to specifications, then bleed clutch system as outlined under "Clutch System Bleed."

CLUTCH SYSTEM BLEED

If any service is performed on the clutch system or air is suspected in the clutch lines, bleed the system.
1. Fill clutch reservoir with suitable brake fluid. **Do not allow fluid to come in contact with painted surfaces.**
2. Check reservoir frequently, add fluid as required.
3. Connect vinyl tube to bleeder plug, then insert other tube end in half full container of brake fluid.
4. Slowly pump clutch pedal several times.
5. While depressing, pedal, loosen bleeder plug until fluid runs out, then close bleeder plug.

6. Repeat procedure until air bubbles are no longer evident in fluid. **Do not reuse fluid.**

CLUTCH

REPLACE

1. **On models with audio coded anti-theft system,** obtain three digit anti-theft code.
2. **On all models,** remove transaxle assembly as outlined under "Transaxle, Replace."
3. Place installation alignment marks on clutch cover and flywheel.
4. Loosen each set bolt one turn at a time until spring tension is released.
5. Remove clutch cover attaching bolts, then remove cover and disc.
6. Remove release bearing, fork and boot.
7. Using suitable calipers, measure clutch disc rivet head depth. Minimum rivet depth should be .020 inch. If not as indicated, replace clutch disc.
8. Using suitable dial indicator, measure flywheel runout. Maximum runout should be .004 inch. If not as indicated, replace flywheel.
9. Measure clutch disc runout, maximum runout is .031 inch. If not as indicated, replace disc.
10. Reverse to install, noting the following:
   a. Using suitable tool, install clutch disc.
   b. Match clutch cover and flywheel alignment marks, then **torque**

cover bolts to 14 ft. lbs. one turn at a time in a criss-cross pattern, ensuring clutch disc and pressure plate remain aligned.

c. Reset audio anti-theft system, if equipped, as outlined under "Precautions."

TRANSAXLE
REPLACE

The transaxle and engine must be replaced as an assembly.

Refer to **Fig. 2,** for transaxle replacement procedure.

TIGHTENING SPECIFICATIONS

Year	Component	Torque, Ft. Lbs.
1996–99	Back-Up Lamp Switch	30
	Bleeder Plug	8
	Bond Cable To Body	14
	Clutch Accumulator	15
	Clutch Cover	14
	Clutch Line Union	11
	Clutch Master Cylinder	9
	Control Shaft Cover	14
	Drain Plug	29
	Driveshaft To Side Gear Shaft	27
	Exhaust Pipe Clamp Bolt	14
	Exhaust Pipe To Converter	32
	Exhaust Pipe To Manifold	46
	Filler Plug	29
	Front Bearing Retainer	8
	Front Engine Mount	64
	Lock Ball Assembly	29
	Lower Ball Joint	47
	Master Cylinder Reservoir Tank	18
	Output Shaft Bearing Lock Plate	8
	Rear Endplate To Transaxle	17
	Release Cylinder To Transaxle	9
	Shift Fork To Set Bolt	12
	Speedometer Driven Gear Lock Plate	8
	Transaxle Case Protector	9
	Transaxle Case To Case Cover	13
	Transaxle Case To Transaxle Case	22
	Transaxle To Engine (10mm)	35
	Transaxle To Engine (12mm)	47
	Transaxle To Starter	29

Rear Axle & Suspension

INDEX

HUB & BEARING
REPLACE

1. Remove brake drum or rotor and check bearing axial play. Play should not exceed .002 inch.
2. Remove ABS speed sensor.
3. **On models with drum brakes,** disconnect brake line from wheel cylinder, **Fig. 1.**
4. **On all models,** remove four bolts holding axle hub to axle carrier and remove axle hub and rear brake assembly.
5. Remove O-ring.
6. Reverse procedure to install. Bleed brake system, then tighten nuts and bolts to specifications.

REAR AXLE CARRIER
REPLACE

1. Remove rear axle hub as outlined.
2. Remove brake hose from strut assembly, then backing plate from rear axle carrier.
3. Loosen three nuts but do not remove bolts.
4. Remove strut rod to rear axle carrier bolt and nut and disconnect strut rod from carrier.
5. Remove three nuts, bolts and carrier.
6. Reverse procedure to install. Tighten nuts and bolts to specifications.

STRUT
REPLACE

1. Remove rear seat cushion and seat back.
2. Remove rear wheel.
3. Disconnect ABS speed sensor wire harness clamp from strut, **Fig. 2.**
4. Remove brake hose retaining clip from strut and disconnect brake line using tool No. 09023–00100, or equivalent.
5. Disconnect stabilizer bar link from strut.
6. Loosen (do not remove) lower strut retaining nuts.
7. Support rear axle carrier with suitable jack.
8. Remove cap from suspension support.
9. Loosen (do not remove) center nut at shock tower in engine compartment, then remove remaining three upper strut retaining nuts. **Center nut should only be loosened if strut is to be disassembled.**
10. Lower rear axle carrier and remove two lower strut retaining bolts.
11. Remove strut assembly.

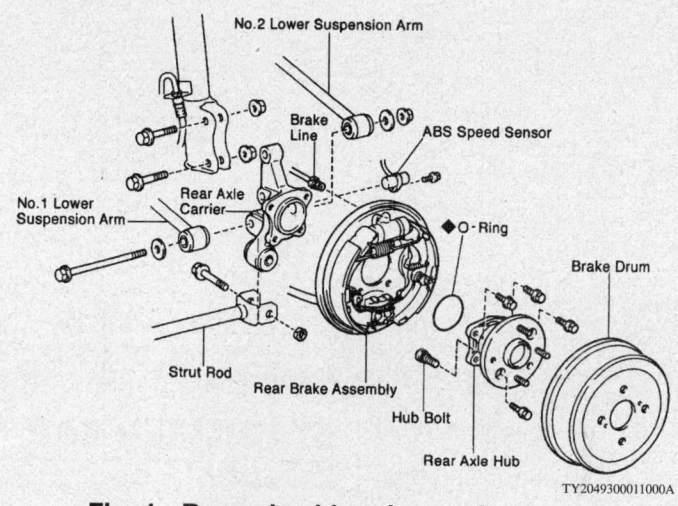

Fig. 1   Rear wheel bearing replacement

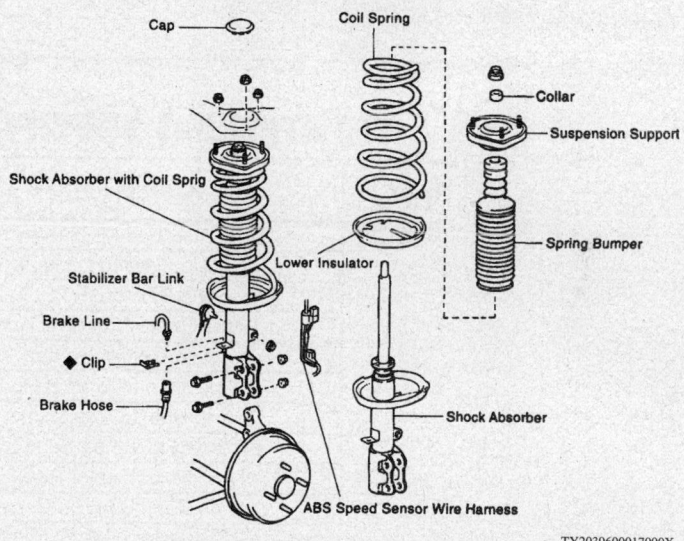

Fig. 2   Rear suspension strut assembly

12. Reverse procedure to install. Tighten to specifications.

STRUT ROD
REPLACE

1. Raise and support rear of vehicle.
2. Remove nut and bolt securing strut rod to axle carrier.
3. Remove nut and bolt securing strut rod to body, then remove strut rod.
4. Reverse procedure to install. Prior to tightening attaching nuts and bolts, lower vehicle to ground and bounce vehicle up and down several times to stabilize suspension, then tighten attaching nuts and bolts to specification with vehicle weight on suspension.

COIL SPRING
REPLACE

1. Remove strut assembly as outlined under "Strut, Replace."
2. Install strut assembly lower bracket bolts and nuts, then place strut assembly in vise so vise grips lower bracket at bolts.
3. Using spring compression tool No.

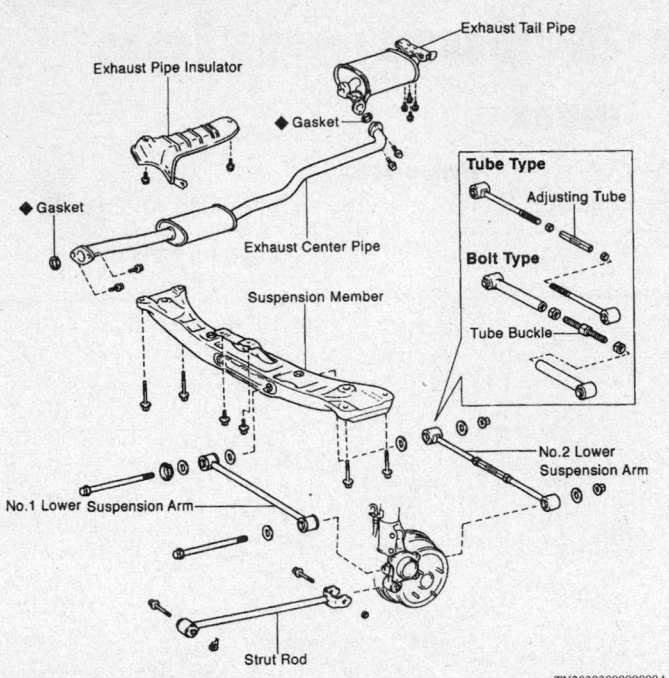

Fig. 3 Rear suspension

TY2039300009000A

09727–30021, or equivalent, compress coil spring.

4. Remove collar and upper strut suspension support retaining nut, **Fig. 2**.
5. Remove coil spring.
6. Reverse procedure to assemble.

2. Remove both stabilizer bar links and bushings.
3. Support fuel tank with a suitable jack stand.
4. Remove left and right fuel tank bands.
5. Lower fuel tank from position.
6. Remove stabilizer bar. Reverse procedure to install, tighten bolts to specifications.

STABILIZER BAR
REPLACE

1. Raise and support rear of vehicle, then remove rear wheels.

SUSPENSION ARM
REPLACE
LOWER

1. Raise and support vehicle, then remove rear tires.
2. Remove two strut rod attaching nuts and bolts, then the strut rod, **Fig. 3**.
3. Disconnect spring from lower arm.
4. Remove No. 2 lower suspension arm attaching nuts, then the suspension arm.
5. Remove stabilizer bar bushing retainer, then the center exhaust pipe and tail pipe.
6. Support suspension member with a suitable jack, remove six nuts, then the left and right suspension member lower stopper.
7. Lower suspension member and remove No. 1 lower suspension arm attaching bolts, then the suspension arm.
8. Reverse procedure to install.

TIGHTENING SPECIFICATIONS

Year	Component	Torque, Ft. Lbs.
1996–99	ABS Speed Sensor	71①
	Axle Bearing Locknut	90
	Axle Bearing Set Bolt	59
	Axle Carrier To Lower Arm	87
	Axle Carrier To Strut	105
	Axle Carrier To Strut Rod	67
	Axle Hub To Axle Carrier	59
	Exhaust Front Pipe Set Clamp	24
	Exhaust Center Pipe	14
	Fuel Tank Band To Body	29
	Nos. 1 & 2 Suspension Arm To Axle Carrier	65
	No. 1 Suspension Arm To Body	65
	No. 2 Suspension Arm To Body	80
	Piston Rod To Suspension Support	36
	Rear Axle Hub	59
	Stabilizer Bar Bracket To Body	14
	Stabilizer Bar Bushing Retainers	14
	Stabilizer Bar Link Set Nuts	33
	Stabilizer Bar To Stabilizer Bar Link	26
	Strut Assembly Suspension Support Retaining Nut	34
	Strut Lower Retaining Bolts	105
	Strut Rod To Body	65

Continued

TIGHTENING
SPECIFICATIONS—Continued

Year	Component	Torque, Ft. Lbs.
1996–99	Strut Rod To Rear Axle Carrier Nuts	67
	Strut Upper Retaining Nuts	29
	Suspension Arm Locknut	41
	Suspension Member To Body	55
	Suspension Upper Support To Body	29
	Suspension Upper Support To Piston Rod	36
	Wheel Lug Nut	76

① — Inch lbs.

Front Suspension & Steering

NOTE: On Air Bag Equipped Models, Refer To "Air Bag System Precautions" Located In The Front Of This Manual For System Disarming & Arming Procedures.

INDEX

PRECAUTIONS

AIR BAG SYSTEMS

Refer to "Air Bag System Precautions" in the front of this manual for system disarming and arming procedures.

AUDIO CODED ANTI-THEFT SYSTEM

Some models are equipped with an audio coded anti-theft system that will disable the radio when the battery cable is disconnected. The system can be identified by the words "ANTI-THEFT SYSTEM" on the cassette tape lid. Obtain three digit customer code for input. Reset system after service as follows:

1. Obtain three digit audio anti-theft code.
2. Depress 1 (PROG) while depressing righthand side of TUNE SEEK button, - - - will appear in tape operation display.
3. To enter the first digit, depress 1 (PROG) button repeatedly until the number of times depressed equals the first digit beginning with zero (depress the 1 button six times if the first digit is five).
4. To enter second digit, depress 2 (APS) button repeatedly until the number of times depressed equals the second digit beginning with zero.
5. To enter third digit, depress 3 (RPT) button repeatedly until the number of times depressed equals the third digit beginning with zero.
6. If - - - is displayed during code input, repeat procedure.
7. When code appears in display, depress and hold SCAN button until SEC appears.
8. When SEC disappears audio system should be operative.
9. If Err is displayed, repeat procedure. **Attempting to input code more than nine times may permanently disable audio system.**

BATTERY GROUND CABLE

Prior to service, disconnect battery ground cable and isolate as required.

WHEEL HUB & STEERING KNUCKLE
REPLACE

1. Remove front wheel.
2. Remove ABS speed sensor, **Fig. 1.**
3. Disconnect brake hose from shock absorber.
4. Check for bearing backlash and axle hub deviation as follows:
   a. Remove brake caliper and disc. Support caliper securely.
   b. Place dial indicator near center of axle hub and check backlash in bearing shaft direction. If backlash measurement exceeds .0020 inch, replace bearing.
   c. Using dial indicator, check deviation at surface of axle hub outside hub bolt. If deviation exceeds .0028 inch, replace axle hub.
   d. Install disc and caliper.
5. Remove driveshaft locknut cotter pin and locknut cap.
6. While depressing brake, remove driveshaft locknut.
7. Remove brake caliper and disc.
8. Loosen lower shock absorber nuts.
9. Remove cotter pin and nut from lower ball joint at steering knuckle.
10. Using tool No. 09628–62011, or equivalent, disconnect tie rod end from steering knuckle.
11. Disconnect lower ball joint from lower suspension arm.
12. Remove two nuts and a bolt from bottom of shock absorber.
13. Remove steering knuckle with axle hub.
14. Reverse procedure to install. Tighten to specifications.

BALL JOINT INSPECTION

1. Remove ball joint as outlined under "Lower Ball Joint, Replace."

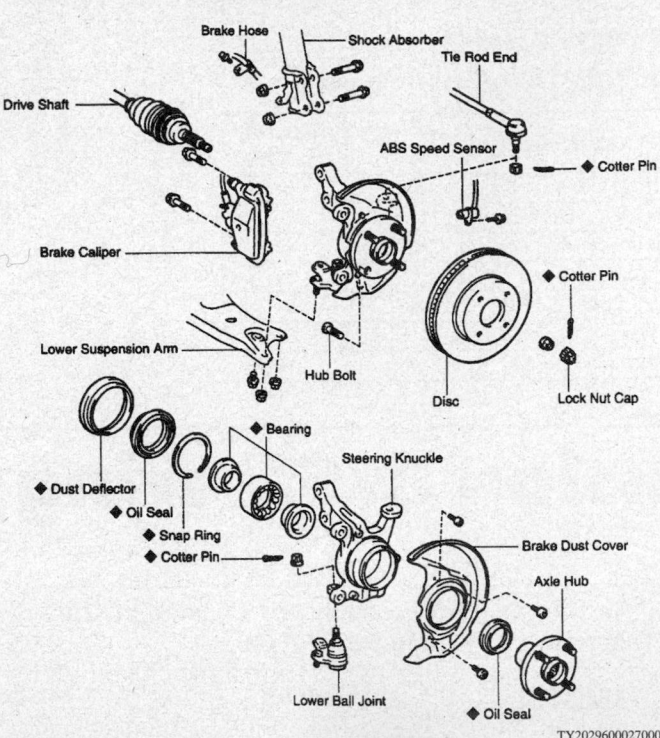

Fig. 1   Front axle hub & steering knuckle replacement

2. Move ball joint stud back and forth five times then install nut.
3. Using tighten wrench, turn nut continuously one turn every two to four seconds, take torque reading on fifth turn.
4. If torque reading is not 8.7–26 inch lbs., replace ball joint.

COIL SPRING
REPLACE

1. Remove strut assembly, **Fig. 2,** as described under "Strut, Replace."
2. Place strut assembly in vise, then using spring compressor tool No. 09727–30021, or equivalent, compress coil spring.
3. Remove upper cap and suspension support from strut assembly using nut removal tool No. 09729–22031, or equivalent.
4. Remove dust seal and spring seat from strut assembly.
5. Remove upper insulator and coil spring.
6. Reverse procedure to assemble strut.

STRUT
REPLACE

1. Remove front wheel and disconnect ABS wire harness clamp.
2. Disconnect brake hose from shock absorber, **Fig. 2.**
3. Remove three nuts on upper side of strut in engine compartment.
4. Remove two nuts and bolts from lower side of strut assembly.
5. Remove strut assembly.
6. Reverse procedure to install. Tighten to specifications.

SHOCK ABSORBER
REPLACE

Refer to "Strut, Replace" for procedure.

LOWER SUSPENSION ARM
REPLACE

1. Raise and support vehicle, then remove front wheel.
2. Remove stabilizer bar, **Fig. 3,** as described under "Stabilizer Bar, Replace."
3. Disconnect lower suspension arm from lower ball joint.
4. Disconnect righthand side of lower suspension arm.
5. Disconnect lefthand side of lower suspension arm and remove front suspension crossmember with lower suspension arm.
6. Remove lower suspension arm from suspension crossmember.
7. Reverse procedure to install, noting the following:
   a. Referring to **Fig. 4, torque** "A" bolt to 161 ft. lbs., "B" bolt to 129 ft. lbs. and "C" bolts to 109 ft. lbs.
   b. Referring to **Fig. 5, torque** "A" bolt to 129 ft. lbs., "B" bolt to 167 ft. lbs. and "C" bolts to 109 ft. lbs. **Torque** nut to 45 ft. lbs.

STABILIZER BAR
REPLACE

1. Remove front wheels.
2. Disconnect exhaust pipe.
3. Disconnect left and right stabilizer bar

links, **Fig. 3.** If ball joint turns together with nut, use a hexagon wrench to hold stud.
4. Remove left and right stabilizer bar brackets and bushing.
5. Remove stabilizer bar.
6. Reverse procedure to install. Referring to **Fig. 6, torque** stabilizer bar bracket "A" bolt to 109 ft. lbs., " B" bolt to 37 ft. lbs. and nut to 14 ft. lbs. Tighten remaining fasteners to specifications.

POWER STEERING GEAR
REPLACE

Refer to **Fig. 7** when replacing power steering gear, noting the following:
1. **On models with audio coded anti-theft system,** obtain three digit anti-theft code.
2. **On all models,** disconnect universal joint as follows:
   a. Position front wheels facing straight ahead.
   b. Using seat belt of driver's seat, fix steering wheel so that it does not turn, **Fig. 8.**
   c. Place alignment marks on universal joint and control valve shaft.
   d. Loosen upper universal joint bolt and remove lower universal joint bolt, then disconnect universal joint.
3. Disconnect tie rod ends using ball joint puller tool No. 09628-62011, or equivalent.
4. Disconnect and connect pressure and return tubes using power steering hose nut wrench set tool No. 09631-22020, or equivalent.
5. Slide gear assembly to righthand side to remove.
6. When connecting universal joint, set gear housing so that it matches dimensions shown in **Fig. 9,** with gear housing at center point.
7. Align marks made during removal and connect universal joint.

POWER STEERING PUMP
REPLACE

Refer to **Fig. 10** when replacing power steering pump, noting the following:
1. Disconnect and connect pressure line using power steering hose nut wrench set tool No. 09631-22020, or equivalent.
2. Bleed power steering system after installation.

POWER STEERING SYSTEM BLEED

1. Ensure fluid in reservoir tank is at proper level.
2. With engine speed below 1000 RPM, turn steering wheel from stop to stop three or four times, keeping at full stop position for two to three seconds.

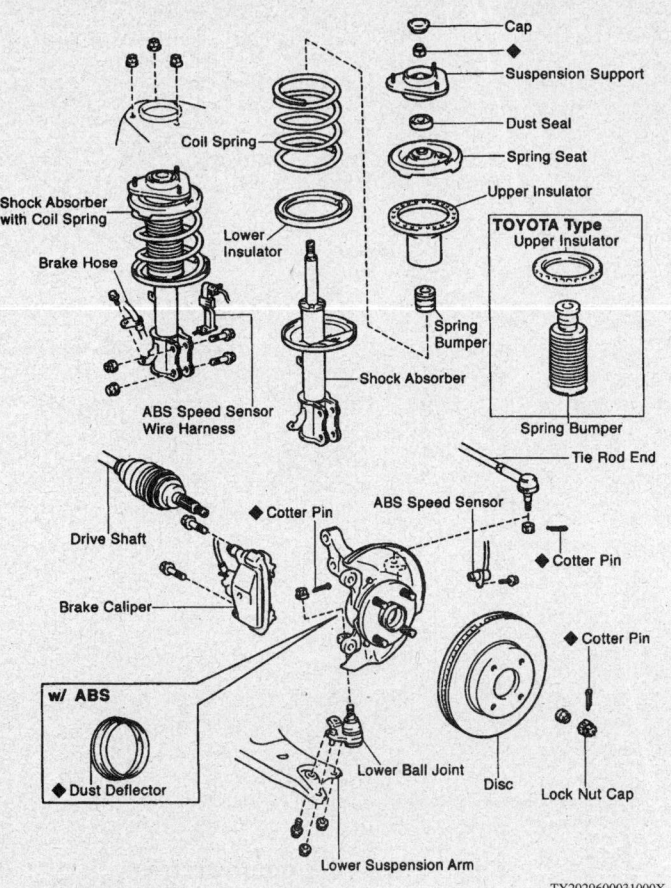

Fig. 2 Front suspension strut assembly

Fig. 3 Front suspension components

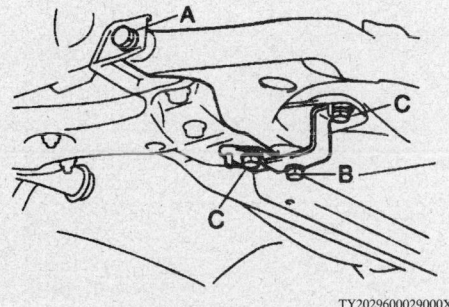

Fig. 4 Righthand side lower suspension arm bolts

3. Ensure fluid is not foamy or cloudy.
4. Measure fluid level with engine running then stop engine and measure fluid level again, **Fig. 11.** Maximum rise of fluid is .20 inch.
5. If a problem is found, proceed as follows:
   a. Disconnect return hose from reservoir tank and drain fluid.
   b. Fill reservoir tank with fresh fluid.
   c. With return hose placed into a suitable container, start engine and run at 1000 RPM. **After 1 or 2 seconds, fluid will begin to discharge from return hose. Stop engine immediately at this time. Ensure some fluid remains in reservoir tank.**
   d. Repeat steps b and c four or five times until there is no more air in fluid.
   e. Connect return hose and correct fluid level.

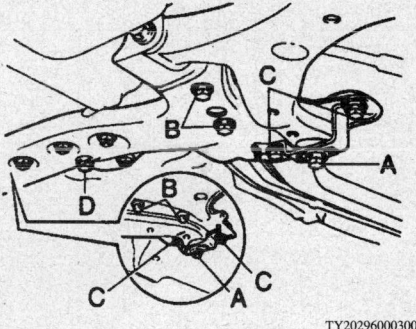

Fig. 5 Crossmember & lefthand side lower suspension arm bolts

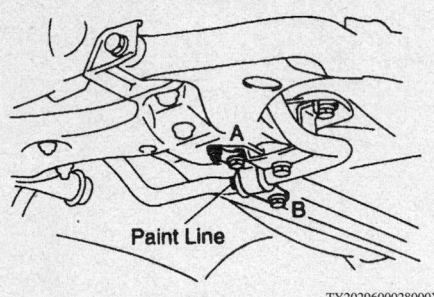

Fig. 6   Stabilizer bar bracket bolts & nut

TY2029600028000X

Paint Line

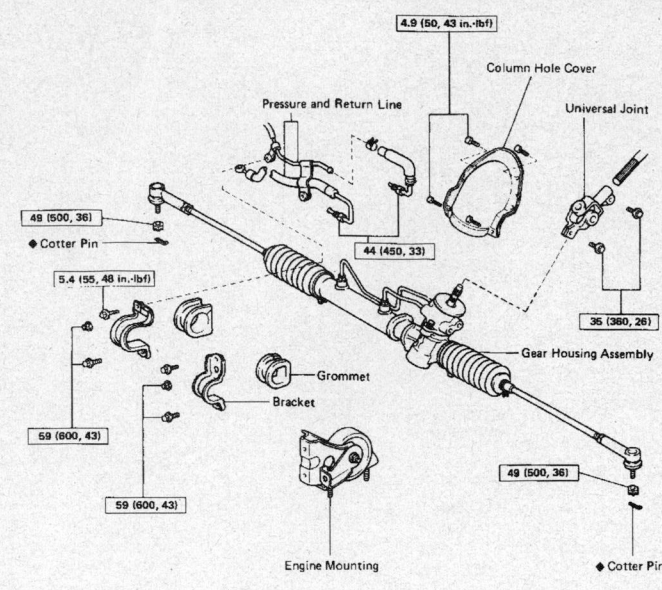

4.9 (50, 43 in.·lbf)

Column Hole Cover

Pressure and Return Line

Universal Joint

49 (500, 36)

◆ Cotter Pin

44 (450, 33)

5.4 (55, 48 in.·lbf)

35 (360, 26)

59 (600, 43)

Grommet

Bracket

59 (600, 43)

Engine Mounting

Gear Housing Assembly

49 (500, 36)

◆ Cotter Pin

N·m (kgf·cm, ft·lbf) : Specified torque
◆ Non-reusable part

TY6029200072000X

Fig. 7   Steering gear removal

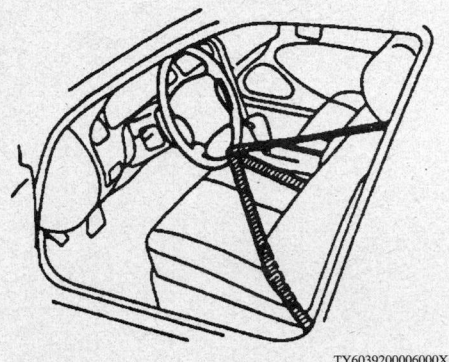

TY6039200006000X

Fig. 8   Steering wheel mounting

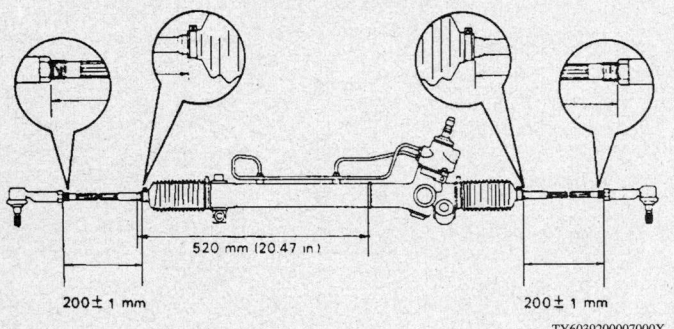

520 mm (20.47 in.)

200 ± 1 mm   200 ± 1 mm

TY6039200007000X

Fig. 9   Steering gear installation

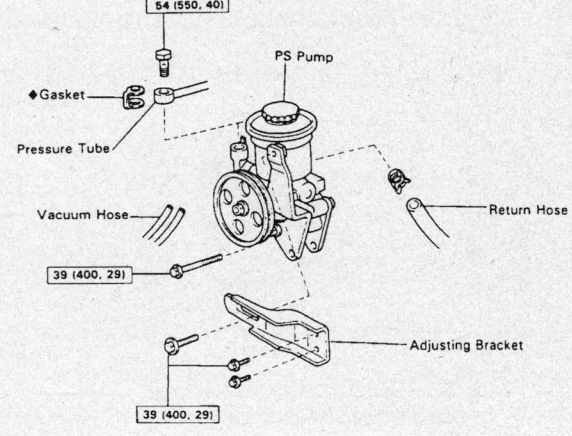

54 (550, 40)

◆ Gasket

PS Pump

Pressure Tube

Vacuum Hose

Return Hose

39 (400, 29)

Adjusting Bracket

39 (400, 29)

N·m (kgf·cm, ft·lbf) : Specified torque
◆ Non-reusable part

TY6039300010000X

Fig. 10   Power steering pump removal

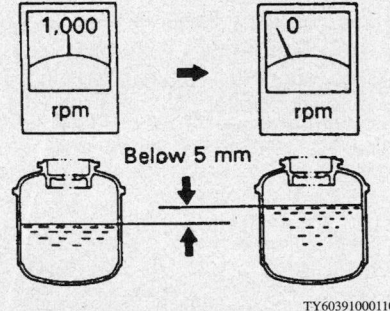

1,000 rpm → 0 rpm

Below 5 mm

TY6039100011000X

Fig. 11   Power steering system bleed

TIGHTENING SPECIFICATIONS

Year	Component	Torque, Ft. Lbs.
1996–99	ABS Speed Sensor	6
	ABS Wire Harness To Shock Absorber	48①
	Axle Hub Nut	159
	Ball Joint To Lower Arm	105
	Ball Joint To Steering Knuckle	87
	Brake Hose To Shock Absorber	22
	Driveshaft Locknut	159
	Engine Mount Bracket To Suspension Crossmember	35
	Front Exhaust Pipe Bracket To Suspension Center Member	14
	Front Exhaust Pipe To Center Exhaust Pipe	32
	Lower Ball Joint To Lower Suspension Arm	105
	Lower Shock Absorber Nuts	203
	Lower Suspension Arm	③
	Stabilizer Bar Brackets	②
	Stabilizer Bar Link Set Nut	33
	Steering Knuckle To Brake Cylinder	65
	Steering Knuckle To Shock Absorber	203
	Steering Knuckle To Tie Rod End	36
	Suspension Crossmember To Body	152
	Suspension Crossmember To Suspension Center Member	45
	Suspension Upper Support To Body	29
	Suspension Upper Support To Piston Rod	34
	Tie Rod End Locknut	41
	Wheel Lug Nuts	76

① — Inch lbs.

② — Refer to "Stabilizer Bar, Replace."

③ — Refer to "Lower Suspension Arm, Replace."

Wheel Alignment

INDEX

PRELIMINARY INSPECTION

1. Check tires for wear and proper inflation.
2. Check wheel runout, .039 (1 mm) inch should be indicated.
3. Check front wheel bearings, front suspension, steering linkage and ball joints for wear or looseness.
4. Ensure front shock absorbers are functioning properly.

FRONT WHEEL ALIGNMENT

CASTER & CAMBER

Camber and caster is not adjustable on these models. If camber and caster angle is not within limits, check for worn or damaged suspension parts and replace as necessary.

TOE-IN

1. Remove clamps from steering gear boots.
2. Loosen tie rod end locknuts.
3. Turn left and right tie rod ends an equal amount to adjust toe-in.
4. Ensure length of both tie rods are equal following adjustment.
5. Following adjustment, install steering gear boot clamps and **torque** tie rod locknuts to 41 ft. lbs.

REAR WHEEL ALIGNMENT

CAMBER

Camber angle is preset and not adjustable. If camber angle is not to specification, inspect and/or replace suspension components as required.

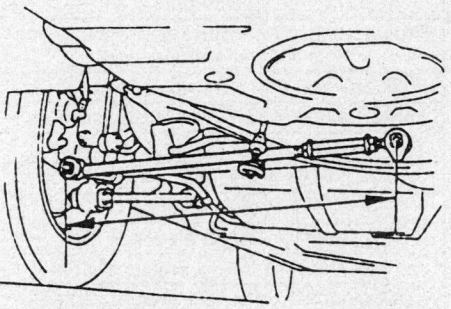

TY2049300016000X

Fig. 1   Rear toe-in adjustment

Tire size	Front	Rear
P175/65R14 81S 175/65R14 82S	185 mm (7.28 in.)	245 mm (9.65 in.)
P185/65R14 85S 185/65R14 85S	190 mm (7.48 in.)	250 mm (9.84 in.)

TY2049300020000X

Fig. 3   Vehicle ride height specifications

TOE-IN

1. Measure length of left and right No. 2 lower suspension arms, **Fig. 1.**
2. Adjust length of lower suspension arms if difference in length is greater than .04 inch.
3. Loosen locknuts and turn left and right adjusting tubes an equal distance to adjust toe-in.
4. One turn of adjusting tube will adjust toe-in approximately .43 inch.
5. Following adjustment, **torque** locknuts to 41 ft. lbs.

Front

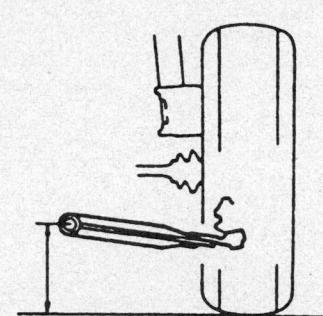

Rear

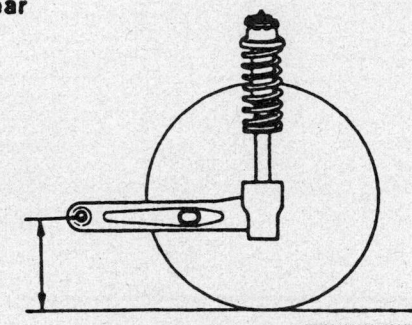

TY2049100017000X

Fig. 2   Vehicle ride height measurement

VEHICLE RIDE HEIGHT

Refer to **Figs. 2 and 3,** for ride height measurements and trim height specifications.

TOYOTA LAND CRUISER, PICKUPS, RAV4, 4RUNNER & TUNDRA

INDEX OF SERVICE OPERATIONS

Specifications

GENERAL ENGINE SPECIFICATIONS

Year	Engine	Fuel System	Bore & Stroke	Compression Ratio	Maximum Brake H.P. @ RPM	Maximum Torque Ft. Lbs. @ RPM	Normal Oil Pressure, psi @ 3000 RPM
1996	2.0L 3S-FE	Fuel Inj.	3.40 x 3.40	9.5	120 @ 5400	125 @ 4600	36-71
	2.4L 2RZ-FE	Fuel Inj.	3.74 x 3.38	9.5	142 @ 5000	160 @ 4000	36-71
	2.7L 3RZ-FE	Fuel Inj.	3.74 x 3.74	9.5	150 @ 4800	177 @ 4000	36-71
	3.4L 5VZ-FE	Fuel Inj.	3.68 x 3.23	9.6	190 @ 4800	220 @ 3600	36-75
	4.5L 1FZ-FE	Fuel Inj.	3.94 x 3.74	9.0	212 @ 4600	275 @ 3200	36-71
1997	2.0L 3S-FE	Fuel Inj.	3.39 x 3.39	9.5	120 @ 5400	125 @ 4600	36-71
	2.4L 2RZ-FE	Fuel Inj.	3.74 x 3.39	9.5	142 @ 5000	160 @ 4000	36-71
	2.7L 3RZ-FE	Fuel Inj.	3.74 x 3.74	9.5	150 @ 4800	177 @ 4000	36-71
	3.4L 5VZ-FE	Fuel Inj.	3.68 x 3.23	9.6	183 @ 4800	217 @ 3600	36-75
	4.5L 1FZ-FE	Fuel Inj.	3.94 x 3.74	9.0	212 @ 4600	275 @ 3200	36-71
1998	2.0L 3S-FE	Fuel Inj.	3.39 x 3.39	9.5	127 @ 5400	132 @ 4600	36-71
	2.4L 2RZ-FE	Fuel Inj.	3.74 x 3.39	9.5	142 @ 5000	160 @ 4000	36-71
	2.7L 3RZ-FE	Fuel Inj.	3.74 x 3.74	9.5	150 @ 4800	177 @ 4000	36-71
	3.4L 5VZ-FE	Fuel Inj.	3.68 x 3.23	9.6	183 @ 4800	177 @ 4000	36-75
	4.7L 2UZ-FE Land Cruiser	Fuel Inj.	3.70 x 3.31	9.6	230 @ 4800	320 @ 3600	36-71
	4.7L 2UZ-FE Tundra	Fuel Inj.	3.70 x 3.31	9.8	245 @ 4800	315 @ 3400	36-71
1999	2.0L 3S-FE	Fuel Inj.	3.39 x 3.39	9.5	127 @ 5400	132 @ 4600	36-71
	2.4L 2RZ-FE	Fuel Inj.	3.74 x 3.39	9.5	142 @ 5000	160 @ 4000	36-71
	2.7L 3RZ-FE	Fuel Inj.	3.74 x 3.74	9.5	150 @ 4800	177 @ 4000	36-71
	3.4L 5VZ-FE	Fuel Inj.	3.68 x 3.23	9.6	183 @ 4800	177 @ 4000	36-75
	4.7L 2UZ-FE Land Cruiser	Fuel Inj.	3.70 x 3.31	9.6	230 @ 4800	320 @ 3600	36-71
	4.7L 2UZ-FE Tundra	Fuel Inj.	3.70 x 3.31	9.8	245 @ 4800	315 @ 3400	36-71

TUNE UP SPECIFICATIONS

The following specifications are published from the latest information available. This data should be used only in the absence of a decal affixed in the engine compartment.

When checking ignition timing, it may be necessary to disconnect certain hoses and/or electrical connectors. Refer to vehicle emission control label for specific instructions.

Before disconnecting spark plug wires from distributor cap, determine location of No. 1 wire in cap, as distributor position may have been altered from that shown.

Year	Engine	Spark Plug Gap, Inch	Ignition			Curb Idle Speed, RPM②		Fuel Pump Pressure, psi	Valve Clearance, Inch	
			Firing Order	Timing, °BTDC①	Timing Mark Fig.	Man. Trans.	Auto. Trans.		Int.	Exh.
1996	2.0L 3S-FE	.043	1-3-4-2	10	B	750	750N	44–50	.007–.011	.011–.015
	2.4L 2RZ-FE	.031	1-3-4-2	5	A	750	750N	38–44	.006–.010	.010–.014
	2.7L 3RZ-FE	.031	1-3-4-2	5	D	700	700N	38–44	.006–.010	.010–.014
	3.4L 5VZ-FE	.043	1-2-3-4-5-6	10	C	700	700N	38–44	.006–.009	.011–.014
	4.5L 1FZ-FE	.031	1-5-3-6-2-4	3	C	650	650N	38–44	.006–.010	.010–.014
1997	2.0L 3S-FE	.043	1-3-4-2	10	B	750	750N	44–50	.007–.011	.011–.015
	2.4L 2RZ-FE	.031	1-3-4-2	5	D	700	700N	38–44	.006–.010	.010–.014
	2.7L 3RZ-FE	.031	1-3-4-2	5	D	700	700N	38–44	.006–.010	.010–.014
	3.4L 5VZ-FE	.043	1-2-3-4-5-6	10	B	700	700N	38–44	.006–.009	.011–.014
	4.5L 1FZ-FE	.031	1-5-3-6-2-4	3	C	650	650N	38–44	.006–.010	.010–.014
1998-99	2.0L 3S-FE	.043	1-3-4-2	10	B	750	750N	44-50	.007-.011	.011-.015
	2.4L 2RZ-FE	.031	1-3-4-2	5	D	700	700N	38-44	.006-.010	.010-.014
	2.7L 3RZ-FE	.031	1-3-4-2	5	D	700	700N	38-44	.006-.010	.010-.014
	3.4L 5VZ-FE	.043	1-2-3-4-5-6	10	B	700	700N	38-44	.006-.009	.011-.014
	4.7L 2UZ-FE Land Cruiser	.043	1-2-3-4-5-6	10	E	700	700N	38-44	.006-.010	.010-.014
	4.7L 2UZ-FE Tundra	.031	1-2-3-4-5-6	10	E	700	700N	38-44	.006-.010	.010-.014

N — Neutral.
BTDC — Before Top Dead Center.
① — Terminals T/Te1 & E1 shorted.

② — When adjusting idle speed, set parking brake & chock drive wheels.

Fig. A

TY1139100122000X

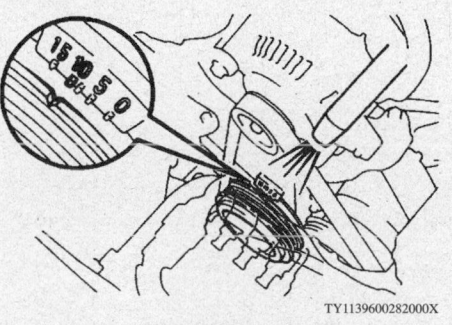

Fig. B

TY1139600282000X

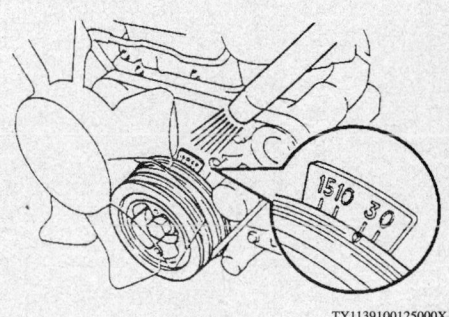

Fig. C

TY1139100125000X

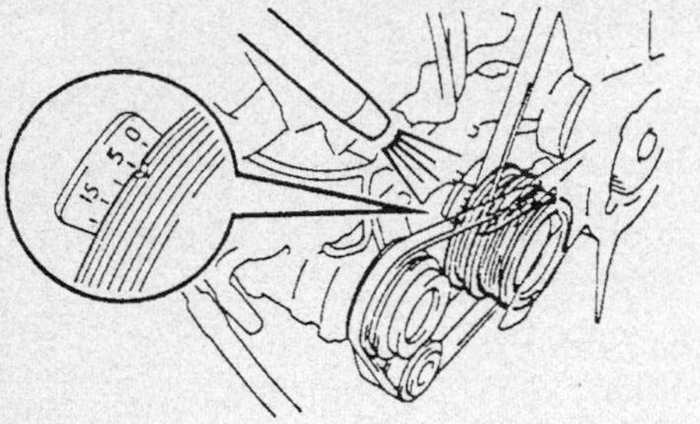

TY1139100126000X

Fig. D

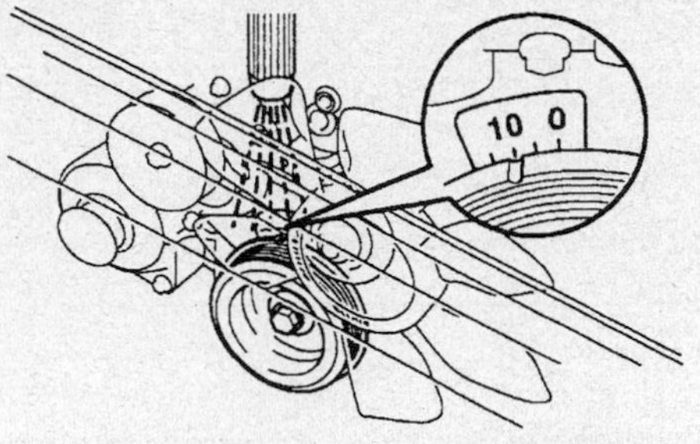

TY1139800357000X

Fig. E

FRONT WHEEL ALIGNMENT SPECIFICATIONS

The specifications listed below are for unloaded vehicles.

LAND CRUISER, RAV4, TACOMA, T100 & 4RUNNER

Year	Model	Caster Angle, Degrees		Camber Angle, Degrees		Toe, Inch①	Toe-Out On Turns, Deg.		Steering Axis Inclination, Deg.	Ball Joint Wear
		Limits	Desired	Limits	Desired		Inner Wheel	Outer Wheel		
1996	Land Cruiser	+2 to +4	+3	+1/4 to +1 3/4	+1	0 to +.32	35	31	13	②
	RAV4 2WD	+1 1/3 to +2 1/4	+1 5/12	-1 1/12 to +5/12	-1/3	-.08 to +.08	33 1/4	28 1/12	11	②
	RAV4 4WD	+5/12 to +2 1/12	+1 1/3	-1 to +1/2	-1/4	-.08 to +.08	33 1/4	28 1/12	10 3/4	②
	Tacoma 2WD	+1 1/12 to +2 7/12	+1 5/6	-3/4 to +3/4	0	-.08 to +.08	36	30 3/4	10	②
	Tacoma 4WD	+2 1/12 to +3 7/12	+2 5/6	-3/4 to +3/4	0	-.08 to +.08	37 1/12	32 1/3	10 3/4	②
	T100 2WD④	⑥	⑦	–1/3 to +1 1/6	+5/12	+.04 to +.20	40 2/3	35 1/6	12 1/12	②
	T100 2WD⑤	+5/6 to +2 1/3	+1 7/12	-1/3 to +1 1/6	+5/12	+.20 to +.36	40 5/12	35 7/12	12 1/6	②
	T100 4WD	⑧	③	-1/12 to +1 5/12	+2/3	+.04 to +.20	32 5/6	30 1/2	12	②
	4Runner⑨	+2 3/5 to +4 3/5	+3 1/3	-1 to +8/15	-1/5	-.02 to +.14	35 1/5	31 11/30	10 29/30	②
	4Runner⑩	+1 9/10 to +3 2/5	+2 19/30	-7/12 to +11/12	+1/6	-.01 to +.15	35 3/4	31 11/12	10 7/12	②

Continued

FRONT WHEEL ALIGNMENT SPECIFICATIONS—Continued

The specifications listed below are for unloaded vehicles.

LAND CRUISER, RAV4, TACOMA, T100 & 4RUNNER

Year	Model	Caster Angle, Degrees		Camber Angle, Degrees		Toe, Inch①	Toe-Out On Turns, Deg.		Steering Axis Inclination, Deg.	Ball Joint Wear
		Limits	Desired	Limits	Desired		Inner Wheel	Outer Wheel		
1997	Land Cruiser	+2 to +4	+3	$+\frac{1}{4}$ to $+1\frac{3}{4}$	+1	0 to +.16	35	31	13	②
	RAV4 2WD	$+1\frac{1}{3}$ to $+2\frac{1}{4}$	$+1\frac{5}{12}$	$-1\frac{1}{12}$ to $+\frac{5}{12}$	$-\frac{1}{3}$	-.08 to +.08	$33\frac{1}{4}$	$28\frac{1}{12}$	11	②
	RAV4 4WD⑪	$+\frac{2}{3}$ to $+2\frac{1}{6}$	$+1\frac{1}{3}$	-1 to $+\frac{1}{2}$	$-\frac{1}{4}$	-.08 to +.08	$33\frac{1}{4}$	$28\frac{1}{12}$	$10\frac{3}{4}$	②
	RAV4 4WD⑫	$+\frac{7}{12}$ to $+2\frac{1}{12}$	$+1\frac{1}{3}$	-1 to $+\frac{1}{2}$	$-\frac{1}{4}$	-.08 to +.08	$33\frac{1}{4}$	$28\frac{1}{12}$	$10\frac{3}{4}$	②
	Tacoma 2WD⑬	$-\frac{1}{6}$ to $+1\frac{1}{3}$	$+\frac{7}{12}$	$-\frac{2}{3}$ to $+\frac{5}{6}$	$\frac{1}{12}$	-.08 to +.08	36	31	10	②
	Tacoma 2WD⑭	$+\frac{1}{2}$ to $+1\frac{7}{12}$	$+\frac{5}{6}$	$-\frac{2}{3}$ to $+\frac{5}{6}$	$\frac{1}{12}$	-.08 to +.08	36	31	10	②
	Tacoma 2WD⑮	$-\frac{1}{12}$ to $+1\frac{5}{12}$	$+\frac{2}{3}$	$-\frac{2}{3}$ to $+\frac{5}{6}$	$\frac{1}{12}$	-.08 to +.08	36	31	10	②
	Tacoma 4WD⑯	$+\frac{5}{6}$ to $+2\frac{1}{3}$	$+1\frac{7}{12}$	$-\frac{1}{2}$ to +1	$+\frac{1}{4}$	-.08 to +.08	$37\frac{1}{5}$	$32\frac{1}{2}$	$10\frac{1}{2}$	②
	Tacoma 4WD⑰	+1 to $+2\frac{1}{2}$	$+1\frac{3}{4}$	$-\frac{5}{12}$ to $+1\frac{1}{12}$	$+\frac{1}{3}$	-.08 to +.08	$37\frac{1}{5}$	$32\frac{1}{2}$	$10\frac{1}{2}$	②
	T100 2WD④	$+1\frac{13}{20}$ to $+3\frac{3}{20}$	$+2\frac{6}{15}$	$-\frac{19}{60}$ to $+1\frac{3}{20}$	$\frac{6}{15}$	+.01 to +.17	$40\frac{2}{3}$	$35\frac{1}{10}$	$12\frac{1}{12}$	②
	T100 2WD⑤	$+1\frac{11}{12}$ to $+2\frac{5}{12}$	$+1\frac{2}{30}$	$-\frac{9}{20}$ to $+1\frac{7}{60}$	$+1\frac{1}{30}$	+.20 to +.36	$40\frac{23}{60}$	$35\frac{19}{60}$	$12\frac{1}{6}$	②
	T100 2WD⑲	$+1\frac{19}{60}$ to $+2\frac{49}{60}$	$+2\frac{1}{15}$	$-\frac{17}{60}$ to $+1\frac{13}{60}$	$+\frac{7}{15}$	+.16 to +.32	$40\frac{5}{6}$	$35\frac{41}{60}$	12	②
	T100 4WD⑱	$+1\frac{1}{3}$ to $+1\frac{5}{6}$	$+1\frac{1}{12}$	$-\frac{1}{12}$ to $+1\frac{5}{12}$	$+\frac{2}{3}$	+.03 to +.18	$32\frac{3}{4}$	$30\frac{31}{60}$	12	②
	T100 4WD⑲	$+1\frac{1}{6}$ to $+1\frac{2}{3}$	$+1\frac{1}{12}$	$-\frac{1}{6}$ to $+1\frac{1}{3}$	$+\frac{7}{12}$	+0 to +.16	$33\frac{7}{60}$	$30\frac{31}{60}$	12	②
	4Runner 2WD	$+2\frac{1}{3}$ to $+3\frac{5}{6}$	$+3\frac{1}{12}$	-1 to $+\frac{1}{2}$	$-\frac{1}{4}$	0 to +.16	35	31	11	②
	4Runner 4WD	$+1\frac{2}{3}$ to $+3\frac{1}{6}$	$+2\frac{5}{12}$	$-\frac{7}{12}$ to $+1\frac{1}{12}$	$+\frac{1}{6}$	0 to +.16	36	32	$10\frac{7}{12}$	②

Continued

FRONT WHEEL ALIGNMENT SPECIFICATIONS—Continued

The specifications listed below are for unloaded vehicles.

LAND CRUISER, RAV4, TACOMA, T100 & 4RUNNER

Year	Model	Caster Angle, Degrees		Camber Angle, Degrees		Toe, Inch①	Toe-Out On Turns, Deg.		Steering Axis Inclination, Deg.	Ball Joint Wear
		Limits	Desired	Limits	Desired		Inner Wheel	Outer Wheel		
1998	Land Cruiser	+1 3/4 to +3 1/4	+2 1/2	-2/3 to +5/6	-1/2	-.04 to +.12	36 7/10	32 3/5	12 1/6	②
	RAV4 2WD	+1 1/3 to +2 1/4	+1 5/12	-1 1/12 to +5/12	-1/3	-.08 to +.08	33 1/4	28 1/12	11	②
	RAV4 4WD⑪	+2/3 to +2 1/6	+1 1/3	-1 to +1/2	-1/4	-.08 to +.08	33 1/4	28 1/12	10 3/4	②
	RAV4 4WD⑫	+7/12 to +2 1/12	+1 1/3	-1 to +1/2	-1/4	-.08 to +.08	33 1/4	28 1/12	10 3/4	②
	Tacoma 2WD⑬	-1/6 to +1 1/3	+7/12	-2/3 to +5/6	1/12	-.08 to +.08	36	31	10	②
	Tacoma 2WD⑭	+1/2 to +1 7/12	+5/6	-2/3 to +5/6	1/12	-.08 to +.08	36	31	10	②
	Tacoma 2WD⑮	-1/12 to +1 5/12	+2/3	-2/3 to +5/6	1/12	-.08 to +.08	36	31	10	②
	Tacoma 4WD⑯	+5/6 to +2 1/3	+1 7/12	-1/2 to +1	+1/4	-.08 to +.08	37 1/5	32 1/2	10 1/2	②
	Tacoma 4WD⑰	+1 to +2 1/2	+1 3/4	-5/12 to +1 1/12	+1/3	-.08 to +.08	37 1/5	32 1/2	10 1/2	②
	T100 2WD④	+1 13/20 to +3 3/20	+2 6/15	-19/60 to +1 3/20	6/15	+.01 to +.17	40 2/3	35 1/10	12 1/12	②
	T100 2WD⑤	+11/12 to +2 5/12	+1 2/30	-9/20 to +1 7/60	+11/30	+.20 to +.36	40 23/60	35 19/60	12 1/6	②
	T100 2WD⑲	+1 19/60 to +2 49/60	+2 1/15	-17/60 to +1 13/60	+7/15	+.16 to +.32	40 5/6	35 41/60	12	②
	T100 4WD⑱	+1/3 to +1 5/6	+1 1/12	-1/12 to +1 5/12	+2/3	+.03 to +.18	32 3/4	30 31/60	12	②
	T100 4WD⑲	+1/6 to +1 2/3	+11/12	-1/6 to +1 1/3	+7/12	+0 to +.16	33 7/60	30 31/60	12	②
	4Runner 2WD	+2 1/3 to +3 5/6	+3 1/12	-1 to +1/2	-1/4	0 to +.16	35	31	11	②
	4Runner 4WD	+1 2/3 to +3 1/6	+2 5/12	-7/12 to +11/12	+1/6	0 to +.16	36	32	10 7/12	②

Continued

FRONT WHEEL ALIGNMENT SPECIFICATIONS—Continued

The specifications listed below are for unloaded vehicles.

LAND CRUISER, RAV4, TACOMA, T100 & 4RUNNER

Year	Model	Caster Angle, Degrees		Camber Angle, Degrees		Toe, Inch①	Toe-Out On Turns, Deg.		Steering Axis Inclination, Deg.	Ball Joint Wear
		Limits	Desired	Limits	Desired		Inner Wheel	Outer Wheel		
1999	Land Cruiser	$+1\frac{3}{4}$ to $+3\frac{1}{4}$	$+2\frac{1}{2}$	$-\frac{2}{3}$ to $+\frac{5}{6}$	$-\frac{1}{2}$	-.04 to +.12	$36\frac{7}{10}$	$32\frac{3}{5}$	$12\frac{1}{6}$	②
	RAV4 2WD	$+1\frac{1}{3}$ to $+2\frac{1}{4}$	$+1\frac{5}{12}$	$-1\frac{1}{12}$ to $+\frac{5}{12}$	$-\frac{1}{3}$	-.08 to +.08	$33\frac{1}{4}$	$28\frac{1}{12}$	11	②
	RAV4 4WD⑪	$+\frac{2}{3}$ to $+2\frac{1}{6}$	$+1\frac{1}{3}$	-1 to $+\frac{1}{2}$	$-\frac{1}{4}$	-.08 to +.08	$33\frac{1}{4}$	$28\frac{1}{12}$	$10\frac{3}{4}$	②
	RAV4 4WD⑫	$+\frac{7}{12}$ to $+2\frac{1}{12}$	$+1\frac{1}{3}$	-1 to $+\frac{1}{2}$	$-\frac{1}{4}$	-.08 to +.08	$33\frac{1}{4}$	$28\frac{1}{12}$	$10\frac{3}{4}$	②
	Tacoma 2WD⑬	$-\frac{1}{6}$ to $+1\frac{1}{3}$	$+\frac{7}{12}$	$-\frac{2}{3}$ to $+\frac{5}{6}$	$\frac{1}{12}$	-.08 to +.08	36	31	10	②
	Tacoma 2WD⑭	$+\frac{1}{2}$ to $+1\frac{7}{12}$	$+\frac{5}{6}$	$-\frac{2}{3}$ to $+\frac{5}{6}$	$\frac{1}{12}$	-.08 to +.08	36	31	10	②
	Tacoma 2WD⑮	$-\frac{1}{12}$ to $+1\frac{5}{12}$	$+\frac{2}{3}$	$-\frac{2}{3}$ to $+\frac{5}{6}$	$\frac{1}{12}$	-.08 to +.08	36	31	10	②
	Tacoma 4WD⑯	$+\frac{5}{6}$ to $+2\frac{1}{3}$	$+1\frac{7}{12}$	$-\frac{1}{2}$ to +1	$+\frac{1}{4}$	-.08 to +.08	$37\frac{1}{5}$	$32\frac{1}{2}$	$10\frac{1}{2}$	②
	Tacoma 4WD⑰	+1 to $+2\frac{1}{2}$	$+1\frac{3}{4}$	$-\frac{5}{12}$ to $+1\frac{1}{12}$	$+\frac{1}{3}$	-.08 to +.08	$37\frac{1}{5}$	$32\frac{1}{2}$	$10\frac{1}{2}$	②
	T100 2WD④	$+1\frac{13}{20}$ to $+3\frac{3}{20}$	$+2\frac{6}{15}$	$-\frac{19}{60}$ to $+1\frac{3}{20}$	$\frac{6}{15}$	+.01 to +.17	$40\frac{2}{3}$	$35\frac{1}{10}$	$12\frac{1}{12}$	②
	T100 2WD⑤	$+1\frac{11}{12}$ to $+2\frac{5}{12}$	$+1\frac{2}{30}$	$-\frac{9}{20}$ to $+1\frac{7}{60}$	$+1\frac{1}{30}$	+.20 to +.36	$40\frac{23}{60}$	$35\frac{19}{60}$	$12\frac{1}{6}$	②
	T100 2WD⑲	$+1\frac{19}{60}$ to $+2\frac{49}{60}$	$+2\frac{1}{15}$	$-\frac{17}{60}$ to $+1\frac{13}{60}$	$+\frac{7}{15}$	+.16 to +.32	$40\frac{5}{6}$	$35\frac{41}{60}$	12	②
	T100 4WD⑱	$+\frac{1}{3}$ to $+1\frac{5}{6}$	$+1\frac{1}{12}$	$-\frac{1}{12}$ to $+1\frac{5}{12}$	$+\frac{2}{3}$	+.03 to +.18	$32\frac{3}{4}$	$30\frac{31}{60}$	12	②
	T100 4WD⑲	$+\frac{1}{6}$ to $+1\frac{2}{3}$	$+1\frac{1}{12}$	$-\frac{1}{6}$ to $+1\frac{1}{3}$	$+\frac{7}{12}$	+0 to +.16	$33\frac{7}{60}$	$30\frac{31}{60}$	12	②
	4Runner 2WD	$+2\frac{1}{3}$ to $+3\frac{5}{6}$	$+3\frac{1}{12}$	-1 to $+\frac{1}{2}$	$-\frac{1}{4}$	0 to +.16	35	31	11	②
	4Runner 4WD	$+1\frac{2}{3}$ to $+3\frac{1}{6}$	$+2\frac{5}{12}$	$-\frac{7}{12}$ to $+1\frac{1}{12}$	$+\frac{1}{6}$	0 to +.16	36	32	$10\frac{7}{12}$	②

① — Toe-in (+); toe-out (-).
② — Refer to "Ball Joint Inspection" in "Front Suspension & Steering."
③ — Standard suspension, $+1\frac{1}{6}$; soft ride suspension, $+1\frac{7}{12}$.
④ — ½ ton models.
⑤ — 1 ton models.
⑥ — Standard suspension, $+1\frac{7}{12}$ to $+3\frac{1}{12}$; soft ride suspension, $+1\frac{11}{12}$ to $+3\frac{5}{12}$.
⑦ — Standard suspension, $+2\frac{1}{3}$; soft ride suspension, $+2\frac{2}{3}$.
⑧ — Standard suspension, $+\frac{5}{12}$ to $+1\frac{11}{12}$; soft ride suspension, $+\frac{5}{6}$ to $+2\frac{1}{3}$.
⑨ — Tire size, 225/75R15.
⑩ — Tire size, 265/70R16.
⑪ — Tire size, 235/60R16.
⑫ — Tire size, 215/70R16.
⑬ — VIN RZN140L.
⑭ — VIN RZN150L.
⑮ — VIN VZN150L.
⑯ — VIN VZN160L & RZN161L.
⑰ — VIN VZN170L & RZN171L.
⑱ — STD. Cab.
⑲ — Extra Cab.

FRONT WHEEL ALIGNMENT SPECIFICATIONS - CONTINUED

The specifications listed below are for unloaded vehicles.

TUNDRA

Year	Model Code	Caster Angle, Deg.①	Camber Angle, Deg.①	Toe, Inch②	Toe-Out on Turns, Deg. Inner Wheel	Toe-Out on Turns, Deg. Outer Wheel	Steering Axis Inclination, Deg.
TWO WHEEL DRIVE MODELS							
2000	UCK30L-ARSLKA	$+1\frac{59}{60}$	$-\frac{2}{15}$	+.08	$34\frac{2}{5}$	$32\frac{3}{10}$	$10\frac{53}{60}$
	UCK30L-ARSSKA	③	$-\frac{1}{12}$	+.06	$34\frac{2}{5}$	$32\frac{3}{10}$	$10\frac{5}{6}$
	VCK30L-ARMSKA	④	$+\frac{1}{30}$	+.08	$34\frac{2}{5}$	$32\frac{3}{10}$	$10\frac{7}{10}$
	VCK30L-ARSLKA	$+1\frac{13}{15}$	$-\frac{1}{30}$	+.08	$34\frac{2}{5}$	$32\frac{3}{10}$	$10\frac{23}{30}$
	VCK30L-ARSSKA	⑤	$+\frac{1}{60}$	⑥	$34\frac{2}{5}$	$32\frac{3}{10}$	$10\frac{11}{15}$
	VCK30L-TRMDKA	$+1\frac{2}{3}$	$-\frac{1}{60}$	+.07	$34\frac{2}{5}$	$32\frac{3}{10}$	$10\frac{23}{30}$
	VCK30L-TRSDKA	$+1\frac{43}{60}$	$-\frac{1}{15}$	+.07	$34\frac{2}{5}$	$32\frac{3}{10}$	$10\frac{49}{60}$
FOUR WHEEL DRIVE MODELS							
2000	UCK40L-ARSLKA	⑦	⑧	+.04	35–38	$32\frac{7}{12}$	⑨
	UCK40L-ARSSKA	⑩	$+\frac{1}{4}$	+.05	35–38	$32\frac{7}{12}$	⑪
	UCK40L-TRSSKA	⑫	$+1\frac{1}{60}$	+.04	35–38	$32\frac{7}{12}$	$10\frac{17}{30}$
	VCK40L-ARMSKA	⑬	⑭	+.07	35–38	$32\frac{7}{12}$	$10\frac{1}{4}$
	VCK40L-ARSLKA	⑮	⑯	+.06	35–38	$32\frac{7}{12}$	$10\frac{7}{15}$
	VCK40L-ARSSKA	⑰	⑱	⑲	35–38	$32\frac{7}{12}$	$10\frac{23}{30}$
	VCK40L-TRMSKA	⑳	$+\frac{17}{60}$	+.08	35–38	$32\frac{7}{12}$	$10\frac{7}{15}$
	VCK40L-TRSSKA	㉑	$+\frac{8}{15}$	+.08	35–38	$32\frac{7}{12}$	$10\frac{29}{60}$

① — Plus or minus $\frac{3}{4}$°.

② — Toe-in (+); toe-out (−).

③ — Models w/P245/70R16 tires, $+1\frac{53}{60}$; w/P265/70R16 tires, $+1\frac{5}{12}$.

④ — Models w/P245/70R16 tires, $+1\frac{43}{60}$; w/P265/70R16 tires, $+1\frac{11}{15}$.

⑤ — Models w/P245/70R16 tires, $+1\frac{23}{30}$; w/P265/70R16 tires, $+1\frac{47}{60}$.

⑥ — Models w/P245/70R16 tires, +.08; w/P265/70R16 tires, +.07.

⑦ — Models w/standard suspension, $+1\frac{17}{60}$; w/Off-Road Package, $+1\frac{1}{3}$.

⑧ — Models w/standard suspension, $+\frac{7}{30}$; w/Off-Road Package, $+\frac{13}{60}$.

⑨ — Models w/standard suspension, $10\frac{31}{60}$; w/Off-Road Package, $10\frac{8}{15}$.

⑩ — Models w/standard suspension w/P245/70R16 tires, $+1\frac{1}{5}$; models w/standard suspension w/P265/70R16 tires, $+1\frac{7}{30}$. Models w/Off-Road Package, $+1\frac{4}{15}$.

⑪ — Models w/standard suspension, $10\frac{1}{2}$; w/Off-Road Package, $10\frac{31}{60}$.

⑫ — Models w/P245/70R16 tires, $+1\frac{1}{12}$; w/P265/70R16 tires, $+1\frac{7}{60}$.

⑬ — Models w/standard suspension w/P245/70R16 tires, $+\frac{29}{30}$; models w/standard suspension w/P265/70R16 tires, $+1\frac{1}{60}$. Models w/Off-Road Package, $+1\frac{1}{20}$.

⑭ — Models w/standard suspension, $+\frac{2}{3}$; w/Off-Road Package, $+\frac{19}{60}$.

⑮ — Models w/standard suspension, $+1\frac{2}{15}$; w/Off-Road Package, $+1\frac{1}{6}$.

⑯ — Models w/standard suspension, $+\frac{17}{60}$; w/Off-Road Package, $+\frac{4}{15}$.

⑰ — Models w/standard suspension w/P245/70R16 tires, $+1\frac{1}{60}$; models w/standard suspension w/P265/70R16 tires, $+1\frac{1}{15}$. Models w/Off-Road Package, $+1\frac{1}{10}$.

⑱ — Models w/standard suspension, $+\frac{3}{10}$; w/Off-Road Package, $+\frac{19}{60}$.

⑲ — Models w/standard suspension, +.08; w/Off-Road Package, +.06.

⑳ — Models w/P245/70R16 tires, $+1\frac{1}{15}$; w/P265/70R16 tires, $+1\frac{1}{10}$.

㉑ — Models w/P245/70R16 tires, $+1\frac{2}{15}$; w/P265/70R16 tires, $+1\frac{1}{6}$.

FLUID CAPACITIES & COOLING SYSTEM DATA

Year	Model	Coolant Capacity, Qts. Less A/C	Coolant Capacity, Qts. With A/C	Radiator Cap Relief Pressure, Lbs.	Thermo. Opening Temp., °F	Fuel Tank, Gals.	Engine Oil Refill, Qts.[3]	5 Speed Man. Trans., Pints	Auto Trans., Qts.	Axle Oil, Pints
1996	Land Cruiser	[23]	[23]	13	180	25.1	7.8	—	11.6[24]	[25]
	RAV4	[31]	[31]	13	180	15.3	4.1	[22]	8.5	2
	Tacoma 2WD w/2RZ-FE	[26]	[26]	13	180	15.1	5.8	5.4	[27]	2.84
	Tacoma 4WD w/3RZ-FE	[28]	[28]	13	180	18	5.7	5.2[20]	[20][27]	[29]
	Tacoma 2WD w/5VZ-FE	[30]	[30]	13	180	15.1	5.7	5.4	[27]	4.38
	Tacoma 4WD w/5VZ-FE	[30]	[30]	13	180	18	5.5	4.6[20]	[20][27]	[29]
	T100 w/3RZ-FE	9.2	9.2	13	180	24	5.8	5.4	8	4.34
	T100 2WD w/5VZ-FE	10.6	10.6	13	180	24	5.5	6.4	8	4.34
	T100 4WD w/5VZ-FE	10.8	10.8	13	180	24	5	4.6[20]	8[20]	[34]
	4Runner 2WD w/3RZ-FE	[9]	[9]	13	180	18.5	5.6	[37]	[39]	[41][33]
	4Runner 4WD w/3RZ-FE	[9]	[9]	13	180	18.5	5.7	[38]	[39][40]	[41][35]
	4Runner 2WD w/5VZ-FE	[36]	[36]	13	180	18.5	5.5	[37]	[39]	[41][33]
	4Runner 4WD w/5VZ-FE	[36]	[36]	13	180	18.5	5.5	[38]	[39][40]	[41][35]
1997	Land Cruiser	[19]	[19]	13	180	25.1	7.5	—	16.3	[25]
	RAV4	[31]	[31]	13	180	15.3	4.1	[22]	[14]	2
	Tacoma w/2RZ-FE	[26]	[26]	13	180	[17]	[6]	[11]	[32]	2.85
	Tacoma w/3RZ-FE	[28]	[28]	13	180	[17]	[6]	[11]	[32]	[41][4]
	Tacoma w/5VZ-FE	[18]	[18]	13	180	[17]	[5]	[11]	[32]	[41][4]
	T100 w/3RZ-FE	9.2	9.2	13	180	24	[2]	5.4	[19]	[1]
	T100 w/5VZ-FE	10.6	10.6	13	180	24	[2]	5.4	[19]	[1]
	4Runner w/3RZ-FE	[9]	[9]	13	180	18.5	[10]	4.6	[12]	[41][7]
	4Runner w/5VZ-FE	[36]	[36]	13	180	18.5	[10]	4.6	[12]	[41][7]

Continued

FLUID CAPACITIES & COOLING SYSTEM DATA—Continued

Year	Model	Coolant Capacity, Qts.		Radiator Cap Relief Pressure, Lbs.	Thermo. Opening Temp., °F	Fuel Tank, Gals.	Engine Oil Refill, Qts. (3)	Transmission/ Transaxle Oil		Axle Oil, Pints
		Less A/C	With A/C					5 Speed Man. Trans., Pints	Auto Trans., Qts.	
1998	Land Cruiser	(21)	(21)	16	180	25.4	7.2	—	12(16)	(15)
	RAV4	(31)	(31)	13	180	15.3	4.1	(22)	(14)	2
	Tacoma w/2RZ-FE	(26)	(26)	13	180	(17)	(6)	(11)	(32)	2.85
	Tacoma w/3RZ-FE	(28)	(28)	13	180	(17)	(6)	(11)	(32)	(41)(4)
	Tacoma w/5VZ-FE	(18)	(18)	13	180	(17)	(5)	(11)	(32)	(41)(4)
	T100 w/3RZ-FE	9.2	9.2	13	180	24	(2)	5.4	(19)	(1)
	T100 w/5VZ-FE	10.6	10.6	13	180	24	(2)	5.4	(19)	(1)
	4Runner w/3RZ-FE	(9)	(9)	13	180	18.5	(10)	4.6	(12)	(41)(7)
	4Runner w/5VZ-FE	(36)	(36)	13	180	18.5	(10)	4.6	(12)	(41)(7)
1999	Land Cruiser	(21)	(21)	16	180	25.4	7.2	—	12(16)	(15)
	RAV4	(31)	(31)	13	180	15.3	4.1	(22)	(14)	2
	Tacoma w/2RZ-FE	(26)	(26)	13	180	(17)	(6)	(11)	(32)	2.85
	Tacoma w/3RZ-FE	(28)	(28)	13	180	(17)	(6)	(11)	(32)	(41)(4)
	Tacoma w/5VZ-FE	(18)	(18)	13	180	(17)	(5)	(11)	(32)	(41)(4)
	T100 w/3RZ-FE	9.2	9.2	13	180	24	(2)	5.4	(19)	(1)
	T100 w/5VZ-FE	10.6	10.6	13	180	24	(2)	5.4	(19)	(1)
	4Runner w/3RZ-FE	(9)	(9)	13	180	18.5	(10)	4.6	(12)	(41)(7)
	4Runner w/5VZ-FE	(36)	(36)	13	180	18.5	(10)	4.6	(12)	(41)(7)
2000	Tundra w/5VZ-FE	10.6	10.6	13	180	26.4	5.5	(13)	10.7	(8)
	Tundra w/2UZ-FE	12.3	12.3	13	180	26.4	6.4		13	(8)

① — Rear axle 2WD, 5.8 pts.; 4WD 6.2 pts.; Front axle 3.9 pts.
② — 2WD 5.5 qts.; 4WD 5 qts.
③ — With filter change.
④ — 4WD 4.33 pts.; short wheel base w/diff. lock 5.59 pts.; long wheel base w/diff. lock, 6.23; w/o diff. lock, 5.38 pts.
⑤ — 2WD 6.6 qts.; 4WD 5.7 qts.
⑥ — 2WD 6.2 qts.; 4WD 5.5 qts.
⑦ — Rear axle 2WD 5.8 pts.; 4WD w/diff. lock 5.8 pts.; w/o diff. lock 5.1 pts.
⑧ — Front, 2.4 pts. Rear, 2WD models, 8 pts.; 4WD models, 7.4 pts.
⑨ — Less rear heater, 10.6 qts.; w/rear heater 11.6 qts.
⑩ — 2WD 5.6 qts.; 4WD 5.7 qts.
⑪ — 2WD 5.4 qts.; 4WD w/R150 4.6pts.; w/W59 5.2 pts.
⑫ — 2WD A340E 7.6 qts.; A340F 8.0 qts.; 4WD 10.9 qts.

⑬ — 2WD models, 5.4 pts.; 4WD models, 4.6 pts.
⑭ — 2WD 8.5 qts.; 4WD 7.4 qts.
⑮ — Front, 3.6 pts.; rear less differential lock, 7 pts.; w/differential lock, 6.8 pts.
⑯ — Tranfer case oil, 2.8 pts.
⑰ — 2WD 14.8 qts.; 4WD 18.0 qts.
⑱ — With manual trans. 10.3 qts.; with automatic trans. 10 qts.
⑲ — Without rear heater 14.4 qts.; with rear heater 15.5 qts.
⑳ — Transfer case oil, 2.4 pts.
㉑ — Front heater only, 15.6 qts.; front and rear heater,16.2 qts.
㉒ — 2WD, 8.2 pts.; 4WD, 10.6 pts.
㉓ — Front heater only, 13.2 qts.; front & rear heater, 14.2 qts.
㉔ — Transfer case oil, 3.6 pts.
㉕ — Front, less differential lock, 6 pts.; w/differential lock, 5.6 pts.; rear, 6.8 pts.

㉖ — Man. trans., 8.5 qts.; auto. trans., 8.2 qts.
㉗ — A43D, 6.9 qts.; A340E, 7.6 qts.; A340F, 10.5 qts.
㉘ — Man. trans., 8.8 qts.; auto. trans., 8.7 qts.
㉙ — Front except ADD, 2.32 pts.; ADD, 2.44 pts.; rear, short wheel base, 4.38 pts.; extra long wheel base, 3.32 pts.
㉚ — Man. trans., 10.7 qts.; auto. trans., 10.5 qts.
㉛ — Man. trans., 8.5 qts.; auto. trans., 8.1 qts.
㉜ — A43D, 6.9 qts.; A340E, 7.6 qts.; A340F, 8 qts.; A340H, 10.8 qts.
㉝ — Rear differential, 5.8 pts.
㉞ — Front, 4 pts.; ADD 4 pts.; rear, 4.34 pts.
㉟ — Rear less differential lock, 5.2 pts.; w/differential lock, 5.8 pts.

㊱ — Less rear heater, 8.5 qts.; w/rear heater, 9.5 qts.
㊲ — W59, 5.4 pts.; R150F, 4.6 pts.

㊳ — W59, 5.2 pts.; R150F, 4.6 pts.
㊴ — A340E, 7.6 qts.; A340F, 9.3 qts.
㊵ — Transfer oil, 2.2 pts.

㊶ — Front except ADD, 2.32 pts.; ADD, 2.44 pts.

LUBRICANT DATA

| Year | Model | Lubricant Type | | | | | |
| | | Transmission | | Transfer Case | Rear Axle | Power Steering | Brake System |
		Manual	Automatic				
1996	Land Cruiser	—	Dexron II	75W-90 GL-4/5	API GL-5	Dexron II/IIE/III	DOT 3
	RAV4	75W-90 GL-4/5	Dexron II	—	API GL-5	Dexron II or III	DOT 3
	Tacoma	75W-90 GL-3/4/5	Dexron II/IIE/III	75W-90 GL-3/4/5	①	Dexron II/IIE/III	DOT 3
	T100	75W-90 GL-4/5	Dexron II/IIE/III	75W-90 GL-4/5	80W-90/90 GL-5	Dexron II/IIE/III	DOT 3
	4Runner	75W-90 GL-4/5	Dexron II/IIE/III	75W-90 GL-4/5	API GL-5	Dexron II or III	DOT 3
1997	Land Cruiser	—	Dexron II	75W-90 GL-4/5	API GL-5	Dexron II/IIE/III	DOT 3
	RAV4	75W-90 GL-4/5	Dexron II	—	API GL-5	Dexron II/III	DOT 3
	Tacoma	75W-90 GL-3/4/5	Dexron II/IIE/III	75W-90 GL-3/4/5	①	Dexron II/IIE/III	DOT 3
	T100	75W-90 GL-4/5	Dexron II/IIE/III	75W-90 GL-4/5	API GL-5	Dexron II/IIE/III	DOT 3
	4Runner	75W-90 GL-4/5	Dexron II/IIE/III	75W-90 GL-4/5	API GL-5		DOT 3
1998	Land Cruiser	—	Dexron II/III	75W-90 GL-4/5	80W-90/90 GL-5	Dexron II/III	DOT 3
	RAV4	75W-90 GL-4/5	Dexron II/III	75W-90 GL-4/5	80W-90/90 GL-5	Dexron II/III	DOT 3
	Tacoma	75W-90 GL-4/5	Dexron II/III	75W-90 GL-4/5	②	Dexron II/III	DOT 3
	T100	75W-90 GL-4/5	Dexron II/III	75W-90 GL-4/5	API GL-5	Dexron II/III	DOT 3
	4Runner	75W-90 GL-4/5	Dexron II/III	75W-90 GL-4/5	②	Dexron II/III	DOT 3
1999	Land Cruiser	—	Dexron II/III	75W-90 GL-4/5	80W-90/90 GL-5	Dexron II/III	DOT 3
	RAV4	75W-90 GL-4/5	Dexron II/III	75W-90 GL-4/5	80W-90/90 GL-5	Dexron II/III	DOT 3
	Tacoma	75W-90 GL-4/5	Dexron II/III	75W-90 GL-4/5	②	Dexron II/III	DOT 3
	4Runner	75W-90 GL-4/5	Dexron II/III	75W-90 GL-4/5	②	Dexron II/III	DOT 3
2000	Tundra	75W-90 GL-4/5	Dexron II/III	75W-90 GL-4/5	API GL-5	Dexron II/III	DOT 3

① — 2WD & 4WD standard differential, 80W-90/90 GL-5; 4WD ADD front differential, 75W-90 GL-5.
② — Front differential less A.D.D., 80W/80W-90 GL-5; front wA.D.D., 75W-90 GL-5. Rear, 80W/80W-90/90 GL-5

Electrical

NOTE: On Air Bag Equipped Models, Refer To "Air Bag System Precautions" Located In The Front Of This Manual For System Disarming & Arming Procedures.

INDEX

PRECAUTIONS

AIR BAG SYSTEMS

Refer to "Air Bag System Precautions" in the front of this manual for system disarming and arming procedures.

AUDIO CODED ANTI-THEFT SYSTEM

Some models are equipped with an audio coded anti-theft system that will disable the radio when the battery cable is disconnected. The system can be identified by the "ANTI-THEFT SYSTEM" on the cassette lid. Obtain three-digit code for input. Reset system after service as follows:

1. Obtain three-digit audio theft code.
2. Depress 1 (PROG) button while depressing righthand side of TUNE SEEK button. Three dashes will appear in tape operation display.
3. To enter first digit, depress 1 (PROG) button repeatedly until number of times depressed equals first digit (depress 1 button six times if first digit is five, first press equals 0).
4. To enter second digit, depress 2 (APS) button repeatedly until number of times depressed equals second digit.
5. To enter third digit, depress 3 (RPT)

button repeatedly until number of times depressed equals third digit.
6. If three dashes are displayed after inputting digits, repeat procedure.
7. When code appears in display, depress and hold SCAN button until SEC appears.
8. When SEC disappears audio system is operative.
9. If Err is displayed, repeat procedure. **Attempting to input code more than nine times may permanently disable audio system.**

BATTERY GROUND CABLE

Prior to service, disconnect battery ground cable and isolate as required.

FUSE PANEL & FLASHER LOCATION

LAND CRUISER

The No. 1 fuse panel is located behind the removable instrument panel cover, to the left of the steering column. The No. 2 fuse panel is located in the lefthand side of the engine compartment, behind the battery. The turn signal/hazard flasher is in the No. 1 relay panel, located at the lefthand side kick panel.

4RUNNER

The No. 1 fuse panel is located behind the lower lefthand side of the instrument panel. Fuse/relay panel No. 2 is located in the lefthand side of the engine compartment, behind the battery. The turn signal/hazard flasher is at fuse panel No. 1.

PICKUP

The No. 1 fuse panel is located behind the lefthand side kick panel. The No. 2 fuse panel is in the righthand side of the engine compartment, behind the battery. Fuse panel No. 3 is on behind the righthand side kick panel. The turn signal/hazard flasher is located behind the instrument cluster.

RAV4

The No. 1 fuse panel is located behind the lefthand side kick panel. The No. 2 fuse panel is in the righthand side of the engine compartment, near the righthand side shock tower. The turn signal/hazard flasher unit is at the No. 1 fuse panel.

TACOMA

The No. 1 fuse panel is located below the lefthand side kick panel. The No. 2 fuse panel is in engine compartment, on the front lefthand side.

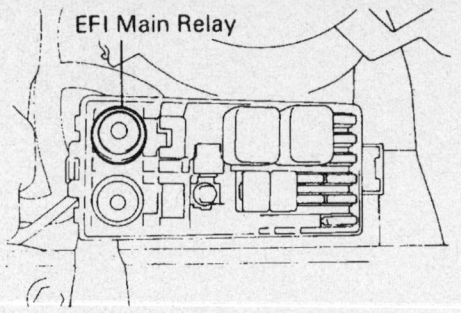

Fig. 1 EFI relay location. Land Cruiser

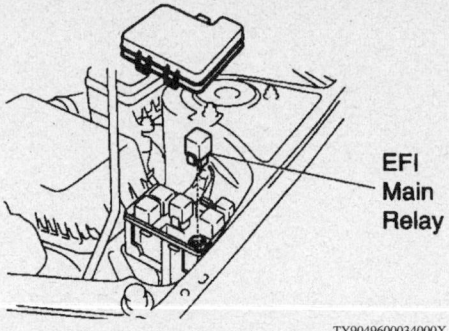

Fig. 2 EFI relay location. RAV4

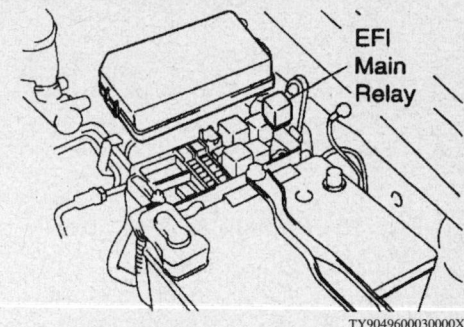

Fig. 3 EFI relay location. Tacoma

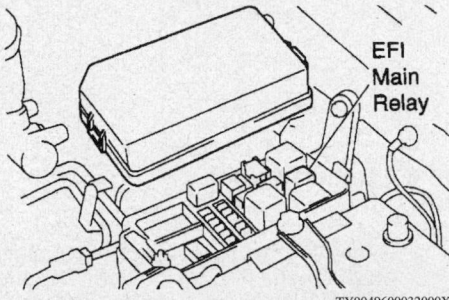

Fig. 4 EFI relay location. 4Runner

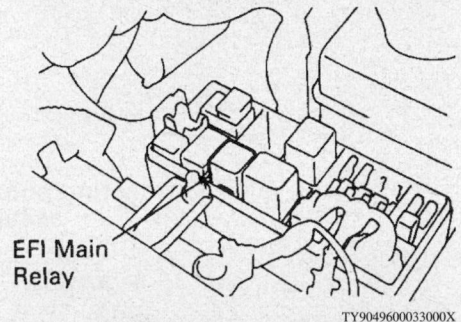

Fig. 5 EFI relay location. T100

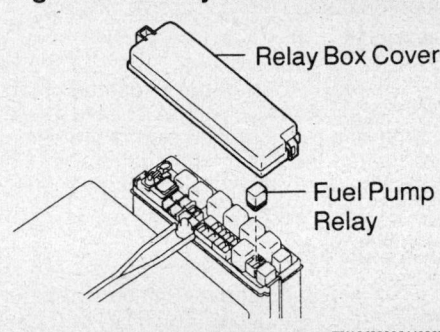

Fig. 6 Fuel pump relay location. Tundra

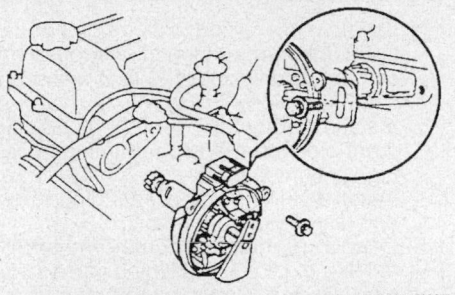

Fig. 7 Distributor flange alignment. Land Cruiser

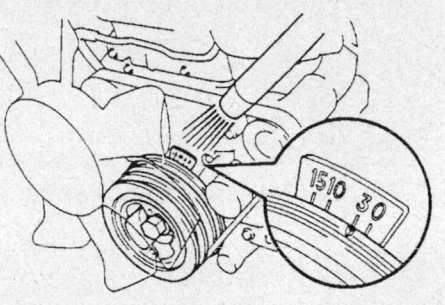

Fig. 8 Ignition timing check. Land Cruiser

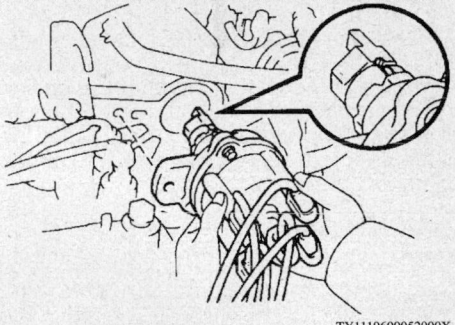

Fig. 9 Distributor rotor alignment. RAV4

T100

The No. 1 fuse panel is located behind the lefthand side kick panel. The No. 2 fuse panel is in the lefthand side of the engine compartment, behind the battery. The turn signal/hazard flasher is located under the instrument panel, below and to the left of the steering column.

TUNDRA

The No. 1 fuse panel is located behind the lower lefthand side of the instrument panel. Fuse/relay panel No. 2 is located in the lefthand side of the engine compartment, behind the battery. The turn signal/hazard flasher is at fuse panel No. 1.

FUEL PUMP RELAY LOCATION

LAND CRUISER

The fuel pump (EFI) relay is located in the engine compartment relay box, **Fig. 1.**

PICKUP

The fuel pump (EFI) relay is located in

the righthand side of the engine compartment, in the fuse/relay box.

RAV4

The fuel pump (EFI) relay is located in the engine compartment fuse/relay box, **Fig. 2.**

TACOMA

The fuel pump (EFI) relay is located in the engine compartment fuse/relay box, lefthand side of engine compartment, **Fig. 3.**

4RUNNER

The fuel pump (EFI) relay is located in the engine compartment relay box, **Fig. 4.**

T100

The fuel pump (EFI) relay is located in the engine compartment relay box, **Fig. 5.**

TUNDRA

The fuel pump (EFI) relay is located in the engine compartment relay box, **Fig. 6.**

RELAY CENTER LOCATION

LAND CRUISER

The No. 1 relay panel is located behind the removable instrument panel cover, to the left of the steering column. The No. 2 relay panel is located in the lefthand side of the engine compartment, behind the battery. The turn signal/hazard flasher is in the No. 1 relay panel, located at the lefthand side kick panel.

4RUNNER

The No. 1 relay panel is located behind the lower lefthand side of the instrument panel. Relay panel No. 2 is located in the lefthand side of the engine compartment, behind the battery. The turn signal/hazard flasher is at fuse panel No. 1.

PICKUP

The No. 1 relay panel is located behind the lefthand side kick panel. The No. 2 relay

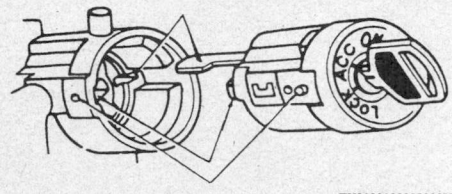

Fig. 10   Ignition lock removal

panel is in the righthand side of the engine compartment, behind the battery. Relay panel No. 3 is on behind the righthand side kick panel. The turn signal/hazard flasher is located behind the instrument cluster.

RAV4

The No. 1 relay panel is located behind the lefthand side kick panel. The No. 2 relay panel is in the righthand side of the engine compartment, near the righthand side shock tower. The turn signal flasher unit is at the No. 1 relay panel.

TACOMA

The No. 1 relay panel is located below the lefthand side kick panel. The No. 2 relay panel is in engine compartment, on the front lefthand side.

T100

The No. 1 relay panel is located behind the lefthand side kick panel. The No. 2 relay panel is in the lefthand side of the engine compartment, behind the battery. The turn signal/hazard flasher is located under the instrument panel, below and left of the steering column.

TUNDRA

The No. 1 relay panel is located behind the lower lefthand side of the instrument panel. Relay panel No. 2 is located in the lefthand side of the engine compartment, behind the battery. The turn signal/hazard flasher is at fuse panel No. 1.

STARTER
REPLACE
EXCEPT 2UZ-FE ENGINE

1. **On models equipped with audio coded anti-theft system,** obtain three-digit system code.
2. **On RAV4 models,** remove engine coolant reservoir.
3. **On all models,** if necessary, remove battery, battery tray and/or igniter bracket.
4. Remove air cleaner assembly, if necessary.
5. Disconnect electrical connectors from starter motor.
6. **On models equipped with automatic transmission,** remove transmission oil filler tube if necessary.
7. **On all models,** remove starter motor attaching bolts, heat shield (if equipped), then the starter motor.
8. Reverse procedure to install. Reset audio coded anti-theft, if equipped, as outlined under "Precautions."

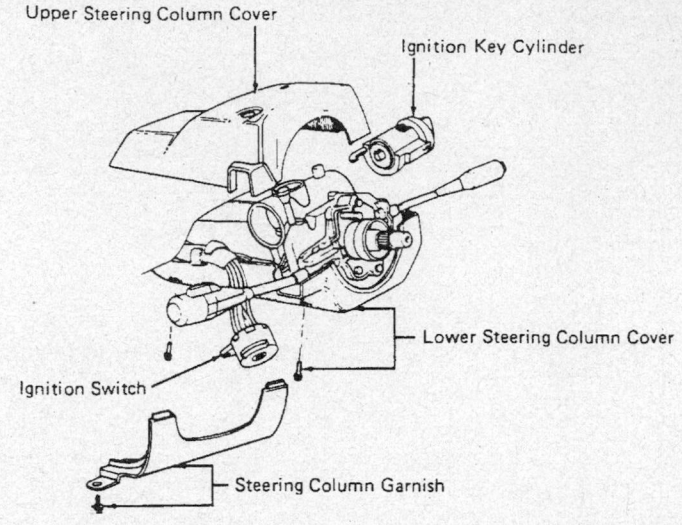

Fig. 11   Steering column & ignition switch assembly

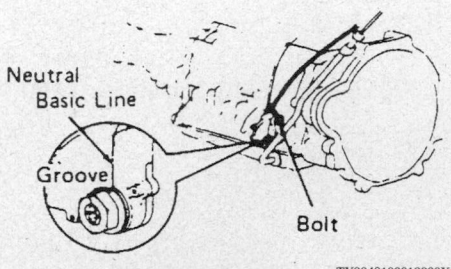

Fig. 12   Neutral safety switch adjustment

2UZ-FE ENGINE

1. Remove V-bank cover, then disconnect accelerator cable.
2. Remove intake air connector, then remove intake manifold as outlined under "Intake Manifold, Replace."
3. Remove starter attaching bolts, then disconnect starter electrical connector.
4. Disconnect starter wire, then remove wire protector and starter.
5. Reverse procedure to install. Tighten all nuts and bolts to specifications.

DISTRIBUTOR
REPLACE
PICKUP, TACOMA & 4RUNNER

2RZ-FE & 3RZ-FE ENGINES
Removal

1. **On models equipped with audio coded anti-theft system,** obtain three-digit system code.
2. **On all models,** disconnect distributor connector, spark plug wires and distributor cap.
3. Set engine to No. 1 cylinder TDC compression stroke. Distributor rotor should point to about 2 o'clock when alignment is correct.

4. Remove two distributor mounting bolts, then the distributor. Discard O-ring.

Installation

1. Install a new O-ring to distributor body. Lubricate O-ring, then align groove on distributor drive gear to protrusion on distributor body.
2. Install distributor, centering adjustment slots on the two mounting bolts. Lightly tighten bolts.
3. Install distributor cap, spark plug wires and distributor connector.
4. Connect suitable tachometer to terminal IG– of DLC1 and timing light to engine. Do not allow tachometer lead to touch ground. Start and run engine until normal operating temperature is reached.
5. Connect a jumper between terminals TE1 and E1 of DLC. Set timing to 5° BTDC at idle with air conditioner off. **Torque** bolts to 14 ft. lbs.
6. Disconnect tachometer and timing light.
7. Reset audio coded anti-theft system, if equipped, as outlined under "Precautions."

LAND CRUISER
REMOVAL

1. **On models equipped with audio coded anti-theft system,** obtain three-digit system code.
2. **On all models,** disconnect distributor connectors, then remove distributor cap with spark plug wires attached.
3. Set No. 1 cylinder to TDC on compression stroke.
4. Remove distributor hold-down bolts and pull out distributor.

INSTALLATION

1. Set No. 1 cylinder to TDC on compression stroke by aligning crankshaft pulley grove with zero mark of timing chain cover.
2. Install new O-ring and align distributor

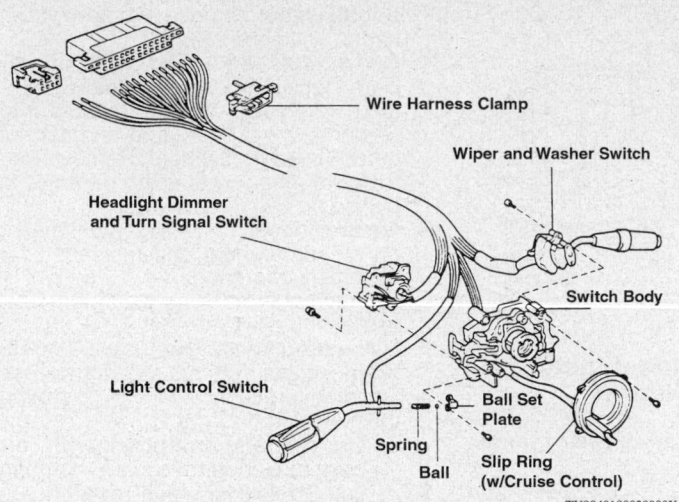

Fig. 13 Combination switch service. Pickup

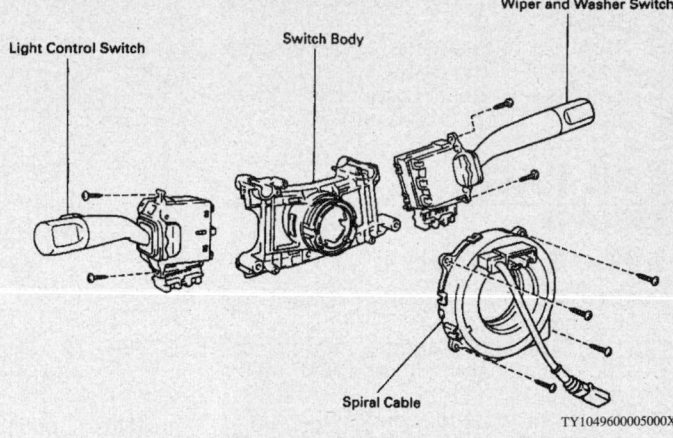

Fig. 14 Combination switch service. RAV4 & 4Runner

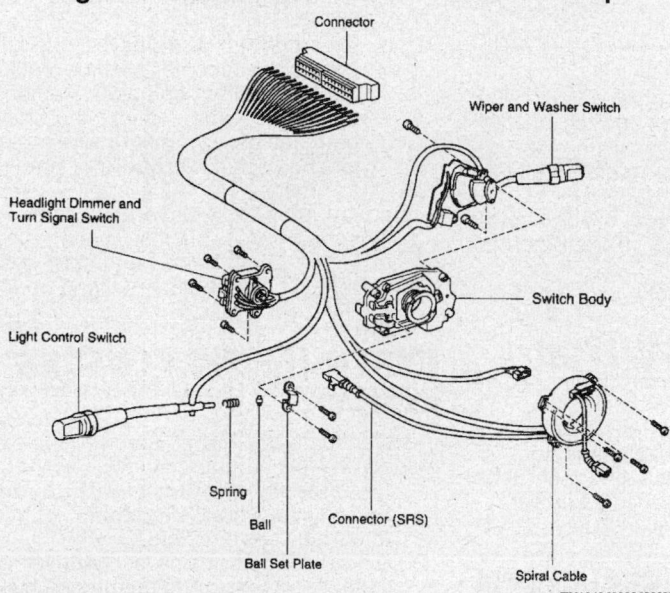

Fig. 15 Combination switch service. Land Cruiser

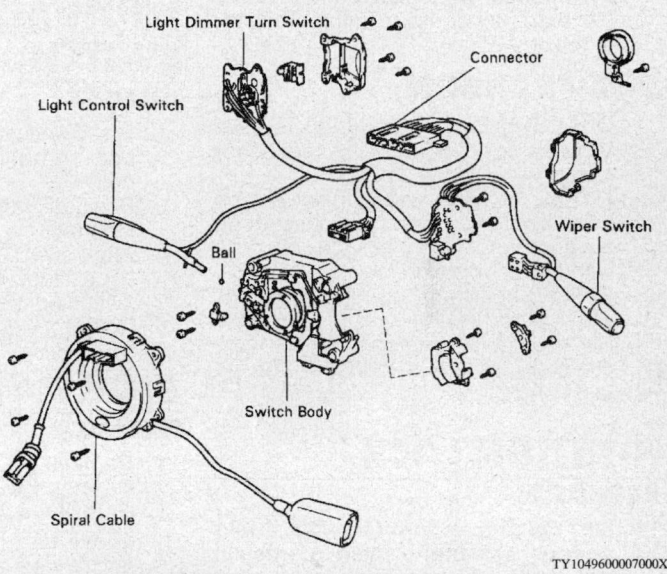

Fig. 16 Combination switch service. Tacoma & T100 less intermittent & mist wipers

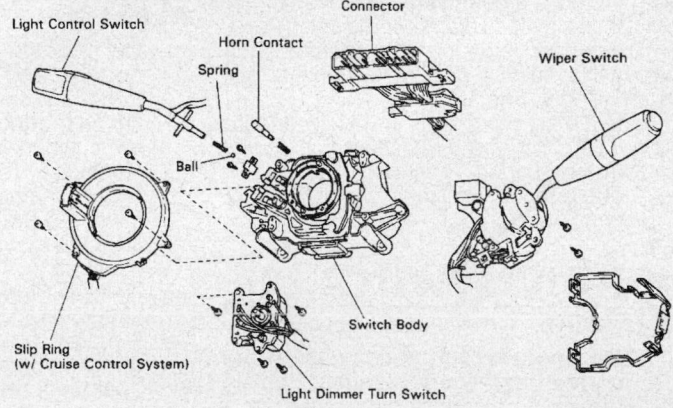

Fig. 17 Combination switch service. T100 w/intermittent & mist wipers

housing with protrusion on driven gear

3. Align center of distributor flange with bolt hole on cylinder head, **Fig. 7,** then install distributor.
4. Install distributor cap and connect distributor connector.
5. Reset audio coded anti-theft system, if equipped, as outlined under "Precautions."
6. Start and warm engine.
7. Connect suitable tachometer and timing light. Do not allow tachometer lead to touch ground. With transmission in neutral and A/C OFF, adjust ignition timing. Ensure timing is 3° BTDC at idle, **Fig. 8.**
8. If no further timing adjusting is necessary, **torque** distributor retaining bolt to 13 ft. lbs.
9. Remove tachometer and timing light.

RAV4
REMOVAL
1. Remove air cleaner cap assembly.
2. Disconnect distributor connector.

3. Disconnect high-tension cord from distributor and spark plugs.
4. Remove distributor mounting bolt and pull out distributor.

INSTALLATION
1. Set No. 1 cylinder to TDC of its compression stroke.
2. Install new distributor O-ring, lightly coated with engine oil.
3. Align cutout of coupling with line of housing, **Fig. 9.**
4. Install distributor, align center of flange with bolt hole on cylinder head.

5. **Torque,** distributor mounting bolt to 14 ft. lbs.
6. Connect high-tension cords to spark pugs and distributor.
7. Connect distributor connector and install air cleaner cap assembly.

COIL PACK
REPLACE
5VZ-FE ENGINE

1. **On 4Runner models,** remove air cleaner hose.
2. **On T100 and Tacoma models,** remove air cleaner cap and MAF meter assembly.
3. **On all models,** disconnect three ignition coil connectors from coils.
4. Remove three bolts and three ignition coils from lefthand side cylinder head.
5. Reverse procedure to install. **Torque,** to 6 ft. lbs.

2UZ-FE ENGINE

1. **On Land Cruiser models,** remove V-bank cover, then the intake air connector.
2. **On all models,** disconnect engine wire from left hand cylinder head cover, then disconnect ignition coils with igniter connectors.
3. Remove bolt, then pull out ignition coils with igniter.
4. Remove ignition coils with igniter.
5. Reverse procedure to install. **Torque** to 6 ft. lbs.

IGNITION LOCK
REPLACE

1. **On models equipped with audio coded anti-theft system,** obtain three-digit system code.
2. **On all models,** turn ignition switch to ACC position.
3. Remove steering column covers.
4. Insert a small diameter rod into hole located on side of lock cylinder, then while holding down pin, remove lock cylinder, **Fig. 10.**
5. Reverse procedure to install. Ensure lock cylinder is in ACC position. Reset audio coded anti-theft system, if equipped, as outlined under "Precautions."

IGNITION SWITCH
REPLACE

1. **On models equipped with audio coded anti-theft system,** obtain three-digit system code.
2. **On all models,** remove steering wheel, if necessary, steering column garnish, if equipped, upper and lower covers, **Fig. 11.**
3. Disconnect electrical connectors from ignition switch.
4. Turn ignition key to ACC position and remove ignition key cylinder.
5. Remove screw and ignition switch.
6. Reverse procedure to install. Reset audio coded anti-theft and air bag sys-

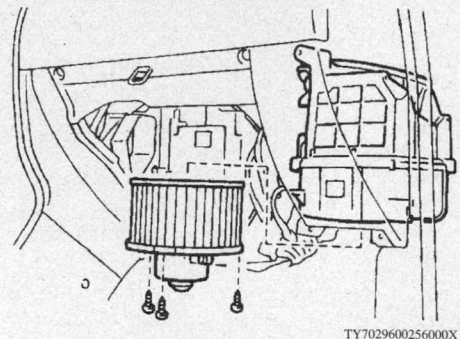

Fig. 18 Front blower motor removal. 4Runner

tem, if equipped, as outlined under "Precautions."

NEUTRAL SAFETY SWITCH
ADJUST

1. Raise and support vehicle.
2. Loosen neutral safety switch bracket bolt.
3. Position transmission shift lever into Neutral.
4. Align switch shaft groove with neutral base line, **Fig. 12,** then retighten switch bracket bolt.
5. Connect electrical connector to switch.

STOP LIGHT SWITCH
REPLACE

1. Remove brake pedal tension spring.
2. Disconnect switch wire connector.
3. Remove switch mounting nut, then slide switch from mounting bracket.
4. Reverse procedure to install.

COMBINATION SWITCH
REPLACE

1. **On models equipped with audio coded anti-theft system,** obtain three-digit system code.
2. **On all models,** remove steering wheel as outlined under "Steering Wheel, Replace."
3. Remove steering column upper and lower covers.
4. Disconnect switch connectors, remove screws and combination switch.
5. Refer to **Figs. 13 through 17** for combination switch disassembly.
6. Reverse procedure to install. Reset audio coded anti-theft system, if equipped, as outlined under "Precautions."

STEERING WHEEL
REPLACE

1. **On models equipped with audio coded anti-theft system,** obtain three-digit system code.
2. **On all models,** remove steering wheel pad.
3. **On models equipped with four**

spoke wheel, remove trim cover from center of steering wheel.
4. **On models equipped with an air bag,** loosen Torx screws holding center pad. These screws are held into steering wheel by a cage and cannot be removed from wheel. Remove pad from steering wheel using care not to pull on air bag wire harness.
5. **On all models,** place alignment marks on steering wheel and mainshaft for assembly reference.
6. Remove nut attaching steering wheel to steering shaft.
7. Using a puller tool No. 09950-50010, or equivalent, remove steering wheel.
8. Reverse procedure to install, noting the following.
   a. **On models equipped with air bag,** center spiral cable by turning counterclockwise until resistance is felt, then turn and additional three turns clockwise and align red marks.
   b. **On models equipped with air bag,** inspect center pad for cracks dents or other damage. Replace damaged pads. Reinstall center pad, use care to ensure wire is not pinched or cut. **Torque** Torx screws to 7 ft. lbs.
   c. **On all models, torque** steering wheel nut to 25 ft. lbs.
   d. Reset audio coded anti-theft system, if equipped, as outlined under "Precautions."

INSTRUMENT CLUSTER
REPLACE

Refer to "Dash Panel Service" for exploded view of instrument panel.
1. **On models equipped with audio coded anti-theft system,** obtain three-digit system code.
2. **On all models,** using screwdriver or suitable tool, remove instrument cluster center finish panel.
3. Remove screws and pull out cluster trim panel. Disconnect connectors, if necessary.
4. Remove cup holder from cluster finish panel, if equipped.
5. Remove cluster attaching screws, then the cluster from instrument panel. Disconnect connectors and speedometer cable, as necessary.
6. Reverse procedure to install. Reset audio coded anti-theft system, if equipped, as outlined under "Precautions."

RADIO
REPLACE
PICKUP, RAV4, TACOMA, TUNDRA, T100 & 4RUNNER

1. **On models equipped with audio coded anti-theft system,** obtain three-digit system code.
2. **On all models,** remove screws and pull out center finish panel. Disconnect connectors.

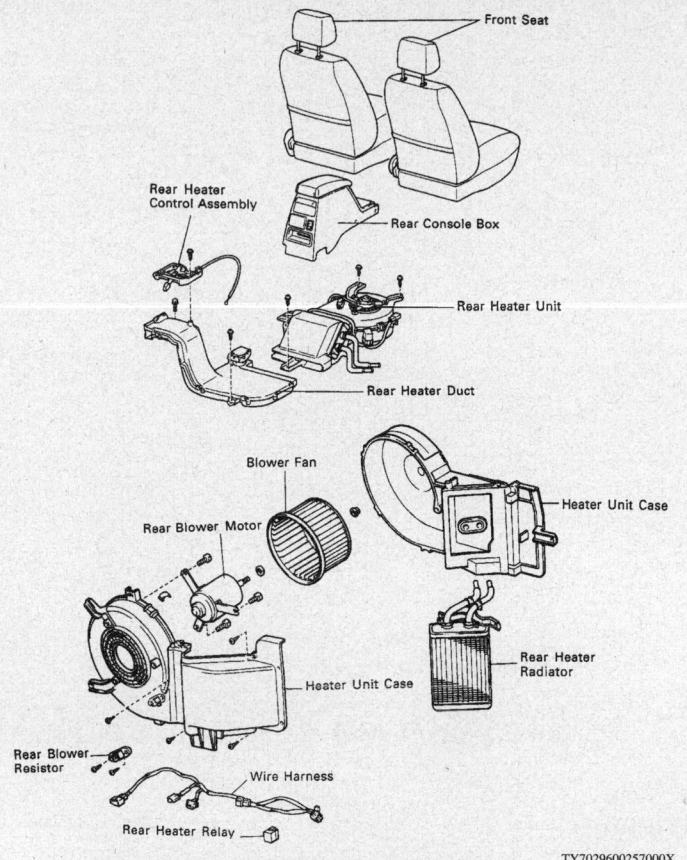

Fig. 19   Rear heater core & blower motor replacement. 4Runner

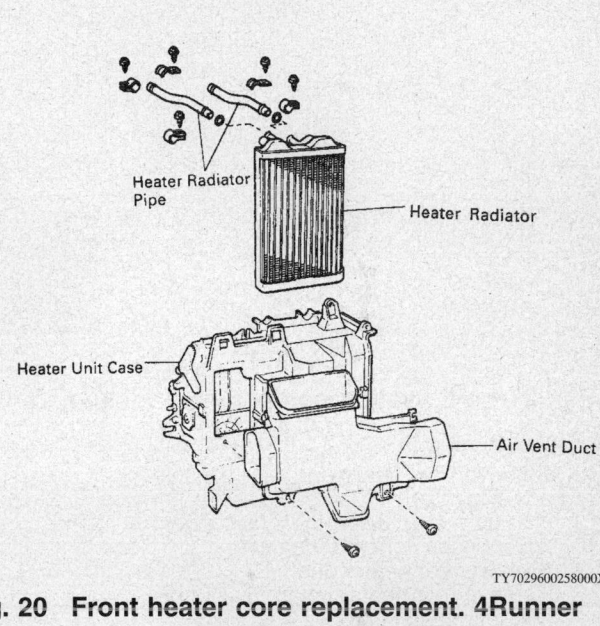

Fig. 20   Front heater core replacement. 4Runner

3. Remove radio retaining screws, then the radio. Disconnect connectors and antenna.
4. Reverse procedure to install. Reset audio coded anti-theft system, if equipped, as outlined under "Precautions."

LAND CRUISER

1. **On models equipped with audio coded anti-theft system,** obtain three-digit system code.
2. **On all models,** remove instrument panel center cluster finish trim.
3. Remove radio and disconnect connectors and antenna.
4. Reverse procedure to install. Reset audio coded anti-theft system, if equipped, as outlined under "Precautions."

WIPER MOTOR

REPLACE

FRONT

1. **On models equipped with audio coded anti-theft system,** obtain three-digit system code.
2. **On all models,** disconnect wiper motor wire connector, then remove wiper motor service cover or cowl vent screen, if equipped.
3. Remove wiper motor attaching bolts.
4. Using a screwdriver disconnect wiper link from wiper motor and remove wiper motor.

5. Reverse procedure to install. Reset audio coded anti-theft system, if equipped, as outlined under "Precautions."

REAR

1. **On models equipped with audio coded anti-theft system,** obtain three-digit system code.
2. **On all models,** remove wiper arm and rear door trim cover.
3. **On RAV4 models,** remove service hole cover.
4. **On all models,** disconnect wiper motor wire connector.
5. Remove wiper motor bracket attaching bolts and wiper motor and bracket.
6. Reverse procedure to install. Reset audio coded anti-theft system, if equipped, as outlined under "Precautions."

WIPER SWITCH

REPLACE

Refer to "Combination Switch Service" and "Combination Switch, Replace" procedures.

BLOWER MOTOR

REPLACE

PICKUP, TUNDRA & T100

1. **On models equipped with audio coded anti-theft system,** obtain three-digit system code.
2. **On all models,** disconnect blower motor and blower resistor connectors.
3. Remove blower motor retaining screws, then the blower motor.
4. Reverse procedure to install. Reset audio coded anti-theft system, if equipped, as outlined under "Precautions."

4RUNNER

FRONT

1. Remove glove compartment.
2. Disconnect blower motor connector.
3. Remove three retaining screws and the blower motor, **Fig. 18.**
4. Reverse procedure to install.

REAR

1. Drain engine coolant.

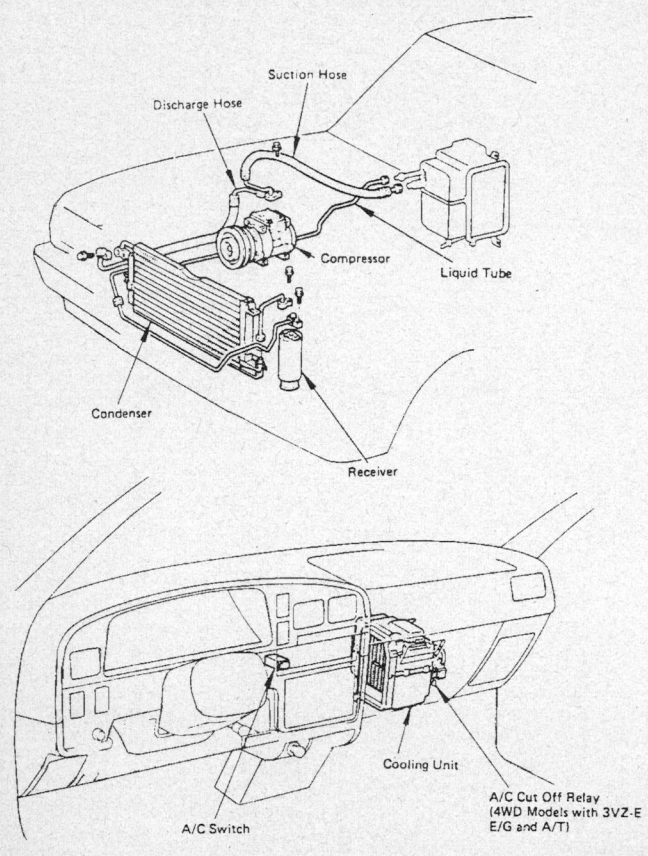

Fig. 21 A/C system components. Pickup, Tundra & 4Runner

2. Remove front seats and rear console box, **Fig. 19.**
3. Roll up floor carpet, then disconnect water hoses from rear heater unit.
4. Remove rear heater duct.
5. Remove rear heater control assembly and rear heater unit.
6. Separate heater unit case halves and remove rear blower motor.
7. Reverse procedure to install.

RAV4 & TACOMA

1. Remove glove compartment.
2. Remove pillar brace.
3. Remove three mounting bolts and the blower unit.
4. Remove three screws from bottom of blower unit, then pull blower motor with fan from blower unit.
5. Reverse procedure to install.

LAND CRUISER

FRONT

1. **On models equipped with audio coded anti-theft system,** obtain three-digit system code.
2. **On all models,** remove righthand scuff plate.
3. Remove blower motor lower cover.
4. Disconnect blower motor connector, then remove blower motor retaining screws and blower motor.

5. Reverse procedure to install. Reset audio coded anti-theft system, if equipped, as outlined under "Precautions."

REAR

1996-97

1. **On models equipped with audio coded anti-theft system,** obtain three-digit system code.
2. **On all models,** remove front righthand seat.
3. Disconnect connectors from blower motor and rear heater relay.
4. Remove rear heater relay and blower motor side cover.
5. Remove upper cover with blower motor.
6. Reverse procedure to install. Reset

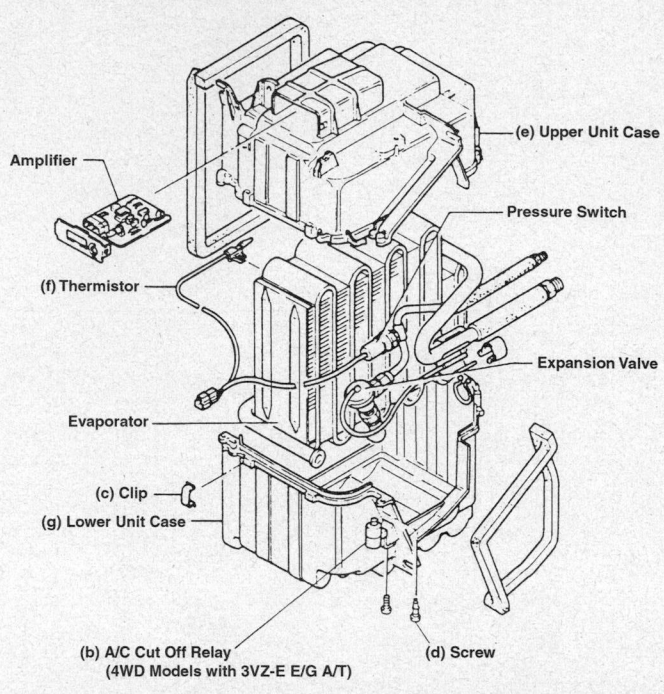

Fig. 22 Exploded view of cooling unit. Pickup

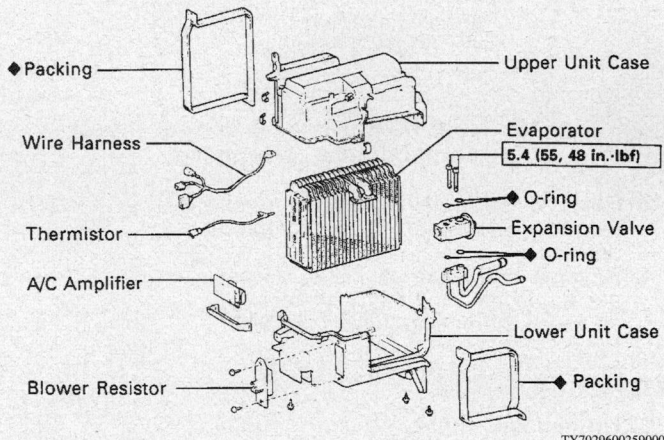

Fig. 23 Exploded view of cooling unit. 4Runner

audio coded anti-theft system, if equipped, as outlined under "Precautions."

1998-99

1. **On models equipped with audio coded anti-theft system,** obtain three-digit system code.
2. **On all models,** remove front righthand seats.
3. Remove rear console box, then front console box cover.
4. remove lower center cluster finish panel, then remove front door scuff plates and cowl side trims.
5. Remove rear door scuff plates, then center pillar garnishes.
6. Slide floor carpet backward, then remove screws and blower motor.
7. Reverse procedure to install. Reset

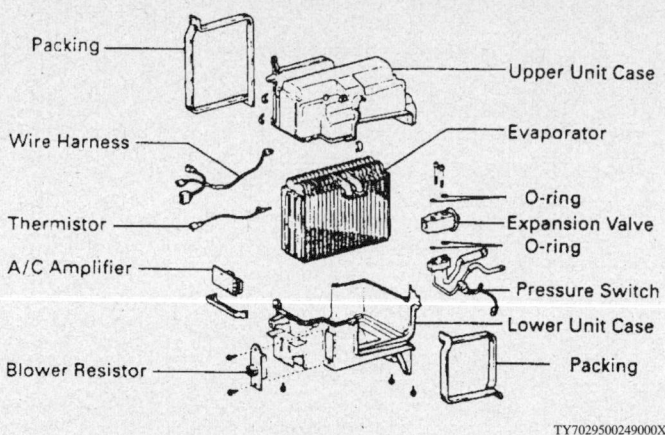

TY7029500249000X

Fig. 24 Exploded view of cooling unit. Tacoma

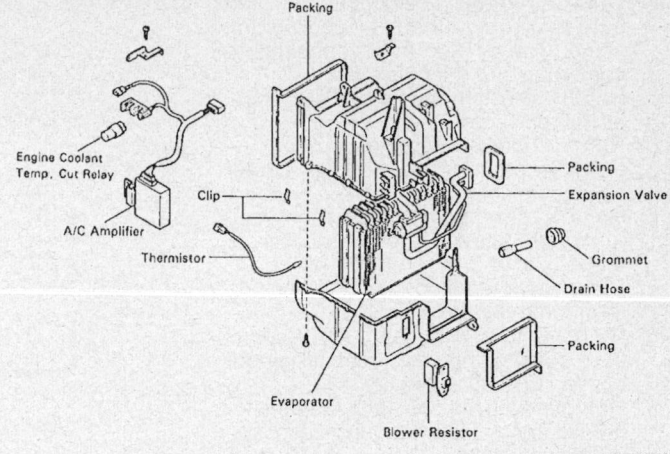

TY7029300233000X

Fig. 25 Exploded view of cooling unit. 1996–97 Land Cruiser

audio coded anti-theft system, if equipped, as outlined under "Precautions."

HEATER CORE
REPLACE
PICKUP, TUNDRA & T100

1. Remove cooling unit as outlined under "Evaporator Core, Replace."
2. Drain engine coolant from radiator.
3. Disconnect water hoses from heater core pipes.
4. Remove instrument panel and reinforcement as outlined under " Dash Panel Service."
5. Disconnect control cables from heater unit.
6. Remove heat duct to register No. 4.
7. Remove heater to register center duct.
8. Remove heater unit.
9. Remove heater air duct.
10. Remove heater core retaining screws and plates.
11. Pull heater core from heater unit.
12. Reverse procedure to install.

4RUNNER
Front

1. Remove cooling unit as outlined under "Evaporator Core, Replace."
2. Drain engine coolant from radiator.
3. Disconnect water hoses from heater radiator pipes.
4. Remove instrument panel and reinforcement as outlined under " Dash Panel Service."
5. Remove defroster nozzle and heater to register duct.
6. Remove heater unit.
7. Remove two plates and clamp, then pull heater core from heater unit, **Fig. 20.**
8. Disconnect heater core inlet and outlet pipes.
9. Reverse procedure to install.

Rear

1. Drain engine coolant.
2. Remove front seats and rear console box, **Fig. 19.**
3. Roll up floor carpet, then disconnect water hoses from rear heater unit.

4. Remove rear heater duct.
5. Remove rear heater control assembly and rear heater unit.
6. Separate heater unit case halves and disconnect heater core pipes from rear heater core.
7. Remove rear heater core.
8. Reverse procedure to install.

RAV4

1. Remove cooling unit as outlined under "Evaporator Core, Replace."
2. Drain engine coolant from radiator.
3. Disconnect water hose from heater unit.
4. Remove rear heater duct, then the heater unit.
5. Remove defroster duct from heater unit.
6. Remove two screws and clips from top of heater unit, then pull heater core from heater unit.
7. Reverse procedure to install.

TACOMA

1. Remove cooling unit as outlined under "Evaporator Core, Replace."
2. Drain engine coolant from radiator.
3. Disconnect water hose from heater unit.
4. Remove instrument panel and reinforcement as outlined in " Dash Panel Service."
5. Remove defroster duct heater to register No. 4, then the heater unit.
6. Remove two screws and clips from top of heater unit, then pull heater core from heater unit.
7. Reverse procedure to install.

LAND CRUISER

1. Remove cooling unit as outlined under "Evaporator Core, Replace."
2. Drain engine coolant from radiator.
3. Disconnect water hoses from heater core.
4. Remove pipe grommets.
5. Remove instrument panel and reinforcement as outlined under " Dash Panel Service."
6. Remove duct heater to register No. 3.
7. Remove heater unit.

8. Remove heater core retaining screws and plates.
9. Pull heater core from heater unit.
10. Reverse procedure to install.

EVAPORATOR CORE
REPLACE
PICKUP, TUNDRA & 4RUNNER

1. **On models equipped with audio coded anti-theft system,** obtain three-digit system code.
2. **On all models,** discharge A/C system as outlined under "Air Conditioning," then disconnect refrigerant lines at cooling unit **Fig. 21,** capping all openings.
3. Remove grommets from inlet and outlet fittings.
4. Remove glove compartment and glove compartment stay.
5. Disconnect A/C switch connector and the connector connected to A/C harness.
6. Remove four attaching screws and bolt, then the cooling unit.
7. Remove four clamps and four screws securing case halves, **Figs. 22 and 23,** then separate case halves and remove evaporator.
8. Pull off clamp and remove thermistor.
9. Remove heat insulator and clamp from outlet tube.
10. Disconnect liquid line tube from inlet fitting of expansion valve.
11. Disconnect expansion valve from inlet fitting of evaporator.
12. Reverse procedure to install, then evacuate the recharge system and check for leaks. If evaporator is replaced, add 1.4–1.7 oz. of new refrigerant oil to compressor. Reset audio coded anti-theft system, if equipped, as outlined under "Precautions."

T100

1. **On models equipped with audio coded anti-theft system,** obtain three-digit system code.

2. **On all models,** disconnect suction tube and liquid tube from cooling unit fitting. Cap or plug fitting openings to keep moisture out of system.
3. Remove two grommets and drain pipe grommet.
4. Remove glove compartment door.
5. Remove instrument panel lower center cover.
6. Remove glove compartment door reinforcement screws, then the reinforcement.
7. Disconnect cooling unit connectors, then remove cooling unit.
8. Remove four clips and four screws from cooling unit case, then the upper cooling unit case, **Fig. 22.**
9. Remove thermistor with thermistor holder, then the lower unit case and evaporator core.
10. Reverse procedure to install, noting the following:
   a. **Torque** liquid tube to cooling unit inlet fitting to 10 ft. lbs.
   b. **Torque** suction tube to cooling unit outlet fitting to 24 ft. lbs.
   c. If evaporator is replaced, add 1.4–1.7 fl. oz. of new refrigerant oil to compressor.
   d. Reset audio coded anti-theft system, if equipped, as outlined under "Precautions."

TACOMA

1. **On models equipped with audio coded anti-theft system,** obtain three-digit system code.
2. **On all models,** disconnect suction tube and liquid tube from cooling unit fitting. Cap or plug fitting openings to keep moisture out of system.
3. Remove two grommets and drain pipe grommet.
4. Remove glove compartment door.
5. Remove instrument panel lower center cover.
6. Remove glove compartment door reinforcement screws, then the reinforcement.
7. Remove A/C amplifier.
8. Disconnect cooling unit connectors, then the cooling unit.
9. Remove three clips and three screws from cooling unit case, then the upper cooling unit case, **Fig. 24.**
10. Remove thermistor and pressure switch, then the lower unit case and evaporator core.
11. Reverse procedure to install, noting the following:

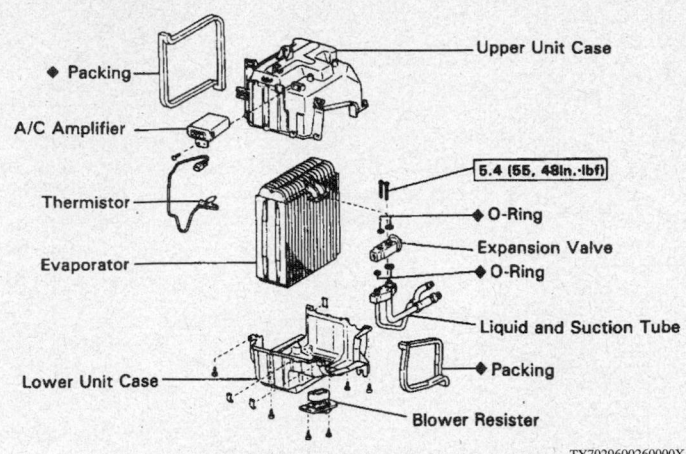

Fig. 26 Exploded view of cooling unit. RAV4

a. **Torque** liquid tube to cooling unit inlet fitting to 10 ft. lbs.
b. **Torque** suction tube to cooling unit outlet fitting to 24 ft. lbs.
c. If evaporator is replaced, add 1.4–1.7 fl. oz. of new refrigerant oil to compressor.
d. Reset audio coded anti-theft system, if equipped, as outlined under "Precautions."

LAND CRUISER

1996-97

1. **On models equipped with audio coded anti-theft system,** obtain three-digit system code.
2. **On all models,** disconnect suction tube and liquid tube from cooling unit fitting. Cap or plug open fittings to prevent moisture in cooling system.
3. Remove glove compartment door.
4. Remove engine control module and disconnect electrical connectors.
5. Remove cooling unit and A/C amplifier.
6. Remove blower speed control relay and magnetic clutch relay.
7. Remove upper and lower cooling unit case, then the evaporator core, **Fig. 25.**
8. Reverse procedure to install, noting the following:
   a. **Torque** cooling unit inlet and outlet tube fittings to 48 inch lbs.
   b. If evaporator is replaced, add 1.4–1.7 fl. oz. of new refrigerant oil to compressor.

c. Reset audio coded anti-theft system, if equipped, as outlined under "Precautions."

1998-99

1. Discharge refrigerant from A/C system, then disconnect liquid and suction tubes from cooling unit.
2. Remove instrument panel as outlined under "Dash Panel Service."
3. Disconnect electrical connector, then remove antenna relay.
4. Disconnect evaporator electrical connector, then the clamp connector.
5. Remove No. 1 cooler cover, then pull out evaporator.
6. Reverse procedure to install.

RAV4

1. Discharge and recover refrigerant from A/C system.
2. Remove glove compartment.
3. Disconnect suction and liquid tubes from rear of engine compartment, at firewall.
4. Remove three screws, three nuts, and the cooling unit from below lefthand side of instrument panel.
5. Separate upper and lower evaporator case by cutting off packing with a sharp knife, **Fig. 26.**
6. Disconnect thermistor and remove evaporator core.
7. Reverse procedure to install. If evaporator is replaced, add 1.4 fl. oz. of new compressor oil to compressor.

3S-FE 2.0L Engine

NOTE: On Air Bag Equipped Models, Refer To "Air Bag System Precautions" Located In The Front Of This Manual For System Disarming & Arming Procedures.

INDEX

PRECAUTIONS

AIR BAG SYSTEMS

Refer to "Air Bag System Precautions"in the front of this manual for system disarming and arming procedures.

AUDIO CODED ANTI-THEFT SYSTEM

Some models are equipped with an audio coded anti-theft system that will disable the radio when the battery cable is disconnected. The system can be identified by the "ANTI-THEFT SYSTEM" on the cassette lid. Obtain three-digit code for input. Reset system after service as follows:
1. Obtain three-digit audio theft code.
2. Depress 1 (PROG) button while depressing righthand side of TUNE SEEK button. Three dashes will appear in tape operation display.
3. To enter first digit, depress 1 (PROG) button repeatedly until number of times depressed equals first digit (depress 1 button six times if first digit is five, first press equals 0).
4. To enter second digit, depress 2 (APS) button repeatedly until number of times depressed equals second digit.
5. To enter third digit, depress 3 (RPT) button repeatedly until number of times depressed equals third digit.
6. If three dashes are displayed after inputting digits, repeat procedure.
7. When code appears in display, depress and hold SCAN button until SEC appears.
8. When SEC disappears audio system is operative.
9. If Err is displayed, repeat procedure. **Attempting to input code more than nine times may permanently disable audio system.**

BATTERY GROUND CABLE

Prior to service, disconnect battery ground cable and isolate as required.

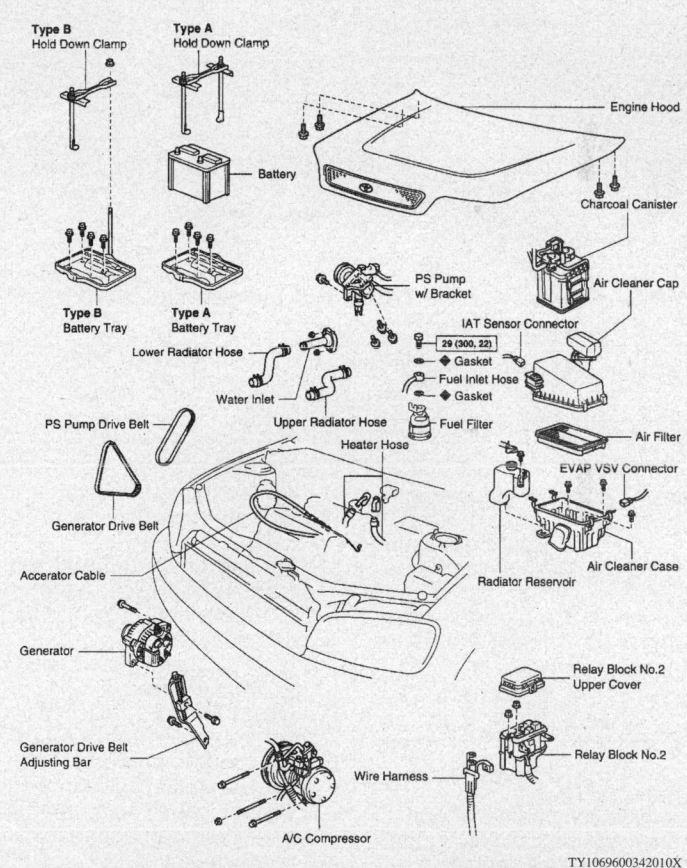

Fig. 1 Engine replacement (Part 1 of 2)

TY1069600342010X

FUEL PRESSURE RELIEF

1. Remove lefthand side rear seat.
2. Remove floor service hole cover.
3. Disconnect fuel pump electrical connector.
4. Start and run engine until it stalls.
5. Turn ignition switch off.

COMPRESSION PRESSURE

1. Start engine and warm to normal operating temperature.
2. Disconnect distributor connector.
3. Disconnect high tension cords from

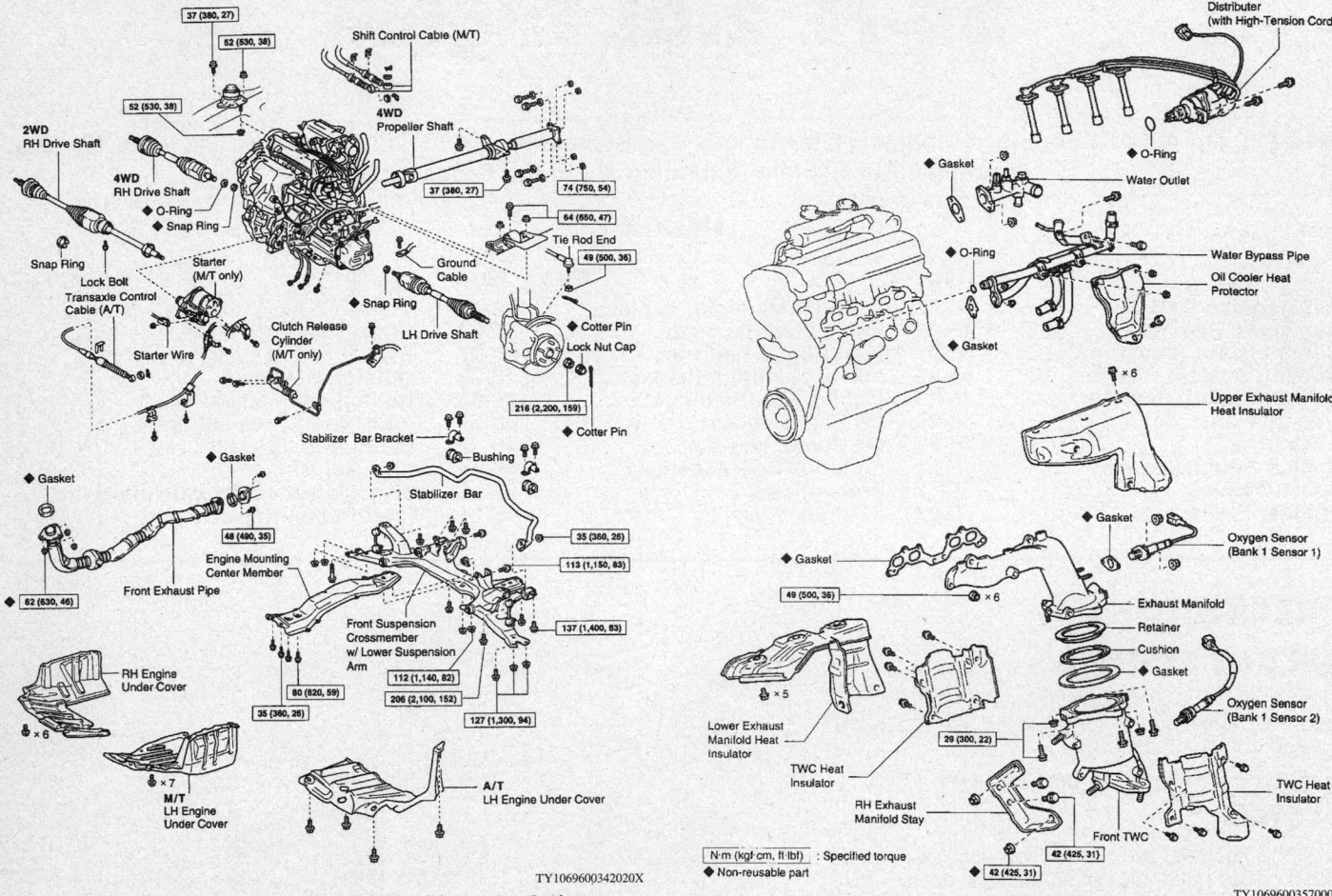

Fig. 1   Engine replacement (Part 2 of 2)

Fig. 2   Exhaust manifold removal

spark plugs and distributor.
4. Remove spark plugs.
5. Insert compression gauge into spark plug hole.
6. Fully open throttle.
7. While cranking engine, measure compression pressure.
8. Standard compression pressure should be 185 psi. Minimum compression is 135 psi.
9. The difference in compression pressure between each cylinder should not exceed 14 psi.

ENGINE

REPLACE

1. Remove battery, **Fig. 1.**
2. Remove engine compartment hood.
3. Remove engine under covers.
4. Drain engine coolant and engine oil.
5. Drain transaxle oil.
6. Remove air cleaner cap and case.
7. Disconnect accelerator cable from throttle body, cable bracket and clamps.
8. Disconnect engine wire from relay block No. 2.
9. Remove charcoal canister.
10. Remove water inlet.
11. Disconnect heater hoses.
12. Remove alternator.
13. Remove radiator upper and lower hoses.

14. Remove water inlet.
15. Disconnect heater hoses.
16. Disconnect fuel inlet hose.
17. **On models equipped with manual transaxle,** remove starter.
18. **On all models,** disconnect ground cable.
19. **On models equipped with manual transaxle,** proceed as follows:
    a. Disconnect back-up lamp switch connector.
    b. Disconnect clutch release cylinder from transaxle.
20. **On all models,** disconnect transaxle control cables from transaxle.
21. **On models equipped with automatic transaxle,** disconnect transaxle control cable from front suspension crossmember and engine mounting center member.
22. **On all models,** disconnect transaxle oil cooler hoses.
23. Disconnect the following connectors:
    a. Vapor pressure sensor.
    b. Igniter.
    c. Ignition coil.
    d. Noise filter.
    e. High-tension cord from ignition coil.
    f. MAP sensor.
    g. MAP sensor vacuum hose from gas filter on intake manifold.
    h. Brake booster hose from intake manifold.

i. Differential lock control solenoid, if equipped.
24. Disconnect ground strap from cowl.
25. Remove righthand scuff plate, righthand cowl side trim and righthand floor carpet center cover.
26. Disconnect engine wire from passenger compartment.
27. Disconnect two ECM connectors and connector from junction box No. 4.
28. Remove front exhaust pipe.
29. Disconnect A/C compressor from engine.
30. Remove propeller shaft, if equipped.
31. Remove front driveshaft.
32. Remove stabilizer.
33. Remove front suspension crossmember.
34. Remove engine mounting center member.
35. Remove drive belt and power steering pump from engine.
36. Install suitable engine hanger, then attach engine sling device to engine hanger.
37. Disconnect lefthand engine mounting bracket from mounting insulator.
38. Disconnect ground strap connector.
39. Disconnect righthand engine mounting bracket from mounting insulator.
40. Slowly lower engine and raise vehicle, ensuring all wiring, hoses and cables are clear.

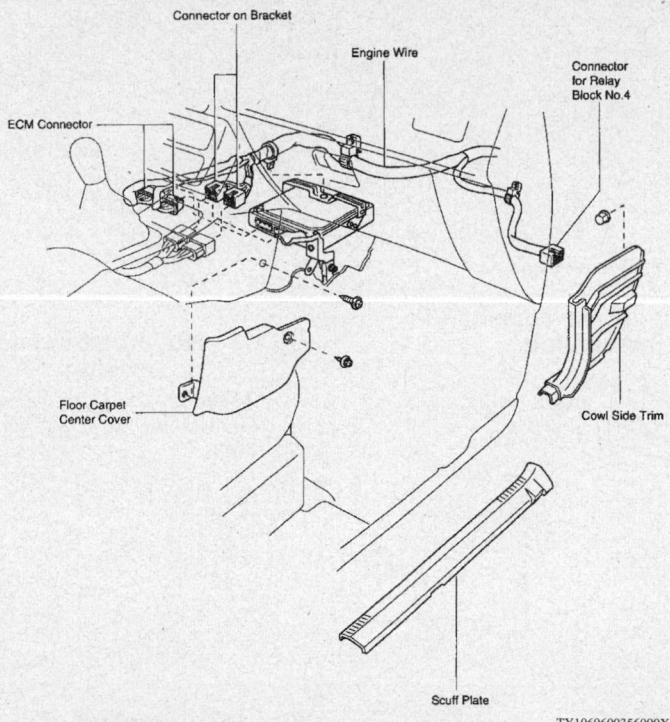

Fig. 3   Engine wire removal

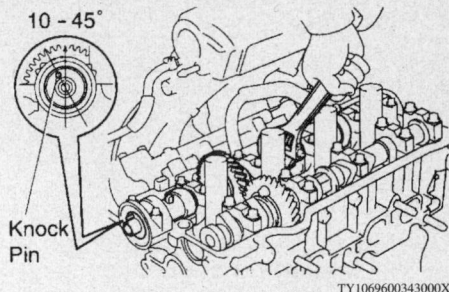

Fig. 4   Intake camshaft knock pin

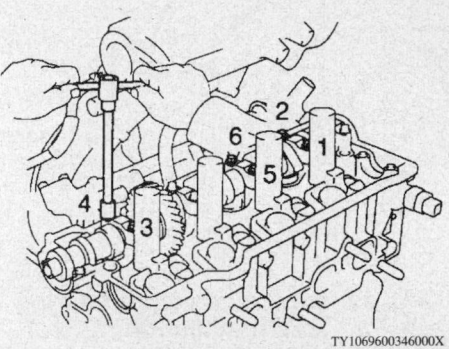

Fig. 7   Intake camshaft bearing cap loosening sequence

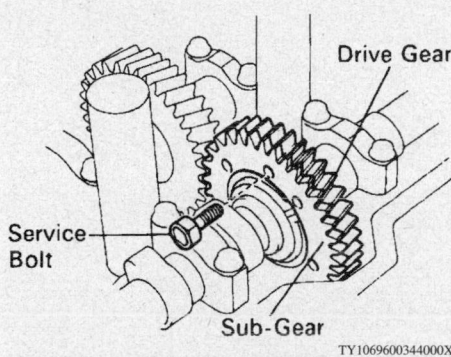

Fig. 5   Service bolt installation

Fig. 6   Exhaust camshaft bearing cap loosening sequence

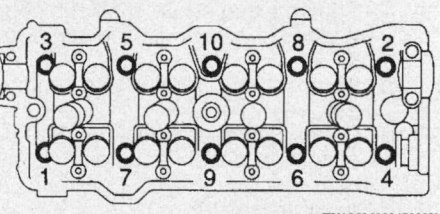

Fig. 8   Cylinder head bolt loosening sequence

41. Place engine and transaxle assembly on stand and separate engine from transaxle.
42. Reverse procedure to install. Tighten to specifications.

INTAKE MANIFOLD
REPLACE

Refer to "Cylinder Head, Replace" for procedure.

EXHAUST MANIFOLD
REPLACE

Refer to "Cylinder Head, Replace" for procedure.

CYLINDER HEAD
REPLACE
REMOVAL

1. Remove righthand side engine under cover.

2. Drain engine coolant.
3. **On models equipped with automatic transaxle,** disconnect throttle cable from throttle body.
4. **On all models,** disconnect accelerator cable from throttle body.
5. Remove air cleaner cap and case.
6. Remove alternator.
7. Remove distributor as outlined under "Distributor, Replace" in "Electrical" section.
8. Remove front exhaust pipe.

9. Disconnect oxygen sensor connectors, (bank 1/sensor 1) and (bank 1/sensor 2), **Fig. 2.**
10. Remove exhaust manifold upper heat insulator.
11. Remove two bolts attaching righthand exhaust manifold stay to cylinder block.
12. Remove exhaust manifold and catalytic converter assembly.
13. Remove oxygen sensor (bank 1/sensor 1) from exhaust manifold.
14. Remove oxygen sensor (bank 1/sensor 2) from catalytic converter.
15. Disconnect oil pressure switch connector.
16. Disconnect ECT sensor and ECT sender connectors.
17. Disconnect radiator hose, water bypass hose, heater water hose and IAC valve water bypass hose from water outlet.
18. Remove water outlet and gasket.
19. Remove water bypass pipe.
20. Disconnect IAC valve water bypass hose from water bypass pipe.
21. Disconnect heater water hose from water bypass pipe.
22. Disconnect two oil cooler water bypass hoses from oil cooler.
23. Disconnect water bypass pipe from water pump cover.
24. Remove water bypass pipe.
25. Disconnect IAC valve and throttle position sensor connectors.
26. Disconnect PCV hose and vacuum hoses from throttle body.
27. Remove throttle body from engine.
28. Disconnect vacuum sensor hose from gas filter on intake manifold.
29. Disconnect brake booster vacuum hose from intake manifold.
30. Disconnect ground strap from intake manifold.

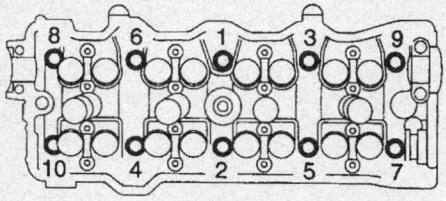

Fig. 9 Cylinder head bolt tightening sequence

TY1069600348000X

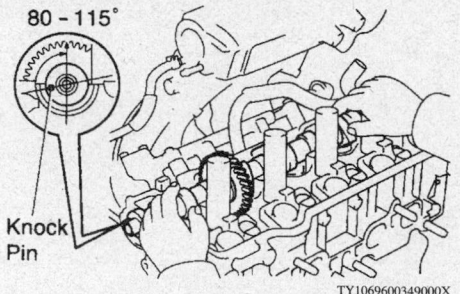

Fig. 10 Intake camshaft installation

TY1069600349000X

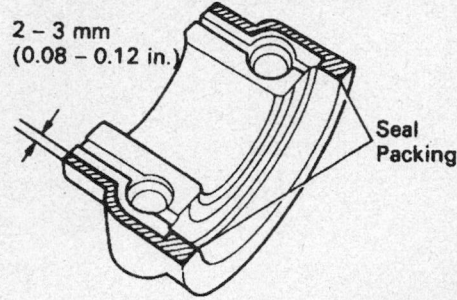

Fig. 11 No. 1 bearing cap seal packing

TY1069600350000X

Fig. 12 Intake camshaft bearing cap installation

TY1069600351000X

Fig. 13 Intake camshaft bearing cap bolt tightening sequence

TY1069600352000X

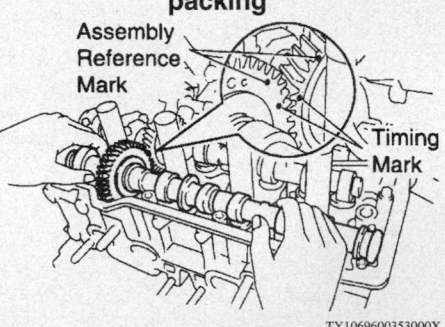

Fig. 14 Camshaft gear timing mark alignment

TY1069600353000X

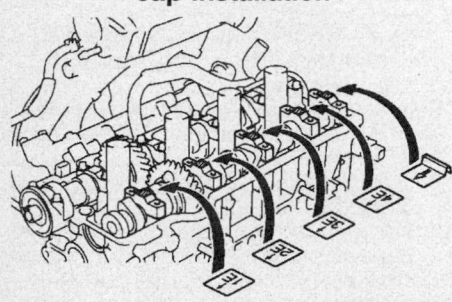

Fig. 15 Exhaust camshaft bearing cap installation

TY1069600354000X

Fig. 16 Exhaust camshaft bearing cap bolt tightening sequence

TY1069600355000X

31. Disconnect fuel inlet hose from fuel filter.
32. Remove EGR valve and vacuum modulator.
33. Remove intake manifold stay.
34. **On models equipped with automatic transaxle,** disconnect throttle control cable from intake manifold.
35. **On all models,** disconnect power steering idle-up air hoses from air tube.
36. Disconnect knock sensor connector.
37. Remove VSV for EGR.
38. Remove two bolts and accelerator cable bracket.
39. Disconnect PCV hose from intake manifold.
40. Disconnect engine wire protector from two mounting bolts of upper (No. 2) timing belt cover.
41. Remove four cylinder head cover nuts, head cover and gasket.
42. Disconnect four fuel injector connectors.
43. Disconnect A/C compressor connector, if equipped.
44. Disconnect crankshaft position sensor connector.
45. Remove righthand scuff plate, righthand cowl side trim and righthand floor carpet center cover, **Fig. 3.**
46. Disconnect engine wire from passen-

ger compartment.
47. Disconnect two ECM connectors and connector from junction box No. 4.
48. Pull engine wire from passenger compartment.
49. Disconnect timing belt from camshaft timing pulley.
50. Remove timing pulley.
51. Remove No. 1 idler pulley and tension spring.
52. Remove camshafts as follows:
   a. Set knock pin of intake camshaft at 10–45° BTDC of camshaft angle, **Fig. 4.** This allows the No. 2 and No. 4 cylinder cam lobes of the exhaust camshaft to push valve lifters evenly.
   b. Secure exhaust camshaft sub gear to drive gear with service bolt, **Fig. 5.**
   c. Remove two bolts and rear bearing cap.
   d. Using sequence shown in **Fig. 6,** uniformly loosen and remove six bolts on No. 1, No. 2 and No. 4 bearing caps.
   e. Remove No. 1, No. 2 and No. 4 bearing caps.
   f. Remove No. 3 bearing cap and exhaust camshaft.
   g. Set knock pin of intake camshaft at 80–115° BTDC of camshaft angle. This allows the No. 1 and No. 3 cylinder cam lobes of the intake camshaft to push valve lifters evenly.
   h. Remove two bolts, front bearing cap and oil seal.
   i. Using sequence shown in **Fig. 7,** uniformly loosen and remove six bolts on No. 1, No. 3 and No. 4 bearing caps.
   j. Remove No. 2 bearing cap and in-

take camshaft.
53. Using sequence shown in **Fig. 8,** uniformly loosen and remove 10 cylinder head bolts.
54. Lift cylinder head from cylinder block dowels.
55. Disconnect air hose from intake manifold, then remove air tube.
56. Remove intake manifold and gasket.
57. Remove delivery pipe and fuel injectors.
58. Remove oil pressure switch.

INSTALLATION

1. Install oil pressure switch. Apply suitable adhesive (Three Bond 1344 or equivalent) to switch threads.
2. Install fuel injectors and delivery pipe.
3. Install air hose for air assist system to cylinder head.
4. Install intake manifold with new gasket to cylinder head. Tighten to specifications.
5. Install air tube and connect air hose to intake manifold.
6. Place cylinder head on engine block

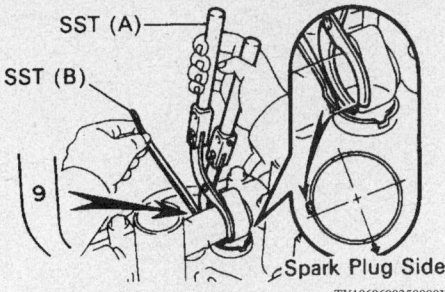

SST (A)
SST (B)
9
Spark Plug Side
TY1069600358000X

Fig. 17 Valve clearance adjustment

Shim No.	Thickness	Shim No.	Thickness
1	2.500 (0.0984)	10	2.950 (0.1161)
2	2.550 (0.1004)	11	3.000 (0.1181)
3	2.600 (0.1024)	12	3.050 (0.1201)
4	2.650 (0.1043)	13	3.100 (0.1220)
5	2.700 (0.1063)	14	3.150 (0.1240)
6	2.750 (0.1083)	15	3.200 (0.1260)
7	2.800 (0.1102)	16	3.250 (0.1280)
8	2.850 (0.1122)	17	3.300 (0.1299)
9	2.900 (0.1142)		

New shim thickness   mm (in.)

TY1069600359000X

Fig. 18 Intake adjustment shims

Shim No.	Thickness	Shim No.	Thickness
1	2.500 (0.0984)	10	2.950 (0.1161)
2	2.550 (0.1004)	11	3.000 (0.1181)
3	2.600 (0.1024)	12	3.050 (0.1201)
4	2.650 (0.1043)	13	3.100 (0.1220)
5	2.700 (0.1063)	14	3.150 (0.1240)
6	2.750 (0.1083)	15	3.200 (0.1260)
7	2.800 (0.1102)	16	3.250 (0.1280)
8	2.850 (0.1122)	17	3.300 (0.1299)
9	2.900 (0.1142)		

New shim thickness   mm (in.)

TY1069600360000X

Fig. 19 Exhaust adjustment shims

with new gasket.

7. Install cylinder head bolts, then using sequence shown in **Fig. 9**, tighten bolts in two steps. First step, **torque** bolts 36 ft. lbs.; second step, tighten bolts an additional 90°.
8. Install spark plug tubes and tighten to specifications.
9. Install camshafts as follows:
   a. Apply MP grease to thrust portion of intake camshaft, then place intake camshaft on cylinder head at 80–115° BTDC, **Fig. 10**.
   b. Install new intake camshaft oil seal.
   c. Apply seal packing, part No. 08826-00080, or equivalent, to No. 1 bearing cap, **Fig. 11**.
   d. Install bearing caps in proper locations, **Fig. 12**.
   e. Uniformly tighten bearing cap bolts to specification using sequence, **Fig. 13**.
   f. Set knock pin of intake camshaft at 10–45° BTDC of camshaft angle, **Fig. 4**.
   g. Apply MP grease to thrust portion of exhaust camshaft, then engage exhaust camshaft gear to intake camshaft gear by aligning timing marks on each gear, **Fig. 14**. Do not use **assembly reference marks shown in illustration.**
   h. Install exhaust camshaft bearing caps in proper locations, **Fig. 15**.
   i. Tighten bearing cap bolts to specification using sequence shown in **Fig. 16**.
10. Check and adjust valve clearance as outlined under " Valve Adjustment."
11. Apply new packing material to semi-circular plugs and install both plugs to cylinder head.
12. Install No. 3 timing belt cover and tighten to specifications.
13. Temporarily install No. 1 idler pulley and tension spring.
14. Install camshaft timing pulley and timing belt as outlined under "Timing Belt, Replace."
15. Install engine wire protector to two brackets on front of intake manifold.
16. Connect four fuel injector connectors. Nos. 1 and 3 connectors are brown, and Nos. 2 and 4 connectors are gray.
17. Install engine wire protector to lefthand side of intake manifold.
18. Push engine wire through cowl panel, **Fig. 3**.
19. Install engine wire clamp to bracket, then connect wire.

20. Connect ECM connectors, junction box No. 4 connector and two bracket connectors.
21. Install righthand floor carpet cover, righthand cowl side trim and righthand scuff plate.
22. Install cylinder head cover with four grommets and tighten bolts to specifications.
23. Install engine wire protector to two mounting bolts of No. 2 timing belt cover.
24. Connect three clamps to No. 2 timing belt cover and alternator belt adjusting bar.
25. Connect crankshaft position sensor connector.
26. Connect A/C compressor connector.
27. Connect PCV hose to intake manifold.
28. Install accelerator cable bracket.
29. Install VSV for EGR.
30. Connect ground cable to intake manifold.
31. Connect knock sensor connector.
32. Connect power steering idle-up air hose to air tube.
33. **On models equipped with automatic transaxle,** connect throttle control cable to intake manifold.
34. **On all models,** install intake manifold stay and tighten to specifications.
35. Install EGR valve and vacuum modulator.
36. Connect two vacuum hoses to VSV for EGR.
37. Connect fuel inlet hose to fuel filter.
38. Install vacuum sensor hose to gas filter on intake manifold.
39. Install brake booster vacuum hose to intake manifold.
40. Install ground strap to intake manifold.
41. Install throttle body.
42. Install water bypass pipe with new gasket and O-ring.
43. Connect IAC valve water bypass hose to water bypass pipe.
44. Connect heater water hose to water bypass pipe.
45. Connect two oil cooler water bypass hoses to oil cooler.
46. Install oil cooler heat protector.
47. Install water outlet, then connect the following hoses:
    a. Radiator.
    b. Water bypass.
    c. Heater water.
    d. IAC valve water bypass.
48. Connect ECT sensor and sender

gauge connectors.
49. Connect oil pressure switch connector.
50. Install catalytic converter to exhaust manifold, then install lower manifold heat insulator.
51. Install two catalytic converter heat insulators.
52. Install oxygen sensor (bank 1/sensor 1) to exhaust manifold.
53. Install oxygen sensor (bank 1/sensor 2) to front of catalytic converter.
54. Install exhaust manifold and front catalytic converter assembly.
55. Connect oxygen sensor electrical connectors, then install front exhaust pipe.
56. Install distributor as outlined under "Distributor, Replace" in "Electrical" section.
57. Install alternator, then the air cleaner case and cap.
58. Connect accelerator cable to throttle body and cable bracket.
59. **On models equipped with automatic transaxle,** connect throttle cable to throttle body and cable bracket.
60. **On all models,** fill engine coolant and oil, then start engine and check for leaks.
61. Install righthand engine under cover.

VALVE CLEARANCE SPECIFICATIONS

Refer to "Tune Up Specifications" for valve clearance.

VALVE ADJUSTMENT

1. Disconnect power steering reservoir.
2. Disconnect accelerator cable from throttle body and clamp on intake manifold.
3. Disconnect accelerator cable from clamp on generator bracket.
4. Disconnect throttle control cable from throttle body.
5. Disconnect PCV hose from air cleaner hose and intake manifold.
6. Disconnect spark plug wires.
7. Remove accelerator cable bracket from intake manifold.
8. Disconnect engine wire protector from two No. 2 timing belt cover mounting bolts.
9. Remove cylinder head cover.
10. Turn crankshaft pulley and align

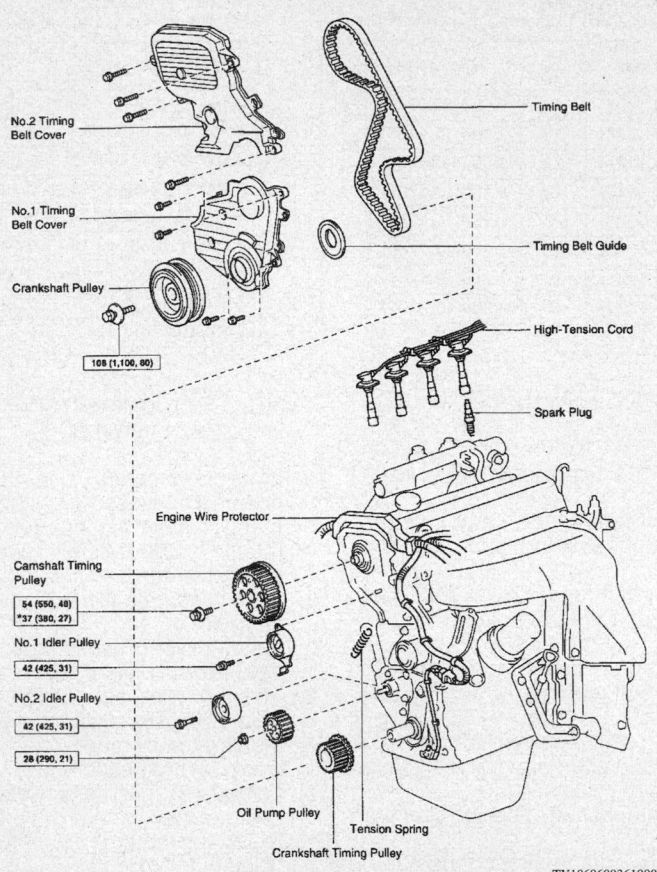

Fig. 20 Timing belt replacement

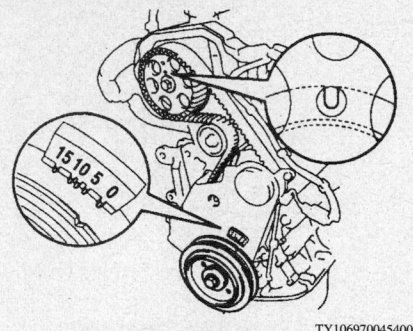

Fig. 21 Timing belt alignment marks

groove with "0" timing mark of timing belt cover. This will set No. 1 cylinder to TDC on compression.

11. Using feeler gauge, measure clearance between valve lifters and camshaft for valve No. 1 intake and exhaust, No. 2 exhaust and No. 3 intake.

12. Turn crankshaft 360° and check clearance of remaining valves.

13. Refer to "Valve Clearance Specifications" for standard cold clearance specifications.

14. If valve clearance falls out of specification, adjust as follows:
  a. Turn crankshaft so that cam lobe on adjusting valve points upward.
  b. Position notch of valve lifter facing spark plug side.
  c. Using tool No. 09248-55040 (A), or equivalent, press down valve lifter and place tool No. 09248-55040 (B), or equivalent, between camshaft and valve lifter, **Fig. 17.**
  d. Remove tool (A).
  e. Remove adjusting shim with screwdriver and magnetic finger.
  f. Using a micrometer, measure thickness of removed shim.
  g. Determine difference between desired and actual valve clearance measurement, then add difference to dimension of measured shim. Refer to shim charts, **Figs. 18 and 19,** to select a replacement shim.
  h. Place new adjusting shim on valve lifter, then remove tool (B).

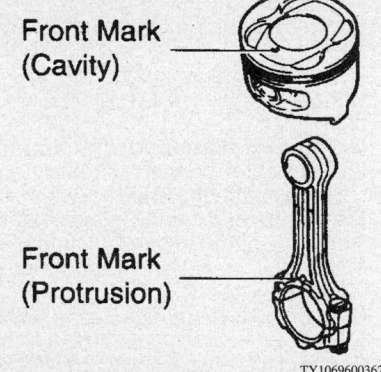

Fig. 22 Piston & rod assembly

  i. Recheck valve clearances.

TIMING BELT
REPLACE

1. Disconnect power steering reservoir and remove reservoir bracket.
2. Disconnect wire harness bracket for DLC1.
3. Remove alternator and bracket.
4. **On models equipped with anti-lock brakes,** remove ABS actuator.
5. **On all models,** remove righthand front wheel and righthand engine under cover.
6. Remove power steering pump drive belt.
7. Place jack under oil pan and raise en-gine enough to remove weight from righthand engine mounting.
8. Remove righthand engine mounting insulator.
9. Remove spark plugs.
10. Using bolt removal tool No. 09213-54015, or equivalent, and bolt (No. 91121-40665), remove crankshaft pulley bolt, **Fig. 20.**
11. Using pulley removal tool No. 09950-50010, or equivalent, remove crankshaft pulley.
12. Remove righthand engine mounting bracket using tool No. 09249-63010, or equivalent.
13. Disconnect engine wire from No. 2 timing belt cover and remove No. 2 timing belt cover.
14. Temporarily install crankshaft pulley with pulley set key aligned with key groove of pulley.
15. Turn crankshaft pulley and align its groove with timing mark " 0" of No. 1 timing belt cover, **Fig. 21.** This will set No. 1 cylinder to TDC on compression.
16. Loosen mounting bolt of No. 1 idler pulley and shift pulley toward left as far as it will go, then temporarily tighten.
17. Remove timing belt from camshaft timing pulley.
18. Using pulley removal tool Nos. 09249-63010 and 09960-10010, or equivalents, remove camshaft timing pulley.
19. Remove crankshaft pulley.
20. Disconnect engine wire from No. 1 timing belt cover, then remove No. 1 timing belt cover.
21. Remove timing belt guide, then the timing belt.
22. Remove both idler pulleys and tension spring.
23. Remove crankshaft timing pulley and oil pump pulley.
24. Reverse procedure to install. Tighten all fasteners to specifications.

CAMSHAFT
REPLACE

Refer to "Cylinder Head, Replace" for procedure.

PISTON & ROD ASSEMBLY

Piston and rod assemblies are marked as shown in **Fig. 22** to indicate the front.

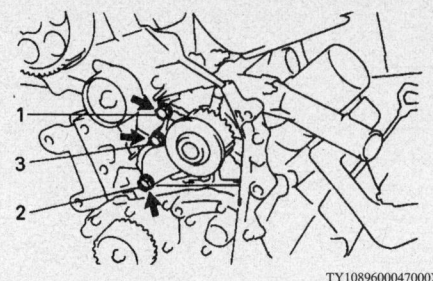

Fig. 23 Water pump bolt removal sequence

Pistons are available in three standard sizes and one oversize. Oversize pistons are available in 3.4004–3.4016 inches. The top of the piston is marked with either a 1, 2 or 3 to indicate standard sizes as follows:
1. Mark "1" (3.3807–3.3811 inches).
2. Mark "2" (3.3811–3.3815 inches).
3. Mark "3" (3.3815–3.3819 inches).

MAIN & ROD BEARINGS

Rod bearings are available in undersizes of .010 inch and three standard sizes marked on connecting rod cap with a 1, 2 or 3. Main bearings are available in standard sizes or in undersizes of .010 inch.

OIL PAN
REPLACE

1. Remove hood and righthand engine under cover.
2. Drain engine oil.
3. Remove front exhaust pipe.
4. Remove stiffener plate.
5. Remove engine oil dipstick.
6. Remove oil pan bolts, cut off applied oil pan sealer material and pry pan loose with suitable tool.
7. Reverse procedure to install. Clear old pan gasket material, apply new gasket and tighten oil pan bolts to specifications.

OIL PUMP
REPLACE

1. Remove oil pan as outlined under "Oil Pan, Replace."
2. Remove oil pan baffle plate and oil strainer.
3. Suspend engine with engine hanger and sling device, tool Nos. 12281-74060 and 91611-B1020, or equivalents.
4. Remove timing belt as outlined under "Timing Belt, Replace."
5. Remove oil pump pulley using pulley removal tool No. 09960-10010, or equivalent.
6. Disconnect crankshaft position sensor connector and remove sensor.

7. Remove oil pump mounting bolts, then the oil pump.
8. Reverse procedure to install. Tighten bolts to specifications.

BELT TENSION DATA

Year	Belt	New, Lbs.	Used, Lbs.
1996	Alternator	140-190①	100-120①
		100-150②	75-115②
	Power Steer.	95-145	60-100
	A/C Comp.	139-192	66-99
1997-99	Alternator	140-190①	100-120①
		100-150②	75-115②
	Power Steer.	95-145	60-100
	A/C Comp.	140-190	100-120

① — With A/C.
② — Less A/C.

COOLING SYSTEM BLEED

These engines do not require a specific bleed procedure. After filling cooling system, run engine to operating temperature with radiator/pressure cap off. Air will then be automatically bled through cap opening.

THERMOSTAT
REPLACE

1. Drain engine coolant.
2. Remove oil filter.
3. Remove two nuts and disconnect water inlet from water pump cover.
4. Remove thermostat and gasket.
5. Reverse procedure to install.

WATER PUMP
REPLACE

1. Remove engine under cover and drain engine coolant.
2. Remove timing belt as outlined under "Timing Belt, Replace."
3. Disconnect lower radiator hose from water inlet.
4. Remove timing belt tension spring and No. 2 idler pulley.
5. Remove alternator drive belt adjusting bar.
6. Remove two nuts attaching water pump to water bypass pipe.
7. Remove three bolts from water pump cover in sequence shown, **Fig. 23**.
8. Disconnect water pump cover from water bypass pipe and remove water pump cover assembly.
9. Remove water pump from water pump cover.
10. Reverse procedure to install. Tighten

pump cover bolts to specifications in reverse order of removal sequence shown in **Fig. 23**.

RADIATOR
REPLACE

1. Remove engine under covers and drain engine coolant.
2. **On models equipped with A/C,** remove condenser core, then disconnect No. 2 cooling fan connector.
3. **On all models,** disconnect No. 1 cooling fan connector, then the ECT switch connector for the electric cooling fan.
4. Disconnect engine wire clamp from No. 1 cooling fan shroud.
5. Disconnect upper and lower radiator hoses.
6. Disconnect radiator overflow reservoir hose from radiator.
7. Disconnect two automatic transaxle oil cooler hoses from oil cooler pipes, if equipped.
8. Remove upper radiator supports, then the radiator.
9. Remove lower radiator supports.
10. **On models equipped with A/C,** remove three No. 2 cooling fan assembly from radiator.
11. **On all models,** remove No. 1 cooling fan from radiator.
12. Reverse procedure to install.

FUEL PUMP
REPLACE

1. Relieve fuel system pressure as outlined under "Precautions."
2. Remove floor service hole cover.
3. Disconnect fuel pump connector.
4. Start engine and wait for engine to shut off on its own before turning ignition switch off. This will relieve fuel system pressure.
5. Disconnect ground strap from fuel pump clamp.
6. Pull off lower side of fuel pump from pump bracket.
7. Disconnect fuel hose from fuel pump, then remove fuel pump.
8. Reverse procedure to install.

FUEL FILTER
REPLACE

1. Relieve fuel system pressure as outlined under "Precautions."
2. Disconnect ground strap from fuel pump clamp.
3. Pull off lower side of fuel pump from pump bracket.
4. Disconnect fuel hose from fuel pump, then remove fuel pump.
5. Using small screwdriver, remove clip at top of fuel pump and pull out pump filter.
6. Reverse procedure to install.

TIGHTENING SPECIFICATIONS

Component	Torque/Ft. Lbs.
Alternator Bracket	31
Camshaft Bearing Cap	14
Catalytic Converter To Exhaust Manifold	22
Crankshaft Pulley Bolt	80
Cylinder Head Bolts	①
Cylinder Head Cover Bolts	17
Distributor Mounting Bolt	14
Exhaust Manifold Mounting Bolts	36
Intake Manifold Bolts	14
Intake Manifold Stay	14
Main Bearing Cap Bolts	43
No. 1 Idler Pulley Bolt	31
No. 2 Idler Pulley Bolt	31
No. 3 Timing Belt Cover	72②
Oil Pump Pulley Bolt	18
Oxygen Sensor (Catalytic Converter)	33
Oxygen Sensor (Exhaust Manifold)	14
Power Steering Pump Adjustment Bolt	39
Power Steering Pump Through Bolt	32
Rear End Plate To Cylinder Block	84②
Rear Oil Seal Retainer	108②
RH Engine Mounting Bracket To Cylinder Block	38
RH Mounting Insulator To Body	47
RH Mounting Insulator To Mounting Bracket	27
Spark Plug Tube	29
Water Bypass Pipe To Engine	14
Water Bypass Pipe To Pump Cover	84②
Water Outlet To Cylinder Head	11

① — Refer to "Cylinder Head, Replace."

② — Inch lbs.

2RZ-FE 2.4L & 3RZ-FE 2.7L Engines

NOTE: On Air Bag Equipped Models, Refer To "Air Bag System Precautions" Located In The Front Of This Manual For System Disarming & Arming Procedures.

INDEX

PRECAUTIONS

AIR BAG SYSTEMS

Refer to "Air Bag System Precautions" in the front of this manual for system disarming and arming procedures.

AUDIO CODED ANTI-THEFT SYSTEM

Some models are equipped with an audio coded anti-theft system that will disable the radio when the battery cable is disconnected. The system can be identified by the "ANTI-THEFT SYSTEM" on the cassette lid. Obtain three-digit code for input. Reset system after service as follows:

1. Obtain three-digit audio theft code.
2. Depress 1 (PROG) button while depressing righthand side of TUNE SEEK button. Three dashes will appear in tape operation display.
3. To enter first digit, depress 1 (PROG) button repeatedly until number of times depressed equals first digit (depress 1 button six times if first digit is five, first press equals 0).
4. To enter second digit, depress 2 (APS) button repeatedly until number of times depressed equals second digit.
5. To enter third digit, depress 3 (RPT) button repeatedly until number of times depressed equals third digit.
6. If three dashes are displayed after inputting digits, repeat procedure.
7. When code appears in display, depress and hold SCAN button until SEC appears.
8. When SEC disappears audio system is operative.
9. If Err is displayed, repeat procedure. **Attempting to input code more than nine times may permanently disable audio system.**

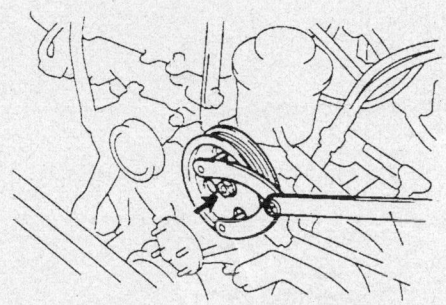

TY1069100230000X

Fig. 1 Power steering pump pulley removal

BATTERY GROUND CABLE

Prior to service, disconnect battery ground cable and isolate as required.

COMPRESSION PRESSURE

1. Start engine and warm to normal operating temperature.
2. Disconnect intake air connector.
3. Disconnect high tension cords from spark plugs and distributor.
4. Remove spark plugs.
5. Insert compression gauge into spark plug hole.
6. Fully open throttle.
7. While cranking engine, measure compression pressure.
8. Standard compression pressure should be 178 psi. Minimum compression is 127 psi.
9. The difference in compression pressure between each cylinder should not exceed 14 psi.

ENGINE

REPLACE

1. **On models equipped with audio coded anti-theft system,** obtain three-digit system code.
2. **On all models,** remove battery, then the engine under covers.
3. Drain engine coolant and oil, drain transmission oil.
4. Make alignment marks on hood hinges, then remove hood.
5. Remove grill and radiator as follows:
   a. Remove two screws holding lefthand and righthand clearance lights, then the lights.
   b. Remove four screws and 11 clips holding grill, then the grill.
   c. Remove radiator hoses, then the radiator reservoir tank.
   d. Remove drive belts, then the cooling fan and fan shroud as a unit.
   e. Remove four radiator mounting bolts, then the radiator.
6. Remove MAF sensor, IAT sensor, air hose and upper air cleaner as a unit, then the lower air cleaner housing.
7. Disconnect throttle cable from throttle body, then remove intake air connector tube.
8. **On models equipped with A/C,** remove compressor without disconnecting hoses or discharging system. Move and secure compressor aside. Remove compressor mount bracket from engine.
9. **On all models,** disconnect heater hoses, brake booster hose and emission system hoses. Disconnect fuel system pressure and return hoses,
10. **On models equipped with power steering,** remove power steering pump pulley using flexible Y wrench, tool No. 09960-10010, or equivalent,

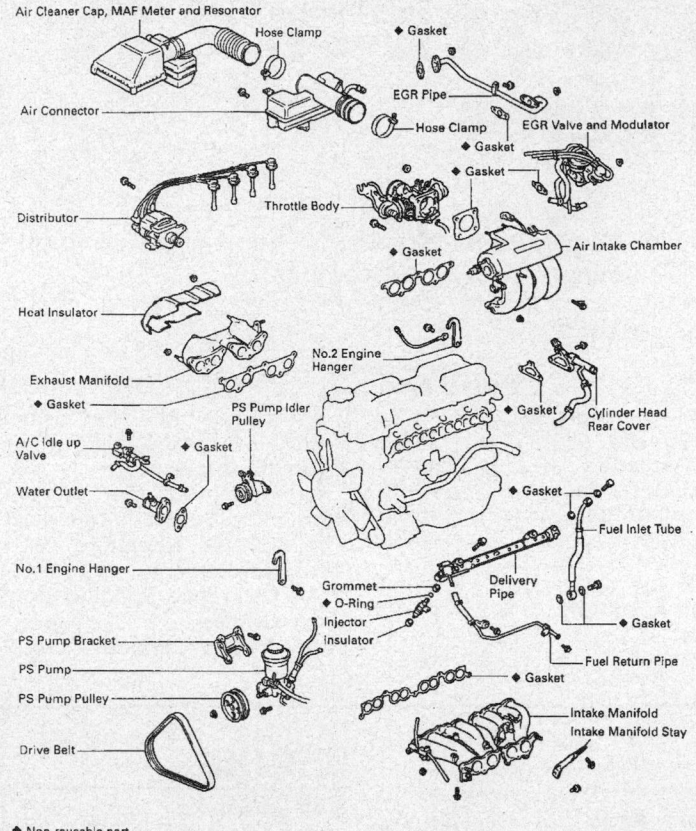

Fig. 3 Crankshaft to No. 1 cylinder TDC alignment

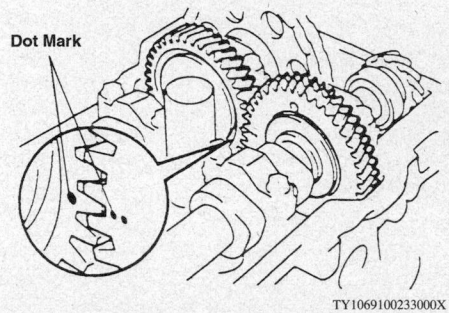

Fig. 4 Camshaft to No. 1 cylinder TDC alignment

Fig. 2 Exploded view of engine components

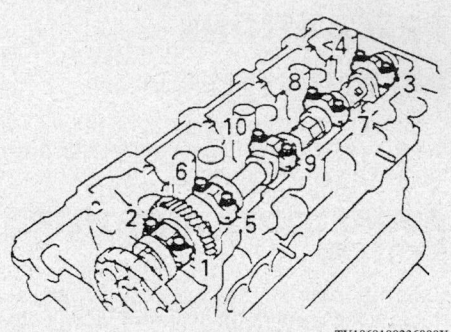

Fig. 7 Intake camshaft bolt loosening sequence

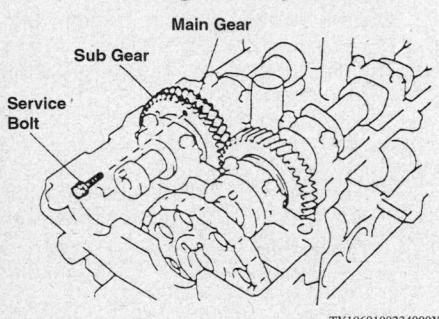

Fig. 5 Service bolt installation

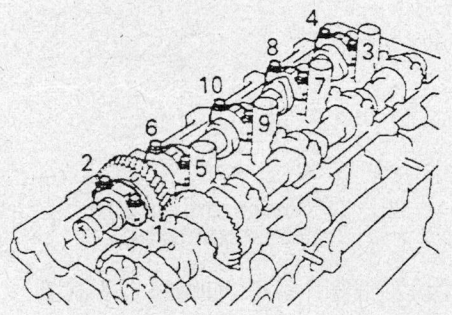

Fig. 6 Exhaust camshaft bolt loosening sequence

to hold pulley, **Fig. 1.** Then, without disconnecting hoses, remove power steering pump and position aside.

11. **On all models,** disconnect wires from alternator.
12. Remove righthand side door scuff plate and kick panel trim. Remove ECM, then disconnect engine compartment wiring, prepare wiring to be pulled through cowl into engine compartment.
13. In engine compartment disconnect engine harness from igniter. Remove ground strap bolt, disconnect harness support clamps, then pull engine harness through firewall.
14. Remove gear shift knob and boot, then the lever by removing six bolts holding shifter housing to transmission.
15. Remove front anti-sway bar, then the complete driveshaft. Place match-marks on driveshaft and differential flanges. Install suitable sealing tool

into transmission tailshaft housing to prevent leakage.
16. Disconnect speedometer cable and both oxygen sensor connectors, then remove front exhaust pipe.
17. Remove clutch slave cylinder, then disconnect starter wiring.
18. Support transmission using suitable equipment, then remove transmission mount bracket from frame and transmission.
19. Attach suitable equipment to engine, remove righthand and lefthand motor mount bolts, then lift engine and transmission from vehicle.
20. Separate engine from transmission.
21. Reverse procedure to install. Reset audio coded anti-theft system, if equipped, as outlined under "Precautions."

INTAKE MANIFOLD
REPLACE

Refer to "Cylinder Head, Replace" for procedure.

CYLINDER HEAD
REPLACE

1. **On models equipped with audio coded anti-theft system,** obtain three-digit system code.
2. **On all models,** drain coolant from engine.
3. Remove MAF sensor, IAT sensor, air hose and upper air cleaner as a unit, then the lower air cleaner housing, **Fig. 2.**
4. Disconnect throttle cable from throttle body, then remove intake air connector tube.
5. **On models equipped with A/C,** remove A/C idle-up valve.
6. **On models equipped with power steering,** proceed as follows:
   a. Remove power steering belt and idler pulley.

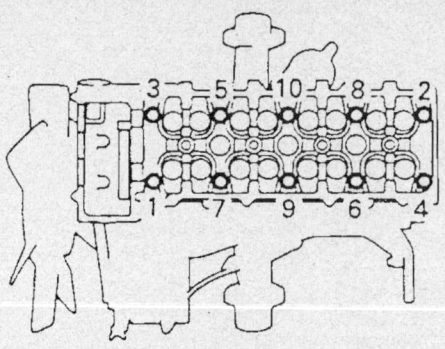

TY1069100237000X

Fig. 8 Cylinder head bolt loosening sequence

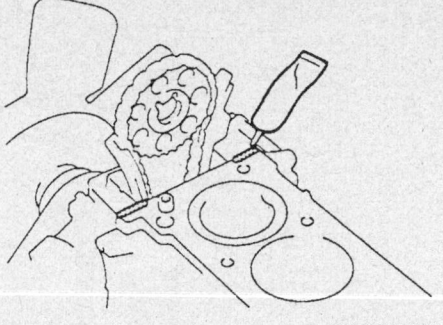

TY1069100238000X

Fig. 9 Cylinder head sealer application

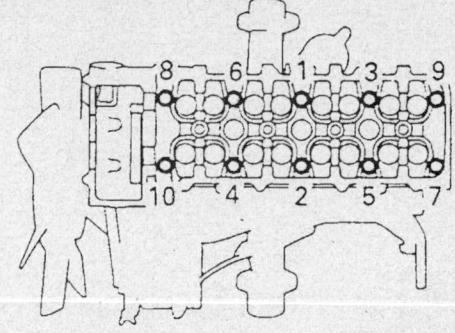

TY1069100239000X

Fig. 10 Cylinder head bolt tightening sequence

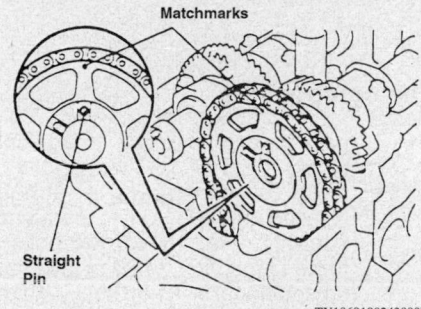

TY1069100240000X

Fig. 11 Intake camshaft bearing cap installation locations

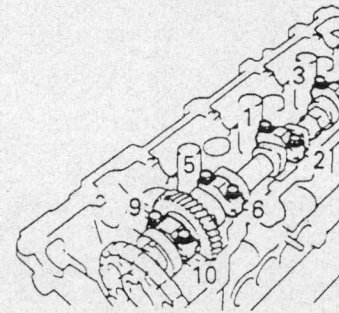

TY1069100241000X

Fig. 12 Intake camshaft bearing cap bolt tightening sequence

Straight Pin

Aligh (Dot Mark)

TY1069100242000X

Fig. 13 Exhaust to intake camshaft timing marks

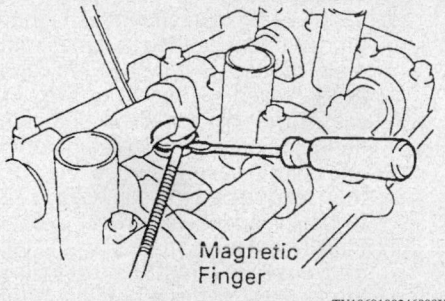

Matchmarks

Straight Pin

TY1069100243000X

Fig. 14 Camshaft alignment marks

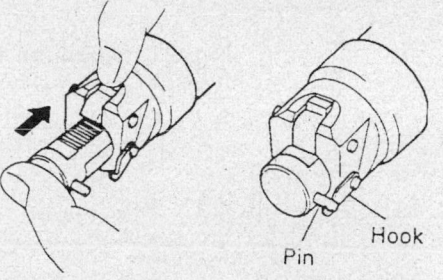

Pin   Hook

TY1069100244000X

Fig. 15 Timing chain tensioner

9

TY1069100245000X

Fig. 16 Valve lifter compressing

Magnetic Finger

TY1069100246000X

Fig. 17 Valve adjustment shim removal

New shim thickness   mm (in.)

Shim No.	Thickness	Shim No.	Thickness
1	2.500 (0.0984)	10	2.950 (0.1161)
2	2.550 (0.1004)	11	3.000 (0.1181)
3	2.600 (0.1024)	12	3.050 (0.1201)
4	2.650 (0.1043)	13	3.100 (0.1220)
5	2.700 (0.1063)	14	3.150 (0.1240)
6	2.750 (0.1083)	15	3.200 (0.1260)
7	2.800 (0.1102)	16	3.250 (0.1280)
8	2.850 (0.1122)	17	3.300 (0.1299)
9	2.900 (0.1142)		

TY1069100247000X

Fig. 18 Intake camshaft shim table

New shim thickness   mm (in.)

Shim No.	Thickness	Shim No.	Thickness
1	2.500 (0.0984)	10	2.950 (0.1161)
2	2.550 (0.1004)	11	3.000 (0.1181)
3	2.600 (0.1024)	12	3.050 (0.1201)
4	2.650 (0.1043)	13	3.100 (0.1220)
5	2.700 (0.1063)	14	3.150 (0.1240)
6	2.750 (0.1083)	15	3.200 (0.1260)
7	2.800 (0.1102)	16	3.250 (0.1280)
8	2.850 (0.1122)	17	3.300 (0.1299)
9	2.900 (0.1142)		

TY1069100248000X

Fig. 19 Exhaust camshaft shim table

b. Remove power steering pump pulley using flexible Y wrench, tool No. 09960-10010, or equivalent, to hold pulley, **Fig. 1.**

c. Then, without disconnecting hoses, remove power steering pump and position aside.

d. Remove power steering pump mounting bracket.

7. **On all models,** disconnect spark plug wires, then disconnect and remove complete distributor.

8. Disconnect and remove water outlet and ECT sender form engine as a unit.

9. Disconnect and remove all connectors and hoses from throttle body, then re-move throttle body.

10. Disconnect all electrical connectors and wiring attached to cylinder head and components.

11. Disconnect heater bypass hose, then

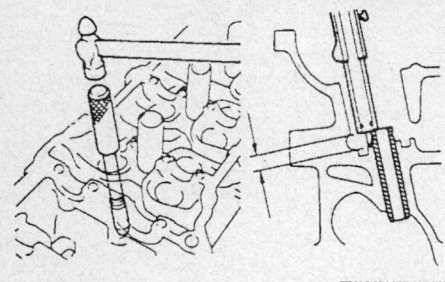

TY1069100249000X

Fig. 20 Valve guide installation

remove cylinder head rear cover.

12. Remove EGR valve, vacuum modulator and connecting pipe, disconnecting necessary water and vacuum lines.

13. Remove intake chamber stay, then the fuel return pipe. When disconnecting fuel lines use a suitable container to collect any spilled fuel, loosen fuel connections slowly to allow pressure to bleed off.

14. Remove bolts to remove intake air chamber from intake manifold, then the fuel inlet tube.

15. Remove fuel delivery pipe and injectors as a unit, then the intake manifold.

16. Disconnect both oxygen sensor connectors, then remove front exhaust pipe.

17. Remove exhaust manifold, then the No. 1 and No. 2 engine hanger hooks.

18. Remove cylinder head cover, then the spark plugs.

19. Turning engine clockwise, set No. 1 cylinder to TDC compression stroke **Figs. 3 and 4.** Remove timing chain tensioner.

20. Remove two rubber semi-circular plugs from head, then place a suitable wrench on the hex part of exhaust camshaft, remove distributor gear and bolt.

21. Place a suitable wrench on hex part of intake camshaft, then remove cam drive sprocket and bolt. Allow chain and sprocket to rest on chain guide rails.

22. Turn exhaust camshaft with a suitable wrench until service bolt hole is accessible, **Fig. 5.** Install a 6 X 1.0 X 16-20 mm bolt into service hole to secure spring loaded sub gear to main exhaust camshaft gear.
    a. Loosen camshaft bearing caps in several stages in sequence shown in **Fig. 6,** then remove bearing caps.
    b. Camshaft must be lifted from head straight and level. **Do not pry or use force. Due to tight tolerances, if cam is not lifted out of cylinder head straight and level, cam or head breakage could occur.** If binding occurs reinstall No. 3 bearing cap, lightly tighten bolts; then while lifting cam gear, loosen bearing cap bolts evenly to allow camshaft to come out of head straight and level.
    c. Repeat steps a and b above to remove intake camshaft, using se-

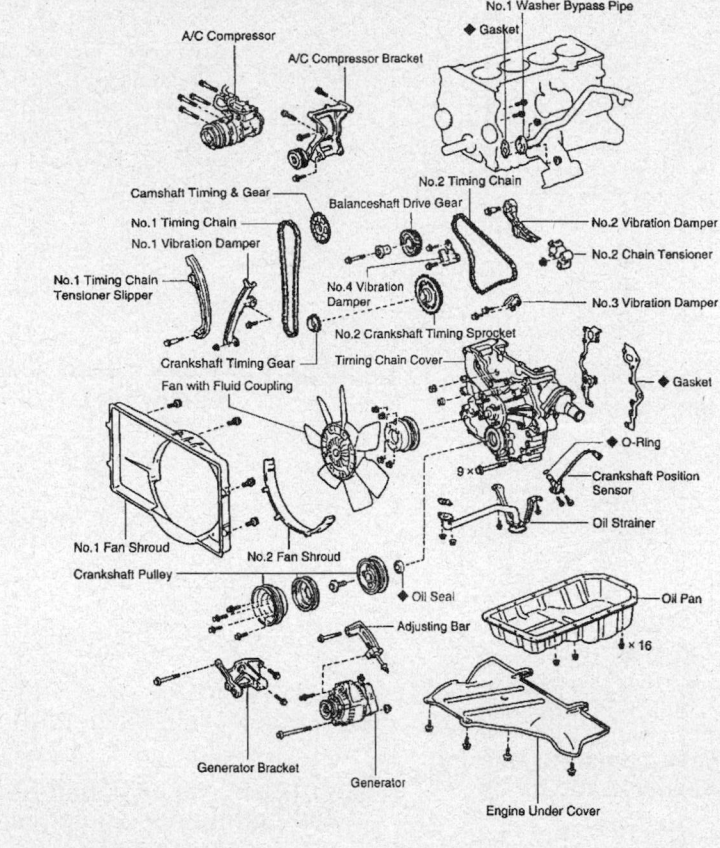

◆ Non-reusable part

TY1069100250000X

Fig. 21 Auxiliary engine components

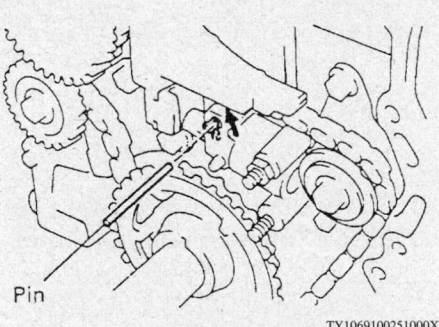

Pin

TY1069100251000X

Fig. 22 Balance shaft timing chain tensioner removal

quence shown in **Fig. 7** to loosen bearing caps.

23. Remove two cylinder head bolts located inside front of cam chain passage, then loosen cylinder head bolts in several stages in sequence shown in **Fig. 8.**

24. Lift cylinder head up off of dowel pins to remove from engine.

25. Remove and store, keeping together in order, lifters, adjustment shims, valves, valve springs and retainers.

26. Reverse procedure to install, noting the following:
    a. Tighten all fasteners to specifications. Before installing head gasket, apply a suitable sealer to areas shown in **Fig. 9,** then place head

gasket and cylinder head onto block.
    b. Install cylinder head bolts with lightly oiled threads. Using sequence shown in **Fig. 10,** torque bolts in three steps: first, to 29 ft. lbs.; then an additional 90°; and finally, an additional 90°.
    c. Install two cylinder head bolts located at front of cam chain well. **Torque** bolts to 15 ft. lbs.
    d. Install intake camshaft first. Lightly grease thrust bearing surfaces with a MP grease. Ensure bearing caps are installed as shown in **Fig. 11** with dowel pin, on drive sprocket flange pointing up. Tighten bearing cap bolts in several stages, **Fig. 12,** then **torque** bearing cap bolts to 12 ft. lbs. in sequence shown.
    e. Install exhaust camshaft using above procedure. Ensure timing marks on camshaft gears are aligned, **Fig. 13.** After bearing cap bolts have been tightened, remove exhaust camshaft gear service bolt.
    f. Set engine to TDC No. 1 cylinder, **Fig. 3.**
    g. Align matchmarks on timing chain to sprocket, then install sprocket to camshaft, **Fig. 14.**
    h. Holding intake camshaft with suitable wrench **torque** sprocket bolt to 54 ft. lbs. Install distributor drive

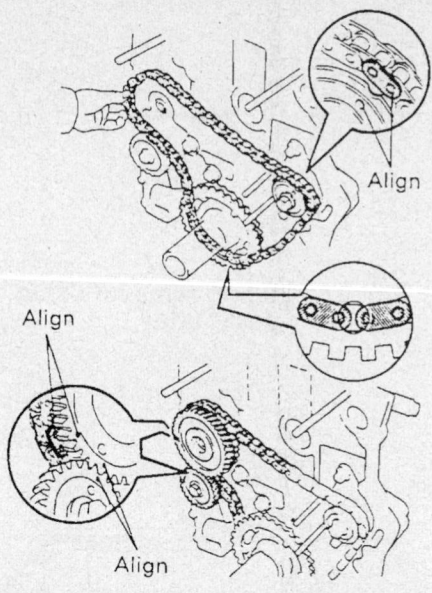

Fig. 23 Balance shaft timing mark alignment

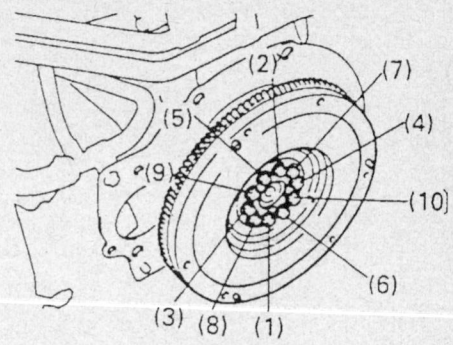

Fig. 24 Piston & rod assembly

Fig. 25 Flywheel bolt tightening sequence

gear, then holding exhaust camshaft with a suitable wrench **torque** drive gear bolt to 34 ft. lbs.

i. Compress and hook chain tensioner pin, **Fig. 15**, then install tensioner. Release tensioner by turning crankshaft counterclockwise or by pressing in on tensioner rail with a screwdriver so that tensioner hook is released.

j. Use new O-rings when installing fuel injectors and distributor. Refer to " Valve Adjustment" for procedures.

k. Reset audio coded anti-theft system, if equipped, as outlined under "Precautions."

VALVE CLEARANCE SPECIFICATIONS

Refer to "Tune Up Specifications" for valve clearance.

VALVE ADJUSTMENT

1. **On models equipped with audio coded anti-theft system,** obtain three-digit system code.
2. **On models equipped with air bag,** disable system as outlined under "Precautions."
3. **On all models,** drain coolant from engine.
4. Remove MAF sensor, IAT sensor, air hose and upper air cleaner as a unit, then the lower air cleaner housing, **Fig. 2.**
5. Disconnect throttle cable from throttle body, then remove intake air connector tube.
6. **On models equipped with A/C,** remove A/C idle-up valve.
7. **On all models,** disconnect spark plug wires.
8. Disconnect and remove all connectors

and hoses from throttle body, then remove throttle body.
9. Disconnect electrical connectors and wiring attached to cylinder head cover, then remove cylinder head cover.
10. With engine cold, set engine to No. 1 cylinder TDC compression stroke by aligning matchmarks shown in **Figs. 3 and 13.**
11. With engine in this position check clearance of the following valves:
    a. No. 1 intake and exhaust valves.
    b. No. 2 intake valves.
    c. No. 3 exhaust valves.
    d. Record these readings.
12. If any measurement was found outside specifications, remove valve adjustment shim using valve lifter cam wrench set tool No. 09248-55040, or equivalent, to depress lifter and a magnet to remove shim, **Figs. 16 and 17.**
13. Using a micrometer measure thickness of removed shim, record this dimension.
14. Determine difference between desired and actual valve clearance measurement, add difference to dimension of measured shim. Refer to shim charts, **Figs. 18 and 19** to select a replacement.
15. Install new shim in lifter, then remove lifter tools. Repeat steps 13 through 16 for any other valves found out of adjustment.
16. Rotate crankshaft pulley two full turns, recheck valves as outlined in steps 11 through 14.
17. Turn crankshaft pulley 360° (one complete revolution) and align timing marks as outlined previously and check the following valves:
    a. No. 2 exhaust valves.
    b. No. 3 intake valves.
    c. No. 4 intake and exhaust valves, record readings, then repeat steps 13 through 16 if necessary.
18. Reverse procedure to install. Reset audio coded anti-theft and air bag system, if equipped, as outlined under "Precautions."

VALVE GUIDES

Valve stem to guide oil clearance should not exceed 0.0031 inch for intake valves

and 0.0039 inch for exhaust. If valve replacement will not bring clearance within standards, guide replacement will be necessary.

1. Using a suitable method, gradually heat cylinder head to 176–212°F.
2. Using valve guide driver tool No. 09201-10000, or equivalent, tap out guide from cylinder side.
3. Using a suitable measuring tool measure bore in cylinder head and select correct guide. Bore measurements between .4331 to .4341 inch. Use a standard guide. Measurements above .4341 require valve guide hole to be rebored to .4350 to .4361 inch and use of an oversize guide.
4. Heat cylinder head as outlined in step 1. Install new valve guide using tool as above and driving in from camshaft side leaving a protrusion of .0323 to .339 inch, **Fig. 20.**
5. Using a sharp .234 inch reamer, ream new valve guide if necessary.

FRONT COVER SEAL
REPLACE

1. Remove crankshaft pulley as outlined under "Oil Pump Replace."
2. Using a suitable tool pry out seal, using care not to damage crankshaft or seal housing.
3. Lubricate lips of new seal, then using seal driver tool No. 09223-50010, or equivalent, drive new seal into place.
4. Reverse procedure to install.

TIMING CHAIN
REPLACE

1. Remove cylinder head as outlined under "Cylinder Head, Replace."
2. Remove front engine cover as outlined under "Oil Pump, Replace."
3. Remove upper timing sprocket and chain, then the crankshaft timing sprocket. If necessary, use gear puller tool No. 09950-20017 with shaft protector tool No. 09213-36020, or equivalents.
4. Reverse procedure to install.

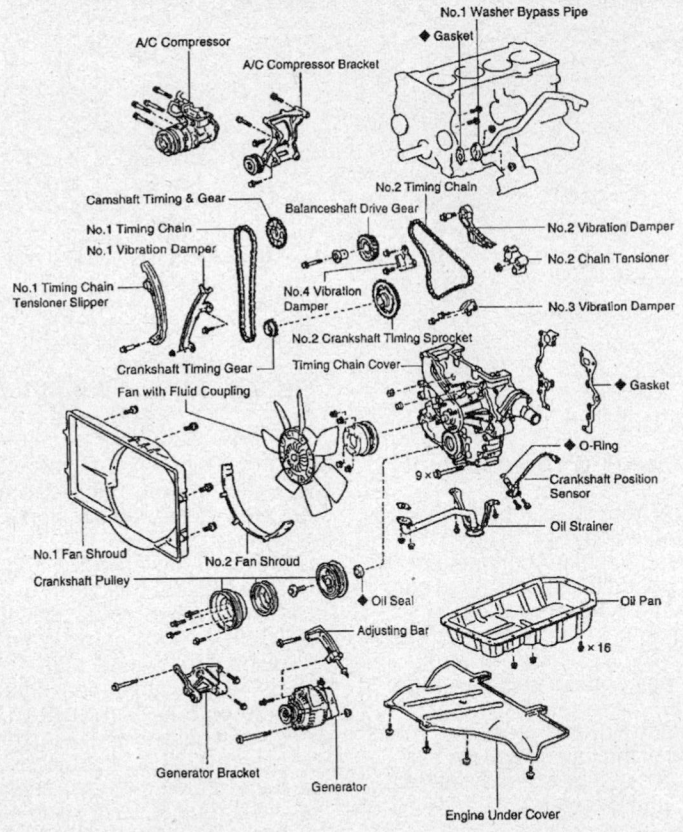

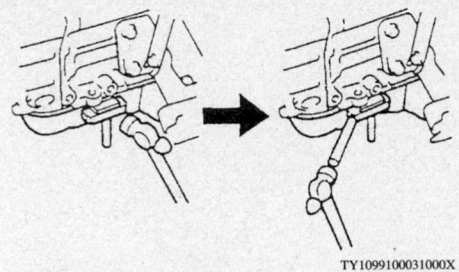

Fig. 27 Oil pan removal using seal cutter

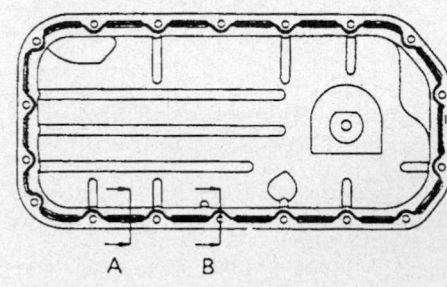

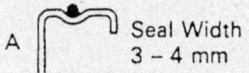

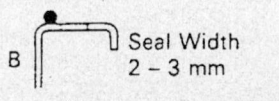

Fig. 30 Oil pan sealer application

♦ Non-reusable part

Fig. 26 Crankshaft position sensor removal

Fig. 28 Water bypass & rear bolts timing chain cover

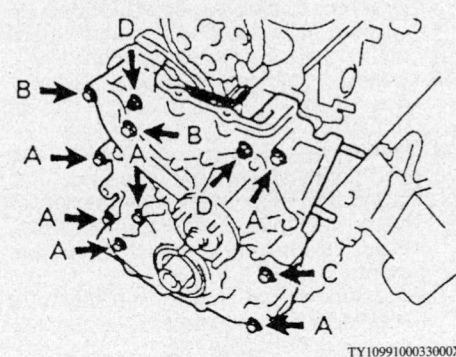

Fig. 29 Bolt tightening, timing chain cover

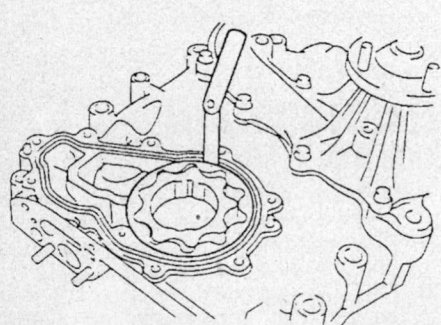

Fig. 31 Oil pump rotor to body measurement

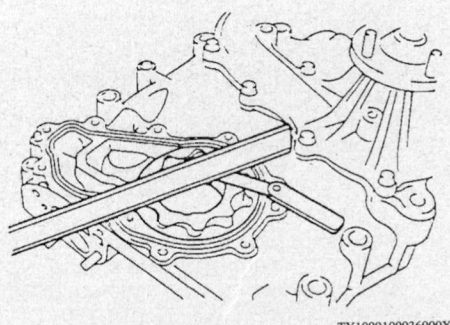

Fig. 32 Oil pump rotor side clearance measurement

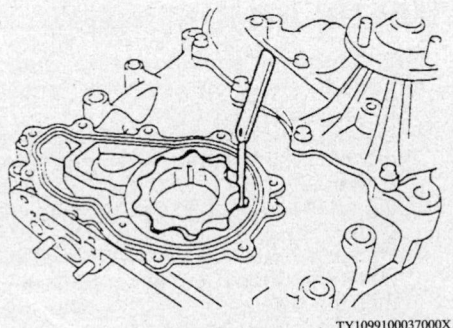

Fig. 33 Oil pump tip clearance measurement

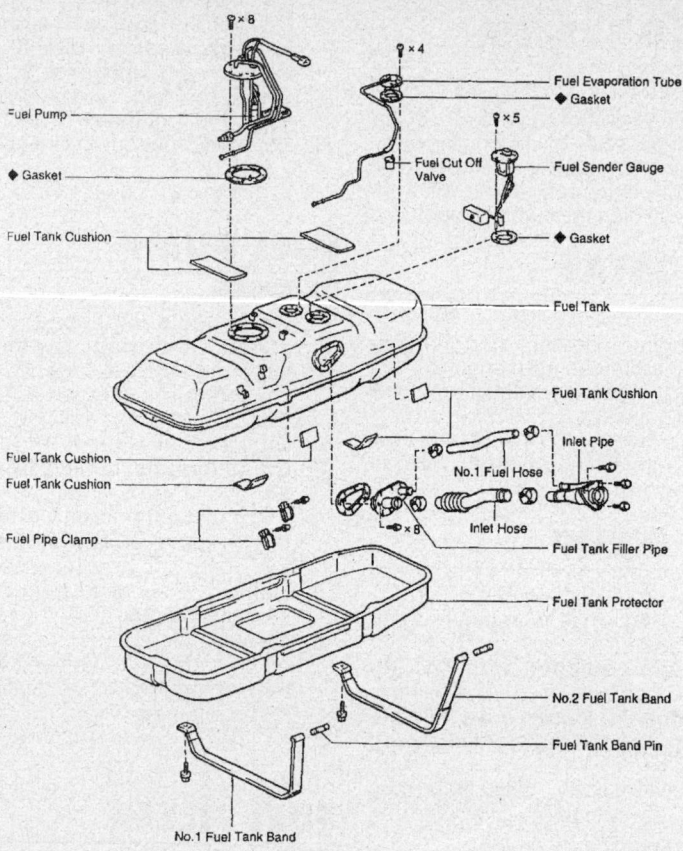

Fig. 34 Fuel tank removal

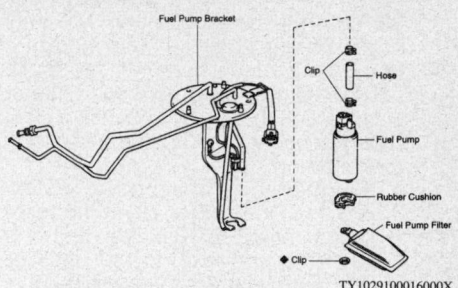

Fig. 35 Fuel pump service

2. Remove clutch as outlined under "Clutch, Replace."
3. Remove flywheel, then using a suitable tool pry out seal, using care not to damage crankshaft or seal housing.
4. Lubricate lips of new seal, then using seal installer tool No. 09223-15030, or equivalent, drive new seal into place.
5. Reverse procedure to install. **Torque** flywheel bolts to 19 ft. lbs. in several stages in pattern shown in **Fig. 25,** then tighten an additional 90° using this pattern. Tighten fasteners to specifications.

OIL PAN
REPLACE

Refer to "Oil Pump, Replace" for procedures.

OIL PUMP
REPLACE

1. Remove cylinder head as outlined under "Cylinder Head, Replace."
2. Remove engine undercover, then the belts.
3. Remove radiator shroud bolts.
4. Remove water pump pulley bolts, then the fan, fan coupling, water pump pulley, and fan shroud.
5. **On models equipped with A/C,** without discharging refrigerant, remove compressor and secure aside, then the compressor mounting bracket.
6. **On all models,** remove alternator, adjusting bracket and mounting bracket.
7. Remove crankshaft position sensor, **Fig. 26.**
8. Remove two engine to transmission stiffener plates, then the oil pan bolts and nuts.
9. Using sealer cutter tool No. 09032-00100, or equivalent, **Fig. 27,** cut sealer to release oil pan. Use caution not to damage flanges.
10. Remove oil strainer and pick-up tube.
11. **On models equipped with A/C,** remove bolts securing V-belt pulley to crankshaft pulley and remove pulley.
12. **On all models,** remove crankshaft pulley nut using holding tool Nos. 09213-54015 and 09330-00021, or equivalents, then the pulley, using gear puller and shaft protector tool Nos. 09213-60017 and 09950-20017, or equivalents, if necessary.
13. Remove two water bypass pipe bolts and two timing chain cover bolts, **Fig.**

CAMSHAFT
REPLACE

Refer to "Cylinder Head, Replace" for camshaft replacement procedures.

BALANCE SHAFT
REPLACE

1. Remove camshaft/No. 1 timing chain as outlined under " Timing Chain, Replace."
2. Remove camshaft/No. 1 timing chain tension slipper and vibration damper, **Fig. 21.**
3. Install a pin into balance shaft/No. 2 timing chain tensioner, **Fig. 22.** Remove No. 2 and No. 3 balance shaft timing chain dampers, **Fig. 21.** Remove tensioner unit.
4. Remove balance shaft drive gear with shaft, lift off chain, slide sprocket off crankshaft.
5. Remove No. 4 balance shaft timing chain dampner.
6. Remove thrust plate retainer bolts, then slide the No. 1 and No. 2 balance shaft from the block.
7. Reverse procedure to install, noting the following:
   a. Fit balance shaft timing chain to crankshaft and balance shaft with sprocket, align match links and marks on sprockets, **Fig. 23.**
   b. Install balance shaft drive gear into chain aligning match link on chain to mark on sprocket part of drive gear, then align match marks of drive gear and balance shaft, **Fig. 23.**
   c. **Torque** drive gear shaft bolt to 18 ft. lbs.
   d. Tighten fasteners to specifications.

PISTON & ROD ASSEMBLY

Pistons are available in standard and one oversize of .020 inch (.50 mm). Place match marks on connecting rod, cap and piston before disassembly. Pistons and rods are marked with a dimple to indicate front, **Fig. 24.**

MAIN & ROD BEARINGS

Main and rod bearings are available in standard and one undersize of .010 inch (.25 mm). Main bearing oil clearance is .0009–.0019 inch for journals 1, 2, 4 and 5 and .0012–.0022 inch for journal 3. Crankshaft thrust clearance is .0008–0.0087 inch. Connecting rod bearing oil clearance is .0012–.0022 inch.

CRANKSHAFT REAR OIL SEAL
REPLACE

1. Remove engine as outlined under "Engine, Replace."

28, then the nine bolts and two nuts holding timing chain cover to block.

14. Using a soft face hammer, tap loose timing chain cover, then slide assembly off crankshaft.

15. Reverse procedure to install, noting the following:
   a. **Torque** timing chain cover fasteners as follows, **Fig. 29**, bolt A to 14 ft. lbs., bolt B to 18 ft. lbs., bolt C to 32 ft. lbs. and nut D to 14 ft. lbs.
   b. Tighten fasteners to specifications.
   c. Apply sealer No. 08826-00080, or equivalent, to oil pan flange as shown in **Fig. 30**.

OIL PUMP SERVICE

1. With timing chain cover removed, remove nine screws holding pump cover to timing chain cover, then the cover, O-ring, drive and driven rotors.
2. Remove oil pressure relief valve snap ring, then the relief valve with spring.
3. Inspect oil relief valve piston and bore for sticking wear. Inspect case and pump cover for wear, cracks or breakage.
4. Measure driven rotor to body clearance, **Fig. 31**. Standard is .0039–.0069 inch, worn is .0118 inch.
5. Measure rotor side clearance, **Fig. 32**. Standard is 0.0012–0.0035 inch, limit is 0.0059 inch.
6. Inspect rotor tip clearance, **Fig. 33**. Standard is .0043–.0094 inch, limit is .0098 inch.
7. Replace worn parts as necessary. Reassemble in reverse order, using a new O-ring.

BELT TENSION DATA

Belt	New, Lbs.	Used, Lbs.
Alternator	145–175	95–135
Power Steer.	135–185	80–120
A/C Comp.	100–150	60–100

COOLING SYSTEM
BLEED

These engines do not require a specific bleed procedure. After filling cooling system, run engine to operating temperature with radiator/pressure cap off. Air will then be automatically bled through cap opening.

THERMOSTAT
REPLACE

1. Drain engine coolant, then remove upper radiator hose from engine.
2. Remove engine water inlet, thermostat and O-ring gasket.
3. Reverse procedure to install. Use new O-ring. Ensure bleed hole or valve is facing upward.

WATER PUMP
REPLACE

1. Drain cooling system, remove upper radiator hose.
2. **On models equipped with A/C,** remove A/C belt.
3. **On all models,** loosen drive belt tension, then remove radiator fan shroud bolts.
4. Remove water pump pulley bolts, then the fan, fan coupling, pulley and fan shroud.
5. Remove water pump ten attaching bolts, then the pump and gasket.
6. Reverse procedure to install. Use new water pump gasket.

RADIATOR
REPLACE

1. Drain engine coolant.
2. Remove radiator grille.
3. Disconnect upper radiator hose.
4. Disconnect coolant reservoir hose.
5. Disconnect lower radiator hose.
6. Remove No. 2 fan shroud.

7. **On models equipped with automatic transmission,** disconnect transmission oil cooler hoses.
8. **On all models,** remove radiator supports and radiator.
9. Reverse procedure to install.

FUEL PUMP
REPLACE

1. **On models equipped with audio coded anti-theft system,** obtain three-digit system code.
2. **On models equipped with air bag,** disable system as outlined under "Precautions."
3. **On all models,** remove fuel tank, **Fig. 34**.
4. Place matchmarks on fuel pump cover, then remove seven bolts and lift out fuel pump and bracket assembly.
5. Remove fuel pump from bracket assembly, **Fig. 35**.
6. Reverse procedure to install. Reset audio coded anti-theft and air bag system, if equipped, as outlined under "Precautions."

FUEL FILTER
REPLACE

1. **On models equipped with audio coded anti-theft system,** obtain three-digit system code.
2. **On all models,** place suitable container under filter to allow fuel drainage.
3. Slowly disconnect fuel hose from fuel filter, use a shop towel to catch any fuel that may spray out under pressure.
4. Remove fuel filter, cap or plug lines.
5. Reverse procedure to install. Reset audio coded anti-theft system, if equipped, as outlined under "Precautions."

TIGHTENING SPECIFICATIONS

Year	Components	Torque/Ft. Lbs.
1996–99	A/C Compressor Bracket	32
	Accessory Pulley Bolt	18
	Air Intake Chamber	15
	Alternator Adjusting Bracket	43
	Alternator Bracket Bolt A	54
	Alternator Bracket Bolt B	13
	Alternator Lock Bolt	54
	Alternator Mounting Bolt	54
	Balance Shaft No. 2 Chain Tensioner	13
	Camshaft Bearing Cap	12
	Camshaft Timing Sprocket	54
	Clutch Cover	14
	Connecting Rod Cap	33②
	Crankshaft Bearing Cap Bolts	29②

Continued

TIGHTENING SPECIFICATIONS—Continued

Year	Components	Torque/Ft. Lbs.
1996–99	Crankshaft Position Sensor	72④
	Crankshaft Pulley	193
	Cylinder Head Bolts	③
	Cylinder Head Rear Cover	10
	Distributor	13
	Distributor Drive Gear	37
	EGR Pipe To Exhaust Manifold	15
	EGR Pipe To Cylinder Head	14
	EGR Valve To Air Intake	14
	EGR Valve To EGR Pipe	14
	Engine Hanger	30
	Engine Mounting Bracket	34
	Exhaust Manifold	36
	Flywheel	19②
	Front Exhaust Pipe To Convertor	29
	Front Exhaust Pipe To Manifold	46
	Fuel Line Banjo Bolts	22
	Intake Manifold	22
	Knock Sensor	27
	Oil Drain Bolt	18
	Oil Pan Bolt & Nut	108④
	Oil Strainer	13
	Power Steering Idler Pulley	14
	Power Steering Pulley Nut	32
	Power Steering Pump Bracket to Head	14
	Power Steering Pump to Bracket	43
	Throttle Body	14
	Timing Chain Cover	①
	Timing/No. 1 Chain Tensioner	13
	Radiator Support	108④
	Rear Oil Seal Retainer	10
	Spark Plug	13
	Water Bypass Pipe	14
	Water Inlet	15
	Water Pump (Long Bolt)	84④
	Water Pump (Short Bolt)	18
	Water Pump Pulley	16

① — Refer to "Timing Chain, Replace."

② — Tighten an additional 90°.

③ — Refer to "Cylinder Head, Replace."

④ — Inch lbs.

NOTE: On Air Bag Equipped Models, Refer To "Air Bag System Precautions" Located In The Front Of This Manual For System Disarming & Arming Procedures.

INDEX

PRECAUTIONS
AIR BAG SYSTEMS

Refer to "Air Bag System Precautions" in the front of this manual for system disarming and arming procedures.

AUDIO CODED ANTI-THEFT SYSTEM

Some models are equipped with an audio coded anti-theft system that will disable the radio when the battery cable is disconnected. The system can be identified by the "ANTI-THEFT SYSTEM" on the cassette lid. Obtain three-digit code for input. Reset system after service as follows:
1. Obtain three-digit audio theft code.
2. Depress 1 (PROG) button while depressing righthand side of TUNE SEEK button. Three dashes will appear in tape operation display.
3. To enter first digit, depress 1 (PROG) button repeatedly until number of times depressed equals first digit (depress 1 button six times if first digit is five, first press equals 0).
4. To enter second digit, depress 2 (APS) button repeatedly until number of times depressed equals second digit.
5. To enter third digit, depress 3 (RPT) button repeatedly until number of times depressed equals third digit.
6. If three dashes are displayed after inputting digits, repeat procedure.
7. When code appears in display, depress and hold SCAN button until SEC appears.
8. When SEC disappears audio system is operative.
9. If Err is displayed, repeat procedure. **Attempting to input code more than nine times may permanently disable audio system.**

BATTERY GROUND CABLE

Prior to service, disconnect battery ground cable and isolate as required.

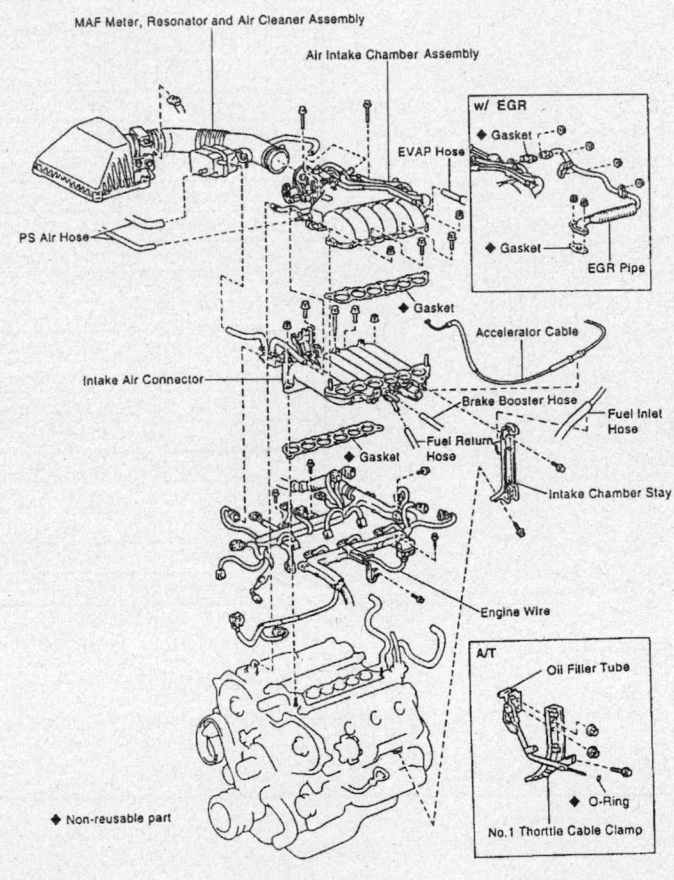

Fig. 1 Exploded view of cylinder head mounted components

COMPRESSION PRESSURE

1. Start engine and warm to normal operating temperature.
2. Remove ignition coils as outlined under "Coil Pack, Replace."
3. Remove spark plugs.
4. Insert compression gauge into spark plug hole.
5. Fully open throttle.

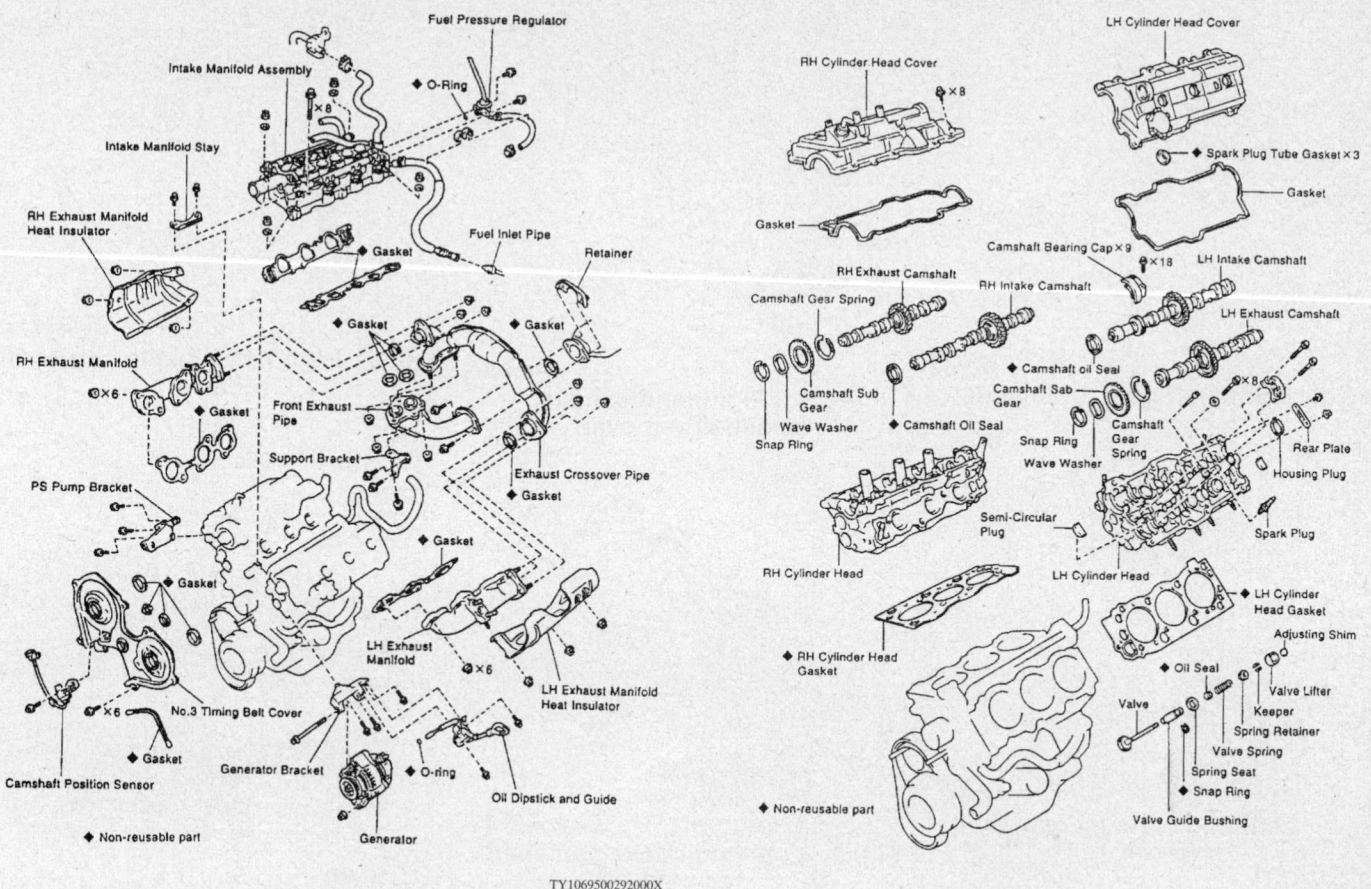

TY1069500292000X

Fig. 2 Exploded view of intake & exhaust components

TY1069500284000X

Fig. 3 Exploded view of cylinder heads

6. While cranking engine, measure compression pressure.
7. Standard compression pressure should be 178 psi. Minimum compression is 127 psi.
8. The difference in compression pressure between each cylinder should not exceed 14 psi.

ENGINE
REPLACE
2WD MODELS

1. **On models equipped with audio coded anti-theft system,** obtain three-digit system code.
2. **On all models,** disconnect battery cables.
3. Scribe hood hinge locations, then remove hood.
4. Remove engine under cover.
5. Drain coolant from radiator and engine.
6. Drain engine oil.
7. Drain transmission fluid.
8. Remove radiator as outlined in "Radiator, Replace."
9. Remove belt drive for power steering pump:
   a. Stretch belt and loosen fan pulley mounting nuts.
   b. Loosen lock bolt, pivot bolt and adjusting bolt, then remove drive belt.

10. **On models equipped with A/C,** loosen compressor idle pulley nut and adjusting bolt, then remove drive belt.
11. **On all models,** loosen alternator lock bolt, pivot bolt and adjusting bolt, then remove drive belt.
12. Remove No. 2 fan shroud.
13. Remove fan with fluid coupling and fan pulleys.
14. Disconnect power steering pump from engine and position aside.
15. **On models equipped with A/C,** disconnect compressor from mounting bracket and position aside. Remove compressor mounting bracket.
16. Remove air cleaner cap, MAF meter and resonator.
17. **On models equipped with cruise control,** disconnect actuator cable.
18. **On all models,** disconnect accelerator cable.
19. **On models equipped with automatic transmission,** disconnect throttle cable.
20. **On all models,** disconnect heater hose.
21. Disconnect brake booster vacuum hose and EVAP hose.
22. Disconnect fuel return and inlet hoses.
23. Disconnect starter harness and connector.
24. Disconnect alternator harness and connector.
25. **On Tacoma, Tundra & 4Runner models,** remove glove compartment

door and lower No. 2 finish panel to disconnect ECM connectors.
26. **On T100 models,** remove front door scuff plate and cowl to disconnect ECM connectors.
27. **On all models,** disconnect igniter connector and ground strap.
28. **On models equipped with manual transmission,** remove shift lever assembly.
29. **On all models,** disconnect propeller shaft.
30. Disconnect speedometer cable.
31. Remove front exhaust pipe.
32. **On models equipped with manual transmission,** remove clutch release cylinder.
33. **On Tacoma and 4Runner models with automatic transmission,** remove control cable.
34. **On T100 models with automatic transmission,** remove cross shaft.
35. **On all models,** place suitable jack under transmission, then remove rear mounting bracket.
36. Attach engine hangers No. 12282–62030, or equivalent, to engine block. Install chain hoist to engine hangers.
37. Remove front engine mounting insulators, then lift engine with transmission out of vehicle.
38. Reverse procedure to install.

4WD MODELS

1. **On models equipped with audio**

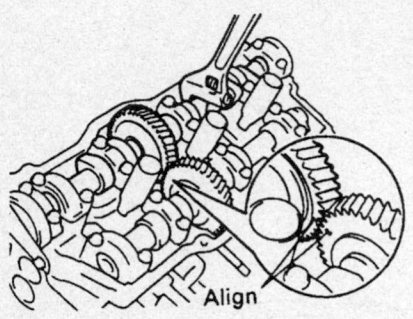

Fig. 4 Camshaft gear alignment

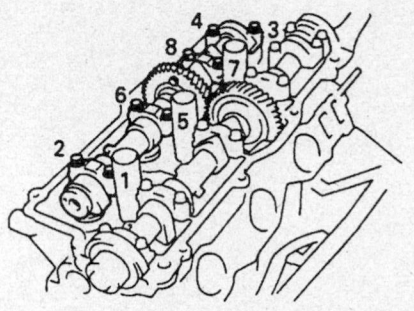

Fig. 5 Righthand exhaust camshaft removal

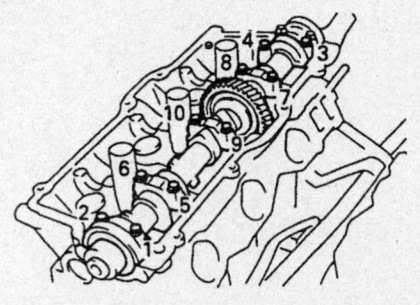

Fig. 6 Righthand intake camshaft removal

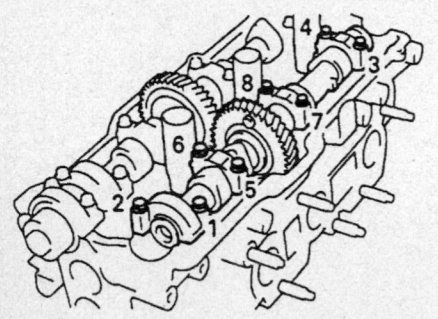

Fig. 7 Lefthand exhaust camshaft removal

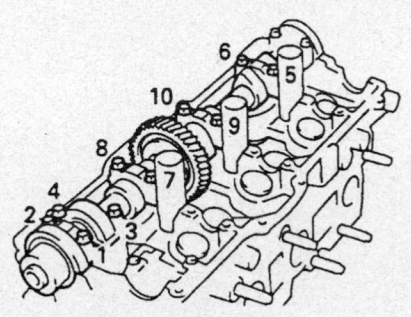

Fig. 8 Lefthand intake camshaft removal

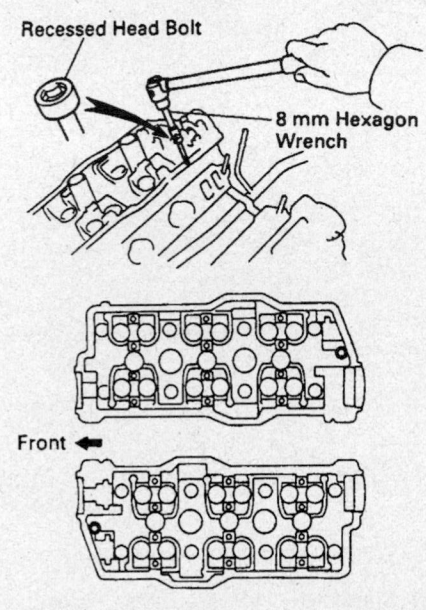

Fig. 9 Recessed head bolt removal

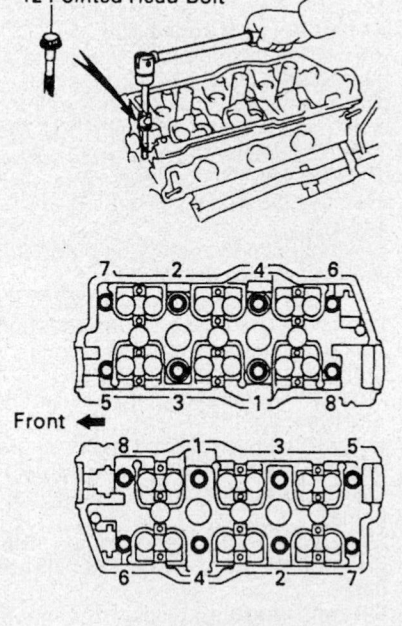

Fig. 10 Cylinder head bolt loosening sequence

coded anti-theft system, obtain three-digit system code.
2. **On all models,** disconnect battery cables.
3. Scribe hood hinge locations, then remove hood.
4. **On Tundra and 4Runner models,** remove transmission as outlined under "Transmission Replace."
5. **On all models,** remove engine under cover.
6. Drain coolant from radiator and engine.
7. Drain engine oil.
8. Remove radiator as outlined in "Radiator, Replace."
9. Remove belt drive for power steering pump:
    a. Stretch belt and loosen fan pulley mounting nuts.
    b. Loosen lock bolt, pivot bolt and adjusting bolt, then remove drive belt.
10. **On models equipped with A/C,** loosen compressor idle pulley nut and adjusting bolt, then remove drive belt.
11. **On all models,** loosen alternator lock bolt, pivot bolt and adjusting bolt, then remove drive belt.
12. Remove fan with fluid coupling and fan pulleys.
13. Disconnect power steering pump from engine and position aside.
14. **On models equipped with A/C,** disconnect compressor from mounting bracket and position aside.
15. **On all models,** remove air cleaner cap, MAF meter and resonator.
16. Remove air cleaner case and filter.

17. **On models equipped with cruise control,** disconnect actuator cable.
18. **On all models,** disconnect accelerator cable.
19. **On models equipped with automat-**

ic transmission, disconnect throttle cable.
20. **On all models,** disconnect heater hose.
21. Disconnect brake booster vacuum hose, automatic disconnect differential vacuum hose and EVAP hose.
22. Disconnect fuel return and inlet hoses.
23. Disconnect starter harness and connector.
24. Disconnect alternator harness and connector.
25. **On Tacoma, Tundra and 4Runner models,** remove glove compartment door and lower No. 2 finish panel to disconnect ECM connectors.
26. **On T100 models,** remove front door scuff plate and cowl to disconnect ECM connectors.
27. **On all models,** disconnect igniter connector and ground strap.
28. **On models equipped with manual transmission,** remove shift lever assembly.
29. **On all models,** disconnect propeller shafts.
30. Disconnect speedometer cable.

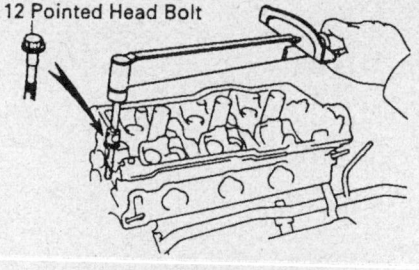

12 Pointed Head Bolt

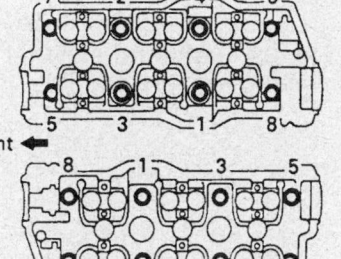

Fig. 11 Cylinder head bolt tightening sequence

TY1069500293000X

Front ←

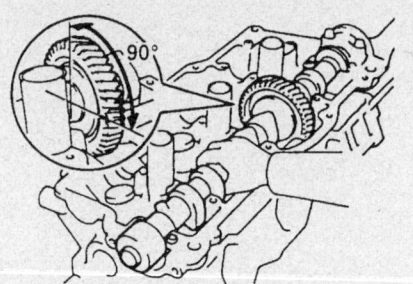

Fig. 12 Righthand intake camshaft installation

TY1069500294000X

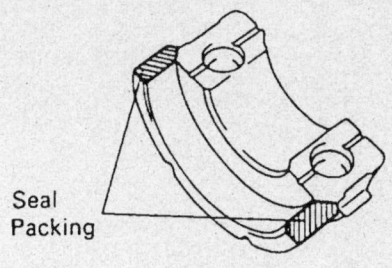

Seal Packing

Fig. 13 No. 1 bearing cap seal packing

TY1069500295000X

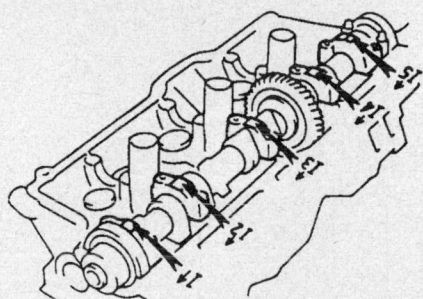

Fig. 14 Righthand intake camshaft bearing cap installation

TY1069500296000X

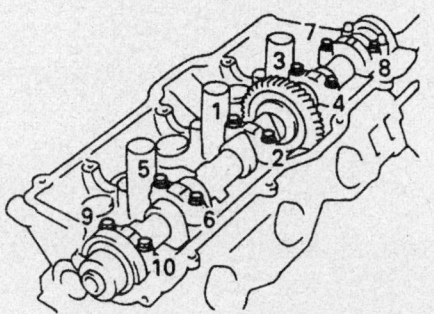

Fig. 15 Righthand intake camshaft bearing cap tightening sequence

TY1069500297000X

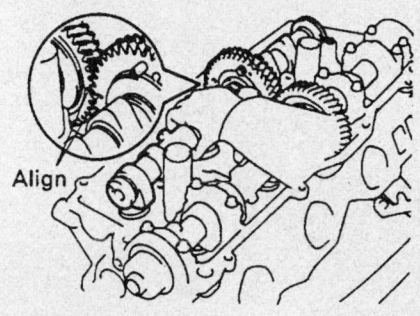

Align

Fig. 16 Righthand exhaust camshaft timing mark alignment

TY1069500298000X

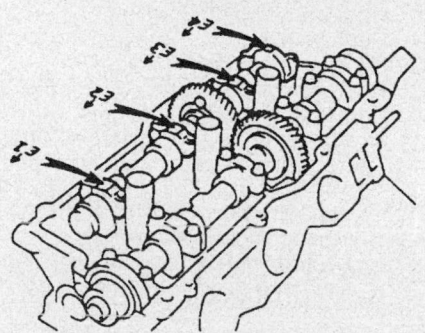

Fig. 17 Righthand exhaust camshaft bearing cap installation

TY1069500299000X

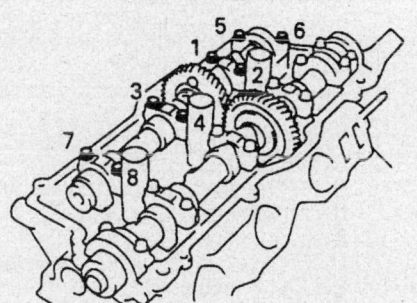

Fig. 18 Righthand exhaust camshaft bearing cap tightening sequence

TY1069500300000X

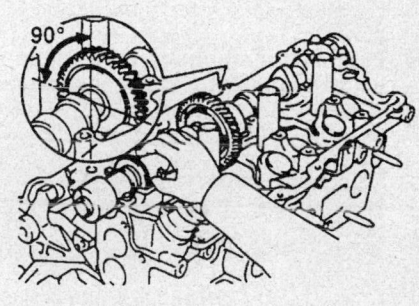

Fig. 19 Lefthand intake camshaft installation

TY1069500301000X

31. Remove front exhaust pipe.
32. **On models equipped with manual transmission,** remove clutch release cylinder.
33. **On Tacoma and 4Runner models with automatic transmission,** re-move control cable.
34. **On T100 models with automatic transmission,** remove cross shaft.
35. **On all models,** place suitable jack under transmission, then remove rear mounting bracket.
36. Attach engine hangers No. 12282–62030, or equivalent, to engine block. Install chain hoist to engine hangers.
37. Remove front engine mounting insulators, then lift engine with transmission out of vehicle.
38. Reverse procedure to install.

CYLINDER HEAD
REPLACE
REMOVAL

1. On models equipped with audio coded anti-theft system, obtain three-digit system code.
2. **On all models,** scribe hood hinge locations, then remove hood.
3. Remove engine under cover.
4. Drain coolant from radiator and engine.
5. Remove front exhaust pipe.
6. Remove air cleaner cap, MAF meter and resonator, **Fig. 1.**
7. **On models equipped with cruise**

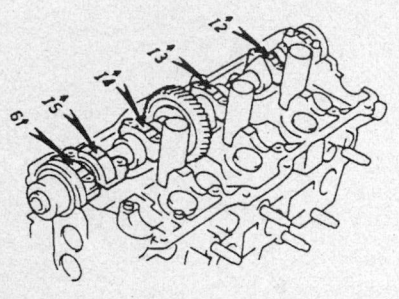

Fig. 20 Lefthand intake camshaft bearing cap installation

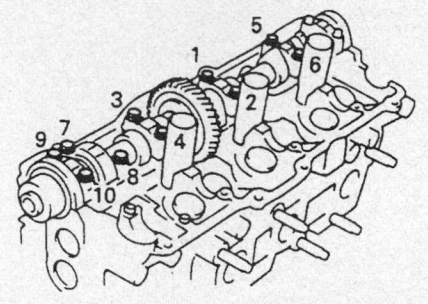

Fig. 21 Lefthand intake camshaft bearing cap tightening sequence

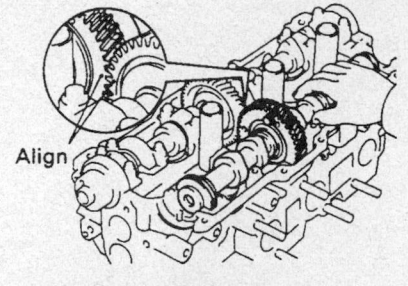

Fig. 22 Lefthand exhaust camshaft installation

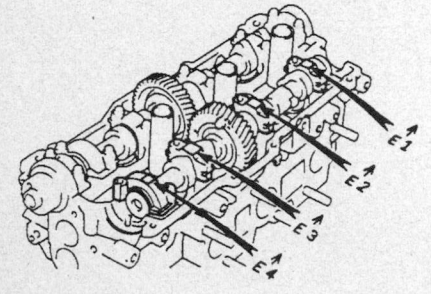

Fig. 23 Lefthand exhaust camshaft bearing cap installation

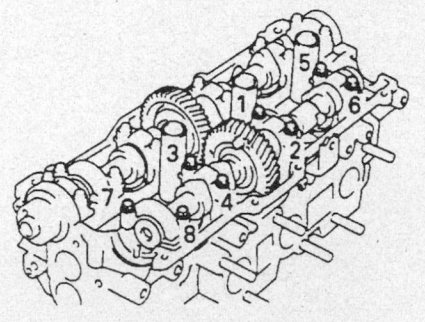

Fig. 24 Lefthand exhaust camshaft bearing cap tightening sequence

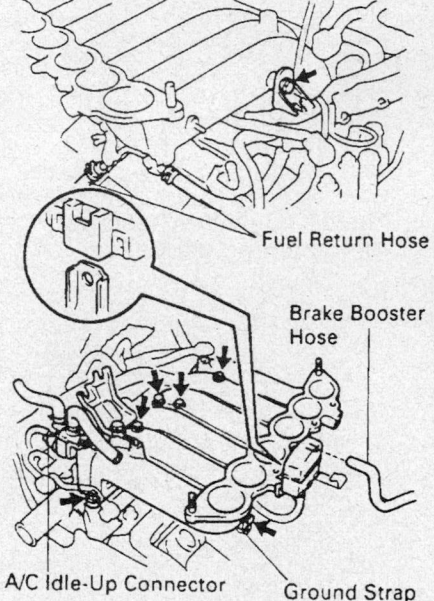

Fig. 25 Intake air connector

control, disconnect actuator cable.
8. **On all models,** disconnect accelerator cable.
9. **On models equipped with automatic transmission,** disconnect throttle cable.
10. **On all models,** disconnect heater hose.
11. Disconnect upper radiator hose.
12. Remove belt drive for power steering pump:
    a. Stretch belt and loosen fan pulley mounting nuts.
    b. Loosen lock bolt, pivot bolt and adjusting bolt, then remove drive belt.
13. Remove spark plug wires with ignition coils, then the spark plugs.
14. Remove timing belt as outlined under "Timing Belt, Replace", then the camshaft timing pulleys.
15. Remove alternator.
16. **On models equipped with EGR,** remove EGR pipe.
17. **On all models,** remove intake chamber stay.
18. Disconnect the following connectors:
    a. VSV connector for fuel pressure control.
    b. Throttle position sensor.
    c. IAC valve
    d. EGR gas temperature sensor and VSV connectors.
19. Disconnect the following hoses:
    a. Two PCV hoses.
    b. Two water bypass hoses.
    c. Air assist hose from throttle body.
    d. Two vacuum sensing hoses from VSV.
    e. EVAP hose.
    f. Air hose from power steering pump.

g. **On models equipped with A/C** air hose from A/C idle-up valve.
20. **On all models,** remove air intake chamber assembly.
21. Remove intake air connector as follows:
    a. Disconnect engine wire harness.
    b. Disconnect fuel return hoses.
    c. Disconnect brake booster vacuum hose from intake air connector.
    d. Disconnect ground strap.
    e. Disconnect data link connector (DLC1) from bracket.
    f. **On models equipped with A/C,** disconnect A/C idle-up valve connector.
    g. **On all models,** disconnect intake air connector and gasket.
22. Disconnect following engine harness connectors:
    a. Oil pressure sensor.
    b. Crankshaft position sensor.
    c. Fuel injectors.
    d. ECT sender gauge.
    e. ECT sensor.
    f. Knock sensor.
    g. Camshaft position sensor.
23. Disconnect engine harness from cylinder head.
24. Remove camshaft position sensor.
25. Remove No. 3 timing belt cover, **Fig. 2.**
26. Remove fuel pressure regulator.
27. Remove intake manifold assembly:
    a. Disconnect fuel inlet hose.
    b. Remove intake manifold stay.
    c. Remove intake manifold with delivery pipes and injectors. Remove gaskets.

28. Remove power steering pump bracket.
29. Remove oil dipstick and tube.
30. Remove alternator bracket.
31. Remove exhaust crossover pipe.
32. Remove exhaust manifolds.
33. Remove cylinder head covers, **Fig. 3.**
34. Remove righthand camshafts:
    a. Rotate righthand driven sub-gear by turning hexagon portion of shaft with a wrench until timing marks (2 dots) are aligned, **Fig. 4,** and service bolt hole is accessible.
    b. Secure righthand exhaust camshaft sub-gear to main gear with a service bolt. **Service bolt is 6 mm thread diameter, 1 mm pitch, 16–20 mm long.**
    c. Uniformly loosen and remove righthand exhaust camshaft bearing cap bolts in sequence, **Fig. 5,** then the righthand exhaust camshaft.
    d. Uniformly loosen and remove righthand intake camshaft bearing cap bolts in sequence, **Fig. 6,** then the oil seal and righthand intake camshaft.
35. Remove lefthand camshafts:

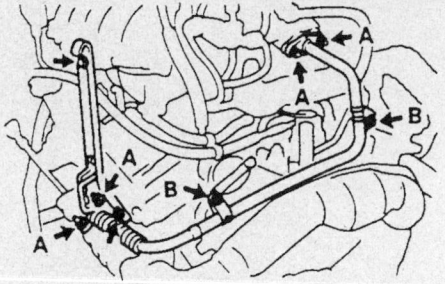

TY1069500308000X

Fig. 26 EGR pipe installation

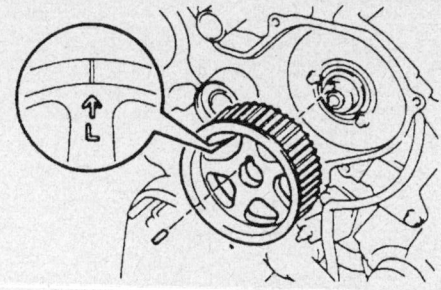

TY1069500309000X

Fig. 27 Lefthand camshaft knock pin alignment

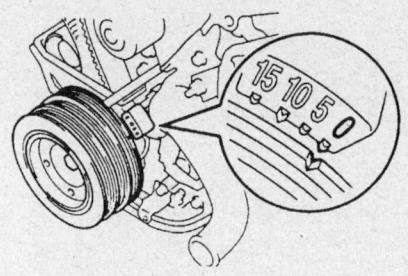

TY1069500310000X

Fig. 28 Timing mark of No. 1 timing belt cover

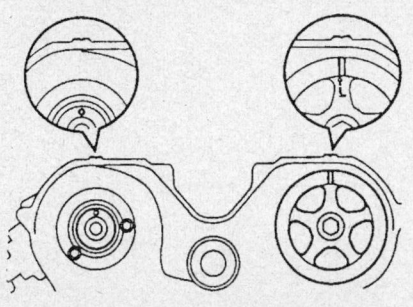

TY1069500311000X

Fig. 29 Camshaft timing positions

a. Rotate lefthand driven sub-gear by turning hexagon portion of shaft with a wrench until timing marks (1 dot) are aligned and service bolt hole is accessible.
b. Secure lefthand exhaust camshaft sub-gear to main gear with a service bolt.
c. Uniformly loosen and remove lefthand exhaust camshaft bearing cap bolts in sequence, **Fig. 7**, then the lefthand exhaust camshaft.
d. Uniformly loosen and remove the lefthand intake camshaft bearing cap bolts in sequence, **Fig. 8**, then the oil seal and lefthand intake camshaft.
e. Using a suitable 8 mm Allen wrench, remove recessed head cylinder head bolts, **Fig. 9**.
f. Uniformly loosen and remove eight cylinder head bolts in sequence, **Fig. 10. These bolts have 12-pointed heads.**
36. Pry cylinder head from engine block dowels using suitable pry bar, ensuring to not damage contact surfaces.

INSPECTION

1. Inspect cylinder head for cracks wear or damage.
2. Using a straightedge and feeler gauge, measure for warpage across contact surface of cylinder head at all angles. If warpage is greater than .0039 inch, replace cylinder head.

INSTALLATION

1. Position new gasket on engine block, then carefully place cylinder head on gasket.
2. Apply a light coat of clean engine oil to

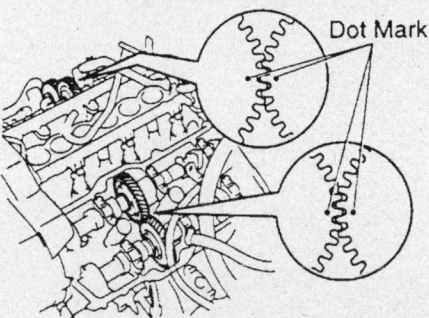

TY1069500312000X

Fig. 30 Camshaft gear alignment

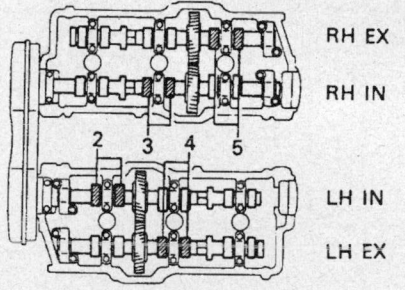

TY1069500314000X

Fig. 32 2nd valve clearance measurement

threads of the eight 12-pointed head bolts and **torque** in several steps to 25 ft. lbs. in sequence, **Fig. 11**.
3. Tighten cylinder head bolts as follows:
a. Place mark on each 12 pointed head bolt.
b. Tighten each bolt in sequence an additional 90°.
c. Retighten each bolt in sequence an additional 90°.
4. Apply a light coat of clean engine oil to threads of 8 mm hexagonal recessed head cylinder head bolts, then **torque** to 13 ft. lbs.
5. Install ground strap.
6. Install righthand intake camshaft:
a. Apply a light coat of clean engine oil to thrust portion and journal of camshaft.
b. Place camshaft at 90° angle of timing mark (2 dots) on cylinder head, **Fig. 12**.
c. Apply suitable grease to lip of new

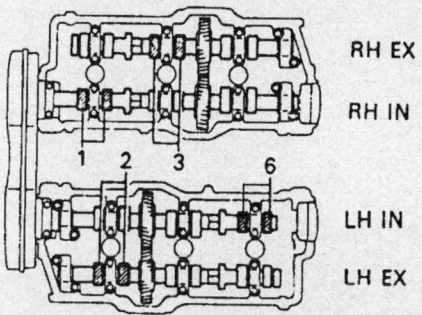

TY1069500313000X

Fig. 31 1st valve clearance measurement

oil seal and install seal to camshaft.
d. Apply seal packing No. 08826-00080, or equivalent, to No. 1 bearing cap, **Fig. 13**.
e. Install bearing caps in their proper locations, **Fig. 14**.
f. Apply a light coat of clean engine oil to threads and under head of bearing cap bolts. Install and **torque** bearing cap bolts in several passes to 12 ft. lbs. in sequence, **Fig. 15**.
7. Install righthand exhaust camshaft:
a. Apply a light coat of clean engine oil to thrust portion and journal of camshaft.
b. Install camshaft and align timing marks (one dot) on gear with timing marks on intake camshaft gear, **Fig. 16**.
c. Install four bearing caps in their proper locations, **Fig. 17**.
d. Apply a light coat of clean engine oil to threads and under head of bearing cap bolts. Install and **torque** bearing cap bolts in several passes to 12 ft. lbs. in sequence, **Fig. 18**.
e. Remove service bolt and adjust alignment of timing marks, if necessary, with wrench.
8. Install lefthand intake camshaft:
a. Apply a light coat of clean engine oil to thrust portion and journal of camshaft.
b. Place camshaft at 90° angle of timing mark (1 dot) on cylinder head, **Fig. 19**.
c. Apply suitable grease to lip of new oil seal and install seal to camshaft.
d. Apply seal packing No. 08826-

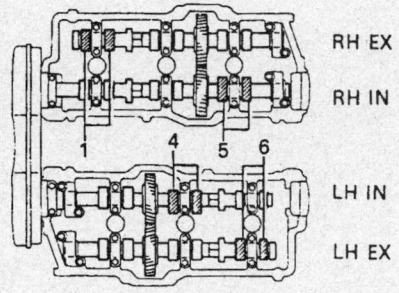

Fig. 33 3rd valve clearance measurement

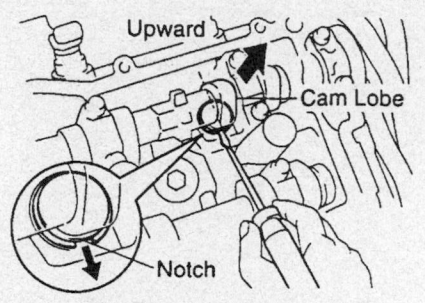

Fig. 34 Cam lobe & lifter positioning

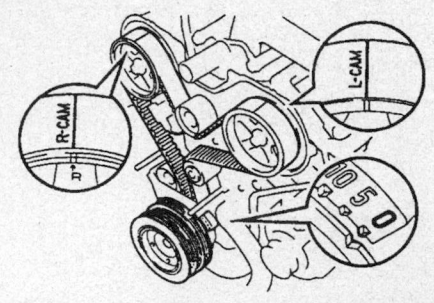

Fig. 35 Timing pulley alignment

00080, or equivalent, to No. 1 bearing cap, **Fig. 13**.

e. Install five bearing caps in their proper locations, **Fig. 20**.

f. Apply a light coat of clean engine oil to threads and under head of bearing cap bolts. Install and **torque** bearing cap bolts in several passes to 12 ft. lbs. in sequence, **Fig. 21**.

9. Install lefthand exhaust camshaft:

a. Apply a light coat of clean engine oil to thrust portion and journal of camshaft.

b. Install camshaft and align timing marks (one dot) on gear with timing marks on intake camshaft gear, **Fig. 22**.

c. Install four bearing caps in their proper locations, **Fig. 23**.

d. Apply a light coat of clean engine oil to threads and under head of bearing cap bolts. Install and **torque** bearing cap bolts in several passes to 12 ft. lbs. in sequence, **Fig. 24**.

e. Remove service bolt and adjust alignment of timing marks, if necessary, with wrench.

f. Check and adjust valves as outlined under "Valve Clearance Specifications" and "Valve Adjustment."

10. Apply seal packing No. 08826–00080, or equivalent, to semi-circular plug grooves in cylinder heads, then install the semi-circular plugs.

11. Apply seal packing No. 08826–00080, or equivalent, to cylinder heads, then install cylinder head covers. Tighten to specification.

12. Install righthand exhaust manifold, using a new gasket. Tighten to specification.

13. Install righthand exhaust manifold heat insulator and tighten to specification.

14. Install lefthand exhaust manifold, using a new gasket. Tighten to specification.

15. Install lefthand exhaust manifold heat insulator and tighten to specification.

16. Install exhaust crossover pipe and tighten to specification.

17. Install alternator bracket and tighten to specification.

18. Install oil dipstick, guide and power steering pump bracket.

19. Install intake manifold assembly and stay. Tighten to specification.

20. Install fuel pressure regulator. Apply a light coat of gasoline to new O-ring be-

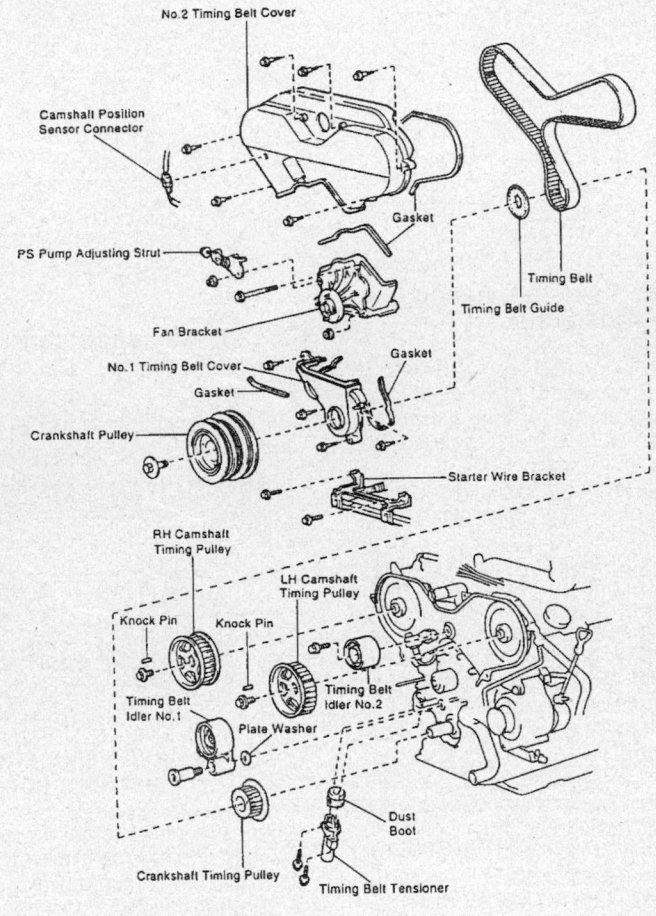

Fig. 36 Exploded view of timing belt assembly

fore installation. Tighten to specification.

21. Inspect No. 3 timing belt cover gaskets for cracks, wear or damage. Replace if necessary. Install cover and tighten to specification.

22. Install camshaft position sensor and tighten to specification.

23. Install engine harness connectors:
a. Oil pressure sensor.
b. Crankshaft position sensor.
c. Fuel injectors.
d. ECT sender gauge.
e. ECT sensor.
f. Knock sensor

g. Camshaft position sensor.

24. Install harness in wire hold down clamps.

25. Install intake air connector, **Fig. 25**:
a. Install new gasket to unit and install. Tighten to specification.
b. Connect DLC1 to bracket.
c. Connect ground strap to intake air connector.
d. Connect brake booster hose to intake air connector.
e. Connect two fuel return hoses.
f. **On models equipped with A/C,** connect A/C idle-up valve connector.

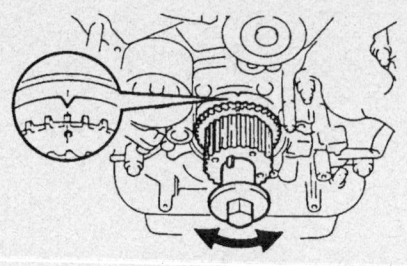

Fig. 37 Crankshaft timing pulley alignment

TY1069500319000X

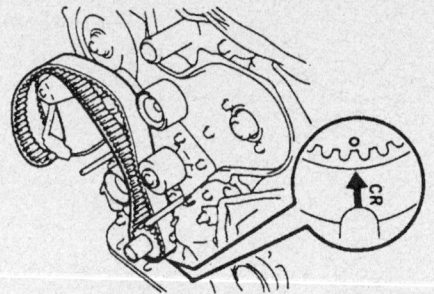

TY1069500320000X

Fig. 38 Timing belt & crankshaft timing pulley alignment

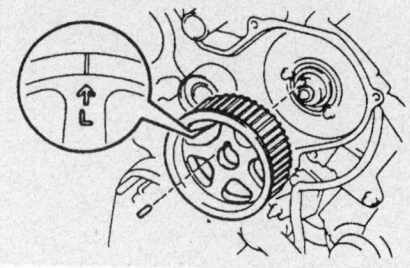

TY1069500321000X

Fig. 39 Lefthand camshaft timing pulley & knock pin groove alignment

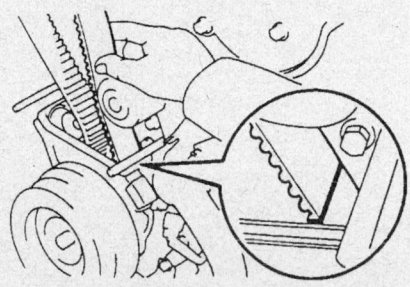

TY1069500322000X

Fig. 40 Timing belt & No. 1 timing belt cover alignment

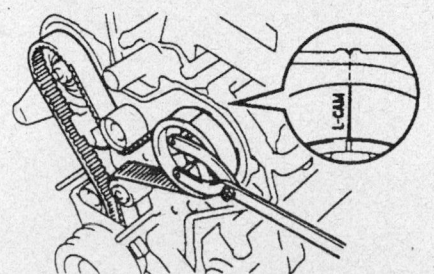

TY1069500323000X

Fig. 41 Timing belt & lefthand camshaft timing pulley alignment

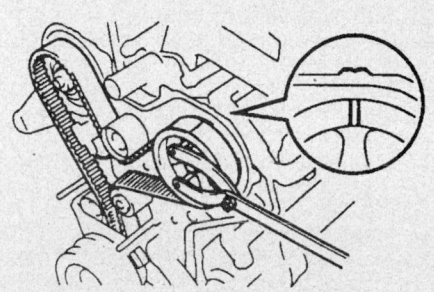

TY1069500324000X

Fig. 42 Lefthand camshaft timing pulley & No. 3 timing belt cover alignment

26. **On all models,** install new gasket to air intake chamber assembly and tighten to specification. Connect the following:
    a. Two PCV hoses
    b. Two water bypass hoses.
    c. Air assist hose to throttle body.
    d. Two vacuum sensing hoses to VSV.
    e. EVAP hose.
    f. Air hose to power steering pump.
    g. Air hose to A/C idle-up valve, if equipped.
    h. VSV connector for fuel pressure control.
    i. Throttle position sensor connector.
    j. IAC valve connector.
    k. Gas temperature sensor connector and VSV connector.
27. Install air intake chamber stay and tighten to specification.
28. Install EGR pipe. **Torque** nuts (A), **Fig. 26,** to 14 ft. lbs., and nuts (B) to 6 ft. lbs.
29. Temporarily install alternator.
30. Install timing belt idler No. 2 and tighten to specification.
31. Install lefthand camshaft timing pulley:
    a. Position pulley, with flange facing outward.
    b. Align knock pin hole of camshaft with knock pin groove of timing pulley, **Fig. 27,** then install knock pin. Using pin wrench tool set No. 09960–10010, or equivalent, tighten pulley bolt to specification.
32. Set No. 1 cylinder to TDC on compression stroke:
    a. Turn crankshaft pulley and align groove with "O" timing mark of No. 1 timing belt cover, **Fig. 28.**
    b. Turn camshaft and align knock pin hole of righthand camshaft with tim-

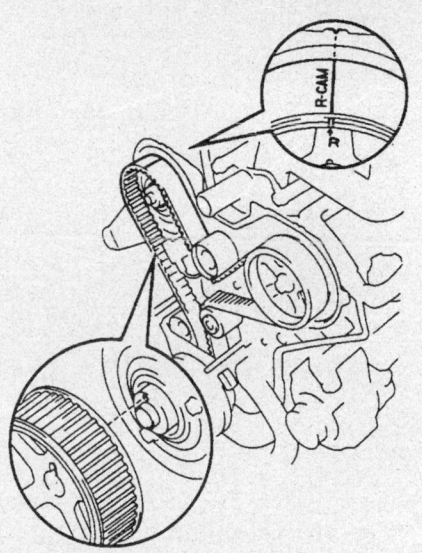

TY1069500325000X

Fig. 43 Righthand camshaft timing pulley & No. 2 idler pulley alignment

ing mark of No. 3 timing belt cover, **Fig. 29.**
    c. Turn camshaft and align timing mark of lefthand camshaft timing pulley with timing mark of No. 3 timing belt cover, **Fig. 29.**
33. Install timing belt as outlined under "Timing Belt, Replace."
34. Install spark plugs.
35. Install spark plug wires with ignition coils.

36. **On models equipped with A/C,** install compressor bracket and connect compressor.
37. **On all models,** install power steering pump.
38. Install fan with fluid coupling and fan pulleys. Tighten to specification.
39. Install No. 2 fan shroud.
40. Install and adjust alternator drive belt.
41. **On models equipped with A/C,** install and adjust compressor drive belt.
42. **On all models,** install and adjust power steering pump drive belt.
43. Connect upper radiator hose and heater hose.
44. **On models equipped with cruise control,** connect actuator cable.
45. **On models equipped with automatic transmission,** connect throttle cable.
46. **On all models,** connect accelerator cable.
47. Install MAF meter, resonator and air cleaner cap.
48. Install front exhaust pipe.
49. Fill radiator with engine coolant. Start engine and check for coolant leaks. Refill coolant as necessary.
50. Install engine under cover.

VALVE CLEARANCE SPECIFICATIONS

Refer to "Tune Up Specifications" for valve clearance.

TY1069500334000X

Fig. 44 Valve timing marks

VALVE ADJUSTMENT

1. Drain engine coolant.
2. Remove intake air connector.
3. Remove cylinder head covers as outlined under "Cylinder Head, Replace."
4. Turn crankshaft pulley and align groove with "O" timing mark of No. 1 timing belt cover, **Fig. 28.**
5. Ensure timing marks (1 dot) of camshaft drive and driven gears are in line, **Fig. 30.**
6. Measure valve clearance:
   a. Using suitable feeler gauge, measure clearance between valve lifter and camshaft. Measure only those valves indicated in **Fig. 31.** Refer to "Valve Clearance Specifications."
   b. Turn crankshaft 360° and measure only those valves indicated in **Fig. 32.**
   c. Turn crankshaft an additional 360° and measure only those valves indicated in **Fig. 33.**
7. Adjust valve clearance:
   a. Remove adjusting shim.
   b. Turn camshaft until cam lobe faces up, **Fig. 34.**
   c. Turn valve lifter with screwdriver until notches are perpendicular to camshaft.
   d. Using valve clearance adjusting tool set No. 09248–55040, or equivalent, remove and replace adjusting shim until proper clearance is obtained. Shims are available in increments of .0020 inch, from .0984 inch to .1299 inch.
8. Install cylinder head cover.
9. Fill cooling system.
10. Install air intake connector.

TIMING BELT
REPLACE
REMOVAL

1. **On models equipped with audio coded anti-theft system,** obtain three-digit system code.
2. **On all models,** remove engine under cover.
3. Drain engine coolant.
4. Disconnect upper radiator hose.
5. Remove belt drive for power steering pump:
   a. Stretch belt and loosen fan pulley mounting nuts.

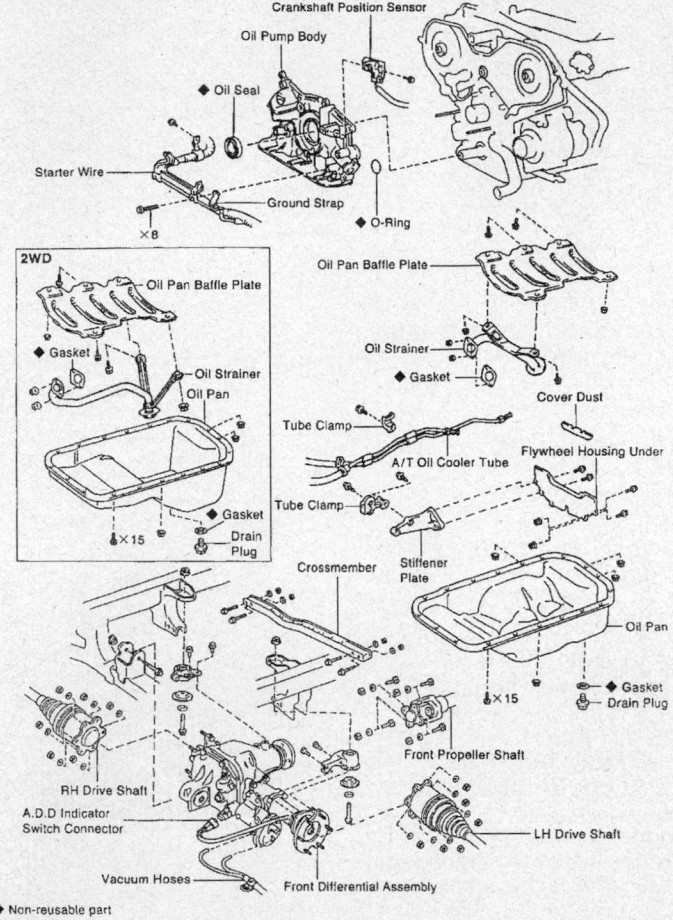

TY1069500335000X

Fig. 45 Lubrication system

◆ Non-reusable part

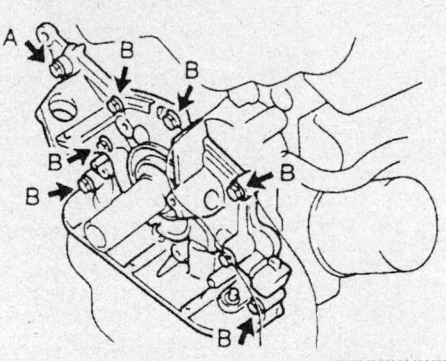

TY1069500336000X

Fig. 46 Oil pump tightening

   b. Loosen lock bolt, pivot bolt and adjusting bolt, then remove drive belt.
6. **On models equipped with A/C,** loosen idle pulley nut and adjusting bolt, then remove drive belt.
7. **On all models,** loosen alternator lock bolt, pivot bolt and adjusting bolt, then remove drive belt.
8. Remove No. 2 fan shroud.
9. Remove fan with fluid coupling and fan pulleys.
10. Disconnect power steering pump from engine and position aside.
11. **On models equipped with A/C,** disconnect compressor from mounting bracket and position aside. Remove compressor mounting bracket.

12. **On all models,** remove No. 2 timing belt cover.
13. Remove fan bracket.
14. Turn crankshaft pulley and align groove with "O" timing mark of No. 1 timing belt cover and ensure timing marks of camshaft timing pulleys and No. 3 timing belt cover are aligned, **Fig. 35.**
15. Remove timing belt tensioner.
16. Remove righthand camshaft timing pulley with using removal wrench tool No. 09962–01000, or equivalent.
17. Remove lefthand camshaft timing pulley using removal wrench tool No. 09962–01000, or equivalent.
18. Remove crankshaft pulley using flange tool No. 09213–54015, or equivalent.
19. Remove starter wire bracket and No. 1 timing belt cover, **Fig. 36.**
20. Remove timing belt guide.
21. Remove timing belt.
22. Remove timing belt idlers No. 1 and No. 2.
23. Remove crankshaft timing pulley using flange tool No. 09950–50010 or equivalent.

INSTALLATION

1. Install crankshaft timing pulley.
2. Install timing belt idlers No. 1 and No. 2. Tighten to specification.
3. Temporarily install timing belt:

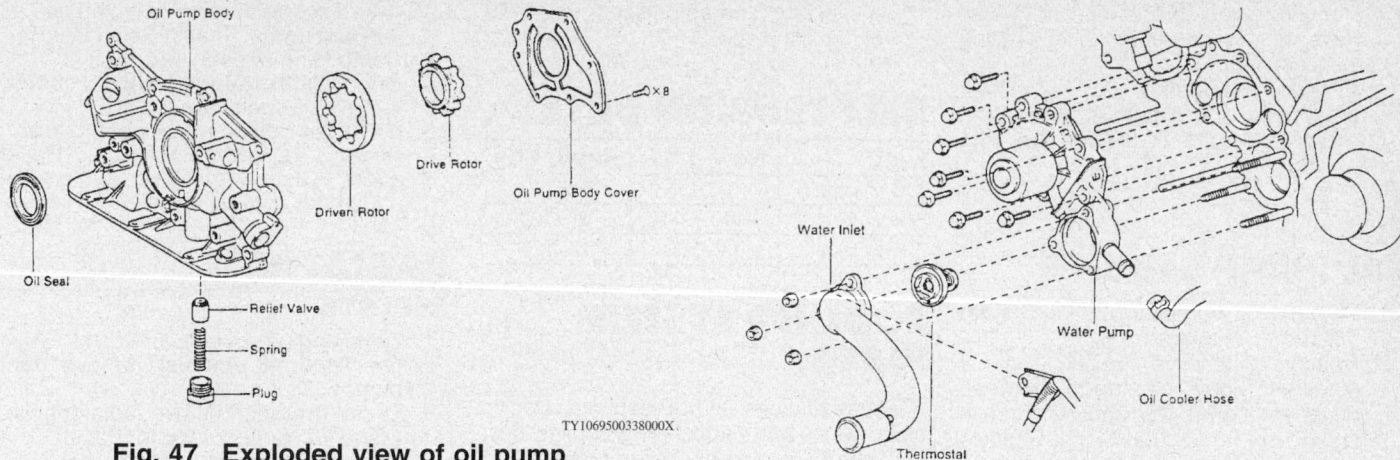

TY1069500338000X

Fig. 47 Exploded view of oil pump

TY1069500339000X

Fig. 48 Water pump removal

a. Ensure engine is cold.
b. Align timing marks on crankshaft timing pulley and oil pump body, **Fig. 37.**
c. Remove any oil or water on pulleys.
d. Align installation mark on timing belt with drilled mark on crankshaft timing pulley, **Fig. 38.**
e. Install timing belt on crankshaft timing pulley, No. 1 idler and water pump pulleys.
4. Install timing belt guide.
5. Install No. 1 timing belt cover and starter wire bracket. Tighten to specification.
6. Install crankshaft pulley using flange tool No. 09213–54015, or equivalent. Tighten to specification.
7. Install lefthand camshaft timing pulley ensuring to align with knock pin groove, **Fig. 39.** Tighten to specification.
8. Turn crankshaft pulley and align groove with "O" timing mark of No. 1 timing belt cover and ensure timing marks of camshaft timing pulleys and No. 3 timing belt cover are aligned, **Fig. 35.**
9. Turn camshaft and align knock pin hole of righthand camshaft with timing mark of No. 3 timing belt cover, **Fig. 29.**
10. Turn camshaft and align timing mark of lefthand camshaft timing pulley with timing mark of No. 3 timing belt cover, **Fig. 29.**
11. Install timing belt to lefthand camshaft timing pulley:
    a. Ensure installation mark on timing belt matches end of No. 1 timing belt cover, **Fig. 40.** If installation mark does not align, shift meshing of timing belt and crankshaft timing pulley until they align.
    b. Remove any oil or water on lefthand camshaft timing pulley.
    c. Using wrench tool No. 09960–10010, or equivalent, slightly turn lefthand camshaft timing pulley clockwise. Align timing mark on timing belt with timing mark on lefthand camshaft timing pulley, **Fig. 41,** and hang timing belt on lefthand camshaft timing pulley.
    d. Using wrench tool No. 09960–10010, or equivalent, align timing

mark of lefthand camshaft pulley and No. 3 timing belt cover, **Fig. 42.**
12. Install righthand camshaft timing pulley and timing belt:
    a. Remove any oil or water on righthand camshaft timing pulley and No. 2 idler pulley.
    b. Align installation mark on timing belt with timing mark on righthand camshaft timing pulley, **Fig. 43.**
    c. Hang timing belt on righthand camshaft timing pulley.
    d. Align timing marks of righthand camshaft timing pulley and No. 3 timing belt cover.
    e. Slide righthand camshaft timing pulley onto camshaft.
    f. Using wrench tool No. 09960–10010, or equivalent, align knock pin hole of camshaft with knock pin groove marked "R" on pulley and install knock pin.
    g. Install pulley bolt and tighten to specification.
13. Install timing belt tensioner:
    a. Using shop press, compress push rod into tensioner body, then insert 1.5 mm hex wrench through collar to retain push rod. Release press.
    b. Install dust boot to tensioner.
    c. Install tensioner and tighten to specification, then remove hex wrench.
14. Check valve timing:
    a. Turn crankshaft two complete revolutions clockwise from TDC to TDC.
    b. Ensure each pulley realigns with timing marks, **Fig. 44. If marks do not realign, remove and reinstall timing belt.**
15. Install fan bracket and power steering pump adjusting bracket.
16. Install No. 2 timing belt cover.
17. **On models equipped with A/C,** install compressor bracket and mount compressor.
18. **On all models,** install power steering pump.
19. Install fan and pulley assembly. Tighten to specification.
20. Install No. 2 fan shroud.
21. Install and adjust drive belt for alternator.

22. **On models equipped with A/C,** install and adjust drive belt for A/C compressor.
23. **On all models,** install and adjust drive belt for power steering pump.
24. Connect upper radiator hose.
25. Fill engine with coolant.
26. Install engine under cover.

CAMSHAFT
REPLACE

Refer to "Cylinder Head, Replace" for camshaft replacement procedure.

OIL PAN
REPLACE

1. Drain engine oil.
2. Remove pan bolts and nuts.
3. Using seal cutter tool No. 09032–00100, or equivalent, remove oil pan from engine block. Ensure to not damage oil pan flange.
4. Remove all remaining seal material from mating surfaces of pan and engine block.
5. Install new seal No. 08826–00080, or equivalent, to oil pan.
6. Install pan to engine and tighten to specification.

OIL PUMP
REPLACE

1. Remove crankshaft timing pulley as outlined under "Timing Belt, Replace."
2. **On 4WD models,** remove front differential.
3. **On models equipped with automatic transmission,** remove transmission fluid cooler lines and clamp.
4. **On all models,** remove stiffener plate, **Fig. 45.**
5. Remove flywheel housing under cover and dust cover.
6. Disconnect starter harness connector.
7. Remove crankshaft position sensor.
8. Remove oil pan as outlined under "Oil Pan, Replace."
9. Remove oil strainer and oil pan baffle plate.

10. Remove oil pump and discard O-ring.
11. Reverse procedure to install, noting the following:
    a. Install new O-ring.
    b. **Torque** oil pump bolts "A" to 15 ft. lbs. and bolts "B" to 31 ft. lbs., **Fig. 46.**

OIL PUMP SERVICE

1. Remove oil pump as outlined under "Oil Pump, Replace."
2. Remove relief valve, **Fig. 47.**
3. Measure body clearance between driven rotor and pump body. Clearance should be .0039–.0069 inch. Replace rotor set or body if not as specified.
4. Measure tip clearance between drive and driven rotors. Clearance should be .0043–.0094 inch. Replace rotor set if not as specified.
5. Using a straight edge, measure side clearance between rotor set and body. Clearance should be .0012–.0035 inch. Replace rotor set and/or body if not as specified.
6. Inspect relief valve for damage or wear. Coat relief valve with engine oil and ensure it falls smoothly into valve hole by its own weight. Replace valve and/or body if not as specified.
7. Replace crankshaft front oil seal.
    a. Using a screwdriver, pry out old seal.
    b. Using seal setting tool No. 09309–37010, or equivalent, and a hammer, install new seal. Seat seal flush with pump body.
    c. Apply multi-purpose grease to seal lip.

8. Install oil pump as outlined under "Oil Pump, Replace."

BELT TENSION DATA

Belt	New, Lbs.	Used, Lbs.
A/C Comp.	135-185	80-120
Alternator	140–180	80–120
Power Steer.	135-180	85-120

COOLING SYSTEM BLEED

These engines do not require a specific bleed procedure. After filling cooling system, run engine to operating temperature with radiator/pressure cap off. Air will then be automatically bled through cap opening.

THERMOSTAT
REPLACE

1. Drain cooling system.
2. Disconnect lower radiator hose.
3. Remove thermostat and gasket.
4. Reverse procedure to install. Use a new thermostat gasket and tighten inlet nuts to specifications.

WATER PUMP
REPLACE

1. **On models equipped with audio coded anti-theft system,** obtain three-digit system code.

2. **On all models,** remove timing belt as outlined under "Timing Belt, Replace."
3. Remove thermostat, **Fig. 48.**
4. **On models equipped with oil cooler,** remove oil cooler hose.
5. **On all models,** remove water pump,
6. Reverse procedure to install. Reset audio coded anti-theft system, if equipped, as outlined under "Precautions."

RADIATOR
REPLACE

1. Drain engine coolant.
2. **On Tacoma models,** remove front bumper filler.
3. **On all models,** remove radiator grille.
4. Disconnect upper radiator hose.
5. Disconnect coolant reservoir hose.
6. Disconnect lower radiator hose.
7. Remove fan shroud No. 2.
8. **On models equipped with automatic transmission,** disconnect transmission oil cooler hoses.
9. **On all models,** remove radiator supports and radiator.
10. Reverse procedure to install.

FUEL PUMP
REPLACE

1. **On models equipped with audio coded anti-theft system,** obtain three-digit system code.
2. **On all models,** remove fuel tank.
3. Remove fuel pump harness connector.
4. Remove fuel pump bracket mounting bolts and pull out pump bracket assembly.
5. Remove and discard gasket.
6. Reverse procedure to install, noting:
    a. Install new gasket.
    b. Reset audio coded anti-theft system, if equipped, as outlined under "Precautions."

FUEL FILTER
REPLACE

1. Remove fuel pump as outlined under "Fuel Pump, Replace."
2. Using a small screwdriver, remove fuel filter clip.
3. Install new filter using new clip.
4. Reverse procedure to install.

TIGHTENING SPECIFICATIONS

Year	Component	Torque/ Ft. Lbs.
1996-99	Air Intake Chamber Assembly	13
	Air Intake Chamber Stay	30
	Alternator Bracket	14
	Alternator Pulley	81
	Camshaft Bearing Cap	②
	Camshaft Position Sensor	72①
	Camshaft Pulley	81
	Clutch Release Cylinder	108①
	Connecting Rod Cap	18⑤
	Crankshaft Main Bearing	45⑤
	Crankshaft Pulley	184
	Cylinder Head Bolts (8 mm Recessed Head)	13
	Cylinder Head Bolts (12 Point)	②
	Cylinder Head Cover	53①
	Cylinder Head Rear Plate	72①
	Drive Plate	61
	EGR Pipe (Nut A)	14
	EGR Pipe (Nut B)	72①
	Engine Front Mounting Bracket	28
	Engine Rear Mounting Bracket	43
	Exhaust Crossover Pipe	33
	Exhaust Manifold	30
	Exhaust Manifold Insulator	72①
	Fan Assembly	48①
	Fan Mounting	48①
	Fuel Pressure Regulator	71①
	Fuel Pump	④
	Fuel Tank Mounting	③
	Intake Air Connector	13
	Intake Manifold & Stay	13
	Knock Sensor	29
	No.1 Idler Pulley	26
	No. 2 Idler Pulley	30
	Oil Dipstick Guide	72①
	Oil Pan	72①
	Oil Pump	②
	Power Steering Pump Bracket	14
	Radiator Support	108①
	Thermostat	14
	Timing Belt Covers	84①
	Timing Belt Idler No. 1	26
	Timing Belt Idler No. 2	30
	Timing Belt Tensioner	20

① — Inch lbs.

② — Refer to "Cylinder Head, Replace."

③ — Tacoma, 45 ft. lbs.; T100, 29 ft. lbs.

④ — Tacoma, 30 inch lbs.; T100, 35 inch lbs.

⑤ — Tighten each bolt an additional 90°.

1FZ-FE 4.5L Engine

NOTE: On Air Bag Equipped Models, Refer To "Air Bag System Precautions" Located In The Front Of This Manual For System Disarming & Arming Procedures.

INDEX

PRECAUTIONS

AIR BAG SYSTEMS

Refer to "Air Bag System Precautions" in the front of this manual for system disarming and arming procedures.

AUDIO CODED ANTI-THEFT SYSTEM

Some models are equipped with an audio coded anti-theft system that will disable the radio when the battery cable is disconnected. The system can be identified by the "ANTI-THEFT SYSTEM" on the cassette lid. Obtain three-digit code for input. Reset system after service as follows:

1. Obtain three-digit audio theft code.
2. Depress 1 (PROG) button while depressing righthand side of TUNE SEEK button. Three dashes will appear in tape operation display.
3. To enter first digit, depress 1 (PROG) button repeatedly until number of times depressed equals first digit (depress 1 button six times if first digit is five, first press equals 0).
4. To enter second digit, depress 2 (APS) button repeatedly until number of times depressed equals second digit.
5. To enter third digit, depress 3 (RPT) button repeatedly until number of times depressed equals third digit.
6. If three dashes are displayed after inputting digits, repeat procedure.
7. When code appears in display, depress and hold SCAN button until SEC appears.
8. When SEC disappears audio system is operative.
9. If Err is displayed, repeat procedure. **Attempting to input code more than nine times may permanently disable audio system.**

BATTERY GROUND CABLE

Prior to service, disconnect battery ground cable and isolate as required.

COMPRESSION PRESSURE

1. Start engine and warm to normal operating temperature.
2. Disconnect distributor connector.
3. Disconnect igniter connector.
4. Disconnect high tension cords from spark plugs.
5. Remove spark plugs, then insert compression gauge into spark plug hole.
6. Fully open throttle.
7. While cranking engine, measure compression pressure.
8. Standard compression pressure should be 171 psi. Minimum compression is 128 psi.
9. The difference in compression pressure between each cylinder should not exceed 14 psi.

ENGINE

REPLACE

1. **On models equipped with audio coded anti-theft system,** obtain three-digit system code.
2. **On all models,** remove battery and battery tray.
3. Drain engine coolant and engine oil.
4. Scribe hood hinge locations, then remove hood.
5. Remove radiator grille.
6. Remove fan with fluid coupling, water pump pulley and fan shroud.
7. Remove drive belts.
8. Disconnect radiator hoses and remove radiator.
9. Disconnect volume airflow meter connector and wire clamp.
10. Loosen No. 2 air hose clamp and disconnect hose.
11. Remove air cleaner cap, resonator and volume airflow meter.
12. Remove air filter and air cleaner case.
13. Disconnect cruise control actuator and accelerator cables from throttle body.
14. Disconnect heater hoses.
15. Disconnect brake booster vacuum hose, EVAP hose and fuel hoses.
16. Disconnect engine wires and connectors.
17. Disconnect A/C compressor and bracket, if equipped. Place compressor aside and suspend it.
18. Disconnect No. 2 radiator hose from water inlet, then remove radiator pipe.
19. Disconnect power steering pressure hose and return hose.
20. Remove heater valve, then disconnect ground strap and engine wire from cowl panel.
21. Remove glove compartment door.
22. Remove ECM retaining screws and disconnect ECM. Disconnect ECM connectors.
23. Disconnect cowl wire connectors, then pull engine wire from cabin.
24. Remove stabilizer bar.
25. Remove front and rear propeller shafts. Put alignment marks on flanges.
26. Remove transmission control rod from shift lever.
27. Remove shift lever knob, console and boot, then the console box.
28. Disconnect shift lever connectors, then remove transmission shift lever assembly.
29. Pull out shift rod pin and disconnect shift rod.
30. Remove hose clamp and transfer shift lever.
31. Remove front exhaust pipe assembly.
32. Disconnect ground strap from heat insulator.
33. Remove transfer undercover.
34. Place jack under transmission, then remove frame crossmember.

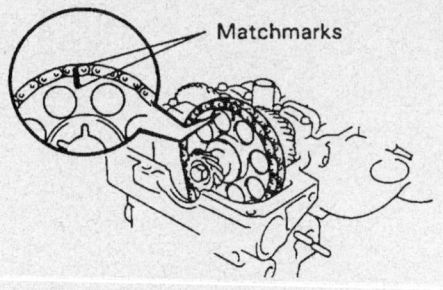
TY1069100270000X

Fig. 1 Camshaft timing gear & chain matchmarks

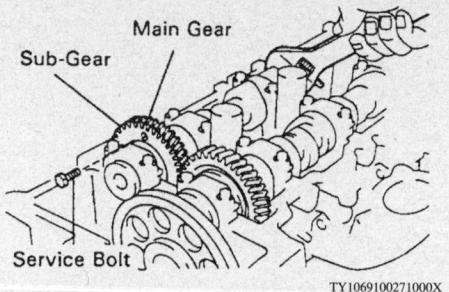
TY1069100271000X

Fig. 2 Service bolt hole

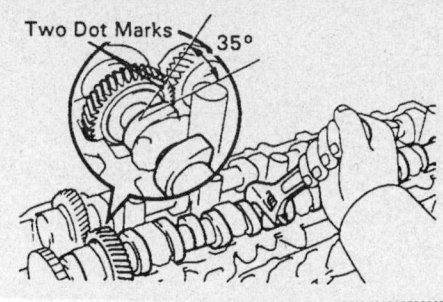
TY1069100272000X

Fig. 3 Camshaft gear timing mark

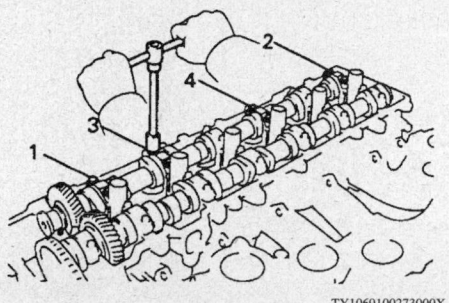
TY1069100273000X

Fig. 4 Bearing cap bolt removal

35. Slowly lift engine with transmission from vehicle. Ensure all cables, hoses and electrical connectors are disconnected during removal.
36. Separate transmission from engine.
37. Reverse procedure to install. Reset audio coded anti-theft system, if equipped, as outlined under "Precautions."

INTAKE MANIFOLD
REPLACE

Refer to "Cylinder Head, Replace" for procedure.

CYLINDER HEAD
REPLACE
REMOVAL

1. **On models equipped with audio coded anti-theft system,** obtain three-digit system code.
2. **On all models,** remove PCV hoses.
3. Remove air cleaner cap, volume air flow meter and resonator.
4. Disconnect cruise control actuator, throttle and accelerator cables from throttle body.
5. Disconnect engine ground straps.
6. Disconnect connector on intake manifold from lefthand fender apron.
7. Disconnect heater hoses.
8. Disconnect heater valve and engine wire from cowl panel.
9. Remove No. 2 and No. 3 cylinder head covers.
10. Disconnect distributor wires and connector, then remove distributor.
11. Disconnect power steering reservoir tank.
12. Disconnect radiator inlet hose.
13. Disconnect No. 3 water bypass hose.

14. Remove generator and generator bracket.
15. Remove water outlet.
16. Disconnect throttle body connectors and remove throttle body.
17. Remove No. 2 water bypass pipe with hoses.
18. Disconnect connector for emission control valve set assembly.
19. Disconnect hoses and connectors from EGR valve, then remove EGR valve and vacuum modulator.
20. Remove heater inlet pipe and air intake chamber retaining bolt.
21. Remove oil dipsticks, engine guides and transmission guides.
22. Remove hoses from air intake chamber, then the air intake chamber.
23. Remove fuel return pipe, No. 1 water bypass hose and No. 1 fuel pipe.
24. Disconnect fuel inlet hose.
25. Remove delivery pipe and injectors.
26. Disconnect engine connectors and engine wire.
27. Remove front exhaust pipe assembly.
28. Remove heater pipe, air pipe and pair reed valve.
29. Remove No. 1 and No. 2 exhaust manifolds.
30. Remove engine hangers.
31. Remove water outlet bypass and pipe.
32. Remove cylinder head cover and spark plugs.
33. Turn crankshaft pulley to set No. 1 cylinder to TDC on compression stroke.
34. Place matchmarks on camshaft timing gear and timing chain, then remove chain tensioner and camshaft timing gear, **Fig. 1.**
35. Remove camshafts as follows:
    a. Turn hexagon portion of intake camshaft with wrench to bring service bolt hole of driven sub-gear upward, **Fig. 2.**
    b. Attach exhaust camshaft sub-gear to driven gear with service bolt.
    c. Set timing mark of camshaft driven gear at a 35° angle by turning hexagon wrench head portion of exhaust camshaft, **Fig. 3.**
    d. Gently push camshaft toward rear of engine. Loosen and remove bearing cap bolts as shown in **Fig. 4.**
    e. Remove two remaining bearing cap bolts and remove exhaust camshaft.
    f. Set timing mark on intake camshaft drive gear at a 25° angle, then lightly push camshaft toward front of engine.

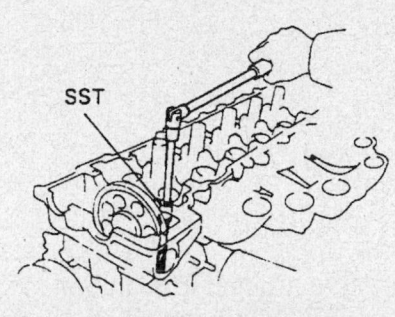

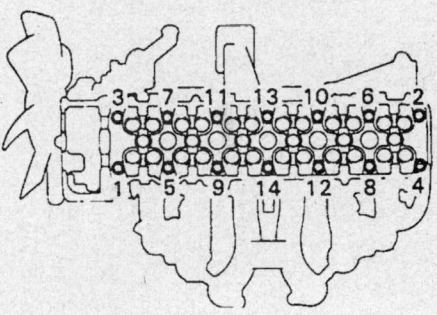
TY1069100274000X

Fig. 5 Cylinder head bolt removal sequence

g. Remove bearing caps and exhaust camshaft.
36. Remove cylinder head bolts in sequence shown in **Fig. 5,** then the cylinder head.
37. Remove heater inlet pipe and hose.
38. Remove intake manifold with fuel filter.

INSTALLATION

1. Install fuel filter and intake manifold. Tighten to specifications.
2. Install heater inlet pipe and hose.
3. Install cylinder head, then using sequence shown in **Fig. 6,** tighten bolts in three steps; first, **torque** cylinder head bolts to 29 ft. lbs.; then tighten an additional 90°; and finally tighten an additional 90°.
4. Install intake and exhaust camshafts and bearing caps. Tighten bearing caps to specifications, then remove service bolt.
5. Set No. 1 cylinder to TDC on compression stroke.
6. Turn camshafts until timing marks align as in **Fig. 7.**
7. Install camshaft gear over straight pin of intake camshaft.
8. Align straight pin of distributor gear with straight pin groove of intake camshaft, **Fig. 8,** then install and tighten

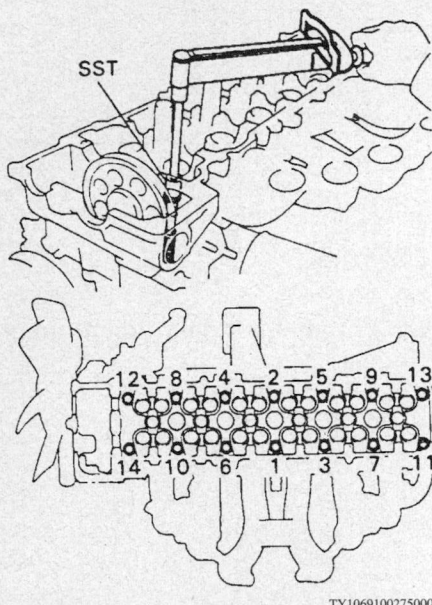

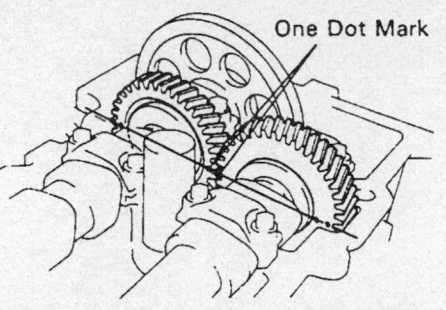

Fig. 7 Camshaft gear alignment

Fig. 8 Distributor gear alignment

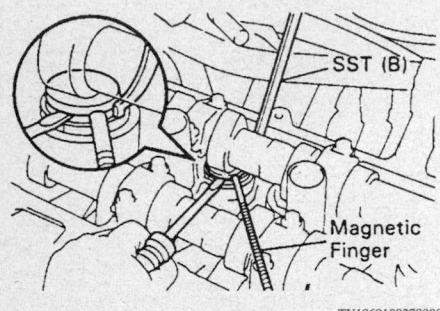

Fig. 6 Cylinder head bolt tightening sequence

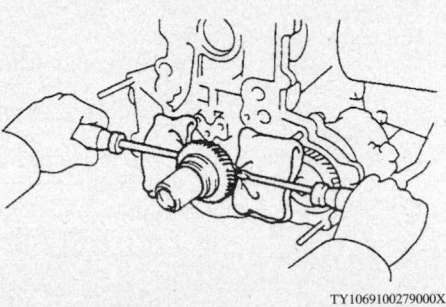

Fig. 10 Driveshaft gear removal

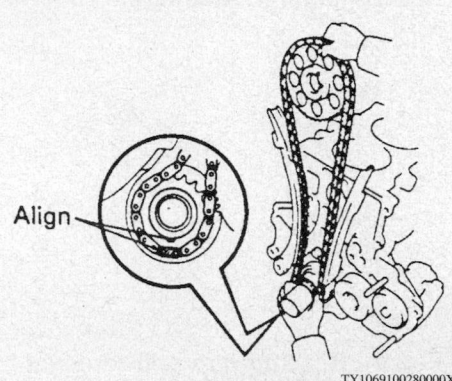

Fig. 11 Crankshaft timing gear alignment

VALVE GUIDES

1. Heat cylinder head to 176–212°F.
2. Using suitable tool and hammer, tap out valve guide bushing.
3. Using suitable tool and hammer, tap in new guide bushing until .323–.339 inch is protruding from cylinder head.

TIMING CHAIN
REPLACE
REMOVAL

1. Drain engine oil and coolant.
2. Remove engine undercover and radiator.
3. Leaving pressure hoses connected, remove A/C compressor and bracket. Position aside.
4. Disconnect radiator hose from water inlet, then remove radiator pipe.
5. Remove water pump retaining bolts and water pump.
6. Remove cylinder head as outlined under "Cylinder Head, Replace."
7. Disconnect oil cooler pipe bracket from No. 1 oil pan.
8. Remove oil level sensor.
9. Remove No. 1 oil pan attaching bolts, then the oil pan.
10. Remove crankshaft pulley and drive belt idler pulley.
11. Remove timing chain cover attaching bolts and drive belt adjusting bar.
12. Remove timing chain cover with oil pump.
13. Remove timing chain and camshaft timing gear.
14. Remove crankshaft timing gear.
15. Remove chain tensioner slipper and vibration damper.

16. Remove oil jet and oil pump driveshaft gear. Position shop towels as shown in **Fig. 10** to prevent damage.

INSTALLATION

1. Rotate crankshaft until set key faces downward.
2. Install pump driveshaft gear.
3. Install oil pump driveshaft gear and oil jet.
4. Install chain tensioner slipper and vibration damper.
5. Install crankshaft timing gear.
6. Install timing chain on camshaft timing gear. Align bright colored link on timing chain with timing mark on camshaft timing gear.
7. Install timing chain on crankshaft timing gear. Align bright colored link on timing chain with timing mark on crankshaft timing gear, **Fig. 11**.
8. Apply seal packing to timing chain cover, then install timing chain cover with oil pump.
9. Install drive belt idler pulley and tighten bolt to specification.
10. Install crankshaft pulley and tighten bolt to specification.
11. Install No. 1 and No. 2 oil pans and tighten bolts to specifications.
12. Install oil level sensor.
13. Connect oil cooler pipe bracket to No. 1 oil pan.
14. Install cylinder head as outlined under "Cylinder Head, Replace."
15. Install water pump and radiator pipe.
16. Install A/C compressor and bracket.
17. Install radiator. Fill engine with oil and check for leaks.

Fig. 9 Valve adjustment shim

bolt to specification.
9. Install and set chain tensioner, then check valve timing.
10. Reverse steps 1 through 32 of removal procedure to complete installation. Reset audio coded anti-theft system, if equipped, as outlined under "Precautions."

VALVE CLEARANCE SPECIFICATIONS

Refer to "Tune Up Specifications" for valve clearance.

VALVE ADJUSTMENT

Valve clearance is adjusted by removing or installing adjusting shims. Shims are removed and inserted with a screwdriver and magnetic finger, **Fig. 9**.
1. Turn crankshaft until No. 1 cylinder is at TDC on compression stroke. Adjust valves of cylinders except No. 6.
2. Before adjusting rear valves of No. 6 cylinder, remove distributor, and camshafts.

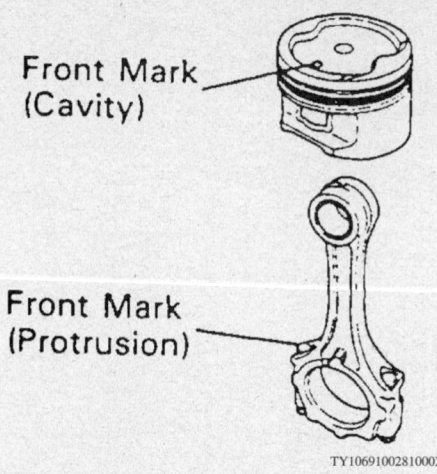

Front Mark (Cavity)

Front Mark (Protrusion)

TY1069100281000X

Fig. 12 Piston & connecting rod

18. Install engine undercover.

CAMSHAFT
REPLACE

Refer to "Cylinder Head, Replace" for camshaft removal procedures.

PISTON & ROD ASSEMBLY

Pistons are available in standard and oversize of .020 (.50 mm) and .040 inch (1.00 mm). When assembling piston onto connecting rod, align front marks of piston and connecting rod, **Fig. 12.** When installing piston and connecting rod assembly, ensure mark on top of piston is facing toward front of engine.

MAIN & ROD BEARINGS

Main and connecting rod bearings are available in standard and undersize of .010 inch (.25 mm) and .020 inch (.50 mm).

OIL PAN
REPLACE

1. Drain engine oil and engine coolant.
2. Remove engine undercover.
3. Remove radiator.
4. Disconnect A/C compressor and bracket. Place compressor aside and suspend it.
5. Disconnect No. 2 radiator hose from water inlet, then remove radiator pipe.
6. Remove water pump.
7. Remove cylinder head as outlined under "Cylinder Head, Replace."
8. Disconnect oil cooler pipe bracket from No. 1 oil pan.
9. Remove oil level sensor.
10. Remove No. 1 oil pan to transmission housing attaching bolts.
11. Remove No. 2 oil pan mounting bolts and oil pan.
12. Remove No. 2 oil pan mounting bolts and oil pan.
13. Remove oil pan baffle plate and oil strainer.

14. Remove crankshaft pulley and drive belt idler pulley.
15. Remove oil pump with timing chain cover.
16. Reverse procedure to install. Tighten oil pump and oil pan mounting bolts to specifications.

OIL PUMP
REPLACE

Refer to "Oil Pan, Replace" for procedure.

OIL PUMP SERVICE
OVERHAUL

1. Remove pump cover, drive rotor, driven rotor and gasket.
2. Remove relief valve plug, gasket and spring.
3. Reverse procedure to assemble.

INSPECTION

1. Check relief valve for scoring or wear. Replace if damaged.
2. Using thickness gauge, measure clearance between driven rotor and body. If clearance is greater than .0118 inch, replace oil pump assembly.
3. Using thickness gauge and straight-edge, measure clearance between rotors and straightedge, **Fig. 13.** If clearance is greater than .0059 inch, replace oil pump assembly.
4. Using thickness gauge, measure clearance between drive and driven rotor tips. If clearance is greater than .0098 inch, replace rotor set.

BELT TENSION DATA

Belt	New, Lbs.	Used, Lbs.
A/C Comp.	100–150	60–100
Generator	100–150	60–100
Power Steer.	100–150	60–100

COOLING SYSTEM BLEED

These engines do not require a specific bleed procedure. After filling cooling system, run engine to operating temperature with radiator/pressure cap off. Air will then be automatically bled through cap opening.

THERMOSTAT
REPLACE

1. Drain engine coolant.
2. Disconnect water inlet and remove thermostat from water pump.
3. Remove gasket and inspect thermostat.
4. Reverse procedure to install.

WATER PUMP
REPLACE

1. Drain engine coolant, then disconnect radiator inlet and water bypass hoses.

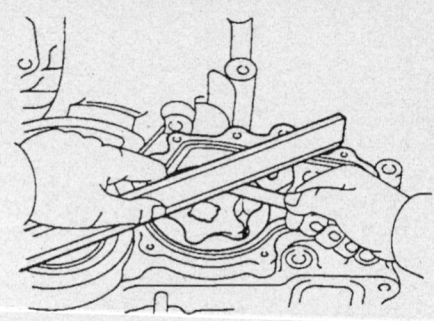

TY1099100041000X

Fig. 13 Oil pump inspection

2. Remove drive belts and fan with fluid coupling, **Fig. 14.**
3. Remove water pump pulley and fan shroud.
4. Remove water pump mounting bolts and water pump.
5. Reverse procedure to install. Tighten water pump mounting bolts to specifications.

RADIATOR
REPLACE

1. Drain engine coolant.
2. Remove battery and tray, **Fig. 15.**
3. Remove radiator grille
4. Disconnect No. 3 water bypass hose.
5. Disconnect radiator inlet hose.
6. Disconnect coolant reservoir hose.
7. Loosen water pump pulley mounting bolts.
8. Loosen lock, pivot and adjusting bolts of alternator and remove drive belts.
9. Disconnect oil cooler hose from clamp on fan shroud, then remove shroud.
10. Remove water pump pulley mounting nuts.
11. Remove fan with fluid coupling, water pump pulley and fan shroud.
12. Disconnect transmission oil cooler hoses.
13. Disconnect radiator outlet hose.
14. Remove radiator brackets, then the radiator.
15. Reverse procedure to install.

FUEL PUMP
REPLACE

1. **On models equipped with audio coded anti-theft system,** obtain three-digit system code.
2. **On all models,** remove rear seats and scuff plate.
3. Remove side garnish and step plate.
4. Remove floor service hole cover, then disconnect fuel pipe and hose from fuel pump bracket.
5. Remove fuel pump bracket mounting bolts and pull out pump bracket assembly.
6. Reverse procedure to install. Reset audio coded anti-theft system, if equipped, as outlined under "Precautions."

FUEL FILTER
REPLACE

1. **On models equipped with audio**

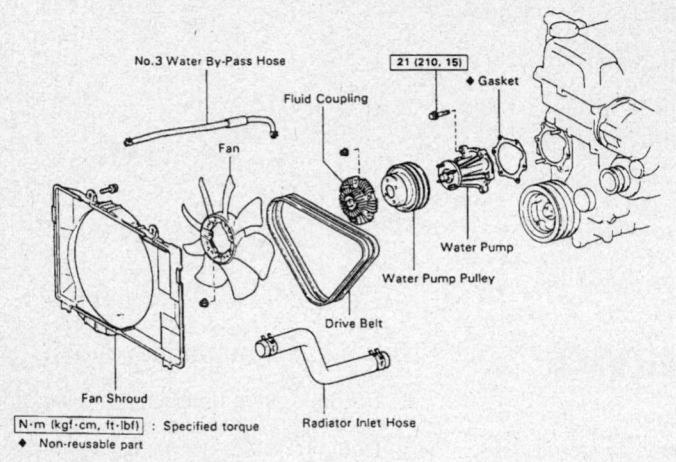

Fig. 14 Water pump removal

coded anti-theft system, obtain three-digit system code.
2. **On all models,** place suitable container under fuel filter to allow fuel drainage.
3. Slowly disconnect fuel pipe and fuel hose from fuel filter. **Place shop towel over connection to avoid fuel spilling on engine.**
4. Remove fuel filter and cap or plug fuel hose.
5. Reverse procedure to install. Reset audio coded anti-theft system, if equipped, as outlined under "Precautions."

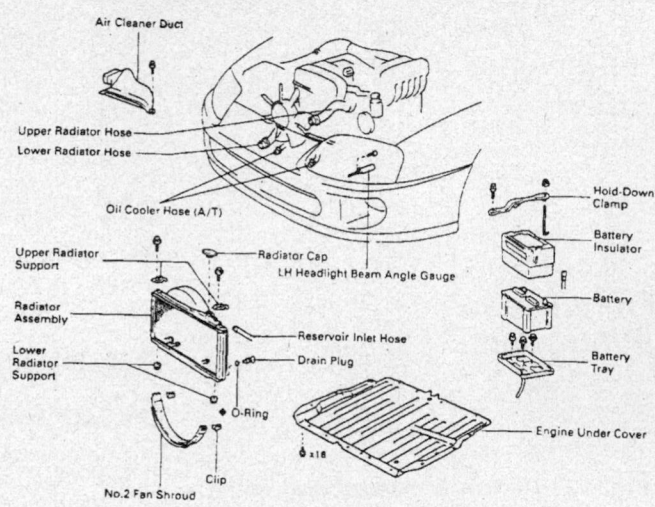

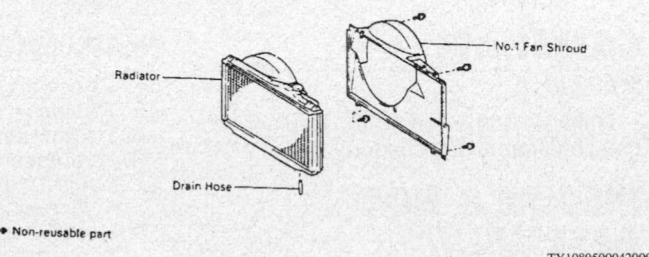

Fig. 15 Radiator removal

TIGHTENING SPECIFICATIONS

Year	Component	Torque/Ft. Lbs.
1996–99	A/C Compressor	18
	Air Intake Chamber	14
	Air Pipe Bolt	14
	Air Pipe Nut	15
	Alternator Bracket	32
	Bearing Cap Bolts	12
	Chain Tensioner Slipper	51
	Crankshaft Pulley	304
	Cylinder Head Bolts	①
	Delivery Pipe To Intake Manifold	15
	Distributor	15
	Drive Belt Idler Pulley	32
	EGR Pipe	15
	EGR Union Nut	47
	EGR Valve	14
	Engine Hanger	30
	Engine To Transmission	43
	Exhaust Manifold	29

Continued

TIGHTENING
SPECIFICATIONS—Continued

Year	Component	Torque/Ft. Lbs.
1996–99	Exhaust Pipe Assembly	46
	Exhaust Pipe Clamp Bolt	14
	Exhaust Pipe Support Bracket	29
	Front Propeller Shaft	54
	Fuel Inlet Hose	22
	Fuel Pipe Bolt	14
	Fuel Pipe To Fuel Pump Bracket	22
	Fuel Pipe Union Bolt	22
	Fuel Return Pipe	14
	Generator Bracket	32
	Heat Insulator Bolts	14
	Heater Inlet Pipe	15
	Heater Pipe Bolt	14
	Heater Pipe Nut	15
	No. 1 Oil Pan To Transmission Housing	53
	No. 1 Oil Pan (12mm Bolts)	14
	No. 1 Oil Pan (14 mm Bolts)	32
	No. 2 Oil Pan Bolts	72②
	No. 2 Oil Pan Nuts	84②
	Oil Jet Bolt	14
	Oil Pan Baffle Plate	69
	Oil Pan Drain Bolt	18
	Oil Pump	15
	Pair Reed Valve	14
	Power Steering Hose	33
	Radiator Bolts	13
	Radiator Nuts	108②
	Radiator Pipe	15
	Rear Propeller Shaft	65
	Starter	29
	Throttle Body	15
	Timing Chain Cover	32
	Timing Chain Tensioner	15
	Torque Converter Clutch	41
	Transfer Shift Lever	13
	Transmission Control Rod	108②
	Transmission Shift Lever	14
	Vibration Damper	14
	Water Bypass Pipe	15
	Water Pump Bolts	15

① — Refer to "Cylinder Head, Replace."
② — Inch lbs.

2UZ-EF 4.7L Engine

NOTE: On Air Bag Equipped Models, Refer To "Air Bag System Precautions" Located In The Front Of This Manual For System Disarming & Arming Procedures.

INDEX

PRECAUTIONS
AIR BAG SYSTEMS

Refer to "Air Bag System Precautions" in the front of this manual for system disarming and arming procedures.

AUDIO CODED ANTI-THEFT SYSTEM

Some models are equipped with an audio coded anti-theft system that will disable the radio when the battery cable is disconnected. The system can be identified by the "ANTI-THEFT SYSTEM" on the cassette lid. Obtain three-digit code for input. Reset system after service as follows:
1. Obtain three-digit audio theft code.
2. Depress 1 (PROG) button while depressing righthand side of TUNE SEEK button. Three dashes will appear in tape operation display.
3. To enter first digit, depress 1 (PROG) button repeatedly until number of times depressed equals first digit (depress 1 button six times if first digit is five, first press equals 0).
4. To enter second digit, depress 2 (APS) button repeatedly until number of times depressed equals second digit.
5. To enter third digit, depress 3 (RPT) button repeatedly until number of times depressed equals third digit.
6. If three dashes are displayed after inputting digits, repeat procedure.
7. When code appears in display, depress and hold SCAN button until SEC appears.
8. When SEC disappears audio system is operative.
9. If Err is displayed, repeat procedure. **Attempting to input code more than nine times may permanently disable audio system.**

BATTERY GROUND CABLE

Prior to service, disconnect battery ground cable and isolate as required.

COMPRESSION PRESSURE

1. Start engine and warm to normal operating temperature.
2. Disconnect high tension cords from spark plugs, then insert compression gauge into spark plug hole.
3. Fully open throttle.
4. While cranking engine, measure compression.
5. Standard compression pressure should be 192 psi. minimum compression is 142 psi.
6. Difference in compression pressure between each cylinder should not exceed 14 psi.

ENGINE
REPLACE
LAND CRUISER

1. **On models equipped with audio coded antitheft system,** obtain three-digit system code.
2. **On all models** remove hood, then the engine under covers.
3. Drain engine coolant and oil into suitable containers.
4. Remove V-bank cover, then the battery.
5. Remove air cleaner cap, then remove intake air connector pipe assembly.
6. Disconnect reservoir hose from radiator , then remove reservoir and grommet.
7. Remove radiator and fan shroud as outlined under " Radiator Replace."
8. Loosen four nuts attaching fluid coupling to fan bracket, then release tensioner and remove drive belt.
9. Remove four nuts, then remove fan, fluid coupling and fan pulley.
10. Remove glove compartment door, then the lower No. 2 panel.
11. Disconnect connector from ECM, then

remove screws and disconnect ECM from body bracket.
12. Disconnect three wire harness connectors.
13. Disconnect accelerator cable from engine, then disconnect two power steering air hoses from hose clamp on No. 3 timing belt cover.
14. Disconnect generator wire, then the connector.
15. Disconnect hose clamp for power steering air hose, then disconnect power steering air hose from upper intake manifold.
16. Disconnect two heater hoses, then engine wire clamp from bracket on cowl panel.
17. Disconnect engine wire grommet from cowl panel, then the ground strap connector.
18. Disconnect fuel main hose and clamps, then fuel return hose and clamp.
19. Disconnect air inlet hose from charcoal canister, then EVAP hose from charcoal canister.
20. Disconnect engine wire from clamp on right fender apron.
21. Disconnect battery cables from right fender apron and relay box.
22. Remove transfer shift lever knob, then the upper console panel.
23. Remove shift lever assembly, then the transfer shift lever boot.
24. Remove transfer shift lever assembly and gasket.
25. Remove front exhaust pipes, then place matchmarks on propeller shaft flange and transfer.
26. Place matchmarks on propeller shaft flange and front differential.
27. Remove attaching nuts and bolts, then remove propeller shaft.
28. Remove lefthand and righthand stabilizer bar links, then remove stabilizer bar.
29. Disconnect A/C compressor electrical connector, then remove compressor

from engine and reposition for clearance.

30. Remove power steering pump from engine and reposition for clearance.
31. Attach engine chain hoist to engine hangers.
32. Remove nuts and bolts holding engine mounting brackets to frame brackets.
33. Remove transfer case protector, then the frame crossmember.
34. Lift engine and transmission slowly and carefully out of vehicle. Ensure engine is clear of all wiring, hoses cables, then place engine and transmission on a suitable stand.
35. Disconnect engine wire from transmission, then remove dipstick guide and dipstick from transmission.
36. Remove oil cooler pipes from transmission, then the flywheel housing under cover.
37. Hold crankshaft pulley with a wrench, then remove torque converter bolts.
38. Remove transmission bolts, then remove transmission and torque converter from engine.
39. Remove attaching bolts, then front spacer, drive plate and rear spacer.
40. Reverse procedure to install. Reset audio coded anti-theft and air bag system, if equipped, as outlined under "Precautions"

TUNDRA

1. **On 4WD models,** proceed as follows:
   a. Remove front and rear propeller shafts.
   b. Remove transmission.
2. **On all models,** remove hood, then the engine under covers.
3. Drain engine coolant and oil into suitable containers.
4. Remove radiator as outlined under "Radiator, Replace."
5. Remove throttle body cover.
6. Disconnect MAF meter connector, then remove air cleaner case.
7. **On models equipped with A/C,** remove suction hose from air intake connector.
8. **On all models,** disconnect power steering air hose, then air inlet hose for EVAP.
9. Disconnect PCV hose and MAF meter wire from air intake connector.
10. Disconnect intake air from throttle body.
11. Disconnect clamp on battery cable from No. 2 relay box.
12. Disconnect battery cables from left fender apron.
13. Loosen four nuts attaching fluid coupling to fan bracket, then loosen adjust lock nut, adjusting bolt, pivot bolt and remove drive belt.
14. Remove four nuts, then remove fan, fluid coupling and fan pulley.
15. Remove glove compartment door, then the lower No. 2 panel.
16. Disconnect connector from ECM, then remove screws and disconnect ECM from body bracket.
17. Disconnect three wire harness connectors, then two wire harness connectors for cassette.
18. Disconnect engine wire from bracket,

then remove bracket.
19. Pull out engine wire from cowl panel.
20. Disconnect accelerator cable from engine, then disconnect two power steering air hoses from hose clamp on No. 3 timing belt cover.
21. Disconnect generator wire, then the connector.
22. Disconnect hose clamp for power steering air hose, then disconnect power steering air hose from upper intake manifold.
23. Disconnect two heater hoses, then engine wire clamp from bracket on cowl panel.
24. Disconnect fuel inlet hose and clamps, then fuel return hose and clamp.
25. Disconnect air inlet hose from charcoal canister, then EVAP hose from charcoal canister.
26. **On models less hydraulic brake booster,** disconnect brake booster tube.
27. **On all models,** remove front exhaust pipes.
28. Remove propeller shaft.
29. Remove nuts, disconnect stabilizer bar links from lower suspension arms.
30. Remove nuts, then the stabilizer bar.
31. Disconnect power steering feed and return tubes from gear, then the transmission control cable from control shift lever.
32. **On models equipped with A/C,** disconnect A/C compressor connector and remove A/C compressor from engine, then reposition for clearance
33. **On all models,** remove power steering pump from engine, then reposition for clearance.
34. Attach engine chain hoist to engine hangers.
35. Remove nuts and bolts holding engine mounting brackets to frame brackets.
36. Place jack under transmission, then remove frame crossmember and engine rear mounting bracket from transmission.
37. Lift engine and transmission slowly and carefully out of vehicle. Ensure engine is clear of all wiring, hoses cables, then place engine and transmission on a suitable stand.
38. Disconnect engine wire from transmission, then remove dipstick guide and dipstick from transmission.
39. Remove oil cooler pipes from transmission, then the flywheel housing under cover.
40. Hold crankshaft pulley with a wrench, then remove torque converter bolts.
41. Remove transmission bolts, then remove transmission and torque converter from engine.
42. Remove attaching bolts, then front spacer, drive plate and rear spacer.
43. Reverse procedure to install.

INTAKE MANIFOLD

REPLACE

Refer to "Cylinder Head, Replace" for procedure

CYLINDER HEAD

REPLACE

REMOVAL

1. Drain engine coolant into a suitable container.
2. **On Tundra models,** remove throttle body cover.
3. **On all models,** disconnect timing belt from camshaft timing pulley as outlined under "Timing Belt Replace."
4. Remove camshaft timing pulleys as outlined under " Camshaft Replace."
5. Remove camshaft position sensor, then remove power steering pump from engine and reposition for clearance.
6. Remove front exhaust pipe from engine, then the oil dipstick and guide.
7. Remove ignition coils, then remove timing belt rear plates. **Ensure not to drop anything inside timing belt cover. Do not allow belt to come in contact with water, oil or dust.**
8. Disconnect fuel inlet hose, then all electrical connectors over intake manifold.
9. Disconnect fuel regulator vacuum from fuel pressure regulator pipe, then the PCV hose from PCV valve on lefthand cylinder head.
10. Disconnect EVAP hose from VSV for EVAP, then from EVAP pipe on intake manifold.
11. Disconnect EVAP hose from intake air connector, then power steering air hose from intake manifold.
12. Disconnect 2 wire clamps from throttle body, then No. 1 water bypass from front water bypass joint.
13. Disconnect 2 wire clamps from wire clamp bracket on righthand delivery pipe.
14. Remove engine wire protector from rear water bypass joint and righthand cylinder head, then remove 2 ground cables from righthand and lefthand cylinder head.
15. Remove bolts, then the engine wire protector from intake manifold.
16. Remove engine wire from engine wire and wire bracket.
17. Remove EVAP pipe from intake manifold.
18. **On Tundra models,** remove nuts, then accelerator cable bracket from intake manifold.
19. **On all models,** remove righthand and lefthand front V-bank cover bracket.
20. Remove bolts, then nuts and intake manifold.
21. Remove water inlet and outlet housing, then the front water bypass joint.
22. Remove rear water bypass joint, then the engine hangers.
23. **On Land Cruiser models,** remove oil dipstick and guide for automatic transmission.
24. **On all models,** remove cylinder head covers. **If necessary, remove semicircular plugs and camshaft housing plugs.**
25. **Since thrust clearance of camshaft is small, camshaft must be kept**

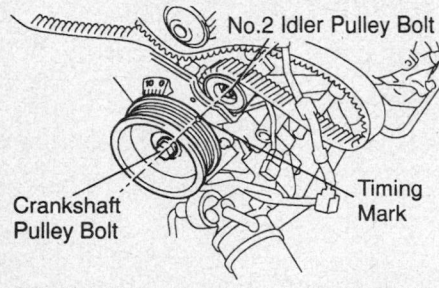

Fig. 1 Crankshaft pulley timing mark

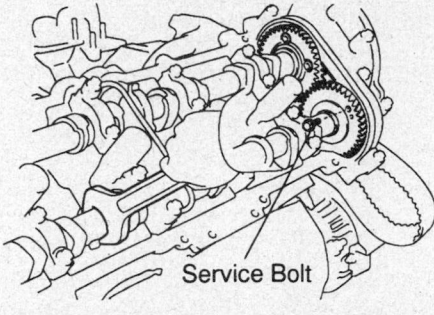

Fig. 2 Righthand service bolt hole

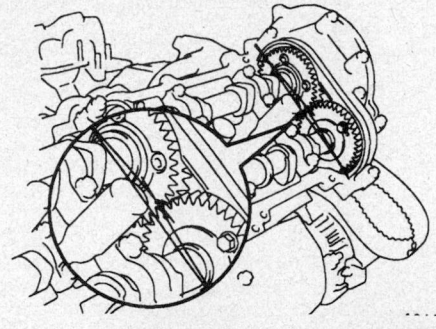

Fig. 3 Righthand camshaft gear timing mark

level while it is being removed. If camshaft is not kept level, portion of cylinder head receiving shaft thrust may crack or be damaged, causing camshaft to seize or break.

26. Check crankshaft pulley position.
27. Ensure that timing mark of crankshaft pulley is aligned with centers of crankshaft pulley bolt and idler pulley bolt, **Fig. 1.**
28. Remove righthand camshafts as follows:
    a. Turn hexagon portion of exhaust camshaft with wrench to bring service bolt hole of sub-gear upward, **Fig. 2.**
    b. Attach sub-gear to driven gear with service bolt.
    c. Set timing mark of camshaft main gear at approximately 10° angle by turning hexagon head portion of exhaust camshaft, **Fig. 3.**
    d. Uniformly loosen and remove bearing caps bolts in several passes, **Fig. 4.**
    e. Remove oil feed pipe, then 9 bearing caps, camshaft timing control valve and camshafts.
29. Remove lefthand camshafts as follows:
    a. Turn hexagon portion of exhaust camshaft with wrench to bring service bolt hole of sub-gear upward, **Fig. 5.**
    b. Attach sub-gear to driven gear with service bolt.
    c. Align timing mark (2 dot marks) of camshaft drive gear by turning hexagon wrench head portion of exhaust camshaft with wrench, **Fig. 6.**
    d. Uniformly loosen bearing cap bolts in several passes, **Fig. 7.**
    e. Remove oil feed pipe, then the 9 bearing caps, camshaft timing oil control valve and camshafts. Arrange bearing caps in correct order.
30. Mount hexagon wrench head portion of camshaft in a vise. **Ensure not to damage camshaft.**
31. Using removal tool No. 09960–10010 or equivalent, turn sub-gear clockwise and remove service bolt.
32. Using ring pliers, remove snap ring.
33. Remove wave washer, camshaft sub-gear and camshaft gear spring. Arrange camshaft sub-gears and gear springs, (righthand and lefthand

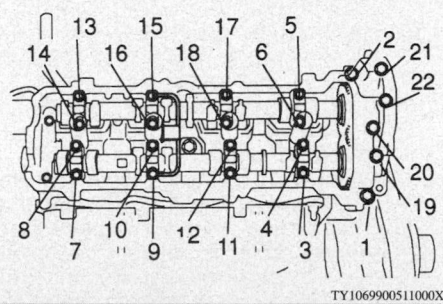

Fig. 4 Righthand bearing cap bolt loosening sequence

sides). **Ensure not to damage camshaft timing tube.**
34. Remove oil seal from intake camshaft, then remove spark plugs.
35. Uniformly loosen cylinder head bolts on one side of each cylinder head in several passes, **Fig. 8.** then do other side.
36. Remove cylinder head bolts and plate washers. **Cylinder head warpage or cracking could result from removing bolts in incorrect order.**
37. Lift cylinder head from dowels on cylinder block, then remove righthand and lefthand exhaust manifolds insulators and gaskets from cylinder heads.

INSTALLATION

1. Install righthand and lefthand exhaust manifolds to cylinder heads.
2. Place 2 new cylinder head gaskets in position on cylinder block.On rear side of cylinder head gaskets are marks to distinguish lefthand and righthand banks, " 2UR" mark for righthand bank and "2UL" for lefthand bank.
3. Place cylinder heads in position on cylinder head gaskets.
4. Apply light coat of engine oil to threads of cylinder head bolts, then install washers to bolts.
5. Install and uniformly tighten cylinder head bolts on one side of cylinder head in several passes, **Fig. 9.** then do other side.
6. **Torque** cylinder head bolts to 24 ft. lbs.
7. Mark front of cylinder head bolt head with paint. Retighten cylinder head

bolts by 180°. Ensure that paint mark is now at a 180° angle to front.
8. Install spark plugs.
9. Install camshaft gear spring, then the sub-gear.
10. Using ring pliers, install snap ring.
11. Mount hexagon wrench portion of camshaft in a vise. **Ensure not to damage camshaft.**
12. Align holes of camshaft main gear and sub-gear by turning camshaft sub-gear counterclockwise, and temporarily install a service bolt.
13. Align gear teeth of main gear and sub-gear using tool No. 09960–10010 or equivalent, then tighten service bolt.
14. Remove any old packing material, apply sealant part No. 08826–00080 or equivalent to camshaft housing plug grooves.
15. Install two camshaft housing plugs to cylinder heads.
16. **Since thrust clearance of camshaft is small, camshaft must be kept level while it is being installed. If camshaft is not kept level, portion of cylinder head receiving shaft thrust may crack or be damaged, causing camshaft to seize or break.**
17. Turn crankshaft pulley clockwise or couterclockwise, put timing mark of crankshaft pulley in line with centers of crankshaft pulley bolt and idler pulley bolt, **Fig. 10.**
18. Install righthand camshafts as follows:
    a. Apply MP grease to thrust portion of intake and exhaust camshafts, then place intake and exhaust camshafts.
    b. Set timing mark (1 dot mark) of camshaft main gear at approximately 10° angle, **Fig. 11.**
    c. Remove any old packing material from front of bearing cap, then apply sealant part No. 08826–00080 or equivalent to front bearing cap, **Fig. 12.** Parts must be assembled within 5 minutes of application, otherwise material must be removed and reapplied.**Do not apply sealant to front bearing cap grooves.**
    d. Install front bearing cap, then install other bearing caps in sequence, **Fig. 13.** with arrow mark facing

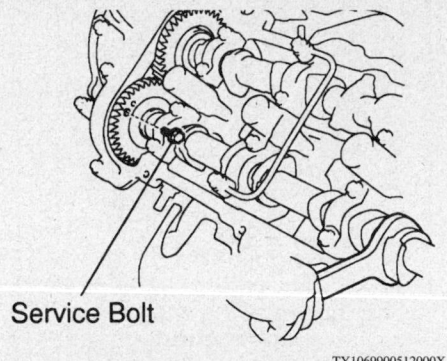

Service Bolt

Fig. 5 Lefthand service bolt hole

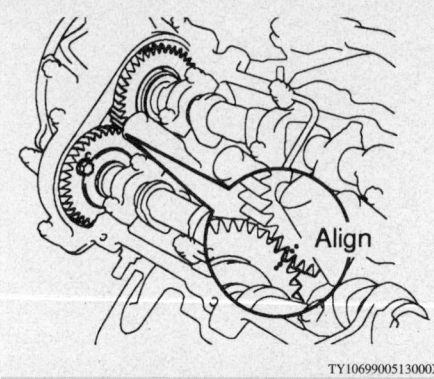

Align

Fig. 6 Lefthand camshaft gear timing mark

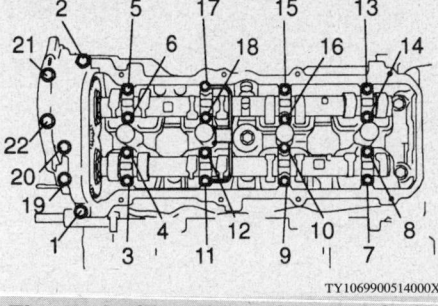

TY1069900514000X

Fig. 7 Lefthand bearing cap bolt loosening sequence

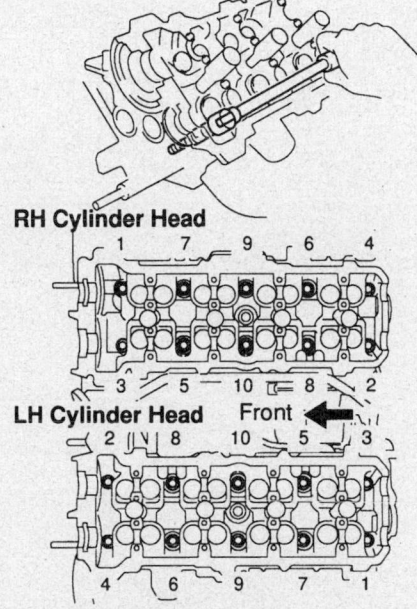

RH Cylinder Head

LH Cylinder Head   Front ←

TY1069900515000X

Fig. 8 Cylinder head bolts loosening sequence

RH Cylinder Head

LH Cylinder Head   Front ←

TY1069900516000X

Fig. 9 Cylinder head bolts tightening sequence

forward.
e. Push in camshaft oil seal, then apply light coat of engine oil on threads and under heads (D and E) of bearing cap bolts, **Fig. 14. Do not apply engine oil under heads of bearing cap bolts (A), (B) and (C).**
f. Install oil feed pipe and 22 bearing cap bolts, then uniformly tighten bolts in several passes, **Fig. 15.** Bearing cap bolt length, 3.70 in. for (A); 2.83 in. for(B); .98 inch for (C); 2.05 in. for (D); 1.50 in. for (E).
g. **Torque** bolt (C) to 69 inch lbs., then others to 12 ft. lbs.
h. Boring service bolt installed in driven sub-gear upward by turning hexagon wrench head portion of camshaft with a wrench, remove service bolt.
19. Install lefthand camshafts as follows:
   a. Apply MP grease to thrust portion of

intake and exhaust camshafts, then place intake and exhaust camshafts.
b. Engage intake to exhaust gear by meeting timing mark (2 dot marks) on each gear, **Fig. 16.**
c. Remove any old packing material from front of bearing cap, then apply sealant part No. 08826–00080 or equivalent to front bearing cap, **Fig. 17.** Parts must be assembled within 5 minutes of application, otherwise material must be removed and reapplied. **Do not apply sealant to front bearing cap grooves.**
d. Install front bearing cap, then install other bearing caps in sequence as shown in, **Fig. 18.** with arrow mark facing forward.
e. Push in camshaft oil seal, then apply light coat of engine oil on threads and under heads (D and E) of bearing cap bolts, **Fig. 19. Do not apply engine oil under heads of bearing cap bolts (A), (B) and (C).**
f. Install oil feed pipe and 22 bearing cap bolts, then uniformly tighten bolts in several passes, **Fig. 20.**
g. **Torque** bolt (C) to 69 inch lbs., then others to 12 ft. lbs.
h. Boring service bolt installed in driven sub-gear upward by turning hexagon wrench head portion of camshaft with a wrench, remove service bolt.
20. Check and adjust valve clearance.
21. Reverse steps 1 through 27 of removal procedure to complete installation.

VALVE CLEARANCE SPECIFICATIONS

Refer to "Tune Up Specifications" for valve clearance.

VALVE ADJUSTMENT

Shims are available in 41 increments of .0008 inch, from .0787 inch to .1102 inch.

1. Drain engine coolant, then remove battery clamp cover.
2. **On Land Cruiser models,** remove V-bank cover.
3. **On all models,** remove air cleaner and intake air connector assembly.
4. Remove No. 3 timing belt cover as outlined under "Timing Belt Replace".
5. Remove ignition coils as outlined under "Coil Pack Replace."
6. Remove righthand and lefthand cylinder head covers as outlined under "Cylinder Head Replace."
7. Rotate crankshaft pulley and align its grooves with timing mark "0" of timing belt cover, **Fig. 21.**
8. Ensure that timing marks of camshaft timing pulley and timing belt rear plates are aligned as in, **Fig. 22.** If not, rotate crankshaft 1 revolution and align mark.
9. Using suitable feeler gauge, measure clearance between valve lifter and camshaft. Measure only those valves

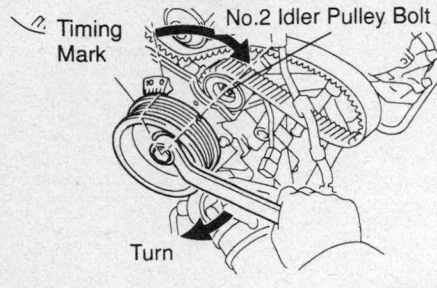

Fig. 10 Crankshaft pulley timing mark

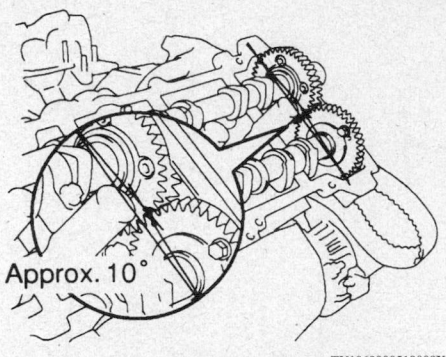

Fig. 11 Righthand camshaft main gear timing mark

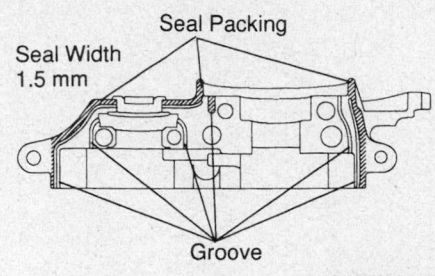

Fig. 12 Bearing cap sealant application

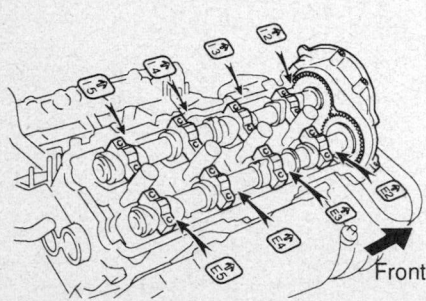

Fig. 13 Righthand cylinder head bearing cap locations

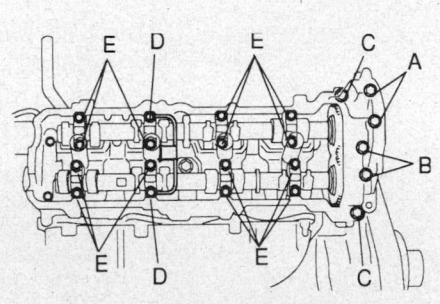

Fig. 14 Righthand cylinder head bearing cap bolt locations

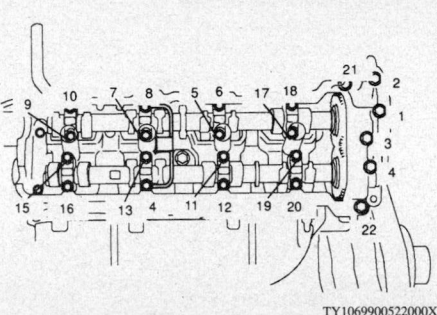

Fig. 15 Righthand cylinder head bearing cap bolts tightening sequence

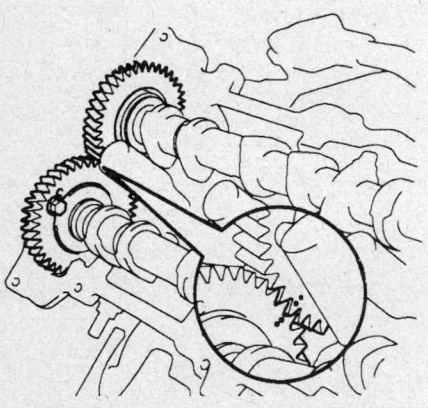

Fig. 16 Lefthand cylinder head intake to exhaust gear timing marks

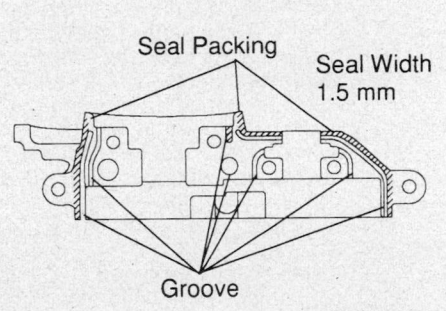

Fig. 17 Bearing cap sealant application

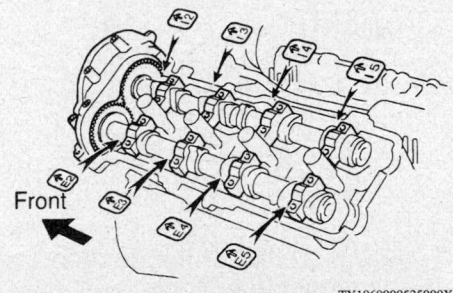

Fig. 18 Lefthand cylinder head bearing cap locations

indicated in **Fig. 23.** Refer to "Valve Clearance Specifications"
10. Turn crankshaft 360° and measure only those valves indicated in **Fig. 24.**
11. Remove timing belt as outlined under "Timing Belt Replace."
12. Remove camshafts as outlined under "Camshaft Replace."
13. Remove valve lifter and adjusting shim.
14. Determine replacement adjusting shim size to chart in, **Figs. 25 and 26.**
15. Using a suitable micrometer, measure thickness of removed shim. Calculate thickness of a new shim so that valve clearance comes within specified value. Select a new shim with a thick-

ness as close as possible to calculated value.
16. Place a new adjusting shim on valve, then place valve lifter.
17. Reinstall camshafts, then timing belt and recheck valve clearance.
18. Reverse procedure to install remaining parts.

TIMING BELT, REPLACE
REMOVAL

1. **On Land Cruiser models,** remove oil pan protector and V-bank cover.
2. **On all models,** remove engine under cover, then drain engine coolant into a suitable container.
3. Remove battery clamp cover, then the air cleaner and intake air connector assembly.

4. Loose bolts holding fluid coupling to fan bracket, then release tensioner and remove drive belt.
5. Remove nuts, then the fan, fluid coupling assembly and fan pulley.
6. **On Land cruiser models,** remove radiator as outlined under "Radiator Replace."
7. **On Tundra models,** remove power steering pump as outlined under "Power Steering Pump Replace."
8. **On all models,** remove drive belt idler pulley.
9. Remove righthand No. 3 timing belt cover.
10. Disconnect engine wire from 2 wire clamps, then remove bolts and nuts from lefthand No. 3 timing belt cover.
11. Disconnect camshaft position sensor from wire clamp on lefthand No. 3 timing belt cover, then sensor connector from bracket.
12. Remove wire grommet from lefthand

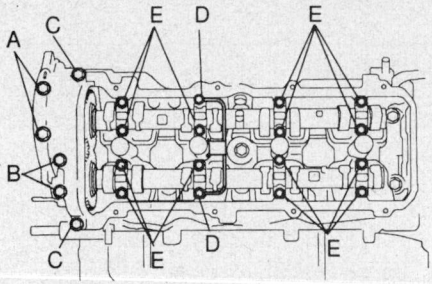

TY1069900526000X

Fig. 19   Lefthand cylinder head bearing cap bolt locations

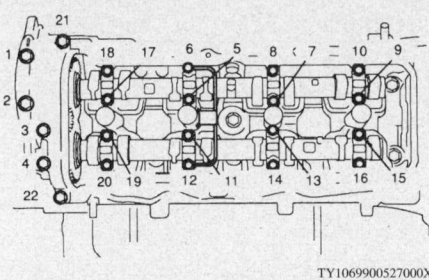

TY1069900527000X

Fig. 20   Lefthand cylinder head bearing cap bolts tightening sequence

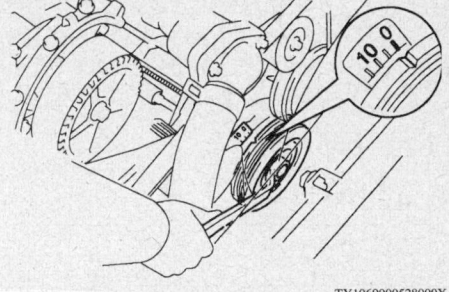

TY1069900528000X

Fig. 21   Crankshaft pulley & No. 1 timing belt cover alignment mark

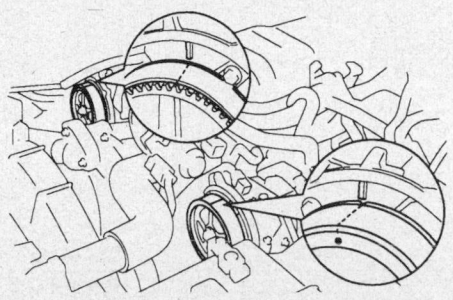

TY1069900529000X

Fig. 22   Camshaft pulleys & timing belt rear plates alignment marks

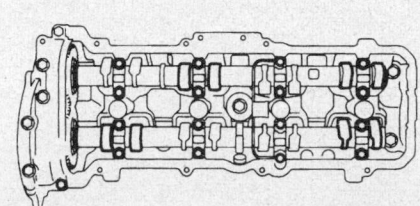

RH Cylinder Head

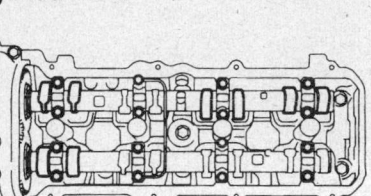

LH Cylinder Head   Front ←

TY1069900530000X

Fig. 23   1st valve clearance measurement

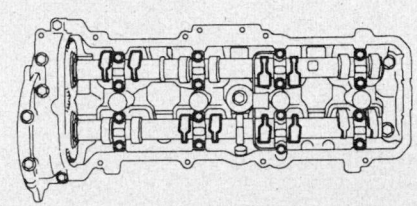

RH Cylinder Head

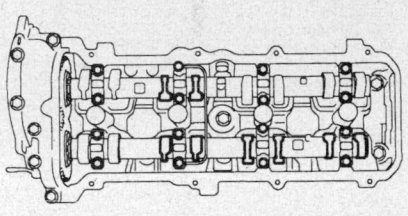

LH Cylinder Head   Front ←

TY1069900531000X

Fig. 24   2nd valve clearance measurement

No. 3 timing belt cover, then remove cover and oil cooler pipe.

13. remove attaching bolts, then the No. 2 timing belt cover.
14. **On models equipped with A/C,** disconnect electrical connector, them bolts and A/C compressor.
15. **On all models,** remove fan bracket.
16. If re-using timing belt, ensure there are installation marks on timing belt, **Fig. 27.** If installation marks have disappeared, place new installation marks on timing belt before removing each part.
17. Loosen crankshaft pulley bolt using pulley holder tool No. 09213–70010 or equivalent.
18. Turn crankshaft pulley and align its grooves with timing mark 0 of No. 1 timing belt cover, **Fig. 28.**
19. Ensure that timing marks of camshaft timing pulleys and timing belt rear plates align, **Fig. 29.**
20. Turn crankshaft pulley approximately 50° clockwise to align timing mark of crankshaft pulley in line with centers of crankshaft pulley bolt and idler pulley bolt, then remove crankshaft pulley bolt. **Do not turn crankshaft pulley.**
21. Remove timing belt tensioner.
22. Using camshaft pulley tool No. 09960–10010 or equivalent, loosen tension between righthand and lefthand camshaft pulleys by slightly turning lefthand camshaft timing pulley clockwise.
23. Disconnect timing belt from camshaft timing pulleys, then remove camshaft timing pulleys.

24. Remove alternator as outlined under "Alternator Replace," then remove drive belt tensioner.
25. Using a crankshaft pulley remover tool No. 09950–50012 or equivalent, remove crankshaft pulley. **Do not turn crankshaft pulley.**
26. Remove No. 1 timing belt cover, then remove timing belt guide and timing belt cover spacer.
27. Remove timing belt, then the Nos. 1 and 2 idler pulleys.
28. Using pulley remover tool No. 09950–50012 or equivalent, remove crankshaft timing pulley. **Do not turn timing pulley.**

INSTALLATION

1. Align timing pulley set key with key groove of pulley, using installation tool No. 09223–46011 or equivalent and a hammer tap in crankshaft timing pulley with flange side facing inward.
2. Apply adhesive part No. 08833–00080 THREE BOND 1334, LOCTITE 242 or equivalent, to 2 or 3 threads of pivot bolt and install Nos. 1 and 2 idler pulleys.

3. Remove any oil or water on crankshaft pulley, oil pump pulley, water pump pulley, Nos. 1 and 2 idler pulleys. **Only wipe pulleys, do not use any cleansing agent.**
4. Align installation mark on timing belt with timing mark on crankshaft timing pulley, **Fig. 30.**
5. Install timing belt on crankshaft timing pulley, Nos. 1 and 2 idler pulleys.
6. Install gasket to cover spacer, then install cover spacer.
7. Install timing belt guide facing cup side outward, then the No. 1 timing belt guide.
8. Using pulley installation tool No. 09223–46011 or equivalent and a hammer, tap in crankshaft pulley.
9. Install drive belt tensioner, then the alternator as outlined under "Alternator Replace."
10. Ensure that timing mark on crankshaft pulley is aligned with centers of crankshaft pulley and idler pulley bolt.
11. Align camshaft knock pin with knock pin groove of timing pulley, and slide on timing pulley.
12. Using installation tool No. 0996010010

Adjusting Shim Selection Chart (Intake)

The chart cross-references the measured valve clearance (left column, mm/in.) against the installed shim thickness (top row, mm/in., ranging from 2.000 (0.0787) to 2.800 (0.1102)) to give the replacement shim number.

Column headers — Installed shim thickness mm (in.): 2.000 (0.0787), 2.020 (0.0795), 2.040 (0.0803), 2.060 (0.0811), 2.080 (0.0819), 2.100 (0.0827), 2.120 (0.0835), 2.140 (0.0843), 2.160 (0.0850), 2.180 (0.0858), 2.200 (0.0866), 2.220 (0.0874), 2.230 (0.0878), 2.240 (0.0882), 2.250 (0.0886), 2.260 (0.0890), 2.270 (0.0894), 2.280 (0.0898), 2.290 (0.0902), 2.300 (0.0906), 2.310 (0.0909), 2.320 (0.0913), 2.330 (0.0917), 2.340 (0.0921), 2.350 (0.0925), 2.360 (0.0929), 2.370 (0.0933), 2.380 (0.0937), 2.390 (0.0941), 2.400 (0.0945), 2.410 (0.0949), 2.420 (0.0953), 2.430 (0.0957), 2.440 (0.0961), 2.450 (0.0965), 2.460 (0.0969), 2.470 (0.0972), 2.480 (0.0976), 2.490 (0.0980), 2.500 (0.0984), 2.510 (0.0988), 2.520 (0.0992), 2.530 (0.0996), 2.540 (0.1000), 2.550 (0.1004), 2.560 (0.1008), 2.570 (0.1012), 2.580 (0.1016), 2.590 (0.1020), 2.600 (0.1024), 2.620 (0.1031), 2.640 (0.1039), 2.660 (0.1047), 2.680 (0.1055), 2.700 (0.1063), 2.720 (0.1071), 2.740 (0.1079), 2.760 (0.1087), 2.780 (0.1094), 2.800 (0.1102)

Row labels — Measured clearance mm (in.):
- 0.000–0.030 (0.0000–0.0012)
- 0.031–0.050 (0.0012–0.0020)
- 0.051–0.070 (0.0020–0.0028)
- 0.071–0.090 (0.0028–0.0035)
- 0.091–0.110 (0.0036–0.0043)
- 0.111–0.130 (0.0044–0.0051)
- 0.131–0.150 (0.0052–0.0059)
- 0.150–0.250 (0.0059–0.0098)
- 0.251–0.270 (0.0099–0.0106)
- 0.271–0.290 (0.0107–0.0114)
- 0.291–0.310 (0.0115–0.0122)
- 0.311–0.330 (0.0122–0.0130)
- 0.331–0.350 (0.0130–0.0138)
- 0.351–0.370 (0.0138–0.0146)
- 0.371–0.390 (0.0146–0.0154)
- 0.391–0.410 (0.0154–0.0161)
- 0.411–0.430 (0.0162–0.0169)
- 0.431–0.450 (0.0170–0.0177)
- 0.451–0.470 (0.0178–0.0185)
- 0.471–0.490 (0.0185–0.0193)
- 0.491–0.510 (0.0193–0.0201)
- 0.511–0.530 (0.0201–0.0209)
- 0.531–0.550 (0.0209–0.0217)
- 0.551–0.570 (0.0217–0.0224)
- 0.571–0.590 (0.0225–0.0232)
- 0.591–0.610 (0.0233–0.0240)
- 0.611–0.630 (0.0241–0.0248)
- 0.631–0.650 (0.0248–0.0256)
- 0.651–0.670 (0.0256–0.0264)
- 0.671–0.690 (0.0264–0.0272)
- 0.691–0.710 (0.0272–0.0280)
- 0.711–0.730 (0.0280–0.0287)
- 0.731–0.750 (0.0288–0.0295)
- 0.751–0.770 (0.0296–0.0303)
- 0.771–0.790 (0.0304–0.0311)
- 0.791–0.810 (0.0311–0.0319)
- 0.811–0.830 (0.0319–0.0327)
- 0.831–0.850 (0.0327–0.0335)
- 0.851–0.870 (0.0335–0.0343)
- 0.871–0.890 (0.0343–0.0350)
- 0.891–0.910 (0.0351–0.0358)
- 0.911–0.930 (0.0359–0.0366)
- 0.931–0.950 (0.0367–0.0374)
- 0.951–0.970 (0.0374–0.0382)
- 0.971–0.990 (0.0382–0.0390)
- 0.991–1.010 (0.0390–0.0398)
- 1.011–1.030 (0.0398–0.0406)
- 1.031–1.050 (0.0406–0.0413)

Intake valve clearance (Cold):
0.15 – 0.25 mm (0.006 – 0.010 in.)
EXAMPLE:
The 2.300 mm (0.0906 in.) shim is installed, and the measured clearance is 0.440 mm (0.0173 in.). Replace the 2.300 mm (0.0906 in.) shim with a No. 54 shim.

New shim thickness mm (in.)

Shim No.	Thickness	Shim No.	Thickness	Shim No.	Thickness
00	2.000 (0.0787)	28	2.280 (0.0898)	56	2.560 (0.1008)
02	2.020 (0.0795)	30	2.300 (0.0906)	58	2.580 (0.1016)
04	2.040 (0.0803)	32	2.320 (0.0913)	60	2.600 (0.1024)
06	2.060 (0.0811)	34	2.340 (0.0921)	62	2.620 (0.1031)
08	2.080 (0.0819)	36	2.360 (0.0929)	64	2.640 (0.1039)
10	2.100 (0.0827)	38	2.380 (0.0937)	66	2.660 (0.1047)
12	2.120 (0.0835)	40	2.400 (0.0945)	68	2.680 (0.1055)
14	2.140 (0.0843)	42	2.420 (0.0953)	70	2.700 (0.1063)
16	2.160 (0.0850)	44	2.440 (0.0961)	72	2.720 (0.1071)
18	2.180 (0.0858)	46	2.460 (0.0969)	74	2.740 (0.1079)
20	2.200 (0.0866)	48	2.480 (0.0976)	76	2.760 (0.1087)
22	2.220 (0.0874)	50	2.500 (0.0984)	78	2.780 (0.1094)
24	2.240 (0.0882)	52	2.520 (0.0992)	80	2.800 (0.1102)
26	2.260 (0.0890)	54	2.540 (0.1000)		

TY1069900532000X

Fig. 25   Intake shim selection chart

or equivalent, install lefthand and righthand pulley bolts.
13. Remove any oil or water on lefthand camshaft timing pulley, and keep it clean.
14. Turn lefthand camshaft timing pulley. Align installation mark on timing belt with timing mark of camshaft timing pulley, and hang timing belt on lefthand timing pulley, **Fig. 31.**
15. Turn lefthand camshaft timing pulley counterclockwise until there is tension between crankshaft timing pulley and lefthand camshaft timing pulley.
16. Remove any oil or water on righthand camshaft timing pulley, and keep it clean.
17. Turn righthand camshaft timing pulley. Align installation mark on timing belt with timing mark of camshaft timing pulley, and hang timing belt on righthand timing pulley, **Fig. 32.**
18. Using a press slowly press in belt tensioner pushrod using 220–2205 ft. lbs. of pressure.
19. Align holes of push rod and housing, pass a 1.27mm hexagon wrench through holes to keep setting position of push rod, **Fig. 33.** Release press,

the install dust booth to belt tensioner.
20. Temporarily install timing belt tensioner and alternately tighten bolts to specification. Using pliers, remove 1.27mm hexagon wrench from belt tensioner.
21. Temporarily install crankshaft pulley bolt. Slowly turn crankshaft pulley 2 revolutions from TDC to TDC. **Always turn crankshaft pulley clockwise.**
22. Ensure that each pulley is aligned with timing marks, **Fig. 34.**
23. Using pulley installation tool Nos. 09213–54015 and 09330–00021 or equivalents, tighten crankshaft pulley bolt to specification.
24. Install fan bracket, then install A/C compressor and connect electrical connector.
25. Install No. 2 timing belt cover, then righthand No. 3 timing belt cover.
26. Install oil cooler pipe and bolt.
27. Install lefthand No. 3 timing belt cover, then install all wiring to bracket and clamps on No. 3 timing belt cover.
28. Install idler pulley and cover plate with bolt.
29. **On Land Cruiser models,** install radi-

ator as outlined under “Radiator Replace.”
30. **On Tundra models,** install power steering pump as outlined under “Power Steering Pump Replace.”
31. **On all models,** temporarily install fan pulley, then the fan and fluid coupling assembly.
32. Release tensioner and install alternator drive belt, the tighten nuts holding fluid coupling to fan bracket to specification.
33. Install air cleaner and intake air connector assembly, then fill with engine coolant.
34. Start engine and check for leaks, then recheck for leaks.
35. **On Land Cruiser model,** install V-bank, then oil pan protector.
36. **On all models,** install battery clamp cover, then install engine under cover.

CAMSHAFT
REPLACE

Refer to “ Cylinder Head Replace” for camshaft replacement procedure.

Adjusting Shim Selection Chart (Exhaust)

The chart cross-references **Installed shim thickness mm (in.)** (columns, from 2.000 (0.0787) through 2.800 (0.1102)) against **Measured clearance mm (in.)** (rows), to give the replacement shim number.

Measured clearance mm (in.)	Installed shim thickness — see chart for shim numbers
0.000–0.030 (0.0000–0.0012)	
0.031–0.050 (0.0012–0.0020)	
0.051–0.070 (0.0020–0.0028)	
0.071–0.090 (0.0028–0.0035)	
0.091–0.110 (0.0036–0.0043)	
0.111–0.130 (0.0044–0.0051)	
0.131–0.150 (0.0052–0.0059)	
0.151–0.170 (0.0059–0.0067)	
0.171–0.190 (0.0067–0.0075)	
0.191–0.210 (0.0075–0.0083)	
0.211–0.230 (0.0083–0.0091)	
0.231–0.249 (0.0091–0.0098)	
0.250–0.350 (0.0098–0.0138)	
0.351–0.370 (0.0138–0.0146)	
0.371–0.390 (0.0146–0.0154)	
0.391–0.410 (0.0154–0.0161)	
0.411–0.430 (0.0162–0.0169)	
0.431–0.450 (0.0170–0.0177)	
0.451–0.470 (0.0178–0.0185)	
0.471–0.490 (0.0185–0.0193)	
0.491–0.510 (0.0193–0.0201)	
0.511–0.530 (0.0201–0.0209)	
0.531–0.550 (0.0209–0.0217)	
0.551–0.570 (0.0217–0.0224)	
0.571–0.590 (0.0225–0.0232)	
0.591–0.610 (0.0233–0.0240)	
0.611–0.630 (0.0241–0.0248)	
0.631–0.650 (0.0248–0.0256)	
0.651–0.670 (0.0256–0.0264)	
0.671–0.690 (0.0264–0.0272)	
0.691–0.710 (0.0272–0.0280)	
0.711–0.730 (0.0280–0.0287)	
0.731–0.750 (0.0288–0.0295)	
0.751–0.770 (0.0296–0.0303)	
0.771–0.790 (0.0304–0.0311)	
0.791–0.810 (0.0311–0.0319)	
0.811–0.830 (0.0319–0.0327)	
0.831–0.850 (0.0327–0.0335)	
0.851–0.870 (0.0335–0.0343)	
0.871–0.890 (0.0343–0.0350)	
0.891–0.910 (0.0351–0.0358)	
0.911–0.930 (0.0359–0.0366)	
0.931–0.950 (0.0367–0.0374)	
0.951–0.970 (0.0374–0.0382)	
0.971–0.990 (0.0382–0.0390)	
0.991–1.010 (0.0390–0.0398)	
1.011–1.030 (0.0398–0.0406)	
1.031–1.050 (0.0406–0.0413)	
1.051–1.070 (0.0414–0.0421)	
1.071–1.090 (0.0422–0.0429)	
1.091–1.110 (0.0430–0.0437)	
1.111–1.130 (0.0437–0.0445)	
1.131–1.150 (0.0445–0.0453)	

Exhaust valve clearance (Cold):
0.25 – 0.35 mm (0.010 – 0.014 in.)

EXAMPLE:
The 2.300 mm (0.0906 in.) shim is installed, and the measured clearance is 0.440 mm (0.0173 in.). Replace the 2.300 mm (0.0906 in.) shim with a No. 44 shim.

New shim thickness — mm (in.)

Shim No.	Thickness	Shim No.	Thickness	Shim No.	Thickness
00	2.000 (0.0787)	28	2.280 (0.0898)	56	2.560 (0.1008)
02	2.020 (0.0795)	30	2.300 (0.0906)	58	2.580 (0.1016)
04	2.040 (0.0803)	32	2.320 (0.0913)	60	2.600 (0.1024)
06	2.060 (0.0811)	34	2.340 (0.0921)	62	2.620 (0.1031)
08	2.080 (0.0819)	36	2.360 (0.0929)	64	2.640 (0.1039)
10	2.100 (0.0827)	38	2.380 (0.0937)	66	2.660 (0.1047)
12	2.120 (0.0835)	40	2.400 (0.0945)	68	2.680 (0.1055)
14	2.140 (0.0843)	42	2.420 (0.0953)	70	2.700 (0.1063)
16	2.160 (0.0850)	44	2.440 (0.0961)	72	2.720 (0.1071)
18	2.180 (0.0858)	46	2.460 (0.0969)	74	2.740 (0.1079)
20	2.200 (0.0866)	48	2.480 (0.0976)	76	2.760 (0.1087)
22	2.220 (0.0874)	50	2.500 (0.0984)	78	2.780 (0.1094)
24	2.240 (0.0882)	52	2.520 (0.0992)	80	2.800 (0.1102)
26	2.260 (0.0890)	54	2.540 (0.1000)		

TY1069900533000X

Fig. 26   Exhaust shim selection chart

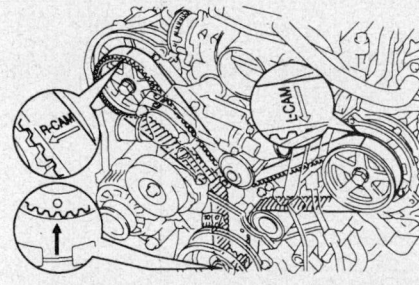

TY1069900534000X

Fig. 27   Timing belt installation marks

TY1069900535000X

Fig. 28   Crankshaft pulley & No. 1 timing belt cover alignment mark

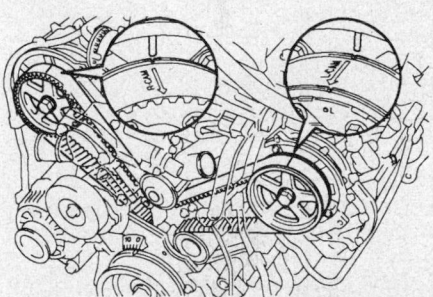

TY1069900536000X

Fig. 29   Camshaft pulleys & timing belt rear plates alignment marks

PISTON & ROD ASSEMBLY

Installation directions of piston and connecting rod are different for lefthand and righthand banks. Lefthand piston is marked with LH and 2L, the right piston with RH and 2R. Align piston holes of piston and connecting rod, and push in piston pin with your thumb, **Fig. 35.**

OIL PAN

REPLACE

1. Remove engine as outlined under "Engine Replace."
2. Install engine on a suitable stand.
3. Remove timing belt, then Nos. 1 and 2 idler pulleys and crankshaft timing pulley as outlined under "Timing Belt Replace."
4. Remove bolts attaching oil dipstick to lefthand cylinder head, then pull out dipstick guide with dipstick from No. 1 oil pan and remove O-ring.
5. Disconnect oil pressure switch connector, then wire from clamp.
6. Turn clamp couterclockwise, and remove clamp from oil filter bracket.
7. Disconnect oil cooler hose from oil

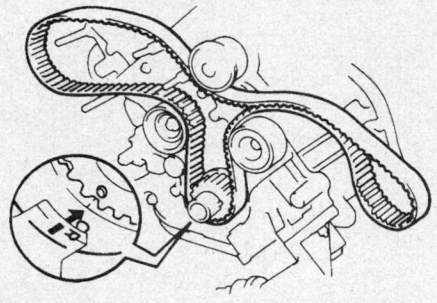

Fig. 30 Timing belt installation marks

TY1069900537000X

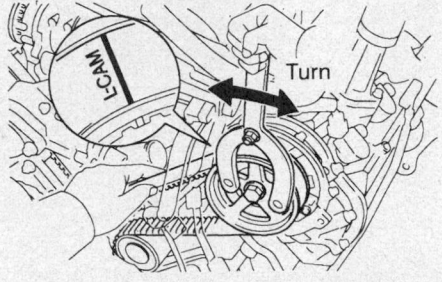

Fig. 31 Lefthand camshaft timing pulley & timing belt installation marks

TY1069900538000X

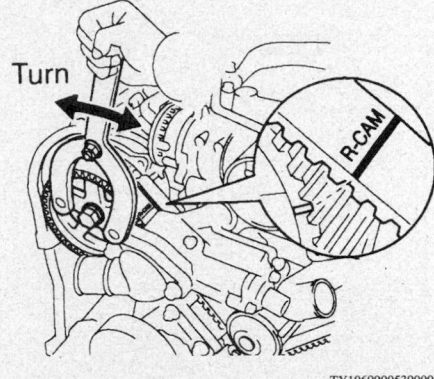

TY1069900539000X

Fig. 32 Righthand camshaft timing pulley & timing belt installation marks

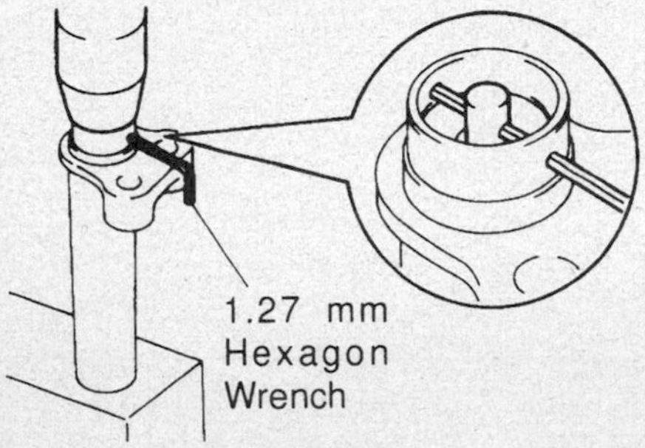

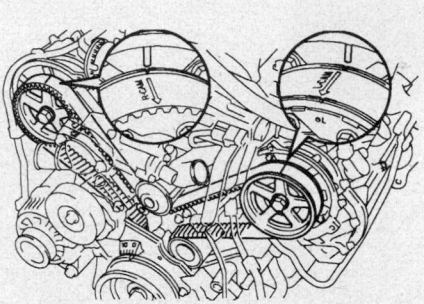

TY1069900540000X

Fig. 33 Belt tensioner push rod setting position

1.27 mm Hexagon Wrench

cooler, then remove oil filter, oil cooler and filter bracket assembly.
8. Remove attaching bolts, then nuts and insert a cutting tool No. 09032–00100 or equivalent between Nos. 1 and 2 oil pans.
9. Cut off applied sealant and remove No. 2 oil pan. **Ensure not to damage No. 2 oil pan contact surface of No. 1 oil pan. Ensure not to damage No. 2 oil pan flange.**
10. Remove oil pan baffle plate, then No. 1 oil pan attaching bolts and nuts.
11. Using a screwdriver, remove No. 1 oil pan by prying between oil pan and cylinder block. **Ensure not to damage contact surface of cylinder block and No. 1 oil pan.**
12. Remove oil strainer and gasket, then remove bolts and pry out oil pump from cylinder block.
13. Reverse procedure to install. Tighten oil pump and oil pans mounting bolts and nuts to specification.

OIL PUMP
REPLACE

Refer to "Oil Pan Replace" for procedure.

BELT TENSION DATA

Vehicle is equipped with automatic belt tensioner.

COOLING SYSTEM BLEED

1. Start engine, then open heater water valve.
2. Maintain engine speed at 2000–2500 RPM, and warm up engine.
3. Stop engine, wait until engine coolant cools down.
4. Refill coolant into reservoir until it is full, then check for leaks.

THERMOSTAT
REPLACE

1. Drain engine coolant into a suitable container.
2. Disconnect water inlet from water inlet housing, then remove thermostat and gasket
3. Reverse procedure to install. Tighten nuts to specification.

WATER PUMP
REPLACE

1. Drain engine coolant into a suitable container.
2. Remove timing belt, then the No. 2 idler pulley as outlined under "Timing Belt, Replace."
3. Disconnect water bypass hose from water inlet housing.
4. Remove bolts attaching water inlet housing to water pump, **Fig. 36.**
5. Disconnect water inlet housing from front water bypass joint, the remove water inlet, inlet housing assembly and O-ring from water inlet housing.
6. Remove water pump, then the gasket and O-ring from water bypass pipe.
7. Reverse procedure to install. Tighten bolts and nuts to specifications.

RADIATOR

1. Remove engine under cover, the drain engine coolant into a suitable container.
2. Disconnect radiator reservoir hose from radiator, then radiator upper hose from radiator.
3. Disconnect radiator lower hose from radiator, then the automatic transmission oil cooler hoses from radiator.

TY1069900541000X

Fig. 34 Camshaft & crankshaft pulley timing marks

4. **On Tundra models,** remove No. 2 fan shroud, then the radiator and No. 1 fan shroud.
5. **On all models,** remove radiator reservoir tank, then the automatic transmission oil cooler hoses from clamp on radiator shroud.
6. Loosen fan pulley mounting nuts holding fluid coupling to fan bracket, then release tensioner and remove alternator drive belt.
7. Remove fan shroud to radiator attaching bolts, then pulley mounting nuts.
8. Pull out fan with fluid coupling, fan pulley and fan shroud.
9. Remove nuts, then bolts and brackets from radiator.
10. Lift out radiator, then remove side supports from radiator.
11. Reverse procedure to install. Tighten bolts and nuts to specifications.

FUEL PUMP
REPLACE

1. **On Land Cruiser models,** remove the following:
   a. No.1 rear seat, then rear door scuff plates.
   b. Rear door seat lock covers, then the floor service hole cover.
2. **On all models,** remove fuel tank.
3. Disconnect fuel pump and sender gauge connector, then the fuel feed and return tubes.

LH Piston

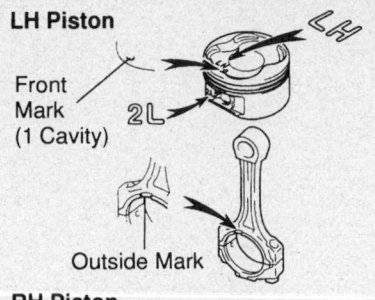

Front Mark (1 Cavity)

Outside Mark

RH Piston

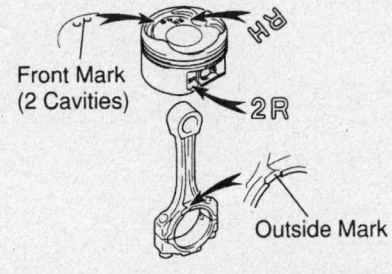

Front Mark (2 Cavities)

Outside Mark

TY1069900542000X

Fig. 35 Piston & connecting rod

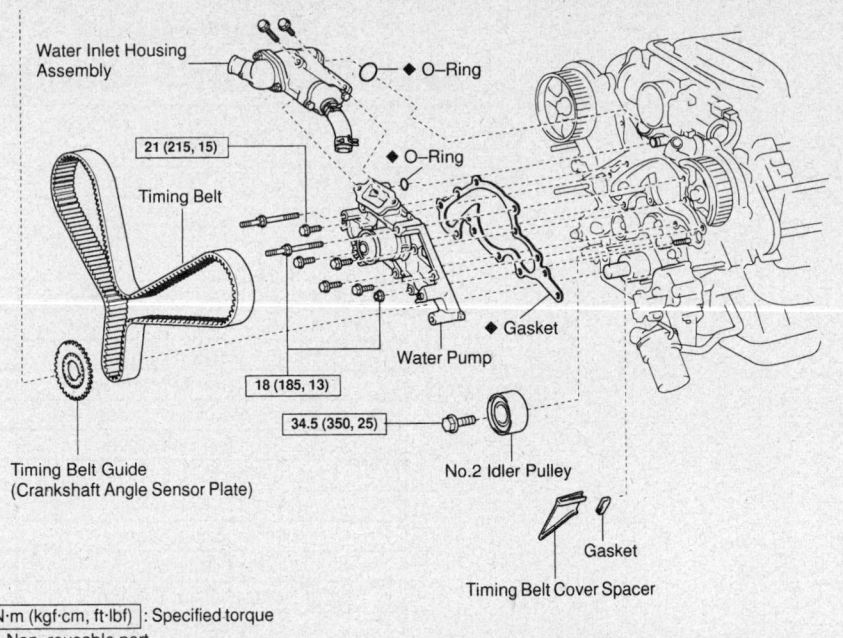

Water Inlet Housing Assembly

◆ O–Ring

21 (215, 15)

◆ O–Ring

Timing Belt

◆ Gasket

Water Pump

18 (185, 13)

34.5 (350, 25)

No.2 Idler Pulley

Timing Belt Guide (Crankshaft Angle Sensor Plate)

Gasket

Timing Belt Cover Spacer

N·m (kgf·cm, ft·lbf) : Specified torque
◆ Non–reusable part

TY1069900543000X

Fig. 36 Exploded view of water pump

4. Remove fuel pump and sender gauge from fuel tank. **Ensure not to damage fuel pump filter and not to bend arm of sender gauge.**
5. Remove gasket from fuel section plate, then the lead wire from fuel pump.
6. Pull out lower side of fuel pump from fuel pump bracket.
7. Disconnect fuel hose from fuel pump, then remove fuel pump and rubber cushion from pump.

8. Using a small screwdriver remove clip, then pull out pump filter.
9. Reverse procedure to install.

FUEL FILTER
REPLACE
1. Place suitable container under fuel filter to allow fuel drainage.

2. Slowly disconnect fuel pipe and fuel hose from fuel filter. **Place shop towel over connection to avoid fuel spilling on engine.**
3. Remove fuel filter and cap or plug fuel hose.
4. Reverse procedure to install.

TIGHTENING SPECIFICATIONS

Year	Component	Torque/Ft. Lbs.
1998-99	A/C Compressor	36
	Alternator Bracket	29
	Accelerator Cable Bracket	13
	Bearing Cap Bolts (C)	72②
	Bearing Cap Bolts	12
	Camshaft Timing Pulley	80
	Connecting Rod Cap	18③
	Crankshaft Pulley	181
	Cylinder Head Bolts	①
	Cylinder Head Cover Bolts	53
	Drive Belt Idler Pulley	27
	Drive Belt Tensioner	12
	Drive Plate To Crankshaft	36③
	Drive Plate To Torque Converter	35
	Engine Coolant Drain Union	36
	Engine Hanger	27
	Engine Mounting Bracket	27
	Engine To Transmission	53
	Exhaust Manifold	33
	Engine Rear Mounting Bracket	48

Continued

TIGHTENING
SPECIFICATIONS—Continued

Year	Component	Torque/Ft. Lbs.
1998-99	Fluid Coupling To Fan Bracket	21
	Flywheel Housing Under Cover	13
	Frame Bracket To Engine Mounting Bracket	28
	Frame Crossmember To Body	53
	Front Exhaust Pipe To Manifold	46
	Heated Oxygen Sensor	14
	Heat Insulator To Manifold	66②
	Main Bearing Cap To Cylinder Head	20③
	No. 2 Timing Belt Cover	12
	No. 3 Timing Belt Cover	66②
	No. 2 Oil Pan Bolts	66②
	Oil Pan Baffle Plate	66②
	Oil Pan Drain Plug	29
	Oil Pump (12mm & 6mm)	11
	Oil Pump (14mm)	22
	Power Steering Pump To Cylinder Head	13
	Radiator Bolts	13
	Radiator To Fan Shroud	44②
	Radiator To Support	108②
	Rear Oil Seal Retainer	71②
	Starter	29
	Throttle Body	66②
	Timing Belt Rear Plate	66②
	Timing Belt Tensioner To Oil Pump	19
	Transmission To Cylinder Block	53
	Transmission To No. 1 Oil Pan	27
	Water Inlet To Housing	14
	Water Pump Bolts	15
	Water Pump Stud Bolt & Nut	13

① — Refer to "Cylinder Head, Replace."

② — Inch lbs.

③ — Tighten each an additional 90°.

Clutch & Manual Transmission/ Transaxle

NOTE: On Air Bag Equipped Models, Refer To "Air Bag System Precautions" Located In The Front Of This Manual For System Disarming & Arming Procedures.

INDEX

PRECAUTIONS

AIR BAG SYSTEMS

Refer to "Air Bag System Precautions" in the front of this manual for system disarming and arming procedures.

AUDIO CODED ANTI-THEFT SYSTEM

Some models are equipped with an audio coded anti-theft system that will disable the radio when the battery cable is disconnected. The system can be identified by the "ANTI-THEFT SYSTEM" on the cassette lid. Obtain three-digit code for input. Reset system after service as follows:

1. Obtain three-digit audio theft code.
2. Depress 1 (PROG) button while depressing righthand side of TUNE SEEK button. Three dashes will appear in tape operation display.
3. To enter first digit, depress 1 (PROG) button repeatedly until number of times depressed equals first digit (depress 1 button six times if first digit is five, first press equals 0).
4. To enter second digit, depress 2 (APS) button repeatedly until number of times depressed equals second digit.
5. To enter third digit, depress 3 (RPT) button repeatedly until number of times depressed equals third digit.
6. If three dashes are displayed after inputting digits, repeat procedure.
7. When code appears in display, depress and hold SCAN button until SEC appears.
8. When SEC disappears audio system is operative.
9. If Err is displayed, repeat procedure. **Attempting to input code more than nine times may permanently disable audio system.**

BATTERY GROUND CABLE

Prior to service, disconnect battery ground cable and isolate as required.

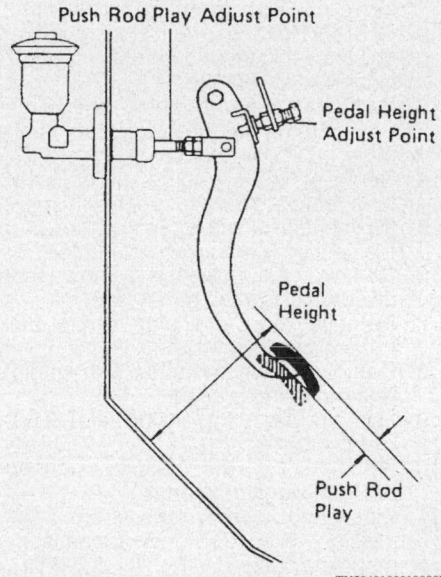

Fig. 1 Clutch pedal adjustments

ADJUSTMENTS

CLUTCH PEDAL

1. Check clutch pedal height, **Fig. 1.** Clutch pedal height should be 6.2 inches. If height is not as specified, loosen locknut, then rotate adjusting bolt until specified height is obtained. Tighten locknut.
2. Check clutch pedal freeplay, **Fig. 1.** Depress clutch pedal until resistance is felt, then measure freeplay distance. Freeplay should be .20–.59 inch.
3. Check clutch cylinder pushrod play at top of pedal. Play should be .039–.197 inch.
4. If clutch pedal freeplay is not as specified, loosen locknut, then rotate pushrod adjusting screw until specified freeplay is obtained.
5. Tighten locknut, then recheck pedal height.

HYDRAULIC SYSTEM SERVICE

CLUTCH MASTER CYLINDER, REPLACE

Pickup, Tacoma, Tundra, T100 & 4Runner

1. Remove pushrod pin.
2. **On Pickup and 4Runner models,** disconnect clutch line using line wrench tool No. 09751-36011, or equivalent.
3. **On Tacoma, Tundra and T100 models,** disconnect clutch line using line wrench tool No. 09023–00100, or equivalent.
4. Remove mounting nuts and master cylinder.
5. Reverse procedure to install. Bleed clutch system.

RAV4

1. **On models equipped with cruise control,** remove cruise control actuator cover and actuator.
2. **On all models,** draw out fluid with syringe.
3. Disconnect reservoir hose from master cylinder.
4. Remove clip and pin.
5. Remove two mounting nuts and pull out master cylinder.
6. Reverse procedure to install.

CLUTCH SLAVE CYLINDER, REPLACE

1. Disconnect clutch line using line wrench tool No. 09751-36011, or equivalent.
2. Remove two bolts and release cylinder.
3. Reverse procedure to install. Bleed clutch system.

CLUTCH SYSTEM BLEED

1. Fill clutch reservoir with fluid. Check reservoir frequently, add if necessary.

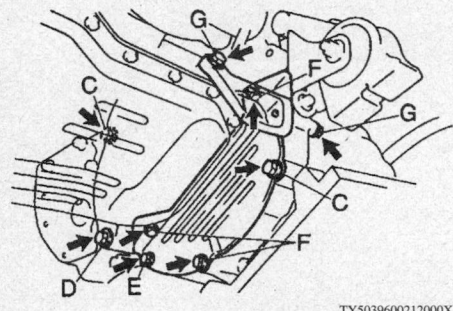

Fig. 2   Rear end plate bolts. 2WD models w/E250 transaxle

2. Connect vinyl tube to bleeder plug, insert opposite end in container half full of fluid.
3. Pump clutch pedal several times. Hold pedal down and open bleeder plug. Close bleeder plug and repeat this step until no more air bubbles are in fluid.

CLUTCH
REPLACE

1. Remove transmission or transaxle from vehicle. Refer to " Transmission, Replace" for procedure.
2. Loosen pressure plate attaching bolts one turn at a time, then remove bolts, pressure plate and clutch disc.
3. Install new clutch disc and pressure plate assembly, checking to ensure disc and plate are properly aligned. Tighten attaching bolts one turn at a time while ensuring clutch disc and pressure plate remain aligned. Refer to "Tightening Specifications" for torque values.
4. Install transmission or transaxle and adjust clutch as outlined under "Adjustments."

TRANSMISSION
REPLACE
PICKUP, TACOMA & 4RUNNER
R150F Transmission

1. **On models equipped with audio coded anti-theft system,** obtain three-digit system code.
2. **On all models,** remove starter upper mount bolt.
3. Remove shift lever from inside vehicle, then, if equipped, the shift lever retainer.
4. Raise and support vehicle, then drain transmission fluid.
5. Disconnect propeller shaft, then the speedometer cable, back-up lamp switch and light switch connector.
6. Remove exhaust pipe clamp and exhaust pipe.
7. Remove clutch release cylinder, tube bracket and lower starter attaching bolt. Position starter aside.
8. Remove four rear engine mount attaching bolts, then slightly raise transmission, using a suitable jack.

9. Remove four attaching bolts from support member, then the rear mount bracket.
10. Remove engine rear mount from transmission.
11. Place a piece of wood, approximately .8 inch (20 mm) thick, between engine oil pan and front crossmember, then lower transmission.
12. Remove exhaust pipe bracket and stiffener plate bolts.
13. Remove remaining transmission attaching bolts.
14. Rotate transmission clockwise approximately 45°, then slide transmission rearward. Lower transmission forward and away from vehicle.
15. Reverse procedure to install. Reset audio coded anti-theft system, if equipped, as outlined under "Precautions."

W5 TRANSMISSION
2WD Models

1. Remove front console box, then remove shift lever boot and retainer.
2. Coat shift lever cap with cloth, pressing down on shift lever cap rotate counterclockwise to remove.
3. Raise and support vehicle, then drain transmission fluid into a suitable container.
4. Remove No. 2 engine under cover, then remove propeller shaft.
5. Disconnect vehicle speed sensor, then the backup light switch connector.
6. Remove clutch release cylinder, then disconnect front exhaust pipe.
7. Remove rear end plate, then jack transmission slightly.
8. Remove cross member with engine rear mounting bracket.
9. Remove starter lower side set bolt with clutch bracket.
10. Disconnect starter electrical connector, then wire and starter.
11. Disconnect wire harness from transmission, then remove transmission mounting bolts.
12. Pull out transmission down and towards rear.
13. Reverse procedure to install. Tighten bolts and nuts to specifications.

4WD Models

1. Remove front console box, then remove shift lever boot and retainer.
2. Using pliers, remove snap ring and pull out transfer shift lever.
3. Raise and support vehicle, then drain transmission fluid into a suitable container
4. Remove Nos. 1 and 2 engine under cover, then remove front propeller shaft.
5. Remove rear propeller shaft, then disconnect vehicle speed sensor.
6. Disconnect 4WD position switch connector, then the back-up light switch.
7. **On models equipped with ABS and or differential lock,** disconnect L4 position switch connector.
8. **On all models,** remove clutch release cylinder.
9. Disconnect front exhaust pipe, then re-

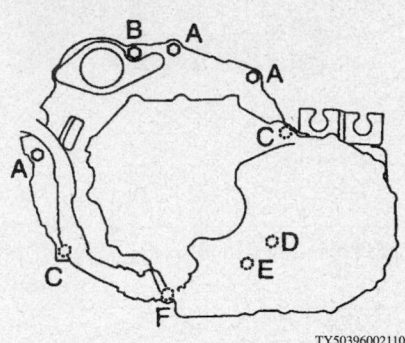

Fig. 3   Transaxle mounting bolts. 4WD models w/E250F transaxle

move rear end plate.
10. Support transmission rear side, then remove crossmember.
11. Remove attaching bolts, then the engine rear mounting from transmission.
12. Jack up transmission slightly, then remove starter set bolts and starter.
13. Disconnect wire harness from transmission, then remove transmission mounting bolts from engine.
14. Pull out transmission with transfer case down and towards rear.
15. Remove transfer adaptor rear mounting bolts, then pull transfer straight up and remove from it from transmission.
16. Reverse procedure to install. Tighten nuts and bolts to specifications.

TRANSAXLE
REPLACE
RAV4
2WD Models w/E250 Transaxle

1. Remove air cleaner case assembly with air hose.
2. Remove engine coolant reservoir tank.
3. Remove engine wire clamp set nut.
4. Remove starter.
5. Remove clutch release cylinder and line.
6. Disconnect ground cable.
7. Disconnect vehicle speed sensor and back-up light switch connector.
8. Disconnect control cable from transaxle housing.
9. Remove four transaxle upper mounting bolts.
10. Remove set bolt and two nuts of engine lefthand mounting insulator.
11. Install engine support fixture.
12. Tie power steering gear assembly to engine support fixture.
13. Remove front wheel, then raise and support vehicle.
14. Remove lefthand and righthand engine under covers.
15. Drain transaxle oil.
16. Remove lefthand and righthand driveshafts.
17. Remove front exhaust pipe.
18. Remove front suspension crossmember with stabilizer bar.
19. Remove engine mounting center member.
20. Slightly raise transaxle.

21. Disconnect lefthand side engine mounting bracket from lefthand side engine mounting insulator.
22. Remove stiffener plate, No. 2 rear end plate and transaxle lower side mounting bolt.
23. Lower engine lefthand side and remove transaxle from engine.
24. Reverse procedure to install. Refer to **Fig. 2** and tighten No. 2 rear end plate bolts as follows:
    a. **Torque** bolt C to 22 ft. lbs.
    b. **Torque** bolt D to 34 ft. lbs.
    c. **Torque** bolt E to 18 ft. lbs.
    d. **Torque** bolt F to 7 ft. lbs.
    e. **Torque** bolt G to 27 ft. lbs.

4WD Models w/E250F Transaxle

1. Remove engine with transaxle as outlined under "Engine, Replace" in "3S-FE 2.0L Engine" section.
2. Remove transaxle case protector.
3. Remove starter.
4. Disconnect differential lock indicator switch, back-up light switch and vehicle speed sensor connector.
5. Remove transfer vacuum actuator bracket.
6. Disconnect vacuum actuator solenoid connectors and remove transfer vacuum actuator assembly.
7. Remove righthand transfer stiffener plate.
8. Remove center transfer stiffener plate.
9. Remove transaxle from engine.
10. Reverse procedure to install. Refer to **Fig. 3,** and tighten transaxle mounting bolts to following specifications:
    a. **Torque** bolt A to 47 ft. lbs.
    b. **Torque** bolt B to 26 ft. lbs.
    c. **Torque** bolt C to 22 ft. lbs.
    d. **Torque** bolt D to 34 ft. lbs.
    e. **Torque** bolt E to 18 ft. lbs.
    f. **Torque** bolt F to 7 ft. lbs.

TIGHTENING SPECIFICATIONS

Year	Component	Torque/Ft. Lbs.
EXCEPT RAV4		
1996-99	Bleeder Plug	96③
	Clutch Line	11
	Crossmember	70
	Engine Rear Mounting	19
	Engine Rear Mounting To Transmission	19
	Flywheel To Crankshaft	①
	Master Cylinder	108③
	No. 2 Crossmember To Frame, 4WD	70
	Pressure Plate	14
	Release Cylinder	108③
	Starter	29
	Stiffener Plate To Transmission	27
	Transfer Vacuum Actuator Bracket	27
	Transmission To Engine	53
2WD RAV4		
1996-97	Clutch Line Union	11
	Clutch Master Cylinder Nut	108③
	Engine LH Mounting Bracket To Mounting Insulator	47
	Flywheel Set Bolt	65
	Starter Bolts	29
	Stiffener Plates To Transaxle	②
	Transaxle Case Protector	18
	Transaxle To Engine Upper Mounting Bolts	47
4WD RAV4		
1996-97	Clutch Line Union	11
	Clutch Master Cylinder Nut	108③
	Flywheel Set Bolt	65
	Starter Bolts	29
	Stiffener Plates To Transaxle	27
	Transaxle Case Protector	18
	Transaxle To Engine	②
	Transfer Vacuum Actuator	27

① — Except 3RZ-FE engine, to 65 ft. lbs.; 3RZ-FE engine, to 19 ft. lbs., then turn an additional 90°.
② — Refer to "Transaxle, Replace."
③ — Inch lbs.

Rear Axle & Suspension

NOTE: On Air Bag Equipped Models, Refer To "Air Bag System Precautions" Located In The Front Of This Manual For System Disarming & Arming Procedures.

INDEX

PRECAUTIONS

AIR BAG SYSTEMS

Refer to "Air Bag System Precautions" in the front of this manual for system disarming and arming procedures.

AUDIO CODED ANTI-THEFT SYSTEM

Some models are equipped with an audio coded anti-theft system that will disable the radio when the battery cable is disconnected. The system can be identified by the "ANTI-THEFT SYSTEM" on the cassette lid. Obtain three-digit code for input. Reset system after service as follows:

1. Obtain three-digit audio theft code.
2. Depress 1 (PROG) button while depressing righthand side of TUNE SEEK button. Three dashes will appear in tape operation display.
3. To enter first digit, depress 1 (PROG) button repeatedly until number of times depressed equals first digit (depress 1 button six times if first digit is five, first press equals 0).
4. To enter second digit, depress 2 (APS) button repeatedly until number of times depressed equals second digit.
5. To enter third digit, depress 3 (RPT) button repeatedly until number of times depressed equals third digit.
6. If three dashes are displayed after inputting digits, repeat procedure.
7. When code appears in display, depress and hold SCAN button until SEC appears.
8. When SEC disappears audio system is operative.
9. If Err is displayed, repeat procedure. **Attempting to input code more than nine times may permanently disable audio system.**

BATTERY GROUND CABLE

Prior to service, disconnect battery ground cable and isolate as required.

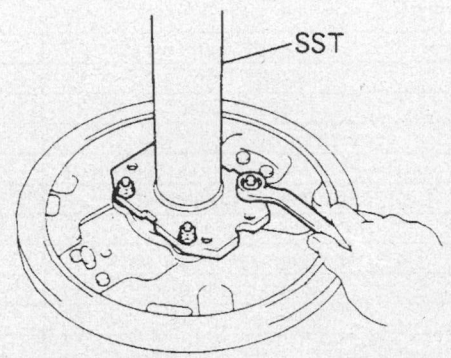

Fig. 1 Backing plate removal (Part 1 of 2). Pickup & 4Runner

REAR AXLE
REPLACE
COIL SPRING

RAV4 & 4Runner

1. Raise and support vehicle.
2. Remove wheel and brake drum.
3. Remove ABS speed sensor.
4. Remove rear brake assembly, then disconnect parking brake cable and brake tube.
5. Remove lock nut and rear axle shaft assembly.
6. Reverse procedure to install.

Land Cruiser

1. Raise and support vehicle.
2. **On models equipped with disc brake,** remove wheel, then brake caliper and disc.
3. **On all models,** remove wheel and brake drum.
4. Remove drain plug and drain differential oil.
5. Remove load sensing proportioning valve shackle bracket from differential cover.
6. Remove parking brake cable clamp and differential cover.
7. Remove pinion shaft and spacer.

8. Remove axle shaft lock and axle shaft, then the oil deflector.
9. Reverse procedure to install.

LEAF SPRING

Pickup, Tacoma, Tundra & T100

1. Raise and support vehicle.
2. Remove wheel and brake drum.
3. **On models equipped with ABS,** remove ABS speed sensor from rear axle housing.
4. **On all models,** disconnect brake tube and parking brake cable.
5. Remove backing plate mounting nuts.
6. Remove axle shaft from rear axle housing.
7. Remove snap ring, then the rear axle shaft from backing plate.
8. Reverse procedure to install.

AXLE SHAFT, BEARING & OIL SEAL
REPLACE
PICKUP & 4RUNNER

1. Raise and support vehicle.
2. Remove rear wheel and brake drum.
3. **On 4Runner models,** remove rear brake assembly.
4. **On all models,** disconnect parking brake cable and using line wrench tool No. 09751-36011, or equivalent, remove brake line.
5. Remove four backing plate mounting bolts and pull out axle.
6. Remove snap ring from axle shaft.
7. Install adapter tool No. 09521-25011, or equivalent, and press axle from backing plate, **Fig. 1.**
8. Pry out outer seal using screwdriver.
9. Using bearing remover tool Nos. 09223-56010 and 09608-35014, or equivalents, press bearing from backing plate.
10. Grind down bearing inner retainer, then cut off using a hammer and chisel.
11. Reverse procedure to install.

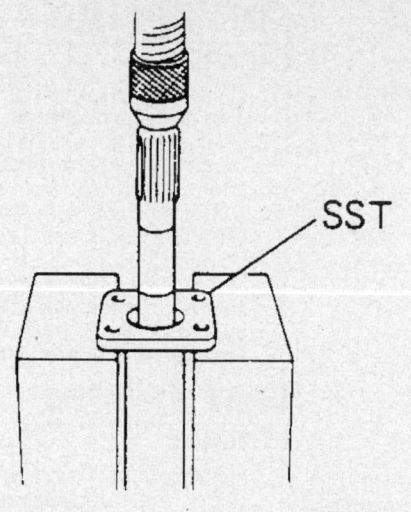

Fig. 1 Backing plate removal (Part 2 of 2). Pickup & 4Runner

TY3039100020020X

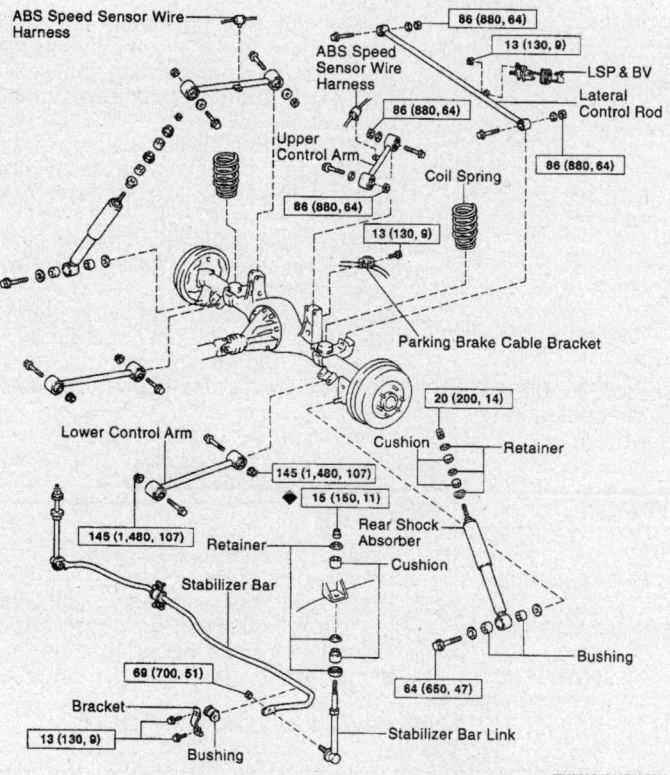

Fig. 3 Exploded view of coil spring rear suspension. 4Runner

TY2039600020000X

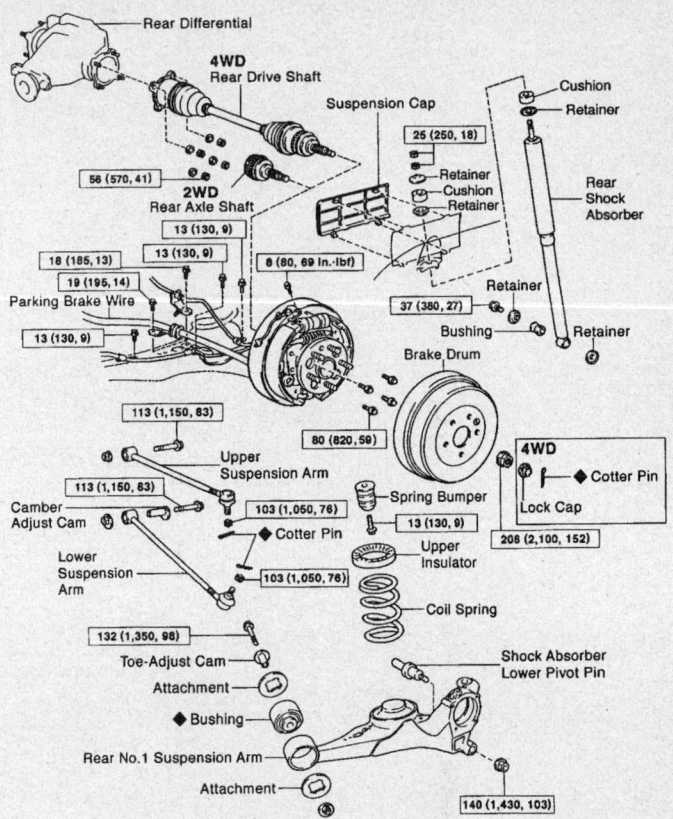

Fig. 2 Exploded view of coil spring rear suspension. RAV4

TY2039600019000X

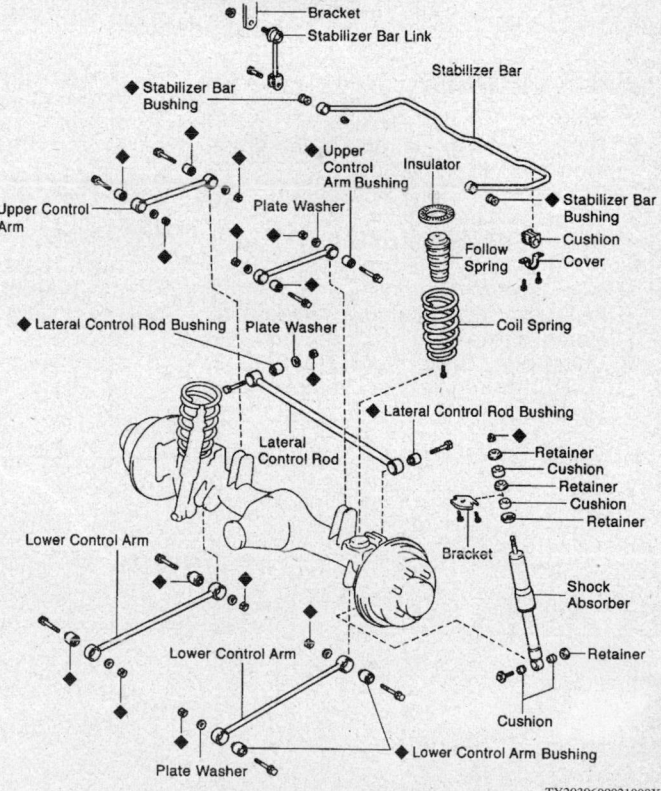

Fig. 4 Exploded view of coil spring rear suspension. Land Cruiser

TY2039600021000X

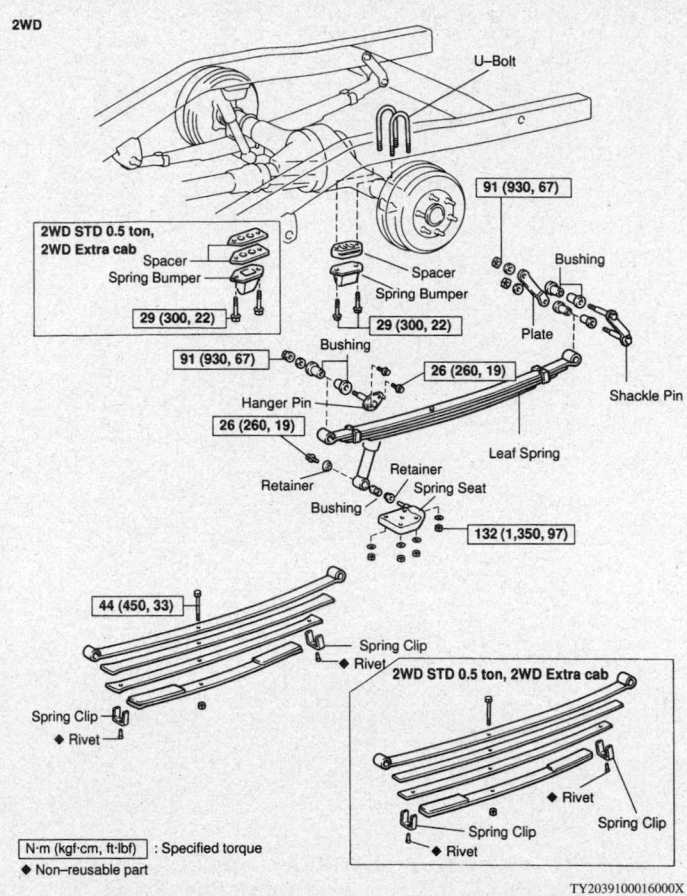

2WD

2WD STD 0.5 ton,
2WD Extra cab
Spacer
Spring Bumper

29 (300, 22)

U–Bolt

91 (930, 67)

Bushing

Spacer
Spring Bumper

29 (300, 22)

Plate

91 (930, 67)

Bushing

26 (260, 19)

Hanger Pin

26 (260, 19)

Shackle Pin

Leaf Spring

Retainer

Retainer
Spring Seat

Bushing

132 (1,350, 97)

44 (450, 33)

Spring Clip
◆ Rivet

Spring Clip
◆ Rivet

2WD STD 0.5 ton, 2WD Extra cab

◆ Rivet

Spring Clip

Spring Clip
◆ Rivet

N·m (kgf·cm, ft·lbf) : Specified torque
◆ Non–reusable part

TY2039100016000X

**Fig. 5   Exploded view of leaf spring rear
suspension**

LAND CRUISER

1. Raise and support vehicle.
2. Remove rear wheel and brake drum, then drain differential oil.
3. Remove LSPV shackle bracket, then the parking brake cable clamp.
4. Remove differential cover.
5. Remove pinion shaft and spacer. Push axle toward differential and remove lock from axle located in differential. Remove axle.
6. Using seal puller tool No. 09308-00010, or equivalent, remove axle seal.
7. Using bearing puller tool No. 09514-35011, or equivalent, remove bearing.
8. Reverse procedure to install.

SHOCK ABSORBER
REPLACE

1. Raise rear of vehicle and support rear axle housing on stands.
2. Disconnect shock absorber from lower mounting.
3. Disconnect shock absorber from upper mounting and remove from vehicle.

COIL SPRING
REPLACE

1. Raise rear of vehicle and support rear axle housing on stands.
2. Disconnect shock absorber from lower mounting, **Figs. 2 through 4,** then the lateral control rod from axle housing.
3. If equipped with rear stabilizer, remove bolts securing stabilizer bar to rear housing.
4. Lower jack until spring tension is relieved, then remove coil spring with insulator.
5. Reverse procedure to install.

LEAF SPRING
REPLACE

1. Raise rear of vehicle and place stands under frame and rear axle housing.
2. Disconnect shock absorber from upper and lower mountings and remove shock absorber from vehicle, **Fig. 5.**
3. Disconnect parking brake equalizer from parking brake intermediate lever.
4. Remove U-bolts and spring seats
5. **On 4WD models,** remove spring bumper.
6. **On all models,** position a suitable jack under rear axle housing and raise housing to relieve weight from rear springs.
7. Remove spring shackle nuts and inner plate, then, using a suitable pry bar, remove spring shackle.
8. Remove two bolts retaining spring bracket and hanger pin nut, then drive out spring hanger pin.
9. Remove spring assembly from vehicle.
10. Reverse procedure to install.

STABILIZER BAR
REPLACE

1. Raise and support rear of vehicle, then remove rear wheels.
2. Disconnect bolts securing stabilizer bar to axle housing, **Figs. 2 through 4.**
3. Disconnect bolts securing stabilizer bar to frame, then remove stabilizer bar.
4. Reverse procedure to install.

TIGHTENING SPECIFICATIONS

4RUNNER

Year	Component	Torque/Ft. Lbs.
1996	Lateral Control Rod To Frame	101
	Lateral Control Rod To Rear Axle Housing	83
	Lower Control Arm To Frame	148
	Lower Control Arm To Rear Axle Housing	148
	Rear Axle Housing To Backing Plate	51
	Shock Absorber To Frame	18
	Shock Absorber To Rear Axle Housing	47
	Stabilizer Bar Bracket To Rear Axle Housing	108①
	Stabilizer Bar Link Stabilizer	70
	Stabilizer Bar Link To Bracket	13
	Upper Control Arm To Frame	148
	Upper Control Arm To Rear Axle Housing	148
	Wheel Lug Nut	76
	Yoke Nut (Max)	253
1997-99	Lateral Control Rod To Frame	64
	Lateral Control Rod To Rear Axle Housing	64
	Lower Control Arm To Frame	107
	Lower Control Arm To Rear Axle Housing	107
	Rear Axle Housing To Backing Plate	48
	Shock Absorber To Frame	18
	Shock Absorber To Rear Axle Housing	47
	Stabilizer Bar Bracket To Rear Axle Housing	14
	Stabilizer Bar Link Stabilizer	64
	Stabilizer Bar Link To Bracket	14
	Upper Control Arm To Frame	64
	Upper Control Arm To Rear Axle Housing	64
	Wheel Lug Nut	83
	Yoke Nut (Max)	253

① — Inch lbs.

PICKUP, TACOMA & T100

Year	Component	Torque/Ft. Lbs.
1996	Differential Carrier To Axle Housing (Double Tire)	23
	Differential Carrier To Axle Housing (Single Tire)	18
	Front Spring Bracket To Hanger Pin (Press Installed Bushing)	116
	Front Spring Bracket To Hanger Pin (Rubber Bushing)	67
	Rear Shock Absorber To Frame (2WD)	19
	Rear Shock Absorber To Frame (4WD)	53
	Rear Shock Absorber To Spring Seat (2WD)	19

PICKUP, TACOMA & T100—Continued

Year	Component	Torque/Ft. Lbs.
1996	Rear Shock Absorber To Spring Seat (4WD)	53
	Rear Spring Shackle To Leaf Spring	67
	Spring Center Bolt	33
	Stabilizer Bar Bracket To Axle Housing	108③
	Stabilizer Bar To Stabilizer Bar Link	26
	U Bolt (½ Ton 2WD)	108
	U Bolt (1 Ton 2WD Cab & Chassis)	90
	U Bolt (4WD)	①
	Wheel Lug Nut	76
	Yoke Nut (Max)	174
1997-99	Bearing Cap To Differential Carrier	83
	Differential Carrier To Axle Housing	54
	Drain Plug	36
	Fill Plug	29
	Hub Nut	76
	Leaf Spring Front Side Bolt To Front Spring Bracket (2WD & 4WD Except 1 Ton)	145
	Leaf Spring Front Side Bolt To Front Spring Bracket (4WD 1 Ton)	67
	Rear Axle Housing To Rear Brake	51
	Rear Shock To Frame	19
	Rear Shock To Spring Seat	19
	Ring Gear To Differential Case	92
	Shackle Pin To Frame	67
	Shackle Pin To Leaf Spring	67
	Wheel Lug Nut	②
	Yoke Nut (Max)	174

① — Regular Cab, 108 ft. lbs.; extra cab, 90 ft. lbs.

② — Tacoma 83 ft. lbs.; T100 76 ft. lbs.

③ — Inch lbs.

LAND CRUISER

Year	Component	Torque/Ft. Lbs.
1996–97	Differential Cover	13
	Lateral Control Rod To Frame	130
	Lateral Control Rod To Rear Axle Housing	181
	Lower Control Arm To Frame	130
	Lower Control Arm To Rear Axle Housing	130
	LSPV Shackle Bracket	108①
	Parking Brake Cable Clamp	108①
	Pinion Nut (Maximum)	325
	Pinion Shaft Pin	20
	Rear Axle Housing To Backing Plate	51
	Shock Absorber To Frame	37
	Shock Absorber To Rear Axle Housing	47
	Stabilizer Bar Bracket To Rear Axle Housing	13
	Stabilizer Bar To Link	19

Continued

LAND CRUISER—Continued

Year	Component	Torque/Ft. Lbs.
1996–97	Stabilizer Link To Frame	11
	Upper Control Arm To Frame	130
	Upper Control Arm To Rear Axle Housing	130
	Wheel Lug Nut	108
	Yoke Nut (Max)	326
1998-99	Differecial Cover	13
	Lateral Control Rod To Frame	111
	Lateral Control Rod To Rear Axle Housing	110
	Lower Control Arm To Frame	111
	Lower Control Arm To Rear Axle Housing	111
	LSPV Shackle Bracket	108①
	Parking Brake Cable Clamp	108①
	Pinion Shaft Pin	20
	Rear Axle Housing To Backing Plate	91
	Shock Absorber To Frame	37
	Shock Absorber To Rear Axle Housing	72
	Stabilizer Bar Bracket To Rear Axle Housing	13
	Stabilizer Bar To Link	19
	Stabilizer Link To Frame	11
	Upper Control Arm To Frame	111
	Upper Control Arm To Rear Axle Housing	111
	Wheel Lug Nut	97

① — Inch lbs.

RAV4

Year	Component	Torque/Ft. Lbs.
1996-99	ABS Speed Sensor	72①
	Axle Hub Bolt	59
	Axle Shaft Lock Nut	159
	Brake Line	11
	Differential Carrier To Differential Case Cover	34
	Differential Carrier To Side Bearing Cap	58
	Differential Rear Mount Cushion	48
	Lower Suspension Arm	83
	Rear No. 1 Suspension Arm To Body	98
	Rear No. 1 Suspension Arm To Brake Line Bracket	13
	Shock Absorber Bolts	18
	Shock Absorber Lower Pivot Pin	103
	Upper Suspension Arm	76
	Wheel Lug Nut	76
	Yoke Nut (Max)	174

① — Inch lbs.

TUNDRA

Year	Component	Torque/Ft. Lbs.
2000	ABS Sensor To Axle Housing	51
	Brake Line Union Nut	11
	Carrier To Axle Housing	54
	Carrier To Bearing Cap	83
	Differetial To Propeller Shaft	56
	Drain Plug & Filler Plug	36
	Hub Nut	81
	Leaf Spring Center Bolt	33
	Leaf Spring Front Side Set Nut	125
	Leaf Spring To Shackle	125
	Rear Axle Housing To Backing Plate	51
	Shock Absorber To Frame	15
	Shock Absorber To Rear Axle Housing	64
	U-Bolt To Spring Seat	98
	U-Bolt To Spring Seat	98

Transfer Case

NOTE: On Air Bag Equipped Models, Refer To "Air Bag System Precautions" Located In The Front Of This Manual For System Disarming & Arming Procedures.

INDEX

PRECAUTIONS

AIR BAG SYSTEMS

Refer to "Air Bag System Precautions" in the front of this manual for system disarming and arming procedures.

AUDIO CODED ANTI-THEFT SYSTEM

Some models are equipped with an audio coded anti-theft system that will disable the radio when the battery cable is disconnected. The system can be identified by the "ANTI-THEFT SYSTEM" on the cassette lid. Obtain three-digit code for input. Reset system after service as follows:

1. Obtain three-digit audio theft code.
2. Depress 1 (PROG) button while depressing righthand side of TUNE SEEK button. Three dashes will appear in tape operation display.
3. To enter first digit, depress 1 (PROG) button repeatedly until number of times depressed equals first digit (depress 1 button six times if first digit is five, first press equals 0).
4. To enter second digit, depress 2 (APS) button repeatedly until number of

times depressed equals second digit.
5. To enter third digit, depress 3 (RPT) button repeatedly until number of times depressed equals third digit.
6. If three dashes are displayed after inputting digits, repeat procedure.
7. When code appears in display, depress and hold SCAN button until SEC appears.
8. When SEC disappears audio system is operative.
9. If Err is displayed, repeat procedure. **Attempting to input code more than nine times may permanently disable audio system.**

BATTERY GROUND CABLE

Prior to service, disconnect battery ground cable and isolate as required.

TRANSFER CASE

REPLACE

LAND CRUISER

Refer to "Automatic Transmission/Transaxles" section for transmission and transfer replacement procedure.

PICKUP, TACOMA, TUNDRA, T100 & 4RUNNER

Manual Transmission

1. **On Pickup, Tacoma, T100 and 4Runner,** remove fan shroud attaching bolts, then fan shroud.
2. **On all models,** using suitable snap ring pliers, remove transfer shift lever snap ring, then remove shift lever from inside vehicle.
3. Raise and support vehicle, then drain transmission fluid.
4. **On models equipped with R150F transmissions,** remove propeller shaft dust cover subassembly.
5. **On all models,** disconnect propeller shaft.
6. Disconnect speedometer cable, back-up lamp switch, light switch connector and transfer indicator switch electrical connector.
7. Remove exhaust pipe clamp and exhaust pipe.
8. Remove clutch release cylinder, tube bracket. **Do not disconnect clutch line.** Remove starter attaching bolt. Position starter aside.
9. Remove eight attaching bolts from

side frame, then remove No. 2 frame crossmember.
10. Place a piece of wood, approximately .8 inch (20 mm) thick, between engine oil pan and front axle, then lower transmission with transfer case.
11. Remove starter.
12. Remove exhaust pipe bracket and stiffener plate bolts.
13. Remove remaining transmission attaching bolts.
14. Pull transmission assembly toward rear of vehicle, then lower transmission and transfer forward and away from vehicle, using care not to damage transfer housing dust deflector.
15. Remove engine rear mount from transfer assembly.
16. **On models equipped with planetary gear transfer,** remove dynamic damper.
17. **On all models,** remove propeller shaft upper dust cover and transfer case from transmission. **Ensure not to damage adapter with transfer case input gear spline.**
18. Reverse procedure to install. Tighten all bolts to specifications. Fill transmission and transfer case with specified quantity of SAE 90 grade gear oil ac-

cording to "Lubricant Data Charts."

Automatic Transmission

1. Refer to "Automatic Transmission/ Transaxles" section for removal procedure, then proceed as follows:
   a. Disconnect breather hose from transfer upper cover and control retainer.
   b. Remove rear engine mount from transfer.
   c. Remove dynamic damper.
2. Reverse procedure to install.

TIGHTENING SPECIFICATIONS

Component	Torque/Ft. Lbs.
LAND CRUISER	
Anti-Lock Brake Retainer	28
Center Diff-Lock Indicator Switch	27
Check Ball, Spring & Screw Plug	14
Front Extension Housing Bolts	27
Motor Actuator	13
Oil Receiver	103①
Oil Strainer	43①
Rear Extension Housing Bolts	27
Rear Transfer Case Cover	27
Shift Lever Locknut	108①
Transfer Case Mounting Bolts	27
4WD Indicator Switch	27
PICKUP, TACOMA, T100, 4RUNNER & TUNDRA w/MANUAL TRNASMISSION	
Clutch Release Cylinder	108①
Crossmember Retaining Bolts	70
Engine Mount To Transfer Bolts	19
Stabilizer Bracket	22
Stiffener Plate Attaching Bolts	27
Transfer Case To Transmission Case Bolts	29
Transmission Mounting Bolts	53
PICKUP & 4RUNNER w/MANUAL TRANSMISSION & COUNTERGEAR TRANSFER	
Ball & Spring Plugs	108①
Companion Flange Nuts	90
Extension Housing Bolts	29
Output Shaft Bearing Retainer	13
Rear Case To Front Case Attaching Bolts	29
Reduction Gear Case Attaching Bolts	29
Shift Lever Retainer	78①
Speed Sensor Retaining Bolt	96①
Transfer Case Cover	78①
Transfer Case Indicator Switch	25
PICKUP, TACOMA, T100, Tundra & 4RUNNER w/MANUAL TRANSMISSION & PLANETARY GEAR TRANSFER	
Ball & Spring Plugs	14
Case Cover & Oil Deflector	13
Companion Flange Locknut	87
Control Retainer	13
Extension Housing To Rear Case Bolts	96①

Continued

TIGHTENING
SPECIFICATIONS—Continued

Component	Torque/Ft. Lbs.
PICKUP, TACOMA, T100, Tundra & 4RUNNER w/MANUAL TRANSMISSION & PLANETARY GEAR TRANSFER	
Front Retainer Bolts	96①
Front To Rear Case Attaching Bolts	27
Oil Pump Body Assembly Bolts	96①
Oil Pump Plate Screws	65①
Oil Strainer Bolts	14
Planetary Ring Gear Plug	14
Speedometer Driven Gear Lock Plate	27
Transfer Indicator Switch	27
Transfer L4 Position Switch	27

① — Inch lbs.

Front Suspension & Steering

NOTE: On Air Bag Equipped Models, Refer To "Air Bag System Precautions" Located In The Front Of This Manual For System Disarming & Arming Procedures.

INDEX

PRECAUTIONS

AIR BAG SYSTEMS

Refer to "Air Bag System Precautions" in the front of this manual for system disarming and arming procedures.

AUDIO CODED ANTI-THEFT SYSTEM

Some models are equipped with an audio coded anti-theft system that will disable the radio when the battery cable is disconnected. The system can be identified by the "ANTI-THEFT SYSTEM" on the cassette lid. Obtain three-digit code for input. Reset system after service as follows:

1. Obtain three-digit audio theft code.

2. Depress 1 (PROG) button while depressing righthand side of TUNE SEEK button. Three dashes will appear in tape operation display.
3. To enter first digit, depress 1 (PROG) button repeatedly until number of times depressed equals first digit (depress 1 button six times if first digit is five, first press equals 0).
4. To enter second digit, depress 2 (APS) button repeatedly until number of times depressed equals second digit.
5. To enter third digit, depress 3 (RPT) button repeatedly until number of times depressed equals third digit.
6. If three dashes are displayed after inputting digits, repeat procedure.
7. When code appears in display, de-

press and hold SCAN button until SEC appears.
8. When SEC disappears audio system is operative.
9. If Err is displayed, repeat procedure. **Attempting to input code more than nine times may permanently disable audio system.**

BATTERY GROUND CABLE

Prior to service, disconnect battery ground cable and isolate as required.

WHEEL BEARING

ADJUST

2WD MODELS

1. Raise and support front of vehicle,

then remove wheel and tire assembly and brake caliper. Wire brake caliper aside without stretching brake hose.

2. Remove hub grease cap, cotter pin and locknut, then loosen hub nut.
3. **Torque** hub nut to 22 ft. lbs., then rotate hub and disc assembly several times to ensure bearings are seated.
4. Loosen hub nut until it can be turned with fingers, then retighten nut finger tight.
5. Using a suitable spring scale, measure frictional force of axle seal and make note of it, **Fig. 1.** Frictional force should be 12.35–30.69 ounces (350–870 g).
6. Tighten hub nut slightly, then measure wheel bearing preload with spring scale. Preload should be 21–64 ounces, in addition to axle seal frictional force measured in step 5.
7. If preload is not as specified, tighten or loosen hub nut as necessary until proper preload is obtained.
8. Install locknut, cotter pin, grease cap, caliper and wheel and tire assembly. **If cotter pin holes do not line up, tighten nut by the least amount possible until holes are aligned.**

4WD MODELS

1. Raise and support vehicle, then remove tire and wheel assembly and brake caliper.
2. Remove manual locking hub as follows:
   a. Place control handle in "Free" position.
   b. Remove cover attaching bolts, then the cover.
   c. Remove axle bolt with washer, then the hub body attaching nuts and washers.
   d. Remove cone washer by tapping on heads of bolts using a hammer and suitable drift.
   e. Remove manual locking hub body.
3. **On models equipped with automatic locking hubs,** remove hub as follows:
   a. Remove hub cover.
   b. Remove axle bolt, then the washer.
   c. Remove hub body attaching nuts.
   d. Remove cone washer by tapping on heads of bolts, using a hammer and suitable drift.
   e. Remove automatic locking hub body.
4. **On models less automatic locking hubs,** remove hub as follows:
   a. Remove grease cap from hub flange.
   b. Remove hub bolt and washer, then the hub flange attaching nuts.
   c. Tap hub flange attaching studs with brass drift and hammer to remove cone washers.
   d. Install two bolts into hub flange opposite from each other, then tighten evenly to remove hub flange.
5. **On models equipped with automatic locking hubs,** proceed as follows:
   a. Release lock washer, then remove locknut and lock washer.
   b. Loosen hub nut.
   c. **Torque** hub nut to 43 ft. lbs., then rotate hub and disc assembly sev-

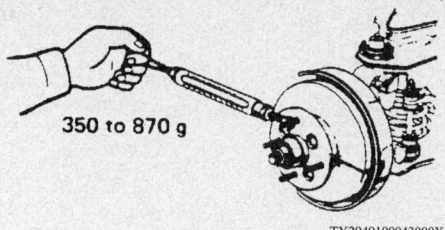

350 to 870 g

TY2049100043000X

Fig. 1   Wheel bearing preload inspection

eral times to ensure bearings are seated.
   d. Loosen hub nut until it can be turned with fingers, then **torque** to 18 ft. lbs.
   e. Using a suitable spring scale, measure wheel bearing starting preload with spring scale, **Fig. 1.** Preload should be 9–17 ft. lbs. If preload is not as specified, tighten or loosen adjusting nut as necessary.
6. **On models less automatic locking hubs,** proceed as follows:
   a. Install lock washer and locknut.
   b. Tighten locknut to specification.
   c. Using a suitable spring scale, measure wheel bearing starting preload with spring scale, **Fig. 1.** Preload should be 9–17 ft. lbs. If preload is not as specified, tighten or loosen adjusting nut as necessary.
   d. If preload is within specifications, bend over lock washer.
7. **On all models,** install freewheeling hub as follows:
   a. Place new gasket on front axle hub.
   b. Install hub body with six cone washers and nuts, then **torque** attaching nuts to 23 ft. lbs.
   c. Install hub bolt with washer, then tighten to specification.
   d. Apply a suitable grease to inner hub splines, then place control handle in "Free" position.
   e. Install new gasket on cover, then install cover on body with follower pawl tabs aligned with non-toothed portions of body.
   f. Install cover attaching bolts and tighten to specification.
8. **On models equipped with automatic locking hubs,** install hub as follows:
   a. Position new gasket on axle hub, then apply suitable multipurpose grease to automatic locking hub splines.
   b. Align spring ends of brake assembly in hub with hub flange alignment pins.
   c. Ensure locking hub outer cam stopper is securely in inner cam groove, then position inner cam protrusion so it is centered between outer cam protrusions and aligned with hub alignment pin holes.
   d. Install locking hub to axle hub ensuring inner cam protrusion is set between ends of hub brake spring.
   e. Install six cone washers and nuts and tighten nuts to specification. **If hub does not fit perfectly on axle hub, remove and reinstall.**

   f. Install cover, then insert attaching bolts and tighten to specification.
9. **On models less automatic locking hubs,** install hubs as follows:
   a. Position new gasket on axle hub, then install hub flange on axle.
   b. Install cone washers and attaching nuts. **Torque** attaching nuts to 23 ft. lbs.
   c. Install grease cap on hub flange.
10. **On all models,** install brake caliper, wheel and tire assembly.

WHEEL HUB & STEERING KNUCKLE
REPLACE
RAV4

1. Remove front wheel and drive shaft locknut, **Fig. 2.**
2. Remove ABS speed sensor and wire harness from steering knuckle.
3. Loosen lower shock absorber nuts.
4. Remove tie rod end cotter pin.
5. Using tie rod end remover tool No. 09610-20012, or equivalent, disconnect lower ball joint from lower arm.
6. Remove steering knuckle with hub.
7. Reverse procedure to install. Tighten to specifications.

BALL JOINT INSPECTION

1. Raise and support vehicle.
2. Ensure front wheels are in straight ahead position and depress and hold brake pedal to eliminate wheel bearing play.
3. Move lower control arm up and down and check that lower ball joint play does not exceed 0 inch.

COIL SPRING
REPLACE

Refer to "Shock Absorber, Replace" for procedure.

SHOCK ABSORBER
REPLACE

1. Raise and support front of vehicle and remove front wheel.
2. Disconnect brake hose and ABS speed sensor from shock absorber.
3. Disconnect shock absorber from upper and lower mountings, **Figs. 3 through 5.**
4. Remove shock absorber with coil spring from vehicle.
5. Reverse procedure to install.

TORSION BAR
REPLACE
PICKUP, TACOMA & T100 w/4WD

1. Remove boots, then mark relative position between torsion bar, anchor arm and torque arm, **Fig. 6.**

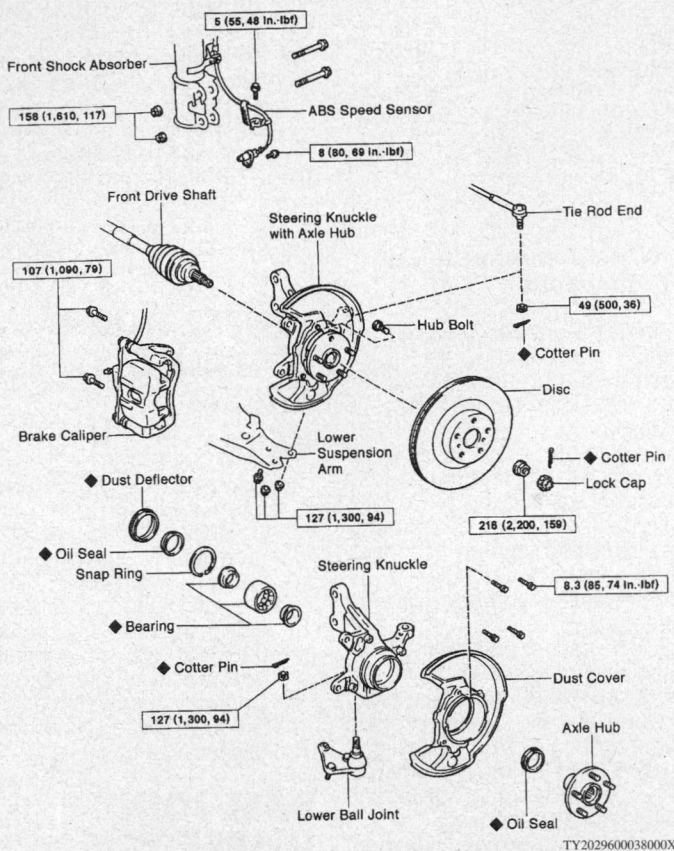

Fig. 2 Exploded view of front axle hub. RAV4

2. Measure protruding bolt end dimension "A," **Fig. 7.**
3. Loosen adjusting nut, then remove anchor arm and torsion bar. **At rear end of torsion bar there are right and left indication marks that are not to be interchanged.**
4. Apply a suitable lubricant to torsion bar spline.
5. Align matchmarks made during removal.
6. Install and tighten adjusting nut to length noted during removal, dimension "A," **Fig. 7.**

PICKUP, TACOMA & T100 w/2WD

Refer to "Control Arm, Replace."

STABILIZER BAR
REPLACE
RAV4

1. Raise and support vehicle, then remove front wheels.
2. Remove both stabilizer bar links.
3. Remove stabilizer bar brackets and bushings.
4. Remove stabilizer bar from righthand side.
5. Reverse procedure to install

PICKUP, TACOMA, TUNDRA, T100 w/4WD & 4RUNNER

1. Remove stabilizer bar to lower suspension arms retaining nuts, cushions and retainers.
2. Disconnect stabilizer bar.
3. Remove stabilizer bar brackets and cushions, then the stabilizer bar.
4. Place stabilizer bar in position, then install new cushion and brackets to frame and insert attaching bolts.
5. Connect stabilizer bar on both sides to lower arms with attaching bolts, retainers and nuts, then **torque** nuts to 19 ft. lbs.
6. **Torque** bracket set bolts to 22 ft. lbs.

PICKUP, TACOMA & T100 w/2WD

1. Remove one torsion bar as outlined under "Control Arm, Replace."
2. Remove stabilizer bar from lower control arms.
3. Remove stabilizer brackets and bushings from frame, then the stabilizer bar.
4. Reverse procedure to install.

LAND CRUISER

1. Raise and support vehicle.
2. Remove stabilizer bar brackets from axle housing, **Fig. 3.**
3. Remove nuts, cushions and bolts retaining both sides of stabilizer bar to frame, then the stabilizer.
4. Reverse procedure to install. Tighten bracket bolts and stabilizer bar to frame nuts to specifications.

STRUT BAR
REPLACE

PICKUP, TACOMA & T100 w/2WD

Mark position of staked nut to strut rod prior to removing strut rod bracket retaining bolt and washers, then disconnect strut bar from frame bracket and lower arm and remove from vehicle. When installing strut rod, check to ensure staked nut is in proper position to strut rod.

CONTROL ARM
REPLACE
LOWER

Pickup, Tacoma & T100 w/2WD

1. Raise and support vehicle.
2. Remove torsion bar boots, then place alignment mark across torsion bar, anchor arm and torque arm, **Fig. 8.**
3. Remove locknut from torsion bar adjusting bolt and measure height of exposed bolt end. Record this value for reference when adjusting vehicle height.
4. Loosen adjusting nut, then remove anchor arm and torsion bar from vehicle.
5. Disconnect stabilizer bar end from lower suspension arm.
6. Disconnect strut bar end from lower suspension arm.
7. Remove shock absorber, refer "Shock Absorber, Replace."
8. Remove bolts securing lower ball joint to lower suspension arm, then separate ball joint from suspension arm.
9. Remove lower arm shaft nut, torque arm and lower arm shaft from lower arm, then the lower suspension arm.
10. To install lower suspension arm, reverse steps 1 through 9. To install torsion bar, follow remaining steps below.
11. If original torsion bar is to be installed, apply suitable grease to splines, then align marks made during removal and install torsion bar. Check to ensure adjusting bolt protrusion is equal to value obtained prior to removal of torsion bar.
12. If new torsion bar is to be installed, position block of wood 7.09–7.87 inches (180–200 mm) under front tire on side of vehicle from which torsion bar was removed.
13. Lower vehicle unit clearance between spring bumper on lower arm and frame is .051 inch (13 mm), **Fig. 9.** Install anchor arm onto torsion bar until adjusting bolt protrusion dimension A is .31–1.10 inch (8–28 mm), **Fig. 10,** on ½ ton models or .43–1.22 inch (11–31 mm) on ¾ ton and Cab and Chassis models. Remove wooden block, then tighten adjusting nut until bolt protrusion dimension B, **Fig. 11,** is 2.72–3.50 inches (69–89 mm).

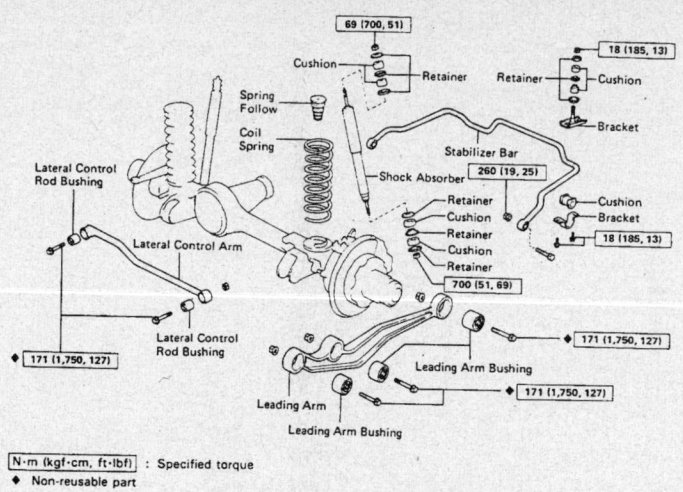

N·m (kgf·cm, ft·lbf) : Specified torque
◆ Non-reusable part

Fig. 3   Exploded view of front suspension components. Land Cruiser

TY2029100019000X

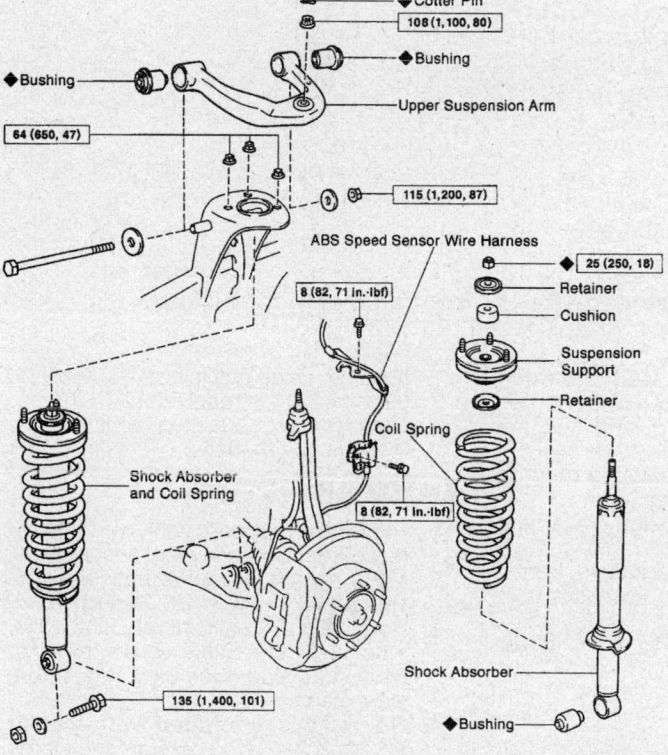

TY2029600040000X

Fig. 5   Exploded view of front suspension components. Pickup, Tacoma, T100 & 4Runner

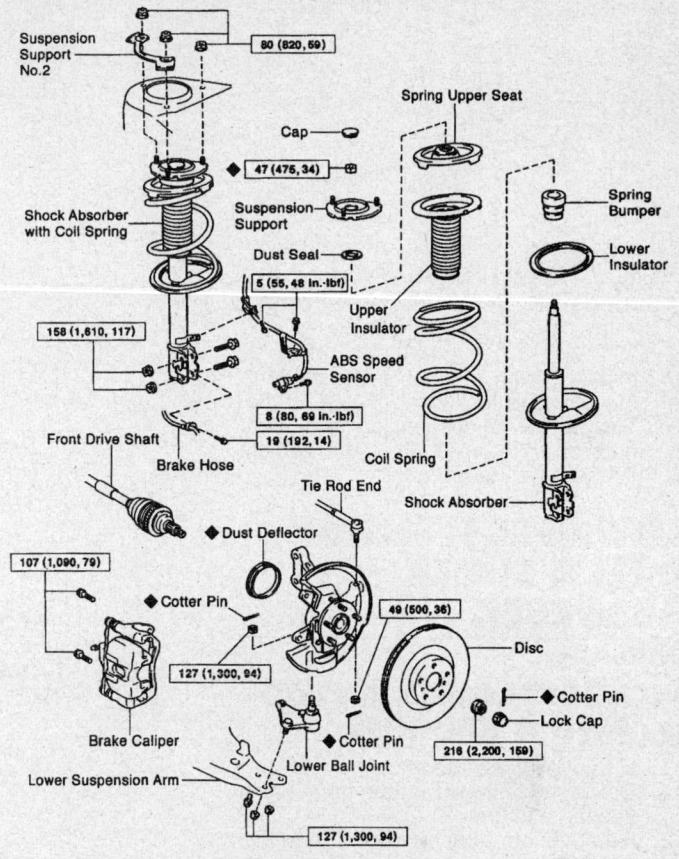

TY2029600039000X

Fig. 4   Exploded view of front suspension components. RAV4

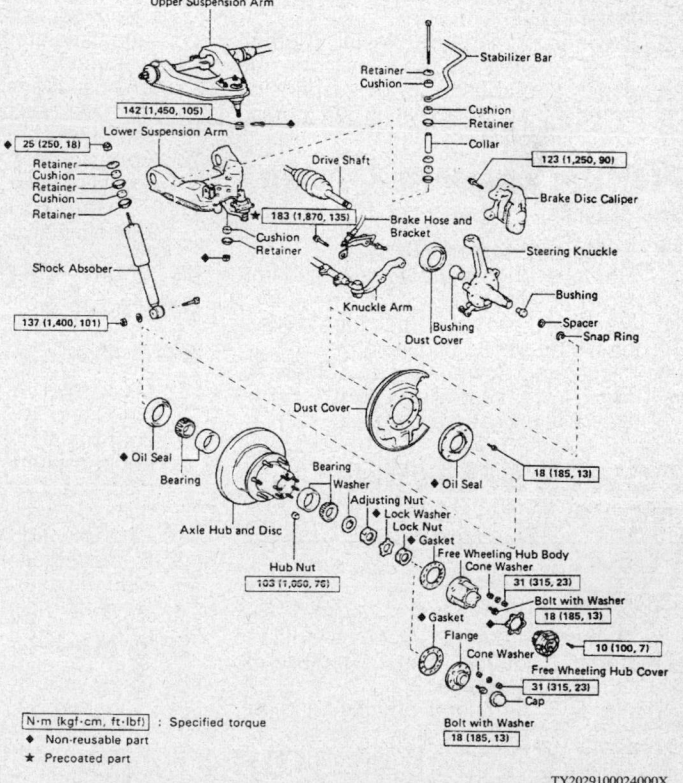

N·m (kgf·cm, ft·lbf) : Specified torque
◆ Non-reusable part
★ Precoated part

TY2029100024000X

Fig. 6   Exploded view of front suspension components. Pickup, Tacoma & T100 w/4WD

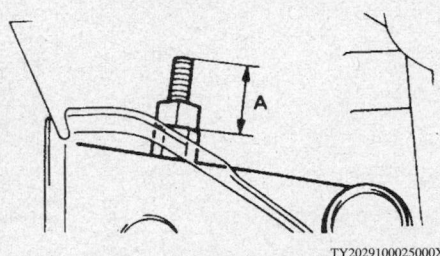

TY2029100025000X

Fig. 7   Measuring protruding bolt dimension "A." Pickup, Tacoma & T100 w/4WD

14. Install torsion bar boots and locknut, then **torque** locknut to 51–65 ft. lbs. **Torque** lower suspension arm shaft nuts to 145–216 ft. lbs. with vehicle suspension loaded.

LOWER SUSPENSION ARM & SHOCK ABSORBER

REPLACE

PICKUP, TACOMA & T100 w/4WD & 4RUNNER

1. Remove shock absorber.
2. Disconnect stabilizer bar from lower suspension arm.
3. Remove four attaching bolts, then disconnect lower suspension arm from lower ball joint.
4. Mark relative position between front and rear adjusting cams, then remove attaching nut, adjusting cams and lower suspension arm.
5. Reverse procedure to install. Tighten lower suspension arm to ball joint nut, shock absorber to lower suspension arm bracket and adjusting cam nuts to specifications.

PICKUP, TACOMA & T100 w/2WD

1. Raise and support vehicle.
2. Remove engine undercover and torsion bar spring.
3. Remove shock absorber, then disconnect strut bar from lower arm.
4. Disconnect lower ball joint, then remove lower suspension arm.
5. Reverse procedure to install.

POWER STEERING GEAR

REPLACE

RAV4

1. Remove steering wheel as outlined under "Steering Wheel, Replace" in "Electrical" section.
2. Remove righthand and lefthand engine under covers.
3. Disconnect righthand and lefthand tie rod ends.
4. Remove front exhaust pipe.
5. Remove stabilizer bar with link.
6. Disconnect No. 2 intermediate shaft.

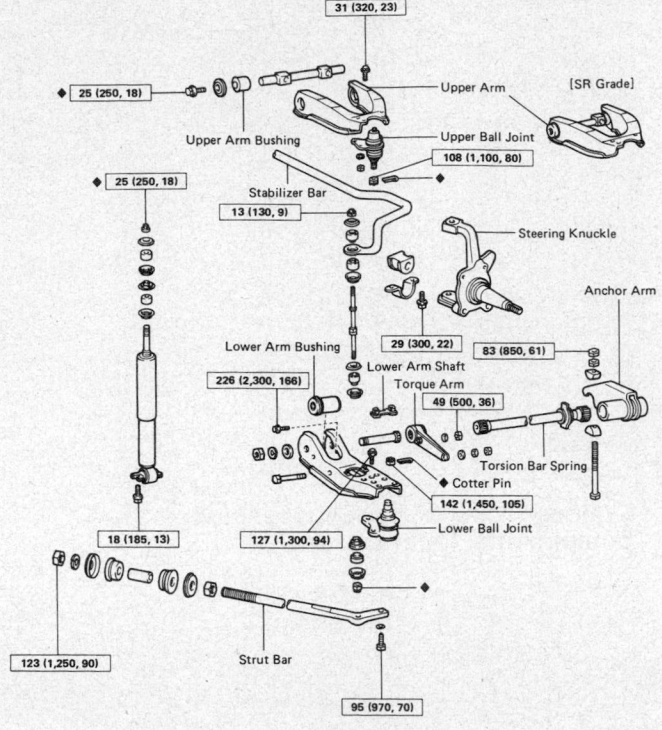

N·m (kgf·cm, ft·lbf) : Specified torque
◆ Non-reusable part

TY2029100020000X

Fig. 8   Exploded view of front suspension. Pickup, Tacoma & T100 w/2WD

7. Disconnect pressure feed and return tubes, then remove tube clamps.
8. Disconnect righthand and lefthand lower suspension arms.
9. Remove two power steering gear assembly set bolts and nuts.
10. Remove front suspension crossmember assembly.
11. Reverse procedure to install. Tighten to specifications.

PICKUP, TACOMA, T100 & 4RUNNER

2WD Models

1. Mark relative position between coupling and worm shaft, then remove coupling attaching bolt.
2. Loosen pitman arm mount nut, then disconnect relay rod from pitman arm, using tie rod end puller tool No. 09611-22012, or equivalent.
3. Remove gear housing attaching bolts, then the gear housing.
4. Reverse procedure to install.

4WD Models

1. Remove joint protector set bolt, then mark relative position between universal joint and worm shaft.
2. Remove two universal joint attaching bolts, then disconnect universal joint from worm shaft.
3. Remove pitman arm set nut, then disconnect pitman arm from steering gear

housing, using ball joint puller tool No. 09628-62011, or equivalent.
4. Remove gear housing attaching bolts, then the gear housing.

LAND CRUISER

1. Raise and support vehicle, then remove front tire and wheel assembly.
2. Make alignment marks between universal joint and worm shaft, **Fig. 12.**
3. Remove universal joint retaining bolts, then slide the intermediate shaft to main shaft side, then disconnect from worm shaft.
4. **On models equipped with power steering,** remove pressure line clamp bolts, then using wrench tool No. 09631-22020, or equivalent, disconnect power steering lines.
5. **On all models,** remove cotter pin and set nut retaining pitman arm onto relay rod, then using ball joint puller tool No. 09628-62011, or equivalent, disconnect pitman arm from relay rod.
6. Remove steering gear retaining bolts, then the steering gear.
7. Reverse procedure to install. Tighten set nut to specification.

TUNDRA

1. Remove steering wheel as outlined under "Steering Wheel, Replace."
2. Disconnect righthand and lefthand tie rod ends.
3. Disconnect No. 2 intermediate shaft.

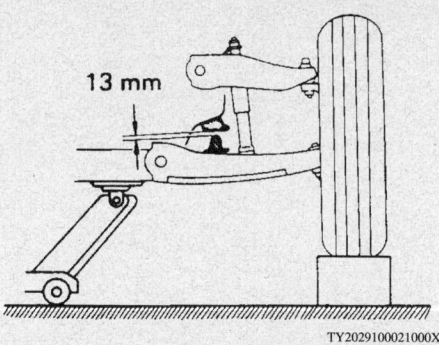

Fig. 9   Front suspension position for torsion bar replacement. Pickup, Tacoma & T100 w/2WD

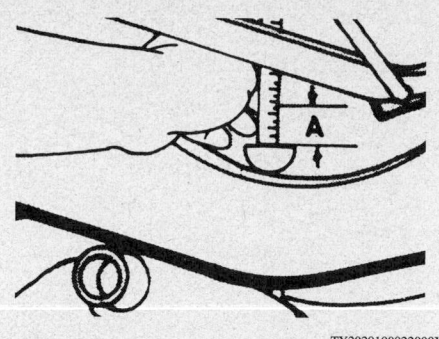

Fig. 10   Torsion bar adjusting bolt height dimension A inspection. Pickup, Tacoma & T100 w/2WD

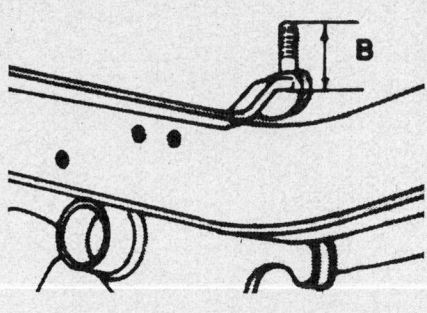

Fig. 11   Torsion bar adjusting bolt height dimension B inspection. Pickup, Tacoma & T100 w/2WD

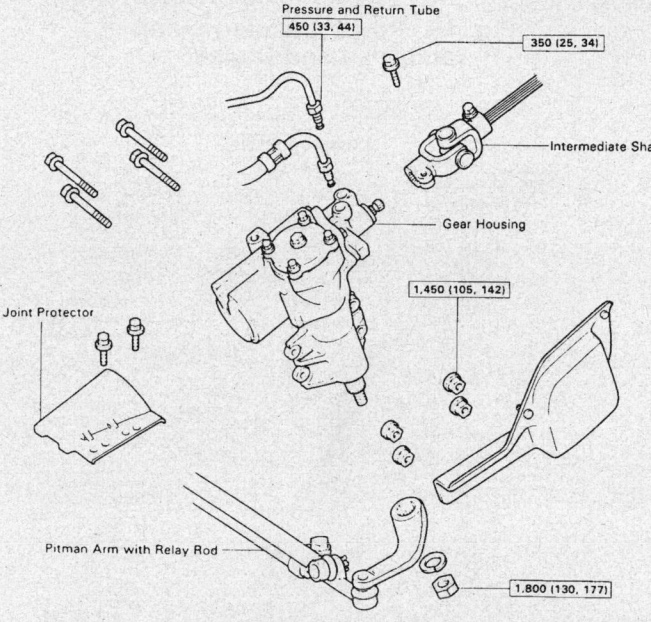

Fig. 12   Exploded view of steering gear components. Land Cruiser

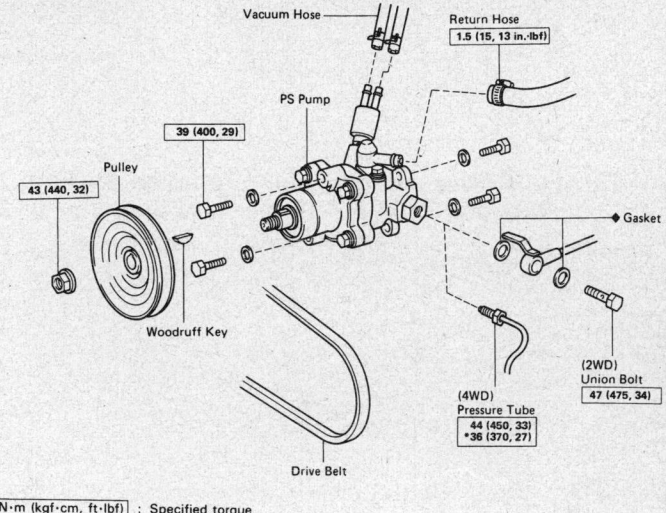

Fig. 13   Power steering pump removal. Pickup, Tacoma, T100, 4Runner & Tundra VZN Series

4. Remove bolt, then disconnect clamp plate.
5. Disconnect pressure feed and return tubes
6. Remove two power steering gear assembly set bolts and nuts.
7. Remove power steering gear, then remove bracket and grommet.
8. Reverse procedure to install. Tighten to specifications.

POWER STEERING PUMP

REPLACE

Refer to **Figs. 13 through 16** for power steering pump replacement.

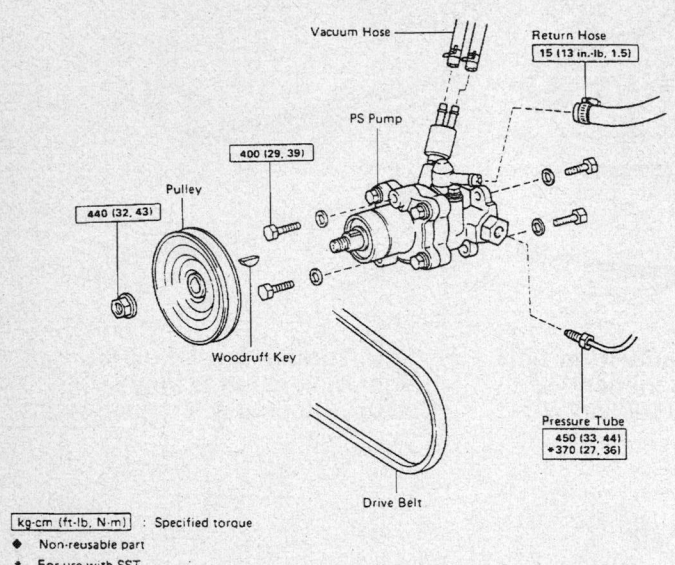

kg·cm (ft-lb, N·m) : Specified torque
◆ Non-reusable part
✦ For use with SST

TY6039100024000X

Fig. 14 Power steering pump removal. Pickup, Tacoma, T100 & 4Runner, RN Series

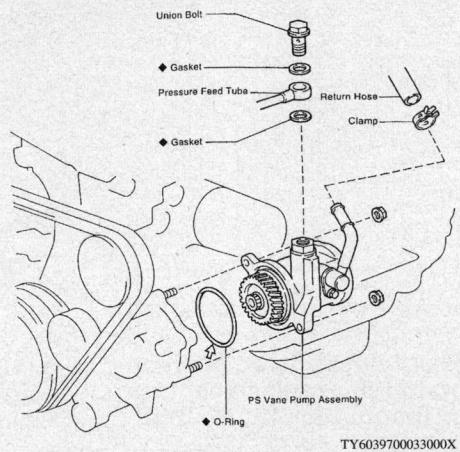

TY6039700033000X

Fig. 15 Power steering pump removal. Land Cruiser

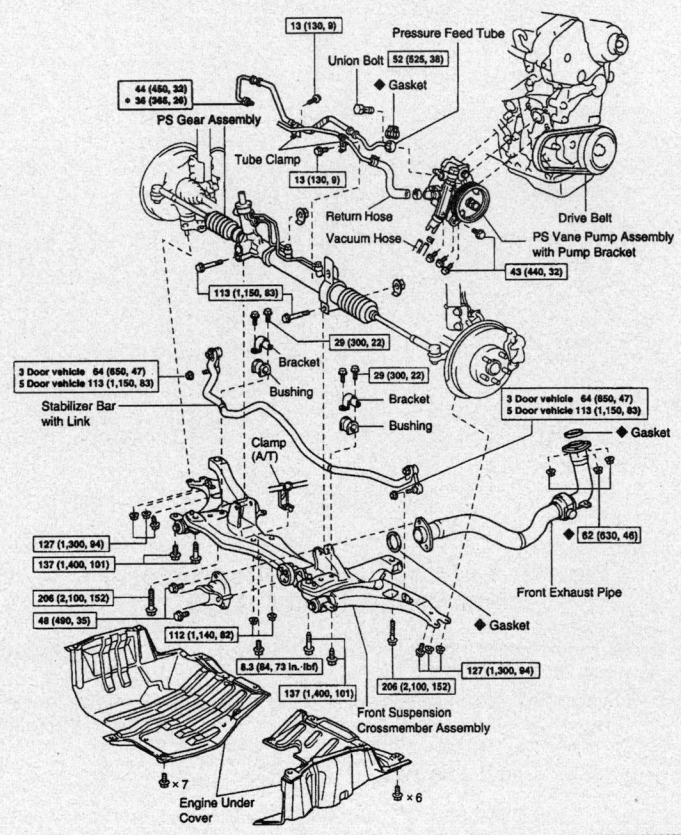

TY6029600055000X

Fig. 16 Power steering pump removal. RAV4

TIGHTENING SPECIFICATIONS

LAND CRUISER

Year	Component	Torque/Ft. Lbs.
1996–99	Brake Line	11
	Disc Brake Cylinder To Axle Hub	90
	Flange To Axle Hub	26
	Front Axle Hub Bearing Locknut	47
	Front Axle Hub To Rotor Disc	47
	Lateral Control Rod	127
	Leading Arm	130
	LH Spring Center Bolt	36
	Propeller Shaft To Companion Flange	65
	Shock Absorber To Axle Housing	51
	Shock Absorber To Frame	51
	Stabilizer Bar Link To Cover	13
	Stabilizer Bar To Link Bracket	76
	Steering Knuckle To Bearing Cap	71
	Steering Knuckle To Knuckle Arm	71
	Tie Rod End	67
	Wheel Lug Nuts	108

PICKUP, TACOMA w/2WD, TUNDRA & T100

Year	Component	Torque/Ft. Lbs.
1996–99	Knuckle Stopper Bolt Locknut	25
	Lower Arm Shaft Nut	166
	Lower Suspension Arm To Lower Ball Joint	94
	Lower Suspension Arm To Shock Absorber	13
	Lower Suspension Arm To Stabilizer Bar	108①
	Lower Suspension Arm To Strut Bar	70
	Shock Absorber To Frame	18
	Stabilizer Bar Bracket To Frame	22
	Steering Knuckle To Lower Ball Joint	105
	Steering Knuckle To Tie Rod	67
	Steering Knuckle To Upper Ball Joint	80
	Strut Bar To Frame	90
	Tie Rod Clamp Bolt	19
	Torsion Bar Spring Locknut	61
	Upper Arm Shaft To Frame	71
	Upper Suspension Arm Set Bolt	93
	Upper Suspension Arm To Upper Ball Joint	23
	Wheel Lug Nut	76

① — Inch lbs.

PICKUP, TACOMA, TUNDRA,T100 & 4RUNNER w/4WD

Year	Component	Torque/ Ft. Lbs.
1996–97	Axle Hub Bearing Locknut	35
	Brake Caliper To Steering Knuckle	90
	Differential Carrier To Carrier Cover	34
	Differential Carrier To Side Bearing Cap	58
	Differential Tube To Bracket	94
	Free Wheeling Hub Body To Axle Hub	23
	Free Wheeling Hub Body To Cover	84①
	Free Wheeling Hub Body To Front Driveshaft	13
	Front Differential Front Mounting Bolt	108
	Front Differential Rear LH Mounting Bolt	123
	Front Differential Rear RH Mounting Bolt	123
	Front Differential To Bracket	94
	Front Driveshaft To Side Gear Shaft	61
	Knuckle Stopper Bolt Locknut	35
	Lower Suspension Arm To Frame	145
	Lower Suspension Arm To Lower Ball Joint	105
	Lower Suspension Arm To Shock Absorber	101
	Lower Suspension Arm To Stabilizer Bar	19
	Ring Gear To Differential Case	71
	Shock Absorber To Frame	18
	Stabilizer Bar Bracket To Frame	22
	Steering Knuckle Arm To Steering Knuckle	135
	Upper Ball Joint To Steering Knuckle	105
	Upper Suspension Arm Shaft Locknut	166
	Upper Suspension Arm Shaft To Frame	131
	Upper Suspension Arm To Torque Arm	64
	Upper Suspension Arm To Upper Ball Joint	18
	Wheel Lug Nut	76

① — Inch lbs.

1997-99 4RUNNER

Year	Component	Torque/ Ft. Lbs.
1997-99	Brake Caliper To Steering Knuckle	90
	Differential Carrier To Differential Tube	77
	Differential Front Mounting Cushion To Differential	80
	Differential Front Mounting Cushion To Frame	101
	Differential Rear Mounting Cushion To Differential	71
	Differential Rear Mounting Cushion To Frame	64
	Drain Plug	48
	Fill Plug	29
	Hub Nut	83
	Lower Suspension Arm To Frame	96
	Lower Suspension Arm To Lower Ball Joint	105
	Rack End Lock Nut	41
	Ring Gear To Differential Case	71
	Shock Absorber To Suspension Support	18
	Stabilizer Bar Bracket To Frame	19
	Stabilizer Bar Bracket To Link	14

Continued

1997-99 4RUNNER—Continued

Year	Component	Torque/Ft. Lbs.
1997-99	Steering Knuckle Arm To Bracket	21
	Steering Knuckle To Lower Ball Joint	67
	Upper Ball Suspension Arm To Ball Joint	80
	Wheel Lug Nut	83

RAV4

Year	Component	Torque/Ft. Lbs.
1996-99	ABS Speed Sensor To Steering Knuckle	72①
	Brake Hose Set Bolt	14
	Center Bearing Bracket Set Bolt	47
	Center Bearing Lock Bolt	24
	Driveshaft Locknut	159
	Lower Ball Joint To Lower Suspension Arm	94
	Lower Ball Joint To Steering Knuckle	94
	Lower Suspension Arm Bracket To Body	101
	Steering Knuckle To Tie Rod End	36
	Suspension Crossmember To Body	152
	Tie Rod End Locknut	41
	Transmission Case Protector Set Bolt	13
	Wheel Lug Nuts	76

① — Inch lbs.

Wheel Alignment

NOTE: On Air Bag Equipped Models, Refer To "Air Bag System Precautions" Located In The Front Of This Manual For System Disarming & Arming Procedures.

INDEX

PRELIMINARY INSPECTION

Prior to checking and resetting front wheel alignment, check tire pressure to ensure it is correct, check wheel bearings for looseness and correct as necessary, check vehicle ride height, and check wheel runout with a dial indicator. Wheel runout should not exceed .047 inch (1.2 mm) on Pickup, .118 inch (3.0 mm) on Land Cruiser, Tacoma, Tundra, T100, and 4Runner, or .039 inch (1.0 mm) on RAV4.

FRONT WHEEL ALIGNMENT

CASTER & CAMBER

Land Cruiser

Caster and camber are not adjustable on these models. If caster and camber are not within limits, check for worn or damaged suspension parts and replace as necessary.

Pickup, Tacoma & T100 w/2WD

Caster and camber are adjusted by increasing or decreasing the number of shims between upper arm shaft and frame mounting surface. The thickness difference between front and rear shim packs should not exceed .16 inch (4 mm).

Pickup, Tacoma & T100 w/4WD

Caster and camber are adjusted by rotating front and/or rear adjusting cams as shown, **Figs. 1 and 2.**

Tundra & 4Runner

Caster and camber are adjusted by rotating front and/or rear adjusting cams as shown, **Fig. 3.**

RAV4

Caster is not adjustable. If caster is out of specification, check for worn or damaged suspension parts.

Adjust front camber as follows:
1. Remove front wheels.
2. Remove two lower shock absorber attaching nuts, then coat threads of nuts with engine oil and temporarily reinstall nuts.
3. Adjust camber by pulling or pushing lower side of shock absorber in direction in which camber adjustment is required.
4. **Torque** two lower shock absorber nuts to 117 ft. lbs. and install front wheels.
5. Check camber. If camber is not within specifications, estimate how much additional camber is required and select adjusting bolt from **Fig. 4.**
6. Repeat procedure, substituting proper adjusting bolt(s) for lower shock absorber bolts.

TOE-IN, ADJUSTMENT

Measure length of tie rod on each side and adjust to be equal. Adjust toe-in by turning adjusting tubes equal amounts. Clamp adjusting tubes after aligning clamps with tube slots. Lock tie rod ends so that inner and outer ends are at right angles to each other.

REAR WHEEL ALIGNMENT

EXCEPT RAV4

Vehicles with solid rear axles are nonadjustable.

RAV4

Camber and toe-in are adjusted by loosening the adjustment cam lock bolt and turning cam, **Fig. 5.**

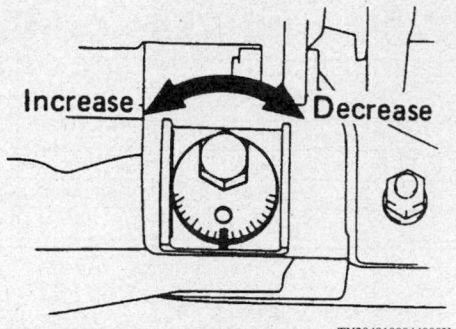

TY2049100044000X

Fig. 1   Front camber angle adjustment. Pickup, Tacoma & T100 w/4WD

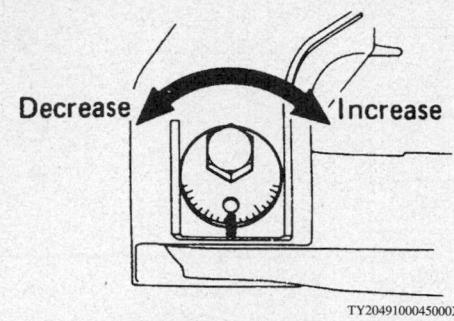

TY2049100045000X

Fig. 2   Rear camber angle adjustment. Pickup, Tacoma & T100 w/4WD

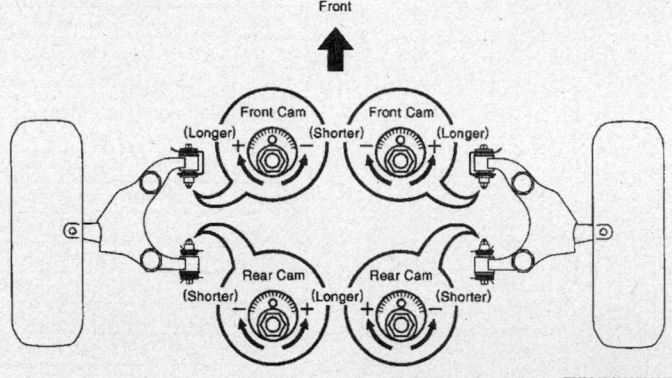

TY2049600070000X

Fig. 3   Caster & camber adjustment cams. Tundra & 4Runner

VEHICLE RIDE HEIGHT

RAV4

Measure front vehicle ride height from ground to the center of the lower suspension arm front mounting bolt. Front vehicle ride height should be 8.94 inches on 2WD models and 9.33 inches on 4WD models.

Measure rear vehicle ride height from ground to the center of the body side No. 1 suspension arm mounting bolt. Rear vehicle ride height should be 13.90 inches on 2WD models and 14.17 inches on 4WD models.

PICKUP, TACOMA & T100

Trim height on these models will vary depending on option package. For measurement, refer to **Figs. 6 and 7.**

4RUNNER

Refer to **Figs. 8 and 9** for ride height check locations. For models with tire size 225/75R15, the front should measure (A-B)=2.740 inches and the rear should measure (C-D)=1.953 inches. For models with tire size 265/70R16, the front should measure (A-B)=1.870 inches and the rear should measure (C-D)=1.157 inches.

LAND CRUISER

Refer to **Figs. 10 and 11** for vehicle ride height check locations. For models with tire size P235/75 R15, the front and rear should measure 13.193 inches. For models with tire size 31x10.50 R15LT (C), the front and rear should measure 14.193 inches.

TUNDRA

Trim height on these models will vary depending on option package. For measurement, refer to **Fig. 12.**

Bolt	Set Bolt	Adjusting Bolt						
	Original	OD=13.9 mm		OD=13.3 mm		OD=12.4 mm		
		1 Dot		2 Dots		3 Dots		
	(11)	(·11)		(··11)		(···11)		
Adjusting Value	① ②	①	②	①	②	①	②	
15'	●		●					
30'	●			●				
45'	●						●	
1°00'		●					●	
1°15'				●			●	
1°30'						●	●	

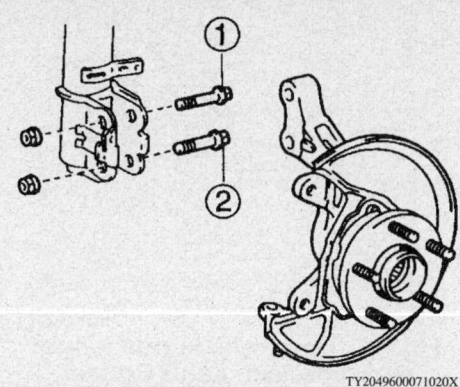

Fig. 4 Front camber adjustment bolt selection (Part 1 of 2). RAV4

Fig. 4 Front camber adjustment bolt selection (Part 2 of 2). RAV4

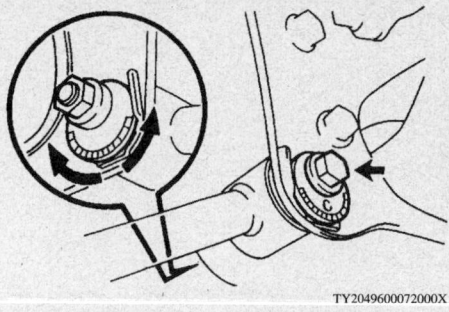

Fig. 5 Rear camber & toe-in adjustment cam. RAV4

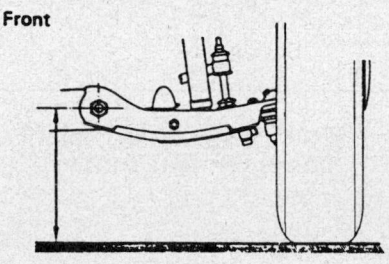

Front

Rear

Fig. 6 Vehicle ride height measurement. Pickup, Tacoma & T100 w/2WD

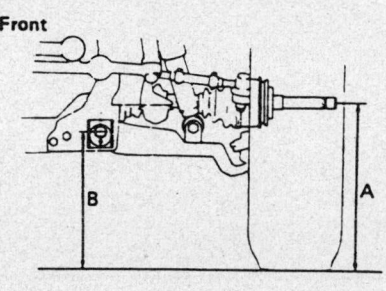

Front

Rear

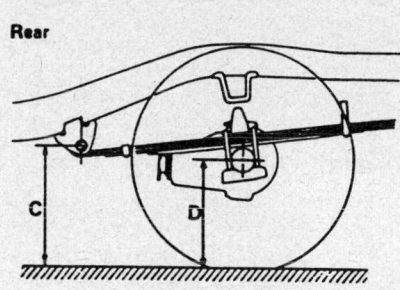

Fig. 7 Vehicle ride height measurement. Pickup, Tacoma & T100 w/4WD

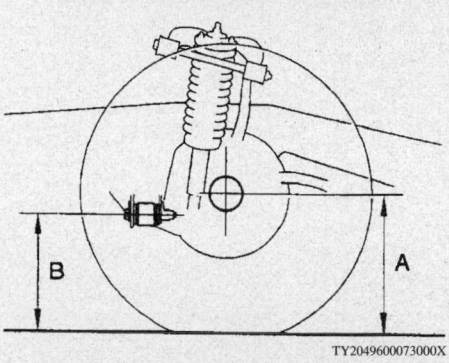

Fig. 8 Front vehicle ride height measurement. 4Runner

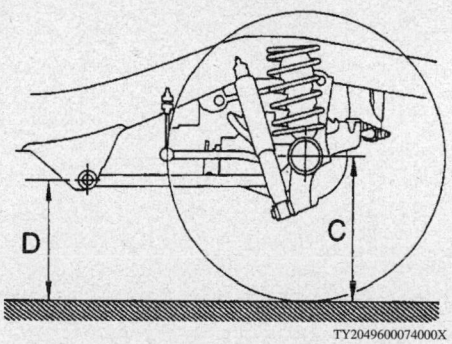

Fig. 9 Rear vehicle ride height measurement. 4Runner

Front

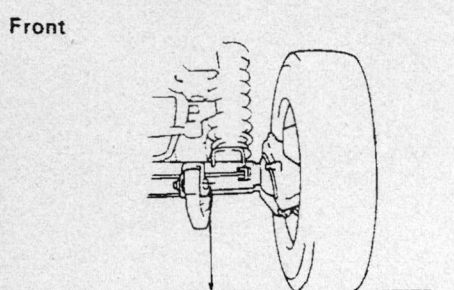

TY2049100049000X

Fig. 10 Front vehicle ride height measurement. Land Cruiser

Rear

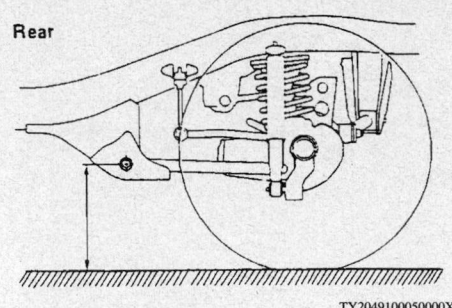

TY2049100050000X

Fig. 11 Rear vehicle ride height measurement. Land Cruiser

Front:

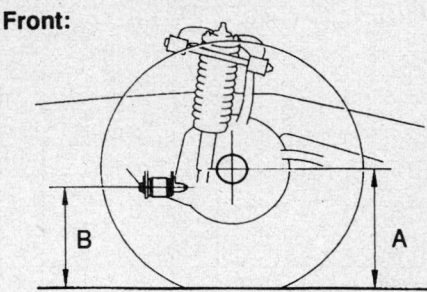

Rear:

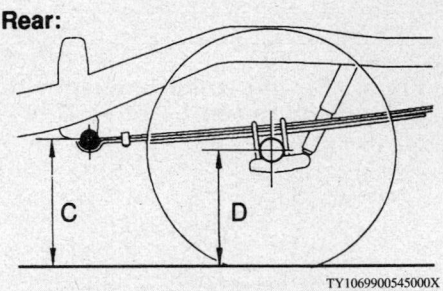

TY1069900545000X

Fig. 12 Vehicle ride height measurement. Tundra

TOYOTA PREVIA

INDEX OF SERVICE OPERATIONS

Specifications

GENERAL ENGINE SPECIFICATIONS

Year	Engine	Fuel System	Bore & Stroke	Compression Ratio	Maximum Brake, H.P. @ RPM	Maximum Torque, Ft. Lbs. @ RPM	Normal Oil Pressure, psi①
1996–97	2.4L 2TZ-FZE	Fuel Inj.	3.74 x 3.39	8.9	161 @ 5000	201 @ 3600	36

① — At 3000 RPM.

TUNE UP SPECIFICATIONS

| Year | Engine | Spark Plug Gap, Inch | Ignition | | | Curb Idle Speed, RPM① | | Fuel Pump Pressure, psi | Valve Clearance, Inch | |
			Firing Order	Timing, °BTDC	Timing Mark, Fig.	Man. Trans.	Auto. Trans.		Int.	Exh.
1996	2.4L	.043	1-3-4-2	5	A	750	750N	38–44	.006–.010	.010–.014
1997	2.4L	.043	1-3-4-2	5	A	750	750N	33–40	.006–.010	.010–.014

BTDC — Before Top Dead Center
N — Neutral

① — Controlled by idle air controller (IAC).

TY1139100120000X

Fig. A

FRONT WHEEL ALIGNMENT SPECIFICATIONS

The following specifications are for unloaded vehicles.

| Year | Model | Caster Angle, Degrees | | Camber Angle, Degrees | | Toe, Inch① | Toe-Out On Turns, Deg. | | Steering Axis Inclination, Deg. | Ball Joint Wear |
		Limits	Desired	Limits	Desired		Outer Wheel	Inner Wheel		
1996	2WD	+4¾ to +6¼	+5½	-⅔ to +⅚	+1/12	.0 to +.16	32¾	35⁷/₁₂	10⁷/₁₂	②
	4WD	+4⁷/₁₂ to +6¹/₁₂	+5⅓	-½ to 1	+¼	+.04 to +.20	33	3⁷/₁₂	10⅓	②
1997	2WD	+4 to +6	+5½	-⁵/₁₂ to +⁷/₁₂	+1/12	.0 to +.16	32¾	35⁷/₁₂	10⁷/₁₂	②
	4WD	+4⅚ to +5⅚	+5⅓	-¼ to ¾	+¼	+.04 to +.20	33	35⁷/₁₂	10⅓	②

① — Toe-in (+); toe-out (-).

② — Refer to "Ball Joint Inspection" under "Front Suspension & Steering."

FLUID CAPACITIES & COOLING SYSTEM DATA

Year	Coolant Capacity, Qts		Radiator Cap Relief Pressure, Lbs.	Thermo. Opening Temp., °F	Fuel Tank, Gals.	Engine Oil Refill, Qts.①	Transmission Oil Qts. (Automatic)	Axle Oil, Pints
	Less A/C	With A/C						
1996	13	13	13	180	19.8	6.1	③	②
1997	12.4	12.4	10.7–14.9	176–183	19.8	6.1	③	②

① — With oil filter change.
② — Front, 2.2 pts.; rear, 3.2 pts.
③ — Drain & refill, 2.5 qts.; dry fill, 6 qts.

LUBRICANT DATA

Year	Model	Lubricant Type				
		Transmission (Automatic)	Transfer Case	Rear Axle	Power Steering	Brake System
1996	All	Dexron II/IIE/III	75W-90 GL-4/5	80W-90 GL-5	Dexron II/IIE/III	DOT 3
1997	All	Dexron II/IIE/III	75W-90 GL-4/5	80W-90 GL-5	Dexron II or III	DOT 3

Electrical

NOTE: On Air Bag Equipped Models, Refer To "Air Bag System Precautions" Located In The Front Of This Manual For System Disarming & Arming Procedures.

INDEX

PRECAUTIONS

AIR BAG SYSTEMS

Refer to "Air Bag System Precautions" in the front of this manual for system disarming and arming procedures.

BATTERY GROUND CABLE

Prior to service, disconnect battery ground cable and isolate as required.

FUSE PANEL & FLASHER LOCATION

The junction block/fuse panel is located behind the center of the instrument panel. The turn signal and hazard flasher are located at the junction block behind the center of the instrument panel.

FUEL PUMP RELAY LOCATION

The fuel pump relay is located on the front righthand side of the engine compartment, **Fig. 1.**

RELAY CENTER LOCATION

The relay center is located behind the upper center of the instrument panel.

STARTER

REPLACE

1. **On 4WD models,** remove front propeller shaft.
2. **On models with manual transmission,** disconnect clutch slave cylinder

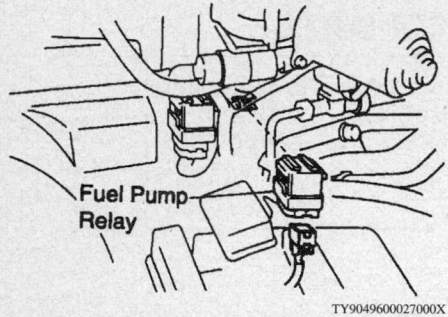

Fig. 1 Fuel pump relay location

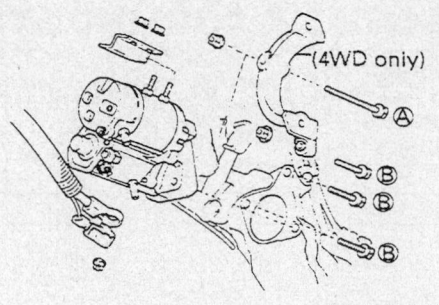

TY1129100001000X

Fig. 2 Starter motor installation

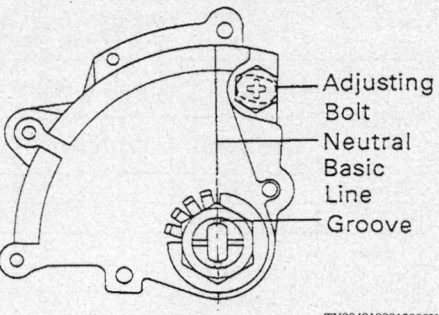

TY9049100012000X

Fig. 3 Neutral start switch adjustment

and position aside. **Do not disconnect clutch line.**
3. **On all models,** remove battery cable to starter attaching nut.
4. Remove starter electrical connector.
5. **On 2WD models,** remove starter attaching nuts and bolt, then the starter.
6. **On 4WD models,** remove center support bracket and starter attaching nuts and bolts, then the starter.
7. **On all models,** reverse procedure to install. **Torque** A starter bolts as shown in **Fig. 2,** to 41 ft. lbs. and B starter bolts to 30 ft. lbs. On 4WD models, **torque** center support bracket to stiffener plate to 43 ft. lbs. and bracket to starter to 12 ft. lbs.
8. Reverse procedure to install.

DISTRIBUTOR
REPLACE

1. Disconnect distributor cap spark plug wires.
2. Disconnect distributor electrical connector.
3. Remove ventilation hoses.
4. Remove distributor cap and packing.
5. Set No. 1 cylinder to TDC, as follows:
   a. Install service nut and bolt to accessory driveshaft.
   b. Turn crankshaft in normal direction until timing mark is aligned with 0 mark on timing chain case.
6. Remove distributor attaching bolts, then the distributor.
7. Reverse procedure to install. **Torque** distributor attaching bolts to 14 ft. lbs.

IGNITION LOCK
REPLACE

1. Turn ignition switch to ACC position.
2. Insert small diameter rod to hole in side of lock cylinder, then holding pin down, remove lock cylinder.
3. Ensure lock cylinder is in ACC position.
4. Reverse procedure to install.

IGNITION SWITCH
REPLACE

1. Remove steering column upper and lower covers.
2. Disconnect ignition switch electrical connectors.
3. Turn ignition key to ACC position, then remove ignition key cylinder.

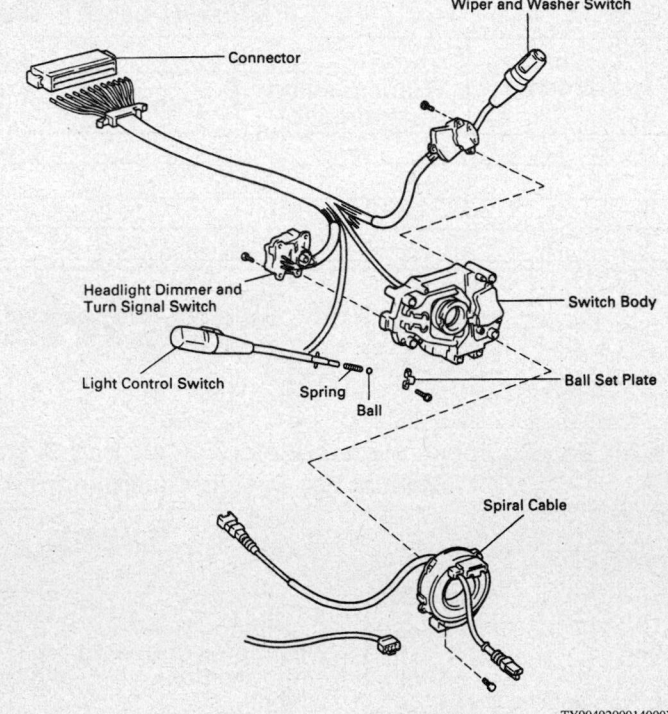

TY9049200014000X

Fig. 4 Combination switch.

4. Remove ignition switch attaching screws, then the ignition switch.
5. Reverse procedure to install.

NEUTRAL SAFETY SWITCH
REPLACE

1. Raise and support vehicle.
2. Disconnect switch electrical connector.
3. Loosen neutral start switch adjusting bolt, **Fig. 3.**
4. Position transmission shift lever in Neutral.
5. Align neutral base line and switch groove.
6. **Torque** adjusting bolt to 48 inch lbs.
7. Bend at least two lock washer tabs.

STOP LIGHT SWITCH
REPLACE

1. Remove brake pedal tension spring.
2. Disconnect switch electrical connector.

3. Remove switch attaching nut, then slide switch from bracket.
4. Reverse procedure to install.

COMBINATION SWITCH
REPLACE
REPLACEMENT

1. Remove steering wheel as outlined under "Steering Wheel, Replace."
2. Remove steering column upper and lower covers.
3. Disconnect combination switch and spiral cable electrical connectors, then remove combination switch.
4. Reverse procedure to install.

SERVICE
Spiral Cable

1. Remove combination switch as outlined previously.
2. Remove spiral cable attaching screws.
3. Separate spiral cable from combination switch body, **Fig. 4.**

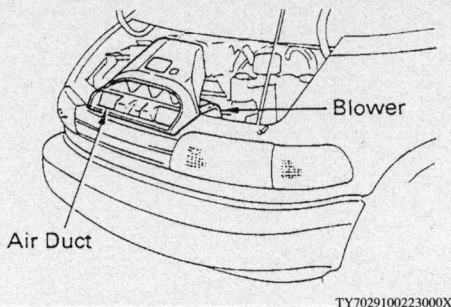

TY7029100223000X

Fig. 5 Front evaporator core replacement

4. Reverse procedure to install. **Ensure spiral cable is in correct mounting position.**

Headlight Dimmer & Turn Signal Switch

1. Remove combination switch as outlined previously.
2. Using suitable small screwdriver, disengage headlight dimmer and turn signal switch wiring from combination switch connector. **Note position of wires.**
3. Remove switch to switch body attaching screws, **Fig. 4.**
4. Reverse procedure to install, noting the following:
   a. Ensure smooth switch operation in all positions.
   b. Install electrical terminals to combination switch in same position as they were removed.

Windshield Wiper/Washer Switch

1. Remove combination switch as outlined previously.
2. Using suitable small screwdriver, disengage headlight dimmer and turn signal switch wiring from combination switch connector. **Note position of wires.**
3. Remove switch to switch body attaching screws, **Fig. 4.**
4. Reverse procedure to install, noting the following:
   a. Ensure smooth switch operation in all positions.
   b. Install electrical terminals to combination switch in same position as they were removed.

Headlamp Switch

1. Remove combination switch as outlined previously.
2. Using suitable small screwdriver, disengage headlight dimmer and turn signal switch wiring from combination switch connector. **Note position of wires.**
3. Remove headlamp switch attaching screws, **Fig. 4.**
4. Remove switch, then the ball and spring assembly.
5. Reverse procedure to install, noting the following:
   a. Ensure smooth switch operation in all positions.

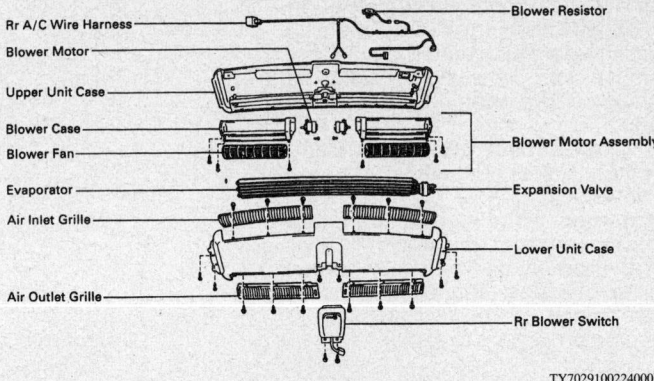

TY7029100224000X

Fig. 6 Exploded view of rear cooling unit. Denso type

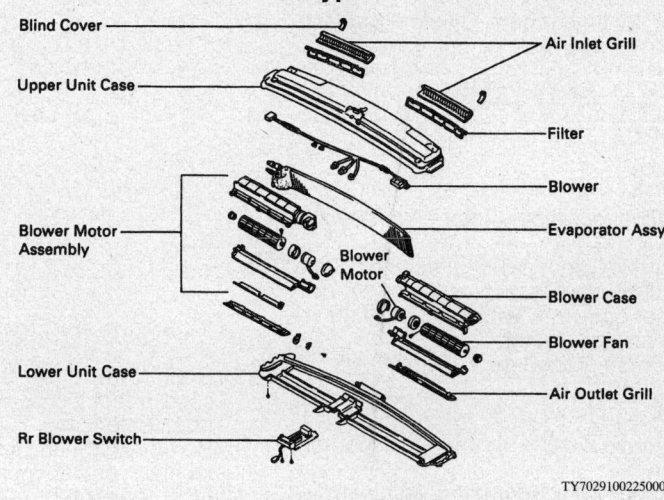

TY7029100225000X

Fig. 7 Exploded view of rear cooling unit. Panasonic type

b. Install electrical terminals to combination switch in same position as they were removed.

STEERING WHEEL
REPLACE

1. **On models with air bag,** remove four wheel pad attaching screws with T30 Torx wrench, then pull pad rearward and disconnect air bag connector.
2. **On models less air bag,** remove steering wheel pad attaching screw, then pull rearward and disconnect electrical connector.
3. Place alignment marks on steering wheel and mainshaft for assembly reference.
4. Remove steering wheel attaching nut.
5. Using steering wheel puller tool No. 09609-20011, or equivalent, remove steering wheel.
6. **Torque** steering wheel attaching bolt to 25 ft. lbs.
7. **On models with air bag, torque** wheel pad attaching screws to 5 ft. lbs. with suitable Torx wrench.
8. **On all models,** reverse procedure to install.

INSTRUMENT CLUSTER
REPLACE

1. Remove steering wheel as outlined under "Steering Wheel, Replace."
2. Remove steering column upper and lower covers.
3. Remove lefthand kick panel.
4. Remove hood release lever attaching screws, then slide forward to remove.
5. Remove instrument cluster lower finish panel attaching screws.
6. Pull cluster finish panel rearward and disconnect electrical connectors, then remove cluster finish panel.
7. Depress cluster finish center upper panel release lock, then pull panel rearward to unclip.
8. Depress sides of console box while pulling rearward to remove.
9. Remove four ash tray and cup holder unit attaching screws.
10. Pull ash tray and cup holder unit rearward and disconnect electrical connectors, then remove ashtray and cup holder unit.
11. Remove cluster finish center panel and radio attaching screws.
12. Pull panel rearward, disconnect electrical connectors and antenna, then remove radio and finish panel as an assembly.

13. Remove instrument cluster upper finish panel attaching screws, then the cluster upper finish panel.
14. Remove four instrument cluster attaching screws, then pull cluster rearward.
15. **On models with automatic transmission,** disconnect cable from control lever.
16. **On models with manual transmission,** disconnect cable from roller.
17. **On all models,** disconnect instrument cluster electrical connectors and remove cluster.
18. Reverse procedure to install.

RADIO
REPLACE

Refer to "Instrument Cluster, Replace" for radio replacement.

WIPER MOTOR
REPLACE
FRONT

1. Disconnect wiper motor electrical connector.
2. Remove wiper motor attaching bolts.
3. Using suitable screwdriver, disconnect wiper link from wiper motor, then remove wiper motor.
4. Reverse procedure to install.

REAR

1. Remove wiper arm and rear door trim cover.
2. Disconnect wiper motor electrical connector.
3. Remove wiper motor bracket attaching bolts, then wiper motor and bracket.
4. Reverse procedure to install.

BLOWER MOTOR
REPLACE
FRONT

1. Remove front air duct, **Fig. 5.**
2. Disconnect blower motor electrical connector.
3. Remove blower motor attaching bolts, then the blower motor.
4. Reverse procedure to install.

REAR
Denso Type

1. Discharge A/C system. Refer to "Air Conditioning" section.
2. Remove right and left air inlet grills and air outlet grills, **Fig. 6.**
3. Remove filter.
4. Remove rear A/C switch.
5. Remove evaporator assembly.
6. Remove right and left blower assemblies.
7. Reverse procedure to install.

Panasonic Type

1. Discharge A/C system. Refer to "Air Conditioning" section.
2. Remove right and left suction grills, register grills and filters, **Fig. 7.**

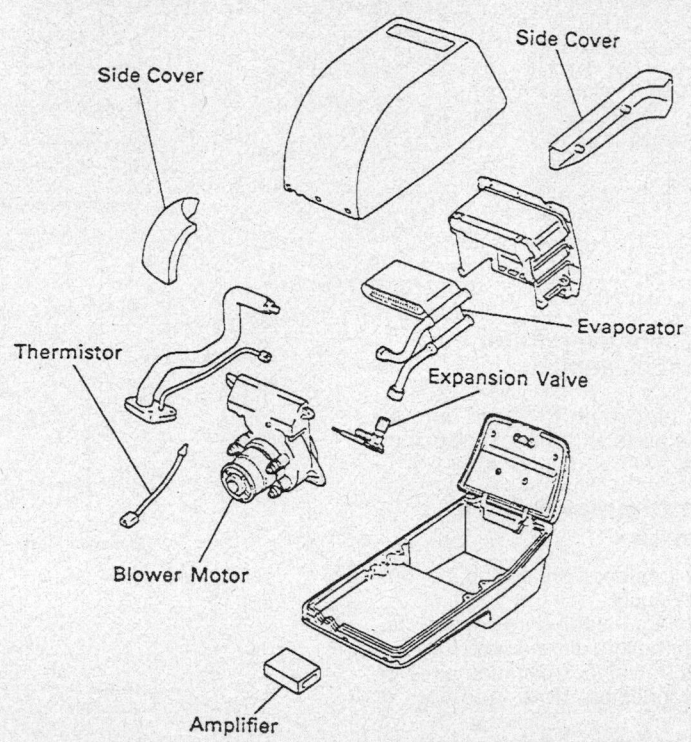

Fig. 8   Exploded view of cool/ice box

3. Drain lower case, then remove lower case attaching screws and separate from upper case.
4. Remove right and left blower motor attaching screws, then disconnect electrical connector.
5. Disengage eight blower motor pawls.
6. Separate upper and lower blower motor case.
7. Remove blower motor attaching screws, then the blower motor with rubber mount.
8. Reverse procedure to install.

COOL/ICE BOX

1. Discharge A/C system as outlined in the "Air Conditioning" section.
2. Remove righthand side kick panels.
3. Disconnect cool/ice box electrical connectors.
4. Disconnect cool/ice box A/C suction and liquid tubes. Refer to "Air Conditioning" section.
5. Remove cool box attaching bolts and then the cool box.
6. Separate cool box upper and lower panels, **Fig. 8.**
7. Remove blower motor.
8. Reverse procedure to install.

EVAPORATOR CORE
REPLACE
FRONT

1. Discharge A/C system as described in the "Air Conditioning" section.
2. Remove front air duct, **Fig. 5.**
3. Remove blower motor.
4. Disconnect evaporator core electrical connectors.

5. Disconnect A/C suction and liquid tubes.
6. Remove evaporator cover attaching nuts, then the cover.
7. Remove evaporator attaching nuts and bolt, then the evaporator.
8. Reverse procedure to install. Rearm air bag system as described under "Precautions."

REAR
Denso Type

1. Discharge A/C system. Refer to "Air Conditioning" section.
2. Remove right and left air inlet grills and air outlet grills, **Fig. 6.**
3. Remove filter.
4. Remove rear A/C switch.
5. Remove evaporator assembly.
6. Remove right and left blower motor assemblies.
7. Using suitable wrench, remove expansion valve to evaporator attaching bolts.
8. Reverse procedure to install.

Panasonic Type

1. Discharge A/C system. Refer to "Air Conditioning" section.
2. Remove right and left suction grills, register grills and filters, **Fig. 7.**
3. Drain lower case, then remove lower case attaching screws and separate from upper case.
4. Remove right and left blower motor attaching screws, then disconnect electrical connector.
5. Disengage and remove eight pawls from blower motor.
6. Remove blower resistor electrical connector, then the attaching screws.

7. Remove rear blower motor switch electrical connector, then the attaching screws.
8. Remove evaporator assembly.
9. Remove heater protective insulators, then liquid line from expansion valve.
10. Separate heat sensing tube from suction tube.
11. Remove expansion valve from evaporator.

12. Reverse procedure to install.

COOL/ICE BOX

1. Discharge A/C system, refer to "Air Conditioning" section.
2. Remove righthand side kick panels.
3. Disconnect cool/ice box electrical connectors.

4. Disconnect cool/ice box A/C suction and liquid tubes.
5. Remove cool/ice box attaching bolts, then the cool/ice box.
6. Separate cool/ice box upper and lower panels, **Fig. 8.**
7. Remove evaporator core.
8. Reverse procedure to install.

2TZ-FZE 2.4L Engine

NOTE: On Air Bag Equipped Models, Refer To "Air Bag System Precautions" Located In The Front Of This Manual For System Disarming & Arming Procedures.

INDEX

PRECAUTIONS

AIR BAG SYSTEMS

Refer to "Air Bag System Precautions" in the front of this manual for system disarming and arming procedures.

BATTERY GROUND CABLE

Prior to service, disconnect battery ground cable and isolate as required.

FUEL SYSTEM PRESSURE RELIEF

1. Place ignition switch in LOCK position.
2. Wait a minimum of 90 seconds before disconnecting any fuel line or component.

COMPRESSION PRESSURE

1. Start engine and warm to normal operating temperature.
2. Disconnect high tension cord from ignition coil.
3. Disconnect high tension cords from spark plugs.
4. Remove spark plugs.
5. Insert compression pressure gauge into spark plug hole.

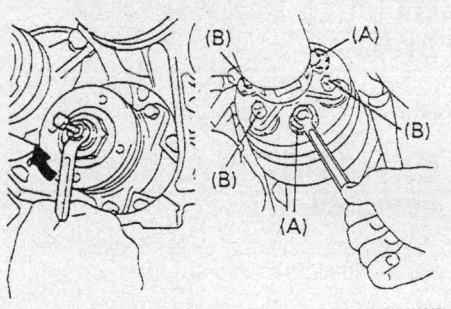

TY1069100164000X

Fig. 1 Accessory driveshaft removal

6. Fully open throttle.
7. While cranking engine, measure compression pressure.
8. Standard compression pressure is 178 psi. Minimum compression pressure should be at least 128 psi.
9. Maximum difference between compression pressures should be 14 psi.

ENGINE

REPLACE

The engine and transmission are removed as an assembly.
1. Remove engine undercovers.

2. Drain coolant and oil using suitable containers.
3. Paint installation alignment marks on accessory driveshaft rear coupling and crankshaft pulley, then disconnect accessory driveshaft from crankshaft pulley.
4. Remove alternator belt, then A/C belt.
5. Install nut and bolt to front of accessory driveshaft, **Fig. 1.**
6. Rotate accessory driveshaft, **Fig. 1,** then remove three A bolts and washers.
7. Remove B bolts, then disconnect driveshaft from pulley, leave driveshaft in same position.
8. Disconnect radiator hose from water inlet, then radiator from water outlet, then heater hose from water pump and oil auto feed hose from No. 1 return pipe.
9. Disconnect accelerator wire from throttle body.
10. Disconnect check, ECU, two cowl and igniter electrical connectors.
11. **On 4WD models,** remove propeller shaft assembly.
12. **On all models,** disconnect water bypass hose from floor pipe and brake booster hose from floor pipe.
13. Disconnect lefthand front engine

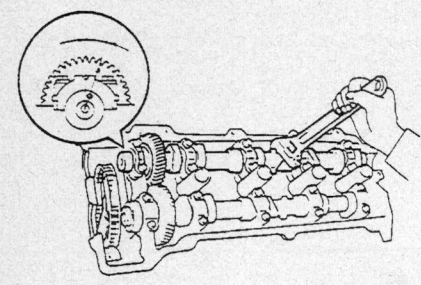

Fig. 2 Setting exhaust camshaft to BTDC

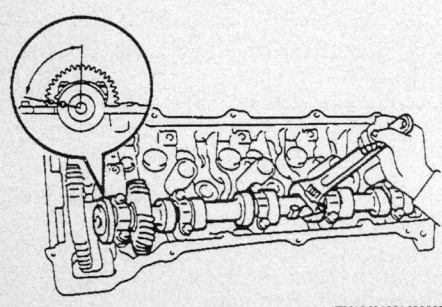

Fig. 5 Setting intake camshaft to BTDC

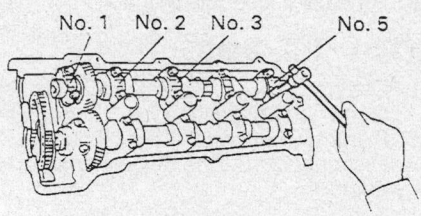

Fig. 3 Exhaust bearing cap Nos. 1, 2, 3 & 5 removal

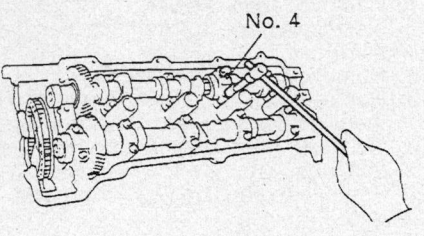

Fig. 4 Exhaust bearing cap No. 4 removal

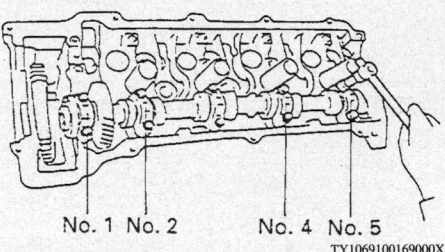

Fig. 6 Intake bearing cap Nos. 1, 2, 4 & 5 removal

ground strap, starter electrical connectors, then hose from intake manifold union.

14. **On models with manual transmission,** remove clutch release cylinder clamp and attaching bolts.
15. **On models with automatic transmission,** remove shift cable as follows:
    a. Remove shift cable to transmission lever attaching nut.
    b. Disconnect shift cable from lever.
    c. Disconnect shift cable from dipstick guide.
    d. Remove cable to floor panel attaching nut.
    e. Remove shift cable from vehicle.
16. **On all models,** disconnect VSV hose from A/C, No. 2 ventilation hose from case, distribution ventilation air hose, ISC valve air hose, then disconnect air intake connector electrical connector.
17. Disconnect VSV fuel pressure control hoses from engine and intake manifold.
18. Disconnect EVAP vacuum hose from charcoal canister, then distributor ventilation air hose from intake manifold.
19. Disconnect IAC valve, cold start injector, throttle position sensor, fuel pressure control VSV and A/C VSV electrical connectors.
20. Remove engine wire to floor panel clamps, then disconnect from floor panel.
21. Disconnect fuel inlet and outlet hoses.
22. Disconnect two oxygen sensors, then remove front exhaust pipe.
23. **On models with automatic transmissions,** disconnect oil cooler hoses from oil cooler lines.
24. **On models with manual transmis-**

sions, disconnect shift cables.
25. **On all models,** disconnect ignition coil and condenser electrical connectors.
26. Disconnect ignition coil high tension cord, then transmission to floor panel ground strap.
27. **On models with manual transmission,** disconnect back-up light switch and speedometer speed sensor connectors.
28. **On models with automatic transmissions,** disconnect speed sensor, neutral start switch, solenoid and A/T oil temperature sensor electrical connectors.
29. **On all models,** remove rear propeller shaft assembly.
30. Install suitable engine lifting equipment, ensure all connectors and hoses are disconnected.
31. Lower vehicle slightly while supporting engine and transmission.
32. Remove righthand and lefthand engine mounts, then rear engine mount.
33. Lower engine and transmission assembly.
34. Reverse procedure to install.

INTAKE MANIFOLD
REPLACE

Refer to "Cylinder Head, Replace" for intake manifold replacement procedure.

EXHAUST MANIFOLD
REPLACE

Refer to "Cylinder Head, Replace" for exhaust manifold replacement.

CYLINDER HEAD
REPLACE

1. Remove engine harness cover attaching bolts, then disconnect.
2. Disconnect pressure regulator vacuum hose.
3. Disconnect the following electrical connectors:
   a. Oil pressure switch.
   b. Oil level sensor.
   c. Distributor connector.
   d. Start injector time switch.
   e. **On California models,** EGR gas temperature sensor.
   f. **On all models,** water temperature sensor and sender gauge.
   g. Knock sensor.
   h. Four injector connectors.
4. Remove No. 2 cylinder head cover.

5. Disconnect No. 2 and 3 air hoses, then remove distributor.
6. Remove EGR valve, pipe and gaskets.
7. Remove delivery pipe and cold start injector union bolts and gaskets.
8. Remove pressure regulator and hose, then the fuel pipe.
9. Remove water outlet and No. 2 water bypass pipe and gasket.
10. Remove PCV hose.
11. Remove delivery pipe.
12. Disconnect water pump hose, the remove intake manifold brackets and manifold.
13. Remove righthand engine mount.
14. Remove exhaust manifold attaching nuts, then the exhaust manifold.
15. Remove righthand engine mount.
16. Remove exhaust manifold heat insulator.
17. Remove No. 1 oil return pipe.
18. Remove No. 1 cylinder head cover, then half circular plugs.
19. Place installation alignment marks on camshaft sprocket and chain.
20. Hold camshaft, then remove cam sprocket bolt.
21. Remove chain tensioner and gasket.
22. Remove cam sprocket and chain. **Do not remove slipper and damper.**
23. Remove No. 6 bearing cap bolt.
24. Remove exhaust camshafts as follows:
    a. **Camshaft must be held level during removal or cylinder head damage may result.**
    b. Set exhaust knock pin hole at 5–30° BTDC, **Fig. 2.**
    c. Install service bolt to camshaft subgear and main gear.
    d. Using sequence shown in **Fig. 3,** alternately and uniformly loosen and remove bearing cap Nos. 1, 2, 3 and 5.
    e. Alternately and uniformly loosen No. 4 bearing cap bolt, **Fig. 4.** Ensure camshaft is being lifted

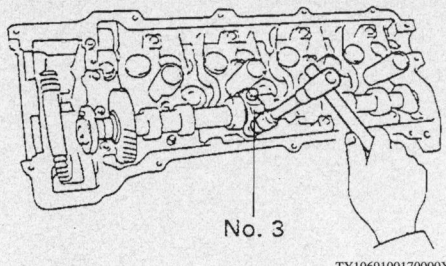

Fig. 7 Intake bearing cap No. 3 removal

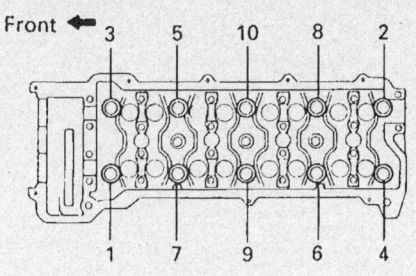

Fig. 8 Cylinder head loosening sequence

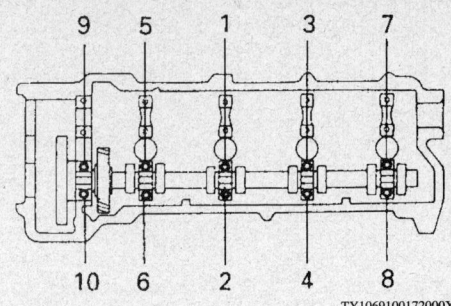

Fig. 9 Intake camshaft tightening sequence

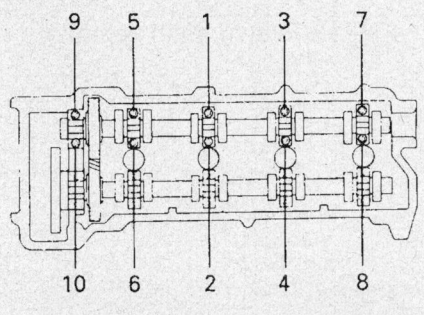

Fig. 10 Exhaust camshaft tightening sequence

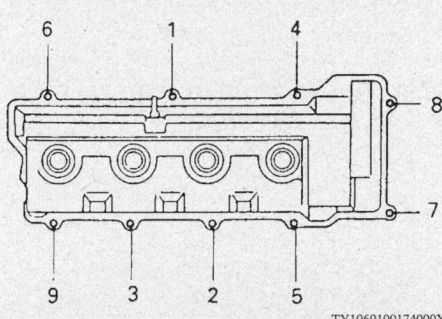

Fig. 11 Cylinder head cover tightening sequence

Fig. 12 Timing mark alignment

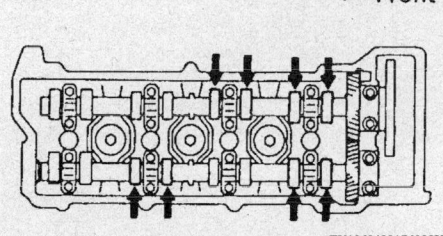

Fig. 13 Valve clearance measurement, Step 1

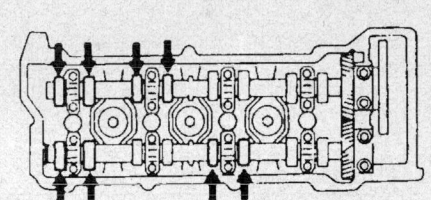

Fig. 14 Valve clearance measurement, Step 2

a. **Torque** cylinder head bolts in reverse order of removal sequence, **Fig. 8**, in three steps to 29 ft. lbs. Mark top front side of each bolt, then tighten an additional 90°, ensure alignment mark is facing sideward. Tighten an additional 90°, ensure alignment mark is facing rearward.

b. **Torque** two front cylinder head bolts to 15 ft. lbs.

c. Using sequence shown in **Fig. 9**, **torque** intake bearing caps in three steps to 12 ft. lbs.

d. Using sequence shown in **Fig. 10**, **torque** exhaust bearing caps in three steps to 12 ft. lbs.

e. Using sequence shown in **Fig. 11**, **torque** cylinder head cover bolts to 6 ft. lbs.

VALVE CLEARANCE SPECIFICATIONS

Year	Stem-To-Guide Clearance	
	intake	Exhaust
1996–97	.006–.010	.010–.014

VALVE ADJUSTMENT

Valve adjustment is accomplished by installing the proper thickness shim to achieve the specified valve clearance. Refer to "Valve Clearance Specifications" for proper clearance. Shims are available in .0020 inch (.050 mm) increments from .0984 inch (2.5 mm) to .1299 inch (3.30 mm).

1. With engine cold, turn accessory driveshaft to TDC alignment mark, then set

straight out, if not, retighten No. 4 cap and reverse camshaft removal procedure. **Do not pry or force camshaft.**

f. Remove No. 4 bearing cap and exhaust camshaft.

25. Remove intake camshafts as follows:
   a. Set exhaust knock pin hole at 75–100° BTDC, **Fig. 5**.
   b. Install service bolt to camshaft subgear and main gear.
   c. Using sequence shown in **Fig. 6**, loosen and remove Nos. 1, 2, 4 and 5 bearing caps.
   d. Loosen No. 3 bearing cap bolt, **Fig. 7**, ensure camshaft is being lifted straight out, if not, retighten No. 3 cap and reverse camshaft removal procedure. **Do not pry or force camshaft.**
   e. Remove No. 3 bearing cap and exhaust camshaft.

26. Remove two front cylinder head bolts, then the remaining cylinder head bolts in two or three steps using sequence shown in **Fig. 8**.

27. Reverse procedure to install, noting the following:

pulley groove to 0.

2. Ensure No. 1 valve lifters are loose and No. 4 valve lifters are tight. If not, turn crankshaft 360° (one complete revolution) and align timing marks, **Fig. 12**.

3. With engine in this position, check clearance of the valves indicated in **Fig. 13**.

4. Check valve clearance and record measurements that are out of specification to determine required replacement shims.

5. Turn equipment driveshaft 360° (one complete revolution), align timing marks, **Fig. 12** and measure the valves indicated in **Fig. 14**.

6. Position notch as shown in **Fig. 15**, then using valve adjusting tool Nos. 09248-55020 (09248-05011 (A), 09248-05021 (B) or equivalents, press down the lifter with A and hold lifter down with B.

7. Remove adjusting shim using a suitable tool and magnet, **Fig. 16**.

8. To determine replacement shim, proceed as follows:
   a. Using a micrometer, measure removed shim.
   b. Calculate the thickness of the new

shim required for specified value, using the variables: T = thickness of used shim, A = measured valve clearance and N = thickness of new shim.

  c. To determine correct intake valve shim, use the formula N = T (A - .008 inch).

  d. To determine correct exhaust valve shim, use the formula N = T (A - .012 inch).

9. Select shim with thickness closest to calculated value.

VALVE GUIDES

1. Using suitable tool and hammer, strike valve guide bushing to break it off cylinder head casting.
2. Heat cylinder head to 176–212°F (80–100°C).
3. Using suitable valve guide removal tool, tap out bushing.
4. Install snap ring on new valve guide, then install new valve guide using toll as above and driving in from the reverse side of removal.
5. Ream valve guide if required. Refer to "Engine Rebuilding Specifications" section for stem clearance.

HYDRAULIC LIFTERS
REPLACE

Check lifters for excessive wear and/or damage. Replace worn or damaged valve lifters as required. Lubricate hydraulic valve lifters before installation.

TIMING CHAIN
REPLACE
REMOVAL

1. Remove engine as outlined under "Engine, Replace."
2. Remove cylinder head as outlined under "Cylinder Head, Replace."
3. Using crankshaft pulley holding tool No. 09213-58012 and flange holding tool No. 09330-00021, or equivalents, remove crankshaft pulley bolt.
4. Using puller set tool No. 09950-20012, or equivalent, remove crankshaft pulley.
5. Remove left engine mount and stay.
6. Remove oil pressure switch.
7. Remove crankcase assembly as follows:
  a. Remove engine oil dipstick.
  b. Remove ventilation case with engine hanger and gasket.
  c. Remove oil dipstick tube and gasket.
  d. Remove crankcase attaching nuts and bolts.
  e. Using seal cutter tool No. 09032-00100, or equivalent, and suitable brass bar, separate crankcase from cylinder block. **Do not damage crankcase flange.**
  f. Remove baffle plate attaching nuts, then the baffle plate.
8. Remove oil filter bracket, **Fig. 17.**
9. Remove timing chain case O-ring.

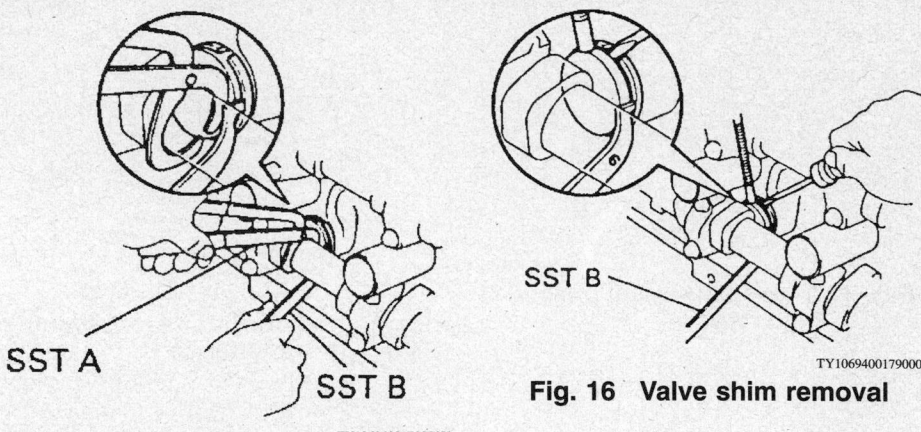

Fig. 15 Valve shim removal tool installation

Fig. 16 Valve shim removal

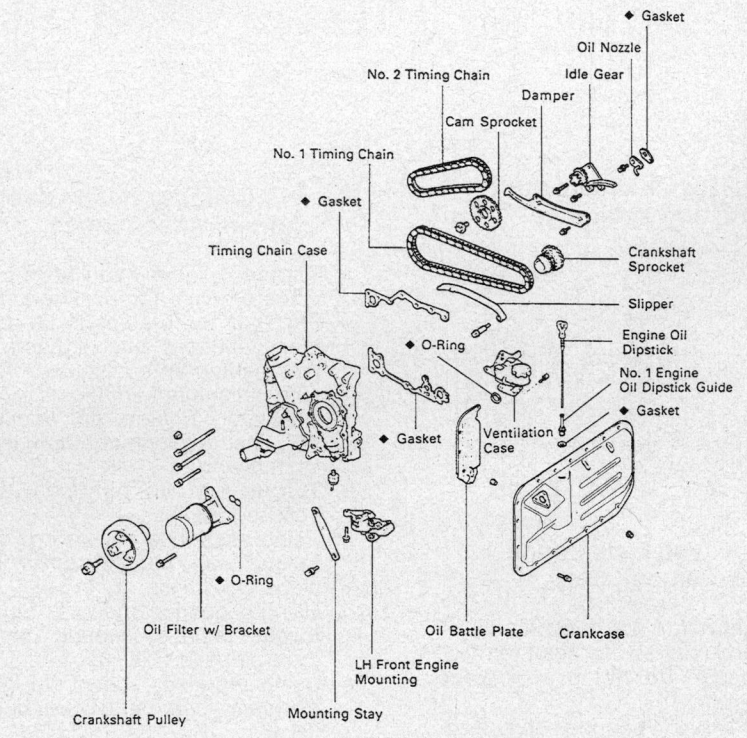

Fig. 17 Exploded view of timing chain

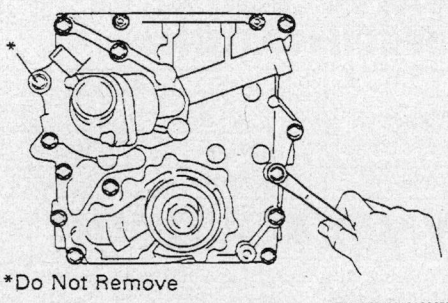

*Do Not Remove

Fig. 18 Timing chain case removal

10. Remove 12 timing chain cover attaching bolts and 2 nuts, **Fig. 18.**
11. Using suitable plastic hammer, loosen timing chain cover, then remove case and two gaskets.
12. Remove chain slipper and damper.
13. Remove oil nozzle and gasket.
14. Loosen idler gear bolts, then pushing idler gear chain guide to left side retighten bolt.
15. Remove idler gear bolts, idler gear and chain assembly.
16. Remove crankshaft sprocket as required.

INSPECTION

1. Measure stretched timing chain length in two places. Measurement at 16 links should be 5.772 inches. Measurement at 18 links should 5.531 inches. If measurement is not as indicated, replace chain.
2. Wrap timing chain around sprocket, then using suitable calipers, measure

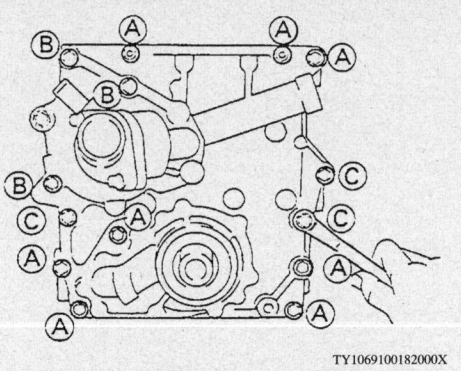

Fig. 19 Timing chain tightening sequence

TY1069100182000X

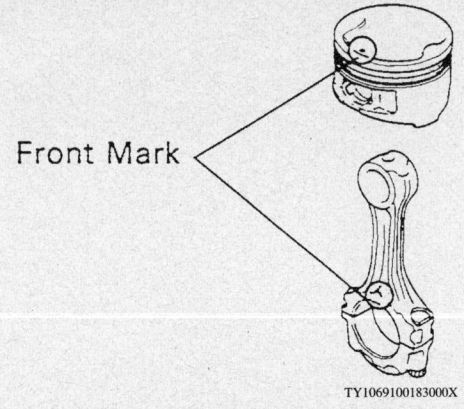

Front Mark

TY1069100183000X

Fig. 20 Piston & connecting rod assembly

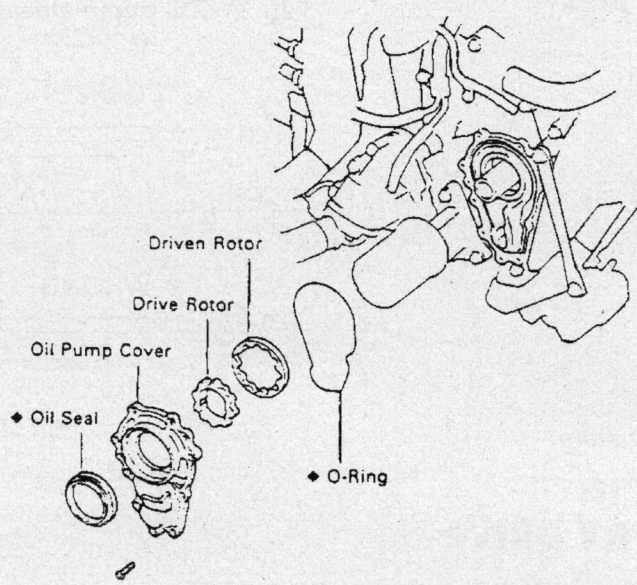

Driven Rotor

Drive Rotor

Oil Pump Cover

◆ Oil Seal

◆ O-Ring

TY1099100019000X

Fig. 21 Oil pump exploded view

outer side of chain rollers. Minimum sprocket width should be as follows:
  a. No. 1 crankshaft sprocket, 2.339 inches.
  b. Camshaft sprocket, 4.480 inches.
  c. No. 2 crankshaft sprocket, 2.752 inches.
  d. Idle sprocket, 2.244 inches.
  e. If measurement is less than minimum, replace sprocket.
3. Using a suitable micrometer, measure chain damper and slipper, maximum wear is .039 inch. If wear is more than .039 inch, replace damper and/or slipper.
4. Check idle sprocket for rough operation or noise, replace as necessary.

INSTALLATION

1. Turn crankshaft until shaft key is at top, then slide sprocket on crankshaft.
2. Install No. 2 timing chain on idler sprocket and crankshaft sprocket, then tighten bolts to specifications.
3. Loosen bolt, ensuring chain guide presses against chain.
4. Depress and release chain guide en-

suring proper operation, then tighten chain guide to specifications.
5. Install oil nozzle.
6. Install chain damper and slipper.
7. Install No. 1 timing chain to camshaft sprocket, ensuring timing mark is between two bright chain links.
8. Install timing chain to crankshaft sprocket, ensuring timing mark is aligned with single bright link.
9. Turn camshaft sprocket counterclockwise to remove slack.
10. Install timing chain case, **torque** A, **Fig. 19,** to 14 ft. lbs., B to 21 ft. lbs. and C to 32 ft. lbs.
11. Install new timing case cover O-ring.
12. Install oil filter bracket.
13. Install baffle plate, crankcase assembly, No. 1 oil dipstick guide, ventilation case and engine hanger.
14. Apply Loctite 242, or equivalent to oil pressure switch first two or three threads, then install oil pressure switch.
15. Install left engine mount and stay.
16. Install crankshaft pulley with spline teeth of pulley engaged with large

teeth of oil pump.
17. Rotate crankshaft pulley to ensure fit, then install crankshaft pulley bolt.
18. Install cylinder head and engine.

CAMSHAFT
REPLACE

Refer to "Cylinder Head, Replace" for camshaft replacement procedure.

PISTON & ROD ASSEMBLY

Pistons are available in standard and oversize of .020 inch (.50 mm). If the piston bore is not within specifications, replace piston and/or cylinder block. When assembling piston onto connecting rod, ensure mark on top of piston and mark on connecting rod are on same side, **Fig. 20.** When installing piston and connecting rod assembly, ensure mark on top of piston is facing toward front of engine.

MAIN & ROD BEARINGS

Undersize bearings are not available. If crankshaft journals or crankpins are worn or scored, the crankshaft must be replaced.

OIL PUMP
REPLACE

1. Disconnect accessory driveshaft from crankshaft pulley.
2. Using crankshaft pulley holder tool No. 09213-58012 and flange holder tool No. 09330-0021, or equivalents, remove crankshaft pulley.
3. Remove oil pump cover attaching bolts, **Fig. 21,** then the oil pump cover.
4. Remove timing chain case as outlined under "Timing Chain, Replace."
5. Remove oil pump attaching bolts, then the oil pump.

OIL PUMP SERVICE

Oil pump inspection may be performed with oil pump cover removed.
1. Using suitable thickness gauge, measure driven rotor and pump body clearance, **Fig. 22.** Maximum clearance is .0118 inch, if clearance is not as indicated, replace rotor set and/or pump body.
2. Using suitable thickness gauge, measure rotor tip clearance, **Fig. 23.** Maximum clearance is .0138 inch, if clearance is not as indicated, replace oil pump rotor set.
3. Using suitable thickness gauge and flat block, measure side clearance, **Fig. 24.** Maximum clearance is .0059 inch, if clearance is not as indicated, replace pump rotor set and/or pump body.

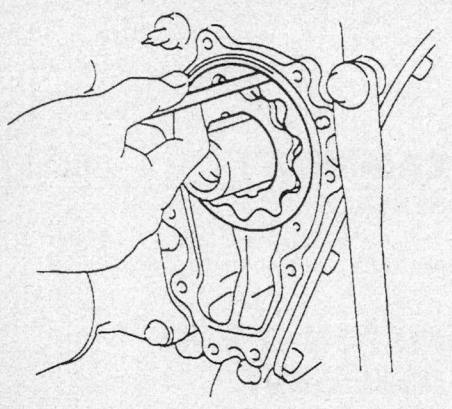

Fig. 22 Oil pump body clearance inspection

TY1099100020000X

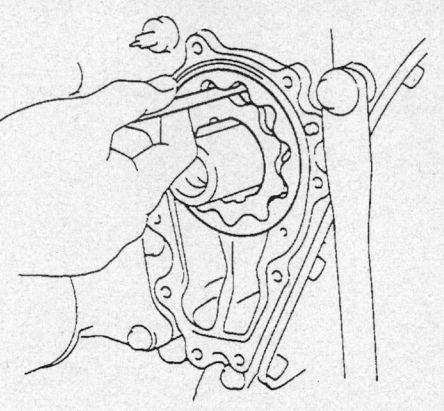

Fig. 23 Oil pump tip clearance inspection

TY1099100021000X

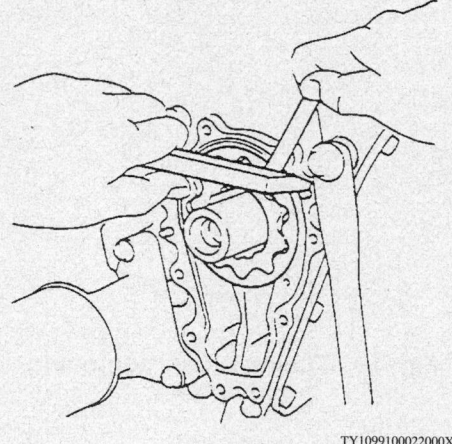

TY1099100022000X

Fig. 24 Oil pump side clearance inspection

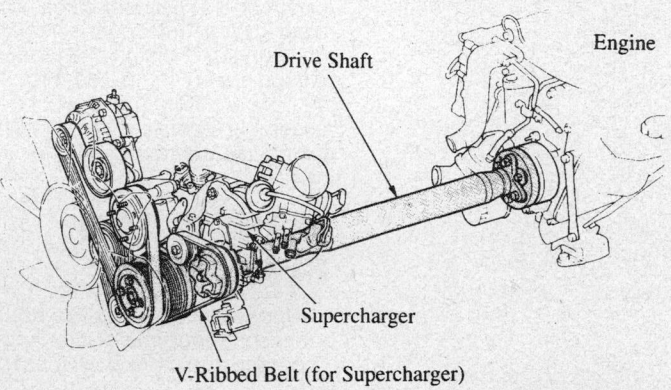

Drive Shaft

Engine

Supercharger

V-Ribbed Belt (for Supercharger)

TY1069600341000X

Fig. 25 Separated accessory drive system

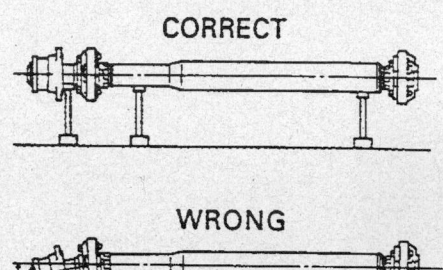

CORRECT

WRONG

TY1069100185000X

Fig. 26 Driveshaft storage

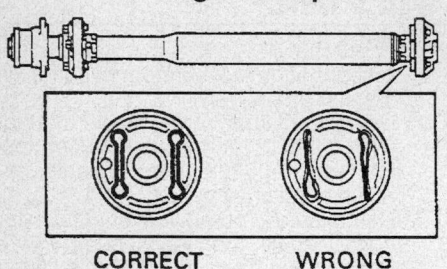

CORRECT WRONG

TY1069100186000X

Fig. 27 Driveshaft coupling

BELT TENSION DATA

Year	Belt	New, lbs.	Used, lbs.
1996	A/C	139–191	66–110
	Alternator	160–180	115–135
	Power Steering	160–180	115–135
	Supercharger	160–180	115–135
1997	A/C	139–191	110–150
	Alternator	160–180	115–135
	Power Steering	160–180	115–135
	Supercharger	160–180	115–135

SEPARATED ACCESSORY DRIVE SYSTEM

DESCRIPTION

The cooling fan, alternator, power steering pump and A/C compressor are remotely driven from the engine's crankshaft through a common driveshaft, **Fig. 25.**

This driveshaft is equipped with a flexible coupling at both ends that compensates for speed variations. The driveshaft and coupling are non-serviceable and should be replaced as a unit.

SERVICE PRECAUTIONS

1. Do not allow rear of driveshaft to hang disconnected. Suspend with suitable sling at horizontal position.
2. Store driveshaft so front coupling is horizontal with shaft, **Fig. 26.**
3. When installing driveshaft, ensure flexible coupling is not malformed, if so, disconnect shaft and install again, **Fig. 27.**
4. When removing driveshaft, do not remove No. 1 and No. 2 equipment drive housing stays unless necessary. If removal is necessary, mark position of stays and install as marked, **Fig. 28.**
5. During installation of driveshaft, using

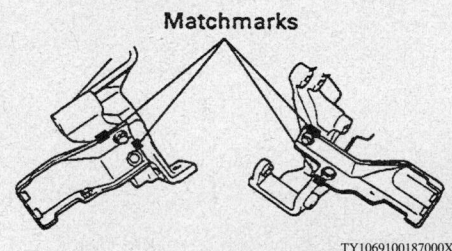

Matchmarks

TY1069100187000X

Fig. 28 Stay matchmarks

appropriate measuring devices, measure installation angle of driveshaft in front of and behind front flexible coupling, **Fig. 29.** If difference in angle between each section is 2° or more, adjust installation angle by adjusting position of No. 1, No. 2 and/or No. 3 equipment drive housing stays.
6. After service, ensure ground straps between equipment drive housing and body and between alternator and battery ground terminal are connected.

ACCESSORY DRIVESHAFT, REPLACE

Removal

1. Remove fluid coupling with cooling fan as follows:
   a. Remove A/C air intake duct.

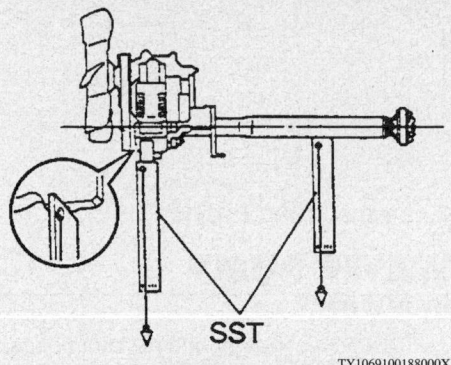

Fig. 29 Driveshaft angle

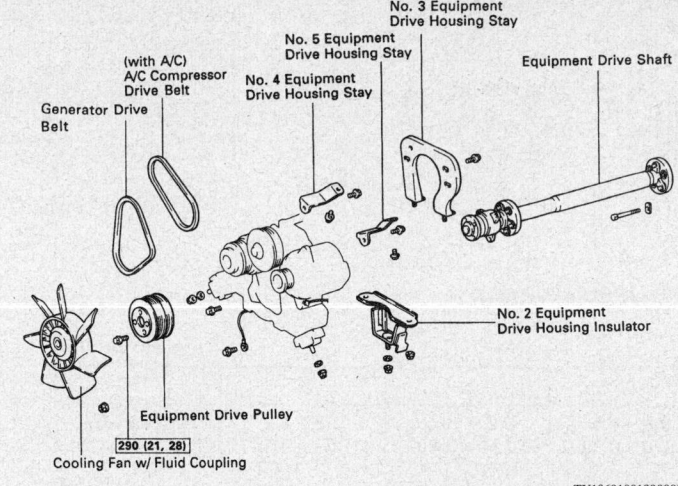

Fig. 30 Exploded view of driveshaft assembly

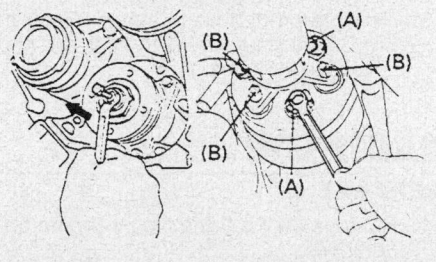

Fig. 31 Driveshaft removal

b. Remove fan shroud.
c. Hold belt down, then loosen nuts of coupling.
d. Remove fluid coupling with cooling fan.
2. Loosen alternator and A/C belt adjusting bolts, then push alternator and A/C compressor as far as possible and remove belts.
3. Remove equipment drive pulley.
4. Remove No. 2 equipment drive housing insulator and No. 3 equipment drive housing stay, **Fig. 30.**
5. Remove No. 4 and No. 5 equipment drive housing stays.
6. Scribe matchmarks on rear flexible coupling flange and crankshaft pulley.
7. Install service bolt and nut to front end of equipment driveshaft, **Fig. 31.**
8. Rotate driveshaft by turning service nut, then remove three A bolts and washers. **Do not remove B bolts.**
9. Remove driveshaft and equipment drive housing retaining bolts, **Fig. 32.**
10. Disconnect equipment drive housing ground strap from body.
11. Remove nuts and washers from No. 1 equipment drive housing insulator and body bracket.
12. Lift up equipment drive housing, then rotate driveshaft approximately 60° clockwise and remove from rear end of driveshaft housing.
13. Lower equipment drive housing, then set in body bracket.

Inspection

1. Check front and rear flexible coupling for cracks and damage.
2. Rotate flange of shaft, ensuring it rotates smoothly without binding or creaking.
3. Using suitable gauge and support,

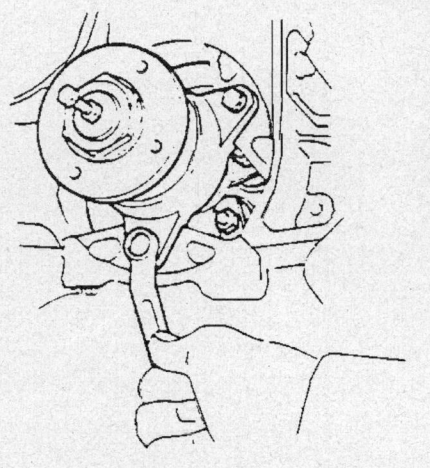

Fig. 32 Driveshaft housing removal

check shaft for runout. Runout should not exceed 0.031 inch.
4. Inspect fluid coupling for leaks.
5. If any of the above criteria is not met, replace the driveshaft.

Installation

1. Lift up equipment drive housing, then insert driveshaft through hole at rear of housing.
2. Align match marks of coupling and pulley, then lower drive housing.
3. Install three front bolts, **torque** to 38 ft. lbs.
4. Install the remaining bolts and **torque** to 25 ft. lbs.
5. Remove the service bolt and nut installed on front end of driveshaft.
6. Secure No. 1 driveshaft housing insulator, then install and **torque** nut to 24 ft. lbs.
7. Install No. 4 and No. 5 driveshaft housing stays.
8. Install the lower bolt, then the upper bolt. **Torque** to 13 ft. lbs.
9. Install No. 2 driveshaft housing insulator.
10. Install No. 3 driveshaft housing stay.

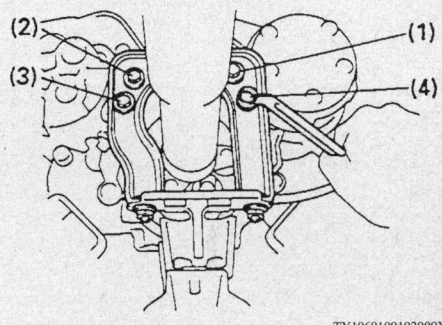

Fig. 33 Stay Installation

11. Install inboard bolt, then the outboard bolt. **Torque** bolts to 18 ft. lbs.
12. Install No. 1 and No. 2 driveshaft housing stay to No. 3 driveshaft housing stay, then **torque** nuts in several passes to 13 ft. lbs., **Fig. 33.**
13. Install washer and nut of body bracket for No. 2 driveshaft housing insulator. **Torque** to 18 ft. lbs.
14. Check installation angle of driveshaft as follows:
a. Using appropriate measuring devices, measure installation angle of driveshaft in front of and behind front flexible coupling, **Fig. 29.**
b. If difference in angle between each section is 2° or more, adjust installation angle by adjusting position of No. 1, No. 2 or No. 3 equipment drive housing stays.
15. Ensure alignment of insulators are correct and gaps are as specified, **Figs. 34 through 36.** Adjust if necessary.
16. Install equipment drive pulley. **Torque** bolts to 21 ft. lbs.
17. Install belts, then the fluid coupling. **Torque** bolts to 10 ft. lbs.
18. Install fan shroud, then A/C air intake duct.
19. Inspect belt tension.

ACCESSORY DRIVESHAFT HOUSING, REPLACE

1. Remove fluid coupling with cooling fan.
2. Remove alternator, A/C compressor

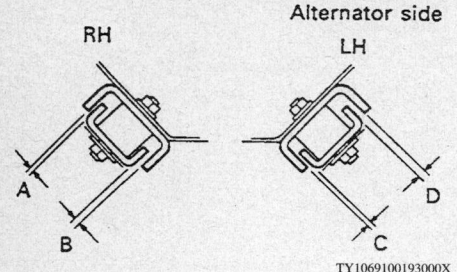

Fig. 34 Insulator gap

	A	B	C	D
with A/C	0.7 – 4.3 (0.028 – 0.169)	4.7 – 8.3 (0.185 – 0.327)	0.4 – 4.0 (0.016 – 0.157)	5.0 – 8.6 (0.197 – 0.339)
without A/C	1.3 – 4.9 (0.051 – 0.193)	4.1 – 7.7 (0.161 – 0.303)		

TY1069100194000X

Fig. 35 Insulator gap specifications. 1996 Previa

A	B	C	D
0.5 – 4.5 (0.020 – 0.177)	6.2 – 10.2 (0.244 – 0.402)	0.2 – 4.2 (0.008 – 0.165)	7.5 – 10.5 (0.295 – 0.413)

TY1069700457000X

Fig. 36 Insulator gap specifications. 1997 Previa

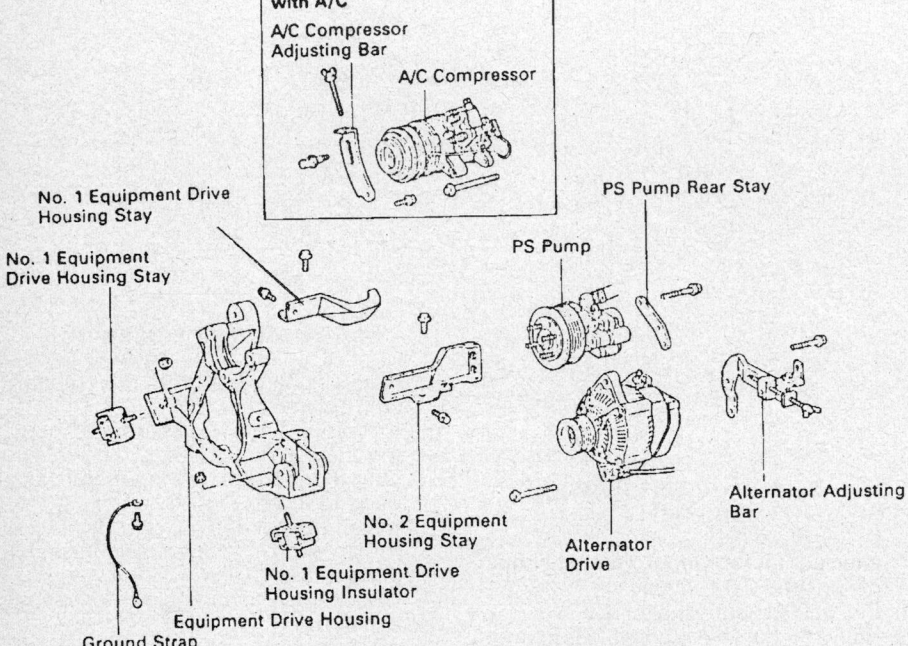

Fig. 37 Driveshaft housing components

and power steering pump with hose.
3. Remove equipment drive pulley.
4. Remove No. 2 equipment driveshaft housing insulator and No. 3 driveshaft housing.
5. Remove No. 4 and No. 5 driveshaft housing stays.
6. Remove driveshaft as outlined under "Accessory Driveshaft Removal."
7. Mark driveshaft housing for installation reference, then remove No. 1 and No. 2 housing stays, **Fig. 37.**
8. Reverse procedure to install, noting the following:
   a. Align marks made during removal.
   b. Ensure lower surface of equipment drive housing and No. 3 stay are flat and aligned.
   c. **Torque** No. 1 and No. 2 housing stay bolts to 13 ft. lbs.
   d. **Torque** insulators to 18 ft. lbs.

COOLING SYSTEM BLEED

This engine does not require a special bleed procedure. After filling cooling system, run engine to operating temperature with radiator/pressure cap off. Air will then automatically bleed through cap opening.

THERMOSTAT
REPLACE

1. Drain coolant into suitable container.
2. Remove hose from thermostat outlet.
3. Remove water inlet from water pump.
4. Remove thermostat from housing.
5. Reverse procedure to install. Ensure thermostat jiggle valve is aligned with protrusion.

WATER PUMP
REPLACE

1. Disconnect heater and radiator hoses.
2. Remove oil filter bracket.
3. Disconnect water pump hose.
4. Remove water pump attaching bolts, then the water pump, **Fig. 38.**
5. Reverse procedure to install. Refer to **Fig. 39. Torque** A bolts to 14 ft. lbs. and B bolts to 21 ft. lbs.

RADIATOR
REPLACE

1. Remove air duct and No. 1 engine undercover.
2. Drain coolant.
3. Remove A/C cooler hoses.
4. Remove radiator outlet hose.
5. Remove power steering reservoir and position aside.
6. Remove radiator inlet hose and reservoir hose.
7. Remove water bypass hose for throttle body.
8. Remove No. 1 and No. 2 radiator fan shrouds.
9. Remove radiator carefully to prevent damage.
10. Reverse procedure to install.

FUEL PUMP
REPLACE

1. Relieve fuel system pressure as described under "Precautions."
2. Drain fuel from tank, then remove tank.
3. Remove fuel pump bracket.
4. Disconnect fuel pump electrical connector.
5. Remove fuel pump attaching bolts, then the fuel pump.
6. Separate fuel filter from fuel pump.
7. Reverse procedure to install. Tighten to specification.

FUEL FILTER
REPLACE

1. Relieve fuel system pressure as described under "Precautions."
2. Place suitable container under fuel filter/hose connection.
3. Slowly loosen fuel hose to fuel filter. **Place shop towel over connection to avoid fuel spillage on engine.**
4. Remove fuel filter, then plug hose connection.
5. Replace gasket.
6. Reverse procedure to install.

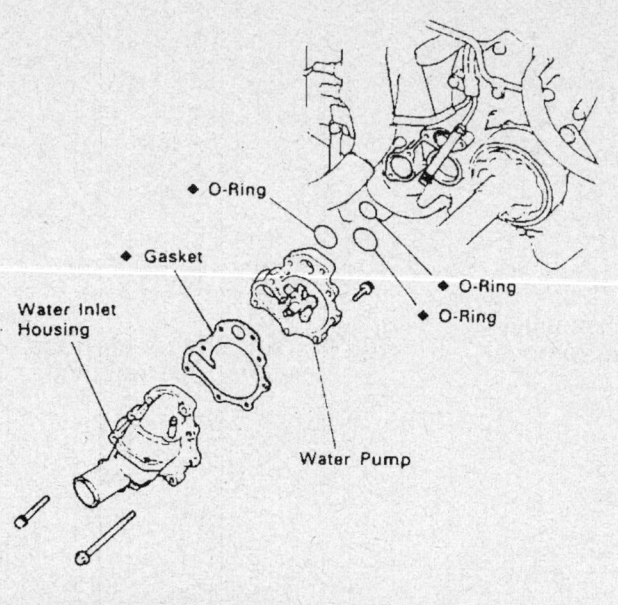

Fig. 38 Exploded view of water pump

TY1089100017000X

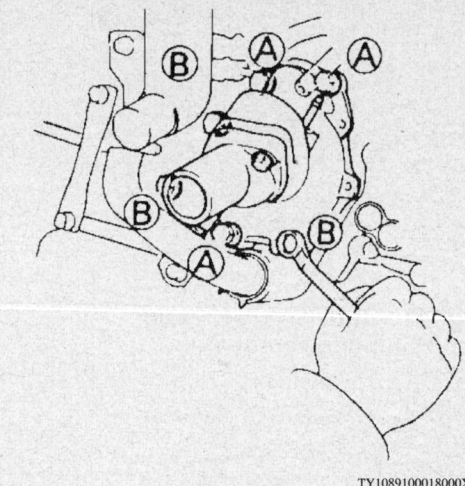

TY1089100018000X

Fig. 39 Water pump installation

SUPERCHARGER
REPLACE

1. Relieve fuel pressure as outlined under "Precautions."
2. Drain engine coolant.
3. Remove air duct, engine coolant reservoir and bracket, **Fig. 40.**
4. Remove air damper case and blower.
5. Disconnect power steering reservoir.
6. Remove radiator and fan shroud.
7. Remove fluid coupling and fan, **Fig. 41.**
8. Disconnect air control valve (ACV) connector and the three ACV hoses, **Fig. 42.**
9. Remove No. 1 engine undercover, then disconnect transmission oil cooler hoses.
10. Disconnect radiator outlet, inlet and bypass hoses, then remove the radiator.
11. Disconnect accelerator cable, A/C idle-up air hose, vent tube and vent pipe, then remove air cleaner hose, **Fig. 43.**
12. Disconnect throttle position sensor and IAC valve electrical connectors.
13. Disconnect the hoses indicated in **Fig. 44,** then remove throttle body.
14. Disconnect two power steering idle-up hoses, clamp and remove power steering pump with power steering hoses attached, **Fig. 45.**
15. Loosen No. 2 idler pulley nut and adjusting bolt, then remove supercharger drive belt, **Fig. 46.**
16. Remove No. 2 idler pulley, **Fig. 47.**
17. Disconnect supercharger bypass valve electrical connector.
18. Disconnect brake booster hose and A/C idle-up air hose, then disconnect supercharger magnetic clutch electrical connector from supercharger and No. 1 hose support bracket, **Fig. 48.**

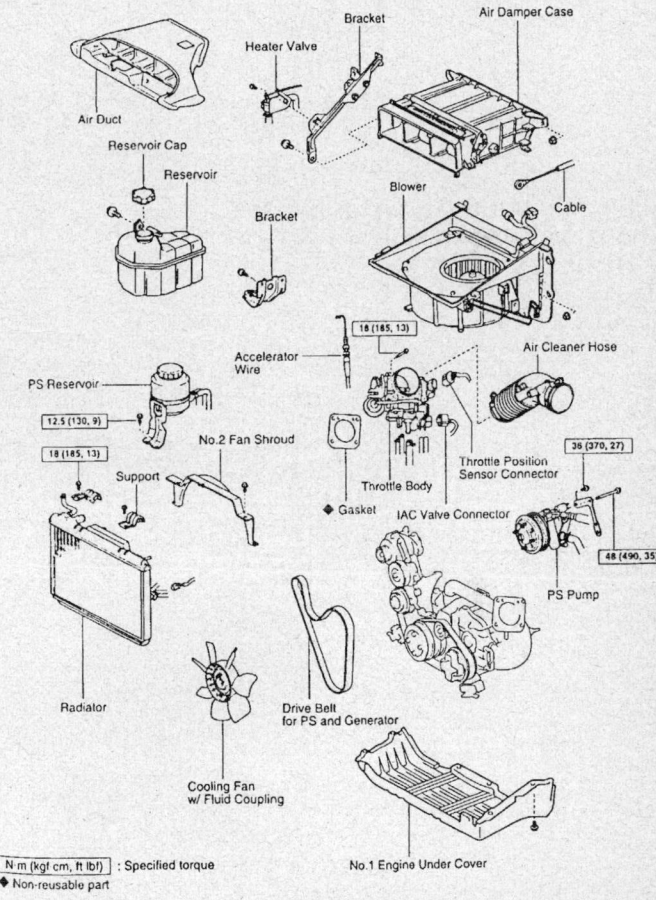

N·m (kgf cm, ft lbf) : Specified torque
◆ Non-reusable part

TY1059100003000X

Fig. 40 Supercharger air duct & blower components

19. Remove lower hoses and three-way connector, **Fig. 49.**
20. Remove supercharger bypass valve from No. 1 air outlet duct, **Fig. 47.**
21. Remove No. 1 air inlet duct and gaskets with supercharger bypass valve, **Fig. 50.**
22. Remove No. 1 idle-up pipe from equipment drive housing, then disconnect the No. 1 air tube from No. 1 air outlet duct.
23. Remove No. 1 intake air connector bracket, **Fig. 47.**
24. Remove supercharger retaining bolts, **Figs. 51 and 52,** then the supercharger and No. 1 air outlet duct.
25. Reverse procedure to install.

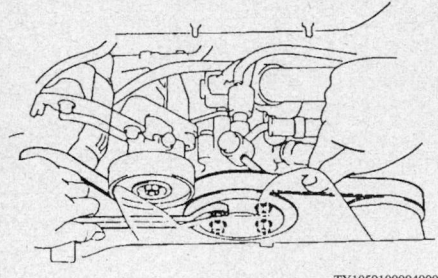

TY1059100004000X

Fig. 41 Supercharger fluid coupling removal

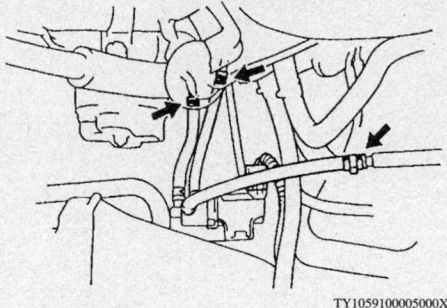

TY1059100005000X

Fig. 42 Air control valve connector & hose removal

TY1059100006000X

Fig. 43 A/C idle-up air hose, vent tube & pipe removal

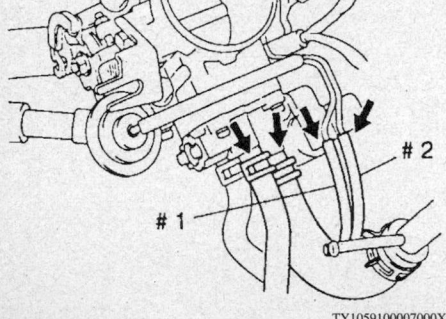

TY1059100007000X

Fig. 44 Air hose, water bypass hose, vacuum hose No. 1 & No. 2 removal

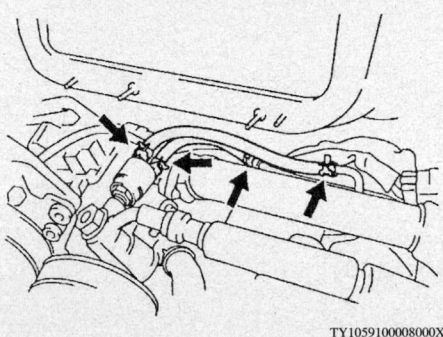

TY1059100008000X

Fig. 45 Power steering idle-up hose removal

TY1059100009000X

Fig. 46 Supercharger drive belt removal

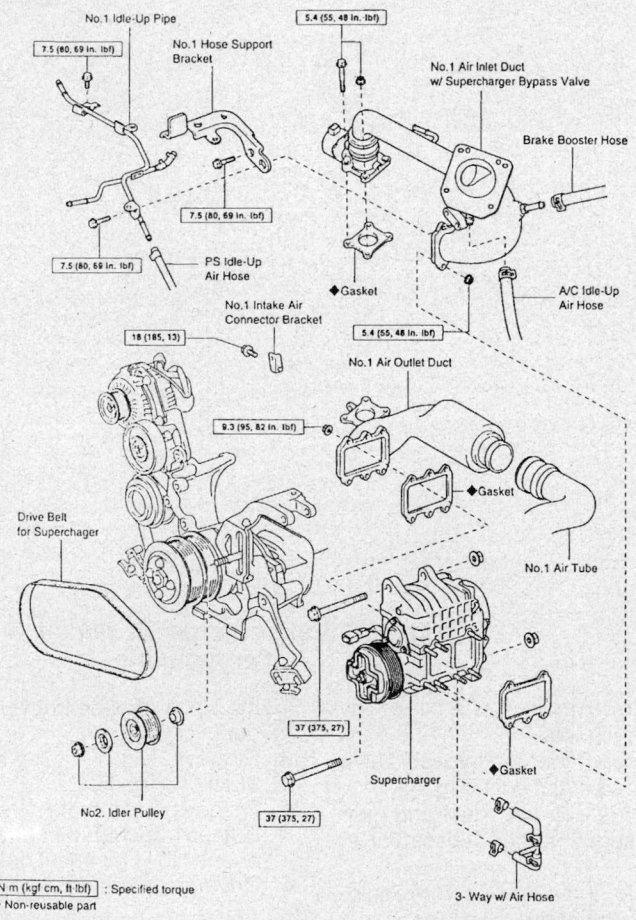

TY1059100010000X

Fig. 47 Supercharger No. 2 idler pulley components

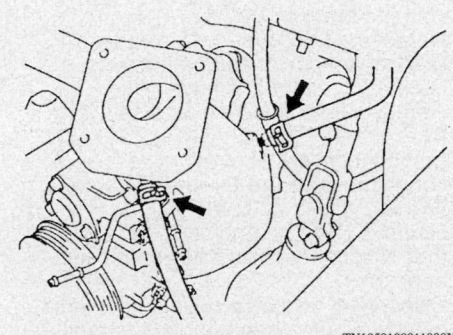

TY1059100011000X

Fig. 48 Brake booster hose, A/C idle-up air hose & magnetic clutch connector

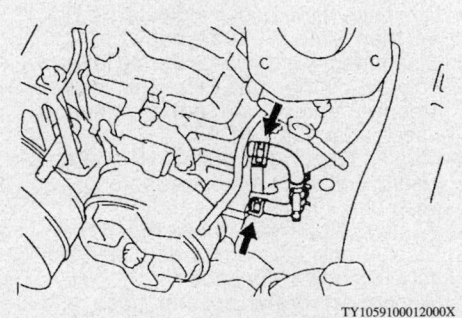

TY1059100012000X

Fig. 49 Air control hoses & three-way connector

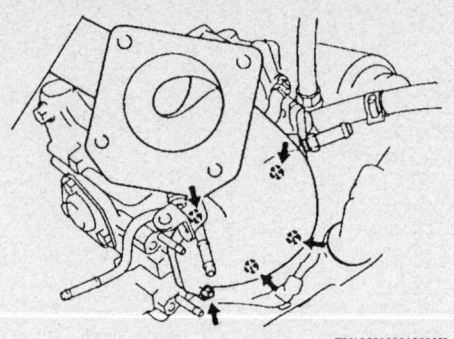

TY1059100013000X

Fig. 50 Supercharger bypass valve

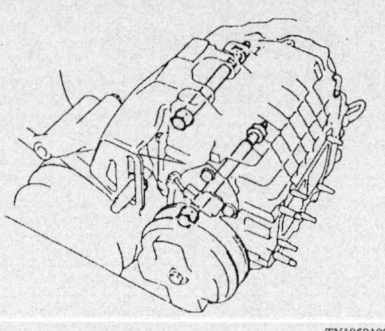

TY1059100014000X

Fig. 51 Supercharger to equipment drive housing removal

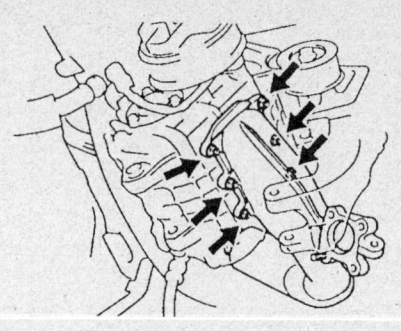

TY1059100015000X

Fig. 52 Supercharger to No. 1 air outlet duct removal

TIGHTENING SPECIFICATIONS

Year	Component	Torque, Ft. Lbs.
1996–97	Crankshaft Pulley To Crankshaft	192
	Crankshaft To Driveplate (A/T)	54
	Cylinder Block To Coolant Drain Cock	18
	Cylinder Block To Crankcase	9
	Cylinder Block To Cylinder Head	②
	Cylinder Block To Damper	13
	Cylinder Block To Engine Mounting Bracket	30
	Cylinder Block To Idle Sprocket	14
	Cylinder Block To No. 2 Engine Hanger	27
	Cylinder Block To Oil Dipstick Guide	13
	Cylinder Block To Oil Nozzle	13
	Cylinder Block To Oil Pan	48①
	Cylinder Block To Oil Strainer	13
	Cylinder Block To Rear Oil Seal Retainer	10
	Cylinder Block To Slipper	20
	Cylinder Head To Camshaft Bearing Cap	12
	Cylinder Head To Chain Tensioner	15
	Cylinder Head To Distributor	14
	Cylinder Head To EGR Pipe	13
	Cylinder Head To Exhaust Manifold	36
	Cylinder Head To Exhaust Manifold Heat Insulator	13
	Cylinder Head To Intake Manifold	15
	Cylinder Head To No. 1 Cylinder Head Cover	6
	Cylinder Head To Oil Return Pipe	15
	Cylinder Head To Spark Plug	14
	Cylinder Head To Water Outlet	15
	Cylinder Head To Water Outlet Stay	13
	EGR Valve To EGR Pipe	58
	EGR Valve To Intake Manifold	13
	Engine Mounting To Mounting Insulator	33
	Fuel Pump Bolt	48①
	Fuel Pump Screws	26①
	No. 1 Camshaft To Camshaft Timing Gear	54
	No. 1 Oil Dipstick Guide To Crankcase	22
	No. 2 Cylinder Head Cover To No. 1 Cylinder Head Cover	48①
	No. 2 Engine Hanger To Ventilation Case	6
	PCV Pipe To Intake Manifold	43①
	Radiator Mounting	13

Continued

TIGHTENING SPECIFICATIONS—Continued

Year	Component	Torque, Ft. Lbs.
1996–97	Radiator Reservoir	9
	Timing Chain Case To Oil Baffle Plate	43①
	Timing Chain Case To Oil Filter Bracket	14
	Timing Chain Case To Water Outlet	14
	Ventilation Case To Crankcase	6
	Water Outlet To No. 2 Water By-Pass Pipe	43①
	Water Outlet To Union Bolt	9
	Water Outlet To Water Outlet Stay	15
	Water Pump to Timing Chain Case	③

① — Inch lbs.
② — Refer to "Cylinder Head, Replace."
③ — Refer to "Water Pump, Replace."

Rear Axle & Suspension

INDEX

REAR AXLE SHAFT

REPLACE

1. Raise and support vehicle, then remove rear wheels.
2. **On models with ABS,** remove speed sensor, **Fig. 1.**
3. **On models with drum brakes,** using brake tube removal tool No. 09751-36011, or equivalent, disconnect brake tube, then remove brake drum, brake shoes and parking brake cable.
4. **On models with disc brakes,** using brake tube removal tool No. 09751-36011, or equivalent, disconnect brake tube, then remove clip, brake hose, cylinder, rotor, parking brake shoes and parking brake cable.
5. **On all models,** remove brake backing plate attaching nuts.
6. Using slide hammer and adapter tool No. 09520-00031, or equivalent, pull out rear axle shaft, then remove backing plate and end gasket.
7. Reverse procedure to install.

AXLE SHAFT BEARING & OIL SEAL

REPLACE

REMOVAL

1. Remove axle shaft as outlined under "Rear Axle Shaft, Replace."
2. **On models with ABS,** using press and bearing holder tool No. 09950-

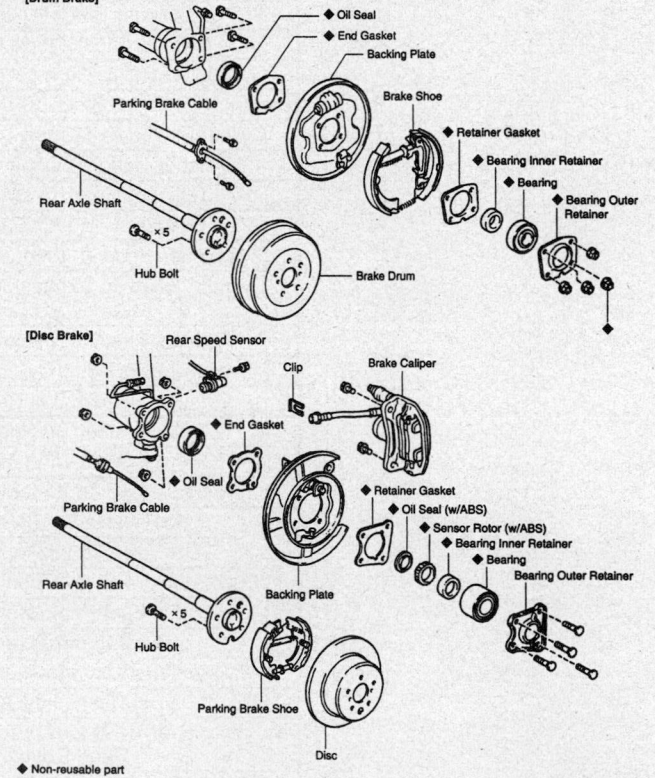

Fig. 1 Exploded view of rear axle shaft

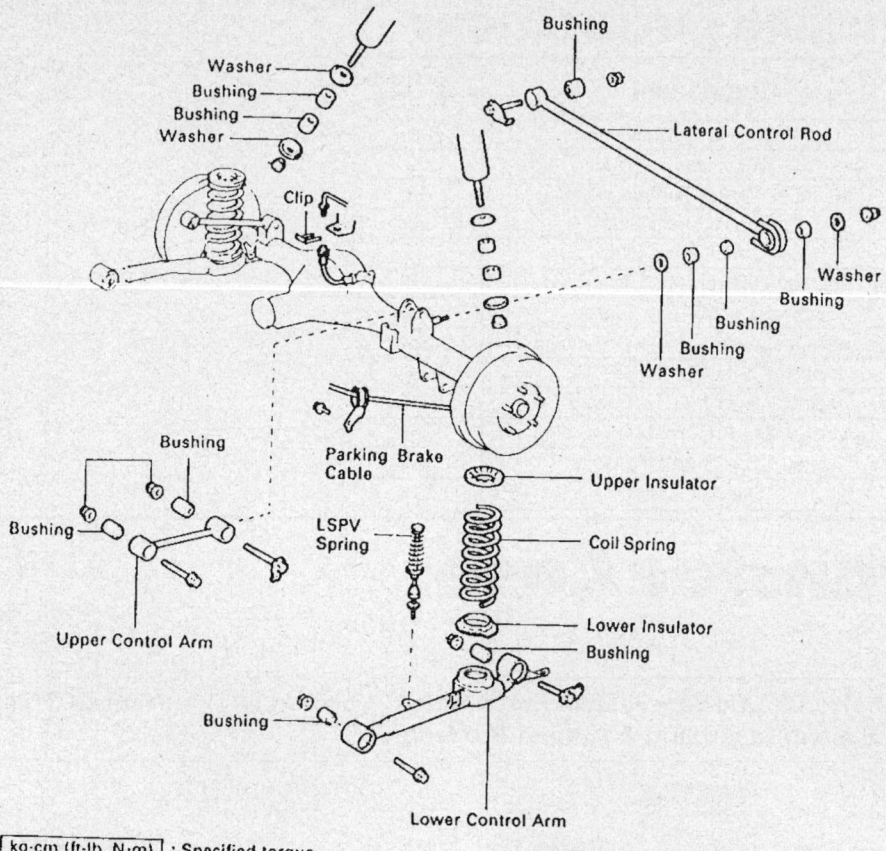

Washer
Bushing
Bushing
Washer
Clip
Bushing
Lateral Control Rod
Washer
Bushing
Washer
Bushing
Bushing
Parking Brake Cable
Upper Insulator
LSPV Spring
Coil Spring
Bushing
Bushing
Lower Insulator
Bushing
Upper Control Arm
Bushing
Lower Control Arm

kg·cm (ft·lb, N·m) : Specified torque
♦ Non-reusable part

TY2039100012000X

Fig. 2 Exploded view of rear suspension

00020, or equivalent, remove oil seal, then using same tool remove speed sensor rotor.

3. **On all models,** grind inner retainer, then using suitable hammer and chisel, cut retainer and remove from shaft.

4. Using bearing housing holder tool No. 09527-30010, or equivalent and suitable press, remove bearing and bearing outer retainer.

5. Using seal removal tool No. 09308-00010, or equivalent, remove oil seal.

INSTALLATION

1. Coat contact surfaces of oil seal with grease, then install oil seal using seal installer tool No. 09517-30010, or equivalent and hammer. Oil seal drive depth for drum brake models is .236 inch and for disc brake models .138 inch.

2. **On models with disc brakes,** assemble bearing outer gasket, retainer and backing plate.

3. **On models with drum brakes,** install bearing outer retainer.

4. **On models with disc brakes,** install backing plate assembly, then using tool No. 09506-30012, or equivalent, and a suitable press, install new bearing.

5. **On all models,** heat inner bearing retainer to about 302°F (150°C) in oil bath, then press inner bearing retainer onto axle shaft with chamfered side facing toward bearing using tool No. 09506-30012, or equivalent.

6. **On models with ABS,** using press and adapter tool No. 09506-30012, or equivalent, and a suitable press, install speed sensor rotor and oil seal.

7. **On all models,** install axle shaft.

SHOCK ABSORBER
REPLACE

1. Raise and support vehicle and support rear axle assembly using suitable jack.
2. Remove rear wheels.
3. Remove shock absorber lower attaching nut.
4. Remove upper shock attaching bolt, then the shock absorber.
5. Reverse procedure to install, noting the following:
   a. Tighten attaching nuts and bolt to specifications.
   b. Tighten lower shock attaching nut until at least .0059 inch of shock bolt protrudes.

COIL SPRING
REPLACE

Refer to "Control Arm, Replace" for coil spring replacement procedure.

CONTROL ARM
REPLACE

1. Raise and support rear of vehicle and rear axle, using suitable jack stands.
2. Using brake tube removal tool No. 09751-36011, or equivalent, disconnect brake tube from brake hose.
3. **On models with ABS,** remove ABS wire harness bracket.
4. **On all models,** disconnect LSPV spring from lower control arm, **Fig. 2**.
5. Remove shock absorber lower attaching nut.
6. Remove lateral control rod attaching nut and bolt, then the lateral control rod with bushings.
7. Disconnect parking brake cable from lower control arm.
8. Lower rear axle assembly, then remove coil spring with upper and lower insulators.
9. Remove lower control arm attaching nuts and bolts, then the lower control arm.
10. Remove upper control arm attaching nuts and bolts, then the upper control arm.
11. Reverse procedure to install.

LATERAL ROD
REPLACE

Refer to "Control Arm, Replace" for lateral rod replacement procedure.

TIGHTENING SPECIFICATIONS

Year	Component	Torque, Ft. Lbs.
1996–97	Adjusting Nut Lock	9
	Backing Plate Set Nut	59
	Differential Carrier To Axle Housing	18
	Differential Drain Plug	36
	Differential Filler Plug	36
	Lateral Control Rod To Body	156
	Lower Control Arm Body	156
	Lower Control Arm To Axle Housing	181
	Propeller Shaft To Differential	54
	Shock Absorber To Body	27
	Upper Control Arm To Axle Housing	156
	Upper Control Arm To Body	156
	Yoke Nut (Max)	174

Transfer Case

NOTE: On Air Bag Equipped Models, Refer To "Air Bag System Precautions" Located In The Front Of This Manual For System Disarming & Arming Procedures.

INDEX

PRECAUTIONS

AIR BAG SYSTEMS

Refer to "Air Bag System Precautions" in the front of this manual for system disarming and arming procedures.

BATTERY GROUND CABLE

Prior to service, disconnect battery ground cable and isolate as required.

TRANSFER CASE

REPLACE

PREVIA

Refer to "Automatic Transmissions" section for automatic transmission and transfer case replacement procedure.

TIGHTENING SPECIFICATIONS

Year	Component	Torque, Ft. Lbs.
1996–97	Companion Flange Locknut	90
	Extension Housing To Rear Case Bolts	9
	Front To Rear Case Attaching Bolts	27
	Oil Assembly	9
	Oil Pump Ball, Spring & Screw Plug	13
	Oil Pump Cover	69①
	Oil Separator & Strainer	43①
	Speedometer Driven Gear	9

① — Inch lbs.

Front Suspension & Steering

NOTE: On Air Bag Equipped Models, Refer To "Air Bag System Precautions" Located In The Front Of This Manual For System Disarming & Arming Procedures.

INDEX

PRECAUTIONS

AIR BAG SYSTEMS

Refer to "Air Bag System Precautions" in the front of this manual for system disarming and arming procedures.

BATTERY GROUND CABLE

Prior to service, disconnect battery ground cable and isolate as required.

HUB, BEARING & SEAL
REPLACE

1. Raise and support vehicle, then remove front wheels.
2. **On models with ABS,** remove speed sensor, **Fig. 1.**
3. **On 2WD models,** remove brake cylinder from steering knuckle, then using suitable wire, hang cylinder aside. Remove brake rotor.
4. **On models with 4WD,** remove cotter pin and lock cap, then with brakes applied, remove locknut. Remove brake cylinder and rotor.
5. **On all models,** loosen lower shock absorber attaching nuts, but do not remove.
6. Loosen lower ball joint attaching bolts, but do not remove.
7. Remove tie rod end cotter pin and nut, then using ball joint puller tool No. 09628-10011, or equivalent, separate tie rod end from steering knuckle.
8. Remove lower ball joint attaching bolts and separate from steering knuckle.
9. Remove shock absorber lower attaching nuts and bolts.
10. Remove steering knuckle and axle hub. **Do not damage speed sensor rotor, oil seal and driveshaft boot.**
11. **On 2WD models,** remove axle hub grease cap, then using suitable chisel and hammer, release nut caulking and remove locknut.
12. **On 2WD models with ABS,** remove speed sensor rotor. **Do not scratch sensor rotor serrations.**
13. **On 2WD models less ABS,** remove spacer.

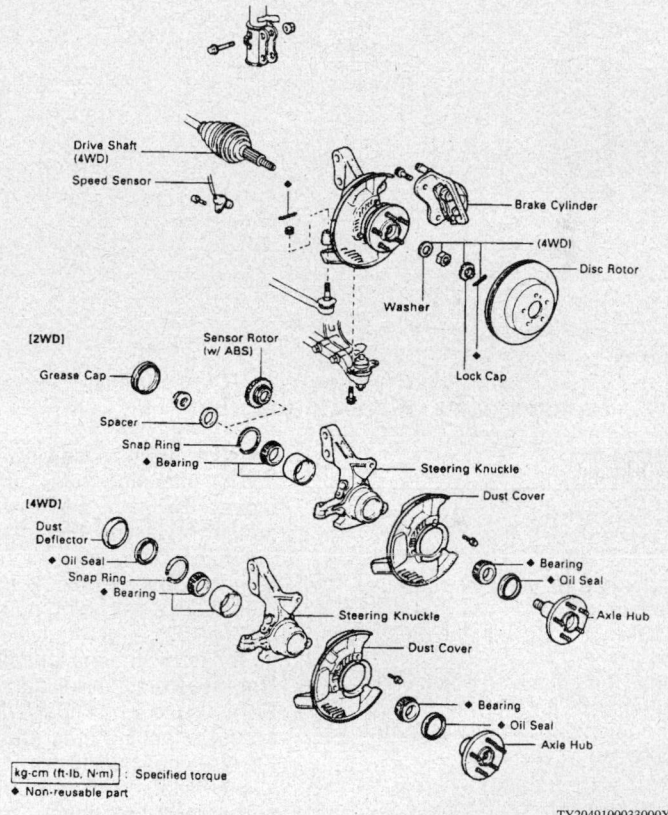

Fig. 1 Exploded view of hub, bearing & seal

14. **On all models,** using axle shaft puller tool No. 09520-00031, or equivalent, remove axle hub.
15. Using bearing remover tool Nos. 09950-00020 (2WD), 09550-10012 (4WD) or 09550-0020 (4WD), or equivalents, and suitable press, remove axle hub bearing.
16. Remove dust cover.
17. **On 4WD models,** remove dust deflector, then using oil seal puller tool No. 09308-00010, or equivalent, remove inner oil seal.
18. **On all models,** remove steering knuckle snap ring, then using bearing replacer tool Nos. 09223-56010 and 09316-60010, or equivalents, remove bearing.
19. Reverse procedure to install.

BALL JOINT INSPECTION

1. Raise and support vehicle.
2. Ensure front wheels are in straight ahead position, then depress and hold brake pedal.
3. Move control arm up and down. If play is evident, replace ball joint.

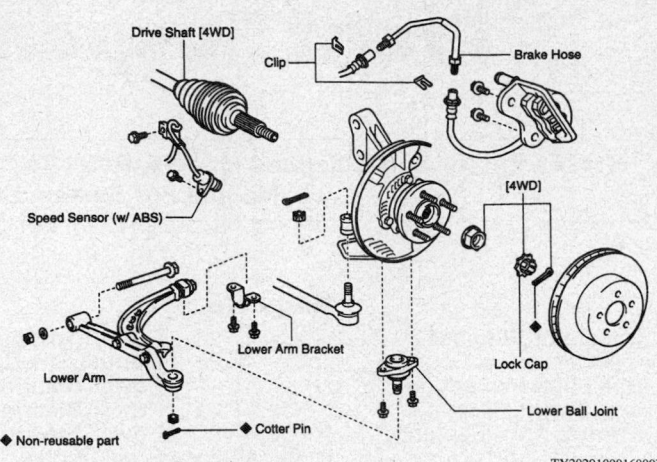

Fig. 3 Exploded view of lower control arm

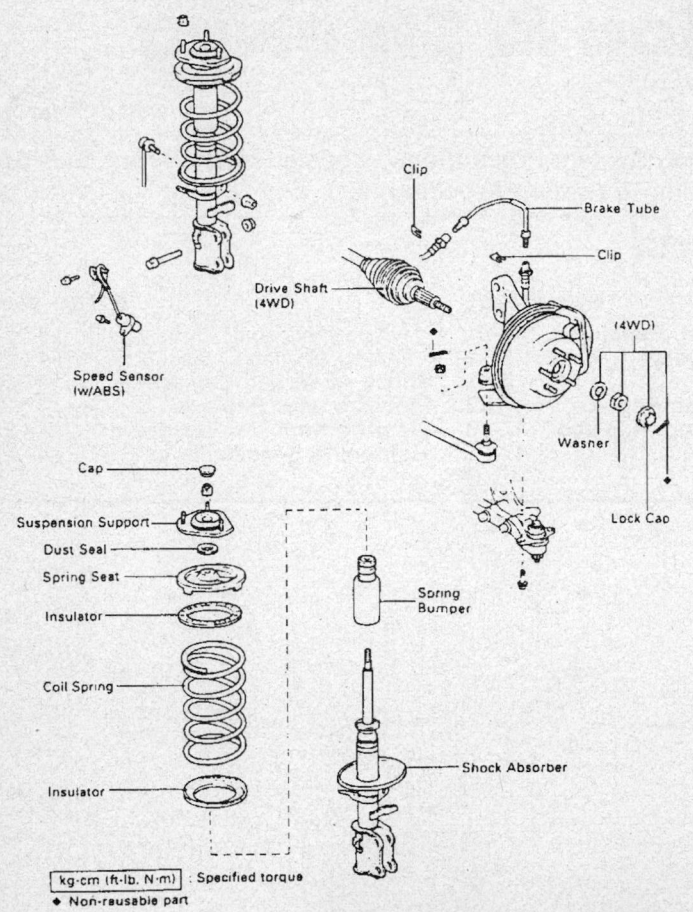

Fig. 2 Exploded view of shock absorber

BALL JOINT
REPLACE
LOWER

1. Raise and support vehicle, then remove front wheels.
2. Remove ball joint cotter pin and attaching nut.
3. Remove ball join attaching bolts.
4. Using ball joint puller tool No. 09628-62011, or equivalent, remove ball joint.
5. Reverse procedure to install.

COIL SPRING
REPLACE

Refer to "Shock Absorber, Replace" for coil spring replacement procedure.

SHOCK ABSORBER
REPLACE

1. Raise and support vehicle, then remove front wheels.
2. **On models with 4WD,** remove driveshaft cotter pin and lock cap, then with brakes applied, remove locknut and washer, **Fig. 2.**
3. **On all models,** disconnect stabilizer bar link from shock assembly.
4. **On models with ABS,** remove speed sensor.

5. **On all models,** loosen lower shock absorber attaching nuts, but do not remove.
6. Loosen lower ball joint attaching bolts, but do not remove.
7. Remove tie rod end cotter pin and nut, then using ball joint puller tool No. 09628-10011, or equivalent, remove tie rod from steering knuckle.
8. Remove lower ball joint attaching nuts.
9. Remove steering knuckle to shock absorber attaching nuts and bolts, then the steering knuckle.
10. Using suitable jack, support shock absorber and coil spring, then remove shock absorber upper attaching nuts.
11. Remove shock absorber and coil spring assembly.
12. Using spring compressor tool No. 09727-30020, or equivalent, compress coil spring.
13. Install bolt and two nuts into shock absorber lower bracket, then install assembly in suitable soft jawed vise.
14. Using upper seat holder tool No. 09729-22031, or equivalent, hold spring seat, then remove nut.
15. Remove suspension support, dust seal, spring seat, upper insulator, coil spring, spring bumper and lower insulator.
16. Reverse procedure to install.

CONTROL ARM
REPLACE
LOWER

1. Raise and support vehicle, then remove front wheels.
2. Remove engine undercover, **Fig. 3.**
3. Remove lower ball joint attaching bolts, then separate from steering knuckle.
4. Remove lower arm bracket attaching bolts.
5. Remove arm shaft attaching nut.
6. Remove lower control arm and lower ball joint assembly.
7. Using ball joint puller tool No. 09628-62011, or equivalent, remove lower ball joint from arm.
8. Reverse procedure to install.

STEERING KNUCKLE
REPLACE

Refer to "Shock Absorber, Replace" for steering knuckle replacement procedure.

STABILIZER BAR
REPLACE

1. Raise and support vehicle, then remove front wheels.
2. Remove engine undercovers.
3. Remove right and left stabilizer bar links.
4. Remove right and left stabilizer bar bracket attaching bolts, then the stabilizer bar.
5. Reverse procedure to install.

POWER STEERING GEAR
REPLACE

1. Refer to **Fig. 4** for steering gear replacement, noting the following:
   a. Using tie rod end puller tool No. 09611-12010, or equivalent, remove tie rod end.
   b. Place installation alignment marks

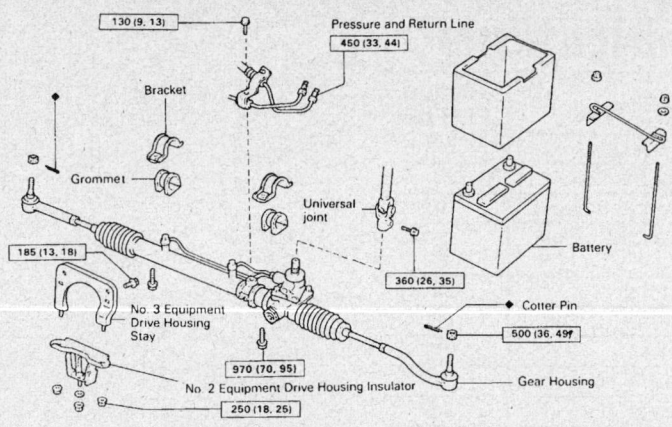

Fig. 4 Steering gear removal

TY6039100017000X

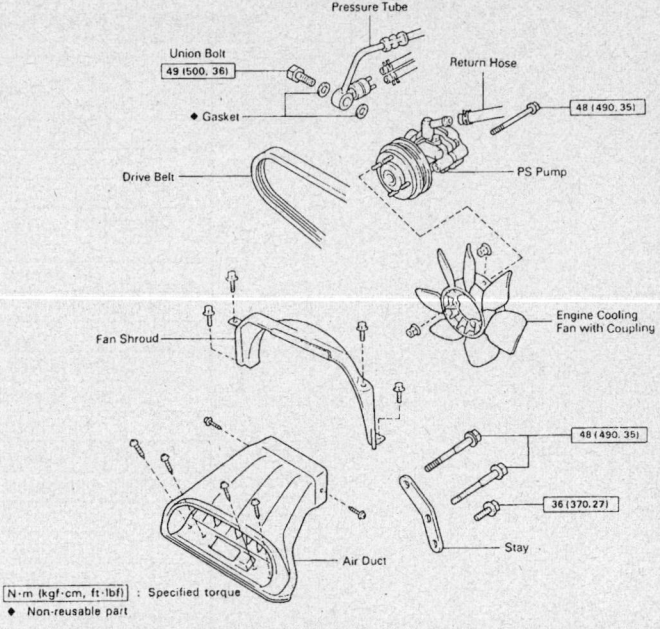

N·m (kgf·cm, ft·lbf) : Specified torque
◆ Non-reusable part

TY6039100018000X

Fig. 5 Power steering pump removal

on universal joint and shaft, then remove joint lower bolt and loosen
upper bolt. Slide joint upward to disconnect.
c. Using hose wrench tool No. 09633-
00020, or equivalent, disconnect
power steering gear pressure and
return lines.

d. Turn gear housing rearward and
slide through left side opening to remove.

POWER STEERING PUMP

REPLACE

Refer to **Fig. 5** for power steering pump
replacement.

TIGHTENING SPECIFICATIONS

Year	Component	Torque, Ft. Lbs.
1996–97	Axle Hub Bearing Locknut	147
	Differential Carrier Cover Set Bolt	34
	Differential Carrier To Differential Support	116
	Differential Carrier To No. 2 Differential Support	48
	Differential Support Bolt	54
	Differential Tube To Differential Carrier	65
	Driveshaft Locknut	152
	Driveshaft To Side Gear Shaft	51
	Front Differential Bearing Cap	58
	Front Differential Drain Plug	36
	Front Differential Filler Plug	29
	Front Differential To Propeller Shaft	31
	Lower Arm Bracket To Body	105
	Lower Ball Joint To Lower Arm	76
	No. 1 Differential Support To Differential Tube	51
	No. 1 Lower Arm To Body	121
	No. 1 Lower Arm To No. 2 Lower Arm	136
	No. 2 Lower Arm To Bushing	80
	Ring Gear To Differential Case	71
	Stabilizer Bar Bracket	14
	Stabilizer Bar Link Nut	76
	Steering Knuckle To Lower Ball Joint	94
	Steering Knuckle To Shock Absorber	232
	Suspension Support To Body	47
	Suspension Support To Shock Absorber	34
	Tie Rod End To Steering Knuckle	36
	Wheel Lug Nut	76

Wheel Alignment

INDEX

PRELIMINARY INSPECTION

Inspect and repair the following prior to adjusting wheel alignment.
1. Check tires for wear and proper inflation.
2. Check front suspension, steering linkage and ball joints for wear or looseness.
3. Check wheel runout with a dial indicator. Wheel runout should not exceed .039 inch (1.0 mm).
4. Ensure front shock absorbers are functioning properly.

FRONT WHEEL ALIGNMENT

CASTER

Caster is not adjustable. If caster is not within specifications, check for worn or damaged suspension parts and replace as required.

CAMBER

1. Remove front wheels.
2. Remove two nuts from lower side of shock absorber.
3. Coat threads of nuts with engine oil and temporarily install.
4. Adjust camber by pushing or pulling lower side of shock absorber in direction in which camber adjustment is required, **Fig. 1**.
5. Tighten nuts, then recheck camber.
6. If camber is not within specifications, estimate how much additional camber adjustment is required and select camber adjusting bolt from chart shown in **Fig. 2**.
7. Install selected bolts and adjust camber by pushing or pulling lower side of shock absorber in direction in which camber adjustment is required.
8. **Torque** set bolt to 232 ft. lbs. and adjusting bolt to 163 ft. lbs.

TOE-IN

1. Rock vehicle up and down to stabilize suspension.
2. Move vehicle forward about 16.4 feet (5 m) with front wheels in straight ahead position on a level surface. **If vehicle is backed up, move forward the same distance.**

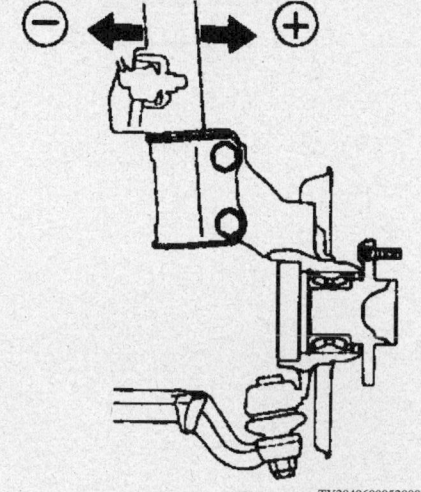

Fig. 1   Camber adjustment

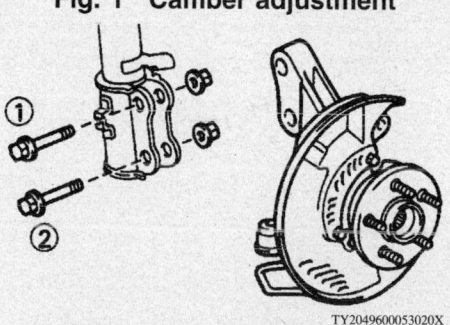

Fig. 2   Camber adjust bolt selection (Part 2 of 2)

3. Mark center of each rear tread and measure distance between marks.
4. Move vehicle forward until marks on rear sides of tires come up to the measuring heights of the gauge on the front side **If tire rolls too far, repeat step 2.**
5. Measure distance between marks on front tires.
6. If toe-in is not to specifications, adjust as follows:
   a. Remove boot clips.
   b. Loosen tie rod end locknut.
   c. Turn left and right tie rod ends an equal amount.
   d. Ensure lengths of left and right tie rod ends are equal.

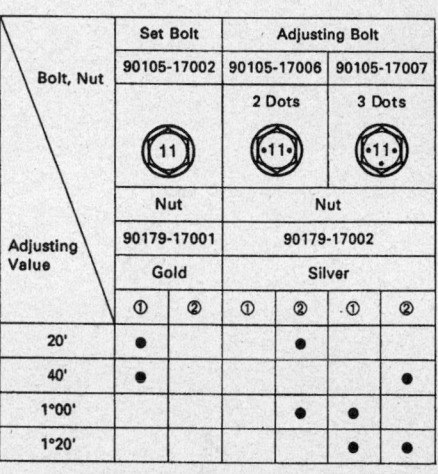

Fig. 2   Camber adjust bolt selection (Part 1 of 2)

STEERING AXIS INCLINATION

Steering axis inclination is not adjustable. If steering axis inclination is not within specifications, check for worn or damaged suspension parts and replace as required.

VEHICLE RIDE HEIGHT

Measure vehicle ride height as shown in **Fig. 3**. Ride height for 2WD models with P205/75 R14 tires, should be 9.37 inches front and 11.06 inches rear. On 2WD models with P215/65 R15 tires, ride height should be 9.33 inches front and 10.98 inches rear.

On 4WD models with P205/75 R14 tires, ride height should be 9.76 inches front and 11.46 inches rear. On 4WD models with P215/65 R15 tires, ride height should be 9.72 inches front and 11.38 inches rear.

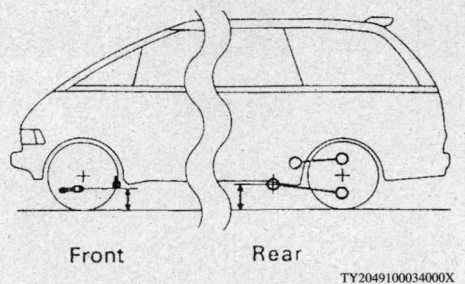

TY2049100034000X

Fig. 3   Vehicle ride height measurement

Specifications

GENERAL ENGINE SPECIFICATIONS

Year	Model	Engine	Fuel System	Bore & Stroke, Inches	Compression Ratio	Maximum Brake H.P. @ RPM	Maximum Torque, Ft. Lbs. @ RPM	Normal Oil Pressure, psi
1996	Paseo	1.5L 5E-FE	Fuel Inj.	2.91 x 3.43	9.4	93 @ 5400	100 @ 4400	①
	Tercel	1.5L 5E-FE	Fuel Inj.	2.91 x 3.43	9.4	93 @ 5400	100 @ 4400	①
1997	Paseo	1.5L 5E-FE	Fuel Inj.	2.91 x 3.43	9.4	93 @ 5400	100 @ 4400	①
	Tercel	1.5L 5E-FE	Fuel Inj.	2.91 x 3.43	9.4	93 @ 5400	100 @ 4400	①
1998	Tercel	1.5L 5E-FE	Fuel Inj.	2.19 x 3.43	9.4	93 @ 5400	100 @ 4400	①

① — 4.3 psi or more @ idle, 36–71 psi @ 3000 RPM.

TUNE UP SPECIFICATIONS

The following specifications are published from the latest information available. This data should be used only in the absence of a decal affixed in the engine compartment.

When checking ignition timing, it may be necessary to disconnect certain hoses and/or electrical connectors. Refer to vehicle emission control label for specific instructions.

Before disconnecting spark plug wires from distributor cap, determine location of No. 1 wire in cap, as distributor position may have been altered from that shown.

Year	Engine	Spark Plug Gap, Inch	Ignition Timing			Idle Speed①②		Fuel Pump Pressure, psi.	Valve Clearance, Inch	
			Firing Order	Timing, °BTDC①	Timing Mark, Fig.	Man. Trans.	Auto. Trans.		Int.	Exh.
1996	1.5L	.043	1-3-4-2	10③	A	750	750N	40.8–41.7	.006–.010	.012–.016
1997	1.5L	.043	1-3-4-2	10③	A	750	750N	44–50	.006–.010	.012–.016
1998	1.5L	.043	1-3-4-2	10③	A	750	750N	44–50	.006–.010	.012–.016

BTDC — Before Top Dead Center
N — Neutral

① — With cooling fan off.
② — Controlled by idle air controller.

③ — With check connector terminals TE1 & E1 connected.

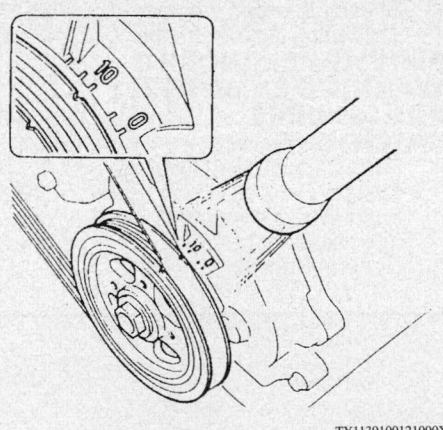

TY1139100121000X

Fig. A

FRONT WHEEL ALIGNMENT SPECIFICATIONS

The specifications listed below are for unloaded vehicles.

| Year | Model | Caster Angle, Degrees | | Camber Angle, Degrees | | Toe-In, Inch① | Toe-Out On Turns, Degrees | | Steering Axis Inclination | Ball Joint Wear |
		Limits	Desired	Limits	Desired		Outer Wheel	Inner Wheel		
1996	Paseo	+2/3 to +2⅙	+1½	-1⅙ to +⅓	-5/12	-.04 to +.12	35¾	32 1/12	12¼	②
	Tercel	+7/12 to +2 1/12	+1⅓	-1 1/12 to +5/12	-⅓	-.04 to +.12	35 11/12	32⅙	12⅙	②
1997	Paseo	-¾ to +2¼	+1½	-1⅙ to +⅓	-5/12	-.04 to +.12	35¾	32 1/12	12¼	②
	Tercel	+7/12 to +2 1/12	+1⅓	-1 1/12 to +5/12	-⅓	-.04 to +.12	35 11/12	32⅙	12⅙	②
1998	Tercel	+7/12 to +2 1/12	+1⅓	-1 1/12 to +5/12	-⅓	-.04 to +.12	35 11/12	32⅙	12⅙	②

① — Toe-in (+); toe-out (-).

② — Refer to "Ball Joint Inspection" under "Front Suspension & Steering."

REAR WHEEL ALIGNMENT SPECIFICATIONS

The specifications listed below are for unloaded vehicles.

| Year | Model | Camber Angle, Degrees | | Toe-In, Inch① |
		Limits	Desired	
1996	Paseo	-1 to 0	-½	0 to +.24
	Tercel	-1¼ to +¼	-½	0 to +.24
1997	Paseo	-1¼ to +¼	-½	0 to +.26
	Tercel	-1¼ to +¼	-13/20	0 to +.24
1998	Tercel	-1¼ to +¼	-13/20	0 to +.24

① — Toe-in (+); toe-out (-).

FLUID CAPACITIES & COOLING SYSTEM DATA

| Year | Model | Cooling Capacity, Qts. | | Radiator Cap Relief Pressure, Lbs. | Thermo. Opening Temp., °F | Fuel Tank, Gals. | Engine Oil Refill, Qts.① | Transmission/Transaxle Oil | | | Axle Oil, Pints |
		Auto Trans.	Manual Trans					4 Speed, Pints	5 Speed, Pints	Auto. Trans., Qts.	
1996	Paseo	5.6	5.6	13	180	11.9	3	—	4.0	7.6	—
	Tercel	5.4	5.4	13	180	11.9	3	—	4.0	②	3
1997	Paseo	5.6	5.6	13	180	11.9	3.0	—	—	7.6	—
	Tercel	5.4	5.4	13	180	11.9	3.0	—	4.0	②	—
1998	Tercel	5.6	5.6	13	180	11.9	3.0	—	4.0	②	3

① — With filter change.

② — A132L, 5.8 qts.; A242L, 7.6 qts.

LUBRICANT DATA

| Year | Model | Lubricant Type | | | | |
| | | Transaxle | | Rear Axle | Power Steering | Brake System |
		Manual	Automatic			
1996	Paseo	75W-90 GL-4/5	Dexron II/IIE/III	—	Dexron II/IIE/III	DOT 3
	Tercel	75W-90 GI-4/5	Dexron II/IIE/III	—	Dexron II/IIE/III	DOT 3
1997	Paseo	75W-90 GL-4/5	Dexron II/IIE/III	—	Dexron II/III	DOT 3
	Tercel	75W-90 GI-4/5	Dexron II/IIE/III	—	Dexron II/III	DOT 3
1998	Tercel	75W-90 GI-4/5	Dexron II/IIE/III	—	Dexron II/III	DOT 3

Electrical

NOTE: On Air Bag Equipped Models, Refer To "Air Bag System Precautions" Located In The Front Of This Manual For System Disarming & Arming Procedures.

INDEX

PRECAUTIONS

AIR BAG SYSTEMS

Refer to "Air Bag System Precautions" in the front of this manual for system disarming and arming procedures.

BATTERY GROUND CABLE

Prior to service, disconnect battery ground cable and isolate as required.

FUSE PANEL & FLASHER LOCATION

There are two fuse panels; the first is on the left front kick panel and the second is forward of the left front shock tower. The turn signal/hazard flasher is under the dash, left of the steering column.

FUEL PUMP RELAY LOCATION

The fuel pump relay is located in the engine compartment relay box, **Fig. 1.**

RELAY CENTER LOCATION

There are two relay centers; one is located on the left front kick panel and the other is located forward of the left front shock tower.

STARTER

REPLACE

1. Remove air cleaner hose and intake manifold stay.
2. Disconnect electrical connectors from starter motor, then remove attaching bolts and starter motor.

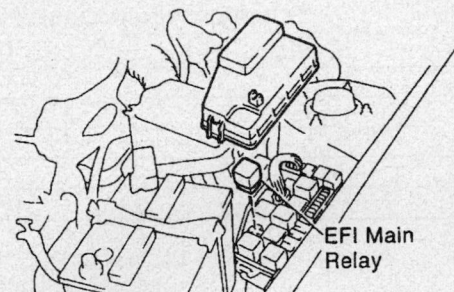

Fig. 1 Fuel pump relay location

3. Reverse procedure to install. **Torque** starter attaching bolts to 29 ft. lbs.

COIL PACK

REPLACE

1. Disconnect high tension cords from ignition coils, **Fig. 2.**
2. Disconnect ignition coil electrical connectors.
3. Remove ignition coil retaining bolts and ignition coils.
4. Reverse procedure to install. **Torque** to 6 ft. lbs.

IGNITION LOCK

REPLACE

1. Turn ignition switch to ACC position.
2. Insert a small diameter rod into hole located on side of lock cylinder, then while holding down pin, remove lock cylinder.
3. Reverse procedure to install. Ensure lock cylinder is in ACC position.

IGNITION SWITCH

REPLACE

1. Remove steering wheel, then upper and lower covers.

2. Disconnect electrical connectors from ignition switch.
3. Turn ignition key to ACC position and remove ignition key cylinder.
4. Remove screw and ignition switch.
5. Reverse procedure to install.

NEUTRAL SAFETY SWITCH

REPLACE

1. Raise and support vehicle.
2. Loosen neutral safety switch bracket bolt.
3. Position transaxle shift lever into Neutral.
4. Align switch shaft groove with neutral base line, **Fig. 3,** then retighten switch bracket bolt. **Torque** bolts to 48 inch lbs.
5. Connect electrical connector to switch.

STOP LIGHT SWITCH

REPLACE

1. Remove brake pedal tension spring.
2. Disconnect switch wire connector.
3. Remove switch mounting nut, then slide switch from mounting bracket.
4. Reverse procedure to install.

COMBINATION SWITCH

REPLACE

REPLACEMENT

1. Remove horn button screws and horn button.
2. Scribe alignment marks on steering wheel and steering shaft.
3. Remove steering wheel nut.
4. Using a steering wheel puller tool No. 09950-50010 or equivalent, remove steering wheel.

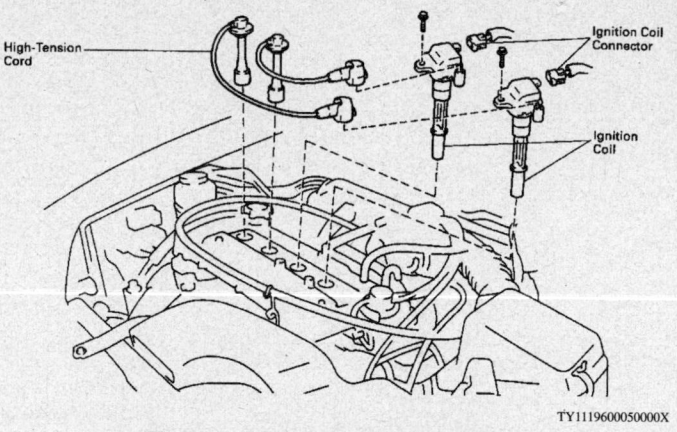

Fig. 2 Coil pack replacement

TY1119600050000X

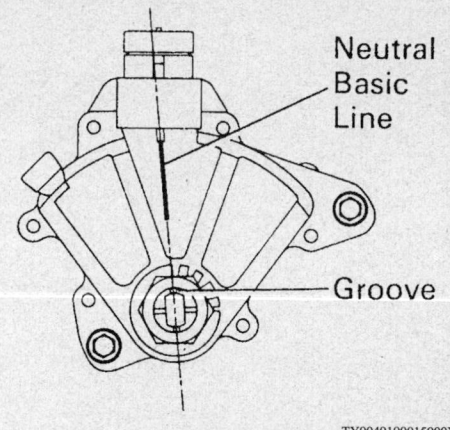

Fig. 3 Neutral safety switch adjustment

TY9049100015000X

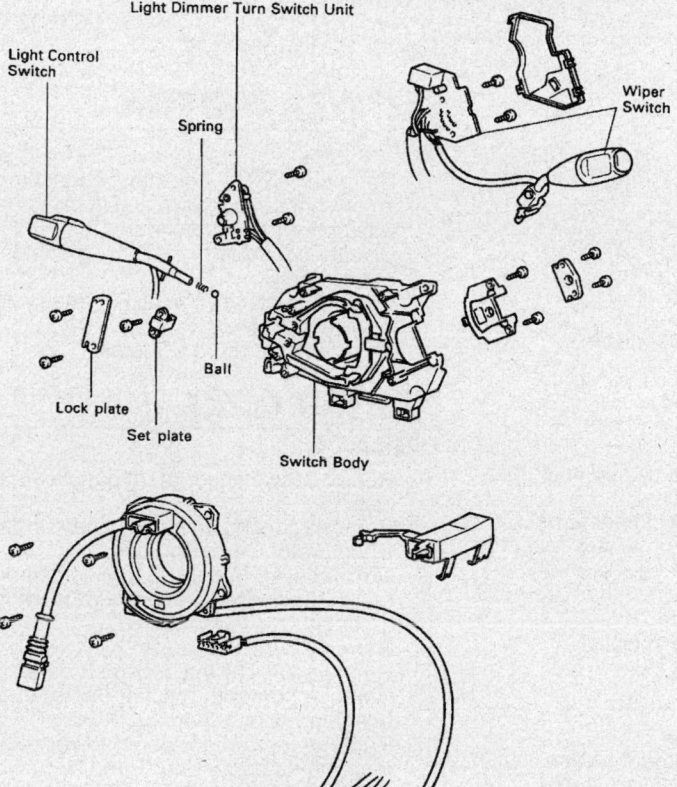

TY9049300017000X

Fig. 4 Exploded view of combination switch

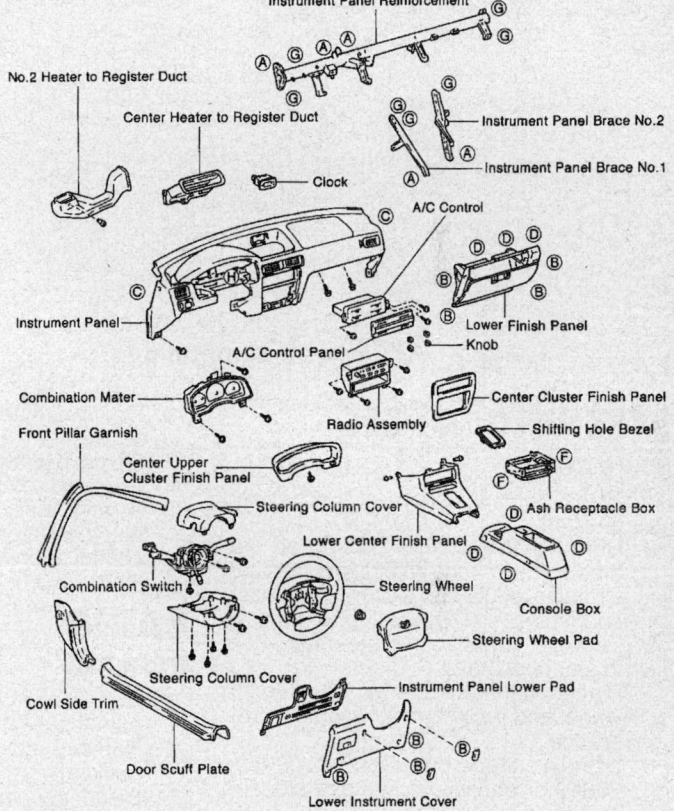

TY9099600094000X

Fig. 5 Exploded view of instrument panel.

5. Remove steering column upper and lower covers.
6. Disconnect combination switch harness.
7. **On models equipped with air bag,** disconnect spiral cable connector.
8. **On all models,** remove combination switch.
9. Reverse procedure to install.

SERVICE

Headlamp & Dimmer Switch

1. Remove combination switch as outlined under "Replacement."
2. Remove four spiral cable attaching screws and separate spiral cable from switch body, **Fig 4**.
3. Remove lock plate and ball set plate from switch body, **Fig. 4.**
4. Remove ball from set plate, then slide out light control switch from switch body.
5. Remove light dimmer turn switch attaching screws and light dimmer turn switch unit.
6. Reverse procedure to install. **Note proper mounting position of spiral cable to combination switch body.**

Windshield Wiper/Washer Switch

1. Remove combination switch as outlined previously.
2. Remove wiper and washer switch attaching screws, then disconnect switch electrical connector and remove switch.
3. Reverse procedure to install.

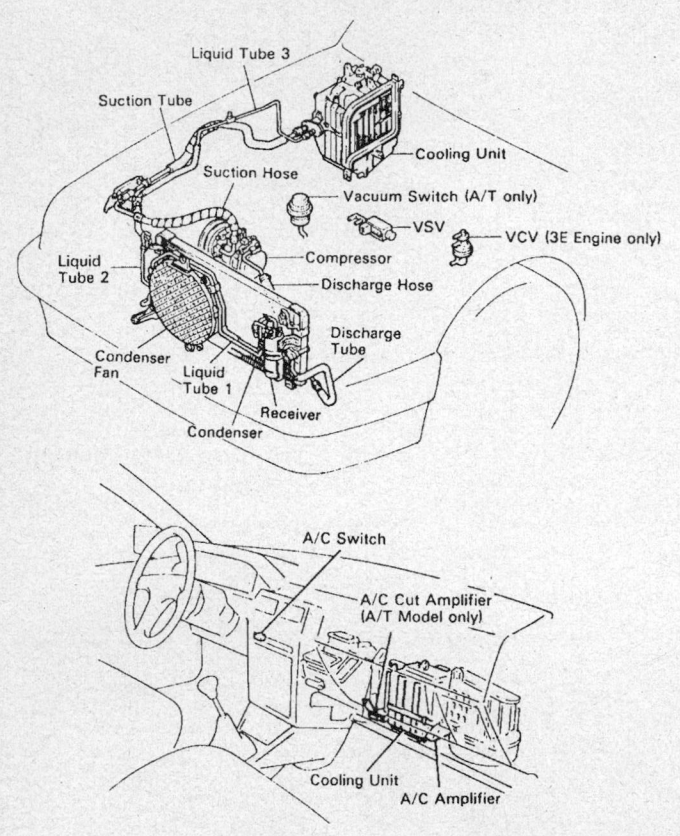

Fig. 6 A/C system components

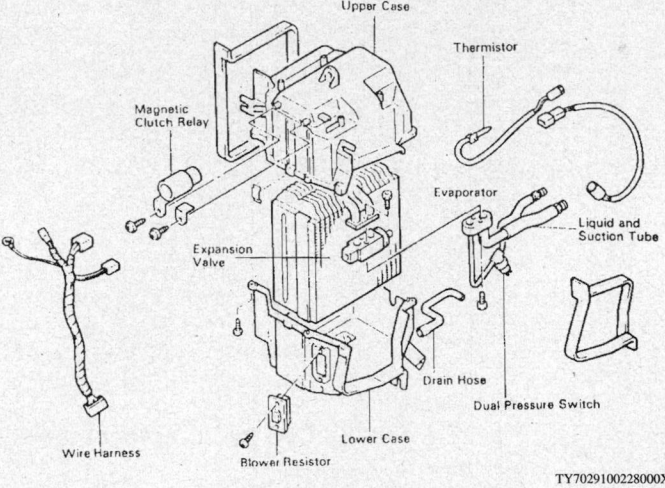

Fig. 7 Cooling unit

STEERING WHEEL
REPLACE

1. Place front wheels in straight-ahead position
2. Remove Torx screws holding air bag module to steering wheel, then remove air bag module and disconnect air bag connector.
3. Remove nut attaching steering wheel to steering shaft.
4. Place alignment marks on steering wheel and mainshaft for assembly reference.
5. Using a suitable puller tool No. 09950–50010 or equivalent, remove steering wheel.
6. Reverse procedure to install, noting:
   a. Realign marks on steering wheel and mainshaft for proper assembly.
   b. **Torque** steering wheel attaching nut to 25 ft. lbs.
7. Rearm air bag system as outlined under "Precautions."

INSTRUMENT CLUSTER
REPLACE

1. Remove steering wheel as outlined under "Steering Wheel, Replace."
2. Remove steering column covers as outlined in **Dash Panel Service** section.
3. Remove console box, if necessary.
4. Remove engine hood release lever.
5. Remove instrument finish lower panel retaining screws and lower panel.

6. Remove instrument cluster finish center panel.
7. Remove instrument cluster panel.
8. Remove combination meter retaining screws, disconnect speedometer and electrical connectors, then remove combination meter.
9. Reverse procedure to install.

RADIO
REPLACE

1. Pull center instrument panel finish panel rearward to remove, **Fig. 5.**
2. Remove radio attaching screws, then pull rearward.
3. Disconnect radio electrical connectors and antenna lead, then remove radio.
4. Reverse procedure to install.

WIPER MOTOR
REPLACE

1. Remove wiper arms, then the cowl louver.
2. Disconnect wiper motor wire connector.
3. Remove wiper motor attaching bolts.
4. Using a suitable screwdriver, disconnect wiper link from wiper motor and remove wiper motor.
5. Reverse procedure to install.

WIPER SWITCH
REPLACE

Refer to "Combination Switch, Replace" for procedure.

BLOWER MOTOR
REPLACE

1. Remove A/C amplifier attaching screws, then position amplifier aside with connectors attached.
2. Disconnect blower motor electrical connector.
3. Remove blower motor attaching screws and blower motor.
4. Reverse procedure to install.

HEATER CORE
REPLACE

1. Remove lower instrument panel safety pad.
2. Remove cooling unit as outlined under "Evaporator Core, Replace."
3. Drain coolant into a suitable container, then disconnect water hoses from radiator pipes.
4. Remove pipe grommets.
5. Remove A/C control assembly.
6. Remove heater to register center duct attaching screws and duct.
7. Remove instrument panel lower reinforcements brace Nos. 1 and 2.
8. Remove heater unit electrical connectors and attaching bolts, then remove unit.
9. Remove two heater core attaching screws and plates, then the heater core.
10. Reverse procedure to install.

EVAPORATOR CORE
REPLACE

1. Discharge and recover A/C system refrigerant as outlined in "Air Conditioning" section.
2. Disconnect refrigerant lines at cooling unit, **Fig. 6,** capping all openings.
3. Remove glove compartment, then lower instrument panel cover.
4. Disconnect A/C electrical connectors and ground strap.
5. Remove ground wire.
6. Remove A/C amplifier and bracket.
7. Remove cooling unit attaching nuts and bolts and cooling unit.

8. Disconnect electrical connector at cooling unit.
9. Remove thermistor.
10. Remove clamps and screws securing lower evaporator case, then the lower evaporator case, **Fig. 7.**

11. Remove two attaching screws, then the upper evaporator case.
12. Reverse procedure to install, then evacuate and recharge system and

check for leaks. If evaporator is replaced, add 1.4–1.7 oz. of new refrigerant oil to compressor.

5E-FE 1.5L Engine

NOTE: On Air Bag Equipped Models, Refer To "Air Bag System Precautions" Located In The Front Of This Manual For System Disarming & Arming Procedures.

INDEX

PRECAUTIONS

AIR BAG SYSTEMS

Refer to "Air Bag System Precautions" in the front of this manual for system disarming and arming procedures.

BATTERY GROUND CABLE

Prior to service, disconnect battery ground cable and isolate as required.

COMPRESSION PRESSURE

1. Start engine and warm to normal operating temperature.
2. Remove spark plugs.
3. Insert compression gauge into spark plug hole.
4. Fully open throttle.
5. While cranking engine, measure compression pressure.
6. Standard compression pressure should be 142–185 psi.
7. Maximum pressure difference between each cylinder should be 14 psi.

ENGINE

REPLACE

PASEO

1. Drain coolant into a suitable container, then remove battery and coolant reservoir tank.

2. Scribe installation reference marks in engine hood hinge area, then remove hood.
3. Remove engine undercovers, then drain transaxle fluid into a suitable container.
4. Remove air cleaner assembly with air intake connector.
5. Remove radiator assembly.
6. **On models equipped with automatic transaxle,** disconnect throttle cable.
7. **On all models,** disconnect accelerator cable.
8. Remove air cleaner bracket.
9. Disconnect ground strap from lefthand fender apron.
10. Remove charcoal canister, then drain case.
11. Position suitable fuel container, disconnect fuel return hoses, then remove union bolt and gaskets and disconnect fuel inlet hose.
12. Disconnect PCV hose, brake booster vacuum hose, vacuum sensor hose, two idle-up vacuum hoses and two idle-up air hoses, as equipped.
13. Disconnect engine wire harness electrical connectors as follows:
    a. Starter.
    b. Fan water temperature switch.
    c. Water temperature sender gauge.
    d. Water temperature sensor.
    e. **On models equipped with automatic transaxle,** water temperature switch, neutral start switch and ECT solenoid.
    f. **On all models,** oxygen sensor.

g. Oil pressure switch.
h. **On with manual transaxle,** back-up light switch.
i. **On all models,** EGR gas temperature sensor.
j. Wiper motor.
k. EGR vacuum switching valve.
l. Throttle opener VSV.
m. Alternator.
n. Fuel injectors.
o. Distributor.
p. ECT solenoid.
14. Disconnect ground straps, then remove eight clamps and engine wiring harness.
15. **On models equipped with cruise control,** remove cruise control actuator.
16. **On all models,** disconnect vacuum switching valve vacuum hoses, then remove ground strap and valve assembly.
17. Disconnect heater hoses from heater radiator pipes.
18. Disconnect speedometer cable and control cables from transaxle.
19. **On models equipped with manual transaxle,** remove clutch release cylinder without disconnecting tube.
20. **On models equipped with power steering,** remove power steering belt, remove power steering pump attaching bolts and position aside, then remove power steering pump adjusting strut.
21. **On models equipped with A/C, less**

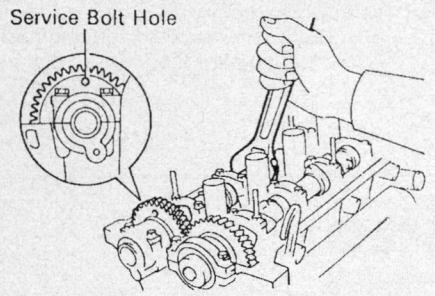

Fig. 1 Intake camshaft positioning

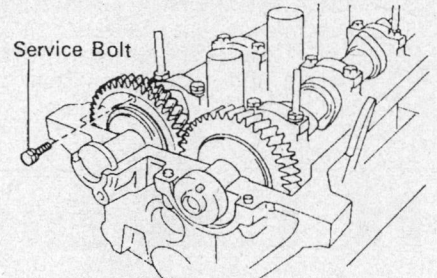

Fig. 2 Service bolt installation

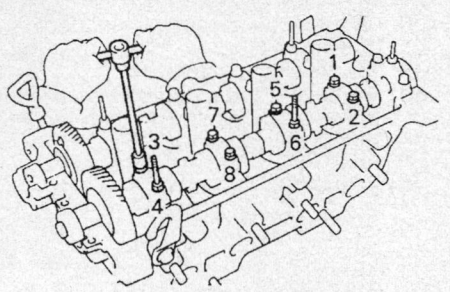

Fig. 3 Exhaust camshaft bolt loosening sequence

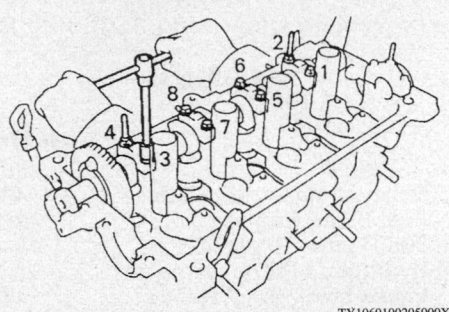

Fig. 4 Intake camshaft bolt loosening sequence

power steering, loosen idler pulley attaching nut, remove compressor belt, then remove idler pulley bracket attaching bolts.

22. **On models equipped with A/C,** disconnect A/C compressor electrical connector, remove compressor attaching bolts and position compressor aside, then remove compressor bracket.
23. **On all models,** remove front exhaust pipe.
24. Remove driveshafts.
25. Install suitable engine lifting equipment, then remove rear engine mount and bracket.
26. Disconnect ground strap, then remove lefthand engine mount.
27. Carefully lift engine from vehicle. Tip transaxle and engine assembly rearward to clear battery carrier support.
28. Position engine and transaxle assembly on suitable stand.
29. Remove engine rear end plate hole cover.
30. Turn crankshaft to gain access to torque converter bolts, then remove six bolts and torque converter assembly.
31. Remove starter assembly.
32. Separate engine and transaxle assembly.
33. Reverse procedure to install. Tighten attaching nuts and bolts to specifications.

TERCEL

1. Remove battery and coolant reserve tank.
2. Scribe reference marks in engine hood hinge area, then remove hood.
3. Remove engine undercovers, then drain transaxle fluid into a suitable container.
4. Drain engine coolant into suitable container.
5. Remove radiator as outlined under "Radiator, Replace."
6. **On models equipped with cruise control,** disconnect control cable and connector, then remove actuator attaching bolts and the actuator.
7. **On all models,** disconnect accelerator cable.
8. Disconnect fuel hoses from fuel pump and plug open ends.
9. Remove charcoal canister.
10. Disconnect heater hoses.
11. Disconnect MAP sensor hose and

brake booster vacuum hose.
12. Disconnect speedometer cable from transaxle.
13. Disconnect vacuum sensor hose and idle-up vacuum transmitting hose.
14. **On models equipped with A/C,** remove A/C idle-up hose.
15. **On models equipped with power steering,** remove power steering idle-up hose.
16. **On all models,** disconnect the following electrical connectors:
    a. Oxygen sensor.
    b. Oil pressure switch.
    c. Engine coolant temperature sender gauge.
    d. Engine coolant temperature sensor.
    e. Camshaft position sensor.
    f. EGR solenoid valve.
    g. Engine coolant temperature switch.
    h. **On models equipped with automatic transaxle,** lock-up solenoid, Park/Neutral position switch, and No. 2 vehicle speed sensor.
    i. **On models equipped with manual transaxle,** back-up light switch.
    j. **On all models,** ground strap.
    k. Throttle position sensor.
    l. IAC valve.
    m. Four injector connectors.
    n. Crankshaft position sensor.
    o. Knock sensor.
    p. Starter and alternator connectors.
17. **On models equipped with manual transaxle,** remove clutch slave cylinder from transaxle and position aside. **Do not disconnect hydraulic lines.**
18. **On all models,** disconnect transaxle control cables from transaxle.
19. **On models equipped with power steering,** remove pump from engine with hoses attached and position aside.

20. **On models equipped with A/C,** remove compressor with hoses attached and position aside.
21. **On all models,** disconnect front exhaust pipe from exhaust manifold.
22. Disconnect driveshafts from transaxle.
23. Attach suitable engine lifting equipment, then remove rear mount through bolt and insulator.
24. Disconnect ground strap.
25. Remove right side mount through bolt and insulator.
26. Remove left side mount attaching bolts, then the mount.
27. Carefully lift engine and transaxle assembly from vehicle and place on suitable stand.
28. Remove starter from engine.
29. **On models equipped with power steering,** remove power steering pump adjusting strut.
30. **On models equipped with A/C,** remove compressor mounting bracket.
31. **On models equipped with automatic transaxle,** remove torque converter clutch mounting bolts.
32. **On all models,** remove transaxle from engine.
33. Reverse procedure to install.

INTAKE MANIFOLD
REPLACE

Refer to "Cylinder Head, Replace" for procedure.

EXHAUST MANIFOLD
REPLACE

Refer to "Cylinder Head, Replace" for procedure.

CYLINDER HEAD
REPLACE
REMOVAL

1. Remove righthand engine undercover.
2. Drain engine coolant.
3. Disconnect front exhaust pipe, then oxygen sensor electrical connector.
4. **On models equipped with automatic transaxle,** disconnect throttle cable.
5. **On all models,** disconnect accelerator cable.
6. Remove PCV hose.
7. Remove air cleaner assembly with air intake connector.
8. Position suitable fuel container, then

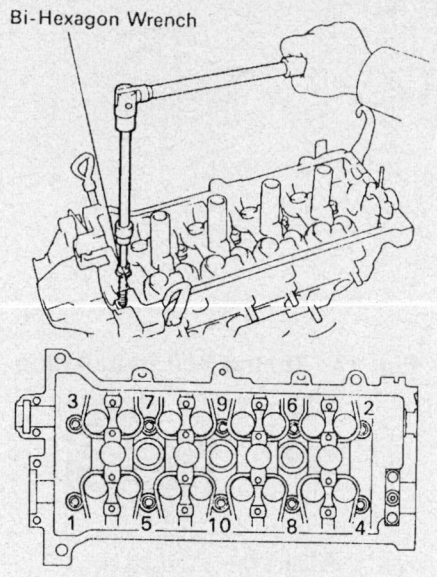

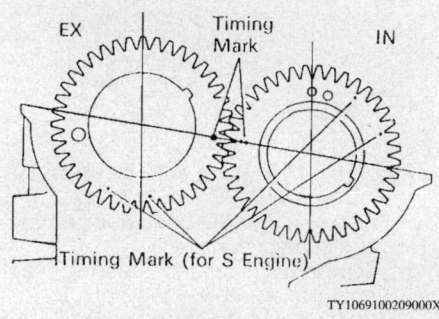

Fig. 5 Cylinder head bolt loosening sequence

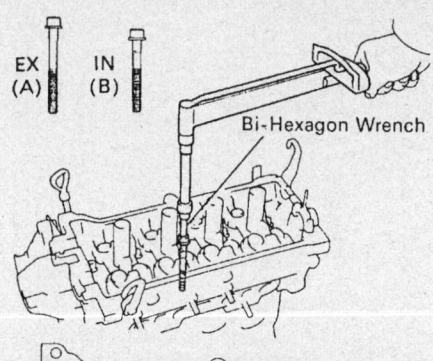

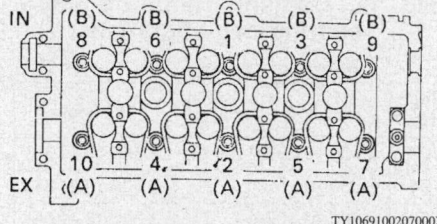

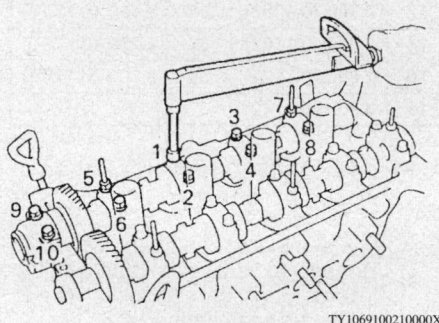

Fig. 6 Cylinder head bolt tightening sequence

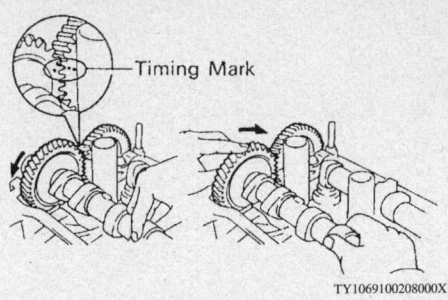

Fig. 7 Intake & exhaust camshaft timing marks

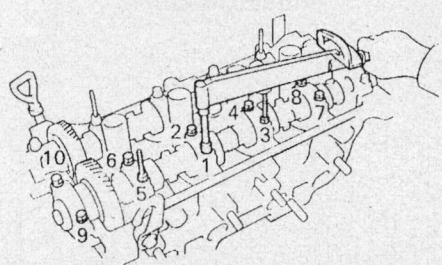

Fig. 10 Exhaust camshaft bolt tightening sequence

Fig. 8 Intake & exhaust camshaft alignment

Fig. 9 Intake camshaft bolt tightening sequence

disconnect fuel return hose. Remove union bolt, gasket and disconnect fuel inlet hose.

9. **On models equipped with power steering,** remove power steering belt, pump attaching bolts and position pump aside. Remove pump bracket.

10. **On models equipped with A/C, less power steering,** loosen idler pulley nut. Remove drive belt, then the idler pulley bracket.

11. **On all models,** remove distributor or ignition coils with spark plug wires.

12. Remove spark plugs.

13. Disconnect vacuum hoses from throttle opener, EGR valve, EGR vacuum modulator, charcoal canister and idle-up vacuum switching valve.

14. Disconnect EGR gas temperature sensor electrical connector, then remove sensor and gasket.

15. Remove EGR vacuum modulator and bracket, then EGR valve and gasket.

16. Disconnect water temperature sender gauge, water temperature sensor, water temperature switch and fan water temperature switch electrical connectors.

17. Disconnect two radiator hoses, water inlet hose, water outlet hose, water by-pass hose and two BVSV vacuum hoses.

18. Remove water inlet and outlet housings.

19. Remove exhaust manifold heat insulator, then manifold and gasket.

20. Disconnect ACV electrical connector and air hose, remove attaching bolts and ground strap, then remove ACV and O-ring.

21. Remove throttle body assembly.

22. Remove delivery pipe and injectors.

23. **On models equipped with power steering,** disconnect two idle-up air hoses from air pipe.

24. **On all models,** remove air pipe attaching bolts and pipe.

25. Remove intake manifold stay, disconnect idle-up vacuum hose, brake booster vacuum hose and vacuum sensor hose, remove intake manifold attaching nuts and bolts, then manifold and gasket.

26. Remove oil filler cap, then the five cylinder head cover attaching cap nuts and seal washers.

27. Remove cover and gasket, then the No. 2 timing belt cover.

28. Loosen alternator pivot and adjusting bolt, then remove belt.

29. Remove No. 3 timing belt cover from No. 1 timing belt cover.

30. If reusing timing belt, place installation alignment marks on timing belt and camshaft timing pulley.

31. Loosen No. 1 idler pulley mount bolt, then shift pulley as far left as possible and temporarily tighten bolt. Remove timing belt.

32. Remove No. 2 idler pulley attaching bolt and pulley. **Support timing belt, ensure crankshaft timing pulley and timing belt do not shift. Do not allow timing belt to come in contact with oil, water or dust.**

33. Hold camshaft hexagonal portion, then remove attaching bolt and timing pulley.

34. Remove camshafts as follows:

  a. **Camshafts must be held level during removal or head or camshaft may be damaged.**

  b. Set intake camshaft, ensuring intake camshaft gear service bolt holes are directly above, **Fig. 1.** Lift exhaust camshaft level and evenly push intake camshaft No. 2 and No. 4 cylinder cam lobes toward valve lifters.

  c. Remove Nos. 1 and 4 bearing caps.

  d. Install service bolt 6 mm thread diameter, 1.0 mm thread pitch and 16–20 mm (.63–.79 inch) long to secure intake camshaft sub-gear to main gear, **Fig. 2.**

  e. Loosen and remove eight No. 3 bearing caps in several passes in sequence shown, **Fig. 3.**

  f. Remove four bearing caps and exhaust camshaft. **Camshaft must be removed straight and level. Do not pry or force camshaft to remove.**

  g. Loosen and remove eight No. 3 bearing caps in several passes in sequence shown, **Fig. 4.**

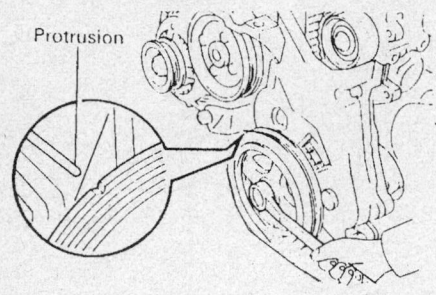

Fig. 11 Timing belt to crankshaft pulley alignment

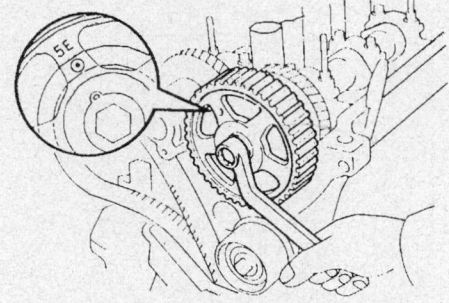

Fig. 12 Camshaft timing pulley to bearing cap alignment

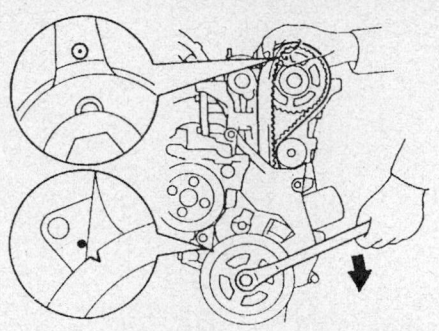

Fig. 13 Timing belt installation

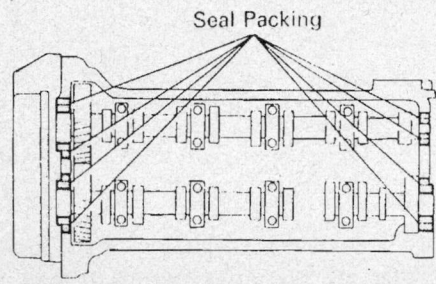

Fig. 14 Cylinder head cover packing locations

New shim thickness		mm (in.)	
Shim No.	Thickness	Shim No.	Thickness
02	2.500 (0.0984)	20	2.950 (0.1161)
04	2.550 (0.1004)	22	3.000 (0.1181)
06	2.600 (0.1024)	24	3.050 (0.1201)
08	2.650 (0.1043)	26	3.100 (0.1220)
10	2.700 (0.1063)	28	3.150 (0.1240)
12	2.750 (0.1083)	30	3.200 (0.1260)
14	2.800 (0.1102)	32	3.250 (0.1280)
16	2.850 (0.1122)	34	3.300 (0.1299)
18	2.900 (0.1142)		

Fig. 15 Valve shim thickness chart

Fig. 16 Piston & rod assembly

h. Remove four bearing caps and intake camshaft. **Camshaft must be removed straight and level. Do not pry or force camshaft to remove.**

35. Using suitable 8 mm bi-hexagon wrench, loosen ten cylinder head bolts in several passes using sequence shown in **Fig. 5.**

36. Lift cylinder head from dowels to remove.

INSTALLATION

1. Thoroughly clean all parts, before installing.
2. Apply clean engine oil to sliding and rotating parts.
3. Replace all gaskets and oil seals.
4. Install cylinder head to block, ensure installation direction is correct.
5. Apply clean engine oil to exhaust and intake bolts, then using suitable 8 mm bi-hexagon wrench, **torque** to 33 ft. lbs. in several passes using sequence shown in **Fig. 6.** Mark front of each bolt with paint, then tighten ten cylinder head bolts an additional 90° in sequence, ensure painted mark is at a 90° angle to front.
6. Install camshafts as follows:
   a. **Camshafts must be held level during installation or head or camshaft may be damaged.**
   b. Apply clean engine oil to trust portion of intake camshaft thrust portion.
   c. Install intake camshaft so intake camshaft gear service bolt is directly above camshaft, **Fig. 7.**
   d. Install four bearing caps, then temporarily tighten bearing caps alternately left and right.
   e. Apply clean engine oil to trust por-

tion of exhaust camshaft.
   f. Engage exhaust camshaft gear to intake gear by aligning timing marks on each gear, **Fig. 8.**
   g. Roll exhaust camshaft down onto bearing journals while engaging gear.
   h. Carefully push exhaust camshaft gear without applying force.
   i. Install four bearing caps, then temporarily tighten bearing caps alternately left and right uniformly, until bearing caps are snug with cylinder head.
   j. Remove service bolt.
   k. Clean No. 2 bearing cap and cylinder head installed surface with suitable cleaner, then apply suitable seal packing to No. 2 bearing cap.
   l. Install No. 2 bearing cap to proper location, ensuring there is no gap between cylinder head and bearing cap contact surface.
   m. Temporarily tighten bearing cap bolts, alternately from right to left uniformly, then install camshaft housing plug.
   n. Install and uniformly **torque** ten bearing cap bolts, in several passes in sequence, **Fig. 9,** to 9 ft. lbs.
   o. Apply suitable MP grease to camshaft oil seal lip, then install as far as deepest part of cylinder head.
   p. Clean No. 1 bearing cap and cylinder head installed surface with suitable cleaner, then apply suitable seal packing to No. 1 bearing cap.
   q. Install No. 1 bearing cap to proper location, ensuring there is no gap

between cylinder head and bearing cap contact surface.
   r. Temporarily tighten bearing cap bolts, alternately from right to left uniformly.
   s. Install and uniformly **torque** ten bearing cap bolts, in several passes in sequence, **Fig. 10,** to 9 ft. lbs.
   t. Turn camshaft one revolution, ensuring camshaft gear timing marks are aligned.
7. Align camshaft knock pin with pulley knock pin groove and slide pulley. Hold camshaft hexagonal portion and install bolt. Tighten to specifications.
8. Install No. 2 idler pulley.
9. Install timing belt as follows:
   a. Turn crankshaft pulley, then holding timing belt, align groove with belt installation protrusion of No. 1 timing belt cover, **Fig. 11.**
   b. Turn camshaft and align camshaft timing pulley hole with bearing cap belt installation mark, **Fig. 12.**
   c. Coil timing belt around camshaft timing pulley, turn crankshaft pulley, then install belt to camshaft timing pulley, **Fig. 13.**
   d. Loosen No. 1 idler pulley mount bolt until pulley is moved slightly by spring tension.
   e. Turn crankshaft pulley two revolutions from TDC to TDC. **Always turn crankshaft clockwise.**
   f. Ensure pulleys align with timing marks.
10. Install No. 3 timing belt cover.
11. Install alternator drive belt.
12. Install No. 2 timing belt cover.

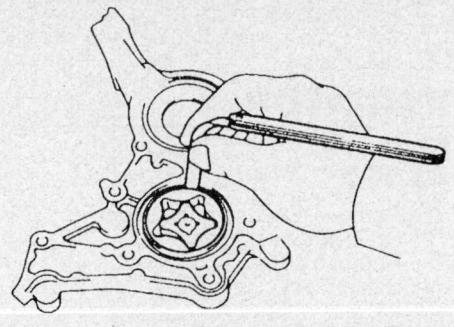

Fig. 17 Oil pump body clearance inspection

TY1099100023000X

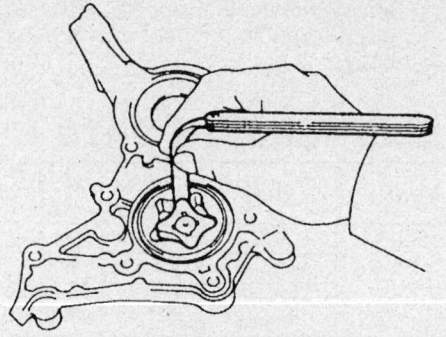

TY1099100024000X

Fig. 18 Oil pump tip clearance inspection

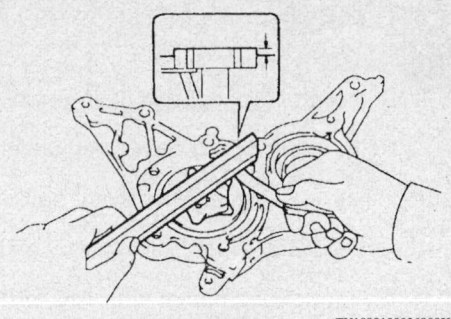

TY1099100026000X

Fig. 19 Oil pump side clearance inspection

13. Apply suitable seal packing to cylinder head cover, **Fig. 14,** then install gasket and cover. Tighten to specifications.
14. Install intake manifold and gasket, connect idle-up vacuum hose, brake booster vacuum hose and vacuum sensor hose, then install manifold stay and tighten attaching nuts and bolts to specifications.
15. Connect two idle-up air hoses, then install air pipe.
16. Install fuel injectors and delivery pipe.
17. Install throttle body.
18. Install ACV.
19. Install exhaust manifold and gasket and heat insulator.
20. Install water inlet and outlet housings, connect two radiator hoses, water inlet hose, heater outlet hose, water bypass hose, BVSV vacuum hose from throttle body P port and from charcoal canister.
21. Connect water temperature sender, water temperature sensor, water temperature switch and fan water temperature switch electrical connectors.
22. Install EGR valve, vacuum modulator and pipe.
23. **On California models,** install EGR temperature sensor and gasket.
24. **On all models,** connect vacuum hose to throttle opener, EGR valve, EGR vacuum modulator, charcoal canister and idle-up vacuum hoses.
25. Install spark plugs. Tighten to specifications.
26. Install distributor, then spark plug wires.
27. **On models equipped with A/C and less power steering,** install idler pulley bracket.
28. **On models equipped with power steering,** install power steering pump bracket and pump, then install belt.
29. **On all models,** connect fuel hoses.
30. Install air cleaner assembly and air intake connector.
31. Install PCV hose.
32. Install accelerator cable and adjust.
33. **On models equipped with automatic transaxle,** connect throttle cable and adjust.
34. **On all models,** connect front exhaust pipe and tighten to specifications.
35. Install righthand engine undercover.

36. Refill engine coolant, then start engine and inspect for leaks.

CAMSHAFT LOBE LIFT SPECIFICATIONS

Year	Cam Height Limit, Inch.	
	Intake	Exhaust
1996	1.6283	1.6205
1997–98	1.6344–1.6383	1.6146–1.6185

VALVE CLEARANCE SPECIFICATIONS

Year	Stem-To-Guide Clearance, Inch	
	Intake	Exhaust
1996–98	.006–.010	.012–.016

VALVE ADJUSTMENT

These engines use an adjusting shim to adjust the valves.
1. With No. 1 piston at TDC on compression stroke, measure and record clearance between valve lifter and camshaft: No. 1 intake and exhaust, No. 2 intake and No. 3 exhaust.
2. Turn crankshaft in normal direction of rotation one full revolution (360°) and measure and record clearance between valve lifter and camshaft: No. 2 exhaust, No. 3 intake and No. 4 intake and exhaust.
3. Turn crankshaft to position camshaft cam lobe on adjusting valve upward.
4. Position valve lifter notch, then using suitable small screwdriver, remove adjusting shim.
5. Using suitable micrometer, measure thickness of removed shim.
6. New shim thickness equals measured valve clearance less .006–.010 inch on intake valves or .012–.016 inch on exhaust valves, plus thickness of used shim.
7. Select new shim with thickness as close as possible to values calculated in step 6, **Fig. 15.**
8. Install new shim, then recheck valve clearance.

VALVE GUIDES

1. Using a suitable tool and hammer, strike valve guide bushing to break it off at cylinder head casting.
2. Heat cylinder head to 176–212°F (80–100°C).
3. Using suitable valve guide removal tool, tap out bushing.
4. Install snap ring on new valve guide, then install new valve guide using tool as outlined above and driving in from the reverse side of removal.
5. Ream new valve guide, if necessary. Refer to "Valve Specifications" for stem clearances.

HYDRAULIC LIFTERS
REPLACE

Check lifters for excessive wear and/or damage. Replace worn or damaged valve lifters as required. Lubricate hydraulic valve lifter before installation.

TIMING BELT
REPLACE

Refer to "Cylinder Head, Replace" for timing belt replacement procedure.

CAMSHAFT
REPLACE

Refer to "Cylinder Head, Replace" for camshaft removal procedures.

PISTON & ROD ASSEMBLY

When assembling piston onto connecting rod, ensure mark on top of piston and mark on connecting rod are on same side, **Fig. 16.** When installing piston and connecting rod assembly, ensure mark on top of piston is facing toward front of engine.

MAIN & ROD BEARINGS

Main and connecting rod bearings are available in standard and undersizes of .010 inch (.25 mm).

OIL PAN
REPLACE

1. Remove oil dipstick and drain engine oil.
2. Remove timing belt as outlined under "Timing Belt Replace."
3. Install suitable engine lifting equipment.
4. Remove crankshaft timing pulley and oil pump pulley.
5. **On models equipped with A/C,** disconnect compressor electrical connector, then remove compressor attaching bolts and position compressor aside. Remove compressor mounting bracket.
6. **On all models,** disconnect oxygen sensor electrical connector, then disconnect front exhaust pipe stay and exhaust pipe.
7. Remove two oil pan attaching nuts and eight bolts, then using suitable tool, cut off oil pan sealer and remove pan.
8. Remove oil strainer and O-ring.
9. Remove pressure regulator valve.
10. Remove oil pump attaching bolts and tension spring bracket.
11. Using suitable soft faced hammer, remove oil pump and O-ring.
12. Reverse procedure to install.

OIL PUMP
REPLACE

Refer to "Oil Pan, Replace" for procedure.

OIL PUMP SERVICE

1. Using a suitable feeler gauge, measure clearance between driven rotor and pump case, **Fig. 17.**
2. Standard clearance should be .0039–.0079 inch. If feeler gauge clearance obtained exceeds specified limits, replace oil pump rotor set and/or pump case.
3. Using a suitable feeler gauge, measure clearance between both rotor tips, **Fig. 18.** Clearance should be .0012–.0079 inch. If feeler gauge clearance obtained exceeds specified limit, replace oil pump rotor set.
4. Place suitable straightedge across pump opening and measure side clearance, **Fig. 19.** Side clearance should be .1145–.1169 inch. If clear-

ance is greater than specifications, replace oil pump rotor set and/or pump body.

BELT TENSION DATA

Year	Belt	New, lbs.	Used, lbs.
1996	A/C	150–180	90–130
	Alternator	140–180	80–120
	Power Steer.	135–185	80–120
1997–98	A/C	140–190	80–120
	Alternator	140–180	80–120
	Power Steer.	140–180	80–120

COOLING SYSTEM BLEED

These engines do not require a specified bleed procedure. After filling cooling system, run engine to operating temperature with radiator/pressure cap off. Air will then be automatically bled through cap opening.

THERMOSTAT
REPLACE

1. **On Paseo models,** remove air intake connector.
2. **On all models,** remove water inlet attaching nuts, then remove inlet, thermostat and gasket.
3. Reverse procedure to install.

WATER PUMP
REPLACE

1. Remove right side undercover, then drain engine coolant into a suitable container.
2. Remove alternator assembly.
3. Remove intake manifold support bracket.
4. Disconnect water inlet, heater inlet and water hoses.
5. Remove dipstick tube.
6. Remove alternator adjusting bracket.
7. Disconnect coolant hose from intake manifold.
8. Remove water pump attaching nuts and bolts, then the water pump.

9. Reverse procedure to install. Tighten water pump mounting bolts to specifications.

RADIATOR
REPLACE
PASEO

1. Remove engine undercovers.
2. Drain engine coolant.
3. Remove air intake connector.
4. Disconnect cooling fan motor connector.
5. Remove oxygen sensor connector.
6. Disconnect coolant reservoir hose.
7. Disconnect radiator hoses.
8. **On models equipped with automatic transaxle,** disconnect transaxle oil cooler hoses.
9. **On all models,** remove radiator supports and radiator with cooling fans.
10. Reverse procedure to install.

TERCEL

1. Remove engine undercovers.
2. Drain engine coolant into a suitable container.
3. Remove air intake connector.
4. Remove coolant reservoir tank assembly and hose.
5. Disconnect No. 1 cooling fan connector.
6. **On models equipped with A/C,** disconnect No. 2 cooling fan connector.
7. **On all models,** disconnect upper radiator hose at radiator and lower radiator hose at water inlet.
8. **On models equipped with automatic transaxle,** disconnect transaxle oil cooler hoses.
9. **On all models,** remove radiator supports, radiator with cooling fans and lower radiator hose attached.
10. Reverse procedure to install.

FUEL PUMP
REPLACE

1. Remove rear seat cushion.
2. Remove floor service hole attaching screws, then remove cover.
3. Disconnect fuel pump electrical connector.
4. Disconnect fuel lines.
5. Remove fuel pump attaching bolts, then the fuel pump.
6. Reverse procedure to install.

FUEL FILTER
REPLACE

1. Place suitable container under fuel filter/hose connection.
2. Slowly disconnect fuel hose from fuel filter outlet. **Place shop towel over fuel hose to prevent fuel spillage on engine.**
3. Remove fuel filter, then plug fuel hose.
4. Replace gasket and reverse procedure to install.

TIGHTENING SPECIFICATIONS

Year	Component	Torque, Ft. Lbs.
1996–98	A/C Compressor	18
	A/C Compressor Bracket	20
	Air Pipe To Intake Manifold	48①
	Alternator Bracket	13
	Camshaft Bearing Cap	108①
	Camshaft Timing Pulley	37
	Clutch Release Cylinder	108①
	Connecting Rod Cap	29
	Crankshaft Pulley	112
	Cylinder Head Bolt	②
	Driveplate To Torque Converter	18
	EGR Pipe Assembly To EGR Valve	29
	EGR Pipe Assembly To Exhaust Manifold	22
	EGR Temperature Sensor	15
	EGR Valve	13
	Exhaust Manifold	35
	Exhaust Pipe Stay	14
	Flywheel To Crankshaft	65
	Front Exhaust Pipe	46
	Fuel Inlet Hose	22
	Fuel Pipe & Hose To Pump Bracket	22
	Fuel Pump Bracket	30①
	Heat Insulator	72①
	Idler Pulley Bracket To Cylinder Block	20
	Idler Pulley Bracket To Cylinder Head	27
	Intake Manifold	14
	Intake Manifold To ACV	72①
	LH Engine Mount Bracket To Engine Mount	35
	LH Engine Mount Bracket To Ground Strap	35
	LH Engine Mount Bracket To Transaxle	47
	Main Bearing Cap	42
	No. 1 Idler Pulley	13
	No. 2 Crankshaft Pulley	14
	No. 2 Idler Pulley	20
	Oil Drain Plug	18
	Oil Filter Union	18
	Oil Pan	72①
	Oil Pressure Regulator Valve	22
	Oil Pump	60①
	Oil Pump Pulley	27
	Oil Strainer	84①
	Power Steering Pump Adjusting Strut To Cylinder Block	15
	Power Steering Pump Adjusting Strut To Pump Housing	29
	Power Steering Pump Bracket	32
	Radiator Support	108①
	Rear Engine Mount Bracket To Engine Mount	47
	Rear Engine Mount Bracket To Transaxle	35
	Rear Oil Seal Retainer	60①
	RH Engine Mount Bracket	43
	RH Engine Mount To Bracket	47

5E-FE 1.5L ENGINE

Continued

TIGHTENING SPECIFICATIONS—Continued

Year	Component	Torque, Ft. Lbs.
1996–98	RH Engine Mount To RH Crossmember	54
	Spark Plug	13
	Valve Cover	60①
	Water Inlet	43①
	Water Outlet Housing	13
	Water Pump	13

① — Inch lbs.
② — Refer to "Cylinder Head, Replace" for procedure.

Clutch & Manual Transaxle

NOTE: On Air Bag Equipped Models, Refer To "Air Bag System Precautions" Located In The Front Of This Manual For System Disarming & Arming Procedures.

INDEX

PRECAUTIONS

AIR BAG SYSTEMS

Refer to "Air Bag System Precautions" in the front of this manual for system disarming and arming procedures.

BATTERY GROUND CABLE

Prior to service, disconnect battery ground cable and isolate as required.

ADJUSTMENTS

CLUTCH PEDAL

1. Measure clutch pedal height as shown, **Fig. 1.**
2. Clutch pedal height should be 5.69–6.08 inches on 4-speed transaxles and 5.51–5.91 inches on 5-speed transaxles, measured from the asphalt sheet.
3. If clutch pedal height is not as specified, loosen clutch pedal locknut, then rotate stopper bolt on models less cruise control or clutch switch on models equipped with cruise control, until specified height is achieved.
4. Tighten locknut.
5. Check clutch pedal freeplay by depressing clutch pedal until resistance is felt. Freeplay should be .197–.591 inch. Pushrod play at top of pedal should be .039–.197 inch.
6. If necessary to adjust freeplay, loosen

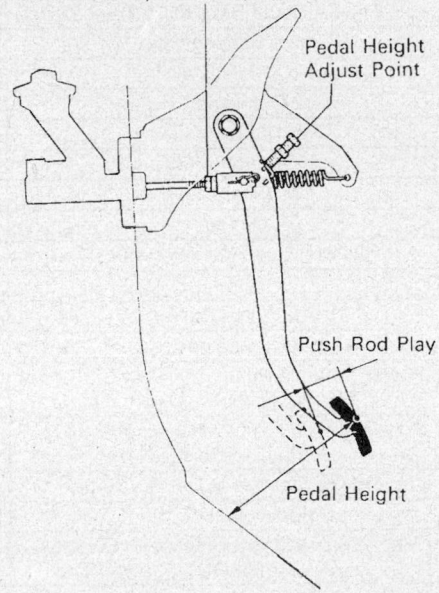

Push Rod Play and Freeplay Adjust Point

Pedal Height Adjust Point

Push Rod Play

Pedal Height

TY5049100018000X

Fig. 1 Clutch pedal adjustment

locknut and rotate pushrod until freeplay is as specified.
7. Tighten locknut.
8. Ensure clutch pedal height and freeplay are as specified, then reinstall air duct and finish panel.

HYDRAULIC SYSTEM SERVICE

CLUTCH SLAVE CYLINDER, REPLACE

1. Place suitable container below slave cylinder.
2. Using tube wrench tool No. 09023-00100, or equivalent, disconnect clutch tube from cylinder.
3. Remove slave cylinder attaching bolts, then the slave cylinder.
4. Reverse procedure to install.

CLUTCH MASTER CYLINDER, REPLACE

1. Remove fluid from cylinder with syringe.
2. Place suitable container below cylinder, then using tube wrench tool No. 09023-00100, or equivalent, disconnect clutch tube from cylinder.
3. Remove clip, clevis pin and wave washer.
4. Remove master cylinder attaching nuts, then pull rearward to remove.
5. Reverse procedure to install.

CLUTCH SYSTEM BLEED

If any service is performed on the clutch system or air is suspected in the clutch lines, bleed the system.
1. Fill clutch reservoir with suitable brake

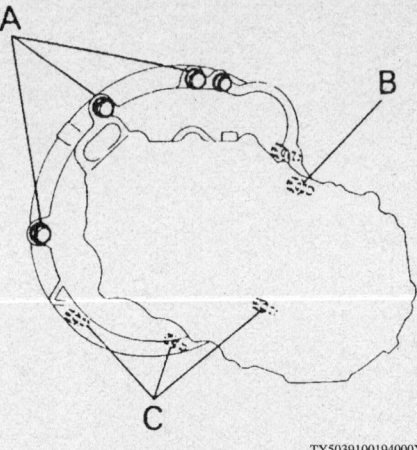

Fig. 3 Transaxle to engine bolt tightening

sure clutch disc and pressure plate remain aligned.

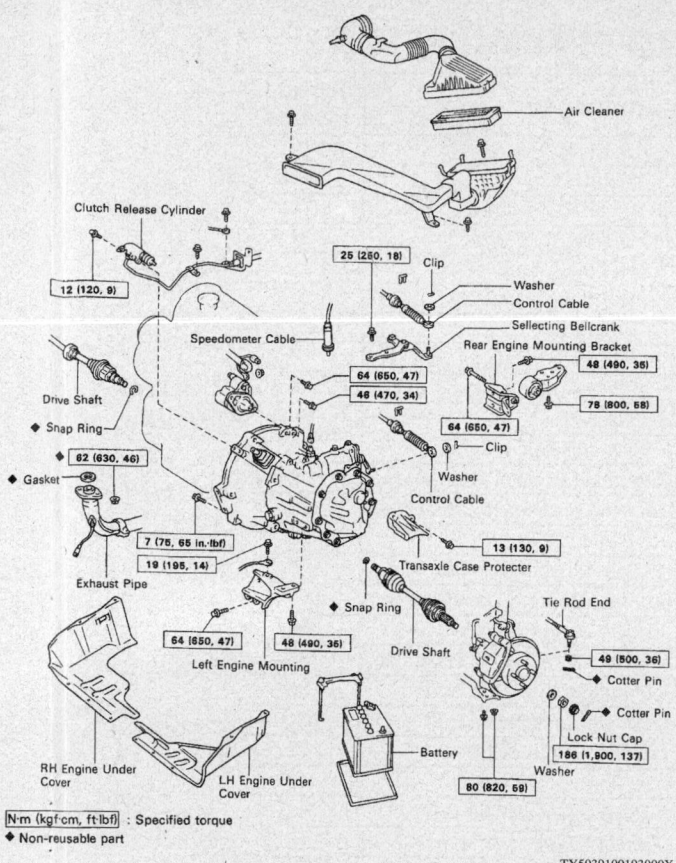

Fig. 2 Exploded view of manual transaxle assembly

fluid. **Do not allow fluid to come in contact with painted surfaces.**

2. Check reservoir frequently and add fluid as required.
3. Connect vinyl tube to bleeder plug, then insert other tube end in half full container of brake fluid.
4. Slowly pump clutch pedal several times.
5. While depressing pedal, loosen bleeder plug until fluid runs out, then close bleeder plug.
6. Repeat procedure until air bubbles are not evident in the fluid. **Do not reuse the fluid that was bled.**

CLUTCH
REPLACE

1. Remove transaxle assembly as outlined under "Transaxle, Replace."
2. Place installation alignment on clutch cover and flywheel.
3. Loosen each set bolt one turn at a time until spring tension is released.
4. Remove clutch cover attaching bolts, then remove cover and disc.
5. Remove release bearing, fork and boot.

6. Using suitable calipers, measure clutch disc rivet head depth. Minimum rivet depth should be .012 inch. If not as indicated, replace clutch disc.
7. Using suitable dial indicator, measure flywheel runout. Maximum runout should be .004 inch. If not as indicated, replace flywheel.
8. Measure clutch disc runout. Maximum runout is .031 inch. If not as indicated, replace disc.
9. Using suitable calipers, measure diaphragm spring depth and width. Maximum depth is .024 inch and maximum width is .0197 inch. If measurements are not as indicated, replace clutch cover.
10. Reverse procedure to install, noting the following:
    a. **On Tercel models,** using clutch guide tool No. 09301–00210 or equivalent, install clutch disc.
    b. **On Paseo models,** using clutch guide tool No. 09301–32010, or equivalent, install clutch disc.
    c. **On all models,** match clutch cover and flywheel alignment marks, then tighten clutch cover bolts to specification in a criss-cross pattern. En-

TRANSAXLE
REPLACE

Refer to **Fig. 2** when replacing manual transaxle.

1. Remove battery, then the air cleaner assembly with hose.
2. Remove clutch release cylinder and tube clamp, then disconnect back-up lamp switch connector.
3. Remove clips and washers, then the control cable retainers.
4. Remove clutch release cylinder bracket with ground strap.
5. Remove upper transaxle mounting bolts.
6. Install engine support fixture.
7. Raise and support vehicle, then remove undercovers.
8. Drain transaxle fluid, then remove front exhaust pipe.
9. Disconnect speedometer cable, then the driveshafts.
10. Remove front and rear engine mounting brackets, then the starter attaching bolts and starter.
11. Slightly raise engine and transaxle assembly, using suitable jacks, then disconnect left engine mount.
12. Remove transaxle to engine attaching bolts, then lower left side of engine and separate transaxle from engine.
13. Reverse procedure to install, noting the following:
    a. Align input shaft spline with clutch disc, then install transaxle to engine.
    b. **Torque** transaxle to engine attaching bolt A to 34 ft. lbs. bolt B, to 17 ft. lbs. and bolt C to 65 inch lbs. **Fig. 3.**

TIGHTENING SPECIFICATIONS

Year	Component	Torque, Ft. Lbs.
1996–98	Back-Up Lamp Switch	30
	Bleeder Plug	72④
	Clutch Cover To Flywheel	14
	Clutch Housing To Engine	34
	Clutch Line Union	11
	Clutch Release Cylinder	108④
	Drain Plug	29
	Drive Axle Bearing Locknut	②
	Exhaust Pipe To Manifold	46
	Filler Plug	29
	Flywheel Bolt	65
	Left Engine Mounting Bracket To Frame	47
	Left Engine Mounting Bracket To Transaxle	35
	Lower Ball Joint To Arm	59
	Master Cylinder Installation Nut	①
	Output Shaft Front Bearing Lock Plate	96④
	Rear Engine Mount Bracket	58
	Rear Engine Mounting Bracket To Transaxle	35
	Rear Engine Mounting Insulator To Body	58
	Release Cylinder Installation Bolt	96④
	Reverse Idler Shaft Lock Bolt	22
	Reverse Shift Arm Bracket	13
	Selecting Bellcrank Mounting Bolt	18
	Shift & Select Lever Assembly	14
	Shift Fork To Shift Fork Shaft	12
	Shift Interlock Plate Lock Bolt	22
	Tie Rod End To Steering Knuckle	36
	Transaxle Case Protector	108④
	Transaxle Case To Case Cover	13
	Transaxle Case To Engine	③
	Transaxle Case To Transaxle	22
	Wheel Lug Nut	76

① — 1996 Paseo, 69 inch lbs.; Tercel & 1997 Paseo, 108 inch lbs.

② — 1996 Tercel, 166 ft. lbs., Paseo & 1997 Tercel, 159 ft. lbs.

③ — Refer to "Transaxle, Replace."

④ — Inch lbs.

Rear Axle & Suspension

INDEX

HUB & BEARING
REPLACE

1. Raise and support rear of vehicle, then remove wheel and tire assembly.
2. Remove grease cap, cotter pin, nut lock and adjusting nut, **Fig. 1.**
3. Remove brake drum/hub assembly with outer bearing and thrust washer from axle shaft.
4. Using a suitable screwdriver, pry oil seal from hub, then remove inner bearing.
5. Inspect inner and outer bearings and races for wear and damage. If necessary, replace race(s) with suitable removal and installation tools.
6. Clean and repack bearings and fill inside of axle hub and grease cap with multi-purpose grease.
7. Install inner bearing in axle hub, then install new oil seal using suitable seal installer. Grease oil seal lips with multi-purpose grease.
8. Install brake drum/hub assembly on axle shaft, then install outer bearing in hub. Apply multi-purpose grease between outer bearing and thrust washer surface, then install thrust washer.
9. Install adjusting nut and tighten to specification, then rotate brake drum/hub assembly to seat bearings. Loosen adjusting nut until hand tight. **Ensure brakes are not dragging.**
10. Attach suitable spring scale to wheel stud and measure oil seal rotation frictional force. Oil seal frictional force should be approximately .9 lbs.
11. With spring scale still attached, tighten adjusting nut until bearing preload is 0–2.6 lbs. above the oil seal frictional force determined in step 10.
12. Install locknut, cotter pin and grease cap. **If cotter pin will not line up with axle shaft hole, tighten adjusting nut to align.**
13. Adjust rear brakes as necessary.

AXLE BEAM
REPLACE

1. Remove rear axle hubs as outlined previously.
2. Remove left and right brake shoes.
3. Disconnect parking brake from backing plate.
4. Using suitable tool, disconnect brake tube from cylinder, then disconnect tube from axle beam.
5. Remove backing plate.

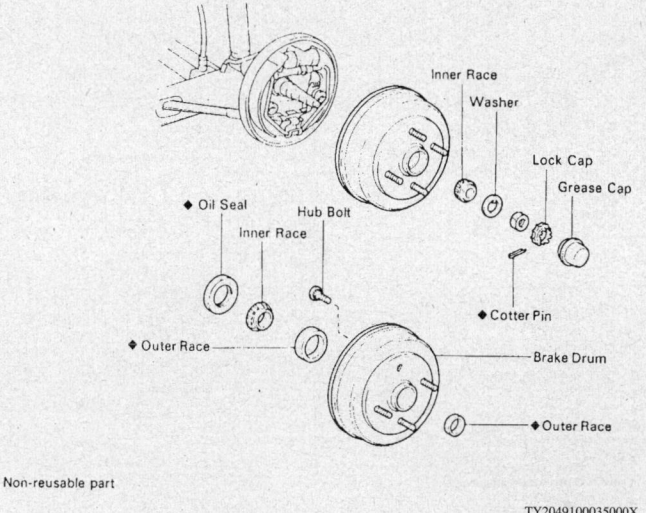

Fig. 1   Exploded view of rear wheel bearing

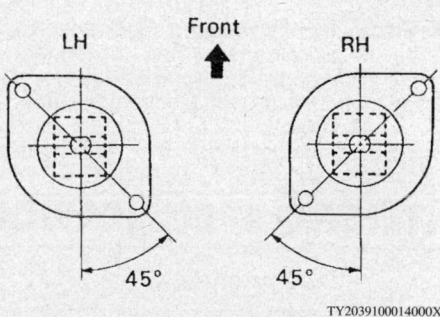

Fig. 2   Suspension support to shock absorber lower bracket alignment. Paseo

6. Remove lateral control rod attaching nut and bolt, then disconnect rod from body.
7. Remove lateral rod from axle beam.
8. Support axle beam, using suitable equipment.
9. Remove shock absorber lower attaching nuts and bolts.
10. Remove axle beam attaching nuts and bolts, then remove beam.
11. Reverse procedure to install.

SHOCK ABSORBER
REPLACE

Refer to "Coil Spring, Replace" for shock absorber replacement procedures.

COIL SPRING
REPLACE
PASEO

1. Remove rear seat cushion, seat back and seat lock striker.
2. Remove quarter trim.
3. Disconnect rear seat belt.
4. Disconnect package tray trim.
5. Remove room partition board.
6. Raise and support rear of vehicle.
7. Remove lower shock attaching nut and bolt, then two upper attaching nuts.
8. Remove shock absorber and coil spring assembly.
9. Using suitable tool, compress coil spring.
10. Remove spring attaching nut, washer, suspension bumper and coil spring.
11. Reverse procedure to install, noting the following:
    a. Align suspension support with shock absorber bracket, **Fig. 2.**
    b. Tighten attaching nuts and bolts to specification.
    c. After repairs, bounce rear of vehicle several time to stabilize suspension.

TERCEL

1. Remove rear seat back and cushion.
2. Working inside vehicle, remove shock absorber cover.
3. Disconnect brake hose from wheel cylinder or caliper, then disconnect brake hose from shock absorber.

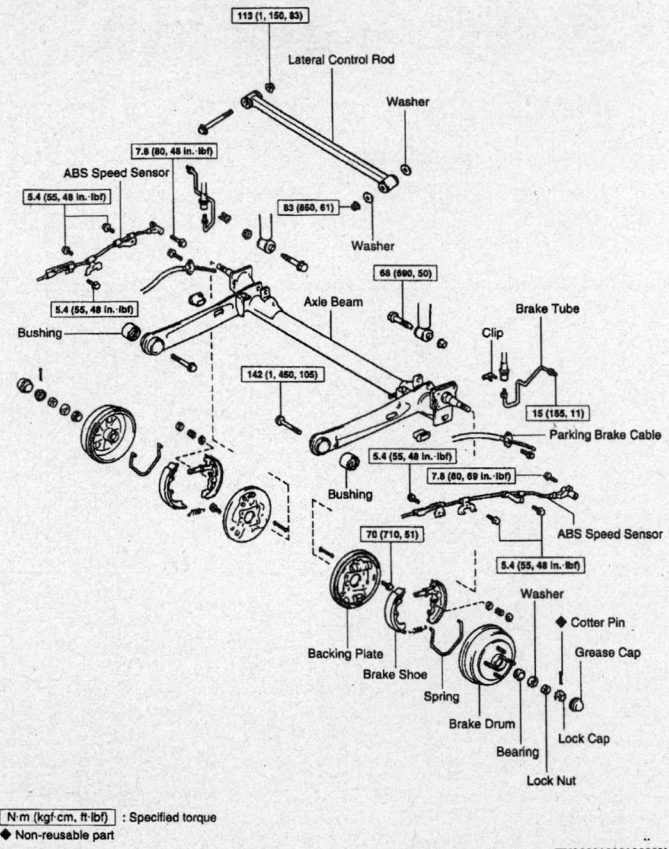

N·m (kgf·cm, ft·lbf) : Specified torque
◆ Non-reusable part

TY2039100013000X

Fig. 3 Exploded view of rear suspension. Tercel

4. Working inside vehicle, loosen nut securing suspension support to shock absorber, **Fig. 3. Do not remove nut at this time.**

5. Remove bolts securing shock absorber to axle carrier, then disconnect shock absorber from carrier.
6. Working inside vehicle, remove nuts securing suspension support to vehicle body, then remove shock absorber.
7. Install a bolt and two nuts in shock absorber lower mounting bracket and clamp unit in a suitable vise using lower mounting bracket as clamping surface.
8. Using a suitable spring compressor, compress coil spring.
9. Remove nut securing suspension support to shock absorber, then remove suspension support, coil spring, insulator and spring bumper. Shock absorber is filled with colorless, odorless and non-poisonous high pressure gas. Upon removal, handle shock absorber with care. Do not score or scratch exposed part of piston rod or allow paint or oil to come in contact with it. Do not rotate piston rod and cylinder assembly with shock absorber fully extended. When discarding shock absorber, drill a small hole in bottom of cylinder to relieve pressure.
10. Reverse procedure to install.

LATERAL CONTROL BAR
REPLACE

1. Raise and support vehicle.
2. Remove lateral control rod attaching nut, retainer and bushing.
3. Disconnect lateral control rod from rear axle beam.
4. Remove bushing and retainer.
5. Remove lateral rod to body attaching nut and bolt, then remove rod.
6. Reverse procedure to install.

TIGHTENING SPECIFICATIONS

Year	Component	Torque, Ft. Lbs.
1996–98	Backing Plate To Axle Beam	51
	Body To Axle Beam	105
	Brake Tube To Flexible Tube	11
	Brake Tube To Wheel Cylinder	11
	Lateral Control Rod To Axle Beam	61
	Lateral Control Rod To Body	83
	Parking Brake Cable To Backing Plate	72①
	Piston Rod To Suspension Support	25
	Shock Absorber To Axle Beam	50
	Suspension Support To Body	29
	Wheel Lug Nut	76

① — Inch lbs.

Front Suspension & Steering

NOTE: On Air Bag Equipped Models, Refer To "Air Bag System Precautions" Located In The Front Of This Manual For System Disarming & Arming Procedures.

INDEX

PRECAUTIONS

AIR BAG SYSTEMS

Refer to "Air Bag System Precautions" in the front of this manual for system disarming and arming procedures.

BATTERY GROUND CABLE

Prior to service, disconnect battery ground cable and isolate as required.

WHEEL HUB & STEERING KNUCKLE

REPLACE

PASEO

1. Raise and support vehicle, then remove front wheels.
2. Remove brake caliper and brake hose from strut.
3. Support caliper with wire, then remove rotor, **Fig. 1.**
4. Place a dial indicator near center of axle hub and check backlash in bearing shaft direction, **Fig. 2.** If backlash is greater than .002 inch, replace bearing.
5. Install rotor and brake caliper, then remove driveshaft locknut while applying brakes.
6. Remove brake caliper and support with wire, then the rotor.
7. Loosen nuts on lower side of shock absorber. **Do not remove bolts at this time.**
8. Disconnect tie rod end from steering knuckle using ball joint puller tool No. 09628-62011, or equivalent, then the lower ball joint from lower suspension arm.
9. Using universal puller tool No. 09950-20017, or equivalent, disconnect driveshaft from steering knuckle.
10. Remove bolts on lower side of shock absorber, then the steering knuckle and hub.

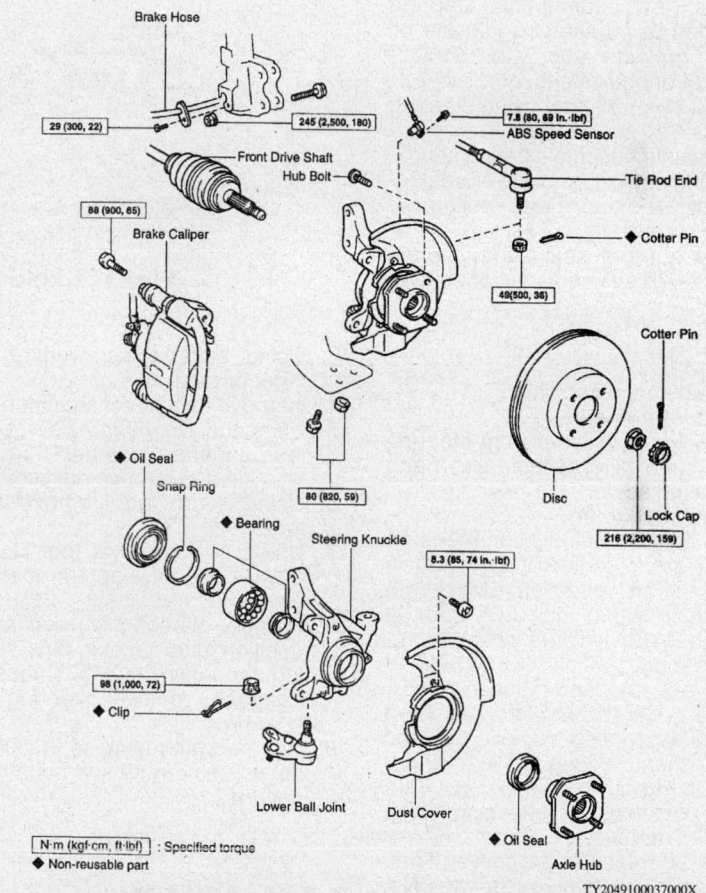

Fig. 1 Exploded view of knuckle, hub & bearing.
Paseo

11. Remove lower ball joint using ball joint puller tool No. 09628-62011, or equivalent.
12. Using a suitable screwdriver, remove inner oil seal.
13. Using a suitable T30 Torx wrench, remove dust cover set bolts.
14. Using universal puller, remove axle hub from steering knuckle, then the dust cover.
15. Remove inner race from axle hub using universal puller, then the outer oil seal from steering knuckle using oil seal puller tool No. 09308-00010, or equivalent.

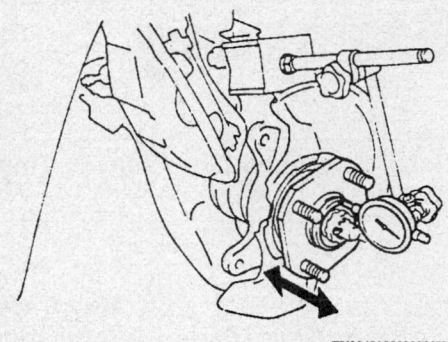

TY2049100038000X

Fig. 2 Bearing backlash measurement. Paseo

16. Remove bearing snap ring from steering knuckle, place inner race on outside of bearing, then using a suitable brass drift and a hammer, drive bearing from steering knuckle.
17. Reverse procedure to install, noting the following:
    a. Press new bearing into steering knuckle using steering knuckle oil seal replacer tool No. 09608-10010, or equivalent.
    b. Install outer oil seal using steering knuckle oil seal replacer.
    c. Press axle hub into steering knuckle using steering knuckle oil seal replacer and universal puller, or equivalents.
    d. Install outer oil seal using steering knuckle oil seal replacer, or equivalent.

TERCEL

1. Raise and support vehicle.
2. Remove front wheels.
3. Remove brake cylinder from steering knuckle, then using suitable wire, hang and position aside.
4. Remove brake rotor.
5. Using suitable dial indicator, measure backlash near center of axle hub in bearing shaft direction. Maximum backlash is .0020 inch (.05 mm). If backlash is greater than indicated, replace bearing.
6. Install brake rotor and cylinder.
7. Remove cotter pin and lock cap, then with brakes applied, remove nut and washer, then remove brake cylinder and rotor, **Fig. 3**.
8. Loosen lower shock attaching bolts, but do not remove.
9. Remove tie rod end cotter pin and nut, then using ball joint puller tool No. 09628-62011, or equivalent, disconnect tie rod end from steering knuckle.
10. Remove lower ball joint to lower arm attaching nuts and bolt, then disconnect joint from arm.
11. Remove lower shock absorber attaching nuts and bolts, then remove steering knuckle with axle hub. **Do not damage driveshaft oil seal.**
12. Place axle hub in suitable vise, then remove ball joint clip and nut. Using ball joint puller tool No. 09628-6201, or equivalent, remove ball joint.

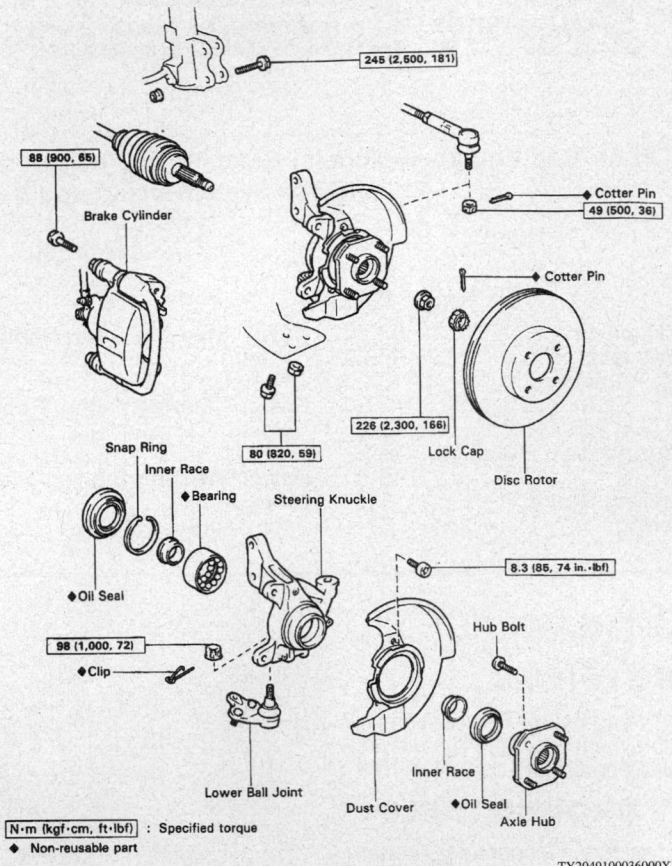

N·m (kgf·cm, ft·lbf) : Specified torque
◆ Non-reusable part

TY2049100036000X

Fig. 3 Exploded view of axle hub & steering knuckle. Tercel

13. Using suitable screwdriver, remove inner oil seal.
14. Remove dust cover attaching bolts.
15. Using tool No. 09950-2001, or equivalent, separate axle hub from steering knuckle and remove dust cover.
16. Using same tool, remove axle hub inner race.
17. Using seal removal tool No. 09308-00010, or equivalent, remove outer oil seal.
18. Remove steering knuckle snap ring, position inner race on outside of bearing, then using suitable brass bar and hammer, remove steering knuckle bearing.
19. Reverse procedure to install. Tighten all attaching nuts and bolts to specifications.

BALL JOINT INSPECTION

1. Remove ball joint as outlined under "Ball Joint, Replace."
2. Move ball joint stud back and forth five times, then install nut.
3. Using a suitable torque wrench, turn nut continuously one turn every two to four seconds and take torque reading on fifth turn.
4. If torque reading is not 9–26 inch lbs., replace ball joint.

BALL JOINT
REPLACE

1. Raise and support vehicle, then remove front wheels.
2. Remove steering knuckle and hub as outlined under "Wheel Hub & Steering Knuckle, Replace."
3. Remove lower ball joint using ball joint puller tool No. 09628-62011, or equivalent.
4. Inspect ball joint as outlined under "Ball Joint Inspection."
5. Reverse procedure to install.

COIL SPRING
REPLACE
PASEO

1. Raise and support vehicle, then remove front wheels.
2. Disconnect brake hose from strut.
3. Remove lower strut attaching nuts and bolts, **Fig. 4,** then disconnect strut from steering knuckle.
4. Remove three nuts holding top of suspension support.
5. Remove strut from body.
6. Using coil spring compressor tool No. 09727-30020, or equivalent, compress coil spring.
7. Install a bolt and two nuts to lower portion of strut shell and secure in vise.
8. Using spring seat holding tool No.

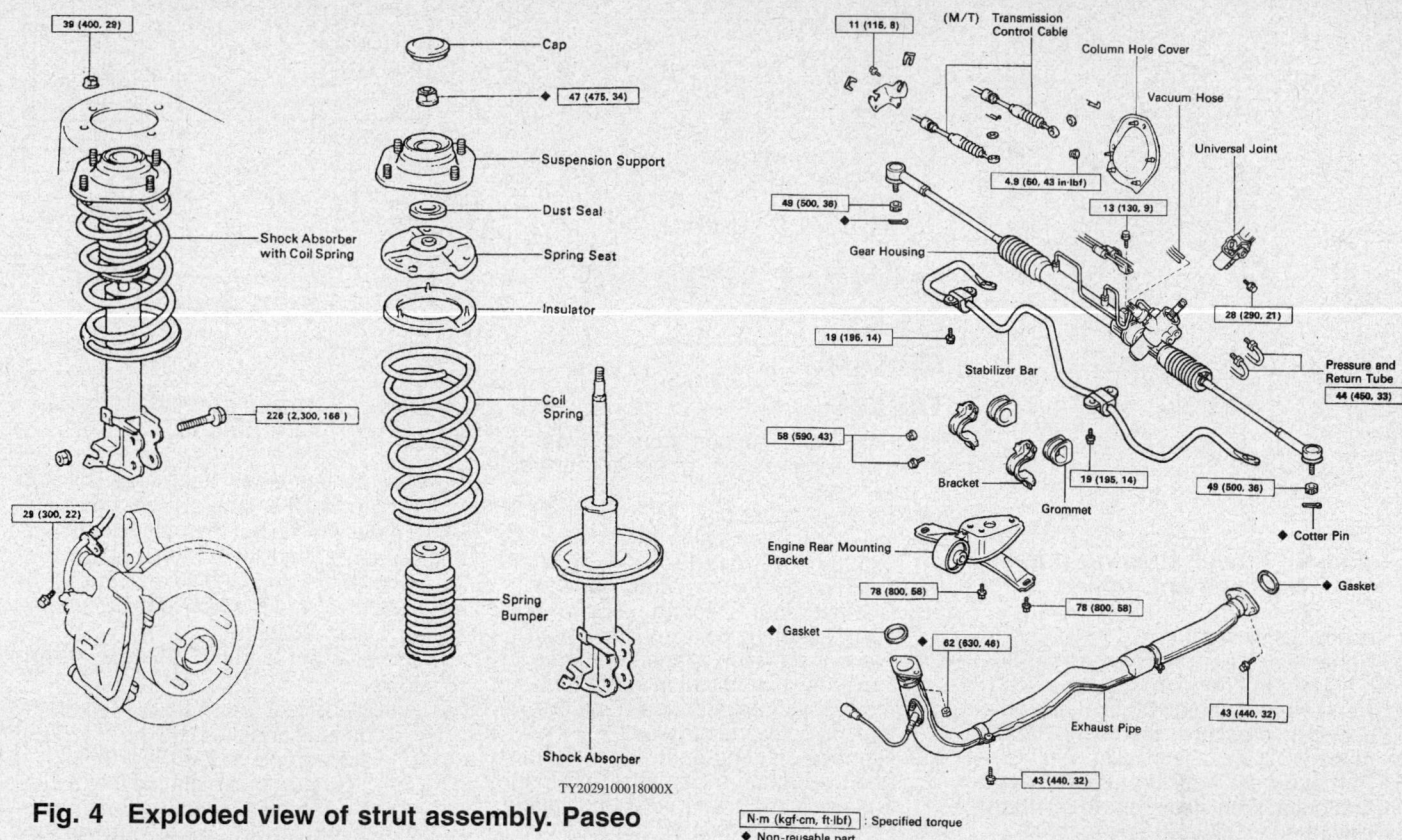

Fig. 4 Exploded view of strut assembly. Paseo

Fig. 5 Power steering gear replacement. Paseo

09729-22031, or equivalent, remove nut, suspension upper support, upper insulator, coil spring, spring bumper and lower insulator. **Do not disassemble spring lower seat.**

9. Reverse procedure to install, noting the following:
   a. Fit lower end of coil spring into gap of lower seat.
   b. Tighten all attaching nuts and bolts to specifications.

TERCEL

1. Raise and support vehicle.
2. Disconnect brake hose to shock absorber attaching bolt.
3. Scribe alignment marks on strut lower bracket and the camber adjusting cam.
4. Remove two bolts and nuts and disconnect from steering knuckle.
5. Remove three nuts attaching strut to body, then remove strut from body. **Cover driveshaft boot with cloth to avoid damage.**
6. Install bolt and nuts on bracket at lower portion of strut shell and secure assembly in suitable vise.
7. Using spring compressor tool No. 09727-30020, or equivalent, compress coil spring.
8. Using front spring upper seat holder tool No. 09729-22031, or equivalent, hold spring seat, then remove support nut.
9. Remove suspension support, spring seat, spring and dust cover.
10. Reverse procedure to install. Tighten all attaching nuts and bolts to specifications.

STRUT
REPLACE

Refer to "Coil Spring, Replace" for procedure.

STABILIZER BAR
REPLACE

1. Disconnect stabilizer bar from front lower suspension arms.
2. Remove stabilizer bar brackets from body structure.
3. Disconnect front exhaust pipe from rings, then remove stabilizer bar.
4. Reverse procedure to install, tighten bolts to specifications.

SUSPENSION ARM
REPLACE

1. Raise and support vehicle.
2. Remove front wheel.
3. Remove lower ball joint to lower arm attaching bolts, then disconnect ball joint.
4. Disconnect stabilizer bar bolt from lower suspension arm.
5. Remove lower arm attaching bolts, then remove arm.
6. Reverse procedure to install, noting the following:
   a. **On Paseo models,** temporarily install lower arm attaching bolts, then lower vehicle, stabilize suspension and tighten attaching bolts to specifications.

POWER STEERING GEAR
REPLACE
PASEO

1. Disconnect tie rod ends using ball joint puller tool No. 09628-62011, or equivalent, **Fig. 5.**
2. Place alignment marks on universal joint and control valve shaft.
3. Loosen upper universal joint bolt and remove lower universal joint bolt, then disconnect universal joint.
4. Disconnect and connect pressure and return tubes using power steering hose nut wrench set tool No. 09631-22020, or equivalent.
5. Slide gear assembly to righthand side, then to lefthand side and remove.
6. Align marks made during removal and connect universal joint.
7. Reverse procedure to install.

TERCEL

1. Raise and support vehicle, then remove front wheel.
2. Remove tie rod end cotter pin and nut, then using ball joint puller tool No. 09628-62011, or equivalent, disconnect tie rod end from steering knuckle.
3. Remove column hole cover attaching bolts, then remove cover.
4. Place installation alignment mark on universal joint and shaft.
5. Loosen upper and lower universal joint set bolt, then pull joint upward from

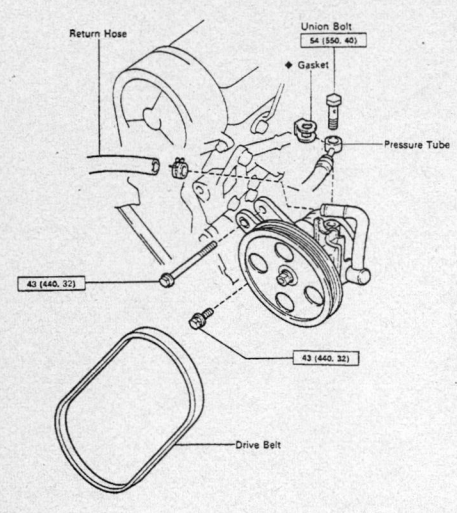

Fig. 6 Power steering pump replacement. Paseo

control valve shaft.

6. Remove exhaust pipe clamp from front bracket, then remove exhaust pipe.
7. Remove rear engine bracket, then disconnect pressure feed and return tubes.
8. Remove gear housing attaching nuts and bolts, then slide gear to righthand side, then to lefthand side to remove.
9. Reverse procedure to install.

POWER STEERING PUMP
REPLACE
PASEO

Refer to **Fig. 6** when replacing power steering pump.

TERCEL

1. Using hose wrench tool No. 09631-22020, or equivalent, remove pressure tube.
2. Disconnect return tube.
3. Loosen power steering adjusting bolt.
4. Remove pump attaching bolts, then the pump.
5. Reverse procedure to install.

MANUAL STEERING GEAR
REPLACE
TERCEL

1. Raise and support front of vehicle, then remove front wheel and tire assemblies.
2. Remove cotter pins and nuts from tie rod ends, then using puller tool No. 09628-62011, or equivalent, separate tie rod ends from steering knuckles.
3. Remove four steering column hole cover attaching bolts and the cover.
4. Place installation alignment marks on universal joint to pinion shaft, then remove steering shaft universal joint attaching bolts and the joint.
5. Remove steering gear attaching nuts and bolts, then slide housing to righthand side and pull through body panel.
6. Reverse procedure to install. Tighten attaching nuts and bolts to specifications.

POWER STEERING SYSTEM BLEED

1. Ensure fluid in reservoir tank is at proper level.
2. With engine speed below 1000 RPM, turn steering wheel from stop to stop

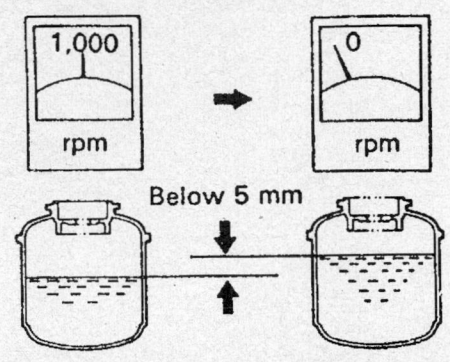

Fig. 7 Power steering system bleed

three or four times, keeping at full stop position for two to three seconds.
3. Ensure fluid is not foamy or cloudy.
4. Measure fluid lever with engine running, then stop engine and measure fluid level again, **Fig. 7.** Maximum rise of fluid is .20 inch.
5. If a problem is found, proceed as follows:
   a. Disconnect return hose from reservoir tank and drain fluid.
   b. Fill reservoir tank with fresh fluid.
   c. With return hose placed into a suitable container, start engine and run at 1000 RPM. **After one or two seconds, fluid will begin to discharge from the return hose. Stop engine immediately at this time. Ensure some fluid remains in the reservoir tank.**
   d. Repeat steps b and c four or five times until there is no more air in fluid.
   e. Connect return hose and correct fluid level.

TIGHTENING SPECIFICATIONS

Year	Component	Torque, Ft. Lbs.
PASEO		
1996–97	Ball Joint To Lower Suspension Arm	59
	Ball Joint To Steering Knuckle	72
	Brake Caliper Bolts	65
	Brake Hose To Strut Bolt	22
	Driveshaft To Axle Hub Nut	159
	Dust Cover To Steering Knuckle	72①
	Front Exhaust Pipe To Converter Nuts	32
	Front Exhaust Pipe To Manifold Nuts	46
	Lower Suspension Arm Bracket Bolts	94
	Lower Suspension Arm Mounting Bolts	105
	Power Steering Pump Mounting Bolts	32
	Power Steering Pump Pressure Tube	40
	Stabilizer Bar Link Nuts	13
	Stabilizer Bar Retainer Bracket Bolts	14
	Steering Rack Line Clamp Nut	108①

Continued

TIGHTENING
SPECIFICATIONS—Continued

Year	Component	Torque, Ft. Lbs.
PASEO		
1996–97	Steering Rack Mounting Bolts	43
	Steering Rack Pressure & Return Tubes	33
	Steering Rack Universal Joint Bolt	21
	Strut Nut	34
	Strut To Steering Knuckle	181
	Strut To Strut Tower	29
	Tie Rod End To Steering Knuckle	35
	Wheel Lug Nut	76
TERCEL		
1996–98	Disc Brake Caliper Union Bolt	22
	Front Axle Bearing Locknut	159
	Lower Ball Joint To Lower Suspension Arm	59
	Lower Ball Joint To Steering Knuckle	72
	Lower Suspension Arm To Body (Front)	105
	Lower Suspension Arm To Body (Rear)	55
	Piston Rod To Suspension Support	34
	Steering Knuckle To Shock Absorber	113
	Steering Knuckle To Tie Rod End	36
	Suspension Support To Body	29
	Tie Rod End Locknut	35
	Wheel Lug Nut	76

① — Inch lbs.

Wheel Alignment

INDEX

PRELIMINARY INSPECTION

1. Check tires for wear and proper inflation.
2. Check wheel runout; .047 inch or less should be indicated.
3. Check front wheel bearings, front suspension, steering linkage and ball joints for wear or looseness.
4. Ensure front shock absorbers are functioning properly.

FRONT WHEEL ALIGNMENT

CASTER & CAMBER

Caster and camber are not adjustable on these models. If caster and camber are not within limits, check for worn or damaged suspension parts and replace as necessary.

TOE-IN

1. Remove clamps from steering gear boots.
2. Loosen tie rod end locknuts.
3. Turn left and right tie rod ends an equal amount to adjust toe-in.
4. Ensure length of both tie rods are equal following adjustment.
5. Following adjustment, install steering boot clamps and **torque** locknut to 35 ft. lbs.

REAR WHEEL ALIGNMENT

CAMBER & TOE-IN

Measure camber angle and toe-in with suitable wheel alignment gauge and adjust to specifications. If reading is not within specification, check for worn or damaged bushings and bent or damaged rear suspension components. Replace parts as necessary.

VEHICLE RIDE HEIGHT

PASEO

Measure vehicle ride height from positions shown in **Fig 1.** Refer to **Fig. 2** for correct height specifications.

TERCEL

Measure vehicle ride height from positions shown in **Fig 1.** Refer to **Fig. 2** for correct height specifications.

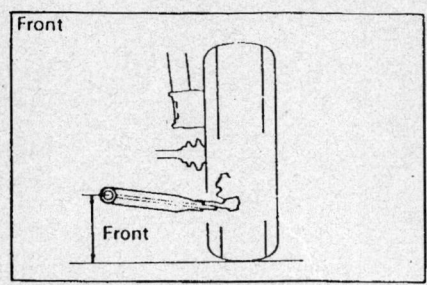

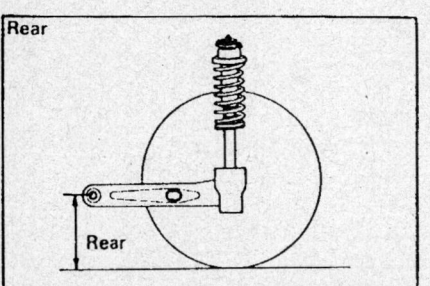

TY2049100039000X

Fig. 1   Vehicle ride height measurement

Year	Model	Tire Size	Height mm (inch)	
			Front	**Rear**
1996	All	175/65 R14	185 (7.28)	244 (9.61)
		185/60 R14	186 (7.32)	245 (9.65)
1997	Paseo	185/60 R14	188 (7.40)	249 (9.80)
	Tercel	155R13	194 (7.63)	252 (9.92)
		175/65 R14	197 (7.76)	253 (9.96)
		185/60 R14	192 (7.56)	250 (9.84)
1998	Tercel	155R13	194 (7.63)	252 (9.92)
		175/65 R14	197 (7.76)	253 (9.96)
		185/60 R14	192 (7.56)	250 (9.84)

Fig. 2   Vehicle ride height

TOYOTA SIENNA
INDEX OF SERVICE OPERATIONS

Specifications

GENERAL ENGINE SPECIFICATIONS

Year	Model	Engine, Liter	Fuel System	Bore & Stroke	Compression Ratio	Maximum Brake H.P. @ RPM	Maximum Torque Ft. Lbs. @ RPM	Normal Oil Pressure, psi
1998-99	1MZ-FE	3.0L	MP-EFI	3.44 x 3.27	10.5	194 @ 5200	209 @ 4400	①

① — 43 psi or more @ idle, 43–78 psi
@ 3000 RPM

TUNE UP SPECIFICATIONS

Year, Model & Engine	Spark Plug Gap Inch	Ignition			Curb Idle Speed		Fuel Pump Pressure, psi	Valve Clearance, Inch	
		Firing Order Fig.	Timing BTDC	Timing Mark Fig.	Man. Trans.	Auto. Trans.		Int.	Exh.
1998-99	.043	1-2-3-4-5-6	8-12①	B	700	700N	44-50②	.006-.010C	.010-.014C

C=Cold

① — Connect data link connector (DLC) No. 1 terminals TE1 & E1 with jumper wire, **Fig. A.**

② — Disconnect battery ground cable and place shop towel under fuel filter. Remove union bolt, gaskets and fuel inlet hose, then connect suitable fuel pressure gauge, inlet hose, gaskets and union bolt. Connect suitable scan tool to data link connector (DLC) No. 3 (or connect positive & negative battery leads to fuel pump connector). Connect battery ground cable, turn ignition switch On & note fuel pressure.

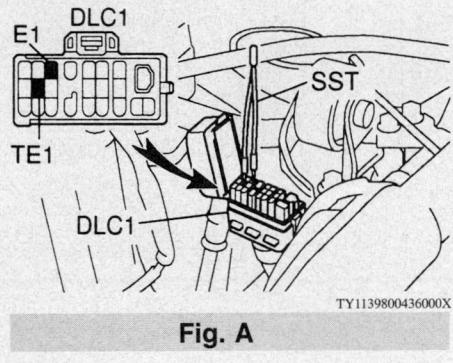

Fig. A

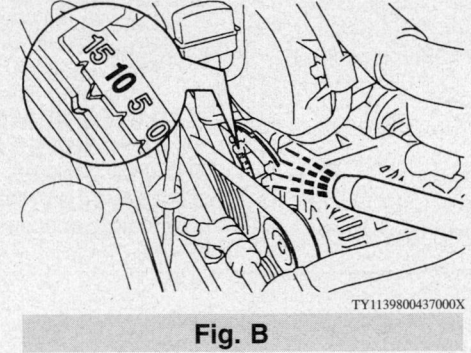

Fig. B

FRONT WHEEL ALIGNMENT SPECIFICATIONS

Year	Model	Caster Angle, Degrees		Camber Angle, Degrees		Toe, Inch	Toe-Out on Turns, Deg.		Steering Axis Inclination, Deg.	Ball Joint Wear
		Limits	Desired	Limits	Desired		Inner Wheel	Outer Wheel		
1998-99	All	$+^{47}/_{60}$ to $+2^9/_{20}$	$+1^8/_{15}$	$-1^{17}/_{60}$ to $+^{13}/_{60}$	$-^8/_{15}$	+.02 to +.18	$34^{19}/_{60}$	$30^{19}/_{60}$	$12^7/_{12}$	0

REAR WHEEL ALIGNMENT SPECIFICATIONS

Year	Model	Camber Angle, Degrees		Toe, Inch
		Limits	Desired	
1998-99	All	1⅔ to -⅙	-¹¹/₁₂	-.03 to +.21

FLUID CAPACITIES & COOLING SYSTEM DATA

Year	Model & Engine	Cooling Capacity Qts.	Radiator Cap Relief Pressure, Lbs.	Thermo. Opening Temp. °F	Fuel Tank Gals.	Engine Oil Refill Qts.	Transaxle Oil		Differential Oil Pts.
							Man. Trans. Pts.	Auto. Trans. Qts.	
1998-99	3.0L	10①	14	180	21	5	—	8	1.6

① — Add 1 qt. if equipped with rear heater.

LUBRICANT DATA

Year	Model	Lubricant Type				
		Transmission		Rear Axle	Power Steering	Brake System
		Manual	Automatic			
1998-99	3.0L	—	Dexron II/III	—	Dexron II/III	DOT 3

Electrical

NOTE: On Air Bag Equipped Models, Refer To " Air Bag System Precautions" Located In The Front Of This Manual For System Disarming & Arming Procedures.

INDEX

PRECAUTIONS

AIR BAG SYSTEMS

Refer to "Air Bag System Precautions" in the front of this manual for system disarming and arming procedures.

AUDIO CODED ANTI-THEFT SYSTEM

Some models are equipped with an audio coded anti-theft system that will dis-able the radio when battery power is removed from the radio. The system can be identified by the "ANTI-THEFT SYSTEM" on the cassette tape lid. Obtain the three digit code from the customer for input before disconnecting battery power to the audio unit. Reset system after service as follows:

1. Obtain three digit code from customer.
2. Depress No. 1 (PROG) button while depressing righthand side of TUNE SEEK button, - - - will appear in tape operation display.
3. Enter code as follows:
   a. To enter first digit, press No. 1 (PROG) button a sufficient number of times, starting with zero, to enter digit (if first digit of code is five press button six times).
   b. To enter second digit, press No. 2 (APS) button a sufficient number of

TOYOTA SIENNA

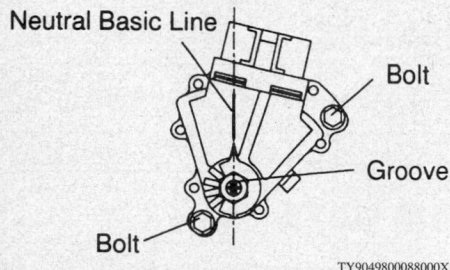

Fig. 1 Park/Neutral position switch neutral basic line

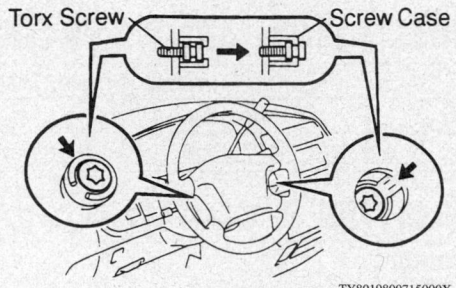

Fig. 2 Driver's air bag removal

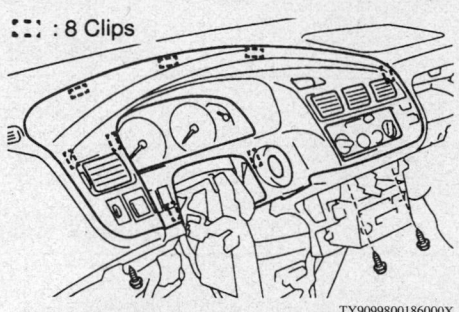

Fig. 3 Cluster finish panel

times, starting with zero, to enter digit.
  c. To enter third digit press, No. 3 (RPT) button a sufficient number of times, starting with zero, to enter digit.
4. If three dashes (- - -) appear in tape operation display during input of digits, restart procedure from beginning.
5. When code digits are correctly input and displayed, press and hold SCAN button until SEC appears in tape operation display.
6. When SEC disappears from display audio unit should be operative.
7. If unit is not operative or Err is displayed, repeat procedure. **Attempting to input code more than nine times may permanently disable audio unit.**

BATTERY GROUND CABLE

Prior to service, disconnect battery ground cable and isolate as required.

FUSE PANEL & FLASHER LOCATION

The interior fuse panel is located under the left hand side of the dash panel. The flasher is located in the under dash fuse panel.

FUEL PUMP RELAY LOCATION

The fuel pump is controlled by the EFI main relay located in the under hood fuse panel

RELAY CENTER LOCATION

The engine relay/fuse panel is located on the left side fender well in the engine compartment area.

STARTER
REPLACE

1. Remove battery and battery tray.
2. **On models equipped with cruise control,** remove cruise control actuator.
3. **On all models,** disconnect A/T shift control cable.

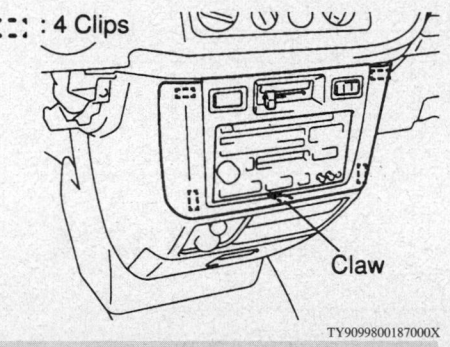

Fig. 4 Center cluster finish panel

4. Disconnect engine wire and starter connector.
5. Remove two mounting bolts, A/T shift control cable clamp and the starter.
6. Reverse procedure to install.

ALTERNATOR
REPLACE

1. Loosen alternator pivot bolt, adjusting lock bolt and adjusting bolt, then remove alternator belt.
2. Remove nut, then disconnect alternator wire.
3. Remove pivot bolt, plate washer, adjusting lock bolt, then the alternator.
4. Reverse procedure to install.

COIL PACK
REPLACE

1. Disconnect high tension cords from ignition coils.
2. Remove mounting bolts, then the ignition coils.
3. Reverse procedure to install.

NEUTRAL SAFETY SWITCH
REPLACE

1. Remove engine lower cover.
2. Disconnect park/neutral position switch connector.
3. Remove nut and disconnect shift control cable.
4. Remove nut, washer and control shaft lever.
5. Pry off lock plate, then remove nut and lockplate.

6. Remove two mounting bolts, then the park/neutral position switch.
7. Reverse procedure to install, adjust switch as follows:
  a. Loosen park/neutral position switch bolt and place selector lever in neutral position.
  b. Align groove and neutral basic line, **Fig. 1.**
  c. Hold in position and tighten bolts to specification.

STEERING WHEEL
REPLACE

1. Disarm airbag system as outlined under "Air Bag System Precautions."
2. Place front wheels in a straight ahead position.
3. Using a suitable Torx socket wrench, loosen two Torx screws until groove along screw circumference catches on screw case, **Fig. 2.**
4. Pull air bag module away from steering wheel and disconnect electrical connector.
5. Remove steering wheel nut set, then mark steering wheel and main shaft assembly for installation reference.
6. Using a suitable steering wheel puller, remove steering wheel.
7. Reverse procedure to install.

INSTRUMENT CLUSTER
REPLACE

1. Remove three screws, then using a suitable screwdriver wrapped in tape, remove dash cluster finish panel, **Fig. 3.**
2. Remove instrument cluster assembly.
3. Reverse procedure to install.

RADIO
REPLACE

1. Using a suitable screwdriver wrapped with tape, remove center cluster finish panel around radio by carefully prying out on attaching clips, **Fig. 4.**
2. Remove radio head assembly from vehicle.
3. Reverse procedure to install.

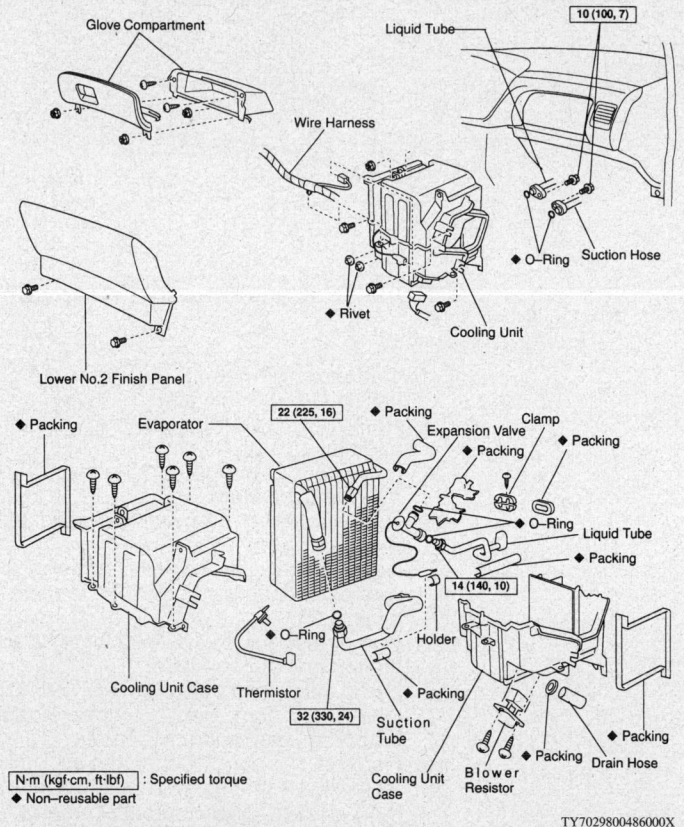

Fig. 5 Exploded view of evaporator assembly

TY7029800486000X

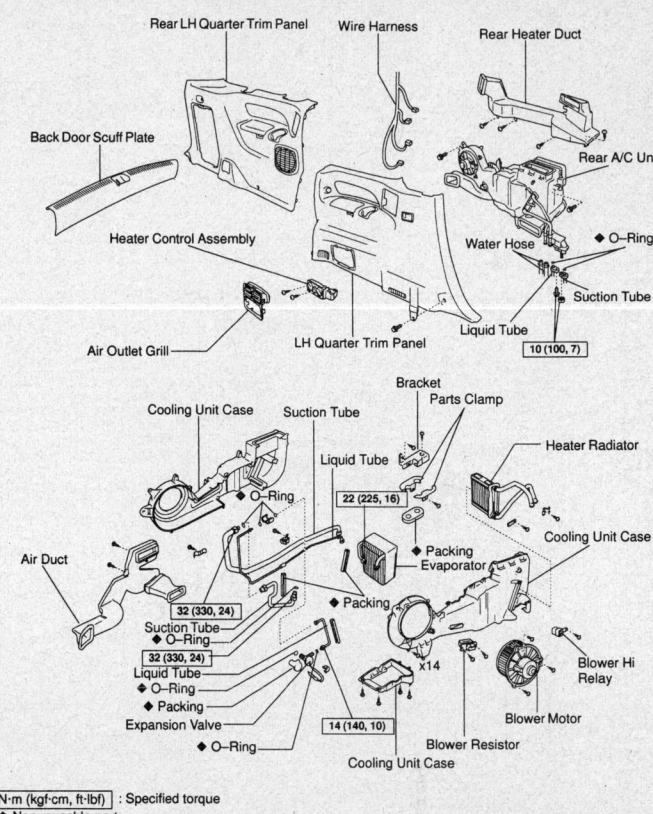

Fig. 6 Rear A/C unit. Four door model

TY7029800488000X

WIPER MOTOR
REPLACE

1. Disconnect wiper motor electrical connector.
2. Remove wiper motor service cover, if equipped.
3. Remove wiper motor attaching bolts.
4. Using a suitable screwdriver, disconnect wiper link from wiper motor, then remove wiper motor.
5. Reverse procedure to install.

BLOWER MOTOR
REPLACE
FRONT

1. Remove lower dash finish panel.
2. Disconnect electrical connectors and three screws, then the ECM.
3. Disconnect blower motor electrical connector, remove three screws, then the blower motor.
4. Reverse procedure to install.

REAR

1. Remove rear seats.
2. Remove left rear quarter trim panel.
3. Remove heater control assembly.
4. Remove left quarter trim panel.
5. Disconnect electrical connector from blower motor, remove three mounting screws, then the motor.
6. Reverse procedure to install.

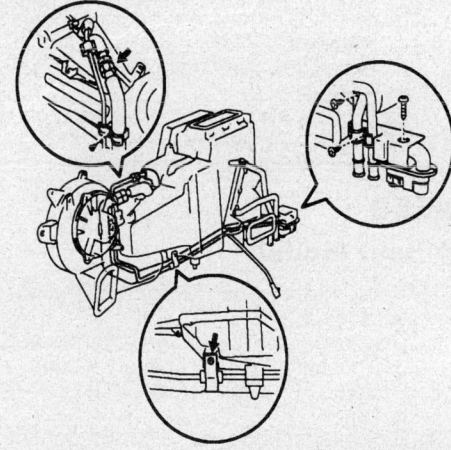

TY7029800487000X

Fig. 7 Liquid tube & suction tube removal. Four door model

HEATER CORE
REPLACE
FRONT

1. Drain engine coolant into suitable container.
2. Remove instrument panel and reinforcement as outlined in "Dash Panel Service" section.
3. Remove defroster nozzle.
4. Remove screw and piping clamp from heater core.
5. Remove two screws, two clamps and two radiator pipes from heater core.
6. Remove heater core, then remove and discard two O-rings from heater radiator pipes.
7. Reverse procedure to install.

REAR

1. Drain engine coolant into suitable container.
2. Using suitable pliers, grip claws of hose clamps and slide up off of pipe connection.
3. Remove water hoses from heater core.
4. Remove front seats, front door scuff plates, cowl side trims, rear door scuff plates, lower door scuff plates, rear console box and left side air outlet grille.
5. Slide floor carpeting backward and remove two clips securing air outlet grille to heater unit.
6. Remove two bolts, two clips and rear air duct.
7. Disconnect connectors, remove three bolts, then the rear heater unit.
8. Remove blower resistor and air mix servo motor.
9. Remove two screws and clamps and any remaining hardware, then remove heater core from heater assembly.
10. Reverse procedure to install.

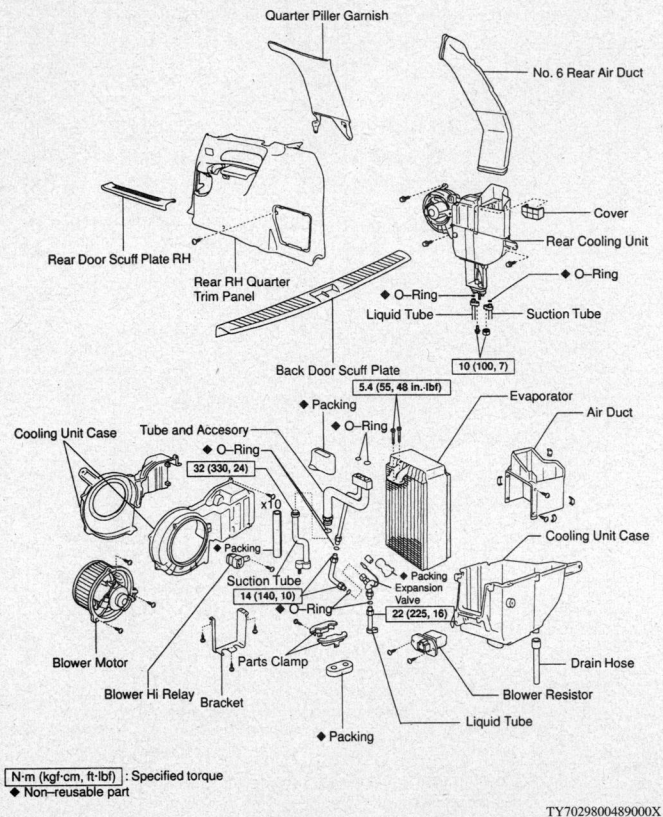

Fig. 8 Rear A/C unit. 5 door model

N·m (kgf·cm, ft·lbf) : Specified torque
◆ Non-reusable part

TY7029800489000X

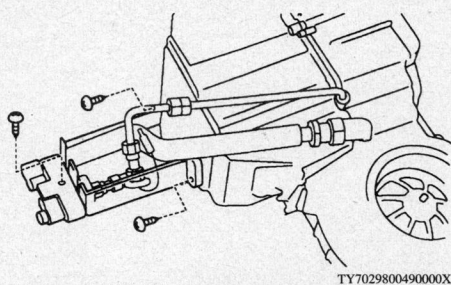

TY7029800490000X

Fig. 9 Expansion valve removal

EVAPORATOR CORE
REPLACE
FRONT

1. Discharge and recover A/C refrigerant using a suitable A/C recovery station.
2. Remove two bolts and disconnect liquid and suction tubes from evaporator assembly.
3. Remove glove compartment and lower finish panel, **Fig. 5.**
4. Disconnect electrical connector and wire harness clamp.
5. Remove two rivets, three bolts, nut, then the evaporator assembly.
6. Remove blower resistor from evaporator case.
7. Using a suitable knife, cut the packing from inlet and outlet ducts.
8. Remove six screws, then separate evaporator case halves.
9. Remove evaporator coil assembly from case.
10. Remove thermister from evaporator coil assembly.
11. Remove and discard packing from around expansion valve.
12. Remove screw and two clamps, then remove holder and disconnect heat sensing tube.
13. Loosen two fittings, then remove expansion valve.
14. Remove suction tube from evaporator.
15. Reverse procedure to install, noting the following:
    a. Install new O-rings on all fittings and lubricate with compressor oil.
    b. Replace removed evaporator rivets with new rivets.
    c. Install new packing on inlet and outlet ducts.
    d. If evaporator assembly is replaced with a new unit, add 1.4 oz. of ND-Oil 8, or equivalent, compressor oil.

REAR
4 Door Models

Refer to **Fig. 6,** when performing the following procedure.
1. Discharge & recover A/C refrigerant using a suitable A/C recovery station.
2. Drain engine coolant into suitable container.
3. Remove bolt and nut, then disconnect liquid and suction tubes.
4. Cap all fittings to prevent system contamination.
5. Remove pipe and grommet.
6. Using suitable pliers, grip claws of hose clamps and move up and off of pipe fitting.
7. Remove water hoses and pipe grommet.
8. Remove rear seats.
9. Remove back door scuff plate, rear left side quarter trim plate, rear heater control assembly, left quarter trim plate, then the rear A/C unit.
10. Disconnect wire harness.
11. Remove two screws, then the rear heater duct.
12. Disconnect remaining connectors,

then remove two bolts and the rear A/C unit.
13. Remove blower motor, blower resistor and blower high relay.
14. Remove heater core as outlined in "Heater Core Replace."
15. Remove three screws and bracket, **Fig. 7.**
16. Pry out packing, remove screw and two parts clamps from tube assemblies.
17. Remove screw and piping clamp, then the nut and suction tube.
18. Using quick joint puller tool No. 09870-00025, or equivalent, remove liquid tube from evaporator assembly.
19. Remove two screws, then the air duct.
20. Remove 14 screws and holding spring, then release claw and separate cooling unit cases.
21. Remove evaporator.
22. Remove packing from around expansion valve, then remove holder and disconnect heat sensing tube from suction tube.
23. Loosen nut, then remove suction tube.
24. Remove expansion valve.
25. Reverse procedure to install

5 Door Models

Refer to **Fig. 8,** when performing the following procedure.
1. Discharge and recover A/C refrigerant using a suitable A/C recovery station.
2. Disconnect liquid and suction tubes.
3. Remove rear seat No. 2, right rear door scuff plate, back door garnish, right rear quarter trim and quarter pillar garnish.
4. Remove No. 6 rear air duct, **Fig. 8.**
5. Disconnect electrical connectors, then remove three bolts and the cooling unit.
6. Remove blower motor and blower resistor.
7. Remove screw and parts clamp, **Fig. 9,** then remove 2 screws and bracket.
8. Pry out packings, then remove holder and disconnect heat sensing tube.
9. Remove expansion valve.
10. Remove liquid and suction tubes, cap all fittings to prevent system contamination.
11. Remove drain hose and air duct.
12. Remove screws, separate evaporator case halves and remove evaporator.
13. Pry out packing, then remove tube assembly.
14. Reverse procedure to install.

1 MZ-FE 3.0L Engine

NOTE: On Air Bag Equipped Models, Refer To "Air Bag System Precautions" Located In The Front Of This Manual For System Disarming & Arming Procedures.

NOTE: For Procedures Not Listed In This Section, Refer To "3.0L Engine" in the "Toyota Avalon, Camry & Camry Solara" Section Of This Manual.

INDEX

PRECAUTIONS

AIR BAG SYSTEMS

Refer to "Air Bag System Precautions" in the front of this manual for system disarming and arming procedures.

AUDIO CODED ANTI-THEFT SYSTEM

Some models are equipped with an audio coded anti-theft system that will disable the radio when battery power is removed from the radio. The system can be identified by the words "ANTI-THEFT SYSTEM" on the cassette tape lid. Obtain the code from the customer for input before disconnecting battery power to the audio unit. Reset system after service as follows:

1. Obtain three digit code from customer.
2. Depress No. 1 (PROG) button while depressing righthand side of TUNE SEEK button, - - - will appear in tape operation display.
3. Enter code as follows:
   a. To enter first digit press No. 1 (PROG) button a sufficient number of times, starting with zero, to enter digit (if first digit of code is five press button six times).
   b. To enter second digit press No. 2 (APS) button a sufficient number of times, starting with zero, to enter digit.
   c. To enter third digit press No. 3 (RPT) button a sufficient number of times, starting with zero, to enter digit.
4. If three dashes (- - -) appear in tape operation display during input of digits, restart procedure from beginning.
5. When code digits are correctly input and displayed, press and hold SCAN button until SEC appears in tape operation display.
6. When SEC disappears from display audio unit should be operative.
7. If unit is not operative or Err is displayed, repeat procedure. **Attempting to input code more than nine times may permanently disable audio unit.**

BATTERY GROUND CABLE

Prior to service, disconnect battery ground cable and isolate as required.

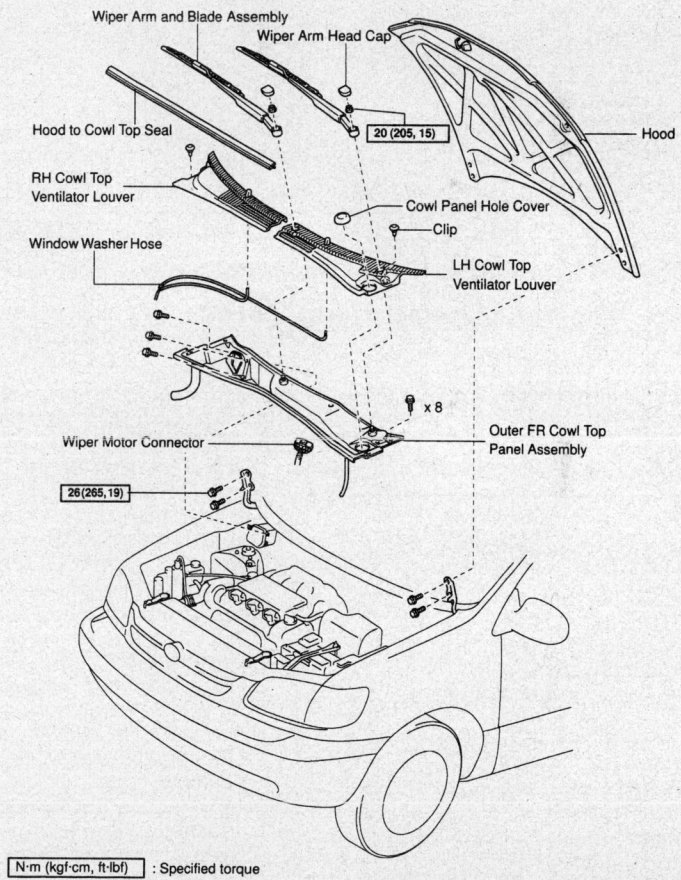

Fig. 1   Engine replacement (Part 1 of 5)

Labels in figure:
- Wiper Arm and Blade Assembly
- Wiper Arm Head Cap
- Hood to Cowl Top Seal
- 20 (205, 15)
- Hood
- RH Cowl Top Ventilator Louver
- Cowl Panel Hole Cover
- Clip
- Window Washer Hose
- LH Cowl Top Ventilator Louver
- x 8
- Wiper Motor Connector
- Outer FR Cowl Top Panel Assembly
- 26 (265, 19)
- N·m (kgf·cm, ft·lbf) : Specified torque
- TY1069800551010X

FUEL SYSTEM PRESSURE RELIEF

Disconnect battery ground cable and place a shop towel under the fuel filter fitting. Loosen union bolt and allow pressurized fuel to escape into shop towel. When

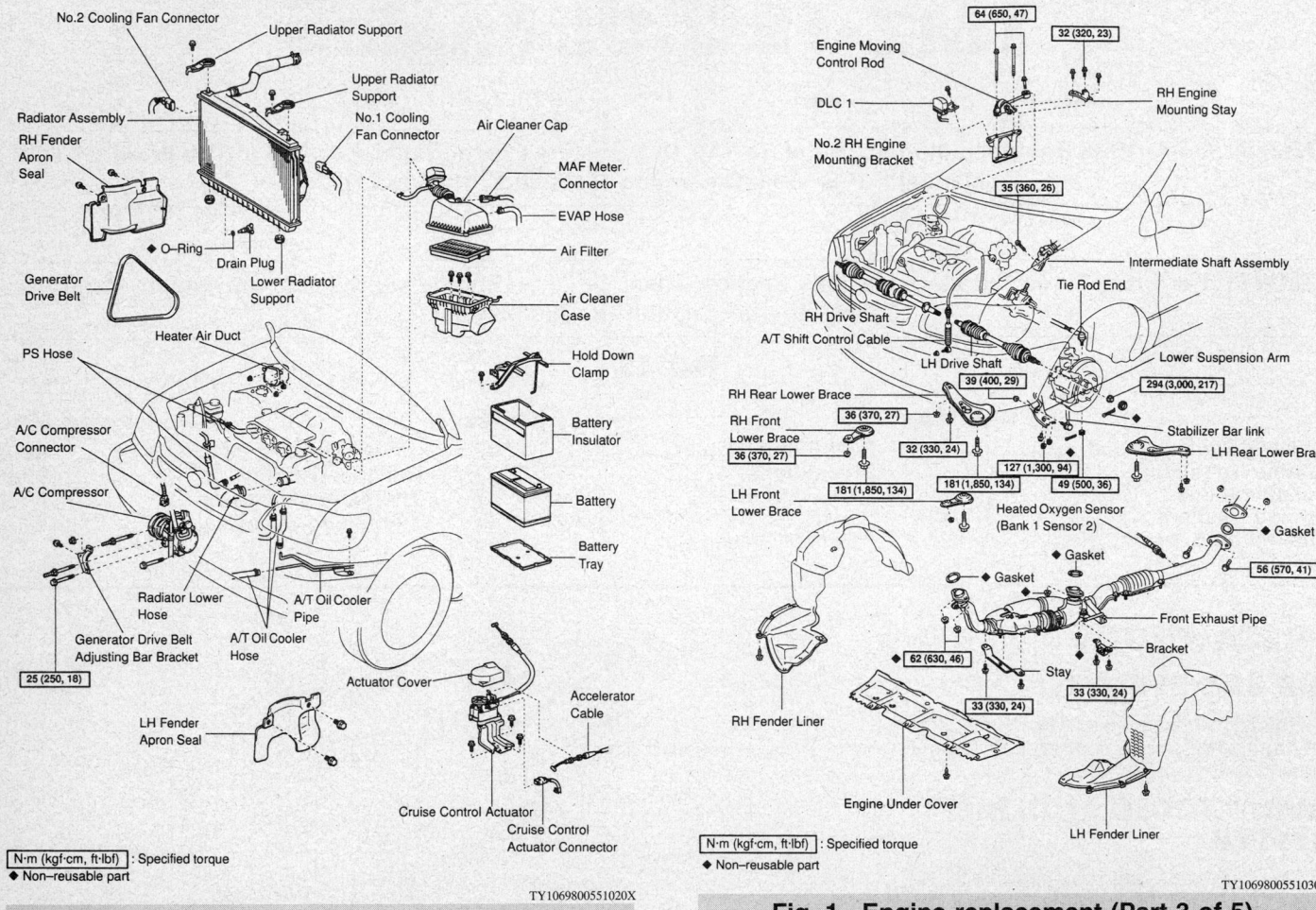

Fig. 1   Engine replacement (Part 2 of 5)

TY1069800551020X

Fig. 1   Engine replacement (Part 3 of 5)

TY1069800551030X

pressure has been relieved, tighten fitting to specification.

ENGINE

REPLACE

Refer to **Fig. 1**, when performing the following procedure.

1. Relieve fuel system pressure as outlined in "Precautions."
2. Remove hood and outer front cowl top panel assembly.
3. Remove wiper arm and blade assemblies.
4. Remove head to cowl top seal and cowl panel hole.
5. Remove clip and disconnect windshield washer hose, then remove cowl top ventilator louver and left and right ventilator louvers.
6. Remove 11 bolts, then disconnect wiper motor connector and remove cowl top ventilator louver.
7. Remove heater air duct and battery and tray.
8. Drain engine coolant and oil into suitable containers.
9. Discharge and recover A/C refrigerant using a suitable A/C recovery station.
10. Disconnect MAF meter connector.

11. Disconnect EVAP hose from charcoal canister and PCV hose from cylinder head cover.
12. Disconnect air cleaner cap from air cleaner case.
13. Disconnect air cleaner hose from throttle body, then remove air cleaner cap with hose.
14. Remove air filter and air cleaner case.
15. Remove cruise control actuator.
16. Remove radiator.
17. Disconnect A/T cooler hose from A/T cooler pipe, then remove cooler pipe from vehicle frame.
18. Disconnect the following components:
    a. Igniter and noise filter connectors on cowl panel.
    b. VSV connector for vapor pressure sensor.
    c. Vapor pressure sensor connector and clamp.
    d. Alternator wire and connector.
    e. Starter wire and connector.
    f. Two ground strap connections from right side fender apron.
    g. Ground strap from left side fender apron.
    h. Brake booster vacuum hose from air intake chamber.
    i. Engine coolant reservoir hose from

water outlet.
    j. Heater hose from intake manifold.
    k. Heater hose from water inlet housing.
    l. Fuel inlet hose from fuel filter.
    m. EVAP hose from pipe on emission control valve set.
    n. Two vacuum hoses from vacuum tank for ACIS.
19. Remove ECM.
20. Disconnect grommet from cowl panel, then pull engine wire harness from cabin.
21. Disconnect and remove A/C compressor.
22. Disconnect A/T shift control cable from transaxle.
23. Disconnect heated oxygen sensor, then remove front exhaust pipe.
24. Remove fender apron seals.
25. Remove drive shafts.
26. Disconnect stabilizer bar links, intermediate shaft assemblies and power steering hose from power steering oil reservoir.
27. Disconnect power steering hose from power steering reservoir pipe.
28. Remove engine under cover, then disconnect fender apron seals.
29. Attach a suitable engine sling device to

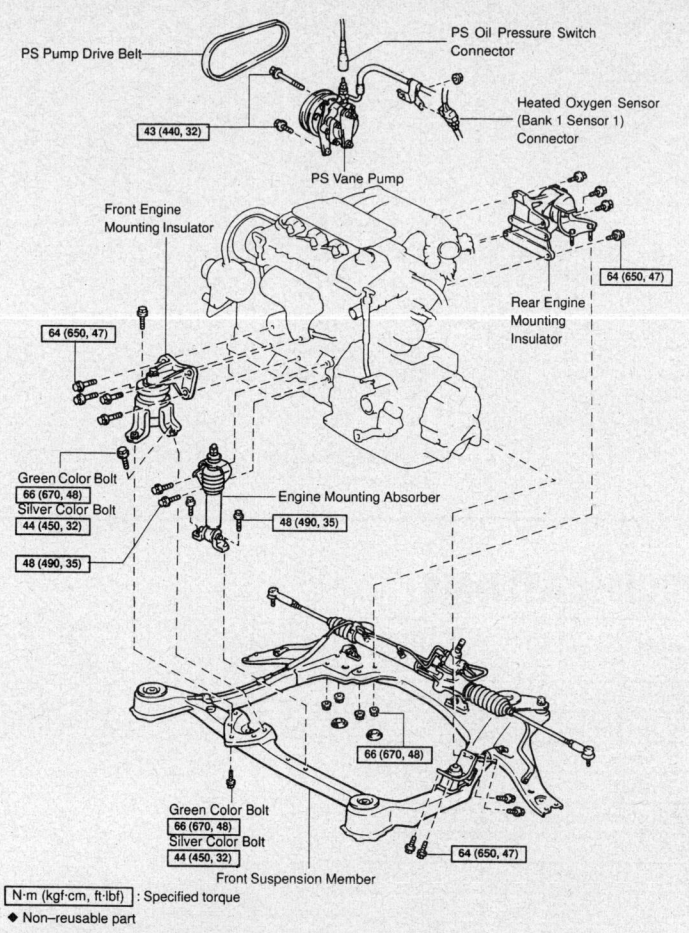

N·m (kgf·cm, ft·lbf) : Specified torque
◆ Non–reusable part

TY1069800551040X

Fig. 1   Engine replacement (Part 4 of 5)

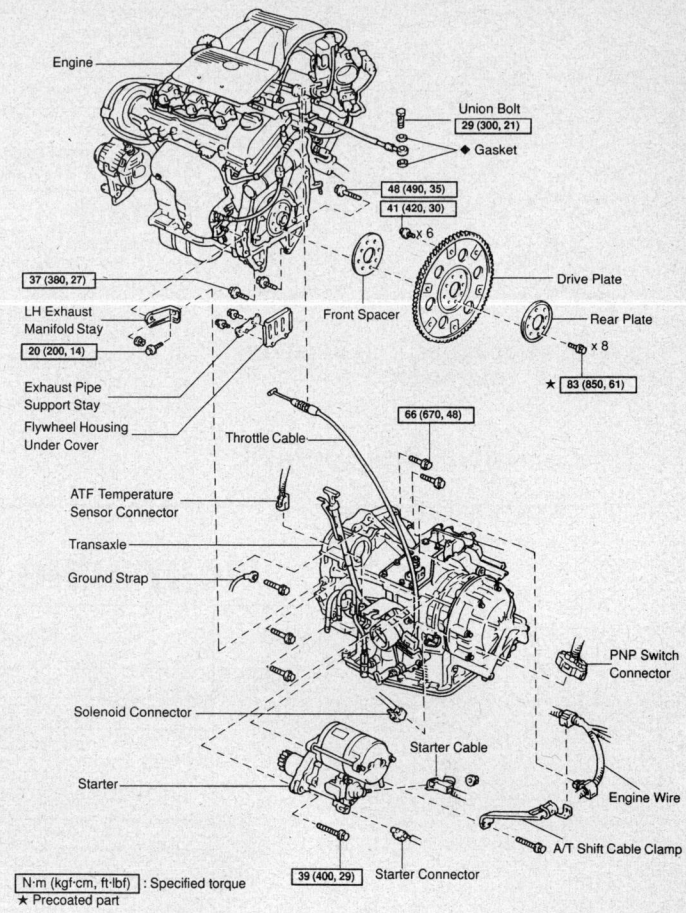

N·m (kgf·cm, ft·lbf) : Specified torque
★ Precoated part

TY1069800551050X

Fig. 1   Engine replacement (Part 5 of 5)

engine hangers, No. 12282-20020, or equivalent.

30. Remove right side engine mounting stay.
31. Remove engine moving control rod and No. 2 right side engine mounting bracket
32. Remove lower braces.
33. Remove engine, transaxle and front suspension member by lowering assembly through bottom of vehicle.
34. Remove power steering pump and front suspension member.
35. Remove front and rear engine mounting insulator.
36. Disconnect throttle cable from throttle body, remove starter, disconnect engine wire harness from transaxle.
37. Remove torque converter clutch mounting bolts, then remove transaxle and drive plate.
38. Reverse procedure to install, noting the following:
    a. Apply adhesive No. 08833-00070, or equivalent, to two or three threads of drive plate bolt ends.
    b. When installing lower braces, **torque** bolts "A" to 134 ft. lbs., bolts "B" to 24 ft. lbs., and bolts "C" to 27 ft. lbs., **Fig. 2.**
    c. When installing A/C compressor, **torque** bolts "A" and "C" to 18 ft. lbs., and bolt "B" to 13 ft. lbs., **Fig. 3.**

COOLING SYSTEM BLEED

1. Engine drain cocks are located at front center and right rear of cylinder block.
2. Remove radiator cap, then drain coolant from engine and radiator drain cocks.
3. Close and tighten drain cocks.
4. Loosen union bolt of water outlet five revolutions.
5. Slowly fill system with coolant, then tighten union bolt to specification.
6. Install radiator cap, then start engine and inspect for leaks.
7. Inspect coolant level and top up as necessary.

THERMOSTAT
REPLACE

1. Drain engine coolant into suitable container.
2. Remove air cleaner cap and hose.
3. Disconnect ECT switch.
4. Disconnect engine wire protector from water inlet and right side cylinder head.
5. Disconnect water inlet pipe from water inlet and left side cylinder head.
6. Remove water inlet and thermostat.
7. Reverse procedure to install.

RADIATOR
REPLACE

1. Drain engine coolant into suitable container.
2. Disconnect No. 1 and No. 2 electric cooling fan connectors.
3. Remove upper radiator hose from radiator.
4. Remove lower radiator hose from water inlet pipe.
5. Remove two oil cooler hoses from oil cooler pipes.
6. Remove two upper radiator supports, then lift out radiator assembly.
7. Remove two lower radiator supports, then the lower radiator hoses and two oil cooler hoses from radiator.
8. Remove No. 1 and No. 2 electric cooling fans from radiator.
9. Reverse procedure to install.

FUEL PUMP
REPLACE

1. Release fuel pressure as outlined in "Fuel System Pressure Relief" under "Precautions."
2. Remove fuel tank assembly.
3. Disconnect fuel tube from pump.
4. Remove eight bolts and fuel tank set

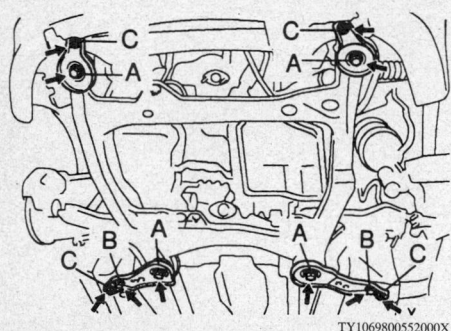

Fig. 2 Lower brace bolt location reference

plate, then the fuel pump from the tank.

5. Remove and discard fuel pump gasket.
6. Reverse procedure to install.

FUEL FILTER
REPLACE

1. Release fuel pressure as outlined in "Fuel System Pressure Relief" under "Precautions."
2. Remove upper union bolt and gaskets from fuel filter.
3. Discard gaskets.
4. Remove lower fuel filter fitting.
5. Remove fuel filter clamp bolt, then the fuel filter.

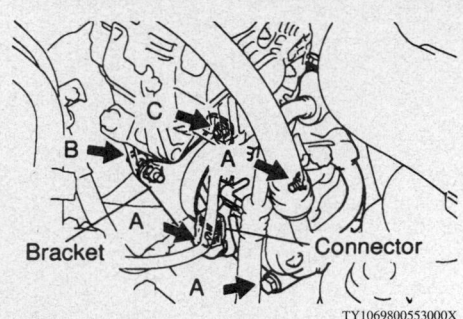

Fig. 3 A/C compressor mounting bolt reference

6. Reverse procedure to install.

TIGHTENING SPECIFICATIONS

Year	Component	Torque/Ft. Lbs.
1998-99	A/C Liquid & Suction Tubes	24
	A/C Suction Tube To Evaporator	24
	Air Bag Torx Screws	78①
	Air Bag Torx Screws	78①
	Alternator Lock Bolt	13
	Alternator Pivot Bolt	41
	Drive Plate Mounting Bolts	61
	Electric Cooling Fan Mounting	44①
	Engine Moving Control Rod & Bracket	47
	Expansion Valve To Evaporator Coil	16
	Expansion Valve To Liquid Tube	10
	Front Engine Mounting Insulator To Frame	②
	Front Suspension Member	48
	Front Exhaust Pipe To Manifold	46
	Fuel Inlet Hose Union Bolts	21
	Fuel Pump Mounting Nuts	35①
	Ignition Coil Mounting Bolt	69①
	Left Engine Mounting Insulator	47
	Park Neutral Position Switch Bolts	48①
	Park Neutral Position Switch Lock Plate Nut	61①
	Power Steering Pump Mounting Bolts	31
	Radiator Support Bolts	108①
	Rear Engine Mounting Insulator	35
	Right Engine Mounting Stay	23
	Shift Control Cable Nut	11
	Steering Wheel Nut Set	25
	Torque Converter Mounting Bolts	30
	Water Inlet Nuts	69①

① — Inch lbs.

② — Green colored bolts, 48 ft. lbs.; silver colored bolts, 32 ft. lbs.

Rear Axle & Suspension

NOTE: On Air Bag Equipped Models, Refer To "Air Bag System Precautions" Located In The Front Of This Manual For System Disarming & Arming Procedures.

INDEX

PRECAUTIONS

AIR BAG SYSTEMS

Refer to "Air Bag System Precautions" in the front of this manual for system disarming and arming procedures.

AUDIO CODED ANTI-THEFT SYSTEM

Some models are with an audio coded anti-theft system that will disable the radio when the battery cable is disconnected. The system can be identified by the words "ANTI-THEFT SYSTEM" on the cassette tape lid. Obtain three digit customer code for input. Reset system after service as follows:

1. Obtain three digit audio anti-theft code.
2. Depress 1 (PROG) while depressing righthand side of TUNE SEEK button, - - - will appear in tape operation display.
3. To enter the first digit, depress 1 (PROG) button repeatedly until the number of times depressed equals the first digit beginning with zero (depress the 1 button six times if the first digit if five).
4. To enter second digit, depress 2 (APS) button repeatedly until the number of times depressed equals the second digit beginning with zero.
5. To enter third digit, depress 3 (RPT) button repeatedly until the number of times depressed equals the third digit beginning with zero.
6. If - - - is displayed during code input, repeat procedure.
7. When code appears in display, depress and hold SCAN button until SEC appears.

8. When SEC disappears audio system should be operative.
9. If Err is displayed, repeat procedure. **Attempting to input code more than nine times may permanently disable audio system.**

BATTERY GROUND CABLE

Prior to service, disconnect battery ground cable and isolate as required.

HUB & BEARING

REPLACE

1. Remove rear wheel and brake drum.
2. Disconnect ABS wheel sensor connector, **Fig. 1.**
3. Remove four nuts, then the rear axle hub assembly.
4. Reverse procedure to install.

COIL SPRING

REPLACE

1. Remove rear wheels and support left and right side of axle beam with suitable jacks.
2. Remove deck trim side board service hole cover.
3. Remove two shock absorber nuts, two retainers and cushions.
4. Remove bolt, washer and shock absorbers from axle beam, **Fig. 2.**
5. Gradually lower jacks and remove springs from upper insulators.
6. Reverse procedure to install.

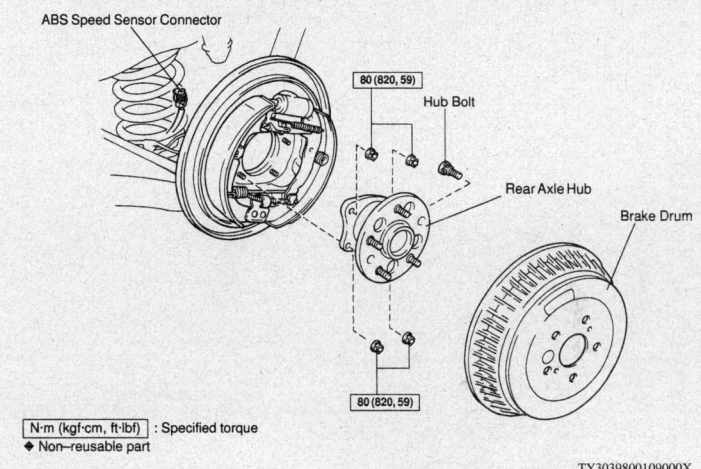

ABS Speed Sensor Connector

80 (820, 59)

Hub Bolt

Rear Axle Hub

Brake Drum

80 (820, 59)

N·m (kgf·cm, ft·lbf) : Specified torque
◆ Non-reusable part

TY3039800109000X

Fig. 1 Rear axle hub replacement

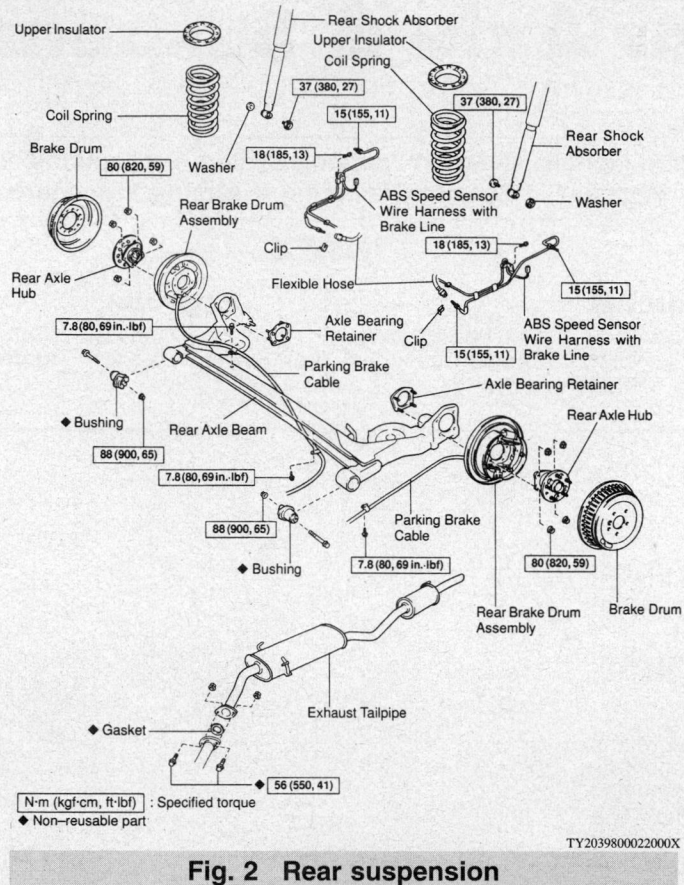

Fig. 2 Rear suspension

Labels in figure:
- Upper Insulator
- Rear Shock Absorber
- Upper Insulator
- Coil Spring
- Coil Spring
- 37 (380, 27)
- 15 (155, 11)
- Rear Shock Absorber
- Brake Drum
- 80 (820, 59)
- Washer
- 18 (185, 13)
- Washer
- Rear Brake Drum Assembly
- ABS Speed Sensor Wire Harness with Brake Line
- Clip
- Rear Axle Hub
- 18 (185, 13)
- Flexible Hose
- 15 (155, 11)
- 7.8 (80, 69 in.-lbf)
- Axle Bearing Retainer
- Clip
- ABS Speed Sensor Wire Harness with Brake Line
- 15 (155, 11)
- Parking Brake Cable
- Axle Bearing Retainer
- Bushing
- Rear Axle Hub
- 88 (900, 65)
- Rear Axle Beam
- 7.8 (80, 69 in.-lbf)
- Parking Brake Cable
- 88 (900, 65)
- 7.8 (80, 69 in.-lbf)
- 80 (820, 59)
- Bushing
- Rear Brake Drum Assembly
- Brake Drum
- Gasket
- Exhaust Tailpipe
- 56 (550, 41)
- N·m (kgf·cm, ft·lbf) : Specified torque
- ◆ Non–reusable part
- TY2039800022000X

TIGHTENING SPECIFICATIONS

Year	Component	Torque/ Ft. Lbs.
1998-99	ABS harness Clamps	13
	Lower Shock Absorber Bolt	27
	Rear Axle Beam Bushing Bolts/Nuts	65
	Rear Axle Hub Nuts	59
	Upper Shock Absorber Nuts	18
	Wheel Lug Nuts	77

Front Suspension & Steering

NOTE: On Air Bag Equipped Models, Refer To "Air Bag System Precautions" Located In The Front Of This Manual For System Disarming & Arming Procedures.

INDEX

PRECAUTIONS

AIR BAG SYSTEMS

Refer to "Air Bag System Precautions" in the front of this manual for system disarming and arming procedures.

AUDIO CODED ANTI-THEFT SYSTEM

Some models are with an audio coded anti-theft system that will disable the radio when the battery cable is disconnected. The system can be identified by the word "ANTI-THEFT SYSTEM" on the cassette tape lid. Obtain three digit customer code for input. Reset system after service as follows:

1. Obtain three digit audio anti-theft code.
2. Depress 1 (PROG) while depressing righthand side of TUNE SEEK button, --- will appear in tape operation display.
3. To enter first digit, depress 1 (PROG) button repeatedly until number of times depressed equals first digit beginning with zero (depress 1 button six times if first digit is five).
4. To enter second digit, depress 2 (APS) button repeatedly until number of times depressed equals the second digit beginning with zero.
5. To enter third digit, depress 3 (RPT) button repeatedly until number of times depressed equals third digit beginning with zero.
6. If --- is displayed during code input, repeat procedure.
7. When code appears in display, depress and hold SCAN button until SEC appears.
8. When SEC disappears audio system should be operative.
9. If Err is displayed, repeat procedure. **Attempting to input code more than nine times may permanently disable audio system.**

BATTERY GROUND CABLE

Prior to service, disconnect battery ground cable and isolate as required.

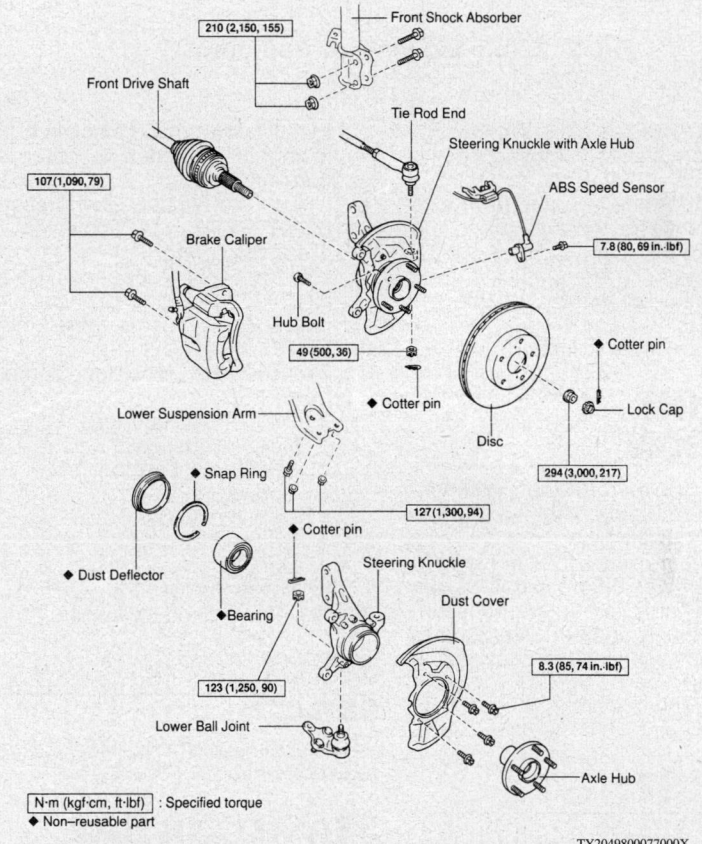

Fig. 1 Exploded view of knuckle, hub & bearing

WHEEL BEARING

ADJUST

These models are equipped with sealed, non-adjustable bearings.

HUB SERVICE

1. Remove front wheel.
2. Remove front brake caliper and disc.
3. Remove drive shaft lock nut, **Fig. 1.**
4. Remove ABS speed sensor and wire harness clamp.
5. Loosen but do not remove, two nuts on lower end of shock absorber.
6. Using a suitable tie rod removal tool, disconnect tie rod from steering knuckle.
7. Disconnect lower ball joint from lower suspension arm.
8. Remove steering knuckle with axle hub.

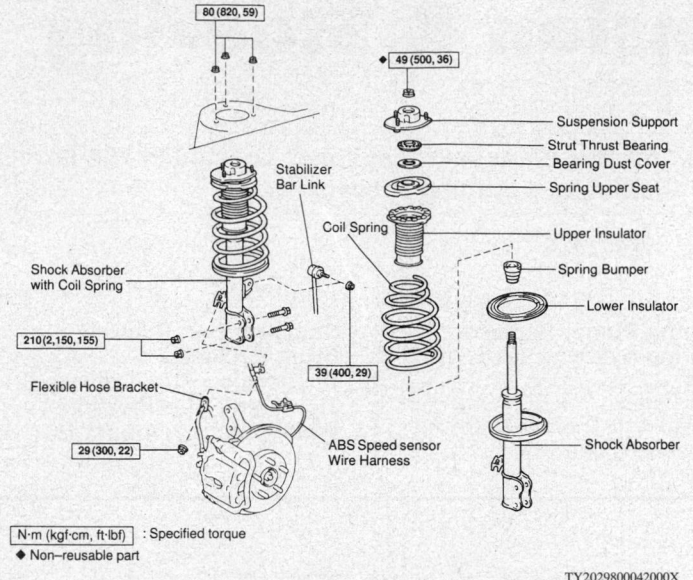

N·m (kgf·cm, ft·lbf) : Specified torque
◆ Non–reusable part

TY2029800042000X

Fig. 2 Exploded view of front strut

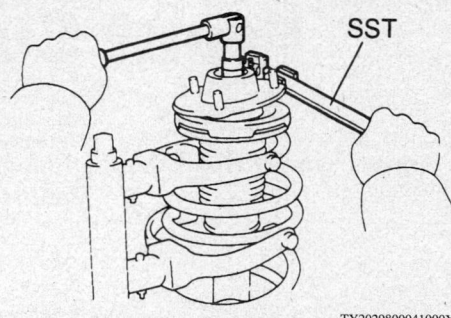

TY2029800041000X

Fig. 3 Suspension support removal

9. Using rear axle shaft puller No. 09520-00031, or equivalent, remove axle hub from knuckle.
10. Remove inner bearing race from axle hub with a suitable hydraulic press and bearing removal tool.
11. Remove snap ring from knuckle, then press bearing out with a suitable hydraulic press.
12. Reverse procedure to install.

BALL JOINT INSPECTION

1. Remove ball joint from steering knuckle with ball joint puller tool No. 09628-62011, or equivalent.
2. Mount ball joint in vise, then move back and forth 5 times before installing nut.
3. Using a suitable torque wrench, turn nut continuously one turn every two to four seconds, then take torque reading on fifth turn.
4. If torque reading is not 9–30 inch lbs., replace ball joint.

BALL JOINT
REPLACE

1. Remove steering knuckle as outlined previously in "Hub Service."
2. Using a suitable screwdriver, remove dust deflector.
3. Remove cotter pin and nut.
4. Using ball joint removal tool No. 09628-62011, or equivalent, remove ball joint.
5. Reverse procedure to install.

COIL SPRING
REPLACE

Refer to **Fig. 2,** when performing the following procedure.
1. Remove strut as outlined in "Strut, Replace."

2. Install two nuts and a bolt to bracket at lower side of shock absorber and secure in a vise.
3. Using coil spring compressor No. 09727-30021, or equivalent, compress coil spring.
4. Use front spring upper seat holder tool No. 09729-22031, or equivalent, to hold support in place, then remove nut, **Fig. 3.**
5. Remove the following components from strut:
   a. Suspension support.
   b. Bearing dust cover.
   c. Strut thrust bearing.
   d. Spring upper seat.
   e. Upper insulator.
   f. Coil spring.
   g. Spring bumper.
   h. Lower insulator.
6. Reverse procedure to install.

STRUT
REPLACE

Refer to "Coil Spring, Replace" for strut replacement procedure.

STABILIZER BAR
REPLACE

1. Remove front wheels.
2. Remove left and right stabilizer bar links.
3. Disconnect tie rod ends from steering knuckle.
4. Remove left and right stabilizer bar brackets and bushings.
5. Remove power steering gear assembly set bolts and nuts.
6. Remove stabilizer bar from left side with power steering gear assembly raised.
7. Reverse procedure to install, noting the following:
   a. Install stabilizer bar with white colored markings on the left side.

b. Inspect stabilizer links rotational torque as outlined in "Ball Joint Inspection" and replace any link that measures more than 48–96 inch lbs.

SUSPENSION ARM
REPLACE

1. Remove front wheel.
2. Disconnect lower suspension arm from lower ball joint, **Fig. 4.**
3. Remove two bolts on front side of lower suspension arm.
4. Remove bolt and nut on rear side of lower suspension arm.
5. Remove lower suspension arm, then the lower suspension arm bushing stopper from lower suspension arm shaft.
6. Reverse procedure to install.

POWER STEERING GEAR
REPLACE

1. Position front wheels straight ahead.
2. Remove driver's air bag and steering wheel as outlined in "Steering Wheel, Replace" in the "Electrical" section.
3. Disconnect right and left tie rod ends.
4. Disconnect intermediate shaft assembly and clamp plates, **Fig. 5.**
5. Disconnect pressure feed and return hoses.
6. Disconnect stabilizer bar.
7. Remove two gear assembly set bolts and nuts, then remove gear assembly from left side of vehicle.
8. Reverse procedure to install.

POWER STEERING PUMP
REPLACE

1. Disconnect power steering return hose and pressure feed tube.
2. Using torque wrench adapter No. 09249-63010, or equivalent, loosen power steering pump pivot bolt "A" and bolt "B," **Fig. 6.**
3. Remove power steering drive belt.
4. Disconnect connector from oil pressure switch, then remove bolt "B" and loosen bolt "A" to allow for removal of pump assembly.

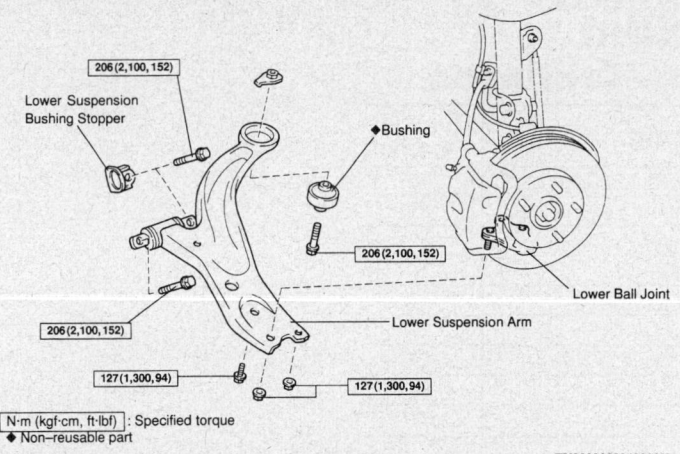

Fig. 4 Front lower suspension arm

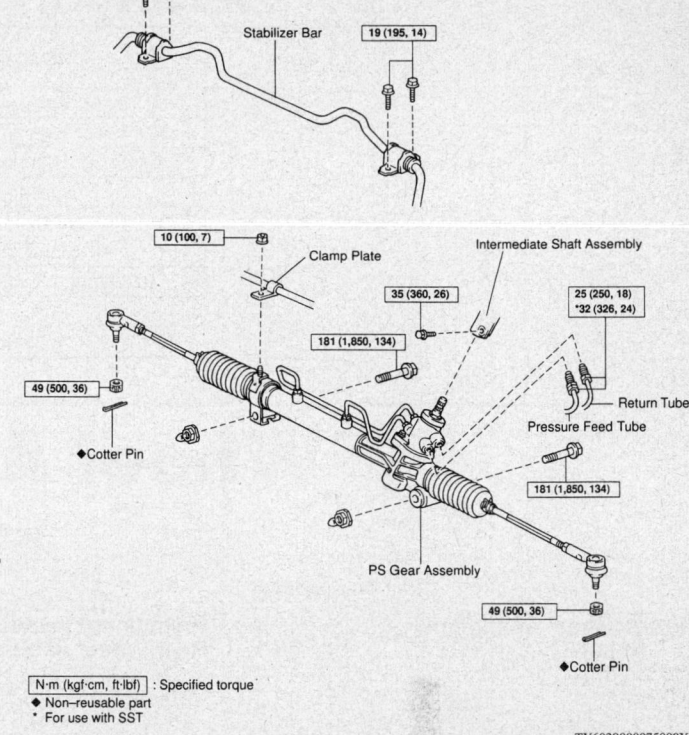

Fig. 5 Power steering gear installation

5. Remove oil pressure switch from union bolt, then the union bolt and gasket.
6. Reverse procedure to install.

POWER STEERING SYSTEM BLEED

1. Raise and support vehicle.
2. With engine stopped, turn steering wheel slowly from lock to lock several times.
3. Lower vehicle, start engine.
4. Run engine at idle for several minutes.
5. With engine idling, turn wheel to left or right full lock position and keep it there for two to three seconds, then turn wheel to opposite full lock position and hold for two to three seconds.
6. Repeat several times.
7. Stop engine and inspect for foaming or emulsification.
8. Inspect fluid level and top up as necessary.

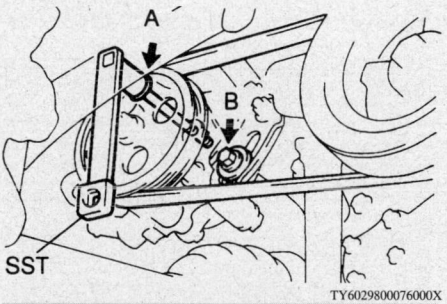

Fig. 6 Power steering pump mounting bolts

TIGHTENING SPECIFICATIONS

Year	Component	Torque/ Ft. Lbs.
1998-99	ABS Sensor Wire Clamp	69①
	Ball Joint Attaching Nuts/Bolt	94
	Drive Shaft Lock Nut	217
	Front Caliper Mounting Bolts	79
	Intermediate Shaft Clamp	26
	Lower Suspension Arm	152
	Power Steering Gear Mounting Bolts	131
	Power Steering Pressure & Return Feed Pipes	18

Continued

TIGHTENING
SPECIFICATIONS—Continued

Year	Component	Torque/Ft. Lbs.
1998-99	Power Steering Pressure Switch	15
	Power Steering Pump "A" Bolt	21
	Power Steering Pump "B" Bolt	32
	Stabilizer Bar Brackets	14
	Stabilizer Bar Clamps	14
	Stabilizer Bar Links	29
	Steering Knuckle Mounting Nuts	155
	Tie Rod Castle Nut	36
	Wheel Lug Nuts	77

① — Inch lbs.

Wheel Alignment

INDEX

PRELIMINARY INSPECTION

1. Inspect tires for proper inflation and for excessive or abnormal wear.
2. Inspect wheel balance.
3. Inspect wheel bearing free play, replace bearing if over .0020 inch.
4. Inspect axle hub deviation, replace hub if over .0020 inch.
5. Inspect front suspension and steering linkage components for looseness.
6. Inspect ball joints for excessive play.
7. Inspect shock absorbers for leaks, bushing wear or excessive bounce.

FRONT WHEEL ALIGNMENT

CASTER

Caster in not adjustable. If caster measurement is not within specification, inspect suspension parts for damage or excessive wear.

CAMBER

After camber is adjusted, inspect toe-in adjustment.
1. Remove front wheels and ABS speed sensor clamp.
2. Remove two nuts on lower side of shock absorber.

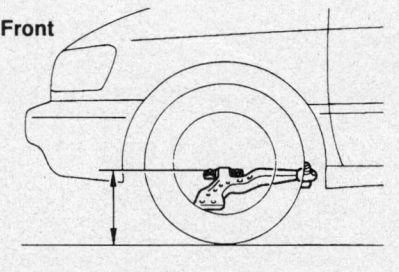

Front

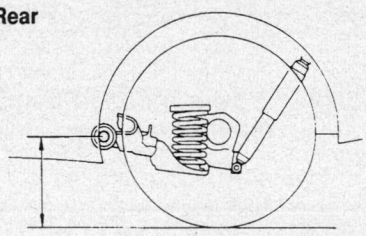

Rear

TY2049800078000X

Fig. 1 Vehicle ride height measurements

3. Coat threads of nuts with engine oil and temporarily install nuts.
4. Adjust camber by pushing or pulling lower side of shock absorber in direction required.
5. Hold in position and tighten nuts to specification.

TOE-IN

1. Remove boot clamps from tie rods.
2. Loosen tie-rod end lock nuts.
3. Turn left and right rack ends an equal amount to adjust toe-in.
4. Ensure length of left and right rack ends are the same.
5. Tighten tie-rod end lock nuts to specification.
6. Ensure boots aren't twisted, then install boot clamps.

REAR WHEEL ALIGNMENT

Before inspecting the wheel alignment, adjust vehicle height to specification.

CAMBER & TOE-IN

Rear camber is not adjustable, if measurements are not within specification, inspect suspension parts for damage or excessive wear. Repair or replace components as necessary to bring alignment into specified range.

VEHICLE RIDE HEIGHT

Refer to **Fig. 1,** for ride height measurements.

TOYOTA SUPRA
INDEX OF SERVICE OPERATIONS

Specifications

ENGINE IDENTIFICATION

Year	Engine Code	Engine, Liter
1996–98	2JZ-GE	3.0L
	2JZ-GTE	3.0L

GENERAL ENGINE SPECIFICATIONS

Year	Engine	Fuel System	Bore & Stroke	Compression Ratio	Maximum Brake H.P. @ RPM	Maximum Torque Ft. Lbs. @ RPM	Normal Oil Pressure, psi @ RPM
1996	3.0L 2JZ-GE①	SFI	3.39 x 3.39	10.0	220 @ 5800	210 @ 4800	47–84 @ 4000
	3.0L 2JZ-GTE②	SFI	3.39 x 3.39	8.5	320 @ 5600	315 @ 4000	47–84 @ 4000
1997	3.0L 2JZ-GE①	SFI	3.39 x 3.39	10.0	220 @ 5800	210 @ 4800	49–84 @ 3000
	3.0L 2JZ-GTE②	SFI	3.39 x 3.39	8.5	320 @ 5600	315 @ 4000	49–84 @ 4000
1998	3.0L 2JZ-GE①	SFI	3.39 x 3.39	10.0	225 @ 6000	220 @ 4000	③
	3.0L 2JZ-GTE②	SFI	3.39 x 3.39	8.5	320 @ 5600	315 @ 4000	③

SFI — Sequential Fuel Injection
① — Non-turbo engine.
② — Turbo engine.
③ — 7.1 psi or more at idle; 47 psi @ 3000 RPM.

TUNE UP SPECIFICATIONS

The following specifications are published from the latest information available. This data should be used only in the absence of a decal affixed in the engine compartment.

When checking ignition timing, it may be necessary to disconnect certain hoses and/or electrical connectors. Refer to vehicle emission control label for specific instructions.

Before disconnecting spark plug wires from distributor cap, determine location of No. 1 wire in cap, as distributor position may have been altered from that shown.

Year	Engine	Spark Plug Gap, Inch	Ignition Timing Firing Order	Ignition Timing Timing, °BTDC	Ignition Timing Timing Mark Fig.	Curb Idle Speed, RPM Man. Trans.	Curb Idle Speed, RPM Auto. Trans.	Fuel Pump Pressure, psi	Valve Clearance, Inch Int.	Valve Clearance, Inch Exh.
1996	3.0L 2JZ-GE	.043	1-5-3-6-2-4	10①	A	700	700N	38–44	.006–.010	.010–.014
	3.0L 2JZ-GTE	.043	1-5-3-6-2-4	10①	A	650	650N	38–44	.006–.010	.010–.014
1997	3.0L 2JZ-GE	.043	1-5-3-6-2-4	10①	A	700	700N	38–44	.006–.010	.010–.014
	3.0L 2JZ-GTE	.043	1-5-3-6-2-4	10①	A	650	650N	33–40	.006–.010	.010–.014
1998	3.0L 2JZ-GE	.043	1-5-3-6-2-4	10①	A	700	700N	44-50	.006–.010	.010–.014
	3.0L 2JZ-GTE	.043	1-5-3-6-2-4	10①	A	650	650N	33-40	.006–.010	.010–.014

BTDC — Before Top Dead Center
N — Neutral
① — With terminals TE1 & E1 connected of DLC1.

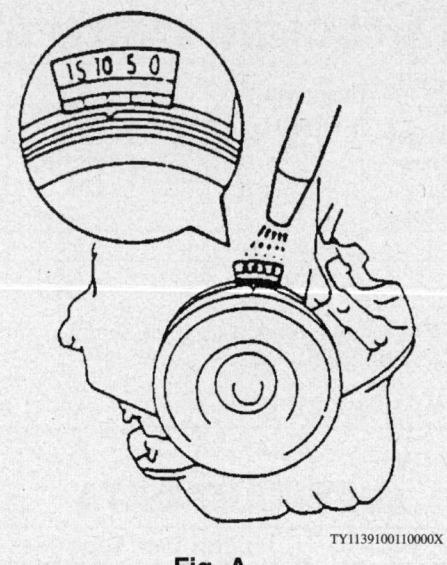

TY1139100110000X

Fig. A

FRONT WHEEL ALIGNMENT SPECIFICATIONS

The specifications listed below are for unloaded vehicles.

Year	Engine	Caster Angle, Degrees		Camber Angle, Degrees		Toe-In, Inch	Toe-Out On Turns, Deg.		Ball Joint Wear
		Limits	Desired	Limits	Desired		Outer Wheel	Inner Wheel	
1996	2JZ-GE	$2\frac{3}{4}$ to $4\frac{1}{4}$	$+3\frac{1}{2}$	$-1\frac{1}{12}$ to $+\frac{5}{12}$	$-\frac{1}{3}$	0	$30\frac{3}{4}$	35	①
	2JZ-GTE	$2\frac{3}{40}$ to $4\frac{1}{4}$	$+3\frac{1}{2}$	$-1\frac{1}{4}$ to $+\frac{1}{4}$	$-\frac{1}{2}$	0	$30\frac{7}{12}$	$34\frac{11}{12}$	①
1997–98	2JZ-GE	$+2\frac{7}{12}$ to $+4\frac{1}{12}$	$+3\frac{1}{3}$	$-1\frac{1}{12}$ to $+\frac{5}{12}$	$-\frac{1}{3}$	-.08 to +.08	$30\frac{3}{4}$	35	①
	2JZ-GTE	$+2\frac{1}{4}$ to $+4\frac{1}{4}$	$+3\frac{1}{2}$	$-1\frac{1}{4}$ to $+\frac{1}{4}$	$-\frac{1}{2}$	-.08 to +.08	$30\frac{7}{12}$	$34\frac{11}{12}$	①

① — Refer to "Ball Joint Inspection" under "Front Suspension & Steering."

REAR WHEEL ALIGNMENT SPECIFICATIONS

The specifications listed below are for unloaded vehicles.

Year	Engine	Camber Angle, Degrees		Toe-In, Inch
		Limits	Desired	
1996	All	$-2\frac{1}{60}$ to $-3\frac{1}{60}$	-1	+.04 to +.20
1997	2JZ-GE	$-2\frac{1}{3}$ to $+\frac{1}{6}$	$-1\frac{7}{12}$	+.04 to +.20
	2JZ-GTE	$-2\frac{1}{4}$ to $-\frac{3}{4}$	$-1\frac{1}{2}$	+.04 to +.20
1998	All	$-2\frac{1}{4}$ to $-\frac{3}{4}$	$-1\frac{1}{2}$	+.04 to +.20

FLUID CAPACITIES & COOLING SYSTEM DATA

Year	Engine	Cooling Capacity, Qts.		Radiator Cap Relief Pressure, Lbs.	Thermo. Opening Temp., °F	Fuel Tank, Gals.	Engine Oil Refill, Qts.①	Transmission/Transaxle Oil			Axle Oil, Pints
		Less A/C	With A/C					4 Speed, Pints	5 & 6 Speed, Pints	Auto. Trans., Qts.	
1996	2JZ-GE	④	④	16	180	18.5	5.6	—	5.4	7.6	2.86
	2JZ-GTE	10	10	16	180	18.5	5.3	—	3.8	8.7	2.86
1997	2JZ-GE	③	③	13.5	176	18.5	5.5	—	5.4	7.6	2.86
	2JZ-GTE	②	②	13.5	176	18.5	5.3	—	3.8	8.7	2.86

Continued

FLUID CAPACITIES & COOLING SYSTEM DATA—Continued

Year	Engine	Cooling Capacity, Qts.		Radiator Cap Relief Pressure, Lbs.	Thermo. Opening Temp., °F	Fuel Tank, Gals.	Engine Oil Refill, Qts.①	Transmission/Transaxle Oil			Axle Oil, Pints
		Less A/C	With A/C					4 Speed, Pints	5 & 6 Speed, Pints	Auto. Trans., Qts.	
1998	2JZ-GE	8.5	8.5	16	180	18.5	5.5	—	3.8	7.6	2.9
	2JZ-GTE	9.4	9.4	16	180	18.5	5.3	—	3.8	8.7	2.9

① — With oil filter change.
② — Manual transaxle, 9.4; automatic transaxle, 9.3.
③ — Manual transaxle, 10; automatic transaxle, 9.9.
④ — Automatic transaxle, 8.8; manual transaxle, 7.7.

LUBRICANT DATA

Year	Lubricant Type					
	Transaxle		Rear Axle	Power Steering	Brake System
	Manual	Automatic			
1996	75W-90 GL-5	Dexron II/IIE/III	80W-90 GL-5	Dexron II/IIE/III	DOT 3
1997	75W-90 GL-5	Dexron II/IIE/III	80W-90 GL-5	Dexron II/IIE/III	DOT 3
1998	①	ATF Type T-1V	80W-90 GL-5	Dexron II/IIE/III	DOT 3

① — Toyota Gear Oil V160, Exxon ATF Dexron D-21065, or equivalent.

Electrical

NOTE: On Air Bag Equipped Models, Refer To "Air Bag System Precautions" Located In The Front Of This Manual For System Disarming & Arming Procedures.

INDEX

PRECAUTIONS

AIR BAG SYSTEMS

Refer to "Air Bag System Precautions" in the front of this manual for system disarming and arming procedures.

BATTERY GROUND CABLE

Prior to service, disconnect battery ground cable and isolate as required.

AUDIO CODED ANTI-THEFT SYSTEM

Some models are equipped with an audio coded anti-theft system that will disable the radio when the battery cable is disconnected. The system can be identified by the "ANTI-THEFT SYSTEM" on the cassette tape lid. Obtain 3 digit customer code for input. Reset system after service as follows:

1. Obtain 3 digit audio anti-theft code.
2. Depress 1 (PROG) while depressing righthand side of TUNE SEEK button, - - will appear in tape operation display.
3. To enter the first digit, depress 1 (PROG) button repeatedly until the number of times depressed equals the first digit beginning with zero (depress the 1 button six times if the first digit if five).
4. To enter second digit, depress 2 (APS) button repeatedly until the number of times depressed equals the second digit beginning with zero.
5. To enter third digit, depress 3 (RPT) button repeatedly until the number of times depressed equals the second digit beginning with zero.
6. If - - - is displayed during code input, repeat procedure.
7. When code appears in display, depress and hold SCAN button until SEC appears.
8. When SEC disappears audio system should be operative.
9. If Err is displayed, repeat procedure. **Attempting to input code more than nine times may permanently disable audio system.**

FUSE PANEL & FLASHER LOCATION

There are three fuse blocks; the first is located on the left front kick panel, the second is on the right front kick panel and the third is next to the battery. On models with ABS brakes, an additional fuse block is located in the engine compartment. The turn signal/hazard flasher is on the left front kick panel fuse block.

FUEL PUMP RELAY LOCATION

The fuel pump relay is located in the engine compartment relay center, **Fig. 1.**

RELAY CENTER LOCATION

The relay center is located at the lefthand front of the engine compartment on the fender apron.

STARTER
REPLACE

1. Obtain audio anti-theft code, if equipped, as outlined in "Precautions."
2. Disconnect electrical connectors from starter motor.

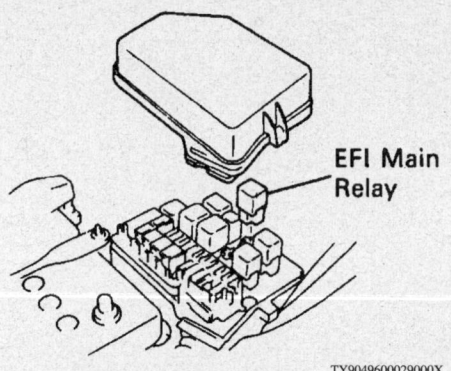

EFI Main Relay

TY9049600029000X

Fig. 1   Fuel pump relay

3. Remove starter attaching bolts, then remove.
4. Reverse to install. Reset audio coded anti-theft, if equipped, as outlined in "Precautions."

DISTRIBUTOR
REPLACE
2JZ-GE ENGINE

1. Disconnect distributor connector.
2. Disconnect high tension cords from distributor.
3. Remove distributor retaining nut and pull out distributor.
4. Remove O-ring from distributor housing.
5. Reverse procedure to install.

COIL PACK
REPLACE
2JZ-GTE ENGINE

1. Remove No. 3 timing belt cover, **Fig. 2.**
2. Remove PCV hoses.
3. Disconnect ignition coil connectors.
4. Remove two bolts and twin ignition coil assembly.
5. Remove rubber boot from ignition coil.
6. Remove two screws and ignition coil from assembly.
7. Reverse procedure to install.

IGNITION LOCK
REPLACE

1. Obtain audio anti-theft code, if equipped, as outlined in "Precautions."
2. Turn ignition switch to ACC position.
3. Insert a small diameter rod into hole located on side of lock cylinder, then while holding down pin, remove lock cylinder.
4. Reverse procedure to install. Ensure lock cylinder is in ACC position.
5. Reset audio coded anti-theft, if equipped, as outlined in "Precautions."

IGNITION SWITCH
REPLACE

1. Obtain audio anti-theft code, if equipped, as outlined in "Precautions."
2. Remove steering wheel as outlined under "Steering Wheel, Replace."

3. Disconnect electrical connectors from ignition switch.
4. Turn ignition key to ACC position and remove ignition key cylinder.
5. Remove screw and ignition switch.
6. Reverse procedure to install. Reset audio coded anti-theft, if equipped, as outlined in "Precautions."

NEUTRAL SAFETY SWITCH
REPLACE

1. Raise and support vehicle.
2. Loosen neutral safety switch bracket bolt.
3. Position transmission shift lever into Neutral.
4. Align switch shaft groove with neutral base line, **Fig. 3,** then retighten switch bracket bolt.
5. Connect electrical connector to switch.

STOP LIGHT SWITCH
REPLACE

1. Remove brake pedal tension spring.
2. Disconnect switch wire connector.
3. Remove switch mounting nut, then slide switch from mounting bracket.
4. Reverse procedure to install.

COMBINATION SWITCH
REPLACE
REPLACEMENT

1. Obtain audio anti-theft code, if equipped, as outlined in "Precautions."
2. Pull wheel pad out from steering wheel and disconnect air bag connector. **When removing wheel pad, take care not to pull air bag wire harness. When storing wheel pad, keep upper surface facing upward. Never disassemble wheel pad.**
3. Remove horn button screws and horn button.
4. Scribe alignment marks on steering wheel and steering shaft.
5. Remove steering wheel nut.
6. Using a steering wheel puller, remove steering wheel.
7. Remove steering column upper and lower covers.
8. Remove combination switch.
9. Reverse procedure to install. Reset audio coded anti-theft, if equipped, as outlined in "Precautions."

SERVICE
Headlight & Dimmer Switch

1. Obtain audio anti-theft code, if equipped, as outlined in "Precautions."
2. Pull wheel pad out from steering wheel and disconnect air bag connector. **When removing wheel pad, take care not to pull air bag wire harness. When storing wheel pad, keep upper surface facing upward. Never disassemble wheel pad.**
3. Remove steering wheel, then upper and lower steering column covers.

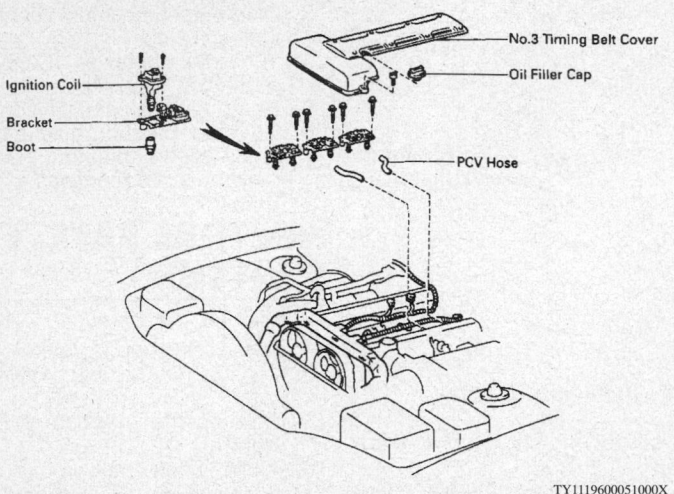

Fig. 2 Ignition coil replacement. 2JZ-GTE engine

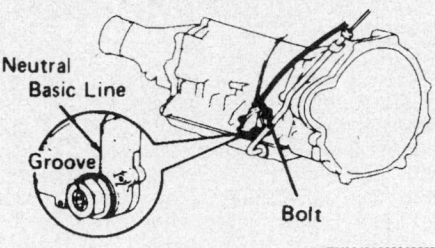

Fig. 3 Neutral safety switch adjustment

4. Disconnect combination switch connector, then using a small screwdriver, disengage headlight and dimmer switch wiring from combination switch connector. **Note position of wires.**
5. **On models with cruise control,** removal of slip ring may be necessary. Remove screws, headlight and dimmer switch, then ball and spring assembly, **Fig. 4.**
6. **On all models,** install headlight and dimmer switch onto combination switch.
7. Insert spring into headlight and dimmer lever, than install lever and screw onto combination switch.
8. Position ball on the spring, **Fig. 5,** and place headlight and dimmer switch lever into HI position. Install screws and clamp, **Fig. 5.**
9. Ensure switch operates smoothly in each position.
10. Install electrical terminals into combination switch connector in the same position as they were removed.
11. Install combination switch connector, then the steering column upper and lower covers and steering wheel.
12. Connect battery ground cable. Reset audio coded anti-theft, if equipped, as outlined in "Precautions."

Hazard & Turn Signal Switch

1. Obtain audio anti-theft code, if equipped, as outlined in "Precautions."
2. Pull wheel pad out from steering wheel and disconnect air bag connector. **When removing wheel pad, take care not to pull air bag wire harness. When storing wheel pad, keep upper surface facing upward. Never disassemble wheel pad.**
3. Remove steering wheel, then the upper and lower steering column covers.
4. Disconnect hazard and turn signal switch connector, then using a small screwdriver, disengage hazard and turn signal switch wiring from combination switch connector. **Note position of wires.**
5. Remove screws, clamp, hazard and turn signal switch assembly from combination switch.
6. Reverse procedure to install. Reset audio coded anti-theft, if equipped, as outlined in "Precautions."

Windshield Wiper/Washer Switch

1. Obtain audio anti-theft code, if equipped, as outlined in "Precautions."
2. Pull wheel pad out from steering wheel and disconnect air bag connector. **When removing wheel pad, take care not to pull air bag wire harness. When storing wheel pad, keep upper surface facing upward. Never disassemble wheel pad.**
3. Remove steering wheel, then upper and lower steering column covers.
4. Remove steering wheel and upper and lower steering column covers.
5. Disconnect wire terminal from horn contact.
6. Disconnect windshield wiper/washer switch connector, then using a small screwdriver, disengage windshield wiper/washer switch wiring from combination switch connector. **Note position of wires.**
7. Remove screw, clamp and windshield wiper/washer switch assembly.
8. Reverse procedure to install. Reset audio coded anti-theft, if equipped, as outlined in "Precautions."

STEERING WHEEL
REPLACE

1. Obtain audio anti-theft code, if equipped, as outlined in "Precautions."
2. Place front wheels in straight ahead position.
3. Pull wheel pad out from steering wheel and disconnect air bag connector. **When removing wheel pad, take care not to pull air bag wire harness. When storing wheel pad, keep upper surface facing upward. Never disassemble wheel pad.**
4. Remove steering wheel pad.
5. Place alignment marks on steering wheel and mainshaft for assembly reference.
6. Remove nut attaching steering wheel to steering shaft.
7. Remove steering wheel using puller tool No. 09950–50010, 09609–20011, or equivalent.
8. Reverse procedure to install. Reset audio coded anti-theft, if equipped, as outlined in "Precautions."

INSTRUMENT CLUSTER
REPLACE

1. Obtain audio anti-theft code, if equipped, as outlined under "Precautions."
2. Remove steering wheel as outlined in "Steering Wheel, Replace."
3. Remove steering column cover.
4. Remove hood release lever attaching bolts, then remove.
5. Remove instrument panel hole cover.
6. Remove I/P left lower panel.
7. Pull lower I/P finish panel rearward, disconnect switch electrical connectors, then remove panel.
8. Remove ash tray assembly, then remove ash tray panel and disconnect electrical connectors.
9. **On models equipped with manual transmission,** remove shift lever knob.
10. **On all models,** remove instrument cluster finish panel attaching screws.
11. Remove instrument cluster attaching screws, then remove.
12. Reverse to install. Reset audio coded anti-theft, if equipped, as outlined under "Precautions."

RADIO
REPLACE

1. Obtain audio anti-theft code, if equipped, as outlined under "Precautions."
2. Pull wheel pad out from steering wheel and disconnect air bag connector. **When removing wheel pad, take care not to pull air bag wire harness. When storing wheel pad, keep upper surface facing upward. Never disassemble wheel pad.**
3. Remove steering wheel, then the upper and lower steering column covers.
4. Remove ashtray and ashtray retainer.

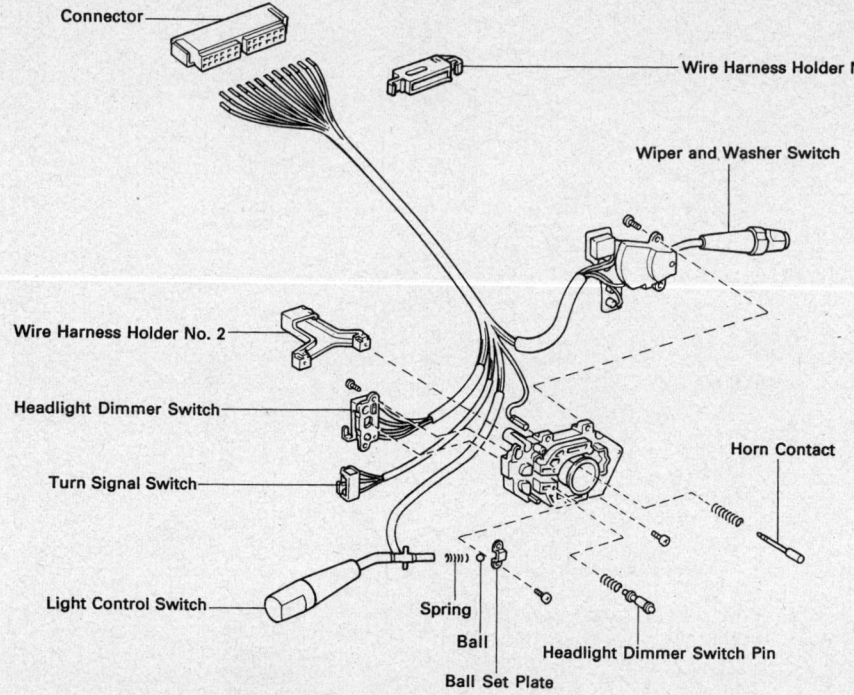

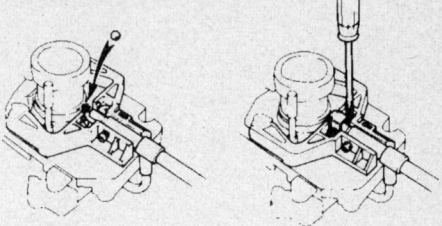

TY9049100003000X

Fig. 5 Positioning ball onto spring

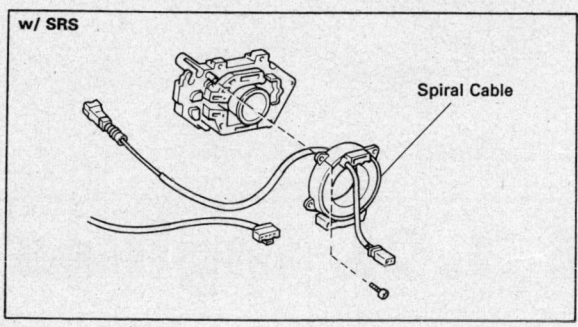

TY9049100002000X

Fig. 4 Exploded view of combination switch

5. **On models equipped with manual transmission,** remove shift lever knob.
6. **On all models,** remove three instrument center cluster finish panel attaching screws, then disconnect the panel electrical connectors and remove the panel.
7. Remove four radio attaching screws, then disconnect electrical connectors and antenna lead and remove radio.
8. Reverse procedure to install. Reset audio coded anti-theft, if equipped, as outlined under "Precautions."

WIPER MOTOR
REPLACE
FRONT

1. Disconnect wiper motor wire connec-

tor, then remove wiper motor service cover, if equipped.
2. Remove wiper motor attaching bolts.
3. Using a screwdriver disconnect wiper link from wiper motor and remove wiper motor.
4. Reverse procedure to install.

REAR

1. Remove wiper arm and rear door trim cover.
2. Disconnect wiper motor wire connector.
3. Remove wiper motor bracket attaching bolts and wiper motor and bracket, **Fig. 6.**

WIPER SWITCH
REPLACE

Refer to "Combination Switch, Replace" procedure.

BLOWER MOTOR
REPLACE

Remove A/C unit as outlined under "Evaporator Core, Replace," then refer to **Fig. 7** to remove blower motor.

HEATER CORE
REPLACE

Remove A/C unit as outlined under "Evaporator Core, Replace," then refer to **Fig. 7** to remove heater core.

EVAPORATOR CORE
REPLACE

1. Obtain audio anti-theft code, if equipped, as outlined under "Precautions," then discharge and recover A/C refrigerant.
2. Drain engine coolant from radiator.
3. Remove engine wire harness bracket mounting bolt.
4. Remove brake tube bracket mounting bolts from dash panel.
5. Disconnect water hose from heater core.
6. Remove insulator retainer.
7. Remove ABS actuator, if equipped.
8. Disconnect liquid and suction tubes from A/C unit.
9. Remove plate cover.
10. Remove instrument panel as outlined under "Dash Panel Service."
11. Remove heater to register No. 3 duct.
12. Disconnect A/C unit connectors and remove A/C unit.
13. Disconnect air inlet servomotor control link and remove air inlet servomotor, **Fig. 7.**
14. Remove blower motor.
15. Remove foot air duct and A/C unit block joint.
16. Remove A/C unit lower case cover and evaporator cover.
17. Pull evaporator out of A/C unit case.
18. Reverse procedure to install. If evaporator was replaced, add 1.4 oz. compressor oil to compressor.

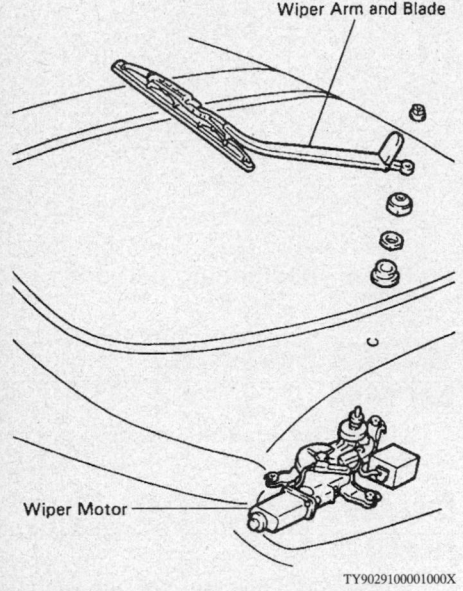

Fig. 6 Exploded view of rear wiper motor

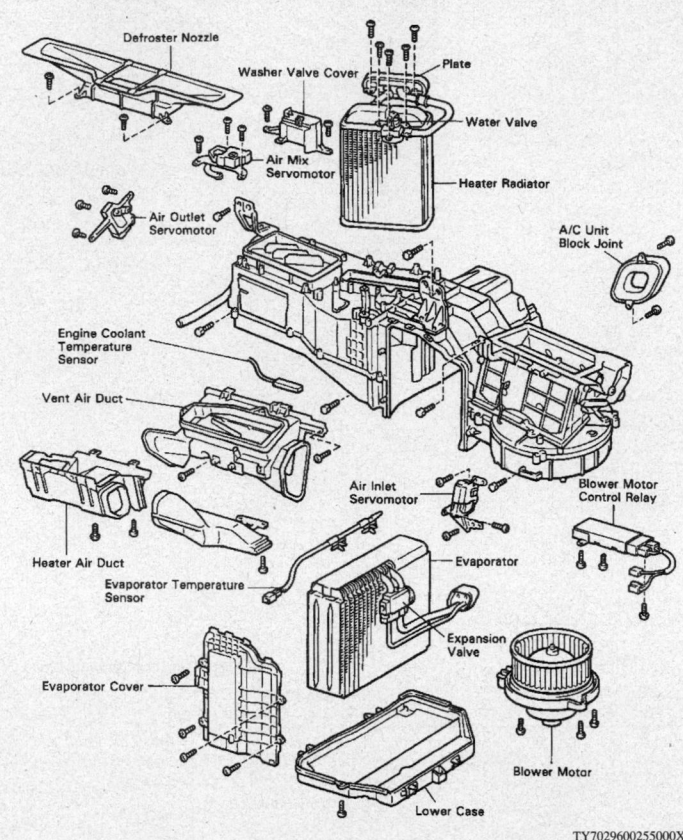

Fig. 7 Exploded view of A/C unit

2JZ-GE & 2JZ-GTE 3.0L Engines

NOTE: On Air Bag Equipped Models, Refer To "Air Bag System Precautions" Located In The Front Of This Manual For System Disarming & Arming Procedures.

INDEX

PRECAUTIONS

AIR BAG SYSTEMS

Refer to "Air Bag System Precautions" in the front of this manual for system disarming and arming procedures.

BATTERY GROUND CABLE

Prior to service, disconnect battery ground cable and isolate as required.

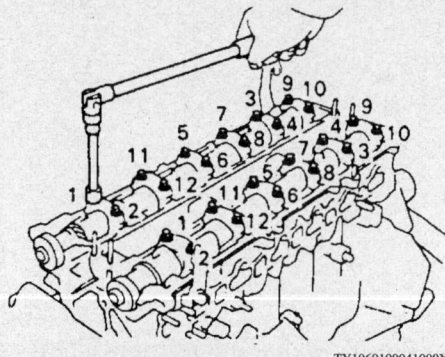

Fig. 1 Camshaft bearing cap loosening sequence. 2JZ-GTE & 1996–97 w/2JZ-GE engines

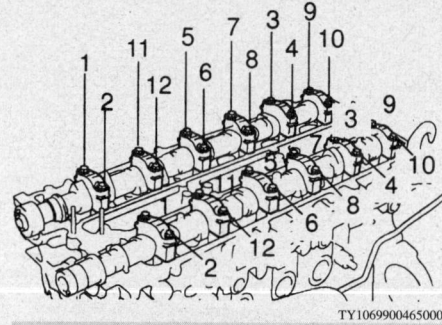

Fig. 2 Camshaft bearing cap loosening sequence. 1998 w/2JZ-GE engine

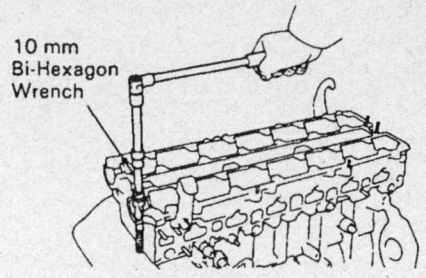

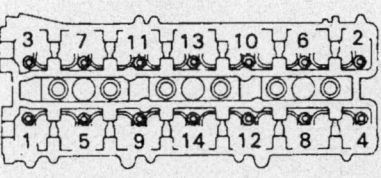

Fig. 3 Cylinder head bolt loosening sequence

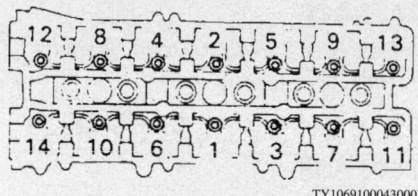

Fig. 4 Cylinder head bolt tightening sequence

AUDIO CODED ANTI-THEFT SYSTEM

Some models are equipped with an audio coded anti-theft system that will disable the radio when the battery cable is disconnected. The system can be identified by the "ANTI-THEFT SYSTEM" on the cassette tape lid. Obtain 3 digit customer code for input. Reset system after service as follows:

1. Obtain 3 digit audio anti-theft code.
2. Depress 1 (PROG) while depressing righthand side of TUNE SEEK button, - - - will appear in tape operation display.
3. To enter the first digit, depress 1 (PROG) button repeatedly until the number of times depressed equals the first digit beginning with zero (depress the 1 button six times if the first digit if five).
4. To enter second digit, depress 2 (APS) button repeatedly until the number of times depressed equals the second digit beginning with zero.
5. To enter third digit, depress 3 (RPT) button repeatedly until the number of times depressed equals the second digit beginning with zero.
6. If - - - is displayed during code input, repeat procedure.
7. When code appears in display, depress and hold SCAN button until SEC appears.
8. When SEC disappears audio system should be operative.
9. If Err is displayed, repeat procedure. **Attempting to input code more than nine times may permanently disable audio system.**

COMPRESSION PRESSURE

1. Start engine and warm to normal operating temperature.
2. **On models equipped with 2JZ-GE engine,** proceed as follows:
   a. Disconnect distributor connector.
   b. Disconnect spark plug wires.
3. **On models equipped with 2JZ-GTE engine,** proceed as follows:
   a. Disconnect camshaft position sensor connectors.
   b. Remove ignition coils as outlined

under "Coil Pack, Replace" in "Electrical" section.
4. **On all models,** remove spark plugs.
5. Insert compression gauge into spark plug hole.
6. While cranking engine, measure compression pressure.
7. **On models equipped with 2JZ-GE engine,** standard compression pressure is 185 psi. Minimum compression pressure is 156 psi.
8. **On models equipped with 2JZ-GTE engine,** standard compression pressure is 156 psi. Minimum compression pressure is 128 psi.
9. **On all models,** maximum compression pressure difference between cylinders should not exceed 14 psi.

ENGINE
REPLACE

1. Obtain audio coded anti-theft code, if equipped, as outlined under "Precautions."
2. Remove battery and battery tray, then the hood.
3. Raise and support vehicle, then re-

move engine undercover, drain coolant, oil and fuel.
4. Lower vehicle and disconnect control cables from throttle body, then remove air cleaner duct.
5. **On models equipped with 2JZ-GTE engine,** remove air cleaner assembly, MAF meter and intake air connector pipe assembly.
6. **On all models,** remove air cleaner assembly, VAF meter and intake air connector pipe assembly.
7. **On models equipped with 2JZ-GTE engine,** remove No. 1, 2 and 5 air tubes.
8. **On all models,** remove No. 2 fan shroud.
9. Remove lefthand headlight beam angle gauge, then the radiator.
10. **On models with automatic transmission,** disconnect oil cooler hoses from cooler tubes and plug hose ends.
11. **On all models,** remove drive belt, fan, fluid coupling assembly and water pump pulley.
12. Remove charcoal canister, then disconnect heater hoses.
13. Disconnect brake booster vacuum hose and EVAP hose.
14. Disconnect all engine wire connectors.
15. Disconnect fuel inlet and return lines. **Put a suitable container or shop towel under fuel pipe support to soak up any spillage.**
16. Remove engine wire bracket, then disconnect power steering pump without disconnecting the hoses.
17. Position power steering pump assembly aside, then disconnect power steering pressure tube from engine.
18. Disconnect air conditioning compressor without disconnecting any hoses and secure aside. **Handle hoses carefully to avoid kinks or other damage.**
19. Disconnect engine wire from cowl panel and from inside vehicle.
20. **On models with manual transmission,** remove upper console panel, shift lever boots and holding bolts, then disconnect clutch release cylinder and

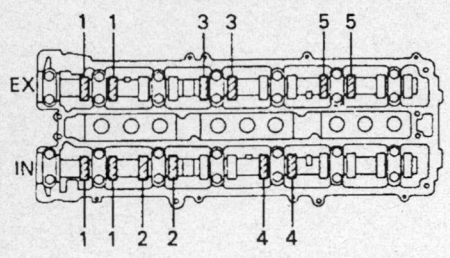

Fig. 5 1st valve adjustment sequence

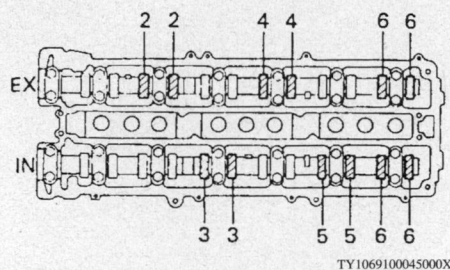

Fig. 6 2nd valve adjustment sequence

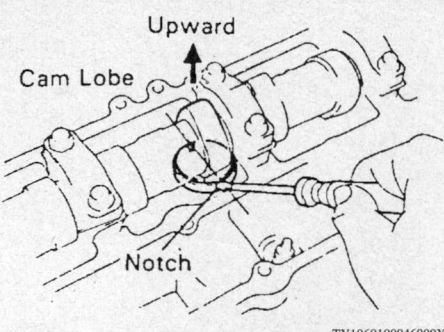

Fig. 7 Valve adjustment shim notch removal

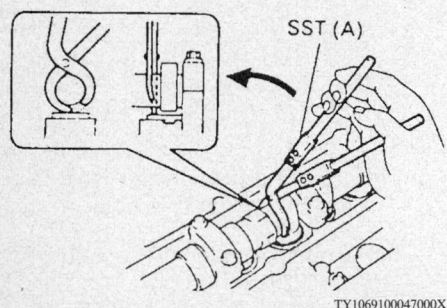

Fig. 8 Valve shim removal tool

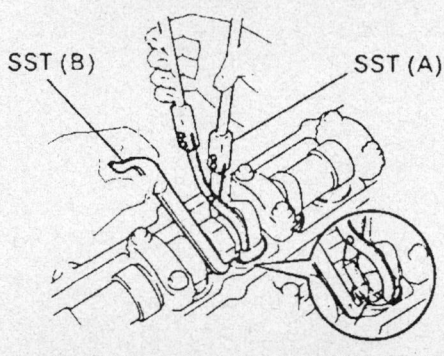

Fig. 9 Valve shim removal

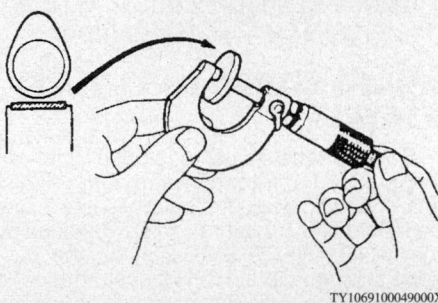

Fig. 10 Valve shim measurement

Shim No.	Thickness	Shim No.	Thickness
1	2.500 (0.0984)	10	2.950 (0.1161)
2	2.550 (0.1004)	11	3.000 (0.1181)
3	2.600 (0.1024)	12	3.050 (0.1201)
4	2.650 (0.1043)	13	3.100 (0.1220)
5	2.700 (0.1063)	14	3.150 (0.1240)
6	2.750 (0.1083)	15	3.200 (0.1260)
7	2.800 (0.1102)	16	3.250 (0.1280)
8	2.850 (0.1122)	17	3.300 (0.1299)
9	2.900 (0.1142)		

New shim thickness   mm (in.)

Fig. 11 Intake valve shim size chart

transmission ground strap.
21. **On models equipped with 2JZ-GTE engine,** disconnect sub-heated oxygen sensor from exhaust.
22. **On all models,** remove No. 2 exhaust pipe from front exhaust pipe.
23. Remove exhaust heat insulator, then the propeller shaft.
24. Disconnect transmission control rod and shift lever.
25. Remove rear engine support member, then attach engine hoist chain and carefully lift engine/transmission assembly from vehicle.
26. Reverse procedure to install. Reset audio coded anti-theft system, if equipped, as outlined under "Precautions."

INTAKE MANIFOLD
REPLACE
Refer to "Cylinder Head, Replace" for procedure.

EXHAUST MANIFOLD
REPLACE
Refer to "Cylinder Head, Replace" for procedure.

CYLINDER HEAD
REPLACE
1. Obtain audio coded anti-theft code, if equipped, as outlined under "Precautions."
2. **On models equipped with 2JZ-GTE engine,** remove turbocharger.
3. **On all models,** raise and support vehicle, then remove lower engine cover and drain coolant.
4. **On models equipped with 2JZ-GE engine,** remove air cleaner duct, air cleaner, VAF meter and intake air pipe assembly.
5. **On all models,** remove drive belt and No. 2 exhaust pipe.
6. Remove exhaust manifold as follows:
   a. Remove manifold heat insulator nuts and the insulator.
   b. Disconnect two main heated oxygen sensor connectors.
   c. **On models equipped with 2JZ-GTE engine,** remove 12 exhaust manifold bolts.

Shim No.	Thickness	Shim No.	Thickness
1	2.500 (0.0984)	10	2.950 (0.1161)
2	2.550 (0.1004)	11	3.000 (0.1181)
3	2.600 (0.1024)	12	3.050 (0.1201)
4	2.650 (0.1043)	13	3.100 (0.1220)
5	2.700 (0.1063)	14	3.150 (0.1240)
6	2.750 (0.1083)	15	3.200 (0.1260)
7	2.800 (0.1102)	16	3.250 (0.1280)
8	2.850 (0.1122)	17	3.300 (0.1299)
9	2.900 (0.1142)		

New shim thickness   mm (in.)

Fig. 12 Exhaust valve shim size chart

   d. **On models equipped with 2JZ-GE engine,** remove 8 nuts then No. 1 and 2 exhaust manifolds.
7. **On all models,** disconnect power steering pump and position aside.
8. Disconnect brake booster vacuum hose and EVAP hose.
9. Remove throttle body and intake air connector assembly.
10. **On models equipped with 2JZ-GTE engine,** disconnect the following connectors:
    a. Six injectors.
    b. Two camshaft position sensors.
    c. Three engine wire clamps from injector holders.

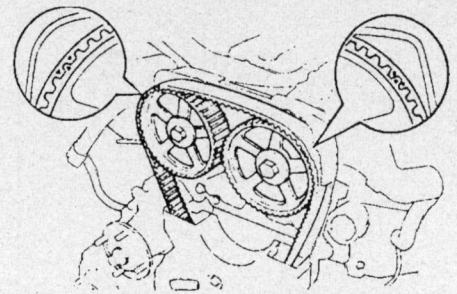

TY1069100052000X

Fig. 13 Timing belt alignment

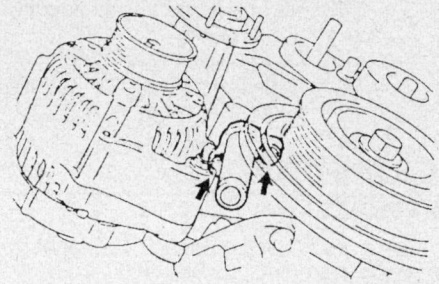

TY1069100053000X

Fig. 14 Timing belt tensioner removal

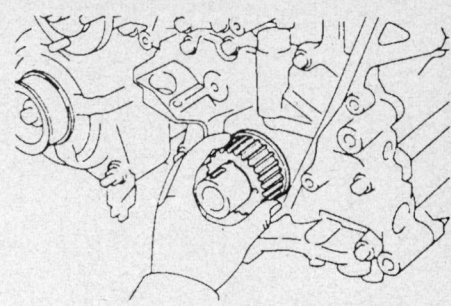

TY1069100054000X

Fig. 15 Crankshaft timing pulley installation

11. **On all models,** remove starter.
12. Remove air intake chamber stays and No. 2 vacuum pipe and VSV assembly.
13. Remove No. 3 timing belt cover and the cylinder head rear cover.
14. Disconnect plug wires from cylinder head covers.
15. Remove distributor and plug wire assembly.
16. Remove spark plugs.
17. Remove timing belt from camshaft timing pulleys.
18. Remove water bypass outlet and No. 1 water bypass pipe
19. Disconnect fuel return lines and plug hose end.
20. Remove engine wire bracket and oil dipstick guide for engine and transmission.
21. Remove air intake chamber and vacuum control valve set.
22. Remove bolt and disconnect engine wire bracket from water pump.
23. **On models equipped with 2JZ-GE engine,** disconnect 2 ground straps from intake manifold and the following connectors:
    a. 6 injectors.
    b. ECT sensor.
    c. ECT sender gauge.
24. **On all models,** remove water outlet and No. 1 bypass hose assembly.
25. Remove intake manifold stay.
26. Remove fuel pressure pulsation damper and fuel inlet pipe.
27. Remove intake manifold and delivery pipe assembly.
28. **On models equipped with 2JZ-GTE engine,** remove ignition coils assemblies, spark plugs, then Nos. 1 and 2 cylinder head covers.
29. **On models equipped with 2JZ-GE engine,** remove Nos. 3, 1 and 2 cylinder head covers.
30. **On all models,** remove camshaft timing pulleys, then the No. 4 timing belt cover.
31. Remove camshafts by uniformly loosening and removing bearing cap bolts in sequence shown, **Figs. 1 and 2.**
32. Remove cylinder head by uniformly loosening and removing cylinder head bolts in sequence shown, **Fig. 3.**
33. Reverse procedure to install, noting the following:
    a. Check cylinder head for warpage on all contact surfaces. Maximum warpage allowed is .0039 inch.
    b. Using sequence shown in **Fig. 4, torque** cylinder head bolts in three

steps; first step to 25 ft. lbs., second step an additional 90°, third step an additional 90.°
    c. Reset audio coded anti-theft system, if equipped, as outlined under "Precautions."

VALVE CLEARANCE SPECIFICATIONS

Year	Stem-To-Guide Clearance	
	Intake	Exhaust
1996–98	.006–.010	.010–.014

VALVE ADJUSTMENT

Valve clearance is adjusted through the use of shims. Shims are available in increments of .0020 inch.
1. Obtain audio coded anti-theft code, if equipped, as outlined under "Precautions."
2. **On models equipped with 2JZ-GE engine,** remove throttle body and intake air connector assembly.
3. **On all models,** remove No. 3 timing belt cover and cylinder head rear cover.
4. Disconnect spark plug wires from cylinder head covers, then remove Nos. 1, 2 and 3 covers.
5. **On models equipped with 2JZ-GTE engines,** proceed as follows:
    a. Remove ignition coils, then disconnect engine wire protector from No. 4 timing belt cover.
    b. Disconnect engine wire protector from cowl top panel and remove IAC valve pipe.
    c. Remove No. 1 and 2 cylinder head covers.
6. **On all models,** set No. 1 cylinder to TDC by turning the crankshaft and align its groove with timing mark "0" on No. 1 timing belt cover. **Always turn crankshaft clockwise.**
7. Ensure timing marks of crankshaft timing pulleys are aligned with timing marks of No. timing belt cover. If not, turn crankshaft one revolution (360°).
8. **Adjust only those valves shown in Fig. 5.** Using a feeler gauge, measure clearance between valve lift and camshaft. Record valve clearance measurement of those out of specification to use later to determine required re-

placement adjusting shim.
9. Turn crank pulley 1 revolution (360°) and align groove with timing mark "0" of No. 1 timing belt cover.
10. **Adjust only those valves shown in Fig. 6** and using a feeler gauge, measure clearance between valve lift and camshaft. Record valve clearance measurement of those out of specification to use later to determine required replacement adjusting shim.
11. To remove adjusting shim turn camshaft so that cam lobe for valve to be adjusted is facing up.
12. Turn valve lifter with screwdriver so notches are perpendicular to camshaft, **Fig. 7.**
13. Using shim removal tool No. 09248-05410, or equivalent, hold camshaft as shown in **Fig. 8,** then press down lifter and place tool between camshaft and valve lifter, **Fig. 9.**
14. Using a screwdriver and magnet, remove adjusting shim.
15. Measure thickness of removed shim, **Fig. 10,** and calculate thickness of new shim so valve clearances meet specifications. Refer **Figs. 11 and 12.**
16. Reset audio coded anti-theft system, if equipped, as outlined under "Precautions."

VALVE GUIDES

1. Using a suitable tool, tap out guide bushing from combustion chamber side.
2. Select new guide and tap in new guide to protrusion height of .484–.500 inch on intake valves and .449–.465 inch on exhaust valves.

TIMING BELT
REPLACE

1. Obtain audio coded anti-theft code, if equipped, as outlined under "Precautions."
2. Remove battery and battery tray.
3. Remove engine undercover.
4. **On models less 2JZ-GTE engine,** remove No. 2 air tube.
5. **On all models,** drain engine coolant and remove air cleaner duct.
6. **On models equipped with 2JZ-GTE engine,** remove No. 5 air hose.
7. **On all models,** remove lefthand headlight beam angle gauge.

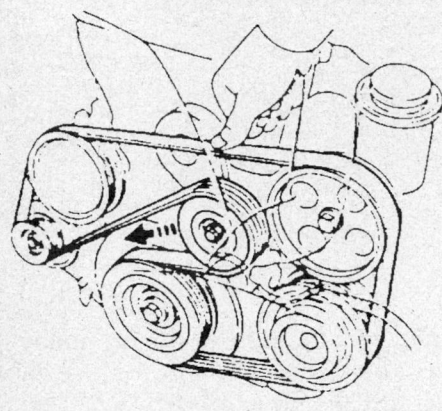

Fig. 16 Drive belt tension inspection

8. Remove No. 2 fan shroud, then the radiator.
9. **On models equipped with 2JZ-GTE engine, with manual transmission,** remove drive belt tensioner damper.
10. **On all models,** remove drive belt, fan fluid coupling assembly and water pump pulley.
11. **On models equipped with 2JZ-GTE engine,** loosen 6 bolts to remove timing belt cover No. 3.
12. **On models equipped with 2JZ-GTE engine,** loosen 10 bolts to remove timing belt cover No. 3.
13. **On all models,** remove timing belt No. 2, then drive belt tensioner.
14. Set No. 1 cylinder to TDC by turning crankshaft and aligning its groove with timing mark "0" on No. 1 timing belt cover.
15. Ensure timing marks of camshaft timing pulley are aligned with timing marks of No. 4 timing belt cover. If not, turn the crankshaft one revolution (360°) clockwise.
16. If using old timing belt, place match marks on belt and camshaft as shown in **Fig. 13. Do not install a timing belt showing signs of wear or stress. Installing a worn or damaged belt will result in serious engine damage.**
17. Alternately loosen two bolts **Fig. 14,** then remove bolts tensioner and dust boot.
18. Disconnect timing belt from camshaft timing pulleys.
19. Remove both timing pulley bolts then pulleys.
20. Using a suitable puller, remove crankshaft pulley.
21. **On models equipped with 2JZ-GE engine,** remove power steering bracket.
22. **On all models,** remove No. 1 timing belt cover.
23. Remove timing belt guide, then the timing belt.
24. Reverse procedure to install, noting the following:
    a. Ensure crankshaft timing pulley set key is with key groove of pulley, **Fig. 15.**
    b. When using old timing belt, align match marks of crankshaft timing pulley and timing belt, then install

belt with arrow pointing in direction of engine rotation.
    c. Reset audio coded anti-theft system, if equipped, as outlined under "Precautions."

CAMSHAFT
REPLACE

Refer to "Cylinder Head, Replace" for camshaft removal procedures.

PISTON & ROD ASSEMBLY

If piston bore is not within specifications, replace piston and/or cylinder block. When assembling piston and rod, ensure mark on top of piston and on connecting rod are the same. Always install in cylinder that assembly originally was removed from.

MAIN & ROD BEARINGS

Undersized rod bearings are available in .0016–.0031 inch. Main bearings are available in .0010–.0024 inch undersizes.

OIL PAN
REPLACE

Refer to "Oil Pump, Replace."

OIL PUMP
REPLACE

1. Obtain audio anti-theft code, if equipped, as outlined under "Precautions," then remove battery and battery tray.
2. Remove engine as outlined under "Engine, Replace."
3. **On models equipped with 2JZ-GTE engine,** remove crankshaft position sensor and alternator.
4. **On all models,** remove timing belt following procedure outlined under "Timing Belt, Replace,"then the idler pulley.
5. **On models equipped with 2JZ-GTE engine,** remove drive belt tensioner bracket then the timing belt plate and crankshaft timing pulley.
6. **On all models,** remove crankshaft timing pulley, then the oil dipstick and tube assembly.
7. Remove oil level sensor, then the No. 2 oil pan.
8. Remove oil strainer, then the oil pan baffle plate.
9. **On models equipped with 2JZ-GTE engine,** remove turbo oil outlet pipe.
10. **On all models,** remove No. 2 oil pan by prying between cylinder block and No. 1 oil pan.
11. Remove crankshaft front oil seal, then the oil pump.
12. Reverse procedure to install. Reset audio coded anti-theft system, if equipped, as outlined under "Precautions."

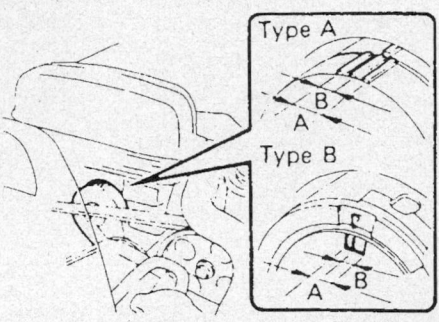

Fig. 17 Drive belt tension for old or new belt

OIL PUMP SERVICE
INSPECTION

1. Remove oil pump relief valve, then the pump body cover, the drive and driven gears.
2. Coat relief valve with engine oil and ensure it falls smoothly into valve hole under its own weight. If not, replace relief valve.
3. Inspect drive and driven rotors by placing in oil pump body. **The marks on the rotors must face up.**
4. Using a feeler gauge, measure clearance between driven rotor and pump housing. Standard tip clearance is .0039–.0069 inch maximum being .0079 inch for 2JZ-GE engines and .0031–.0053 inch, maximum being .0063 inch for 2JZ-GTE engines. If the body clearance is greater than maximum, replace rotors as a set. If necessary, replace oil pump assembly.

BELT TENSION DATA

Check that belt tensioner moves downward when drive belt is pressed down at points in **Fig. 16** with approximately 22 ft. lbs.

Check that arrow mark on belt tensioner falls within area A in **Fig. 17.** If new belt is installed, it should be within area B.

COOLING SYSTEM BLEED

These engines do not require a specific bleed procedure. After filling cooling system, run engine to operating temperature with radiator/pressure cap off. Air will then be automatically bled through cap opening.

THERMOSTAT
REPLACE

1. Obtain audio anti-theft code, if equipped, as outlined under "Precautions."
2. Remove engine undercover and drain coolant.
3. **On models equipped with 2JZ-GTE engine,** disconnect water inlet from water pump and remove thermostat.
4. **On models equipped with 2JZ-GE**

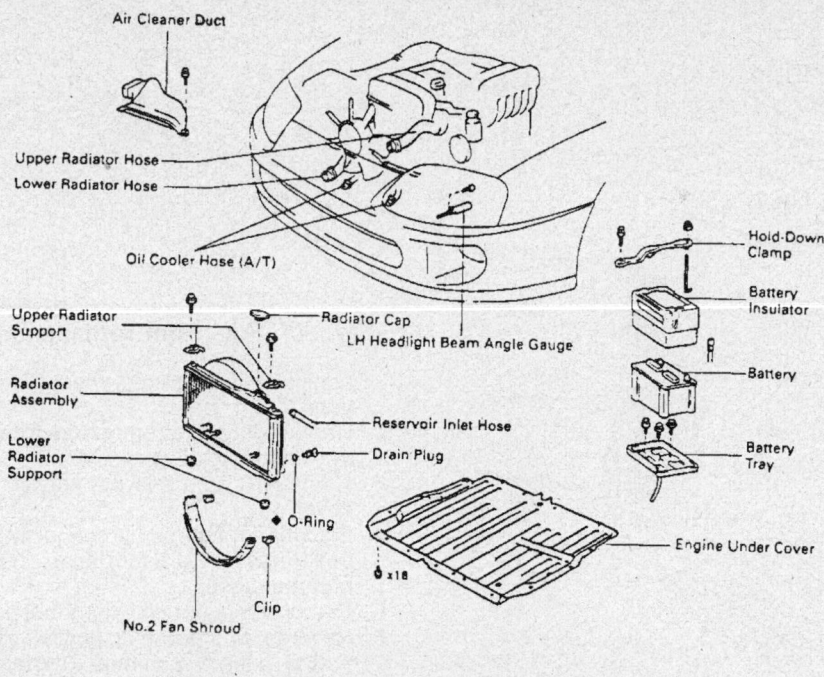

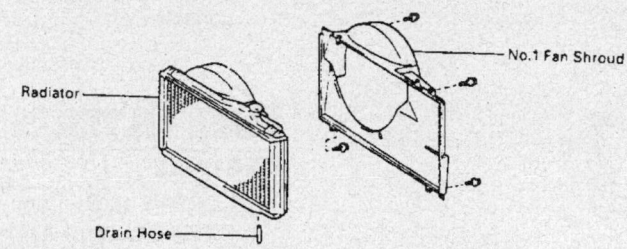

Fig. 18 Radiator replacement. 2JZ-GE engine

engine, remove water inlet, lower radiator hose assembly, then the thermostat.

5. **On all models,** reverse procedure to install. Reset audio coded anti-theft system, if equipped, as outlined under "Precautions."

WATER PUMP

REPLACE

2JZ-GE ENGINE

1. Obtain audio coded anti-theft code, if equipped, as outlined under "Precautions."
2. Remove battery and battery tray, then the engine undercover.
3. Drain coolant, then remove air cleaner, VAF meter and intake air connector pipe assembly.
4. Remove lefthand headlight beam angle gauge.
5. Remove No. 2 fan shroud, than the radiator assembly.
6. **On models with automatic transmissions,** remove two cooler hoses and plug hose ends.
7. **On all models,** remove drive belt, fan, fluid coupling assembly and water pump pulley.

8. Remove water inlet, lower radiator hose assembly and thermostat.
9. Remove timing belt as outlined under "Timing Belt, Replace."
10. Remove exhaust manifold heat insulator, then the water bypass outlet and No. 1 water bypass pipe.
11. Remove mounting bolt and disconnect engine wire bracket. Loosen alternator mounting nut and disconnect from water pump.
12. Remove six water pump attaching bolts, then the water pump.
13. Reverse procedure to install. Reset audio coded anti-theft system, if equipped, as outlined under "Precautions."

2JZ-GTE ENGINE

1. Obtain audio coded anti-theft code, if equipped, as outlined under "Precautions."
2. Remove battery and battery tray, then the engine undercover.
3. Remove No. 1 and No. 2 air tubes, then drain coolant.
4. Remove air cleaner and MAF meter assembly, then the No. 5 air hose.
5. Remove lefthand headlight beam angle gauge.
6. Remove No. 2 fan shroud, than the ra-

diator assembly.

7. **On models with automatic transmissions,** remove two cooler hoses and plug hose ends.
8. **On all models,** remove drive belt tensioner damper.
9. Remove drive belt, fan, fluid coupling assembly and water pump pulley.
10. Remove water inlet, lower radiator hose assembly and thermostat.
11. Remove timing belt as outlined under "Timing Belt, Replace."
12. Remove alternator, then disconnect turbo water hoses from water outlet and remove water outlet and No. 1 water bypass valve.
13. Disconnect No. 3 turbo water hose from water pump.
14. Remove six water pump attaching bolts, then the water pump.
15. Reverse procedure to install. Reset audio coded anti-theft system, if equipped, as outlined under "Precautions."

RADIATOR

REPLACE

2JZ-GE ENGINE

1. Remove engine under cover, **Fig. 18.**
2. Remove battery and battery tray.
3. Drain coolant.
4. Remove No. 2 fan shroud.
5. Remove air cleaner duct.
6. Remove lefthand headlight beam angle gauge.
7. Disconnect radiator hoses.
8. **On models with automatic transmission,** disconnect transmission oil cooler hoses.
9. **On all models,** disconnect coolant reservoir hose.
10. Remove upper radiator support, then the radiator with No. 1 shroud attached.
11. Reverse procedure to install.

2JZ-GTE ENGINE

1. Remove engine under cover, **Fig. 19.**
2. Remove battery and battery tray.
3. Drain coolant.
4. Remove No. 2 air tube.
5. Remove No. 2 fan shroud.
6. Remove air cleaner duct.
7. Remove No. 5 air hose.
8. Remove lefthand headlight beam angle gauge.
9. Disconnect radiator hoses.
10. **On models with automatic transmission,** disconnect transmission oil cooler hoses.
11. **On all models,** disconnect coolant reservoir hose.
12. Disconnect electric cooling fan connector and engine coolant temperature switch connector.
13. Remove upper radiator support, then the radiator with No. 1 shroud attached.
14. Reverse procedure to install.

FUEL PUMP

REPLACE

1. Obtain audio anti-theft code, if

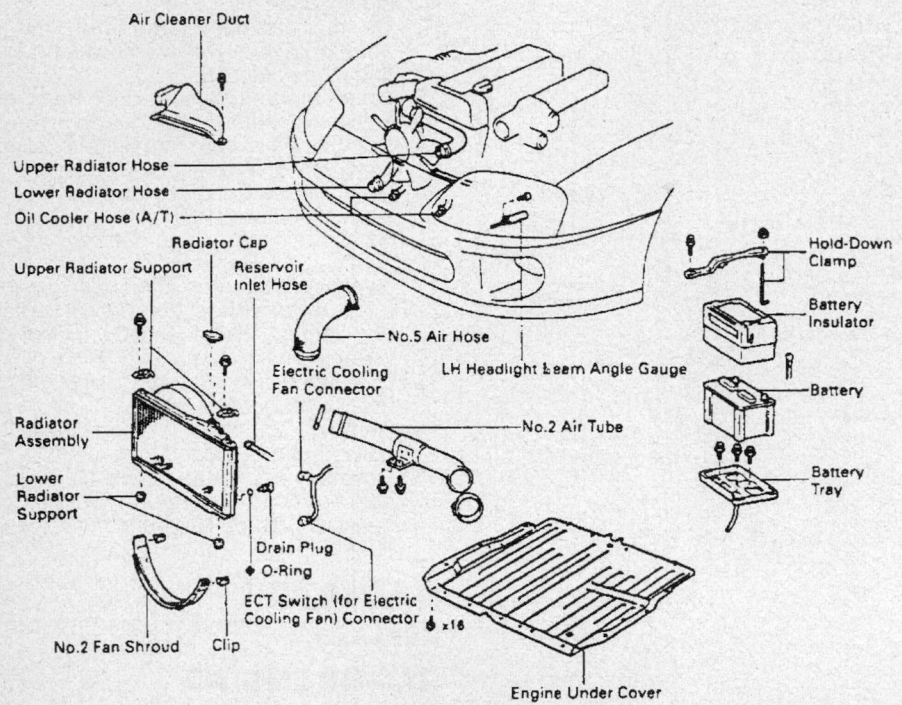

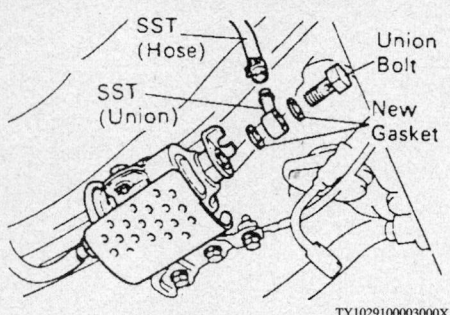

Fig. 20 Fuel filter replacement

equipped, as outlined under "Precautions."
2. Remove luggage compartment carpet, then spare wheel and cover.
3. Remove 6 nuts and the service hole cover.
4. Disconnect fuel pump connector, fuel outlet hose, fuel return hose and fuel breather hose.
5. Remove retainer clip, then fuel pump.
6. Reverse procedure to install. Reset audio coded anti-theft system, if equipped, as outlined under "Precautions."

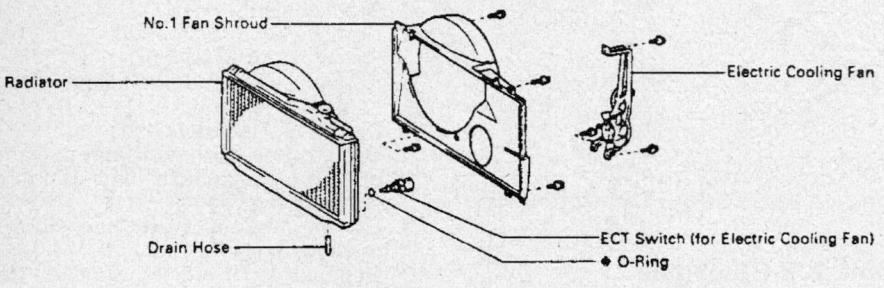

♦ Non-reusable part

Fig. 19 Radiator replacement. 2JZ-GTE engine

FUEL FILTER
REPLACE

1. Obtain audio anti-theft code, if equipped, as outlined in "Precautions."
2. Remove union bolt and 2 gaskets, **Fig. 20.**
3. Disconnect fuel inlet and outlet hoses.
4. Reverse procedure to install. Install new gaskets. Reset audio coded anti-theft system, if equipped, as outlined under "Precautions."

TIGHTENING SPECIFICATIONS

Year	Component	Torque, Ft. Lbs.
1996–97	A/C Compressor To Power Steering Pump Bracket	43
	Camshaft Bearing Cap To Cylinder Head	14
	Camshaft Timing Pulley	59
	Crankshaft Mains	33③
	Crankshaft Pulley To Crankshaft	239
	Cylinder Head To Cylinder Block	①
	Cylinder Head Cover	②
	Driveplate	25
	Drive Belt Tensioner To Oil Pump	15
	ECT Switch	5
	EGR Cooler To Cylinder Head	6
	Engine Hanger To Cylinder Head	29
	Engine Mount Bracket To Cylinder Block	43
	Exhaust Manifold To Cylinder Head	29
	Flywheel	26③
	Front Suspension Crossmember To Engine Mount	43
	Fuel Inlet Hose To Fuel Pipe Support	22
	Fuel Inlet Pipe To Intake Manifold	6
	Idler Pulley	25
	Intake Manifold	④
	Main Bearing Cap to Cylinder Block	33③
	No. 2 Exhaust Pipe To Front Exhaust	43
	No. 2 Water Bypass Pipe To Water Pump	15
	No. 2 Water Bypass Pipe to Cylinder Block	15
	Oil Pump Pulley	25
	Power Steering Pump Bracket	43
	Rear Support Member To Body	19
	Rear Support Member To Engine Rear Mount	10
	Spark Plugs	13
	Timing Belt Tensioner To Oil Pump	20
	Upper Radiator Support	11
	Water Outlet	15
1998	A/C Compressor To Power Steering Pump Bracket	43
	Camshaft Bearing Cap To Cylinder Head	14
	Camshaft Timing Pulley	60
	Crankshaft Mains	33③
	Crankshaft Pulley To Crankshaft	243
	Cylinder Head To Cylinder Block	①
	Cylinder Head Cover	⑤
	Driveplate	25
	Drive Belt Tensioner To Oil Pump	15
	ECT Switch	5
	EGR Cooler To Cylinder Head	6
	Engine Hanger To Cylinder Head	30
	Engine Mount Bracket To Cylinder Block	44
	Exhaust Manifold To Cylinder Head	30
	Flywheel	36③
	Front Suspension Crossmember To Engine Mount	44
	Fuel Inlet Hose To Fuel Pipe Support	30
	Fuel Inlet Pipe To Intake Manifold	6
	Idler Pulley	26
	Intake Manifold	21

Continued

TIGHTENING
SPECIFICATIONS—Continued

Year	Component	Torque, Ft. Lbs.
1998	Main Bearing Cap To Cylinder Head Block	33③
	No. 2 Exhaust Pipe To Front Exhaust	43
	No. 2 Water Bypass Pipe To Water Pump	15
	No. 2 Water Bypass Pipe To Cylinder Block	15
	Oil Pump Pulley	26
	Power Steering Pump Bracket	43
	Rear Support Member To Body	19
	Rear Support Member To Engine Rear Mount	10
	Spark Plugs	13
	Timing Belt Tensioner To Oil Pump	20
	Upper Radiator Support	11
	Water Outlet	15

① — Refer to "Cylinder Head, Replace" for tightening procedure.
② — 2JZ-GE engine, 74 inch lbs.; 2JZ-GTE engine, 48 inch lbs.
③ — Tighten bolts an additional 90.°
④ — 2JZ-GE engine, 15 ft. lbs.; 2JZ-GTE engine, 20 ft. lbs.
⑤ — 2JZ-GE engine, 75 inch lbs.; 2JZ-GTE engine, 49 inch lbs.

Clutch & Manual Transmission

NOTE: On Air Bag Equipped Models, Refer To "Air Bag System Precautions" Located In The Front Of This Manual For System Disarming & Arming Procedures.

INDEX

PRECAUTIONS
AIR BAG SYSTEMS

Refer to "Air Bag System Precautions" in the front of this manual for system disarming and arming procedures.

BATTERY GROUND CABLE

Prior to service, disconnect battery ground cable and isolate as required.

AUDIO CODED ANTI-THEFT SYSTEM

Some models are equipped with an audio coded anti-theft system that will disable the radio when the battery cable is disconnected. The system can be identified by the "ANTI-THEFT SYSTEM" on the cassette tape lid. Obtain 3 digit customer code for input. Reset system after service as follows:

1. Obtain 3 digit audio anti-theft code.
2. Depress 1 (PROG) while depressing righthand side of TUNE SEEK button, - - - will appear in tape operation display.
3. To enter the first digit, depress 1 (PROG) button repeatedly until the number of times depressed equals the first digit beginning with zero (depress the 1 button six times if the first digit if five).
4. To enter second digit, depress 2 (APS) button repeatedly until the number of times depressed equals the second digit beginning with zero.
5. To enter third digit, depress 3 (RPT) button repeatedly until the number of times depressed equals the second digit beginning with zero.
6. If - - - is displayed during code input, repeat procedure.
7. When code appears in display, depress and hold SCAN button until SEC appears.
8. When SEC disappears audio system should be operative.
9. If Err is displayed, repeat procedure. **Attempting to input code more than nine times may permanently disable audio system.**

ADJUSTMENTS
CLUTCH PEDAL HEIGHT

1. Check clutch pedal height, **Fig. 1.**
2. Clutch pedal height should be 5.76–6.15 inches.
3. If clutch pedal height is not as specified, loosen locknut and turn adjusting bolt until specified clutch pedal height is obtained, then tighten adjusting bolt locknut.
4. Clutch freeplay should be .197–.591

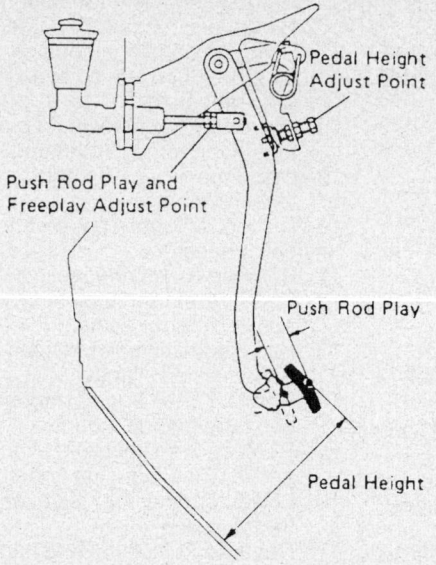

Fig. 1 Clutch pedal adjustment

inch. Pushrod play at pedal should be .039–.197 inch.

5. If clutch pedal freeplay is not as specified, loosen locknut and turn pushrod adjusting screw until specified pedal freeplay is obtained.
6. Tighten locknut, then recheck clutch pedal height.

HYDRAULIC SYSTEM SERVICE

CLUTCH SYSTEM BLEED

If any service is performed on the clutch system or air is suspected in the clutch lines, bleed the system.

1. Fill clutch reservoir with suitable brake fluid. **Do not allow fluid to come in contact with painted surfaces.**
2. Check reservoir frequently, add fluid as required.
3. Connect vinyl tube to bleeder plug, then insert other tube end in half full container of brake fluid.
4. Slowly pump clutch pedal several times.
5. While depressing, pedal, loosen bleeder plug until fluid runs out, then close bleeder plug.
6. Repeat procedure until air bubbles are evident in the fluid. **Do not reuse the fluid that was bled.**

CLUTCH SLAVE CYLINDER, REPLACE

1. Remove clutch slave cylinder hose or tube.
2. Remove slave cylinder.
3. Reverse procedure to install. Tighten bolts to specifications.
4. Bleed clutch system.

CLUTCH

REPLACE

1. Remove transaxle assembly as outlined under "Transmission, Replace."

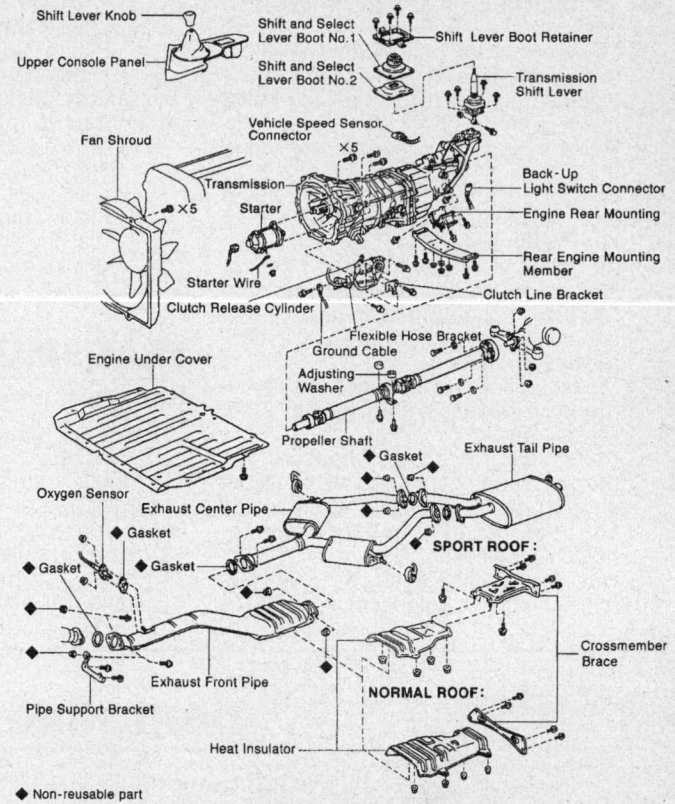

◆ Non-reusable part

Fig. 2 Transmission replacement. W58 transmission

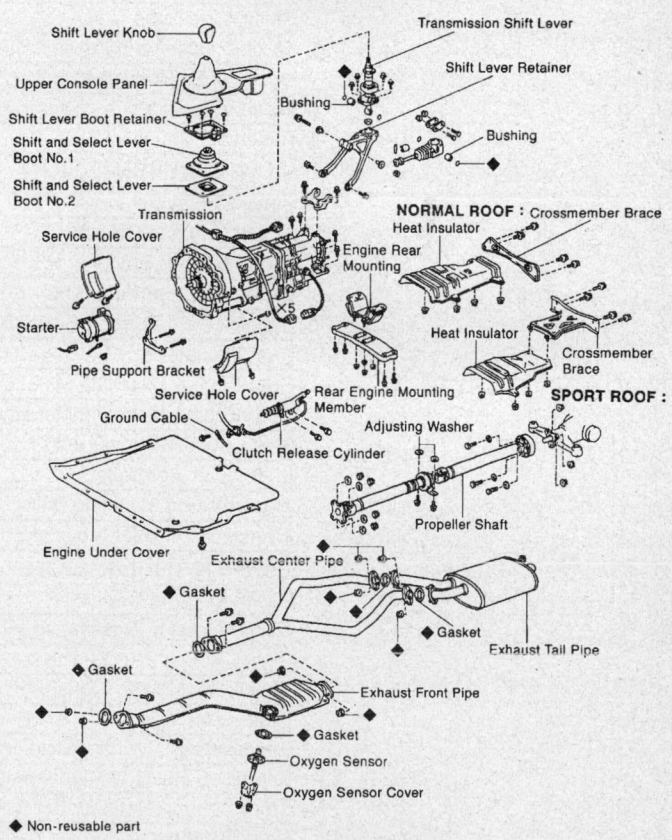

◆ Non-reusable part

Fig. 3 Transmission replacement. V160 transmission

2. Place installation alignment on clutch cover and flywheel.
3. Loosen each set bolt one turn at a time until spring tension is released.
4. Remove clutch cover attaching bolts, then cover and disc.
5. Remove release bearing, fork and boot.
6. Using suitable calipers, measure clutch disc rivet head depth. Minimum rivet depth should be .012 inch. If not as indicated, replace clutch disc.
7. Using suitable dial indicator, measure flywheel runout. Maximum runout should be .008 inch. If not as indicated, replace flywheel.
8. Measure clutch disc runout, maximum runout is .031 inch. If not as indicated, replace disc.
9. Using suitable calipers, measure diaphragm spring depth and width. Depth should be 0.024 inch and width should be 0.197 inch. If not as indicated, replace clutch cover.
10. Reverse to install, noting the following:
   a. Using clutch guide tool No. 09301–

17010 or 093201–20020, or equivalent, install clutch disc.
   b. Match clutch cover and flywheel alignment marks, then tighten cover bolts to specifications, one turn at a time in a criss-cross pattern, ensuring clutch disc and pressure plate remain aligned.
   c. Using suitable dial indicator, check diaphragm spring tip alignment, .020 inch is maximum allowable out of alignment.

TRANSMISSION

REPLACE

Refer to **Figs. 2 and 3** when replacing transmission.
1. Obtain audio anti-theft code, if equipped, as outlined in "Precautions."
2. Remove upper console panel.
3. Remove shift lever from inside vehicle.
4. Raise and support vehicle, then drain transmission fluid.
5. Remove engine undercover.
6. Remove crossmember brace.
7. Using extension housing tool No. 09325–20010, or equivalent, remove propeller shaft.
8. Disconnect front exhaust pipe from tail pipe, then remove exhaust pipe.
9. Disconnect back-up light switch electrical connector.
10. Disconnect rear speed sensor electrical connector.
11. Remove clutch release cylinder.
12. Remove starter attaching bolts, then position starter aside.
13. Using suitable transmission jack, raise transmission slightly.
14. Remove rear engine mounting member, then engine mount.
15. Remove transmission attaching bolts and flywheel housing undercover.
16. Lower engine rear side and remove transmission.
17. Reverse to install. Reset audio coded anti-theft, if equipped, as outlined in "Precautions."

TIGHTENING SPECIFICATIONS

Component	Torque, Ft. Lbs.
CLUTCH	
Bleeder Plug	8
Clutch Cover To Flywheel Bolts	14
Clutch Line Tube Union	11
Flexible Hose To Release Cylinder	17②
Flywheel To Crankshaft Bolts	54③
Release Cylinder To Clutch Housing Mounting Bolts	9
Reservoir Mounting Bolts	18
V160 TRANSMISSION	
Clutch Cover Set Bolt	9
Clutch Release Cylinder	14
Crossmember Brace	9
Exhaust Center Pipe Bolts	14
Exhaust Pipe Support Bracket To Clutch Housing	27
Heat Insulator	48①
Rear Engine Mounting Member Bolt	19
Rear Engine Mounting Member Nut	10
Shift Lever Retaining Bolts	14
Shift Lever Set Bolts	6
Transmission Mounting Bolts	53
Transmission Rear Mounting Bolts	18
W58 TRANSMISSION	
Back-Up Lamp Switch	30
Center Bearing Retainer To Intermediate Plate	9
Clutch Housing To Engine	29
Clutch Housing To Transmission Case	27
Drain Filler Plug	30
Engine Rear Mounting Bolts	18
Extension Housing To Intermediate Plate	27
Front Bearing Retainer Set Bolts	18
Restrict Pin	30
Reverse Idler Gear Shaft Stopper Bolt	18
Shift Fork Set Bolt	9

Continued

TIGHTENING
SPECIFICATIONS—Continued

Component	Torque, Ft. Lbs.
W58 TRANSMISSION	
Shift Lever Housing To Shift & Select Lever Shaft	29
Shift Lever Retainer To Extension Housing	13
Stiffener Plate Bolt	27
Straight Screw Plug	18

① — Inch lbs.
② — For 1998 tighten to 9 ft. lbs.
③ — For 1998 tighten to 36 ft. lbs.

Rear Axle & Suspension

NOTE: On Air Bag Equipped Models, Refer To "Air Bag System Precautions" Located In The Front Of This Manual For System Disarming & Arming Procedures.

INDEX

PRECAUTIONS

AIR BAG SYSTEMS

Refer to "Air Bag System Precautions" in the front of this manual for system disarming and arming procedures.

BATTERY GROUND CABLE

Prior to service, disconnect battery ground cable and isolate as required.

HUB & BEARING
REPLACE
REMOVAL

1. Raise and support rear of vehicle, then remove wheel and tire assembly.
2. Remove brake caliper from axle carrier and suspend with wire.
3. Remove brake disc, then install suitable dial indicator and measure axial hub bearing play. If play is within .002 inch play is satisfactory. If play exceeds .002 inch, disassemble and inspect axle hub.
4. Check axle flange runout. If runout exceeds .002 inch, replace axle shaft.
5. Remove axle shaft.
6. Remove parking brake assembly.
7. **On models with ABS,** disconnect

speed sensor.
8. **On all models,** remove No. 1 lower suspension arm attaching nut from axle carrier, then using suitable puller, disconnect suspension arm, **Figs. 1 and 2,**
9. Disconnect No. 2 lower suspension arm and strut rod from axle carrier.
10. Disconnect shock absorber from axle carrier.
11. Disconnect upper control arm from body, then remove axle carrier and upper control arm as an assembly.
12. Remove upper arm-to-axle carrier attaching nut, then separate components.
13. Remove brake backing plate from axle carrier.
14. If bearing replacement is required, proceed as follows:
    a. Remove dust deflector.
    b. Place carrier in a suitable vise.
    c. Using hub removal tool No. 09520-00031, or equivalent, remove axle hub from carrier.
    d. Using puller set No. 09950-40010, or equivalent, remove bearing race from axle hub.
    e. Remove inner and outer oil seals using puller tool No. 09308-00010, or equivalent.
    f. Using a suitable pair of snap ring

pliers, remove snap ring from carrier.
    g. Remove bearing from carrier using a suitable press and bearing tool Nos. 09950-60010 and 09950-70010, or equivalent.
    h. Install new bearing using bearing installation tool Nos. 09527-17011 and 09608-32010, or equivalent.
    i. Install snap ring using a suitable pair of snap ring pliers.
    j. Install inner race.
    k. Install new oil seal using seal installer tool No. 09608-32010, or equivalent and a suitable hammer.
    l. Temporarily install backing plate.
    m. Install inner race using a suitable press and race installation tool Nos. 09608-32010, 09950-60010 and 09950-70010, or equivalents.
    n. Install new inner oil seal using a suitable hammer and seal installation tool No. 09223-15020, or equivalent.
    o. Using a suitable press and press tool Nos. 09950-60020 and 09950-70010, or equivalents, install dust deflector.

INSTALLATION

1. Install upper control arm to body. Do

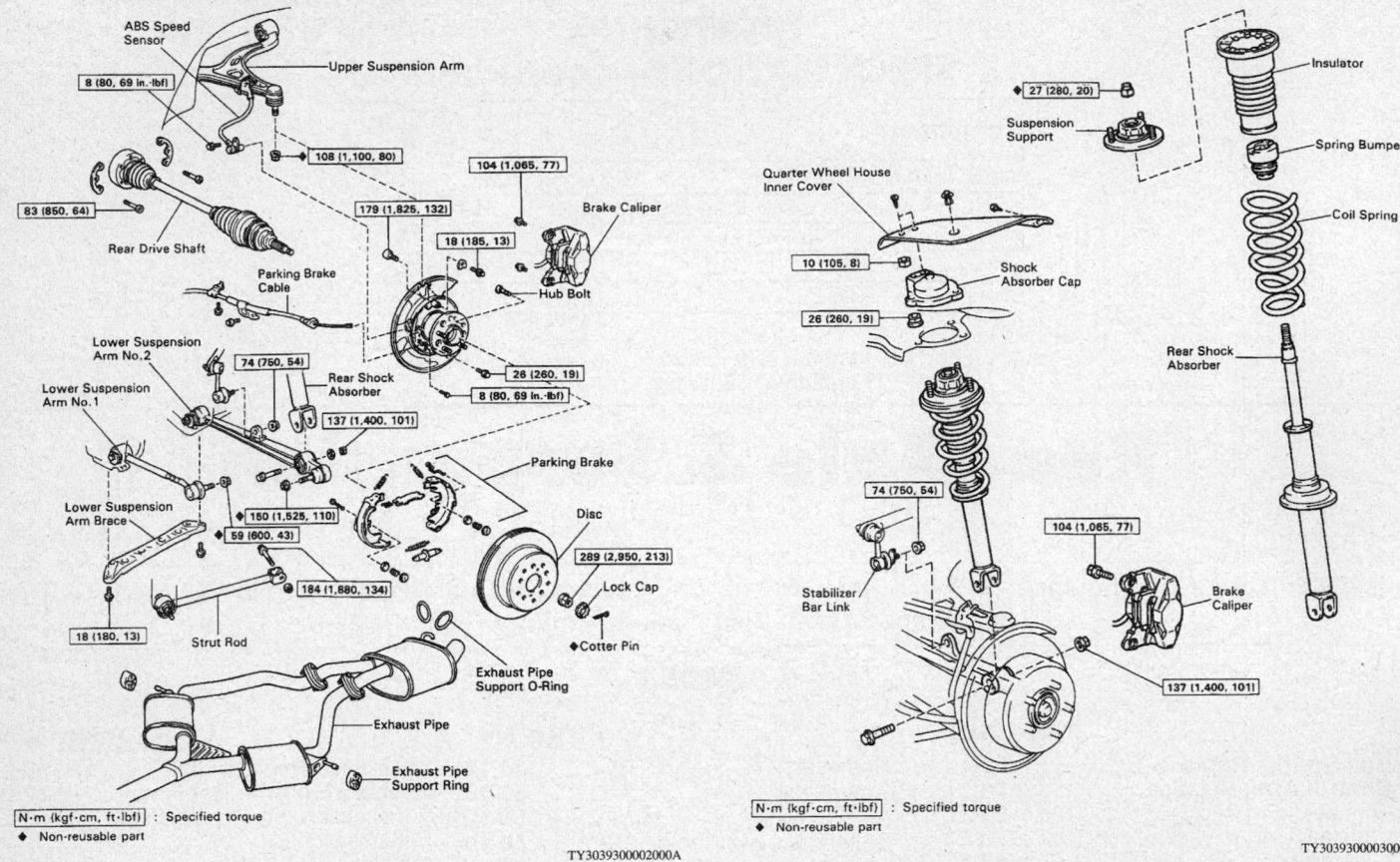

Fig. 1 Exploded view of rear axle hub

Fig. 2 Exploded view of rear suspension components

not tighten attaching nuts at this time.

2. Install axle carrier on upper control arm and install new nut. Do not tighten at this time.
3. Install No. 1 suspension arm on axle carrier. Tighten attaching nut to specification.
4. Install No. 2 suspension arm on axle carrier. Do not tighten attaching nut at this time.
5. Install strut rod on axle carrier. Do not tighten attaching nut at this time.
6. Tighten upper control arm-to-axle carrier attaching nut to specification.
7. Install shock absorber on axle carrier. Tighten attaching nut to specification.
8. Install parking brake assembly and brake disc.
9. Install axle shaft.
10. Install brake caliper. Tighten attaching bolts to specification.
11. Lower vehicle to ground, then bounce vehicle up and down several times to stabilize suspension.
12. With vehicle weight on suspension, tighten upper control arm-to-body attaching nuts, No. 2 lower suspension arm-to-axle carrier attaching nut and strut rod-to-axle carrier attaching nut to specifications.

STRUT ROD
REPLACE

1. Raise and support rear of vehicle.

2. Remove strut rod-to-axle carrier attaching nut, then the bolt and strut rod.
3. Remove strut rod-to-body attaching bolt, then the strut rod.
4. Reverse procedure to install. Prior to tightening attaching parts, lower vehicle to ground and bounce vehicle several times to stabilize suspension. Tighten strut rod attaching nuts and bolts to specification.

SHOCK ABSORBER
REPLACE

1. Raise and support rear of vehicle, then remove wheel and tire assembly.
2. Remove rear brake caliper and secure aside with wire.
3. Disconnect rear stabilizer link from lower suspension arm No. 2, then remove lower shock mounting bolt. Lower vehicle.
4. Remove speaker grille above shock absorber being replaced.
5. **On models equipped with Toyota Electronically Modulated Suspension (TEMS)**, remove quarter panel trim.
6. **On all models**, remove shock absorber to axle carrier attaching nut and bolt, **Fig. 2**.
7. Working inside vehicle, remove shock absorber cap, then on models equipped with TEMS, the TEMS actuator.

8. Remove three upper shock absorber attaching nuts, then the shock absorber and spring assembly. Install shock absorber and spring assembly in suitable vise, positioning vise jaws at lower shock mount.
9. Remove coil spring as follows:
   a. Using front coil spring compressor tool No. 09727-22032, or equivalent, compress coil spring.
   b. Remove suspension support nut, then the suspension support.
   c. Remove coil spring and bumper.
10. Reverse procedure to install, noting the following:
    a. Install bumper and coil spring on shock.
    b. Align coil spring end with lower seat hollow.
    c. Tighten attaching nuts and bolts to specifications.
    d. Tighten upper shock absorber attaching nuts to specification.
    e. Tighten shock absorber-to-axle carrier attaching bolts to specification.

COIL SPRING
REPLACE

Refer to "Shock Absorber, Replace" procedure for coil spring replacement procedures.

CONTROL ARM

REPLACE

REMOVAL

Refer to "Hub, Replace" for upper control arm replacement procedures.

INSPECTION

1. Flip ball joint stud back and forth five times, then install nut.
2. Using torque wrench, turn nut continuously one turn each 2–4 seconds and take torque reading on fifth turn.
3. If turning torque is not 9–30 inch lbs., replace upper control arm.

INSTALLATION

Refer to "Hub, Replace" for upper control arm installation procedures.

STABILIZER BAR

REPLACE

1. Raise and support rear of vehicle.
2. Disconnect two exhaust support rings and secure exhaust pipe aside with wire.
3. Disconnect both stabilizer bar links, **Fig. 2.**
4. Remove both stabilizer bar bracket attaching bolts, then the stabilizer bar.
5. Remove stabilizer bar links from bar.
6. Reverse procedure to install. Tighten stabilizer bar bracket attaching bolts and stabilizer link-to-No. 1 lower suspension arm attaching bolts to specifications.

SUSPENSION ARM

REPLACE

REMOVAL

1. Raise and support rear of vehicle, disconnect brake caliper and secure aside with wire.
2. Disconnect ABS speed sensor and wire harness.
3. Remove axle shaft, then the No. 1 suspension arm-to-axle carrier attaching nut.
4. Remove suspension arm No. 1 tie rod end from axle carrier, then disconnect parking brake cable.
5. Scribe reference marks between suspension arm No. 1 adjusting cam and crossmember, then remove arm pivot nut, bolt, cams and arm.
6. Remove suspension arm No. 2 to axle carrier attaching nut and bolt, then disconnect arm from carrier.
7. Scribe reference marks between suspension arm No. 2 adjusting cam and crossmember, then remove arm pivot nut, bolt, cams and arm.

INSPECTION

1. Flip tie rod end stud back and forth five times, then install nut.
2. Using torque wrench, turn nut continuously one turn each 2–4 seconds and take torque reading on fifth turn.
3. If turning torque is not 7–30 inch lbs., replace No. 1 suspension arm.

INSTALLATION

Reverse procedure to install. Prior to tightening attaching parts, lower vehicle to ground and bounce vehicle several times to stabilize suspension. Tighten No. 1 suspension arm-to-axle carrier attaching nut, suspension arms-to-crossmember attaching nuts and suspension arm-to-axle carrier attaching nuts to specifications.

TIGHTENING SPECIFICATIONS

Year	Component	Torque, Ft. Lbs.
1996–98	Axle Hub Locknuts	147
	Brake Hose Bracket To Steering Knuckle	14
	Disc Brake Caliper To Steering Knuckle	77
	Front & Rear Adjusting Cam Bolts	177
	Front Shock Absorber To Body	26
	Front Shock Absorber To Lower Suspension Arm	106
	Lower Ball Joint To Lower Suspension Arm	94
	Lower Ball Joint To Steering Knuckle	92
	Piston Rod Locknut	22
	Speed Sensor Set Bolt	14
	Stabilizer Bar Bracket To Body	13
	Stabilizer Link To Lower Suspension Arm	47
	Stabilizer Link To Stabilizer Bar	47
	Steering Knuckle To Upper Suspension Arm	76
	Tie Rod End Clamp Bolt	14
	Tie Rod End To Steering Knuckle	36
	Upper Suspension Arm Mounting Nut	121
	Wheel Lug Nut	76

Front Suspension & Steering

NOTE: On Air Bag Equipped Models, Refer To "Air Bag System Precautions" Located In The Front Of This Manual For System Disarming & Arming Procedures.

INDEX

PRECAUTIONS

AIR BAG SYSTEMS

Refer to "Air Bag System Precautions" in the front of this manual for system disarming and arming procedures.

BATTERY GROUND CABLE

Prior to service, disconnect battery ground cable and isolate as required.

WHEEL BEARING

ADJUST

Supra incorporates lubed for life, sealed front wheel bearings with no provision for adjustment.

HUB & BEARING

REPLACE

1. Raise and support front of vehicle, then remove tire and wheel assembly.
2. Remove speed sensor and brake hose bracket from steering knuckle, **Fig. 1.**
3. Remove brake caliper from steering knuckle and suspend out of way.
4. Remove rotor disc, then ensure bearing play in axial direction does not exceed .002 inch.
5. Remove cotter pin and nut from steering knuckle, then using suitable tool, disconnect tie rod end from steering gear knuckle.
6. Remove cotter pin and nut, then using suitable tool, disconnect steering knuckle from upper suspension arm.
7. Remove clip and nut, then using suitable tool, remove steering knuckle from the upper suspension arm, then axle hub.
8. Using a suitable tool, remove hub bearing cap.
9. Secure axle hub in vice, then using a hammer and chisel, loosen the staked part of the luck nut, then remove.
10. Using a suitable tool, remove axle hub from axle bearing.
11. Using a suitable tool, remove hub bearing inner race (outside) from axle hub.

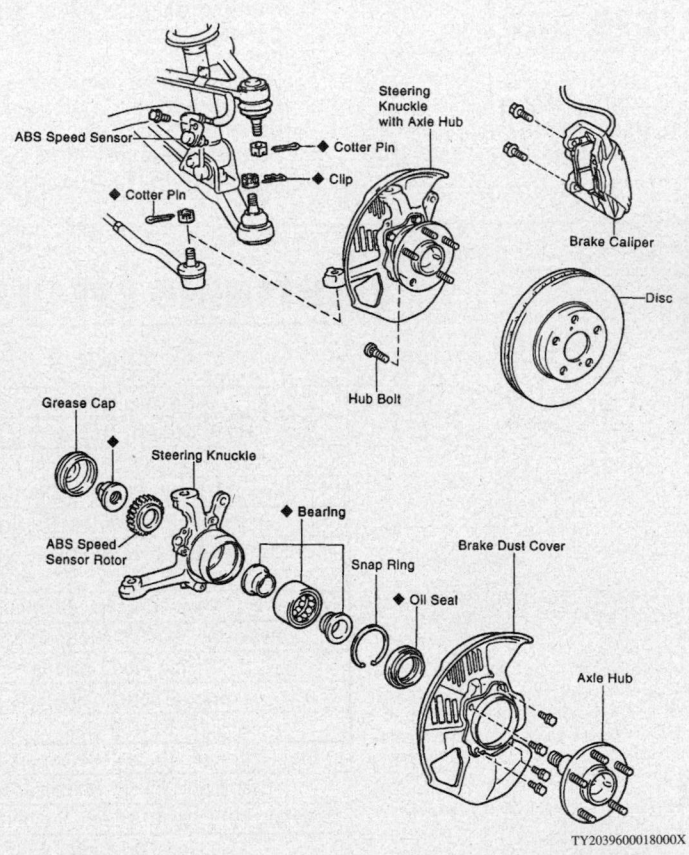

Fig. 1 Exploded view of axle hub & steering knuckle

12. Remove dust cover retaining bolts, then the dust cover from steering knuckle.
13. Using a screwdriver, remove outer oil seal from steering knuckle.
14. Using snap ring pliers, remove the hole snap rings.
15. Temporarily install hub bearing inner race (outside) to the hub bearing, then using suitable tool and hammer, remove hub bearing from steering knuckle.
16. Using a suitable tool, press new bearing into steering knuckle.
17. Install the hole snap ring, then using steering knuckle seal tool No. 09608–32010, or equivalent, install the hub bearing inner race (outside) to the hub bearing then, using axle hub tool set No. 09608–35014, or equivalent, press the oil seal into the steering knuckle.
18. Install disc brake dust cover.
19. Install hub bearing inner race (inside) to the hub bearing, then using a suitable tool install axle hub to steering knuckle.
20. Install and tighten new axle hub locknut to specification, then using punch and hammer stake the locknut.

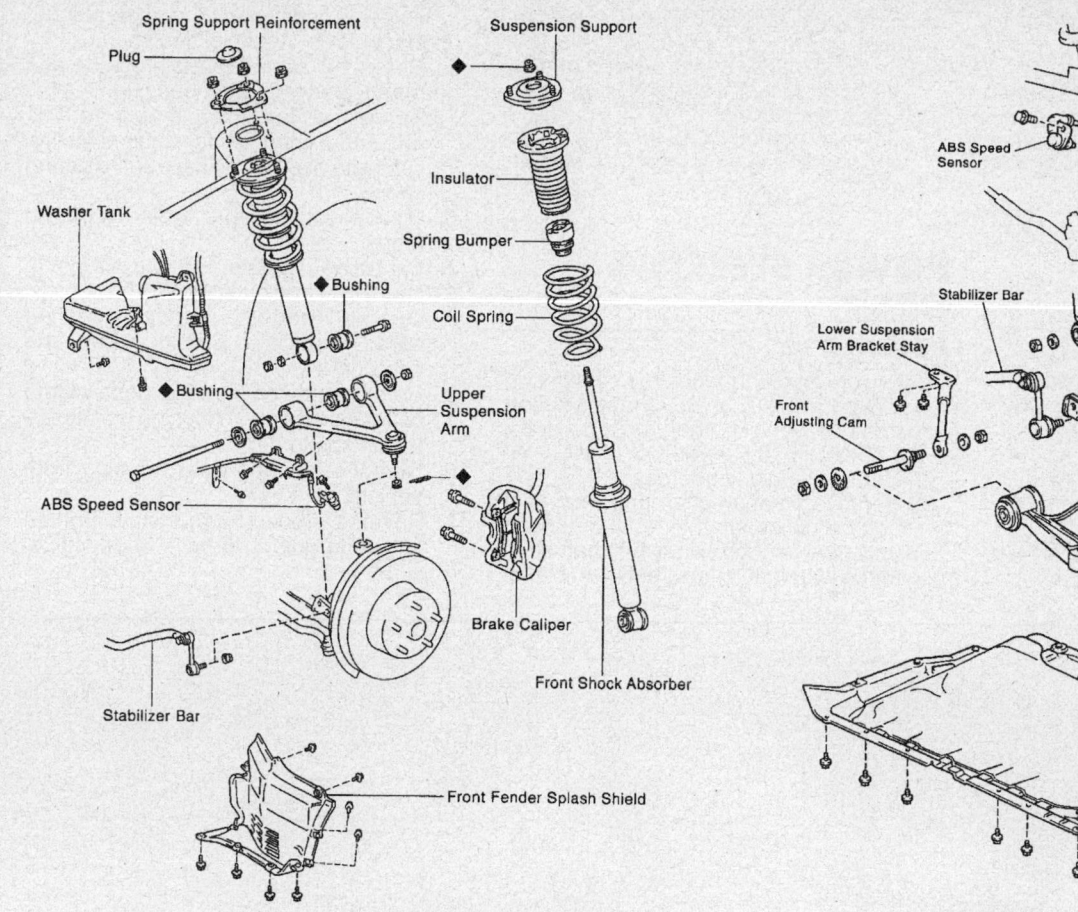

TY2029600032000X

Fig. 2 Front suspension strut & coil spring components

TY2029600002000A

Fig. 3 Exploded view of front suspension

21. Install hub bearing cap.
22. Reverse procedure to install. Tighten attaching nuts and bolts to specifications.

BALL JOINT INSPECTION

1. Raise front of vehicle and place a 7–8 inch block under one tire.
2. Lower vehicle until the front springs are about half loaded. Place stands under vehicle.
3. Ensure front wheels are in a straight forward position, then chock front wheels.
4. Using suitable lever, move lower control arm up and down and check ball joint for excessive play. If any ball joint play is observed, replace ball joint.
5. Repeat procedure for opposite ball joint.

COIL SPRING
REPLACE

1. Raise and support vehicle, then remove wheel.
2. Remove brake caliper from steering knuckle, **Fig. 2.** Suspend caliper aside with suitable wire. **Leave brake hose attached.**
3. **On models equipped with Toyota**

Electronically Modulated Suspension (TEMS), remove TEMS actuator cover and actuator from top of strut.
4. **On all models,** loosen piston rod locknut enough that it can be turned by hand.
5. Remove upper suspension arm to vehicle body attaching nuts and bolts, then disconnect suspension arm from body.
6. Remove three strut assembly to vehicle body attaching nuts.
7. Remove strut to lower suspension arm attaching nut and bolt, then the strut.
8. Place strut in suitable holding devise, then compress coil spring with spring compressing tool No. 09727-30020, or equivalent.
9. Remove top strut support center nut, then suspension support, coil spring and spring bumper.
10. Reverse procedure to install. Tighten strut to vehicle attaching nuts and strut to lower suspension arm attaching nut to specifications. Temporarily install upper suspension arm, then lower vehicle and bounce several times to stabilize suspension. With vehicle weight on suspension, tighten upper suspension arm to vehicle body attaching nuts and piston rod locknut specifications.

STRUT
REPLACE

Refer to "Coil Spring, Replace" for procedure.

CONTROL ARM
REPLACE
LOWER

1. Raise and support vehicle, remove lower engine cover and brake caliper, then secure caliper aside with wire.
2. Disconnect stabilizer bar link from lower suspension arm, **Fig. 3.**
3. Remove lower ball joint locknut, then using suitable puller, disconnect ball joint from steering knuckle.
4. Remove shock absorber-to-lower suspension arm attaching nut and bolt, then disconnect shock absorber from arm.
5. Make reference marks between lower suspension arm alignment cams and their mounting surfaces, then remove nuts, alignment cams, bolts and suspension arm.
6. Reverse procedure to install, noting the following:
   a. Tighten lower suspension arm-to-ball joint attaching nuts and bolts to specification.

b. Install lower suspension arm. Do not tighten alignment cams at this time.

c. When installing ball joint to steering knuckle, install conventional nut first and tighten to specification, then install locking nut and tighten to specification.

d. Tighten shock absorber lower mounting nut and bolt, stabilizer link attaching nut to specification.

e. Lower vehicle and allow the weight to rest on suspension. Bounce vehicle several times to settle suspension, then align marks made on cams. Tighten adjusting cam nuts to specification with vehicle weight on suspension.

STABILIZER BAR
REPLACE

1. Disconnect stabilizer link from stabilizer bar, **Fig. 3.**

2. Remove stabilizer link from lower suspension arm.

3. Remove stabilizer bar bracket attaching bolts, then the stabilizer bar, cushions and brackets.

4. Reverse procedure to install. Tighten all attaching nuts and bolts to specification.

POWER STEERING GEAR
REPLACE

1. Ensure steering wheel in center and locked into place. Raise and support front of vehicle, then position front wheels straight ahead.

2. Remove engine undercover.

3. Remove steering shaft universal joint bolt on pinion shaft side, then loosen universal joint bolt on main shaft side. Make alignment marks between pinion shaft and universal joint, then pull out universal joint from pinion shaft.

4. Remove power steering pressure and return lines from gear housing.

5. Remove cotter pins and nuts from tie rod ends, then using suitable puller, separate tie rod ends from steering knuckles.

6. Disconnect pressure feed and return tubes.

7. **On turbo models,** remove air intake connector and air hose.

8. **On all models,** remove steering damper attaching bolts, then the damper.

9. Remove power steering hose clamp bolts, then the gear housing bracket attaching bolts.

10. Remove steering gear housing from vehicle.

11. Reverse procedure to install. Tighten attaching nuts and bolts to specifications.

TIGHTENING SPECIFICATIONS

Year	Component	Torque, Ft. Lbs.
1996–97	Axle Carrier To Backing Plate (Bolt)	19
	Axle Carrier To Backing Plate (Nut)	43
	Axle Carrier To Driveshaft	203
	Axle Carrier To No. 1 Suspension Arm	43
	Axle Carrier To No. 2 Suspension Arm	121
	Axle Carrier To Shock Absorber	101
	Axle Carrier To Strut Rod	121
	Axle Carrier To Torque Plate	34
	Axle Carrier To Upper Arm	80
	Carrier To Carrier Cover	34
	Companion Flange To Propeller Shaft	54
	Differential Front Bolts To Body	122
	Differential Nuts To Body	67
	Differential Rear Bolts To Body	67
	Differential Stud Bolts To Body	58
	Drain Plug	36
	Filler Plug	36
	No. 1 Suspension Arm To Body	136
	No. 2 Suspension Arm To Body	136
	Shock Absorber To Suspension Support	20
	Side Bearing Cap To Carrier	58
	Stabilizer Bar Bracket To Body	21
	Stabilizer Bar To Link	26
	Strut Rod To Body	121
	Suspension Support To Body	10
	Upper Arm To Body	121
	Wheel Lug Nuts	76
1998	Axle Carrier To Backing Plate (Bolt)	19
	Axle Carrier To Backing Plate (Nut)	43
	Axle Carrier To Drivshaft	213
	Axle Carrier To No. 1 Suspension Arm	43
	Axle Carrier To No. 2 Suspension Arm	110
	Axle Carrier To Shock Absorber	101
	Axle Carrier To Strut Rod	136
	Axle Carrier To Torque Plate	34
	Axle Carrier To Upper Arm	80
	Carrier To Carrier Cover	34
	Companion Flange To Propeller Shaft	58
	Differential Mounting Bolts (Front)	108
	Differential Mounting Bolts (Rear)	105
	Drain Plug	36
	Filler Plug	36
	No. 1 Suspension Arm To Body	136
	No. 2 Suspension Arm To Body	136
	Shock Absorber To Suspension Support	20
	Side Bearing Cap To Carrier	58
	Stabilizer Bar Bracket To Body	23
	Stabilizer Bar To Link	54
	Strut Rod To Body	136
	Suspension Support To Body	10
	Upper Arm To Body	121
	Wheel Lug Nuts	76

Wheel Alignment

INDEX

PRELIMINARY INSPECTION

Prior to checking and resetting front wheel alignment, check wheel runout with a dial indicator. Wheel runout should not exceed .055 inch (1.4 mm).

Inspect the following prior to adjusting wheel alignment.
1. Check tires for wear and proper inflation pressure.
2. Check front wheel bearings, front suspension, steering linkage and ball joints for wear or looseness.
3. Ensure front shock absorbers are functioning properly.

FRONT WHEEL ALIGNMENT

CASTER & CAMBER

Caster and camber are adjusted by rotating front and/or rear adjusting cams as shown, **Fig. 1.** Take measurements of vehicle front caster and camber, then plot measurements on adjustment charts, **Figs. 2 and 3,** to obtain the amount that adjusting cams should be turned.

TOE-IN

Measure length of tie rod end on each side and adjust to be equal. Adjust toe-in by turning tubes equal amounts. Clamp adjusting tubes after aligning clamps with tube slots. Lock tie rod ends so that inner and outer ends are at right angles to each other.

REAR WHEEL ALIGNMENT

CAMBER & TOE-IN

1. Measure length of lower suspension arm No. 1 and No. 2 as shown in **Fig. 4.**

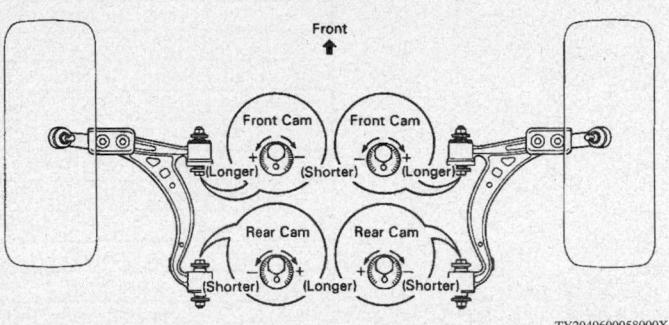

TY2049600058000X

Fig. 1   Front camber/caster adjustment cams

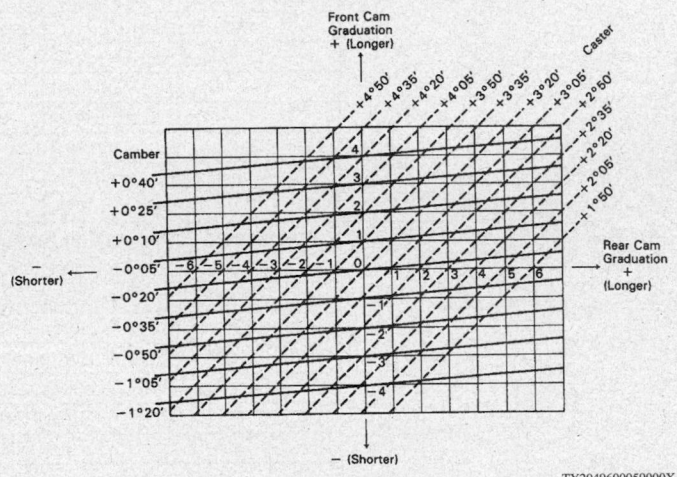

TY2049600059000X

Fig. 2   Front caster & camber adjustment chart. 2JZ-GE engine

2. If (E-F) or (F-E) is greater than 4 mm, length of arms must be adjusted by turning adjusting cam(s).
3. Measure camber and toe-in, then plot measurements on adjustment chart, **Fig. 5.**
4. Read from chart the amounts to turn adjusting cams, **Fig. 6.**

VEHICLE RIDE HEIGHT

Refer to **Figs. 7 through 9,** for trim height and specifications.

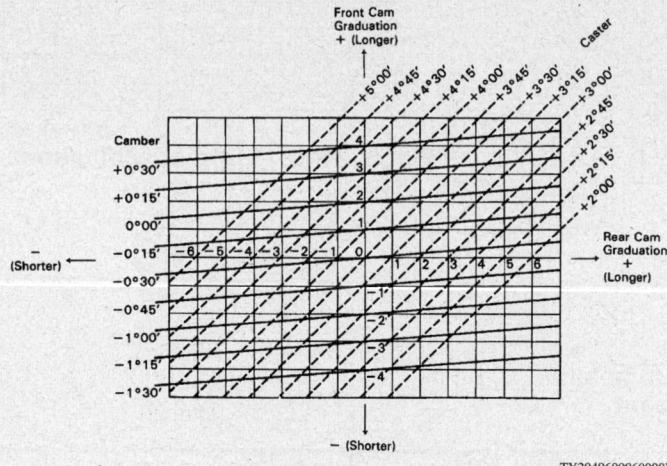

TY2049600060000X

Fig. 3   Front caster & camber adjustment chart. 2JZ-GTE engine

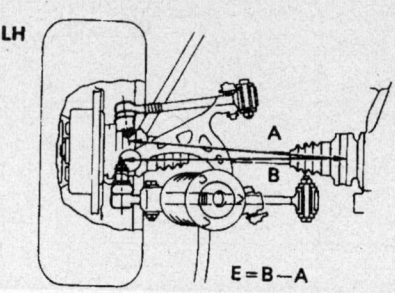

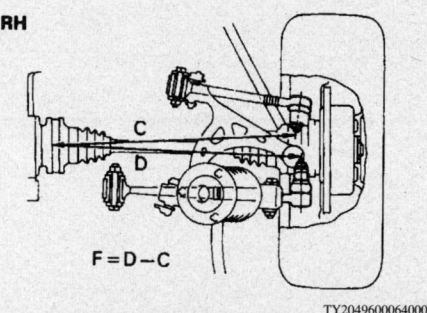

$E = B - A$

$F = D - C$

TY2049600064000X

Fig. 4   Rear camber & toe-in measurement

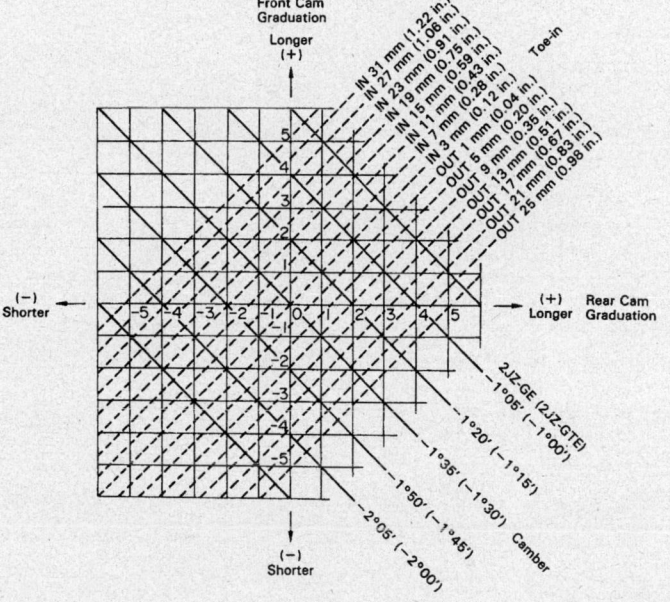

TY2049600065000X

Fig. 5   Rear camber & toe-in adjustment chart

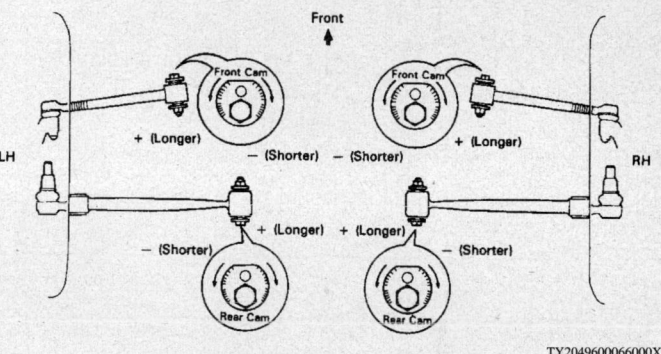

TY2049600066000X

Fig. 6   Rear camber & toe-in adjustment cams

TY2049100007000X

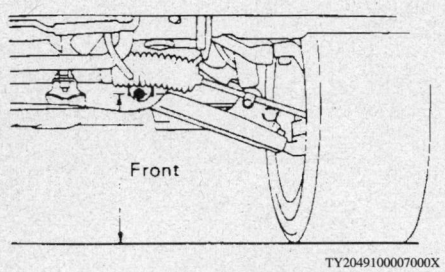

Fig. 7 Front ride height measurement

TY2049100008000X

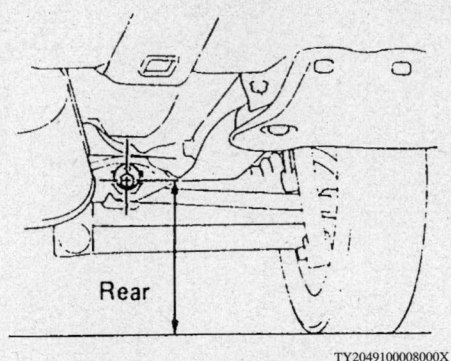

Fig. 8 Rear ride height measurement

Tire size	Front	Rear
P235/45ZR17	187 mm (7.36 in.)	251 mm (9.88 in.)
Tire size	Front	Rear
P225/50ZR16	185 mm (7.28 in.)	250 mm (9.84 in.)

TY2049300010000X

Fig. 9 Ride height specifications

TOYOTA UNIT REPAIR

TABLE OF CONTENTS

Air Conditioning

INDEX

PRECAUTIONS

AIR BAG SYSTEMS

Refer to "Air Bag System Precautions" in the front of this manual for system disarming & arming procedures.

BATTERY GROUND CABLE

Prior to service, disconnect battery ground cable and isolate as required.

AUDIO CODED ANTI-THEFT SYSTEM

Some models are equipped with an audio coded anti-theft system that will disable the radio when the battery cable is disconnected. The system can be identified by the "ANTI-THEFT SYSTEM" on the cassette tape lid. Obtain 3 digit customer code for input. Reset system after service as follows:

1. Obtain 3 digit audio anti-theft code.
2. Depress 1 (PROG) while depressing righthand side of TUNE SEEK button, - - will appear in tape operation display.
3. To enter the first digit, depress 1 (PROG) button repeatedly until the number of times depressed equals the first digit beginning with zero (depress the 1 button six times if the first digit if five).
4. To enter second digit, depress 2 (APS) button repeatedly until the number of times depressed equals the second digit beginning with zero.
5. To enter third digit, depress 3 (RPT) button repeatedly until the number of times depressed equals the third digit beginning with zero.
6. If - - - is displayed during code input, repeat procedure.
7. When code appears in display, depress and hold SCAN button until SEC appears.
8. When SEC disappears audio system should be operative.
9. If Err is displayed, repeat procedure.

Attempting to input code more than nine times may permanently disable audio system.

R-134A SYSTEMS

R-134a is a non-toxic, non-flammable, clear, odorless, liquified gas.

R-134a refrigerant is not compatible with R-12 refrigerant. Even small amounts of R-12 in a R134a system can cause lubricant contamination, improper A/C performance or compressor failure. Never add R-12 to a R-134a system.

New service ports have been added to the compressor to prevent charging the system with R-12 refrigerant. **R-134a systems require a special compressor lubricant. Use ND8 PAG compressor oil part No. 82300102, or equivalent, when servicing system.**

Avoid breathing A/C refrigerant and lubricant vapor and mist. Exposure may irritate eyes, nose and throat. Use only approved service equipment to discharge R-134a systems.

CLEANLINESS

Air conditioning systems are extremely

sensitive to moisture and dirt. The importance of clean working conditions is extremely important, as the smallest particle of foreign matter in an air conditioning system will contaminate the refrigerant, causing rust, ice or damage to the compressor. For this reason, all replacement parts are sold in vacuum sealed containers and should not be opened until they are to be installed in the system. If, for any reason, a part has been removed from its container for any length of time, the part must be completely flushed using only refrigerant to remove any dust or moisture that may have accumulated during storage. In cases of collision repairs where the system has been open for any length of time, the entire system must be purged completely and a new receiver-dehydrator must be installed because the element of the existing unit will have become saturated and unable to remove any moisture from the system once the system is recharged.

When making gauge connections, purge the gauge lines first by cracking the charging valve and allowing a small amount of refrigerant to flow through the lines, then connect the lines immediately.

Cleanliness is especially important when servicing compressors because of the very close tolerances used in these units. Consequently, repairs to the compressor itself should not be attempted unless all proper tools are at hand and a virtually spotless work area is provided.

GENERAL SERVICE

Use care when disconnecting or connecting refrigerant lines; always use a back-up wrench and be careful not to over-tighten any connection. Over-tightening will result inline and flare seat distortion and a system leak.

When making pressure checks on systems having service valves, be sure valve is in the intermediate position. If turned in too far, the hose connection will be closed, a position used for isolating the compressor. When closing the gauge port, do not over-tighten the valve or damage to the seat will result.

After disconnecting gauge lines, check the valve areas to be sure service valves are correctly seated and Schraeder valves, if used, are not leaking.

DESCRIPTION

AUTOMATIC SYSTEM

The automatic A/C system automatically controls operation of the A/C compressor, air inlet door, water valve and blower fan in order to maintain passenger compartment temperature within the range selected by the operator.

The system control circuit consists of a feedback potentiometer, temperature control rheostat and ambient and in-car temperature sensors which are connected in series to provide a variable resistance to system input voltage. The output voltage of this control circuit is applied to an amplifier which transforms the control signal into an operating voltage that is proportional to the control circuit voltage signal. The amplifier

output voltage is converted to a modulated vacuum signal in the vacuum valve, the vacuum signal is applied to the power servo, and the power servo controls system operation.

TROUBLESHOOTING

AUTOMATIC SYSTEM

BLOWER MOTOR DOES NOT OPERATE

1. Blown circuit breaker or fuse.
2. Faulty blower motor.
3. Faulty blower relay.
4. Faulty blower or A/C cutoff relay.
5. Faulty blower switch.
6. Faulty A/C auto relay.
7. Faulty water temperature switch.
8. Faulty blower resistor.
9. Faulty wiring connection.
10. Faulty power transistor.
11. Faulty ambient temperature sensor.
12. Faulty A/C control assembly.
13. Faulty air flow mode control servo.
14. Faulty A/C amplifier.
15. Faulty heater relay circuit.

NO BLOWER MOTOR CONTROL

1. Faulty blower motor resistor.
2. Faulty blower switch.
3. Faulty in-car and/or ambient sensors.
4. Faulty rheostat.
5. Faulty servo motor.
6. Faulty vacuum valves.
7. Faulty blower control relay.
8. Faulty amplifier.
9. Faulty heater mode switch.
10. Faulty coolant temperature switch.
11. Faulty wiring or ground connections.
12. Faulty vacuum circuit.
13. Faulty blower motor.
14. Faulty A/C control assembly.

INTERIOR TEMPERATURE DOES NOT LOWER

1. Blown fuse or circuit breaker.
2. Faulty magnetic clutch.
3. Faulty compressor.
4. Faulty pressure switch.
5. Faulty expansion valve.
6. Faulty EPR valve.
7. Insufficient refrigerant in system.
8. Faulty A/C switch.
9. Faulty temperature sensors.
10. Faulty rheostat.
11. Faulty servo motor.
12. Faulty vacuum valves.
13. Faulty A/C amplifier.
14. Faulty magnetic clutch relay.
15. Faulty wiring or ground connections.
16. Faulty vacuum circuit.
17. Faulty water valve.

INTERIOR TEMPERATURE DOES NOT RISE

1. Faulty water valve.
2. Faulty temperature sensors.
3. Faulty rheostat.
4. Faulty power servo motor.
5. Faulty vacuum valves.
6. Faulty A/C amplifier.
7. Faulty wiring or ground connections.
8. Faulty vacuum circuit.

UNSTABLE SYSTEM OPERATION

1. Faulty vacuum circuit.
2. Improperly connected rheostat.
3. Faulty power servo motor.
4. Faulty vacuum valves.
5. Faulty A/C amplifier.
6. Faulty wiring or ground connection.

IMPROPER SHIFTING OF DAMPER DOORS

1. Control damper or rod improperly adjusted.
2. Faulty vacuum circuit.
3. Faulty dampers.
4. Faulty vacuum valves.

NO COOL AIR COMES OUT

1. Incorrect volume of refrigerant.
2. Fault in cooling fan system.
3. Faulty revolution detecting sensor.
4. Faulty pressure switch.
5. Faulty magnetic clutch.
6. Faulty igniter circuit.
7. Faulty A/C amplifier.
8. Fault in A/C control assembly.
9. Faulty room temperature sensor.
10. Faulty air mix control servo motor.
11. Faulty ambient temperature sensor.
12. Faulty evaporator temperature sensor circuit.
13. Faulty engine coolant temperature sensor circuit.
14. Faulty compressor lock sensor circuit.
15. Faulty air mix damper control sensor circuit.
16. Faulty temperature set dial circuit.
17. Improper drive belt tension.

NO WARM AIR COMES OUT

1. Faulty air mix control servo motor.
2. Faulty ambient temperature sensor.
3. Faulty room temperature sensor.
4. Faulty evaporator temperature sensor.
5. Fault in A/C control assembly.
6. Fault in A/C amplifier.
7. Faulty air mix damper position sensor circuit.
8. Faulty temperature set dial circuit.

OUTPUT AIR DIFFERS FROM SET TEMPERATURE OR RESPONSE IS SLOW

1. Improper refrigerant volume.
2. Improper drive belt tension.
3. Faulty ambient temperature sensor.
4. Faulty room temperature sensor.
5. Faulty evaporator temperature sensor.
6. Faulty air mix control servo motor.
7. Fault in A/C control assembly.
8. Faulty A/C amplifier.
9. Faulty compressor, condenser, evaporator or receiver.
10. Fault in heater core.
11. Faulty expansion valve.
12. Faulty engine coolant temperature circuit.
13. Faulty compressor lock sensor circuit.
14. Faulty pressure switch circuit.
15. Faulty air mix damper position sensor circuit.
16. Faulty temperature set dial circuit.
17. Faulty solar sensor circuit.
18. Faulty air inlet damper control servo motor circuit.
19. Faulty electric cooling fan.

NO AIR TEMPERATURE CONTROL (ONLY PROVIDES MAX COOL & MAX WARM)

1. Faulty air mix control servo motor.
2. Fault in A/C control assembly.
3. Faulty A/C amplifier.
4. Faulty room temperature sensor circuit.
5. Faulty ambient temperature sensor circuit.
6. Faulty air mix damper position sensor circuit.
7. Faulty temperature set dial circuit.

NO AIR INLET CONTROL

1. Faulty air inlet control servo motor.
2. Fault in A/C control assembly.
3. Faulty A/C amplifier.

NO AIR OUTLET CONTROL

1. Faulty air outlet control servo motor.
2. Fault in A/C control assembly.
3. Faulty A/C amplifier.
4. Faulty air outlet damper position sensor circuit.

ENGINE IDLE-UP DOES NOT OCCUR, OR IS CONTINUOUS

1. Fault in A/C control assembly.
2. Faulty igniter circuit.
3. Faulty magnetic clutch.
4. Faulty A/C amplifier.

BLINKING OF A/C INDICATOR

1. Faulty revolution detecting sensor.
2. Fault in A/C control assembly.
3. Faulty compressor lock sensor circuit.
4. Faulty A/C amplifier.
5. Faulty compressor circuit.

NO ENGINE IDLE-UP WHEN A/C TURNED ON

1. A/C amplifier.
2. Idle control system.
3. Wire harness.

MANUAL SYSTEM

System Cools Intermittently

1. Slipping magnetic clutch.
2. Faulty expansion valve.
3. Faulty wiring connections.
4. Excess moisture in system.
5. Faulty revolution detecting sensor.
6. Faulty A/C amplifier.
7. Improper refrigerant volume.
8. Improper drive belt tension.
9. Faulty evaporator temperature sensor.
10. Faulty evaporator.
11. Faulty thermistor.
12. Faulty compressor.
13. Faulty receiver.

Insufficient Cooling At High Speeds

1. Faulty thermistor.

System Cools At High Speeds Only

1. Condenser fins partially clogged.
2. Slipping compressor drive belt.
3. Faulty compressor.
4. Insufficient or excess refrigerant in system.
5. Air in system.

6. Faulty revolution detecting sensor.
7. Faulty A/C amplifier.
8. Faulty evaporator temperature sensor.
9. Faulty expansion valve.

Insufficient Cooling (All Speeds)

1. Clogged condenser fins.
2. Slipping compressor drive belt.
3. Slipping magnetic clutch.
4. Faulty compressor.
5. Faulty expansion valve.
6. Improperly adjusted temperature control lever.
7. Faulty thermistor.
8. Faulty temperature control resistor (if equipped).
9. Air or excessive compressor oil in system.
10. Clogged receiver.
11. Faulty vent mode switch.
12. Water valve cable set faulty.
13. Improper refrigerant volume.
14. Faulty pressure switch.
15. Faulty evaporator temperature sensor.
16. Faulty A/C fan relays.
17. Faulty condenser fan motor.
18. Faulty A/C amplifier.
19. Faulty evaporator.
20. Faulty air mix servo motor.

Insufficient Velocity Of Cool Air

1. Blocked air inlet.
2. Clogged evaporator fins.
3. Frosted evaporator.
4. Air leakage from cooling unit or air duct.
5. Faulty blower motor.
6. Faulty wiring connections.

System Produces Little Or No Heat

1. Faulty water valve.
2. Improperly adjusted temperature control lever.
3. Disconnected control wire.
4. Insufficient coolant.
5. Clogged heater core.
6. Clogged or collapsed heater hoses.
7. Faulty vacuum switching valve.
8. Faulty air mix servo motor.

Improper Shifting Of Damper Doors

1. Improperly adjusted control lever.
2. Disconnected control wire.

Noisy System Operation

1. Piping noise:
   a. Loose or broken piping clamp.
   b. Faulty compressor.
   c. Faulty expansion valve.
2. Blower noise:
   a. Blower touching case.
   b. Faulty blower motor bearing.
3. Compressor noise:
   a. Compressor mount or mounting bolts loose or broken.
   b. Faulty compressor.
   c. Improper amount of compressor oil.
   d. Insufficient amount of refrigerant.
4. Magnetic clutch noise:
   a. Seized or worn bearings.

   b. Insufficient clearance between pressure plate and rotor.
5. Compressor drive belt noise:
   a. Loose drive belt.
6. Idle pulley noise:
   a. Seized or worn bearing.

Engine Overheats

1. Loose or broken fan belt.
2. Clogged radiator or condenser fins.
3. Faulty radiator cap.
4. Faulty water pump.
5. Incorrect ignition timing.
6. Low coolant level.
7. Faulty thermostat.
8. Cracked block.
9. Cracked cylinder head.

No Blower Operation With Fan On

1. Blown heater fuse.
2. Faulty heater relay.
3. Faulty heater blower switch.
4. Faulty heater blower resistor.
5. Faulty heater blower motor.
6. Faulty wiring or ground.
7. Fault in A/C control assembly.

Incorrect Water Temperature Output

1. Broken or binding control cables.
2. Leaking or clogged heater hoses.
3. Faulty water valve.
4. Broken air dampers.
5. Clogged air ducts.
6. Leaking or clogged heater core.
7. Faulty heater control unit.

A/C Switch Indicator Flashing

1. Slipping compressor drive belt.
2. Faulty revolution sensor.
3. Faulty A/C amplifier.

EXERCISE SYSTEM

An important fact most car owners ignore is that A/C systems must be used periodically. Car manufacturers recommend that when the air conditioner is not used regularly, particularly during cold months, it should be turned on for a few minutes once every two or three weeks while the engine is running. This keeps the system in good operating condition.

Checking out the system for the effects of disuse before the onset of summer is one of the most important aspects of A/C system servicing.

First clean out the condenser core. All obstructions, such as leaves, bugs and dirt, must be removed as they will reduce heat transfer and impair the efficiency of the system. Make sure the space between the condenser and the radiator also is free of foreign matter.

Make certain the evaporator water drain is open. Certain systems have two evaporators, one in the engine compartment and one in the trunk. The evaporator cools and dehumidifies the air before it enters the car; there the refrigerant is changed from a liquid to a vapor. As the core cools the air, moisture condenses on it but is prevented from collecting in the evaporator by the water drain.

PERFORMANCE TEST

1. Connect manifold gauge set as follows:
   a. Connect charging hoses to manifold gauge set.
   b. Connect quick connectors to charging hoses.
   c. Close both hand valves of manifold gauge set.
   d. Remove caps from service valves on refrigerant line.
   e. Connect quick connectors to service valves.
2. Read manifold gauge pressure when the following conditions are established:
   a. Temperature at air inlet with the switch set at RECIRC is 86–95°F.
   b. Engine running at 1,500 RPM .
   c. Blower speed control switch set at high.
   d. Temperature control set at MAX COOL.
3. For a normally functioning refrigeration system, the gauge reading should be 21–35 psi for the low pressure side, and 198–228 psi for the high pressure side.
4. Refer to **Figs. 1 through 8** for problems that may cause abnormal gauge readings.

LEAK TEST

R-134A SYSTEMS

When servicing R-134a air conditioning systems always use the R-134a manifold gauges, gas leak detector assembly, tool No. 07116-38360, or equivalent, and vacuum pump adapter. Use R-134a manifold gauges to prevent R12 and R12 compressor oil contaminating the R-134a system. The R12 leak detector is not sufficiently sensitive, always use the R-134a gas leak detector assembly tool. By adapting a vacuum pump adapter, the vacuum pump can be used for both R-134a and R-12 air conditioning systems. The vacuum pump adapter has an internal magnetic valve. When evacuation is completed and the vacuum pump switch is turned off, the magnetic valve opens allowing atmospheric air into the manifold gauges to prevent the back flow of oil from the vacuum pump into the gauge hose. Be sure to turn off manifold gauge immediately after evacuating system. If not, the line will temporarily open to atmosphere.

System Empty

Do not pressure test the R-134a system with compressed air. Some mixtures of R-134a refrigerant have been shown be to combustible at higher pressures. Use gas leak detector assembly, tool No. 07116-38360, or equivalent, designed for R-134a systems.
1. Evacuate A/C system.
2. Charge system until low pressure gauge reads 14 psi. Refer to "Charging System" for procedure.

3. With engine Off, use the gas leak detector assembly, tool No. 07116-38360, or equivalent, designed for R-134a system and inspect for leaks. Fittings, lines or components that appear to be oily may indicate a refrigerant leak. To inspect the evaporator core for leaks, it is possible to insert the leak detector probe into the recirculating air door opening. With the blower at low speed and the selector in FLOOR and RECIRC mode check for leaks at left and right heater outlets. If no leak is present, fill system as outlined under "Charging System."

Low Level

1. Start engine with A/C On for five minutes to allow system to reach operating temperature and pressure.
2. With engine Off, use the gas leak detector assembly, tool No. 07116-38360, or equivalent, designed for R-134a system and inspect for leaks. Fittings, lines or components that appear to be oily may indicate a refrigerant leak. To inspect the evaporator core for leaks, it is possible to insert the leak detector probe into the recirculating air door opening. With the blower at low speed and the selector in FLOOR and RECIRC mode check for leaks at left and right heater outlets. If no leak is present, fill system as outlined under "Charging System."

DISCHARGING SYSTEM

REFRIGERANT RECOVERY

The use of refrigerant recovery and recycling stations allows the recovery and reuse of refrigerant after contaminants and moisture have been removed.

When using a recovery or recycling station, follow manufacturer's operating instructions, while noting the following:
1. **Use extreme caution and observe all safety and service precautions related to the use of refrigerant.**
2. Connect refrigerant recycling station hose(s) to vehicle A/C service port(s) and recovery station inlet fitting. Hoses should have shutoff devices within 12 inches of hose ends to minimize introduction of air into recycling station and to minimize amount of refrigerant release when hose(s) are disconnected.
3. Turn on recycling station to start recovery process. Allow recycling station to pump refrigerant from A/C system until station pressure gauge indicates vacuum.
4. After vehicle A/C system has been evacuated, close station inlet valve, if equipped.
5. Turn off station. On some stations the pump will automatically be turned off by a low pressure switch.
6. Allow vehicle A/C system to remain closed for about two minutes. Observe vacuum level indicated on gauge. If

pressure does not rise, disconnect recycling station hose(s).
7. If system pressure rises, repeat steps 3 through 6 until vacuum level remains stable for two minutes.
8. Service A/C system as necessary, then evacuate and recharge A/C system.

EVACUATING SYSTEM

R-134a Systems

Keep all R-134a components capped to prevent moisture from entering the system. If the refrigerant system has been opened to the atmosphere, it must be evacuated.

The system must be completely discharged before it can be evacuated. Damage to the vacuum pump may result if pressurized refrigerant is allowed to enter.
1. Connect suitable charging station, refrigerant recovery machine and a manifold gauge set with vacuum pump.
2. Open suction and discharge valves and start vacuum pump. The vacuum pump should run a minimum of 45 minutes before charging to eliminate all moisture in system. When suction gauge reads 26 inches Hg or greater for 45 minutes, close all valves and turn off vacuum pump. If system fails to reach specified vacuum, refrigerant system likely has a leak that must be corrected. If refrigerant system maintains specified vacuum for at least 30 minutes, start vacuum pump and open discharge and suction valves, and allow system to evacuate for an additional 10 minutes.
3. Close all valves, turn off and disconnect pump and charge with refrigerant.

SYSTEM FLUSH

Several factors, particularly compressor failure can cause contamination of the A/C system. If the A/C system is suspected of being contaminated, or if any system components have been stored in open air for extended periods, the entire system should be flushed. If contamination or moisture is minimal, the system can be flushed with nitrogen. If contamination is more extensive, the system should be flushed with refrigerant. The receiver drier or accumulator should be replaced and a full charge of oil should be added any time the system is flushed.

CHARGING SYSTEM

To charge system using a charging station, use manufacturers instructions provided with the unit. Observe the following precautions:
1. Do not connect high pressure line to A/C system.
2. Always keep high pressure valve on charging station closed.
3. Perform all evacuation and charging through low side pressure service fitting.

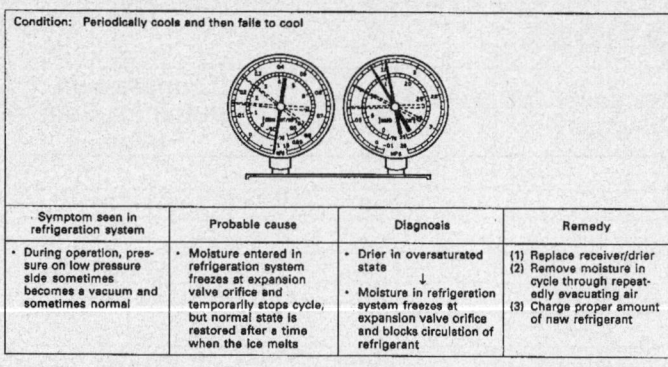

Condition: Periodically cools and then fails to cool

Symptom seen in refrigeration system	Probable cause	Diagnosis	Remedy
• During operation, pressure on low pressure side sometimes becomes a vacuum and sometimes normal	• Moisture entered in refrigeration system freezes at expansion valve orifice and temporarily stops cycle, but normal state is restored after a time when the ice melts	• Drier in oversaturated state ↓ • Moisture in refrigeration system freezes at expansion valve orifice and blocks circulation of refrigerant	(1) Replace receiver/drier (2) Remove moisture in cycle through repeatedly evacuating air (3) Charge proper amount of new refrigerant

TY7029100237000X

Fig. 1 Moisture present in refrigeration system

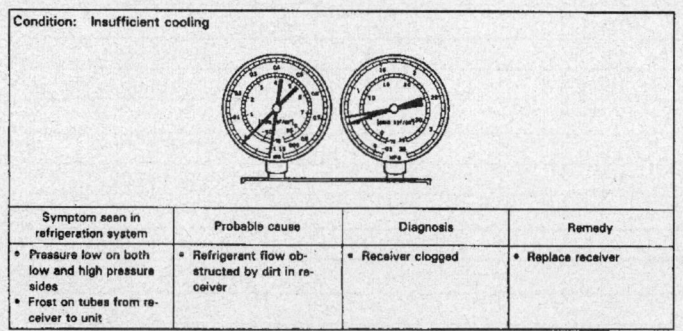

Condition: Insufficient cooling

Symptom seen in refrigeration system	Probable cause	Diagnosis	Remedy
• Pressure low on both low and high pressure sides • Frost on tubes from receiver to unit	• Refrigerant flow obstructed by dirt in receiver	• Receiver clogged	• Replace receiver

TY7029100239000X

Fig. 3 Poor recirculation of refrigerant

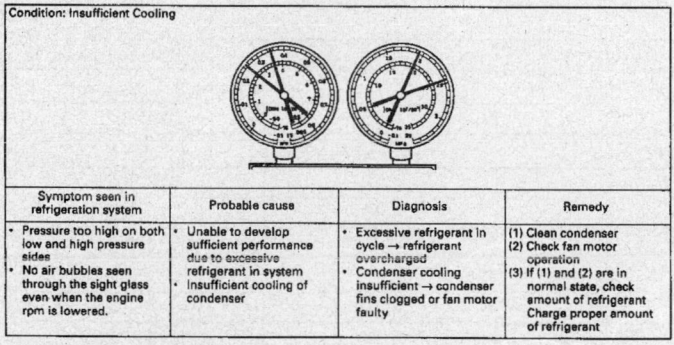

Condition: Insufficient Cooling

Symptom seen in refrigeration system	Probable cause	Diagnosis	Remedy
• Pressure too high on both low and high pressure sides • No air bubbles seen through the sight glass even when the engine rpm is lowered.	• Unable to develop sufficient performance due to excessive refrigerant in system • Insufficient cooling of condenser	• Excessive refrigerant in cycle → refrigerant overcharged • Condenser cooling insufficient → condenser fins clogged or fan motor faulty	(1) Clean condenser (2) Check fan motor operation (3) If (1) and (2) are in normal state, check amount of refrigerant Charge proper amount of refrigerant

TY7029100241000X

Fig. 5 Refrigerant overcharge or insufficient cooling of condenser

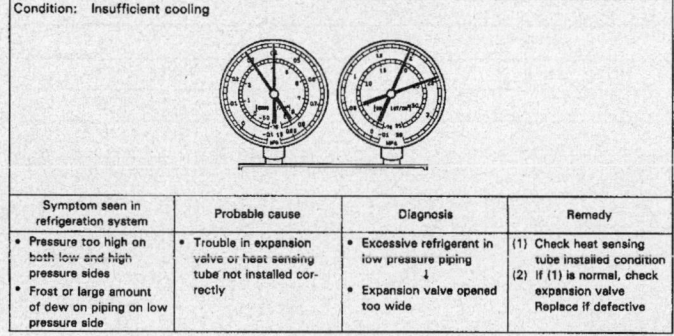

Condition: Insufficient cooling

Symptom seen in refrigeration system	Probable cause	Diagnosis	Remedy
• Pressure too high on both low and high pressure sides • Frost or large amount of dew on piping on low pressure side	• Trouble in expansion valve or heat sensing tube not installed correctly	• Excessive refrigerant in low pressure piping ↓ • Expansion valve opened too wide	(1) Check heat sensing tube installed condition (2) If (1) is normal, check expansion valve Replace if defective

TY7029100243000X

Fig. 7 Expansion valve improperly mounted/heat sensing tube faulty

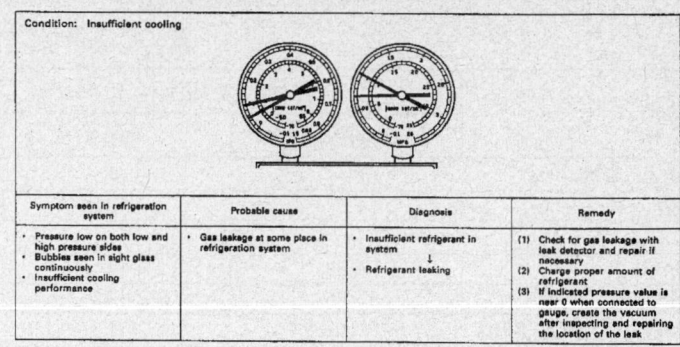

Condition: Insufficient cooling

Symptom seen in refrigeration system	Probable cause	Diagnosis	Remedy
• Pressure low on both low and high pressure sides • Bubbles seen in sight glass continuously • Insufficient cooling performance	• Gas leakage at some place in refrigeration system	• Insufficient refrigerant in system ↓ • Refrigerant leaking	(1) Check for gas leakage with leak detector and repair if necessary (2) Charge proper amount of refrigerant (3) If indicated pressure value is near 0 when connected to gauge, create the vacuum after inspecting and repairing the location of the leak

TY7029100238000X

Fig. 2 Insufficient refrigerant

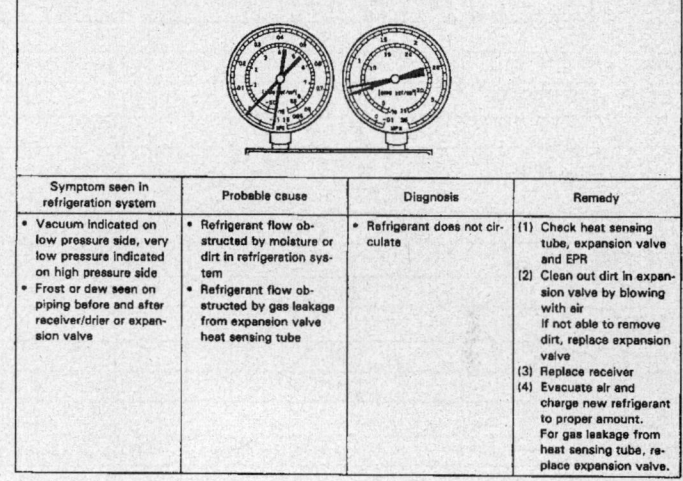

Condition: Does not cool (Cools from time to time in some cases)

Symptom seen in refrigeration system	Probable cause	Diagnosis	Remedy
• Vacuum indicated on low pressure side, very low pressure indicated on high pressure side • Frost or dew seen on piping before and after receiver/drier or expansion valve	• Refrigerant flow obstructed by moisture or dirt in refrigeration system • Refrigerant flow obstructed by gas leakage from expansion valve heat sensing tube	• Refrigerant does not circulate	(1) Check heat sensing tube, expansion valve and EPR (2) Clean out dirt in expansion valve by blowing with air If not able to remove dirt, replace expansion valve (3) Replace receiver (4) Evacuate air and charge new refrigerant to proper amount. For gas leakage from heat sensing tube, replace expansion valve.

TY7029100240000X

Fig. 4 Refrigerant does not circulate

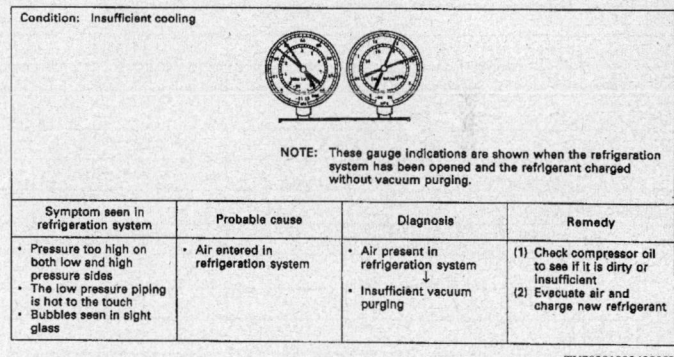

Condition: Insufficient cooling

NOTE: These gauge indications are shown when the refrigeration system has been opened and the refrigerant charged without vacuum purging.

Symptom seen in refrigeration system	Probable cause	Diagnosis	Remedy
• Pressure too high on both low and high pressure sides • The low pressure piping is hot to the touch • Bubbles seen in sight glass	• Air entered in refrigeration system	• Air present in refrigeration system ↓ • Insufficient vacuum purging	(1) Check compressor oil to see if it is dirty or insufficient (2) Evacuate air and charge new refrigerant

TY7029100242000X

Fig. 6 Air present in refrigeration system

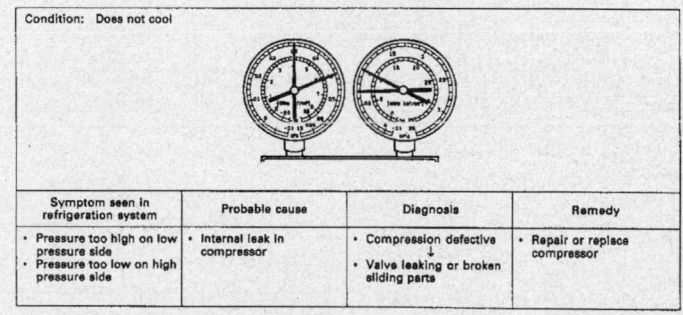

Condition: Does not cool

Symptom seen in refrigeration system	Probable cause	Diagnosis	Remedy
• Pressure too high on low pressure side • Pressure too low on high pressure side	• Internal leak in compressor	• Compression defective ↓ • Valve leaking or broken sliding parts	• Repair or replace compressor

TY7029100244000X

Fig. 8 Faulty compression compressor

A/C SPECIFICATIONS

Year	Refrigerant		Compressor Oil Viscosity	Total System Oil Capacity, Oz.	Compressor Clutch Air Gap, Inch
	Capacity, Lbs.	Type			
AVALON					
1996–99	1.87	R-134a	③	4.10	.014–.026
CAMRY					
1996	1.88	R-134a	③	4.90	.014–.026
1997–99	1.76	R-134a	③	4.10	.014–.026
CAMRY SOLARA					
1999	1.76	R-134a	③	4.10	.014–.026
CELICA					
1996–99	1.43	R-134a	③	4.10	.014–.026
COROLLA					
1996–98	1.54	R-134a	③	4.10	.014–.026
1999	1.43	R-134a	③	4.10	.014–.026
LAND CRUISER					
1996–97	1.87	R-134a	③	4.10	.014–.026
1998–99	①	R-134a	③	—	.014–.026
PASEO					
1996–97	1.32	R-134a	③	4.10	.014–.026
PREVIA					
1996–97	④	R-134a	③	—	.014–.026
RAV4					
1996	1.56	R-134a	③	4.10	.014–.026
1997–99	1.54	R-134a	③	4.10	.014–.026
SIENNA					
1998–99	②	R-134a	③	4.10	.014–.026
SUPRA					
1996–98	1.56	R-134a	③	4.80	.014–.026
TACOMA					
1996	1.32	R-134a	③	4.10	.014–.026
1997	1.32	R-134a	③	4.80	.014–.026
1998–99	1.32	R-134a	③	—	.014–.026
TERCEL					
1996–97	1.43	R-134a	③	4.10	.014–.026
1998	.99	R-134a	③	4.10	.014–.026
TUNDRA					
2000	1.32	R-134a	③	—	.014–.026
T-100					
1996–98	1.43	R-134a	③	4.80	.014–.026
4RUNNER					
1996	1.43	R-134a	③	4.10	.014–.026
1997–99	1.43	R-134a	③	—	.014–.026

① — Single A/C, 1.76 lbs.; dual A/C, 2.40 lbs.
② — Single A/C, 1.76 lbs.; 4 door models w/dual A/C, 2.76 lbs.; 5 door models w/dual A/C, 2.98 lbs.
③ — ND Oil 8, or equivalent.
④ — Front A/C, 1.98 lbs.; dual A/C, 2.54 oz.

BELT TENSION

Engine	Belt Tension, Lbs.	
	New	Used
1996-97		
1FZ-FE & 3VZ-E	100–150	60–100
1MZ-FE	140–190	99-121

Continued

BELT TENSION—Continued

Engine	Belt Tension, Lbs.	
	New	Used
1996-97		
2JZ-GE & 2JZ-GTE	①	①
2RZ-FE	④	④
2TZ-FE &2TZ-FZE	139-191	③
3RZ-FE & 3S-GTE	135–185	80–120
3S-FE	139–192	⑤
3VZ-E	100–150	60–100
4A-FE	135–185	80–120
5E-FE	②	80-120
5S-FE	⑥	⑦
5VZ-FE	135–185	80–120
7A-FE	135–180	80–120
1998–99		
1MZ-FE	⑧	⑨
1ZZ-FE	⑩	⑩
2JZ-GE	①	①
2JZ-GTE	①	①
2RZ-FE	④	④
2UZ-FE	⑪	⑪
3RZ-FE	135-185	80-120
3S-FE	135-185	80-120
5E-FE	135-185	80-120
5S-FE	⑥	⑦
5VZ-FE	135-185	75-125

① — Belt tension should be within the "A" range on the auto tensioner scale, Fig. A.
② — 1996 Tercel, 140–180; 1997 Tercel, 135–185; Paseo, 135–185.
③ — 1996; 110–150, 1997; 80–120.
④ — 1996–97; New, 135–185; Used, 80–120.
⑤ — 1996, 66–99; 1997, 100–120.
⑥ — Camry, 139–191; Celica, 170–180.
⑦ — Celica, 88–132; Camry, 99–121.
⑧ — Avalon, 143–187; Camry & Sienna, 139–191.
⑨ — Avalon & Sienna, 66–110; Camry, 99–121.
⑩ — Equipped with automatic tensioner.
⑪ — If tension is not within "A" range, **Fig. B,** replace belt tensioner.

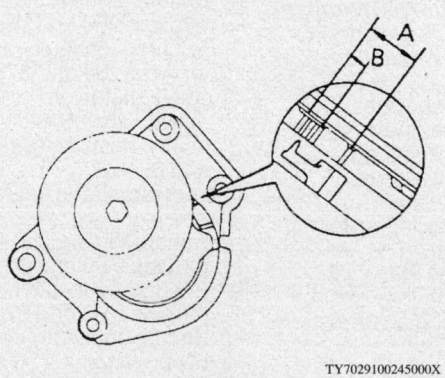

TY7029100245000X

Fig. A

2UZ–FE:

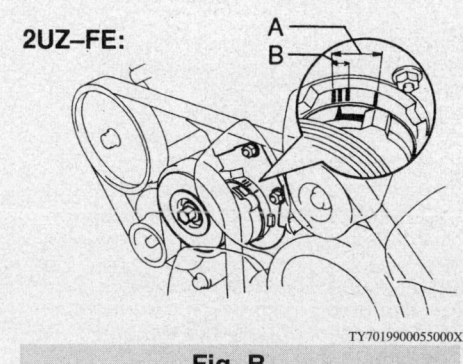

TY7019900055000X

Fig. B

Cooling Fans

INDEX

PRECAUTIONS

AIR BAG SYSTEMS

Refer to "Air Bag System Precautions" in the front of this manual for system disarming & arming procedures.

BATTERY GROUND CABLE

Prior to service, disconnect battery ground cable and isolate as required.

AUDIO CODED ANTI-THEFT SYSTEM

Some models are equipped with an audio coded anti-theft system that will disable the radio when the battery cable is disconnected. The system can be identified by the "ANTI-THEFT SYSTEM" on the cassette tape lid. Obtain 3 digit customer code for input. Reset system after service as follows:

1. Obtain 3 digit audio anti-theft code.
2. Depress 1 (PROG) while depressing righthand side of TUNE SEEK button, - - - will appear in tape operation display.
3. To enter the first digit, depress 1 (PROG) button repeatedly until the number of times depressed equals the first digit beginning with zero (depress the 1 button six times if the first digit is five).
4. To enter second digit, depress 2 (APS) button repeatedly until the number of times depressed equals the second digit beginning with zero.
5. To enter third digit, depress 3 (RPT) button repeatedly until the number of times depressed equals the second digit beginning with zero.
6. If - - - is displayed during code input, repeat procedure.
7. When code appears in display, depress and hold SCAN button until SEC appears.

8. When SEC disappears audio system should be operative.
9. If Err is displayed, repeat procedure. **Attempting to input code more than nine times may permanently disable audio system.**

TROUBLESHOOTING

Avalon

ON-VEHICLE INSPECTION

1. Check cooling fan operation with temperature below 190°F as follows:
   a. Turn ignition switch to On.
   b. Check that cooling fan stops. If not, check cooling fan relay and ECT switch and check for separated connector or severed wire between cooling fan relay and ECT switch.
   c. Disconnect No. 1 ECT switch connector.
   d. Check that cooling fan operates. If not, check the fuses, engine main relay, cooling fan relay, cooling fan and check for a short between cooling fan relay and ECT switch.
   e. Reconnect No.1 ECT switch connector.
2. Check cooling fan operation with high temperature above 208°F as follows:
   a. Start engine and raise coolant temperature to above 208°F.
   b. Check that cooling fan operates. If not, replace No. 1 ECT switch.

NO. 1 COOLING FAN MOTOR INSPECTION

1. Disconnect cooling fan connector.
2. Connect battery and ammeter to connector, **Fig. 1.**
3. **On 1996–97 models,** ensure cooling fan rotates smoothly and reading on ammeter is 6.1–7.3 amps.
4. **On 1998–99 models,** ensure cooling fan rotates smoothly and reading on ammeter is 5.1–6.3 amps.

NO. 2 COOLING FAN MOTOR INSPECTION

1. Disconnect cooling fan connector.
2. Connect battery and ammeter to connector, **Fig. 2.**
3. Ensure cooling fan rotates smoothly and reading on ammeter is 9.2–11.0 amps.

COOLING FAN RELAY INSPECTION

1. Inspect No. 1 cooling fan relay as follows:
   a. Ensure continuity exists between terminals 85 and 86, **Fig. 3.**
   b. Ensure continuity exists between terminals 30 and 87.
   c. Apply battery voltage across terminals 85 and 86, then ensure no continuity exists between terminals 30 and 87.
2. Inspect No. 2 cooling fan relay as follows:
   a. Ensure continuity exists between terminals 85 and 86, **Fig. 4.**
   b. Ensure continuity exists between terminals 30 and 87_a.
   c. Ensure continuity does not exist between terminals 30 and 87.
   d. Apply battery voltage across terminals 85 and 86.
   e. Ensure continuity does not exist between terminals 30 and 87_a.
   f. Ensure continuity exists between terminals 30 and 87.
3. Inspect No. 3 cooling fan relay as follows:
   a. Ensure continuity exists between

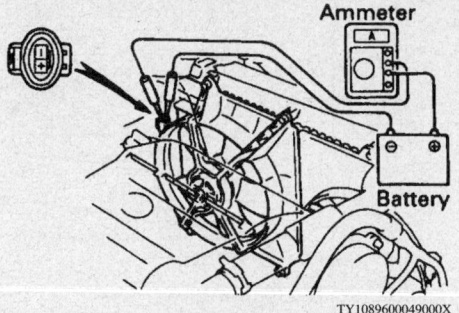

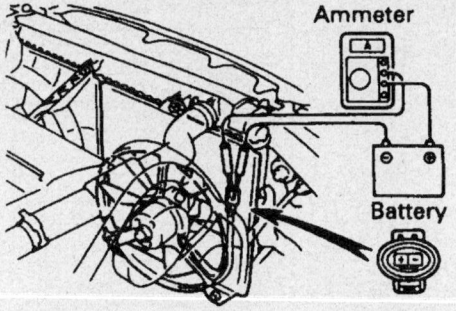

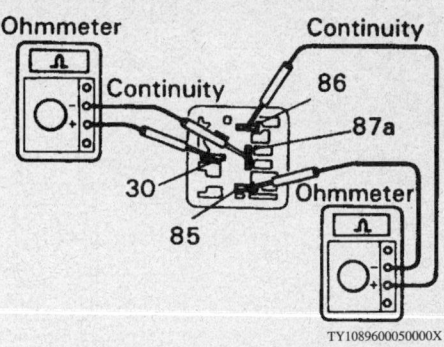

Fig. 1 No. 1 fan motor inspection. Avalon, Camry & Camry Solara w/1MZ-FE Engine

Fig. 2 No. 2 fan inspection. Avalon, Camry & Camry Solara w/1MZ-FE engine

Fig. 3 No. 1 cooling fan relay inspection. Avalon

terminals 85 and 86, **Fig. 5.**
  b. Ensure continuity does not exist between terminals 30 and 87.
  c. Apply battery voltage across terminals 85 and 86.
  d. Ensure continuity exists between terminals 30 and 87.

Camry & Camry Solara

1MZ-FE ENGINE

ON-VEHICLE INSPECTION

Refer to "Avalon" for troubleshooting procedures.

NO. 1 COOLING FAN MOTOR INSPECTION

Refer to "Avalon" for troubleshooting procedures.

NO. 2 COOLING FAN MOTOR INSPECTION

Refer to "Avalon" for troubleshooting procedures.

COOLING FAN RELAY INSPECTION

1. Inspect No. 1 cooling fan relay as follows:
   a. Ensure continuity exists between terminals 1 and 2, **Fig. 6.**
   b. Ensure continuity exists between terminals 3 and 4.
   c. Apply battery voltage across terminals 1 and 2.
   d. Ensure continuity does not exist between terminals 3 and 4.
   e. If continuity is not as specified, replace relay.
2. Inspect No. 2 cooling fan relay as follows:
   a. Ensure continuity exists between terminals 1 and 2, **Figs. 7 and 8.**
   b. Ensure continuity exists between terminals 3 and 4.
   c. Ensure continuity does not exist between terminals 3 and 5
   d. Apply battery voltage across terminals 1 and 2.
   e. Ensure continuity does not exist between terminals 3 and 4.
   f. Ensure continuity exists between terminals 3 and 5.

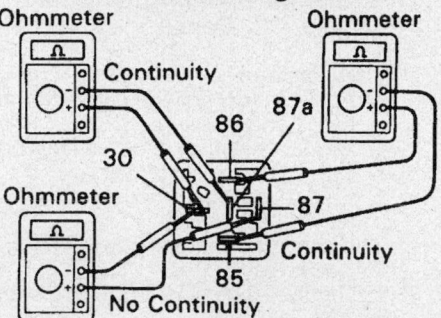

Fig. 4 No. 2 cooling fan relay inspection. Avalon

   g. If continuity is not as specified, replace relay.
3. Inspect No. 3 cooling fan relay as follows:
   a. Ensure continuity exists between terminals 1 and 2, **Fig. 9.**
   b. Ensure continuity does not exist between terminals 3 and 5.
   c. Apply battery voltage across terminals 1 and 2.
   d. Ensure continuity exists between terminals 3 and 5.
   e. If continuity is not as specified, replace relay.

5S-FE ENGINE

ON-VEHICLE INSPECTION

1. If coolant temperature is low (below 181°F), proceed as follows:
   a. Turn ignition switch on and check that cooling fan does not operate.
   b. If fan is operating, check for faulty fan relay and/or temperature switch. Check too for separated electrical connectors or severed wire between fan relay and temperature switch.
   c. Disconnect temperature switch wire, then check that fan rotates.
   d. If fan does not rotate, check fan relay, fan motor, engine main relay and fuse. Check also for short circuit between fan relay and temperature switch.
   e. Connect temperature switch connector.
2. If coolant temperature is high (above 199°F), proceed as follows:
   a. Raise engine temperature to at

least 200°F, then check that fan rotates.
  b. If fan does not rotate, replace temperature switch.

COOLING FAN INSPECTION

1. Disconnect cooling fan electrical connector.
2. Connect battery and ammeter to cooling fan connector.
3. Ensure cooling fan operates smoothly and reading on measurement is 5.8–7.4 amps.

COOLING FAN RELAY INSPECTION

1. Ensure continuity exists between terminals 1 and 2, **Fig. 10.**
2. Ensure continuity exists between terminals 3 and 4.
3. Apply battery voltage across terminals 1 and 2.
4. Ensure continuity does not exist between terminals 3 and 4.
5. If continuity is not as specified, replace relay.

Celica

ON-VEHICLE INSPECTION

1. If coolant temperature is low (below 181°F), proceed as follows:
   a. Turn on ignition switch and check that cooling fan is not operating.
   b. If fan is operating, check for faulty fan relay and/or temperature switch. Check too for separated electrical connectors or severed wire between relay and temperature switch.
   c. Disconnect temperature switch wire, then check that fan rotates.
   d. If fan does not rotate, check fan relay, fan motor, engine main relay and fuse. Check also for short circuit between fan relay and temperature switch.
   e. Connect temperature switch wire.
2. Raise engine temperature at least 200°F, then check that fan rotates. If fan does not rotate, replace temperature switch.

NO. 1 COOLING FAN INSPECTION

1. Disconnect cooling fan electrical connector.

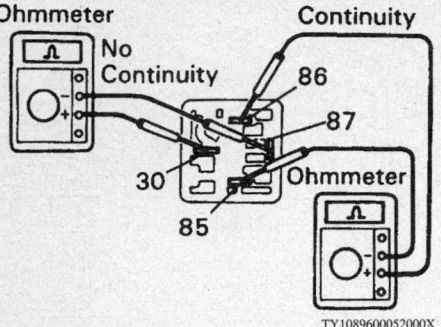

Fig. 5 No. 3 cooling fan relay inspection. Avalon

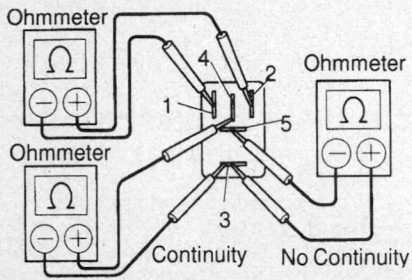

Fig. 8 No. 2 cooling fan relay inspection. Camry Solara, Sienna & 1997–99 Camry w/1MZ-FE engine

2. Connect battery and ammeter to cooling fan connector.
3. Ensure cooling fan operates smoothly and reading on measurement is 5.8–7.4 amps.

NO. 2 COOLING FAN INSPECTION

1. Disconnect cooling fan electrical connector.
2. Connect battery and ammeter to cooling fan connector.
3. Ensure cooling fan operates smoothly and reading on measurement is 5.7–7.7 amps.

COOLING FAN RELAY INSPECTION

1. Inspect No. 1 cooling fan relay as follows:
   a. Ensure continuity exists between terminals 1 and 2, **Fig. 6.**
   b. Ensure continuity exists between terminals 3 and 4.
   c. Apply battery voltage across terminals 1 and 2.
   d. Ensure continuity does not exist between terminals 3 and 4.
   e. If continuity is not as specified, replace relay.
2. Inspect No. 2 cooling fan relay as follows:
   a. Ensure continuity exists between terminals 1 and 2, **Fig. 7.**
   b. Ensure continuity exists between terminals 3 and 4.
   c. Ensure continuity does not exist be-

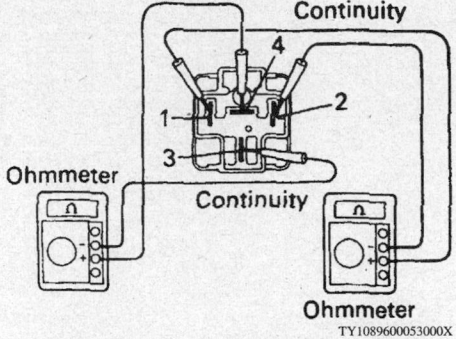

Fig. 6 No. 1 cooling fan relay inspection. Camry, Camry Solara & Sienna w/1MZ-FE engine & Celica

   tween terminals 3 and 5
   d. Apply battery voltage across terminals 1 and 2.
   e. Ensure continuity does not exist between terminals 3 and 4.
   f. Ensure continuity exists between terminals 3 and 5.
   g. If continuity is not as specified, replace relay.
3. Inspect No. 3 cooling fan relay as follows:
   a. Ensure continuity exists between terminals 1 and 2, **Fig. 9.**
   b. Ensure continuity does not exist between terminals 3 and 5.
   c. Apply battery voltage across terminals 1 and 2.
   d. Ensure continuity exists between terminals 3 and 5.
   e. If continuity is not as specified, replace relay.

Corolla

ON-VEHICLE INSPECTION

1. If coolant temperature is low (below 181°F), proceed as follows:
   a. Turn ignition switch on and check that cooling fan does not operate. If fan runs, check for faulty fan relay and/or temperature switch (ECT). Check too for separated electrical connectors or severed wire between relay and temperature switch (ECT).
   b. Disconnect temperature switch wire, then check that fan rotates. If fan does not run, check fan relay, fan motor, ignition relay and temperature switch (ECT).
   c. Connect temperature switch wire.
2. If coolant temperature is high (above 199°F), proceed as follows:
   a. Raise engine temperature to at least 200°F, then confirm that fan rotates.
   b. If fan does not rotate, replace temperature switch (ECT).

COOLING FAN INSPECTION

1. Disconnect cooling fan electrical connector.
2. Connect battery and ammeter to cooling fan connector.
3. Ensure cooling fan operates smoothly

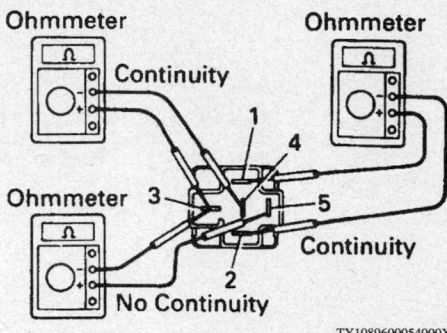

Fig. 7 No. 2 cooling fan relay inspection. Celica & 1996 Camry w/1MZ-FE engine

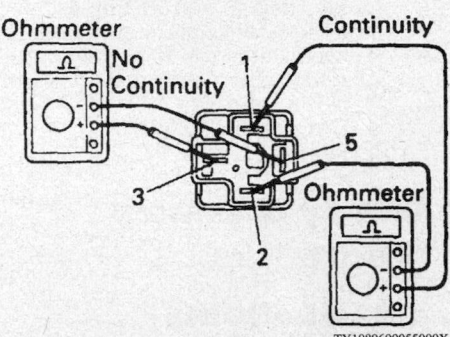

Fig. 9 No. 3 cooling fan relay inspection. Camry, Camry Solara & Sienna w/1MZ-FE engine & Celica

and reading on measurement is 5.7–7.7 amps.

COOLING FAN RELAY INSPECTION

COROLLA

Nippondenso

1. Using an ohmmeter, check relay continuity. If in either case continuity is absent, replace relay. Check for continuity first between terminals 1 and 2, then between terminals 3 and 4, **Fig. 11.**
2. Apply battery voltage across terminals 1 and 2, then confirm that continuity is not present between terminals 3 and 4. If continuity is found, replace relay.

Bosch

1. Using an ohmmeter, check relay continuity. If in either case continuity is absent, replace relay. Check for continuity first between terminals 86 and 85, then between terminals 30 and 87a, **Fig. 12.**
2. Apply battery voltage across terminals 86 and 85, then confirm that continuity is not present between terminals 30 and 87a. If continuity is found, replace relay.

Paseo

ON-VEHICLE INSPECTION

1. If coolant temperature is low (below

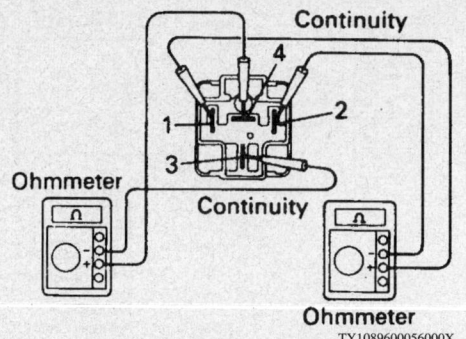

Fig. 10   Cooling fan relay inspection. Camry & Camry Solara w/5S-FE engine

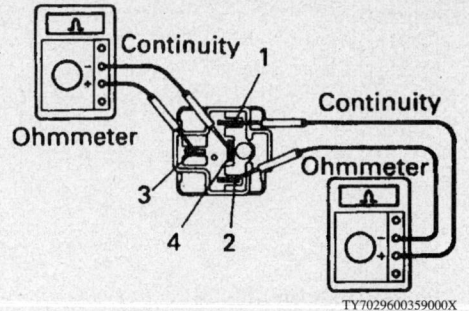

Fig. 11   Cooling fan relay inspection (Nippondenso). Corolla

TY7029600359000X

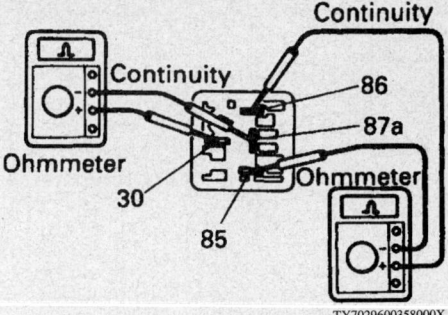

Fig. 12   Cooling fan relay inspection (Bosch). Corolla

TY7029600358000X

181°F), proceed as follows:

a. Turn ignition switch On and check cooling fan does not operate.

b. If fan runs, check for fan motor relay and/or water temperature switch failure. Check for separated connectors or broken wire between fan motor relay and temperature switch.

c. Disconnect water temperature switch connector, then check that fan runs.

d. If fan does not operate, check cooling fan, fan motor relays, engine main relay and fuse. Check for short circuit between fan motor relay and water temperature switch.

2. If coolant temperature is high (above 199°F), check that cooling fan rotates. If fan does not operate, replace water temperature switch.

NO. 1 FAN INSPECTION

1. Disconnect cooling fan electrical connector.

2. Connect battery and ammeter to cooling fan connector.

3. Ensure cooling fan operates smoothly and reading on measurement is 5.7–7.7 amps on models equipped with manual transaxle and 8.8–10.8 amps on models equipped with automatic transaxle.

NO. 2 FAN INSPECTION

1. Disconnect cooling fan electrical connector.

2. Connect battery and ammeter to cooling fan connector.

3. Ensure cooling fan operates smoothly and reading on measurement is 6.0–7.4 amps.

COOLING FAN RELAY INSPECTION

1. Inspect No. 1 cooling fan relay as follows:

a. Ensure continuity exists between terminals 85 and 86, **Fig. 13.**

b. Ensure continuity exists between terminals 30 and 87a.

c. Apply battery voltage across terminals 85 and 86.

d. Ensure continuity does not exist between terminals 30 and 87a.

e. If continuity is not as specified, replace relay.

2. Inspect No. 2 cooling fan relay as follows:

a. Ensure continuity exists between terminals 85 and 86, **Fig. 14.**

b. Ensure continuity exists between terminals 30 and 87a.

c. Ensure continuity does not exist between terminals 30 and 87.

d. Apply battery voltage across terminals 85 and 86.

e. Ensure continuity does not exist between terminals 30 and 87a.

f. Ensure continuity exists between terminals 30 and 87.

g. If continuity is not as specified, replace relay.

3. Inspect No. 3 cooling fan relay as follows:

a. Ensure continuity exists between terminals 85 and 86, **Fig. 15.**

b. Ensure continuity does not exist between terminals 30 and 87.

c. Apply battery voltage across terminals 85 and 86.

d. Ensure continuity exists between terminals 30 and 87.

e. If continuity is not as specified, replace relay.

RAV4

ON-VEHICLE INSPECTION

1. If coolant temperature is low (below 181°F), proceed as follows:

a. Turn ignition switch On and check that cooling fan does not operate.

b. If fan runs, check for fan motor relay and/or engine coolant temperature (ECT) switch failure. Check for separated connectors or broken wire between fan motor relay and temperature switch.

c. Disconnect ECT switch connector, then ensure fan runs.

d. If fan does not operate, check cooling fan, fan motor relays, engine main relay and fuse. Check for short circuit between fan motor relay and ECT switch.

2. If coolant temperature is high (above 199°F), check that cooling fan rotates. If fan does not operate, replace ECT switch.

NO. 1 FAN INSPECTION

1. Disconnect cooling fan electrical connector.

2. Connect battery and ammeter to cooling fan connector.

3. Ensure cooling fan operates smoothly and reading on measurement is 10.9–13.9 amps.

NO. 2 FAN INSPECTION

1. Disconnect cooling fan electrical connector.

2. Connect battery and ammeter to cooling fan connector.

3. Ensure cooling fan operates smoothly and reading on measurement is 9.1–11.1 amps.

COOLING FAN RELAY INSPECTION

1. Inspect No. 1 cooling fan relay as follows:

a. Ensure continuity exists between terminals 1 and 2, **Fig. 16.**

b. Ensure continuity exists between terminals 3 and 4.

c. Apply battery voltage across terminals 1 and 2.

d. Ensure continuity does not exist between terminals 3 and 4.

2. Inspect No. 2 cooling fan relay as follows:

a. Ensure continuity exists between terminals 1 and 2, **Fig. 17.**

b. Ensure continuity exists between terminals 3 and 4.

c. Ensure continuity does not exist between terminals 3 and 5.

d. Apply battery voltage across terminals 1 and 2.

e. Ensure continuity does not exist between terminals 3 and 4.

f. Ensure continuity exists between terminals 3 and 5.

3. Inspect No. 3 cooling fan relay as follows:

a. Ensure continuity exists between terminals 1 and 2, **Fig. 18.**

b. Ensure continuity does not exist between terminals 3 and 5.

c. Apply battery voltage across terminals 1 and 2.

d. Ensure continuity exists between terminals 3 and 5.

4. If continuity is not as specified, replace relay.

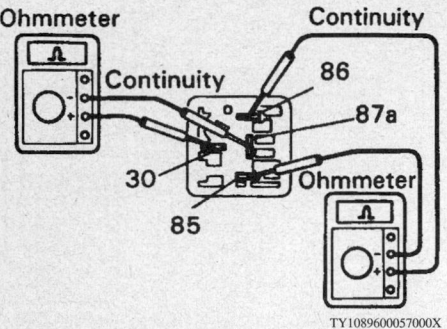

Fig. 13 No. 1 cooling fan relay inspection. Paseo & Tercel

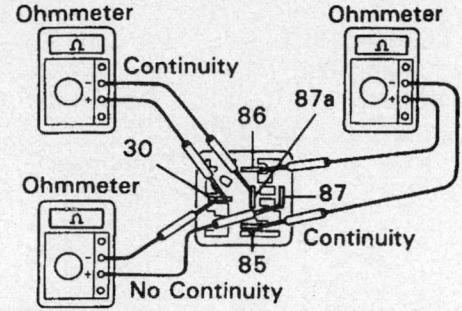

Fig. 14 No. 2 cooling fan relay inspection. Paseo & Tercel

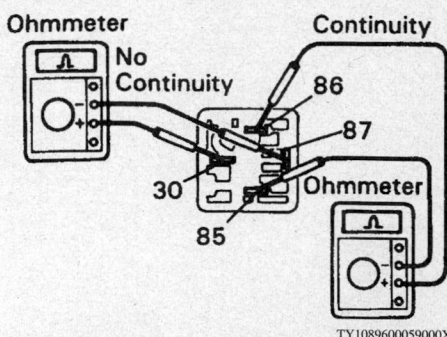

Fig. 15 No. 3 cooling fan relay inspection. Paseo & Tercel

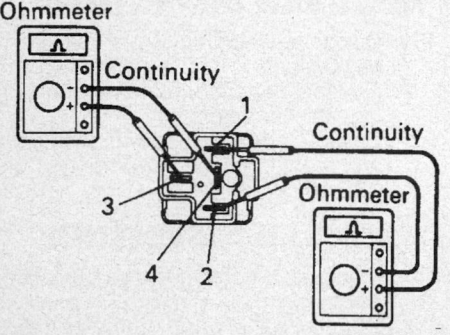

Fig. 16 No. 1 cooling fan relay inspection. RAV4

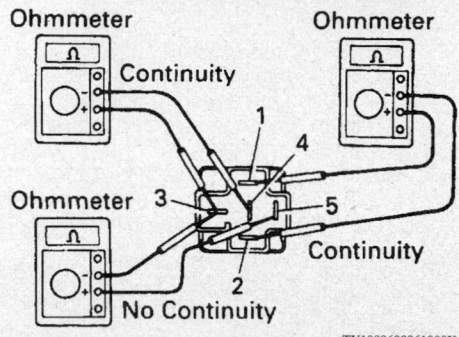

Fig. 17 No. 2 cooling fan relay inspection. RAV4

Sienna

ON-VEHICLE INSPECTION

Refer to "Avalon" for troubleshooting procedures.

NO. 1 COOLING FAN MOTOR INSPECTION

1. Start engine and raise coolant temperature to above 208°F.
2. Stop engine, then disconnect cooling fan connector.
3. Connect battery and ammeter to cooling fan connector, **Fig. 19.**
4. Refer to **Fig. 19.** for cooling fan identification mark location.
5. Ensure cooling fan rotates smoothly and ammeter reads as follows:
   a. **On models equipped with cooling fan identification S1,** 11.5 amps at 68°F.
   b. **On models equipped with cooling fan identification T1,** 14–20 amps at 68°F.
6. Reconnect cooling fan connector.

NO. 2 COOLING FAN MOTOR INSPECTION

1. Start engine and raise coolant temperature to above 208°F.
2. Stop engine, then disconnect cooling fan connector.
3. Connect battery and ammeter to cooling fan, **Fig. 19.**
4. Refer to **Fig. 19.**
5. Ensure cooling fan rotates smoothly and ammeter reads as follows:
   a. **On models equipped with cool-**

ing fan identification S2, 11.5 amps at 68°F.
   b. **On models equipped with cooling fan identification T2,** 14–20 amps at 68°F.

COOLING FAN RELAY INSPECTION

For cooling fan No.1, 2 and 3 inspection, refer to " Camry & Camry Solara" "1MZ-FE Engine."

Supra

2JZ-GTE ENGINE

ON-VEHICLE INSPECTION

1. If coolant temperature is below 190°F, proceed as follows:
   a. Turn ignition switch on and ensure cooling fan is not operating.
   b. If fan is operating, check for faulty fan relay and/or temperature (ECT) switch. Check too for separated electrical connectors or severed wire between radiator fan relay and temperature switch.
   c. Disconnect temperature switch wire, then check that fan rotates.
   d. If fan does not rotate, check No. 1 radiator fan relay, No. 2 radiator fan relay, cooling fan and fuses. Check also for short circuit between No. 1 fan relay and temperature switch.
   e. Connect temperature switch connector.
2. If coolant temperature is above 207°F, proceed as follows:
   a. Raise engine temperature above 207°F, then check that fan rotates.
   b. If fan does not rotate, replace temperature (ECT) switch.
   c. Allow coolant temperature to drop below 190°F. Fan should stop rotating.
   d. If fan does not stop rotating, replace temperature (ECT) switch.

COOLING FAN INSPECTION

1. Disconnect cooling fan electrical connector.
2. Connect battery and ammeter to cooling fan connector.
3. Ensure cooling fan operates smoothly and reading on measurement is 2.5–4.5 amps.

COOLING FAN RELAY INSPECTION

1. Disconnect No. 1 cooling fan relay electrical connector and remove relay from mounting clip, then inspect as follows:
   a. Ensure continuity exists between terminals 3 and 4, **Fig. 20.**
   b. Ensure continuity does not exists between terminals 1 and 2.
   c. Apply battery voltage across terminals 3 and 4.
   d. Ensure continuity exists between terminals 1 and 2.
2. Disconnect No. 2 cooling fan relay electrical connector and remove relay from mounting clip, then inspect as follows:
   a. Ensure continuity exists between terminals 1 and 6, **Fig. 21.**
   b. Ensure continuity exists between terminals 3 and 5.
   c. Ensure continuity does not exist between terminals 2 and 5.
   d. Apply battery voltage across terminals 1 and 6.
   e. Ensure continuity does not exist between terminals 3 and 5.
   f. Ensure continuity exists between terminals 2 and 5.
3. If continuity is not as specified, replace relay.

Tercel

ON-VEHICLE INSPECTION

1. If coolant temperature is below 181°F, proceed as follows:
   a. Turn ignition switch on and ensure

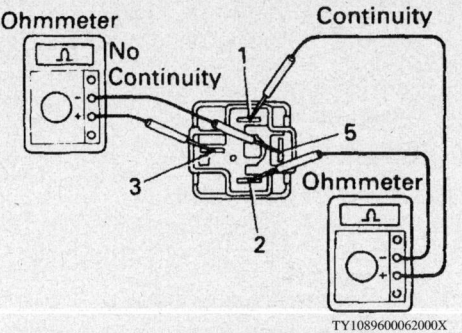

TY1089600062000X

Fig. 18   No. 3 cooling fan relay inspection. RAV4

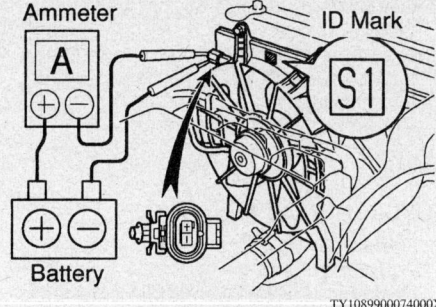

TY1089900074000X

Fig. 19   Cooling fan inspection. Sienna

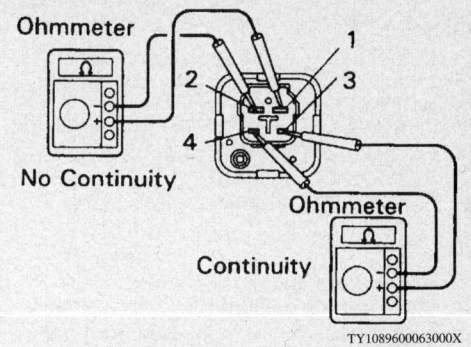

TY1089600063000X

Fig. 20   No. 1 cooling fan relay inspection. Supra w/2JZ-GTE engine

cooling fan is not operating.

b. If fan is operating, check for faulty fan relay and/or temperature switch. Inspect for separated electrical connectors or severed wire between relay and temperature switch.

c. Disconnect temperature switch wire, then check that fan rotates.

d. If fan does not rotate, check fan relay, fan motor, engine main relay and fuse. Check also for short circuit between fan relay and temperature switch.

e. Connect temperature switch wire.

2. Inspect cooling fan with engine temperature above 201°F as follows:

a. Raise engine temperature above 201°F, then check that fan rotates.

b. If fan does not rotate, replace temperature switch.

c. Allow coolant temperature to drop below 181°F. Fan should stop rotating.

d. If fan does not stop rotating, replace temperature switch.

COOLING FAN INSPECTION

1. Disconnect cooling fan electrical connector.
2. Connect battery and ammeter to cooling fan connector.
3. Ensure cooling fan operates smoothly and reading on measurement for No. 1 cooling fan is 5.7–7.7 amps on models equipped with manual transaxle and 8.6–11.6 amps on models equipped with automatic transaxle.
4. Ensure measurement for No. 2 cooling fan is 5.7–7.7 amps.

COOLING FAN RELAY INSPECTION

1. Inspect No. 1 cooling fan relay as follows:
a. Ensure continuity exists between terminals 85 and 86, **Fig. 13.**
b. Ensure continuity exists between terminals 30 and 87.
c. Apply battery voltage across terminals 85 and 86.
d. Ensure continuity does not exist between terminals 30 and 87.
e. If continuity is not as specified, replace relay.
2. Inspect No. 2 cooling fan relay as follows:
a. Ensure continuity exists between

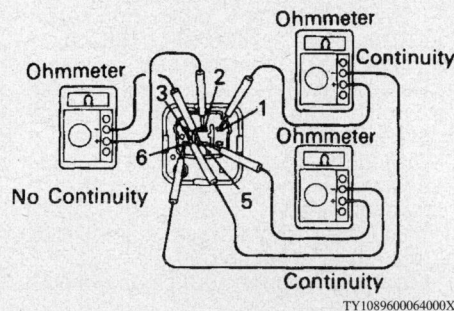

TY1089600064000X

Fig. 21   No. 2 cooling fan relay inspection. Supra w/2JZ-GTE engine

terminals 85 and 86, **Fig. 14.**

b. Ensure continuity exists between terminals 30 and 87ₐ.
c. Ensure continuity does not exist between terminals 30 and 87.
d. Apply battery voltage across terminals 85 and 86.
e. Ensure continuity does not exist between terminals 30 and 87ₐ.
f. Ensure continuity exists between terminals 30 and 87.
g. If continuity is not as specified, replace relay.

3. Inspect No. 3 cooling fan relay as follows:
a. Ensure continuity exists between terminals 85 and 86, **Fig. 15.**
b. Ensure continuity does not exist between terminals 30 and 87.
c. Apply battery voltage across terminals 85 and 86.
d. Ensure continuity exists between terminals 30 and 87.
e. If continuity is not as specified, replace relay.

COMPONENT REPLACEMENT

Cooling Fan/Motor

AVALON

NO. 1 COOLING FAN

1. Remove battery and tray as necessary.
2. Disconnect cruise control actuator from body.

3. Remove No. 1 cooling fan from left hand side of engine compartment.
4. Disconnect cruise control actuator wire from clamp on fan shroud.
5. Disconnect cooling fan connector.
6. Remove four retaining bolts from cooling fan assembly.
7. Remove fan blade attaching nut and fan.
8. Remove three fan motor to assembly attaching screws and remove motor.
9. Reverse procedure to install, **torque** fan assembly bolts to 44 inch. lbs. and fan blade attaching nut to 55 inch. lbs.

NO. 2 COOLING FAN

1. Drain engine coolant.
2. Disconnect upper radiator hose from radiator.
3. Remove three attaching bolts and No. 2 cooling fan assembly.
4. Disconnect cooling fan connector.
5. Remove clip from fan blade.
6. Remove three motor to fan assembly attaching screws and motor.
7. Reverse procedure to install, **torque** fan assembly bolts to 44 inch. lbs.

CAMRY & CAMRY SOLARA

1996

1. Drain engine coolant.
2. **On models equipped with cruise control,** remove cruise control actuator cover if necessary.
3. **On all models,** disconnect cooling fan motor electrical connectors from both fan assemblies.
4. Remove cooling fan assembly attaching screws, then the fan assembly.
5. Reverse procedure to install.

1997-99

No. 1 Cooling Fan

1. Disconnect cooling fan connector.
2. If necessary, drain engine coolant into a suitable container and disconnect upper radiator hose.
3. Disconnect relay block for daytime running lamps, if equipped.
4. Disconnect No. 1 ECT switch wire connector, then the ECT wire clamps.
5. Remove cooling fan attaching bolts, then the cooling fan.
6. Reverse procedure to install.

No. 2 Cooling Fan

1. If necessary, drain engine coolant into a suitable container and disconnect upper radiator hose.
2. Disconnect cooling fan connector.
3. Remove cooling fan attaching bolts, then the cooling fan.
4. Reverse procedure to install.

CELICA

1. Remove engine undercovers.
2. Drain engine coolant.
3. Disconnect engine relay box from battery.
4. Disconnect coolant reservoir hose from radiator.
5. Disconnect upper radiator hose from radiator.
6. Disconnect cooling fan electrical connector.
7. Remove three fan mounting bolts and the cooling fan.
8. Reverse procedure to install.

COROLLA

1. Disconnect electrical connector from fan motor.
2. Remove reservoir tank.
3. Drain coolant, then remove upper radiator hose.
4. Remove front grille.
5. Remove cooling fan assembly.
6. Remove attaching nut, then separate fan blade and spacer from motor.
7. Remove bushings and attaching screws, then separate fan motor from shroud.
8. Reverse procedure to assemble and install.

PASEO

1. Remove righthand and lefthand engine undercovers.
2. Drain engine coolant, then remove three bolts and air intake connector.
3. Remove three bolts and exhaust manifold heat shield.

4. Disconnect radiator inlet hose from radiator.
5. Disconnect oxygen sensor and cooling fan connectors, then remove four bolts and cooling fan.
6. Reverse procedure to install.

RAV4

COOLING FAN NO. 1

1. Remove engine under cover if equipped.
2. Drain coolant into a suitable container.
3. Remove A/C condenser as follows:
   a. Discharge A/C system as outlined under "Air Conditioning."
   b. Disconnect liquid tube and discharge hose. Cap fittings to prevent system contamination.
   c. Remove condenser attaching bolts, then the condenser.
4. Remove radiator as outlined under "Land Cruiser, Pickups, RAV4, Tundra & 4Runner."
5. Disconnect cooling fan electrical connector, then the ECT switch connector for cooling fan.
6. Disconnect engine wire clamp from No. 1 cooling fan shroud.
7. Disconnect upper and lower radiator hoses.
8. Remove reservoir hose from radiator.
9. **On models equipped with automatic transmission,** disconnect transmission cooler lines from radiator.
10. **On all models,** remove upper radiator supports, then the radiator and lower supports.
11. Remove cooling fan attaching bolts, then the cooling fan.
12. Reverse procedure to install.

COOLING FAN NO. 2

1. Remove righthand under cover if equipped.
2. Remove A/C condenser as outlined under "Cooling Fan No. 1."
3. Remove upper radiator supports.
4. Disconnect cooling fan connector.

5. Push radiator toward front bumper.
6. Remove cooling fan attaching bolts.
7. Push No. 2 cooling fan toward radiator and pull upward and out.
8. Reverse procedure to install.

SIENNA

NO. 1 COOLING FAN

1. Disconnect cooling fan connector.
2. Remove cooling fan attaching bolts, then the cooling fan.
3. Reverse procedure to install.

NO. 2 COOLING FAN

1. Drain coolant into a suitable container.
2. Disconnect upper radiator hose from radiator.
3. Disconnect cooling fan electrical connector.
4. Remove cooling fan attaching bolts, then the cooling fan.
5. Reverse procedure to install.

SUPRA

2JZ-GTE ENGINE

1. Remove engine under cover.
2. Disconnect cooling fan connector.
3. Remove three bolts and cooling fan shroud with fan attached.
4. Remove three attaching screws and separate fan motor from fan shroud.
5. Reverse procedure to install.

TERCEL

1. Remove righthand and lefthand engine undercovers.
2. Drain engine coolant, then remove three bolts and air intake connector.
3. Remove upper radiator hose if necessary.
4. Remove three bolts and exhaust manifold heat shield.
5. Disconnect radiator inlet hose from radiator.
6. Disconnect oxygen sensor and cooling fan connectors, then remove cooling fan.
7. Reverse procedure to install.

Dash Gauges

NOTE: Refer To The "Dash Panel Service" Section For Dash Panel Removal Procedures.

NOTE: On Air Bag Equipped Models, Refer To "Air Bag System Precautions" Located In The Front Of This Manual For System Disarming & Arming Procedures.

INDEX

PRECAUTIONS

AIR BAG SYSTEMS

Refer to "Air Bag System Precautions" in the front of this manual for system disarming & arming procedures.

BATTERY GROUND CABLE

Prior to service, disconnect battery ground cable and isolate as required.

AUDIO CODED ANTI-THEFT SYSTEM

Some models are equipped with an audio coded anti-theft system that will disable the radio when the battery cable is disconnected. The system can be identified by the "ANTI-THEFT SYSTEM" on the cassette tape lid. Obtain 3 digit customer code for input. Reset system after service as follows:

1. Obtain 3 digit audio anti-theft code.
2. Depress 1 (PROG) while depressing righthand side of TUNE SEEK button, - - - will appear in tape operation display.
3. To enter the first digit, depress 1 (PROG) button repeatedly until the number of times depressed equals the first digit beginning with zero (depress the 1 button six times if the first digit if five).
4. To enter second digit, depress 2 (APS) button repeatedly until the number of times depressed equals the second digit beginning with zero.
5. To enter third digit, depress 3 (RPT) button repeatedly until the number of times depressed equals the third digit beginning with zero.
6. If - - - is displayed during code input, repeat procedure.
7. When code appears in display, depress and hold SCAN button until SEC appears.
8. When SEC disappears audio system should be operative.
9. If Err is displayed, repeat procedure. **Attempting to input code more than nine times may permanently disable audio system.**

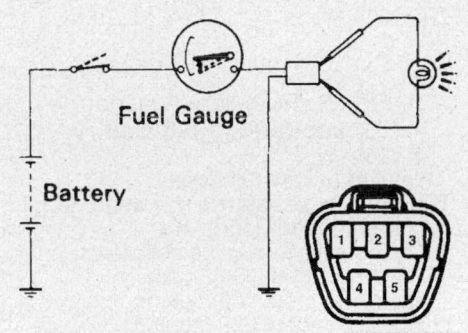

TY9099700108000X

Fig. 1 Fuel receiver gauge inspection. Avalon, Camry Solara, Celica, Sienna, Supra, Tacoma, Corolla, Previa, 1997–99 4Runner & Camry

GAUGES

FUEL

Avalon

1. Disconnect connector from sender gauge.
2. Turn ignition switch to On position, then check receiver gauge needle indicates Empty.
3. Connect terminals 2 and 3 on wire harness side connector through a 3.4W test bulb, **Fig. 1.**
4. Turn ignition switch On, then ensure bulb lights and receiver gauge needle moves toward full side.
5. Measure resistance between terminals A, B and C, **Fig. 2.** Resistance should be as follows:
   a. A–B: about 151 ohms.
   b. A–C: about 306 ohms.
   c. B–C: about 154 ohms.
   d. If resistance is not as specified, replace receiver gauge.
6. Measure resistance between terminal 2 and 3 for each float position, **Fig. 3.**
7. Ensure resistance rises between terminals 2 and 3 as the float is moved from top to bottom position.
8. Measure resistance between termi-

nals 2 and 3 for each float position. Resistance should be as follows:
   a. Full position: about 3.0 ohms.
   b. Half position: about 30.8 ohms.
   c. Empty position: about 110.0 ohms.
   d. If resistance is not as specified, replace sender gauge.
9. Inspect fuel level warning lamp switch as follows:
   a. Apply battery voltage between terminals 1 and 3 through of fuel sender through a 3.4 watt test bulb ensuring bulb lights up, **Fig. 4.**
   b. Submerge switch in fuel, **Fig. 5.** Lamp should go out.
   c. If operation is not as specified, replace sender gauge.

Camry & Camry Solara

1. Disconnect connector from sender gauge.
2. Turn ignition switch to On position, then check receiver gauge needle indicates Empty.
3. Connect terminals 2 and 3 on wire harness side connector through a 3.4W test bulb, **Figs. 1 and 6.**
4. Turn ignition switch On, then ensure bulb lights and receiver gauge needle moves toward full side.
5. Measure resistance between terminals A, B and C, **Figs. 7 and 8.** Resistance should be as follows:
   a. A–B: about 126 ohms.
   b. A–C: about 281 ohms.
   c. B–C: about 154 ohms.
   d. If resistance is not as specified, replace receiver gauge.
6. **On 1996 models,** proceed as follows:
   a. Connect a series of three 1.5 volt dry cell batteries.
   b. Connect the positive lead from the dry cell batteries to terminal 2 through a 3.4W test bulb and the negative lead to terminal 3, **Fig. 9.**
   c. Ensure voltage rises between terminals 2 and 3 as the float is moved from top to bottom position.
7. **On all models,** measure resistance between terminals 2 and 3 for each

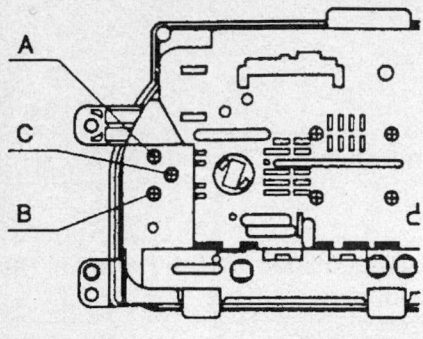

Fig. 2 Fuel gauge terminal locations. Avalon

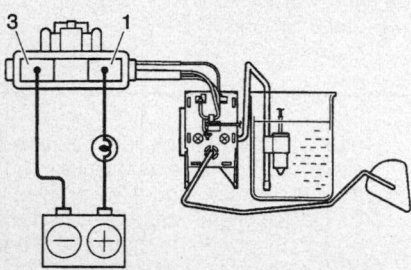

Fig. 5 Fuel level warning lamp switch wet inspection. Avalon

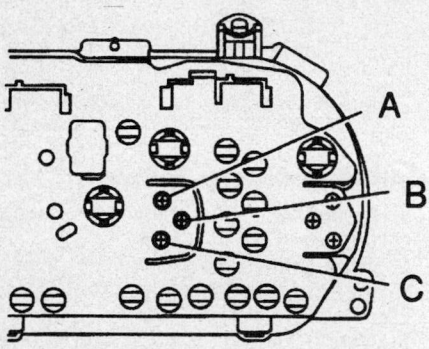

Fig. 8 Fuel gauge terminal locations. Camry Solara & 1997–99 Camry

float position. Resistance should be as follows:
a. Full position: about 3.0 ohms.
b. Empty position: about 110.0 ohms.
c. If resistance is not as specified, replace sender gauge.

Celica

1. Disconnect connector from sender gauge.
2. Turn ignition switch to On position, then check receiver gauge needle indicates Empty.
3. Connect terminals 2 and 3 on wire harness side connector through a 3.4W test bulb, **Fig. 1.**
4. Turn ignition switch On, then ensure bulb lights and receiver gauge needle

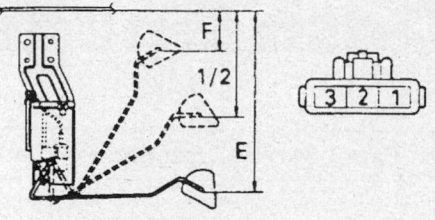

Fig. 3 Fuel sender gauge inspection. Avalon

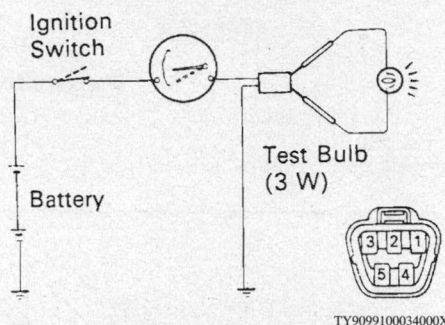

Fig. 6 Fuel receiver gauge inspection. 1996 Camry

moves toward full side.
5. Measure resistance between terminals A, B and C, **Fig. 10.**
6. Resistance should be as follows:
a. A–B: about 154.3 ohms.
b. A–C: about 126.2 ohms.
c. B–C: about 280.5 ohms.
7. If resistance is not as specified, replace fuel receiver gauge.
8. Measure resistance between terminals 2 and 3 for each float position. Resistance should be as follows:
a. Full position: about 3.0 ohms.
b. ½ position: about 31.6 ohms.
c. Empty position: about 110.0 ohms.
d. If resistance is not as specified, replace sender gauge.

Corolla

1. Disconnect connector from sender gauge.
2. Turn ignition switch to On position, then check receiver gauge needle indicates Empty.
3. Connect terminals 1 and 3 on wire harness side connector through a 3.4W test bulb, **Figs. 11 and 1.**
4. Turn ignition switch On, then ensure bulb lights and receiver gauge needle moves toward full side.
5. If gauge does not operate as specified, check receiver gauge resistance.
6. Measure resistance between terminals A, B and C, **Figs. 12 and 13.**
7. **On 1996 models with tachometer,** resistance should be as follows:
a. A–B: about 154.3 ohms.
b. A–C: about 107.2 ohms.
c. B–C: about 261.5 ohms.
d. If resistance is not as specified, replace receiver gauge.
8. **On 1997 models with tachometer,** resistance should be as follows:
a. A–B: about 256.3 ohms.

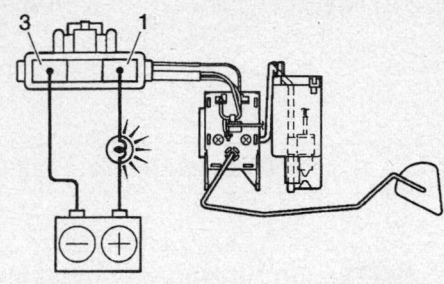

Fig. 4 Fuel level warning lamp switch dry inspection. Avalon

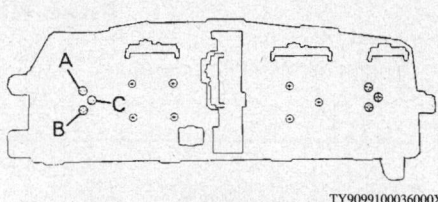

Fig. 7 Fuel gauge terminal locations. 1996 Camry

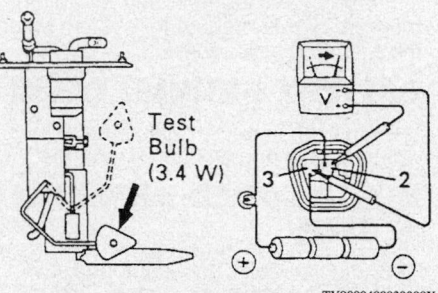

Fig. 9 Fuel sender gauge inspection. 1996 Camry

b. A–C: about 106.0 ohms.
c. B–C: about 150.3 ohms.
d. If resistance is not as specified, replace receiver gauge.
9. **On 1998 models with tachometer,** resistance should be as follows:
a. A–B: about 108.3 ohms.
b. A–C: about 233.3 ohms.
c. B–C: about 125.0 ohms.
d. If resistance is not as specified, replace receiver gauge.
10. **On 1996 models less tachometer,** resistance should be as follows:
a. A–B: about 280.5 ohms.
b. A–C: about 126.2 ohms.
c. B–C: about 154.3 ohms.
d. If resistance is not as specified, replace receiver gauge.
11. **On 1997 models less tachometer,** resistance should be as follows:
a. A–B: about 125.0 ohms.
b. A–C: about 108.3 ohms.
c. B–C: about 233.3 ohms.
d. If resistance is not as specified, replace receiver gauge.
12. **On 1998 models less tachometer,** resistance should be as follows:
a. A–B: about 106.0 ohms.
b. A–C: about 256.0 ohms.
c. B–C: about 150.3 ohms.

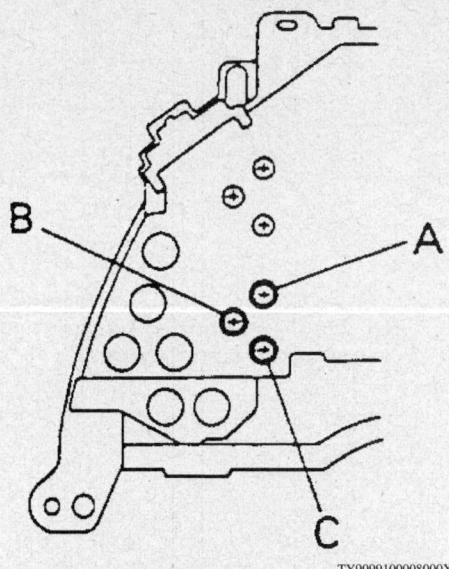

Fig. 10 Fuel gauge terminal locations. Celica

w/ Tachometer

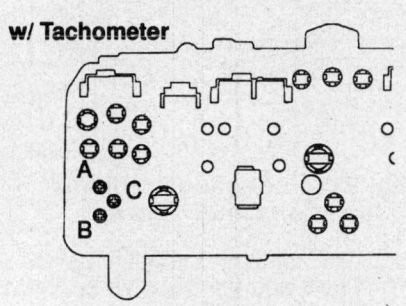

w/o Tachometer

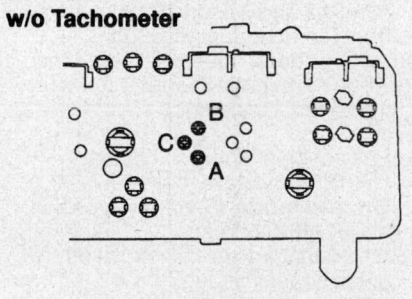

Fig. 13 Fuel gauge terminal locations. 1998 Corolla

d. If resistance is not as specified, replace receiver gauge.

13. **On 1996 models,** check fuel sender gauge as follows:
   a. Connect a series of three 1.5 volt dry cell batteries.
   b. Connect positive lead from dry cell batteries to terminal 2 through a 3.4W test bulb, **Fig. 14.**
   c. Connect negative lead from dry cell batteries to terminal 3.
   d. Connect positive lead from voltmeter to terminal 1 and negative lead to terminal 3.
   e. Ensure voltage rises between terminals as float is moved from top to

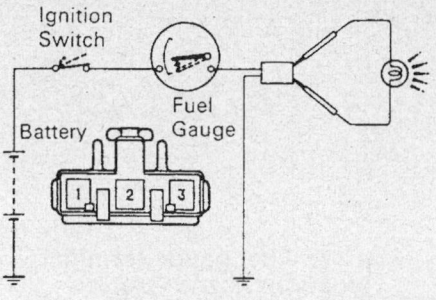

Fig. 11 Fuel receiver gauge inspection. 1996 Corolla

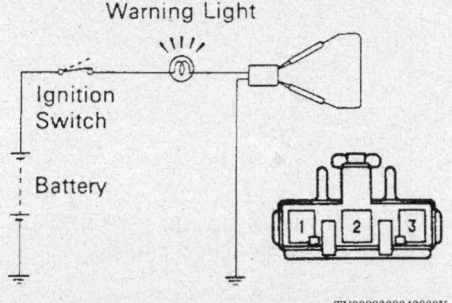

Fig. 14 Fuel sender gauge inspection (terminals 1 & 3). 1996 Corolla

bottom position.
   f. If voltage does not rise as specified, replace fuel sender gauge.
14. **On 1996 models,** measure resistance between terminals 2 and 3 for each float position.
15. **On 1997–99 models,** measure resistance between terminals 1 and 2 for each float position, **Fig. 15.**
16. Resistance should be as follows:
   a. Full position: about 4.0 ohms.
   b. Half position: about 55.0 ohms.
   c. Empty position: about 111.0 ohms.
   d. If resistance is not as specified, replace sender gauge.

Land Cruiser

1. Disconnect connector from sender gauge.
2. Turn ignition switch to On position, then check receiver gauge needle indicates Empty.
3. Connect terminals 4 and 5 on wire harness side connector through a 3.4W test bulb, **Fig. 16.**
4. Turn ignition switch On, ensure bulb lights and receiver gauge needle moves towards Full.
5. If gauge does not operate as specified, check receiver gauge resistance.
6. Measure resistance between terminals A, B and C, **Fig. 17.** Resistance should be as follows:
   a. A–B: about 85.5–105.5 ohms.
   b. A–C: about 126.0–150.0 ohms.
   c. B–C: about 90.0–110.0 ohms.
   d. If resistance is not as specified, replace receiver gauge.
7. Connect a series of three 1.5 volt dry cell batteries, then connect the positive lead from the dry cell batteries to termi-

w/ Tachometer

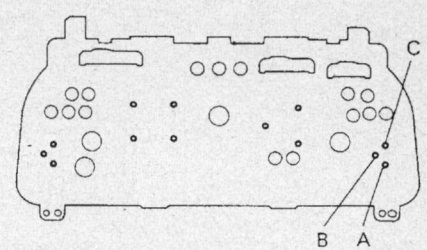

w/o Tachometer

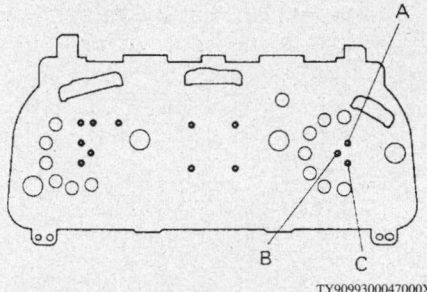

Fig. 12 Fuel gauge terminal locations. Corolla

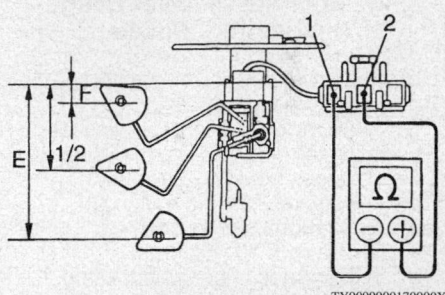

Fig. 15 Fuel sending unit inspection. 1997-99 Corolla

nal 4 through a 3.4W test bulb and the negative lead to terminal 5, **Fig. 18.**
8. Connect the positive lead from the voltmeter to terminal 5 and the negative lead to terminal 4.
9. Ensure voltage rises between terminals as float is moved from top to bottom position.
10. Measure resistance between terminals 4 and 5 for each float position. Resistance should be as follows:
   a. Full position: about 3.0 ohms.
   b. Empty position: about 110.0 ohms.
   c. If resistance is not as specified, replace sender gauge.

Paseo

1. Disconnect connector from sender gauge.
2. Turn ignition switch to On position, then check receiver gauge needle indicates Empty.
3. **On 1996 models,** connect terminals 1 and 4 on wire harness side connector through a 3.4W test bulb, **Fig. 19.**
4. **On 1997 models,** connect terminals 3 and 4 on wire harness side connector through a 3.4W test bulb, **Fig. 19.**
5. Turn ignition switch On, then ensure

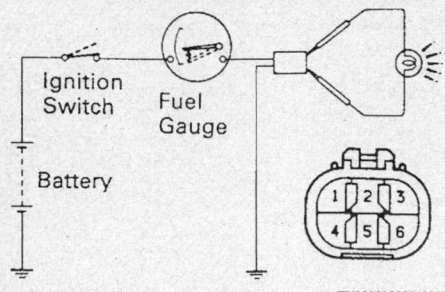

Fig. 16 Fuel receiver gauge inspection. Land Cruiser

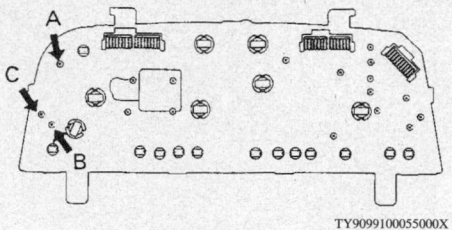

TY9099100055000X

Fig. 17 Fuel gauge terminal locations. Land Cruiser

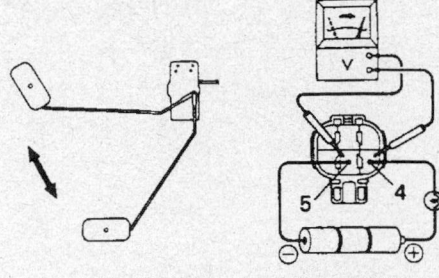

TY9099100056000X

Fig. 18 Fuel sender gauge inspection. Land Cruiser

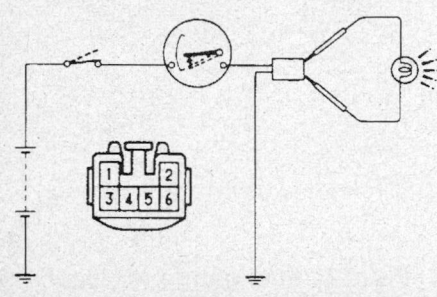

TY9099100016000X

Fig. 19 Fuel receiver gauge inspection. Paseo

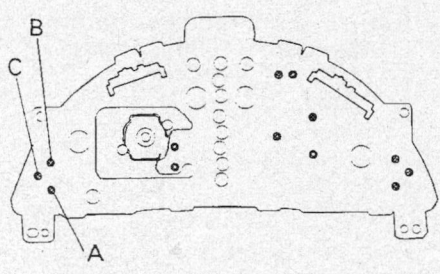

TY9099100017000X

Fig. 20 Fuel gauge terminal locations. 1996 Paseo

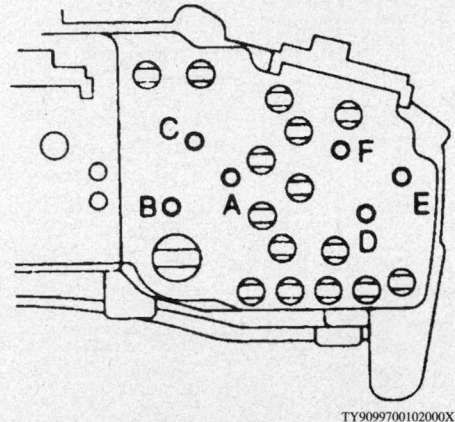

TY9099700102000X

Fig. 21 Fuel gauge terminal locations. 1997 Paseo

bulb lights and receiver gauge needle moves toward full side.

6. **On 1996 models,** measure resistance between terminals A, B and C, **Fig. 20.** Resistance should be as follows:
   a. A–B: about 101.9 ohms.
   b. A–C: about 203.4 ohms.
   c. B–C: about 101.5 ohms.
   d. If resistance is not as specified, replace receiver gauge.
7. **On 1997 models,** measure resistance between terminals A, B and C, **Fig. 21.** Resistance should be as follows:
   a. A–B: about 115.8 ohms.
   b. A–C: about 177.2 ohms.
   c. B–C: about 61.4 ohms.
   d. If resistance is not as specified, replace receiver gauge.
8. **On 1996 models,** proceed as follows:
   a. Connect a series of three 1.5 volt dry cell batteries, then connect the positive lead from the dry cell batteries to terminal 1 through a 3.4W test bulb and the negative lead to terminal 4, **Fig. 22.**
   b. Connect positive lead from voltmeter to terminal and negative lead to terminal. Ensure voltage rises between terminals 1 and 4 as the float is moved from top to bottom position.
   c. Measure resistance between terminals 1 and 4 for each float position. Resistance should be 2.0–4.0 ohms at full position.
   d. Resistance should be 25.0–34.0 ohms at half position, and 103.0–117.0 ohms at the empty position.
   e. If resistance is not as specified, replace sender gauge.
9. **On 1997 models,** measure resistance between red and black cables and ensure readings are as follows:

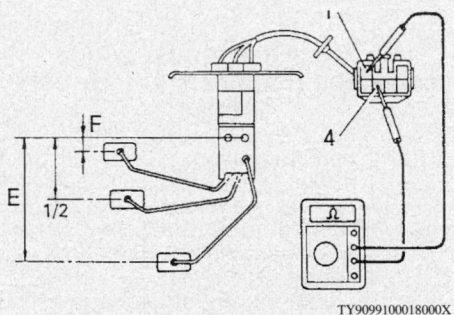

TY9099100018000X

Fig. 22 Fuel sender gauge inspection. 1996 Paseo

   a. Full position: 2–4 ohms.
   b. Half position: 24.2–33.8 ohms.
   c. Empty position: 102.3–117.7 ohms.
   d. If resistance is not as specified, replace sender gauge.

Previa

1. Disconnect connector from sender gauge.
2. Turn ignition switch to On position, then check receiver gauge needle indicates Empty.
3. Connect terminals 2 and 3 on wire harness side connector through a 3.4W test bulb, **Figs. 1 and 23.**
4. Turn ignition switch On, then ensure bulb lights and receiver gauge needle moves toward full side.
5. Measure resistance between terminals A, B and C, **Fig. 24.** Resistance should be as follows:
   a. A–B: about 101.3 ohms.
   b. A–C: about 101.9 ohms.
   c. B–C: about 203.2 ohms.
   d. If resistance is not as specified, replace receiver gauge.
6. **On 1996 models,** proceed as follows:
   a. Connect a series of three 1.5 volt dry cell batteries, then connect the positive lead from the dry cell bat-

teries to terminal 3 through a 3.4W test bulb and the negative lead to terminal 2, **Fig. 25.**
   b. Ensure voltage rises between terminals 2 and 3 as the float is moved from top to bottom position.
7. **On all models,** measure resistance between terminals 2 and 3 for each float position. Resistance should be as follows:
   a. Full position: about 3.0 ohms.
   b. **On 1997 models,** half: 27.7–37.3.
   c. **On all models,** empty position: about 110.0 ohms.
   d. If resistance is not as specified, replace sender gauge.

RAV4

1. Disconnect connector from main fuel sender gauge assembly.
2. Turn ignition switch On and ensure receiver gauge needle indicates Empty, **Figs. 26 and 27.**
3. Connect main sender gauge, then disconnect sub sender gauge assembly connector.
4. Turn ignition switch On and ensure receiver gauge needle indicates Empty, **Figs. 28 and 29.**
5. Disconnect main sender gauge.
6. **On 1996 models,** connect terminals 3 of main sender gauge and A of sub sender gauge, on harness side connectors, through a 3.4W test bulb, **Fig. 30.**
7. **On 1997–99 models,** connect terminals 3 of main sender gauge and 1 of sub sender gauge on harness side

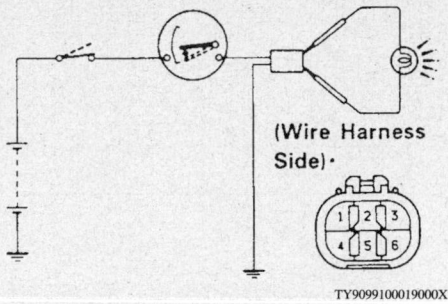

Fig. 23 Fuel receiver gauge inspection. 1996 Previa

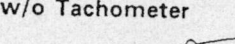
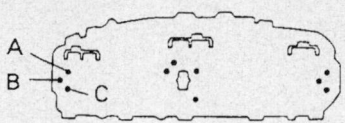
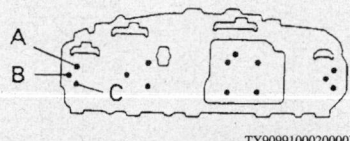

Fig. 24 Fuel gauge terminal locations. Previa

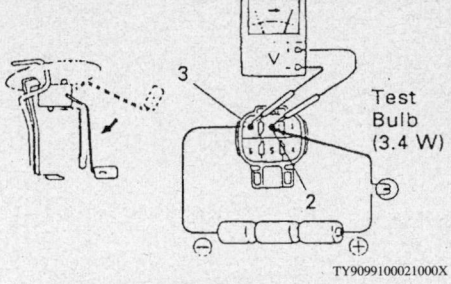

Fig. 25 Fuel sender gauge inspection. Previa

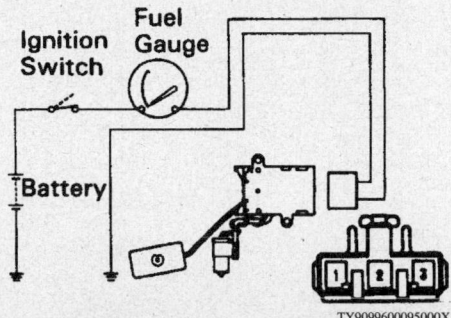

Fig. 26 Main fuel sender gauge inspection. 1996 RAV4

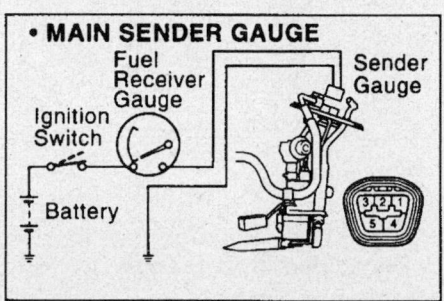

Fig. 27 Main fuel sender gauge inspection. 1997–99 RAV4

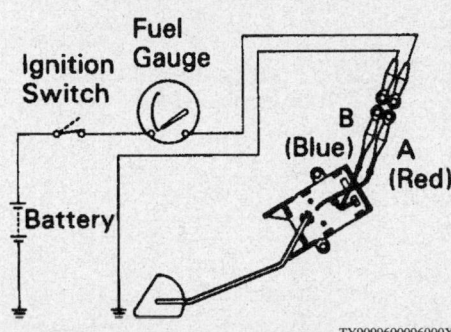

Fig. 28 Sub fuel sender gauge inspection. 1996 RAV4

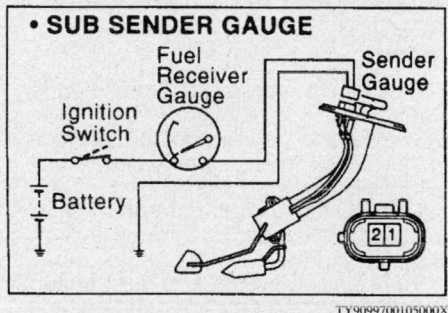

Fig. 29 Sub fuel sender gauge inspection. 1997–99 RAV4

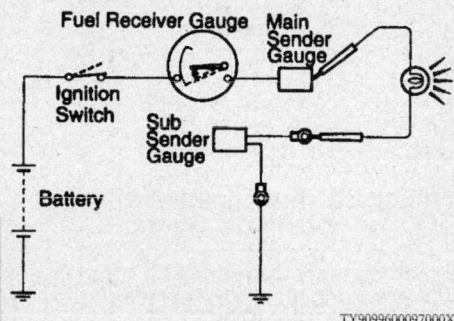

Fig. 30 Fuel gauge test bulb check. RAV4

---

connectors through a 3.4W test bulb, **Fig. 30.**

8. **On all models,** turn ignition switch On and ensure bulb illuminates and receiver gauge needle moves toward full side.
9. Inspect receiver gauge resistance by measuring between terminal locations, **Fig. 31.** Resistance should be as follows:
   a. A-B: about 106 ohms.
   b. A-C: about 256.3 ohms.
   c. B-C: about 150.3 ohms.
10. Inspect main sender gauge resistance by measuring between terminals 2 and 3 on 1996 models and 1 and 2 on 1997–99 models, with float in high and low position. Resistance should be about 2 ohms with float in full position and about 74 ohms with float in empty position.
11. Inspect sub sender gauge resistance by measuring resistance between terminals with float in high position and low position. Resistance should be about 2 ohms with float in high position and about 74 ohms with float in high position

and about 32.9 ohms with float in low position.
12. If resistance is not as specified, replace sender gauge.

Sienna

1. Inspect fuel gauge operation as follows:
   a. Disconnect electrical connector from fuel gauge.
   b. Turn ignition switch on. Ensure fuel gauge indicates empty.
   c. Turn ignition switch off.
   d. Connect terminals 1 and 2 of fuel sender wire harness connector through a 3.4 watt test bulb, **Fig. 1.**
   e. Turn ignition switch on. Ensure test bulb illuminates and receiver gauge needle moves towards full side.
   f. If operation is not as specified, inspect receiver gauge resistance.
2. Measure resistance of fuel gauge terminals A, B and C, **Fig. 32,** as follows:
   a. A–B: 262 ohms.
   b. A–C: 107 ohms.
   c. B–C: 154 ohms.
   d. If resistance is not as specified, replace gauge.
   e. If resistance is as specified, inspect fuel sender resistance.
3. Measure resistance between terminals 2 and 3 of fuel sending unit, **Fig. 33.** Ensure resistance is as follows:
   a. Full: 3 ohms.
   b. Half: 32 ohms.
   c. Empty: 110 ohms.
   d. If resistance is not as specified, replace sending unit.

Supra

1. Disconnect connector from sender gauge.
2. Turn ignition switch to On position, then check receiver gauge needle indicates Empty.
3. Connect terminals 2 and 3 on wire harness side connector through a 3.4W test bulb, **Fig. 1.**
4. Turn ignition switch On, then ensure bulb lights and receiver gauge needle moves toward full side.
5. Measure resistance between terminals A, B and C, **Fig. 34.** Resistance should be as follows:
   a. A–B: about 269.7 ohms.
   b. A–C: about 123.5 ohms.
   c. B–C: about 146.2 ohms.
6. If resistance is not as specified, replace receiver gauge.
7. **On 1996 models,** connect a series of three 1.5 volt dry cell batteries, then connect the positive lead from the dry

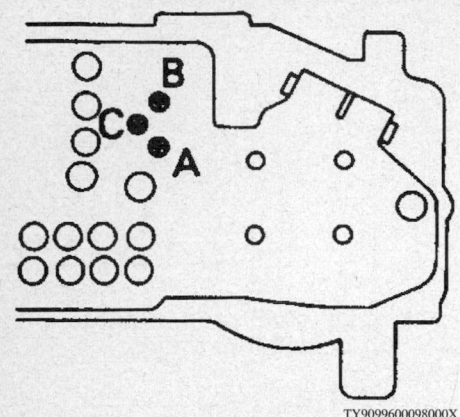

Fig. 31 Fuel gauge terminal locations. RAV4

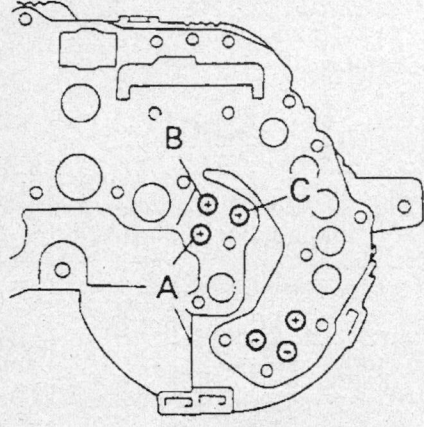

Fig. 34 Fuel gauge terminal locations. Supra

w/o Tachometer:

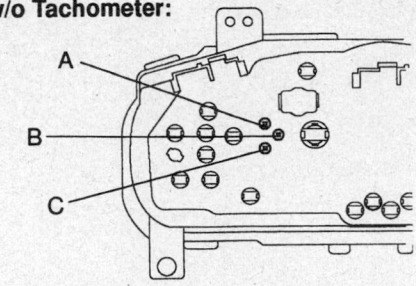

w/ Tachometer:

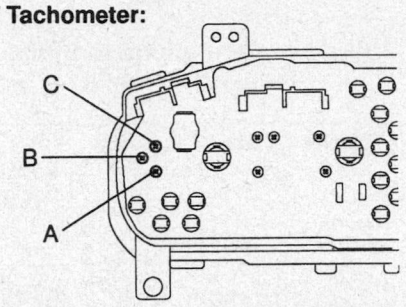

Fig. 32 Fuel gauge terminal locations. Sienna

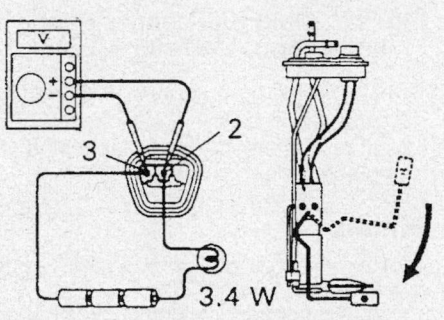

Fig. 35 Fuel sender gauge inspection. Supra

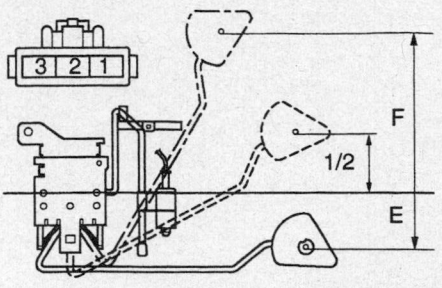

Fig. 33 Fuel sending unit terminal locations. Sienna

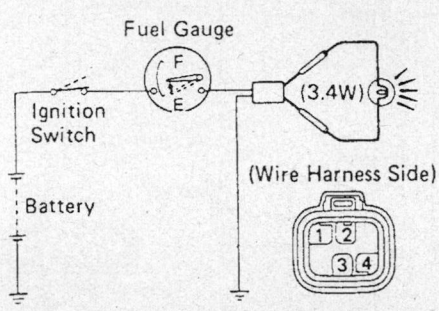

Fig. 36 Fuel receiver gauge inspection. T100 & 1996 4Runner

cell batteries to terminal 2 through a 3.4W test bulb and the negative lead to terminal 3, **Fig. 35.**

8. **On 1996 models,** ensure voltage rises between terminals 2 and 3 as the float is moved from top to bottom position.

9. **On all models,** measure resistance between terminals 2 and 3 for each float position, **Fig. 35.** Resistance should be as follows:
   a. Full position: about 4.0 ohms.
   b. ½ position: about 55.0 ohms.
   c. Empty position: about 107.0 ohms.

10. If resistance is not as specified, replace sender gauge.

T100

1. Disconnect connector from sender gauge.
2. Turn ignition switch to On position, then check receiver gauge needle indicates Empty.
3. Connect terminals 1 and 3 on wire harness side connector through a 3.4W test bulb, **Fig. 36.**
4. Turn ignition switch On, then ensure bulb lights and receiver gauge needle moves toward full side.
5. Measure resistance between terminals A, B and C, **Fig. 37.** Resistance should be as follows with tachometer:
   a. A–B: about 137 ohms.

b. A–C: about 123 ohms.
   c. B–C: about 260 ohms.
6. Resistance should be as follows without tachometer:
   a. A–B: about 150 ohms.
   b. A–C: about 80 ohms.
   c. B–C: about 55 ohms.
   d. If resistance is not as specified, replace receiver gauge.
7. Connect a series of three 1.5 volt dry cell batteries, then connect the positive lead from the dry cell batteries to terminal 2 through a 3.4W test bulb and the negative lead to terminal 1, **Fig. 38.**
8. Connect positive lead from voltmeter to terminal 2 and negative lead to terminal 1. Ensure voltage rises between terminals 1 and 2 as the float is moved from top to bottom position.
9. Measure resistance between terminals 1 and 2 for each float position. Resistance should be as follows:
   a. Full position: about 3.0 ohms.
   b. Half position: about 32.5 ohms.
   c. Empty position: about 110.0 ohms.
   d. If resistance is not as specified, replace sender gauge.

Tacoma

1. Disconnect connector from sender gauge.
2. Turn ignition switch to On position, then check receiver gauge needle indicates Empty.
3. Connect terminals 1 and 3 on wire harness side connector through a 3.4W test bulb, **Fig. 1.**
4. Turn ignition switch On, then ensure bulb lights and receiver gauge needle moves toward full side.
5. Measure resistance between terminals A, B and C, **Fig. 39.**
6. **On 1996 models,** resistance should be as follows using a tachometer:
   a. A–B: about 137 ohms.
   b. A–C: about 123 ohms.
   c. B–C: about 260 ohms.
7. **On 1997–99 models,** resistance should be as follows using a tachometer:
   a. A–B: about 140–158 ohms.
   b. A–C: about 233–271 ohms.
   c. B–C: about 92–114 ohms.
8. **On 1996 models** resistance should be as follows without using a tachometer:
   a. A–B: about 150 ohms.
   b. A–C: about 80 ohms.
   c. B–C: about 55 ohms.
   d. If resistance is not as specified, replace receiver gauge.
9. **On 1997–99 models,** resistance should be as follows without using a tachometer:
   a. A–B: about 115–130 ohms.
   b. A–C: about 208–244 ohms.
   c. B–C: about 92–114 ohms.
   d. If resistance is not as specified, replace receiver gauge.
10. **On 1996 models,** proceed as follows:

w/ Tachometer

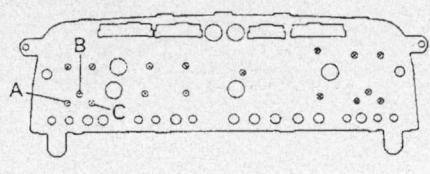

w/o Tachometer

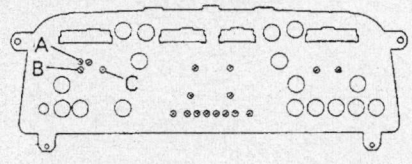

TY9099100029000X

Fig. 37   Fuel gauge terminal locations. T100

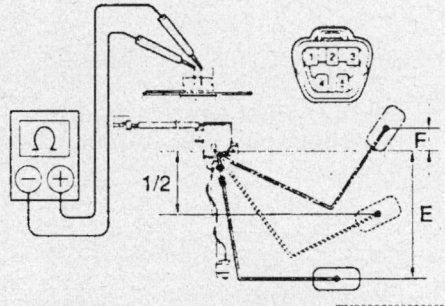

TY9099500092000X

Fig. 40   Fuel sender gauge inspection. Tacoma

a. Connect a series of three 1.5 volt dry cell batteries, then connect the positive lead from the dry cell batteries to terminal 2 through a 3.4W test bulb and the negative lead to terminal 1, **Fig. 40**.

b. Connect positive lead from voltmeter to terminal 2 and negative lead to terminal 1. Ensure voltage rises between terminals 1 and 2 as the float is moved from top to bottom position.

c. Measure resistance between terminals 1 and 2 for each float position.

11. **On 1997–99 models,** measure resistance between terminals 2 and 3 for each float position. Resistance should be as follows:
   a. Full position: about 3.0 ohms.
   b. Half position: about 32.5 ohms.
   c. Empty position: about 110.0 ohms.
   d. If resistance is not as specified, replace sender gauge.

Tercel

1. Disconnect connector from sender gauge.
2. Turn ignition switch to On position, ensure gauge needle indicates Empty.
3. **On 1996 models,** connect terminals 3 and 4 on wire harness side of the connector through a 3.4W test bulb, **Fig. 41**.

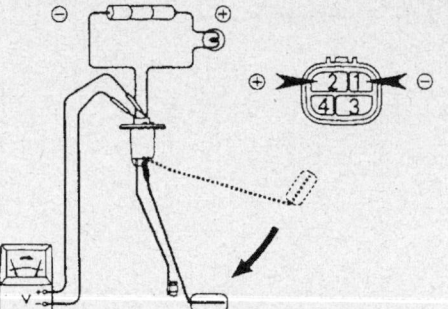

TY9099100030000X

Fig. 38   Fuel sender gauge inspection. T100

4. **On 1997 models,** connect terminals 5 and 6 on wire harness side of the connector through a 3.4W test bulb, **Fig. 41.**

5. **On 1998 models,** connect terminals 2 and 3 on wire harness side connector through a 3.4 watt test lamp, **Fig. 42.**

6. **On all models,** turn ignition switch On, ensure bulb lights and gauge needle moves towards Full.

7. If gauge does not operate as specified, check receiver gauge resistance.

8. Measure resistance between terminals A, B and C, **Figs. 43 through 46.**

9. **On 1996 models with tachometer,** resistance should be as follows:
   a. A–B: about 101.9 ohms.
   b. A–C: about 203.4 ohms.
   c. B–C: about 101.5 ohms.
   d. If resistance is not as specified, replace receiver gauge.

10. **On 1997–98 models with tachometer,** resistance should be as follows:
   a. A–B: about 115.8 ohms.
   b. A–C: about 177.2 ohms.
   c. B–C: about 61.4 ohms.
   d. If resistance is not as specified, replace receiver gauge.

11. **On 1996 models less tachometer,** resistance should be as follows:
   a. A–B: about 55 ohms.
   b. A–C: about 70 ohms.
   c. B–C: about 125 ohms.
   d. If resistance is not as specified, replace receiver gauge.

12. **On 1997–98 models less tachometer,** resistance should be as follows:
   a. A–B: about 171.2 ohms.
   b. A–C: about 272.8 ohms.
   c. B–C: about 101.6 ohms.
   d. If resistance is not as specified, replace receiver gauge.

13. **On all models,** connect an ohmmeter between red and black cable terminals of fuel gauge sender connector, **Figs. 47 and 48.**

14. **On 1996–97 models,** resistance for each float position should be as follows:
   a. Full position: about 2.0–4.0 ohms.
   b. **On 1997 models,** half position: 24.2–32.8 ohms.
   c. **On all models,** empty position: about 102.3–117.7 ohms.
   d. If resistance is not as specified, replace sender gauge.

15. **On 1998 models,** resistance for each float position should be as follows:

w/ Tachometer

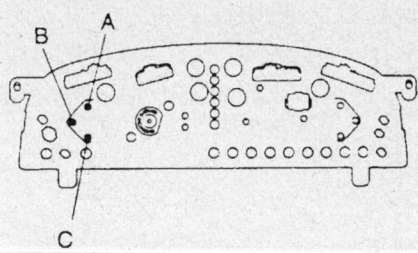

w/o Tachometer

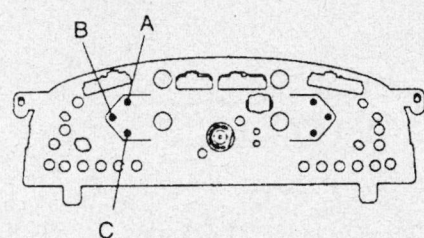

TY9099500091000X

Fig. 39   Fuel gauge terminal locations. Tacoma

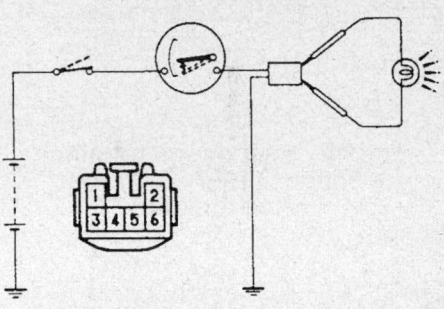

TY9099100050000X

Fig. 41   Fuel receiver gauge inspection. Tercel

   a. Full position: 6.5 ohms.
   b. Half position: 32.5 ohms.
   c. Empty position: 95 ohms.

Tundra

1. Inspect fuel gauge operation as follows:
   a. Disconnect fuel gauge.
   b. Turn ignition switch to on position. Ensure gauge indicates empty.
   c. Connect terminals 1 and 3 on wire harness side of connector through a 3.4 watt test lamp, **Fig. 49.**
   d. Turn ignition switch to on position. Ensure test lamp illuminates and gauge indicates full. Due to gauge construction, a short period will be needed for gauge to move to full position.
   e. If operation is not as specified, replace gauge.

2. Inspect fuel gauge resistance as follows referring to **Figs. 50 and 51:**
   a. Terminals A–B, 83 ohms.
   b. Terminals A–C, 268 ohms.
   c. Terminals B–C, 160 ohms.
   d. If resistance is not as specified, replace gauge.

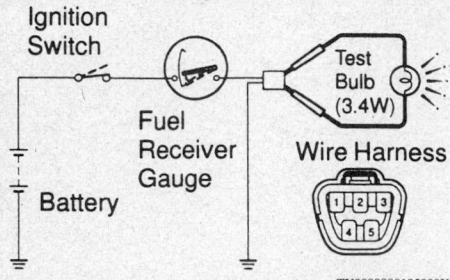

Fig. 42 Fuel receiver gauge inspection. 1998 Tercel

w/ Tachometer

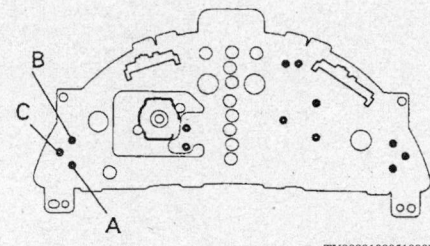

Fig. 43 Fuel gauge terminal locations. 1996 Tercel w/tachometer

w/o Tachometer

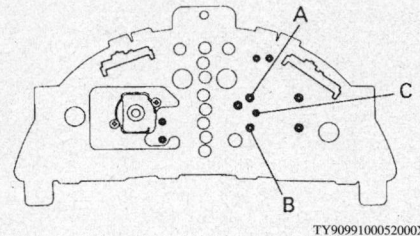

Fig. 44 Fuel gauge terminal locations. 1996 Tercel less tachometer

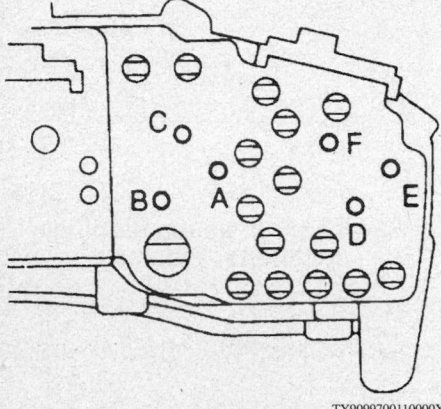

Fig. 45 Fuel gauge terminal locations. 1997–98 Tercel w/tachometer

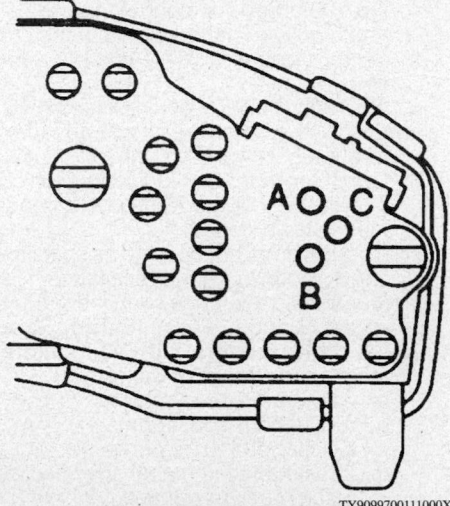

Fig. 46 Fuel gauge terminal locations. 1997–98 Tercel less tachometer

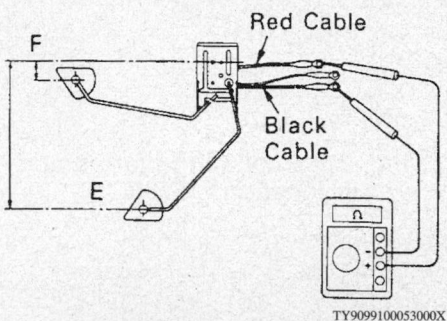

Fig. 47 Fuel sender gauge inspection. 1996 Tercel

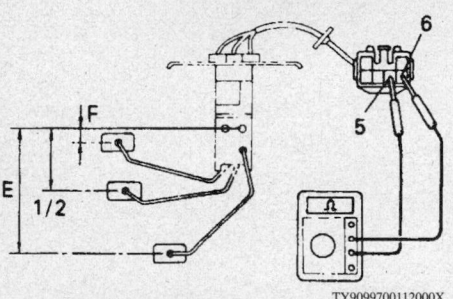

Fig. 48 Fuel sender gauge inspection. 1997–98 Tercel

a. Apply battery voltage through a 3.4 watt test lamp and across terminals 1 and 3 of sending unit wiring harness connector, **Fig. 54.**
b. Fuel level warning lamp should now illuminate.
c. Submerge switch in fuel, **Fig. 55.**
d. Warning lamp should now go out.
e. If lamp operation is not as specified, replace sending unit.

4Runner

1. Disconnect connector from sender gauge.
2. Turn ignition switch to On position, then check receiver gauge needle indicates Empty.
3. **On 1996 models,** connect terminals 2 and 4 on wire harness side connector through a 3.4W test bulb, **Fig. 36.**
4. **On 1997–99 models,** connect terminals 2 and 3 on wire harness side connector through a 3.4W test bulb, **Fig. 1.**
5. **On all models,** turn ignition switch On, then ensure bulb lights and receiver gauge needle moves toward full side.
6. **On 1996 models,** measure resistance between terminals A, B and C, **Fig. 56.** Resistance should be as follows:
   a. A–B: about 123 ohms.
   b. A–C: about 260 ohms.

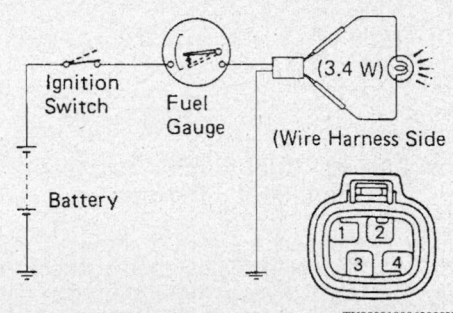

Fig. 49 Fuel gauge inspection. Tundra

c. B–C: about 137 ohms.
d. If resistance is not as specified, replace receiver gauge.
7. **On 1997–99 models,** measure resistance between terminals A, B and C, **Fig. 57.** Resistance should be as follows:
   a. A–B: about 151 ohms.
   b. A–C: about 254 ohms.
   c. B–C: about 103 ohms.
   d. If resistance is not as specified, replace receiver gauge.
8. **On 1996 models,** connect a series of three 1.5 volt dry cell batteries, then connect the positive lead from the dry cell batteries to terminal 4 through a 3.4W test bulb and the negative lead to terminal 2, **Fig. 58.**
9. **On all models,** connect positive lead from voltmeter to terminal 4 and negative lead to terminal 2. Ensure voltage rises between terminals 2 and 4 as the

3. Inspect fuel sender resistance of terminals 1 and 2, **Fig. 52,** as follows:
   a. Full position: 3 ohms.
   b. Half position: 32.5 ohms.
   c. Empty position: 110 ohms.
   d. If resistance is not as specified, replace sending unit.
4. Inspect fuel level warning lamp as follows:
   a. Disconnect fuel gauge connector.
   b. Connector terminals 1 and 3 on wire harness side connector, **Fig. 53.**
   c. Turn ignition switch on. Ensure warning lamp illuminates.
   d. If warning lamp operation is not as specified, test bulb or inspect wiring harness.
5. Inspect fuel level warning switch as follows:

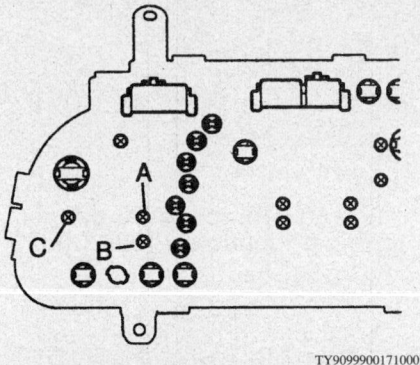

Fig. 50 Fuel gauge resistance check. Tundra w/tachometer

Fig. 51 Fuel gauge resistance check. Tundra less tachometer

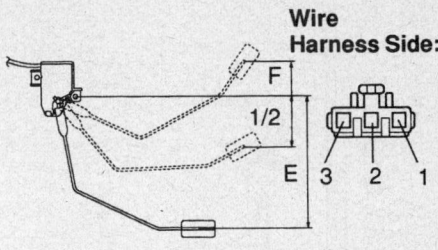

Fig. 52 Fuel sending unit resistance check. Tundra

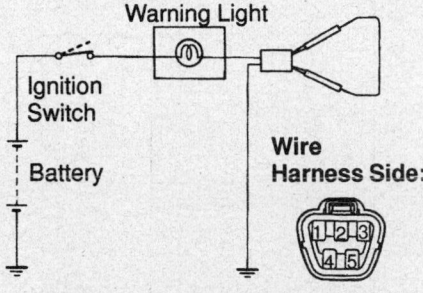

Fig. 53 Fuel warning lamp inspection. Tundra

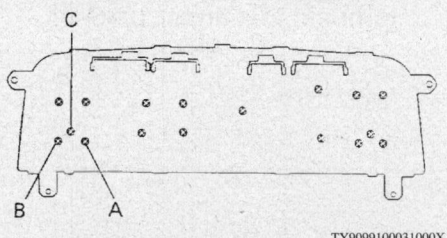

Fig. 54 Fuel level warning switch inspection (less fuel). Tundra

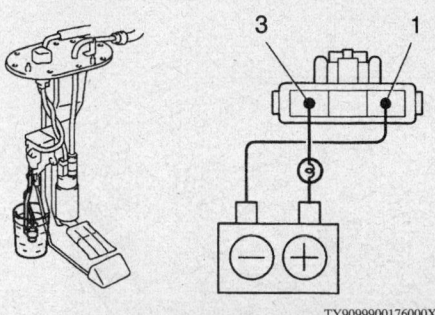

Fig. 55 Fuel level warning switch inspection (w/fuel). Tundra

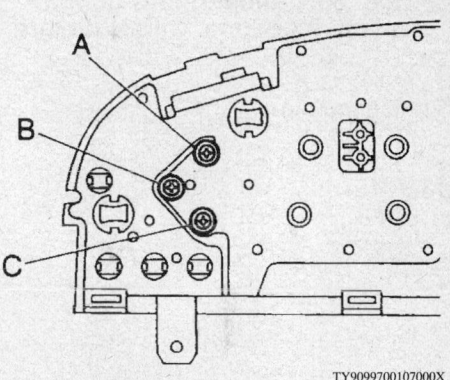

Fig. 56 Fuel gauge terminal locations. 1996 4Runner

float is moved from top to bottom position.

10. Measure resistance between terminals 2 and 4 on 1996 models, and terminals 2 and 3 on 1997 models, for each float position. Resistance should be as follows:
   a. Full position: about 3.0 ohms.
   b. Half position: about 32.5 ohms.
   c. Empty position: about 110.0 ohms.
   d. If resistance is not as specified, replace sender gauge.

ENGINE COOLANT TEMPERATURE

Refer to **Figs. 59 through 79** for terminal locations on engine coolant temperature gauges.

1. Disconnect connector from sender gauge.
2. Turn ignition switch On, then check receiver gauge needle indicates COOL.
3. Ground terminal on wire harness side

connector through a 3.4W test bulb, **Fig. 80.**

4. Turn ignition switch On, then check bulb lights up and receiver gauge needle moves toward hot side.
5. If operation is as specified, replace sender gauge, then recheck system.
6. If operation is not as specified, measure receiver gauge resistance between gauge terminals as indicated in following steps.
7. **On Avalon and 1996 Camry models,** resistance should be as follows:
   a. A–B: 54 ohms.
   b. A–C: 176 ohms.
   c. B–C: 230 ohms.
8. **On Camry Solara and 1997–99 Camry models,** resistance should be as follows:
   a. A–B: 175.7 ohms.
   b. A–C: 54.0 ohms.
   c. B–C: 229.7 ohms.
9. **On Celica models,** resistance should be as follows:
   a. A–B: 230 ohms.
   b. A–C: 54 ohms.
   c. B–C: 176 ohms.
10. **On 1996–97 Corolla models less tachometer,** resistance should be as follows:
   a. A–B: 176 ohms.
   b. A–C: 54 ohms.
   c. B–C: 230 ohms.
11. **On 1996–97 Corolla models with tachometer,** resistance should be as follows:
   a. A–B: 230 ohms.

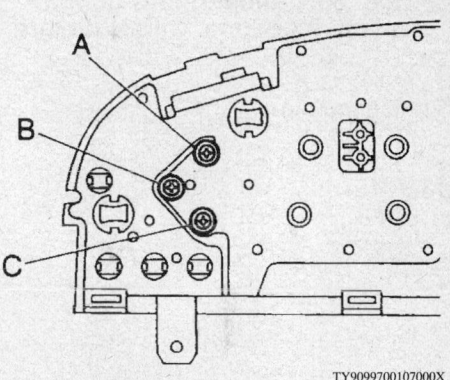

Fig. 57 Fuel gauge terminal locations. 1997–99 4Runner

   b. A–C: 54 ohms.
   c. B–C: 176 ohms.
12. **On 1998–99 Corolla models,** resistance should be as follows:
   a. A–B: 54.0 ohms.
   b. A–C: 175.7 ohms.
   c. B–C: 229.7 ohms
13. **On Land Cruiser models,** resistance should be as follows:
   a. A–B: 71–79 ohms.
   b. A–C: 117–141 ohms.
   c. B–C: 185–215 ohms.
14. **On 1996 Paseo models,** resistance should be as follows:
   a. A–B: 54 ohms.
   b. A–C: 146 ohms.
   c. B–C: 200 ohms.
15. **On 1997 Paseo models,** resistance should be as follows:
   a. D–E: 51.0 ohms.
   b. D–F: 152.8 ohms.
   c. E–F: 203.8 ohms.

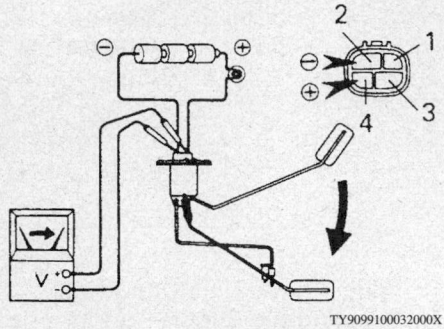

Fig. 58   Fuel sender gauge inspection. 1996 4Runner

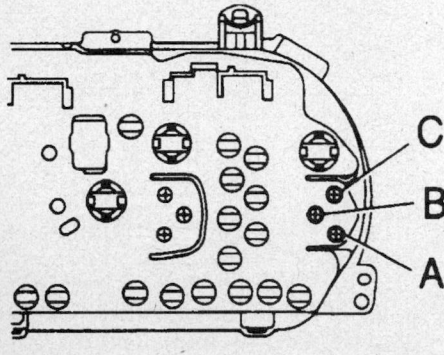

Fig. 61   Temperature gauge terminal locations. Camry Solara & 1997–99 Camry

w/ Tachometer

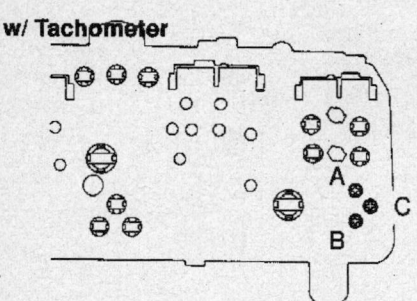

w/o Tachometer

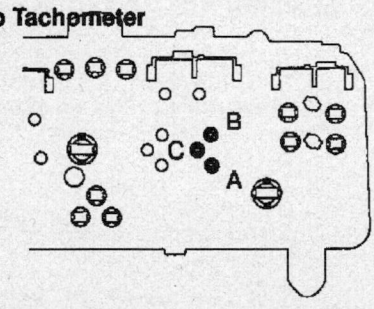

Fig. 64   Temperature gauge terminal locations. 1998–99 Corolla

16. **On Previa models,** resistance should be as follows:
    a. A–B: 200 ohms.
    b. A–C: 54 ohms.
    c. B–C: 146 ohms.

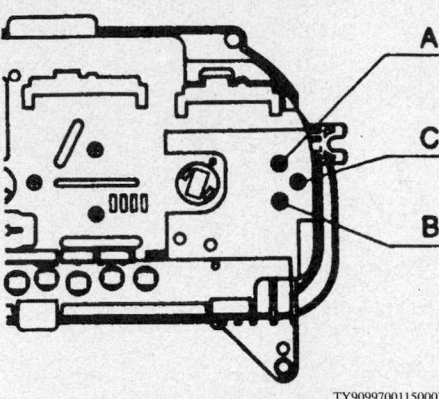

Fig. 59   Temperature gauge terminal locations. Avalon

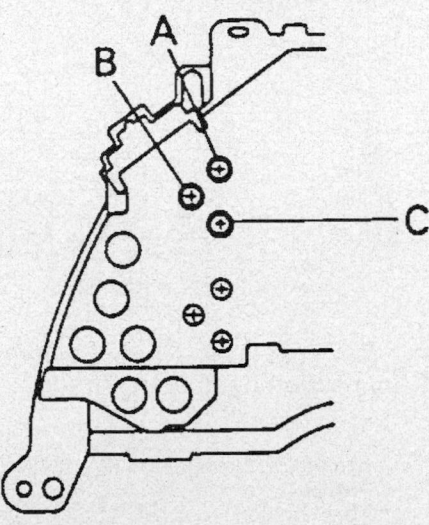

Fig. 62   Temperature gauge terminal locations. Celica

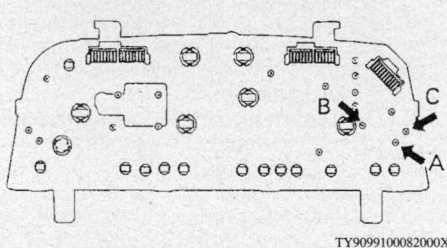

Fig. 65   Temperature gauge terminal locations. Land Cruiser

17. **On RAV4 models,** resistance should be as follows:
    a. A–B: 54 ohms.
    b. A–C: 175.7 ohms.
    c. B–C: 229.7 ohms.
18. **On Sienna models,** resistance should be as follows:
    a. A–B: 176 ohms.
    b. A–C: 54 ohms.
    c. B–C: 230 ohms.
19. **On Supra models,** measure resistance between terminals A, B and C. Resistance should be as follows:
    a. A–B: 229.7 ohms.
    b. A–C: 54.0 ohms.
    c. B–C: 175.7 ohms.

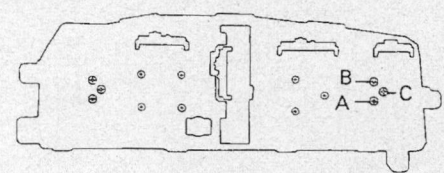

Fig. 60   Temperature gauge terminal locations. 1996 Camry

w/ Tachometer

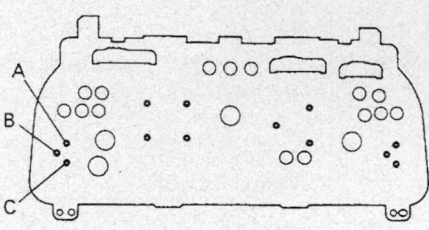

w/o Tachometer

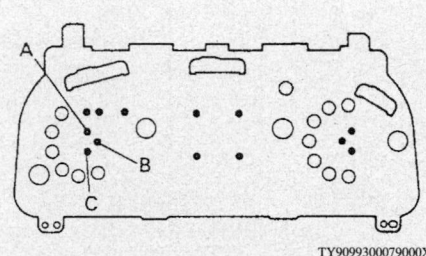

Fig. 63   Temperature gauge terminal locations. 1996–97 Corolla

w/ Tachometer

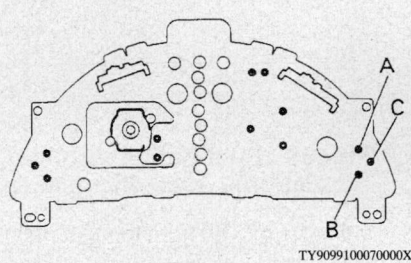

Fig. 66   Temperature gauge terminal locations. 1996 Paseo

20. **On 1996 Previa models,** measure resistance between terminals A, B and C. Resistance should be as follows:
    a. A–B: 200.3 ohms.
    b. A–C: 54.0 ohms.
    c. B–C: 146.3 ohms.
21. **On Tercel models with tachometer,** resistance should be as follows:
    a. D–E: 51 ohms.
    b. D–F: 149 ohms.
    c. E–F: 200 ohms.
22. **On Tercel models less tachometer,** resistance should be as follows:
    a. A–B: 54 ohms.
    b. A–C: 176 ohms.
    c. B–C: 230 ohms.
23. **On Tacoma models with tachometer,** resistance should be as follows:

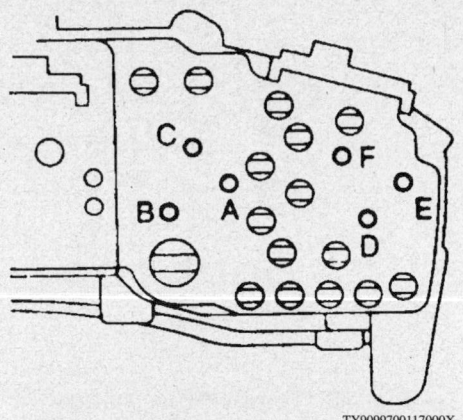

Fig. 67   Temperature gauge terminal locations. 1997 Paseo

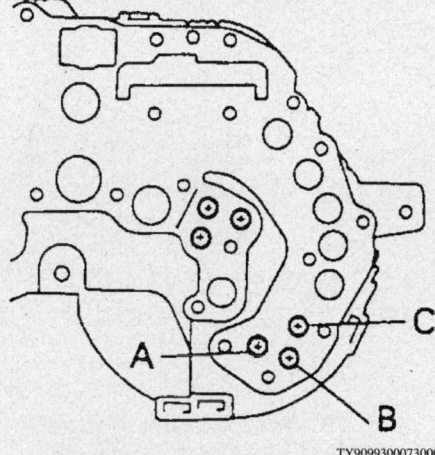

Fig. 70   Temperature gauge terminal locations. Supra

    a. A–B: 85–95 ohms.
    b. A–C: 158–192 ohms.
    c. B–C: 215–255 ohms.

24. **On Tacoma models less tachometer,** resistance should be as follows:
    a. A–B: 85–95 ohms.
    b. A–C: 158–192 ohms.
    c. B–C: 215–255 ohms.
25. **On Tundra models with tachometer,** resistance should be as follows:
    a. A–B: 55.9 ohms.
    b. A–C: 136 ohms.
    c. B–C: 211 ohms.
26. **On Tundra models less tachometer,** resistance should be as follows:
    a. A–B: 54.5 ohms.
    b. A–C: 139 ohms.
    c. B–C: 214 ohms.
27. **On T100 models with tachometer,** resistance should be as follows:
    a. A–B: 150 ohms.
    b. A–C: 54 ohms.
    c. B–C: 138 ohms.
28. **On T100 models less tachometer,** resistance should be as follows:
    a. A–B: 25 ohms.
29. **On 1996 4Runner models,** resistance should be as follows:
    a. A–B: 57 ohms.
    b. A–C: 135 ohms.
    c. B–C: 217 ohms.

w/o Tachometer

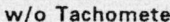
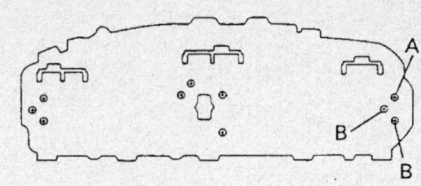

w/ Tachometer

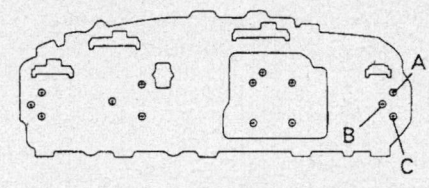

Fig. 68   Temperature gauge terminal locations. Previa

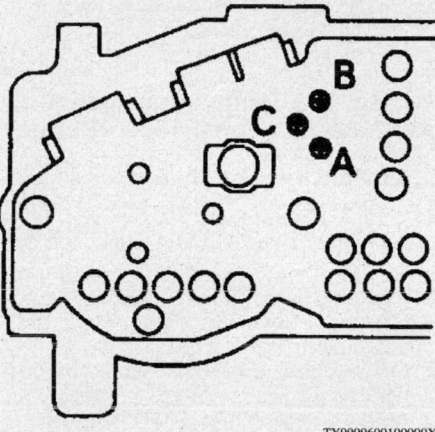

Fig. 71   Temperature gauge terminal locations. RAV4

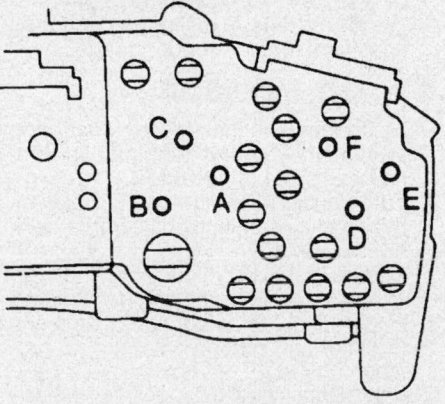

Fig. 73   Temperature gauge terminal locations. Tercel w/tachometer

w/o Tachometer:

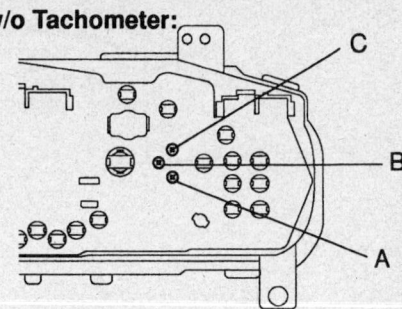

w/ Tachometer:

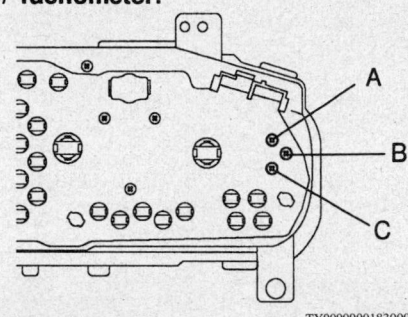

Fig. 69   Temperature gauge terminal locations. Sienna

w/ Tachometer

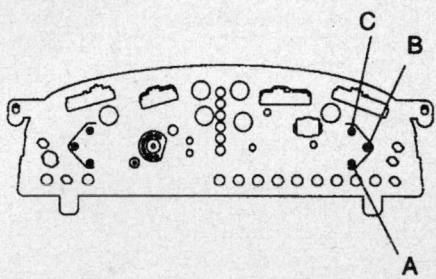

w/o Tachometer

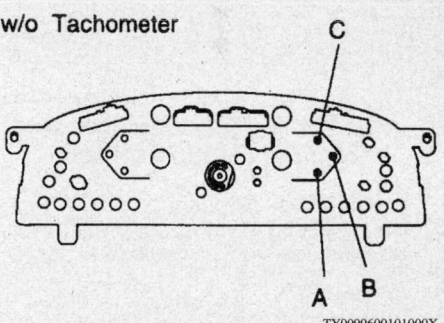

Fig. 72   Temperature gauge terminal locations. Tacoma

30. **On 1997–99 4Runner models,** resistance should be as follows:
    a. A–B: 90 ohms.
    b. A–C: 170 ohms.
    c. B–C: 230 ohms.
31. **On all models,** if resistance is not as specified, replace receiver gauge.
32. Measure sender resistance between terminal and ground.
33. **On 1996 models,** resistance should read as follows:
    a. 122°F: 160–314 ohms.

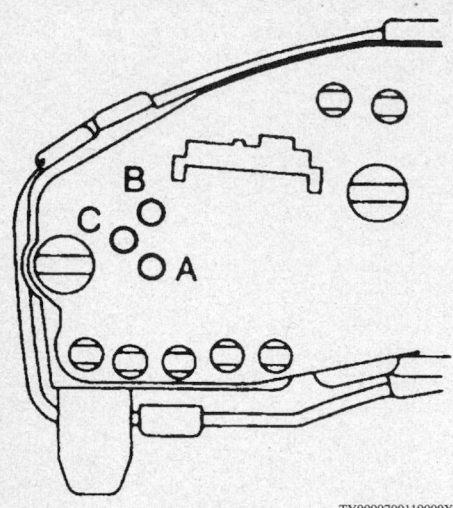

Fig. 74 Temperature gauge terminal locations. Tercel less tachometer

w/ Tachometer

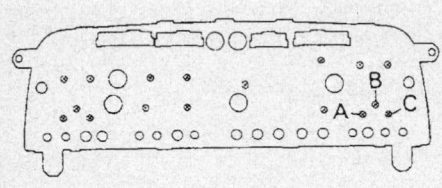

w/o Tachometer

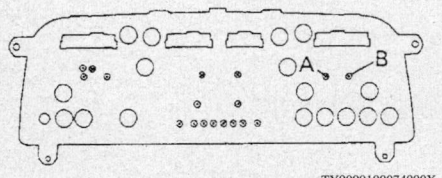

Fig. 77 Temperature gauge terminal locations. T100

b. 248°F: 17–30 ohms.
34. **On 1997–99 Avalon and 4Runner models,** resistance should read as follows:
    a. 122°F: 234–314 ohms.
    b. 248°F: 24–30.5 ohms.
35. **On 1997–99 Camry models,** resistance should read as follows:
    a. 122°F: approximately 274 ohms.
    b. 248°F: approximately26.4 ohms.
36. **On Camry Solara and Sienna models,** resistance should be as follows:
    a. 122°F: 160–240 ohms.
    b. 248°F: 17–21 ohms.
37. **On Celica, RAV4, Supra and 1998–99 Corolla models,** resistance should read as follows:
    a. 122°F: 160–240 ohms.
    b. 248°F: 17.1–21.2 ohms.

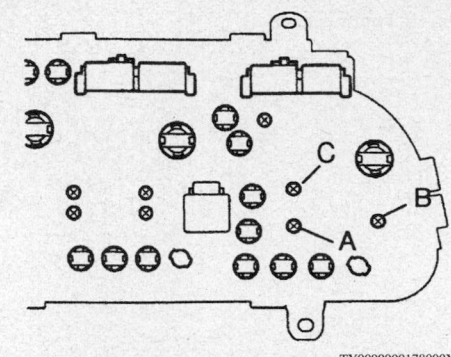

Fig. 75 Temperature gauge terminal locations. Tundra w/tachometer

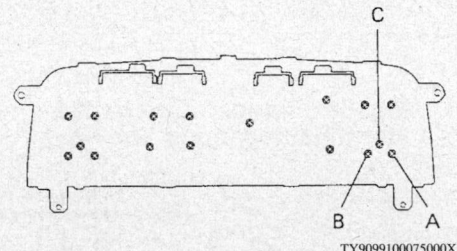

Fig. 78 Temperature gauge terminal locations. 1996 4Runner

38. **On Previa models,** resistance should read as follows:
    a. 122°F: 200.0 ohms.
    b. 248°F: 19.4 ohms.
39. Sending unit resistance values not available for 1997–99 Corolla, Land Cruiser, Paseo, Tacoma, T100 and 1997–98 Tercel.
40. **On Tundra models,** install jumper wire as shown in **Fig. 81.** Adjust ammeter pointer to read "0" using rheostat, then read rheostat indication. Resistance should be as follows:
    a. 122°F: 160–240 ohms.
    b. 248°F: 17.1–21.2 ohms.
41. **On all models,** if resistance is not as specified, replace sender gauge.

LOW OIL PRESSURE

1. Disconnect connector from warning switch and ground terminal on wire harness side connector.
2. Turn ignition switch to On position, then check warning light illuminates. If not, test bulb.
3. Ensure there is continuity between terminal and ground with engine stopped.
4. Ensure there is no continuity between terminal and ground with engine running.
5. If operation is not as specified, replace switch.
6. **On Land Cruiser, 1996 4Runner and 1997–98 T100 models,** proceed as follows:

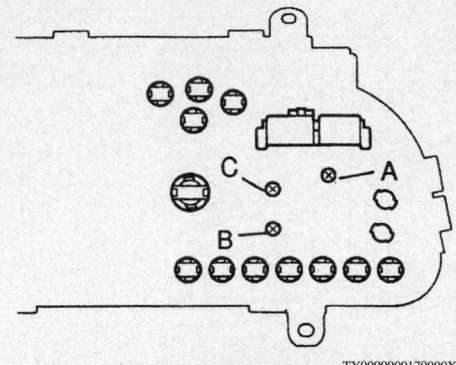

Fig. 76 Temperature gauge terminal locations. Tundra less tachometer

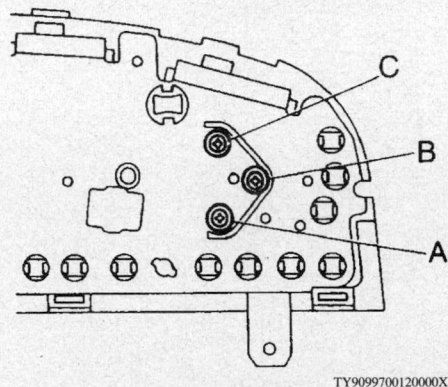

Fig. 79 Temperature gauge terminal locations. 1997–99 4Runner

a. Disconnect connector from sender gauge.
b. Turn ignition switch to On position, then check receiver gauge needle indicates Low.
c. Ground terminal on wire harness side connector through a 3.4W test bulb.
d. Turn ignition switch to On position, then check bulb illuminates and receiver gauge needle moves to high side.
e. If operation is not as specified, measure receiver gauge resistance.
7. **On 1996 4Runner and 1997–98 T100 models,** measure resistance between terminals A and B. Resistance should be 25.0 ohms. If not as specified, replace receiver gauge.
8. **On Land Cruiser models,** measure resistance between terminals. Resistance should be 40.0–48.0 ohms. If not as specified, replace receiver gauge.
9. **On all models,** if resistance is not as specified, replace sender gauge.

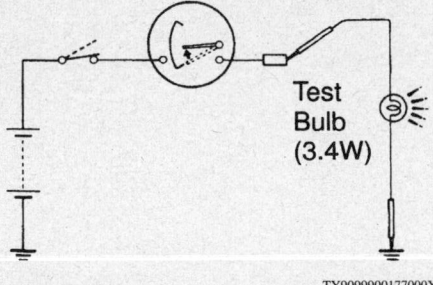

Fig. 80   Temperature gauge ground terminal inspection

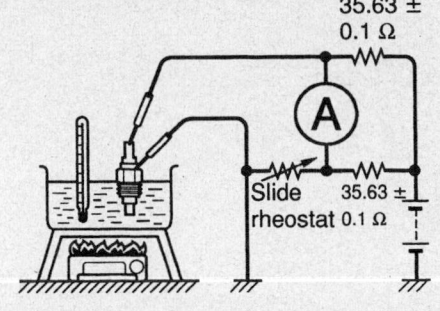

Fig. 81   Temperature sending unit inspection. Tundra

Starter Motors

INDEX

PRECAUTIONS

AIR BAG SYSTEMS

Refer to "Air Bag System Precautions" in the front of this manual for system disarming & arming procedures.

BATTERY GROUND CABLE

Prior to service, disconnect battery ground cable and isolate as required.

AUDIO CODED ANTI-THEFT SYSTEM

Some models are equipped with an audio coded anti-theft system that will disable the radio when the battery cable is disconnected. The system can be identified by the "ANTI-THEFT SYSTEM" on the cassette tape lid. Obtain 3 digit customer code for input. Reset system after service as follows:

1. Obtain 3 digit audio anti-theft code.
2. Depress 1 (PROG) while depressing righthand side of TUNE SEEK button, - - - will appear in tape operation display.
3. To enter the first digit, depress 1 (PROG) button repeatedly until the number of times depressed equals the first digit beginning with zero (depress the 1 button six times if the first digit if five).
4. To enter second digit, depress 2 (APS) button repeatedly until the number of times depressed equals the second digit beginning with zero.
5. To enter third digit, depress 3 (RPT) button repeatedly until the number of times depressed equals the third digit beginning with zero.
6. If - - - is displayed during code input, repeat procedure.
7. When code appears in display, depress and hold SCAN button until SEC appears.
8. When SEC disappears audio system should be operative.
9. If Err is displayed, repeat procedure. **Attempting to input code more than nine times may permanently disable audio system.**

DESCRIPTION

Refer to **Figs. 1 through 14** for reduction type starter, and **Fig. 15** for planetary starter.

TROUBLESHOOTING

Before beginning any troubleshooting procedures, ensure all connections are tight and theft deterrent system, if equipped, is operating properly.

ENGINE WILL NOT CRANK

1. Low battery charge.
2. Battery cables loose or corroded.
3. **On models equipped with manual transaxle,** faulty clutch start switch.
4. **On models equipped with automatic transaxle,** faulty neutral start switch.
5. **On models equipped with manual transaxle,** faulty starter relay.
6. **On all models,** blown fusible link.
7. Faulty starter.
8. Faulty ignition switch.

ENGINE CRANKS SLOWLY

1. Low battery charge.
2. Battery cables loose, corroded or worn.
3. Faulty starter.

STARTER KEEPS RUNNING

1. Faulty starter.
2. Faulty ignition switch.
3. Electrical wiring short or open.

STARTER SPINS, ENGINE WILL NOT CRANK

1. Faulty starter.
2. Broken pinion gear teeth.
3. **On models equipped with manual transaxle,** broken flywheel teeth.
4. **On models equipped with automatic transaxle,** broken driveplate teeth.

DIAGNOSIS & TESTING

BENCH TEST

These tests must be performed within 3 to 5 seconds to avoid burning out the coil.

Pull-In Test

1. Disconnect field coil wire from terminal C.
2. Connect negative battery voltage to both magnetic switch body and terminal C.
3. Connect positive battery voltage to starter terminal 50, **Fig. 16.**
4. Ensure pinion gear moves outward.

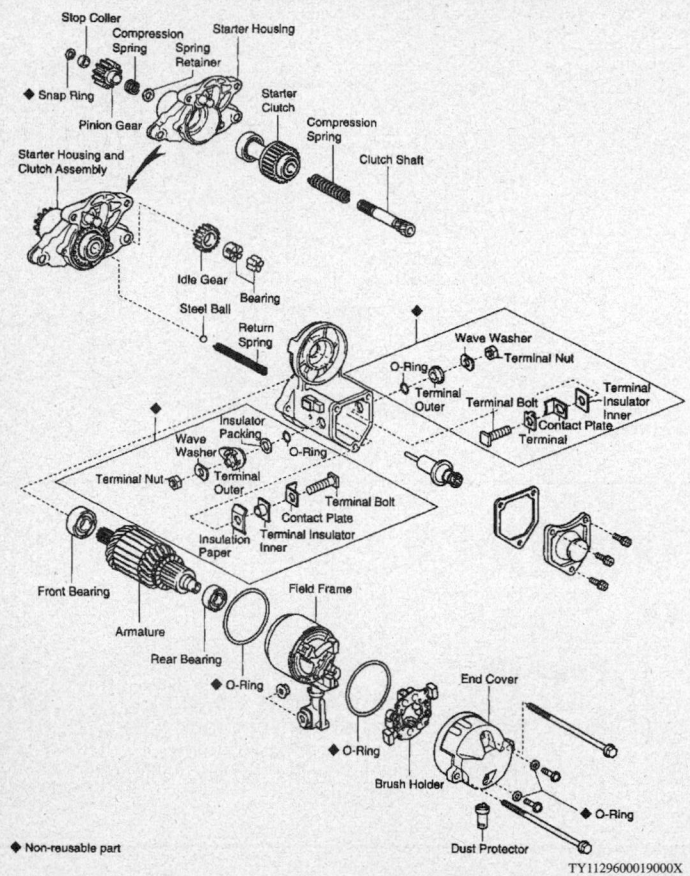

Fig. 1 Exploded view of reduction type starter. Avalon, Camry, Camry Solara, RAV4, Sienna & 1996–97 Celica w/5S-FE engine

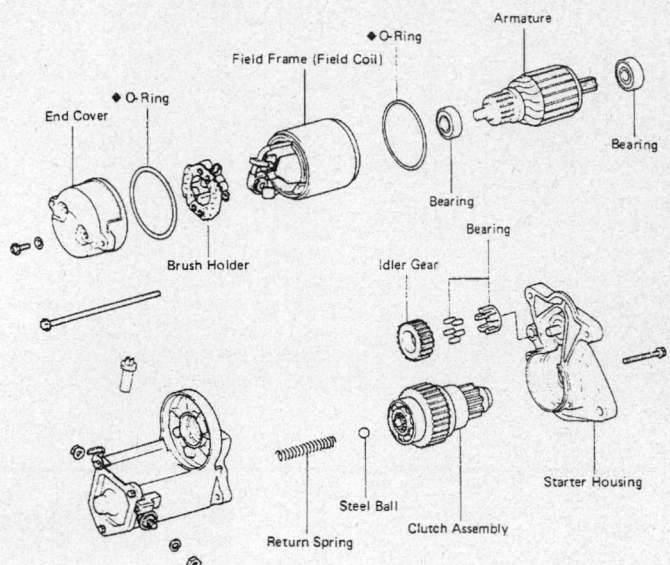

Fig. 2 Exploded view of reduction type starter. Paseo & 1996 Corolla, Land Cruiser, Previa, Supra, T100, Tercel & 4Runner

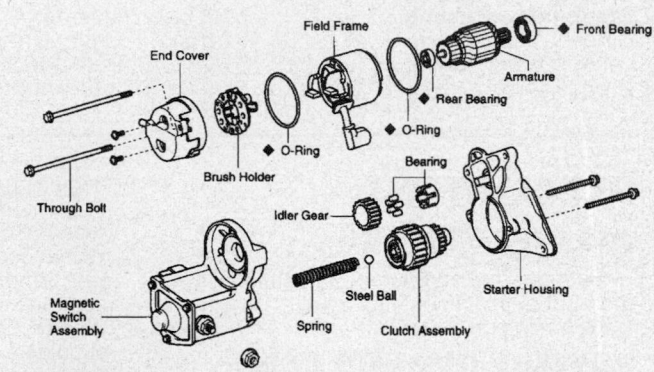

Fig. 3 Exploded view of reduction type starter. Tundra w/5VZ-FE engine & 1997–99 Corolla

5. If pinion gear movement is not as indicated, replace magnetic switch.

Hold-In Test

1. Install test equipment as outlined under "Pull-In Test."
2. With pinion gear out, disconnect negative lead from terminal C.
3. Ensure pinion gear remains out.
4. If pinion gear returns inward, replace magnetic switch.

Plunger Return

1. Install test equipment as outlined under "Pull-In Test."
2. Disconnect negative lead from magnetic switch body.
3. Ensure pinion gear moves inward.
4. If pinion gear movement is not as indicated, replace magnetic switch.

No-Load Performance

1. Connect suitable ammeter negative lead to terminals both 30 and 50.
2. Connect ammeter positive terminal to positive battery terminal.
3. Ensure starter rotates smoothly and steadily with pinion gear moving out.
4. Refer to "Starter Specifications" for standard amperage.

COMPONENT TESTING

Starter Relay

1. **On Avalon, Camry, Camry Solara and Sienna models,** starter relay is located in the engine compartment relay box.
2. **On Celica models,** starter relay is located in the front lefthand side of the engine compartment, at relay block No. 2.
3. **On Corolla and T100 models,** starter relay is located behind the lefthand side kick panel.
4. **On RAV4, Tundra and 1996 Land Cruiser models,** starter relay is located in engine compartment relay box.
5. **On 1996 4Runner models,** the starter

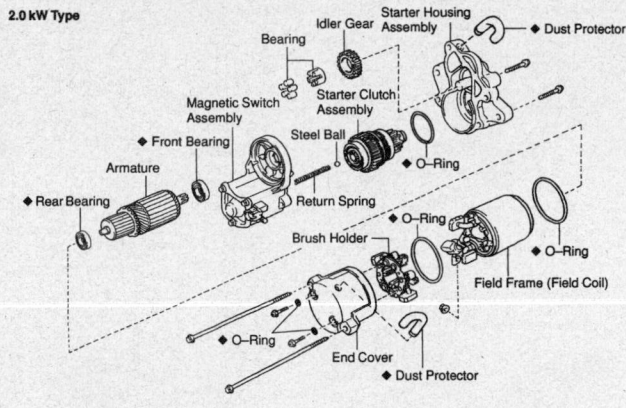

2.0 kW Type

1.0 kW Type

1.4, 1.6 kW Type

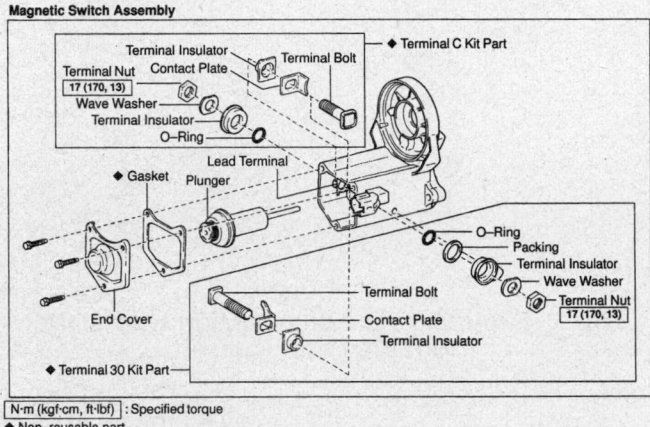

Magnetic Switch Assembly

N·m (kgf·cm, ft·lbf) : Specified torque

◆ Non-reusable part

TY1129900037000X

◆ Non-reusable part

TY1129100002000X

Fig. 4   Exploded view of reduction type starter. Tundra w/2UZ-FE engine

Fig. 5   Exploded view of reduction type starter. 1996 Previa, Tacoma, T100 & 4Runner

relay is located in the righthand front of the engine compartment, in the No. 2 relay box.

6. **On Tacoma and 1997 4Runner models,** starter relay is located in relay box on left side of engine compartment.

7. **On 1996 Paseo and Tercel models,** starter relay is located behind the lower lefthand side of the center dash cluster, behind radio.

8. **On 1997 Paseo and Tercel models,** starter relay is located in engine compartment fuse box near battery.

9. **On 1996 Previa models,** starter relay is located below the lefthand side of instrument panel.

10. **On 1997 Previa models,** starter relay is located near center of instrument cluster.

11. **On Supra and Tacoma models,** starter relay is located in the lefthand side of the engine compartment, at relay block No. 2.

12. **On Previa models,** using a suitable ohmmeter, check relay continuity as follows:
    a. Ensure continuity between terminal Nos. 1 and 3, **Fig. 17.**
    b. No continuity should exist between terminal Nos. 2 and 4.
    c. If continuity is not as indicated, replace relay.

13. **On Previa models,** using a suitable ohmmeter, inspect relay operation as follows:
    a. Apply battery voltage across terminal Nos. 1 and 3.
    b. Using suitable ohmmeter, ensure continuity exists between terminal Nos. 2 and 4.
    c. If continuity is not as indicated, replace relay.

14. **On 1996 Paseo and Tercel models,** using a suitable ohmmeter, check relay continuity as follows:
    a. Ensure continuity exists between

terminals 85 and 86, **Fig. 18.**
    b. Ensure continuity exists between terminals 30 and 87.
    c. Apply battery voltage across terminals 85 and 86.
    d. Ensure continuity does not exist between terminals 30 and 87.
    e. If continuity is not as specified, replace relay.

15. **On models except Previa and 1996 Paseo and Tercel,** using a suitable ohmmeter, check relay continuity as follows:
    a. Ensure continuity exists between terminals 1 and 2, **Fig. 19.**
    b. Ensure continuity does not exist between terminals 3 and 5.
    c. Apply battery voltage across terminals 1 and 2.
    d. Ensure continuity exists between terminals 3 and 5.
    e. If measurements are not as specified, replace relay.

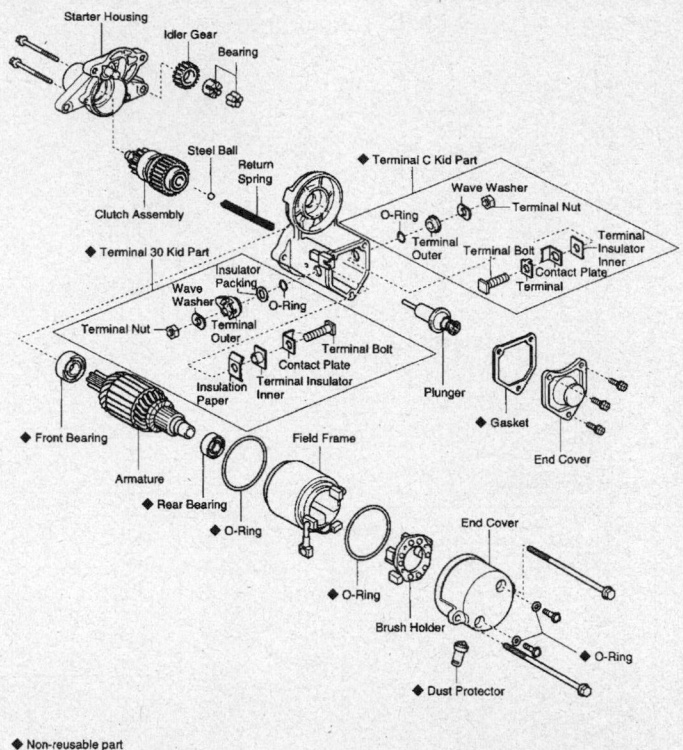

Fig. 7   Exploded view of reduction type starter. 1997–99 Land Cruiser

◆ Non-reusable part

TY1129700022000X

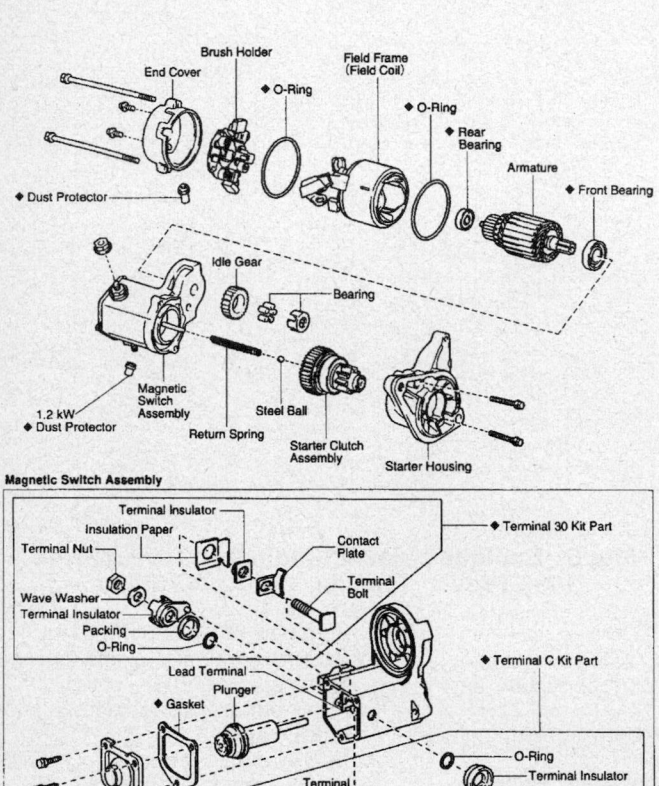

Fig. 6   Exploded view of reduction type starter. 1996–97 Celica w/7A-FE engine

◆ Non-reusable part

TY1129700030000X

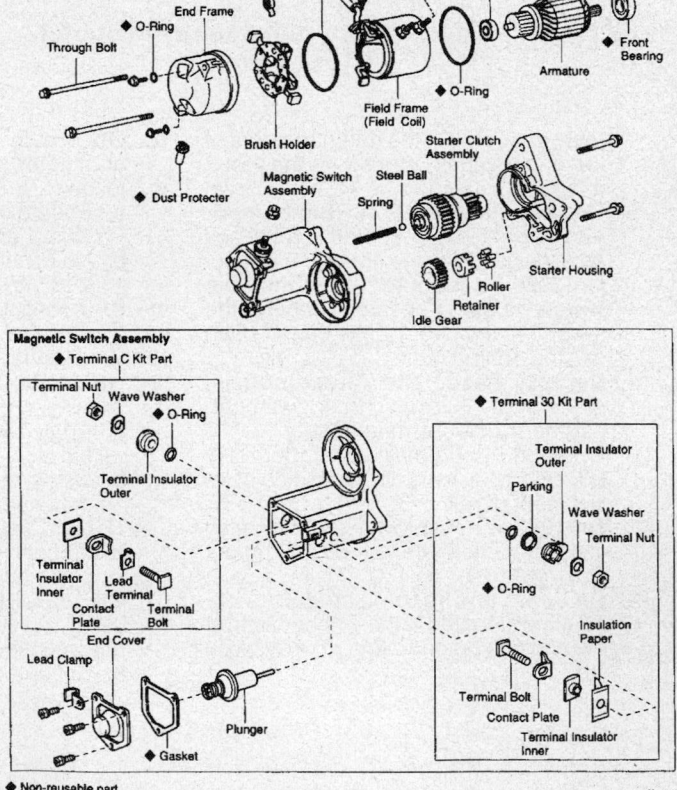

Fig. 8   Exploded view of reduction type starter. 1997 Previa w/1.4 kilowatts

◆ Non-reusable part

TY1129700023000X

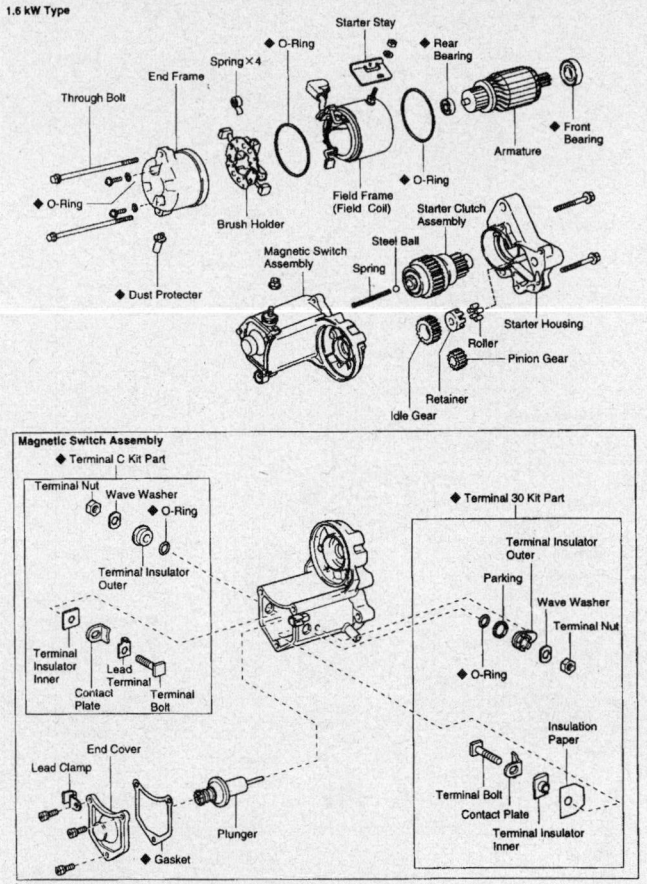

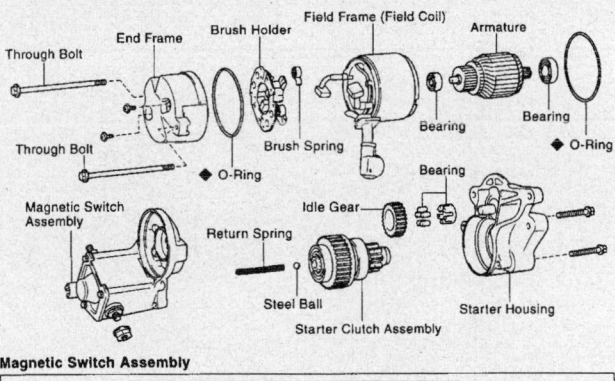

Fig. 9 Exploded view of reduction type starter. 1997 Previa 1.6 kilowatts

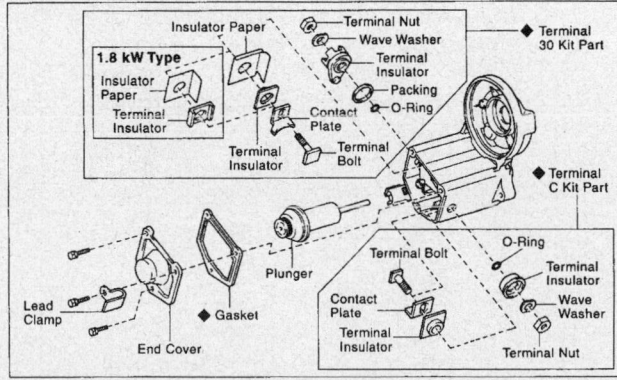

Fig. 11 Exploded view of reduction type starter. 1997–99 Tacoma w/1.8 kilowatt

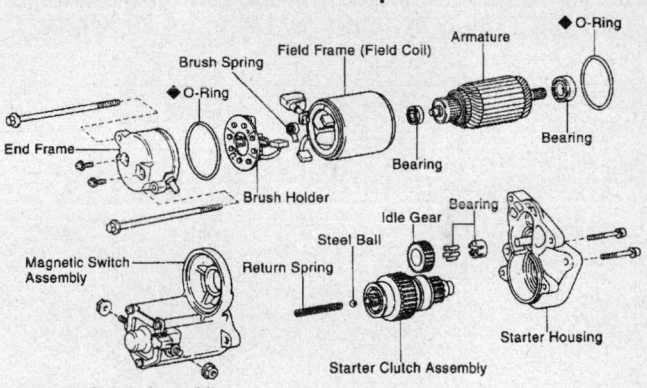

Fig. 10 Exploded view of reduction type starter. 1997–98 Supra

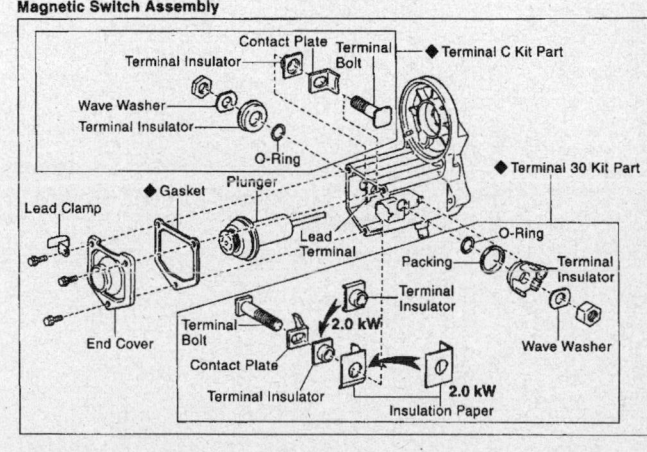

Fig. 12 Exploded view of reduction type starter. 1997–99 Tacoma w/2.0 kilowatt

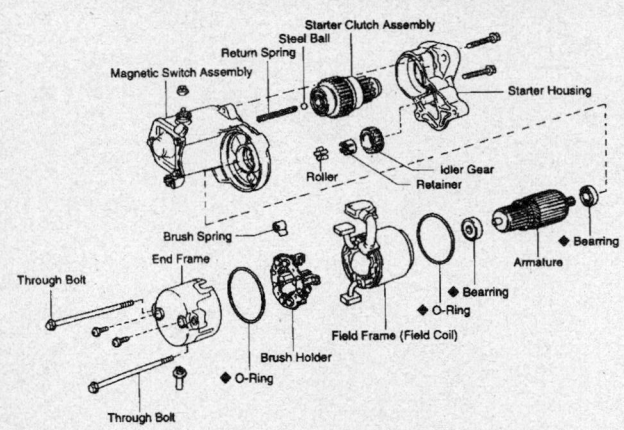

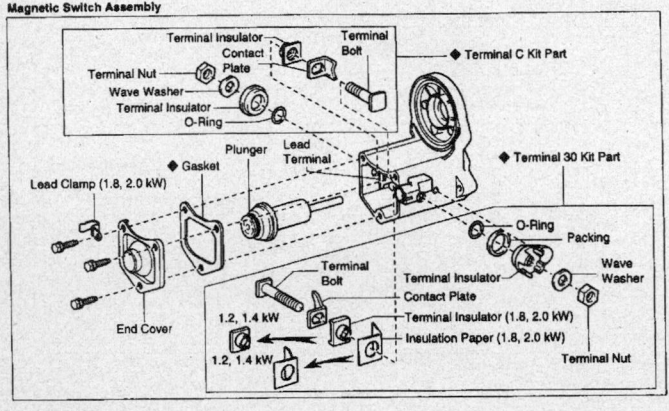

Fig. 13 Exploded view of reduction type starter. 1997–98 T100 & 4Runner w/1.2 or 1.4 kilowatts

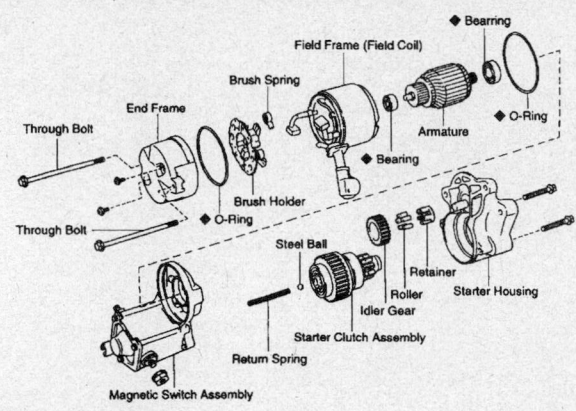

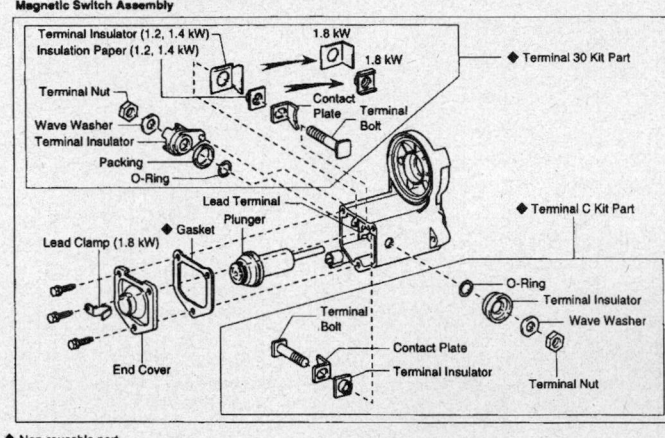

Fig. 14 Exploded view of reduction type starter. 4Runner & 1997–98 T100 w/1.8 or 2.0 kilowatts

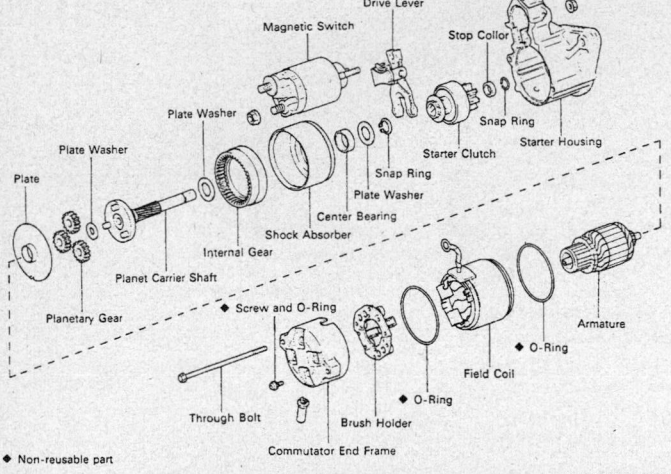

Fig. 15 Exploded view of planetary starter. Paseo & Tercel

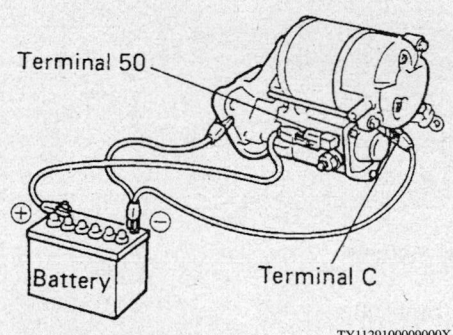

Fig. 16 Bench test connectors

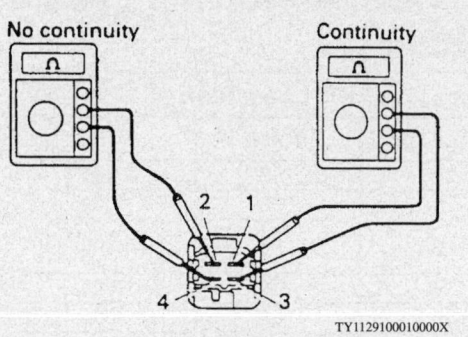

Fig. 17 Starter relay inspection. Previa

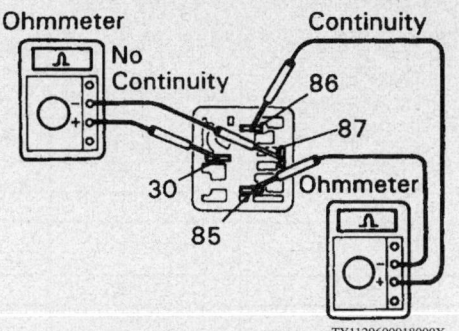

Fig. 18 Starter relay inspection. 1996 Paseo & Tercel

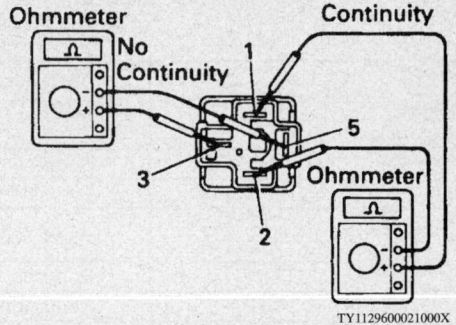

Fig. 19 Starter relay inspection. Except Previa & 1996 Paseo & Tercel

STARTER SPECIFICATIONS

Year	Engine	Starter Type	Kilowatt Rating	Brush Spring Tension, Ounces	No Load Test		
					Amperes	Volts	RPM
1996	1FZ-FE	Reduction	1.4	62–84	90	11.5	3000
	1FZ-FE	Reduction	2.0	43–84	100	11.5	2500
	1MZ-FE	Reduction	1.4	62–84	90	11.5	3000
	2JZ-GE, 2JZ-GTE	Reduction	1.4	62–84	90	11.5	3000
	2TZ-FZE	Reduction	1.4	62–85	90	11.5	3000
	2TZ-FZE	Reduction	1.6	62–85	90	11.5	3500
	2RZ-FE	Reduction	1.0	42–72	90	11.5	3000
	2RZ-FE	Reduction	1.4	34–60	90	11.5	3000
	2RZ-FE	Reduction	2.0	43–85	100	11.5	2500
	3RZ-FE	Reduction	1.2	34–60	90	11.5	3000
	3RZ-FE	Reduction	1.8	43–85	100	11.5	2500
	3S-FE	Reduction	1.2 or 1.4	49–70	90	11.5	3000
	4A-FE	Reduction	1.0	62–85	90	11.5	3000
	4A-FE	Reduction	1.4	62–85	90	11.5	3500
	5E-FE	Planetary	.8	56	90	11.5	3000
	5E-FE	Reduction	1.0	62–85	90	11.5	3000
	5S-FE	Reduction	1.4 or 1.6	62–85	90	11.5	3500
	5S-FE	Compact Reduction	1.4	62–85	90	11.5	3000
	5VZ-FE	Reduction	1.4	33–60	90	11.5	3000
	5VZ-FE	Reduction	1.8	43–85	100	11.5	2500
	7A-FE	Reduction	1.4	64–85	90	11.5	3000

Continued

STARTER SPECIFICATIONS—Continued

Year	Engine	Starter Type	Kilowatt Rating	Brush Spring Tension, Ounces	No Load Test		
					Amperes	Volts	RPM
1997	1FZ-FE	Reduction	1.4	64–85	90	11.5	3000
	1MZ-FE	Reduction	1.4	62–84	90	11.5	3000
	2JZ-GE, 2JZ-GTE	Reduction	1.4	62–84	90	11.5	3000
	2TZ-FZ	Reduction	1.4 or 1.6	64–85	90	11.5	3000
	2RZ-FE	Reduction	1.4	62-85	90	11.5	3000
	3RZ-FE	Reduction	1.4	64-85	90	11.5	3000
	3RZ-FE	Reduction	1.2	50-70	90	11.5	3000
	3RZ-FE	Reduction	1.4	62-85	90	11.5	3000
	3S-FE	Reduction	1.4	63-84	90	11.5	3000
	3S-FE	Reduction	1.2	49–70	90	11.5	3000
	4A-FE	Reduction	1.4	64–85	90	11.5	3000
	5E-FE	Planetary	.8	50-64	90	11.5	3000
	5E-FE	Reduction	1.0	62–85	90	11.5	3000
	5S-FE	Reduction	1.4	64–85	90	11.5	3000
	5VZ-FE	Reduction	1.2	50-70	90	11.5	3000
	5VZ-FE	Reduction	1.4	64-85	90	11.5	3000
	5VZ-FE	Reduction	1.8	78-99	100	11.5	2500
	7A-FE	Reduction	1.4	64–85	90	11.5	3000
	7A-FE	Reduction	1.2	50-70	90	11.5	3000
1998	1MZ-FE	Reduction	1.4	64-84	90	11.5	3000
	1ZZ-FE	Reduction	1.2	50-74	90	11.5	3000
	1ZZ-FE	Reduction	1.4	64-84	90	11.5	3000
	2JZ-GE	Reduction	1.4	62-85	90	11.5	3000
	2JZ-GTE	Reduction	1.4	62-85	90	11.5	3000
	2RZ-FE	Reduction	1.4	62-85	90	11.5	3000
	2RZ-FE	Reduction	2.0	78-99	100	11.5	2500
	2UZ-FE	Reduction	2.0	77-99	100	11.5	2500
	3RZ-FE	Reduction	1.4	62-85	90	11.5	3000
	3RZ-FE	Reduction	2.0	78=-99	100	11.5	2500
	3S-FE	Reduction	1.2	49-70	90	11.5	3000
	3S-FE	Reduction	1.4	63-84	90	11.5	3000
	5E-FE	Planetary	1	49-64	90	11.5	3000
	5S-FE	Reduction	1.2	48-70	90	11.5	3000
	5S-FE	Reduction	1.4	62-85	90	11.5	3000
	5VZ-FE	Reduction	1.4	64-85	90	11.5	3000
	5VZ-FE	Reduction	1.8	78-99	100	11.5	2500
1999	1MZ-FE	Reduction	1.4	64-84	90	11.5	3000
	1ZZ-FE	Reduction	1.2	50-74	90	11.5	3000
	1ZZ-FE	Reduction	1.4	64-84	90	11.5	3000
	2RZ-FE	Reduction	1.4	62-85	90	11.5	3000
	2RZ-FE	Reduction	2.0	78-99	100	11.5	2500
	2UZ-FE	Reduction	1.4	64-85	90	11.5	3000
	2UZ-FE	Reduction	2.0	77-99	100	11.5	2500
	3RZ-FE	Reduction	1.4	62-85	90	11.5	3000
	3RZ-FE	Reduction	2.0	78-99	100	11.5	2500
	3S-FE	Reduction	1.2	49-70	90	11.5	3000
	3S-FE	Reduction	1.4	63-84	90	11.5	3000
	5S-FE	Reduction	1.2	48-70	90	11.5	3000
	5S-FE	Reduction	1.4	62-85	90	11.5	3000
	5VZ-FE	Reduction	1.2	49-70	90	11.5	3000
	5VZ-FE	Reduction	1.4	64-85	90	11.5	3000
	5VZ-FE	Reduction	1.8	78-85	100	11.5	2500

Alternators

INDEX

PRECAUTIONS

AIR BAG SYSTEMS

Refer to "Air Bag System Precautions" in the front of this manual for system disarming & arming procedures.

BATTERY GROUND CABLE

Prior to service, disconnect battery ground cable and isolate as required.

AUDIO CODED ANTI-THEFT SYSTEM

Some models are equipped with an audio coded anti-theft system that will disable the radio when the battery cable is disconnected. The system can be identified by the "ANTI-THEFT SYSTEM" on the cassette tape lid. Obtain 3 digit customer code for input. Reset system after service as follows:

1. Obtain 3 digit audio anti-theft code.
2. Depress 1 (PROG) while depressing righthand side of TUNE SEEK button, - - will appear in tape operation display.
3. To enter the first digit, depress 1 (PROG) button repeatedly until the number of times depressed equals the first digit beginning with zero (depress the 1 button six times if the first digit if five).
4. To enter second digit, depress 2 (APS) button repeatedly until the number of times depressed equals the second digit beginning with zero.
5. To enter third digit, depress 3 (RPT) button repeatedly until the number of times depressed equals the third digit beginning with zero.
6. If - - - is displayed during code input, repeat procedure.
7. When code appears in display, depress and hold SCAN button until SEC appears.
8. When SEC disappears audio system should be operative.
9. If Err is displayed, repeat procedure. **Attempting to input code more than nine times may permanently disable audio system.**

DESCRIPTION

Refer to **Figs. 1 through 9,** for alternator exploded views.

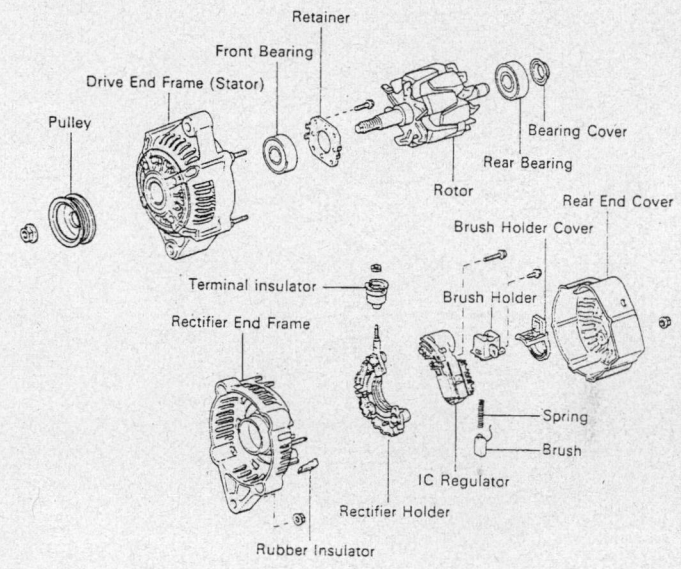

TY1129100014000X

Fig. 1 Exploded view of alternator. 1996 60 & 70 amp

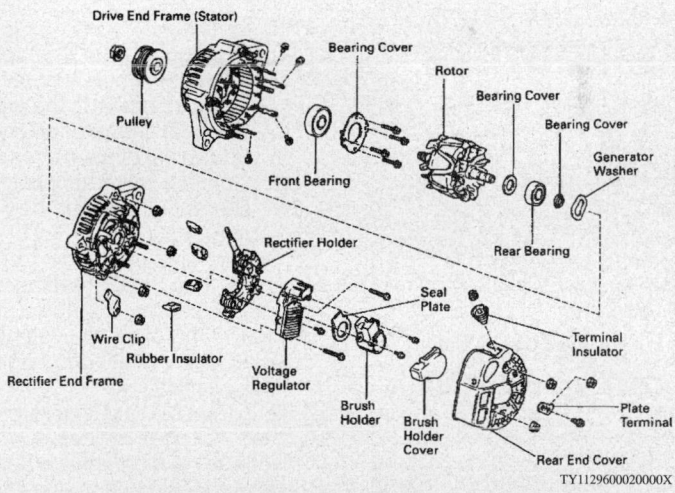

TY1129600020000X

Fig. 2 Exploded view of alternator. Avalon, Camry, Camry Solara, RAV4, Sienna & Supra w/70, 80, 90 & 100 amp

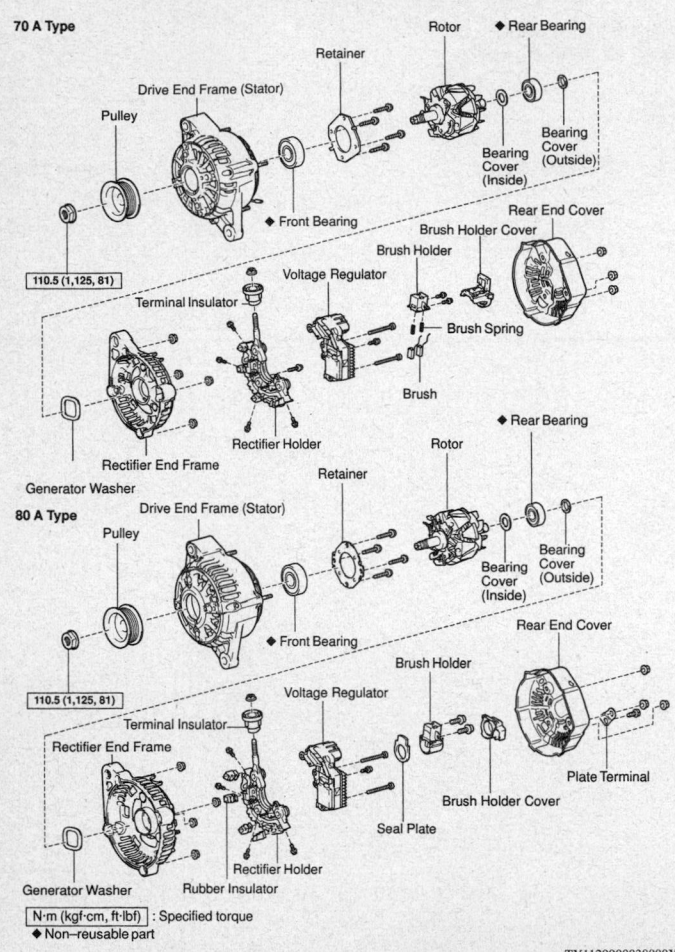

Fig. 3 Exploded view of alternator. Tundra w/70 & 80 amp & 5VZ-FE engine

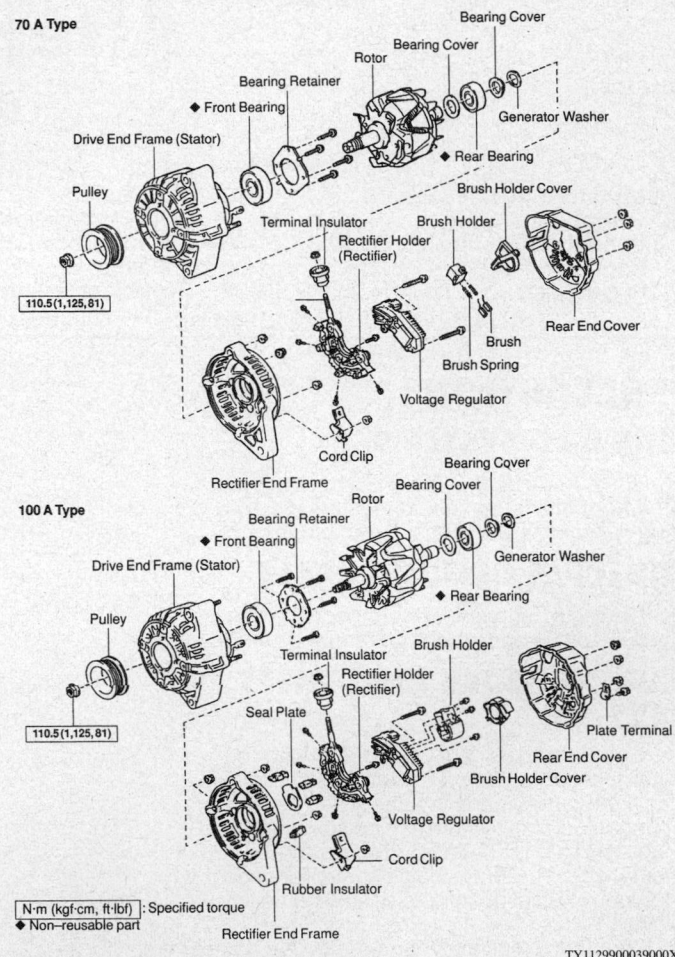

Fig. 4 Exploded view of alternator. Tundra w/70 & 100 amp & 2UZ-FE engine

TROUBLESHOOTING

WARNING LIGHT DOES NOT LIGHT w/IGNITION ON & ENGINE OFF

1. Blown fuse.
2. Lamp burned out.
3. Loose electrical connection.
4. Faulty main ignition relay.
5. Faulty IC regulator.

WARNING LIGHT DOES NOT GO OUT w/ENGINE RUNNING

1. Worn or loose drive belt.
2. Loose, corroded or worn battery cables.
3. Blown fuse.
4. Faulty alternator.
5. Faulty IC regulator.
6. Faulty wiring.

DIAGNOSIS & TESTING

SYSTEM TEST

1. Connect ammeter and voltmeter as follows:

a. Disconnect wire from terminal B of alternator, then connect ammeter negative probe to the wire.
b. Connect ammeter positive probe to B terminal of alternator.
c. Connect voltmeter positive probe to B terminal and the negative probe to ground.

2. Start engine and allow to run at 2000 RPM, then check reading of ammeter and voltmeter. Ammeter should read less than 10 amps. Voltmeter should read to specifications under "Alternator Specifications."

3. If voltage reading is greater than specified voltage, replace IC regulator. If voltage reading is less than specified, check IC regulator and alternator as follows:

a. With engine running and F terminal grounded, check voltage reading at B terminal.
b. If voltage is greater than specified, replace IC regulator. If voltage reading is less than specified, check alternator.

4. With engine running at 2000 RPM, turn on high beam headlights and place heater in HI position.

5. Check ammeter reading. If reading is less than 30 amps, repair alternator.

REGULATOR TEST

1. Connect voltmeter and fast charger to battery.
2. Turn ignition switch On and slowly increase charge rate. Indicator lamp in vehicle will begin to dim when voltage setting is reached.
3. Observe voltmeter, light should dim at 13.5–16.9 volts.
4. If no voltage is present, replace voltage regulator.

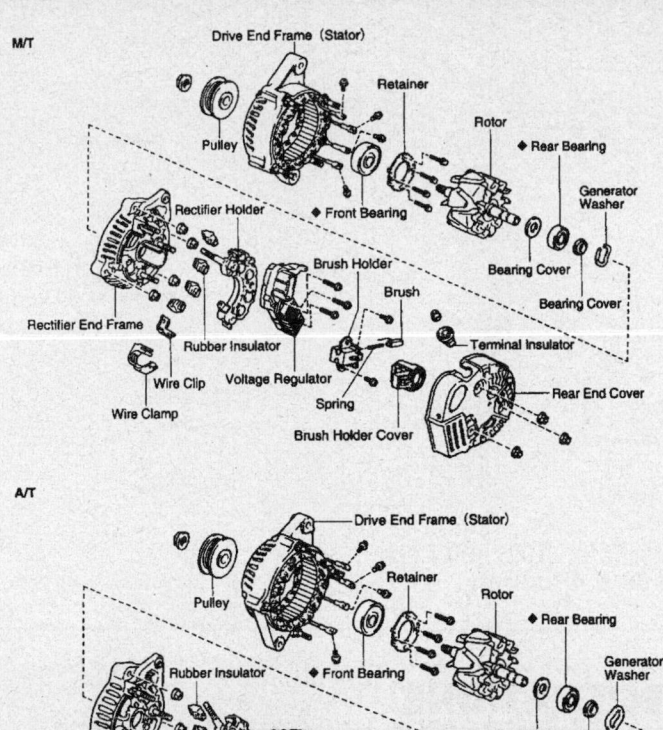

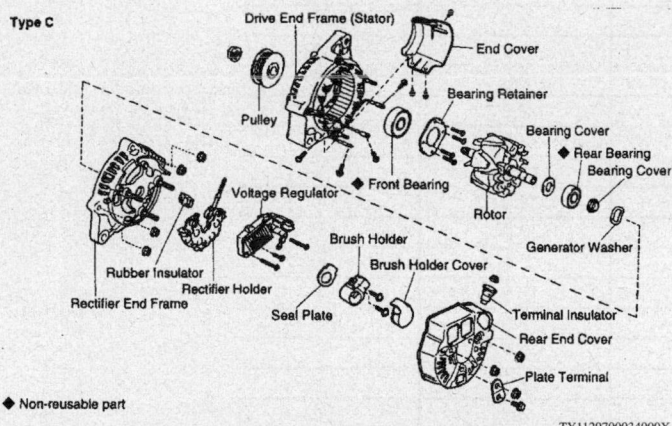

Fig. 5   Exploded view of alternator. 1997–99 Celica & Corolla

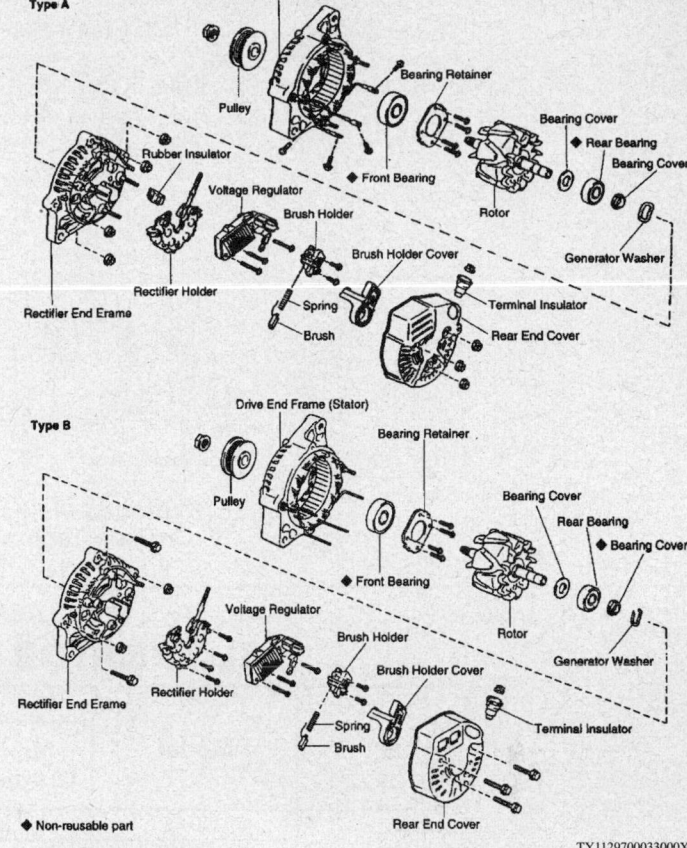

Fig. 6   Exploded view of alternator (Type A & B). 1997–98 Paseo & Tercel

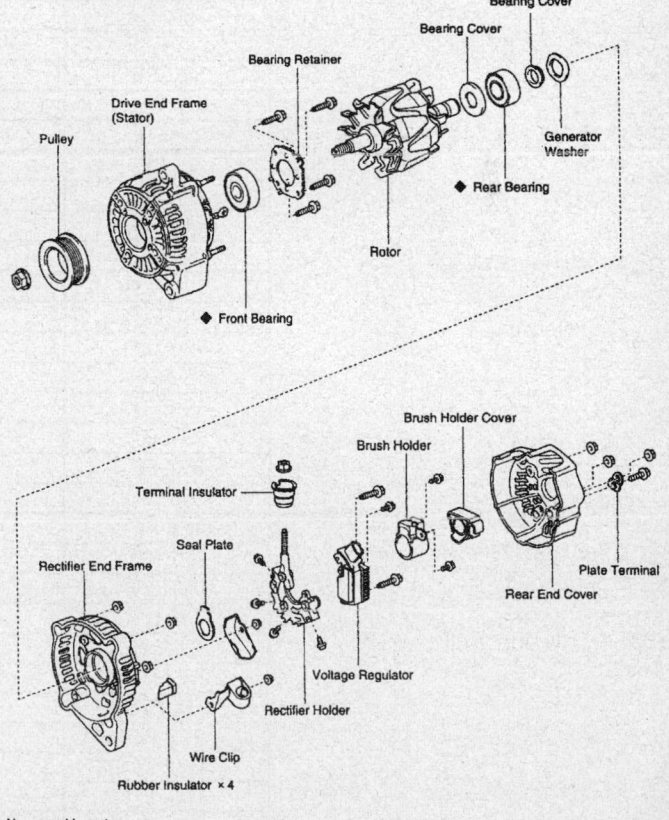

Fig. 7   Exploded view of alternator (Type C). 1997–98 Paseo & Tercel

Fig. 8   Exploded view of alternator. 1997 Previa

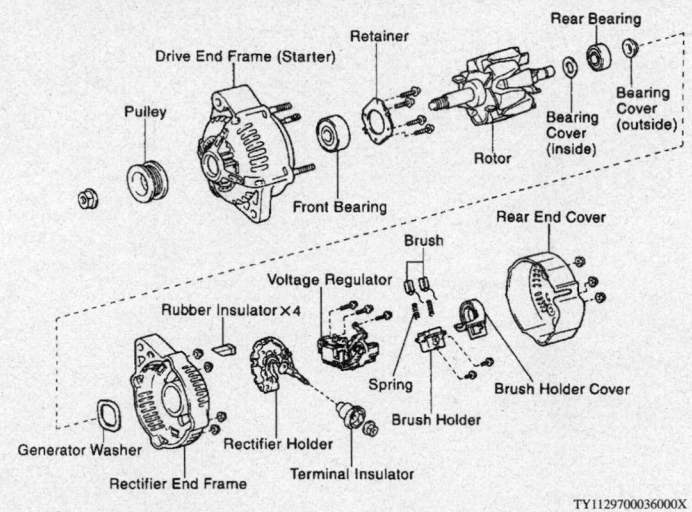

Fig. 9   Exploded view of alternator. 1997–99 Land Cruiser, Tacoma, T100 & 4Runner

ALTERNATOR SPECIFICATIONS

Year	Model	Alternator		Voltage Regulator Voltage
		Maximum Output Amps	Rotor Coil Resistance Ohms	
1996	1FZ-FE	80	2.9	②
	1MZ-FE	80	2.9	②
	2JZ-GE	80	2.9	④
	2JZ-GTE	80	2.9	④
	2RZ-FE	60	2.9	②
	2TZ-FZE	70	2.9	③
	3RZ-FE	60	2.9	②
	3S-GTE	70	2.9	③
	3S-GTE	80	2.9	③
	3S-FE	80	2.9	②
	4A-FE⑦	70	2.9	③
	4A-FE⑤	80	2.9	③
	5E-FE	70	2.9	③
	5S-FE⑤	70	2.9	③
	5S-FE⑥	70	2.9	③
	5S-FE⑧	70	2.9	②
	5S-FE⑤	80	2.9	③
	5S-FE⑥	80	2.9	③
	5S-FE⑥	90	2.9	③
	5VZ-FE	60	2.9	③
	7A-FE⑥	70	2.9	②
1997	1FZ-FE	80	2.7-3.1	13.5-15.1
	1MZ-FE	80	2.1-2.5	13.5-15.1
	1MZ-FE⑫	80	2.2-2.4	13.2-15.8
	2JZ-GE	80	2.7-3.1	13.2-14.8
	2JZ-GTE	90	2.7-3.1	13.2-14.8
	2JZ-GTE	100	2.7-3.1	13.2-14.8
	2TZ-FZE	70	2.7-3.1	13.5-15.1
	2RZ-FE	70	2.1-2.5	13.2-14.8
	3RZ-FE⑬	60	2.1-2.5	13.2-14.8
	3RZ-FE⑥	70	2.1-2.5	13.2-14.8
	3S-FE	80	2.7-3.1	13.5-15.1
	4A-FE	70	2.7-3.1	13.5-15.1

Continued

ALTERNATOR SPECIFICATIONS—Continued

Year	Model	Alternator		Voltage Regulator Voltage
		Maximum Output Amps	Rotor Coil Resistance Ohms	
1997	5E-FE	60	2.1-2.5	13.5-15.1
	5E-FE	70	2.7-3.1	13.5-15.1
	5S-FE	70	2.7-3.1	13.5-15.1
	5S-FE	80	2.7-3.1	13.5-15.1
	5VZ-FE⑬	60	2.1-2.5	13.2-14.8
	5VZ-FE⑥	70	2.1-2.5	13.2-14.8
	7A-FE	70	2.7-3.1	13.5-15.1
1998	1MZ-FE⑧	80	2.1-2.5	13.5-15.1
	1MZ-FE⑫	80	2.1-2.5	13.2-14.8
	1MZ-FE⑮	100	2.1-2.5	13.2-14.8
	1ZZ-FE	80	2.7-3.1	13.5-15.1
	2JZ-GE	80	2.7-3.1	13.2-14.8
	2JZ-GTE⑩	90	2.7-3.1	13.2-14.8
	2JZ-GTE⑨	100	2.7-3.1	13.2-14.8
	2RZ-FE	70	2.1-2.5	13.2-14.8
	2UZ-FE	80	2.1-2.5	13.2-14.8
	2UZ-FE	100	2.1-2.5	13.2-14.8
	3RZ-FE⑬	60	2.1-2.5	13.2-14.8
	3RZ-FE⑥	70	2.1-2.5	13.2-14.8
	3S-FE	80	2.7-3.1	②
	5E-FE	60	⑪	⑪
	5E-FE	70	⑪	13.5-15.1
	5S-FE	70	2.7-3.1	13.5-15.1
	5S-FE	80	2.7-3.1	13.5-15.1
	5VZ-FE⑬	60	2.1-2.5	13.2-14.8
	5VZ-FE⑥	70	2.1-2.5	13.2-14.8
1999	1MZ-FE⑧⑭	80	2.1-2.5	13.5-15.1
	1MZ-FE⑫	80	2.1-2.5	13.2-14.8
	1MZ-FE⑮	100	2.1-2.5	13.2-14.8
	1ZZ-FE	80	2.7-3.1	13.5-15.1
	2RZ-FE	70	2.1-2.5	13.2-14.8
	2UZ-FE	70	2.1-2.5	13.2-14.8
	2UZ-FE	100	2.1-2.5	13.2-14.8
	3RZ-FE⑬	60	2.1-2.5	13.2-14.8
	3RZ-FE⑥	70	2.1-2.5	13.2-14.8
	3S-FE	80	2.7-3.1	①
	5S-FE	70	2.7-3.1	13.5-15.1
	5S-FE	80	2.7-3.1	13.5-15.1
	5VZ-FE	70	2.1-2.5	④
	5VZ-FE	80	2.1-2.5	④

① — 14–15 volts at 77°F; 13.5–14.3 volts at 239°F.
② — 14–15 volts at 77°F, 13.5–14.3 volts at 239°F.
③ — 13.9–15.1 volts at 77°F, 13.5–14.3 volts at 239°F.
④ — 13.6–14.8 volts at 77°F, 13.2–14.0 volts at 239°F.
⑤ — Celica.
⑥ — Tacoma or 4Runner.
⑦ — Corolla.
⑧ — Camry.
⑨ — Manual Transmission.
⑩ — Automatic Transmission.
⑪ — Type A, 2.1–2.5 ohms; Types B and C, 2.7–3.1 ohms.
⑫ — Avalon.
⑬ — T100 or 4Runner.
⑭ — Camry Solara.
⑮ — Sienna.

Speed Control Systems

INDEX

PRECAUTIONS

AIR BAG SYSTEMS

Refer to "Air Bag System Precautions" in the front of this manual for system disarming & arming procedures.

BATTERY GROUND CABLE

Prior to service, disconnect battery ground cable and isolate as required.

AUDIO CODED ANTI-THEFT SYSTEM

Some models are equipped with an audio coded anti-theft system that will disable the radio when the battery cable is disconnected. The system can be identified by the "ANTI-THEFT SYSTEM" on the cassette tape lid. Obtain 3 digit customer code for input. Reset system after service as follows:

1. Obtain 3 digit audio anti-theft code.
2. Depress 1 (PROG) while depressing righthand side of TUNE SEEK button, - - - will appear in tape operation display.
3. To enter the first digit, depress 1 (PROG) button repeatedly until the number of times depressed equals the first digit beginning with zero (depress the 1 button six times if the first digit if five).
4. To enter second digit, depress 2 (APS) button repeatedly until the number of times depressed equals the second digit beginning with zero.
5. To enter third digit, depress 3 (RPT) button repeatedly until the number of times depressed equals the third digit beginning with zero.

6. If - - - is displayed during code input, repeat procedure.
7. When code appears in display, depress and hold SCAN button until SEC appears.
8. When SEC disappears audio system should be operative.
9. If Err is displayed, repeat procedure. **Attempting to input code more than nine times may permanently disable audio system.**

SYSTEM DIAGNOSIS & TESTING

When performing cruise control system diagnosis, proceed as follows:
1. Ensure cruise indicator lamp is operational, if equipped, then check and clear DTC's.
2. Confirm problem symptoms. If problem symptoms are confirmed, access diagnostic trouble codes as outlined under "Accessing Diagnostic Trouble Codes." If problem symptoms are not confirmed, refer to "Symptom Simulation" under "Component Diagnosis & Testing."
3. If normal DTC's are output, **Fig. 1** refer to "Problem Symptoms Table" under "Diagnostic Tests."

Accessing Diagnostic Trouble Codes

If a fault occurs in the speed control system during cruise control driving, the ECU actuates "AUTO CANCEL" of the cruise control and turns the "CRUISE MAIN" indicator lamp on and off to inform the driver of a fault. At the same time, fault is stored in memory as a DTC.

Before checking for DTC's, proceed as follows:
1. Turn ignition switch on.
2. Ensure "CRUISE MAIN" indicator light comes on when main cruise control switch is turned on. Ensure lamp goes off when switch is turned off.
3. If indicator operation is not as specified, inspect indicator circuit.

AVALON, CAMRY & CAMRY SOLARA

1. Turn ignition switch on.
2. Using jumper wire tool No. 09843–18020 or equivalent, connect terminals T_C and E_1 of DLC 2, **Fig. 2.**
3. Read DTC on "CRUISE MAIN" indicator light.
4. If DTC is not output, inspect diagnosis circuit.
5. If DTC is output, refer to DTC interpretation and "Diagnostic Chart Index" for diagnostic tests.

PASEO, PREVIA & 1996–97 RAV4

1. Turn ignition switch on.
2. Using jumper wire tool No. 09843–18020 or equivalent, connect terminals T_C and E_1 of DLC1, **Fig. 3.**
3. Read DTC output on "CRUISE MAIN" indicator lamp.
4. If DTC is not output, inspect diagnosis circuit.
5. If DTC is output refer to **Figs. 4**

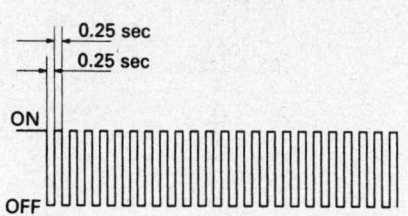

Fig. 1 Normal DTC output code

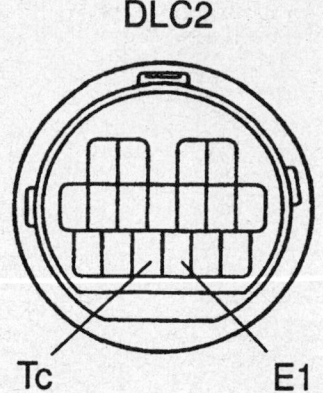

Fig. 2 DLC 2. Avalon, Camry, Camry Solara, 1996 Supra

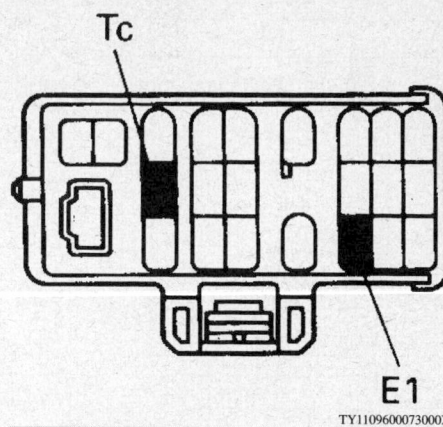

Fig. 3 DLC1 terminal location. Celica, Paseo, Previa & 1996–97 RAV4

through **9** for DTC interpretation and "Diagnostic Chart Index" for diagnostic tests.

COROLLA, SIENNA, TACOMA, T100, 4RUNNER & 1996–97 LAND CRUISER & 1998–99 RAV4

1. Using jumper wire tool No. 09843–18020 or equivalent, connect terminals T_C and E_1 of DLC1, **Figs. 10 and 11.**
2. Read DTC on cruise main indicator light.
3. If DTC is not output, inspect diagnosis circuit.
4. If DTC is output, refer to **Figs. 44 and 12 through 24** for DTC interpretation and "Diagnostic Chart Index" for diagnostic tests.

1998–99 LAND CRUISER

1. Turn ignition switch on.
2. Using jumper wire tool No. 09843–18020 or equivalent, connect terminals T_C and E_1 of DLC3, **Fig. 25.**
3. Read DTC on "CRUISE MAIN" indicator lamp.
4. If DTC is not output, inspect diagnosis circuit.
5. If DTC is output, refer to **Fig. 26** for DTC interpretation and "Diagnostic Chart Index" for diagnostic tests.

SUPRA

Except 1998 w/2JZ-GE Engine

1. Turn ignition switch on.
2. **On 1996 models,** using jumper wire tool No. 09843–18020 or equivalent, connect terminals T_C and E_1 of DLC 2, **Fig. 2.**
3. **On 1997–98 models,** using jumper wire tool No. 09843–18020 or equivalent, connect terminals T_C and E_1 of DLC 1, **Fig. 11.**
4. **On all models,** read DTC on "CRUISE MAIN" indicator lamp.
5. If DTC is not output, inspect diagnosis circuit.
6. If DTC is output, refer to **Figs. 27 and 28** for DTC interpretation and "Diagnostic Chart Index" for diagnostic tests.

1998 w/2JZ-GE Engine

1. Turn ignition switch on.
2. Using jumper wire tool No. 09843–18020 or equivalent, connect terminals T_C and E_1 of DLC3, **Fig. 25.**
3. Read DTC on "CRUISE MAIN" indicator lamp.
4. If DTC is not output, inspect diagnosis circuit.
5. If DTC is output, refer to **Fig. 29** for DTC interpretation and "Diagnostic Chart Index" for diagnostic tests.

TUNDRA

1. Turn ignition switch to on position.
2. Using jumper wire tool No. 09843–

18020 or equivalent, connect terminals T_C and E_1 of DLC1, **Fig. 30.**
3. Read DTC output from "CRUISE MAIN" indicator lamp.
4. If DTC is not output, inspect diagnosis circuit.
5. If DTC is output, refer to **Figs. 31 and 32** for DTC interpretation and "Diagnostic Chart Index" for diagnostic tests.

Diagnostic Trouble Code Interpretation

Refer to **Figs. 33 and 35** for DTC interpretation

DTC No.	Detection Item	Trouble Area
11	• Actuator Motor Circuit	• Actuator motor • Harness or connector between cruise control ECU and actuator motor • Cruise control ECU
12	• Actuator Magnetic Clutch Circuit	• STOP Fuse • Stop light switch • Actuator magnetic clutch • Harness or connector between cruise control ECU and actuator magnetic clutch, actuator magnetic clutch and body ground • Cruise control ECU
13	• Actuator Position Sensor Circuit	• Actuator motor • Harness or connector between actuator position sensor and body ground. • Harness or connector between cruise control ECU and actuator. • Cruise control ECU
14	• Actuator Motor Circuit • Actuator Position Sensor Circuit	• Actuator motor • Harness or connector between actuator position sensor and body ground. • Harness or connector between cruise control ECU and actuator. • Cruise control ECU
*21	• Vehicle Speed Sensor Circuit	• Combination meter • Harness or connector between cruise control ECU and combination meter, combination meter and vehicle speed sensor • Vehicle speed sensor • Cruise control ECU
*23	• Actuator Control Cable • Vehicle Speed Sensor Circuit	• Actuator • Vehicle speed sensor • Harness or connector in OD and SPD circuit (Open or short intermittently) • Cruise control ECU
32	• Control Switch Circuit	• Cruise control switch • Harness or connector between cruise control ECU and cruise control switch, cruise control switch and body ground • Cruise control ECU
41	• Cruise Control ECU	• Cruise control ECU
42	• Source Voltage Drop	• Battery
43	• Cruise Control ECU	• Cruise control ECU

HINT:
*When the vehicle speed decreases on uphill roads, the speed can be set again and drive can be continued. (This is not a malfunction.)

Fig. 4 DTC interpretation. Celica

Indication code	Diagnosis
	Normal
11	Excessive current flowed to motor drive circuit.
12	• Excessive current flowed to magnetic clutch drive circuit. • Open circuit magnetic clutch circuit.
13	• Position sensor circuit abnormal. • Open circuit in motor.
21	Vehicle speed signal not sent for 140 msec. or longer.
23	Vehicle speed has decreased by 16 km/h (10 mph) or more from the set speed during cruising.
32	Short circuit in control switch circuit.
34	Control switch does not turn off before switching
41	ECU malfunction.

• If the set speed can be maintained when the speed control switch is again set at SET/COAST, there is no malfunction.

TY1109900354000X

Fig. 5 DTC interpretation. 1996 Previa

Code No.	CRUISE MAIN Indicator Light Blinking Pattern	Diagnosis
—	ON / OFF	Normal
11	ON / OFF	• Over current (short) in motor circuit.
12	ON / OFF	• Over current (short) in magnetic clutch circuit power. • Open in magnetic clutch circuit for 0.8 sec.
13	ON / OFF	• Open in potentiometer circuit. • Short in potentiometer circuit.
14	ON / OFF	• Mechanical trouble (Including open in motor circuit.)
15	ON / OFF	• Close side open trouble (Including motor disconnection.)
21	ON / OFF	• Open in vehicle speed sensor signal circuit.
23	ON / OFF	• Vehicle speed signal abnormally.
32	ON / OFF	• Earth short in cruise control switch circuit.
41	ON / OFF	• Continuous electric current in motor open side.
42	ON / OFF	• Mechanical trouble at low voltage.
43	ON / OFF	• Actuator power supply abnormally.

TY1109700090000X

Fig. 6 DTC interpretation. 1997 Previa

DTC No.	Detection Item	Trouble Area
—	• Normal	
11	• Actuator Motor Circuit	• Cruise control actuator motor • Harness or connector between actuator motor and ECU • ECU
12	• Actuator Magnetic Clutch Circuit	• Cruise control actuator magnetic clutch • Harness or connector between ECU and magnetic clutch, magnetic clutch and body ground • ECU • STOP Fuse
13	• Actuator Position Sensor Circuit	• Cruise control actuator position sensor • Harness or connector between actuator position sensor and ECU • ECU
14	• Actuator Motor Circuit • Actuator Position Sensor Circuit	• Cruise control actuator motor • Cruise control actuator position sensor • Harness or connector between actuator position sensor and body ground • Harness or connector between actuator motor and ECU • ECU
21, 23	• Vehicle Speed Sensor Circuit	• Vehicle speed sensor • Combination meter • Harness or connector between vehicle speed sensor and combination meter, combination meter and ECU • ECU
32	• Control Switch Circuit (Cruise Control Switch)	• Cruise control switch • Harness and connector between control switch and ECU • ECU
41	• Cruise Control ECU	• ECU
42	• Source Voltage Drop	• Battery

TY1109700092000X

Fig. 7 DTC interpretation. 1996-97 RAV4

DTC No.	Detection Item	Trouble Area
—	• Normal	
11	• Actuator Motor Circuit • Actuator Magnet Clutch Circuit	• Cruise control actuator motor • Harness or connector between actuator motor and ECU • ECU
12	• Actuator Magnetic Clutch Circuit	• Cruise control magnetic clutch. • Harness or connector between ECU and magnetic clutch, magnetic clutch and body ground • ECU
13	• Actuator Motor Circuit • Actuator Position Sensor Circuit	• Cruise control actuator motor. • Cruise control actuator position sensor. • Harness or connector between actuator position sensor and body ground. • ECU
14	• Actuator Motor Circuit • Actuator Magnet Clutch Circuit • Actuator Position Sensor Circuit	• Harness or connector between actuator motor and ECU. • ECU
21	• Vehicle Speed Sensor Circuit	• Vehicle Speed Sensor • Combination meter • Harness or connector between speed sensor and combination meter, combination meter and ECU • ECU
*23	• Actuator Control Cable • Vehicle Speed Sensor Circuit • Actuator Motor Circuit	• STOP Fuse • Actuator • Vehicle Speed Sensor • Harness or connector in OD and SPD circuit (Open or short intermittently) • ECU
32	• Control Switch Circuit	• Cruise control switch • Harness or connector between control switch and ECU • ECU

When 41, 42 code is indicated, replace the cruise control ECU.

HINT:
1. When 2 or more codes are indicated, the lowest numbered code will be displayed first.
2. If the instruction "Proceed to next circuit inspection shown on matrix chart" is given in the flow chart for each circuit, proceed to the circuit with the next highest number in the table to continue the check.
3. If the trouble still reappears even though there are no abnormalities in any of the other circuits, then check or replace the Cruise control ECU as the last step.
(*) When the vehicle speed is reduced on uphill roads, the speed can be set again and driving continued. (This is not a malfunction.)

TY1109900190000X

Fig. 8 DTC interpretation. 1996 Paseo

Road Test

1. Push main switch to on position.
2. Drive vehicle at 25 mph or higher.
3. Press control switch to "SET/COAST" position.
4. After releasing switch, ensure vehicle cruises at desired speed.
5. Ensure vehicle speed increases as "RES/ACC" switch is pressed. Vehicle speed should increase by 1 mph when "RES/ACC" switch is momentarily pressed.
6. Press "SET/COAST" switch and ensure vehicle speed decreases. Vehicle speed should decrease by 1 mph when "SET/COAST" switch is momentarily pressed.
7. Ensure cruise control is canceled when one of the following conditions is met:
   a. Brake pedal depressed.
   b. **On models equipped with automatic transmission,** shift to except "D" position.
   c. **On models equipped with manual transmission,** depress clutch pedal.
   d. **On all models,** push main switch off.
   e. Place cruise control switch to "CANCEL" position.

DTC No.	Detection Item	Trouble Area
11, 15	• Short in actuator motor circuit. • Open in actuator motor circuit.	• Cruise control actuator. • Harness or connector between actuator and cruise control ECU. • Cruise control ECU.
12	• Short in magnetic clutch circuit. • Open (0.8 sec.) in magnetic clutch circuit.	• Cruise control actuator magnetic clutch. • Harness or connector between ECU and magnetic clutch, magnetic clutch and body ground. • Cruise control ECU.
14	• Actuator mechanical malfunction.	• Cruise control actuator. • Harness or connector between actuator and cruise control ECU. • Cruise control ECU.
21	• Speed signal is not input to the cruise control ECU while cruise control is set.	• Vehicle speed sensor. • Combination meter. • Harness or connector between vehicle speed sensor and combination meter, combination meter. • Cruise control ECU.
23	• Actual vehicle speed has dropped either by 16 km/h (10 mph) or more below the set speed, or by 20 % or more of the set speed. • Vehicle speed sensor pulse is abnormal. (When speed signal is not input to the ECU below 0.2 sec., code will be displayed.)	• Vehicle speed sensor. • Harness or connector in SPD circuit. • Cruise control ECU.
32	• Short in control switch circuit.	• Cruise control switch. • Harness or connector between control switch and cruise control ECU. • Cruise control ECU.
41	• Cruise control ECU.	• Cruise control ECU.
42	• Source voltage drop.	• Power sourse.
51	• Short in idle signal circuit.	• Throttle position sensor. • Harness or connector between cruise control ECU and throttle position sensor. • Cruise control ECU.

TY1109900206000X

Fig. 9   DTC interpretation. 1997 Paseo

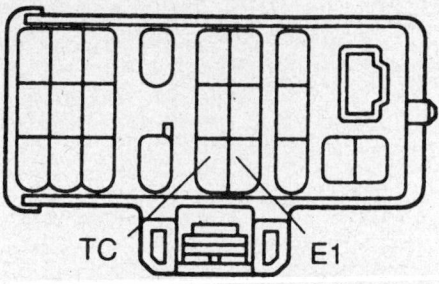
TY1109900148000X

Fig. 10   DLC1 terminal location. Sienna

DTC No.	Circuit Inspection	Trouble Area
11, 15	Actuator Motor Circuit	• Actuator motor • Harness or connector between cruise control ECU and actuator motor • Cruise control ECU
12	Actuator Magnetic Clutch Circuit	• STOP Fuse • Stop light switch • Actuator magnetic clutch • Harness or connector between cruise control ECU and actuator magnetic clutch, actuator magnetic clutch and body ground • Cruise control ECU
14	Actuator Mechanical Malfunction	• Actuator motor (actuator lock: motor, arm) • Cruise control ECU
21	Open in Vehicle Speed Sensor Circuit	• Combination meter • Harness or connector between cruise control ECU and combination meter, combination meter and vehicle speed sensor • Vehicle speed sensor • Cruise control ECU
23	Vehicle Speed Signal Abnormal	• Vehicle speed sensor • Cruise control ECU
41	Cruise Control ECU	• Cruise control ECU
42	Source Voltage Drop	• Power source
43	Actuator Source Voltage Abnormal	• Cruise control ECU • Harness or connector between control ECU and actuator

TY1109900154000X

Fig. 12   DTC interpretation. 1998–99 RAV4

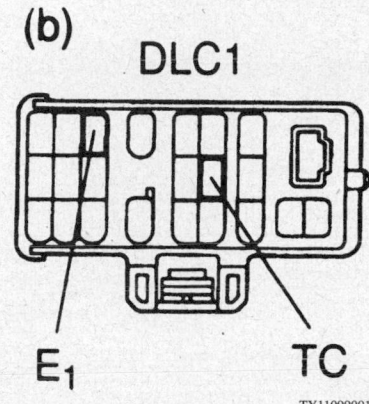
TY1109900150000X

Fig. 11   DLC1 terminal location. Corolla, Sienna (clearing codes), 1997 Supra w/2JZ–GE & 2JZ–GTE & 1998 w/2JZ-GTE engine, Tacoma, T100, 4Runner, 1996–97 Land Cruiser & 1998–99 RAV4

LAND CRUISER, PASEO, SUPRA EXCEPT 1998 w/2JZ-GE ENGINE, TACOMA, T100 & 4RUNNER

1. **For checks 1–2, Fig. 37,** ensure ignition switch is turned on.
2. **For check 3,** turn ignition switch on and shift to "D" position.
3. **For check 4,** raise and support vehicle, start engine and shift to "D" position.
4. **For checks 1–4,** press control switch to "SET/COAST" or "RES/ACC" position and hold button down or up.
5. Push main switch on.
6. Ensure "CRUISE MAIN" indicator lamp blinks 2 or 3 times repeatedly after 3 seconds.
7. Turn "SET/COAST" or "RES/ACC" switch off.
8. Operate each switch as listed in **Fig. 37.**
9. Read blinking pattern of "CRUISE MAIN" indicator lamp.
10. After performing inspection, turn main switch off. When 2 or more signals are input to ECU, only lowest numbered

8. After cruise control has been canceled, press "RESUME" button and ensure vehicle returns to previous vehicle speed. When testing "RESUME" function, ensure vehicle speed is greater than 25 mph.
9. If cruise control switch operation is not as specified, refer to "Input Signal Check."

Input Signal Check

AVALON, CAMRY SOLARA, CELICA, COROLLA, RAV4, SIENNA & 1997–99 CAMRY

1. **For checks 1–3, Figs. 36 and 37** ensure ignition switch is turned on.
2. **For check 4, Figs. 36 and 37** proceed as follows:
   a. Raise and support vehicle.
   b. Start engine, then shift to "D" position.
3. **For checks 1–4,** pull cruise control switch to "SET/COAST" or "RES/ACC" position and hold up or down.
4. Push main switch to on position.
5. Ensure "CRUISE MAIN" indicator lamp blinks 2 or 3 times repeatedly after 3 seconds.
6. Turn "SET/COAST" or "RES/ACC" switch off.
7. Operate each switch as listed in **Figs. 36 and 37.**
8. Read blinking pattern of "CRUISE MAIN" indicator light.
9. After performing inspection, turn main cruise control switch off. When 2 or more signals are input to the ECU, lowest numbered code will be displayed first.

Code No.	CRUISE MAIN Indicator Light Blinking Pattern	Diagnosis
—	ON / OFF (normal pattern)	Normal
11	ON / OFF	• Duty ratio of 100 % output to motor acceleration side. • Overcurrent (short) in motor circuit.
12	ON / OFF	• Overcurrent (short) in magnet clutch circuit. • Open in magnet clutch circuit for 0.8 sec.
13	ON / OFF	• Open in actuator motor circuit. • Position sensor detects abnormal voltage. • Position sensor signal value does not change when the motor operates.
21	ON / OFF	• Speed signal is not input to the ECU while cruise control is set.
*23	ON / OFF	• Actual vehicle speed has dropped by 16 km/h (10 mph) or more below the set speed.
32	ON / OFF	• Short in control switch circuit.
34	ON / OFF	• Voltage abnormality in control switch.
41	ON / OFF	• When 41 code is indicated, replace the cruise control ECU.

HINT: When 2 or more codes are indicated, the lowest numbered code will be displayed first.
(*) When the vehicle speed is reduced on uphill roads, the speed can be set again and driving continued. (This is not a malfunction.)

TY1109900542000X

Fig. 13 DTC interpretation. 1996 Land Cruiser

Code No.	CRUISE MAIN Indicator Light Blinking Pattern	Diagnosis
—	ON / OFF (normal pattern)	Normal
11	ON / OFF	• Over current (short) in motor circuit.
12	ON / OFF	• Over current (short) in magnetic clutch circuit power. • Open in magnetic clutch circuit for 0.8 sec.
13	ON / OFF	• Open in potentiometer circuit. • Short in potentiometer circuit.
14	ON / OFF	• Mechanical trouble (Including open in motor circuit.)
15	ON / OFF	• Close side open trouble (Including motor disconnection.)
21	ON / OFF	• Open in vehicle speed sensor signal circuit.
*23	ON / OFF	• Vehicle speed signal abnormal.
32	ON / OFF	• Earth short in cruise control switch circuit.
41	ON / OFF	• Continuous electric current in motor open side.
42	ON / OFF	• Mechanical trouble at low voltage.
51	ON / OFF	• Short in idle signal circuit.

TY1109700087000X

Fig. 14 DTC interpretation. 1997 Land Cruiser

DTC No.	Detection Item	Trouble Area
11, 15*1	Actuator Motor Circuit	• Cruise control actuator motor • Harness or connector between actuator motor and ECU • ECU
12	Actuator Magnetic Clutch Circuit	• Cruise control magnetic clutch • Harness or connector between ECU and magnetic clutch, magnetic clutch and body ground • ECU
13*2	Actuator Position Sensor Circuit	• Cruise control actuator motor • Cruise control actuator position sensor • Harness or connector between actuator position sensor and body ground • Harness or connector between actuator motor and ECU • ECU
14	Actuator Motor Circuit Actuator Position Sensor	• Cruise control actuator motor • Cruise control actuator position sensor • Harness or connector between actuator position sensor and body ground • Harness or connector between actuator motor and ECU • ECU
21	Vehicle Speed Sensor Circuit	• Vehicle speed sensor • ECM • Combination meter • Harness or connector between vehicle speed sensor and ECM, ECM and combination meter, combination meter and ECU • ECU
23	Actuator Control Cable Vehicle Speed Sensor Circuit	• Cruise control actuator motor • Cruise control actuator control cable • Vehicle speed sensor • Harness or connector (OD, SPD) • ECU
32	Control Switch Circuit (Cruise Control Switch)	• Cruise control switch • Harness or connector between control switch and ECU • ECU
41	Cruise Control ECU	• Cruise control ECU
42	Source voltage drop	• Power source
51*3	Idle switch circuit	• Throttle position sensor • Harness or connector between cruise control ECU and throttle position sensor • Cruise control ECU

*1, *3: Only 5VZ–FE engine
*2: Only 3RZ–FE engine

TY1109900572000A

Fig. 15 DTC interpretation. 1996–97 4Runner

DTC No.	Detection Item	Trouble Area
11	Actuator Motor Circuit	• Cruise control actuator motor • Harness or connector between actuator motor and ECU • ECU
12	Actuator Magnetic Clutch Circuit	• Cruise control magnetic clutch • Harness or connector between ECU and magnetic clutch, magnetic clutch and body ground • ECU
14	Actuator Mechanical Malfunction	• Cruise control actuator motor • Harness or connector between actuator motor and ECU • ECU
15	Actuator Motor Circuit	• Cruise control actuator motor • Harness or connector between actuator motor and ECU • ECU
21	Vehicle Speed Sensor Circuit	• Vehicle speed sensor • ECM • Combination meter • Harness or connector between vehicle speed sensor and ECM, ECM and combination meter, combination meter and ECU • ECU
23	Vehicle Speed Sensor Circuit	• Vehicle speed sensor • Harness or connector (SPD) • ECU
32	Control Switch Circuit (Cruise Control Switch)	• Cruise control switch • Harness or connector between control switch and ECU • ECU
41	Cruise Control ECU	• Cruise control ECU
42	Source voltage drop	• Power source
51	Idle Signal Circuit	• Throttle position sensor • Harness or connector between ECM and throttle position sensor • Harness or connector between ECU and throttle position sensor, throttle position sensor and body ground • ECM • ECU

TY1109900593000X

Fig. 16 DTC interpretation. 1998–99 4Runner w/Denso cruise control

code is displayed.

PREVIA

1. For checks 1–2, **Fig. 38,** ensure ignition switch is on.
2. For checks 3–5, proceed as follows:
   a. Raise and support vehicle.
   b. Start engine and shift to "D" position.
3. Press cruise control switch to "SET/COAST" or "RES/ACC" position and hold it down.
4. Place main switch in on position.
5. Ensure "CRUISE MAIN" indicator lamp blinks 2 or 3 times repeatedly after 3 seconds.
6. Turn "SET/COAST" or "RES/ACC" switch off.
7. Operate each switch as shown in **Fig. 38.**
8. Read blinking pattern of "CRUISE MAIN" indicator lamp.
9. After input signal check, turn ignition switch off. When 2 or more signals are

DTC No.	Detection Item	Trouble Area
12	Actuator Circuit	• Connector of cruise control actuator and ECU • STOP fuse and stop light switch • Cruise control actuator and ECU
14	Actuator Mechanical Malfunction	• Connector of cruise control actuator and ECU • Cruise control actuator and ECU
21	Open in Vehicle Speed Sensor Circuit	• Harness or connector between vehicle speed sensor and combination meter, combination meter and cruise control actuator and ECU • Speed sensor (in combination meter) • Combination meter • Cruise control actuator and ECU
23	Vehicle Speed Signal abnormal	• Speed sensor (in combination meter) • Combination meter cable • Cruise control actuator and ECU
32	Control Switch Circuit	• Harness or connector between control switch and cruise control actuator and ECU • Cruise control switch • Cruise control actuator and ECU

TY1109900612000X

Fig. 17 DTC interpretation. 1998–99 4Runner w/Ford cruise control

DTC No. (See page)	Detection Item	Trouble Area
11	• Short in Actuator Motor Circuit	• Wire harness or connector between actuator and cruise control ECU • Cruise control actuator • Cruise control ECU
12	• Short in Magnetic Clutch Circuit • Open (0.8 sec.) in Magnetic Clutch	• Wire harness or connector between cruise control ECU and magnetic clutch, magnetic clutch and body ground • STOP fuse and Stop light switch • Cruise control actuator magnetic clutch • Cruise control ECU
13	• Position Sensor Detects Abnormal Voltage	• Wire harness or connector between actuator position sensor and body ground • Wire harness or connector between actuator motor and cruise control ECU • Cruise control actuator • Cruise control actuator position sensor • Cruise control ECU
14	• Open in Actuator Motor Circuit • Position Sensor Signal signal value does not change when the motor operates	• Cruise control actuator • Cruise control actuator position sensor • Wire harness or connector between actuator position sensor and body ground • Wire harness or connector between actuator and cruise control ECU • Cruise control ECU
21	• Speed signal is not input to the cruise control ECU while cruise control is set	• Vehicle speed sensor • ECM • Combination meter • Wire harness or connector between vehicle speed sensor and ECM, ECM and combination meter, combination meter and cruise control ECU • Cruise control ECU
23	• Vehicle speed sensor pulse is abnormal	• Vehicle speed sensor • Cruise control ECU
32	• Short in control switch circuit	• Wire harness or connector between control switch and cruise control ECU • Cruise control switch • Cruise control ECU
41	• Cruise Control ECU	• Cruise control ECU
42	• Source voltage drop	• Power source

TY1109900640000X

Fig. 19 DTC interpretation. 1997 Tacoma w/Denso cruise control

DTC No.	Detection Item	Trouble Area
—	• Normal	
11	• Actuator Motor Circuit	• Cruise control actuator motor • Harness or connector between actuator motor and Cruise control ECU • Cruise Control ECU
12	• Actuator Magnetic Clutch Circuit	• Cruise control magnetic clutch • Harness or connector between Cruise Control ECU and magnetic clutch and body ground • Cruise Control ECU
13	• Actuator Position Sensor Circuit • Open in STOP Fuse	• Cruise control actuator motor • Cruise control actuator position sensor • Harness or connector between actuator position sensor and body ground • Harness or connector between actuator motor and Cruise Control ECU • Cruise Control ECU
14	• Actuator Motor Circuit • Actuator Position Sensor Circuit	
21	• Vehicle Speed Sensor	• Vehicle speed sensor • Combination meter • Harness or connector between vehicle speed sensor and combination meter, combination meter and Cruise Control ECU • Cruise Control ECU
*23	• Actuator Control Cable • Vehicle Speed Sensor Circuit	• Actuator • Vehicle speed sensor • Harness or connector in OD and SPD circuit (Open or short intermittently) • Cruise Control ECU
32, 34	• Control Switch Circuit (Cruise Control Switch)	• Cruise control switch • Harness or connector between control switch and Cruise Control ECU • Cruise Control ECU
41	• Cruise Control ECU	• Cruise Control ECU
42	• Source Voltage Drop	• Battery

HINT:
1. When 2 or more codes are indicated, the lowest numbered code will be displayed first.
2. If the inspection "Proceed to next circuit inspection shown on matrix chart" is given in the flow chart for each circuit, proceed to the circuit with the next highest number in the table to continue check.
3. If the trouble still reappears even though there are no abnormalities in any of the other circuits, then check or replace the cruise control ECU as the last step.
   (*): When the vehicle speed decreases on uphill roads, the speed can be set again and driving continued.
   (This is not a malfunction.)

TY1109900321000X

Fig. 18 DTC interpretation. 1996 Tacoma

DTC No.	Detection Item	Trouble Area
11	Actuator Motor Circuit	• Cruise control actuator motor • Harness or connector between actuator motor and ECU • ECU
12	Actuator Magnetic Clutch Circuit	• Cruise control magnetic clutch • Harness or connector between ECU and magnetic clutch, magnetic clutch and body ground • ECU
14	Actuator Motor Circuit	• Cruise control actuator motor • Harness or connector between actuator motor and ECU • ECU
15	Actuator Motor Circuit	• Cruise control actuator motor • Harness or connector between actuator motor and ECU • ECU
21	Vehicle Speed Sensor Circuit	• Vehicle speed sensor • ECM • Combination meter • Harness or connector between vehicle speed sensor and ECM, ECM and combination meter, combination meter and ECU • ECU
23	Vehicle Speed Sensor Circuit	• Vehicle speed sensor • Harness or connector (SPD) • ECU
32	Control Switch Circuit (Cruise Control Switch)	• Cruise control switch • Harness or connector between control switch and ECU • ECU
41	Cruise Control ECU	• Cruise control ECU
42	Source voltage drop	• Power source

TY1109900247000X

Fig. 20 DTC interpretation. 1998–99 Tacoma w/Denso cruise control

DTC No.	Detection Item	Trouble Area
12	Actuator Circuit	• Connector of cruise control actuator and ECU • STOP fuse and stop light switch • Cruise control actuator and ECU
14	Actuator Mechanical Malfunction	• Connector of cruise control actuator and ECU • Cruise control actuator and ECU
21	Open in Vehicle Speed Sensor Circuit	• Harness or connector between vehicle speed sensor and combination meter, combination meter and cruise control actuator and ECU • Speed sensor (in combination meter) • Combination meter • Cruise control actuator and ECU
23	Vehicle Speed Signal abnormal	• Speed sensor (in combination meter) • Combination meter cable • Cruise control actuator and ECU
32	Control Switch Circuit	• Harness or connector between control switch and cruise control actuator and ECU • Cruise control switch • Cruise control actuator and ECU

TY1109900267000X

Fig. 21   DTC interpretation. 1997–99 Tacoma w/Ford cruise control

Code No.	CRUISE MAIN Indicator Light Blinking Pattern	Diagnosis
–	ON / OFF	Normal
11	ON / OFF	• Duty ratio of 100% output to motor acceleration side. • Overcurrent (short) in motor circuit.
12	ON / OFF	• Overcurrent (short) in magnet clutch circuit. • Open in magnet clutch circuit.
13	ON / OFF	• Open in actuator motor circuit. • Position sensor detects abnormal voltage. • Position sensor signal value does not change when the motor operates.
21	ON / OFF	• Speed signal is not input to the Cruise Control ECU.
*23	ON / OFF	• Actual vehicle speed has dropped by 16 km/h (10 mph)or more below the set speed during crusing.
32	ON / OFF	• Short in control switch circuit.
34	ON / OFF	• Voltage abnormality in control switch circuit.
41	ON / OFF	• When 41 code is indicated, replace the cruise control ECU.

TY1109900511000X

Fig. 22   DTC interpretation. 1996 T100

DTC No.	Detection Item	Trouble Area
12	Actuator Circuit	• Connector of cruise control actuator with ECU • Stop fuse and stop light switch • Cruise control actuator with ECU
14	Actuator Motor Circuit Actuator Position Sensor	• Connector of cruise control actuator with ECU • Cruise control actuator with ECU
21	Vehicle Speed Sensor Circuit	• Harness or connector between vehicle speed sensor and combination meter, combination meter and cruise control actuator with ECU • Speed sensor (in combination meter) • Combination meter • Cruise control actuator with ECU
23	Vehicle Speed Sensor Circuit	• Speed sensor (in combination meter) • Combination meter cable • Cruise control actuator with ECU
32	Control Switch Circuit (Cruise Control Switch)	• Harness or connector between control switch and cruise control actuator with ECU • Cruise control switch • Cruise control actuator with ECU

TY1109900524000X

Fig. 23   DTC interpretation. 1997–98 T100

input to ECU, only lowers numbered code is displayed.

1998 SUPRA w/2JZ-GE ENGINE

Connect Toyota Hand Held Tester or equivalent to DLC 3 and monitor cruise control switch inputs as switch is actuated.

TUNDRA

5VZ-FE Engine

1. **For checks 1 and 2, Fig. 37,** ensure ignition switch is on.
2. **For check 3,** ensure ignition switch is on and transmission is in D position.
3. **For check 4,** proceed as follows:
   a. Raise and support vehicle.
   b. Start engine and shift transmission to D position.
4. **For checks 1–4,** press cruise control switch to "SET/COAST" or "RES/ACC" position and hold up or down 1 inch.
5. Push main switch on.
6. Ensure "CRUISE MAIN" indicator blinks 2 or 3 times repeatedly after 3 seconds.
7. Turn "SET/COAST" or "RES/ACC" off.
8. Operate each switch as listed in **Fig. 37.**
9. Read blinking pattern of "CRUISE MAIN" indicator lamp.
10. After performing check, turn main switch off. If 2 or more signals are input to cruise control ECU, lowest numbered code will be displayed first.

DTC No.	Detection Item	Trouble Area
–	• Normal.	
11	• Actuator Motor Circuit.	• Cruise control actuator motor. • Harness or connector between actuator motor and Cruise Control ECU. • Cruise Control ECU.
12	• Actuator Magnetic Clutch Circuit.	• Cruise control magnetic clutch. • Harness or connector between Cruise Control ECU and magnetic clutch, magnetic clutch and body ground. • Stop light switch. • Cruise Control ECU.
13	• Actuator Position Sensor Circuit.	• Cruise control actuator motor. • Cruise control actuator position sensor. • Harness or connector between actuator position sensor and body ground.
14	• Actuator Motor Circuit. • Actuator Position Sensor Circuit.	• Harness or connector between actuator motor and Cruise Control ECU. • Cruise Control ECU.
21	• Vehicle Speed Sensor Circuit.	• Vehicle Speed Sensor. • Combination meter. • Harness or connector between vehicle speed sensor and combination meter, combination meter and Cruise Control ECU. • Cruise Control ECU.
23	• Actuator Control Cable. • Vehicle Speed Sensor Circuit. • Actuator Motor Circuit.	• Actuator. • Actuator control cable. • Vehicle Speed Sensor. • Harness or connector in OD and SPD circuit. (Open or short intermittently) • Cruise Control ECU.
32, 34	• Control Switch Circuit. (Cruise Control Switch)	• Cruise control switch. • Harness or connector between control switch and Cruise Control ECU. • Cruise Control ECU.
41	• Cruise Control ECU.	• Cruise Control ECU.
42	• Source Voltage Drop.	• Battery.
43	• Actuator Motor Circuit. • Actuator Magnetic Clutch Circuit.	• Cruise control actuator motor. • Cruise control magnetic clutch. • Harness or connector cruise control ECU and magnetic clutch and body ground.

TY1109700083000X

Fig. 24   DTC interpretation. 1996–97 Corolla

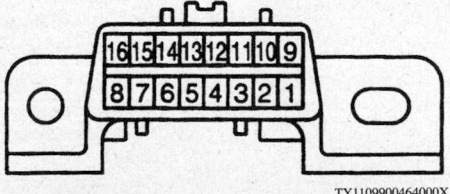

TY1109900464000X

Fig. 25   DLC 3 terminal location. 1998 Supra w/2JZ-GE engine & 1998–99 Land Cruiser

2UZ-FE Engine

Connect Toyota Hand-Held Tester or equivalent to DLC1 and inspect input signals from main cruise control switch.

1996 CAMRY

1. **For checks 1–2, Fig. 39,** ensure ignition switch is in on position.

2. **For checks 3–6,** ensure ignition switch is on and transaxle is in D position.
3. **For checks 1–6,** press control switch to "SET/COAST" or "RES/ACC" position and hold it up or down.
4. Push main switch to on position. Ensure "CRUISE MAIN" indicator light blinks 2 or 3 times repeatedly after 3 seconds.
5. Turn "SET/COAST" or "RES/ACC" switch off.
6. Operate each switch as outlined in **Fig. 39.**
7. Read blinking pattern of "CRUISE MAIN" indicator lamp.
8. After performing checks, turn main switch off. When 2 or more DTC's are input to ECU, only lowest numbered code is displayed.

DTC No.	Circuit Inspection	Trouble Area
P0500/ 21,23	Vehicle Speed Signal Abnormal	• Harness or connector between ECM and vehicle speed sensor • Vehicle speed sensor • ECM
P1520/ 52	Short in Stop Light Switch Circuit	• Stop light switch • Harness or connector between ECM and stop light switch circuit • ECM
P1565/ 32	Short in Cruise Control Switch Circuit	• Cruise control switch • Harness or connector between ECM and cruise control switch circuit • ECM
P1566/ 54	Input Signal Circuit	• ECM

TY1109900555000X

Fig. 26   DTC interpretation. 1998–99 Land Cruiser

DTC No.	Detection Item	Trouble Area
11, 15	• Actuator Motor Circuit	• Cruise control actuator motor • Harness or connector between actuator motor and ECU • ECU
12	• Actuator Magnetic Clutch Circuit	• Cruise control magnetic clutch • Harness or connector between ECU and magnetic clutch, magnetic clutch and body ground • ECU
14	• Actuator Motor Circuit	• Cruise control actuator motor • Harness or connector between actuator motor and ECU • ECU
21	• Vehicle Speed Sensor Circuit	• Vehicle speed sensor • ECM • Combination meter • Harness or connector between vehicle speed sensor and ECM, ECM and combination meter, combination meter and ECU • ECU
23	• Vehicle Speed Sensor Circuit	• Vehicle speed sensor • Harness or connector (SPD) • ECU
32	• Control Switch Circuit (Cruise Control Switch)	• Cruise control switch • Harness or connector between control switch and ECU • ECU
41	• Cruise Control ECU	• ECU
42	• Source voltage drop	• Power source
51	• Idle switch circuit	• Throttle position sensor • Harness or connector between cruise control ECU and throttle position sensor • ECU

HINT:
1. When 2 or more codes are indicated, the lowest numbered code will be displayed first.
2. If the inspection "Proceed to next circuit inspection shown on problem symptoms table" is given in the flow chart for each circuit, proceed to the circuit with the next highest number in the table to continue check.
3. If the trouble still reappears even though there are no abnormalities in any of the other circuit, then check or replace the cruise control ECU as the last step.
(*) When the vehicle speed decrease on uphill roads, the speed can be set again and driving continued. (This is not a malfunction.)

TY1109900439000X

Fig. 28   DTC interpretation. 1997 Supra & 1998 w/2JZ-GTE engine

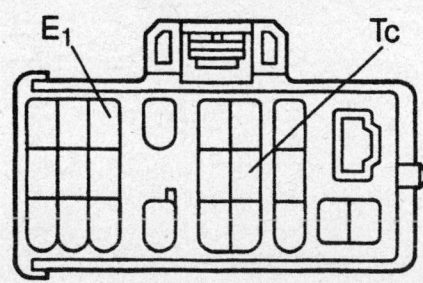

TY1109900113000X

Fig. 30   DLC1 terminal location. Camry Solara, Tundra & 1999 Camry

DTC No.	Ditection Item	Trouble Area
—	• Normal	—
11		
14	• Actuator Motor Circuit	• Cruise control actuator motor. • Harness of connector between actuator motor and ECU. • ECU
12	• Actuator Magnetic Clutch Circuit	• Cruise control magnet clutch. • Harness or connector between ECU and magnetic clutch magnetic clutch and body ground. • ECU
13		
14	• Actuator Position Sensor Circuit	• Cruise control actuator position sensor. • Harness or connector between actuator position sensor and ECU. • ECU
21	• Vehicle Speed Sensor Circuit	• Vehicle speed sensor • Combination meter. • Harness or connector between vehicle speed sensor and combination meter, combination meter and ECU. • ECU
23	• Vehicle Speed Sensor Circuit	• Vehicle speed sensor • Harness or connector in SPD circuit. (Open or short intermittently) • ECU
32		
34	• Control Switch Circuit. (Cruise control switch)	• Circuit control switch. • Harness or connector between control switch and ECU. • ECU
41	• Actuator Motor Circuit	• ECU

HINT:
1. If the instruction "Proceed to next circuit inspection shown on **problem symptoms chart** is given in the flow chart for each circuit, proceed to the circuit with the next highest number in the table to continue check.
2. If the trouble still reappears even though there are no abnormalities in any of the other circuits, then check or replace the cruise control ECU as the last step.

TY1109900465000X

Fig. 27   DTC interpretation. 1996 Supra

DTC No.	Circuit Inspection	Trouble Area
P0500/ 21, 23	Vehicle Speed Sensor Circuit	• Harness or connector between ECM and vehicle speed sensor • Vehicle speed sensor • ECM
P01520/ 52	Stop Light Switch Circuit	• Stop light switch • Harness or connector between ECM and stop light switch circuit • ECM
P01565/ 32	Control Switch Circuit (Cruise Control Switch)	• Cruise control switch • Harness or connector between ECM and cruise control switch, cruise control switch and body ground • ECM
P1566/ 54	Input Signal Circuit Abnormal	• ECM

TY1109900430000X

Fig. 29   DTC interpretation. 1998 Supra w/2JZ-GE engine

DTC No.	Detection Item	Trouble Area
12	Actuator Circuit	• Connector of cruise control actuator with ECU • Stop fuse and stop light switch • Cruise control actuator with ECU
14	Actuator Motor Circuit Actuator Position Sensor	• Connector of cruise control actuator with ECU • Cruise control actuator with ECU
21	Vehicle Speed Sensor Circuit	• Harness or connector between vehicle speed sensor and combination meter, combination meter and cruise control actuator with ECU • Speed sensor (in combination meter) • Combination meter • Cruise control actuator with ECU
23	Vehicle Speed Sensor Circuit	• Speed sensor (in combination meter) • Combination meter cable • Cruise control actuator with ECU
32	Control Switch Circuit (Cruise Control Switch)	• Harness or connector between control switch and cruise control actuator with ECU • Cruise control switch • Cruise control actuator with ECU

TY1109900100000X

Fig. 31   DTC interpretation. Tundra w/5VZ-FE engine

DTC No.	Circuit Inspection	Trouble Area
P0500/ 21,23	Vehicle Speed Signal Abnormal	• Harness or connector between ECM and vehicle speed sensor • Vehicle speed sensor • ECM
P1520/ 52	Short in Stop Light Switch Circuit	• Stop light switch • Harness or connector between ECM and stop light switch circuit • ECM
P1565/ 32	Short in Cruise Control Switch Circuit	• Cruise control switch • Harness or connector between ECM and cruise control switch circuit • ECM
P1566/ 54	Input Signal Circuit	• ECM

TY1109900115000X

Fig. 32 DTC interpretation. Tundra w/2UZ-FE engine

DTC No.	Detection Item	Trouble Area
—	• Normal	—
11	• Actuator Motor Circuit	• Cruise control actuator motor. • Harness or connector between actuator motor and ECU. • ECU
12	• Actuator Magnetic Clutch Circuit	• Cruise control magnetic clutch. • Harness or connector between ECU and magnetic clutch, magnetic clutch and body ground. • ECU
13	• Actuator Position Sensor Circuit	• Cruise control actuator position sensor. • Harness or connector between actuator position sensor and body ground. • ECU
14	• Actuator Motor Circuit	• Actuator motor circuit. • Actuator
21	• Vehicle Speed Sensor Circuit	• Vehicle Speed Sensor. • Combination meter. • Harness or connector between vehicle speed sensor and combination meter, combination meter and ECU. • ECU
*23	• Actuator Control Cable • Vehicle Speed Sensor Circuit • Actuator Motor Circuit	• Actuator • Actuator control cable. • Vehicle Speed Sensor. • Harness or connector in OD and SPD circuit. (Open or short intermittently) • ECU
32	• Control Switch Circuit. (cruise control switch)	• Cruise control switch. • Harness or connector between control switch and ECU. • ECU
34		
42	• Actuator Motor Circuit	• Battely positive voltage.

When 41, 43 code is indicated, replace the cruise control ECU.

HINT:
1. When 2 or more codes are indicated, the lowest numbered code will be displayed first.
2. If the instruction "Proceed to next circuit inspection shown on matrix chart" is given in the flow chart for each circuit, proceed to the circuit with the next highest number in the table to continue the check.
3. If the trouble still reappears even though there are no abnormalities in any of the other circuits, then check or replace the cruise control ECU as the last step.
(*) When the vehicle speed is reduced on uphill roads, the speed can be set again and driving continued. (This is not a malfunction.)

TY1109900132000X

Fig. 34 DTC interpretation. 1996 Camry

DTC No.	Detection Item	Trouble area
—	• Normal	—
11	• Actuator Motor Circuit • Actuator Magnet Clutch Circuit	• Cruise control actuator motor • Harness or connector between actuator motor and ECU • ECU
12	• Actuator Magnet Clutch Circuit	• Cruise control magnetic clutch. • Harness or connector between ECU and magnetic clutch, magnetic clutch and body ground. • ECU
13	• Actuator Motor Circuit • Actuator Position Sensor Circuit	• Cruise control actuator motor. • Cruise control actuator position sensor. • Harness or connector between actuator position sensor and body ground. • ECU
14	• Actuator Motor Circuit • Actuator Magnet Clutch Circuit • Actuator Position Sensor Circuit	• Harness or connector between actuator motor and ECU. • ECU
21	• Speed Sensor Circuit	• Vehicle speed sensor • Combination meter • Harness or connector between speed sensor and combination meter, combination meter and ECU. • ECU
*23	• Actuator Control Cable • Speed Sensor Circuit • Actuator Motor Circuit	• Actuator • Vehicle speed sensor • Harness or connector in OD and SPD circuit (Open or short intermittently) • ECU
32	• Control Switch Circuit	• Cruise control switch. • Harness or connector between control switch and ECU. • ECU
34		

When 41 code is indicated, replace the cruise control ECU.

HINT:
1. When 2 or more codes are indicated, the lowest numbered code will be displayed first.
2. If the instruction "Proceed to next circuit inspection shown on matrix chart" is given in the flow chart for each circuit, proceed to the circuit with the next highest number in the table to continue the check.
3. If the trouble still reappears even though there are no abnormalities in any of the other circuits, then check or replace the Cruise control ECU as the last step.
(*) When the vehicle speed is reduced on uphill roads, the speed can be set again and driving continued. (This is not a malfunction.)

TY9099900150000X

Fig. 33 DTC interpretation. 1996 Avalon

DTC No.	Circuit Inspection	Trouble Area
11, 15	• Actuator Motor Circuit	• Actuator motor • Harness or connector between cruise control ECU and actuator motor • Cruise control ECU
12	• Actuator Magnetic Clutch Circuit	• STOP Fuse • Stop light switch • Actuator magnetic clutch • Harness or connector between cruise control ECU and actuator magnetic clutch, actuator magnetic clutch and body ground • Cruise control ECU
14	• Actuator Mechanical Malfunction	• Actuator motor (actuator lock: motor, arm) • Cruise control ECU
21	• Open in Vehicle Speed Sensor Circuit	• Combination meter • Harness or connector between cruise control ECU and combination meter, combination meter and vehicle speed sensor • Vehicle speed sensor • Cruise control ECU
23	• Vehicle Speed Signal Abnormal	• Vehicle speed sensor • Cruise control ECU
32	• Control Switch Circuit	• Cruise control switch • Harness or connector between cruise control ECU and cruise control switch, cruise control switch and body ground • Cruise control ECU
41	• Cruise control ECU	• Cruise control ECU
42	• Source voltage drop	• Power source
51	• Idle Signal Circuit	• Throttle position sensor • Harness or connector between ECM and throttle position sensor • Harness or connector between cruise control ECU and ECM, throttle position sensor and body ground • Cruise control ECU

TY9099900130000X

Fig. 35 DTC interpretation. Camry Solara, Sienna, 1997–99 Avalon & Camry & 1998–99 Corolla

No.	Operation Method	CRUISE MAIN Indicator Light Blinking Pattern	Diagnosis
1	Turn SET/COAST switch ON	Light ON / OFF	SET/COAST switch circuit is normal
2	Turn RES/ACC switch ON	Light ON / OFF	RES/ACC switch circuit is normal
3	Turn CANCEL switch ON	ON / OFF Switch OFF / Switch ON	CANCEL switch circuit is normal
	Turn stop light switch ON Depress brake pedal		Stop light switch circuit is normal
	Turn PNP switch OFF (Shift to except D position)	Light ON / OFF Switch ON / Switch OFF	PNP switch circuit is normal
4	Drive at about 40 km/h (25 mph) or higher	Light ON / OFF	Vehicle Speed Sensor is normal
	Drive at about 40 km/h (25 mph) or below	Light ON / OFF	

TY9099900149000X

Fig. 36 Input signal check. Avalon

No.	Operation Method	CRUISE MAIN Indicator Light Blinking Pattern	Diagnosis
1	Turn SET/COAST switch ON	Light ON / OFF	SET/COAST switch circuit is normal
2	Turn RES/ACC switch ON	Light ON / OFF	RES/ACC switch circuit is normal
3	Turn CANCEL switch ON	ON Switch OFF / OFF Switch ON	CANCEL switch circuit is normal
	Turn stop light switch ON Depress brake pedal		Stop light switch circuit is normal
	Turn Park/Neutral Position switch OFF (Shift to except D position)	Light ON Switch ON / OFF Switch OFF	Park/Neutral Position switch circuit is normal
	Turn clutch switch OFF (Depress clutch pedal)		Clutch switch circuit is normal
4	Drive at about 40 km/h (25 mph) or higher	Light ON / OFF	Vehicle Speed Sensor is normal
	Drive at about 40 km/h (25 mph) or below	Light ON / OFF	

TY1109900099000X

Fig. 37 Input signal check. Camry Solara, Celica, Corolla, Paseo, RAV4, Sienna, Supra, Tacoma, Tundra w/5VZ-FE engine & 1997–99 Camry

No.	Conditions	Indication code	Diagnosis
1	Turn the control switch to SET/COAST position	ON / OFF BE1931	SET/COAST circuit is normal.
2	Turn the control switch to RES/ACC position.	ON / OFF BE1932	RES/ACC circuit is normal.
3	Each cancel switch is turned ON. • Control switch (to CANCEL) • Stop light switch • Parking brake switch • Park/Neutral Position switch (to N or P position)	ON / OFF BE1935	Each cancel switch is normal.
4	Drive approx. 40 km/h (25 mph) or below.	ON / OFF BE1938	Speed sensor circuit is normal.
5	Drive approx. 40 km/h (25 mph) or over. (w/o ECT)	ON / OFF BE1937	Speed sensor (in meter) circuit is normal.

HINT:
• Indication codes appear in order from No.1.
• If there in no indication code, perform troubleshooting and inspection.
• Indication is stopped when the MAIN switch is repushed.

TY1109900342000X

Fig. 38 Input signal check. Previa

No.	Operation Method	CRUISE MAIN Indicator Light Blinking Pattern	Diagnosis
1	Turn SET/COAST switch ON.	Light ON / OFF	SET/COAST switch circuit is normal.
2	Turn RES/ACC switch ON.	Light ON / OFF	RES/ACC switch circuit is normal.
3	Turn CANCEL switch ON.		CANCEL switch circuit is normal.
4	Turn stop light switch ON. (Depress brake pedal)	Light ON switch OFF / OFF switch ON	Stop light switch circuit is normal.
5	Turn park/neutral position switch ON. (Shift to N or P position)		Park/Neutral Position switch circuit is normal.
6	Turn clutch start switch ON (Depress clutch pedal.)		Clutch switch circuit is normal.
7	Drive at 40 km/h (25 mph) or higher.	Light ON / OFF	Speed sensor is normal.
8	Drive at 40 km/h (25 mph) or below.	Light ON / OFF	

TY1109900133000X

Fig. 39 Input signal check. 1996 Camry

Wiring Diagrams

Refer to **Figs. 40 through 72** for wiring diagrams.

Diagnostic Tests

AVALON, CAMRY, CAMRY SOLARA, SIENNA & TUNDRA

Refer to **Figs. 83 through 86** for problem symptoms tables and **Figs. 83 through 116** for diagnostic tests.

CELICA

Refer to **Fig. 136** for problem symptoms table and **Figs. 142 through 158** for diagnostic tests.

COROLLA

Refer to **Fig. 159** for problem symptoms chart and **Figs. 160 through 190** for diagnostic tests.

LAND CRUISER

Refer to **Figs. 191 and 192** for problem symptoms tables and **Figs. 193 through 216** for diagnostic tests.

1996 PASEO

Refer to **Fig. 217** for problem symptoms chart and **Figs. 218 through 231** for diagnostic tests.

1997 PASEO

Refer to **Fig. 232** for problem symptoms table and **Figs. 233 through 249** for diagnostic tests.

PREVIA

Refer to **Figs. 250 and 251** for problem symptoms table and **Figs. 252 through 261** for diagnostic tests.

RAV4

Refer to **Fig. 262** for problem symptoms table and **Figs. 263 through 294** for diagnostic tests.

SUPRA EXCEPT 1998 w/2JZ-GE ENGINE

Refer to **Fig. 294** for problem symptoms table and **Figs. 294 through 324** for diagnostic tests.

1998 SUPRA w/2JZ-GE ENGINE

Refer to **Fig. 325** for problem symptoms table and **Figs. 326 through 332** for diagnostic tests.

TACOMA

Refer to **Fig. 333** for problem symptoms chart and **Figs. 334 through 397** for diagnostic tests.

T100

Refer to **Figs. 398 and 399** for problem symptoms tables and **Figs. 400 through 424** for diagnostic tests.

4RUNNER

Refer to **Figs. 425 and 426** for problem symptoms table and **Figs. 427 through 476** for diagnostic tests.

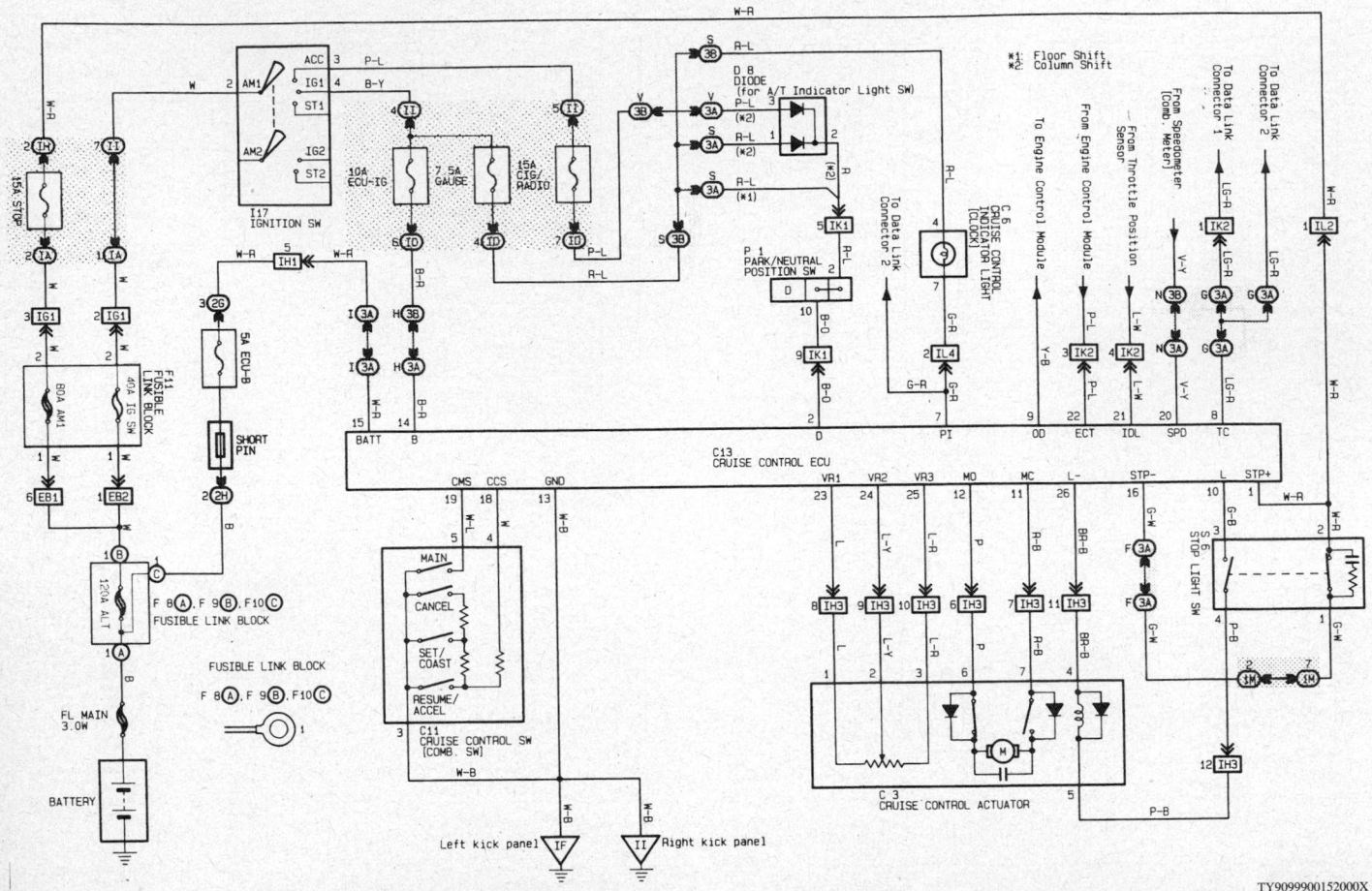

Fig. 40 Cruise control wiring diagram. 1996 Avalon

TY9099900152000X

Clearing Diagnostic Trouble Codes

AVALON

1996-97

To clear codes, remove the ECU-B fuse for at least 10 seconds with ignition switch off. Ensure normal code is displayed after connecting fuse.

1998-99

1. Drive vehicle at 10 mph or below.
2. Using jumper wire tool No. 09843–18020 or equivalent, connect terminals T_C and E_1 of DLC1, **Fig. 477.**
3. Pull cruise control switch to "CANCEL," then turn on cruise control main switch 5 times within 3 seconds. Ensure normal code is displayed after DTC clearance.

CAMRY

1996

Trouble codes may be cleared by removing the "STOP" fuse for at least 10 seconds with ignition switch off. After DTC clearance, ensure normal code is displayed after connecting the fuse.

1997-98

Trouble codes may be cleared by removing the "ECU–B fuse" for at least 10 seconds with ignition switch off. After DTC clearance, ensure normal code is displayed after connecting fuse.

1999

1. Connect terminals T_C and E_1 of DLC1 using jumper wire tool No. 09843–18020 or equivalent, **Fig. 30.**
2. Turn on cruise control switch 5 times within 3 seconds while holding switch in "CANCEL" position.
3. Verify normal DTC output.

CAMRY SOLARA

1. Connect terminals T_C and E_1 of DLC1 using jumper wire tool No. 09843–18020 or equivalent, **Fig. 30.**
2. Turn on cruise control switch 5 times within 3 seconds while holding switch in "CANCEL" position.
3. Verify normal DTC output.

CELICA, PREVIA & 1996-97 COROLLA

To clear DTC's, remove "ECU-B" fuse for at least 10 seconds with ignition switch off. Ensure normal code is displayed after DTC clearance.

1998-99 COROLLA

1. Drive vehicle at 10 mph or less.
2. Using jumper wire tool No. 09843–18020 or equivalent, connect terminals T_C and E_1 of DLC 1, **Fig. 11.**
3. While holding cruise control switch in "CANCEL" position, turn on cruise control switch 5 times within 3 seconds.
4. Verify DTC's have been cleared.

LAND CRUISER

1996

To clear DTC's, remove "DOME" fuse for at least 10 seconds with ignition switch off. Ensure normal code is displayed after DTC clearance.

1997

To clear DTC's, remove "ECU-R" fuse for at least 10 seconds with ignition switch off. Ensure normal code is displayed after DTC clearance.

1998-99

Diagnostic trouble codes may be cleared by one of the following methods; connect a suitable scan tool to DLC3 and follow scan tool instructions, or; disconnect battery terminals or "EFI" fuse. After codes have been cleared, ensure normal DTC is output.

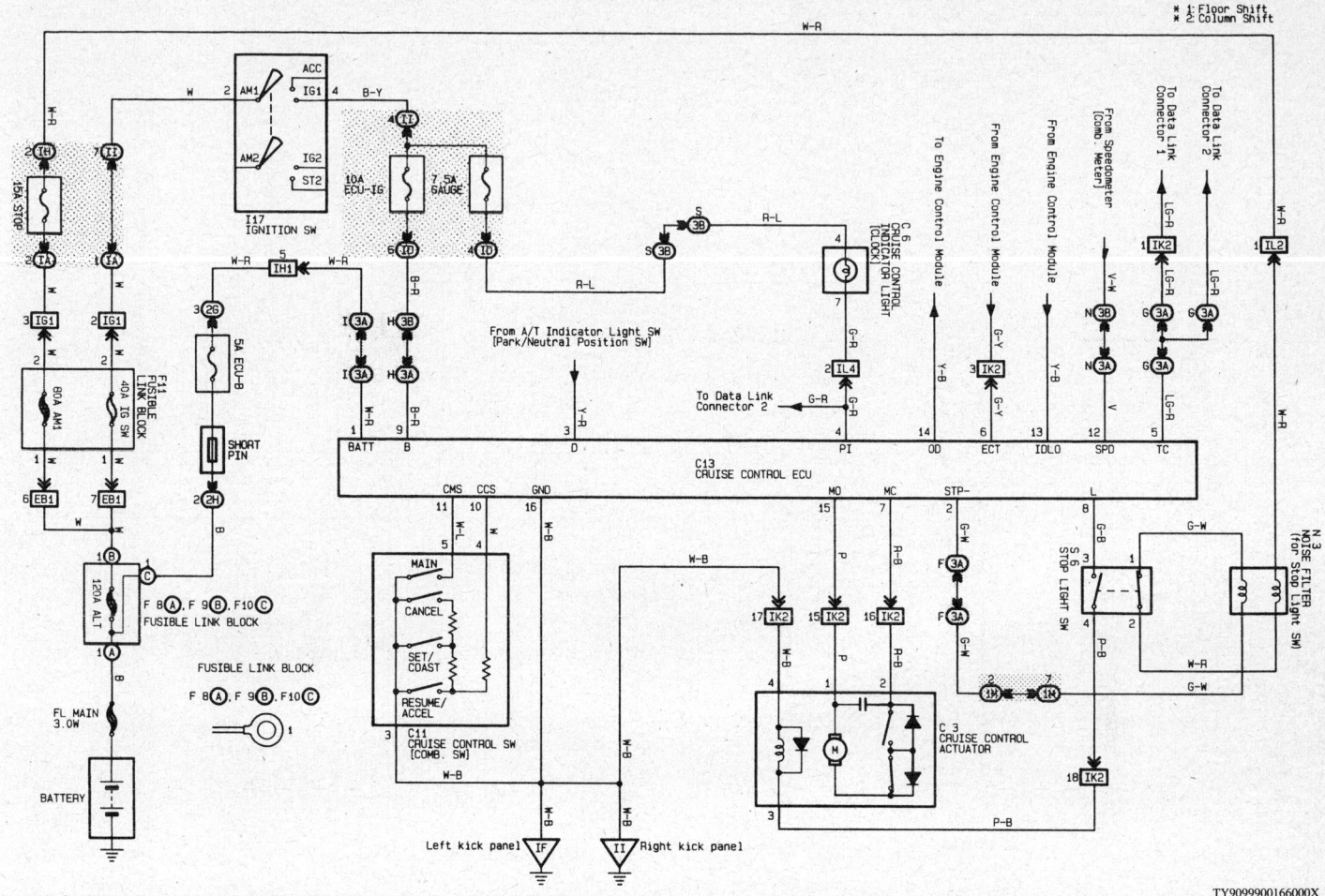

Fig. 41   Cruise control wiring diagram. 1997 Avalon

PASEO

To clear DTC's, remove "ECU-IG" fuse for at least 10 seconds with ignition switch off. Ensure normal code is displayed after DTC clearance.

RAV4

1996-97

To clear DTC's, remove "ECU-IG" fuse for at least 10 seconds with ignition switch off. Ensure normal code is displayed after DTC clearance.

1998-99

1. Drive vehicle at 10 mph or less.
2. Using jumper wire tool No. 09843–18020 or equivalent, connect terminals T_C and E_1 of DLC 1, **Fig. 11.**
3. While holding cruise control switch in "CANCEL" position, turn on cruise control switch 5 times within 3 seconds.
4. Verify DTC's have been cleared.

SIENNA

1998

After completing service, DTC can be cleared by removing the "ECU-B" fuse from engine room junction box No. 2 for at least 10 seconds with ignition switch off. Ensure normal DTC is displayed.

1999

1. Drive vehicle at 15 mph.
2. Using jumper wire tool No. 09843–18020 or equivalent, connect terminals T_C and E_1 or DLC1, **Fig. 11.**
3. While holding cruise control switch in cancel position, turn on cruise control main switch 5 times within 3 seconds.
4. Verify DTC's have been cleared.

SUPRA

1996

To clear DTC's, remove the "ECU-IB" fuse for at least 10 seconds with ignition switch off. Ensure normal code is displayed after DTC clearance.

1997 w/2JZ-GE & 2JZ-GTE & 1998 w/2JZ-GTE Engine

To clear DTC's, remove "DOME" fuse for at least 10 seconds with ignition switch off. Ensure normal code is displayed after DTC clearance.

1998 w/2JZ-GE Engine

Connect Toyota Hand Held Tester or equivalent to DLC 3 and follow scan tool instructions to clear DTC's. An alternate method of clearing codes is to disconnect the battery terminals or remove "EFI" fuse. Ensure normal code is displayed after DTC clearance.

TACOMA

1996 & 1997 w/Denso Cruise Control

To clear DTC's, remove the "ECU-B" fuse for at least 10 seconds with ignition switch off. Ensure normal code is displayed after DTC clearance.

1998-99 w/Denso Cruise Control

To clear DTC's, remove the "DOME" fuse for at least 10 seconds with ignition switch off. Ensure normal code is displayed after DTC clearance.

1997-98 w/Ford Cruise Control

1. Using jumper wire tool No. 09843–18020 or equivalent, connect terminals T_C and OP3 of DLC 1, **Fig. 478.**
2. Hold cruise control switch to "SET/COAST" position and hold switch down or up.

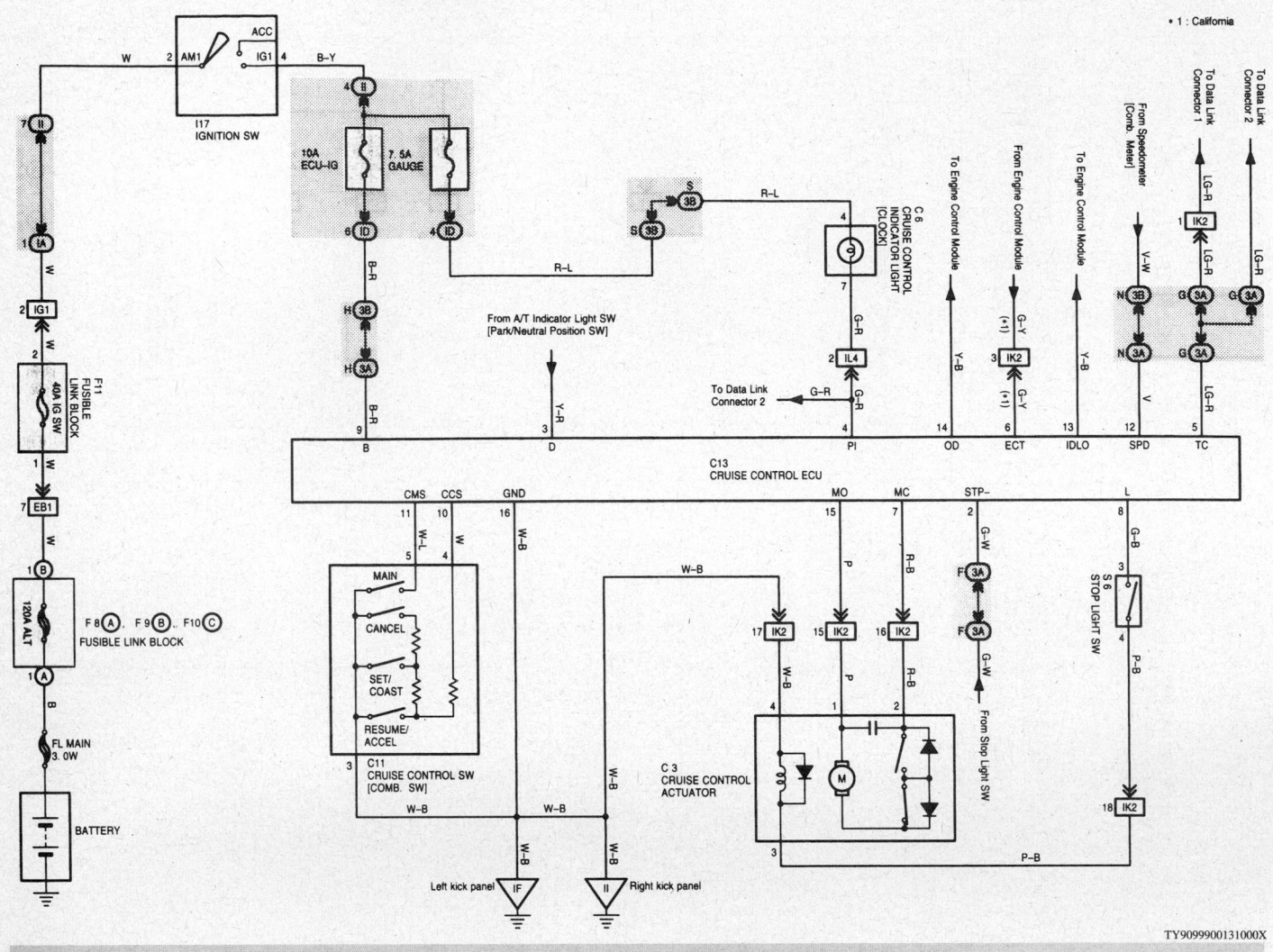

Fig. 42 Cruise control wiring diagram. 1998–99 Avalon

3. Place main cruise control switch to on position.
4. Ensure "CRUISE MAIN" indicator blinks 2 or 3 times repeatedly after 3 seconds.
5. Turn "SET/COAST" switch off.

1999 w/Ford Cruise Control

1. Drive vehicle at 10 mph or less.
2. Connect terminals TC and E1 of DLC 1, **Fig. 11,** using jumper wire tool No. 09843–18020 or equivalent.
3. Hold cruise control switch in "CANCEL" position.
4. Turn cruise control main switch on 5 times within 3 seconds.

TUNDRA

5VZ-FE Engine

1. Ensure engine is not running.
2. Using jumper wire tool No. 09843–18020 or equivalent, connect terminals T_C and OP3 of DLC1, **Fig. 478.**
3. Pull cruise control switch to "CANCEL."
4. Turn on cruise control main switch 5 times within 3 seconds. Ensure normal

code is displayed after DTC clearance.

2UZ-FE Engine

Diagnostic trouble codes can be cleared using one of the following methods:

1. Install Toyota Hand-Held Tester or equivalent and follow scan tool instructions.
2. Disconnect battery terminals or remove EFI fuse.
3. After completing repairs, DTC retained in memory can be cleared by removing ECU-B fuse for 10 seconds or more with ignition switch off. Ensure normal code is displayed after connecting fuse.

T100

1996

To clear codes, remove the ECU-B fuse for at least 10 seconds with ignition switch off. Ensure normal code is displayed after connecting fuse.

1997-98

1. Using jumper wire tool No. 09843–18020 or equivalent, connect termi-

nals T_C and OP3 of DLC 1, **Fig. 478.**
2. Hold cruise control switch to "SET/COAST" position and hold switch down or up.
3. Place main cruise control switch to on position.
4. Ensure "CRUISE MAIN" indicator blinks 2 or 3 times repeatedly after 3 seconds.
5. Turn "SET/COAST" switch off.

4RUNNER

1996-97

To clear DTC's, remove "DOME" fuse for at least 10 seconds with ignition switch off. Ensure normal code is displayed after DTC clearance.

1998-99

1. Drive vehicle at 10 mph or less.
2. Connect terminals TC and E1 of DLC 1, **Fig. 11,** using jumper wire tool No. 09843–18020 or equivalent.
3. Hold cruise control switch in "CANCEL" position.
4. Turn cruise control main switch on 5 times within 3 seconds.

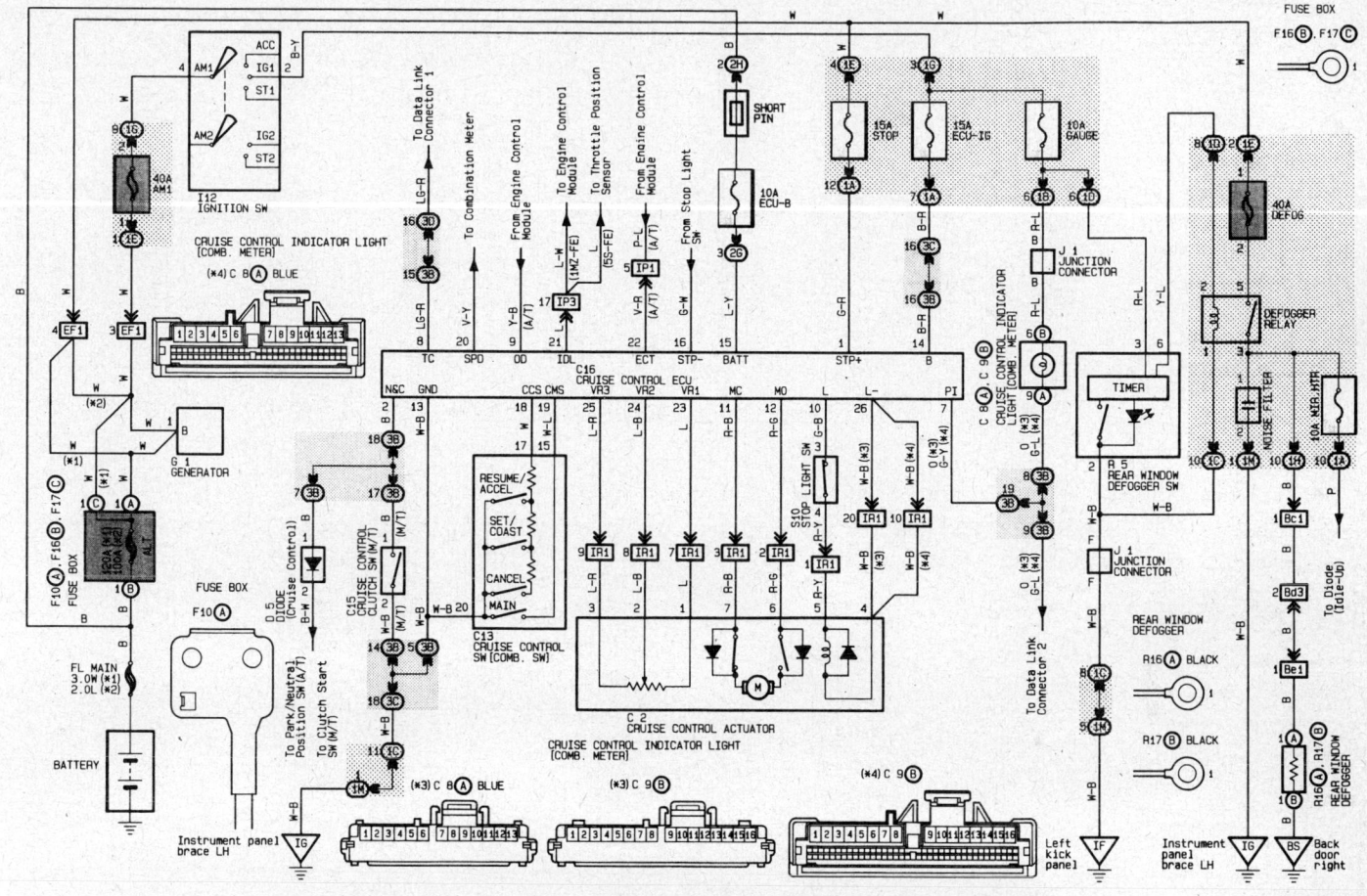

Fig. 43 Cruise control wiring diagram. 1996 Camry

TY1109900129000X

Component Diagnosis & Testing

SYMPTOM SIMULATION

Vibration Method

If the system fault occurs when vibration is present, inspect system wiring, connectors and related parts for obvious signs of damage. Apply vibration to system components, then lightly shake and vibrate system connectors and wiring harnesses.

Heat Method

If system fault occurs when the suspect area is heated, heat the likely component using a suitable heat gun. **Ensure components are not heated to more than 140°F and do not apply heat directly to parts in the ECU.**

Water Method

If a system fault occurs during damp or high humidity conditions, apply water to ve-

hicle and inspect to see if fault occurs. **Do not apply water into engine compartment or directly to electronic components.**

Load Method

When a fault occurs when electrical load is excessive, turn on all electrical loads including heater blower, headlamps, and rear window defogger and inspect for occurrence of fault.

TY1109900130000X

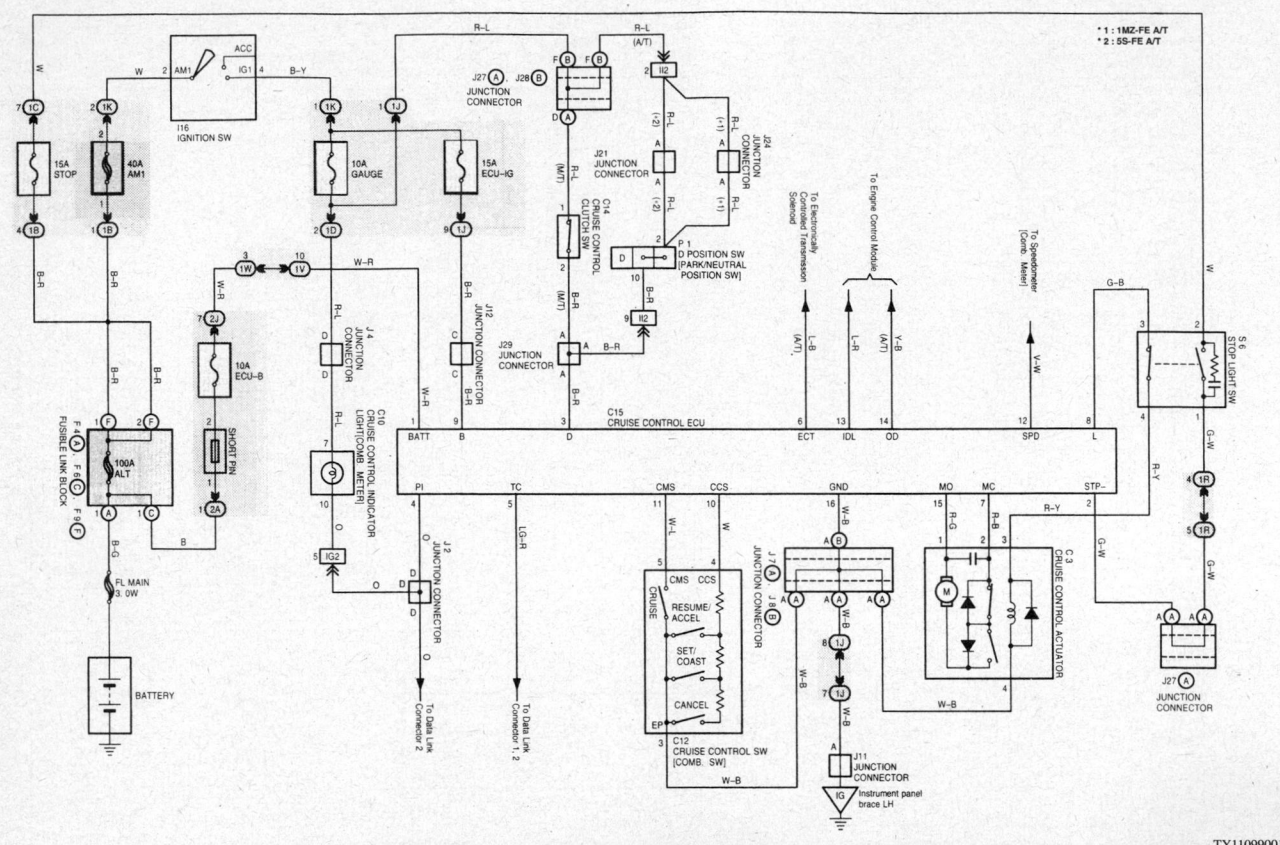

Fig. 44 Cruise control wiring diagram. 1997–98 Camry

TY1109900131000X

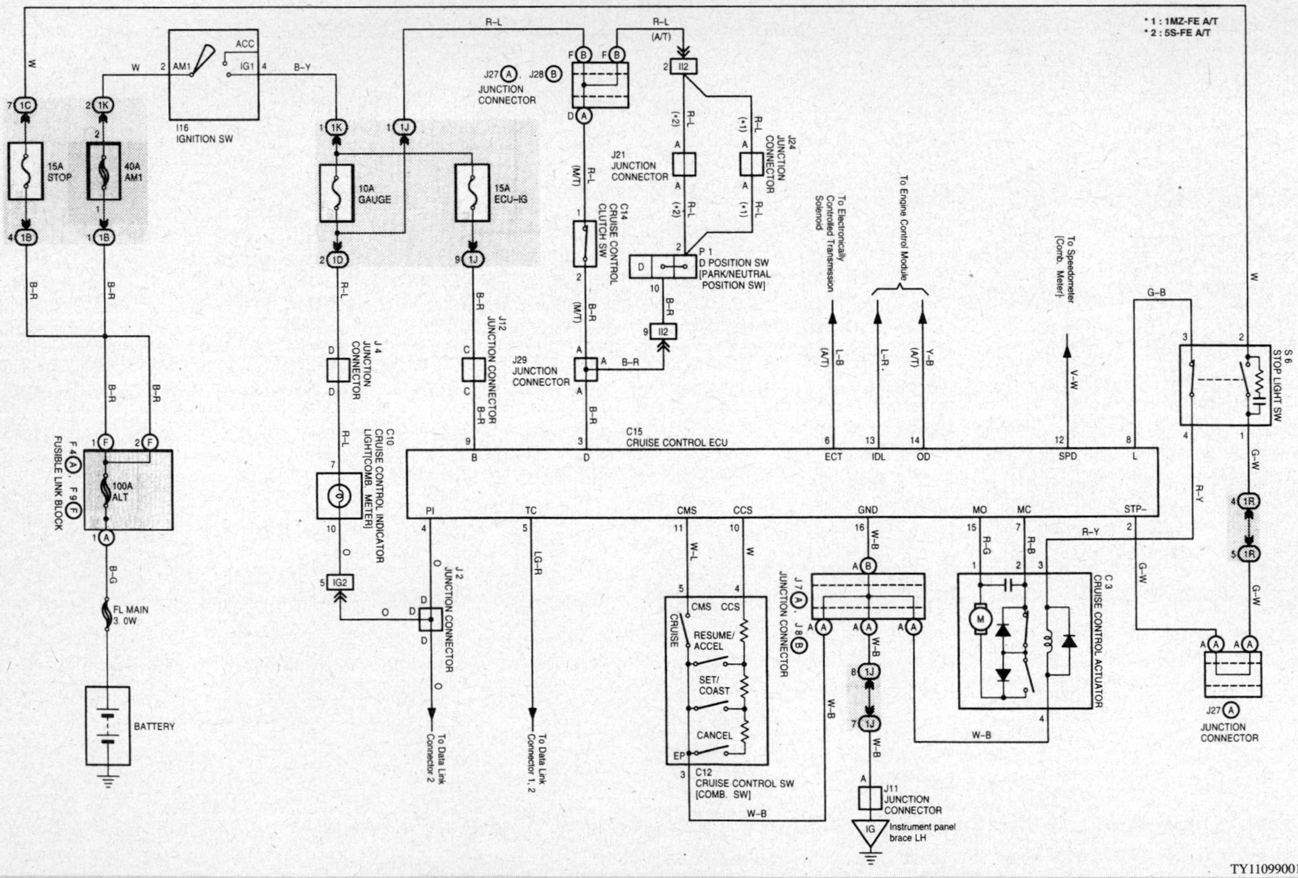

Fig. 45 Cruise control wiring diagram. 1999 Camry

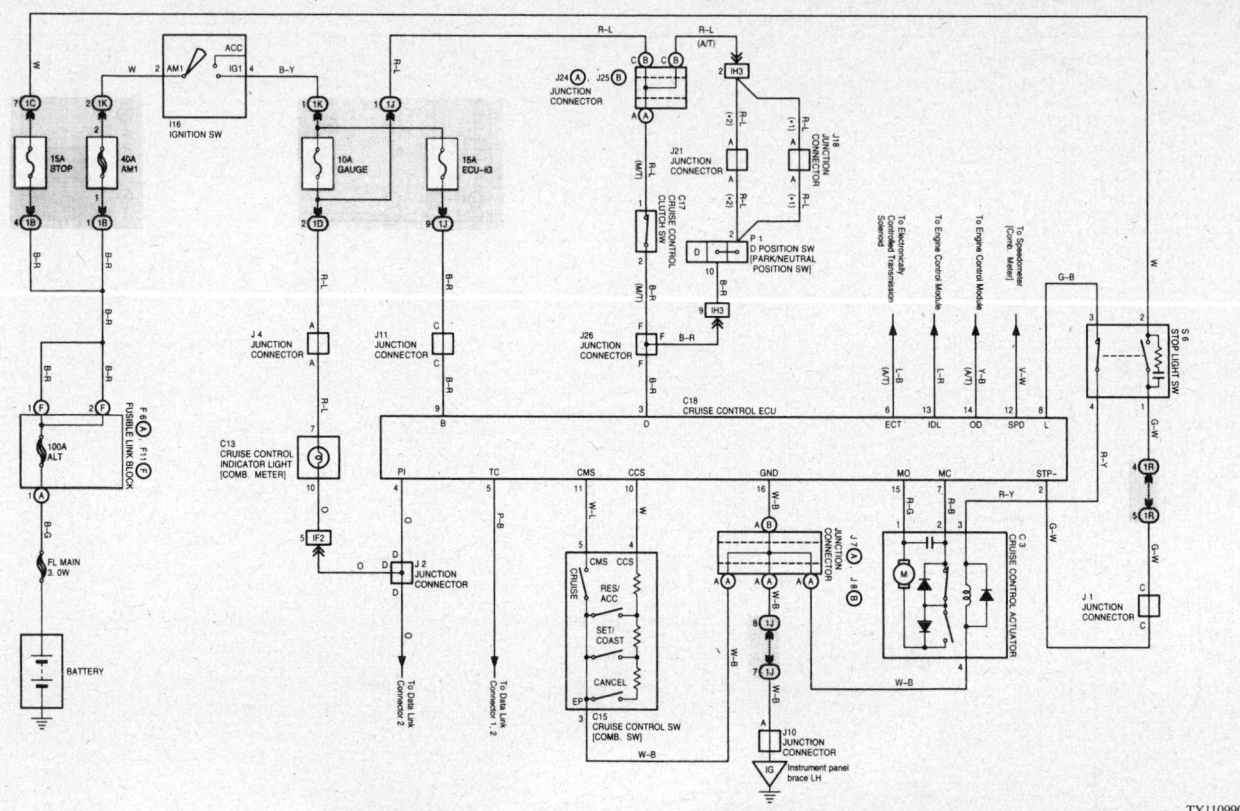

Fig. 46 Cruise control wiring diagram. Camry Solara

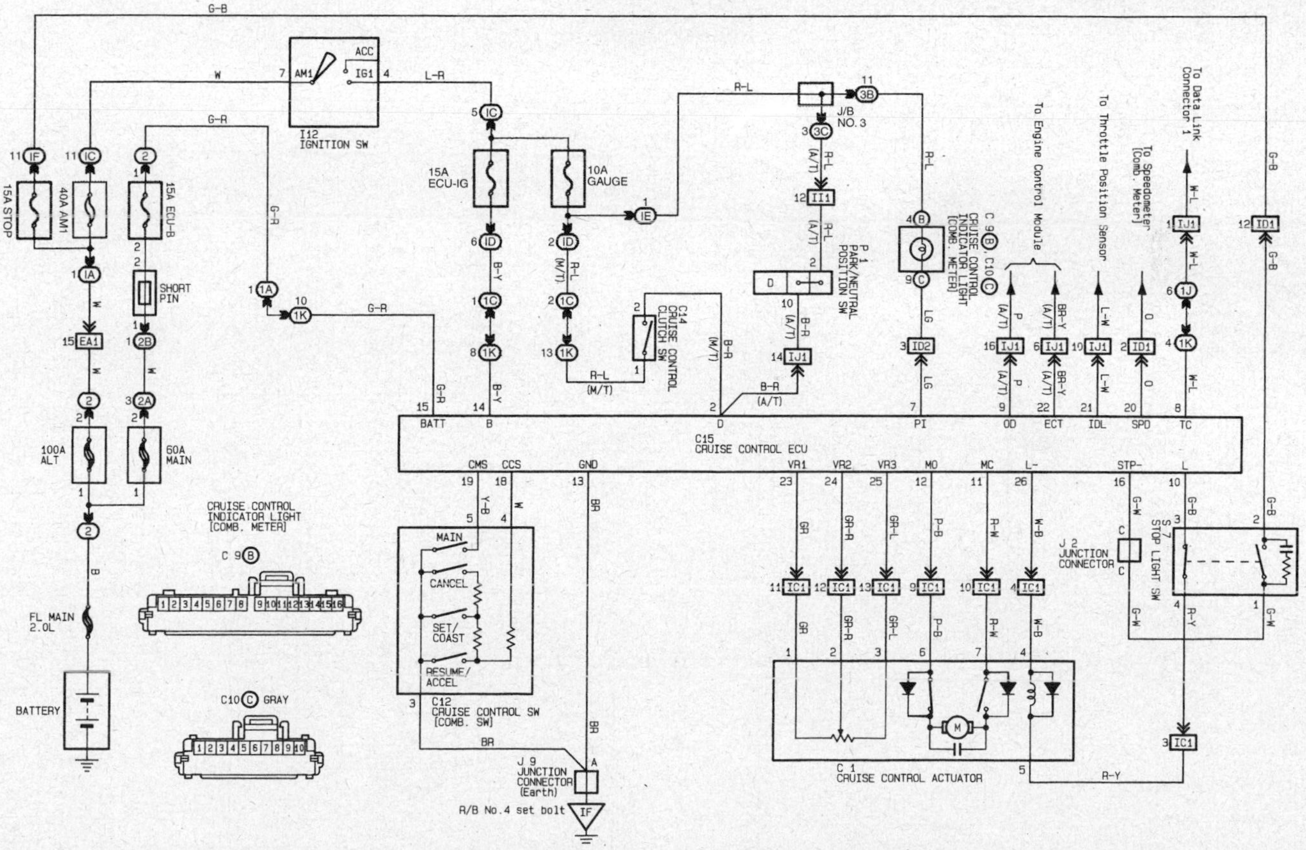

TY1109900145000X

Fig. 47 Cruise control wiring diagram. Celica

TY1109900489000X

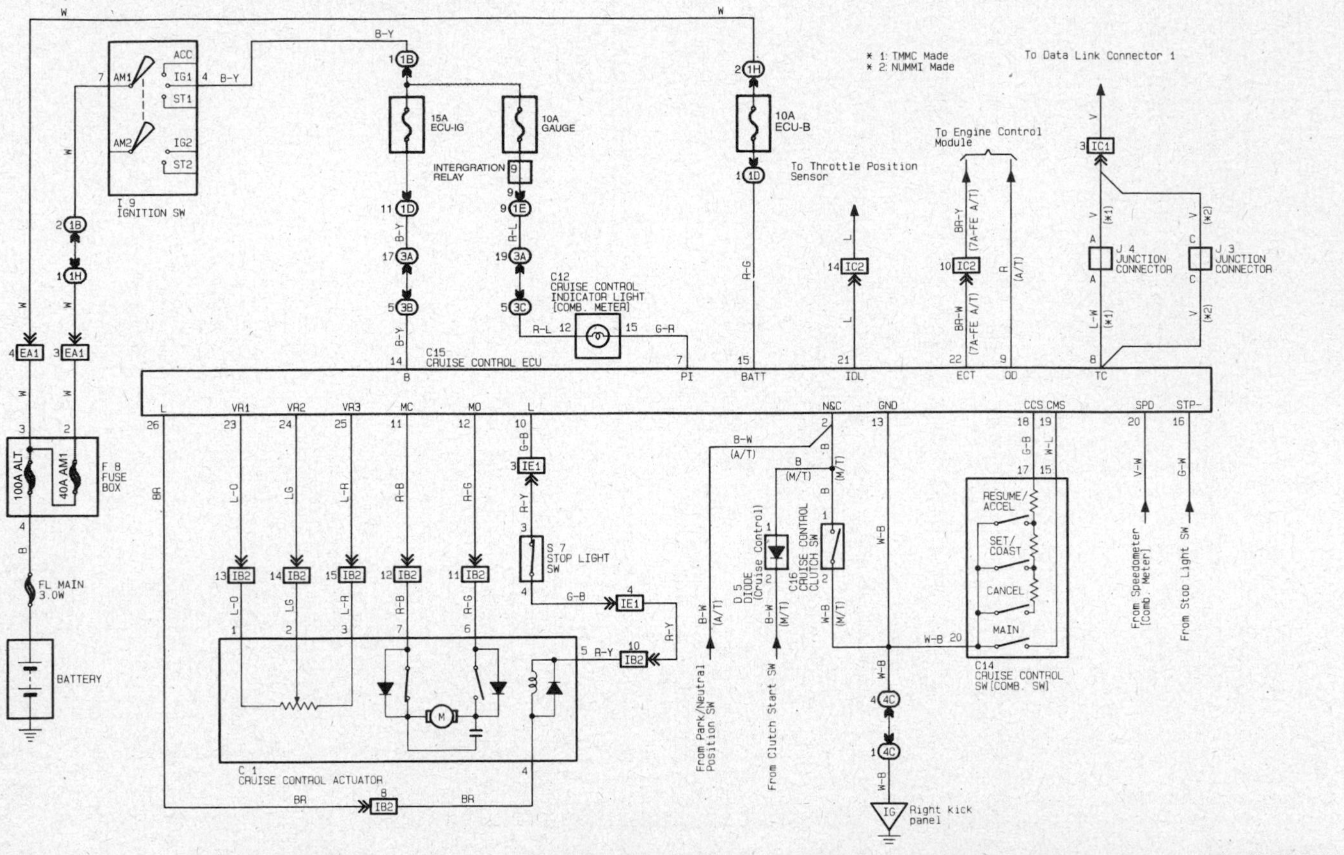

Fig. 48   Cruise control wiring diagram. 1996–97 Corolla

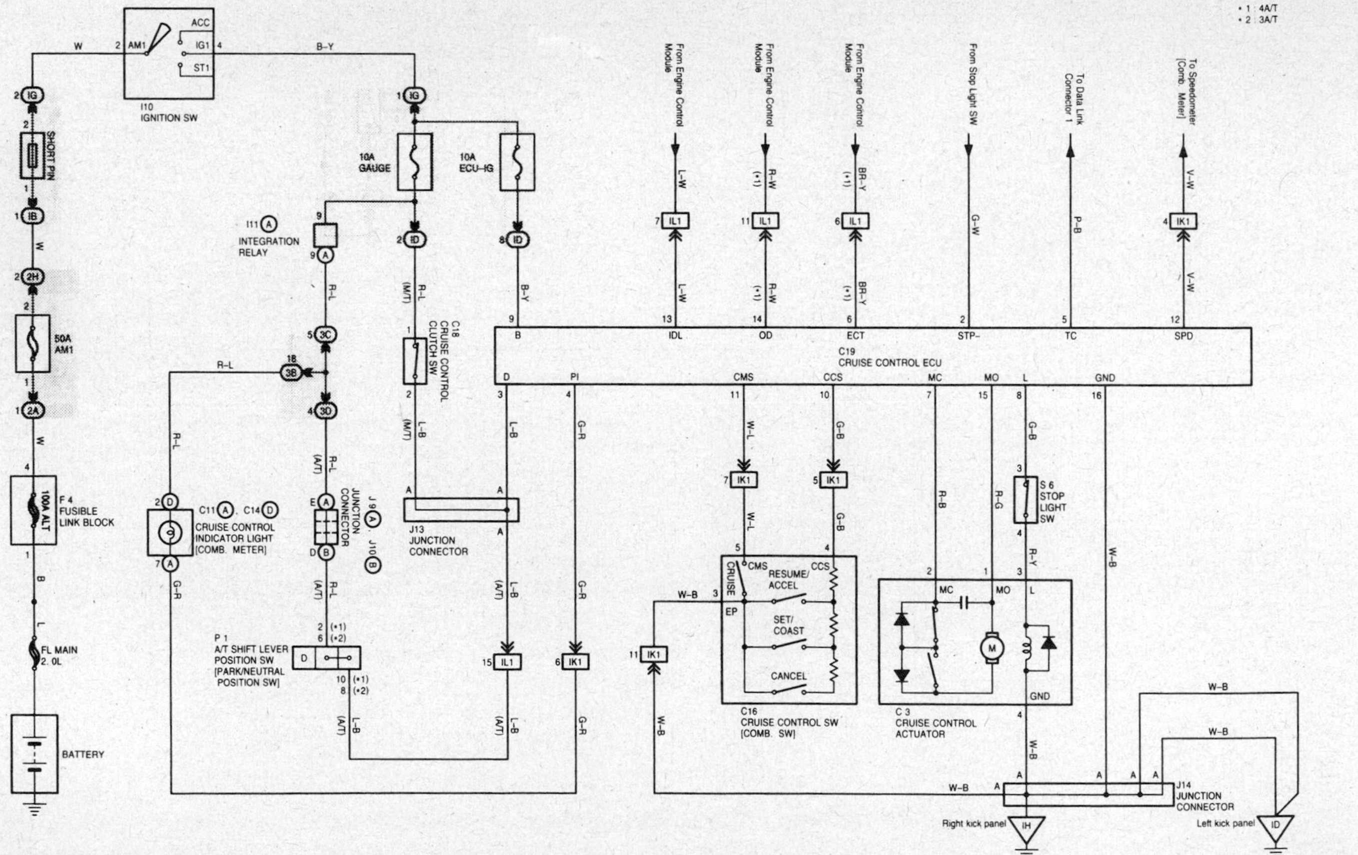

TY1109900356000X

Fig. 49   Cruise control wiring diagram. 1998–99 Corolla

TY1109900357000X

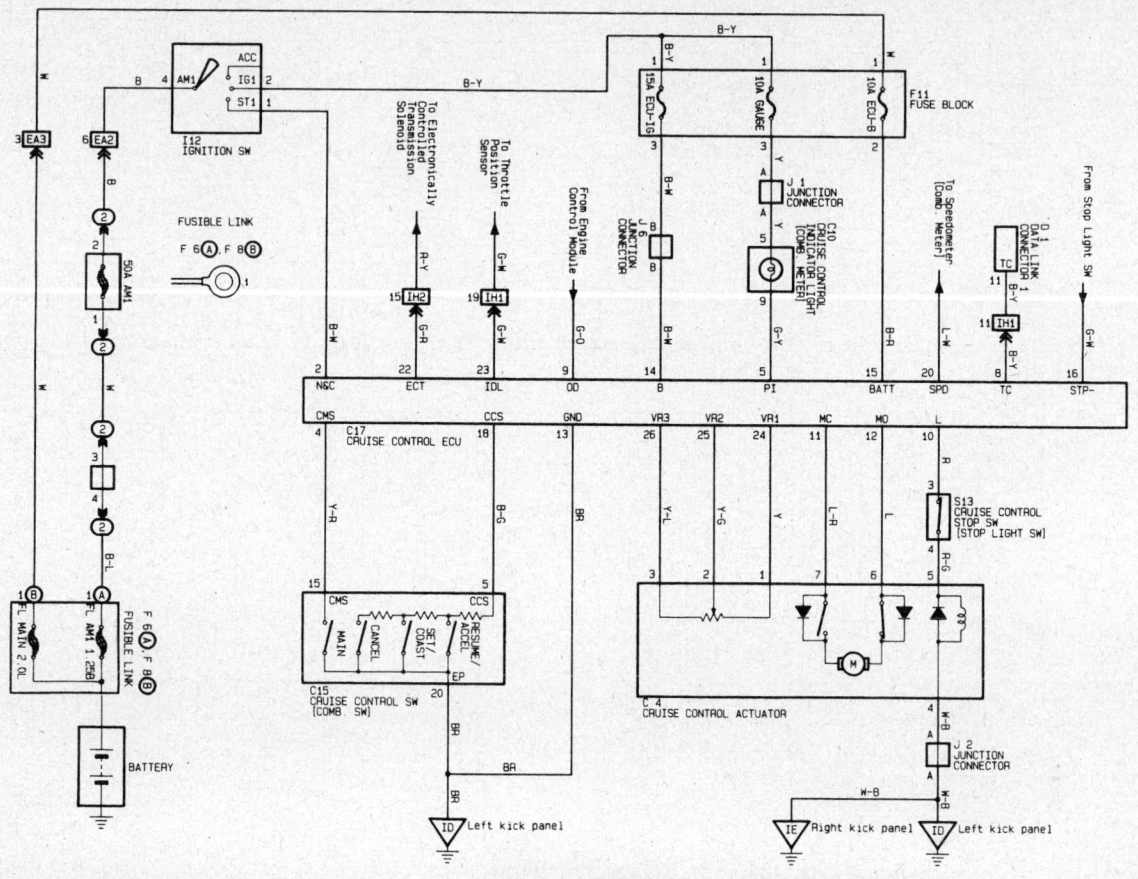

Fig. 50 Cruise control wiring diagram. 1996 Land Cruiser

TY1109900358000X

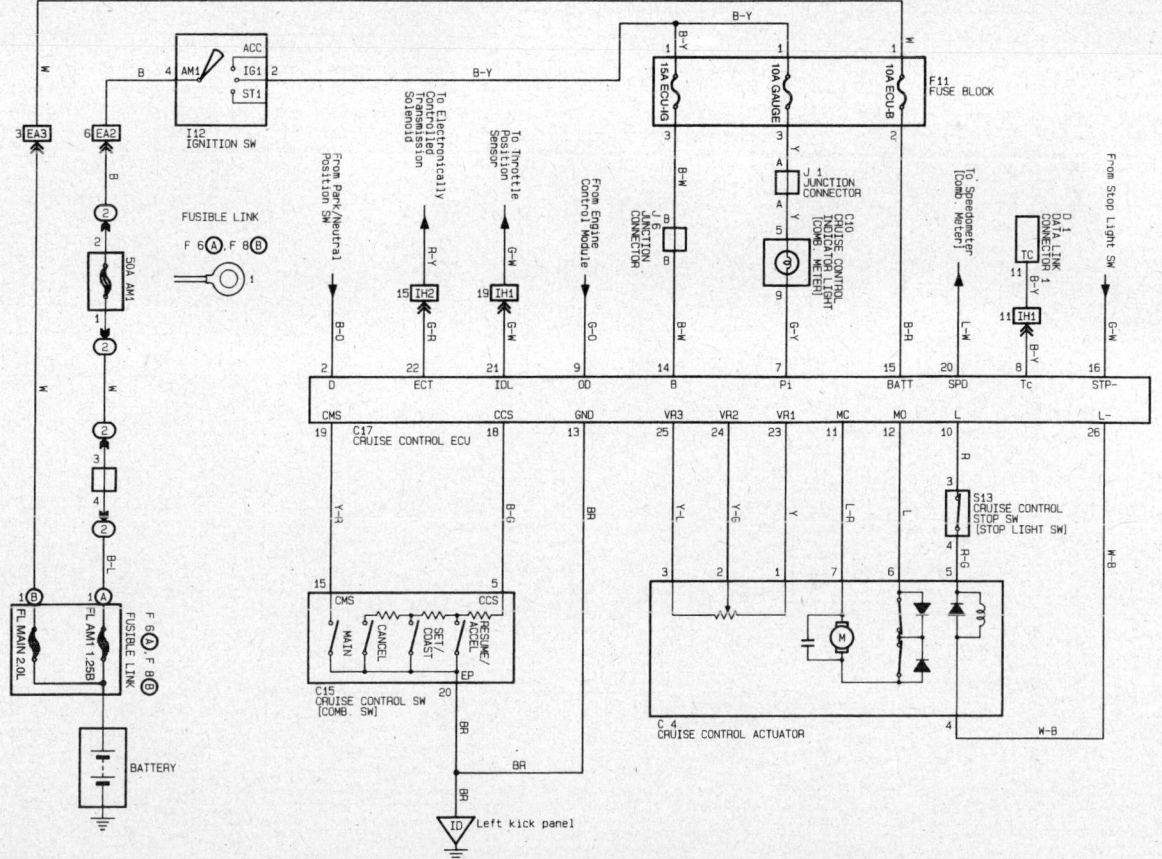

Fig. 51 Cruise control wiring diagram. 1997 Land Cruiser

TY1109900359000X

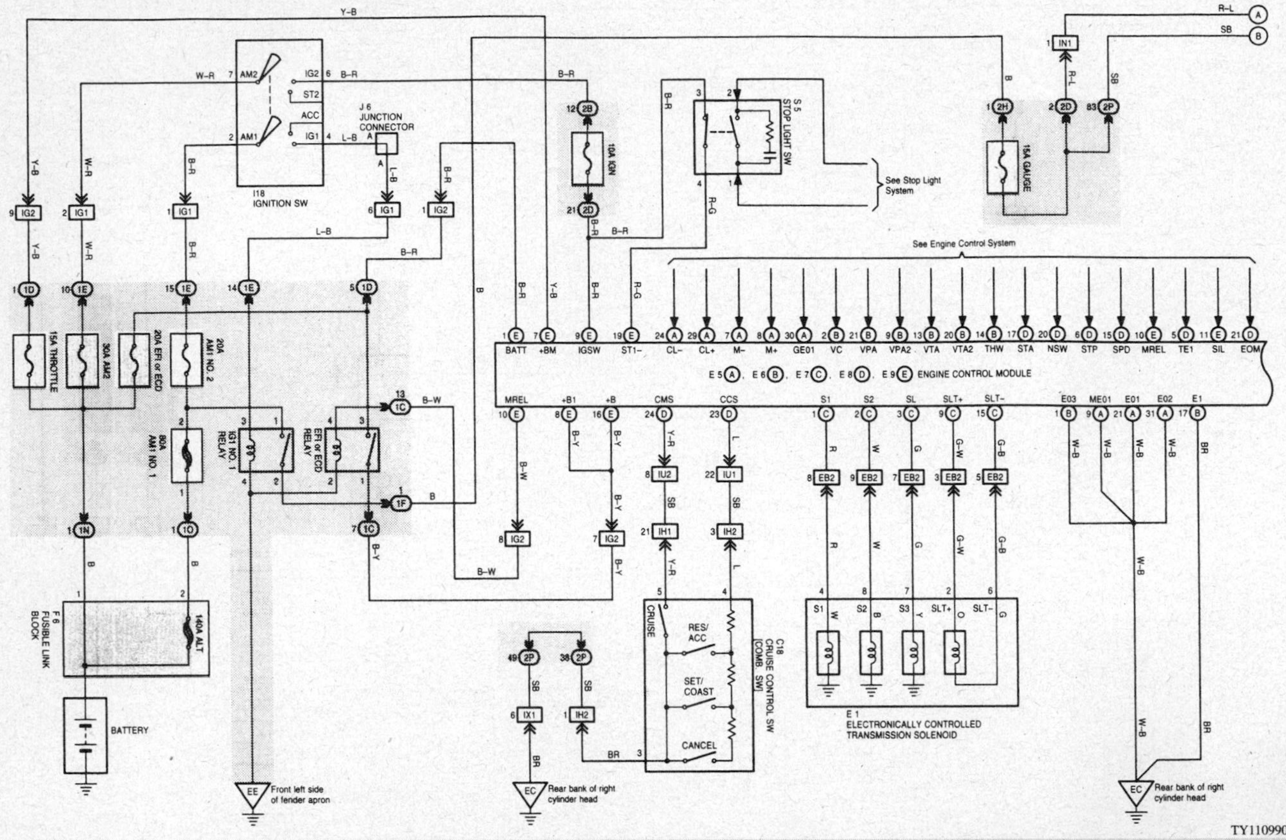

Fig. 52 Cruise control wiring diagram. 1998–99 Land Cruiser

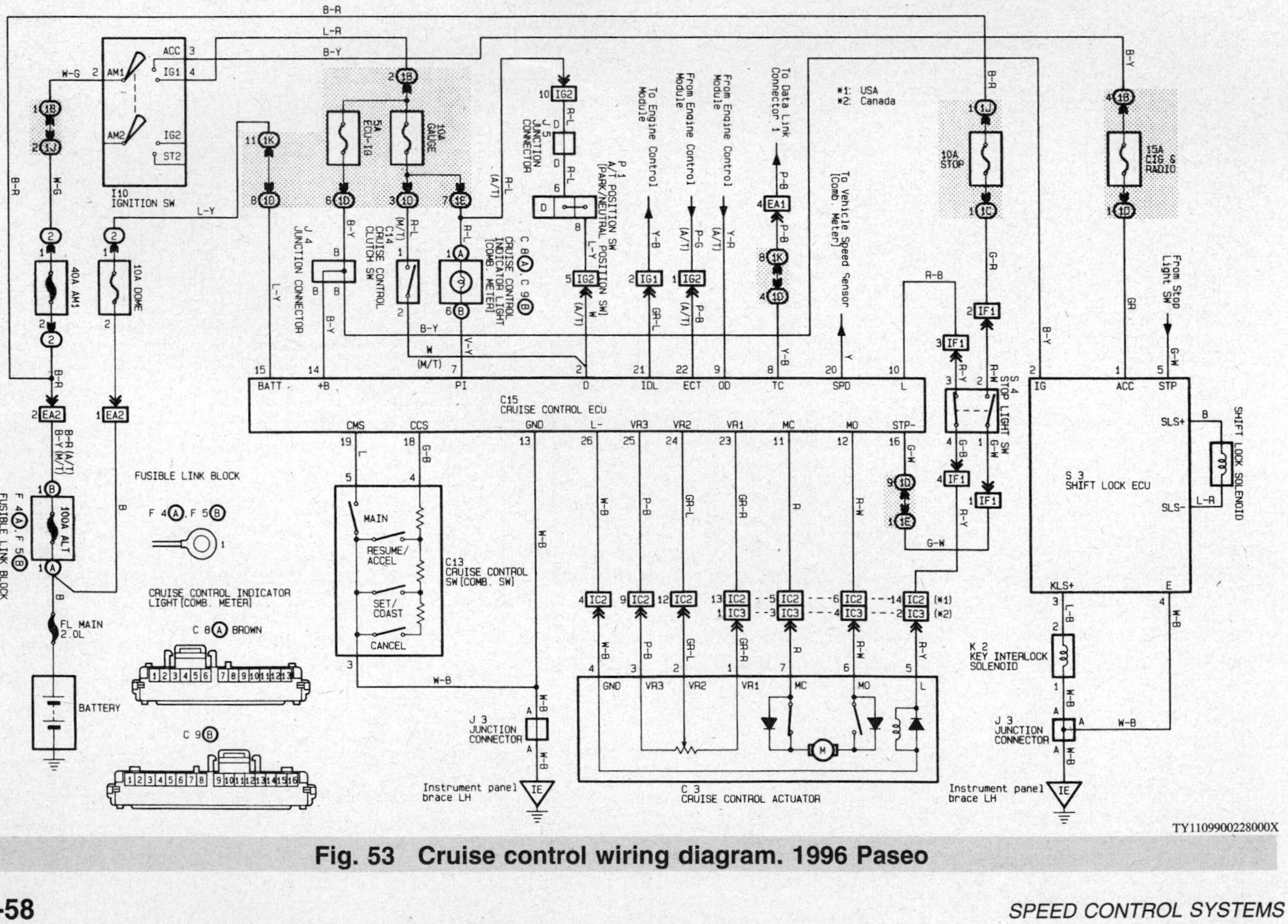

Fig. 53 Cruise control wiring diagram. 1996 Paseo

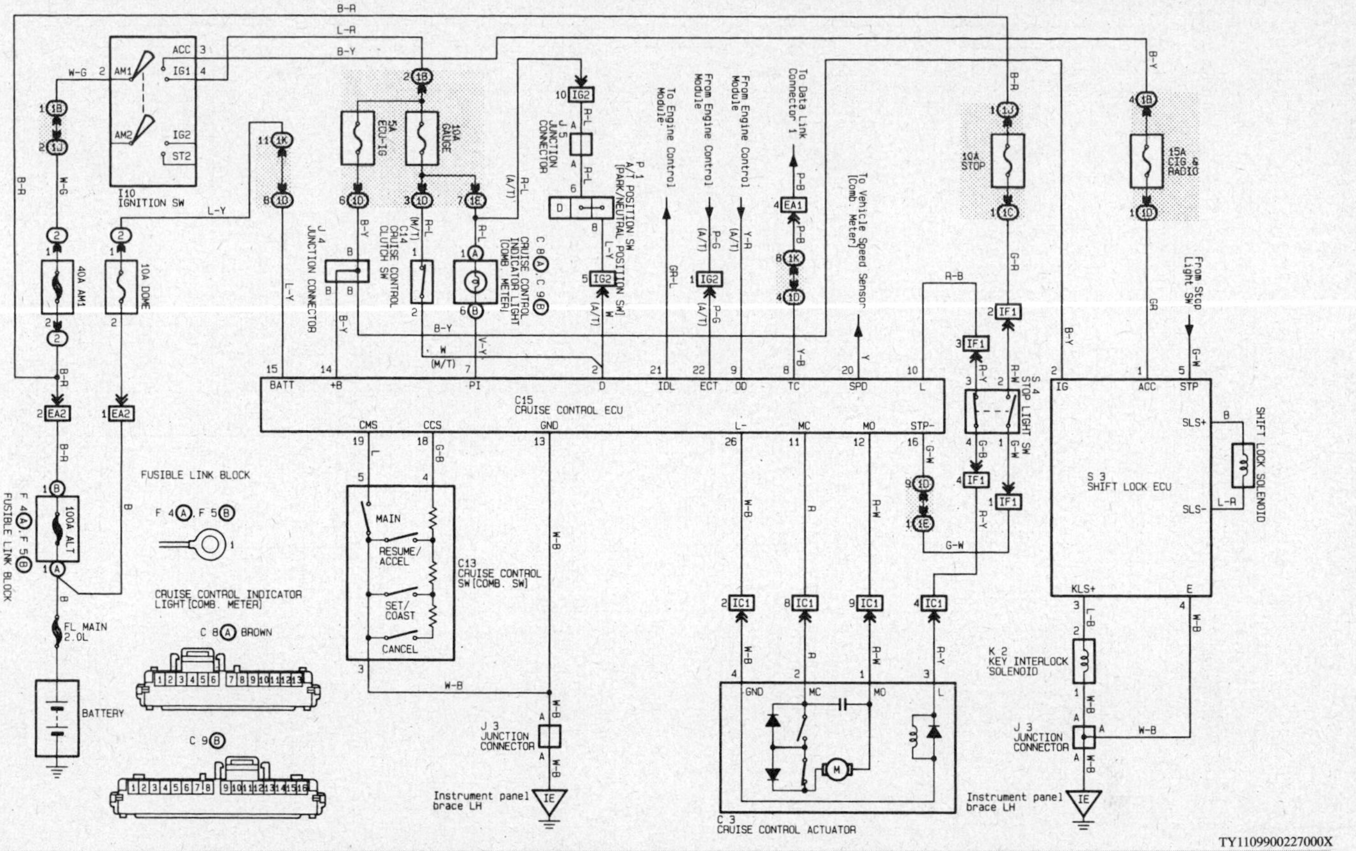

Fig. 54   Cruise control wiring diagram. 1997 Paseo

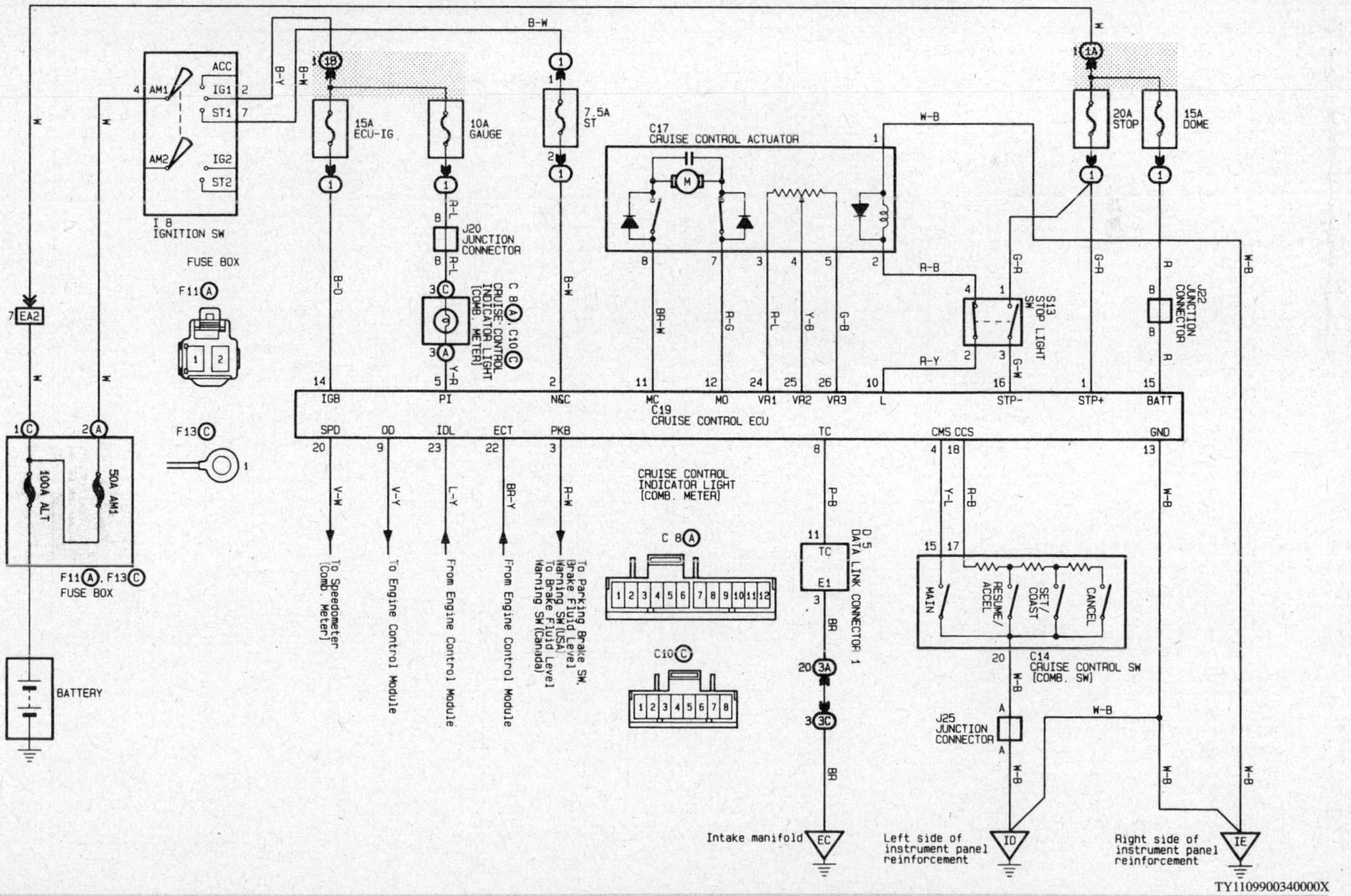

TY1109900227000X

Fig. 55   Cruise control wiring diagram. 1996 Previa

TY1109900340000X

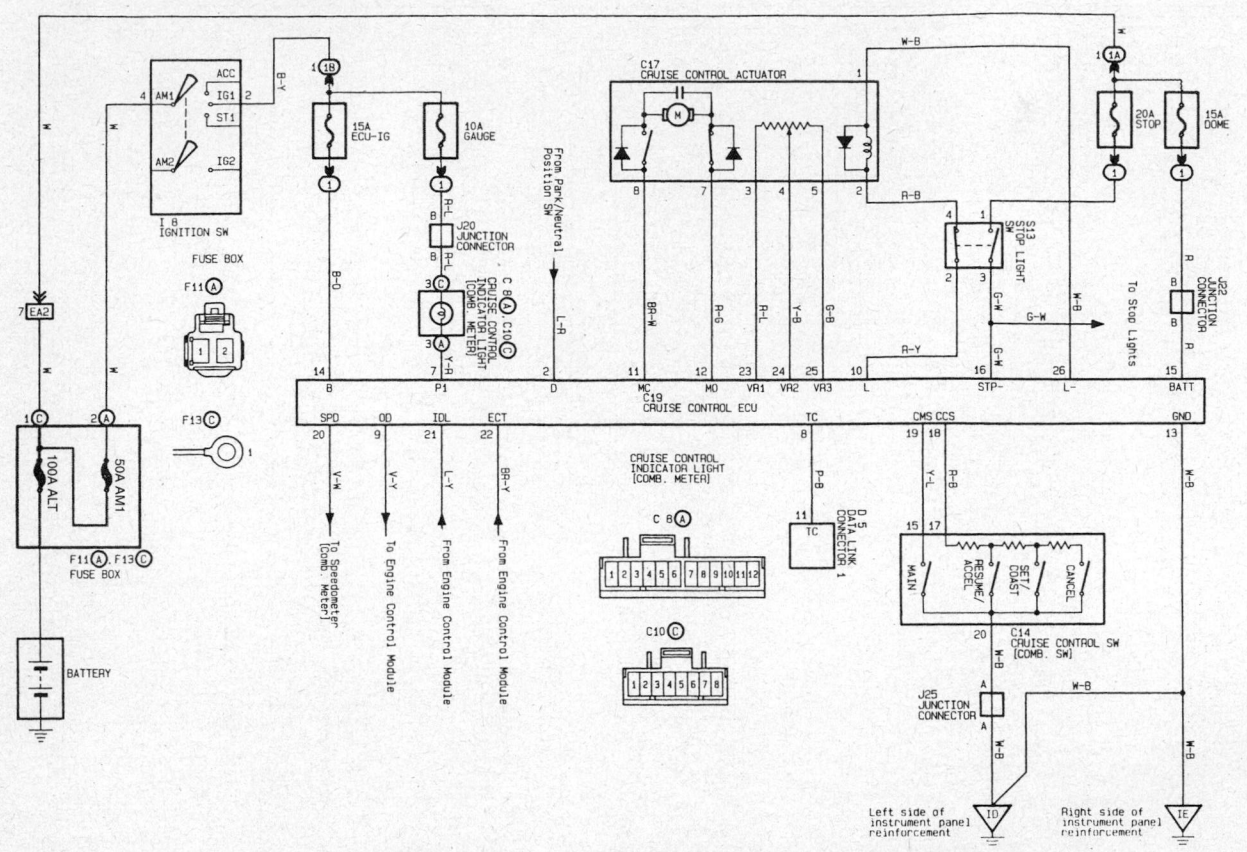

Fig. 56 Cruise control wiring diagram. 1997 Previa

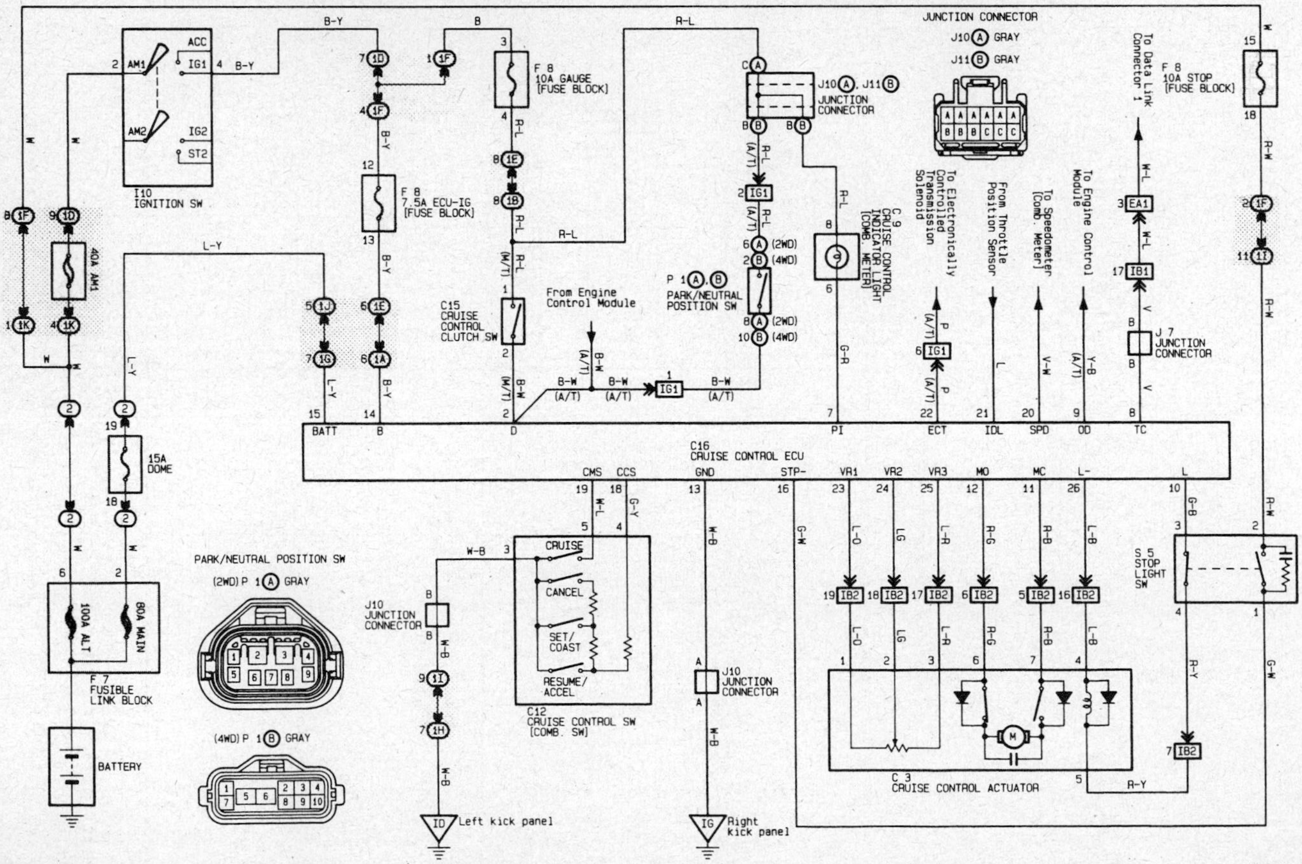

TY1109900341000X

Fig. 57 Cruise control wiring diagram. 1996–97 RAV4

TY1109900172000X

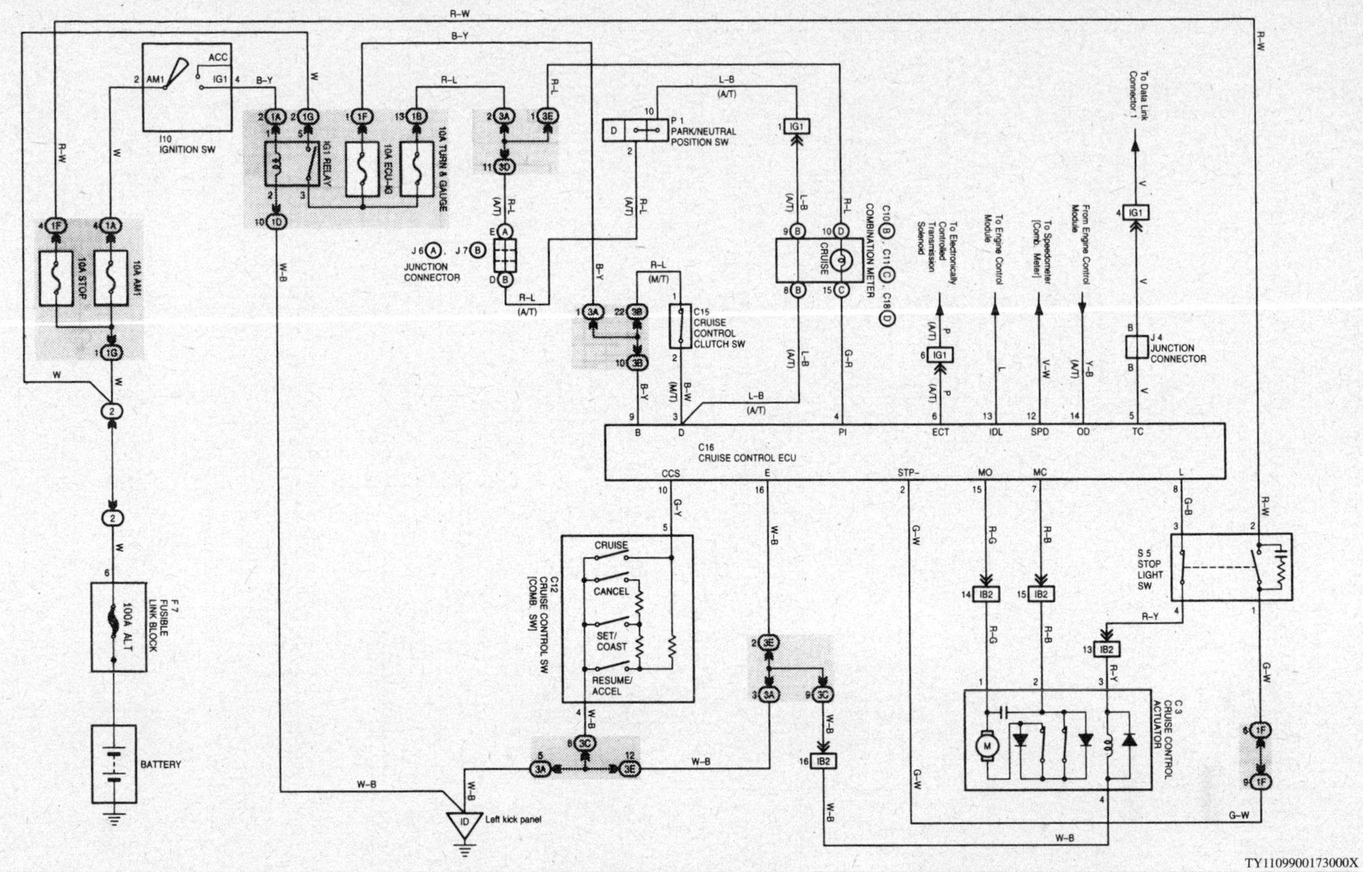

Fig. 58 Cruise control wiring diagram. 1998–99 RAV4

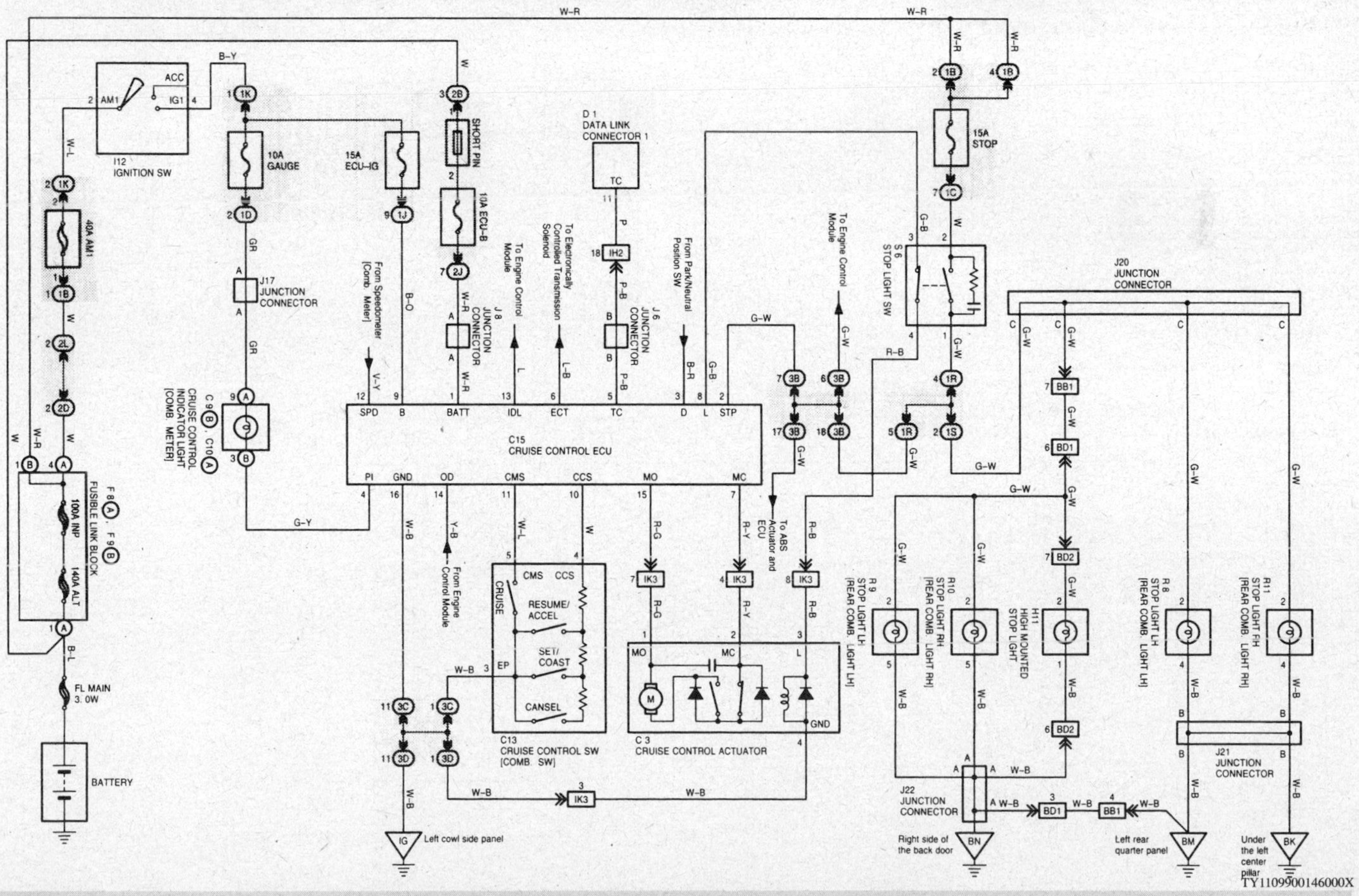

Fig. 59 Cruise control wiring diagram. 1998 Sienna

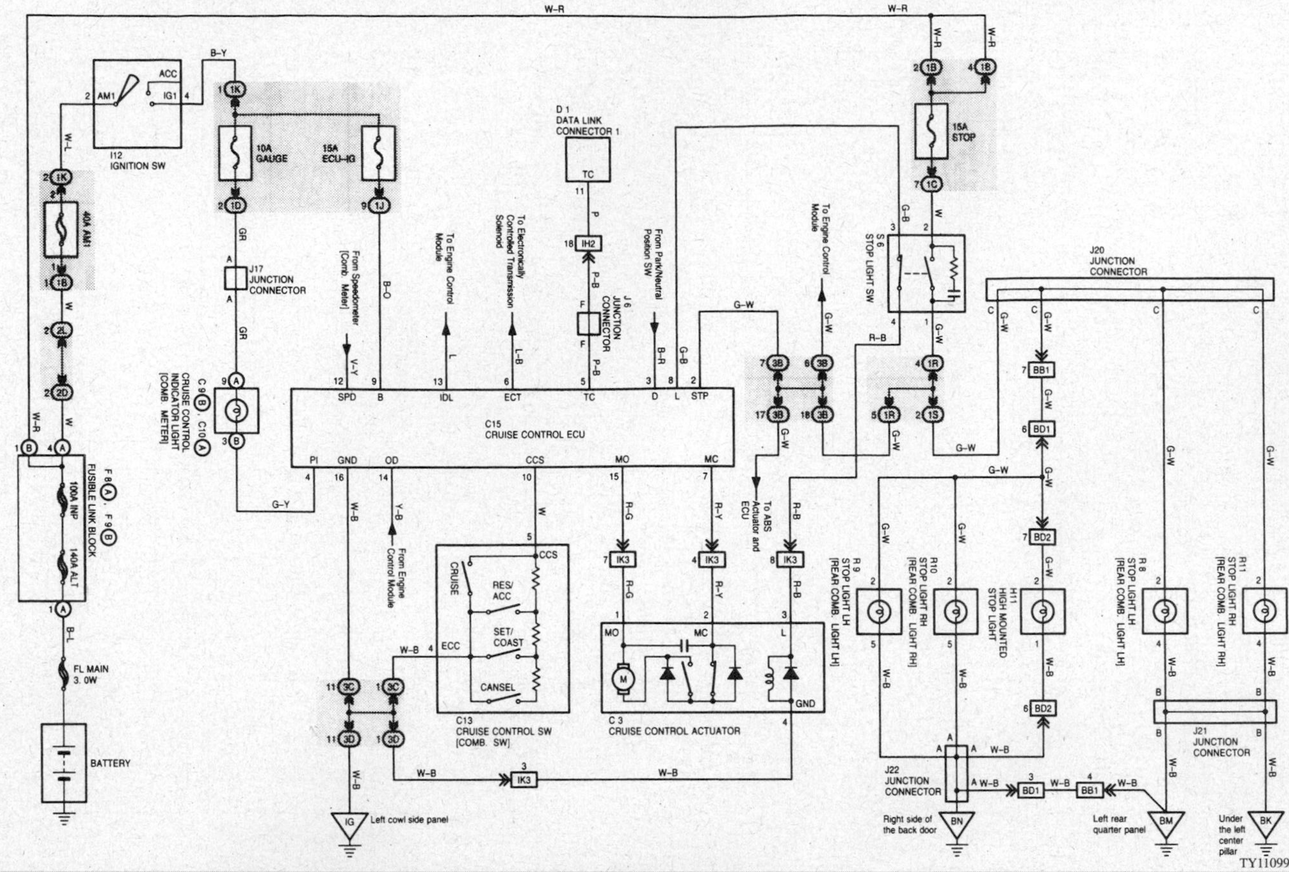

TY1109900147000X

Fig. 60 Cruise control wiring diagram. 1999 Sienna

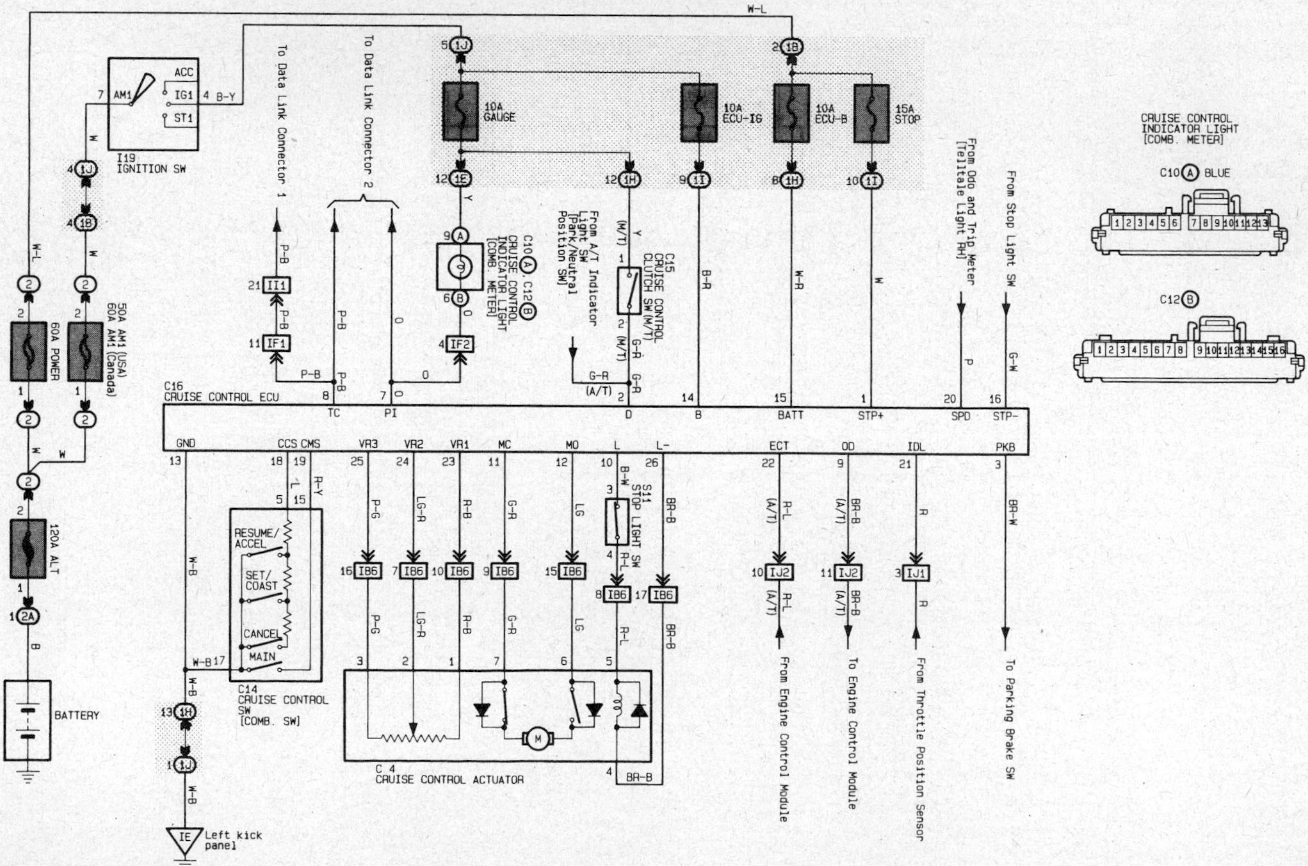

TY1109900462000X

Fig. 61 Cruise control wiring diagram. 1996 Supra

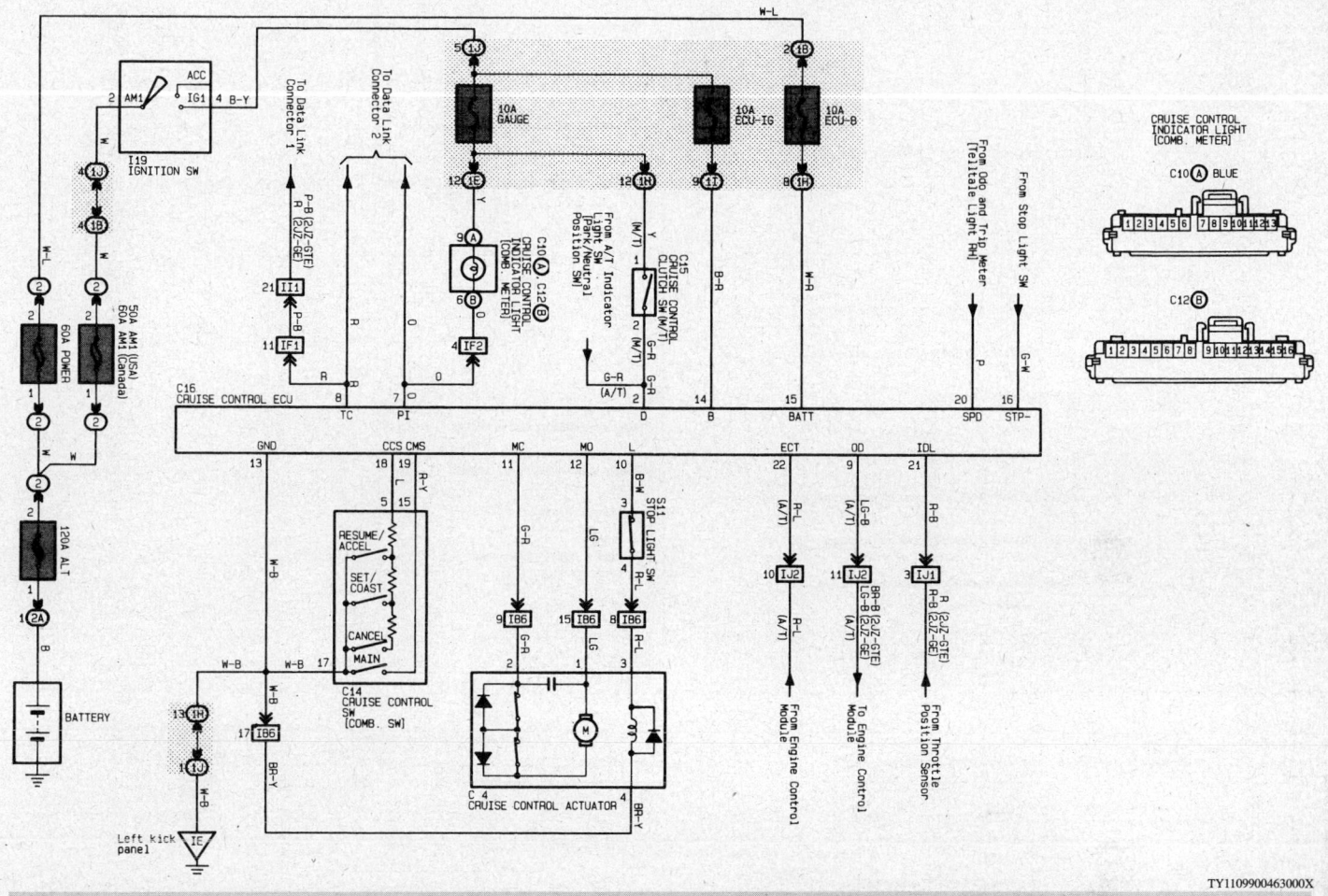

Fig. 62 Cruise control wiring diagram. 1997 Supra

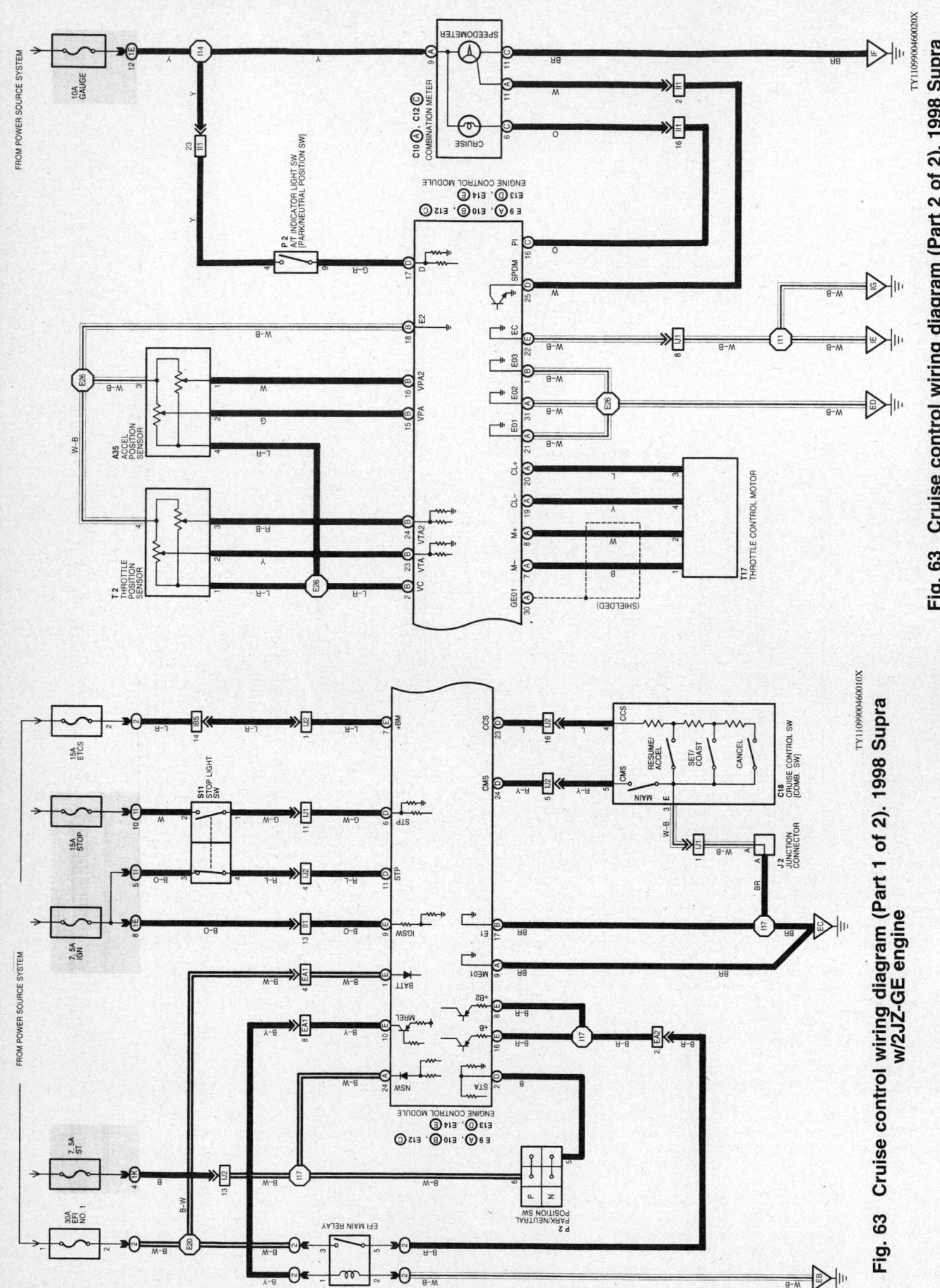

Fig. 63 Cruise control wiring diagram (Part 2 of 2). 1998 Supra w/2JZ-GE engine

Fig. 63 Cruise control wiring diagram (Part 1 of 2). 1998 Supra w/2JZ-GE engine

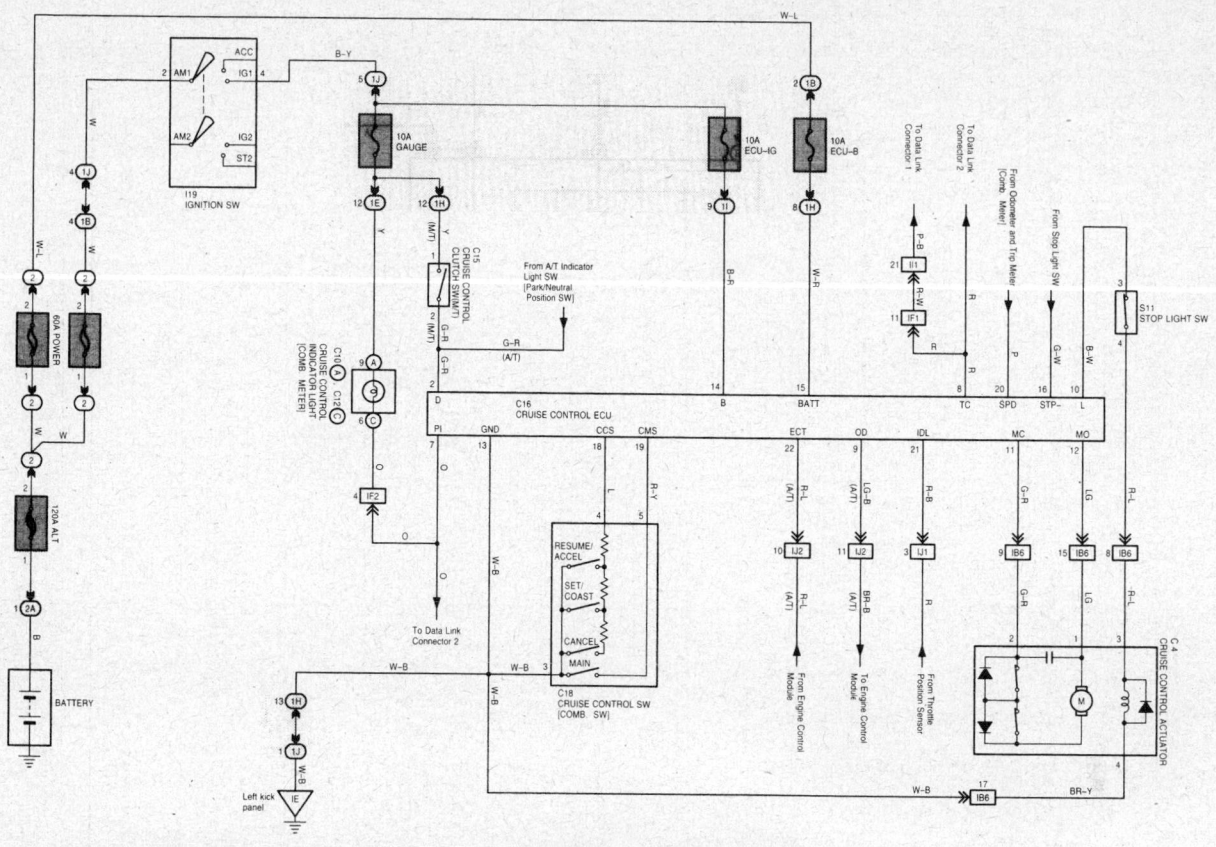

TY1109900461000X

Fig. 64   Cruise control wiring diagram. 1998 Supra w/2JZ-GTE engine

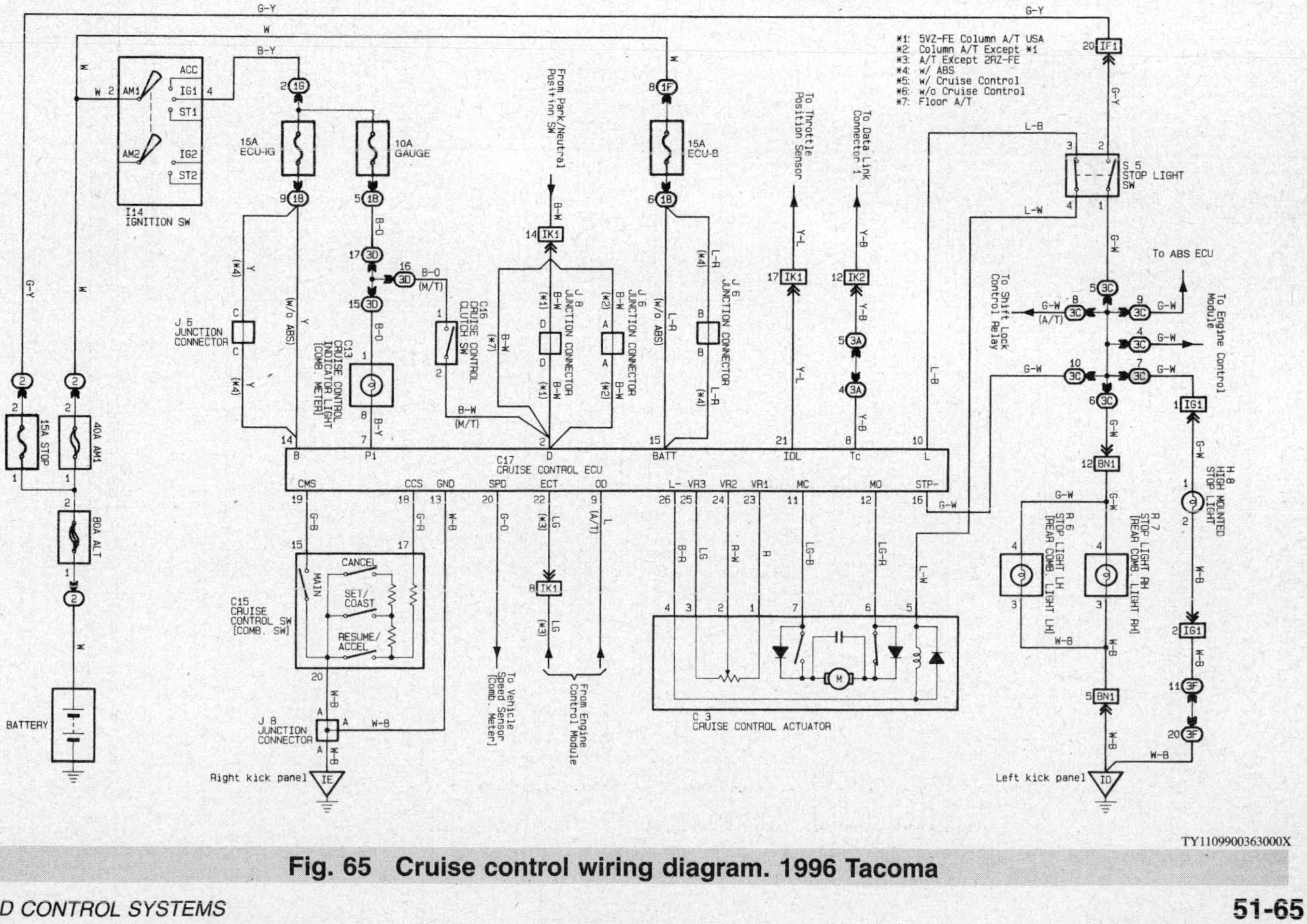

TY1109900363000X

Fig. 65   Cruise control wiring diagram. 1996 Tacoma

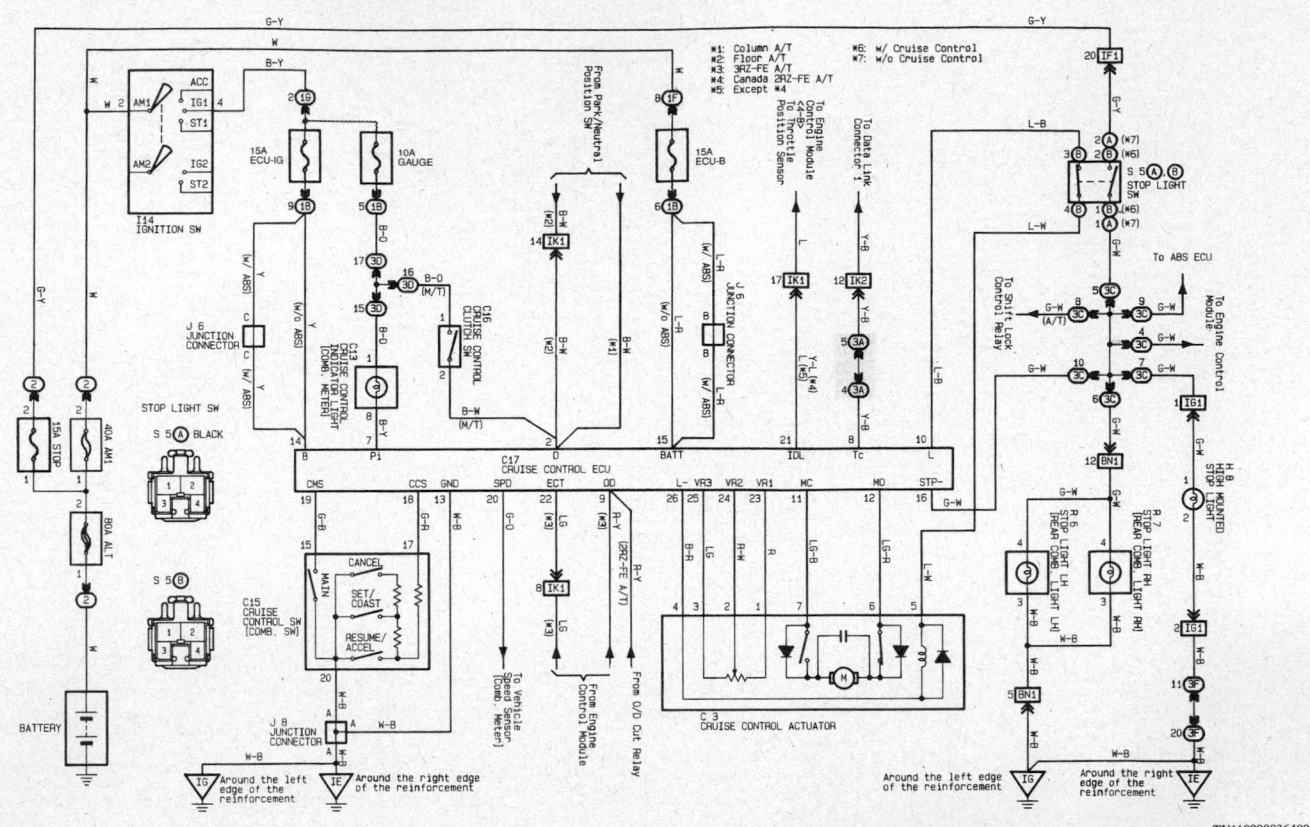

Fig. 66 Cruise control wiring diagram. 1997 Tacoma w/2RZ-FE & 3RZ-FE engines

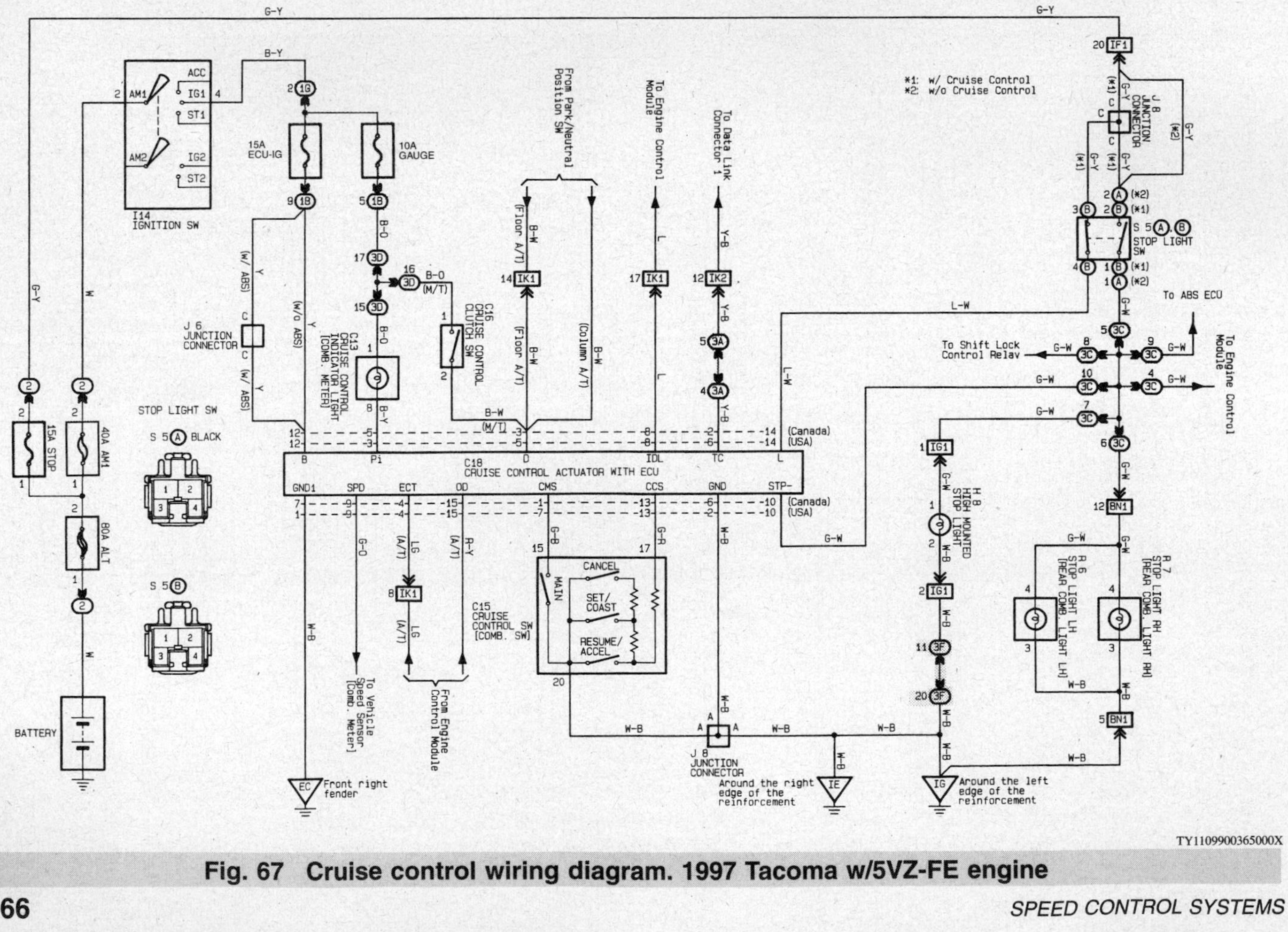

TY1109900364000X

Fig. 67 Cruise control wiring diagram. 1997 Tacoma w/5VZ-FE engine

TY1109900365000X

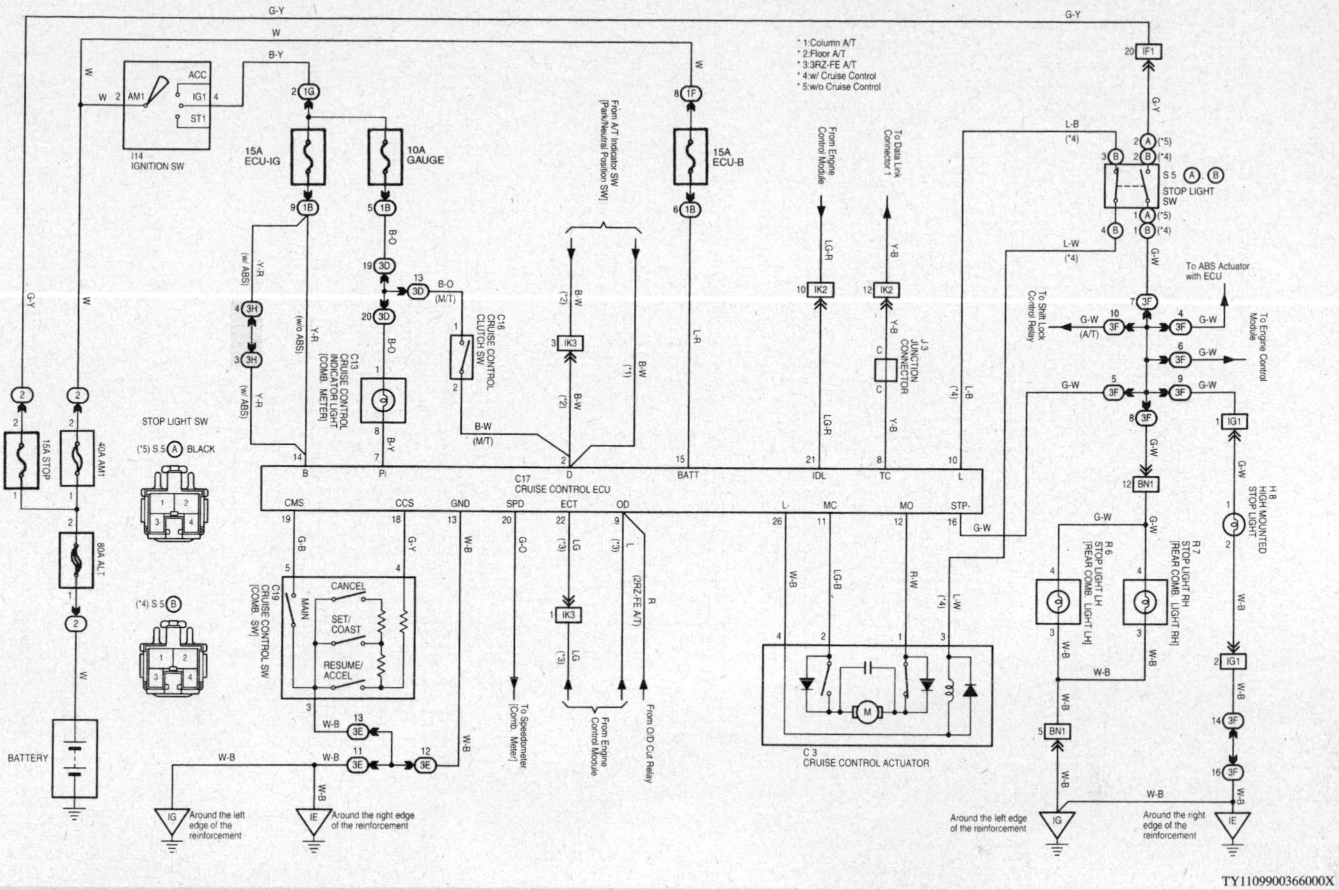

Fig. 68 Cruise control wiring diagram. 1998 Tacoma w/2RZ-FE & 3RZ-FE engines

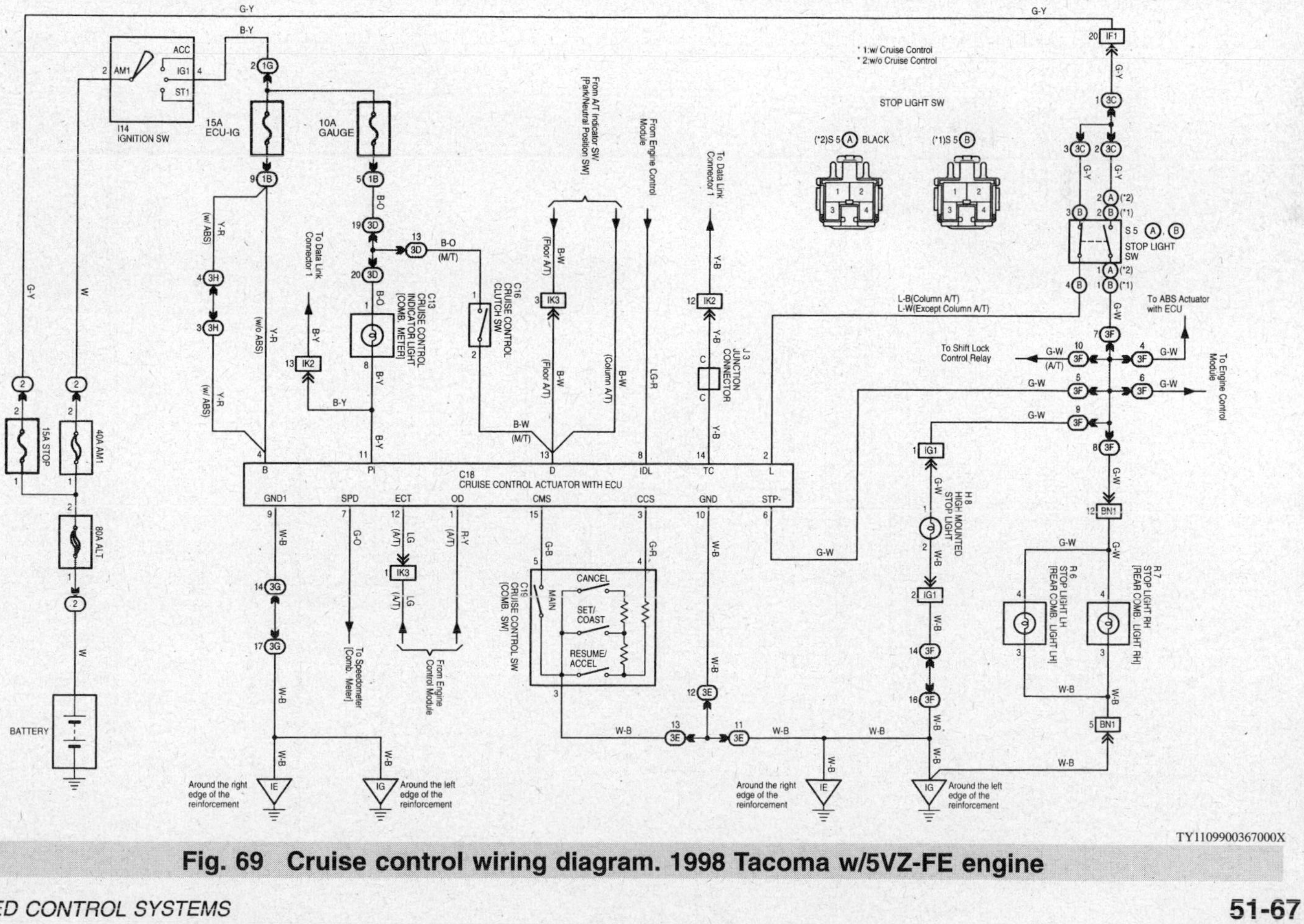

Fig. 69 Cruise control wiring diagram. 1998 Tacoma w/5VZ-FE engine

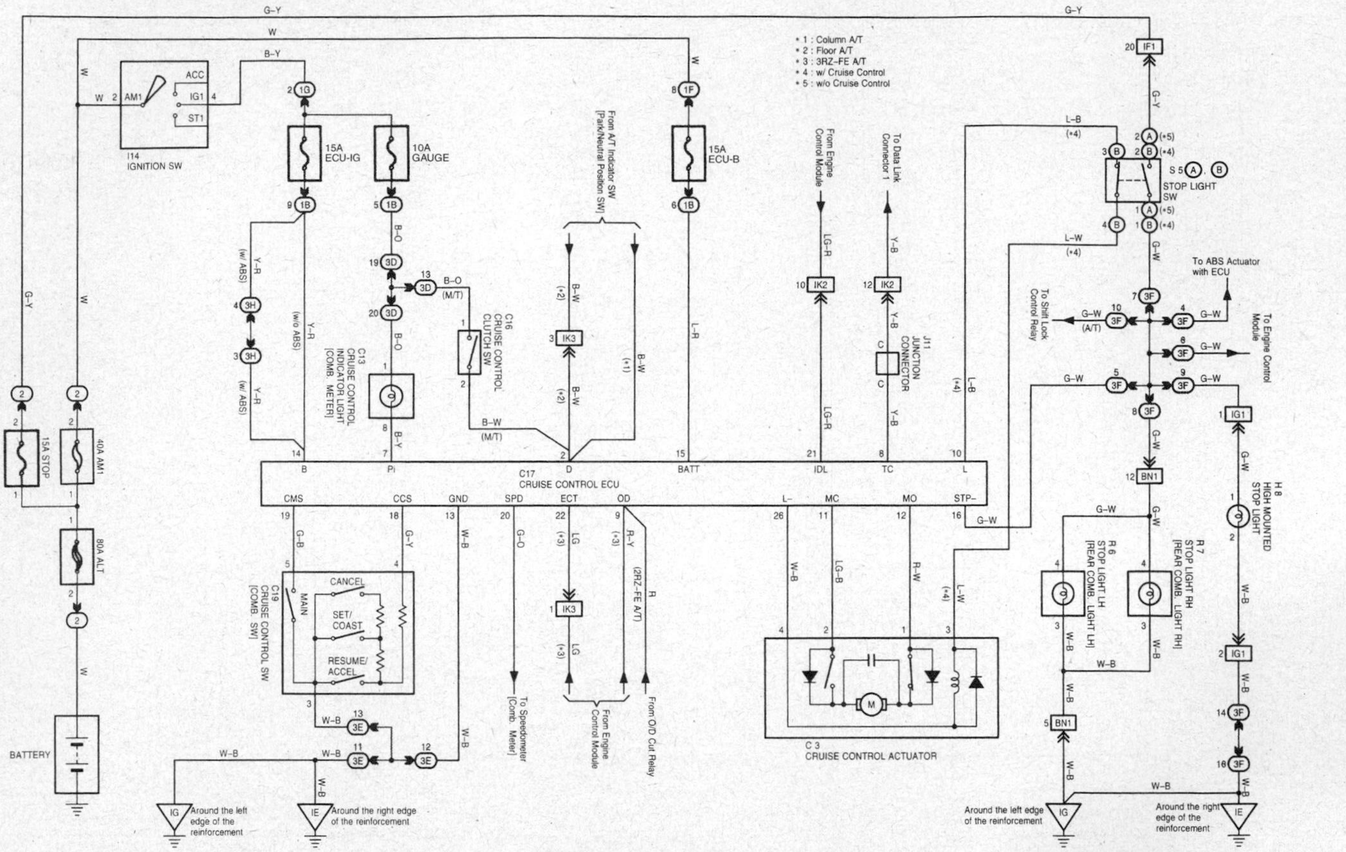

Fig. 70 Cruise control wiring diagram. 1999 Tacoma w/2RZ-FE & 3RZ-FE engines

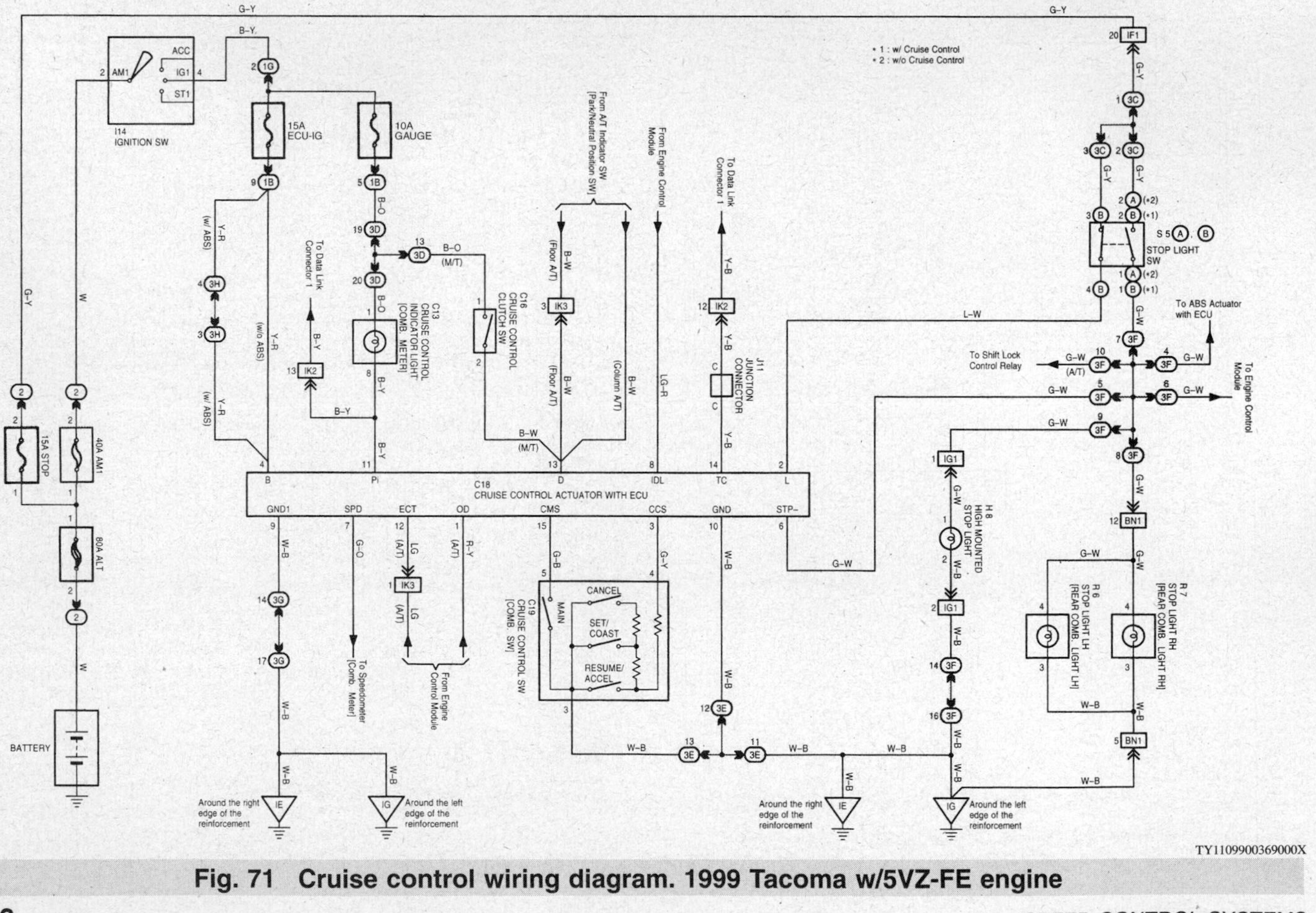

Fig. 71 Cruise control wiring diagram. 1999 Tacoma w/5VZ-FE engine

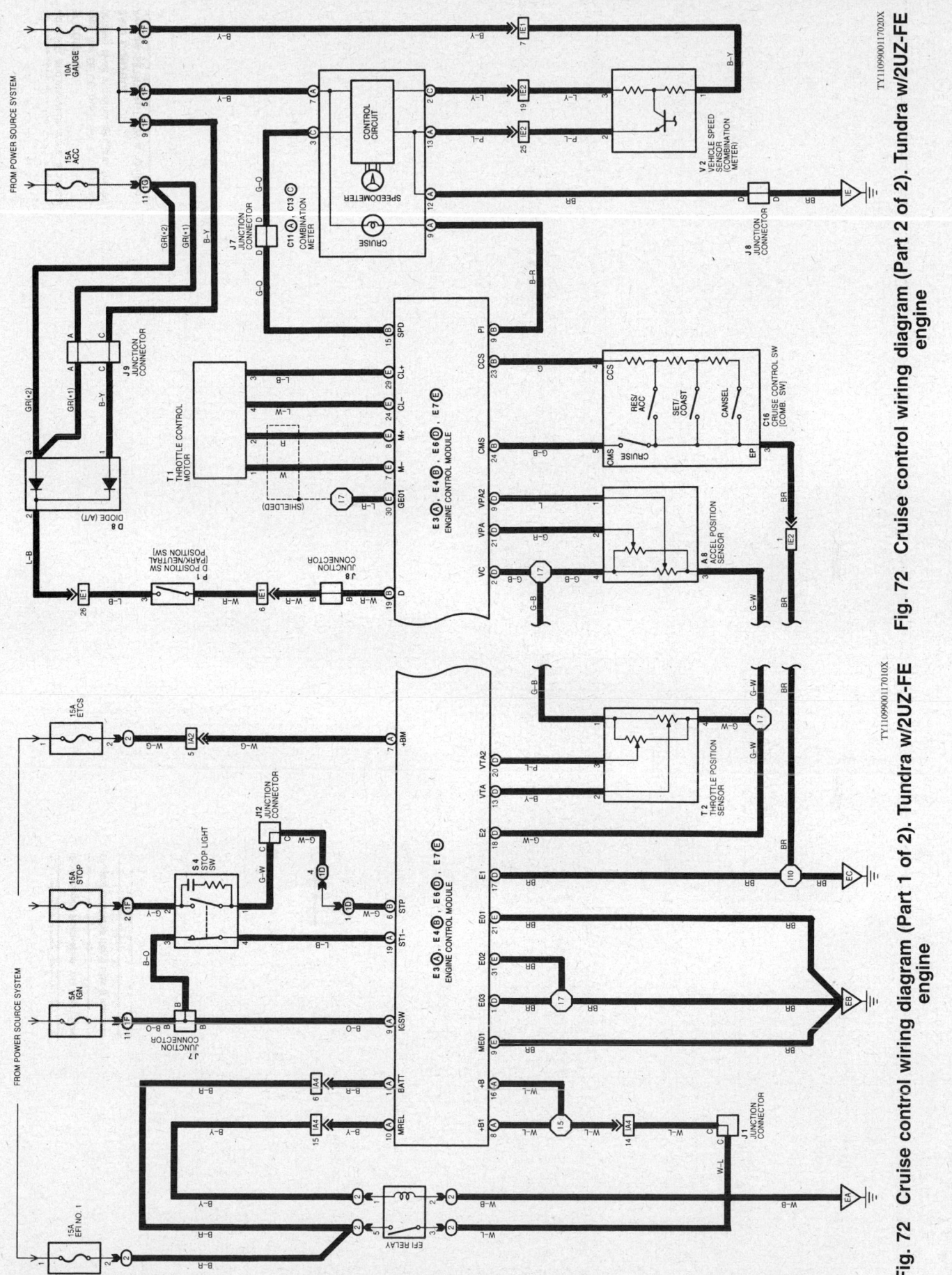

Fig. 72 Cruise control wiring diagram (Part 2 of 2). Tundra w/2UZ-FE engine

Fig. 72 Cruise control wiring diagram (Part 1 of 2). Tundra w/2UZ-FE engine

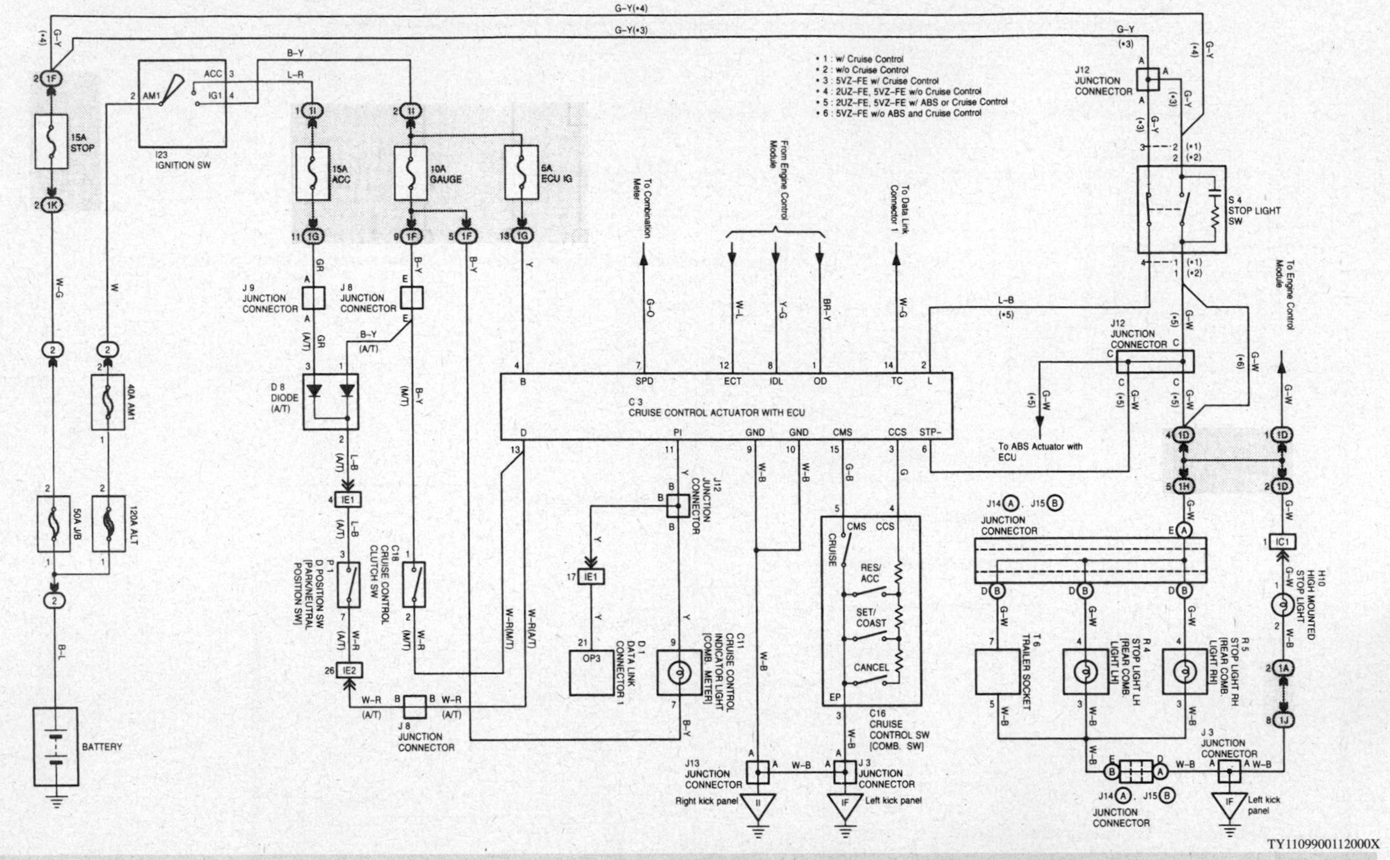

Fig. 73 Cruise control wiring diagram. Tundra w/5VZ-FE engine

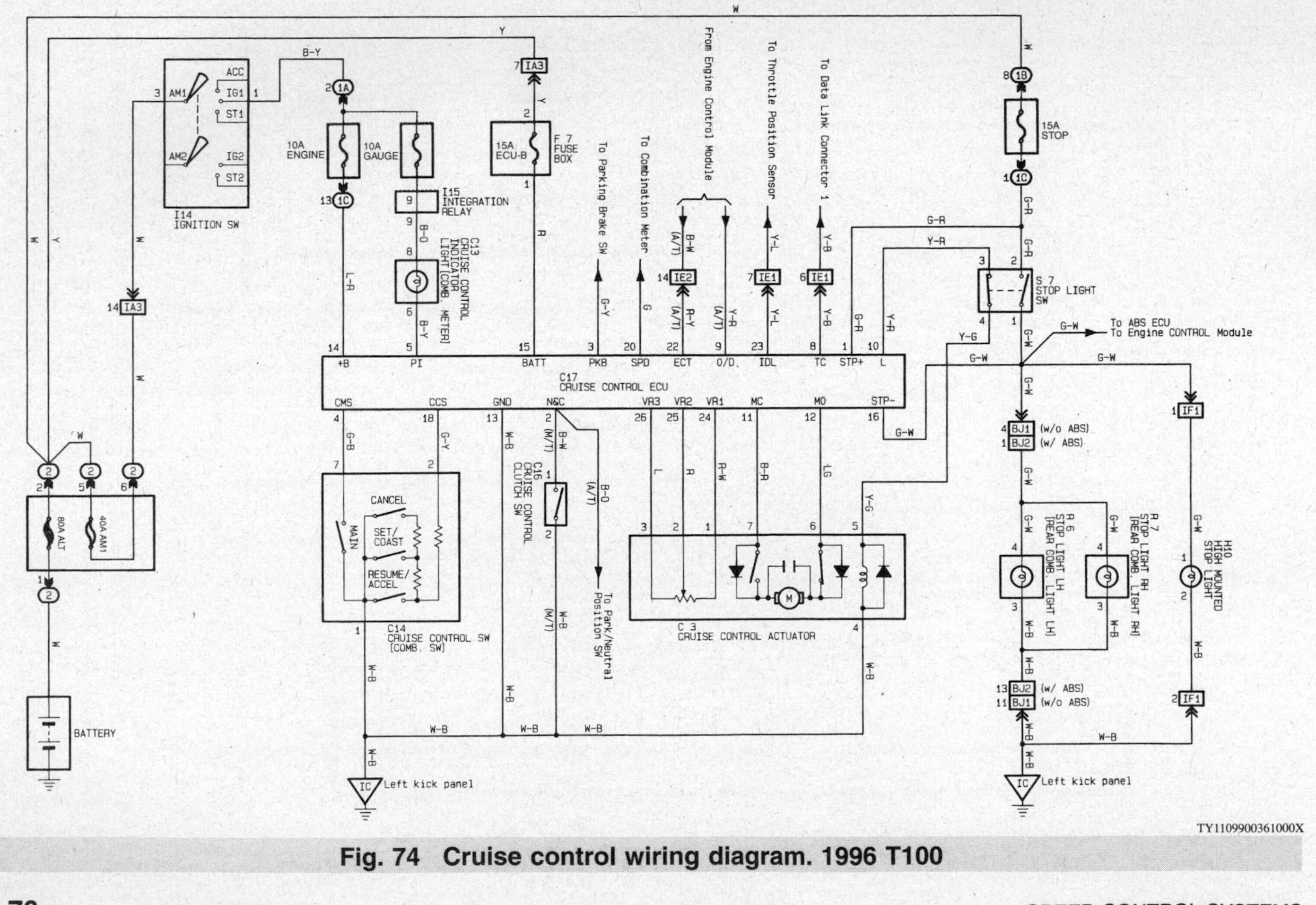

Fig. 74 Cruise control wiring diagram. 1996 T100

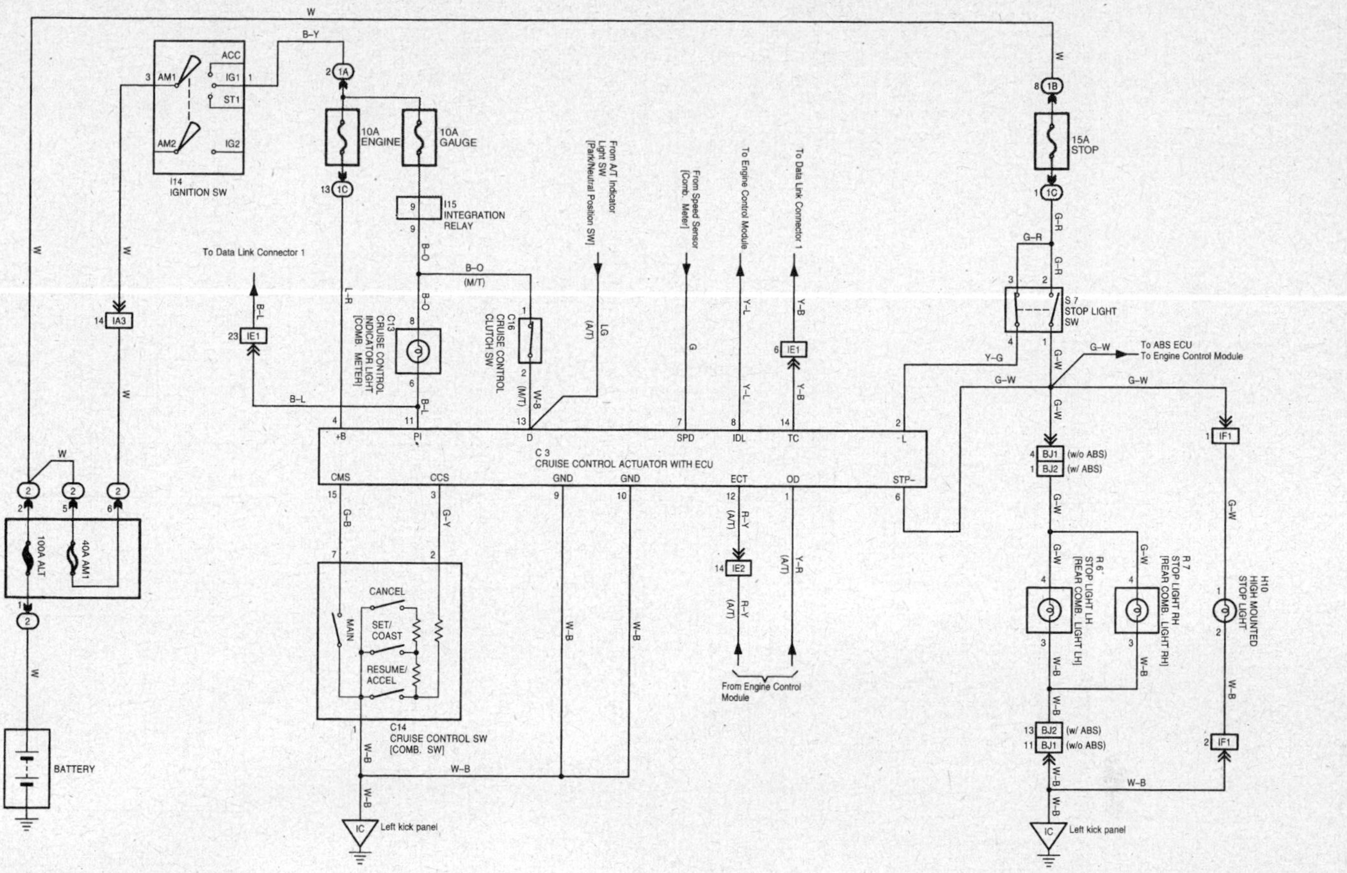

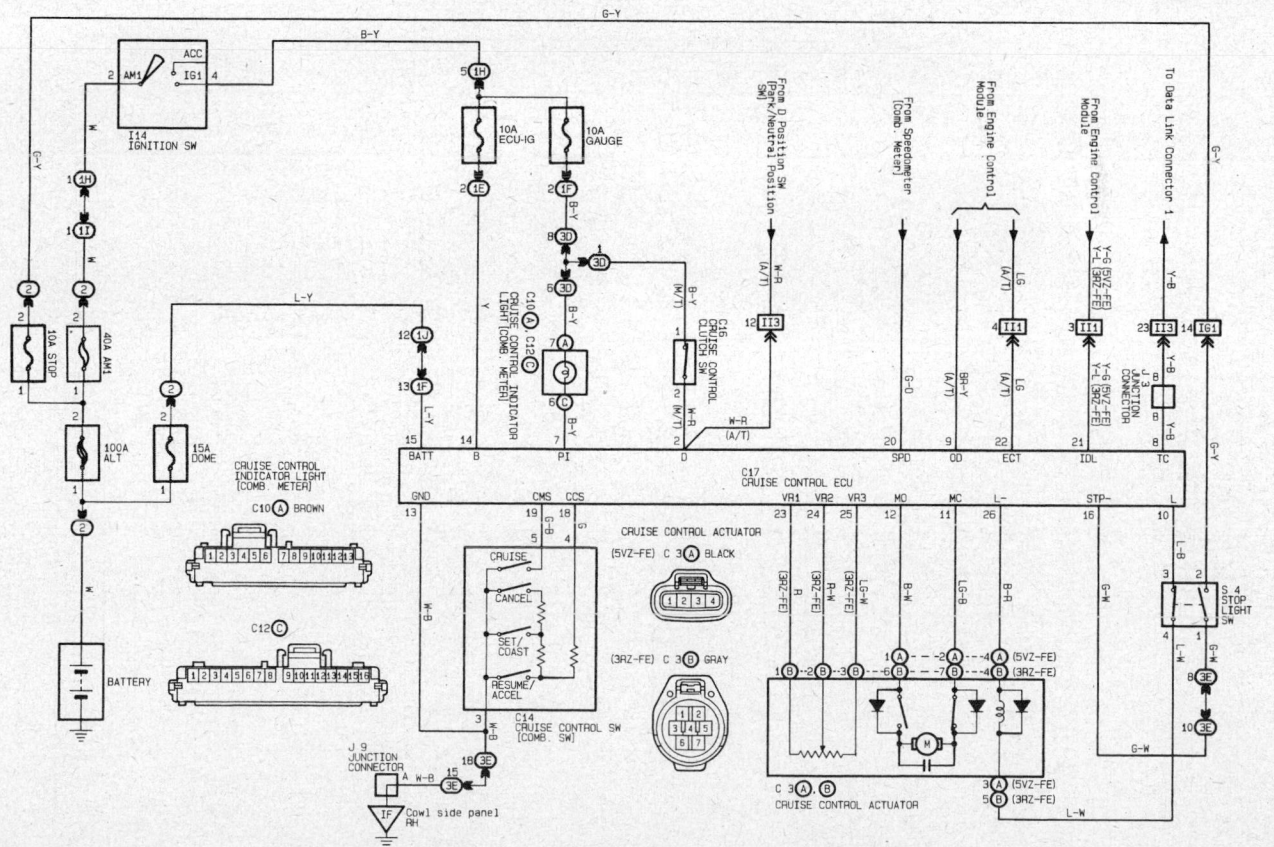

Fig. 75 Cruise control wiring diagram. 1997–98 T100

TY1109900362000X

Fig. 76 Cruise control wiring diagram. 1996 4Runner

TY1109900370000X

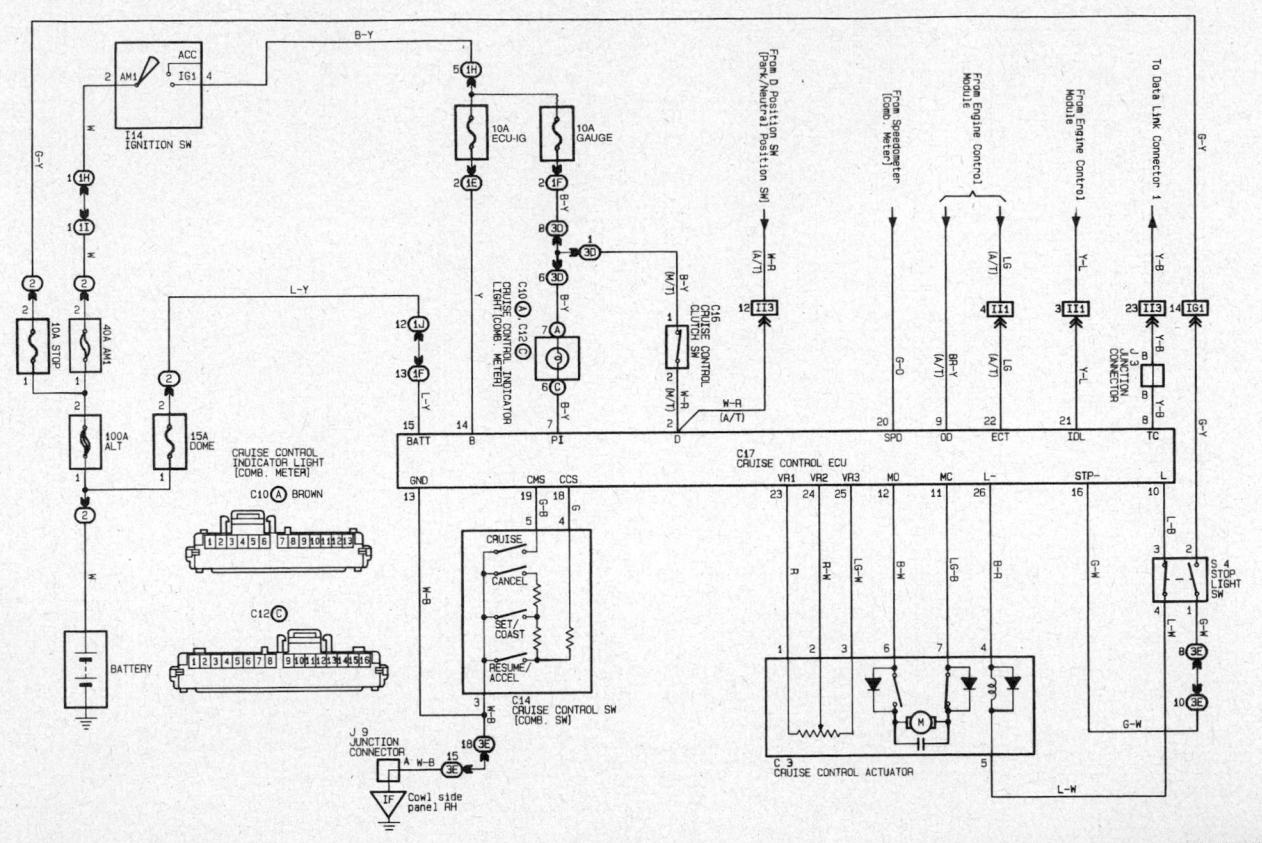

Fig. 77 Cruise control wiring diagram. 1997 4Runner w/3RZ-FE engine

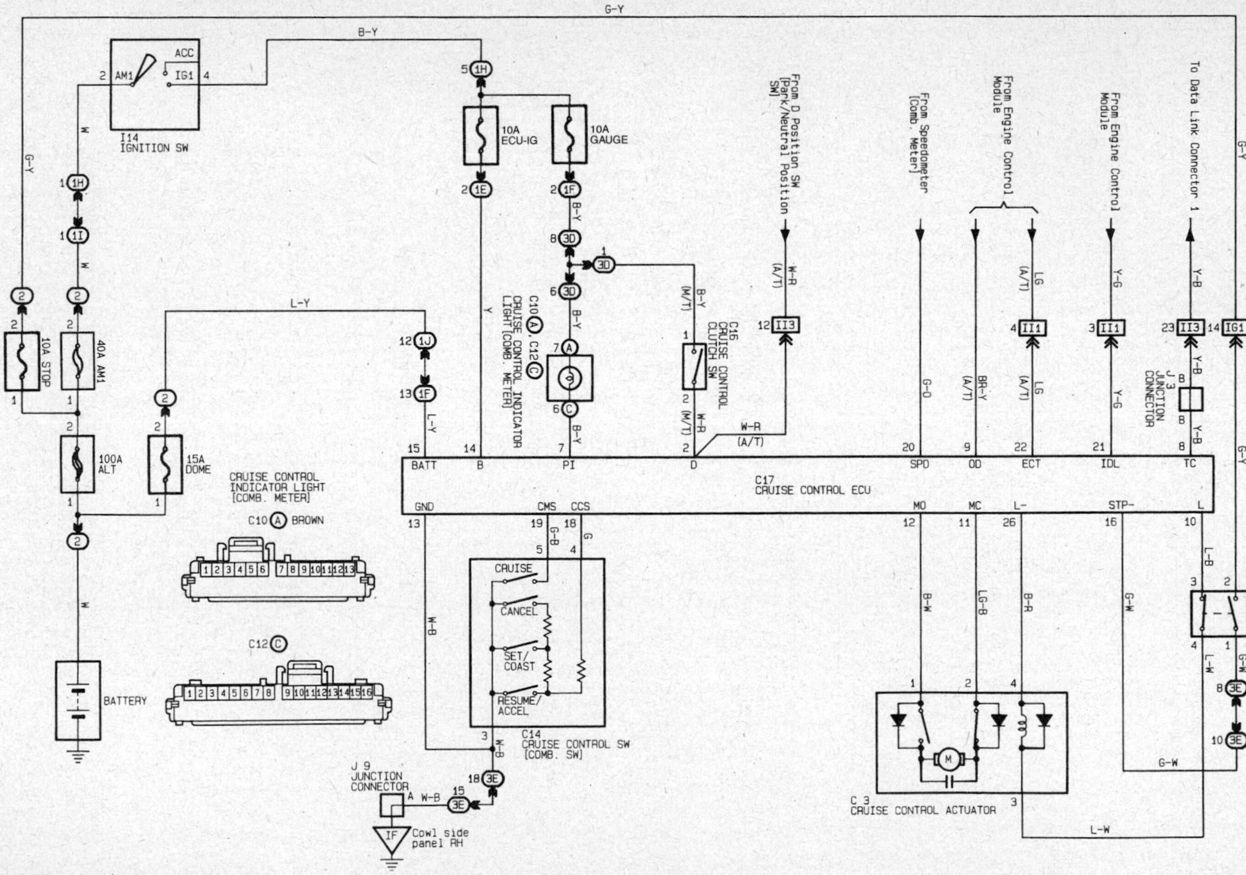

TY1109900371000X

Fig. 78 Cruise control wiring diagram. 1997 4Runner w/5VZ-FE engine

TY1109900372000X

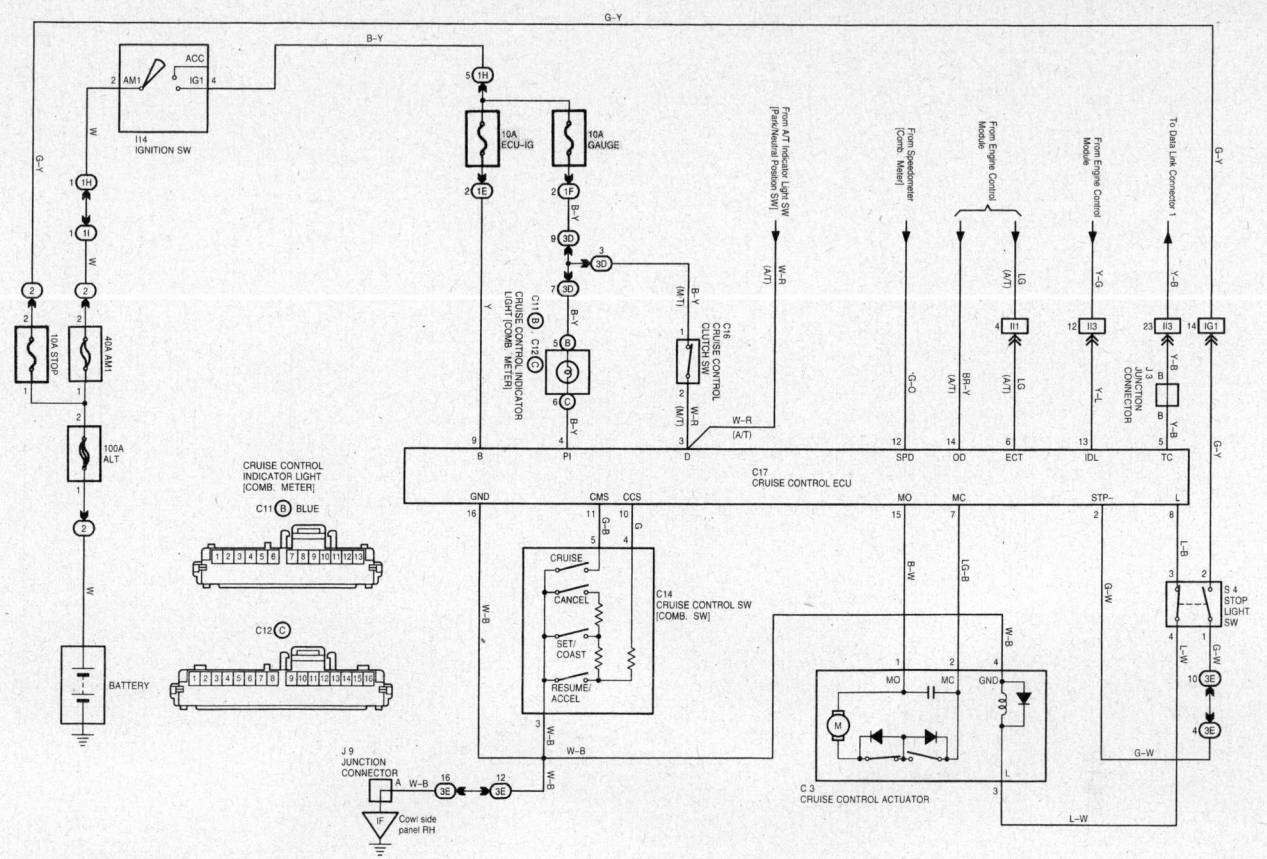

Fig. 79   Cruise control wiring diagram. 1998 4Runner w/3RZ-FE engine

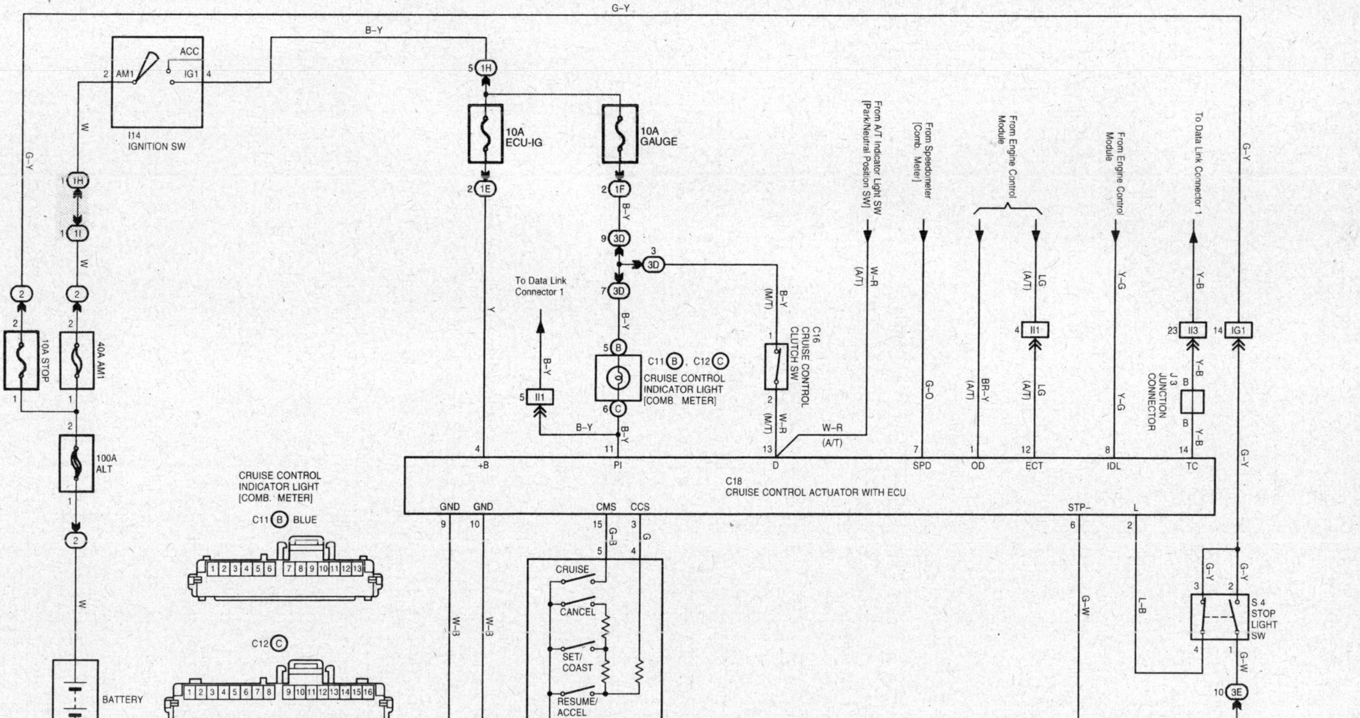

TY1109900373000X

Fig. 80   Cruise control wiring diagram. 1998 4Runner w/5VZ-FE engine

TY1109900374000X

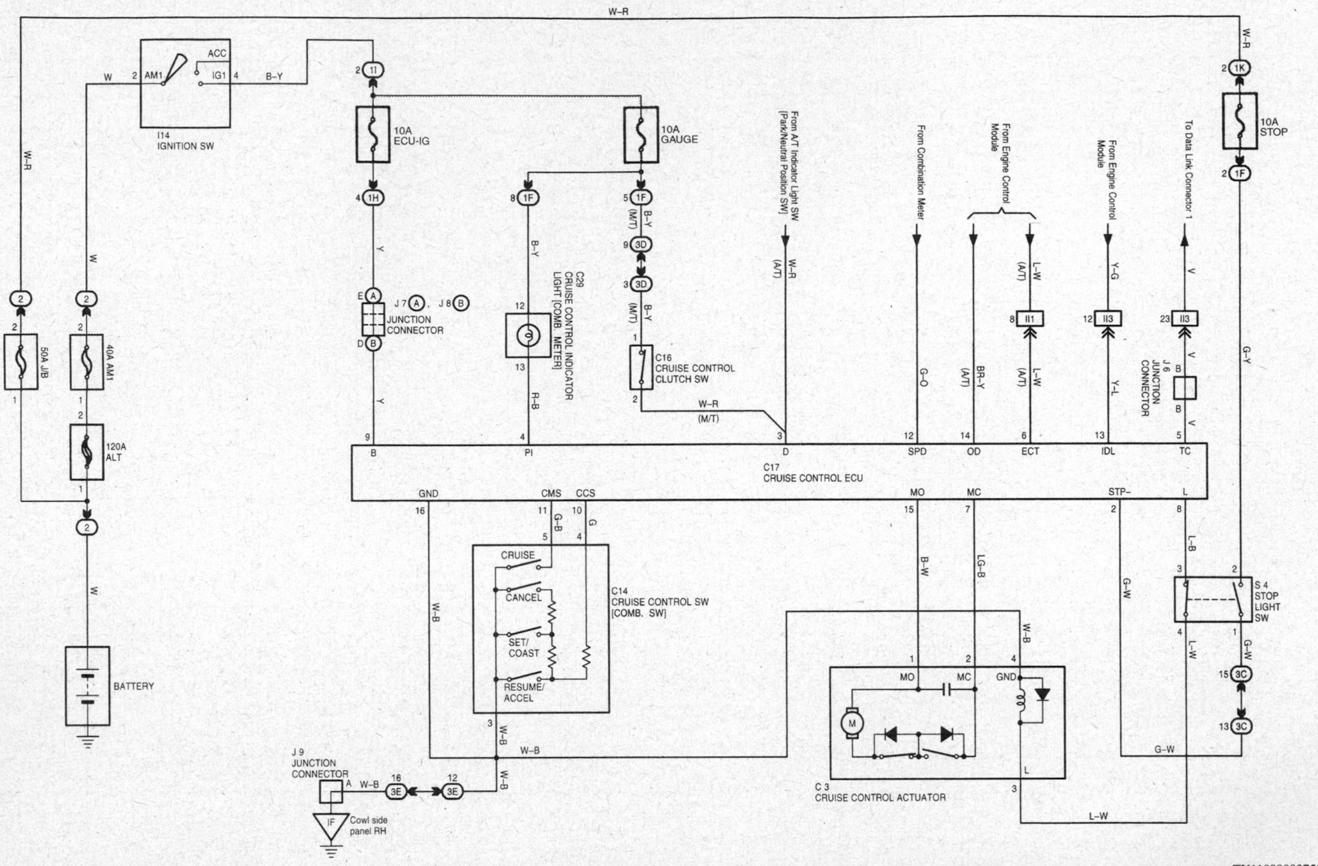

TY1109900375000X

Fig. 81 Cruise control wiring diagram. 1999 4Runner w/3RZ-FE engine

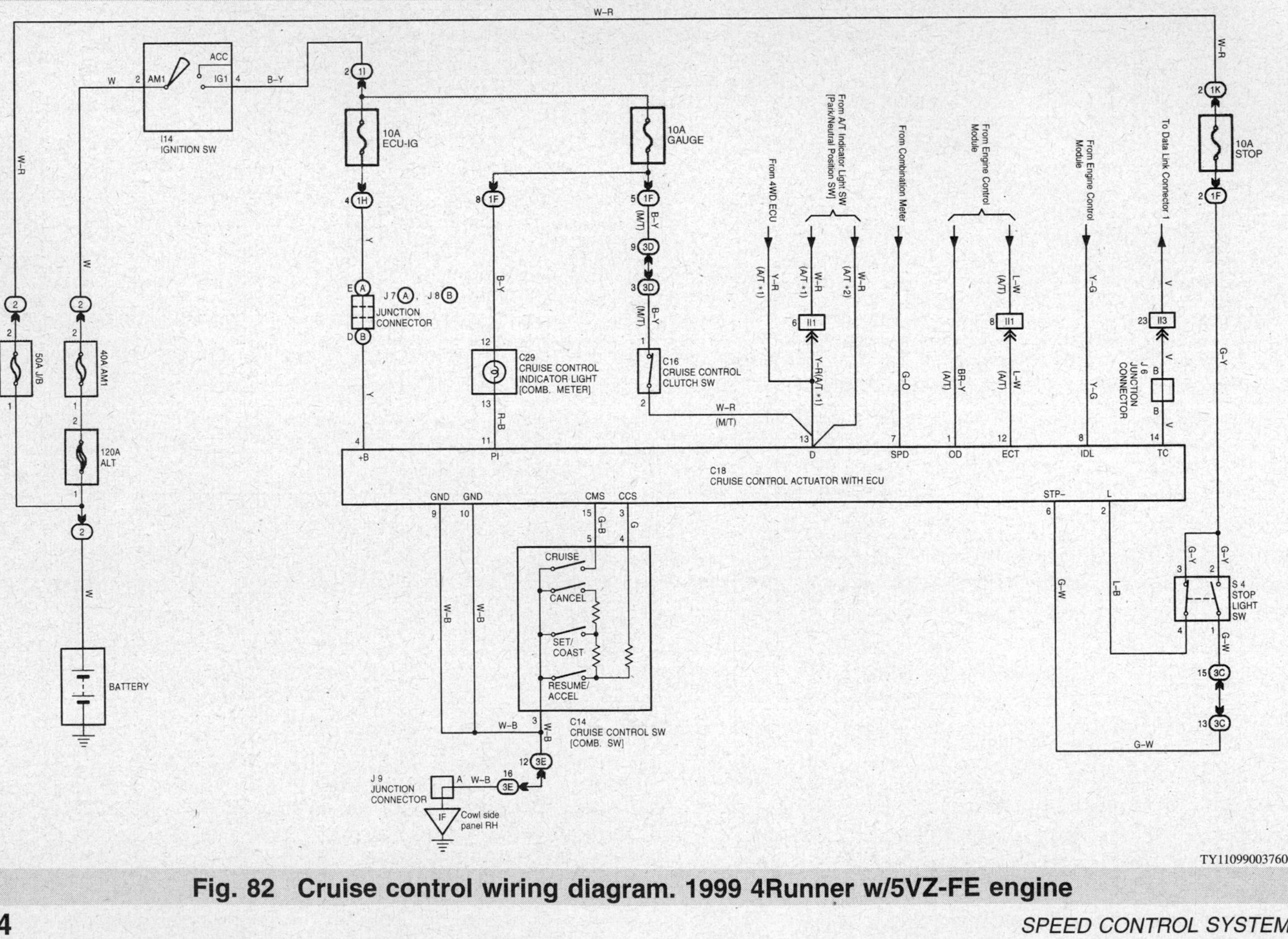

TY1109900376000X

Fig. 82 Cruise control wiring diagram. 1999 4Runner w/5VZ-FE engine

DIAGNOSTIC CHART INDEX

Code/Test	Description/Test	Page No.	Fig. No.
1996 AVALON			
—	Problem Symptoms Table	51-84	83
—	Actuator Control Cable	51-99	116
—	Back-Up Power Source Circuit	51-90	96
—	Cruise Control Switch Circuit	51-90	97
—	Electronically Controlled Transaxle Communication Circuit	51-88	94
—	Idle Switch Circuit	51-88	93
—	Park/Neutral Position Switch Circuit	51-89	95
—	Stop Lamp Switch Circuit	51-88	92
—	T_C Circuit	51-90	98
Code 11	Actuator Motor Circuit	51-85	87
Code 12	Actuator Magnetic Clutch Circuit	51-86	88
Code 13	Actuator Position Sensor Circuit	51-86	89
Code 14	Actuator Motor Circuit	51-85	87
Code 14	Actuator Position Sensor Circuit	51-86	89
Code 21	Vehicle Speed Sensor Circuit	51-86	90
Code 23	Vehicle Speed Sensor Circuit	51-86	90
Code 32	Control Switch Circuit	51-87	91
Code 34	Control Switch Circuit	51-87	91
Code 41	Actuator Motor Circuit	51-85	87
1996 CAMRY			
—	Problem Symptoms Table	51-84	84
—	Actuator Control Cable	51-99	116
—	Back-Up Power Source Circuit	51-90	96
—	Clutch Switch Circuit	51-101	120
—	Cruise Control Switch Circuit	51-90	97
—	Electronically Controlled Transaxle Communication Circuit	51-88	94
—	Idle Switch Circuit	51-88	93
—	Park/Neutral Position Switch Circuit	51-100	119
—	Stop Lamp Switch Circuit	51-88	92
—	T_c Circuit	51-101	121
Code 11	Actuator Motor Circuit	51-100	117
Code 12	Actuator Magnetic Clutch Circuit	51-86	88
Code 13	Actuator Position Sensor Circuit	51-100	118
Code 14	Actuator Motor Circuit	51-100	117
Code 21	Vehicle Speed Sensor Circuit	51-86	90
Code 23	Vehicle Speed Sensor Circuit	51-86	90
Code 32	Control Switch Circuit	51-87	91
Code 34	Control Switch Circuit	51-87	91
Code 42	Actuator Motor Circuit	51-100	117
CAMRY SOLARA, SIENNA & 1997–99 AVALON & CAMRY			
—	Problem Symptoms Table (Avalon & Sienna)	51-84	83
—	Problem Symptoms Table (Camry & Camry Solara)	51-84	84
—	Actuator Control Cable	51-99	116
—	Cruise Control Main Switch Circuit Fault	51-98	113
—	Cruise Main Indicator Lamp Circuit	51-98	114
—	Diagnosis Circuit	51-99	115
—	ECU Power Source Circuit	51-97	112
—	Electronically Controlled Transmission Communication Circuit	51-96	110
—	Park/Neutral Position Switch Circuit	51-97	111
—	Stop Lamp Switch Circuit Fault	51-95	109
Code 11	Actuator Motor Circuit	51-90	99
Code 12	Actuator Magnetic Clutch Circuit	51-91	100
Code 14	Actuator Mechanical Fault	51-92	101
Code 15	Actuator Motor Circuit	51-90	99
Code 21	Open In Vehicle Speed Sensor Circuit (Camry Solara & 1997–99 Avalon & Camry)	51-92	103
Code 21	Open In Vehicle Speed Sensor Circuit (Sienna)	51-93	104

Continued

DIAGNOSTIC CHART INDEX—Continued

Code/Test	Description/Test	Page No.	Fig. No.
CAMRY SOLARA, SIENNA & 1997–99 AVALON & CAMRY			
Code 23	Vehicle Speed Signal Fault	51-94	105
Code 32	Cruise Control Switch Circuit Fault	51-94	106
Code 51	Idle Signal Circuit Fault	51-94	107
PREVIA			
—	Problem Symptoms Table (1996)	51-155	250
—	Problem Symptoms Table (1997)	51-155	251
Test A	Power Source Circuit	51-155	252
Test B	Cruise Control Indicator Circuit	51-155	253
Test C	Control Switch Circuit	51-156	254
Test D	Actuator Circuit	51-156	255
Test E	Speed Sensor Circuit	51-156	256
Test F	Stop Lamp Switch Circuit	51-157	257
Test G	Parking Brake Switch Circuit	51-157	258
Test H	Park/Neutral Position Switch Circuit	51-158	259
Test I	ECT Solenoid No. 2 Circuit	51-158	260
Test J	IDL Signal Circuit	51-158	261
TUNDRA w/2UZ-FE ENGINE			
—	Problem Symptoms Table	51-85	86
—	Cruise Main Indicator Lamp	51-107	135
—	Main Switch Circuit	51-106	134
Code 21	Vehicle Speed Sensor Signal Abnormal	51-104	130
Code 23	Vehicle Speed Sensor Signal Abnormal	51-104	130
Code 32	Cruise Control Switch Circuit	51-106	132
Code 52	Stop Lamp Switch Circuit	51-105	131
Code 54	Input Signal Circuit	51-106	133
Code P0500	Vehicle Speed Sensor Signal Abnormal	51-104	130
Code P1520	Stop Lamp Switch Circuit	51-105	131
Code P1565	Cruise Control Switch Circuit	51-106	132
Code P1566	Input Signal Circuit	51-106	133
TUNDRA w/5VZ-FE ENGINE			
—	Problem Symptoms Table	51-85	85
—	Actuator Control Cable	51-104	129
—	Clutch Switch Circuit	51-104	128
—	Cruise Main Indicator Lamp Circuit	51-98	114
—	Cruise Control Main Switch Circuit Fault	51-98	113
—	Diagnosis Circuit	51-99	115
—	ECU Power Source Circuit	51-97	112
—	Electronically Controlled Transmission Communication Circuit	51-96	110
—	Idle Switch Circuit	51-103	127
—	Park/Neutral Position Switch Circuit	51-97	111
—	Stop Lamp Switch Circuit Fault	51-95	109
Code 12	Actuator Circuit Fault	51-102	122
Code 14	Actuator Mechanical Fault	51-102	123
Code 21	VSS Circuit Open	51-102	124
Code 23	VSS Signal Abnormal	51-103	125
Code 32	Control Switch Circuit	51-103	126
1996 LAND CRUISER			
—	Problem Symptoms Table	51-133	191
Test A	Power Source Circuit	51-134	193
Test B	Cruise Control Indicator Circuit	51-134	194
Test C	Actuator Circuit	51-134	195
Test D	Control Switch Circuit	51-135	196
Test E	No. 1 Vehicle Speed Sensor Circuit.	51-135	197
Test F	Stop Lamp Switch Circuit	51-135	198
Test G	Park/Neutral Position Switch Circuit	51-136	199

Continued

DIAGNOSTIC CHART INDEX—Continued

Code/Test	Description/Test	Page No.	Fig. No.
1996 LAND CRUISER			
Test H	No. 2 Solenoid Circuit	51-136	200
Test I	IDL Signal Circuit	51-136	201
1997 LAND CRUISER			
—	Problem Symptoms Table	51-133	191
Test A	Power Source Circuit	51-137	202
Test B	Cruise Control Indicator Circuit	51-137	203
Test C	Actuator Circuit	51-137	204
Test D	Control Switch Circuit	51-138	205
Test E	No. 1 Vehicle Speed Sensor Circuit	51-138	206
Test F	Stop Lamp Switch Circuit	51-138	207
Test G	Park/Neutral Position Switch Circuit	51-139	208
Test H	No. 2 Solenoid Circuit	51-139	209
Test I	IDL Signal Circuit	51-139	210
1998–99 LAND CRUISER			
—	Problem Symptoms Table	51-134	192
—	Cruise Main Indicator Lamp Circuit	51-142	216
—	Main Switch Circuit	51-141	215
Code 21	Vehicle Speed Sensor Fault	51-139	211
Code 23	Vehicle Speed Sensor Fault	51-139	211
Code 32	Control Switch Circuit	51-140	213
Code 52	Stop Lamp Switch Circuit	51-140	212
Code 54	Input Signal Circuit	51-141	214
Code P0500	Vehicle Speed Sensor Fault	51-139	211
Code P1520	Stop Lamp Switch Circuit	51-140	212
Code P1565	Control Switch Circuit	51-140	213
Code P1566	Input Signal Circuit	51-141	214
1996 PASEO			
—	Problem Symptoms Table	51-142	217
—	Actuator Control Cable Inspection	51-148	231
—	Back-Up Power Source Circuit	51-147	228
—	Cruise Control Switch Circuit	51-148	229
—	Idle Switch Circuit	51-145	224
—	ECU Power Source Circuit	51-147	227
—	Electronically Controlled Transaxle Communication Circuit	51-146	225
—	Park/Neutral Position Switch Circuit	51-146	226
—	Stop Light Switch Circuit	51-145	223
—	T_C Circuit	51-148	230
Code 11	Actuator Motor Circuit	51-142	218
Code 12	Actuator Magnetic Clutch Circuit	51-143	219
Code 13	Actuator Position Sensor Circuit	51-143	220
Code 14	Actuator Motor Circuit	51-142	218
Code 14	Actuator Position Sensor Circuit	51-143	220
Code 21	Vehicle Speed Sensor Circuit	51-144	221
Code 23	Vehicle Speed Sensor Circuit	51-144	221
Code 32	Control Switch Circuit	51-144	222
Code 41	Actuator Motor Circuit	51-142	218
Code 42	Actuator Motor Circuit	51-142	218
Code 42	Actuator Position Sensor Circuit	51-143	220
1997 PASEO			
—	Problem Symptoms Table	51-148	232
—	Actuator Control Cable Inspection	51-154	249
—	Back-Up Power Source Circuit	51-153	245
—	Clutch Switch Circuit	51-152	243
—	Cruise Main Indicator Light Circuit	51-154	247
—	Diagnosis Circuit	51-154	248

Continued

DIAGNOSTIC CHART INDEX—Continued

Code/Test	Description/Test	Page No.	Fig. No.
1997 PASEO			
—	ECU Power Source Circuit	51-153	244
—	Electronically Controlled Transaxle Communication Circuit	51-151	241
—	Main Cruise Control Switch Circuit	51-154	246
—	Park/Neutral Position Switch Circuit	51-152	242
—	Stop Lamp Switch Circuit	51-151	240
Code 11	Actuator Motor Circuit	51-149	233
Code 15	Actuator Motor Circuit	51-149	233
Code 12	Actuator Magnetic Clutch Circuit	51-149	234
Code 14	Actuator Mechanical Fault	51-149	235
Code 21	Vehicle Speed Sensor Open Circuit	51-150	236
Code 23	Vehicle Speed Signal Abnormal	51-150	237
Code 32	Cruise Control Switch Circuit	51-150	238
Code 51	Idle Signal Circuit	51-151	239
1996 SUPRA			
—	Problem Symptoms Table	51-173	293
—	Back-Up Power Source Circuit	51-179	305
—	ECU Power Source Circuit	51-179	304
—	Electronically Controlled Transmission Communication Circuit	51-177	301
—	Idle Switch Circuit	51-177	300
—	Main Switch Circuit	51-180	306
—	Parking Brake Switch Circuit	51-178	302
—	Park Neutral Position/Clutch Switch Circuit	51-178	303
—	Stop Lamp Switch Circuit	51-176	299
—	T_C Circuit	51-180	307
Code 11	Actuator Motor Circuit	51-173	294
Code 12	Actuator Magnetic Clutch Circuit	51-174	295
Code 13	Actuator Position Sensor Circuit	51-174	296
Code 14	Actuator Motor Circuit	51-173	294
Code 14	Actuator Position Sensor Circuit	51-174	296
Code 21	Vehicle Speed Sensor Circuit	51-175	297
Code 23	Vehicle Speed Sensor Circuit	51-175	297
Code 32	Control Switch Circuit	51-175	298
Code 34	Control Switch Circuit	51-175	298
Code 41	Actuator Motor Circuit	51-173	294
1996 TACOMA			
—	Problem Symptoms Table	51-191	333
—	Actuator Control Cable Inspection	51-197	348
—	Back-Up Power Source Circuit	51-196	345
—	Clutch Switch Circuit	51-195	343
—	ECU Power Source Circuit	51-196	344
—	Electronically Controlled Transmission Communication Circuit	51-194	341
—	Idle Switch Circuit	51-194	340
—	Main Switch Circuit	51-197	346
—	Park/Neutral Position Switch Circuit	51-195	342
—	Stop Lamp Switch Circuit	51-194	339
—	T_C Circuit	51-197	347
Code 11	Actuator Motor Circuit	51-192	334
Code 12	Actuator Magnetic Clutch Circuit	51-192	335
Code 13	Actuator Position Sensor Circuit	51-192	336
Code 14	Actuator Motor Circuit	51-192	334
Code 14	Actuator Position Sensor Circuit	51-192	336
Code 21	Vehicle Speed Sensor Circuit	51-193	337
Code 23	Vehicle Speed Sensor Circuit	51-193	337
Code 32	Control Switch Circuit	51-193	338
Code 34	Control Switch Circuit	51-193	338

Continued

DIAGNOSTIC CHART INDEX—Continued

Continued

DIAGNOSTIC CHART INDEX—Continued

Code/Test	Description/Test	Page No.	Fig. No.
1996 T100			
—	Problem Symptoms Table	51-222	398
Test A	Power Source Circuit	51-222	400
Test B	Cruise Control Indicator Circuit	51-222	401
Test C	Speed Control Switch Circuit Inspection	51-223	402
Test D	Actuator Circuit	51-223	403
Test E	Speed Sensor Circuit	51-223	404
Test F	Stop Lamp Switch Circuit	51-224	405
Test G	Parking Brake Circuit	51-224	406
Test H	Clutch Start Switch Circuit	51-224	407
Test I	Park/Neutral Position Switch Circuit	51-224	408
Test J	IDL Signal Circuit	51-225	409
1997–98 T100			
—	Problem Symptoms Table	51-222	399
—	Actuator Control Cable Inspection	51-231	424
—	Clutch Switch Circuit	51-229	419
—	Cruise Main Indicator Lamp	51-230	422
—	Diagnosis Circuit	51-231	423
—	ECU Power Source Circuit	51-229	420
—	Electronically Controlled Transmission Communication Circuit	51-228	417
—	Idle Switch Circuit	51-227	416
—	Main Switch Circuit	51-230	421
—	Park/Neutral Position Switch Circuit	51-228	418
—	Stop Lamp Switch Circuit	51-227	415
Code 12	Actuator Circuit	51-225	410
Code 14	Actuator Mechanical Fault	51-225	411
Code 21	Open In Vehicle Speed Sensor Circuit	51-225	412
Code 23	Vehicle Speed Sensor Abnormal	51-226	413
Code 32	Control Switch Circuit	51-226	414
1996-97 CELICA			
—	Problem Symptoms Table	51-107	136
—	Actuator Control Cable Inspection	51-118	158
—	Back-Up Power Source Circuit	51-117	155
—	Clutch Switch Circuit	51-116	152
—	ECU Power Source Circuit	51-116	153
—	Electronically Controlled Transaxle Communication Circuit	51-114	150
—	Idle Switch Circuit	51-113	148
—	Main Switch Circuit	51-118	156
—	Park/Neutral Position Switch Circuit	51-115	151
—	Stop Lamp Switch Circuit	51-113	147
—	T_C Circuit	51-118	157
Code 11	Actuator Motor Circuit	51-107	137
Code 12	Actuator Magnetic Clutch Circuit	51-108	138
Code 13	Actuator Position Sensor Circuit	51-108	139
Code 14	Actuator Motor Circuit	51-107	137
Code 14	Actuator Position Sensor Circuit	51-108	139
Code 21	Vehicle Speed Sensor Circuit	51-109	140
Code 23	Vehicle Speed Sensor Circuit	51-109	140
Code 32	Control Switch Circuit	51-109	141
1998–99 CELICA			
—	Problem Symptoms Table	51-107	136
—	Actuator Control Cable Inspection	51-118	158
—	Back-Up Power Source Circuit	51-117	155
—	Clutch Switch Circuit	51-116	152
—	ECU Power Source Circuit	51-117	154
—	Electronically Controlled Transaxle Communication Circuit	51-114	150
—	Idle Switch Circuit	51-114	149

Continued

SPEED CONTROL SYSTEMS

DIAGNOSTIC CHART INDEX—Continued

Code/Test	Description/Test	Page No.	Fig. No.
1998–99 CELICA			
—	Main Switch Circuit	51-118	156
—	Park/Neutral Position Switch Circuit	51-115	151
—	Stop Lamp Switch Circuit	51-113	147
—	T_C Circuit	51-118	157
Code 11	Actuator Motor Circuit	51-110	142
Code 12	Actuator Magnetic Clutch Circuit	51-110	143
Code 13	Actuator Position Sensor Circuit	51-111	144
Code 14	Actuator Motor Circuit	51-110	142
Code 14	Actuator Position Sensor Circuit	51-111	144
Code 21	Vehicle Speed Sensor Circuit	51-111	145
Code 23	Vehicle Speed Sensor Circuit	51-111	145
Code 32	Control Switch Circuit	51-112	146
1996–97 COROLLA			
—	Problem Symptoms Table	51-119	159
—	Actuator Control Cable Inspection	51-125	174
—	Back-Up Power Source Circuit	51-124	171
—	Clutch Switch Circuit	51-123	169
—	Cruise Control ECU Power Source Circuit	51-124	170
—	Electronically Controlled Transaxle Communication Circuit	51-122	167
—	Idle Switch Circuit	51-122	166
—	Main Switch Circuit	51-124	172
—	Park/Neutral Position Switch Circuit	51-123	168
—	Stop Lamp Switch Circuit	51-121	165
—	T_C Circuit	51-125	173
Code 11	Actuator Motor Circuit	51-119	160
Code 12	Actuator Magnetic Clutch Circuit	51-119	161
Code 13	Actuator Position Sensor Circuit	51-120	162
Code 14	Actuator Motor Circuit	51-119	160
Code 14	Actuator Position Sensor Circuit	51-120	162
Code 21	Vehicle Speed Sensor Circuit	51-120	163
Code 23	Vehicle Speed Sensor Circuit	51-120	163
Code 32	Control Switch Circuit	51-121	164
Code 34	Control Switch Circuit	51-121	164
1998–99 COROLLA			
—	Problem Symptoms Table	51-119	159
—	Actuator Control Cable	51-133	190
—	Clutch Switch Circuit	51-131	185
—	Cruise Main Indicator Lamp Circuit	51-132	188
—	Diagnosis Circuit	51-133	189
—	ECU Power Source Circuit	51-131	186
—	Electronically Controlled Transmission Communication Circuit	51-130	183
—	Main Switch Circuit	51-132	187
—	Park/Neutral Position Switch Circuit	51-130	184
—	Stop Lamp Switch Circuit	51-129	182
Code 11	Actuator Motor Circuit	51-125	175
Code 12	Actuator Magnetic Clutch Circuit	51-126	176
Code 14	Actuator Mechanical Fault	51-126	177
Code 15	Actuator Motor Circuit	51-125	175
Code 21	Open In Vehicle Speed Sensor Circuit	51-127	178
Code 23	Vehicle Speed Signal Abnormal	51-127	179
Code 32	Control Switch Circuit	51-128	180
Code 51	Idle Signal Circuit	51-128	181
1996–97 RAV4			
—	Problem Symptoms Table	51-158	262
—	Actuator Control Cable Inspection	51-165	277
—	Back-Up Power Source Circuit	51-164	274

Continued

DIAGNOSTIC CHART INDEX—Continued

Code/Test	Description/Test	Page No.	Fig. No.
1996–97 RAV4			
—	Clutch Switch Circuit	51-163	272
—	Cruise Control Main Switch Circuit	51-164	275
—	ECU Power Source Circuit	51-163	273
—	Electronically Controlled Transaxle Communication Circuit	51-162	270
—	Idle Switch Circuit	51-162	269
—	Park/Neutral Position Switch Circuit	51-163	271
—	Stop Lamp Switch Circuit	51-161	268
—	T_C Circuit	51-165	276
Code 11	Actuator Motor Circuit	51-159	263
Code 12	Actuator Magnetic Clutch Circuit	51-159	264
Code 13	Actuator Position Sensor Circuit	51-160	265
Code 14	Actuator Motor Circuit	51-159	263
Code 14	Actuator Position Sensor Circuit	51-160	265
Code 21	Vehicle Speed Sensor Circuit	51-160	266
Code 32	Cruise Control Switch Circuit	51-160	267
1998–99 RAV4			
—	Problem Symptoms Table	51-158	262
—	Actuator Control Cable	51-173	292
—	Clutch Switch Circuit	51-171	288
—	Cruise Control Main Indicator Lamp Circuit	51-172	290
—	Cruise Control Switch Circuit	51-168	283
—	Diagnosis Circuit	51-172	291
—	ECU Power Source Circuit	51-171	289
—	Electronically Controlled Transmission Communications Circuit	51-170	286
—	Idle Signal Circuit	51-169	285
—	Park/Neutral Position Switch	51-170	287
—	Stop Light Switch Circuit	51-169	284
Code 11	Actuator Motor Circuit	51-165	278
Code 12	Actuator Magnetic Clutch Circuit	51-166	279
Code 14	Actuator Mechanical Fault	51-166	280
Code 15	Actuator Motor Circuit	51-165	278
Code 21	Open In Vehicle Speed Sensor Circuit	51-167	281
Code 23	Vehicle Speed Signal Abnormal	51-167	282
1996–97 4RUNNER			
—	Problem Symptoms Table	51-231	425
—	Actuator Control Cable	51-241	445
—	Back-Up Power Source Circuit	51-239	441
—	Clutch Switch Circuit	51-238	439
—	Cruise Main Indicator Lamp Circuit	51-240	443
—	Diagnosis Circuit	51-240	444
—	ECU Power Source Circuit	51-239	440
—	Electronically Controlled Transmission Communication Circuit	51-237	437
—	Idle Switch Circuit	51-236	436
—	Main Switch Circuit	51-240	442
—	Park/Neutral position Switch Circuit	51-238	438
—	Stop Lamp Switch Circuit	51-236	435
Code 11	Actuator Motor Circuit	51-232	427
Code 12	Magnetic Clutch Circuit	51-233	428
Code 13	Actuator Position Sensor Circuit	51-233	429
Code 14	Actuator Mechanical Fault	51-233	430
Code 15	Actuator Motor Circuit	51-232	427
Code 21	Open In Vehicle Speed Sensor Circuit	51-234	431
Code 23	Vehicle Speed Sensor Abnormal	51-235	432
Code 32	Control Switch Circuit	51-235	433
Code 51	Idle Signal Circuit	51-235	434

Continued

DIAGNOSTIC CHART INDEX—Continued

Code/Test	Description/Test	Page No.	Fig. No.
1998–99 4RUNNER w/DENSO CRUISE CONTROL			
—	Problem Symptoms Table	51-231	425
—	Actuator Control Cable	51-248	461
—	Clutch Switch Circuit	51-246	456
—	Cruise Main Indicator Lamp Circuit	51-247	459
—	Diagnosis Circuit	51-248	460
—	ECU Power Source Circuit	51-246	457
—	Electronically Controlled Transmission Communication Circuit	51-245	454
—	Main Switch Circuit	51-247	458
—	Park/Neutral Position Switch Circuit	51-245	455
—	Stop Lamp Switch Circuit	51-244	453
Code 11	Actuator Motor Circuit	51-241	446
Code 12	Magnetic Clutch Circuit	51-241	447
Code 14	Actuator Mechanical Fault	51-242	448
Code 15	Actuator Motor Circuit	51-241	446
Code 21	Open In Vehicle Speed Sensor Circuit	51-242	449
Code 23	Vehicle Speed Sensor Abnormal	51-243	450
Code 32	Control Switch Circuit	51-243	451
Code 51	Idle Switch Circuit	51-244	452
1998-99 4RUNNER w/FORD CRUISE CONTROL			
—	Problem Symptoms Table	51-232	426
—	Actuator Control Cable	51-255	476
—	Clutch Switch Circuit	51-253	471
—	Cruise Main Indicator Lamp Circuit	51-254	474
—	Diagnosis Circuit	51-255	475
—	ECU Power Source Circuit	51-253	472
—	Electronically Controlled Transmission Communication Circuit	51-252	469
—	Idle Switch Circuit	51-251	468
—	Main Switch Circuit	51-254	473
—	Park/Neutral Position Switch Circuit	51-252	470
—	Stop Lamp Switch Circuit	51-250	467
Code 12	Actuator Circuit	51-248	462
Code 14	Actuator Mechanical Fault	51-249	463
Code 21	Open In Vehicle Speed Sensor Circuit	51-249	464
Code 23	Vehicle Speed Signal Abnormal	51-250	465
Code 32	Control Switch Circuit	51-250	466
1997 SUPRA & 1998 w/2JZ-GTE ENGINE			
—	Actuator Control Cable	51-188	324
—	Back-Up Power Source Circuit	51-186	320
—	Clutch Switch Circuit	51-186	318
—	Cruise Main Indicator Lamp Circuit	51-187	322
—	Diagnosis Circuit	51-187	323
—	Electronically Controlled Transmission Communication Circuit	51-184	316
—	Main Switch Circuit	51-187	321
—	Park/Neutral Position Switch Circuit	51-185	317
—	Power Source Circuit	51-186	319
—	Problem Symptoms Table	51-173	293
—	Stop Lamp Switch Circuit	51-183	315
Code 11	Actuator Motor Circuit	51-180	308
Code 12	Magnetic Clutch Circuit	51-181	309
Code 14	Actuator Mechanical Fault	51-181	310
Code 15	Actuator Motor Circuit	51-180	308
Code 21	Open In Vehicle Speed Sensor Circuit	51-182	311
Code 23	Vehicle Speed Signal Fault	51-182	312
Code 32	Control Switch Circuit	51-182	313
Code 51	Idle Signal Circuit	51-183	314

Continued

DIAGNOSTIC CHART INDEX—Continued

Code/Test	Description/Test	Page No.	Fig. No.
1998 SUPRA w/2JZ-GE ENGINE			
—	Cruise Main Indicator Lamp	51-191	332
—	Main Switch Circuit	51-190	330
—	Problem Symptoms Table	51-188	325
Code P0500	Stop Lamp Switch Circuit	51-189	327
Code P0500	Vehicle Speed Sensor Fault	51-188	326
Code P1565	Control Switch Circuit	51-189	328
Code P1566	Input Signal Circuit Fault	51-190	329
Code 21	Vehicle Speed Sensor Fault	51-188	326
Code 23	Vehicle Speed Sensor Fault	51-188	326
Code 32	Control Switch Circuit	51-189	328
Code 52	Stop Lamp Switch Circuit	51-189	327
Code 54	Input Signal Circuit Fault	51-190	329

Symptom	Suspect Area
SET not occurring or CANCEL occurring. (DTC is Normal)	1. Main Switch Circuit (Cruise control switch) 2. Vehicle Speed Sensor 3. Control Switch Circuit (Cruise control switch) 4. Stop Light Switch Circuit 5. Park/Neutral Position Switch Circuit 6. Actuator Motor Circuit 7. Cruise Control Cable 8. Cruise Control ECU
SET not occurring or CANCEL occurring. (DTC dose not output)	1. ECU Power Source Circuit 2. Cruise Control ECU
Actual vehicle speed deviates above or below the set speed.	1. Cruise Control Cable 2. Vehicle Speed Signal Abnormal 3. Electronically Controlled Transmission Communication Circuit 4. Actuator Motor Circuit 5. Idle Signal Circuit (Main throttle position sensor) 6. Cruise Control ECU
Gear shifting frequent between 3rd O/D when driving on uphill road. (Hurting)	1. Electronically Controlled Transmission Communication Circuit 2. Cruise Control ECU
Cruise control not cancelled, even when brake pedal is depressed.	1. Cruise Control Cable 2. Stop Light Switch Circuit 3. Actuator Motor Circuit 4. Cruise Control ECU
Cruise control not cancelled, even when transmission is shifted to "N" position.	1. Cruise Control Cable 2. Park/Neutral Position Switch Circuit 3. Actuator Motor Circuit 4. Cruise Control ECU
Control switch does not operate. (SET/COAST, ACC/RES, CANCEL not possible)	1. Cruise Control Cable 2. Control Switch Circuit 3. Actuator Motor Circuit 4. Cruise Control ECU
SET possible at 40 km/h (25 mph) or less, or CANCEL does not operate at 40 km/h (25 mph) or less.	1. Cruise Control Cable 2. Vehicle Speed Signal Abnormal 3. Actuator Motor Circuit 4. Cruise Control ECU
Poor response is in ACCEL and RESUME modes.	1. Cruise Control Cable 2. Electronically Controlled Transmission Communication Circuit 3. Actuator Motor Circuit 4. Cruise Control ECU
O/D does not resume, even though the road is not uphill.	1. Electronically Controlled Transmission Communication Circuit 2. Cruise Control ECU
DTC memory is erased.	1. Back-up Power Source Circuit 2. Cruise Control ECU
DTC is not output, or is output when should not be.	1. Diagnosis Circuit 2. Cruise Control ECU
Cruise MAIN indicator light remains ON or falls to light up.	1. Cruise MAIN Indicator Light Switch Circuit

TY9099900133000X

Fig. 83 Problem Symptoms Table. Avalon & Sienna

Symptom	Suspect Area
SET not occourring or CANCEL occurring. (DTC is Normal)	1. Main Switch Circuit (Cruise control switch) 2. Vehicle Speed Sensor 3. Control Switch Circuit (Cruise control switch) 4. Stop Light Switch Circuit 5. Park/Neutral Position Switch Circuit 6. Clutch Switch 7. Actuator Motor Circuit 8. Cruise Control Cable 9. Cruise Control ECU
SET not occurring or CANCEL occurring. (DTC dose not output)	1. ECU Power Source Circuit 2. Cruise Control ECU
Actual vehicle speed deviates above or below the set speed.	1. Cruise Control Cable 2. Vehicle Speed Signal Abnormal 3. Electronically Controlled Transmission Communication Circuit 4. Actuator Motor Circuit 5. Idle Signal Circuit (Main throttle position sensor) 6. Cruise Control ECU
Gear shifting frequent between 3rd O/D when driving on uphill road. (Hurting)	1. Electronically Controlled Transmission Communication Circuit 2. Cruise Control ECU
Cruise control not cancelled, even when brake pedal is depressed.	1. Cruise Control Cable 2. Stop Light Switch Circuit 3. Actuator Motor Circuit 4. Cruise Control ECU
Cruise control not cancelled, even when transmission is shifted to "N" postion.	1. Cruise Control Cable 2. Park/Neutral Position Switch Circuit 3. Actuator Motor Circuit 4. Cruise Control ECU
Cruise control not cancelled, even when clutch pedal is depressed.	1. Cruise Control Cable 2. Clutch Switch Circuit 3. Actuator Motor Circuit 4. Cruise Control ECU
Control switch does not operate. (SET/COAST, ACC/RES, CANCEL not possible)	1. Cruise Control Cable 2. Control Switch Circuit 3. Actuator Motor Circuit 4. Cruise Control ECU
SET possible at 40 km/h (25 mph) or less, or CANCEL does not operate at 40 km/h (25 mph) or less.	1. Cruise Control Cable 2. Vehicle Speed Signal Abnormal 3. Actuator Motor Circuit 4. Cruise Control ECU
Poor response is in ACCEL and RESUME modes.	1. Cruise Control Cable 2. Electronically Controlled Transmission Communication Circuit 3. Actuator Motor Circuit 4. Cruise Control ECU
O/D does not resume, even though the road is not uphill.	1. Electronically Controlled Transmission Communication Circuit 2. Cruise Control ECU

TY1109900127010X

Fig. 84 Problem Symptoms Table (Part 1 of 2). Camry & Camry Solara

DTC memory is erased.	1. Cruise Control ECU
DTC is not output, or is output when should not be.	1. Diagnosis Circuit 2. Cruise Control ECU
Cruise MAIN indicator light remains ON or falls to light up.	1. Cruise MAIN Indicator Light Switch Circuit

TY1109900127020X

Fig. 84 Problem Symptoms Table (Part 2 of 2). Camry & Camry Solara

Symptom	Suspect Area
SET not occouring or CANCEL occurring. (DTC is Normal)	1. Main Switch Circuit (Cruise control switch) 2. Vehicle Speed Sensor Circuit 3. Control Switch Circuit (Cruise control switch) 4. Stop Light Switch Circuit 5. PNP Switch (A/T) Clutch Switch Circuit (M/T) 6. Cruise Control Actuator with ECU
SET not occurring or CANCEL occurring. (DTC does not output)	1. ECU Power Source Circuit 2. Cruise Control Actuator with ECU
Actual vehicle speed deviates above or below the set speed.	1. Vehicle Speed Signal Abnormal 2. Electronically Controlled Transmission Communication Circuit 3. Idle Signal Circuit (Main throttle position sensor) 4. Cruise Contorl Actuator with ECU
Gear shifting frequent between 3rd O/D when driving on uphill road. (Hurting)	1. Electronically Controlled Transmission Communication Circuit 2. Cruise Control Actuator with ECU
Cruise control not cancelled, even when brake pedal is depressed.	1. Stop Light Switch Circuit 2. Cruise Control Actuator with ECU
Cruise control not cancelled, even when transmission is shifted to "N" position.	1. Park/Neutral Position Switch Circuit 2. Cruise Control Actuator with ECU
Cruise control not cancelled, even when clutch pedal is depressed.	1. Clutch Switch Circuit 2. Cruise Control Actuator with ECU
Control switch does not operate. (SET/COAST, ACC/RES, CANCEL not possible)	1. Contorl Switch Circuit (Cruise Control Switch) 2. Cruise Control Actuator with ECU
SET possible at 40 km/h (25 mph) or less, or CANCEL does not operate at 40 km/h (25 mph) or less.	1. Vehicle Speed Signal Abnormal 2. Cruise Control Actuator with ECU
Poor response is ACCEL and RESUME modes.	1. Electronically Controlled Transmission Communication Circuit 2. Cruise Control Actuator with ECU
O/D does not RESUME, even through the road is uphill.	1. Electronically Controlled Transmission Communication Circuit 2. Cruise Control Actuator with ECU
DTC memory is erased.	1. ECU Power Source Circuit 2. Cruise Control Actuator with ECU
DTC is not output, or is output when is should not be.	1. Diagnosis Circuit 2. Cruise Control Actuator with ECU
Cruise MAIN indicator light remains ON or fall to light up.	1. Cruise MAIN Indicator Light Switch Circuit

TY1109900102000X

Fig. 85   Problem Symptoms Table. Tundra w/5VZ-FE engine

CIRCUIT DESCRIPTION

The actuator motor is operated by signals from the ECU. Acceleration and deceleration signals are transmitted by changes in the Duty Ratio (See note below).

Duty Ratio

The duty ratio is the ratio of the period of continuity in one cycle. For example, if A is period of continuity in one cycle, and B is the period of non-continuity, then

$$\text{Duty Ratio} = \frac{A}{A + B} \times 100 \ (\%)$$

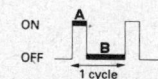

Code No.	Diagnosis	Trouble area
11	• Overcurrent (short) in motor circuit.	• Cruise control actuator motor • Harness or connector between actuator motor and ECU • ECU
14	• Open in actuator motor circuit	
41	• Duty ratio of 100 % output to motor acceleration side.	

TY9099900153010X

Fig. 87   Codes 11, 14 & 41: Actuator Motor Circuit (Part 1 of 2). 1996 Avalon

Symptom	Suspect Area
SET not occurring or CANCEL occurring. (DTC is Normal)	1. Input Signal Circuit 2. Vehicle Speed Sensor Circuit 3. Stop Light Switch Circuit 4. Park/Neutral Position Switch Circuit 5. ECM
SET not occurring or CANCEL occurring. (DTC is not output)	ECM
Actual vehicle speed deviates above or below the set speed.	1. Input Signal Circuit 2. ECM
Gear shifting occurs frequently between 3rd and O/D when driving on uphill road. (Hurting)	ECM
Cruise control not cancelled, even when brake pedal is depressed.	1. Stop Light Switch Circuit 2. ECM
Cruise control not cancelled, even when transmission is shifted to "N" position.	1. Park/Neutral Position Switch Circuit 2. ECM
Cruise control not cancelled, even when clutch pedal is depressed.	ECM
Control switch does not operate. (SET/COAST, ACC/RES, CANCEL not possible)	1. Cruise Control Switch Circuit 2. ECM
SET possible at 40 km/h (25 mph) or less, or CANCEL does not operate at 40 km/h (25 mph) or less.	1. Input Signal Circuit 2. ECM
Poor response is ACCEL and RESUME modes.	ECM
O/D does not resume, even though the road is not uphill.	ECM
DTC memory is erased.	ECM
DTC is not output, or is output when should not be.	1. Diagnosis Circuit 2. ECM
Cruise MAIN indicator light remains ON or falls to light up.	1. Input Signal Circuit 2. ECM

TY1109900119000X

Fig. 86   Problem Symptoms Table. Tundra w/2UZ-FE engine

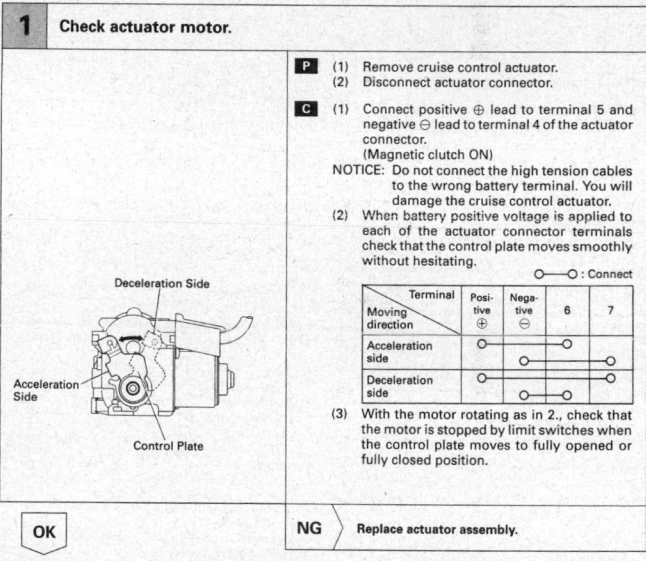

1   Check actuator motor.

P (1) Remove cruise control actuator.
(2) Disconnect actuator connector.

C (1) Connect positive ⊕ lead to terminal 5 and negative ⊖ lead to terminal 4 of the actuator connector.
(Magnetic clutch ON)
NOTICE: Do not connect the high tension cables to the wrong battery terminal. You will damage the cruise control actuator.
(2) When battery positive voltage is applied to each of the actuator connector terminals check that the control plate moves smoothly without hesitating.

○—○ : Connect

Moving direction \ Terminal	Positive ⊕	Negative ⊖	6	7
Acceleration side	○			○
		○	○	
Deceleration side	○		○	
		○		○

(3) With the motor rotating as in 2., check that the motor is stopped by limit switches when the control plate moves to fully opened or fully closed position.

OK ▷

NG ▷ Replace actuator assembly.

2   Check harness and connector between cruise control ECU and actuator motor

OK ▷

NG ▷ Repair or replace harness or connector.

Proceed to next circuit inspection shown on matrix chart
However, when DTC 11, 14, 41 is displayed, check and replace cruise control ECU.

TY9099900153020X

Fig. 87   Codes 11, 14 & 41: Actuator Motor Circuit (Part 2 of 2). 1996 Avalon

CIRCUIT DESCRIPTION

This circuit turns on the magnetic clutch inside the actuator during cruise control operation according to the signal from the ECU. If a malfunction occurs in the actuator or speed sensor, etc. during cruise control, the rotor shaft between the motor and control plate is released.

When the brake pedal is depressed, the stoplight switch turns on, supplying electrical power to the stoplight. Power supply to the magnetic clutch is mechanically cut and the magnetic clutch is turned OFF.

When driving downhill, if the vehicle speed exceeds the set speed by 15 km/h (9 mph), the ECU turns the magnetic clutch OFF. If the vehicle speed later drops to within 10 km/h (6 mph) above the set speed, then cruise control at the set speed is resumed.

Code No.	Diagnosis	Trouble area
12	• Overcurrent (short) in magnetic clutch circuit. • Open (0.8 sec) in magnetic clutch circuit.	• Cruise control magnetic clutch. • Harness or connector between ECU and magnetic clutch, magnetic clutch and body ground. • ECU

TY9099900154010X

Fig. 88 Code 12: Actuator Magnetic Clutch Circuit (Part 1 of 2). 1996 Avalon & Camry

CIRCUIT DESCRIPTION

This circuit detects the rotation position of the actuator control plate and sends signal to the ECU.

Code No.	Diagnosis	Trouble area
13	• Position sensor detects abnormal voltage.	• Cruise control actuator motor. • Cruise control actuator position sensor. • Harness or connector between actuator position sensor and body ground.
14	• Open in actuator motor circuit. • Position sensor signal value does not change when the motor operates.	• Harness or connector between actuator motor and ECU. • ECU

TY9099900155010X

Fig. 89 Codes 13 & 14: Actuator Position Sensor Circuit (Part 1 of 2). 1996 Avalon

INSPECTION PROCEDURE

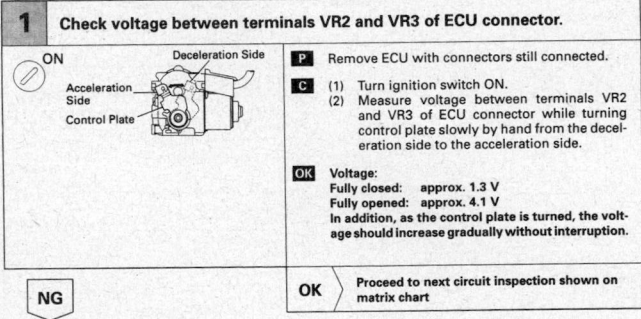

1	Check voltage between terminals VR2 and VR3 of ECU connector.

P	Remove ECU with connectors still connected.
C	(1) Turn ignition switch ON. (2) Measure voltage between terminals VR2 and VR3 of ECU connector while turning control plate slowly by hand from the deceleration side to the acceleration side.
OK	**Voltage:** Fully closed: approx. 1.3 V Fully opened: approx. 4.1 V In addition, as the control plate is turned, the voltage should increase gradually without interruption.

NG | OK | Proceed to next circuit inspection shown on matrix chart

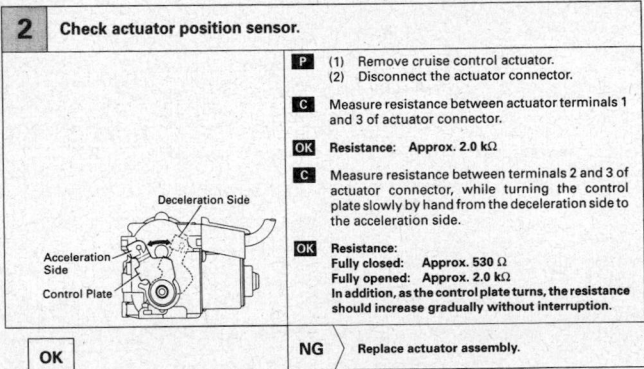

2	Check actuator position sensor.

P	(1) Remove cruise control actuator. (2) Disconnect the actuator connector.
C	Measure resistance between actuator terminals 1 and 3 of actuator connector.
OK	**Resistance: Approx. 2.0 kΩ**
C	Measure resistance between terminals 2 and 3 of actuator connector, while turning the control plate slowly by hand from the deceleration side to the acceleration side.
OK	**Resistance:** Fully closed: Approx. 530 Ω Fully opened: Approx. 2.0 kΩ In addition, as the control plate turns, the resistance should increase gradually without interruption.

OK | NG | Replace actuator assembly.

3	Check for open short in harness and connector between ECU and actuator position sensor

OK | NG | Repair or replace harness or connector.

Check harness and connector for loose connection.
If connection is normal check and replace ECU.

TY9099900155020X

Fig. 89 Codes 13 & 14: Actuator Position Sensor Circuit (Part 2 of 2). 1996 Avalon

INSPECTION PROCEDURE

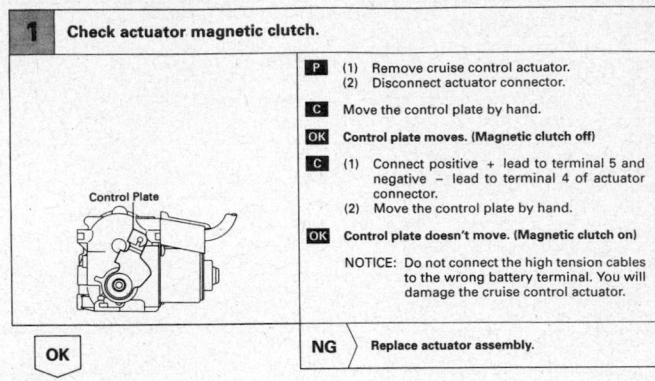

1	Check actuator magnetic clutch.

P	(1) Remove cruise control actuator. (2) Disconnect actuator connector.
C	Move the control plate by hand.
OK	**Control plate moves. (Magnetic clutch off)**
C	(1) Connect positive + lead to terminal 5 and negative − lead to terminal 4 of actuator connector. (2) Move the control plate by hand.
OK	**Control plate doesn't move. (Magnetic clutch on)**

NOTICE: Do not connect the high tension cables to the wrong battery terminal. You will damage the cruise control actuator.

OK | NG | Replace actuator assembly.

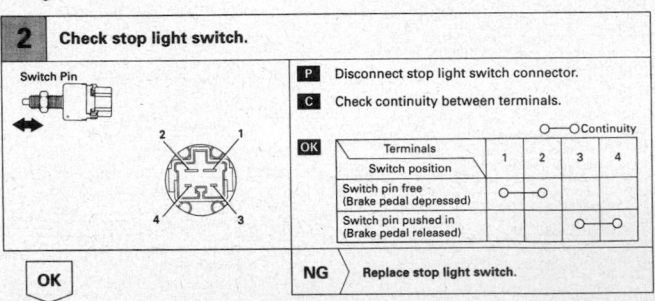

2	Check stop light switch.

| P | Disconnect stop light switch connector. |
| C | Check continuity between terminals. |

OK	Terminals / Switch position	1	2	3	4
	Switch pin free (Brake pedal depressed)	○—○			
	Switch pin pushed in (Brake pedal released)			○—○	

OK | NG | Replace stop light switch.

3	Check for open and short in harness and connectors between ECU and stop light switch, stop light switch and magnetic clutch, magnetic clutch and body ground

OK | NG | Repair or replace harness or connector.

Proceed to next circuit inspection shown on matrix chart
However, when DTC 12 is displayed, check harness and connector for loose connection.
If connection is normal, check and replace ECU.

TY9099900154020X

Fig. 88 Code 12: Actuator Magnetic Clutch Circuit (Part 2 of 2). 1996 Avalon & Camry

CIRCUIT DESCRIPTION

The vehicle speed sensor signal is sent to cruise control ECU as vehicle speed signal.
The rotor shaft is driven by the gear of the transmission.
For each rotation of the shaft, the vehicle speed sensor sends a 4-pulse signal to the combination meter.
This signal is converted inside the combination meter and sent as a 4-pulse signal to the cruise control ECU. The ECU calculates the vehicle speed from this pulse frequency.

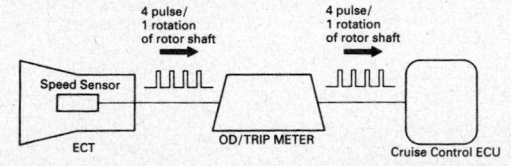

Code No.	Diagnosis	Trouble area
21	Speed signal is not input to the ECU while cruise control is set.	• Vehicle speed sensor • Combination meter • Harness or connector between speed sensor and combination meter, combination meter and ECU. • ECU
23	• Vehicle speed decrease 16 km/h or more than preset speed. • Vehicle speed sensor pulse is abnormal.	• Actuator • Vehicle speed sensor • Harness or connector in OD and SPD circuit (Open or short intermittently) • ECU

TY9099900156010X

Fig. 90 Codes 21 & 23: Vehicle Speed Sensor Circuit (Part 1 of 2). 1996 Avalon & Camry

INSPECTION PROCEDURE

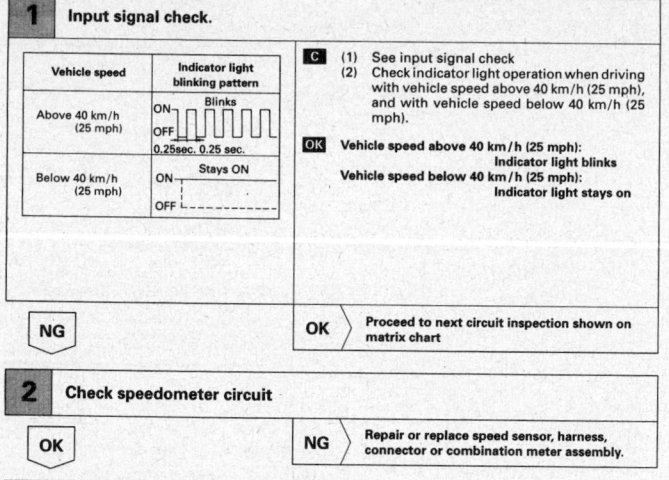

1 Input signal check.

Vehicle speed	Indicator light blinking pattern
Above 40 km/h (25 mph)	ON / OFF — Blinks — 0.25sec. 0.25 sec.
Below 40 km/h (25 mph)	ON — Stays ON / OFF

C
(1) See input signal check
(2) Check indicator light operation when driving with vehicle speed above 40 km/h (25 mph), and with vehicle speed below 40 km/h (25 mph).

OK
Vehicle speed above 40 km/h (25 mph):
Indicator light blinks
Vehicle speed below 40 km/h (25 mph):
Indicator light stays on

NG ↓

OK ▷ Proceed to next circuit inspection shown on matrix chart

2 Check speedometer circuit

OK ↓

NG ▷ Repair or replace speed sensor, harness, connector or combination meter assembly.

Check harness and connector for loose connection. If connection is normal, check and replace ECU.

TY9099900156020X

Fig. 90   Codes 21 & 23: Vehicle Speed Sensor Circuit (Part 2 of 2). 1996 Avalon & Camry

---

CIRCUIT DESCRIPTION

This circuit carries the SET/COAST, RESUME/ACCEL and CANCEL signals (each voltage) to the ECU.

Code No.	Diagnosis	Trouble area
32	Short in, control switch circuit.	• Cruise control switch. • Harness or connector between control switch and ECU.
34	Voltage abnormality in control switch.	• ECU

INSPECTION PROCEDURE

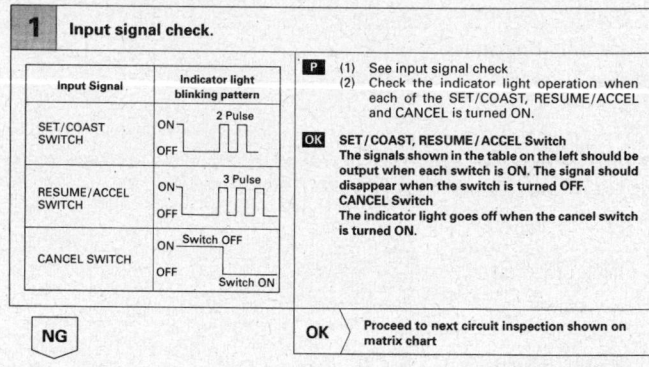

1 Input signal check.

Input Signal	Indicator light blinking pattern
SET/COAST SWITCH	ON / OFF — 2 Pulse
RESUME/ACCEL SWITCH	ON / OFF — 3 Pulse
CANCEL SWITCH	ON Switch OFF / OFF Switch ON

P
(1) See input signal check
(2) Check the indicator light operation when each of the SET/COAST, RESUME/ACCEL and CANCEL is turned ON.

OK
SET/COAST, RESUME/ACCEL Switch
The signals shown in the table on the left should be output when each switch is ON. The signal should disappear when the switch is turned OFF.
CANCEL Switch
The indicator light goes off when the cancel switch is turned ON.

NG ↓

OK ▷ Proceed to next circuit inspection shown on matrix chart

TY9099900157010X

Fig. 91   Codes 32 & 34: Control Switch Circuit (Part 1 of 2). 1996 Avalon & Camry

---

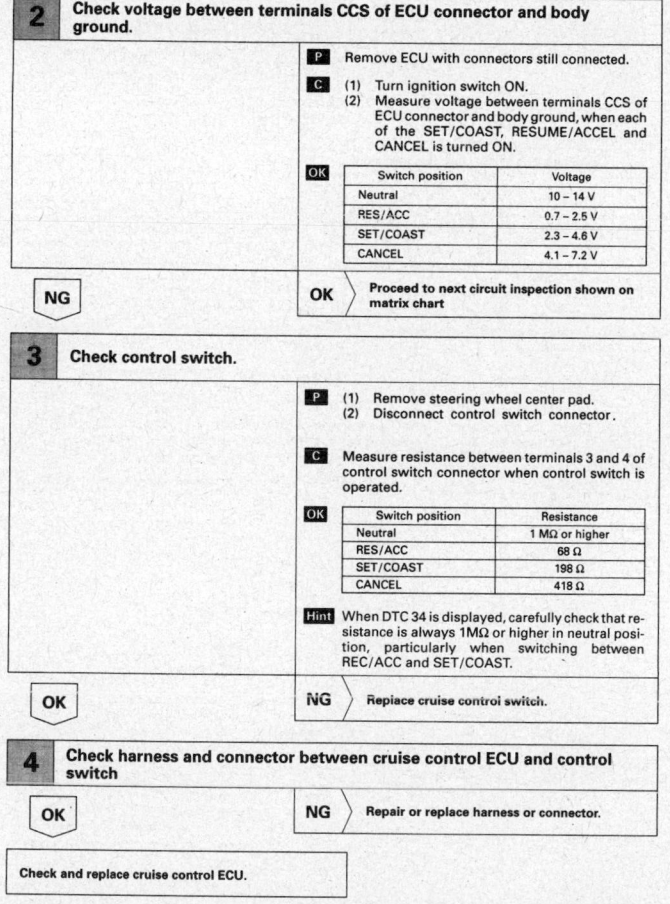

2 Check voltage between terminals CCS of ECU connector and body ground.

P Remove ECU with connectors still connected.

C
(1) Turn ignition switch ON.
(2) Measure voltage between terminals CCS of ECU connector and body ground, when each of the SET/COAST, RESUME/ACCEL and CANCEL is turned ON.

OK
Switch position	Voltage
Neutral	10 – 14 V
RES/ACC	0.7 – 2.5 V
SET/COAST	2.3 – 4.6 V
CANCEL	4.1 – 7.2 V

NG ↓

OK ▷ Proceed to next circuit inspection shown on matrix chart

3 Check control switch.

P
(1) Remove steering wheel center pad.
(2) Disconnect control switch connector.

C Measure resistance between terminals 3 and 4 of control switch connector when control switch is operated.

OK
Switch position	Resistance
Neutral	1 MΩ or higher
RES/ACC	68 Ω
SET/COAST	198 Ω
CANCEL	418 Ω

Hint When DTC 34 is displayed, carefully check that resistance is always 1MΩ or higher in neutral position, particularly when switching between REC/ACC and SET/COAST.

OK ↓

NG ▷ Replace cruise control switch.

4 Check harness and connector between cruise control ECU and control switch

OK ↓

NG ▷ Repair or replace harness or connector.

Check and replace cruise control ECU.

TY9099900157020X

Fig. 91   Codes 32 & 34: Control Switch Circuit (Part 2 of 2). 1996 Avalon

---

2 Check voltage between terminal CCS of cruise control ECU connector and body ground.

P Remove the cruise control ECU with connectors still connected.

C
1. Turn the ignition switch ON.
2. Measure the voltage between terminal CCS of cruise control ECU connector and body ground, when each of the SET/COAST, RESUME/ACCEL and CANCEL is turned ON.

OK
Switch position	Voltage
Neutral	10 – 14 V
RES/ACC	0.7 – 2.5 V
SET/COAST	2.3 – 4.6 V
CANCEL	4.1 – 7.2 V

NG ↓

OK ▷ Proceed to next circuit inspection shown on Problem Symptom Chart.

3 Check control switch.

P
1. Remove the steering wheel center pad.
2. Disconnect the control switch connector.

C Measure resistance between terminals 3 and 4 of the control switch connector when the switch is operated.

OK
Switch position	Resistance
Neutral	1 MΩ or higher
RES/ACC	60–80 Ω
SET/COAST	190–210 Ω
CANCEL	410–430 Ω

Hint When DTC 34 is displayed, carefully check that resistance is always 1 MΩ or higher in neutral position, particularly when switching between REC/ACC and SET/COAST.

OK ↓

NG ▷ Replace cruise control switch.

4 Check harness and connector between cruise control ECU and control switch.

OK ↓

NG ▷ Repair or replace harness or connector.

Check and replace cruise control ECU.

TY1109900137000X

Fig. 91   Codes 32 & 34: Control Switch Circuit (Part 2 of 2). 1996 Camry

CIRCUIT DESCRIPTION

When the brake is on, battery positive voltage normally applies through the stop fuse and stop switch to terminal STP– of the ECU, and the ECU turns the cruise control off.

A fail-safe function is provided so that cancel functions normally, even if there is a malfunction in the stop light signal circuit.

① If the harness connected to terminal STP– has an open, terminal STP– will have battery positive voltage and the cruise control will be turned off, also SET not occurring.

② If the stop fuse is open, terminal STP+ becomes approx. 0 V when the brake is turned on, so the ECU performs cancel function normally.

Also, when the brake is on, the magnetic clutch is cut mechanically by the stop light switch, turning the cruise control off.

INSPECTION PROCEDURE

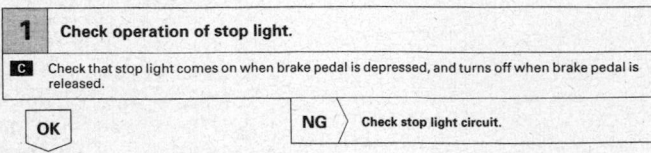

Fig. 92 Stop Lamp Switch Circuit (Part 1 of 2). 1996 Avalon & Camry

CIRCUIT DESCRIPTION

When the idle switch is turned ON, a signal is sent to the ECU. The ECU uses this signal to correct the discrepancy between the throttle valve position and the actuator position sensor value to enable accurate cruise control at the set speed. If the idle switch is malfunctioning, problem symptoms also occur in the engine, so also inspect the engine.

INSPECTION PROCEDURE

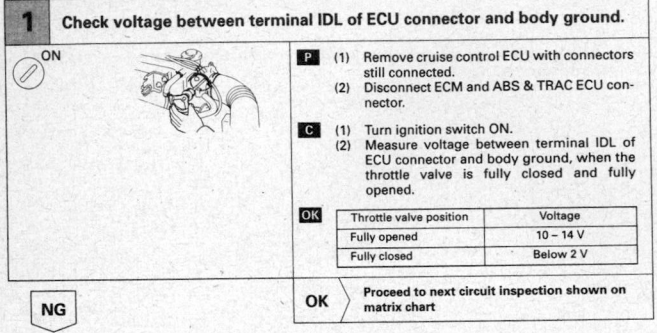

Fig. 93 Idle Switch Circuit (Part 1 of 2). 1996 Avalon & Camry

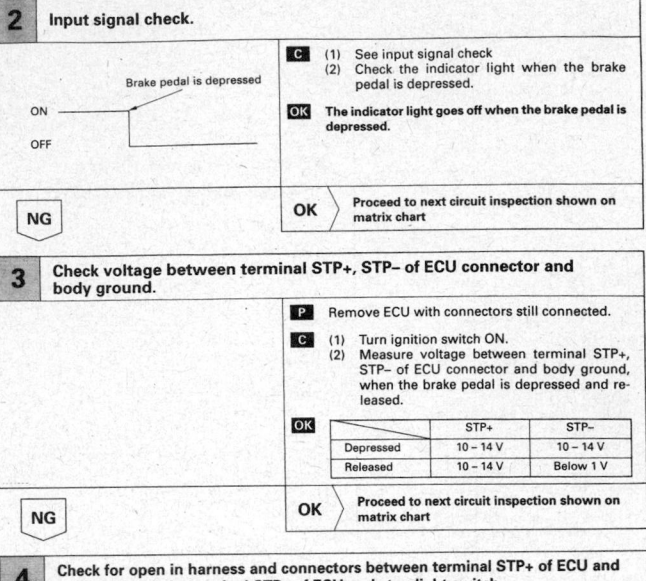

Fig. 92 Stop Lamp Switch Circuit (Part 2 of 2). 1996 Avalon & Camry

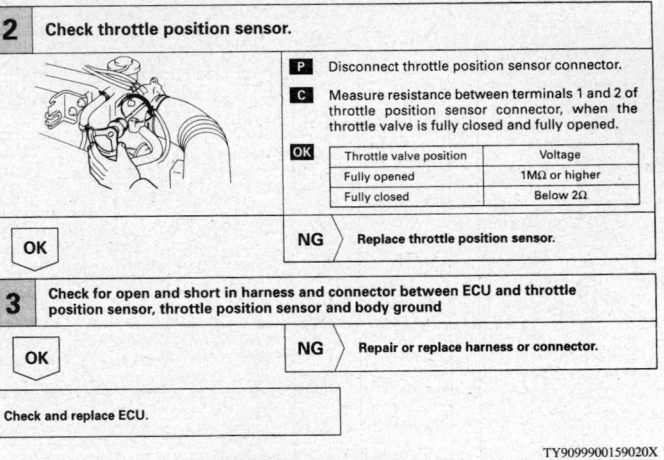

Fig. 93 Idle Switch Circuit (Part 2 of 2). 1996 Avalon & Camry

CIRCUIT DESCRIPTION

When driving uphill under cruise control, in order to reduce shifting due to ON-OFF overdrive operation and to provide smooth driving, when down shifting in the electronic controlled transaxle occurs, a signal to prevent upshift until the end of the uphill slope is sent from the cruise control ECU to the electronic controlled transaxle.

Terminal ECT of the cruise control ECU detects the shift change signal (output to electronic controlled transaxle No.2 solenoid) from the electronically controlled transaxle.

If vehicle speed down, also when terminal electronically controlled transaxle of the cruise control ECU receives down shifting signal, it sends a signal from terminal OD to OD1 to cut overdrive until the end of the uphill slope, and the gear shifts are reduced and gear shift points in the electronically controlled transaxle are changed.

Fig. 94 Electronically Controlled Transaxle Communication Circuit (Part 1 of 3). 1996 Avalon & Camry

INSPECTION PROCEDURE

1 Check operation of overdrive.

P Test drive after engine warm up.

C Check that overdrive ON ↔ OFF occurs with operation of OD switch ON-OFF.

OK → **NG** | Check and Repair Electronically controlled transmission

2 Check voltage between terminal OD of harness side connector of ECU and body ground.

ON

P Remove ECU with connector still connected.

C
(1) Disconnect ECU connector.
(2) Turn ignition switch ON.
(3) Measure voltage between terminal OD of harness side connector of ECU and body ground.

OK Voltage: 10 – 14 V

OK → **NG** | Go to step **5**

3 Check voltage between terminal ECT of cruise control ECU connector and body ground (On test drive).

P
(1) Connect ECU connector.
(2) Test drive after engine warm up.

C Check voltage between terminal ECT of cruise control ECU connector and body ground when OD switch is on and off.

OK

Gear Position	Voltage
O/D	Below 1 V
3rd	10 – 14 V

NG → **OK** | Proceed to next circuit inspection shown on matrix chart

4 Check for open and short in harness and connector between terminal ECT of cruise control ECU and electronically controlled transmission solenoid

OK → **NG** | Repair or replace harness or connector.

Check and repair ECU.

TY9099900160020X

Fig. 94 Electronically Controlled Transaxle Communication Circuit (Part 2 of 3). 1996 Avalon & Camry

CIRCUIT DESCRIPTION

When the shift position is put in except D position, a signal is sent from the park/neutral position switch to the ECU. When this signal is input during cruise control driving, the ECU cancels the cruise control.

TY9099900161010X

Fig. 95 Park/Neutral Position Switch Circuit (Part 1 of 2). 1996 Avalon

5 Check for open and short in harness and connector between terminal OD of ECU and terminal OD1 of ECM

OK → **NG** | Repair or replace harness or connector.

Check and replace ECM.

TY9099900160030X

Fig. 94 Electronically Controlled Transaxle Communication Circuit (Part 3 of 3). 1996 Avalon & Camry

INSPECTION PROCEDURE

1 Check operation of starter.

C Check that the starter operates normally and that the engine starts.

OK → **NG** | Proceed to engine troubleshooting

2 Input signal Check.

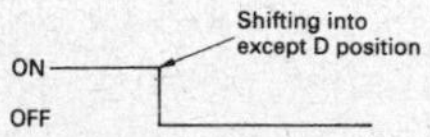

ON
OFF

Shifting into except D position

P
(1) See input signal check
(2) Check the indicator light when shifting into except D position.

OK The indicator light goes off when shifting into except D position.

NG → **OK** | Proceed to next circuit inspection shown on matrix chart

3 Check voltage between terminal D of ECU connector and body ground.

ON

P Remove ECU with connectors still connected.

C
(1) Turn ignition switch ON.
(2) Measure voltage between terminal D of ECU connector and body ground, when shifting into D position and other positions.

OK

Shift Position	Voltage
D position	10 – 14 V
Other positions	Below 1 V

NG → **OK** | Proceed to next circuit inspection shown on matrix chart

4 Check for open in harness and connector between ECU and GAUGE fuse.

OK → **NG** | Repair or replace harness or connector.

Check and replace ECU.

TY9099900161020X

Fig. 95 Park/Neutral Position Switch Circuit (Part 2 of 2). 1996 Avalon

CIRCUIT DESCRIPTION

The ECU back-up power source provides power even when the ignition switch is off and is used for DTC memory, etc.

INSPECTION PROCEDURE

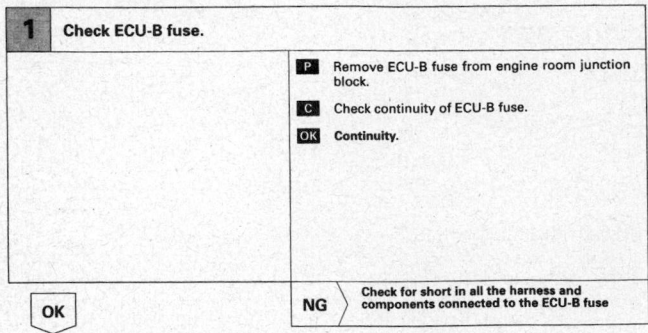

1	Check ECU-B fuse.
	P Remove ECU-B fuse from engine room junction block.
	C Check continuity of ECU-B fuse.
	OK Continuity.
OK	**NG** Check for short in all the harness and components connected to the ECU-B fuse

TY9099900162010X

Fig. 96 Back-Up Power Source Circuit (Part 1 of 2). Sienna, 1996–97 Avalon & 1996–98 Camry

CIRCUIT DESCRIPTION

When the cruise control main switch is turned off, the cruise control does not operate.

TY9099900163010X

Fig. 97 Cruise Control Switch Circuit (Part 1 of 2). 1996 Avalon & Camry

CIRCUIT DESCRIPTION

This circuit sends a signal to the ECU that diagnostic code output is required.

INSPECTION PROCEDURE

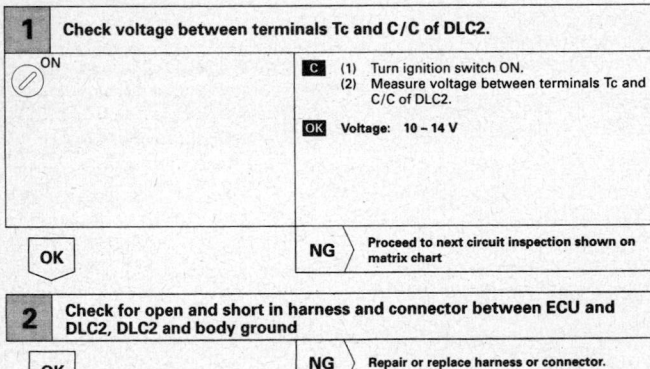

1	Check voltage between terminals Tc and C/C of DLC2.
ON	**C** (1) Turn ignition switch ON. (2) Measure voltage between terminals Tc and C/C of DLC2.
	OK Voltage: 10 – 14 V
OK	**NG** Proceed to next circuit inspection shown on matrix chart

2	Check for open and short in harness and connector between ECU and DLC2, DLC2 and body ground
OK	**NG** Repair or replace harness or connector.

Check and replace ECU.

TY9099900164000X

Fig. 98 T$_C$ Circuit. 1996 Avalon

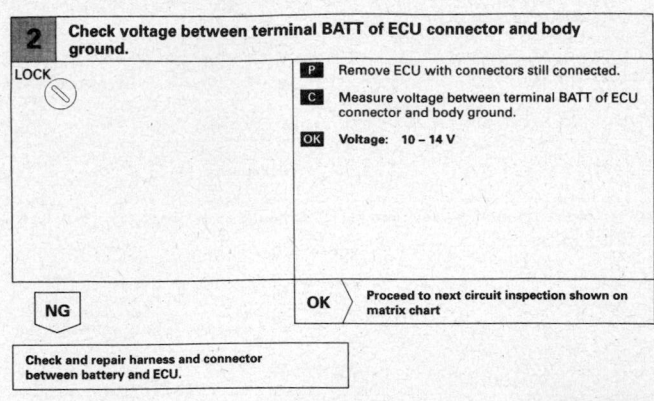

2	Check voltage between terminal BATT of ECU connector and body ground.
LOCK	**P** Remove ECU with connectors still connected.
	C Measure voltage between terminal BATT of ECU connector and body ground.
	OK Voltage: 10 – 14 V
NG	**OK** Proceed to next circuit inspection shown on matrix chart

Check and repair harness and connector between battery and ECU.

TY9099900162020X

Fig. 96 Back-Up Power Source Circuit (Part 2 of 2). Sienna, 1996–97 Avalon & 1996–98 Camry

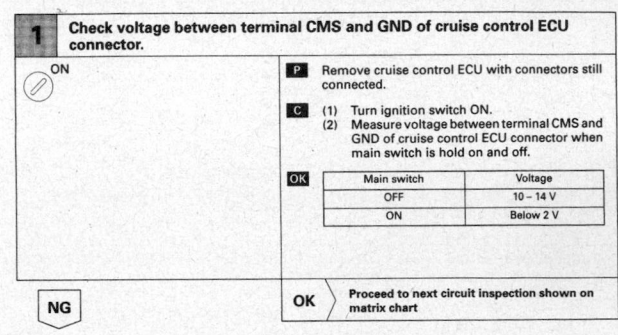

1	Check voltage between terminal CMS and GND of cruise control ECU connector.
ON	**P** Remove cruise control ECU with connectors still connected.
	C (1) Turn ignition switch ON. (2) Measure voltage between terminal CMS and GND of cruise control ECU connector when main switch is hold on and off.

OK	Main switch	Voltage
	OFF	10 – 14 V
	ON	Below 2 V

NG	**OK** Proceed to next circuit inspection shown on matrix chart

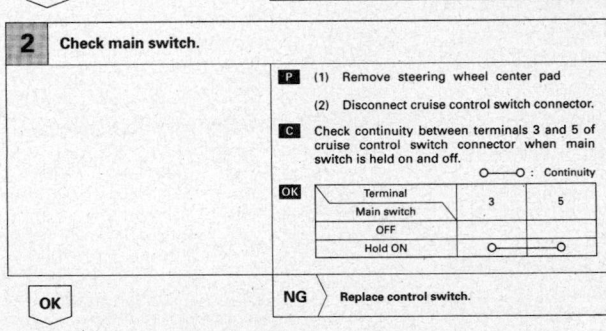

2	Check main switch.
	P (1) Remove steering wheel center pad (2) Disconnect cruise control switch connector.
	C Check continuity between terminals 3 and 5 of cruise control switch connector when main switch is held on and off.

OK		o——o : Continuity
Terminal Main switch	3	5
OFF		
Hold ON	o——	——o

OK	**NG** Replace control switch.

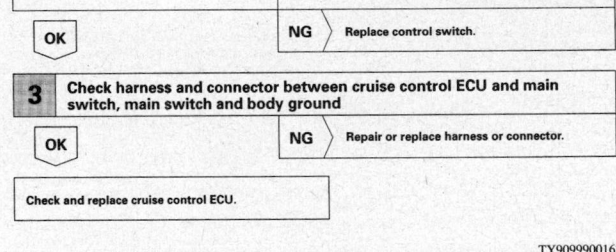

3	Check harness and connector between cruise control ECU and main switch, main switch and body ground
OK	**NG** Repair or replace harness or connector.

Check and replace cruise control ECU.

TY9099900163020X

Fig. 97 Cruise Control Switch Circuit (Part 2 of 2). 1996 Avalon & Camry

CIRCUIT DESCRIPTION

The actuator motor is operated by signals from the ECU. Acceleration and deceleration signals are transmitted according to changes in the Duty Ratio (See below).

Duty Ratio
The duty ratio is the ratio of the period of continuity in one cycle. For example, if A is the period of continuity in one cycle, and B is the period of non–continuity.

$$\text{Duty Ratio} = \frac{A}{A + B} \times 100 \ (\%)$$

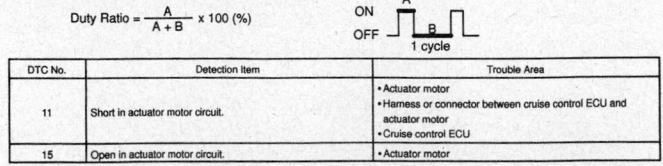

DTC No.	Detection Item	Trouble Area
11	Short in actuator motor circuit.	• Actuator motor • Harness or connector between cruise control ECU and actuator motor • Cruise control ECU
15	Open in actuator motor circuit.	• Actuator motor

TY9099900134010X

Fig. 99 Codes 11 & 15: Actuator Motor Circuit (Part 1 of 2). Camry Solara, Sienna & 1997–99 Avalon & Camry

INSPECTION PROCEDURE

1 Check resistance between terminals MO and MC of actuator motor.

PREPARATION:
(a) Turn ignition switch OFF.
(b) Disconnect the actuator connector.
CHECK:
Measure resistance between terminals 1 and 2.
HINT:
If control plate is in fully opened or fully closed positions, resistance can not be measured.
OK:
Resistance: more than 4.2 Ω

NG ▷ **Replace cruise control actuator.**

OK

2 Check for open and short in harness and connectors between cruise control ECU and actuator motor

NG ▷ **Repair or replace harness or connector.**

OK

Check and replace cruise control ECU

TY9099900134020X

Fig. 99   Codes 11 & 15: Actuator Motor Circuit (Part 2 of 2). Camry Solara, Sienna & 1997–99 Avalon & Camry

INSPECTION PROCEDURE

1 Check STOP fuse.

PREPARATION:
(a) Turn ignition switch OFF.
(b) Remove the STOP fuse from instrument panel junction block.
CHECK:
Check fuse continuity.
OK:
There is continuity.

NG ▷ **Replace STOP fuse.**

OK

2 Check stop light switch.

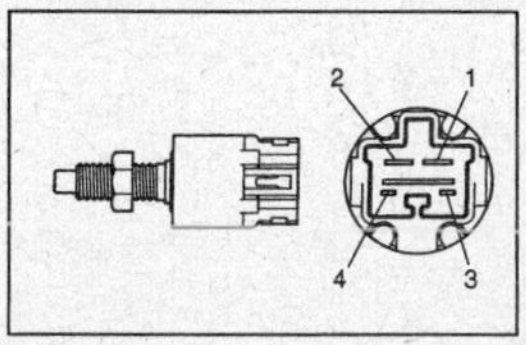

PREPARATION:
Disconnect the stop light switch connector.
CHECK:
Check continuity between terminals.

Switch position	Continuity
Switch pin free (Brake pedal depressed)	1 – 2
Switch pin pushed in (Brake pedal released)	3 – 4

NG ▷ **Replace stop light switch.**

OK

TY9099900135020X

Fig. 100   Code 12: Actuator Magnetic Clutch Circuit (Part 2 of 3). Camry Solara, Sienna & 1997–99 Avalon & Camry

CIRCUIT DESCRIPTION

This circuit turns on the magnetic clutch inside the actuator during cruise control operation according to the signal from the ECU. If a malfunction occurs in the actuator or speed sensor, etc. during cruise control operation, the rotor shaft between the motor and control plate is released.
When the brake pedal is depressed, the stop light switch turns on, supplying electrical power to the stop light. Power supply to the magnetic clutch is mechanically cut and the magnetic clutch is turned OFF.
When driving downhill, if the vehicle speed exceeds the set speed by 15 km/h (9 mph), the ECU turns the safety magnet clutch OFF. If the vehicle speed later drops to within 10 km/h (6 mph), cruise control at the set speed is resumed.

DTC No.	Detection Item	Trouble Area
12	Short in actuator magnetic clutch circuit. Open (0.8 sec.) in actuator magnetic clutch circuit.	• STOP Fuse • Stop light switch • Actuator magnetic clutch • Harness or connector between cruise control ECU and actuator magnetic clutch, actuator magnetic clutch and body ground • Cruise control ECU

TY9099900135010X

Fig. 100   Code 12: Actuator Magnetic Clutch Circuit (Part 1 of 3). Camry Solara, Sienna & 1997–99 Avalon & Camry

3 Check resistance between terminals L and GND of actuator magnetic clutch.

PREPARATION:
(a) Turn ignition switch OFF.
(b) Disconnect the actuator connector.
CHECK:
Measure resistance between terminals 3 and 4.
OK:
Resistance: 34.65 – 42.35 Ω

NG ▷ **Replace cruise control actuator.**

OK

4 Check for open and short in harness and connectors between cruise control ECU and actuator magnetic clutch, actuator magnetic clutch and body ground

NG ▷ **Repair or replace harness or connector.**

OK

Check and replace cruise control ECU

TY9099900135030X

Fig. 100   Code 12: Actuator Magnetic Clutch Circuit (Part 3 of 3). Camry Solara, Sienna & 1997–99 Avalon & Camry

CIRCUIT DESCRIPTION

The circuit detects the rotation position of the actuator control plate and sends a signal to the ECU.

DTC No.	Detection Item	Trouble Area
14	• Open in actuator motor circuit.	• Actuator lock: (motor, arm) • Actuator motor • Cruise control ECU

INSPECTION PROCEDURE

1 Check cruise control actuator arm locking operation

PREPARATION:
(a) Turn ignition switch OFF.
(b) Disconnect the actuator connector.
CHECK:
Connect the positive (+) lead from the battery to the terminal 3 of actuator and the negative (–) lead to terminal 4.
NOTICE:
Do not connect the high tension cables to the wrong battery terminal. The cruise control actuator will be damaged.
Move the control plate by hand.
OK:
   Control plate doesn't move.

NG ▷ Replace cruise control actuator.

OK ▽

TY9099900136010X

Fig. 101   Code 14: Actuator Mechanical Fault (Part 1 of 2). Camry Solara, Sienna & 1997–99 Avalon & Camry

2 Check cruise control actuator operation.

PREPARATION:
(a) Turn ignition switch OFF.
(b) Disconnect the actuator connector.
CHECK:
Connect the positive (+) lead from the battery to terminals 1 and 3 of actuator, connect the negative (–) lead to terminals 2 and 4 of actuator.
OK:
   Control arm moves to fully open side
CHECK:
Connect the positive (+) lead from the battery to terminals 2 and 3 of actuator, connect the negative (–) lead to terminals 1 and 4 of actuator.
OK:
   Control arm moves to fully close side

NG ▷ Replace cruise control actuator.

OK ▽

3 Check harness and connector between cruise control ECU and cruise control actuator

NG ▷ Repair or replace harness or connector.

OK ▽

Check and replace cruise control ECU

TY9099900136020X

Fig. 102   Code 14: Actuator Mechanical Fault (Part 2 of 2). Camry Solara, Sienna & 1998–99 Avalon & Camry

2 Check cruise control actuator operation.

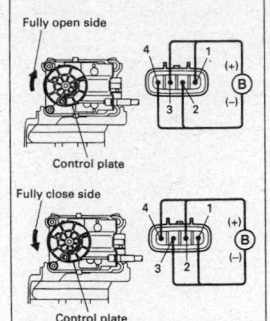

Fully open side

Control plate

Fully close side

Control plate

PREPARATION:
(a) Turn ignition switch OFF.
(b) Disconnect the actuator connector.
CHECK:
Connect the positive (+) lead from the battery to terminals 1 and 4 of actuator, connect the negative (–) lead to terminals 2 and 3 of actuator.
OK:
   Control arm moves to full open side
CHECK:
Connect the positive (+) lead from the battery to terminals 1 and 4 of actuator, connect the negative (–) lead to terminals 2 and 3 of actuator.
OK:
   Control arm moves to full close side

OK ▽   NG ▷ Replace cruise control actuator.

3 Check harness and connector between cruise control ECU and cruise control actuator

OK ▽   NG ▷ Repair or replace harness or connector.

Check and replace cruise control ECU.

TY9099900165000X

Fig. 102   Code 14: Actuator Mechanical Fault (Part 2 of 2). 1997 Avalon

CIRCUIT DESCRIPTION

The signal from the vehicle speed sensor circuit is sent to cruise control ECU as vehicle speed signal.
The rotor shaft is driven by the gear of the transmission.
For each rotation of the shaft, the vehicle speed sensor sends a 4–pulse signal through the combination meter to the cruise control ECU (See the following installation).
This signal is converted inside the combination meter and sent as a 4–pulse signal to the cruise control ECU.
The ECU calculates the vehicle speed from this pulse frequency.

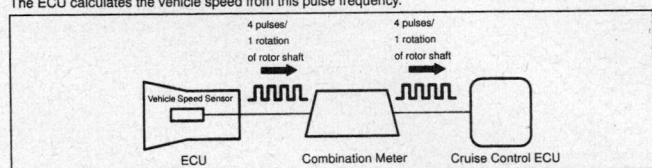

DTC No.	Detection Item	Trouble Area
21	Speed signal is not input to the cruise control ECU while cruise control is set.	• Combination meter • Harness or connector between cruise control ECU and combination meter, combination meter and vehicle speed sensor • Vehicle speed sensor • Cruise control ECU

TY9099900137010X

Fig. 103   Code 21: Open In Vehicle Speed Sensor Circuit (Part 1 of 3). Camry Solara & 1997–99 Avalon & Camry

INSPECTION PROCEDURE

1	Input signal check.

Input Signal	Indicator Light Blinking Pattern
Drive at about 40 km/h (25 mph) or below	Light ON ⎯⎯ / OFF -----
Drive at about 40 km/h (25 mph) or higher	Light ON ⎍⎍⎍ / OFF

CHECK:
(a) Input signal check.
(b) Check indicator light operation when driving with vehicle speed above 40 km/h (25 mph), and with vehicle speed below 40 km/h (25 mph).

OK:
Vehicle speed above 40 km/h (25 mph):
    Indicator light blinks
Vehicle speed below 40 km/h (25 mph):
    Indicator light stays on

OK ▷ Check and replace cruise control ECU

NG ⬡

2	Check speedometer circuit

NG ▷ Repair or replace harness, connector or combination meter assembly.

OK ⬡

3	Check harness and connector between cruise control ECU and combination meter, combination meter and vehicle speed sensor

NG ▷ Repair or replace harness or connector.

OK ⬡

TY9099900137020X

Fig. 103   Code 21: Open In Vehicle Speed Sensor Circuit (Part 2 of 3). Camry Solara & 1997–99 Avalon & Camry

CIRCUIT DESCRIPTION

The vehicle speed sensor circuit send the vehicle speed signal to the cruise control ECU. For each rotation of the shaft, the vehicle speed sensor sends a signal through the combination meter to the cruise control ECU (See the following). The ECU calculates the vehicle speed from this pulse frequency.

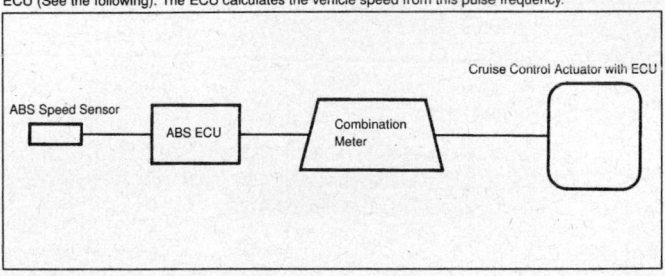

DTC No.	Detection Item	Trouble Area
21	Speed signal is not input to the cruise control ECU while cruise control is set.	• Combination meter • Harness or connector between cruise control ECU and combination meter, combination meter and vehicle speed sensor • Vehicle speed sensor • Cruise control ECU

TY1109900149010X

Fig. 104   Code 21: Open In Vehicle Speed Sensor Circuit (Part 1 of 2). Sienna

---

4	Check vehicle speed sensor

NG ▷ Replace vehicle speed sensor.

OK ⬡

Check and replace cruise control ECU

TY9099900137030X

Fig. 103   Code 21: Open In Vehicle Speed Sensor Circuit (Part 3 of 3). Camry Solara & 1997–99 Avalon & Camry

INSPECTION PROCEDURE

1	Input signal check.

Input Signal	Indicator Light Blinking Pattern
Drive at about 40 km/h (25 mph) or below	Light ON ⎯⎯ / OFF -----
Drive at about 40 km/h (25 mph) or higher	Light ON ⎍⎍⎍ / OFF

CHECK:
(a) See input signal check on page DI-427.
(b) Check indicator light operation when driving with vehicle speed above 40 km/h (25 mph), and with vehicle speed below 40 km/h (25 mph).

OK:
Vehicle speed above 40 km/h (25 mph):
    Indicator light blinks
Vehicle speed below 40 km/h (25 mph):
    Indicator light stays on

OK ▷ Check and replace cruise control ECU

NG ⬡

2	Check speedometer circuit

NG ▷ Repair or replace harness, connector or combination meter assembly.

OK ⬡

3	Check harness and connector between cruise control ECU and combination meter, combination meter and ABS ECU

NG ▷ Repair or replace harness or connector.

OK ⬡

Check and replace cruise control ECU

TY1109900149020X

Fig. 104   Code 21: Open In Vehicle Speed Sensor Circuit (Part 2 of 2). Sienna

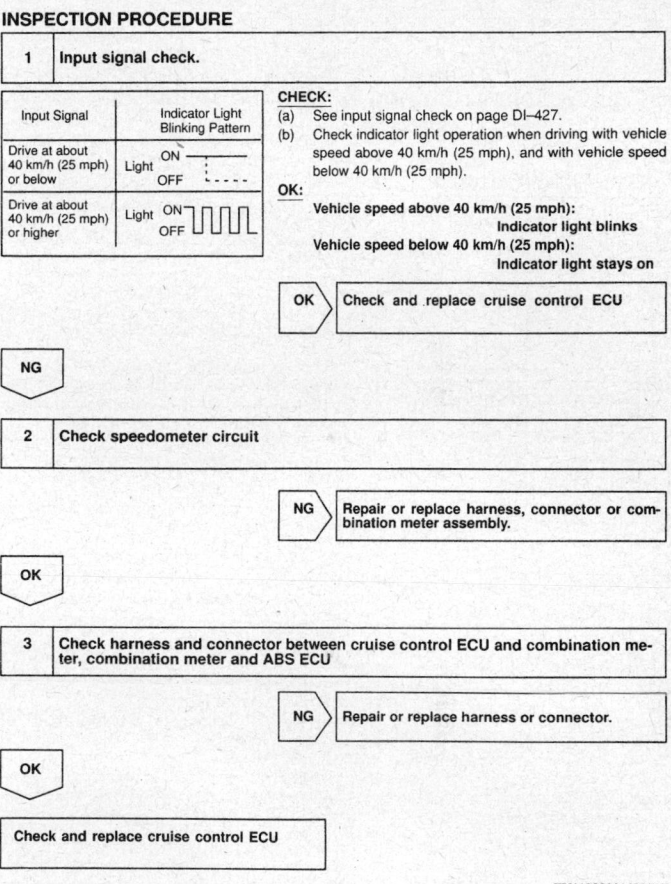

CIRCUIT DESCRIPTION

DTC No.	Detection Item	Trouble Area
23	Vehicle speed sensor pulse is abnormal.	• Vehicle speed sensor • Cruise control ECU

INSPECTION PROCEDURE

1	Check vehicle speed sensor

NG	Replace vehicle speed sensor.

OK

Check and replace cruise control ECU

TY9099900138000X

Fig. 105   Code 23: Vehicle Speed Signal Fault. Camry Solara, Sienna & 1997–99 Avalon & Camry

INSPECTION PROCEDURE

1	Input signal check.

PREPARATION:
Input signal check
CHECK:
Check the indicator light operation when each of the SET/COAST, RESUME/ACCEL and CANCEL is turned on.
OK:

SET/COAST, RESUME/ACCEL switch
The signals shown in the table on the left should be output when each switch is ON. The signal should disappear when the switch is turned OFF.
CANCEL switch
The indicator light goes off when the cancel switch is turned ON.

Input Signal	Indicator Light Blinking Pattern
SET/COAST switch	ON / OFF — 2 Pulses
RESUME/ACCEL switch	ON / OFF — 3 Pulses
CANCEL switch	ON / OFF — SW OFF / SW ON

OK	Wait and see.

NG

2	Check voltage between terminals CCS of cruise control ECU connector and body ground.

PREPARATION:
(a)   Remove the ECU with connector still connected.
(b)   Turn ignition switch ON.
CHECK:
Measure voltage between terminals 18 of ECU connector and body ground, when each of the SET/COAST, RESUME/ACCEL and CANCEL is turned ON.

Switch position	Resistance (V)
Neutral	10 – 16 V
RES/ACC	0.8 – 3.7 V
SET/COAST	2.5 – 6.3 V
CANCEL	4.2 – 8.8 V

NG	Proceed to next circuit inspection shown in problem symptom table

OK

TY9099900139020X

Fig. 106   Code 32: Cruise Control Switch Circuit Fault (Part 2 of 3). Camry Solara, Sienna & 1997–99 Avalon & Camry

CIRCUIT DESCRIPTION

This circuit carries the SET/COAST, RESUME/ACCEL and CANCEL signals (each voltage) to the ECU.

DTC No.	Detection Item	Trouble Area
32	Short in control switch circuit.	• Cruise control switch • Harness or connector between cruise control ECU and cruise control switch, cruise control switch and body ground • Cruise control ECU

TY9099900139010X

Fig. 106   Code 32: Cruise Control Switch Circuit Fault (Part 1 of 3). Camry Solara, Sienna & 1997–99 Avalon & Camry

3	Check control switch.

PREPARATION:
(a)   Remove steering wheel center pad.
(b)   Disconnect the control switch connector.
CHECK:
Measure resistance between terminals 3 and 4 of control switch connector when control switch is operated.

Switch position	Resistance (Ω)
Neutral	∞ (No continuity)
RES/ACC	50 – 80
SET/COAST	180 – 220
CANCEL	400 – 440

NG	Replace control switch.

OK

4	Check harness and connector between cruise control ECU and cruise control switch, cruise control switch and body ground

NG	Repair or replace harness or connector.

OK

5	Input signal check (See step 1).

OK	Wait and see.

NG

Check and replace cruise control ECU

TY9099900139030X

Fig. 106   Code 32: Cruise Control Switch Circuit Fault (Part 3 of 3). Camry Solara, Sienna & 1997–99 Avalon & Camry

CIRCUIT DESCRIPTION

When the idle switch is turned ON, a signal is sent to the ECU. The ECU uses this signal to correct the discrepancy between the throttle valve position and the actuator position sensor value to enable accurate cruise control at the set speed. If the idle switch is malfunctioning, problem symptoms also occur in the engine, so also inspect the engine.

DTC No.	Detection Item	Trouble Area
51	Short in idle signal circuit.	• Harness or connector between ECM and throttle position sensor • Throttle position sensor • Harness or connector between cruise control ECU and ECM, throttle position sensor and body ground • Cruise control ECU

TY9099900140010X

Fig. 107   Code 51: Idle Signal Circuit Fault (Part 1 of 3). Camry Solara, Sienna & 1997–99 Avalon & Camry

INSPECTION PROCEDURE

1 | Check voltage between terminal IDL of cruise control ECU connector and body ground.

PREPARATION:
(a) Remove the ECU with connector still connected.
(b) Disconnect the ECM connector.
(c) Turn ignition switch ON.
CHECK:
Measure voltage between terminal IDLO of ECU connector and body ground when the throttle valve is fully closed and fully opened.
OK:

Throttle valve position	Voltage
Fully opened	10 – 14 V
Fully closed	Below 2 V

OK ▷ Proceed to next circuit inspection shown in problem symptom table

NG

2 | Check harness and connector between ECM and throttle position sensor

NG ▷ Repair or replace harness or connector.

OK

3 | Check throttle position sensor circuit

NG ▷ Replace throttle position sensor.

OK

TY9099900140020X

Fig. 107 Code 51: Idle Signal Circuit Fault (Part 2 of 3). Camry Solara, Sienna & 1997–99 Avalon & Camry

4 | Check throttle position sensor.

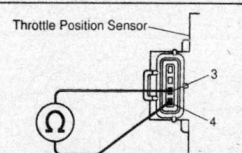

PREPARATION:
Disconnect the throttle position sensor connector.
CHECK:
Measure resistance between terminals 3 and 4 of throttle position sensor connector when the throttle valve is fully closed and fully opened.
OK:

Throttle valve position	Resistance
Fully opened	1 MΩ or higher
Fully closed	Below 2.3 kΩ

NG ▷ Replace throttle position sensor.

OK

5 | Check for open and short in harness and connector between cruise control ECU and ECM

NG ▷ Repair or replace harness or connector.

OK

Check and replace cruise control ECU

TY1109900128000X

Fig. 107 Code 51: Idle Signal Circuit Fault (Part 3 of 3). 1997–99 Camry

4 | Check throttle position sensor.

PREPARATION:
Disconnect the throttle position sensor connector.
CHECK:
Measure resistance between terminals 3 and 4 of throttle position sensor connector when the throttle valve is fully closed and fully opened.
OK:

Throttle valve position	Resistance
Fully opened	1 MΩ or higher
Fully closed	Below 2.3 kΩ

NG ▷ Replace throttle position sensor.

OK

5 | Check for open and short in harness and connector between cruise control ECU and throttle position sensor, throttle position sensor and body ground

NG ▷ Repair or replace harness or connector.

OK

Check and replace cruise control ECU

TY9099900140030X

Fig. 107 Code 51: Idle Signal Circuit Fault (Part 3 of 3). Sienna & 1997–99 Avalon

4 | Check throttle position sensor.

NG ▷ Replace throttle position sensor.

OK

5 | Check for open and short in harness and connector between cruise control ECU and ECM

NG ▷ Repair or replace harness or connector.

OK

Check and replace cruise control ECU

TY1109900144000X

Fig. 108 Code 51: Idle Signal Circuit Fault (Part 3 of 3). Camry Solara

CIRCUIT DESCRIPTION

When the brake pedal is depressed, the stop light switch sends a signal to the ECU. When the ECU receives this signal, it cancels the cruise control.
A fail–safe function is provided so that the cancel functions normally, even if there is a malfunction in the stop light signal circuit.
The cancel conditions are: Battery positive voltage at terminal STP–
When the brake is ON, battery positive voltage normally is applied through the STOP fuse and stop light switch to terminal STP– of the ECU, and the ECU turns the cruise control OFF.
If the harness connected to terminal STP– has an open circuit, terminal STP– will have battery positive voltage and the cruise control will be turned OFF.
Also, when the brake is ON, the magnetic clutch circuit is cut mechanically by the stop light switch, turning the cruise control OFF

TY9099900141010X

Fig. 109 Stop Lamp Switch Circuit Fault (Part 1 of 3). Camry Solara, Sienna, Tundra w/5VZ-FE engine & 1997–99 Avalon & Camry

INSPECTION PROCEDURE

1 Check operation of stop light.

CHECK:
Check that stop light comes ON when brake pedal is depressed, and turns OFF when brake pedal is released.

NG ▷ Check stop light system

OK

2 Input signal check.

CHECK:
(a) Input signal check
(b) Check the indicator light when the brake pedal is depressed.

OK:
The indicator light goes OFF when the brake pedal is depressed.

Input Signal	Indicator Light Blinking Pattern
Stop Light switch ON	OFF SW OFF Light ON ----- SW ON

OK ▷ Proceed to next circuit inspection shown in problem symptom table

NG

TY9099900141020X

Fig. 109 Stop Lamp Switch Circuit Fault (Part 2 of 3). Camry Solara, Sienna, Tundra w/5VZ-FE engine & 1997–99 Avalon & Camry

CIRCUIT DESCRIPTION

When driving uphill under the cruise control, in order to reduce shifting due to ON–OFF overdrive operation and to provide smooth driving, when down shifting in the electronically controlled transmission occurs, a signal to prevent upshift until the end of the uphill slope is sent from the cruise control ECU to the electronically controlled transmission.

Terminal ECT of the cruise control ECU detects the shift change signal (output to electronically controlled transmission No. 2 solenoid) from the ECM.

If the vehicle speeds down, also when terminal ECT of the cruise control ECU receives down shifting signal, it sends a signal from terminal OD to ECM to cut overdrive until the end of the uphill slope, and the gear shifts are reduced and gear shift points in the electronically controlled transmission are changed.

TY9099900142010X

Fig. 110 Electronically Controlled Transmission Communication Circuit (Part 1 of 3). Camry Solara, Sienna, Tundra w/5VZ-FE engine & 1997–99 Avalon & Camry

3 Check voltage between terminal STP– of cruise control ECU connector and body ground.

PREPARATION:
(a) Remove the ECU with connectors still connected.
(b) Turn ignition switch ON.

CHECK:
Measure voltage between terminal STP– of cruise control ECU connector and body ground, when the brake pedal is depressed and released.

OK:

Depressed	10 – 14 V
Released	Below 1 V

OK ▷ Proceed to next circuit inspection shown in problem symptom table

NG

4 Check for open in harness and connectors between terminal STP– of cruise control ECU and stop light switch

NG ▷ Repair or replace harness or connector.

OK

Check and replace cruise control ECU

TY9099900141030X

Fig. 109 Stop Lamp Switch Circuit Fault (Part 3 of 3). Camry Solara, Sienna, Tundra w/5VZ-FE engine & 1997–99 Avalon & Camry

INSPECTION PROCEDURE

1 Check operation of overdrive.

PREPARATION:
Test drive after engine warms up.

CHECK:
Check that overdrive ON ↔ OFF occurs by operation of OD switch ON–OFF.

NG ▷ Check and repair electronically controlled transmission

OK

2 Check voltage between terminal OD of harness side connector of cruise control ECU and body ground.

PREPARATION:
(a) Remove the ECU with connector still connected.
(b) Turn ignition switch ON.
(c) Disconnect the ECU connector.

CHECK:
Measure voltage between terminal OD of harness side connector of ECU and body ground.

OK:
Voltage: 10 – 14 V

NG ▷ Go to step 5.

OK

TY9099900142020X

Fig. 110 Electronically Controlled Transmission Communication Circuit (Part 2 of 3). Camry Solara, Sienna, Tundra w/5VZ-FE engine & 1997–99 Avalon & Camry

3 Check voltage between terminal ECT of cruise control ECU connector and body ground (On test drive).

PREPARATION:
(a) Connect the ECU connector.
(b) Test drive after engine warms up.
CHECK:
Check voltage between terminal ECT of ECU connector and body ground when OD switch is ON and OFF.
OK:

OD switch position	Voltage
ON	8 – 14 V
OFF	Below 0.5 V

OK ⟩ Proceed to next circuit inspection shown in problem symptom table

NG

4 Check harness and connector between terminal ECT of cruise control ECU and electronically controlled transmission solenoid

NG ⟩ Repair or replace harness or connector.

OK

Check and replace cruise control ECU.

5 Check harness and connector between terminal OD of cruise control ECU and terminal OD1 of ECM

NG ⟩ Repair or replace harness or connector.

OK

Check and replace cruise control ECU

TY9099900142030X

Fig. 110 Electronically Controlled Transmission Communication Circuit (Part 3 of 3). Camry Solara, Sienna, Tundra w/5VZ-FE engine & 1997–99 Avalon & Camry

INSPECTION PROCEDURE

1 Check starter operation.

CHECK:
Check that the starter operates normally and that the engine starts.

NG ⟩ Proceed to engine troubleshooting

OK

2 Input signal check.

Input Signal	Indicator Light Blinking Pattern
Turn PNP switch OFF (Shift to positions except D)	Light ON SW ON / OFF SW OFF

PREPARATION:
Input signal check
CHECK:
Check the indicator light when shifting into positions except D.
OK:
The indicator light goes off when shifting into positions except D.

OK ⟩ Proceed to next circuit inspection shown in problem symptom table

NG

TY9099900143020X

Fig. 111 Park/Neutral Position Switch Circuit (Part 2 of 3). Camry Solara, Sienna, Tundra w/5VZ-FE engine & 1997–99 Avalon & Camry

CIRCUIT DESCRIPTION

When the shift position is except D, a signal is sent from the park/neutral position switch to the ECU. When this signal is input during cruise control driving, the ECU cancels the cruise control.

TY9099900143010X

Fig. 111 Park/Neutral Position Switch Circuit (Part 1 of 3). Camry Solara, Sienna, Tundra w/5VZ-FE engine & 1997–99 Avalon & Camry

3 Check voltage between terminal D of cruise control ECU connector and body ground.

PREPARATION:
Turn ignition switch ON.
CHECK:
Measure voltage between terminal D of ECU connector and body ground when shifting into D position and other positions.
OK:

Shift Position	Voltage
D position	10 – 14 V
Other positions	Below 1 V

OK ⟩ Proceed to next circuit inspection shown in problem symptom table

NG

4 Check harness and connector between cruise control ECU and park/neutral position switch

NG ⟩ Repair or replace harness or connector.

OK

Check and replace cruise control ECU

TY9099900143030X

Fig. 111 Park/Neutral Position Switch Circuit (Part 3 of 3). Camry Solara, Sienna, Tundra w/5VZ-FE engine & 1997–99 Avalon & Camry

CIRCUIT DESCRIPTION

The ECU power source supplies power to the actuator and sensors, etc, when terminal GND and the cruise control ECU case are grounded.

TY9099900144010X

Fig. 112 ECU Power Source Circuit (Part 1 of 3). Avalon, Camry, Camry Solara, Sienna, & Tundra w/5VZ-FE engine

INSPECTION PROCEDURE

1 | Check ECU–IG fuse.

PREPARATION:
Remove the ECU–IG fuse from instrument panel junction block.
CHECK:
Check continuity of ECU–IG fuse.
OK:
    Continuity

NG > Check for short in all the harness and components connected to ECU–IG fuse.

OK

2 | Check voltage between terminals B and GND of cruise control ECU connector.

PREPARATION:
(a)   Remove the ECU with connector still connected.
(b)   Turn ignition switch ON.
CHECK:
Measure voltage between terminals B and GND of ECU connector.
OK:
    10 – 14 V

OK > Proceed to next circuit inspection shown in problem symptom table

NG

TY9099900144020X

Fig. 112   ECU Power Source Circuit (Part 2 of 3). Avalon, Camry, Camry Solara, Sienna, & Tundra w/5VZ-FE engine

CIRCUIT DESCRIPTION
When the cruise control main switch is turned OFF, the cruise control does not operate.

INSPECTION PROCEDURE

1 | Check voltage between terminal CMS of cruise control ECU connector and body ground.

PREPARATION:
(a)   Remove the ECU with connector still connected.
(b)   Turn ignition switch ON.
CHECK:
Measure voltage between terminal CMS of cruise control ECU connector when main switch is held ON and OFF.
OK:

Main switch	Voltage
OFF	10 – 14 V
ON	Below 0.5 V

OK > Proceed to next circuit inspection shown in problem symptom table

NG

TY9099900145010X

Fig. 113   Cruise Control Main Switch Circuit Fault (Part 1 of 2). Camry Solara, Sienna, Tundra w/5VZ-FE engine & 1997–99 Avalon & Camry

3 | Check resistance between terminal GND of cruise control ECU connector and body ground.

CHECK:
Measure resistance between terminal GND of ECU connector and body ground.
OK:
    Resistance: Below 1 Ω

NG > Repair or replace harness or connector.

OK

Check and repair harness and connector between cruise control ECU and battery

TY9099900144030X

Fig. 112   ECU Power Source Circuit (Part 3 of 3). Avalon, Camry, Camry Solara, Sienna, & Tundra w/5VZ-FE engine

2 | Check main switch continuity.

PREPARATION:
(a)   Remove steering wheel center pad (See page SR–12).
(b)   Disconnect the control switch connector.
CHECK:
Check continuity between terminals 3 and 5 of control switch connector when main switch is held ON and OFF.
OK:

Switch position	Tester connection	Specified condition
OFF	3 – 5	No continuity
Hold ON	3 – 5	Continuity

NG > Replace control switch.

OK

3 | Check harness and connector between cruise control ECU and main switch

NG > Repair or replace harness or connector.

OK

Check and replace cruise control ECU

TY9099900145020X

Fig. 113   Cruise Control Main Switch Circuit Fault (Part 2 of 2). Camry Solara, Sienna, Tundra w/5VZ-FE engine & 1997–99 Avalon & Camry

CIRCUIT DESCRIPTION
When the cruise control main switch is turned ON, CRUISE MAIN indicator light lights up.

TY9099900146010X

Fig. 114   Cruise Main Indicator Lamp Circuit (Part 1 of 2). Camry Solara, Sienna, Tundra w/5VZ-FE engine & 1997–99 Avalon & Camry

INSPECTION PROCEDURE

1	Check voltage between terminals PI and GND of cruise control ECU connector.

PREPARATION:
Tun ignition switch ON.
CHECK:
Measure voltage between terminals PI and GND of cruise control ECU connector when main switch is ON and OFF.
OK:

Switch position	Voltage
OFF	10 – 16 V
ON	Below 1.2 V

OK	Proceed to next circuit inspection shown in problem symptom table

NG

2	Check combination meter

NG	Replace combination meter.

OK

Check and replace cruise control ECU

TY9099900146020X

Fig. 114 Cruise Main Indicator Lamp Circuit (Part 2 of 2). Camry Solara, Sienna, Tundra w/5VZ-FE engine & 1997–99 Avalon & Camry

INSPECTION PROCEDURE

1	Check voltage between terminals Tc and E_1 of DLC1.

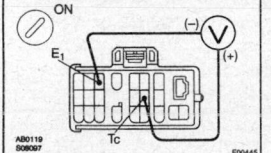

CHECK:
(a) Turn ignition switch ON.
(b) Measure voltage between terminals Tc and E_1 of DLC1.
OK:

Voltage: 10 – 14 V

OK	Proceed to next circuit inspection shown on problem symptoms table

NG

2	Check harness and connector between cruise control actuator with ECU and DLC1, DLC1 and body ground

NG	Repair or replace harness or connector.

OK

Check and replace cruise control actuator with ECU

TY1109900110000X

Fig. 115 Diagnosis Circuit (Part 2 of 2). Tundra w/5VZ-FE engine

CIRCUIT DESCRIPTION

This circuit sends a signal to the ECU that outputs DTC.

TY9099900147010X

Fig. 115 Diagnosis Circuit (Part 1 of 2). Camry Solara, Sienna, Tundra w/5VZ-FE engine & 1997–99 Avalon & Camry

INSPECTION PROCEDURE

1	Check voltage between terminals Tc and E_1 of DLC2.

PREPARATION:
Turn ignition switch ON.
CHECK:
Measure voltage between terminals Tc and E_1 of DLC2.
OK:
Voltage: 10 – 14 V

OK	Proceed to next circuit inspection shown in problem symptom table

NG

2	Check harness and connector between cruise control ECU and DLC2, DLC2 and body ground

NG	Repair or replace harness or connector.

OK

Check and replace cruise control ECU

TY9099900147020X

Fig. 115 Diagnosis Circuit (Part 2 of 2). Camry Solara, Sienna, & 1997–99 Avalon & Camry

INSPECTION PROCEDURE

1	Actuator control cable inspection

OK:
(a) Check that the actuator and control cable throttle link are properly installed and that the cable and link are connected correctly.
(b) Check that the actuator and bell crank operate smoothly.
(c) Check that the cable is not loose or too tight.
OK:
Freeplay: less than 10 mm
HINT:
• If the control cable is very loose, the vehicle's loss of speed going uphill will be large.
• If the control cable is too tight, the idle RPM will become high.

TY9099900148000X

Fig. 116 Actuator Control Cable. Avalon, Camry, Camry Solara & Sienna,

CIRCUIT DESCRIPTION

The actuator motor is operated by signals from the ECU. Acceleration and deceleration signals are transmitted by changes in the Duty Ratio (See note below).

Duty Ratio
The duty ratio is the ratio of the period of continuity in one cycle. For example, if A is the period of continuity in one cycle, and B is the period of non-continuity, then

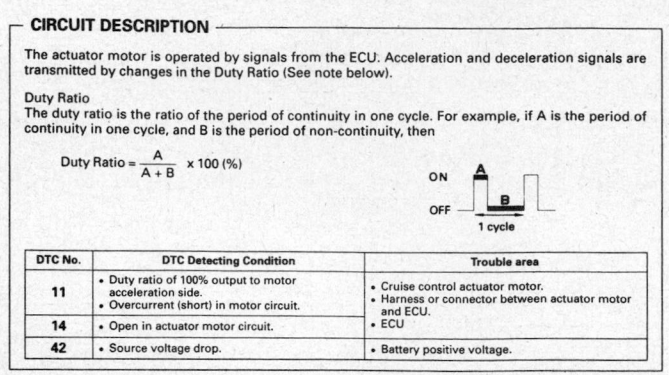

$$\text{Duty Ratio} = \frac{A}{A + B} \times 100 \ (\%)$$

DTC No.	DTC Detecting Condition	Trouble area
11	• Duty ratio of 100% output to motor acceleration side. • Overcurrent (short) in motor circuit.	• Cruise control actuator motor. • Harness or connector between actuator motor and ECU. • ECU
14	• Open in actuator motor circuit.	
42	• Source voltage drop.	• Battery positive voltage.

TY1109900135010X

Fig. 117   Codes 11, 14 & 42: Actuator Motor Circuit (Part 1 of 2). 1996 Camry

CIRCUIT DESCRIPTION

This circuit detects the rotation position of the actuator control plate and sends signal to the ECU.

DTC No.	DTC Detection Condition	Trouble area
13	• Position sensor detects abnormal voltage. • Position sensor signal value does not change when the motor operates.	• Cruise control actuator position sensor. • Harness or connector between actuator position sensor and body ground. • ECU

INSPECTION PROCEDURE

1   Check voltage between terminals VR2 and VR3 of cruise control ECU connector.

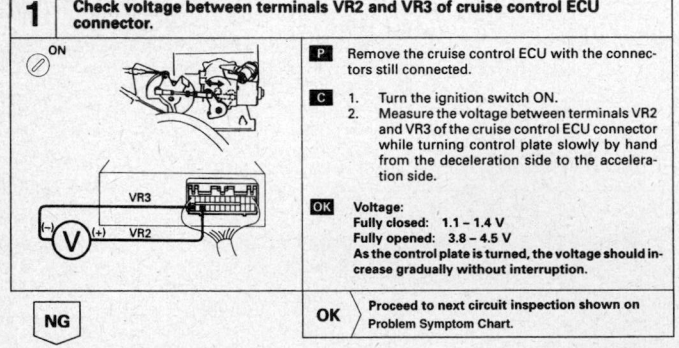

P Remove the cruise control ECU with the connectors still connected.

C 1. Turn the ignition switch ON.
2. Measure the voltage between terminals VR2 and VR3 of the cruise control ECU connector while turning control plate slowly by hand from the deceleration side to the acceleration side.

OK Voltage:
Fully closed: 1.1 – 1.4 V
Fully opened: 3.8 – 4.5 V
As the control plate is turned, the voltage should increase gradually without interruption.

NG ▷

OK ▷ Proceed to next circuit inspection shown on Problem Symptom Chart.

TY1109900136010X

Fig. 118   Code 13: Actuator Position Sensor Circuit (Part 1 of 2). 1996 Camry

INSPECTION PROCEDURE

1   Check actuator motor.

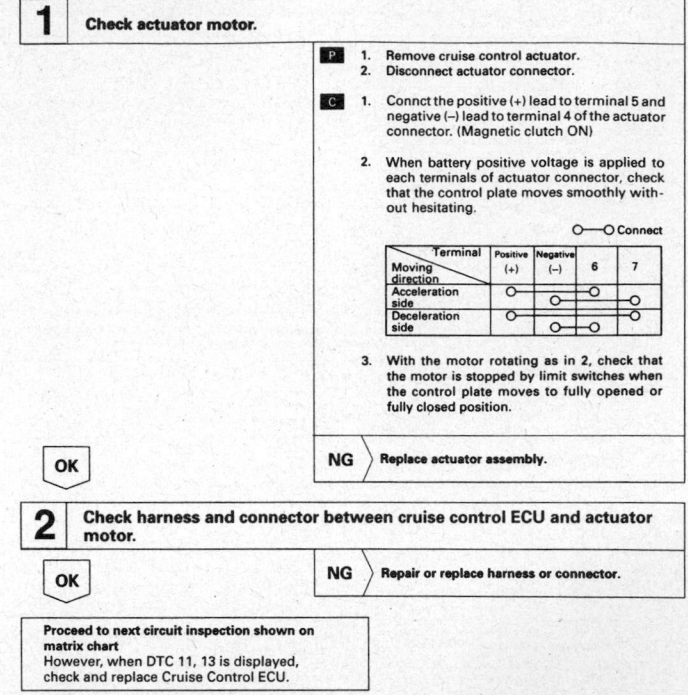

P 1. Remove cruise control actuator.
2. Disconnect actuator connector.

C 1. Connct the positive (+) lead to terminal 5 and negative (–) lead to terminal 4 of the actuator connector. (Magnetic clutch ON)
2. When battery positive voltage is applied to each terminals of actuator connector, check that the control plate moves smoothly without hesitating.

○——○ Connect

Terminal Moving direction	Positive (+)	Negative (–)	6	7
Acceleration side	○	○		
Deceleration side	○		○	

3. With the motor rotating as in 2, check that the motor is stopped by limit switches when the control plate moves to fully opened or fully closed position.

OK ▷

NG ▷ Replace actuator assembly.

2   Check harness and connector between cruise control ECU and actuator motor.

OK ▷

NG ▷ Repair or replace harness or connector.

Proceed to next circuit inspection shown on matrix chart
However, when DTC 11, 13 is displayed, check and replace Cruise Control ECU.

TY1109900135020X

Fig. 117   Codes 11, 14 & 42: Actuator Motor Circuit (Part 2 of 2). 1996 Camry

2   Check actuator position sensor.

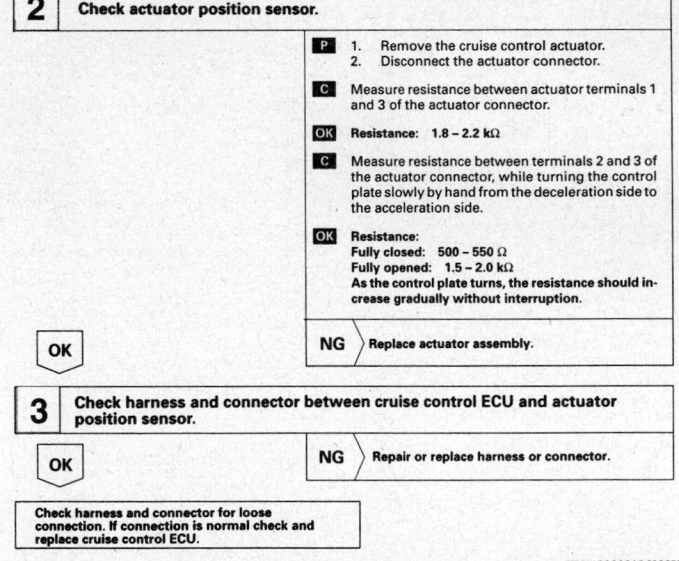

P 1. Remove the cruise control actuator.
2. Disconnect the actuator connector.

C Measure resistance between actuator terminals 1 and 3 of the actuator connector.

OK Resistance: 1.8 – 2.2 kΩ

C Measure resistance between terminals 2 and 3 of the actuator connector, while turning the control plate slowly by hand from the deceleration side to the acceleration side.

OK Resistance:
Fully closed: 500 – 550 Ω
Fully opened: 1.5 – 2.0 kΩ
As the control plate turns, the resistance should increase gradually without interruption.

OK ▷

NG ▷ Replace actuator assembly.

3   Check harness and connector between cruise control ECU and actuator position sensor.

OK ▷

NG ▷ Repair or replace harness or connector.

Check harness and connector for loose connection. If connection is normal check and replace cruise control ECU.

TY1109900136020X

Fig. 118   Code 13: Actuator Position Sensor Circuit (Part 2 of 2). 1996 Camry

CIRCUIT DESCRIPTION

When the shift position is put in P or N, a signal is sent from the park/neutral position switch to the ECU.
When this signal is input during cruise control driving, the ECU cancels the cruise control.

TY1109900138010X

Fig. 119   Park/Neutral Position Switch Circuit (Part 1 of 2). 1996 Camry

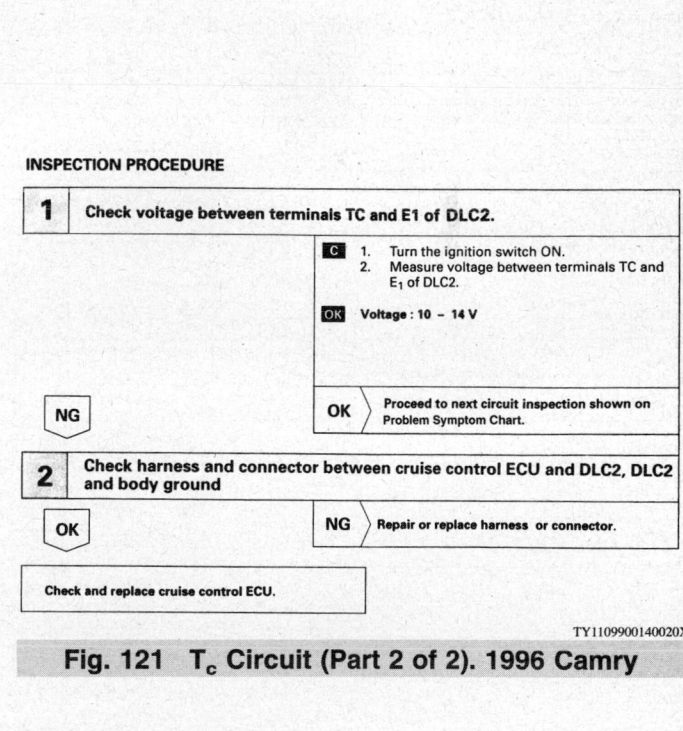

INSPECTION PROCEDURE

1 Check operation of starter.

C Check that the starter operates normally and that the engine starts.

OK | NG ▷ DIAGNOSE STARTING SYSTEM

2 Input signal check.

Shifting into P or N position

ON ┐
OFF ┘

C
1. See the input signal check.
2. Check the indicator light when shifting into P position or N position.

OK The indicator light goes off when shifting into P position or N position.

NG | OK ▷ Proceed to next circuit inspection shown on Problem Symptom Chart.

3 Check voltage between terminal N & C of cruise control ECU connector and body ground.

P Remove cruise control ECU with the connectors still connected.

C
1. Turn the ignition switch ON.
2. Measure voltage between terminal N & C of cruise control ECU connector and body ground, when shifting into P, N position and other positions.

OK

Switch Position	Voltage
P or N position	Below 1 V
Other positions	10 – 14 V

NG | OK ▷ Proceed to next circuit inspection shown on Problem Symptom Chart.

4 Check for open in harness and connector between cruise control ECU and ST fuse

OK | NG ▷ Repair or replace harness or connector.

Check and replace cruise control ECU.

TY1109900138020X

Fig. 119 Park/Neutral Position Switch Circuit (Part 2 of 2). 1996 Camry

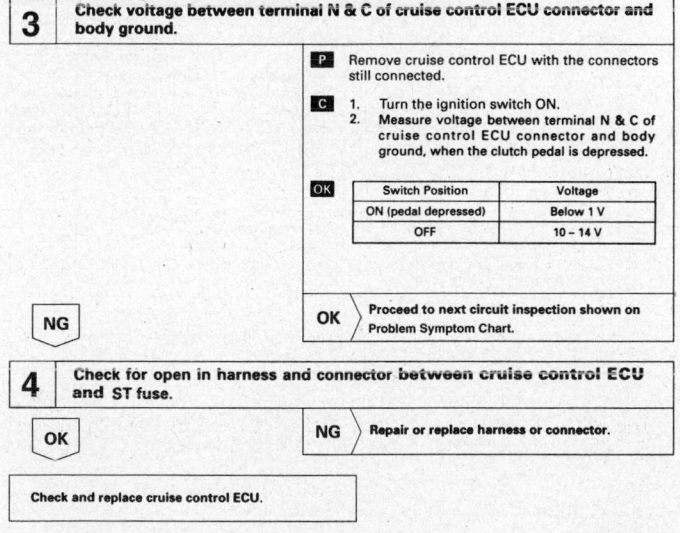

3 Check voltage between terminal N & C of cruise control ECU connector and body ground.

P Remove cruise control ECU with the connectors still connected.

C
1. Turn the ignition switch ON.
2. Measure voltage between terminal N & C of cruise control ECU connector and body ground, when the clutch pedal is depressed.

OK

Switch Position	Voltage
ON (pedal depressed)	Below 1 V
OFF	10 – 14 V

NG | OK ▷ Proceed to next circuit inspection shown on Problem Symptom Chart.

4 Check for open in harness and connector between cruise control ECU and ST fuse.

OK | NG ▷ Repair or replace harness or connector.

Check and replace cruise control ECU.

TY1109900139020X

Fig. 120 Clutch Switch Circuit (Part 2 of 2). 1996 Camry w/5S-FE

CIRCUIT DESCRIPTION

When the clutch pedal is depressed, the clutch switch sends a signal to the ECU, when this signal is input to the ECU during cruise control driving, the ECU cancels cruise control.

INSPECTION PROCEDURE

1 Check operation of starter.

C Check that the starter operates normally and that the engine starts.

OK | NG ▷ DIAGNOSE STARTING SYSTEM

2 Input signal check.

Clutch pedal is depressed

ON ┐
OFF ┘

C
1. See input signal check
2. Check the indicator light when shifting into P range or N position.

OK The indicator light goes off when the clutch pedal is depressed.

NG | OK ▷ Proceed to next circuit inspection shown on Problem Symptom Chart.

TY1109900139010X

Fig. 120 Clutch Switch Circuit (Part 1 of 2). 1996 Camry w/5S-FE

CIRCUIT DESCRIPTION

This circuit sends a signal to the ECU that DTC output is required.

TY1109900140010X

Fig. 121 T$_c$ Circuit (Part 1 of 2). 1996 Camry

INSPECTION PROCEDURE

1 Check voltage between terminals TC and E1 of DLC2.

C
1. Turn the ignition switch ON.
2. Measure voltage between terminals TC and E$_1$ of DLC2.

OK Voltage : 10 – 14 V

NG | OK ▷ Proceed to next circuit inspection shown on Problem Symptom Chart.

2 Check harness and connector between cruise control ECU and DLC2, DLC2 and body ground

OK | NG ▷ Repair or replace harness or connector.

Check and replace cruise control ECU.

TY1109900140020X

Fig. 121 T$_c$ Circuit (Part 2 of 2). 1996 Camry

CIRCUIT DESCRIPTION

This circuit turns on the magnetic clutch inside the actuator during cruise control operation according to the signal from the ECU. If a malfunction occurs in the actuator or speed sensor, etc. during cruise control operation, the rotor shaft between the motor and control plate is released.

When the brake pedal is depressed, the stop light switch turns on, supplying electrical power to the stop light. Power supply to the magnetic clutch is mechanically cut and the magnetic clutch is turned OFF.

When driving downhill, if the vehicle speed exceeds the set speed by 15 km/h (6 mph) above the set speed, then cruise control at the set speed is resumed.

DTC No.	Detection Item	Trouble Area
12	• Short in actuator with ECU circuit • Open in actuator with ECU circuit	• Connector of cruise control actuator with ECU • Stop fuse and stop light switch • cruise control actuator with ECU

TY1109900103010X

Fig. 122   Code 12: Actuator Circuit Fault (Part 1 of 2). Tundra w/5VZ-FE engine

CIRCUIT DESCRIPTION

The circuits detects the rotation position of the actuator contorl plate and sends a signal to the ECU.

DTC No.	Detection Item	Trouble Area
14	• Cruise contorl actuator motor open and shout.	• Connector of cruise control actuator with ECU • Cruise control actuator with ECU

INSPECTION PROCEDURE

1	Check connector of cruise control actuator with ECU

NG > Repair or replace connector.

OK

Check and replace cruise control actuator with ECU

TY1109900104000X

Fig. 123   Code 14: Actuator Mechanical Fault. Tundra w/5VZ-FE engine

CIRCUIT DESCRIPTION

The combination meter sends the vehicle speed signal to the cruise control ECU. The cruise control ECU calculates the vehicle speed by of the vehicle speed signal sent from the combination meter.

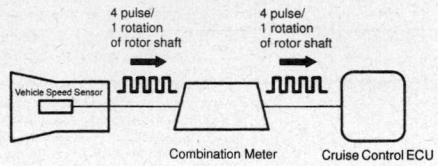

DTC No.	Detection Item	Trouble Area
21	Speed signal is not input to cruise control ECU while cruise control is set.	• Harness or connector between combination meter and cruise control actuator with ECU • Speed sensor (in combination meter) • Combination meter • Cruise control actuator with ECU

TY1109900105010X

Fig. 124   Code 21: VSS Circuit Open (Part 1 of 2). Tundra w/5VZ-FE engine

INSPECTION PROCEDURE

1	Check STOP fuse.

PREPARATION:
Remove STOP fuse from driverside J/B.
CHECK:
Check fuse continuity.
OK:
There is continuity.

NG > Replace STOP fuse.

OK

2	Check stop light switch.

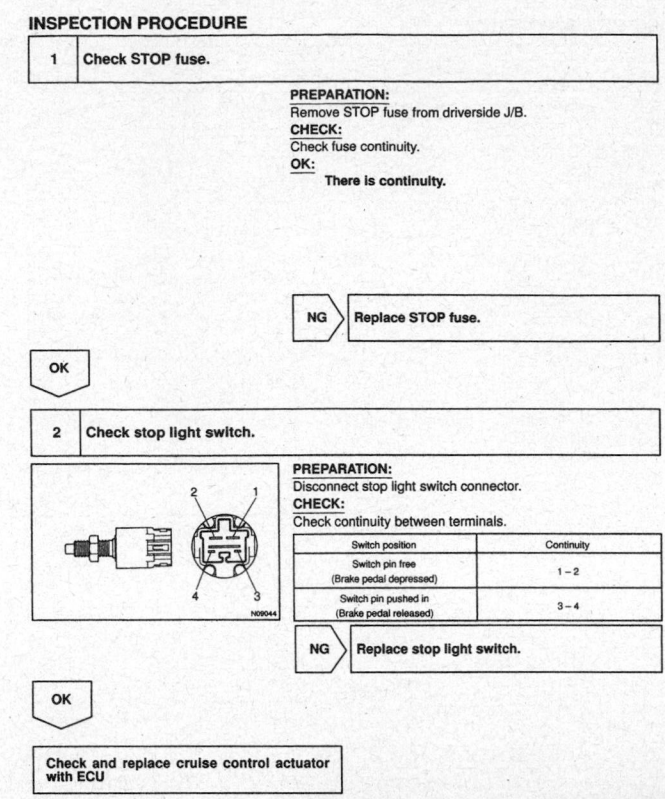

PREPARATION:
Disconnect stop light switch connector.
CHECK:
Check continuity between terminals.

Switch position	Continuity
Switch pin free (Brake pedal depressed)	1 – 2
Switch pin pushed in (Brake pedal released)	3 – 4

NG > Replace stop light switch.

OK

Check and replace cruise control actuator with ECU

TY1109900103020X

Fig. 122   Code 12: Actuator Circuit Fault (Part 2 of 2). Tundra w/5VZ-FE engine

INSPECTION PROCEDURE

1	Input signal check.

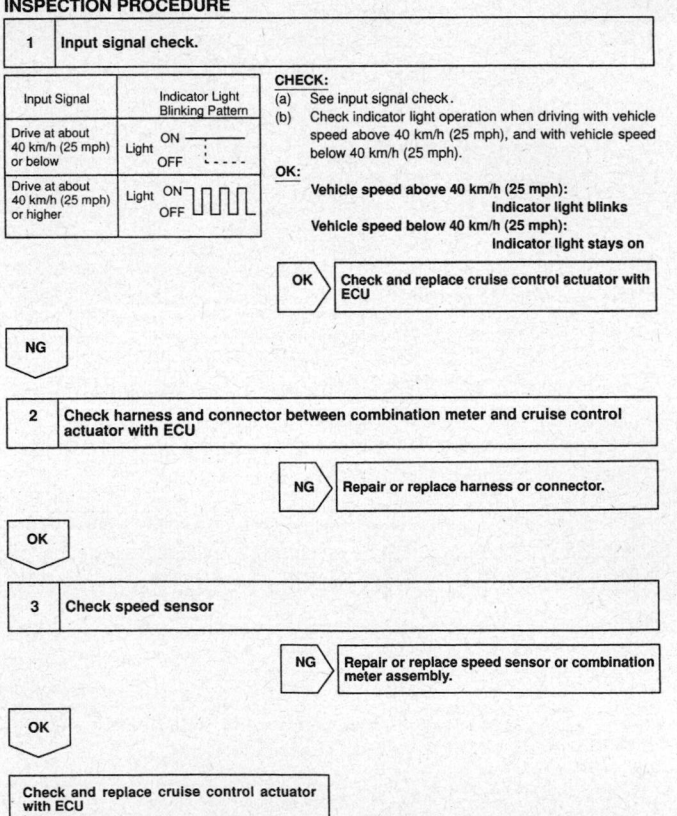

CHECK:
(a)   See input signal check.
(b)   Check indicator light operation when driving with vehicle speed above 40 km/h (25 mph), and with vehicle speed below 40 km/h (25 mph).
OK:
   Vehicle speed above 40 km/h (25 mph):
         Indicator light blinks
   Vehicle speed below 40 km/h (25 mph):
         Indicator light stays on

OK > Check and replace cruise control actuator with ECU

NG

2	Check harness and connector between combination meter and cruise control actuator with ECU

NG > Repair or replace harness or connector.

OK

3	Check speed sensor

NG > Repair or replace speed sensor or combination meter assembly.

OK

Check and replace cruise control actuator with ECU

TY1109900105020X

Fig. 124   Code 21: VSS Circuit Open (Part 2 of 2). Tundra w/5VZ-FE engine

CIRCUIT DESCRIPTION

DTC No.	Detection Item	Trouble Area
23	• Actuator vehicle speed has dropped either by 16 km/h (10 mph) or more below the set speed, or by 20% or more of the set speed.	• Speed sensor (in combination meter) • Cruise control actuator with ECU

WIRING DIAGRAM

INSPECTION PROCEDURE

1	Check speedometer circuit

NG → Repair or replace speed sensor or combination meter assembly.

OK

Check and replace cruise control actuator with ECU

TY1109900106000X

Fig. 125   Code 23: VSS Signal Abnormal. Tundra w/5VZ-FE engine

INSPECTION PROCEDURE

1	Input signal check.

Input Signal	Indicator Light Blinking Pattern
SET/COAST switch	ON / OFF — 2 Pulses
RES/ACC switch	ON / OFF — 3 Pulses
CANCEL switch	ON / OFF — SW OFF / SW ON

PREPARATION:
See input signal check
CHECK:
Check the indicator light operation when each of the SET/COAST, RES/ACC and CANCEL is turned on.
OK:
    SET/COAST, RES/ACC switch
    The signals shown in the table on the left should be output when each switch is ON. The signal should disappear when the switch is turned OFF.
    CANCEL switch
    The indicator light goes off when the cancel switch is turned ON.

OK → Wait and see.

NG

2	Check control switch.

PREPARATION:
(a) Remove steering wheel center pad.
(b) Disconnect control switch connector.
CHECK:
Measure resistance between terminals 3 and 4 of control switch connector when control switch is operated.

Switch position	Resistance (Ω)
Neutral	∞ (No continuity)
RES/ACC	50 – 80
SET/COAST	180 – 220
CANCEL	400 – 440

OK → Replace control switch.

NG

TY1109900107020X

Fig. 126   Code 32: Control Switch Circuit (Part 2 of 3). Tundra w/5VZ-FE engine

CIRCUIT DESCRIPTION

When the "IDLO" terminal of ECM is turned ON, a signal is sent to the ECU. The ECU uses this signal to correct the discrepancy between the throttle valve position and the actuator position sensor valve to enable accurate cruise control at the set speed. If the idle switch is malfunctioning, problem symptoms also occur in the engine, so also inspect engine.

TY1109900108010X

Fig. 127   Idle Switch Circuit (Part 1 of 3). Tundra w/5VZ-FE engine

CIRCUIT DESCRIPTION

This circuit carries the SET/COAST, RES/ACC and CANCEL signals (each voltage) to the ECU.

DTC No.	Detection Item	Trouble Area
32	Short in control switch circuit	• Harness or connector between control switch and cruise control actuator with ECU • Cruise control switch • Cruise control actuator with ECU

TY1109900107010X

Fig. 126   Code 32: Control Switch Circuit (Part 1 of 3). Tundra w/5VZ-FE engine

3	Check harness and connector between cruise control switch and cruise control actuator with ECU

NG → Repair or replace harness or connector.

OK

4	Input signal check (See step 1).

OK → Wait and see.

NG

Check and replace cruise control actuator with ECU

TY1109900107030X

Fig. 126   Code 32: Control Switch Circuit (Part 3 of 3). Tundra w/5VZ-FE engine

INSPECTION PROCEDURE

1	Check voltage between terminal IDL of ECU connector and body ground.

PREPARATION:
(a) Remove cruise control ECU with connector still connected.
(b) Disconnect ECM and ABS ECU connectors.
(c) Turn ignition switch ON.
CHECK:
Measure voltage between terminal IDL of ECU connector and body ground when the throttle valve is fully closed and fully opened.
OK:

Throttle valve position	Voltage
Fully opened	10 – 14 V
Fully closed	Below 2 V

OK → Proceed to next circuit inspection shown on problem symptoms table

NG

2	Check throttle position sensor.

PREPARATION:
Disconnect throttle position sensor connector.
CHECK:
Measure resistance between terminals 3 and 4 of throttle position sensor connector when the throttle valve is fully closed and fully opened.
OK:

Throttle valve position	Resistance
Fully opened	1 MΩ or higher
Fully closed	Below 2.3 kΩ

NG → Replace throttle position sensor.

OK

TY1109900108020X

Fig. 127   Idle Switch Circuit (Part 2 of 3). Tundra w/5VZ-FE engine

3 | Check for open and short in harness and connector between ECU and ECM

NG > Repair or replace harness or connector.

OK

Check and replace cruise control actuator with ECU

TY1109900108030X

Fig. 127 Idle Switch Circuit (Part 3 of 3). Tundra w/5VZ-FE engine

3 | Check voltage between terminal D of cruise control actuator with ECU and body ground.

PREPARATION:
Turn ignition switch ON.
CHECK:
Measure voltage between terminal D of cruise control ECU connector and body ground when clutch pedal depressed and pushed in.
OK:

Shift Position	Voltage
Clutch pedal depressed	10 – 14 V
Clutch pedal pushed in	Below 1 V

OK > Proceed to next circuit inspection shown on problem symptoms table

NG

4 | Check for open in harness and connector between cruise control actuator with ECU and GAUGE fuse

NG > Repair or replace harness or connector.

OK

Check and replace cruise control actuator with ECU

TY1109900109020X

Fig. 128 Clutch Switch Circuit (Part 2 of 2). Tundra w/5VZ-FE engine & 1997–99 Camry

CIRCUIT DESCRIPTION
When the clutch pedal is depressed, the clutch switch sends a signal to the cruise control ECU. When the signal is input to the cruise control ECU during cruise control driving, the cruise control ECU cancels cruise control.

INSPECTION PROCEDURE

1 | Check starter operation.

CHECK:
Check that the starter operates normally and that the engine starts.

NG > Proceed to engine troubleshooting

OK

2 | Input signal check.

Input Signal	Indicator Light Blinking Pattern
Clutch switch OFF (Depress clutch pedal)	

PREPARATION:
See input signal check
CHECK:
Check the indicator light when clutch pedal depressed.
OK:
The indicator light goes off when clutch pedal depressed.

OK > Proceed to next circuit inspection shown on problem symptoms table

NG

TY1109900109010X

Fig. 128 Clutch Switch Circuit (Part 1 of 2). Tundra w/5VZ-FE engine & 1997–99 Camry

INSPECTION PROCEDURE

1 | Check actuator control cable.

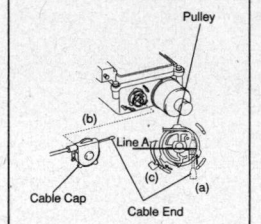

PREPARATION:
(a) Remove actuator control cable.
  (1) Insert the inner cable end into the pulley and pull it up to the line "A", show in the illustration.
    The end of the spring prevents to pulley from slipping out.
  (2) Install the cable cap to the fit it with the actuator.
  (3) Turn the cable cap clockwise to lock.
(b) Install actuator control cable.
  Installation in the reverse order of removal.
CHECK:
(a) Check that the actuator, control cable throttle link are properly installed and that the cable and link are connected correctly.
(b) Check that the actuator and bell crank are operating smoothly.
(c) Check that the cable is not loose or too tight.
OK:
Freeplay: less than 10 mm
HINT:
• If the control cable is very loose, the vehicle's loss of speed going uphill will be large.
• If the control cable is too tight, the idle RPM will become high.

TY1109900111000X

Fig. 129 Actuator Control Cable. Tundra w/5VZ-FE engine

CIRCUIT DESCRIPTION
The vehicle speed sensor outputs a 4–pulse signal for every revolution of the rotor shaft, which is rotated by the transmission output shaft via the driven gear. After this signal is converted into a more precise rectangular waveform by the waveform shaping circuit inside the combination meter, it is then transmitted to the engine ECU. The ECM determines the vehicle speed based on the frequency of these pulse signals.

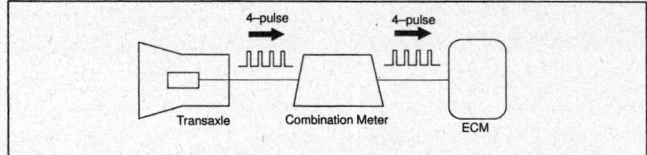

DTC No.	DTC Detecting Condition	Trouble Area
P0500	No vehicle speed sensor signal to ECM under following conditions (a) and (b): (2 trip detection logic) (a) Park/neutral position switch is OFF (b) Vehicle is being driven	• Combination meter • Open or short in vehicle speed sensor circuit • Vehicle speed sensor • ECM

TY1109900118010X

Fig. 130 Code P0500/21 & 23: Vehicle Speed Sensor Signal Abnormal (Part 1 of 3). Tundra w/2UZ-FE engine

INSPECTION PROCEDURE

HINT:
Read freeze frame data using TOYOTA hand–held tester or OBD II scan tool. Because freeze frame records the engine conditions when the malfunction is detected. When troubleshooting it is useful for determining whether the vehicle was running or stopped, the engine was warmed up or not, the air–fuel ratio was lean or rich, etc. at the time of the malfunction.

1	Check operation of speedometer.

CHECK:
Drive the vehicle and check if the operation of the speedometer in the combination meter is normal.
HINT:
The vehicle speed is operating normally if the speedometer display is normal.

> NG → Check speedometer circuit. See combination meter troubleshooting

OK

2	Check voltage between terminal SPD of ECM connector and body ground.

PREPARATION:
(a) Remove the glove compartment
(b) Shift the shift lever to neutral.
(c) Jack up a rear wheel on one side.
(d) Turn the ignition switch ON.

CHECK:
Measure the voltage between terminal SPD of the ECM connector and body ground when the wheel is turned slowly.

OK:

Voltage is generated intermittently.

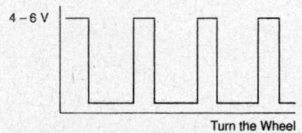

4 – 6 V

Turn the Wheel

> NG → Check and repair harness and connector between combination meter and ECM.

TY1109900118020X

Fig. 130   Code P0500/21 & 23: Vehicle Speed Sensor Signal Abnormal (Part 2 of 3). Tundra w/2UZ-FE engine

CIRCUIT DESCRIPTION

When the brake pedal is depressed, the stop light switch sends a signal to the ECM. When the ECM receives this signal, it cancels the cruise control.
A fail–safe function is provided so that the cancel functions normally, even if there is a malfunction in the stop light signal circuit.
The cancel condition is that battery positive voltage is supplied to terminal STP.
When the brake is on, battery positive voltage is normally applied through the STOP fuse and stop light switch to terminal STP of the ECM, and the ECM turns the cruise control OFF.
If the harness connected to terminal STP has an open circuit, terminal STP will have battery positive voltage and the cruise control will be turned OFF.

DTC No.	Detection Item	Trouble Area
52	Stop light switch circuit.	• Stop light switch • Harness or connector between ECM and stop light switch circuit • ECM

TY1109900120010X

Fig. 131   Code P1520/52: Stop Lamp Switch Circuit (Part 1 of 4). Tundra w/2UZ-FE engine

OK

	Check and replace ECM

TY1109900118030X

Fig. 130   Code P0500/21 & 23: Vehicle Speed Sensor Signal Abnormal (Part 3 of 3). Tundra w/2UZ-FE engine

INSPECTION PROCEDURE

HINT:
In case of using the TOYOTA hand–held tester, start the inspection from step 1 and in case of not using the TOYOTA hand–held tester, start from step 2.

1	Check stop light switch using TOYOTA hand–held tester.

PREPARATION:
Connect the TOYOTA hand–held tester to the DLC1.
CHECK:
Check the stop light switch using DATALIST.
OK:

Condition	Stop light switch 1 (Sub CPU)	Stop light switch 2 (Sub CPU)	Stop light switch 2 (Main CPU)
Depressed	ON	ON	ON
Released	OFF	OFF	OFF

HINT:
• Stop light SW 1 has a function to disconnect the connection (OFF) when depressing the pedal, however, ECM controls by the logic rivers, so with the TOYOTA hand–held tester, it displays ON.
• Stop light SW 1 indicates the input of ST1–terminal and Stop light SW 2 indicates the input of STP terminal.

> OK → Proceed to next circuit inspection shown in problem symptom table

NG

2	Check operation of stop light.

CHECK:
Check that stop light comes on when brake pedal is depressed, and turns off when brake pedal is released.

> NG → Check stop light system

OK

TY1109900120020X

Fig. 131   Code P1520/52: Stop Lamp Switch Circuit (Part 2 of 4). Tundra w/2UZ-FE engine

3	Check voltage between terminal STP of ECM connector and body ground.

PREPARATION:
(a) Remove the ECM with connectors still connected.
(b) Turn ignition switch ON.
CHECK:
Measure voltage between terminal STP of ECM connector and body ground, when the brake pedal is depressed and released.
OK:

Depressed	7.5 – 14 V
Released	0 – 1.5 V

> OK → Proceed to next circuit inspection shown in problem symptom table

NG

TY1109900120030X

Fig. 131   Code P1520/52: Stop Lamp Switch Circuit (Part 3 of 4). Tundra w/2UZ-FE engine

4	Check voltage between terminal ST1– of ECM connector and body ground.

PREPARATION:
(a) Remove the ECM with connectors still connected.
(b) Turn ignition switch ON.
CHECK:
Measure voltage between terminal ST1– of ECM connector and body ground, when the brake pedal is depressed and released.
OK:

Depreased	Below 1 V
Released	7.5 – 14 V

OK ▷ Proceed to next circuit inspection shown in problem symptoms table

NG ▽

5	Check wire harness and connector between terminal STP of ECM and stop light switch, and terminal ST1– of ECM and stop light switch

NG ▷ Repair or replace harness or connector.

OK ▽

Check and replace ECM

TY1109900120040X

Fig. 131 Code P1520/52: Stop Lamp Switch Circuit (Part 4 of 4). Tundra w/2UZ-FE engine

3	Check harness and connector between ECM and cruise control switch, cruise control switch and body ground.

NG ▷ Repair or replace harness or connector.

OK ▽

4	Check cruise control indicator light.

NG ▷ Replace combination meter.

OK ▽

Check and replace ECM.

TY1109900121030X

Fig. 132 Code P1565/32: Cruise Control Switch Circuit (Part 3 of 3). Tundra w/2UZ-FE engine

DTC	P1566/54	Input Signal Circuit

CIRCUIT DESCRIPTION

DTC No.	Detection Item	Trouble Area
P1566/54	Input signal abnormal.	ECM

INSPECTION PROCEDURE

Check and replace ECM

TY1109900122000X

Fig. 133 Code P1566/54: Input Signal Circuit. Tundra w/2UZ-FE engine

CIRCUIT DESCRIPTION
This circuit carries the SET/COAST, RESUME/ACCEL and CANCEL signals (each voltage) to the ECM.

DTC No.	Detection Item	Trouble Area
P1565/32	Short in control switch circuit.	• Cruise control switch • Harness or connector between ECM and cruise control switch, cruise control switch and body ground • ECM

TY1109900121010X

Fig. 132 Code P1565/32: Cruise Control Switch Circuit (Part 1 of 3). Tundra w/2UZ-FE engine

INSPECTION PROCEDURE

1	Check voltage between terminals CCS of ECM connector and body ground.

PREPARATION:
(a) Remove the ECM with connector still connected.
(b) Turn ignition switch ON.
CHECK:
Measure voltage between terminals CCS of ECM connector and body ground, when each of the SET/COAST, RESUME/ACCEL and CANCEL is turned ON.

Switch position	Resistance (V)
Neutral	9 – 14 V
RES/ACC	1.3 – 2.1 V
SET/COAST	3.0 – 4.7 V
CANCEL	4.6 – 7.3 V

NG ▷ Proceed to next circuit inspection shown in problem symptoms table

OK ▽

2	Check control switch continuity.

PREPARATION:
(a) Remove steering wheel center pad.
(b) Disconnect the control switch connector.
CHECK:
Measure resistance between terminals 4 and 5 of control switch connector when control switch is operated.

Switch position	Resistance (Ω)
Neutral	∞ (No continuity)
RES/ACC	60 – 70
SET/COAST	180 – 220
CANCEL	380 – 460

NG ▷ Replace control switch.

OK ▽

TY1109900121020X

Fig. 132 Code P1565/32: Cruise Control Switch Circuit (Part 2 of 3). Tundra w/2UZ-FE engine

CIRCUIT DESCRIPTION
When the cruise control main switch is turned off, the cruise control does not operate.

INSPECTION PROCEDURE

1	Check voltage between terminal CMS of ECM connector and body ground.

PREPARATION:
(a) Remove the ECM with connector still connected.
(b) Turn ignition switch ON.
CHECK:
Measure voltage between terminal CMS of ECM connector when main switch is held on and off.
OK:

Main switch	Voltage
OFF	7.5 – 14 V
ON	0 – 1.5 V

OK ▷ Proceed to next circuit inspection shown on problem symptom table

NG ▽

TY1109900123010X

Fig. 134 Main Switch Circuit (Part 1 of 2). Tundra w/2UZ-FE engine

2	Check main switch continuity.

PREPARATION:
(a) Remove steering wheel center pad
(b) Disconnect the control switch connector.

CHECK:
Check continuity between terminals 3 and 5 of control switch connector when main switch is held on and off.

OK:

Switch position	Tester connection	Specified condition
OFF	3 – 5	No continuity
ON	3 – 5	Continuity

NG ▷ Replace control switch.

OK

3	Check harness and connector between ECM and main switch

NG ▷ Repair or replace harness or connector.

OK

Check and replace ECM

TY1109900123020X

Fig. 134   Main Switch Circuit (Part 2 of 2). Tundra w/2UZ-FE engine

INSPECTION PROCEDURE

1	Check voltage between terminals PI and GND of ECM connector.

PREPARATION:
Tun ignition switch ON.

CHECK:
Measure voltage between terminals PI and GND of ECM connector when main switch is held on and off.

OK:

Switch position	Voltage
OFF	9 – 14 V
ON	0 – 3 V

OK ▷ Proceed to next circuit inspection shown on problem symptom table

NG

2	Check combination meter

NG ▷ Replace combination meter.

OK

Check and replace ECM

TY1109900124020X

Fig. 135   Cruise Main Indicator Lamp (Part 2 of 2). Tundra w/2UZ-FE engine

CIRCUIT DESCRIPTION

When the cruise control main switch is turned ON, CRUISE MAIN indicator light lights up.

TY1109900124010X

Fig. 135   Cruise Main Indicator Lamp (Part 1 of 2). Tundra w/2UZ-FE engine

Symptom	Suspect Area
SET not occourring or CANCEL occurring. (DTC is Normal)	1. Main Switch Circuit (Cruise control switch) 2. Vehicle Speed Sensor 3. Control Switch Circuit (Cruise control switch) 4. Stop Light Switch Circuit 5. Park/Neutral Position Switch Circuit 6. Actuator Motor Circuit 7. Cruise Control Cable 8. Cruise Control ECU
SET not occurring or CANCEL occurring. (DTC is not output)	1. ECU Power Source Circuit 2. Cruise Control ECU
Actual vehicle speed deviates above or below the set speed.	1. Cruise Control Cable 2. Vehicle Speed Signal Abnormal 3. Electronically Controlled Transmission Communication Circuit 4. Actuator Motor Circuit 5. Idle Signal Circuit (Main throttle position sensor) 6. Cruise Control ECU
Gear shifting frequent between 3rd and O/D when driving on uphill road. (Hurting)	1. Electronically Controlled Transmission Communication Circuit 2. Cruise Control ECU
Cruise control not cancelled, even when brake pedal is depressed.	1. Cruise Control Cable 2. Stop Light Switch Circuit 3. Actuator Motor Circuit 4. Cruise Control ECU
Cruise control not cancelled, even when transmission is shifted to "N" postion.	1. Cruise Control Cable 2. Park/Neutral Position Switch Circuit 3. Actuator Motor Circuit 4. Cruise Control ECU
Control switch does not operate. (SET/COAST, ACC/RES, CANCEL not possible)	1. Cruise Control Cable 2. Control Switch Circuit 3. Actuator Motor Circuit 4. Cruise Control ECU
SET possible at 40 km/h (25 mph) or less, or CANCEL does not operate at 40 km/h (25 mph) or less.	1. Cruise Control Cable 2. Vehicle Speed Signal Abnormal 3. Actuator Motor Circuit 4. Cruise Control ECU
Poor response in ACCEL and RESUME modes.	1. Cruise Control Cable 2. Electronically Controlled Transmission Communication Circuit 3. Actuator Motor Circuit 4. Cruise Control ECU
O/D does not resume, even though the road is not uphill.	1. Electronically Controlled Transmission Communication Circuit 2. Cruise Control ECU
DTC memory is erased.	1. Back-up Power Source Circuit 2. Cruise Control ECU
DTC is not output, or is output when it should not be.	1. Tc Circuit 2. Cruise Control ECU
Cruise MAIN indicator light remains ON or fails to light up.	1. Cruise MAIN Indicator Light Switch Circuit

TY1109900231000X

Fig. 136   Problem Symptoms Table. Celica

CIRCUIT DESCRIPTION

The actuator motor is operated by signals from the ECU. Acceleration and deceleration signals are transmitted by changes in the Duty Ratio (See note below).

Duty Ratio
The duty ratio is the ratio of the period of continuity in one cycle. For example, if A is the period of continuity in one cycle, and B is the period of non-continuity, then

$$\text{Duty Ratio} = \frac{A}{A + B} \times 100 \ (\%)$$

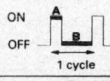

1 cycle

DTC No.	DTC Detecting Condition	Trouble area
11	• Short in motor circuit.	• Cruise control actuator motor • Harness or connector between actuator motor and ECU • ECU
14	• Open in actuator motor circuit	• ECU

TY1109900482010X

Fig. 137   Codes 11 & 14: Actuator Motor Circuit (Part 1 of 2). 1996–97 Celica

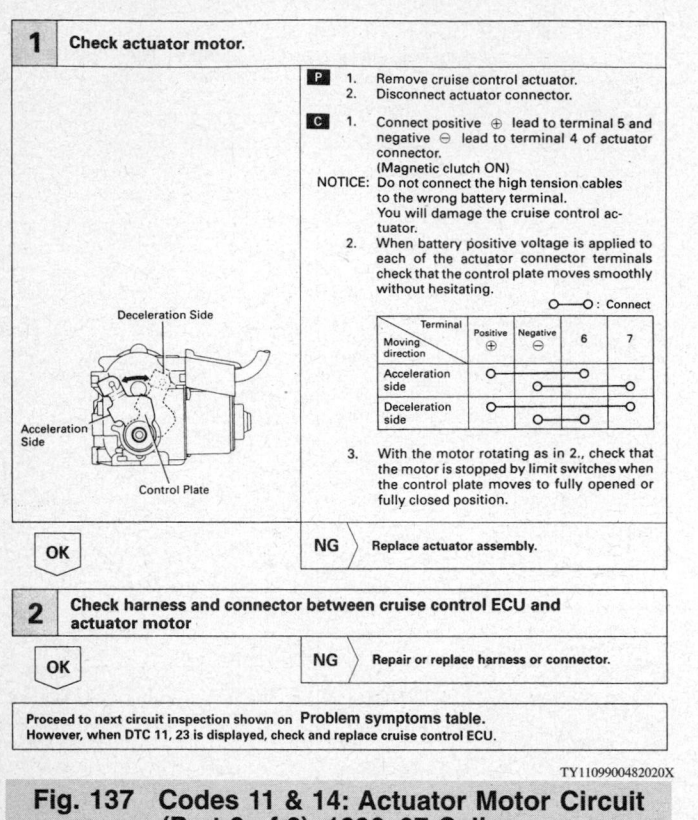

1 Check actuator motor.

P	1. Remove cruise control actuator.
	2. Disconnect actuator connector.
C	1. Connect positive ⊕ lead to terminal 5 and negative ⊖ lead to terminal 4 of actuator connector. (Magnetic clutch ON)
	NOTICE: Do not connect the high tension cables to the wrong battery terminal. You will damage the cruise control actuator.
	2. When battery positive voltage is applied to each of the actuator connector terminals check that the control plate moves smoothly without hesitating.

○——○ : Connect

Terminal / Moving direction	Positive ⊕	Negative ⊖	6	7
Acceleration side	○		○	
Deceleration side		○		○

3. With the motor rotating as in 2., check that the motor is stopped by limit switches when the control plate moves to fully opened or fully closed position.

| **OK** | | **NG** ▷ Replace actuator assembly. |

2 Check harness and connector between cruise control ECU and actuator motor

| **OK** | | **NG** ▷ Repair or replace harness or connector. |

Proceed to next circuit inspection shown on **Problem symptoms table**. However, when DTC 11, 23 is displayed, check and replace cruise control ECU.

TY1109900482020X

Fig. 137 Codes 11 & 14: Actuator Motor Circuit (Part 2 of 2). 1996–97 Celica

INSPECTION PROCEDURE

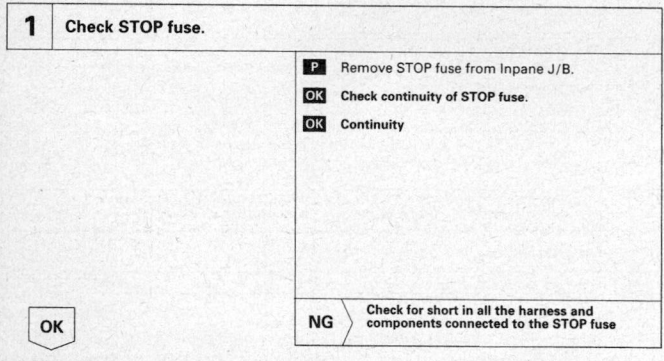

1 Check STOP fuse.

P	Remove STOP fuse from Inpane J/B.
OK	Check continuity of STOP fuse.
OK	Continuity

| **OK** | | **NG** ▷ Check for short in all the harness and components connected to the STOP fuse |

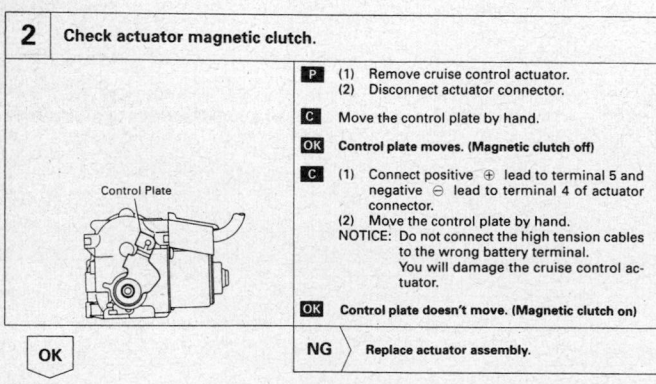

2 Check actuator magnetic clutch.

P	(1) Remove cruise control actuator.
	(2) Disconnect actuator connector.
C	Move the control plate by hand.
OK	Control plate moves. (Magnetic clutch off)
C	(1) Connect positive ⊕ lead to terminal 5 and negative ⊖ lead to terminal 4 of actuator connector.
	(2) Move the control plate by hand.
	NOTICE: Do not connect the high tension cables to the wrong battery terminal. You will damage the cruise control actuator.
OK	Control plate doesn't move. (Magnetic clutch on)

| **OK** | | **NG** ▷ Replace actuator assembly. |

TY1109900483020X

Fig. 138 Code 12: Actuator Magnetic Clutch Circuit (Part 2 of 3). 1996–97 Celica

CIRCUIT DESCRIPTION

This circuit turns on the magnetic clutch inside the actuator during cruise control operation according to the signal from the ECU. If a malfunction occurs in the actuator or vehicle speed sensor, etc. during cruise control, the rotor shaft between the motor and control plate is released.

When the brake pedal is depressed, the stop light switch turns on, supplying electrical power to the stop light. Power supply to the magnetic clutch is mechanically cut and the magnetic clutch is turned OFF.

When driving downhill, if the vehicle speed exceeds the set speed by 15 km/h (9 mph), the ECU turns the magnetic clutch OFF. If the vehicle speed later drops to within 10 km/h (6 mph) above the set speed, then cruise control at the set speed is resumed.

DTC No.	DTC Detecting Condition	Trouble area
12	• Short in magnetic clutch circuit. • Open (0.8 sec) in magnetic clutch circuit.	• Cruise control magnetic clutch. • Harness or connector between ECU and magnetic clutch, magnetic clutch and body ground. • ECU • STOP Fuse

TY1109900483010X

Fig. 138 Code 12: Actuator Magnetic Clutch Circuit (Part 1 of 3). 1996–97 Celica

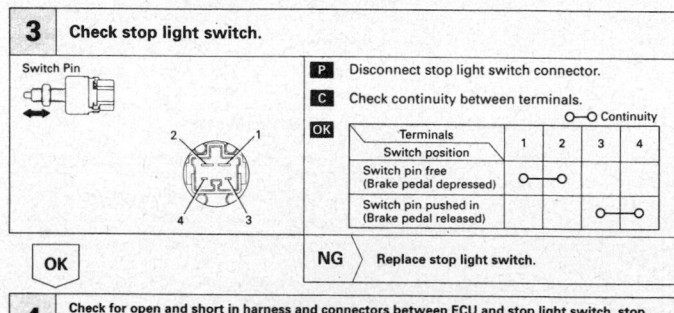

3 Check stop light switch.

Switch Pin

| **P** | Disconnect stop light switch connector. |
| **C** | Check continuity between terminals. |

○——○ Continuity

Terminals / Switch position	1	2	3	4
Switch pin free (Brake pedal depressed)	○	○		
Switch pin pushed in (Brake pedal released)			○	○

| **OK** | | **NG** ▷ Replace stop light switch. |

4 Check for open and short in harness and connectors between ECU and stop light switch, stop light switch and magnetic clutch, magnetic clutch and body ground

| **OK** | | **NG** ▷ Repair or replace harness or connector. |

Proceed to next circuit inspection shown **Problem symptoms table**. However, when DTC 12 is displayed, check harness and connector for loose connection. If connection is normal, check and replace ECU.

TY1109900483030X

Fig. 138 Code 12: Actuator Magnetic Clutch Circuit (Part 3 of 3). 1996–97 Celica

CIRCUIT DESCRIPTION

The circuit detects the rotation position of the actuator control plate and sends a signal to the ECU.

DTC No.	DTC Detecting Condition	Trouble area
13	• Position sensor detects abnormal voltage.	• Cruise control actuator motor. • Cruise control actuator position sensor. • Harness or connector between actuator position sensor and body ground. • Harness or connector between actuator motor and ECU. • ECU
14	• Open in actuator motor circuit. • Position sensor signal value does not change when the motor operates.	

TY1109900484010X

Fig. 139 Codes 13 & 14: Actuator Position Sensor Circuit (Part 1 of 2). 1996–97 Celica

INSPECTION PROCEDURE

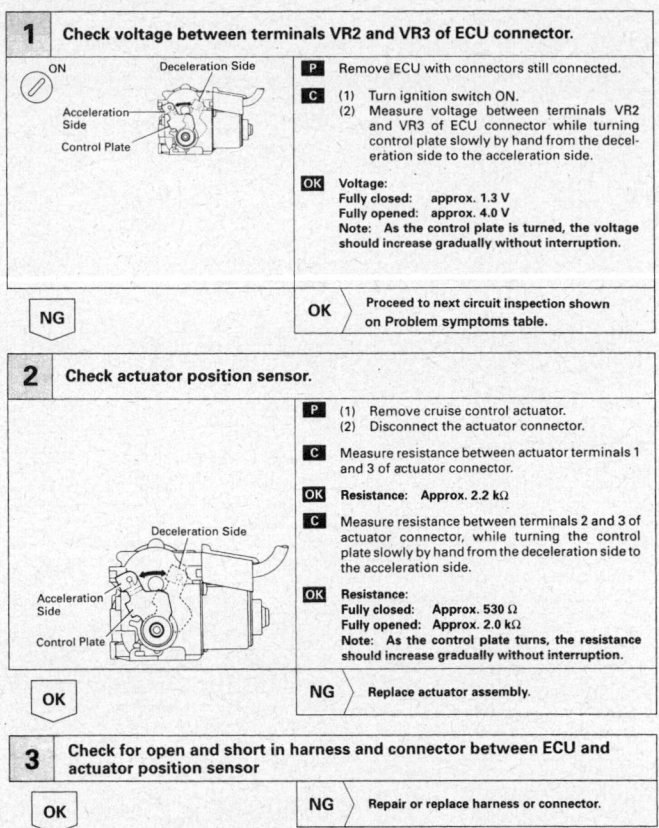

1 | Check voltage between terminals VR2 and VR3 of ECU connector.

P Remove ECU with connectors still connected.

C
(1) Turn ignition switch ON.
(2) Measure voltage between terminals VR2 and VR3 of ECU connector while turning control plate slowly by hand from the deceleration side to the acceleration side.

OK Voltage:
Fully closed: approx. 1.3 V
Fully opened: approx. 4.0 V
Note: As the control plate is turned, the voltage should increase gradually without interruption.

NG | **OK** Proceed to next circuit inspection shown on Problem symptoms table.

2 | Check actuator position sensor.

P
(1) Remove cruise control actuator.
(2) Disconnect the actuator connector.

C Measure resistance between actuator terminals 1 and 3 of actuator connector.

OK Resistance: Approx. 2.2 kΩ

C Measure resistance between terminals 2 and 3 of actuator connector, while turning the control plate slowly by hand from the deceleration side to the acceleration side.

OK Resistance:
Fully closed: Approx. 530 Ω
Fully opened: Approx. 2.0 kΩ
Note: As the control plate turns, the resistance should increase gradually without interruption.

OK | **NG** Replace actuator assembly.

3 | Check for open and short in harness and connector between ECU and actuator position sensor

OK | **NG** Repair or replace harness or connector.

Check harness and connector for loose connection.
If connection is normal check and replace ECU.

TY1109900484020X

Fig. 139   Codes 13 & 14: Actuator Position Sensor Circuit (Part 2 of 2). 1996–97 Celica

INSPECTION PROCEDURE

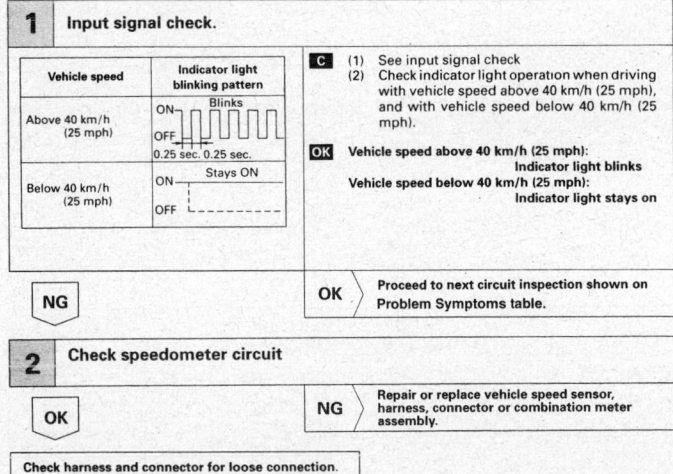

1 | Input signal check.

Vehicle speed	Indicator light blinking pattern
Above 40 km/h (25 mph)	Blinks ON/OFF 0.25 sec. 0.25 sec.
Below 40 km/h (25 mph)	Stays ON ON/OFF

C
(1) See input signal check
(2) Check indicator light operation when driving with vehicle speed above 40 km/h (25 mph), and with vehicle speed below 40 km/h (25 mph).

OK Vehicle speed above 40 km/h (25 mph):
Indicator light blinks
Vehicle speed below 40 km/h (25 mph):
Indicator light stays on

NG | **OK** Proceed to next circuit inspection shown on Problem Symptoms table.

2 | Check speedometer circuit

OK | **NG** Repair or replace vehicle speed sensor, harness, connector or combination meter assembly.

Check harness and connector for loose connection.
If connection is normal, check and replace ECU.

TY1109900485020X

Fig. 140   Codes 21 & 23: Vehicle Speed Sensor Circuit (Part 2 of 2). 1996–97 Celica

CIRCUIT DESCRIPTION

The vehicle speed sensor signal is sent to the cruise control ECU as the vehicle speed signal.
The rotor shaft is driven by the gear of the transaxle.
For each rotation of the shaft, the speed sensor sends a 4-pulse signal to the combination meter.
This signal is converted inside the combination meter and sent as a 4-pulse signal to the cruise control ECU. The ECU calculates the vehicle speed from this pulse frequency.

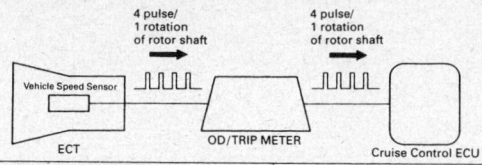

DTC No.	DTC Detecting Condition	Trouble area
21	Speed signal is not input to the ECU while cruise control is set.	• Speed sensor • Combination meter • Harness or connector between speed sensor and combination meter, combination meter and ECU. • ECU
23	Vehicle speed sensor pulse is abnormal.	• Actuator • Speed sensor • Harness or connector in OD and SPD circuit (Open or short intermittently) • ECU

TY1109900485010X

Fig. 140   Codes 21 & 23: Vehicle Speed Sensor Circuit (Part 1 of 2). 1996–97 Celica

CIRCUIT DESCRIPTION

This circuit carries the SET/COAST, RESUME/ACCEL and CANCEL signals (each voltage) to the ECU.

DTC No.	DTC Detecting Condition	Trouble area
32	Short in, control switch circuit. Voltage abnormality in control switch.	• Cruise control switch. • Harness or connector between control switch and ECU. • ECU

TY1109900486010X

Fig. 141   Code 32: Control Switch Circuit (Part 1 of 3). 1996–97 Celica

INSPECTION PROCEDURE

1 | Input signal check.

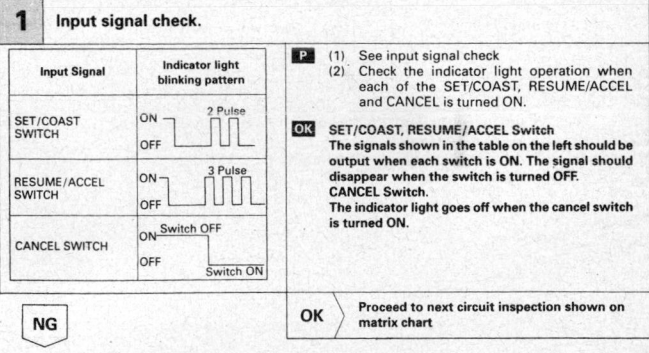

Input Signal	Indicator light blinking pattern
SET/COAST SWITCH	2 Pulse ON/OFF
RESUME/ACCEL SWITCH	3 Pulse ON/OFF
CANCEL SWITCH	Switch OFF ON/OFF Switch ON

P
(1) See input signal check
(2) Check the indicator light operation when each of the SET/COAST, RESUME/ACCEL and CANCEL is turned ON.

OK SET/COAST, RESUME/ACCEL Switch
The signals shown in the table on the left should be output when each switch is ON. The signal should disappear when the switch is turned OFF.
CANCEL Switch
The indicator light goes off when the cancel switch is turned ON.

NG | **OK** Proceed to next circuit inspection shown on matrix chart

TY1109900486020X

Fig. 141   Code 32: Control Switch Circuit (Part 2 of 3). 1996–97 Celica

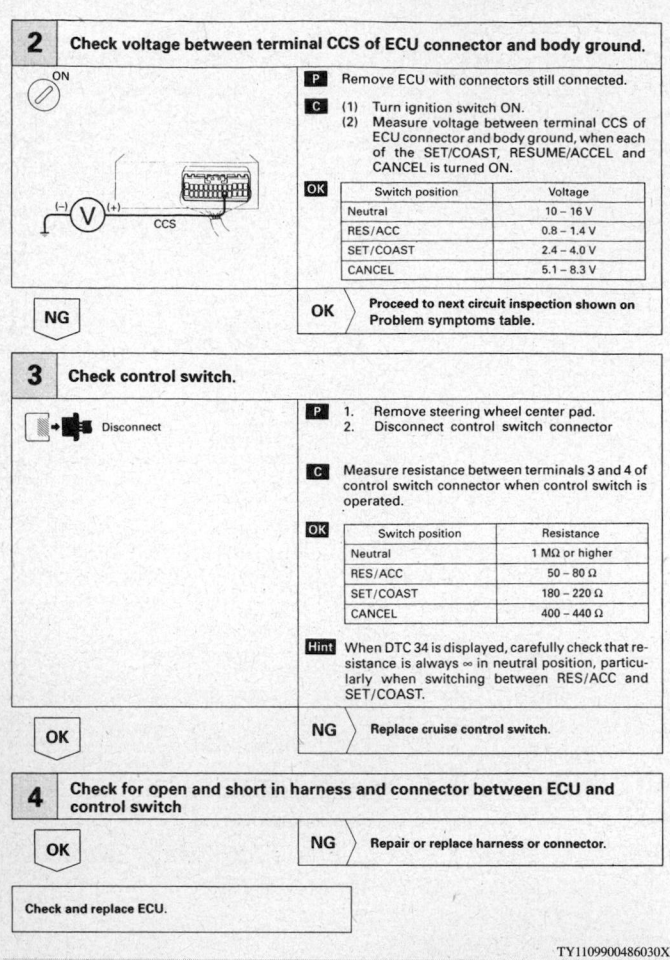

2 | Check voltage between terminal CCS of ECU connector and body ground.

P Remove ECU with connectors still connected.

C
(1) Turn ignition switch ON.
(2) Measure voltage between terminal CCS of ECU connector and body ground, when each of the SET/COAST, RESUME/ACCEL and CANCEL is turned ON.

OK

Switch position	Voltage
Neutral	10 – 16 V
RES/ACC	0.8 – 1.4 V
SET/COAST	2.4 – 4.0 V
CANCEL	5.1 – 8.3 V

NG

OK Proceed to next circuit inspection shown on Problem symptoms table.

3 | Check control switch.

Disconnect

P
1. Remove steering wheel center pad.
2. Disconnect control switch connector

C Measure resistance between terminals 3 and 4 of control switch connector when control switch is operated.

OK

Switch position	Resistance
Neutral	1 MΩ or higher
RES/ACC	50 – 80 Ω
SET/COAST	180 – 220 Ω
CANCEL	400 – 440 Ω

Hint When DTC 34 is displayed, carefully check that resistance is always ∞ in neutral position, particularly when switching between RES/ACC and SET/COAST.

OK

NG Replace cruise control switch.

4 | Check for open and short in harness and connector between ECU and control switch

OK

NG Repair or replace harness or connector.

Check and replace ECU.

TY1109900486030X

Fig. 141 Code 32: Control Switch Circuit (Part 3 of 3). 1996–97 Celica

INSPECTION PROCEDURE

1 | Check resistance between terminals MO and MC of actuator motor.

PREPARATION:
(a) Turn ignition switch OFF.
(b) Disconnect the actuator connector.
CHECK:
Measure resistance between terminals 6 and 7.
HINT:
If control plate position is fully opened or fully closed, resistance can not be measured.
OK:
Resistance: more than 4.2 Ω

NG Replace cruise control actuator.

OK

2 | Check for open and short in harness and connectors between cruise control ECU and actuator motor

NG Repair or replace harness or connector.

OK

Check and replace cruise control ECU.

TY1109900232020X

Fig. 142 Codes 11 & 14: Actuator Motor Circuit (Part 2 of 2). 1998–99 Celica

CIRCUIT DESCRIPTION

The actuator motor is operated by signals from the ECU. Acceleration and deceleration signals are transmitted by changes in the Duty Ratio (See note below).

Duty Ratio

The duty ratio is the ratio of the period of continuity in one cycle. For example, if A is the period of continuity in one cycle, and B is the period of non–continuity, then.

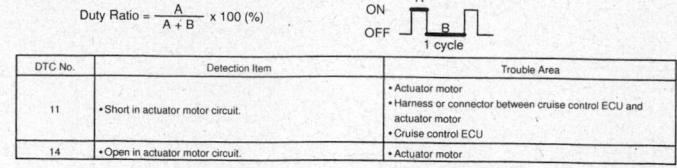

$$\text{Duty Ratio} = \frac{A}{A + B} \times 100 \ (\%)$$

DTC No.	Detection Item	Trouble Area
11	• Short in actuator motor circuit.	• Actuator motor • Harness or connector between cruise control ECU and actuator motor • Cruise control ECU
14	• Open in actuator motor circuit.	• Actuator motor

TY1109900232010X

Fig. 142 Codes 11 & 14: Actuator Motor Circuit (Part 1 of 2). 1998–99 Celica

CIRCUIT DESCRIPTION

This circuit turns on the magnetic clutch inside the actuator during cruise control operation according to the signal from the ECU. If a malfunction occurs in the actuator or speed sensor, etc. during cruise control operation, the rotor shaft between the motor and control plate is released.

When the brake pedal is depressed, the stop light switch turns ON, supplying electrical power to the stop light. Power supply to the magnetic clutch is mechanically cut and the magnetic clutch is turned OFF.

When driving downhill, if the vehicle speed exceeds the set speed by 15 km/h (9 mph), the ECU turns the safety magnet clutch OFF. If the vehicle speed later drops to within 10 km/h (6 mph) above the set speed, then cruise control at the set speed is resumed.

DTC No.	Detection Item	Trouble Area
12	• Short in actuator magnetic clutch circuit. • Open (0.8 sec.) in actuator magnetic clutch circuit.	• STOP Fuse • Stop light switch • Actuator magnetic clutch • Harness or connector between cruise control ECU and actuator magnetic clutch, actuator magnetic clutch and body ground • Cruise control ECU

TY1109900233010X

Fig. 143 Code 12: Actuator Magnetic Clutch Circuit (Part 1 of 3). 1998–99 Celica

INSPECTION PROCEDURE

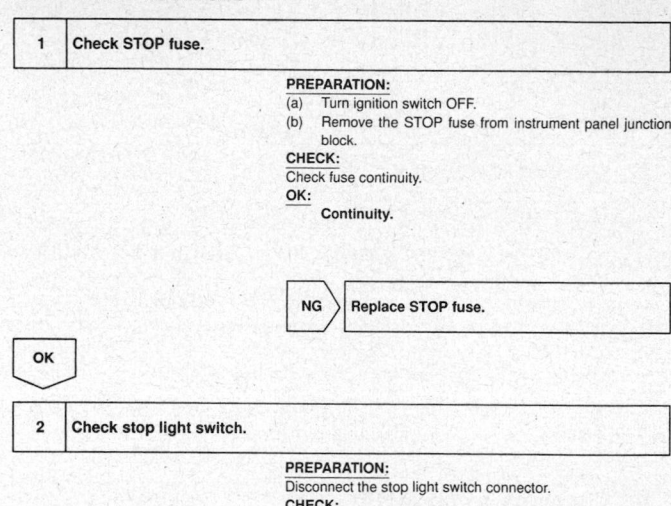

1 | Check STOP fuse.

PREPARATION:
(a) Turn ignition switch OFF.
(b) Remove the STOP fuse from instrument panel junction block.
CHECK:
Check fuse continuity.
OK:
Continuity.

NG Replace STOP fuse.

OK

2 | Check stop light switch.

PREPARATION:
Disconnect the stop light switch connector.
CHECK:
Check continuity between terminals.

Switch position	Continuity
Switch pin free (Brake pedal depressed)	1 – 2
Switch pin pushed in (Brake pedal released)	3 – 4

NG Replace stop light switch.

OK

TY1109900233020X

Fig. 143 Code 12: Actuator Magnetic Clutch Circuit (Part 2 of 3). 1998–99 Celica

3	Check resistance between terminal L and GND of actuator magnetic clutch.

PREPARATION:
(a) Turn ignition switch OFF.
(b) Disconnect the actuator connector.
CHECK:
Measure resistance between terminals 4 and 5.
OK:
  Resistance: 34.65 ~ 42.35 Ω.

NG ⟩ Replace cruise control actuator.

OK

4	Check for open and short in harness and connectors between cruise control ECU and actuator magnetic clutch, actuator magnetic clutch and body ground

NG ⟩ Repair or replace harness or connector.

OK

Check and replace cruise control ECU

TY1109900233030X

Fig. 143 Code 12: Actuator Magnetic Clutch Circuit (Part 3 of 3). 1998–99 Celica

INSPECTION PROCEDURE

1	Check resistance between terminals VR2 and VR3 of cruise control ECU connector.

PREPARATION:
(a) Remove the ECU with connectors still connected.
(b) Turn ignition switch OFF.
CHECK:
Measure voltage between terminals VR2 and VR3 of ECU connector while turning control plate slowly by hand from the deceleration side to the acceleration side.
OK:
  Voltage:
  Fully closed: Approx. 1.3 V
  Fully opened: Approx. 4.0 V
  As the control plate is turned, the voltage should increase gradually without interruption.

NG ⟩ Proceed to next circuit inspection shown in problem symptoms table

OK

2	Check resistance between terminals VR1 and VR3 of actuator position sensor.

PREPARATION:
(a) Turn ignition switch OFF.
(b) Disconnect the actuator connector.
CHECK:
Measure resistance between actuator terminals 1 and 3 of actuator connector.
OK:
  Resistance: Approx. 2.2 kΩ (25 °C)

NG ⟩ Replace cruise control actuator.

OK

TY1109900234020X

Fig. 144 Codes 13 & 14: Actuator Position Sensor Circuit (Part 2 of 3). 1998–99 Celica

CIRCUIT DESCRIPTION

The circuit detects the rotation position of the actuator control plate and sends a signal to the ECU.

DTC No.	Detection Item	Trouble Area
13	• Position sensor detects abnormal voltage.	• Actuator motor • Actuator position sensor • Harness or connector between cruise control ECU and actuator position sensor • Cruise control ECU

TY1109900234010X

Fig. 144 Codes 13 & 14: Actuator Position Sensor Circuit (Part 1 of 3). 1998–99 Celica

3	Check voltage between terminals VR2 and VR3 of actuator position sensor.

PREPARATION:
(a) Turn ignition switch ON.
(b) Connect the actuator connector.
CHECK:
Measure voltage between terminals 2 and 3 of actuator connector while turning control plate slowly by hand from the deceleration side to the acceleration side.
OK:
  Voltage: 1.3 ~4.0 V
HINT:
As the control plate is turned, the voltage should increase gradually without interruption.

NG ⟩ Replace cruise control actuator.

OK

4	Check for open and short in harness and connector between cruise control ECU and actuator position sensor

NG ⟩ Repair or replace harness or connector.

OK

Check and replace cruise control ECU

TY1109900234030X

Fig. 144 Codes 13 & 14: Actuator Position Sensor Circuit (Part 3 of 3). 1998–99 Celica

CIRCUIT DESCRIPTION

The vehicle speed siggnal is sent to cruise control ECU from the vehicle speed sensor.
The rotor shaft is driven by the gear of the transmission.
For each rotation of the shaft, the vehicle speed sensor sends a 4–pulse signal through the combination meter to the cruise control ECU (See the following).
This signal is converted inside the combination meter and sent as a 4–pulse signal to the cruise control ECU.
The ECU calculates the vehicle speed from this pulse frequency.

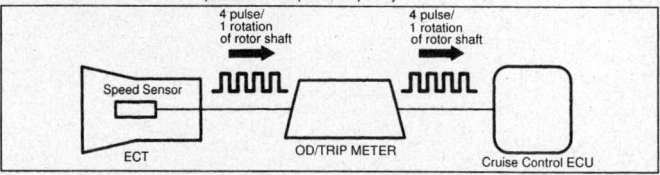

DTC No.	Detection Item	Trouble Area
21	• Speed signal is not input to the cruise control ECU while cruise control is set.	• Combination meter • Harness or connector between cruise control ECU and combination meter, combination meter and vehicle speed sensor • Vehicle speed sensor • Cruise control ECU

TY1109900235010X

Fig. 145 Codes 21 & 23: Vehicle Speed Sensor Circuit (Part 1 of 3). 1998–99 Celica

INSPECTION PROCEDURE

1 | Input signal check.

Input Signal	Indicator Light Blinking Pattern
Drive at about 40 km/h (25 mph) or below	Light ON ————— OFF - - - - -
Drive at about 40 km/h (25 mph) or higher	Light ON ⊓⊓⊓⊓ OFF

CHECK:
(a) See input signal check on page DI–312.
(b) Check indicator light operation when driving at vehicle speed above 40 km/h (25 mph), and at vehicle speed below 40 km/h (25 mph).

OK:
Vehicle speed above 40 km/h (25 mph):
    Indicator light blinks
Vehicle speed below 40 km/h (25 mph):
    Indicator light stays on

OK ⟩ Check and replace cruise control ECU

NG ▽

2 | Check speedometer circuit

NG ⟩ Repair or replace harness, connector or combination meter assembly.

OK ▽

3 | Check harness and connector between cruise control ECU and combination meter, combination meter and vehicle speed sensor

NG ⟩ Repair or replace harness or connector.

OK ▽

TY1109900235020X

Fig. 145   Codes 21 & 23: Vehicle Speed Sensor Circuit (Part 2 of 3). 1998–99 Celica

CIRCUIT DESCRIPTION

This circuit sends the SET/COAST, RESUME/ACCEL and CANCEL signals (each voltage) to the ECU.

DTC No.	Detection Item	Trouble Area
32	• Short in control switch circuit.	• Cruise control switch • Harness or connector between cruise control ECU and cruise control switch, cruise control switch and body ground • Cruise control ECU

TY1109900236010X

Fig. 146   Code 32: Control Switch Circuit (Part 1 of 3). 1998–99 Celica

4 | Check vehicle speed sensor

NG ⟩ Replace vehicle speed sensor.

OK ▽

Check and replace cruise control ECU

TY1109900235030X

Fig. 145   Codes 21 & 23: Vehicle Speed Sensor Circuit (Part 3 of 3). 1998–99 Celica

INSPECTION PROCEDURE

1 | Input signal check.

Input Signal	Indicator Light Blinking Pattern
SET/COAST switch	ON ⊓⊓ 2 Pulses OFF
RESUME/ACCEL switch	ON ⊓⊓⊓ 3 Pulses OFF
CANCEL switch	ON ‾‾SW OFF‾ OFF ___SW ON

PREPARATION:
See input signal check
CHECK:
Check the indicator light operation when each of the SET/COAST, RESUME/ACCEL and CANCEL is turned ON.
OK:
SET/COAST, RESUME/ACCEL switch
The signals shown in the table on the left should be output when each switch is ON. The signal should disappear when the switch is turned OFF.
CANCEL switch
The indicator light goes off when the cancel switch is turned ON.

OK ⟩ Wait and see.

NG ▽

2 | Check voltage between terminal CCS of cruise control ECU connector and body ground.

PREPARATION:
(a) Remove the ECU with connector still connected.
(b) Turn ignition switch ON.
CHECK:
Measure voltage between terminal CCS of ECU connector and body ground, when each of the SET/COAST, RESUME/ACCEL and CANCEL is turned ON.

Switch position	Voltage (V)
Neutral	10 – 16
RES/ACC	0.8 – 14 V
SET/COAST	2.4 – 4.0 V
CANCEL	5.1 – 8.3 V

NG ⟩ Proceed to next circuit inspection shown in problem symptom table

OK ▽

TY1109900236020X

Fig. 146   Code 32: Control Switch Circuit (Part 2 of 3). 1998–99 Celica

3 | Check control switch.

PREPARATION:
(a) Remove steering wheel center pad.
(b) Disconnect the control switch connector.

CHECK:
Measure resistance between terminals 3 and 4 of control switch connector when control switch is operated.

Switch position	Resistance (Ω)
Neutral	∞ (No continuity)
RES/ACC	50 – 80
SET/COAST	180 – 220
CANCEL	400 – 440

NG ⟩ Replace control switch.

OK

4 | Check harness and connector between cruise control ECU and cruise control switch, cruise control switch and body ground

NG ⟩ Repair or replace harness or connector.

OK

5 | Input signal check (See step 1).

OK ⟩ Wait and see.

NG

Check and replace cruise control ECU

TY1109900236030X

Fig. 146   Code 32: Control Switch Circuit (Part 3 of 3). 1998–99 Celica

INSPECTION PROCEDURE

1 | **Check operation of stop light.**

CHECK:
Check that stop light comes on when brake pedal is depressed, and turns off when brake pedal is released.

NG ⟩ Check stop light system

OK

2 | **Input signal check.**

Input Signal	Indicator Light Blinking Pattern
Stop Light switch ON	Light ON — SW OFF / OFF — SW ON

CHECK:
(a) See input signal check.
(b) Check the indicator light when the brake pedal is depressed.

OK:
The indicator light goes off when the brake pedal is depressed.

OK ⟩ Proceed to next circuit inspection shown in problem symptoms table

NG

TY1109900237020X

Fig. 147   Stop Lamp Switch Circuit (Part 2 of 3). Celica

CIRCUIT DESCRIPTION

When the brake pedal is depressed, the stop light switch sends a signal to the ECU. When the ECU receives this signal, it cancels the cruise control.
A fail–safe function is provided so that the cancel functions normally, even if there is a malfunction in the stop light signal circuit.
The cancel conditions are: Battery positive voltage at terminal STP–
When the brake is ON, battery positive voltage is normally applied through the STOP fuse and stop light switch to terminal STP– of the ECU, and the ECU turns the cruise control OFF.
If the harness connected to terminal STP– has an open circuit, terminal STP– will have battery positive voltage and the cruise control will be turned OFF.
Also, when the brake is ON, the magnetic clutch circuit is cut mechanically by the stop light switch, turning the cruise control OFF.

TY1109900237010X

Fig. 147   Stop Lamp Switch Circuit (Part 1 of 3). Celica

3 | Check voltage between terminal STP– of cruise control ECU connector and body ground.

PREPARATION:
(a) Remove the ECU with connectors still connected.
(b) Turn ignition switch ON.

CHECK:
Measure voltage between terminal STP– of cruise control ECU connector and body ground, when the brake pedal is depressed and released.

OK:

Depressed	10 – 16 V
Released	Below 1 V

OK ⟩ Proceed to next circuit inspection shown in problem symptoms table

NG

4 | Check for open in harness and connectors between terminal STP– of cruise control ECU and stop light switch

NG ⟩ Repair or replace harness or connector.

OK

Check and replace cruise control ECU

TY1109900237030X

Fig. 147   Stop Lamp Switch Circuit (Part 3 of 3). Celica

CIRCUIT DESCRIPTION

When the idle switch is turned ON, a signal is sent to the ECU. The ECU uses this signal to correct the discrepancy between the throttle valve position and the actuator position sensor value to enable accurate cruise control at the set speed. If the idle switch is malfunctioning, problem symptoms also occur in the engine, so also inspect the engine.

INSPECTION PROCEDURE

1 | **Check voltage between terminal IDL of ECU connector and body ground.**

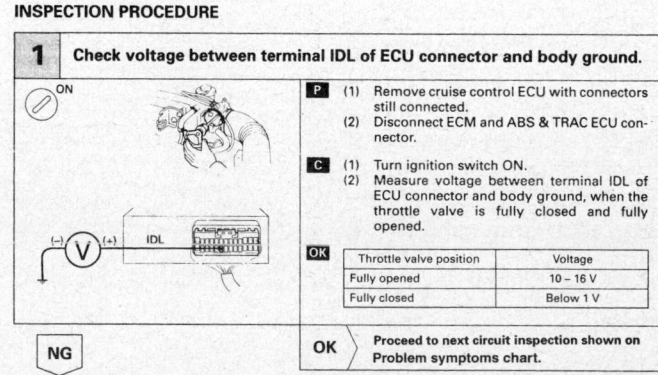

P (1) Remove cruise control ECU with connectors still connected.
(2) Disconnect ECM and ABS & TRAC ECU connector.

C (1) Turn ignition switch ON.
(2) Measure voltage between terminal IDL of ECU connector and body ground, when the throttle valve is fully closed and fully opened.

OK

Throttle valve position	Voltage
Fully opened	10 – 16 V
Fully closed	Below 1 V

NG

OK ⟩ Proceed to next circuit inspection shown on Problem symptoms chart.

TY1109900487010X

Fig. 148   Idle Switch Circuit (Part 1 of 2). 1996–97 Celica

2 | **Check throttle position sensor.**

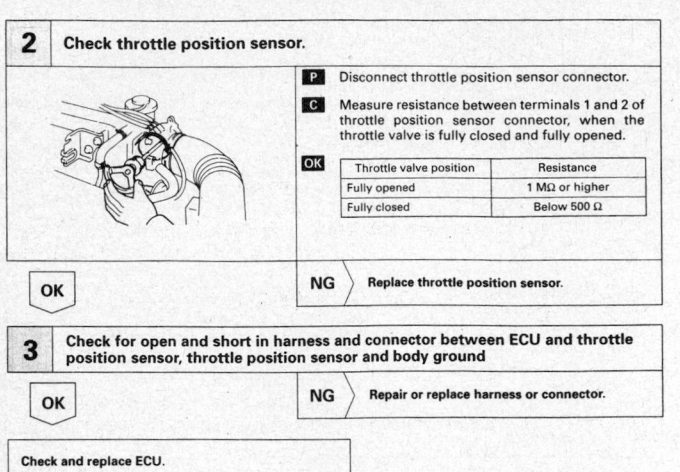

P Disconnect throttle position sensor connector.

C Measure resistance between terminals 1 and 2 of throttle position sensor connector, when the throttle valve is fully closed and fully opened.

OK

Throttle valve position	Resistance
Fully opened	1 MΩ or higher
Fully closed	Below 500 Ω

OK

NG > Replace throttle position sensor.

3 | **Check for open and short in harness and connector between ECU and throttle position sensor, throttle position sensor and body ground**

OK

NG > Repair or replace harness or connector.

Check and replace ECU.

TY1109900487020X

Fig. 148 Idle Switch Circuit (Part 2 of 2). 1996–97 Celica

INSPECTION PROCEDURE

1 | **Check voltage between terminal IDL of cruise control ECU connector and body ground.**

PREPARATION:
(a) Remove the ECU with connector still connected.
(b) Disconnect the ECM and ABS ECU connectors.
(c) Turn ignition switch ON.

CHECK:
Measure voltage between terminal IDL of ECU connector and body ground when the throttle valve is fully closed and fully opened.

OK:

Throttle valve position	Voltage
Fully opened	10 – 16 V
Fully closed	Below 1 V

OK > Proceed to next circuit inspection shown in problem symptoms table

NG

2 | **Check harness and connector between ECM and throttle position sensor**

NG > Repair or replace harness or connector.

OK

3 | **Check throttle position sensor circuit**

NG > Replace throttle position sensor.

OK

TY1109900238020X

Fig. 149 Idle Switch Circuit (Part 2 of 3). 1998–99 Celica

CIRCUIT DESCRIPTION

When the idle switch is turned ON, a signal is sent to the ECU. The ECU uses this signal to correct the discrepancy between the throttle valve position and the actuator position sensor value to enable accurate cruise control at the set speed. If the idle switch is malfunctioning, problem symptoms also occur in the engine, so also inspect the engine.

TY1109900238010X

Fig. 149 Idle Switch Circuit (Part 1 of 3). 1998–99 Celica

4 | **Check throttle position sensor.**

PREPARATION:
Disconnect the throttle position sensor connector.

CHECK:
Measure resistance between terminals 1 and 2 of throttle position sensor connector when the throttle valve is fully closed and fully opened.

OK:

Throttle valve position	Resistance
Fully opened	1 MΩ or higher
Fully closed	Below 500 Ω

NG > Replace throttle position sensor.

OK

5 | **Check for open and short in harness and connector between cruise control ECU and throttle position sensor, throttle position sensor and body ground**

NG > Repair or replace harness or connector.

OK

Check and replace cruise control ECU

TY1109900238030X

Fig. 149 Idle Switch Circuit (Part 3 of 3). 1998–99 Celica

CIRCUIT DESCRIPTION

When driving uphill under cruise control, in order to reduce shifting due to ON–OFF overdrive operation and to provide smooth driving, when down shifting in the electronically controlled transmission occurs, a signal to prevent upshift until the end of the up hill slope is sent from the cruise control ECU to the electronically controlled transmission.

Terminal ECT of the cruise control ECU detects the shift change signal (output to electronically controlled transmission No. 2 solenoid) from the ECM.

If vehicle speed down, also when terminal ECT of the cruise control ECU receives down shifting signal, it sends a signal from terminal OD to ECM to cut overdrive until the end of the uphill slope, and the gear shifts are reduced and gear shift points in the electronically controlled transmission are changed.

TY1109900239010X

Fig. 150 Electronically Controlled Transaxle Communication Circuit (Part 1 of 3). Celica

INSPECTION PROCEDURE

1	Check operation of overdrive.

PREPARATION:
Test drive after engine warms up.
CHECK:
Check that overdrive ON ↔ OFF occurs with operation of OD switch ON–OFF.

NG ⟩ Check and repair electronically controlled transmission

OK

2	Check voltage between terminal OD of harness side connector of cruise control ECU and body ground.

PREPARATION:
(a) Remove the ECU with connector still connected.
(b) Turn ignition switch ON.
(c) Disconnect the ECU connector.
CHECK:
Measure voltage between terminal OD of ECU connector on the harness side and body ground.
OK:
   Voltage: 10 – 16 V

NG ⟩ Go to step 5.

OK

TY1109900239020X

Fig. 150 Electronically Controlled Transaxle Communication Circuit (Part 2 of 3). Celica

CIRCUIT DESCRIPTION

When the shift position is in except D position, a signal is sent from the park/neutral position switch to the ECU. When this signal is input during cruise control driving, the ECU cancels the cruise control.

TY1109900240010X

Fig. 151 Park/Neutral Position Switch Circuit (Part 1 of 3). Celica

3	Check voltage between terminal ECT of cruise control ECU connector and body ground (On test drive).

PREPARATION:
(a) Connect the ECU connector.
(b) Test drive after engine warms up.
CHECK:
Check voltage between terminal ECT of ECU connector and body ground when OD switch is ON and OFF.
OK:

OD switch position	Voltage
ON	Below 1 V
OFF	10 – 16 V

OK ⟩ Proceed to next circuit inspection shown in problem symptoms table

NG

4	Check harness and connector between terminal ECT of cruise control ECU and electronically controlled transmission solenoid

NG ⟩ Repair or replace harness or connector.

OK

Check and replace cruise control ECU.

5	Check harness and connector between terminal OD of cruise control ECU and terminal OD1 of ECM

NG ⟩ Repair or replace harness or connector.

OK

Check and replace cruise control ECU

TY1109900239030X

Fig. 150 Electronically Controlled Transaxle Communication Circuit (Part 3 of 3). Celica

INSPECTION PROCEDURE

1	Check starter operation.

CHECK:
Check that the starter operates normally and that the engine starts.

NG ⟩ Proceed to engine troubleshooting.

OK

2	Input signal check.

Input Signal	Indicator Light Blinking Pattern
Turn PNP switch OFF (Shift to except D position)	Light ON ⎍ SW ON / OFF- - - ⎍SW OFF

PREPARATION:
See input signal check.
CHECK:
Check the indicator light when shifting into except D position.
OK:
   The indicator light goes off when shifting into except D position.

OK ⟩ Proceed to next circuit inspection shown in problem symptoms table

NG

TY1109900240020X

Fig. 151 Park/Neutral Position Switch Circuit (Part 2 of 3). Celica

3	Check voltage between terminal D of cruise control ECU connector and body ground.

PREPARATION:
Turn ignition switch ON.
CHECK:
Measure each voltage between terminal D of ECU connector and body ground when shifting into D position and other positions.
OK:

Shift Position	Voltage
D position	10 – 16 V
Other positions	Below 1 V

OK	Proceed to next circuit inspection shown in problem symptoms table

NG

4	Check harness and connector between cruise control ECU and park/neutral position switch

NG	Repair or replace harness or connector.

OK

Check and replace cruise control ECU

TY1109900240030X

Fig. 151   Park/Neutral Position Switch Circuit (Part 3 of 3). Celica

INSPECTION PROCEDURE

1	Check starter operation.

CHECK:
Check that the starter operates normally and that the engine starts.

NG	Proceed to engine troubleshooting

OK

2	Input signal check.

Input Signal	Indicator Light Blinking Pattern
Clutch switch OFF (Depress clutch pedal)	Light ON ‾‾‾SW ON‾‾‾ OFF - - - - - SW OFF

PREPARATION:
See input signal check .
CHECK:
Check the indicator light when clutch pedal is depressed.
OK:
The indicator light goes off when depressing the clutch pedal .

OK	Proceed to next circuit inspection shown in problem symptoms table

NG

TY1109900241020X

Fig. 152   Clutch Switch Circuit (Part 2 of 3). Celica

CIRCUIT DESCRIPTION

The ECU power source supplies power to the actuator and sensors, etc., Terminal GND and the cruise control ECU case are grounded.

TY1109900488010X

Fig. 153   ECU Power Source Circuit (Part 1 of 3). 1996–97 Celica

CIRCUIT DESCRIPTION

When the clutch pedal is depressed, the clutch switch sends a signal to the cruise control ECU. When the signal is input to the cruise control ECU during cruise control driving, the cruise control ECU cancels cruise control.

TY1109900241010X

Fig. 152   Clutch Switch Circuit (Part 1 of 3). Celica

3	Check voltage between terminal D of cruise control ECU and body ground.

PREPARATION:
Turn ignition switch ON.
CHECK:
Measure voltage between terminal D of cruise control ECU connector and body ground when clutch pedal is depressed and released.
OK:

Shift Position	Voltage
Clutch pedal released	Below 1 V
Clutch pedal depressed	10 – 16 V

OK	Proceed to next circuit inspection shown in problem symptoms table

NG

4	Check for open in harness and connector between ECU and GAUGE fuse

NG	Repair or replace harness or connector.

OK

Check and replace cruise control ECU

TY1109900241030X

Fig. 152   Clutch Switch Circuit (Part 3 of 3). Celica

INSPECTION PROCEDURE

1	Check ECU-IG fuse.

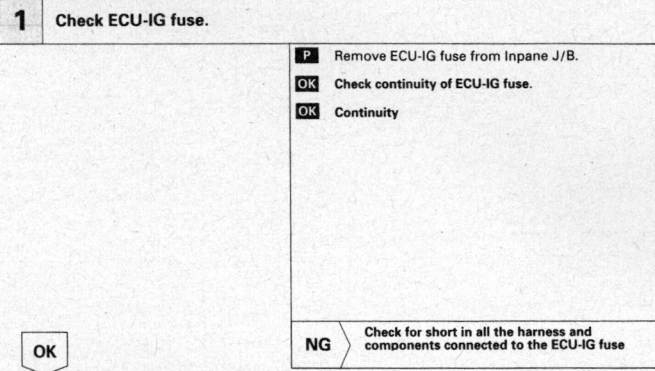

P	Remove ECU-IG fuse from Inpane J/B.
OK	Check continuity of ECU-IG fuse.
OK	Continuity

NG	Check for short in all the harness and components connected to the ECU-IG fuse

OK

TY1109900488020X

Fig. 153   ECU Power Source Circuit (Part 2 of 3). 1996–97 Celica

2 | Check voltage between terminals B and GND of ECU connector.

P	Remove ECU with connectors still connected.
C	(1) Turn ignition switch ON. (2) Measure voltage between terminals B and GND of ECU connector.
OK	Voltage: 10 – 16 V

NG |

| **OK** | Proceed to next circuit inspection shown on Problem symptoms chart. |

3 | Check continuity between terminal GND of ECU connector and body ground.

| **C** | Measure resistance between terminal GND of cruise control ECU connector and body ground. |
| **OK** | Resistance: 1 Ω or loss |

OK |

| **NG** | Repair or replace harness or connector. |

Check and repair harness and connector between battery and ECU.

TY1109900488030X

Fig. 153 ECU Power Source Circuit (Part 3 of 3). 1996–97 Celica

INSPECTION PROCEDURE

1 | Check ECU–IG fuse.

PREPARATION:
Remove the ECU–IG fuse from instrument panel junction block.
CHECK:
Check continuity of ECU–IG fuse.
OK:
  Continuity

| **NG** | Check for short in all the harness and components connected to ECU–IG fuse. |

OK |

2 | Check voltage between terminals B and GND of cruise control ECU connector.

PREPARATION:
(a) Remove the ECU with connector still connected.
(b) Turn ignition switch ON.
CHECK:
Measure voltage between terminals B and GND of ECU connector.
OK:
  10 – 16 V

| **OK** | Proceed to next circuit inspection shown in problem symptoms table |

NG |

TY1109900242020X

Fig. 154 ECU Power Source Circuit (Part 2 of 3). 1998–99 Celica

CIRCUIT DESCRIPTION

The ECU back–up power source provides power even when the ignition is OFF, and it is used for DTC memory, etc..

TY1109900243010X

Fig. 155 Back Up Power Source Circuit (Part 1 of 2). Celica

CIRCUIT DESCRIPTION

The ECU power source supplies power to the actuator and sensors, etc. when terminal GND and the cruise control ECU case are grounded.

TY1109900242010X

Fig. 154 ECU Power Source Circuit (Part 1 of 3). 1998–99 Celica

3 | Check resistance between terminal GND of cruise control ECU connector and body ground

CHECK:
Measure resistance between terminal GND of ECU connector and body ground.
OK:
  Resistance: Below 1 Ω

| **NG** | Repair or replace harness or connector. |

OK |

Check and repair harness and connector between cruise control ECU and battery

TY1109900242030X

Fig. 154 ECU Power Source Circuit (Part 3 of 3). 1998–99 Celica

1 | Check ECU–B fuse.

PREPARATION:
Remove the ECU–B fuse from relay block No.1.
CHECK:
Check continuity of ECU–B fuse.
OK:
  Continuity

| **NG** | Check for short in all the harness and components connected to the ECU–B fuse. |

OK |

2 | Check voltage between terminal BATT of cruise control ECU connector and body ground

PREPARATION:
Remove the ECU with connector still connected.
CHECK:
Measure voltage between terminal BATT of ECU connector and body ground.
OK:
  Voltage: 10 – 16 V

| **OK** | Proceed to next circuit inspection shown in problem symptoms table |

NG |

Check and repair harness and connector between battery and cruise control ECU

TY1109900243020X

Fig. 155 Back Up Power Source Circuit (Part 2 of 2). Celica

CIRCUIT DESCRIPTION

When the cruise control main switch is turned OFF, the cruise control does not operate.

INSPECTION PROCEDURE

| 1 | Check voltage between terminal CMS of cruise control ECU connector and body ground. |

PREPARATION:
(a) Remove the ECU with connector still connected.
(b) Turn ignition switch ON.
CHECK:
Measure voltage between terminal CMS of cruise control ECU connector when main switch is held ON and OFF.
OK:

Main switch	Voltage
OFF	10 – 16 V
ON	Below 1 V

OK ▷ Proceed to next circuit inspection shown in problem symptoms table

NG

TY1109900244010X

Fig. 156 Main Switch Circuit (Part 1 of 2). Celica

CIRCUIT DESCRIPTION

This circuit sends a signal to the ECU that DTC output is required.

TY1109900245010X

Fig. 157 T$_C$ Circuit (Part 1 of 2). Celica

| 2 | Check main switch continuity. |

PREPARATION:
(a) Remove steering wheel center pad. (See SR section)
(b) Disconnect the control switch connector.
CHECK:
Check continuity between terminals 2 and 4 of control switch connector when main switch is held ON and OFF.
OK:

Switch position	Tester connection	Specified condition
OFF	2 – 4	No continuity
Hold ON	2 – 4	Continuity

NG ▷ Replace control switch.

OK

| 3 | Check harness and connector between cruise control ECU and main switch |

NG ▷ Repair or replace harness or connector.

OK

| Check and replace cruise control ECU |

TY1109900244020X

Fig. 156 Main Switch Circuit (Part 2 of 2). Celica

| 1 | Check voltage between terminals Tc and E$_1$ of DLC1. |

PREPARATION:
Turn ignition switch ON.
CHECK:
Measure voltage between terminals Tc and E$_1$ of DLC1.
OK:
Voltage: 10 – 16 V

OK ▷ Proceed to next circuit inspection shown in problem symptoms table

NG

| 2 | Check harness and connector between cruise control ECU and DLC1, DLC1 and body ground |

NG ▷ Repair or replace harness or connector.

OK

| Check and replace cruise control ECU |

TY1109900245020X

Fig. 157 T$_C$ Circuit (Part 2 of 2). Celica

INSPECTION PROCEDURE

| 1 | Actuator control cable inspection |

CHECK:
(a) Check that the actuator and control cable throttle link are properly installed and that the cable and **link** are connected correctly.
(b) Check that the actuator and bell crank are operating smoothly.
(c) Check that the cable is not loose or too tight.
OK:
Freeplay: less than 10 mm
HINT:
• If the control cable is very loose, the vehicle's loss of speed going uphill will be large.
• If the control cable is too tight, the idle RPM will become high.

TY1109900481000X

Fig. 158 Actuator Control Cable Inspection. Celica

Symptom	Suspect Area
SET not occurring or CANCEL occurring. (DTC is Normal)	1. Main Switch Circuit (Cruise control switch) 2. Vehicle Speed Sensor 3. Control Switch Circuit (Cruise control switch) 4. Stop Light Switch Circuit 5. Park/Neutral Position Switch Circuit 6. Clutch Switch 7. Actuator Motor Circuit 8. Cruise Control Cable 9. Cruise Control ECU
SET not occurring or CANCEL occurring. (DTC dose not output)	1. ECU Power Source Circuit 2. Cruise Control ECU
Actual vehicle speed deviates above or below the set speed.	1. Cruise Control Cable 2. Vehicle Speed Signal Abnormal 3. Electronically Controlled Transmission Communication Circuit 4. Actuator Motor Circuit 5. Idle Signal Circuit (Main throttle position sensor) 6. Cruise Control ECU
Gear shifting frequent between 3rd O/D when driving on uphill road. (Hurting)	1. Electronically Controlled Transmission Communication Circuit 2. Cruise Control ECU
Cruise control not cancelled, even when brake pedal is depressed.	1. Cruise Control Cable 2. Stop Light Switch Circuit 3. Actuator Motor Circuit 4. Cruise Control ECU
Cruise control not cancelled, even when transmission is shifted to "N" position.	1. Cruise Control Cable 2. Park/Neutral Position Switch Circuit 3. Actuator Motor Circuit 4. Cruise Control ECU
Cruise control not cancelled, even when clutch pedal is depressed.	1. Cruise Control Cable 2. Clutch Switch Circuit 3. Actuator Motor Circuit 4. Cruise Control ECU
Control switch does not operate. (SET/COAST, ACC/RES, CANCEL not possible)	1. Cruise Control Cable 2. Control Switch Circuit 3. Actuator Motor Circuit 4. Cruise Control ECU
SET possible at 40 km/h (25 mph) or less, or CANCEL does not operate at 40 km/h (25 mph) or less.	1. Cruise Control Cable 2. Vehicle Speed Signal Abnormal 3. Actuator Motor Circuit 4. Cruise Control ECU
Poor response is ACCEL and RESUME modes.	1. Cruise Control Cable 2. Electronically Controlled Transmission Communication Circuit 3. Actuator Motor Circuit 4. Cruise Control ECU
O/D does not RESUME, even though the road is not uphill.	1. Electronically Controlled Transmission Communication Circuit 2. ruise Control ECU
DTC memory is erased.	1. Cruise Control ECU

TY1109900287010X

Fig. 159   Problem Symptoms Table (Part 1 of 2). Corolla

CIRCUIT DESCRIPTION

The actuator motor is operated by signals from the cruise control ECU. Acceleration and deceleration signals are transmitted by changes in the Duty Ratio (See note below).

Duty Ratio
The duty ratio is the ratio of the period of continuity in one cycle. For example, if A is the period of continuity in one cycle, and B is the period of non-continuity, then

$$\text{Duty Ratio} = \frac{A}{A + B} \times 100 \,(\%)$$

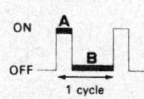

DTC No.	DTC Detecting Condition	Trouble Area
11	• Continuous output to motor acceleration side. • Overcurrent (short) in motor circuit.	• Cruise control actuator motor. • Harness or connector between actuator motor and Cruise Control ECU. • Cruise Control ECU.
14	• Open in actuator motor circuit.	

TY1109900306010X

Fig. 160   Codes 11 & 14: Actuator Motor Circuit (Part 1 of 2). 1996–97 Corolla

DTC is not output, or is output when is should not be.	1. Diagnosis Circuit 2. Cruise Control ECU
Cruise MAIN indicator light remains ON or fail to light up.	1. Cruise MAIN Indicator Light Switch Circuit 2. Cruise Control ECU

TY1109900287020X

Fig. 159   Problem Symptoms Table (Part 2 of 2). Corolla

INSPECTION PROCEDURE

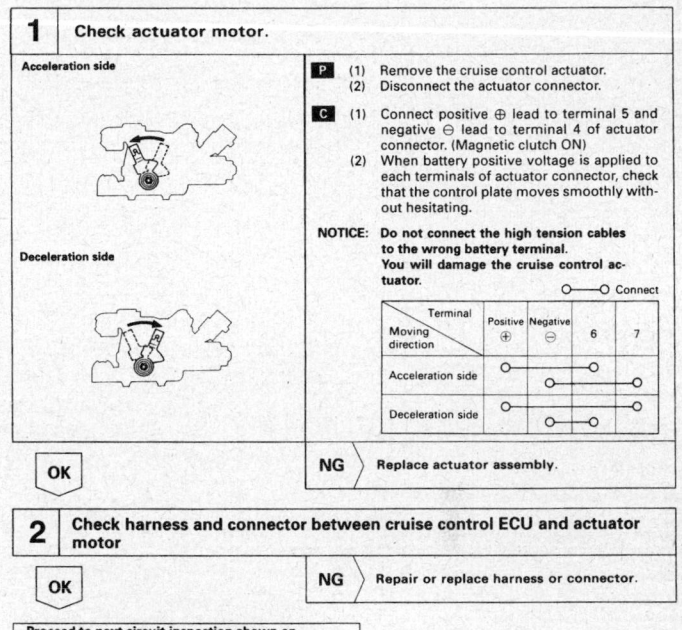

TY1109900306020X

Fig. 160   Codes 11 & 14: Actuator Motor Circuit (Part 2 of 2). 1996 Corolla

CIRCUIT DESCRIPTION

This circuit turns on the magnetic clutch inside the actuator during cruise control operation according to the signal from the cruise control ECU. If a malfunction occurs in the actuator or vehicle speed sensor, etc. during cruise control, the rotor shaft between the motor and control plate is released.

When the brake pedal is depressed, the stoplight switch turns on supplying electrical power to the stoplight. Power supply to the magnetic clutch is mechanically cut and the magnetic clutch is turned OFF.

When driving downhill, if the vehicle speed exceeds the set speed by 15 km/h (9 mph), the cruise control ECU turns the magnetic clutch OFF. If the vehicle speed later drops to within 10 km/h (6 mph) above the set speed, then cruise control at the set speed is resumed.

DTC No.	DTC Detecting Condition	Trouble Area
12	• Overcurrent (short) in magnetic clutch circuit. • Open in magnetic clutch circuit for 0.8 seconds.	• Cruise control magnetic clutch. • Harness or connector between Cruise Control ECU and magnetic clutch, magnetic clutch and body ground. • Stop light switch. • Cruise control ECU.

TY1109900307010X

Fig. 161   Code 12: Actuator Magnetic Clutch Circuit (Part 1 of 2). 1996–97 Corolla

INSPECTION PROCEDURE

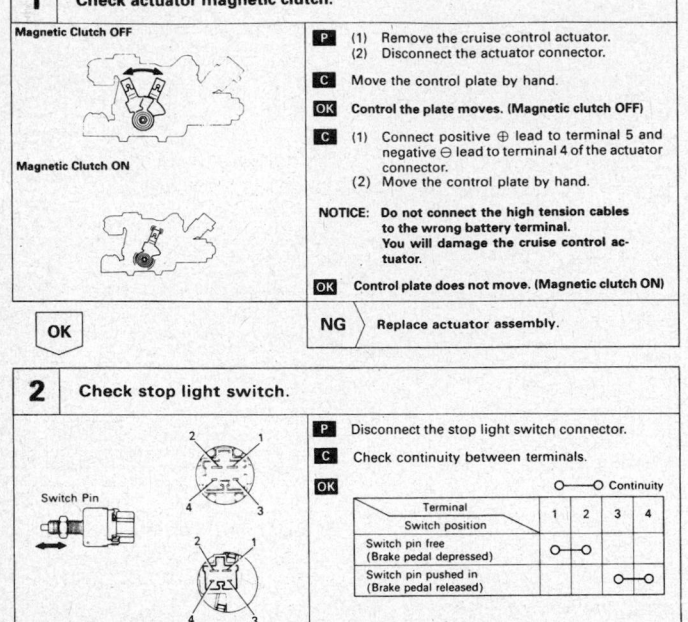

1 | Check actuator magnetic clutch.

Magnetic Clutch OFF

P (1) Remove the cruise control actuator.
(2) Disconnect the actuator connector.

C Move the control plate by hand.

OK Control the plate moves. (Magnetic clutch OFF)

Magnetic Clutch ON

C (1) Connect positive ⊕ lead to terminal 5 and negative ⊖ lead to terminal 4 of the actuator connector.
(2) Move the control plate by hand.

NOTICE: Do not connect the high tension cables to the wrong battery terminal. You will damage the cruise control actuator.

OK Control plate does not move. (Magnetic clutch ON)

OK | **NG** > Replace actuator assembly.

2 | Check stop light switch.

Switch Pin

P Disconnect the stop light switch connector.

C Check continuity between terminals.

OK

Terminal Switch position	1	2	3	4
Switch pin free (Brake pedal depressed)	○—	—○		
Switch pin pushed in (Brake pedal released)			○—	—○

○——○ Continuity

OK | **NG** > Replace stop light switch.

3 | Check harness and connectors between cruise control ECU and stop light switch, stop light switch and magnetic clutch, magnetic clutch and body ground

OK | **NG** > Repair or replace harness or connector.

Proceed to next circuit inspection shown on Problem Symptoms table. However, when diag code 12 is dispalyed, check harness and connector for loose connection. If connection is normal, check and replace Cruise Control ECU.

TY1109900307020X

Fig. 161   Code 12: Actuator Magnetic Clutch Circuit (Part 2 of 2). 1996–97 Corolla

CIRCUIT DESCRIPTION

This circuit detects the rotation position of the actuator control plate and sends signal to the Cruise Control ECU.

DTC No.	DTC Detecting Condition	Trouble Area
13	• Position sensor detects abnormal voltage.	• Cruise control actuator motor. • Cruise control actuator position sensor. • Harness or connector between actuator position sensor and body ground.
14	• Open in actuator motor circuit. • Position sensor signal value does not change when the motor operates.	• Harness or connector between actuator motor and ECU. • ECU.

TY1109900308010X

Fig. 162   Codes 13 & 14: Actuator Position Sensor Circuit (Part 1 of 2). 1996–97 Corolla

INSPECTION PROCEDURE

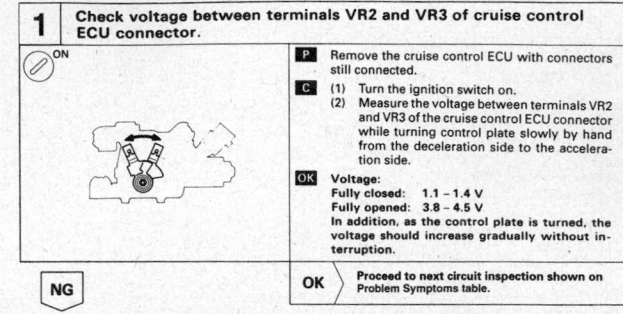

1 | Check voltage between terminals VR2 and VR3 of cruise control ECU connector.

ON

P Remove the cruise control ECU with connectors still connected.

C (1) Turn the ignition switch on.
(2) Measure the voltage between terminals VR2 and VR3 of the cruise control ECU connector while turning control plate slowly by hand from the deceleration side to the acceleration side.

OK Voltage:
Fully closed: 1.1 – 1.4 V
Fully opened: 3.8 – 4.5 V
In addition, as the control plate is turned, the voltage should increase gradually without interruption.

NG | **OK** > Proceed to next circuit inspection shown on Problem Symptoms table.

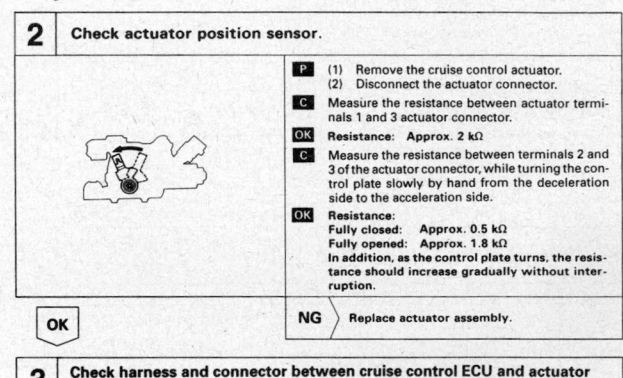

2 | Check actuator position sensor.

P (1) Remove the cruise control actuator.
(2) Disconnect the actuator connector.

C Measure the resistance between actuator terminals 1 and 3 actuator connector.

OK Resistance: Approx. 2 kΩ

C Measure the resistance between terminals 2 and 3 of the actuator connector, while turning the control plate slowly by hand from the deceleration side to the acceleration side.

OK Resistance:
Fully closed: Approx. 0.5 kΩ
Fully opened: Approx. 1.8 kΩ
In addition, as the control plate turns, the resistance should increase gradually without interruption.

OK | **NG** > Replace actuator assembly.

3 | Check harness and connector between cruise control ECU and actuator position sensor

OK | **NG** > Repair or replace harness or connector.

Check harness and connector for loose connection. If connection is normal, check and replace cruise control ECU.

TY1109900308020X

Fig. 162   Codes 13 & 14: Actuator Position Sensor Circuit (Part 2 of 2). 1996–97 Corolla

CIRCUIT DESCRIPTION

The vehicle speed sensor signal is sent to cruise control ECU as vehicle speed signal.

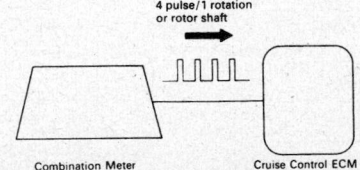

4 pulse/1 rotation or rotor shaft

Combination Meter   Cruise Control ECM

DTC No.	DTC Detecting Condition	Trouble Area
21	Vehicle speed sensor signal is not input to the cruise control ECU.	• Vehicle Speed Sensor. • Combination meter. • Harness or connector between vehicle speed sensor and combination meter, combination meter and Cruise Control ECU. • Cruise Control ECU.
22	Actual vehicle speed has dropped by 16 km/h (10 mph) or more below the set speed during cruising. HINT: When vehicle speed sensor circuit is opened intermittently (Below 0.2 sec), code 23 is output. Vehicle speed sensor pulse is abnormal. HINT: In the vehicle speed pulse is detected 3 times with in 2 sec.	• Actuator. • Actuator control cable. • Vehicle Speed Sensor. • Harness or connector in OD and SPD circuit. (Open or short intermittently) • Cruise Control ECU.

TY1109900309010X

Fig. 163   Codes 21 & 23: Vehicle Speed Sensor Circuit (Part 1 of 2). 1996–97 Corolla

INSPECTION PROCEDURE

1 | **Input signal check.**

Vehicle speed	Indicator light blinking pattern
Above 40 km/h (25 mph)	ON **Blinks** OFF 0.25 sec ⟷ 0.25 sec
Below 40 km/h (25 mph)	ON **Stays ON** OFF - - - - - - - - -

C (1) See the input signal check
(2) Check the indicator light operation when driving with vehicle speed above 40 km/h (25 mph), and with vehicle speed below 40 km/h (25 mph).

OK Vehicle speed above 40 km/h (25 mph)
: Indicator light blinks
Vehicle speed below 40 km/h (25 mph)
: Indicator light stays on

NG ↓ | **OK** > Proceed to next circuit inspection shown on Problem Symptoms table.

2 | **Check speedometer circuit**

OK ↓ | **NG** > Repair or replace vehicle speed sensor, harness, connector or combination meter assembly.

Check harness and connector for loose connection. If connection is normal, check and replace cruise control ECU.

TY1109900309020X

Fig. 163 Codes 21 & 23: Vehicle Speed Sensor Circuit (Part 2 of 2). 1996–97 Corolla

INSPECTION PROCEDURE

1 | **Input signal check**

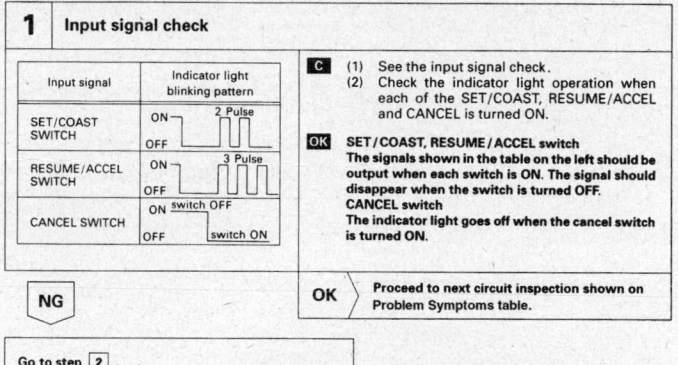

Input signal	Indicator light blinking pattern
SET/COAST SWITCH	ON **2 Pulse** OFF
RESUME/ACCEL SWITCH	ON **3 Pulse** OFF
CANCEL SWITCH	ON **switch OFF** OFF **switch ON**

C (1) See the input signal check.
(2) Check the indicator light operation when each of the SET/COAST, RESUME/ACCEL and CANCEL is turned ON.

OK SET/COAST, RESUME/ACCEL switch
The signals shown in the table on the left should be output when each switch is ON. The signal should disappear when the switch is turned OFF.
CANCEL switch
The indicator light goes off when the cancel switch is turned ON.

NG ↓ | **OK** > Proceed to next circuit inspection shown on Problem Symptoms table.

Go to step **2** .

TY1109900310020X

Fig. 164 Codes 32 & 34: Control Switch Circuit (Part 2 of 3). 1996–97 Corolla

CIRCUIT DESCRIPTION

This circuit carries the SET/COAST, RESUME/ACCEL and CANCEL signals (each voltage) to the cruise control ECU.

DTC No.	DTC Detecting Condition	Trouble Area
32	Short in, control switch circuit.	• Cruise control switch. • Harness or connector between control switch and Cruise Control ECU. • Cruise Control ECU.
34	Voltage abnormality in control switch circuit.	

TY1109900310010X

Fig. 164 Codes 32 & 34: Control Switch Circuit (Part 1 of 3). 1996–97 Corolla

2 | **Check voltage between terminal CCS of cruise control ECU connector and body ground.**

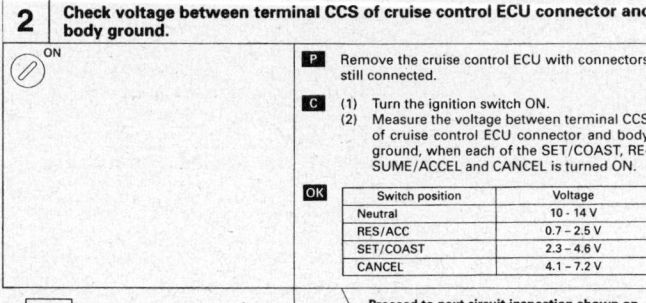

P Remove the cruise control ECU with connectors still connected.

C (1) Turn the ignition switch ON.
(2) Measure the voltage between terminal CCS of cruise control ECU connector and body ground, when each of the SET/COAST, RESUME/ACCEL and CANCEL is turned ON.

OK

Switch position	Voltage
Neutral	10 - 14 V
RES/ACC	0.7 – 2.5 V
SET/COAST	2.3 – 4.6 V
CANCEL	4.1 – 7.2 V

NG ↓ | **OK** > Proceed to next circuit inspection shown on Problem Symptoms table.

3 | **Check control switch.**

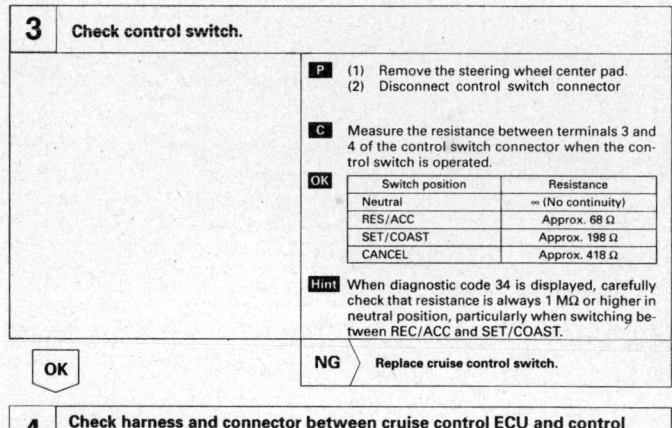

P (1) Remove the steering wheel center pad.
(2) Disconnect control switch connector

C Measure the resistance between terminals 3 and 4 of the control switch connector when the control switch is operated.

OK

Switch position	Resistance
Neutral	∞ (No continuity)
RES/ACC	Approx. 68 Ω
SET/COAST	Approx. 198 Ω
CANCEL	Approx. 418 Ω

Hint When diagnostic code 34 is displayed, carefully check that resistance is always 1 MΩ or higher in neutral position, particularly when switching between REC/ACC and SET/COAST.

OK ↓ | **NG** > Replace cruise control switch.

4 | **Check harness and connector between cruise control ECU and control switch**

OK ↓ | **NG** > Repair or replace harness or connector.

Check and replace cruise control ECU.

TY1109900310030X

Fig. 164 Codes 32 & 34: Control Switch Circuit (Part 3 of 3). 1996–97 Corolla

CIRCUIT DESCRIPTION

When the brake is on, battery positive voltage normally applies through the stop fuse and stop switch to terminal STP– of the cruise control ECU, and the cruise control ECU turns the cruise control off.

A fail-safe function is provided so that the cancel functions normally, even if there is a malfunction in the stop light signal circuit.

If the harness connected to terminal STP– has an open, terminal STP– will have battery positive voltage and the cruise control will be turned off, also SET not occurring.

Also, shown the brake is on, the magnetic clutch circuit is cut mechanically by the stop light switch, turning the cruise control off.

TY1109900311010X

Fig. 165 Stop Lamp Switch Circuit (Part 1 of 2). 1996–97 Corolla

INSPECTION PROCEDURE

1 | Check operation of stop light.

C Check that the stop light comes on when the brake pedal is depressed, and turns off when the brake pedal is released.

OK ↓

NG > Check stop light circuit.

2 | Input signal check.

C (1) See the input signal check
(2) Check the indicator light when the brake pedal is depressed.

Brake pedal is depressed

ON
OFF

OK The indicator light goes off when the brake pedal is depressed.

NG ↓

OK > Proceed to next circuit inspection shown on Problem Symptoms table.

3 | Check voltage between terminal STP– of cruise control ECU connector and body ground.

ON

P Remove the cruise control ECU with connectors still connected.
C (1) Turn the ignition switch ON.
(2) Measure the voltage between terminal STP– of cruise control ECU connector and body ground, when the brake pedal is depressed and released.

OK

	STP–
Depressed	10 – 14 V
Released	Below 1 V

NG ↓

OK > Proceed to next circuit inspection shown on Problem Symptoms table.

4 | Check for open in harness and connectors between terminal STP– of cruise control ECU and stop light switch

OK ↓

NG > Repair or replace harness or connector.

Check and replace cruise control ECU.

TY1109900311020X

Fig. 165 Stop Lamp Switch Circuit (Part 2 of 2). 1996–97 Corolla

2 | Check throttle position sensor.

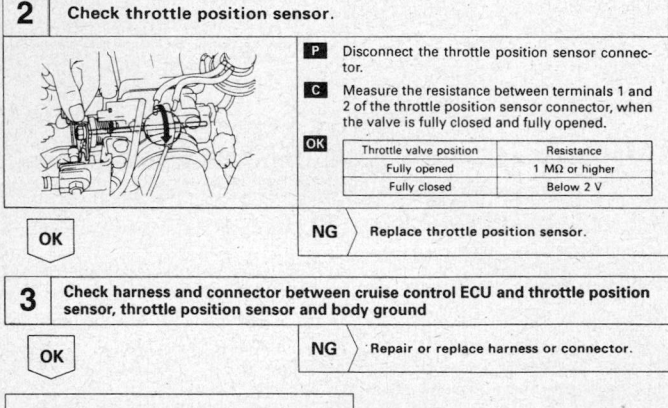

P Disconnect the throttle position sensor connector.
C Measure the resistance between terminals 1 and 2 of the throttle position sensor connector, when the valve is fully closed and fully opened.

OK

Throttle valve position	Resistance
Fully opened	1 MΩ or higher
Fully closed	Below 2 V

OK ↓

NG > Replace throttle position sensor.

3 | Check harness and connector between cruise control ECU and throttle position sensor, throttle position sensor and body ground

OK ↓

NG > Repair or replace harness or connector.

Check and replace cruise control ECU.

TY1109900312020X

Fig. 166 Idle Switch Circuit (Part 2 of 2). 1996–97 Corolla

CIRCUIT DESCRIPTION

When the idle switch is turned ON, a signal is sent to the cruise control ECU. The cruise control ECU uses this signal to enable accurate cruise control at the set speed quickly. If the idle switch is malfunctioning, problem symptoms also occur in the engine, so also inspect the engine.

INSPECTION PROCEDURE

1 | Check voltage between terminal IDL of cruise control ECU connector and body ground.

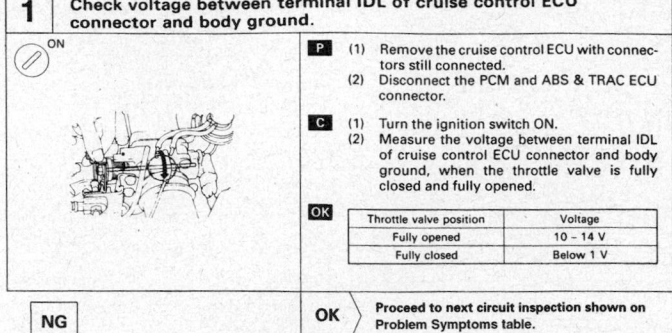

P (1) Remove the cruise control ECU with connectors still connected.
(2) Disconnect the PCM and ABS & TRAC ECU connector.
C (1) Turn the ignition switch ON.
(2) Measure the voltage between terminal IDL of cruise control ECU connector and body ground, when the throttle valve is fully closed and fully opened.

OK

Throttle valve position	Voltage
Fully opened	10 – 14 V
Fully closed	Below 1 V

NG ↓

OK > Proceed to next circuit inspection shown on Problem Symptoms table.

TY1109900312010X

Fig. 166 Idle Switch Circuit (Part 1 of 2). 1996–97 Corolla

CIRCUIT DESCRIPTION

When driving uphill under cruise control, in order to reduce shifting due to ON-OFF overdrive operation and to provide smooth driving, when down shifting in the electronically controlled transaxle occurs, a signal to prevent upshift until the end of the uphill slope is sent from the cruise control ECU to the ECU.

Terminal ECT of the cruise control ECU detects the shift change signal (output to Electronically Controlled Transaxle No.2 solenoid) from the ECU.

If vehicle speed down and terminal ECT of the cruise control ECU receives down shifting signal, it sends a signal from terminal OD to ECU to cut overdrive until the end of the uphill slope, and the gear shifts are reduced.

TY1109900313010X

Fig. 167 Electronically Controlled Transaxle Communication Circuit (Part 1 of 3). 1996–97 Corolla

INSPECTION PROCEDURE

1 | **Check operation of overdrive.**

P Test drive after engine warm up.

C Check that overdrive ON ↔ OFF occurs with operation of OD switch ON-OFF.

OK → NG → **Check and Repair Electronically Controlled Transaxle**

Go to step **2** .

2 | **Check voltage between terminal OD of harness side connector of cruise control ECU and body ground.**

ON

P Remove the cruise control ECU with connectors still connected.

C (1) Disconnect the cruise control ECU connector.
(2) Turn the ignition switch ON.
(3) Measure the voltage between terminal OD of harness side connector of cruise control ECU and body ground.

OK Voltage: 10 – 14 V

OK → NG → Go to step **5** .

TY1109900313020X

Fig. 167 Electronically Controlled Transaxle Communication Circuit (Part 2 of 3). 1996–97 Corolla

CIRCUIT DESCRIPTION

When the parking brake is operating, the parking brake switch sends a signal to the cruise control ECU. When this signal is input to the cruise control ECU during cruise control driving, the cruise control ECU cancels cruise control.

TY1109900314010X

Fig. 168 Park/Neutral Position Switch Circuit (Part 1 of 3). 1996–97 Corolla

3 | **Check voltage between terminal PKB of cruise control ECU connector and body ground.**

ON

P Remove the cruise control ECU with connectors still connected.

C (1) Turn the ignition switch ON.
(2) Measure the voltage between terminal PKB of cruise control ECU connector and body ground, when the parking brake lever is operating.

OK

Switch Position	Voltage
ON (lever pulled)	Below 1 V
OFF (lever released)	10 – 14 V

NG → OK → **Proceed to next circuit inspection shown on Problem Symptoms table.**

4 | **Check for open in harness and connector between cruise control ECU and ST fuse**

OK → NG → **Repair or replace harness or connector.**

Check and replace cruise control ECU.

TY1109900314030X

Fig. 168 Park/Neutral Position Switch Circuit (Part 3 of 3). 1996–97 Corolla

3 | **Check voltage between terminal ECT of cruise control ECU connector and body ground (On test drive).**

P (1) Connect the cruise control ECU connector.
(2) Test drive after engine warm up.

C Check the voltage between terminal ECT of the cruise control ECU connector and body ground when the OD switch is on all off.

OK

Gear Position	Voltage
O/D	Below 1V
3rd	10 – 14 V

NG → OK → **Proceed to next circuit inspection shown on Problem Symptoms table.**

4 | **Check harness and connector between terminal ECT of cruise control ECU and Electronically Controlled Transaxle solenoid**

OK → NG → **Repair or replace harness or connector.**

Check and repair cruise control ECU.

5 | **Check harness and connector between terminal OD of cruise control ECU and terminal OD1 of ECU**

OK → NG → **Repair or replace harness or connector.**

Check and replace ECU.

TY1109900313030X

Fig. 167 Electronically Controlled Transaxle Communication Circuit (Part 3 of 3). 1996–97 Corolla

INSPECTION PROCEDURE

1 | **Check operation of starter.**

C Check that the starter operates normally and that the engine starts.

OK → NG → **Diagnose starting system.**

2 | **Input signal check.**

Shifting into P or N position

ON

OFF

C (1) See the input signal check
(2) Check the indicator light when shifting into the P position or N position.

OK The indicator light goes off when shifting into the P position or N position.

NG → OK → **Proceed to next circuit inspection shown on Problem Symptoms table.**

TY1109900314020X

Fig. 168 Park/Neutral Position Switch Circuit (Part 2 of 3). 1996–97 Corolla

CIRCUIT DESCRIPTION

When the clutch pedal is depressed, the clutch switch sends a signal to the cruise control ECU, when this signal is input to the cruise control ECU during cruise control driving, the cruise control ECU cancels cruise control.

TY1109900315010X

Fig. 169 Clutch Switch Circuit (Part 1 of 3). 1996–97 Corolla

INSPECTION PROCEDURE

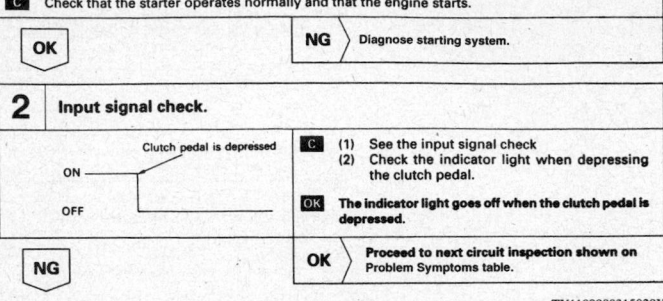

Fig. 169   Clutch Switch Circuit (Part 2 of 3).
1996–97 Corolla

CIRCUIT DESCRIPTION

The cruise control ECU power source supplies power to the actuator. Terminal GND and the cruise control ECU case the grounded.

TY1109900316010X

Fig. 170   Cruise Control ECU Power Source Circuit (Part 1 of 3). 1996–97 Corolla

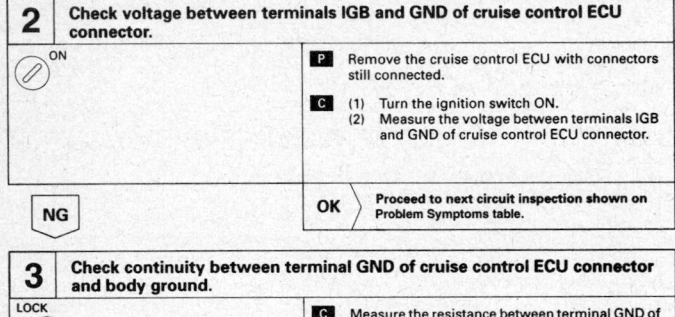

Fig. 170   Cruise Control ECU Power Source Circuit (Part 3 of 3). 1996–97 Corolla

INSPECTION PROCEDURE

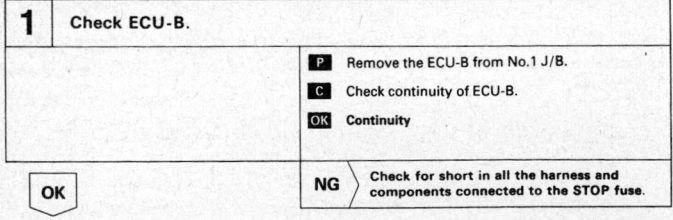

TY1109900317020X

Fig. 171   Back Up Power Source Circuit (Part 2 of 3). 1996–97 Corolla

3 Check voltage between terminal N & C of cruise control ECU connector and body ground.

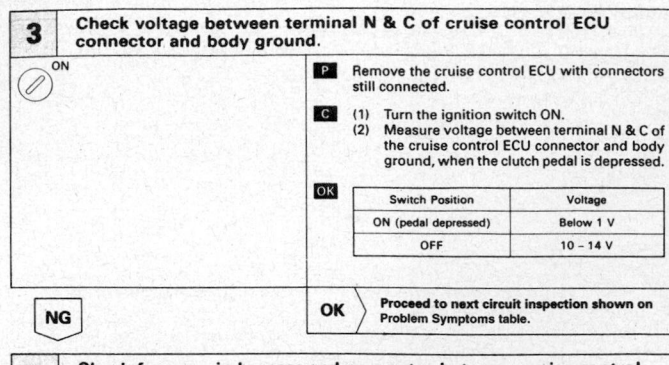

P Remove the cruise control ECU with connectors still connected.

C (1) Turn the ignition switch ON.
(2) Measure voltage between terminal N & C of the cruise control ECU connector and body ground, when the clutch pedal is depressed.

OK

Switch Position	Voltage
ON (pedal depressed)	Below 1 V
OFF	10 – 14 V

NG

OK Proceed to next circuit inspection shown on Problem Symptoms table.

4 Check for open in harness and connector between cruise control ECU and fuse.

OK

NG Repair or replace harness or connector.

Check and replace cruise control ECU.

TY1109900315030X

Fig. 169   Clutch Switch Circuit (Part 3 of 3). 1996–97 Corolla

INSPECTION PROCEDURE

1 Check ECU-IG fuse.

P Remove the ECU-IG fuse from No.1 J/B.

C Check continuity of ECU-IG fuse.

OK Continuity

OK

NG Check for short in all the harness and components connected to the ECU-IG fuse

TY1109900316020X

Fig. 170   Cruise Control ECU Power Source Circuit (Part 2 of 3). 1996–97 Corolla

CIRCUIT DESCRIPTION

The cruise control ECU back-up power source provides power even when the ignition switch is off and is used for diagnostic code memory, etc.

TY1109900317010X

Fig. 171   Back Up Power Source Circuit (Part 1 of 3). 1996–97 Corolla

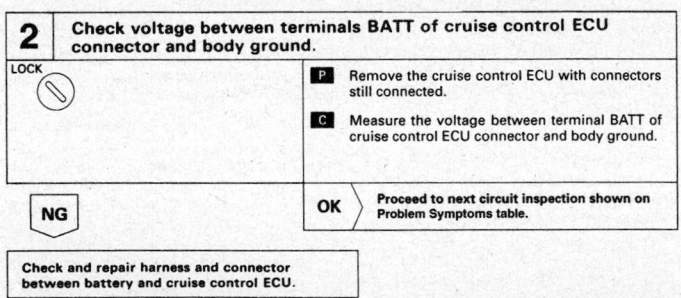

TY1109900317030X

Fig. 171   Back Up Power Source Circuit (Part 3 of 3). 1996–97 Corolla

CIRCUIT DESCRIPTION

When the cruise control main switch is turned off, the cruise control does not operate.

TY1109900318010X

Fig. 172   Main Switch Circuit (Part 1 of 2). 1996–97 Corolla

INSPECTION PROCEDURE

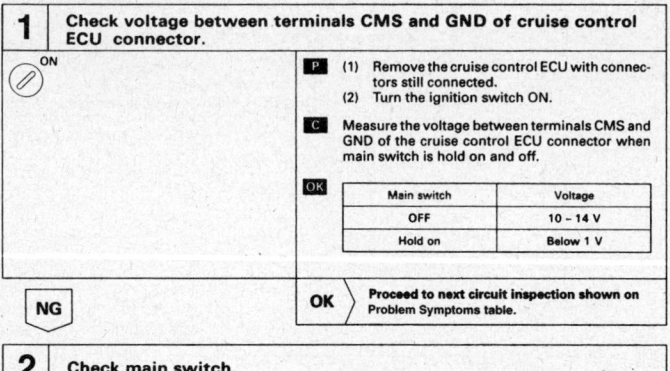

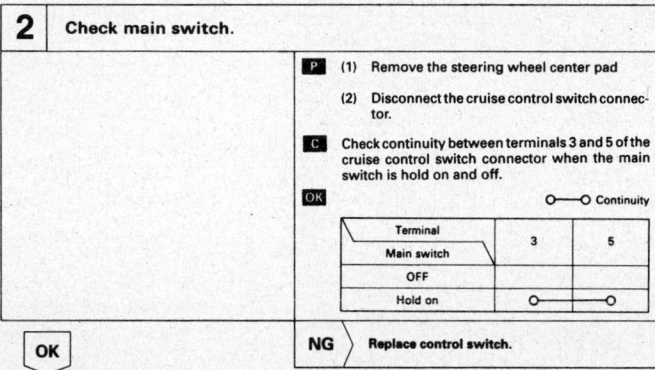

Fig. 172   Main Switch Circuit (Part 2 of 2). 1996–97 Corolla

TY1109900318020X

Actuator Control Cable Inspection

C (1) Check that the actuator, control cable and throttle link are properly installed and that the cable and link are connected correctly.
(2) Check that the actuator and throttle link are operating smoothly.
(3) Check that the cable is not loose or too tight.

Hint (1) If the control cable is very loose, the vehicle's loss of speed going uphill will be large.
(2) If the control cable is too tight, the idle rpm will become high.

TY1109900320000X

Fig. 174   Actuator Control Cable Inspection. 1996–97 Corolla

CIRCUIT DESCRIPTION

The actuator motor is operated by signals from the ECU. Acceleration and deceleration signals are transmitted by changes in the Duty Ratio (See note below).

Duty Ratio
The duty ratio is the ratio of the period of continuity in one cycle. For example, if A is the period of continuity in one cycle, and B is the period of non–continuity, then.

$$\text{Duty Ratio} = \frac{A}{A + B} \times 100 \, (\%)$$

DTC No.	Detection Item	Trouble Area
11	Short in actuator motor circuit.	• Actuator motor • Harness or connector between cruise control ECU and actuator motor • Cruise control ECU
15	Open in actuator motor circuit.	• Actuator motor

TY1109900288010X

Fig. 175   Codes 11 & 15: Actuator Motor Circuit (Part 1 of 2). 1998–99 Corolla

CIRCUIT DESCRIPTION

This circuit sends a signal to the ECU that DTC output is required.

TY1109900319010X

Fig. 173   T$_C$ Circuit (Part 1 of 2). 1996–97 Corolla

INSPECTION PROCEDURE

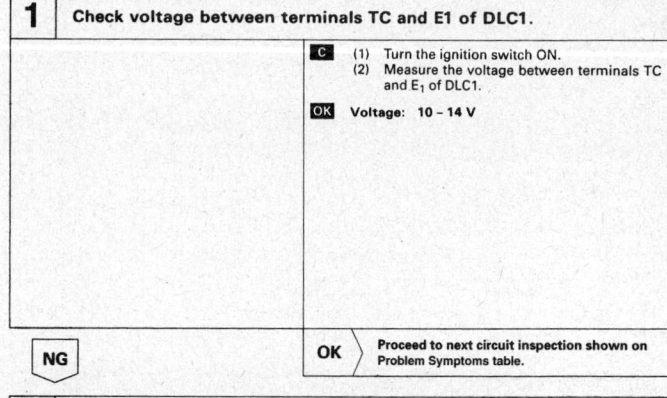

2 Check harness and connector between cruise control ECU and DLC1, DLC1 and body ground.

OK | NG > Repair or replace harness or connector.

Check and replace cruise control ECU.

TY1109900319020X

Fig. 173   T$_C$ Circuit (Part 2 of 2). 1996–97 Corolla

INSPECTION PROCEDURE

1 Check resistance between terminals MO and MC of actuator motor.

PREPARATION:
(a) Turn ignition switch OFF.
(b) Disconnect the actuator connector.
CHECK:
Measure resistance between terminals 1 and 2.
HINT:
If control plate position is fully opened or fully closed, resistance can not measure.
OK:
Resistance: more than 4.2 Ω

NG > Replace cruise control actuator.

2 Check for open and short in harness and connectors between cruise control ECU and actuator motor

NG > Repair or replace harness or connector.

Check and replace cruise control ECU

TY1109900288020X

Fig. 175   Codes 11 & 15: Actuator Motor Circuit (Part 2 of 2). 1998–99 Corolla

CIRCUIT DESCRIPTION

This circuit turns on the magnetic clutch inside the actuator during cruise control operation according to the signal from the ECU. If a malfunction occurs in the actuator or speed sensor, etc. during cruise control operation, the rotor shaft between the motor and control plate is released.

When the brake pedal is depressed, the stop light switch turns on, supplying electrical power to the stop light. Power supply to the magnetic clutch is mechanically cut and the magnetic clutch is turned OFF.

When driving downhill, if the vehicle speed exceeds the set speed by 8 km/h (5 mph), the ECU turns the safety magnet clutch OFF. If the vehicle speed later drops to within 5 km/h (3 mph) above the set speed, then cruise control at the set speed is resumed.

DTC No.	Detection Item	Trouble Area
12	Short in actuator magnetic clutch circuit. Open (0.8 sec.) in actuator magnetic clutch circuit.	• STOP Fuse • Stop light switch • Actuator magnetic clutch • Harness or connector between cruise control ECU and actuator magnetic clutch, actuator magnetic clutch and body ground • Cruise control ECU

TY1109900289010X

Fig. 176   Code 12: Actuator Magnetic Clutch Circuit (Part 1 of 3). 1998–99 Corolla

---

3	Check resistance between terminals L and GND of actuator magnetic clutch.

PREPARATION:
(a) Turn ignition switch OFF.
(b) Disconnect the actuator connector.
CHECK:
Measure resistance between terminals 3 and 4.
OK:
Resistance: 34.65 – 42.35 Ω.

NG ▷ Replace cruise control actuator.

OK

4	Check for open and short in harness and connectors between cruise control ECU and actuator magnetic clutch, actuator magnetic clutch and body ground

NG ▷ Repair or replace harness or connector.

OK

Check and replace cruise control ECU

TY1109900289030X

Fig. 176   Code 12: Actuator Magnetic Clutch Circuit (Part 3 of 3). 1998–99 Corolla

---

INSPECTION PROCEDURE

1	Check STOP fuse.

PREPARATION:
(a) Turn ignition switch OFF.
(b) Remove the STOP fuse from instrument panel junction block.
CHECK:
Check fuse continuity.
OK:
   There is continuity.

NG ▷ Replace STOP fuse.

OK

2	Check stop light switch.

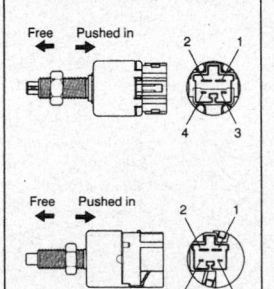

PREPARATION:
Disconnect the stop light switch connector.
CHECK:
Check continuity between terminals.

Switch position	Continuity
Switch pin free (Brake pedal depressed)	1 – 2
Switch pin pushed in (Brake pedal released)	3 – 4

NG ▷ Replace stop light switch.

OK

TY1109900289020X

Fig. 176   Code 12: Actuator Magnetic Clutch Circuit (Part 2 of 3). 1998–99 Corolla

---

CIRCUIT DESCRIPTION

The circuit detects the rotation position of the actuator control plate and sends a signal to the ECU.

DTC No.	Detection Item	Trouble Area
14	Cruise control actuator mechanical malfunction.	• Actuator lock: (motor, arm) • Actuator motor • Cruise control ECU

INSPECTION PROCEDURE

1	Check cruise control actuator arm locking operation.

PREPARATION:
(a) Turn ignition switch OFF.
(b) Disconnect the actuator connector.
CHECK:
Connect the positive (+) lead from the battery to the terminal 3 of actuator and the negative (–) lead to terminal 4.
NOTICE:
Do not connect the high tension cables to the wrong battery terminal. You will damage the cruise control actuator.
Move the control plate by hand.
OK:
   Control plate doesn't move.

NG ▷ Replace cruise control actuator.

OK

TY1109900290010X

Fig. 177   Code 14: Actuator Mechanical Fault (Part 1 of 2). 1998–99 Corolla

2	Check cruise control actuator operation.

PREPARATION:
(a) Turn ignition switch OFF.
(b) Disconnect the actuator connector.

CHECK:
Connect the positive (+) lead from the battery to terminals 1 and 3 of actuator, connect the negative (−) lead to terminals 2 and 4 of actuator.
OK:
   Control arm moves to full open side

CHECK:
Connect the positive (+) lead from the battery to terminals 2 and 4 of actuator, connect the negative (−) lead to terminals 1 and 3 of actuator.
OK:
   Control arm moves to full close side

NG > Replace cruise control actuator.

OK

3	Check harness and connector between cruise control ECU and cruise control actuator

NG > Repair or replace harness or connector.

OK

Check and replace cruise control ECU

TY1109900290020X

Fig. 177   Code 14: Actuator Mechanical Fault (Part 2 of 2). 1998–99 Corolla

INSPECTION PROCEDURE

1	Input signal check.

Input Signal	Indicator Light Blinking Pattern	
Drive at about 40 km/h (25 mph) or below	Light ON / OFF	
Drive at about 40 km/h (25 mph) or higher	Light ON / OFF	

CHECK:
(a) See input signal check
(b) Check indicator light operation when driving with vehicle speed above 40 km/h (25 mph), and with vehicle speed below 40 km/h (25 mph).
OK:
   Vehicle speed above 40 km/h (25 mph):
      Indicator light blinks
   Vehicle speed below 40 km/h (25 mph):
      Indicator light stays on

OK > Check and replace cruise control ECU

NG

2	Check speedometer circuit

NG > Repair or replace harness, connector or combination meter assembly.

OK

3	Check harness and connector between cruise control ECU and combination meter, combination meter and vehicle speed sensor

NG > Repair or replace harness or connector.

OK

TY1109900291020X

Fig. 178   Code 21: Open In Vehicle Speed Sensor Circuit (Part 2 of 3). 1998–99 Corolla

CIRCUIT DESCRIPTION

The vehicle speed sensor circuit is sent to cruise control ECU as vehicle speed signal.
The rotor shaft is driven by the gear of the transmission.
For each rotation of the shaft, the vehicle speed sensor sends a 4 pulse signal through the combination meter to the cruise control ECU (See the following).
This signal is converted inside the combination meter and sent as a 4–pulse signal to the cruise control ECU.
The ECU calculates the vehicle speed from this pulse frequency.

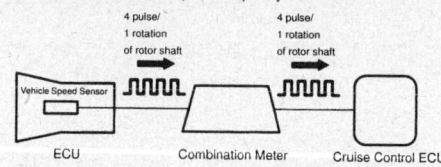

DTC No.	Detection Item	Trouble Area
21	Speed signal is not input to the cruise control ECU while cruise control is set.	• Combination meter • Harness or connector between cruise control ECU and combination meter, combination meter and vehicle speed sensor • Vehicle speed sensor • Cruise control ECU

TY1109900291010X

Fig. 178   Code 21: Open In Vehicle Speed Sensor Circuit (Part 1 of 3). 1998–99 Corolla

4	Check vehicle speed sensor

NG > Replace vehicle speed sensor.

OK

Check and replace cruise control ECU

TY1109900291030X

Fig. 178   Code 21: Open In Vehicle Speed Sensor Circuit (Part 3 of 3). 1998–99 Corolla

CIRCUIT DESCRIPTION

DTC No.	Detection Item	Trouble Area
23	Vehicle speed sensor pulse is abnormal.	• Vehicle speed sensor • Cruise control ECU

INSPECTION PROCEDURE

1	Check vehicle speed sensor

NG > Replace vehicle speed sensor.

OK

Check and replace cruise control ECU

TY1109900292000X

Fig. 179   Code 23: Vehicle Speed Signal Abnormal. 1998–99 Corolla

CIRCUIT DESCRIPTION

This circuit carries the SET/COAST, RESUME/ACCEL and CANCEL signals (each voltage) to the ECU.

DTC No.	Detection Item	Trouble Area
32	Short in control switch circuit.	• Cruise control switch • Harness or connector between cruise control ECU and cruise control switch, cruise control switch and body ground • Cruise control ECU

TY1109900293010X

Fig. 180   Code 32: Control Switch Circuit (Part 1 of 3). 1998–99 Corolla

3   Check control switch.

PREPARATION:
(a)   Remove steering wheel center pad.
(b)   Disconnect the control switch connector.
CHECK:
Measure resistance between terminals 3 and 4 of control switch connector when control switch is operated.

Switch position	Resistance (Ω)
Neutral	∞ (No continuity)
RES/ACC	50 – 80
SET/COAST	180 – 220
CANCEL	400 – 440

NG ▷ **Replace control switch.**

OK

4   Check harness and connector between cruise control ECU and cruise control switch, cruise control switch and body ground

NG ▷ **Repair or replace harness or connector.**

OK

5   Input signal check (See step 1).

OK ▷ **Wait and see.**

NG

Check and replace cruise control ECU

TY1109900293030X

Fig. 180   Code 32: Control Switch Circuit (Part 3 of 3). 1998–99 Corolla

INSPECTION PROCEDURE

1   Input signal check.

Input Signal	Indicator Light Blinking Pattern	
SET/COAST switch	ON OFF	2 Pulses
RESUME/ACCEL switch	ON OFF	3 Pulses
CANCEL switch	ON OFF	SW OFF SW ON

PREPARATION:
See input signal check
CHECK:
Check the indicator light operation when each of the SET/COAST, RESUME/ACCEL and CANCEL is turned on.
OK:

SET/COAST, RESUME/ACCEL switch
The signals shown in the table on the left should be output when each switch is ON. The signal should disappear when the switch is turned OFF.
CANCEL switch
The indicator light goes off when the cancel switch is turned ON.

OK ▷ **Wait and see.**

NG

2   Check voltage between terminals CCS of cruise control ECU connector and body ground.

PREPARATION:
(a)   Remove the ECU with connector still connected.
(b)   Turn ignition switch ON.
CHECK:
Measure voltage between terminals CCS (10) of ECU connector and body ground, when each of the SET/COAST, RESUME/ACCEL and CANCEL is turned ON.

Switch position	Resistance (V)
Neutral	10 – 16 V
RES/ACC	0.6 – 2.3 V
SET/COAST	1.9 – 4.7 V
CANCEL	3.4 – 7.2 V

NG ▷ **Proceed to next circuit inspection shown on problem symptom table**

OK

TY1109900293020X

Fig. 180   Code 32: Control Switch Circuit (Part 2 of 3). 1998–99 Corolla

CIRCUIT DESCRIPTION

When the idle switch in turned ON, a signal is sent to the ECU. The ECU uses this signal to correct the discrepancy between the throttle valve position and the actuator position sensor value to enable accurate cruise control at the set speed. If the idle switch is malfunctioning, problem symptoms also occur in the engine, so also inspect the engine.

DTC No.	Detection Item	Trouble Area
51	Short in idle signal circuit.	• Harness or connector between ECM and throttle position sensor • Throttle position sensor • Harness or connector between cruise control ECU and ECM • Cruise control ECU

TY1109900294010X

Fig. 181   Code 51: Idle Signal Circuit (Part 1 of 3). 1998–99 Corolla

INSPECTION PROCEDURE

1	Check voltage between terminal IDL of cruise control ECU connector and body ground.

PREPARATION:
(a) Remove the ECU with connector still connected.
(b) Disconnect the ECM connector.
(c) Turn ignition switch ON.

CHECK:
Measure voltage between terminal IDL (13) of ECU connector and body ground when the throttle valve is fully closed and fully opened.

OK:

Throttle valve position	Voltage
Fully opened	10 – 14 V
Fully closed	Below 1.5 V

OK	Proceed to next circuit inspection shown on problem symptom table

NG

2	Check harness and connector between ECM and throttle position sensor

NG	Repair or replace harness or connector.

OK

3	Check throttle position sensor circuit

NG	Replace throttle position sensor.

OK

TY1109900294020X

Fig. 181   Code 51: Idle Signal Circuit (Part 2 of 3). 1998–99 Corolla

CIRCUIT DESCRIPTION

When the brake pedal is depressed, the stop light switch sends a signal to the ECU. When the ECU receives this signal, it cancels the cruise control.

A fail–safe function is provided so that the cancel functions normally, even if there is a malfunction in the stop light signal circuit.

The cancel conditions are: Battery positive voltage at terminal STP–

When the brake is on, battery positive voltage normally applies through the STOP fuse and stop light switch to terminal STP– of the ECU, and the ECU turns the cruise control off.

If the harness connected to terminal STP– has an open circuit, terminal STP– will have battery positive voltage and the cruise control will be turned off.

Also, when the brake is on, the magnetic clutch circuit is cut mechanically by the stop light switch, turning the cruise control off.

TY1109900295010X

Fig. 182   Stop Lamp Switch Circuit (Part 1 of 3). 1998–99 Corolla

4	Check throttle position sensor.

PREPARATION:
Disconnect the throttle position sensor connector.
CHECK:
Measure resistance between terminals 1, 3 and 2 of throttle position sensor connector.
OK:

Terminals	Throttle valve	Resistance
1 – 2	–	2.5 – 5.9 kΩ
2 – 3	Fully closed	0.2 – 6.3 kΩ
2 – 3	Fully opened	2.0 – 10.2 kΩ

NG	Replace throttle position sensor.

OK

5	Check for open and short in harness and connector between cruise control ECU and ECM

NG	Repair or replace harness or connector.

OK

Check and replace cruise control ECU

TY1109900294030X

Fig. 181   Code 51: Idle Signal Circuit (Part 3 of 3). 1998–99 Corolla

INSPECTION PROCEDURE

1	Check operation of stop light.

CHECK:
Check that stop light comes on when brake pedal is depressed, and turns off when brake pedal is released.

NG	Check stop light system

OK

2	Input signal check.

Input Signal	Indicator Light Blinking Pattern
Stop Light switch ON	Light ON — SW OFF OFF ----- SW ON

CHECK:
(a) See input signal check
(b) Check the indicator light when the brake pedal is depressed.
OK:

The indicator light goes off when the brake pedal is depressed.

OK	Proceed to next circuit inspection shown on problem symptom table

NG

TY1109900295020X

Fig. 182   Stop Lamp Switch Circuit (Part 2 of 3). 1998–99 Corolla

3 Check voltage between terminal STP– of cruise control ECU connector and body ground.

PREPARATION:
(a) Remove the ECU with connectors still connected.
(b) Turn ignition switch ON.
CHECK:
Measure voltage between terminal STP– (2) of cruise control ECU connector and body ground, when the brake pedal is depressed and released.
OK:

Depressed	10 – 14 V
Released	Below 1 V

OK ▷ Proceed to next circuit inspection shown on problem symptom table

NG ▽

4 Check for open in harness and connectors between terminal STP– of cruise control ECU and stop light switch

NG ▷ Repair or replace harness or connector.

OK ▽

Check and replace cruise control ECU

TY1109900295030X

INSPECTION PROCEDURE

1 Check operation of overdrive.

PREPARATION:
Test drive after engine warms up.
CHECK:
Check that overdrive ON ↔ OFF occurs with operation of OD switch ON–OFF.

NG ▷ Check and repair electronically controlled transmission

OK ▽

2 Check voltage between terminal OD of harness side connector of cruise control ECU and body ground.

PREPARATION:
(a) Remove the ECU with connector still connected.
(b) Turn ignition switch ON.
(c) Disconnect the ECU connector.
CHECK:
Measure voltage between terminal OD (14) of harness side connector of ECU and body ground.
OK:
Voltage: 10 – 14 V

NG ▷ Go to step 5.

OK ▽

TY1109900296020X

Fig. 183 Electronically Controlled Transmission Communication Circuit (Part 2 of 3). 1998–99 Corolla

CIRCUIT DESCRIPTION

When driving uphill under cruise control, in order to reduce shifting due to ON–OFF overdrive operation and to provide smooth driving, when down shifting in the electronically controlled transmission occurs, a signal to prevent upshift until the end of the up hill slope is sent from the cruise control ECU to the electronically controlled transmission.
Terminal ECT of the cruise control ECU detects the shift change signal (output to electronically controlled transmission No. 2 solenoid) from the ECM.
If vehicle speed down, also when terminal ECT of the cruise control ECU receives down shifting signal, it sends a signal from terminal OD to ECM to cut overdrive until the end of the uphill slope, and the gear shifts are reduced and gear shift points in the electronically controlled transmission are changed.

TY1109900296010X

Fig. 183 Electronically Controlled Transmission Communication Circuit (Part 1 of 3). 1998–99 Corolla

3 Check voltage between terminal ECT of cruise control ECU connector and body ground (On test drive).

PREPARATION:
(a) Connect the ECU connector.
(b) Test drive after engine warms up.
CHECK:
Check voltage between terminal ECT (6) of ECU connector and body ground when OD switch is ON and OFF.
OK:

OD switch position	Voltage
ON	8 – 14 V
OFF	Below 0.5 V

OK ▷ Proceed to next circuit inspection shown on problem symptom table

NG ▽

4 Check harness and connector between terminal ECT of cruise control ECU and electronically controlled transmission solenoid

NG ▷ Repair or replace harness or connector.

OK ▽

Check and replace cruise control ECU.

5 Check harness and connector between terminal OD of cruise control ECU and terminal OD1 of ECM

NG ▷ Repair or replace harness or connector.

OK ▽

Check and replace cruise control ECU

TY1109900296030X

Fig. 183 Electronically Controlled Transmission Communication Circuit (Part 3 of 3). 1998–99 Corolla

CIRCUIT DESCRIPTION

When the shift position is put in except D position, a signal is sent from the park/neutral position switch to the ECU. When this signal is input during cruise control driving, the ECU cancels the cruise control.

TY1109900297010X

Fig. 184 Park/Neutral Position Switch Circuit (Part 1 of 3). 1998–99 Corolla

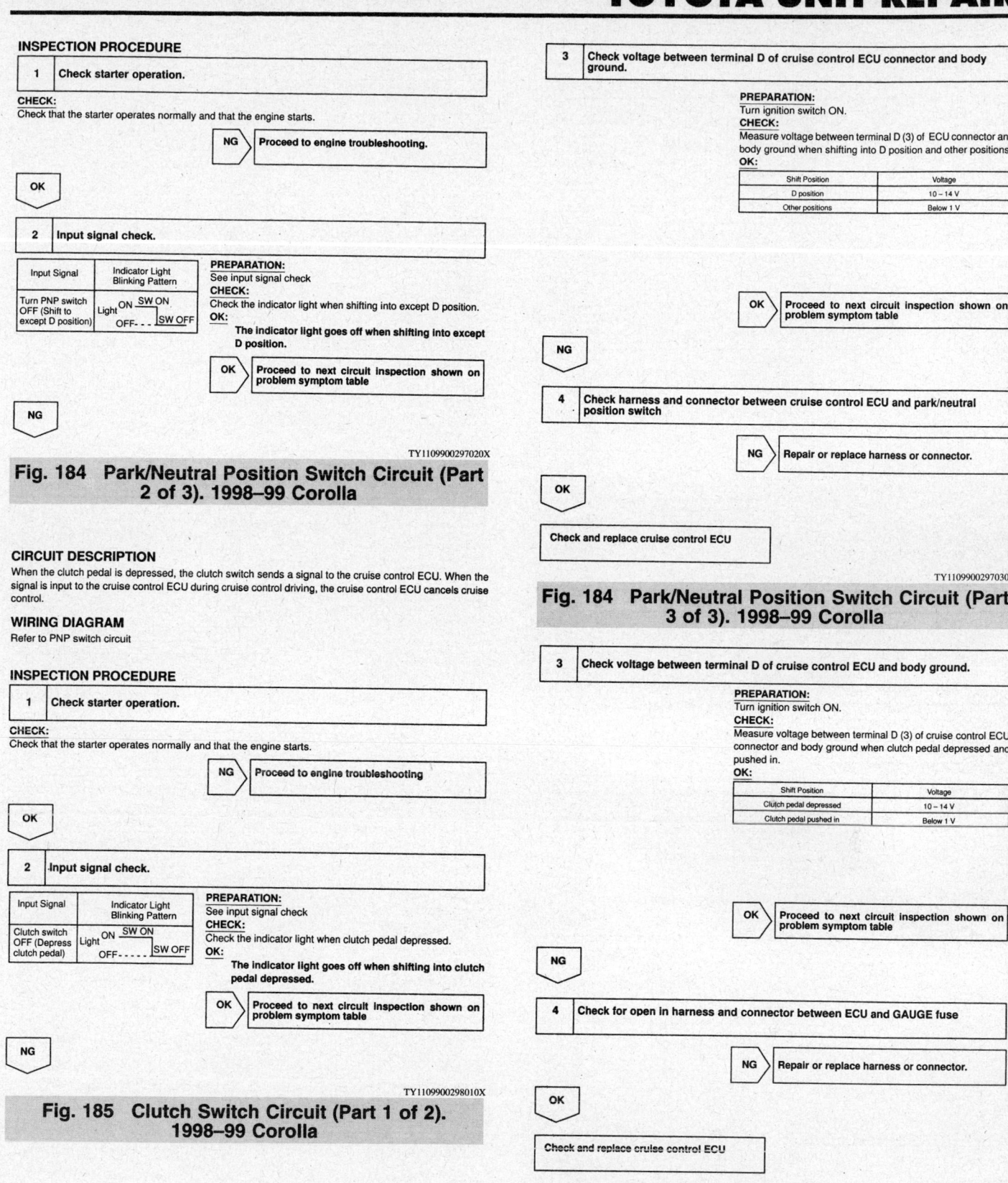

INSPECTION PROCEDURE

1	Check starter operation.

CHECK:
Check that the starter operates normally and that the engine starts.

NG → Proceed to engine troubleshooting.

OK

2	Input signal check.

Input Signal	Indicator Light Blinking Pattern
Turn PNP switch OFF (Shift to except D position)	Light ON ⎡SW ON⎤ OFF --- ⎣SW OFF⎦

PREPARATION:
See input signal check
CHECK:
Check the indicator light when shifting into except D position.
OK:
The indicator light goes off when shifting into except D position.

OK → Proceed to next circuit inspection shown on problem symptom table

NG

TY1109900297020X

Fig. 184   Park/Neutral Position Switch Circuit (Part 2 of 3). 1998–99 Corolla

CIRCUIT DESCRIPTION

When the clutch pedal is depressed, the clutch switch sends a signal to the cruise control ECU. When the signal is input to the cruise control ECU during cruise control driving, the cruise control ECU cancels cruise control.

WIRING DIAGRAM
Refer to PNP switch circuit

INSPECTION PROCEDURE

1	Check starter operation.

CHECK:
Check that the starter operates normally and that the engine starts.

NG → Proceed to engine troubleshooting

OK

2	Input signal check.

Input Signal	Indicator Light Blinking Pattern
Clutch switch OFF (Depress clutch pedal)	Light ON ⎡SW ON⎤ OFF ----- ⎣SW OFF⎦

PREPARATION:
See input signal check
CHECK:
Check the indicator light when clutch pedal depressed.
OK:
The indicator light goes off when shifting into clutch pedal depressed.

OK → Proceed to next circuit inspection shown on problem symptom table

NG

TY1109900298010X

Fig. 185   Clutch Switch Circuit (Part 1 of 2). 1998–99 Corolla

3	Check voltage between terminal D of cruise control ECU connector and body ground.

PREPARATION:
Turn ignition switch ON.
CHECK:
Measure voltage between terminal D (3) of ECU connector and body ground when shifting into D position and other positions.
OK:

Shift Position	Voltage
D position	10 – 14 V
Other positions	Below 1 V

OK → Proceed to next circuit inspection shown on problem symptom table

NG

4	Check harness and connector between cruise control ECU and park/neutral position switch

NG → Repair or replace harness or connector.

OK

Check and replace cruise control ECU

TY1109900297030X

Fig. 184   Park/Neutral Position Switch Circuit (Part 3 of 3). 1998–99 Corolla

3	Check voltage between terminal D of cruise control ECU and body ground.

PREPARATION:
Turn ignition switch ON.
CHECK:
Measure voltage between terminal D (3) of cruise control ECU connector and body ground when clutch pedal depressed and pushed in.
OK:

Shift Position	Voltage
Clutch pedal depressed	10 – 14 V
Clutch pedal pushed in	Below 1 V

OK → Proceed to next circuit inspection shown on problem symptom table

NG

4	Check for open in harness and connector between ECU and GAUGE fuse

NG → Repair or replace harness or connector.

OK

Check and replace cruise control ECU

TY1109900298020X

Fig. 185   Clutch Switch Circuit (Part 2 of 2). 1998–99 Corolla

CIRCUIT DESCRIPTION

The ECU power source supplies power to the actuator and sensors, etc.. When terminal GND and the cruise control ECU case are grounded.

TY1109900299010X

Fig. 186   ECU Power Source Circuit (Part 1 of 3). 1998–99 Corolla

INSPECTION PROCEDURE

1 Check ECU–IG fuse.

PREPARATION:
Remove the ECU–IG fuse from instrument panel junction block.
CHECK:
Check continuity of ECU–IG fuse.
OK:
Continuity

NG Check for short in all the harness and components connected to ECU–IG fuse.

OK

2 Check voltage between terminals B and GND of cruise control ECU connector.

PREPARATION:
(a) Remove the ECU with connector still connected.
(b) Turn ignition switch ON.
CHECK:
Measure voltage between terminals B (9) and GND (16) of ECU connector.
OK:
10 – 14 V

OK Proceed to next circuit inspection shown on problem symptom table

NG

TY1109900299020X

Fig. 186 ECU Power Source Circuit (Part 2 of 3). 1998–99 Corolla

CIRCUIT DESCRIPTION

When the cruise control main switch is turned off, the cruise control does not operate.

INSPECTION PROCEDURE

1 Check voltage between terminal CMS of cruise control ECU connector and body ground.

PREPARATION:
(a) Remove the ECU with connector still connected.
(b) Turn ignition switch ON.
CHECK:
Measure voltage between terminal CMS (11) of cruise control ECU connector when main switch is held on and off.
OK:

Main switch	Voltage
OFF	10 – 14 V
ON	Below 0.5 V

OK Proceed to next circuit inspection shown on problem symptom table

NG

TY1109900300010X

Fig. 187 Main Switch Circuit (Part 1 of 2). 1998–99 Corolla

---

3 Check resistance between terminal GND of cruise control ECU connector and body ground.

CHECK:
Measure resistance between terminal GND (16) of ECU connector and body ground.
OK:
Resistance: Below 1 Ω

NG Repair or replace harness or connector.

OK

Check and repair harness and connector between cruise control ECU and battery

TY1109900299030X

Fig. 186 ECU Power Source Circuit (Part 3 of 3). 1998–99 Corolla

2 Check main switch continuity.

PREPARATION:
(a) Remove steering wheel center pad.
(b) Disconnect the control switch connector.
CHECK:
Check continuity between terminals 3 and 5 of control switch connector when main switch is held on and off.
OK:

Switch position	Tester connection	Specified condition
OFF	3 – 5	No continuity
ON	3 – 5	Continuity

NG Replace control switch.

OK

3 Check harness and connector between cruise control ECU and main switch

NG Repair or replace harness or connector.

OK

Check and replace cruise control ECU

TY1109900300020X

Fig. 187 Main Switch Circuit (Part 2 of 2). 1998–99 Corolla

CIRCUIT DESCRIPTION

When the cruise control main switch is turned ON, CRUISE MAIN indicator light lights up.

TY1109900301010X

Fig. 188 Cruise Main Indicator Lamp Circuit (Part 1 of 2). 1998–99 Corolla

INSPECTION PROCEDURE

1	Check voltage between terminals PI and GND of cruise control ECU connector.

PREPARATION:
Tun ignition switch ON.
CHECK:
Measure voltage between terminals PI (4) and GND of cruise control ECU connector when main switch ON and OFF.
OK:

Switch position	Voltage
OFF	10 – 16 V
ON	Below 1.2 V

OK >	Proceed to next circuit inspection shown on problem symptom table

NG

2	Check combination meter

NG >	Replace combination meter.

OK

Check and replace cruise control ECU

TY1109900301020X

Fig. 188   Cruise Main Indicator Lamp Circuit (Part 2 of 2). 1998–99 Corolla

INSPECTION PROCEDURE

1	Check voltage between terminals Tc and E₁ of DLC1.

PREPARATION:
Turn ignition switch ON.
CHECK:
Measure voltage between terminals Tc and E₁ of DLC1.
OK:
Voltage: 10 – 14 V

OK >	Proceed to next circuit inspection shown on problem symptom table

NG

2	Check harness and connector between cruise control ECU and DLC1, DLC1 and body ground

NG >	Repair or replace harness or connector.

OK

Check and replace cruise control ECU

TY1109900302020X

Fig. 189   Diagnosis Circuit (Part 2 of 2). 1998–99 Corolla

CIRCUIT DESCRIPTION

This circuit sends a signal to the ECU that DTC output is required.

TY1109900302010X

Fig. 189   Diagnosis Circuit (Part 1 of 2). 1998–99 Corolla

INSPECTION PROCEDURE

1	Actuator control cable inspection

OK:
(a)   Check that the actuator, control cable throttle link are properly installed and that the cable and link are connected correctly.
(b)   Check that the actuator and bell crank are operating smoothly.
(c)   Check that the cable is not loose or too tight.
OK:
Freeplay: less than 10 mm
HINT:
• If the control cable is very loose, the vehicle's loss of speed going uphill will be large.
• If the control cable is too tight, the idle RPM will become high.

TY1109900303000X

Fig. 190   Actuator Control Cable. 1998–99 Corolla

Chart No.			C	D	D	F	G, H	E	H	I		
Inspection Item												
Problem / DTC	Type B	Type A	CC ECU	Actuator	Main Switch (in Control Switch)	Control Switch	Stop Light Switch	Park/Neutral Position Switch	No.1 Vehicle Speed Sensor	No.2 Solenoid	Throttle Position Sensor (IDL)	Speed Control Cable, Control Link	Other Parts
11	2			1									
12	3			1			2						
13	2			1									
21	2								1				
23				3					2			1	
32	2					1							
34	2					1							
41	2												
Normal OK		4	8	7	1	2	3	4				6	9*
Normal NG			2								1		
Set speed deviates on high or low side.			4	3						1		2	
Large speed increase or speed drop when control switch turned to SET.			3	2							1		
Vehicle speed fluctuates when speed control switch turned to SET.			4	3						1		2	
Set speed does not cancel when brake pedal depressed. OK	3		3	1			2						
Set speed does not cancel when brake pedal depressed. NG			2				1						
Set speed does not cancel when shifted to "N" position. OK	3		2	1									
Set speed does not cancel when shifted to "N" position. NG			2					1					
Vehicle speed does not decrease when speed control switch turned to COAST. OK	1		4	1						3		2	
Vehicle speed does not decrease when speed control switch turned to COAST. NG			2			1							
Vehicle speed does not accelerate when speed control switch turned to ACCEL. OK	2			1						3	4	5	2
Vehicle speed does not accelerate when speed control switch turned to ACCEL. NG			2			1							
Vehicle speed does not return to memorized speed when control switch turned on RESUME. OK	2		4	1						3		2	
Vehicle speed does not return to memorized speed when control switch turned on RESUME. NG			2			1							
Set speed does not cancel when speed control switch turned to CANCEL. OK	3		2	1									
Set speed does not cancel when speed control switch turned to CANCEL. NG			2			1							
Speed can be set below about 40 km/h (25 mph). OK	4		2	1									
Speed can be set below about 40 km/h (25 mph). NG			2								1		
Cruise control will not disengage even at about 40 km/h (25 mph). OK	4		2	1									
Cruise control will not disengage even at about 40 km/h (25 mph). NG			2								1		
Acceleration response is sluggish when speed control switch turned to "ACCEL" or "RESUME".			6	3	1					4	5	2	

*:   Inspect wire harness.

TY1109900544000X

Fig. 191   Problem Symptoms Table. 1996–97 Land Cruiser

Symptom	Suspect Area
SET not occurring or CANCEL occurring. (DTC is Normal)	1. Input Signal Circuit 2. Vehicle Speed Sensor Circuit 3. Stop Light Switch Circuit 4. Park/Neutral Position Switch Circuit 5. ECM
SET not occurring or CANCEL occurring. (DTC is not output)	1. ECM
Actual vehicle speed deviates above or below the set speed.	1. Input Signal Circuit 2. ECM
Gear shifting occurs frequently between 3rd and O/D when driving on uphill road. (Hurting)	1. ECM
Cruise control not cancelled, even when brake pedal is de-pressed.	1. Stop Light Switch Circuit 2. ECM
Cruise control not cancelled, even when transmission is shifted to "N" position.	1. Park/Neutral Position Switch Circuit 2. ECM
Cruise control not cancelled, even when clutch pedal is de-pressed.	1. ECM
Control switch does not operate. (SET/COAST, ACC/RES, CANCEL not possible)	1. Cruise Control Switch Circuit
SET possible at 40 km/h (25 mph) or less, or CANCEL does not operate at 40 km/h (25 mph) or less.	1. Input Signal Circuit 2. ECM
Poor response is ACCEL and RESUME modes.	1. ECM
O/D does not resume, even though the road is not uphill.	1. ECM
DTC memory is erased.	1. ECM
DTC is not output, or is output when should not be.	1. Diagnosis Circuit 2. ECM
Cruise MAIN indicator light remains ON or falls to light up.	1. Input Signal Circuit 2. CM

TY1109900557000X

Fig. 192   Problem Symptoms Table. 1998–99 Land Cruiser

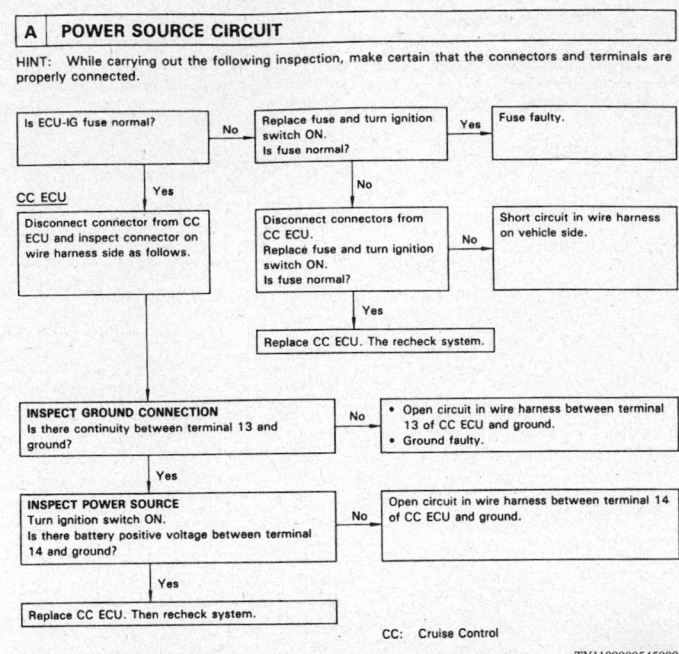

TY1109900545000X

Fig. 193   Test A: Power Source Circuit. 1996 Land Cruiser

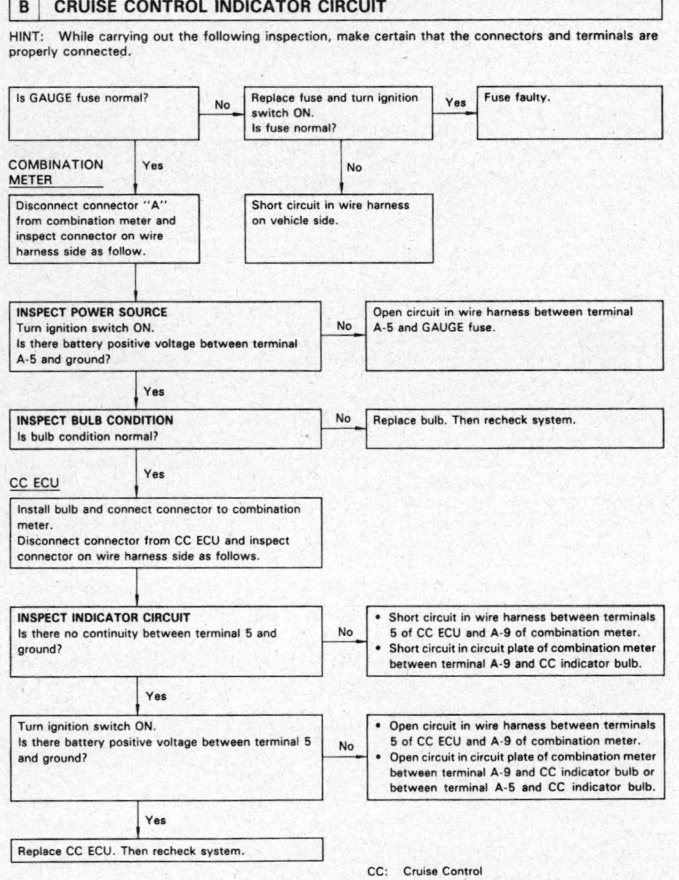

TY1109900546000X

Fig. 194   Test B: Cruise Control Indicator Circuit. 1996 Land Cruiser

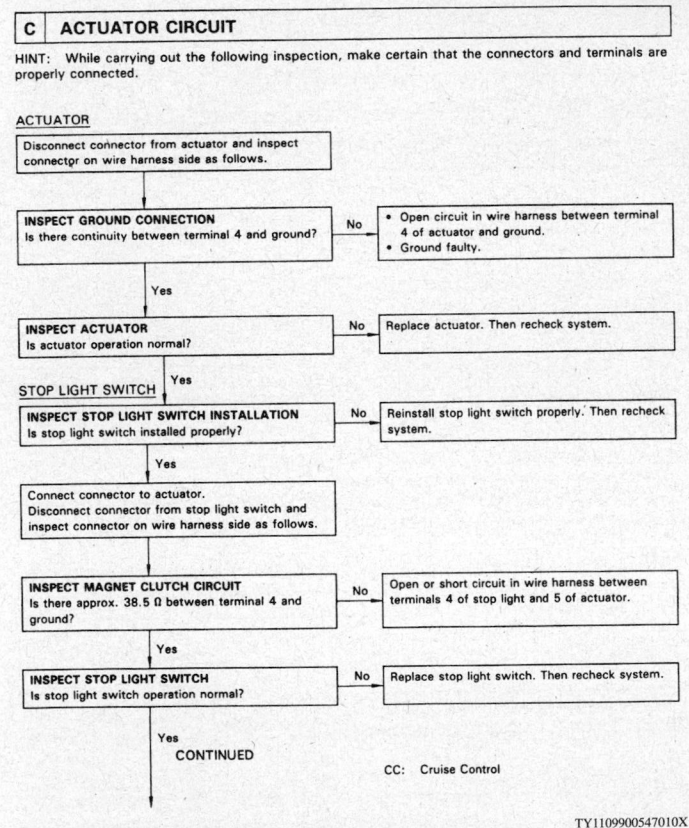

TY1109900547010X

Fig. 195   Test C: Actuator Circuit (Part 1 of 2). 1996 Land Cruiser

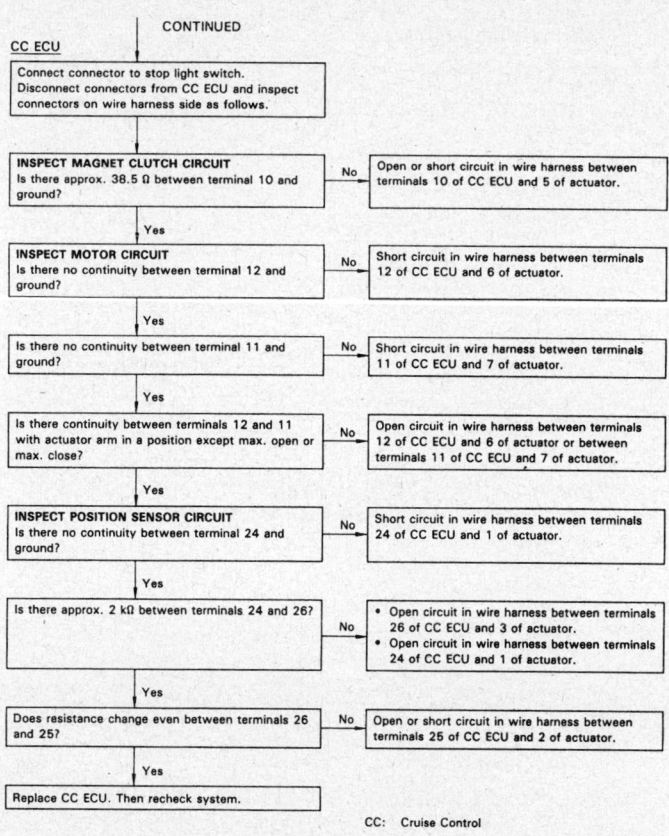

CC ECU

CONTINUED

Connect connector to stop light switch. Disconnect connectors from CC ECU and inspect connectors on wire harness side as follows.

INSPECT MAGNET CLUTCH CIRCUIT
Is there approx. 38.5 Ω between terminal 10 and ground?

— No → Open or short circuit in wire harness between terminals 10 of CC ECU and 5 of actuator.

↓ Yes

INSPECT MOTOR CIRCUIT
Is there no continuity between terminal 12 and ground?

— No → Short circuit in wire harness between terminals 12 of CC ECU and 6 of actuator.

↓ Yes

Is there no continuity between terminal 11 and ground?

— No → Short circuit in wire harness between terminals 11 of CC ECU and 7 of actuator.

↓ Yes

Is there continuity between terminals 12 and 11 with actuator arm in a position except max. open or max. close?

— No → Open circuit in wire harness between terminals 12 of CC ECU and 6 of actuator or between terminals 11 of CC ECU and 7 of actuator.

↓ Yes

INSPECT POSITION SENSOR CIRCUIT
Is there no continuity between terminal 24 and ground?

— No → Short circuit in wire harness between terminals 24 of CC ECU and 1 of actuator.

↓ Yes

Is there approx. 2 kΩ between terminals 24 and 26?

— No → • Open circuit in wire harness between terminals 26 of CC ECU and 3 of actuator.
• Open circuit in wire harness between terminals 24 of CC ECU and 1 of actuator.

↓ Yes

Does resistance change even between terminals 26 and 25?

— No → Open or short circuit in wire harness between terminals 25 of CC ECU and 2 of actuator.

↓ Yes

Replace CC ECU. Then recheck system.

CC: Cruise Control

TY1109900547020X

Fig. 195   Test C: Actuator Circuit (Part 2 of 2). 1996 Land Cruiser

---

D   CONTROL SWITCH CIRCUIT

HINT: While carrying out the following inspection, make certain that the connectors and terminals are properly connected.

CONTROL SWITCH

Disconnect connector from control switch and inspect connector on wire harness side as follows.

INSPECT GROUND CONNECTION
Is there continuity between terminal 3 and ground?

— No → • Open circuit in wire harness between terminal 3 of control switch and ground.
• Ground faulty.

↓ Yes

INSPECT CONTROL SWITCH
Is control switch operation normal?

— No → Replace control switch. Then recheck system.

↓ Yes

CC ECU

Connect connector to control switch. Disconnect connectors from CC ECU and inspect connectors on wire harness side as follows.

INSPECT MAIN SWITCH CIRCUIT
Is there no continuity between terminal 4 and ground with main switch OFF?

— No → Short circuit in wire harness between terminals 4 of CC ECU and 5 of control switch.

↓ Yes

Is there continuity between terminal 4 and ground with main switch ON?

— No → Open circuit in wire harness between terminals 4 of CC ECU and 5 of control switch.

↓ Yes

INSPECT CONTROL SWITCH CIRCUIT
Is there no continuity between terminal 18 and ground with control switch OFF?

— No → Short circuit in wire harness between terminals 18 of CC ECU and 4 of control switch.

↓ Yes

Is there resistance as shown in table below between terminal 18 and ground when control switch is turned to each position?

Position	Resistance (Ω)
RES/ACC	Approx. 68
SET/COAST	Approx. 198
CANCEL	Approx. 418

— No → Open circuit in wire harness between terminals 18 of CC ECU and 4 of control switch.

↓ Yes

Replace CC ECU. Then recheck system.

CC: Cruise Control

TY1109900548000X

Fig. 196   Test D: Control Switch Circuit. 1996 Land Cruiser

E   NO.1 VEHICLE SPEED SENSOR CIRCUIT

HINT: While carrying out the following inspection, make certain that the connectors and terminals are properly connected.

NO.1 VEHICLE SPEED SENSOR

Disconnect connector from No.1 vehicle speed sensor and inspect connector on wire harness side as follows.

INSPECT GROUND CONNECTION
Is there continuity between terminal 3 and ground?

— No → • Open circuit in wire harness between terminal 3 of No.1 vehicle speed sensor and ground.
• Ground faulty.

↓ Yes

INSPECT NO.1 VEHICLE SPEED SENSOR
Is No.1 vehicle speed sensor operation normal?

— No → Replace No.1 vehicle speed sensor. Then recheck system.

↓ Yes

CC ECU

Connect connector to No.1 vehicle speed sensor. Disconnect connector from CC ECU and inspect connector on wire harness side as follows.

INSPECT NO.1 VEHICLE SPEED SENSOR CIRCUIT
Is there continuity repeatedly between terminal 20 and ground?

— No → • Open or short circuit in wire harness between terminals 20 of CC ECU and 2 of No.1 vehicle speed sensor.

↓ Yes

Replace CC ECU. Then recheck system.

CC: Cruise Control

TY1109900549000X

Fig. 197   Test E: No. 1 Vehicle Speed Sensor Circuit. 1996 Land Cruiser

---

F   STOP LIGHT SWITCH CIRCUIT

HINT: While carrying out the following inspection, make certain that the connectors and terminals are properly connected.

INSPECT STOP LIGHT SYSTEM
Is stop light system operation normal?

— Yes → Inspect CC ECU

↓ No

Is STOP fuse normal?

→ Replace fuse. Is fuse normal?

— Yes → Fuse faulty.

↓ No

Disconnect connector from CC ECU and replace fuse. Is fuse normal?

— No → • Short circuit in wire harness between terminal 1 of stop light switch and STOP fuse.
• Short circuit in wire harness between terminal 16 of CC ECU and STOP fuse.

↓ Yes

Replace fuse and depress brake pedal. Is fuse normal?

— No → • Short circuit in wire harness between terminal 3 of stop light switch and stop light.
• Short circuit in wire harness between terminals 1 of CC ECU and 3 of stop light switch.

↓ Yes

Replace CC ECU. Then recheck system.

↓ Yes (from Is STOP fuse normal?)

STOP LIGHT SWITCH

INSPECT STOP LIGHT SWITCH INSTALLATION
Is stop light switch installed properly?

— No → Reinstall stop light switch properly. Then recheck system.

↓ Yes

CONTINUED

CC: Cruise Control

TY1109900550010X

Fig. 198   Test F: Stop Lamp Switch Circuit (Part 1 of 2). 1996 Land Cruiser

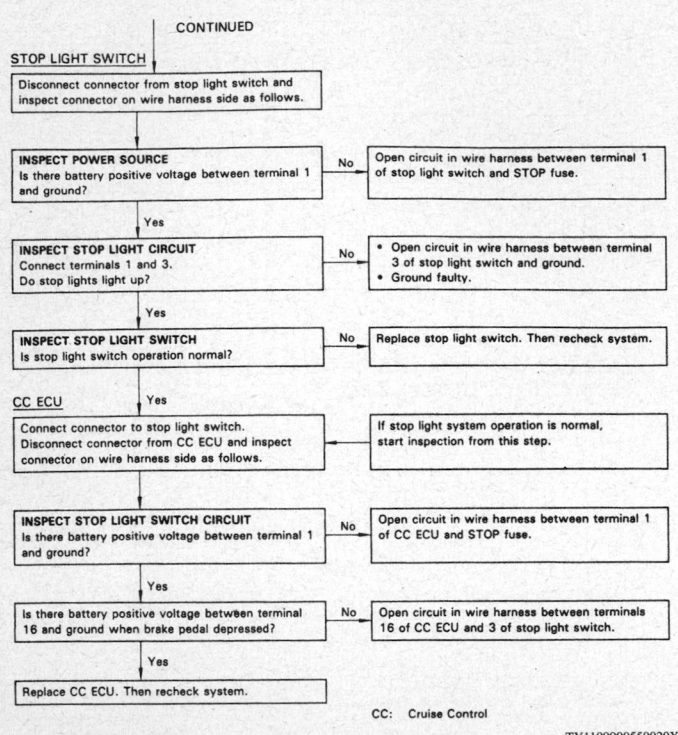

Fig. 198 Test F: Stop Lamp Switch Circuit (Part 2 of 2). 1996 Land Cruiser

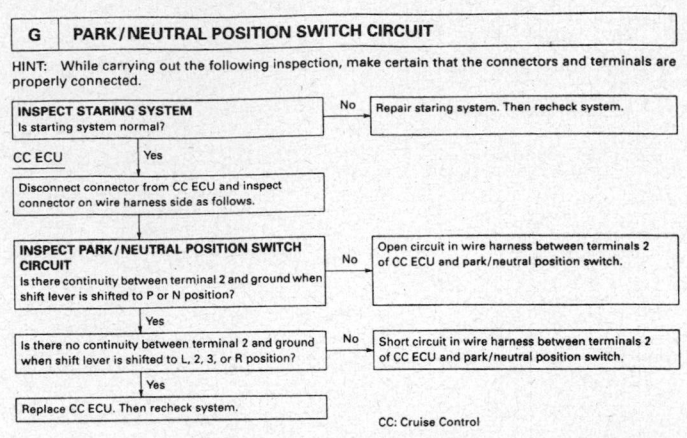

Fig. 199 Test G: Park/Neutral Position Switch Circuit. 1996 Land Cruiser

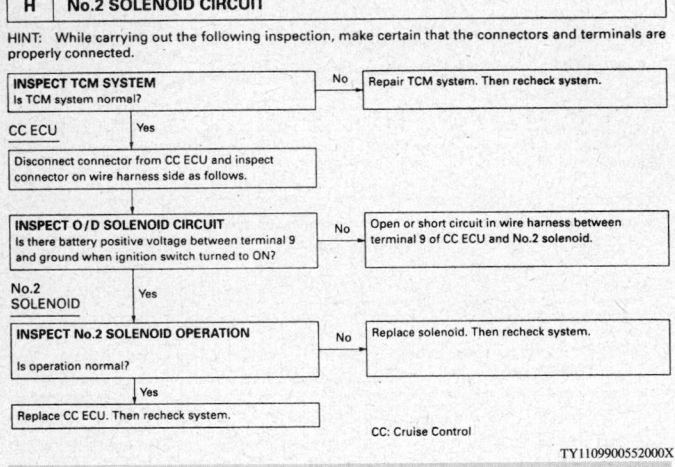

Fig. 200 Test H: No. 2 Solenoid Circuit. 1996 Land Cruiser

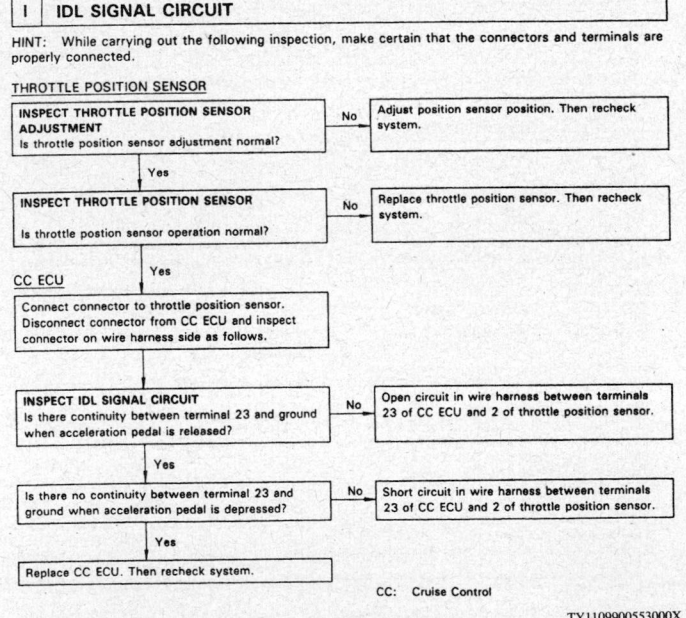

Fig. 201 Test I: IDL Signal Circuit. 1996 Land Cruiser

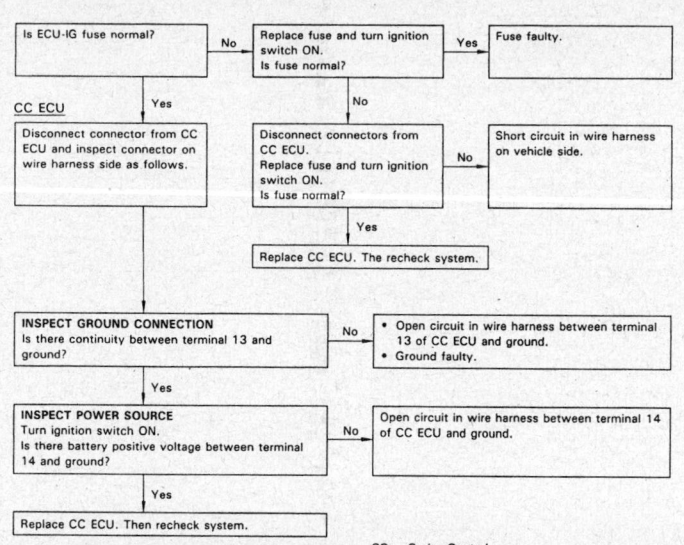

A POWER SOURCE CIRCUIT

HINT: While carrying out the following inspection, make certain that the connectors and terminals are properly connected.

CC: Cruise Control

TY1109900563000X

Fig. 202 Test A: Power Source Circuit. 1997 Land Cruiser

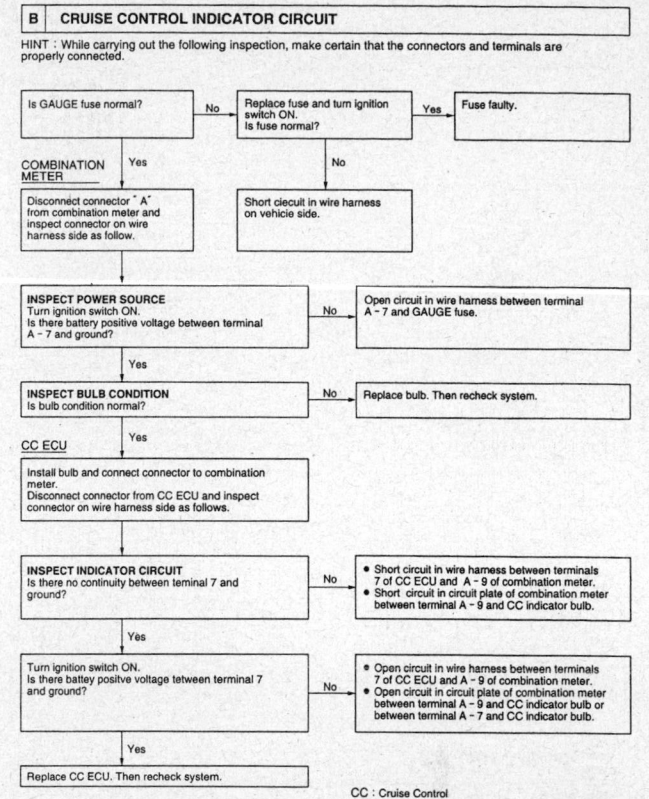

B CRUISE CONTROL INDICATOR CIRCUIT

HINT: While carrying out the following inspection, make certain that the connectors and terminals are properly connected.

CC : Cruise Control

TY1109900564000X

Fig. 203 Test B: Cruise Control Indicator Circuit. 1997 Land Cruiser

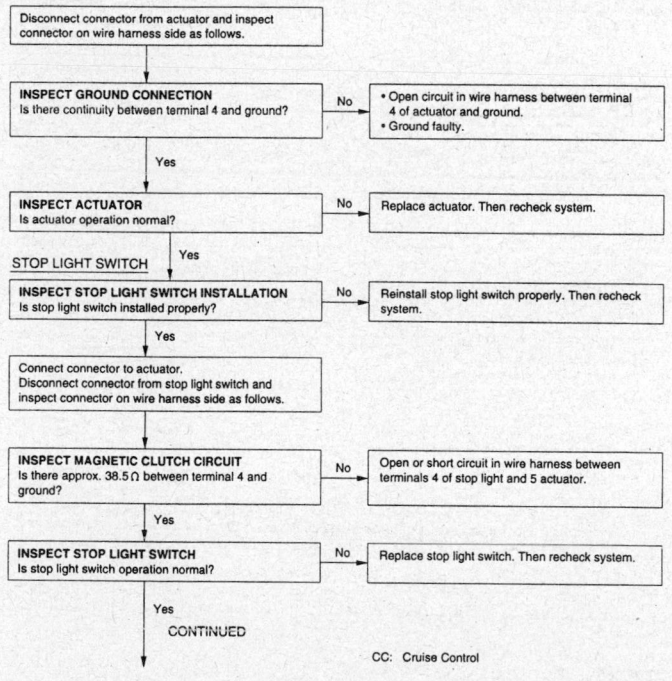

C ACTUATOR CIRCUIT

HINT: While carrying out the following inspection, make certain that the connectors and terminals are properly connected.

CC: Cruise Control

TY1109900565010X

Fig. 204 Test C: Actuator Circuit (Part 1 of 2). 1997 Land Cruiser

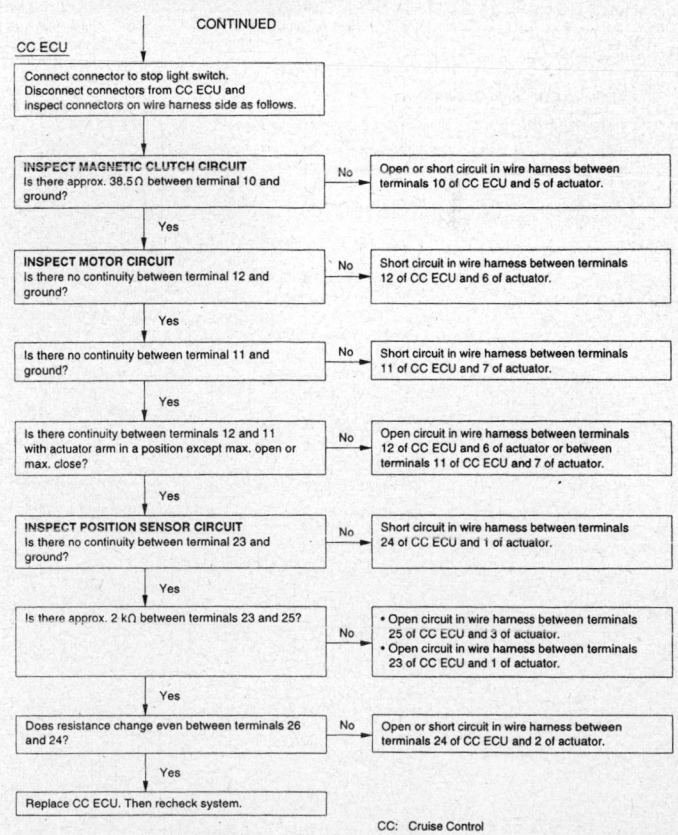

CC : Cruise Control

TY1109900565020X

Fig. 204 Test C: Actuator Circuit (Part 2 of 2). 1997 Land Cruiser

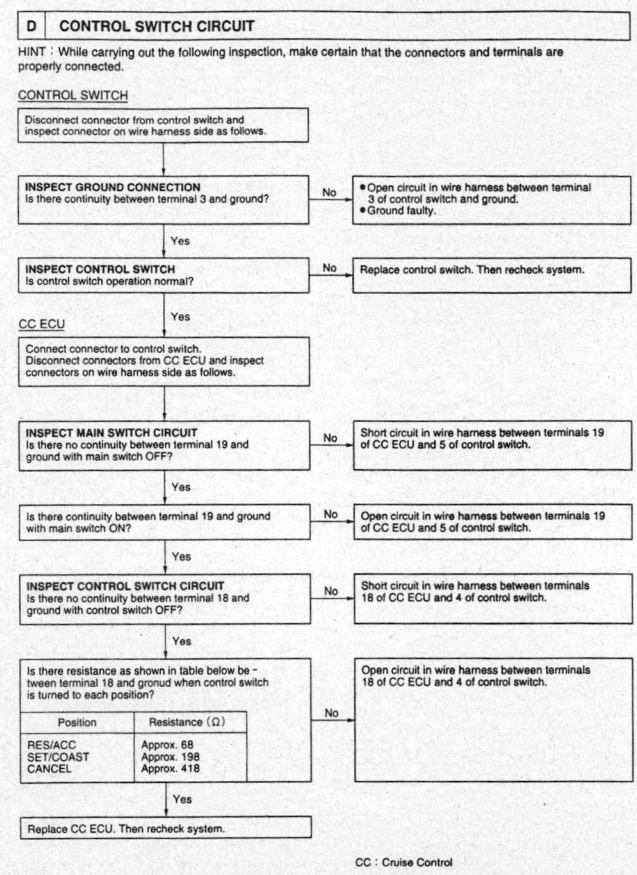

Fig. 205   Test D: Control Switch Circuit. 1997 Land Cruiser

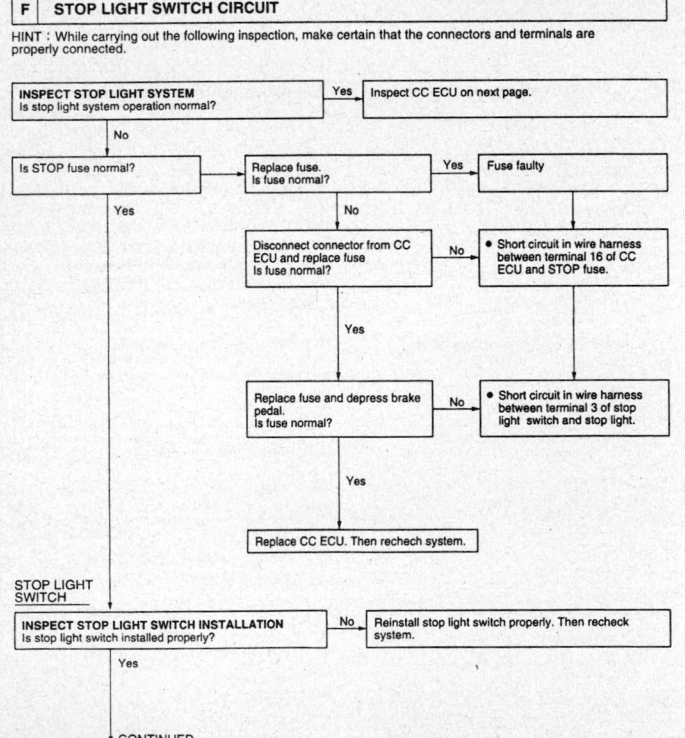

Fig. 207   Test F: Stop Lamp Switch Circuit (Part 1 of 2). 1997 Land Cruiser

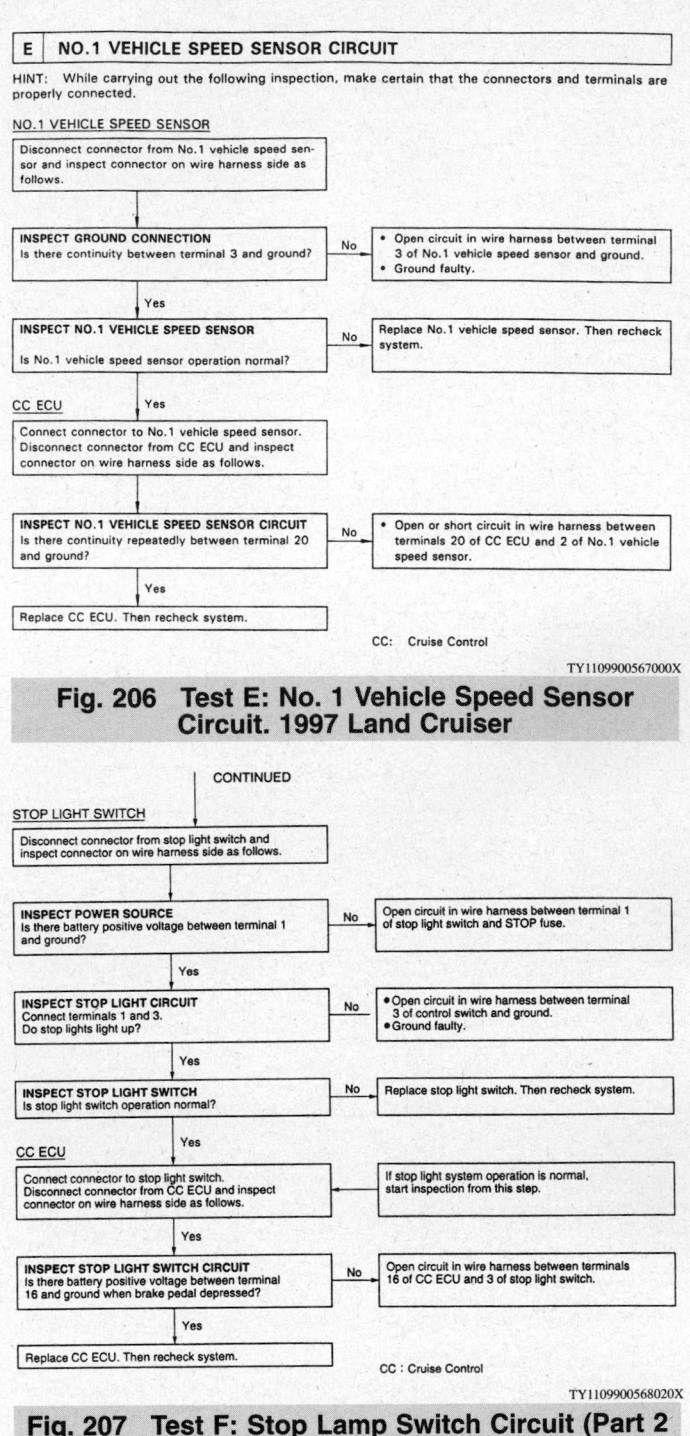

Fig. 206   Test E: No. 1 Vehicle Speed Sensor Circuit. 1997 Land Cruiser

Fig. 207   Test F: Stop Lamp Switch Circuit (Part 2 of 2). 1997 Land Cruiser

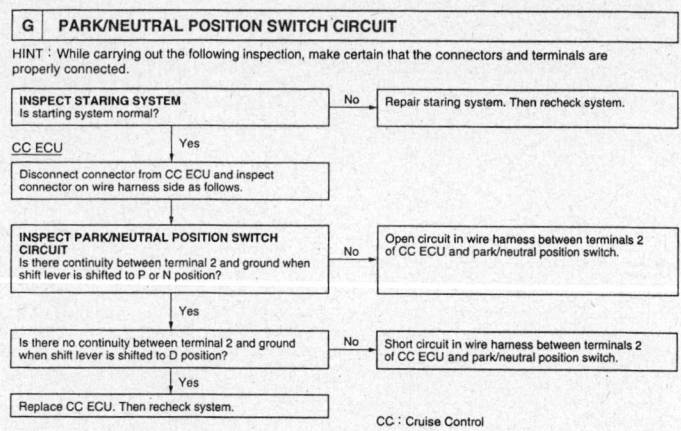

Fig. 208 Test G: Park/Neutral Position Switch Circuit. 1997 Land Cruiser

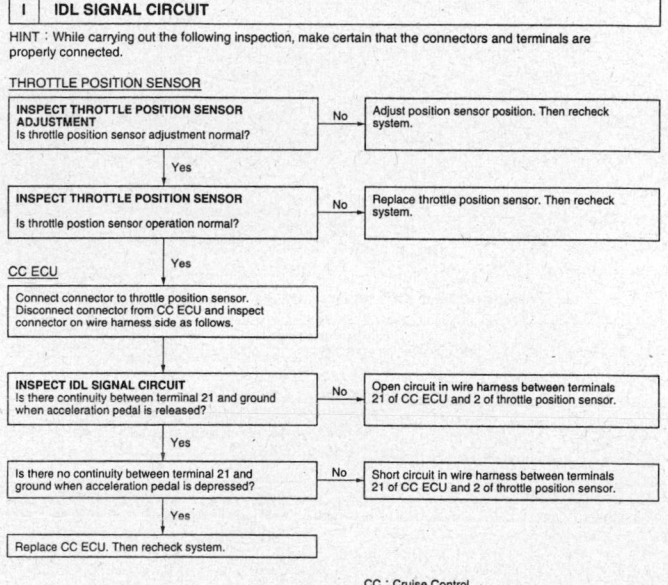

Fig. 210 Test I: IDL Signal Circuit. 1997 Land Cruiser

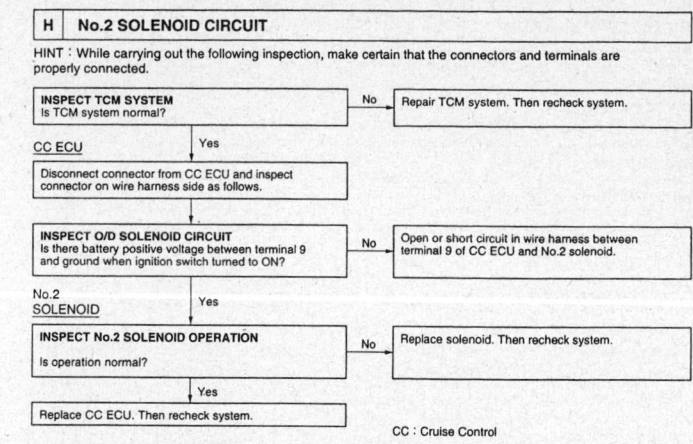

Fig. 209 Test H: No. 2 Solenoid Circuit. 1997 Land Cruiser

CIRCUIT DESCRIPTION

The No.1 vehicle speed sensor outputs a 4–pulse signal for every revolution of the rotor shaft, which is rotated by the transmission output shaft via the driven gear. After this signal is converted into a more precise rectangular waveform by the waveform shaping circuit inside the combination meter, it is then transmitted to the ECM. The ECM determines the vehicle speed based on the frequency of these pulse signals.

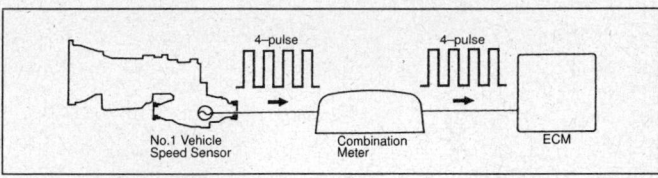

DTC No.	DTC Detecting Condition	Trouble Area
P0500	No vehicle speed sensor signal to ECM under following conditions (a) and (b): (2 trip detection logic) (a) Park/neutral position switch is OFF (b) Vehicle is being driven	• Open or short in No.1 vehicle speed sensor circuit • No.1 vehicle speed sensor • Combination meter • ECM

Fig. 211 Code P0500/21 & 23: Vehicle Speed Sensor Fault (Part 1 of 3). 1998–99 Land Cruiser

INSPECTION PROCEDURE

HINT:
Read freeze frame data using TOYOTA hand–held tester or OBD II scan tool. Because freeze frame records the engine conditions when the malfunction is detected, when troubleshooting it is useful for determining whether the vehicle was running or stopped, the engine warmed up or not, the air–fuel ratio lean or rich, etc. at the time of the malfunction.

1	Check operation of speedometer.

CHECK:
Drive the vehicle and check if the operation of the speedometer in the combination meter is normal.
HINT:
The vehicle speed is operating normally if the speedometer display is normal.

> NG ▷ Check speedometer circuit. See combination meter troubleshooting

▽ OK

Fig. 211 Code P0500/21 & 23: Vehicle Speed Sensor Fault (Part 2 of 3). 1998–99 Land Cruiser

2	Check voltage between terminal SPD of ECM connector and body ground.

PREPARATION:
(a) Remove the glove compartment door.
(b) Shift the shift lever to neutral.
(c) Jack up a rear wheel on one side.
(d) Turn the ignition switch ON.
CHECK:
Measure voltage between terminal SPD of the ECM connector and body ground when the wheel is turned slowly.
OK:
Voltage is generated intermittently.

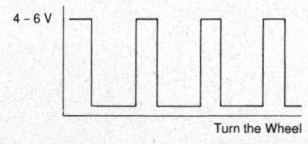

Turn the Wheel

> NG ▷ Check and repair harness and connector between combination meter and ECM.

▽ OK

Check and replace ECM

Fig. 211 Code P0500/21 & 23: Vehicle Speed Sensor Fault (Part 3 of 3). 1998–99 Land Cruiser

CIRCUIT DESCRIPTION

When the brake pedal is depressed, the stop light switch sends a signal to the ECM. When the ECM receives this signal, it cancels the cruise control.

A fail–safe function is provided so that the cancel functions normally, even if there is a malfunction in the stop light signal circuit.

The cancel condition is that battery positive voltage is supplied to terminal STP.

When the brake is on, battery positive voltage is normally applied through the STOP fuse and stop light switch to terminal STP of the ECM, and the ECM turns the cruise control OFF.

If the harness connected to terminal STP has an open circuit, terminal STP will have battery positive voltage and the cruise control will be turned OFF.

DTC No.	Detection Item	Trouble Area
52	Stop light switch circuit.	• Stop light switch • Harness or connector between ECM and stop light switch circuit • ECM

TY1109900559010X

Fig. 212   Code P1520/52: Stop Lamp Switch Circuit (Part 1 of 4). 1998–99 Land Cruiser

INSPECTION PROCEDURE

HINT:
In case of using the TOYOTA hand–held tester, start the inspection from step 1 and in case of not using the TOYOTA hand–held tester, start from step 2.

1	Check stop light switch using TOYOTA hand–held tester.

PREPARATION:
Connect the TOYOTA hand–held tester to the DLC3.
CHECK:
Check the stop light switch using DATALIST.
OK:

Condition	Stop light switch 1 (Sub CPU)	Stop light switch 2 (Sub CPU)	Stop light switch 2 (Main CPU)
Depressed	ON	ON	ON
Released	OFF	OFF	OFF

HINT:
• Stop light SW 1 has a function to disconnect the connection (OFF) when depressing the pedal, however, ECM controls by the logic rivers, so with the TOYOTA hand–held tester, it displays ON.
• Stop light SW 1 indicates the input of ST1–terminal and Stop light SW 2 indicates the input of STP terminal.

OK ⟩ Proceed to next circuit inspection shown in problem symptom table

NG

2	Check operation of stop light.

CHECK:
Check that stop light comes on when brake pedal is depressed, and turns off when brake pedal is released.

NG ⟩ Check stop light system

OK

TY1109900559020X

Fig. 212   Code P1520/52: Stop Lamp Switch Circuit (Part 2 of 4). 1998–99 Land Cruiser

3	Check voltage between terminal STP of ECM connector and body ground.

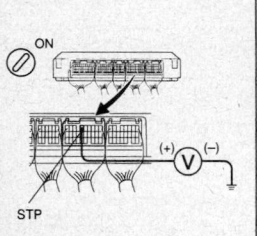

PREPARATION:
(a)   Remove the ECM with connectors still connected.
(b)   Turn ignition switch ON.
CHECK:
Measure voltage between terminal STP of ECM connector and body ground, when the brake pedal is depressed and released.
OK:

Depressed	10 – 14 V
Released	Below 1 V

OK ⟩ Proceed to next circuit inspection shown in problem symptom table

NG

TY1109900559030X

Fig. 212   Code P1520/52: Stop Lamp Switch Circuit (Part 3 of 4). 1998–99 Land Cruiser

4	Check voltage between terminal ST1– of ECM connector and body ground.

PREPARATION:
(a)   Remove the ECM with connectors still connected.
(b)   Turn ignition switch ON.
CHECK:
Measure voltage between terminal ST1– of ECM connector and body ground, when the brake pedal is depressed and released.
OK:

Depressed	Below 1 V
Released	10 – 14 V

OK ⟩ Proceed to next circuit inspection shown in problem symptoms table

NG

5	Check wire harness and connector between terminal STP of ECM and stop light switch, and terminal ST1– of ECM and stop light switch

NG ⟩ Repair or replace harness or connector.

OK

Check and replace ECM

TY1109900559040X

Fig. 212   Code P1520/52: Stop Lamp Switch Circuit (Part 4 of 4). 1998–99 Land Cruiser

CIRCUIT DESCRIPTION

This circuit carries the SET/COAST, RESUME/ACCEL and CANCEL signals (each voltage) to the ECM.

DTC No.	Detection Item	Trouble Area
P1565/32	Short in control switch circuit.	• Cruise control switch • Harness or connector between ECM and cruise control switch, cruise control switch and body ground • ECM

TY1109900560010X

Fig. 213   Code P1565/32: Control Switch Circuit (Part 1 of 3). 1998–99 Land Cruiser

INSPECTION PROCEDURE

1 | Check voltage between terminals CCS of ECM connector and body ground.

PREPARATION:
(a) Remove the ECM with connector still connected.
(b) Turn ignition switch ON.

CHECK:
Measure voltage between terminals CCS of ECM connector and body ground, when each of the SET/COAST, RESUME/ACCEL and CANCEL is turned ON.

Switch position	Resistance (V)
Neutral	10 – 16 V
RES/ACC	0.6 – 2.3 V
SET/COAST	1.9 – 4.7 V
CANCEL	3.4 – 7.2 V

NG ▷ Proceed to next circuit inspection shown in problem symptoms table

OK

2 | Check control switch continuity.

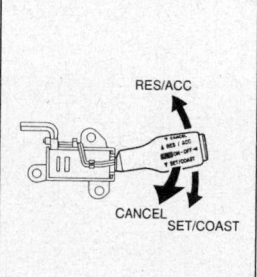

RES/ACC

CANCEL   SET/COAST

PREPARATION:
(a) Remove steering wheel center pad.
(b) Disconnect the control switch connector.

CHECK:
Measure resistance between terminals 4 and 5 of control switch connector when control switch is operated.

Switch position	Resistance (Ω)
Neutral	∞ (No continuity)
RES/ACC	60 – 70
SET/COAST	180 – 220
CANCEL	380 – 460

NG ▷ Replace control switch.

OK

TY1109900560020X

Fig. 213   Code P1565/32: Control Switch Circuit (Part 2 of 3). 1998–99 Land Cruiser

CIRCUIT DESCRIPTION

DTC No.	Detection Item	Trouble Area
P1566/ 54	• Input signal abnormal.	• ECM

INSPECTION PROCEDURE

Check and replace ECM

TY1109900561000X

Fig. 214   Code P1566/54: Input Signal Circuit. 1998–99 Land Cruiser

3 | Check harness and connector between ECM and cruise control switch, cruise control switch and body ground

NG ▷ Repair or replace harness or connector.

OK

4 | Check cruise control indicator light

NG ▷ Replace combination meter.

OK

Check and replace ECM

TY1109900560030X

Fig. 213   Code P1565/32: Control Switch Circuit (Part 3 of 3). 1998–99 Land Cruiser

CIRCUIT DESCRIPTION

When the cruise control main switch is turned off, the cruise control does not operate.

INSPECTION PROCEDURE

1 | Check voltage between terminal CMS of ECM connector and body ground.

PREPARATION:
(a) Remove the ECM with connector still connected.
(b) Turn ignition switch ON.

CHECK:
Measure voltage between terminal CMS of ECM connector when main switch is held on and off.

OK:

Main switch	Voltage
OFF	10 – 14 V
ON	Below 0.5 V

OK ▷ Proceed to next circuit inspection shown on problem symptom table

NG

TY1109900562010X

Fig. 215   Main Switch Circuit (Part 1 of 2). 1998–99 Land Cruiser

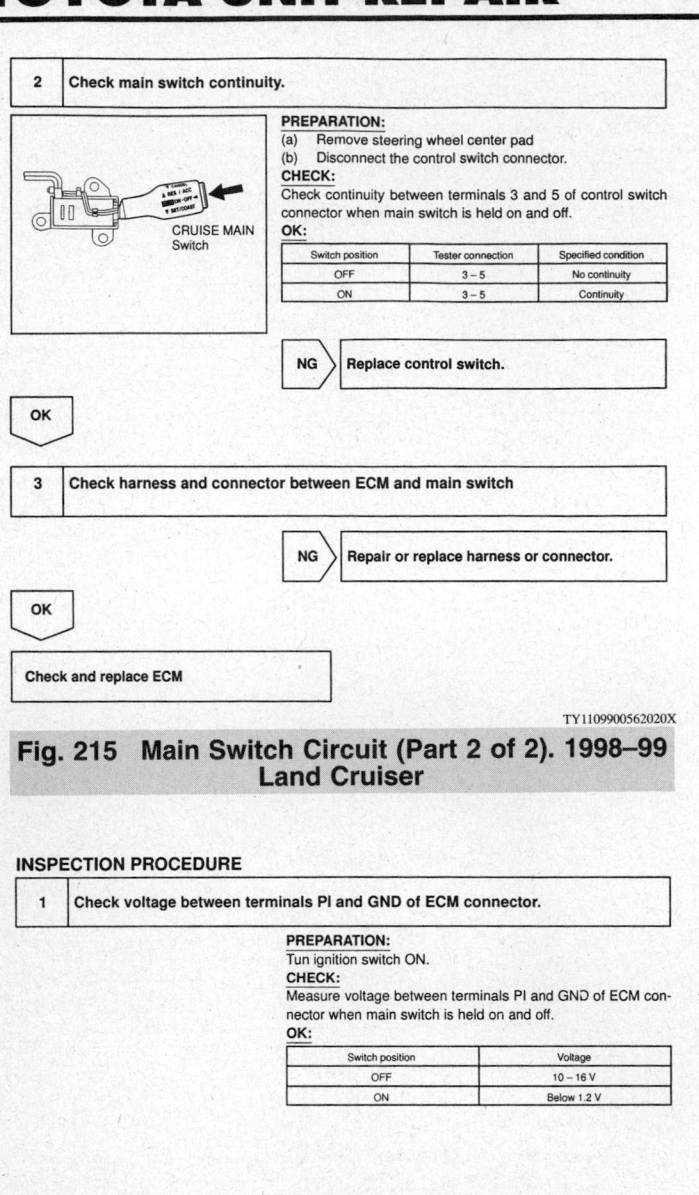

2 Check main switch continuity.

CRUISE MAIN Switch

PREPARATION:
(a) Remove steering wheel center pad
(b) Disconnect the control switch connector.
CHECK:
Check continuity between terminals 3 and 5 of control switch connector when main switch is held on and off.
OK:

Switch position	Tester connection	Specified condition
OFF	3 – 5	No continuity
ON	3 – 5	Continuity

NG ▷ Replace control switch.

OK

3 Check harness and connector between ECM and main switch

NG ▷ Repair or replace harness or connector.

OK

Check and replace ECM

TY1109900562020X

Fig. 215 Main Switch Circuit (Part 2 of 2). 1998–99 Land Cruiser

INSPECTION PROCEDURE

1 Check voltage between terminals PI and GND of ECM connector.

PREPARATION:
Turn ignition switch ON.
CHECK:
Measure voltage between terminals PI and GND of ECM connector when main switch is held on and off.
OK:

Switch position	Voltage
OFF	10 – 16 V
ON	Below 1.2 V

OK ▷ Proceed to next circuit inspection shown on problem symptom table

NG

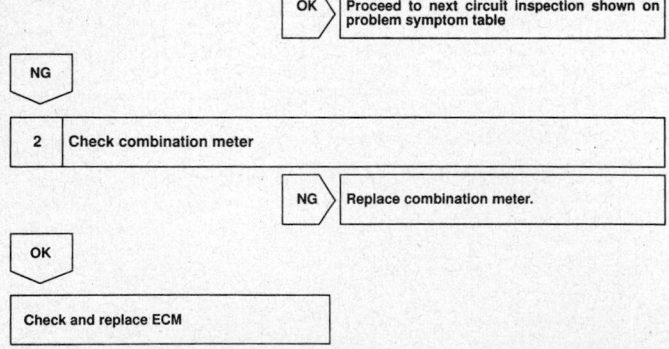

2 Check combination meter

NG ▷ Replace combination meter.

OK

Check and replace ECM

TY1109900563020X

Fig. 216 Cruise Main Indicator Lamp Circuit (Part 2 of 2). 1998–99 Land Cruiser

CIRCUIT DESCRIPTION

When the cruise control main switch is turned ON, CRUISE MAIN indicator light lights up.

TY1109900563010X

Fig. 216 Cruise Main Indicator Lamp Circuit (Part 1 of 2). 1998–99 Land Cruiser

Symptom / Suspect Area	Actuator	Vehicle Speed Sensor	Control Switch Circuit (Cruise Control Switch)	Stop Light Switch Circuit	Idle Switch Circuit (main throttle position sensor)	Electrically Controlled Transaxle Comunication Circuit	Park / Neutral Position Switch Circuit	ECU Power Source Circuit	Back-up Power Source Circuit	Main Switch Circuit (Cruise Control Switch)	Tc Terminal Circuit	Actuator Control Cable	Cruise Control ECU
SET not occurring or CANCEL occurring. (DTC is Normal)	6	2	3	4			5			1			7
SET not occurring or CANCEL occurring. DTC does not output.								1					2
Actual vehicle speed deviates above or below the set speed.	4	2			5	3						1	6
Gear shifting is frequent between 3rd and OD when driving on uphill road. (Hunting)						1							3
Cruise control not cancelled, even when clutch pedal is depressed.	2												1
Cruise control not cancelled, even when transaxle is shifted to "N" position.	3						1						2
Control switch does not operate. (SET/COAST, ACC/RES, CANCEL not possible)	3		1										2
SET possible at 40 km/h (25 mph) or less, CANCEL does not operate at 40 km/h (25 mph) or less.	3	1											2
Poor response in ACCEL and RESUME modes.	3					2						1	4
O/D does not resume, even though the road is not uphill.						1							2
DTC memory is erased.											1		2
DTC is not output, or is output when should not be.												1	2
Cruise MAIN indicator light remains ON or fails to light up.	Combination meter troubleshooting												

TY1109900225000X

Fig. 217 Problem Symptoms Table. 1996 Paseo

CIRCUIT DESCRIPTION

The actuator motor is operated by signals from the ECU. Acceleration and deceleration signals are transmitted by changes in the Duty Ratio (See note below).
Duty Ratio
The duty ratio is the ratio of the period of continuity in one cycle. For example, if A is period of continuity in one cycle, and B is the period of non-continuity, then

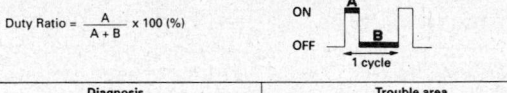

$$\text{Duty Ratio} = \frac{A}{A+B} \times 100\ (\%)$$

Code No.	Diagnosis	Trouble area
11	• Overcurrent (short) in motor circuit.	
14	• Open in actuator motor circuit.	• Cruise control actuator motor
41	• Duty ratio of 100 % output to motor acceleration side.	• Harness or connector between actuator motor and ECU
42	• Source voltage drop.	• ECU

TY1109900192010X

Fig. 218 Codes 11, 14, 41 & 42: Actuator Motor Circuit (Part 1 of 2). 1996 Paseo

1 Check actuator motor.

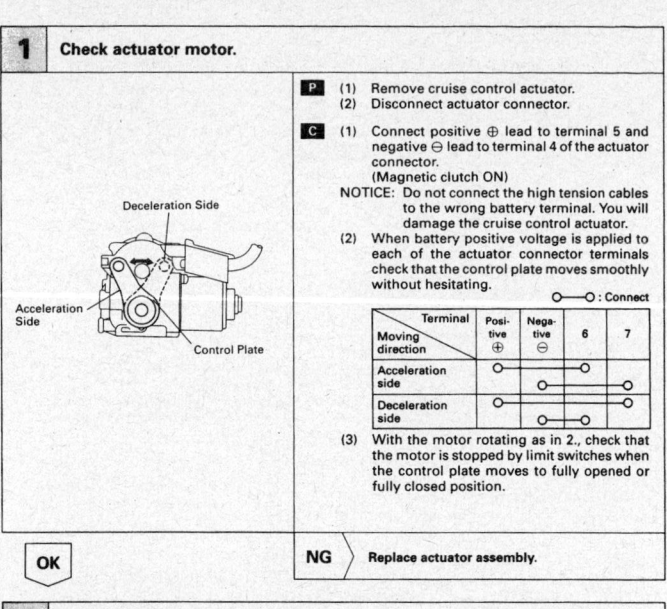

P
(1) Remove cruise control actuator.
(2) Disconnect actuator connector.

C
(1) Connect positive ⊕ lead to terminal 5 and negative ⊖ lead to terminal 4 of the actuator connector.
(Magnetic clutch ON)
NOTICE: Do not connect the high tension cables to the wrong battery terminal. You will damage the cruise control actuator.
(2) When battery positive voltage is applied to each of the actuator connector terminals check that the control plate moves smoothly without hesitating.

○—○ : Connect

Terminal / Moving direction	Positive ⊕	Negative ⊖	6	7
Acceleration side	○			○
		○		○
Deceleration side	○		○	
		○	○	

(3) With the motor rotating as in 2., check that the motor is stopped by limit switches when the control plate moves to fully opened or fully closed position.

OK | **NG** ⟩ Replace actuator assembly.

2 Check harness and connector between cruise control ECU and actuator motor

OK | **NG** ⟩ Repair or replace harness or connector.

Proceed to next circuit inspection shown on Problem Symptoms chart.
However, when DTC 11, 14, 41 is displayed, check and replace cruise control ECU.

TY1109900192020X

Fig. 218 Codes 11, 14, 41 & 42: Actuator Motor Circuit (Part 2 of 2). 1996 Paseo

INSPECTION PROCEDURE

1 Check actuator magnetic clutch.

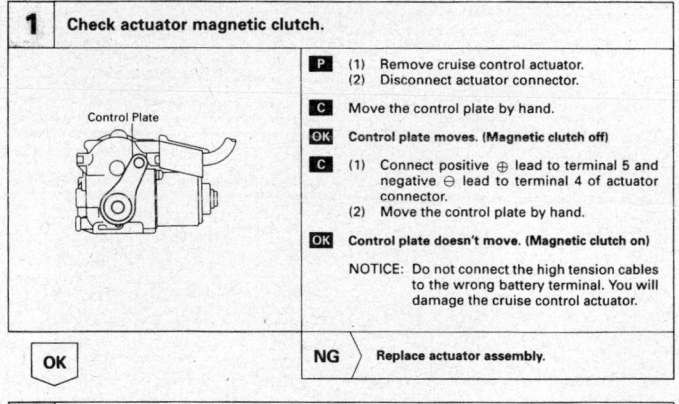

P
(1) Remove cruise control actuator.
(2) Disconnect actuator connector.

C Move the control plate by hand.

OK Control plate moves. (Magnetic clutch off)

C
(1) Connect positive ⊕ lead to terminal 5 and negative ⊖ lead to terminal 4 of actuator connector.
(2) Move the control plate by hand.

OK Control plate doesn't move. (Magnetic clutch on)

NOTICE: Do not connect the high tension cables to the wrong battery terminal. You will damage the cruise control actuator.

OK | **NG** ⟩ Replace actuator assembly.

2 Check stop light switch.

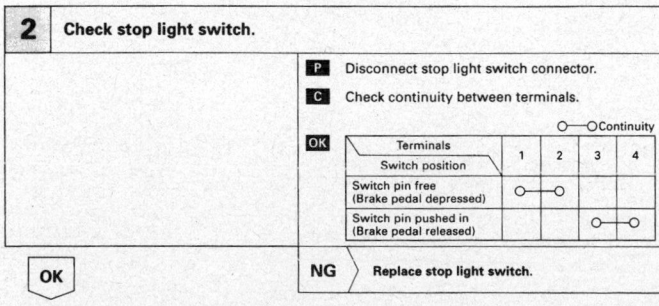

P Disconnect stop light switch connector.

C Check continuity between terminals.

○—○Continuity

OK

Terminals / Switch position	1	2	3	4
Switch pin free (Brake pedal depressed)	○	○		
Switch pin pushed in (Brake pedal released)			○	○

OK | **NG** ⟩ Replace stop light switch.

3 Check for open and short in harness and connectors between ECU and stop light switch, stop light switch and magnetic clutch, magnetic clutch and body ground

OK | **NG** ⟩ Repair or replace harness or connector.

Proceed to next circuit inspection shown on Problem Symptoms chart.
However, when DTC 12 is displayed, check harness and connector for loose connection.
If connection is normal, check and replace ECU.

TY1109900193020X

Fig. 219 Code 12: Actuator Magnetic Clutch Circuit (Part 2 of 2). 1996 Paseo

CIRCUIT DESCRIPTION

This circuit turns on the magnetic clutch inside the actuator during cruise control operation according to the signal from the ECU. If a malfunction occurs in the actuator or speed sensor, etc. during cruise control, the rotor shaft between the motor and control plate is released.

When the brake pedal is depressed, the stoplight switch turns on, supplying electrical power to the stoplight. Power supply to the magnetic clutch is mechanically cut and the magnetic clutch is turned OFF.

When driving downhill, if the vehicle speed exceeds the set speed by 15 km/h (9 mph), the ECU turns the magnetic clutch OFF. If the vehicle speed later drops to within 10 km/h (6 mph) above the set speed, then cruise control at the set speed is resumed.

DTC No.	Diagnosis	Trouble Area
12	• Overcurrent (short) in magnetic clutch circuit. • Open (0.8 sec) in magnetic clutch circuit.	• Cruise control magnetic clutch. • Harness or connector between ECU and magnetic clutch, magnetic clutch and body ground. • STOP fuse open. • ECU.

TY1109900193010X

Fig. 219 Code 12: Actuator Magnetic Clutch Circuit (Part 1 of 2). 1996 Paseo

CIRCUIT DESCRIPTION

This circuit detects the ratation position of the actuator control plate and sends signal to the ECU.

Code No.	Diagnosis	Trouble area
13	• Position sensor detects abnormal voltage.	• Cruise control actuator motor. • Cruise control actuator position sensor. • Harness or connector between actuator position sensor and body ground. • harness or connector between actuator motor and ECU. • ECU
14	• Open in actuator motor circuit. • Position sensor signal value does not change when the motor operates.	
42	• Source voltage drop.	

TY1109900194010X

Fig. 220 Code 13, 14 & 42: Actuator Position Sensor Circuit (Part 1 of 2). 1996 Paseo

INSPECTION PROCEDURE

1 Check voltage between terminals VR2 and VR3 of ECU connector.

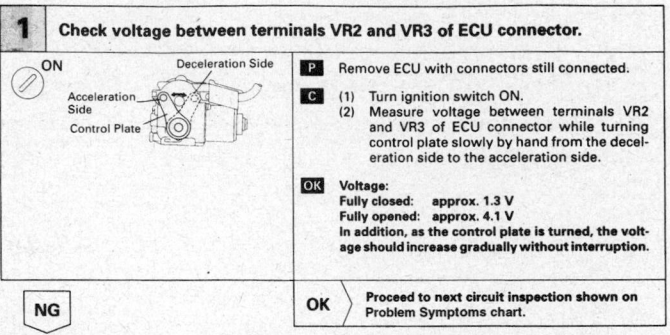

P Remove ECU with connectors still connected.

C (1) Turn ignition switch ON.
(2) Measure voltage between terminals VR2 and VR3 of ECU connector while turning control plate slowly by hand from the deceleration side to the acceleration side.

OK Voltage:
Fully closed: approx. 1.3 V
Fully opened: approx. 4.1 V
In addition, as the control plate is turned, the voltage should increase gradually without interruption.

NG / **OK** Proceed to next circuit inspection shown on Problem Symptoms chart.

2 Check actuator position sensor.

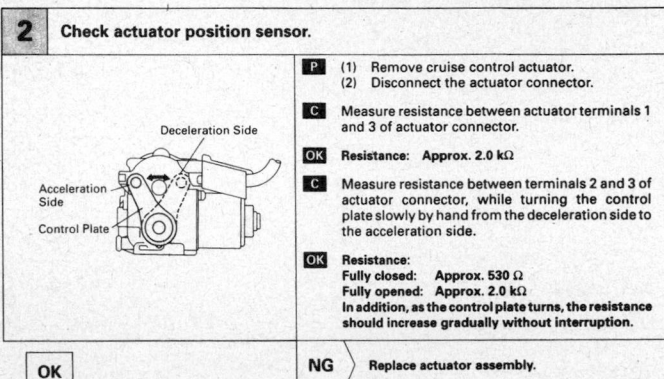

P (1) Remove cruise control actuator.
(2) Disconnect the actuator connector.

C Measure resistance between actuator terminals 1 and 3 of actuator connector.

OK Resistance: Approx. 2.0 kΩ

C Measure resistance between terminals 2 and 3 of actuator connector, while turning the control plate slowly by hand from the deceleration side to the acceleration side.

OK Resistance:
Fully closed: Approx. 530 Ω
Fully opened: Approx. 2.0 kΩ
In addition, as the control plate turns, the resistance should increase gradually without interruption.

OK / **NG** Replace actuator assembly.

3 Check for open short in harness and connector between ECU and actuator position sensor

OK / **NG** Repair or replace harness or connector.

Check harness and connector for loose connection.
If connection is normal check and replace ECU.

TY1109900194020X

Fig. 220   Code 13, 14 & 42: Actuator Position Sensor Circuit (Part 2 of 2). 1996 Paseo

INSPECTION PROCEDURE

1 Input signal check.

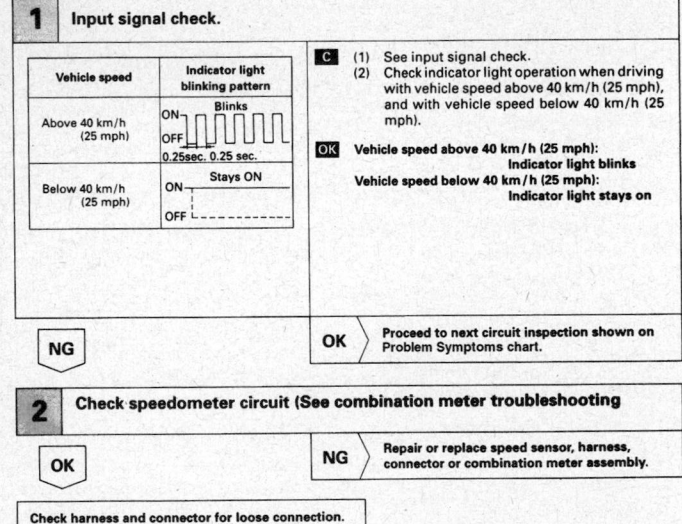

C (1) See input signal check.
(2) Check indicator light operation when driving with vehicle speed above 40 km/h (25 mph), and with vehicle speed below 40 km/h (25 mph).

OK Vehicle speed above 40 km/h (25 mph):
Indicator light blinks
Vehicle speed below 40 km/h (25 mph):
Indicator light stays on

NG / **OK** Proceed to next circuit inspection shown on Problem Symptoms chart.

2 Check speedometer circuit (See combination meter troubleshooting

OK / **NG** Repair or replace speed sensor, harness, connector or combination meter assembly.

Check harness and connector for loose connection.
If connection is normal, check and replace ECU.

TY1109900195020X

Fig. 221   Codes 21 & 23: Vehicle Speed Sensor Circuit (Part 2 of 2). 1996 Paseo

CIRCUIT DESCRIPTION

The vehicle speed sensor signal is sent to cruise control ECU as vehicle speed signal.

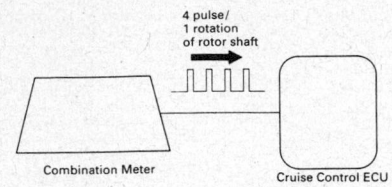

Code No.	Diagnosis	Trouble Area
21	Speed signal is not input to the ECU while cruise control is set.	• Vehicle speed sensor • Combination meter • Harness or connector between speed sensor and combination meter, combination meter and ECU. • ECU
23	Vehicle speed sensor pulse is abnormal.	• Vehicle speed sensor • Harness or connector in OD and SPD circuit (Open or short intermittently) • ECU

TY1109900195010X

Fig. 221   Codes 21 & 23: Vehicle Speed Sensor Circuit (Part 1 of 2). 1996 Paseo

CIRCUIT DESCRIPTION

This circuit carries the SET/COAST, RESUME/ACCEL and CANCEL signals (each voltage) to the ECU.

Code No.	Diagnosis	Trouble Area
32	Short in, control switch circuit.	• Cruise control switch. • Harness or connector between control switch and ECU. • ECU

INSPECTION PROCEDURE

1 Input signal check.

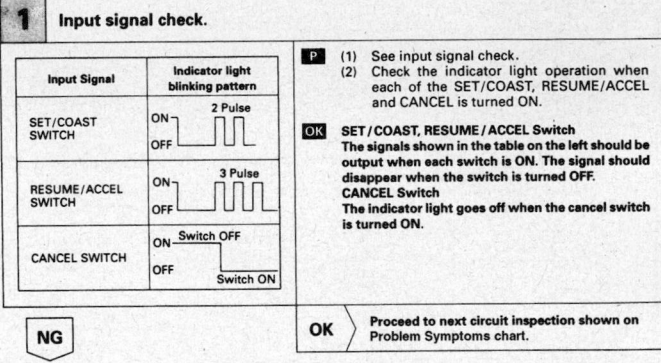

P (1) See input signal check.
(2) Check the indicator light operation when each of the SET/COAST, RESUME/ACCEL and CANCEL is turned ON.

OK SET / COAST, RESUME / ACCEL Switch
The signals shown in the table on the left should be output when each switch is ON. The signal should disappear when the switch is turned OFF.
CANCEL Switch
The indicator light goes off when the cancel switch is turned ON.

NG / **OK** Proceed to next circuit inspection shown on Problem Symptoms chart.

TY1109900196010X

Fig. 222   Code 32: Control Switch Circuit (Part 1 of 2). 1996 Paseo

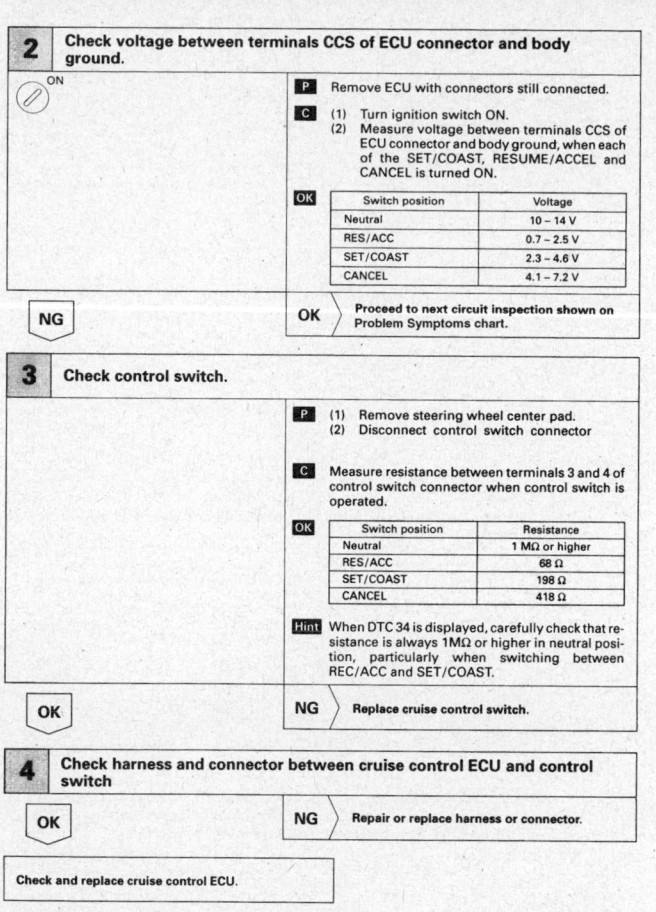

2 Check voltage between terminals CCS of ECU connector and body ground.

| P | Remove ECU with connectors still connected. |

| C | (1) Turn ignition switch ON.
(2) Measure voltage between terminals CCS of ECU connector and body ground, when each of the SET/COAST, RESUME/ACCEL and CANCEL is turned ON. |

| OK |

Switch position	Voltage
Neutral	10 – 14 V
RES/ACC	0.7 – 2.5 V
SET/COAST	2.3 – 4.6 V
CANCEL	4.1 – 7.2 V

NG |

OK > Proceed to next circuit inspection shown on Problem Symptoms chart.

3 Check control switch.

| P | (1) Remove steering wheel center pad.
(2) Disconnect control switch connector |

| C | Measure resistance between terminals 3 and 4 of control switch connector when control switch is operated. |

| OK |

Switch position	Resistance
Neutral	1 MΩ or higher
RES/ACC	68 Ω
SET/COAST	198 Ω
CANCEL	418 Ω

| Hint | When DTC 34 is displayed, carefully check that resistance is always 1MΩ or higher in neutral position, particularly when switching between REC/ACC and SET/COAST. |

OK |

NG > Replace cruise control switch.

4 Check harness and connector between cruise control ECU and control switch

OK |

NG > Repair or replace harness or connector.

Check and replace cruise control ECU.

TY1109900196020X

Fig. 222   Code 32: Control Switch Circuit (Part 2 of 2). 1996 Paseo

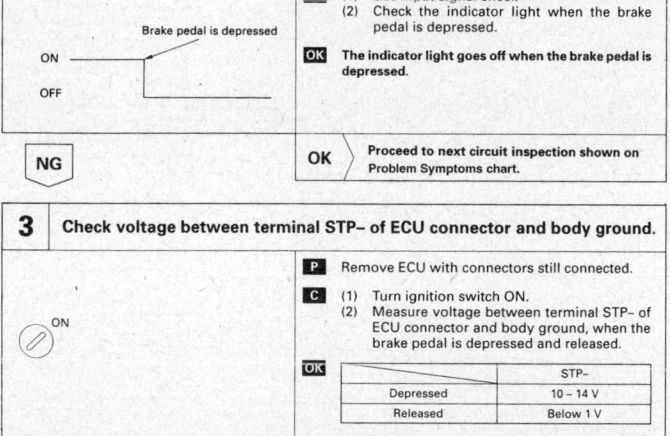

2 Input signal check.

| C | (1) See input signal check
(2) Check the indicator light when the brake pedal is depressed. |

| OK | The indicator light goes off when the brake pedal is depressed. |

NG |

OK > Proceed to next circuit inspection shown on Problem Symptoms chart.

3 Check voltage between terminal STP– of ECU connector and body ground.

| P | Remove ECU with connectors still connected. |

| C | (1) Turn ignition switch ON.
(2) Measure voltage between terminal STP– of ECU connector and body ground, when the brake pedal is depressed and released. |

| OK |

	STP–
Depressed	10 – 14 V
Released	Below 1 V

NG |

OK > Proceed to next circuit inspection shown on Problem Symptoms chart.

4 Check for open in harness and connectors between terminal STP– of ECU and stop light switch

OK |

NG > Repair or replace harness or connector.

Check and replace ECU.

TY1109900197020X

Fig. 223   Stop Light Switch Circuit (Part 2 of 2). 1996 Paseo

CIRCUIT DESCRIPTION

When the brake is on, battery positive voltage normally applies through the stop fuse and stop switch to terminal STP– of the ECU, and the ECU turns the cruise control off.

A fail-safe function is provided so that cancel functions normally, even if there is a malfunction in the stop light signal circuit.

If the harness connected to terminal STP– has an open, terminal STP– will have battery positive voltage and the cruise control will be turned off, also SET not occurring.

Also, when the brake is on, the magnetic clutch is cut mechanically by the stop light switch, turning the cruise control off.

INSPECTION PROCEDURE

1 Check operation of stop light.

| C | Check that stop light comes on when brake pedal is depressed, and turns off when brake pedal is released. |

OK |

NG > Check stop light circuit.

TY1109900197010X

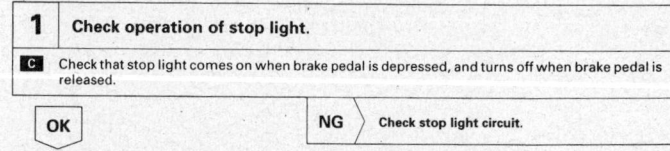

Fig. 223   Stop Light Switch Circuit (Part 1 of 2). 1996 Paseo

CIRCUIT DESCRIPTION

When the idle switch is turned ON, a signal is sent to the ECU. The ECU uses this signal to correct the discrepancy between the throttle valve position and the actuator position sensor value to enable accurate cruise control at the set speed. If the idle switch is malfunctioning, problem symptoms also occur in the engine, so also inspect the engine.

INSPECTION PROCEDURE

1 Check voltage between terminal IDL of ECU connector and body ground.

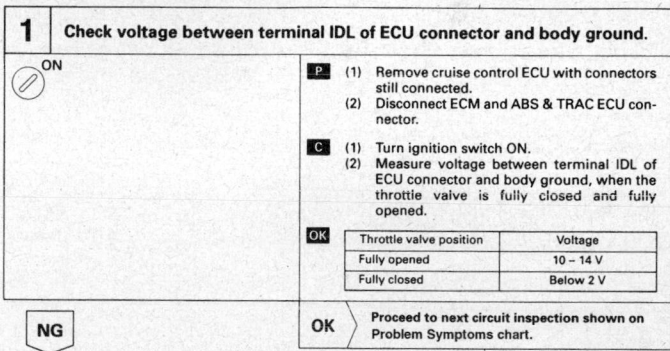

| P | (1) Remove cruise control ECU with connectors still connected.
(2) Disconnect ECM and ABS & TRAC ECU connector. |

| C | (1) Turn ignition switch ON.
(2) Measure voltage between terminal IDL of ECU connector and body ground, when the throttle valve is fully closed and fully opened. |

| OK |

Throttle valve position	Voltage
Fully opened	10 – 14 V
Fully closed	Below 2 V

NG |

OK > Proceed to next circuit inspection shown on Problem Symptoms chart.

TY1109900198010X

Fig. 224   Idle Switch Circuit (Part 1 of 2). 1996 Paseo

2 Check throttle position sensor.

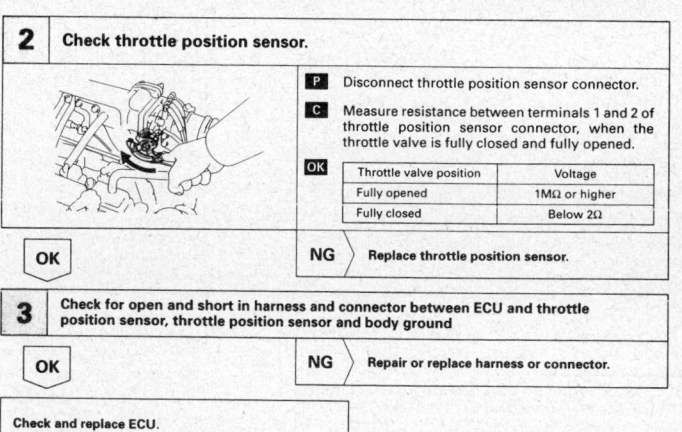

| P | Disconnect throttle position sensor connector. |

| C | Measure resistance between terminals 1 and 2 of throttle position sensor connector, when the throttle valve is fully closed and fully opened. |

| OK |

Throttle valve position	Voltage
Fully opened	1MΩ or higher
Fully closed	Below 2Ω

OK |

NG > Replace throttle position sensor.

3 Check for open and short in harness and connector between ECU and throttle position sensor, throttle position sensor and body ground

OK |

NG > Repair or replace harness or connector.

Check and replace ECU.

TY1109900198020X

Fig. 224   Idle Switch Circuit (Part 2 of 2). 1996 Paseo

TOYOTA UNIT REPAIR

CIRCUIT DESCRIPTION

When driving uphill under cruise control, in order to reduce shifting due to ON-OFF overdrive operation and to provide smooth driving, when down shifting in the electronic controlled transaxle occurs, a signal to prevent upshift until the end of the uphill slope is sent from the cruise control ECU to the electronic controlled transaxle.

Terminal ECT of the cruise control ECU detects the shift change signal (output to electronic controlled transaxle No.2 solenoid) from the electronically controlled transaxle.

If vehicle speed down, also when terminal electronically controlled transaxle of the cruise control ECU receives down shifting signal, it sends a signal from terminal OD to OD1 to cut overdrive until the end of the uphill slope, and the gear shifts are reduced and gear shift points in the electronically controlled transaxle are changed.

TY1109900199010X

Fig. 225 Electronically Controlled Transaxle Communication Circuit (Part 1 of 3). 1996 Paseo

---

5 | Check for open and short in harness and connector between terminal OD of ECU and terminal OD1 of ECM

| OK | | NG | Repair or replace harness or connector. |

Check and replace ECM.

TY1109900199030X

Fig. 225 Electronically Controlled Transaxle Communication Circuit (Part 3 of 3). 1996 Paseo

---

INSPECTION PROCEDURE

1 | Check operation of overdrive.

P Test drive after engine warm up.

C Check that overdrive ON ↔ OFF occurs with operation of O/D switch ON-OFF.

| OK | | NG | Check and Repair Electronically controlled transmission |

2 | Check voltage between terminal OD of harness side connector of ECU and body ground.

ON

P Remove ECU with connector still connected.

C
(1) Disconnect ECU connector.
(2) Turn ignition switch ON.
(3) Measure voltage between terminal OD of harness side connector of ECU and body ground.

OK Voltage: 10 – 14 V

| OK | | NG | Go to step **5** . |

3 | Check voltage between terminal ECT of cruise control ECU connector and body ground (On test drive).

P
(1) Connect ECU connector.
(2) Test drive after engine warm up.

C Check voltage between terminal ECT of cruise control ECU connector and body ground when OD switch is on and off.

OK

Gear Position	Voltage
O/D	Below 1 V
3rd	10 – 14 V

| NG | | OK | Proceed to next circuit inspection shown on Problem Symptoms chart. |

4 | Check for open and short in harness and connector between terminal ECT of cruise control ECU and electronically controlled transmission solenoid

| OK | | NG | Repair or replace harness or connector. |

Check and repair ECU.

TY1109900199020X

Fig. 225 Electronically Controlled Transaxle Communication Circuit (Part 2 of 3). 1996 Paseo

CIRCUIT DESCRIPTION

When the shift position is put in except D position, a signal is sent from the park/neutral position switch to the ECU. When this signal is input during cruise control driving, the ECU cancels the cruise control.

TY1109900200010X

Fig. 226 Park/Neutral Position Switch Circuit (Part 1 of 2). 1996 Paseo

INSPECTION PROCEDURE

1 | **Check operation of starter.**

C Check that the starter operates normally and that the engine starts.

OK ↓ | NG > Proceed to engine troubleshooting

2 | **Input signal Check.**

P (1) See input signal check on page BE-193.
(2) Check the indicator light when shifting into except D position.

Shifting into except D position

ON —
OFF —

OK The indicator light goes off when shifting into except D position.

NG ↓ | OK > Proceed to next circuit inspection shown on Problem Symptoms chart.

3 | **Check voltage between terminal D of ECU connector and body ground.**

ON

P Remove ECU with connectors still connected.
C (1) Turn ignition switch ON.
(2) Measure voltage between terminal D of ECU connector and body ground, when shifting into D position and other positions.

OK

Shift Position	Voltage
D position	10 – 14 V
Other positions	Below 1 V

NG ↓ | OK > Proceed to next circuit inspection shown on Problem Symptoms chart.

4 | **Check for open in harness and connector between ECU and GAUGE fuse**

OK ↓ | NG > Repair or replace harness or connector.

Check and replace ECU.

TY1109900200020X

Fig. 226   Park/Neutral Position Switch Circuit (Part 2 of 2). 1996 Paseo

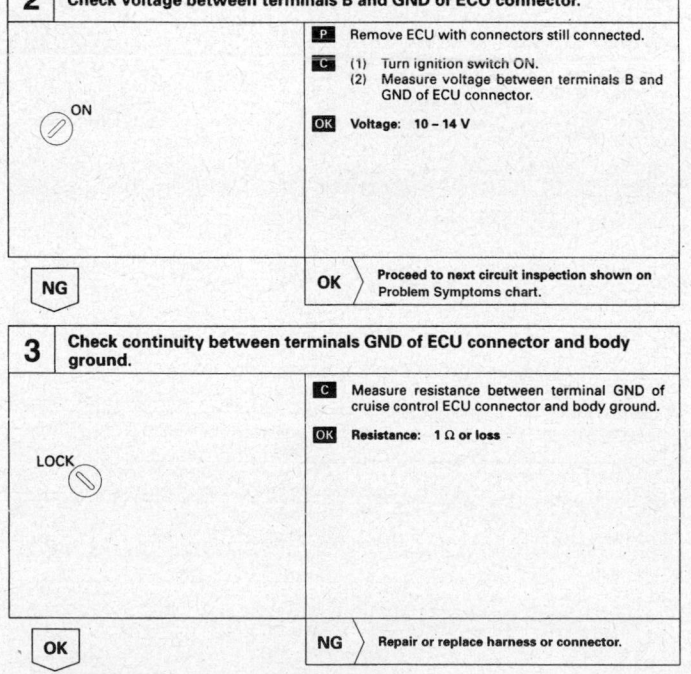

2 | **Check voltage between terminals B and GND of ECU connector.**

ON

P Remove ECU with connectors still connected.
C (1) Turn ignition switch ON.
(2) Measure voltage between terminals B and GND of ECU connector.

OK Voltage: 10 – 14 V

NG ↓ | OK > Proceed to next circuit inspection shown on Problem Symptoms chart.

3 | **Check continuity between terminals GND of ECU connector and body ground.**

LOCK

C Measure resistance between terminal GND of cruise control ECU connector and body ground.
OK Resistance: 1 Ω or loss

OK ↓ | NG > Repair or replace harness or connector.

Check and repair harness and connector between battery and ECU.

TY1109900201020X

Fig. 227   ECU Power Source Circuit (Part 2 of 2). 1996 Paseo

CIRCUIT DESCRIPTION

The ECU power source supplies power to the actuator and sensors, etc., when the terminal GND and the cruise control ECU case are grounded.

INSPECTION PROCEDURE

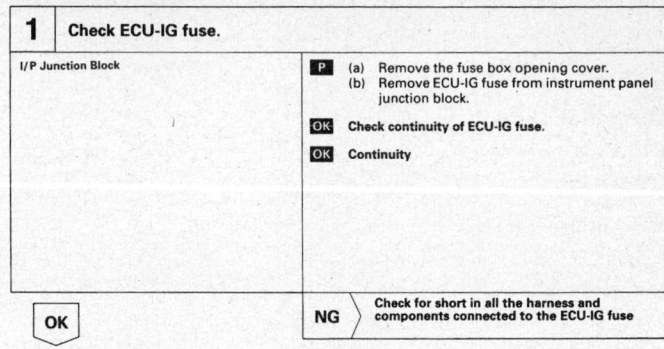

1 | **Check ECU-IG fuse.**

I/P Junction Block

P (a) Remove the fuse box opening cover.
(b) Remove ECU-IG fuse from instrument panel junction block.
OK Check continuity of ECU-IG fuse
OK Continuity

OK ↓ | NG > Check for short in all the harness and components connected to the ECU-IG fuse

TY1109900201010X

Fig. 227   ECU Power Source Circuit (Part 1 of 2). 1996 Paseo

CIRCUIT DESCRIPTION

The ECU back-up power source provides power even when the ignition switch is off and is used for DTC memory, etc.

INSPECTION PROCEDURE

1 | **Check ECU-B fuse.**

● Engine Room Junction Block

P Remove DOME fuse from engine room junction block.
C Check continuity of DOME fuse.
OK Continuity.

OK ↓ | NG > Check for short in all the harness and components connected to the DOME fuse

TY1109900202010X

Fig. 228   Back Up Power Source Circuit (Part 1 of 2). 1996 Paseo

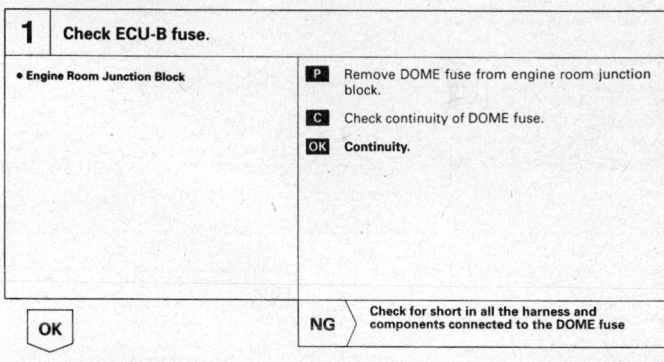

2 | **Check voltage between terminal BATT of ECU connector and body ground.**

LOCK

P Remove ECU with connectors still connected.
C Measure voltage between terminal BATT of ECU connector and body ground.
OK Voltage: 10 – 14 V

NG ↓ | OK > Proceed to next circuit inspection shown on Problem Symptoms chart.

Check and repair harness and connector between battery and ECU.

TY1109900202020X

Fig. 228   Back Up Power Source Circuit (Part 2 of 2). 1996 Paseo

CIRCUIT DESCRIPTION

When the cruise control main switch is turned off, the cruise control does not operate.

TY1109900203010X

Fig. 229   Cruise Control Switch Circuit (Part 1 of 2). 1996 Paseo

CIRCUIT DESCRIPTION

This circuit sends a signal to the ECU that diagnostic code output is required.

INSPECTION PROCEDURE

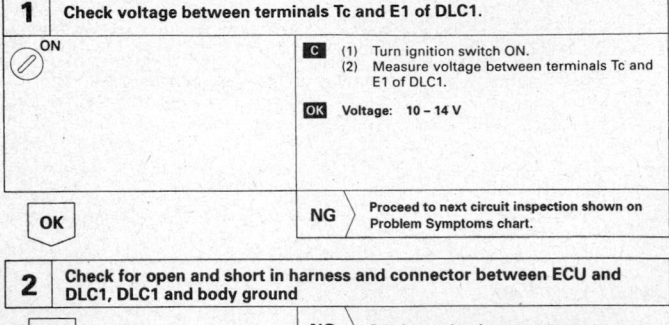

1	Check voltage between terminals Tc and E1 of DLC1.

	C (1) Turn ignition switch ON. (2) Measure voltage between terminals Tc and E1 of DLC1. OK Voltage: 10 – 14 V

OK		NG	Proceed to next circuit inspection shown on Problem Symptoms chart.

2	Check for open and short in harness and connector between ECU and DLC1, DLC1 and body ground

OK		NG	Repair or replace harness or connector.

Check and replace ECU.

TY1109900204000X

Fig. 230   T$_C$ Circuit. 1996 Paseo

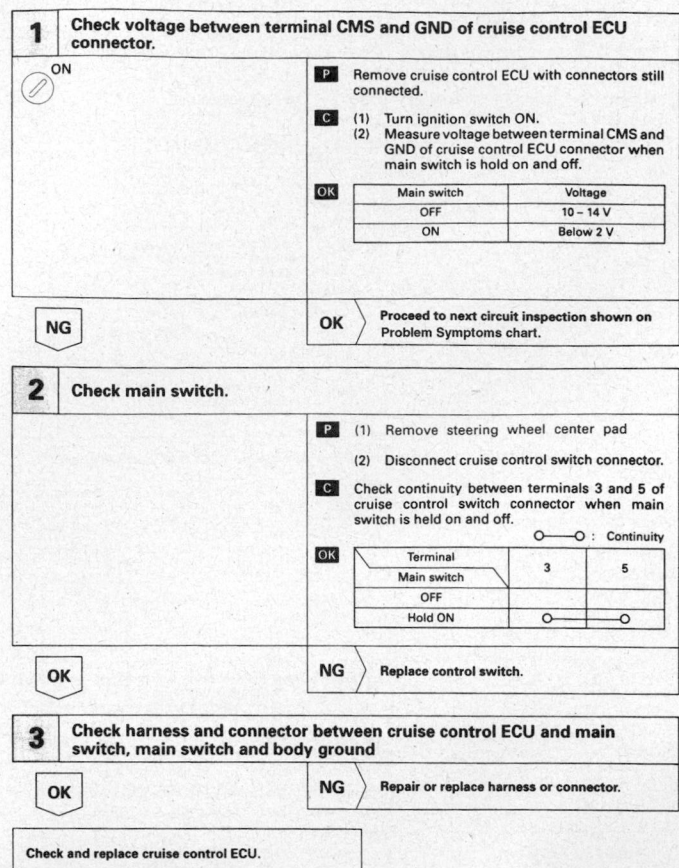

1	Check voltage between terminal CMS and GND of cruise control ECU connector.

	P Remove cruise control ECU with connectors still connected. C (1) Turn ignition switch ON. (2) Measure voltage between terminal CMS and GND of cruise control ECU connector when main switch is hold on and off.

OK	Main switch	Voltage
	OFF	10 – 14 V
	ON	Below 2 V

NG		OK	Proceed to next circuit inspection shown on Problem Symptoms chart.

2	Check main switch.

	P (1) Remove steering wheel center pad (2) Disconnect cruise control switch connector. C Check continuity between terminals 3 and 5 of cruise control switch connector when main switch is held on and off. OK ○——○ : Continuity

OK	Terminal Main switch	3	5
	OFF		
	Hold ON	○	○

OK		NG	Replace control switch.

3	Check harness and connector between cruise control ECU and main switch, main switch and body ground

OK		NG	Repair or replace harness or connector.

Check and replace cruise control ECU.

TY1109900203020X

Fig. 229   Cruise Control Switch Circuit (Part 2 of 2). 1996 Paseo

Actuator Control Cable Inspection

C (1) Check that the actuator, control cable and throttle link are properly installed and that the cable and link are connected correctly.
(2) Check that the actuator and bell crank are operating smoothly.
(3) Check that the cable is not loose or too tight.

Hint (1) If the control cable is very loose, the vehicle's loss of speed going uphill will be large.
(2) If the control cable is too tight, the idle RPM will become high.

TY1109900205000X

Fig. 231   Actuator Control Cable Inspection. 1996 Paseo

Symptom	Suspect Area

SET not occuring or CANCEL occurring.
(DTC is Normal)
	1. Main Switch Circuit.
	   (Cruise Control Switch)
	2. Vehicle Speed Signal Abnormal.
	3. Control Switch Circuit.
	   (Cruise Control Switch)
	4. Stop Light Switch Circuit.
	5. Park/Neutral Position Switch Circuit.
	6. Actuator Motor Circuit.
	7. Cruise Control ECU.

SET not occuring or CANCEL occuring. (DTC does not output)	1. ECU Power Source Circuit. 2. Cruise Control ECU.
Actual vehicle speed deviates above or below the set speed.	1. Vehicle Speed Signal Abnormal. 2. Electronically Controlled Transmission Communication Circuit. 3. Actuator Motor Circuit. 4. Idle Signal Circuit. (Main Throttle Position Sensor) 5. Cruise Control ECU.
Gear shifting frequent between 3rd O/D when driving on uphill road. (Hurting)	1. Electronically Controlled Transmission Communication Circuit. 2. Cruise Control ECU.
Cruise control not cancelled, even brake pedal is depressed.	1. Stop Light Switch Circuit. 2. Actuator Motor Circuit. 3. Cruise Control ECU.
Cruise control not cancelled, even when transmission is shifted to "N" position.	1. Park/Neutral Position Switch Circuit. 2. Actuator Motor Circuit. 3. Cruise Control ECU.
Cruise control not cancelled, even when clutch pedal is depressed.	1. Clutch Switch Circuit. 2. Actuator Motor Circuit. 3. Cruise Control ECU.
Control switch does not operate. (SET/COAST, ACC/RES, CANCEL not possible)	1. Control Switch Circuit. (Cruise Control Switch) 2. Actuator Motor Circuit. 3. Cruise Control ECU.
SET possible at 40 km/h (25 mph) or less, or CANCEL does not operate at 40 km/h (25 mph) or less.	1. Vehicle Speed Signal Abnormal. 2. Actuator Motor Circuit. 3. Cruise Control ECU.

TY1109900226010X

Fig. 232   Problem Symptoms Table (Part 1 of 2). 1997 Paseo

Symptom	Suspect Area
Poor response is ACCEL and RESUME modes.	1. Electronically Controlled Transmission Communication Circuit. 2. Actuator Motor Circuit 3. Cruise Control ECU.
O/D does not RESUME, even though the road is not uphill.	1. Electronically Controlled Transmission Communication Circuit. 2. Cruise Control ECU.
DTC memory is erased.	1. Back-up Power Source Circuit. 2. Cruise Control ECU.
DTC is not output, or is output when it should not be.	1. Diagnosis Circuit. 2. Cruise Control ECU.
Cruise MAIN indicator light remains ON or fall to light up.	1. Cruise MAIN Indicator Light Switch Circuit.

TY1109900226020X

Fig. 232   Problem Symptoms Table (Part 2 of 2). 1997 Paseo

CIRCUIT DESCRIPTION

The actuator motor is operated by signals from the ECU. Acceleration and deceleration signals are transmitted by changes in the Duty Ratio

Duty Ratio

The duty ratio is the ratio of the period of continuity in one cycle. For example, if A is the period of continuity in one cycle, and B is the period of non-continuity, then:

$$\text{Duty Ratio} = \frac{A}{A+B} \times 100 \ (\%)$$

DTC No.	Diagnosis	Trouble Area
11	Short in actuator motor circuit	• Cruise control actuator • Harness or connector between actuator and cruise control ECU • Cruise control ECU
15	Open in actuator motor circuit	• Cruise control actuator

TY1109900208010X

Fig. 233   Codes 11 & 15: Actuator Motor Circuit (Part 1 of 2). 1997 Paseo

CIRCUIT DESCRIPTION

This circuit turns on the magnetic clutch inside the actuator during cruise control operation according to the signal from the ECU. If a malfunction occurs in the actuator or speed sensor, etc. during cruise control, the rotor shaft between the motor and control plate is released.

When the brake pedal is depressed, the stop light switch turns on, supplying electrical power to the stop light. Power supply to the magnetic clutch is mechanically cut and the magnetic clutch is turned OFF.

When driving downhill, if the vehicle speed exceeds the set speed by 15 km/h (9 mph), the ECU turns the magnetic clutch OFF. If the vehicle speed later drops to within 10 km/h (6 mph) above the set speed, then cruise control at the set speed is resumed.

DTC No.	Diagnosis	Trouble Area
12	• Short in magnetic clutch circuit. • Open (0.8 sec.) in magnetic clutch circuit.	• Cruise control actuator magnetic clutch • Harness or connector between ECU and magnetic clutch, magnetic clutch and body ground • Cruise control ECU

TY1109900209010X

Fig. 234   Code 12: Actuator Magnetic Clutch Circuit (Part 1 of 2). 1997 Paseo

INSPECTION PROCEDURE

1   Check actuator arm locking operation.

P   (1) Ignition switch OFF.
(2) Disconnect actuator connector.

C   (1) Connect the positive (+) lead from the battery to the terminal 3 of actuator and the negative (–) lead to terminal 4.
NOTICE: Do not connect the high tension cables to the wrong battery terminal. You will damage the cruise control actuator.
(2) Move the control plate by hand.

OK   Control plate doesn't move. (Magnetic clutch on)

OK

NG > Replace cruise control actuator.

2   Check actuator operation.

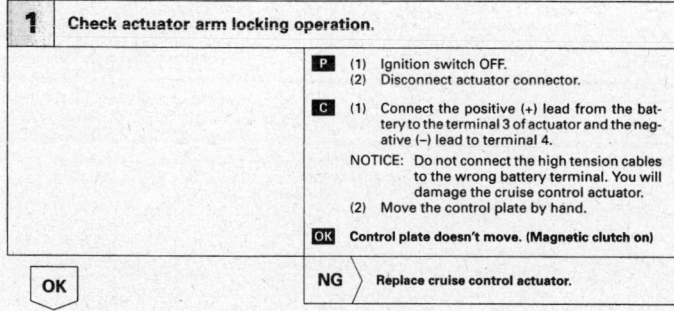

Full open side

Control plate

Fully close side

Control plate

P   Disconnect the actuator connector.

C   Connect the positive (+) lead from the battery to terminals 3 and 1 of actuator, connect the negative (–) lead to terminals 4 and 2 of actuator.

OK   Control arm moves to full open side.

C   Connect the positive (+) lead from the battery to terminals 4 and 2 of actuator, connect the negative (–) lead to terminals 3 and 1 of actuator.

OK   Control arm moves to full close side.

OK

NG > Replace actuator.

TY1109900210010X

Fig. 235   Code 14: Actuator Mechanical Fault (Part 1 of 2). 1997 Paseo

INSPECTION PROCEDURE

1   Check resistance between terminals MO and MC of cruise control actuator.

P   (1) Ignition switch ON.
(2) Disconnect actuator connector.

C   Measure resistance between terminals 1 and 2.
HINT:
If control plate position is fully opened or fully closed, resistance can not measure.

OK   Resistance: more than 4.2 Ω

OK

NG > Replace actuator assembly.

2   Check wire harness and connector between terminals MO of cruise control ECU and MO of cruise control actuator

OK

NG > Repair or replace harness or connector.

Replace cruise control ECU.

TY1109900208020X

Fig. 233   Codes 11 & 15: Actuator Motor Circuit (Part 2 of 2). 1997 Paseo

INSPECTION PROCEDURE

1   Check STOP fuse.

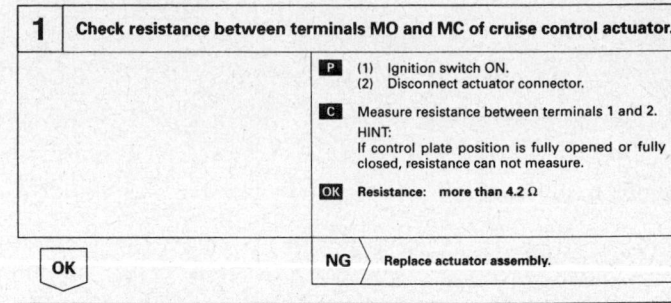

Instrument Panel Junction Block

P   (a) Remove the fuse box opening cover.
(b) Remove STOP fuse from instrument panel junction block.

OK   Check continuity of STOP fuse.

OK   Continuity

OK

NG > Replace STOP fuse.

2   Check harness and connector between actuator and cruise control actuator

OK

NG > Repair or replace harness or connector.

Check and replace cruise control ECU

TY1109900209020X

Fig. 234   Code 12: Actuator Magnetic Clutch Circuit (Part 2 of 2). 1997 Paseo

3   Check harness and connector between actuator and cruise control ECU

OK

NG > Repair or replace harness or connector.

Check and replace cruise control ECU

TY1109900210020X

Fig. 235   Code 14: Actuator Mechanical Fault (Part 2 of 2). 1997 Paseo

CIRCUIT DESCRIPTION

The vehicle speed sensor circuit is sent to cruise control ECU as vehicle speed signal. For each rotation of the shaft, the vehicle speed sensor sends a signal through the combination meter to the cruise control ECU (See the following). The ECU calculates the vehicle speed from this pulse frequency.

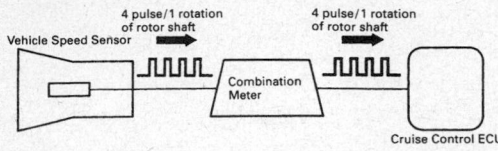

DTC No.	Diagnosis	Trouble Area
21	Speed signal is not input to the cruise control ECU while cruise control is set.	• Vehicle speed sensor • Combination meter • Cruise control ECU

TY1109900211010X

Fig. 236 Code 21: Vehicle Speed Sensor Open Circuit (Part 1 of 2). 1997 Paseo

CIRCUIT DESCRIPTION

DTC No.	Diagnosis	Trouble Area
23	• Actual vehicle speed has dropped either by 16 km/h (10 mph) or more below the set speed, or by 20 % or more of the set speed. • Vehicle speed sensor pulse is abnormal. (When speed signal is not input to the ECU below 0.2 sec., code will be displayed.)	• Vehicle speed sensor • Harness or connector in SPD circuit • Cruise control ECU

INSPECTION PROCEDURE

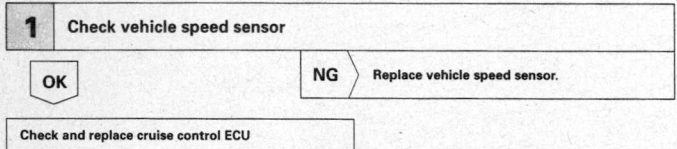

1 Check vehicle speed sensor

| OK | | NG | Replace vehicle speed sensor. |

Check and replace cruise control ECU

TY1109900212000X

Fig. 237 Code 23: Vehicle Speed Signal Abnormal. 1997 Paseo

CIRCUIT DESCRIPTION

This circuit carries the SET/COAST, RESUME/ACCEL and CANCEL signals (each voltage) to the ECU.

Code No.	Diagnosis	Trouble Area
32	Short in control switch circuit.	• Cruise control switch • Harness or connector between control switch and cruise control ECU • Cruise control ECU

INSPECTION PROCEDURE

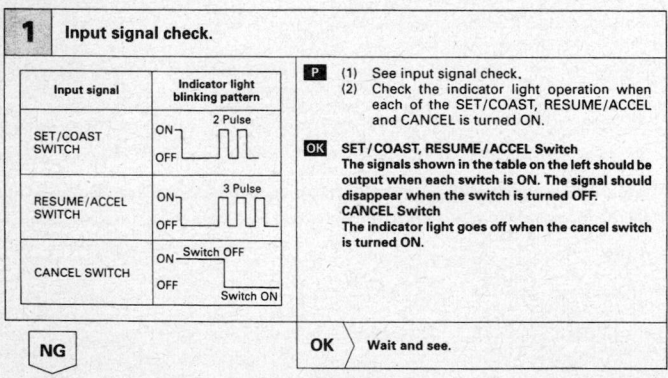

1 Input signal check.

P (1) See input signal check.
(2) Check the indicator light operation when each of the SET/COAST, RESUME/ACCEL and CANCEL is turned ON.

OK **SET/COAST, RESUME/ACCEL Switch**
The signals shown in the table on the left should be output when each switch is ON. The signal should disappear when the switch is turned OFF.
CANCEL Switch
The indicator light goes off when the cancel switch is turned ON.

| NG | | OK | Wait and see. |

TY1109900213010X

Fig. 238 Code 32: Cruise Control Switch Circuit (Part 1 of 2). 1997 Paseo

INSPECTION PROCEDURE

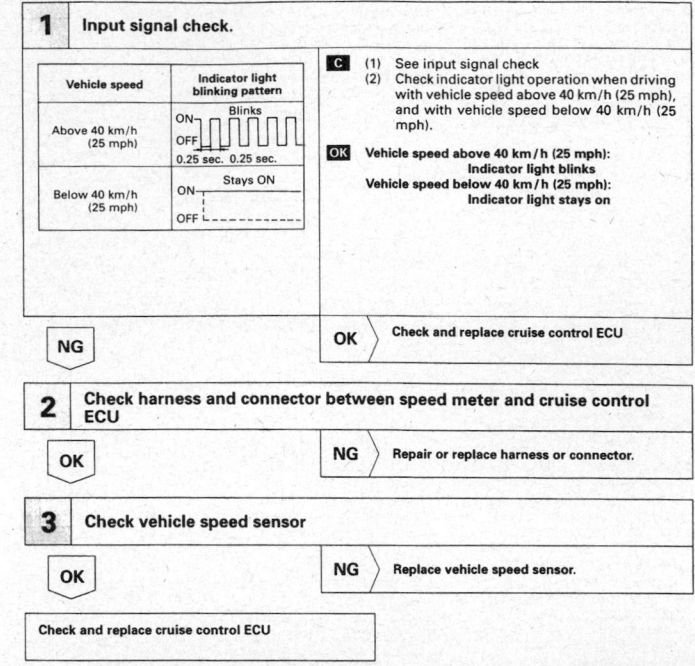

1 Input signal check.

C (1) See input signal check
(2) Check indicator light operation when driving with vehicle speed above 40 km/h (25 mph), and with vehicle speed below 40 km/h (25 mph).

OK Vehicle speed above 40 km/h (25 mph):
Indicator light blinks
Vehicle speed below 40 km/h (25 mph):
Indicator light stays on

| NG | | OK | Check and replace cruise control ECU |

2 Check harness and connector between speed meter and cruise control ECU

| OK | | NG | Repair or replace harness or connector. |

3 Check vehicle speed sensor

| OK | | NG | Replace vehicle speed sensor. |

Check and replace cruise control ECU

TY1109900211020X

Fig. 236 Code 21: Vehicle Speed Sensor Open Circuit (Part 2 of 2). 1997 Paseo

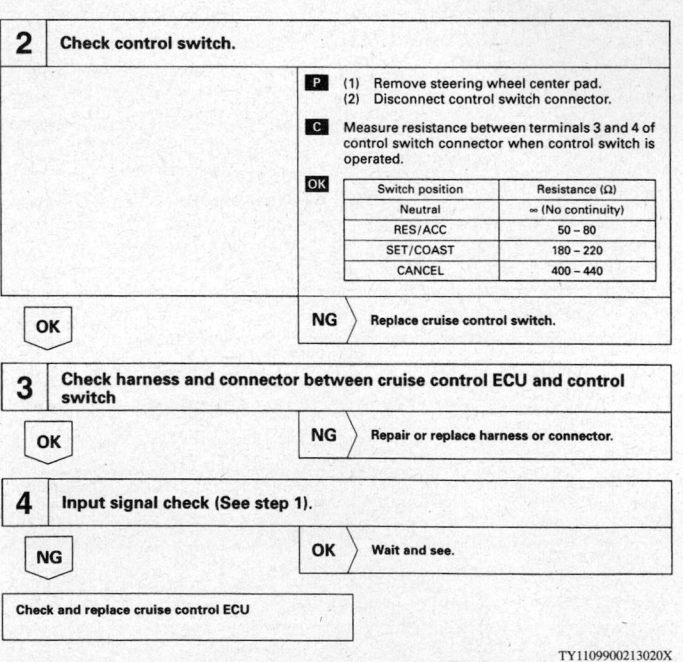

2 Check control switch.

P (1) Remove steering wheel center pad.
(2) Disconnect control switch connector.

C Measure resistance between terminals 3 and 4 of control switch connector when control switch is operated.

OK

Switch position	Resistance (Ω)
Neutral	∞ (No continuity)
RES/ACC	50 – 80
SET/COAST	180 – 220
CANCEL	400 – 440

| OK | | NG | Replace cruise control switch. |

3 Check harness and connector between cruise control ECU and control switch

| OK | | NG | Repair or replace harness or connector. |

4 Input signal check (See step 1).

| NG | | OK | Wait and see. |

Check and replace cruise control ECU

TY1109900213020X

Fig. 238 Code 32: Cruise Control Switch Circuit (Part 2 of 2). 1997 Paseo

CIRCUIT DESCRIPTION

When the idle switch in turned ON, a signal is sent to the ECU. The ECU uses this signal to correct the discrepancy between the throttle valve position and the actuator position sensor value to enable accurate cruise control at the set speed. If the idle switch is malfunctioning, problem symptoms also occur in the engine, so also inspect the engine.

DTC No.	Diagnosis	Trouble Area
51	Short in idle signal circuit.	• Harness or connector between cruise control ECU and throttle position sensor • Throttle position sensor • Cruise control ECU

INSPECTION PROCEDURE

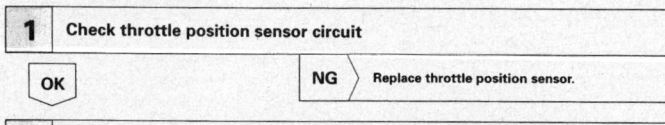

1 | Check throttle position sensor circuit

OK | NG ▷ Replace throttle position sensor.

2 | Check harness and connector between ECM and throttle position sensor

OK | NG ▷ Repair or replace harness or connector.

TY1109900214010X

**Fig. 239   Code 51: Idle Signal Circuit (Part 1 of 2).
1997 Paseo**

CIRCUIT DESCRIPTION

When the brake is on, battery positive voltage normally applies through the stop fuse and stop switch to terminal STP– of the ECU, and the ECU turns the cruise control off.
A fail-safe function is provided so that cancel functions normally, even if there is a malfunction in the stop light signal circuit.
If the harness connected to terminal STP– has an open, terminal STP– will have battery positive voltage and the cruise control will be turned off, also SET not occurring.
Also, when the brake is on, the magnetic clutch is cut mechanically by the stop light switch, turning the cruise control off.

INSPECTION PROCEDURE

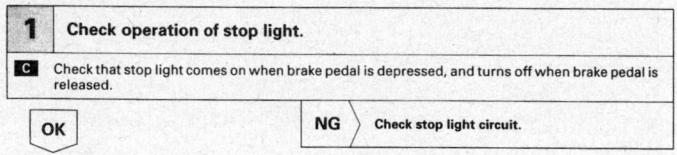

1 | Check operation of stop light.

C | Check that stop light comes on when brake pedal is depressed, and turns off when brake pedal is released.

OK | NG ▷ Check stop light circuit.

TY1109900215010X

**Fig. 240   Stop Lamp Switch Circuit (Part 1 of 2).
1997 Paseo**

---

3 | Check harness and connector between cruise control ECU and throttle position sensor

OK | NG ▷ Repair or replace harness or connector.

Check and replace cruise control ECU

TY1109900214020X

**Fig. 239   Code 51: Idle Signal Circuit (Part 2 of 2).
1997 Paseo**

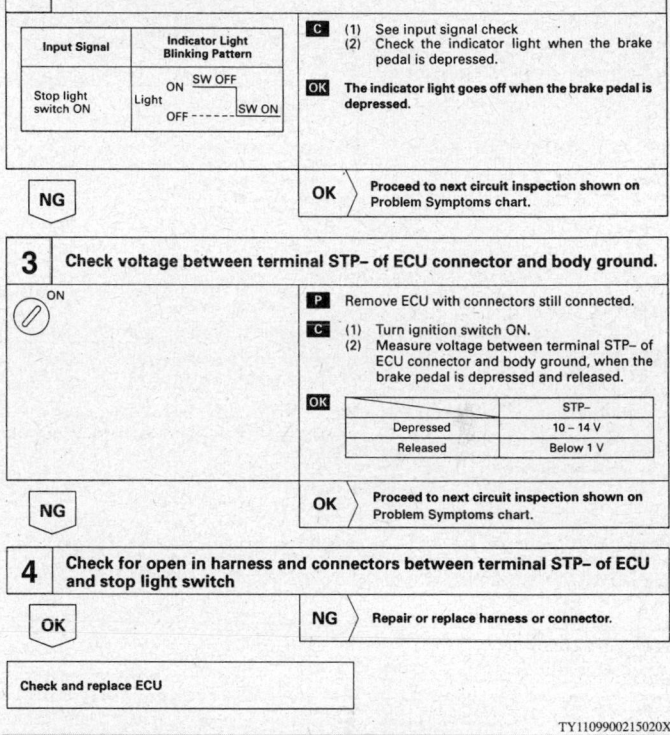

2 | Input signal check.

Input Signal	Indicator Light Blinking Pattern
Stop light switch ON	Light ON/OFF pattern

C | (1) See input signal check
(2) Check the indicator light when the brake pedal is depressed.

OK | The indicator light goes off when the brake pedal is depressed.

NG | OK ▷ Proceed to next circuit inspection shown on Problem Symptoms chart.

3 | Check voltage between terminal STP– of ECU connector and body ground.

P | Remove ECU with connectors still connected.

C | (1) Turn ignition switch ON.
(2) Measure voltage between terminal STP– of ECU connector and body ground, when the brake pedal is depressed and released.

OK |
	STP–
Depressed	10 – 14 V
Released	Below 1 V

NG | OK ▷ Proceed to next circuit inspection shown on Problem Symptoms chart.

4 | Check for open in harness and connectors between terminal STP– of ECU and stop light switch

OK | NG ▷ Repair or replace harness or connector.

Check and replace ECU

TY1109900215020X

**Fig. 240   Stop Lamp Switch Circuit (Part 2 of 2).
1997 Paseo**

CIRCUIT DESCRIPTION

When driving uphill under cruise control, in order to reduce shifting due to ON-OFF overdrive operation and to provide smooth driving, when down shifting in the electronic controlled transaxle occurs, a signal to prevent upshift until the end of the uphill slope is sent from the cruise control ECU to the electronic controlled transaxle.
Terminal ECT of the cruise control ECU detects the shift change signal (output to electronic controlled transaxle No.2 solenoid) from the electronically controlled transaxle.
If vehicle speed down, also when terminal electronically controlled transaxle of the cruise control ECU receives down shifting signal, it sends a signal from terminal OD to OD1 to cut overdrive until the end of the uphill slope, and the gear shifts are reduced and gear shift points in the electronically controlled transaxle are changed.

INSPECTION PROCEDURE

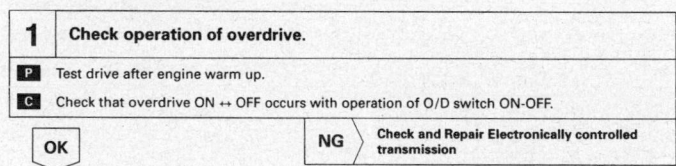

1 | Check operation of overdrive.

P | Test drive after engine warm up.

C | Check that overdrive ON ↔ OFF occurs with operation of O/D switch ON-OFF.

OK | NG ▷ Check and Repair Electronically controlled transmission

TY1109900216010X

**Fig. 241   Electronically Controlled Transaxle
Communication Circuit (Part 1 of 3). 1997 Paseo**

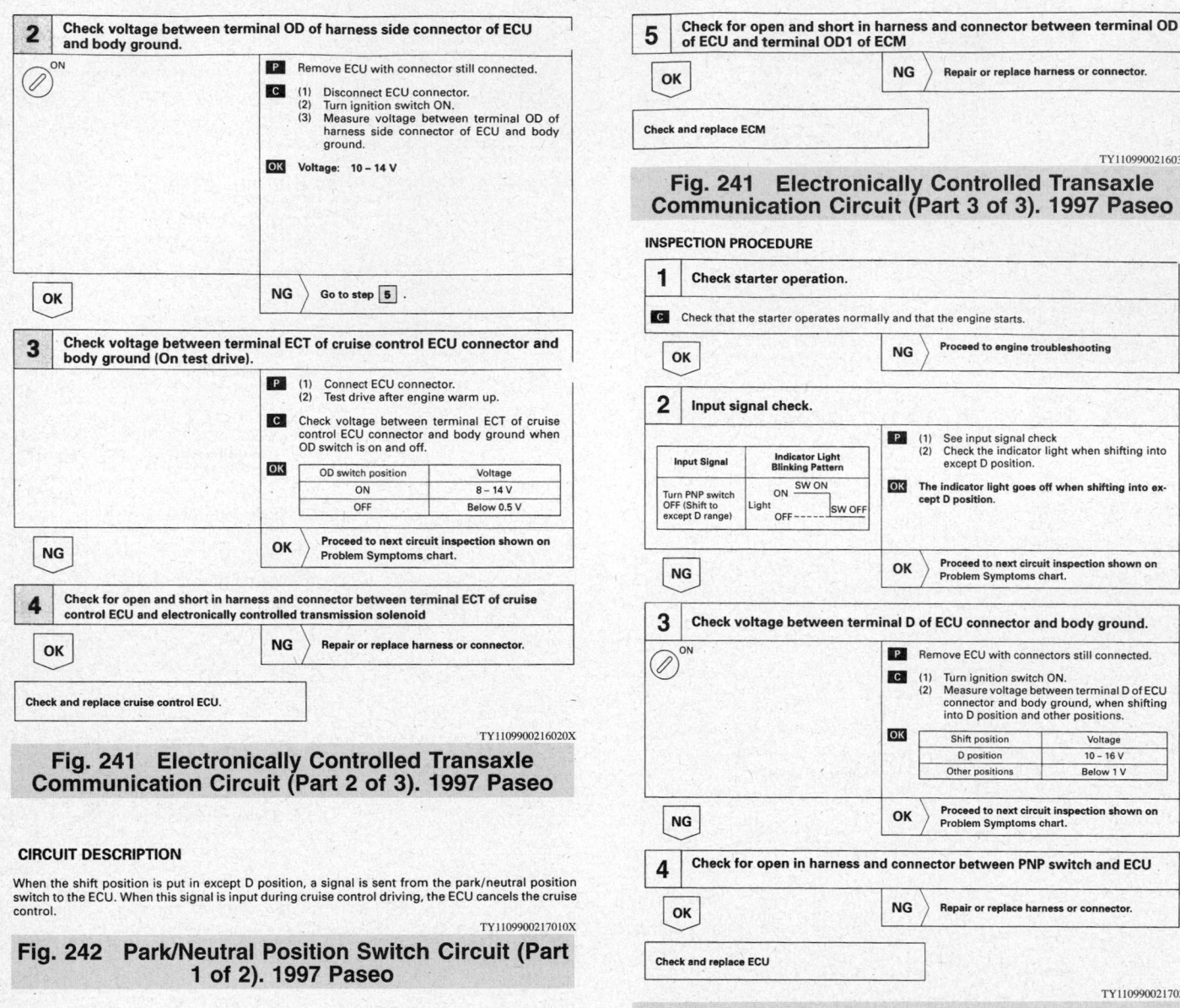

2 | Check voltage between terminal OD of harness side connector of ECU and body ground.

P Remove ECU with connector still connected.

C
(1) Disconnect ECU connector.
(2) Turn ignition switch ON.
(3) Measure voltage between terminal OD of harness side connector of ECU and body ground.

OK Voltage: 10 – 14 V

OK

NG > Go to step **5** .

3 | Check voltage between terminal ECT of cruise control ECU connector and body ground (On test drive).

P
(1) Connect ECU connector.
(2) Test drive after engine warm up.

C Check voltage between terminal ECT of cruise control ECU connector and body ground when OD switch is on and off.

OK

OD switch position	Voltage
ON	8 – 14 V
OFF	Below 0.5 V

NG

OK > Proceed to next circuit inspection shown on Problem Symptoms chart.

4 | Check for open and short in harness and connector between terminal ECT of cruise control ECU and electronically controlled transmission solenoid

OK

NG > Repair or replace harness or connector.

Check and replace cruise control ECU.

TY1109900216020X

Fig. 241 Electronically Controlled Transaxle Communication Circuit (Part 2 of 3). 1997 Paseo

CIRCUIT DESCRIPTION

When the shift position is put in except D position, a signal is sent from the park/neutral position switch to the ECU. When this signal is input during cruise control driving, the ECU cancels the cruise control.

TY1109900217010X

Fig. 242 Park/Neutral Position Switch Circuit (Part 1 of 2). 1997 Paseo

5 | Check for open and short in harness and connector between terminal OD of ECU and terminal OD1 of ECM

OK

NG > Repair or replace harness or connector.

Check and replace ECM

TY1109900216030X

Fig. 241 Electronically Controlled Transaxle Communication Circuit (Part 3 of 3). 1997 Paseo

INSPECTION PROCEDURE

1 | Check starter operation.

C Check that the starter operates normally and that the engine starts.

OK

NG > Proceed to engine troubleshooting

2 | Input signal check.

Input Signal	Indicator Light Blinking Pattern
Turn PNP switch OFF (Shift to except D range)	ON _SW ON_ Light OFF _____ SW OFF

P
(1) See input signal check
(2) Check the indicator light when shifting into except D position.

OK The indicator light goes off when shifting into except D position.

NG

OK > Proceed to next circuit inspection shown on Problem Symptoms chart.

3 | Check voltage between terminal D of ECU connector and body ground.

P Remove ECU with connectors still connected.

C
(1) Turn ignition switch ON.
(2) Measure voltage between terminal D of ECU connector and body ground, when shifting into D position and other positions.

OK

Shift position	Voltage
D position	10 – 16 V
Other positions	Below 1 V

NG

OK > Proceed to next circuit inspection shown on Problem Symptoms chart.

4 | Check for open in harness and connector between PNP switch and ECU

OK

NG > Repair or replace harness or connector.

Check and replace ECU

TY1109900217020X

Fig. 242 Park/Neutral Position Switch Circuit (Part 2 of 2). 1997 Paseo

CIRCUIT DESCRIPTION

When the clutch pedal is depressed, the clutch switch sends a signal to the cruise control ECU. When the signal is input to the cruise control ECU during cruise control driving, the cruise control ECU cancels cruise control.

INSPECTION PROCEDURE

1 | Check starter operation.

C Check that the starter operates normally and that the engine starts.

OK

NG > Proceed to engine troubleshooting

2 | Input signal check.

Input Signal	Indicator Light Blinking Pattern
Clutch switch OFF (Depress clutch pedal)	SW ON ON Light OFF _____ SW OFF

P See input signal check

C Check the indicator light when the clutch pedal is depressed.

OK The indicator light goes off when the clutch pedal is depressed.

OK

OK > Proceed to next circuit inspection shown on Problem Symptoms chart.

TY1109900218010X

Fig. 243 Clutch Switch Circuit (Part 1 of 2). 1997 Paseo

3	Check voltage between terminal D of cruise control ECU and body ground.

⊘ ON	**P** Turn ignition switch ON.
	C Measure voltage between terminal D of ECU connector and body ground, when the clutch pedal is depressed.
	OK

Switch position	Voltage
ON (Pedal depressed)	Below 1 V
OFF	10 – 16 V

NG ▽	OK ▷	Proceed to next circuit inspection shown on Problem Symptoms chart.

4	Check for open in harness and connector between ECU and GAUGE fuse

OK ▽	NG ▷	Repair or replace harness or connector.

Check and replace cruise control ECU

TY1109900218020X

Fig. 243   Clutch Switch Circuit (Part 2 of 2). 1997 Paseo

INSPECTION PROCEDURE

1	Check ECU-IG fuse.

Instrument Panel Junction Block	**P** (a) Remove the fuse box opening cover.
	(b) Remove ECU-IG fuse from instrument panel junction block.
	C Check continuity of ECU-IG fuse.
	OK Continuity

OK ▽	NG ▷	Check for short in all the harness and components connected to the ECU-IG fuse

2	Check voltage between terminals B and GND of ECU connector.

⊘ ON	**P** Remove ECU with connectors still connected.
	C (1) Turn ignition switch ON.
	(2) Measure voltage between terminals B and GND of ECU connector.
	OK Voltage: 10 – 14 V

NG ▽	OK ▷	Proceed to next circuit inspection shown on Problem Symptoms chart.

TY1109900219020X

Fig. 244   ECU Power Source Circuit (Part 2 of 3). 1997 Paseo

CIRCUIT DESCRIPTION

The ECU back-up power source provides power even when the ignition switch is off and is used for DTC memory, etc.

TY1109900220010X

Fig. 245   Back Up Power Source Circuit (Part 1 of 2). 1997 Paseo

CIRCUIT DESCRIPTION

The ECU power source supplies power to the actuator and sensors, etc., when the terminal GND and the cruise control ECU case are grounded.

TY1109900219010X

Fig. 244   ECU Power Source Circuit (Part 1 of 3). 1997 Paseo

3	Check resistance between terminals GND of ECU connector and body ground.

⊘ LOCK	**C** Measure resistance between terminal GND of cruise control ECU connector and body ground.
	OK Resistance: Below 1 Ω

OK ▽	NG ▷	Repair or replace harness or connector.

Check and repair harness and connector between battery and ECU

TY1109900219030X

Fig. 244   ECU Power Source Circuit (Part 3 of 3). 1997 Paseo

INSPECTION PROCEDURE

1	Check DOME fuse.

• Engine Room Junction Block	**P** Remove DOME fuse from engine room junction block.
	C Check continuity of DOME fuse.
	OK Continuity.

OK ▽	NG ▷	Check for short in all the harness and components connected to the DOME fuse.

2	Check voltage between terminal BATT of ECU connector and body ground.

⊘ LOCK	**P** Remove ECU with connectors still connected.
	C Measure voltage between terminal BATT of ECU connector and body ground.
	OK Voltage: 10 – 14 V

NG ▽	OK ▷	Proceed to next circuit inspection shown on Problem Symptoms chart.

Check and repair harness and connector between battery and ECU.

TY1109900220020X

Fig. 245   Back Up Power Source Circuit (Part 2 of 2). 1997 Paseo

CIRCUIT DESCRIPTION

When the cruise control main switch is turned off, the cruise control does not operate.

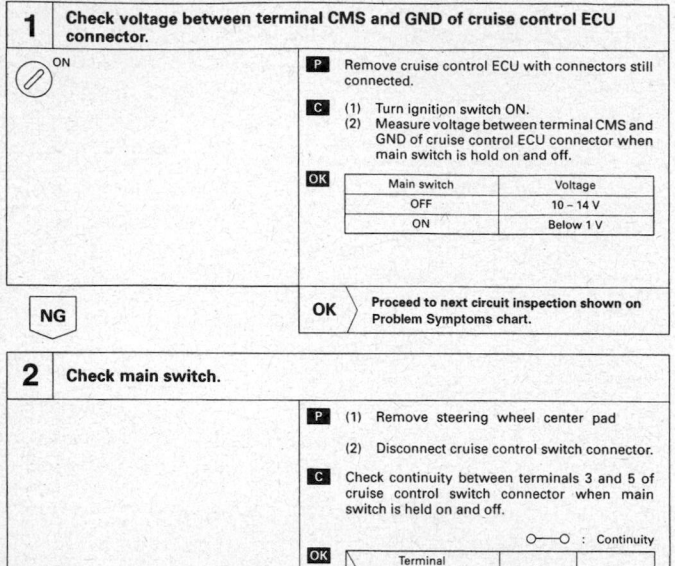

1	Check voltage between terminal CMS and GND of cruise control ECU connector.

P — Remove cruise control ECU with connectors still connected.

C —
(1) Turn ignition switch ON.
(2) Measure voltage between terminal CMS and GND of cruise control ECU connector when main switch is hold on and off.

OK

Main switch	Voltage
OFF	10 – 14 V
ON	Below 1 V

NG

OK — Proceed to next circuit inspection shown on Problem Symptoms chart.

2	Check main switch.

P —
(1) Remove steering wheel center pad
(2) Disconnect cruise control switch connector.

C — Check continuity between terminals 3 and 5 of cruise control switch connector when main switch is held on and off.

OK — ○—○ : Continuity

Terminal Main switch	3	5
OFF		
Hold ON	○——○	

OK

NG — Replace control switch.

TY1109900221010X

Fig. 246   Main Cruise Control Switch Circuit (Part 1 of 2). 1997 Paseo

CIRCUIT DESCRIPTION

When the cruise control main switch is turned ON, CRUISE MAIN indicator light lights up.

TY1109900222010X

Fig. 247   Cruise Main Indicator Light Circuit (Part 1 of 2). 1997 Paseo

CIRCUIT DESCRIPTION

This circuit sends a signal to the ECU that diagnostic code output is required.

TY1109900223010X

Fig. 248   Diagnosis Circuit (Part 1 of 2). 1997 Paseo

3	Check harness and connector between cruise control ECU and main switch, main switch and body ground

OK

NG — Repair or replace harness or connector.

Check and replace cruise control ECU

TY1109900221020X

Fig. 246   Main Cruise Control Switch Circuit (Part 2 of 2). 1997 Paseo

INSPECTION PROCEDURE

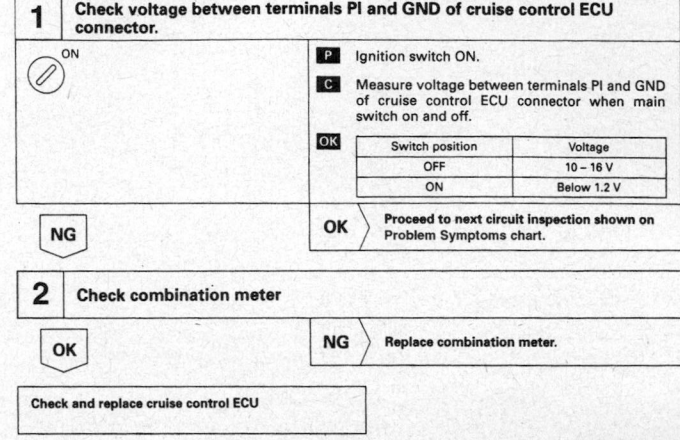

1	Check voltage between terminals PI and GND of cruise control ECU connector.

P — Ignition switch ON.

C — Measure voltage between terminals PI and GND of cruise control ECU connector when main switch on and off.

OK

Switch position	Voltage
OFF	10 – 16 V
ON	Below 1.2 V

NG

OK — Proceed to next circuit inspection shown on Problem Symptoms chart.

2	Check combination meter

OK

NG — Replace combination meter.

Check and replace cruise control ECU

TY1109900222020X

Fig. 247   Cruise Main Indicator Light Circuit (Part 2 of 2). 1997 Paseo

INSPECTION PROCEDURE

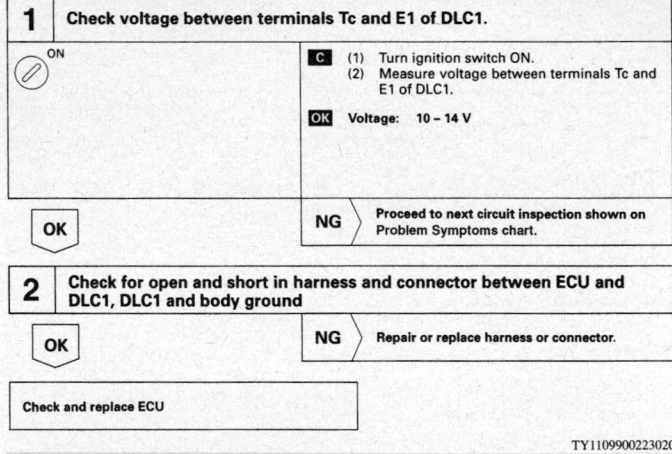

1	Check voltage between terminals Tc and E1 of DLC1.

C —
(1) Turn ignition switch ON.
(2) Measure voltage between terminals Tc and E1 of DLC1.

OK — Voltage: 10 – 14 V

OK

NG — Proceed to next circuit inspection shown on Problem Symptoms chart.

2	Check for open and short in harness and connector between ECU and DLC1, DLC1 and body ground

OK

NG — Repair or replace harness or connector.

Check and replace ECU

TY1109900223020X

Fig. 248   Diagnosis Circuit (Part 2 of 2). 1997 Paseo

Actuator Control Cable Inspection

C —
(1) Check that the actuator, control cable and throttle link are properly installed and that the cable and link are connected correctly.
(2) Check that the actuator and bell crank are operating smoothly.
(3) Check that the cable is not loose or too tight.

OK — Freeplay: less than 10 mm

Hint —
(1) If the control cable is very loose, the vehicle's loss of speed going uphill will be large.
(2) If the control cable is too tight, the idle RPM will become high.

TY1109900224000X

Fig. 249   Actuator Control Cable Inspection. 1997 Paseo

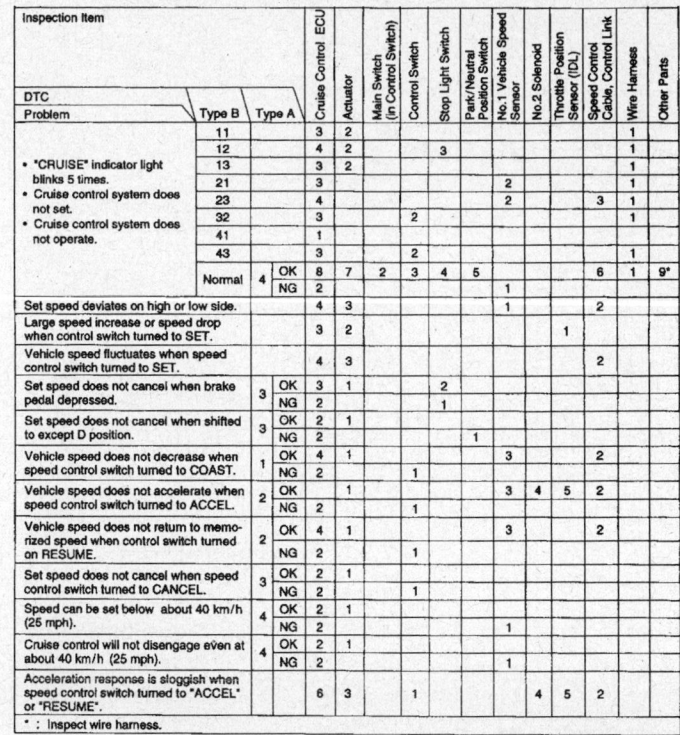

Fig. 250 — Problem Symptoms Table. 1996 Previa (left)

Inspection Item / Problem	DTC Type A	DTC Type B	Cruise Control ECU	Actuator (D)	Main Switch (in Control Switch) (C)	Control Switch (C)	Stop Light Switch (F)	Park./Neutral Position Switch (H)	Parking Brake Switch (G)	Vehicle Speed Sensor (E)	Speed Control Cable Function	Throttle Position Sensor (IDL) (J)	Wire Harness	Indicator Light (B)
• "CRUISE" indicator light blinks 5 times. • Cruise control system goes not set. • Cruise control system does not operate.	11	–	3	2										1
	12	–	4	2			3							1
	13	–	3	2										1
	21	–	3							2				1
	23	–	4	3						2	1			
	32	–	3			2								1
	34	–	3			2								1
	41	–	1											
Indicator light does not light up.			3										1	1
Large speed drop when the cruise control switch turned to SET.				4	3						1	2		
Vehicle speed fluctuates when cruise control switch turned to SET.				4	3						1	2		
Cruise control system goes not set. / Cruise control system does not operate.	OK		9	8	2	3	4	5	6				7	1
	NG									1				
Set speed deviates on high or low side.	OK		4	3							1	2		
	NG		1											
Acceleration response is sluggish when cruise control switch turned to "ACCEL" or "RESUME".	OK		4	3							2	1		
	NG		1											
Set speed does not cancel when brake pedal depressed.	OK		1											
	NG						2							
Set speed does not cancel when parking brake lever pulled.	OK		1											
	NG								2					
Cruise control not cancelled, even when transmission is shifted to "P" or "N".	OK		1											
	NG							2						
Set speed does not cancel when clutch pedal depressed.	OK		1											
	NG							2						
Set speed does not cancel when cruise control switch pushed to CANCEL.	OK		1											
	NG					2								
Vehicle speed does not decrease when cruise control switch pushed to COAST.	OK		4	1							3	2		
	NG					2								
Speed does not accelerate when cruise control switch pushed to ACCEL.	OK		4	1										
	NG					2								
Vehicle speed does not return to memorized cruise when control switch pushed to RESUME.	OK		4	1							3	2		
	NG					2								
Speed can be set below about 40 km/h (25 mph.)	OK		4											
	NG										1			
Cruise control does not disengage even at about 40 km/h (25 mph) or less.	OK		4	2	1									
	NG										1			

TY1109900355000X

Fig. 250 — Problem Symptoms Table. 1996 Previa

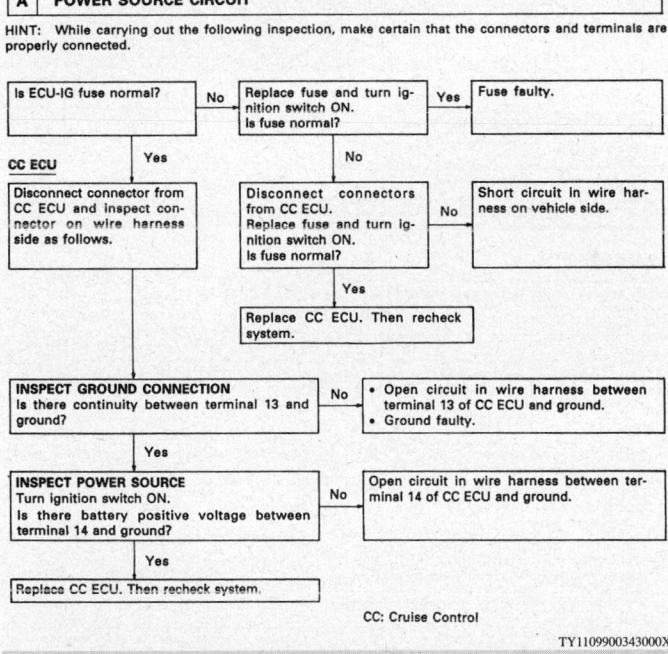

Fig. 251 — Problem Symptoms Table. 1997 Previa (right)

DTC / Problem	Type B	Type A	Cruise Control ECU	Actuator	Main Switch (in Control Switch)	Control Switch	Stop Light Switch	Park/Neutral Position Switch	No.1 Vehicle Speed Sensor	No.2 Solenoid	Throttle Position Sensor (IDL)	Speed Control Cable, Control Link	Wire Harness	Other Parts
• "CRUISE" indicator light blinks 5 times. • Cruise control system does not set. • Cruise control system does not operate.	11		3	2									1	
	12		4	2			3						1	
	13		3	2									1	
	21		3						2				1	
	23		4						2			3	1	
	32		3			2							1	
	41		1											
	43		3			2							1	
Normal		4	OK	8	7	2	3	4	5				6	1	9*
			NG								1				
Set speed deviates on high or low side.			4	3							1		2	
Large speed increase or speed drop when control switch turned to SET.			3	2							1			
Vehicle speed fluctuates when speed control switch turned to SET.			4	3								2		
Set speed does not cancel when brake pedal depressed.	3	OK	3	1			2							
		NG	2				1							
Set speed does not cancel when shifted to except D position.	3	OK	2	1										
		NG	2					1						
Vehicle speed does not decrease when speed control switch turned to COAST.	1	OK	4	1						3		2		
		NG	2		1									
Vehicle speed does not accelerate when speed control switch turned to ACCEL.	2	OK	4	1						3	4	5	2	
		NG	2		1									
Vehicle speed does not return to memorized speed when control switch turned on RESUME.	2	OK	4	1						3		2		
		NG	2		1									
Set speed does not cancel when speed control switch turned to CANCEL.	3	OK	4	1										
		NG	2		1									
Speed can be set below about 40 km/h (25 mph).	4	OK	2	1										
		NG									1			
Cruise control will not disengage even at about 40 km/h (25 mph).	4	OK	2	1										
		NG									1			
Acceleration response is sluggish when speed control switch turned to "ACCEL" or "RESUME".			6	3		1					4	5	2	

* : inspect wire harness.

TY1109700091000X

Fig. 251 — Problem Symptoms Table. 1997 Previa

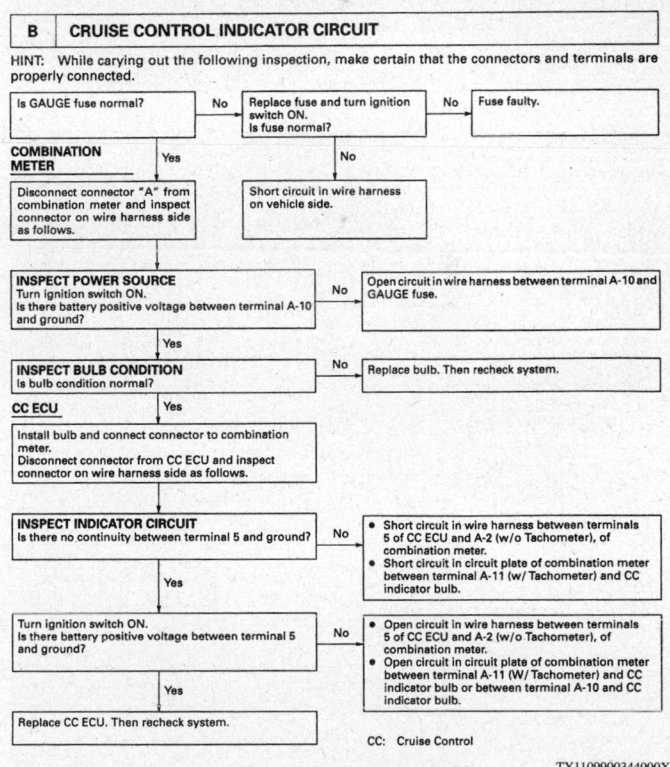

A — POWER SOURCE CIRCUIT

HINT: While carrying out the following inspection, make certain that the connectors and terminals are properly connected.

- Is ECU-IG fuse normal?
  - No → Replace fuse and turn ignition switch ON. Is fuse normal?
    - Yes → Fuse faulty.
    - No → Disconnect connectors from CC ECU. Replace fuse and turn ignition switch ON. Is fuse normal?
      - No → Short circuit in wire harness on vehicle side.
      - Yes → Replace CC ECU. Then recheck system.
  - Yes → **CC ECU** — Disconnect connector from CC ECU and inspect connector on wire harness side as follows.
    - **INSPECT GROUND CONNECTION** — Is there continuity between terminal 13 and ground?
      - No → • Open circuit in wire harness between terminal 13 of CC ECU and ground. • Ground faulty.
      - Yes → **INSPECT POWER SOURCE** — Turn ignition switch ON. Is there battery positive voltage between terminal 14 and ground?
        - No → Open circuit in wire harness between terminal 14 of CC ECU and ground.
        - Yes → Replace CC ECU. Then recheck system.

CC: Cruise Control

TY1109900343000X

Fig. 252 — Test A: Power Source Circuit. Previa

B — CRUISE CONTROL INDICATOR CIRCUIT

HINT: While carrying out the following inspection, make certain that the connectors and terminals are properly connected.

- Is GAUGE fuse normal?
  - No → Replace fuse and turn ignition switch ON. Is fuse normal?
    - No → Fuse faulty.
    - Yes → Short circuit in wire harness on vehicle side.
  - Yes → **COMBINATION METER** — Disconnect connector "A" from combination meter and inspect connector on wire harness side as follows.
    - **INSPECT POWER SOURCE** — Turn ignition switch ON. Is there battery positive voltage between terminal A-10 and ground?
      - No → Open circuit in wire harness between terminal A-10 and GAUGE fuse.
      - Yes → **INSPECT BULB CONDITION** — Is bulb condition normal?
        - No → Replace bulb. Then recheck system.
        - Yes → **CC ECU** — Install bulb and connect connector to combination meter. Disconnect connector from CC ECU and inspect connector on wire harness side as follows.
          - **INSPECT INDICATOR CIRCUIT** — Is there no continuity between terminal 5 and ground?
            - No → • Short circuit in wire harness between terminals 5 of CC ECU and A-2 (w/o Tachometer), of combination meter. • Short circuit in circuit plate of combination meter between terminal A-11 (w/ Tachometer) and CC indicator bulb.
            - Yes → Turn ignition switch ON. Is there battery positive voltage between terminal 5 and ground?
              - No → • Open circuit in wire harness between terminals 5 of CC ECU and A-2 (w/o Tachometer), of combination meter. • Open circuit in circuit plate of combination meter between terminal A-11 (W/ Tachometer) and CC indicator bulb or between terminal A-10 and CC indicator bulb.
              - Yes → Replace CC ECU. Then recheck system.

CC: Cruise Control

TY1109900344000X

Fig. 253 — Test B: Cruise Control Indicator Circuit. Previa

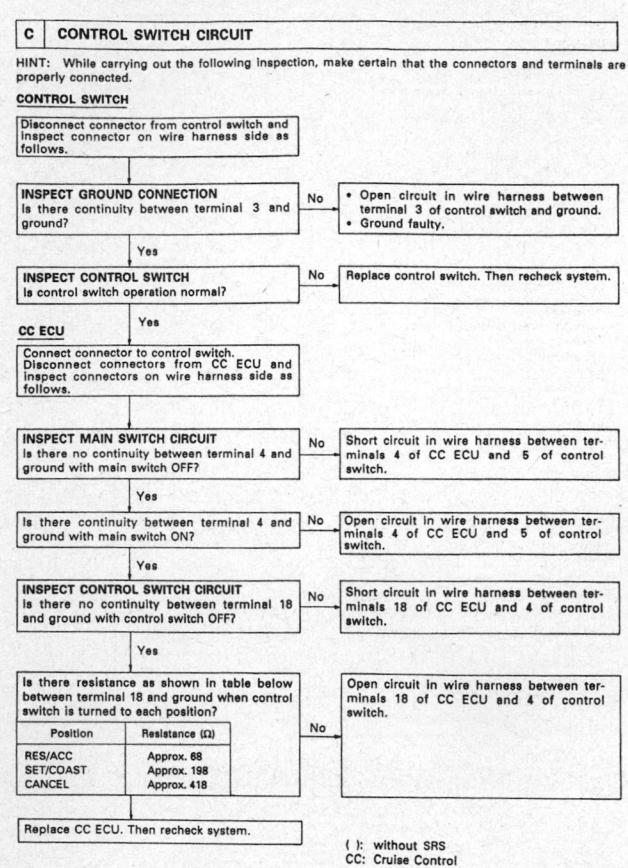

Fig. 254   Test C: Control Switch Circuit. Previa

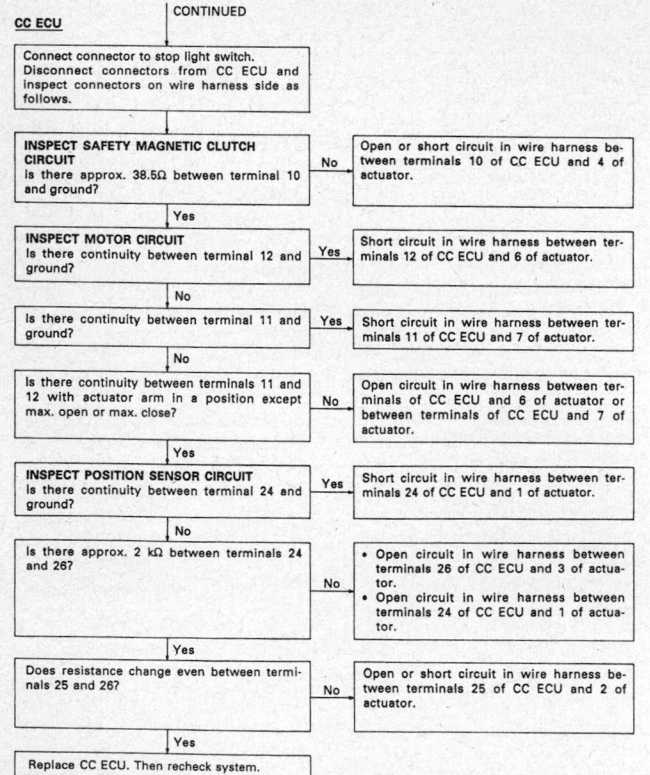

Fig. 255   Test D: Actuator Circuit (Part 2 of 2). Previa

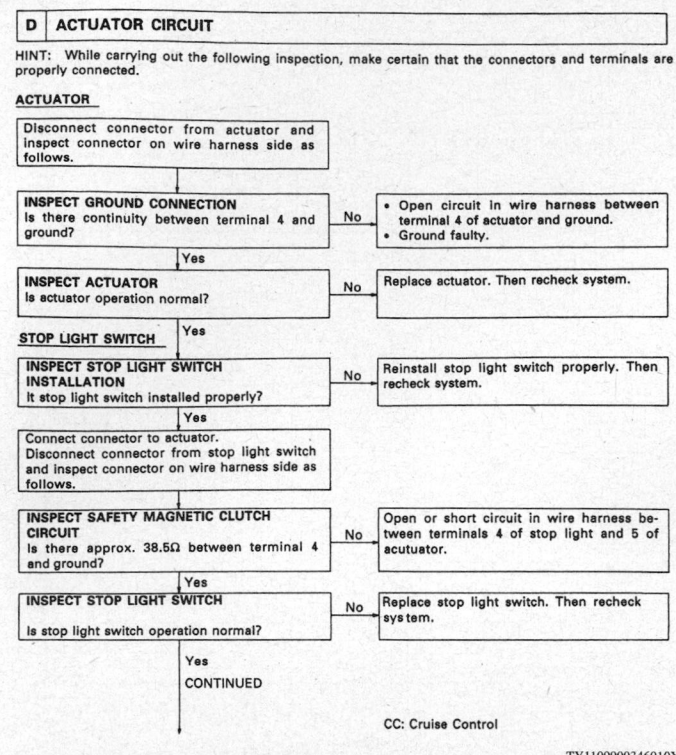

Fig. 255   Test D: Actuator Circuit (Part 1 of 2). Previa

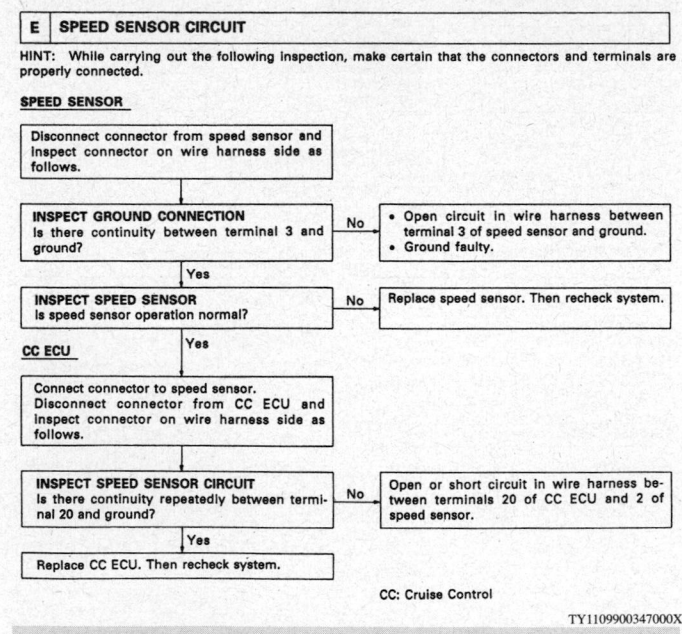

Fig. 256   Test E: Speed Sensor Circuit. Previa

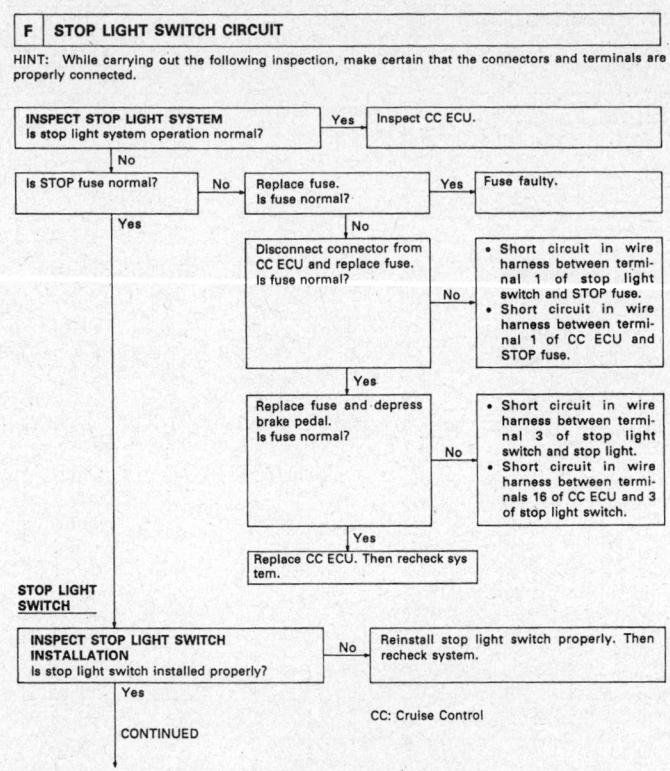

Fig. 257   Test F: Stop Lamp Switch Circuit (Part 1 of 2). Previa

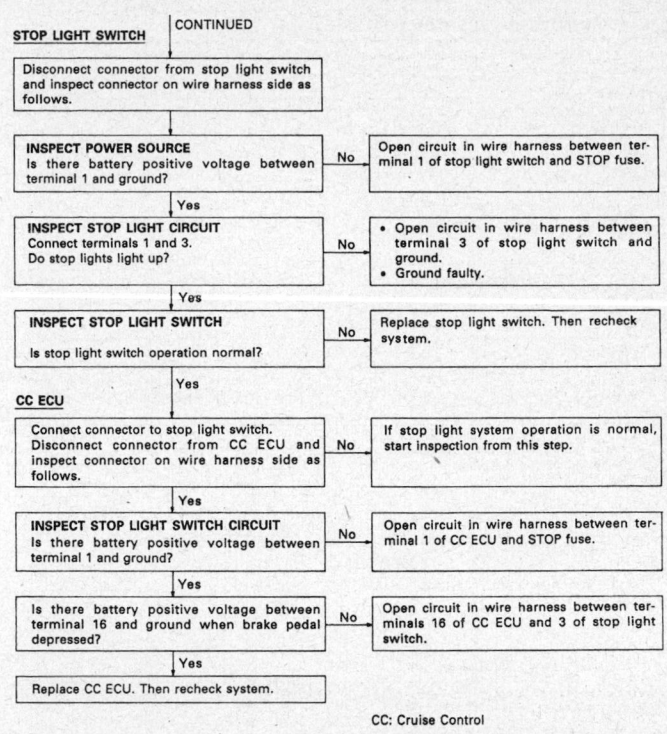

Fig. 257   Test F: Stop Lamp Switch Circuit (Part 2 of 2). Previa

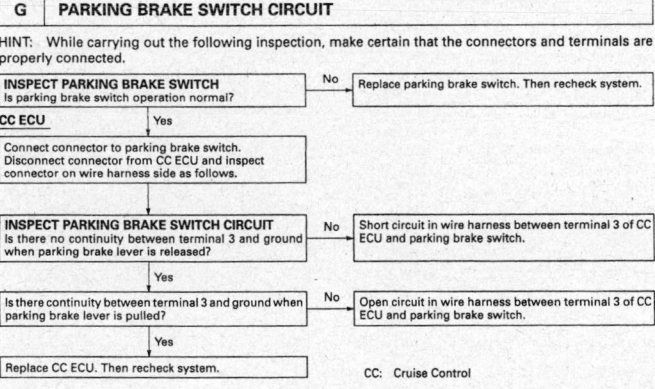

Fig. 258   Test G: Parking Brake Switch Circuit. Previa

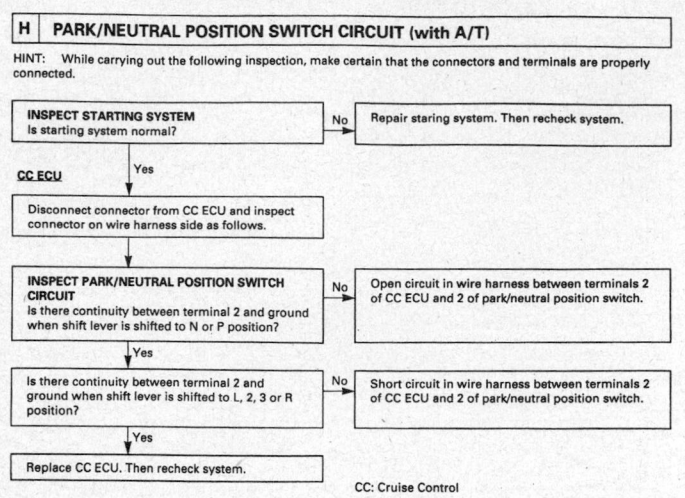

Fig. 259   Test H: Park/Neutral Position Switch Circuit. Previa

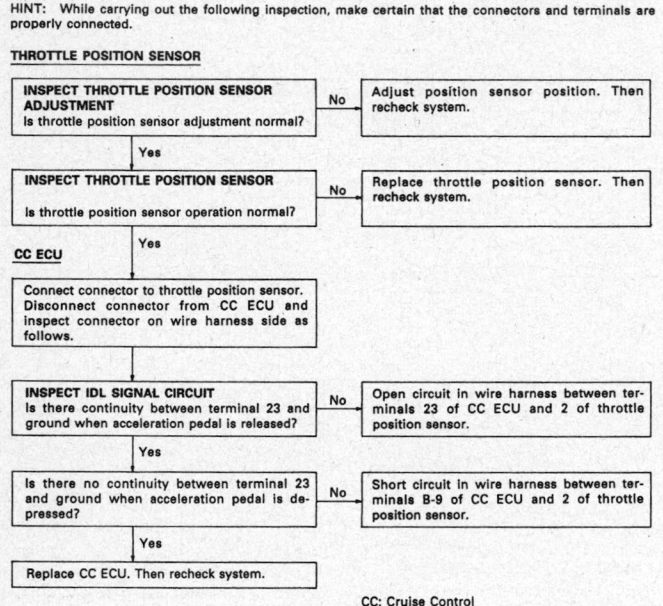

Fig. 261   Test J: IDL Signal Circuit. Previa

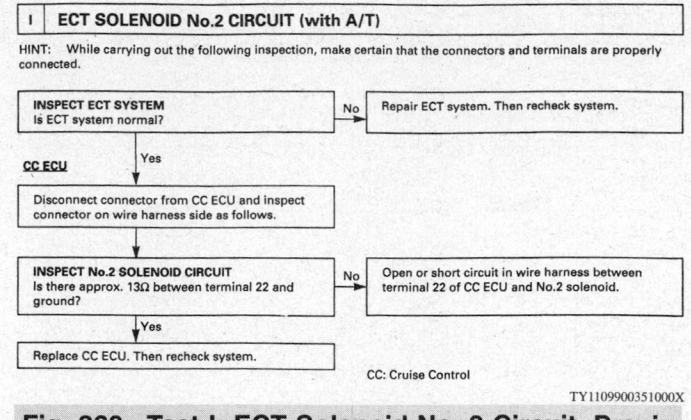

Fig. 260   Test I: ECT Solenoid No. 2 Circuit. Previa

Symptom	Suspect Area
SET not occurring or CANCEL occurring. (DTC is Normal)	1. Main Switch Circuit (Cruise control switch) 2. Vehicle Speed Sensor 3. Control Switch Circuit (Cruise control switch) 4. Stop Light Switch Circuit 5. Park/Neutral Position Switch Circuit 6. Clutch Switch 7. Actuator Motor Circuit 8. Cruise Control Cable 9. Cruise Control ECU
SET not occurring or CANCEL occurring. (DTC dose not output)	1. ECU Power Source Circuit 2. Cruise Control ECU
Actual vehicle speed deviates above or below the set speed.	1. Cruise Control Cable 2. Vehicle Speed Signal Abnormal 3. Electronically Controlled Transmission Communication Circuit 4. Actuator Motor Circuit 5. Idle Signal Circuit (main throttle position sensor) 6. Cruise Control ECU
Gear shifting frequent between 3rd O/D when driving on uphill road. (Hurting)	1. Electronically Controlled Transmission Communication Circuit 2. Cruise Control ECU
Cruise control not cancelled, even when brake pedal is depressed.	1. Cruise Control Cable 2. Stop Light Switch Circuit 3. Actuator Motor Circuit 4. Cruise Control ECU
Cruise control not cancelled, even when transmission is shifted to "N" position.	1. Cruise Control Cable 2. Park/Neutral Position Switch Circuit 3. Actuator Motor Circuit 4. Cruise Control ECU
Cruise control not cancelled, even when clutch pedal is depressed.	1. Cruise Control Cable 2. Clutch Switch Circuit 3. Actuator Motor Circuit 4. Cruise Control ECU
Control switch does not operate. (SET/COAST, ACC/RES, CANCEL not possible)	1. Cruise Control Cable 2. Control Switch Circuit 3. Actuator Motor Circuit 4. Cruise Control ECU
SET possible at 40 km/h (25 mph) or less, or CANCEL does not operate at 40 km/h (25 mph) or less.	1. Cruise Control Cable 2. Vehicle Speed Signal Abnormal 3. Actuator Motor Circuit 4. Cruise Control ECU
Poor response is ACCEL and RESUME modes.	1. Cruise Control Cable 2. Electronically Controlled Transmission Communication Circuit 3. Actuator Motor Circuit 4. Cruise Control ECU
O/D does not resume, even though the road is not uphill.	1. Electronically Controlled Transmission Communication Circuit 2. Cruise Control ECU

Fig. 262   Problem Symptoms Table (Part 1 of 2). RAV4

DTC memory is erased.	1. Cruise Control ECU
DTC is not output, or is output when should not be.	1. Diagnosis Circuit 2. Cruise Control ECU
Cruise MAIN indicator light remains ON or fails to light up.	1. Cruise MAIN Indicator Light Switch Circuit 2. Cruise Control ECU

Fig. 262   Problem Symptoms Table (Part 2 of 2). RAV4

CIRCUIT DESCRIPTION

The actuator motor is operated by signals from the ECU. Acceleration and deceleration signals are transmitted by changes in the Duty Ratio (See note below).

Duty Ratio

The duty ratio is the ratio of the period of continuity in one cycle. For example, if A is the period of continuity in one cycle, and B is the period of non-continuity, then

$$Duty\ Ratio = \frac{A}{A+B} \times 100\ (\%)$$

DTC No.	DTC Detecting Condition	Trouble area
11	• Short in motor circuit.	• Cruise control actuator motor • Harness or connector between actuator motor and ECU • ECU
14	• Open in actuator motor circuit	

TY1109900174010X

Fig. 263   Codes 11 & 14: Actuator Motor Circuit (Part 1 of 2). 1996–97 RAV4

CIRCUIT DESCRIPTION

This circuit turns on the magnetic clutch inside the actuator during cruise control operation according to the signal from the ECU. If a malfunction occurs in the actuator or vehicle speed sensor, etc. during cruise control, the rotor shaft between the motor and control plate is released.

When the brake pedal is depressed, the stop light switch turns on, supplying electrical power to the stop light. Power supply to the magnetic clutch is mechanically cut and the magnetic clutch is turned OFF.

When driving downhill, if the vehicle speed exceeds the set speed by 15 km/h (9 mph), the ECU turns the magnetic clutch OFF. If the vehicle speed later drops to within 10 km/h (6 mph) above the set speed, then cruise control at the set speed is resumed.

DTC No.	DTC Detecting Condition	Trouble area
12	• Short in magnetic clutch circuit. • Open (0.8 sec) in magnetic clutch circuit.	• Cruise control magnetic clutch. • Harness or connector between ECU and magnetic clutch, magnetic clutch and body ground. • ECU • STOP Fuse

TY1109900175010X

Fig. 264   Code 12: Actuator Magnetic Clutch Circuit (Part 1 of 3). 1996–97 RAV4

INSPECTION PROCEDURE

1   Check STOP fuse.

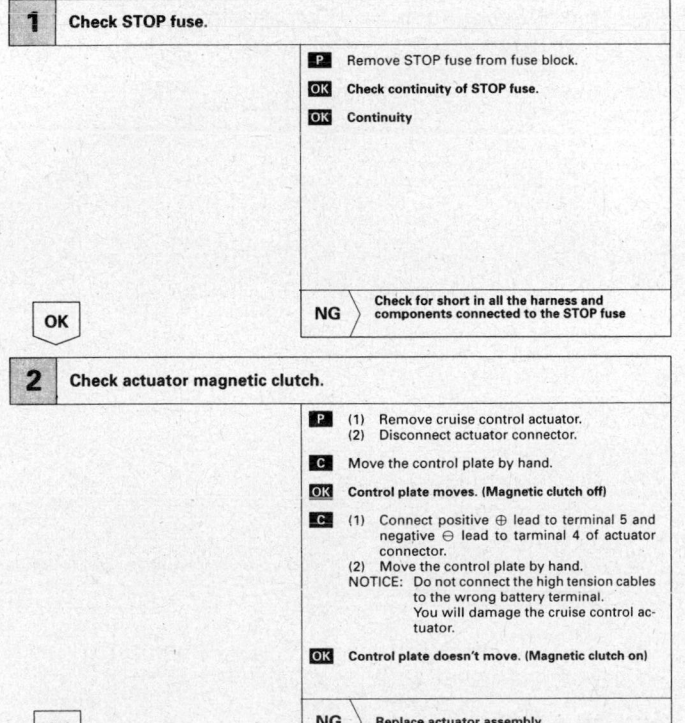

P	Remove STOP fuse from fuse block.
OK	Check continuity of STOP fuse.
OK	Continuity

OK ↓

NG ▷ Check for short in all the harness and components connected to the STOP fuse

2   Check actuator magnetic clutch.

P	(1) Remove cruise control actuator. (2) Disconnect actuator connector.
C	Move the control plate by hand.
OK	Control plate moves. (Magnetic clutch off)
C	(1) Connect positive ⊕ lead to terminal 5 and negative ⊖ lead to terminal 4 of actuator connector. (2) Move the control plate by hand. NOTICE: Do not connect the high tension cables to the wrong battery terminal. You will damage the cruise control actuator.
OK	Control plate doesn't move. (Magnetic clutch on)

OK ↓

NG ▷ Replace actuator assembly.

TY1109900175020X

Fig. 264   Code 12: Actuator Magnetic Clutch Circuit (Part 2 of 3). 1996–97 RAV4

INSPECTION PROCEDURE

1   Check actuator motor.

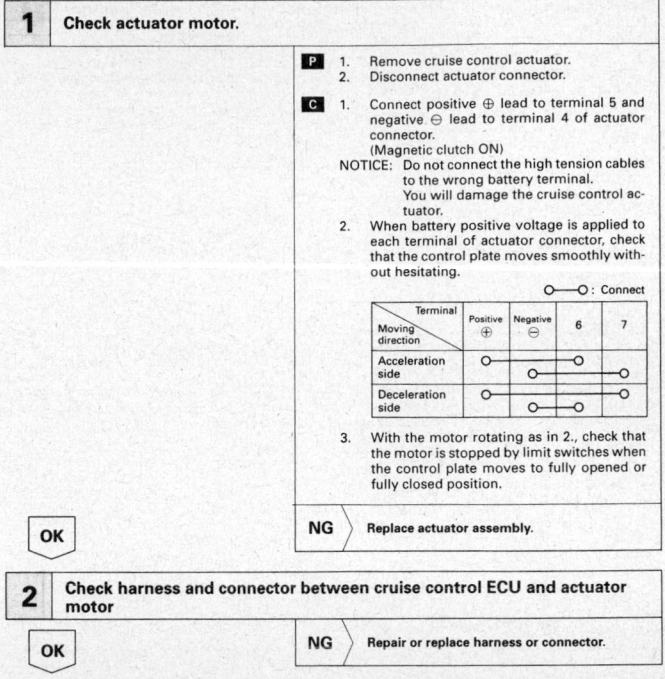

| **P** | 1. Remove cruise control actuator.
2. Disconnect actuator connector. |
| **C** | 1. Connect positive ⊕ lead to terminal 5 and negative ⊖ lead to terminal 4 of actuator connector. (Magnetic clutch ON)
NOTICE: Do not connect the high tension cables to the wrong battery terminal. You will damage the cruise control actuator.
2. When battery positive voltage is applied to each terminal of actuator connector, check that the control plate moves smoothly without hesitating. |

			○—○ : Connect	
Terminal Moving direction	Positive ⊕	Negative ⊖	6	7
Acceleration side	○		○	
Deceleration side	○			○

3. With the motor rotating as in 2., check that the motor is stopped by limit switches when the control plate moves to fully opened or fully closed position.

OK ↓

NG ▷ Replace actuator assembly.

2   Check harness and connector between cruise control ECU and actuator motor

OK ↓

NG ▷ Repair or replace harness or connector.

Proceed to next circuit inspection shown on problem symptoms chart.
However, when DTC 11, 14 is displayed, check and replace cruise control ECU.

TY1109900174020X

Fig. 263   Codes 11 & 14: Actuator Motor Circuit (Part 2 of 2). 1996–97 RAV4

3   Check stop light switch.

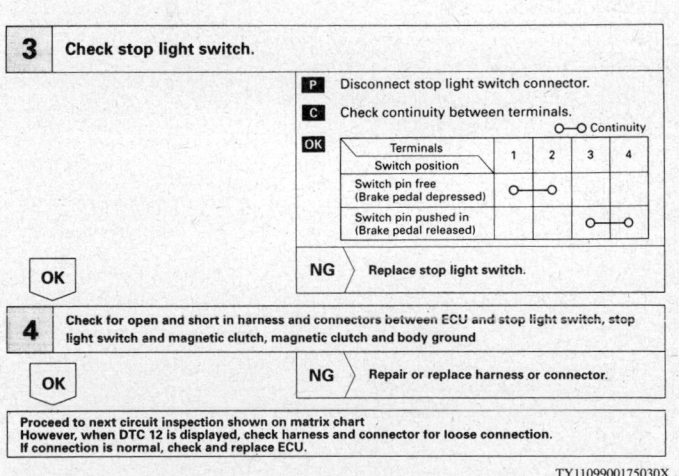

| **P** | Disconnect stop light switch connector. |
| **C** | Check continuity between terminals. |

		○—○ Continuity		
Terminals Switch position	1	2	3	4
Switch pin free (Brake pedal depressed)	○	○		
Switch pin pushed in (Brake pedal released)			○	○

OK ↓

NG ▷ Replace stop light switch.

4   Check for open and short in harness and connectors between ECU and stop light switch, stop light switch and magnetic clutch, magnetic clutch and body ground

OK ↓

NG ▷ Repair or replace harness or connector.

Proceed to next circuit inspection shown on matrix chart
However, when DTC 12 is displayed, check harness and connector for loose connection.
If connection is normal, check and replace ECU.

TY1109900175030X

Fig. 264   Code 12: Actuator Magnetic Clutch Circuit (Part 3 of 3). 1996–97 RAV4

CIRCUIT DESCRIPTION

The circuit detects the rotation position of the actuator control plate and sends a signal to the ECU.

DTC No.	DTC Detecting Condition	Trouble area
13	• Position sensor detects abnormal voltage.	• Cruise control actuator motor. • Cruise control actuator position sensor. • Harness or connector between actuator position sensor and body ground.
14	• Open in actuator motor circuit. • Position sensor signal value does not change when the motor operates.	• Harness or connector between actuator motor and ECU. • ECU

TY1109900176010X

Fig. 265   Codes 13 & 14: Actuator Position Sensor Circuit (Part 1 of 2). 1996–97 RAV4

CIRCUIT DESCRIPTION

The vehicle speed sensor signal is sent to the cruise control ECU as the vehicle speed signal.
The rotor shaft is driven by the gear of the transaxle.
For each rotation of the shaft, the speed sensor sends a 4-pulse signal to the combination meter. This signal is converted inside the combination meter and sent as a 4-pulse signal to the cruise control ECU. The ECU calculates the vehicle speed from this pulse frequency.

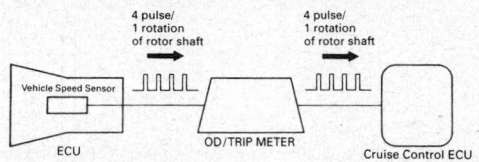

DTC No.	DTC Detecting Condition	Trouble area
21	Speed signal is not input to the ECU while cruise control is set.	• Vehicle speed sensor • Combination meter • Harness or connector between speed sensor and combination meter, combination meter and ECU. • ECU
23	Vehicle speed sensor pluse is abnormal.	• Vehicle speed sensor • Harness or connector (SPD) • ECU

TY1109900177010X

Fig. 266   Code 21: Vehicle Speed Sensor Circuit (Part 1 of 2). 1996–97 RAV4

INSPECTION PROCEDURE

1   Input signal check.

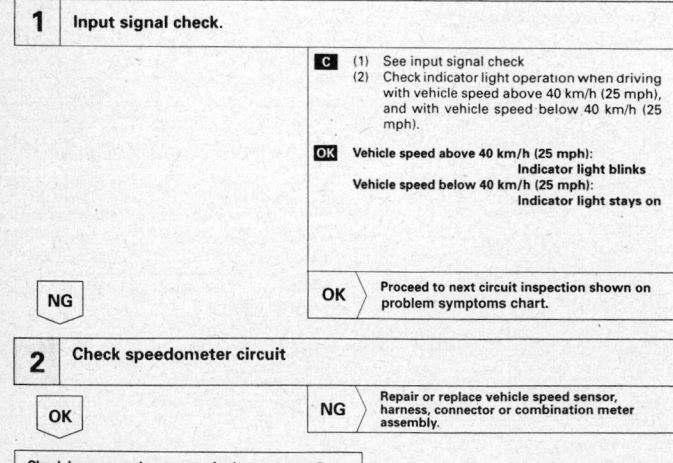

C	(1) See input signal check (2) Check indicator light operation when driving with vehicle speed above 40 km/h (25 mph), and with vehicle speed below 40 km/h (25 mph).
OK	Vehicle speed above 40 km/h (25 mph): Indicator light blinks Vehicle speed below 40 km/h (25 mph): Indicator light stays on
OK	Proceed to next circuit inspection shown on problem symptoms chart.

NG

2   Check speedometer circuit

OK		
	NG	Repair or replace vehicle speed sensor, harness, connector or combination meter assembly.

Check harness and connector for loose connection.
If connection is normal, check and replace ECU.

TY1109900177020X

Fig. 266   Code 21: Vehicle Speed Sensor Circuit (Part 2 of 2). 1996–97 RAV4

INSPECTION PROCEDURE

1   Check voltage between terminals VR2 and VR3 of ECU connector.

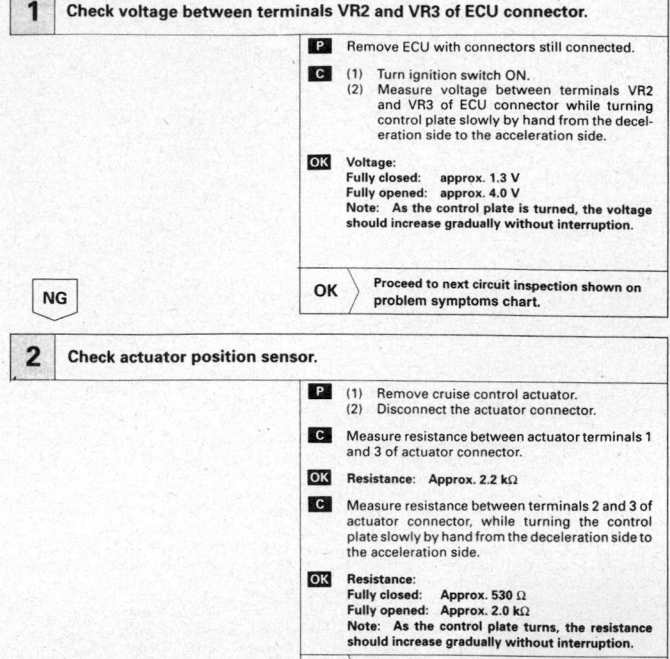

P	Remove ECU with connectors still connected.
C	(1) Turn ignition switch ON. (2) Measure voltage between terminals VR2 and VR3 of ECU connector while turning control plate slowly by hand from the deceleration side to the acceleration side.
OK	Voltage: Fully closed: approx. 1.3 V Fully opened: approx. 4.0 V Note: As the control plate is turned, the voltage should increase gradually without interruption.

NG   OK | Proceed to next circuit inspection shown on problem symptoms chart.

2   Check actuator position sensor.

P	(1) Remove cruise control actuator. (2) Disconnect the actuator connector.
C	Measure resistance between actuator terminals 1 and 3 of actuator connector.
OK	Resistance: Approx. 2.2 kΩ
C	Measure resistance between terminals 2 and 3 of actuator connector, while turning the control plate slowly by hand from the deceleration side to the acceleration side.
OK	Resistance: Fully closed: Approx. 530 Ω Fully opened: Approx. 2.0 kΩ Note: As the control plate turns, the resistance should increase gradually without interruption.

OK   NG | Replace actuator assembly.

3   Check for open and short in harness and connector between ECU and actuator position sensor

OK   NG | Repair or replace harness or connector.

Check harness and connector for loose connection.
If connection is normal check and replace ECU.

TY1109900176020X

Fig. 265   Codes 13 & 14: Actuator Position Sensor Circuit (Part 2 of 2). 1996–97 RAV4

CIRCUIT DESCRIPTION

This circuit carries the SET/COAST, RESUME/ACCEL and CANCEL signals (each voltage) to the ECU.

DTC No.	DTC Detecting Condition	Trouble area
32	Short in, control switch circuit. Voltage abnormality in control switch.	• Cruise control switch. • Harness or connector between control switch and ECU. • ECU

TY1109900178010X

Fig. 267   Code 32: Cruise Control Switch Circuit (Part 1 of 3). 1996–97 RAV4

INSPECTION PROCEDURE

1 Input signal check.

Input Signal	Indicator light blinking pattern
SET/COAST SWITCH	ON — 2 Pulse / OFF
RESUME/ACCEL SWITCH	ON — 3 Pulse / OFF
CANCEL SWITCH	ON Switch OFF / OFF Switch ON

P (1) See input signal check on
(2) Check the indicator light operation when each of the SET/COAST, RESUME/ACCEL and CANCEL is turned ON.

OK SET/COAST, RESUME/ACCEL Switch
The signals shown in the table on the left should be output when each switch is ON. The signal should disappear when the switch is turned OFF.
CANCEL Switch.
The indicator light goes off when the cancel switch is turned ON.

NG

OK Proceed to next circuit inspection shown on matrix chart

TY1109900178020X

Fig. 267 Code 32: Cruise Control Switch Circuit (Part 2 of 3). 1996–97 RAV4

CIRCUIT DESCRIPTION

When the brake is on, battery positive voltage normally applies through the stop fuse and stop light switch to terminal STP- of the ECU, and the ECU turns the cruise control off.
A fail-safe function is provided so that cancel functions normally, even if there is a malfunction in the stop light signal circuit.
If the harness connected to terminal STP- has an open, terminal STP- will have battery positive voltage and the cruise control will be turned off, also SET not occurring.
Also, when the brake is on, the magnetic clutch is cut electrically by the stop light switch, turning the cruise control off.

INSPECTION PROCEDURE

1 Check operation of stop light.

C Check that stop light comes on when brake pedal is depressed, and turns off when brake pedal is released.

OK

NG Check stop light circuit.

TY1109900179010X

Fig. 268 Stop Lamp Switch Circuit (Part 1 of 2). 1996–97 RAV4

---

2 Check voltage between terminal CCS of ECU connector and body ground.

P Remove ECU with connectors still connected.

C (1) Turn ignition switch ON.
(2) Measure voltage between terminal CCS of ECU connector and body ground, when each of the SET/COAST, RESUME/ACCEL and CANCEL is turned ON.

OK

Switch position	Voltage
Neutral	10 – 16 V
RES/ACC	0.8 – 1.4 V
SET/COAST	2.4 – 4.0 V
CANCEL	5.1 – 8.3 V

NG

OK Proceed to next circuit inspection shown on problem symptoms chart.

3 Check control switch.

P 1. Remove steering wheel center pad.
2. Disconnect control switch connector

C Measure resistance between terminals 3 and 4 of control switch connector when control switch is operated.

OK

Switch position	Resistance
Neutral	1 MΩ or higher
RES/ACC	50 – 80 Ω
SET/COAST	180 – 220 Ω
CANCEL	400 – 440 Ω

Hint When DTC 34 is displayed, carefully check that resistance is always ∞ in neutral position, particularly when switching between RES/ACC and SET/COAST.

OK

NG Replace cruise control switch.

4 Check for open and short in harness and connector between ECU and control switch

OK

NG Repair or replace harness or connector.

Check and replace ECU.

TY1109900178030X

Fig. 267 Code 32: Cruise Control Switch Circuit (Part 3 of 3). 1996–97 RAV4

---

2 Input signal check.

C (1) See input signal check
(2) Check the indicator light when the brake pedal is depressed.

OK The indicator light goes off when the brake pedal is depressed.

NG

OK Proceed to next circuit inspection shown on problem symptoms chart.

3 Check voltage between terminal, STP– of ECU connector and body ground.

P Remove ECU with connectors still connected.

C (1) Turn ignition switch ON.
(2) Measure voltage between terminsl STP– of ECU connector and body ground, when the brake pedal is depressed and released.

OK

	STP–
Depressed	10 – 16 V
Released	Below 1 V

NG

OK Proceed to next circuit inspection shown on problem symptoms chart.

4 Check for open in harness and connectors between terminal STP– of ECU and stop light switch

OK

NG Repair or replace harness or connector.

Check and replace ECU.

TY1109900179020X

Fig. 268 Stop Lamp Switch Circuit (Part 2 of 2). 1996–97 RAV4

CIRCUIT DESCRIPTION

When the idle switch is turned ON, a signal is sent to the ECU. The ECU uses this signal to correct the discrepancy between the throttle valve position and the actuator position sensor value to enable accurate cruise control at the set speed. If the idle switch is malfunctioning, problem symptoms also occur in the engine, so also inspect the engine.

INSPECTION PROCEDURE

1 Check voltage between terminal IDL of ECU connector and body ground.

P
(1) Remove cruise control ECU with connectors still connected.
(2) Disconnect ECM and ABS & TRAC ECU connector.

C
(1) Turn ignition switch ON.
(2) Measure voltage between terminal IDL of ECU connector and body ground, when the throttle valve is fully closed and fully opened.

OK

Throttle valve position	Voltage
Fully opened	10 – 16 V
Fully closed	Below 1 V

NG

OK Proceed to next circuit inspection shown on matrix chart

TY1109900180010X

Fig. 269 Idle Switch Circuit (Part 1 of 2). 1996–97 RAV4

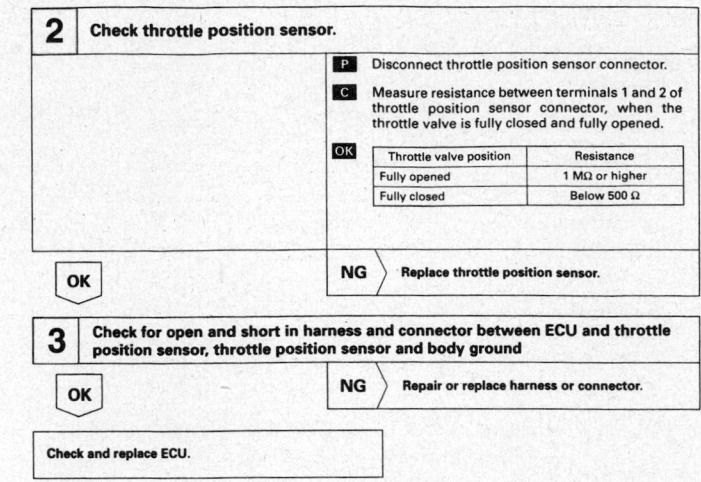

2 Check throttle position sensor.

P Disconnect throttle position sensor connector.

C Measure resistance between terminals 1 and 2 of throttle position sensor connector, when the throttle valve is fully closed and fully opened.

OK

Throttle valve position	Resistance
Fully opened	1 MΩ or higher
Fully closed	Below 500 Ω

OK

NG Replace throttle position sensor.

3 Check for open and short in harness and connector between ECU and throttle position sensor, throttle position sensor and body ground

OK

NG Repair or replace harness or connector.

Check and replace ECU.

TY1109900180020X

Fig. 269 Idle Switch Circuit (Part 2 of 2). 1996–97 RAV4

CIRCUIT DESCRIPTION

When driving uphill under cruise control, in order to reduce shifting due to ON-OFF overdrive operation and to provide smooth driving, when down shifting in the electronically controlled transaxle occurs, a signal to prevent upshift until the end of the uphill slope is sent from the cruise control ECU to the electronically controlled transaxle.

Terminal ECM of the cruise control ECU detects the shift change signal (output to electronically controlled transaxle No.2 solenoid) from the electronically controlled transaxle.

If vehicle speed down, also when terminal electronically controlled transaxle of the cruise control ECU receives down shifting signal, it sends a signal from terminal OD to OD1 to cut overdrive until the end of the uphill slope, and the gear shifts are reduced and gear shift points in the electronically controlled transaxle are changed.

TY1109900181010X

Fig. 270 Electronically Controlled Transaxle Communication Circuit (Part 1 of 3). 1996–97 RAV4

INSPECTION PROCEDURE

1 Check operation of overdrive.

P Test drive after engine warm up.

C Check that overdrive ON ↔ OFF occurs with operation of OD switch ON-OFF.

OK

NG Check and repair electronically controlled transaxle

2 Check voltage between terminal OD of harness side connector of ECU and body ground.

P Remove ECU with connector still connected.

C
(1) Disconnect ECU connector.
(2) Turn ignition switch ON.
(3) Measure voltage between terminal OD of harness side connector of ECU and body ground.

OK Voltage: 10 – 16 V

OK

NG Go to step **5**

TY1109900181020X

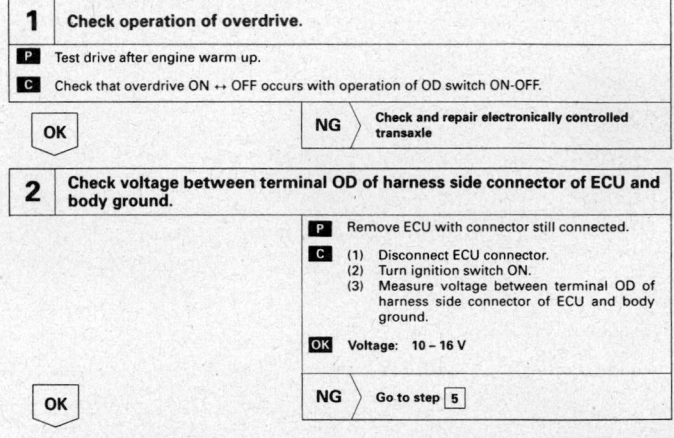

Fig. 270 Electronically Controlled Transaxle Communication Circuit (Part 2 of 3). 1996–97 RAV4

3	Check voltage between terminal ECT of cruise control ECU connector and body ground (On test drive).

P
(1) Connect ECU connector.
(2) Test drive after engine warm up.

C Check voltage between terminal ECT of cruise control ECU connector and body ground when OD switch is on and off.

OK

Gear Position	Voltage
O/D	Below 1 V
3rd	10 – 16 V

NG

OK Proceed to next circuit inspection shown on problem symptoms chart.

4	Check for open and short in harness and connector between terminal ECT of cruise control ECU and electronically controlled transaxle solenoid

OK

NG Repair or replace harness or connector.

Check and repair ECU.

5	Check for open and short in harness and connector between terminal OD of ECU and terminal OD1 of ECM

OK

NG Repair or replace harness or connector.

Check and replace ECM.

TY1109900181030X

Fig. 270 Electronically Controlled Transaxle Communication Circuit (Part 3 of 3). 1996–97 RAV4

INSPECTION PROCEDURE

1	Check operation of starter.

C Check that the starter operates normally and that the engine starts.

OK

NG Diagnose starting system.

2	Input signal check.

P
(1) See input signal check
(2) Check the indicator light when shifting into except D position.

OK The indicator light goes off when shifting into except D position.

NG

OK Proceed to next circuit inspection shown on problem symptoms chart.

TY1109900182020X

Fig. 271 Park/Neutral Position Switch Circuit (Part 2 of 3). 1996–97 RAV4

CIRCUIT DESCRIPTION

When the clutch pedal is depressed, the clutch switch sends a signal to the cruise control ECU, when this signal is input to the cruise control ECU during cruise control driving, the cruise control ECU cancels cruise control.

TY1109900183010X

Fig. 272 Clutch Switch Circuit (Part 1 of 2). 1996–97 RAV4

CIRCUIT DESCRIPTION

When the shift position is put in except D position, a signal is sent from the park/neutral position switch to the ECU. When this signal is input during cruise control driving, the ECU cancels the cruise control.

TY1109900182010X

Fig. 271 Park/Neutral Position Switch Circuit (Part 1 of 3). 1996–97 RAV4

INSPECTION PROCEDURE

3	Check voltage between terminal D of ECU connector and body ground.

P Remove ECU with connectors still connected.

C
(1) Turn ignition switch ON.
(2) Measure voltage between terminal D of ECU connector and body ground, when shifting into D position and other ranges.

OK

Shift Position	Voltage
D position	10 – 16 V
Other positions	Below 1 V

NG

OK Proceed to next circuit inspection shown on problem symptoms chart.

4	Check for open in harness and connector between ECU and GAUGE fuse

OK

NG Repair or replace harness or connector.

Check and replace ECU.

TY1109900182030X

Fig. 271 Park/Neutral Position Switch Circuit (Part 3 of 3). 1996–97 RAV4

INSPECTION PROCEDURE

1	Check operation of starter.

C Check that the starter operates normally and that the engine starts.

OK

NG Diagnose starting system.

2	Input signal check.

C
(1) See input signal check on page BE-95.
(2) Check the indicator light when the clutch pedal is depressed.

OK The indicator light goes off when the clutch pedal is depressed.

NG

OK Proceed to next circuit inspection shown on problem symptoms chart.

3	Check voltage between terminal D of ECU connector and body ground.

P Remove ECU with connectors still connected.

C
(1) Turn ignition switch ON.
(2) Measure voltage between terminal D of ECU connector and body ground, when the clutch pedal is depressed.

OK

Switch Position	Voltage
ON (pedal depressed)	Below 1 V
OFF	10 – 16 V

NG

OK Proceed to next circuit inspection shown on problem symptoms chart.

4	Check for open in harness and connector between ECU and GAUGE fuse

OK

NG Repair or replace harness or connector.

Check and replace ECU.

TY1109900183020X

Fig. 272 Clutch Switch Circuit (Part 2 of 2). 1996–97 RAV4

CIRCUIT DESCRIPTION

The ECU power source supplies power to the actuator and sensors, etc., Terminal GND and the cruise control ECU case are grounded.

TY1109900184010X

Fig. 273 ECU Power Source Circuit (Part 1 of 3). 1996–97 RAV4

INSPECTION PROCEDURE

1 | Check ECU-IG fuse.

P Remove ECU-IG fuse from fuse block.

OK Check continuity of ECU-IG fuse.

OK Continuity

OK

NG > Check for short in all the harness and components connected to the ECU-IG fuse

TY1109900184020X

Fig. 273 ECU Power Source Circuit (Part 2 of 3). 1996–97 RAV4

CIRCUIT DESCRIPTION

The ECU back-up power source provides power even when the ignition switch is off and is used for DTC memory, etc.

TY1109900185010X

Fig. 274 Back-Up Power Source Circuit (Part 1 of 3). 1996–97 RAV4

INSPECTION PROCEDURE

1 | Check DOME fuse.

P Remove DOME fuse from R/B No.2.

C Check continuity of DOME fuse.

OK Continuity

OK

NG > Check for short in all the harness and components connected to the DOME fuse

TY1109900185030X

Fig. 274 Back-Up Power Source Circuit (Part 2 of 3). 1997 RAV4

2 | Check voltage between terminals B and GND of ECU connector.

P Remove ECU with connectors still connected.

C (1) Turn ignition switch ON.
(2) Measure voltage between terminals B and GND of ECU connector.

OK Voltage: 10 – 16 V

NG

OK > Proceed to next circuit inspection shown on matrix chart

3 | Check continuity between terminal GND of ECU connector and body ground.

C Measure resistance between terminal GND of cruise control ECU connector and body ground.

OK Resistance: 1 Ω or loss

OK

NG > Repair or replace harness or connector.

Check and repair harness and connector between battery and ECU.

TY1109900184030X

Fig. 273 ECU Power Source Circuit (Part 3 of 3). 1996–97 RAV4

INSPECTION PROCEDURE

1 | Check ECU-B fuse.

P Remove ECU-B fuse from R/B No.2.

C Check continuity of ECU-B fuse.

OK Continuity

OK

NG > Check for short in all the harness and components connected to the ECU-B fuse

TY1109900185020X

Fig. 274 Back-Up Power Source Circuit (Part 2 of 3). 1996 RAV4

2 | Check voltage between terminal BATT of ECU connector and body ground.

P Remove ECU with connectors still connected.

C Measure voltage between terminal BATT of ECU connector and body ground.

OK Voltage: 10 – 16 V

NG

OK > Proceed to next circuit inspection shown on matrix chart

Check and repair harness and connector between battery and ECU.

TY1109900185040X

Fig. 274 Back-Up Power Source Circuit (Part 3 of 3). 1996–97 RAV4

CIRCUIT DESCRIPTION

When the cruise control main switch is turned off, the cruise control does not operate.

TY1109900186010X

Fig. 275 Cruise Control Main Switch Circuit (Part 1 of 2). 1996–97 RAV4

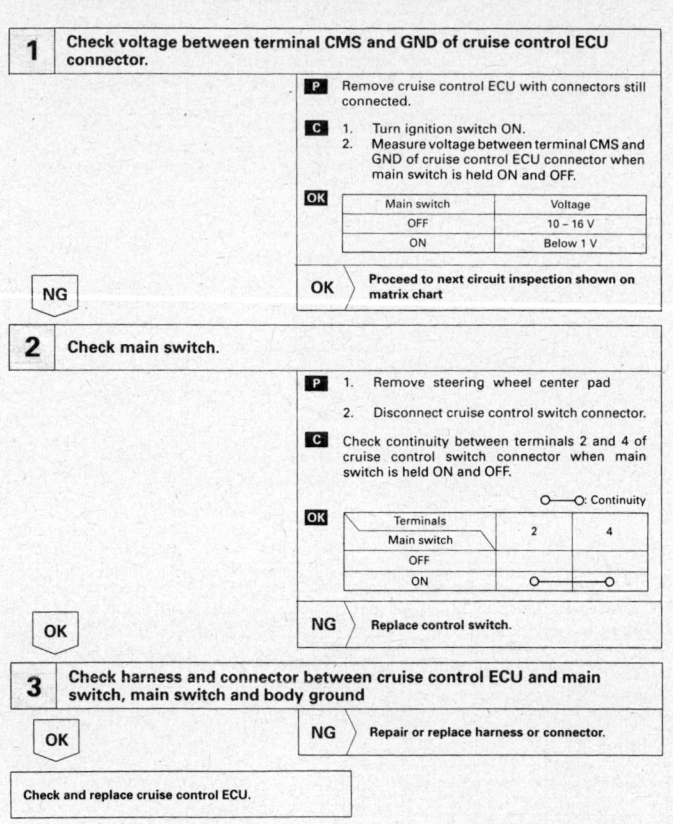

1 Check voltage between terminal CMS and GND of cruise control ECU connector.

P Remove cruise control ECU with connectors still connected.

C
1. Turn ignition switch ON.
2. Measure voltage between terminal CMS and GND of cruise control ECU connector when main switch is held ON and OFF.

OK

Main switch	Voltage
OFF	10 – 16 V
ON	Below 1 V

NG

OK Proceed to next circuit inspection shown on matrix chart

2 Check main switch.

P
1. Remove steering wheel center pad
2. Disconnect cruise control switch connector.

C Check continuity between terminals 2 and 4 of cruise control switch connector when main switch is held ON and OFF.

○—○: Continuity

OK

Terminals		
Main switch	2	4
OFF		
ON	○	○

NG Replace control switch.

OK

3 Check harness and connector between cruise control ECU and main switch, main switch and body ground

OK

NG Repair or replace harness or connector.

Check and replace cruise control ECU.

TY1109900186020X

Fig. 275   Cruise Control Main Switch Circuit (Part 2 of 2). 1996–97 RAV4

CIRCUIT DESCRIPTION

This circuit sends a signal to the ECU that DTC output is required.

TY1109900187010X

Fig. 276   T$_C$ Circuit (Part 1 of 2). 1996–97 RAV4

INSPECTION PROCEDURE

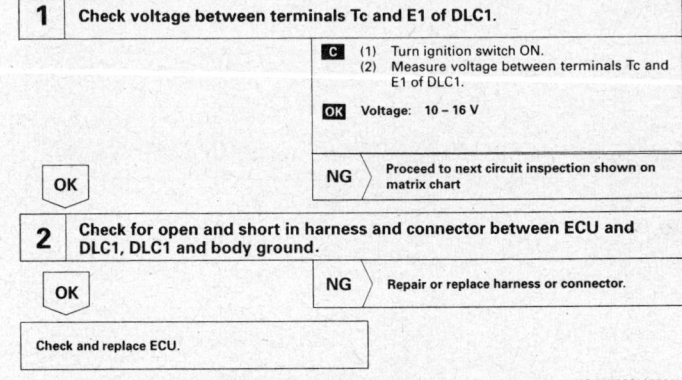

1 Check voltage between terminals Tc and E1 of DLC1.

C
(1) Turn ignition switch ON.
(2) Measure voltage between terminals Tc and E1 of DLC1.

OK Voltage: 10 – 16 V

OK

NG Proceed to next circuit inspection shown on matrix chart

2 Check for open and short in harness and connector between ECU and DLC1, DLC1 and body ground.

OK

NG Repair or replace harness or connector.

Check and replace ECU.

TY1109900187020X

Fig. 276   T$_C$ Circuit (Part 2 of 2). 1996–97 RAV4

Actuator Control Cable Inspection

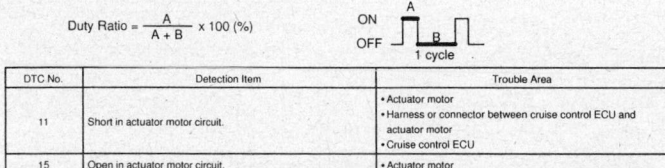

C
1. Check that the actuator, control cable and throttle link are properly installed and that the cable and link are connected correctly.
2. Check that the actuator and bell crank are operating smoothly.
3. Check that the cable is not loose or too tight.

Hint
1. If the control cable is very loose, the vehicle's loss of speed going uphill will be large.
2. If the control cable is too tight, the idle RPM will become high.

TY1109900188000X

Fig. 277   Actuator Control Cable Inspection. 1996–97 RAV4

CIRCUIT DESCRIPTION

The actuator motor is operated by signals from the ECU. Acceleration and deceleration signals are transmitted by changes in the Duty Ratio (See note below).

Duty Ratio

The duty ratio is the ratio of the period of continuity in one cycle. For example, if A is the period of continuity in one cycle, and B is the period of non–continuity, then.

$$\text{Duty Ratio} = \frac{A}{A + B} \times 100 \ (\%)$$

DTC No.	Detection Item	Trouble Area
11	Short in actuator motor circuit.	• Actuator motor • Harness or connector between cruise control ECU and actuator motor • Cruise control ECU
15	Open in actuator motor circuit.	• Actuator motor

TY1109900156010X

Fig. 278   Codes 11 & 15: Actuator Motor Circuit (Part 1 of 2). 1998–99 RAV4

INSPECTION PROCEDURE

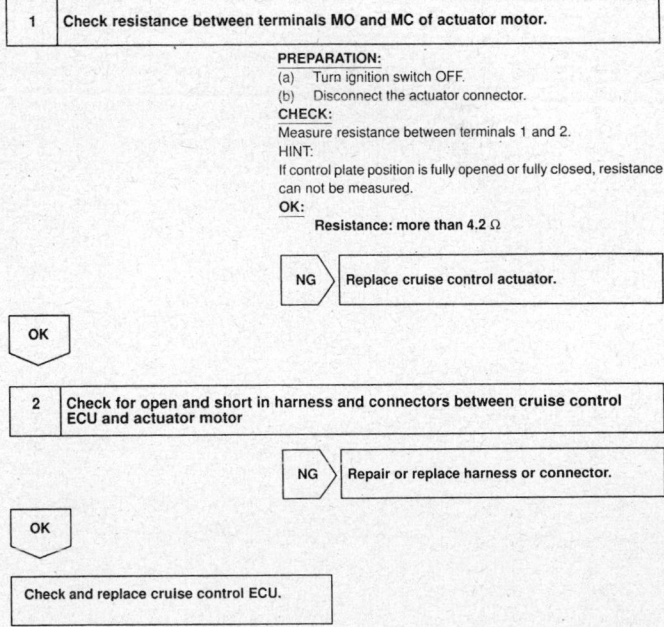

1 Check resistance between terminals MO and MC of actuator motor.

PREPARATION:
(a) Turn ignition switch OFF.
(b) Disconnect the actuator connector.

CHECK:
Measure resistance between terminals 1 and 2.

HINT:
If control plate position is fully opened or fully closed, resistance can not be measured.

OK:
Resistance: more than 4.2 Ω

NG Replace cruise control actuator.

OK

2 Check for open and short in harness and connectors between cruise control ECU and actuator motor

NG Repair or replace harness or connector.

OK

Check and replace cruise control ECU.

TY1109900156020X

Fig. 278   Codes 11 & 15: Actuator Motor Circuit (Part 2 of 2). 1998–99 RAV4

CIRCUIT DESCRIPTION

This circuit turns on the magnetic clutch inside the actuator during cruise control operation according to the signal from the ECU. If a malfunction occurs in the actuator or speed sensor, etc. during cruise control operation, the rotor shaft between the motor and control plate is released.

When the brake pedal is depressed, the stop light switch turns on, supplying electrical power to the stop light. Power supply to the magnetic clutch is mechanically cut and the magnetic clutch is turned OFF.

When driving downhill, if the vehicle speed exceeds the set speed by 8 km/h (5 mph), the ECU turns the safety magnet clutch OFF. If the vehicle speed later drops to within 5 km/h (3 mph) above the set speed, then cruise control at the set speed is resumed.

DTC No.	Detection Item	Trouble Area
12	Short in actuator magnetic clutch circuit. Open (0.8 sec.) in actuator magnetic clutch circuit.	• STOP Fuse • Stop light switch • Actuator magnetic clutch • Harness or connector between cruise control ECU and actuator magnetic clutch, actuator magnetic clutch and body ground • Cruise control ECU

TY1109900157010X

Fig. 279   Code 12: Actuator Magnetic Clutch Circuit (Part 1 of 4). 1998–99 RAV4

---

2 | Check stop light switch.

PREPARATION:
Disconnect the stop light switch connector.
CHECK:
Check continuity between terminals.

Switch position	Continuity
Switch pin free (Brake pedal depressed)	1 – 2
Switch pin pushed in (Brake pedal released)	3 – 4

NG > Replace stop light switch.

OK

3 | Check resistance between terminals L and GND of actuator magnetic clutch.

PREPARATION:
(a) Turn ignition switch OFF.
(b) Disconnect the actuator connector.
CHECK:
Measure resistance between terminals 3 and 4.
OK:
   Resistance: 34.65 ~ 42.35 Ω.

NG > Replace cruise control actuator.

OK

TY1109900157030X

Fig. 279   Code 12: Actuator Magnetic Clutch Circuit (Part 3 of 4). 1998–99 RAV4

INSPECTION PROCEDURE

1 | Check STOP fuse.

PREPARATION:
(a) Turn ignition switch OFF.
(b) Remove the STOP fuse from instrument panel junction block.
CHECK:
Check fuse continuity.
OK:
   Continuity exists.

NG > Replace STOP fuse.

OK

TY1109900157020X

Fig. 279   Code 12: Actuator Magnetic Clutch Circuit (Part 2 of 4). 1998–99 RAV4

---

4 | Check for open and short in harness and connectors between cruise control ECU and actuator magnetic clutch, actuator magnetic clutch and body ground

NG > Repair or replace harness or connector.

OK

Check and replace cruise control ECU

TY1109900157040X

Fig. 279   Code 12: Actuator Magnetic Clutch Circuit (Part 4 of 4). 1998–99 RAV4

CIRCUIT DESCRIPTION

The circuit detects the rotation position of the actuator control plate and sends a signal to the ECU.

DTC No.	Detection Item	Trouble Area
14	Cruise control actuator mechanical malfunction.	• Actuator lock: (motor, arm) • Actuator motor • Cruise control ECU

INSPECTION PROCEDURE

1 | Check cruise control actuator arm locking operation

PREPARATION:
(a) Turn ignition switch OFF.
(b) Disconnect the actuator connector.
CHECK:
Connect the positive (+) lead from the battery to the terminal 3 of actuator and the negative (–) lead to terminal 4.
NOTICE:
Do not connect the high tension cable to the wrong battery terminal. You will damage the cruise control actuator.
Move the control plate by hand.
OK:
   Control plate does not move.

NG > Replace cruise control actuator.

OK

TY1109900158010X

Fig. 280   Code 14: Actuator Mechanical Fault (Part 1 of 2). 1998–99 RAV4

2	Check cruise control actuator operation.

PREPARATION:
(a) Turn ignition switch OFF.
(b) Disconnect the actuator connector.
CHECK:
Connect the positive (+) lead from the battery to terminals 1 and 3 of actuator, connect the negative (−) lead to terminals 2 and 4 of actuator.
OK:
Control arm moves to full open side

CHECK:
Connect the positive (+) lead from the battery to terminals 2 and 4 of actuator, connect the negative (−) lead to terminals 1 and 3 of actuator.
OK:
Control arm moves to fully closed side

NG ▷ Replace cruise control actuator.

OK

3	Check harness and connector between cruise control ECU and cruise control actuator

NG ▷ Repair or replace harness or connector.

OK

Check and replace cruise control ECU

TY1109900158020X

Fig. 280   Code 14: Actuator Mechanical Fault (Part 2 of 2). 1998–99 RAV4

INSPECTION PROCEDURE

1	Input signal check.

Input Signal	Indicator Light Blinking Pattern
Drive at about 40 km/h (25 mph) or below	Light ON / OFF
Drive at about 40 km/h (25 mph) or higher	Light ON / OFF

CHECK:
(a) See input signal check
(b) Check indicator light operation when driving at vehicle speed above 40 km/h (25 mph), and at vehicle speed below 40 km/h (25 mph).
OK:
Vehicle speed above 40 km/h (25 mph): Indicator light blinks
Vehicle speed below 40 km/h (25 mph): Indicator light stays on

OK ▷ Check and replace cruise control ECU

NG

2	Check speedometer circuit

NG ▷ Repair or replace harness, connector or combination meter assembly.

OK

3	Check harness and connector between cruise control ECU and combination meter, combination meter and vehicle speed sensor

NG ▷ Repair or replace harness or connector.

OK

TY1109900159020X

Fig. 281   Code 21: Open In Vehicle Speed Sensor Circuit (Part 2 of 3). 1998–99 RAV4

CIRCUIT DESCRIPTION

The vehicle speed sensor circuit sends vehicle speed signal to cruise control ECU.
The rotor shaft is driven by the gear of the transmission.
For each rotation of the shaft, the vehicle speed sensor sends a 4 pulse signal through the combination meter to the cruise control ECU (See the following).
This signal is converted inside the combination meter and sent as a 4–pulse signal to the cruise control ECU.
The ECU calculates the vehicle speed from this pulse frequency.

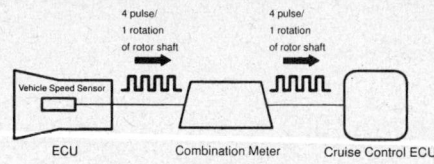

DTC No.	Detection Item	Trouble Area
21	Speed signal is not input to the cruise control ECU while cruise control is set.	• Combination meter • Harness or connector between cruise control ECU and combination meter, combination meter and vehicle speed sensor • Vehicle speed sensor • Cruise control ECU

TY1109900159010X

Fig. 281   Code 21: Open In Vehicle Speed Sensor Circuit (Part 1 of 3). 1998–99 RAV4

4	Check vehicle speed sensor

NG ▷ Replace vehicle speed sensor.

OK

Check and replace cruise control ECU

TY1109900159030X

Fig. 281   Code 21: Open In Vehicle Speed Sensor Circuit (Part 3 of 3). 1998–99 RAV4

CIRCUIT DESCRIPTION

DTC No.	Detection Item	Trouble Area
23	Vehicle speed sensor pulse is abnormal.	• Vehicle speed sensor • Cruise control ECU

INSPECTION PROCEDURE

1	Check vehicle speed sensor

NG ▷ Replace vehicle speed sensor.

OK

Check and replace cruise control ECU

TY1109900160000X

Fig. 282   Code 23: Vehicle Speed Signal Abnormal. 1998–99 RAV4

CIRCUIT DESCRIPTION

This circuit carries the SET/COAST, RESUME/ACCEL and CANCEL signals (each voltage) to the ECU.

TY1109900161010X

**Fig. 283   Cruise Control Switch Circuit (Part 1 of 4).
1998–99 RAV4**

---

3   Check control switch.

PREPARATION:
(a)   Remove steering wheel center pad.
(b)   Disconnect the control switch connector.
CHECK:
Measure resistance between terminals 2 and 3 of control switch connector when control switch is operated.

Switch position	Resistance (Ω)
Neutral	∞ (No continuity)
RES/ACC	50 – 80
SET/COAST	180 – 220
CANCEL	400 – 440

NG ⟩ Replace control switch.

OK

TY1109900161030X

**Fig. 283   Cruise Control Switch Circuit (Part 3 of 4).
1998–99 RAV4**

INSPECTION PROCEDURE

1   Input signal check.

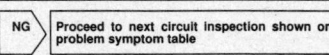

Input Signal	Indicator Light Blinking Pattern	
SET/COAST switch	ON OFF	2 Pulses
RESUME/ACCEL switch	ON OFF	3 Pulses
CANCEL switch	ON OFF	SW OFF / SW ON

PREPARATION:
See input signal check
CHECK:
Check the indicator light operation when each of the SET/COAST, RESUME/ACCEL and CANCEL is turned on.
OK
    SET/COAST, RESUME/ACCEL switch
    The signals shown in the table on the left should be output when each switch is ON. The signal should disappear when the switch is turned OFF.
    CANCEL switch
    The indicator light goes off when the cancel switch is turned ON.

OK ⟩ Wait and see.

NG

2   Check voltage between terminals CCS of cruise control ECU connector and body ground.

PREPARATION:
(a)   Remove the ECU with connector still connected.
(b)   Turn ignition switch ON.
CHECK:
Measure voltage between terminals CCS (10) of ECU connector and body ground, when each of the SET/COAST, RESUME/ACCEL and CANCEL is turned ON.

Switch position	Voltage (V)
Neutral	10 – 16
RES/ACC	0.6 – 2.3
SET/COAST	1.9 – 4.7
CANCEL	3.4 – 7.2

NG ⟩ Proceed to next circuit inspection shown on problem symptom table

OK

TY1109900161020X

**Fig. 283   Cruise Control Switch Circuit (Part 2 of 4).
1998–99 RAV4**

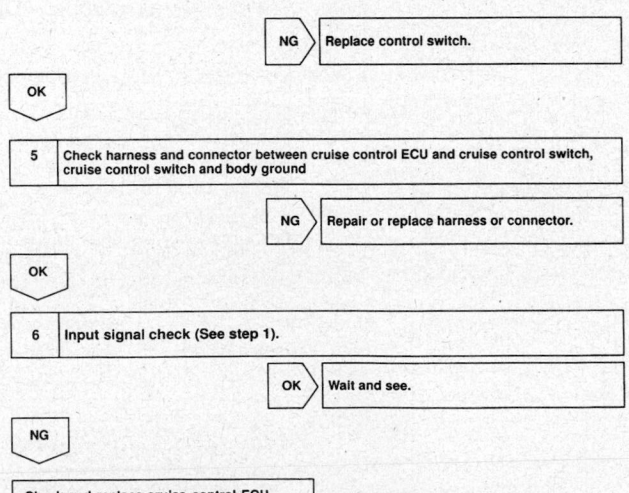

4   Check main switch continuity.

PREPARATION:
(a)   Remove steering wheel center pad.
(b)   Disconnect the control switch connector.
CHECK:
Check continuity between terminals 4 and 5 of control switch connector when main switch is held ON and OFF.
OK:

Switch position	Tester connection	Specified condition
OFF	4 – 5	No continuity
Hold ON	4 – 5	Continuity

NG ⟩ Replace control switch.

OK

5   Check harness and connector between cruise control ECU and cruise control switch, cruise control switch and body ground

NG ⟩ Repair or replace harness or connector.

OK

6   Input signal check (See step 1).

OK ⟩ Wait and see.

NG

Check and replace cruise control ECU

TY1109900161040X

**Fig. 283   Cruise Control Switch Circuit (Part 4 of 4).
1998–99 RAV4**

CIRCUIT DESCRIPTION

When the brake pedal is depressed, the stop light switch sends a signal to the ECU. When the ECU receives this signal, it cancels the cruise control.

A fail–safe function is provided so that the cancel functions normally, even if there is a malfunction in the stop light signal circuit.

The cancel conditions are: Battery positive voltage at terminal STP–

When the brake is ON, battery positive voltage normally applies through the STOP fuse and stop light switch to terminal STP– of the ECU, and the ECU turns the cruise control OFF.

If the harness connected to terminal STP– has an open circuit, terminal STP– will have battery positive voltage and the cruise control will be turned OFF.

Also, when the brake is ON, the magnetic clutch circuit is cut mechanically by the stop light switch, turning the cruise control OFF.

TY1109900162010X

Fig. 284   Stop Light Switch Circuit (Part 1 of 3). 1998–99 RAV4

| 3 | Check voltage between terminal STP– of cruise control ECU connector and body ground. |

PREPARATION:
(a)   Remove the ECU with connectors still connected.
(b)   Turn ignition switch ON.

CHECK:
Measure voltage between terminal STP– (2) of cruise control ECU connector and body ground, when the brake pedal is depressed and released.

OK:

| Depressed | 10 – 14 V |
| Released | Below 1 V |

| OK | Proceed to next circuit inspection shown in problem symptom table |

NG

| 4 | Check for open in harness and connectors between terminal STP– of cruise control ECU and stop light switch |

| NG | Repair or replace harness or connector. |

OK

| Check and replace cruise control ECU |

TY1109900162030X

Fig. 284   Stop Light Switch Circuit (Part 3 of 3). 1998–99 RAV4

INSPECTION PROCEDURE

| 1 | Check operation of stop light. |

CHECK:
Check that stop light comes on when brake pedal is depressed, and turns off when brake pedal is released.

| NG | Check stop light system |

OK

| 2 | Input signal check. |

| Input Signal | Indicator Light Blinking Pattern |
| Stop Light switch ON | Light ON ___ SW OFF
OFF - - - - SW ON |

CHECK:
(a)   See input signal check.
(b)   Check the indicator light when the brake pedal is depressed.

OK:
The indicator light goes off when the brake pedal is depressed.

| OK | Proceed to next circuit inspection shown in problem symptom table |

NG

TY1109900162020X

Fig. 284   Stop Light Switch Circuit (Part 2 of 3). 1998–99 RAV4

CIRCUIT DESCRIPTION

When the idle switch in turned ON, a signal is sent to the ECU. The ECU uses this signal to correct the discrepancy between the throttle valve position and the actuator position sensor value to enable accurate cruise control at the set speed. If the idle switch is malfunctioning, problem symptoms also occur in the engine, so also inspect the engine.

TY1109900163010X

Fig. 285   Idle Signal Circuit (Part 1 of 3). 1998–99 RAV4

INSPECTION PROCEDURE

| 1 | Check voltage between terminal IDL of cruise control ECU connector and body ground. |

PREPARATION:
(a)   Remove the ECU with connector still connected.
(b)   Disconnect the ECM connector.
(c)   Turn ignition switch ON.

CHECK:
Measure voltage between terminal IDL (13) of ECU connector and body ground when the throttle valve is fully closed and fully opened.

OK:

Throttle valve position	Voltage
Fully opened	10 – 14 V
Fully closed	Below 1.5 V

| OK | Proceed to next circuit inspection shown on problem symptom table |

NG

| 2 | Check harness and connector between ECM and throttle position sensor |

| NG | Repair or replace harness or connector. |

OK

TY1109900163020X

Fig. 285   Idle Signal Circuit (Part 2 of 3). 1998–99 RAV4

3 | Check throttle position sensor.

PREPARATION:
Disconnect the throttle position sensor connector.
CHECK:
Measure resistance between terminals 1, 3 and 2 of throttle position sensor connector.
OK:

Terminals	Throttle valve	Resistance
1 – 2	–	2.5 – 5.9 kΩ
2 – 3	Fully closed	0.2 – 6.3 kΩ
2 – 3	Fully opened	2.0 – 10.2 kΩ

NG ▷ Replace throttle position sensor.

OK

4 | Check for open and short in harness and connector between cruise control ECU and ECM

NG ▷ Repair or replace harness or connector.

OK

Check and replace cruise control ECU

TY1109900163030X

Fig. 285   Idle Signal Circuit (Part 3 of 3). 1998–99 RAV4

INSPECTION PROCEDURE

1 | Check operation of overdrive.

PREPARATION:
Test drive after engine warms up.
CHECK:
Check that overdrive ON ↔ OFF occurs with operation of OD switch ON–OFF.

NG ▷ Check and repair electronically controlled transmission

OK

2 | Check voltage between terminal OD of harness side connector of cruise control ECU and body ground.

PREPARATION:
(a)   Remove the ECU with connector still connected.
(b)   Turn ignition switch ON.
(c)   Disconnect the ECU connector.
CHECK:
Measure voltage between terminal OD (14) of harness side connector of ECU and body ground.
OK:
   Voltage: 10 – 14 V

NG ▷ Go to step 5.

OK

TY1109900164020X

Fig. 286   Electronically Controlled Transmission Communications Circuit (Part 2 of 3). 1998–99 RAV4

CIRCUIT DESCRIPTION

When driving uphill under cruise control, in order to reduce shifting due to ON–OFF overdrive operation and to provide smooth driving, when down shifting in the electronically controlled transmission occurs, a signal to prevent upshift until the end of the uphill slope is sent from the cruise control ECU to the electronically controlled transmission.
Terminal ECT of the cruise control ECU detects the shift change signal (output to electronically controlled transmission No. 2 solenoid) from the ECM.
If vehicle speeds down, also when terminal ECT of the cruise control ECU receives down shifting signal, it sends a signal from terminal OD to ECM to cut overdrive until the end of the uphill slope, and the gear shifts are reduced and gear shift points in the electronically controlled transmission are changed.

TY1109900164010X

Fig. 286   Electronically Controlled Transmission Communications Circuit (Part 1 of 3). 1998–99 RAV4

3 | Check voltage between terminal ECT of cruise control ECU connector and body ground (On test drive).

PREPARATION:
(a)   Connect the ECU connector.
(b)   Test drive after engine warms up.
CHECK:
Check voltage between terminal ECT (6) of ECU connector and body ground when OD switch is ON and OFF.
OK:

OD switch position	Voltage
ON	8 – 14 V
OFF	Below 0.5 V

OK ▷ Proceed to next circuit inspection shown in problem symptom table

NG

4 | Check harness and connector between terminal ECT of cruise control ECU and electronically controlled transmission solenoid

NG ▷ Repair or replace harness or connector.

OK

Check and replace cruise control ECU

5 | Check harness and connector between terminal OD of cruise control ECU and terminal OD1 of ECM.

NG ▷ Repair or replace harness or connector.

OK

Check and replace cruise control ECU

TY1109900164030X

Fig. 286   Electronically Controlled Transmission Communications Circuit (Part 3 of 3). 1998–99 RAV4

CIRCUIT DESCRIPTION

When the shift position is put in except D position, a signal is sent from the park/neutral position switch to the ECU. When this signal is input during cruise control driving, the ECU cancels the cruise control.

TY1109900165010X

Fig. 287   Park/Neutral Position Switch (Part 1 of 3). 1998–99 RAV4

INSPECTION PROCEDURE

1	Check starter operation.

CHECK:
Check that the starter operates normally and that the engine starts.

NG	Proceed to engine troubleshooting.

OK

2	Input signal check.

Input Signal	Indicator Light Blinking Pattern
Turn PNP switch OFF (Shift to except D position)	Light ON — SW ON OFF - - - SW OFF

PREPARATION:
See input signal check on
CHECK:
Check the indicator light when shifting into except D position.
OK:
The indicator light goes off when shifting into except D position.

OK	Proceed to next circuit inspection shown in problem symptom table

NG

TY1109900165020X

Fig. 287   Park/Neutral Position Switch (Part 2 of 3). 1998–99 RAV4

CIRCUIT DESCRIPTION

When the clutch pedal is depressed, the clutch switch sends a signal to the cruise control ECU. When the signal is input to the cruise control ECU during cruise control driving, the cruise control ECU cancels cruise control.

TY1109900166010X

Fig. 288   Clutch Switch Circuit (Part 1 of 3). 1998–99 RAV4

3	Check voltage between terminal D of cruise control ECU and body ground.

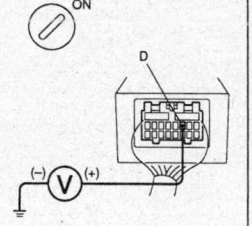

PREPARATION:
Turn ignition switch ON.
CHECK:
Measure voltage between terminal D (3) of cruise control ECU connector and body ground when clutch pedal is depressed and pushed in.
OK:

Shift Position	Voltage
Clutch pedal depressed	10 – 14 V
Clutch pedal pushed in	Below 1 V

OK	Proceed to next circuit inspection shown in problem symptom table .

NG

4	Check for open in harness and connector between ECU and GAUGE fuse .

NG	Repair or replace harness or connector.

OK

Check and replace cruise control ECU .

TY1109900166030X

Fig. 288   Clutch Switch Circuit (Part 3 of 3). 1998–99 RAV4

3	Check voltage between terminal D of cruise control ECU connector and body ground.

PREPARATION:
Turn ignition switch ON.
CHECK:
Measure voltage between terminal D (3) of ECU connector and body ground when shifting into D position and other positions.
OK:

Shift Position	Voltage
D position	10 – 14 V
Other positions	Below 1 V

OK	Proceed to next circuit inspection shown in problem symptom table

NG

4	Check harness and connector between cruise control ECU and park/neutral position switch

NG	Repair or replace harness or connector.

OK

Check and replace cruise control ECU

TY1109900165030X

Fig. 287   Park/Neutral Position Switch (Part 3 of 3). 1998–99 RAV4

INSPECTION PROCEDURE

1	Check starter operation.

CHECK:
Check that the starter operates normally and that the engine starts.

NG	Proceed to engine troubleshooting

OK

2	Input signal check.

Input Signal	Indicator Light Blinking Pattern
Clutch switch OFF (Depress clutch pedal)	Light ON — SW ON OFF - - - - SW OFF

PREPARATION:
See input signal check.
CHECK:
Check the indicator light when clutch pedal is depressed.
OK:
The indicator light goes off when shifting into clutch pedal depressed.

OK	Proceed to next circuit inspection shown in problem symptom table

NG

TY1109900166020X

Fig. 288   Clutch Switch Circuit (Part 2 of 3). 1998–99 RAV4

CIRCUIT DESCRIPTION

The ECU power source supplies power to the actuator and sensors, etc.. When terminal GND and the cruise control ECU case are grounded.

TY1109900167010X

Fig. 289   ECU Power Source Circuit (Part 1 of 3). 1998–99 RAV4

INSPECTION PROCEDURE

| 1 | Check TURN & GAUGE fuse. |

PREPARATION:
Remove the TURN &GAUGE fuse from instrument panel junction block.
CHECK:
Check continuity of TURN &GAUGE fuse.
OK:
    Continuity

NG ▷ Check for short in all the harness and components connected to TURN & GAUGE fuse.

OK

TY1109900167020X

Fig. 289 ECU Power Source Circuit (Part 2 of 3). 1998–99 RAV4

CIRCUIT DESCRIPTION

When the cruise control main switch is turned ON, CRUISE MAIN indicator light lights up.

TY1109900168010X

Fig. 290 Cruise Control Main Indicator Lamp Circuit (Part 1 of 2). 1998–99 RAV4

INSPECTION PROCEDURE

| 1 | Check voltage between terminals PI and GND of cruise control ECU connector. |

PREPARATION:
Tun ignition switch ON.
CHECK:
Measure voltage between terminals PI (4) and GND of cruise control ECU connector when main switch is held ON and OFF.
OK:

Switch position	Voltage
OFF	10 – 16 V
ON	Below 1.2 V

OK ▷ Proceed to next circuit inspection shown in problem symptom table.

NG

| 2 | Check combination meter. |

NG ▷ Replace combination meter.

OK

Check and replace cruise control ECU

TY1109900168020X

Fig. 290 Cruise Control Main Indicator Lamp Circuit (Part 2 of 2). 1998–99 RAV4

| 2 | Check voltage between terminals B and GND of cruise control ECU connector. |

PREPARATION:
(a) Remove the ECU with connector still connected.
(b) Turn ignition switch ON.
CHECK:
Measure voltage between terminals B (9) and GND (16) of ECU connector.
OK:
    10 – 14 V

OK ▷ Proceed to next circuit inspection shown in problem symptom table

NG

| 3 | Check resistance between terminal GND of cruise control ECU connector and body ground. |

CHECK:
Measure resistance between terminal GND (16) of ECU connector and body ground.
OK:
    Resistance: Below 1 Ω

NG ▷ Repair or replace harness or connector.

OK

Check and repair harness and connector between cruise control ECU and battery

TY1109900167030X

Fig. 289 ECU Power Source Circuit (Part 3 of 3). 1998–99 RAV4

CIRCUIT DESCRIPTION

This circuit sends a signal to the ECU that DTC output is required.

TY1109900169010X

Fig. 291 Diagnosis Circuit (Part 1 of 2). 1998–99 RAV4

INSPECTION PROCEDURE

| 1 | Check voltage between terminals Tc and E_1 of DLC1. |

PREPARATION:
Turn ignition switch ON.
CHECK:
Measure voltage between terminals Tc and E_1 of DLC1.
OK:
    Voltage: 10 – 14 V

OK ▷ Proceed to next circuit inspection shown in problem symptom table

NG

| 2 | Check harness and connector between cruise control ECU and DLC1, DLC1 and body ground |

NG ▷ Repair or replace harness or connector.

OK

Check and replace cruise control ECU

TY1109900169020X

Fig. 291 Diagnosis Circuit (Part 2 of 2). 1998–99 RAV4

INSPECTION PROCEDURE

1	Actuator control cable inspection

OK:
(a) Check that the actuator and control cable throttle link are properly installed and that the cable and link are connected correctly.
(b) Check that the actuator and bell crank are operating smoothly.
(c) Check that the cable is not loose or too tight.

OK:
Freeplay: less than 10 mm

HINT:
- If the control cable is very loose, the vehicle's loss of speed going uphill will be large.
- If the control cable is too tight, the idle RPM will become high.

TY1109900170000X

Fig. 292   Actuator Control Cable. 1998–99 RAV4

Symptom	Suspect Area
Cruise control does not cancel when clutch pedal depressed.	Input signal check No.3: OK 1. Cruise Control ECU Input signal check No.3: NG 1. Clutch Switch Circuit 2. Cruise Control ECU
Cruise control does not cancel when cruise control switch turned to CANCEL.	Input signal check No.3: OK 1. Cruise Control ECU Input signal check No.3: NG 1. Control Switch Circuit 2. Cruise Control ECU
Vehicle speed does not decrease when cruise control switch turned to COAST.	Input signal check No.1: OK 1. Actuator Motor Circuit 2. Actuator Control Cable 3. Vehicle Speed Sensor Circuit 4. Cruise Control ECU Input signal check No.1: NG 1. Control Switch Circuit 2. Cruise Control ECU
Vehicle speed does not accelerate when cruise control switch turned to ACCEL.	Input signal check No.2: OK 1. Actuator Motor Circuit 2. Actuator Control Cable 3. Vehicle Speed Sensor Circuit 4. Cruise Control ECU Input signal check No.2: NG 1. Control Switch Circuit 2. Cruise Control ECU
Vehicle speed does not return to memorized speed when cruise control switch turned to RESUME.	Input signal check No.2: OK 1. Actuator Motor Circuit 2. Actuator Control Cable 3. Vehicle Speed Sensor Circuit 4. Cruise Control ECU Input signal check No.2: NG 1. Control Switch Circuit 2. Cruise Control ECU
Speed can be set below about 40 km/h (25 mph).	Input signal check No.4: OK 1. Cruise Control ECU Input signal check No.4: NG 1. Vehicle Speed Sensor Circuit 2. Cruise Control ECU
Cruise control does not cancel when speed is less than 40 km/h (25 mph).	Input signal check No.4: OK 1. Actuator Motor Circuit 2. Cruise Control ECU Input signal check No.4: NG 1. Vehicle Speed Sensor Circuit 2. Cruise Control ECU

TY1109900441020X

Fig. 293   Problem Symptoms Table (Part 2 of 2). 1996–97 Supra & 1998 w/2JZ-GTE engine

Symptom	Suspect Area
• Cruise control system does not set. • Cruise control system does not operate.	Input signal check No.4: OK 1. ECU Power Source Circuit 2. Wire Harness 3. Main Switch Circuit 4. Control Switch Circuit 5. Stop Light Switch Circuit 6. PNP Switch or Clutch Switch Circuit 7. Actuator Control Cable 8. Actuator Motor Circuit 9. Cruise Control ECU Input signal check No.4: NG 1. Vehicle Speed Sensor Circuit 2. Cruise Control ECU
Indicator light does not light up.	1. Wire Harness 2. CRUISE MAIN Indicator Light Circuit 3. Cruise Control ECU
Vehicle speed drop when the cruise control switch turned to SET.	1. Actuator Control Cable 2. ECU Power Source Circuit 3. Idle Signal Circuit 4. Actuator Motor Circuit 5. Cruise Control ECU
Set speed deviates on high or low side.	Input signal check No.4: OK 1. Vehicle Speed Sensor Circuit 2. Actuator Control Cable 3. ECU Power Source Circuit 4. Actuator Motor Circuit 5. Cruise Control ECU Input signal check No.4: NG 1. Cruise Control ECU
Vehicle speed fluctuates when cruise control switch turn to SET.	1. Vehicle Speed Sensor Circuit 2. Actuator Control Cable 3. Idle Signal Circuit 4. ECT Communication Circuit 5. Actuator Motor Circuit 6. Cruise Control ECU
Acceleration response is sluggish when cruise control switch turn to "ACCEL" or "RESUME".	Input signal check No.4: OK 1. Actuator Control Cable 2. Vehicle Speed Sensor Circuit 3. Actuator Motor Circuit 4. Cruise Control ECU Input signal check No.4: NG 1. Control Switch Circuit 2. Cruise Control ECU
Set speed does not cancel when brake pedal depressed.	Input signal check No.3: OK 1. Cruise Control ECU Input signal check No.3: NG 1. Stop Light Switch Circuit 2. Cruise Control ECU
Cruise control does not cancel when transmission is shifted to except D position. (A/T)	Input signal check No.3: OK 1. Cruise Control ECU Input signal check No.3: NG 1. PNP Switch Circuit 2. Cruise Control ECU

TY1109900441010X

Fig. 293   Problem Symptoms Table (Part 1 of 2). 1996–97 Supra & 1998 w/2JZ-GTE engine

CIRCUIT DESCRIPTION

The actuator motor is operated by signals from the ECU. Acceleration and deceleration signals are transmitted by changes in the Duty Ratio (See note below).

Duty Ratio

The duty ratio is the ratio of the period of continuity in one cycle. For example, if A is the period of continuity in one cycle, and B is the period of non-continuity, then

$$\text{Duty Ratio} = \frac{A}{A + B} \times 100 \, (\%)$$

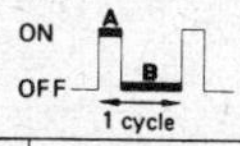

DTC No.	DTC Detecting Condition	Trouble area
11	• Overcurrent (short) in motor circuit.	• Cruise control actuator motor. • Harness or connector between actuator motor and ECU. • ECU
14	• Open in actuator motor circuit.	
41	• Duty ratio of 100% output to motor acceleration side.	• ECU

TY1109900467010X

Fig. 294   Codes 11, 14 & 41: Actuator Motor Circuit (Part 1 of 2). 1996 Supra

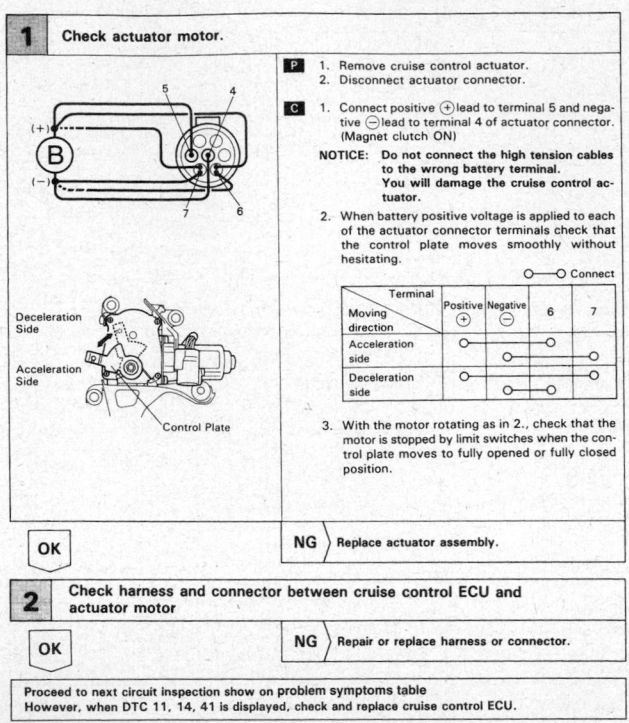

1 Check actuator motor.

P 1. Remove cruise control actuator.
   2. Disconnect actuator connector.

C 1. Connect positive ⊕ lead to terminal 5 and negative ⊖ lead to terminal 4 of actuator connector. (Magnet clutch ON)

NOTICE: Do not connect the high tension cables to the wrong battery terminal. You will damage the cruise control actuator.

   2. When battery positive voltage is applied to each of the actuator connector terminals check that the control plate moves smoothly without hesitating.

○——○ Connect

Terminal Moving direction	Positive ⊕	Negative ⊖	6	7
Acceleration side	○			○
Deceleration side	○		○	

   3. With the motor rotating as in 2., check that the motor is stopped by limit switches when the control plate moves to fully opened or fully closed position.

OK | **NG** ⟩ Replace actuator assembly.

2 Check harness and connector between cruise control ECU and actuator motor

OK | **NG** ⟩ Repair or replace harness or connector.

Proceed to next circuit inspection show on problem symptoms table
However, when DTC 11, 14, 41 is displayed, check and replace cruise control ECU.

TY1109900467020X

Fig. 294 Codes 11, 14 & 41: Actuator Motor Circuit (Part 2 of 2). 1996 Supra

INSPECTION PROCEDURE

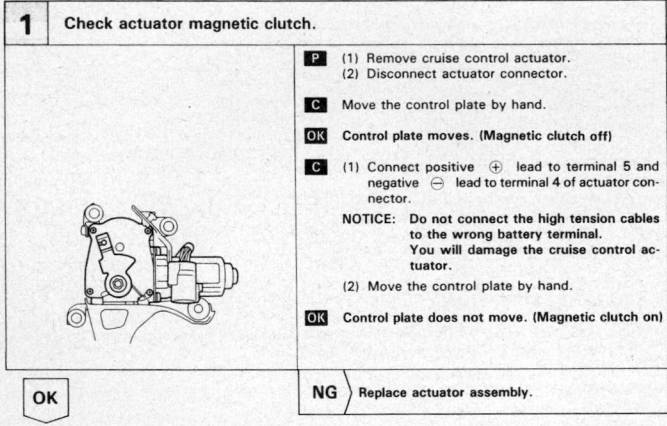

1 Check actuator magnetic clutch.

P (1) Remove cruise control actuator.
   (2) Disconnect actuator connector.

C Move the control plate by hand.

OK Control plate moves. (Magnetic clutch off)

C (1) Connect positive ⊕ lead to terminal 5 and negative ⊖ lead to terminal 4 of actuator connector.

NOTICE: Do not connect the high tension cables to the wrong battery terminal. You will damage the cruise control actuator.

   (2) Move the control plate by hand.

OK Control plate does not move. (Magnetic clutch on)

OK | **NG** ⟩ Replace actuator assembly.

2 Check stop light switch.

P Disconnect stop light switch connector.

C Check continuity between terminals.

OK ○——○ Continuity

Terminals Switch position	1	2	3	4
Switch pin free (Brake pedal depressed)	○	○		
Switch pin pushed in (Brake pedal released)			○	○

OK | **NG** ⟩ Replace stop light switch.

3 Check for open and short in harness and connectors between ECU and stop light switch, stop light switch and magnetic clutch, magnetic clutch and body ground.

OK | **NG** ⟩ Repair or replace harness or connector.

Proceed to next circuit inspection shown on problem symptoms chart
However, when DTC 12 is displayed, check harness and connector for loose connection. If connection is normal, check and replace ECU.

TY1109900468020X

Fig. 295 Code 12: Actuator Magnetic Clutch Circuit (Part 2 of 2). 1996 Supra

CIRCUIT DESCRIPTION

This circuit turns on the magnetic clutch inside the actuator during cruise control operation according to the signal from the ECU. If a malfunction occurs in the actuator or speed sensor, etc. during cruise control, the rotor shaft between the motor and control plate is released.

When the brake pedal is depressed, the stoplight switch turns on, supplying electrical power to the stoplight. Power supply to the magnetic clutch is mechanically cut and the magnetic clutch is turned OFF.

When driving downhill , if the vehicle speed exceeds the set speed by 15 km/h (9 mph), the ECU turns the magnetic clutch OFF. If the vehicle speed later drops to within 10 km/h (6 mph) above the set speed, then cruise control at the set speed is resumed.

DTC No.	DTC Detecting Condition	Trouble area
12	• Overcurrent (short) in magnetic clutch circuit. • Open (0.8 sec) in magnetic clutch circuit.	• Cruise control magnetic clutch. • Harness or connector between ECU and magnetic clutch, magnetic clutch and body ground. • ECU

TY1109900468010X

Fig. 295 Code 12: Actuator Magnetic Clutch Circuit (Part 1 of 2). 1996 Supra

CIRCUIT DESCRIPTION

This circuit detects the rotation position of the actuator control plate and sends a signal to the ECU.

DTC No.	DTC Detecting Condition	Trouble area
13	• Position sensor detects abnormal voltage.	• Cruise control actuator position sensor. • Harness or connector between actuator position sensor and ECU. • ECU
14	• Position sensor signal value does not change when the motor operates.	

INSPECTION PROCEDURE

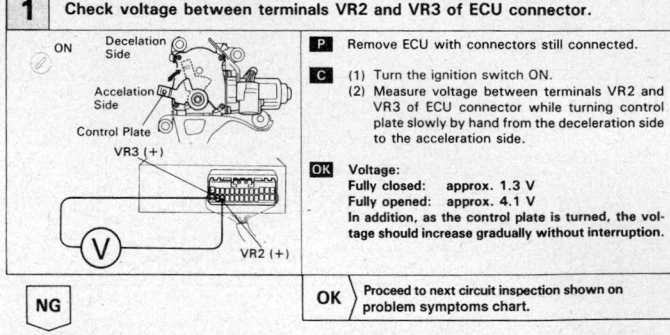

1 Check voltage between terminals VR2 and VR3 of ECU connector.

P Remove ECU with connectors still connected.

C (1) Turn the ignition switch ON.
   (2) Measure voltage between terminals VR2 and VR3 of ECU connector while turning control plate slowly by hand from the deceleration side to the acceleration side.

OK Voltage:
Fully closed: approx. 1.3 V
Fully opened: approx. 4.1 V
In addition, as the control plate is turned, the voltage should increase gradually without interruption.

NG | **OK** ⟩ Proceed to next circuit inspection shown on problem symptoms chart.

TY1109900469010X

Fig. 296 Codes 13 & 14: Actuator Position Sensor Circuit (Part 1 of 2). 1996 Supra

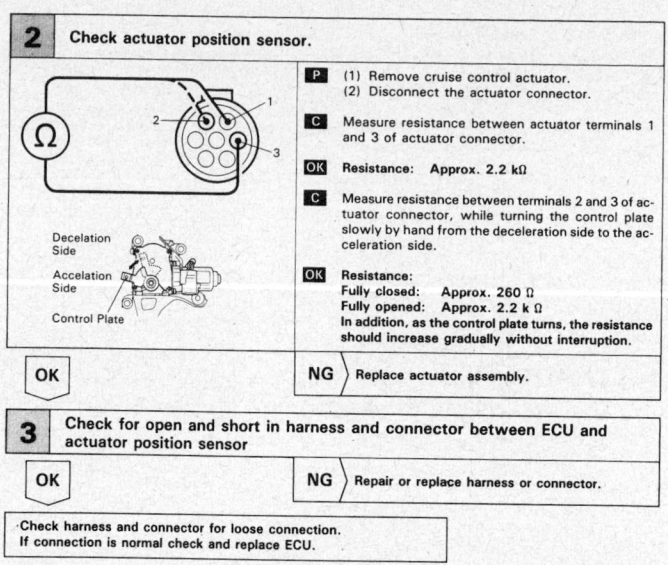

2	Check actuator position sensor.

P	(1) Remove cruise control actuator. (2) Disconnect the actuator connector.
C	Measure resistance between actuator terminals 1 and 3 of actuator connector.
OK	Resistance: Approx. 2.2 kΩ
C	Measure resistance between terminals 2 and 3 of actuator connector, while turning the control plate slowly by hand from the deceleration side to the acceleration side.
OK	Resistance: Fully closed: Approx. 260 Ω Fully opened: Approx. 2.2 kΩ In addition, as the control plate turns, the resistance should increase gradually without interruption.

OK	NG	Replace actuator assembly.

3	Check for open and short in harness and connector between ECU and actuator position sensor

OK	NG	Repair or replace harness or connector.

Check harness and connector for loose connection.
If connection is normal check and replace ECU.

TY1109900469020X

Fig. 296   Codes 13 & 14: Actuator Position Sensor Circuit (Part 2 of 2). 1996 Supra

CIRCUIT DESCRIPTION

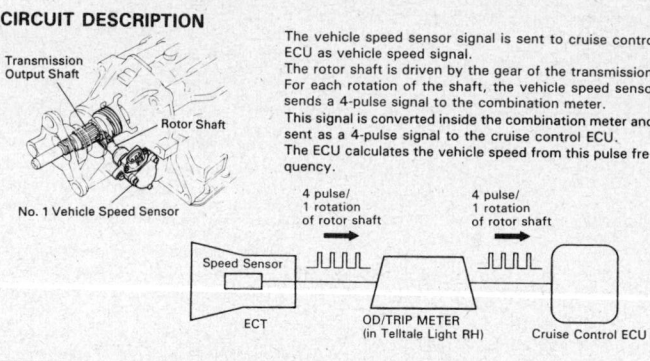

The vehicle speed sensor signal is sent to cruise control ECU as vehicle speed signal.
The rotor shaft is driven by the gear of the transmission. For each rotation of the shaft, the vehicle speed sensor sends a 4-pulse signal to the combination meter.
This signal is converted inside the combination meter and sent as a 4-pulse signal to the cruise control ECU.
The ECU calculates the vehicle speed from this pulse frequency.

DTC No.	DTC Detecting Condition	Trouble area
21	Speed signal is not input to the ECU while cruise control is set.	• Vehicle speed sensor • Combination meter • Harness or connector between vehicle speed sensor and combination meter, combination meter and ECU. • ECU
23	Vehicle speed decrease 16 km/h or more than preset speed. Vehicle speed sensor pulse is abnormal.	• Vehicle speed sensor • Harness or connector in SPD circuit (Open or short intermittently). • ECU

TY1109900470010X

Fig. 297   Codes 21 & 23: Vehicle Speed Sensor Circuit (Part 1 of 2). 1996 Supra

INSPECTION PROCEDURE

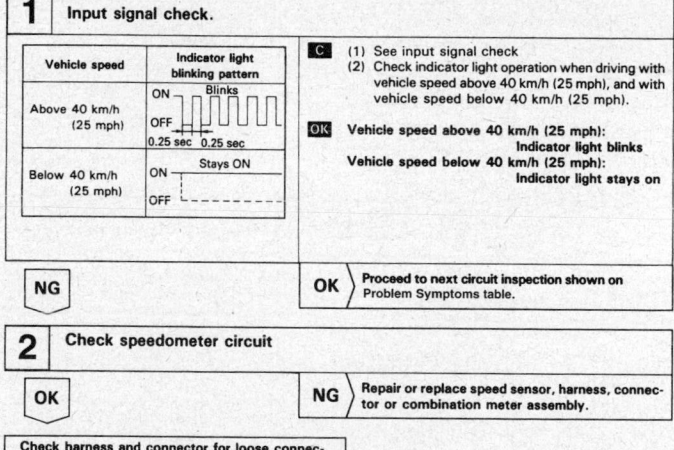

1	Input signal check.

Vehicle speed	Indicator light blinking pattern
Above 40 km/h (25 mph)	ON Blinks OFF 0.25 sec 0.25 sec
Below 40 km/h (25 mph)	ON Stays ON OFF

C	(1) See input signal check (2) Check indicator light operation when driving with vehicle speed above 40 km/h (25 mph), and with vehicle speed below 40 km/h (25 mph).
OK	Vehicle speed above 40 km/h (25 mph): Indicator light blinks Vehicle speed below 40 km/h (25 mph): Indicator light stays on

NG	OK	Proceed to next circuit inspection shown on Problem Symptoms table.

2	Check speedometer circuit

OK	NG	Repair or replace speed sensor, harness, connector or combination meter assembly.

Check harness and connector for loose connection. If connection is normal, check and replace ECU.

TY1109900470020X

Fig. 297   Codes 21 & 23: Vehicle Speed Sensor Circuit (Part 2 of 2). 1996 Supra

CIRCUIT DESCRIPTION

This circuit carries the SET/COAST, RESUME/ACCEL and CANCEL signals (each voltage) to the ECU.

DTC No.	DTC Detecting Condition	Trouble area
32	Short in, control switch circuit.	• Cruise control switch. • Harness or connector between control switch and ECU. • ECU
34	Voltage abnormality in control switch	

TY1109900471010X

Fig. 298   Codes 32 & 34: Control Switch Circuit (Part 1 of 3). 1996 Supra

INSPECTION PROCEDURE

1	Input signal check.

Input Signal	Indicator light blinking pattern		P	(1) See input signal check (2) Check the indicator light operation when each of the SET/COAST, RESUME/ACCEL and CANCEL is turned ON.
SET/COAST SWITCH	ON OFF	2 Pulses	OK	**SET/COAST, RESUME/ACCEL Switch** The signals shown in the table on the left should be output when each switch is ON. The signal should disappear when the switch is turned OFF. **CANCEL Switch.** The indicator light goes off when the cancel switch is turned ON.
RESUME/ACCEL SWITCH	ON OFF	3 Pulses		
CANCEL SWITCH	ON OFF	Switch OFF Switch ON		

NG		OK	Proceed to next circuit inspection shown on problem symptoms chart.

TY1109900471020X

Fig. 298   Codes 32 & 34: Control Switch Circuit (Part 2 of 3). 1996 Supra

CIRCUIT DESCRIPTION

When the brake is on, battery positive voltage normally applies through the stop fuse and stop switch to terminal STP— of the ECU, and the ECU turns the cruise control off.

A fail-safe function is provied so that cancel functions normally, if there is a malfunction in the stop light signal circuit.

① If the harness connected to terminal STP — has an open, terminal STP — will have battery positive voltage and the cruise control will be turned off, also SET not occurring.

② If the stop fuse is open, terminal STP + becomes approx. 0 V when the brake is turned on, so the ECU performs cancel function normally.

Also, when the brake is on, the magnetic clutch is cut mechanically by the stop light switch, turning the cruise control off.

INSPECTION PROCEDURE

1	**Check operation of stop light.**

C	Check that stop light comes on when brake pedal is depressed, and turns off when brake pedal is released.

OK		NG	Check stop light circuit.

TY1109900472010X

Fig. 299   Stop Lamp Switch Circuit (Part 1 of 2). 1996 Supra

2	Check voltage between terminal CCS of ECU connector and body ground.

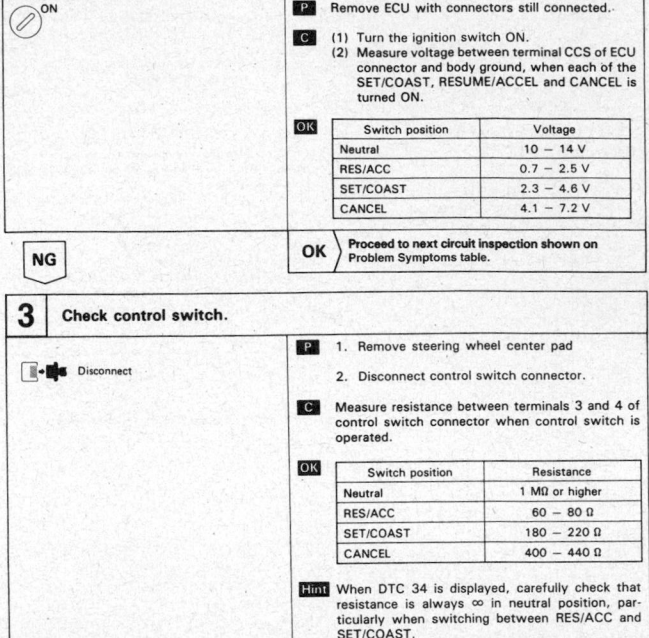

P	Remove ECU with connectors still connected.
C	(1) Turn the ignition switch ON. (2) Measure voltage between terminal CCS of ECU connector and body ground, when each of the SET/COAST, RESUME/ACCEL and CANCEL is turned ON.

OK	Switch position	Voltage
	Neutral	10 — 14 V
	RES/ACC	0.7 — 2.5 V
	SET/COAST	2.3 — 4.6 V
	CANCEL	4.1 — 7.2 V

NG		OK	Proceed to next circuit inspection shown on Problem Symptoms table.

3	Check control switch.

Disconnect

P	1. Remove steering wheel center pad 2. Disconnect control switch connector.
C	3. Measure resistance between terminals 3 and 4 of control switch connector when control switch is operated.

OK	Switch position	Resistance
	Neutral	1 MΩ or higher
	RES/ACC	60 — 80 Ω
	SET/COAST	180 — 220 Ω
	CANCEL	400 — 440 Ω

Hint	When DTC 34 is displayed, carefully check that resistance is always ∞ in neutral position, particularly when switching between RES/ACC and SET/COAST.

OK		NG	Replace cruise control switch.

4	**Check for open and short in harness and connector between ECU and control switch**

OK		NG	Repair or replace harness or connector.

Check and replace ECU.

TY1109900471030X

Fig. 298   Codes 32 & 34: Control Switch Circuit (Part 3 of 3). 1996 Supra

2	Input signal check.

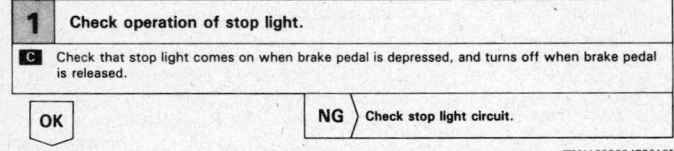

Brake pedal is depressed

ON
OFF

C	(1) See input signal check (2) Check the indicator light when the brake pedal is depressed.
OK	The indicator light goes off when the brake pedal is depressed.

NG		OK	Proceed to next circuit inspection shown on problem symptoms chart.

3	Check voltage between terminal STP +, STP— of ECU connector and body ground.

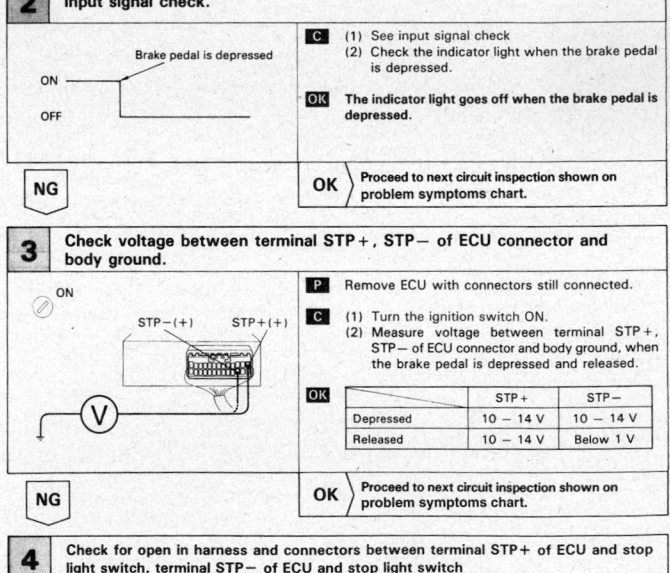

ON

STP—(+)   STP+(+)

V

P	Remove ECU with connectors still connected.
C	(1) Turn the ignition switch ON. (2) Measure voltage between terminal STP +, STP— of ECU connector and body ground, when the brake pedal is depressed and released.

OK		STP+	STP—
	Depressed	10 — 14 V	10 — 14 V
	Released	10 — 14 V	Below 1 V

NG		OK	Proceed to next circuit inspection shown on problem symptoms chart.

4	**Check for open in harness and connectors between terminal STP + of ECU and stop light switch, terminal STP — of ECU and stop light switch**

OK		NG	Repair or replace harness or connector.

Check and replace ECU.

TY1109900472020X

Fig. 299   Stop Lamp Switch Circuit (Part 2 of 2). 1996 Supra

SPEED CONTROL SYSTEMS

CIRCUIT DESCRIPTION

When the idle switch is turned ON, a signal is sent to the ECU. The ECU uses this signal to correct the discrepancy between the throttle valve position and the actuator position sensor value to enable accurate cruise control at the set speed. If the idle switch is malfunctioning, problem symptoms also occur in the engine, so also inspect the engine.

INSPECTION PROCEDURE

1	**Check voltage between terminal IDL of ECU connector and body ground.**

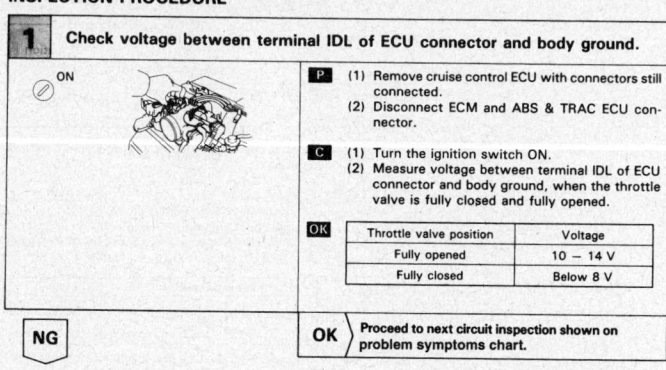

ON

P	(1) Remove cruise control ECU with connectors still connected.
	(2) Disconnect ECM and ABS & TRAC ECU connector.
C	(1) Turn the ignition switch ON.
	(2) Measure voltage between terminal IDL of ECU connector and body ground, when the throttle valve is fully closed and fully opened.

OK	Throttle valve position	Voltage
	Fully opened	10 — 14 V
	Fully closed	Below 8 V

NG		OK	Proceed to next circuit inspection shown on problem symptoms chart.

TY1109900473010X

Fig. 300 Idle Switch Circuit (Part 1 of 2). 1996 Supra

2	**Check throttle position sensor.**

P	Disconnect throttle position sensor connector.
C	Measure resistance between terminals 1 and 2 of throttle position sensor connector, when the throttle valve is fully closed and fully opened.

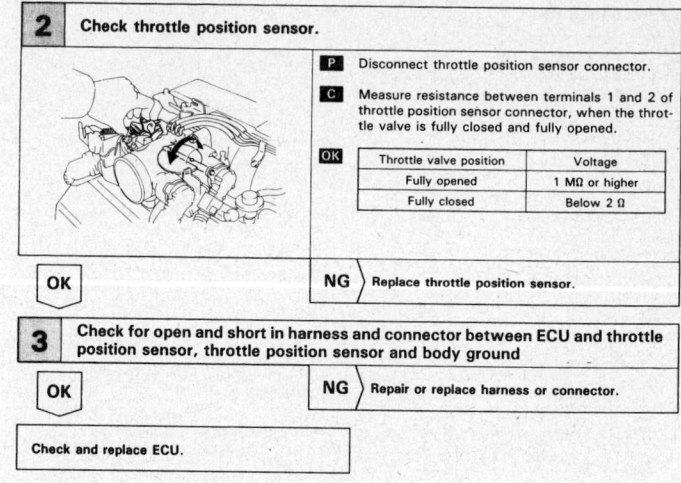

OK	Throttle valve position	Voltage
	Fully opened	1 MΩ or higher
	Fully closed	Below 2 Ω

OK		NG	Replace throttle position sensor.

3	**Check for open and short in harness and connector between ECU and throttle position sensor, throttle position sensor and body ground**

OK		NG	Repair or replace harness or connector.

Check and replace ECU.

TY1109900473020X

Fig. 300 Idle Switch Circuit (Part 2 of 2). 1996 Supra

CIRCUIT DESCRIPTION

When driving uphill under cruise control, in order to reduce shifting due to ON-OFF overdrive operation and to provide smooth driving, when down shifting in the electronically controlled transmission occurs, a signal to prevent upshift until the end of the uphill slope is sent from the cruise control ECU to the electronically controlled transmission.

Terminal ECM of the cruise control ECU detects the shift change signal (output to electronically controlled transmission No.2 solenoid) from the electronically controlled transmission.

If vehicle speed down, also when terminal ECT of the cruise control ECU receives down shifting signal, it sends a signal from terminal OD to ECM to cut overdrive until the end of the uphill slope, and the gear shifts are reduced and gear shift points in the electronically controlled transmission are changed.

TY1109900474010X

Fig. 301 Electronically Controlled Transmission Communication Circuit (Part 1 of 3). 1996 Supra

---

INSPECTION PROCEDURE

1	**Check operation of overdrive.**

P	Test drive after engine warm up.
C	Check that overdrive ON ↔ OFF occurs with operation of OD switch ON-OFF.

OK		NG	Check and Repair Electronically controlled transmission

2	**Check voltage between terminal OD of harness side connector of ECU and body ground.**

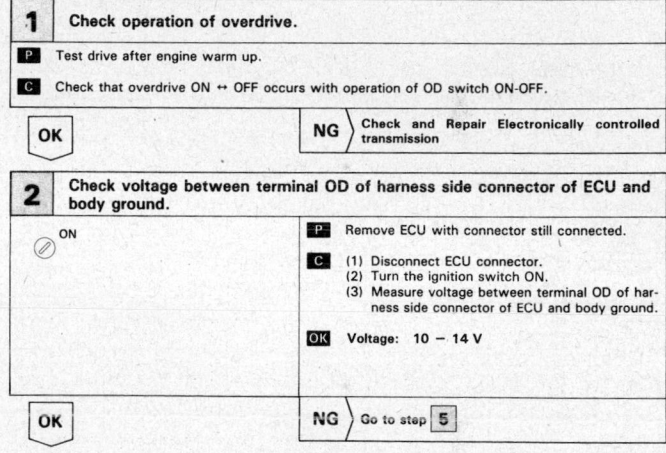

ON

P	Remove ECU with connector still connected.
C	(1) Disconnect ECU connector.
	(2) Turn the ignition switch ON.
	(3) Measure voltage between terminal OD of harness side connector of ECU and body ground.
OK	Voltage: 10 — 14 V

OK		NG	Go to step 5

TY1109900474020X

Fig. 301 Electronically Controlled Transmission Communication Circuit (Part 2 of 3). 1996 Supra

3 Check voltage between terminal ECT of cruise control ECU connector and body ground (On test drive).

P
(1) Connect ECU connector.
(2) Test drive after engine warm up.

C Check voltage between terminal ECT of cruise control ECU connector and body ground when OD switch is on and off.

OK

Gear Position	Voltage
O/D	Below 1 V
3rd	10 — 14 V

NG

OK Proceed to next circuit inspection shown on problem symptoms chart

4 Check for open and short in harness and connector between terminal ECT of cruise control ECU and electronically controlled transmission solenoid

OK

NG Repair or replace harness or connector.

Check and repair ECU.

5 Check for open and short in harness and connector between terminal OD of ECU and terminal OD1 of ECM

OK

NG Repair or replace harness or connector.

Check and replace ECM.

TY1109900474030X

Fig. 301 Electronically Controlled Transmission Communication Circuit (Part 3 of 3). 1996 Supra

INSPECTION PROCEDURE

1 Check operation of brake warning light.

C Check that the brake warning light in the instrument panel comes on when the parking brake lever is pulled up with the engine running, and the light goes off when the parking brake lever is released.

OK

NG Check brake warning light circuit

2 Input signal check.

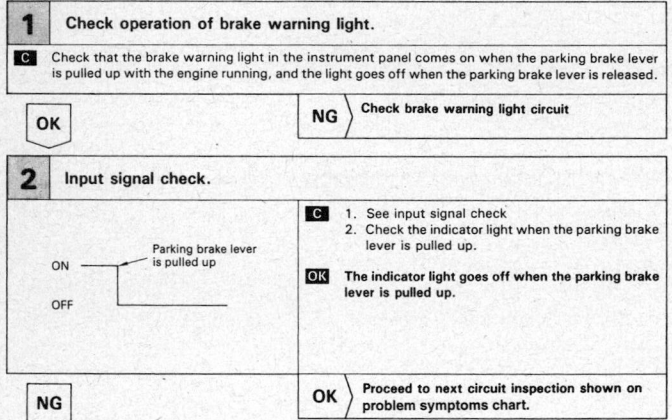

C
1. See input signal check
2. Check the indicator light when the parking brake lever is pulled up.

OK The indicator light goes off when the parking brake lever is pulled up.

NG

OK Proceed to next circuit inspection shown on problem symptoms chart.

TY1109900475020X

Fig. 302 Parking Brake Switch Circuit (Part 2 of 3). 1996 Supra

CIRCUIT DESCRIPTION

(A/T)
When the shift position is put in EXCEPT D position, a signal is sent from the park/neutral position switch to the ECU. When this signal is input during cruise control driving, the ECU cancels the cruise control.

(M/T)
When the clutch pedal is depressed, the clutch switch sends a signal to the ECU, When this signal is input to the ECU during cruise control driving, the ECU cancels cruise control.

TY1109900476010X

Fig. 303 Park Neutral Position/Clutch Switch Circuit (Part 1 of 3). 1996 Supra

CIRCUIT DESCRIPTION

When the parking brake pedal is depressed, the parking brake switch sends a signal to the ECU. When this signal is input to the ECU during cruise control driving, the ECU cancels cruise control.

TY1109900475010X

Fig. 302 Parking Brake Switch Circuit (Part 1 of 3). 1996 Supra

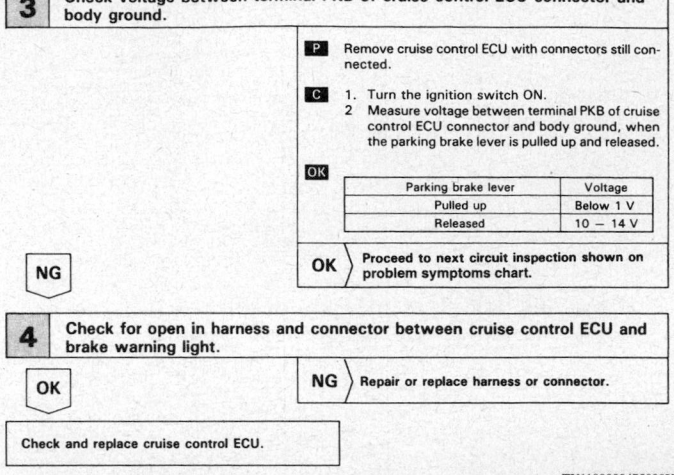

3 Check voltage between terminal PKB of cruise control ECU connector and body ground.

P Remove cruise control ECU with connectors still connected.

C
1. Turn the ignition switch ON.
2 Measure voltage between terminal PKB of cruise control ECU connector and body ground, when the parking brake lever is pulled up and released.

OK

Parking brake lever	Voltage
Pulled up	Below 1 V
Released	10 — 14 V

NG

OK Proceed to next circuit inspection shown on problem symptoms chart.

4 Check for open in harness and connector between cruise control ECU and brake warning light.

OK

NG Repair or replace harness or connector.

Check and replace cruise control ECU.

TY1109900475030X

Fig. 302 Parking Brake Switch Circuit (Part 3 of 3). 1996 Supra

INSPECTION PROCEDURE

1 Check operation of starter.

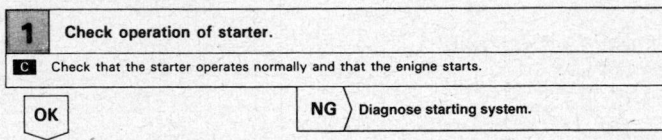

C Check that the starter operates normally and that the enigne starts.

OK

NG Diagnose starting system.

TY1109900476020X

Fig. 303 Park Neutral Position/Clutch Switch Circuit (Part 2 of 3). 1996 Supra

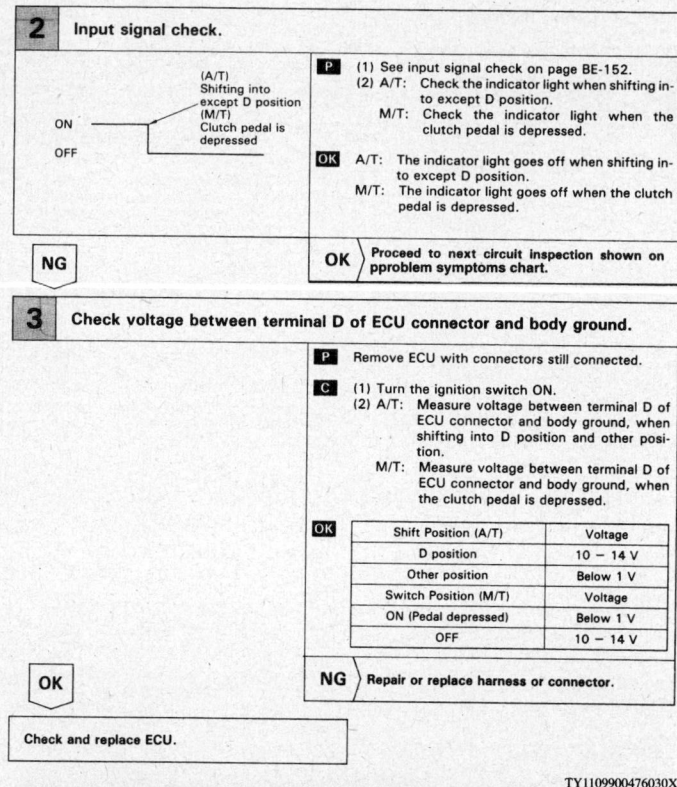

2 Input signal check.

ON — OFF
(A/T) Shifting into except D position
(M/T) Clutch pedal is depressed

P (1) See input signal check on page BE-152.
(2) A/T: Check the indicator light when shifting into except D position.
M/T: Check the indicator light when the clutch pedal is depressed.

OK A/T: The indicator light goes off when shifting into except D position.
M/T: The indicator light goes off when the clutch pedal is depressed.

NG | **OK** Proceed to next circuit inspection shown on pproblem symptoms chart.

3 Check voltage between terminal D of ECU connector and body ground.

P Remove ECU with connectors still connected.

C (1) Turn the ignition switch ON.
(2) A/T: Measure voltage between terminal D of ECU connector and body ground, when shifting into D position and other position.
M/T: Measure voltage between terminal D of ECU connector and body ground, when the clutch pedal is depressed.

OK

Shift Position (A/T)	Voltage
D position	10 – 14 V
Other position	Below 1 V
Switch Position (M/T)	Voltage
ON (Pedal depressed)	Below 1 V
OFF	10 – 14 V

NG Repair or replace harness or connector.

OK

Check and replace ECU.

TY1109900476030X

Fig. 303   Park Neutral Position/Clutch Switch Circuit (Part 3 of 3). 1996 Supra

INSPECTION PROCEDURE

1 Check ECU-IG fuse.

P Remove ECU-IG fuse from J/B No.1.

OK Check continuity of ECU-IG fuse.

OK Continuity

OK | **NG** Check for short in all the harness and components connected to the ECU-IG fuse

TY1109900477020X

Fig. 304   ECU Power Source Circuit (Part 2 of 3). 1996 Supra

CIRCUIT DESCRIPTION

The ECU power source supplies power to the actuator and sensors, etc. Terminal GND and the cruise control ECU case are grounded.

TY1109900477010X

Fig. 304   ECU Power Source Circuit (Part 1 of 3). 1996 Supra

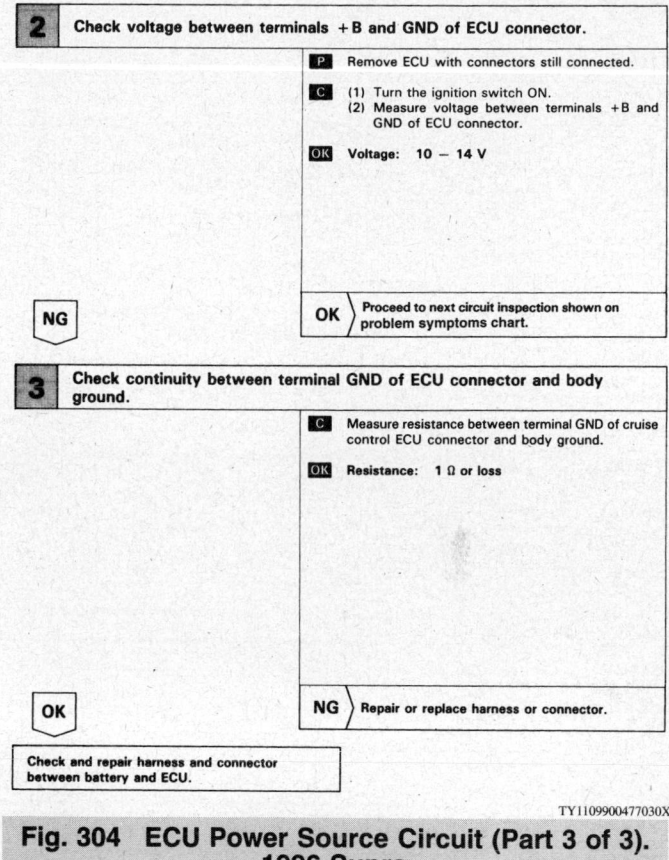

2 Check voltage between terminals +B and GND of ECU connector.

P Remove ECU with connectors still connected.

C (1) Turn the ignition switch ON.
(2) Measure voltage between terminals +B and GND of ECU connector.

OK Voltage: 10 – 14 V

NG | **OK** Proceed to next circuit inspection shown on problem symptoms chart.

3 Check continuity between terminal GND of ECU connector and body ground.

C Measure resistance between terminal GND of cruise control ECU connector and body ground.

OK Resistance: 1 Ω or loss

OK | **NG** Repair or replace harness or connector.

Check and repair harness and connector between battery and ECU.

TY1109900477030X

Fig. 304   ECU Power Source Circuit (Part 3 of 3). 1996 Supra

CIRCUIT DESCRIPTION

The ECU back-up power source provides power even when the ignition switch is off and is used for DTC memory, etc.

TY1109900478010X

Fig. 305   Back Up Power Source Circuit (Part 1 of 2). 1996 Supra

INSPECTION PROCEDURE

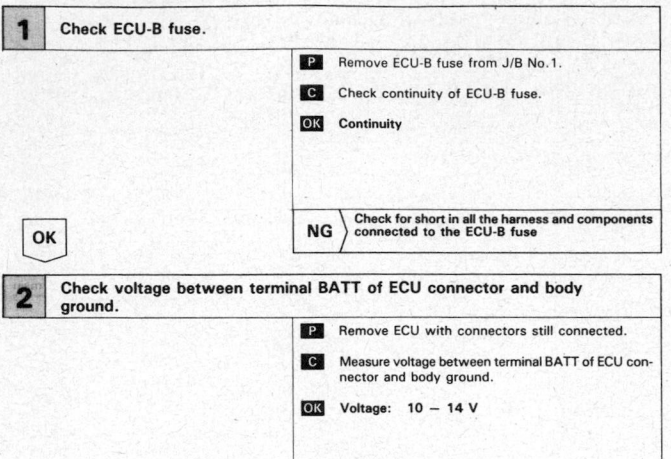

1 Check ECU-B fuse.

P	Remove ECU-B fuse from J/B No.1.
C	Check continuity of ECU-B fuse.
OK	Continuity

OK

| NG | Check for short in all the harness and components connected to the ECU-B fuse |

2 Check voltage between terminal BATT of ECU connector and body ground.

P	Remove ECU with connectors still connected.
C	Measure voltage between terminal BATT of ECU connector and body ground.
OK	Voltage: 10 – 14 V

NG

| OK | Proceed to next circuit inspection shown on problem symptoms chart. |

Check and repair harness and connector between battery and ECU.

TY1109900478020X

Fig. 305 Back Up Power Source Circuit (Part 2 of 2). 1996 Supra

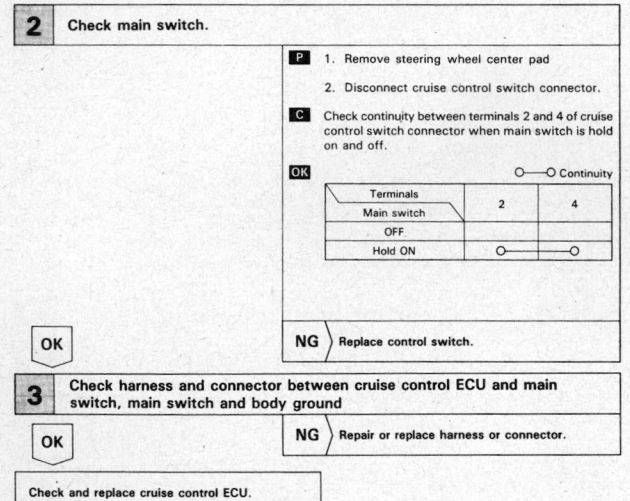

2 Check main switch.

P	1. Remove steering wheel center pad
	2. Disconnect cruise control switch connector.
C	Check continuity between terminals 2 and 4 of cruise control switch connector when main switch is hold on and off.
OK	

Terminals Main switch	2	4
OFF		
Hold ON	o———	———o

o———o Continuity

OK

| NG | Replace control switch. |

3 Check harness and connector between cruise control ECU and main switch, main switch and body ground

OK

| NG | Repair or replace harness or connector. |

Check and replace cruise control ECU.

TY1109900479020X

Fig. 306 Main Switch Circuit (Part 2 of 2). 1996 Supra

INSPECTION PROCEDURE

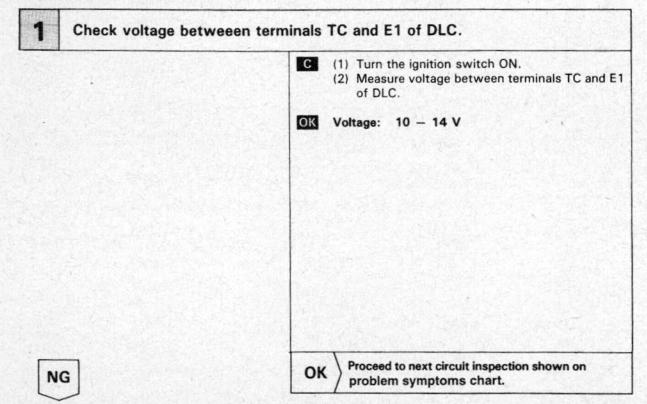

1 Check voltage betweeen terminals TC and E1 of DLC.

C	(1) Turn the ignition switch ON.
	(2) Measure voltage between terminals TC and E1 of DLC.
OK	Voltage: 10 – 14 V

NG

| OK | Proceed to next circuit inspection shown on problem symptoms chart. |

TY1109900480020X

Fig. 307 T_C Circuit (Part 2 of 3). 1996 Supra

CIRCUIT DESCRIPTION

When the cruise control main switch is turned off, the cruise control does not operate.

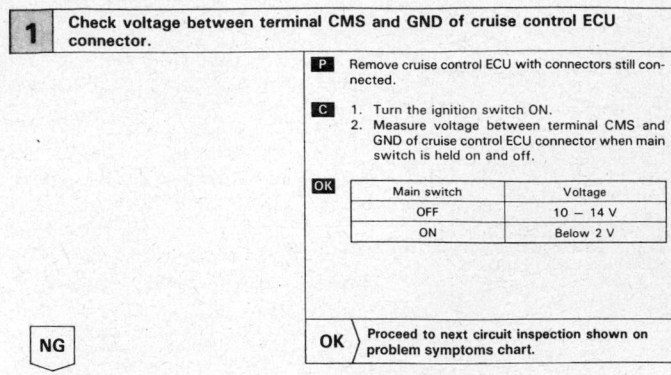

1 Check voltage between terminal CMS and GND of cruise control ECU connector.

P	Remove cruise control ECU with connectors still connected.
C	1. Turn the ignition switch ON.
	2. Measure voltage between terminal CMS and GND of cruise control ECU connector when main switch is held on and off.
OK	

Main switch	Voltage
OFF	10 – 14 V
ON	Below 2 V

NG

| OK | Proceed to next circuit inspection shown on problem symptoms chart. |

TY1109900479010X

Fig. 306 Main Switch Circuit (Part 1 of 2). 1996 Supra

CIRCUIT DESCRIPTION

This circuit sends a signal to the ECU that diagnostic code output is required.

TY1109900480010X

Fig. 307 T_C Circuit (Part 1 of 3). 1996 Supra

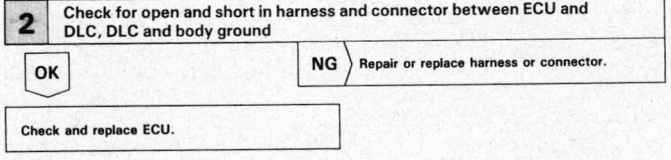

2 Check for open and short in harness and connector between ECU and DLC, DLC and body ground

OK

| NG | Repair or replace harness or connector. |

Check and replace ECU.

TY1109900480030X

Fig. 307 T_C Circuit (Part 3 of 3). 1996 Supra

CIRCUIT DESCRIPTION

The actuator motor is operated by signals from the ECU. Acceleration and deceleration signals are transmitted by changes in the Duty Ratio (See note below).
Duty Ratio
The duty ratio is the ratio of the period of continuity in one cycle. For example, if A is the period of continuity in one cycle, and B is the period of non–continuity, then

$$\text{Duty Ratio} = \frac{A}{A + B} \times 100 \ (\%)$$

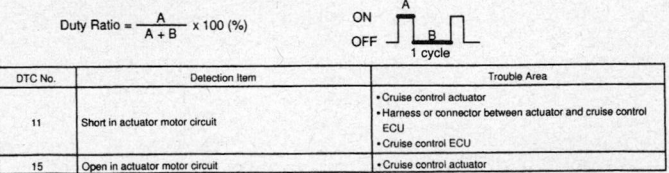

DTC No.	Detection Item	Trouble Area
11	Short in actuator motor circuit	• Cruise control actuator • Harness or connector between actuator and cruise control ECU • Cruise control ECU
15	Open in actuator motor circuit	• Cruise control actuator

TY1109900442010X

Fig. 308 Codes 11 & 15: Actuator Motor Circuit (Part 1 of 2). 1997 Supra & 1998 w/2JZ-GTE engine

INSPECTION PROCEDURE

| 1 | Check resistance between terminals MO and MC of cruise control actuator. |

PREPARATION:
(a) Ignition switch ON.
(b) Disconnect actuator connector.
CHECK:
Measure resistance between terminals 1 and 2.
HINT:
If control plate position is fully opened or fully closed, resistance can not measure.
OK:
Resistance: more than 4.2 Ω

| NG > | Replace cruise control actuator. |

| OK |

| 2 | Check wire harness and connector between terminals MO of cruise control ECU and MO of cruise control actuator |

| NG > | Repair or replace harness or connector. |

| OK |

| Replace cruise control ECU |

TY1109900442020X

Fig. 308   Codes 11 & 15: Actuator Motor Circuit (Part 2 of 2). 1997 Supra & 1998 w/2JZ-GTE engine

INSPECTION PROCEDURE

| 1 | Check STOP fuse. |

PREPARATION:
Remove STOP fuse from J/B No.1.
CHECK:
Check fuse continuity.
OK:
There is continuity.

| NG > | Replace STOP fuse. |

| OK |

| 2 | Check harness and connector between actuator and cruise control actuator |

| NG > | Repair or replace harness or connector. |

| OK |

| Check and replace cruise control ECU |

TY1109900443020X

Fig. 309   Code 12: Magnetic Clutch Circuit (Part 2 of 2). 1997 Supra & 1998 w/2JZ-GTE engine

CIRCUIT DESCRIPTION

This circuit turns on the magnetic clutch inside the actuator during cruise control operation according to the signal from the ECU. If a malfunction occurs in the actuator or speed sensor, etc. during cruise control operation, the rotor shaft between the motor and control plate is released.
When the brake pedal is depressed, the stoplight switch turns on, supplying electrical power to the stoplight. Power supply to the magnetic clutch is mechanically cut and the magnetic clutch is turned OFF.
When driving downhill, if the vehicle speed exceeds the set speed by 15 km/h (6 mph) above the set speed, then cruise control at the set speed is resumed.

DTC No.	Detection Item	Trouble Area
12	Short in magnetic clutch circuit Open (0.8 sec.) in magnetic clutch circuit	• Cruise control actuator magnetic clutch • Harness or connector between ECU and magnetic clutch, magnetic clutch and body ground • Cruise control ECU

TY1109900443010X

Fig. 309   Code 12: Magnetic Clutch Circuit (Part 1 of 2). 1997 Supra & 1998 w/2JZ-GTE engine

INSPECTION PROCEDURE

| 1 | Check actuator arm locking operation. |

PREPARATION:
(a) Ignition switch OFF.
(b) Disconnect actuator connector.
CHECK:
(a) Connect the positive ⊕ lead from the battery to the terminal 3 of actuator and the negative ⊖ lead to terminal 4.
NOTICE:
Do not connect the high tension cables to the wrong battery terminal. You will damage the cruise control actuator.
(b) Move the control plate by hand.
OK:
Control plate does not move.

| NG > | Replace cruise control actuator. |

| OK |

TY1109900444010X

Fig. 310   Code 14: Actuator Mechanical Fault (Part 1 of 2). 1997 Supra & 1998 w/2JZ-GTE engine

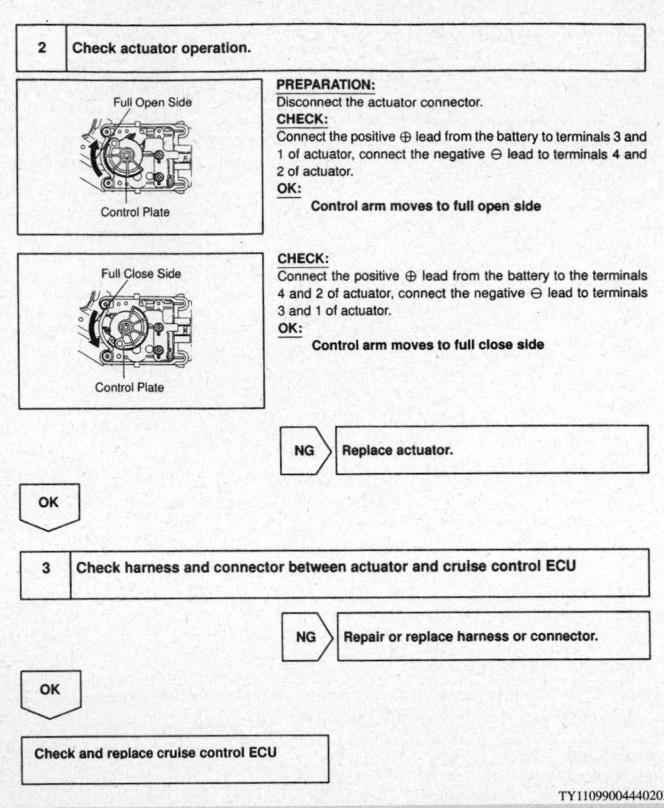

2	Check actuator operation.

PREPARATION:
Disconnect the actuator connector.
CHECK:
Connect the positive ⊕ lead from the battery to terminals 3 and 1 of actuator, connect the negative ⊖ lead to terminals 4 and 2 of actuator.
OK:
Control arm moves to full open side

CHECK:
Connect the positive ⊕ lead from the battery to the terminals 4 and 2 of actuator, connect the negative ⊖ lead to terminals 3 and 1 of actuator.
OK:
Control arm moves to full close side

NG ➤ Replace actuator.

OK

3	Check harness and connector between actuator and cruise control ECU

NG ➤ Repair or replace harness or connector.

OK

Check and replace cruise control ECU

TY1109900444020X

Fig. 310   Code 14: Actuator Mechanical Fault (Part 2 of 2). 1997 Supra & 1998 w/2JZ-GTE engine

INSPECTION PROCEDURE

1	Input signal check.

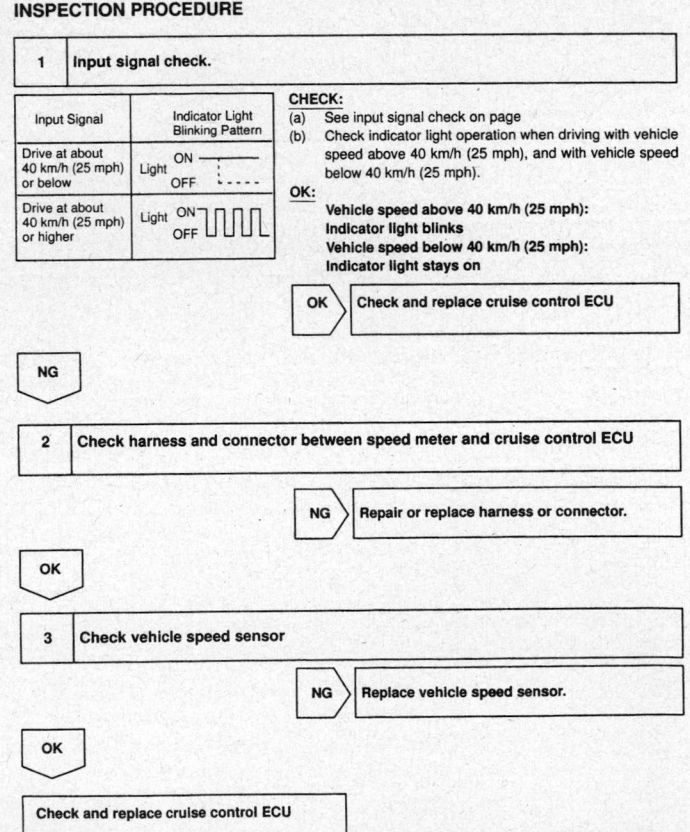

Input Signal	Indicator Light Blinking Pattern
Drive at about 40 km/h (25 mph) or below	Light ON / OFF
Drive at about 40 km/h (25 mph) or higher	Light ON / OFF

CHECK:
(a) See input signal check on page
(b) Check indicator light operation when driving with vehicle speed above 40 km/h (25 mph), and with vehicle speed below 40 km/h (25 mph).
OK:
Vehicle speed above 40 km/h (25 mph):
Indicator light blinks
Vehicle speed below 40 km/h (25 mph):
Indicator light stays on

OK ➤ Check and replace cruise control ECU

NG

2	Check harness and connector between speed meter and cruise control ECU

NG ➤ Repair or replace harness or connector.

OK

3	Check vehicle speed sensor

NG ➤ Replace vehicle speed sensor.

OK

Check and replace cruise control ECU

TY1109900445020X

Fig. 311   Code 21: Open In Vehicle Speed Sensor Circuit (Part 2 of 2). 1997 Supra & 1998 w/2JZ-GTE engine

CIRCUIT DESCRIPTION

The vehicle speed sensor circuit is sent to cruise control ECU as vehicle speed signal. For each rotation of the shaft, the vehicle speed sensor sends a signal through the combination meter to the cruise control ECU (See the following). The ECU calculates the vehicle speed from this pulse frequency.

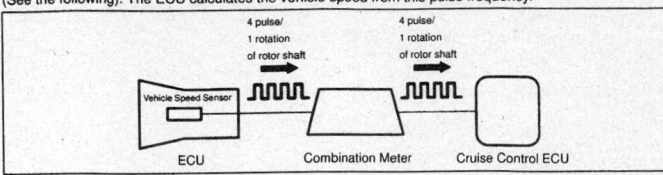

DTC No.	Detection Item	Trouble Area
21	Speed signal is not input to the cruise control ECU while cruise control is set.	• Vehicle speed sensor • Combination meter • Cruise control ECU

TY1109900445010X

Fig. 311   Code 21: Open In Vehicle Speed Sensor Circuit (Part 1 of 2). 1997 Supra & 1998 w/2JZ-GTE engine

CIRCUIT DESCRIPTION

DTC No.	Detection Item	Trouble Area
23	• Vehicle speed sensor pulse is abnormal. (When speed signal is not input to the ECU below 0.2 sec., code will be displayed.)	• Vehicle speed sensor • Cruise control ECU

INSPECTION PROCEDURE

1	Check vehicle speed sensor

NG ➤ Replace vehicle speed sensor.

OK

Check and replace cruise control ECU

TY1109900446000X

Fig. 312   Code 23: Vehicle Speed Signal Fault. 1997 Supra & 1998 w/2JZ-GTE engine

CIRCUIT DESCRIPTION

This circuit carries the SET/COAST, RESUME/ACCEL and CANCEL signals (each voltage) to the ECU.

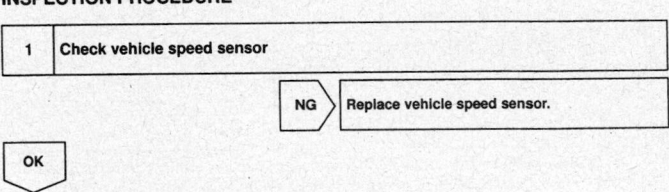

DTC No.	Detection Item	Trouble Area
32	Short in control switch circuit	• Cruise control switch • Harness or connector between control switch and cruise control ECU. • Cruise control ECU

TY1109900447010X

Fig. 313   Code 32: Control Switch Circuit (Part 1 of 3). 1997 Supra & 1998 w/2JZ-GTE engine

INSPECTION PROCEDURE

1	Input signal check.

Input Signal	Indicator Light Blinking Pattern	
SET/COAST switch	ON OFF	2 Pulses
RESUME/ACCEL switch	ON OFF	3 Pulses
CANCEL switch	ON OFF	SW OFF SW ON

PREPARATION:
See input signal check
CHECK:
Check the indicator light operation when each of the SET/COAST, RESUME/ACCEL and CANCEL is turned on.
OK:
    SET/COAST, RESUME/ACCEL switch
    The signals shown in the table on the left should be output when each switch is ON. The signal should disappear when the switch is turned OFF.
    CANCEL switch
    The indicator light goes off when the cancel switch is turned on.

OK > Wait and see.

NG

2	Check control switch.

PREPARATION:
(a) Remove steering wheel center pad
(b) Disconnect control switch connector.
CHECK:
Measure resistance between terminals 3 and 4 of control switch connector when control switch is operated.

Switch position	Resistance (Ω)
Neutral	∞ (No continuity)
RES/ACC	50 – 80
SET/COAST	180 – 220
CANCEL	400 – 440

OK > Repair control switch.

NG

TY1109900448020X

Fig. 313 Code 32: Control Switch Circuit (Part 2 of 3). 1997 Supra & 1998 w/2JZ-GTE engine

CIRCUIT DESCRIPTION

When the idle switch in turned ON, a signal is sent to the ECU. The ECU uses this signal to correct the discrepancy between the throttle valve position and the actuator position sensor value to enable accurate cruise control at the set speed. If the idle switch is malfunctioning, problem symptoms also occur in the engine, so also inspect the engine.

DTC No.	Detection Item	Trouble Area
51	Short in idle signal circuit	• Harness or connector between cruise control ECU and throttle position sensor • Throttle position sensor • Cruise control ECU

TY1109900449010X

Fig. 314 Code 51: Idle Signal Circuit (Part 1 of 2). 1997 Supra & 1998 w/2JZ-GTE engine

3	Check harness and connector between cruise control switch and cruise control ECU

NG > Repair or replace harness or connector.

OK

4	Input signal check (See step 1).

OK > Wait and see.

NG

Check and replace cruise control ECU

TY1109900448030X

Fig. 313 Code 32: Control Switch Circuit (Part 3 of 3). 1997 Supra & 1998 w/2JZ-GTE engine

INSPECTION PROCEDURE

1	Check throttle position sensor circuit

NG > Replace throttle position sensor.

OK

2	Check harness and connector between ECM and throttle position sensor

NG > Repair or replace harness or connector.

OK

3	Check harness and connector between cruise control ECU and throttle position sensor

NG > Repair or replace harness or connector.

OK

Check and replace cruise control ECU

TY1109900449020X

Fig. 314 Code 51: Idle Signal Circuit (Part 2 of 2). 1997 Supra & 1998 w/2JZ-GTE engine

CIRCUIT DESCRIPTION

When the brake is on, battery positive voltage normally applies through the STOP fuse and stop light switch to terminal STP– of the ECU, and the ECU turns the cruise control off.
A fail–safe function is provided so that cancel functions normally, even if there is a malfunction in the stop light signal circuit.
If the harness connected to terminal STP– has an open circuit, terminal STP– will have battery positive voltage and the cruise control will be turned off.
Also, when the brake is on, the magnetic clutch is cut mechanically by the stop light switch, turning the cruise control off.

TY1109900450010X

Fig. 315 Stop Lamp Switch Circuit (Part 1 of 3). 1997 Supra & 1998 w/2JZ-GTE engine

INSPECTION PROCEDURE

1	Check operation of stop light.

CHECK:
Check that stop light comes on when brake pedal is depressed, and turns off when brake pedal is released.

NG ▷ Check stop light system.

OK ▽

2	Input signal check.

Input Signal	Indicator Light Blinking Pattern
Stop Light switch ON	Light OFF SW OFF / ON ----- SW ON

CHECK:
(a) See input signal check .
(b) Check the indicator light when the brake pedal is depressed.

OK:
The indicator light goes off when the brake pedal is depressed.

OK ▷ Proceed to next circuit inspection shown on problem symptoms table

NG ▽

TY1109900450020X

Fig. 315 Stop Lamp Switch Circuit (Part 2 of 3). 1997 Supra & 1998 w/2JZ-GTE engine

CIRCUIT DESCRIPTION

When driving uphill under cruise control, in order to reduce shifting due to ON–OFF overdrive operation and to provide smooth driving, when down shifting in the electronically controlled transmission occurs, a signal to prevent upshift until the end of the uphill slope is sent from the cruise control ECU to the electronically controlled transmission.

Terminal ECM of the cruise control ECU detects the shift change signal (output to electronically controlled transmission No.2 solenoid) from the electronically controlled transmission.

If vehicle speed down, also when terminal electronically controlled transmission of the cruise control ECU receive down shifting signal, it sends a signal from terminal OD to ECM to cut overdrive until the end of the uphill slope, and the gear shifts are reduced and gear shift points in the electronically controlled transmission are changed.

TY1109900451010X

Fig. 316 Electronically Controlled Transmission Communication Circuit (Part 1 of 4). 1997 Supra & 1998 w/2JZ-GTE engine

3	Check voltage between terminal STP– of cruise control ECU connector and body ground.

PREPARATION:
Remove cruise control ECU with connectors still connected.

CHECK:
(a) Turn ignition switch ON.
(b) Measure voltage between terminal STP– of cruise control ECU connector and body ground, when the brake pedal is depressed and released.

OK:

Depressed	10 – 14 V
Released	Below 1 V

OK ▷ Proceed to next circuit inspection shown on problem symptoms table

NG ▽

4	Check for open in harness and connectors between terminal STP– of cruise control ECU and stop light switch

NG ▷ Repair or replace harness or connector.

OK ▽

Check and replace cruise control ECU

TY1109900450030X

Fig. 315 Stop Lamp Switch Circuit (Part 3 of 3). 1997 Supra & 1998 w/2JZ-GTE engine

INSPECTION PROCEDURE

1	Check operation of overdrive.

PREPARATION:
Test drive after engine warms up.

CHECK:
Check that overdrive ON ↔ OFF occurs with operation of OD switch ON ↔ OFF.

NG ▷ Check and repair electronically controlled transmission

OK ▽

2	Check voltage between terminal OD of harness side connector of cruise control ECU and body ground.

PREPARATION:
Remove cruise control ECU with connector still connected.

CHECK:
(a) Disconnect cruise control ECU connector.
(b) Turn ignition switch ON.
(c) Measure voltage between terminal OD of harness side connector of cruise control ECU and body ground.

OK:
Voltage: 10 – 14 V

NG ▷ Go to step 5.

OK ▽

TY1109900451020X

Fig. 316 Electronically Controlled Transmission Communication Circuit (Part 2 of 4). 1997 Supra & 1998 w/2JZ-GTE engine

3	Check voltage between terminal ECT of cruise control ECU connector and body ground (On test drive).

PREPARATION:
(a) Connect cruise control ECU connector.
(b) Test drive after engine warms up.
CHECK:
Check voltage between terminal ECT of cruise control ECU connector and body ground when OD switch is ON and OFF.
OK:

OD switch position	Voltage
ON	8 – 14 V
OFF	Below 0.5 V

> **OK** → Proceed to next circuit inspection shown on problem symptoms table

NG ↓

4	Check harness and connector between terminal ECT of cruise control ECU and electronically controlled transmission solenoid

> **NG** → Repair or replace harness or connector.

OK ↓

Check and replace cruise control ECU.

TY1109900451030X

Fig. 316 Electronically Controlled Transmission Communication Circuit (Part 3 of 4). 1997 Supra & 1998 w/2JZ-GTE engine

CIRCUIT DESCRIPTION

When the shift position is put in except D position, a signal is sent from the park/neutral position switch to the ECU. When this signal is input during cruise control driving, the ECU cancels the cruise control.

INSPECTION PROCEDURE

1	Check starter operation.

CHECK:
Check that the starter operates normally and that the engine starts.

> **NG** → Diagnose starting system.

OK ↓

TY1109900452010X

Fig. 317 Park/Neutral Position Switch Circuit (Part 1 of 3). 1997 Supra & 1998 w/2JZ-GTE engine

5	Check harness and connector between terminal OD of cruise control ECU and terminal OD1 of ECM

> **NG** → Repair or replace harness or connector.

OK ↓

Check and replace cruise control ECU

TY1109900451040X

Fig. 316 Electronically Controlled Transmission Communication Circuit (Part 4 of 4). 1997 Supra & 1998 w/2JZ-GTE engine

2	Input signal check.

Input Signal	Indicator Light Blinking Pattern
Turn PNP switch OFF (Shift to except D position)	Light ON — SW ON / OFF --- SW OFF

PREPARATION:
See input signal check
CHECK:
Check the indicator light when shifting into except D position.
OK:
The indicator light goes off when shifting into except D position.

> **OK** → Proceed to next circuit inspection shown on problem symptoms table

NG ↓

3	Check voltage between terminal D of cruise control ECU and body ground.

PREPARATION:
Turn ignition switch ON.
CHECK:
Measure voltage between terminal D of cruise control ECU connector and body ground when shifting into D position and other positions.
OK:

Shift Position	Voltage
D position	10 – 14 V
Other positions	Below 1 V

> **OK** → Proceed to next circuit inspection shown on problem symptoms table

NG ↓

TY1109900452020X

Fig. 317 Park/Neutral Position Switch Circuit (Part 2 of 3). 1997 Supra & 1998 w/2JZ-GTE engine

4	Check harness and connector between PNP switch and cruise control ECU

> **NG** → Repair or replace harness or connector.

OK ↓

Check and replace cruise control ECU

TY1109900452030X

Fig. 317 Park/Neutral Position Switch Circuit (Part 3 of 3). 1997 Supra & 1998 w/2JZ-GTE engine

CIRCUIT DESCRIPTION

When the clutch pedal is depressed, the clutch switch sends a signal to the cruise control ECU. When the signal is input to the cruise control ECU during cruise control driving, the cruise control ECU cancels cruise control.

INSPECTION PROCEDURE

1	Check starter operation.

CHECK:
Check that the starter operates normally and that the engine starts.

> NG → Diagnose starting system.

> OK

2	Input signal check.

Input Signal	Indicator Light Blinking Pattern
Clutch switch OFF (Depress clutch pedal)	Light — ON SW ON / OFF ----- SW OFF

PREPARATION:
See input signal check
CHECK:
Check the indicator light when the clutch pedal is depressed.
OK:
The indicator light goes off when the clutch pedal is depressed.

> OK → Proceed to next circuit inspection shown on problem symptoms table

> NG

TY1109900453010X

Fig. 318   Clutch Switch Circuit (Part 1 of 2). 1997 Supra & 1998 w/2JZ-GTE engine

CIRCUIT DESCRIPTION

The ECU power source supplies power to the actuator and sensors, etc.. When terminal GND and the cruise control ECU case are grounded.

TY1109900454010X

Fig. 319   Power Source Circuit (Part 1 of 3). 1997 Supra & 1998 w/2JZ-GTE engine

3	Check resistance between terminal GND of cruise control ECU connector and body ground

CHECK:
Measure resistance between terminal GND of cruise control ECU connector and body ground.
OK:
Resistance: Below 1 Ω

> NG → Repair or replace harness or connector.

> OK

Check and repair harness and connector between battery and cruise control ECU

TY1109900454030X

Fig. 319   Power Source Circuit (Part 3 of 3). 1997 Supra & 1998 w/2JZ-GTE engine

3	Check voltage between terminal D of cruise control ECU and body ground.

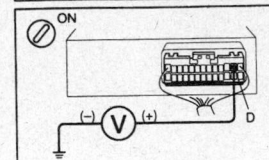

PREPARATION:
Turn ignition switch ON.
CHECK:
Measure voltage between terminal D of cruise control ECU connector and body ground when the clutch pedal is depressed.
OK:

Shift Position	Voltage
ON (Pedal depressed)	Below 1 V
OFF	10 – 14 V

> OK → Proceed to next circuit inspection shown on problem symptoms table

> NG

4	Check for open in harness and connector between ECU and GAUGE fuse

> NG → Repair or replace harness or connector.

> OK

Check and replace cruise control ECU

TY1109900453020X

Fig. 318   Clutch Switch Circuit (Part 2 of 2). 1997 Supra & 1998 w/2JZ-GTE engine

INSPECTION PROCEDURE

1	Check ECU–IG fuse.

PREPARATION:
Remove ECU–IG fuse from junction block No.1.
CHECK:
Check continuity of ECU–IG fuse.
OK:
Continuity

> NG → Check for short in all the harness and components connected to ECU–IG fuse.

> OK

2	Check voltage between terminals B and GND of cruise control ECU connector.

PREPARATION:
Remove cruise control ECU with connector still connected.
CHECK:
(a) Turn ignition switch ON.
(b) Measure voltage between terminals B and GND of cruise control ECU connector.
OK:
10 – 14 V

> OK → Proceed to next circuit inspection shown on problem symptoms table

> NG

TY1109900454020X

Fig. 319   Power Source Circuit (Part 2 of 3). 1997 Supra & 1998 w/2JZ-GTE engine

CIRCUIT DESCRIPTION

The ECU back–up power source provides power even when the ignition is off and is used for DTC memory, etc..

TY1109900455010X

Fig. 320   Back Up Power Source Circuit (Part 1 of 2). 1997 Supra & 1998 w/2JZ-GTE engine

INSPECTION PROCEDURE

1	Check DOME fuse.

PREPARATION:
Remove DOME fuse from relay block No.2.
CHECK:
Check continuity of DOME fuse.
OK:
  Continuity

NG → Check for short in all the harness and components connected to the DOME fuse.

OK

2	Check voltage between terminal BATT of cruise control ECU connector and body ground

PREPARATION:
Remove cruise control ECU with connector still connected.
CHECK:
Measure voltage between terminal BATT of cruise control ECU connector and body ground.
OK:
  Voltage: 10 – 14 V

OK → Proceed to next circuit inspection shown on problem symptoms table

NG

Check and repair harness and connector between battery and cruise control ECU

TY1109900455020X

Fig. 320 Back Up Power Source Circuit (Part 2 of 2). 1997 Supra & 1998 w/2JZ-GTE engine

2	Check main switch continuity.

PREPARATION:
(a) Remove steering wheel center pad
(b) Disconnect cruise control switch connector.
CHECK:
Check continuity between terminals 3 and 5 of cruise control switch connector when main switch is held on and off.
OK:

Switch position	Tester connection	Specified condition
OFF	3 – 5	No continuity
Hold ON	3 – 5	Continuity

NG → Replace control switch.

OK

3	Check harness and connector between cruise control ECU and main switch

NG → Repair or replace harness or connector.

OK

Check and replace cruise control ECU

TY1109900456020X

Fig. 321 Main Switch Circuit (Part 2 of 2). 1997 Supra & 1998 w/2JZ-GTE engine

CIRCUIT DESCRIPTION

When the cruise control main switch is turned off, the cruise control does not operate.

INSPECTION PROCEDURE

1	Check voltage between terminal CMS of cruise control ECU connector and body ground.

PREPARATION:
Remove cruise control ECU with connector still connected.
CHECK:
(a) Turn ignition switch ON.
(b) Measure voltage between terminal CMS of cruise control ECU connector when main switch is held on and off.
OK:

Main switch	Voltage
OFF	10 – 14 V
ON	Below 1 V

OK → Proceed to next circuit inspection shown on problem symptoms table

NG

TY1109900456010X

Fig. 321 Main Switch Circuit (Part 1 of 2). 1997 Supra & 1998 w/2JZ-GTE engine

CIRCUIT DESCRIPTION

When the cruise control main switch is turned ON, CRUISE MAIN indicator light lights up.

TY1109900457010X

Fig. 322 Cruise Main Indicator Lamp Circuit (Part 1 of 2). 1997 Supra & 1998 w/2JZ-GTE engine

INSPECTION PROCEDURE

1	Check voltage between terminals PI and GND of cruise control ECU connector.

PREPARATION:
Ignition switch ON.
CHECK:
Measure voltage between terminals PI and GND of cruise control ECU connector when main switch on and off.
OK:

Switch position	Voltage
OFF	10 – 16 V
ON	Below 1.2 V

OK → Proceed to next circuit inspection shown on problem symptoms table

NG

2	Check combination meter

NG → Replace combination meter.

OK

Check and replace cruise control ECU

TY1109900457020X

Fig. 322 Cruise Main Indicator Lamp Circuit (Part 2 of 2). 1997 Supra & 1998 w/2JZ-GTE engine

CIRCUIT DESCRIPTION

This circuit sends a signal to the ECU that DTC output is required.

TY1109900458010X

Fig. 323 Diagnosis Circuit (Part 1 of 2). 1997 Supra & 1998 w/2JZ-GTE engine

INSPECTION PROCEDURE

1	Check voltage between terminals Tc and E₁ of DLC1.

CHECK:
(a) Turn ignition switch ON.
(b) Measure voltage between terminals Tc and E_1 of DLC1.
OK:
  Voltage: 10 – 14 V

> **OK** | Proceed to next circuit inspection shown on problem symptoms table

NG

2	Check harness and connector between cruise control ECU and DLC1, DLC1 and body ground

> **NG** | Repair or replace harness or connector.

OK

Check and replace cruise control ECU

TY1109900458020X

Fig. 323 Diagnosis Circuit (Part 2 of 2). 1997 Supra & 1998 w/2JZ-GTE engine

Symptom	Suspect Area
SET not occurring or CANCEL occurring. (DTC is Normal)	1. Input Signal Circuit 2. Main Switch Circuit (Cruise control switch) 3. Control Switch Circuit (Cruise control switch) 4. Vehicle Speed Sensor Circuit 5. Stop Light Switch Circuit 6. Park/Neutral Position Switch Circuit 7. ECM
SET not occurring or CANCEL occurring. (DTC dose not output)	1. ECM
Actual vehicle speed deviates above or below the set speed.	1. Vehicle Speed Sensor Circuit 2. ECM
Gear shifting frequent between 3rd O/D when driving on uphill road. (Hurting)	1. ECM
Cruise control not cancelled, even when brake pedal is depressed.	1. Stop Light Switch Circuit 2. ECM
Cruise control not cancelled, even when transmission is shifted to "N" position.	1. Park/Neutral Position Switch Circuit 2. ECM
Cruise control not cancelled, even when clutch pedal is depressed.	1. ECM
Control switch does not operate. (SET/COAST, ACC/RES, CANCEL not possible)	1. Control Switch Circuit (Cruise control switch) 2. ECM
SET possible at 40 km/h (25 mph) or less, or CANCEL does not operate at 40 km/h (25 mph) or less.	1. Vehicle Speed Sensor Circuit 2. ECM
Poor response is ACCEL and RESUME modes.	1. ECM
O/D does not RESUME, even though the road is not uphill.	1. ECM
DTC memory is erased.	1. ECM
DTC is not output, or is output when is should not be.	1. Diagnosis Circuit 2. ECM
Cruise MAIN indicator light remains ON or fail to light up.	1. Cruise MAIN Indicator Light Circuit 2. ECM

TY1109900432000X

Fig. 325 Problem Symptoms Table. 1998 Supra w/2JZ-GE engine

INSPECTION PROCEDURE

1	Actuator control cable inspection.

CHECK:
(a) Check that the actuator, control cable throttle link are properly installed and that the cable and link are connected correctly.
(b) Check that the actuator and bell crank are operating smoothly.
(c) Check that the cable is not loose or too tight.
OK:
  Freeplay: less than 10 mm
HINT:
• If the control cable is very loose, the vehicle's loss of speed going uphill will be large.
• If the control cable is too tight, the idle RPM will become high.

TY1109900459000X

Fig. 324 Actuator Control Cable. 1997 Supra & 1998 w/2JZ-GTE engine

CIRCUIT DESCRIPTION

The vehicle speed sensor detects the rotation speed of the transmission output shaft and sends signals to the ECM. The ECM determines the vehicle speed based on these signals. An AC voltage is generated in the vehicle speed sensor coil as the rotor mounted on the output shaft rotates, and this voltage is sent to the ECM.

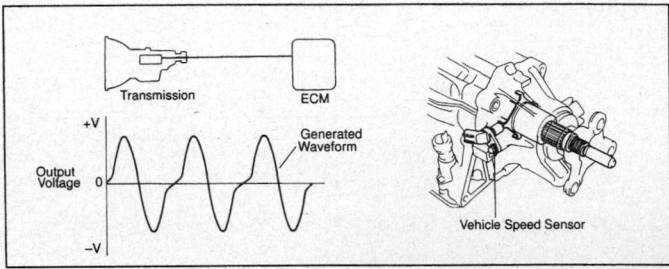

DTC No.	DTC Detecting Condition	Trouble Area
P0500	No vehicle speed sensor signal to ECM under conditions (a) and (b): (a) Park/neutral position switch is OFF (b) Vehicle is being driven	• Open or short in vehicle speed sensor circuit • Vehicle speed sensor • ECM

TY1109900433010X

Fig. 326 Code P0500/21, 23: Vehicle Speed Sensor Fault (Part 1 of 4). 1998 Supra w/2JZ-GE engine

INSPECTION PROCEDURE

HINT:
Read freeze frame data using TOYOTA hand–held tester or OBD II scan tool. Because freeze frame records the engine conditions when the malfunction is detected, when troubleshooting it is useful for determining whether the vehicle was running or stopped, the engine warmed up or not, the air–fuel ratio lean or rich, etc. at the time of the malfunction.

1	Connect OBD II scan tool or TOYOTA hand–held tester and read value of vehicle speed value.

PREPARATION:
(a) Connect the OBD II scan tool or TOYOTA hand–held tester to the DLC3.
(b) Start the engine and the OBD II scan tool or TOYOTA hand–held tester main switch ON.
CHECK:
Drive the vehicle and read vehicle speed value.
OK:
  Vehicle speed matches tester speed value

> **NG** | Check and replace ECM

OK

2	Check speedometer circuit

> **NG** | Repair or replace speedometer circuit.

OK

TY1109900433020X

Fig. 326 Code P0500/21, 23: Vehicle Speed Sensor Fault (Part 2 of 4). 1998 Supra w/2JZ-GE engine

3	Check resistance between terminals SP2+ and SP2– of ECM connector.

PREPARATION:
(a) Remove the scuff plate
(b) Disconnect the E12 connector of the ECM.
CHECK:
Check resistance between terminals SP2+ and SP2– of the
ECM connector.
OK:

> **Resistance: 560 ~ 680 Ω**

OK	Check and replace ECM

NG

4	Check vehicle speed sensor.

PREPARATION:
Remove the vehicle speed sensor from the transmission.
CHECK:
Measure resistance between terminals 1 and 2 of the speed
sensor.
OK:

> **Resistance: 560 ~ 680 Ω**
Reference
Check vehicle speed sensor's function.
CHECK:
Check voltage between terminals 1 and 2 of the vehicle speed
sensor when a magnet is put close to front end of the vehicle
speed sensor then taken away quickly.
OK:

> **Voltage is generated intermittently.**
HINT:
Voltage generated is extremely low.

TY1109900433030X

Fig. 326   Code P0500/21, 23: Vehicle Speed Sensor Fault (Part 3 of 4). 1998 Supra w/2JZ-GE engine

CIRCUIT DESCRIPTION

When the brake pedal is depressed, the stop light switch sends a signal to the ECM. When the ECM receives
this signal, it cancels the cruise control.
A fail–safe function is provided so that the cancel functions normally, even if there is a malfunction in the stop
light signal circuit.
The cancel conditions are: Battery positive voltage at terminal STP–
When the brake is on, battery positive voltage normally applies through the STOP fuse and stop light switch
to terminal STP– of the ECM, and the ECM turns the cruise control off.
If the harness connected to terminal STP– has an open circuit, terminal STP– will have battery positive volt-
age and the cruise control will be turned off.

DTC No.	Detection Item	Trouble Area
52	Stop light switch circuit.	• Stop light switch • Harness or connector between ECM and stop light switch circuit • ECM

TY1109900434010X

Fig. 327   Code P0500/52: Stop Lamp Switch Circuit (Part 1 of 3). 1998 Supra w/2JZ-GE engine

3	Check wire harness and connector between terminal STP of ECM and stop light switch, and terminal ST1–of ECM and stop light switch

NG	Repair or replace harness or connector.

OK

Check and replace ECM

TY1109900434030X

Fig. 327   Code P0500/52: Stop Lamp Switch Circuit (Part 3 of 3). 1998 Supra w/2JZ-GE engine

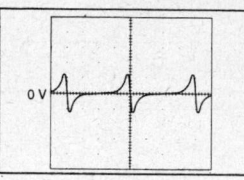

Reference INSPECTION USING OSCILLOSCOPE
Waveform between terminals SP2+ and SP2– When the vehicle speed is approx. 60 km/h (37 mph).

NG	Replace vehicle speed sensor.

OK

Check and repair harness and connector between ECM and vehicle speed sensor

TY1109900433040X

Fig. 326   Code P0500/21, 23: Vehicle Speed Sensor Fault (Part 4 of 4). 1998 Supra w/2JZ-GE engine

INSPECTION PROCEDURE

HINT:
In case of using the TOYOTA hand–held tester, start the inspection from step 1 and in case of not using the
LEXUS hand–held tester, start from step 2.

1	Check stop light switch using TOYOTA hand–held tester.

PREPARATION:
Connect the TOYOTA hand–held tester to the DLC3.
CHECK:
Check the stop light switch using DATALIST.
OK:

Condition	Stop light switch 1 (Sub CPU)	Stop light switch 2 (Sub CPU)	Stop light switch 2 (Main CPU)
Depressed	ON	ON	ON
Released	OFF	OFF	OFF

HINT:
• Stop light SW 1 has a function to disconnect the connection (OFF) when depressing the pedal, however, ECM controls by the logic rivers, so with the TOYOTA hand–held tester, it displays ON.
• Stop light SW 1 indicates the input of ST1–terminal and Stop light SW 2 indicates the input of STP
   terminal.

OK	Proceed to next circuit inspection shown on problem symptom table

NG

2	Check stop light switch

NG	Replace stop light switch.

OK

TY1109900434020X

Fig. 327   Code P0500/52: Stop Lamp Switch Circuit (Part 2 of 3). 1998 Supra w/2JZ-GE engine

CIRCUIT DESCRIPTION

This circuit carries the SET/COAST, RESUME/ACCEL and CANCEL signals (each voltage) to the ECM.

DTC No.	Detection Item	Trouble Area
P1565/32	Short in control switch circuit.	• Cruise control switch • Harness or connector between ECM and cruise control switch, cruise control switch and body ground • ECM

TY1109900435010X

Fig. 328   Code P1565/32: Control Switch Circuit (Part 1 of 3). 1998 Supra w/2JZ-GE engine

INSPECTION PROCEDURE

1	Check voltage between terminals CCS of ECM connector and body ground.

PREPARATION:
(a) Remove the ECM with connector still connected.
(b) Turn ignition switch ON.

CHECK:
Measure voltage between terminals CCS of ECM connector and body ground, when each of the SET/COAST, RESUME/ACCEL and CANCEL is turned ON.

Switch position	Resistance (V)
Neutral	10 – 16 V
RES/ACC	0.6 – 2.3 V
SET/COAST	1.9 – 4.7 V
CANCEL	3.4 – 7.2 V

NG >	Proceed to next circuit inspection shown on problem symptom table

OK

2	Check control switch.

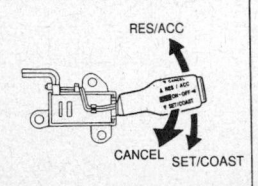

PREPARATION:
(a) Remove steering wheel center pad.
(b) Disconnect the control switch connector.

CHECK:
Measure resistance between terminals 3 and 4 of control switch connector when control switch is operated.

Switch position	Resistance (Ω)
Neutral	∞ (No continuity)
RES/ACC	50 – 80
SET/COAST	180 – 220
CANCEL	400 – 440

NG >	Replace control switch.

OK

TY1109900435020X

Fig. 328 Code P1565/32: Control Switch Circuit (Part 2 of 3). 1998 Supra w/2JZ-GE engine

CIRCUIT DESCRIPTION

DTC No.	Detection Item	Trouble Area
54	• Stop light switch input signal abnormal. • Cruise control switch input signal abnormal.	• ECM

INSPECTION PROCEDURE

Check and replace ECM

TY1109900436000X

Fig. 329 Code P1566/54: Input Signal Circuit Fault. 1998 Supra w/2JZ-GE engine

3	Check harness and connector between ECM and cruise control switch, cruise control switch and body ground

NG >	Repair or replace harness or connector.

OK

Check and replace ECM

TY1109900435030X

Fig. 328 Code P1565/32: Control Switch Circuit (Part 3 of 3). 1998 Supra w/2JZ-GE engine

CIRCUIT DESCRIPTION

When the cruise control main switch is turned off, the cruise control does not operate.

INSPECTION PROCEDURE

1	Check voltage between terminal CMS of ECM connector and body ground.

PREPARATION:
(a) Remove the ECM with connector still connected.
(b) Turn ignition switch ON.

CHECK:
Measure voltage between terminal CMS of ECM connector when main switch is held on and off.

OK:

Main switch	Voltage
OFF	10 – 14 V
ON	Below 0.5 V

OK >	Proceed to next circuit inspection shown on problem symptom table

NG

TY1109900437010X

Fig. 330 Main Switch Circuit (Part 1 of 2). 1998 Supra w/2JZ-GE engine

2	Check main switch continuity.

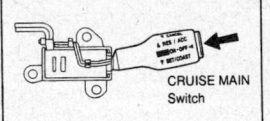

CRUISE MAIN Switch

PREPARATION:
(a) Remove steering wheel center pad.
(b) Disconnect the control switch connector.

CHECK:
Check continuity between terminals 3 and 5 of control switch connector when main switch is held on and off.

OK:

Switch position	Tester connection	Specified condition
OFF	3 – 5	No continuity
Hold ON	3 – 5	Continuity

NG >	Replace control switch.

OK

3	Check harness and connector between ECM and main switch

NG >	Repair or replace harness or connector.

OK

Check and replace ECM

TY1109900437020X

Fig. 331 Main Switch Circuit (Part 2 of 2). 1998 Supra w/2JZ-GE engine

CIRCUIT DESCRIPTION

When the cruise control main switch is turned ON, CRUISE MAIN indicator light lights up.

TY1109900438010X

**Fig. 332   Cruise Main Indicator Lamp (Part 1 of 2).
1998 Supra w/2JZ-GE engine**

Symptom	Suspect Area
• Cruise control system does not set. • Cruise control system does not operate.	Input signal check No.4: OK 1. ECU Power Source Circuit 2. Wire Harness 3. Cruise Control Main Switch Circuit 4. Cruise Control Switch Circuit 5. Stop Light Switch Circuit 6. PNP Switch or Clutch Switch Circuit 7. Cable 8. Cruise Control Actuator Circuit 9. Cruise Control ECU Input signal check No.4: NG 1. Vehicle Speed Sensor Circuit 2. Cruise Control ECU
Indicator light does not light up.	1. Wire Harness 2. Indicator Light Circuit 3. Cruise Control ECU
Vehicle speed drop when the cruise control switch turned to SET.	1. Cable 2. ECU Power Source Circuit 3. Throttle Position Sensor (IDL) Circuit 4. Cruise Control Actuator Circuit 5. Cruise Control ECU
Set speed deviates on high or low side.	Input signal check No.4: OK 1. Vehicle Speed Sensor Circuit 2. Cable 3. ECU Power Source Circuit 4. Cruise Control Actuator Circuit 5. Cruise Control ECU Input signal check No.4: NG 1. Cruise Control ECU
Vehicle speed fluctuates when cruise control switch is turned SET.	1. Vehicle Speed Sensor Circuit 2. Cable 3. Throttle Position Sensor Circuit 4. ECT Communecation Circuit 5. Cruise Control Actuator Circuit 6. Cruise Control ECU
Acceleration response is sluggish when cruise control switch is turned "ACCEL" or "RESUME".	Input signal check No.4: OK 1. Cable 2. Vehicle Speed Sensor Circuit 3. Cruise Control Actuator Circuit 4. Cruise Control ECU Input signal check No.4: NG 1. Cruise Control Switch Circuit 2. Cruise Control ECU
Set speed does not cancel when brake pedal depressed.	Input signal check No.3: OK 1. Cruise Control ECU Input signal check No.3: NG 1. Stop Light Switch Circuit 2. Cruise Control ECU
Cruise control does not cancel when transmission is shifted to ranges except D. (A/T)	Input signal check No.3: OK 1. Cruise Control ECU Input signal check No.3: NG 1. PNP Switch Circuit 2. Cruise Control ECU

TY1109900249010X

**Fig. 333   Problem Symptoms Table (Part 1 of 2).
Tacoma**

INSPECTION PROCEDURE

1	Check voltage between terminals PI and GND of ECM connector.

PREPARATION:
Tun ignition switch ON.
CHECK:
Measure voltage between terminals PI and GND of ECM connector when main switch on and off.
OK:

Switch position	Voltage
OFF	10 – 16 V
ON	Below 1.2 V

OK → Proceed to next circuit inspection shown on problem symptom table

NG

2	Check combination meter

NG → Replace combination meter.

OK

Check and replace ECM

TY1109900438020X

**Fig. 332   Cruise Main Indicator Lamp (Part 2 of 2).
1998 Supra w/2JZ-GE engine**

Symptom	Suspect Area
Cruise control does not cancel when clutch pedal is depressed.	Input signal check No.3: OK 1. Cruise Control ECU Input signal check No.3: NG 1. Clutch Switch Circuit 2. Cruise Control ECU
Cruise control does not cancel when cruise control switch is turned to CANCEL.	Input signal check No.3: OK 1. Cruise Control ECU Input signal check No.3: NG 1. Cruise Control Switch Circuit 2. Cruise Control ECU
Vehicle Speed does not decrease when cruise control switch is turned to COAST.	Input signal check No.1: OK 1. Cruise Control Actuator Circuit 2. Cable 3. Vehicle Speed Sensor Circuit 4. Cruise Control ECU Input signal check No.1: NG 1. Cruise Control Switch Circuit 2. Cruise Control ECU
Vehicle speed does not accelerate when cruise control switch is turned to ACCEL.	Input signal check No.2: OK 1. Cruise Control Actuator Circuit 2. Cable 3. Vehicle Speed Sensor Circuit 4. Cruise Control ECU Input signal check No.2: NG 1. Cruise Control Switch Circuit 2. Cruise Control ECU
Vehicle speed does not return to memorized speed when cruise control switch is turned to RESUME.	Input signal check No.2: OK 1. Cruise Control Actuator Circuit 2. Cable 3. Vehicle Speed Sensor Circuit 4. Cruise Control ECU Input signal check No.2: NG 1. Cruise Control Switch Circuit 2. Cruise Control ECU
Speed can be set below about 40 km/h (25 mph).	Input signal check No.4: OK 1. Cruise Control ECU Input signal check No.4: NG 1. Vehicle Speed Sensor Circuit 2. Cruise Control ECU
Cruise control does not cancel when speed is less than 40 km/h (25 mph).	Input signal check No.4: OK 1. Cruise Control Actuator Circuit 2. Cruise Control ECU Input signal check No.4: NG 1. Vehicle Speed Sensor Circuit 2. Cruise Control ECU

TY1109900249020X

**Fig. 333   Problem Symptoms Table (Part 2 of 2).
Tacoma**

CIRCUIT DESCRIPTION

The actuator motor is operated by signals from the ECU. Acceleration and deceleration signals are transmitted by changes in the Duty Ratio (See note below).

Duty Ratio
The duty ratio is the ratio of the period of continuity in one cycle. For example, if A is the period of continuity in one cycle, and B is the period of non-continuity, then

$$\text{Duty Ratio} = \frac{A}{A+B} \times 100 \ (\%)$$

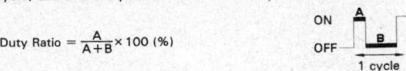

DTC No.	DTC Detecting Condition	Trouble area
11	• Short in motor circuit	• Cruise control actuator motor
14	• Open in actuator motor circuit	• Harness or connector between actuator motor and ECU • ECU

TY1109900324010X

Fig. 334   Codes 11 & 14: Actuator Motor Circuit (Part 1 of 2). 1996 Tacoma

CIRCUIT DESCRIPTION

This circuit turns on the magnetic clutch inside the actuator during cruise control operation according to the signal from the ECU. If a malfunction occurs in the actuator or vehicle speed sensor, etc. during cruise control, the rotor shaft between the motor and control plate is released.

When the brake pedal is depressed, the stoplight switch turns on, supplying electrical power to the stoplight. Power supply to the magnetic clutch is mechanically cut and the magnetic clutch is turned OFF.

When driving downhill, if the vehicle speed exceeds the set speed by 15 km/h (9 mph), the ECU turns the magnetic clutch OFF. If the vehicle speed later drops to within 10 km/h (6 mph) above the set speed, then cruise control at the set speed is resumed.

DTC No.	DTC Detecting Condition	Trouble area
12	• Short in magnetic clutch circuit. • Open (0.8 sec) in magnetic clutch circuit. • Open in STOP Fuse.	• Cruise control magnetic clutch. • Harness or connector between ECU and magnetic clutch, magnetic clutch and body ground. • ECU

TY1109900325010X

Fig. 335   Code 12: Actuator Magnetic Clutch Circuit (Part 1 of 2). 1996 Tacoma

INSPECTION PROCEDURE

1   Check actuator magnetic clutch.

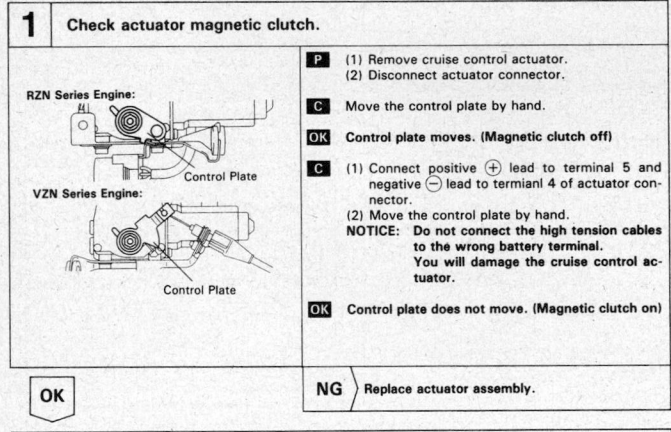

P (1) Remove cruise control actuator.
(2) Disconnect actuator connector.

C Move the control plate by hand.

OK Control plate moves. (Magnetic clutch off)

C (1) Connect positive (+) lead to terminal 5 and negative (−) lead to terminal 4 of actuator connector.
(2) Move the control plate by hand.
NOTICE: Do not connect the high tension cables to the wrong battery terminal. You will damage the cruise control actuator.

OK Control plate does not move. (Magnetic clutch on)

OK ⟶

NG ⟩ Replace actuator assembly.

2   Check stop light switch.

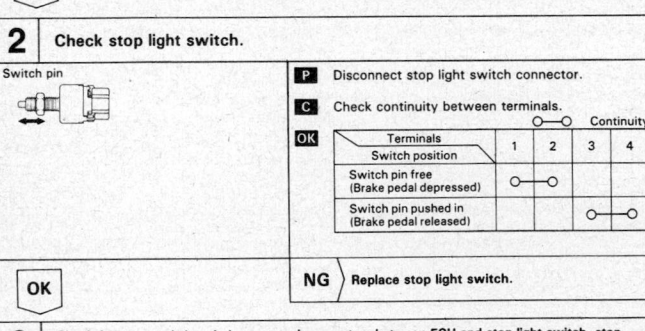

P Disconnect stop light switch connector.

C Check continuity between terminals.

Terminals Switch position	1	2	3	4	Continuity
Switch pin free (Brake pedal depressed)	○	○			
Switch pin pushed in (Brake pedal released)			○	○	

OK ⟶

NG ⟩ Replace stop light switch.

3   Check for open and short in harness and connectors between ECU and stop light switch, stop light switch and magnetic clutch, magnetic clutch and body ground

OK ⟶

NG ⟩ Repair or replace harness or connector.

Proceed to next circuit inspection shown on Problem Symptoms table.
However, when DTC 12 is displayed, check harness and connector for loose connection.
If connection is normal, check and replace ECU.

TY1109900325020X

Fig. 335   Code 12: Actuator Magnetic Clutch Circuit (Part 2 of 2). 1996 Tacoma

---

1   Check actuator motor.

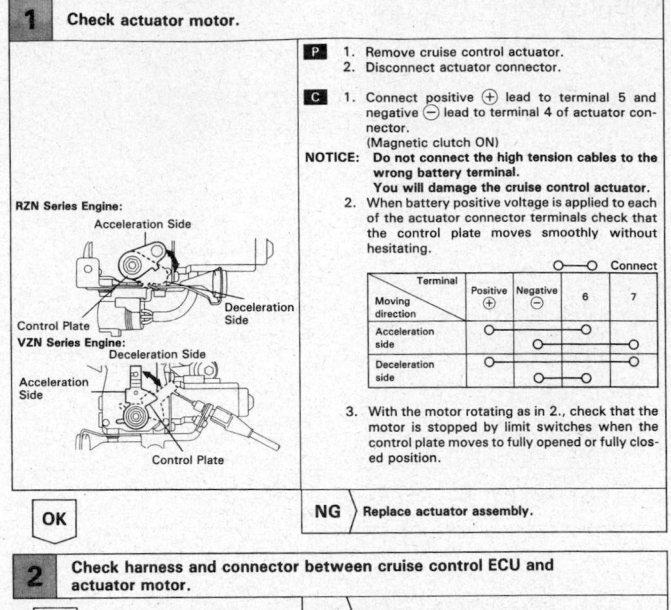

P 1. Remove cruise control actuator.
2. Disconnect actuator connector.

C 1. Connect positive (+) lead to terminal 5 and negative (−) lead to terminal 4 of actuator connector.
(Magnetic clutch ON)
NOTICE: Do not connect the high tension cables to the wrong battery terminal. You will damage the cruise control actuator.
2. When battery positive voltage is applied to each of the actuator connector terminals check that the control plate moves smoothly without hesitating.

Terminal Moving direction	Positive (+)	Negative (−)	6	7	Connect
Acceleration side	○	○			
Deceleration side		○	○	○	

3. With the motor rotating as in 2., check that the motor is stopped by limit switches when the control plate moves to fully opened or fully closed position.

OK ⟶

NG ⟩ Replace actuator assembly.

2   Check harness and connector between cruise control ECU and actuator motor.

OK ⟶

NG ⟩ Repair or replace harness or connector.

Proceed to next circuit inspection shown on problem symptoms table.
However, when DTC 11, 23 is displayed, check and replace cruise control ECU.

TY1109900324020X

Fig. 334   Codes 11 & 14: Actuator Motor Circuit (Part 2 of 2). 1996 Tacoma

CIRCUIT DESCRIPTION

The circuit detects the rotation position of the actuator control plate and sends a signal to the ECU.

DTC No.	DTC Detecting Condition	Trouble area
13	• Position sensor detects abnormal voltage.	• Cruise control actuator motor. • Cruise control actuator position sensor. • Harness or connector between actuator position sensor and body ground.
14	• Open in actuator motor circuit. • Position sensor signal value does not change when the motor operates.	• Harness or connector between actuator motor and ECU. • ECU

TY1109900326010X

Fig. 336   Codes 13 & 14: Actuator Position Sensor Circuit (Part 1 of 3). 1996 Tacoma

1   Check voltage between terminals VR2 and VR3 of ECU connector.

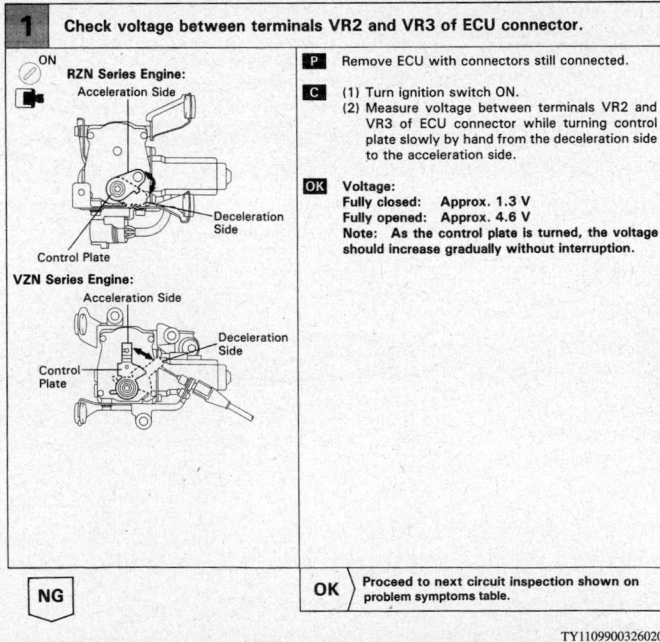

P Remove ECU with connectors still connected.

C (1) Turn ignition switch ON.
(2) Measure voltage between terminals VR2 and VR3 of ECU connector while turning control plate slowly by hand from the deceleration side to the acceleration side.

OK Voltage:
Fully closed: Approx. 1.3 V
Fully opened: Approx. 4.6 V
Note: As the control plate is turned, the voltage should increase gradually without interruption.

NG ⟶

OK ⟩ Proceed to next circuit inspection shown on problem symptoms table.

TY1109900326020X

Fig. 336   Codes 13 & 14: Actuator Position Sensor Circuit (Part 2 of 3). 1996 Tacoma

SPEED CONTROL SYSTEMS

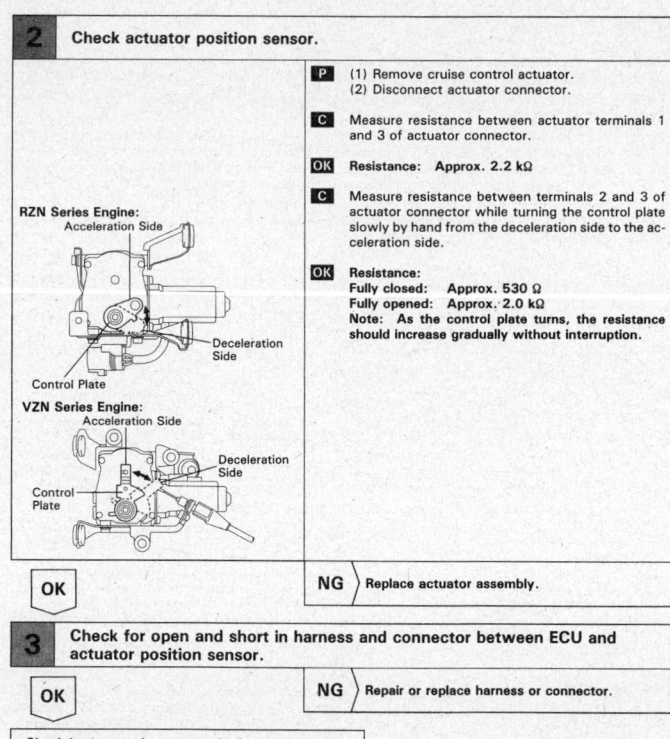

2 Check actuator position sensor.

P	(1) Remove cruise control actuator. (2) Disconnect actuator connector.
C	Measure resistance between actuator terminals 1 and 3 of actuator connector.
OK	Resistance: Approx. 2.2 kΩ
C	Measure resistance between terminals 2 and 3 of actuator connector while turning the control plate slowly by hand from the deceleration side to the acceleration side.
OK	Resistance: Fully closed: Approx. 530 Ω Fully opened: Approx. 2.0 kΩ Note: As the control plate turns, the resistance should increase gradually without interruption.

OK	NG > Replace actuator assembly.

3 Check for open and short in harness and connector between ECU and actuator position sensor.

OK	NG > Repair or replace harness or connector.

Check harness and connector for loose connection.
If connection is normal check and replace ECU.

TY1109900326030X

Fig. 336 Codes 13 & 14: Actuator Position Sensor Circuit (Part 3 of 3). 1996 Tacoma

INSPECTION PROCEDURE

1 Input signal check.

Vehicle speed	Indicator light blinking pattern
Above 40 km/h (25 mph)	ON OFF Blinks 0.25 sec. 0.25 sec.
Below 40 km/h (25 mph)	ON OFF Stays ON

C	(1) See input signal check (2) Check indicator light operation when driving with vehicle speed above 40 km/h (25 mph), and with vehicle speed below 40 km/h (25 mph).
OK	Vehicle speed above 40 km/h (25 mph): Indicator light blinks Vehicle speed below 40 km/h (25 mph): Indicator light stays on

NG	OK > Proceed to next circuit inspection shown on Problem Symptoms table.

2 Check speedometer circuit (See combination meter troubleshooting

OK	NG > Repair or replace speed sensor, harness, connector or combination meter assembly.

Check harness and connector for loose connection.
If connection is normal, check and replace ECU.

TY1109900327020X

Fig. 337 Codes 21 & 23: Vehicle Speed Sensor Circuit (Part 2 of 2). 1996 Tacoma

CIRCUIT DESCRIPTION

The vehicle speed sensor signal is sent to the cruise control ECU as the vehicle speed signal.
The rotor shaft is driven by the gear of the transmission.
For each rotation of the shaft, the vehicle speed sensor sends a 4-pulse signal to the combination meter. This signal is converted inside the combination meter and sent as a 4-pulse signal to the cruise control ECU. The ECU calculates the vehicle speed from this pulse frequency.

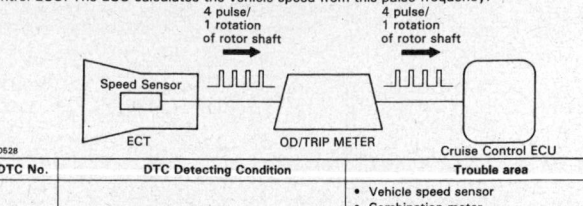

DTC No.	DTC Detecting Condition	Trouble area
21	Speed signal is not input to the ECU while cruise control is set.	• Vehicle speed sensor • Combination meter • Harness or connector between speed sensor and combination meter, combination meter and ECU • ECU
23	• Vehicle speed decrease 16 km/h or more than preset speed. • Vehicle speed sensor pulse is abnormal.	• Actuator • Vehicle speed sensor • Harness or connector in OD and SPD circuit (Open or short intermittently) • ECU

TY1109900327010X

Fig. 337 Codes 21 & 23: Vehicle Speed Sensor Circuit (Part 1 of 2). 1996 Tacoma

CIRCUIT DESCRIPTION

This circuit carries the SET/COAST, RESUME/ACCEL and CANCEL signals (each voltage) to the ECU.

DTC No.	DTC Detecting Condition	Trouble area
32	Short in, control switch circut	• Cruise control switch. • Harness or connector between control switch and ECU • ECU
34	Voltage abnormality in control switch	

TY1109900328010X

Fig. 338 Codes 32 & 34: Control Switch Circuit (Part 1 of 3). 1996 Tacoma

INSPECTION PROCEDURE

1 Input signal check.

Input Signal	Indicator light blinking pattern
SET/COAST SWITCH	ON OFF 2 Pulse
RESUME/ACCEL SWITCH	ON OFF 3 Pulse
CANCEL SWITCH	ON OFF Switch OFF / Switch ON

P	(1) See input signal check (2) Check the indicator light operation when each of the SET/COAST, RESUME/ACCEL and CANCEL is turned. ON.
OK	SET/COAST, RESUME/ACCEL Switch The signals shown in the table on the left should be output when each switch is ON. The signal should disappear when the switch is turned OFF. CANCEL Switch. The indicator light goes off when the cancel switch is turned ON.

NG	OK > Proceed to next circuit inspection shown on Problem Symptoms table.

2 Check voltage between terminal CCS of ECU connector and body ground.

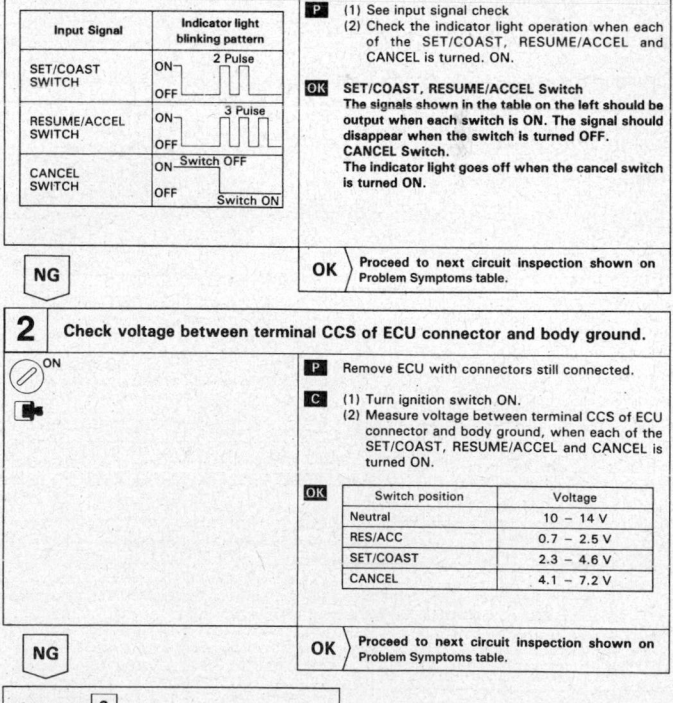

P	Remove ECU with connectors still connected.
C	(1) Turn ignition switch ON. (2) Measure voltage between terminal CCS of ECU connector and body ground, when each of the SET/COAST, RESUME/ACCEL and CANCEL is turned ON.

OK	Switch position	Voltage
	Neutral	10 – 14 V
	RES/ACC	0.7 – 2.5 V
	SET/COAST	2.3 – 4.6 V
	CANCEL	4.1 – 7.2 V

NG	OK > Proceed to next circuit inspection shown on Problem Symptoms table.

Go to step **3** .

TY1109900328020X

Fig. 338 Codes 32 & 34: Control Switch Circuit (Part 2 of 3). 1996 Tacoma

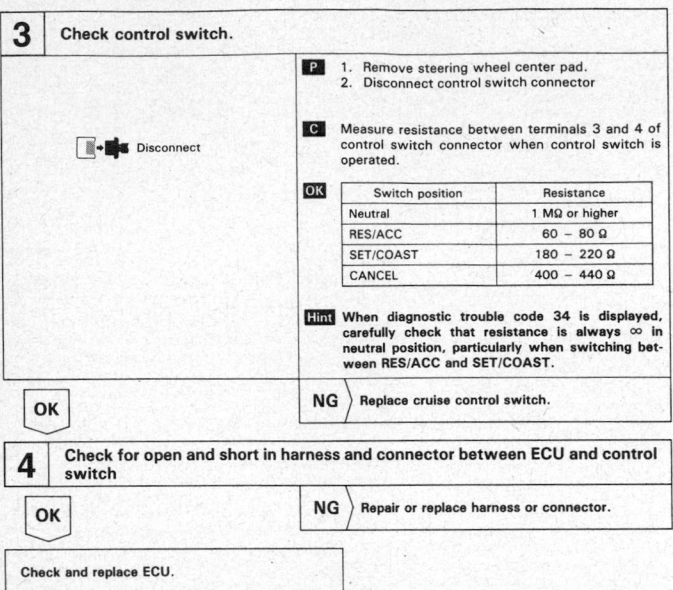

<table>
<tr><td>3</td><td>Check control switch.</td></tr>
</table>

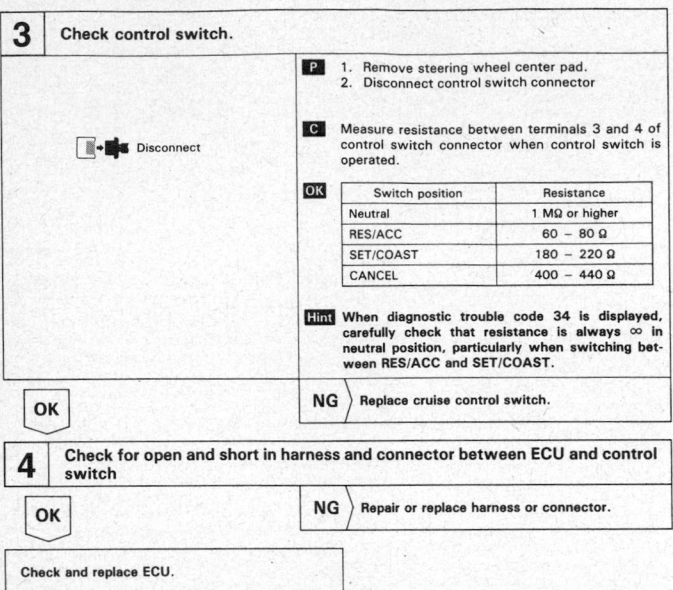 Disconnect	**P** 1. Remove steering wheel center pad. 2. Disconnect control switch connector.
	C Measure resistance between terminals 3 and 4 of control switch connector when control switch is operated.

OK

Switch position	Resistance
Neutral	1 MΩ or higher
RES/ACC	60 – 80 Ω
SET/COAST	180 – 220 Ω
CANCEL	400 – 440 Ω

Hint When diagnostic trouble code 34 is displayed, carefully check that resistance is always ∞ in neutral position, particularly when switching between RES/ACC and SET/COAST.

OK → **NG** Replace cruise control switch.

4	Check for open and short in harness and connector between ECU and control switch

OK → **NG** Repair or replace harness or connector.

Check and replace ECU.

TY1109900328030X

Fig. 338 Codes 32 & 34: Control Switch Circuit (Part 3 of 3). 1996 Tacoma

INSPECTION PROCEDURE

1	Check operation of stop light.
	C Check that stop light comes on when brake pedal is depressed, and turns off when brake pedal is released.

OK → **NG** Check stop light circuit.

TY1109900329020X

Fig. 339 Stop Lamp Switch Circuit (Part 2 of 3). 1996 Tacoma

CIRCUIT DESCRIPTION

When the idle switch is turned ON, a signal is sent to the ECU. The ECU uses this signal to correct the discrepancy between the throttle valve position and the actuator position sensor value to enable accurate cruise control at the set speed. If the idle switch is malfunctioning, problem symptoms also occur in the engine, so also inspect the engine.

TY1109900330010X

Fig. 340 Idle Switch Circuit (Part 1 of 3). 1996 Tacoma

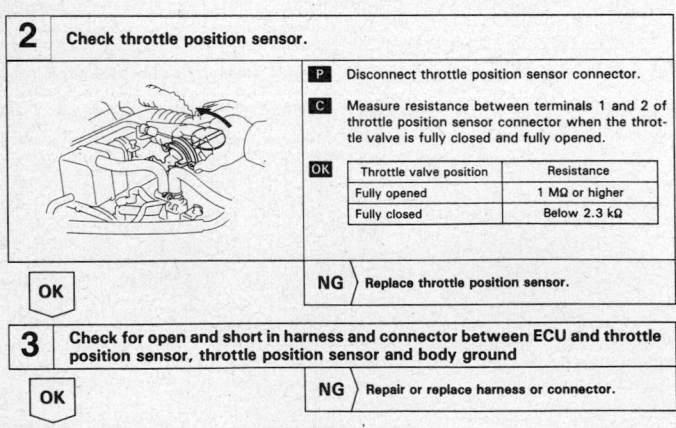

2	Check throttle position sensor.
	P Disconnect throttle position sensor connector.
	C Measure resistance between terminals 1 and 2 of throttle position sensor connector when the throttle valve is fully closed and fully opened.

OK

Throttle valve position	Resistance
Fully opened	1 MΩ or higher
Fully closed	Below 2.3 kΩ

OK → **NG** Replace throttle position sensor.

3	Check for open and short in harness and connector between ECU and throttle position sensor, throttle position sensor and body ground

OK → **NG** Repair or replace harness or connector.

Check and replace ECU.

TY1109900330030X

Fig. 340 Idle Switch Circuit (Part 3 of 3). 1996 Tacoma

CIRCUIT DESCRIPTION

When the brake is on, battery voltage normally applies through the stop fuse and stop switch to terminal STP− of the ECU, and the ECU turns the cruise control off.

A fail-safe function is provided so that cancel functions normally even if there is a malfunction in the stop light signal circuit.

① If the harness connected to terminal STP− has an open, terminal STP− will have battery positive voltage and the cruise control will be turned off, also SET not occurring.

② The STP signal is not input because of the fuse disconnection, the clutch disconnecting signal is detected by the cruise control ECU and 1−2 code is output.
Thus, 1−2 code also means the STP fuse disconnection.

Also, when the brake is on, the magnetic clutch is cut electrically by the stop light switch, turning the cruise control off.

TY1109900329010X

Fig. 339 Stop Lamp Switch Circuit (Part 1 of 3). 1996 Tacoma

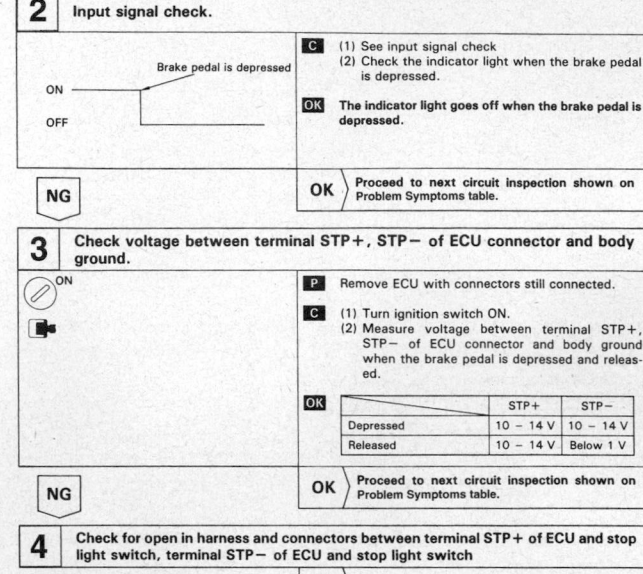

2	Input signal check.
Brake pedal is depressed ON OFF	**C** (1) See input signal check (2) Check the indicator light when the brake pedal is depressed. **OK** The indicator light goes off when the brake pedal is depressed.

NG **OK** Proceed to next circuit inspection shown on Problem Symptoms table.

3	Check voltage between terminal STP+, STP− of ECU connector and body ground.
ON	**P** Remove ECU with connectors still connected. **C** (1) Turn ignition switch ON. (2) Measure voltage between terminal STP+, STP− of ECU connector and body ground when the brake pedal is depressed and released.

OK

	STP+	STP−
Depressed	10 – 14 V	10 – 14 V
Released	10 – 14 V	Below 1 V

NG **OK** Proceed to next circuit inspection shown on Problem Symptoms table.

4	Check for open in harness and connectors between terminal STP+ of ECU and stop light switch, terminal STP− of ECU and stop light switch

OK → **NG** Repair or replace harness or connector.

Check and replace ECU.

TY1109900329030X

Fig. 339 Stop Lamp Switch Circuit (Part 3 of 3). 1996 Tacoma

INSPECTION PROCEDURE

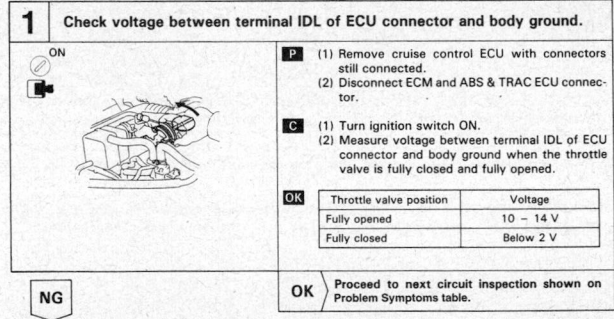

1	Check voltage between terminal IDL of ECU connector and body ground.
ON	**P** (1) Remove cruise control ECU with connectors still connected. (2) Disconnect ECM and ABS & TRAC ECU connector. **C** (1) Turn ignition switch ON. (2) Measure voltage between terminal IDL of ECU connector and body ground when the throttle valve is fully closed and fully opened.

OK

Throttle valve position	Voltage
Fully opened	10 – 14 V
Fully closed	Below 2 V

NG **OK** Proceed to next circuit inspection shown on Problem Symptoms table.

TY1109900330020X

Fig. 340 Idle Switch Circuit (Part 2 of 3). 1996 Tacoma

CIRCUIT DESCRIPTION

While the vehicle is climbing uphill under cruise control, when downshift occurs in the electronically controlled transmission, a signal is sent from the cruise control ECU to the electronically controlled transmission to prevent upshift until the end of the uphill slope. This is for smooth driving by reducing shifting due to ON/OFF operations of the overdrive.

Terminal ECT of the cruise control ECU detects the shift change signal from the electronically controlled transmission. (The signal is caused by the output to the electronically controlled transmission No.2 solenoid.)

While the vehicle speed is being reduced, when terminal ECT of the cruise control ECU detects downshift signal, terminal OD of the cruise control ECU sends a signal to OD1 of ECM to cut overdrive until the end of the uphill slope.

Then the gear shifts are reduced and gear shift points in the electronically controlled transmission are changed.

TY1109900331010X

Fig. 341 Electronically Controlled Transmission Communication Circuit (Part 1 of 4). 1996 Tacoma

INSPECTION PROCEDURE

1	Check operation of overdrive.
P	Test drive after engine warm up.
C	Check that overdrive ON ↔ OFF occurs with operation of OD switch ON-OFF.

OK	NG	Check and repair electronically controlled transmission

TY1109900331020X

Fig. 341 Electronically Controlled Transmission Communication Circuit (Part 2 of 4). 1996 Tacoma

---

1	Check for open and short in harness and connector between terminal OD of ECU and terminal OD1 of ECM

OK	NG	Repair or replace harness or connector.

Check and replace ECM.

TY1109900331040X

Fig. 341 Electronically Controlled Transmission Communication Circuit (Part 4 of 4). 1996 Tacoma

---

INSPECTION PROCEDURE

1	Check operation of starter.
C	Check that the starter operates normally and that the engine starts.

OK	NG	Diagnose starting system.

2	Input signal check.

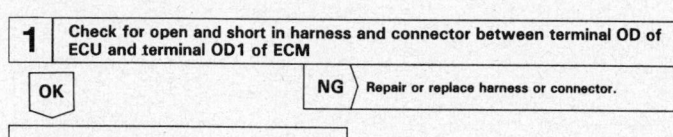

P	(1) See input signal check (2) Check the indicator light when shifting into except D position.
OK	The indicator light goes off when shifting into except D position.

NG	OK	Proceed to next circuit inspection shown on Problem Symptoms table.

3	Check voltage between terminal D of ECU connector and body ground.

P	Remove ECU with connectors still connected.
C	(1) Turn ignition switch ON. (2) Measure voltage between terminal D of ECU connector and body ground when shifting into D position and other ranges.

OK	Shift Position	Voltage
	D position	10 − 14 V
	Other positions	Below 1 V

NG	OK	Proceed to next circuit inspection shown on Problem Symptoms table.

4	Check for open in harness and connector between ECU and GAUGE fuse

OK	NG	Repair or replace harness or connector.

Check and replace ECU.

TY1109900332020X

Fig. 342 Park/Neutral Position Switch Circuit (Part 2 of 2). 1996 Tacoma

---

2	Check voltage between terminal OD of harness side connector of ECU and body ground.

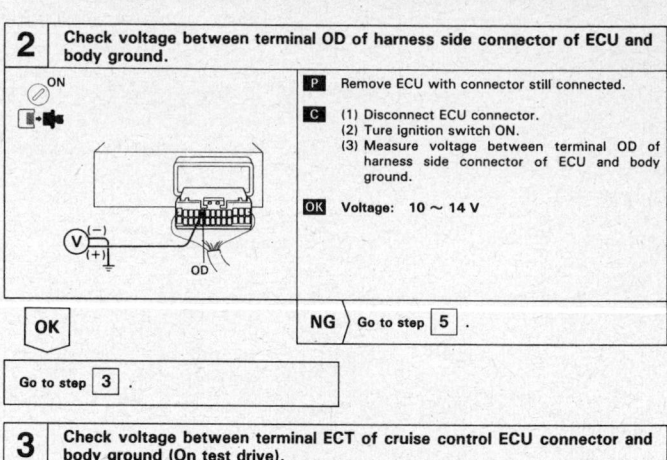

P	Remove ECU with connector still connected.
C	(1) Disconnect ECU connector. (2) Ture ignition switch ON. (3) Measure voltage between terminal OD of harness side connector of ECU and body ground.
OK	Voltage: 10 ~ 14 V

OK	NG	Go to step 5 .

Go to step 3 .

3	Check voltage between terminal ECT of cruise control ECU connector and body ground (On test drive).

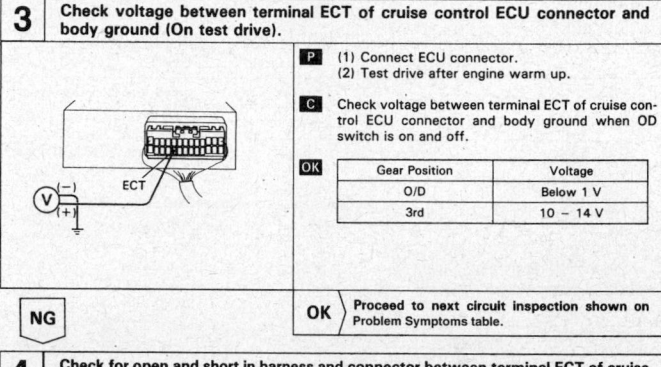

P	(1) Connect ECU connector. (2) Test drive after engine warm up.
C	Check voltage between terminal ECT of cruise control ECU connector and body ground when OD switch is on and off.

OK	Gear Position	Voltage
	O/D	Below 1 V
	3rd	10 − 14 V

NG	OK	Proceed to next circuit inspection shown on Problem Symptoms table.

4	Check for open and short in harness and connector between terminal ECT of cruise control ECU and electronically controlled transmission solenoid

OK	NG	Repair or replace harness or connector.

Check and repair ECU.

TY1109900331030X

Fig. 341 Electronically Controlled Transmission Communication Circuit (Part 3 of 4). 1996 Tacoma

CIRCUIT DESCRIPTION

When the shift position is put in except D position, a signal is sent from the park/neutral position switch to the ECU. When this signal is input during cruise control driving, the ECU cancels the cruise control.

TY1109900332010X

Fig. 342 Park/Neutral Position Switch Circuit (Part 1 of 2). 1996 Tacoma

CIRCUIT DESCRIPTION

When the clutch pedal is depressed, the clutch switch sends a signal to the cruise control ECU. When the signal is input to the cruise control ECU during cruise control driving, the cruise control ECU cancels cruise control.

INSPECTION PROCEDURE

1	Check operation of starter.

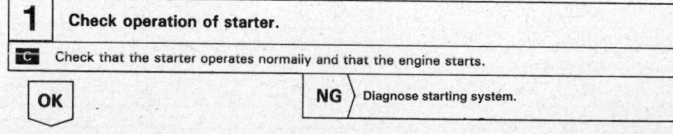

	Check that the starter operates normally and that the engine starts.

OK	NG	Diagnose starting system.

TY1109900333010X

Fig. 343 Clutch Switch Circuit (Part 1 of 2). 1996 Tacoma

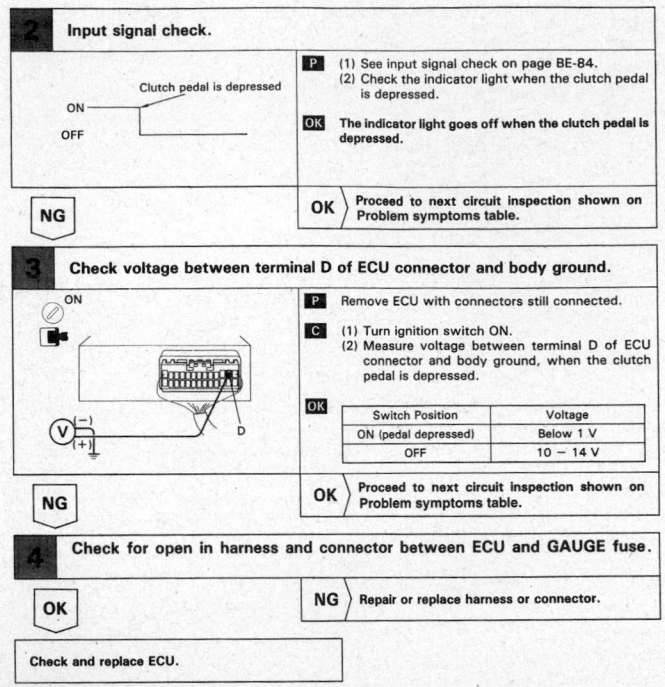

2	Input signal check.		
	Clutch pedal is depressed ON OFF	**P**	(1) See input signal check on page BE-84. (2) Check the indicator light when the clutch pedal is depressed.
		OK	The indicator light goes off when the clutch pedal is depressed.

NG		**OK**	Proceed to next circuit inspection shown on Problem symptoms table.

3	Check voltage between terminal D of ECU connector and body ground.		
	P	Remove ECU with connectors still connected.	
ON	**C**	(1) Turn ignition switch ON. (2) Measure voltage between terminal D of ECU connector and body ground, when the clutch pedal is depressed.	
	OK		

Switch Position	Voltage
ON (pedal depressed)	Below 1 V
OFF	10 — 14 V

NG		**OK**	Proceed to next circuit inspection shown on Problem symptoms table.

4	Check for open in harness and connector between ECU and GAUGE fuse.

OK		**NG**	Repair or replace harness or connector.

Check and replace ECU.

TY1109900333020X

Fig. 343 Clutch Switch Circuit (Part 2 of 2). 1996 Tacoma

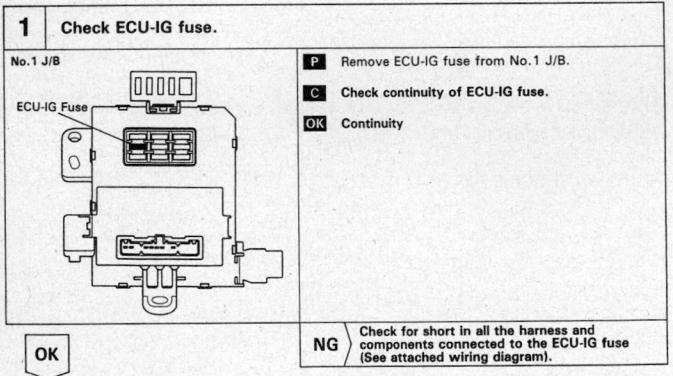

1	Check ECU-IG fuse.		
No.1 J/B ECU-IG Fuse	**P**	Remove ECU-IG fuse from No.1 J/B.	
	C	Check continuity of ECU-IG fuse.	
	OK	Continuity	

OK		**NG**	Check for short in all the harness and components connected to the ECU-IG fuse (See attached wiring diagram).

TY1109900334020X

Fig. 344 ECU Power Source Circuit (Part 2 of 3). 1996 Tacoma

CIRCUIT DESCRIPTION

The ECU power source supplies power to the actuator and sensors, etc., Terminal GND and the cruise control ECU case are grounded.

TY1109900334010X

Fig. 344 ECU Power Source Circuit (Part 1 of 3). 1996 Tacoma

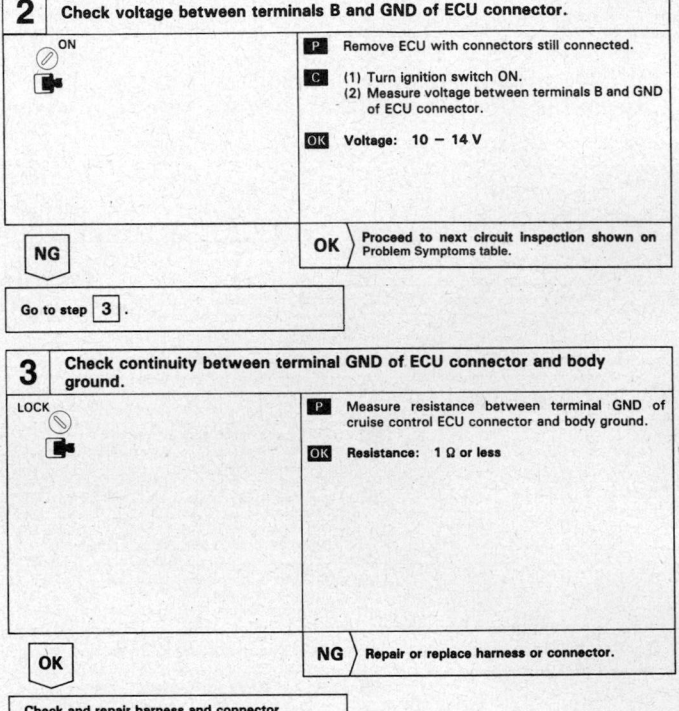

2	Check voltage between terminals B and GND of ECU connector.		
ON	**P**	Remove ECU with connectors still connected.	
	C	(1) Turn ignition switch ON. (2) Measure voltage between terminals B and GND of ECU connector.	
	OK	Voltage: 10 — 14 V	

NG		**OK**	Proceed to next circuit inspection shown on Problem Symptoms table.

Go to step [3] .

3	Check continuity between terminal GND of ECU connector and body ground.		
LOCK	**P**	Measure resistance between terminal GND of cruise control ECU connector and body ground.	
	OK	Resistance: 1 Ω or less	

OK		**NG**	Repair or replace harness or connector.

Check and repair harness and connector between battery and ECU.

TY1109900334030X

Fig. 344 ECU Power Source Circuit (Part 3 of 3). 1996 Tacoma

CIRCUIT DESCRIPTION

The ECU back-up power source provides power even when the ignition switch is off and is used for diagnostic code memory, etc.

TY1109900335010X

Fig. 345 Back Up Power Source Circuit (Part 1 of 3). 1996 Tacoma

INSPECTION PROCEDURE

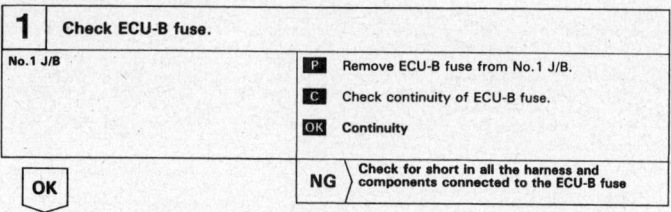

Fig. 345   Back Up Power Source Circuit (Part 2 of 3). 1996 Tacoma

CIRCUIT DESCRIPTION

When the cruise control main switch is turned off, the cruise control does not operate.

TY1109900336010X

Fig. 346   Main Switch Circuit (Part 1 of 2). 1996 Tacoma

INSPECTION PROCEDURE

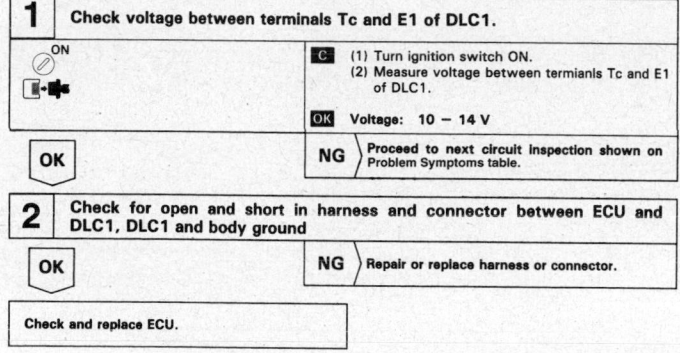

Fig. 347   T$_C$ Circuit. 1996 Tacoma

Actuator Control Cable Inspection

C 1. Check that the actuator, control cable and throttle link are properly installed and that the cable and link are connected correctly.
2. Check that the actuator and bell crank are operating smoothly.
3. Check that the cable is not loose or too tight.

Hint 1. If the control cable is very loose, the vehicle's loss of speed going uphill will be large.
2. If the control cable is too tight, the idle RPM will become high.

TY1109900338000X

Fig. 348   Actuator Control Cable Inspection. 1996 Tacoma

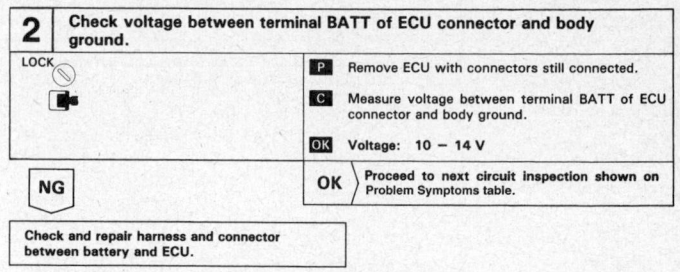

Fig. 345   Back Up Power Source Circuit (Part 3 of 3). 1996 Tacoma

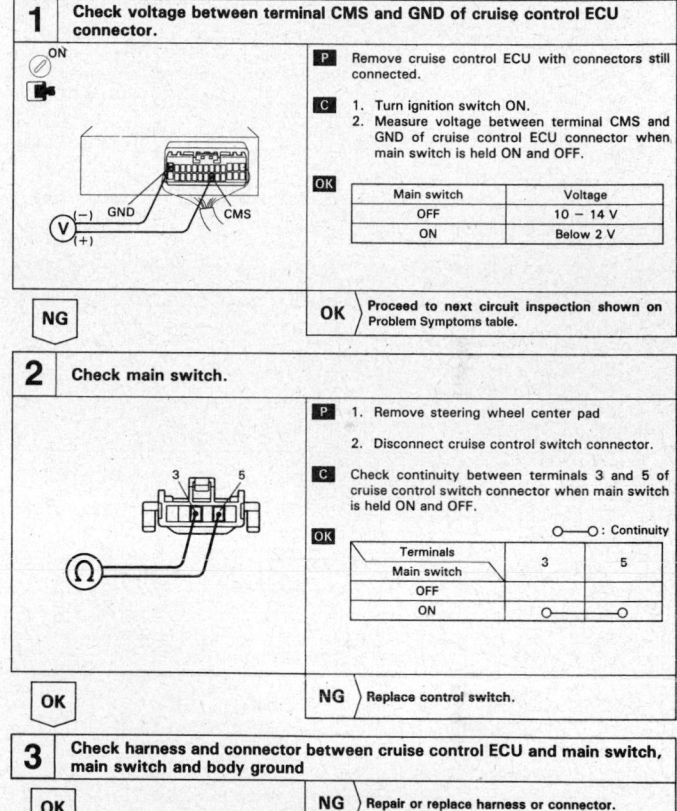

Fig. 346   Main Switch Circuit (Part 2 of 2). 1996 Tacoma

CIRCUIT DESCRIPTION

The actuator motor is operated by signals from the ECU. Acceleration and deceleration signals are transmitted by changes in the Duty Ratio

Duty Ratio
The duty ratio is the ratio of the period of continuity in one cycle. For example, if A is the period of continuity in one cycle, and B is the period of non-continuity, then

$$\text{Duty Ratio} = \frac{A}{A + B} \times 100 \ (\%)$$

DTC No.	Detection Item	Trouble Area
11	Short in actuator motor circuit	• Wire harness or connector between actuator and cruise control ECU • Cruise control actuator • Cruise control ECU

TY1109900493010X

Fig. 349   Code 11: Actuator Motor Circuit (Part 1 of 2). 1997 Tacoma w/Denso cruise control

INSPECTION PROCEDURE

1 Check resistance between terminals MO and MC of cruise control actuator.

PREPARATION:
(a) Ignition switch ON.
(b) Disconnect actuator connector.

CHECK:
Measure resistance between terminals 6 and 7.

HINT:
If control plate position is fully opened or fully closed, resistance can not measure.

OK:
Resistance: more than 4.2 Ω

> NG ⟩ Replace cruise control actuator.

OK

2 Check wire harness and connector between terminals MO of cruise control ECU and MO of cruise control actuator

> NG ⟩ Repair or replace harness or connector.

OK

Replace cruise control ECU.

TY1109900493020X

Fig. 349   Code 11: Actuator Motor Circuit (Part 2 of 2). 1997 Tacoma w/Denso cruise control

INSPECTION PROCEDURE

1 Check STOP fuse.

PREPARATION:
Remove STOP fuse from Relay Block No.2.

CHECK:
Check fuse continuity.

OK:
There is continuity

> NG ⟩ Replace STOP fuse.

OK

2 Check stop light switch.

PREPARATION:
Disconnect stop light switch connector.

CHECK:
Check continuity between terminals.

OK:

Switch position	Continuity
Switch pin free (Brake pedal depressed)	1 − 2
Switch pin pushed in (Brake pedal released)	3 − 4

> NG ⟩ Replace stop light switch.

OK

TY1109900494020X

Fig. 350   Code 12: Magnetic Clutch Circuit (Part 2 of 3). 1997 Tacoma w/Denso cruise control

CIRCUIT DESCRIPTION

This circuit turns on the magnetic clutch inside the actuator during cruise control operation according to the signal from the ECU. If a malfunction occurs in the actuator or speed sensor, etc. during cruise control operation, the rotor shaft between the motor and control plate is released.
When the brake pedal is depressed, the stop light switch turns on, supplying electrical power to the stop light. Power supply to the magnetic clutch is mechanically cut and the magnetic clutch is turned OFF.
When driving downhill, if the vehicle speed exceeds the set speed by 15 km/h (6 mph) above the set speed, then cruise control at the set speed is resumed.

DTC No.	Detection Item	Trouble Area
12	• Short in magnetic clutch circuit • Open (0.8 sec.) in magnetic clutch circuit	• Wire harness or connector between cruise control ECU and magnetic clutch, magnetic clutch and body ground • STOP fuse and stop light switch • Cruise control actuator magnetic clutch • Cruise control ECU

TY1109900494010X

Fig. 350   Code 12: Magnetic Clutch Circuit (Part 1 of 3). 1997 Tacoma w/Denso cruise control

3 Check harness and connector between actuator and cruise control actuator

> NG ⟩ Repair or replace harness or connector.

OK

Check and replace cruise control ECU

TY1109900494030X

Fig. 350   Code 12: Magnetic Clutch Circuit (Part 3 of 3). 1997 Tacoma w/Denso cruise control

CIRCUIT DESCRIPTION

The circuit detects the rotation position of the actuator control plate and sends a signal to the ECU.

DTC No.	Detection Item	Trouble Area
13	• Position sensor detects abnormal voltage.	• Wire harness or connector between actuator position sensor and body ground • Wire harness or connector between actuator motor and cruise control ECU • Cruise control actuator • Cruise control actuator position sensor • Cruise control ECU

TY1109900495010X

Fig. 351   Code 13: Actuator Position Sensor Circuit (Part 1 of 3). 1997 Tacoma w/Denso cruise control

INSPECTION PROCEDURE

1 Check resistance between terminals VR1 and VR3 of actuator.

PREPARATION:
Disconnect the actuator connector.

CHECK:
Measure resistance between actuator terminal 1 and 3 of actuator connector.

OK:
Resistance: 1.8 ~ 2.2 kΩ (25°C)

NG ▷ Replace actuator.

OK

2 Check voltage between terminals VR2 and VR3 of cruise control actuator.

PREPARATION:
Turn ignition switch ON.

CHECK:
Measure voltage between terminals 2 and 3 of actuator connector while turning control plate slowly by hand from the deceleration side to the acceleration side.

OK:
Voltage:
Fully closed: Approx. 1.3 V
Fully opened: Approx. 4.6 V
HINT:
As the control plate is turned, the voltage should increase gradually without interruption.

NG ▷ Replace cruise control actuator.

OK

TY1109900495020X

Fig. 351   Code 13: Actuator Position Sensor Circuit (Part 2 of 3). 1997 Tacoma w/Denso cruise control

CIRCUIT DESCRIPTION

The circuits detects the rotation position of the actuator control plate and sends a signal to the ECU.

DTC No.	Detection Item	Trouble Area
14	• Open in actuator motor circuit • Position sensor signal value does not change when the motor operates	• Cruise control actuator • Cruise control actuator position sensor position sensor and body ground • Wire harness or connector between actuator position sensor and body ground • Wire harness or connector between actuator motor and cruise control ECU • Cruise control ECU

INSPECTION PROCEDURE

1 Check actuator arm locking operation

PREPARATION:
(a) Ignition switch OFF.
(b) Disconnect actuator connector.

CHECK:
(a) Connect the positive (+) lead from the battery to the terminal 5 of actuator and the negative (−) lead to terminal 4.
NOTICE:
Do not connect the high tension cables to the wrong battery terminal. You will damage the cruise control actuator.
(b) Move the control plate by hand.

OK:
Control plate doesn't move.

NG ▷ Replace cruise control actuator.

OK

TY1109900496010X

Fig. 352   Code 14: Actuator Mechanical Fault (Part 1 of 2). 1997 Tacoma w/Denso cruise control

---

3 Check for open and short in harness and connector between ECU and actuator position sensor

NG ▷ Repair or replace harness or connector.

OK

Check and replace cruise control ECU

TY1109900495030X

Fig. 351   Code 13: Actuator Position Sensor Circuit (Part 3 of 3). 1997 Tacoma w/Denso cruise control

2 Check actuator operation.

PREPARATION:
Disconnect the actuator connector.

CHECK:
Connect the positive (+) lead from the battery to terminals 5 and 6 of actuator, connect the negative (−) lead to terminals 4 and 7 of actuator.

OK:
Control arm moves to full open side

CHECK:
Connect the positive (+) lead from the battery to terminals 4 and 7 of actuator, connect the negative (−) lead to terminals 5 and 6 of actuator.

OK:
Control arm moves to full close side

NG ▷ Replace actuator.

OK

3 Check harness and connector between actuator and cruise control ECU

NG ▷ Repair or replace harness or connector.

OK

Check and replace cruise control ECU

TY1109900496020X

Fig. 352   Code 14: Actuator Mechanical Fault (Part 2 of 2). 1997 Tacoma w/Denso cruise control

CIRCUIT DESCRIPTION

The vehicle speed sensor circuit is sent to cruise control ECU as vehicle speed signal. For each rotation of the shaft, the vehicle speed sensor sends a signal through the combination meter to the cruise control ECU (See the following). The ECU calculates the vehicle speed from this pulse frequency.

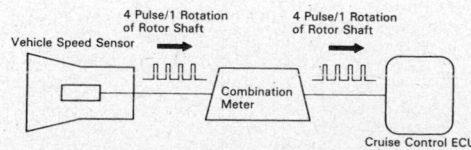

DTC No.	Detection Item	Trouble Area
21	Speed signal is not input to the cruise control ECU while cruise control is set	• Vehicle speed sensor • Combination meter • Wire harness or connector between vehicle speed sensor and combination meter, combination meter and cruise control ECU • Cruise control ECU

TY1109900497010X

Fig. 353   Code 21: Open In Vehicle Speed Sensor Circuit (Part 1 of 2). 1997 Tacoma w/Denso cruise control

INSPECTION PROCEDURE

| 1 | Input signal check. |

Input Signal	Indicator Light Blinking Pattern
Drive at about 40 km/h (25 mph) or below	Light ON ‾‾‾ OFF - - - -
Drive at about 40 km/h (25 mph) or higher	Light ON ⊓⊔⊓⊔ OFF

CHECK:
(a) See input signal check
(b) Check indicator light operation when driving with vehicle speed above 40 km/h (25 mph), and with vehicle speed below 40 km/h (25 mph).

OK:
Vehicle speed above 40 km/h (25 mph):
　　　　Indicator light blinks
Vehicle speed below 40 km/h (25 mph):
　　　　Indicator light stays on

OK ▷ Check and replace cruise control ECU

NG ▽

| 2 | Check harness and connector between speed meter and cruise control ECU |

NG ▷ Repair or replace harness or connector.

OK ▽

| 3 | Check vehicle speed sensor |

NG ▷ Replace vehicle speed sensor.

OK ▽

Check and replace cruise control ECU

TY1109900497020X

Fig. 353   Code 21: Open In Vehicle Speed Sensor Circuit (Part 2 of 2). 1997 Tacoma w/Denso cruise control

CIRCUIT DESCRIPTION

This circuit carries the SET/COAST, RESUME/Accel and CANCEL signals (each voltage) to the ECU.

DTC No.	Detection Item	Trouble Area
32	Short in control switch circuit	• Wire harness or connector between control switch and cruise control ECU • Cruise control switch • Cruise control ECU

TY1109900499010X

Fig. 355   Code 32: Control Switch Circuit (Part 1 of 3). 1997 Tacoma w/Denso cruise control

---

CIRCUIT DESCRIPTION

DTC No.	Detection Item	Trouble Area
23	• Vehicle speed sensor pulse is abnormal.	• Vehicle speed sensor • Cruise control ECU

INSPECTION PROCEDURE

| 1 | Check vehicle speed sensor |

NG ▷ Replace vehicle speed sensor.

OK ▽

Check and replace cruise control ECU

TY1109900498000X

Fig. 354   Code 23: Vehicle Speed Signal Abnormal. 1997 Tacoma w/Denso cruise control

INSPECTION PROCEDURE

| 1 | Input signal check. |

Input Signal	Indicator Light Blinking Pattern
SET/COAST switch	ON ⊓⊓ 2 Pulses OFF
RESUME/ACCEL switch	ON ⊓⊓⊓ 3 Pulses OFF
CANCEL switch	ON ‾SW OFF‾ OFF ＿SW ON＿

PREPARATION:
See input signal check

CHECK:
Check the indicator light operation when each of the SET/COAST, RESUME/ACCEL and CANCEL is turned on.

OK:
SET/COAST, RESUME/ACCEL switch:
The signals shown in the table on the left should be output when each switch is ON. The signal should disappear when the switch is turned OFF.
CANCEL switch:
The indicator light goes off when the cancel switch is turned ON.

OK ▷ Wait and see.

NG ▽

| 2 | Check control switch. |

PREPARATION:
(a) Remove steering wheel center pad.
(b) Disconnect control switch connector.

CHECK:
Measure resistance between terminals 3 and 4 of control switch connector when control switch is operated.

Switch position	Resistance (Ω)
Neutral	∞ (No continuity)
RES/ACC	50 – 80
SET/COAST	180 – 220
CANCEL	400 – 440

OK ▷ Replace control switch.

NG ▽

TY1109900499020X

Fig. 355   Code 32: Control Switch Circuit (Part 2 of 3). 1997 Tacoma w/Denso cruise control

3	Check harness and connector between cruise control switch and cruise control ECU

NG → Repair or replace harness or connector.

OK

4	Input signal check

OK → Wait and see.

NG

Check and replace cruise control ECU

Fig. 355   Code 32: Control Switch Circuit (Part 3 of 3). 1997 Tacoma w/Denso cruise control

TY1109900499030X

INSPECTION PROCEDURE

1	Check operation of stop light.

CHECK:
Check that stop light comes on when brake pedal is depressed, and turns off when brake pedal is released.

NG → Check stop light system.

OK

2	Input signal check.

Input Signal	Indicator Light Blinking Pattern	
Stop Light Switch ON	ON Light OFF	SW OFF SW ON

CHECK:
(a) See input signal check
(b) Check the indicator light when the brake pedal is depressed.

OK:
The indicator light goes off when the brake pedal is depressed.

OK → Proceed to next circuit inspection shown on problem symptom table

NG

TY1109900500020X

Fig. 356   Stop Lamp Switch Circuit (Part 2 of 3). 1997 Tacoma w/Denso cruise control

---

CIRCUIT DESCRIPTION

When the brake is on, battery positive voltage normally applies through the STOP fuse and stop light switch to terminal STP− of the ECU, and the ECU turns the cruise control off.
A fail-safe function is provided so that cancel functions normally, even if there is a malfunction in the stop light signal circuit.
   If the harness connected to terminal STP− has an open circuit, terminal STP− will have battery positive voltage and the cruise control will be turned off.
Also, when the brake is on, the magnetic clutch is cut mechanically by the stop light switch, turning the cruise control off. (See page BE-94 for operation of the magnetic clutch)

TY1109900500010X

Fig. 356   Stop Lamp Switch Circuit (Part 1 of 3). 1997 Tacoma w/Denso cruise control

3	Check voltage between terminal STP− of cruise control ECU connector and body ground.

PREPARATION:
Remove cruise control ECU with connectors still connected.

CHECK:
(a) Turn ignition switch ON.
(b) Measure voltage between terminal STP− of cruise control ECU connector and body ground, when the brake pedal is depressed and released.

OK:

Brake pedal position	Voltage
Depressed	10 − 14 V
Released	Below 1 V

OK → Proceed to next circuit inspection shown on problem symptom table

NG

4	Check for open in harness and connectors between terminal STP− of cruise control ECU and stop light switch

NG → Repair or replace harness or connector.

OK

Check and replace cruise control ECU

TY1109900500030X

Fig. 356   Stop Lamp Switch Circuit (Part 3 of 3). 1997 Tacoma w/Denso cruise control

CIRCUIT DESCRIPTION

When the idle switch is turned ON, a signal is sent to the ECU. The ECU uses this signal to correct the discrepancy between the throttle valve position and the actuator position sensor valve to enable accurate cruise control at the set speed. If the idle switch is malfunctioning, problem symptoms also occur in the engine, so also inspect engine.

TY1109900501010X

Fig. 357   Idle Switch Circuit (Part 1 of 3). 1997 Tacoma w/Denso cruise control

INSPECTION PROCEDURE

1 | Check voltage between terminal IDL of ECU connector and body ground.

PREPARATION:
(a) Remove cruise control ECU with connector still connected.
(b) Disconnect ECM and ABS ECU connectors.
(c) Ignition switch ON.

CHECK:
Measure voltage between terminal IDL of ECU connector and body ground when the throttle valve is fully closed and fully opened.

OK:

Throttle valve position	Voltage
Fully opened	10 – 14 V
Fully closed	Below 2 V

OK ⟩ Proceed to next circuit inspection shown on problem symptom table

NG

2 | Check throttle position sensor.

PREPARATION:
Disconnect throttle position sensor connector.

CHECK:
Measure resistance between terminals 3 and 4 of throttle position sensor connector when the throttle valve is fully closed and fully opened.

OK:

Throttle valve position	Resistance
Fully opened	1 MΩ or higher
Fully closed	Below 2.3 kΩ

NG ⟩ Replace throttle position sensor.

OK

TY1109900501020X

Fig. 357   Idle Switch Circuit (Part 2 of 3). 1997 Tacoma w/Denso cruise control

CIRCUIT DESCRIPTION

When driving uphill under cruise control, in order to reduce shifting due to ON-OFF overdrive operation and to provide smooth driving, when down shifting in the electronically controlled transmission occurs, a signal to prevent upshift until the end of the up hill slope is sent from the cruise control ECU to the electronically controlled transmission.
Terminal ECT of the cruise control ECU detects the shift change signal (output to electronically controlled transmission No.2 solenoid) from the electronically controlled transmission.
If vehicle speed down, also when terminal electronically controlled transmission of the cruise control ECU receives down shifting signal, it sends a signal from terminal OD to ECM to cut overdrive until the end of the uphill slope, and the gear shifts are reduced and gear shift points in the electronically controlled transmission are changed.

TY1109900502010X

Fig. 358   Electronically Controlled Transmission Communication Circuit (Part 1 of 3). 1997 Tacoma w/Denso cruise control

3 | Check for open and short in harness and connector between ECU and throttle position sensor, throttle position sensor and body ground

NG ⟩ Repair or replace harness or connector.

OK

Check and replace cruise control ECU

TY1109900501030X

Fig. 357   Idle Switch Circuit (Part 3 of 3). 1997 Tacoma w/Denso cruise control

INSPECTION PROCEDURE

1 | Check operation of overdrive.

PREPARATION:
Test drive after engine warms up.

CHECK:
Check that overdrive ON ↔ OFF occurs with operation of OD switch ON – OFF.

NG ⟩ Check and repair electronically controlled transmission

OK

2 | Check voltage between terminal OD of harness side connector of cruise control ECU and body ground.

PREPARATION:
Remove cruise control ECU with connector still connected.

CHECK:
(a) Disconnect cruise control ECU connector.
(b) Turn ignition switch ON.
(c) Measure voltage between terminal OD of harness side connector of cruise control ECU and body ground.

OK:
Voltage: 10 – 14 V

NG ⟩ Go to step 5.

OK

TY1109900502020X

Fig. 358   Electronically Controlled Transmission Communication Circuit (Part 2 of 3). 1997 Tacoma w/Denso cruise control

3 Check voltage between terminal ECT of cruise control ECU connector and body ground (On test drive).

PREPARATION:
(a) Connect cruise control ECU connector.
(b) Test drive after engine warms up.

CHECK:
Check voltage between terminal ECT of cruise control ECU connector and body ground when OD switch is ON and OFF.

OK:

OD switch position	Voltage
ON	8 – 14 V
OFF	Below 0.5 V

OK ⟩ Proceed to next circuit inspection shown on problem symptom table

NG

4 Check harness and connector between terminal ECT of cruise control ECU and electronically controlled transmission solenoid

NG ⟩ Repair or replace harness or connector.

OK

Check and replace cruise control ECU.

5 Check harness and connector between terminal OD of cruise control ECU and terminal OD1 of ECM

NG ⟩ Repair or replace harness or connector.

OK

Check and replace cruise control ECU

TY1109900502030X

Fig. 358 Electronically Controlled Transmission Communication Circuit (Part 3 of 3). 1997 Tacoma w/Denso cruise control

INSPECTION PROCEDURE

1 Check starter operation.

CHECK:
Check that the starter operates normally and that the engine starts.

NG ⟩ Proceed to engine troubleshooting.

OK

2 Input signal check.

Input Signal	Indicator Light Blinking Pattern
Turn PNP switch OFF (Shift to except D position)	ON SW ON / Light / OFF SW OFF

PREPARATION:
See input signal check

CHECK:
Check the indicator light when shifting into except D position.

OK:
The indicator light goes off when shifting into except D position.

OK ⟩ Proceed to next circuit inspection shown on problem symptom table

NG

TY1109900503020X

Fig. 359 Park/Neutral Position Switch Circuit (Part 2 of 3). 1997 Tacoma w/Denso cruise control

CIRCUIT DESCRIPTION

When the shift position is put in except D position, a signal is sent from the park/neutral position switch to the ECU. When this signal is input during cruise control driving, the ECU cancels the cruise control.

TY1109900503010X

Fig. 359 Park/Neutral Position Switch Circuit (Part 1 of 3). 1997 Tacoma w/Denso cruise control

3 Check voltage between terminal D of cruise control ECU and body ground.

PREPARATION:
Turn ignition switch ON.

CHECK:
Measure voltage between terminal D of cruise control ECU connector and body ground when shifting into D position and other positions.

OK:

Shift Position	Voltage
D position	10 – 14 V
Other positions	Below 1 V

OK ⟩ Proceed to next circuit inspection shown on problem symptom table

NG

4 Check harness and connector between PNP switch and cruise control ECU

NG ⟩ Repair or replace harness or connector.

OK

Check and replace cruise control ECU

TY1109900503030X

Fig. 359 Park/Neutral Position Switch Circuit (Part 3 of 3). 1997 Tacoma w/Denso cruise control

CIRCUIT DESCRIPTION

When the clutch pedal is depressed, the clutch switch sends a signal to the cruise control ECU. When the signal is input to the cruise control ECU during cruise control driving, the cruise control ECU cancels cruise control.

INSPECTION PROCEDURE

1 Check starter operation.

CHECK:
Check that the starter operates normally and that the engine starts.

NG ⟩ Proceed to engine troubleshooting

OK

2 Input signal check.

Input Signal	Indicator Light Blinking Pattern
Clutch switch OFF (Depress clutch pedal)	ON SW ON / Light / OFF SW OFF

PREPARATION:
See input signal check

CHECK:
Check the indicator light when clutch pedal depressed.

OK:
The indicator light goes off when clutch pedal depressed.

OK ⟩ Proceed to next circuit inspection shown on problem symptom table

NG

TY1109900504010X

Fig. 360 Clutch Switch Circuit (Part 1 of 2). 1997 Tacoma w/Denso cruise control

3 | Check voltage between terminal D of cruise control ECU and body ground.

PREPARATION:
Turn ignition switch ON.

CHECK:
Measure voltage between terminal D of cruise control ECU connector and body ground when clutch pedal depressed and pushed in.

OK:

Shift Position	Voltage
Clutch pedal depressed	10 – 14 V
Clutch pedal pushed in	Below 1 V

OK > Proceed to next circuit inspection shown on problem symptom table

NG

4 | Check for open in harness and connector between ECU and GAUGE fuse

NG > Repair or replace harness or connector.

OK

Check and replace cruise control ECU

TY1109900504020X

Fig. 360 Clutch Switch Circuit (Part 2 of 2). 1997 Tacoma w/Denso cruise control

INSPECTION PROCEDURE

1 | Check ECU-IG fuse.

PREPARATION:
Remove ECU-IG fuse from junction block No.1.

CHECK:
Check continuity of ECU-IG fuse.

OK:
Continuity

NG > Check for short in all the harness and components connected to ECU-IG fuse.

OK

2 | Check voltage between terminals B and GND of cruise control ECU connector.

PREPARATION:
Remove cruise control ECU with connector still connected.

CHECK:
(a) Turn ignition switch ON.
(b) Measure voltage between terminals B and GND of cruise control ECU connector.

OK:
10 – 14 V

OK > Proceed to next circuit inspection shown on problem symptom table

NG

TY1109900505020X

Fig. 361 ECU Power Source Circuit (Part 2 of 3). 1997 Tacoma w/Denso cruise control

CIRCUIT DESCRIPTION

The ECU power source supplies power to the actuator and sensors, etc.. When terminal GND and the cruise control ECU case are grounded.

TY1109900505010X

Fig. 361 ECU Power Source Circuit (Part 1 of 3). 1997 Tacoma w/Denso cruise control

3 | Check resistance between terminal GND of cruise control ECU connector and body ground

CHECK:
Measure resistance between terminal GND of cruise control ECU connector and body ground.

OK:
Resistance: Below 1Ω

NG > Repair or replace harness or connector.

OK

Check and repair harness and connector between battery and cruise control ECU

TY1109900505030X

Fig. 361 ECU Power Source Circuit (Part 3 of 3). 1997 Tacoma w/Denso cruise control

CIRCUIT DESCRIPTION

The ECU back-up power source provides power even when the ignition is off and is used for DTC memory, etc..

TY1109900506010X

Fig. 362 Back Up Power Source Circuit (Part 1 of 2). 1997 Tacoma w/Denso cruise control

INSPECTION PROCEDURE

1 | Check ECU-B fuse.

PREPARATION:
Remove ECU-B fuse from relay block No.2.

CHECK:
Check continuity of ECU-B fuse.

OK:
Continuity

NG > Check for short in all the harness and components connected to the ECU-B fuse.

OK

2 | Check voltage between terminal BATT of cruise control ECU connector and body ground

PREPARATION:
Remove cruise control ECU with connector still connected.

CHECK:
Measure voltage between terminal BATT of cruise control ECU connector and body ground.

OK:
Voltage: 10 – 14 V

OK > Proceed to next circuit inspection shown on problem symptom table

NG

Check and repair harness and connector between battery and cruise control ECU

TY1109900506020X

Fig. 362 Back Up Power Source Circuit (Part 2 of 2). 1997 Tacoma w/Denso cruise control

CIRCUIT DESCRIPTION

When the cruise control main switch is turned off, the cruise control does not operate.

INSPECTION PROCEDURE

| 1 | Check voltage betweem terminal CMS of cruise control ECU connector and body ground. |

PREPARATION:

Remove cruise control ECU with connector still connected.

CHECK:

(a) Turn ignition switch ON.
(b) Measure voltage between terminal CMS of cruise control ECU connector when main switch is held on and off.

OK:

Main switch	Voltage
OFF	10 ~ 14 V
ON	Below 1 V

OK ▷ Proceed to next circuit inspection shown on problem symptom table

NG

TY1109900507010X

Fig. 363   Main Switch Circuit (Part 1 of 2). 1997 Tacoma w/Denso cruise control

| 2 | Check main switch continuity. |

PREPARATION:

(a) Remove steering wheel center pad
(b) Disconnect cruise control switch connector.

CHECK:

Check continuity between terminals 3 and 5 of cruise control switch connector when main switch is held on and off.

OK:

Switch position	Tester connection	Specified condition
OFF	3 — 5	No continuity
Hold ON	3 — 5	Continuity

NG ▷ Replace control switch.

OK

| 3 | Check harness and connector between cruise control ECU and main switch |

NG ▷ Repair or replace harness or connector.

OK

Check and replace cruise control ECU

TY1109900507020X

Fig. 363   Main Switch Circuit (Part 2 of 2). 1997 Tacoma w/Denso cruise control

INSPECTION PROCEDURE

| 1 | Check voltage between terminals PI and GND of cruise control ECU connector. |

PREPARATION:

Ignition switch ON.

CHECK:

Measure voltage between terminals PI and GND of cruise control ECU connector when main switch on and off.

OK:

Switch position	Voltage
OFF	10 ~ 16 V
ON	Below 1.2 V

OK ▷ Proceed to next circuit inspection shown on problem symptom table

NG

| 2 | Check combination meter |

NG ▷ Replace combination meter.

OK

Check and replace cruise control ECU

TY1109900508020X

Fig. 364   Cruise Main Indicator Lamp Circuit (Part 2 of 2). 1997 Tacoma w/Denso cruise control

CIRCUIT DESCRIPTION

When the cruise control main switch is turned ON, CRUISE MAIN indicator light lights up.

TY1109900508010X

Fig. 364   Cruise Main Indicator Lamp Circuit (Part 1 of 2). 1997 Tacoma w/Denso cruise control

CIRCUIT DESCRIPTION

This circuit sends a signal to the ECU that DTC output is required.

TY1109900509010X

Fig. 365   Diagnosis Circuit (Part 1 of 2). 1997 Tacoma w/Denso cruise control

INSPECTION PROCEDURE

1 Check voltage between terminals Tc and E₁ of DLC1.

CHECK:
(a) Turn ignition switch ON.
(b) Measure voltage between terminals Tc and E₁ of DLC1.

OK:
Voltage: 10 – 14 V

OK ⟩ Proceed to next circuit inspection shown on problem symptom table

NG

2 Check harness and connector between cruise control ECU and DLC1, DLC1 and body ground

NG ⟩ Repair or replace harness or connector.

OK

Check and replace cruise control ECU

TY1109900509020X

Fig. 365 Diagnosis Circuit (Part 2 of 2). 1997 Tacoma w/Denso cruise control

CIRCUIT DESCRIPTION

The actuator motor is operated by signals from the ECU. Acceleration and deceleration signals are transmitted according to changes in the Duty Ratio (See below).
Duty Ratio
The duty ratio is the ratio of the period of continuity in one cycle. For example, if A is the period of continuity in one cycle, and B is the period of non–continuity.

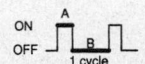

$$\text{Duty Ratio} = \frac{A}{A + B} \times 100 \ (\%)$$

DTC No.	Detection Item	Trouble Area
11	Short in actuator motor circuit	• Harness or connector between actuator and cruise control ECU • Cruise control actuator • Cruise control ECU
15	Open in actuator	• Actuator motor

TY1109900250010X

Fig. 367 Codes 11 & 15: Actuator Motor Circuit (Part 1 of 2). 1998–99 Tacoma w/Denso cruise control

INSPECTION PROCEDURE

1 Actuator control cable inspection.

CHECK:
(a) Check that the actuator, control cable throttle link are properly installed and that the cable and link are connected correctly.
(b) Check that the actuator and bell crank are operating smoothly.
(c) Check that the cable is not loose or too tight.

OK:
Freeplay: less than 10 mm
HINT:
• If the control cable is very loose, the vehicle's loss of speed going uphill will be large.
• If the control cable is too tight, the idle RPM will become high.

TY1109900510000X

Fig. 366 Actuator Control Cable Inspection. 1997 Tacoma w/Denso cruise control

INSPECTION PROCEDURE

1 Check resistance between terminals MO and MC of cruise control actuator.

PREPARATION:
(a) Ignition switch ON.
(b) Disconnect actuator connector.
CHECK:
Measure resistance between terminals 1 and 2.
HINT:
If control plate position is fully opened or fully closed, resistance can not be measured.
OK:
Resistance: more than 4.2 Ω

NG ⟩ Replace cruise control actuator.

OK

2 Check wire harness and connector between terminals MO of cruise control ECU and MO of cruise control actuator.

NG ⟩ Repair or replace harness or connector.

OK

Replace cruise control ECU.

TY1109900250020X

Fig. 367 Codes 11 & 15: Actuator Motor Circuit (Part 2 of 2). 1998–99 Tacoma w/Denso cruise control

CIRCUIT DESCRIPTION

This circuit turns on the magnetic clutch inside the actuator during cruise control operation according to the signal from the ECU. If a malfunction occurs in the actuator or speed sensor, etc. during cruise control operation, the rotor shaft between the motor and control plate is released.
When the brake pedal is depressed, the stop light switch turns on, supplying electrical power to the stop light. Power supply to the magnetic clutch is mechanically cut and the magnetic clutch is turned OFF.
When driving downhill, if the vehicle speed exceeds the set speed by 15 km/h (6 mph), cruise control at the set speed is resumed.

DTC No.	Detection Item	Trouble Area
12	• Short in magnetic clutch circuit. • Open (0.8 sec.) in magnetic clutch circuit	• Harness or connector between ECU and magnetic clutch, magnetic clutch and body ground • STOP fuse and stop light switch • Cruise control actuator magnetic clutch • Cruise control ECU

TY1109900251010X

Fig. 368 Code 12: Magnetic Clutch Circuit (Part 1 of 3). 1998–99 Tacoma w/Denso cruise control

1 | Check STOP fuse.

PREPARATION:
Remove STOP fuse from Relay Block No.2.
CHECK:
Check fuse continuity.
OK:
    There is continuity.

NG > Replace STOP fuse.

OK

2 | Check stop light switch.

PREPARATION:
Disconnect stop light switch connector.
CHECK:
Check continuity between terminals.
OK:

Switch position	Continuity
Switch pin free (Brake pedal depressed)	1 – 2
Switch pin pushed in (Brake pedal released)	3 – 4

NG > Replace stop light switch.

OK

TY1109900251020X

Fig. 368   Code 12: Magnetic Clutch Circuit (Part 2 of 3). 1998–99 Tacoma w/Denso cruise control

CIRCUIT DESCRIPTION

DTC No.	Detection Item	Trouble Area
14	• Open in actuator motor circuit. • Position sensor signal valve does not change when the motor operates.	• Cruise control actuator motor • Harness or connector between actuator motor and ECU • Harness or connector between actuator position sensor and body ground • Cruise control actuator position sensor • Cruise control ECU

INSPECTION PROCEDURE

1 | Check actuator arm locking operation

PREPARATION:
(a)   Ignition switch OFF.
(b)   Disconnect actuator connector.
CHECK:
(a)   Connect the positive (+) lead from the battery to the terminal 3 of actuator and the negative (–) lead to terminal 4.
NOTICE:
Do not connect the high tension cables to the wrong battery terminal. The cruise control actuator will be damaged.
(b)   Move the control plate by hands.
OK:
    Control plate doesn't move.

NG > Replace cruise control actuator.

OK

TY1109900252010X

Fig. 369   Code 14: Actuator Mechanical Fault (Part 1 of 2). 1998–99 Tacoma w/Denso cruise control

3 | Check harness and connector between actuator and cruise control actuator.

NG > Repair or replace harness or connector.

OK

Check and replace cruise control ECU.

TY1109900251030X

Fig. 368   Code 12: Magnetic Clutch Circuit (Part 3 of 3). 1998–99 Tacoma w/Denso cruise control

2 | Check actuator operation.

PREPARATION:
Disconnect the actuator connector.
CHECK:
Connect the positive (+) lead from the battery to terminals 1 and 3 of actuator, connect the negative (–) lead to terminals 2 and 4 of actuator.
OK:
    Control arm moves to fully open side
CHECK:
Connect the positive (+) lead from the battery to terminals 2 and 4 of actuator, connect the negative (–) lead to terminals 1 and 3 of actuator.
OK:
    Control arm moves to fully close side

NG > Replace actuator.

OK

3 | Check harness and connector between actuator and cruise control ECU.

NG > Repair or replace harness or connector.

OK

Check and replace cruise control ECU.

TY1109900252020X

Fig. 369   Code 14: Actuator Mechanical Fault (Part 2 of 2). 1998–99 Tacoma w/Denso cruise control

CIRCUIT DESCRIPTION

The signal from the vehicle speed sensor circuit is sent to cruise control ECU as vehicle speed signal. For each rotation of the shaft, the vehicle speed sensor sends a signal through the combination meter to the cruise control ECU (See the following illustration). The ECU calculates the vehicle speed from this pulse frequency.

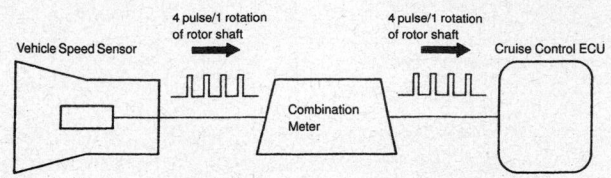

DTC No.	Detection Item	Trouble Area
21	Speed signal is not input to the cruise control ECU while cruise control is set.	• Vehicle speed sensor • Combination meter • Harness or connector between vehicle speed sensor and combination meter, combination meter and cruise control ECU • Cruise control ECU

TY1109900253010X

Fig. 370   Code 21: Open In Vehicle Speed Sensor Circuit (Part 1 of 3). 1998–99 Tacoma w/Denso control

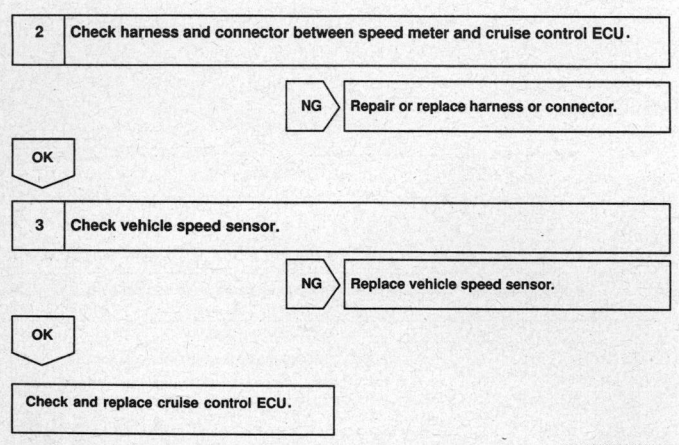

2   Check harness and connector between speed meter and cruise control ECU.

NG Repair or replace harness or connector.

OK

3   Check vehicle speed sensor.

NG Replace vehicle speed sensor.

OK

Check and replace cruise control ECU.

TY1109900253030X

Fig. 370   Code 21: Open In Vehicle Speed Sensor Circuit (Part 3 of 3). 1998–99 Tacoma w/Denso cruise control

INSPECTION PROCEDURE

1   Input signal check.

Input Signal	Indicator Light Blinking Pattern	
Drive at about 40 km/h (25 mph) or below	Light	ON ——— OFF - - - -
Drive at about 40 km/h (25 mph) or higher	Light	ON ⊓⊓⊓⊓ OFF

CHECK:
(a) See input signal check.
(b) Check indicator light operation when driving with vehicle speed above 40 km/h (25 mph), and with vehicle speed below 40 km/h (25 mph).

OK:
Vehicle speed above 40 km/h (25 mph):
 Indicator light blinks
Vehicle speed below 40 km/h (25 mph):
 Indicator light stays on

OK Check and replace cruise control ECU.

NG

TY1109900253020X

Fig. 370   Code 21: Open In Vehicle Speed Sensor Circuit (Part 2 of 3). 1998–99 Tacoma w/Denso cruise control

CIRCUIT DESCRIPTION

DTC No.	Detection Item	Trouble Area
23	Vehicle speed sensor pulse is abnormal.	• Vehicle speed sensor • Cruise control ECU

INSPECTION PROCEDURE

1   Check vehicle speed sensor.

NG Replace vehicle speed sensor.

OK

Check and replace cruise control ECU.

TY1109900254000X

Fig. 371   Code 23: Vehicle Speed Signal Abnormal. 1998–99 Tacoma w/Denso cruise control

CIRCUIT DESCRIPTION

This circuit carries the SET/COAST, RESUME/ACCEL and CANCEL signals (each voltage) to the ECU.

DTC No.	Detection Item	Trouble Area
32	Short in control switch circuit	• Harness or connector between control switch and cruise control ECU. • Cruise control switch • Cruise control ECU

TY1109900255010X

Fig. 372   Code 32: Control Switch Circuit (Part 1 of 3). 1998–99 Tacoma w/Denso cruise control

INSPECTION PROCEDURE

1	Input signal check.

PREPARATION:
See input signal check.

CHECK:
Check the indicator light operation when each of the SET/COAST, RESUME/ACCEL and CANCEL is turned on.

Input Signal	Indicator Light Blinking Pattern
SET/COAST switch	ON / OFF — 2 Pulses
RESUME/ACCEL switch	ON / OFF — 3 Pulses
CANCEL switch	ON / OFF — SW OFF / SW ON

OK:
SET/COAST, RESUME/ACCEL switch
The signals shown in the table on the left should be output when each switch is ON. The signal should disappear when the switch is turned OFF.
CANCEL switch
The indicator light goes off when the cancel switch is turned ON.

OK	Wait and see.

NG

2	Check control switch.

PREPARATION:
(a) Remove steering wheel center pad.
(b) Disconnect control switch connector.

CHECK:
Measure resistance between terminals 3 and 4 of control switch connector when control switch is operated.

Switch position	Resistance (Ω)
Neutral	∞ (No continuity)
RES/ACC	50 – 80
SET/COAST	180 – 220
CANCEL	400 – 440

OK	Replace control switch.

NG

TY1109900255020X

Fig. 372   Code 32: Control Switch Circuit (Part 2 of 3). 1998–99 Tacoma w/Denso cruise control

CIRCUIT DESCRIPTION

When the brake pedal is on depressed, battery positive voltage normally applies through the STOP fuse and stop light switch to terminal STP– of the ECU, and the ECU turns the cruise control off.

A fail–safe function is provided so that cancel functions normally, even if there is a malfunction in the stop light signal circuit.

If the harness connected to terminal STP– has an open circuit, terminal STP– will have battery positive voltage and the cruise control will be turned off.

Also, when the brake is on, the magnetic clutch is cut mechanically by the stop light switch, turning the cruise control off.

TY1109900256010X

Fig. 373   Stop Lamp Switch Circuit (Part 1 of 3). 1998–99 Tacoma w/Denso cruise control

---

3	Check harness and connector between cruise control switch and cruise control ECU.

NG	Repair or replace harness or connector.

OK

4	Input signal check (See step 1).

OK	Wait and see.

NG

Check and replace cruise control ECU.

TY1109900255030X

Fig. 372   Code 32: Control Switch Circuit (Part 3 of 3). 1998–99 Tacoma w/Denso cruise control

INSPECTION PROCEDURE

1	Check operation of stop light.

CHECK:
Check that stop light comes on when brake pedal is depressed, and turns off when brake pedal is released.

NG	Check stop light system.

OK

2	Input signal check.

Input Signal	Indicator Light Blinking Pattern
Stop light switch ON	Light ON / OFF — SW OFF / SW ON

CHECK:
(a) See input signal check.
(b) Check the indicator light when the brake pedal is depressed.

OK:
The indicator light goes off when the brake pedal is depressed.

OK	Proceed to next circuit inspection shown on problem symptoms table.

NG

TY1109900256020X

Fig. 373   Stop Lamp Switch Circuit (Part 2 of 3). 1998–99 Tacoma w/Denso cruise control

3	Check voltage between terminal STP– of cruise control ECU connector and body ground.

PREPARATION:
Remove cruise control ECU with connectors still connected.
CHECK:
(a) Turn ignition switch ON.
(b) Measure voltage between terminal STP– of cruise control ECU connector and body ground, when the brake pedal is depressed and released.
OK:

Brake pedal position	Voltage
Depressed	10 – 14 V
Released	Below 1 V

> **OK** | Proceed to next circuit inspection shown on problem symptoms table.

> **NG**

4	Check for open in harness and connectors between terminal STP– of cruise control ECU and stop light switch.

> **NG** | Repair or replace harness or connector.

> **OK**

Check and replace cruise control ECU.

TY1109900256030X

Fig. 373 Stop Lamp Switch Circuit (Part 3 of 3). 1998–99 Tacoma w/Denso cruise control

INSPECTION PROCEDURE

1	Check voltage between terminal IDL of ECU connector and body ground.

PREPARATION:
(a) Remove cruise control ECU with connector still connected.
(b) Disconnect ECM and ABS ECU connectors.
(c) Ignition switch ON.
CHECK:
Measure voltage between terminal IDL of ECU connector and body ground when the throttle valve is fully closed and fully opened.
OK:

Throttle valve position	Voltage
Fully opened	10 – 14 V
Fully closed	Below 2 V

> **OK** | Proceed to next circuit inspection shown on problem symptoms table.

> **NG**

2	Check for open and short in harness and connector between ECU and throttle position sensor, throttle position sensor and body ground.

> **NG** | Repair or replace harness or connector.

> **OK**

Check and replace cruise control ECU.

TY1109900257020X

Fig. 374 Idle Switch Circuit (Part 2 of 2). 1998–99 Tacoma w/Denso cruise control

CIRCUIT DESCRIPTION

When the idle switch is turned ON, a signal is sent to the ECU. The ECU uses this signal to correct the discrepancy between the throttle valve position and the actuator position sensor valve to enable accurate cruise control at the set speed. If the idle switch is malfunctioning, problem symptoms also occur in the engine, so also inspect the engine.

TY1109900257010X

Fig. 374 Idle Switch Circuit (Part 1 of 2). 1998–99 Tacoma w/Denso cruise control

CIRCUIT DESCRIPTION

When driving uphill under the cruise control, in order to reduce shifting due to ON–OFF overdrive operation and to provide smooth driving, when down shifting in the electronically controlled transmission occurs, a signal to prevent upshift until the end of the uphill slope is sent from the cruise control ECU to the electronically controlled transmission.
Terminal ECT of the cruise control ECU detects the shift change signal (output to electronically controlled transmission No. 2 solenoid) from the electronically controlled transmission.
If a or the vehicle speeds down, also when terminal electronically controlled transmission of the cruise control ECU receives down shifting signal, it sends a signal from terminal OD to ECM to cut overdrive until the end of the uphill slope, and the gear shifts are reduced and gear shift points in the electronically controlled transmission are changed.

TY1109900258010X

Fig. 375 Electronically Controlled Transmission Communication Circuit Fault (Part 1 of 3). 1998–99 Tacoma w/Denso cruise control

INSPECTION PROCEDURE

1	Check operation of overdrive.

PREPARATION:
Test drive after engine warms up.
CHECK:
Check that overdrive ON ↔ OFF occurs with operation of OD switch ON–OFF.

> **NG** | Check and repair electronically controlled transmission (See page DI–306).

> **OK**

2	Check voltage between terminal OD of harness side connector of cruise control ECU and body ground.

PREPARATION:
Remove cruise control ECU with connector still connected.
CHECK:
(a) Disconnect cruise control ECU connector.
(b) Turn ignition switch ON.
(c) Measure voltage between terminal OD of harness side connector of cruise control ECU and body ground.
OK:

Voltage: 10 – 14 V

> **NG** | Go to step 5.

> **OK**

TY1109900258020X

Fig. 375 Electronically Controlled Transmission Communication Circuit Fault (Part 2 of 3). 1998–99 Tacoma w/Denso cruise control

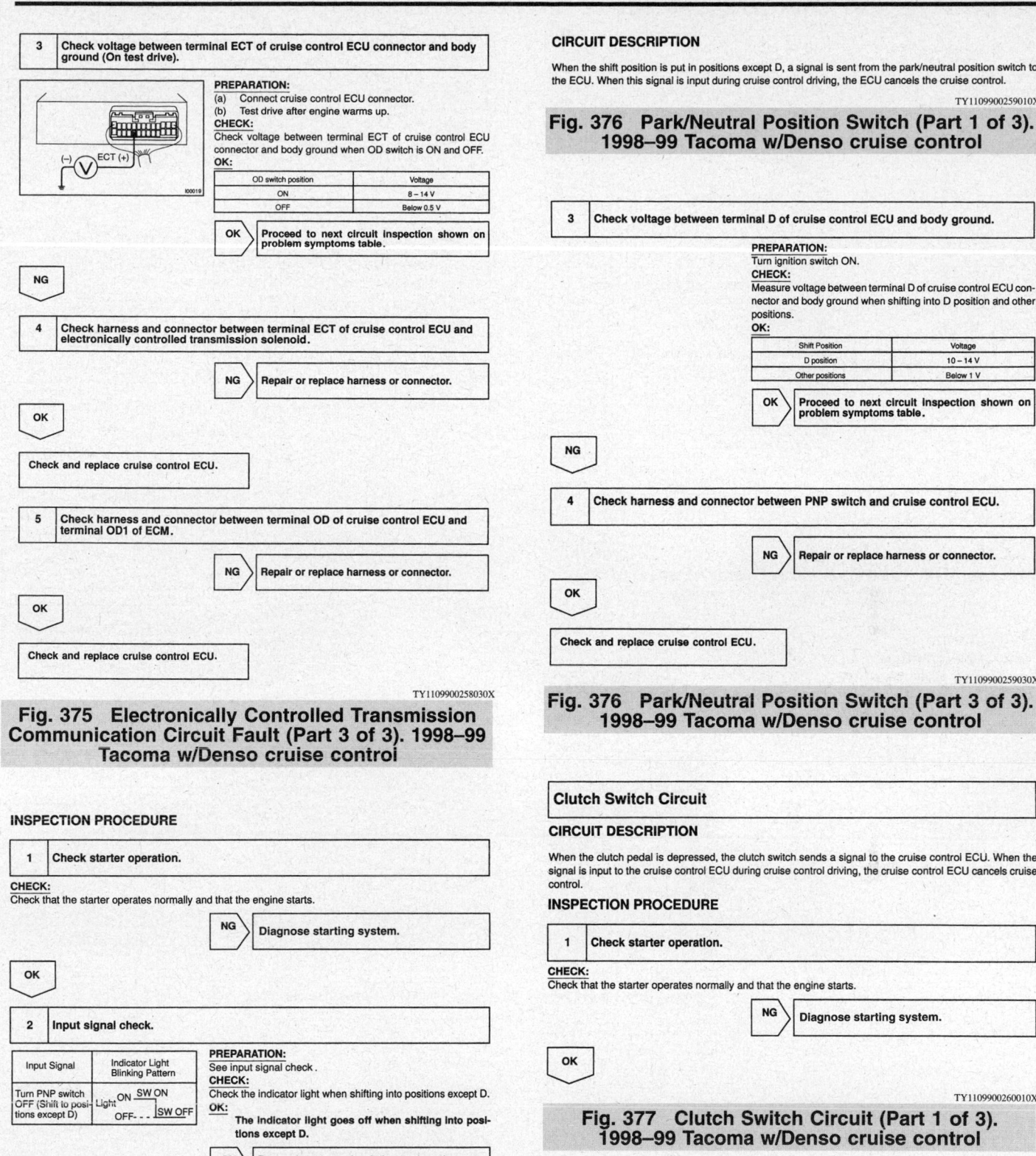

3 Check voltage between terminal ECT of cruise control ECU connector and body ground (On test drive).

PREPARATION:
(a) Connect cruise control ECU connector.
(b) Test drive after engine warms up.
CHECK:
Check voltage between terminal ECT of cruise control ECU connector and body ground when OD switch is ON and OFF.
OK:

OD switch position	Voltage
ON	8 – 14 V
OFF	Below 0.5 V

OK → Proceed to next circuit inspection shown on problem symptoms table.

NG

4 Check harness and connector between terminal ECT of cruise control ECU and electronically controlled transmission solenoid.

NG → Repair or replace harness or connector.

OK

Check and replace cruise control ECU.

5 Check harness and connector between terminal OD of cruise control ECU and terminal OD1 of ECM.

NG → Repair or replace harness or connector.

OK

Check and replace cruise control ECU.

TY1109900258030X

Fig. 375 Electronically Controlled Transmission Communication Circuit Fault (Part 3 of 3). 1998–99 Tacoma w/Denso cruise control

INSPECTION PROCEDURE

1 Check starter operation.

CHECK:
Check that the starter operates normally and that the engine starts.

NG → Diagnose starting system.

OK

2 Input signal check.

Input Signal	Indicator Light Blinking Pattern
Turn PNP switch OFF (Shift to positions except D)	Light ON SW ON / OFF SW OFF

PREPARATION:
See input signal check .
CHECK:
Check the indicator light when shifting into positions except D.
OK:
The indicator light goes off when shifting into positions except D.

OK → Proceed to next circuit inspection shown on problem symptoms table.

NG

TY1109900259020X

Fig. 376 Park/Neutral Position Switch (Part 2 of 3). 1998–99 Tacoma w/Denso cruise control

CIRCUIT DESCRIPTION

When the shift position is put in positions except D, a signal is sent from the park/neutral position switch to the ECU. When this signal is input during cruise control driving, the ECU cancels the cruise control.

TY1109900259010X

Fig. 376 Park/Neutral Position Switch (Part 1 of 3). 1998–99 Tacoma w/Denso cruise control

3 Check voltage between terminal D of cruise control ECU and body ground.

PREPARATION:
Turn ignition switch ON.
CHECK:
Measure voltage between terminal D of cruise control ECU connector and body ground when shifting into D position and other positions.
OK:

Shift Position	Voltage
D position	10 – 14 V
Other positions	Below 1 V

OK → Proceed to next circuit inspection shown on problem symptoms table.

NG

4 Check harness and connector between PNP switch and cruise control ECU.

NG → Repair or replace harness or connector.

OK

Check and replace cruise control ECU.

TY1109900259030X

Fig. 376 Park/Neutral Position Switch (Part 3 of 3). 1998–99 Tacoma w/Denso cruise control

Clutch Switch Circuit

CIRCUIT DESCRIPTION

When the clutch pedal is depressed, the clutch switch sends a signal to the cruise control ECU. When the signal is input to the cruise control ECU during cruise control driving, the cruise control ECU cancels cruise control.

INSPECTION PROCEDURE

1 Check starter operation.

CHECK:
Check that the starter operates normally and that the engine starts.

NG → Diagnose starting system.

OK

TY1109900260010X

Fig. 377 Clutch Switch Circuit (Part 1 of 3). 1998–99 Tacoma w/Denso cruise control

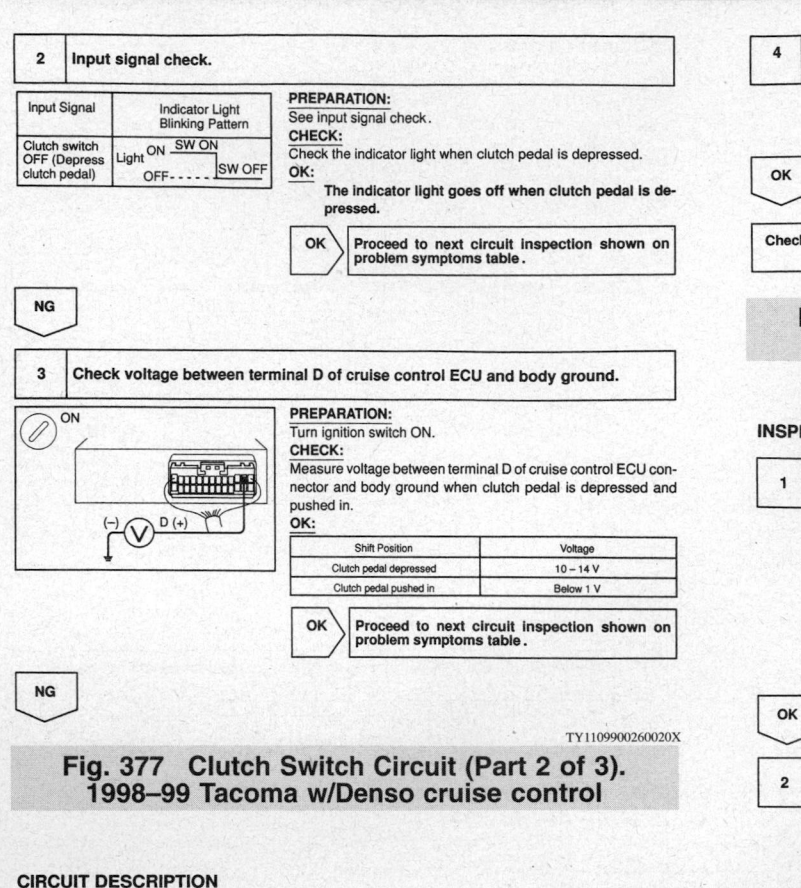

2	Input signal check.

Input Signal	Indicator Light Blinking Pattern
Clutch switch OFF (Depress clutch pedal)	Light ─ ON ─ SW ON / OFF ─ ─ ─ ─ SW OFF

PREPARATION:
See input signal check.
CHECK:
Check the indicator light when clutch pedal is depressed.
OK:
The indicator light goes off when clutch pedal is depressed.

OK ▷ Proceed to next circuit inspection shown on problem symptoms table.

NG ▽

3	Check voltage between terminal D of cruise control ECU and body ground.

PREPARATION:
Turn ignition switch ON.
CHECK:
Measure voltage between terminal D of cruise control ECU connector and body ground when clutch pedal is depressed and pushed in.
OK:

Shift Position	Voltage
Clutch pedal depressed	10 – 14 V
Clutch pedal pushed in	Below 1 V

OK ▷ Proceed to next circuit inspection shown on problem symptoms table.

NG ▽

TY1109900260020X

Fig. 377   Clutch Switch Circuit (Part 2 of 3).
1998–99 Tacoma w/Denso cruise control

CIRCUIT DESCRIPTION

The ECU power source supplies power to the actuator and sensors, etc., when terminal GND and the cruise control ECU case are grounded.

TY1109900261010X

Fig. 378   ECU Power Source Circuit (Part 1 of 3).
1998–99 Tacoma w/Denso cruise control

4	Check for open in harness and connector between ECU and GAUGE fuse.

NG ▷ Repair or replace harness or connector.

OK ▽

Check and replace cruise control ECU.

TY1109900260030X

Fig. 377   Clutch Switch Circuit (Part 3 of 3).
1998–99 Tacoma w/Denso cruise control

INSPECTION PROCEDURE

1	Check ECU–IG fuse.

PREPARATION:
Remove ECU–IG fuse from junction block No.1.
CHECK:
Check continuity of ECU–IG fuse.
OK:
Continuity

NG ▷ Check for short in all the harness and components connected to ECU–IG fuse.

OK ▽

2	Check voltage between terminals B and GND of cruise control ECU connector.

PREPARATION:
Remove cruise control ECU with connector still connected.
CHECK:
(a)   Turn ignition switch ON.
(b)   Measure voltage between terminals B and GND of cruise control ECU connector.
OK:
10 – 14 V

OK ▷ Proceed to next circuit inspection shown on problem symptoms table.

NG ▽

TY1109900261020X

Fig. 378   ECU Power Source Circuit (Part 2 of 3).
1998–99 Tacoma w/Denso cruise control

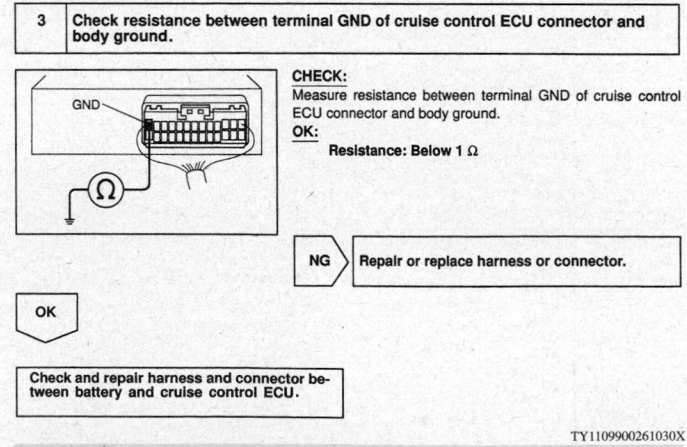

3	Check resistance between terminal GND of cruise control ECU connector and body ground.

CHECK:
Measure resistance between terminal GND of cruise control ECU connector and body ground.
OK:
Resistance: Below 1 Ω

NG ▷ Repair or replace harness or connector.

OK ▽

Check and repair harness and connector between battery and cruise control ECU.

TY1109900261030X

Fig. 378   ECU Power Source Circuit (Part 3 of 3).
1998–99 Tacoma w/Denso cruise control

Main Switch Circuit (Cruise Control Switch)

CIRCUIT DESCRIPTION

When the cruise control main switch is turned off, the cruise control does not operate.

INSPECTION PROCEDURE

| 1 | Check voltage between terminal CMS of cruise control ECU connector and body ground. |

PREPARATION:
Remove cruise control ECU with connector still connected.
CHECK:
(a) Turn ignition switch ON.
(b) Measure voltage between terminal CMS of cruise control ECU connector when main switch is held on and off.
OK:

Main switch	Voltage
OFF	10 – 14 V
ON	Below 1 V

| OK | Proceed to next circuit inspection shown on problem symptoms table. |

NG

Fig. 379   Main Switch Circuit (Part 1 of 2). 1998–99 Tacoma w/Denso cruise control

TY1109900263010X

CIRCUIT DESCRIPTION

When the cruise control main switch is turned ON, CRUISE MAIN indicator light lights up.

TY1109900264010X

Fig. 380   Cruise Main Indicator Lamp Circuit (Part 1 of 2). 1998–99 Tacoma w/Denso cruise control

| 2 | Check main switch continuity. |

PREPARATION:
(a) Remove steering wheel center pad.
(b) Disconnect cruise control switch connector.
CHECK:
Check continuity between terminals 3 and 5 of cruise control switch connector when main switch is held on and off.
OK:

Switch position	Tester connection	Specified condition
OFF	3 – 5	No continuity
Hold ON	3 – 5	Continuity

| NG | Replace control switch. |

OK

| 3 | Check harness and connector between cruise control ECU and main switch. |

| NG | Repair or replace harness or connector. |

OK

| Check and replace cruise control ECU. |

TY1109900263020X

Fig. 379   Main Switch Circuit (Part 2 of 2). 1998–99 Tacoma w/Denso cruise control

INSPECTION PROCEDURE

| 1 | Check voltage between terminals PI and GND of cruise control ECU connector. |

PREPARATION:
Ignition switch ON.
CHECK:
Measure voltage between terminals PI and GND of cruise control ECU connector when main switch is on and off.
OK:

Switch position	Voltage
OFF	10 – 16 V
ON	Below 1.2 V

| OK | Proceed to next circuit inspection shown on problem symptoms table. |

NG

| 2 | Check combination meter. |

| NG | Replace combination meter. |

OK

| Check and replace cruise control ECU. |

TY1109900264020X

Fig. 380   Cruise Main Indicator Lamp Circuit (Part 2 of 2). 1998–99 Tacoma w/Denso cruise control

CIRCUIT DESCRIPTION

This circuit sends a signal to the ECU that outputs DTC.

TY1109900265010X

Fig. 381   Diagnosis Circuit (Part 1 of 2). 1998–99 Tacoma w/Denso cruise control

INSPECTION PROCEDURE

1	Check voltage between terminals Tc and E₁ of DLC1.

CHECK:
(a) Turn ignition switch ON.
(b) Measure voltage between terminals Tc and E₁ of DLC1.
OK:
    Voltage: 10 – 14 V

> **OK** → Proceed to next circuit inspection shown on problem symptoms table.

NG ↓

2	Check harness and connector between cruise control ECU and DLC1, DLC1 and body ground.

> **NG** → Repair or replace harness or connector.

OK ↓

Check and replace cruise control ECU.

TY1109900265020X

Fig. 381 Diagnosis Circuit (Part 2 of 2). 1998–99 Tacoma w/Denso cruise control

CIRCUIT DESCRIPTION

This circuit turns on the magnetic clutch inside the actuator during cruise control operation according to the signal from the ECU. If a malfunction occurs in the actuator or speed sensor, etc. during cruise control operation, the rotor shaft between the motor and control plate is released.
When the brake pedal is depressed, the stop light switch turns on, supplying electrical power to the stop light. Power supply to the magnetic clutch is mechanically cut and the magnetic clutch is turned OFF.
When driving downhill, if the vehicle speed exceeds the set speed by 15 km/h (6 mph) above the set speed, then cruise control at the set speed is resumed.

DTC No.	Detection Item	Trouble Area
12	• Short in actuator and ECU circuit • Open in actuator and ECU circuit	• Connector of cruise control actuator and ECU • STOP fuse and stop light switch • Cruise control actuator and ECU

TY1109900270010X

Fig. 383 Code 12: Actuator Circuit (Part 1 of 3). 1997–99 Tacoma w/Ford cruise control

3	Check harness and connector between actuator and cruise control actuator.

> **NG** → Repair or replace harness or connector.

OK ↓

Check and replace cruise control actuator and ECU.

TY1109900270030X

Fig. 383 Code 12: Actuator Circuit (Part 3 of 3). 1997–99 Tacoma w/Ford cruise control

INSPECTION PROCEDURE

1	Actuator control cable inspection

CHECK:
(a) Check that the actuator, control cable throttle link are properly installed and that the cable and link are connected correctly.
(b) Check that the actuator and bell crank operate smoothly.
(c) Check that the cable is not loose or too tight.
OK:
    Freeplay: Less than 10 mm
HINT:
• If the control cable is very loose, the vehicle's loss of speed going uphill will be large.
• If the control cable is too tight, the idle RPM will become high.

TY1109900266000X

Fig. 382 Actuator Control Cable. 1998–99 Tacoma w/Denso cruise control

INSPECTION PROCEDURE

1	Check STOP fuse.

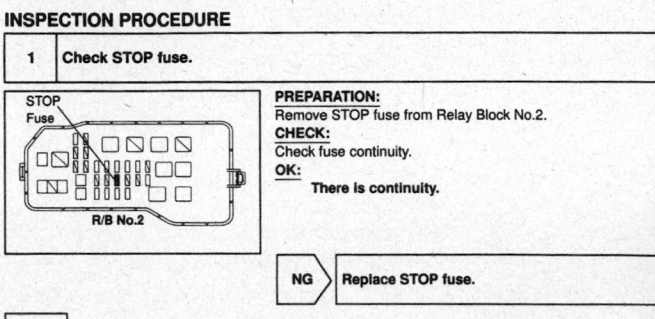

PREPARATION:
Remove STOP fuse from Relay Block No.2.
CHECK:
Check fuse continuity.
OK:
    There is continuity.

> **NG** → Replace STOP fuse.

OK ↓

2	Check stop light switch.

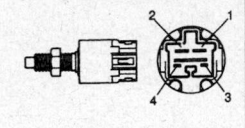

PREPARATION:
Disconnect stop light switch connector.
CHECK:
Check continuity between terminals.
OK:

Switch position	Continuity
Switch pin free (Brake pedal depressed)	1 – 2
Switch pin pushed in (Brake pedal released)	3 – 4

> **NG** → Replace stop light switch.

OK ↓

TY1109900270020X

Fig. 383 Code 12: Actuator Circuit (Part 2 of 3). 1997–99 Tacoma w/Ford cruise control

CIRCUIT DESCRIPTION

The circuit detects the rotation position of the actuator control plate and sends a signal to the ECU.

DTC No.	Detection Item	Trouble Area
14	• Cruise control actuator motor open and short	• Connector of cruise control actuator and ECU • Cruise control actuator and ECU

INSPECTION PROCEDURE

1	Check connector of cruise control actuator and ECU.

> **NG** → Repair or replace connector.

OK ↓

Check and replace cruise control actuator and ECU.

TY1109900271000X

Fig. 384 Code 14: Actuator Mechanical Fault. 1997–99 Tacoma w/Ford cruise control

CIRCUIT DESCRIPTION

The vehicle speed sensor circuit is sent to cruise control ECU as vehicle speed signal. For each rotation of the shaft, the vehicle speed sensor sends a signal through the combination meter to the cruise control ECU (See the following illustration). The ECU calculates the vehicle speed from this pulse frequency.

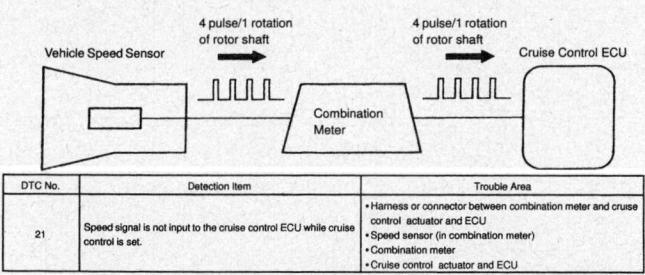

DTC No.	Detection Item	Trouble Area
21	Speed signal is not input to the cruise control ECU while cruise control is set.	• Harness or connector between combination meter and cruise control actuator and ECU • Speed sensor (in combination meter) • Combination meter • Cruise control actuator and ECU

TY1109900272010X

Fig. 385   Code 21: Open In Vehicle Speed Sensor Circuit (Part 1 of 2). 1997–99 Tacoma w/Ford cruise control

CIRCUIT DESCRIPTION

DTC No.	Detection Item	Trouble Area
23	• Actual vehicle speed has dropped either by 16 km/h (10 mph) or more below the set speed, or by 20% or more of the set speed.	• Speed sensor (in combination meter) • Cruise control actuator and ECU

WIRING DIAGRAM

INSPECTION PROCEDURE

1	Check speedometer circuit.

NG → Repair or replace speed sensor or combination meter assembly.

OK

Check and replace cruise control actuator and ECU.

TY1109900273000X

Fig. 386   Code 23: Vehicle Speed Sensor Abnormal. 1997–99 Tacoma w/Ford cruise control

INSPECTION PROCEDURE

1	Input signal check.

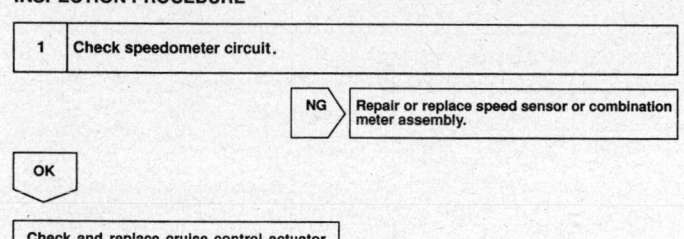

CHECK:
(a) See input signal check.
(b) Check indicator light operation when driving with vehicle speed above 40 km/h (25 mph), and with vehicle speed below 40 km/h (25 mph).

OK:

Vehicle speed above 40 km/h (25 mph):
Indicator light blinks
Vehicle speed below 40 km/h (25 mph):
Indicator light stays on

OK → Check and replace cruise control actuator and ECU.

NG

2	Check harness and connector between combination meter and cruise control actuator and ECU.

NG → Repair or replace harness or connector.

OK

3	Check speedometer circuit.

NG → Repair or replace speed sensor or combination meter assembly.

OK

Check and replace cruise control actuator and ECU.

TY1109900272020X

Fig. 385   Code 21: Open In Vehicle Speed Sensor Circuit (Part 2 of 2). 1997–99 Tacoma w/Ford cruise control

CIRCUIT DESCRIPTION

This circuit carries the SET/COAST, RESUME/Accel and CANCEL signals (each voltage) to the ECU.

DTC No.	Detection Item	Trouble Area
32	Short in control switch circuit	• Harness or connector between control switch and cruise control actuator and ECU. • Cruise control switch • Cruise control actuator and ECU

TY1109900274010X

Fig. 387   Code 32: Control Switch Circuit (Part 1 of 3). 1997–99 Tacoma w/Ford cruise control

INSPECTION PROCEDURE

1	Input signal check.

PREPARATION:
See input signal check.

CHECK:
Check the indicator light operation when each of the SET/COAST, RESUME/ACCEL and CANCEL is turned on.

OK:

SET/COAST, RESUME/ACCEL switch
The signals shown in the table on the left should be output when each switch is ON. The signal should disappear when the switch is turned OFF.

CANCEL switch
The Indicator light goes off when the cancel switch is turned ON.

Input Signal	Indicator Light Blinking Pattern	
SET/COAST switch	ON	2 Pulses
	OFF	
RESUME/ACCEL switch	ON	3 Pulses
	OFF	
CANCEL switch	ON	SW OFF
	OFF	SW ON

OK	Wait and see.

NG

2	Check control switch.

PREPARATION:
(a)   Remove steering wheel center pad.
(b)   Disconnect control switch connector.

CHECK:
Measure resistance between terminals 3 and 4 of control switch connector when control switch is operated.

Switch position	Resistance (Ω)
Neutral	∞ (No continuity)
RES/ACC	50 – 80
SET/COAST	180 – 220
CANCEL	400 – 440

OK	Replace control switch.

NG

TY1109900274020X

Fig. 387   Code 32: Control Switch Circuit (Part 2 of 3). 1997–99 Tacoma w/Ford cruise control

CIRCUIT DESCRIPTION

When the brake is on, battery positive voltage normally applies through the STOP fuse and stop light switch to terminal STP– of the ECU, and the ECU turns the cruise control off.
A fail-safe function is provided so that cancel functions normally, even if there is a malfunction in the stop light signal circuit.

If the harness connected to terminal STP– has an open circuit, terminal STP– will have battery positive voltage and the cruise control will be turned off.

Also, when the brake is on, the magnetic clutch is cut mechanically by the stop light switch, turning the cruise control off.

TY1109900275010X

Fig. 388   Stop Lamp Switch Circuit (Part 1 of 3). 1997–99 Tacoma w/Ford cruise control

---

3	Check harness and connector between cruise control switch and cruise control actuator and ECU.

NG	Repair or replace harness or connector.

OK

4	Input signal check (See step 1).

OK	Wait and see.

NG

Check and replace cruise control actuator and ECU.

TY1109900274030X

Fig. 387   Code 32: Control Switch Circuit (Part 3 of 3). 1997–99 Tacoma w/Ford cruise control

INSPECTION PROCEDURE

1	Check operation of stop light.

CHECK:
Check that stop light comes on when brake pedal is depressed, and turns off when brake pedal is released.

NG	Check stop light system.

OK

2	Input signal check.

Input Signal	Indicator Light Blinking Pattern	
Stop light switch ON	Light ON	SW OFF
	OFF	SW ON

CHECK:
(a)   See input signal check.
(b)   Check the indicator light when the brake pedal is depressed.

OK:
The indicator light goes off when the brake pedal is depressed.

OK	Proceed to next circuit inspection shown on problem symptoms table.

NG

TY1109900275020X

Fig. 388   Stop Lamp Switch Circuit (Part 2 of 3). 1997–99 Tacoma w/Ford cruise control

3 | Check voltage between terminal STP– of cruise control actuator and ECU connector and body ground.

PREPARATION:
Remove cruise control ECU with connectors still connected.
CHECK:
(a) Turn ignition switch ON.
(b) Measure voltage between terminal STP– of cruise control ECU connector and body ground, when the brake pedal is depressed and released.
OK:

Brake pedal position	Voltage
Depressed	10 – 14 V
Released	Below 1 V

OK ▷ Proceed to next circuit inspection shown on problem symptoms table.

NG

4 | Check for open in harness and connectors between terminal STP– of cruise control actuator and ECU and stop light switch.

NG ▷ Repair or replace harness or connector.

OK

Check and replace cruise control actuator and ECU.

TY1109900275030X

Fig. 388   Stop Lamp Switch Circuit (Part 3 of 3). 1997–99 Tacoma w/Ford cruise control

INSPECTION PROCEDURE

1 | Check voltage between terminal IDL of ECU connector and body ground.

PREPARATION:
(a) Remove the cruise control ECU with connector still connected.
(b) Disconnect ECM and ABS ECU connectors.
(c) Ignition switch ON.
CHECK:
Measure voltage between terminal IDL of ECU connector and body ground when the throttle valve is fully closed and fully opened.
OK:

Throttle valve position	Voltage
Fully opened	10 – 14 V
Fully closed	Below 2 V

OK ▷ Proceed to next circuit inspection shown on problem symptoms table.

NG

2 | Check throttle position sensor.

PREPARATION:
Disconnect throttle position sensor connector.
CHECK:
Measure resistance between terminals 3 and 4 of throttle position sensor connector when the throttle valve is fully closed and fully opened.
OK:

Throttle valve position	Resistance
Fully opened	1 MΩ or higher
Fully closed	Below 2.3 kΩ

NG ▷ Replace throttle position sensor.

OK

TY1109900276020X

Fig. 389   Idle Switch Circuit (Part 2 of 3). 1997–99 Tacoma w/Ford cruise control

CIRCUIT DESCRIPTION

When the idle switch is turned ON, a signal is sent to the ECU. The ECU uses this signal to correct the discrepancy between the throttle valve position and the actuator position sensor valve to enable accurate cruise control at the set speed. If the idle switch is malfunctioning, problem symptoms also occur in the engine, so also inspect the engine.

TY1109900276010X

Fig. 389   Idle Switch Circuit (Part 1 of 3). 1997–99 Tacoma w/Ford cruise control

3 | Check for open and short in harness and connector between ECU and throttle position sensor, throttle position sensor and body ground.

NG ▷ Repair or replace harness or connector.

OK

Check and replace cruise control actuator and ECU.

TY1109900276030X

Fig. 389   Idle Switch Circuit (Part 3 of 3). 1997–99 Tacoma w/Ford cruise control

CIRCUIT DESCRIPTION

When driving uphill under the cruise control, in order to reduce shifting due to ON–OFF overdrive operation and to provide smooth driving, when down shifting in the electronically controlled transmission occurs, a signal to prevent upshift until the end of the up hill slope is sent from the cruise control ECU to the electronically controlled transmission.
Terminal ECM of the cruise control ECU detects the shift change signal (output to electronically controlled transmission No. 2 solenoid) from the electronically controlled transmission.
If vehicle speeds down, also when terminal electronically controlled transmission of the cruise control ECU receives down shifting signal, it sends a signal from terminal OD to ECM to cut overdrive until the end of the uphill slope, and the gear shifts are reduced and gear shift points in the electronically controlled transmission are changed.

TY1109900277010X

Fig. 390   Electronically Controlled Transmission Communication Circuit (Part 1 of 4). 1997–99 Tacoma w/Ford cruise control

INSPECTION PROCEDURE

1	Check operation of overdrive.

PREPARATION:
Test drive after engine warms up.
CHECK:
Check that overdrive ON ↔ OFF occurs with operation of OD switch ON–OFF.

NG ▷ Check and repair electronically controlled transmission.

OK

2	Check voltage between terminal OD of harness side connector of cruise control actuator and ECU and body ground.

PREPARATION:
Remove cruise control ECU with connector still connected.
CHECK:
(a) Disconnect cruise control ECU connector.
(b) Turn ignition switch ON.
(c) Measure voltage between terminal OD of harness side connector of cruise control ECU and body ground.
OK:
Voltage: 10 – 14 V

NG ▷ Go to step 5.

OK

TY1109900277020X

Fig. 390   Electronically Controlled Transmission Communication Circuit (Part 2 of 4). 1997–99 Tacoma w/Ford cruise control

5	Check harness and connector between terminal OD of cruise control actuator and ECU and terminal OD1 of ECM.

NG ▷ Repair or replace harness or connector.

OK

Check and replace cruise control actuator and ECU.

TY1109900277040X

Fig. 390   Electronically Controlled Transmission Communication Circuit (Part 4 of 4). 1997–99 Tacoma w/Ford cruise control

3	Check voltage between terminal ECT of cruise control actuator and ECU connector and body ground (On test drive).

PREPARATION:
(a)   Connect cruise control ECU connector.
(b)   Test drive after engine warms up.
CHECK:
Check voltage between terminal ECT of cruise control ECU connector and body ground when OD switch is ON and OFF.
OK:

OD switch position	Voltage
ON	8 – 14 V
OFF	Below 0.5 V

OK ▷ Proceed to next circuit inspection shown on problem symptoms table.

NG

4	Check harness and connector between terminal ECT of cruise control actuator and ECU and electronically controlled transmission solenoid.

NG ▷ Repair or replace harness or connector.

OK

Check and replace cruise control actuator and ECU.

TY1109900277030X

Fig. 390   Electronically Controlled Transmission Communication Circuit (Part 3 of 4). 1997–99 Tacoma w/Ford cruise control

CIRCUIT DESCRIPTION

When the shift position is put in positions except D, a signal is sent from the park/neutral position switch to the ECU. When this signal is input during cruise control driving, the ECU cancels the cruise control.

TY1109900278010X

Fig. 391   Park/Neutral Position Switch Circuit (Part 1 of 3). 1997–99 Tacoma w/Ford cruise control

INSPECTION PROCEDURE

1	Check starter operation.

CHECK:
Check that the starter operates normally and that the engine starts.

NG ▷ Diagnose starting system.

OK

2	Input signal check.

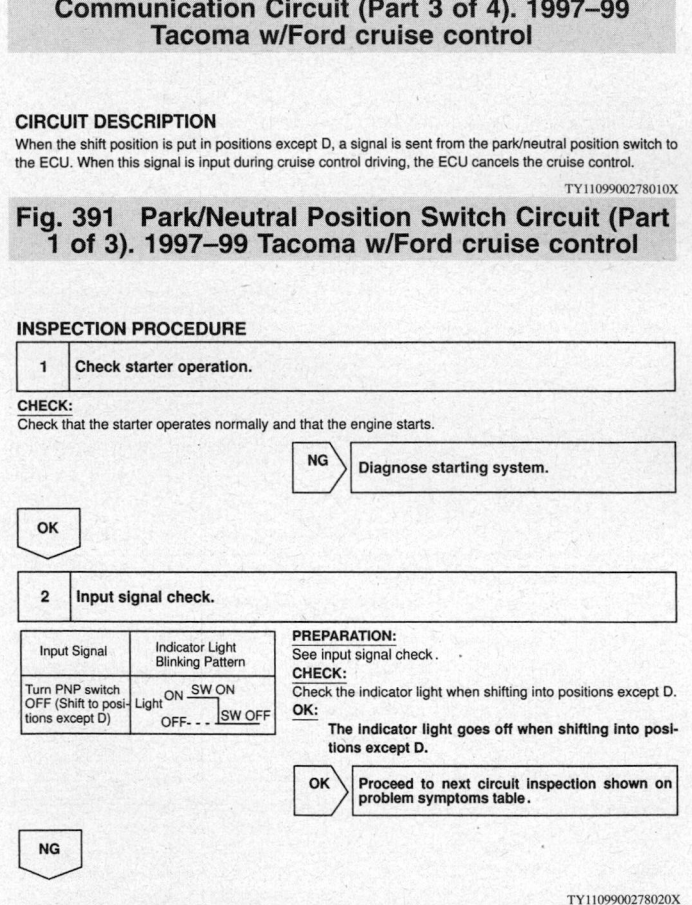

Input Signal	Indicator Light Blinking Pattern
Turn PNP switch OFF (Shift to positions except D)	Light ON ⎍ SW ON / OFF--- SW OFF

PREPARATION:
See input signal check.
CHECK:
Check the indicator light when shifting into positions except D.
OK:
The indicator light goes off when shifting into positions except D.

OK ▷ Proceed to next circuit inspection shown on problem symptoms table.

NG

TY1109900278020X

Fig. 391   Park/Neutral Position Switch Circuit (Part 2 of 3). 1997–99 Tacoma w/Ford cruise control

3 | Check voltage between terminal D of cruise control actuator and ECU and body ground.

PREPARATION:
Turn ignition switch ON.
CHECK:
Measure voltage between terminal D of cruise control ECU connector and body ground when shifting into D position and other positions.
OK:

Shift Position	Voltage
D position	10 – 14 V
Other positions	Below 1 V

OK > Proceed to next circuit inspection shown on problem symptoms table.

NG

4 | Check harness and connector between PNP switch and cruise control actuator and ECU.

NG > Repair or replace harness or connector.

OK

Check and replace cruise control actuator and ECU.

TY1109900278030X

Fig. 391 Park/Neutral Position Switch Circuit (Part 3 of 3). 1997–99 Tacoma w/Ford cruise control

INSPECTION PROCEDURE

1 | Check starter operation.

CHECK:
Check that the starter operates normally and that the engine starts.

NG > Diagnose starting system.

OK

2 | Input signal check.

Input Signal	Indicator Light Blinking Pattern
Clutch switch OFF (Depress clutch pedal)	Light ON ‾‾‾ SW ON / OFF - - - - SW OFF

PREPARATION:
See input signal check.
CHECK:
Check the indicator light when clutch pedal depressed.
OK:
The indicator light goes off when clutch pedal depressed.

OK > Proceed to next circuit inspection shown on problem symptoms table.

NG

TY1109900279020X

Fig. 392 Clutch Switch Circuit (Part 2 of 3). 1997–99 Tacoma w/Ford cruise control

CIRCUIT DESCRIPTION

When the clutch pedal is depressed, the clutch switch sends a signal to the cruise control ECU. When the signal is input to the cruise control ECU during cruise control driving, the cruise control ECU cancels cruise control.

TY1109900279010X

Fig. 392 Clutch Switch Circuit (Part 1 of 3). 1997–99 Tacoma w/Ford cruise control

3 | Check voltage between terminal D of cruise control actuator and ECU and body ground.

PREPARATION:
Turn ignition switch ON.
CHECK:
Measure voltage between terminal D of cruise control ECU connector and body ground when clutch pedal depressed and pushed in.
OK:

Shift Position	Voltage
Clutch pedal depressed	10 – 14 V
Clutch pedal pushed in	Below 1 V

OK > Proceed to next circuit inspection shown on problem symptoms table.

NG

4 | Check for open in harness and connector between cruise control actuator and ECU and GAUGE fuse.

NG > Repair or replace harness or connector.

OK

Check and replace cruise control actuator and ECU.

TY1109900279030X

Fig. 392 Clutch Switch Circuit (Part 3 of 3). 1997–99 Tacoma w/Ford cruise control

CIRCUIT DESCRIPTION

The ECU power source supplies power to the actuator and sensors, etc.. When terminal GND and the cruise control ECU case are grounded.

TY1109900280010X

Fig. 393 ECU Power Source Circuit (Part 1 of 3). 1997–99 Tacoma w/Ford cruise control

INSPECTION PROCEDURE

1	Check ECU–IG fuse.

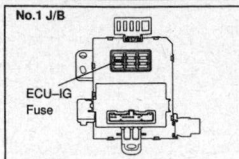

No.1 J/B

ECU–IG Fuse

PREPARATION:
Remove ECU–IG fuse from junction block No.1.
CHECK:
Check continuity of ECU–IG fuse.
OK:
   Continuity

NG ▷ Check for short in all the harness and components connected to ECU–IG fuse.

OK

2	Check voltage between terminals B and GND of cruise control actuator and ECU connector.

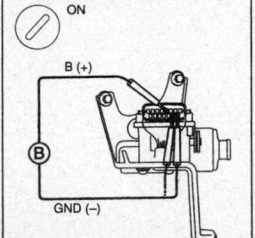

ON

B (+)

B

GND (−)

PREPARATION:
Remove cruise control ECU with connector still connected.
CHECK:
(a) Turn ignition switch ON.
(b) Measure voltage between terminals B and GND of cruise control ECU connector.
OK:
   10 – 14 V

OK ▷ Proceed to next circuit inspection shown on problem symptoms table.

NG

TY1109900280020X

**Fig. 393 ECU Power Source Circuit (Part 2 of 3).
1997–99 Tacoma w/Ford cruise control**

CIRCUIT DESCRIPTION
When the cruise control main switch is turned off, the cruise control does not operate.

INSPECTION PROCEDURE

1	Check voltage between terminal CMS of cruise control actuator and ECU connector and body ground.

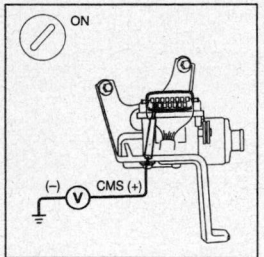

ON

(−) CMS (+)

V

PREPARATION:
Remove the cruise control ECU with connector still connected.
CHECK:
(a) Turn ignition switch ON.
(b) Measure voltage between terminal CMS of cruise control ECU connector when main switch is held on and off.
OK:

Main switch	Voltage
OFF	10 – 14 V
ON	Below 1 V

OK ▷ Proceed to next circuit inspection shown on problem symptoms table.

NG

TY1109900281010X

**Fig. 394 Main Switch Circuit (Part 1 of 2). 1997–99
Tacoma w/Ford cruise control**

3	Check resistance between terminal GND of cruise control actuator and ECU connector and body ground.

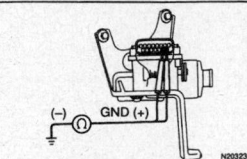

(−) GND (+)

N20323

CHECK:
Measure resistance between terminal GND of cruise control ECU connector and body ground.
OK:
   Resistance: Below 1 Ω

NG ▷ Repair or replace harness or connector.

OK

Check and repair harness and connector between battery and cruise control actuator and ECU.

TY1109900280030X

**Fig. 393 ECU Power Source Circuit (Part 3 of 3).
1997–99 Tacoma w/Ford cruise control**

2	Check main switch continuity.

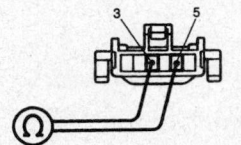

3   5

PREPARATION:
(a) Remove the steering wheel center pad.

(b) Disconnect the cruise control switch connector.
CHECK:
Check continuity between terminals 3 and 5 of cruise control switch connector when main switch is held on and off.
OK:

Switch position	Tester connection	Specified condition
OFF	3 – 5	No continuity
Hold ON	3 – 5	Continuity

NG ▷ Replace control switch.

OK

3	Check harness and connector between cruise control actuator and ECU and main switch.

NG ▷ Repair or replace harness or connector.

OK

Check and replace cruise control actuator and ECU.

TY1109900281020X

**Fig. 394 Main Switch Circuit (Part 2 of 2). 1997–99
Tacoma w/Ford cruise control**

CIRCUIT DESCRIPTION
When the cruise control main switch is turned ON, CRUISE MAIN indicator light lights up.

TY1109900282010X

**Fig. 395 Cruise Main Indicator Lamp Circuit (Part 1
of 2). 1997–99 Tacoma w/Ford cruise control**

INSPECTION PROCEDURE

1 Check voltage between terminals PI and GND of cruise control actuator and ECU connector.

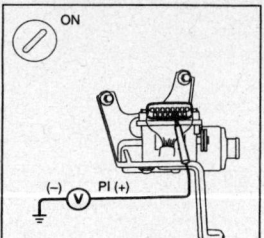

PREPARATION:
Ignition switch ON.
CHECK:
Measure voltage between terminals PI and GND of cruise control ECU connector when the main switch on and off.
OK:

Switch position	Voltage
OFF	10 ~ 16 V
ON	Below 1.2 V

OK ▷ Proceed to next circuit inspection shown on problem symptoms table.

NG ▽

2 Check combination meter.

NG ▷ Replace combination meter.

OK ▽

Check and replace cruise control actuator and ECU.

TY1109900282020X

Fig. 395 Cruise Main Indicator Lamp Circuit (Part 2 of 2). 1997–99 Tacoma w/Ford cruise control

INSPECTION PROCEDURE

1 Check voltage between terminals Tc and E₁ of DLC1.

CHECK:
(a) Turn the ignition switch ON.
(b) Measure voltage between terminals Tc and E₁ of DLC1.
OK:
Voltage: 10 – 14 V

OK ▷ Proceed to next circuit inspection shown on problem symptoms table.

NG ▽

2 Check harness and connector between cruise control actuator and ECU and DLC1, DLC1 and body ground.

NG ▷ Repair or replace harness or connector.

OK ▽

Check and replace cruise control actuator and ECU.

TY1109900283020X

Fig. 396 Diagnosis Circuit (Part 2 of 2). 1997–99 Tacoma w/Ford cruise control

CIRCUIT DESCRIPTION

This circuit sends a signal to the ECU that DTC output is required.

TY1109900283010X

Fig. 396 Diagnosis Circuit (Part 1 of 2). 1997–99 Tacoma w/Ford cruise control

INSPECTION PROCEDURE

1 Actuator control cable removal and installation

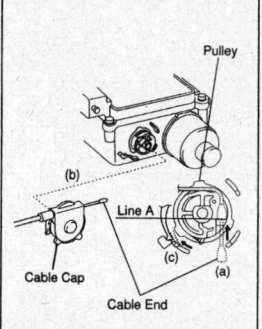

CHECK:REMOVE:
(a) Insert the inner cable end into the pulley and pull it up to the line "A", shown in the illustration.
The end of the spring prevents the pulley from slipping out.
(b) Install the cable cap to fit it with the actuator.
(c) Turn the cable cap clockwise to lock.
CHECK:INSTALL:
Installation is in the reverse order of removal.

2 Actuator control cable inspection

CHECK:
(a) Check that the actuator and control cable throttle link are properly installed and that the cable and the link are connected correctly.
(b) Check that the actuator and bell crank are operating smoothly.
(c) Check that the cable is not loose or too tight.
OK:
Freeplay: Less than 10 mm
HINT:
• If the control cable is very loose, the vehicle's loss of speed going uphill will be large.
• If the control cable is too tight, the idle RPM will become high.

TY1109900284000X

Fig. 397 Actuator Control Cable. 1997–99 Tacoma w/Ford cruise control

Inspection Item		TEST NO. →	D		C	C	F	H,I		G	E		J		
Diagnosis Trouble Code / Problem	Type A	Type B	Cruise Control ECU	Actuator	Main Switch (in Control Switch)	Control Switch	Stop Light Switch	Clutch Start Switch or Park/Neutral Position Switch	Parking Brake Switch	Vehicle Speed Sensor	Speed Control Cable Function	Throttle Position Sensor (IDL)	Wire Harness	Indicator Light
• "CRUISE" Indicator light blinks. • Cruise control system does not set. • Cruise control system does not operate.	11	–	3	2										1
	12	–	4	2			3							1
	13	–	3	2										1
	21	–	3							2				1
	23	–	4							2	3			1
	32	–	3			2								1
	34	–	3			2								1
	41	–	1											
Indicator light does not light up.			3										1	2
Large speed drop when the cruise control switch turned to SET.			4	3						1	2			
Vehicle speed fluctuates when cruise control SET.			4	3						1	2			
Set speed deviates on high or low side.	4	OK	4	3						1	2			
		NG		1										
Acceleration response is sluggish when cruise control switch turned to "ACCEL" or "RESUME"	4	OK	4	3						2	1			
		NG		1										
Cruise control system does not set. Cruise control system does not operate.	4	OK	9	8	2	3	4	5	6		7			
		NG		2						1				
Set speed does no cancel when brake pedal depressed.	3	OK	1											
		NG		2			1							
Set speed does not cancel when parking brake lever pulled.	3	OK	1											
		NG		2					1					
Cruise control not cancelled, even when transmission is shifted to EXCEPT D RANGE.	3	OK	1											
		NG		2				1						
Set speed does not cancel when clutch pedal depressed.	3	OK	1											
		NG		2				1						
Set speed does not cancel when cruise control switch to CANCEL.	3	OK	1											
		NG		2		1								
Vehicle speed does not decrease when cruise control switch turned to COAST.	1	OK	4	1						3	2			
		NG		2							1			
Vehicle speed does not accelerate when cruise control switch turned to ACCEL.	2	OK	4	1						3	2			
		NG		2		1								
Vehicle speed does not return to memorized cruise when control switch turned to RESUME.	2	OK	4	1						3	2			
		NG		2		1								
Speed can be set below about 40 km/h (25 mph).	4	OK	1											
		NG		2						1				
Cruise control does not disengage even at about 40 km/h (25 mph) or less.	4	OK	2	1										
		NG		2						1				

TY1109900512000X

Fig. 398   Problem Symptoms Table. 1996 T100

Symptom	Suspect Area
SET not occurring or CANCEL occurring. (DTC is Normal)	1. Main Switch Circuit (Cruise control switch) 2. Vehicle Speed Sensor Circuit 3. Control Switch Circuit (Cruise control switch) 4. Stop Light Switch Circuit 5. PNP Switch or Clutch Switch Circuit 6. Cruise Control Actuator with ECU
SET not occurring or CANCEL occurring. (DTC does not output)	1. ECU Power Source Circuit 2. Cruise Control Actuator with ECU
Actual vehicle speed deviates above or below the set speed.	1. Vehicle Speed Signal Abnormal 2. Electronically Controlled Transmission Communication Circuit 3. Idle Signal Circuit (Main throttle position sensor) 4. Cruise Control Actuator with ECU
Gear shifting frequent between 3rd O/D when driving on uphill road. (Hurting)	1. Electronically Controlled Transmission Communication Circuit 2. Cruise Control Actuator with ECU
Cruise control not cancelled, even when brake pedal is depressed.	1. Stop Light Switch Circuit 2. Cruise Control Actuator with ECU
Cruise control not cancelled, even when transmission is shifted to "N" position.	1. Park/Neutral Position Switch Circuit 2. Cruise Control Actuator with ECU
Cruise control not cancelled, even when clutch pedal is depressed.	1. Clutch Switch Circuit 2. Cruise Control Actuator with ECU
Control switch does not operate. (SET/COAST, ACC/RES, CANCEL not possible)	1. Control Switch Circuit (Cruise Control Switch) 2. Cruise Control Actuator with ECU
SET possible at 40 km/h (25 mph) or less, or CANCEL does not operate at 40 km/h (25 mph) or less.	1. Vehicle Speed Signal Abnormal 2. Cruise Control Actuator with ECU
Poor response is ACCEL and RESUME modes.	1. Electronically Controlled Transmission Communication Circuit 2. Cruise Control Actuator with ECU
O/D does not RESUME, even through the road is uphill.	1. Electronically Controlled Transmission Communication Circuit 2. Cruise Control Actuator with ECU
DTC memory is erased.	1. ECU Power Source Circuit 2. Cruise Control Actuator with ECU
DTC is not output, or is output when is should not be.	1. Diagnosis Circuit 2. Cruise Control Actuator with ECU
Cruise MAIN indicator light remains ON or fall to light up.	1. Cruise MAIN indicator Light Switch Circuit

TY1109900526000X

Fig. 399   Problem Symptoms Table. 1997–98 T100

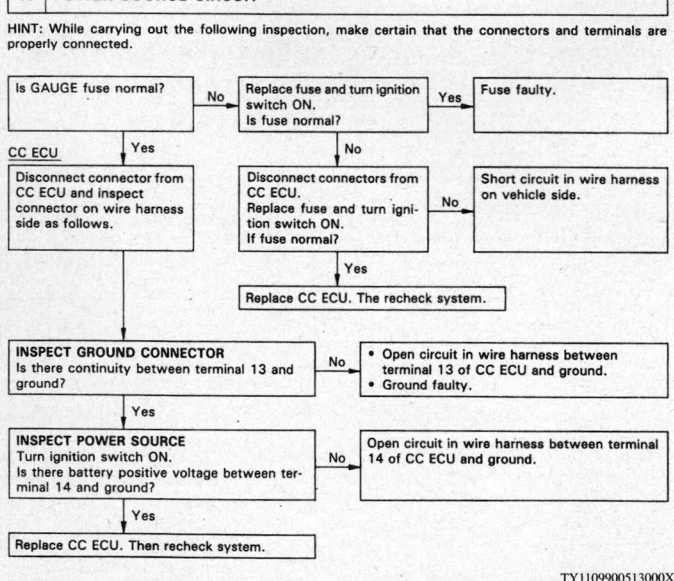

A   POWER SOURCE CIRCUIT

HINT: While carrying out the following inspection, make certain that the connectors and terminals are properly connected.

TY1109900513000X

Fig. 400   Test A: Power Source Circuit. 1996 T100

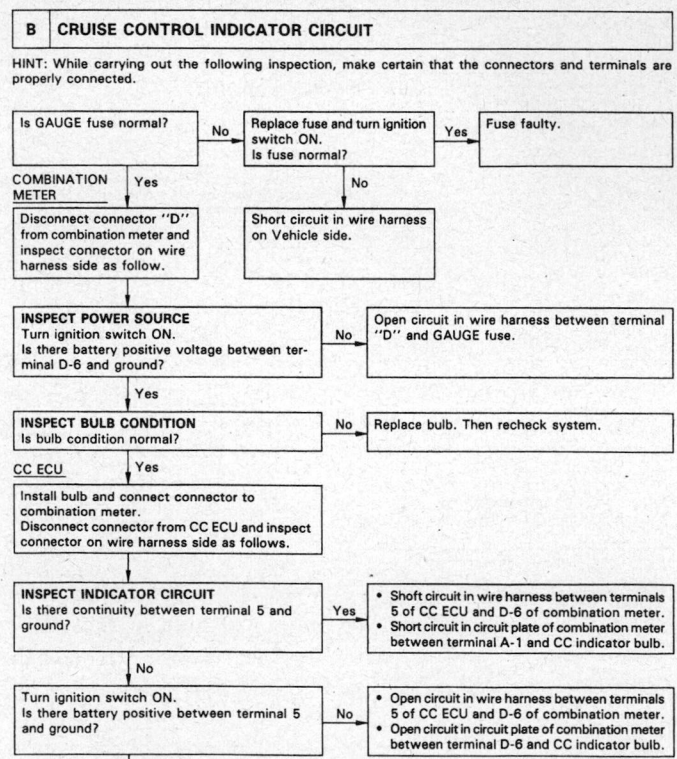

B   CRUISE CONTROL INDICATOR CIRCUIT

HINT: While carrying out the following inspection, make certain that the connectors and terminals are properly connected.

TY1109900514000X

Fig. 401   Test B: Cruise Control Indicator Circuit. 1996 T100

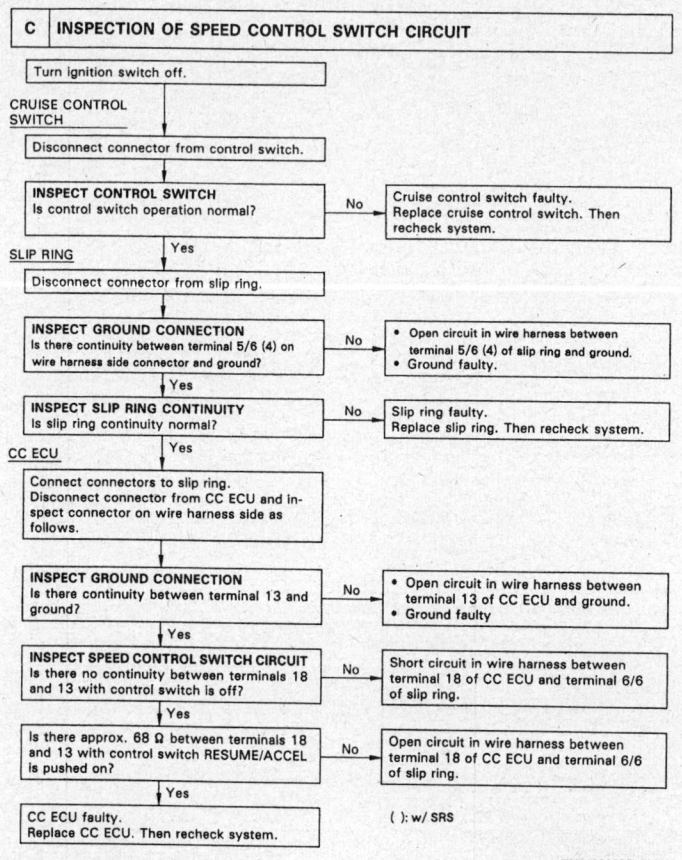

Fig. 402   Test C: Speed Control Switch Circuit Inspection. 1996 T100

TY1109900515000X

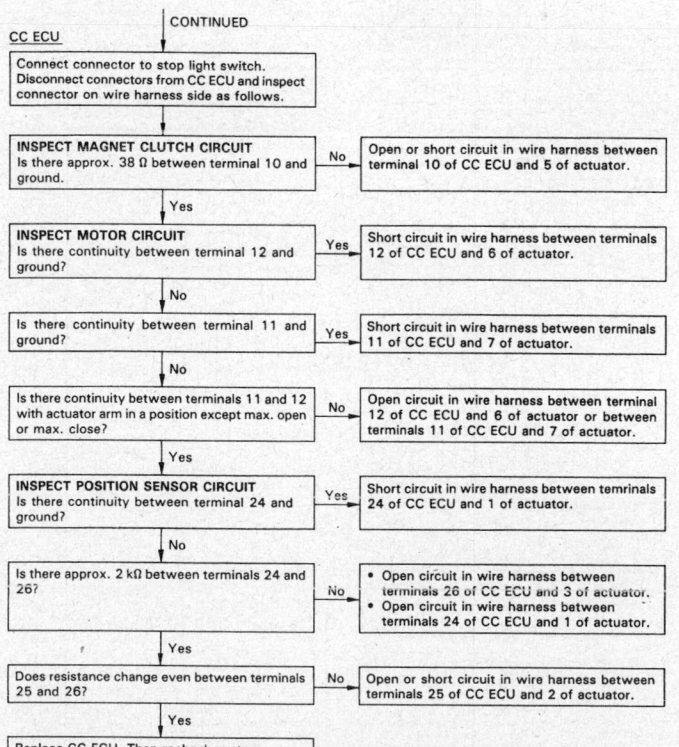

CC: Cruise Control

TY1109900516020X

Fig. 403   Test D: Actuator Circuit (Part 2 of 2). 1996 T100

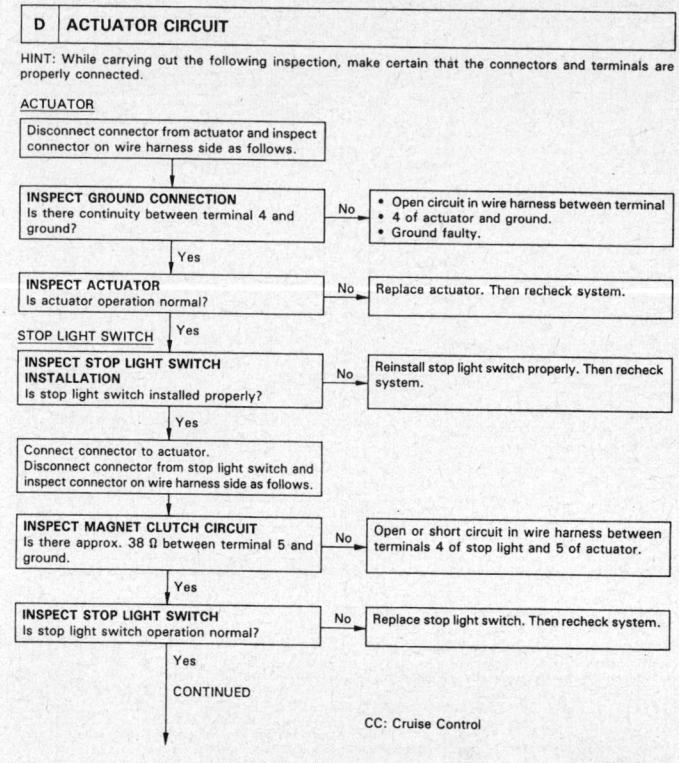

TY1109900516010X

Fig. 403   Test D: Actuator Circuit (Part 1 of 2). 1996 T100

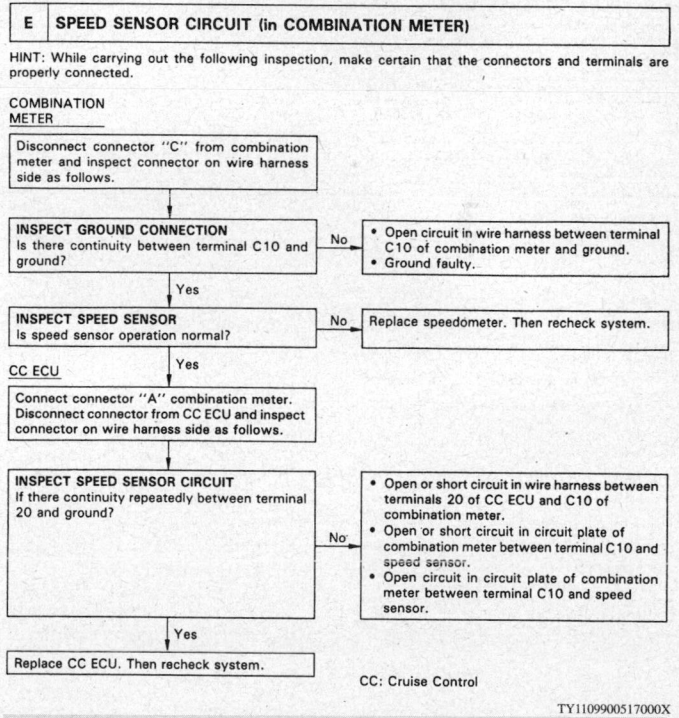

CC: Cruise Control

TY1109900517000X

Fig. 404   Test E: Speed Sensor Circuit. 1996 T100

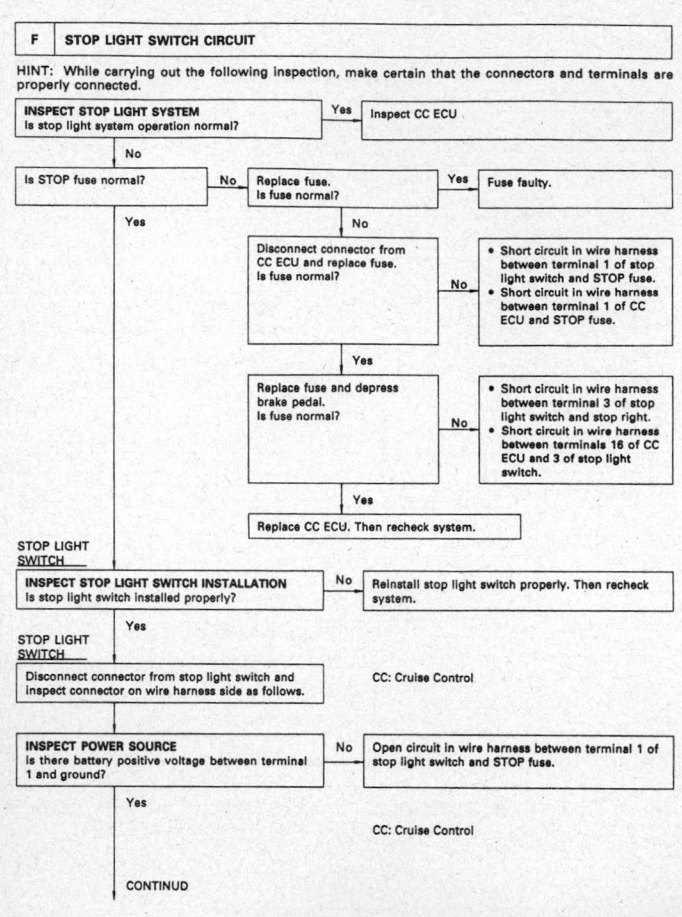

Fig. 405   Test F: Stop Lamp Switch Circuit (Part 1 of 2). 1996 T100

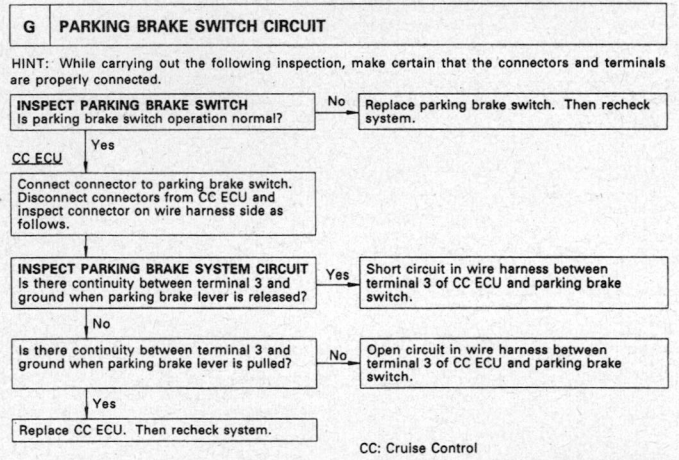

Fig. 406   Test G: Parking Brake Circuit. 1996 T100

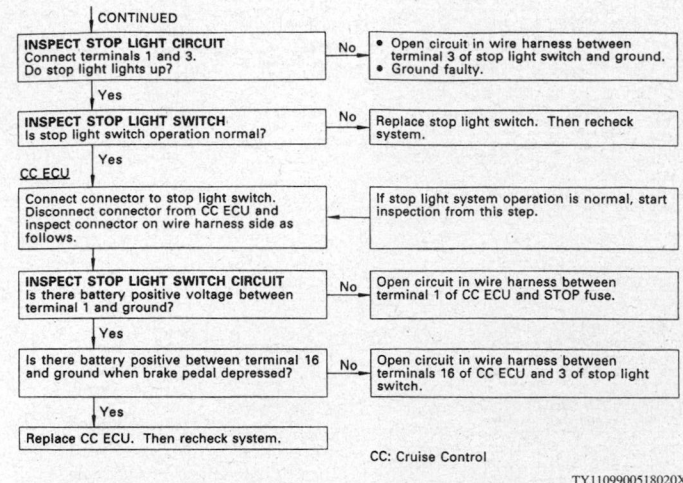

Fig. 405   Test F: Stop Lamp Switch Circuit (Part 2 of 2). 1996 T100

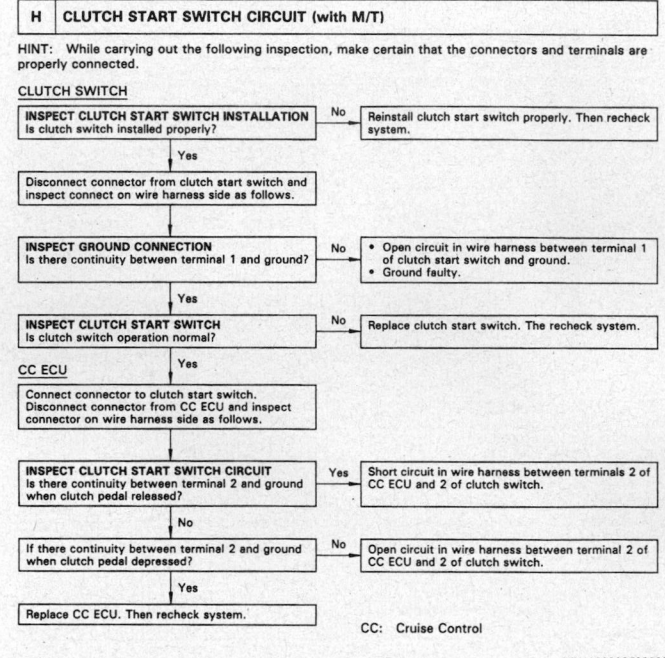

Fig. 407   Test H: Clutch Start Switch Circuit. 1996 T100

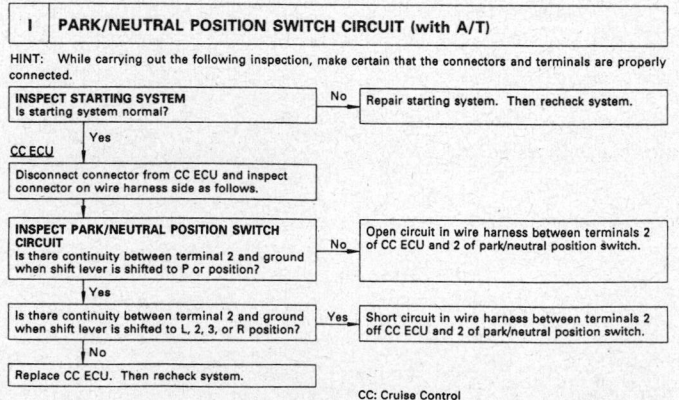

Fig. 408   Test I: Park/Neutral Position Switch Circuit. 1996 T100

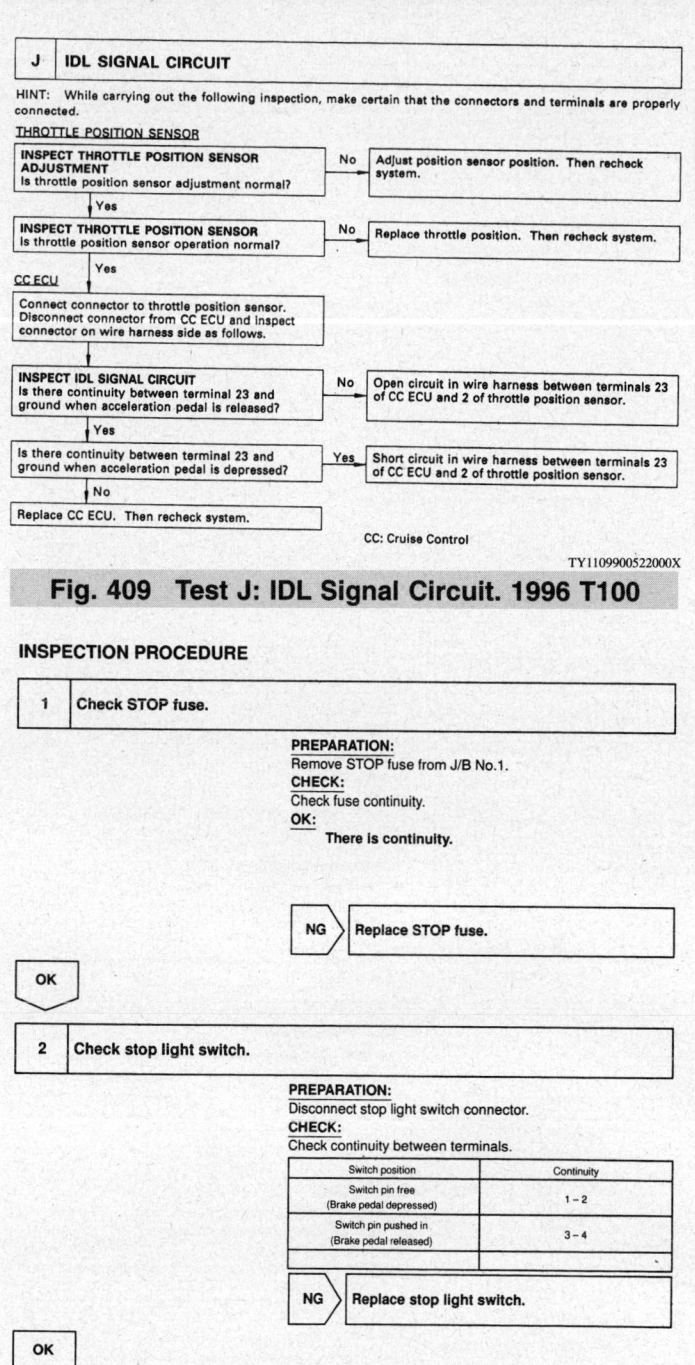

J IDL SIGNAL CIRCUIT

HINT: While carrying out the following inspection, make certain that the connectors and terminals are properly connected.

THROTTLE POSITION SENSOR

INSPECT THROTTLE POSITION SENSOR ADJUSTMENT	No	Adjust position sensor position. Then recheck
Is throttle position sensor adjustment normal?	→	system.

↓ Yes

INSPECT THROTTLE POSITION SENSOR	No	Replace throttle position. Then recheck system.
Is throttle position sensor operation normal?	→	

↓ Yes

CC ECU

Connect connector to throttle position sensor.
Disconnect connector from CC ECU and inspect connector on wire harness side as follows.

INSPECT IDL SIGNAL CIRCUIT	No	Open circuit in wire harness between terminals 23
Is there continuity between terminal 23 and ground when acceleration pedal is released?	→	of CC ECU and 2 of throttle position sensor.

Is there continuity between terminal 23 and ground when acceleration pedal is depressed?	Yes	Short circuit in wire harness between terminals 23 of CC ECU and 2 of throttle position sensor.

↓ No

Replace CC ECU. Then recheck system.

CC: Cruise Control

TY1109900522000X

Fig. 409 Test J: IDL Signal Circuit. 1996 T100

INSPECTION PROCEDURE

1	Check STOP fuse.

PREPARATION:
Remove STOP fuse from J/B No.1.
CHECK:
Check fuse continuity.
OK:
　　There is continuity.

NG ▷ Replace STOP fuse.

OK

2	Check stop light switch.

PREPARATION:
Disconnect stop light switch connector.
CHECK:
Check continuity between terminals.

Switch position	Continuity
Switch pin free (Brake pedal depressed)	1 – 2
Switch pin pushed in (Brake pedal released)	3 – 4

NG ▷ Replace stop light switch.

OK

Check and replace cruise control actuator with ECU

TY1109900527020X

Fig. 410 Code 12: Actuator Circuit (Part 2 of 2). 1997–98 T100

CIRCUIT DESCRIPTION

This circuit turns on the magnetic clutch inside the actuator during cruise control operation according to the signal from the ECU. If a malfunction occurs in the actuator or speed sensor, etc. during cruise control operation, the rotor shaft between the motor and control plate is released.
When the brake pedal is depressed, the stop light switch turns on, supplying electrical power to the stop light. Power supply to the magnetic clutch is mechanically cut and the magnetic clutch is turned OFF.
When driving downhill, if the vehicle speed exceeds the set speed by 15 km/h (6 mph) above the set speed, then cruise control at the set speed is resumed.

DTC No.	Detection Item	Trouble Area
12	• Short in actuator with ECU circuit • Open in actuator with ECU circuit	• Connector of cruise control actuator with ECU • Stop fuse and stop light switch • cruise control actuator with ECU

TY1109900527010X

Fig. 410 Code 12: Actuator Circuit (Part 1 of 2). 1997–98 T100

CIRCUIT DESCRIPTION

The circuits detects the rotation position of the actuator contorl plate and sends a signal to the ECU.

DTC No.	Detection Item	Trouble Area
14	• Cruise contorl actuator motor open and shout.	• Connector of cruise control actuator with ECU • Cruise control actuator with ECU

INSPECTION PROCEDURE

1	Check connector of cruise control actuator with ECU

NG ▷ Repair or replace connector.

OK

Check and replace cruise control actuator with ECU

TY1109900528000X

Fig. 411 Code 14: Actuator Mechanical Fault. 1997–98 T100

CIRCUIT DESCRIPTION

The combination meter sends the vehicle speed signal to the cruise control ECU. The cruise control ECU calculates the vehicle speed by of the vehicle speed signal sent from the combination meter.

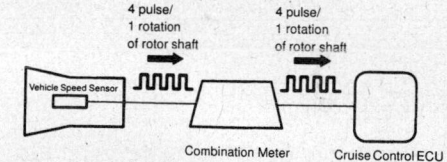

DTC No.	Detection Item	Trouble Area
21	Speed signal is not input to cruise control ECU while cruise control is set.	• Harness or connector between combination meter and cruise control actuator with ECU • Speed sensor (in combination meter) • Combination meter • Cruise control actuator with ECU

TY1109900529010X

Fig. 412 Code 21: Open In Vehicle Speed Sensor Circuit (Part 1 of 2). 1997–98 T100

INSPECTION PROCEDURE

1	Input signal check.

Input Signal	Indicator Light Blinking Pattern
Drive at about 40 km/h (25 mph) or below	Light ON / OFF
Drive at about 40 km/h (25 mph) or higher	Light ON / OFF

CHECK:
(a) See input signal check
(b) Check indicator light operation when driving with vehicle speed above 40 km/h (25 mph), and with vehicle speed below 40 km/h (25 mph).

OK:
Vehicle speed above 40 km/h (25 mph):
Indicator light blinks
Vehicle speed below 40 km/h (25 mph):
Indicator light stays on

OK	Check and replace cruise control actuator with ECU

NG

2	Check harness and connector between combination meter and cruise control actuator with ECU

NG	Repair or replace harness or connector.

OK

3	Check speed sensor

NG	Repair or replace speed sensor or combination meter assembly.

OK

	Check and replace cruise control actuator with ECU

TY1109900529020X

Fig. 412   Code 21: Open In Vehicle Speed Sensor Circuit (Part 2 of 2). 1997–98 T100

CIRCUIT DESCRIPTION

This circuit carries the SET/COAST, RES/ACC and CANCEL signals (each voltage) to the ECU.

DTC No.	Detection Item	Trouble Area
32	Short in control switch circuit	• Harness or connector between control switch and cruise control actuator with ECU • Cruise control switch • Cruise control actuator with ECU

TY1109900531010X

Fig. 414   Code 32: Control Switch Circuit (Part 1 of 3). 1997–98 T100

CIRCUIT DESCRIPTION

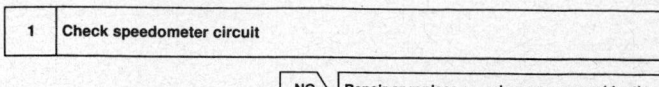

DTC No.	Detection Item	Trouble Area
23	• Actuator vehicle speed has dropped either by 16 km/h (10 mph) or more below the set speed, or by 20% or more of the set speed.	• Speed sensor (in combination meter) • Cruise control actuator with ECU

INSPECTION PROCEDURE

1	Check speedometer circuit

NG	Repair or replace speed sensor or combination meter assembly.

OK

	Check and replace cruise control actuator with ECU

TY1109900530000X

Fig. 413   Code 23: Vehicle Speed Sensor Abnormal. 1997–98 T100

INSPECTION PROCEDURE

1	Input signal check.

Input Signal	Indicator Light Blinking Pattern
SET/COAST switch	ON / OFF 2 Pulses
RES/ACC switch	ON / OFF 3 Pulses
CANCEL switch	ON / OFF SW OFF / SW ON

PREPARATION:
See input signal check
CHECK:
Check the indicator light operation when each of the SET/COAST, RES/ACC and CANCEL is turned on.
OK:
SET/COAST, RES/ACC switch
The signals shown in the table on the left should be output when each switch is ON. The signal should disappear when the switch is turned OFF.
CANCEL switch
The indicator light goes off when the cancel switch is turned ON.

OK	Wait and see.

NG

2	Check control switch.

PREPARATION:
(a)   Remove steering wheel center pad.
(b)   Disconnect control switch connector.
CHECK:
Measure resistance between terminals 3 and 4 of control switch connector when control switch is operated.

Switch position	Resistance (Ω)
Neutral	∞ (No continuity)
RES/ACC	50 – 80
SET/COAST	180 – 220
CANCEL	400 – 440

OK	Replace control switch.

NG

TY1109900531020X

Fig. 414   Code 32: Control Switch Circuit (Part 2 of 3). 1997–98 T100

3 Check harness and connector between cruise control switch and cruise control actuator with ECU

NG > Repair or replace harness or connector.

OK

4 Input signal check (See step 1).

OK > Wait and see.

NG

Check and replace cruise control actuator with ECU

TY1109900531030X

Fig. 414   Code 32: Control Switch Circuit (Part 3 of 3). 1997–98 T100

3 Check voltage between terminal STP– of cruise control actuator with ECU connector and body ground.

PREPARATION:
Remove cruise control ECU with connectors still connected.
CHECK:
(a) Turn ignition switch ON.
(b) Measure voltage between terminal STP– of cruise control ECU connector and body ground when the brake pedal is depressed and released.
OK:

Depressed	10 – 14 V
Released	Below 1 V

OK > Proceed to next circuit inspection shown on problem symptoms table

NG

4 Check for open in harness and connectors between terminal STP– of cruise control actuator with ECU and stop light switch

NG > Repair or replace harness or connector.

OK

Check and replace cruise control ECU actuator with

TY1109900532020X

Fig. 415   Stop Lamp Switch Circuit (Part 2 of 2). 1997–98 T100

CIRCUIT DESCRIPTION

When the "IDLO" terminal of ECM is turned ON, a signal is sent to the ECU. The ECU uses this signal to correct the discrepancy between the throttle valve position and the actuator position sensor valve to enable accurate cruise control at the set speed. If the idle switch is malfunctioning, problem symptoms also occur in the engine, so also inspect engine.

TY1109900533010X

Fig. 416   Idle Switch Circuit (Part 1 of 3). 1997–98 T100

CIRCUIT DESCRIPTION

When the brake is on, battery positive voltage normally applies through the STOP fuse and stop light switch to terminal STP– of the ECU, and the ECU turns the cruise control off.
A fail–safe function is provided so that cancel functions normally, even if there is a malfunction in the stop light signal circuit.
If the harness connected to terminal STP– has an open circuit, terminal STP– will have battery positive voltage and the cruise control will be turned off.
Also, when the brake is on, the magnetic clutch is cut mechanically by the stop light switch, turning the cruise control off.

INSPECTION PROCEDURE

1 Check operation of stop light.

CHECK:
Check that stop light comes on when brake pedal is depressed, and turns off when brake pedal is released.

NG > Check stop light system.

OK

2 Input signal check.

Input Signal	Indicator Light Blinking Pattern	
Stop light switch ON	Light	ON ⸺ SW OFF
		OFF - - - - ⸺ SW ON

CHECK:
(a) See input signal check
(b) Check the indicator light when the brake pedal is depressed.
OK:
The indicator light goes off when the brake pedal is depressed.

OK > Proceed to next circuit inspection shown on problem symptoms table

NG

TY1109900532010X

Fig. 415   Stop Lamp Switch Circuit (Part 1 of 2). 1997–98 T100

INSPECTION PROCEDURE

1 Check voltage between terminal IDL of ECU connector and body ground.

PREPARATION:
(a) Remove cruise control ECU with connector still connected.
(b) Disconnect ECM and ABS ECU connectors.
(c) Turn ignition switch ON.
CHECK:
Measure voltage between terminal IDL of ECU connector and body ground when the throttle valve is fully closed and fully opened.
OK:

Throttle valve position	Voltage
Fully opened	10 – 14 V
Fully closed	Below 2 V

OK > Proceed to next circuit inspection shown on problem symptoms table

NG

2 Check throttle position sensor.

PREPARATION:
Disconnect throttle position sensor connector.
CHECK:
Measure resistance between terminals 3 and 4 of throttle position sensor connector when the throttle valve is fully closed and fully opened.
OK:

Throttle valve position	Resistance
Fully opened	1 MΩ or higher
Fully closed	Below 2.3 kΩ

NG > Replace throttle position sensor.

OK

TY1109900533020X

Fig. 416   Idle Switch Circuit (Part 2 of 3). 1997–98 T100

3	Check for open and short in harness and connector between ECU and ECM

NG ▷ Repair or replace harness or connector.

OK

Check and replace cruise control actuator with ECU

TY1109900533030X

Fig. 416   Idle Switch Circuit (Part 3 of 3). 1997–98 T100

INSPECTION PROCEDURE

1	Check operation of overdrive.

PREPARATION:
Test drive after engine warms up.
CHECK:
Check that overdrive ON ↔ OFF occurs with operation of OD switch ON–OFF.

NG ▷ Check and repair electronically controlled transmission

OK

2	Check voltage between terminal OD of harness side connector of cruise control actuator with ECU and body ground.

PREPARATION:
Remove cruise control ECU with connector still connected.
CHECK:
(a)   Disconnect cruise control ECU connector.
(b)   Turn ignition switch ON.
(c)   Measure voltage between terminal OD of harness side connector of cruise control ECU and body ground.
OK:
Voltage: 10 – 14 V

NG ▷ Go to step 5.

OK

TY1109900534020X

Fig. 417   Electronically Controlled Transmission Communication Circuit (Part 2 of 4). 1997–98 T100

Check and replace cruise control actuator with ECU

TY1109900534040X

Fig. 417   Electronically Controlled Transmission Communication Circuit (Part 4 of 4). 1997–98 T100

CIRCUIT DESCRIPTION

When driving uphill under cruise control, in order to reduce shifting due to ON–OFF overdrive operation and to provide smooth driving, when down shifting in the electronically controlled transmission occurs, a signal to prevent upshift until the end of the up hill slope is sent from the cruise control ECU to the electronically controlled transmission.
Terminal ECT of the cruise control ECU detects the shift change signal (output to electronically controlled transmission No. 2 solenoid) from the electronically controlled transmission.
If vehicle speed down, also when terminal electronically controlled transmission of the cruise control ECU receives down shifting signal, it sends a signal from terminal OD to ECM to cut overdrive until the end of the uphill slope, and the gear shifts are reduced and gear shift points in the electronically controlled transmission are changed.

TY1109900534010X

Fig. 417   Electronically Controlled Transmission Communication Circuit (Part 1 of 4). 1997–98 T100

3	Check voltage between terminal ECT of cruise control actuator with ECU connector and body ground (On test drive).

PREPARATION:
(a)   Connect cruise control ECU connector.
(b)   Test drive after engine warms up.
CHECK:
Check voltage between terminal ECT of cruise control ECU connector and body ground when OD switch is ON and OFF.
OK:

OD switch position	Voltage
ON	8 – 14 V
OFF	Below 0.5 V

OK ▷ Proceed to next circuit inspection shown on problem symptoms table

NG

4	Check harness and connector between terminal ECT of cruise control actuator with ECU and electronically controlled transmission solenoid

NG ▷ Repair or replace harness or connector.

OK

Check and replace cruise control actuator with ECU

5	Check harness and connector between terminal OD of cruise control actuator with ECU and terminal OD1 of ECM

NG ▷ Repair or replace harness or connector.

OK

TY1109900534030X

Fig. 417   Electronically Controlled Transmission Communication Circuit (Part 3 of 4). 1997–98 T100

CIRCUIT DESCRIPTION

When the shift position is put in except D position, a signal is sent from the park/neutral position switch to the ECU. When this signal is input during cruise control driving, the ECU cancels the cruise control.

INSPECTION PROCEDURE

1	Check starter operation.

CHECK:
Check that the starter operates normally and that the engine starts.

NG ▷ Proceed to engine troubleshooting.

OK

TY1109900535010X

Fig. 418   Park/Neutral Position Switch Circuit (Part 1 of 3). 1997–98 T100

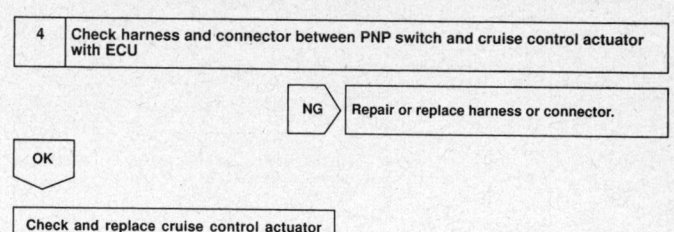

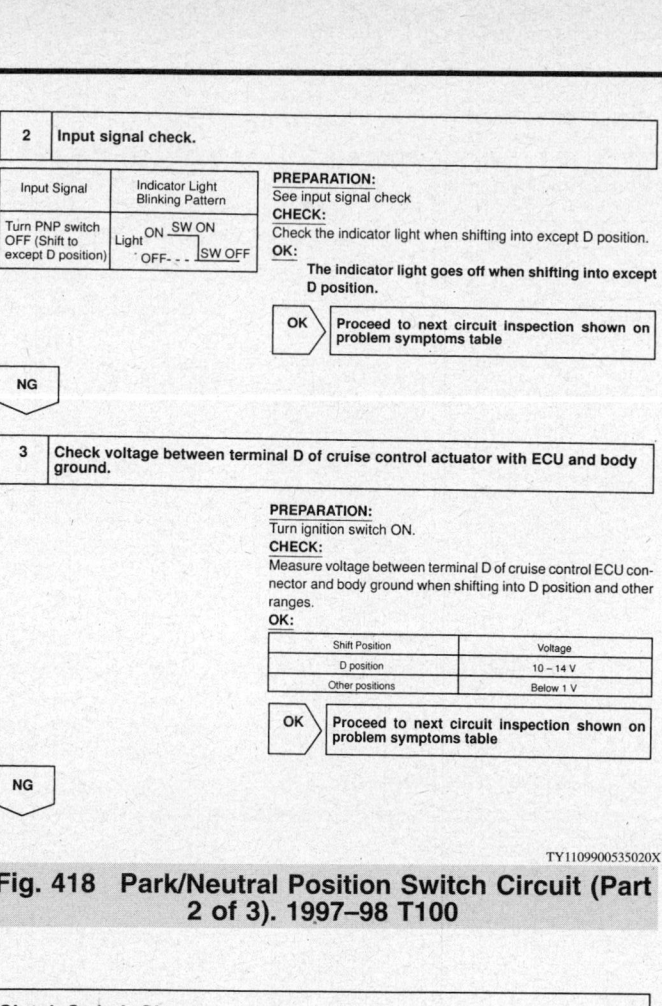

2	Input signal check.

Input Signal	Indicator Light Blinking Pattern
Turn PNP switch OFF (Shift to except D position)	Light ON — SW ON / OFF - - - SW OFF

PREPARATION:
See input signal check
CHECK:
Check the indicator light when shifting into except D position.
OK:

The indicator light goes off when shifting into except D position.

OK ⟩ Proceed to next circuit inspection shown on problem symptoms table

NG

3	Check voltage between terminal D of cruise control actuator with ECU and body ground.

PREPARATION:
Turn ignition switch ON.
CHECK:
Measure voltage between terminal D of cruise control ECU connector and body ground when shifting into D position and other ranges.
OK:

Shift Position	Voltage
D position	10 – 14 V
Other positions	Below 1 V

OK ⟩ Proceed to next circuit inspection shown on problem symptoms table

NG

TY1109900535020X

Fig. 418   Park/Neutral Position Switch Circuit (Part 2 of 3). 1997–98 T100

Clutch Switch Circuit

CIRCUIT DESCRIPTION

When the clutch pedal is depressed, the clutch switch sends a signal to the cruise control ECU. When the signal is input to the cruise control ECU during cruise control driving, the cruise control ECU cancels cruise control.

INSPECTION PROCEDURE

1	Check starter operation.

CHECK:
Check that the starter operates normally and that the engine starts.

NG ⟩ Proceed to engine troubleshooting

OK

2	Input signal check.

Input Signal	Indicator Light Blinking Pattern
Clutch switch OFF (Depress clutch pedal)	Light ON — SW ON / OFF - - - - - SW OFF

PREPARATION:
See input signal check
CHECK:
Check the indicator light when clutch pedal depressed.
OK:

The indicator light goes off when clutch pedal depressed.

OK ⟩ Proceed to next circuit inspection shown on problem symptoms table

NG

TY1109900536010X

Fig. 419   Clutch Switch Circuit (Part 1 of 2). 1997–98 T100

4	Check harness and connector between PNP switch and cruise control actuator with ECU

NG ⟩ Repair or replace harness or connector.

OK

Check and replace cruise control actuator with ECU

TY1109900535030X

Fig. 418   Park/Neutral Position Switch Circuit (Part 3 of 3). 1997–98 T100

3	Check voltage between terminal D of cruise control actuator with ECU and body ground.

PREPARATION:
Turn ignition switch ON.
CHECK:
Measure voltage between terminal D of cruise control ECU connector and body ground when clutch pedal depressed and pushed in.
OK:

Shift Position	Voltage
Clutch pedal depressed	10 – 14 V
Clutch pedal pushed in	Below 1 V

OK ⟩ Proceed to next circuit inspection shown on problem symptoms table

NG

4	Check for open in harness and connector between cruise control actuator with ECU and GAUGE fuse

NG ⟩ Repair or replace harness or connector.

OK

Check and replace cruise control actuator with ECU

TY1109900536020X

Fig. 419   Clutch Switch Circuit (Part 2 of 2). 1997–98 T100

CIRCUIT DESCRIPTION

The ECU power source supplies power to the actuator and sensors, etc. When terminal GND and the cruise control ECU case are grounded.

INSPECTION PROCEDURE

1	Check ECU–IG fuse.

PREPARATION:
Remove ECU–IG fuse from J/B No.1.
CHECK:
Check continuity of ECU–IG fuse.
OK:

Continuity

NG ⟩ Check for short in all harness and components connected to ECU–IG fuse.

OK

TY1109900537010X

Fig. 420   ECU Power Source Circuit (Part 1 of 2). 1997–98 T100

2	Check voltage between terminals B and GND of cruise control actuator with ECU connector.

PREPARATION:
Remove cruise control ECU with connector still connected.
CHECK:
(a) Turn ignition switch ON.
(b) Measure voltage between terminals B and GND of cruise mcontrol ECU connector.
OK:
10 – 14 V

OK >	Proceed to next circuit inspection shown on problem symptoms table

NG

3	Check resistance between terminal GND of cruise control actuator with ECU connector and body ground

CHECK:
Measure resistance between terminal GND of cruise control ECU connector and body ground.
OK:
Resistance: Below 1 Ω

NG >	Repair or replace harness or connector.

OK

Check and repair harness and connector between battery and cruise control actuator with ECU

TY1109900537020X

Fig. 420 ECU Power Source Circuit (Part 2 of 2). 1997–98 T100

2	Check main switch continuity.

PREPARATION:
(a) Remove steering wheel center pad
(b) Disconnect cruise control switch connector.
CHECK:
Check continuity between terminals 3 and 5 of cruise control switch connector when main switch is held on and off.
OK:

Switch position	Tester connection	Specified condition
OFF	3 – 5	No continuity
Hold ON	3 – 5	Continuity

NG >	Replace control switch.

OK

3	Check harness and connector between cruise control actuator with ECU and main switch

NG >	Repair or replace harness or connector.

OK

Check and replace cruise control actuator with ECU

TY1109900538020X

Fig. 421 Main Switch Circuit (Part 2 of 2). 1997–98 T100

CIRCUIT DESCRIPTION

When the cruise control main switch is turned off, the cruise control does not operate.

INSPECTION PROCEDURE

1	Check voltage between terminal CMS of cruise control actuator with ECU connector and body ground.

PREPARATION:
Remove cruise control ECU with connector still connected.
CHECK:
(a) Turn ignition switch ON.
(b) Measure voltage between terminal CMS of cruise control ECU connector and body ground when main switch is held on and off.
OK:

Main switch	Voltage
OFF	10 – 14 V
ON	Below 1 V

OK >	Proceed to next circuit inspection shown on problem symptoms table

NG

TY1109900538010X

Fig. 421 Main Switch Circuit (Part 1 of 2). 1997–98 T100

CIRCUIT DESCRIPTION

When the cruise control main switch is turned ON, CRUISE MAIN indicator light lights up.

INSPECTION PROCEDURE

1	Check voltage between terminals PI of cruise control actuator with ECU connector and body ground.

PREPARATION:
Turn ignition switch ON.
CHECK:
Measure voltage between terminals PI of cruise control ECU connector and body ground when main switch on and off.
OK:

Switch position	Voltage
OFF	10 – 16 V
ON	Below 1.2 V

OK >	Proceed to next circuit inspection shown on problem symptoms table

NG

TY1109900539010X

Fig. 422 Cruise Main Indicator Lamp (Part 1 of 2). 1997–98 T100

2	Check combination meter

NG >	Replace combination meter.

OK

Check and replace cruise control actuator with ECU

TY1109900539020X

Fig. 422 Cruise Main Indicator Lamp (Part 2 of 2). 1997–98 T100

CIRCUIT DESCRIPTION

This circuit sends a signal to the ECU that DTC output is required.

INSPECTION PROCEDURE

1	Check voltage between terminals Tc and E₁ of DLC1.

CHECK:
(a) Turn ignition switch ON.
(b) Measure voltage between terminals Tc and E₁ of DLC1.
OK:
Voltage: 10 – 14 V

| OK | Proceed to next circuit inspection shown on problem symptoms table |

| NG |

TY1109900540010X

Fig. 423   Diagnosis Circuit (Part 1 of 2). 1997–98 T100

INSPECTION PROCEDURE

1	Check actuator control cable.

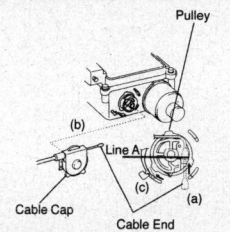

PREPARATION:
1. Remove actuator control cable.
(a) Insert the inner cable end into the pulley and pull it up to the line "A", show in the illustration.
   The end of the spring prevents to pulley from slipping out.
(b) Install the cable cap to the fit it with the actuator.
(c) Turn the cable cap clockwise to lock.
2. Install actuator control cable.
Installation in the reverse order of removal.
CHECK:
(a) Check that the actuator, control cable throttle link are properly installed and that the cable and link are connected correctly.
(b) Check that the actuator and bell crank are operating smoothly.
(c) Check that the cable is not loose or too tight.
OK:
Freeplay: less than 10 mm
HINT:
• If the control cable is very loose, the vehicle's loss of speed going uphill will be large.
• If the control cable is too tight, the idle RPM will become high.

TY1109900541000X

Fig. 424   Actuator Control Cable Inspection. 1997–98 T100

2	Check harness and connector between cruise control actuator with ECU and DLC1, DLC1 and body ground

| NG | Repair or replace harness or connector. |

| OK |

| Check and replace cruise control actuator with ECU |

TY1109900540020X

Fig. 423   Diagnosis Circuit (Part 2 of 2). 1997–98 T100

Symptom	Suspect Area
• Cruise control system does not set. • Cruise control system does not operate.	Input signal check No.4: OK 1. ECU Power Source Circuit 2. Wire Harness 3. Cruise Control Main Switch Circuit 4. Cruise Control Switch Circuit 5. Stop Light Switch Circuit 6. PNP Switch or Clutch Switch Circuit 7. Cable 8. Cruise Control Actuator Circuit 9. Cruise Control ECU Input signal check No.4: NG 1. Vehicle Speed Sensor Circuit 2. Cruise Control ECU
Indicator light does not light up.	1. Wire Harness 2. Indicator Light Circuit 3. Cruise Control ECU
Vehicle speed drop when the cruise control switch turned to SET.	1. Cable 2. ECU Power Source Circuit 3. Throttle Position Sensor (IDL) Circuit 4. Cruise Control Actuator Circuit 5. Cruise Control ECU
Set speed deviates on high or low side.	Input signal check No.4: OK 1. Vehicle Speed Sensor Circuit 2. Cable 3. ECU Power Source Circuit 4. Cruise Control Actuator Circuit 5. Cruise Control ECU Input signal check No.4: NG 1. Cruise Control ECU
Vehicle speed fluctuates when cruise control switch turn to SET.	1. Vehicle Speed Sensor Circuit 2. Cable 3. Throttle Position Sensor Circuit 4. ECT Communecation Circuit 4. Cruise Control Actuator Circuit 5. Cruise Control ECU
Acceleration response is sluggish when cruise control switch turn to "ACCEL" or "RESUME".	Input signal check No.4: OK 1. Cable 2. Vehicle Speed Sensor Circuit 3. Cruise Control Actuator Circuit 4. Cruise Control ECU Input signal check No.4: NG 1. Cruise Control Switch Circuit 2. Cruise Control ECU
Set speed does not cancel when brake pedal depressed.	Input signal check No.3: OK 1. Cruise Control ECU Input signal check No.3: NG 1. Stop Light Switch Circuit 2. Cruise Control ECU
Cruise control does not cancel when transmission is shifted to except D range. (A/T)	Input signal check No.3: OK 1. Cruise Control ECU Input signal check No.3: NG 1. PNP Switch Circuit 2. Cruise Control ECU

TY1109900630010X

Fig. 425   Problem Symptoms Table (Part 1 of 2). 4Runner except Ford cruise control

Symptom	Suspect Area
Cruise control does not cancel when clutch pedal depressed.	Input signal check No.3: OK 1. Cruise control ECU Input signal check No.3: NG 1. Clutch Switch Circuit 2. Cruise Control ECU
Cruise control does not cancel when cruise control switch turned to CANCEL.	Input signal check No.3: OK 1. Cruise Control ECU Input signal check No.3: NG 1. Cruise Control Switch Circuit 2. Cruise Control ECU
Vehicle Speed does not decrease when cruise control switch turned to COAST.	Input signal check No.1: OK 1. Cruise Control Actuator Circuit 2. Cable 3. Vehicle Speed Sensor Circuit 4. Cruise Control ECU Input signal check No.1: NG 1. Cruise Control Switch Circuit 2. Cruise Control ECU
Vehicle speed does not accelerate when cruise control switch turned to ACCEL.	Input signal check No.2: OK 1. Cruise Control Actuator Circuit 2. Cable 3. Vehicle Speed Sensor Circuit 4. Cruise Control ECU Input signal check No.2: NG 1. Cruise Control Switch Circuit 2. Cruise Control ECU
Vehicle speed does not return to memorized speed when cruise control switch turned to RESUME.	Input signal check No.2: OK 1. Cruise Control Actuator Circuit 2. Cable 3. Vehicle Speed Sensor Circuit 4. Cruise Control ECU Input signal check No.2: NG 1. Cruise Control Switch Circuit 2. Cruise Control ECU
Speed can be set below about 40 km/h (25 mph).	Input signal check No.4: OK 1. Cruise Control ECU Input signal check No.4: NG 1. Vehicle Speed Sensor Circuit 2. Cruise Control ECU
Cruise control does not cancel when speed is less than 40 km/h (25 mph).	Input signal check No.4: OK 1. Cruise Control Actuator Circuit 2. Cruise Control ECU Input signal check No.4: NG 1. Vehicle Speed Sensor Circuit 2. Cruise Control ECU

TY1109900630020X

Fig. 425   Problem Symptoms Table (Part 2 of 2). 4Runner except Ford cruise control

CIRCUIT DESCRIPTION

The actuator motor is operated by signals from the ECU. Acceleration and deceleration signals are transmitted by changes in the Duty Ratio (See note below).

Duty Ratio

The duty ratio is the ratio of the period of continuity in one cycle. For example, if A is the period of continuity in one cycle, and B is the period of non–continuity, then.

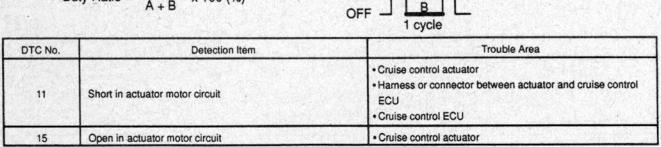

$$\text{Duty Ratio} = \frac{A}{A + B} \times 100 \ (\%)$$

DTC No.	Detection Item	Trouble Area
11	Short in actuator motor circuit	• Cruise control actuator • Harness or connector between actuator and cruise control ECU • Cruise control ECU
15	Open in actuator motor circuit	• Cruise control actuator

TY1109900574010X

Fig. 427   Codes 11 & 15: Actuator Motor Circuit (Part 1 of 2). 1996–97 4Runner

Symptom	Suspect Area
• SET not occurring or CANCEL occurring. (DTC is Normal)	1. Main Switch Circuit(Cruise control switch) 2. Vehicle Speed Sensor 3. Control Switch Circuit (Cruise control switch) 4. Stop Light Switch Circuit 5. PNP Switch or Clutch Switch Circuit 6. Cruise Control Actuator and ECU
SET not occurring or CANCEL occurring. (DTC does not output)	1. ECU Power Source Circuit 2. Cruise Control Actuator and ECU
Actual vehicle speed deveates above or below the set speed.	1. Vehicle Speed Signal Abnormal 2. Electronically Controlled Transmission Communication Circuit 3. dle Signal (Main throttle position sensor) 4. Cruise Control Actuator and ECU
Gear shifting frequent between 3rd O/D when driving on uphill road. (Hunting)	1. Electronically Controlled Transmission Communication Circuit 2. Cruise Control Actuator and ECU
Cruise control not cancelled, even when brake pedal is depressed.	1. Stop Light Switch Circuit 2. Cruise Control Actuator and ECU
Cruise control not cancelled, even when transmission is shifted to "N" position.	1. PNP Switch Circuit 2. Cruise Control Actuator and ECU
Cruise control is not canceled when clutch pedal depressed.	1. Clutch Switch Circuit 2. Cruise Control Actuator and ECU
Control switch dose not operate. (SET/COAST, ACC/RES, CANCEL not possible)	1. Control Switch Circuit (Cruise Control Switch) 2. Cruise Control Actuator and ECU
SET possible at 40km/h (25 mph) or less, or CANCEL does not operate at 40km/h (25 mph) or less.	1. Vehicle Speed Signal Abnormal 2. Cruise Control Actuator and ECU
Poor response in ACCEL and RESUME modes.	1. Electronically Controlled Transmission Communication Circuit 2. Cruise Control Actuator and ECU
O/D does not resume, even though the road is not uphill.	1. Electronically Controlled Transmission Communication Circuit 2. Cruise Control Actuator and ECU
DTC memory is erased.	1. ECU Power Souce Circuit 2. Cruise Control Actuator and ECU
DTC is not output, or is output when it should not be.	1. Diagnosis Circuit 2. Cruise Control Actuator and ECU
Cruise MAIN indicator light remains ON or fails to light up.	1. Cruise MAIN Indicator Light Switch Circuit

TY1109900614000X

Fig. 426   Problem Symptoms Table. 4Runner w/Ford cruise control

INSPECTION PROCEDURE

1   Check resistance between terminals MO and MC of cruise control actuator.

PREPARATION:
(a)   Ignition switch ON.
(b)   Disconnect actuator connector.
CHECK:
Measure resistance between terminals 5 (1) and 6 (2).
( ): 5VZ Engine
HINT:
If control plate position is fully opened or fully closed, resistance can not measure.
OK:
Resistance: more than 4.2 Ω

NG ▷ Replace cruise control actuator.

OK

2   Check wire harness and connector between terminals MO of cruise control ECU and MO of cruise control actuator

NG ▷ Repair or replace harness or connector.

OK

Replace cruise control ECU.

TY1109900574020X

Fig. 427   Codes 11 & 15: Actuator Motor Circuit (Part 2 of 2). 1996–97 4Runner

A

CIRCUIT DESCRIPTION

This circuit turns on the magnetic clutch inside the actuator during cruise control operation according to the signal from the ECU. If a malfunction occurs in the actuator or speed sensor, etc. during cruise control operation, the rotor shaft between the motor and control plate is released.
When the brake pedal is depressed, the stoplight switch turns on, supplying electrical power to the stoplight. Power supply to the magnetic clutch is mechanically cut and the magnetic clutch is turned OFF.
When driving downhill, if the vehicle speed exceeds the set speed by 15 km/h (6 mph) above the set speed, then cruise control at the set speed is resumed.

DTC No.	Detection Item	Trouble Area
12	• Short in magnetic clutch circuit. • Open (0.8 sec.) in magnetic clutch circuit	• Cruise control actuator magnetic clutch • Harness or connector between ECU and magnetic clutch, magnetic clutch and body ground • Cruise control ECU

TY1109900575010X

Fig. 428   Code 12: Magnetic Clutch Circuit (Part 1 of 2). 1996–97 4Runner

CIRCUIT DESCRIPTION

The circuit detects the rotation position of the actuator control plate and sends a signal to the ECU.

DTC No.	Detection Item	Trouble Area
13	• Position Sensor detects abnormal voltage.	• Cruise control actuator motor • Cruise control actuator position sensor
14	• Open in actuator motor circuit. • Position sensor signal valve does not change when the motor operates.	• Harness or connector between actuator position sensor and body ground • Harness or connector between actuator motor and ECU • ECU

TY1109900576010X

Fig. 429   Code 13: Actuator Position Sensor Circuit (Part 1 of 3). 1996–97 4Runner w/3RZ-FE engine

INSPECTION PROCEDURE

1   Check resistance between terminals VR1 and VR3 of actuator.

PREPARATION:
Disconnect the actuator connector.
CHECK:
Measure resistance between actuator terminal 1 and 3 of actuator connector.
OK:
    Resistance: 1.8 ~ 2.2 kΩ (25 °C)

NG ▷ Replace actuator.

OK

2   Check voltage between terminals VR2 and VR3 of cruise control actuator.

PREPARATION:
Turn ignition switch ON.
CHECK:
Measure voltage between terminals 2 and 3 of actuator connector while turning control plate slowly by hand from the deceleration side to the acceleration side.
OK:
    Voltage:
    Fully closed: Approx. 1.3 V
    Fully opened: Approx. 4.6 V
HINT:
As the control plate is turned, the voltage should increase gradually without interruption.

NG ▷ Replace cruise control actuator.

OK

TY1109900576020X

Fig. 429   Code 13: Actuator Position Sensor Circuit (Part 2 of 3). 1996–97 4Runner w/3RZ-FE engine

INSPECTION PROCEDURE

1   Check actuator arm locking operation

TY1109900577010X

Fig. 430   Code 14: Actuator Mechanical Fault (Part 1 of 3). 1996–97 4Runner w/3RZ-FE engine

INSPECTION PROCEDURE

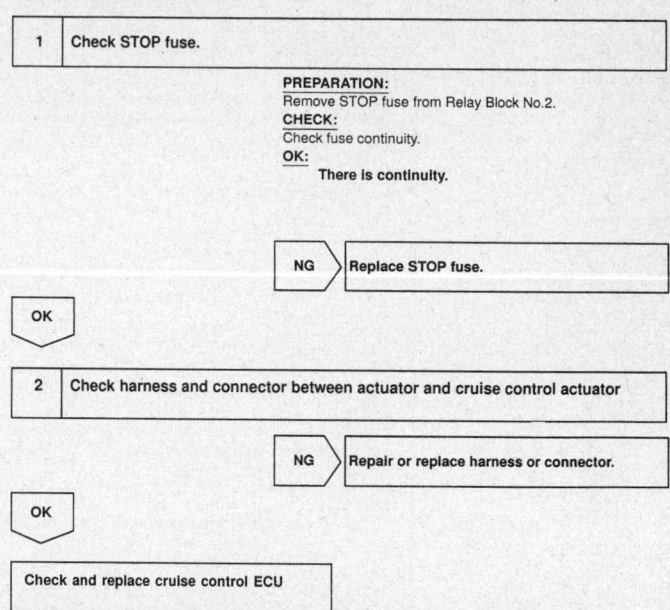

1   Check STOP fuse.

PREPARATION:
Remove STOP fuse from Relay Block No.2.
CHECK:
Check fuse continuity.
OK:
    There is continuity.

NG ▷ Replace STOP fuse.

OK

2   Check harness and connector between actuator and cruise control actuator

NG ▷ Repair or replace harness or connector.

OK

Check and replace cruise control ECU

TY1109900575020X

Fig. 428   Code 12: Magnetic Clutch Circuit (Part 2 of 2). 1996–97 4Runner

3   Check for open and short in harness and connector between ECU and actuator position sensor

NG ▷ Repair or replace harness or connector.

OK

Check and replace cruise control ECU

TY1109900576030X

Fig. 429   Code 13: Actuator Position Sensor Circuit (Part 3 of 3). 1996–97 4Runner w/3RZ-FE engine

2	Check actuator operation.

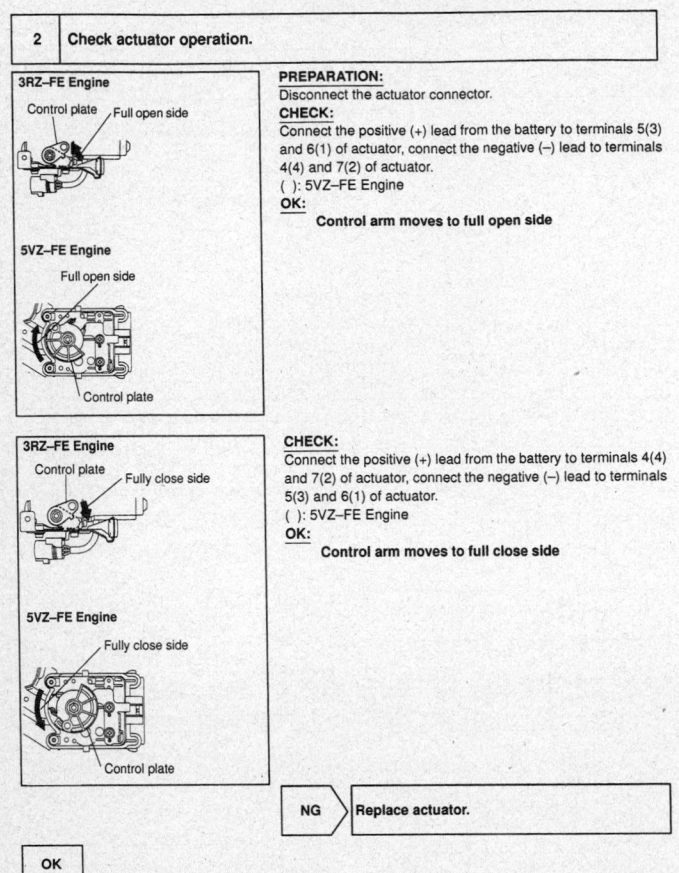

3RZ–FE Engine
Control plate / Full open side

5VZ–FE Engine
Full open side
Control plate

PREPARATION:
Disconnect the actuator connector.
CHECK:
Connect the positive (+) lead from the battery to terminals 5(3) and 6(1) of actuator, connect the negative (–) lead to terminals 4(4) and 7(2) of actuator.
( ): 5VZ–FE Engine
OK:
    Control arm moves to full open side

3RZ–FE Engine
Control plate / Fully close side

5VZ–FE Engine
Fully close side
Control plate

CHECK:
Connect the positive (+) lead from the battery to terminals 4(4) and 7(2) of actuator, connect the negative (–) lead to terminals 5(3) and 6(1) of actuator.
( ): 5VZ–FE Engine
OK:
    Control arm moves to full close side

NG	Replace actuator.

OK

TY1109900577020X

Fig. 430 Code 14: Actuator Mechanical Fault (Part 2 of 3). 1996–97 4Runner w/3RZ-FE engine

CIRCUIT DESCRIPTION

The vehicle speed sensor circuit is sent to cruise control ECU as vehicle speed signal. For each rotation of the shaft, the vehicle speed sensor sends a signal through the combination meter (5VZ–FE: ABS ECU and combination meter) to the cruise control ECU (See the following). The ECU calculates the vehicle speed from this pulse frequency.

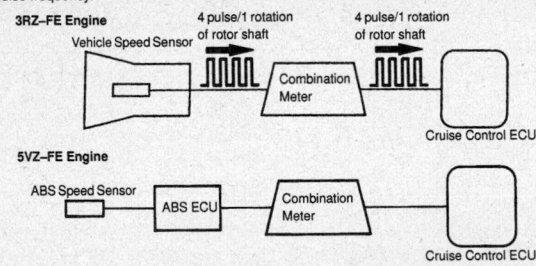

3RZ–FE Engine
Vehicle Speed Sensor — 4 pulse/1 rotation of rotor shaft — Combination Meter — 4 pulse/1 rotation of rotor shaft — Cruise Control ECU

5VZ–FE Engine
ABS Speed Sensor — ABS ECU — Combination Meter — Cruise Control ECU

DTC No.	Detection Item	Trouble Area
21	Speed signal is not input to the cruise control ECU while cruise control is set.	• Vehicle speed sensor • ABS speed sensor (5VZ–FE) • ABS ECU (5VZ–FE) • Combination meter • Harness or connector between ABS speed sensor and ABS ECU, ABS ECU and combination meter, combination meter and cruise control ECU (5VZ–FE) • Harness or connector between vehicle speed sensor and combination meter, combination meter and cruise control ECU (3RZ–FE) • Cruise control ECU

TY1109900578010X

Fig. 431 Code 21: Open In Vehicle Speed Sensor Circuit (Part 1 of 3). 1996–97 4Runner

3	Check harness and connector between actuator and cruise control ECU

NG	Repair or replace harness or connector.

OK

Check and replace cruise control ECU

TY1109900577030X

Fig. 430 Code 14: Actuator Mechanical Fault (Part 3 of 3). 1996–97 4Runner w/3RZ-FE engine

INSPECTION PROCEDURE

1	Input signal check.

Input Signal	Indicator Light Blinking Pattern
Drive at about 40 km/h (25 mph) or below	Light ON ___ OFF -----
Drive at about 40 km/h (25 mph) or higher	Light ON ⊓⊓⊓ OFF

CHECK:
(a) See input signal check.
(b) Check indicator light operation when driving with vehicle speed above 40 km/h (25 mph), and with vehicle speed below 40 km/h (25 mph).
OK:
    Vehicle speed above 40 km/h (25 mph):
        Indicator light blinks
    Vehicle speed below 40 km/h (25 mph):
        Indicator light stays on

OK	Check and replace cruise control ECU

NG

TY1109900578020X

Fig. 431 Code 21: Open In Vehicle Speed Sensor Circuit (Part 2 of 3). 1996–97 4Runner

2	Check harness and connector between speed meter and cruise control ECU

NG	Repair or replace harness or connector.

OK

3	Check vehicle speed sensor

NG	Replace vehicle speed sensor.

OK

Check and replace cruise control ECU

TY1109900578030X

Fig. 431 Code 21: Open In Vehicle Speed Sensor Circuit (Part 3 of 3). 1996–97 4Runner

CIRCUIT DESCRIPTION

DTC No.	Detection Item	Trouble Area
23	• Actual vehicle speed has dropped either by 16 km/h (10 mph) or more below the set speed, or by 20 % or more of the set speed. • Vehicle speed sensor pulse is abnormal. (When speed signal is not input to the ECU below 0.2 sec., code will be displayed.)	• Vehicle speed sensor • Cruise control ECU

INSPECTION PROCEDURE

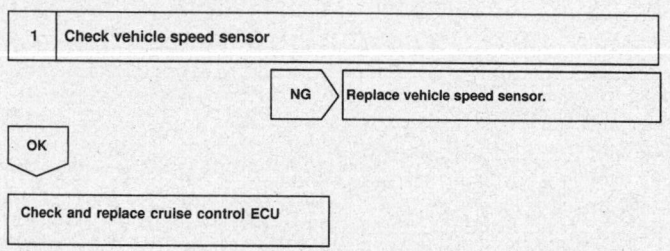

1	Check vehicle speed sensor

NG → Replace vehicle speed sensor.

OK

Check and replace cruise control ECU

TY1109900579000X

Fig. 432   Code 23: Vehicle Speed Sensor Abnormal. 1996–97 4Runner

INSPECTION PROCEDURE

1	Input signal check.

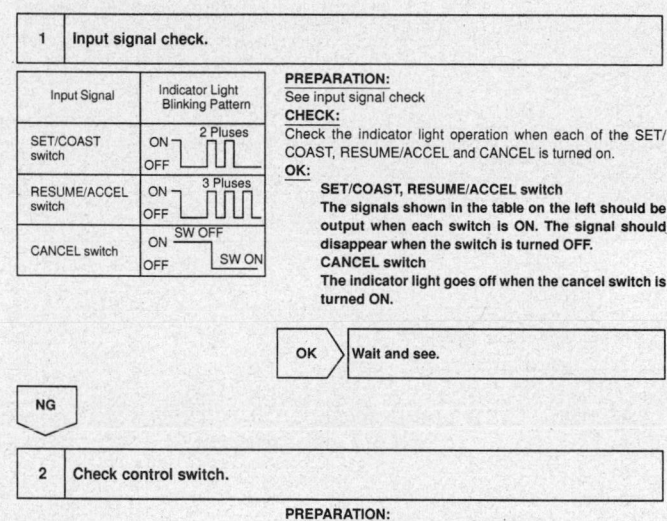

Input Signal	Indicator Light Blinking Pattern
SET/COAST switch	ON ⎍⎍ 2 Pluses / OFF
RESUME/ACCEL switch	ON ⎍⎍⎍ 3 Pluses / OFF
CANCEL switch	ON SW OFF / OFF SW ON

PREPARATION:
See input signal check
CHECK:
Check the indicator light operation when each of the SET/COAST, RESUME/ACCEL and CANCEL is turned on.
OK:
SET/COAST, RESUME/ACCEL switch
The signals shown in the table on the left should be output when each switch is ON. The signal should disappear when the switch is turned OFF.
CANCEL switch
The indicator light goes off when the cancel switch is turned ON.

OK → Wait and see.

NG

2	Check control switch.

PREPARATION:
(a) Remove steering wheel center pad.
(b) Disconnect control switch connector.
CHECK:
Measure resistance between terminals 3 and 4 of control switch connector when control switch is operated.

Switch position	Resistance (Ω)
Neutral	∞ (No continuity)
RES/ACC	50 – 80
SET/COAST	180 – 220
CANCEL	400 – 440

OK → Replace control switch.

NG

TY1109900580020X

Fig. 433   Code 32: Control Switch Circuit (Part 2 of 3). 1996–97 4Runner

CIRCUIT DESCRIPTION

This circuit carries the SET/COAST, RESUME/Accel and CANCEL signals (each voltage) to the ECU.

DTC No.	Detection Item	Trouble Area
32	Short in control switch circuit	• Cruise control switch • Harness or connector between control switch and cruise control ECU. • Cruise control ECU

TY1109900580010X

Fig. 433   Code 32: Control Switch Circuit (Part 1 of 3). 1996–97 4Runner

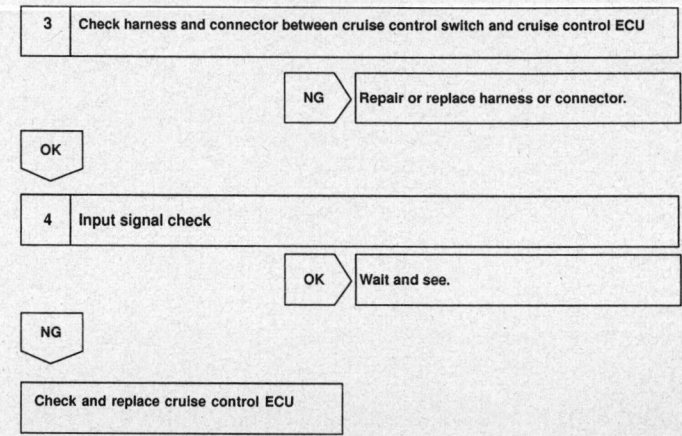

3	Check harness and connector between cruise control switch and cruise control ECU

NG → Repair or replace harness or connector.

OK

4	Input signal check

OK → Wait and see.

NG

Check and replace cruise control ECU

TY1109900580030X

Fig. 433   Code 32: Control Switch Circuit (Part 3 of 3). 1996–97 4Runner

CIRCUIT DESCRIPTION

When the idle switch in turned ON, a signal is sent to the ECU. The ECU uses this signal to correct the discrepancy between the throttle valve position and the actuator position sensor value to enable accurate cruise control at the set speed. If the idle switch is malfunctioning, problem symptoms also occur in the engine, so also inspect the engine.

DTC No.	Detection Item	Trouble Area
51	Short in idle signal circuit	• Harness or connector between cruise control ECU and throttle position sensor • Throttle position sensor • Cruise control ECU

TY1109900581010X

Fig. 434   Code 51: Idle Signal Circuit (Part 1 of 2). 1996–97 4Runner

INSPECTION PROCEDURE

```
┌─────────────────────────────────────────────┐
│ 1  Check throttle position sensor circuit      │
└─────────────────────────────────────────────┘
          NG ▷ Replace throttle position sensor.

    OK

┌─────────────────────────────────────────────┐
│ 2  Check harness and connector between ECM and │
│    throttle position sensor                     │
└─────────────────────────────────────────────┘
          NG ▷ Repair or replace harness or connector.

    OK

┌─────────────────────────────────────────────┐
│ 3  Check harness and connector between cruise   │
│    control ECU and throttle position sensor     │
└─────────────────────────────────────────────┘
          NG ▷ Repair or replace harness or connector.

    OK

┌─────────────────────────────────────────────┐
│ Check and replace cruise control ECU            │
└─────────────────────────────────────────────┘
```

TY1109900581020X

**Fig. 434   Code 51: Idle Signal Circuit (Part 2 of 2).
1996–97 4Runner**

INSPECTION PROCEDURE

```
┌─────────────────────────────────────────────┐
│ 1  Check operation of stop light.              │
└─────────────────────────────────────────────┘
```
CHECK:
Check that stop light comes on when brake pedal is depressed, and turns off when brake pedal is released.

```
          NG ▷ Check stop light system.

    OK

┌─────────────────────────────────────────────┐
│ 2  Input signal check.                          │
└─────────────────────────────────────────────┘
```

Input Signal	Indicator Light Blinking Pattern
Stop Light switch ON	Light ON ─┐ SW OFF OFP - - - -┘ SW ON

CHECK:
(a) See input signal check
(b) Check the indicator light when the brake pedal is depressed.
OK:
The indicator light goes off when the brake pedal is depressed.

```
          OK ▷ Proceed to next circuit inspection shown on
                matrix chart

    NG
```

TY1109900582020X

**Fig. 435   Stop Lamp Switch Circuit (Part 2 of 3).
1996–97 4Runner**

CIRCUIT DESCRIPTION

When the brake is on, battery positive voltage normally applies through the STOP fuse and stop light switch to terminal STP– of the ECU, and the ECU turns the cruise control off.
A fail–safe function is provided so that cancel functions normally, even if there is a malfunction in the stop light signal circuit.
  If the harness connected to terminal STP– has an open circuit, terminal STP– will have battery positive voltage and the cruise control will be turned off.
Also, when the brake is on, the magnetic clutch is cut mechanically by the stop light switch, turning the cruise control off.

TY1109900582010X

**Fig. 435   Stop Lamp Switch Circuit (Part 1 of 3).
1996–97 4Runner**

```
┌─────────────────────────────────────────────┐
│ 3  Check voltage between terminal STP– of cruise│
│    control ECU connector and body ground.       │
└─────────────────────────────────────────────┘
```
PREPARATION:
Remove cruise control ECU with connectors still connected.
CHECK:
(a) Turn ignition switch ON.
(b) Measure voltage between terminal STP– of cruise control ECU connector and body ground, when the brake pedal is depressed and released.
OK:

Depressed	10 – 14 V
Released	Below 1 V

```
          OK ▷ Proceed to next circuit inspection shown on
                matrix chart

    NG

┌─────────────────────────────────────────────┐
│ 4  Check for open in harness and connectors     │
│    between terminal STP– of cruise con-         │
│    trol ECU  and stop light switch              │
└─────────────────────────────────────────────┘
          NG ▷ Repair or replace harness or connector.

    OK

┌─────────────────────────────────────────────┐
│ Check and replace cruise control ECU            │
└─────────────────────────────────────────────┘
```

TY1109900582030X

**Fig. 435   Stop Lamp Switch Circuit (Part 3 of 3).
1996–97 4Runner**

CIRCUIT DESCRIPTION

When the idle switch is turned ON, a signal is sent to the ECU. The ECU uses this signal to correct the discrepancy between the throttle valve position and the actuator position sensor valve to enable accurate cruise control at the set speed. If the idle switch is malfunctioning, problem symptoms also occur in the engine, so also inspect engine.

TY1109900583010X

**Fig. 436   Idle Switch Circuit (Part 1 of 3). 1996–97
4Runner w/3RZ-FE engine**

INSPECTION PROCEDURE

1	Check voltage between terminal IDL of ECU connector and body ground.

PREPARATION:
(a) Remove cruise control ECU with connector still connected.
(b) Disconnect ECM and ABS ECU connectors.
(c) Ignition switch ON.
CHECK:
Measure voltage between terminal IDL of ECU connector and body ground when the throttle valve is fully closed and fully opened.
OK:

Throttle valve position	Voltage
Fully opened	10 – 14 V
Fully closed	Below 2 V

> **OK** → Proceed to next circuit inspection shown on matrix chart

NG ↓

2	Check throttle position sensor.

PREPARATION:
Disconnect throttle position sensor connector.
CHECK:
Measure resistance between terminals 3 and 4 of throttle position sensor connector when the throttle valve is fully closed and fully opened.
OK:

Throttle valve position	Resistance
Fully opened	1 MΩ or higher
Fully closed	Below 2.3 kΩ

> **NG** → Replace throttle position sensor.

OK ↓

TY1109900583020X

Fig. 436   Idle Switch Circuit (Part 2 of 3). 1996–97 4Runner w/3RZ-FE engine

CIRCUIT DESCRIPTION

When driving uphill under cruise control, in order to reduce shifting due to ON–OFF overdrive operation and to provide smooth driving, when down shifting in the electronically controlled transmission occurs, a signal to prevent upshift until the end of the up hill slope is sent from the cruise control ECU to the electronically controlled transmission.
Terminal ECM of the cruise control ECU detects the shift change signal (output to electronically controlled transmission No. 2 solenoid) from the electronically controlled transmission.
If vehicle speed down, also when terminal electronically controlled transmission of the cruise control ECU receives down shifting signal, it sends a signal from terminal OD to ECM to cut overdrive until the end of the uphill slope, and the gear shifts are reduced and gear shift points in the electronically controlled transmission are changed.

TY1109900584010X

Fig. 437   Electronically Controlled Transmission Communication Circuit (Part 1 of 3). 1996–97 4Runner

3	Check for open and short in harness and connector between ECU and throttle position sensor, throttle position sensor and body ground

> **NG** → Repair or replace harness or connector.

OK ↓

Check and replace cruise control ECU

TY1109900583030X

Fig. 436   Idle Switch Circuit (Part 3 of 3). 1996–97 4Runner w/3RZ-FE engine

INSPECTION PROCEDURE

1	Check operation of overdrive.

PREPARATION:
Test drive after engine warms up.
CHECK:
Check that overdrive ON ↔ OFF occurs with operation of OD switch ON–OFF.

> **NG** → Check and repair electronically controlled transmission

OK ↓

2	Check voltage between terminal OD of harness side connector of cruise control ECU and body ground.

PREPARATION:
Remove cruise control ECU with connector still connected.
CHECK:
(a) Disconnect cruise control ECU connector.
(b) Turn ignition switch ON.
(c) Measure voltage between terminal OD of harness side connector of cruise control ECU and body ground.
OK:
Voltage: 10 – 14 V

> **NG** → Go to step 5.

OK ↓

TY1109900584020X

Fig. 437   Electronically Controlled Transmission Communication Circuit (Part 2 of 3). 1996–97 4Runner

3 Check voltage between terminal ECT of cruise control ECU connector and body ground (On test drive).

PREPARATION:
(a) Connect cruise control ECU connector.
(b) Test drive after engine warms up.
CHECK:
Check voltage between terminal ECT of cruise control ECU connector and body ground when OD switch is ON and OFF.
OK:

OD switch position	Voltage
ON	8 – 14 V
OFF	Below 0.5 V

OK → Proceed to next circuit inspection shown on matrix chart

NG ↓

4 Check harness and connector between terminal ECT of cruise control ECU and electronically controlled transmission solenoid

NG → Repair or replace harness or connector.

OK ↓

Check and replace cruise control ECU.

5 Check harness and connector between terminal OD of cruise control ECU and terminal OD1 of ECM

NG → Repair or replace harness or connector.

OK ↓

Check and replace cruise control ECU

TY1109900584030X

Fig. 437 Electronically Controlled Transmission Communication Circuit (Part 3 of 3). 1996–97 4Runner

INSPECTION PROCEDURE

1 Check starter operation.

CHECK:
Check that the starter operates normally and that the engine starts.

NG → Proceed to engine troubleshooting.

OK ↓

2 Input signal check.

Input Signal	Indicator Light Blinking Pattern
Turn PNP switch OFF (Shift to except D range)	Light ON — SW ON / OFF - - - - SW OFF

PREPARATION:
See input signal check
CHECK:
Check the indicator light when shifting into except D range.
OK:
The indicator light goes off when shifting into except D range.

OK → Proceed to next circuit inspection shown on matrix chart

NG ↓

TY1109900585020X

Fig. 438 Park/Neutral position Switch Circuit (Part 2 of 3). 1996–97 4Runner

CIRCUIT DESCRIPTION

When the shift position is put in except D position, a signal is sent from the park/neutral position switch to the ECU. When this signal is input during cruise control driving, the ECU cancels the cruise control.

TY1109900585010X

Fig. 438 Park/Neutral position Switch Circuit (Part 1 of 3). 1996–97 4Runner

3 Check voltage between terminal D of cruise control ECU and body ground.

PREPARATION:
Turn ignition switch ON.
CHECK:
Measure voltage between terminal D of cruise control ECU connector and body ground when shifting into D position and other ranges.
OK:

Shift Position	Voltage
D range	10 – 14 V
Other ranges	Below 1 V

OK → Proceed to next circuit inspection shown on matrix chart

NG ↓

4 Check harness and connector between PNP switch and cruise control ECU

NG → Repair or replace harness or connector.

OK ↓

Check and replace cruise control ECU

TY1109900585030X

Fig. 438 Park/Neutral position Switch Circuit (Part 3 of 3). 1996–97 4Runner

CIRCUIT DESCRIPTION

When the clutch pedal is depressed, the clutch switch sends a signal to the cruise control ECU. When the signal is input to the cruise control ECU during cruise control driving, the cruise control ECU cancels cruise control.

INSPECTION PROCEDURE

1 Check starter operation.

CHECK:
Check that the starter operates normally and that the engine starts.

NG → Proceed to engine troubleshooting.

OK ↓

2 Input signal check.

Input Signal	Indicator Light Blinking Pattern
Clutch switch OFF (Depress clutch pedal)	Light ON — SW ON / OFF - - - - SW OFF

PREPARATION:
See input signal check
CHECK:
Check the indicator light when shifting into except D range.
OK:
The indicator light goes off when shifting into except D range.

OK → Proceed to next circuit inspection shown on matrix chart

NG ↓

TY1109900586010X

Fig. 439 Clutch Switch Circuit (Part 1 of 2). 1996–97 4Runner

3 Check voltage between terminal D of cruise control ECU and body ground.

PREPARATION:
Turn ignition switch ON.
CHECK:
Measure voltage between terminal D of cruise control ECU connector and body ground when shifting into D position and other ranges.
OK:

Shift Position	Voltage
D range	10 – 14 V
Other ranges	Below 1 V

OK ▷ Proceed to next circuit inspection shown on matrix chart

NG

4 Check for open in harness and connector between ECU and GAUGE fuse.

NG ▷ Repair or replace harness or connector.

OK

Check and replace cruise control ECU

TY1109900586020X

Fig. 439 Clutch Switch Circuit (Part 2 of 2). 1996–97 4Runner

INSPECTION PROCEDURE

1 Check ECU–IG fuse.

PREPARATION:
Remove ECU–IG fuse from junction block No.1.
CHECK:
Check continuity of ECU–IG fuse.
OK:
Continuity

NG ▷ Check for short in all the harness and components connected to ECU–IG fuse.

OK

2 Check voltage between terminals B and GND of cruise control ECU connector.

PREPARATION:
Remove cruise control ECU with connector still connected.
CHECK:
(a) Turn ignition switch ON.
(b) Measure voltage between terminals B and GND of cruise control ECU connector.
OK:
10 – 14 V

OK ▷ Proceed to next circuit inspection shown on matrix chart

NG

TY1109900587020X

Fig. 440 ECU Power Source Circuit (Part 2 of 3). 1996–97 4Runner

CIRCUIT DESCRIPTION

The ECU back–up power source provides power even when the ignition is off and is used for DTC memory, etc..

TY1109900588010X

Fig. 441 Back Up Power Source Circuit (Part 1 of 2). 1996–97 4Runner

CIRCUIT DESCRIPTION

The ECU power source supplies power to the actuator and sensors, etc.. When terminal GND and the cruise control ECU case are grounded.

TY1109900587010X

Fig. 440 ECU Power Source Circuit (Part 1 of 3). 1996–97 4Runner

3 Check resistance between terminal GND of cruise control ECU connector and body ground

CHECK:
Measure resistance between terminal GND of cruise control ECU connector and body ground.
OK:
Resistance: Below 1 Ω

NG ▷ Repair or replace harness or connector.

OK

Check and repair harness and connector between battery and cruise control ECU

TY1109900587030X

Fig. 440 ECU Power Source Circuit (Part 3 of 3). 1996–97 4Runner

INSPECTION PROCEDURE

1 Check DOME fuse.

PREPARATION:
Remove DOME fuse from relay block No.2.
CHECK:
Check continuity of DOME fuse.
OK:
Continuity

NG ▷ Check for short in all the harness and components connected to the DOME fuse.

OK

2 Check voltage between terminal BATT of cruise control ECU connector and body ground

PREPARATION:
Remove cruise control ECU with connector still connected.
CHECK:
Measure voltage between terminal BATT of cruise control ECU connector and body ground.
OK:
Voltage: 10 – 14 V

OK ▷ Proceed to next circuit inspection shown on matrix chart

NG

Check and repair harness and connector between battery and cruise ECU

TY1109900588020X

Fig. 441 Back Up Power Source Circuit (Part 2 of 2). 1996–97 4Runner

Main Switch Circuit (Cruise Control Switch)

CIRCUIT DESCRIPTION

When the cruise control main switch is turned off, the cruise control does not operate.

INSPECTION PROCEDURE

| 1 | Check voltage between terminal CMS of cruise control ECU connector and body ground. |

PREPARATION:
Remove cruise control ECU with connector still connected.
CHECK:
(a) Turn ignition switch ON.
(b) Measure voltage between terminal CMS of cruise control ECU connector when main switch is held on and off.
OK:

Main switch	Voltage
OFF	10 – 14 V
ON	Below 1 V

| OK | Proceed to next circuit inspection shown on matrix chart. |

| NG |

Fig. 442 Main Switch Circuit (Part 1 of 2). 1996–97 4Runner

TY1109900589010X

CIRCUIT DESCRIPTION

When the cruise control main switch is turned ON, CRUISE MAIN indicator light lights up.

TY1109900590010X

Fig. 443 Cruise Main Indicator Lamp Circuit (Part 1 of 2). 1996–97 4Runner

| 2 | Check main switch continuity. |

PREPARATION:
(a) Remove steering wheel center pad.
(b) Disconnect cruise control switch connector.
CHECK:
Check continuity between terminals 3 and 5 of cruise control switch connector when main switch is held on and off.
OK:

Switch position	Tester connection	Specified condition
OFF	3 – 5	No continuity
Hold ON	3 – 5	Continuity

| NG | Replace control switch. |

| OK |

| 3 | Check harness and connector between cruise control ECU and main switch. |

| NG | Repair or replace harness or connector. |

| OK |

Check and replace cruise control ECU.

TY1109900589020X

Fig. 442 Main Switch Circuit (Part 2 of 2). 1996–97 4Runner

| 1 | Check voltage between terminals PI and GND of cruise control ECU connector. |

PREPARATION:
Ignition switch ON.
CHECK:
Measure voltage between terminals PI and GND of cruise control ECU connector when main switch on and off.
OK:

Switch position	Voltage
OFF	10 – 16 V
ON	Below 1.2 V

| OK | Proceed to next circuit inspection shown on matrix chart. |

| NG |

| 2 | Check combination meter. |

| NG | Replace combination meter. |

| OK |

Check and replace cruise control ECU.

TY1109900590020X

Fig. 443 Cruise Main Indicator Lamp Circuit (Part 2 of 2). 1996–97 4Runner

CIRCUIT DESCRIPTION

This circuit sends a signal to the ECU that DTC output is required.

TY1109900591010X

Fig. 444 Diagnosis Circuit (Part 1 of 2). 1996–97 4Runner

INSPECTION PROCEDURE

1	Check voltage between terminals Tc and E_1 of DLC2.

CHECK:
(a) Turn ignition switch ON.
(b) Measure voltage between terminals Tc and E_1 of DLC2.
OK:
Voltage: 10 – 14 V

OK >	Proceed to next circuit inspection shown on matrix chart.

NG

2	Check harness and connector between cruise control ECU and DLC2, DLC2 and body ground.

NG >	Repair or replace harness or connector.

OK

Check and replace cruise control ECU.

TY1109900591020X

Fig. 444 Diagnosis Circuit (Part 2 of 2). 1996–97 4Runner

CIRCUIT DESCRIPTION

The actuator motor is operated by signals from the ECU. Acceleration and deceleration signals are transmitted by changes in the Duty Ratio (See below).
Duty Ratio:
The duty ratio is the ratio of the period of continuity in one cycle. For example, if A is the period of continuity in one cycle, and B is the period of non–continuity, then.

$$\text{Duty Ratio} = \frac{A}{A + B} \times 100 \ (\%)$$

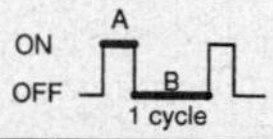

DTC No.	Detection Item	Trouble Area
11	Short in actuator motor circuit	• Cruise control actuator • Harness or connector between actuator and cruise control ECU • Cruise control ECU
15	Open in actuator motor circuit	• Cruise control actuator

TY1109900596010X

Fig. 446 Code 11 & 15: Actuator Motor Circuit (Part 1 of 2). 1998–99 4Runner w/Denso cruise control

INSPECTION PROCEDURE

1	Actuator control cable inspection

CHECK:
(a) Check that the actuator, control cable throttle link are properly installed and that the cable and link are connected correctly.
(b) Check that the actuator and bell crank are operating smoothly.
(c) Check that the cable is not loose or too tight.
OK:
Freeplay: less than 10 mm
HINT:
• If the control cable is very loose, the vehicle's loss of speed going uphill will be large.
• If the control cable is too tight, the idle RPM will become high.

TY1109900592000X

Fig. 445 Actuator Control Cable. 1996–97 4Runner

INSPECTION PROCEDURE

1	Check resistance between terminals MO and MC of cruise control actuator.

PREPARATION:
(a) Ignition switch ON.
(b) Disconnect actuator connector.
CHECK:
Measure resistance between terminals 1 and 2.
HINT:
If control plate position is fully opened or fully closed, resistance can not be measured.
OK:
Resistance: more than 4.2 Ω

NG >	Replace cruise control actuator.

OK

2	Check wire harness and connector between terminals MO of cruise control ECU and MO of cruise control actuator.

NG >	Repair or replace harness or connector.

OK

Replace cruise control ECU.

TY1109900596020X

Fig. 446 Code 11 & 15: Actuator Motor Circuit (Part 2 of 2). 1998–99 4Runner w/Denso cruise control

CIRCUIT DESCRIPTION

This circuit turns on the magnetic clutch inside the actuator during cruise control operation according to the signal from the ECU. If a malfunction occurs in the actuator or speed sensor, etc. during cruise control operation, the rotor shaft between the motor and control plate is released.
When the brake pedal is depressed, the stop light switch turns ON, supplying electrical power to the stop light. Power supply to the magnetic clutch is mechanically cut and the magnetic clutch is turned OFF.
When driving downhill, if the vehicle speed exceeds the set speed by 15 km/h (6 mph) above the set speed, cruise control at the set speed is resumed.

DTC No.	Detection Item	Trouble Area
12	• Short in magnetic clutch circuit. • Open (0.8 sec.) in magnetic clutch circuit	• Cruise control actuator magnetic clutch • Harness or connector between ECU and magnetic clutch, magnetic clutch and body ground • Cruise control ECU

TY1109900597010X

Fig. 447 Code 12: Magnetic Clutch Circuit (Part 1 of 2). 1998–99 4Runner w/Denso cruise control

TOYOTA UNIT REPAIR

INSPECTION PROCEDURE

1 | Check STOP fuse.

PREPARATION:
Remove STOP fuse from No.1 J/B.
CHECK:
Check fuse continuity.
OK:
There is continuity.

NG ▷ Replace STOP fuse.

OK

2 | Check harness and connector between actuator and cruise control actuator.

NG ▷ Repair or replace harness or connector.

OK

Check and replace cruise control ECU.

TY1109900597020X

Fig. 447 Code 12: Magnetic Clutch Circuit (Part 2 of 2). 1998–99 4Runner w/Denso cruise control

2 | Check actuator operation.

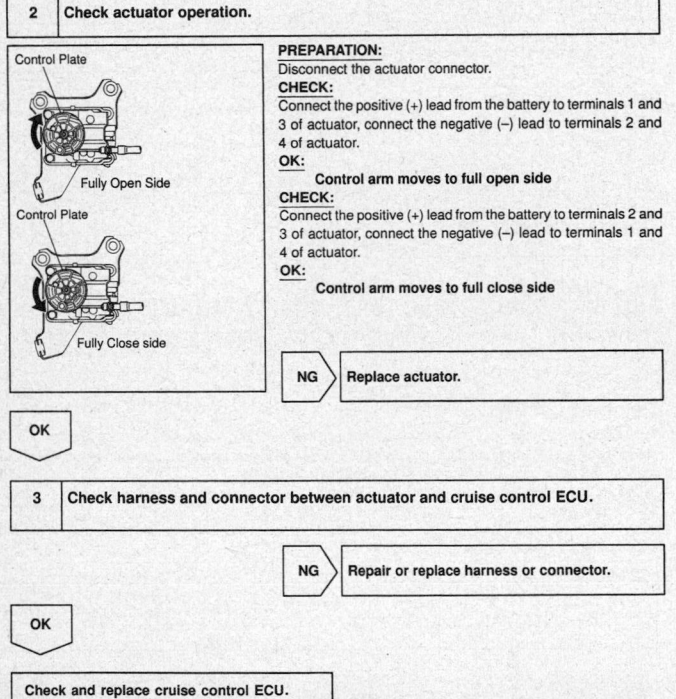

PREPARATION:
Disconnect the actuator connector.
CHECK:
Connect the positive (+) lead from the battery to terminals 1 and 3 of actuator, connect the negative (–) lead to terminals 2 and 4 of actuator.
OK:
Control arm moves to full open side
CHECK:
Connect the positive (+) lead from the battery to terminals 2 and 3 of actuator, connect the negative (–) lead to terminals 1 and 4 of actuator.
OK:
Control arm moves to full close side

NG ▷ Replace actuator.

OK

3 | Check harness and connector between actuator and cruise control ECU.

NG ▷ Repair or replace harness or connector.

OK

Check and replace cruise control ECU.

TY1109900598020X

Fig. 448 Code 14: Actuator Mechanical Fault (Part 2 of 2). 1998–99 4Runner w/Denso cruise control

CIRCUIT DESCRIPTION

DTC No.	Detection Item	Trouble Area
14	Actuator mechanical malfunction	• Cruise control actuator motor • Harness or connector between actuator motor and ECU • ECU

INSPECTION PROCEDURE

1 | Check actuator arm locking operation

PREPARATION:
(a) Ignition switch OFF.
(b) Disconnect actuator connector.
CHECK:
(a) Connect the positive (+) lead from the battery to the terminal 4 of actuator and the negative (–) lead to terminal 3.
NOTICE:
Do not connect the high tension cables to the wrong battery terminal. You will damage the cruise control actuator.
(b) Move the control plate by hand.
OK:
Control plate doesn't move.

NG ▷ Replace cruise control actuator.

OK

TY1109900598010X

Fig. 448 Code 14: Actuator Mechanical Fault (Part 1 of 2). 1998–99 4Runner w/Denso cruise control

CIRCUIT DESCRIPTION

The vehicle speed sensor circuit is sent to cruise control ECU as vehicle speed signal. For each rotation of the shaft, the vehicle speed sensor sends a signal through the combination meter (5VZ–FE: ABS ECU and combination meter) to the cruise control ECU (See the following). The ECU calculates the vehicle speed from this pulse frequency.

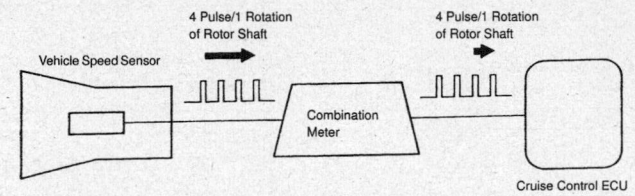

DTC No.	Detection Item	Trouble Area
21	Speed signal is not input to the cruise control ECU while cruise control is set.	• Vehicle speed sensor • Combination meter • Harness or connector between vehicle speed sensor and combination meter, combination meter and cruise control ECU • Cruise control ECU

TY1109900599010X

Fig. 449 Code 21: Open In Vehicle Speed Sensor Circuit (Part 1 of 3). 1998–99 4Runner w/Denso cruise control

SPEED CONTROL SYSTEMS

INSPECTION PROCEDURE

1	Input signal check.

Input Signal	Indicator Light Blinking Pattern
Drive at about 40 km/h (25 mph) or below	Light ON ——— OFF - - - -
Drive at about 40 km/h (25 mph) or higher	Light ON ⊓⊓⊓⊓ OFF

CHECK:
(a) See input signal check.
(b) Check indicator light operation when driving with vehicle speed above 40 km/h (25 mph), and with vehicle speed below 40 km/h (25 mph).
OK:

Vehicle speed above 40 km/h (25 mph):
  Indicator light blinks
Vehicle speed below 40 km/h (25 mph):
  Indicator light stays on

> **OK** | Check and replace cruise control ECU.

NG ▽

TY1109900599020X

Fig. 449   Code 21: Open In Vehicle Speed Sensor Circuit (Part 2 of 3). 1998–99 4Runner w/Denso cruise control

CIRCUIT DESCRIPTION

DTC No.	Detection Item	Trouble Area
23	Vehicle speed sensor pulse is abnormal.	• Vehicle speed sensor • Cruise control ECU

INSPECTION PROCEDURE

1	Check vehicle speed sensor.

> **NG** | Replace vehicle speed sensor.

OK ▽

> Check and replace cruise control ECU.

TY1109900600000X

Fig. 450   Code 23: Vehicle Speed Sensor Abnormal. 1998–99 4Runner w/Denso cruise control

---

2	Check harness and connector between speed meter and cruise control ECU.

> **NG** | Repair or replace harness or connector.

OK ▽

3	Check vehicle speed sensor.

> **NG** | Replace vehicle speed sensor.

OK ▽

> Check and replace cruise control ECU.

TY1109900599030X

Fig. 449   Code 21: Open In Vehicle Speed Sensor Circuit (Part 3 of 3). 1998–99 4Runner w/Denso cruise control

CIRCUIT DESCRIPTION

This circuit carries the SET/COAST, RESUME/ACCEL and CANCEL signals (each voltage) to the ECU.

DTC No.	Detection Item	Trouble Area
32	Short in control switch circuit	• Cruise control switch • Harness or connector between control switch and cruise control ECU. • Cruise control ECU

TY1109900601010X

Fig. 451   Code 32: Control Switch Circuit (Part 1 of 3). 1998–99 4Runner w/Denso cruise control

INSPECTION PROCEDURE

1	Input signal check.

Input Signal	Indicator Light Blinking Pattern
SET/COAST switch	ON ⊓⊓ 2 Pulses OFF
RESUME/ACCEL switch	ON ⊓⊓⊓ 3 Pulses OFF
CANCEL switch	ON SW OFF OFF SW ON

PREPARATION:
See input signal check.
CHECK:
Check the indicator light operation when each of the SET/COAST, RESUME/ACCEL and CANCEL is turned on.
OK:

SET/COAST, RESUME/ACCEL switch
The signals shown in the table on the left should be output when each switch is ON. The signal should disappear when the switch is turned OFF.
CANCEL switch
The indicator light goes off when the cancel switch is turned ON.

> **OK** | Wait and see.

NG ▽

2	Check control switch.

PREPARATION:
(a) Remove steering wheel center pad.
(b) Disconnect control switch connector.
CHECK:
Measure resistance between terminals 3 and 4 of control switch connector when control switch is operated.

Switch position	Resistance (Ω)
Neutral	∞ (No continuity)
RES/ACC	50 – 80
SET/COAST	180 – 220
CANCEL	400 – 440

> **OK** | Replace control switch.

NG ▽

TY1109900601020X

Fig. 451   Code 32: Control Switch Circuit (Part 2 of 3). 1998–99 4Runner w/Denso cruise control

3 | Check harness and connector between cruise control switch and cruise control ECU.

NG ▷ Repair or replace harness or connector.

OK

4 | Input signal check (See step 1).

OK ▷ Wait and see.

NG

Check and replace cruise control ECU.

TY1109900601030X

Fig. 451   Code 32: Control Switch Circuit (Part 3 of 3). 1998–99 4Runner w/Denso cruise control

INSPECTION PROCEDURE

1 | Check voltage between terminal IDL of ECU connector and body ground.

PREPARATION:
(a) Remove cruise control ECU with connector still connected.
(b) Disconnect ECM and ABS ECU connectors.
(c) Ignition switch ON.
CHECK:
Measure voltage between terminal IDL of ECU connector and body ground when the throttle valve is fully closed and fully opened.
OK:

Throttle valve position	Voltage
Fully opened	10 – 14 V
Fully closed	Below 2 V

OK ▷ Proceed to next circuit inspection shown in problem symptoms table.

NG

2 | Check throttle position sensor.

PREPARATION:
Disconnect throttle position sensor connector.
CHECK:
Measure resistance between terminals 1,2 and 3 of throttle position sensor connector when the throttle valve is fully closed and fully opened.
OK:

Terminals	Throttle valve	Resistance
1 – 2	–	2.5 – 5.9 kΩ
1 – 3	Fully closed	0.2 – 5.7 kΩ
1 – 3	Fully open	2.0 –10.2 kΩ

NG ▷ Replace throttle position sensor.

OK

TY1109900602020X

Fig. 452   Code 51: Idle Switch Circuit (Part 2 of 3). 1998–99 4Runner w/Denso cruise control

CIRCUIT DESCRIPTION

When the brake is on, battery positive voltage normally is applied through the STOP fuse and stop light switch to terminal STP– of the ECU, and the ECU turns the cruise control OFF.

A fail-safe function is provided so that cancel functions normally, even if there is a malfunction in the stop light signal circuit.

If the harness connected to terminal STP– has an open circuit, terminal STP– will have battery positive voltage and the cruise control will be turned OFF.

Also, when the brake is ON, the magnetic clutch is cut mechanically by the stop light switch, turning the cruise control OFF.

TY1109900603010X

Fig. 453   Stop Lamp Switch Circuit (Part 1 of 3). 1998–99 4Runner w/Denso cruise control

CIRCUIT DESCRIPTION

When the idle switch is turned ON, a signal is sent to the ECU. The ECU uses this signal to correct the discrepancy between the throttle valve position and the actuator position sensor valve to enable accurate cruise control at the set speed. If the idle switch is malfunctioning, problem symptoms also occur in the engine, so also inspect the engine.

TY1109900602010X

Fig. 452   Code 51: Idle Switch Circuit (Part 1 of 3). 1998–99 4Runner w/Denso cruise control

3 | Check for open and short in harness and connector between ECU and throttle position sensor, throttle position sensor and body ground.

NG ▷ Repair or replace harness or connector.

OK

Check and replace cruise control ECU.

TY1109900602030X

Fig. 452   Code 51: Idle Switch Circuit (Part 3 of 3). 1998–99 4Runner w/Denso cruise control

INSPECTION PROCEDURE

1 | Check operation of stop light.

CHECK:
Check that stop light comes ON when brake pedal is depressed, and turns OFF when brake pedal is released.

NG ▷ Check stop light system.

OK

2 | Input signal check.

Input Signal	Indicator Light Blinking Pattern	
Stop light switch ON	Light	ON ‾‾‾ SW OFF OFF ----- SW ON

CHECK:
(a) See input signal check.
(b) Check the indicator light when the brake pedal is depressed.
OK:
The indicator light goes off when the brake pedal is depressed.

OK ▷ Proceed to next circuit inspection shown in problem symptoms table.

NG

TY1109900603020X

Fig. 453   Stop Lamp Switch Circuit (Part 2 of 3). 1998–99 4Runner w/Denso cruise control

3	Check voltage between terminal STP– of cruise control ECU connector and body ground.

PREPARATION:
Remove cruise control ECU with connectors still connected.
CHECK:
(a) Turn ignition switch ON.
(b) Measure voltage between terminal STP– of cruise control ECU connector and body ground, when the brake pedal is depressed and released.
OK:

Depressed	10 – 14 V
Released	Below 1 V

OK → Proceed to next circuit inspection shown in problem symptoms table.

NG

4	Check for open in harness and connectors between terminal STP– of cruise control ECU and stop light switch.

NG → Repair or replace harness or connector.

OK

Check and replace cruise control ECU.

TY1109900603030X

Fig. 453 Stop Lamp Switch Circuit (Part 3 of 3). 1998–99 4Runner w/Denso cruise control

INSPECTION PROCEDURE

1	Check operation of overdrive.

PREPARATION:
Test drive after engine warms up.
CHECK:
Check that overdrive ON ↔ OFF occurs with operation of OD switch ON–OFF.

NG → Check and repair electronically controlled transmission.

OK

2	Check voltage between terminal OD of harness side connector of cruise control ECU and body ground.

PREPARATION:
Remove cruise control ECU with connector still connected.
CHECK:
(a) Disconnect cruise control ECU connector.
(b) Turn ignition switch ON.
(c) Measure voltage between terminal OD of harness side connector of cruise control ECU and body ground.
OK:
Voltage: 10 – 14 V

NG → Go to step 5.

OK

TY1109900604020X

Fig. 454 Electronically Controlled Transmission Communication Circuit (Part 2 of 3). 1998–99 4Runner w/Denso cruise control

CIRCUIT DESCRIPTION

When driving uphill under cruise control, in order to reduce shifting due to ON–OFF overdrive operation and to provide smooth driving, when down shifting in the electronically controlled transmission occurs, a signal to prevent upshift until the end of the uphill slope is sent from the cruise control ECU to the electronically controlled transmission.

Terminal ECM of the cruise control ECU detects the shift change signal (output to electronically controlled transmission No. 2 solenoid) from the electronically controlled transmission.

If vehicle speeds down, also when terminal electronically controlled transmission of the cruise control ECU receives down shifting signal, it sends a signal from terminal OD to ECM to cut overdrive until the end of the uphill slope, and the gear shifts are reduced and gear shift points in the electronically controlled transmission are changed.

TY1109900604010X

Fig. 454 Electronically Controlled Transmission Communication Circuit (Part 1 of 3). 1998–99 4Runner w/Denso cruise control

3	Check voltage between terminal ECT of cruise control ECU connector and body ground (On test drive).

PREPARATION:
(a) Connect cruise control ECU connector.
(b) Test drive after engine warms up.
CHECK:
Check voltage between terminal ECT of cruise control ECU connector and body ground when OD switch is ON and OFF.
OK:

OD switch position	Voltage
ON	8 – 14 V
OFF	Below 0.5 V

OK → Proceed to next circuit inspection shown in problem symptoms table.

NG

4	Check harness and connector between terminal ECT of cruise control ECU and electronically controlled transmission solenoid.

NG → Repair or replace harness or connector.

OK

Check and replace cruise control ECU.

5	Check harness and connector between terminal OD of cruise control ECU and terminal OD1 of ECM.

NG → Repair or replace harness or connector.

OK

Check and replace cruise control ECU.

TY1109900604030X

Fig. 454 Electronically Controlled Transmission Communication Circuit (Part 3 of 3). 1998–99 4Runner w/Denso cruise control

CIRCUIT DESCRIPTION

When the shift position is put in except D position, a signal is sent from the park/neutral position switch to the ECU. When this signal is input during cruise control driving, the ECU cancels the cruise control.

TY1109900605010X

Fig. 455 Park/Neutral Position Switch Circuit (Part 1 of 3). 1998–99 4Runner w/Denso cruise control

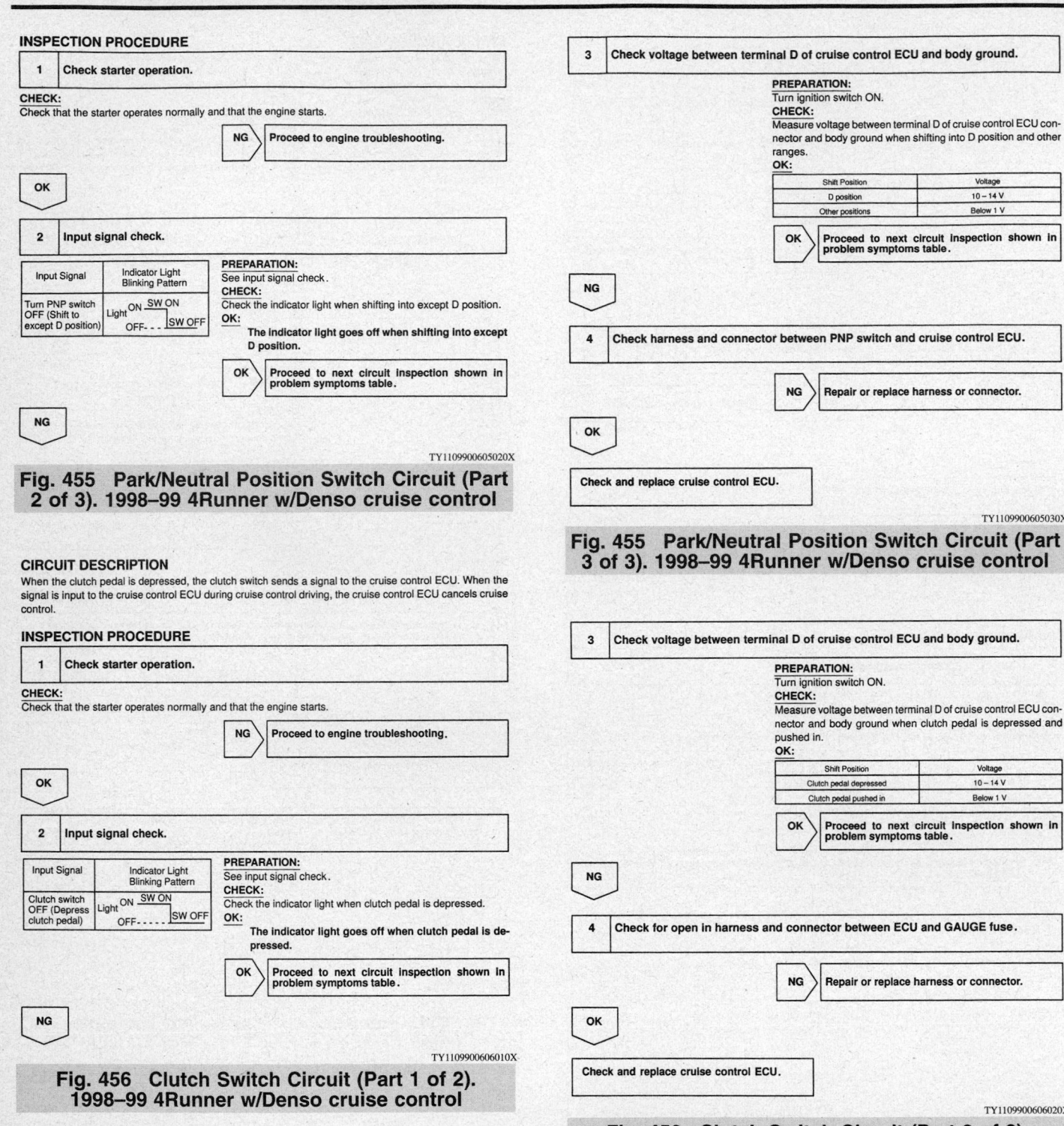

INSPECTION PROCEDURE

1	Check starter operation.

CHECK:
Check that the starter operates normally and that the engine starts.

NG → Proceed to engine troubleshooting.

OK

2	Input signal check.

Input Signal	Indicator Light Blinking Pattern
Turn PNP switch OFF (Shift to except D position)	Light ON — SW ON OFF---- SW OFF

PREPARATION:
See input signal check.
CHECK:
Check the indicator light when shifting into except D position.
OK:
The indicator light goes off when shifting into except D position.

OK → Proceed to next circuit inspection shown in problem symptoms table.

NG

TY1109900605020X

Fig. 455   Park/Neutral Position Switch Circuit (Part 2 of 3). 1998–99 4Runner w/Denso cruise control

CIRCUIT DESCRIPTION

When the clutch pedal is depressed, the clutch switch sends a signal to the cruise control ECU. When the signal is input to the cruise control ECU during cruise control driving, the cruise control ECU cancels cruise control.

INSPECTION PROCEDURE

1	Check starter operation.

CHECK:
Check that the starter operates normally and that the engine starts.

NG → Proceed to engine troubleshooting.

OK

2	Input signal check.

Input Signal	Indicator Light Blinking Pattern
Clutch switch OFF (Depress clutch pedal)	Light ON — SW ON OFF----- SW OFF

PREPARATION:
See input signal check.
CHECK:
Check the indicator light when clutch pedal is depressed.
OK:
The indicator light goes off when clutch pedal is depressed.

OK → Proceed to next circuit inspection shown in problem symptoms table.

NG

TY1109900606010X

Fig. 456   Clutch Switch Circuit (Part 1 of 2). 1998–99 4Runner w/Denso cruise control

3	Check voltage between terminal D of cruise control ECU and body ground.

PREPARATION:
Turn ignition switch ON.
CHECK:
Measure voltage between terminal D of cruise control ECU connector and body ground when shifting into D position and other ranges.
OK:

Shift Position	Voltage
D position	10 – 14 V
Other positions	Below 1 V

OK → Proceed to next circuit inspection shown in problem symptoms table.

NG

4	Check harness and connector between PNP switch and cruise control ECU.

NG → Repair or replace harness or connector.

OK

Check and replace cruise control ECU.

TY1109900605030X

Fig. 455   Park/Neutral Position Switch Circuit (Part 3 of 3). 1998–99 4Runner w/Denso cruise control

3	Check voltage between terminal D of cruise control ECU and body ground.

PREPARATION:
Turn ignition switch ON.
CHECK:
Measure voltage between terminal D of cruise control ECU connector and body ground when clutch pedal is depressed and pushed in.
OK:

Shift Position	Voltage
Clutch pedal depressed	10 – 14 V
Clutch pedal pushed in	Below 1 V

OK → Proceed to next circuit inspection shown in problem symptoms table.

NG

4	Check for open in harness and connector between ECU and GAUGE fuse.

NG → Repair or replace harness or connector.

OK

Check and replace cruise control ECU.

TY1109900606020X

Fig. 456   Clutch Switch Circuit (Part 2 of 2). 1998–99 4Runner w/Denso cruise control

CIRCUIT DESCRIPTION

The ECU power source supplies power to the actuator and sensors, etc., when terminal GND and the cruise control ECU case are grounded.

TY1109900607010X

Fig. 457   ECU Power Source Circuit (Part 1 of 3). 1998–99 4Runner w/Denso cruise control

INSPECTION PROCEDURE

1	Check ECU–IG fuse.

PREPARATION:
Remove ECU–IG fuse from junction block No.1.
CHECK:
Check continuity of ECU–IG fuse.
OK:

    Continuity

NG ⟩ Check for short in all the harness and components connected to ECU–IG fuse.

OK

2	Check voltage between terminals B and GND of cruise control ECU connector.

PREPARATION:
Remove cruise control ECU with connector still connected.
CHECK:
(a) Turn ignition switch ON.
(b) Measure voltage between terminals B and GND of cruise control ECU connector.
OK:

    10 – 14 V

OK ⟩ Proceed to next circuit inspection shown in problem symptoms table.

NG

TY1109900607020X

Fig. 457 ECU Power Source Circuit (Part 2 of 3). 1998–99 4Runner w/Denso cruise control

CIRCUIT DESCRIPTION

When the cruise control main switch is turned OFF, the cruise control does not operate.

INSPECTION PROCEDURE

1	Check voltage between terminal CMS of cruise control ECU connector and body ground.

PREPARATION:
Remove cruise control ECU with connector still connected.
CHECK:
(a) Turn ignition switch ON.
(b) Measure voltage between terminal CMS of cruise control ECU connector when main switch is held ON and OFF.
OK:

Main switch	Voltage
OFF	10 – 14 V
ON	Below 0.5 V

OK ⟩ Proceed to next circuit inspection shown in problem symptoms table.

NG

TY1109900608010X

Fig. 458 Main Switch Circuit (Part 1 of 2). 1998–99 4Runner w/Denso cruise control

3	Check resistance between terminal GND of cruise control ECU connector and body ground.

CHECK:
Measure resistance between terminal GND of cruise control ECU connector and body ground.
OK:

    Resistance: Below 1 Ω

NG ⟩ Repair or replace harness or connector.

OK

Check and repair harness and connector between battery and cruise control ECU.

TY1109900607030X

Fig. 457 ECU Power Source Circuit (Part 3 of 3). 1998–99 4Runner w/Denso cruise control

2	Check main switch continuity.

PREPARATION:
(a) Remove steering wheel center pad.
(b) Disconnect cruise control switch connector.
CHECK:
Check continuity between terminals 3 and 5 of cruise control switch connector when main switch is held ON and OFF.
OK:

Switch position	Tester connection	Specified condition
OFF	3 – 5	No continuity
Hold ON	3 – 5	Continuity

NG ⟩ Replace control switch.

OK

3	Check harness and connector between cruise control ECU and main switch.

NG ⟩ Repair or replace harness or connector.

OK

Check and replace cruise control ECU.

TY1109900608020X

Fig. 458 Main Switch Circuit (Part 2 of 2). 1998–99 4Runner w/Denso cruise control

CIRCUIT DESCRIPTION

When the cruise control main switch is turned ON, CRUISE MAIN indicator light lights up.

TY1109900609010X

Fig. 459 Cruise Main Indicator Lamp Circuit (Part 1 of 2). 1998–99 4Runner w/Denso cruise control

INSPECTION PROCEDURE

1	Check voltage between terminals PI and GND of cruise control ECU connector.

PREPARATION:
Ignition switch ON.
CHECK:
Measure voltage between terminals PI and GND of cruise control ECU connector when main switch is held ON and OFF.
OK:

Switch position	Voltage
OFF	10 – 16 V
ON	Below 1.2 V

OK	Proceed to next circuit inspection shown in problem symptoms table.

NG

2	Check combination meter.

NG	Replace combination meter.

OK

Check and replace cruise control ECU.

TY1109900609020X

Fig. 459   Cruise Main Indicator Lamp Circuit (Part 2 of 2). 1998–99 4Runner w/Denso cruise control

INSPECTION PROCEDURE

1	Check voltage between terminals Tc and E₁ of DLC2.

CHECK:
(a) Turn ignition switch ON.
(b) Measure voltage between terminals Tc and E₁ of DLC2.
OK:
Voltage: 10 – 14 V

OK	Proceed to next circuit inspection shown in problem symptoms table.

NG

2	Check harness and connector between cruise control ECU and DLC2, DLC2 and body ground.

NG	Repair or replace harness or connector.

OK

Check and replace cruise control ECU.

TY1109900610020X

Fig. 460   Diagnosis Circuit (Part 2 of 2). 1998–99 4Runner w/Denso cruise control

CIRCUIT DESCRIPTION

This circuit sends a signal to the ECU that DTC output is required.

TY1109900610010X

Fig. 460   Diagnosis Circuit (Part 1 of 2). 1998–99 4Runner w/Denso cruise control

INSPECTION PROCEDURE

1	Actuator control cable inspection

OK:
(a) Check that the actuator, and control cable throttle link are properly installed and that the cable and link are connected correctly.
(b) Check that the actuator and bell crank are operating smoothly.
(c) Check that the cable is not loose or too tight.
OK:
Freeplay: less than 10 mm
HINT:
• If the control cable is very loose, the vehicle's loss of speed going uphill will be large.
• If the control cable is too tight, the idle RPM will become high.

TY1109900611000X

Fig. 461   Actuator Control Cable. 1998–99 4Runner w/Denso cruise control

CIRCUIT DESCRIPTION

This circuit turns on the magnetic clutch inside the actuator during cruise control operation according to the signal from the ECU. If a malfunction occurs in the actuator or speed sensor, etc. during cruise control operation, the rotor shaft between the motor and control plate is released.
When the brake pedal is depressed, the stop light switch turns ON, supplying electrical power to the stop light. Power supply to the magnetic clutch is mechanically cut and the magnetic clutch is turned OFF.
When driving downhill, if the vehicle speed exceeds the set speed by 15 km/h (6 mph) above the set speed, then cruise control at the set speed is resumed.

DTC No.	Detection Item	Trouble Area
12	• Short in actuator and ECU circuit • Open in actuator and ECU circuit	• Connector of cruise control actuator and ECU • STOP fuse and stop light switch • Cruise control actuator and ECU

TY1109900615010X

Fig. 462   Code 12: Actuator Circuit (Part 1 of 3). 1998–99 4Runner w/Ford cruise control

INSPECTION PROCEDURE

1	Check STOP fuse.

PREPARATION:
Remove STOP fuse from Relay Block No.2.
CHECK:
Check fuse continuity.
OK:
There is continuity.

NG ▷ Replace STOP fuse.

OK

2	Check stop light switch.

PREPARATION:
Disconnect stop light switch connector.
CHECK:
Check continuity between terminals.
OK:

Switch position	Continuity
Switch pin free (Brake pedal depressed)	1 – 2
Switch pin pushed in (Brake pedal released)	3 – 4

NG ▷ Replace stop light switch.

OK

TY1109900615020X

Fig. 462 Code 12: Actuator Circuit (Part 2 of 3). 1998–99 4Runner w/Ford cruise control

CIRCUIT DESCRIPTION

The circuit detects the rotation position of the actuator control plate and sends a signal to the ECU.

DTC No.	Detection Item	Trouble Area
14	• Open on short in actuator motor circuite	• Connector of cruise control actuator and ECU • Cruise control actuator and ECU

INSPECTION PROCEDURE

1	Check connector of cruise control actuator and ECU.

NG ▷ Repair or replace connector.

OK

Check and replace cruise control actuator and ECU.

TY1109900616000X

Fig. 463 Code 14: Actuator Mechanical Fault. 1998–99 4Runner w/Ford cruise control

3	Check harness and connector between actuator and cruise control actuator.

NG ▷ Repair or replace harness or connector.

OK

Check and replace cruise control actuator and ECU.

TY1109900615030X

Fig. 462 Code 12: Actuator Circuit (Part 3 of 3). 1998–99 4Runner w/Ford cruise control

CIRCUIT DESCRIPTION

The vehicle speed sensor circuit is sent to cruise control ECU as vehicle speed signal. For each rotation of the shaft, the vehicle speed sensor sends a signal through the combination meter to the cruise control ECU (See the following). The ECU calculates the vehicle speed from this pulse frequency.

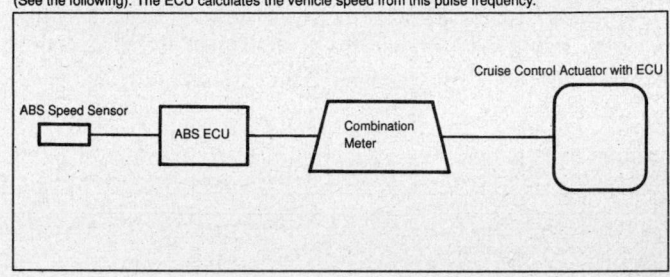

DTC No.	Detection Item	Trouble Area
21	Speed signal is not input to the cruise control ECU while cruise control is set.	• Harness or connector between combination meter and cruise control actuator and ECU • Speed sensor (in combination meter) • Combination meter • Cruise control actuator and ECU

TY1109900617010X

Fig. 464 Code 21: Open In Vehicle Speed Sensor Circuit (Part 1 of 3). 1998–99 4Runner w/Ford cruise control

INSPECTION PROCEDURE

1	Input signal check.

Input Signal	Indicator Light Blinking Pattern
Drive at about 40 km/h (25 mph) or below	Light ON
Drive at about 40 km/h (25 mph) or higher	Light ON OFF

CHECK:
(a) See input signal check.
(b) Check indicator light operation when driving with vehicle speed above 40 km/h (25 mph), and with vehicle speed below 40 km/h (25 mph).
OK:
Vehicle speed above 40 km/h (25 mph):
Indicator light blinks
Vehicle speed below 40 km/h (25 mph):
Indicator light stays ON

OK ▷ Check and replace cruise control actuator and ECU.

NG

TY1109900617020X

Fig. 464 Code 21: Open In Vehicle Speed Sensor Circuit (Part 2 of 3). 1998–99 4Runner w/Ford cruise control

2 | Check harness and connector between combination meter and cruise control actuator and ECU.

NG ▷ Repair or replace harness or connector.

OK

3 | Check speedometer circuit.

NG ▷ Repair or replace speed sensor or combination meter assembly.

OK

Check and replace cruise control actuator and ECU.

TY1109900617030X

Fig. 464   Code 21: Open In Vehicle Speed Sensor Circuit (Part 3 of 3). 1998–99 4Runner w/Ford cruise control

CIRCUIT DESCRIPTION

This circuit carries the SET/COAST, RESUME/ACCEL and CANCEL signals (each voltage) to the ECU.

DTC No.	Detection Item	Trouble Area
32	Short in control switch circuit	• Harness or connector between control switch and cruise control actuator and ECU. • Cruise control switch • Cruise control actuator and ECU

TY1109900619010X

Fig. 466   Code 32: Control Switch Circuit (Part 1 of 3). 1998–99 4Runner w/Ford cruise control

3 | Check harness and connector between cruise control switch and cruise control actuator and ECU.

NG ▷ Repair or replace harness or connector.

OK

4 | Input signal check (See step 1).

OK ▷ Wait and see.

NG

Check and replace cruise control actuator and ECU.

TY1109900619030X

Fig. 466   Code 32: Control Switch Circuit (Part 3 of 3). 1998–99 4Runner w/Ford cruise control

CIRCUIT DESCRIPTION

DTC No.	Detection Item	Trouble Area
23	• Actual vehicle speed has dropped either by 16 km/h (10 mph) or more below the set speed, or by 20% or more of the set speed.	• Speed sensor (in combination with meter) • Cruise control actuator and ECU

INSPECTION PROCEDURE

1 | Check speedometer circuit.

NG ▷ Repair or replace speed sensor or combination meter assembly.

OK

Check and replace cruise control actuator and ECU.

TY1109900618000X

Fig. 465   Code 23: Vehicle Speed Signal Abnormal. 1998–99 4Runner w/Ford cruise control

INSPECTION PROCEDURE

1 | Input signal check.

Input Signal	Indicator Light Blinking Pattern
SET/COAST switch	ON / OFF 2 Pulses
RESUME/ACCEL switch	ON / OFF 3 Pulses
CANCEL switch	ON SW OFF / OFF SW ON

PREPARATION:
See input signal check.
CHECK:
Check the indicator light operation when each of the SET/COAST, RESUME/ACCEL and CANCEL is turned on.
OK:
SET/COAST, RESUME/ACCEL switch
The signals shown in the table on the left should be output when each switch is ON. The signal should disappear when the switch is turned OFF.
CANCEL switch
The indicator light goes off when the cancel switch is turned ON.

OK ▷ Wait and see.

NG

2 | Check control switch.

PREPARATION:
(a)   Remove steering wheel center pad.
(b)   Disconnect control switch connector.
CHECK:
Measure resistance between terminals 3 and 4 of control switch connector when control switch is operated.

Switch position	Resistance (Ω)
Neutral	∞ (No continuity)
RES/ACC	50 – 80
SET/COAST	180 – 220
CANCEL	400 – 440

OK ▷ Replace control switch.

NG

TY1109900619020X

Fig. 466   Code 32: Control Switch Circuit (Part 2 of 3). 1998–99 4Runner w/Ford cruise control

CIRCUIT DESCRIPTION

When the brake is ON, battery positive voltage normally is applied through the STOP fuse and stop light switch to terminal STP– of the ECU, and the ECU turns the cruise control OFF.
A fail–safe function is provided so that cancel functions normally, even if there is a malfunction in the stop light signal circuit.
   If the harness connected to terminal STP– has an open circuit, terminal STP– will have battery positive voltage and the cruise control will be turned OFF.
Also, when the brake is ON, the magnetic clutch is cut mechanically by the stop light switch, turning the cruise control OFF.

TY1109900620010X

Fig. 467   Stop Lamp Switch Circuit (Part 1 of 3). 1998–99 4Runner w/Ford cruise control

SPEED CONTROL SYSTEMS

INSPECTION PROCEDURE

| 1 | Check operation of stop light. |

CHECK:
Check that stop light comes on when brake pedal is depressed, and turns off when brake pedal is released.

→ NG → | Check stop light system. |

↓ OK

| 2 | Input signal check. |

Input Signal	Indicator Light Blinking Pattern
Stop light switch ON	Light ON — SW OFF / OFF - - - - - SW ON

CHECK:
(a) See input signal check.
(b) Check the indicator light when the brake pedal is depressed.

OK:
The indicator light goes off when the brake pedal is depressed.

→ OK → | Proceed to next circuit inspection shown in problem symptoms table. |

↓ NG

TY1109900620020X

Fig. 467 Stop Lamp Switch Circuit (Part 2 of 3). 1998–99 4Runner w/Ford cruise control

CIRCUIT DESCRIPTION

When the idle switch is turned ON, a signal is sent to the ECU. The ECU uses this signal to correct the discrepancy between the throttle valve position and the actuator position sensor valve to enable accurate cruise control at the set speed. If the idle switch is malfunctioning, problem symptoms also occur in the engine, so also inspect the engine.

TY1109900621010X

Fig. 468 Idle Switch Circuit (Part 1 of 3). 1998–99 4Runner w/Ford cruise control

INSPECTION PROCEDURE

| 1 | Check voltage between terminal IDL of ECU connector and body ground. |

PREPARATION:
(a) Remove cruise control ECU with connector still connected.
(b) Disconnect ECM and ABS ECU connectors.
(c) Ignition switch ON.

CHECK:
Measure voltage between terminal IDL of ECU connector and body ground when the throttle valve is fully closed and fully opened.

OK:

Throttle valve position	Voltage
Fully opened	10 – 14 V
Fully closed	Below 2 V

→ OK → | Proceed to next circuit inspection shown on problem symptoms table. |

↓ NG

| 2 | Check throttle position sensor. |

PREPARATION:
Disconnect throttle position sensor connector.

CHECK:
Measure resistance between terminals 3 and 4 of throttle position sensor connector when the throttle valve is fully closed and fully opened.

OK:

Throttle valve position	Resistance
Fully opened	1 MΩ or higher
Fully closed	Below 2.3 kΩ

→ NG → | Replace throttle position sensor. |

↓ OK

TY1109900621020X

Fig. 468 Idle Switch Circuit (Part 2 of 3). 1998–99 4Runner w/Ford cruise control

| 3 | Check voltage between terminal STP– of cruise control actuator and ECU connector and body ground. |

PREPARATION:
Remove cruise control ECU with connectors still connected.

CHECK:
(a) Turn ignition switch ON.
(b) Measure voltage between terminal STP– of cruise control ECU connector and body ground, when the brake pedal is depressed and released.

OK:

Brake pedal position	Voltage
Depressed	10 – 14 V
Released	Below 1 V

→ OK → | Proceed to next circuit inspection shown in problem symptoms table. |

↓ NG

| 4 | Check for open in harness and connectors between terminal STP– of cruise control actuator and ECU and stop light switch. |

→ NG → | Repair or replace harness or connector. |

↓ OK

| Check and replace cruise control actuator and ECU. |

TY1109900620030X

Fig. 467 Stop Lamp Switch Circuit (Part 3 of 3). 1998–99 4Runner w/Ford cruise control

| 3 | Check for open and short in harness and connector between ECU and throttle position sensor, throttle position sensor and body ground. |

→ NG → | Repair or replace harness or connector. |

↓ OK

| Check and replace cruise control actuator and ECU. |

TY1109900621030X

Fig. 468 Idle Switch Circuit (Part 3 of 3). 1998–99 4Runner w/Ford cruise control

CIRCUIT DESCRIPTION

When driving uphill under cruise control, in order to reduce shifting due to ON–OFF overdrive operation and to provide smooth driving, when down shifting in the electronically controlled transmission occurs, a signal to prevent upshift until the end of the uphill slope is sent from the cruise control ECU to the electronically controlled transmission.

Terminal ECM of the cruise control ECU detects the shift change signal (output to electronically controlled transmission No. 2 solenoid) from the electronically controlled transmission.

If vehicle speeds down, also when terminal electronically controlled transmission of the cruise control ECU receives down shifting signal, it sends a signal from terminal OD to ECM to cut overdrive until the end of the uphill slope, and the gear shifts are reduced and gear shift points in the electronically controlled transmission are changed.

TY1109900622010X

Fig. 469 Electronically Controlled Transmission Communication Circuit (Part 1 of 3). 1998–99 4Runner w/Ford cruise control

---

3 | Check voltage between terminal ECT of cruise control actuator and ECU connector and body ground (On test drive).

PREPARATION:
(a) Connect cruise control ECU connector.
(b) Test drive after engine warms up.

CHECK:
Check voltage between terminal ECT of cruise control ECU connector and body ground when OD switch is ON and OFF.

OK:

OD switch position	Voltage
ON	8 – 14 V
OFF	Below 0.5 V

OK > Proceed to next circuit inspection shown in problem symptoms table.

NG

4 | Check harness and connector between terminal ECT of cruise control actuator and ECU and electronically controlled transmission solenoid.

NG > Repair or replace harness or connector.

OK

Check and replace cruise control actuator and ECU.

5 | Check harness and connector between terminal OD of cruise control actuator and ECU and terminal OD1 of ECM.

NG > Repair or replace harness or connector.

OK

Check and replace cruise control actuator and ECU.

TY1109900622030X

Fig. 469 Electronically Controlled Transmission Communication Circuit (Part 3 of 3). 1998–99 4Runner w/Ford cruise control

---

INSPECTION PROCEDURE

1 | Check operation of overdrive.

PREPARATION:
Test drive after engine warms up.

CHECK:
Check that overdrive ON ↔ OFF occurs with operation of OD switch ON–OFF.

NG > Check and repair electronically controlled transmission.

OK

2 | Check voltage between terminal OD of harness side connector of cruise control actuator and ECU and body ground.

PREPARATION:
Remove cruise control ECU with connector still connected.

CHECK:
(a) Disconnect cruise control ECU connector.
(b) Turn ignition switch ON.
(c) Measure voltage between terminal OD of harness side connector of cruise control ECU and body ground.

OK:
Voltage: 10 – 14 V

NG > Go to step 5.

OK

TY1109900622020X

Fig. 469 Electronically Controlled Transmission Communication Circuit (Part 2 of 3). 1998–99 4Runner w/Ford cruise control

---

CIRCUIT DESCRIPTION

When the shift position is put in except D position, a signal is sent from the park/neutral position switch to the ECU. When this signal is input during cruise control driving, the ECU cancels the cruise control.

TY1109900623010X

Fig. 470 Park/Neutral Position Switch Circuit (Part 1 of 3). 1998–99 4Runner w/Ford cruise control

---

INSPECTION PROCEDURE

1 | Check starter operation.

CHECK:
Check that the starter operates normally and that the engine starts.

NG > Proceed to engine troubleshooting.

OK

2 | Input signal check.

Input Signal	Indicator Light Blinking Pattern
Turn PNP switch OFF (Shift to except D position)	ON SW ON / Light OFF- - - SW OFF

PREPARATION:
See input signal check

CHECK:
Check the indicator light when shifting into except D position.

OK:
The indicator light goes off when shifting into except D position.

OK > Proceed to next circuit inspection shown in problem symptoms table.

NG

TY1109900623020X

Fig. 470 Park/Neutral Position Switch Circuit (Part 2 of 3). 1998–99 4Runner w/Ford cruise control

| 3 | Check voltage between terminal D of cruise control actuator and ECU and body ground. |

PREPARATION:
Turn ignition switch ON.
CHECK:
Measure voltage between terminal D of cruise control ECU connector and body ground when shifting into D position and other positions.
OK:

Shift Position	Voltage
D position	10 – 14 V
Other positions	Below 1 V

OK Proceed to next circuit inspection shown in problem symptoms table.

NG

| 4 | Check harness and connector between PNP switch and cruise control actuator and ECU. |

NG Repair or replace harness or connector.

OK

Check and replace cruise control actuator and ECU.

TY1109900623030X

Fig. 470   Park/Neutral Position Switch Circuit (Part 3 of 3). 1998–99 4Runner w/Ford cruise control

| 3 | Check voltage between terminal D of cruise control actuator and ECU and body ground. |

PREPARATION:
Turn ignition switch ON.
CHECK:
Measure voltage between terminal D of cruise control ECU connector and body ground when clutch pedal is depressed and pushed in.
OK:

Shift Position	Voltage
Clutch pedal depressed	10 – 14 V
Clutch pedal pushed in	Below 1 V

OK Proceed to next circuit inspection shown in problem symptoms table.

NG

| 4 | Check for open in harness and connector between cruise control actuator and ECU and GAUGE fuse. |

NG Repair or replace harness or connector.

OK

Check and replace cruise control actuator and ECU.

TY1109900624020X

Fig. 471   Clutch Switch Circuit (Part 2 of 2). 1998–99 4Runner w/Ford cruise control

CIRCUIT DESCRIPTION

When the clutch pedal is depressed, the clutch switch sends a signal to the cruise control ECU. When the signal is input to the cruise control ECU during cruise control driving, the cruise control ECU cancels cruise control.

INSPECTION PROCEDURE

| 1 | Check starter operation. |

CHECK:
Check that the starter operates normally and that the engine starts.

NG Proceed to engine troubleshooting.

OK

| 2 | Input signal check. |

Input Signal	Indicator Light Blinking Pattern
Clutch Switch OFF (Depress clutch pedal)	

PREPARATION:
See input signal check.
CHECK:
Check the indicator light when clutch pedal is depressed.
OK:
The indicator light goes off when clutch pedal is depressed.

OK Proceed to next circuit inspection shown in problem symptoms table.

NG

TY1109900624010X

Fig. 471   Clutch Switch Circuit (Part 1 of 2). 1998–99 4Runner w/Ford cruise control

CIRCUIT DESCRIPTION

The ECU power source supplies power to the actuator and sensors, etc., when terminal GND and the cruise control ECU case are grounded.

TY1109900625010X

Fig. 472   ECU Power Source Circuit (Part 1 of 3). 1998–99 4Runner w/Ford cruise control

INSPECTION PROCEDURE

1 | Check ECU–IG fuse.

PREPARATION:
Remove ECU–IG fuse from junction block No.1.
CHECK:
Check continuity of ECU–IG fuse.
OK:
Continuity

NG > Check for short in all the harness and components connected to ECU–IG fuse.

OK

2 | Check voltage between terminals B and GND of cruise control actuator and ECU connector.

PREPARATION:
Remove cruise control ECU with connector still connected.
CHECK:
(a) Turn ignition switch ON.
(b) Measure voltage between terminals B and GND of cruise control ECU connector.
OK:
10 – 14 V

OK > Proceed to next circuit inspection shown in problem symptoms table.

NG

TY1109900625020X

Fig. 472 ECU Power Source Circuit (Part 2 of 3). 1998–99 4Runner w/Ford cruise control

CIRCUIT DESCRIPTION
When the cruise control main switch is turned OFF, the cruise control does not operate.

INSPECTION PROCEDURE

1 | Check voltage between terminal CMS of cruise control actuator and ECU connector and body ground.

PREPARATION:
Remove cruise control ECU with connector still connected.
CHECK:
(a) Turn ignition switch ON.
(b) Measure voltage between terminal CMS of cruise control ECU connector when main switch is held ON and OFF.
OK:

Main switch	Voltage
OFF	10 – 14 V
ON	Below 1 V

OK > Proceed to next circuit inspection shown in problem symptoms table.

NG

TY1109900626010X

Fig. 473 Main Switch Circuit (Part 1 of 2). 1998–99 4Runner w/Ford cruise control

3 | Check resistance between terminal GND of cruise control actuator and ECU connector and body ground.

CHECK:
Measure resistance between terminal GND of cruise control ECU connector and body ground.
OK:
Resistance: Below 1 Ω

NG > Repair or replace harness or connector.

OK

Check and repair harness and connector between battery and cruise control actuator and ECU.

TY1109900625030X

Fig. 472 ECU Power Source Circuit (Part 3 of 3). 1998–99 4Runner w/Ford cruise control

2 | Check main switch continuity.

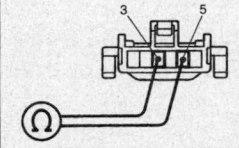

PREPARATION:
(a) Remove steering wheel center pad.
(b) Disconnect cruise control switch connector.
CHECK:
Check continuity between terminals 3 and 5 of cruise control switch connector when main switch is held ON and OFF.
OK:

Switch position	Tester connection	Specified condition
OFF	3 – 5	No continuity
Held ON	3 – 5	Continuity

NG > Replace control switch.

OK

3 | Check harness and connector between cruise control actuator and ECU and main switch.

NG > Repair or replace harness or connector.

OK

Check and replace cruise control actuator and ECU.

TY1109900626020X

Fig. 473 Main Switch Circuit (Part 2 of 2). 1998–99 4Runner w/Ford cruise control

CIRCUIT DESCRIPTION
When the cruise control main switch is turned ON, CRUISE MAIN indicator light lights up.

TY1109900627010X

Fig. 474 Cruise main Indicator Lamp Circuit (Part 1 of 2). 1998–99 4Runner w/Ford cruise control

INSPECTION PROCEDURE

1	Check voltage between terminals PI and GND of cruise control actuator and ECU connector.

PREPARATION:
Ignition switch ON.
CHECK:
Measure voltage between terminals PI and GND of cruise control ECU connector when main switch is ON and OFF.
OK:

Switch position	Voltage
OFF	10 – 16 V
ON	Below 1.2 V

OK	Proceed to next circuit inspection shown in problem symptoms table.

NG

2	Check combination meter.

NG	Replace combination meter.

OK

Check and replace cruise control actuator and ECU.

TY1109900627020X

Fig. 474 Cruise main Indicator Lamp Circuit (Part 2 of 2). 1998–99 4Runner w/Ford cruise control

INSPECTION PROCEDURE

1	Check voltage between terminals Tc and E_1 of DLC1.

CHECK:
(a)   Turn ignition switch ON.
(b)   Measure voltage between terminals Tc and E_1 of DLC1.
OK:
Voltage: 10 – 14 V

OK	Proceed to next circuit inspection shown in problem symptoms table.

NG

2	Check harness and connector between cruise control actuator and ECU and DLC1, DLC1 and body ground.

NG	Repair or replace harness or connector.

OK

Check and replace cruise control actuator and ECU.

TY1109900628020X

Fig. 475   Diagnosis Circuit (Part 2 of 2). 1998–99 4Runner w/Ford cruise control

CIRCUIT DESCRIPTION

This circuit sends a signal to the ECU that DTC output is required.

TY1109900628010X

Fig. 475   Diagnosis Circuit (Part 1 of 2). 1998–99 4Runner w/Ford cruise control

INSPECTION PROCEDURE

1	Actuator control cable removal and installation

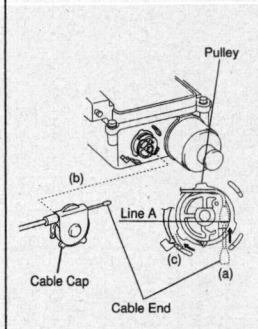

CHECK:REMOVE:
(a)   Insert the inner cable end into the pulley and pull it up to the line "A", shown in the illustration.
The end of the spring prevents the pulley from slipping out.
(b)   Install the cable cap to the fit it with the actuator.
(c)   Turn the cable cap clockwise to lock.
CHECK:INSTALL:
Installation is in the reverse order of removal.

2	Actuator control cable inspection

CHECK:
(a)   Check that the actuator and control cable throttle link are properly installed and that the cable and link are connected correctly.
(b)   Check that the actuator and bell crank are operating smoothly.
(c)   Check that the cable is not loose or too tight.
OK:
Freeplay: Less than 10 mm
HINT:
•   If the control cable is very loose, the vehicle's loss of speed going uphill will be large.
•   If the control cable is too tight, the idle RPM will become high.

TY1109900629000X

Fig. 476   Actuator Control Cable. 1998–99 4Runner w/Ford cruise control

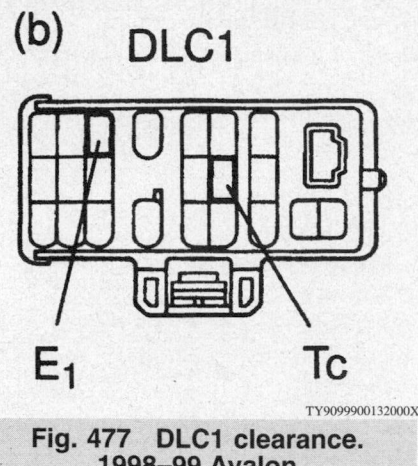

(b) DLC1

Fig. 477 DLC1 clearance. 1998–99 Avalon

TY9099900132000X

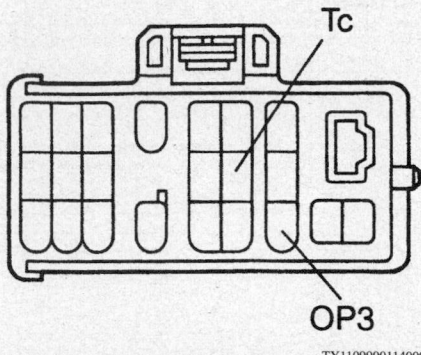

Fig. 478 DTC clearance. Tundra, T100 & 1997–98 Tacoma w/Ford cruise control

TY1109900114000X

Wiper Systems

INDEX

PRECAUTIONS

AIR BAG SYSTEMS

Refer to "Air Bag System Precautions" in the front of this manual for system disarming & arming procedures.

BATTERY GROUND CABLE

Prior to service, disconnect battery ground cable and isolate as required.

AUDIO CODED ANTI-THEFT SYSTEM

Some models are equipped with an audio coded anti-theft system that will disable the radio when the battery cable is disconnected. The system can be identified by the "ANTI-THEFT SYSTEM" on the cassette tape lid. Obtain 3 digit customer code for input. Reset system after service as follows:

1. Obtain 3 digit audio anti-theft code.
2. Depress 1 (PROG) while depressing righthand side of TUNE SEEK button, - - - will appear in tape operation display.
3. To enter the first digit, depress 1 (PROG) button repeatedly until the number of times depressed equals the first digit beginning with zero (depress the 1 button six times if the first digit is five).
4. To enter second digit, depress 2 (APS) button repeatedly until the number of times depressed equals the second digit beginning with zero.
5. To enter third digit, depress 3 (RPT) button repeatedly until the number of times depressed equals the second digit beginning with zero.
6. If - - - is displayed during code input, repeat procedure.
7. When code appears in display, depress and hold SCAN button until SEC appears.
8. When SEC disappears audio system should be operative.
9. If Err is displayed, repeat procedure. **Attempting to input code more than nine times may permanently disable audio system.**

TROUBLESHOOTING

FRONT WIPER

Wiper Does Not Operate Or Return To Off Position

1. Wiper fuse blown.
2. Wiper motor faulty.
3. Wiper switch faulty.
4. Wiring or ground faulty.

Wiper Does Not Operate In Mist Position

1. Wiper motor faulty.
2. Wiper switch faulty.
3. Wiring or ground faulty.
4. Wiper relay faulty.

REAR WIPER

On 4Runner models, ensure there is no fault in the back door power window control system.

Wiper Does Not Operate Or Return To Off Position

1. Circuit breaker off.
2. Wiper fuse blown.
3. Wiper motor faulty.
4. Rear door power window and wiper relay faulty.
5. Wiring or ground faulty.

Wiper Does Not Operate In Intermittent Position

1. Wiper motor faulty.
2. Wiper switch faulty.
3. Wiring or ground faulty.
4. Wiper relay faulty.

COMPONENT DIAGNOSIS & TESTING

FRONT WIPER & WASHER SWITCH

1. Using suitable ohmmeter, inspect continuity between terminals, **Figs. 1 through 14.**
2. If continuity is not as indicated, replace switch.

INTERMITTENT & WASHER SWITCH

Camry Solara, Sienna, 1997–99 Camry & Supra

1. Inspect wiper switch operation as follows:
   a. Place wiper switch to INT position.
   b. Place INT switch to FAST position.
   c. Connect positive battery lead to terminal 16 and negative lead to terminal 2.
   d. Connect positive voltmeter lead to terminal 7 and negative lead to terminal 2.
   e. Ensure voltmeter indicates battery positive voltage.
   f. Connect terminal 16 to terminal 17, then terminal 17 to terminal 2.
   g. Ensure voltage rises from 0 volts to battery voltage as indicated in **Figs. 15 and 16**.
   h. If operation is not as specified, replace wiper switch.
2. Inspect washer switch operation as follows:
   a. Connect jumper wires and voltmeter as outlined under steps C and D of intermittent switch test.
   b. Place washer switch to closed position and ensure voltage is as shown in **Fig. 17**.
   c. If operation is not as specified, replace wiper switch.

Previa, Land Cruiser, Tacoma, 1996 Avalon, Camry & Celica & 1997 Supra

1. Inspect intermittent switch operation as follows:
   a. Place wiper switch in INT position.
   b. **On models equipped with variable type,** place INT switch to Fast position.
   c. **On all models,** connect battery positive lead to terminal (B)18 and negative lead to terminal (B)16.
   d. Connect voltmeter positive lead to terminal (B)7 and negative lead to terminal (B)16, needle sweep indicates battery voltage.
   e. Using suitable wire, connect terminals (B)4 and (B)18, then connect terminal (B)16.
   f. Battery voltage should rise from zero volts to battery voltage, as shown in **Figs. 15 and 16.**
   g. If operation is not as indicated, replace wiper and washer switch.
2. Inspect washer switch operation as follows:
   a. Connect positive battery lead to terminal (B)18 and negative to terminal (B)16.
   b. Connect voltmeter positive lead to terminal (B)7 and negative to terminal (B)16.
   c. Depress washer switch, ensuring voltage is as indicated in **Fig. 17**.
   d. If operation is not as indicated, replace wiper and washer switch.

RAV4

1. Use the following procedure to inspect intermittent switch operation:
   a. Place wiper switch in INT position.
   b. Place INT switch to Fast position.
   c. Connect battery positive lead to terminal 17 and negative lead to terminal 16.
   d. Connect voltmeter positive lead to terminal 7 and negative lead to terminal 16, needle sweep indicates battery voltage.
   e. Using suitable wire, connect terminals 2 and 17, then connect terminal 16.
   f. Battery voltage should rise from zero volts to battery voltage, as shown in **Fig. 16.**
   g. If operation is not as specified, replace wiper/washer switch.

Tundra

1. Inspect intermittent switch operation as follows:
   a. Place wiper switch in "INT" position.
   b. Place wiper time control switch to "FAST" position.
   c. Apply battery positive voltage to terminal 16 of wiper switch, **Fig. 7.**
   d. Apply battery ground to terminal 2 of wiper switch.
   e. Connect voltmeter positive lead to terminal 7 and negative lead to terminal 2. Ensure meter needle indicates battery positive. In " FAST" position, voltmeter needle should fluctuate from zero to battery voltage every 1–3 seconds. In "SLOW" position, voltmeter needle should fluctuate from zero to battery voltage every 10–15 seconds.

T100

1. Inspect intermittent switch operation as follows:
   a. Place wiper switch in INT position.
   b. **On models equipped with variable type,** place INT switch to Fast position.
   c. **On all models,** connect battery positive lead to terminal (A)4 and negative lead to terminal (A)1.
   d. Connect voltmeter positive lead to terminal (A)8 and negative lead to terminal (A)1, needle sweep indicates battery voltage.
   e. Using suitable wire, connect terminals (A)7 and (A)4, then connect terminal (A)1.
   f. Battery voltage should rise from zero volts to battery voltage, as shown in **Fig. 18.**
   g. if operation is not as indicated, replace wiper and washer switch.

1996 Supra

1. Inspect intermittent switch operation as follows:
   a. Connect battery positive lead to terminal 5 and negative lead to terminal 7, **Fig. 19.**
   b. Using suitable wire, connect terminals 7 and 8, check continuity between terminals 1 and 5, as shown in **Fig. 20.**
2. Inspect washer circuit relay as follows:
   a. Connect battery positive lead to terminal 5 and negative lead to terminal 7.
   b. Check continuity between terminals 1 and 5 as shown in **Fig. 21.**
   c. If operation is not as indicated, replace relay.

1996–97 Corolla

1. Inspect intermittent switch operation as follows:
   a. Place wiper switch in INT position.
   b. Connect battery positive lead to terminal (B)18 and negative lead to terminal (B)16.
   c. Connect voltmeter positive lead to terminal (B)13 and negative lead to terminal (B)16, needle sweep indicates battery voltage.
   d. Using suitable wire, connect terminals (B)4 and (B)16, then connect terminal (B)18.
   e. Battery voltage should rise from zero volts to battery voltage as indicated, **Fig. 22.**
   f. If operation is not as indicated, replace wiper and washer switch.

1996–97 Paseo

1. Inspect intermittent switch operation as follows:
   a. Place wiper switch in INT position.
   b. Connect battery positive lead to terminal 17 and negative lead to terminal 2.
   c. Connect voltmeter positive lead to terminal 16 and negative lead to terminal 7, needle sweep indicates battery voltage.
   d. Using suitable wire, connect terminals 16 and 17, then connect terminals 16 and 2.
   e. Battery voltage should rise from zero volts to battery voltage as shown in **Fig. 23.**
   f. If operation is not as indicated, replace switch.

Tercel

1. Inspect intermittent switch operation as follows:
   a. Place wiper switch in INT position.
   b. Connect battery positive lead to terminal 17 and negative lead to terminal 2.
   c. Connect voltmeter positive lead to terminal 7 and negative lead to terminal 2, needle sweep indicates battery voltage.
   d. Using suitable wire, connect terminals 16 and 17, then connect terminals 17 and 2.
   e. Battery voltage should rise from zero volts to battery voltage as shown in **Fig. 22.**
   f. If operation is not as indicated, replace switch.

1996–97 4Runner

1. Inspect intermittent switch operation as follows:
   a. Place wiper switch in INT position.
   b. Place INT switch to Fast position.
   c. Connect battery positive lead to terminal 16 and negative lead to terminal 2.

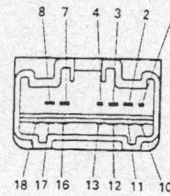

Switch position	Tester connection to terminal number	Specified condition
Wiper OFF	7 – 16	Continuity
Wiper INT	7 – 16	Continuity
Wiper LO	7 – 17	Continuity
Wiper HI	8 – 17	Continuity
Washer ON	2 – 11	Continuity

TY9029500038000X

Fig. 1   Front wiper & washer switch inspection. Avalon, Camry Solara, Celica, RAV4, Sienna, Tercel less intermittent wiper, 1996–97 Paseo, 1997–99 Camry & 1998 Supra

d. Connect voltmeter positive lead to terminal 7 and negative lead to terminal 2, needle sweep indicates battery voltage.
e. Battery voltage should rise from zero volts to battery voltage, as shown in **Fig. 16.**
f. If operation is not as specified, replace wiper/washer switch.

1997-99 Celica

1. Inspect intermittent switch operation as follows:
   a. Place wiper switch to INT position.
   b. Turn intermittent time control switch to FAST position.
   c. Connect positive battery lead to terminal 17, then the negative lead to terminal 16.
   d. Connect positive lead of voltmeter to terminal 7, then the negative lead to terminal 16.
   e. Connect terminal 17 to terminal 2.
   f. Connect terminal 16 to terminal 2.
   g. Ensure voltage rises from 0 volts to battery voltage, **Fig. 15.**
   h. If operation is not as specified, replace switch.

1997-99 Avalon

1. Inspect intermittent switch operation as follows:
   a. Place wiper switch to INT position.
   b. Place INT time control to FAST position.
   c. Install jumper wire from battery positive to wiper switch terminal 17.
   d. Install jumper wire from battery negative to terminal 2 of wiper switch.
   e. Connect voltmeter positive lead to terminal 7 and negative lead to terminal 2.
   f. Connect terminal 16 and 2 to terminal 17.
   g. Ensure voltage increases from 0 volts to battery voltage in 2.3–4.3 second rhythm.
   h. If operation is not as specified, replace switch.
2. Inspect washer switch as follows:

Switch position	Tester connection	Specified condition
Wiper OFF	B4 – B7	Continuity
Wiper INT	B4 – B7	Continuity
Wiper LO	B7 – B18	Continuity
Wiper HI	B13 – B18	Continuity
Washer OFF	–	No continuity
Washer ON	B8 – B16	Continuity

TY9029600042000X

Fig. 2   Front wiper & washer switch inspection. Land Cruiser

a. Connect jumper wires and voltmeter as outlined under steps C-E of intermittent switch test.
b. Position washer switch to closed position.
c. Ensure voltage is as outlined in **Fig. 17.**
d. If operation is not as specified, replace switch.

1998-99 Corolla

1. Inspect intermittent switch operation as follows:
   a. Place wiper switch to INT position.
   b. Place INT time control to FAST position.
   c. Connect positive lead from battery to terminal 16 and negative lead to terminal 2.
   d. Connect positive lead from voltmeter to terminal 7 and negative lead to terminal 2.
   e. Ensure voltmeter indicates battery voltage.
   f. Connect terminal 16 to 17, then 2 to 17. Ensure voltage rises from 0 to battery voltage in 2–3 seconds.
   g. Place INT time control to SLOW position. Ensure voltage rises from 0 to battery voltage in 10–15 seconds.
   h. If operation is not as specified, replace wiper switch.
2. Inspect washer switch operation as follows:
   a. Connect positive lead from battery to terminal 16 and negative lead to terminal 2.
   b. Connect positive lead from voltmeter to terminal 7 and negative lead to terminal 2.
   c. Activate washer switch and ensure battery voltage is indicated.
   d. If operation is not as specified, replace switch.

WIPER RELAY

Land Cruiser

1. Inspect rear wiper relay operation as follows:
   a. Ensure no continuity exists between terminals 1 and 3.
   b. Continuity should exist between terminals 2 and 3.
   c. If continuity is not as indicated, replace relay.
   d. Connect positive battery lead to terminal 1 and negative to terminal 6.
   e. Connect voltmeter positive lead to terminal 2 and negative to terminal

Switch position	Tester connection	Specified condition
Wiper OFF	B4 – B7	Continuity
Wiper INT	B4 – B7 / B12 – B16	Continuity
Wiper LO	B7 – B18	Continuity
Wiper HI	B13 – B18	Continuity
Washer ON	B8 – B16	Continuity

TY9029600041000X

Fig. 3   Front wiper & washer switch inspection. Previa

6, ensure meter indicates zero volts.
f. Connect voltmeter positive lead to terminal 3 and negative to terminal 6, ensure meter indicates battery voltage volts.
g. Connect positive battery lead to terminal 2 and negative to terminal 4.
h. Connect voltmeter positive lead to terminal 3 and negative to terminal 4.
i. Disconnect positive lead from terminal 2, then connect to terminal 1, ensure meter needle rises from zero volts to battery voltage within 6–10 seconds.
j. If operation is not as indicated, replace relay.

Previa

1. Inspect front wiper relay for continuity between terminals 1 and 4, no continuity should be indicated.
2. Ensure continuity between terminals 1 and 3, **Fig. 24.**
3. If continuity is not as indicated, replace relay.
4. Inspect front wiper relay operation as follows:
   a. Connect battery positive lead to terminal 4 and negative lead to terminal 5.
   b. Connect voltmeter positive lead to terminal 3 and negative to terminal 5.
   c. Connect battery negative lead to terminal 6, ensure voltage changes from battery voltage to no voltage.
   d. Disconnect negative lead from terminal 6, ensure voltage changes from no voltage to battery voltage in about 2.5 seconds.
   e. If operation is not as indicated, replace relay.

Sienna

1. Inspect rear wiper relay as follows:
   a. Ensure no continuity is present between terminals 3 and 4 of relay, **Fig. 25.**
   b. Ensure continuity exists between terminals 4 and 5.
   c. Connect battery voltage to terminal 3 and battery ground to terminal 6.
   d. Connect positive voltmeter lead to terminal 5 and negative lead to terminal 6.
   e. Ensure voltmeter indicates 0 volts.
   f. Connect positive lead from voltmeter to terminal 4 and negative lead to terminal 6.

Switch position	Tester connection to terminal number	Specified value
Wiper OFF	B4 – B7	Continuity
Wiper OFF and MIST	B7 – B18	Continuity
Wiper INT	B4 – B7	Continuity
Wiper INT and MIST	B7 – B18	Continuity
Wiper LO	B7 – B18	Continuity
Wiper LO and MIST	B7 – B18	Continuity
Wiper HI	B13 – B18	Continuity
Wiper HI and MIST	B7 – B13 B13 – B18	Continuity
Washer ON	B8 – B16	Continuity

TY9029300011000X

Fig. 4   Front wiper & washer switch inspection. 1996–97 Supra

Connector "A"   Connector "B"

Terminal (Color) Switch position		B-4 (L-R)	B-7 (L-B)	B-13 (L-O)	B-18 (L-W)	B-8 (L)	B-16 (B)
Wiper	MIST		O				
	OFF	O—O					
	INT	O—O					
	LO		O—O				
	HI			O—O			
Washer	OFF						
	ON					O—O	

TY9029100002000X

Fig. 5   Front wiper & washer switch inspection. Tacoma & 1996–97 Corolla

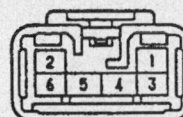

Terminal Switch position		1	2	5	6	3	4
Wiper	OFF	O—		—O			
	INT	O—		—O			
	LO	O—	—O				
	HI			O—	—O		
Washer	OFF						
	ON					O—	—O

TY9029100014000X

Fig. 6   Front wiper & washer switch inspection. Tercel w/intermittent wiper

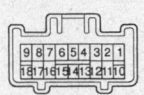

w/ MIST:

Switch position	Tester connection	Specified condition
OFF	7 – 16	Continuity
MIST	7 – 17	Continuity
LO	7 – 17	Continuity
HI	8 – 17	Continuity
Washer ON	2 – 11	Continuity

w/ INTERMITTENT:

Switch position	Tester connection	Specified condition
OFF	7 – 16	Continuity
INT	7 – 16	Continuity
LO	7 – 17	Continuity
HI	8 – 17	Continuity
Washer ON	2 – 11	Continuity

TY9029900059000X

Fig. 7   Front wiper & washer switch inspection. Tundra

Connector "A"   Connector "B"

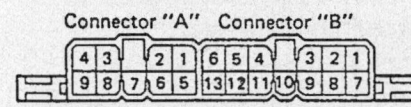

Terminal (Color) Switch position		A-1 (B)	A-2 (L)	A-4 (L-W)	A-7 (L-R)	A-8 (L-B)	A-9 (L-O)
Wiper	MIST			O—O			
	OFF				O—O		
	LO			O—O			
	HI					O—O	
Washer	OFF						
	ON	O—O					

TY9029100006000X

Fig. 8   Front wiper & washer switch inspection. T100 w/mist wiper

Connector "A"   Connector "B"

Switch position	Tester connection	Specified condition
Wiper OFF	B4 – B7	Continuity
Wiper OFF and MIST	B4 – B7 B16 – B18	Continuity
Wiper INT	B4 – B7 B14 – B16	Continuity
Wiper INT and MIST	B4 – B7 B14 – B16 – B18	Continuity
Wiper LO	B7 – B18	Continuity
Wiper LO and MIST	B7 – B18	Continuity
Wiper HI	B6 – B16 B13 – B16	Continuity
Wiper HI and MIST	B6 – B16 B13 – B18	Continuity
Washer ON	B8 – B16	Continuity

TY9029600040000X

Fig. 9   Front wiper & washer switch inspection. 1996 Camry

Connector "A"   Connector "B"

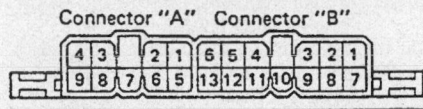

Terminal (Color) Switch position		A-1 (B)	A-2 (L)	A-4 (L-W)	A-7 (L-R)	A-8 (L-B)	A-9 (L-O)
Wiper	MIST			O—O			
	INT			O—O			
	LO			O—O			
	HI			O—O			—O
Washer	OFF						
	ON	O—O					

TY9029100007000X

Fig. 10   Front wiper & washer switch inspection. 1996 T100 w/intermittent wiper

g. Ensure voltmeter indicates battery voltage.

h. Connect positive lead from battery to terminal 5 and negative lead to terminal 2 for more than two seconds.

i. Connect positive lead from voltmeter to terminal 4 and negative lead to terminal 2.

j. After disconnecting positive lead from terminal 5, connect it to terminal 3, then check voltmeter reading within 9 to 15 seconds.

k. Replace relay if operation is not as specified.

FRONT WIPER MOTOR

Camry Solara

1. Inspect low speed operation as follows:

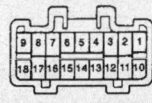

Switch position	Tester connection	Specified condition
OFF	7 – 16	Continuity
INT	7 – 16	Continuity
LO	7 – 17	Continuity
HI	8 – 17	Continuity
Washer ON	2 – 11	Continuity

TY9029600044000X

Fig. 11   Front wiper & washer switch inspection. 4Runner w/intermittent wiper

Switch position	Tester connection	Specified condition
OFF	7 – 8	Continuity
INT	7 – 8	Continuity
LO	4 – 8	Continuity
HI	4 – 9	Continuity

TY9029700055000X

Fig. 13   Front wiper & washer switch inspection. 1997–98 T100 w/intermittent wiper

a. Connect battery positive lead to terminal 1 of wiper motor connector, **Fig. 26.**

b. Connect battery negative lead to terminal 5 of wiper motor connector.

c. If wiper motor does not operate at low speed, replace.

2. Inspect high speed operation as follows:

a. Connect positive lead from battery

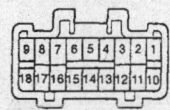

Switch position	Tester connection	Specified condition
OFF	7 – 16	Continuity
MIST	7 – 17	Continuity
LO	7 – 17	Continuity
HI	8 – 17	Continuity
Washer ON	2 – 11	Continuity

TY9029600043000X

Fig. 12   Front wiper & washer switch inspection. 4Runner w/mist wiper

to terminal 4 of wiper motor.

b. Connect negative lead from battery to terminal 5 of wiper motor.

c. If wiper motor does not operate at high speed, replace.

3. Inspect wiper motor stop circuit as follows:

a. Operate wiper motor at low speed.

b. Stop motor in any position except stop position by disconnecting positive lead from terminal 1 of motor connector.

c. Connect terminals 1 and 3.

d. Connect positive lead from battery to terminal 2, then the negative lead to terminal 5.

e. If motor does not return to stop position, replace.

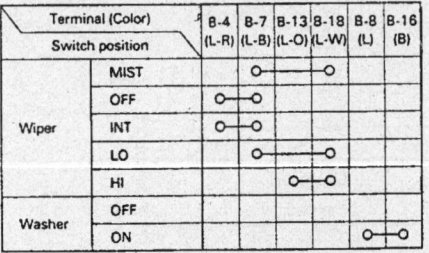

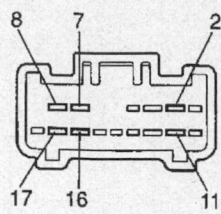

Switch position	Tester connection	Specified condition
OFF	7 – 16	Continuity
MIST (w/ Mist wiper)	3 – 11	Continuity
INT (w/ Intermittent wiper)	7 – 16	Continuity
LO	7 – 17	Continuity
HI	8 – 17	Continuity
Washer ON	2 – 11	Continuity

TY9029800058000X

Fig. 14   Front wiper & washer switch inspection. 1998–99 Corolla

INT time control switch position	Voltage
FAST	Approx. 1 – 3 sec. Battery positive voltage / 0 volt
SLOW	Approx. 10 – 15 sec. Battery positive voltage / 0 volt

TY9029600045000X

Fig. 16   Wiper intermittent switch inspection. RAV4, Sienna, 4Runner & Supra

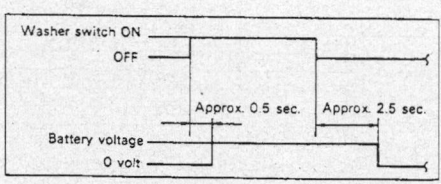

TY9029100016000X

Fig. 17   Washer intermittent switch inspection. Avalon, Camry, Celica, Previa, Land Cruiser, Supra & Tacoma

INT time control switch position	Voltage
FAST	Approx. 2 sec. Battery voltage / 0 volt
SLOW	10.7 ± 5 sec. Battery voltage / 0 volt
Non variable type	3.3 ± 1 sec. Battery voltage / 0 volt

TY9029100015000X

Fig. 15   Wiper intermittent switch inspection. Camry, Camry Solara, Celica, Land Cruiser, Previa, Tacoma & 1996 Avalon

Non Variable Type

Switch position	Specifed value	
INT	3.3 ± 1 sec.	Battery voltage / 0 volts

Variable Type

Switch position		Specifed value	
INT	FAST	1.6 ± 1 sec.	Battery voltage / 0 volts
	LOW	10.7 ± 5 sec.	Battery voltage / 0 volts

TY9029100022000X

Fig. 18   Wiper & washer intermittent switch inspection. T100

1996 Avalon, Camry, Paseo, RAV4, Supra, Tercel & 4Runner

1. Inspect low speed motor operation as follows:
   a. Disconnect wiper motor electrical connector.
   b. Connect positive battery lead to terminal 2 and negative to motor body, **Fig. 27.**
   c. Ensure motor operates at low speed.
2. Inspect high speed motor operation as follows:
   a. Connect positive battery lead to terminal 1 and negative to motor body.
   b. Ensure motor operates at high speed.
3. Inspect motor operation, stopping at stop position, as follows:
   a. Operate motor at low speed.
   b. Disconnect terminal 2 to stop motor operation.
   c. Connect terminals 2 and 3.
   d. Connect battery positive lead to terminal 4.
   e. Ensure motor stops running in Off position after motor operates again.
4. If motor operation is not as indicated, replace motor.

Celica, Corolla, Previa, Land Cruiser, Tacoma, T100, 1997 Paseo & Tercel, 1997–98 Avalon & Supra & 1997–99 RAV4

1. Inspect low speed motor operation as follows:
   a. Disconnect wiper motor electrical connector.
   b. **On all models except 1997 Previa and T100,** connect positive battery lead to terminal 3 and negative to terminal 1.
   c. **On 1997 Previa and T100 models,** connect positive battery lead to terminal 3, then the negative lead to wiper motor ground strap.
   d. **On all models,** refer to **Figs. 28 through 30** and **Fig. 34** for connector pin locations.
   e. Ensure motor operates at low speed.
2. Inspect high speed motor operation as follows:
   a. **On all models except 1997 Previa and T100,** connect positive battery

lead to terminal 2 and negative to terminal 1.
   b. **On 1997 Previa and T100 models,** connect positive battery lead to terminal, then the negative lead to wiper motor ground strap.
   c. **On all models,** ensure motor operates at high speed.
3. Inspect motor stop operation, as follows:
   a. Operate motor at low speed.
   b. Disconnect positive lead from terminal 3 to stop motor operation.
   c. **On Previa models,** connect terminals 3 and 4.
   d. **On 1996 Previa models,** connect battery positive lead to terminal 5 and negative lead to terminal 1.
   e. **On 1997 Previa models,** connect battery positive lead to terminal 5 and negative lead to terminal wiper motor ground strap.
   f. **On Celica, 1997 Corolla, Land Cruiser, Paseo, 1997–99 RAV4, Tacoma, Tercel, T100, and 1997–98 Avalon and Supra models,** connect terminals 3 and 5.
   g. **On models except 1997 T100,** connect battery positive lead to terminal 6 and negative lead to terminal 1.
   h. **On 1997–98 T100 models,** connect positive battery lead to terminal 6, then the negative lead to motor body.
   i. **On all models,** ensure motor stops running in Off position after motor

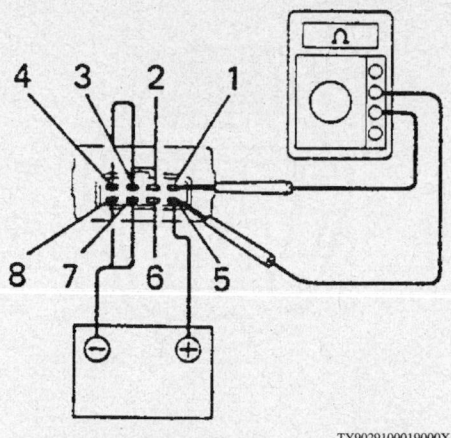

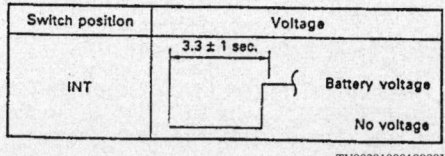

TY9029100019000X

Fig. 19 Wiper relay. 1996 Supra

Switch position	Voltage	
INT	3.3 ± 1 sec.	Battery voltage
		No voltage

TY9029100018000X

Fig. 22 Wiper intermittent switch inspection. Tercel & 1996–97 Corolla

operates again.
4. If motor operation is not as indicated, replace motor.

Sienna

1. Inspect low speed wiper operation as follows:
   a. Connect battery positive lead to terminal 5 of wiper motor, **Fig. 31.**
   b. Connect battery negative to terminal 1.
   c. If motor does not operate at low speed, replace.
2. Inspect wiper motor high speed operation as follows:
   a. Connect battery positive lead to terminal 4 of wiper motor.
   b. Connect battery negative lead to terminal 1.
   c. If motor does not operate at high speed, replace.
3. Inspect motor stop circuit as follows:
   a. Operate motor on low speed.
   b. Disconnect terminal 5 from wiper motor in any position except park.
   c. Connect terminals 2 and 5 using a suitable jumper wire.
   d. Connect battery positive lead to terminal 3 and negative lead to terminal 1.
   e. If motor does not stop at park position, replace.

Tundra

1. Inspect low speed operation as follows:
   a. Connect battery positive lead to wiper motor terminal 5 and negative lead to terminal 4, **Fig. 32.**
   b. If motor does not operate at low speed, replace.
2. Inspect high speed operation as follows:

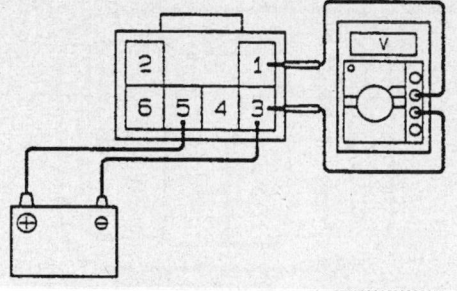

TY9029100020000X

Fig. 20 Wiper relay intermittent operation inspection. 1996 Supra

   a. Connect battery positive lead to wiper motor terminal 3.
   b. Connect battery negative lead to motor body or terminal 4.
   c. If motor does not operate at high speed, replace.
3. Inspect wiper motor park position as follows:
   a. Operate motor at low speed, then stop motor operation anywhere except stop position by disconnecting positive lead from terminal 5.
   b. Connect terminals 1 and 5.
   c. Connect battery positive lead to terminal 2 and negative lead to terminal 4 or motor body.
   d. If motor does not stop running and return to park position, replace motor.

1997–99 4Runner

1. Inspect low speed operation as follows:
   a. Connect positive battery lead to terminal 3, then the negative lead to motor body, **Fig. 33.**
   b. Ensure wiper motor operates on low speed.
   c. If operation is not as described, replace motor.
2. Inspect high speed operation as follows:
   a. Connect positive battery lead to terminal 2, then the negative lead to motor body.
   b. Ensure motor operates on high speed.
   c. If operation is not as described, replace motor.
3. Inspect motor stop position operation as follows:
   a. Operate motor at low speed, then disconnect terminal 2 and ensure motor does not stop at park position.
   b. Connect terminals 2 and 3.
   c. Connect positive battery lead to terminal 4, then the negative lead to motor body.
   d. Ensure motor returns to park position.
   e. If operation is not as specified, replace motor.

1997–99 Camry

1. Inspect low speed motor operation as follows:
   a. Connect battery positive lead to terminal 5, then the negative lead to

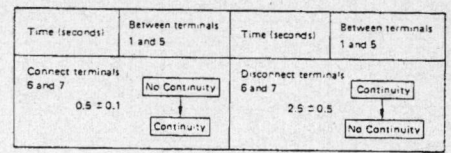

Time (seconds)	Between terminals 1 and 5	Time (seconds)	Between terminals 1 and 5
Connect terminals 6 and 7		Disconnect terminals 6 and 7	
0.5 ± 0.1	No Continuity → Continuity	2.5 ± 0.5	Continuity → No Continuity

TY9029100021000X

Fig. 21 Wiper relay washer circuit inspection. 1996 Supra

Switch position	Specified value	
INT	4.1 ± 1 sec.	Battery voltage 0 volts

TY9029600046000X

Fig. 23 Wiper intermittent switch inspection. 1996–97 Paseo

terminal 4, **Figs. 26 and 34.**
   b. Ensure motor operates at low speed.
   c. If operation is not as specified, replace motor.
2. Inspect high speed motor operation as follows:
   a. Connect positive battery lead to terminal 3, then the negative lead to terminal 4.
   b. Ensure motor operates at high speed.
   c. If operation is not as specified, replace motor.
3. Inspect motor stop operation as follows:
   a. Operate motor at low speed, then disconnect positive lead from terminal 5. Ensure motor does not come to rest in stop position.
   b. Connect terminals 3 and 5.
   c. Connect battery positive lead to terminal 2, then the negative lead to terminal 4.
   d. Ensure motor returns to stop position.
   e. If operation is not as specified, replace motor.

1998 Tercel

1. Inspect low speed operation as follows:
   a. Connect positive lead from battery to terminal 5 and negative lead to terminal 4, **Fig. 34.**
   b. Ensure motor operates on low speed
2. Inspect high speed operation as follows:
   a. Connect positive lead from battery to terminal 3 and negative lead to terminal 4.
   b. Ensure motor operates on high speed.
3. Inspect wiper motor stop operation as follows:
   a. Operate motor at low speed.
   b. Stop motor at any position except park by disconnecting positive lead from terminal 5.
   c. Connect terminals 1 and 5.
   d. Connect positive lead from battery to terminal 2 and negative lead to terminal 4.
   e. Ensure motor stops running at stop position after motor operates again.

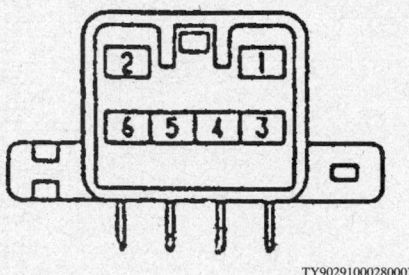

Fig. 24 Wiper relay. Previa

TY9029100028000X

4. If operation is not as specified, replace motor.

1999 Avalon

1. Inspect low speed operation as follows:
   a. Connect positive lead from battery to terminal 3.
   b. Connect negative lead from battery to terminal 1.
   c. Ensure motor operates at low speed.
   d. If motor operation is not as specified, replace motor.
2. Inspect high speed motor operation as follows:
   a. Connect positive lead from battery to terminal 2.
   b. Connect negative lead from battery to terminal 1.
   c. Ensure motor operates at high speed.
   d. If operation is not as specified, replace motor.

WASHER MOTOR

Avalon, Camry, Camry Solara, Corolla, Land Cruiser, Paseo, Previa, Sienna, Supra, 4Runner, T100 & Tercel & Celica Less Rear Wiper

Perform test within 20 seconds to prevent coil damage.
1. Connect battery positive lead to terminal 2 and negative to terminal 1.
2. Ensure motor operates.
3. If motor operation is not as indicated, replace motor.

Celica w/Rear Wiper

Perform test within 20 seconds to prevent coil damage.
1. Connect battery positive lead to terminal 2 and negative to terminal 1.
2. Ensure motor operates.
3. Disconnect negative lead from terminal 1 and connect to terminal 3.
4. Ensure motor operates.
5. If motor operation is not as indicated, replace motor.

REAR WIPER & WASHER SWITCH

1. Inspect for continuity as shown in **Figs. 35 through 40.**
2. If continuity is not as indicated, replace switch.

TY9029900061000X

Fig. 25 Rear wiper relay terminal identification. Sienna

REAR MOTOR & RELAY

Celica & Supra

1. Inspect relay and motor operation as follows:
   a. Connect battery positive lead to terminal 1 and negative to terminal 3 and motor body, **Fig. 41.**
   b. Ensure motor operation.
2. Inspect motor operation, stopping at stop position, as follows:
   a. Connect battery positive lead to terminal 1 and negative to both terminal 3 and motor body to start motor operation.
   b. **On models except 1996 Celica,** disconnect terminal 1 to stop motor operation.
   c. **On 1997–99 Celica,** disconnect negative lead from terminal 3.
   d. **On all models,** connect battery positive lead to terminal 1 and negative lead to motor body.
   e. **On all models,** ensure motor stops running at stop position after motor operates again.
   f. If operation is not as indicated, replace motor.
3. Inspect intermittent relay operation as follows:
   a. Connect battery positive lead to terminal 1 and negative to terminal 2 and motor body.
   b. Ensure motor operates intermittently for 9–15 seconds.
   c. If operation is not as indicated, replace relay.

Corolla

1. Inspect motor operation as follows:
   a. Connect battery positive lead to terminal 2 and negative to motor body.
   b. Ensure motor operation.
2. Inspect motor operation, stopping at stop position, as follows:
   a. Operate motor, then disconnect terminal 2 to stop motor operation.
   b. Connect terminals 2 and 3.
   c. Connect battery positive lead to terminal 1 and negative lead to motor body.
   d. Ensure motor stops running at stop position after motor operates again.
   e. If operation is not as indicated, replace motor.

TY9029800057000X

Fig. 26 Wiper motor connector. Camry Solara & 1998–99 Camry

Previa & Land Cruiser

1. Inspect low speed motor operation as follows:
   a. Connect battery positive lead to terminal 3 and negative to terminal 2.
   b. Ensure motor operation.
2. Inspect motor operation, stopping at stop position, as follows:
   a. Operate motor, then disconnect terminal 3 to stop motor operation.
   b. Connect terminals 3 and 4.
   c. Connect battery positive lead to terminal 1 and negative lead to terminal 2.
   d. Ensure motor stops running at stop position after motor operates again.
   e. If operation is not as indicated, replace motor.

RAV4

1. Inspect motor operation as follows:
   a. Connect battery positive lead to terminal 4 and negative battery lead to motor, **Fig. 42.**
   b. Ensure motor operates.
   c. Inspect motor operation, stopping at stop position.
   d. Operate motor, then disconnect terminal 4 to stop motor operation.
   e. Connect terminals 2 and 4.
   f. Connect battery positive lead to terminal 1 and negative lead to motor body.
   g. Ensure motor stops running at stop position after motor operates again.
   h. If operation is not as indicated, replace motor.
2. Inspect rear wiper relay continuity as follows:
   a. Ensure no continuity is present between terminals 3 and 4, **Fig. 43.**
   b. Ensure continuity exists between terminals 4 and 5.
3. Inspect rear wiper relay operation as follows:
   a. Connect positive lead from battery to terminal 3 and negative lead from battery to terminal 6.
   b. Connect positive lead from voltmeter to terminal 5 and negative lead to terminal 6. Ensure voltmeter indicates 0 volts.

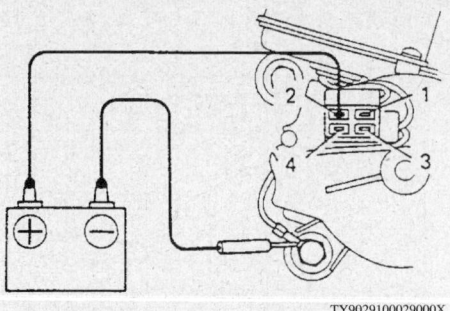

Fig. 27 Front wiper motor connector. 1996 Avalon, Camry, Paseo, RAV4, Supra, Tercel & 4Runner

Fig. 28 Wiper motor connector. Celica, Corolla, Previa, Land Cruiser, Tacoma, T100, 1997 Paseo & Tercel, 1997–98 Avalon & Supra & 1997–99 Rav4

Fig. 29 Front wiper motor connector. 1996 Previa

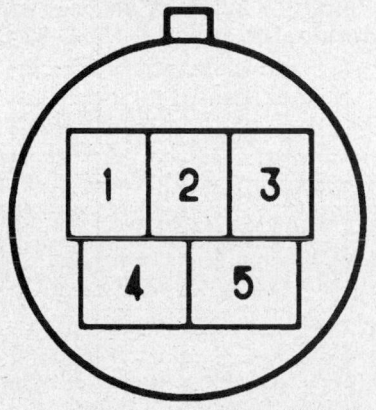

Fig. 30 Front wiper motor connector. 1997 Previa

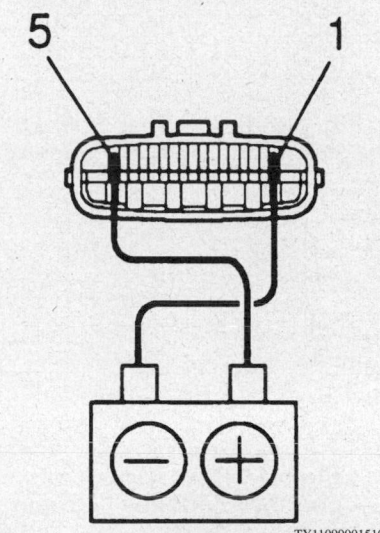

Fig. 31 Wiper motor harness connector. Sienna

Fig. 32 Wiper motor harness connector. Tundra

c. Connect positive lead from voltmeter to terminal 4 and negative lead to terminal 6. Ensure voltmeter indicates battery positive voltage.
4. Inspect rear wiper relay operation as follows:
   a. Connect positive lead from battery to terminal 5 and negative lead to terminal 2 for more than 2 seconds.
   b. Connect positive lead from voltmeter to terminal 4 and negative lead to terminal 2.
   c. After disconnecting positive lead from terminal 5, connect it to terminal 3. Voltmeter should rise from 0 volts to battery positive voltage in 9–15 seconds.
5. Inspect rear washer operation as follows:
   a. Connect battery positive lead to terminal 2 and negative lead to terminal 1.
   b. Ensure motor operates.

Fig. 33 Front wiper motor connector. 1997–99 4Runner

4Runner

1. Inspect low speed motor operation as follows:
   a. Connect battery positive lead to terminal 1 and negative to terminal 3, **Fig. 44**.
   b. Ensure motor turns clockwise.
   c. Reverse polarity, ensure motor turn counterclockwise.
   d. If operation is not as indicated, replace motor.
2. Inspect motor continuity as follows:
   a. Connect battery positive lead to terminal 3 and negative to terminal 1, inspect continuity between terminals, **Fig. 45**.
   b. If continuity is not as indicated, replace motor.

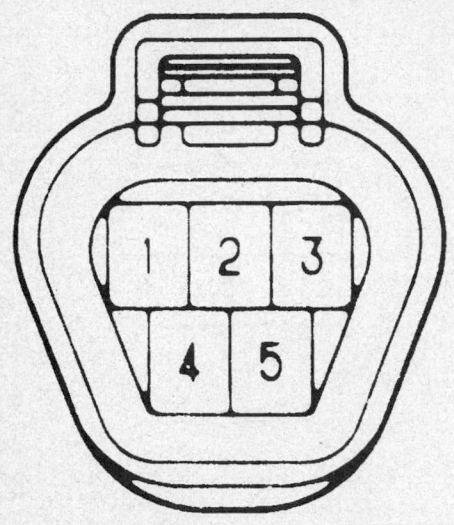

Fig. 34 Wiper motor connector. 1997–98 Tercel & 1997 Camry & Paseo

Switch position	Tester connection	Specified condition
Wiper OFF	–	No continuity
Wiper INT	2 – 13	Continuity
Wiper ON	2 – 10	Continuity
Washer ON	2 – 12	Continuity

Fig. 37 Rear wiper & washer continuity test. 1997–99 Celica

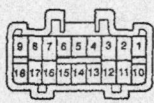

Switch position	Tester connection	Specified condition
Washer 1	2 – 12	Continuity
Wiper OFF	–	No continuity
Wiper INT	2 – 13	Continuity
Wiper ON	2 – 10	Continuity
Washer 2	2 – 10 – 12	Continuity

Fig. 40 Rear wiper & washer switch. Sienna, 4Runner & 1998 Supra

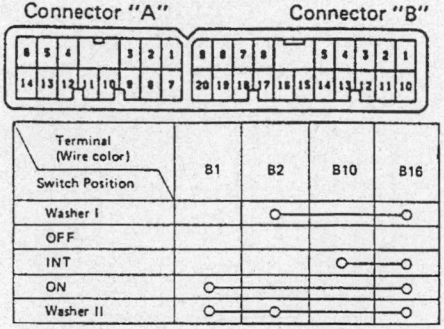

Terminal (Wire color) / Switch Position	B1	B2	B10	B16
Washer I		○———		———○
OFF				
INT			○———	———○
ON	○———			———○
Washer II	○———			———○

Fig. 35 Rear wiper & washer switch. Land Cruiser, Previa & 1996 Celica & RAV4 & 1996–97 Supra

Switch position	Tester connection	Specified condition
Washer 1	2 – 16	Continuity
Wiper OFF	–	No continuity
Wiper INT	10 – 16	Continuity
Wiper ON	1 – 16	Continuity
Washer 2	1 – 2 – 16	Continuity

Fig. 38 Rear wiper & washer continuity test. 1997–98 RAV4

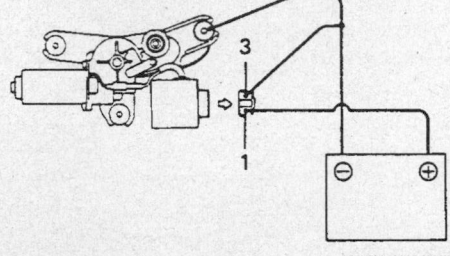

Fig. 41 Rear wiper motor connector. Celica & Supra

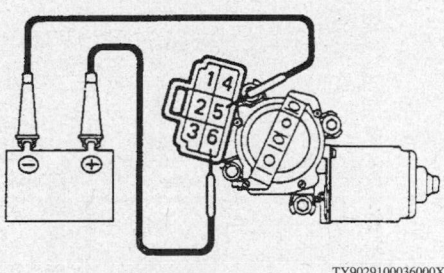

Fig. 44 Rear wiper motor connector. 4Runner

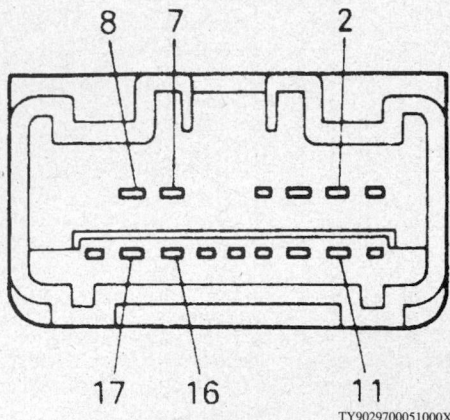

Fig. 36 Wiper & washer switch connector. RAV4 & 1997–99 Celica

Terminal / Switch position		1	2	10	16
Washer 1			○———		———○
Wiper	OFF				
	INT			○———	———○
	ON	○———			———○
Washer 2		○———		———○	———○

Fig. 39 Rear wiper & washer switch. Corolla

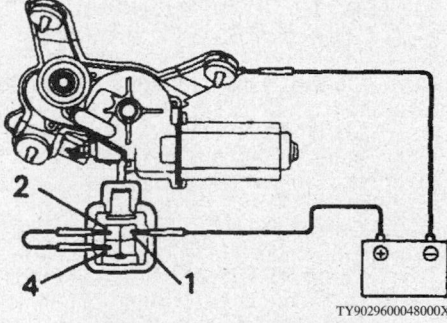

Fig. 42 Rear wiper motor connector. RAV4

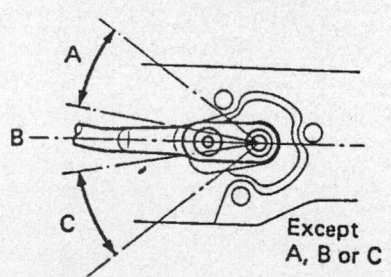

Terminal / Motor link position	4	5	6
A		○———	———○
B	○———	———○	
C		○———	———○
Except A, B or C			

Fig. 45 Rear wiper motor inspection. 4Runner

Fig. 43 Rear wiper relay terminal identification. RAV4

Air Bag System

INDEX

PRECAUTIONS

BATTERY GROUND CABLE

Prior to service, disconnect battery ground cable and isolate as required.

AUDIO CODED ANTI-THEFT SYSTEM

Some models are equipped with an audio coded anti-theft system that will disable the radio when the battery cable is disconnected. The system can be identified by the "ANTI-THEFT SYSTEM" on the cassette tape lid. Obtain 3 digit customer code for input. Reset system after service as follows:

1. Obtain 3 digit audio anti-theft code.
2. Depress 1 (PROG) while depressing righthand side of TUNE SEEK button, - - - will appear in tape operation display.
3. To enter the first digit, depress 1 (PROG) button repeatedly until the number of times depressed equals the first digit beginning with zero (depress the 1 button six times if the first digit is five).
4. To enter second digit, depress 2 (APS) button repeatedly until the number of times depressed equals the second digit beginning with zero.
5. To enter third digit, depress 3 (RPT) button repeatedly until the number of times depressed equals the second digit beginning with zero.
6. If - - - is displayed during code input, repeat procedure.
7. When code appears in display, depress and hold SCAN button until SEC appears.
8. When SEC disappears audio system should be operative.
9. If Err is displayed, repeat procedure. **Attempting to input code more than nine times may permanently disable audio system.**

AIR BAG SYSTEM DISARMING & ARMING

Disarming

1. Note radio station settings before disconnecting battery, as all vehicle memory will be lost.
2. Turn ignition switch to Lock position, then disconnect battery ground cable.
3. **Wait at least 90 seconds after disconnection before proceeding with any service procedures.** The Supplemental Restraint System (SRS) incorporates back-up energy source that can maintain sufficient deployment voltage for up to 90 seconds after ignition has been turned Off and battery disconnected.
4. Never use backup power source.

Arming

1. Ensure ignition switch is in the Lock position.
2. Reconnect battery ground cable.
3. **Wait at least 10 seconds before turning the ignition switch from the Lock position.**
4. Place ignition switch in the Acc or On position. Ensure the air bag light illuminates. After approximately 6 seconds, the light should go off. If not, there is a code stored in the system memory.

DESCRIPTION & OPERATION

The Supplemental Restraint System (SRS) works together with seat belts to protect driver and, if equipped, front seat passenger by deploying air bag(s) during certain frontal collisions. The SRS consists of a series of sensors, air bag module(s), spiral cable, steering wheel pad, diagnosis system, ignition control, drive circuit, SRS warning lamp, connectors and wires, **Figs. 1 through 28.**

Sensors are set in line. They work in separate, redundant circuits. Power supply and ground circuits also have built-in redundancy.

Air bag deployment occurs instantaneously when a safing sensor and a front air bag sensor and/or air bag sensor simultaneously detect deceleration greater than a specified valve. When a deceleration force acts on sensors, electric current is sent through air bag squib to igniter. This generates gas, rapidly increasing pressure inside bag. The inflated bag breaks open steering wheel pad or instrument panel. Inflation ends as gas discharges through rear and/or side bag holes and the air bag deflates.

Some models are equipped with side impact air bags and seat belt pretensioners. The side air bag system consists of side air bag assemblies, side sensors and on some models, door side sensors. The seat belt pretensioner is a component of the front seat outer belt and contains a squib, gas generant, wire and piston. These systems is used in conjunction with the front driver and passenger air bag system.

SYSTEM COMPONENTS

AIR BAG MODULE

Driver

Inflator and air bag are stored in steering wheel pad that cannot be disassembled. Inflator contains a squib, igniter charge and gas generant. When sensors detect sufficient impact, electric current is sent through squib in inflator. This heats filament and sets off igniter, which ignites chemical packed around squib. The burning chemical generates a very large amount of gas,

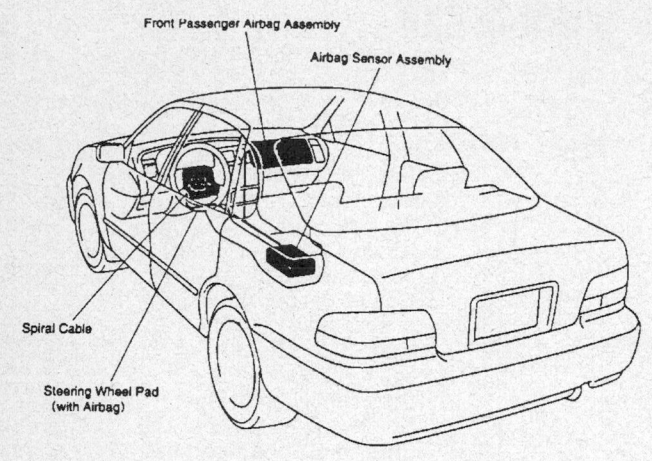

Fig. 1 SRS component locations. 1996–97 Avalon

TY8019500140000X

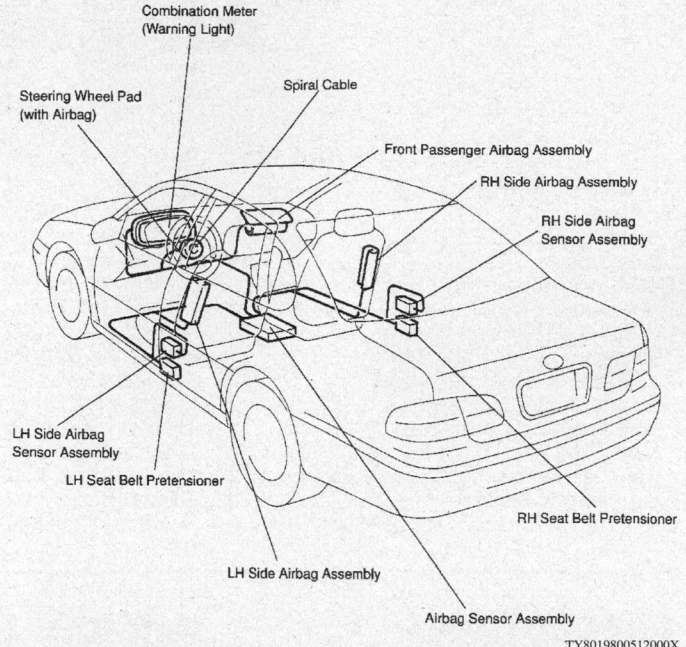

Fig. 2 SRS component locations. 1998 Avalon

TY8019800512000X

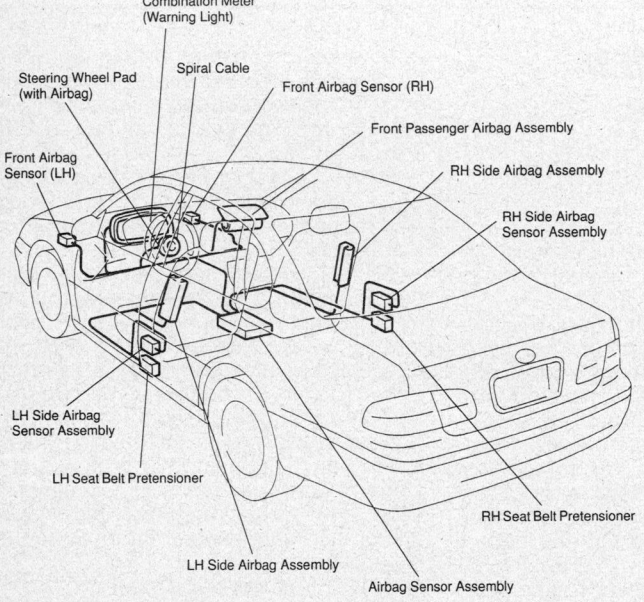

Fig. 3 SRS component locations. 1999 Avalon

TY8019900674000X

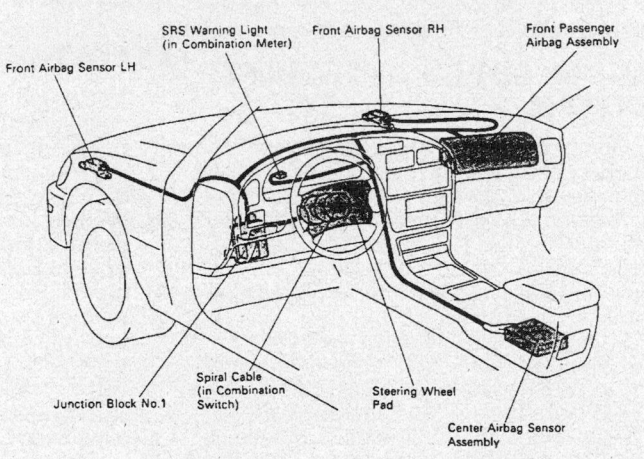

Fig. 4 SRS component locations. 1996 Camry

TY8019400141000X

which flows through a filter into the air bag, inflating it within .1 second.

Passenger

Inflator and air bag are stored in passenger side instrument panel. Passenger's air bag module cannot be disassembled. Inflator contains a squib, igniter charge and gas generant. When sensors detect sufficient impact, electric current is sent through squib in inflator. This heats filament and sets off igniter, which ignites chemical packed around driver's squib. The burning chemical generates a very large amount of gas, which flows through a filter into the air bag, inflating it within .1 second.

Side

Inflator and bag are stored in the driver and passenger seats. Side impact air bags cannot be disassembled. The inflator con-

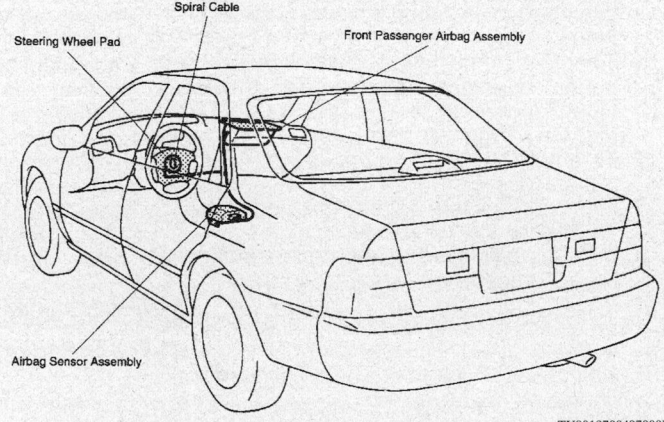

Fig. 5 SRS component locations. 1997 Camry

TY8019700497000X

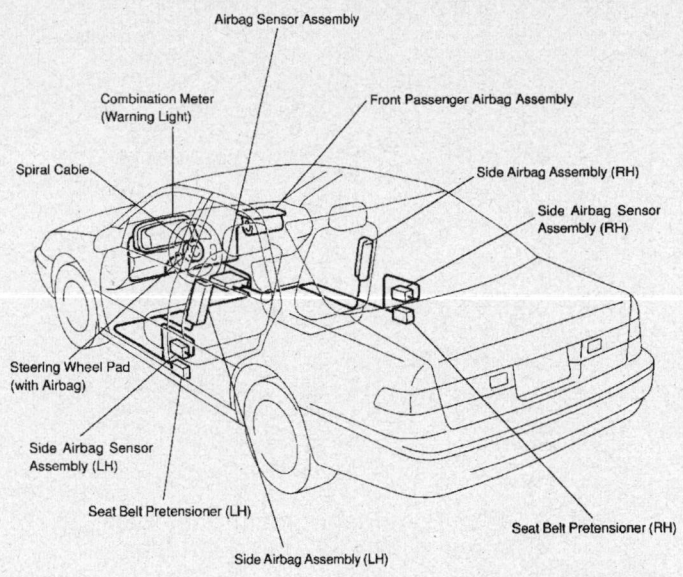

Fig. 6   SRS component locations. 1998 Camry

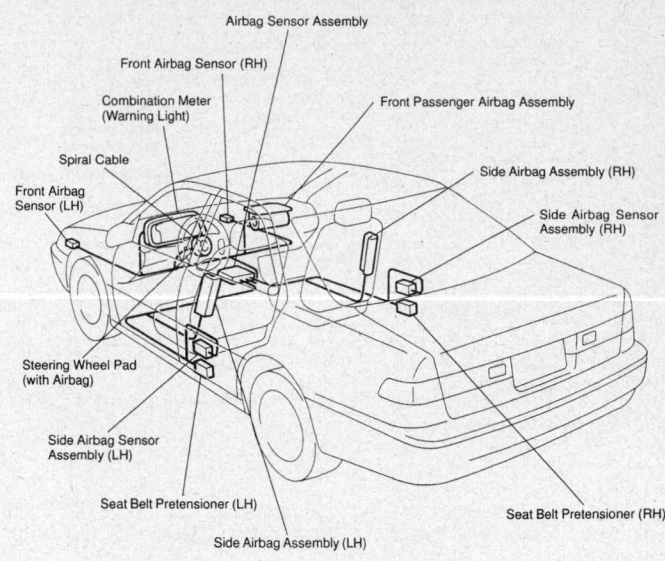

Fig. 7   SRS component locations. 1999 Camry

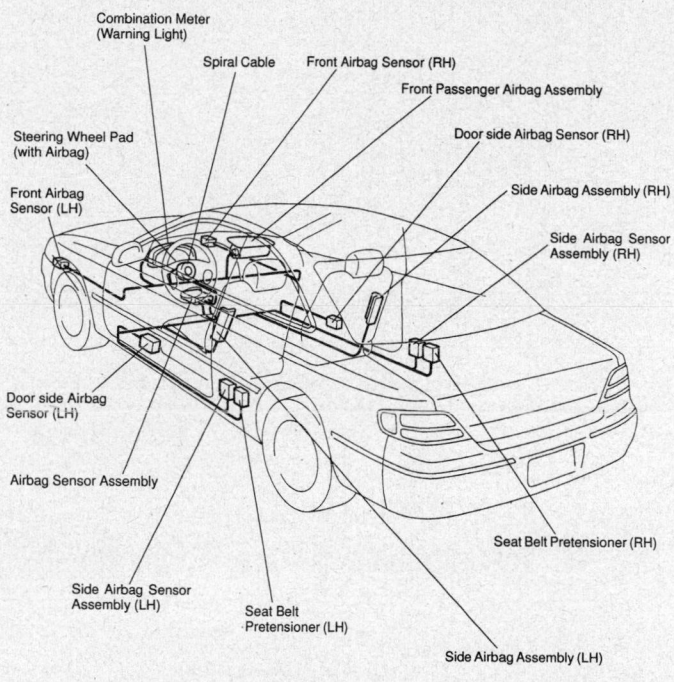

Fig. 8   SRS component locations. Camry Solara

Fig. 9   SRS component locations. Celica

Fig. 10   SRS component locations. 1996–97 Corolla

tains a squib, igniter charge and gas generant. When the side impact sensor detects sufficient impact, air bag is deployed.

SEAT BELT PRETENSIONER

The seatbelt pretensioner system is a component of the front seat outer belt. The pretensioner contains a squib, gas generator, wire and piston and operates in the event of a frontal collision.

AIR BAG ON-OFF SWITCH

When activated, this switch allows the passenger's air bag to be disabled. This switch should only be utilized when people of certain risk groups are seated in the passenger's seat. Consult vehicle owner's manual for proper use of this switch.

SPIRAL CABLE

The spiral cable is an electrical joint between vehicle body side and steering wheel. It is located in steering column combination switch.

SENSOR

Sensor detect impacts severe enough to set off inflator, varying with collision type and vehicle speed. G sensors measure

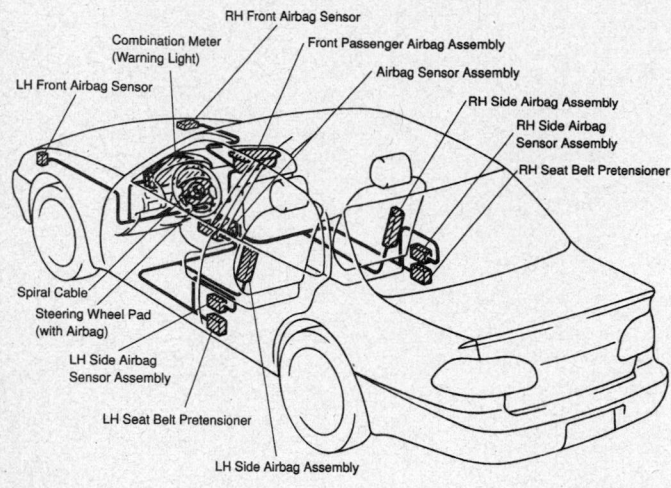

Fig. 11 SRS component locations. 1998–99 Corolla

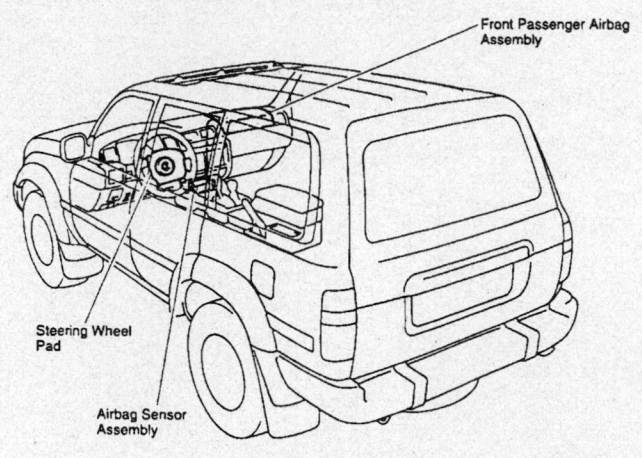

Fig. 12 SRS component locations. 1996–98 4Runner & 1996–97 Land Cruiser

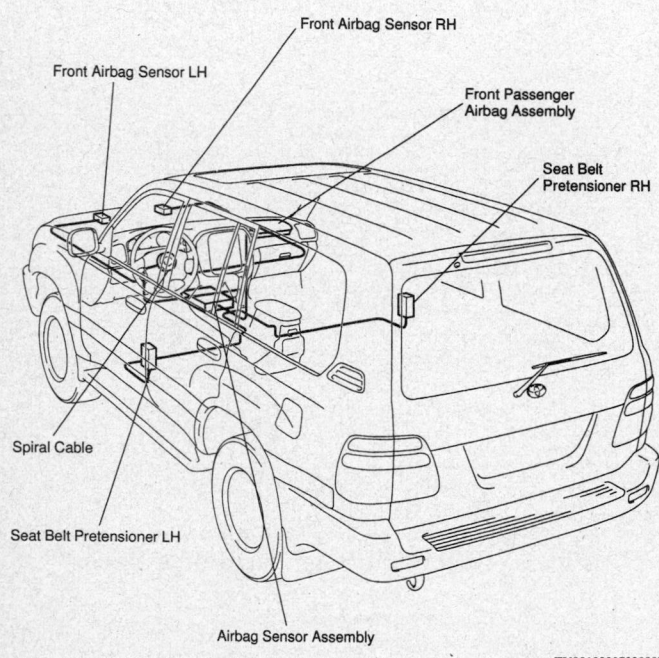

Fig. 13 SRS component locations. 1998–99 Land Cruiser

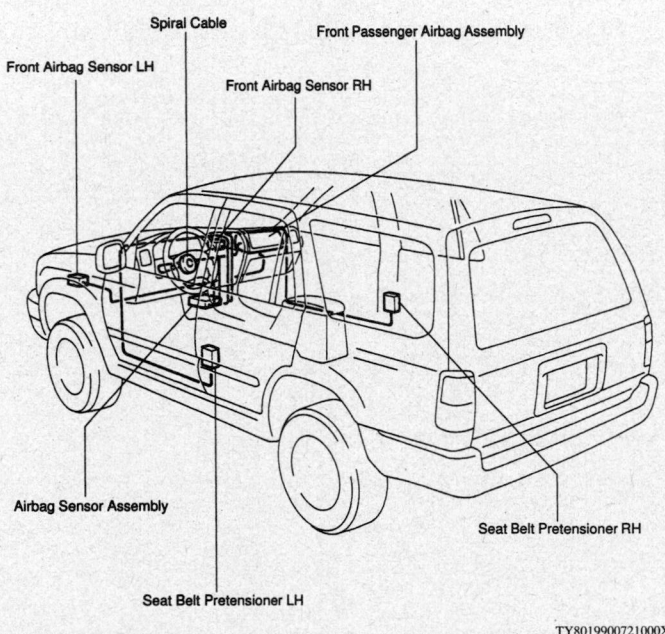

Fig. 14 SRS component locations. 1999 4Runner

speed and degree of deceleration to determine whether or not to send signal to inflator. Mechanical sensors utilize sprung masses, while analog sensors use electrical circuitry for calculations.

Front Air Bag Sensor

The front air bag sensor unit is a mechanical G sensor that cannot be disassembled. The G sensor is an eccentric mass rotating on a fixed axis and held in place by a spring. If deceleration exceeds a predetermine value, the rotor moves and at a certain point turns a switch On. If the safety switch is also On, the air bag inflator is ignited.

Front sensors are placed in a case filled with potting material to protect them from

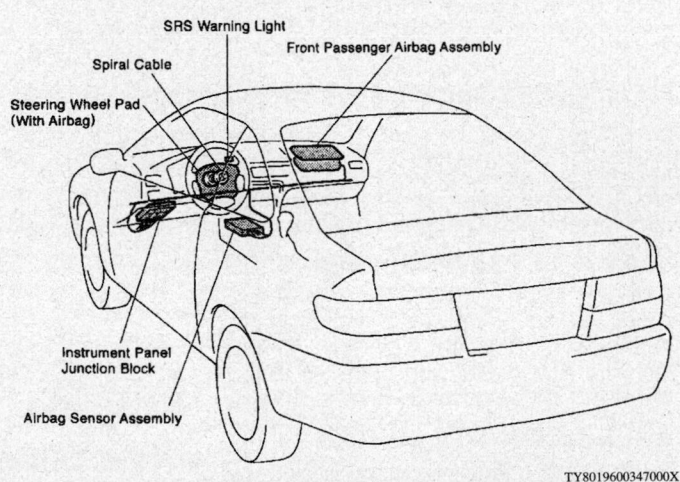

Fig. 15 SRS component locations. Paseo

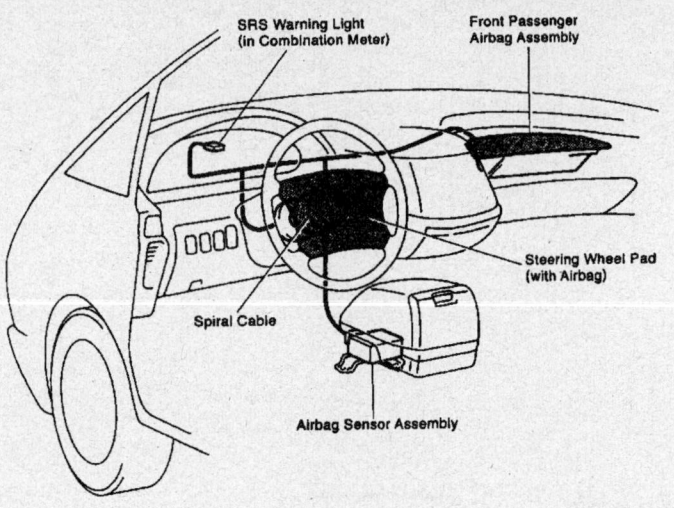

TY8019600348000X

Fig. 16 SRS component locations. Previa

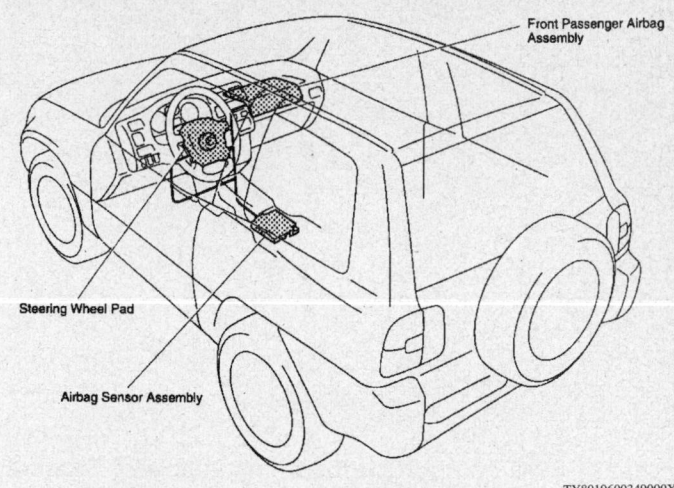

TY8019600349000X

Fig. 17 SRS component locations. 1996–97 RAV4

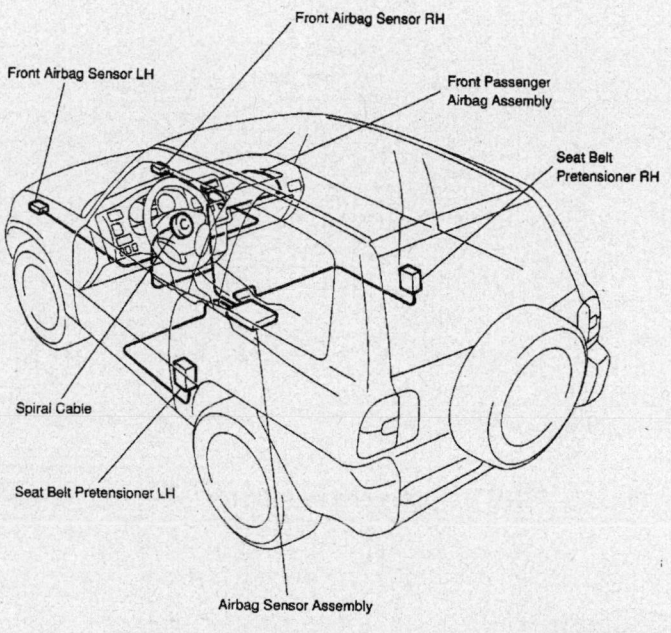

TY8019800516000X

Fig. 18 SRS component locations. 1998–99 RAV4

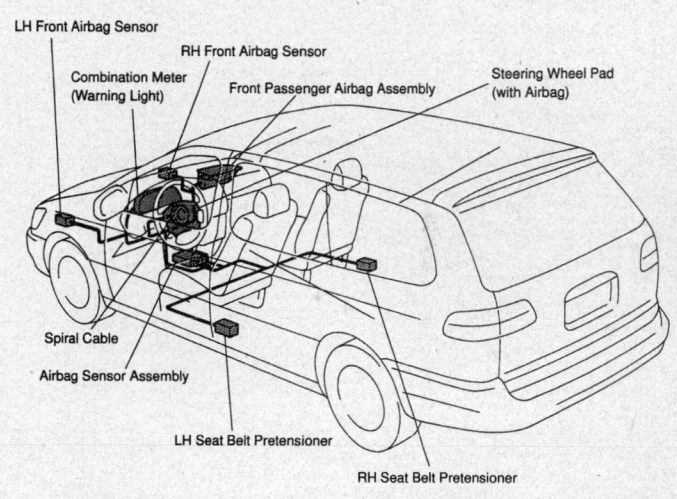

TY8019900700000X

Fig. 19 SRS component locations. Sienna

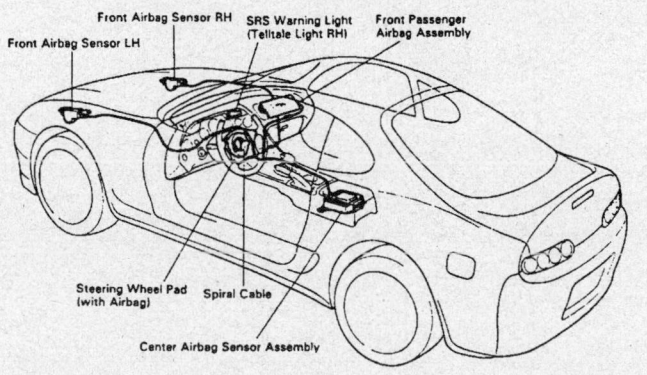

TY8019400148000X

Fig. 20 SRS component locations. 1996 Supra

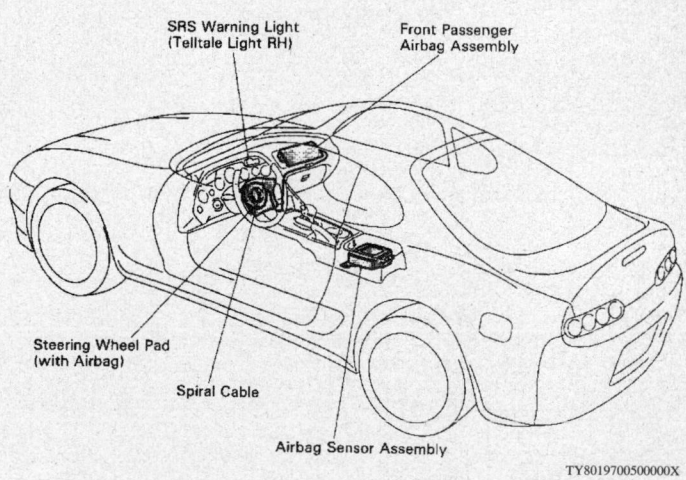

TY8019700500000X

Fig. 21 SRS component locations. 1997 Supra

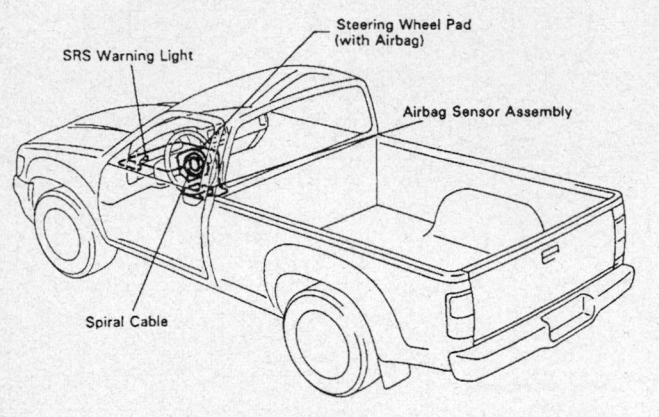

Fig. 22 SRS component locations. 1996–97 Tacoma

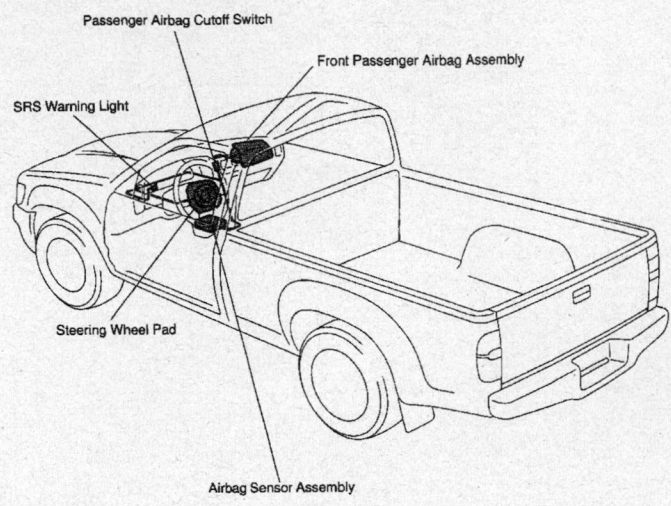

Fig. 23 SRS component locations. 1998 Tacoma

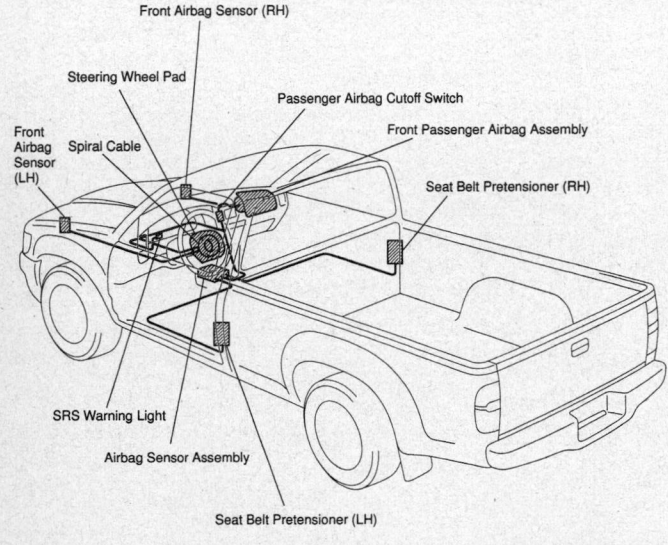

Fig. 24 SRS component locations. 1999 Tacoma

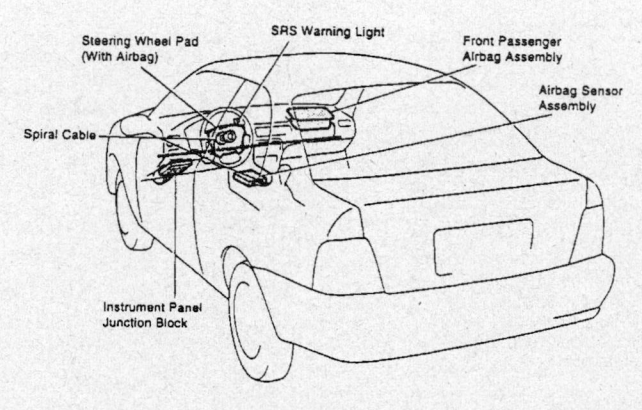

Fig. 25 SRS component locations. 1996–97 Tercel

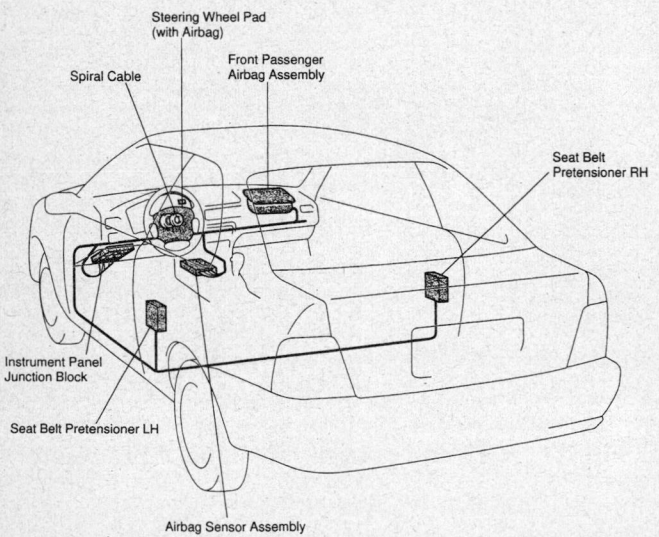

Fig. 26 SRS component locations. 1998 Tercel

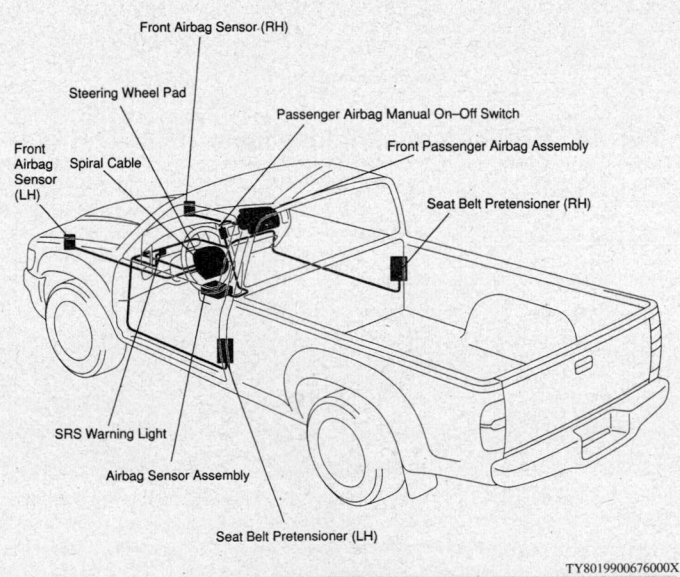

Fig. 27 SRS component locations. Tundra

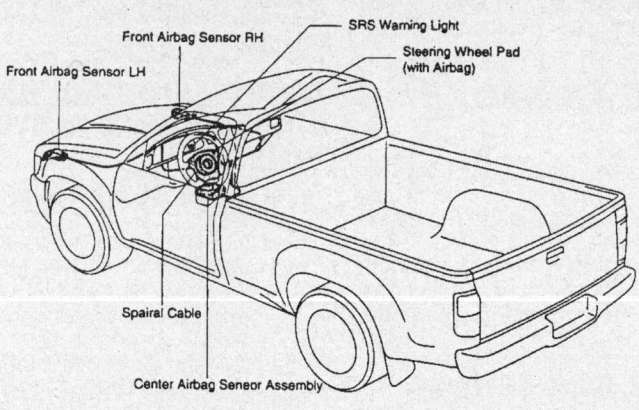

Fig. 28 SRS component locations. T100

the elements and ensure reliability. The switch is gold-plated for reliability.

The front sensor is equipped with an electrical connection check mechanism. Ensure this mechanism is securely locked when connecting connector. If connector is not locked, SRS malfunction or diagnostic trouble codes (DTC's) will be generated.

Air Bag Sensor Assembly

The air bag sensor assembly consists of an air bag sensor, safing sensor, ignition control, drive circuit and diagnostic circuit. The assembly receives signals from air bag sensors, judges whether air bag must be activated or not and diagnoses air bag system malfunctions.

The air bag sensor use semiconductors to detect deceleration rate. A semiconductor acceleration sensor has a silicon base with a lever on one side. Resistance bridges detect lever change amounts and an amplifier circuit boosts output for readability. Even if there is a circuitry breakdown, the safety sensor will not complete the circuit and send the igniter signal to the squib unless there is an actual collision.

Side Air Bag Sensor

The side air bag sensors are mounted in the lefthand and righthand center pillars. The sensor consists of a lateral deceleration sensor, safing sensor and diagnosis circuit. Air bag activation is based on signals received from the air bag sensors.

Door Side Air Bag Sensor

The door side air bag sensor is mounted on each door inside panel. The sensor unit is a mechanical type. When the sensor detects deceleration force above a predetermined specification, contact is made in the sensor and a signal is sent to the air bag sensor assembly.

SRS WARNING LAMP

SRS warning lamp is located in instrument cluster and lights to alert driver if a malfunction is detected by air bag sensor assembly self-diagnosis feature. In normal operating conditions, when ignition is turned to Acc or On positions, the lamp goes on for about six seconds, then goes off.

DIAGNOSIS CIRCUIT

When ignition is turned on, diagnosis circuit lights SRS warning lamp for about six seconds while running primary check of every part of system. If system operation is normal, the circuit turns the lamp off. The diagnosis circuit continues to check system functions during operation. If anything is amiss, the circuit turns the SRS warning lamp on and memorizes the problem as a diagnostic trouble code (DTC).

AIR BAG CONNECTORS

SRS wire harness is integrated with cowl wire harness and luggage compartment wire harness assembly. SRS harnesses are encased in a yellow corrugated tube. All SRS wiring connectors are yellow colored. Connectors having special functions and specifically designed for air bags are used in these locations to ensure high reliability. These connectors use durable gold plated terminals.

PRECAUTIONS

AUDIO CODED ANTI-THEFT SYSTEM

Some models are equipped with an audio coded anti-theft system that will disable the radio when the battery cable is disconnected. The system can be identified by the "ANTI-THEFT SYSTEM" on the cassette tape lid. Obtain 3 digit customer code for input. Reset system after service as follows:

1. Obtain 3 digit audio anti-theft code.
2. Depress 1 (PROG) while depressing righthand side of TUNE SEEK button, - - - will appear in tape operation display.
3. To enter the first digit, depress 1 (PROG) button repeatedly until the number of times depressed equals the first digit beginning with zero (depress the 1 button six times if the first digit if five).
4. To enter second digit, depress 2 (APS) button repeatedly until the number of times depressed equals the second digit beginning with zero.
5. To enter third digit, depress 3 (RPT) button repeatedly until the number of

times depressed equals the second digit beginning with zero.
6. If - - - is displayed during code input, repeat procedure.
7. When code appears in display, depress and hold SCAN button until SEC appears.
8. When SEC disappears audio system should be operative.
9. If Err is displayed, repeat procedure. **Attempting to input code more than nine times may permanently disable audio system.**

AIR BAG MODULE

Driver's

Refer to the following steps when working with driver's, passenger and side air bag modules.

1. Never measure air bag squib resistance.
2. Grease or oil should not be applied to steering wheel pad, nor should it be cleaned with detergents.
3. Do not paint air bag to correct cosmetic flaws. It must be replaced.
4. Steering wheel pad should not be exposed to ambient temperatures above 200°F.
5. Disconnect air bag 2-pin yellow electrical connector located under steering column, near combination switch connector, prior to using electric arc welding equipment.
6. When disposing of a vehicle or steering wheel pad, air bag must be deployed using special service tool No. 09082-00700, or equivalent.
7. Never use SRS parts from another vehicle. When replacing parts, replace them with new components.
8. Never disassemble and repair SRS system components.
9. If SRS system components have been dropped, or if there are cracks, dents or other defects in the case, bracket or connector, replace parts with new ones.
10. When diagnosing SRS electrical circuits, use a volt/ohmmeter with high impedance of 10,000 ohms or greater.
11. After work on SRS system is completed, perform SRS light check.
12. If vehicle is equipped with a mobile communication system, ensure all system components are kept away from SRS components. Do not install powerful communications systems.

Passenger's

1. When removing passenger's air bag or handling a replacement, it should be placed with door surface facing upward.
2. Never measure air bag squib resistance.
3. Grease or oil should not be applied to air bag door, nor should it be cleaned with detergents.
4. Air bag assembly should not be exposed to ambient temperatures above 200°F.
5. Disconnect air bag 2-pin yellow electrical connector prior to using electric arc welding equipment.

6. When disposing of vehicle or passenger's air bag, air bag must be deployed using special service tool No. 09082-00700, or equivalent.
7. Never use SRS parts from another vehicle. When replacing parts, replace them with new components.
8. Never disassemble and repair SRS system components.
9. If SRS system components have been dropped, or if there are cracks, dents or other defects in the case, bracket or connector, replace parts with new ones.
10. When diagnosing SRS electrical circuits, use a volt/ohmmeter with high impedance of 10,000 ohms or greater.
11. After work on SRS system is completed, perform SRS light check.
12. If vehicle is equipped with a mobile communication system, ensure all system components are kept away from SRS components. Do not install powerful communications systems.

Side

1. When removing passenger's air bag or handling a replacement, it should be placed with door surface facing upward.
2. Never measure air bag squib resistance.
3. Grease or oil should not be applied to air bag door, nor should it be cleaned with detergents.
4. Air bag assembly should not be exposed to ambient temperatures above 200°F.
5. When disposing of vehicle or passenger's air bag, air bag must be deployed using special service tool No. 09082-00700, or equivalent.
6. Disconnect air bag electrical connector prior to using arc welding equipment.
7. Never use SRS parts from another vehicle. When replacing parts, replace them with new components.
8. Never disassemble and repair SRS system components.
9. If SRS system components have been dropped, or if there are cracks, dents or other defects in the case, bracket or connector, replace parts with new ones.
10. When diagnosing SRS electrical circuits, use a volt/ohmmeter with high impedance of 10,000 ohms or greater.
11. After work on SRS system is completed, perform SRS light check.
12. If vehicle is equipped with a mobile communication system, ensure all system components are kept away from SRS components. Do not install powerful communications systems.

CENTER AIR BAG SENSOR ASSEMBLY

The center air bag sensor assembly contains mercury, after replacement or service, do not destroy old part, dispose of as toxic waste. Do not disassemble center air bag sensor assembly. When disconnecting sensor assembly electrical connectors, en-

sure assembly is properly mounted to floor or accidental air bag deployment may occur.

DOOR SIDE AIR BAG SENSOR

Never reuse door air bag sensors that have been involved in a collision when the air bag has been deployed. Do not disassemble air bag sensors. Ensure air bag sensor is installed with correct up and front orientation. Sensor connectors should only be connected or disconnected when sensor is mounted in place.

FRONT AIR BAG SENSOR

Never reuse front air bag sensors that have been involved in a collision when the air bag has been deployed. Do not disassemble front air bag sensors. Install the front air bag sensor with the arrow on the sensor facing toward the front of the vehicle. Sensor connectors should only be connected or disconnected when sensor is mounted in place. The front air bag sensor set bolts and nuts have been anti-rust treated, when then sensor is removed, always replace set bolt and nut.

SEAT BELT PRETENSIONER

1. Never measure resistance of seat belt pretensioner.
2. Do not disassemble pretensioner or install into another vehicle.
3. Always store belt pretensioner where ambient temperature remains below 176°F.
4. When using electrical welding equipment, disconnect air bag sensors before starting work.
5. When disposing of vehicle or tensioner, pretensioner must be activated.
6. After activation, pretensioner must be allowed to cool for at least 30 minutes.

SPIRAL CABLE

The spiral cable must be installed in the neutral position for air bag deployment may occur.

WIRE HARNESS & CONNECTOR REPAIR

Wires for air bag wiring harness are encased in a yellow conduit, with yellow electrical connectors.

When required, replace either wiring harness or connector. If harness has been damaged, replace entire harness assembly. If only connector has been damaged, replace only connector.

DIAGNOSIS & TESTING

Refer to **MOTOR'S** "Air Bag Manual" for complete diagnosis and testing information.

COLLISION INSPECTION

DRIVER SIDE AIR BAG, SPIRAL CABLE & STEERING WHEEL

1. **If air bag did not deploy,** proceed as follows:
   a. Inspect SRS system as outlined in **MOTOR's "Air Bag Manual."**
   b. Remove air bag unit from steering wheel as outlined under "Component Service."
   c. Inspect air bag unit for cuts, cracks and discoloration, and replace as necessary.
   d. Inspect horn button contact plate on steering wheel for deformation and replace if needed.
   e. Inspect air bag unit to steering wheel mounting. Clearance between these should be uniform.
2. **If air bag deployment has taken place,** proceed as follows:
   a. Inspect SRS system as outlined in **MOTOR's "Air Bag Manual."**
   b. Remove air bag unit from steering wheel as outlined under "Component Service."
   c. Inspect horn button contact plate on steering wheel for deformation and replace as necessary.
   d. Inspect spiral cable wiring and connector for damage and replace if required.
   e. Install a new air bag unit, then inspect unit to steering wheel mounting. Clearance between these should be uniform.

PASSENGER SIDE AIR BAG

1. **If air bag did not deploy,** proceed as follows:
   a. Inspect SRS system as outlined in **MOTOR's "Air Bag Manual."**
   b. Inspect air bag unit for cuts, cracks and discoloration, and replace as necessary.
   c. Inspect air bag unit to instrument panel mounting and all mounting points, including brackets.
2. **If air bag deployment has taken place,** proceed as follows:
   a. Inspect SRS system as outlined in **MOTOR's "Air Bag Manual."**
   b. Inspect instrument panel for cracks and other damage.
   c. Install a new air bag unit.
   d. Inspect air bag unit to instrument panel mounting and all mounting points, including brackets.

SIDE AIR BAG ASSEMBLY

1. **If air bag did not deploy,** proceed as follows:
   a. Inspect SRS system as outlined in **MOTOR'S "Air Bag Manual."**
   b. Remove seatback frame from vehicle as outlined under "Air Bag Module, Replace", "Side."
   c. Inspect seatback frame assembly for deformity. If damage is present, **do not repair seatback, replace with new unit.**

d. Inspect side air bag assembly for cuts, cracks or marked discoloration of side airbag assembly.
e. Inspect related wiring harnesses for cuts and cracks.
f. Inspect connectors for damage.
2. **If air bag did deploy,** proceed as follows:
 a. Inspect SRS system as outlined in **MOTOR's "Air Bag Manual."**
 b. Remove seatback frame from vehicle as outlined under "Air Bag Module, Replace", "Side."
 c. Inspect side air bag to seat frame mounting surfaces. If damage is present, **do not repair seatback, replace with new unit.**
 d. Inspect related wiring harnesses for cuts and cracks.
 e. Inspect connectors for damage.

SEAT BELT PRETENSIONER

Avalon & Camry

1. **If seat belt pretensioner has not been activated,** proceed as follows:
 a. Inspect SRS system as outlined in **MOTOR's "Air Bag Manual."**
 b. Remove front seat outer belt from vehicle.
 c. Inspect for cuts, cracks or marked discoloration of center pillar lower garnish.
 d. Inspect for cuts and cracks in wire harnesses and damage to connectors.
 e. Inspect for deformation of center pillar.
2. **If seat belt pretensioner has been activated,** proceed as follows:
 a. Inspect SRS system as outlined in **MOTOR's "Air Bag Manual."**
 b. Remove front outer seat belt from vehicle.
 c. Inspect center pillar for deformation.
 d. Inspect wiring harnesses and connectors for damage.
3. Seat belt pretensioner should be replaced if any of the following apply: activation has occurred, flaws found during collision inspection or if unit is dropped.

Camry Solara

1. **If seat belt pretensioner has not been activated,** proceed as follows:
 a. Inspect SRS system as outlined in **MOTOR's "Air Bag Manual."**
 b. Remove front seat outer belt from vehicle.
 c. Inspect for cuts, cracks or marked discoloration on quarter trim panel.
 d. Inspect for cuts and cracks in wire harness.
 e. Inspect for chipping of wiring connectors.
 f. Inspect for deformation of quarter panel.
2. **If seat belt pretensioner has been activated,** proceed as follows:
 a. Inspect SRS system as outlined in **MOTOR's "Air Bag Manual."**
 b. Remove front seat outer belt from vehicle.

c. Inspect for deformation of quarter panel.
d. Inspect for damage to wire harness and connectors.

Tundra

1. **If seat belt pretensioner has not been activated,** proceed as follows:
 a. Inspect SRS system as outlined in **MOTOR's "Air Bag Manual."**
 b. Remove front seat outer belt from vehicle.
 c. **On standard cab models,** inspect for cuts, cracks or marked discoloration on quarter trim and deformation of quarter panel.
 d. **On access cab models,** inspect for cuts, cracks or marked discoloration on front door rear scuff plate and deformation of ELR bracket.
 e. **On all models,** inspect for damage to wiring harness and connectors.
2. **If seat belt pretensioner has been activated,** proceed as follows:
 a. Inspect SRS system as outlined in **MOTOR's "Air Bag Manual."**
 b. Remove front outer seat belt from vehicle.
 c. **On standard cab models,** inspect for deformation of quarter panel.
 d. **On access cab models,** inspect for deformation of ELR bracket.
 e. **On all models,** inspect for damage to wiring harness and connectors.
3. Seat belt pretensioner should be replaced if any of the following apply: activation has occurred, flaws found during collision inspection or if unit is dropped.

DOOR SIDE AIR BAG SENSOR

1. **If vehicle has not been involved in a collision,** perform diagnostic system check as outlined in **MOTOR's "Air Bag Manual."**
2. **If vehicle has been involved in a collision,** proceed as follows:
 a. Perform diagnostic system check as outlined in **MOTOR's "Air Bag Manual."**
 b. Inspect bracket for deformation or peeling paint.
 c. Cracks dents or chips in case.
 d. Cracks, dents, chipping and scratches in connector.
 e. Peeling off of label or damage to serial number.
3. Sensors should be replaced if any of the following have occurred:
 a. Side air bag has been deployed.
 b. Sensor found to be faulty.
 c. Sensor has been dropped.
 d. Flaws found during collision inspection.

FRONT AIR BAG SENSORS

1. **If air bag did not deploy,** proceed as follows:
 a. Inspect SRS system as outlined in **MOTOR's "Air Bag Manual."**
 b. Inspect front sensor and bracket dents, cracks, chips, deformation and other damage, and replace as necessary.

c. Inspect air bag mounting surface for damage and misalignment, and repair if needed.
2. **If air bag deployment has taken place or if sensor has been dropped,** replace both front sensors, then inspect SRS as outlined under "Diagnosis & Testing."

AIR BAG SENSOR ASSEMBLY

1. Inspect SRS system as outlined in **MOTOR's "Air Bag Manual."**
2. **If air bag deployment has taken place, or sensor dropped,** replace air bag sensor assembly, then inspect SRS as outlined in **MOTOR's "Air Bag Manual."**

COMPONENT SERVICE
AIR BAG MODULE, REPLACE
DRIVER'S
Removal

1. Disarm SRS as outlined under "Air Bag System Disarming & Arming."
2. Position front wheels in straight-ahead position.
3. Remove steering wheel lower covers and scuff plates if necessary.
4. Using a suitable Torx socket wrench, loosen Torx screws until screw circumference grooves catch screw case, **Figs. 29 through 39.** On Sienna models, loosen bolts until screw opening is aligned in screw case.
5. Pull steering pad rearward, then disconnect air bag electrical connector.
6. Remove air bag module and store with pad facing upward.

Installation

1. Connect air bag electrical connector.
2. Ensure Torx screw circumference grooves are caught in screw case, then install air bag module.
3. Ensure wiring does not interfere with other parts and is not pinched, then tighten mounting screws to specifications.
4. Install steering wheel lower covers.
5. Ensure steering wheel is centered.
6. Arm SRS as outlined under "Air Bag System Disarming & Arming."

PASSENGER
1996-97 Avalon

1. Disarm SRS as outlined under "Air Bag System Disarming & Arming."
2. Remove glove compartment door finish plate.
3. Disconnect passenger air bag electrical connector.
4. Remove instrument panel, **Fig. 40.**
5. Remove passenger air bag mounting nuts.
6. Carefully remove passenger air bag module.
7. Remove screws and air bag door.
8. Reverse procedure to install, and tighten to specifications.

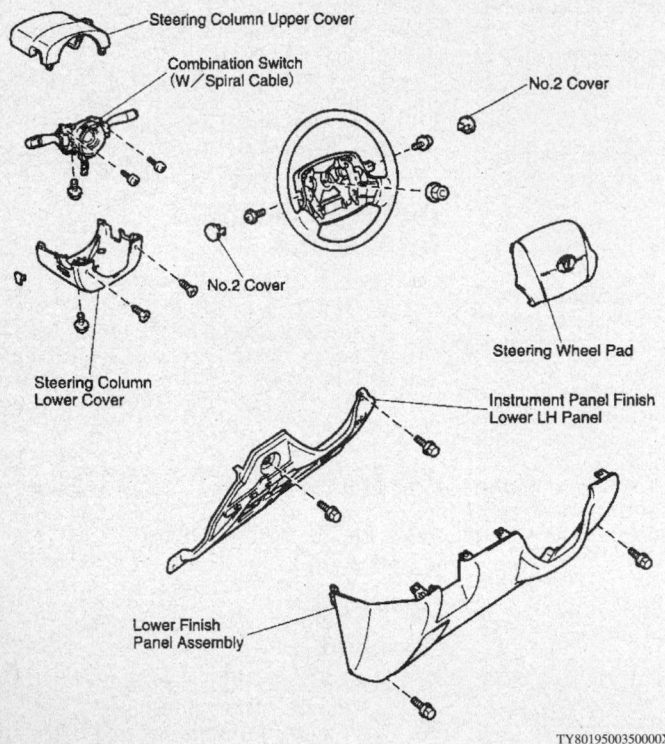

Fig. 29   Driver side air bag module replacement. Avalon

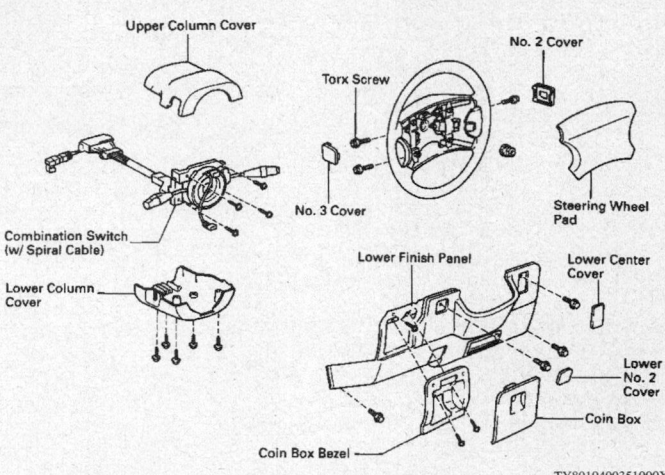

Fig. 30   Driver side air bag module replacement. Camry & Camry Solara

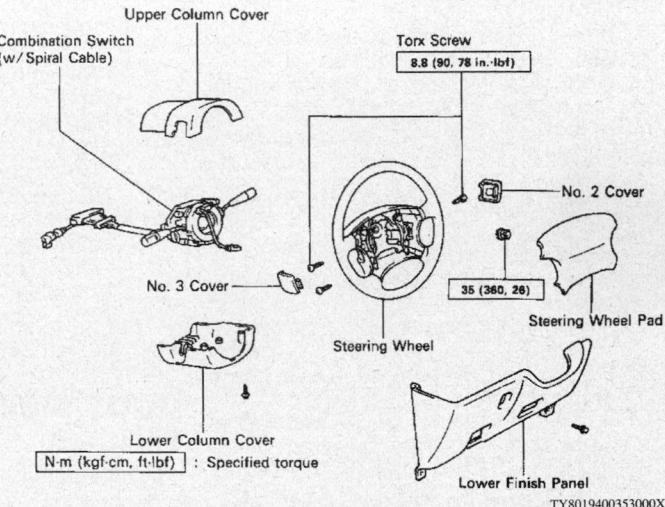

Fig. 32   Driver side air bag module replacement. Corolla

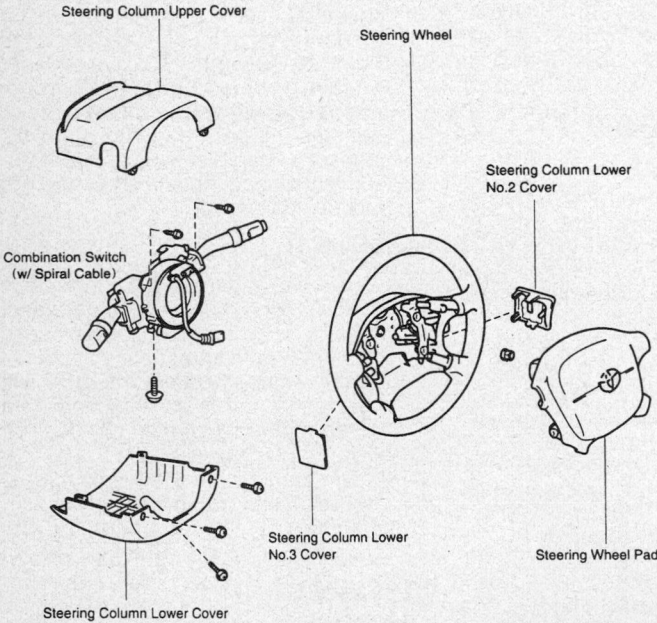

Fig. 31   Driver side air bag module replacement. Celica, RAV4, Sienna & Tundra

1998-99 Avalon

1. Disarm SRS as outlined under "Air Bag System Disarming & Arming."
2. Remove cowl side trim, then the No. 2 under cover, **Fig. 40.**
3. Remove instrument panel finish panel, **Fig. 40.**
4. Using a suitable screwdriver, pry out glove compartment door finish plate from inside of glove box.

5. Remove electrical connector from glove compartment door finish plate.
6. Disconnect air bag electrical connector.
7. Remove glove compartment door attaching nuts, then the door.
8. Remove glove compartment attaching screws, then disconnect glove box lamp connector.
9. Remove glove compartment.

10. Remove passenger's air bag mounting nuts.
11. Carefully remove passenger's air bag module.
12. Remove screws and air bag door.
13. Reverse procedure to install. Tighten nuts and bolts to specifications.

1996 Camry

1. Disarm SRS as outlined under "Air Bag System Disarming & Arming."
2. Remove glove compartment door finish plate.
3. Remove driver side air bag module as outlined under "Air Bag Module, Replace."
4. Remove steering wheel as outlined under "Spiral Cable, Replace."
5. Remove under cover No. 2, instrument lower panel, glove compartment panel and door, combination switch, center cluster finish panel, radio, cluster finish panel and heater control panel, **Fig. 42.**
6. Remove passenger side air bag module righthand side mounting bolt, then

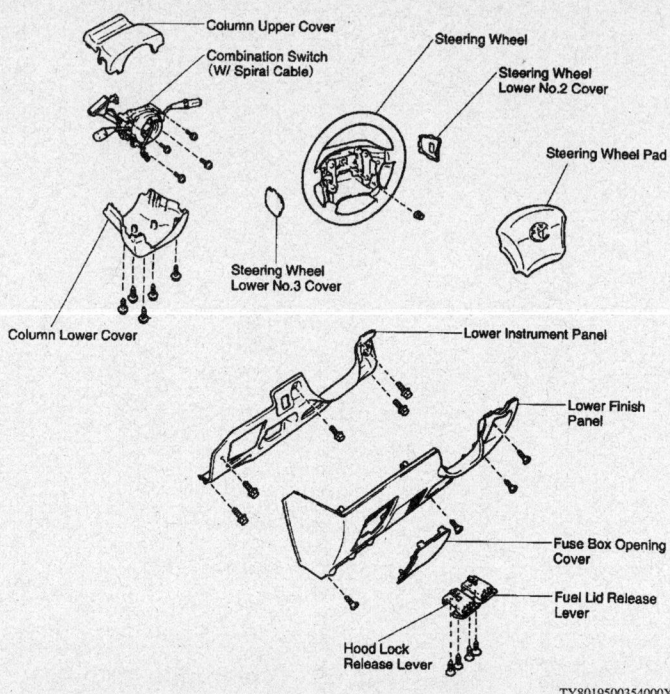

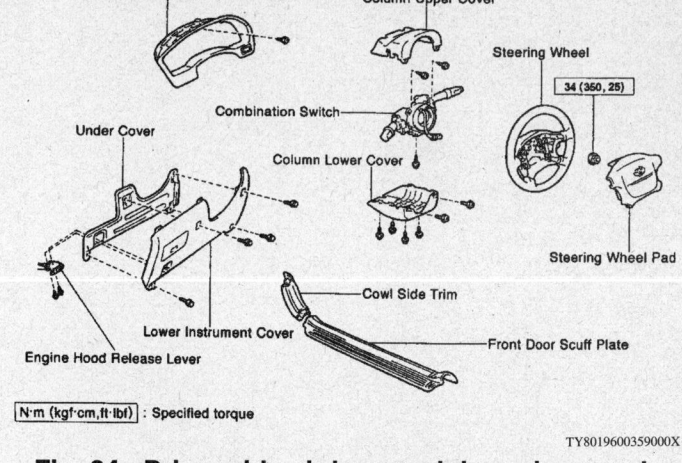

Fig. 34 Driver side air bag module replacement. Paseo & Tercel

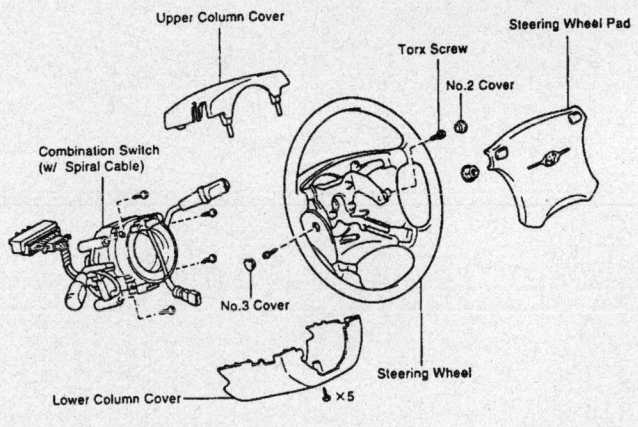

Fig. 33 Driver side air bag module replacement. Land Cruiser

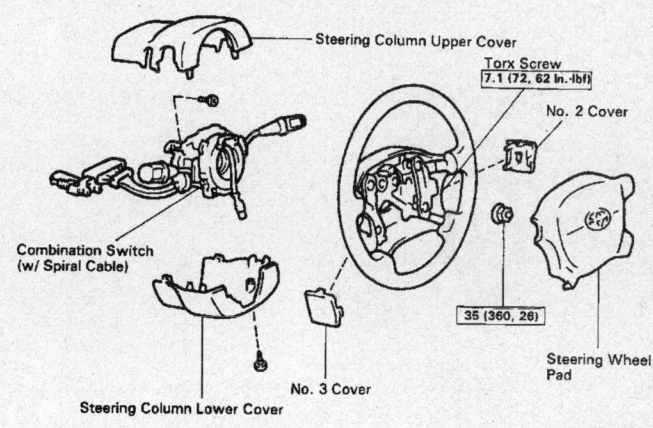

Fig. 35 Driver side air bag module removal. Previa

remove remaining air bag module mounting bolts.

7. Remove air bag module and store with air bag door facing up.

8. Reverse procedure to install and tighten bolts to specifications.

1997-99 Camry

1. Disarm SRS as outlined under "Air Bag System Disarming & Arming."
2. Remove glove compartment door finish plate.
3. Disconnect air bag connector.
4. Remove front door scuff plate, cowl side trim, and glove compartment box, **Fig. 43**.
5. Remove air bag mounting bolts and nuts.
6. Remove air bag module and store with air bag door facing up.
7. Reverse procedure to install and tighten bolts to specifications.

en bolts to specifications.

Camry Solara

1. Disarm SRS as outlined under "Air Bag System Disarming & Arming."
2. Using a suitable screwdriver, pry out glove compartment door finish plate inside lower panel.
3. Remove air bag electrical connector from finish plate.
4. Disconnect air bag electrical connector.

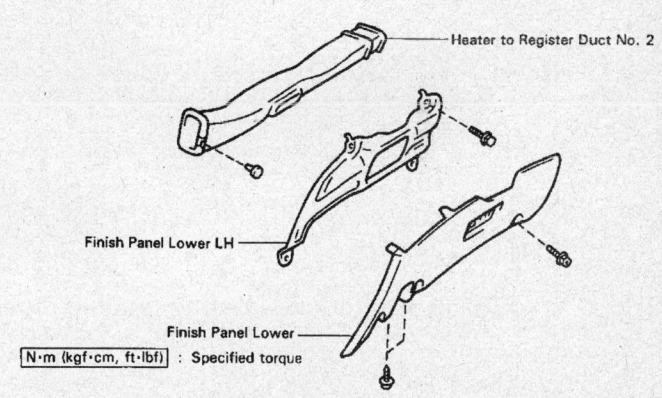

Fig. 36 Driver side air bag module replacement. Supra

5. Remove door scuff plate, then the cowl side trim, **Fig. 44**.
6. Remove front door opening cover trim, then the No. 2 undercover.
7. Remove bolt, 4 screws and lower panel.
8. Remove thermistor connector clamp.
9. Remove 2 nuts connecting front passenger air bag assembly to instrument panel.
10. Remove 2 air bag attaching bolts, then the No. 1 air bag mounting bracket

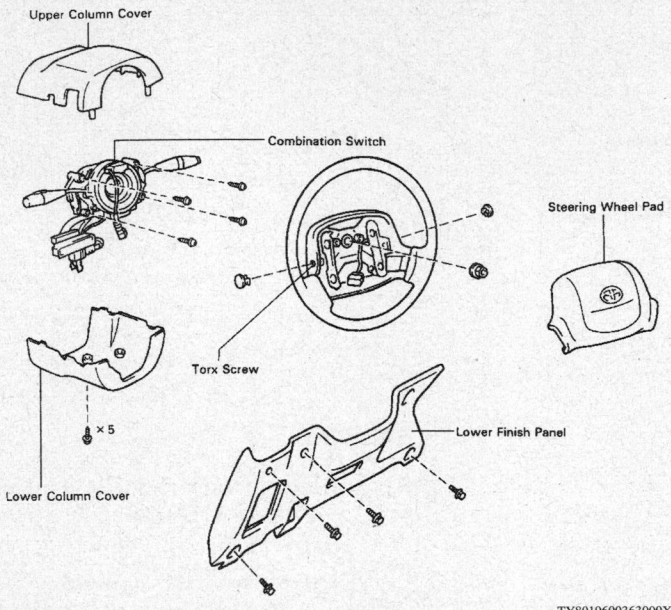

Fig. 37   Driver side air bag module replacement. Tacoma

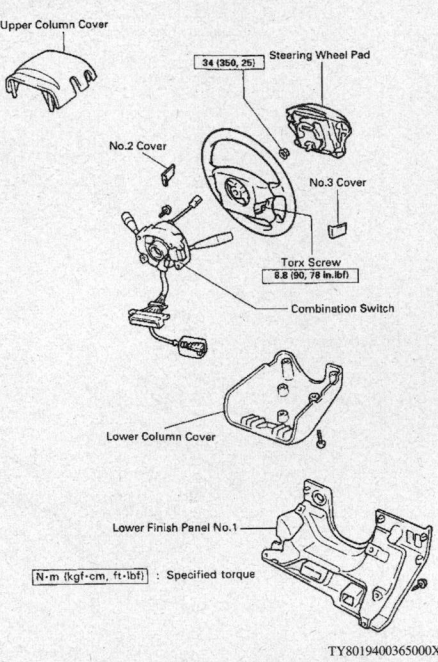

Fig. 38   Driver side air bag module replacement. T100

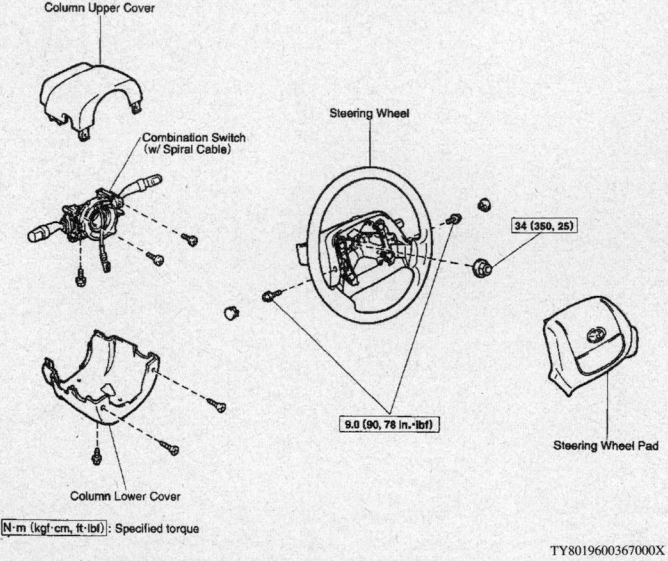

Fig. 39   Driver side air bag module replacement. 4Runner

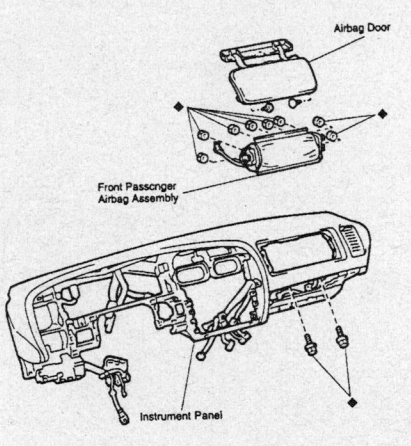

Fig. 40   Passenger air bag module replacement. 1996–97 Avalon

bolts with brackets.
11. Remove air bag straps, **Fig. 45,** as follows:
  a. Remove nut, then the air bag strap from outer side.
  b. Slide air bag assembly to outer side of vehicle.
  c. Remove nut and air bag strap form inner side.
12. Remove air bag module and store with air bag door facing up.
13. Reverse procedure to install and tighten bolts to specifications.

Celica

1. Disarm SRS as outlined under "Air Bag System Disarming & Arming."
2. Remove glove compartment door finish plate.

3. Disconnect passenger air bag electrical connector, **Figs. 46 and 47.**
4. Remove instrument panel and outlined under "Dash Panel Service."
5. Remove passenger air bag mounting bolts and nuts.
6. Remove screws and air bag door.
7. Carefully remove passenger's air bag module.
8. Reverse procedure to install, and tighten to specifications.

Corolla

1. Disarm SRS as outlined under "Air Bag System Disarming & Arming."
2. Remove glove compartment door finish plate.
3. Disconnect passenger air bag electrical connector.

4. Remove glove compartment door, **Fig. 48.**
5. Remove front passenger air bag module mounting bolts and clips, then module.
6. Reverse procedure to install and tighten bolts to specifications.

Land Cruiser

1. Disarm SRS as outlined under "Air Bag System Disarming & Arming."
2. Remove glove compartment door.
3. Remove air bag electrical connector from bracket and disconnect
4. Remove instrument panel, **Figs. 49 and 50**
5. Remove front passenger air bag mounting nuts and bolts, then assembly.
6. Remove clips and air bag door.

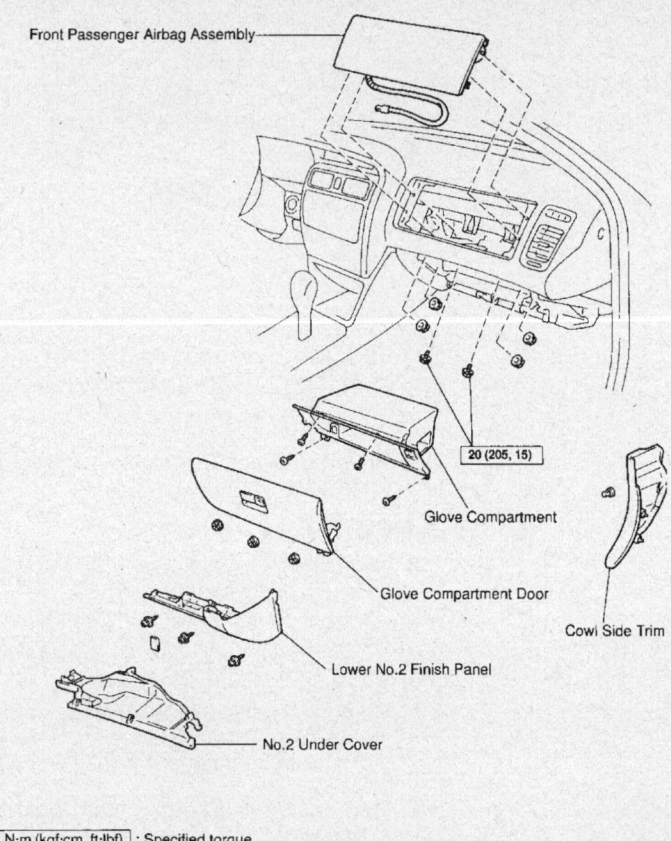

Code	Shape	Size	Code	Shape	Size
Ⓐ		φ = 8 (0.32) L = 18 (0.71)	Ⓑ		φ = 6 (0.24) L = 16 (0.63)

mm (in.)

N·m (kgf·cm, ft·lbf) : Specified torque

TY8019800628000X

Fig. 41 Passenger's air bag module replacement. 1998–99 Avalon

7. Reverse procedure to install, and tighten bolts and nuts to specifications.

Paseo

1. Disarm SRS as outlined under "Air Bag System Disarming & Arming."
2. Remove lower finish panel
3. Disconnect air bag electrical connector.
4. Remove instrument panel reinforcement bolts and instrument panel, **Fig. 51.**
5. Remove front passenger air bag mounting nuts and bolts, then assembly.
6. Remove air bag door.
7. Reverse procedure to install, and tighten to specifications.

Previa

1. Disarm SRS as outlined under "Air Bag System Disarming & Arming."
2. Remove glove compartment door finish plate.
3. Disconnect air bag connector.
4. Remove glove compartment door and lock striker, **Fig. 52.**
5. Remove passenger air bag module mounting bolts and nuts.
6. Remove air bag module and store with air bag door facing up.
7. Reverse procedure to install, and tighten to specifications.

RAV4 & 4Runner

1. Disarm SRS as outlined under "Air Bag System Disarming & Arming."
2. Remove glove compartment door.
3. Remove air bag electrical connector from bracket and disconnect

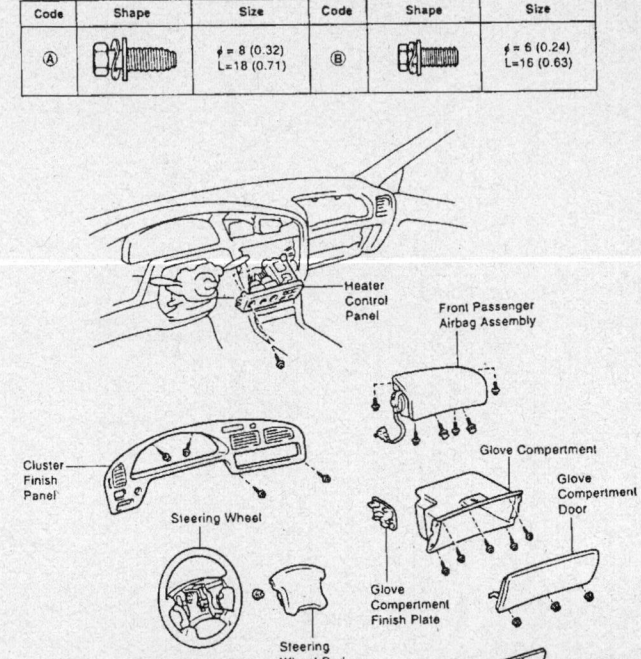

TY8019400295000X

Fig. 42 Passenger air bag module replacement. 1996 Camry

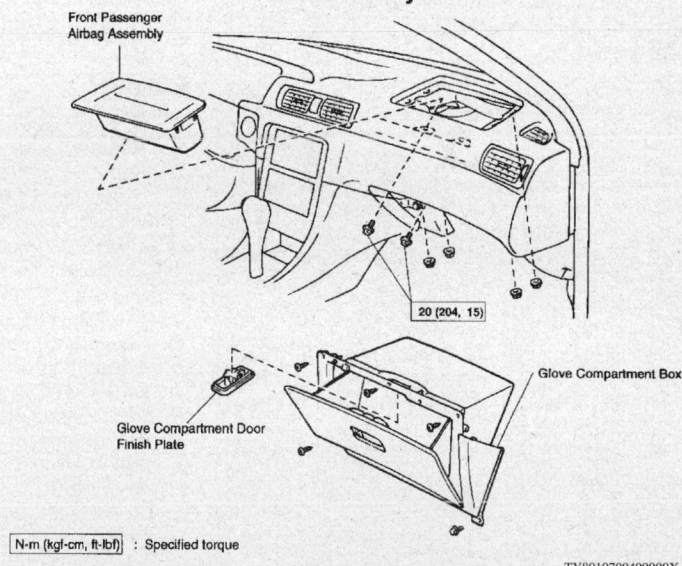

N·m (kgf·cm, ft·lbf) : Specified torque

TY8019700499000X

Fig. 43 Passenger's air bag module replacement. 1997–99 Camry

4. Remove instrument panel, **Fig. 53.**
5. Remove front passenger air bag mounting bolts, then assembly.
6. Remove bolts and pry off clips, then remove air bag door.

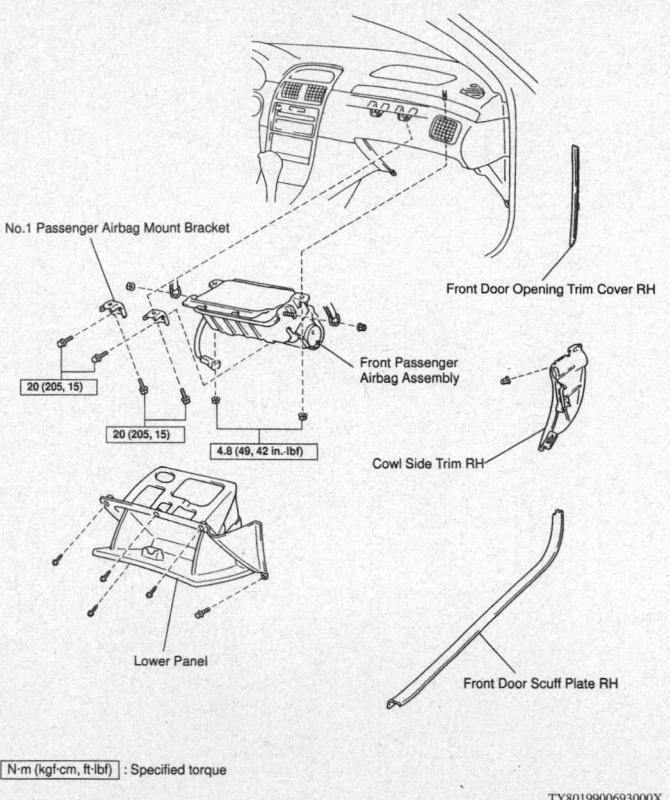

No.1 Passenger Airbag Mount Bracket

Front Door Opening Trim Cover RH

20 (205, 15)

20 (205, 15)

4.8 (49, 42 in.-lbf)

Front Passenger Airbag Assembly

Cowl Side Trim RH

Lower Panel

Front Door Scuff Plate RH

N·m (kgf-cm, ft-lbf) : Specified torque

TY8019900693000X

Fig. 44   Passenger's air bag module replacement. Camry Solara

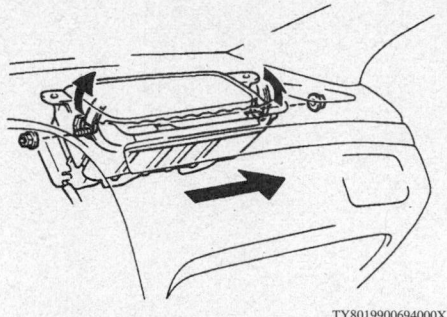

TY8019900694000X

Fig. 45   Passenger air bag removal. Camry Solara

7. Reverse procedure to install, and tighten to specifications.

1998 Tercel

1. Disarm SRS as outlined under "Air Bag System Disarming & Arming."
2. Remove 7 lower finish panel attaching screws, then the lower finish panel subassembly, **Fig. 59.**
3. Disconnect air bag connector.
4. Remove 2 bolts, 2 nuts and passenger air bag assembly. Ensure air bag is stored with deployment side facing upward.
5. Reverse procedure to install. Tighten to specifications.

Tundra

1. Using a suitable clip remover, disengage connector clamp and disconnect air bag connector, **Fig. 60.**
2. Remove front door scuff plates, **Fig. 61.**
3. Remove glove compartment door, then the cowl side trim panels.
4. Remove No. 2 lower finish panel, then the lower center cover.
5. Remove lower finish panel and lower instrument cover.
6. Remove 2 air bag to instrument panel attaching bolts.
7. Remove 2 air bag to instrument panel reinforcement bolts, then the air bag.
8. **Store air bag with deployment side facing up.**
9. Reverse procedure to install. Tighten to specifications. Ensure no foreign objects are trapped between airbag and module.

SIDE
Avalon

1. Disarm SRS as outlined under "Air Bag System Disarming & Arming."
2. Remove seat track covers, then the seat attaching bolts.
3. Disconnect side air bag and power seat electrical connectors.
4. Remove front seat.
5. Remove center armrest if equipped.
6. Remove headrest, then the seatback board in order as shown in **Fig. 62.**
7. Disengage seatback hooks, then remove seatback assembly.
8. Disconnect side air bag electrical connector.

7. Reverse procedure to install and tighten bolts to specifications.

Sienna

1. Disarm SRS as outlined under "Air Bag System Disarming & Arming."
2. Open glove compartment door.
3. Using a suitable screwdriver, remove finish plate from glove compartment.
4. Pull connector from glove compartment door finish plate.
5. Disconnect air bag assembly connector.
6. Remove instrument panel as outlined under "Dash Panel Service."
7. Remove No. 2 heater to register duct.
8. Remove 9 air bag attaching bolts, **Fig. 54,** then the air bag from instrument panel.
9. Store air bag with deployment side facing upward.
10. Reverse procedure to install. Tighten to specifications.

Supra

1. Disarm SRS as outlined under "Air Bag System Disarming & Arming."
2. Remove glove compartment door finish plate.
3. Disconnect passenger air bag electrical connector.
4. Remove glove compartment panel and heater to register duct No. 4, **Fig. 55.**
5. Remove passenger air bag mounting bolts.

6. Carefully remove passenger air bag module.
7. Reverse procedure to install and tighten bolts to specifications.

Tacoma

1. Disarm SRS as outlined under "Air Bag System Disarming & Arming."
2. Remove glove compartment door.
3. Disconnect passenger's air bag module electrical connector.
4. Remove instrument panel, **Fig. 56.**
5. Remove two passenger's air bag module attaching screws, then the air bag module, **Fig. 57.**
6. Remove three instrument panel stay attaching bolts and screws, then the instrument panel stay.
7. Remove air bag door.
8. Reverse procedure to install, noting the following:
   a. Tighten passenger's air bag module nuts and bolts to specifications.
   b. Arm SRS as outlined under "Air Bag System Disarming & Arming."

1996–97 Tercel

1. Disarm SRS as outlined under "Air Bag System Disarming & Arming."
2. Remove lower finish panel
3. Disconnect air bag electrical connector.
4. Remove instrument panel, **Fig. 58.**
5. Remove front passenger air bag mounting nuts and bolts, then assembly.
6. Remove air bag door.

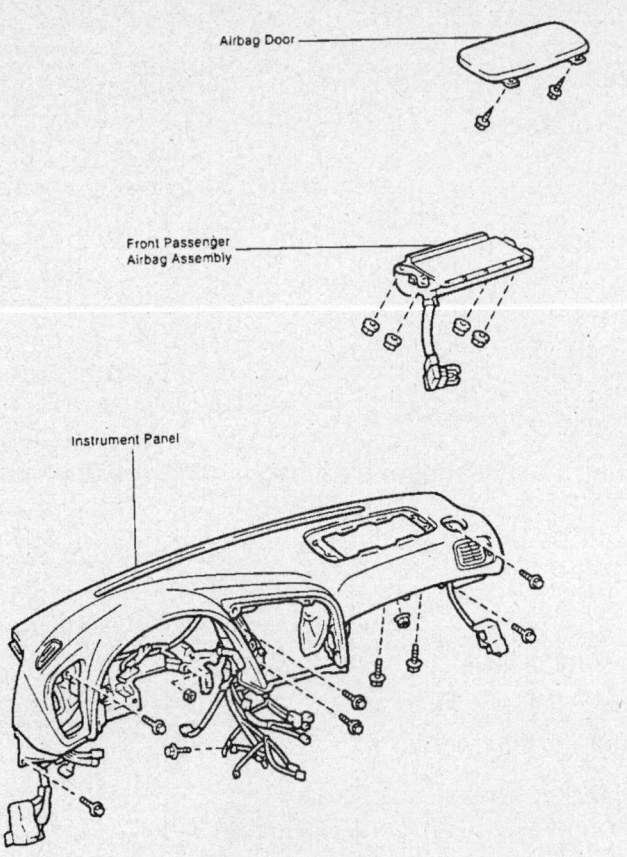

Fig. 46   Passenger air bag module replacement. 1996 Celica

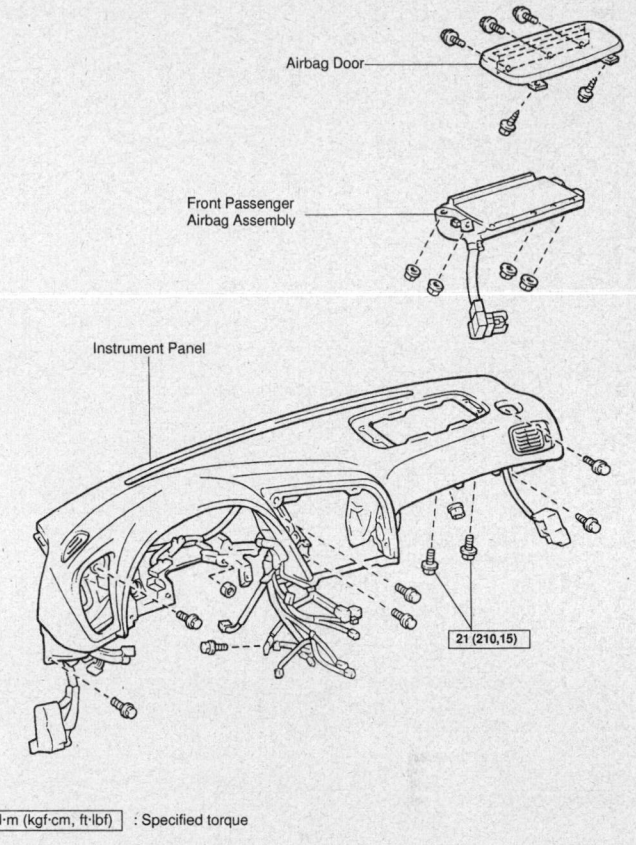

N·m (kgf·cm, ft·lbf) : Specified torque

Fig. 47   Passenger air bag module replacement. 1997–99 Celica

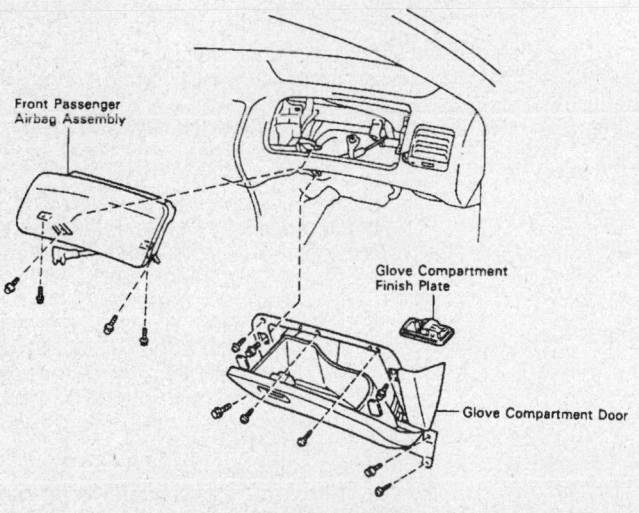

Fig. 48   Passenger side air bag replacement. Corolla

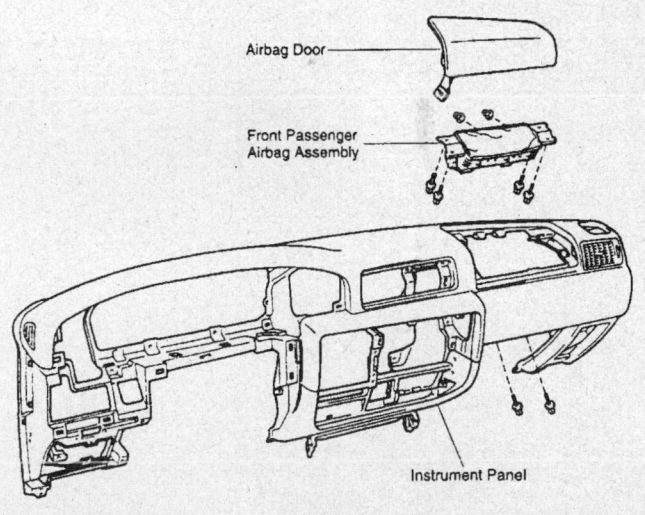

Fig. 49   Passenger air bag replacement. 1996–97 Land Cruiser

9. Remove seat cover retaining rings, then disengage hooks from seatback frame.
10. Remove four bolts and seatback assembly.
11. Remove seatback cover attaching rings, then the headrest supports.
12. Remove lumbar support lever if equipped.

13. Remove seatback frame assembly from seatback cover with pad.
14. Reverse procedure to install.

Camry w/TMMK Air Bag

1. Disarm SRS as outlined under "Air Bag System Disarming & Arming."

2. Remove seat track covers, then the 4 attaching bolts, **Figs. 63 and 64.**
3. Disconnect power seat if equipped.
4. Disconnect side air bag electrical connector.
5. Remove front seat.
6. Remove seat cushion lower shield.

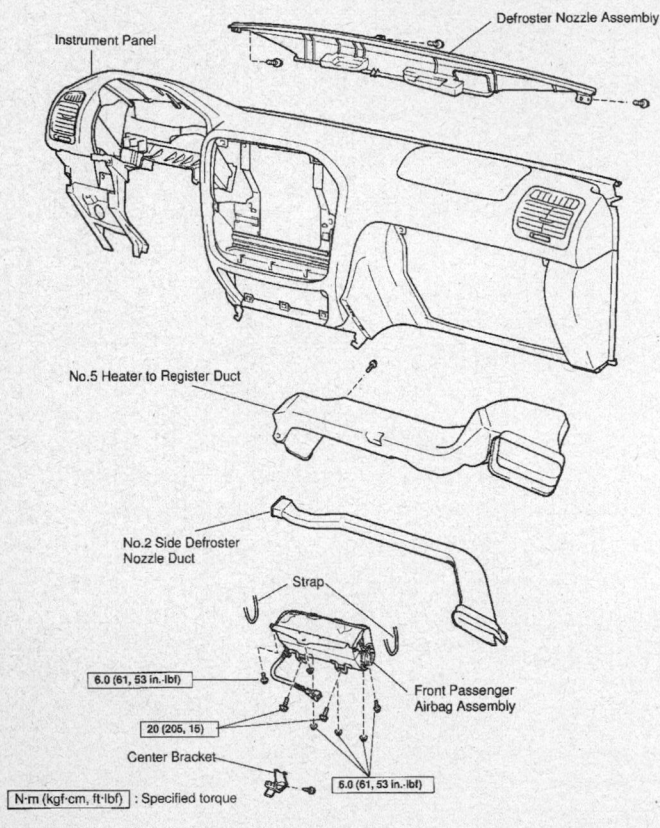

Fig. 50 Passenger air bag replacement. 1998–99 Land Cruiser

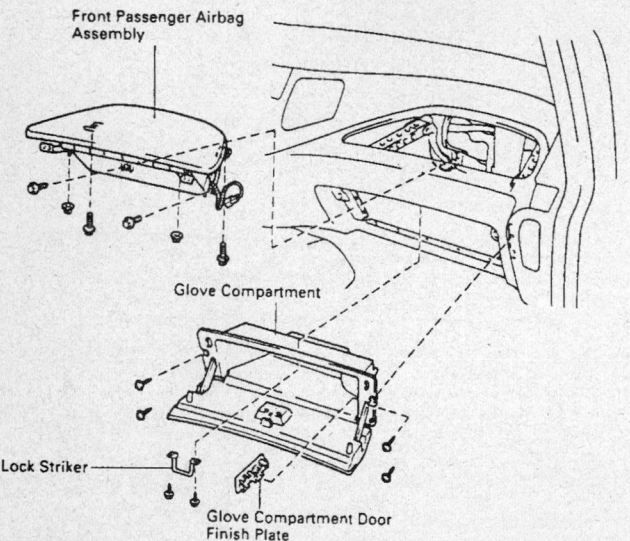

Fig. 52 Passenger air bag replacement. Previa

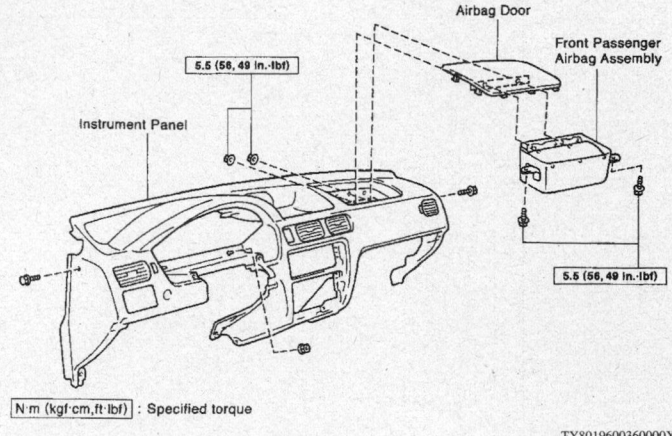

Fig. 51 Passenger's air bag module replacement. Paseo

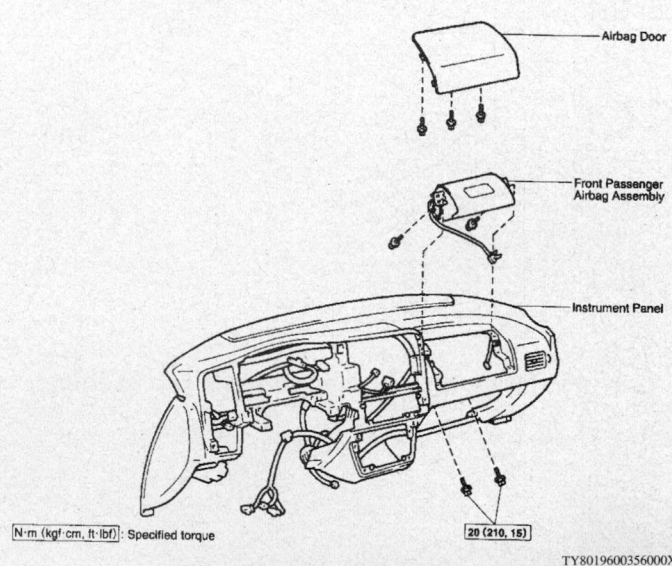

Fig. 53 Passenger air bag module replacement. RAV4 & 4Runner

a. Remove headrest and supports.
b. Remove lumbar support lever, then the hook from seatback frame.
c. Remove seatback cover with pad from seatback frame.
d. Remove side air bag attaching bolts, then the air bag. **Do not store air bag assembly with deployment side facing down. Never disassemble air bag assembly.**
15. **On all models,** reverse procedure to install noting the following:
a. Ensure air bag is tightened to specifications.
b. During installation, ensure air bag is not pinched between parts or incorrect deployment may result.
c. Ensure hook is attached securely to seatback.

Camry w/TMC Air Bag

1. Disarm SRS as outlined under "Air Bag System Disarming & Arming."
2. Remove 2 seat track covers, then the seat attaching bolts, **Figs. 65 and 66.**

7. **On models less power seat,** remove release handle, then the vertical adjusting knob.
8. **On models equipped with power seat,** disconnect electrical connector from power seat switch.
9. **On all models,** remove seat cushion shield.
10. Remove four seatback attaching bolts, then the hog rings.
11. Disconnect side air bag connector at side air bag assembly side.
12. Disconnect sub wire harness clips, then remove sub wire harness.
13. Remove seat back assembly.
14. **On 1998 models,** proceed as follows:

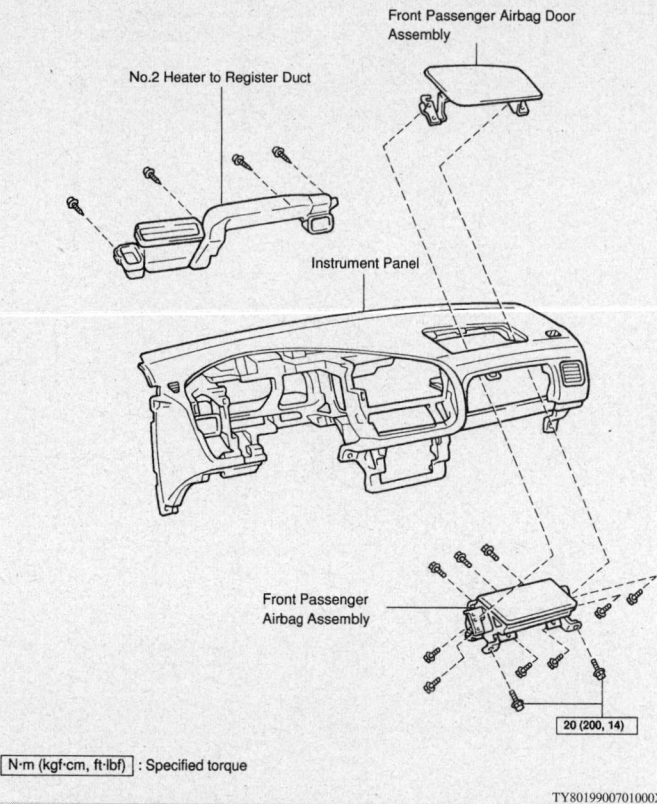

Fig. 54   Passenger air bag module replacement. Sienna

N·m (kgf·cm, ft·lbf) : Specified torque

TY8019900701000X

Code	Shape	Size	Code	Shape	Size
Ⓐ		⌀ = 8 (0.32) L = 18 (0.71)	Ⓑ		⌀ = 6 (0.24) L = 22 (0.87)

mm (in.)

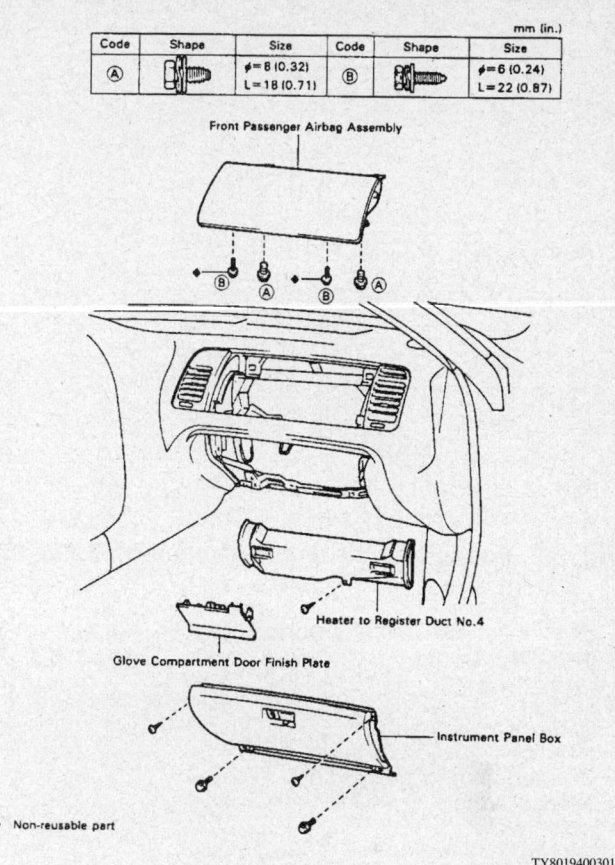

♦ Non-reusable part

TY8019400301000X

Fig. 55   Passenger air bag replacement. Supra

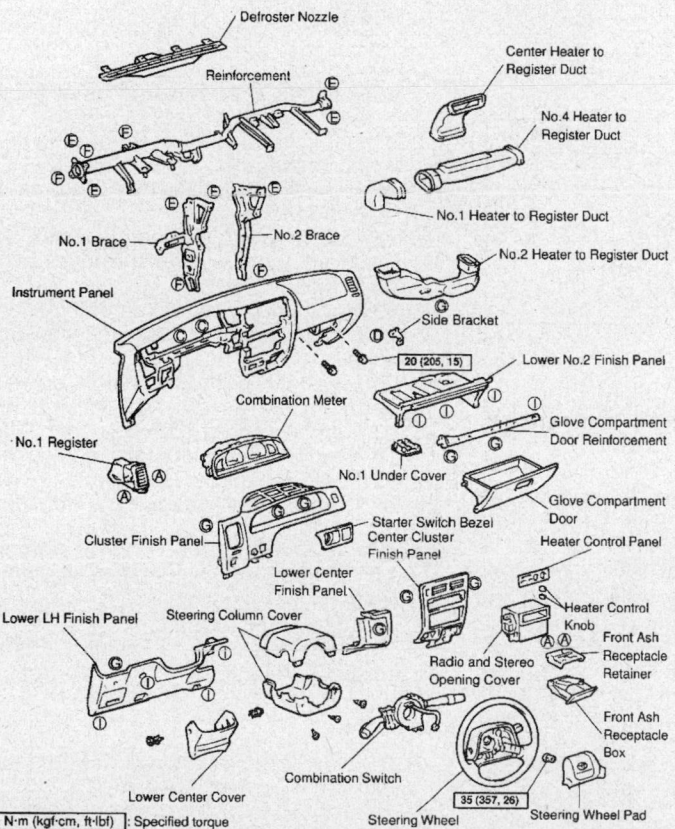

N·m (kgf·cm, ft·lbf) : Specified torque

TY8019800634000X

Fig. 56   Passenger air bag replacement. Tacoma

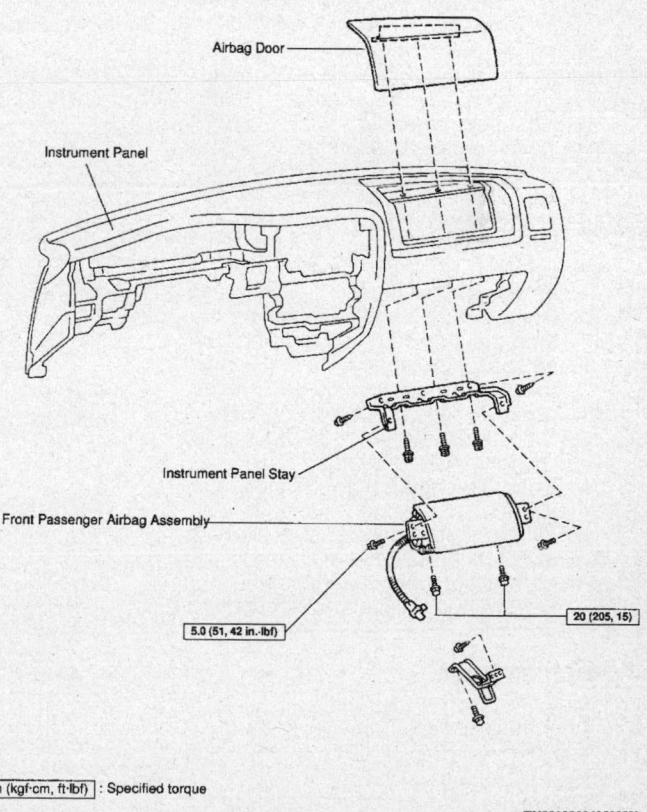

N·m (kgf·cm, ft·lbf) : Specified torque

TY8019800635000X

Fig. 57   Passenger's air bag module removal. Tacoma

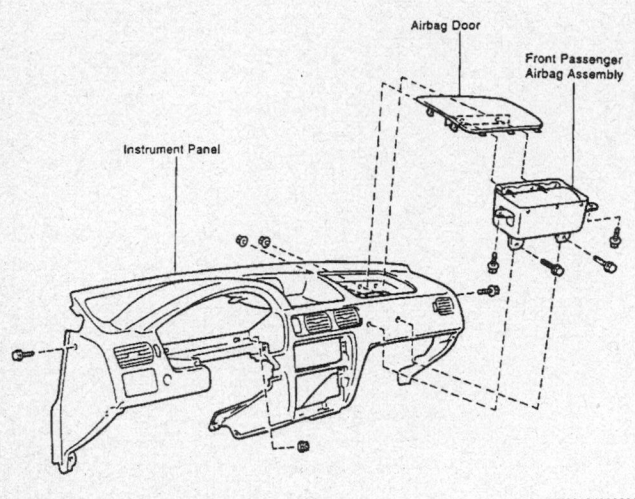

Fig. 58 Passenger air bag replacement. 1996–97 Tercel

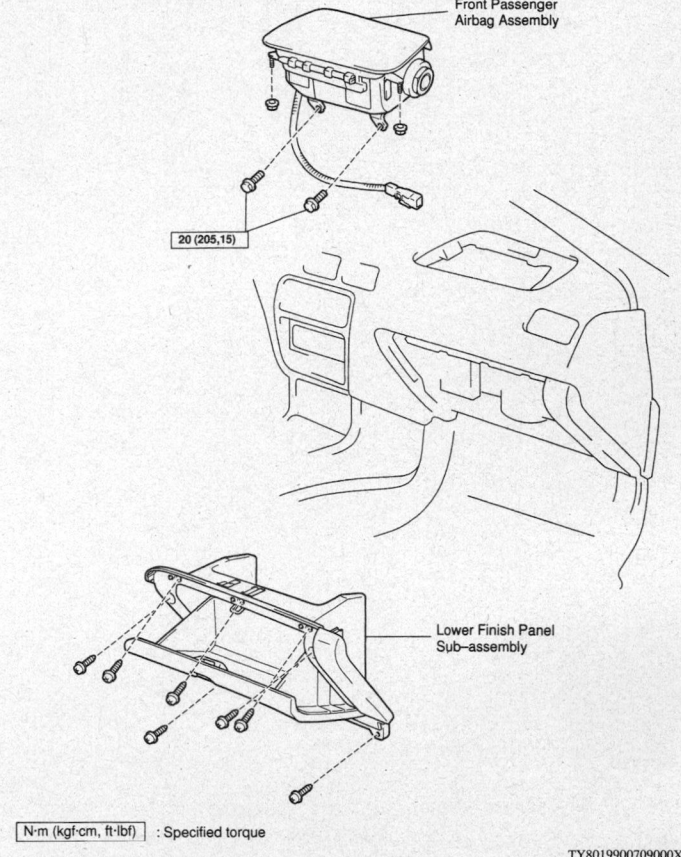

N·m (kgf·cm, ft·lbf) : Specified torque

TY8019900709000X

Fig. 59 Passenger side air bag replacement. 1998 Tercel

3. Disconnect power seat electrical connector if equipped.
4. Disconnect side air bag electrical connector.
5. Remove front seat.
6. Remove seat cushion lower shield.
7. **On models less power seat,** remove release handle, then the vertical adjuster knob.
8. **On models equipped with power seat,** disconnect electrical connector from seat switch.
9. **On all models,** remove front seat cushion shield.
10. Remove cushion inner shield.
11. Remove headrest, then the supports.
12. Remove seatback attaching bolts, then the hog rings.
13. Remove seatback assembly.
14. **On 1998 models,** proceed as follows:
    a. Remove lumbar support lever.
    b. With seatback cover turned up, remove hook from seatback frame.
    c. Remove seatback cover with pad from seatback frame.
    d. Remove side airbag attaching nuts, then the side air bag. **Do not store air bag assembly with deployment side facing down. Never disassemble air bag assembly.**
15. **On all models,** reverse procedure to install noting the following:
    a. Ensure air bag is tightened to specifications.
    b. During installation, ensure air bag is not pinched between parts or incorrect deployment may result.
    c. Ensure hook is attached securely to seatback.

Camry Solara

1. Disarm SRS as outlined under "Air Bag System Disarming & Arming."
2. Remove seat track covers, then the seat attaching bolts, **Fig. 67.**
3. Disconnect power seat if equipped.
4. Disconnect side air bag connector.
5. Remove front seat, then the headrest and adjuster knob.

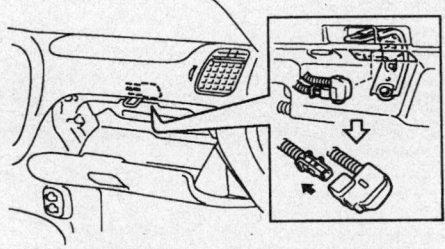

TY8019900684000X

Fig. 60 Passenger air bag connector location. Tundra

6. Remove front seat cushion shield.
7. **On models equipped with power seat,** proceed as follows:
    a. Remove seat belt warning light connector clamp, then the bolt and inner belt.
    b. Remove 2 screws and inner front seat cushion shield.
    c. Remove wire harness of side air bag assembly.
    d. Remove wire harness of power seat from seat cushion assembly.
    e. Remove 4 bolts and seat cushion assembly.
8. **On models less power seat,** proceed as follows:

a. Remove 2 screws and inner front seat cushion shield.
b. Remove wire harness of side air bag assembly.
c. Remove 4 bolts, then the seat cushion.
9. **On all models,** disengage hook of seatback cover, then remove hog rings.
10. Remove seatback attaching bolts, then move seatback assembly upward slightly.
11. **On models equipped with power seat,** proceed as follows:
    a. Remove screw and separate lefthand reclining adjuster inside cover from seat adjuster assembly.
    b. Remove lefthand reclining adjuster inside cover.
12. **On all models,** separate wire harness of side air bag assembly from reclining adjuster inside cover.
13. Remove seatback assembly.
14. Reverse procedure to install. Tighten to specifications.

Corolla

1. Disarm SRS as outlined under "Air Bag System Disarming & Arming."
2. Remove seat track covers and seat attaching bolts.

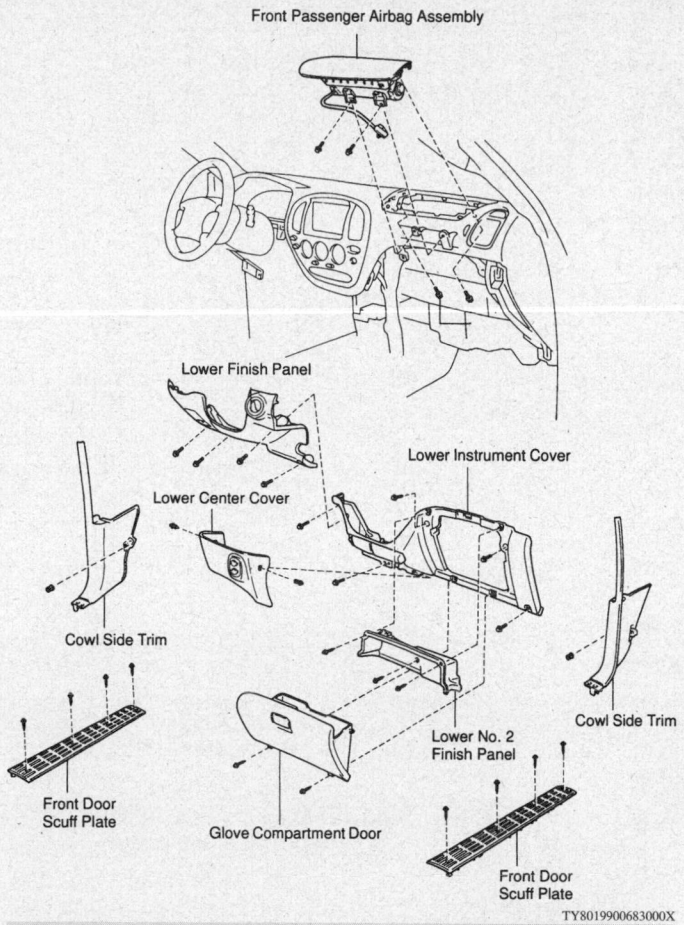

Fig. 61 Passenger air bag replacement. Tundra

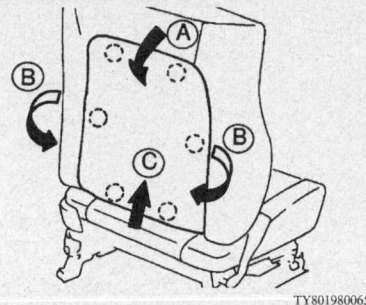

Fig. 62 Seatback board removal. Avalon

3. Disconnect side air bag electrical connector, then remove seat.
4. Remove headrest, reclining adjuster release handle and front cushion shields.
5. Remove air bag harness from harness protector on rear of seat.
6. Remove hog rings from rear of seat.
7. Remove seatback attaching bolts, then the seatback.
8. Remove hook and hog rings from seatback, then the headrest supports.
9. Remove seatback frame from seatback cover.
10. Remove air bag attaching bolts, then the air bag. **Do not store air bag assembly with deployment side facing down. Never disassemble air bag assembly.**
11. Reverse procedure to install noting the following:
    a. Ensure air bag is tightened to specifications.
    b. During installation, ensure air bag is not pinched between parts or incorrect deployment may result.
    c. Ensure hook is attached securely to seatback.

SEAT BELT PRETENSIONER

AVALON & CAMRY

1. Disarm SRS as outlined under "Air Bag System Disarming & Arming."

2. Remove door scuff plate.
3. Using a suitable screwdriver, remove center pillar lower garnish.
4. Remove anchor cap, then the bolt and shoulder anchor.
5. Disconnect pretensioner connector as shown in **Fig. 68.**
6. Remove seat belt attaching bolts, then the seat belt.
7. Reverse procedure to install. Tighten to specifications and ensure wiring harness is not pinched between other parts.

CAMRY SOLARA

1. Disarm SRS as outlined under "Air Bag System Disarming & Arming."
2. Remove front door scuff plate.
3. Pull up on front portion of rear seat cushion and remove.
4. Remove rear seatback as follows:
    a. Release seatback assembly, then fold seatback assembly.
    b. Remove three clips, then the two bolts and seatback assembly.
    c. Perform same procedure for opposite side if necessary.
5. Remove seatback side hinges.
6. Using a suitable screwdriver, open screw covers of rear assist grip.
7. Remove front seat belt floor anchor, then the assist grip.
8. Remove rear quarter trim panel, then

the front seat outer belt shoulder anchor.
9. Disconnect retractor switch connector.
10. Disconnect pretensioner as shown in **Fig. 69.**
11. Remove retractor attaching bolts, then the retractor of front seat outer belt.
12. Reverse procedure to install. Tighten to specifications.

COROLLA

1. Disarm SRS as outlined under "Air Bag System Disarming & Arming."
2. Remove front door scuff plate, then the center pillar lower garnish.
3. Remove bolt, then the front seat outer belt floor anchor.
4. Remove shoulder anchor cap, then the shoulder anchor.
5. **When removing lefthand pretensioner,** disconnect retractor switch connector.
6. **When removing either pretensioner,** disconnect pretensioner connector as shown in **Fig. 70.**
7. Remove retractor attaching bolts, then the retractor
8. Reverse procedure to install. Tighten to specifications.

LAND CRUISER

1. Disarm SRS as outlined under "Air Bag System Disarming & Arming."
2. Remove front door scuff plate, then the door opening trim.
3. Remove rear door scuff plate and opening trim.
4. Remove center pillar lower garnish cover, then the lower garnish.
5. Remove front seat outer belt shoulder anchor.
6. Remove front seat outer belt floor anchor.
7. Disconnect seatbelt pretensioner in order "A" and "B" as shown in **Fig. 71.**
8. Remove bolt and retractor of front seat outer belt.
9. Reverse procedure to install. Tighten to specifications.

RAV4
1998

1. **On two door models,** proceed as follows:
    a. Remove rear seat.
    b. Remove floor finish plate, then the front door scuff plate.

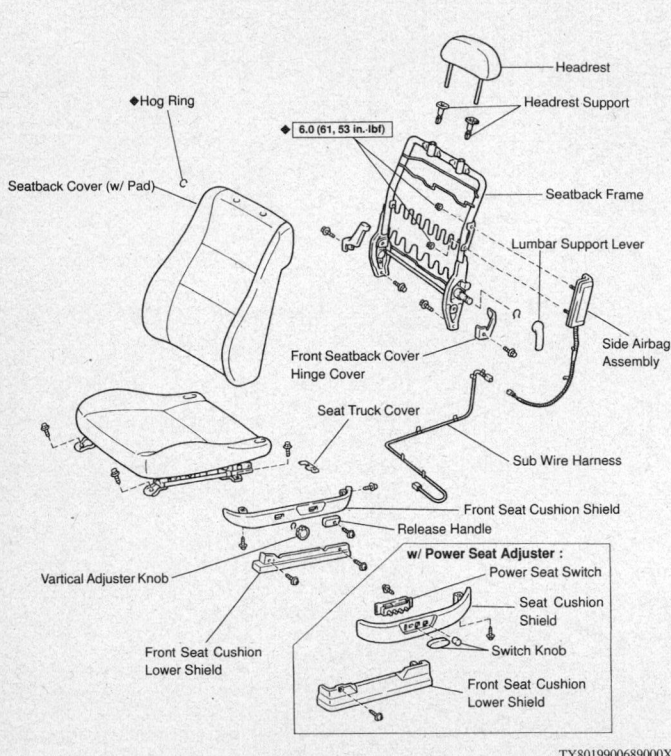

Fig. 63 Side air bag components. 1998 Camry w/TMMK air bag

TY8019900689000X

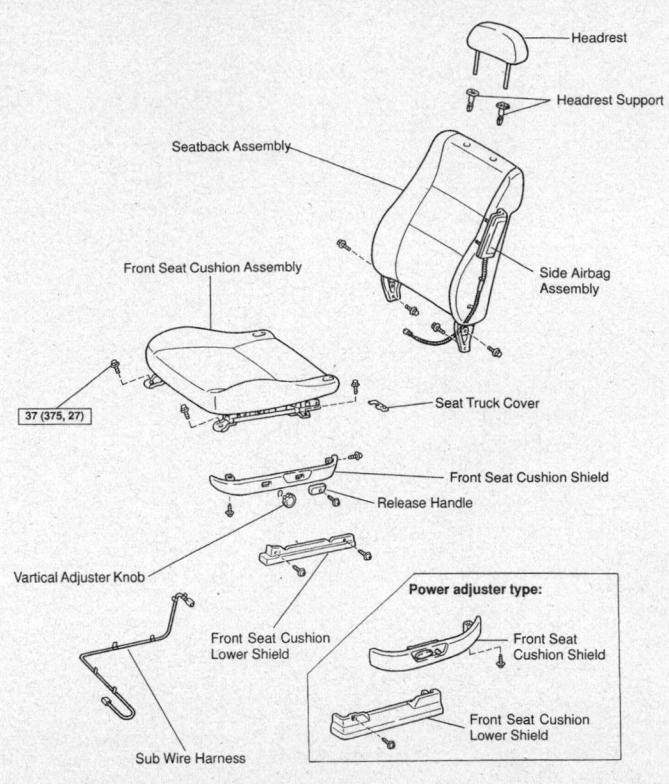

Fig. 64 Side air bag components. 1999 Camry w/TMMK air bag

TY8019900688000X

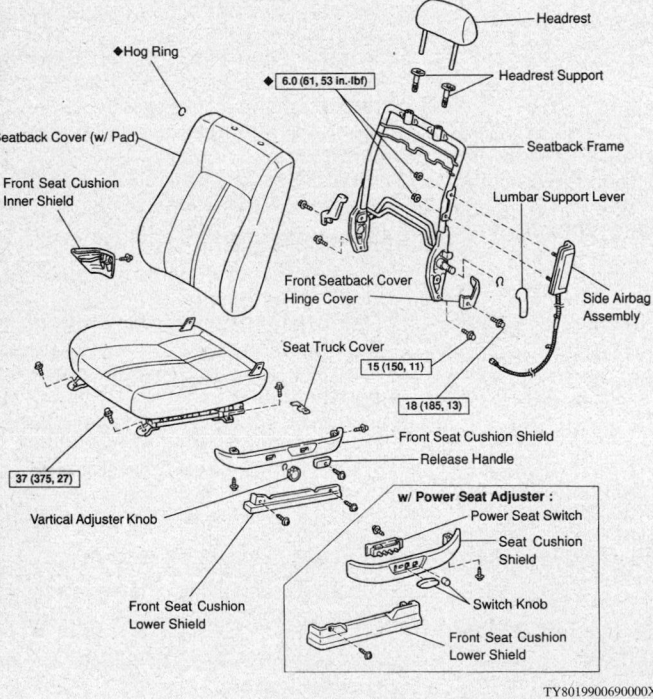

Fig. 65 Side air bag components. 1998 Camry w/TMC air bag

TY8019900690000X

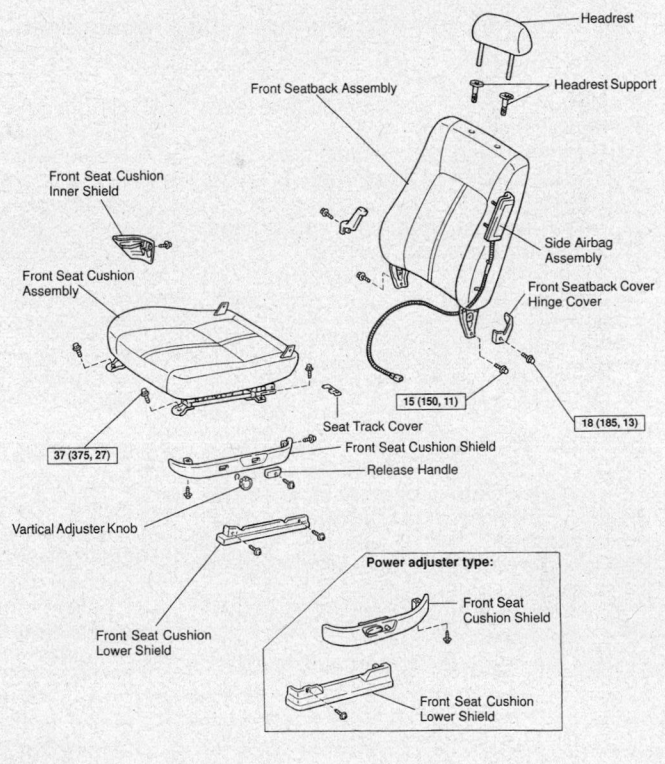

N·m (kgf·cm, ft·lbf) : Specified torque

Fig. 66 Side air bag components. 1999 Camry w/TMC air bag

TY8019900691000X

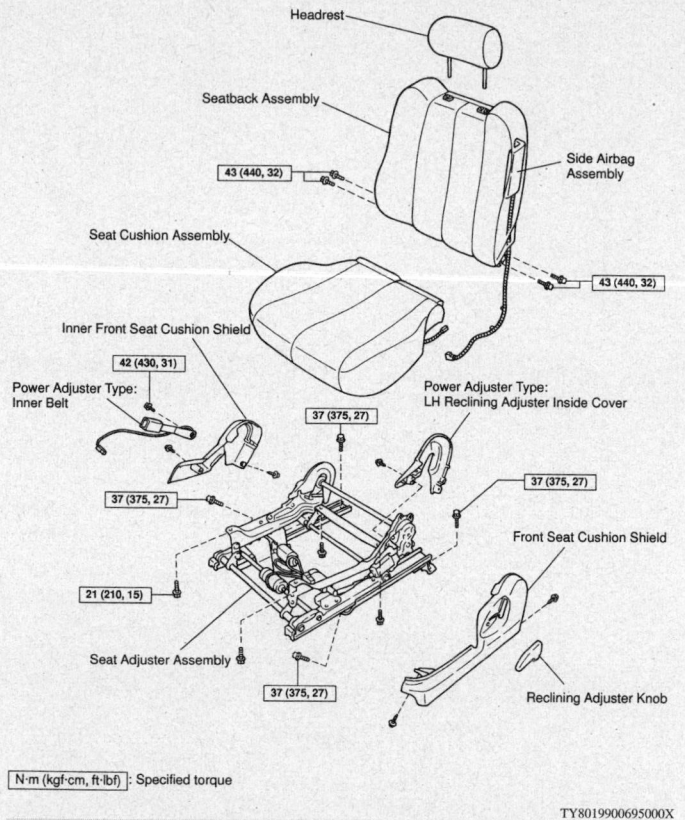

Fig. 67 Side air bag components. Camry Solara

N·m (kgf·cm, ft·lbf) : Specified torque

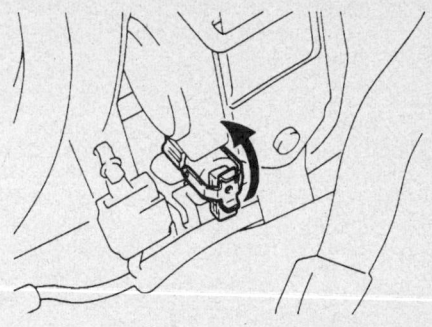

Fig. 68 Seat belt pretensioner removal. Avalon & Camry

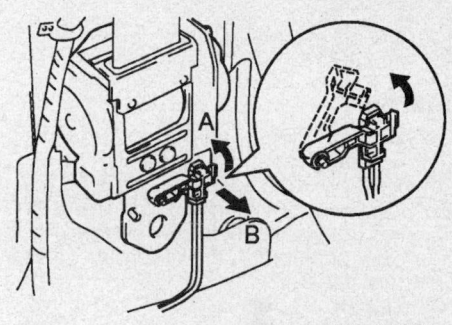

Fig. 71 Seat belt tension removal. Land Cruiser

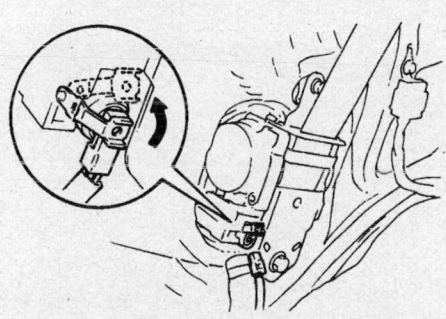

Fig. 69 Seat belt pretensioner removal. Camry Solara

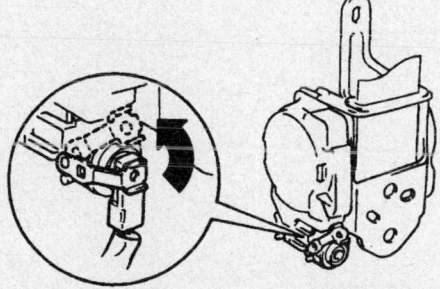

Fig. 70 Pretensioner removal. Corolla

c. Remove quarter, then the roof side inner garnish.
2. **On four door models,** proceed as follows:
   a. Remove front and rear door scuff plates.
   b. Remove center pillar lower garnish.
3. **On all models,** remove bolts and floor anchor.
4. Remove anchor caps, then the bolt and shoulder anchor.
5. Disconnect pretensioner as shown in **Figs. 72 and 73.**
6. Disconnect retractor switch connector if equipped.
7. Remove front seat outer belt.
8. Reverse procedure to install.

1999

1. Disarm SRS as outlined under "Air Bag System Disarming & Arming."
2. **On models equipped with soft top, Fig. 74,** proceed as follows:
   a. Remove back window glass.
   b. Remove right and left quarter window glass.
   c. Disengage hooks on bottom of top cover assembly.
   d. Fold down top cover rearward.
   e. Remove 4 torx screws and top cover assembly.
   f. Remove screw and rear end cover.
   g. Using a suitable screwdriver, remove front end cover.

h. Remove right and left quarter belt molding and body.
i. Remove right and left rear quarter outside molding.
j. Remove left and right pivot brackets, then the side panel retainers.
k. Remove outer weatherstrip and top molding.
l. Remove back door opening trim, then the tailgate bar.
m. Remove auxiliary catches.
n. Remove rear seat, then the rear floor finish plate.
o. Remove front door scuff plate.
p. Remove outer belt floor anchor, then the quarter trim.
q. Remove assist grip, then the front seat outer belt shoulder anchor.
r. Remove roof side inner garnish.
s. Remove retractor of front seat outer belt.
t. Disconnect pretensioner as shown in **Fig. 72.**
u. Remove front outer seat belt retractor.
3. **On two door models,** proceed as follows:
   a. Remove rear seat, then the rear floor finish plate.
   b. Remove front door scuff plate, then the rear seat outer belt floor anchor.
   c. Remove rear quarter trim.
   d. Remove rear seat outer belt shoulder anchor, then the front seat outer belt shoulder anchor.

e. Remove roof side inner garnish.
f. Remove retractor from front seat outer belt.
g. Disconnect pretensioner as shown in **Fig. 72**.
h. Remove front seat belt retractor.
4. **On four door models,** proceed as follows:
 a. Remove front and rear door scuff plates.
 b. Remove front seat outer belt floor anchor.
 c. Pull center pillar lower garnish upward, then remove.
 d. Remove front seat outer belt shoulder anchor.
 e. Disconnect pretensioner as shown in **Fig. 73**.
 f. Remove front seat outer belt retractor.
5. **On all models,** reverse procedure to install.

SIENNA

1. Disarm SRS as outlined under "Air Bag System Disarming & Arming."
2. Remove front door scuff plate.
3. **On four door models,** when removing left front seat outer belt, remove back door scuff plate, then the rear quarter trim panel.
4. **On all models,** remove anchor cap, then the bolt and rear No. 1 seat outer belt shoulder anchor, **Fig. 75**.
5. **On four door models,** when removing left front seat outer belt, remove front quarter trim panel.
6. **On all models,** when removing right front seat outer belt, remove sliding door scuff plate.
7. Remove bolt and front seat outer belt floor anchor, then the lower center pillar garnish.
8. Disconnect pretensioner as shown in **Fig. 76**.
9. Disconnect retractor switch connector if equipped.
10. Remove front seat outer belt attaching bolts, then the belt.
11. Reverse procedure to install. Tighten to specifications.

TACOMA

Regular Cab

1. Disarm SRS as outlined under "Air Bag System Disarming & Arming."
2. Remove front seat outer belt floor anchor, then the shoulder anchor.
3. Remove retractor cover.
4. Remove retractor of front seat outer belt.
5. Disconnect pretensioner as shown in **Fig. 77**.
6. Remove retractor from front seat outer belt.
7. Reverse procedure to install. Tighten to specifications.

Extended Cab

1. Disarm SRS as outlined under "Air Bag System Disarming & Arming."
2. Remove door scuff plate.
3. Remove back panel upper garnish.
4. Remove back panel trim, then the back panel lower garnish.

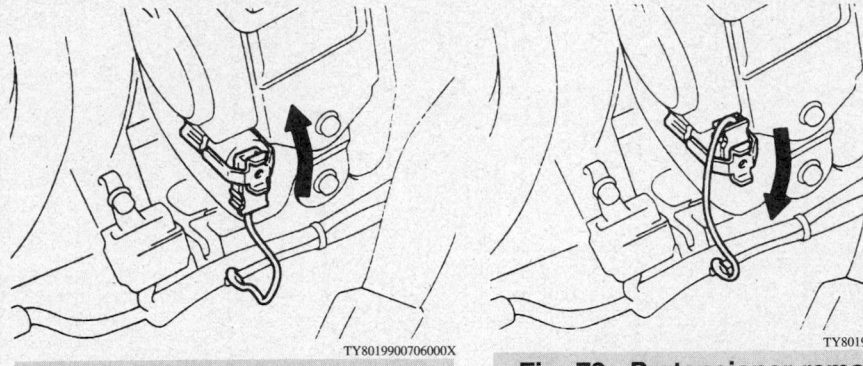

Fig. 72 Pretensioner removal. 1999 RAV4 w/soft top & two door

TY8019900706000X

Fig. 73 Pretensioner removal. RAV4 w/four door

TY8019900707000X

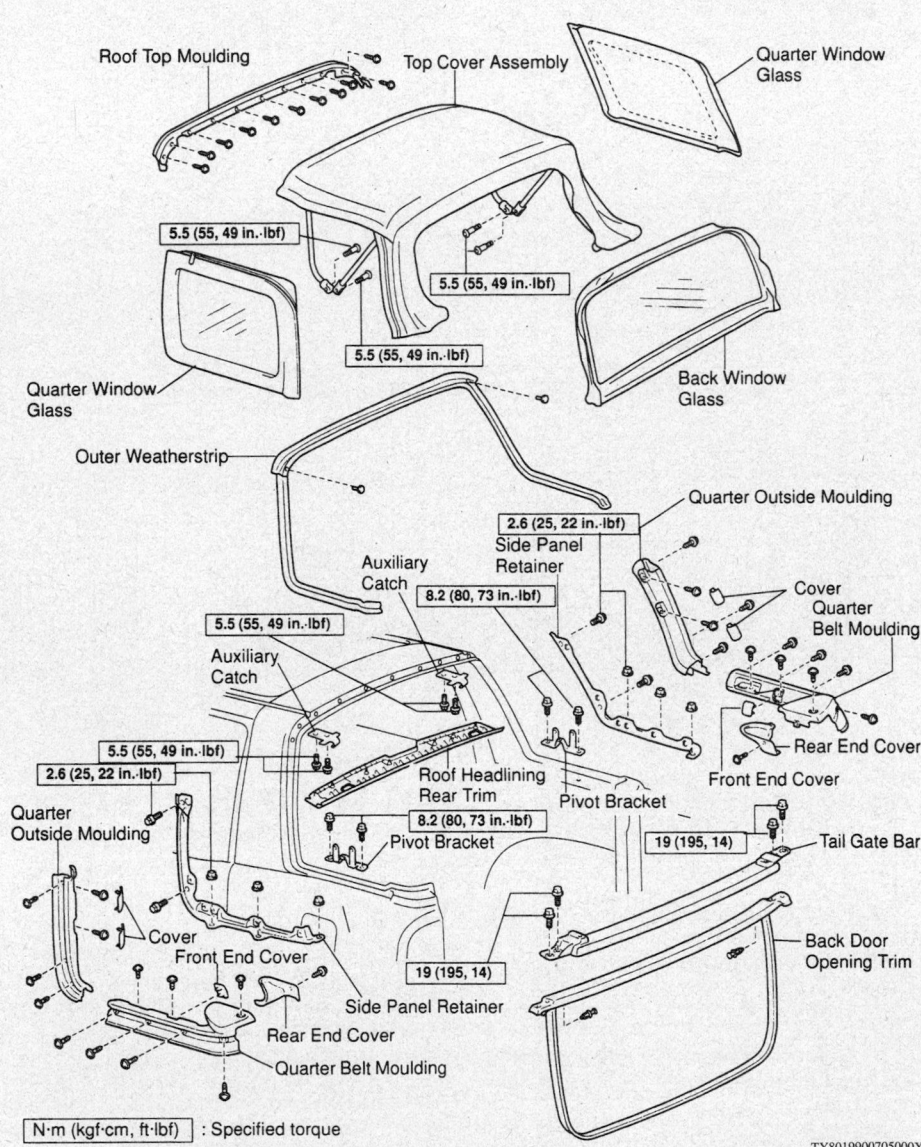

N·m (kgf·cm, ft·lbf) : Specified torque

TY8019900705000X

Fig. 74 Exploded view of soft top components. 1999 RAV4

5. Remove rear seat cushions, then the front and rear seat outer belt shoulder anchors.
6. Remove lock handle.
7. Remove outer belt shoulder anchors,

then the coat hook.
8. Remove quarter trim.
9. Disconnect retractor switch connector.
10. Disconnect pretensioner as shown in **Fig. 78**.

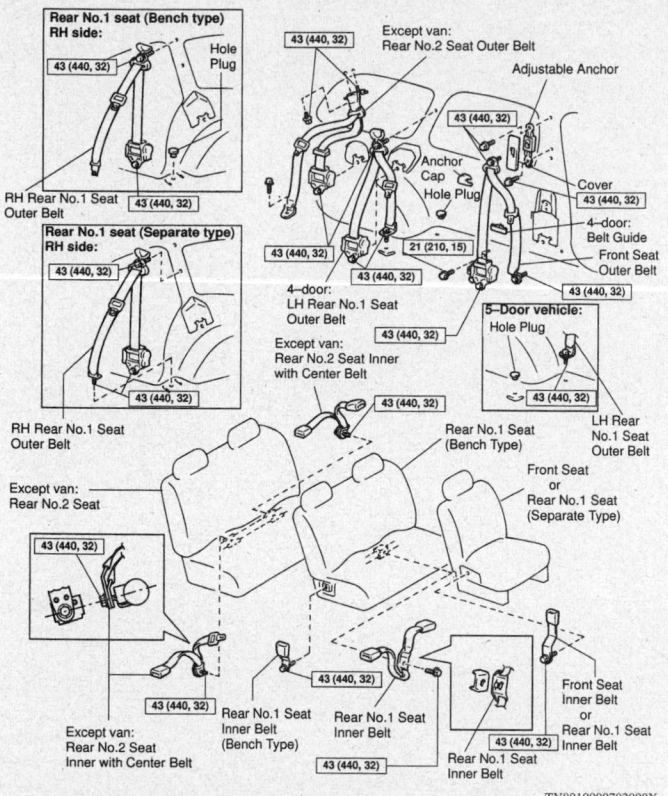

Fig. 75   Seat belt components. Sienna

TY8019900702000X

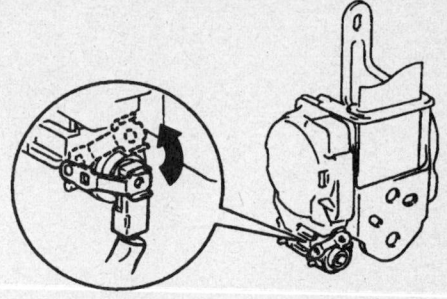

TY8019900703000X

Fig. 76   Seat belt pretensioner removal. Sienna

the front seat outer belt floor anchor.
 c. Remove shoulder belt anchor bolt cap, then the shoulder anchor.
 d. Remove screw covers, then the assist grip and side rail garnish.
 e. Remove front door rear scuff plate and cover.
 f. Remove retractor of front seat outer belt. **Do not disassemble front seat outer belt.**
 g. Disconnect pretensioner as shown in **Fig. 83.**
 h. Remove bolt and retractor of outer belt.
4. Reverse procedure to install. Tighten to specifications.

4RUNNER

1. Disarm SRS as outlined under "Air Bag System Disarming & Arming."
2. Remove front and rear door scuff plate.
3. Remove center pillar lower garnish.
4. Remove front seat outer belt floor anchor.
5. Remove front seat outer belt shoulder anchor.
6. Disconnect pretensioner connector as shown in **Fig. 85.**
7. Remove front seat outer belt.
8. Reverse procedure to install. Tighten to specifications.

SPIRAL CABLE, REPLACE

REMOVAL

1. Ensure front wheels are straight-ahead.
2. Disarm SRS as outlined under "Air Bag System Disarming & Arming."
3. Remove air bag module as outlined under "Air Bag Module, Replace."
4. Disconnect connector and remove steering wheel set nut.
5. Place alignment marks on steering wheel and steering shaft for use during installation.
6. Remove steering wheel with suitable puller tool.
7. Remove steering column covers.
8. **On RAV4 models,** remove instrument panel lower finish panel and insert as necessary.
9. **On all models,** remove combination switch.
10. Remove mounting screws and spiral

11. Remove retractor attaching bolts, then the retractor.
12. Reverse procedure to install. Tighten to specifications.

TERCEL

Refer to **Figs. 79 and 80** when servicing seat belt pretensioner system.
1. **On two door models,** remove the following components:
 a. Rear seat.
 b. Front door scuff plate.
 c. Package tray trim side cover.
 d. Quarter trim.
2. **On four door models,** remove front door scuff plate, then the center pillar lower garnish.
3. **On all models,** remove floor anchor.
4. Using a suitable screwdriver, remove anchor caps.
5. Remove shoulder anchor, then disconnect pretensioner as shown in **Fig. 81.**
6. Remove front seat outer belt.
7. Reverse procedure to install. Tighten to specifications.

TUNDRA

1. Disarm SRS as outlined under "Air Bag System Disarming & Arming."
2. **On standard cab models,** proceed as follows:
 a. Remove 5 attaching screws, then the front door scuff plate.
 b. Remove screw covers, **Fig. 82.**
 c. Remove torx screws, then the assist grip.
 d. Remove front pillar garnish.
 e. Remove back panel upper garnish.

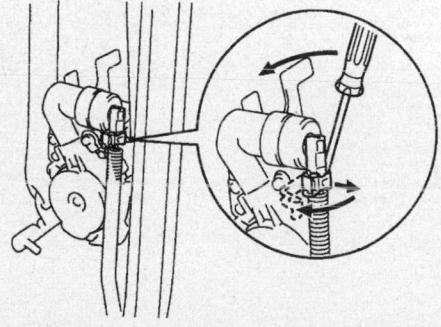

TY8019900719000X

Fig. 77   Pretensioner removal. Tacoma

 f. Remove bolt and front seat outer belt floor anchor.
 g. Remove quarter trim belt hole cover.
 h. Remove shoulder harness cap.
 i. Remove bolt and front seat belt shoulder harness anchor.
 j. Remove quarter trim panel.
 k. Remove retractor from front seat outer belt. **Do not disassemble front seat outer belt.**
 l. Disconnect pretensioner connector as shown in **Fig. 83.**
3. **On access cab models,** proceed as follows:
 a. Remove front door scuff plate, **Fig. 84.**
 b. Remove rear door scuff plate, then

Fig. 78 Pretensioner removal. Tacoma

TY8019900720000X

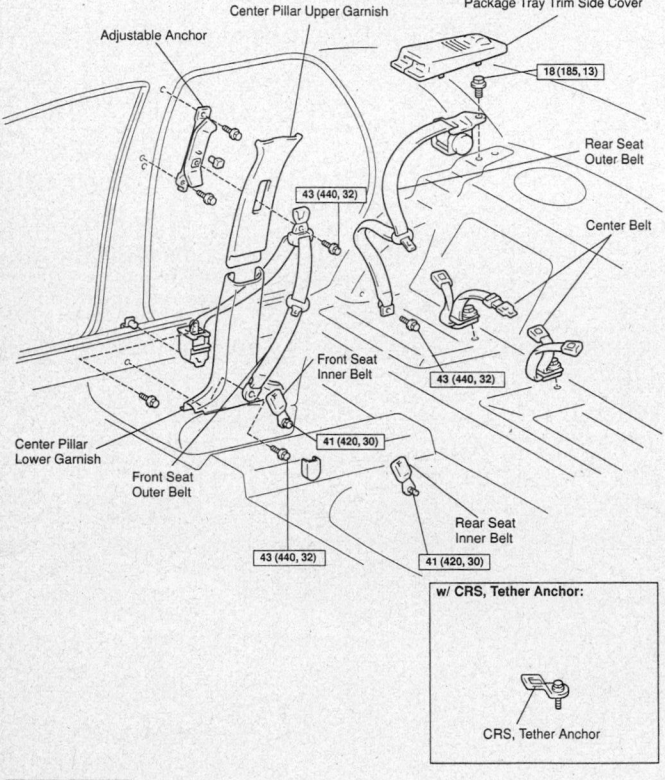

Adjustable Anchor

Center Pillar Upper Garnish

Package Tray Trim Side Cover

18 (185, 13)

43 (440, 32)

Rear Seat Outer Belt

Center Belt

Front Seat Inner Belt

43 (440, 32)

41 (420, 30)

Center Pillar Lower Garnish

Front Seat Outer Belt

Rear Seat Inner Belt

43 (440, 32)

41 (420, 30)

w/ CRS, Tether Anchor:

CRS, Tether Anchor

N·m (kgf·cm, ft·lbf) : Specified torque

TY8019900711000X

Fig. 80 Seat belt pretensioner components (4door). Tercel

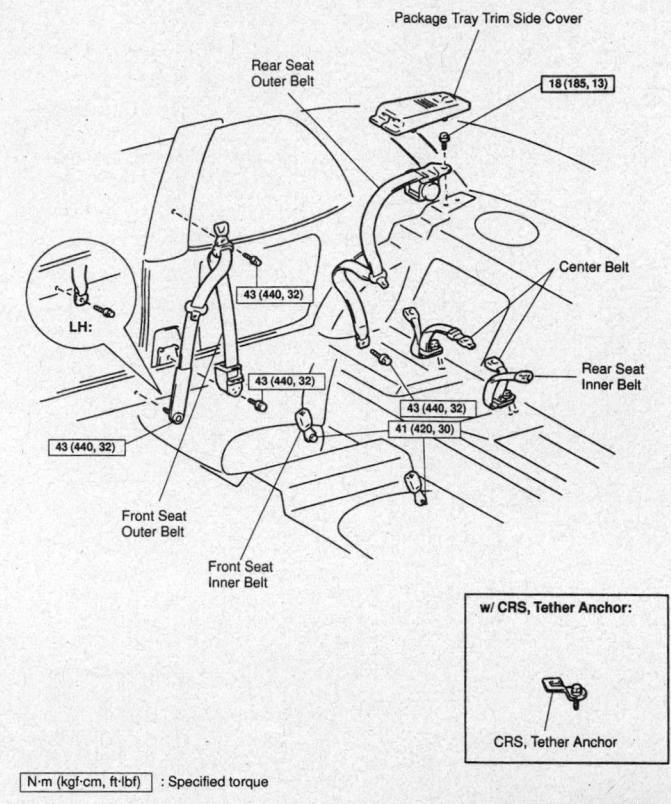

Package Tray Trim Side Cover

18 (185, 13)

Rear Seat Outer Belt

43 (440, 32)

Center Belt

LH:

43 (440, 32)

Rear Seat Inner Belt

43 (440, 32)

41 (420, 30)

Front Seat Outer Belt

Front Seat Inner Belt

43 (440, 32)

w/ CRS, Tether Anchor:

CRS, Tether Anchor

N·m (kgf·cm, ft·lbf) : Specified torque

TY8019900710000X

Fig. 79 Seat belt pretensioner components (2 door). Tercel

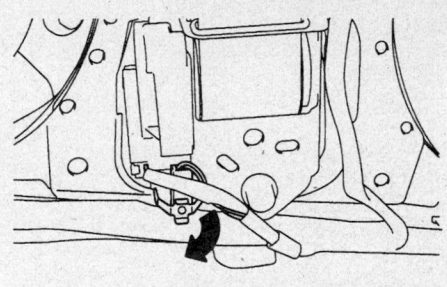

TY8019900712000X

Fig. 81 Seatbelt pretensioner removal. Tercel

cable from combination switch.

INSTALLATION

1. Ensure front wheel are in straight-ahead position.
2. Install spiral cable.
3. Turn spiral cable counterclockwise by hand until cable becomes difficult to turn.
4. **On Avalon, Camry, Camry Solara, Celica, Corolla, Land Cruiser, Previa, Sienna, Supra, Tacoma and T100, and 1996 4Runner models,** turn spiral cable clockwise approximately 2 ½–3 turns to align mark, **Figs. 86 through 88** Spiral cable will rotate about three turns either left or right of center.
5. **On RAV4, Tercel and 1996–97 Paseo models,** turn spiral cable clockwise approximately two and one-half turns to align mark, **Figs. 86 through 88.** Spiral cable will rotate about 2½ turns either left or right of center.
6. **On Tundra models,** turn cable clockwise 2½ turns to align mark, **Fig. 87.**
7. **On all models,** install combination switch.
8. **On RAV4 models,** install instrument panel No. 1 lower finish panel and insert.
9. **On all models,** install steering column covers.
10. Align steering wheel and steering shaft marks, then install steering wheel mounting nut and tighten to specifications.
11. Install air bag module as outlined

under "Air Bag Module, Replace."
12. Arm SRS system as outlined under "Air Bag System Disarming & Arming."

FRONT AIR BAG SENSOR, REPLACE

AVALON

1. Disarm SRS as outlined under "Air Bag System Disarming & Arming."
2. Remove radiator grille.
3. Remove right and left turn signal lamps.
4. Remove right and left headlamps.
5. Disconnect air bag sensors attaching bolts, then the sensors, **Fig. 89.**
6. Reverse procedure to install. Tighten to specification and ensure arrow on

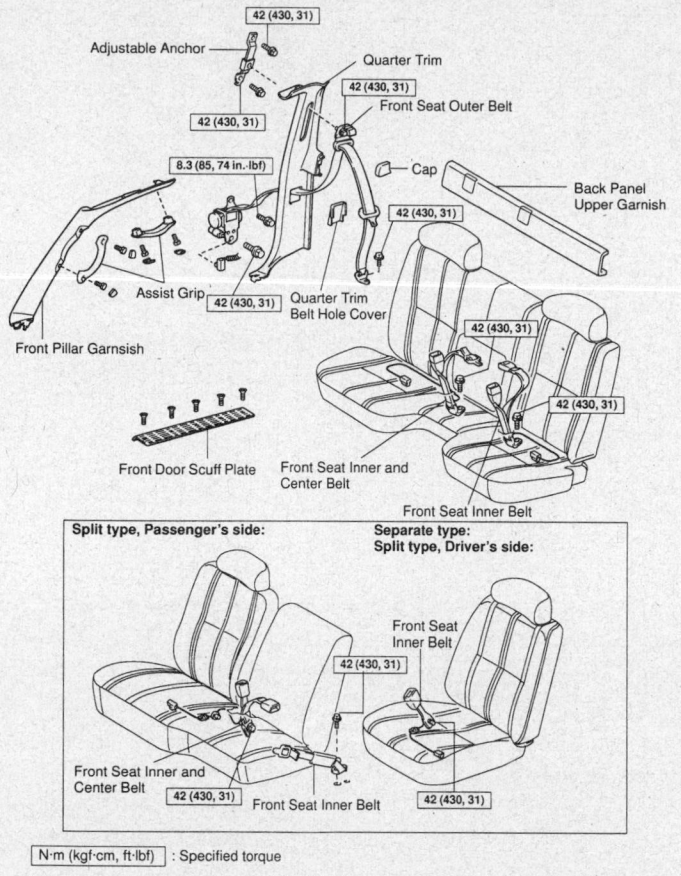

Fig. 82 Seat belt components. Tundra w/standard cab

Fig. 83 Seat belt pretensioner removal. Tundra

sensor is pointing toward front of vehicle. Arm SRS system as outlined under "Air Bag System Disarming & Arming."

1996 CAMRY & SUPRA

1. Disarm SRS as outlined under "Air Bag System Disarming & Arming."
2. Remove inner fender liners, **Figs. 90 through 94.**
3. **On Supra models,** remove headlamps.
4. **On all models,** disconnect sensor electrical connectors.
5. Remove sensor mounting bolt and sensor.
6. Reverse procedure to install, noting following:
   a. Ensure sensor arrow points toward vehicle front.
   b. Tighten new mounting bolts to specifications. **Do not reuse old mounting bolts.**
   c. Shake sensor and ensure there is no looseness.
   d. Lock electrical connection check mechanism securely or diagnosis circuit may generate diagnostic trouble code (DTC).

1999 CAMRY

1. Disarm SRS as outlined under "Air Bag System Disarming & Arming."
2. Remove turn signals, then the head lamps.

3. Disconnect air bag sensor electrical connectors.
4. Remove air bag sensor attaching bolts, then the sensors.
5. Reverse procedure to install noting the following:
   a. Ensure sensor is installed with arrow pointing toward front of vehicle.
   b. Connect sensor electrical connector after sensor is installed.
   c. Tighten to specifications.

CAMRY SOLARA

1. Disarm SRS as outlined under "Air Bag System Disarming & Arming."
2. Remove turn signal lamps.
3. Remove radiator grille.
4. Remove headlamps, then disconnect air bag sensor electrical connectors.
5. Remove sensor attaching bolts, then the sensors.
6. Reverse procedure to install. Ensure arrow on sensor points toward front of vehicle. Tighten to specifications.

CELICA

1. Disarm SRS as outlined under "Air Bag System Disarming & Arming."
2. Remove under engine under cover and front fender liners.
3. Remove front bumper cover, **Fig. 92.**
4. Remove condenser bolt and nut.
5. Disconnect front air bag sensor electri-

cal connectors.
6. Tilt radiator and condenser back.
7. Remove sensor mounting screws with suitable Torx wrench tool, then sensor.
8. Reverse procedure to install, ensure sensor arrow points toward vehicle front and tighten screws to specifications.

COROLLA

1. Disarm SRS as outlined under "Air Bag System Disarming & Arming."
2. For lefthand front air bag sensor, remove lefthand engine under cover, **Fig. 93.**
3. For righthand front air bag sensor, remove front turn signal lamp and headlamp.
4. Disconnect front air bag sensor electrical connector.
5. Remove front air bag sensor retaining bolts, then the sensor.
6. Reverse procedure to install, noting the following:
   a. Ensure arrow points toward vehicle front.
   b. When install front air bag sensor, install sensor before connecting electrical connector.
   c. Tighten front air bag sensor bolts to specifications.
   d. Arm SRS as outlined under "Air Bag System Disarming & Arming."

LAND CRUISER

Left

1. Disarm SRS as outlined under "Air Bag System Disarming & Arming."
2. Remove battery carrier and battery.
3. Disconnect air bag sensor.
4. Move windshield washer tank as necessary to gain access to sensor bolts.
5. Remove sensor attaching bolts, then the sensor.
6. Reverse procedure to install. Tighten to specification ensuring arrow on sensor is pointing toward front of vehicle.

Right

1. Disarm SRS as outlined under "Air Bag System Disarming & Arming."
2. Disconnect air bag sensor.
3. Remove sensor attaching bolts, then the sensor.
4. Reverse procedure to install. Tighten to specification ensuring arrow on sensor is pointing toward front of vehicle.

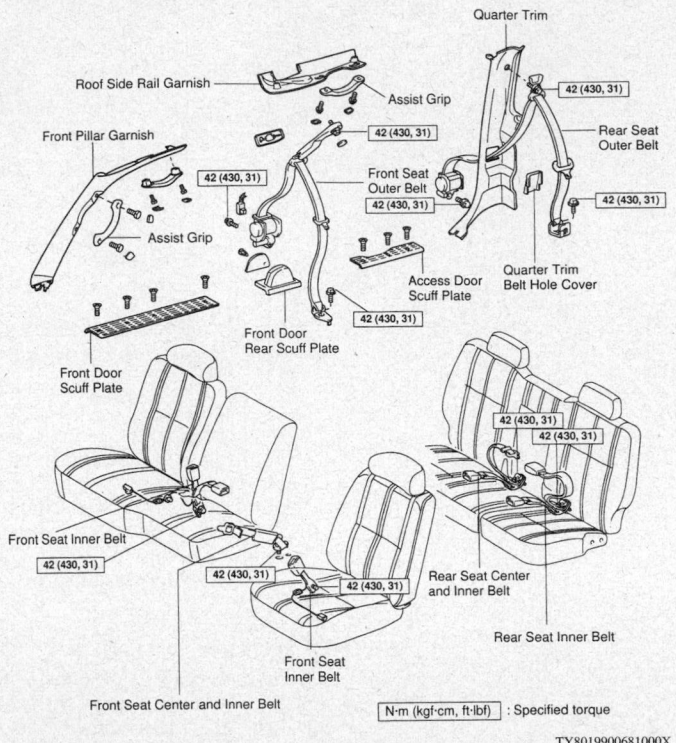

Fig. 84   Seat belt components. Tundra w/access cab

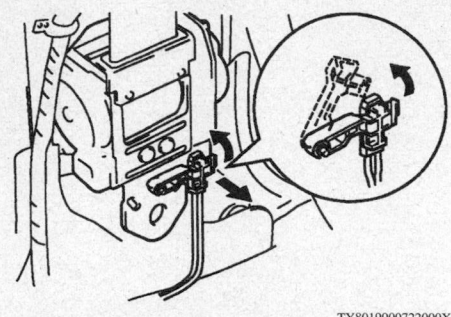

Fig. 85   Pretensioner removal. 4Runner

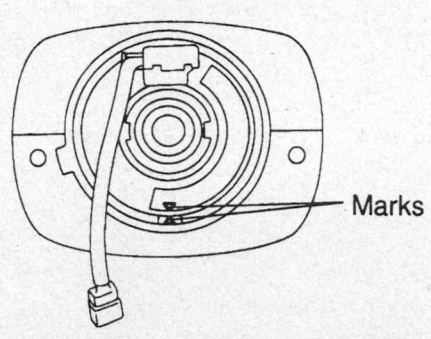

Fig. 88   Spiral cable alignment marks. 1998 Supra & Tercel

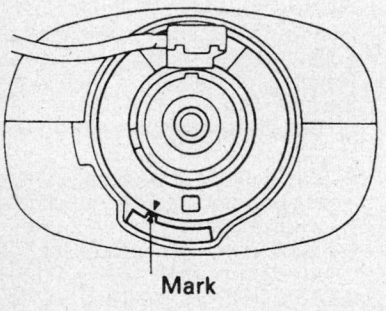

Fig. 86   Spiral cable alignment marks. Except Tundra, 1998 Supra & Tercel, 1997–99 RAV4 & 1998–99 Land Cruiser

RAV4

Left

1. Disarm SRS as outlined under "Air Bag System Disarming & Arming."
2. Remove front end panel, then the headlamp assemblies.
3. Disconnect front air bag sensors.
4. Remove 3 bolts to slip resonator and ensure socket is inserted in sensor installation bolt.
5. Remove air bag sensor attaching bolts, then the sensor.
6. Reverse procedure to install. Tighten to specifications.

Right

1. Disarm SRS as outlined under "Air Bag System Disarming & Arming."

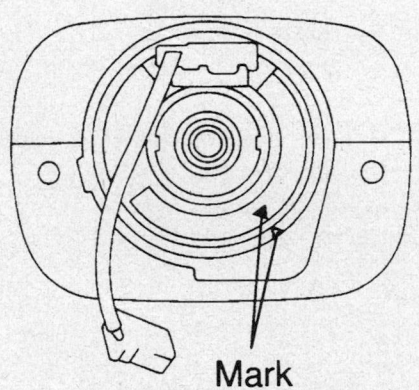

Fig. 87   Spiral cable alignment marks. Tundra, 1997–99 RAV4 & 1998–99 Land Cruiser

2. Remove front end panel, then the headlamp assembly.
3. Disconnect front air bag sensor connector.
4. Remove air bag sensor attaching bolts, then the sensor.
5. Reverse procedure to install. Tighten to specifications.

SIENNA

Left

1. Disarm SRS as outlined under "Air Bag System Disarming & Arming."
2. Disconnect air bag sensor electrical connector.

3. Remove sensor attaching bolts, then the sensor.
4. Reverse procedure to install. Ensure arrow on sensor is pointing toward front of vehicle and tighten to specifications.

Right

1. Disarm SRS as outlined under "Air Bag System Disarming & Arming."
2. Remove 2 fender liner set screws.
3. Disconnect air bag sensor electrical connector.
4. Remove sensor attaching bolts, then the sensor.
5. Reverse procedure to install. Ensure arrow on sensor is pointing toward front of vehicle and tighten to specifications.

TACOMA

1. Disarm SRS as outlined under "Air Bag System Disarming & Arming."
2. Remove battery clamp, then the battery and battery carrier.
3. Disconnect air bag sensor electrical connector.
4. Remove sensor attaching bolts, then the sensor.
5. Reverse procedure to install. Ensure arrow on sensor is pointing toward front of vehicle and tighten to specifications.

LH:

RH:

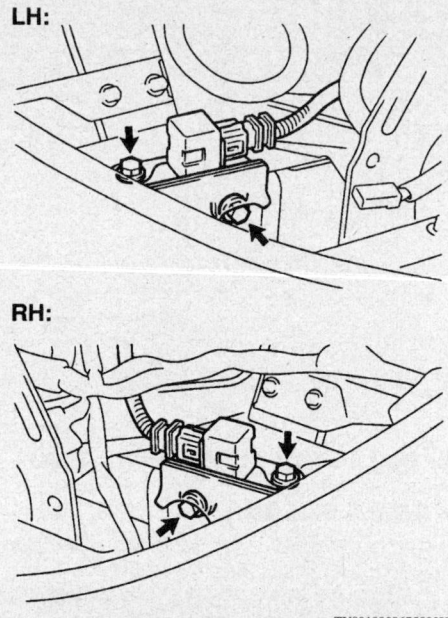

Fig. 89 Front air bag sensor replacement. 1999 Avalon

TY8019900675000X

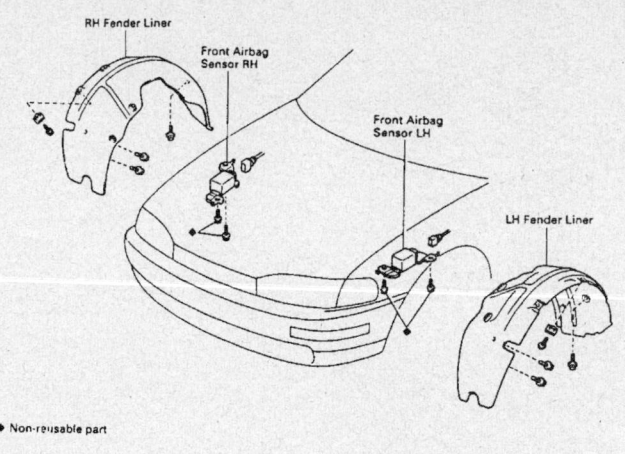

◆ Non-reusable part

TY8019400303000X

Fig. 90 Front air bag sensor replacement. 1996 Camry

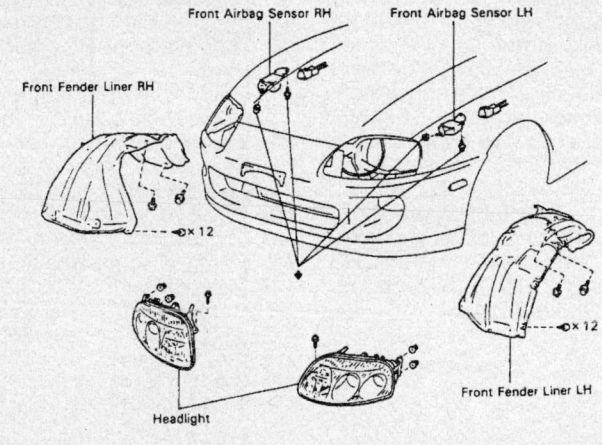

◆ Non-reusable part

TY8019400306000X

Fig. 91 Front air bag sensor replacement. 1996 Supra

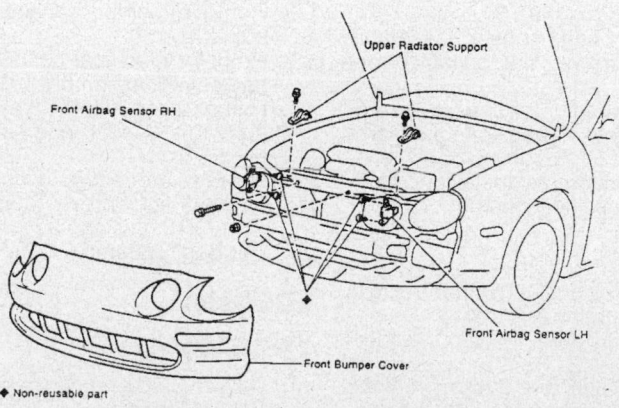

◆ Non-reusable part

TY8019400308000X

Fig. 92 Front air bag sensor replacement. Celica

TUNDRA

Left

1. Disarm SRS as outlined under "Air Bag System Disarming & Arming."
2. Remove battery carrier, battery and tray as necessary.
3. Disconnect air bag sensor connector.
4. Remove sensor attaching bolts, then the sensor.
5. Reverse procedure to install noting the following:
   a. Ensure arrow on sensor is pointing toward front of vehicle.
   b. Connect sensor after it has been installed.
   c. Ensure connector lock is secure after installation.

Right

1. Disarm SRS as outlined under "Air Bag System Disarming & Arming."
2. Remove air cleaner assembly.
3. Disconnect air bag sensor connector.
4. Remove sensor attaching bolts, then the sensor.
5. Reverse procedure to install noting the following:
   a. Ensure arrow on sensor is pointing toward front of vehicle.
   b. Connect sensor after it has been installed.
   c. Ensure connector lock is secure after installation.

T100

1. Disarm SRS as outlined under "Air Bag System Disarming & Arming."
2. Remove battery and air cleaner assembly, Fig. 94.
3. Disconnect sensor electrical connectors.
4. Loosen sensor mounting screws with suitable Torx wrench and remove sensor.
5. Reverse procedure to install, noting following:
   a. Ensure sensor arrow points toward vehicle front.
   b. Tighten mounting screws to specifications.
   c. Shake sensor and ensure there is

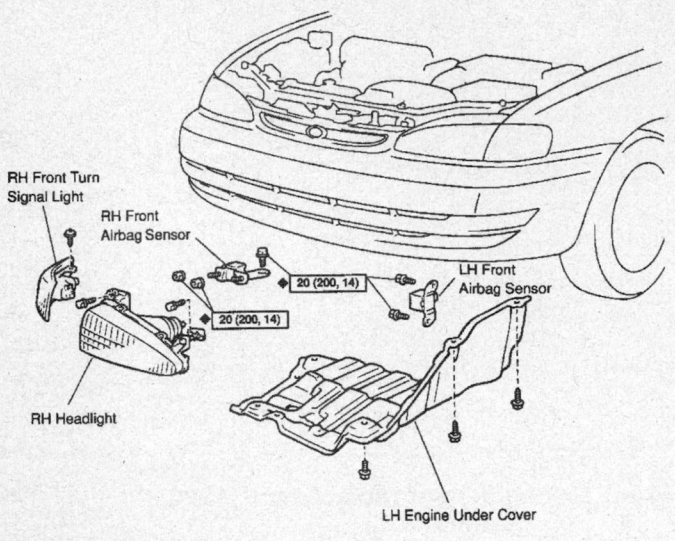

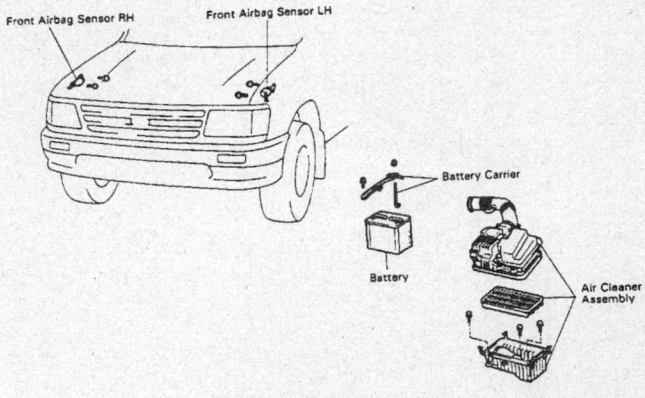

TY8019400307000X

Fig. 94 Front air bag sensor replacement. T100

N·m (kgf·cm, ft·lbf) : Specified torque
◆ Non–reusable part

TY8019800639000X

Fig. 93 Front air bag sensor replacement. Corolla

no looseness.
d. Lock electrical connection check mechanism securely or diagnosis circuit may generate diagnostic trouble code (DTC).
e. Arm SRS system as outlined under "Air Bag System Disarming & Arming."

4RUNNER

Left

1. Disarm SRS as outlined under "Air Bag System Disarming & Arming."
2. Remove battery and battery tray.
3. Disconnect air bag sensor connector.
4. Remove sensor attaching bolts, then the sensor.
5. Reverse procedure to install. Ensure arrow on sensor is pointing toward front of vehicle and tighten to specifications.

Right

1. Disarm SRS as outlined under "Air Bag System Disarming & Arming."
2. Remove air cleaner assembly with hose.
3. Disconnect air bag sensor connector.
4. Remove sensor attaching bolts, then the sensor.
5. Reverse procedure to install. Ensure arrow on sensor is pointing toward front of vehicle and tighten to specifications.

CENTER AIR BAG SENSOR ASSEMBLY, REPLACE

AVALON

1. Disarm SRS as outlined under "Air Bag System Disarming & Arming."
2. **On models equipped with floor shift,** remove front seat, upper console box, center cluster finish panel, lower finish panel assembly, lower No. 2 finish panel, glove compartment door, glove compartment and front

console box, **Fig. 95.**
3. **On models equipped with column shift,** remove front seat, center seat belt, center cluster finish panel, lower No. 2 finish panel, glove compartment door, glove compartment, finish panel, center pillar garnish, cowl side trim, front door inside scuff plate and protector, then peel back floor carpet, **Fig. 96.**
4. **On all models,** remove connector for sensor assembly, then remove mounting screws with suitable Torx wrench and remove air bag sensor assembly.
5. Reverse procedure to install and tighten bolts to specifications. Arm SRS system as outlined under "Air Bag System Disarming & Arming."

CAMRY

1996

1. Disarm SRS as outlined under "Air Bag System Disarming & Arming."
2. Remove front door inside scuff plate and opening cover, cowl side trim, coin box and bezel, lower center cover, No. 2 cover and finish panel, console upper panel, rear console box and front console box, **Fig. 97.**
3. Loosen air bag sensor assembly mounting screws with suitable Torx wrench.
4. Remove connector for sensor assembly and remove air bag sensor assembly.
5. Reverse procedure to install and tighten bolts to specifications.

1997-99

1. Disarm SRS as outlined under "Air Bag System Disarming & Arming."
2. Disconnect air bag sensor electrical connectors.
3. Using a suitable torx socket, remove sensor attaching screws, then the sensor, **Fig. 98.**
4. Reverse procedure to install.

CAMRY SOLARA

1. Disarm SRS as outlined under "Air Bag System Disarming & Arming."
2. Remove lefthand scuff plate, then the clip and cowl side trim, **Fig. 99.**
3. Remove left front door opening trim cover.
4. Remove bolt, nut and lower No. 1 panel.
5. Disconnect hood release cable.
6. Remove righthand door scuff plate, then the clip and cowl side trim.
7. Remove right front door opening trim cover.
8. Remove No. 2 undercover.
9. Remove bolt, nut and lower panel.
10. Remove upper console panel.
11. Remove 2 bolts, 2 screws and rear console box.
12. Remove center cluster finish panel and disconnect connector.
13. Remove center cluster finish panel.
14. Remove front console box.
15. Remove sensor heater protector, then disconnect sensor electrical connectors.
16. Using a suitable torx wrench, remove sensor attaching bolts, then the sensor.
17. Reverse procedure to install. Tighten to specifications.

CELICA

1. Disarm SRS as outlined under "Air Bag System Disarming & Arming."
2. Remove center console panel and box, **Fig. 100.**
3. Remove electrical connector from air bag sensor assembly.
4. Remove mounting screws with suitable Torx wrench and sensor assembly.
5. Reverse procedure to install and tighten mounting screws to specifications. Arm SRS system as outlined under "Air Bag System Disarming & Arming."

COROLLA

1996-97

1. Disarm SRS as outlined under "Air Bag System Disarming & Arming."
2. Remove console box, **Fig. 101.**
3. Loosen air bag sensor assembly

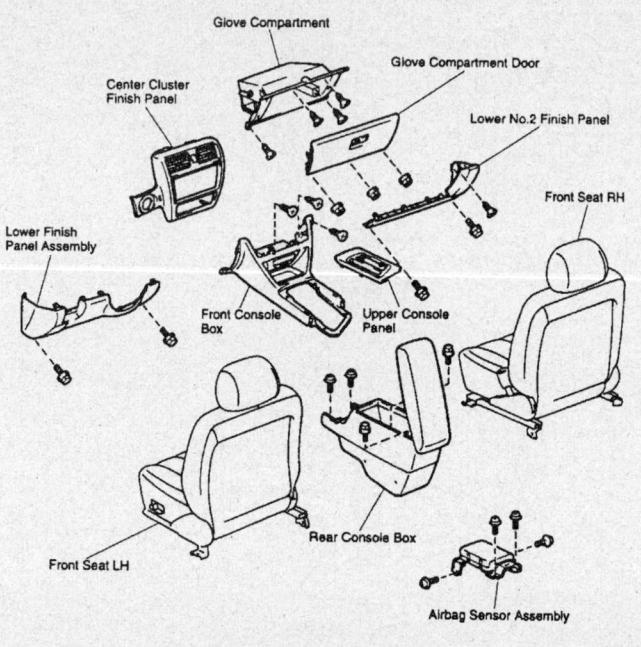

Fig. 95 Air bag sensor assembly replacement. Avalon w/floor shift

TY8019500311000X

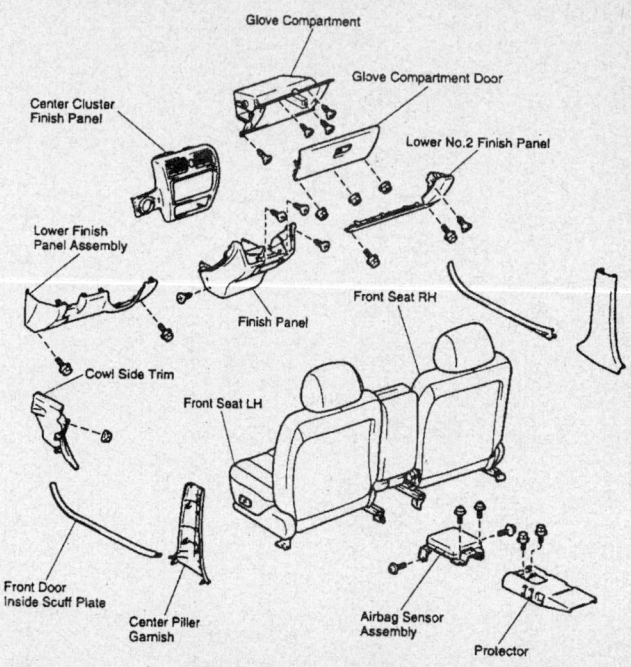

Fig. 96 Air bag sensor assembly replacement. Avalon w/column shift

TY8019500312000X

mounting screws with suitable Torx wrench.
4. Remove electrical connector for air bag sensor assembly, then remove assembly.
5. Reverse procedure to install and tighten mounting screws to specifications.

1998-99

1. Remove front door scuff plates, then the cowl side trims and lower finish panel, **Fig. 102.**
2. Remove lower lefthand insert, then the lower panels.
3. Remove center cluster finish panel, then the stereo opening cover.
4. **On models equipped with automatic transaxle,** remove shifter hole bezel.
5. **On models equipped with manual transaxle,** remove shifter hole cover.
6. **On all models,** remove rear console box, then the lower center finish panel.
7. Disconnect air bag sensor electrical connectors, then remove sensor attaching screws and sensor.
8. Reverse procedure to install and tighten mounting screws to specifications. Arm SRS system as outlined under "Air Bag System Disarming & Arming."

LAND CRUISER

1996-97

1. Disarm SRS as outlined under "Air Bag System Disarming & Arming."
2. Remove transfer shift knob and front console box, **Fig. 103.**
3. Remove air bag sensor assembly electrical connector.
4. Remove assembly mounting screws with suitable Torx wrench, then remove assembly.
5. Reverse procedure to install and tight-

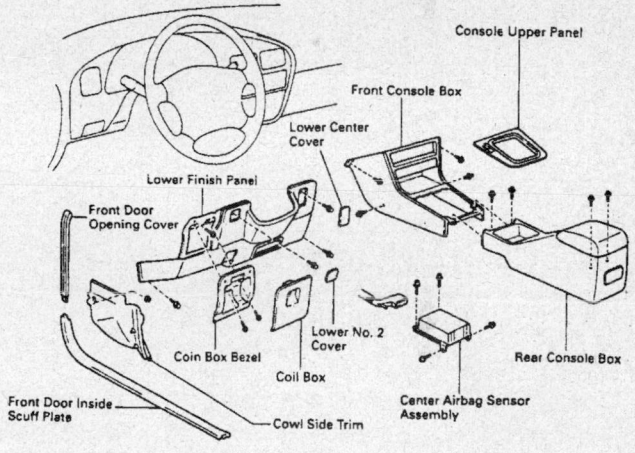

Fig. 97 Air bag sensor assembly replacement. 1996 Camry

TY8019400313000X

en mounting screws to specifications. Arm SRS system as outlined under "Air Bag System Disarming & Arming."

1998-99

1. Disarm SRS as outlined under "Air Bag System Disarming & Arming."
2. Remove components shown in **Fig. 104.**
3. Remove air bag sensor assembly electrical connector.
4. Remove sensor assembly mounting screws with suitable Torx T40 wrench, then sensor assembly.
5. Reverse procedure to install and tighten screws to specifications. Arm SRS system as outlined under "Air Bag System Disarming & Arming."

PASEO

1. Disarm SRS as outlined under "Air Bag System Disarming & Arming."
2. Remove console box center cluster finish panel, rear air duct No. 3, and lower center finish panel, **Fig. 105.**
3. Remove air bag sensor assembly electrical connector.
4. Loosen assembly screws with suitable Torx wrench and remove assembly.
5. Reverse procedure to install and tighten mounting screws to specifications. Arm SRS system as outlined under "Air Bag System Disarming & Arming."

PREVIA

1. Disarm SRS as outlined under "Air Bag System Disarming & Arming."

LH side:

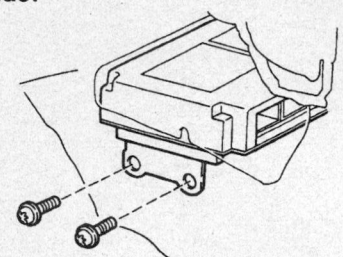

RH side:

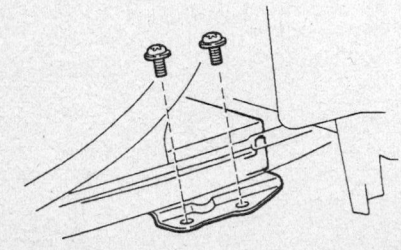

TY8019900692000X

Fig. 98 Air bag sensor assembly replacement. 1997–99 Camry

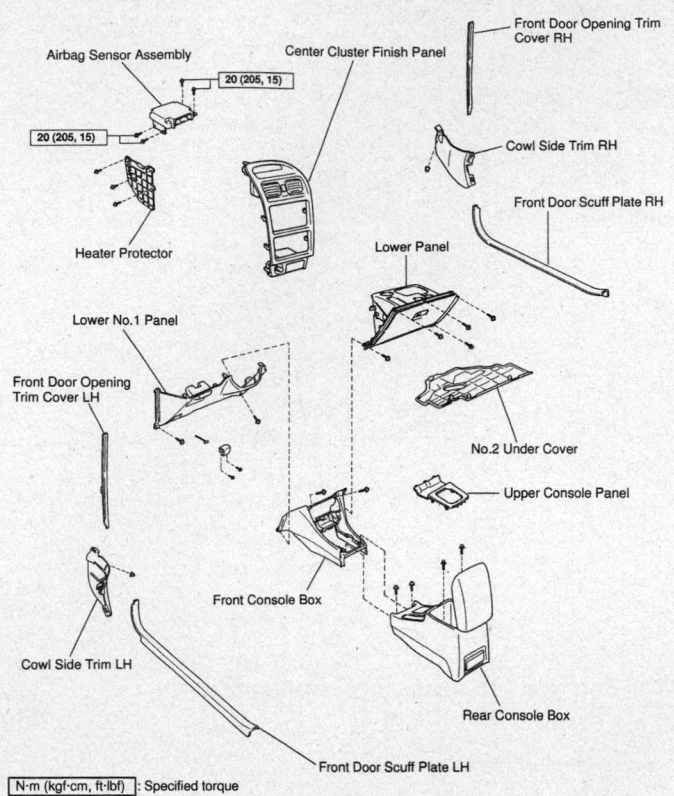

Airbag Sensor Assembly
Center Cluster Finish Panel
Front Door Opening Trim Cover RH
20 (205, 15)
20 (205, 15)
Cowl Side Trim RH
Front Door Scuff Plate RH
Heater Protector
Lower Panel
Lower No.1 Panel
Front Door Opening Trim Cover LH
No.2 Under Cover
Upper Console Panel
Cowl Side Trim LH
Front Console Box
Rear Console Box
Front Door Scuff Plate LH

N·m (kgf·cm, ft·lbf) : Specified torque

TY8019900698000X

Fig. 99 Air bag sensor replacement. Camry Solara

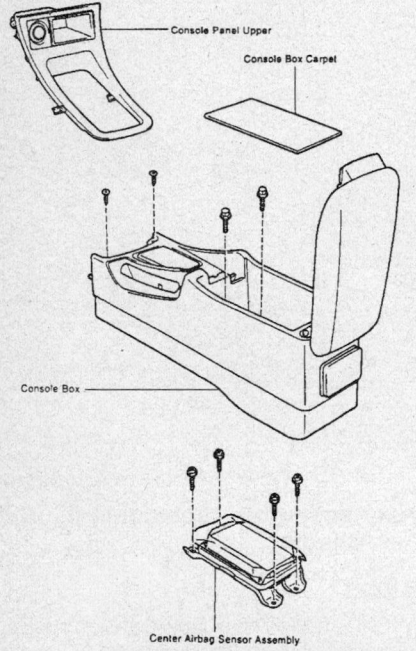

Console Panel Upper
Console Box Carpet
Console Box
Center Airbag Sensor Assembly

TY8019400314000X

Fig. 100 Air bag sensor assembly replacement. Celica

2. Remove cool or console box, **Fig. 106.**
3. Remove side cover.
4. Loosen air bag sensor assembly mounting screws with suitable Torx wrench.
5. Remove air bag sensor assembly electrical connector and assembly.
6. Reverse procedure to install and tighten mounting screws to specifications. Arm SRS system as outlined under "Air Bag System Disarming & Arming."

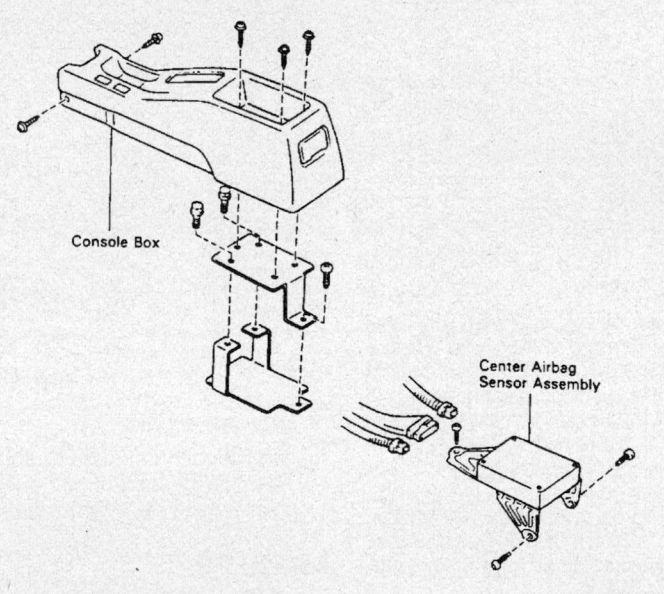

Console Box
Center Airbag Sensor Assembly

TY8019400315000X

Fig. 101 Air bag sensor assembly replacement. 1996–97 Corolla

RAV4

1. Disarm SRS as outlined under "Air Bag System Disarming & Arming."
2. Remove shift lever knob, shifting hole cover, console box hole cover and console box, **Fig. 107.**
3. Remove air bag sensor assembly electrical connector.
4. Remove sensor assembly mounting screws with suitable Torx wrench, then assembly.
5. Reverse procedure to install and tighten screws to specifications. Arm SRS

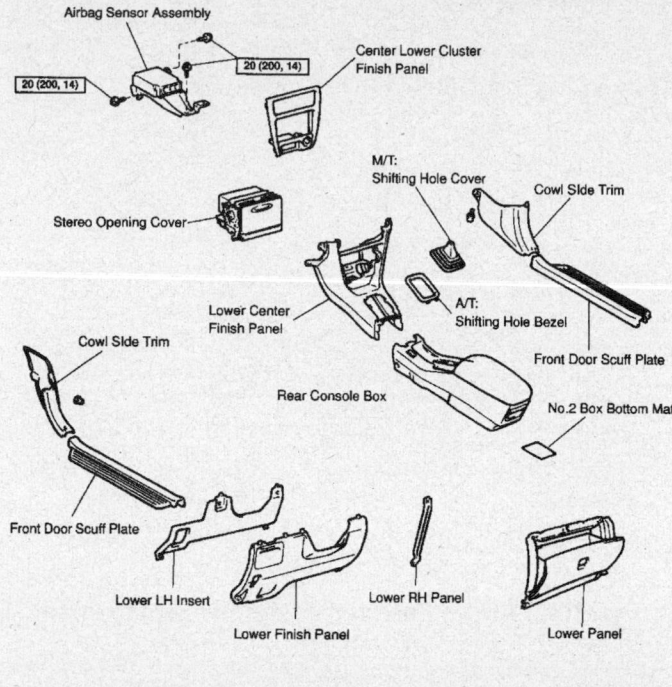

N·m (kgf·cm, ft·lbf) : Specified torque

TY801980064000AX

**Fig. 102 Air bag sensor assembly replacement.
1998–99 Corolla**

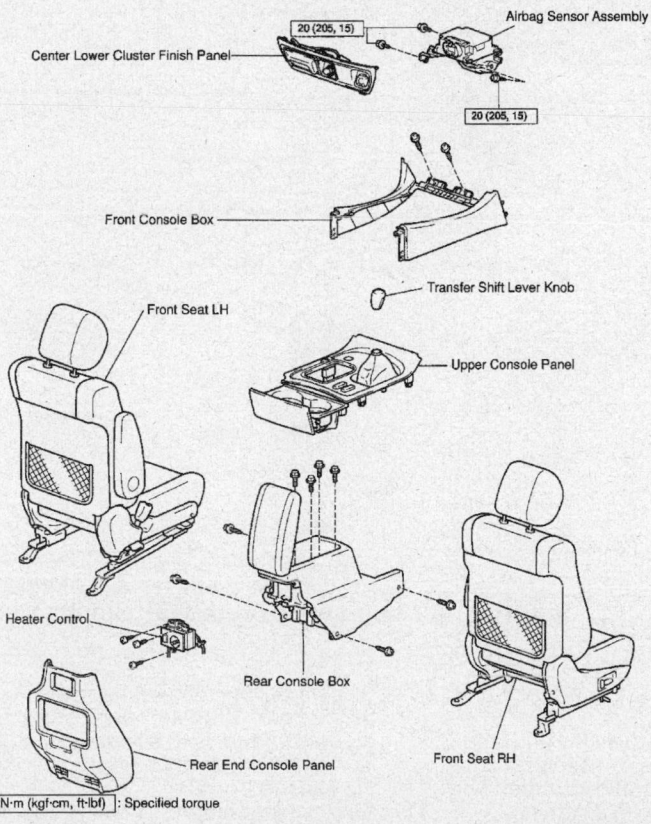

N·m (kgf·cm, ft·lbf) : Specified torque

TY8019800657000X

**Fig. 104 Air bag sensor assembly replacement.
1998–99 Land Cruiser**

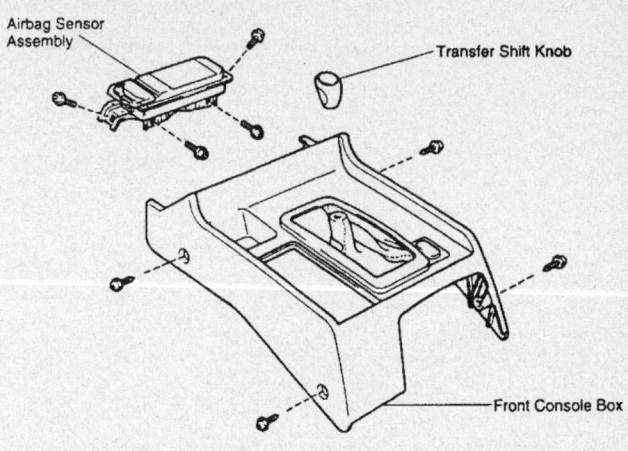

TY8019400316000X

**Fig. 103 Air bag sensor assembly replacement.
1996–97 Land Cruiser**

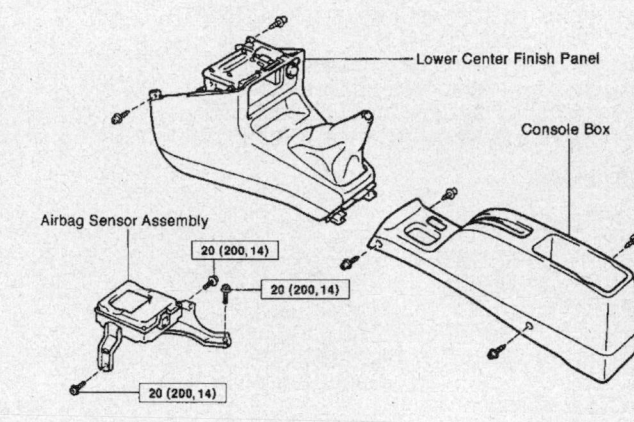

N·m (kgf·cm, ft·lbf) : Specified torque

TY8019600361000X

**Fig. 105 Air bag sensor assembly replacement.
Paseo**

system as outlined under "Air Bag System Disarming & Arming."

SIENNA

1. Remove Front door scuff plates, then the cowl side boards, **Fig. 108.**
2. Remove No. 2 finish panel, glove compartment and glove compartment finish plate.
3. Remove lower finish panel, then the No. 1 safety pad insert.
4. Remove center cluster finish panel, front ash tray and ash tray retainer.
5. Remove radio, then the lower center cluster finish panel.
6. Disconnect air bag sensor electrical connectors.
7. Remove air bag sensor attaching screws, then the sensor.
8. Reverse procedure to install. Tighten to specifications.

SUPRA

1. Disarm SRS as outlined under "Air Bag System Disarming & Arming."
2. Remove console panel upper and console box, **Fig. 109.**
3. Remove air bag sensor assembly

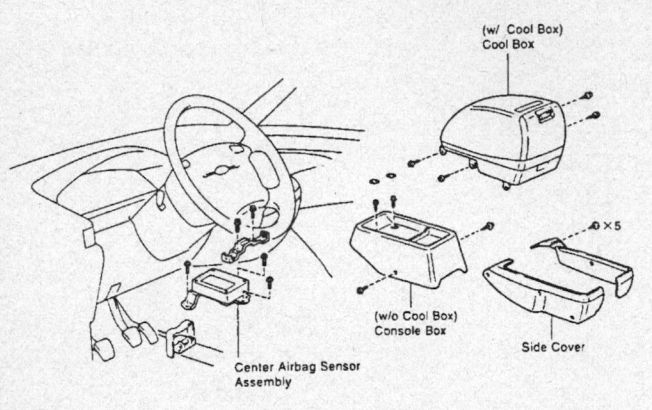

Fig. 106 Air bag sensor assembly replacement. Previa

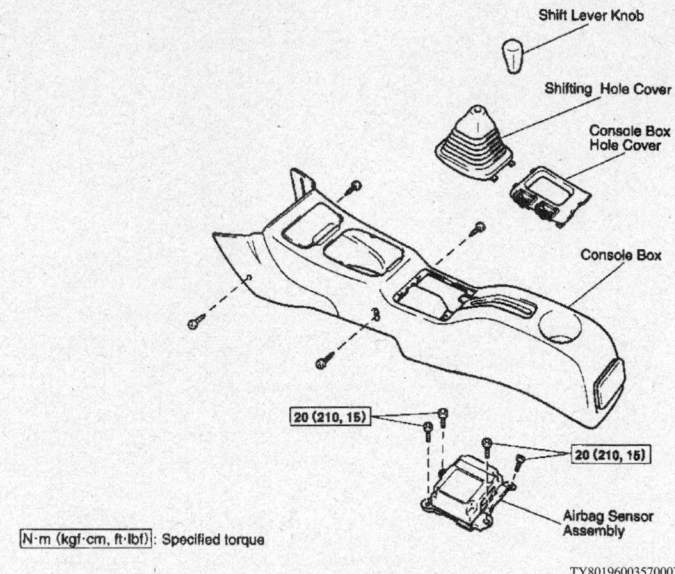

Fig. 107 Air bag sensor assembly replacement. RAV4

electrical connector.
4. Remove air bag sensor assembly mounting screws with suitable Torx wrench and assembly.
5. Reverse procedure to install and tighten mounting screws to specifications. Arm SRS system as outlined under "Air Bag System Disarming & Arming."

TACOMA

1996-97

1. Disarm SRS as outlined under "Air Bag System Disarming & Arming."
2. Remove lower center cover and antilock brake system (ABS) electrical control unit (ECU), **Fig. 110.**
3. Remove air bag sensor assembly electrical connector.
4. Remove air bag sensor assembly mounting screws with suitable Torx wrench and assembly.
5. Reverse procedure to install and tighten mounting screws to specifications. Arm SRS system as outlined under "Air Bag System Disarming & Arming."

1998-99

1. Disarm SRS as outlined under "Air Bag System Disarming & Arming."
2. Remove shift lever knobs.
3. Remove four front console box retaining screws, then the console box.
4. Remove two lower center cover attaching screws, the cover.
5. Disconnect air bag sensor assembly electrical connector.
6. Remove air bag sensor assembly mounting screws with suitable Torx T40 wrench, then the sensor assembly.
7. Reverse procedure to install and tighten mounting screws to specifications. Arm SRS system as outlined under "Air Bag System Disarming & Arming."

TERCEL

1. Disarm SRS as outlined under "Air Bag System Disarming & Arming."
2. Remove console box, center cluster and lower center finish panels, and rear air duct No. 3, **Fig. 111.**
3. Remove electrical connector.
4. Remove air bag sensor assembly

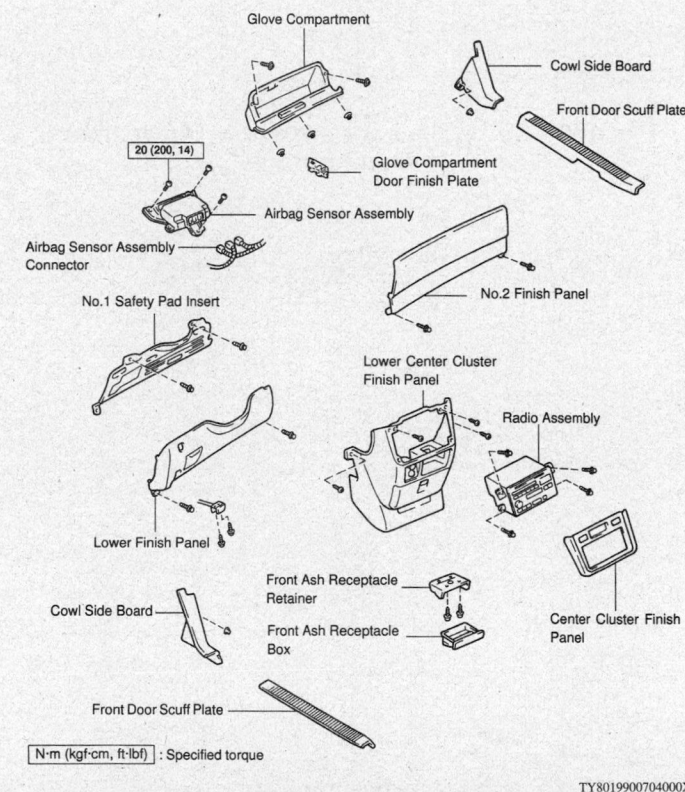

Fig. 108 Air bag sensor removal. Sienna

screws with suitable Torx wrench and assembly.
5. Reverse procedure to install and tighten mounting screws to specifications, then arm SRS as outlined under "Air Bag System Disarming & Arming."

TUNDRA

1. Disarm SRS as outlined under "Air Bag System Disarming & Arming."
2. Remove two clips and lower center cover, **Fig. 112.**

3. Disconnect air bag sensor electrical connectors. **Ensure connectors are disconnected with sensor installed.**
4. Remove sensor attaching bolts, then the sensor.
5. Reverse procedure to install. Tighten to specifications.

T100

1. Disarm SRS as outlined under "Air Bag System Disarming & Arming."
2. Remove lower center cover and cruise

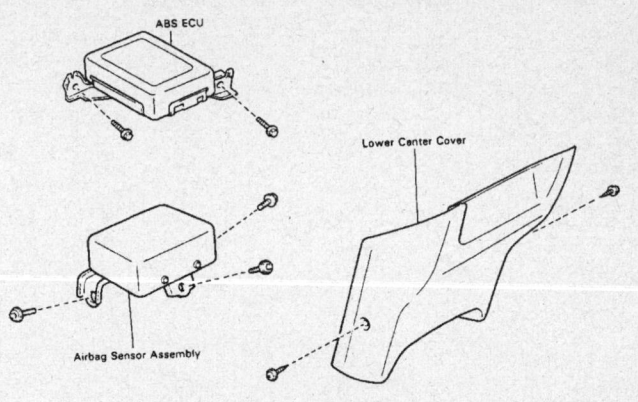

ABS ECU

Lower Center Cover

Airbag Sensor Assembly

TY8019500321000X

**Fig. 110 Air bag sensor assembly replacement.
Tacoma**

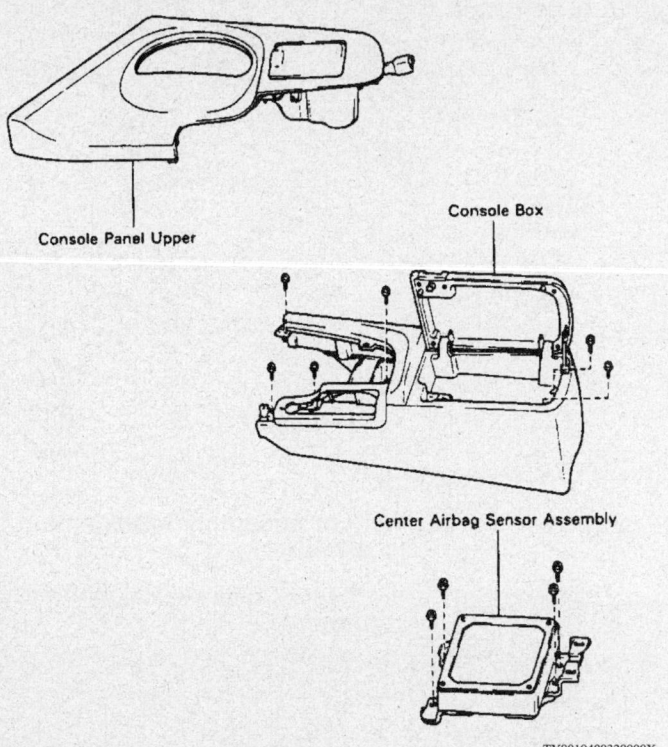

Console Panel Upper

Console Box

Center Airbag Sensor Assembly

TY8019400320000X

**Fig. 109 Air bag sensor assembly replacement.
Supra**

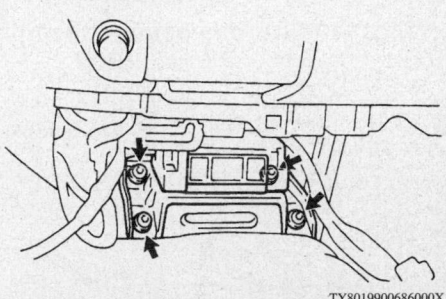

TY8019900686000X

**Fig. 112 Lower panel removal.
Tundra**

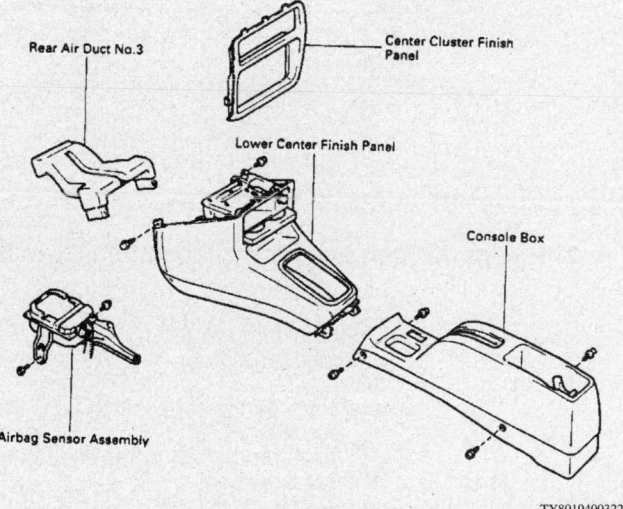

Rear Air Duct No.3

Center Cluster Finish Panel

Lower Center Finish Panel

Console Box

Airbag Sensor Assembly

TY8019400322000X

**Fig. 111 Air bag sensor assembly replacement.
Tercel**

control electrical control unit (ECU), **Fig. 113.**
3. Remove air bag sensor assembly mounting screws with suitable Torx wrench, then remove assembly.
4. Reverse procedure to install and tighten mounting screws to specifications. Arm SRS system as outlined under "Air Bag System Disarming & Arming."

4RUNNER
1. Disarm SRS as outlined under "Air Bag System Disarming & Arming."
2. Remove upper console panel, rear

console box, console panel garnish, ash tray, heater control panel and center cluster finish panel, **Fig. 114.**
3. Disconnect air bag sensor assembly connector.
4. Remove air bag sensor assembly mounting screws with suitable Torx wrench, then remove assembly.
5. Reverse procedure to install and tighten mounting screws to specifications. Arm SRS system as outlined under "Air Bag System Disarming & Arming."

SIDE AIR BAG SENSOR ASSEMBLY, REPLACE

AVALON, CAMRY & COROLLA
1. Disarm SRS as outlined under "Air Bag System Disarming & Arming."
2. Remove front door scuff plate, then the center pillar lower garnish, **Figs. 115 and 116.**
3. Disconnect seat belt pretensioner connector, then the retractor switch connector if equipped.
4. Remove retractor attaching bolts, then the retractor.
5. Disconnect side air bag sensor electrical connector.
6. Remove sensor attaching screws, then the sensor.
7. Reverse procedure to install, noting the following:
   a. When installing side air bag sensor, install sensor before connecting electrical connector.
   b. Tighten side air bag sensor bolts to specifications.
   c. Arm SRS as outlined under "Air Bag System Disarming & Arming."

CAMRY SOLARA
1. Disarm SRS as outlined under "Air Bag System Disarming & Arming."
2. Remove rear seat cushion.
3. Remove seat back attaching bolts, then the seat back.

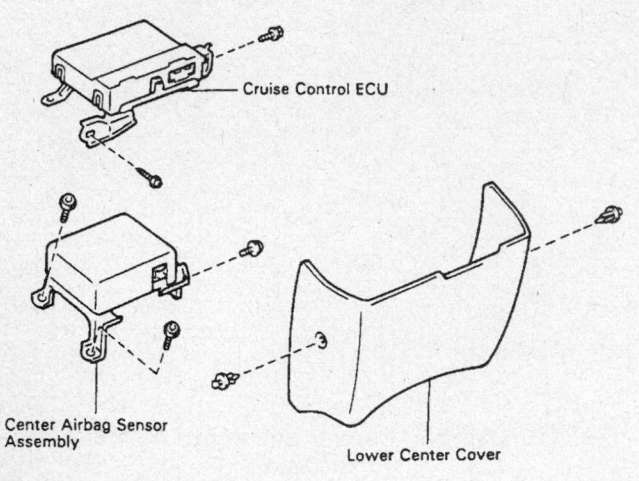

Fig. 113   Air bag sensor assembly replacement. T100

TY8019400323000X

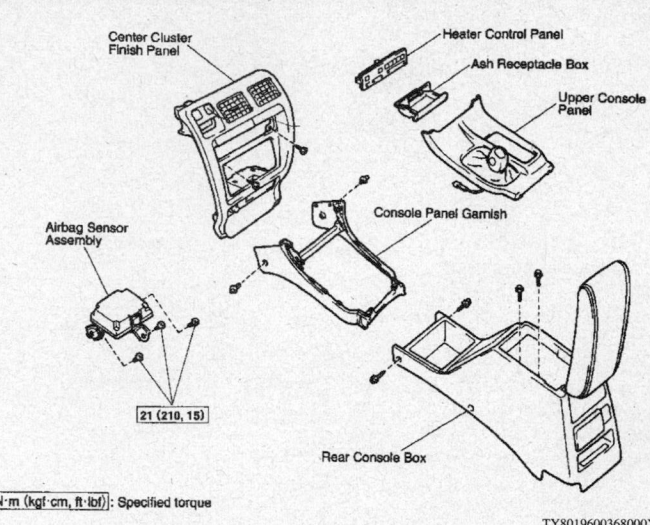

N·m (kgf·cm, ft·lbf): Specified torque

Fig. 114   Air bag sensor assembly replacement. 4Runner

TY8019600368000X

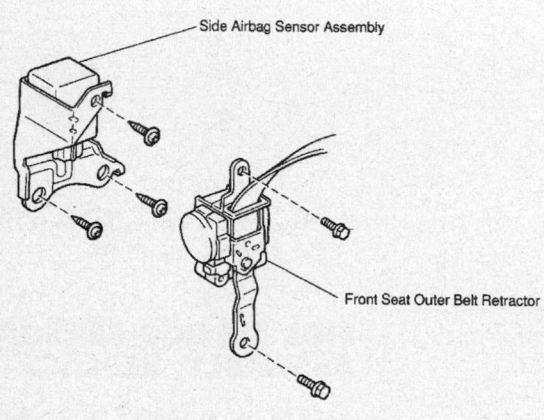

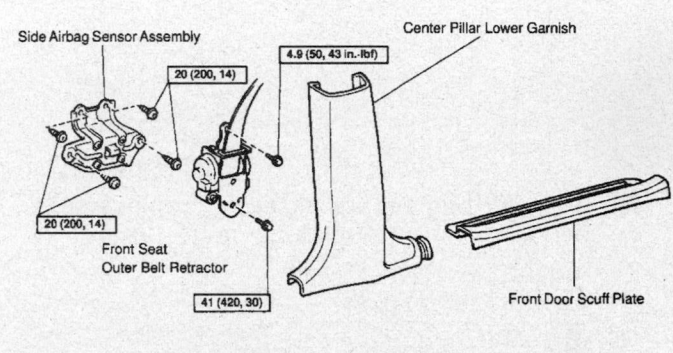

N·m (kgf·cm, ft·lbf) : Specified torque

TY8019800649000X

Fig. 116   Side air bag sensor replacement. Corolla

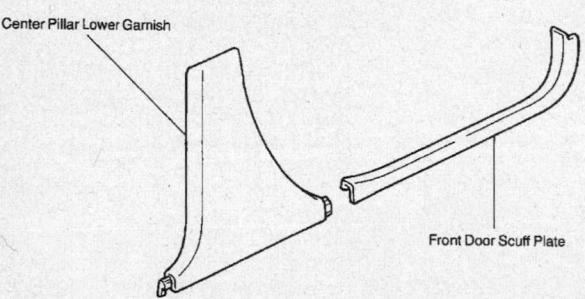

TY8019800644000X

Fig. 115   Side air bag sensor removal. Avalon & Camry

4. Remove front door scuff plate.
5. Remove assist grip screw covers, then the screws and assist grip.
6. Remove lower quarter trim panel.
7. Disconnect sensor electrical connector.
8. Remove sensor attaching nuts, then the sensor.
9. Reverse procedure to install. Tighten to specification.

DOOR SIDE AIR BAG SENSOR

CAMRY SOLARA

1. Disarm SRS as outlined under "Air Bag System Disarming & Arming."
2. Remove door inside handle bezel.
3. Remove power window switch.
4. Remove lower frame bracket garnish,

then the door trim.
5. Disconnect sensor electrical connector.
6. Remove sensor attaching nuts, then the sensor.
7. Reverse procedure to install. Tighten to specifications.

AIR BAG ASSEMBLY DISPOSAL

When handling a deployed air bag assembly, a face shield and rubber gloves should be worn. Vehicle interior and HVAC ducts should be vacuumed. If sinus or throat irritation is encountered during air bag removal, exit vehicle and breath fresh air. If skin irritation is encountered, flush affected area with cool water. If sinus, throat, skin or any other type of irritation continues, consult a physician. Wash hands and rinse thoroughly with water after handling a deployed air bag assembly.

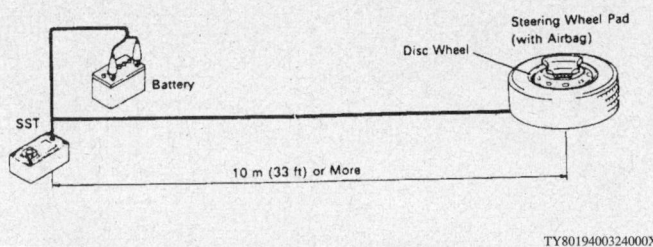

TY8019400324000X

Fig. 117 Driver side air bag disposal outside vehicle

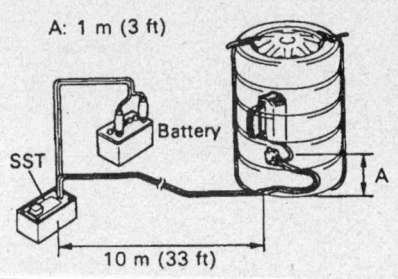

TY8019400325000X

Fig. 118 Passenger air bag disposal outside vehicle

All deployed air bag units must be removed as outlined under "Air Bag Module, Replace." After unit has been removed, it should be placed in a heavy duty plastic bag, sealed securely, then discarded with automotive scrap.

An undeployed air bag unit must be deployed prior to disposal.

After an air bag has been deployed, it should be allowed to cool for at least 30 minutes before final disposal.

If vehicle is not being scrapped, air bag assembly should be deployed outside of vehicle. If vehicle is to be scrapped, air bag may be deployed while still installed.

DRIVER SIDE AIR BAG

Outside Vehicle Deployment

1. Disarm SRS as outlined under "Air Bag System Disarming & Arming."
2. Remove driver's air bag as outlined under "Air Bag Module, Replace."
3. Using bolts and washers, mount driver's air bag to a discarded tire and rim.
4. Using three pieces of thick wire, wrap wire at least two times around each air bag bolt. Wrap harness through wheel lug holes and securely tie off, **Fig. 117.**
5. Connect deployment tool No. 09082-00700, or equivalent, to air bag connector from underneath wheel. Move deployment tool at least 33 feet away from wheel.
6. Ensure wheel pad is facing upward. Cover wheel and pad with a large cardboard box. Weigh box down in four places.
7. Ensure no people, animals or objects are within 33 feet of air bag.
8. Connect deployment tool's battery terminals to a fully charged 12 volt battery.
9. Press deployment button and deploy air bag.
10. If air bag assembly does not deploy, consult Toyota for disposal procedures.

Inside Vehicle Deployment

If a vehicle with an undeployed air bag is to be scrapped, air bag must be deployed before scrapping.
1. Disarm SRS as outlined under "Air Bag System Disarming & Arming."
2. Remove No. 1 undercover and disconnect air bag connector from spiral cable.
3. Connect deployment tool No. 09082-

00700, or equivalent, to spiral cable connector.
4. Close all vehicle doors and windows.
5. Move deployment tool at least 33 feet from vehicle.
6. Ensure no people, animals or objects are within 33 feet of air bag.
7. Connect deployment tool's battery terminals to a fully charged 12 volt battery.
8. Press deployment button and deploy air bag.
9. If air bag assembly does not deploy, consult Toyota for disposal procedures.

PASSENGER AIR BAG

Outside Vehicle Deployment

1. Disarm SRS as outlined under "Air Bag System Disarming & Arming."
2. Remove passenger air bag as outlined under "Air Bag Module, Replace."
3. Using thick wire, secure passenger air bag to a discarded tire and wheel, **Fig. 118.**
4. Position tire with air bag on top of two tires, then place two more tires on top of tires containing air bag.
5. Use thick wire to secure tires together.
6. Connect deployment tool No. 09082-00700, or equivalent, to air bag connector from underneath wheel. Move deployment tool at least 33 feet away from wheel.
7. Ensure no people, animals or objects are within 33 feet of air bag.
8. Connect battery terminals of deployment tool to battery source.
9. Press deployment button and deploy air bag.
10. If air bag assembly does not deploy, consult Toyota for disposal procedures.

Inside Vehicle Deployment

If a vehicle with an undeployed air bag is to be scrapped, air bag must be deployed before scrapping.
1. Disarm SRS as outlined under "Air Bag System Disarming & Arming."
2. Remove glove compartment door trim plate, then disconnect passenger air bag connector.
3. Connect air bag deployment tool No. 09082-00700, or equivalent, to air bag connector, **Fig. 119.**
4. Close all vehicle doors and windows.
5. Move deployment tool at least 33 feet from vehicle.

6. Ensure no people, animals or objects are within 33 feet of air bag.
7. Connect deployment tool's battery terminals to a fully charged 12 volt battery.
8. Press deployment button and deploy air bag.
9. If air bag assembly does not deploy, consult Toyota for disposal procedures.

SIDE AIR BAG

Outside Vehicle Deployment

1. Remove side air bag assembly as outlined under "Air Bag Module, Replace."
2. Install 2 attaching nuts to air bag module.
3. Using thick wire, secure side air bag to a discarded tire. Wrap wire at least 3 times around studs and attach to a suitable tire that has at least a 7.28 inch width and 14.17 inch inner diameter as shown in **Figs. 120 and 121.**
4. Ensure wire attachment is tight. Attach air bag with deployment door facing inside.
5. Confirm operation of deployment tool No. 09082–00700 or equivalent.
6. Connect deployment tool to air bag connector.
7. Position tire as shown in **Fig. 122.** Tie all tires together using suitable thick wire. Top tire should have wheel installed.
8. Connect deployment tool to a suitable battery and ensure area around tire is clear for 33 ft.
9. Press deployment button and deploy air bag.
10. If air bag assembly does not deploy, consult Toyota for disposal procedures.

Inside Vehicle Deployment

If a vehicle with an undeployed air bag is to be scrapped, air bag must be deployed before scrapping.
1. Disarm SRS as outlined under "Air Bag System Disarming & Arming."
2. Disconnect side air bag electrical connector.
3. Install deployment tool No. 09082–00700 or equivalent to air bag module harness. To avoid damage to tool connector and wiring, do not lock secondary lock of twin lock.
4. Place deployment tool at least 33 ft.

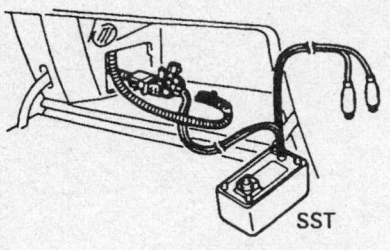

Fig. 119 Passenger air bag disposal inside vehicle

TY8019400326000X

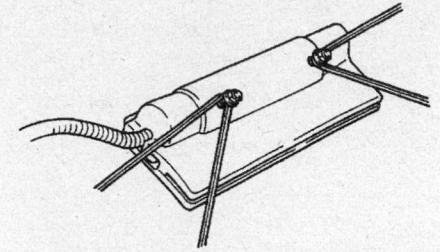

TY8019800645000X

Fig. 120 Service wire installation

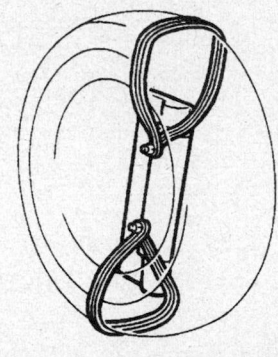

TY8019800646000X

Fig. 121 Side air bag to tire installation

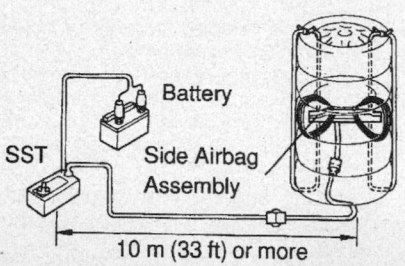

TY8019800647000X

Fig. 122 Side air bag disposal outside of vehicle

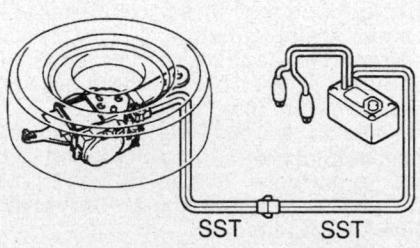

TY8019900679000X

Fig. 123 Pretensioner deployment (outside vehicle)

from vehicle. Ensure all doors are closed and windows are up.
5. Connect deployment tool to a suitable battery.
6. Press deployment button and deploy air bag. Vehicle may be scrapped with side air bag assembly still installed. If air bag fails to deploy, consult Toyota for disposal procedure.

SEAT BELT PRETENSIONER DISPOSAL

The seat belt pretensioner produces a large exploding sound when it activates. Disposal should not be performed indoors. Never dispose of an outer seatbelt which has inactivated pretensioner.

When activating pretensioner, always use specified SRS air bag deployment tool. Perform disposal in an area clear from electrical noise.

Always use gloves and safety glasses when handling a front seat outer belt with activated pretensioner. Wash hands with water after completing operation.

Do not apply water to front seat outer belt with activated pretensioner.

When pretensioner is activated, it becomes very hot and should be left alone for 30 minutes.

OUTSIDE VEHICLE DEPLOYMENT

When disposing of seat belt pretensioner, never use customers vehicle to activate pretensioner.
1. Remove pretensioner as outlined under "Component Service."
2. Connect air bag deployment tool No. 09082–00700 or equivalent to a suitable battery.
3. Press deployment tool activation switch. Ensure LED illuminates. **If LED illuminates without activation switch being pressed, activation tool is faulty and should not be used.**
4. Disconnect deployment tool from battery.
5. Connect air bag deployment wire tool No. 09082–00740 or equivalent to pretensioner and to deployment tool. **To avoid damage to air bag deployment tool, do not lock secondary lock of twin lock.**
6. Place pretensioner on ground and cover with a suitable wheel and tire.
7. Place deployment tool 33 ft. away from pretensioner as shown in **Fig. 123.**
8. Connect deployment tool to battery.
9. Ensure no one is within 33 ft. of pretensioner.
10. Activate pretensioner, then dispose of tensioner.

INSIDE VEHICLE DEPLOYMENT

If a vehicle with an undeployed seat belt pretensioner is to be scrapped, pretensioner must be deployed before scrapping.
1. Disarm SRS as outlined under "Air Bag System Disarming & Arming."
2. Connect air bag deployment tool No. 09082–00700 or equivalent to a suitable battery.
3. Press deployment tool activation switch. Ensure LED illuminates. **If LED illuminates without activation switch being pressed, activation tool is faulty and should not be used.**

4. Disconnect deployment tool from battery.
5. Remove front door scuff plate.
6. Remove center pillar lower garnish.
7. Disconnect pretensioner connector.
8. Buckle front seat belt and ensure there is no looseness and slack in the inner or outer belts.
9. Connect air bag deployment wire tool No. 09082–00740 or equivalent to pretensioner and to deployment tool. **To avoid damage to air bag deployment tool, do not lock secondary lock of twin lock.**
10. Move deployment tool at least 33 ft. away from front of vehicle.
11. Close all doors and windows of vehicle.
12. Connect deployment tool to battery.
13. Confirm no one is inside vehicle or within 33 ft. of vehicle.
14. Press activation switch and activate seat belt pretensioner.
15. Dispose of seat belt pretensioner.

TIGHTENING SPECIFICATIONS

Year	Component	Torque/Ft. Lbs
AVALON		
1996	Center Air Bag Sensor	15
	Front Air Bag Sensor	19
	Front Passenger Air Bag To Instrument Panel Reinforcement Screws	15
	Front Passenger Air Bag To Instrument Panel Screws	52①
	Steering Wheel Retaining Nut	26
	Steering Wheel Side Torx Screws	78①
1997	Air Bag Module Nuts, Passenger's	15
	Air Bag Module Screws, Driver's	78①
	Air Bag Sensor Assembly Mounting Screws	15
	Instrument Panel Reinforcement Bolts	15
	Steering Wheel Nut	26
1998	Air Bag Module Nuts, Passenger's	15
	Air Bag Module Screws, Driver's	78①
	Air Bag Sensor Assembly Mounting Screws	15
	Instrument Panel Reinforcement Bolts	15
	Side Air Bag Sensor	15
	Steering Wheel Nut	26
1999	Air Bag Module Nuts, Passenger's	15
	Air Bag Module Screws, Driver's	78①
	Air Bag Sensor Assembly Mounting Screws	15
	Front Air Bag Sensor	15
	Pretensioner Lower Bolt	30
	Pretensioner Upper Bolt	65①
	Side Air Bag Sensor	15
	Shoulder Anchor Bolt	30
	Steering Wheel Nut	26
CAMRY		
1996	Center Air Bag Sensor	15
	Front Air Bag Sensor	19
	Front Passenger Air Bag To Instrument Panel Reinforcement Screws	15
	Front Passenger Air Bag To Instrument Panel Screws	52①
	Steering Wheel Retaining Nut	26
	Steering Wheel Side Torx Screws	78①
1997	Air Bag Module Bolts, Passenger's	15
	Air Bag Module Screws, Driver's	62①
	Air Bag Sensor Assembly Mounting Screws	14
	Steering Wheel Nut	26

Continued

TIGHTENING
SPECIFICATIONS—Continued

Year	Component	Torque/Ft. Lbs
CAMRY		
1998–99	Air Bag Module Bolts, Passenger's	15
	Air Bag Module Screws, Driver's	60①
	Air Bag Sensor Assembly Mounting Screws	15
	Front Seat Outer Belt Retractor Lower Bolt	31
	Front Seat Outer Belt Retractor Lower Bolt	66①
	Seatback Frame Set Bolt (A)	13
	Seatback Frame Set Bolt (B)	11
	Side Air Bag To Seat Frame	53①
	Steering Wheel Nut	26
CAMRY SOLARA		
1999	Air Bag Sensor Assembly	15
	Door Side Air Bag Sensor	15
	Driver's Air Bag	63①
	Front Air Bag Sensor	15
	Front Seat Attaching Bolt	27
	Inner Belt To Seat Adjuster Assembly	31
	Instrument Panel Reinforcement To No. 1 Mount Bracket	15
	Passenger's Air Bag To Instrument Panel	42①
	Passenger's Air Bag To No. 1 Mount Bracket	15
	Side Air Bag Sensor	15
	Steering Wheel	26
CELICA		
1996	Center Air Bag Sensor	15
	Front Air Bag Sensor	22
	Front Passenger Air Bag Assembly	15
	Steering Wheel Retaining Nut	25
	Steering Wheel Side Torx Screws	80①
1997–99	Air Bag Module Bolts, Passenger's	15
	Air Bag Module Screws, Driver's	80①
	Air Bag Sensor Assembly Mounting Screws	15
	Front Sensor Mounting Screws	22
	Instrument Panel Reinforcement Bolts	15
	Steering Wheel Nut	25
COROLLA		
1996	Air Bag Sensor Assembly Mounting Screws	15
	Front Passenger Air Bag To Instrument Panel Reinforcement Screws	15
	Front Passenger Air Bag To Instrument Panel Screws	49①
	Steering Wheel Retaining Nut	26
	Steering Wheel Side Torx Screws	78①

TIGHTENING
SPECIFICATIONS—Continued

Year	Component	Torque/Ft. Lbs
COROLLA		
1997	Air Bag Module Bolts, Passenger's	③
	Air Bag Module Screws, Driver's	78①
	Air Bag Sensor Assembly Mounting Screws	15
	Steering Wheel Nut	26
1998	Air Bag Module Bolts, Passenger	15
	Air Bag Module Bolts, Driver	78①
	Air Bag Module Bolts, Side	48①
	Air Bag Sensor Assembly	14
	Floor Anchor To Body	30
	Front Air Bag Sensor	14
	Front Seat Outer Belt Retractor (Lower Bolt)	31
	Front Seat Outer Belt Retractor (Upper Bolt)	43①
	Side Air Bag Sensor Assembly	14
	Steering Wheel Nut	26
1999	Air Bag Module Bolts, Passenger	15
	Air Bag Module Bolts, Driver	78①
	Air Bag Module Bolts, Side	48①
	Air Bag Sensor Assembly	15
	Floor Anchor To Body	30
	Front Air Bag Sensor	15
	Front Seat Outer Belt Retractor (Lower Bolt)	30
	Front Seat Outer Belt Retractor (Upper Bolt)	43①
	Side Air Bag Sensor Assembly	15
	Steering Wheel Nut	25
LAND CRUISER		
1996	Center Air Bag Sensor	15
	Front Air Bag Sensor	22
	Passenger Air Bag assembly	80①
	Steering Wheel Retaining Nut	25
	Steering Wheel Side Torx Screws	78①
1997	Air Bag Module Bolts, Passenger's	15
	Air Bag Module Screws, Driver's	78①
	Air Bag Sensor Assembly Mounting Screws	15
	Instrument Panel Reinforcement Bolts	15
	Steering Wheel Nut	25
1998–99	Center Air Bag Sensor	15
	Driver's Air Bag	78①
	Front Air Bag Sensor	15
	Passenger Air Bag To Instrument Panel	53①
	Passenger Air Bag To Instrument Panel Reinforcement	15
	Steering Wheel Nut	25
PASEO		
1996	Center Air Bag Sensor	14
	Front Air Bag Sensor	22
	Steering Wheel Retaining Nut	26
	Steering Wheel Side Torx Screws	78①

Continued

TIGHTENING
SPECIFICATIONS—Continued

Year	Component	Torque/Ft. Lbs
PASEO		
1997	Air Bag Module Bolts, Passenger's	49①
	Air Bag Module Screws, Driver's	78①
	Air Bag Sensor Assembly Mounting Screws	14
	Instrument Panel Reinforcement Bolts	14
	Steering Wheel Nut	25
PREVIA		
1996	Center Air Bag Sensor	14
	Front Air Bag Sensor	22
	Front Passenger Air Bag Assembly Bolts	14
	Front Passenger Air Bag Assembly Nuts	52①
	Steering Wheel Retaining Nut	26
	Steering Wheel Side Torx Screws	78①
1997	Air Bag Module Bolts, Passenger's	15
	Air Bag Module Nuts, Passenger's	52①
	Air Bag Module Screws, Driver's	78①
	Air Bag Sensor Assembly Mounting Screws	15
	Steering Wheel Nut	26
RAV4		
1996	Air Bag Module Bolts (Passenger)	②
	Air Bag Module Screws (Driver)	78①
	Air Bag Sensor Assembly Mounting Screws	15
	Instrument Panel Reinforcement Bolts	15
	Steering Wheel Nut	26
1997-99	Air Bag Module Bolts, Passenger's	15
	Air Bag Module Screws, Driver's	78①
	Air Bag Sensor Assembly Mounting Screws	15
	Instrument Panel Reinforcement Bolts	15
	Steering Wheel Nut	25
SIENNA		
1998–99	Adjustable Anchor To Body	32
	Air Bag Sensor To Body	14
	Driver's Air Bag	78①
	Floor Anchor To Body	32
	Front Air Bag Sensor	14
	Passenger's Air Bag To Instrument Panel	14
	Retractor To Body (Lower)	32
	Retractor To Body (Upper)	15
	Shoulder Anchor To Body	32
	Steering Wheel	25

TIGHTENING
SPECIFICATIONS—Continued

Year	Component	Torque/Ft. Lbs
SUPRA		
1996	Center Air Bag Sensor	15
	Front Air Bag Sensor	22
	Front Passenger Air Bag To Instrument Panel Reinforcement Screws	15
	Front Passenger Air Bag To Instrument Panel Screws	78①
	Steering Wheel Retaining Nut	26
	Steering Wheel Side Torx Screws	62①
1997	Air Bag Module Bolts, Passenger's	78①
	Air Bag Module Screws, Driver's	62①
	Air Bag Sensor Mounting Screws	15
	Passenger's Air Bag To Instrument Panel Reinforcement	15
	Steering Wheel Nut	26
1998	Air Bag Sensor	15
	Driver's Air Bag Module	78①
	Passenger's Air Bag To Instrument Panel	75①
	Passenger's Air Bag To Instrument Panel Reinforcement	15
	Steering Wheel	26
TACOMA		
1996	Center Air Bag Sensor	15
	Front Air Bag Sensor	22
	Passenger Air Bag assembly	80①
	Steering Wheel Retaining Nut	25
	Steering Wheel Side Torx Screws	78①
1997	Air Bag Module, Driver's	78①
	Air Bag Sensor Assembly Mounting Screws	15
	Steering Wheel Nut	26
1998	Air Bag Sensor	15
	Driver's Air Bag	78①
	Passenger's Air Bag To Instrument Panel	42①
	Passenger's Air Bag To Instrument Panel Reinforcement	15
	Steering Wheel	26
1999	Air Bag Sensor	15
	Driver's Air Bag	78①
	Front Air Bag Sensor To Body	108①
	Front Seat Outer Belt Shoulder Anchor To Body	32
	Front Seat Outer Belt Retractor To Body (Lower Bolt)	43①
	Front Seat Outer Belt Retractor To Body (Upper Bolt)	32
	Passenger's Air Bag To Instrument Panel	42①
	Passenger's Air Bag To Instrument Panel Reinforcement	15
	Steering Wheel	26

Continued

AIR BAG SYSTEM

TOYOTA UNIT REPAIR

TIGHTENING
SPECIFICATIONS—Continued

Year	Component	Torque/Ft. Lbs
TERCEL		
1996	Center Air Bag Sensor	14
	Front Air Bag Sensor	22
	Steering Wheel Retaining Nut	26
	Steering Wheel Side Torx Screws	78①
1997	Air Bag Module Bolts, Passenger's	14
	Air Bag Module Screws, Driver's	78①
	Air Bag Sensor Assembly Mounting Screws	14
	Instrument Panel Bracket Bolts	14
	Steering Wheel Nut	26
1998	Air Bag Sensor	15
	Driver's Air Bag	78①
	Front Seat Inner Belt To Front Seat	30
	Front Seat Outer Belt Floor Anchor To Body	32
	Front Seat Outer Belt Shoulder Anchor To Body	32
	Passenger's Air Bag To Instrument Panel Reinforcement	15
	Retractor To Body	32
	Steering Wheel	25
TUNDRA		
2000	Center Air Bag Sensor	15
	Driver's Air Bag Module	78①
	Front Air Bag Sensor	15
	Passenger Air Bag Module To Instrument Panel	44①
	Passenger Air Bag Module To Instrument Panel Reinforcement	15
	Steering Wheel	26
T100		
1996	Center Air Bag Sensor	15
	Front Air Bag Sensor	22
	Passenger Air Bag assembly	80①
	Steering Wheel Retaining Nut	25
	Steering Wheel Side Torx Screws	78①
1997–98	Air Bag Module, Driver's	78①
	Air Bag Sensor Assembly Mounting Screws	15
	Front Sensor Assembly Mounting Screws	22
	Steering Wheel Nut	26
4RUNNER		
1996	Air Bag Module Screws (Driver)	78①
	Air Bag Module Bolts (Passenger)	②
	Air Bag Sensor Assembly Mounting Screws	15
	Instrument Panel Reinforcement Bolts	15
	Steering Wheel Nut	26

Continued

AIR BAG SYSTEM

TIGHTENING
SPECIFICATIONS—Continued

Year	Component	Torque/Ft. Lbs
4RUNNER		
1997	Air Bag Module Bolts, Passenger's	48①
	Air Bag Module Screws, Driver's	78①
	Air Bag Sensor Assembly Mounting Screws	15
	Instrument Panel Reinforcement Bolts	14
	Steering Wheel Nut	26
1998	Air Bag Sensor	15
	Driver's Air Bag	78①
	Passenger's Air Bag To Instrument Panel Reinforcement	14
	Steering Wheel	25
1999	Air Bag Sensor	15
	Driver's Air Bag	78①
	Front Air Bag Sensor	15
	Front Seat Outer Shoulder Belt Anchor To Body	31
	Front Seat Outer Belt Floor Anchor To Body	31
	Front Seat Outer Belt Retractor To Body (Lower Bolt)	31
	Front Seat Outer Belt Retractor To Body (Upper Bolt)	74①
	Passenger's Air Bag To Instrument Panel	48①
	Passenger's Air Bag To Instrument Panel Reinforcement	14
	Steering Wheel	25

① — Inch lbs.

② — 6 mm, 6.5 ft. lbs.; 8 mm, 15 ft. lbs.

③ — 6mm, 49 inch lbs.; 8mm, 15 ft. lbs.

Dash Panel Service

NOTE: On Air Bag Equipped Models, Refer To "Air Bag System Precautions" Located In The Front Of This Manual For System Disarming & Arming Procedures.

NOTE: Refer To The "Dash Gauges" Section For Related Information.

INDEX

PRECAUTIONS

AIR BAG SYSTEMS

Refer to "Air Bag System Precautions" in the front of this manual for system disarming & arming procedures.

BATTERY GROUND CABLE

Prior to service, disconnect battery ground cable and isolate as required.

AUDIO CODED ANTI-THEFT SYSTEM

Some models are equipped with an audio coded anti-theft system that will disable the radio when the battery cable is disconnected. The system can be identified by the "ANTI-THEFT SYSTEM" on the cassette tape lid. Obtain 3 digit customer code for input. Reset system after service as follows:

1. Obtain 3 digit audio anti-theft code.
2. Depress 1 (PROG) while depressing righthand side of TUNE SEEK button, - - will appear in tape operation display.
3. To enter the first digit, depress 1 (PROG) button repeatedly until the number of times depressed equals the first digit beginning with zero (depress the 1 button six times if the first digit if five).
4. To enter second digit, depress 2 (APS) button repeatedly until the number of times depressed equals the second digit beginning with zero.
5. To enter third digit, depress 3 (RPT) button repeatedly until the number of times depressed equals the third digit beginning with zero.
6. If - - - is displayed during code input, repeat procedure.
7. When code appears in display, depress and hold SCAN button until SEC appears.
8. When SEC disappears audio system should be operative.
9. If Err is displayed, repeat procedure.

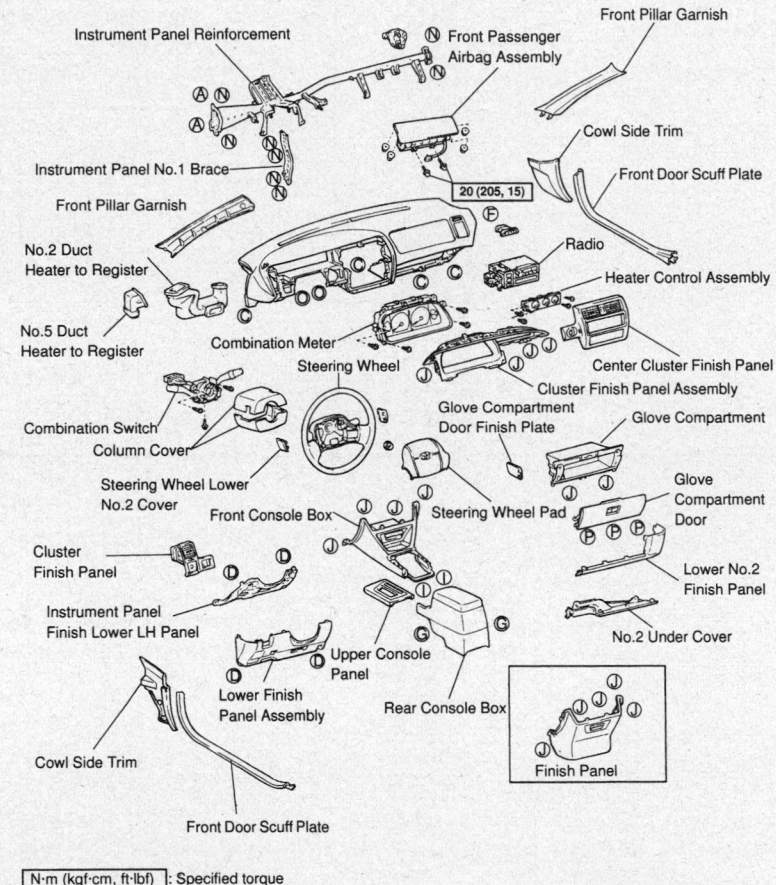

Instrument Panel Reinforcement
Front Passenger Airbag Assembly
Front Pillar Garnish
Cowl Side Trim
Front Door Scuff Plate
20 (205, 15)
Instrument Panel No.1 Brace
Front Pillar Garnish
Radio
No.2 Duct Heater to Register
Heater Control Assembly
No.5 Duct Heater to Register
Combination Meter
Center Cluster Finish Panel
Steering Wheel
Cluster Finish Panel Assembly
Combination Switch
Glove Compartment Door Finish Plate
Glove Compartment
Column Cover
Steering Wheel Lower No.2 Cover
Glove Compartment Door
Front Console Box
Steering Wheel Pad
Cluster Finish Panel
Lower No.2 Finish Panel
Instrument Panel Finish Lower LH Panel
No.2 Under Cover
Upper Console Panel
Lower Finish Panel Assembly
Rear Console Box
Cowl Side Trim
Finish Panel
Front Door Scuff Plate

N·m (kgf·cm, ft·lbf) : Specified torque

TY9149500023010X

Fig. 1   Exploded view of instrument panel (Part 1 of 2). Avalon

Attempting to input code more than nine times may permanently disable audio system.

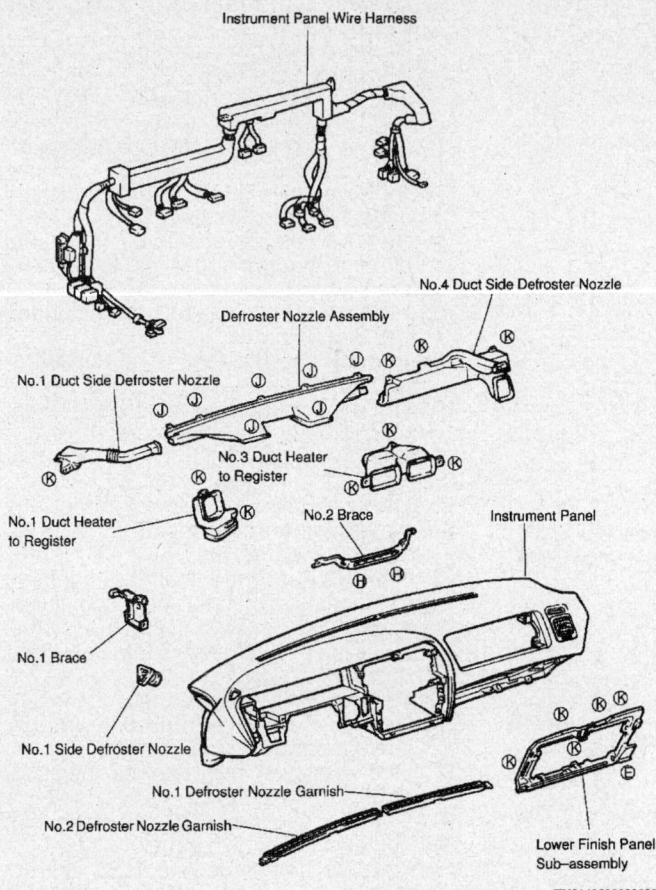

Fig. 1 Exploded view of instrument panel (Part 2 of 2). Avalon

TY9149500023020X

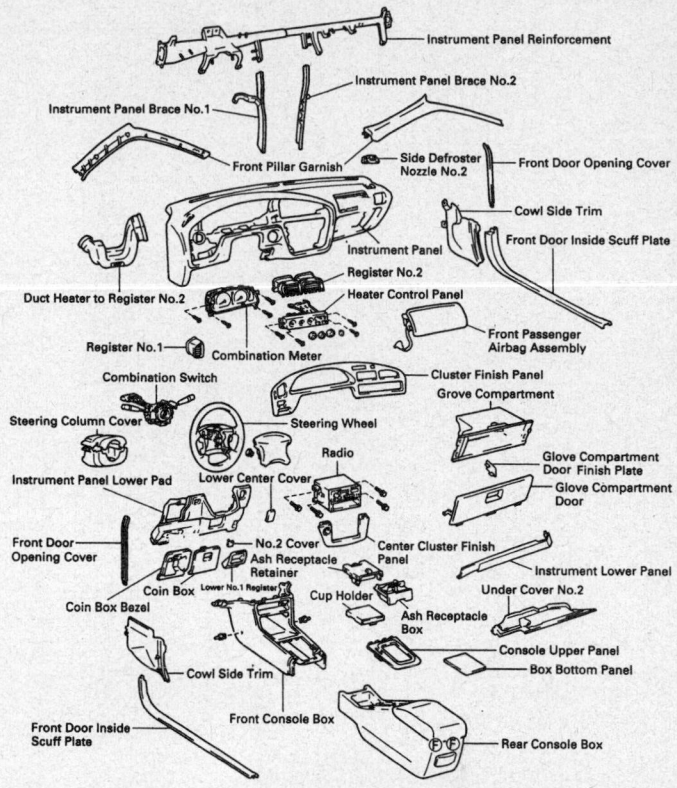

TY914940001101BX

Fig. 2 Exploded view of instrument panel (Part 1 of 2). 1996 Camry

DASH PANEL
REPLACE
AVALON

1. Remove front pillar garnish and door inside scuff plate, **Fig. 1.**
2. Remove hood lock release lever and cowl side trim.
3. Remove steering wheel, steering column cover and combination switch.
4. Remove lower finish panel assembly and instrument panel finish lower left-hand panel.
5. Remove fuse box bolt and parking brake release lever.
6. Remove No. 2 duct heater to register and No. 2 under cover and lower finish panel.
7. Remove glove compartment door and glove compartment.
8. Remove glove compartment door finish plate inside instrument panel box.
9. Pull up and disconnect air bag connector.
10. Remove four screws and compartment by pulling and disconnect the connectors.
11. Remove center cluster finish panel, radio and heater control assembly.
12. **On models equipped with floor shift,** remove the following parts:
    a. Upper console panel.
    b. Rear console box.
    c. Front console box.
13. **On models equipped with column shift,** remove finish panel.
14. **On all models**, remove steering column.
15. Remove cluster finish panel, assembly and combination meter.
16. Remove and disconnect attaching bolts and connectors, then remove instrument panel from vehicle.
17. Remove instrument panel reinforcement.
18. Reverse procedure to install.

CAMRY
1996

1. Pry out front pillar garnish retaining clips, then remove garnish by pulling upwards by hand.
2. Remove front door inside scuff plate, **Fig. 2.**
3. Remove front door opening cover.
4. Remove engine hood release lever attaching screws, then the lever.
5. Remove cowl side trim.
6. Remove steering wheel.
7. Remove steering column upper and lower covers.
8. Remove console upper panel.
9. Remove rear console box.
10. Remove coil box and bezel.
11. Remove instrument panel lower pad.
12. Remove combination switch.
13. Remove No. 2 undercover.
14. Remove instrument lower panel.
15. Remove front console box.
16. Remove glove compartment door.
17. **On models equipped with passenger side air bag,** remove glove compartment door finish plate, then pull up and disconnect air bag connector.
18. **On all models,** remove glove compartment attaching screws, then pull out glove compartment.
19. Remove center cluster finish panel.
20. Remove four cluster finish panel attaching screws, pry panel rearward, disconnect electrical connectors, then remove panel.
21. Remove register No. 1 and 2 attaching screws, then remove registers.
22. Remove radio attaching screws, disconnect electrical connector, then remove radio.
23. Remove instrument cluster attaching screws, disconnect electrical connector, then remove cluster.
24. Remove heater control knobs, remove heater control attaching screws, disconnect air mix damper control cable, then remove heater control.
25. Remove duct heater to register No. 2.
26. **On models equipped with passenger side air bag,** remove front passenger air bag assembly.
27. **On all models,** remove side defroster nozzle No. 2.
28. Disconnect instrument panel right and left electrical connectors, remove connector holder attaching bolt, then remove connector holder.

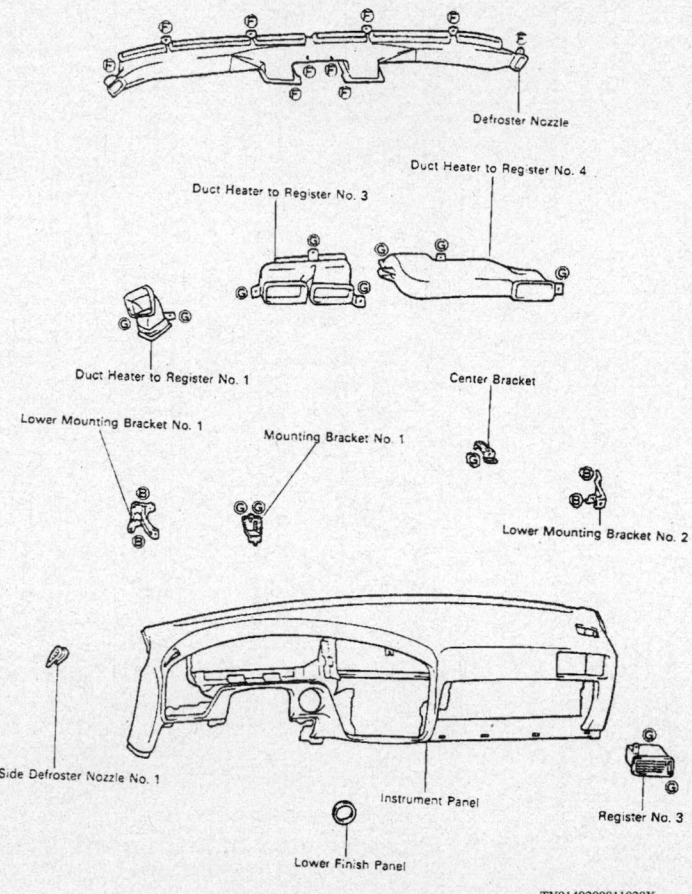

Fig. 2 Exploded view of instrument panel (Part 2 of 2). 1996 Camry

TY9149200011020X

29. Remove instrument panel six attaching bolts and three nuts, then remove instrument panel.
30. Reverse procedure to install, noting the following:
   a. **Torque** passenger air bag assembly to instrument panel reinforcement screws to 15 ft. lbs.
   b. **Torque** passenger air bag assembly to instrument panel screws to 69 inch lbs.

1997-99

1. Remove front door inside scuff plate, **Fig. 3.**
2. Remove cowl side trim.
3. Remove front pillar garnish.
4. Remove front door opening cover.
5. Remove lower instrument finish panel.
6. Remove steering wheel and steering column covers.
7. Remove combination switch.
8. Remove hood lock release lever.
9. Remove No. 1 lower instrument panel.
10. Remove No. 2 lower cover and instrument lower panel.
11. Remove glove compartment door finish plate.
12. Disconnect passenger side air bag connector.
13. Remove five screws, then the glove compartment assembly.
14. Remove console upper panel.
15. Remove two screws, two bolts, then the console box.
16. Remove center cluster finish panel.
17. Remove four screws, two bolts, then remove front console box assembly.
18. Remove radio assembly.
19. Remove heater control assembly as follows:
   a. Remove the four mounting screws.
   b. Disconnect air mix damper control cable, air temperature adjusting cable and four connectors.
   c. Remove heater control head.
20. Remove instrument cluster finish panel.
21. Remove remote control mirror hole base.
22. Remove lefthand lower instrument panel.
23. Remove two bolts, four nuts, then the front passenger side air bag.
24. Remove No. 1 and No. 2 instrument panel brackets.
25. Remove No. 2 side defroster nozzle.
26. Disconnect electrical connectors from left and righthand connector holders.
27. Remove bolts holding ground wires to body.
28. Remove bolts, nut and screws, then the instrument panel, **Fig. 4.**
29. Reverse procedure to install.

CAMRY SOLARA

1. Disarm SRS as outlined under "Air Bag Systems."

2. Remove right and left door scuff plates, **Fig. 5.**
3. Remove front door opening covers.
4. Disconnect clip from right and left cowl side trim pieces, then slide trim rearward and remove.
5. Remove right and left front pillar garnish.
6. Remove driver's air bag as outlined under "Air Bag Systems."
7. Remove steering wheel, then the steering column upper and lower covers.
8. Remove spiral cable as outlined under "Air Bag Systems."
9. Remove hood release lever from No. 1 panel.
10. Disconnect cable from release lever, then remove No. 1 lower panel.
11. Remove lower panel insert, then the No. 2 under cover.
12. Using a suitable screwdriver, pry out glove compartment door finish plate inside lower panel.
13. Remove passenger's air bag connector from glove compartment door finish plate.
14. Disconnect passengers air bag connector.
15. Remove No. 2 lower panel.
16. Remove passenger's air bag as outlined under "Air Bag Systems."
17. Remove lower finish panel, then the upper console panel.
18. Remove ash tray and clip, then the center cluster finish panel.
19. Remove heater control assembly as follows:
   a. Remove A/C control assembly attaching screws.
   b. Pull out control assembly with undertray.
   c. Disconnect A/C control electrical connectors.
   d. Remove mounting brackets from control assembly, then separate from instrument panel undertray.
20. Remove carpet from bottom of rear console box.
21. Remove console box attaching screws, then the console box.
22. Remove front console box.
23. Remove cluster finish panel, then the instrument cluster.
24. Remove lower No. 1 retainers.
25. Remove steering column as follows:
   a. Place alignment marks on intermediate shaft and control valve shaft.
   b. Disconnect intermediate shaft from steering column shaft.
   c. Disconnect steering column electrical connectors.
   d. Remove 4 steering column attaching nuts, then the steering column.
26. Remove No. 2 side defroster nozzle.
27. Using a suitable screwdriver, remove bolt cap.
28. Disconnect electrical connectors as necessary.
29. Remove junction block attaching bolts.
30. Remove instrument panel safety pad attaching nuts, then the safety pad.
31. Remove junction block from reinforcement.
32. Remove No.1 and No. 2 braces, then the instrument panel reinforcement.

33. Remove reinforcement bracket, then the instrument panel.
34. Reverse procedure to install.

CELICA

Refer to **Fig. 6,** when performing the following procedure.
1. Remove front pillar lower garnish and front pillar garnish.
2. Remove front door inside scuff plate.
3. Remove cowl side trim board.
4. Remove steering column cover.
5. Remove upper console panel and console box.
6. Remove lower finish panel No. 1.
7. Remove finish panel.
8. Remove heater to register duct No. 2.
9. Remove combination switch.
10. Remove lower cluster finish panel.
11. Remove heater register No. 1 and combination meter.
12. Remove center cluster finish panel.
13. Remove audio receiver assembly.
14. Disconnect cable to air mix damper control.
15. Disconnect cable to water valve in engine compartment.
16. Remove A/C control assembly.
17. Remove glove compartment door finish plate, then pull up and disconnect passenger side air bag connector.
18. Remove glove compartment.
19. Remove lower center finish panel.
20. Remove side defroster No. 2.
21. Remove steering column.
22. Disconnect instrument panel electrical connectors, then remove instrument panel.
23. Remove center console bracket No. 1.
24. Remove instrument panel brace No. 2.
25. Remove brake spring and center console bracket support.
26. Remove cowl top inner brace.
27. Reverse procedure to install, noting the following:
    a. **Torque** steering column attaching bolts to 19 ft. lbs.
    b. **Torque** passenger air bag assembly bolts to 15 ft. lbs.
    c. **Torque** steering wheel set nut to 25 ft. lbs.
    d. **Torque** steering wheel pad to 80 inch lbs.

COROLLA

1. Remove front pillar garnish and door scuff plate.
2. Remove steering wheel and steering column covers, **Figs. 7 and 8.**
3. Remove shifting hole bezel, hood release lever and rear console box.
4. Remove lower finish panel, combination switch and glove compartment door.
5. Remove center cluster finish lower panel.
6. Remove heater control knobs, then remove center cluster finish panel.
7. Remove radio and heater control.
8. Remove two attaching screws and dash cluster finish panel.
9. Remove finish lower center panel, then remove defroster nozzle No. 2 and heat ducts.
10. **On models equipped with passenger side air bag,** disconnect air bag

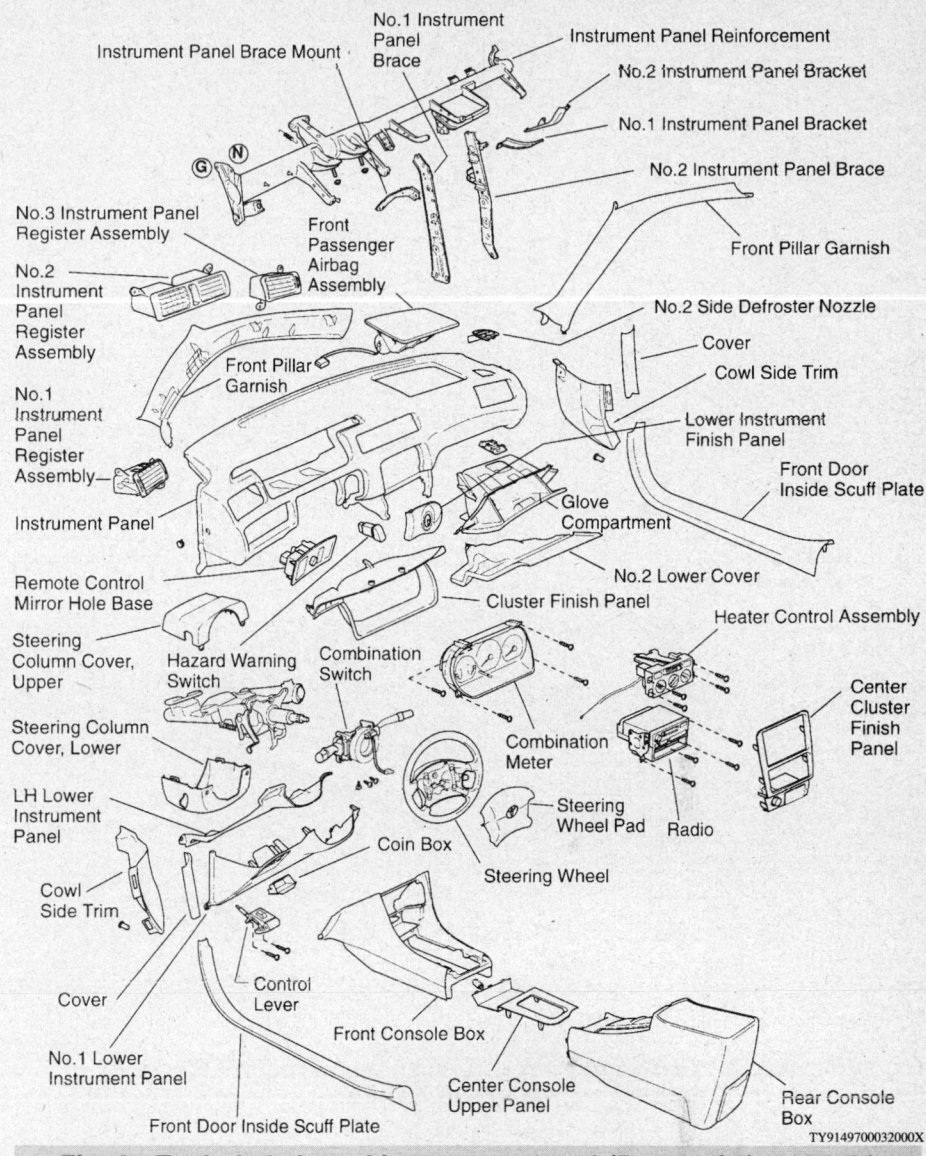

Fig. 3 Exploded view of instrument panel (Part 1 of 2). 1997–99 Camry

electrical connector, remove attaching bolts and clips, then pull out passenger air bag assembly.
11. **On all models,** disconnect instrument panel electrical connectors, then remove instrument panel and panel reinforcement.
12. Reverse procedure to install.

LAND CRUISER

1. Remove driver side air bag assembly, steering wheel, combination switch and turn signal bracket as outlined in the "Electrical" section. Refer to **Figs. 9 and 10.**
2. Apply protection tape to roof pillars.
3. Remove hood and fuel filler release levers. Then remove lower finish and instrument panels.
4. Remove No. 2 heater to register duct.
5. Loosen DLC 3 and fuse block.
6. Remove ashtray, ashtray receptacle and No. 2 instrument cluster center finish panel and clock.
7. Remove instrument cluster finish panel and combination meter.
8. Remove instrument cluster. Then remove heater control unit and radio. Disconnect necessary connectors.
9. Remove front console box, then instrument panel speaker. Disconnect connectors.
10. Remove glove compartment door. Then remove engine ECU.
11. Disconnect passenger air bag electrical connector and remove air bag module.
12. Remove nine bolts, five screws and instrument panel.
13. Reverse procedure to install, noting the following:
    a. **Torque** steering column attaching bolts to 19 ft. lbs.
    b. **Torque** passenger air bag assembly bolts to 15 ft. lbs.
    c. **Torque** steering wheel set nut to 25 ft. lbs.

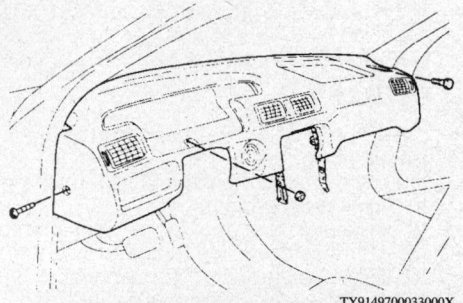

Fig. 4 Instrument panel removal. 1997–99 Camry

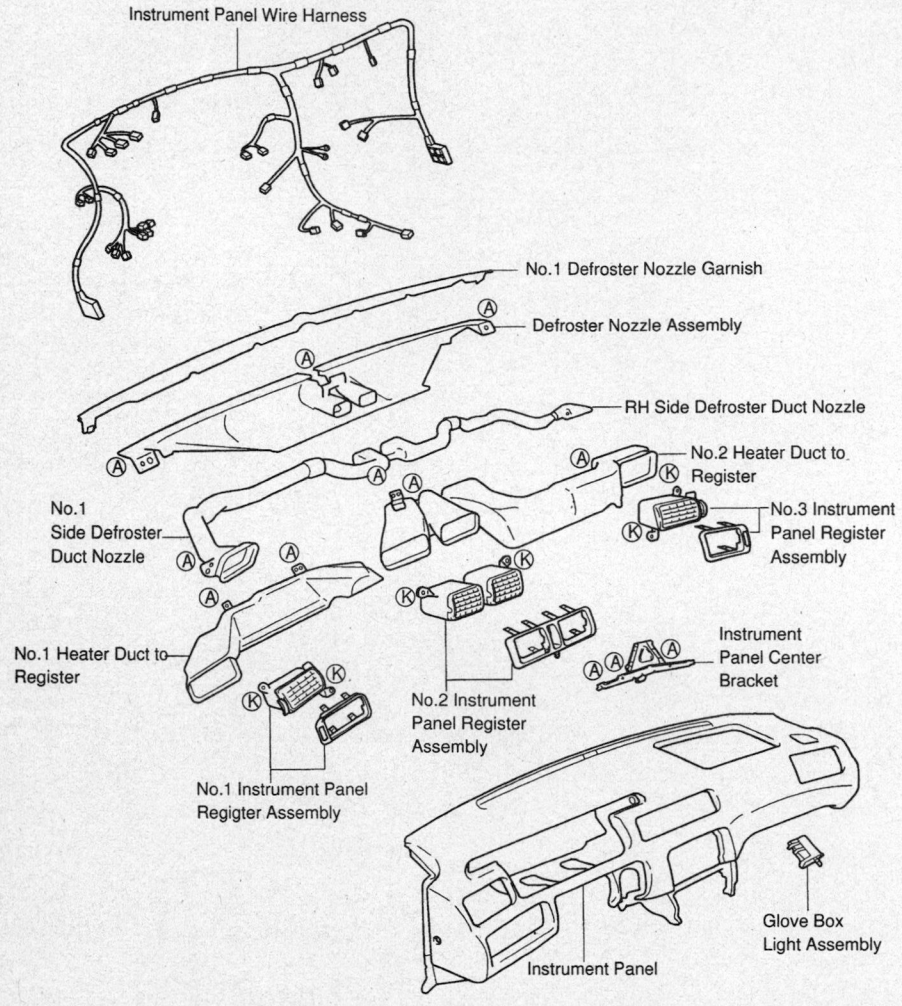

Instrument Panel Wire Harness

No.1 Defroster Nozzle Garnish

Defroster Nozzle Assembly

RH Side Defroster Duct Nozzle

No.2 Heater Duct to Register

No.3 Instrument Panel Register Assembly

No.1 Side Defroster Duct Nozzle

No.1 Heater Duct to Register

No.2 Instrument Panel Register Assembly

Instrument Panel Center Bracket

No.1 Instrument Panel Register Assembly

Instrument Panel

Glove Box Light Assembly

TY9149900039000X

Fig. 3 Exploded view of instrument panel (Part 2 of 2). 1997–99 Camry

d. **Torque** steering wheel pad to 80 inch lbs.

PASEO

1. Disarm anti-theft system as outlined under "Precautions."
2. Remove front garnish clip, **Fig. 11.**
3. Remove door scuff plate.
4. Remove steering wheel.
5. Remove steering column cover.
6. Remove console box.
7. Remove hood lever release.
8. Using suitable screwdriver with taped tip, remove lower No. 1 finish panel opening covers, then remove lower No. 1 finish panel.
9. Remove combination switch.
10. Remove cluster finish center upper panel.
11. Remove instrument cluster attaching bolt and screws, pull cluster rearward, disconnect electrical connectors, then remove cluster.
12. Using suitable screwdriver with taped tip, remove lower No. 2 finish panel opening covers, then remove lower No. 2 finish panel.
13. Remove center cluster finish panel.

14. Remove radio.
15. Remove lower center finish panel.
16. Remove clock.
17. Remove heater control knobs.
18. **On models equipped with A/C,** pry out A/C switch.
19. **On all models,** pry out heater control plate, then remove heater control.
20. Remove duct heater to register No. 2 duct.
21. Remove junction block No. 1.
22. Remove instrument panel attaching bolt and three nuts, then remove instrument panel.
23. Reverse procedure to install.

PREVIA

1. Remove assist grips, front pillar garnish and side defroster nozzle, **Fig. 12.**
2. Remove steering wheel and steering column cover.
3. Remove front door scuff plate, side panel, hood release lever and cluster finish lower panel.
4. Remove knee panel.
5. Remove combination switch with spiral cable and turn signal bracket.
6. Remove cluster finish center upper

panel. Then remove console box, ash receptacle retainer and cup holder.
7. Remove cluster finish center panel with radio. Remove cluster finish end panel.
8. Remove cluster finish panel and combination meter.
9. Remove glove compartment door finish plate, then pull up and disconnect air bag connector.
10. Remove glove compartment lock striker.
11. Remove glove compartment door.
12. Remove passenger air bag assembly, then the heater control.
13. Remove No. 1 junction and relay block.
14. Remove two bolts and the detent plate. Then remove the through bolt, nut and the shift lever. Disconnect connectors.
15. Remove ten bolts, three screws, three nuts and the instrument panel.
16. **On 1997 models,** proceed as follows:
    a. Remove instrument panel reinforcement, then the instrument panel No. 1 brace.
    b. Remove finish panel No. 3 retainer and the center instrument panel reinforcement, then the center No. 1 brace.
    c. Remove center No. 2 brace, then the Center instrument panel bracket.
17. **On all models,** reverse procedure to install.

RAV4

1. Remove door scuff plate and cowl side trim board, **Fig. 13.**
2. Remove steering wheel.
3. Remove steering column cover.
4. Remove cluster finish panel and combination meter.
5. Remove hood lock release lever.
6. Remove lower finish panel.
7. Remove instrument panel lower finish panel and lower insert.
8. Remove No. 2 heater to register duct.
9. Remove steering column assembly as outlined under "Steering Columns."
10. Remove center cluster finish panel.
11. Remove heater control knobs and the heater control name plate.
12. Pry off cluster instrument panel, then remove three screws from heater control assembly.
13. Disconnect connectors, then remove cluster panel.

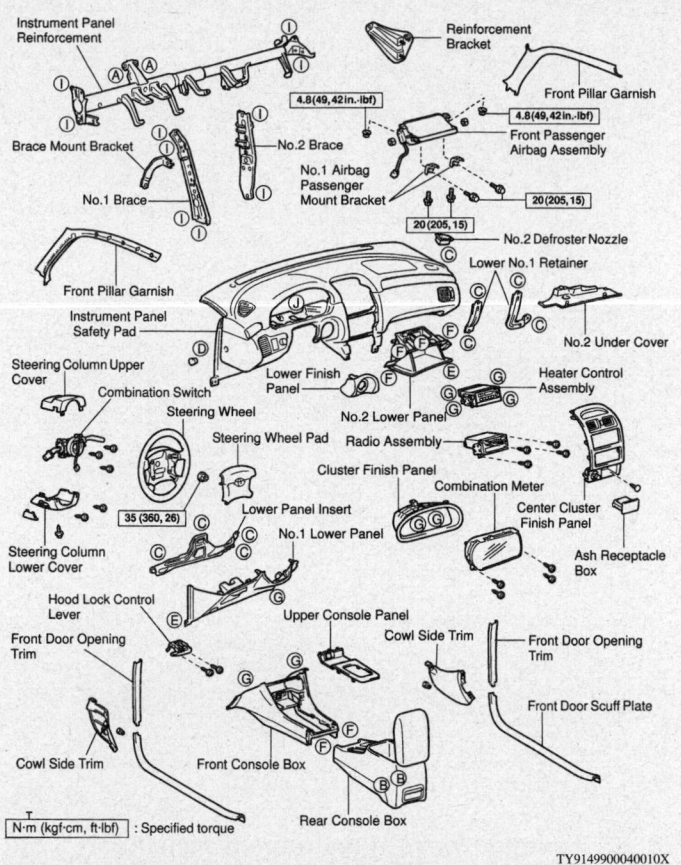

Fig. 5   Exploded view of instrument panel (Part 1 of 2). Camry Solara

TY9149900040010X

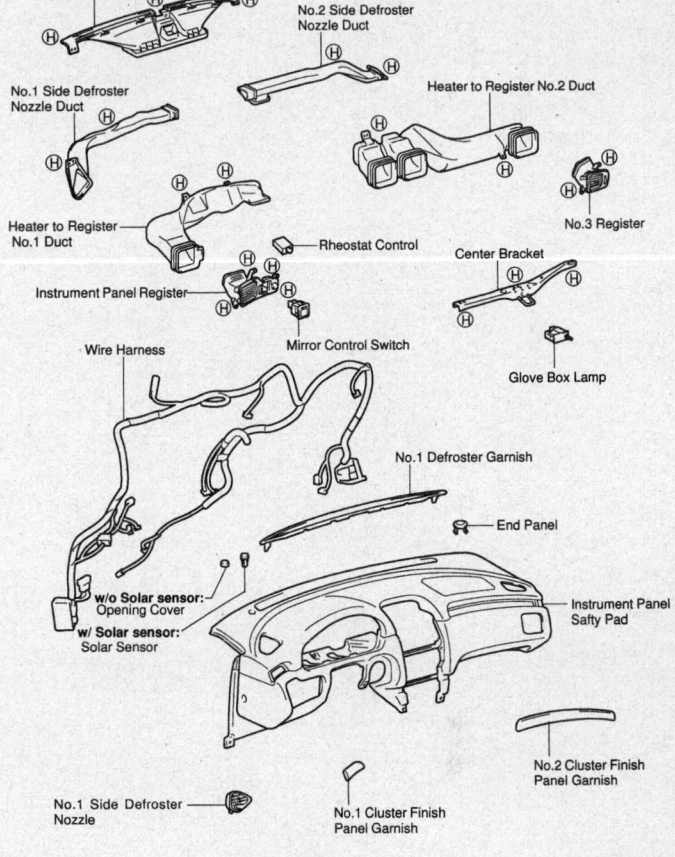

Fig. 5   Exploded view of instrument panel (Part 2 of 2). Camry Solara

TY9149900040020X

14. Remove heater control and accessory assembly.
15. Remove radio and console box.
16. Remove lower center cluster finish panel.
17. Remove stereo opening cover.
18. Remove two mounting screws and glove compartment door.
19. Remove kick panel covers.
20. Remove instrument panel retaining screws and nuts.
21. Disconnect instrument panel electrical connectors and remove instrument panel.
22. Remove instrument panel reinforcement.
23. Reverse procedure to install.

SIENNA

1. Disarm SRS as outlined under "Air Bag Systems."
2. Remove front door scuff plates, **Fig. 14.**
3. Remove cowl side boards, then the front door opening trim covers.
4. Remove right and left front pillar garnish.
5. Remove driver's air bag as outlined under "Air Bag System."
6. Remove steering column cover, then the combination switch.
7. Remove hood release lever from finish panel.
8. Remove lower finish panel, then the No. 1 safety pad insert.

9. Remove No. 2 finish panel, then pry out glove compartment door finish plate.
10. Remove air bag connector from glove compartment door finish plate.
11. Disconnect passenger's air bag connector.
12. Remove glove compartment, then the center cluster finish panel.
13. Remove lower center cluster finish panel and disconnect connector.
14. Remove ash tray, then the ash tray retainer from panel.
15. Remove instrument cluster finish panel, then disconnect panel connector.
16. Remove clock, then the No. 1 and No. 2 registers from finish panel.
17. Remove instrument cluster, then the radio.
18. Remove heater control assembly as follows:
    a. Remove control instrument cluster finish panel.
    b. Disconnect heater control cables, **Fig. 15.**
    c. Remove heater control assembly, then disconnect connectors.
19. Remove 2 bolts from passenger's air bag assembly.
20. Remove 5 bolts, nut and instrument panel, then disconnect connectors as necessary.

21. Remove radio amplifier, then the No. 1 and No. 2 braces.
22. Remove No. 2 cowl brace, then the instrument panel reinforcement.
23. Reverse procedure to install.

SUPRA

1. Remove front pillar garnishes with assist grip.
2. Remove foot rest and front door scuff inside plates.
3. Remove air bag, steering wheel and steering column cover.
4. Remove console upper panel, **Fig. 16.**
5. Remove parking brake hole cover.
6. Remove console box.
7. Remove lower finish panel, below steering column.
8. Remove center, lefthand and righthand dash gauge finish panels.
9. Remove combination meter.
10. Remove heater to register duct No. 2.
11. Remove combination switch.
12. Remove audio receiver assembly and computer cover.
13. Remove glove compartment door finish plate.
14. Pull up and disconnect passenger air bag connector.
15. Remove glove compartment and finish panel mounting brackets.
16. Remove heater to register duct No. 4.

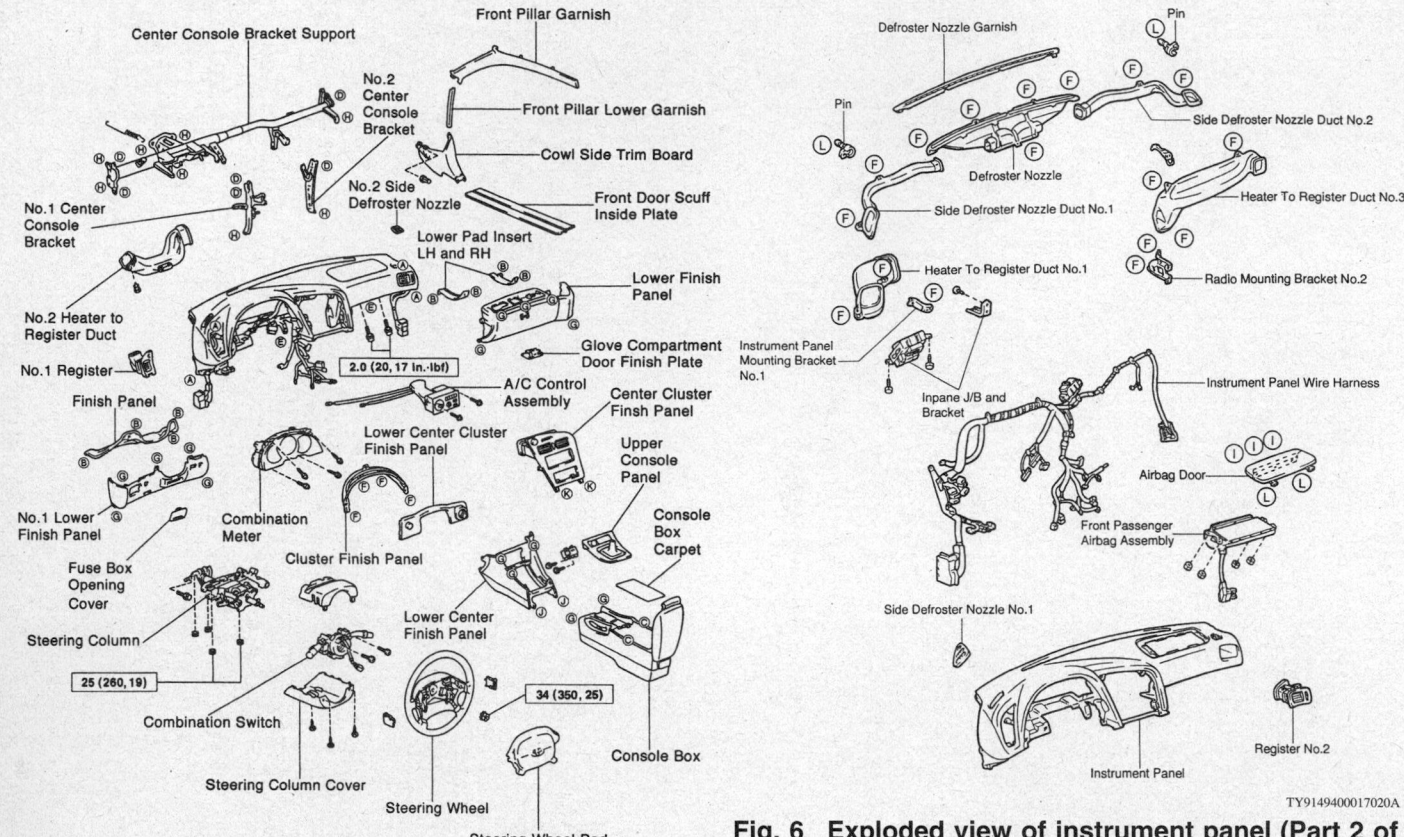

Fig. 6 Exploded view of instrument panel (Part 1 of 2). Celica

N·m (kgf·cm,ft·lbf) : Specified torque

TY9149400017010A

Fig. 6 Exploded view of instrument panel (Part 2 of 2). Celica

TY9149400017020A

Fig. 6 Exploded view of instrument panel (Part 1 of 2). Celica

17. Remove front passenger air bag assembly.
18. Remove parking brake lever, steering column and side defroster nozzle No. 2.
19. Disconnect instrument panel electrical connectors, then remove instrument panel and instrument panel reinforcement.
20. Remove instrument panel brace No. 1 and side bracket No. 3.
21. Reverse procedure to install, noting the following:
   a. **Torque** steering column bolts to 19 ft. lbs.
   b. **Torque** passenger air bag assembly to instrument panel reinforcement screws to 15 ft. lbs.
   c. **Torque** passenger air bag assembly to instrument panel screws to 78 inch lbs.
   d. **Torque** steering wheel set nut to 26 ft. lbs.
   e. **Torque** steering wheel pad to 62 inch lbs.

TACOMA

1996-97

1. Disarm SRS as outlined under "Air Bag Systems."
2. Remove air bag, steering wheel, column cover and combination switch, **Fig. 17.**

3. Remove hood lock release lever and fuse box opening cover.
4. Remove four bolts, one screw and lower left hand finish panel.
5. Remove starter switch bezel.
6. Remove No. 2 heater to register duct.
7. Remove steering column.
8. Remove clock.
9. Remove the center cluster finish panel as follows:
   a. Remove cup holder and heater control knobs.
   b. Using a screwdriver, or equivalent, remove heater control panel.
   c. Disconnect hazard connector.
   d. Remove two screws and center cluster finish panel.
   e. Remove heater control and radio.
10. Remove three screws and three clips, then cluster finish panel.
11. Remove and disconnect four screws, four connectors, speedometer cable and combination meter.
12. Remove No. 1 register and No. 1 heater to register duct.
13. Remove two screws and glove compartment door.
14. Remove two screws, bolt and glove compartment door reinforcement.
15. Remove two clips and lower center instrument cover.
16. Remove three screws and lower No. 2 finish panel.

17. Remove ash receptacle box and retainer.
18. Remove and disconnect stereo opening cover, screw, cigar lighter connector and center lower cluster finish panel.
19. Remove instrument panel side bracket, two nuts and instrument panel.
20. Remove instrument panel No. 1 and No. two brace.
21. Remove center heater to register duct and defroster nozzle.
22. Remove four nuts, three bolts and instrument panel reinforcement.
23. Reverse procedure to install.

1998-99

1. Remove spiral cable as outlined under "Air Bag Systems."
2. Remove hood lock release lever, then the fuse box opening cover, **Fig. 18.**
3. Remove lower lefthand finish panel.
4. Remove rear console box if equipped.
5. Remove front console box.
6. Remove upper console box mounting bracket.
7. Remove lower center cover, then the No. 2 heater to register duct.
8. Remove heater control knobs, then the heater control panel.
9. Remove center cluster finish panel.
10. Disconnect all electrical connectors as necessary.
11. Remove cigar lighter bezel from center cluster finish panel, then the ash tray.
12. Remove starter switch bezel.
13. Remove cluster finish panel, then the

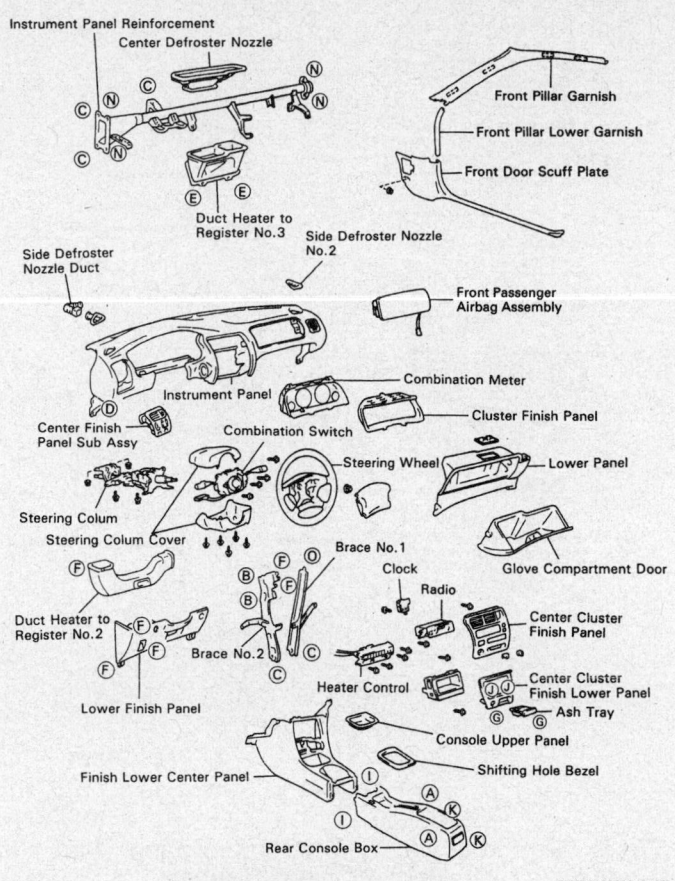

Fig. 7   Exploded view of instrument panel (Part 1 of 2). 1996–97 Corolla

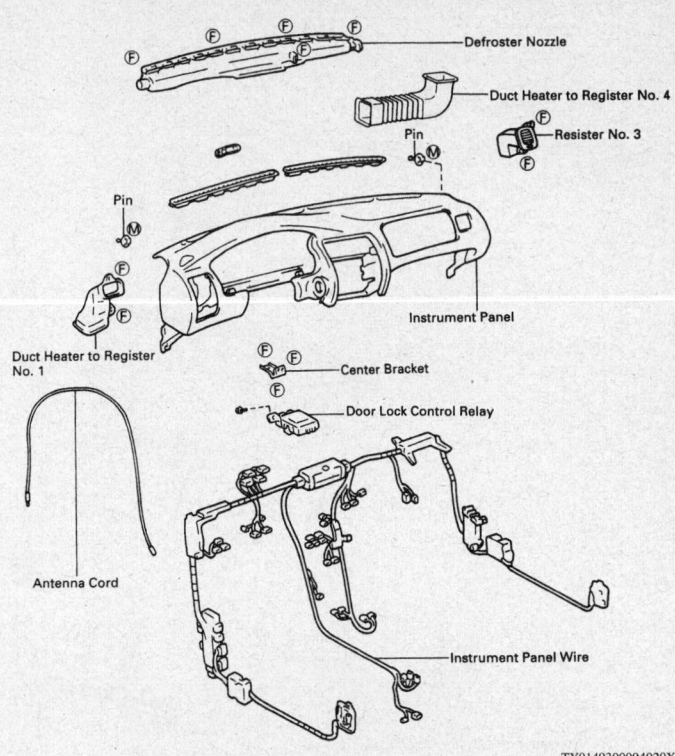

Fig. 7   Exploded view of instrument panel (Part 2 of 2). 1996–97 Corolla

radio opening cover.

14. Remove instrument cluster, then the No. 1 heater to register duct.
15. Remove steering column.
16. Remove glove compartment door, then the glove compartment reinforcement.
17. Remove No. 4 heater to register duct.
18. Remove No. 1 under cover, then pull up and disconnect air bag connector.
19. Remove lower No. 2 finish panel.
20. Remove heater control attaching screws, then the lower center finish panel.
21. Remove two bolts, two nuts, then the instrument panel.
22. Remove No. 1 and No. 2 braces, then the center heater to register duct.
23. Remove defroster nozzle, then the instrument panel reinforcement and side bracket.
24. Reverse procedure to install.

TERCEL

Refer to **Fig. 19,** for assistance in the following procedure.

1. Disarm anti-theft system as outlined under "Precautions."
2. Remove front pillar garnishes by pulling.
3. Remove cowl side trim and door scuff plates.
4. Remove drivers side air bag and steering wheel as outlined in the "Electrical" section.

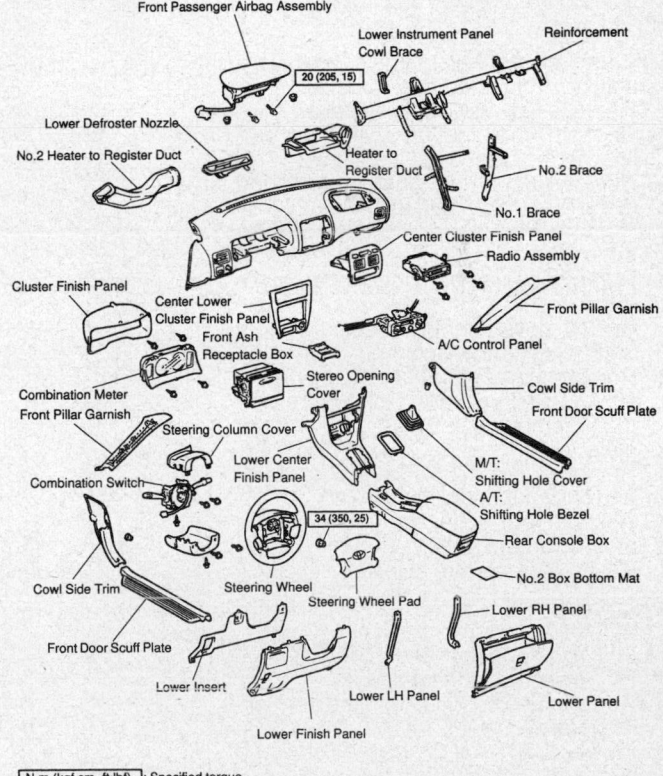

Fig. 8   Exploded view of instrument panel (Part 1 of 2). 1998–99 Corolla

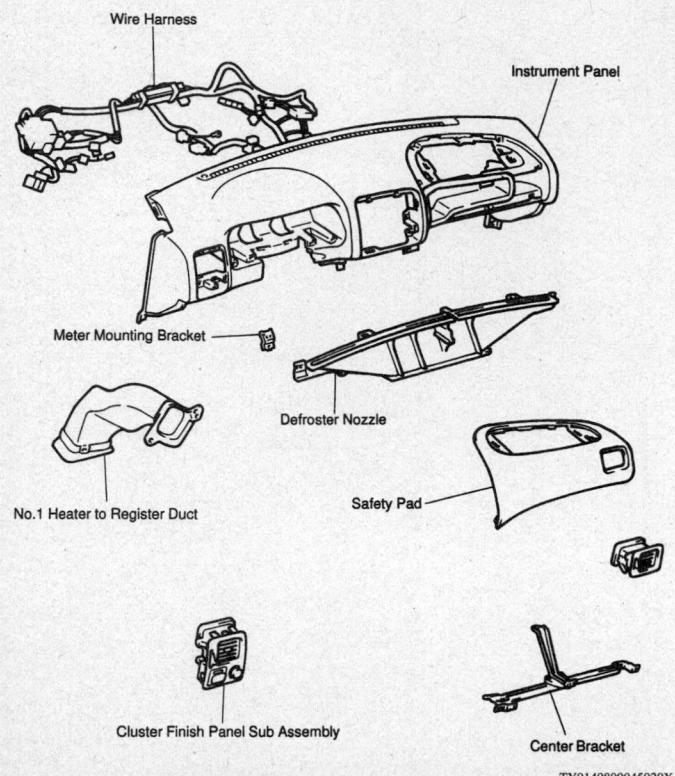

Fig. 8   Exploded view of instrument panel (Part 2 of 2). 1998–99 Corolla

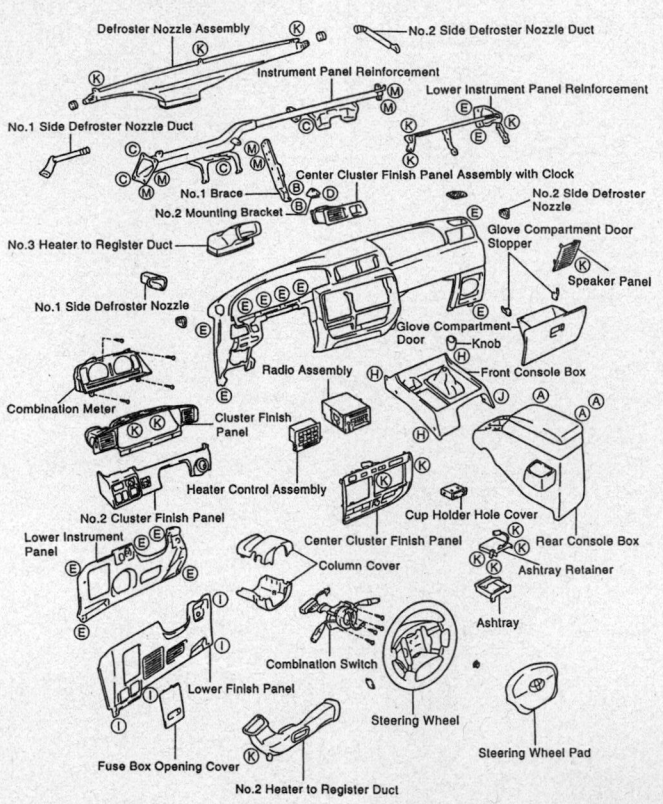

Fig. 9   Exploded view of instrument panel (Part 1 of 2). 1996–97 Land Cruiser

5. Remove steering column covers, console box and hood release lever.
6. Remove No. 1 lower finish panel.
7. Remove combination switch as outlined in the "Electrical" section.
8. Remove instrument cluster as outlined in the "Electrical" section.
9. Remove No. 2 lower finish panel, then the radio.
10. Remove passenger side air bag module.
11. Remove lower center finish panel. Remove clock and disconnect connector.
12. Remove heater control plate by prying off A/C switch, pulling off knobs and then removing screws and heater plate.
13. Remove heater to register duct No. 2 and No. 1 junction block.
14. Remove four bolts, two nuts and then the instrument panel.
15. Reverse procedure to install.

TUNDRA

1. Remove door scuff plates, **Fig. 20.**
2. Remove cowl side trim panel.
3. Remove assist grips, then the front pillar garnish.
4. Remove driver's air bag as outlined under "Air Bag System."
5. Remove steering wheel as outlined under "Electrical" section.
6. Remove steering column covers, then the combination switch.
7. Remove hood lock release lever, then the lower finish panel.
8. Lift switch base up, then remove it.
9. Remove No. 2 heater to register duct.

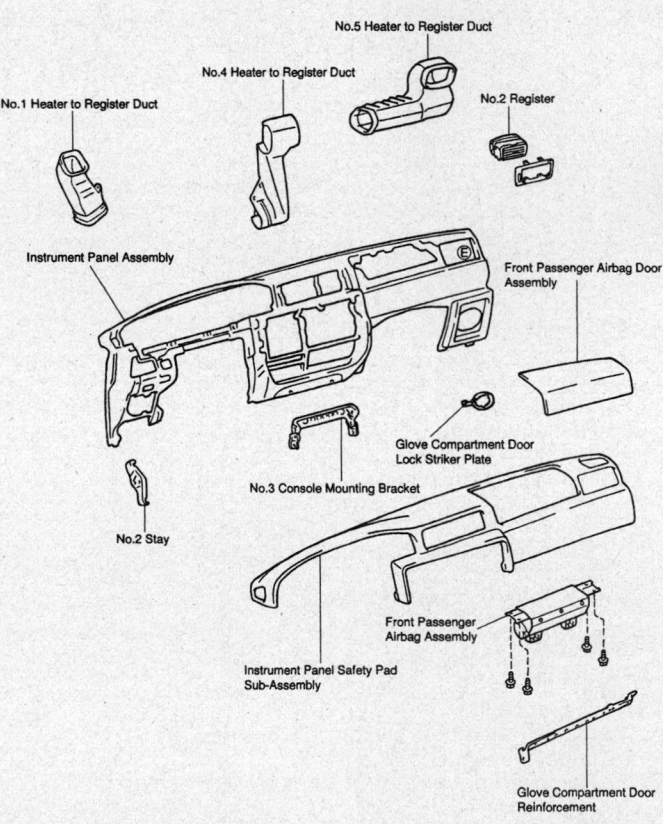

Fig. 9   Exploded view of instrument panel (Part 2 of 2). 1996–97 Land Cruiser

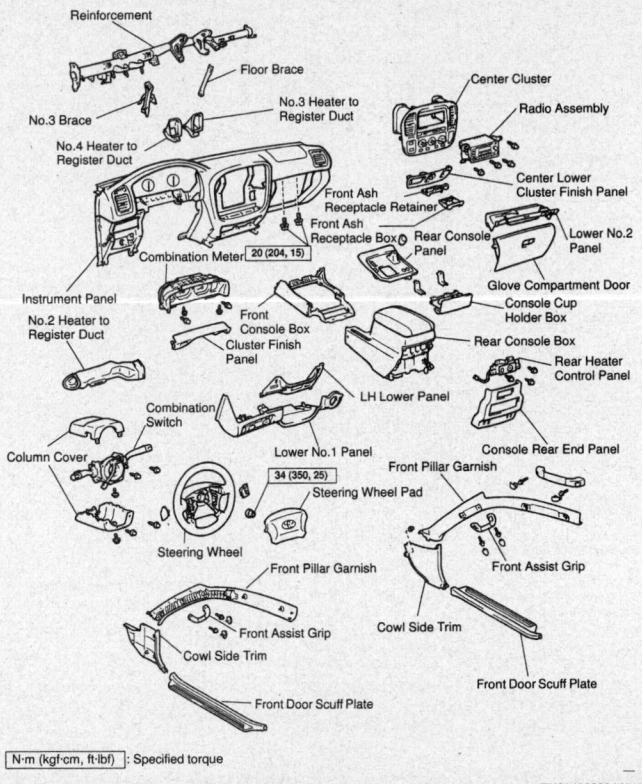

Fig. 10 Exploded view of instrument panel (Part 1 of 2). 1998–99 Land Cruiser

N·m (kgf·cm, ft·lbf) : Specified torque

TY9149800046010X

Fig. 10 Exploded view of instrument panel (Part 2 of 2). 1998–99 Land Cruiser

N·m (kgf·cm, ft·lbf) : Specified torque

TY9149800046020X

10. Remove steering column as follows:
    a. Remove lower lefthand finish panel.
    b. Remove brake pedal return spring.
    c. Place alignment marks on No. 2 universal joint assembly and No. 2 intermediate shaft assembly.
    d. Remove "A" bolt, **Fig. 21.**
    e. Place alignment marks on No. 2 intermediate shaft assembly and control valve shaft.
    f. Remove "B" bolt, **Fig. 21.**
    g. Slide No. 2 intermediate shaft assembly and remove.
    h. Remove column hole cover No. 2, **Fig. 22.**
    i. **On models equipped with automatic transmission,** disconnect cable from column shift lever.
    j. **On all models,** disconnect steering column electrical connectors, then remove steering column attaching nuts and steering column.
11. Remove instrument cluster finish panel, then the instrument cluster.
12. Remove integration control panel as follows:
    a. Remove 3 control knobs, then the 5 panel attaching screws.
    b. Remove control panel by pulling in area shown in **Fig. 23.**
    c. Disconnect control panel electrical connectors, then remove panel.
13. Remove radio, then the heater control assembly as follows:
    a. Remove glove compartment door, then the lower No. 2 finish panel.

    b. Remove heater to register duct No. 4.
    c. Disconnect heater control cables, **Fig. 24.**
    d. Remove heater control assembly, then disconnect electrical connectors.
14. Remove passenger's air bag as outlined under "Air Bag System."
15. Remove lower center cover, then the lower instrument cover.
16. **On models equipped with rear console box,** remove rear console box.
17. **On all models,** remove nut from center of instrument cluster opening in instrument panel.
18. Disconnect remaining electrical connectors, then remove instrument panel.
19. Reverse procedure to install.

T100

1. Disarm anti-theft system as outlined under "Precautions."
2. Remove pillar garnish, scuff plate and cowl side trim.
3. Remove steering wheel and steering column covers.
4. Remove hood release lever, lower finish panels, lower center cover and glove compartment door, **Fig. 25.**
5. Remove combination switch and heater control knobs.
6. Remove center cluster finish panel, then remove radio and heater control.
7. Remove center cluster lower finish panel.

8. Remove dash cluster finish panel. Remove heating ducts and registers as necessary.
9. Reverse procedure to install.

4RUNNER

1. Remove steering wheel, **Fig. 26.**
2. Remove cowl side trim and front door scuff plate.
3. Remove hood and fuel tank release lever.
4. Remove lower finish panel.
5. Remove starter switch bezel.
6. Remove No. 1 and No. 2 heater register ducts.
7. Remove four screws and instrument cluster finish panel.
8. Disconnect combination meter connectors and remove combination meter.
9. Remove A/C switch, heater control knob and heater control panel.
10. Remove center cluster finish panel and disconnect A/C control cable.
11. Remove glove compartment door.
12. Remove lower No. 2 finish panel.
13. Remove glove compartment door reinforcement.
14. Remove No. 4 heater to register duct.
15. Remove radio and side bracket.
16. Disconnect air bag connector, then remove instrument panel.
17. Remove defroster nozzle.
18. Remove instrument panel reinforcement No. 1 and No. 2 brace.
19. Remove steering column assembly.
20. Remove center heater to register duct.
21. Remove instrument panel reinforcement.
22. Reverse procedure to install.

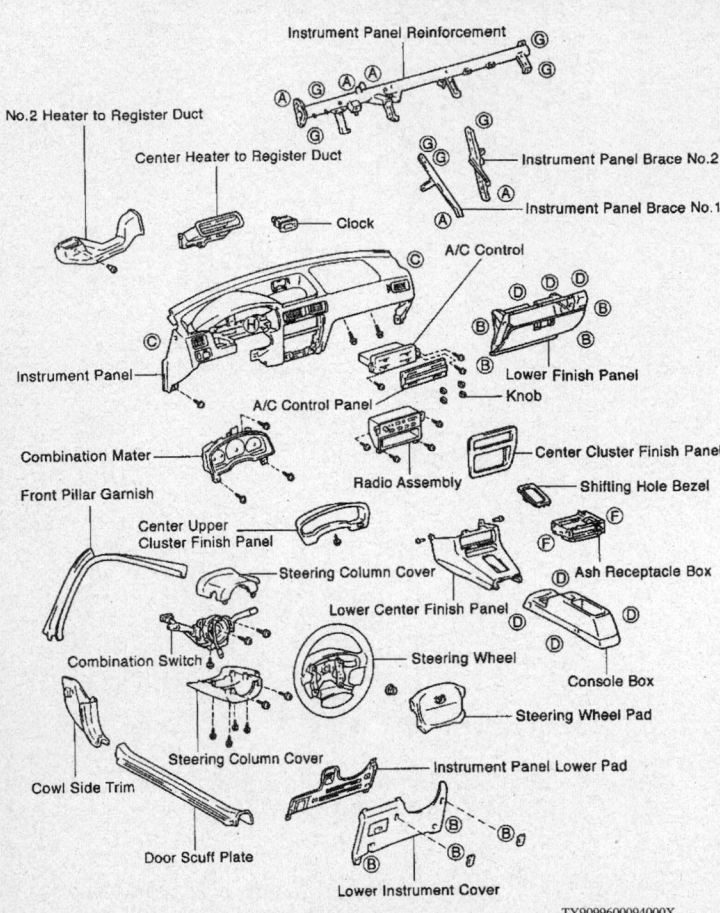

Fig. 11   Exploded view of instrument panel. Paseo

TY9099600094000X

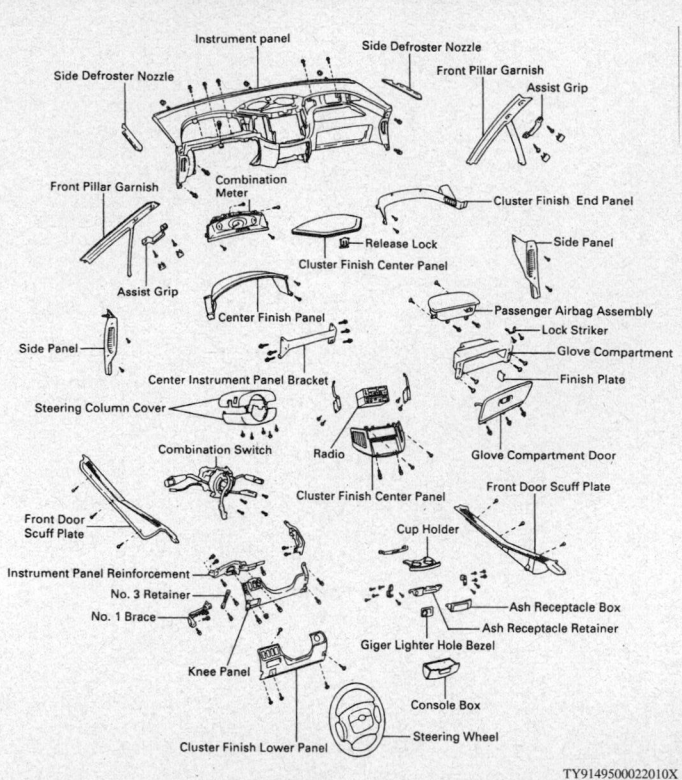

Fig. 12   Exploded view of instrument panel (Part 1 of 2). Previa

TY9149500022010X

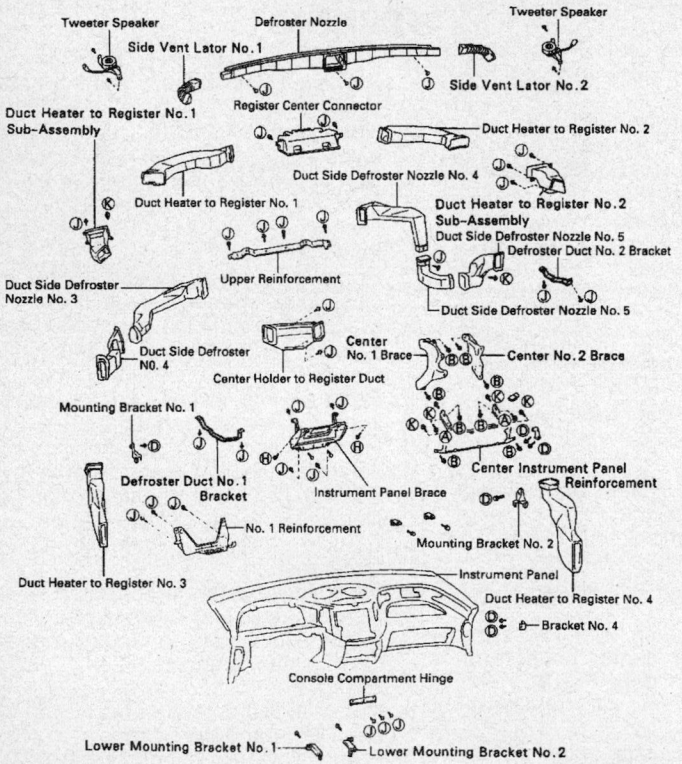

Fig. 12   Exploded view of instrument panel (Part 2 of 2). Previa

TY9149500022020X

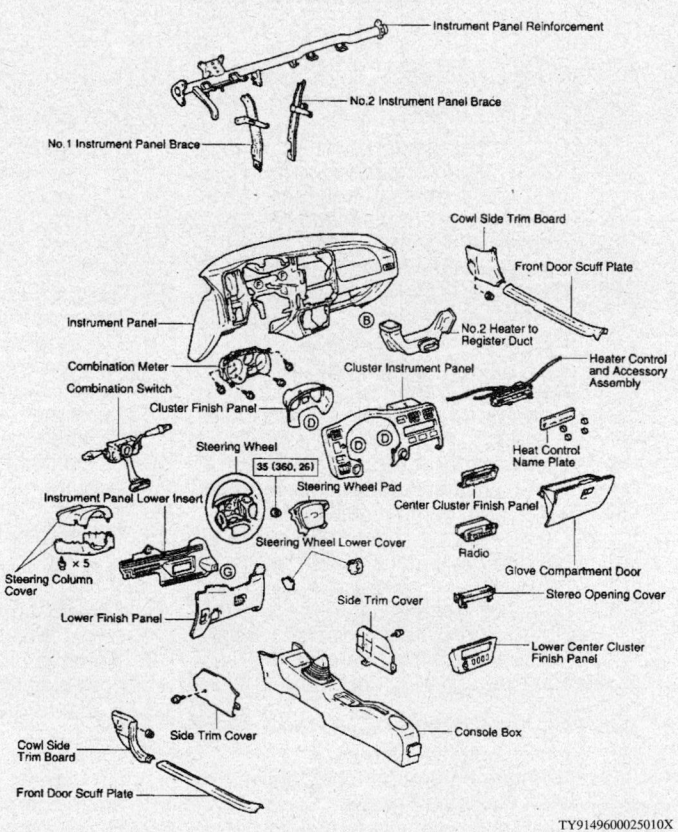

Fig. 13   Exploded view of instrument panel (Part 1 of 2). RAV4

TY9149600025010X

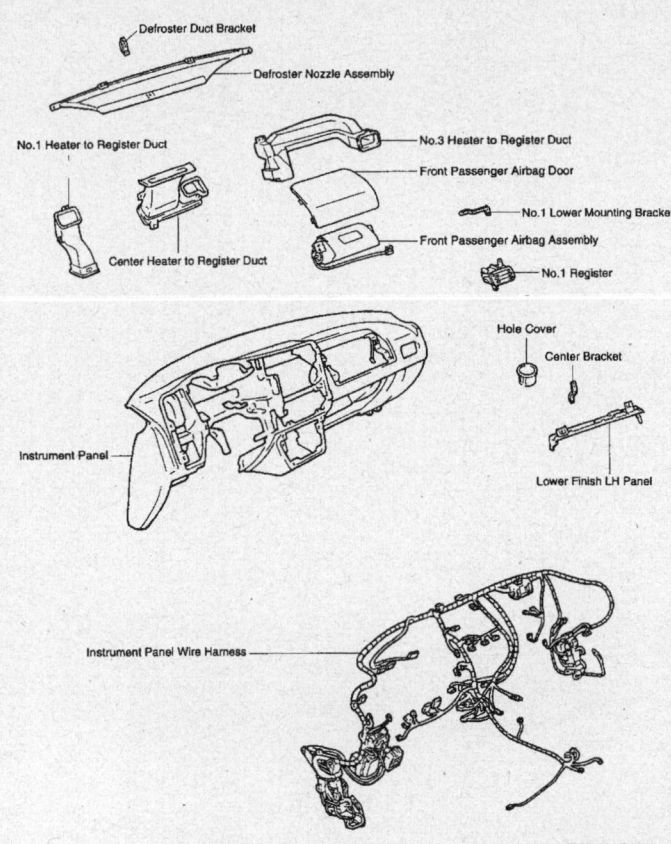

Fig. 13 Exploded view of instrument panel (Part 2 of 2). RAV4

TY9149600025020X

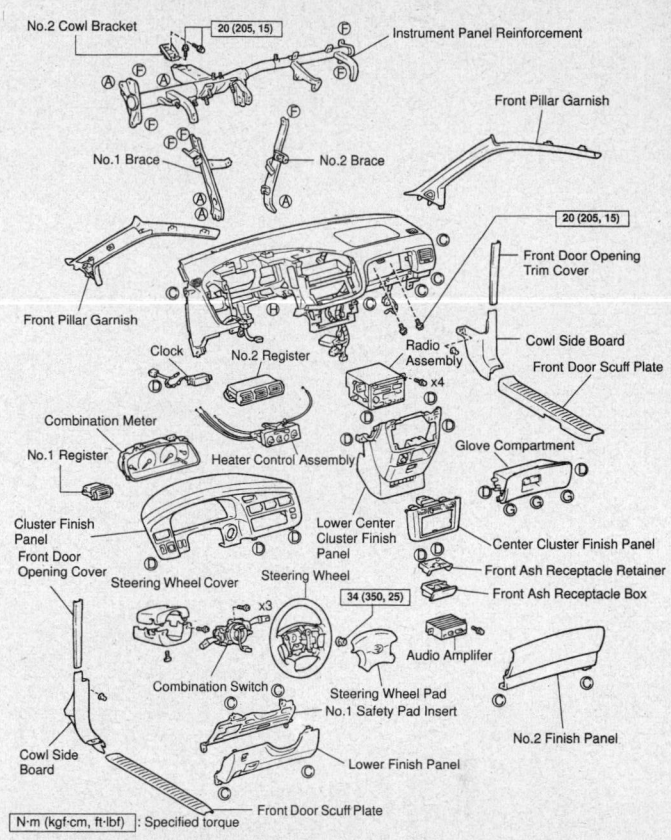

Fig. 14 Exploded view of instrument panel (Part 1 of 2). Sienna

N·m (kgf·cm, ft·lbf) : Specified torque

TY9149900042010X

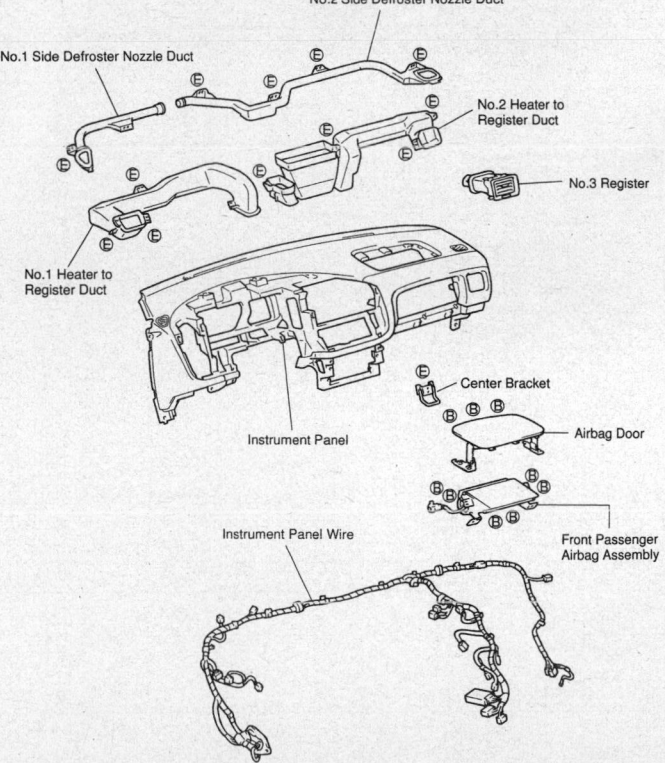

Fig. 14 Exploded view of instrument panel (Part 2 of 2). Sienna

TY9149900042020X

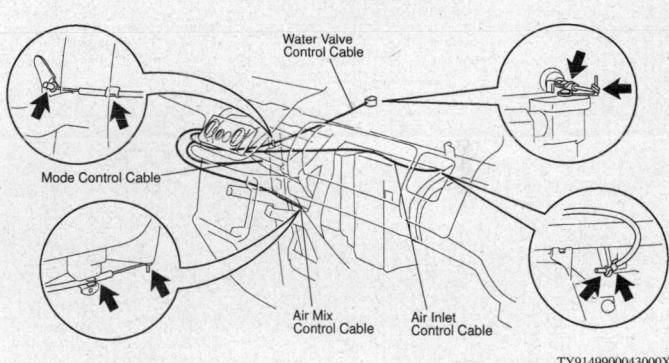

Fig. 15 Heater control cable location. Sienna

TY9149900043000X

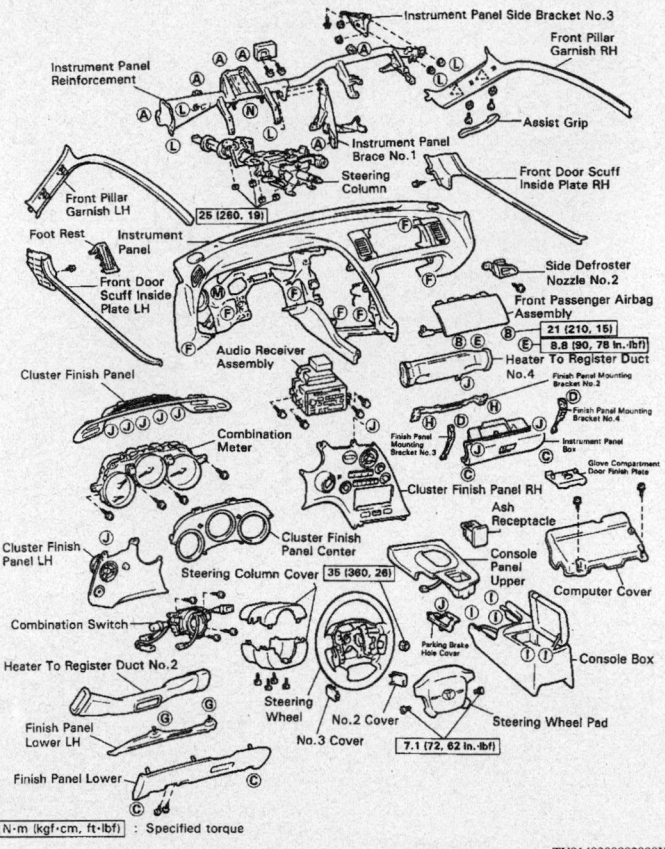

Fig. 16 Exploded view of instrument panel. Supra

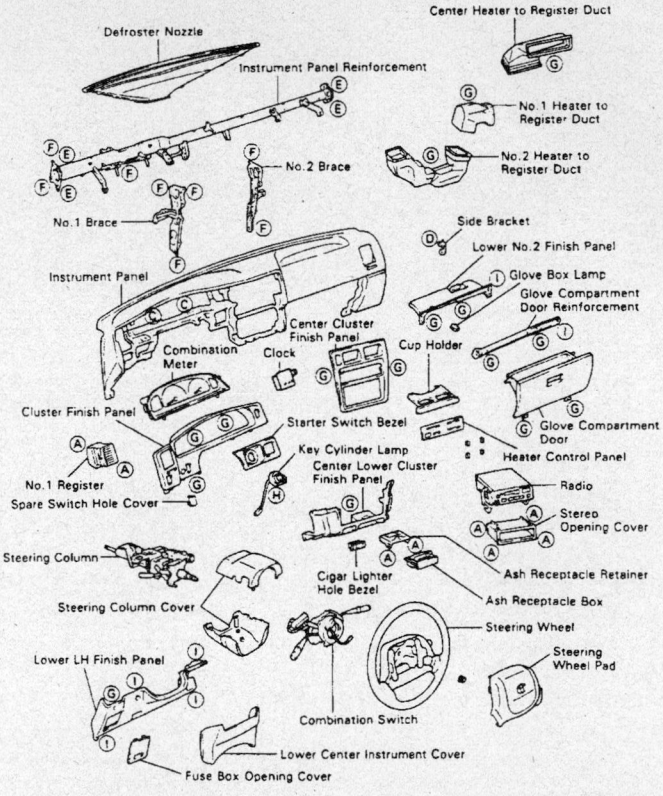

Fig. 17 Exploded view of instrument panel (Part 1 of 2). 1996–97 Tacoma

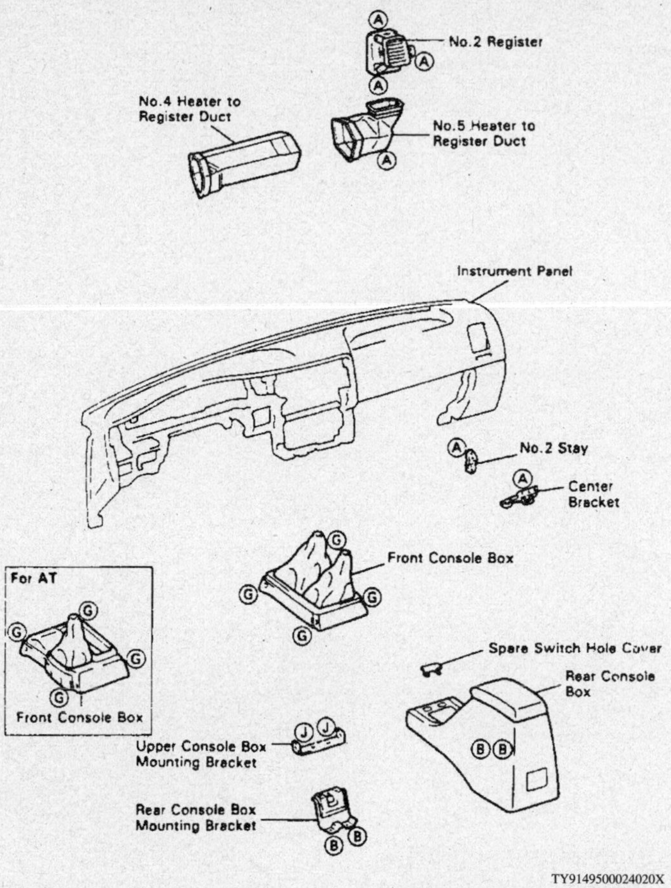

No.4 Heater to Register Duct

No.2 Register

No.5 Heater to Register Duct

Instrument Panel

No.2 Stay

Center Bracket

For AT

Front Console Box

Front Console Box

Upper Console Box Mounting Bracket

Rear Console Box Mounting Bracket

Spare Switch Hole Cover

Rear Console Box

TY9149500024020X

Fig. 17   Exploded view of instrument panel (Part 2 of 2). 1996–97 Tacoma

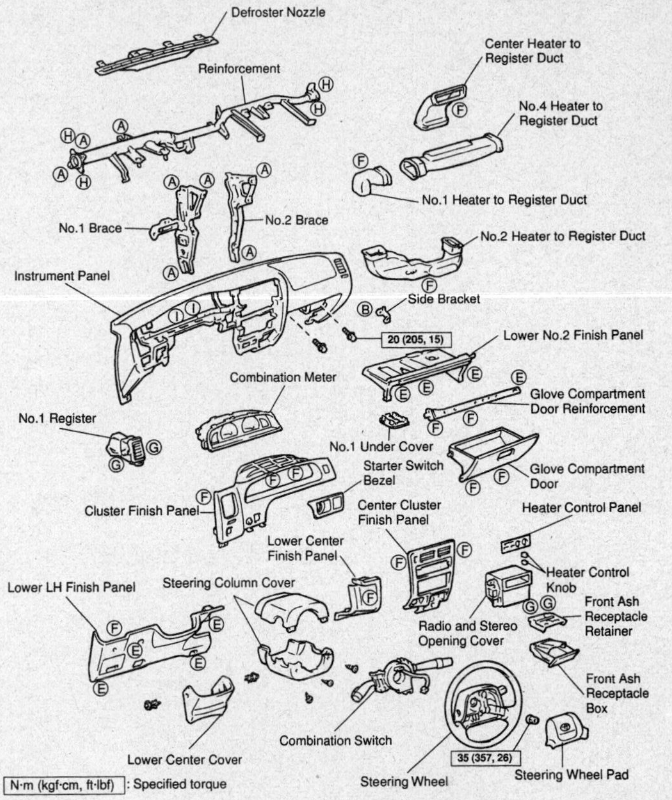

Defroster Nozzle

Reinforcement

Center Heater to Register Duct

No.4 Heater to Register Duct

No.1 Heater to Register Duct

No.2 Heater to Register Duct

No.1 Brace

No.2 Brace

Instrument Panel

Side Bracket

20 (205, 15)

Lower No.2 Finish Panel

Combination Meter

Glove Compartment Door Reinforcement

No.1 Register

Glove Compartment Door

No.1 Under Cover

Starter Switch Bezel

Cluster Finish Panel

Center Cluster Finish Panel

Heater Control Panel

Lower Center Finish Panel

Heater Control Knob

Lower LH Finish Panel

Steering Column Cover

Radio and Stereo Opening Cover

Front Ash Receptacle Retainer

Front Ash Receptacle Box

Lower Center Cover

Combination Switch

35 (357, 26)

N·m (kgf·cm, ft·lbf) : Specified torque

Steering Wheel

Steering Wheel Pad

TY9149900044010X

Fig. 18   Exploded view of instrument panel (Part 1 of 3). 1998–99 Tacoma

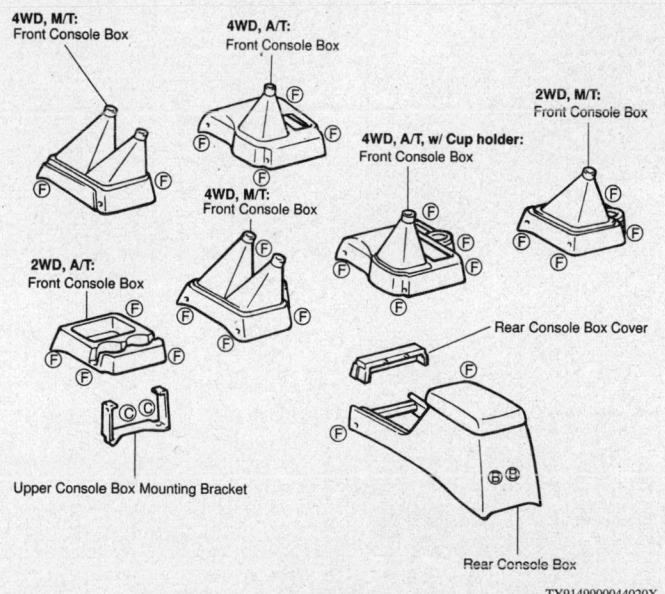

4WD, M/T: Front Console Box

4WD, A/T: Front Console Box

4WD, A/T, w/ Cup holder: Front Console Box

2WD, M/T: Front Console Box

4WD, M/T: Front Console Box

2WD, A/T: Front Console Box

Rear Console Box Cover

Upper Console Box Mounting Bracket

Rear Console Box

TY9149900044020X

Fig. 18   Exploded view of instrument panel (Part 2 of 3). 1998–99 Tacoma

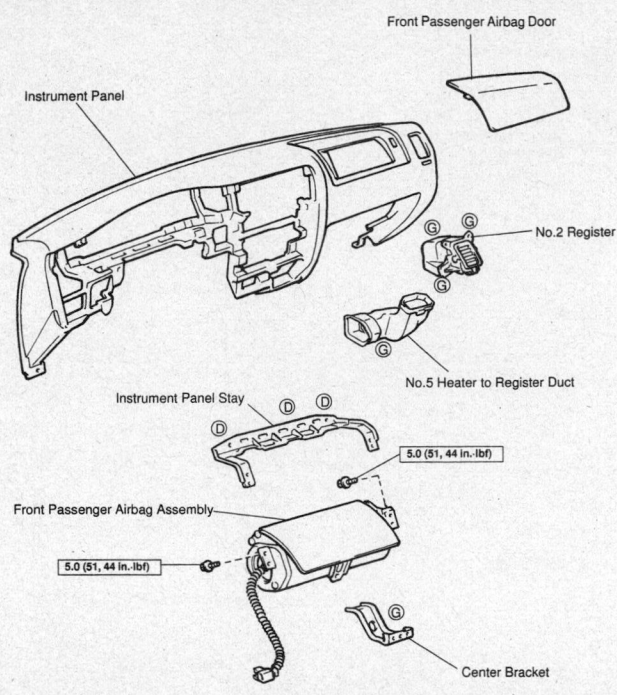

Fig. 18   Exploded view of instrument panel (Part 3 of 3). 1998–99 Tacoma

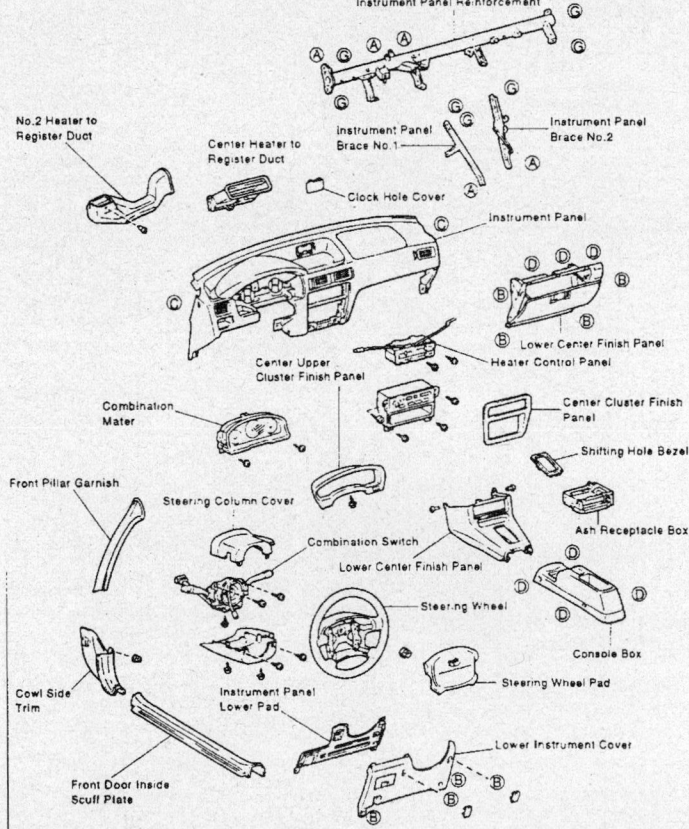

Fig. 19   Exploded view of instrument panel. Tercel

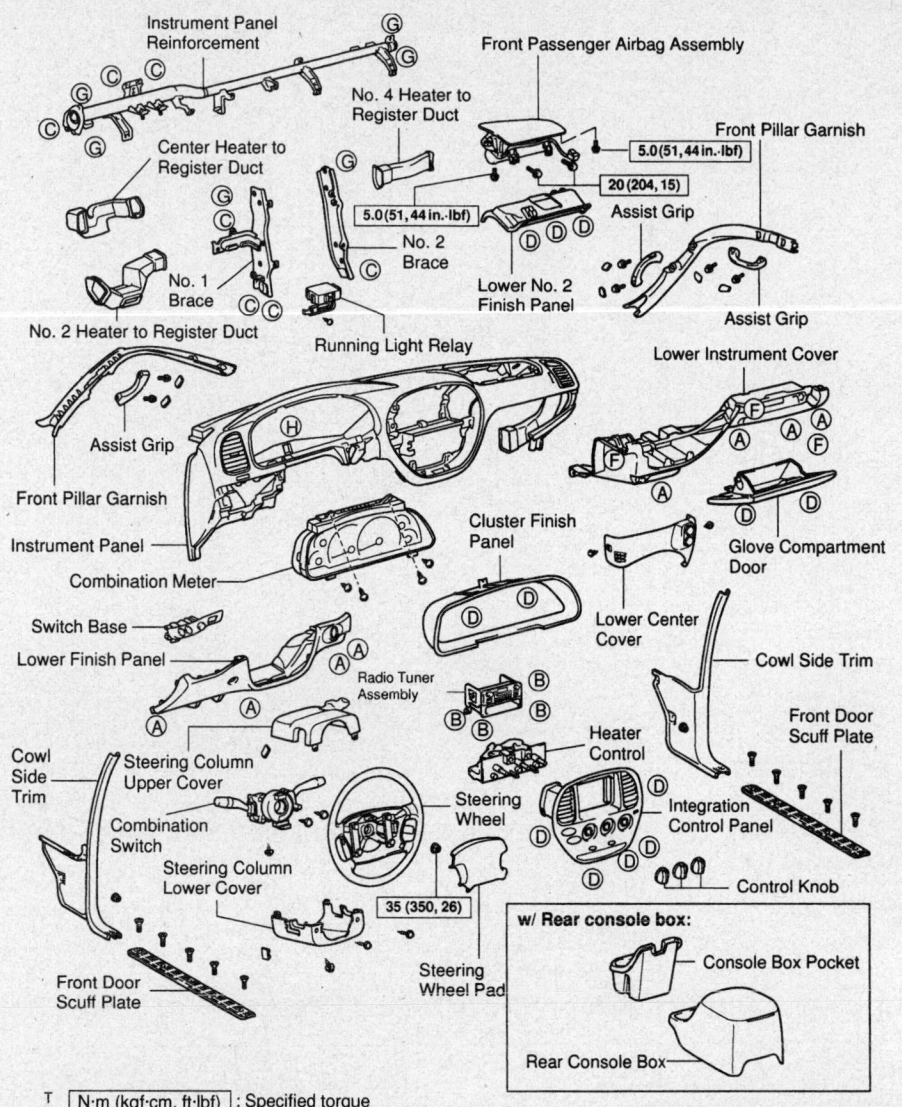

Instrument Panel Reinforcement

No. 4 Heater to Register Duct

Front Passenger Airbag Assembly

Center Heater to Register Duct

Front Pillar Garnish

5.0 (51, 44 in.·lbf)

20 (204, 15)

5.0 (51, 44 in.·lbf)

No. 2 Brace

Assist Grip

No. 2 Brace

No. 1 Brace

Lower No. 2 Finish Panel

Assist Grip

No. 2 Heater to Register Duct

Running Light Relay

Lower Instrument Cover

Assist Grip

Front Pillar Garnish

Instrument Panel

Combination Meter

Cluster Finish Panel

Glove Compartment Door

Switch Base

Lower Finish Panel

Radio Tuner Assembly

Lower Center Cover

Cowl Side Trim

Front Door Scuff Plate

Cowl Side Trim

Steering Column Upper Cover

Combination Switch

Steering Column Lower Cover

Steering Wheel

Heater Control

Integration Control Panel

35 (350, 26)

Control Knob

Front Door Scuff Plate

Steering Wheel Pad

w/ Rear console box:

Console Box Pocket

Rear Console Box

T N·m (kgf·cm, ft·lbf) : Specified torque

TY9149900034000X

Fig. 20   Exploded view of instrument panel. Tundra

A Matchmarks

B

Matchmarks

TY9149900035000X

Fig. 21   Steering column bolt locations. Tundra

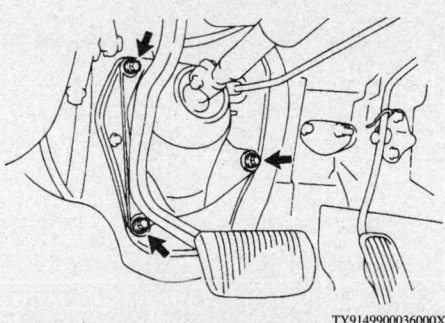

TY9149900036000X

Fig. 22   Column cover removal. Tundra

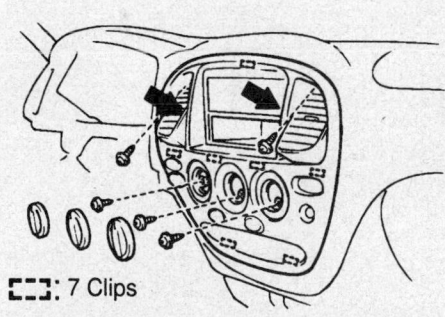

⊏⊐: 7 Clips

TY9149900037000X

Fig. 23   Integration control panel replacement. Tundra

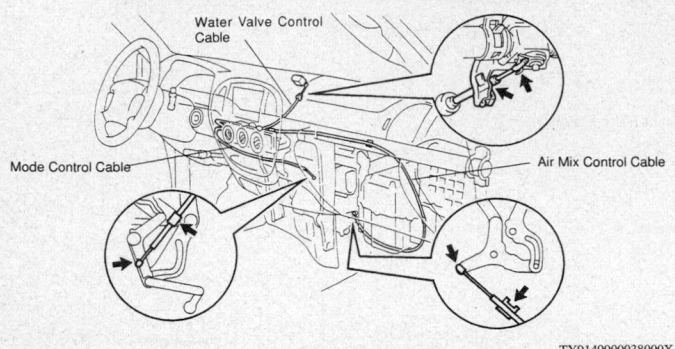

Fig. 24   Heater control cable locations. Tundra

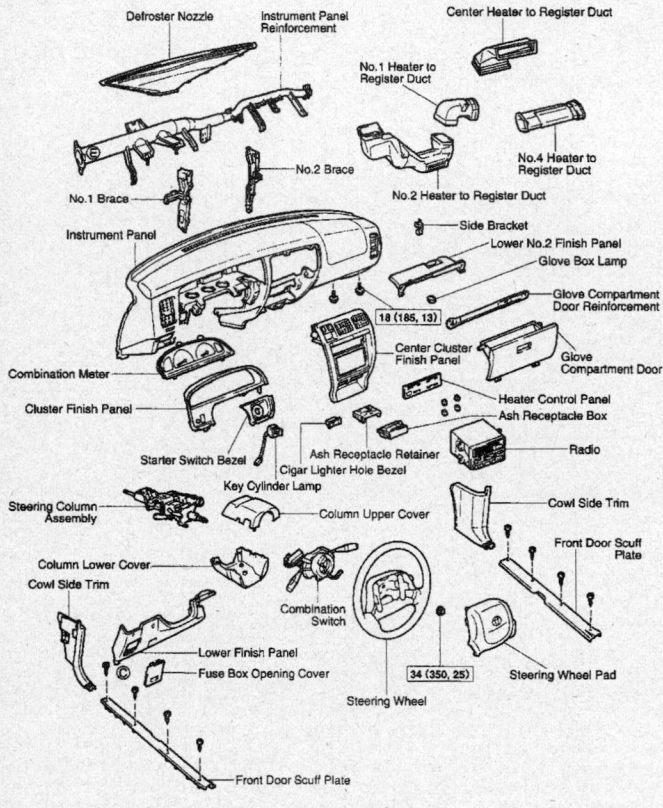

Fig. 26   Exploded view of instrument panel (Part 1 of 2). 4Runner

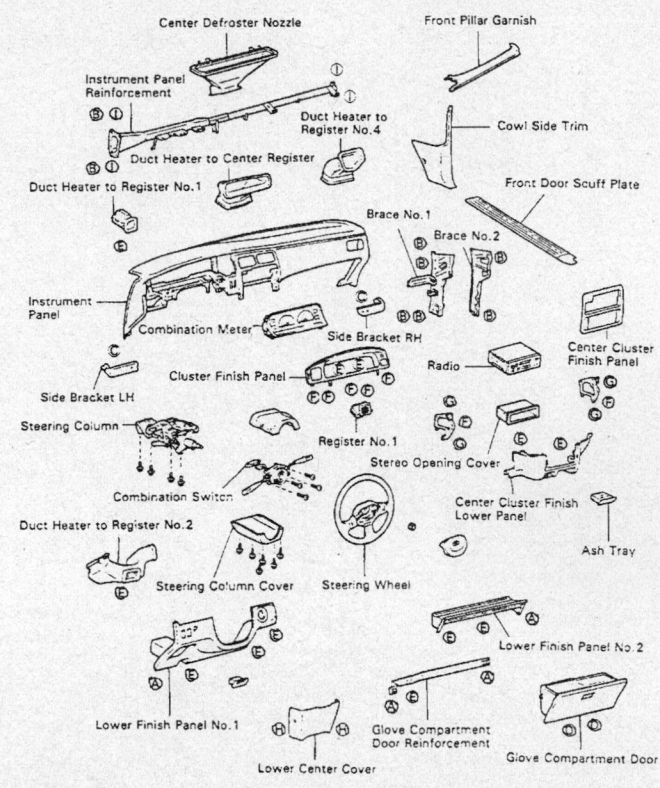

Fig. 25   Exploded view of instrument panel. T100

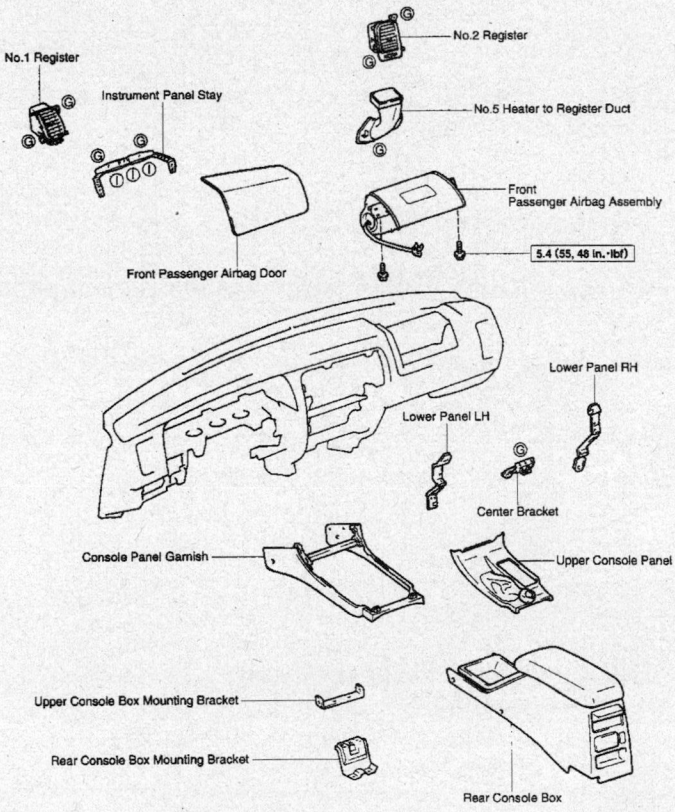

Fig. 26   Exploded view of instrument panel (Part 2 of 2). 4Runner

Steering Columns

NOTE: On Air Bag Equipped Models, Refer To "Air Bag System Precautions" Located In The Front Of This Manual For System Disarming & Arming Procedures.

INDEX

PRECAUTIONS

AIR BAG SYSTEMS

Refer to "Air Bag System Precautions" in the front of this manual for system disarming & arming procedures.

BATTERY GROUND CABLE

Prior to service, disconnect battery ground cable and isolate as required.

AUDIO CODED ANTI-THEFT SYSTEM

Some models are equipped with an audio coded anti-theft system that will disable the radio when the battery cable is disconnected. The system can be identified by the "ANTI-THEFT SYSTEM" on the cassette tape lid. Obtain 3 digit customer code for input. Reset system after service as follows:

1. Obtain 3 digit audio anti-theft code.
2. Depress 1 (PROG) while depressing righthand side of TUNE SEEK button, - - - will appear in tape operation display.
3. To enter the first digit, depress 1 (PROG) button repeatedly until the number of times depressed equals the first digit beginning with zero (depress the 1 button six times if the first digit if five).
4. To enter second digit, depress 2 (APS) button repeatedly until the number of times depressed equals the second digit beginning with zero.
5. To enter third digit, depress 3 (RPT) button repeatedly until the number of times depressed equals the third digit beginning with zero.
6. If - - - is displayed during code input, repeat procedure.
7. When code appears in display, depress and hold SCAN button until SEC appears.
8. When SEC disappears audio system should be operative.
9. If Err is displayed, repeat procedure.

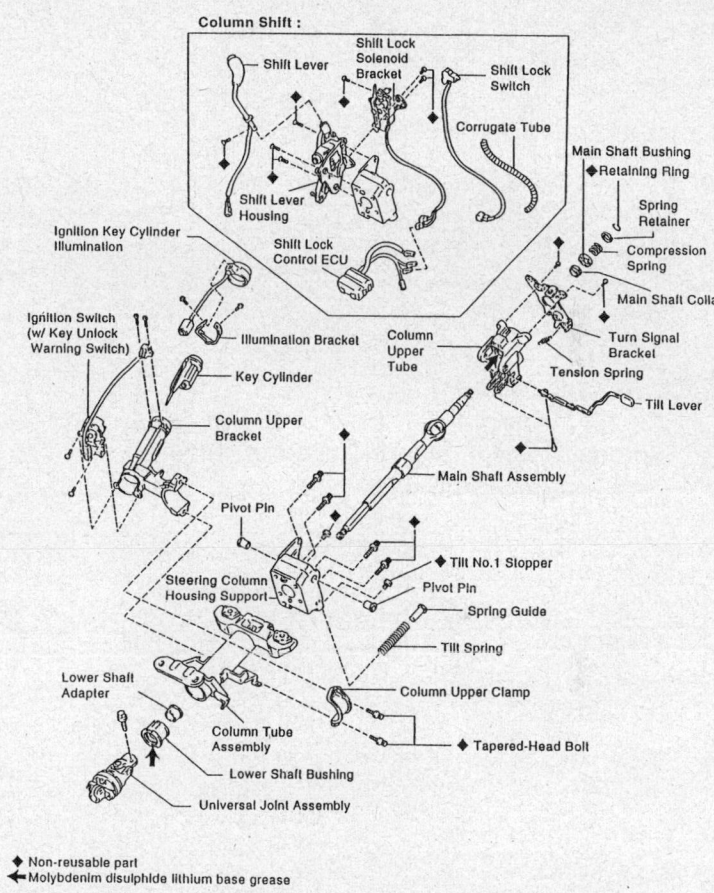

Fig. 1   Exploded view of steering column. 1996–97 Avalon

Attempting to input code more than nine times may permanently disable audio system.

STEERING COLUMN SERVICE

On models equipped with air bags and/ or anti-theft system, disarm systems as outlined under "Precautions." For steering column service, refer to **Figs. 1 through 29.**

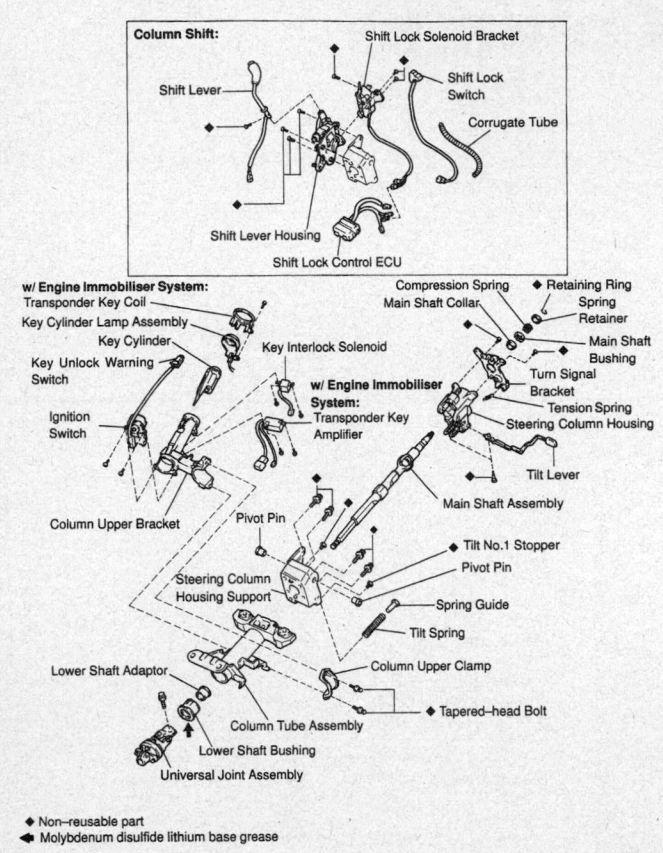

Fig. 2   Exploded view of steering column. 1998–99 Avalon

◆ Non-reusable part
◄ Molybdenum disulfide lithium base grease

TY6049800031000X

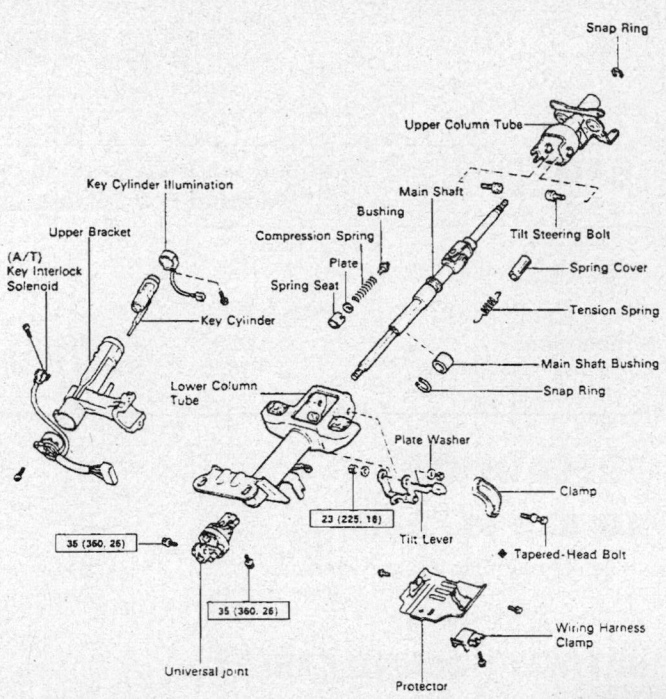

Fig. 3   Exploded view of steering column. 1996 Camry

TY6049200002000X

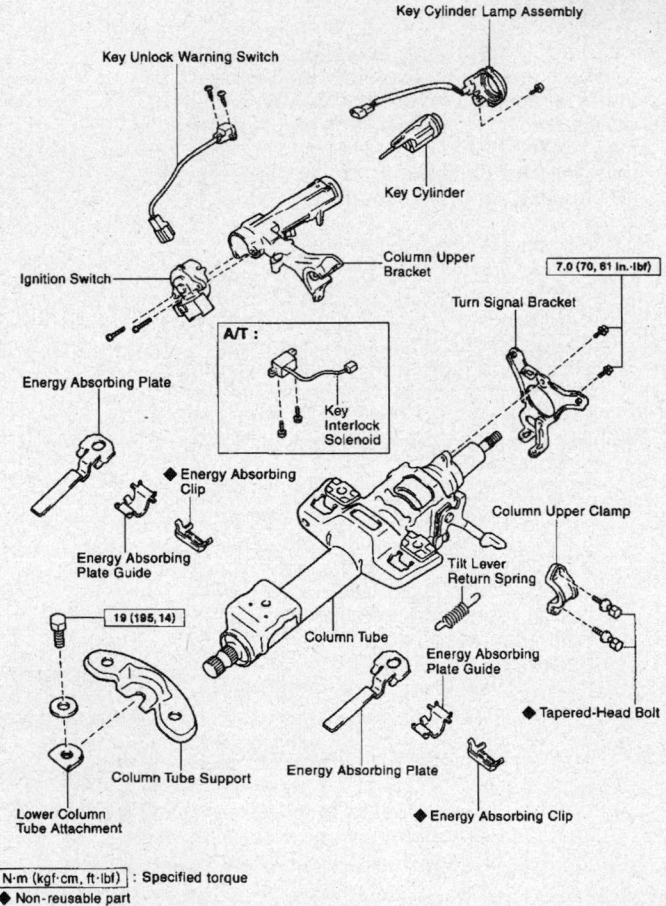

N·m (kgf·cm, ft·lbf) : Specified torque
◆ Non-reusable part

TY6049700027000X

Fig. 4   Exploded view of steering column. 1997 Camry

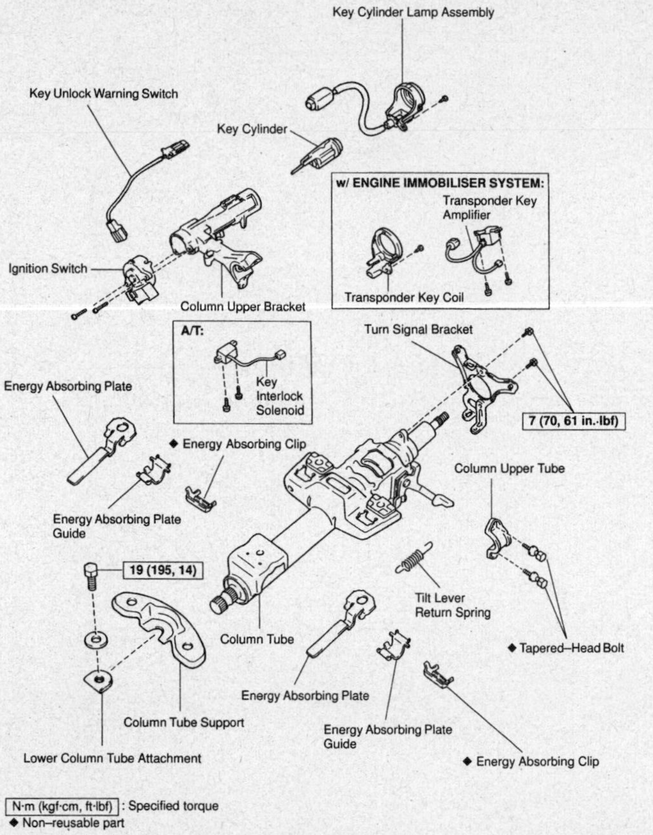

Fig. 5   Exploded view of steering column. Camry Solara & 1998–99 Camry

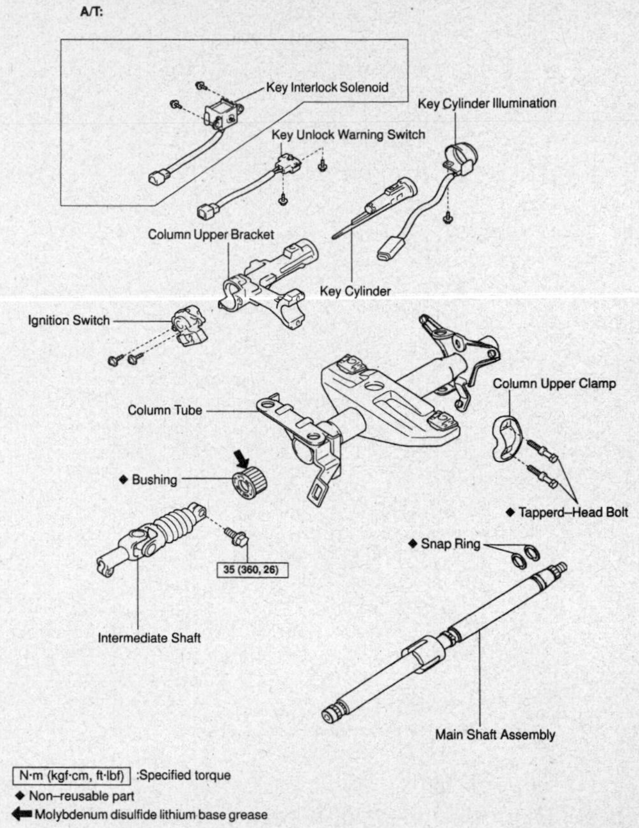

Fig. 6   Exploded view of steering column. Celica less tilt column

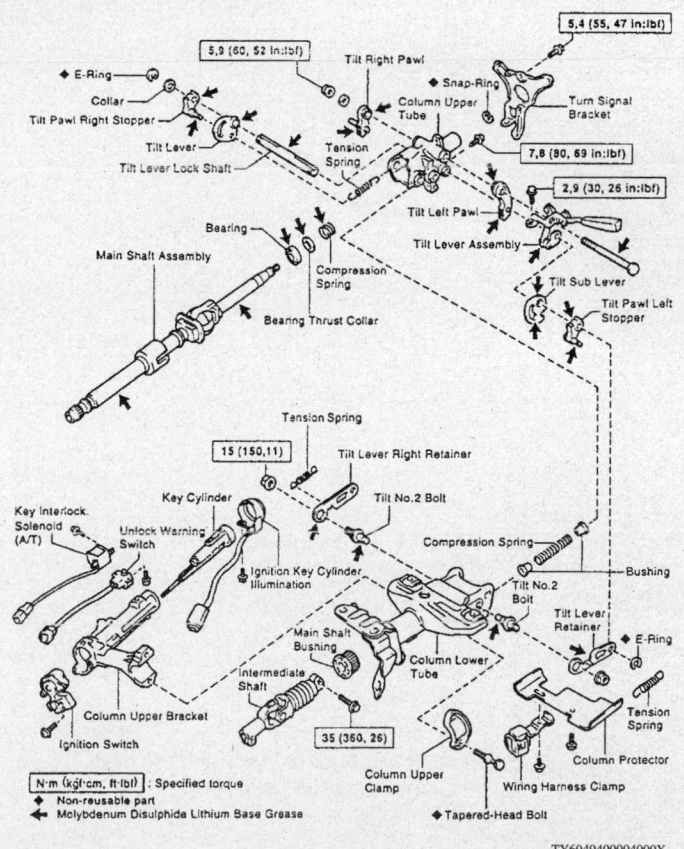

Fig. 7   Exploded view of steering column. Celica w/tilt column

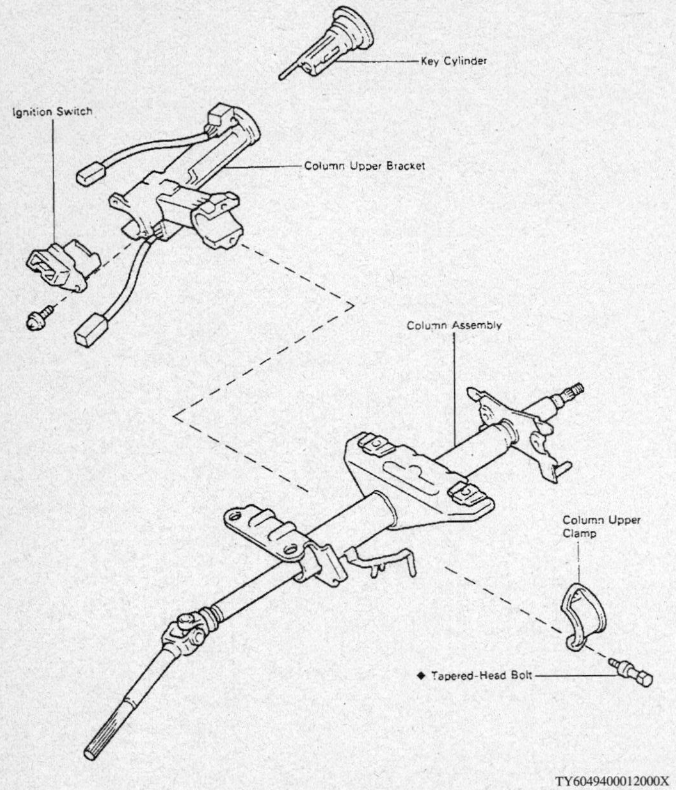

Key Cylinder

Ignition Switch

Column Upper Bracket

Column Assembly

Column Upper Clamp

◆ Tapered-Head Bolt

TY6049400012000X

Fig. 8   Exploded view of steering column (Nastech). Corolla less tilt column

Key Cylinder

Column Upper Clamp

Column Tube

Ignition Switch

Column Upper Clamp

◆ Tapered-Head Bolt

Main Shaft Bushing

Main Shaft Assembly

◆ Snap Ring

TY6049400013000X

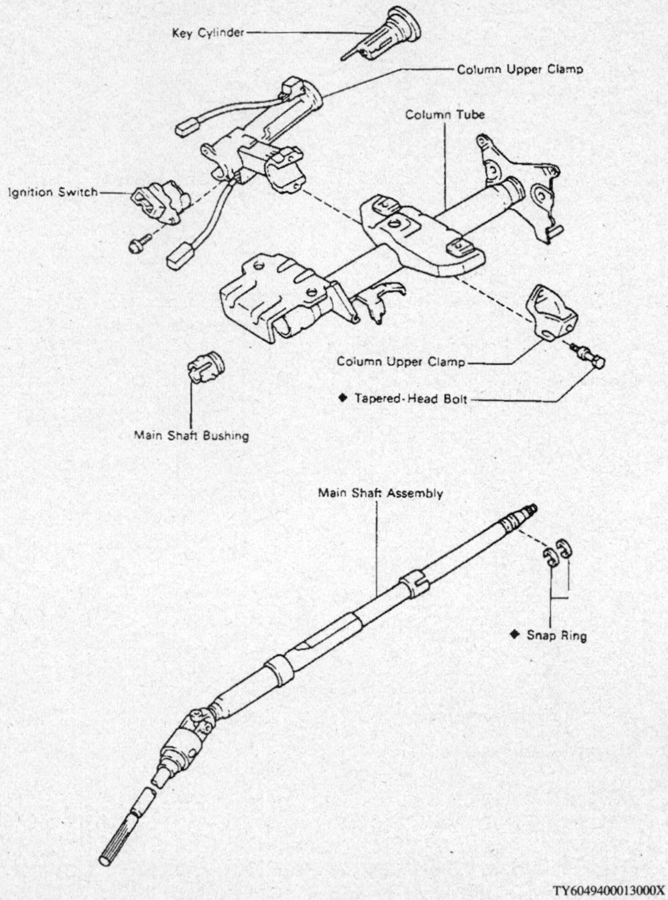

Fig. 9   Exploded view of steering column (Toyota). Corolla less tilt column

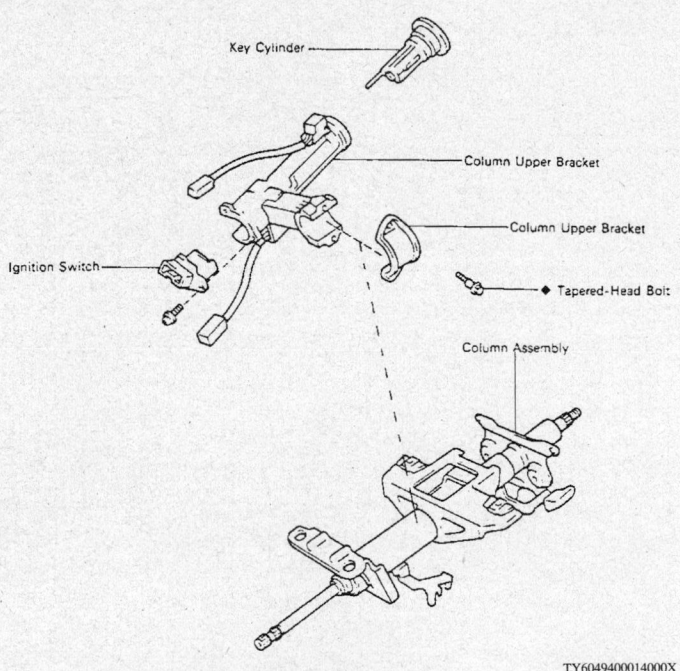

Key Cylinder

Column Upper Bracket

Column Upper Bracket

◆ Tapered-Head Bolt

Ignition Switch

Column Assembly

TY6049400014000X

Fig. 10   Exploded view of steering column. 1996 Corolla w/tilt column

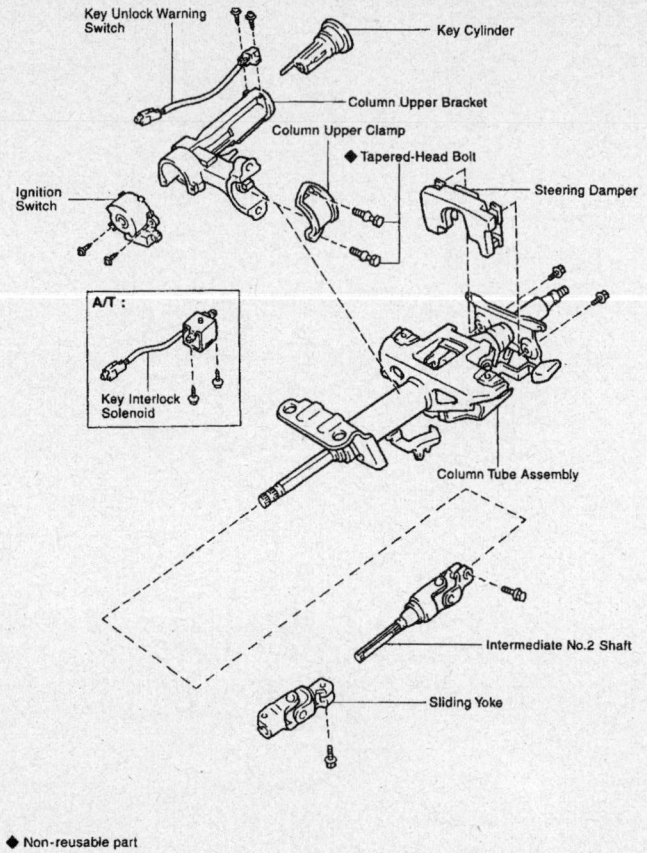

Key Unlock Warning Switch

Key Cylinder

Column Upper Bracket

Column Upper Clamp

◆ Tapered-Head Bolt

Steering Damper

Ignition Switch

A/T :

Key Interlock Solenoid

Column Tube Assembly

Intermediate No.2 Shaft

Sliding Yoke

◆ Non-reusable part

TY6049700028000X

Fig. 11 Exploded view of steering column. 1997–99 Corolla w/tilt column

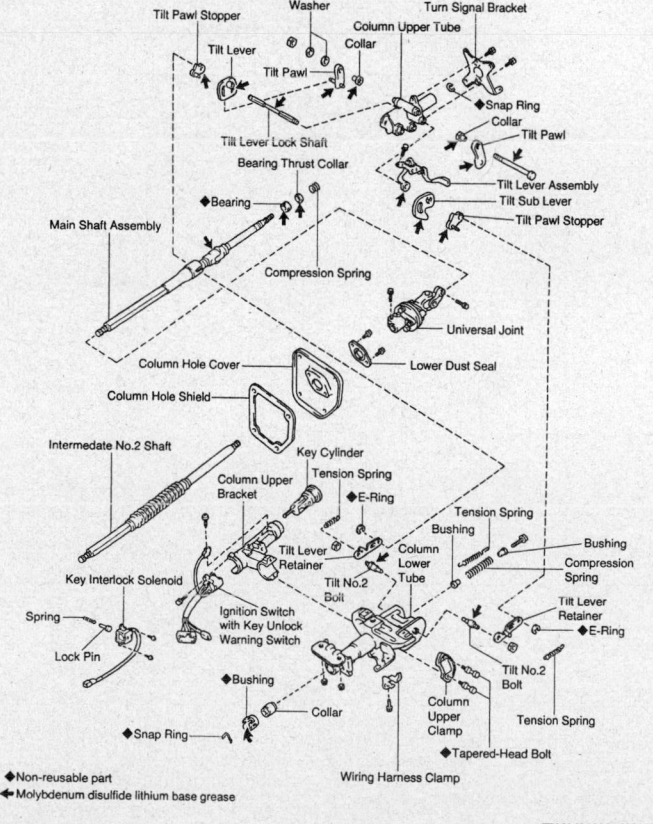

Tilt Pawl Stopper

Washer

Turn Signal Bracket

Tilt Lever

Collar

Column Upper Tube

Tilt Pawl

◆Snap Ring

Collar

Tilt Pawl

Tilt Lever Lock Shaft

Bearing Thrust Collar

Tilt Lever Assembly

Tilt Sub Lever

Tilt Pawl Stopper

Main Shaft Assembly

◆Bearing

Compression Spring

Universal Joint

Column Hole Cover

Lower Dust Seal

Column Hole Shield

Intermediate No.2 Shaft

Key Cylinder

Tension Spring

Column Upper Bracket

◆E-Ring

Tension Spring

Bushing

Bushing

Compression Spring

Key Interlock Solenoid

Tilt Lever Retainer

Column Lower Tube

Spring

Tilt No.2 Bolt

Tilt Lever Retainer

Lock Pin

◆E-Ring

Ignition Switch with Key Unlock Warning Switch

Tilt No.2 Bolt

◆Bushing

Tension Spring

Collar

Column Upper Clamp

◆Snap Ring

◆Tapered-Head Bolt

Wiring Harness Clamp

◆Non-reusable part
◄ Molybdenum disulfide lithium base grease

TY6049100016000X

Fig. 12 Exploded view of steering column. 1996–97 Land Cruiser

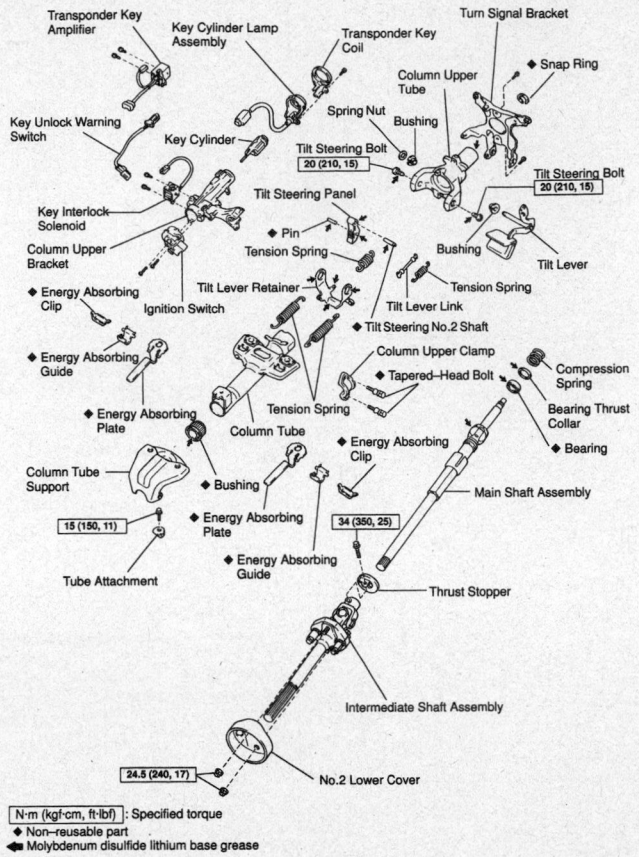

Fig. 13   Exploded view of steering column. 1998–99 Land Cruiser

TY6049800038000X

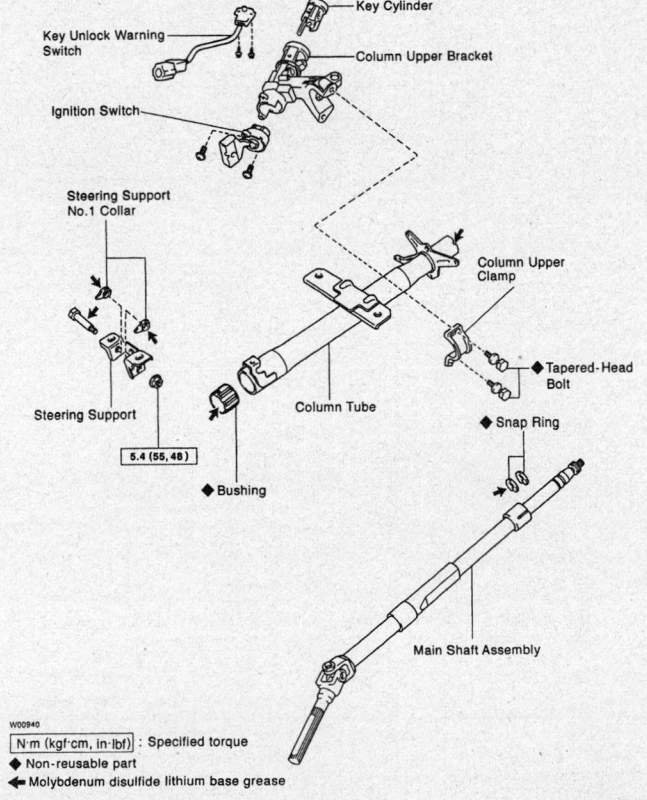

W00940

Fig. 14   Exploded view of steering column. 1996 Paseo

TY6049100018000A

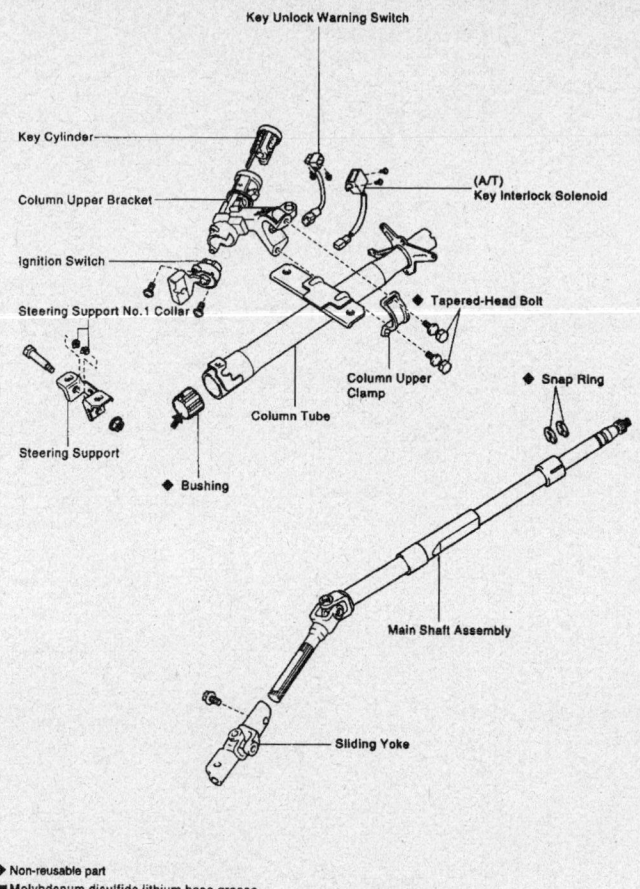

Fig. 15 Exploded view of steering column. 1997 Paseo

◆ Non-reusable part
◆— Molybdenum disulfide lithium base grease

TY6049700029000X

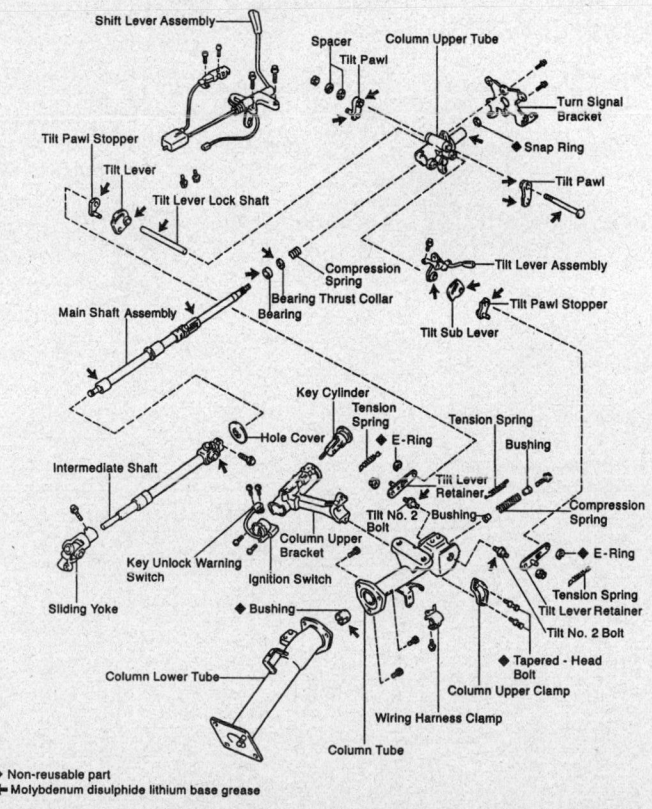

Fig. 16 Exploded view of steering column. Previa

◆ Non-reusable part
◆— Molybdenum disulphide lithium base grease

TY6049400022000X

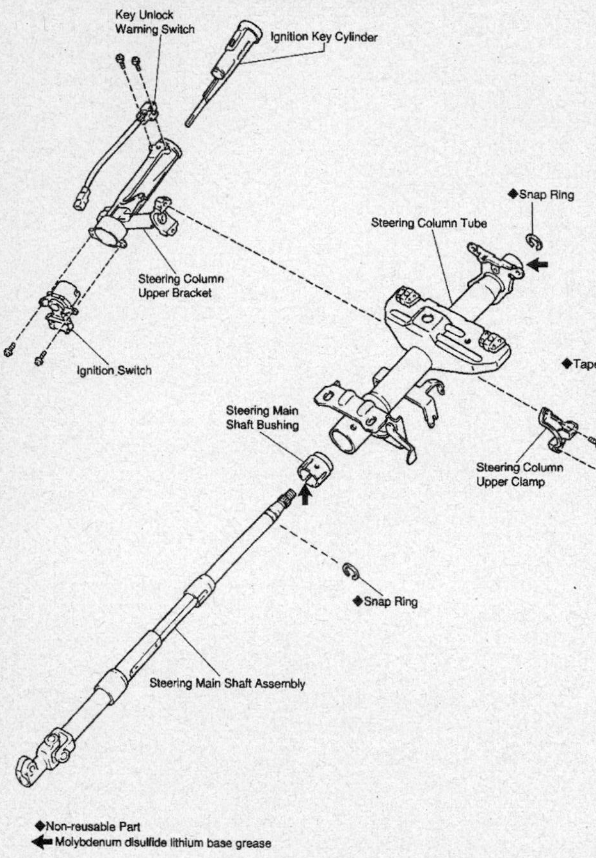

Key Unlock Warning Switch

Ignition Key Cylinder

◆ Snap Ring

Steering Column Tube

Steering Column Upper Bracket

Ignition Switch

Steering Main Shaft Bushing

◆ Taperd-Head Bolt

Steering Column Upper Clamp

◆ Snap Ring

Steering Main Shaft Assembly

◆ Non-reusable Part
◄ Molybdenum disulfide lithium base grease

TY6049600024000X

Fig. 17 Exploded view of steering column. RAV4 less tilt column

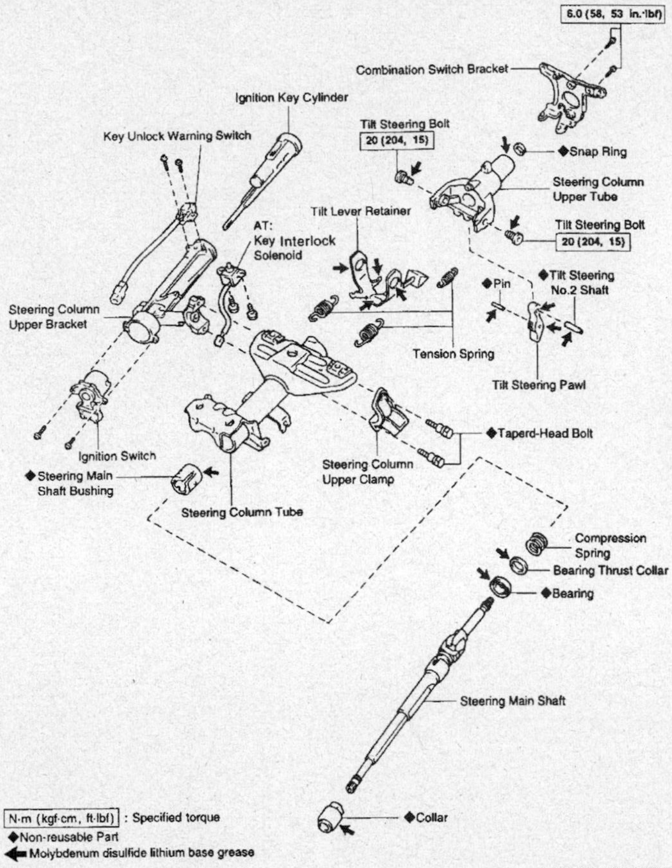

6.0 (58, 53 in.·lbf)

Combination Switch Bracket

Ignition Key Cylinder

Key Unlock Warning Switch

Tilt Steering Bolt
20 (204, 15)

◆ Snap Ring

Steering Column Upper Tube

Tilt Steering Bolt
20 (204, 15)

AT: Key Interlock Solenoid

Tilt Lever Retainer

◆ Pin

◆ Tilt Steering No.2 Shaft

Steering Column Upper Bracket

Tension Spring

Tilt Steering Pawl

Ignition Switch

◆ Taperd-Head Bolt

◆ Steering Main Shaft Bushing

Steering Column Upper Clamp

Steering Column Tube

Compression Spring

Bearing Thrust Collar

◆ Bearing

Steering Main Shaft

◆ Collar

N·m (kgf·cm, ft·lbf) : Specified torque
◆ Non-reusable Part
◄ Molybdenum disulfide lithium base grease

TY6049700030000X

Fig. 18 Exploded view of steering column. RAV4 w/tilt column

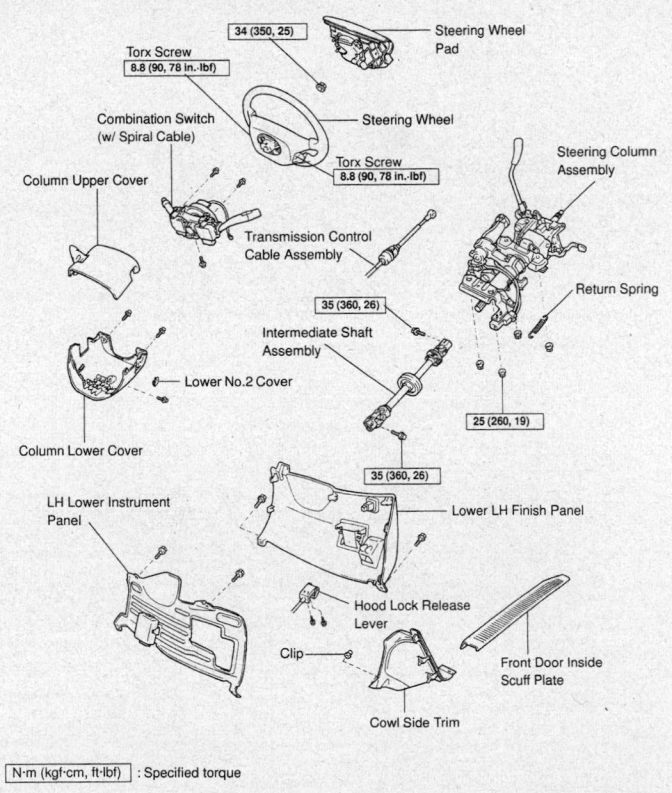

34 (350, 25)

Steering Wheel Pad

Torx Screw
8.8 (90, 78 in.·lbf)

Steering Wheel

Combination Switch (w/ Spiral Cable)

Column Upper Cover

Torx Screw
8.8 (90, 78 in.·lbf)

Steering Column Assembly

Transmission Control Cable Assembly

Return Spring

35 (360, 26)

Intermediate Shaft Assembly

25 (260, 19)

Lower No.2 Cover

Column Lower Cover

35 (360, 26)

LH Lower Instrument Panel

Lower LH Finish Panel

Hood Lock Release Lever

Clip

Front Door Inside Scuff Plate

Cowl Side Trim

N·m (kgf·cm, ft·lbf) : Specified torque

TY6049900036010X

Fig. 19 Exploded view of steering column (Part 1 of 2). Sienna

---

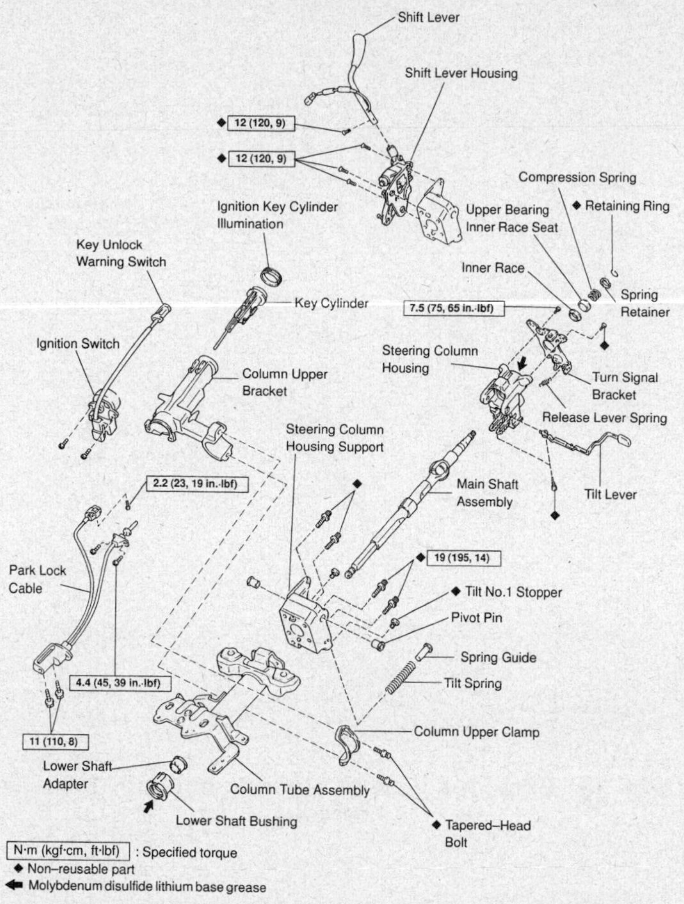

Fig. 19 Shift Lever
Shift Lever Housing
12 (120, 9)
12 (120, 9)
Ignition Key Cylinder Illumination
Compression Spring
◆ Retaining Ring
Upper Bearing Inner Race Seat
Key Unlock Warning Switch
Key Cylinder
Inner Race
Spring Retainer
Ignition Switch
7.5 (75, 65 in.·lbf)
Column Upper Bracket
Steering Column Housing
Turn Signal Bracket
Release Lever Spring
Steering Column Housing Support
Tilt Lever
2.2 (23, 19 in.·lbf)
Main Shaft Assembly
◆ Tilt No.1 Stopper
Park Lock Cable
◆ 19 (195, 14)
Pivot Pin
Spring Guide
Tilt Spring
4.4 (45, 39 in.·lbf)
Column Upper Clamp
11 (110, 8)
Lower Shaft Adapter
Column Tube Assembly
Lower Shaft Bushing
◆ Tapered-Head Bolt

N·m (kgf·cm, ft·lbf) : Specified torque
◆ Non-reusable part
◀ Molybdenum disulfide lithium base grease

TY6049900036020X

Fig. 19   Exploded view of steering column (Part 2 of 2). Sienna

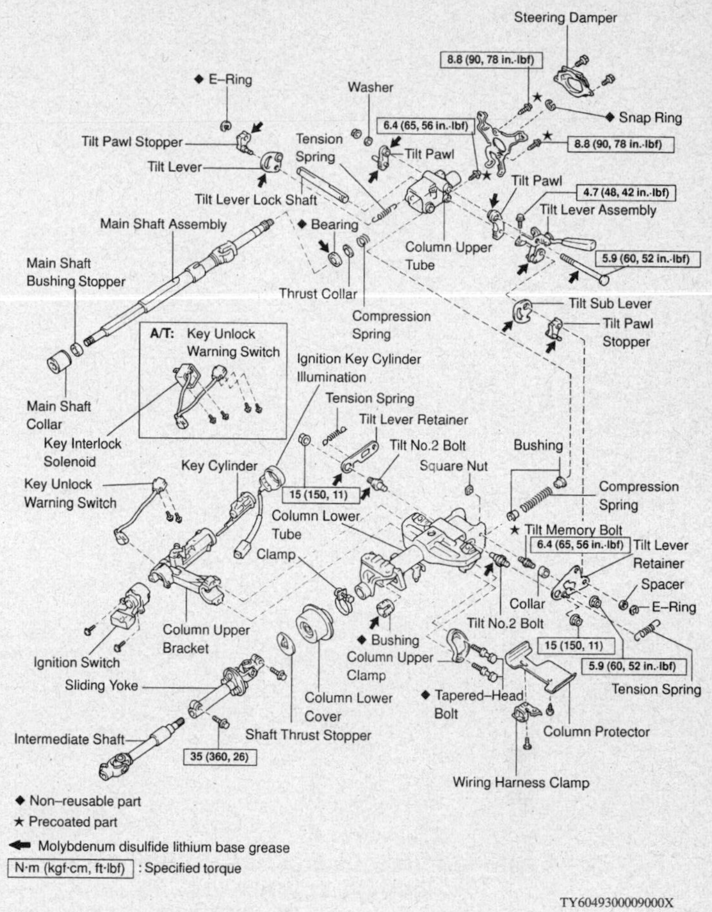

◆ E-Ring
Steering Damper
8.8 (90, 78 in.·lbf)
Washer
6.4 (65, 56 in.·lbf)
Tilt Pawl Stopper
Tension Spring
Tilt Pawl
◆ Snap Ring
Tilt Lever
8.8 (90, 78 in.·lbf)
Tilt Lever Lock Shaft
Main Shaft Assembly
Tilt Pawl
4.7 (48, 42 in.·lbf)
Main Shaft Bushing Stopper
◆ Bearing
Tilt Lever Assembly
Column Upper Tube
5.9 (60, 52 in.·lbf)
Thrust Collar
A/T: Key Unlock Warning Switch
Compression Spring
Tilt Sub Lever
Tilt Pawl Stopper
Main Shaft Collar
Ignition Key Cylinder Illumination
Tension Spring
Key Interlock Solenoid
Tilt Lever Retainer
Bushing
Key Cylinder
Key Unlock Warning Switch
Tilt No.2 Bolt
Square Nut
Compression Spring
15 (150, 11)
★ Tilt Memory Bolt
Column Lower Tube Clamp
6.4 (65, 56 in.·lbf)
Tilt Lever Retainer
Ignition Switch
Column Upper Bracket
Collar
Spacer
◆ E-Ring
Sliding Yoke
◆ Bushing
Tilt No.2 Bolt
15 (150, 11)
Column Column Upper Clamp
5.9 (60, 52 in.·lbf)
Intermediate Shaft
Column Lower Cover
◆ Tapered-Head Bolt
Tension Spring
35 (360, 26)
Shaft Thrust Stopper
Column Protector
Wiring Harness Clamp

◆ Non-reusable part
★ Precoated part
◀ Molybdenum disulfide lithium base grease
N·m (kgf·cm, ft·lbf) : Specified torque

TY6049300009000X

Fig. 20   Exploded view of steering column. Supra

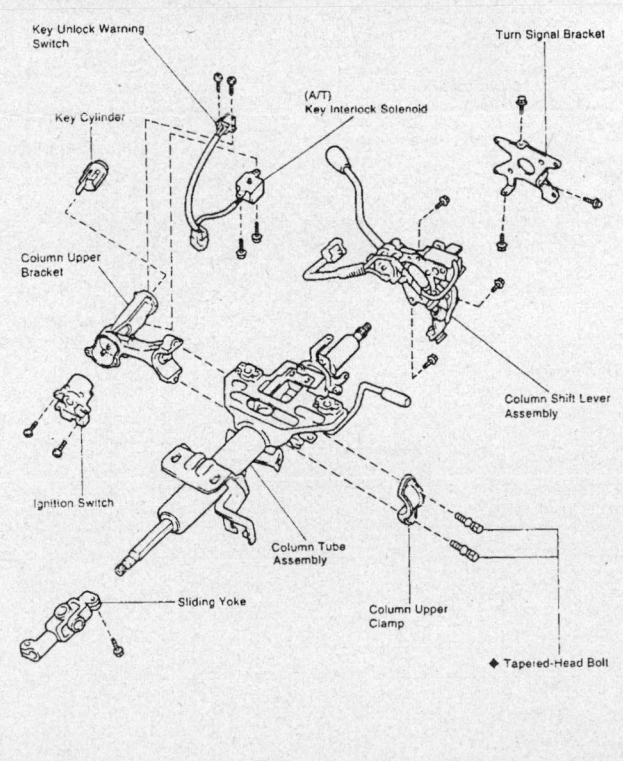

Key Unlock Warning Switch
Turn Signal Bracket
Key Cylinder
(A/T) Key Interlock Solenoid
Column Upper Bracket
Column Shift Lever Assembly
Ignition Switch
Column Tube Assembly
Sliding Yoke
Column Upper Clamp
◆ Tapered-Head Bolt

◆ Non-reusable part

TY6049500004000X

Fig. 21   Exploded view of steering column. Tacoma w/tilt column

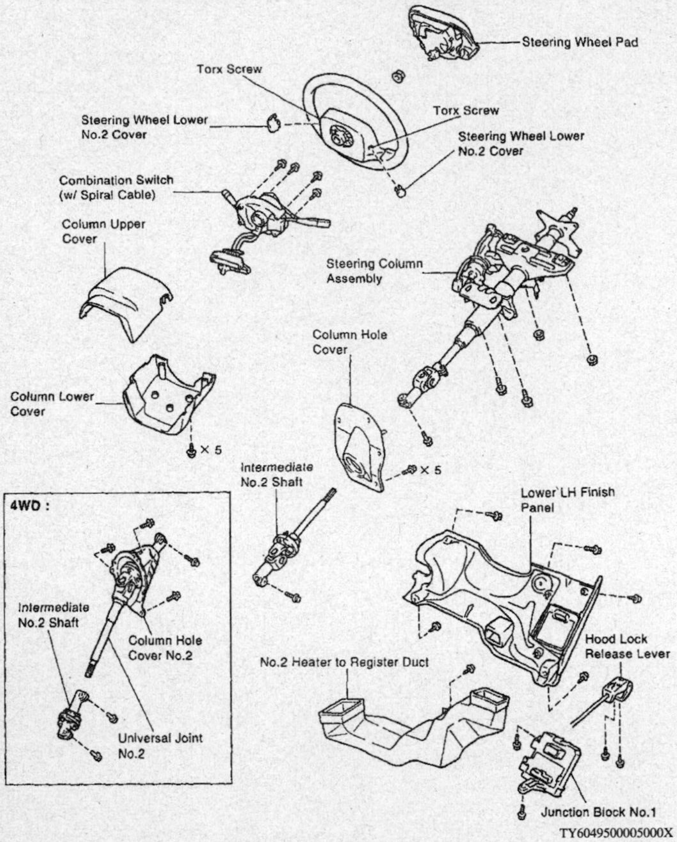

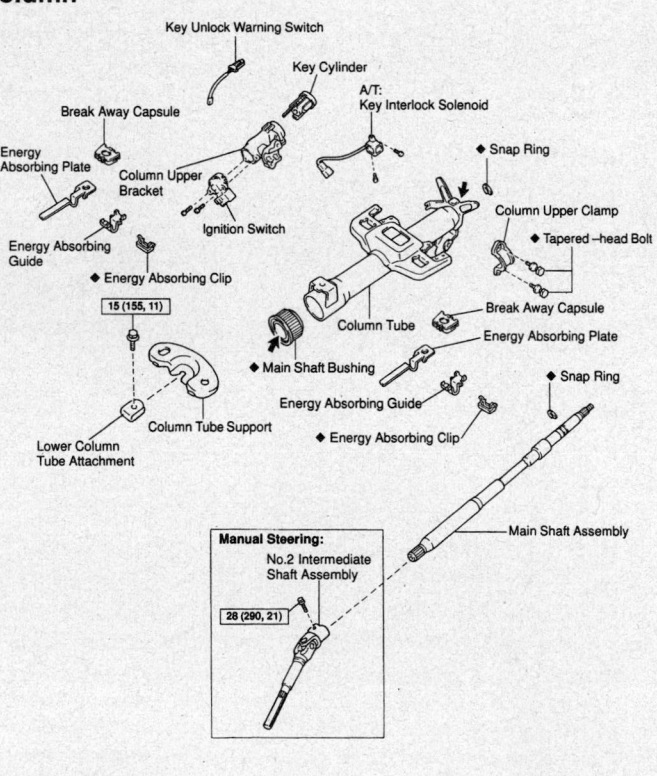

Steering Wheel Pad

Torx Screw

Steering Wheel Lower
No.2 Cover

Torx Screw

Steering Wheel Lower
No.2 Cover

Combination Switch
(w/ Spiral Cable)

Column Upper
Cover

Steering Column
Assembly

Column Hole
Cover

Column Lower
Cover

× 5

× 5

4WD:

Intermediate
No.2 Shaft

Column Hole
Cover No.2

Intermediate
No.2 Shaft

Universal Joint
No.2

Lower LH Finish
Panel

Hood Lock
Release Lever

No.2 Heater to Register Duct

Junction Block No.1

TY6049500005000X

Fig. 22 Exploded view of steering column. Tacoma less tilt column

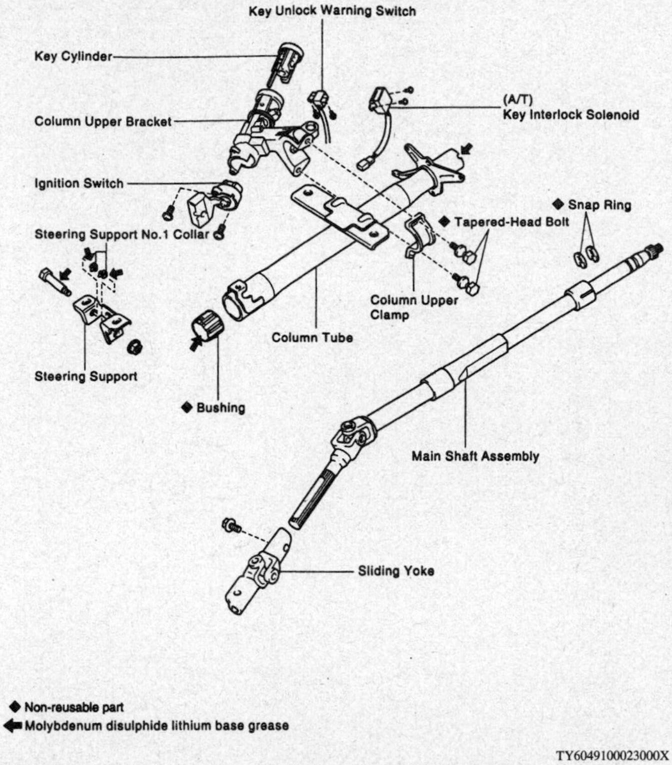

Key Unlock Warning Switch

Key Cylinder

Column Upper Bracket

(A/T)
Key Interlock Solenoid

Ignition Switch

◆ Snap Ring

Steering Support No.1 Collar

◆ Tapered-Head Bolt

Column Upper
Clamp

Column Tube

Steering Support

◆ Bushing

Main Shaft Assembly

Sliding Yoke

◆ Non-reusable part

◀ Molybdenum disulphide lithium base grease

TY6049100023000X

Fig. 23 Exploded view of steering column. 1996–97 Tercel

Key Unlock Warning Switch

Key Cylinder

Break Away Capsule

A/T:
Key Interlock Solenoid

Energy
Absorbing Plate

Column Upper
Bracket

Ignition Switch

◆ Snap Ring

Energy Absorbing
Guide

Column Upper Clamp

◆ Tapered–head Bolt

◆ Energy Absorbing Clip

15 (155, 11)

Break Away Capsule

Main Shaft Bushing

Energy Absorbing Plate

Column Tube

Lower Column
Tube Attachment

Column Tube Support

Energy Absorbing Guide

◆ Energy Absorbing Clip

◆ Snap Ring

Manual Steering:

No.2 Intermediate
Shaft Assembly

Main Shaft Assembly

28 (290, 21)

N·m (kgf·cm, ft·lbf) : Specified torque

◆ Non–reusable part

◀ Molybdenum disulfide lithium base grease

TY6049900037000X

Fig. 24 Exploded view of steering column. 1998 Tercel

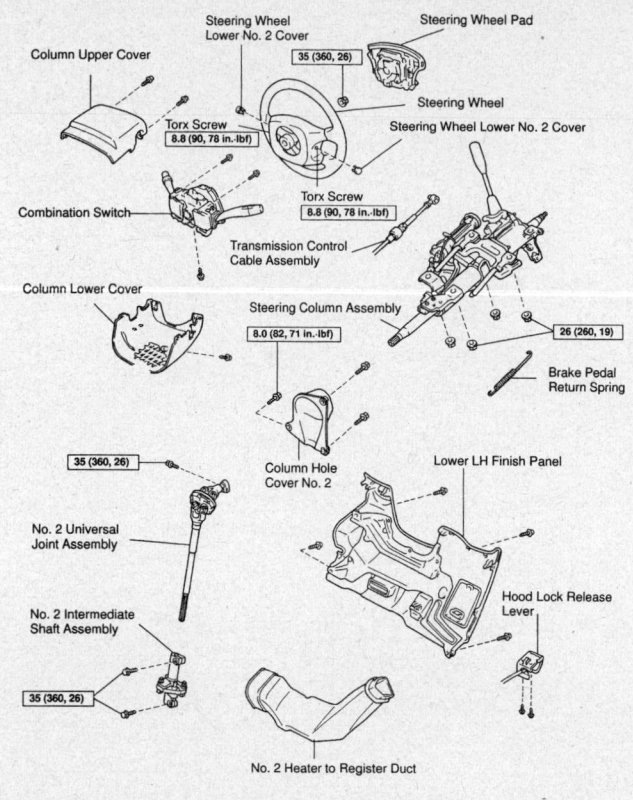

Fig. 24 Exploded view of steering column (Part 1 of 2). Tundra w/non-tilt & automatic transmission

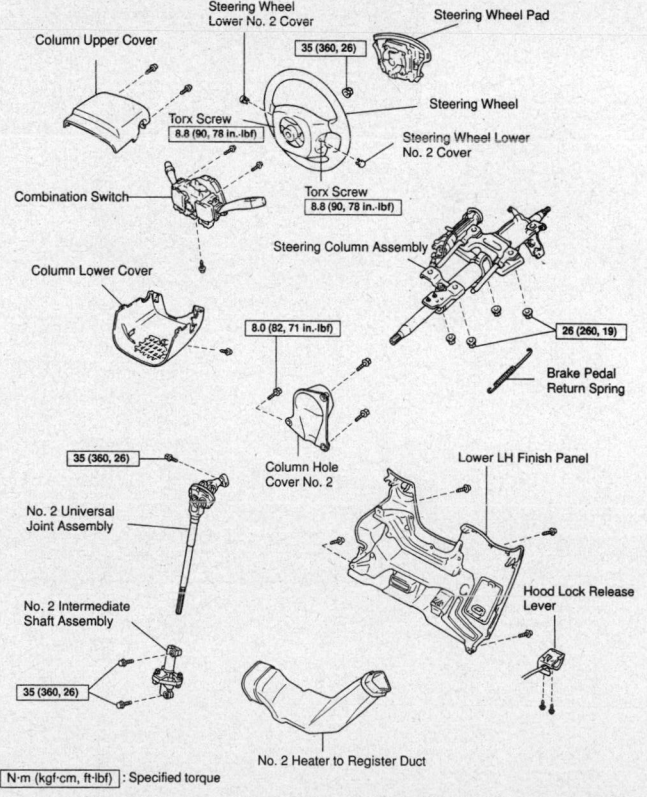

Fig. 24 Exploded view of steering column (Part 1 of 2). Tundra w/non-tilt & manual transmission

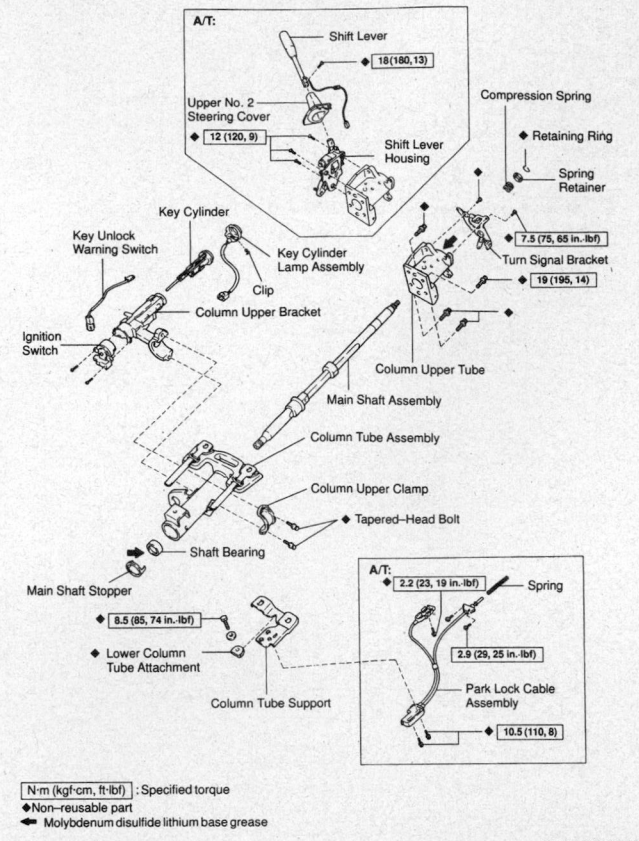

Fig. 24 Exploded view of steering column (Part 2 of 2). Tundra w/non-tilt

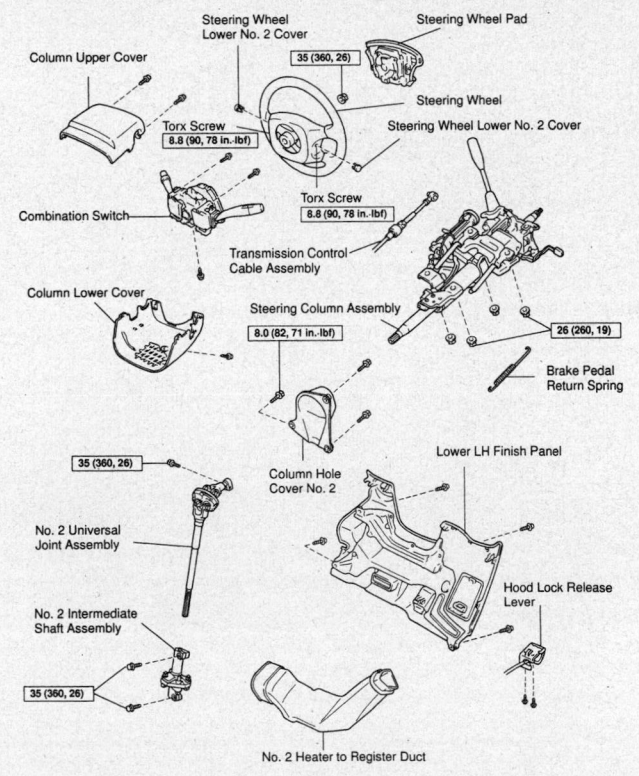

Fig. 25 Exploded view of steering column (Part 1 of 2). Tundra w/tilt & automatic transmission

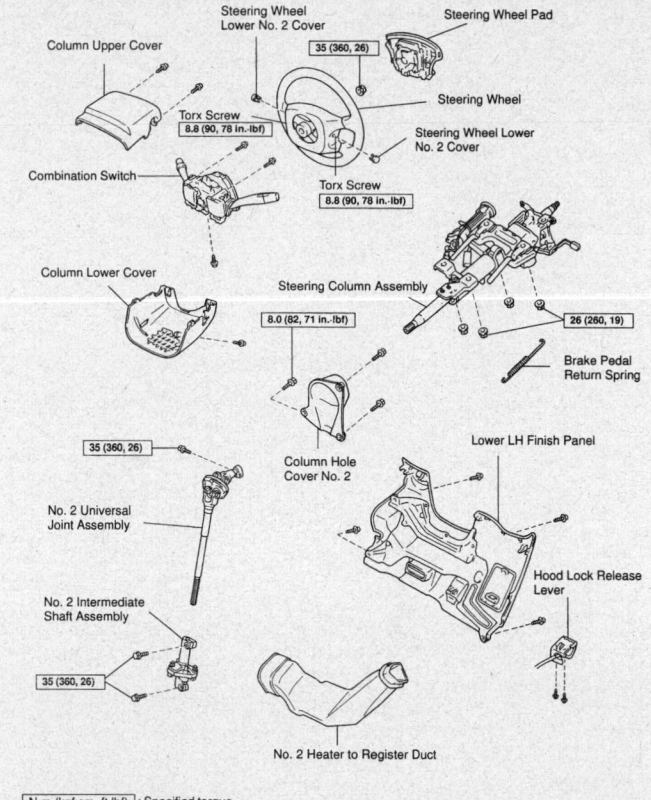

Column Upper Cover

Steering Wheel Lower No. 2 Cover

Steering Wheel Pad

35 (360, 26)

Torx Screw
8.8 (90, 78 in.·lbf)

Steering Wheel

Combination Switch

Steering Wheel Lower No. 2 Cover

Torx Screw
8.8 (90, 78 in.·lbf)

Column Lower Cover

Steering Column Assembly

8.0 (82, 71 in.·lbf)

26 (260, 19)

Brake Pedal Return Spring

35 (360, 26)

Column Hole Cover No. 2

Lower LH Finish Panel

No. 2 Universal Joint Assembly

No. 2 Intermediate Shaft Assembly

Hood Lock Release Lever

35 (360, 26)

No. 2 Heater to Register Duct

N·m (kgf·cm, ft·lbf) : Specified torque

TY6049900033010X

Fig. 25 Exploded view of steering column (Part 1 of 2). Tundra w/tilt & manual transmission

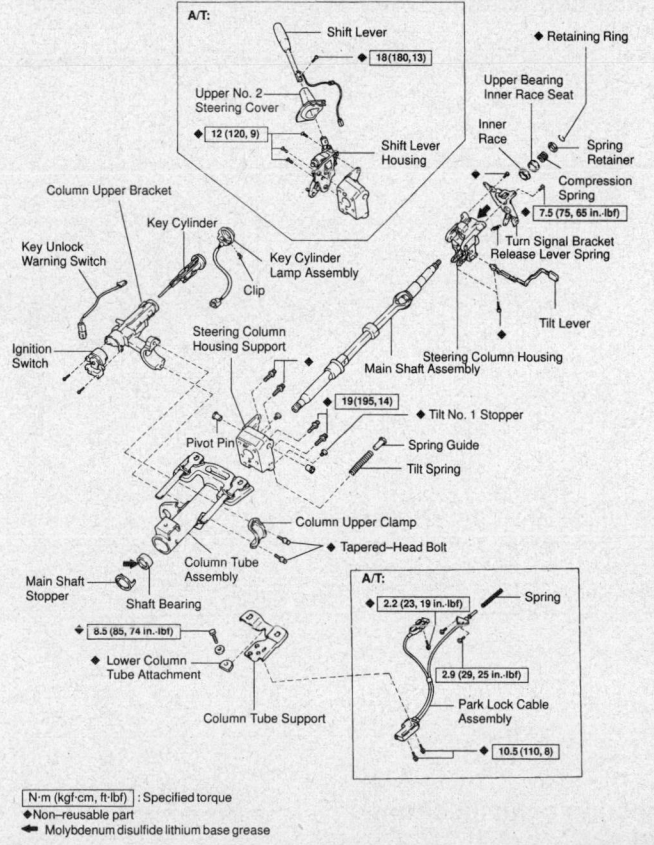

A/T:

Shift Lever

18 (180, 13)

Retaining Ring

Upper No. 2 Steering Cover

Upper Bearing Inner Race Seat

12 (120, 9)

Inner Race

Shift Lever Housing

Spring Retainer

Compression Spring

Column Upper Bracket

7.5 (75, 65 in.·lbf)

Key Cylinder

Turn Signal Bracket Release Lever Spring

Key Unlock Warning Switch

Key Cylinder Lamp Assembly

Clip

Tilt Lever

Ignition Switch

Steering Column Housing Support

Steering Column Housing

Main Shaft Assembly

19 (195, 14)

Tilt No. 1 Stopper

Pivot Pin

Spring Guide

Tilt Spring

Column Upper Clamp

Tapered–Head Bolt

Main Shaft Stopper

Column Tube Assembly

A/T:

2.2 (23, 19 in.·lbf)

Spring

Shaft Bearing

8.5 (85, 74 in.·lbf)

2.9 (29, 25 in.·lbf)

Lower Column Tube Attachment

Park Lock Cable Assembly

Column Tube Support

10.5 (110, 8)

N·m (kgf·cm, ft·lbf) : Specified torque
◆ Non–reusable part
◀ Molybdenum disulfide lithium base grease

TY6049900033030X

Fig. 25 Exploded view of steering column (Part 2 of 2). Tundra w/tilt

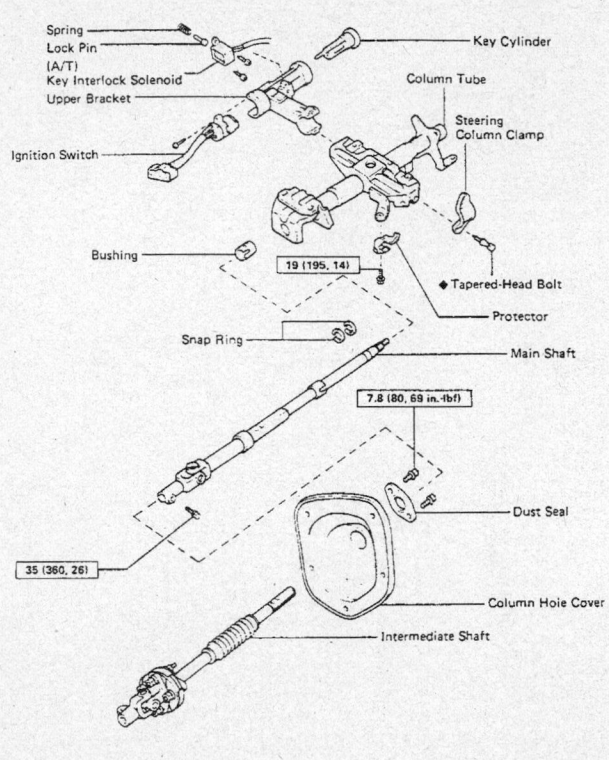

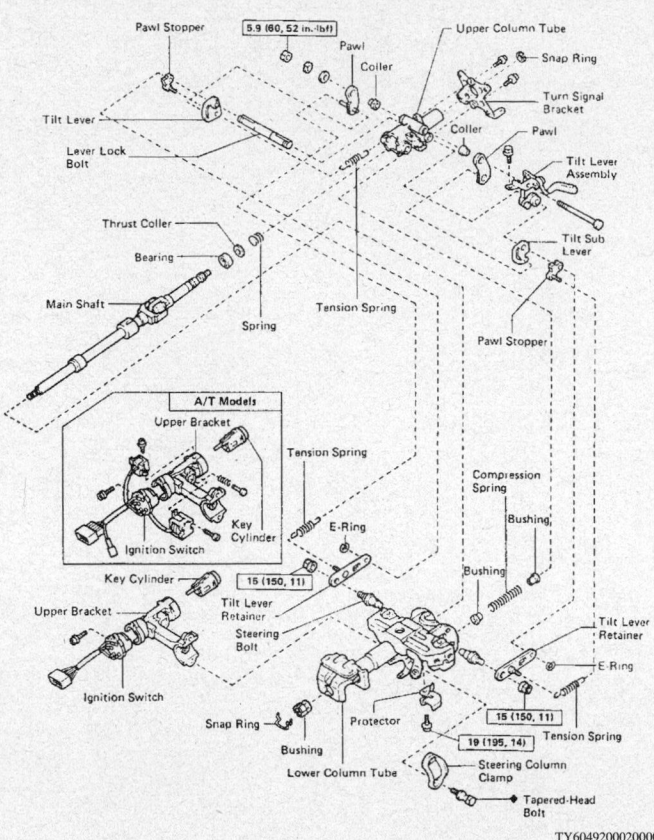

N·m (kgf·cm, ft·lbf) : Specified torque
◆ Non-reusable part

TY6049100019000X

Fig. 26   Exploded view of steering column. T100 less tilt column

TY6049200020000X

Fig. 27   Exploded view of steering column. T100 w/tilt column

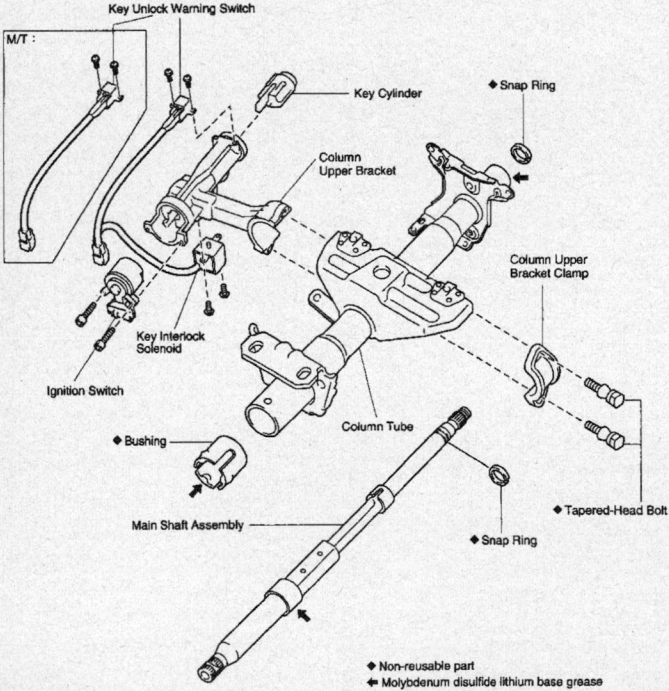

◆ Non-reusable part
← Molybdenum disulfide lithium base grease

TY6049600025000X

Fig. 28   Exploded view of steering column. 4Runner less tilt column

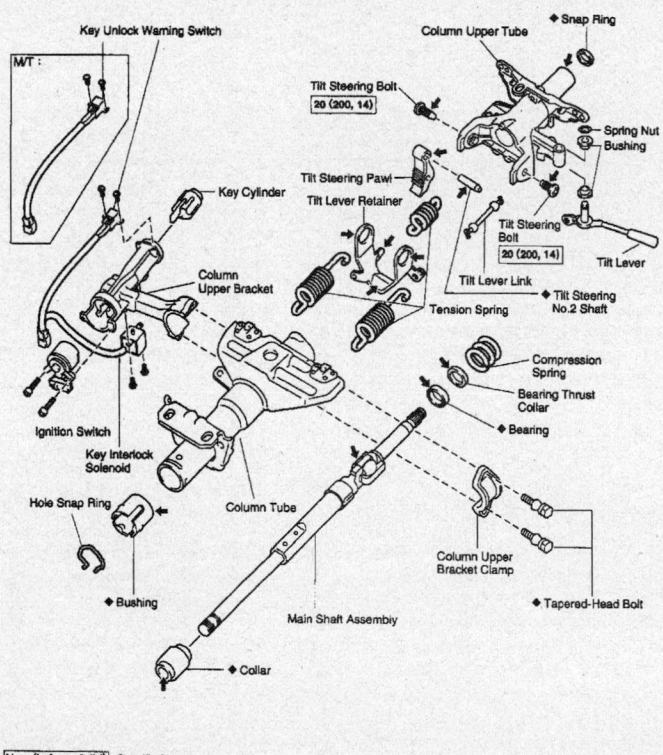

N·m (kgf·cm, ft·lbf) : Specified torque
◆ Non-reusable part
← Molybdenum disulfide lithium base grease

TY6049600026000X

Fig. 29   Exploded view of steering column. 4Runner w/tilt column

Manual Steering Gears

INDEX

PRECAUTIONS

AIR BAG SYSTEMS

Refer to "Air Bag System Precautions" in the front of this manual for system disarming & arming procedures.

BATTERY GROUND CABLE

Prior to service, disconnect battery ground cable and isolate as required.

AUDIO CODED ANTI-THEFT SYSTEM

Some models are equipped with an audio coded anti-theft system that will disable the radio when the battery cable is disconnected. The system can be identified by the "ANTI-THEFT SYSTEM" on the cassette tape lid. Obtain 3 digit customer code for input. Reset system after service as follows:

1. Obtain 3 digit audio anti-theft code.
2. Depress 1 (PROG) while depressing righthand side of TUNE SEEK button, - - - will appear in tape operation display.
3. To enter the first digit, depress 1 (PROG) button repeatedly until the number of times depressed equals the first digit beginning with zero (depress the 1 button six times if the first digit is five).
4. To enter second digit, depress 2 (APS) button repeatedly until the number of times depressed equals the second digit beginning with zero.
5. To enter third digit, depress 3 (RPT) button repeatedly until the number of times depressed equals the second digit beginning with zero.
6. If - - - is displayed during code input, repeat procedure.
7. When code appears in display, depress and hold SCAN button until SEC appears.
8. When SEC disappears audio system should be operative.
9. If Err is displayed, repeat procedure. **Attempting to input code more than nine times may permanently disable audio system.**

INSPECTION

TACOMA & COROLLA

1. Check rack teeth and back for wear or damage.
2. Ensure rack runout does not exceed .012 inch (.3 mm).

3. Inspect pinion bearings.

TERCEL

1. Inspect rack boot, rack end dust seal and rack clamp for damage and wear.
2. Check for excessive play in rack end ball joint.
3. Inspect rack guide for damage or wear.
4. Inspect pinion tooth surface for damage or wear. Check oil seal and dust cover for damage or wear.

STEERING GEAR SERVICE

RACK & PINION MANUAL STEERING GEAR

TERCEL

Disassemble

1. Place steering assembly in suitable vise, then mark position of tie rod and rack end for reference during assembly. Remove tie rod ends, **Fig. 1.**
2. Remove clip and clamp, then remove rack boot.
3. Remove rack end dust seal, then remove claw washer. Remove rack end using suitable tool and a wrench. Use caution not to scratch outside of rack with wrench.
4. Remove rack guide spring cap locknut, rack guide spring cap and spring.
5. Remove rack guide, dust cover, locknut and pinion bearing adjusting screw.
6. Pull rack from rack housing side and align rack notched portion with pinion. Remove pinion, upper bearing and washer.
7. Remove rack from pinion side, using caution not to rotate rack as it is being removed.

Assemble

1. To replace pinion upper bearing, remove and install using suitable puller and press. Check to ensure spacer is installed before installing bearing.
2. To replace lower bearing, heat rack housing to above 176°F, then tap bearing from shaft. Heat housing again when installing bearing.
3. Measure rack runout using dial indicator. Runout should be no more than .012 inch (.3 mm).
4. Apply suitable grease to pinion lower bearing, and rack bushing. Install rack

into rack housing. Position rack notched area so that pinion can be installed.
5. Apply grease to pinion bearing and tooth surfaces, then install pinion and spacer.
6. Install pinion bearing adjusting screw and adjust preload to 3.2 inch lbs. on all vehicles. Loosen adjusting screw until preload is 2–2.9 inch lbs. on all vehicles.
7. Install adjusting screw locknut and tighten to specifications.
8. Apply grease to rack guide, then install spring and rack guide spring cap. **Torque** spring cap to 43 inch lbs.
9. Install locknut and tighten to specifications. Recheck preload as outlined in step 13.
10. Install dust cover and claw washer, aligning claw on washer with rack groove, then tighten rack end to specifications. Stake claw washer in position.
11. Install rack end seal and dust boot. Check to ensure tube hole is not blocked.
12. Install rack boot clamp with tapered edge toward tube side. Install rack boot clip.
13. Install tie rod end aligning marks made during disassembly.

COROLLA

1. Clamp steering gear housing in soft jawed vise, **Fig. 2.**
2. Remove tie rod ends after making alignment marks.
3. Remove clips, clamps and rack boots.
4. Unstake claw washers and remove rack ends using suitable tools. Mark left and right ends and remove claw washers.
5. Using suitable tool, remove locknut and rack guide spring cap.
6. Remove rack guide spring, rack guide with spacer, then dust cover.
7. Using suitable tool, remove locknut and pinion bearing adjusting screw.
8. Pull rack fully from housing side and align pinion with notched portion of rack. Remove pinion and upper bearing as an assembly.
9. Remove rack from pinion side without turning it.
10. Reverse procedure to assemble, noting the following:
    a. If necessary, replace pinion upper bearing using suitable tools.
    b. If necessary, replace lower pinion bearing by heating rack housing to

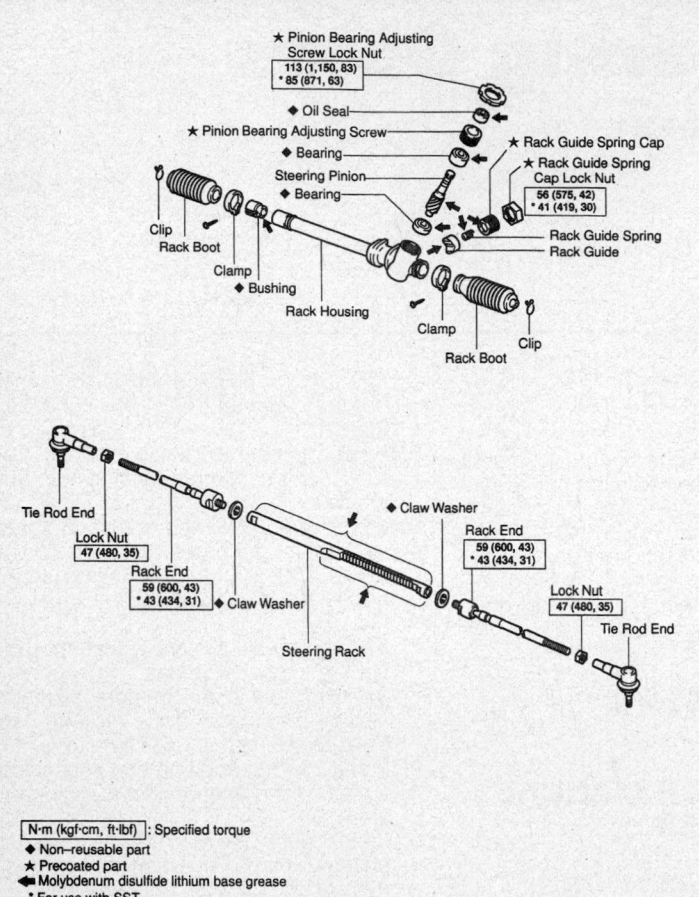

N·m (kgf·cm, ft·lbf): Specified torque
◆ Non–reusable part
★ Precoated part
◀ Molybdenum disulfide lithium base grease
* For use with SST

TY6039100028000X

Fig. 1 Rack & pinion manual steering gear assembly. Tercel

N·m (kgf·cm, ft·lbf) : Specified torque
◆ Non-reusable part
★ Precoated part
* For use with SST
◀ Molybdenum Disulphide Lithium Base Grease
◇ Power Steering Fluid

TY6039300030000X

Fig. 2 Rack & pinion manual steering gear assembly. Corolla

over 176 °F and using a plastic hammer to tap housing and free bearing. Then reheat rack housing to over 176 °F and using a suitable tool, install new lower bearing, noting correct bearing direction.

c. If necessary, replace rack bushing using suitable tools. **Ensure tube hole is not blocked with grease.**

TACOMA

1. Using vise mounted steering gear assembly holder tool No. 09612–00012, or equivalent, and two bolts, secure gear assembly in a vise, or clamp steering gear housing in soft jawed vise, being careful not to damage the gear housing.
2. Remove tie rod ends and lock nuts, after making alignment marks, **Fig. 3.**

3. Remove clips, clamps and rack boots.
4. Unstake claw washers and remove rack ends using suitable tools. Mark left and right ends and remove claw washers.
5. Remove rack housing No. 2 bracket and grommet after placing alignment marks on rack and housing.
6. Using suitable tool, remove locknut and rack guide spring cap.
7. Remove rack guide spring, rack guide with spacer, rack guide seat, then dust cover.
8. Using suitable tool, remove locknut and pinion bearing adjusting screw.
9. Pull rack fully from housing side and align pinion with notched portion of rack. Remove pinion and upper bearing as an assembly.

10. Remove rack from pinion side without turning it.
11. Reverse procedure to assemble, noting the following:
   a. If necessary, replace pinion upper bearing using suitable tools.
   b. If necessary, replace lower pinion bearing by heating rack housing to over 176 °F and using a plastic hammer to tap housing and free bearing. Then reheat rack housing to over 176 °F and using a suitable tool, install new lower bearing, noting correct bearing direction.
   c. If necessary, replace rack bushing using suitable tools. **Ensure tube hole is not blocked with grease.**

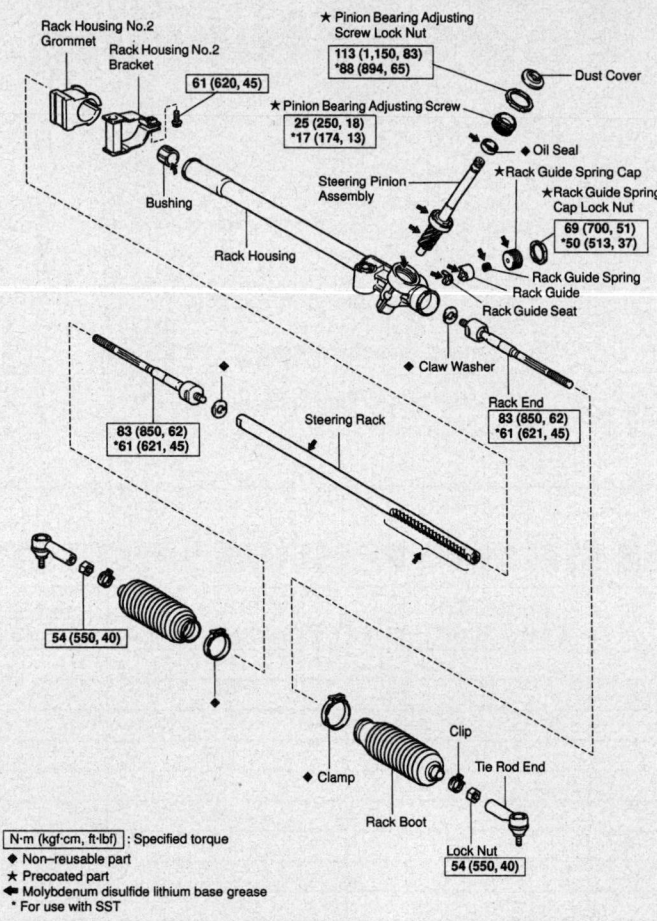

Rack Housing No.2 Grommet

Rack Housing No.2 Bracket

61 (620, 45)

★ Pinion Bearing Adjusting Screw Lock Nut
113 (1,150, 83)
*88 (894, 65)

Dust Cover

★ Pinion Bearing Adjusting Screw
25 (250, 18)
*17 (174, 13)

◆ Oil Seal

★ Rack Guide Spring Cap

★ Rack Guide Spring Cap Lock Nut
69 (700, 51)
*50 (513, 37)

Steering Pinion Assembly

Bushing

Rack Housing

Rack Guide Spring

Rack Guide

Rack Guide Seat

◆ Claw Washer

Steering Rack

83 (850, 62)
*61 (621, 45)

Rack End
83 (850, 62)
*61 (621, 45)

54 (550, 40)

Clip

Tie Rod End

◆ Clamp

Rack Boot

Lock Nut
54 (550, 40)

N·m (kgf·cm, ft·lbf) : Specified torque
◆ Non–reusable part
★ Precoated part
◀ Molybdenum disulfide lithium base grease
* For use with SST

TY6039500032000X

Fig. 3 Rack & pinion manual steering gear assembly. Tacoma

Power Steering

INDEX

POWER STEERING PRESSURE SPECIFICATIONS

Model	Year	Maximum Oil Level Rise, Inch	Minimum Oil Pressure, psi①	Maximum Oil Pressure, psi①	Steering Effort
Avalon	1996–99	.2	1138	—	52②
Camry	1996	.2	⑥	—	52②
	1997–99	.2	1138	—	52②
Camry Solara	1999	.2	1138	—	52②
Celica	1996–99	.2	⑤	—	61②
Corolla	1996	.2	924	—	11④
	1997	.2	924	—	7④
	1998–99	.2	925	—	43②
Land Cruiser	1996–99	.2	1351	—	73②
Paseo	1996–97	.2	925	—	69②
4Runner	1996–99	.2	1209	—	43②
Previa	1996	.2	1067	—	8.8④
	1997	.2	1067	—	50②
RAV4	1996–99	.2	1067	—	52②
Sienna	1998–99	.2	1138	—	52②
Supra	1996	.2	1140	—	9.0④
	1997–98	.2	1067	—	61②
Tacoma	1996–99	.2	1209	—	43②
Tercel	1996–97	.2	925	—	69②
	1998	.2	996	—	69②
Tundra	2000	.2	1209	—	43②
T100	1996–99	.2	③	—	73②
4Runner	1996–99	.2	1209	—	43②

① — SV models, 924 psi, VZV models, 1067 psi.
② — Inch lbs.
③ — 2WD models, 1138 psi, 4WD models, 1209 psi.
④ — Ft. lbs.
⑤ — 7A-FE, 996 psi, 5S-FE, 1280 psi.
⑥ — 1MZ-FE, 1138 psi, 5S-FE, 1209 psi.

PRECAUTIONS

AIR BAG SYSTEMS

Refer to "Air Bag System Precautions" in the front of this manual for system disarming & arming procedures.

BATTERY GROUND CABLE

Prior to service, disconnect battery ground cable and isolate as required.

AUDIO CODED ANTI-THEFT SYSTEM

Some models are equipped with an audio coded anti-theft system that will disable the radio when the battery cable is disconnected. The system can be identified by the "ANTI-THEFT SYSTEM" on the cassette tape lid. Obtain 3 digit customer code for input. Reset system after service as follows:

1. Obtain 3 digit audio anti-theft code.
2. Depress 1 (PROG) while depressing righthand side of TUNE SEEK button, - - - will appear in tape operation display.
3. To enter the first digit, depress 1 (PROG) button repeatedly until the number of times depressed equals the first digit beginning with zero (depress the 1 button six times if the first digit is five).
4. To enter second digit, depress 2 (APS) button repeatedly until the number of times depressed equals the second

5. To enter third digit, depress 3 (RPT) button repeatedly until the number of times depressed equals the second digit beginning with zero.
6. If - - - is displayed during code input, repeat procedure.
7. When code appears in display, depress and hold SCAN button until SEC appears.
8. When SEC disappears audio system should be operative.
9. If Err is displayed, repeat procedure. **Attempting to input code more than nine times may permanently disable audio system.**

MAINTENANCE

OIL PRESSURE CHECK

Avalon, Camry, Camry Solara & Sienna

1. Disconnect pressure tube from power steering pump.
2. Connect gauge side of pressure gauge to power steering pump side and valve side to gear housing side.
3. Bleed power steering system as outlined under "Power Steering System Bleed."
4. Start engine, turn steering wheel from lock to lock three or four times, ensure proper fluid level.
5. Allow fluid temperature to reach at least 176°F.
6. Start engine and allow to idle.
7. Close pressure valve and observe valve reading. **Do not keep valve closed for more then 10 seconds. Do not allow fluid temperature to become too high.**
8. If observed pressure is below specifications, replace power steering pump.
9. Open valve fully.
10. Check and record pressure reading at 1000 RPM and 3000 RPM, less then 71 psi difference should be indicated from 1000 RPM to 3000 RPM . If difference is higher than indicated, repair or replace power steering pump flow control valve.
11. Ensure valve is fully open with engine at idle, check pressure with steering wheel at full lock. **Do not maintain full lock position for more than 10 seconds. Do not allow fluid temperature to become too high.**
12. If pressure is below specifications, internal gear housing leak is indicated and must be repaired or replaced.
13. Center steering wheel and allow engine to idle.
14. Using suitable spring scale, measure steering effort in both directions. If steering effort is above specifications,

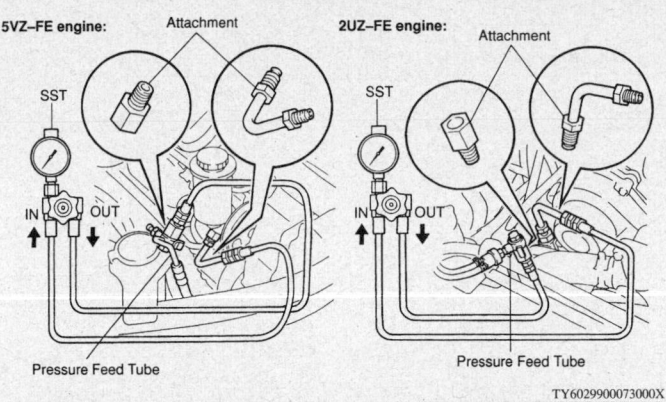

Fig. 1   Power steering pressure test. Tundra

repair power steering unit.

Celica, Corolla, Paseo, RAV4, Supra & Tercel

1. Disconnect pressure feed tube from power steering pump.
2. Connect gauge side of pressure gauge to power steering pump side and valve side to gear housing side.
3. Bleed power steering system as outlined under "Power Steering System Bleed."
4. Start engine, turn steering wheel from lock to lock three or four times, ensuring proper fluid level.
5. Allow fluid temperature to reach at least 176°F.
6. Start engine and allow to idle.
7. Close pressure valve and observe valve reading. **Do not keep valve closed for more then 10 seconds. Do not allow fluid temperature to become too high.**
8. If observed pressure is below specifications, replace power steering pump.
9. Open valve fully.
10. Check and record pressure reading at 1000 RPM and 3000 RPM, less then 71 psi difference should be indicated from 1000 RPM to 3000 RPM. If difference is higher than indicated, repair or replace power steering pump flow control valve.
11. Ensure valve is fully open with engine at idle, check pressure with steering wheel at full lock. **Do not maintain full lock position for more than 10 seconds. Do not allow fluid temperature to become too high.**
12. If pressure is below specifications, internal gear housing leak is indicated and must be repaired or replaced.
13. Center steering wheel and allow engine to idle.
14. Using suitable spring scale, measure

steering effort in both directions. If steering effort is above specifications, repair power steering unit.

Land Cruiser, T100, Tacoma & 4Runner

1. Using suitable tool, disconnect pressure line from power steering pump.
2. Connect gauge side of pressure gauge to power steering pump side and valve side to pressure line side.
3. Bleed power steering system as outlined under "Power Steering System Bleed."
4. Start engine, turn steering wheel from lock to lock three or four times, ensuring proper fluid level.
5. Allow fluid temperature to reach at least 176°F.
6. Start engine and allow to idle.
7. Close pressure valve and observe valve reading. **Do not keep valve closed for more then 10 seconds. Do not allow fluid temperature to become too high.**
8. If observed pressure is below specifications, replace power steering pump.
9. Open valve fully.
10. Check and record pressure reading at 1000 RPM and 3000 RPM, less then 71 psi difference should be indicated from 1000 RPM to 3000 RPM. If difference is higher than indicated, repair or replace power steering pump flow control valve.
11. **On models equipped with standard power steering,** proceed as follows:
   a. Ensure valve is fully open with engine at idle, check pressure with steering wheel at full lock. **Do not maintain full lock position for more than 10 seconds. Do not allow fluid temperature to become too high.**
   b. If pressure is below specifications,

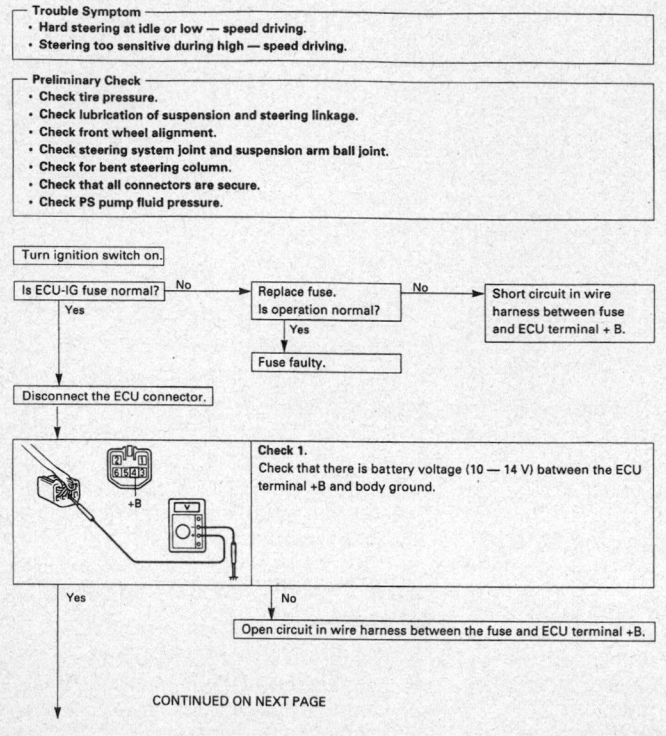

Trouble Symptom
- Hard steering at idle or low — speed driving.
- Steering too sensitive during high — speed driving.

Preliminary Check
- Check tire pressure.
- Check lubrication of suspension and steering linkage.
- Check front wheel alignment.
- Check steering system joint and suspension arm ball joint.
- Check for bent steering column.
- Check that all connectors are secure.
- Check PS pump fluid pressure.

Turn ignition switch on.

Is ECU-IG fuse normal? —No→ Replace fuse. Is operation normal? —No→ Short circuit in wire harness between fuse and ECU terminal + B.

Yes ↓ / Yes ↓ Fuse faulty.

Disconnect the ECU connector.

Check 1.
Check that there is battery voltage (10 — 14 V) between the ECU terminal +B and body ground.

Yes ↓ / No → Open circuit in wire harness between the fuse and ECU terminal +B.

CONTINUED ON NEXT PAGE

TY6029700066010X

Fig. 2   PPS troubleshooting (Part 1 of 3). Supra

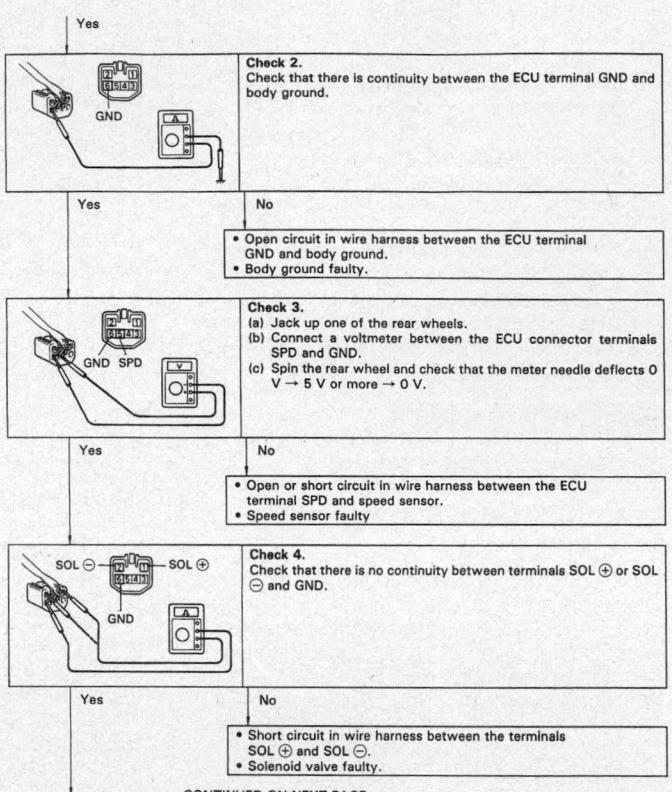

Check 2.
Check that there is continuity between the ECU terminal GND and body ground.

Yes ↓ / No →
- Open circuit in wire harness between the ECU terminal GND and body ground.
- Body ground faulty.

Check 3.
(a) Jack up one of the rear wheels.
(b) Connect a voltmeter between the ECU connector terminals SPD and GND.
(c) Spin the rear wheel and check that the meter needle deflects 0 V → 5 V or more → 0 V.

Yes ↓ / No →
- Open or short circuit in wire harness between the ECU terminal SPD and speed sensor.
- Speed sensor faulty

Check 4.
Check that there is no continuity between terminals SOL ⊕ or SOL ⊖ and GND.

Yes ↓ / No →
- Short circuit in wire harness between the terminals SOL ⊕ and SOL ⊖.
- Solenoid valve faulty.

CONTINUED ON NEXT PAGE

TY6029700066020X

Fig. 2   PPS troubleshooting (Part 2 of 3). Supra

internal gear housing leak is indicated and must be repaired or replaced.

12. **On models equipped with Progressive Power Steering (PPS),** proceed as follows:
    a. Turn steering wheel to full lock, disconnect solenoid electrical connector, ensure pressure gauge valve is fully opened and engine is running at 1000 RPM.
    b. If pressure is below specifications, internal gear housing leak or faulty solenoid is indicated.
    c. Apply battery voltage to solenoid. **Do not apply voltage for more than 30 seconds to avoid burning out solenoid.** Inspect oil pressure, maximum pressure should be 569 psi., if pressure is high, inspect solenoid.
    d. Connect solenoid electrical connector, then inspect oil pressure. If pressure is below specifications, PPS system is faulty.
13. **On all models,** center steering wheel and allow engine to idle. Using suitable spring scale, measure steering effort in both directions. If steering effort is above specifications, repair power steering unit.
14. **On models equipped with PPS,** apply battery voltage to solenoid. **Do not apply voltage for more than 30 seconds to avoid burning out solenoid.** Recheck steering effort. Maximum steering effort should be 26 ft. lbs.
15. **On models equipped with PPS,** if steering effort is not heavier then specification, inspect solenoid.

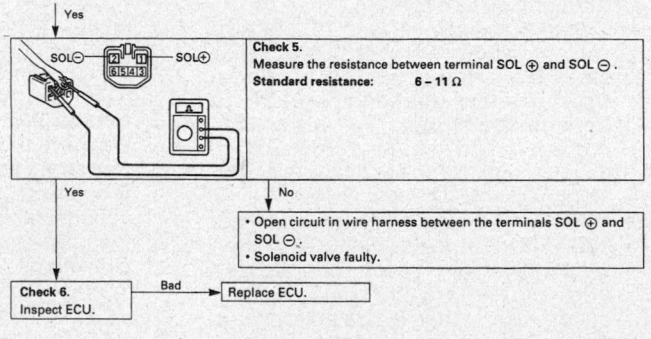

Check 5.
Measure the resistance between terminal SOL ⊕ and SOL ⊖.
Standard resistance: 6 – 11 Ω

Yes ↓ / No →
- Open circuit in wire harness between the terminals SOL ⊕ and SOL ⊖.
- Solenoid valve faulty.

Check 6.
Inspect ECU. —Bad→ Replace ECU.

TY6029700066030X

Fig. 2   PPS troubleshooting (Part 3 of 3). Supra

Tundra

1. Remove air cleaner assembly.
2. Disconnect pressure feed tube at power steering pump.
3. Connect power steering pressure test kit tool No. 09640–10010 or equivalent as shown in **Fig. 1.**
4. Ensure valve of pressure tester in open position.
5. Bleed power steering system as outlined under "Power Steering System Bleed."
6. Start engine and operate at idle.
7. Turn steering wheel from lock to lock several times to boost fluid temperature. Fluid temperature should reach 176°F.
8. With engine at idle, close valve of pressure tester and observe reading. **Do not close valve for more than 10 seconds or let fluid temperature become too high.** Ensure fluid pressure is with specifications.
9. With engine at idle, open valve fully.
10. Measure fluid pressure at engine speeds of 1000–3000 RPM. **Do not turn steering wheel.**
11. Ensure fluid pressure difference is not more than 71 psi.
12. With engine at idle, turn steering wheel from lock to lock. Ensure pressure is within specifications.

TROUBLESHOOTING
AVALON, CAMRY, CAMRY SOLARA & SIENNA

Hard Steering

1. Improperly inflated tires.
2. Incorrect front wheel alignment.

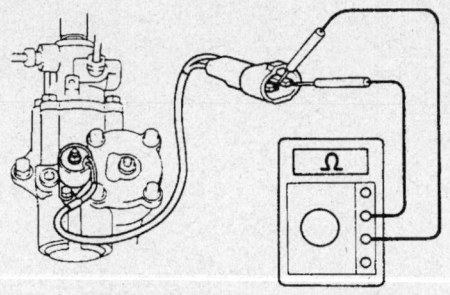

TY6029100020000X

Fig. 3 Solenoid valve inspection. 4Runner

3. Worn steering system joints.
4. Worn lower arm ball joints.
5. Steering column binding.
6. Steering gear housing.
7. Improperly adjusted power steering belt.
8. Low reservoir fluid level.

Poor Return

1. Improperly inflated tires.
2. Incorrect wheel alignment.
3. Steering column binding.
4. Steering gear out of adjustment or faulty.

Excessive Play

1. Worn steering system joints.
2. Worn suspension ball joints.
3. Worn sliding yoke.
4. Worn front wheel bearing.
5. Steering gear housing.

Abnormal Noise

1. Low reservoir fluid level.
2. Worn steering system joints.
3. Steering gear housing.

CELICA

Hard Steering

1. Improperly inflated tires.
2. Insufficient front end lubrication.
3. Excessive caster.
4. Worn steering system joints.
5. Worn lower arm ball joints.
6. Steering column binding.
7. Steering gear out of adjustment or faulty.
8. Improperly adjusted power steering belt.
9. Low reservoir fluid level.
10. Faulty power steering unit.

Poor Return

1. Improperly inflated tires.
2. Insufficient front end lubrication.
3. Incorrect wheel alignment.
4. Steering column binding.
5. Steering gear out of adjustment or faulty.

Excessive Play

1. Worn front wheel bearing.
2. Worn main shaft yoke or intermediate shaft yoke.
3. Worn lower ball joints.
4. Worn steering system joints.

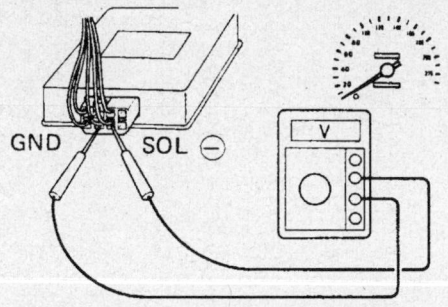

TY6029100021000X

Fig. 4 ECU connector inspection. 4Runner

5. Steering gear out of adjustment or faulty.

Abnormal Noise

1. Loose steering linkage.
2. Worn steering system joints.
3. Steering gear out of adjustment or faulty.

COROLLA

Hard Steering

1. Improperly inflated tires.
2. Insufficient front end lubrication.
3. Excessive caster.
4. Worn steering system joints.
5. Worn lower arm ball joints.
6. Steering column binding.
7. Steering gear out of adjustment or faulty.
8. Improperly adjusted power steering belt.
9. Low reservoir fluid level.
10. Faulty power steering unit.

Poor Return

1. Improperly inflated tires.
2. Insufficient front end lubrication.
3. Incorrect wheel alignment.
4. Steering column binding.
5. Steering gear out of adjustment or faulty.

Excessive Play

1. Worn front wheel bearing.
2. Worn main shaft yoke or intermediate shaft yoke.
3. Worn lower ball joints.
4. Worn steering system joints.
5. Steering gear out of adjustment or faulty.

Abnormal Noise

1. Loose steering linkage.
2. Worn steering system joints.
3. Steering gear out of adjustment or faulty.

LAND CRUISER

Hard Steering

1. Improperly inflated tires.
2. Insufficient front end lubrication.
3. Excessive caster.
4. Worn steering system joints.
5. Worn lower arm ball joints.
6. Steering column binding.

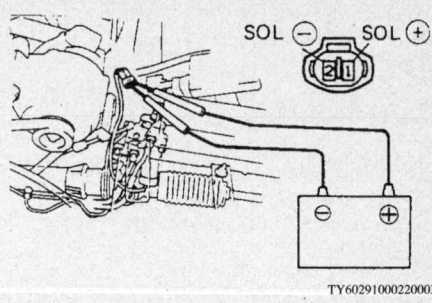

TY6029100022000X

Fig. 5 Solenoid valve inspection. Supra

7. Steering gear out of adjustment or faulty.
8. Improperly adjusted power steering belt.
9. Low reservoir fluid level.
10. Faulty power steering unit.

Poor Return

1. Improperly inflated tires.
2. Insufficient front end lubrication.
3. Incorrect wheel alignment.
4. Steering column binding.
5. Steering gear out of adjustment or faulty.

Excessive Play

1. Worn front wheel bearing.
2. Worn main shaft yoke or intermediate shaft yoke.
3. Worn lower ball joints.
4. Worn steering system joints.
5. Steering gear out of adjustment or faulty.

Abnormal Noise

1. Loose steering linkage.
2. Worn steering system joints.
3. Steering gear out of adjustment or faulty.

PASEO

Hard Steering

1. Improperly inflated tires.
2. Incorrect front wheel alignment.
3. Worn steering system joints.
4. Worn lower arm ball joints.
5. Steering column binding.
6. Steering gear housing.
7. Improperly adjusted power steering belt.
8. Low reservoir fluid level.

Poor Return

1. Improperly inflated tires.
2. Incorrect wheel alignment.
3. Steering column binding.
4. Steering gear out of adjustment or faulty.

Excessive Play

1. Worn steering system joints.
2. Worn suspension ball joints.
3. Worn sliding yoke.
4. Worn front wheel bearing.
5. Steering gear housing.

Abnormal Noise

1. Low reservoir fluid level.

2. Worn steering system joints.
3. Steering gear housing.

PREVIA

Hard Steering

1. Improperly inflated tires.
2. Incorrect front wheel alignment.
3. Worn steering system joints.
4. Worn lower arm ball joints.
5. Steering column binding.
6. Steering gear housing.
7. Improperly adjusted power steering belt.
8. Low reservoir fluid level.

Poor Return

1. Improperly inflated tires.
2. Incorrect wheel alignment.
3. Steering column binding.
4. Steering gear out of adjustment or faulty.

Excessive Play

1. Worn steering system joints.
2. Worn suspension ball joints.
3. Worn sliding yoke.
4. Worn front wheel bearing.
5. Steering gear housing.

Abnormal Noise

1. Low reservoir fluid level.
2. Worn steering system joints.
3. Steering gear housing.

RAV4 & 4RUNNER

Hard Steering

1. Improperly inflated tires.
2. Low power steering fluid level.
3. Loose drive belt.
4. Incorrect front wheel alignment.
5. Worn steering system joints.
6. Worn suspension arm ball joints.
7. Binding steering column.
8. Faulty power steering vane pump.
9. Faulty power steering gear.

Poor Return

1. Improperly inflated tires.
2. Incorrect front wheel alignment.
3. Binding steering column.
4. Faulty power steering gear.

Excessive Play

1. Worn steering system joints.
2. Worn suspension arm ball joints.
3. Worn intermediate shaft or sliding yoke.
4. Faulty power steering gear.
5. Worn front wheel bearing.

Abnormal Noise

1. Low power steering fluid level.
2. Worn steering system joints.
3. Faulty power steering vane pump.
4. Faulty power steering gear.

SUPRA

Hard Steering

1. Improperly inflated tires.
2. Insufficient front end lubrication.
3. Excessive caster.
4. Worn steering system joints.

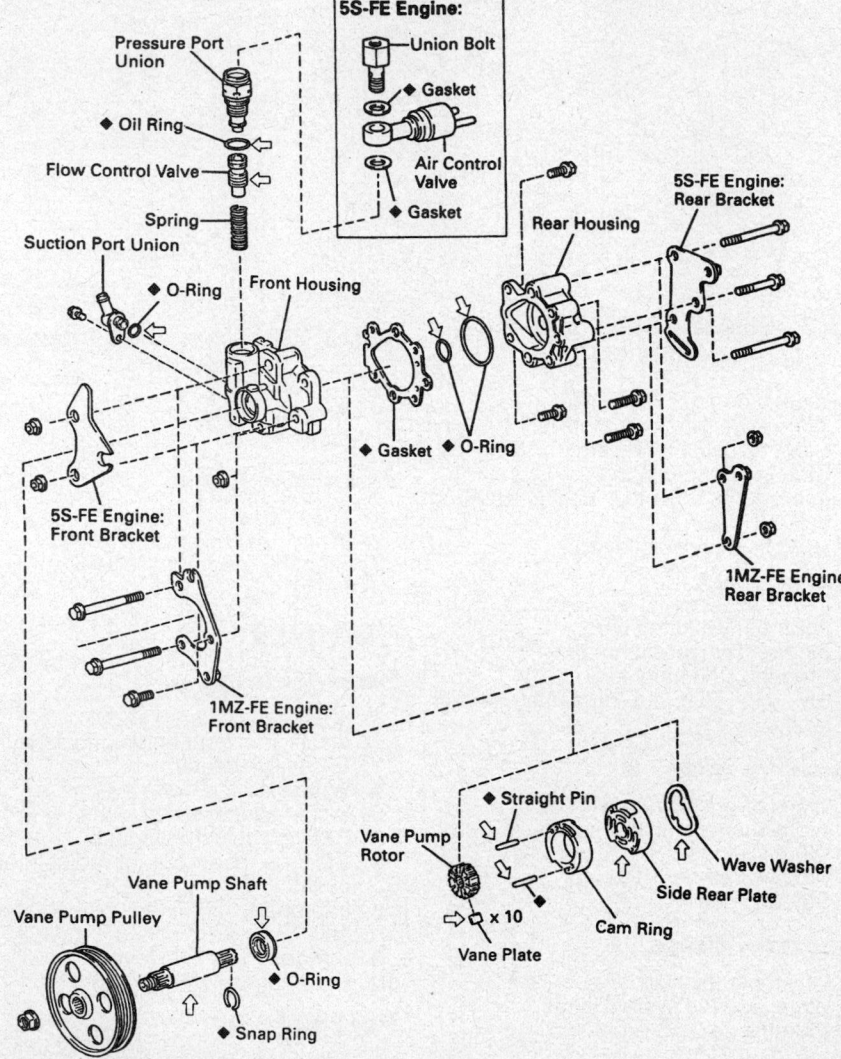

Fig. 6 Exploded view of power steering pump. Avalon, Camry, Camry Solara & Sienna

5. Worn lower arm ball joints.
6. Steering column binding.
7. Steering gear out of adjustment or faulty.
8. Improperly adjusted power steering belt.
9. Low reservoir fluid level.
10. Faulty power steering unit.

Poor Return

1. Improperly inflated tires.
2. Insufficient front end lubrication.
3. Incorrect wheel alignment.
4. Steering column binding.
5. Steering gear out of adjustment or faulty.

Excessive Play

1. Worn front wheel bearing.
2. Worn main shaft yoke or intermediate shaft yoke.
3. Worn lower ball joints.
4. Worn steering system joints.

5. Steering gear out of adjustment or faulty.

Abnormal Noise

1. Loose steering linkage.
2. Worn steering system joints.
3. Steering gear out of adjustment or faulty.

PPS System

Refer to **Fig. 2,** for troubleshooting procedures.

TACOMA & T100

Hard Steering

1. Improperly inflated tires.
2. Incorrect front wheel alignment.
3. Worn steering system joints.
4. Worn lower arm ball joints.
5. Steering column binding.
6. Steering gear out of adjustment of faulty.

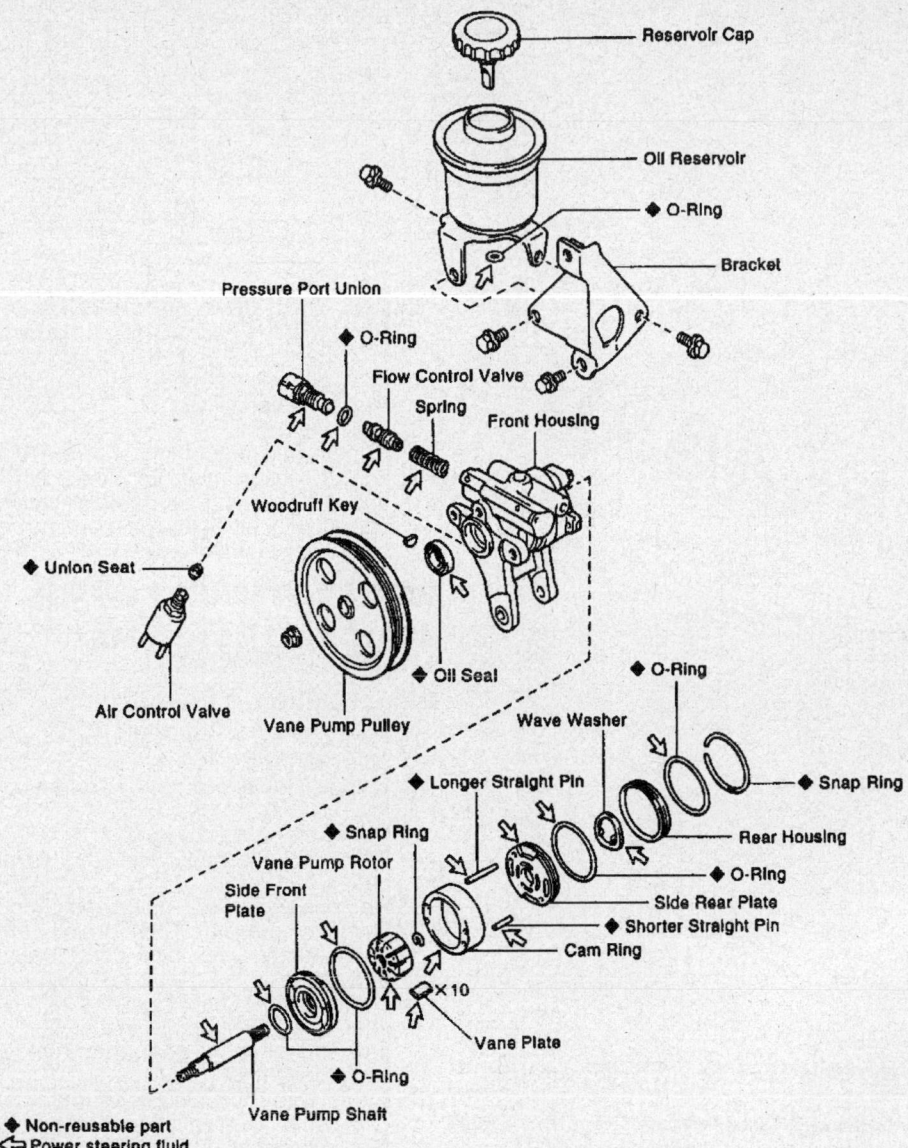

Fig. 7 Exploded view of power steering pump. Celica w/7A-FE engine

7. Improperly adjusted power steering belt.
8. Low reservoir fluid level.
9. Insufficient front end lubrication.
10. Faulty power steering unit.
11. Faulty solenoid valve.
12. Faulty electronic control.

Poor Return
1. Improperly inflated tires.
2. Incorrect wheel alignment.
3. Steering column binding.
4. Steering gear out of adjustment or faulty.
5. Insufficient front end lubrication.

Excessive Play
1. Worn steering system joints.
2. Worn lower arm ball joints.
3. Worn main shaft yoke or intermediate shaft yoke.
4. Worn front wheel bearing.
5. Steering gear out of adjustment or faulty.

Abnormal Noise
1. Loose steering linkage.
2. Worn steering system joints.
3. Steering gear out of adjustment or faulty.

TERCEL

Hard Steering
1. Improperly inflated tires.
2. Incorrect front wheel alignment.
3. Worn steering system joints.
4. Worn lower arm ball joints.
5. Steering column binding.
6. Steering gear housing.
7. Improperly adjusted power steering belt.
8. Low reservoir fluid level.

Poor Return
1. Improperly inflated tires.
2. Incorrect wheel alignment.
3. Steering column binding.

4. Steering gear out of adjustment or faulty.

Excessive Play
1. Worn steering system joints.
2. Worn suspension ball joints.
3. Worn sliding yoke.
4. Worn front wheel bearing.
5. Steering gear housing.

Abnormal Noise
1. Low reservoir fluid level.
2. Worn steering system joints.
3. Steering gear housing.

TUNDRA

Abnormal Noise
1. Low power steering fluid.
2. Steering system joints worn.
3. Power steering pump.
4. Power steering gear.

Excessive Play
1. Steering system joints worn.
2. Intermediate shaft or sliding yoke worn.
3. Front wheel bearings worn.
4. Power steering gear.

Hard Steering
1. Improperly inflated tires.
2. Power steering fluid low.
3. Loose drive belt.
4. Incorrect front wheel alignment.
5. Steering system joints worn.
6. Steering column binding.
7. Power steering pump.
8. Power steering gear.

Poor Return
1. Improperly inflated tires.
2. Incorrect front wheel alignment.
3. Steering column binding.
4. Power steering gear.

DIAGNOSIS & TESTING

Progressive Power Steering (PPS) System

4RUNNER

Solenoid Valve
1. Disconnect solenoid electrical connector.
2. Measure resistance between terminals SOL+ and SOL-, **Fig. 3.**
3. Reconnect electrical connector.

Solenoid Operation
1. Remove solenoid valve from gear housing.
2. Connect positive battery voltage to solenoid terminal SOL+.
3. Connect negative battery voltage to solenoid terminal SOL-.
4. Needle valve should withdraw .79 inch during step 2 and 3, if not as indicated, replace solenoid valve.
5. Install solenoid valve and bleed power steering line.

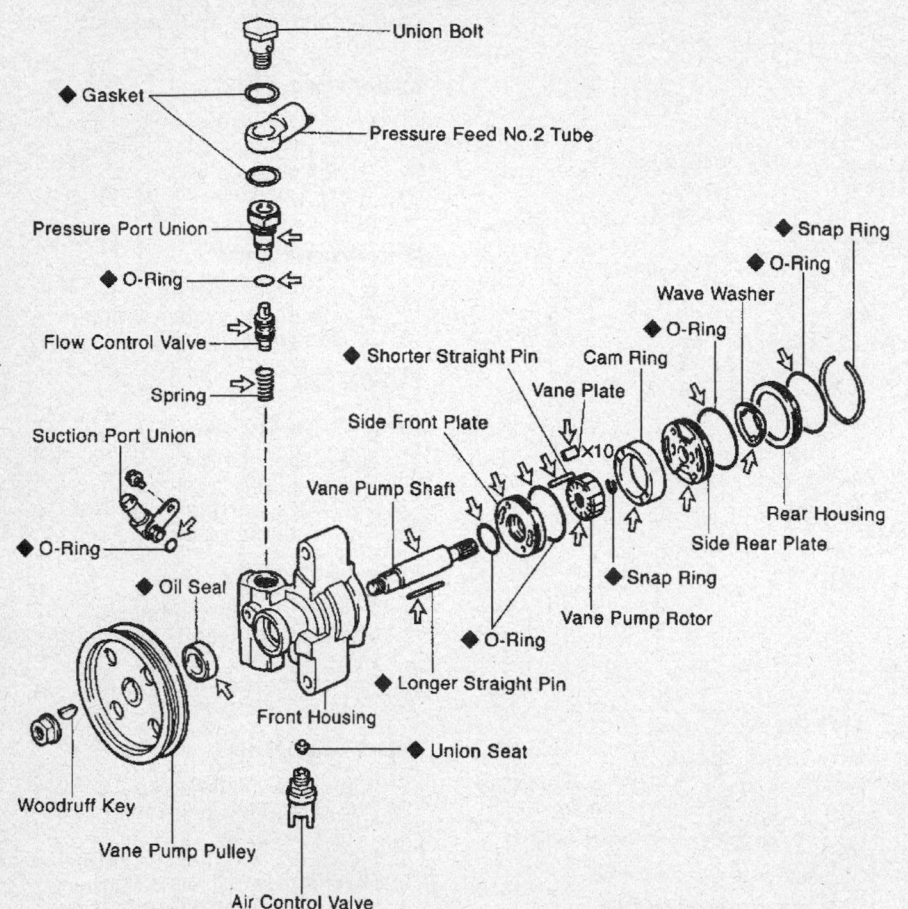

Fig. 8 Exploded view of power steering pump. Celica w/5S–FE engine

◆ Non-reusable part
⇐ Power steering fluid

TY6029700059000X

Rotor and cam ring mark	Vane plate part number	Vane plate length mm (in.)
None	44345−12010	14.996−14.998 (0.59039−0.59047)
1	44345−12020	14.994−14.996 (0.59032−0.59039)
2	44345−12030	14.992−14.994 (0.59024−0.59032)
3	44345−12040	14.990−14.992 (0.59016−0.59024)
4	44345−12050	14.988−14.990 (0.59008−0.59016)

TY6029700060000X

Fig. 9 Vane plate specifications. Celica w/7A-FE & 5S-FE engine

tion and keep it there for 2–3 seconds. Repeat several times.
6. Turn engine off.
7. Inspect fluid for foaming or emulsification. If system must be bled 2 times due to foaming or emulsification, check fluid level and inspect power steering system for leaks.

POWER STEERING PUMP

AVALON, CAMRY, CAMRY SOLARA & SIENNA

Disassemble

1. Position power steering pump in suitable soft-jawed vise.
2. Using suitable tool, remove pump pulley.
3. Remove end plate, **Fig. 6.**
4. Remove air control valve and union seat.
5. Remove suction port union and O-ring.
6. Remove pressure port union and O-ring, then remove flow control valve and spring.
7. Using suitable snap ring pliers, remove snap ring, temporarily install bolt to flow control spring seat, then remove seat and O-ring.
8. Remove rear housing snap ring, then using suitable plastic hammer, tap out rear housing, wave washer and O-ring.
9. Using suitable plastic hammer, tap out end shaft, then remove rear side plate and O-ring.
10. Remove pump shaft, cam ring and vane plates.
11. Using suitable screwdriver, remove pump shaft snap ring, remove rotor and front plate from pump shaft.
12. Remove front plate O-rings, then using suitable pin punch and hammer, drive out straight pin.

Inspection & Repair

1. Using suitable micrometer and calipers, measure oil clearance between shaft and bushing, .0028 inch or less should be indicated, if not replace entire power steering pump.
2. Using suitable micrometer, measure height, thickness and length of vane plates. Minimum height should be .315 inch, thickness, .0697 inch and length .5894 inch.
3. Using suitable feeler gauge, measure clearance between rotor groove and vane plate, maximum indicated should be .0012 inch.
4. If measurements are not as indicated

Power Steering ECU

1. Using suitable stands, raise and support vehicle.
2. Remove center console. **Do not disconnect ECU electrical connector.**
3. Start engine.
4. Using suitable voltmeter, measure voltage between terminals GND and SOL− with engine at idle, **Fig. 4,** 0−.05 volts should be indicated.
5. Place transmission in gear and while running at 31 mph, measure voltage between terminals GND and SOL−.
6. Total voltage should be voltage measured in step 4 plus an additional .12−.24 volts.
7. If no voltage is indicated, replace ECU.
8. Install center console and lower vehicle.

SUPRA

Solenoid Valve

1. Disconnect solenoid electrical connector.
2. Measure resistance between terminals SOL+ and SOL−, **Fig. 5,** resistance should be 6.0−11.0 ohms.
3. Reconnect electrical connector.

Solenoid Operation

1. Connect positive battery voltage to solenoid terminal SOL+.
2. Connect negative battery voltage to solenoid terminal SOL−.
3. Solenoid valve should click, if not as indicated, replace pressure control valve with solenoid. **Do not apply voltage for more than 30 seconds to avoid burning out solenoid.**
4. Connect electrical connector.

POWER STEERING SYSTEM SERVICE

POWER STEERING SYSTEM BLEED

1. Ensure power steering fluid is at proper level.
2. Raise and support front of vehicle.
3. With engine stopped, slowly turn wheel from lock to lock several times.
4. Lower vehicle, then start engine and run at idle for 5 minutes.
5. Turn wheel to left or right full lock posi-

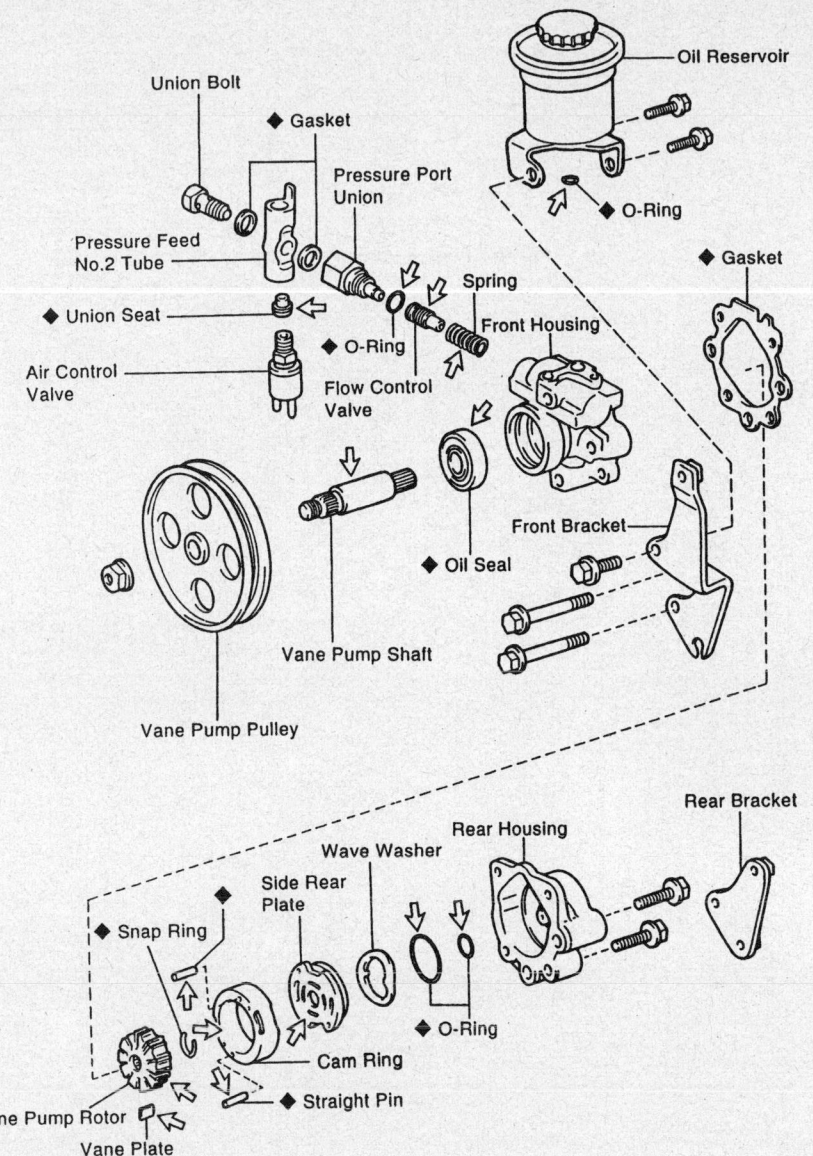

Fig. 10 Exploded view of power steering pump. 1996–97 Corolla

◆ Non-reusable part
⇦ Power Steering Fluid

TY6029500051000X

in steps 2 and 3, replace vane plate and/or rotor with one having the same mark stamped on cam ring.
5. Coat flow control valve with power steering fluid, ensure it falls smoothly into valve hole.
6. Close one flow control valve hole, then apply compressed air (57–71 psi) to opposite side, ensure air does not come out end holes.
7. If inspections are not as indicated in steps 6 and 7, replace flow control valve with one having same letter as on front housing.
8. Using suitable scale, measure flow control spring free length, 1.42–1.49 inch should be indicated, if not replace spring.
9. If required, replace oil seal as follows:
   a. Using suitable screwdriver, pry out oil seal.
   b. Using suitable socket and hammer, drive in new oil seal.

Assemble

1. Coat all sliding surfaces with power steering fluid.
2. Using suitable plastic hammer, drive short straight pin to front plate.
3. Install O-rings to front plate, then install front plate, rotor and snap ring to pump shaft.
4. Coat oil seal lip with MP grease, install long straight pin to front housing, align front plate hole and straight pin, then using suitable plastic hammer, tap in pump shaft. **Do not damage oil seal and O-rings.**
5. Align cam ring holes with straight pins, then install cam ring with inscribed marks facing outward.

6. Install vane plates with round end facing outward.
7. Install side plate O-ring, then align side plate holes with pins and install side plate.
8. Install rear housing wave washer, O-ring, then using suitable plastic hammer, tap in rear housing, install snap ring.
9. Ensure pump shaft rotates smoothly without abnormal noise.
10. Temporarily install pulley nut and check rotating torque. Ensure 2.4 inch lbs. or less is indicated.
11. Install O-ring to flow control spring seat, install spring seat with bolt hole facing outward to housing, then install snap ring.
12. Install spring, flow control valve, O-ring and pressure port union, tighten to specifications.
13. Install suction port O-ring and suction port union to housing, tightening to specifications.
14. Install air control valve.
15. Install woodruff key to power steering pulley shaft, then install pulley and nut, tighten to specifications.
16. Install end plate.

CELICA w/7A-FE & 5S-FE ENGINE

Refer to **Figs. 7 and 8** when performing the following service procedures.

Disassemble

1. Position power steering pump in a suitable soft-jawed vise.
2. Using a suitable torque wrench, measure rotational torque of pump.
3. Ensure pump rotates quietly and smoothly.
4. Ensure rotational torque is 2.4 inch lbs. or less.
5. Using tool Nos. 09960–10010, 09962–01000, and 09963–01000, or equivalent, hold pulley and remove pulley retaining nut.
6. Remove key from pump shaft.
7. Remove air control valve and union seat.
8. **On models equipped with 7A-FE engine,** remove bracket and oil reservoir.
9. **On models equipped with 5S-FE engine,** remove pressure feed No. 2 tube and suction port union.
10. **On all models,** remove pressure port union.
11. Remove flow control valve and spring.
12. Using two suitable screwdrivers, remove rear housing snap ring.
13. Wrap pump shaft with suitable vinyl tape.
14. Tap pump shaft with a suitable plastic hammer until wave washer and rear housing are removed.
15. Remove O-ring from housing.
16. Remove side rear plate using a suitable plastic hammer.
17. Remove O-ring from housing.
18. Remove cam ring and plates. Ensure vane plates are not dropped.
19. Remove vane pump shaft together with vane pump rotor and side front plate.

20. Remove longest straight pin from housing.
21. Using a suitable screwdriver, remove vane pump shaft snap ring.
22. Remove O-rings from plate.
23. Remove pin from side front plate.

Inspection

1. Using a suitable micrometer and caliper gauge, measure oil clearance between pump shaft and bushing. Ensure clearance does not exceed .0028 inch.
2. If clearance exceeds specification, replace front housing and vane pump shaft.
3. Using a suitable micrometer, measure vane plates and replace as necessary. Ensure measurements are as follows:
   a. Height: .319 inch.
   b. Thickness: .0707 inch.
   c. Length: .5901 inch.
4. Using a suitable feeler gauge, measure clearance between rotor groove and plate.
5. If clearance exceeds .0012 inch, replace plate or rotor as necessary.
6. Ensure replacement plate or rotor has same mark as stamped on cam ring. Refer to **Fig. 9** for vane plate specifications.
7. Coat flow control valve with power steering fluid ensuring it falls smoothly into valve hole.
8. Close on flow control valve hole, then apply 57–71 psi of compressed air into opposite hole.
9. Ensure air does not exit from end hole. If flow control valve does not pass compressed air check, replace valve with one having same letter as stamped on front housing.
10. Using a suitable caliper, measure spring free length.
11. If measurement is below 1.42 inches, replace spring.
12. If seal replacement is required, pry oil seal out using a suitable screwdriver with tapped end.
13. Apply suitable clean power steering fluid to lip of new seal.
14. Using tool Nos. 09950–60010 and 09950–70010, or equivalent, install seal.

Assemble

1. Coat all sliding surfaces with suitable power steering fluid.
2. Install new short straight pin to side front plate.
3. Coat new O-rings with suitable power steering fluid, then install to plate.
4. Install plate to vane pump shaft.
5. Install vane pump rotor. Ensure inscribed mark faces outward.
6. Install new snap ring on vane pump shaft.
7. Install new long straight pin to front housing.
8. Wrap suitable vinyl tape around vane pump shaft to prevent oil seal lip damage during installation.
9. Align hole of plate and longer straight pin, then tap into place using a suitable plastic hammer.

10. Align holes of cam ring and straight pins, then install ring with inscribed mark facing outward.
11. Install plates with round end facing outward.
12. Apply suitable power steering fluid to new O-ring and install to plate.
13. Align holes of plate and straight pins.
14. Install wave washer. Ensure protrusions of washer are installed into slots of side rear plate.
15. Apply suitable power steering fluid to rear housing and install into housing.
16. Install rear housing, then the snap ring.
17. Install spring, then the flow control valve.
18. Apply suitable power steering fluid to new pressure port union O-ring and install to pressure port union.
19. Install pressure port union.
20. **On models equipped with 7A-FE engine,** proceed as follows:
    a. Apply suitable power steering fluid to new reservoir O-ring, then install to oil reservoir.
    b. Install oil reservoir and tighten to specification.
21. **On models equipped with 5S-FE engine,** proceed as follows:
    a. Apply suitable power steering fluid to suction port union O-ring, then install to suction port union.
    b. Install suction port union and tighten to specification.
    c. Install pressure feed No. 2 tube with new gaskets at each side of tube. **Pressure tube installation angel is 35°.**
22. **On all models,** install new union seat, then the air control valve.
23. Install key to pump shaft, then the pulley.

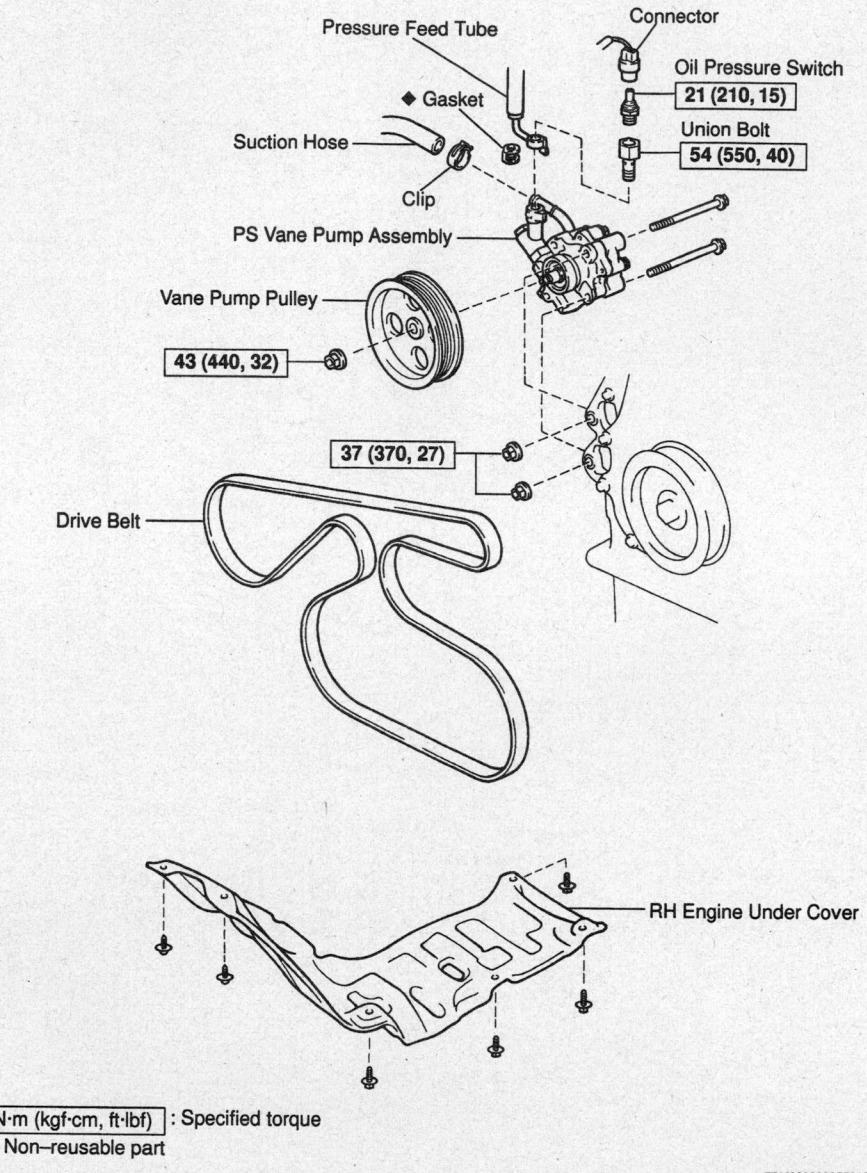

Pressure Feed Tube
Connector
◆ Gasket
Oil Pressure Switch
21 (210, 15)
Suction Hose
Union Bolt
54 (550, 40)
Clip
PS Vane Pump Assembly
Vane Pump Pulley
43 (440, 32)
37 (370, 27)
Drive Belt
RH Engine Under Cover

N·m (kgf·cm, ft·lbf) : Specified torque
◆ Non–reusable part

TY6029800077010X

Fig. 11 Exploded view of power steering pump (Part 1 of 2). 1998–99 Corolla

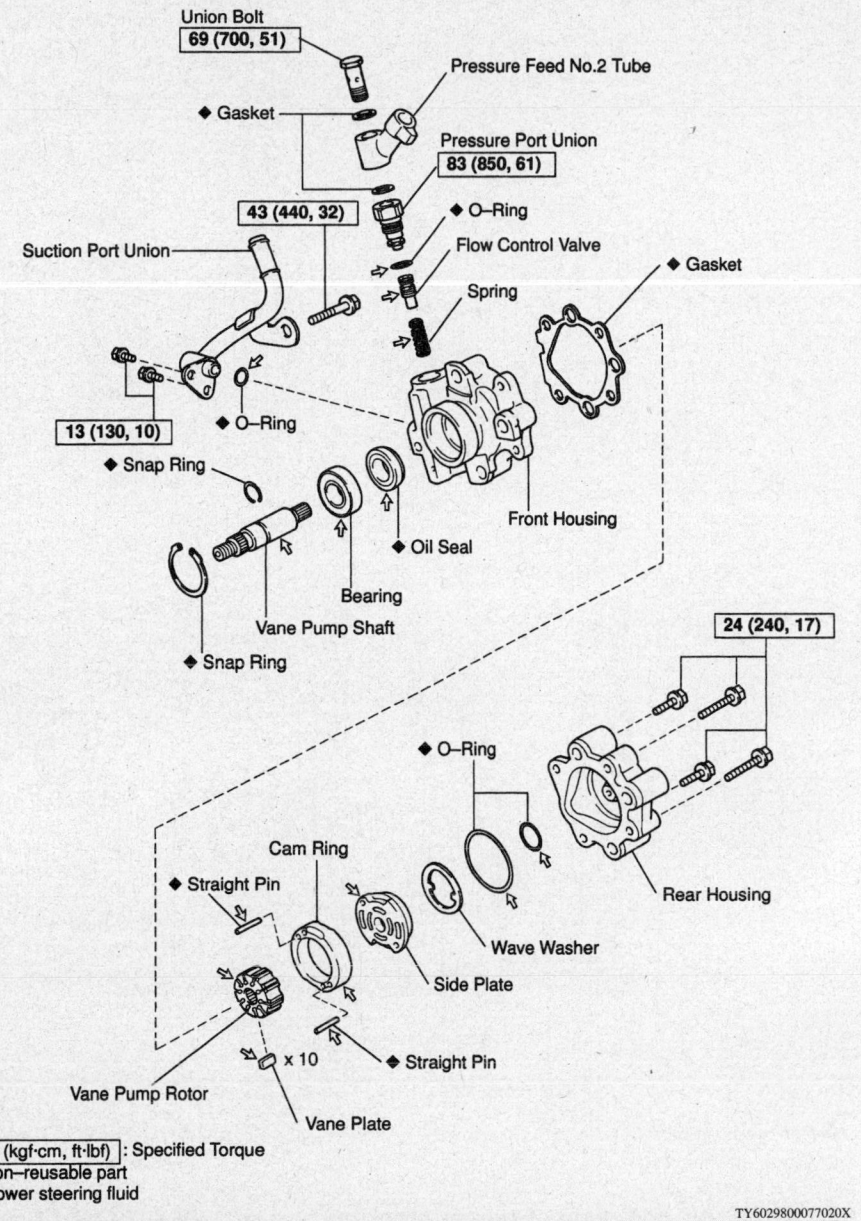

Fig. 11   Exploded view of power steering pump (Part 2 of 2). 1998–99 Corolla

Labels in figure:
- Union Bolt **69 (700, 51)**
- Pressure Feed No.2 Tube
- ◆ Gasket
- Pressure Port Union **83 (850, 61)**
- **43 (440, 32)**
- ◆ O–Ring
- Suction Port Union
- Flow Control Valve
- Spring
- ◆ Gasket
- **13 (130, 10)**
- ◆ O–Ring
- Front Housing
- ◆ Snap Ring
- ◆ Oil Seal
- Vane Pump Shaft
- Bearing
- ◆ Snap Ring
- **24 (240, 17)**
- ◆ O–Ring
- Rear Housing
- Cam Ring
- ◆ Straight Pin
- Wave Washer
- Side Plate
- Vane Pump Rotor
- ◆ Straight Pin
- Vane Plate
- x 10

N·m (kgf·cm, ft·lbf) : Specified Torque
◆ Non–reusable part
⇐ Power steering fluid

TY6029800077020X

---

tire power steering pump.

2. Using suitable micrometer, measure height, thickness and length of vane plates. Minimum height should be .339 inch, thickness, .055 inch and length .5902 inch.
3. Using suitable feeler gauge, measure clearance between rotor groove and vane plate, maximum indicated should be .014 inch.
4. If measurements are not as indicated in steps 2 and 3, replace vane plate and/ or rotor with one having the same mark stamped on cam ring.
5. Coat flow control valve with power steering fluid, ensuring it falls smoothly into valve hole.
6. Close one flow control valve hole, then apply compressed air (57–71 psi) to opposite side, ensuring air does not come out end holes.
7. If inspections are not as indicated in steps 6 and 7, replace flow control valve with one having same letter as on front housing.
8. Using suitable scale, measure flow control spring free length. Length should be 1.28–1.34 inches.
9. If required, replace oil seal as follows:
   a. Using suitable screwdriver, pry out oil seal.
   b. Using suitable socket and hammer, drive in new oil seal.

Assemble

1. Coat all sliding surfaces with power steering fluid.
2. Using suitable plastic hammer, drive short straight pin to front plate.
3. Install O-rings to front plate, then install front plate, rotor and snap ring to pump shaft.
4. Coat oil seal lip with MP grease, install long straight pin to front housing, align front plate hole and straight pin, then using suitable plastic hammer, tap in pump shaft. **Do not damage oil seal and O-rings.**
5. Align cam ring holes with straight pins, then install cam ring with inscribed marks facing outward.
6. Install vane plates with round end facing outward.
7. Install side plate O-ring, then align side plate holes with pins and install side plate.
8. Install rear housing wave washer, O-ring, then using suitable plastic hammer, tap in rear housing, install snap ring.
9. Ensure pump shaft rotates smoothly without abnormal noise.
10. Temporarily install pulley nut and check rotating torque. Ensure 2.2 or less is indicated.
11. Install spring, flow control valve, O-ring and pressure port union, tighten to specifications.
12. Install reservoir tank O-ring, tank and bracket, tighten to specifications.
13. Install air control valve.
14. Install woodruff key to power steering pulley shaft, then install pulley and nut, tighten to specifications.

---

24. Using tool Nos. 09960–10010, 09962–01000, and 09963–01000, or equivalent, tighten pulley nut to specification.
25. Ensure pump rotational torque is within specification.

COROLLA

Disassemble

1. Position power steering pump in suitable soft-jawed vise.
2. Using suitable tool, remove pump pulley.
3. Remove air control valve, **Figs. 10 and 11.**
4. Remove reservoir tank, bracket and O-ring.
5. Remove pressure port union and O-ring, then remove flow control valve and spring.
6. Remove rear housing snap ring, then using suitable plastic hammer, tap out rear housing, wave washer and O-ring.
7. Using suitable plastic hammer, tap out shaft end, rear side plate and O-ring.
8. Remove pump shaft, cam ring and vane plates.
9. Using suitable screwdriver, remove pump shaft snap ring, remove rotor and front plate from pump shaft.
10. Remove front plate O-rings, then using suitable pin punch and hammer, drive out straight pin.

Inspection

1. Using suitable micrometer and calipers, measure oil clearance between shaft and bushing, .0028 inch or less should be indicated, if not replace en-

---

LAND CRUISER

Disassemble

1. Position power steering pump in suitable soft-jawed vise.
2. Remove reservoir tank and O-ring.
3. Remove pressure port union and O-ring, then remove flow control valve and spring, **Figs. 12 and 13.**
4. Remove rear housing snap ring, then using suitable plastic hammer, tap out rear housing, wave washer and O-ring.
5. Using suitable plastic hammer, tap shaft end, rear side plate and O-ring.
6. Using suitable snap ring pliers, remove snap ring, temporarily install bolt to flow control spring seat, then remove seat and O-ring.
7. Remove pump shaft, cam ring and vane plates.
8. Using suitable screwdriver, remove pump shaft snap ring, remove rotor and front plate from pump shaft.
9. Remove front plate O-rings, then remove straight pin.

Inspection

1. Using suitable micrometer and calipers, measure oil clearance between shaft and bushing, .0028 inch or less should be indicated, if not replace entire power steering pump.
2. Using suitable micrometer, measure height, thickness and length of vane plates. Minimum height should be .319 inch, thickness, .0707 inch and length .5901 inch.
3. Using suitable feeler gauge, measure clearance between rotor groove and vane plate, maximum indicated should be .0011 inch.
4. If measurements are not as indicated in steps 2 and 3, replace vane plate and/or rotor with one having the same mark stamped on cam ring.
5. Coat flow control valve with power steering fluid, ensuring it falls smoothly into valve hole.
6. Close one flow control valve hole, then apply compressed air (57–71 psi) to opposite side, ensuring air does not come out end holes.
7. If inspections are not as indicated in steps 6 and 7, replace flow control valve with one having same letter as on front housing.
8. Using suitable scale, measure flow control spring free length, 1.38–1.46 inch should be indicated, if not replace spring.
9. If required, replace oil seal as follows:
   a. Using suitable screwdriver, pry out oil seal.
   b. Using suitable socket and hammer, drive in new oil seal.

Assemble

1. Coat all sliding surfaces with power steering fluid.
2. Using suitable plastic hammer, drive short straight pin to front plate.
3. Install O-rings to front plate, install front plate to pump shaft, then rotor to pump shaft with inscribed mark facing outward, then install snap ring.

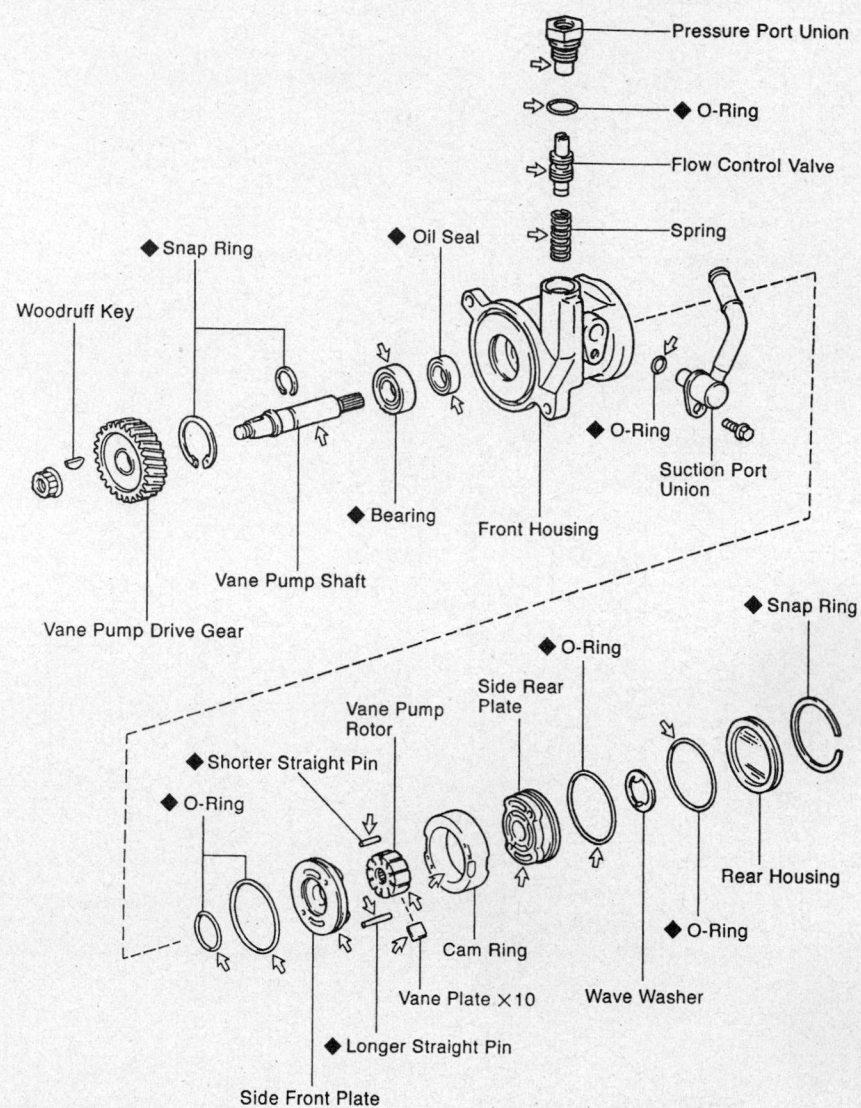

Fig. 12 Exploded view of power steering pump. 1996–97 Land Cruiser

◆ Non-reusable part
⇐ Power steering fluid

TY6029500052000X

4. Coat oil seal lip with MP grease, install long straight pin to front housing, align front plate hole and straight pin, then using suitable plastic hammer, tap in pump shaft. **Do not damage oil seal and O-rings.**
5. Align cam ring holes with straight pins, then install cam ring with inscribed marks facing outward.
6. Install vane plates with round end facing outward.
7. Install side plate O-ring, then align rear plate holes with pins and install rear plate.
8. Install rear housing wave washer, O-ring, then using suitable plastic hammer, tap in rear housing, install snap ring.
9. Ensure pump shaft rotates smoothly without abnormal noise.
10. Temporarily install pulley nut and check rotating torque. Ensure 2.4 inch lbs. or less is indicated.
11. Install O-ring to flow control spring seat, install spring seat with bolt hole facing outward to housing, then install snap ring.
12. Install spring, flow control valve, O-ring and pressure port union, tighten to specifications.
13. Install reservoir tank and O-ring.
14. Install suction port O-ring and suction port union to housing, tightening to specifications.

PREVIA

Disassemble

1. Position power steering pump in suitable soft-jawed vise.
2. Using suitable tool, remove pump pulley.
3. Remove suction port union and O-ring, **Fig. 14.**
4. Remove pressure port union and

should be indicated, if not replace spring.
8. If required, replace oil seal as follows:
   a. Using suitable tool, pry out oil seal.
   b. Using suitable socket and hammer, drive in new oil seal.

Assemble

1. Coat all sliding surfaces with power steering fluid.
2. Install pump shaft with bearing into front housing.
3. Using suitable plastic hammer, drive short straight pin to front plate.
4. Align cam ring holes with straight pins and install cam ring with inscribed mark facing upward.
5. Install rotor with inscribed marks facing outward.
6. Coat vane plates with power steering fluid, then install vane plates with round end facing outward.
7. Install rear plate O-ring, then align rear plate holes with pins and install rear plate.
8. Install suction port union.
9. Install spring, flow control valve, O-ring and pressure port union, tighten to specifications.
10. Install suction port O-ring and suction port union to housing, tightening to specifications.
11. Using tool No. 09613-00012, or equivalent, press pulley to pump shaft until .071–.087 inch of shaft is above pulley.
12. Ensure pump shaft rotates smoothly without abnormal noise.
13. Install pulley nut and check rotating torque. Ensure 2.4 inch lbs. or less is indicated.

RAV4

Disassemble

1. Position power steering pump in suitable soft-jawed vise.
2. Remove pump front bracket and pump bracket, **Fig. 15**.
3. Using tool No. 09960-10010, or equivalent, remove pump pulley set bolt and pulley.
4. Remove O-ring from pulley.
5. Remove woodruff key from pump shaft.
6. Remove air control valve.
7. Remove pressure feed No. 2 tube.
8. Remove union set bolt, union and union O-ring.
9. Remove pressure port union.
10. Remove flow control valve and spring.
11. Using snap ring pliers, remove flow control snap ring.
12. Partially install a 6 mm normal diameter bolt (Part No. 91651-60650, or equivalent) into flow control spring seat, then remove bolt and spring seat from front pump housing.
13. Remove O-ring from flow control spring seat.
14. Using a plastic hammer, tap out rear housing, wave washer and side rear plate.
15. Remove cam ring and 10 vane plates.
16. Remove vane pump shaft with vane pump rotor and side front plate.
17. Using pliers, remove shorter straight

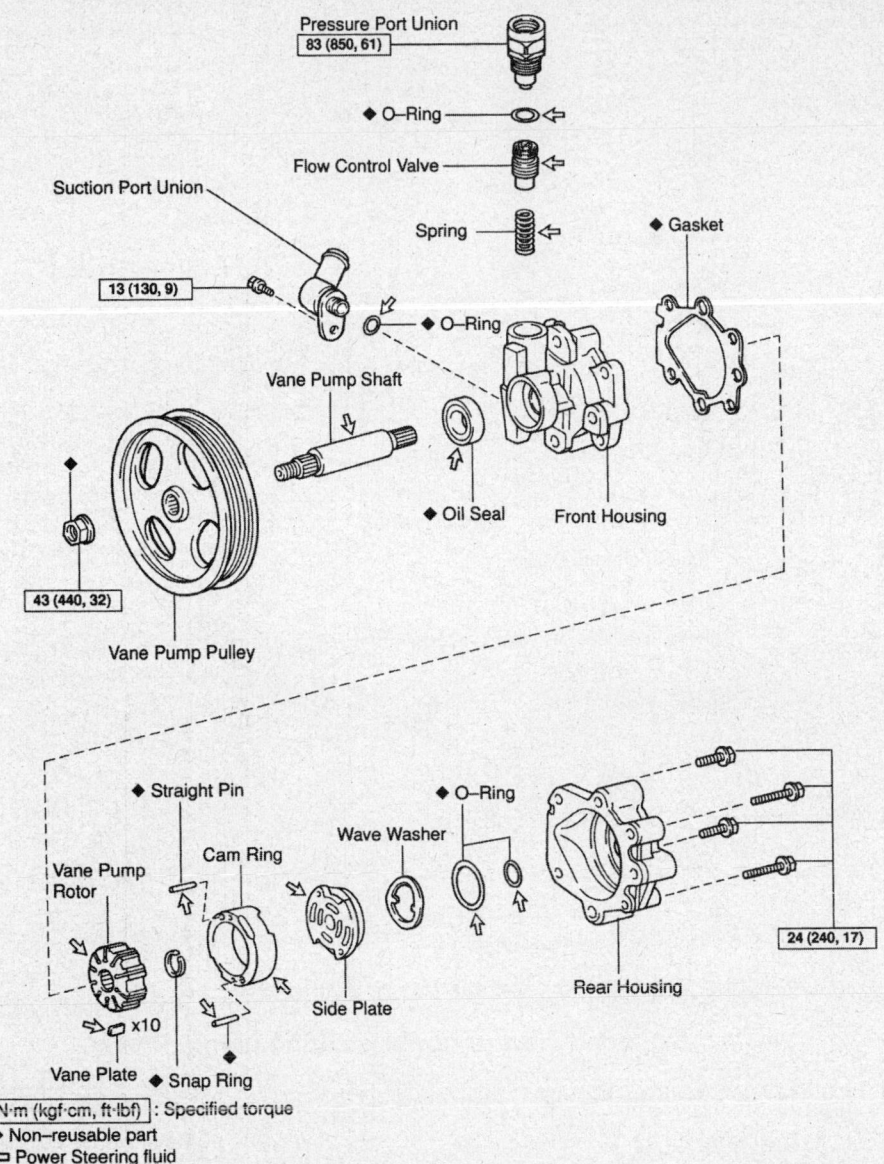

TY6029800078000X

Fig. 13 Exploded view of power steering pump. 1998–99 Land Cruiser

O-ring, then remove flow control valve and spring.
5. Place installation alignment marks on front and rear housing, then remove rear housing attaching bolts, O-rings and gasket.
6. Remove wave washer and rear plate.
7. Remove cam ring, rotor and vane plates.
8. Using suitable pliers, remove straight pins from front housing.
9. Using suitable pliers, remove bearing wire.
10. Using tool No. 09515-21010, or equivalent, and an extension bar, press out pump shaft with bearing. Do not allow assembly to drop.

Inspection & Repair

1. Using suitable micrometer, measure height, thickness and length of vane plates. Minimum height should be .315

inch, thickness, .0697 inch and length .5894 inch.
2. Using suitable feeler gauge, measure clearance between rotor groove and vane plate, maximum indicated should be .0012 inch.
3. If measurements are not as indicated in steps 1 and 2, replace vane plate and/ or rotor with one having the same mark stamped on cam ring.
4. Coat flow control valve with power steering fluid, ensuring it falls smoothly into valve hole.
5. Close one flow control valve hole, then apply compressed air (57–71 psi) to opposite side, ensuring air does not come out end holes.
6. If inspections are not as indicated in steps 4 and 5, replace flow control valve with one having same letter as on front housing.
7. Using suitable scale, measure flow control spring free length, 1.42 inch

pin from side front plate and longer straight pin from front housing.

Inspection

1. Using a micrometer and caliper gauge, measure oil clearance between vane pump shaft and bushing.
2. Standard oil clearance should be .0012–.0020 inch. Maximum oil clearance is .0028 inch.
3. Using a micrometer, measure the height, thickness and length of 10 pump plates. Height should be .319 inch. Thickness should be .0707 inch and plate length should be .59008 inch.
4. Using a feeler gauge, measure clearance between rotor groove and plate. Maximum clearance should be .0012 inch.
5. If plate and/or rotor must be replaced, use replacement part with the same mark inscribed on cam ring (1, 2, 3, 4 or none).
6. Inspect flow control valve by coating with power steering fluid and ensuring it falls smoothly into valve hole by its own weight.
7. Check flow control valve for leakage by closing one hole and applying compressed air into opposite side.
8. If necessary, replace valve with one having the same letter inscribed (A, B, C, D, E or F).
9. Using calipers, measure free length of spring.
10. Spring length should be at least 1.42 inches.

Assemble

1. Coat parts with power steering fluid.
2. Using plastic hammer, tap new long straight pin into front pump housing.
3. Using plastic hammer, tap new short straight pin into side front plate.
4. Place new O-rings on side front plate and install plate to pump shaft.
5. Install rotor to pump shaft with inscribed mark facing outward.
6. Using snap ring pliers, install new snap ring to vane pump shaft.
7. Align hole of plate and longer straight pin, then tap in shaft with plastic hammer.
8. Align holes of cam ring and two straight pins, then install ring with inscribed mark facing outward.
9. Install 10 vane plates with round end facing outward.
10. Align holes of side rear plate and two straight pins, then install side rear plate.
11. Install wave washer so that its protrusions fit into slots in side rear plate.
12. Using plastic hammer, tap rear housing to front housing and install new snap ring.
13. Install flow control spring seat into rear housing, then remove bolt.
14. Install spring and flow control valve.
15. Install pressure port union and **torque** to 51 ft. lbs.
16. Install suction port union and **torque** to 9 ft. lbs.
17. Install pressure feed No. 2 tube.

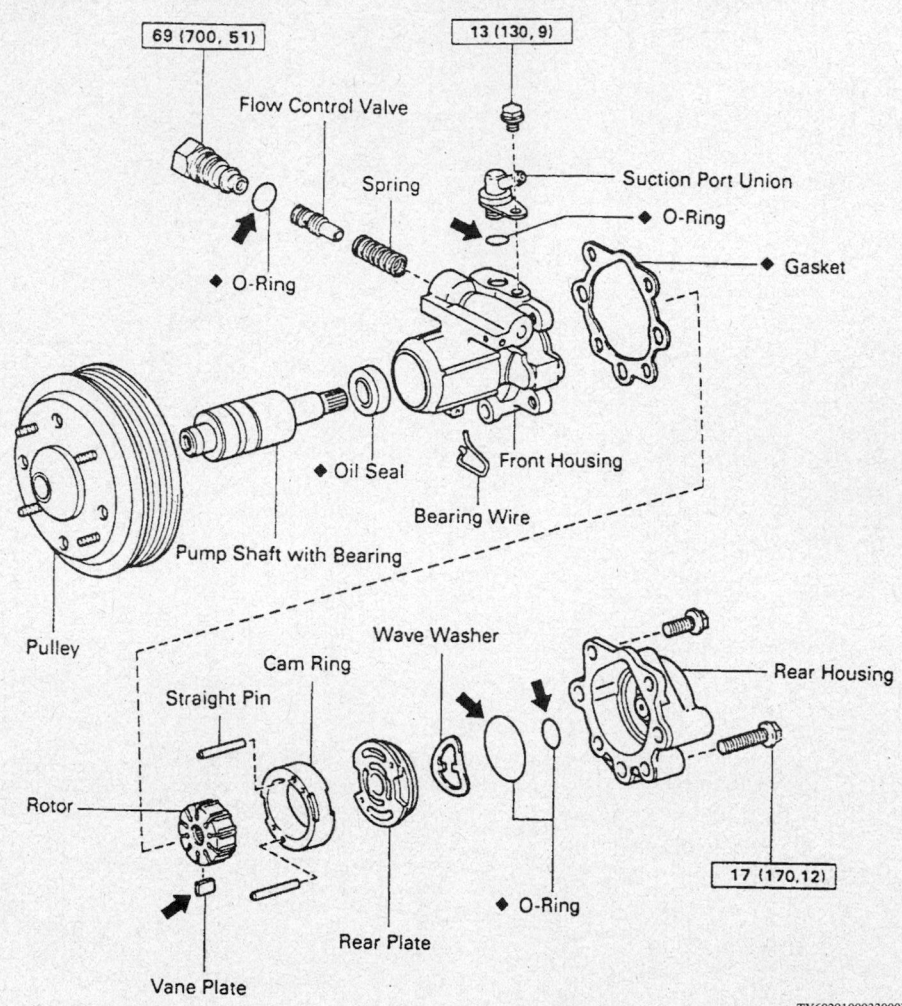

Fig. 14 Exploded view of power steering pump. Previa

18. Install air control valve. **Torque** to 27 ft. lbs.
19. Install woodruff key to vane pump shaft.
20. Using tool No. 09960-10010, or equivalent, install pump pulley and **torque** set nut to 32 ft. lbs.
21. Install pump bracket and pump front bracket.

SUPRA

Disassemble

1. Remove power steering pump pulley using holding tool No. 09960–10010, or equivalent, and a suitable wrench.
2. Install pulley set nut, then measure pump rotational torque using a suitable torque wrench.
3. Ensure pump rotational torque is 2.2 inch lbs. or less.
4. **On non-turbo models,** remove oil reservoir.
5. **On turbo models,** remove suction port union.
6. **On all models,** remove pressure port union, **Fig. 16.**
7. Remove rear housing.
8. Remove cam ring, vane pump rotor and vane plates.

9. Remove two straight pins, then the gasket.
10. Remove vane pump shaft with bearing as follows:
    a. Using a suitable pair of snap rig pliers, remove snap ring from front housing.
    b. Apply suitable vinyl tape to pump shaft.
    c. Using a suitable press, press out shaft with bearing.
11. Remove side plate and wave washer.
12. Remove two O-rings from rear housing.

Inspection & Repair

1. Using suitable micrometer and calipers, measure oil clearance between shaft and bushing, .0028 inch or less should be indicated, if not, replace vane pump shaft and front housing.
2. Using suitable micrometer, measure height, thickness and length of vane plates. Minimum height should be .339 inch, thickness, .0551 inch and length .5902 inch.
3. Using suitable feeler gauge, measure clearance between rotor groove and vane plate, maximum indicated should be .0014 inch.
4. If measurements are not as indicated

7. Install vane pump rotor with inscribed mark facing outward.
8. Install vane plates with rounded edge facing outward.
9. Install new gasket to front housing.
10. Install side plate, then the wave washer.
11. Install rear housing O-rings, then the rear housing.
12. Install spring, flow control valve, and pressure port union.
13. **On non-turbo models,** install suction port union.
14. **On turbo models,** install oil reservoir.
15. **On all models,** install pulley set nut, then check pump rotational torque using a suitable torque wrench. Ensure torque is 2.2 inch lbs. or less.
16. Install vane pump pulley. Tighten nut to specification.

TACOMA & T100 (VZ SERIES) & 4RUNNER (VZ SERIES)

Disassemble

1. Position power steering pump in suitable soft-jawed vise.
2. Remove air control valve, then remove reservoir tank and O-ring.
3. Remove suction port union and O-ring, then remove flow control valve and spring **Fig. 17.**
4. Remove rear housing snap ring, then using suitable plastic hammer, tap out rear housing, wave washer and O-ring.
5. Using suitable plastic hammer, tap shaft end, rear side plate and O-ring.
6. Remove pump shaft, cam ring and vane plates.
7. Using suitable screwdriver, remove pump shaft snap ring, remove rotor and front plate from pump shaft.
8. Remove front plate O-rings, then remove straight pin.
9. Remove adjusting stay.

Inspection

1. Using suitable micrometer and calipers, measure oil clearance between shaft and bushing, .0028 inch or less should be indicated, if not replace entire power steering pump.
2. Using suitable micrometer, measure height, thickness and length of vane plates. Minimum height should be .319 inch, thickness, .0707 inch and length .5901 inch.
3. Using suitable feeler gauge, measure clearance between rotor groove and vane plate, maximum indicated should be .0012 inch.
4. If measurements are not as indicated in steps 2 and 3, replace vane plate and/ or rotor with one having the same mark stamped on cam ring.
5. Coat flow control valve with power steering fluid, ensuring it falls smoothly into valve hole.
6. Close one flow control valve hole, then apply compressed air (57–71 psi) to opposite side, ensuring air does not come out end holes.
7. If inspections are not as indicated in steps 6 and 7, replace flow control valve with one having same letter as on front housing.

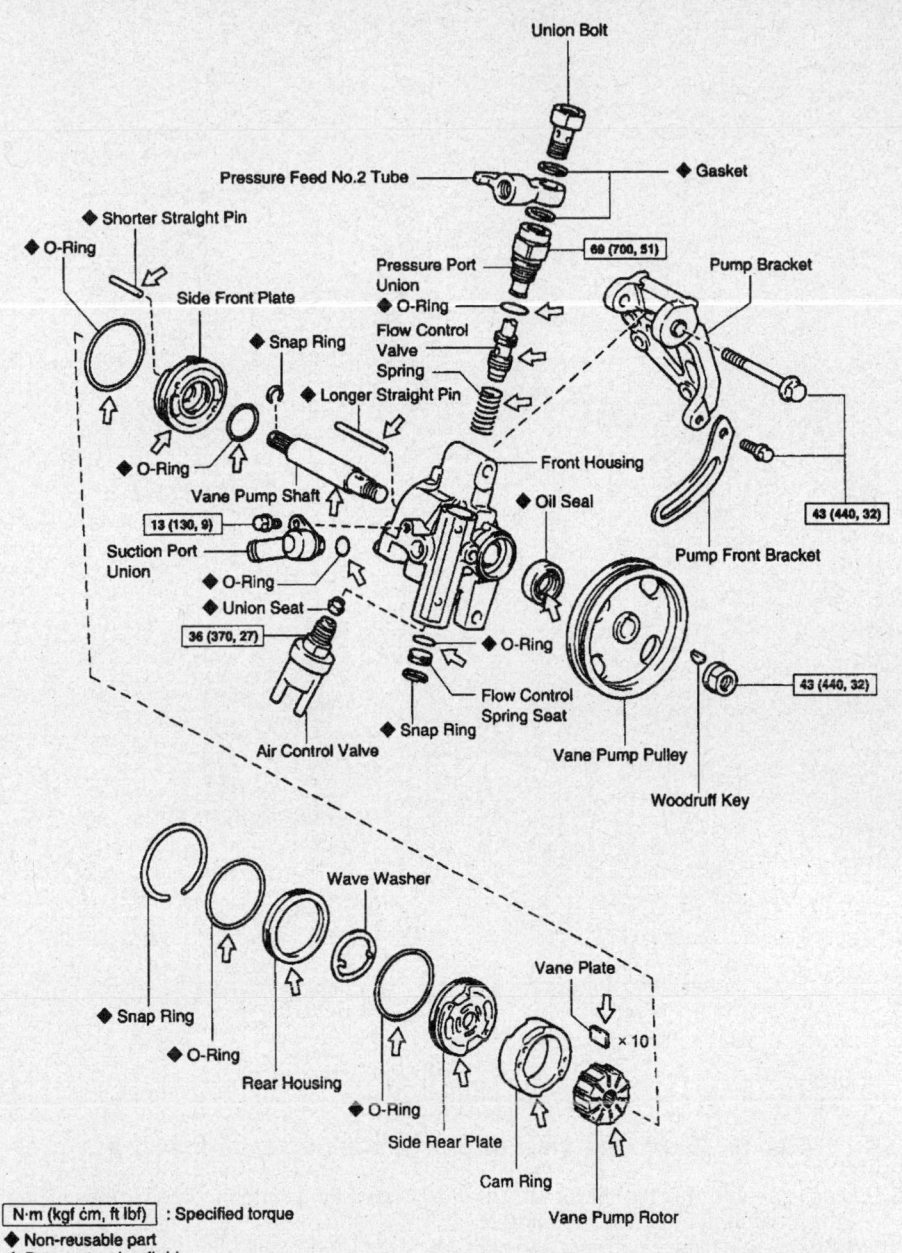

Fig. 15 Exploded view of power steering pump. RAV4

in steps 2 and 3, replace vane plate and/or rotor with one having the same mark stamped on cam ring.
5. Coat flow control valve with power steering fluid, ensuring it falls smoothly into valve hole.
6. Close one flow control valve hole, then apply compressed air (57–71 psi) to opposite side, ensuring air does not come out end holes.
7. If inspections are not as indicated in steps 6 and 7, replace flow control valve with one having same letter as on front housing.
8. Using suitable scale, measure flow control spring free length, minimum 1.30 inch should be indicated, if not replace spring.
9. If required, replace oil seal as follows:
   a. Using seal removal tool No. 09631–

10030, or equivalent, remove seal.
   b. Apply power steering fluid to new seal, then install using a suitable 24 mm socket and press.

Assemble

1. Apply power steering fluid to all seals and O-rings before installation.
2. Apply vinyl tape to pump shaft.
3. Install pump shaft to front housing using shaft installer tool No. 09608–04031, or equivalent, and a suitable press.
4. Using a suitable pair of snap ring pliers, install snap ring to front housing.
5. Install 2 new straight pins to front housing using a suitable plastic hammer.
6. Align holes of cam ring and straight pins, then install ring with inscribed mark facing outward.

8. Using suitable scale, measure flow control spring free length, 1.38–1.46 inch should be indicated, if not replace spring.
9. If required, replace oil seal as follows:
   a. Using suitable screwdriver, pry out oil seal.
   b. Using suitable socket and hammer, drive in new oil seal.

Assemble

1. Coat all sliding surfaces with power steering fluid, then install adjusting stay.
2. Using suitable plastic hammer, drive short straight pin to front plate.
3. Install O-rings to front plate, install front plate to pump shaft, then rotor to pump shaft with inscribed mark facing outward, then install snap ring.
4. Coat oil seal lip with MP grease, install long straight pin to front housing, align front plate hole and straight pin, then using suitable plastic hammer, tap in pump shaft. **Do not damage oil seal and O-rings.**
5. Align cam ring holes with straight pins, then install cam ring with inscribed marks facing outward.
6. Install vane plates with round end facing outward.
7. Install side plate O-ring, then align rear plate holes with pins and install rear plate.
8. Install rear housing wave washer, O-ring, then using suitable plastic hammer, tap in rear housing, install snap ring.
9. Ensure pump shaft rotates smoothly without abnormal noise.
10. Temporarily install pulley nut and check rotating torque. Ensure 2.4 inch lbs. or less is indicated.
11. Install O-ring to flow control spring seat, install spring seat with bolt hole facing outward to housing, then install snap ring.
12. Install spring, flow control valve, O-ring and pressure port union, tighten to specifications.
13. Install reservoir tank and O-ring.
14. Install air control valve and tighten to specifications.

TACOMA & T100 & 4RUNNER (RZ SERIES)

Disassemble

1. Position power steering pump in suitable soft-jawed vise.
2. Remove air control valve and union seat.
3. Remove suction port union and O-ring, **Fig. 18.**
4. Remove front housing attaching bolts, place installation alignment mark on front and rear housing, then using suitable plastic hammer, tap off front housing. **Do not allow vane plates, rotor or cam ring to fall out.**
5. Remove cam ring, rotor and vane plates.
6. Position front housing in suitable soft jawed vise.
7. Using suitable hammer and chisel, pry off oil seal, then remove snap ring.

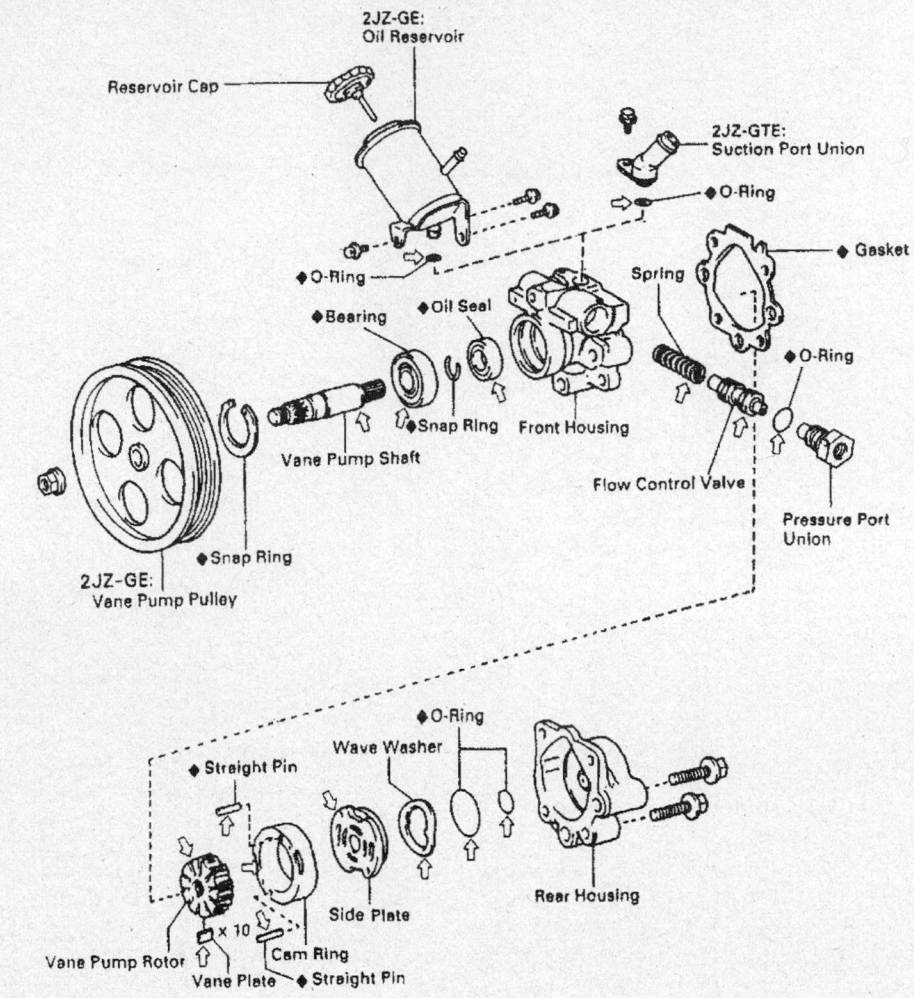

◆ Non-reusable part   ⇐ : Power steering fluid

TY6029700065000X

Fig. 16   Exploded view of power steering pump. Supra

8. Using suitable plastic hammer, remove rotor shaft from front housing.
9. Using suitable plastic hammer, tap bottom end of rear housing and remove rear plate and spring. **Do not grip rear plate with pliers as damage may occur.**
10. Temporarily install bolt to spring seat, using suitable snap ring pliers, remove snap ring, pull out bolt, using suitable tool, remove spring seat, then remove O-ring.

Inspection & Repair

1. Using suitable micrometer and calipers, measure oil clearance between shaft and bushing, .0028 inch or less should be indicated, if not replace entire power steering pump.
2. If required, replace rotor shaft bearing as follows:
   a. Using suitable snap ring pliers, remove snap ring.
   b. Using suitable press, press out bearing.
   c. Using suitable press, press in bearing.
   d. Using suitable snap ring pliers, install snap ring.
3. Using suitable feeler gauge, measure cam ring clearance, maximum should be .0024 inch, if difference is not as indicated, replace cam ring with one with same letter as on rotor.
4. Using suitable micrometer, measure height, thickness and length of vane plates. Minimum height should be .319 inch, thickness, .0707 inch and length .5901 inch.
5. Using suitable feeler gauge, measure clearance between rotor groove and vane plate, maximum indicated should be .0012 inch.
6. If measurements are not as indicated in steps 5 and 6; replace vane plate and/ or rotor with one having the same mark stamped on cam ring.
7. Coat flow control valve with power steering fluid, ensuring it falls smoothly into valve hole.
8. Close one flow control valve hole, then apply compressed air (57–71 psi) to

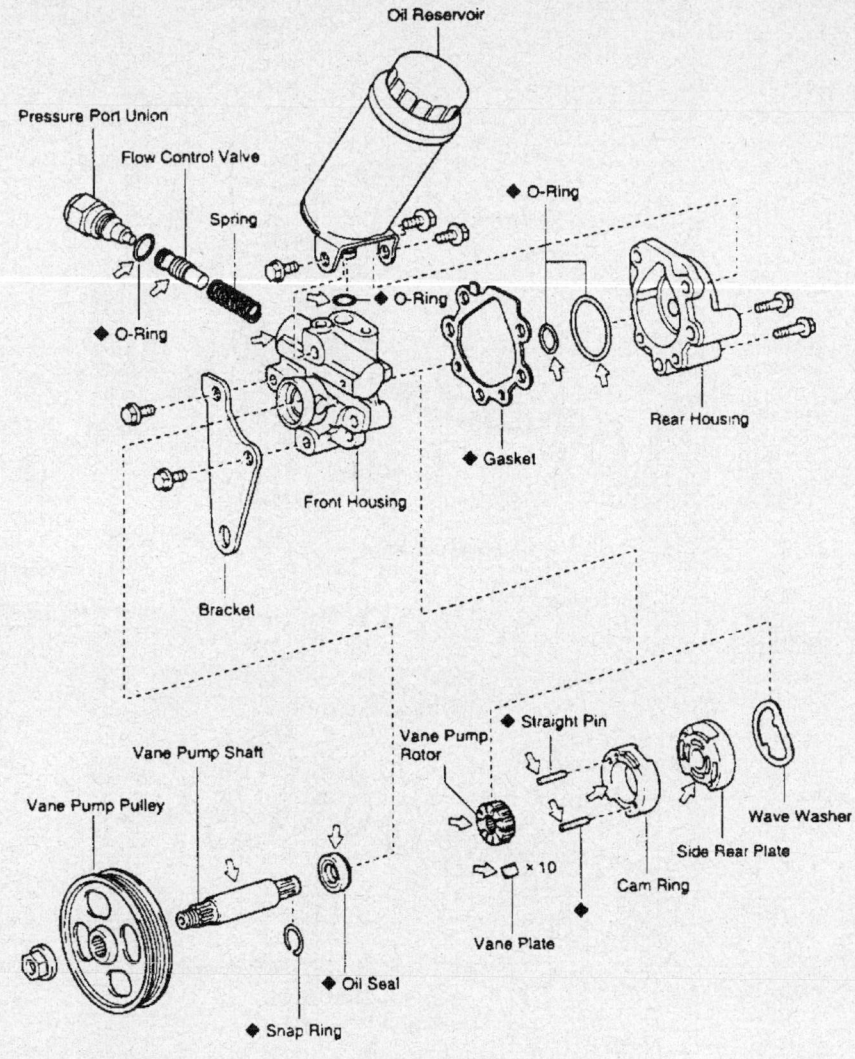

Fig. 17 Exploded view of power steering pump. Tacoma & T100 & 4Runner (VZ series)

◆ Non-reusable part
⇦ Power steering fluid

TY6029500054000X

opposite side, ensuring air does not come out end holes.

9. If inspections are not as indicated in steps 8 and 9, replace flow control valve with one having same letter as on front housing.

10. Using suitable scale, measure flow control spring free length, 1.38–1.46 inch should be indicated, if not replace spring.

Assemble

1. Coat all sliding surfaces with power steering fluid.

2. Install O-ring to flow control spring seat, install spring seat to housing, then install snap ring.

3. Install spring, flow control valve, O-ring and pressure port union, tighten to specifications.

4. Using suitable plastic hammer, tap in rotor shaft to front housing, then install snap ring.

5. Coat oil seal lip with MP grease, using suitable tool and hammer, install oil seal.

6. Install O-ring and pin to front housing.

7. Align and install cam ring fluid passages and front housing and install cam ring.

8. Install rotor with inscribed letters facing upward.

9. Install vane plates with round end facing outward.

10. Install rear plate O-ring, then align rear plate fluid passages with cam ring and install rear plate and spring.

11. Align front and rear housing matchmarks, install reservoir tank and O-ring, install and temporarily tighten front housing bolts.

12. Position rear housing in suitable soft jawed vise, then tighten housing attaching bolts uniformly in several passes to specifications.

13. Install suction port union and O-ring and tighten to specifications.

14. Install new union seat, then air control valve.

15. Temporarily install pulley nut and check rotating torque. Ensure 2.4 inch lbs. or less is indicated.

TUNDRA w/5VZ-FE ENGINE
Disassemble

1. Ensure pump rotates smoothly without noise.

2. Ensure pump rotational torque is 2.4 inch lbs. or less.

3. Remove oil reservoir, then the O-ring from reservoir, **Fig. 19.**

4. Remove pressure port union, flow control valve and spring, then the O-ring from pressure port union.

5. Remove bracket from pump.

6. Remove rear housing and 2 O-rings.

7. Remove wave washer, then the side plate.

8. Remove gasket from housing.

9. Using a suitable screwdriver, remove snap ring from vane pump shaft.

10. Remove cam ring, vane plates and pump rotor.

11. Remove vane pump shaft with pulley, then the straight pins.

Inspection

1. Ensure oil clearance between vane pump shaft and front housing is no more than .0028 inch. If clearance is greater than specified, replace shaft and housing.

2. Using a suitable micrometer, measure vane pump plate thickness. Thickness should be as follows:
   a. Minimum height, .339 inch.
   b. Minimum thickness, .055 inch.
   c. Minimum length, .59 inch.

3. Using a suitable feeler gauge, measure clearance between rotor groove and plate. Clearance should be no more than .0013 inch.

4. If rotor clearance is not as specified, replace with new part having same mark stamped on cam ring and rotor.

5. Apply clean power steering fluid to flow control valve and ensure it falls smoothly into valve bore by its own weight.

6. Inspect control valve for leakage as follows:
   a. Close one hole of valve and apply 57–71 psi into opposite side hole.
   b. Ensure air does not leak from end holes.
   c. If leakage is present, replace as necessary. Ensure replacement valve has same letter as stamped on housing.

7. Measure spring free length. Minimum free length is 1.307 inch.

8. If spring free length is not as specified, replace as necessary.

9. If seal replacement is required, proceed as follows:
   a. Using a suitable screwdriver with vinyl tape applied to blade end, remove seal from housing.
   b. Apply power steering fluid to lip of new seal.
   c. Using seal replacer tool No.

09951–00330 and handle tool No. 09951–07100 or equivalents, install new seal.

Assemble

1. Apply clean power steering fluid to parts as indicated in **Fig. 19.**
2. Install straight pins.
3. Install pump shaft with pulley.
4. Align cam ring with straight pins and install with inscribed mark facing outward.
5. Install pump rotor with inscribed mark facing outward.
6. Install new snap ring to vane pump shaft.
7. Install vane plates with round edge facing outward.
8. Install new gasket to front housing.
9. Install side plate while aligning straight pins.
10. Install wave washer ensuring protrusions fit into slots in side plate.
11. Install rear housing with O-rings.
12. Install spring, flow control valve and pressure port union.
13. Install bracket, then the reservoir.
14. Measure pump rotational torque as outlined under "Disassemble."

1996 PASEO & TERCEL
Disassemble

1. Position power steering pump in suitable soft-jawed vise.
2. Using suitable tool, remove pump pulley and woodruff key.
3. Remove suction port union and O-ring, **Fig. 20.**
4. Remove pressure port union, O-ring, flow control valve and spring.
5. Remove rear housing snap ring, place suitable vinyl tape on pump shaft, then using suitable plastic hammer, tap out rear housing, wave washer and O-ring.
6. Using suitable plastic hammer, tap out shaft end, then remove rear side plate and O-ring.
7. Remove pump shaft, cam ring and vane plates.
8. Remove long straight pin from front housing.
9. Using suitable snap ring pliers, remove pump shaft snap ring, remove rotor and front plate from pump shaft.
10. Remove front plate O-rings.

Inspection

1. Using suitable micrometer and calipers, measure oil clearance between shaft and bushing, .0028 inch or less should be indicated, if not replace entire power steering pump.
2. Using suitable micrometer, measure height, thickness and length of vane plates. Minimum height should be .315 inch, thickness, .0697 inch and length .5894 inch.
3. Measurements should be as follows:
   a. Height, .315 inch.
   b. Thickness, .0697 inch.
   c. Length, .5894 inch.
4. Using suitable feeler gauge, measure clearance between rotor groover and vane plate, maximum indicated should be .0012 inch.

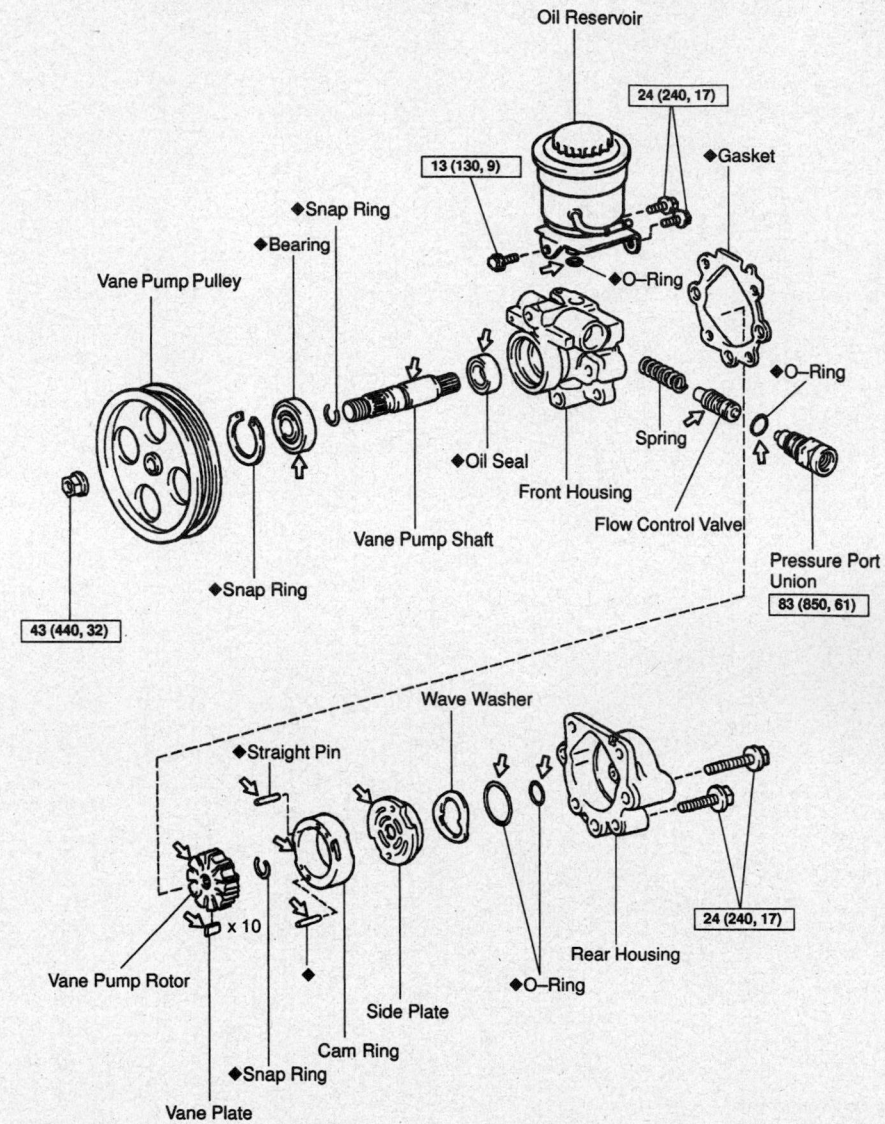

Fig. 18 **Exploded view of power steering pump. Tacoma & T100 & 4Runner (RZ Series)**

5. If measurements are not as indicated in steps 2 and 3, replace vane plate and/ or rotor with one having the same mark stamped on cam ring.
6. Coat flow control valve with power steering fluid, ensuring it falls smoothly into valve hole.
7. Close one flow control valve hole, then apply compressed air (57–71 psi) to opposite side, ensuring air does not come out end holes.
8. If inspections are not as indicated in steps 6 and 7, replace flow control valve with one having same letter as on front housing.
9. Using suitable scale, measure flow control spring free length, 1.42–1.49 inch should be indicated, if not replace spring.
10. If required, replace oil seal as follows:
   a. Using suitable screwdriver, pry out oil seal.
   b. Using suitable socket and hammer, drive in new oil seal.

Assemble

1. Coat all sliding surfaces with power steering fluid.
2. Using suitable plastic hammer, drive longer straight pin to front plate.
3. Install O-rings to front plate, then install front plate, rotor with inscribed mark facing toward rear and snap ring to pump shaft.
4. Coat oil seal lip with MP grease, install straight pin to front housing, place suitable vinyl tape on pump shaft, align front plate hole and straight pin, then using suitable plastic hammer, tap in

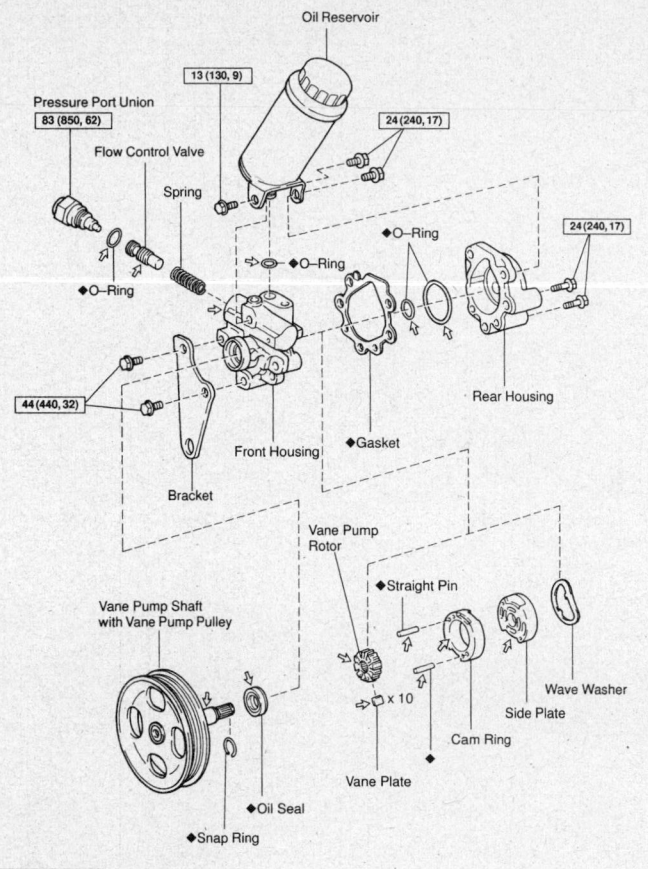

N·m (kgf·cm, ft·lbf) : Specified torque
◆Non-reusable part
↦ Power steering fluid

TY6029900074000X

**Fig. 19   Exploded view of power steering pump.
Tundra w/5VZ-FE engine**

TY6029100035000X

**Fig. 20   Exploded view of power steering pump.
1996 Paseo & Tercel**

---

pump shaft. **Do not damage oil seal and O-rings.**

5. Align cam ring holes with long straight pins, then install cam ring with inscribed marks facing outward.
6. Install vane plates with round end facing outward.
7. Install rear side plate O-ring, then align rear side plate wide hole with long straight pins and install rear side plate.
8. Install rear housing wave washer so washer protrusions fit into slots on rear side of plate, O-ring, then using suitable press, install rear housing, press wave washer hard enough to compress it, then install snap ring.
9. Ensure pump shaft rotates smoothly without abnormal noise.
10. Temporarily install pulley nut and check rotating torque. Ensure 2.4 inch lbs. or less is indicated.
11. Install spring, flow control valve, O-ring and pressure port union, tighten to specifications.
12. Install suction port union O-ring and union, tighten to specifications.
13. Install woodruff key to power steering pulley shaft, then install pulley and nut to shaft, using suitable tool, hold pulley and tighten attaching nut to specifications.

1997 TERCEL & 1997-98 PASEO

Disassemble

1. Measure pump rotational torque using a suitable torque wrench. Ensure torque is 2.2 inch lbs. or less.
2. Using variable pin wrench tool No. 09960–10010, or equivalent, remove pulley.
3. Remove front and rear brackets.
4. Remove protector retaining bolts, then the protector, **Fig. 21.**
5. Remove oil reservoir and O-ring.
6. Remove pressure feed No. 2 tube.
7. Remove pressure port union, then the flow control valve and compression spring.
8. Remove rear housing, then the 2 O-rings from housing.
9. Remove wave washer and skid plate.
10. Remove gasket, then the cam ring, vane plates, and vane pump rotor.
11. Remove straight pins from front housing.
12. Remove vane pump shaft as follows:
   a. Using a suitable pair of snap ring pliers, remove snap ring from front housing.
   b. Apply suitable vinyl tape to pump shaft.
   c. Using a suitable press, remove shaft with bearing.

Inspection

1. Using a suitable caliper and micrometer, measure oil clearance between pump shaft and bushing. Ensure clearance does not exceed .0028. If measurement is not as specified, replace front housing and pump shaft.
2. Using a suitable micrometer, measure vane plates. Measurements should be as follows:
   a. Height, .339 inch.
   b. Thickness, .0550 inch.
   c. Length, .5902 inch.
3. Using a suitable feeler gauge, measure clearance between vane plate and rotor groove. Ensure measurement does not exceed .00138 inch. If clearance is not as specified, replace plate and/or rotor with new part having same number as stamped on cam ring.
4. Inspect flow control valve as follows:
   a. Apply power steering fluid to valve and ensure fluid falls smoothly into valve hole.
   b. Check valve for leakage by closing one side hole and applying 57–71 psi of compressed air to opposite hole. Ensure air does not leak from end holes.
   c. If valve requires replacement, ensure new part has same letter as stamped on front housing.
5. Inspect free length of spring. Ensure

measurement is not below 1.30 inches.

6. If necessary, replace oil seal as follows:
   a. Using seal remover tool No. 09631–10030, or equivalent, remove seal from housing.
   b. Apply power steering fluid to new seal.
   c. Using a suitable press and seal installer tool Nos. 09950–60010 and 09950–70010, install seal.
7. If bearing replacement is required, proceed as follows:
   a. Apply suitable vinyl tape to end of pump shaft.
   b. Remove bearing using a suitable press.
   c. Replace snap ring.
   d. Apply power steering fluid to bearing, then install using a suitable press.

Assemble

1. When replacing seals, O-rings and bearings, coat with power steering fluid before installation.
2. Apply suitable vinyl tape to pump shaft, then install using a suitable press and bearing installer tool No. 09608–04031, or equivalent.
3. Using a suitable pair of snap ring pliers, install snap ring to front housing.
4. Install two straight pins using a suitable plastic hammer.
5. Install cam ring with stamped mark facing outward.
6. Install vane pump rotor with inscribed mark facing outward.
7. Install snap ring to pump shaft using a suitable pair of snap ring pliers.
8. Install vane plates, then the gasket and side plate.
9. Install wave washer.
10. Install rear housing O-rings, then the rear housing.
11. Install compression spring, flow control valve, and pressure port union.
12. Install pressure feed No. 2 tube.
13. Install oil reservoir O-ring, then the reservoir.
14. Install protector, then the front and rear brackets.
15. Install pump pulley, then measure pump rotational torque as outlined under "Disassemble."

POWER STEERING GEAR

AVALON, CAMRY, CAMRY SOLARA & SIENNA

Disassemble

1. Position rack in suitable soft jawed vise.
2. Using suitable tool, remove turn tubes and O-rings, **Fig. 22.**
3. Loosen tie rod end locknut, then place installation alignment marks on tie rod end and rack end, remove tie rod end.
4. Remove back boots. **Do not damage rack boots or rack housing.**
5. Unstake claw washers, then using suitable tool, remove rack ends, mark right and left rack ends and remove claw washers.

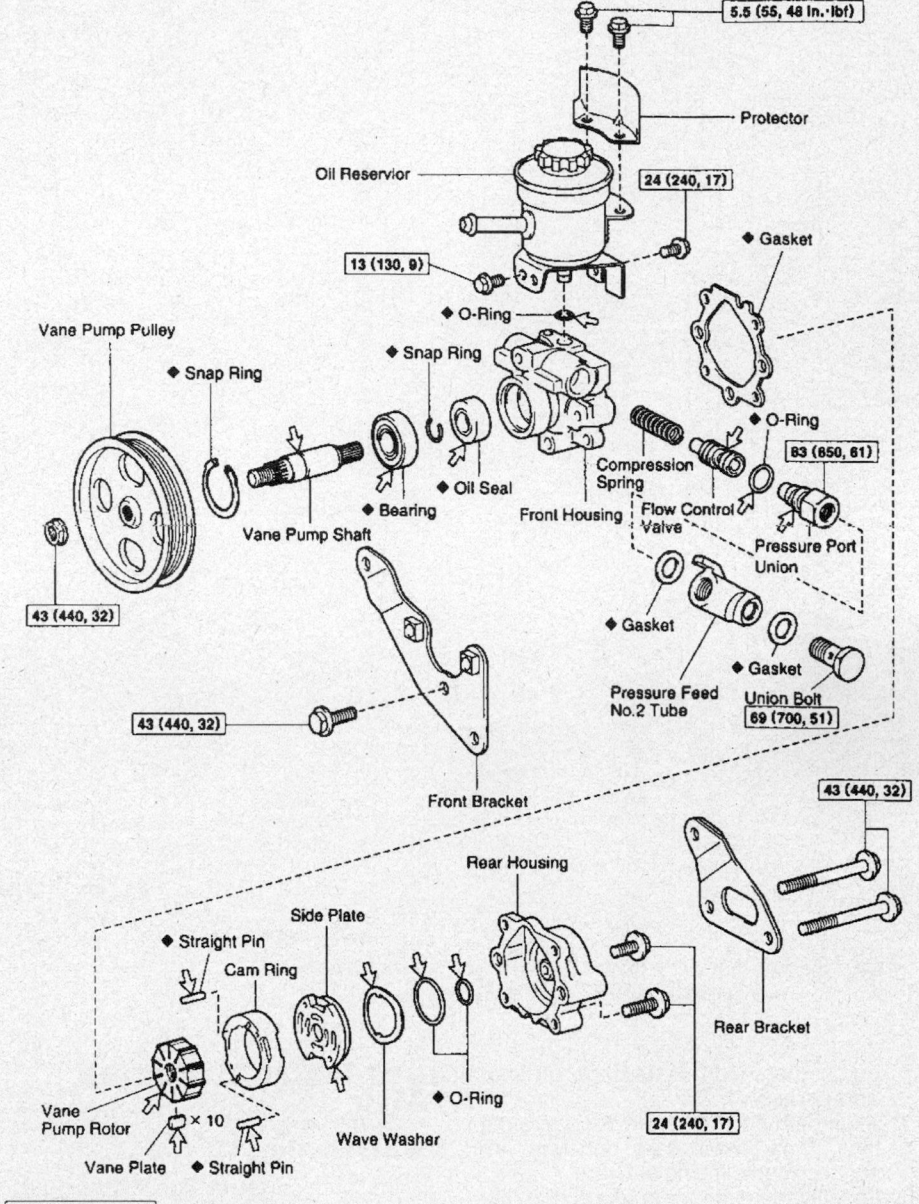

Fig. 21 Exploded view of power steering pump. 1997 Tercel & 1997–98 Paseo

6. Using suitable tool, remove rack guide spring cap locknut.
7. Using suitable tool, remove rack guide spring cap.
8. Remove rack guide spring, rack guide and seat.
9. Remove rack housing cap.
10. Using suitable tool to hold control valve, remove self locking nut.
11. Remove control valve housing dust cover, place installation alignment marks on valve and rack housing, remove valve housing, valve and rack housing gasket.
12. Tap out control valve and oil seal.
13. Place installation alignment marks on No. 2 bracket and rack housing, then using suitable screwdriver, pry No. 2

bracket clasp apart, remove bushing and bracket.
14. Using suitable tool, turn cylinder end stopper clockwise until wire end comes out, then turn cylinder end stopper counterclockwise and remove wire.
15. Using suitable brass bar, tap out rack with rack bushing and remove O-ring.
16. Using suitable tool and brass bar, drive out oil seal and spacer.

Inspection & Repair

1. Using suitable dial indicator, inspect rack for runout and tooth wear or damage. Maximum runout is .012 inch, if measurement is not as indicated or damaged, replace rack.

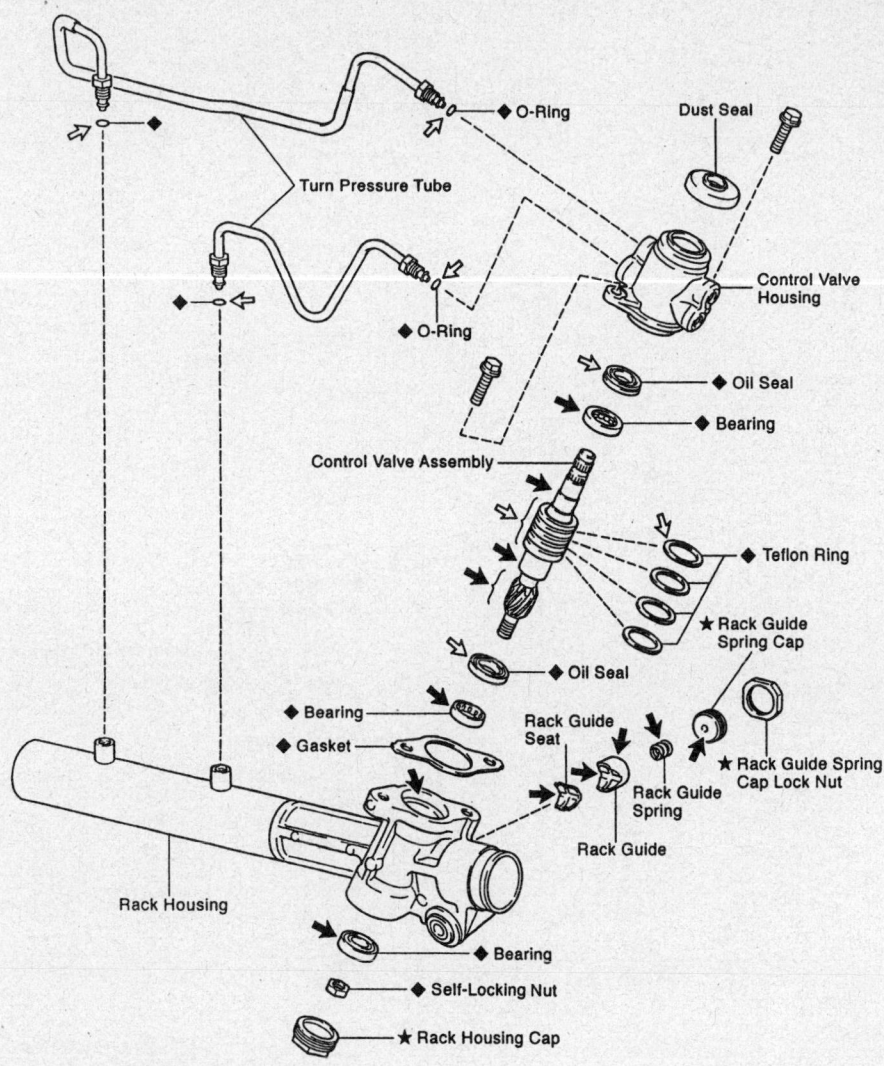

◆ Non-reusable part
★ Precoated part
◀ Molybdenum disulphide lithium base grease
⇦ Power steering fluid

TY6029200041000X

Fig. 22 Exploded view of power steering gear. Avalon, Camry, Camry Solara & Sienna

2. If required, replace control valve housing oil seal and upper bearing.
3. If required, replace control valve lower bearing and center bearing.
4. If required, replace rack bushing oil seal, using suitable tool, remove oil seal, coat new oil seal with power steering fluid, then install.
5. If required, replace Teflon ring and O-ring as follows:
   a. Remove Teflon ring and O-ring. **Do not damage steering rack.**
   b. Coat new O-ring with power steering fluid, then install.
   c. Coat new Teflon ring with power steering fluid.
   d. Install Teflon ring to tool No. 09630-24013, or equivalent, then expand ring.
   e. Install expanded ring to steering rack and snug down by hand to fit tightly in groove.
6. If required, replace control valve Teflon ring as follows:
   a. Using suitable screwdriver, remove Teflon ring. **Do not damage control valve.**
   b. Install new rings to tool No. 09631-20070, or equivalent, then expand rings.
   c. Install expanded rings to control valve and snug down by hand.
   d. Coat ring with power steering fluid, then carefully slide tapered end of tool No. 09631-20081, or equivalent, over rings to seat rings.

Assemble

1. Coat cylinder side oil seal lip with power steering fluid, then press in cylinder side oil seal and spacer.
2. Install tool No. 09631-33010, or equiv-

alent, to rack, scrape burrs from rack teeth end and burnish as required, coat tool with power steering fluid, the install rack to cylinder, remove tool.
3. Install rack bushing and cylinder end stopper pushing in until wire installation hole appears.
4. Install wire end to hole, then using suitable tool, turn cylinder end stopper clockwise until wire end disappears.
5. Install suitable vacuum tool to cylinder housing unions, apply 15.75 inch Hg. vacuum for about 30 seconds, ensure no change in vacuum, if change is indicated, inspect rack housing oil seal installation.
6. Install No. 2 bracket and bushing, aligning matchmarks.
7. Place suitable vinyl tape on control valve, coat Teflon rings with power steering fluid, then install control valve into housing and press in new oil seal.
8. Position new gasket on rack housing, align valve and rack housing matchmarks, install attaching bolts and tighten to specifications, then install dust cover.
9. Using suitable tool, hold control valve, install new self locking nut and tighten to specifications.
10. Apply Loctite 242, or equivalent, to two or three rack housing cap threads, then install cap, using suitable center punch, stake housing in two places.
11. Install rack guide seat, rack guide and spring.
12. Apply Loctite 242, or equivalent, to two or three spring cap threads, then install cap, tighten to specifications.
13. Return rack guide spring cap 12°, turn control valve shaft right and left one or two times, loosen spring cap until rack guide compression spring is not functioning, then using suitable tool, tighten rack guide spring cap until turning preload of 6.9–12.2 ft. lbs. is indicated.
14. Apply Loctite 242, or equivalent, to two or three rack guide spring cap locknut threads, then install locknut, tighten to specifications, then recheck preload as outlined in step 13.
15. Install claw washer and rack ends, then using suitable brass bar and hammer, stake claw washer.
16. Ensure tube hole is not clogged, then install rack boots.
17. Install tie rod ends, align matchmarks.
18. Install right and left turn pressure tubes.

CELICA

Disassemble

Refer to **Fig. 23** during service procedures.
1. Install power steering gear in fixture tool No. 09612–00012, or equivalent, then place fixture in a suitable vise.
2. Remove pressure tubes using wrench tool No. 09633–00020, or equivalent.
3. Loosen locknut, then mark relative position between tie rod end and rack end. Remove tie rod end and locknut.
4. Remove rack boot clips and clamps, then the rack boots.
5. Unstake claw washer, then remove

rack ends using wrench tool No. 09922–10010, or equivalent. Mark left and right ends respectively, then remove claw washers.

6. Using wrench tool No. 09922–10010, or equivalent, remove rack guide spring cap lock nut.
7. Using a suitable 24 mm hexagon wrench, remove rack guide spring cap.
8. Remove rack guide spring, then the rack guide and seat.
9. Remove rack housing cap locknut using wrench tool No. 0922–10010, or equivalent.
10. Remove rack housing cap using a suitable 24 mm hexagon wrench.
11. Remove bearing from rack housing.
12. Remove dust cover.
13. Mark relative position between valve housing and rack housing, then remove two retaining bolts. Pull out valve with valve housing, then remove O-ring from rack housing.
14. Wrap suitable vinyl tape around valve shaft to prevent damage to oil seal, then using a suitable plastic hammer, tap valve assembly from valve housing.
15. Mark relative position between rack housing and No. 2 bracket, then remove bracket and grommet.
16. Using a suitable pair of snap ring pliers, remove snap ring from rack housing.
17. Remove stopper from housing.
18. Using seal remover tool Nos. 09950–60010 and 09950–70010, or equivalent, remove oil seal(s) from rack.

Inspection & Repair

1. Inspect rack for excessive runout, tooth wear, or damage and replace as necessary. Maximum runout should be .0118 inch.
2. If necessary to replace control valve housing oil seal and bearing, use seal driver tool Nos. 09950–60010 and 09950–70010, or equivalent, to drive seal and bearing from housing.
3. Apply power steering fluid to new seal lip, then install seal and bearing using seal installer tool Nos. 09950–60010, 09952–06010, and 09950–70010, or equivalent.
4. If necessary, to replace rack housing oil seal, pry out oil seal, using a suitable tool, then install new seal using tool Nos. 09950–60010, 09952–06010, and 09950–70010, or equivalent.
5. Inspect control valve bearing rotation and check for abnormal noise. If problem is indicated, replace control valve.
6. If necessary to replace Teflon ring and O-ring, proceed as follows:
   a. Remove Teflon ring and O-ring.
   b. Install new Teflon ring onto suitable tool to expand it.
   c. Insert tool with ring onto rack, then install ring onto piston.
   d. Apply a suitable lubricant to Teflon ring, then ensure proper installation position.
7. If necessary to replace control valve Teflon ring, proceed as follows:

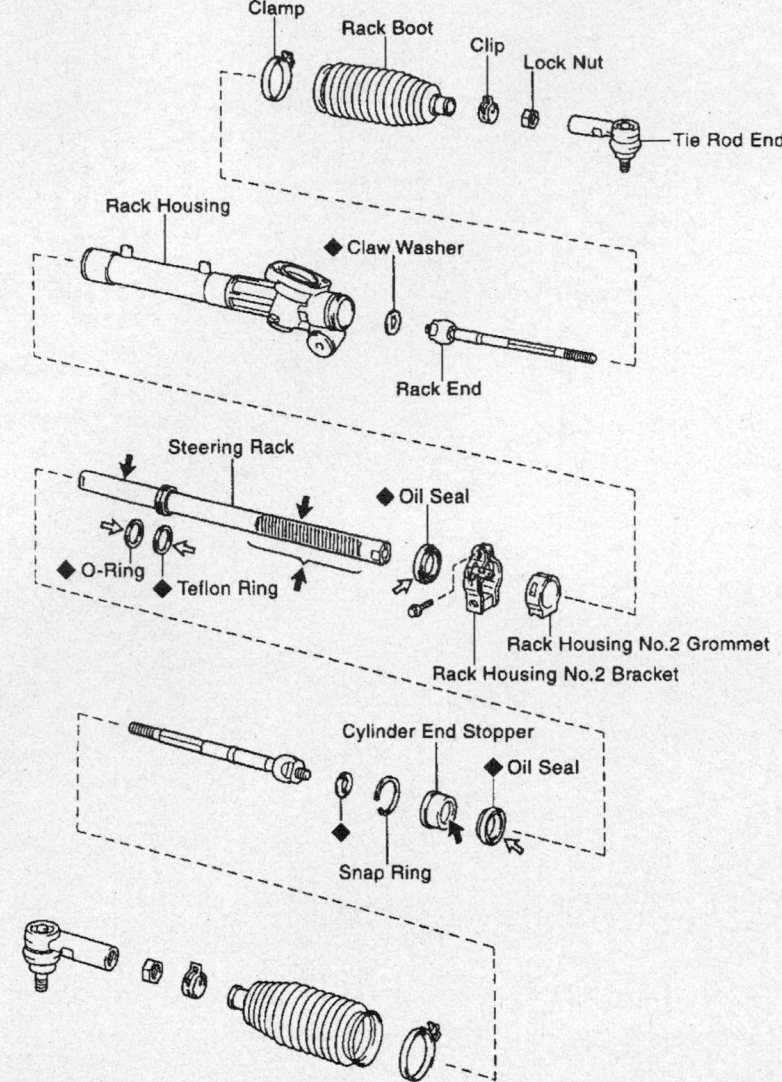

- ◆ Non-reusable part
- ⬅ Molybdenum disulfide lithium base grease
- ⬅ Power steering fluid

TY6029700061010X

Fig. 23 Exploded view of rack & pinion power steering gear (Part 1 of 2). Celica

a. Remove ring, using a suitable screwdriver.
b. Expand new rings before installation. Ensure not to over expand rings.
c. Install rings onto control valve assembly, then ensure proper installation position.
d. Apply a suitable lubricant to Teflon ring, then slide tapered end of Teflon ring installation tool No. 09631–20081, or equivalent, over rings to seat them.
8. If necessary to replace union seat, remove it with suitable screw extractor, then tap new union seat into place, using a suitable hammer and drift.

Assemble

During assembly, coat all moving parts, bearings, and bushings with molybdenum disulfide lithium based grease, and all O-rings and Teflon rings with power steering fluid.

1. Apply power steering fluid to oil seal, then install seal using seal installer tool Nos. 09950–60010, 09952–06010, and 09950–70010, or equivalent.
2. Install tool No. 09631–20100, or equivalent, onto rack, then apply a suitable lubricant. Insert rack into cylinder.
3. Apply power steering fluid to oil seal, then install seal.
4. Install stopper to rack housing, then the snap ring.
5. Ensure cylinder is air tight. Connect tool No. 09631-12070, or equivalent, to union of cylinder housing, then apply 15.75 inches of vacuum for approximately 30 seconds. There should be no drop in vacuum.
6. Install No.2 rack grommet and bracket.
7. Apply a suitable lubricant to Teflon

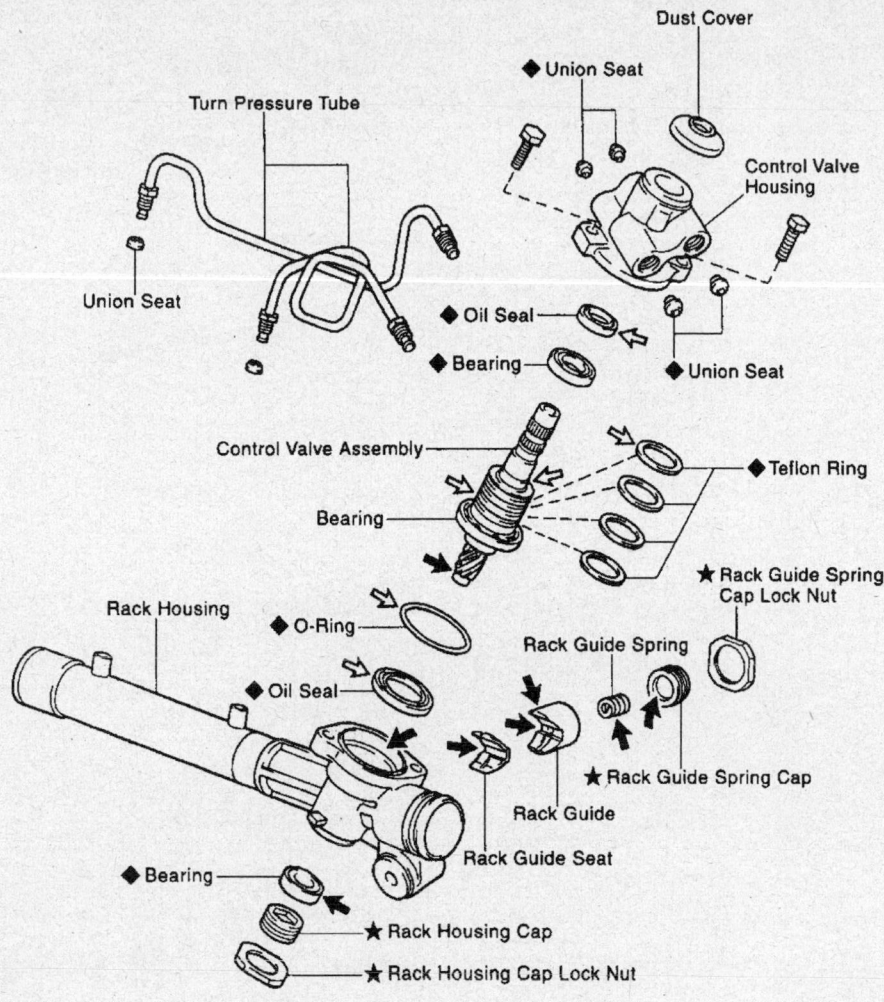

◆ Non-reusable part
★ Precoated part
◀ Molybdenum disulfide lithium base grease
⇦ Power steering fluid

TY6029700061020X

Fig. 23 Exploded view of rack & pinion power steering gear (Part 2 of 2). Celica

ring, then insert control valve into housing.

8. Apply power steering fluid to O-ring, then install into housing.

9. Align match marks on valve housing and rack housing, then insert two attaching bolts and tighten specifications.

10. Install dust cover.

11. Install control valve bearing, then apply a suitable sealant to 2 or 3 threads of bearing guide nut. Install nut, then tighten to specifications. Using a suitable torque meter, loosen guide nut until preload of 0.9–1.7 inch lbs. is obtained.

12. Apply Loctite 242, or equivalent, to 2 or 3 threads of bearing guide locknut, then install locknut and tighten to specifications. Install rack guide seat, rack guide, then the rack guide spring.

13. Apply a suitable sealant to 2 or 3 threads of spring cap, then tighten cap to specifications.

14. Adjust total preload as follows:
    a. Temporarily install rack ends to prevent rack teeth from damaging oil seal lip.
    b. Using a suitable 24 mm hexagon wrench, **torque** rack guide spring cap to 18 ft. lbs.
    c. Back off spring cap 12°, then rotate control valve shaft right and left two to three times.
    d. Loosen spring cap until rack guide compression spring is not functional.
    e. Tighten rack guide spring cap until preload of 10.4–13.0 inch lbs. is obtained.

15. Apply a suitable sealant to 2 or 3 threads of locknut, then install rack guide spring cap locknut and tighten to specifications. Recheck total preload.

16. Install new claw washer, then the rack ends. Tighten rack end to specifications. Stake claw washer using a suitable hammer and drift.

17. Install rack boots, clamps and clips, ensuring holes in tube are not clogged, and that clip ends face outward.

18. Screw locknuts and tie rod ends onto rack ends until match marks are aligned.

19. Install new union seats. Install turn tubes, then tighten fittings to specifications.

COROLLA w/KOYO TYPE
Disassemble

Refer to **Fig. 24** when performing the following procedures.

1. Remove right and left turn pressure lines.
2. Mount steering gear housing in soft jawed vise.
3. Remove tie rod ends.
4. Remove clips, clamps and rack boots.
5. Remove rack ends and claw washers.
6. Using suitable tool, remove rack guide spring cap locknut.
7. Using suitable tool, remove rack guide spring cap.
8. Remove rack guide spring, rack guide, and seat.
9. Remove dust cover.
10. Remove rack housing cap.
11. Using suitable tool, remove self-locking nut.
12. Remove dust cover.
13. Mark relative position between valve housing and rack housing, then remove valve housing retaining bolts.
14. Remove control valve housing with control valve.
15. Apply suitable vinyl tape to valve shaft.
16. Using a suitable plastic hammer, remove valve assembly from valve housing with oil seal.
17. Using cylinder end stopper positioning tool No. 09631–10021, or equivalent, turn cylinder end stopper clockwise until wire end is visible through service hole.
18. Turn stopper counterclockwise and remove wire.
19. Remove rack with bushing from rack housing.
20. Remove bushing and O-ring from rack.
21. Using seal remover tool Nos. 09950–60010 and 09950–70010, or equivalent, press out oil seal and spacer.

Inspection & Assemble

During assembly procedure, coat all moving parts, bearings, and bushings with molybdenum disulfide lithium base grease, and all O-rings and Teflon rings with power steering fluid.

1. Check back surface of rack or teeth for wear or damage.
2. Ensure rack runout does not exceed .012 inch (.3 mm).
3. If necessary, replace bearing and oil seal as follows:
    a. Remove oil seal and bearing using remover tool Nos. 09950–60010

and 09950–70010, or equivalent.
  b. Coat oil seal lip with power steering fluid.
  c. Install new seal using seal installer tool Nos. 09950–60010, 09952–06010, and 09950–70010, or equivalent. Ensure oil seal faces correct direction.
  d. Press bearing into place using press tool Nos. 09950–60010 and 09950–70010, or equivalent.
4. If necessary replace bearings as follows:
  a. Using a suitable brass bar and hammer or removal tool No. 09950–70010, or equivalent, tap bearings from rack housing.
  b. Press new bearings into place using bearing installation tool Nos. 09950–60010, 09950–70010, and 09952–06010, or equivalents.
5. If necessary, replace Teflon ring and O-ring as follows:
  a. Remove Teflon ring and O-ring.
  b. Install new O-ring.
  c. Expand new Teflon ring with fingers. Ensure not to over stretch ring.
  d. Position ring into piston ring groove of rack.
  e. Snug down Teflon ring with fingers so it fits tightly in groove.
6. If necessary, replace control valve Teflon rings as follows:
  a. Remove Teflon rings from control valve using a suitable screwdriver.
  b. Expand new Teflon rings with fingers. Ensure not to overstretch rings.
  c. Apply power steering fluid to rings, then install rings to control valve and snug into grooves with fingers.
  d. Install ring seat tool No. 09631–20081, or equivalent, to properly seat rings.
7. If union seats require replacement, use a suitable screw extractor to remove seats.
8. Using a suitable extension bar and hammer, install new seats.
9. Using seal installer tool Nos. 09950–60010, 09952–06010, and 09950–70010, or equivalents, install new oil seal and spacer.
10. Install seal protector tool No. 09631–16020, or equivalent, on rack. If tool can not be inserted smoothly, remove any burrs on rack with fine emery cloth.
11. Coat service tool with power steering fluid and insert rack into cylinder.
12. Remove service tool.
13. Apply suitable vinyl tape to rack end, then install new O-ring, bushing and oil seal.
14. Install cylinder end stop as follows:
  a. Align installation hole for stopper wire with rack housing access hole.
  b. Install new wire into stopper.
  c. Turn stopper clockwise 400–500°.
15. Check seal tightness as follows:
  a. Install air tightness check tool No. 09631–12071, or equivalent, to fluid fittings on cylinder housing.
  b. Apply 15.75 inches of (400 mm Hg) of vacuum for about 30 seconds.
  c. Ensure there is no drop in vacuum

for approximately 30 seconds.
  d. If vacuum change occurs, check oil seals.
16. Place control valve in housing.
17. Using suitable tool, install upper bearing with press.
18. Install oil seal using suitable tool.
19. Install dust cover.
20. Install self-locking nut on control valve shaft. **Torque** nut to 18 ft. lbs.
21. Apply liquid seal to threads of new housing cap. Install and **torque** cap to 43 ft. lbs.
22. Install rack guide seat, rack guide, conical spring, and rack guide spring.
23. Apply suitable liquid sealer to threads of spring cap.
24. Using suitable tool, temporarily install spring cap.
25. Adjust total preload as follows:
  a. To prevent damage to rack seals, temporarily install right and left rack ends.
  b. Using suitable tool, **torque** rack guide spring cap to 18 ft. lbs.
  c. Turn rack guide spring cap back 12°.
  d. Turn control valve shaft right and left a few times. Then, using suitable tools, and suitable torque

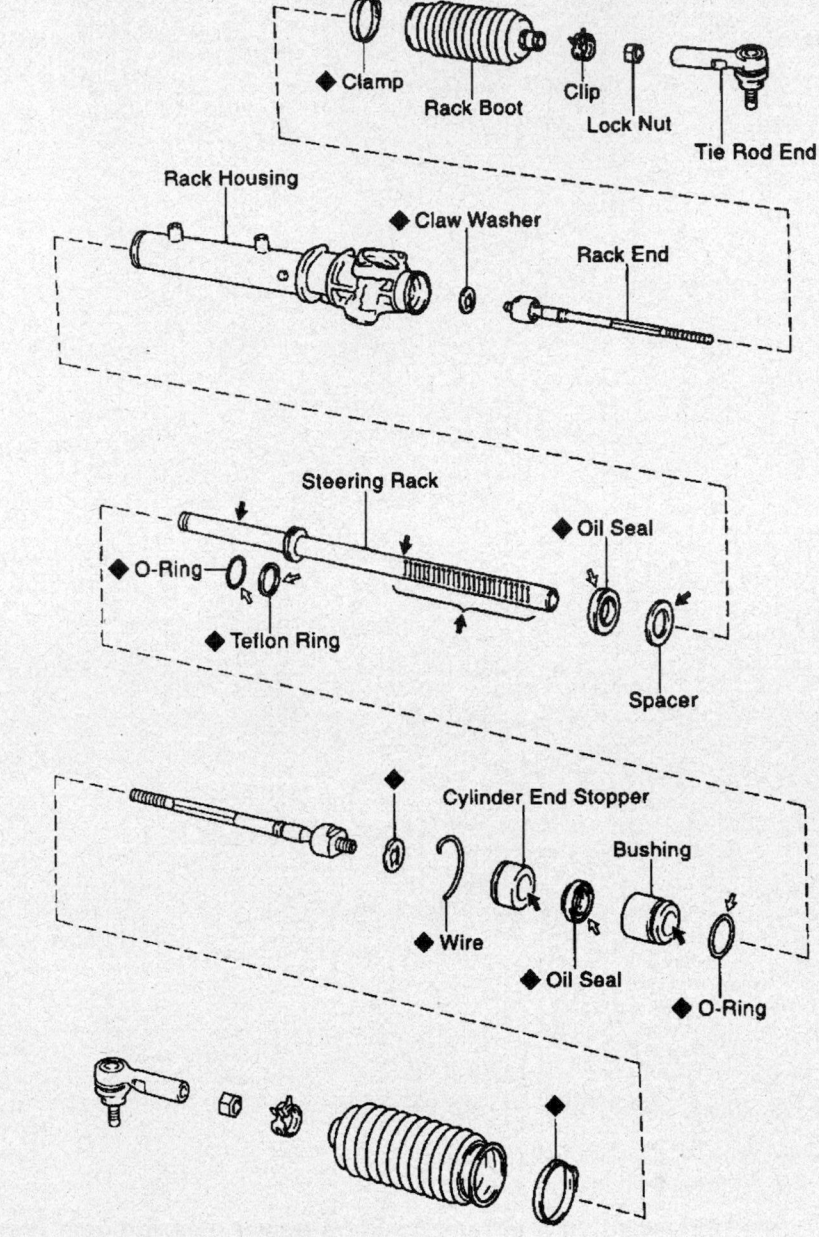

◆ Non-reusable part
◀ Molybdenum disulfide lithium base grease
◁ Power steering fluid

TY6029700062010X

Fig. 24 Exploded view of power steering gear (Part 1 of 2). Corolla w/Koyo gear

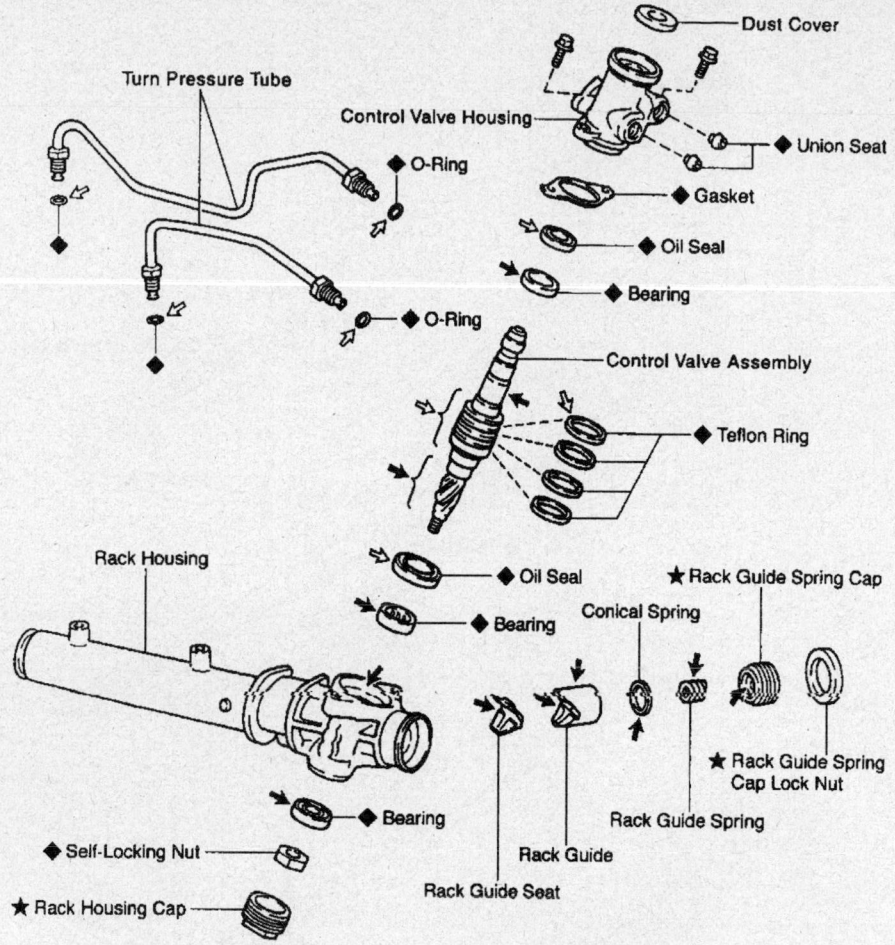

Fig. 24   Exploded view of power steering gear (Part 2 of 2). Corolla w/Koyo gear

Labels in figure: Dust Cover, Turn Pressure Tube, Control Valve Housing, ◆ O-Ring, ◆ Union Seat, ◆ Gasket, ◆ Oil Seal, ◆ Bearing, ◆ O-Ring, Control Valve Assembly, ◆ Teflon Ring, Rack Housing, ◆ Oil Seal, ◆ Bearing, ★ Rack Guide Spring Cap, Conical Spring, ★ Rack Guide Spring Cap Lock Nut, ◆ Bearing, ★ Rack Guide Spring, Rack Guide, Rack Guide Seat, ◆ Self-Locking Nut, ★ Rack Housing Cap

TY6029700062020X

◆ Non-reusable part
★ Precoated part
◀ Molybdenum disulfide lithium base grease
⇐ Power steering fluid

wrench, loosen rack guide spring cap until preload is 6.9–12.2 inch lbs.
26. Apply liquid sealer to threads of spring cap lock nut. **Torque** to 32 ft. lbs.
27. Recheck preload, and adjust if necessary.
28. Install claw washer, and rack end. Tighten rack end to specifications.
29. Stake claw washer.
30. Ensure rack hole is not clogged with grease. Install rack boots, clamps, and clips. Make sure that open ends of clips face outward to avoid damage to boots.
31. Install tie rod ends onto rack ends and align marks. After adjusting toe-in, tighten locknut to specifications.
32. Install right and left turn pressure lines. Using tool 09633-00020, or equivalent, tighten nuts to specifications.

COROLLA w/TOYOTA TYPE

Disassemble

Refer to **Fig. 25** when performing the following procedures.
1. Using tool 09631-22020, or equivalent, remove pressure lines.
2. Mount steering gear housing in soft jawed vise using rack mount tool No. 09612-00012, or equivalent.
3. Remove tie rod ends.
4. Using screwdriver, loosen staked part of clamp and remove clamps. Remove clips and rack boots.
5. Remove rack ends and claw washers.
6. Remove rack guide spring cap lock nut using tool 09922-10010, or equivalent.
7. Remove rack guide spring cap, rack guide spring, conical spring, rack guide and rack guide seat.
8. Remove rack housing cap.

9. Using tool 09616-00010, or equivalent, remove self-locking nut.
10. Remove snap ring from rack housing using a suitable pair of snap ring pliers.
11. Using removal tool No. 09613-12010, or equivalent, remove control valve assembly with bearing and oil seal.
12. Remove oil seal and bearing from control valve.
13. Using a suitable brass bar and hammer, remove bearing from rack housing.
14. Remove steering rack and oil seal using a suitable brass bar and hammer.
15. Using a suitable hammer and seal remover tool No. 09950-70010, or equivalent, remove rack seal.

Inspection & Assemble

During assembly, coat all moving parts, bearings, and bushings with molybdenum disulfide lithium base grease, and all seals, O-rings and Teflon rings with power steering fluid.
1. Check back surface of rack and teeth for wear or damage.
2. Ensure rack runout does not exceed .012 inch (.3 mm).
3. Using suitable micrometer and cylinder gauge, measure shaft O.D. and bushing I.D. Shaft O.D. should be 1.0925 inch and bushing I.D. should be 1.1102 inch.
4. If necessary, replace bushing and oil seal as follows:
   a. Remove bushing from rack housing using remover tool No. 09612-24014, or equivalent.
   b. Using a suitable screwdriver, remove oil seal from rack housing.
   c. Install new seal and bushing using installer tool Nos. 09950-60010, 09952-06010, and 09950-70010, or equivalent.
5. If necessary, replace Teflon ring and O-ring as follows:
   a. Remove Teflon ring and O-ring.
   b. Install new O-ring.
   c. Using fingers only, stretch new Teflon ring just enough to install into groove of rack.
   d. Using fingers, smooth Teflon ring down so it fits tightly in groove.
6. If necessary replace control valve Teflon rings as follows:
   a. Using a suitable screwdriver, remove Teflon rings from control valve.
   b. Expand new rings with fingers.
   c. Coat rings with power steering fluid and install rings to control valve assembly.
   d. Press rings into grooves with fingers, then install seal protector tool No. 09631-20081, or equivalent.
7. If union seats require replacement, proceed as follows:
   a. Using a suitable screw extractor, remove union seats.
   b. Install new union seats using a suitable extension bar and hammer.
8. Install rack seal using installer tool

Nos. 09950–60010, 09950–70010, and 09952–06010, or equivalent.

9. Mount tool 09631-16020 on end of rack.
10. Coat tool with power steering fluid.
11. Insert rack into cylinder.
12. Remove tool.
13. Apply suitable vinyl tape to rack end, then install outer rack seal.
14. Using installer tool No. 09612–22011, or equivalent, install cylinder end stopper.
15. Using a suitable pair of snap ring pliers, install snap ring.
16. Check seal tightness as follows:
    a. Install air tightness check tool No. 09631–12071, or equivalent, to fluid fittings on cylinder housing.
    b. Apply 15.75 inches of (400 mm Hg) of vacuum for about 30 seconds.
    c. Ensure there is no drop in vacuum for approximately 30 seconds.
    d. If vacuum change occurs, check oil seals.
17. Install control valve into rack housing.
18. Install bearing and seal using installer tool No. 09612–22011, or equivalent.
19. Install holding tool No. 09616–00010, or equivalent, to control valve, then **torque** lock nut to 9 ft. lbs.
20. Install adjustment tool No. 09613-12020, or equivalent, **Fig. 26,** to control valve and proceed as follows:
    a. Turn "C" of tool to measure dimension "A," then place tool as shown.
    b. Dimension "A" should be .65–.67 inch.
    c. Stake nut by turning "B" until it touches spacer of tool.
21. Apply suitable sealant to threads of rack housing cap, then install cap and **torque** to 51 ft. lbs.
22. Install rack guide seat, rack guide, conical spring and rack guide spring.
23. Apply suitable sealant to rack guide spring cap, then install cap.
24. Adjust rack preload as follows:
    a. Temporarily install right and left rack ends.
    b. Using a suitable wrench, **torque** rack guide spring cap to 18 ft. lbs.
    c. Turn cap 12° counterclockwise.
    d. Using control valve adapter tool No. 09616–00010, or equivalent, turn control valve shaft right and left 2 times.
    e. Using a suitable wrench, loosen cap until rack guide spring is not functioning.
    f. Tighten cap until preload is 6.9–15.6 inch lbs.
25. Apply suitable sealant to rack guide spring cap locknut, then install and **torque** to 23 ft. lbs.
26. Recheck total preload, adjust if necessary.
27. Install new claw washers, then the rack ends.
28. Using a suitable spanner wrench and tightening tool No. 09922–10010, or equivalent, tighten rack ends to specification.
29. Stake claw washers in place.
30. Install right and left rack boots, clamps, and clips. Ensure steering rack hole is not clogged with grease.

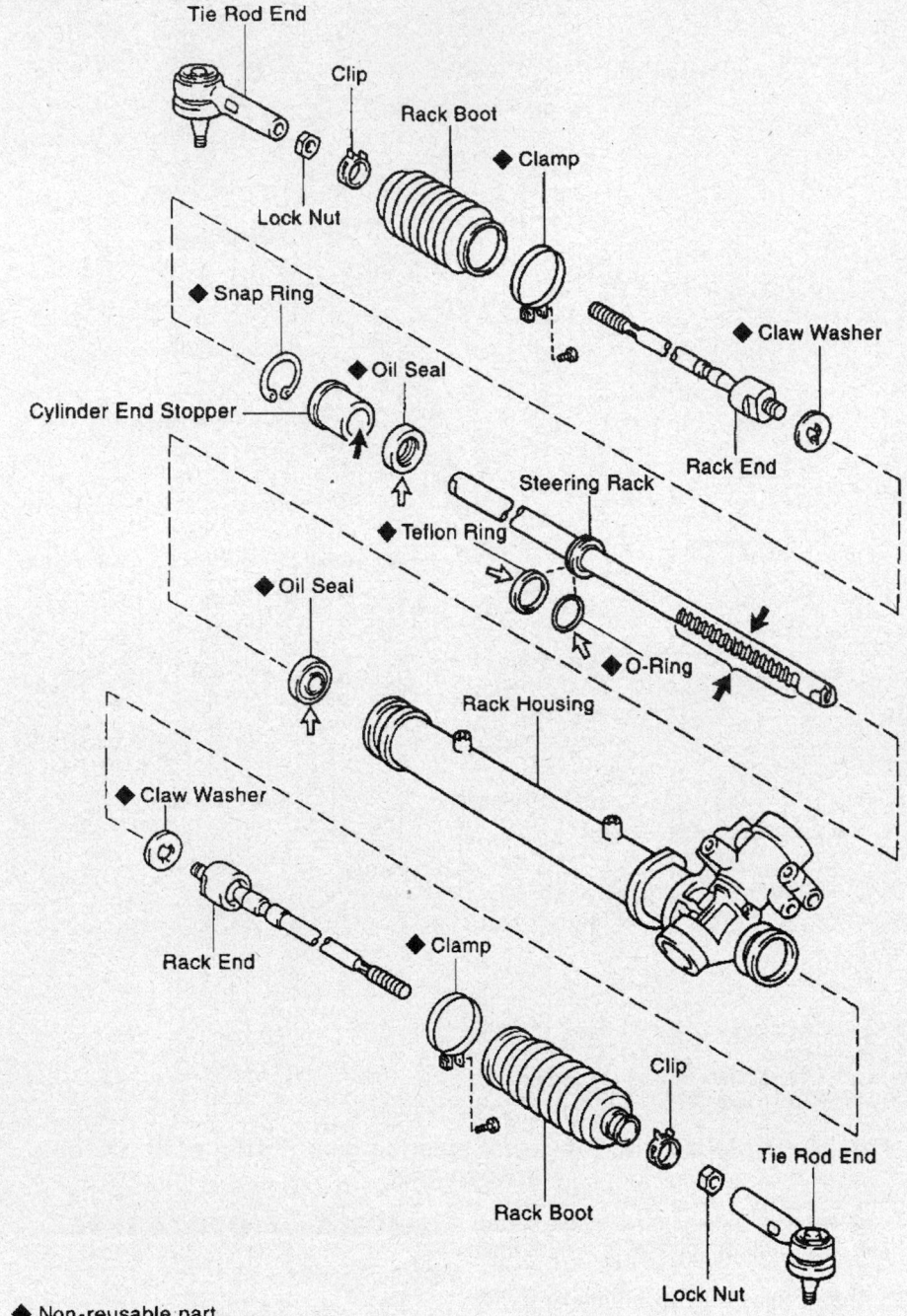

◆ Non-reusable part
◀ Molybdenum disulfide lithium base grease
⇐ Power steering fluid

TY6029700063010X

Fig. 25 Exploded view of power steering gear (Part 1 of 2). Corolla w/Toyota gear

31. Install right and left tie rods and locknuts.
32. Install turn pressure tubes and tighten to specification using wrench tool No. 09633–00020, or equivalent.

LAND CRUISER

Disassemble

1. Place gear in suitable soft jawed vise.
2. Remove end cover adjusting screw locknut and seal washer, remove end cover attaching bolts, **Fig. 27,** screw in adjusting screw until cover is removed.
3. Using suitable plastic hammer, tap out cross shaft end and remove shaft.
4. Using tool No. 09043-38100, or equivalent, remove plunger guide nut, then remove spring, plunger, plunger guide and O-ring.
5. Remove four valve body cap bolts, then using tool No. 09616-00010, or equivalent, turn shaft clockwise to disconnect worm gear valve body from gear housing.
6. Hold power piston so it cannot move,

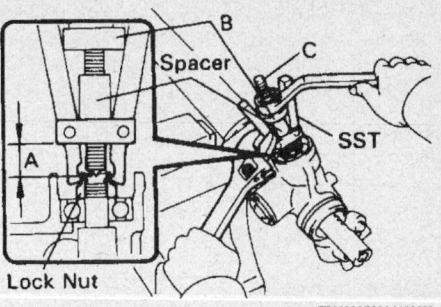

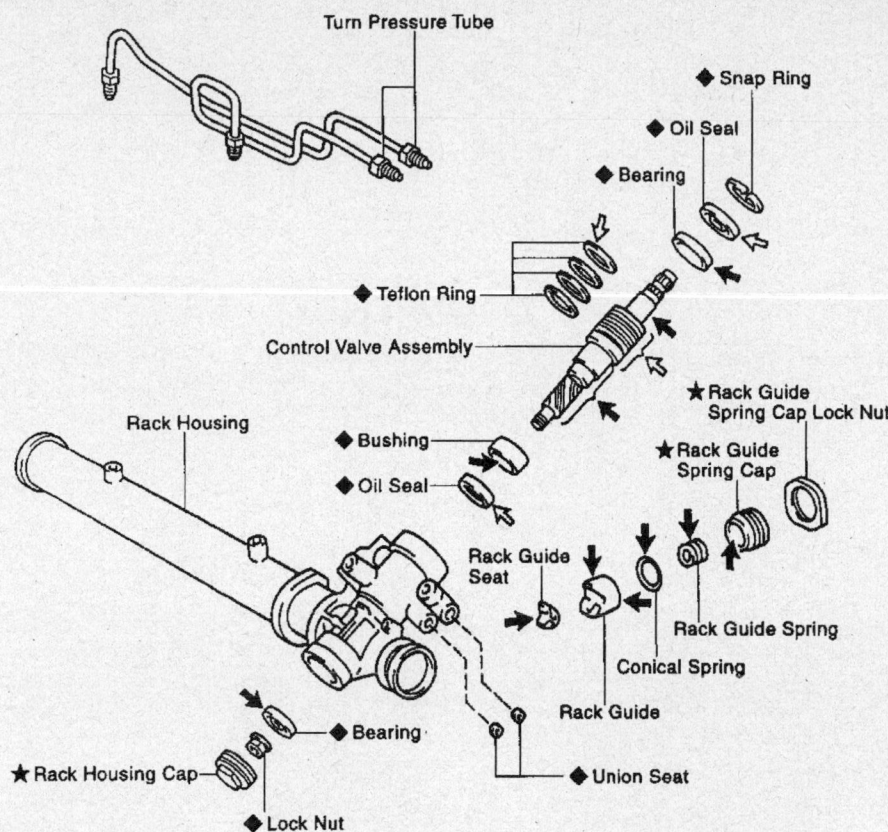

Turn Pressure Tube

◆ Snap Ring
◆ Oil Seal
◆ Bearing
◆ Teflon Ring
Control Valve Assembly
Rack Housing
◆ Bushing
◆ Oil Seal
★ Rack Guide Spring Cap Lock Nut
★ Rack Guide Spring Cap
Rack Guide Seat
Rack Guide Spring
Conical Spring
Rack Guide
◆ Bearing
◆ Union Seat
★ Rack Housing Cap
◆ Lock Nut

◆ Non-reusable part
★ Precoated part
◀ Molybdenum disulfide lithium base grease
◁ Power steering fluid

TY6029700063020X

Fig. 25 Exploded view of power steering gear (Part 2 of 2). Corolla w/Toyota gear

TY6029700064000X

Fig. 26 Control valve adjustment. Corolla w/Toyota type

turn wormshaft clockwise, then remove valve body and power piston assembly and O-ring. **Ensure power piston nut does not come off with worm shaft.**

Inspection & Repair

1. Place valve body in suitable soft jawed vise, using suitable dial indicator, inspect ball clearance, moving worm gear up and down, maximum ball clearance should be .00059 inch, if clearance is not as indicated, replace power control valve assembly.
2. Place cross shaft in suitable soft jawed vise, then using suitable dial indicator, measure thrust clearance, .0012–.0020 inch should be indicated, is not as indicated, adjust thrust clearance.
3. Adjust thrust clearance as follows:
   a. Using suitable hammer and chisel, remove locknut stake.
   b. Using tool No. 09630–00012, or equivalent, loosen locknut.
   c. Turn adjusting screw for correct

thrust clearance, then tighten locknut.
   d. Stake locknut.
4. If required, replace needle roller bearings as follows:
   a. Using suitable screw driver, remove oil seal.
   b. Using suitable snap ring pliers, remove snap ring.
   c. Remove metal spacer, O-ring and Teflon ring.
   d. Using tool No. 09630–00012, or equivalent, press out bearings.
   e. Install new lower bearing, ensuring it is positioned .909 inch away from lower end of housing.
   f. Press in new upper bearing, ensuring top end is installed so it aligns with end of housing hole.
   g. Install O-ring and metal spacer.
   h. Using suitable snap ring pliers, install snap ring.
   i. Form Teflon ring into heart shape and install with fingers.
   j. Using tool No. 09630–00012, or equivalent, form Teflon ring, Teflon

ring must be formed before sector shaft installation or damage may occur.
   k. Drive in new oil seal, then apply MP grease to oil seal lip.
5. If required, replace control valve Teflon rings as follows:
   a. Using suitable screwdriver, remove Teflon ring and O-ring. **Do not damage control valve.**
   b. Install new O-ring.
   c. Expand Teflon ring by hand, do not over expand Teflon ring.
   d. Install Teflon ring.
   e. Coat Teflon ring with power steering fluid and snug down with piston ring compressor for 5–7 minutes.
6. If required, replace union set as follows:
   a. Using suitable screw extractor, remove union seat.
   b. Using suitable plastic hammer and extension bar, tap in new union seat.

Assemble

1. Install O-rings to gear housing and valve body, mount gear housing to tool No. 09630–00012, or equivalent, then install tool to suitable soft jawed vise. Install worm gear valve body. **Do not damage Teflon ring.**
2. Hold power piston nut to prevent turning, then using tool No. 09616-00010, or equivalent, check worm gear preload, starting preload should be 2.6–4.8 inch lbs. If preload is not as indicated, replace worm gear assembly.
3. Install plunger, plunger guide and spring.
4. Install plunger guide nut O-ring, then using tool No. 09043-38100, or equivalent, install plunger guide nut and tighten specifications.
5. Install end cover O-ring, fully loosen adjusting screw, using suitable screwdriver, assemble cross shaft to end cover.
6. Set worm gear at center of gear housing.
7. Install and push cross shaft into gear housing so center teeth mesh together, install four cap bolts tightening to specifications in diagonal pattern.
8. Using tool No. 09616-00010, or equivalent, turn worm shaft to full lock in both directions to determine exact center, place matchmarks on worm shaft

and housing to show neutral position.

9. Install tool No. 09616-0010, or equivalent, with suitable torque meter to worm shaft, turn adjusting screw while measuring preload, total starting preload should be 6.5–9.6 inch lbs.
10. Install washer, then install and tighten locknut while holding adjusting screw.
11. Recheck total preload.

PASEO & TERCEL

Disassemble

1. Place steering gear in suitable vice, then remove pressure lines using wrench tool No. 09633-00020, or equivalent, **Fig. 28.**
2. Remove the air control valve.
3. Mark position of tie-rod and rack end for reference during assembly, then remove tie-rods.
4. Remove rack boots, then unstake claw washer.
5. Using adjustable wrench tool No. 09922-10010, or equivalent, remove rack ends, then the claw washer.
6. Using adjustable wrench tool No. 09922-10010, or equivalent, remove rack guide spring cap locknut.
7. Remove rack guide spring cap, using suitable 21 mm hexagon wrench.
8. Remove rack guide spring, rack guide, rack guide seat, and rack housing cap.
9. Remove self locking nut.
10. Remove control valve with seal and bearing as follows:
    a. Using a suitable pair of snap ring pliers, remove snap ring from housing.
    b. Remove control valve with bearing and seal using control valve puller tool No. 09613-12010, or equivalent.
    c. Remove oil seal from control valve.
    d. Using bearing remover set tool No. 09950-40010, or equivalent, remove bearing from control valve.
11. Using a suitable brass bar and hammer, remove bearing from rack housing.
12. Using cylinder end stopper tool No. 09631-20090, or equivalent, remove cylinder end stopper.
13. Remove bushing from stopper.
14. Using rack remover tool No. 09612-24014, or equivalent, and a suitable press, remove rack with oil seal from rack housing.
15. Remove inner rack seal from rack housing using a suitable press and press tool kit No. 09950-60010, or equivalent.

Inspection & Repair

1. Check rack for damage, wear or excessive runout. If runout exceeds .012 inch, replace rack.
2. Using a suitable micrometer and cylinder gauge, measure oil clearance between control valve and bushing. Ensure clearance does not exceed .0049 inch.
3. If necessary replace bushing and oil seal as follows:
    a. Using puller tool No. 09612-65014, or equivalent, remove bushing from rack housing.

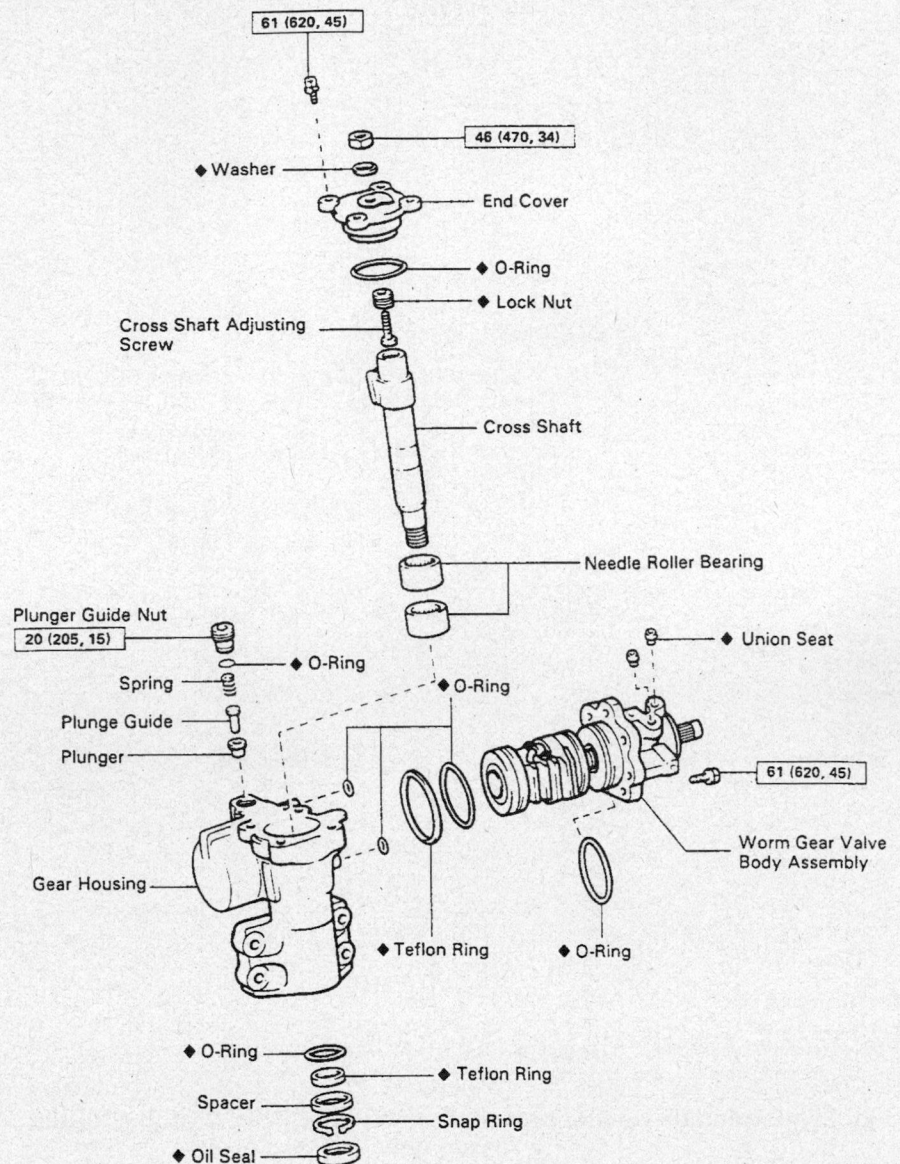

Fig. 27 **Exploded view of power steering gear. Land Cruiser**

Labels: 61 (620, 45); 46 (470, 34); ◆ Washer; End Cover; ◆ O-Ring; ◆ Lock Nut; Cross Shaft Adjusting Screw; Cross Shaft; Needle Roller Bearing; Plunger Guide Nut 20 (205, 15); ◆ O-Ring; Spring; ◆ O-Ring; Plunge Guide; Plunger; Union Seat; 61 (620, 45); Gear Housing; Worm Gear Valve Body Assembly; ◆ Teflon Ring; ◆ O-Ring; ◆ O-Ring; ◆ Teflon Ring; Spacer; Snap Ring; ◆ Oil Seal

TY6029100042000X

    b. Remove oil seal from rack housing using a suitable brass bar and hammer.
    c. Apply power steering fluid to new seal.
    d. Using a suitable press and press tool kit No. 09950-60010, or equivalent, install seal and bushing into rack housing.
4. If necessary, replace rack Teflon ring and O-ring, coating Teflon ring with power steering fluid.
5. If necessary, replace control valve Teflon ring as follows:
    a. Pry off Teflon ring with suitable screwdriver.
    b. Expand new Teflon rings using fingers.
    c. Apply power steering fluid to new rings, then install to control valve.
    d. Push rings into groove using fingers, then install seal protector tool No. 09631–20081, or equivalent, to control valve.

Assemble

During assembly, coat all moving parts, bearings and bushings with molybdenum disulfide lithium base grease, and all O-rings and Teflon rings with power steering fluid.

1. Install oil seal and spacer using installer kit tool No. 09950-60010, or equivalent.
2. Install seal protector to steering rack, then install rack into housing.
3. Remove seal protector, then apply vinyl tape to rack end.
4. Install outer rack seal into rack housing.
5. Install new bushing to cylinder end stopper.
6. Using cylinder end stopper nut tool No. 09631-20090, or equivalent, install stopper to rack housing.
7. Ensure cylinder is air tight. Connect

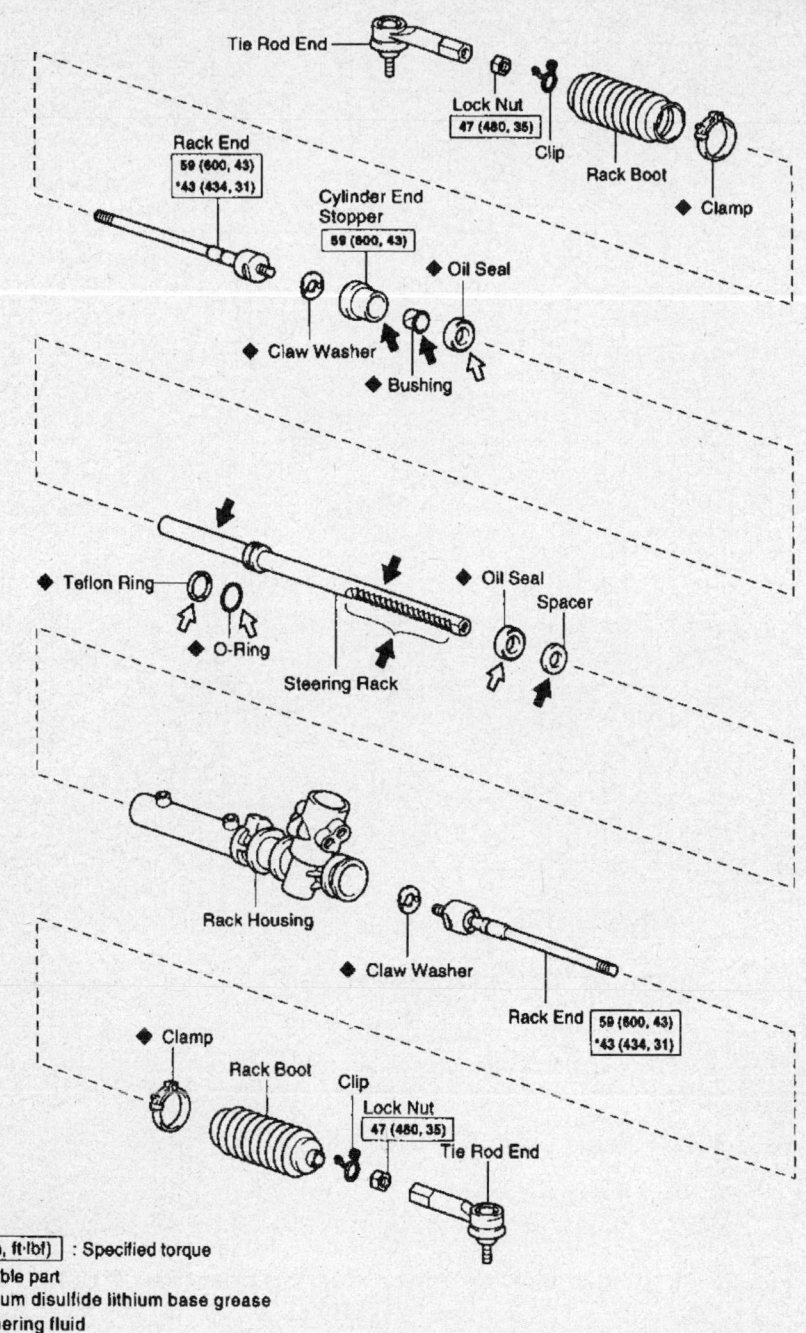

N·m (kgf·cm, ft·lbf) : Specified torque
◆ Non-reusable part
◀ Molybdenum disulfide lithium base grease
◁ Power steering fluid
* For use with SST

TY6029700071010X

Fig. 28 Exploded view of power steering gear (Part 1 of 2). Paseo & Tercel

suitable tool, to union of cylinder housing, then apply 15.75 inches Hg vacuum for at least 30 seconds. There should be no drop in vacuum.

8. Install control valve assembly as follows:
   a. Push control valve into housing.
   b. Using suitable tool, press in new bearing.
   c. Using suitable tool press in oil seal until snug with bearing.
   d. Install snap ring using suitable snap ring pliers.
9. Using suitable tool, install self-locking nut into lower control valve housing. Tighten nut to specifications.

10. Apply Loctite 242, or equivalent, to rack housing cap, then install cap, tighten to specifications. Using a center punch, stake the housing cap at opposite ends of cap.
11. Install rack guide seat, rack guide, and rack guide spring.
12. Temporarily install right and left inner tie rods.
13. Apply suitable sealant to 3 threads of spring cap, then adjust preload as follows:
    a. **Torque** spring cap to 18 ft. lbs.
    b. Turn cap counterclockwise 12°, then turn rack right and left 2 times.
    c. Loosen cap until guide spring is not functioning.
    d. Tighten cap until preload is 6.9–12.2 inch lbs.
14. Install rack guide spring cap locknut and recheck preload. Ensure preload is 6.9–12.2 inch lbs.
15. Remove right and left rack ends.
16. Install new rack end claw washers, then rack ends. Tighten rack ends to specifications.
17. Stake claw washers into position, then ensuring that tube hole is not clogged with grease, install rack boots, clamps and clips. Ensure clip ends face outward.
18. Install tie-rod ends, ensuring marks made during disassembly are aligned. After adjusting toe-in, tighten locknuts to specifications.
19. Install new pressure line O-rings, then the pressure lines. Tighten to specifications.
20. Install air control valve. Tighten to specifications.

PREVIA

Disassemble

1. Connect a suitable holding fixture to gear housing, then place fixture in a suitable vise, **Fig. 29.**
2. Remove right and left turn pressure tubes, using tool No. 09633-00020, or equivalent.
3. Loosen locknut, then mark relative position between tie rod end and rack end. Remove tie rod end and locknut.
4. Remove rack boots clips and clamps, then the rack boots.
5. Unstake claw washers, then remove rack ends. Mark left and right ends respectively, then remove claw washer.
6. Remove rack guide spring cap locknut, then the rack guide spring cap.
7. Remove rack guide, spring, then the rack guide seat.
8. Mark relative position between valve housing and rack housing, then remove two attaching bolts. Remove control valve with housing, then the O-rings.
9. Remove cylinder end stopper nut, using tool No. 09631-20120, or equivalent.
10. Using tool No. 09612-24013, or equivalent, and a suitable press, remove rack and oil seal. Pull out steering rack with oil seal and rack end guide from cylinder.

Inspection & Repair

1. Inspect rack for runout, tooth wear and damage and replace as necessary. Maximum runout should be .012 inch.
2. Check needle roller bearing for wear or damage and replace cylinder housing assembly as necessary.
3. If necessary to replace control valve bearing oil seal, press out oil seal and bearing, using tool Nos. 09630-24013 and 09631-12020. Press in new oil seal, using tool Nos. 09631-12020 and 09630-24013 and a suitable press.
4. If necessary, replace rack Teflon ring

and O-ring coating with fluid and snug down.

5. If necessary to replace control valve Teflon ring, proceed as follows:
   a. Remove ring, using a suitable tool.
   b. Place new ring onto tool No. 09631-20070, or equivalent, to expand it.
   c. Install rings onto control valve, then ensure proper installation position.
   d. Apply a suitable lubricant to Teflon ring, then slide tapered end of tool over ring and seat ring.
6. If necessary to replace union seat, remove it, using a suitable screw extractor, then tap new union seat into place, using a hammer and suitable drift.

Assemble

During assembly, coat all moving parts, bearings, and bushings with molybdenum disulfide lithium based grease, and all O-rings and Teflon rings with power steering fluid.

1. Install spacer to rack housing, then using tool No. 09631-12020, or equivalent, tap in new seal horizontally.
2. Coat tool No. 09631-20111, or equivalent, with power steering fluid, then insert rack and tool into cylinder and remove tool.
3. Coat tool No. 09631-20111, or equivalent, with power steering fluid, then insert rack into opposite end and install oil seal by pushing over tool horizontally.
4. Secure rack onto vise, then install O-ring to end stopper and tap into rack housing using a block of wood and hammer.
5. Using tool No. 09631-20120, or equivalent, install stopper. Tighten to specifications, then stake rack housing.
6. Install new O-ring into control valve, then apply a suitable lubricant to Teflon ring and O-ring. Carefully push control valve into housing, then install bearing guide nut and tighten to specification.
7. Fill bottom of housing cavity with suitable grease, then align matchmarks and install control valve assembly onto rack housing.
8. Install rack guide, then rack guide spring and rack guide spring cap. Tighten to specifications.
9. Adjust total preload as follows:
   a. Back off spring cap 30°, then rotate control valve shaft right and left two to three times.
   b. Loosen spring cap until rack guide compression spring is not functional.
   c. Tighten rack guide spring cap until preload of 6.1–11.3 inch lbs. is obtained.
10. Apply a suitable sealant to spring cap screws, then install and tighten locknut to specifications. Recheck total preload. Stake locknut and cap.
11. Install claw washers, rack and rack ends. Tighten rack ends to specifications. Stake claw washer.
12. Install rack boots, clamp and clips. Ensure rack hole is not clogged with grease, and that open end of clips face outward.

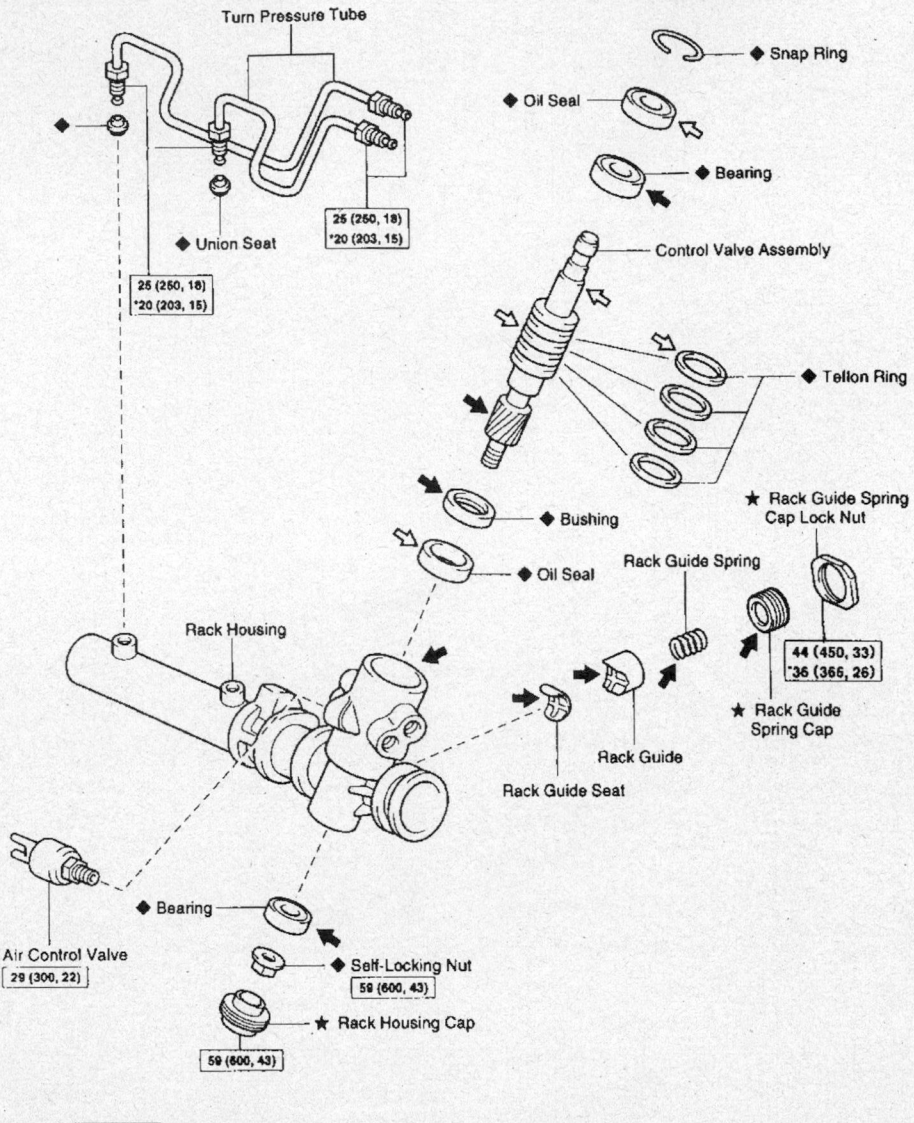

Fig. 28 Exploded view of power steering gear (Part 2 of 2). Paseo & Tercel

13. Install tie rods, aligning match marks, then adjust toe-in.
14. Install right and left turn pressure tubes, then tighten to specifications.

RAV4
Disassemble

1. Secure power steering gear in suitable soft-jawed vise.
2. Remove two turn pressure tubes using tool No. 09633-00020, or equivalent, **Fig. 30.**
3. Place matchmarks on tie rod end and rack end, then remove righthand and lefthand tie rod ends and lock nuts.
4. Remove righthand and lefthand clips, rack boots and clamps.
5. Using tool No. 09922-10010, or equivalent, remove rack ends and claw washers. Use a spanner to hold steering rack steady.
6. Place matchmarks on rack housing No. 1 bracket and rack housing.
7. Remove grommet from rack housing No. 1 bracket.
8. Remove rack guide spring cap lock nut using tool No. 09922-10010, or equivalent.
9. Remove rack guide spring cap, spring, guide and guide seat.
10. Remove rack housing cap.
11. Using tool No. 09616-00010, or equivalent, to stop control valve shaft rotation, remove nut.
12. Remove dust cover.
13. Using snap ring pliers, remove snap ring from rack housing.

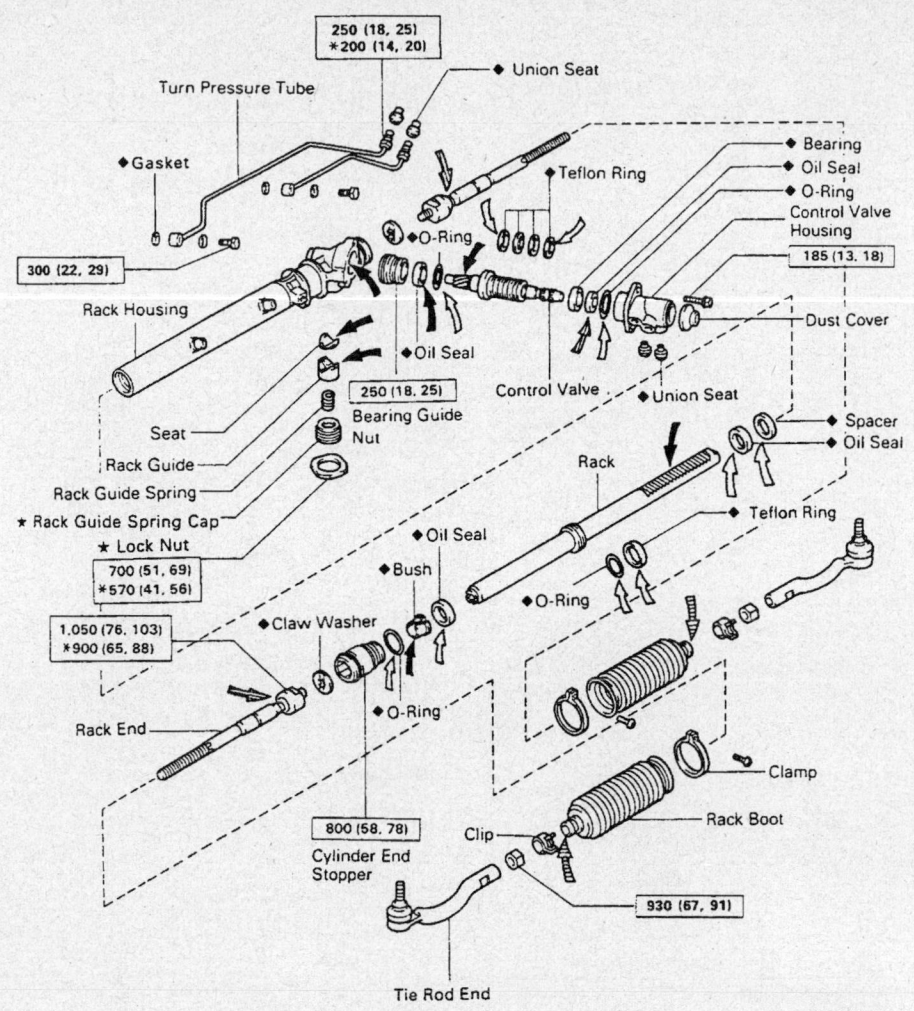

250 (18, 25)
*200 (14, 20)

Turn Pressure Tube

◆ Union Seat

◆ Gasket

◆ Bearing
◆ Oil Seal
◆ O-Ring
Control Valve Housing

◆ Teflon Ring

O-Ring

300 (22, 29)

185 (13, 18)

Rack Housing

◆ Oil Seal

Dust Cover

Control Valve

◆ Union Seat

Seat

250 (18, 25)

◆ Spacer
◆ Oil Seal

Rack Guide

Bearing Guide Nut

Rack

Rack Guide Spring

★ Rack Guide Spring Cap

◆ Oil Seal

◆ Teflon Ring

★ Lock Nut

◆ Bush

700 (51, 69)
*570 (41, 56)

1,050 (76, 103)
*900 (65, 88)

◆ O-Ring

◆ Claw Washer

Rack End

◆ O-Ring

800 (58, 78)

Clip

Cylinder End Stopper

Clamp

Rack Boot

930 (67, 91)

Tie Rod End

TY6029100046000X

Fig. 29 Exploded view of power steering gear. Previa

14. Using tool No. 09613-12010, or equivalent, remove control valve with oil seal and bearing.
15. Remove oil seal and bearing from control valve.
16. Remove bearing and spacer from rack housing.
17. Using tool No. 09612-10093, or equivalent, press out steering rack and end stopper.
18. Press oil seat from steering rack using tool Nos. 09950-60010 and 09950-70010, or equivalents.

Inspection

1. Using a dial indicator, check rack for runout. Maximum runout is .0118 inch.
2. Check rack teeth for wear and damage.
3. Check back surface for wear and damage.
4. Using a cylinder gauge and micrometer, measure inside diameter of bushing and outside diameter of valve assembly.
5. Maximum inside diameter of bushing should be 1.11 inches. Minimum outside diameter of valve assembly should be 1.0925 inches.

Assemble

1. Using tool Nos. 09950-60010 and 09950-70010, or equivalents, install new oil seal.
2. Install tool No. 09631-16020, or equivalent, to steering rack, then install rack into rack housing and remove tool.
3. Install oil seal into rack housing.
4. Install cylinder end stopper and new snap ring to rack housing.
5. Install control valve assembly.
6. Using tool No. 09612-22011, or equivalent, press in new bearing.
7. Install dust cover, spacer and new bearing into rack housing.
8. Using tool No. 09616-00010, or equivalent, to stop control valve shaft rotation, install lock nut and tighten to specifications.
9. Install rack housing cap with suitable sealant.
10. Install rack guide seat, rack guide, spring and spring cap.
11. Adjust preload as follows:
    a. Using hexagon wrench, **torque** rack guide spring cap to 18 ft. lbs., then turn cap back 12°.
    b. Temporarily install righthand and lefthand rack ends to prevent steer-

ing rack teeth from damaging oil seal lip.
    c. Using tool No. 09616-00010, or equivalent, turn control valve shaft left and right a few times.
    d. Loosen rack guide spring cap until rack guide spring is not functioning.
    e. Using tool No. 09616-00010, or equivalent, and a hexagon wrench, tighten cap until preload is 6.9–11.3 inch lbs.
12. Install rack guide spring cap lock nut and tighten to specification.
13. Remove righthand and lefthand rack ends.
14. Install new washer and lefthand and righthand rack ends.
15. Install grommet to rack housing No. 1 bracket. Align matchmarks on bracket and housing.
16. Install righthand and lefthand rack boots, clamps and clips.
17. Install righthand and lefthand tie rod ends and lock nuts. Align matchmarks on tie rod end and rack.
18. Install turn pressure tubes and tighten to specifications.

SUPRA

Disassemble

1. Position rack in suitable soft jawed vise.
2. Using suitable tool, remove turn tubes and O-rings, **Fig. 31.**
3. Loosen tie rod end locknut, then place installation alignment marks on tie rod end and rack end, remove tie rod end.
4. Remove back boots. **Do not damage rack boots or rack housing.**
5. Unstake claw washers, then using suitable tool, remove rack ends, mark right and left rack ends and remove claw washers.
6. Using suitable tool, remove rack guide spring cap locknut.
7. Using suitable tool, remove rack guide spring cap.
8. Remove rack guide spring, rack guide and seat.
9. Remove rack housing gap.
10. Using suitable tool to hold control valve, remove self locking nut.
11. Remove control valve housing dust cover, place installation alignment marks on valve and rack housing, remove valve housing, valve and rack housing gasket.
12. Tap out control valve and oil seal.
13. Remove lower bearing and spacer.
14. Using suitable tool, remove snap ring, then using suitable tool, press rack until end stopper slightly touches press block, pull out rack with cylinder end stopper, two spacers and oil seal.
15. Using suitable tool, tap cylinder housing oil seal and spacer.

Inspection & Repair

1. Using suitable dial indicator, inspect rack for runout and tooth wear or damage. Maximum runout is .012 inch, if measurement is not as indicated or damaged, replace rack.
2. If required, replace rack housing oil seal and bearing.

3. If required, replace control valve housing oil seal and bearing.
4. If required, replace rack bushing oil seal, using suitable tool, remove oil seal, coat new oil seal with power steering fluid, then install.
5. If required, replace Teflon ring and O-ring as follows:
   a. Remove Teflon ring and O-ring. **Do not damage steering rack.**
   b. Coat new O-ring with power steering fluid, then install.
   c. Coat new Teflon ring with power steering fluid.
   d. Install Teflon ring then expand ring by hand.
   e. Install expanded ring to steering rack and snug down by hand to fit tightly in groove.
6. If required, replace control valve Teflon ring as follows:
   a. Using suitable screwdriver, remove Teflon ring. **Do not damage control valve.**
   b. Install new rings to tool No. 09631-20070, or equivalent, then expand rings.
   c. Install expanded rings to control valve and snug down by hand.
   d. Coat ring with power steering fluid, then carefully slide tapered end of tool No. 09631-20081, or equivalent, over rings to seat rings.
7. If required, replace hydraulic reaction chamber Teflon rings and O-rings as follows:
   a. Remove Teflon ring and O-rings. **Do not damage control valve.**
   b. Install new O-rings.
   c. Expand Teflon rings by hand. **Do not over expand Teflon rings.**
   d. Install expanded Teflon rings to control valve.
   e. Coat Teflon rings with power steering fluid and snug down by hand.
   f. Slide tapered end of tool No. 09631-32020, or equivalent, over Teflon rings to seat rings.
8. If required, replace pressure control valve.

Assemble

1. Coat cylinder housing oil seal lip with power steering fluid, then using suitable tool, tap in cylinder housing oil seal and spacer.
2. Install tool No. 09631-20102 equivalent, to rack, scrape burrs from rack teeth end and burnish as required, coat tool with power steering fluid, the install rack to cylinder, remove tool.
3. Install cylinder end stopper, oil seal and spacers as follows:
   a. Apply suitable vinyl tape to steering rack end to prevent oil seal lip damage.
   b. Push oil seal into cylinder without tilting seal.
   c. Install two spacers.
   d. Using tool No. 09620-30010, or equivalent, drive in cylinder end stopper.
   e. Using suitable snap ring pliers, install snap ring.
4. Install tool No. 09631-12070 or 09631-12071 equivalent, to cylinder housing,

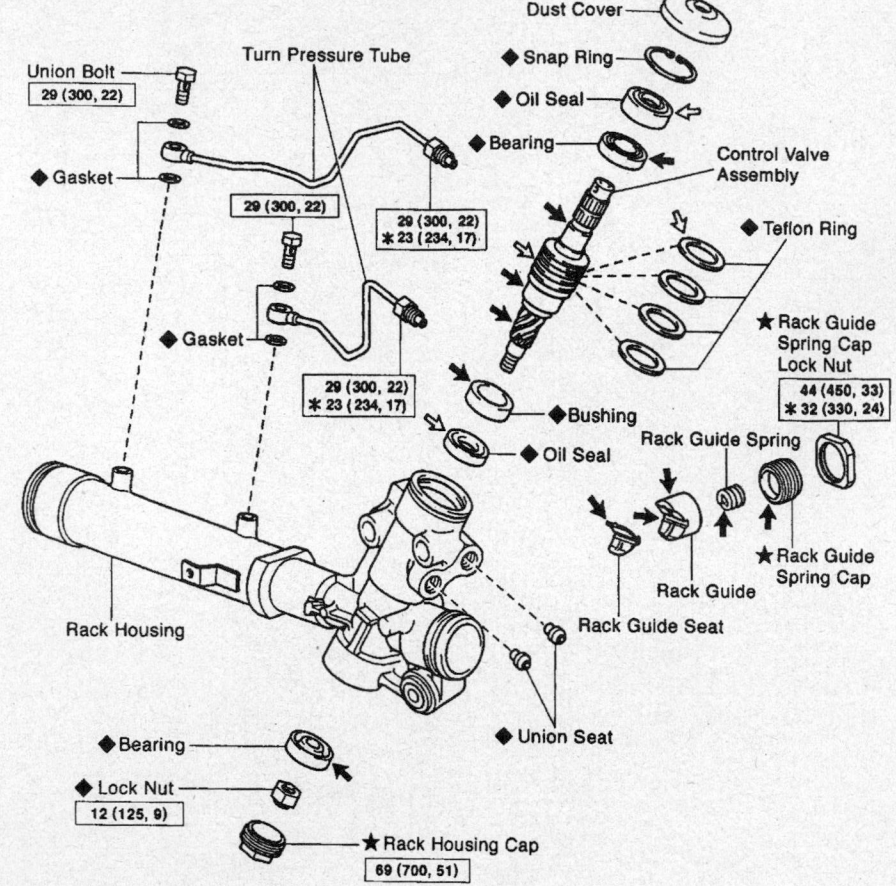

Fig. 30 Exploded view of power steering gear (Part 1 of 2). RAV4

apply 15.75 inches Hg vacuum for about 30 seconds, ensure no change in vacuum, if vacuum changes, inspect oil seal installation.
5. Coat Teflon rings with power steering fluid, then install control valve into housing.
6. Coat O-ring with power steering fluid and install, align valve and rack housing matchmarks, install attaching bolts and tighten to specifications.
7. Install lower bearing and spacer.
8. Using suitable tool, install new self locking nut and tighten to specifications.
9. Apply Loctite 242, or equivalent, to two or three rack housing cap threads, then install cap, using suitable center punch, stake housing in two places.
10. Install rack guide seat, rack guide and spring.
11. Apply Loctite 242, or equivalent, to two or three spring cap threads, then install spring cap, tighten to specifications.
12. Return rack guide spring cap 15°, turn control valve shaft right and left one or two times, loosen spring cap until rack guide compression spring is not func-

tioning, then using suitable tool, tighten rack guide spring cap until turning preload of 7.8–10.4 ft. lbs. is indicated.
13. Apply Loctite 242, or equivalent, to two or three rack guide spring cap locknut threads, then install locknut, tighten to specifications, then recheck preload as outlined in step 13.
14. Install dust cover, install claw washer and rack ends, then using suitable brass bar and hammer, stake claw washer.
15. Ensure tube hole is not clogged, then install rack boots.
16. Install tie rod ends, align matchmarks.
17. Install right and left turn pressure tubes.

TUNDRA & 2WD TACOMA

Disassemble

1. Remove 2 turn pressure tubes using wrench tool No. 09633–00020, or equivalent.
2. Mount power steering gear in housing stand tool No. 09612–00012, or equivalent.
3. Place housing stand in suitable vise.

16. Using seal removal tool Nos. 09950–60010 and 09950–70010, or equivalent, remove oil seal and spacer from rack housing.

Inspection & Repair

1. Using a suitable dial indicator inspect rack runout and check teeth for wear and damage. Ensure runout does not exceed .0118 inch.
2. Inspect back surface of rack for wear and damage.
3. Inspect needle roller bearing for wear or damage.
4. If necessary, replace oil seal as follows:
   a. Using a suitable hammer and seal remover tool Nos. 09950–60010 and 09950–70010, or equivalent, drive seal from bearing guide nut.
   b. Apply power steering fluid to seal lip.
   c. Install seal using seal installer tool Nos. 09950–60010, 09950–70010 and 09952–06010, or equivalent.
5. If necessary, replace control valve housing oil seal and bearing as follows:
   a. Using seal remover tool Nos. 09950–60010 and 09950–70010, or equivalent, press oil seal and bearing from control valve housing.
   b. Apply power steering fluid to seal lip.
   c. Install seal using seal installer tool Nos. 09950–60010, 09950–70010 and 09952–06010, or equivalent.
   d. Apply molybdenum disulfide lithium grease to bearing, then press into place using bearing installation tool Nos. 09950–60010 and 09970–70010, or equivalent.
6. Inspect control valve roller bearing for wear or damage.
7. If necessary replace Teflon ring and O-ring as follows:
   a. Using a suitable screwdriver, remove Teflon ring and O-ring front steering rack.
   b. Apply power steering fluid to O-ring and install.
   c. Expand new Teflon ring using fingers, then coat with power steering fluid.
   d. Install O-ring to rack and push into groove with fingers.
8. If necessary, replace union seats as follows:
   a. Using a suitable screw extractor, remove two seats from control valve housing.
   b. Install new seats using a suitable plastic hammer and sliding handle.

Assemble

1. Apply power steering fluid to all seals and O-rings before installation.
2. Apply molybdenum disulfide grease to all bushings and bearings before installation.
3. Install oil seal and spacer using installation tool Nos. 09950-60010, 09952-06010, and 09950-70010, or equivalent.
4. Install steering rack cover tool No.

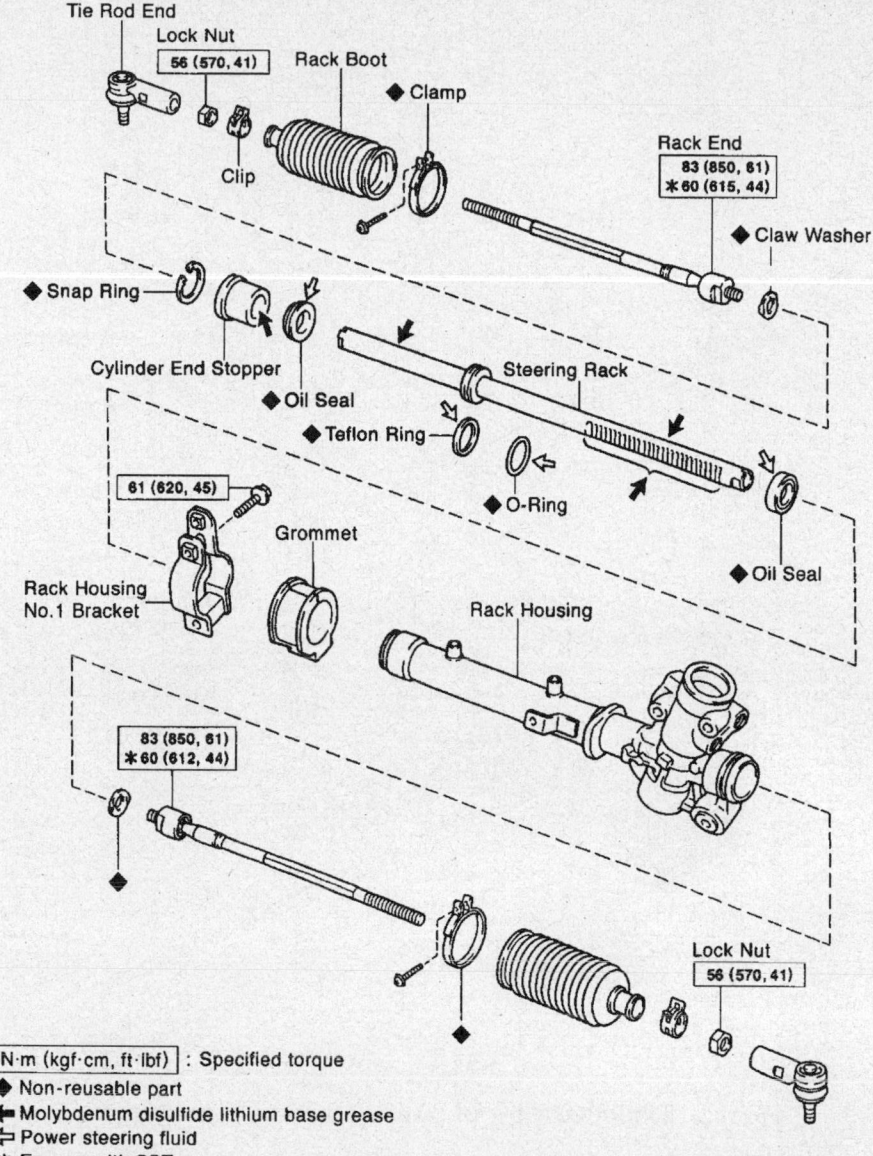

```
N·m (kgf·cm, ft·lbf) : Specified torque
◆ Non-reusable part
◄ Molybdenum disulfide lithium base grease
⇦ Power steering fluid
✱ For use with SST
```

TY6029600057020X

Fig. 30   Exploded view of power steering gear (Part 2 of 2). RAV4

4. Place alignment marks on both outer tie rods, then remove.
5. Remove right and left clips, rack boots and clamps.
6. Remove left and right inner tie rods and claw washers as follows:
   a. Using a suitable screwdriver and hammer, unstake washer.
   b. Use a suitable spanner to hold steering rack, then remove inner tie rod using wrench tool No. 09922–10010, or equivalent.
7. Place alignment marks on bracket and rack housing, then remove bracket, **Fig. 32.**
8. Using wrench tool No. 09922–10010, or equivalent, remove rack guide spring cap locknut.
9. Remove rack guide spring cap, then the guide spring, guide and guide seat.
10. Remove dust cover, then place alignment marks on valve housing and steering gear.

11. Remove valve housing retaining bolts, then the control valve housing and valve assembly.
12. Remove control valve as follows:
    a. Loosen bearing guide nut using bearing guide wrench tool No. 09631–20060, or equivalent.
    b. Apply suitable vinyl tape to control valve shaft.
    c. Using a suitable plastic hammer, drive control valve from housing with nut attached. Ensure oil seal lip is not damaged when removing control valve.
    d. Remove nut from control valve, then remove O-ring from nut.
13. Using cylinder end stopper wrench tool No. 09631–20090, or equivalent, remove cylinder end stopper.
14. Remove steering rack and oil seal using a suitable extension bar and socket wrench.
15. Remove oil seal from rack.

09631-20102, or equivalent, to power steering rack and coat with power steering fluid.

5. Remove burrs from rack teeth as necessary.
6. Install rack into housing, then remove rack cover.
7. Install steering rack cover tool No. 09631-20102, or equivalent, to opposite end of steering rack and coat with power steering fluid.
8. Install rack seal then remove rack cover.
9. Install new O-ring to rack cylinder end stopper then install using a suitable hammer and block of wood.
10. Using cylinder end stopper wrench, tighten rack stopper to specification.
11. Using a suitable hammer and punch, stake rack housing.
12. Install seal test tool No. 09631-12071, or equivalent, to rack housing unions.
13. Apply 15.75 in. Hg for 30 seconds. Ensure no change in vacuum is indicated. If change occurs, check oil seals.
14. Apply vinyl tape to control valve shaft.
15. Install control valve into control valve housing.
16. Install bearing guide nut O-ring.
17. Using bearing guide nut wrench tool No. 09631-20060, or equivalent, tighten bearing guide nut to specification.
18. Install O-ring to control valve housing.
19. Install control valve housing and position to alignment marks. Tighten to specification.
20. Install dust cover.
21. Install rack guide seat, rack guide and rack guide spring.
22. Apply suitable sealant to two or three threads of cap.
23. Install cap and adjust preload as follows:
    a. Temporarily install right and left inner tie rods.
    b. **Torque** rack guide spring cap to 18 ft. lbs.
    c. Turn cap 12° counterclockwise.
    d. Using pinion socket tool No. 09616-00010, or equivalent, turn control valve shaft right and left 2 times.
    e. Loosen cap until rack guide spring is not functioning.
    f. Using pinion socket tool No. 09616-00010, or equivalent, and a suitable torque wrench, tighten cap until preload is 4.3–14.3 inch lbs.
24. Apply suitable sealant to three threads of guide spring cap locknut.
25. Using a suitable wrench, hold rack guide spring cap. **Torque** locknut to 37 ft. lbs. using adjustable wrench tool No. 09922–10010, or equivalent.
26. Recheck preload and adjust as necessary.
27. Remove right and left inner tie rods.
28. Install rack housing bracket and insulator.
29. Install claw washers, then the right and left inner tie rods.
30. Tighten inner tie rods to specifications using a suitable spanner and adjustable wrench tool No. 09922–10010, or equivalent.
31. Using a suitable brass bar and hammer, stake washers.

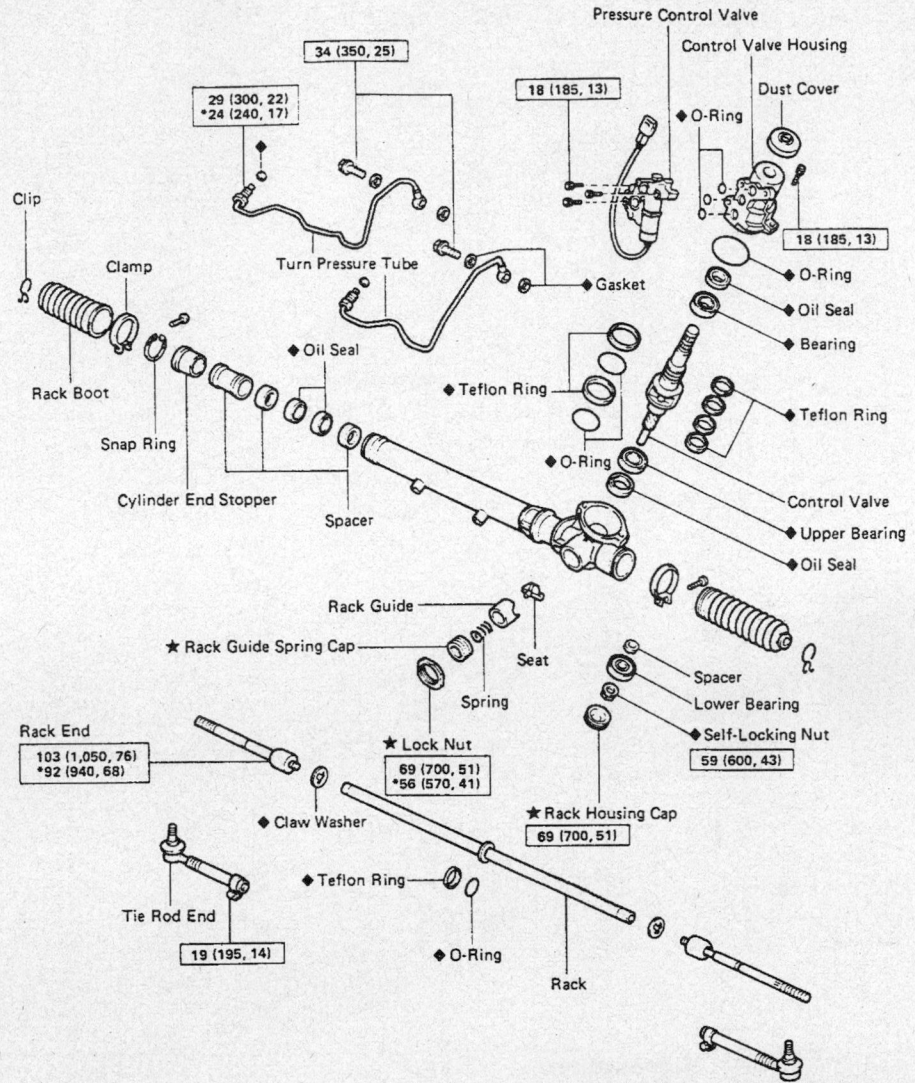

Fig. 31 Exploded view of power steering gear. Supra

32. Install right and left rack boots, clamps and clips.
33. Install left and right outer tie rods and locknuts.
34. Install new union seats, then the turn pressure tubes.

4RUNNER & 4WD TACOMA
Disassemble

1. Remove two turn pressure tubes using wrench tool No. 09633-00020, or equivalent.
2. Mount power steering gear in housing stand tool No. 09612-00012, or equivalent.
3. Place housing stand in suitable vise.
4. Place alignment marks on both outer tie rods, then remove.
5. Remove right and left clips, rack boots and clamps.
6. Remove left and right inner tie rods and claw washers as follows:
    a. Using a suitable screwdriver and hammer, unstake washer.
    b. Use a suitable spanner to hold steering rack, then remove inner tie rod using wrench tool No. 09922–

10010, or equivalent.
7. Remove rack guide spring cap lock nut using adjustable wrench tool No. 09922-10010 or equivalent, **Fig. 33.**
8. Remove rack guide spring cap, then the guide spring and rack guide.
9. Remove dust cover, then place alignment marks on valve housing and steering gear.
10. Remove valve housing retaining bolts, then the control valve housing and valve assembly.
11. Remove control valve as follows:
    a. Loosen bearing guide nut using bearing guide wrench tool No. 09631-20060, or equivalent.
    b. Apply suitable vinyl tape to control valve shaft.
    c. Using a suitable plastic hammer, drive control valve from housing with nut attached. Ensure oil seal lip is not damaged when removing control valve.
    d. Remove nut from control valve, then remove O-ring from nut.
12. Using adjustable wrench tool No. 09922-10010, or equivalent, remove

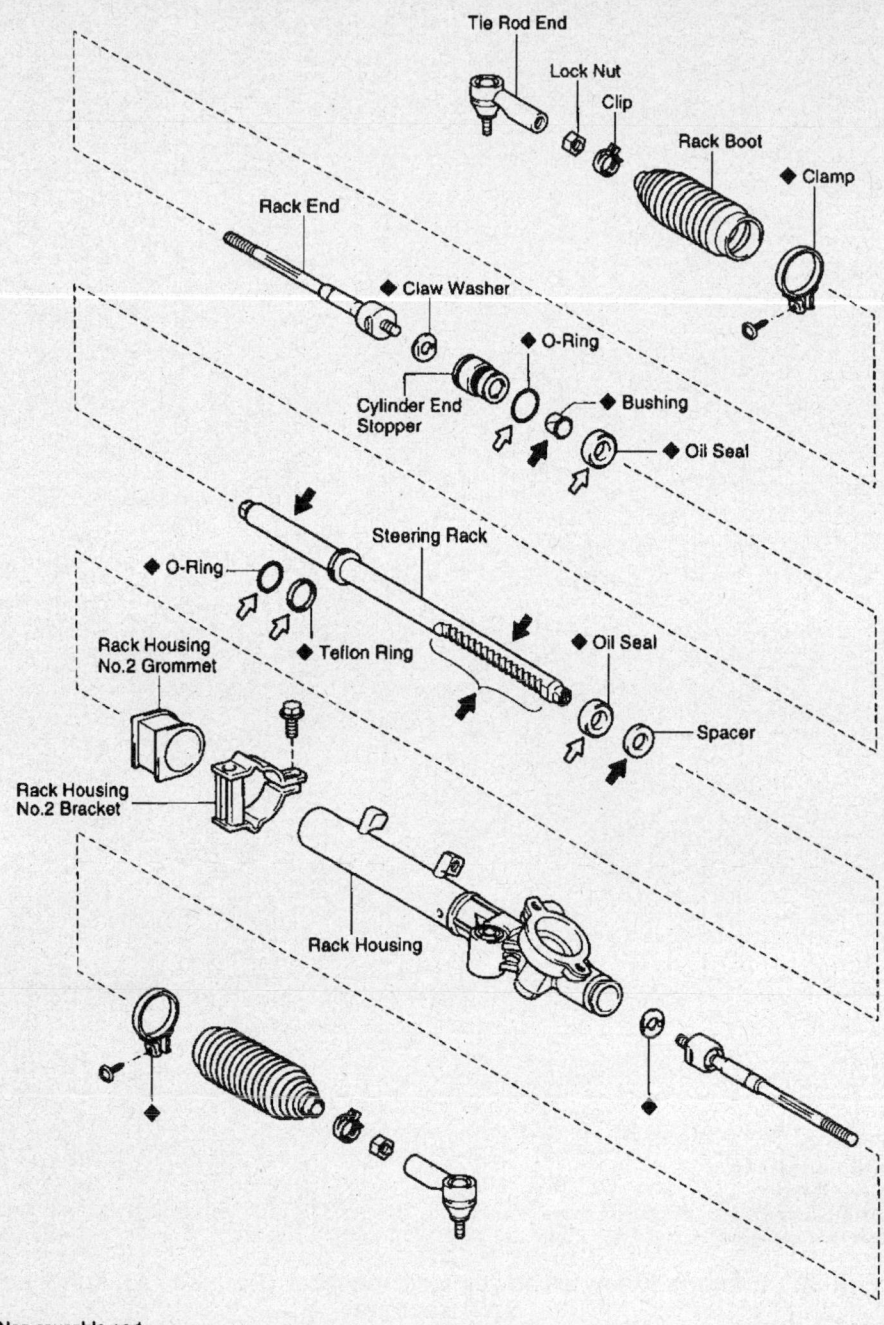

Fig. 32 Exploded view of power steering gear (Part 1 of 2). Tundra & 2WD Tacoma

◆ Non-reusable part
◀ Molybdenum disulfide lithium base grease
◁ Power steering fluid

TY6029700067010X

Nos. 09950-60010, 09950-70010 and 09952-06010, or equivalent.

5. If necessary, replace control valve housing oil seal and bearing as follows:
   a. Using seal remover tool Nos. 09950-60010 and 09950-70010, or equivalent, press oil seal and bearing from control valve housing.
   b. Apply power steering fluid to seal lip.
   c. Install seal using seal installer tool Nos. 09950–60010, 09950–70010 and 09952–06010, or equivalent.
   d. Apply molybdenum disulfide lithium grease to bearing, then press into place using bearing installation tool Nos. 09950-60010 and 09970-70010, or equivalent.
6. Inspect control valve roller bearing for wear or damage.
7. If necessary replace Teflon ring and O-ring as follows:
   a. Using a suitable screwdriver, remove Teflon ring and O-ring front steering rack.
   b. Apply power steering fluid to O-ring and install.
   c. Expand new Teflon ring using fingers, then coat with power steering fluid.
   d. Install O-ring to rack and push into groove with fingers.
8. If necessary, replace union seats as follows:
   a. Using a suitable screw extractor, remove 2 seats from control valve housing.
   b. Install new seats using a suitable plastic hammer and sliding handle.

Assemble

1. Apply power steering fluid to all seals and O-rings before installation.
2. Apply molybdenum disulfide grease to all bushings and bearings before installation.
3. Install oil seal and spacer using installation tool Nos. 09951-60010, 09952-06010, and 09951-70010, or equivalent.
4. Install steering rack cover tool No. 09631-00350, or equivalent, to power steering rack and coat with power steering fluid.
5. Remove burrs from rack teeth as necessary.
6. Install rack into housing, then remove rack cover.
7. Install steering rack cover tool No. 09631-00350, or equivalent, to opposite end of steering rack and coat with power steering fluid.
8. Install rack seal then remove rack cover.
9. Install new O-ring to cylinder end stopper.
10. Install cylinder end stopper using adjustable wrench tool No. 09922-10010, or equivalent.
11. Using a suitable hammer and punch, stake rack housing.
12. Install seal test tool No. 09631-12071, or equivalent, to rack housing unions.
13. Apply 15.75 in. Hg for 30 seconds. Ensure no change in vacuum is indicated.

cylinder end stopper.
13. Remove O-ring from stopper.
14. Using a suitable extension bar and socket, remove rack and oil seal.
15. Remove oil seal from rack.
16. Remove oil seal and spacer from rack housing using seal remover tool Nos. 09950–60010 and 09950–70010, or equivalent.

Inspection & Repair

1. Using a suitable dial indicator inspect rack runout and check teeth for wear and damage. Ensure runout does not

exceed .0118 inch.
2. Inspect back surface of rack for wear and damage.
3. Inspect needle roller bearing for wear or damage.
4. If necessary, replace oil seal as follows:
   a. Using a suitable hammer and seal remover tool Nos. 09950–60010 and 09950–70010, or equivalent, drive seal from bearing guide nut.
   b. Apply power steering fluid to seal lip.
   c. Install seal using seal installer tool

If change occurs, check oil seals.
14. Apply vinyl tape to control valve shaft.
15. Install control valve into control valve housing.
16. Install bearing guide nut O-ring.
17. Using bearing guide nut wrench tool No. 09631-20060, or equivalent, tighten bearing guide nut to specification.
18. Install O-ring to control valve housing.
19. Install control valve housing and position to alignment marks. Tighten to specification.
20. Install dust cover.
21. Install rack guide and rack guide spring.
22. Apply suitable sealant to 2 or 3 threads of cap.
23. Install cap and adjust preload as follows:
    a. Temporarily install right and left inner tie rods.
    b. **Torque** rack guide spring cap to 18 ft. lbs.
    c. Turn cap 19° counterclockwise.
    d. Using pinion socket tool No. 09616-00010, or equivalent, turn control valve shaft right and left 2 times.
    e. Loosen cap until rack guide spring is not functioning.
    f. Using pinion socket tool No. 09616-00010, or equivalent, and a suitable torque wrench, tighten cap until preload is 4.3–14.3 inch lbs.
24. Apply suitable sealant to 3 threads of guide spring cap locknut.
25. Using a suitable wrench, hold rack guide spring cap. **Torque** locknut to 37 ft. lbs. using adjustable wrench tool No. 09922–10010, or equivalent.
26. Recheck preload and adjust as necessary.
27. Remove right and left inner tie rods.
28. Install claw washers, then the right and left inner tie rods.
29. Tighten inner tie rods using a suitable spanner and adjustable wrench tool No. 09922-10010, or equivalent.
30. Using a suitable brass bar and hammer, stake washers.
31. Install right and left rack boots, clamps and clips.
32. Install left and right outer tie rods and locknuts.
33. Install new union seats, then the turn pressure tubes.

2WD T100

Disassemble

1. Remove turn pressure tube bracket, then using power steering hose nut wrench tool No. 09633-00020, or equivalent, remove turn pressure tubes and O-rings.
2. Secure gear housing in a vise.
3. Loosen locknut and place matchmarks on tie rod and rack ends, then remove tie rod ends and locknuts.
4. Remove rack boot clips and clamps, then rack boots. Mark left and right boots accordingly.
5. Unstake claw washers, **avoid any impact to rack,** using variable open wrench tool No. 09922-10010, remove rack ends, **Fig. 34.**
6. Mark left and right rack ends accord-

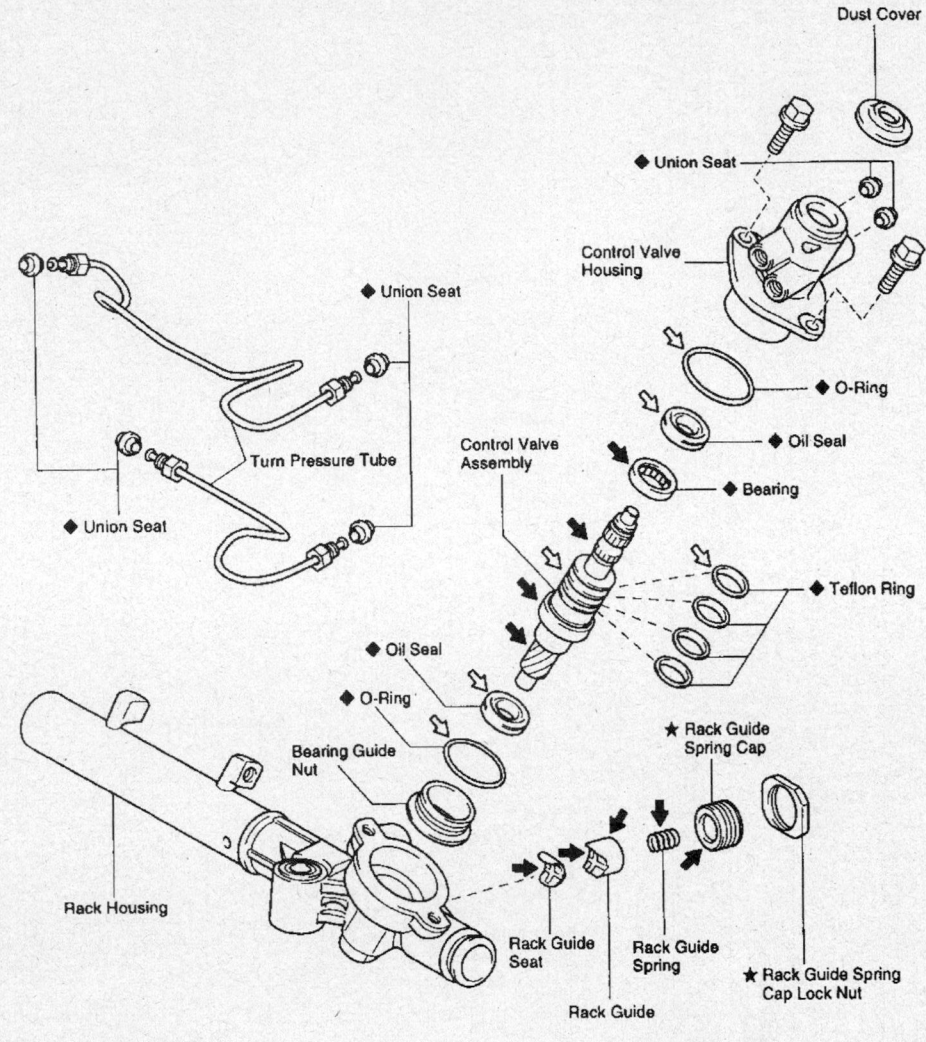

♦ Non-reusable part
★ Precoated part
◄ Molybdenum disulfide lithium base grease
⇦ Power steering fluid

TY6029700067020X

Fig. 32   Exploded view of power steering gear (Part 2 of 2). Tundra & 2WD Tacoma

ingly, then remove claw washers.
7. Remove rack guide spring cap locknut, then rack guide spring cap.
8. Remove rack guide spring cap and rack guide, then O-ring from rack guide.
9. Remove rack housing cap.
10. Using steering worm bearing adjusting socket tool No. 09616-00010, or equivalent, to hold control valve, remove self-locking nut.
11. Remove control valve housing as follows:
    a. Place matchmarks on valve housing and rack housing, then remove dust cover and two bolts.
    b. Pull out valve with valve housing.
    c. Remove gasket from rack housing.
    d. Remove control valve housing and oil seal.

12. Using cylinder end stopper nut wrench tool No. 09631-16010, or equivalent, turn cylinder end stopper clockwise until wire end comes out, then turn cylinder end stopper counterclockwise and remove wire.
13. Using a brass bar, tap out rack with rack bushing and remove O-ring from bushing.
14. Using steering gearbox replacer set tool No. 09620-30010, or equivalent, and a brass bar, drive out oil seal.

Inspection & Repair

1. Check rack runout; maximum runout is .012 inch. Check back surface for wear or damage; if faulty, replace rack.
2. If necessary, replace control valve housing oil seal and upper bearing as follows:

a. Using steering gearbox replacer set tool No. 09620-30010, or equivalent, tap out oil seal and upper bearing.

b. Coat new seal lip with MP grease.

c. Using steering gearbox replacer set tool No. 09620-3001, or equivalent, press in oil seal. the install new upper bearing in valve housing.

d. Using steering gearbox replacer set tool No. 09620-30010, or equivalent, press in new upper bearing.

3. If necessary, replace control valve lower bearing as follows:

a. Using a brass bar, drive out lower bearing.

b. Using steering gear housing overhaul set tool No. 09612-24014, or equivalent, remove center bearing.

c. Using steering gearbox replacer set tool No. 09620-30010, or equivalent, press in new center bearing.

d. Using steering gear rack oil tool set tool No. 09630-24013, or equivalent, press in new lower bearing.

4. If necessary, replace rack bushing oil seal as follows:

a. Using water pump overhaul set tool No. 09236-00101, or equivalent, remove oil seal.

b. Coat new seal with power steering fluid.

c. Using oil seal replacer tool No. 09631-32010, or equivalent, press in new oil seal.

5. If necessary, replace Teflon ring and O-ring as follows:

a. Remove Teflon ring and O-ring. **Ensure not to damage steering rack.**

b. Coat with power steering fluid, then install new O-ring.

c. Expand new Teflon ring. **Ensure not to over-expand ring.**

d. Install Teflon ring to steering rack, then coat Teflon ring with power steering fluid and snug it down with fingers.

6. If necessary, replace control valve Teflon ring as follows:

a. Using a screwdriver, remove Teflon rings. **Ensure not to damage control valve.**

b. Install new Teflon rings to seal ring guide No. 09631-20070 and expand them.

c. Install expanded Teflon rings to control valve and snug them down with fingers, then carefully slide tapered end of tool over Teflon rings to seat them.

Assemble

1. Coat new cylinder housing seal with power steering fluid, install seal onto front hub and drive pinion bearing replacer set tool No. 09608-12010, or equivalent, and press seal in.

2. Install rack as follows:

a. Install rack to steering rack cover "I" tool No. 09631-33010, or equivalent, then coat tool with power steering fluid.

b. Insert rack into cylinder.

c. Remove tool.

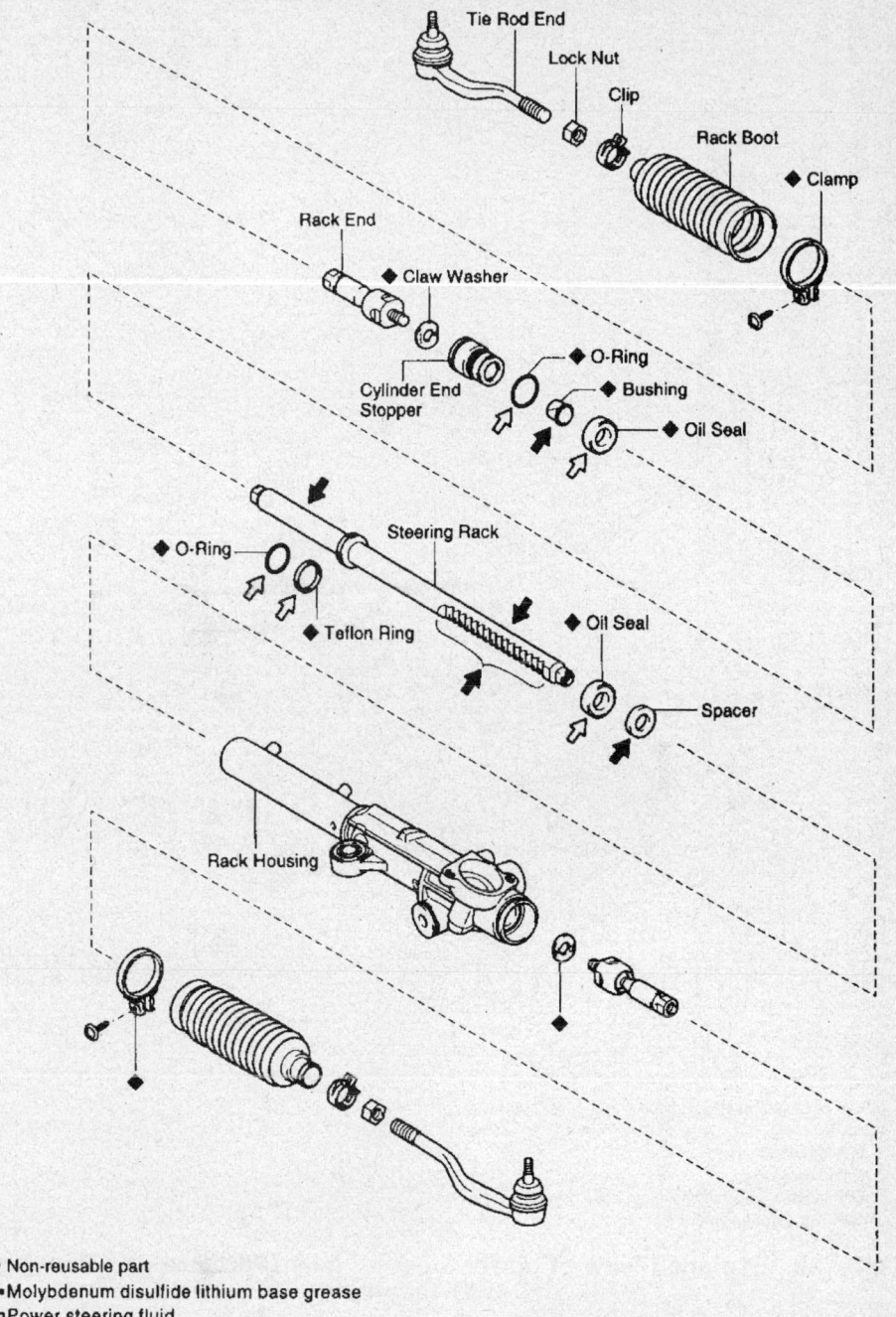

◆ Non-reusable part
◄ Molybdenum disulfide lithium base grease
◁ Power steering fluid

TY6029700068010X

Fig. 33   Exploded view of power steering gear (Part 1 of 2). 4Runner & 4WD Tacoma

3. To prevent damage to oil seal lip, wrap vinyl tape around steering rack end and apply power steering fluid.

4. Coat new O-ring with power steering fluid and install it to rack bushing. Push rack bushing and cylinder end stopper until wire installation hole appears.

5. Insert a new wire into hole, then using cylinder end stopper wrench tool No. 09631-16010, or equivalent, turn cylinder end clockwise until wire end disappears.

6. Install suitable hand vacuum pump to unions of cylinder housing, then apply 15.75 inches of vacuum for about 30 seconds. Ensure of no change in vacuum; if vacuum changes, check installation of rack housing oil seal.

7. Wind vinyl tape on control valve and coat Teflon rings with power steering fluid. Push control valve into housing, **ensure not to damage Teflon rings and oil seal. Using tilt bearing handle replacer tool No. 09612-22011, or equivalent, press in new oil seal.**

8. Install new control valve housing gasket on rack housing, then control valve housing and two bolts and dust cover. Tighten housing bolts to specifications.

9. Using steering worm bearing adjusting

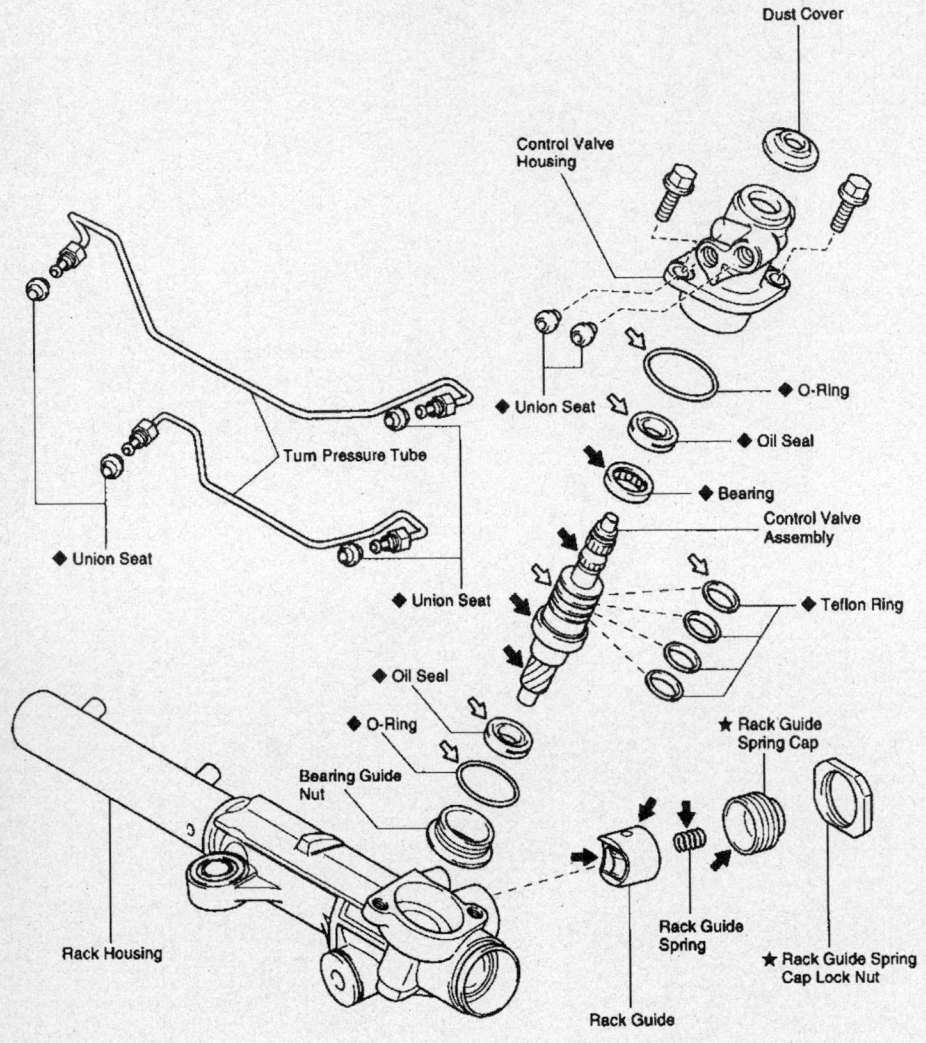

◆ Non-reusable part
★ Precoated part
◄ Molybdenum disulfide lithium base grease
⟵ Power steering fluid

TY60297000⌀68020X

Fig. 33 Exploded view of power steering gear (Part 2 of 2). 4Runner & 4WD Tacoma

socket tool No. 09616-00010, or equivalent, to hold control valve, install new self-locking nut. Tighten to specifications.

10. Apply sealant (Loctite 242, or equivalent) to two or three threads of housing cap, then install cap. Using a center punch, stake housing at two places.

11. Install O-ring to rack guide, then install rack guide and spring.

12. Adjust total preload as follows:
   a. Apply sealant (Loctite 242, or equivalent) to two or three threads of spring cap, then install spring cap.
   b. Set rack at rack stroke center.
   c. Using steering gear housing overhaul set tool No. 09612-24014, or equivalent, install and tighten spring cap to specifications.
   d. Using steering gear housing overhaul set tool No. 09612-24014, or equivalent, return rack guide spring cap 10° to 12°.
   e. Using steering worm bearing adjusting socket tool No. 09616-00010, or equivalent, and torque meter, check total preload; preload (turning) should be 11.3 inch lbs. or less. If preload is 11.3 inch lbs. or more, return rack guide spring cap another 5°.

13. Install rack guide spring cap locknut as follows:
   a. Apply sealant (Loctite 242, or equivalent) to two or three threads of locknut, then using steering gear housing overhaul tool set tool No. 09612-24014, or equivalent, install and tighten locknut to specifica-

tions; use torque wrench with a fulcrum length of 13.39 inches.
   b. Recheck total preload.

14. Install rack ends as follows:
   a. Install a new claw washer.
   b. Using variable open wrench tool No. 09922-10010, or equivalent, install rack ends; use torque wrench with a fulcrum length of 13.39 inches.
   c. Using a brass bar and a hammer, stake claw washers.

15. Install rack boots as follows:
   a. Ensure tube hole is not clogged with grease. If tube hole is clogged, pressure inside boot will change after it is assembled and steering wheel is turned.
   b. Install boots. **Ensure not to damage to twist boots.**
   c. Install clips and clamps.

16. Screw locknuts and tie rod ends onto rack ends until matchmarks are aligned. After adjusting toe-in, tighten locknut to specifications.

17. Install right and left turn pressure tubes as follows:
   a. Install new O-rings to tube.
   b. Using power steering hose nut wrench tool No. 09633-0020, or equivalent, install and tighten tubes to specifications; use torque wrench with a fulcrum length of 11.81 inches.
   c. Install turn pressure tube bracket.

4WD T100

Disassemble

1. Place gear in suitable soft jawed vise.
2. Remove end cover adjusting screw locknut and seal washer, remove end cover attaching bolts and No. 1 hose support bracket, **Fig. ,** screw in adjusting screw until cover is removed.
3. Using suitable plastic hammer, tap out cross shaft end and remove shaft.
4. Using tool No. 09043-38100, or equivalent, remove plunger guide nut, then remove spring, plunger, plunger guide and O-ring.
5. Remove four valve body cap bolts, then using tool No. 09616-00010, or equivalent, turn shaft clockwise to disconnect worm gear valve body from gear housing.
6. Hold power piston so it cannot move, turn wormshaft clockwise, then remove valve body and power piston assembly and O-ring. **Ensure power piston nut does not come off with worm shaft.**

Inspection & Repair

1. Place valve body in suitable soft jawed vise, using suitable dial indicator, inspect ball clearance, moving worm gear up and down, maximum ball clearance should be .00059 inch, if clearance is not as indicated, replace power control valve assembly.
2. Place cross shaft in suitable soft jawed vise, then using suitable dial indicator, measure thrust clearance, .0012–.0020 inch should be indicated, is not as indicated, adjust thrust clearance.

3. Adjust thrust clearance as follows:
   a. Using suitable hammer and chisel, remove locknut stake.
   b. Using tool No. 09630-00012, or equivalent, loosen locknut.
   c. Turn adjusting screw for correct thrust clearance, then tighten locknut.
   d. Stake locknut.
4. If required, replace needle roller bearings as follows:
   a. Using suitable screw driver, remove oil seal.
   b. Using suitable snap ring pliers, remove snap ring.
   c. Remove metal spacer, O-ring and Teflon ring.
   d. Using tool No. 09630-00012, or equivalent, press out bearings.
   e. Install new lower bearing, ensuring it is positioned .909 inch away from lower end of housing.
   f. Press in new upper bearing, ensuring top end is installed so it aligns with housing end surface.
   g. Install O-ring and metal spacer.
   h. Using suitable snap ring pliers, install snap ring.
   i. Form Teflon ring into heart shape and install with fingers.
   j. Using tool No. 09630-00012, or equivalent, form Teflon ring, Teflon ring must be formed before sector shaft installation or damage may occur.
   k. Drive in new oil seal.
5. If required, replace control valve Teflon rings as follows:
   a. Using suitable screwdriver, remove Teflon ring and O-ring. **Do not damage control valve.**
   b. Install new O-ring.
   c. Expand Teflon ring by hand, do not over expand Teflon ring.
   d. Install Teflon ring.
   e. Coat Teflon ring with power steering fluid and snug down with piston ring compressor for 5–7 minutes.
6. If required, replace union set as follows:
   a. Using suitable screw extractor, remove union seat.
   b. Using suitable plastic hammer and extension bar, tap in new union seat.

Assemble

1. Install O-rings to gear housing and valve body, mount gear housing to tool No. 09630-00012, or equivalent, then install tool to suitable soft jawed vise. Install worm gear valve body. **Do not damage Teflon ring.**
2. Hold power piston nut to prevent turning, then using tool No. 09616-00010, or equivalent, check worm gear preload, starting preload should be 2.6–

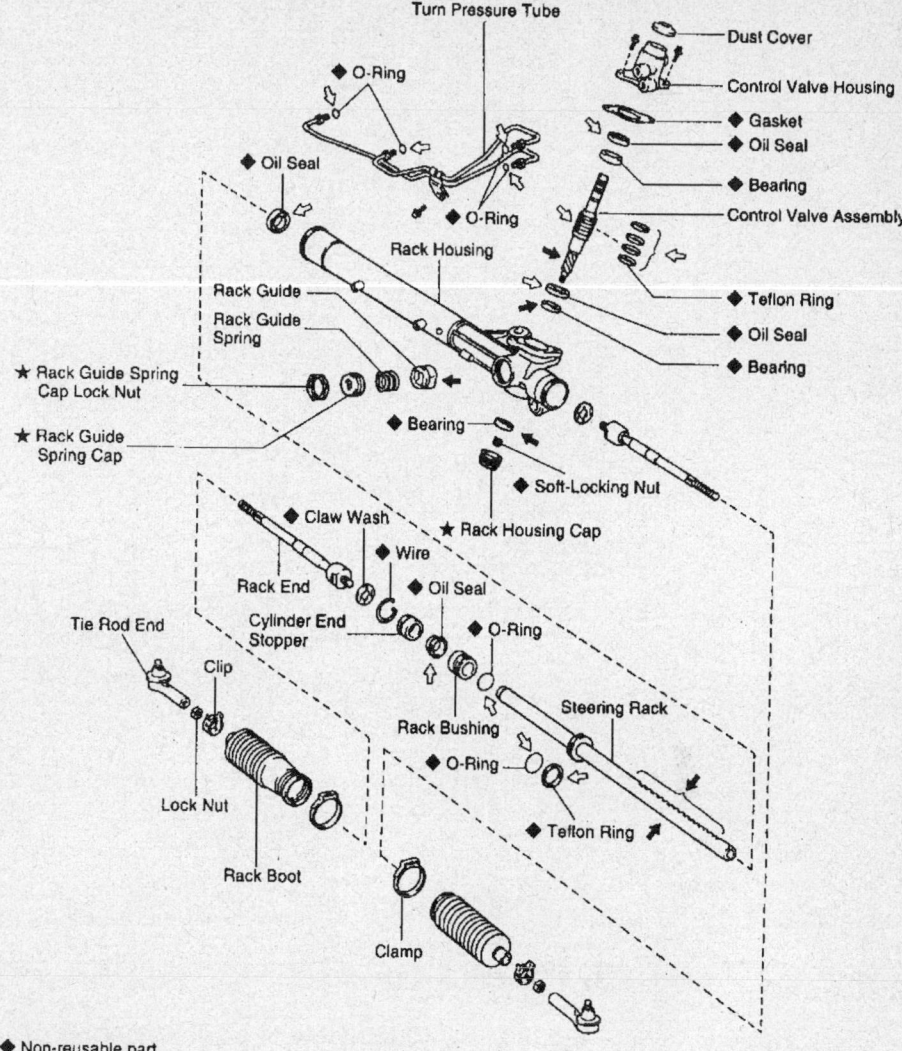

Fig. 34 Exploded view of power steering gear. 2WD T100

◆ Non-reusable part
★ Precoated part
⬅ Molybdenum disulphide lithium base grease
⇦ Power steering fluid

TY6029500069010X

4.8 inch lbs. If preload is not as indicated, replace worm gear assembly.
3. Install plunger, plunger guide and spring.
4. Install plunger guide nut O-ring, then using tool No. 09043-38100, or equivalent, install plunger guide nut and tighten specifications.
5. Install end cover O-ring, fully loosen adjusting screw, using suitable screwdriver, assemble cross shaft to end cover.
6. Set worm gear at center of gear housing.
7. Install and push cross shaft into gear

housing so center teeth mesh together, install four cap bolts tightening to specifications in diagonal pattern.
8. Using tool No. 09616-00010, or equivalent, turn worm shaft to full lock in both directions to determine exact center, place matchmarks on worm shaft and housing to show neutral position.
9. Install tool No. 09616-0010, or equivalent, with suitable torque meter to worm shaft, turn adjusting screw while measuring preload, total starting preload should be 4.3–8.3 inch lbs.
10. Install washer, then install and tighten locknut while holding adjusting screw.
11. Recheck total preload.

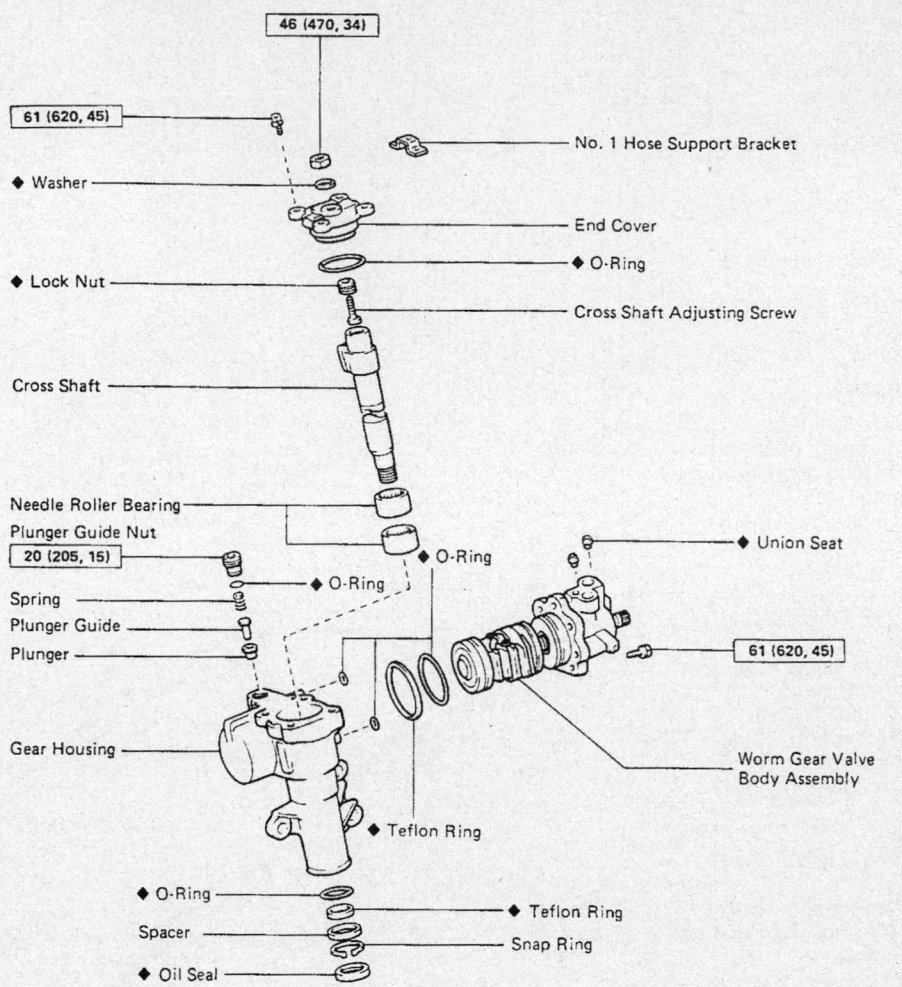

Fig. 35 Exploded view of power steering gear. 4WD T100

TY6029100045000X

TIGHTENING SPECIFICATIONS

Year	Component	Torque/Ft. Lbs.
AVALON, CAMRY, CAMRY SOLARA & SIENNA		
1996–99	Control Valve Housing To Rack Housing	13
	Control Valve Self-Locking Nut	18
	Control Valve Shaft To Universal Joint	26
	Gear Housing To Sub Frame	134
	Pressure & Return Tube To Gear Housing	18
	Pressure Port Union To Pump Housing	③
	Power Steering Pump Adjusting Bolt	29
	Power Steering Pump Through Bolt	32
	Power Steering Pump To Pressure Tube	38
	Pump Pulley To Pump Shaft	32
	Rack Housing Cap	43
	Rack To Rack End	④
	Suction Port Union To Pump Housing	108①
	Tie Rod End Locknut	54
	Tie Rod End To Steering Knuckle	36
	Turn Pressure Tube Union Nut	96①
CELICA		
1996–99	Air Control Valve	27
	Bracket Set Bolt (7A-FE)	⑤
	Bracket Set Bolt (5S-FE)	32
	Control Valve Housing Set Bolt	23
	Control Valve Shaft To Intermediate Shaft No. 2	26
	Drive Belt Adjusting Bolt (7A-FE)	29
	Drive Belt Adjusting Bolt (5S-FE)	32
	Power Steering Gear Assembly Set Bolt	94
	Pressure Feed And Return Tubes To Control Valve Housing	32
	Pressure Port Union	51
	Pump Assembly Set Bolt (7A-FE)	29
	Pump Assembly Set Bolt (5S-FE)	32
	Rack End	61
	Rack Guide Spring Cap Lock Nut	50
	Rack Housing Cap Lock Nut	50
	Rack Housing No. 2 Bracket Set Bolt	29
	Reservoir To Front Housing	⑥
	Suction Port Union Set Bolt	108①
	Tie Rod End Lock Nut	41
	Tie Rod End To Steering Knuckle	36
	Tube Clamp Bracket Set Bolt	108①
	Turn Pressure Tube Union Nut	18
	Union Bolt	38
	Vane Pump Pulley Set Nut	32

Continued

TIGHTENING
SPECIFICATIONS—Continued

Year	Component	Torque/Ft. Lbs.
COROLLA		
1996–99	Adjusting Bracket Set Bolt	29
	Air Control Valve	27
	Control Valve Lock Nut (Toyota)	108①
	Control Valve Self-Locking Nut	18
	Control Valve Shaft To Universal Joint	26
	Drive Pulley To Rotor Shaft	31
	Front Bracket To Rear Bracket	⑧
	Front Housing To Rear Housing	12
	Oil Reservoir Set Bolt	12
	Pressure Feed Tube Set Union Bolt	40
	Pressure Port Union To Pump Housing	51
	Pressure Tube To Pressure Port Union	40
	Rack Guide Spring Cap Locknut	43
	Rack Guide Spring Cap Locknut (Toyota)	32
	Rack Housing Cap (TKS)	43
	Rack Housing Cap (Toyota)	51
	Rack To Rack End	61
	Steering Main Shaft To Universal Joint	26
	Tie Rod End Locknut	41
	Tie Rod End To Steering Knuckle	36
	Turn Pressure Tube (Toyota)	⑦
	Turn Pressure Tube (TKS)	108①
	Vane Pump Pulley Set Nut	31
LAND CRUISER		
1996–99	Adjusting Screw Lock Nut	34
	Cross Shaft Side Cover Lock Bolt	45
	Gear Housing To Body	105
	Pitman Arm To Cross Shaft	130
	Plunger Guide Nut	15
	Power Steering Pump To Bracket	27
	Pressure & Return Tube	33
	Pressure Port Union	51
	Pressure Tube To Power Steering Pump	42
	Tie Or Relay Rod Clamp	27
	Tie Rod To Knuckle Arm	67
	Universal Joint	25
	Worm Gear Valve Body Set Bolt	45

Continued

POWER STEERING

TIGHTENING
SPECIFICATIONS—Continued

Year	Component	Torque/Ft. Lbs.
PASEO & TERCEL		
1996	Air Control Valve To Gear Housing	22
	Control Valve Self-Locking Nut	43
	Control Valve Shaft To Universal Joint	19
	Cylinder End Stopper	43
	Drive Pulley To Rotor Shaft	32
	Gear Housing Bracket To Body	43
	Pressure & Return Tube Clamp To Gear Housing	108①
	Pressure & Return Tube To Gear Housing	33
	Pressure Port Union To Pump Housing	51
	Pressure Tube To Pressure Port Union	40
	PS Pump Installation Bolt	32
	Rack Guide Spring Cap Locknut	33
	Rack Housing Cap	43
	Rack To Rack End	43
	Steering Main Shaft To Universal Joint	19
	Suction Port Union To Pump Housing	108①
	Tie Rod End Locknut	35
	Tie Rod End To Steering Knuckle	36
	Turn Pressure Tube Union Nut	18
1997-98	Air Control Valve	22
	Control Valve Shaft To Sliding Yoke	19
	Cylinder End Stopper	43
	Oil Reservoir Set Bolt	⑩
	Pressure Feed & Return Tubes To Control Valve	33
	Pressure Port Union To Front Housing	61
	Protector Set Bolt	48①
	PS Gear Bracket To Body	43
	PS Pump Set Bolt	32
	Pulley Set Nut	32
	Rack Guide Spring Cap Lock Nut	33
	Rack Housing Cap	43
	Rear Housing To Front Housing	17
	Rack To Rack End	43
	Self Locking Nut	43
	Tie Rod End Locknut	35
	Tube Clamp Set Bolt	108①
	Turn Pressure Tube Union Nut	18
	Union Bolt To PS Pump	40
	Union Bolt To Pressure Port Union	51

TIGHTENING
SPECIFICATIONS—Continued

Year	Component	Torque/Ft. Lbs.
PREVIA		
1996–97	Bearing Guide Nut	18
	Control Valve Housing To Rack Housing	13
	Cylinder End Stopper	58
	Front Differential To Body	54
	Front Differential To Driveshaft	50
	Front Differential To Propeller Shaft	31
	Gear Housing Set Bolt	70
	No. 2 Equipment Drive Housing Insulator	18
	No. 2 Equipment Drive Housing Mount	13
	Pressure & Return Lines	33
	PS Pump Bracket To Stay	27
	PS Pump Front To Rear Housing	12
	PS Pump Pressure Port Union	61
	PS Pump Set Bolt	35
	PS Pump Suction Port Union	108①
	PS Pump Union	36
	Rack Guide Spring Cap Locknut	51
	Return & Pressure Line To Gear Housing	33
	Steering Rack To Rack End	76
	Tie Rod End Locknut	67
	Tie Rod End To Knuckle	36
	Torque Shaft To Pinion Shaft	26
	Turn Pressure Tubes (Control Valve Side)	14
	Turn Pressure Tubes (Rack Housing Guide)	22
	Universal Joint	26
RAV4		
1996-99	Air Control Valve	27
	Drive Belt Adjusting Bolt	32
	Pressure Feed Tube Union Bolt	38
	Pressure Port Union	51
	Pump Bracket Set Bolt	32
	Pump Suction Port Union Set Bolt	108①
	Rack Guide Spring Cap	18
	Rack Guide Spring Cap Lock Nut	33
	Rack Housing No. 1 Bracket Set Bolt	45
	Tie Rod End Lock Nut	41
	Turn Pressure Tube	22

Continued

POWER STEERING

TIGHTENING
SPECIFICATIONS—Continued

Year	Component	Torque/Ft. Lbs.
SUPRA		
1996-97	Control Valve Housing Set Bolt	13
	Control Valve Housing To Pressure Control Valve Assembly	13
	Control Valve Self-Locking Nut (w/PPS)	43
	Control Valve Shaft To Universal Joint	24
	Front Housing To Rear Housing	12
	Gear Housing To Body	55
	Oil Reservoir Set Bolt	⑨
	Pressure Control Valve To Control Valve Housing (w/PPS)	13
	Pressure Feed And Return Tube Set Union Bolts	36
	Pressure Port Union To Pump Housing	61
	PS Pump Pulley To Rotor Shaft	32
	PS Pump To Pressure Tube	36
	PS Vane Set Bolt	42
	Rack Guide Spring Cap Locknut	51
	Rack Housing Cap (w/PPS)	50
	Rack To Rack End	76
	Self Locking Nut	29
	Suction Port Union To Pump Housing	108①
	Tie Rod End Lock Nut	41
	Tie Rod End To Steering Knuckle	36
	Turn Pressure Tube Union Bolt	25
	Turn Pressure Tube Union Nut	22
1998	Control Valve Housing Set Bolt	13
	Gear Housing Set Bolt & Nut	55
	Intermediate Shaft To Sliding Yoke	26
	Power Steering Pump Front Housing To Rear Housing	12
	Power Steering Pump Pressure Port Union	61
	Power Steering Pump Set Nut	32
	Pressure Control Valve Assembly To Control Valve Housing	13
	Pressure Feed And Return Tube Set Union Bolts	36
	Rack End	74
	Rack Guide Spring Cap Lock Nut	51
	Rack Housing Cap	50
	Sliding Yoke To Control Valve Shaft	26
	Tie Rod End Lock Nut	41
	Tie Rod End To Steering Knuckle	36
	Turn Pressure Tube Union Nut	22
	Turn Pressure Tube Union Bolt	25

TIGHTENING
SPECIFICATIONS—Continued

Year	Component	Torque/Ft. Lbs.
TACOMA		
1996-99	Bearing Guide Nut	18
	Bracket To Pump (5VZ-FE)	32
	Control Housing Set Bolt	13
	Control Valve Shaft To Intermediate No. 2 Shaft	27
	Cylinder End Stopper	43
	Power Steering Gear Set Bolt (2WD)	148
	Power Steering Gear Set Bolt (4WD)	123
	Pressure Feed Tube To Control Valve Housing	33
	Pressure Port Union To Pump Housing	61
	Power Steering Pump Pulley Set Nut	32
	Power Steering Pump Set Bolt (2RZ-FE & 3RZ-FE)	32
	Power Steering Pump Set Bolt & Nut (5VZ-FE)	29
	Rack Guide Spring Cap	18
	Rack Guide Spring Cap Lock Nut	51
	Rack Housing No. 2 Bracket Set Bolt	29
	Rack To Rack End	76
	Rear Housing Set Bolt	17
	Return Tube To Control Valve Housing	36
	Sliding Yoke To Intermediate No. 2 Shaft	27
	Tie Rod End Lock Nut	40
	Turn Pressure Tube Union Nut	18
TUNDRA		
2000	Intermediate Shaft To Steering Gear	26
	Power Steering Bracket To Pump	32
	Power Steering Pump Rear Housing	17
	Power Steering Rack Mounting Bolts	123
	Pressure Line To Steering Gear	18
	Pressure Port Union	62
	Reservoir Front Bolt	108①
	Reservoir Rear Bolts	17
	Return Line To Steering Gear	18
	Tie Rod To Steering Knuckle	67

Continued

TIGHTENING
SPECIFICATIONS—Continued

Year	Component	Torque/Ft. Lbs.
T100		
1996-98	Air Control Valve To Rear Housing	27
	Bleeder Plug	34
	Control Valve Housing	13
	Cross Shaft Adjusting Screw Locknut	34
	Cross Shaft End Cover To Gear Housing	34
	Cross Shaft End Cover To Gear Housing	72②
	Front Housing To Rear Housing	34
	Gear Housing To Body	87
	Idler Arm Bracket To Frame	87
	Idler Arm To Idler Arm Bracket	58
	Knuckle Arm To Steering Knuckle	80
	Pitman Arm To Relay Rod	67
	Pitman Arm To Sector Shaft	130
	Plunger Guide Nut	69①
	Power Steering Pump Pulley To Rotor Shaft	32
	Power Steering Pump To Bracket	29
	Pressure Port Union To Rear Housing	51
	Pressure Tube To Pressure Port Union	27
	Rack Ends	44
	Rack Guide Spring Cap Locknut	35
	Rack Housing Cap	51
	Relay Rod To Idler Arm	43
	Return Hose Clamp (RN Series)	13①
	Return Hose Clamp (VZN Series)	35①
	Self Locking Nut	18
	Steering Damper To Frame	108①
	Steering Damper To Relay Rod	43
	Suction Port Union To Rear Housing	108①
	Tie Rod End Clamp Bolt	19
	Tie Rod Ends	41
	Tie Rod To Knuckle Arm	67
	Tie Rod To Relay Rod	67
	Turn Pressure Tubes	96①
	Worm Gear Valve Body To Gear Housing	34
	Worm Gear Valve Body To Gear Housing	45②

Continued

TIGHTENING
SPECIFICATIONS—Continued

Year	Component	Torque/Ft. Lbs.
4RUNNER		
1996-99	Bearing Guide Nut	18
	Control Housing Set Bolt	13
	Control Valve Shaft To Intermediate No. 2 Shaft	27
	Cylinder End Stopper	43
	Power Steering Gear Set Bolt	123
	Power Steering Pump Pulley Set Nut	32
	Power Steering Pump Set Bolt	32
	Pressure Feed Tube To Control Valve Housing	33
	Pressure Port Union To Pump Housing	61
	Rack Guide Spring Cap	18
	Rack Guide Spring Cap Lock Nut	51
	Rack Housing No. 2 Bracket Set Bolt	29
	Rack To Rack End	76
	Rear Housing Set Bolt	17
	Return Tube To Control Valve Housing	36
	Sliding Yoke To Intermediate No. 2 Shaft	27
	Tie Rod End Lock Nut	40
	Turn Pressure Tube Union Nut	18

① — Inch lbs.

② — T100.

③ — 1996 models, 51 ft. lbs.; 1997–99 models, 62 ft. lbs.

④ — 1996 models, 53 ft. lbs.; 1997–99 models, 62 ft. lbs.

⑤ — 12 mm bolt, 14 ft. lbs.; 14 mm bolt, 29 ft. lbs.

⑥ — 12 mm bolt, 9 ft. lbs.; 14 mm bolt, 30 ft. lbs.

⑦ — 1996 models, 18 ft. lbs.; 1997–99 models, 22 ft. lbs.

⑧ — 12 mm bolt, 15 ft. lbs.; 14 mm bolt, 32 ft. lbs.

⑨ — Front bolts, 9 ft. lbs.; Rear bolts, 12 ft. lbs.

⑩ — Front bolts, 9 ft. lbs.; Rear bolts, 17 ft. lbs.

Disc Brakes

TABLE OF CONTENTS

Front Disc Brakes

INDEX

PRECAUTIONS

AIR BAG SYSTEMS

Refer to "Air Bag System Precautions" in the front of this manual for system disarming & arming procedures.

BATTERY GROUND CABLE

Prior to service, disconnect battery ground cable and isolate as required.

AUDIO CODED ANTI-THEFT SYSTEM

Some models are equipped with an audio coded anti-theft system that will disable the radio when the battery cable is disconnected. The system can be identified by the "ANTI-THEFT SYSTEM" on the cassette tape lid. Obtain 3 digit customer code for input. Reset system after service as follows:

1. Obtain 3 digit audio anti-theft code.
2. Depress 1 (PROG) while depressing righthand side of TUNE SEEK button, - - - will appear in tape operation display.
3. To enter the first digit, depress 1 (PROG) button repeatedly until the number of times depressed equals the first digit beginning with zero (depress the 1 button six times if the first digit is five).
4. To enter second digit, depress 2 (APS) button repeatedly until the number of times depressed equals the second digit beginning with zero.
5. To enter third digit, depress 3 (RPT) button repeatedly until the number of times depressed equals the second digit beginning with zero.
6. If - - - is displayed during code input, repeat procedure.
7. When code appears in display, depress and hold SCAN button until SEC appears.
8. When SEC disappears audio system should be operative.
9. If Err is displayed, repeat procedure. **Attempting to input code more than nine times may permanently disable audio system.**

BRAKE PAD SERVICE

AVALON, CAMRY, CAMRY SOLARA, COROLLA, CELICA & SIENNA

1. Remove front wheel and reinstall lug nuts to locate disc temporarily.
2. Remove caliper from torque plate and suspend so brake hose is not under tension. Do not disconnect brake hose.
3. Refer to **Figs. 1 and 2** and remove the following components:
   a. Brake pads.
   b. Anti-squeal shims.
   c. Pad wear indicator plates.
   d. Support plates.
   e. Anti-squeal springs.
4. Install new pad support plates.
5. Install new pad wear indicator plates on each pad with arrow pointing in direction of disc rotation.
6. Install new anti-squeal shims on each pad.
7. Install each brake pad on to each support plate.
8. Install anti-squeal springs.
9. Siphon out a small amount of brake fluid from reservoir and press caliper piston in with hammer handle. Change one brake pad at a time to prevent chance of opposite piston from flying out.
10. Install caliper taking care not to wedge dust boot.
11. Install wheel and check that brake fluid level is at MAX line.

LAND CRUISER, 4WD TACOMA & T100

1. Raise and support front of vehicle, then remove tire and wheel assembly.
2. Remove clip and hole pins, **Fig. 3**.
3. Remove anti-rattle spring and shim(s) if equipped, then remove brake pads.
4. Lubricate caliper housing with suitable brake grease at pad contact points.
5. Reverse procedure to install.

Disc, Replace

1. Remove caliper.
2. Remove cap and snap ring, **Fig. 4**, then remove cone washers with tapered punch.
3. Insert suitable length bolts into flange bolt holes, then tighten bolts evenly and remove flanges.
4. Remove free wheel hub cover and snap ring, then remove nut, spring washer and cone washer with suitable tapered punch.
5. Remove free wheel hub body and gasket.

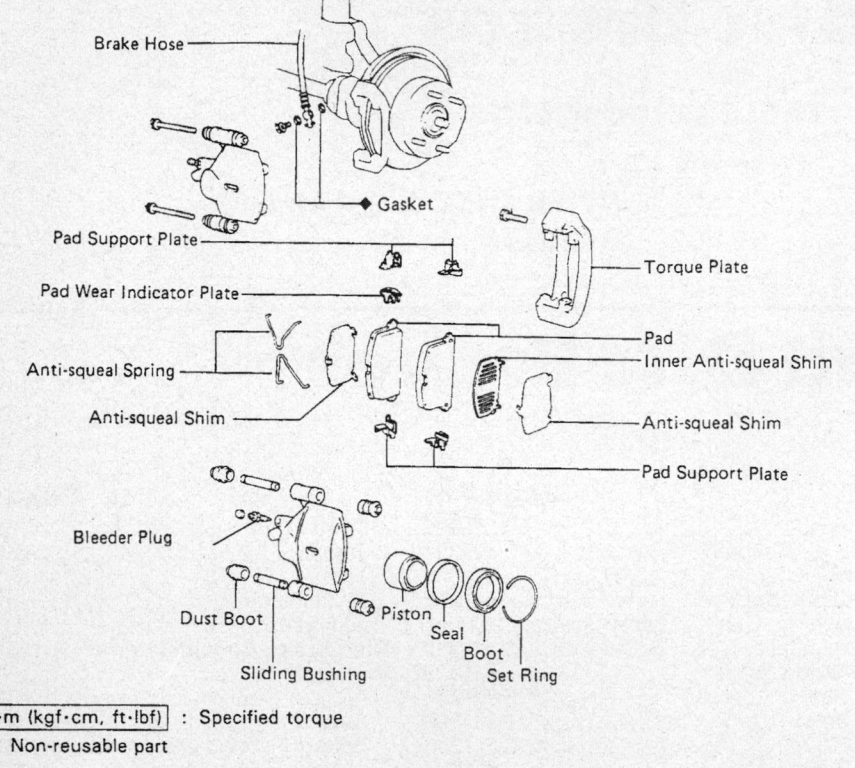

N·m (kgf·cm, ft·lbf) : Specified torque
◆ Non-reusable part

TY4079100011000X

Fig. 1 Exploded view of single piston disc brake assembly. Avalon, Camry, Camry Solara, Celica, Corolla & Sienna

6. Remove locknut, lock washer and adjusting nut.
7. Remove axle hub and brake disc as an assembly.
8. Remove oil seal and inner bearing from hub.
9. Reverse procedure to install. **Torque** adjusting nut to 43 ft. lbs., then back off nut. **Torque** nut to 18 ft. lbs. Using spring scale attached to hub bolt, check that preload is 1.4–12.6. Install lockwasher and locknut, if equipped. **Torque** locknut to 35 ft. lbs., and re-check preload. Secure lockwasher by bending one tab inward and one tab outward.

PASEO

1. Raise and support vehicle, then remove wheel and tire assembly.
2. Reinstall two wheel lug nuts to retain disc.
3. Remove two attaching bolts and the caliper from torque plate, **Fig. 5,** then suspend from chassis.
4. Remove brake pads, anti-squeal shims, pad wear indicator plates and support plates.
5. Reverse procedure to install, **torque** caliper attaching bolts to 18 ft. lbs.

PREVIA

1. Raise and support front of vehicle, then remove tire and wheel assembly. Temporarily install lug nuts to hold rotor in place.
2. Remove brake hose bracket attaching bolts from steering knuckle, if necessary.

3. While holding the sliding bushing, remove cylinder installation bolt, **Figs. 6 and 7.**
4. Rotate caliper upwards and remove. Suspend caliper with suitable wire using caution not to stretch brake hose.
5. Remove pads and anti-squeal shim(s).
6. Remove anti-rattle springs, support and pad guide plates.
7. Install new anti-rattle springs, support and pad guide plates.
8. Siphon a small amount of fluid from master cylinder reservoir.
9. Slowly force piston into caliper bore.
10. Install new pads and anti-squeal shim(s). **If pads are equipped with wear indicators, install outside pad so indicator is at top side of caliper.**
11. Rotate caliper into place, then install cylinder installation bolt and tighten to specifications.
12. Install brake hose bracket attaching bolts. **Torque** attaching bolts to 14 ft. lbs.
13. Fill master cylinder, then pump brake pedal until a firm pedal is obtained.

RAV4

1. Raise and support vehicle, then remove front wheel.
2. Inspect brake pad lining thickness. Minimum thickness should be .039 inch.
3. Lift caliper and remove flexible hose bracket, **Fig. 8.**
4. Hold sliding pin on bottom and loosen installation bolt.
5. Remove installation bolt.

6. Lift and suspend caliper with brake hose attached.
7. Remove brake pads, anti-squeal shims and pad support plates.
8. Reverse procedure to install. If caliper pistons are difficult to push in, loosen bleeder plug and let some brake fluid escape.

SUPRA

1. Raise and support front of vehicle, then remove tire and wheel assembly. Temporarily install lug nuts to hold rotor in place.
2. While holding sliding pin in place, remove installation bolt.
3. Lift and support caliper.
4. **On non-turbo models,** remove anti-squeal springs, brake pads, anti-squeal shims, and support plates, **Fig. 9.**
5. **On turbo models,** remove clip and pins, then the anti-rattle spring, pads, pad spacers, and anti-squeal shims, **Fig. 10.**
6. **On all models,** reverse procedure to install noting the following:
   a. Remove a small amount of brake fluid from master cylinder.
   b. Press caliper piston in using a suitable hammer handle.
   c. If piston is difficult to move, loosen bleeder screw and push piston in allowing fluid to escape.
   d. Tighten caliper to specification.

TERCEL

1. Raise and support front of vehicle, then remove wheel and tire assembly.
2. Remove two caliper mounting bolts, then remove caliper. **Do not allow caliper to hang by brake hose.**
3. Remove inner pad, then remove outer pad and anti-squeal shim(s), **Fig. 11.**
4. Remove anti-rattle spring and pad guide plate.
5. Remove pad support plate and anti-squeal shim(s).
6. Reverse procedure to install.

TUNDRA

1. Raise and support vehicle.
2. Remove front wheels.
3. Inspect pad minimum thickness. If pad is less than .039 inch, replace.
4. Remove clip, two pins and anti-rattle spring, **Fig. 12.**
5. Remove two pads, then the four anti-squeal shims.
6. Inspect anti-rattle spring and clip. Ensure parts are clean and they have sufficient rebound, no deformation, cracks or wear.
7. Ensure brake disc thickness and runout are within specifications.
8. Proceed as follows to install new pads:
   a. Remove a small amount of brake fluid from brake reservoir.
   b. Press in brake pistons. If piston is difficult to move in, loosen bleeder plug and push piston in while letting fluid out.
   c. Install anti-squeal shims to new pads.
   d. Apply suitable disc brake grease to

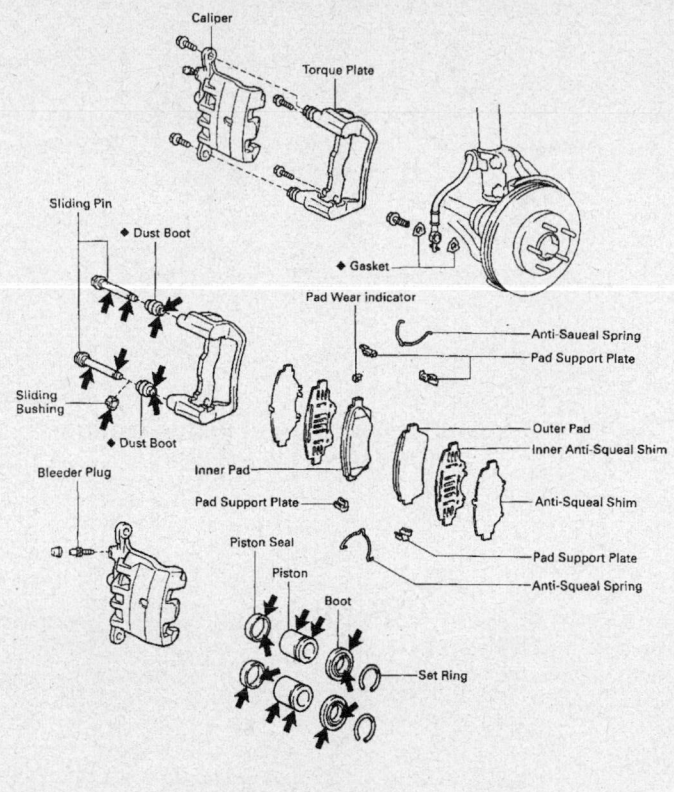

Fig. 2   Exploded view of dual piston disc brake assembly. Avalon & Camry

◆ Non-reusable part
♦ Lithium Soap Base Glycol Grease

TY4079700034000X

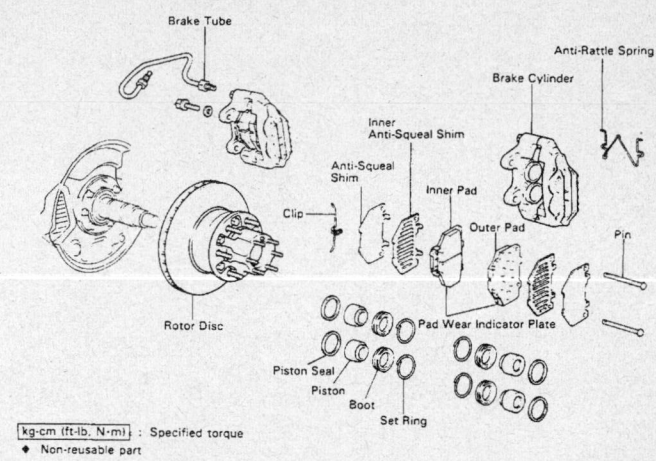

kg-cm (ft-lb, N·m) : Specified torque
◆ Non-reusable part

TY4079100007000X

Fig. 3   Exploded view of disc brake assembly. Land Cruiser, 4WD Tacoma & T100

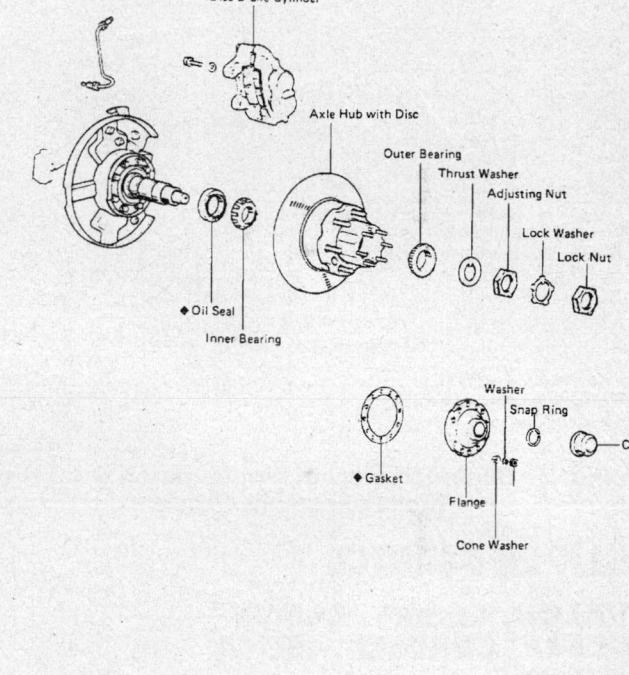

kg-cm (ft-lb, N·m) : Specified torque
◆ Non-reusable part

TY4079100008000X

Fig. 4   Exploded view of front axle hub. Land Cruiser

both sides of inner anti-squeal shims.
e. Install new pads ensuring grease does not come into contact with braking surfaces.
f. Install anti-rattle spring and two pins, then the clip and front wheel.
g. Depress brake pedal several times and ensure brake fluid is at proper level.

T100

1. Raise and support vehicle and remove tire and wheel assembly.
2. Remove caliper attaching bolts, **Figs. 13 and 14**, and the caliper, supporting caliper out of way so that brake hose is not stretched.
3. Remove two anti-rattle springs, brake pads, anti-squeal shims and the four support plates.
4. Reverse procedure to install, **torque** caliper mounting bolts to 29 ft. lbs.

2WD TACOMA

1. Check that pad thickness is no less than .039 inch. Replace pads if thinner.
2. Raise and support vehicle and remove front wheel.
3. Remove caliper pin on sub-pin side, **Fig. 15.**

4. Pivot caliper up and support, leaving brake hose connected.
5. Remove brake pads, anti-squeal shim(s), pad wear indicator plate and four support plates.
6. Reverse procedure to install.

4RUNNER

1. Raise and support vehicle, then remove front wheel.

2. Inspect brake pad lining thickness. Minimum thickness should be .039 inch.
3. Remove pad retaining clip and two pins, **Fig. 16.**
4. Remove anti-rattle spring, brake pads and four anti-squeal shims.
5. Reverse procedure to install.

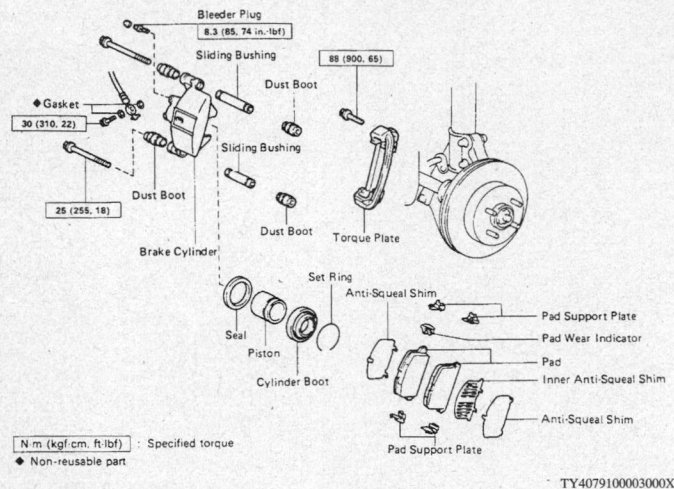

N·m (kgf·cm, ft·lbf) : Specified torque
◆ Non-reusable part

TY4079100003000X

Fig. 5   Exploded view of disc brake assembly. Paseo

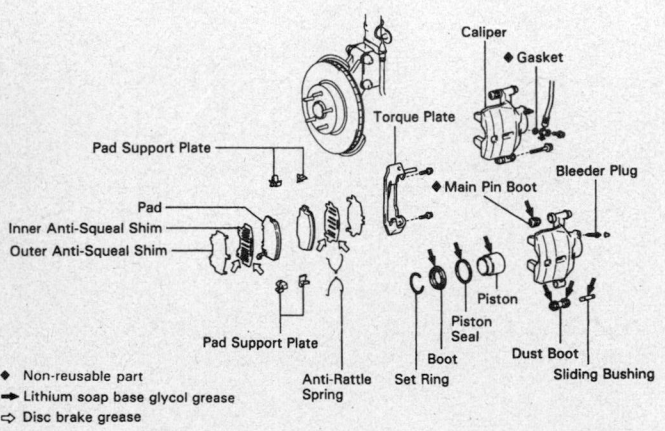

◆ Non-reusable part
➡ Lithium soap base glycol grease
⇨ Disc brake grease

TY4079100010000A

Fig. 7   Exploded view of single piston front disc brake assembly. Previa

CALIPER SERVICE

AVALON, CAMRY, CAMRY SOLARA, COROLLA, CELICA & SIENNA

Replace

1. Raise and support vehicle and remove front wheel.
2. Remove union bolt and disconnect brake hose. Use suitable container to catch brake fluid.
3. Remove caliper, **Figs. 1 and 2.**
4. Remove anti-squeal shims and brake pad wear indicator plates.
5. Remove support plates.
6. Reverse procedure to install.

Overhaul

1. Remove caliper.
2. Remove the following parts:
   a. Caliper slide bushings.
   b. Dust boots.
   c. Collars.
3. Using screwdriver, remove caliper boot set ring and boot.
4. Place suitable rag between caliper and piston and using compressed air, re-

move pistons.
5. Using screwdriver, remove piston seal.
6. Apply suitable lubricant to following parts: boot, piston seal, piston, slide bushing, collar, and dust boot.
7. Install piston seal(s) and piston(s) in caliper.
8. Install caliper boot and set ring in caliper.
9. Install collar and dust boots in caliper.
10. Check that boots are firmly seated in caliper grooves.
11. Install bushing into boots.
12. Check that boots are firmly secured to each bushing groove.

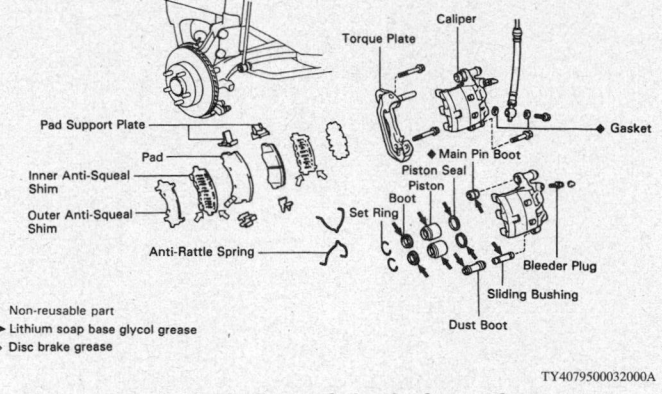

◆ Non-reusable part
➡ Lithium soap base glycol grease
⇨ Disc brake grease

TY4079500032000A

Fig. 6   Exploded view of dual piston front disc brake assembly. Previa

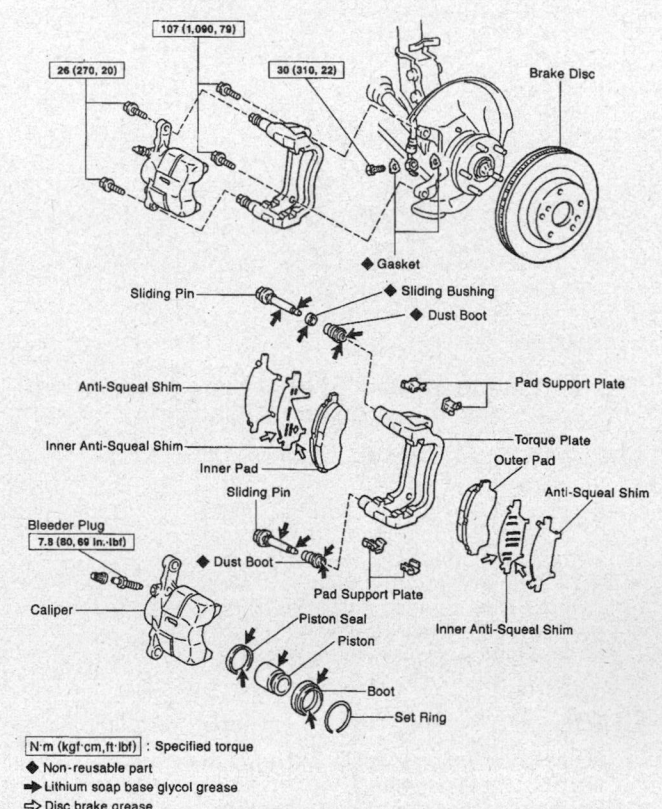

N·m (kgf·cm, ft·lbf) : Specified torque
◆ Non-reusable part
➡ Lithium soap base glycol grease
⇨ Disc brake grease

TY4079600028000X

Fig. 8   Exploded view of disc brake assembly. RAV4

LAND CRUISER

Replace

1. Remove pads as outlined under "Brake Pad Service."
2. Disconnect brake hydraulic line from caliper.
3. Remove caliper retaining bolts, then the caliper.
4. Reverse procedure to install, then bleed brake system.

Overhaul

1. Remove caliper.
2. Fabricate block of wood to dimensions

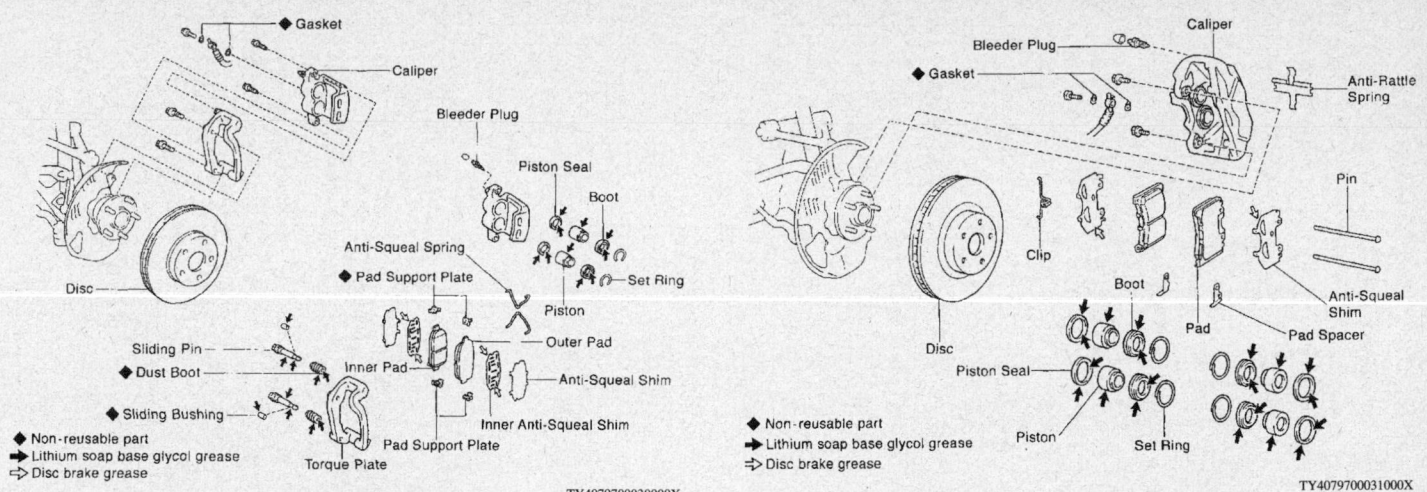

Fig. 9 Exploded view of disc brake assembly. Supra w/2JZ-GE engine

Fig. 10 Exploded view of disc brake assembly. Supra w/2JZ-GTE engine

Fig. 11 Exploded view of disc brake assembly. Tercel

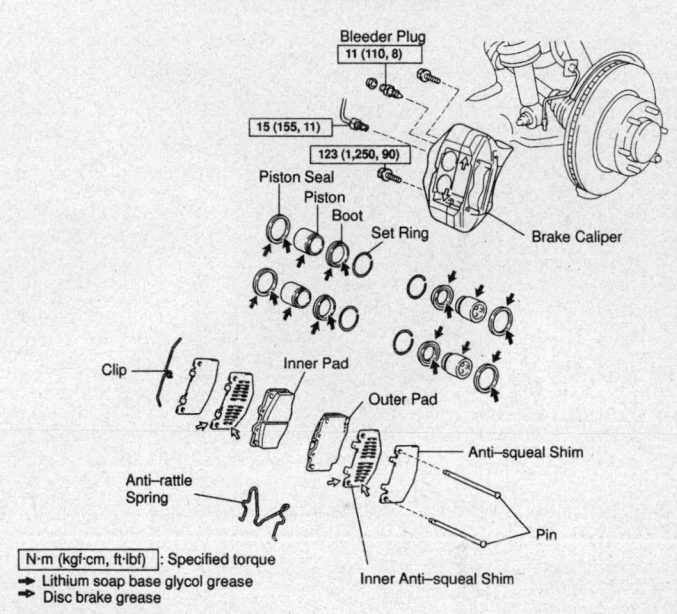

Fig. 12 Exploded view of disc brake assembly. Tundra

shown in **Fig. 17.**
3. Remove snap ring and boot, **Fig. 3.**
4. Position block of wood between pistons, then remove pistons using compressed air.
5. Remove piston seals.
6. Lubricate piston and seal with suitable grease, then reverse procedure to assemble.

PASEO

Replace

Remove caliper as in "Brake Pad Service" and remove brake line union.

Overhaul

1. Remove caliper as in "Brake Pad Service."
2. Remove two caliper siding bushings and four dust boots.
3. Using screwdriver, remove cylinder boot set ring and cylinder boot.
4. Place a piece of cloth between piston and cylinder and using compressed air, remove piston from cylinder.

5. Using screwdriver, remove piston seal.
6. Apply lithium soap base glycol grease to all movable parts.
7. Install piston seal and piston in cylinder.
8. Install cylinder boot and set ring in cylinder.
9. Install collar and dust boot, ensuring that boot is secured firmly to bushing groove.

PREVIA

Replace

1. Disconnect brake hydraulic hose at frame bracket, then at caliper.
2. Remove caliper attaching bolts, then lift caliper up and pull away from torque plate main pin, removing brake pads and components in the process, **Figs. 6 and 7.**

3. Reverse procedure to install.

Overhaul

1. Remove caliper.
2. Remove pads, anti-squeal shims, anti-rattle springs, support and pad guide plates.
3. Remove sliding bushing and boot, **Figs. 6 and 7.**
4. Remove main pin boot.
5. Remove caliper boot and set ring from caliper.
6. Remove piston using compressed air. **When using compressed air to remove piston, keep fingers clear of piston to avoid injury.**
7. Remove piston seal using a suitable screwdriver.
8. Reverse procedure to install. Lubricate

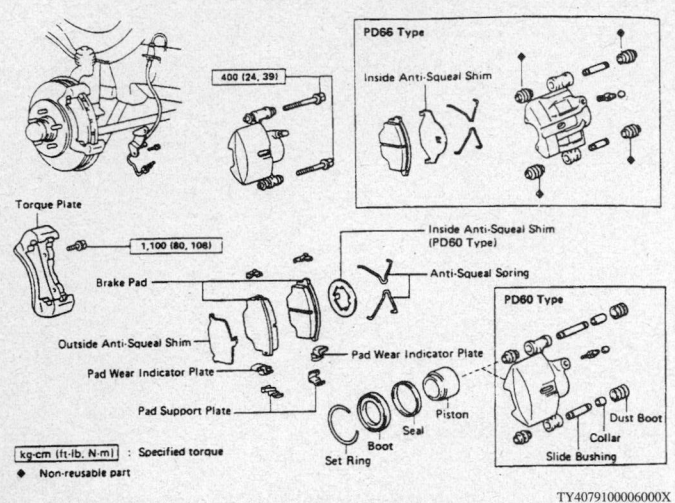

Fig. 13 Exploded view of PD60 & PD66 disc brake assembly. T100

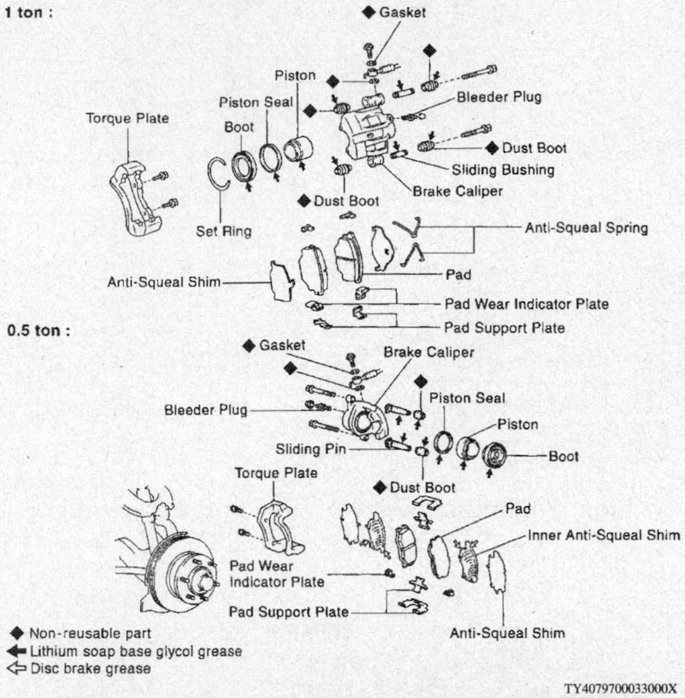

TY4079100006000X

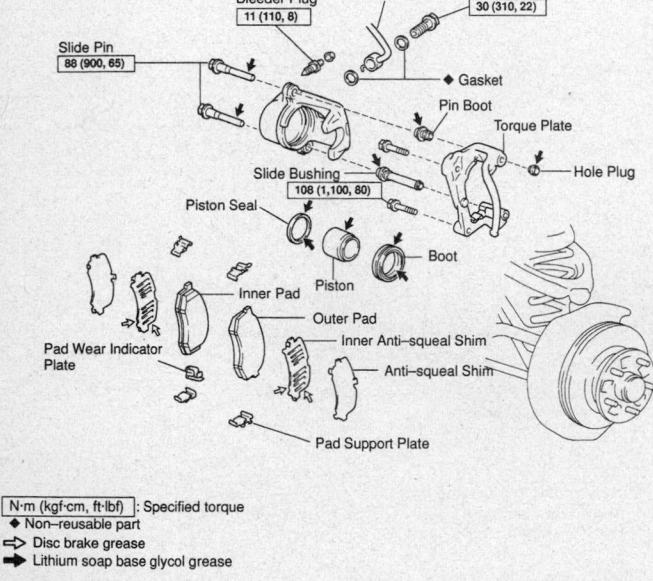

Fig. 15 Exploded view of disc brake assembly. 2WD Tacoma

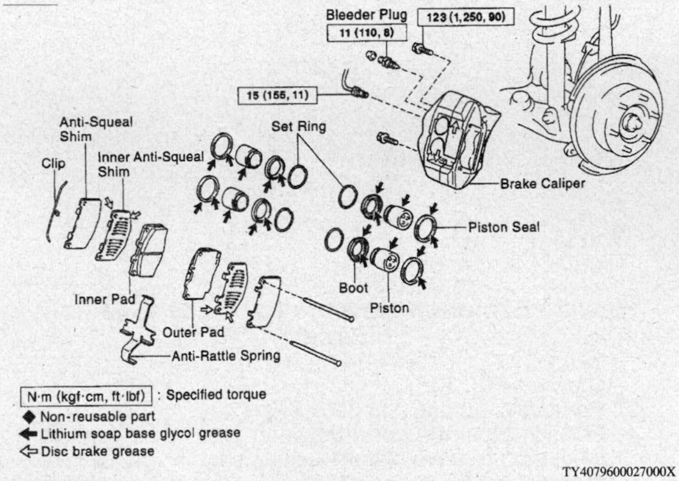

TY4079500024000X

Fig. 14 Exploded view of disc brake assembly. 1997–98 T100

TY4079700033000X

Fig. 16 Exploded view of disc brake assembly. 4Runner

TY4079600027000X

main pin boot, sliding pin and boot, piston seal and boot and dust boot with suitable brake lubricant.

RAV4

Replace

1. Disconnect flexible brake hose from caliper and drain brake fluid into suitable container.
2. Hold sliding pin and loosen installation bolts, **Fig. 8.**
3. Remove installation bolts and caliper from torque plate.
4. Remove brake pads and support plates as outlined under " Brake Pad Service."
5. Reverse procedure to install.

Overhaul

1. Remove caliper.

2. Remove cylinder boot set ring.
3. Place a piece of cloth between piston and caliper, then use compressed air to remove piston from cylinder.
4. Remove piston seal.
5. Remove sliding pins and dust boots.
6. Reverse procedure to assemble. Apply lithium soap base glycol grease to all movable parts.

SUPRA

Replace

1. Raise and support vehicle, then remove front wheel.
2. Remove brake hose from caliper.
3. **On models equipped with normally aspirated engine,** refer to **Fig. 9** and proceed as follows:

a. Hold sliding pin, then remove caliper attaching bolts.
b. Remove caliper from torque plate.
c. Remove anti-squeal springs, then the brake pads and anti-squeal shims.
4. **On models equipped with turbocharged engine,** refer to **Fig. 10** and proceed as follows:
a. Remove caliper mounting bolts, then the caliper.
b. Remove clip, then the two pins.
c. Remove anti-rattle spring, brake pads, spacers, and anti-squeal shims.
5. **On all models,** reverse procedure to install, then bleed brake system.

Overhaul

1. Using a suitable screwdriver, remove cylinder boot set rings and boots from cylinder.
2. Place a suitable wooden block between pistons and outer caliper housing.
3. Remove pistons from caliper using compressed air.
4. Using a suitable screwdriver, remove piston seals from cylinder.
5. Remove sliding pins and dust boots.
6. Reverse procedure to install.

TERCEL

Replace

1. Raise and support front of vehicle, then remove wheel and tire assembly.
2. Disconnect brake hydraulic line from frame bracket and from caliper using line wrench tool No. 09751-36011, or equivalent.
3. Remove caliper mounting bolts, then the caliper.
4. Reverse procedure to install and bleed brake system.

Overhaul

1. Remove caliper.
2. Remove anti-squeal shim(s) and cylinder boot set ring, **Fig. 11**.
3. Remove cylinder boot, then remove piston using compressed air.
4. Remove piston seal, caliper sliding bolt, dust boot, collar and union.
5. Install union onto caliper and tighten to specification.
6. Apply rubber grease to piston seal, then install piston seal onto piston.
7. Apply rubber grease to piston, then install piston into caliper.
8. Install cylinder boot and set ring, then lubricate collar and dust boot and assemble onto caliper.
9. Install caliper sliding bolt and anti-squeal shim(s).

TUNDRA

Replace

1. Raise and support vehicle, then remove front wheel.
2. Attach brake disc to hub using wheel nuts.
3. Disconnect caliper brake line and catch fluid in a suitable container.
4. Remove caliper attaching bolts, then the caliper.
5. Reverse procedure to install.

Overhaul

1. Using a suitable screwdriver, remove 4 cylinder boot set rings and boots, **Fig. 12**.
2. Fabricate a wooden block as shown in **Fig. 17**.
3. Place wooden block between pistons and insert pad at one side.

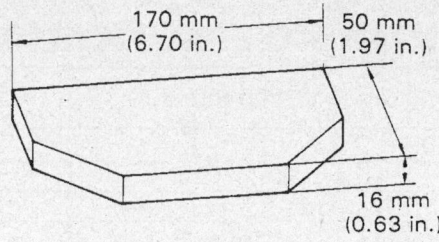

Fig. 17 Dimensions for fabricating block of wood for piston removal. Land Cruiser, Tundra, 4Runner & T100

4. Using compressed air, remove pistons alternately from cylinder.
5. Using a suitable screwdriver, remove 4 piston seals from cylinder.
6. Reverse procedure to assemble caliper. Fill brake system with suitable brake fluid, then bleed brake system.

T100

Replace

1. Raise and support vehicle and remove tire and wheel assembly.
2. Disconnect brake line at caliper.
3. Remove bracket from caliper.
4. Remove two caliper attaching bolts and the caliper.
5. Remove anti-rattle springs, brake pads, anti-squeal shims and support plates.
6. Reverse procedure to install. **Torque** bracket attaching bolts to 13 ft. lbs. and the brake line to 11 ft. lbs.

Overhaul

1. Remove caliper as previously described.
2. Remove two cylinder slide bushings, four dust boots and two collars.
3. Using screwdriver, remove cylinder boot set ring and boot.
4. Place a piece of cloth between piston and cylinder and, using compressed air, remove piston from cylinder.
5. Using screwdriver, remove piston seal from brake cylinder.
6. Apply lithium soap base glycol grease to all movable components.
7. Install piston seal and piston in cylinder.
8. Install cylinder boot and set ring in cylinder.
9. Install collar and dust boot in caliper, ensuring that boots are secured firmly to each brake cylinder groove.
10. Install bushing into boots, ensuring boots are secured firmly to each bushing groove.

4RUNNER

Replace

1. Raise and support vehicle, then re-

move front wheel.
2. Disconnect brake line from caliper, **Fig. 16**.
3. Remove caliper mounting bolts and caliper.
4. Remove clip, pins, anti-rattle spring, pads and anti-squeal shims as outlined under "Brake Pad Service."
5. Reverse procedure to install.

Overhaul

1. Remove caliper and brake pads.
2. Using a screwdriver, remove cylinder boot set rings and boots.
3. Fabricate wooden block, **Fig. 17**, to hold pistons, then place block between pistons and insert a brake pad on side of block opposite pistons.
4. Use compressed air to remove pistons from cylinder.
5. Remove piston seals from cylinder.
6. Reverse procedure to assemble. Apply lithium soap base glycol grease to all movable parts.

2WD TACOMA

Replace

1. Raise and support vehicle and remove front wheel.
2. Disconnect brake hose and use suitable container to catch brake fluid.
3. Remove bracket from caliper.
4. Remove 2 slide pins and caliper.
5. Remove brake pads, anti-squeal shim(s), pad wear indicator plate and 4 support plates.
6. If necessary, remove slide bushing and pin boots.

Overhaul

1. Remove caliper.
2. Using screwdriver, remove cylinder boot set ring and boot.
3. Place suitable rag or block between caliper and piston. Using compressed air, remove piston.
4. Using screwdriver, remove piston seal.
5. Apply lithium soap base glycol grease to caliper boot, piston, piston seal, and both slide pins.
6. Install piston seal and piston in caliper.
7. Install caliper boot and set ring in cylinder.
8. Install pin boots to torque plate of main pin side.
9. Using a suitable driver, install slide bushing into torque plate of sub-pin side.

DISC BRAKE SPECIFICATIONS

Refer to the disc brake specifications under "Rear Disc & Parking Brakes" for rotor thickness and lateral runout specifications.

TIGHTENING SPECIFICATIONS

Year	Component	Torque/Ft. Lbs.
AVALON		
1996-99	Bleeder Plug	72⑤
	Caliper To Torque Plate	25
	Flexible Hose	21
	Torque Plate	79
	Union Nut	11
CAMRY		
1996–99	Bleeder Plug	72⑤
	Flexible Hose	22
	Front Caliper Bolt	25
	Front Torque Plate	79
	Union Nut	①
CAMRY SOLARA		
1999	Bleeder Plug	72⑤
	Flexible Hose	21
	Front Caliper Bolt	25
	Front Torque Plate	79
	Union Nut (10 mm)	11
	Union Nut (12 mm)	14
CELICA		
1996–99	Bleeder Plug	72⑤
	Flexible Hose	22
	Front Caliper Bolt	②
	Front Torque Plate	79
	Union Nut	11
COROLLA		
1996–99	Bleeder Plug	72⑤
	Flexible Hose	22
	Front Caliper Bolt	③
	Front Torque Plate	65
	Union Nut	11
LAND CRUISER		
1996–99	Bleeder Plug	96⑤
	Caliper Bolts	90
	Disc To Hub	④
	Union Nut	11
PASEO		
1996–97	Bleeder Plug	72⑤
	Flexible Hose	22
	Front Caliper Bolt	18
	Front Torque Plate	65
	Union Nut	11
PREVIA		
1996–97	Bleeder Plug	72⑤
	Front Brake Hose	22
	Front Caliper Bolt	27
	Front Torque Plate	65
1996-99	Bleeder Plug	72⑤
	Brake Line Union Nut	11
	Front Brake Hose	22
	Front Caliper Bolt	20
	Torque Plate	79

TIGHTENING SPECIFICATIONS—Continued

51-397

Year	Component	Torque/Ft. Lbs.
SIENNA		
1998–99	Bleeder Plug	74⑤
	Caliper Installation Bolt	25
	Flex Hose To Caliper	21
	Torque Plate To Steering Knuckle	79
SUPRA		
1996–98	Bleeder Plug	96⑤
	Caliper To Steering Knuckle (2JZ-GTE)	87
	Caliper To Torque Plate	25
	Flexible Hose	22
	Torque Plate (2JZ-GE)	87
	Union Nut	11
TACOMA		
1996–99	Bleeder Plug	96⑤
	Caliper Bolts To Steering Knuckle (4WD)	90
	Caliper Sliding Pin	65
	Disc To Hub	47
	Torque Plate	80
	Union Nut	11
TERCEL		
1996-98	Bleeder Plug	72⑤
	Caliper Bolt	18
	Flexible Hose	22
	Torque Plate	65
	Union Nut	11
TUNDRA		
2000	Bleeder Plug	96⑤
	Brake Line To Caliper	11
	Caliper To Steering Knuckle	90
T100		
1996–98	Bleeder Plug	96⑤
	Caliper Bolts To Steering Knuckle (4WD)	90
	Caliper To Torque Plate (2WD)	29
	Disc To Hub	47
	Flexible Hose To Caliper	11
	Torque Plate	80
	Union Nut	11
4RUNNER		
1996-99	Bleeder Plug	96⑤
	Front Brake Hose	11
	Front Caliper Bolts	90

① — 1996–97 models, 11 ft. lbs.; 1998–99 models w/10 mm nut, 11 ft. lbs., 12 mm nut, 14 ft. lbs.
② — 13 inch wheel, 18 ft. lbs.; 14 & 15 inch wheel, 29 ft. lbs.; 1997 models, 25 ft. lbs.
③ — 1996 models, 18 ft. lbs.; 1997–98 models, 25 ft. lbs.
④ — 1996 models, 34 ft. lbs.; 1997 models, 54 ft. lbs.
⑤ — Inch lbs.

Rear Disc & Parking Brakes

INDEX

BRAKE PAD SERVICE

AVALON & SUPRA

1. Raise and support rear of vehicle, then remove tire and wheel assembly.
2. Remove caliper attaching bolts, then the caliper, **Figs. 1 through 3.** Do not allow caliper to hang unsupported or damage to the brake hose may occur.
3. Remove pads and anti-squeal shim(s).
4. Remove anti-rattle springs, pad guide plates and support plate.
5. Reverse procedure to install. Tighten caliper attaching bolts to specifications.

CAMRY, CAMRY SOLARA & PREVIA

1. Raise and support rear of vehicle, then remove tire and wheel assembly.
2. Remove caliper attaching bolts, then the caliper, **Fig. 4.** Do not allow caliper to hang unsupported or damage to the brake hose may occur.
3. Remove pads and anti-squeal shim(s).
4. Remove anti-rattle springs, pad guide plates and support plate.
5. Reverse procedure to install. Tighten caliper attaching bolts to specifications.

CELICA

1. Raise and support vehicle, then remove rear wheel.
2. Remove brake flex hose bracket.
3. Remove installation bolt, **Fig. 5.**
4. Lift caliper and suspend securely.
5. Remove brake pads, then the anti squeal shims and pad support plates.
6. Reverse procedure to install. Tighten caliper to specification.

LAND CRUISER

1. Raise and support rear of vehicle, then remove tire and wheel assembly.
2. Check pad thickness through caliper inspection hole and replace pads if measured thickness is less than .039 inch.
3. Remove caliper sliding main pin and sliding sub pin, **Fig. 6.**
4. Remove brake caliper and suspend it so hose is not stretched. **Do not disconnect brake hose.**
5. Remove brake pads, anti-squeal shim, support plates and pad wear indicators, **Fig. 6.**
6. Reverse procedure to install. Tighten

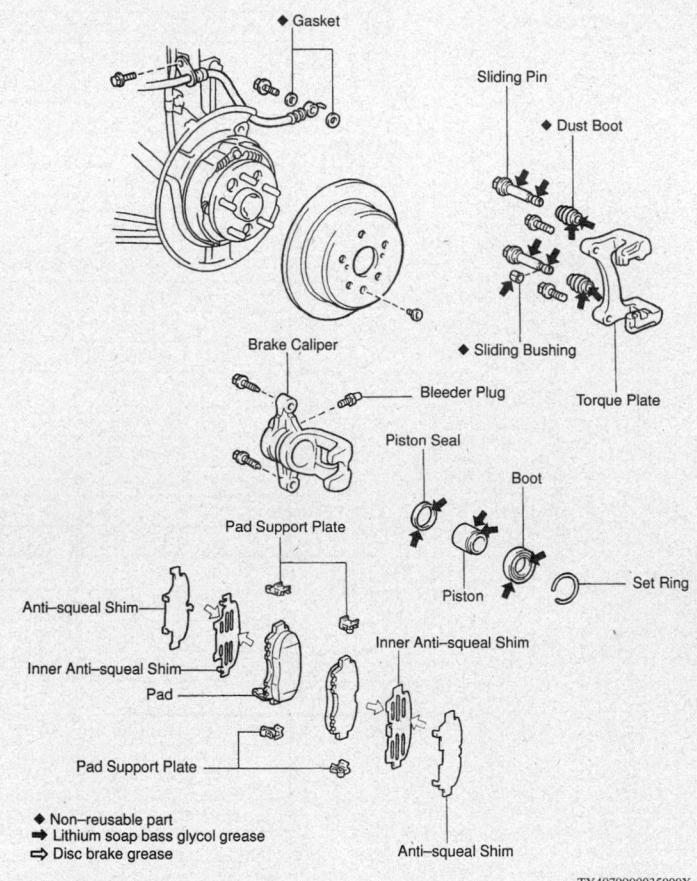

Fig. 1 Exploded view of rear disc brake caliper assembly. Avalon

caliper sliding main pin and sliding sub pin to specifications.

CALIPER SERVICE

AVALON & SUPRA

Replace

1. Raise and support rear of vehicle, then remove tire and wheel assembly.
2. Disconnect brake hose from brake tube and caliper using a suitable tool.
3. Remove caliper attaching bolts, then the caliper, **Figs. 1 through 3.**
4. Remove anti-squeal shim(s), brake

pad, anti-rattle spring, pad guide plate and pad support plate.
5. Reverse procedure to install, then bleed brake system.

Overhaul

1. Remove sliding bushing and boot, **Figs. 2 and 3.**
2. Remove main pin boot using a suitable chisel.
3. Remove piston using compressed air. **When using air pressure to remove caliper piston, place a shop towel over piston to prevent it from flying out.**
4. Remove caliper boot, set ring and piston seal from caliper.

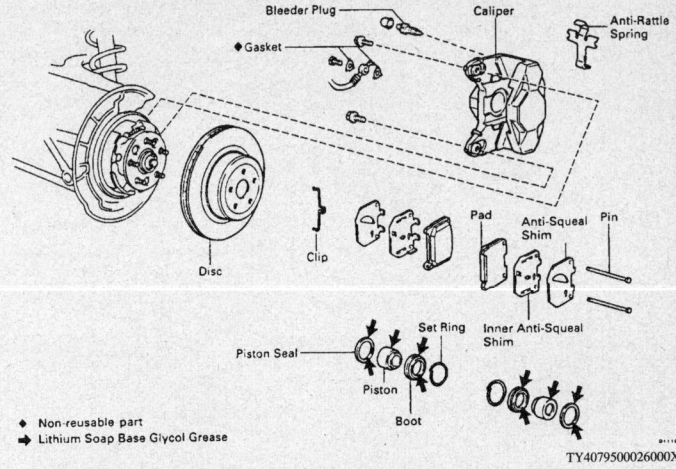

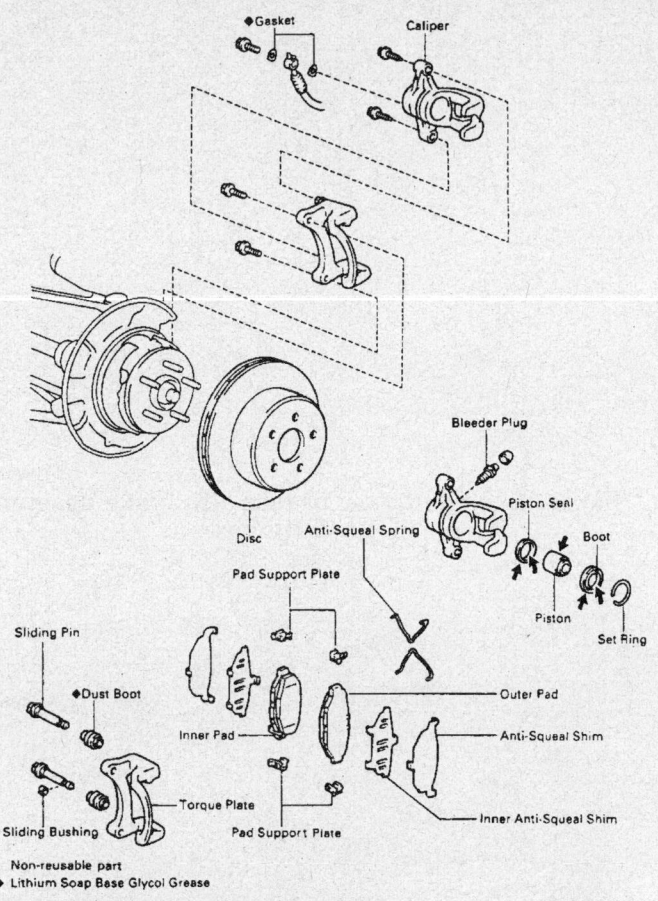

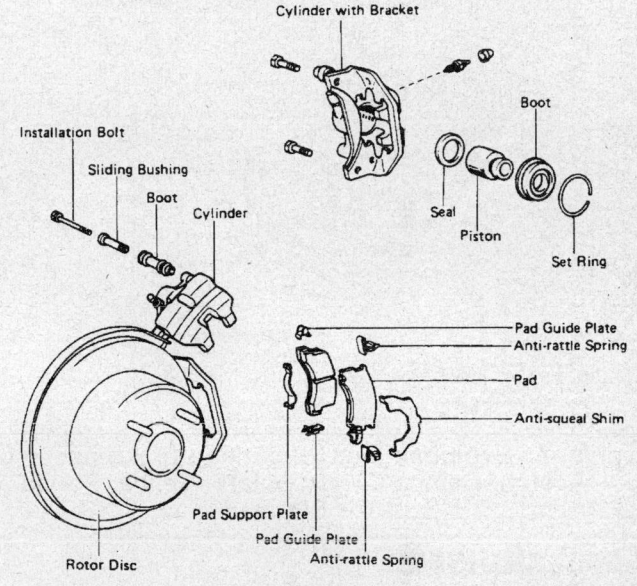

Fig. 2   Exploded view of rear disc brake caliper assembly. Supra w/2JZ-GE engine

Fig. 3   Exploded view of rear disc brake caliper assembly. Supra w/2JZ-GTE engine

Fig. 4   Exploded view of rear disc brake caliper assembly. Camry, Camry Solara & Previa

5. Reverse procedure to install, noting the following:
   a. Apply suitable grease to the main pin boot, sliding pin and boot, piston seal and piston and dust boot.
   b. Install main pin boot using a press and suitable socket.
   c. Ensure dust boot does not fold under during installation.

CAMRY, CAMRY SOLARA & PREVIA

Replace

1. Raise and support rear of vehicle, then remove tire and wheel assembly.
2. Disconnect brake hose from brake tube and caliper using a suitable tool.
3. Remove caliper attaching bolts, then the caliper, **Fig. 4.**
4. Remove anti-squeal shim(s), brake pad, anti-rattle spring, pad guide plate and pad support plate.
5. Reverse procedure to install, then bleed brake system.

Overhaul

1. Remove sliding bushing and boot, **Fig. 4.**
2. Remove main pin boot using a suitable chisel.
3. Remove piston using compressed air. **When using air pressure to remove caliper piston, place a shop towel**

over piston to prevent it from flying out.
4. Remove caliper boot, set ring and piston seal from caliper.
5. Reverse procedure to install, noting the following:
   a. Apply suitable grease to the main pin boot, sliding pin and boot, piston seal and piston and dust boot.
   b. Install main pin boot using a press and suitable socket.
   c. Ensure dust boot does not fold under during installation.

CELICA

Replace

1. Raise and support vehicle, then remove rear wheel.
2. Disconnect brake flex hose from caliper.
3. Remove caliper attaching bolt, then the caliper, **Fig. 5.**

4. Remove brake pads, then the pad support plates.
5. Remove main pin.
6. Reverse procedure to install, then bleed brake system.

Overhaul

1. Remove sliding bushing and dust boots.
2. Remove main pin boot.
3. Using a suitable screwdriver, remove cylinder boot set ring and boot from cylinder.
4. Remove piston using compressed air. **When using air pressure to remove caliper piston, place a shop towel over piston to prevent it from flying out.**
5. Using a suitable screwdriver, remove piston seal.
6. Reverse procedure to install. Apply suitable lithium soap base grease to piston, seal, and boot before installation.

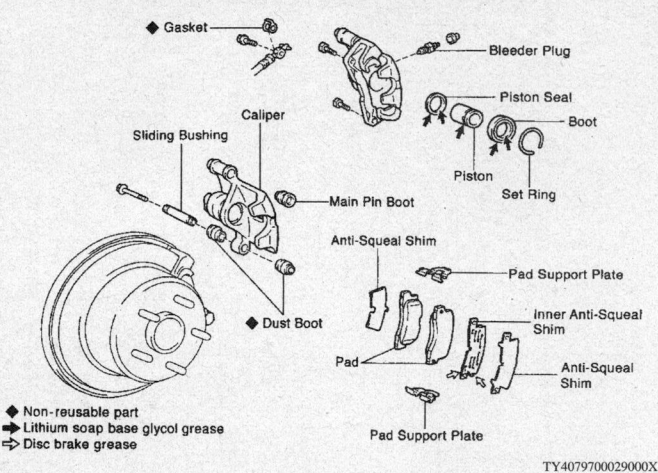

Fig. 5 Exploded view of rear disc brake assembly. Celica

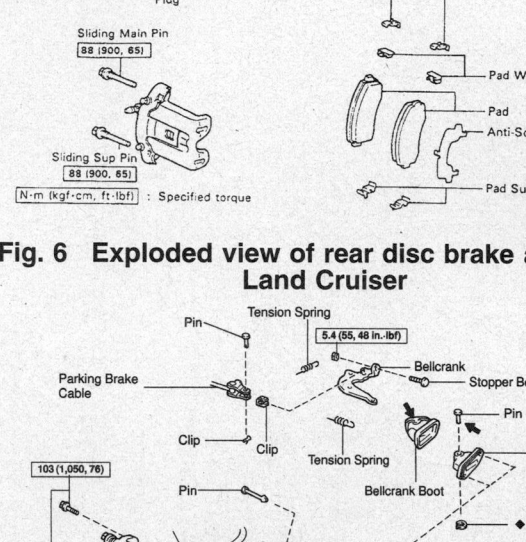

Fig. 6 Exploded view of rear disc brake assembly. Land Cruiser

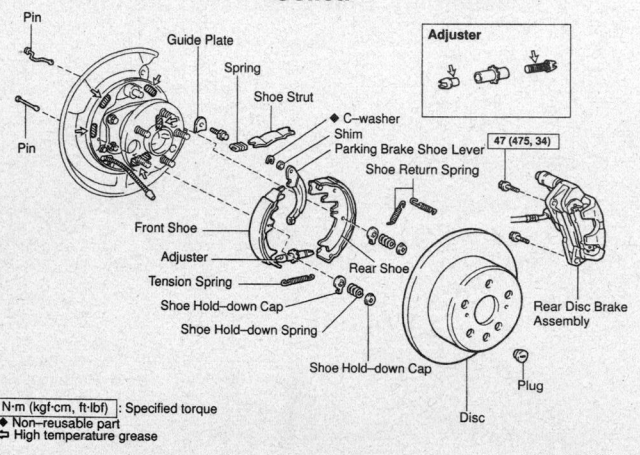

Fig. 7 Exploded view of parking brake assembly. Avalon, Camry, Camry Solara, Celica, Previa & Supra

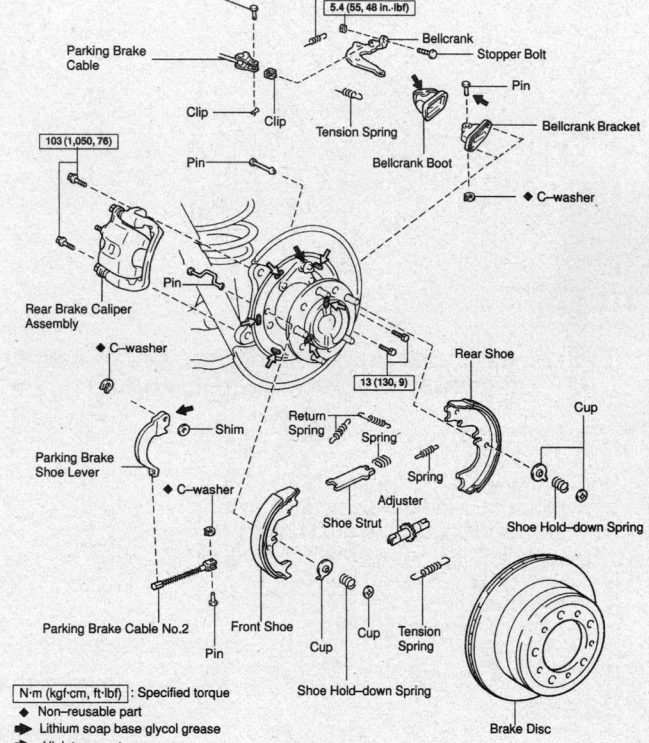

Fig. 8 Exploded view of rear disc brake parking brake assembly. Land Cruiser

LAND CRUISER

Replace

1. Remove union bolt and gaskets from brake caliper, then disconnect flexible hose. **Use suitable container to catch brake fluid.**
2. Remove caliper sliding pins, then the caliper.
3. Reverse procedure to install, Tighten caliper mounting bolt to specification.

Overhaul

1. Using suitable screwdriver, remove cylinder boot from caliper.
2. Place cloth between piston and caliper, then use compressed air to remove piston from caliper.
3. Using suitable screwdriver, remove piston seal from caliper.
4. Remove pin boot and sliding bushing using screwdriver and suitable hammer.

PARKING BRAKE SERVICE

AVALON, PREVIA, SUPRA, CAMRY, CAMRY SOLARA & CELICA

Shoes, Replace

1. Raise and support rear of vehicle, then remove tire and wheel assembly.

2. Remove rear caliper.
3. Remove rotor disc.
4. Remove shoe return springs, **Fig. 7.**
5. Using strut remover 09717–20010, or equivalent, remove shoe strut and spring.
6. Slide front shoe from under shoe hold-down spring, then remove shoe adjusting screw, tension spring and remove shoe.
7. Slide rear from shoe hold-down spring, then disconnect parking brake cable

from shoe lever.

8. Apply non-melting grease on brake backing plate shoe flats, then on shoe sliding surface.
9. Lubricate adjusting screw with non-melting lubricant.
10. Connect parking brake lever to cable.
11. Slide rear shoe into position under shoe hold-down spring, then install tension spring.
12. Install adjusting screw on rear shoe and partially install on front shoe.
13. Slide front shoe into position under shoe hold-down spring. Ensure adjusting screw and tension spring are positioned properly.
14. Install front shoe return spring, then rear return spring.
15. Lightly sand brake drum inner surface, then align the service hole on disc with groove on axle shaft and install disc.

16. Install caliper, then adjust parking brake.

LAND CRUISER

1. Raise and support rear of vehicle, then remove tire and wheel assembly.
2. Remove rear disc brake assembly.
3. Place matchmarks on disc and rear hub, then remove disc, **Fig 8**.
4. Remove tension spring using suitable pliers.
5. Remove shoe return springs.
6. Remove shoe strut with spring.
7. Remove rear shoe, adjuster and tension spring, **Fig 8**.
8. Remove front shoe hold-down spring cups, springs and pin.
9. Slide out front shoe.
10. Disconnect parking brake cable from parking brake shoe lever.

11. Measure clearance between parking brake shoe and lever. If clearance is greater than .0138 inch, replace shim to obtain correct clearance.
12. Apply high temperature grease to the backing plate, adjusting screw and sliding surfaces of the shoe.
13. Install parking brake cable to front shoe using suitable pliers.
14. Install front shoe pin to backing plate, then slide in front shoe.
15. Install front shoe hold-down spring and cups.
16. Install tension spring, rear shoe and adjuster.
17. Install front shoe hold-down spring and cups.
18. Install strut with spring.
19. Install shoe return springs.
20. Install disc brake assembly.

DISC BRAKE SPECIFICATIONS

Model	Year	Front Disc Brake				Rear Disc Brake			
		Rotor Nominal Thickness Inch	Min. Thickness Inch	Rotor Thickness Variation Parallelism Inch	Rotor Lateral Run Out (T.I.R.) Inch	Rotor Nominal Thickness Inch	Rotor Min. Refinish Thickness Inch	Rotor Thickness Variation Parallelism Inch	Rotor Lateral Run-Out (T.I.R.) Inch
Avalon	1996–99	1.102	1.024	—	.002	.354	.315	—	.0059
Camry	1996–99	1.102	1.024	—	.002	.394	.354	—	.0059
Camry Solara	1999	1.102	1.024	—	.002	.394	.354	—	.0059
Celica w/5S-FE Engine	1996	1.102	1.024	—	.002	.394	.354	—	.0059
	1997-98	1.102	1.024	—	.002	.354	.315	—	.0059
	1999	1.102	1.024	—	.002	.354	.314	—	.0059
Celica w/7A-FE Engine	1996	.984	.906	—	.002	.394	.354	—	.0059
	1997	.984	.906	—	.002	.354	.315	—	.0059
Corolla	1996–99	.866	.787	—	.002	—	—	—	—
4Runner	1996–99	.866	.787	—	.0028	—	—	—	—
Land Cruiser	1996–97	1.260	1.181	—	.0059	.709	.630	—	.0059
	1998–99	1.260	1.181	—	.0028	.709	.630	—	.0039
Paseo	1996–97	.709	.669	—	.002	—	—	—	—
Previa②	1996	③	④	—	.0028	—	—	—	—
	1997	.866	.787	—	.0028	—	—	—	—
Previa①	1996	③	④	—	.0028	.709	.630	—	.0039
	1997	.866	.787	—	.0028	.709	.650	—	.0039
RAV4	1997–99	.709	.630	—	.002	—	—	—	—
Sienna	1998–99	1.102	1.024	—	.002	—	—	—	—
Supra w/2JZ-GE Engine	1996–98	1.260	1.181	—	.002	.630	.591	—	.002
Supra w/2JZ-GTE Engine	1996–98	1.181	1.102	—	.002	.630	.591	—	.002
Tacoma 2WD	1996–99	.886	.787	—	.0028	—	—	—	—
Tacoma 4WD	1996–99	.886	.787	—	.0028	—	—	—	—
Tercel	1996	.709	.669	—	.0035	—	—	—	—
	1997	.709	.630	—	.0028	—	—	—	—
	1998	.709	.630	—	.0020	—	—	—	—
T-100	1996–98	.984	.906	—	.0028	—	—	—	—
Tundra	2000	1.102	1.024	—	.0028	—	—	—	—

TOYOTA UNIT REPAIR

① — Models w/4 wheel disc brakes.
② — Models w/front disc & rear drum brakes.

③ — Single piston, .866 inch; dual piston, .984 inch.

④ — Single piston, .787 inch; dual piston, .906 inch.

TIGHTENING SPECIFICATIONS

Year	Component	Torque/Ft.Lbs.
AVALON		
1996–99	Bleeder Plug	72③
	Flexible Hose	21
	Rear Caliper Bolt	25
	Rear Speed Sensor Bolt	6
	Rear Torque Plate	34
	Union Nut	①
CAMRY		
1996–99	Bleeder Plug	72③
	Flexible Hose	22
	Rear Caliper Bolt	14
	Rear Torque Plate	34
	Union Nut	②
CAMRY SOLARA		
1999	Bleeder Plug	72③
	Flexible Hose	21
	Rear Caliper Bolt	14
	Rear Torque Plate	34
	Union Nut (10 mm)	11
	Union Nut (12 mm)	14
CELICA		
1996–99	Bleeder Plug	72③
	Flexible Hose	22
	Rear Caliper Bolt	14
	Rear Torque Plate	34
	Union Nut	11
LAND CRUISER		
1996–99	Bleeder Plug	96③
	Caliper Bolts	65
	Disc To Hub	76
	Torque Plate	76
	Union Nut	11
PREVIA		
1996–97	Bleeder Plug	72③
	Rear Brake Hose	22
	Rear Caliper Bolt	18
	Rear Torque Plate	65
SUPRA		
1996–98	Bleeder Plug	96③
	Flexible Hose Union Bolt	22
	Rear Caliper To Axle Carrier (2JZ-GTE)	77
	Rear Caliper To Torque Plate (2JZ-GE)	25
	Rear Torque Plate	77
4RUNNER		
1996	Bleeder Plug	96③
	Caliper Bolts (PD60 & 66, 2WD)	24
	Caliper Bolts (S12 & 12, 4WD)	90
	Caliper Sliding Pin (FS17 & 18, 2WD)	65

Continued

REAR DISC & PARKING BRAKES

TIGHTENING
SPECIFICATIONS—Continued

Year	Component	Torque/ Ft.Lbs.
4RUNNER		
1996	Disc To Hub	47
	Torque Plate (PD60 & 66, 2WD)	80
	Union Nut	11

① — 1996–97 models, 11 ft. lbs.; 1998–99 models w/10 mm
    nut, 11 ft. lbs.; 12 mm nut, 15 ft. lbs.
② — 1996–97 models, 11 ft. lbs.; 1998–99 models w/10 mm
    nut, 11 ft. lbs.; 12 mm nut, 14 ft. lbs.
③ — Inch lbs.

Drum Brakes

INDEX

APPLICATION CHART

Model	Type
Camry	7
Camry Solara	7
Celica	6
Corolla	6
Land Cruiser	4
Paseo	3
Previa	5
RAV4	1
Sienna	8
Tercel	3
Tundra	4
2WD Tacoma	2
4WD Tacoma	4
2WD T100	2
4WD T100	4
4Runner	4

PRECAUTIONS

AIR BAG SYSTEMS

Refer to "Air Bag System Precautions" in the front of this manual for system disarming & arming procedures.

BATTERY GROUND CABLE

Prior to service, disconnect battery ground cable and isolate as required.

AUDIO CODED ANTI-THEFT SYSTEM

Some models are equipped with an audio coded anti-theft system that will disable the radio when the battery cable is disconnected. The system can be identified by the "ANTI-THEFT SYSTEM" on the cassette tape lid. Obtain 3 digit customer code for input. Reset system after service as follows:

1. Obtain 3 digit audio anti-theft code.
2. Depress 1 (PROG) while depressing righthand side of TUNE SEEK button, - - - will appear in tape operation display.
3. To enter the first digit, depress 1 (PROG) button repeatedly until the number of times depressed equals the first digit beginning with zero (depress the 1 button six times if the first digit if five).
4. To enter second digit, depress 2 (APS) button repeatedly until the number of times depressed equals the second digit beginning with zero.
5. To enter third digit, depress 3 (RPT) button repeatedly until the number of times depressed equals the third digit beginning with zero.
6. If - - - is displayed during code input, repeat procedure.
7. When code appears in display, depress and hold SCAN button until SEC appears.
8. When SEC disappears audio system should be operative.
9. If Err is displayed, repeat procedure.

Attempting to input code more than nine times may permanently disable audio system.

BRAKE SERVICE
TYPE 1
Removal

1. Raise and support vehicle, then remove rear wheel.
2. Remove brake drum. If drum cannot easily be removed, insert bent wire through hole in drum and hold automatic adjusting lever away from adjuster.
3. Remove front shoe return spring using tool No. 09703-30010, or equivalent, **Fig. 1**.
4. Using tool No. 09718-00010, or equivalent, remove front shoe hold-down spring, cups and pin.
5. Disconnect anchor spring from front shoe and remove front shoe.
6. Using tool No. 09718-00010, or equivalent, remove rear shoe hold-down spring, cups and pin.
7. Using a screwdriver, disconnect parking cable from anchor plate.
8. Using pliers, disconnect parking brake cable from lever and remove rear shoe together with adjuster.
9. Remove adjusting lever spring and adjuster from rear shoe.
10. Disconnect brake line from wheel cylinder using tool No. 09023-00100, or equivalent.

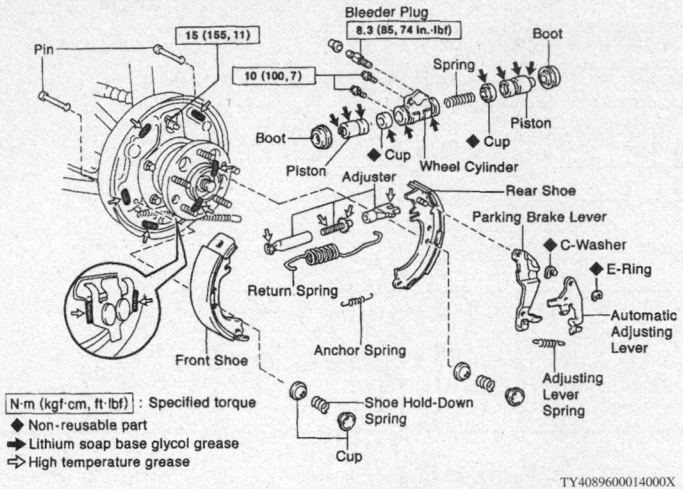

Fig. 1   Exploded view of type 1 drum brake assembly

TY4089600014000X

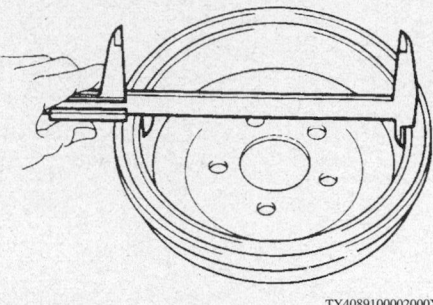

TY4089100002000X

Fig. 2   Brake drum inside diameter measurement

11.   Remove wheel cylinder.

Inspection

1.   Inspect parts for wear, rust or damage.
2.   Using vernier calipers, measure inside drum diameter, **Fig. 2.** Standard diameter should be 9 inches. Maximum inner diameter is 9.08 inches.
3.   Using a ruler, measure brake shoe lining, **Fig. 3.** Standard thickness is .197 inch. Minimum thickness is .039 inch.
4.   If brake drum is scored or worn, it may be lathed to maximum inside diameter.
5.   Inspect brake lining and drum for proper contact and replace drum or shoes as necessary.

Installation

1.   Reverse removal procedure to install, noting the following:
  a.   Move parking brake lever of rear shoe back and forth. Ensure adjuster turns.
  b.   If adjuster does not turn, check for incorrect installation of rear brakes.
  c.   Adjust length of adjuster to shortest length possible.
  d.   Check clearance between brake shoes and drum, **Fig. 4.** Clearance should be .024 inch.

TYPE 2 (2WD LEADING/ TRAILING TYPE)

Removal

1.   Raise and support rear of vehicle, then remove wheel and tire assembly.
2.   Remove brake drum. If brake drum cannot be remove easily, insert a suitable screwdriver through hole in backing plate, then push adjuster lever away from adjuster and back of adjustment tension.
3.   Remove return spring adjuster, using a suitable tool, then the front shoe hold-down spring and pin, **Fig. 5.**
4.   Remove front brake shoe, then the anchor spring.
5.   Remove hold-down spring and pin, then the rear shoe, using a suitable tool.

6.   Remove strut and spring from parking brake lever, then the adjusting lever spring.
7.   Remove parking brake cable from parking brake lever.

Inspection

1.   Measure brake drum inside diameter. Inside diameter should be 10.00 inches, **Fig. 2.**
2.   Measure brake shoe lining thickness, **Fig. 3.** Minimum thickness should be .04 inch.
3.   Inspect brake lining and drum for proper contact and replace drum or shoes as necessary.
4.   Inspect wheel cylinder for corrosion or damage.
5.   Inspect backing plate for wear or damage.
6.   Apply a suitable lubricant to backing plate contact areas.

Installation

1.   Apply a suitable lubricant to adjuster bolt threads and end.
2.   Connect parking brake cable, then assemble strut and return spring to lever. Install adjusting lever spring using a suitable tool.
3.   Position rear shoe in place with one end of shoe inserted in wheel cylinder and the other end in anchor plate. Using a suitable tool, install pin and shoe hold-down spring.
4.   Insert anchor spring between front and rear shoes, then position front shoe in place with end of shoe in wheel cylinder and strut in place. Using a suitable tool, install pin and shoe hold-down spring.
5.   Install return spring.
6.   Pull adjusting lever cable upward, then release and ensure adjusting bolt rotates. If bolt does not rotate, check for improper installation of rear brakes.
7.   Adjust strut to shortest possible length, then install drum.
8.   Pull parking brake lever fully upward. Repeat process several times.
9.   Remove drum, then check for proper

clearance, **Fig. 4.** Clearance should be .024 inch. If clearance is not as specified, check parking brake system.
10.   Install brake drum, then bleed and refill brake system.
11.   Install wheel and tire assembly, then lower vehicle.

TYPE 3

Removal

1.   Raise and support rear of vehicle, then remove wheel and tire assembly.
2.   Remove brake drum. If brake drum cannot be remove easily, insert a suitable screwdriver through hole in backing plate, then push adjuster lever away from adjuster and back of adjustment tension.
3.   Remove shoe return spring, using suitable tool, then remove return spring clamp, **Fig. 6.**
4.   Remove front shoe hold-down spring, retainers and pin.
5.   Disconnect anchor spring, then remove front brake shoe and anchor spring.
6.   Remove rear shoe hold-down spring, retainers and pin using suitable tool.
7.   Disconnect parking brake cable from lever, then remove rear shoe with strut.
8.   Remove adjusting lever spring and strut from rear shoe.
9.   Remove C-washer, then the shims, parking brake lever and automatic adjusting lever from rear shoe.
10.   Position a suitable container to catch fluid, then disconnect brake line.
11.   Remove two attaching bolts, then the wheel cylinder.
12.   Remove two boots, two pistons, two piston cups and spring from wheel cylinder.

Inspection

1.   Measure brake drum inside diameter. Inside diameter should be 7.09 inches, **Fig. 2.**
2.   Measure brake shoe lining thickness, **Fig. 3.** Minimum thickness should be .04 inch.
3.   Inspect brake lining and drum for proper contact and replace drum or shoes as necessary.
4.   Inspect wheel cylinder for corrosion or damage.
5.   Inspect backing plate for wear or damage.
6.   Inspect bellcrank components for

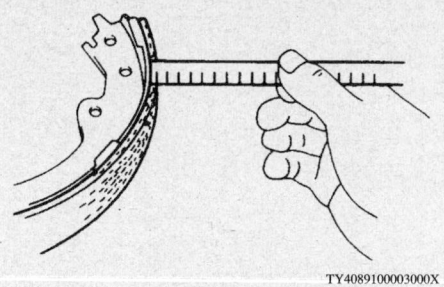

Fig. 3 Brake shoe lining thickness measurement

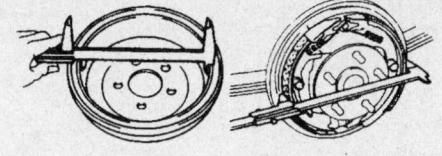

Fig. 4 Clearance between shoes & drum measurement

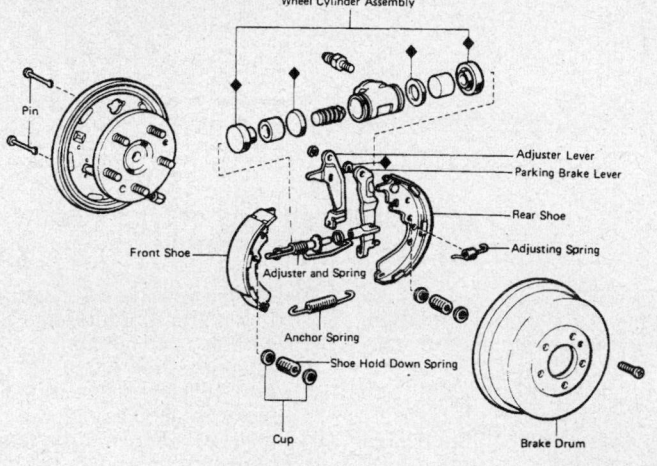

Fig. 5 Exploded view of type 2 (2WD leading/ trailing) brake assembly

bending, wear or damage.
7. Apply a suitable lubricant to backing plate contact areas.

Installation

1. Apply a suitable lubricant to pistons and cups, then install spring and two piston cups into wheel cylinder. Apply a suitable lubricant to inside of boots, then insert them into cylinder, **Fig. 6.**
2. Install wheel cylinder onto backing plate, then insert attaching bolts and **torque** to 7 ft. lbs.
3. Connect brake tube to wheel cylinder, then **torque** nut to 11 ft. lbs.
4. Apply a suitable lubricant to adjuster bolt contact points, then install levers, shim and new C-washer.
5. Measure clearance between shoe and lever. Clearance should be .014 inch. If clearance is not as specified, select a suitable shim to bring clearance to specified value.
6. Place strut and return spring on rear shoe, then install adjusting lever spring.
7. Connect parking brake cable to lever, then position one end of rear shoe in wheel cylinder and the other end in anchor plate.
8. Install rear shoe pin and hold-down spring.
9. Insert anchor spring between front and rear shoes, then position end of front shoe in wheel cylinder with strut in place.
10. Install front shoe hold-down spring, re-

tainers and pin.
11. Install shoe return spring clamp, then the shoe return spring.
12. Ensure adjusting bolt rotates while pulling parking brake upward. If bolt does not turn, check installation of rear brakes.
13. Adjust strut to shortest possible length, then install drum.
14. Pull parking brake lever fully upward then repeat step several times.
15. Remove drum, then check for proper clearance, **Fig. 4.** Clearance should be .024 inch. If clearance is not as specified, check parking brake system.
16. Install brake drum, then bleed and refill brake system.
17. Install wheel and tire assembly, then lower vehicle.

TYPE 4

EXCEPT TUNDRA

Removal

1. Raise and support rear of vehicle, then remove wheel and tire assembly.
2. Remove brake drum. If brake drum cannot be removed easily, insert a suitable screwdriver through hole in backing plate, then push adjuster lever away from adjuster and back of adjustment tension.
3. Remove tension spring, using a suitable tool, then remove rear shoe hold-down spring and pin. Remove rear brake shoe and anchor spring, **Fig. 7.**

4. **On Land Cruiser models,** remove front hold-down spring using a suitable tool, then disconnect the parking brake cable from the parking brake bellcrank, **Fig. 7.**
5. **On 4Runner, 4WD T100 and 4WD Tacoma models,** remove front shoe hold-down spring and pin, using a suitable tool, then disconnect No. 1 parking brake cable from No. 3 parking brake bellcrank.
6. **On 2WD T100 models,** proceed as follows:
   a. Remove E-ring, then automatic adjusting lever and C-washer, then parking brake lever. Disconnect brake line from wheel cylinder using a suitable container to catch fluid.
   b. Remove wheel cylinder. Remove following parts from wheel cylinder: two boots, two pistons, two pistons cups and spring.
7. **On models except 2WD T100,** remove front brake with strut, then disconnect parking brake cable from front shoe. Remove parking brake cable No. 2.
8. **On all models,** remove adjusting lever spring, then the adjuster from front shoe.

Inspection

1. Measure brake drum inside diameter. Inside diameter should be 11.61 inches, **Fig. 2.**
2. Measure brake shoe lining thickness, **Fig. 3.** Minimum thickness should be .04 inch on models except on T100 models and .039 inch on T100 models.
3. Inspect brake lining and drum for proper contact and replace drum or shoes as necessary.
4. Inspect wheel cylinder for corrosion or damage.
5. Inspect backing plate for wear or damage.
6. Inspect bellcrank components for bending, wear or damage.
7. Apply a suitable lubricant to backing plate contact areas.

Installation

1. **On 2WD T100 models,** proceed as follows:
   a. Apply lithium soap base glycol grease to piston cups, pistons and boots.
   b. Assemble and install wheel cylinder.
   c. Connect brake line to cylinder.
2. **On all models,** apply high temperature grease to following parts:
   a. Backing plate and brake shoe contact points.
   b. Anchor plate and brake shoe contact points.
   c. Adjusting bolt.
   d. Adjuster and brake shoe contact points.
3. Apply a suitable lubricant to adjuster bolt threads and end.
4. Assemble adjuster to lever, then install adjuster lever spring.
5. **On Land Cruiser models,** install parking brake lever cable to parking

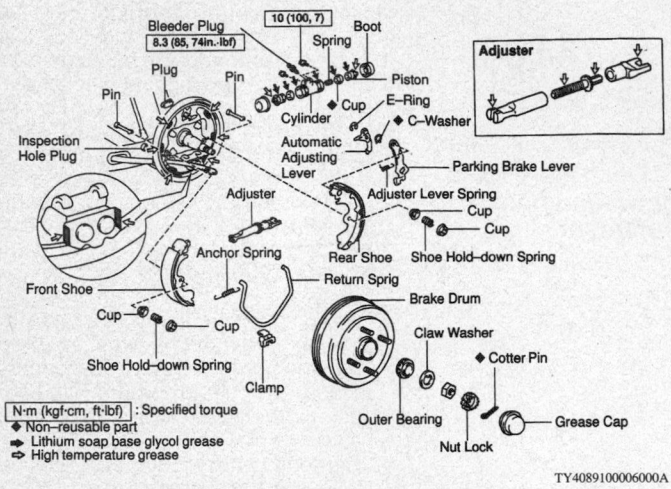

**Fig. 6 Exploded view of type 3 brake assembly.
Tercel & Paseo**

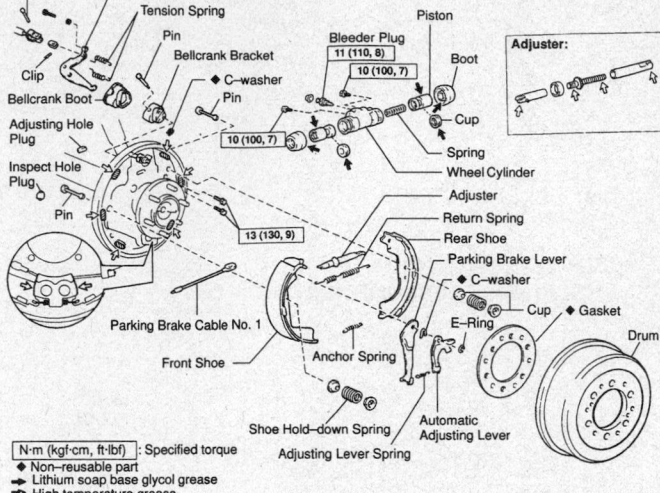

**Fig. 7 Exploded view of type 4 drum brake
assembly**

brake shoe, then attach cable to bellcrank.

6. **On 4Runner, 4WD T100 and 4WD Tacoma models,** install No. 1 parking brake cable to parking brake lever shoe, then attach the other side of cable to No. 3 bellcrank.
7. **On all models,** position front shoe in place with end of shoe inserted into piston, then install shoe hold-down spring and pin using a suitable tool.
8. Assemble anchor spring to front and rear shoe, then install rear shoe with end inserted in piston.
9. Install rear shoe hold-down spring and pin, then the tension spring.
10. If necessary, adjust bellcrank as follows:
    a. Lightly pull bellcrank in direction "A," **Fig. 8,** until there is no slack in part "B."
    b. Rotate adjusting bolt until dimension "C" is .016–.031 inch.
    c. Lock adjusting bolt with locknut, when connect parking brake cable to bellcrank.
    d. Install tension spring.
11. Ensure proper parking brake travel.
12. Pull adjusting lever cable upward, then release and ensure adjusting bolt rotates. If bolt does not rotate, check for improper installation of rear brakes.
13. Adjust strut to shortest possible length, then install drum.
14. Pull parking brake lever fully upward. Repeat process several times.
15. Remove drum, then check for proper clearance, **Fig. 4.** Clearance should be .024 inch. If clearance is not as specified, check parking brake system.
16. Install brake drum, then bleed and refill brake system.
17. Install wheel and tire assembly, then lower vehicle.

TUNDRA

Replace

1. Remove inspection cover and inspect shoe lining thickness. If thickness is .039 inch or less, replace shoes.
2. Raise and support vehicle, then re-

move rear wheels.
3. Release parking brake lever or pedal, then remove brake drum. If drum cannot be removed, proceed as follows:
   a. Remove adjusting hole plug from backing plate.
   b. Insert a screwdriver through hole and hold automatic adjusting lever away from adjusting bolt.
   c. Using another screwdriver, reduce brake shoe adjustment by turning adjusting bolt.
4. Using brake spring tool No. 07703–30010 or equivalent, remove return spring from both shoes, **Fig. 7.**
5. Using hold down spring tool No. 09718–00010 or equivalent, remove anchor springs from both shoes.
6. Disconnect parking brake cable No. 1 from parking brake bellcrank, then from front shoe.
7. Remove adjuster and lever spring from front shoe.
8. Remove automatic adjusting lever and parking brake lever from shoe.
9. Remove and disassemble parking brake bellcrank as follows:
   a. Remove clip and pin, then disconnect parking brake cable.
   b. Remove 2 tension springs, then the bolts and bellcrank.
   c. Remove c-washer and pin, then the bracket and boot.
10. Disconnect wheel cylinder brake line using union nut wrench tool No. 09023–00100 or equivalent.
11. Remove wheel cylinder attaching bolts, then the wheel cylinder.
12. Remove wheel cylinder boots, then the pistons, cups and spring.
13. Reverse procedure to install. Apply lithium soap base glycol grease and high temperature grease to parts during assembly as shown in **Fig. 7.**

Inspection

1. Inspect all disassembled parts for wear, rust or damage.

2. Using a suitable drum gauge, measure drum inner diameter and ensure drum is within specifications.
3. Measure shoe lining thickness. Standard thickness is .236 inch, minimum thickness is .039 inch.
4. If shoe lining is less than minimum thickness or shows signs of uneven wear, replace.
5. Inspect shoe and drum for even contact, **Fig. 9.**

TYPE 5

Removal

1. Raise and support rear of vehicle, then remove wheel and tire assembly.
2. Remove brake drum. If brake drum cannot be remove easily, insert a suitable screwdriver through hole in backing plate, then push adjuster lever away from adjuster and back of adjustment tension.
3. Remove tension spring, using a suitable tool, then remove rear shoe hold-down spring and pin. Remove rear brake shoe and anchor spring, **Fig. 10.**
4. Remove rear shoe hold-down spring and pin, using suitable tool, then disconnect parking brake cable from lever.
5. Remove adjusting lever spring and strut from rear shoe.
6. Position a suitable container to catch fluid, then remove two boots, two pistons, two piston cups and spring from wheel cylinder.

Inspection

1. Measure brake drum inside diameter. Inside diameter should be 9.00 inches, **Fig. 2.**
2. Measure brake shoe lining thickness, **Fig. 3.** Minimum thickness should be .04 inch.
3. Inspect brake lining and drum for proper contact and replace drum or shoes as necessary.

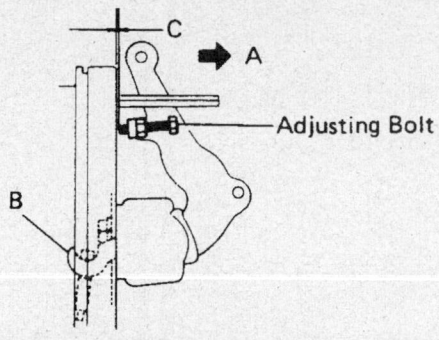

Fig. 8 Bellcrank adjustment. Land Cruiser, 4WD 4Runner, 4WD Tacoma & T100

4. Inspect wheel cylinder for corrosion or damage.
5. Inspect backing plate for wear or damage.
6. Apply a suitable lubricant to backing plate contact areas.

Installation

1. Apply a suitable lubricant to piston cups, then insert spring and two piston cups into wheel cylinder. Apply a suitable lubricant to inside of boots, then insert them into cylinder, **Fig. 10.**
2. Apply a suitable lubricant to adjuster bolt threads and end, then install strut and adjusting lever spring.
3. Connect parking brake cable to lever, then position one end of rear shoe in wheel cylinder and the other end in anchor plate.
4. Install rear shoe pin and hold-down spring.
5. Insert anchor spring between front and rear shoes, then position end of front shoe in wheel cylinder with strut in place.
6. Install front shoe hold-down spring and pin.
7. Install tension spring.
8. Ensure adjusting bolt rotates while pulling parking brake upward. If bolt does not turn, check installation of rear brakes.
9. Adjust strut to shortest possible length, then install drum.
10. Pull parking brake lever fully upward then repeat step several times.
11. Remove drum, then check for proper clearance, **Fig. 4.** Clearance should be .024 inch. if clearance is not as specified, check parking brake system.
12. Install brake drum, then bleed and refill brake system.
13. Install wheel and tire assembly, then lower vehicle.

TYPE 6

Removal

1. Raise and support rear of vehicle, then remove wheel and tire assembly.
2. Remove brake drum. If brake drum cannot be remove easily, insert a suitable screwdriver through hole in backing plate, then push automatic adjuster

lever away from adjuster and back of adjustment tension.
3. Disconnect return spring, using a suitable tool, then remove front shoe hold-down spring, retainers and pin.
4. Disconnect anchor spring, then remove front brake shoe and anchor spring, **Fig. 11.**
5. Remove rear shoe hold-down spring, retainers and pin, using suitable a tool, then disconnect parking brake cable from anchor plate.
6. Disconnect parking brake cable from lever, then remove rear shoe with strut.
7. Remove adjusting lever spring, strut and return spring from rear shoe.
8. Remove C-washer, then the shims, parking brake lever and automatic adjusting lever from rear shoe.
9. Position a suitable container to catch fluid, then disconnect brake line.
10. Remove two attaching bolts, then the wheel cylinder.
11. Remove two boots, two pistons, two piston cups and spring from wheel cylinder.

Inspection

1. Measure brake drum inside diameter. Inside diameter should be 7.87 inches, **Fig. 2.**
2. Measure brake shoe lining thickness, **Fig. 3.** Minimum thickness should be .04 inch.
3. Inspect brake lining and drum for proper contact and replace drum or shoes as necessary.
4. Inspect wheel cylinder for corrosion or damage.
5. Inspect backing plate for wear or damage.
6. Inspect bellcrank components for bending, wear or damage.
7. Apply a suitable lubricant to backing plate contact areas.

Installation

1. Apply a suitable lubricant to pistons and cups, then install spring and two piston cups into wheel cylinder. Apply a suitable lubricant to inside of boots, then insert them into cylinder, **Fig. 11.**
2. Install wheel cylinder onto backing plate, then insert attaching bolts and **torque** to 7 ft. lbs.
3. Connect brake tube to wheel cylinder, then **torque** nut to 11 ft. lbs.
4. Apply a suitable lubricant to adjuster bolt contact points, then install levers, shim and new C-washer.
5. Measure clearance between shoe and lever. Clearance should be .014 inch. If clearance is not as specified, select a suitable shim to bring clearance to specified value.
6. Place strut and return spring on rear shoe, then install adjusting lever spring.
7. Connect parking brake cable to lever, then insert cable through notch in anchor plate.
8. Position one end of rear shoe in wheel cylinder and the other end in anchor plate.
9. Install rear shoe pin and hold-down

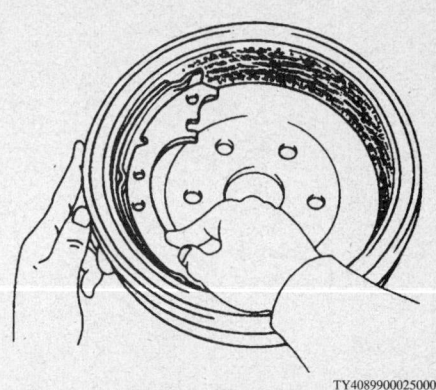

Fig. 9 Shoe contact inspection. Tundra

spring and retainers.
10. Insert anchor spring between front and rear shoes, then position end of front shoe in wheel cylinder with strut in place.
11. Install front shoe hold-down spring, retainers and pin.
12. Install return spring.
13. Ensure adjusting bolt rotates while pulling parking brake upward. If bolt does not turn, check installation of rear brakes.
14. Adjust strut to its shortest possible length, then install drum.
15. Pull parking brake lever fully upward, then repeat step several times.
16. Remove drum, then check for proper clearance, **Fig. 4.** Clearance should be .024 inch. If clearance is not as specified, check parking brake system.
17. Install brake drum, then bleed and refill brake system.
18. Install wheel and tire assembly, then lower vehicle.

TYPE 7

Removal

1. Raise and support rear of vehicle, then remove wheel and tire assembly.
2. Remove brake drum. If brake drum cannot be remove easily, insert a suitable screwdriver through hole in backing plate, then push adjuster lever away from adjuster and back of adjustment tension.
3. Disconnect return spring, using a suitable tool, then remove front shoe hold-down spring, retainers and pin.
4. Disconnect anchor spring, then remove front brake shoe and anchor spring, **Fig. 12.**
5. Remove rear shoe hold-down spring, retainers and pin, using suitable tool, then disconnect parking brake cable from anchor plate.
6. Disconnect parking brake cable from lever, then remove rear shoe with strut.
7. Remove adjusting lever spring, strut and return spring from rear shoe.
8. Remove C-washer, then the shims, parking brake lever and automatic adjusting lever from rear shoe.
9. Position a suitable container to catch fluid, then disconnect brake line.

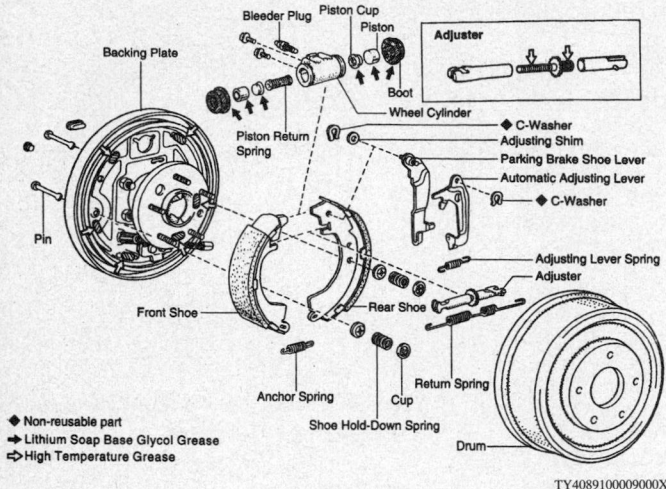

Fig. 10 Exploded view of type 5 drum brake assembly

◆ Non-reusable part
➡ Lithium Soap Base Glycol Grease
⇨ High Temperature Grease

TY4089100009000X

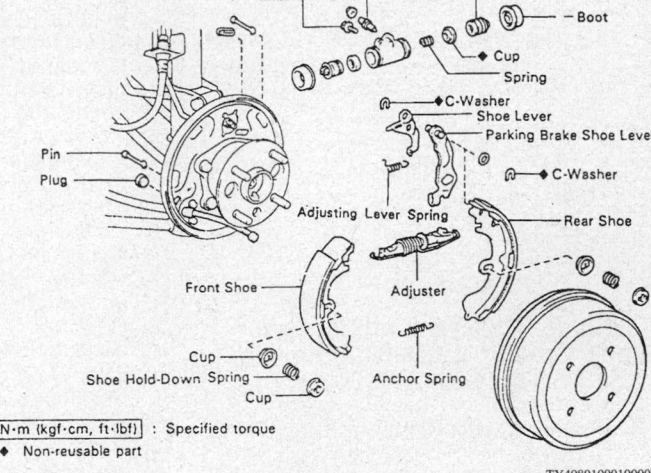

N·m (kgf·cm, ft·lbf) : Specified torque
◆ Non-reusable part

TY4089100010000X

Fig. 11 Exploded view of type 6 drum brake assembly

10. Remove two attaching bolts, then the wheel cylinder.
11. Remove two boots, two pistons, two piston cups and spring from wheel cylinder.

Inspection

1. Measure brake drum inside diameter. Inside diameter should be 7.87 inches, **Fig. 2.**
2. Measure brake shoe lining thickness, **Fig. 3.** Minimum thickness should be .04 inch.
3. Inspect brake lining and drum for proper contact and replace drum or shoes as necessary.
4. Inspect wheel cylinder for corrosion or damage.
5. Inspect backing plate for wear or damage.
6. Inspect bellcrank components for bending, wear or damage.
7. Apply a suitable lubricant to backing plate contact areas.

Installation

1. Apply a suitable lubricant to pistons and cups, then install spring and two piston cups into wheel cylinder. Apply a suitable lubricant to inside of boots, then insert them into cylinder, **Fig. 12.**
2. Install wheel cylinder onto backing plate, then insert attaching bolts and **torque** to 7 ft. lbs.
3. Connect brake tube to wheel cylinder, then **torque** nut to 11 ft. lbs.
4. Apply a suitable lubricant to adjuster bolt contact points, then install levers, shim and new C-washer.
5. Measure clearance between shoe and lever. Clearance should be .014 inch. If clearance is not as specified, select a suitable shim to bring clearance to specified value.
6. Place strut and return spring on rear shoe, then install adjusting lever spring.
7. Connect parking brake cable to lever, then insert cable through notch in anchor plate.
8. Position one end of rear shoe in wheel

cylinder and the other end in anchor plate.
9. Install rear shoe pin and hold-down spring and retainers.
10. Insert anchor spring between front and rear shoes, then position end of front shoe in wheel cylinder with strut in place.
11. Install front shoe hold-down spring, retainers and pin.
12. Install return spring.
13. Ensure adjusting bolt rotates while pulling parking brake upward. If bolt does not turn, check installation of rear brakes.
14. Adjust strut to its shortest possible length, then install drum.
15. Pull parking brake lever fully upward then repeat step several times.
16. Remove drum, then check for proper clearance, **Fig. 4.** Clearance should be .024 inch. If clearance is not as specified, check parking brake system.
17. Install brake drum, then bleed and refill brake system.
18. Install wheel and tire assembly, then lower vehicle.

TYPE 8

Replace

1. Remove brake drum plug, **Fig. 13.**
2. Hold automatic adjusting lever away from adjuster.
3. Reduce brake shoe adjuster by turning with a suitable screwdriver.
4. Remove brake drum.
5. Using suitable pliers, disconnect return spring from automatic adjusting lever.
6. Remove return spring from rear shoe.
7. Remove automatic adjusting lever.
8. Using hold down spring tool No. 09718–00010 or equivalent, remove shoe hold down spring, cup and pin from front shoe.
9. Using spring brake shoe return spring tool No. 09703–30010 or equivalent, disconnect anchor spring from front

shoe and remove shoe.
10. Remove adjuster, then the anchor spring from rear shoe.
11. Using hold down spring tool No. 09718–00010 or equivalent, remove shoe hold down spring, cup and pin from rear shoe.
12. Using a suitable pair of pliers, disconnect parking brake cable from parking brake lever and remove rear shoe.
13. Remove "C" washer and shim from parking brake lever, then remove lever.
14. Reverse procedure to install noting the following:
    a. Apply lithium soap base glycol grease and high temperature grease to parts as indicated in **Fig. 13.**
    b. Measure brake drum inside diameter and diameter of brake shoes. Ensure difference is .020 inch. If clearance is not as specified, inspect parking brake system.

Inspection

1. Inspect disassembled parts for wear, rust or damage.
2. Measure brake shoe lining thickness. Standard thickness is .236 inch. Minimum thickness is .039 inch. Replace as necessary.
3. Measure brake drum inside diameter. Refer to "Drum Brake Specifications" for proper brake drum inside diameter and service as necessary. Replace drum if scored or worn beyond limit.
4. Inspect brake linings and drum for proper contact. If contact between drum and shoe is improper, repair lining using a brake shoe grinder or replace shoe assembly.

ADJUSTMENTS
PARKING BRAKE
Celica, Corolla, Paseo, Previa, Tercel

1. Apply parking brake and count number

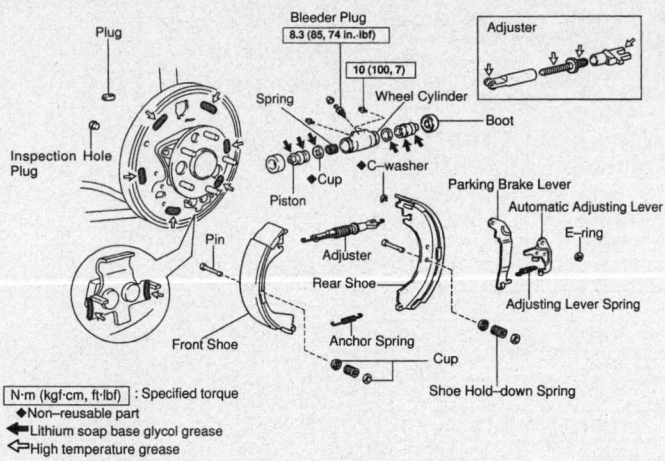

Fig. 12 Exploded view of type 7 drum brake assembly

TY4089100011000X

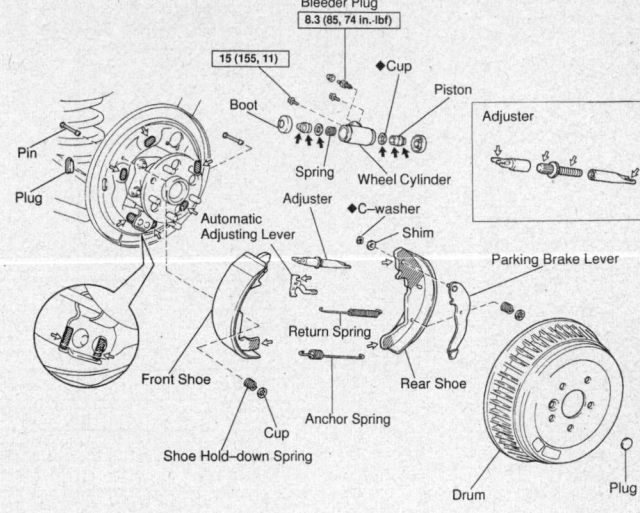

N·m (kgf·cm, ft·lbf) : Specified torque
◆ Non–reusable part
➡ Lithium soap base glycol grease
➪ High temperature grease

TY4089900027000X

Fig. 13 Exploded view of type 8 drum brake assembly

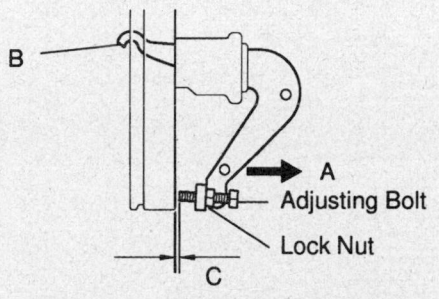

TY4089900026000X

Fig. 14 Bellcrank adjustment. Tundra

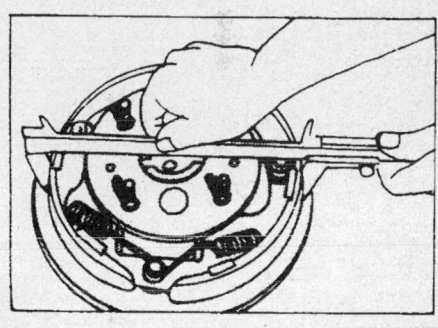

TY4089100013000X

Fig. 15 Brake shoe to brake drum clearance measurement. Land Cruiser, Tacoma, Tundra, T100 & 4Runner

of notches on parking brake sector. Specified number of notches should be as follows: 4–7 for Celica, 5–8 for Corolla, 4–5 for Previa, 5–8 for Tercel sedans and 6–8 for Tercel wagons.

2. **On Camry, Camry Solara, Celica, Corolla and Tercel,** adjust parking brake as follows:
   a. Remove console box, and if necessary, the shift knob.
   b. Loosen locknut and turn adjustment screw until lever travel is correct.
   c. Tighten locknut and reinstall console.

3. **On Previa models,** proceed as follows:
   a. Raise and support vehicle.
   b. Tighten or loosen adjusting nut at parking brake equalizer as necessary to bring parking brake adjustment within specifications.
   c. Lower vehicle.

Tundra

1. Pull bellcrank in direction "A," **Fig. 14,** until there is no slack at "B."
2. Turn adjusting bolt until dimension "C" is .016–.031 inch.
3. Lock adjusting bolt with lock nut.

4. Connect parking brake cable to parking brake bellcrank and install pin and clip.
5. Install 2 tension springs.

2WD T100, Tacoma & 4Runner

1. Release parking brake and check to ensure warning light switch is off. If adjustment is required, loosen parking brake warning light switch bracket and position switch.
2. Adjust nut at parking brake cable equalizer so that there is no looseness at No. 2 and No. 3 parking brake cables. Check to ensure both rear wheels rotate freely.
3. After adjusting, apply parking brake lever and count number of notches on brake lever. Specified number of notches should be 10–16.

4WD Land Cruiser, T100, Tacoma & 4Runner

1. Tighten bellcrank stopper screw until there is no play in rear brake link. Back off screw one turn, then tighten screw locknut.
2. Tighten one intermediate lever adjusting nut while loosening the other until lever travel of 9–17 clicks is obtained. Tighten both adjusting nuts.
3. Check to ensure bellcrank stopper screw contacts backing plate.

SHOE ADJUSTMENT

Land Cruiser, Tacoma, Tundra, T100 & 4Runner

Measure brake drum inside diameter

and maximum diameter of brake shoes using brake shoe clearance gauge, **Fig. 15.** **On Land Cruiser, Tacoma, T100 & 4Runner models,** turn adjuster so that brake shoe diameter will be .012–.024 inch (.3–.6 mm) smaller than brake drum inner diameter. On Tundra models, turn adjuster so that brake shoe clearance will be .020 inch.

Raise and support rear of vehicle, ensure rear wheels move freely. Remove brake shoe adjusting hole plug from backing plate, then using a suitable brake tool, expand adjuster until wheel is locked. Working through backing plate, insert a narrow tool to move self-adjuster lever away from adjuster, then loosen adjuster wheel approximately 10–12 notches. Install brake shoe adjusting hole plug.

DRUM BRAKE SPECIFICATIONS

Model	Year	Brake Drum	
		Drum Nom- inal Inside Dia- meter Inch	Drum Max. Re- finish Inside Dia- meter Inch
Camry	1996–99	9	9.079
Camry Solara	1999	9	9.079
Celica	1996	7.874	7.913
	1997	7.874	7.913
Corolla	1996–99	7.874	7.913
4Runner	1996–99	11.614	11.693
Land Cruiser	1998–99	9.06	9.09
Paseo	1996–97	7.087	7.126
Previa	1996	10	10.18
	1997	10	10.18
RAV4	1997–99	9	9.079
Sienna	1998–99	9.843	9.921
Tacoma 2WD	1996–99	10	10.079
Tacoma 4WD	1996–99	11.614	11.693
Tercel	1996	7.087	7.126
	1997	7.087	7.126
	1998–99	7.087	7.126
T-100	1996–98	11.614	11.693
Tundra	2000	11.614	11.693

TIGHTENING SPECIFICATIONS

Year	Component	Torque/Ft.Lbs.
CAMRY		
1996–99	Bleeder Plug	74①
	Union Nut	11
	Wheel Cylinder	84①
CAMRY SOLARA		
1999	Bleeder Plug	74①
	Union Nut	11
	Wheel Cylinder	84①
CELICA		
1996–97	Bleeder Plug	74①
	Union Nut	11
	Wheel Cylinder	84①
COROLLA		
1996–99	Bleeder Plug	74①
	Union Nut	11
	Wheel Cylinder	84①
PASEO		
1996–97	Bleeder Plug	74①
	Union Nut	11
	Wheel Cylinder	84①
PREVIA		
1996–97	Bleeder Plug	74①
	Union Nut	11
	Wheel Cylinder	84①

Continued

DRUM BRAKES

TIGHTENING
SPECIFICATIONS—Continued

Year	Component	Torque/Ft.Lbs.
RAV4		
1996-99	Bleeder Plug	74①
	Union Nut	11
	Wheel Cylinder	84①
SIENNA		
1998–99	Bleeder Plug	74①
	Union Nut	11
	Wheel Cylinder	11
TERCEL		
1996–98	Bleeder Plug	74①
	Union Nut	11
	Wheel Cylinder	84①
T100, TACOMA & TUNDRA		
1996–99	Bleeder Plug	96①
	Parking Brake Bellcrank Bracket To Backing Plate	108①
	Union Nut	11
	Wheel Cylinder	84①
4RUNNER		
1996–99	Bleeder Plug	96①
	Union Nut	11
	Wheel Cylinder (Duo Servo Brakes)	10
	Wheel Cylinder (Leading-Trailing Brakes)	84①

① — Inch lbs.

Hydraulic Brake Systems

NOTE: On Vehicles Equipped With Anti-Lock Brakes Refer To "Anti-Lock Brakes" Section Of This Manual.

INDEX

PRECAUTIONS

AIR BAG SYSTEMS

Refer to "Air Bag System Precautions" in the front of this manual for system disarming & arming procedures.

BATTERY GROUND CABLE

Prior to service, disconnect battery ground cable and isolate as required.

AUDIO CODED ANTI-THEFT SYSTEM

Some models are equipped with an audio coded anti-theft system that will disable the radio when the battery cable is disconnected. The system can be identified by the "ANTI-THEFT SYSTEM" on the cassette tape lid. Obtain 3 digit customer code for input. Reset system after service as follows:

1. Obtain 3 digit audio anti-theft code.
2. Depress 1 (PROG) while depressing righthand side of TUNE SEEK button, - - - will appear in tape operation display.
3. To enter the first digit, depress 1 (PROG) button repeatedly until the number of times depressed equals the first digit beginning with zero (depress the 1 button six times if the first digit is five).
4. To enter second digit, depress 2 (APS) button repeatedly until the number of times depressed equals the second digit beginning with zero.
5. To enter third digit, depress 3 (RPT) button repeatedly until the number of times depressed equals the second digit beginning with zero.
6. If - - - is displayed during code input, repeat procedure.
7. When code appears in display, depress and hold SCAN button until SEC appears.
8. When SEC disappears audio system should be operative.
9. If Err is displayed, repeat procedure.
Attempting to input code more than nine times may permanently disable audio system.

DESCRIPTION

When the brake pedal is depressed, a vacuum builds up in the booster which amplifies the pedal force, pressing on the piston in the master cylinder. The piston raises the hydraulic pressure in the cylinder. This hydraulic pressure is then applied to each respective brake caliper, and acts to press the brake pads and shoes against the rotating discs and drums. The resulting friction converts the rotational energy to thermal energy, stopping the vehicle.

TROUBLESHOOTING

Refer to **Fig. 1** for general troubleshooting of the brake system.

COMPONENT REPLACEMENT

MASTER CYLINDER

Except Sienna

1. Remove brake fluid with syringe.
2. **On RAV4 models,** remove air cleaner cover with air cleaner hose.
3. **On all models,** label and disconnect brake lines using line wrench 09751-36011, 09023-00100, or equivalent. Then cap brake lines from master cylinder.
4. Disconnect wire connector from brake pressure switch and then disconnect level warning switch connector, if equipped.
5. Remove master cylinder to brake unit attaching nuts, then remove master cylinder, wire clamp, gasket and 3-way union, as needed.
6. Reverse procedure to install. Bleed brake system.

Sienna

1. Remove air cleaner assembly.
2. Disconnect level warning switch connector.
3. Remove fluid from reservoir using a suitable syringe.
4. Remove reservoir tank with bracket, **Fig. 2.**
5. Using brake line wrench tool No.

09023-00100 or equivalent, disconnect brake lines from master cylinder and label for installation reference.
6. Remove master cylinder attaching bolts, then the master cylinder with gasket.
7. Reverse procedure to install. Bleed brake system.

WHEEL CYLINDERS

1. Remove brake shoes as outlined under "Drum Brakes."
2. Disconnect brake line using line wrench 09751-36011, or equivalent. Then remove two wheel cylinder attaching bolts and wheel cylinder.
3. Reverse procedure to install. Tighten to specifications and bleed brakes.

PROPORTIONING VALVE

EXCEPT LAND CRUISER, & 4RUNNER

Models w/Load Sensing Proportioning Valve (LSPV)

1. Disconnect brake lines using line wrench 09751-36011, or equivalent.
2. Remove proportioning valve adjusting nut, then the spring from rear suspension arm.
3. Remove bolts and proportioning valve from mounting assembly.
4. Reverse procedure to install. Bleed brakes.

Models w/Proportioning & Bypass Valve (P-BV)

The proportioning valve is located next to the master cylinder. Remove brake lines with line wrench 09751-36011, or equivalent. Then remove attaching bolts and valve. Reverse necessary steps to install, then bleed system.

LAND CRUISER, & 4RUNNER

1. Disconnect shackle No. 2 from bracket.
2. Disconnect brake lines using line wrench 09751-36011, or equivalent.
3. Remove mounting bolts and valve.
4. Reverse procedure to install. Bleed system.

Symptom	CAUSE
Low pedal or spongy pedal	1. Fluid leaks for brake system 2. Air in brake system 3. Piston seals (Worn or damaged) 4. Rear brake shoe clearance (Out of adjustment) 5. Master cylinder (Faulty) 6. Booster push rod (Out of adjustment)
Brake drag	1. Brake pedal freeplay (Minimal) 2. Parking brake lever travel (Out of adjustment) 3. Parking brake wire (Sticking) 4. Rear brake shoe clearance (Out of adjustment) 5. Pad or lining (Cracked or distorted) 6. Piston (Stuck) 7. Piston (Frozen) 8. Anchor or return spring (Faulty) 9. Booster push rod (Out of adjustment) 10. Vacuum leaks for booster system 11. Master cylinder (Faulty)
Brake pull	1. Piston (Stuck) 2. Pad or lining (Oily) 3. Piston (Frozen) 4. Disc (Scored) 5. Pad or lining (Cracked or distorted)
Hard pedal but brake inefficient	1. Fluid leaks for brake system 2. Air in brake system 3. Pad or lining (Worn) 4. Pad or lining (Cracked or distorted) 5. Rear brake shoe clearance (Out of adjustment) 6. Pad or lining (Oily) 7. Pad or lining (Glazed) 8. Disc (Scored) 9. Booster push rod (Out of adjustment) 10. Vacuum leaks for booster system
Noise from brakes	1. Pad or lining (Cracked or distorted) 2. Installation bolt (Loose) 3. Disc (Scored) 4. Pad support plate (Loose) 5. Sliding pin (Worn) 6. Pad or lining (Dirty) 7. Pad or lining (Glazed) 8. Anchor or return spring (Faulty) 9. Anti–squeal shim (Damaged) 10. Shoe hold–down spring (Damaged)

TY4099500006000X

Fig. 1 Troubleshooting chart

COMPONENT SERVICE

MASTER CYLINDER

EXCEPT SIENNA

Disassemble

For the following procedures, refer to **Fig. 3** for assistance.

1. Remove master cylinder boot.
2. Remove setscrew and then reservoir tank. Remove cap and strainer from reservoir.
3. Remove two grommets. Then place cylinder in vise.
4. Push piston in and remove stopper bolt, **Fig. 4**.
5. Push pistons in and remove snap ring.

Then carefully remove No. 1 piston by hand.
6. Place cylinder on edges of two wooden blocks and tap on cylinder until No. 2 piston comes out.

Inspection

Clean parts with compressed air. Inspect cylinder bore for rust and scoring. Also, inspect for wear or damage to bore. If necessary, replace. Refer to **Fig. 5** for master cylinder lubrication locations.

Assemble

1. Install two grommets.
2. Install reservoir, while pushing down on reservoir, install setscrew. **Torque** setscrew to 15.2 inch lbs.
3. Install master cylinder boot, then the master cylinder as previously described.

SIENNA

Overhaul

Refer to **Fig. 2** when servicing master cylinder.
1. Remove reservoir from bracket.
2. Disconnect two reservoir hoses from reservoir.
3. Remove cap and strainer from reservoir.
4. Disconnect two reservoir hoses from master cylinder.
5. Remove screw and pull out inlet union.
6. Remove two grommets, then place cylinder in a suitable vise.
7. Using a suitable screwdriver, push pistons in fully and remove piston stopper bolt and gasket.
8. Push in piston with screwdriver and remove snap ring using suitable pair of snap ring pliers.
9. Remove No. 1 piston and spring by pulling straight out. **If removed at an angle, cylinder bore may become damaged.**
10. Place a shop towel and two wooden blocks an work table and tap cylinder flange against block edges until remaining piston is removed.
11. Reverse procedure to assemble. Apply lithium soap base glycol grease to rubber parts indicated by arrows, **Fig. 2.**

Inspection

1. Clean disassembled parts using compressed air.
2. Inspect cylinder bore for rust or scoring.
3. Replace or clean cylinder as necessary.
4. Inspect cylinder for wear or damage and replace as necessary.

WHEEL CYLINDERS

Refer to **Fig. 6** for disassembled view of a typical wheel cylinder.
1. Remove boots, pistons, piston cups and spring from wheel cylinder.
2. Clean all parts using suitable brake cleaner. Inspect cylinder bore for rust, scoring or wear. If necessary, replace cylinder.

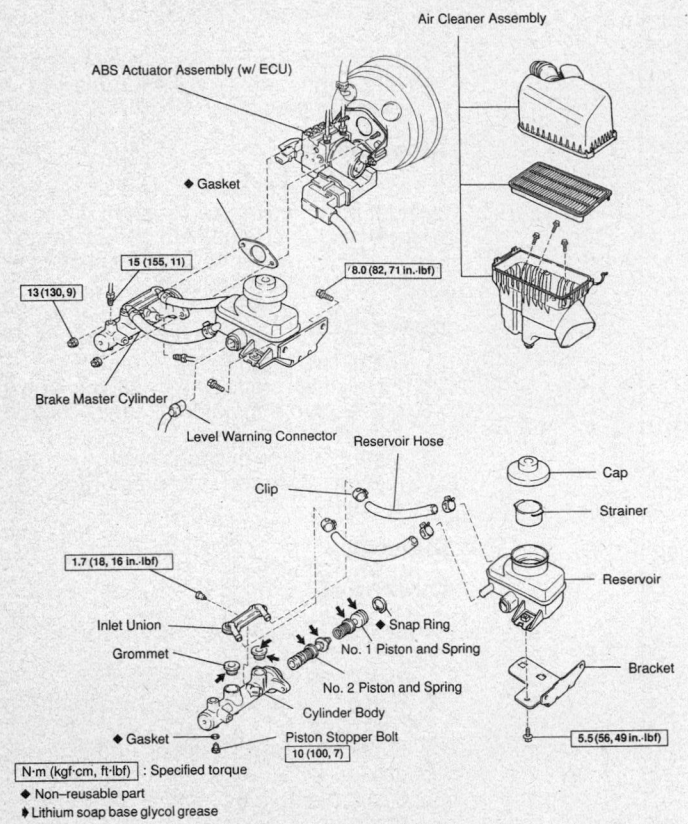

Fig. 2   Master cylinder removal. Sienna

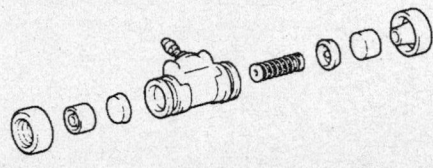

Fig. 3   Exploded view of typical master cylinder. Except Sienna

Fig. 6   Exploded view of wheel cylinder. Typical

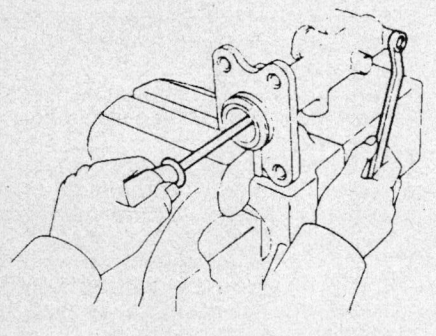

Fig. 4   Piston stopper bolt removal

3. Apply suitable grease to all rubber parts and mating surfaces.
4. Install piston cups to pistons. Then install spring and pistons into wheel cyl-

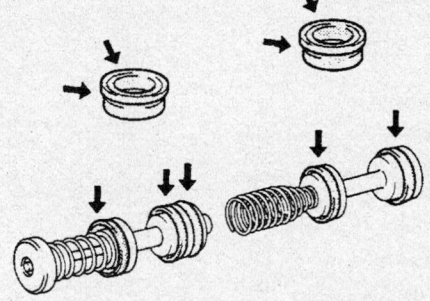

Fig. 5   Typical master cylinder lubrication locations

inder. **Ensure flanges of cups are pointed upward.** Install boots.

BRAKE SYSTEM BLEED

MASTER CYLINDER

1. Fill reservoir with fluid.
2. Disconnect tubes from master cylinder. Then slowly depress brake pedal and hold.
3. Block off outlet holes with fingers, and release pedal. Repeat three or four times.

BRAKE LINES

Bleed wheel with longest brake line first, then work your way back to the master cylinder according to brake line length.
1. Connect tube to brake cylinder.
2. Depress pedal several times and hold. Loosen bleeder plug.
3. When fluid stops coming out, tighten bleeder plug and release pedal. Repeat several times.
4. Repeat entire procedure for each wheel. Fill reservoir.

TIGHTENING SPECIFICATIONS

Year	Component	Torque/ Ft. Lbs.
1996–2000	Brake Line To Master Cylinder Union Nuts	11
	Master Cylinder Bolts	108①
	Piston Stopper Bolt	72-84①
	Reservoir Set Screw	13–15.5①
	Wheel Cylinder Bolts	②

① — Inch Lbs.
② — Except Sienna, 7 ft. lbs; Sienna, 11 ft. lbs.

Power Brake Units

NOTE: On Air Bag Equipped Models, Refer To "Air Bag System Precautions" Located In The Front Of This Manual For System Disarming & Arming Procedures.

INDEX

PRECAUTIONS

AIR BAG SYSTEMS

Refer to "Air Bag System Precautions" in the front of this manual for system disarming & arming procedures.

BATTERY GROUND CABLE

Prior to service, disconnect battery ground cable and isolate as required.

AUDIO CODED ANTI-THEFT SYSTEM

Some models are equipped with an audio coded anti-theft system that will disable the radio when the battery cable is disconnected. The system can be identified by the "ANTI-THEFT SYSTEM" on the cassette tape lid. Obtain 3 digit customer code for input. Reset system after service as follows:

1. Obtain 3 digit audio anti-theft code.
2. Depress 1 (PROG) while depressing righthand side of TUNE SEEK button, - - - will appear in tape operation display.
3. To enter the first digit, depress 1 (PROG) button repeatedly until the number of times depressed equals the first digit beginning with zero (depress the 1 button six times if the first digit if five).
4. To enter second digit, depress 2 (APS) button repeatedly until the number of times depressed equals the second digit beginning with zero.
5. To enter third digit, depress 3 (RPT) button repeatedly until the number of times depressed equals the third digit beginning with zero.
6. If - - - is displayed during code input, repeat procedure.
7. When code appears in display, depress and hold SCAN button until SEC appears.
8. When SEC disappears audio system should be operative.
9. If Err is displayed, repeat procedure. **Attempting to input code more than nine times may permanently disable audio system.**

DESCRIPTION

When the brake pedal is depressed, a vacuum builds up in the booster which amplifies the pedal force, pressing on the piston in the master cylinder. The piston raises the hydraulic pressure in the cylinder. This hydraulic pressure is then applied to each respective brake cylinder, and acts to press the brake pads against the rotating rotor discs. the resulting friction converts the rotational energy to thermal energy, stopping the vehicle.

TROUBLESHOOTING

Refer to "Hydraulic Brake Systems" for general brake system troubleshooting charts.

DIAGNOSIS & TESTING

BRAKE BOOSTER OPERATIONAL TEST

Operating Check

1. Depress brake pedal several times with engine stopped, and ensure pedal reserve distance has no change, **Fig. 1.**
2. Depress brake pedal and start engine. If pedal drops slightly, operation is normal.

Air Tightness Check

1. Start engine and stop after one or two minutes.
2. Depress brake pedal several times slowly. If pedal drops the most on the first time, but gradually rises after the second or third time, booster is air tight, **Fig. 2.**
3. Depress brake pedal with engine running, then while depressing brake pedal stop engine. If there is no change in pedal reserve travel after holding pedal for 30 seconds, the booster is air tight.

ADJUSTMENTS

BRAKE PEDAL HEIGHT & FREEPLAY

Refer to **Fig. 3** for pedal height and freeplay references.

1. Loosen stop light switch, then the clevis locknut.
2. Adjust pedal height by turning pushrod.
3. Tighten locknut and adjust stop light switch .02–.09 inch from pedal stopper.
4. Depress pedal several times to relieve vacuum.
5. Push pedal until beginning of resistance is felt. Adjust freeplay by turning pushrod, if necessary.

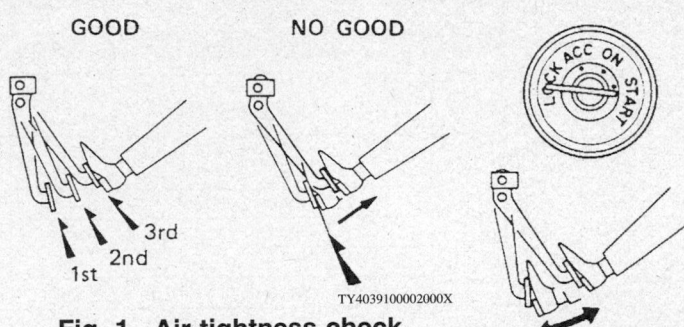

Fig. 1 Air tightness check

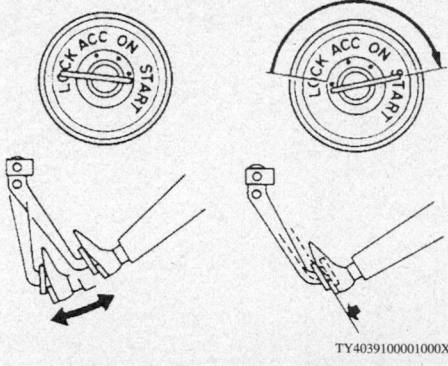

Fig. 2 Operational test

POWER BRAKE UNIT SERVICE

BRAKE BOOSTER, REPLACE
EXCEPT TUNDRA & SIENNA
Removal

1. Remove master cylinder as outlined under "Master Cylinder, Replace" in the "Hydraulic Brake Systems" section.
2. Remove charcoal vapor canister as necessary.
3. Remove brake booster vacuum hose.
4. **On 1997–98 Supra models,** remove pedal bracket stay.
5. **On 1996 Supra models,** remove cruise actuator.
6. **On 1996 Supra and Celica models,** remove lower finish panel or lower pad as outlined in "Dash Panel Service."
7. **On all models,** remove pedal return spring, clip, clevis pin and clevis locknut, **Fig. 4.**
8. **On 1996 Celica models,** proceed as follows:
   a. Remove ignition coil and igniter.
   b. Using a suitable wrench and service tool No. 09751-36011, or equivalent, disconnect brake line from lefthand front brake hose, then remove brake line grommet from wheelhouse.
9. **On all models,** remove brake booster nuts. Pull out booster and gasket.

Installation

1. Adjust length of booster pushrod as follows:
   a. Install gasket on master cylinder.
   b. Install brake booster pushrod gauge tool No. 09737-00010, or equivalent, on gasket.
   c. Lower pin until its tip slightly touches the piston.
   d. Turn gauge tool upside down and set it on booster.
   e. Measure clearance between booster pushrod and pin head of gauge tool.
   f. Adjust booster pushrod length until the pushrod slightly touches the pin head.
2. Install booster and gasket.
3. Install clevis to operating rod.
4. Install clevis pin into clevis and brake pedal then install clip to clevis pin.
5. **On Celica models,** connect vacuum hose to brake booster.
6. Install lower finish panel and undercover.

Model	Year	Pedal Height, Inch	Pedal Freeplay, Inch
Avalon	1996	5.81–6.20	.04–.24
	1997–99	5.98–6.37	.04–.24
Camry	1996	5.81–6.20	.04–.24
	1997–99	5.98–6.37	.04–.24
Camry Solara	1999	5.98–6.37	.04–.24
Celica	1996	5.98–6.37	.02–.09
	1997–99	5.35–5.75	.04–.24
Corolla	1996–97	5.65–6.05	.04–.24
	1998–99	5.85–6.24	.04–.24
Land Cruiser	1996–99	6.59–6.99	.12–.24
Paseo	1996–97	5.45–5.85	.04–.24
Previa	1996	5.71–6.10	.04–.24
	1997	5.76–6.16	.04–.24
RAV4	1996-99	6.19–6.58	.04–.24
Sienna	1998–99	6.28–6.67	.04–.24
Supra	1996	5.92–6.31	.04–.24
	1997–98	6.07–6.46	.04–.24
Tacoma	1996	6.34–6.74	.12–.24
	1997–99	6.26–6.65	.12–.24
Tercel (Base Model)	1996–98	5.63–6.02	.04–.24
Tercel (Except Base Model)	1996–98	5.51–5.91	.04–.24
Tundra	2000	6.46–6.85	.04–.24
T100 Std.	1996	6.06	.12–.24
T100 SR5	1996	5.91	.12–.24
T100 Extra Cab 4WD	1997–98	5.77–6.16	.12–.24
T100 Except Extra Cab 4WD	1997–98	5.89–6.28	.12–.24
4Runner	1996	6.22–6.62	.12–.24
	1997–99	6.34–6.73	.12–.24

Fig. 3 Brake pedal height & freeplay chart

7. **On Supra models,** install cruise actuator.
8. **On all models,** install master cylinder, fill and bleed brake system as outlined under "Hydraulic Brake System."
9. Check and adjust pedal height and freeplay.
10. Ensure brake system is operating correctly.

TUNDRA
Removal

1. Remove master cylinder as outlined under "Master Cylinder, Replace" in the "Hydraulic Brake Systems" section.
2. Disconnect vacuum hose from booster.
3. Remove scuff plate and cowl trim from left side of vehicle.
4. Remove lefthand lower finish panel, then the No. 2 heater to register duct.
5. Remove pedal return spring.
6. Remove clip and clevis pin.
7. Remove four nuts, then the clevis.
8. Pull out brake booster and gasket.
9. Remove stopper rings, brake booster bracket and gasket from booster.

Installation

1. Install new gasket to brake booster.
2. Install brake booster bracket and 2 stopper rings to brake booster.

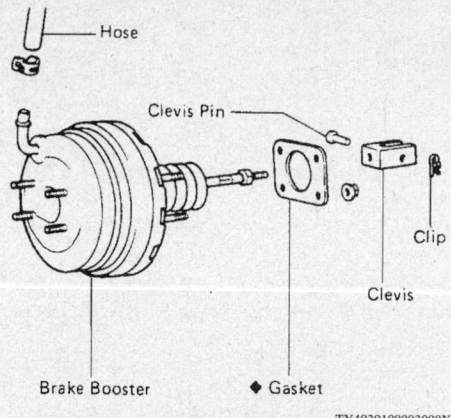

Fig. 4 Brake booster pushrod connections. Typical

3. Install booster with gasket.
4. Install clevis pin to operating rod.
5. **Torque** booster attaching nuts to 9 ft. lbs.
6. Attach clevis pin to clevis and brake pedal.
7. Connect vacuum hose to brake booster.
8. Install No. 2 heater to register duct, finish panel, cowl trim and scuff plate.
9. Adjust length of booster push rod as follows:
   a. Install brake booster push rod gauge tool No. 09737-00011 or equivalent on master cylinder and lower pin until tip slightly touches piston.
   b. Turn push rod gauge upside down and place on booster.
   c. Measure clearance between booster pushrod and pin head. Clearance should be 0.
   d. Using booster push rod wrench tool No. 09737-00020 or equivalent, adjust booster push rod length until rod lightly touches pin head.
10. Install master cylinder as outlined under "Master Cylinder, Replace" in the "Hydraulic Brake Systems" section.
11. Inspect system for fluid leaks.
12. Adjust brake pedal as outlined under "Adjustments."
13. Ensure proper booster operation.

SIENNA

Removal

1. Remove two cowl top ventilator louvers and outer front cowl top panel, **Fig. 5.**
2. Remove master cylinder as outlined under "Hydraulic Brake Systems."
3. Remove ABS actuator assembly as outlined under "Anti-Lock Brakes."
4. Disconnect vacuum hose from brake booster.

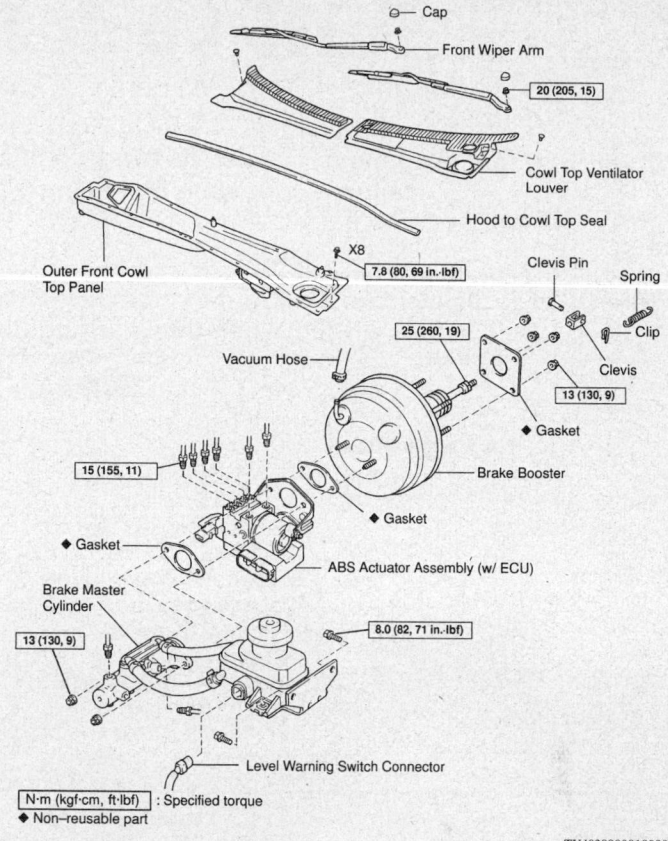

Fig. 5 Brake booster removal. Sienna

5. Remove lower finish panel and No. 1 safety pad insert.
6. Remove cruise control ECU, then the pedal return spring, clip and clevis pin.
7. Remove four brake booster attaching nuts and clevis, then pull out booster with gasket.

Installation

1. Install brake booster with new gasket.
2. Install clevis to operating rod.
3. **Torque** booster attaching nuts to 9 ft. lbs.
4. Insert clevis pin to clevis and brake pedal, then install clevis clip to pin.
5. Install pedal return spring, then the cruise control ECU.
6. Adjust length of booster push rod as follows:
   a. Install gasket on master cylinder.
   b. Place brake booster push rod gauge tool No. 09737-00010 or equivalent on gasket and lower pin until tip slightly touches piston.
   c. Set gasket and ABS actuator bracket on booster and tighten two bracket nuts.
   d. Turn push rod gauge tool upside down and place on booster.
   e. Measure clearance between booster pushrod and pin head. Adjust clearance to .014 inch.
   f. Adjust booster pushrod until push rod slightly touches pin head.
7. Install ABS actuator as outlined under "Anti-Lock Brakes."
8. Install master cylinder as outlined under "Hydraulic Brake Systems."
9. Connect vacuum hose to booster.
10. Install outer front cowl top panel and two cowl top ventilator louvers.
11. Fill brake reservoir with brake fluid and bleed system as outlined under "Hydraulic Brake Systems."
12. Inspect brake system for leaks, then check and adjust brake pedal as outlined under "Power Brake Units."

BRAKE BOOSTER OVERHAUL

The brake booster on these models cannot be overhauled and must be replaced as a complete unit.

Anti-Lock Brakes

NOTE: On Air Bag Equipped Models, Refer To "Air Bag System Precautions" Located In The Front Of This Manual For System Disarming & Arming Procedures.

NOTE: Wire Color Code Identification And Symbol Identification Located In The Front Of This Manual May Be Used As An Aid When Using Wiring Circuits Found In This Section.

INDEX

PRECAUTIONS

AIR BAG SYSTEMS

Refer to "Air Bag System Precautions" in the front of this manual for system disarming and arming procedures.

AUDIO CODED ANTI-THEFT SYSTEM

Some models are equipped with an audio coded anti-theft system that will disable the radio when the battery cable is disconnected. The system can be identified by the "ANTI-THEFT SYSTEM" on the cassette lid. Obtain 3 digit code for input. Reset system after service as follows:

1. Obtain 3 digit audio theft code.
2. Depress 1 (PROG) while depressing righthand side of TUNE SEEK button, - - - will appear in tape operation display.
3. To enter the first digit, depress 1 (PROG) button repeatedly until the number of times depressed equals the first digit (depress the 1 button six times if the first digit if five, first press equals 0).
4. To enter second digit, depress 2 (APS) button repeatedly until the number of times depressed equals the second digit.
5. To enter third digit, depress 3 (RPT) button repeatedly until the number of times depressed equals the third digit.
6. If - - - is displayed after inputting digits, repeat procedure.
7. When code appears in display, depress and hold SCAN button until SEC appears.
8. When SEC disappears audio system is operative.

9. If Err is displayed, repeat procedure. **Attempting to input code more than 9 times may permanently disable audio system.**

BATTERY GROUND CABLE

Prior to service, disconnect battery ground cable and isolate as required.

DESCRIPTION

ANTI-LOCK BRAKE SYSTEM

By use of a micro-computer, this anti-lock brake system controls brake fluid pressure to prevent wheel lock. With this system, directional stability is improved and steerability maintained even at panic braking on wet, sandy, snowy or icy road conditions.

TRACTION CONTROL SYSTEM (TRAC)

The traction control system controls the engine torque and rear wheel braking. It helps avoid wheel slippage and maintain optimal driving force according to road surface conditions.

TROUBLESHOOTING

Refer to **Figs. 1 through 8** for troubleshooting of the anti-lock brake system.

Symptoms	Inspection Circuit
ABS does not operate.	Only when 1. ~ 4. are all normal and the problem is still occurring, replace the ABS ECU. 1. Check the DTC reconfirming that the normal code is output. 2. +BS power source circuit. 3. Speed sensor circuit. 4. Check the hydraulic circuit for leakage.
ABS does not operate efficiently.	Only when 1. ~ 4. are all normal and the problem is still occurring, replace the ABS ECU. 1. Check the DTC reconfirming that the normal code is output. 2. Speed sensor circuit. 3. Stop light switch circuit. 4. Check the hydraulic circuit for leakage.
ABS warning light abnormal.	1. ABS warning light circuit. 2. ABS ECU.
DTC check cannot be done.	Only when 1. and 2. are all normal and the problem is still occurring, replace the ABS ECU. 1. ABS warning light circuit. 2. Tc terminal circuit.
Speed sensor signal check cannot be done.	1. Ts terminal circuit. 2. ABS ECU.

TY4029600190000X

Fig. 1 Troubleshooting. Avalon & Camry w/Bosch ABS, Camry Solara less traction control & Sienna

DIAGNOSIS & TESTING
WIRING DIAGRAMS

Refer to wiring circuits **Figs. 9 through 41** when diagnosing anti-lock brake system.

SELF DIAGNOSTIC SYSTEM

The anti-lock brake system is equipped with a self diagnosis system capable of reading and storing specific diagnostic trouble codes, which may indicate component failure or system malfunction.

DIAGNOSTIC SYSTEM INSPECTION

1. Ensure battery voltage is about 12 volts.
2. Turn ignition switch on.
3. Ensure "ANTI-LOCK" warning light turns On for three seconds. If not, service ABS system.

ACCESSING DIAGNOSTIC TROUBLE CODES
Less Toyota Hand-Held Tester

1. **On Land Cruiser models,** ensure center differential is free.
2. **On all models,** turn ignition switch to On position.
3. Disconnect short pin from data link connector 1 (DLC1).
4. Connect terminals Tc and E1 of DLC1 using tool No. 09843–18020, or equivalent, **Figs. 42 and 43.**
5. Read and record number of times the "ANTI-LOCK" warning light flashes.
6. If the system is operation properly, (no faults) the warning light will blink once every .5 seconds.
7. Connect actuator check connector and ensure proper operation.

With Toyota Hand-Held Tester

1. **On all models except Tundra, 1997–99 Avalon and Camry Solara,** hook up tester and breakout box to vehicle harness.
2. **On 1997–99 Avalon and Camry Solara models,** install Toyota hand held tester to DLC 2.
3. **On Tundra models,** install Toyota hand held tester to DLC 3.
4. **On all models,** read ECU codes and input/output values by following prompts on tester screen.

DIAGNOSTIC TROUBLE CODE INTERPRETATION

Refer to **Figs. 44 through 70,** to diagnosis light pattern and possible trouble area.

CLEARING DIAGNOSTIC TROUBLE CODES

1. Turn ignition switch to On position.
2. Disconnect actuator check connector.
3. Using suitable jumper wire, connect check terminals Tc and E1 of DLC 1.
4. Clear diagnostic trouble codes stored in memory by depressing the brake pedal eight or more times within three seconds.

5. Ensure warning light shows normal code.
6. Connect actuator connector.
7. Ensure warning light goes Off.

CIRCUIT TESTS
Stop Light Switch

Refer to **Figs. 71 through 85** for stop light switch inspection and testing procedure.

ABS Warning Light

Refer to **Figs. 86 through 104,** for ABS warning light inspection and testing procedure.

Traction Control Warning Light

Refer to **Figs. 105 through 111** for traction control lamp inspection and testing procedures.

Tc Terminal

Refer to **Figs. 112 through 127** for Tc terminal inspection and testing procedure.

Ts Terminal

Refer to **Figs. 128 through 143** for Ts inspection and terminal testing procedure.

DIAGNOSTIC TESTS

Refer to **Figs. 144 through 339** for diagnostic testing procedures.

SYSTEM SERVICE
SPEED SENSOR DIAGNOSTIC SYSTEM
EXCEPT LAND CRUISER, PREVIA, TACOMA, TUNDRA, T100 & 4RUNNER

1. Turn ignition switch to OFF.
2. Connect terminals E1 and Ts of data link connector (DLC1).
3. Start engine and ensure ABS warning light blinks.
4. Drive vehicle straight ahead at least 28 mph for several seconds, then stop vehicle.
5. Connect terminals E1 and Tc of DLC1.
6. Read number of blinks of ABS warning light to obtain diagnostic trouble codes, **Figs. 340 and 341.**
7. After performing check, remove DLC1 terminal connections, then turn ignition off.

LAND CRUISER, PREVIA, TACOMA, T100 & 4RUNNER

1. Turn ignition switch on and ensure ABS warning lamp turns on for 3 seconds then turns off.
2. Turn ignition switch off.
3. Connect terminals E1 and Ts of data link connector (DLC1), then start engine.
4. Check that ABS warning light blinks about 4 times every second.
5. Inspect speed sensor signal change by driving vehicle at least 28 mph for several seconds.
6. Check ABS warning light signal. If

warning light signal is abnormal, stop vehicle. Warning light will begin to blink.
7. Read number of blinks of ABS warning light to obtain diagnostic trouble codes, **Fig. 342.**
8. If the system is operating normally, the light will blink once every .5 seconds.
9. After any malfunctioning component has been repaired, clear diagnostic trouble codes from ECU, then remove DLC1 terminal connections.

TUNDRA
Less Toyota Hand Held Tester

1. Turn ignition switch off.
2. Using jumper wire tool No. 09843–18020 or equivalent, connect terminals Ts and E1 of DLC 1, **Fig. 343.**
3. Start engine and ensure ABS warning lamp blinks.
4. Drive vehicle in forward direction faster than 28 mph for several seconds.
5. Stop vehicle and connect terminals Tc and E1 of DLC 1.
6. Read number of blinks from ABS warning lamp.
7. If all sensors are normal, a normal code is output (cycle of .25 seconds on, .25 seconds off) is repeated.
8. If 2 or more faults are present, lowest number code will be displayed first, **Fig. 344.**
9. After completing check, remove jumper wires from DLC 1 and turn ignition switch off.

With Toyota Hand Held Tester

1. Install Toyota hand held tester or equivalent to DLC 3.
2. Start engine and drive vehicle in forward direction faster than 28 mph for several seconds.
3. Stop vehicle and read DTC by following scan tool instructions. Refer to **Fig. 344** for DTC identification.

BRAKE ACTUATOR

1. Ensure battery voltage is approximately 12 volts.
2. Disconnect actuator connectors.
3. **On 1997–99 Avalon models,** connect actuator checker tool Nos. 09990–00150, 09990–00250, 09990–00360 and 09990–00450, or equivalents, to actuator.
4. **On Camry, Celica and 1997–98 Supra with 2JZ-GTE engine,** connect actuator checker tool Nos. 09990–00150, 09990–00250, 09990–00300 and 09990–00360, or equivalents, to actuator.
5. **On Corolla, T100, 1997 Paseo, 4Runner, Previa, RAV4, 1997–98 Supra with 2JZ-GE engine and Tercel models,** connect actuator checker tool Nos. 09990–00150, 09990–00200 and 09990–00300, or equivalents, to actuator.
6. **On Land Cruiser models,** connect actuator checker tool Nos. 09990–00150, 09990–00200 and 09990–00210, or equivalents, to actuator.
7. **On all models except Camry, Celica, Corolla, Land Cruiser, T100, 1997–**

Symptoms	Inspection Circuit
TRAC does not operate.	Only when inspection circuits for each problem symptom are all normal and the problem is still occurring, replace the ABS & TRAC ECU. 1. Check the DTC, reconfirming that the normal code is output. 2. IG power source circuit. 3. Check the hydraulic circuit for leakage. 4. Speed sensor circuit.
SLIP indicator light abnormal.	SLIP indicator light circuit.
TRAC OFF indicator light abnormal.	Only when inspection circuits for each problem symptom are all normal and the problem is still occurring, replace the ABS & TRAC ECU. 1. TRAC OFF indicator light circuit. 2. TRAC cut switch circuit.
DTC check cannot be done.	Only when inspection circuits for each problem symptom are all normal and the problem is still occurring, replace the ABS & TRAC ECU. 1. TRAC OFF indicator light circuit. 2. Tc terminal circuit.

TY4029700238000X

Fig. 2 Troubleshooting. Avalon w/Traction Control

99 Avalon, 4Runner, Previa, RAV4, Supra, Tercel and Paseo, connect actuator checker, tool Nos. 09990–00150, 09990–00200, 09990–00205 or 09990–00210 or equivalents, to actuator.

8. **On all models,** inspect as follows:
   a. Connect checker to sub-wire harness.
   b. Connect red cable of checker to battery positive terminal and black to negative terminal. Connect black cable of sub-wire harness to battery negative terminal or body ground.
   c. **On Celica, Corolla, Camry with traction control and 1997 Paseo & Previa, 1997–98 Tercel, and 1997–99 Avalon and RAV4 models,** place checker "Sheet A" tool No. 09990–00163, or equivalent, on actuator checker.
   d. **On Camry models less traction control system,** place checker "Sheet P" tool No. 09990–00430, or equivalent, on actuator checker.
   e. **On Tacoma models,** place checker "Sheet L" tool No. 09990–00370, or equivalent, on actuator checker.
   f. **On 1997–99 4Runner and 1997–98 T100 models,** place checker "Sheet M" tool No. 09990–00400, or equivalent, on actuator checker.
   g. **On 1997–98 Supra models with 2JZ-GE engine,** place checker "Sheet O" tool No. 09990–00420, or equivalent, on actuator checker.
   h. **On 1997–98 Supra models with 2JZ-GTE engine,** place checker "Sheet N" tool No. 09990–00410, or equivalent, on actuator checker.
   i. **On 1996 Supra models,** substitute "motor" for "sub-motor," and "solenoid" for "main" switch on actuator when referring to following steps.
   j. **On all models,** start engine and run at idle.
   k. **On models with four wheel ABS,** turn selector switch of actuator checker to "Front RH" position.
   l. **On models with four wheel ABS,** press and hold in "motor" switch for a few seconds, then press brake pedal and hold it for 15 seconds. Press motor switch for a few seconds and ensure brake pedal does not pulsate.
   m. **On models equipped with rear wheel ABS,** turn selector switch to "Rear" position.
   n. **On all models,** depress brake pedal and hold, then press power switch, ensure brake pedal does not go down. **Do not press power switch for more than 10 seconds.** Release power switch, ensure brake pedal goes down, then press motor or sub motor switch, ensuring pedal returns.
   o. Release pedal.
   p. Repeat steps for remaining wheels.
   q. After testing has been completed remove test sheet from actuator checker and sub-wire harness from actuator. Connect actuator and/or control relay connectors.

Symptom	Suspect Area
ABS does not operate.	Only when 1. ~ 4. are all normal and the problem is still occurring, replace the ABS & TRAC ECU. 1. Check the DTC reconfirming that the normal code is output. 2. IG power source circuit. 3. Speed sensor circuit. 4. Check the ABS & TRAC actuator with a checker. If abnormal, check the hydraulic circuit for leakage.
ABS does not operate efficiently.	Only when 1. ~ 4. are all normal and the problem is still occurring, replace the ABS & TRAC ECU. 1. Check the DTC reconfirming that the normal code is output. 2. Speed sensor circuit. 3. Stop light switch circuit. 4. Check the ABS & TRAC actuator with a checker. If abnormal, check the hydraulic circuit for leakage.
ABS warning light abnormal.	1. ABS warning light circuit 2. ABS & TRAC ECU
DTC check cannot be done.	Only when 1. and 2. are all normal and the problem is still occurring, replace the ABS & TRAC ECU. 1. ABS warning light circuit 2. TRAC OFF indicator light circuit 3. Tc terminal circuit
Speed sensor signal check cannot be done.	1. Ts terminal circuit 2. ABS & TRAC ECU
TRAC does not operate.	Only when inspection circuits for each problem symptom are all normal and the problem is still occurring, replace the ABS & TRAC ECU. 1. Check the DTC, reconfirming that the normal code is output. 2. IG power source circuit 3. Check the hydraulic circuit for leakage. 4. Speed sensor circuit.
SLIP indicator light abnormal	SLIP indicator light circuit
TRAC OFF indicator light abnormal.	Only when inspection circuits for each problem symptom are all normal and the problem is still occurring, replace the ABS & TRAC ECU. 1. TRAC OFF indicator light circuit 2. TRAC cut switch circuit

TY4029900601000X

Fig. 3 Troubleshooting. Camry Solara w/traction control

Symptoms	Inspection Circuit
ABS does not operate.	Only when 1. ~ 4. are all normal and the problem is still occuring, replace the ABS ECU. 1. Check the DTC reconfirming that the normal code is output. 2. IG power source circuit. 3. Speed sensor circuit. 4. Check the ABS actuator with a checker. If abnormal, check the hydraulic circuit for leakage.
ABS does not operate efficiently	Only when 1. ~ 4. are all normal and the problem is still occuring, replace the ABS ECU. 1. Check the DTC reconfirming that the normal code is output. 2. Speed sensor circuit. 3. Stop light switch circuit. 4. Check the ABS actuator with a checker. If abnormal, check the hydraulic circuit for leakage.
ABS warning light abnormal.	1. ABS warning light circuit. 2. ABS ECU.
DTC check cannot be done	Only when 1. and 2. are all normal and the problem is still occuring, replace the ABS ECU. 1. ABS warning light circuit. 2. Tc terminal circuit.
Speed sensor signal check cannot be done	1. Ts terminal circuit. 2. ABS ECU.

TY4029600189000X

Fig. 4 Troubleshooting. Celica, Corolla, RAV4, Tacoma, Tundra, Camry w/Nippondenso ABS, Camry w/Traction Control, & 1996–97 Paseo, 4Runner & Tercel

r. Clear diagnostic trouble codes.

ANTI-LOCK BRAKE SYSTEM CIRCUIT CHECK

1. Remove ABS control unit.
2. Using a multimeter with high impedance (10,000 ohms minimum), measure voltage and resistance at each terminal shown in **Figs. 345 through 381,** and body ground.
3. Ensure results are as shown.

Brake System Bleed

MASTER CYLINDER

1. Fill reservoir with fluid.
2. Disconnect tubes from master cylinder. Then slowly depress brake pedal and hold.
3. Block off outlet holes with fingers and release pedal. Repeat three or four times.

BRAKE LINES

Bleed wheel with longest brake line first, then work your way back to the master cylinder according to brake line length.
1. Connect tube to brake cylinder.
2. Depress pedal several times and hold. Loosen bleeder plug.
3. When fluid stops coming out, tighten bleeder plug and release pedal. Repeat several times.
4. Repeat entire procedure for each wheel. Fill reservoir.

Component Replacement

BRAKE ACTUATOR

Except RAV4, Sienna & Tundra

1. Remove brake fluid from actuator using a suitable tool.
2. **On Avalon, Camry and Camry Solara models,** remove right front fender splash shield, then the A/C tube clamp bolt.
3. **On Paseo and Tercel models,** remove right front fender splash shield.
4. **On 1997–98 Supra models,** remove cruise control actuator.

5. **On 1996 4Runner models,** remove battery.
6. **On all models,** disconnect connectors from actuator.
7. Remove brake tubes from actuator using suitable wrench.
8. Remove actuator bracket attaching bolt, then remove actuator and bracket assembly.
9. Remove actuator mounting nuts and actuator.
10. Reverse procedure to install, noting the following:
    a. **On all models, except Paseo and 4Runner, torque** actuator mounting nuts to 48 inch lbs.
    b. **On Paseo models, torque** actuator mounting nuts to 69 inch lbs.
    c. **On 1996 4Runner models, torque** actuator mounting nuts to 9 ft. lbs.
    d. **On Camry, Camry Solara, Celica, Corolla, Land Cruiser, Paseo, Previa, Supra, Tacoma, T100, Tercel and 1997–99 Avalon and 4Runner, torque** actuator bracket to 14 ft. lbs.
    e. **On all models except Camry, Camry Solara, Celica, Corolla, Land Cruiser, Paseo, Previa, Supra, Tacoma, T100, Tercel and 1997–99 Avalon, torque** actuator bracket bolt to 21 ft. lbs.
    f. **On all models, torque** brake lines to 11 ft. lbs.
    g. Fill brake fluid reservoir and bleed brakes.
    h. Check for fluid leakage and proper brake operation.

RAV4

1. Disconnect brake lines from ABS actuator using tool No. 09023-00100, or equivalent.
2. Disconnect power steering fluid reservoir.
3. Remove ABS actuator assembly.
4. Remove ABS actuator from bracket.
5. Remove three holders and cushions.
6. Reverse procedure to install, noting the following:
    a. **Torque** brake lines to 11 ft. lbs.
    b. **Torque** ABS actuator to bracket nuts to 48 inch lbs.
    c. **Torque** actuator assembly retain-

ing bolts to 14 ft. lbs.

Sienna

1. Remove air cleaner.
2. Using brake line wrench tool No. 09023–00100 or equivalent, disconnect brake lines from actuator.
3. Disconnect actuator electrical connector.
4. Remove actuator attaching nuts, then the actuator from bracket.
5. Reverse procedure to install noting the following:
    a. **Torque** brake actuator to 10 ft. lbs.
    b. **Torque** brake lines to 11 ft. lbs.
    c. Bleed brake system.

Tundra

1. Remove brake line cover.
2. Disconnect actuator electrical connector.
3. Using brake line wrench tool No. 09023–00100 or equivalent, disconnect brake lines.
4. Remove actuator attaching nuts, then the actuator from bracket.
5. Reverse procedure to install noting the following:
    a. **Torque** actuator to 14 ft. lbs.
    b. **Torque** brake lines to 11 ft. lbs.
    c. Bleed brake system.

ABS COMPUTER

The ABS computer is integral with the brake actuator on some models. Refer to "Brake Actuator, Replace" for replacement procedures.
1. **On models equipped with CD player,** remove audio power amplifier attaching screws, then remove.
2. **On 4Runner and T100 models,** remove glove box assembly.
3. **On all models,** remove computer cover, as required, then the computer retaining screws.
4. Pull out wire harness from clamp on bracket, then pull out connector from clamp on bracket.
5. Disconnect electrical connectors, then remove computer.
6. Reverse procedure to install.

	Problem	No.
"ABS" warning light	Always comes on after ignition switch is turned ON.	1
	Does not come on for 3 seconds after ignition switch ON.	2
	Goes on and off.	3
	Comes on while running.	1
	Does not light up when the transfer is in L (center differential lock) position.	6
Brake condition	Brakes pull.*	4
	Braking inefficient.*	4
	ABS operates during normal braking.	4
	ABS operates just before stopping during normal braking.	4
	Brake pedal pulsates abnormally while ABS is operating.	4
	Skidding noise occurs while ABS operating. (ABS operates inefficiently)	5
	When the transfer is in L (center differential lock) position, the ABS operates.	6

* Also check the parts of the brake system (brake cylinders, pads, hydraulic lines, etc.) not specifically part of the ABS.

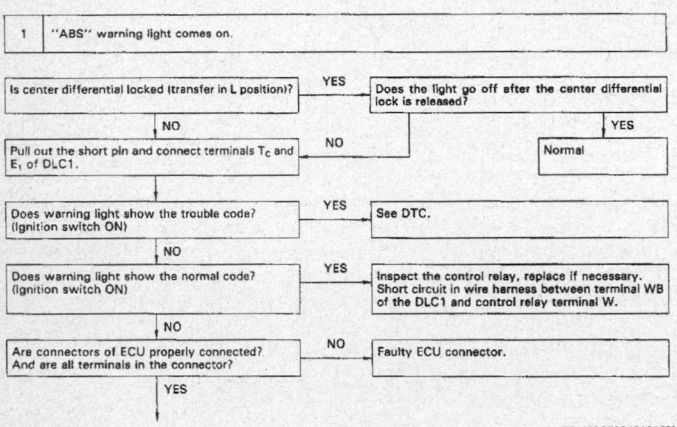

1 "ABS" warning light comes on.

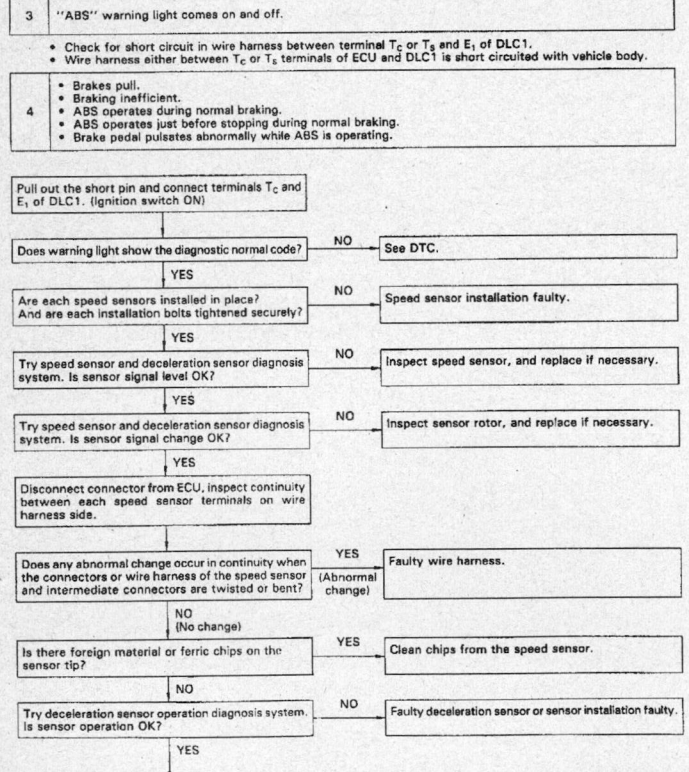

TY4029700401010X

Fig. 5 Troubleshooting (Part 1 of 4). Land Cruiser

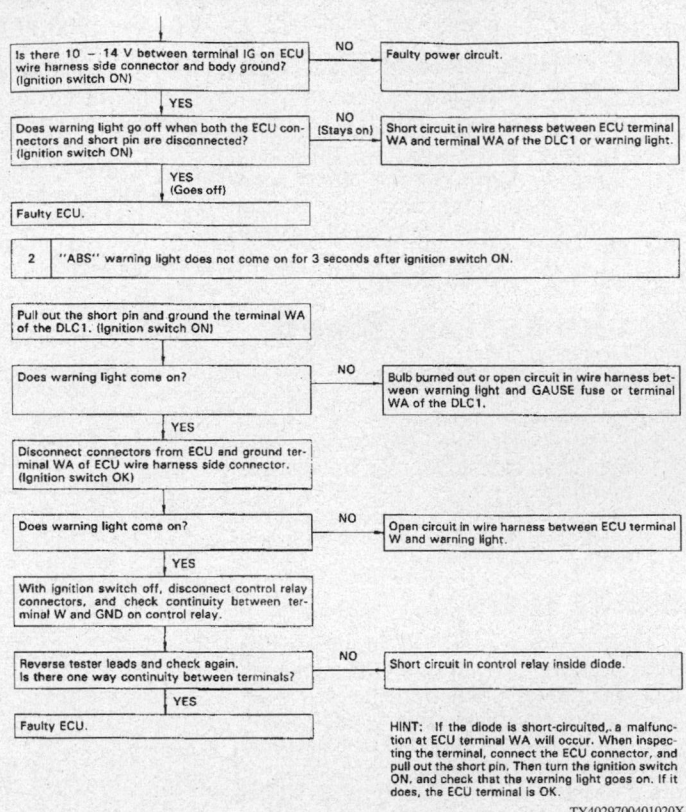

2 "ABS" warning light does not come on for 3 seconds after ignition switch ON.

TY4029700401020X

Fig. 5 Troubleshooting (Part 2 of 4). Land Cruiser

3 "ABS" warning light comes on and off.

- Check for short circuit in wire harness between terminal T_C or T_S and E_1 of DLC1.
- Wire harness either between T_C or T_S terminals of ECU and DLC1 is short circuited with vehicle body.

4
- Brakes pull.
- Braking inefficient.
- ABS operates during normal braking.
- ABS operates just before stopping during normal braking.
- Brake pedal pulsates abnormally while ABS is operating.

TY4029700401030X

Fig. 5 Troubleshooting (Part 3 of 4). Land Cruiser

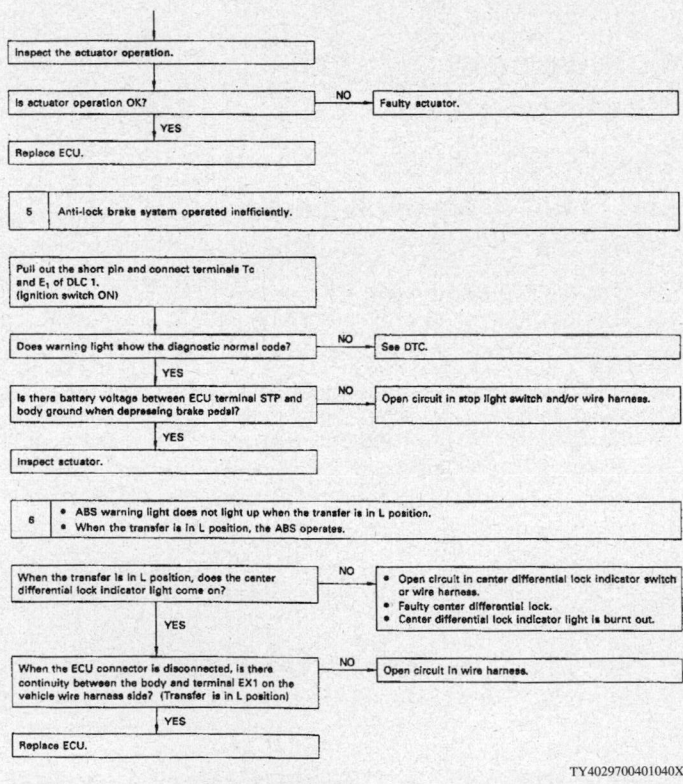

TY4029700401040X

Fig. 5 Troubleshooting (Part 4 of 4). Land Cruiser

ANTI-LOCK BRAKES

Problem		No.
"ABS" warning light	Always comes on after ignition switch is turned on.	1
	Does not come on for 3 seconds after ignition switched on.	2
	Goes on and off.	3
	Comes on while running.	1
Brake condition	Brakes pull. ※	4
	Braking inefficient. ※	4
	ABS operates during normal braking.	4
	ABS operates just before stopping during normal braking.	4
	Brake pedal pulsates abnormally while ABS is operating.	4
	Skidding noise occurs while ABS operating. (ABS operates inefficiently)	5

※ Also check the parts of the brake system (brake cylinders, pads, hydraulic lines, etc.) not specifically part of the ABS.

TY4029400020010X

Fig. 6 Troubleshooting (Part 1 of 5). 1996 Previa

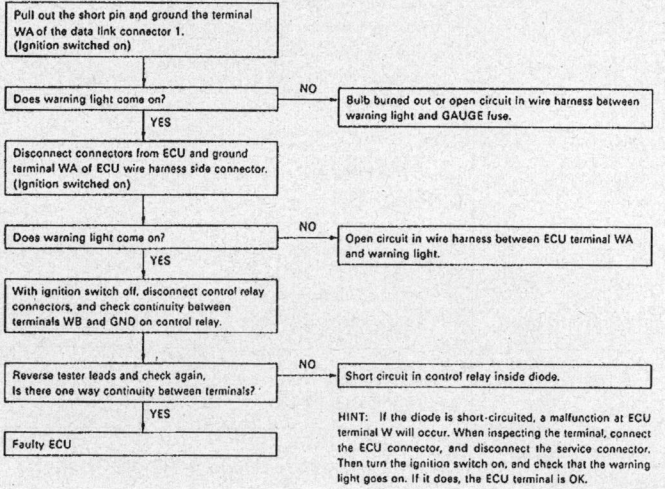

TY4029400020030X

Fig. 6 Troubleshooting (Part 3 of 5). 1996 Previa

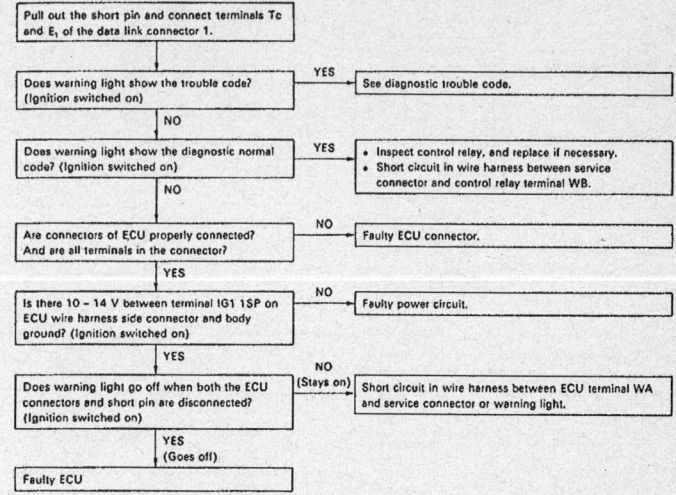

TY4029400020020X

Fig. 6 Troubleshooting (Part 2 of 5). 1996 Previa

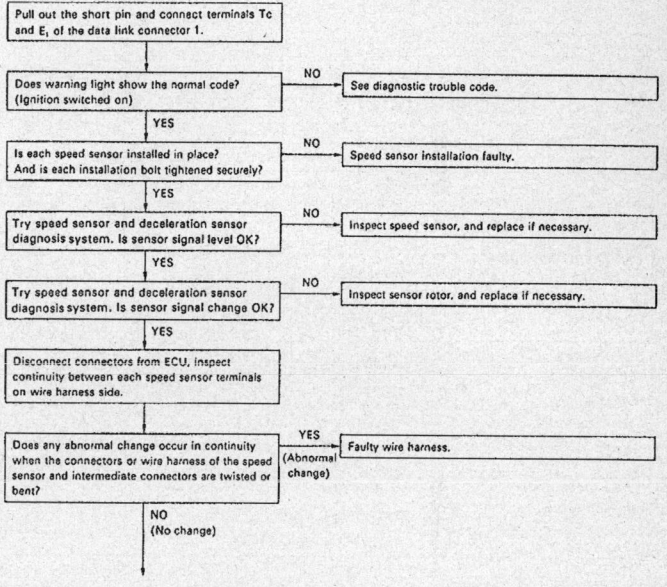

TY4029400020040X

Fig. 6 Troubleshooting (Part 4 of 5). 1996 Previa

TOYOTA UNIT REPAIR

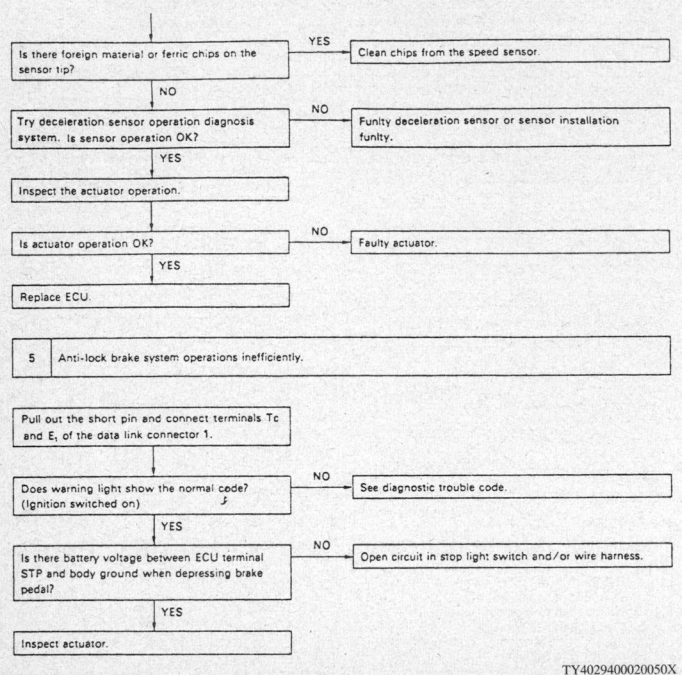

Fig. 6 Troubleshooting (Part 5 of 5). 1996 Previa

Symptoms	Inspection Circuit
TRAC does not operate.	Only when inspection circuits for each problem symptom are all normal and the problem is still occurring, replace the throttle control ECU. 1. Check the DTC, reconfirming that the normal code is output. 2. Power source circuit. 3. Speed sensor circuit.
SLIP indicator light abnormal.	SLIP indicator light circuit.
SNOW indicator light abnormal.	1. SNOW indicator light circuit. 2. SNOW mode switch circuit.
TRAC OFF indicator light abnormal.	Only when inspection circuits for each problem symptom are all normal and the problem is still occurring, replace the throttle control ECU. 1. TRAC OFF indicator light circuit. 2. TRAC OFF switch circuit.
DTC check cannot be done.	Only when inspection circuits for each problem symptom are all normal and the problem is still occurring, replace the throttle control ECU. 1. TRAC OFF indicator light circuit. 2. Tc terminal circuit.

TY4029700411000X

Fig. 7 Troubleshooting (Part 2 of 2). Supra

Symptoms	Inspection Circuit
ABS does not operate.	Only when 1. ~ 4. are all normal and the problem is still occuring, replace the ABS (& TRAC) ECU. 1. Check the DTC, reconfirming that the normal code is output. 2. IG power source circuit. 3. Speed sensor circuit. 4. Check the ABS actuator with a checker. If abnormal, check the hydraulic circuit for leakage.
ABS does not operate efficiently.	Only when 1. ~ 4. are all normal and the problem is still occuring, replace the ABS (& TRAC) ECU. 1. Check the DTC, reconfirming that the normal code is output. 2. Speed sensor circuit. 3. Stop light switch circuit. 4. Check the ABS actuator with a checker. If abnormal, check the hydraulic circuit for leakage.
ABS warning light abnormal.	1. ABS warning light circuit. 2. ABS (& TRAC) ECU.
DTC check cannot be done.	Only when 1. and 2. are all normal and the problem is still occuring, replace the ABS (& TRAC) ECU. 1. ABS warning light circuit. 2. Tc terminal circuit.
Speed sensor signal check cannot be done.	1. Ts terminal circuit. 2. ABS (& TRAC) ECU.

TY4029600188000X

Fig. 7 Troubleshooting (Part 1 of 2). Supra

Problem		No.
"ABS" warning light	Always comes on after ignition switched ON.	1
	Does not come on for 3 seconds after ignition switched ON.	2
	Goes on and off.	3
	Comes on while running.	1
Brake condition	Brakes pull. ※	4
	Braking inefficient. ※	4
	ABS operates during normal braking.	4
	ABS operates just before stopping during normal braking.	4
	Brake pedal pulsates abnormally while ABS is operating.	4
	Skidding noise occurs while ABS operating. (ABS operates inefficiently)	5

※ Also check the parts of the brake system (brake cylinders, pads, hydraulic lines, etc.) not specifically part of the ABS.

TY4029500146010X

Fig. 8 Troubleshooting (Part 1 of 5). T100

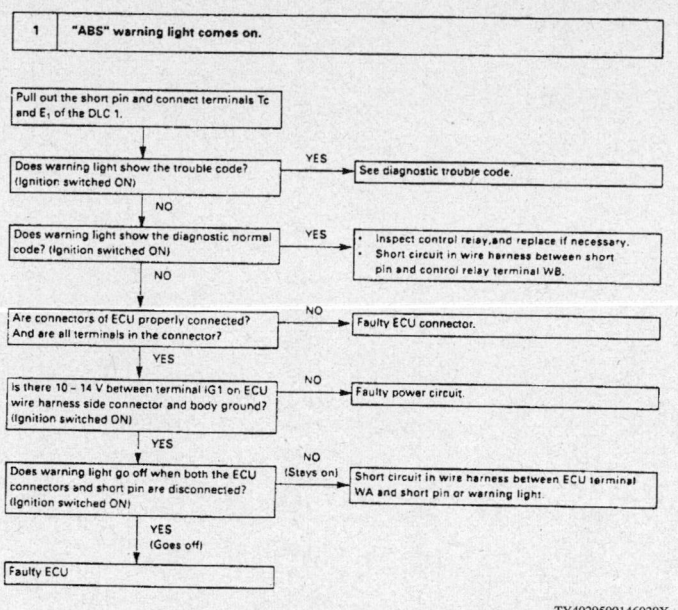

Fig. 8   Troubleshooting (Part 2 of 5). T100

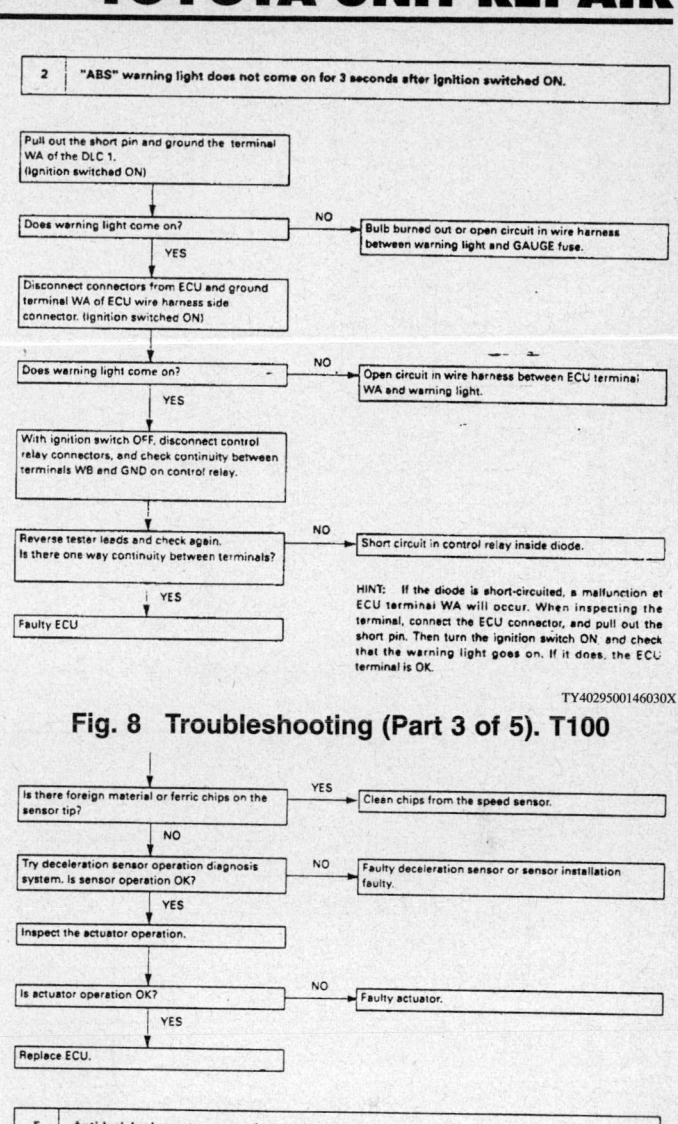

Fig. 8   Troubleshooting (Part 3 of 5). T100

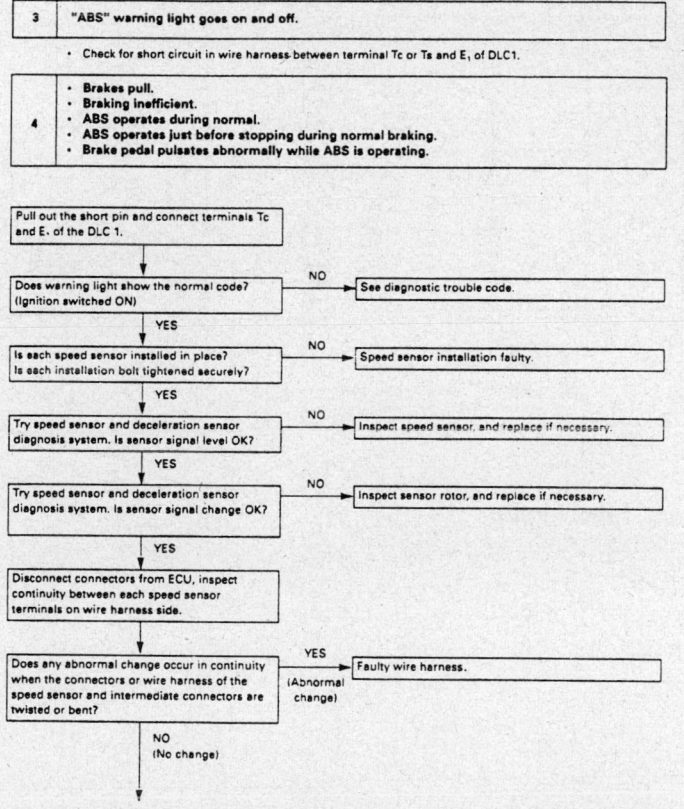

Fig. 8   Troubleshooting (Part 4 of 5). T100

Fig. 8   Troubleshooting (Part 5 of 5). T100

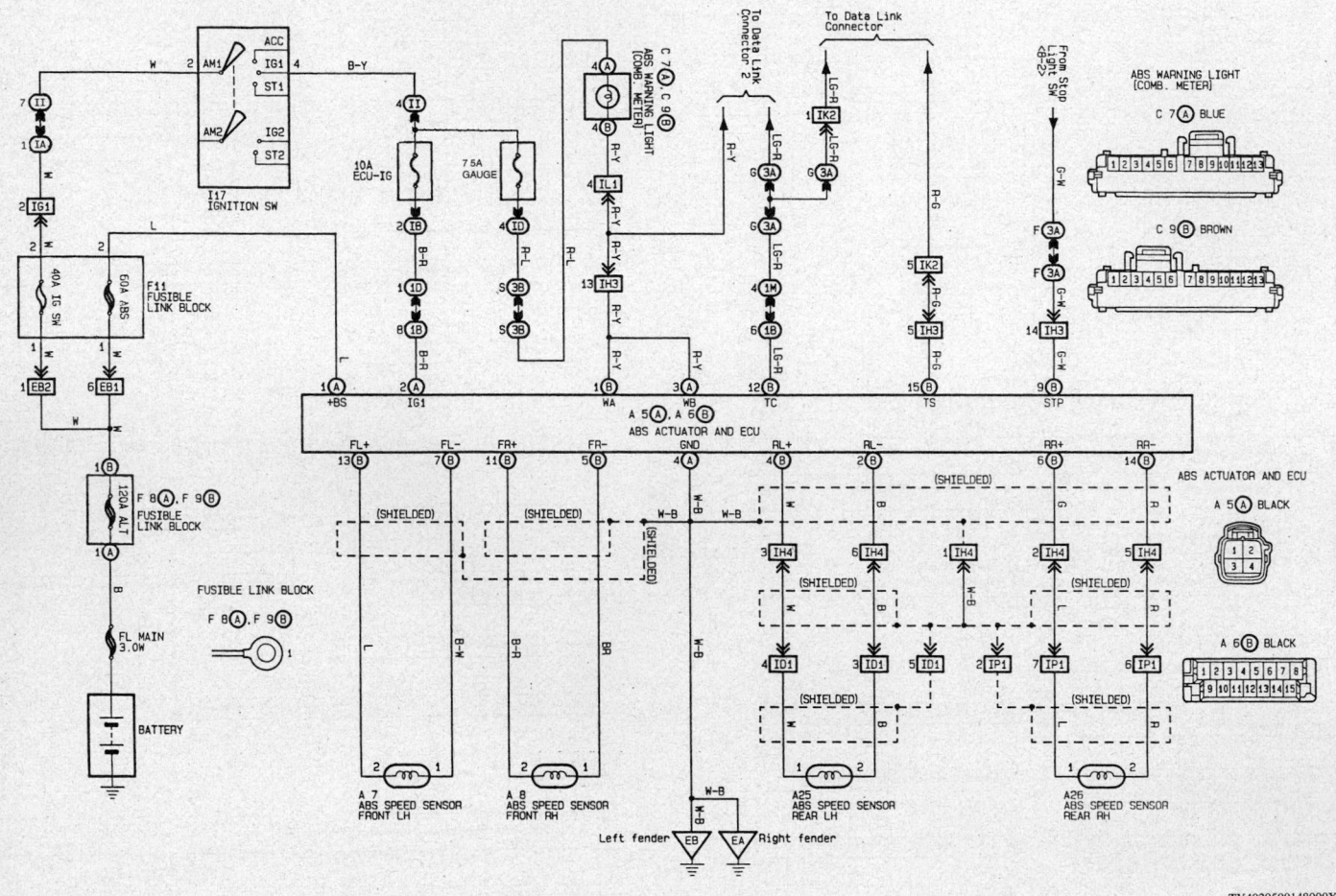

Fig. 9 Wiring diagram. 1996 Avalon

TY4029500148000X

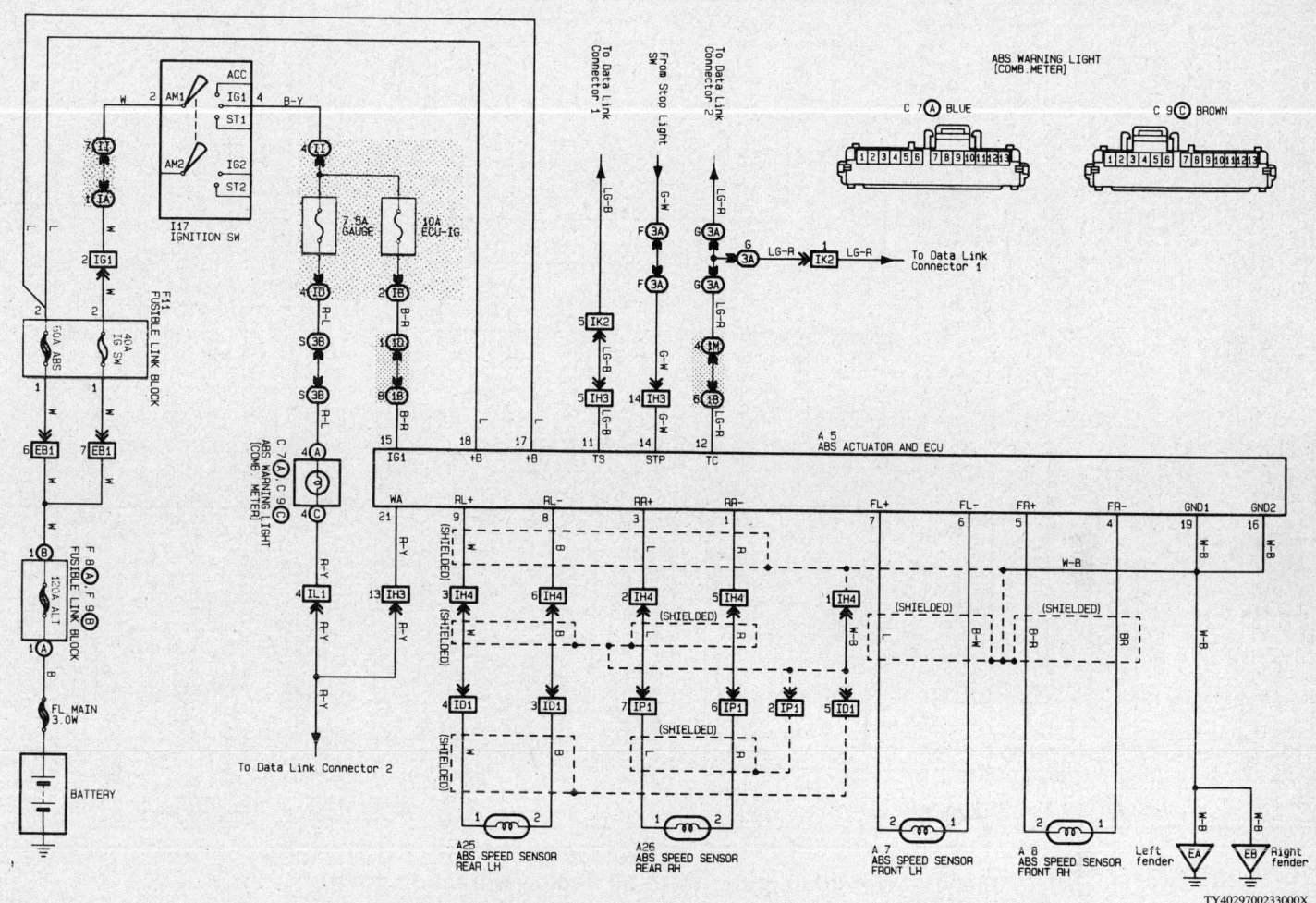

Fig. 10 Wiring diagram. 1997–99 Avalon less traction control

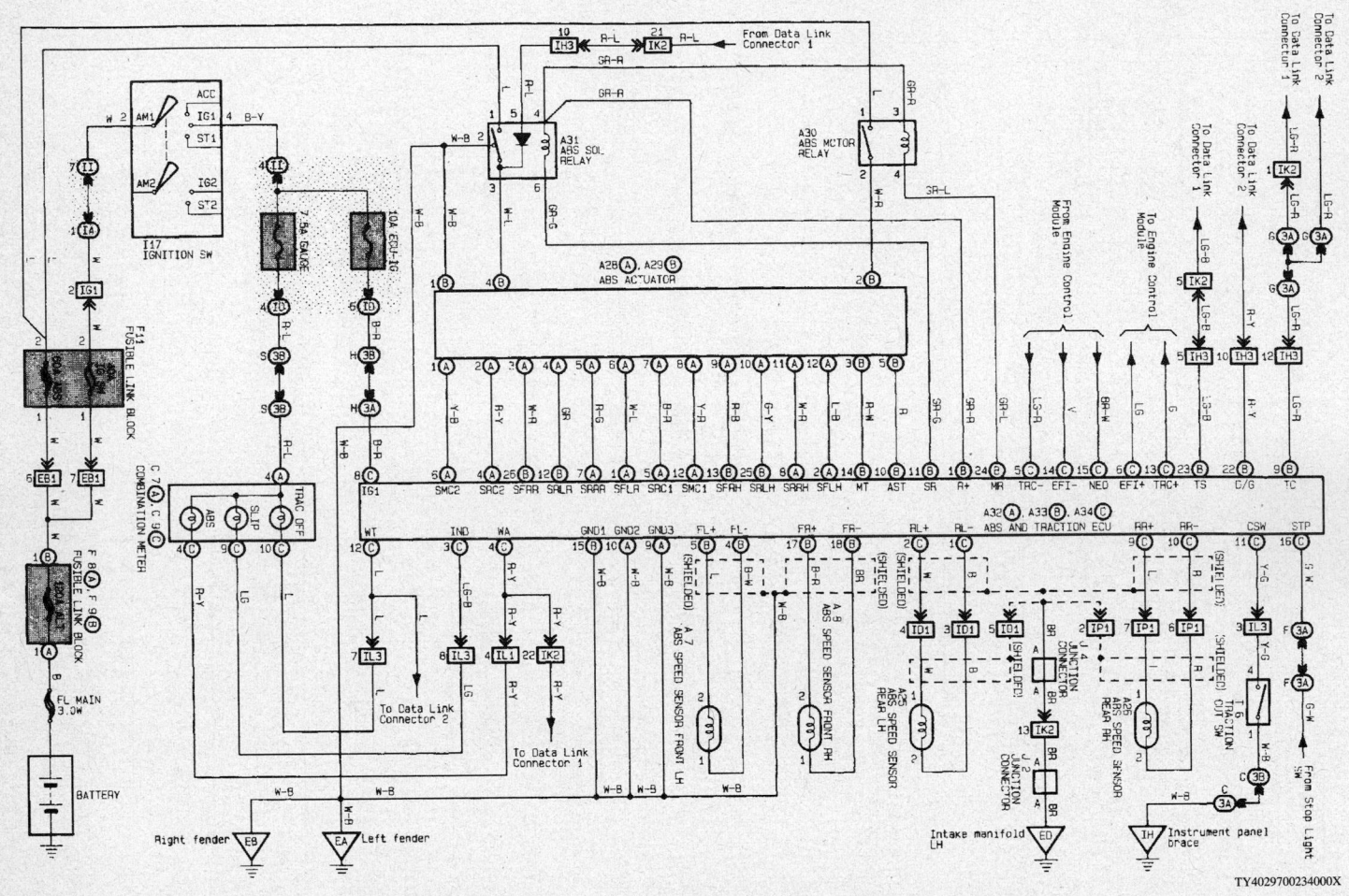

Fig. 11   Wiring diagram. 1997–99 Avalon w/traction control

TY4029700234000X

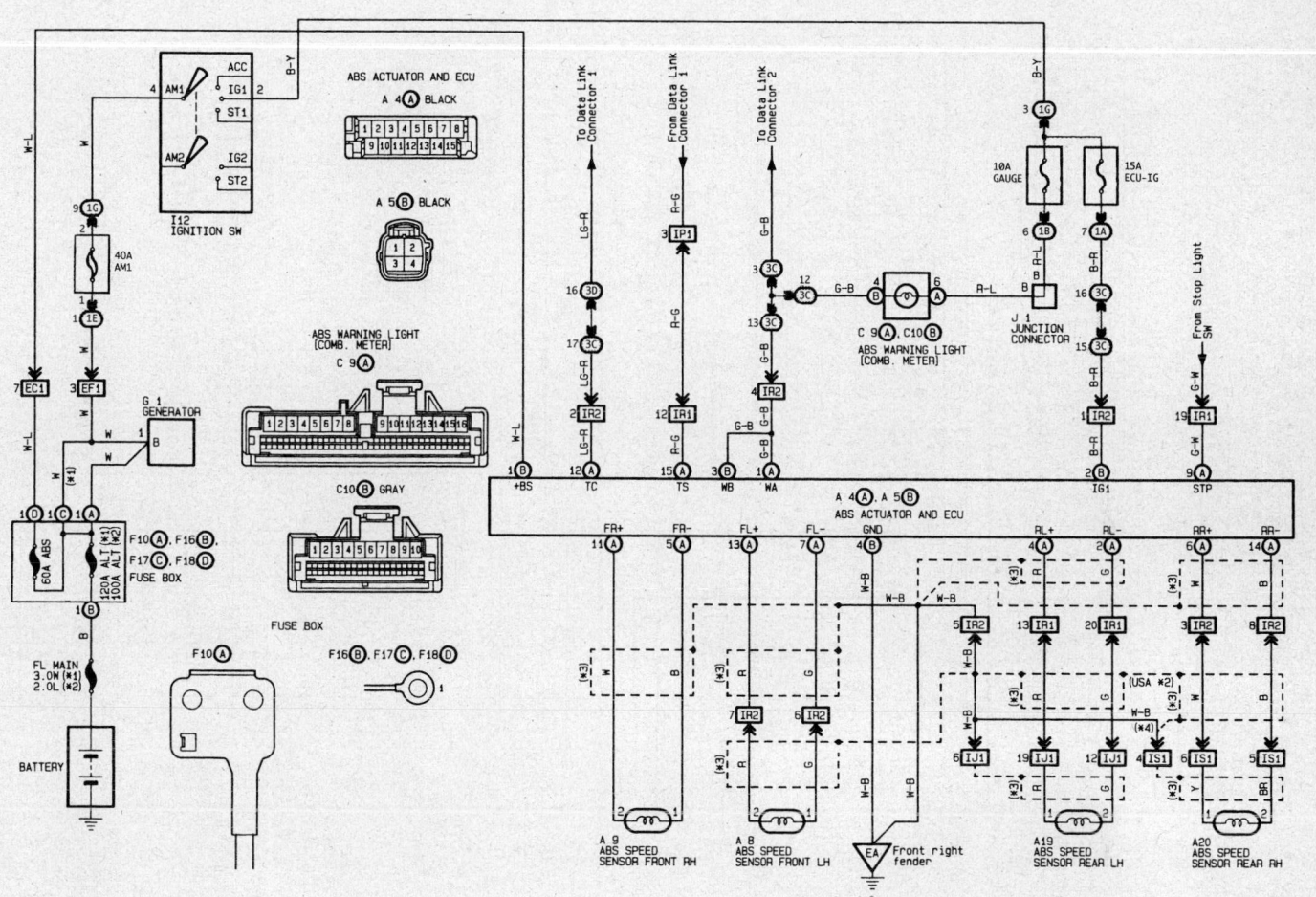

Fig. 12 Wiring diagram. 1996 Camry w/Bosch ABS

TY4029500333000X

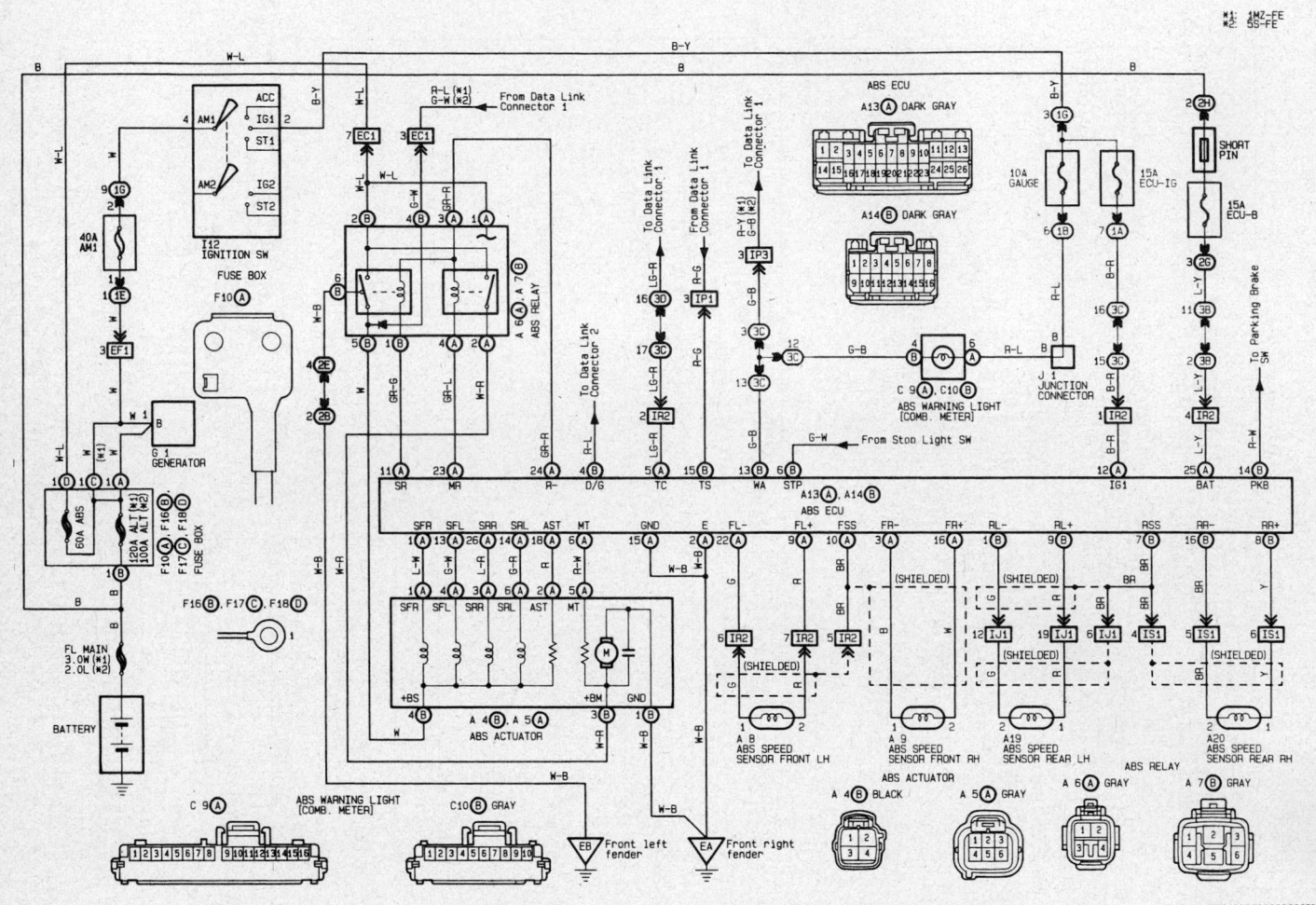

Fig. 13   Wiring diagram. 1996 Camry w/Nippondenso ABS

TY4029500332000X

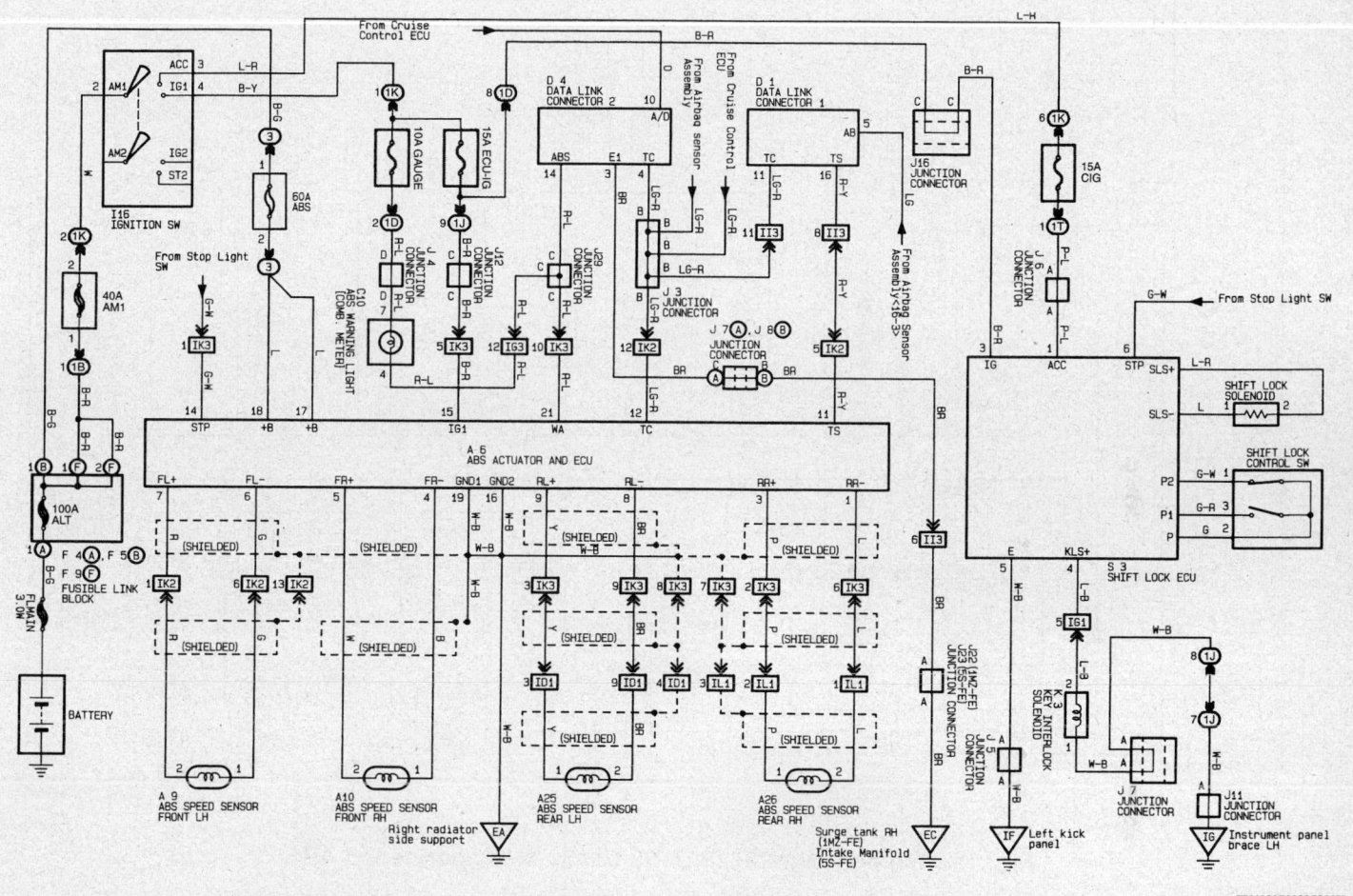

Fig. 14   Wiring diagram. 1997–99 Camry w/Bosch ABS

TY4029700335000X

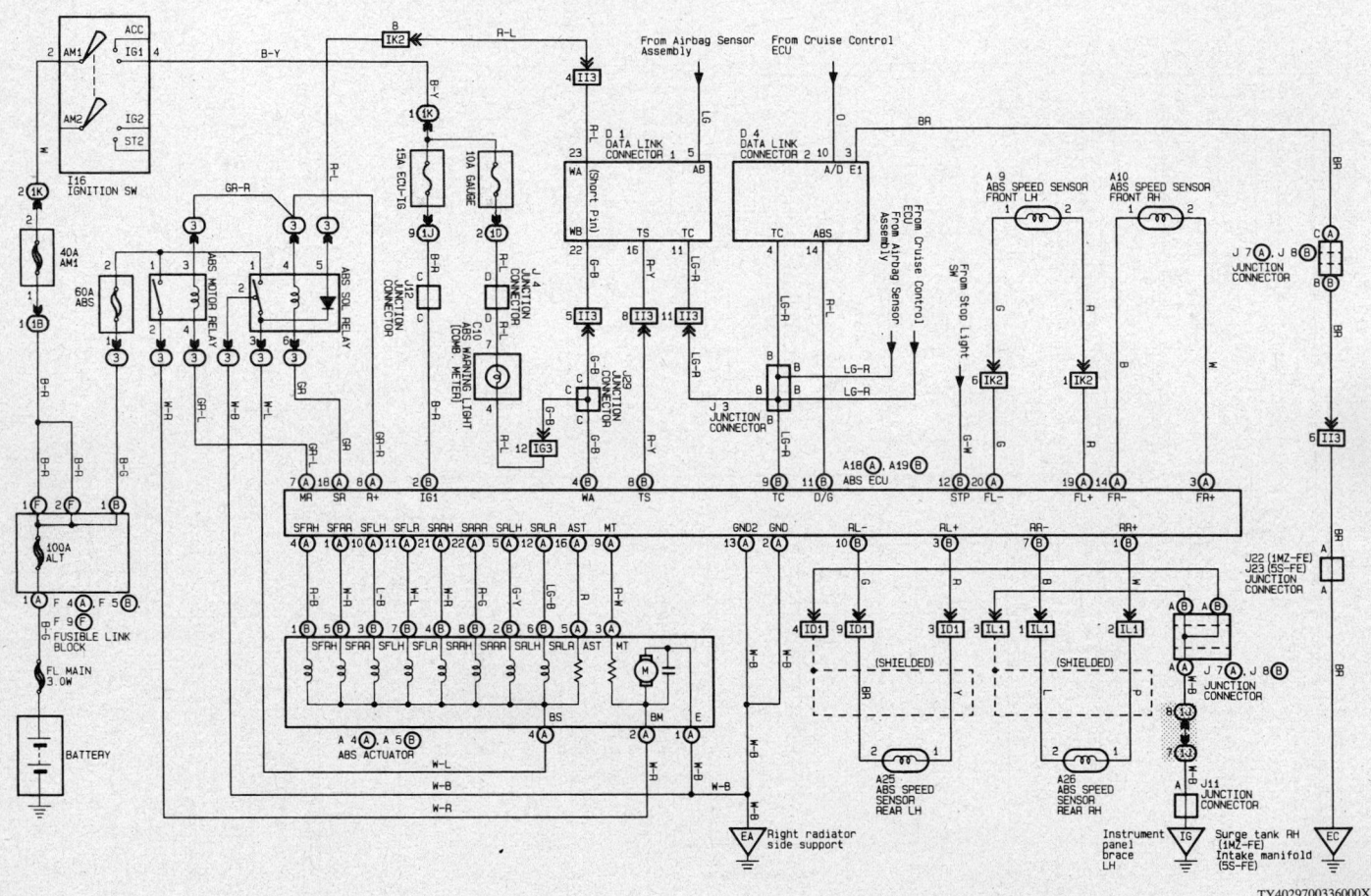

Fig. 15 Wiring diagram. 1997–99 Camry w/Nippondenso ABS

TY4029700336000X

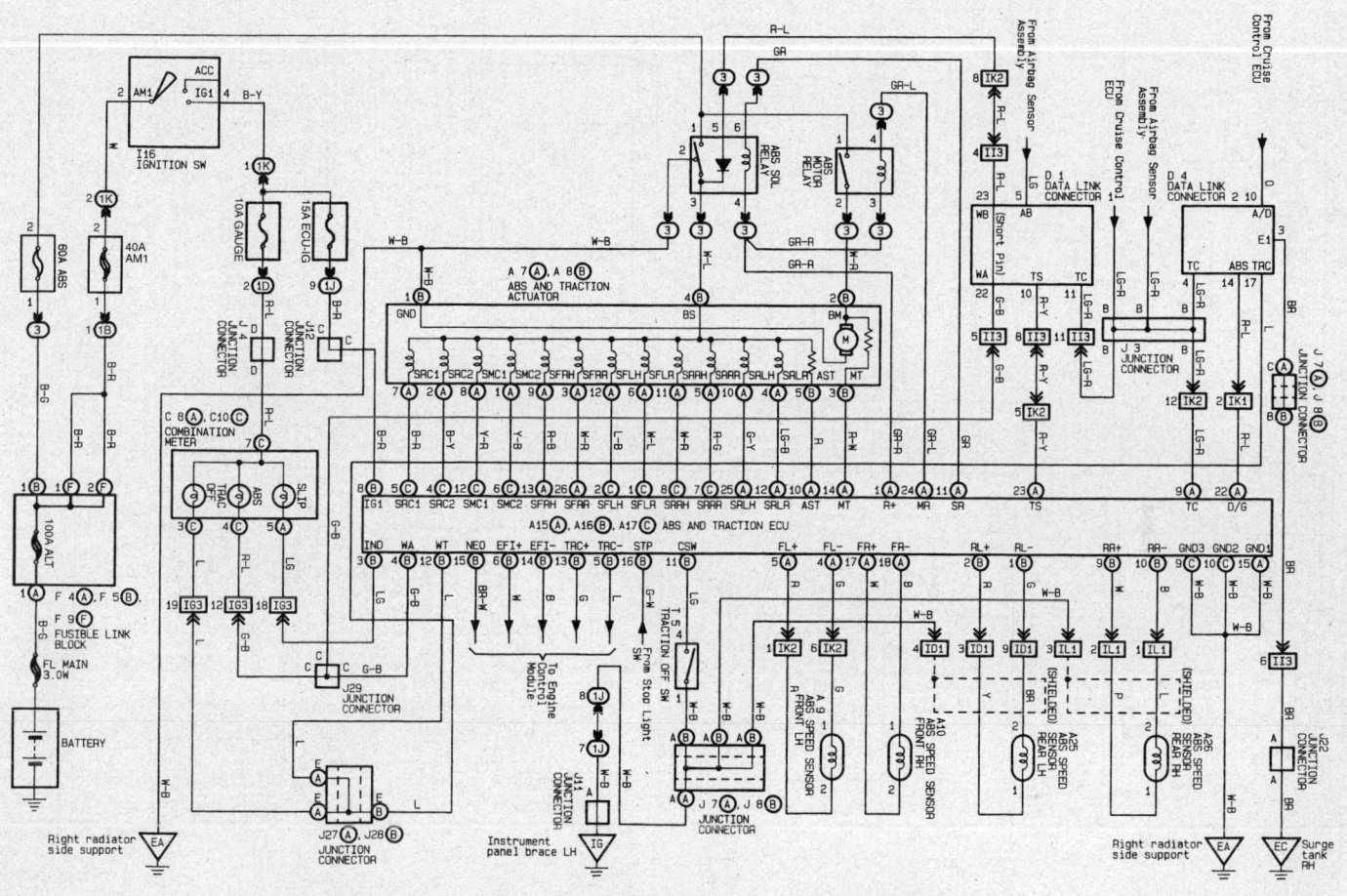

Fig. 16   Wiring diagram. 1997–99 Camry w/traction control

TY4029700334000X

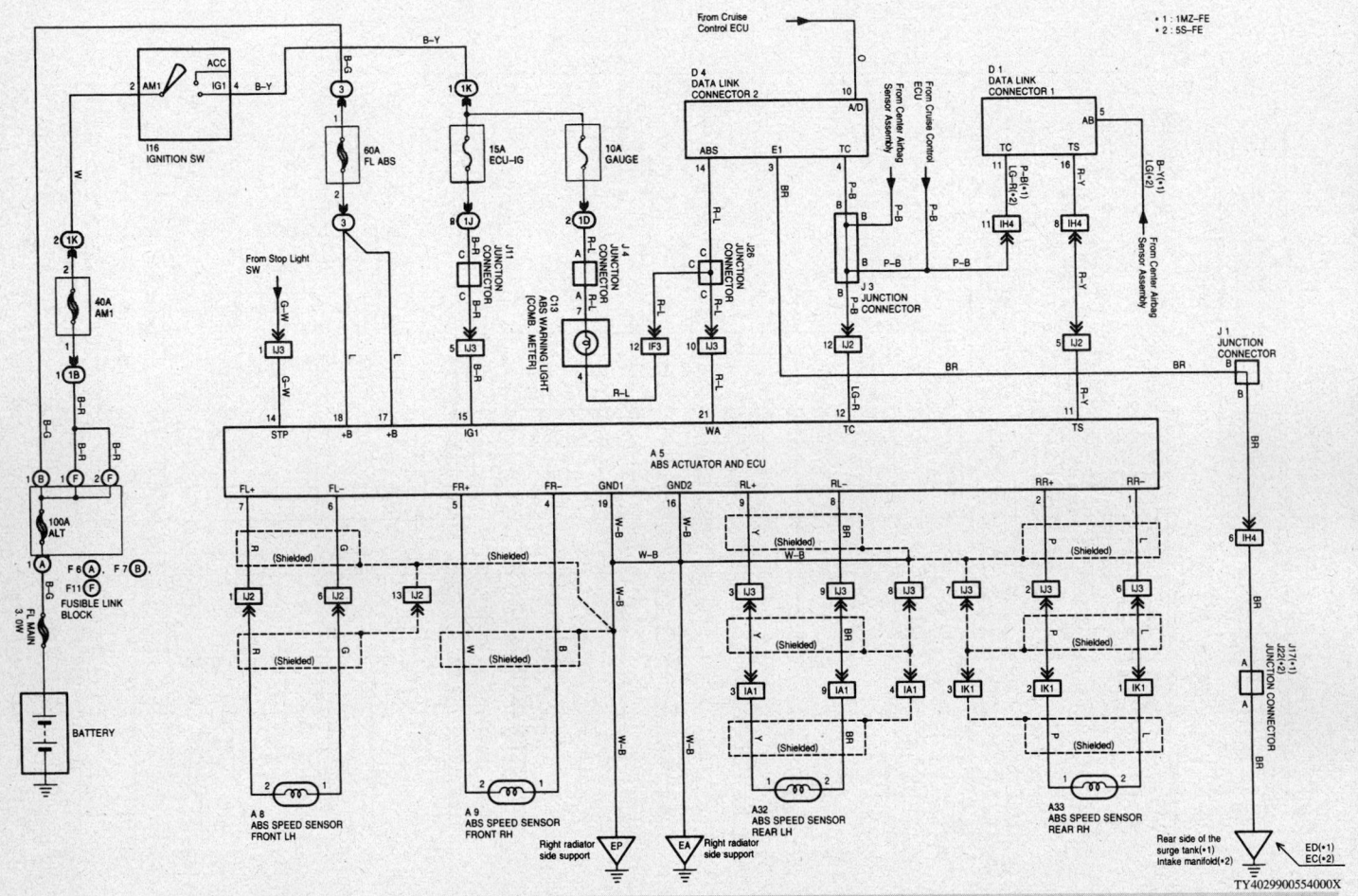

Fig. 17 Wiring diagram. Camry Solara w/ABS less traction control

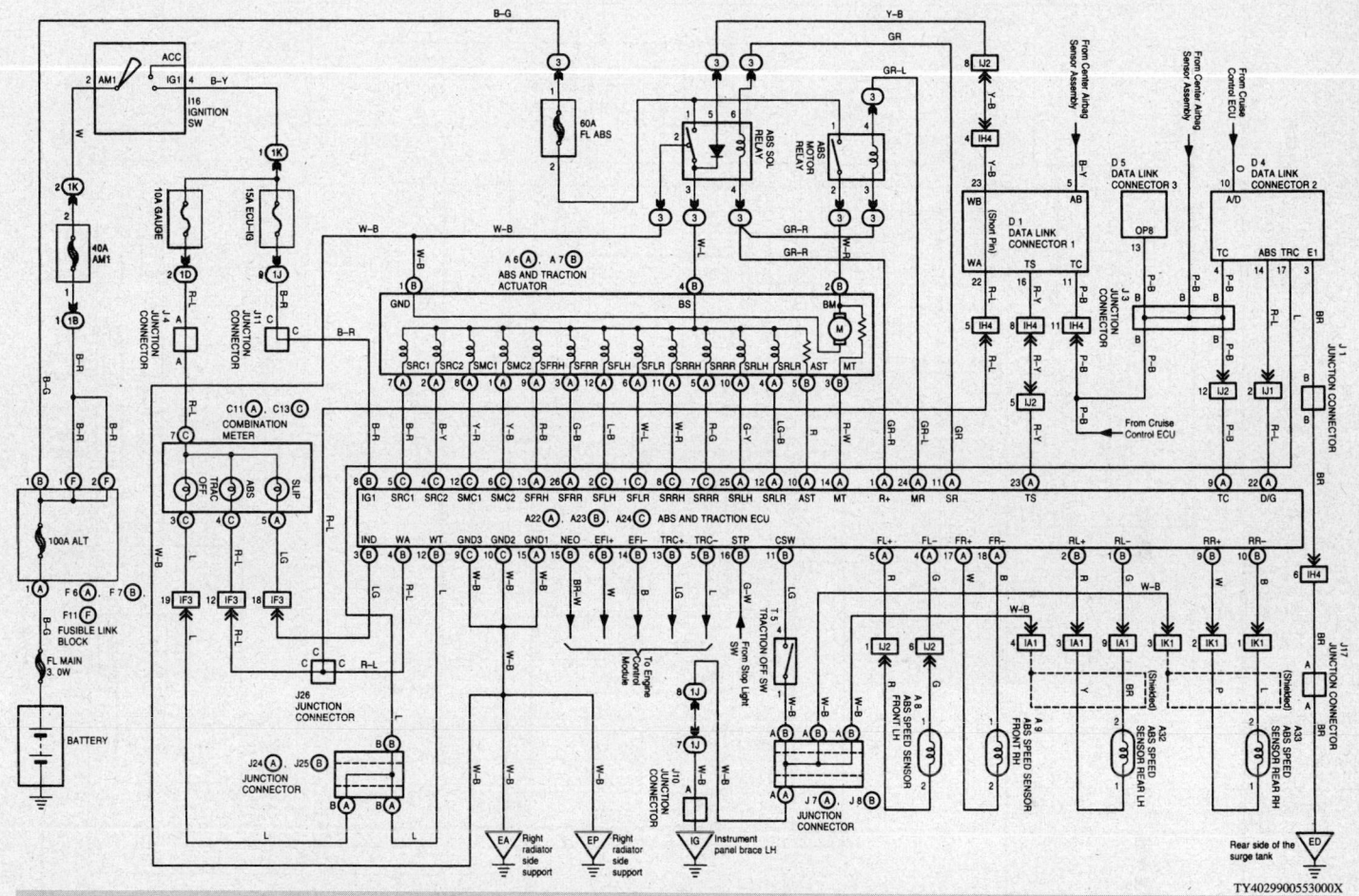

Fig. 18 Wiring diagram. Camry Solara w/ABS & traction control

TY4029900553000X

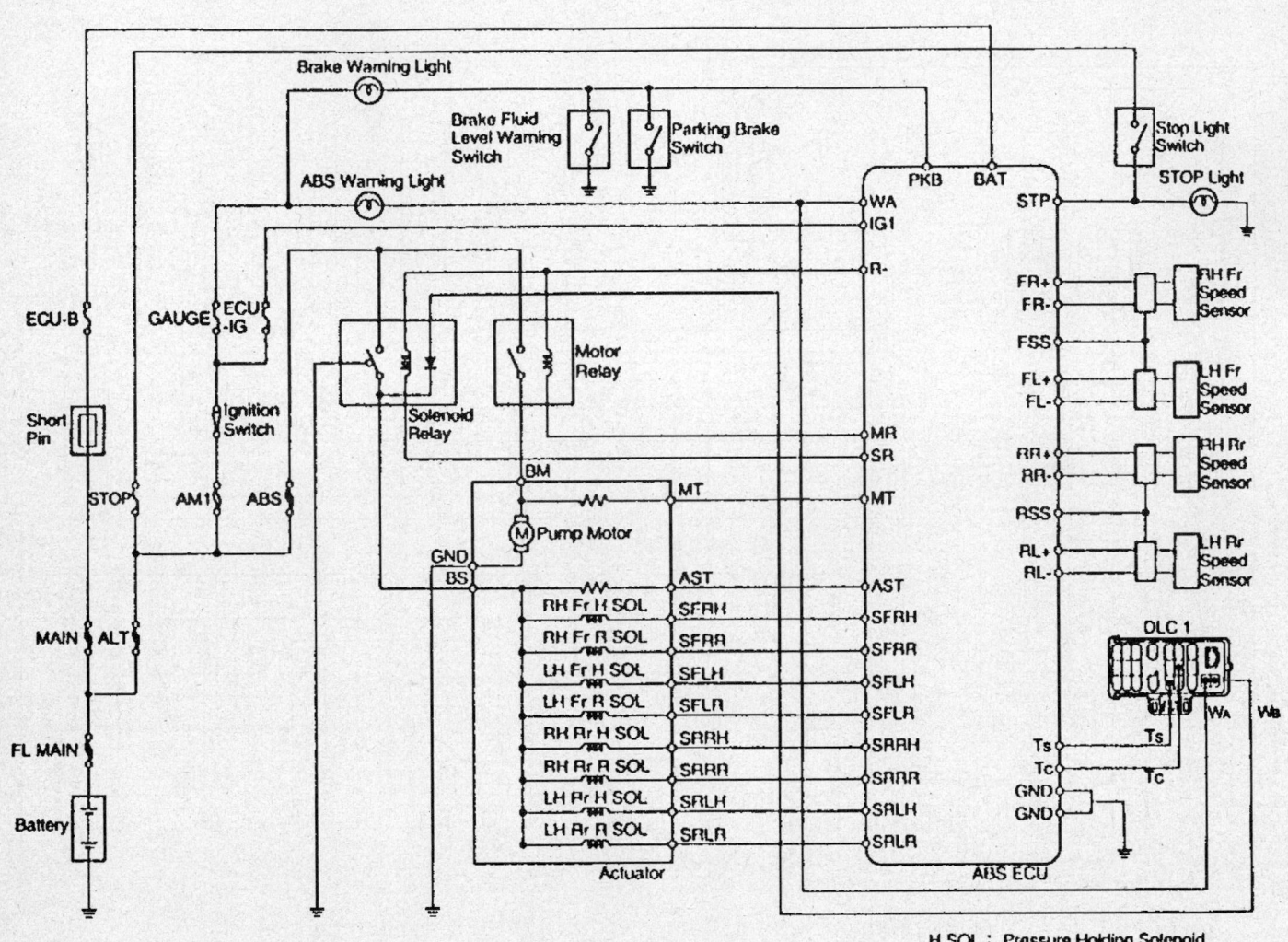

Fig. 19   Wiring diagram. 1996 Celica

TY4029400028000X

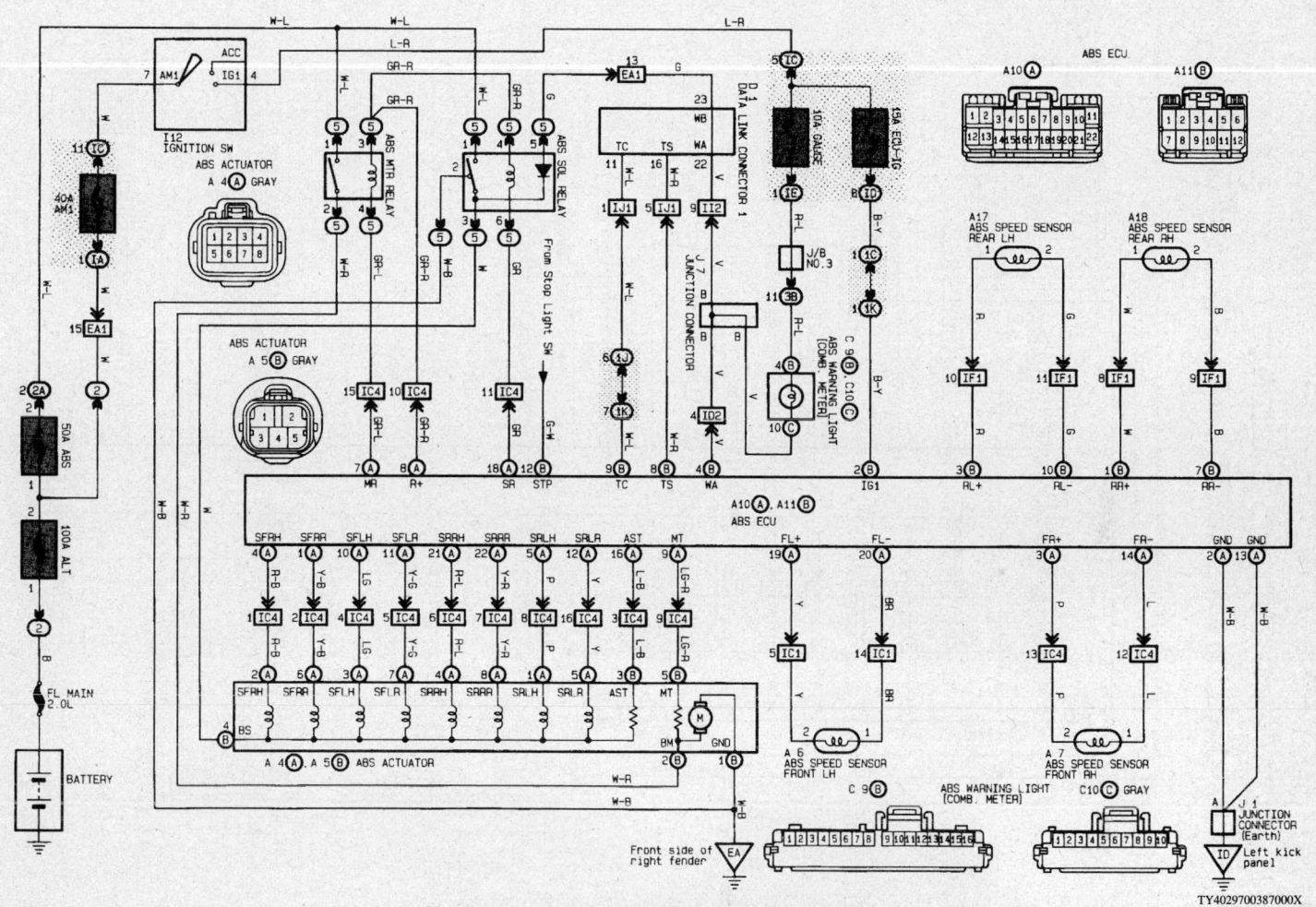

Fig. 20 Wiring diagram. 1997–99 Celica

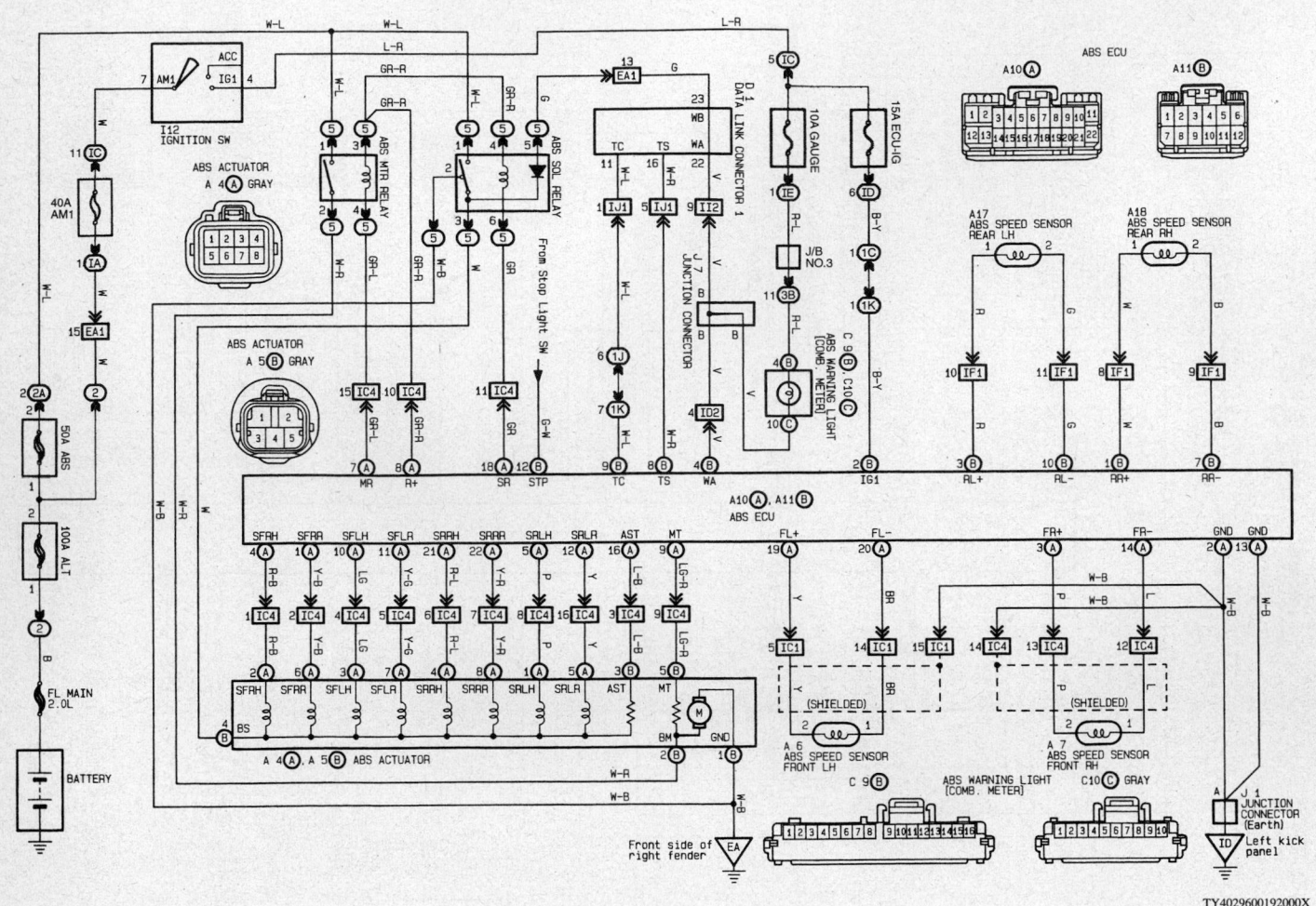

Fig. 21 Wiring diagram. Corolla

TY4029600192000X

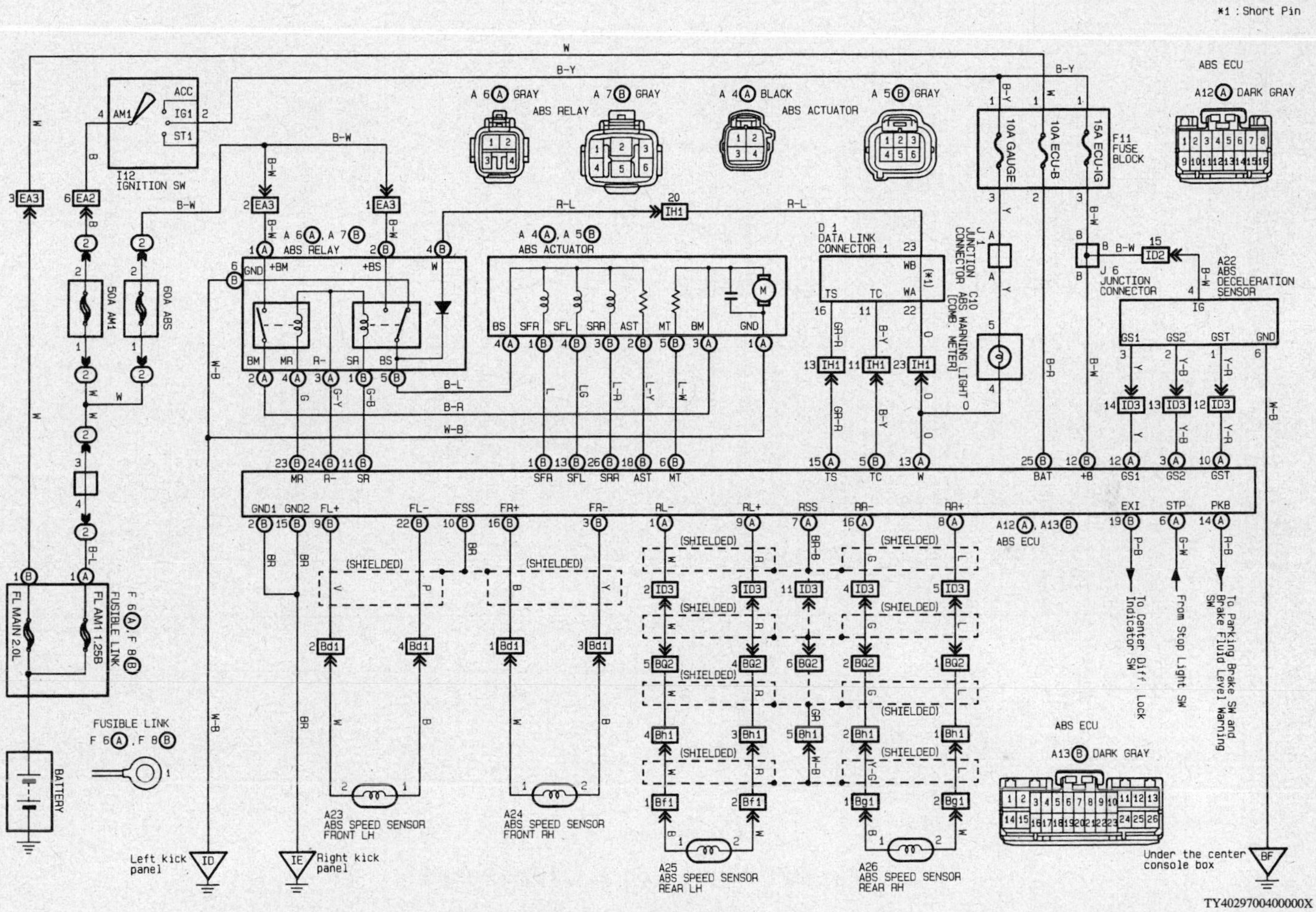

*1 : Short Pin

Fig. 22 Wiring diagram. Land Cruiser

TY4029700400000X

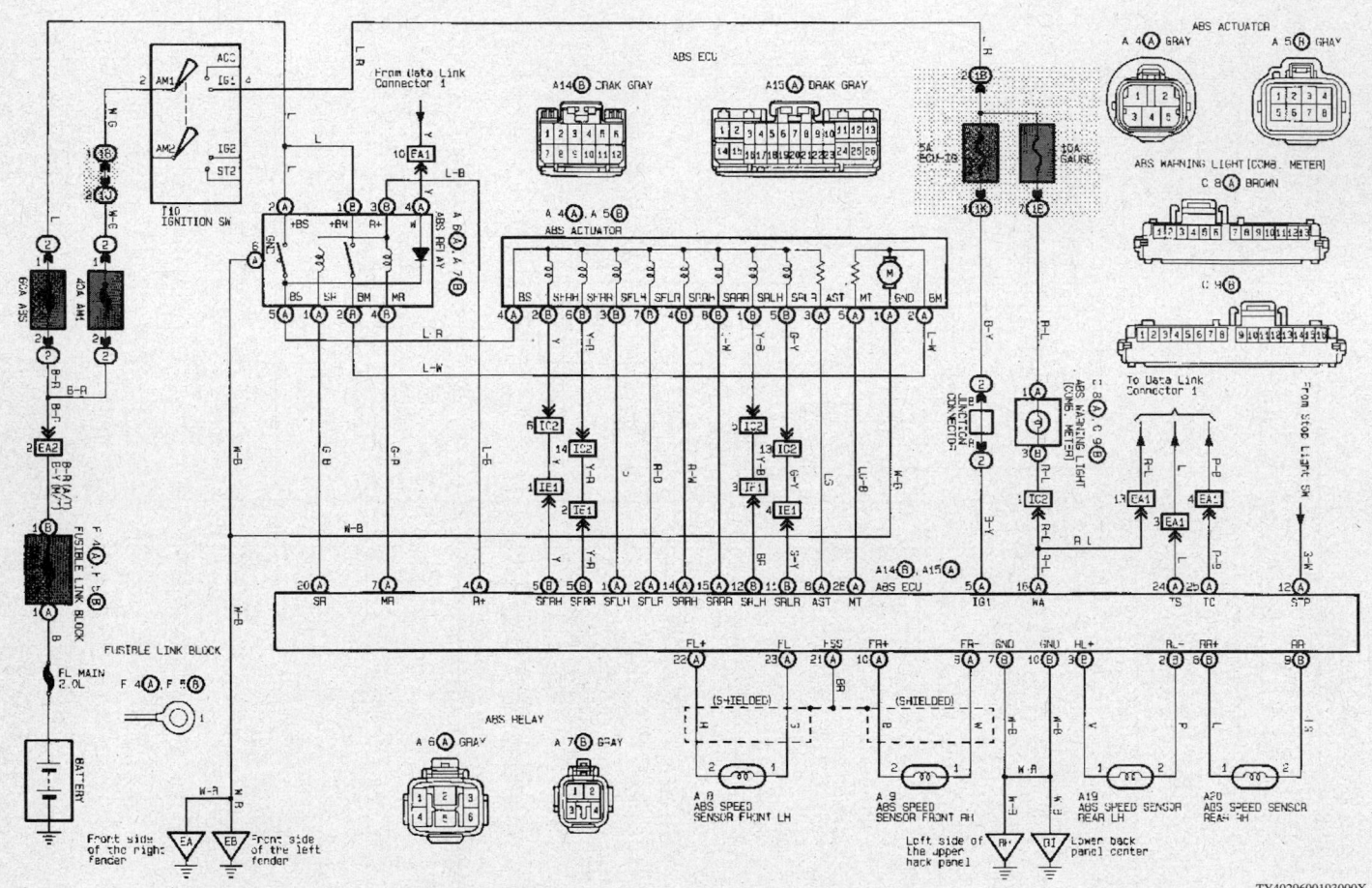

Fig. 23 Wiring diagram. 1996 Paseo

TY4029600193000X

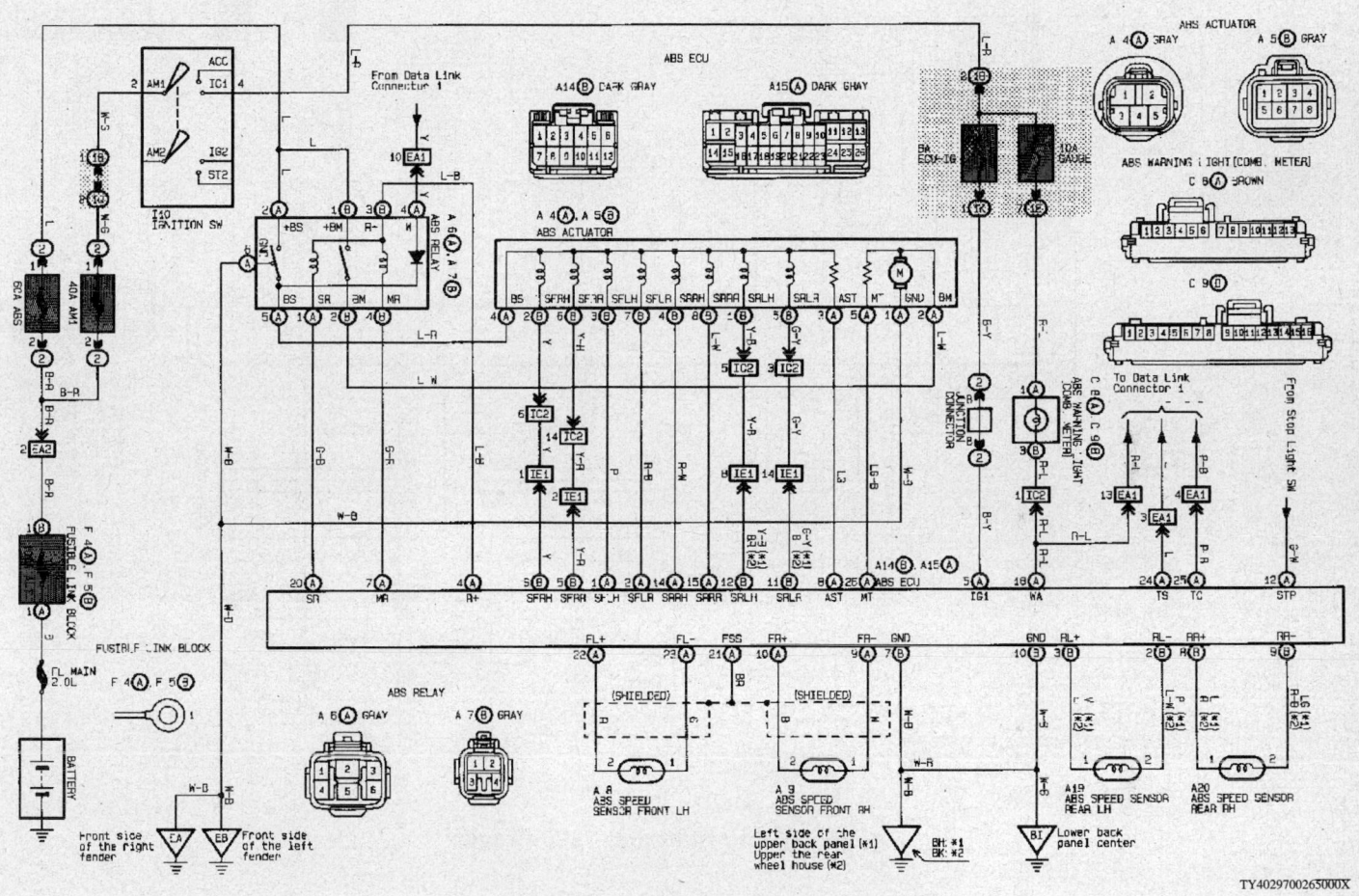

Fig. 24   Wiring diagram. 1997 Paseo

TY4029700265000X

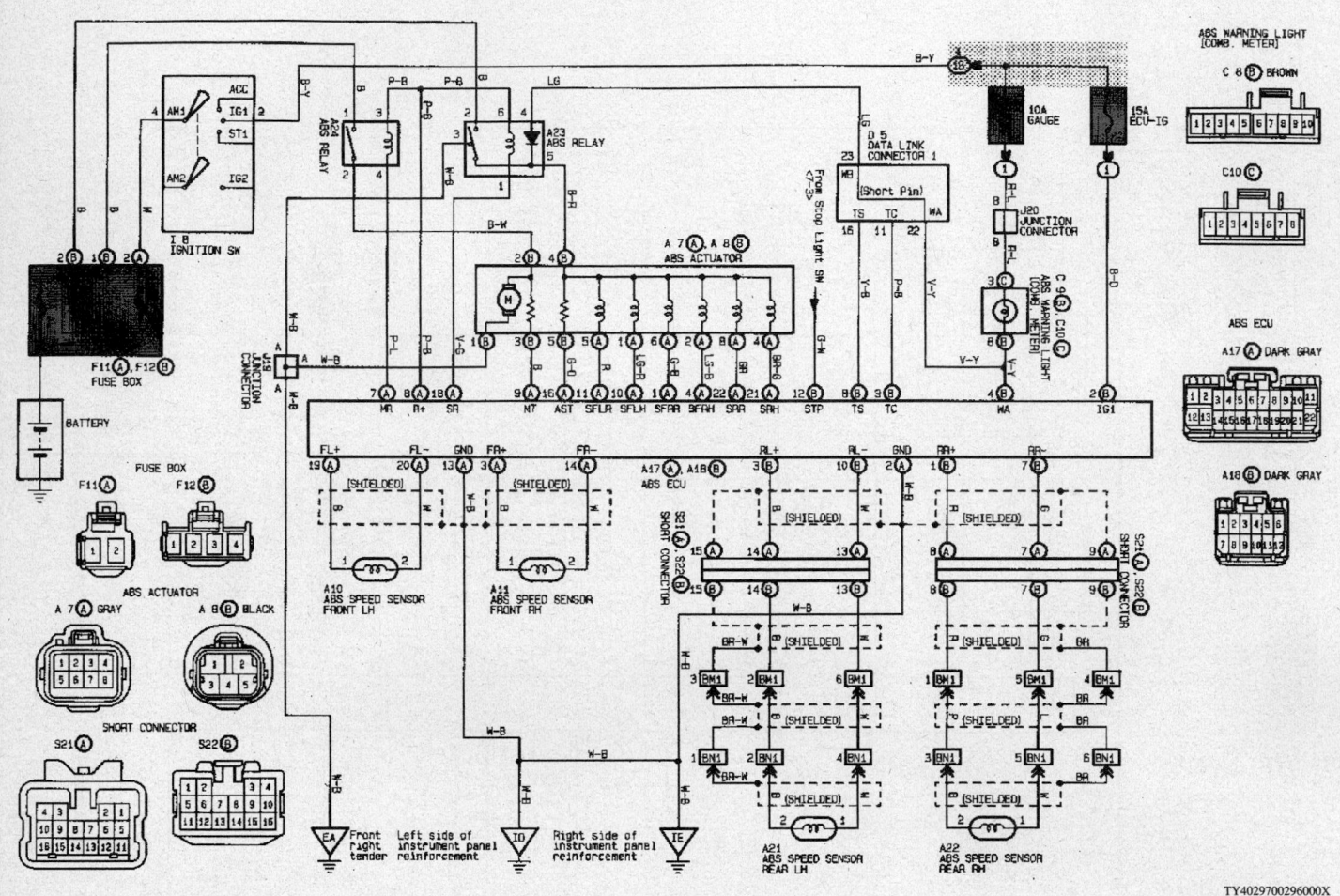

Fig. 25 Wiring diagram. 1996 Previa

TY4029700296000X

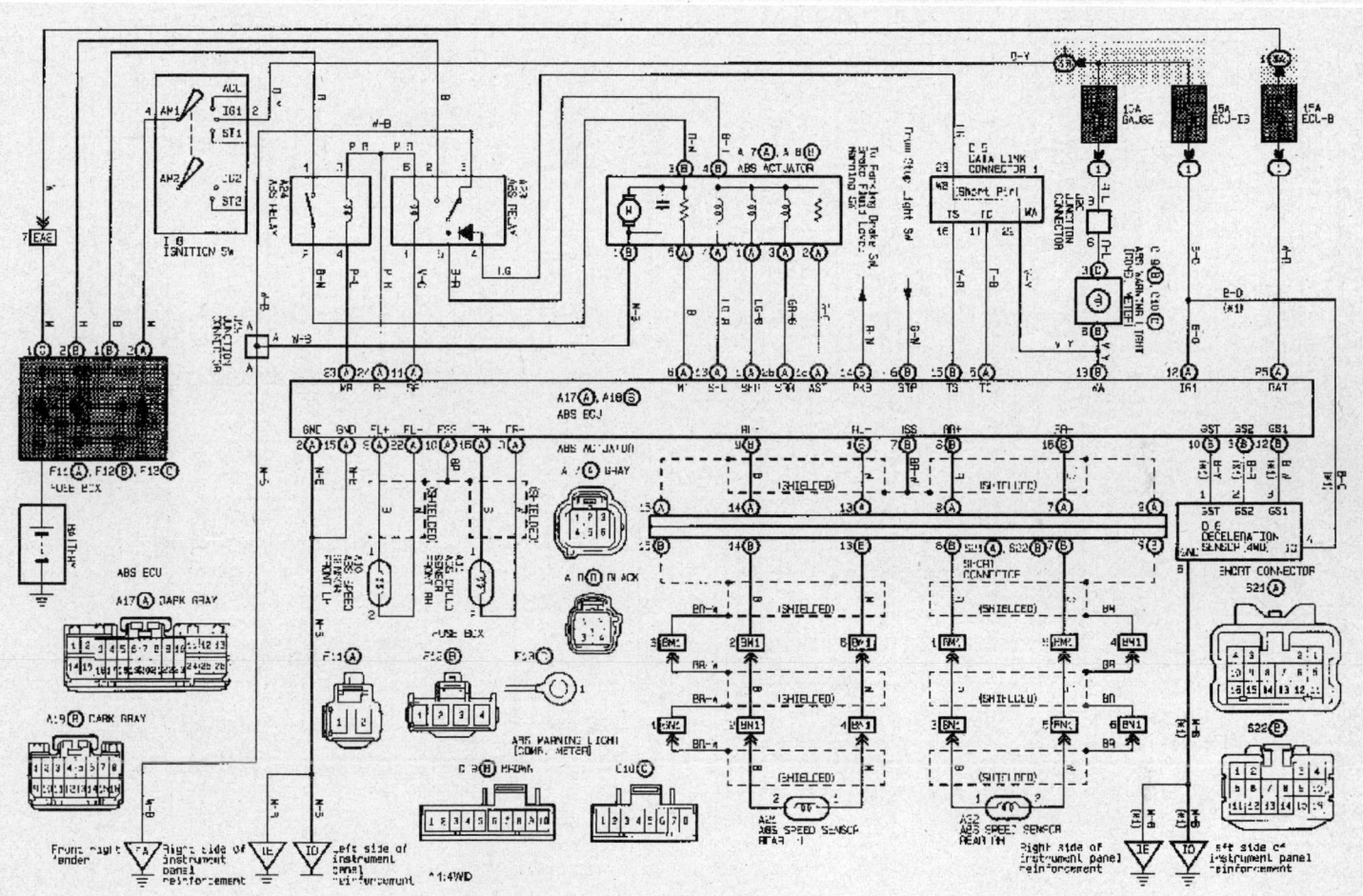

Fig. 26   Wiring diagram. 1997 Previa w/2TZ-FZE Engine

TY4029700297000X

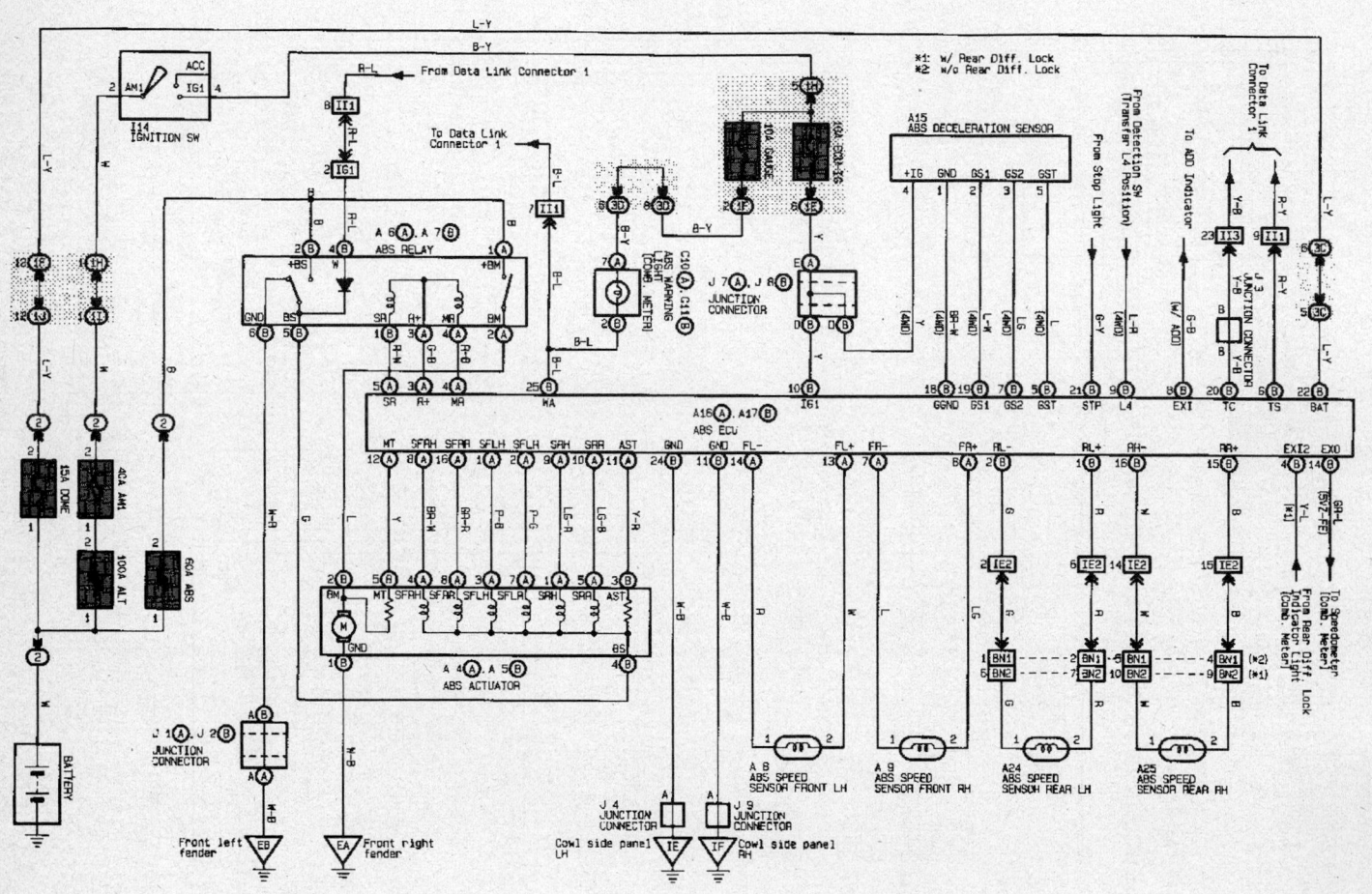

Fig. 27 Wiring diagram. 4Runner

TY4029600194000X

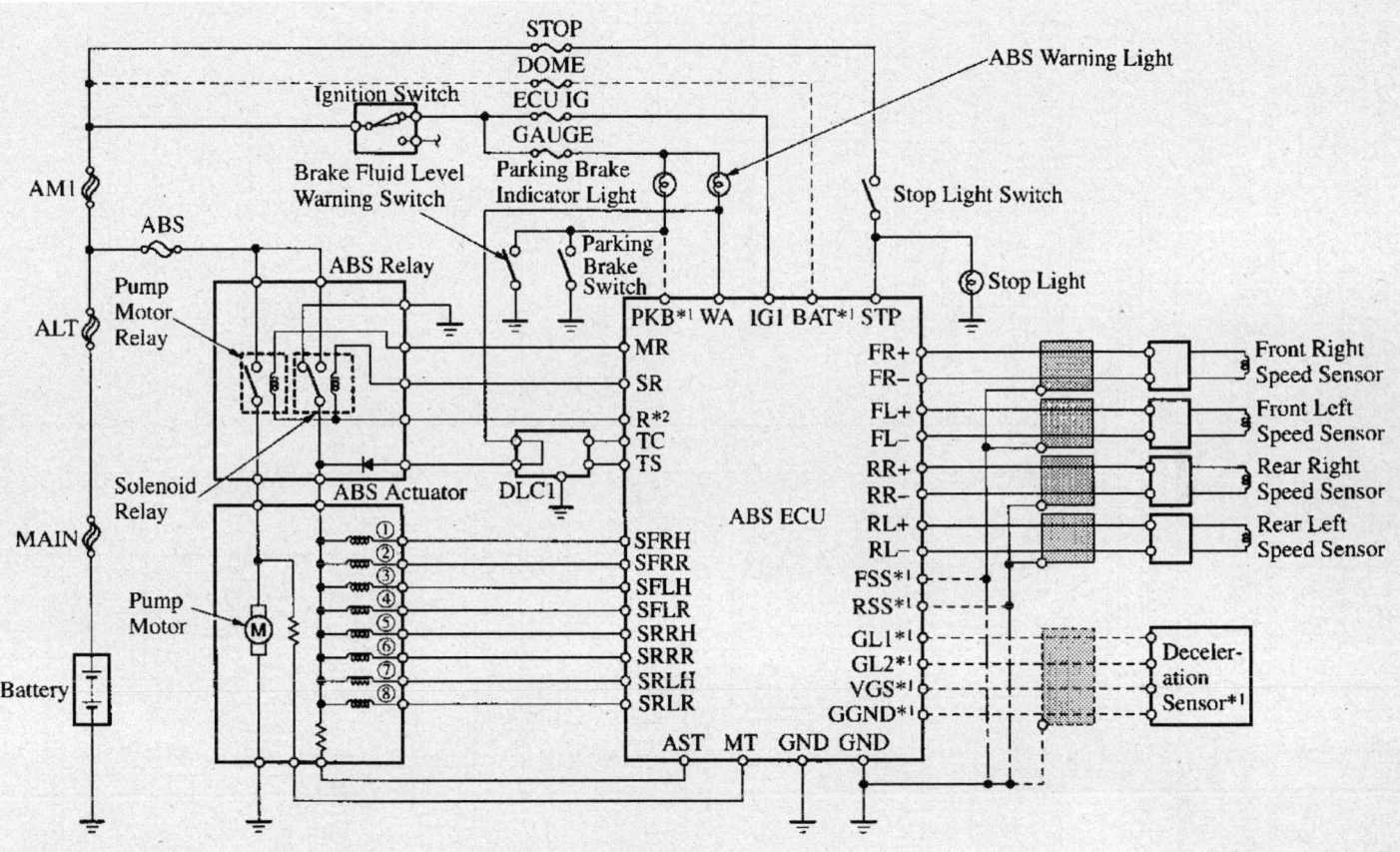

① Front Right Pressure Holding Valve
② Front Right Pressure Reduction Valve
③ Front Left Pressure Holding Valve
④ Front Left Pressure Reduction Valve
⑤ Rear Right Pressure Holding Valve
⑥ Rear Right Pressure Reduction Valve
⑦ Rear Left Pressure Holding Valve
⑧ Rear Left Pressure Reduction Valve

*1 : Only 4WD Model
*2 : 2WD Model : R+, 4WD Model: R−
−·−·− : Only 2WD Model
−−−−− : Only 4WD Model

TY4029600191000X

Fig. 28 Wiring diagram. 1996 RAV4

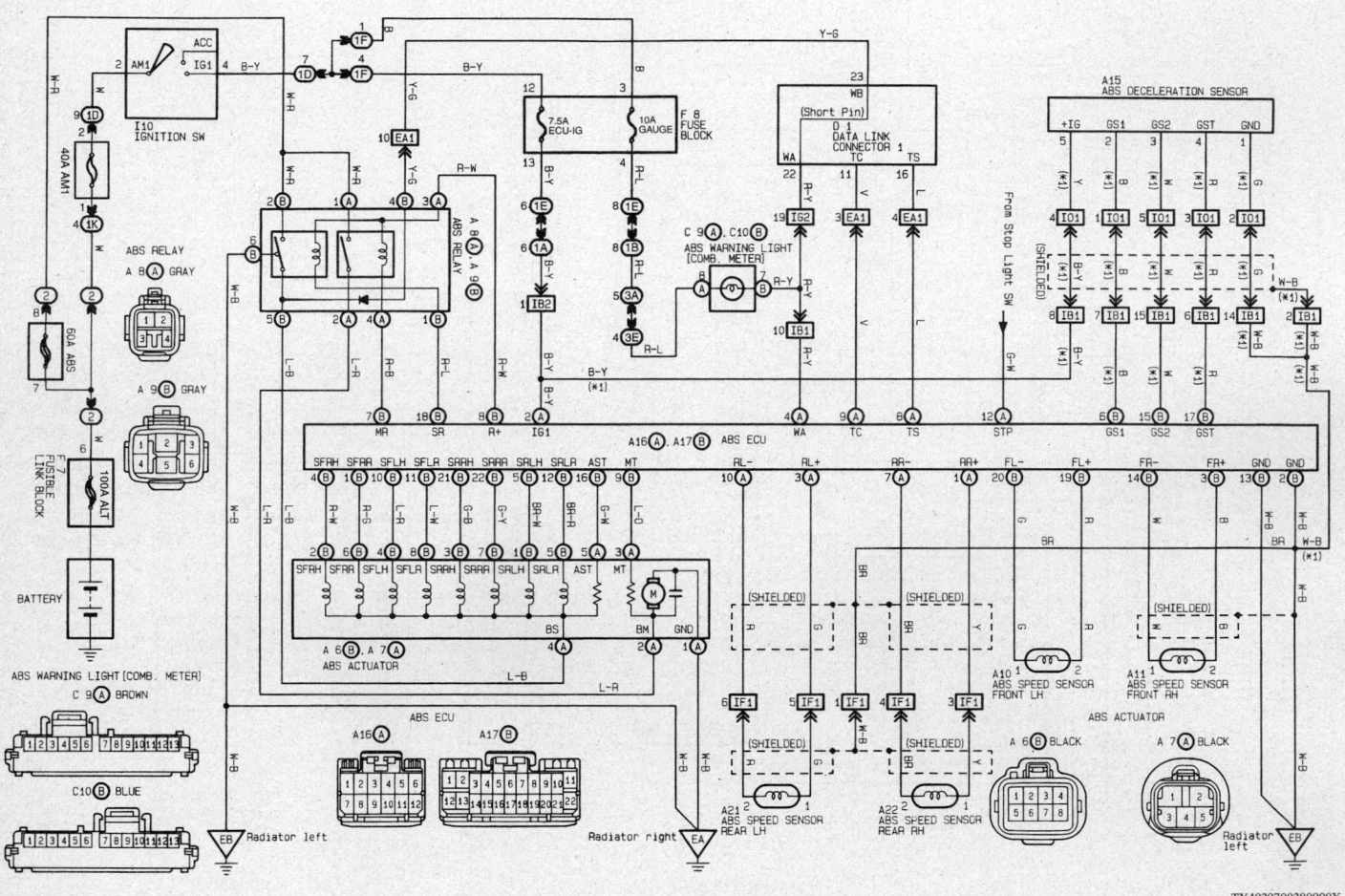

Fig. 29 Wiring diagram. 1997–99 2WD RAV4 w/4 Door

TY4029700280000X

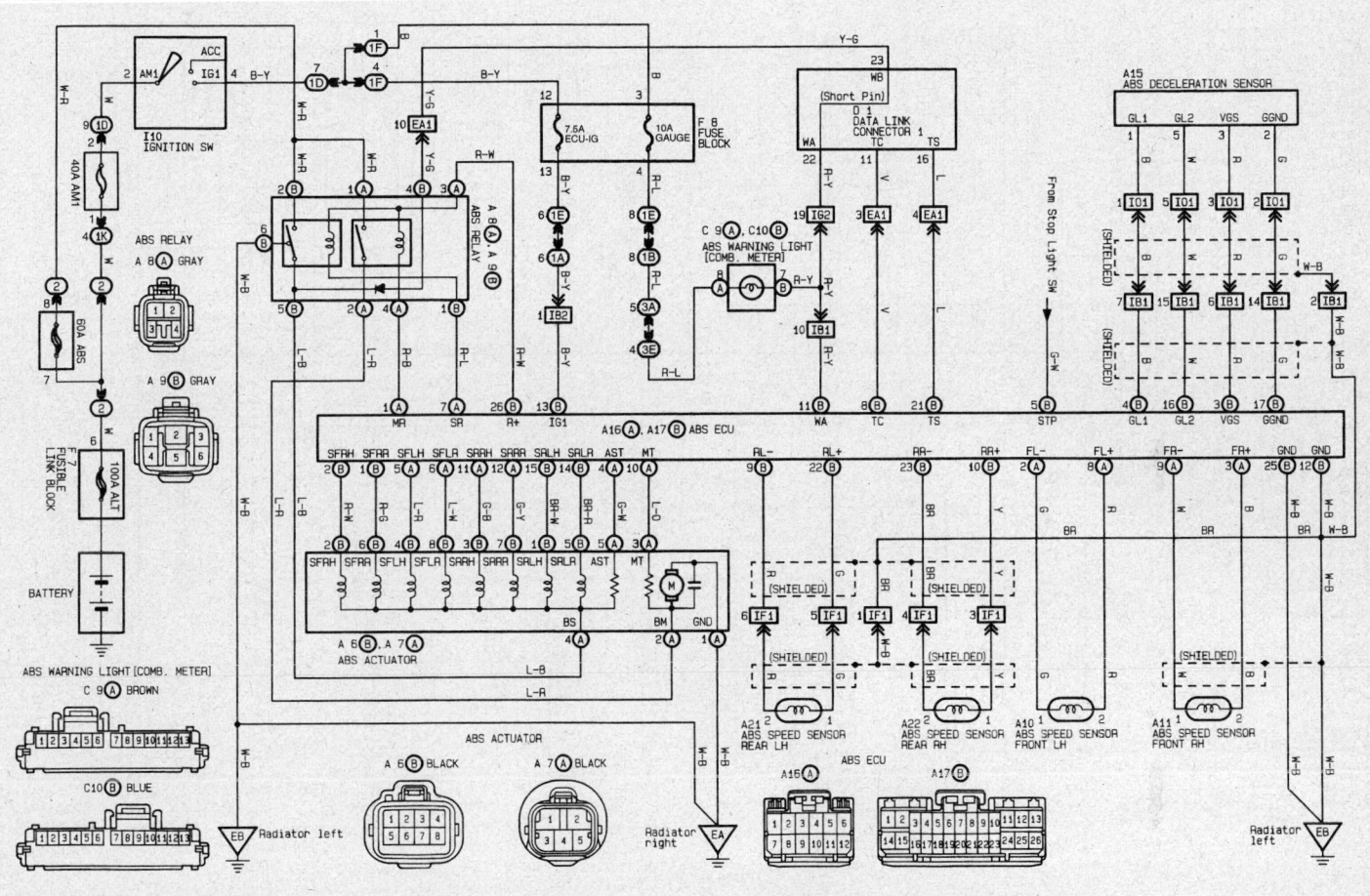

Fig. 30   Wiring diagram. 1997–99 4WD RAV4 w/4 Door

TY4029700279000X

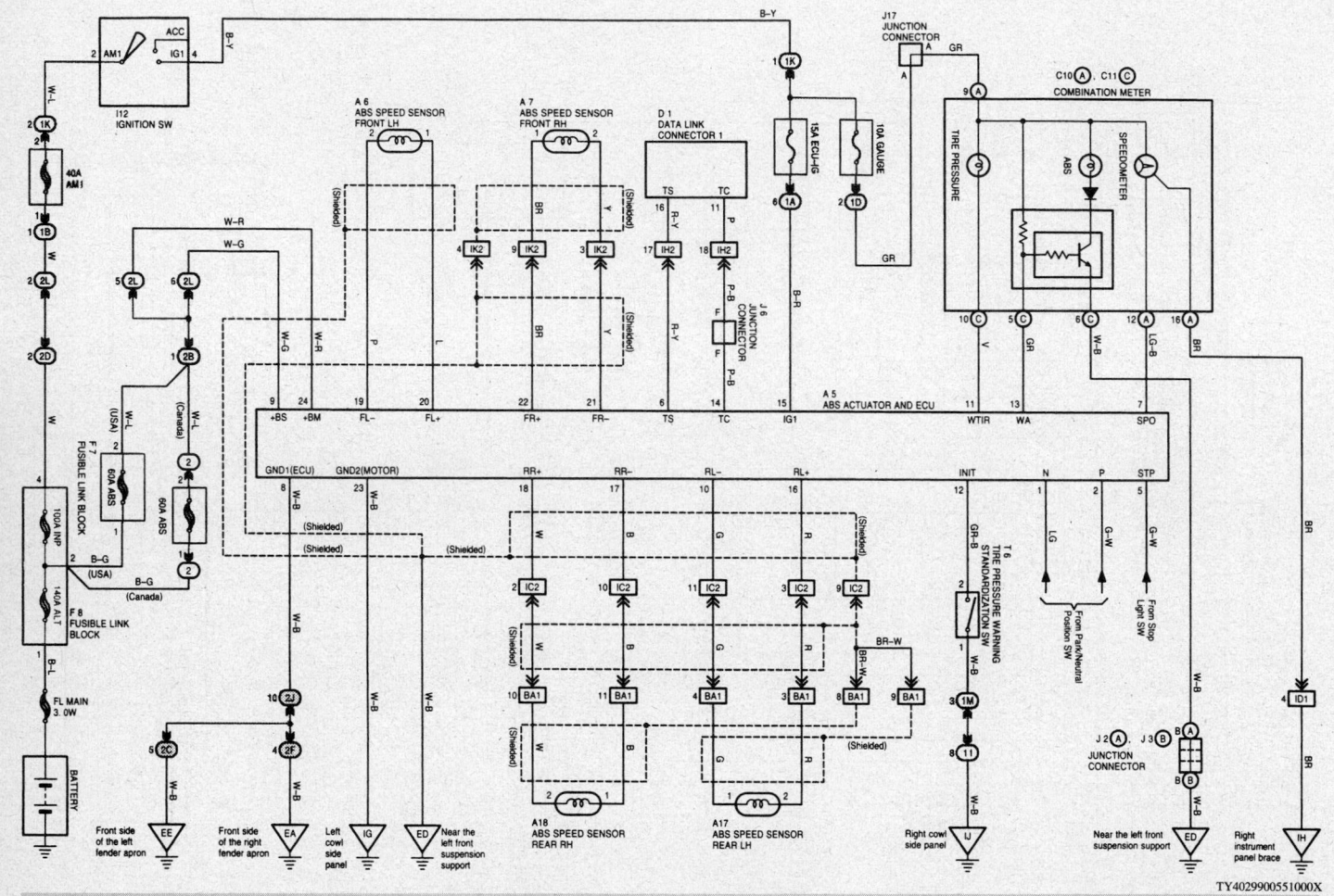

Fig. 31 Wiring diagram. Sienna

TY402990055I000X

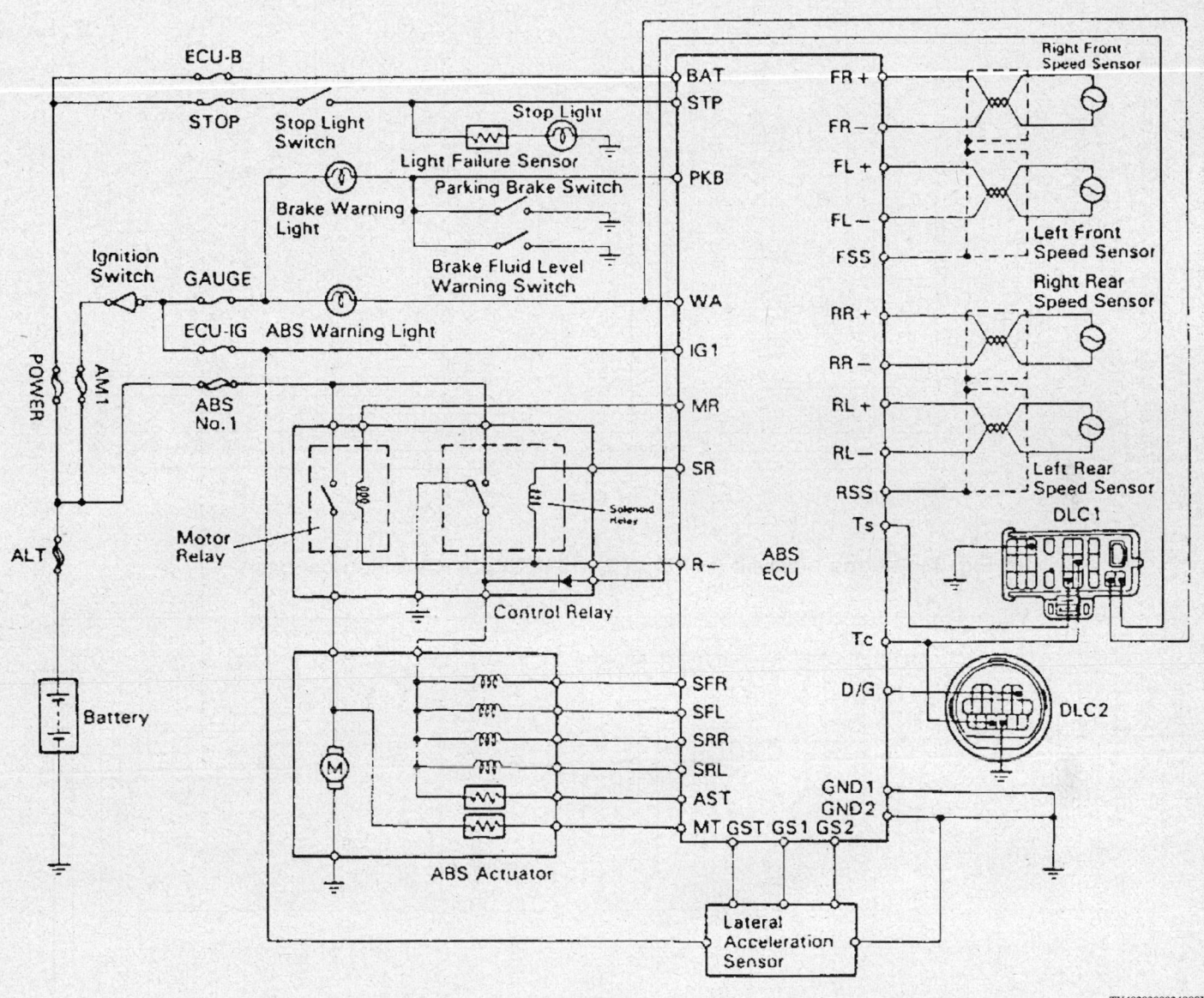

Fig. 32   Wiring diagram. 1996 Supra less traction control

TY4029300024000X

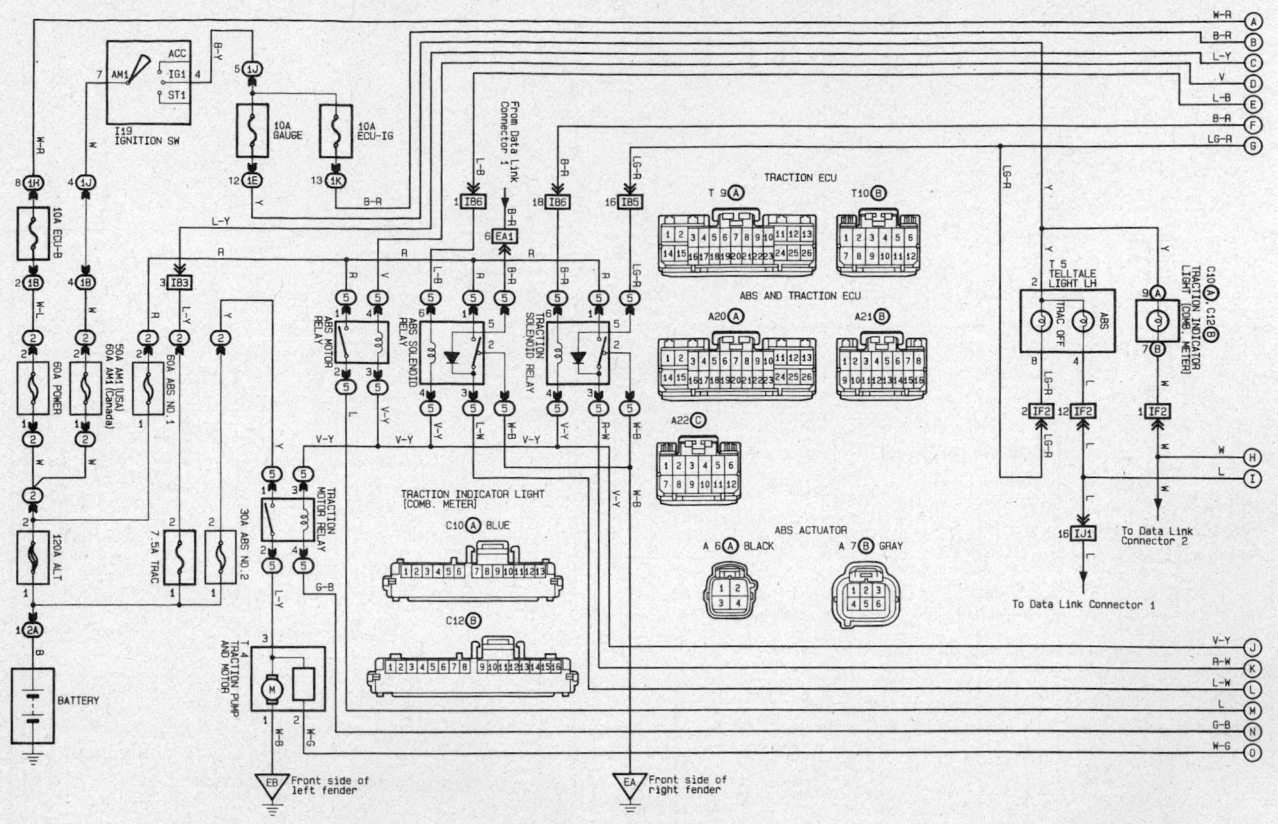

Fig. 33   Wiring diagram (Part 1 of 2). 1996 Supra w/traction control

TY4029300025010X

Fig. 33   Wiring diagram (Part 2 of 2). 1996 Supra w/traction control

TY4029300025020X

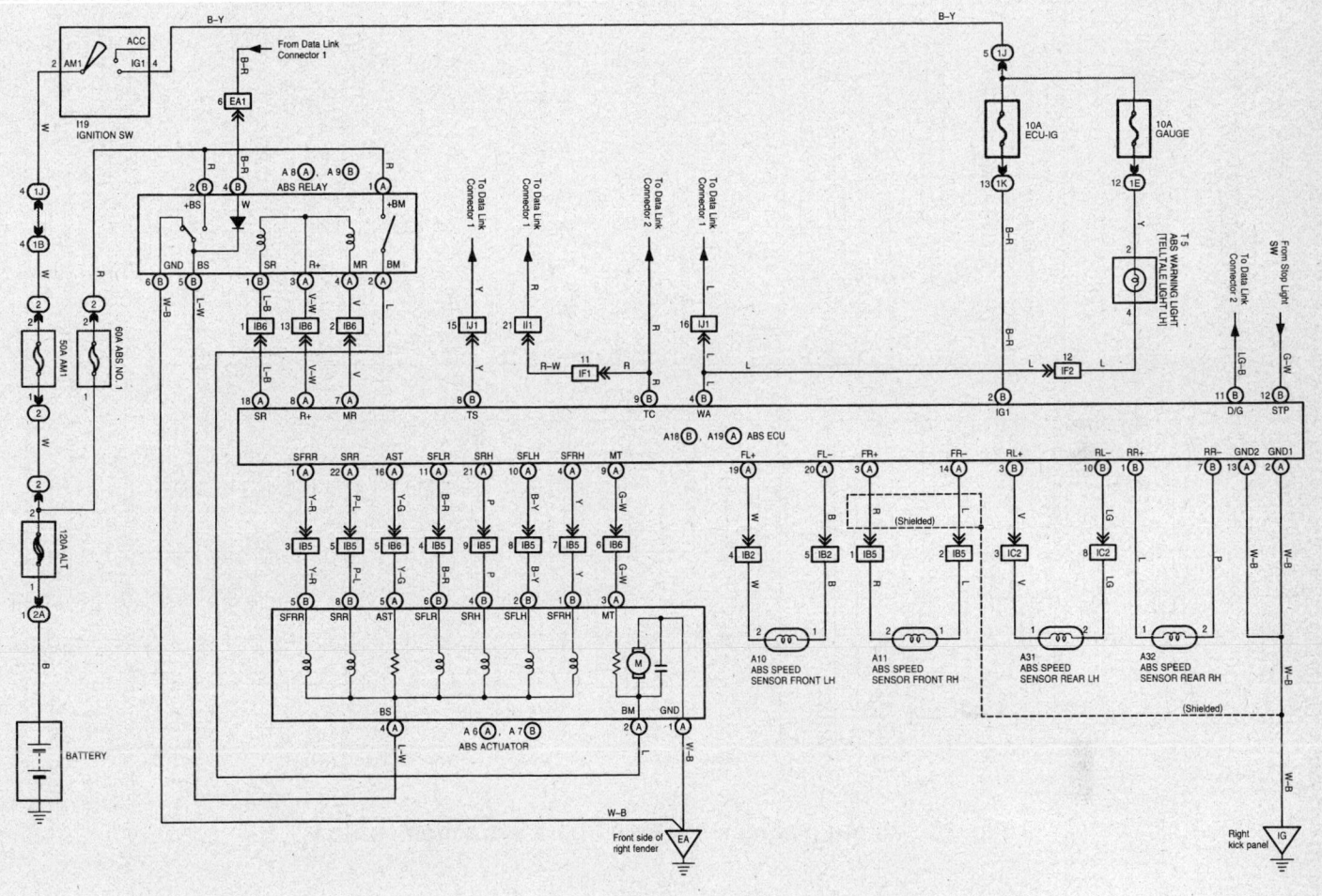

Fig. 34   Wiring diagram. 1997–98 Supra less traction control

TY4029700402000A

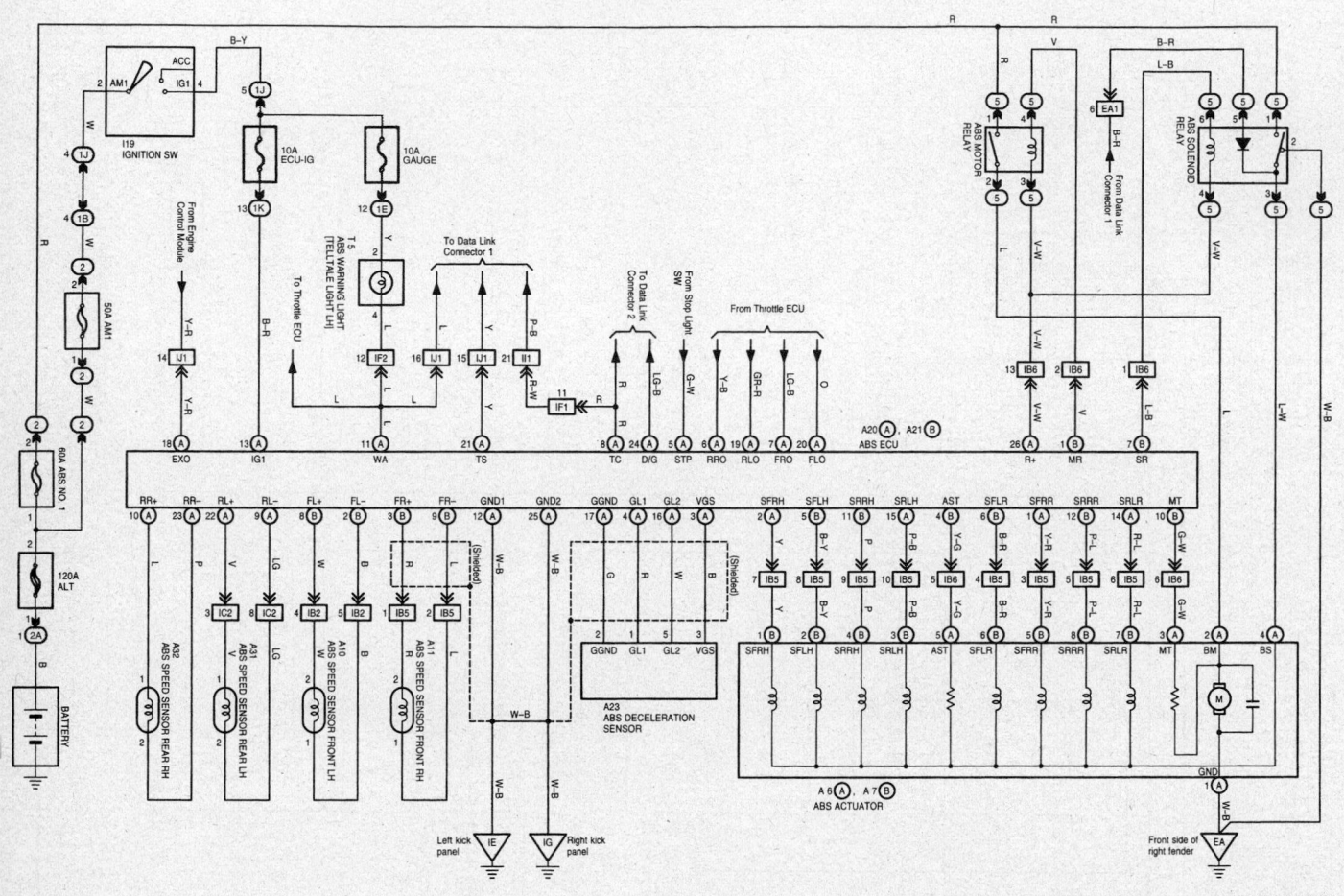

Fig. 35   Wiring diagram. 1997–98 Supra w/traction control

TY4029700403000AX

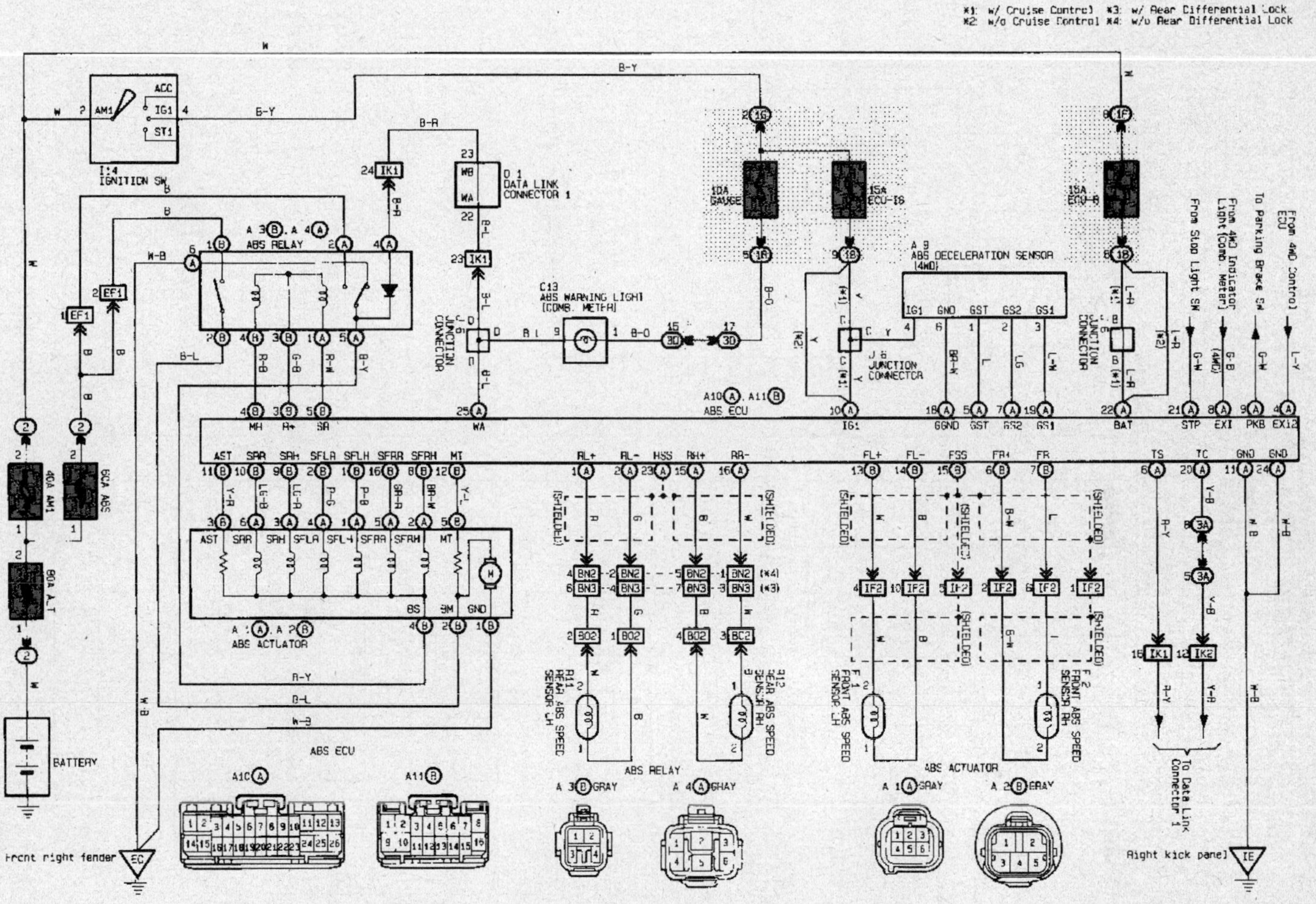

Fig. 36 Wiring diagram. 1996 Tacoma

TY4029600308000X

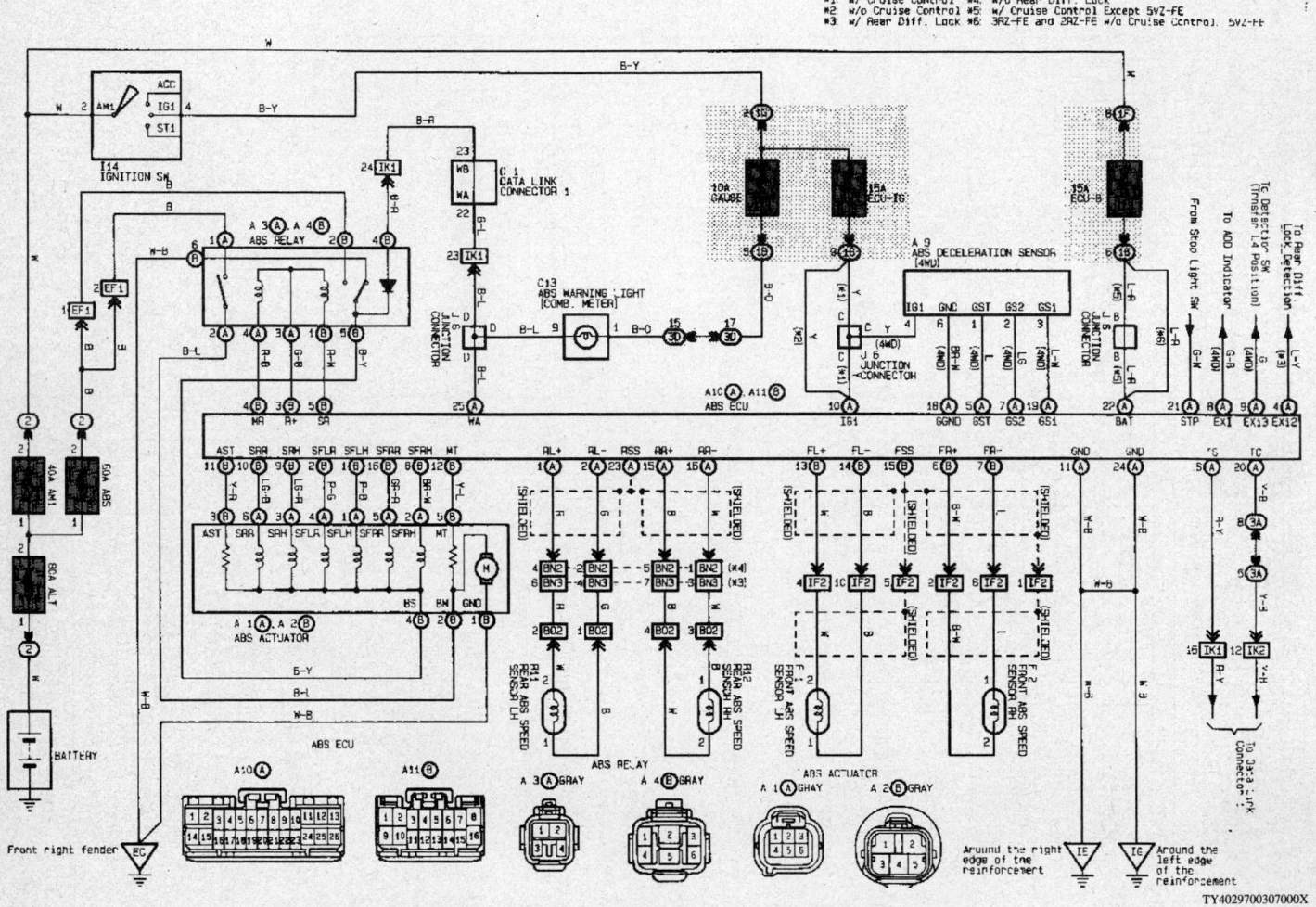

Fig. 37 Wiring diagram. 1997–99 Tacoma

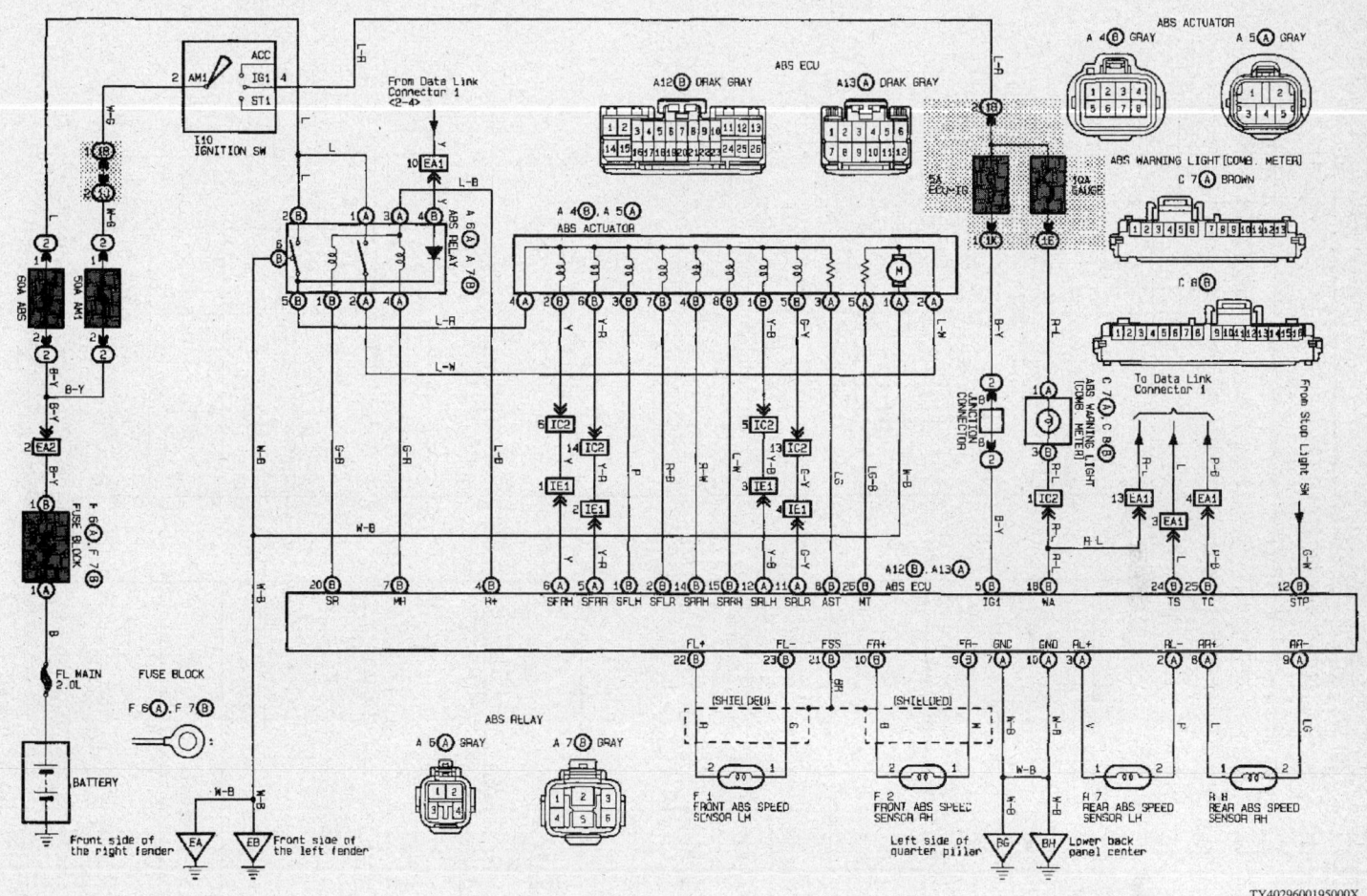

Fig. 38   Wiring diagram. Tercel

TY4029600195000X

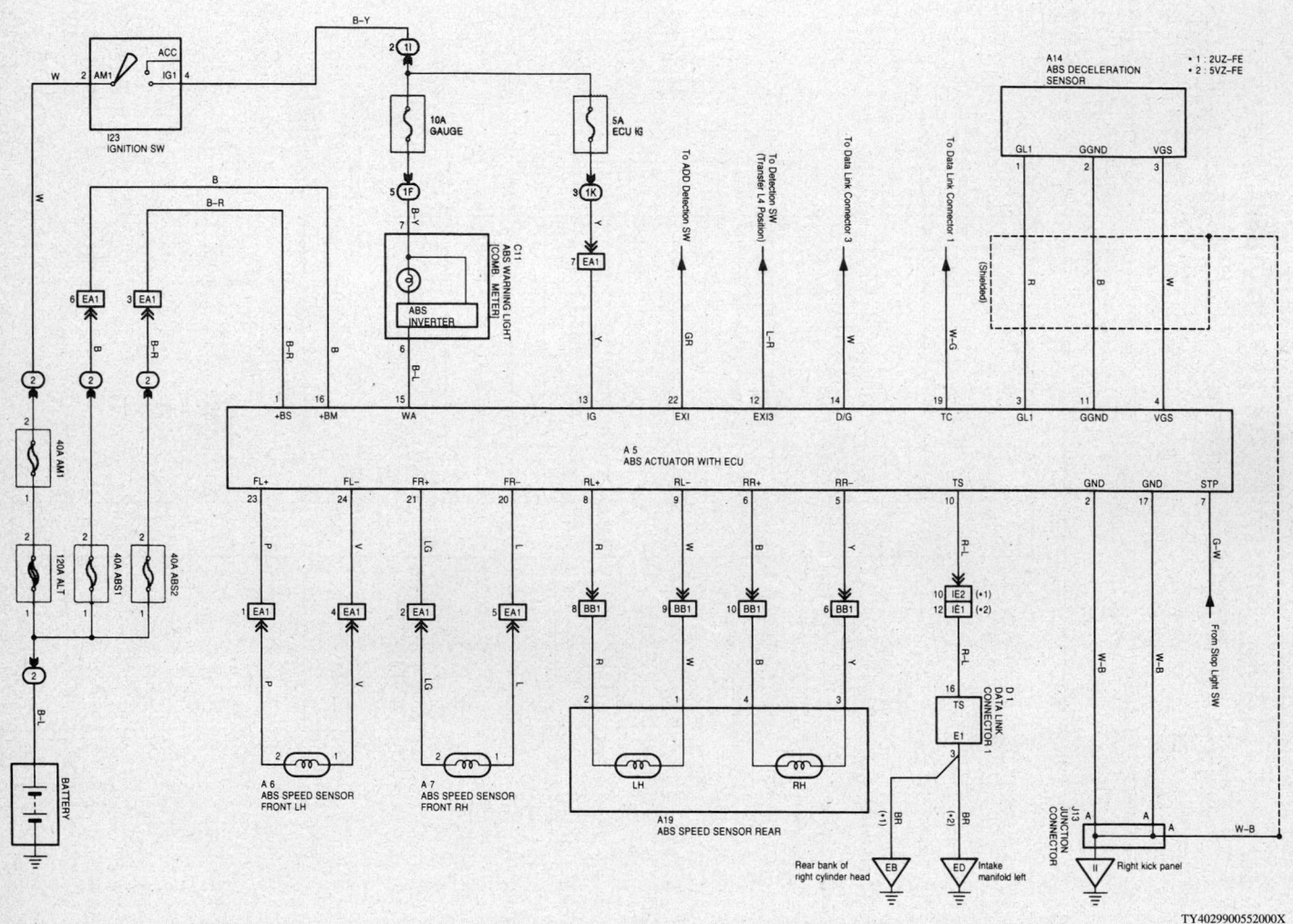

Fig. 39   Wiring diagram. Tundra

TY4029900552000X

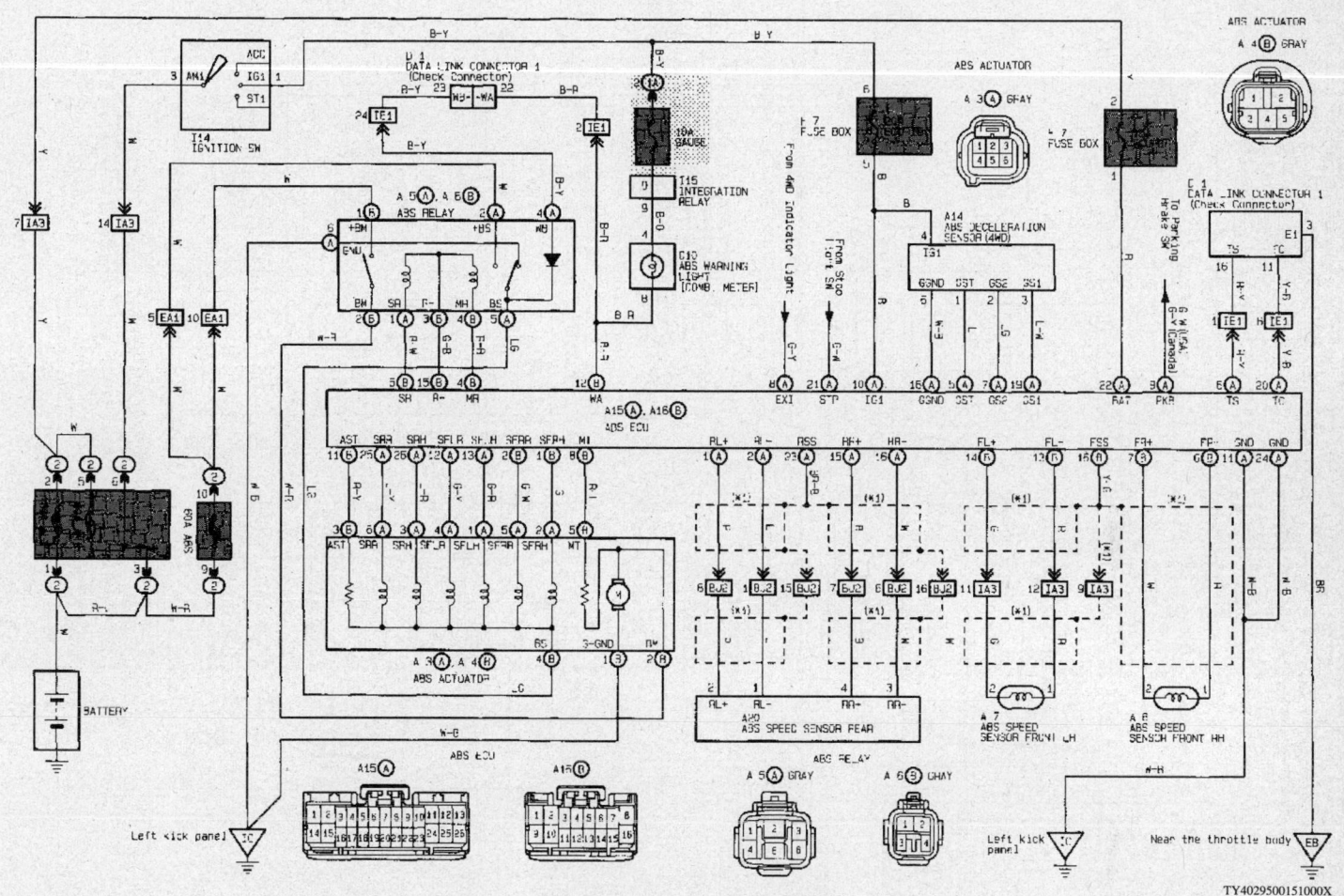

Fig. 40 Wiring diagram. 1996 T100

TY4029500151000X

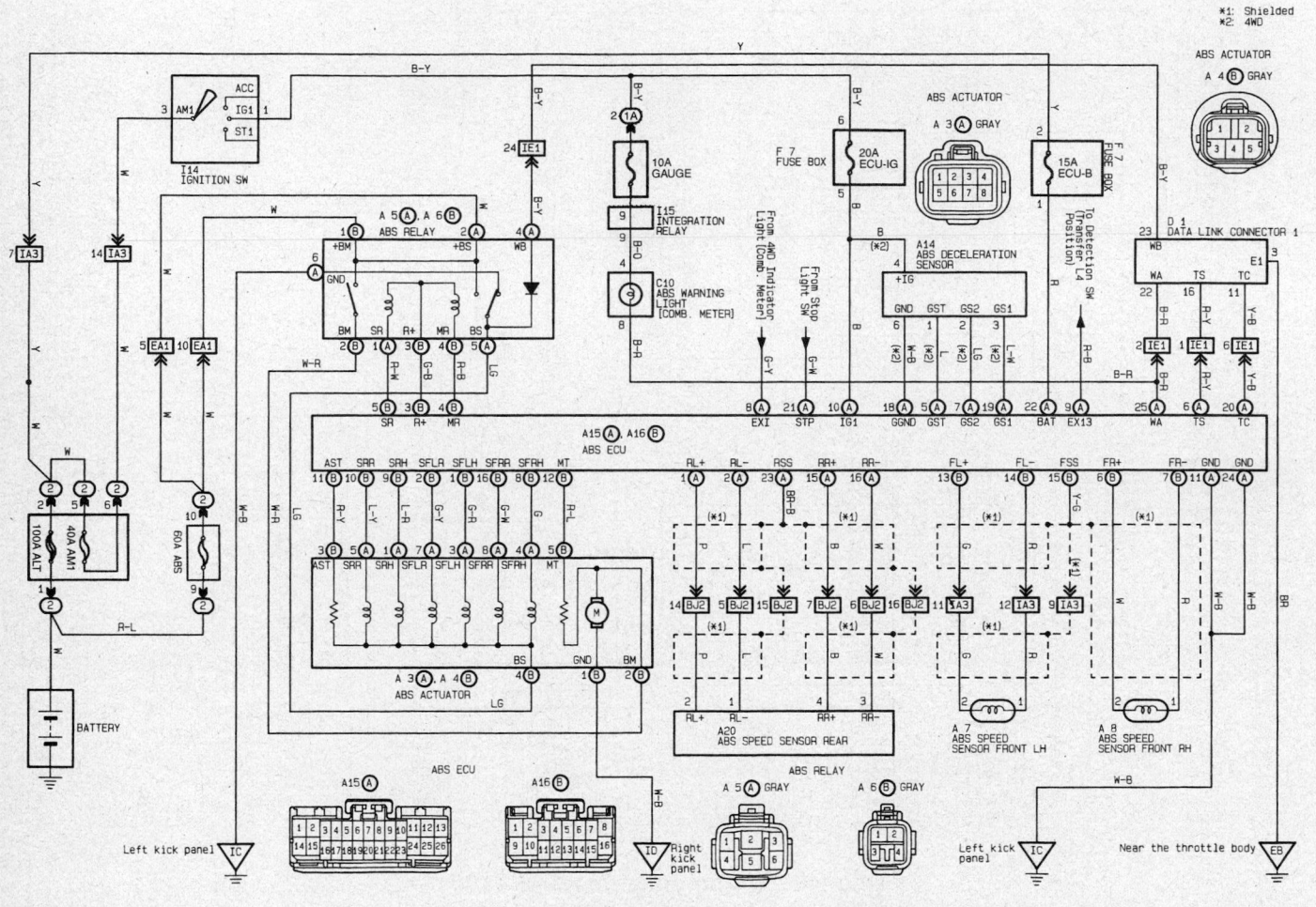

Fig. 41   Wiring diagram. 1997–98 T100

TY4029700301000X

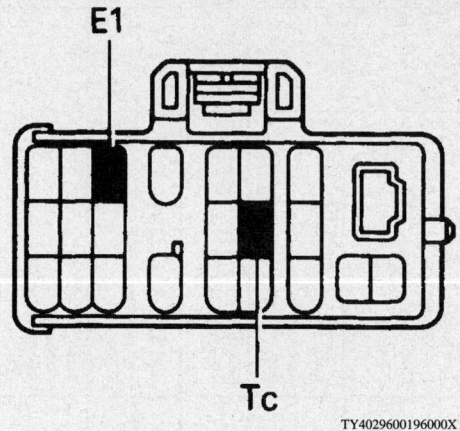

E1

Tc

TY4029600196000X

**Fig. 42   Data link connector
(DLC1). Except Tundra**

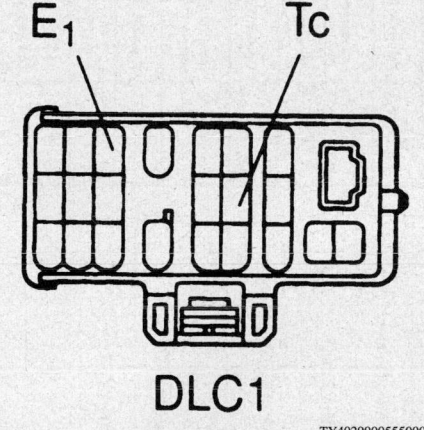

E_1 Tc

DLC1

TY4029900555000X

**Fig. 43   Data link connector
(DLC1). Tundra**

Code	ABS Warning Light Blinking Pattern	Diagnosis
11		Open or short circuit in ABS solenoid relay circuit
13		Open or short circuit in ABS motor relay circuit
21		Open or short circuit in 3-position solenoid circuit for right front wheel
22		Open or short circuit in 3-position solenoid circuit for left front wheel
23		Open or short circuit in 3-position solenoid circuit for rear wheels
31		Right front wheel speed sensor signal malfunction
32		Left front wheel speed sensor signal malfunction
33		Right rear wheel speed sensor signal malfunction
34		Left rear wheel speed sensor signal malfunction
35		Open circuit in right front speed sensor circuit
36		Open circuit in left front speed sensor circuit
37		Faulty front or rear speed sensor rotor
38		Open circuit in right rear speed sensor circuit
39		Open circuit in left rear speed sensor circuit
41		Low battery positive voltage
51		Pump motor is locked Open in pump motor circuit in actuator
62		Malfunction in ECU

TY4029500152000X

Fig. 44 Diagnostic trouble codes. 1996 Avalon

DTC No.	Detection Item	Trouble Area
11	ABS solenoid valve relay faulty	• ABS solenoid valve relay • Valve supply voltage • ECU
13	ABS pump motor faulty	• ABS motor relay • Pump motor voltage • Pump motor lead disconnected • ECU
21	Right front solenoid valves faulty	• ABS actuator (right front inlet or outlet solenoid valve)
22	Left front solenoid valves faulty	• ABS actuator (left front inlet or outlet solenoid valve)
23	Right rear solenoid valves faulty	• ABS actuator (right rear inlet or outlet solenoid valve)
24	Left rear solenoid valves faulty	• ABS actuator (left rear inlet or outlet solenoid valve)
31	Right front wheel speed sensor signal malfunction	• Right front, left front, right rear and left rear speed sensor
32	Left front wheel speed sensor signal malfunction	• Each speed sensor circuit • Sensor installation • ECU
33	Right rear wheel speed sensor signal malfunction	
34	Left rear wheel speed sensor signal malfunction	
35	Open circuit in right front wheel speed sensor circuit	• Right front, left front speed sensor • Each speed sensor circuit • ECU
36	Open circuit in left front wheel speed sensor circuit	
37	Speed sensor rotor is wrong number of teeth on one of the 4 wheels	• Speed sensor • Sensor rotor • ECU
38	Open circuit in right rear wheel speed sensor circuit	• Right rear, left rear speed sensor • Each speed sensor circuit • ECU
39	Open circuit in left rear wheel speed sensor circuit	
41	Low battery positive voltage	• Battery • IC regulator • Power source circuit • ECU
58	Open circuit in stop light switch circuit	• Stop light switch • Stop light switch circuit • ECU
62	Malfunction in ECU	• ECU

TY4029700236000X

Fig. 45 Diagnostic trouble codes. 1997–99 Avalon less traction control

ANTI-LOCK BRAKES

DTC No.	Detection Item	Trouble Area
49	Open circuit in stop light switch circuit	• Stop light switch • Stop light switch circuit • ECU
51	Pump motor is locked	• ABS pump motor • ECU
Always ON	Malfunction in ECU	• ECU

TY40297002390200X

Fig. 46 Diagnostic trouble codes (Part 2 of 3). 1997–99 Avalon w/traction control

DTC No.	Detection Item	Trouble Area
11	Open circuit in ABS solenoid relay circuit	• ABS solenoid relay • ABS solenoid relay circuit • ECU
12	Short circuit in ABS solenoid relay circuit	
13	Open circuit in ABS motor relay circuit	• ABS motor relay • ABS motor relay circuit • ECU
14	Short circuit in ABS motor relay circuit	
21	Open or short circuit in right front solenoid circuit	• ABS & TRAC actuator • SFRR or SFRH circuit • ECU
22	Open or short circuit in left front solenoid circuit	• ABS & TRAC actuator • SFLR or SFLH circuit • ECU
23	Open or short circuit in right rear solenoid circuit	• ABS & TRAC actuator • SRRR or SRRH circuit • ECU
24	Open or short circuit in left rear solenoid circuit	• ABS & TRAC actuator • SRLR or SRLH circuit • ECU
25	Open or short circuit in SMC1 circuit	• ABS & TRAC actuator • SMC1 circuit • ECU
26	Open or short circuit in SMC2 circuit	• ABS & TRAC actuator • SMC2 circuit • ECU
27	Open or short circuit in SRC1 circuit	• ABS & TRAC actuator • SRC1 circuit • ECU
28	Open or short circuit in SRC2 circuit	• ABS & TRAC actuator • SRC2 circuit • ECU
31	Right front wheel speed sensor signal malfunction	• Right front, left front, right rear and left rear speed sensor • Each speed sensor circuit • Speed sensor rotor • ECU
32	Left front wheel speed sensor signal malfunction	
33	Right rear wheel speed sensor signal malfunction	
34	Left rear wheel speed sensor signal malfunction	
41	Low battery positive voltage or abnormally high battery positive voltage	• Battery • IC regulator • Power source circuit • ECU

TY40297002390110X

Fig. 46 Diagnostic trouble codes (Part 1 of 3). 1997–99 Avalon w/traction control

DTC No.	Detection Item	Trouble Area
11	ABS solenoid valve relay faulty	• ABS solenoid valve relay • Valve supply voltage • ECU
13	ABS pump motor faulty	• ABS motor relay • Pump motor voltage • Pump motor lead disconnected • ECU
21	Right front solenoid valves faulty	• ABS actuator (right front inlet or outlet solenoid valve)
22	Left front solenoid valves faulty	• ABS actuator (left front inlet or outlet solenoid valve)
23	Right rear solenoid valves faulty	• ABS actuator (right rear inlet or outlet solenoid valve)
24	Left rear solenoid valves faulty	• ABS actuator (left rear inlet or outlet solenoid valve)
31	Right front wheel speed sensor signal malfunction	• Right front, left front, right rear and left rear speed sensor • Each speed sensor circuit • Sensor installation • ECU
32	Left front wheel speed sensor signal malfunction	
33	Right rear wheel speed sensor signal malfunction	
34	Left rear wheel speed sensor signal malfunction	
35	Open circuit in right front wheel speed sensor circuit	• Right front, left front speed sensor • Each speed sensor circuit • ECU
36	Open circuit in left front wheel speed sensor circuit	
37	Speed sensor rotor is wrong number of teeth on one of the 4 wheels	• Speed sensor • Sensor rotor • ECU
38	Open circuit in right rear wheel speed sensor circuit	• Right rear, left rear speed sensor • Each speed sensor circuit • ECU
39	Open circuit in left rear wheel speed sensor circuit	
41	Low battery positive voltage	• Battery • Charging system • Power source circuit • ECU
58	Open circuit in stop light switch circuit	• Stop light switch • Stop light switch circuit • ECU
62	Malfunction in ECU	• ECU

Fig. 47 Diagnostic trouble codes. Camry Solara less traction control

DTC No.	Detection Item	Trouble Area
43	Malfunction in ABS control system	• ABS control system
44	Open or short circuit in NE signal circuit	• NEO circuit • ECM • ECU
53	Malfunction in ECM communication circuit	• TRC+ or TRC – circuit • EFI+ or EFI– circuit • ECM • ECU
61	Malfunction in engine control system	• Engine control system
Always ON	Malfunction in ECU	• ECU

Fig. 46 Diagnostic trouble codes (Part 3 of 3). 1997–99 Avalon w/traction control

DTC No.	Detection Item	Trouble Area
43*	Malfunction in ABS control system	• ABS control system
44*	Open or short circuit in NE signal circuit	• NEO circuit • ECM • ECU
49	Open circuit in stop light switch circuit	• Stop light switch • Stop light switch circuit • ECU
51	Pump motor is locked	• ABS pump motor
53*	Malfunction in ECM communication circuit	• TRC+ or TRC – circuit • EFI+ or EFI– circuit • ECM • ECU
61*	Malfunction in engine control system	• Engine control system
Always ON	Malfunction in ECU	• ECU

*: TRAC OFF indicator light blinking

TY4029005570020X

Fig. 48 Diagnostic trouble codes (Part 2 of 2). Camry Solara w/traction control

DTC No.	Detection Item	Trouble Area
11	Open circuit in ABS & TRAC solenoid relay circuit	• ABS & TRAC solenoid relay • ABS & TRAC solenoid relay circuit • ECU
12	Short circuit in ABS & TRAC solenoid relay circuit	
13	Open circuit in ABS & TRAC motor relay circuit	• ABS & TRAC motor relay • ABS & TRAC motor relay circuit • ECU
14	Short circuit in ABS & TRAC motor relay circuit	
21	Open or short circuit in right front solenoid circuit	• ABS & TRAC actuator • SFRR or SFRH circuit • ECU
22	Open or short circuit in left front solenoid circuit	• ABS & TRAC actuator • SFLR or SFLH circuit • ECU
23	Open or short circuit in right rear solenoid circuit	• ABS & TRAC actuator • SRRR or SRRH circuit • ECU
24	Open or short circuit in left rear solenoid circuit	• ABS & TRAC actuator • SRLR or SRLH circuit • ECU
25	Open or short circuit in SMC1 circuit	• ABS & TRAC actuator • SMC1 circuit • ECU
26	Open or short circuit in SMC2 circuit	• ABS & TRAC actuator • SMC2 circuit • ECU
27	Open or short circuit in SRC1 circuit	• ABS & TRAC actuator • SRC1 circuit • ECU
28	Open or short circuit in SRC2 circuit	• ABS & TRAC actuator • SRC2 circuit • ECU
31	Right front wheel speed sensor signal malfunction	• Right front, left front, right rear and left rear speed sensor • Each speed sensor circuit • Speed sensor rotor • ECU
32	Left front wheel speed sensor signal malfunction	
33	Right rear wheel speed sensor signal malfunction	
34	Left rear wheel speed sensor signal malfunction	
41	Low battery positive voltage or abnormally high battery positive voltage	• Battery • Charging system • Power source circuit • ECU

TY4029005570010X

Fig. 48 Diagnostic trouble codes (Part 1 of 2). Camry Solara w/traction control

DTC No.	Detection Item	Trouble Area
11	Open circuit in ABS control (solenoid) relay circuit	• ABS control (solenoid) relay • Open or short in ABS control (solenoid) relay circuit • ECU
12	Short circuit in ABS control (solenoid) relay circuit	• ABS control (solenoid) relay • B+ short in ABS control (solenoid) relay circuit • ECU
13	Open circuit in ABS control (motor) relay circuit	• ABS control (motor) relay • Open or short in ABS control (motor) relay circuit • ECU
14	Short circuit in ABS control (motor) relay circuit	• ABS control (motor) relay • B+ short in ABS control (motor) relay circuit • ECU
21	Open or short circuit in 2-position solenoid circuit for right front wheel	• ABS actuator • Open or short in SFRR or SFRH circuit • ECU
22	Open or short circuit in 2-position solenoid circuit for left front wheel	• ABS actuator • Open or short in SFLR or SFLH circuit • ECU
23	Open or short circuit in 2-position solenoid circuit for rear wheel	• ABS actuator • Open or short in SRR or SRH circuit • ECU
31	Right front wheel speed sensor signal malfunction	
32	Left front wheel speed sensor signal malfunction	• Right front, left front, right rear and left rear speed sensor • Open or short in each speed sensor circuit • ECU
33	Right rear wheel speed sensor signal malfunction	
34	Left rear wheel speed sensor signal malfunction	
37	Neither front speed sensor rotor missing	• Front axle hub • Right front, left front speed sensor • Wire harness for sensor system • ECU
37	Some tire is different size from the other tires	• Tire size • ECU
41	Low battery positive voltage or abnormally high battery positive voltage	• Battery • IC regulator • Open or short in power source circuit • ECU
43*1	Malfunction in deceleration sensor	• Deceleration sensor • Wire harness for deceleration sensor circuit • ECU
44*1	Open or short in deceleration sensor circuit	• Deceleration sensor • Open or short in deceleration sensor circuit • ECU

Fig. 49 Diagnostic trouble codes (Part 1 of 2). 4Runner

48*2	Open or short circuit in rear differential lock circuit Rear differential is locking	• Rear differential lock • ECU
51	Pump motor is locked Open in pump motor ground	• ABS pump motor
Always ON	Malfunction in ECU	• ECU

*1: 4WD models
*2: w/ Rear differential lock

Fig. 49 Diagnostic trouble codes (Part 2 of 2). 4Runner

Code	ABS Warning Light Blinking Pattern	Indicator			Diagnosis
		ABS Warning Light	TRAC Indicator Light	TRAC OFF Light	
11	(pattern)	ON	OFF	ON	Open or short in ABS solenoid relay circuit
12	(pattern)	ON	OFF	ON	B+ short in ABS solenoid relay circuit
13	(pattern)	ON	OFF	ON	Open or short in ABS motor relay circuit
14	(pattern)	ON	OFF	ON	B+ short in ABS motor relay circuit
(15)	(pattern)	ON	ON	ON	Open or short in TRAC solenoid relay circuit
16	(pattern)	ON	ON	OFF	B+ short in TRAC solenoid relay circuit
17	(pattern)	OFF*	ON	ON	Open or short in TRAC motor relay circuit
18	(pattern)	OFF*	ON	ON	B+ short in TRAC motor relay circuit
21	(pattern)	ON	OFF	ON	Open or short in ABS actuator solenoid circuit (SFR circuit)
22	(pattern)	ON	OFF	ON	Open or short in ABS actuator solenoid circuit (SFL circuit)
23	(pattern)	ON	OFF	ON	Open or short in ABS actuator solenoid circuit (SRR circuit)
24	(pattern)	ON	OFF	ON	Open or short in ABS actuator solenoid circuit (SRL circuit)
(25)	(pattern)	ON	ON	ON	Open or short in TRAC actuator solenoid circuit (SMC circuit)
(27)	(pattern)	ON	OFF	ON	Open or short in TRAC actuator solenoid circuit (SRC circuit)
31	(pattern)	ON	ON	ON	Right front wheel speed sensor signal malfunction
32	(pattern)	ON	OFF	ON	Left front wheel speed sensor signal malfunction
33	(pattern)	ON	OFF	ON	Right rear wheel speed sensor signal malfunction
34	(pattern)	ON	OFF	ON	Left rear wheel speed sensor signal malfunction

Fig. 50 Diagnostic trouble codes (Part 1 of 2). 1996 Supra

TY402930004 6010X

Code	ABS Warning Light Blinking Pattern	Indicator			Diagnosis
		ABS Warning Light	TRAC Indicator Light	TRAC OFF Light	
35	(pattern)	ON	OFF	ON	Open circuit in left front or right rear speed sensor circuit
36	(pattern)	ON	OFF	ON	Open circuit in right front or left rear speed sensor circuit
41	(pattern)	ON	OFF	ON	Low battery positive voltage or abnormally high battery positive voltage
44	(pattern)	ON	OFF	OFF	Open or short in lateral acceleration sensor circuit
51	(pattern)	ON	OFF	ON	ABS pump motor is locked / Open in ABS pump motor ground
(55)	(pattern)	OFF*	ON	ON	Brake fluid reservoir level low
(58)	(pattern)	OFF*	ON	ON	Open circuit in TRAC pump motor circuit
(61)	(pattern)	OFF*	ON	ON	TRAC ECU communication abnormal
(62)	(pattern)	OFF*	ON	ON	Wheel speed sensor signal malfunction
Always ON	(pattern)	ON	ON	ON	Malfunction in ABS (& TRAC) ECU

C: Only vehicles with TRAC

*: When a malfunction causing code No. 17, 18, 55, 58, 61 or 62 is detected, the ABS warning light does not light up, but the TRAC indicator light does. However, when checking the DTC, check the blinking pattern of the ABS warning light.

Fig. 50 Diagnostic trouble codes (Part 2 of 2). 1996 Supra

TY402930004 6020X

DTC No.	Detection Item	Trouble Area
11	Open circuit in ABS solenoid relay circuit	• ABS solenoid relay • Open or short in ABS solenoid relay circuit
12	Short circuit in ABS solenoid relay circuit	• ABS solenoid relay • B+ short in ABS solenoid relay circuit
*13	Open circuit in ABS motor relay circuit	• ABS motor relay • Open or short in ABS motor relay circuit
14	Short circuit in ABS motor relay circuit	• ABS motor relay • B+ short in ABS motor relay circuit
21	Open or short circuit in 2-position solenoid circuit for right front wheel	• ABS actuator • Open or short in SFRH or SFRR circuit
22	Open or short circuit in 2-position solenoid circuit for left front wheel	• ABS actuator • Open or short in SFLH or SFLR circuit
23	Open or short circuit in 2-position solenoid circuit for right rear wheel	• ABS actuator • Open or short in SRH (SRRH) or SRR (SRRR) circuit
㉔	Open or short circuit in 2-position solenoid circuit for left rear wheel	• ABS actuator • Open or short in SRLH or SRLR circuit
*31	Right front wheel speed sensor signal malfunction	• Right front, left front, right rear and left rear speed sensor • Open or short in each speed sensor circuit • Speed sensor rotor
*32	Left front wheel speed sensor signal malfunction	
*33	Right rear wheel speed sensor signal malfunction	
*34	Left rear wheel speed sensor signal malfunction	
41	Low battery positive voltage	• Battery • IC regulator • Open or short in power source circuit
㊸	Malfunction in deceleration sensor (constant output)	• Deceleration sensor • Wire harness for deceleration sensor system
㊹	Open or short in deceleration sensor circuit	• Deceleration sensor • Open or short in deceleration sensor circuit
㊺	Malfunction in deceleration sensor	• Deceleration sensor • Wire harness for deceleration sensor system
49	Open circuit in stop light switch circuit	• Open in stop light circuit
*51	Pump motor is locked Open in pump motor ground	• ABS pump motor
Always ON	Malfunction in ECU IG power source circuit	• Battery • IC regulator • Open or short in power source circuit

○: Sport ABS (2JZ-GTE Engine) only

*: As the DTC cannot be erased by replacing parts alone, do either of the following operations.
1. Clear DTC.
2. At the vehicle speed of 20 km/h (12 mph), drive the vehicle for 30 sec. or more.

TY402970040400X

Fig. 52   Diagnostic trouble codes. 1997–98 Supra less traction control

Code	TRAC Indicator Light Blinking Pattern	Diagnosis
24		Open or short in sub-throttle actuator circuit
25		Step motor does not move to a position decided by ECU
26		Sub-throttle valve does not move even when the sub-throttle valve is controlled to fully open position by ECU
31		Right front wheel speed sensor signal malfunction
32		Left front wheel speed sensor signal malfunction
33		Right rear wheel speed sensor signal malfunction
34		Left rear wheel speed sensor signal malfunction
41		Low battery positive voltage or abnormally high battery positive voltage
43*1		Malfunction in ABS or TRAC (BRAKE) control system
44		Open or short in NE signal circuit
45		Main throttle position sensor circuit malfunction
46*2		Open or short in main throttle position sensor circuit
47		Sub-throttle position sensor circuit malfunction
48		Open or short in sub-throttle position sensor circuit
51*3		Engine & ECT system malfunction
53*4		ECM communication circuit malfunction
61		ABS & TRAC ECU communication circuit malfunction
Always ON		Malfunction in TRAC ECU

TY402950043800X

*1: If a malfunction is detected in ABS, the TRAC OFF indicator light lights up instead of the TRAC indicator light.
*2: The TRAC indicator light does not light up even if an error is detected.
*3: If a malfunction is detected, the TRAC OFF indicator light lights up instead of the TRAC indicator light.
*4: Depending on the malfunction, the TRAC indicator light does not light up.

Fig. 51   Diagnostic trouble codes. 1996 Supra w/traction control

ANTI-LOCK BRAKES

DTC No.	Detection Item	Trouble Area
52	Power source voltage down	• Battery • IC regulator • Wire harness and connector (+B and E01 circuit) • Throttle control ECU
61	Right front speed sensor circuit	• Right front, left front, right rear and left rear speed sensor • Wire harness and connector (FRO, FLO, RRO and RLO circuit) • Throttle control ECU
62	Left front speed sensor circuit	
63	Right rear speed sensor circuit	
64	Left rear speed sensor circuit	
71	Emergency fuel cut (sub-throttle motor circuit malfunction)	• Sub-throttle valve motor • Sub-throttle valve • Throttle control ECU
72	Emergency fuel cut	
81	ABS ECU malfunction	• Wire harness and connector (WA circuit) • ABS ECU • Throttle control ECU
Always ON	• Throttle control ECU malfunction • TRAC OFF switch ON	• Throttle control ECU

Fig. 53 Diagnostic trouble codes (Part 2 of 2). 1997–98 Supra w/traction control

TY402970044050020X

DTC No.	Detection Item	Trouble Area
11	Throttle control relay circuit open	• Throttle control relay • TRAC fuse • Wire harness and connector (throttle control relay circuit) • Throttle control ECU
12	Throttle control relay circuit short	• Throttle control relay • Wire harness and connector (throttle control relay circuit) • Throttle control ECU
21	Sub-throttle valve motor circuit open or short	• Sub-throttle valve motor • Wire harness and connector (sub-throttle valve motor and E01 circuit) • Throttle control ECU
22	Sub-throttle valve motor malfunction	• Sub-throttle valve motor • Sub-throttle valve • Sub-throttle position sensor • Wire harness and connector (E1 circuit) • Throttle control ECU
23	Throttle body malfunction	• Sub-throttle valve • Sub-throttle position sensor • Throttle control ECU
24	Sub-throttle position sensor leakage/sub-throttle valve stuck	• Sub-throttle valve • Sub-throttle position sensor • Wire harness and connector (E1 circuit) • Throttle control ECU
31	Throttle position sensor signal malfunction	• Throttle position sensor • Wire harness and connector (throttle position sensor and E1 circuit) • Throttle control ECU
32	Sub-throttle position sensor signal malfunction	• Sub-throttle position sensor • Sub-throttle valve motor • Sub-throttle valve • Wire harness and connector (sub-throttle position sensor and E1 circuit) • Throttle control ECU
41	Engine revolution signal open or short	• Wire harness and connector (NE circuit) • ECM • Throttle control ECU
42	ECM malfunction	• Wire harness and connector (EFIF circuit) • ECM • Throttle control ECU
43	ECM communication circuit malfunction	• Wire harness and connector (EFI+ and EFI− circuit) • ECM • Throttle control ECU
51	Power source voltage down (sub-throttle valve in a bad condition)	• Wire harness and connector (+B and E01 circuit) • Throttle control ECU

Fig. 53 Diagnostic trouble codes (Part 1 of 2). 1997–98 Supra w/traction control

TY402970040405010X

Code	ABS Warning Light Blinking Pattern	Diagnosis
11	BE3931	Open circuit in ABS control (solenoid) relay circuit
12	BE3931	Short circuit in ABS control (solenoid) relay circuit
13	BE3931	Open circuit in ABS control (motor) relay circuit
14	BE3931	Short circuit in ABS control (motor) relay circuit
21	BE3932	Open or short circuit in 2-position solenoid circuit for right front wheel
22	BE3932	Open or short circuit in 2-position solenoid circuit for left front wheel
23	BE3932	Open or short circuit in 2-position solenoid circuit for rear wheel
31	BE3933	Right front wheel speed sensor signal malfunction
32	BE3933	Left front wheel speed sensor signal malfunction
33	BE3933	Right rear wheel speed sensor signal malfunction
34	BE3933	Left rear wheel speed sensor signal malfunction
35	BE3933	Open circuit in left front or right rear speed sensor circuit
36	BE3933	Open circuit in right front or left rear speed sensor circuit
41	BE3934	Low battery positive voltage or abnormally high battery positive voltage
*43	BE3934	Malfunction in deceleration sensor
*44	BE3934	Open or short in deceleration sensor circuit
51	BE3935	Pump motor is locked / Open in pump motor ground
Always ON		Malfunction in ECU

*: 4WD models

Fig. 54 Diagnostic trouble codes. 1996 Previa

TY40292000049000X

DTC No.	Detection Item	Trouble Area
11	Open circuit in ABS solenoid relay circuit	• Actuator inside wire harness • ABS solenoid relay • Wire harness and connector of solenoid relay circuit
12	Short circuit in ABS solenoid relay circuit	• Actuator inside wire harness • ABS solenoid relay • Wire harness and connector of solenoid relay circuit
13	Open circuit in ABS motor relay circuit	• Actuator inside wire harness • ABS motor relay • Wire harness and connector of motor relay circuit
14	Short circuit in ABS motor relay circuit	• Actuator inside wire harness • ABS motor relay • Wire harness and connector of motor relay circuit
21	Open or short circuit in 2 position solenoid of right front wheel	• Actuator solenoid • Wire harness and connector of actuator solenoid circuit
22	Open or short circuit in 2 position solenoid of left front wheel	• Actuator solenoid • Wire harness and connector of actuator solenoid circuit
23	Open or short circuit in 2 position solenoid of rear wheel	• Actuator solenoid • Wire harness and connector of actuator solenoid circuit
31	Right front wheel speed sensor signal malfunction	• Speed sensor • Sensor rotor • Wire harness and connector of speed sensor
32	Left front wheel speed sensor signal malfunction	• Speed sensor • Sensor rotor • Wire harness and connector of speed sensor
33	Right rear wheel speed sensor signal malfunction	• Speed sensor • Sensor rotor • Wire harness and connector of speed sensor
34	Left rear wheel speed sensor signal malfunction	• Speed sensor • Sensor rotor • Wire harness and connector of speed sensor
41	Low battery positive voltage	• Battery • Voltage regulator
49	Open circuit in stop light circuit	• Wire harness and connector of stop light circuit
51	Pump motor is locked / Open in pump motor ground	• Pump motor, relay and battery • Wire harness, connector and ground bolt or actuator pump motor circuit
Always ON	Malfunction in ECU / Abnormally high battery positive voltage	• Battery • Voltage regulator • ECU

TY40297003000000X

Fig. 55 Diagnostic trouble codes. 1997 Previa

Fig. 57 Diagnostic trouble codes. Paseo & Tercel

DTC No.	Detection Item	Trouble Area
11	Open circuit in ABS control (solenoid) relay circuit	• ABS control (solenoid) relay • Solenoid relay • Open or short in ABS control (solenoid) relay circuit • ECU
12	Short circuit in ABS control (solenoid) relay circuit	• ABS control (solenoid) relay • B+ short in ABS control (solenoid) relay circuit • ECU
13	Open circuit in ABS control (motor) relay circuit	• ABS control (motor) relay • Open or short in ABS control (motor) relay circuit • ECU
14	Short circuit in ABS control (motor) relay circuit	• ABS control (motor) relay • B+ short in ABS control (motor) relay circuit • ECU
21	Open or short circuit in solenoid circuit for right front wheel	• ABS actuator • Open or short in SFR circuit • ECU
22	Open or short circuit in solenoid circuit for left front wheel	• ABS actuator • Open or short in SFL circuit • ECU
23	Open or short circuit in solenoid circuit for right rear wheel	• ABS actuator • Open or short in SRR circuit • ECU
24	Open or short circuit in solenoid circuit for left rear wheel	• ABS actuator • Open or short in SRL circuit • ECU
31	Right front wheel speed sensor signal malfunction	• Right front, left front, right rear and left rear speed sensor • Open or short in each speed sensor circuit • ECU
32	Left front wheel speed sensor signal malfunction	
33	Right rear wheel speed sensor signal malfunction	
34	Left rear wheel speed sensor signal malfunction	
41	Low battery positive voltage or abnormally high battery positive voltage	• Battery • IC regulator • Open or short in power source circuit • ECU
51	Pump motor is locked Open in pump motor ground	• ABS pump motor
Always ON	Malfunction in ECU	• ECU

TY40296002000000X

Fig. 56 Diagnostic trouble codes. Land Cruiser

Code No.	Light Pattern	Diagnosis	Trouble Part
11	(light pattern)	Open circuit in solenoid relay circuit	• Actuator inside wire harness • Solenoid relay • Wire harness and connector of solenoid relay circuit (Include AST circuit)
12	(light pattern)	Short circuit in solenoid relay circuit	
13	(light pattern)	Open circuit in pump motor relay circuit	• Actuator inside wire harness • Pump motor relay • Wire harness and connector of pump motor relay circuit (Include MT circuit)
14	(light pattern)	Short circuit in pump motor relay circuit	
21	(light pattern)	Open or short circuit in 3 position solenoid of front right wheel	• Actuator solenoid • Wire harness and connector of actuator solenoid circuit
22	(light pattern)	Open or short circuit in 3 position solenoid of front left wheel	
23	(light pattern)	Open or short circuit in 3 position solenoid of rear wheel	
31	(light pattern)	Front right wheel speed sensor signal malfunction	• Speed sensor • Sensor rotor • Wire harness and connector of speed sensor
32	(light pattern)	Front left wheel speed sensor signal malfunction	
33	(light pattern)	Rear right wheel speed sensor signal malfunction	
34	(light pattern)	Rear left wheel speed sensor signal malfunction	
35	(light pattern)	Open circuit in front left or rear right wheel speed sensor	
36	(light pattern)	Open circuit in front right or rear left wheel speed sensor	
41	(light pattern)	Abnormally high or low battery voltage	• Battery • Voltage regulator
43	(light pattern)	Malfunction in deceleration sensor	• Deceleration sensor • Deceleration sensor installation • Wire harness and connector of deceleration sensor
44	(light pattern)	Open or short circuit in deceleration sensor	
48	(light pattern)	Open or short circuit on center differential lock indicator	• Center differential lock • Center differential lock indicator light • Center differential lock switch • Wire harness and connector of center differential lock
51	(light pattern)	Pump motor of actuator locked or open circuit in pump motor circuit in actuator	• Pump motor, relay and battery • Wire harness, connector and ground bolt or actuator pump motor circuit (Include MT circuit) • ECU
Always on	(light pattern)	Malfunction in ECU	• ECU

TY40293000500000X

DTC No.	Detection Item	Trouble Area
11	Open circuit in ABS solenoid relay circuit	• ABS solenoid relay • ABS solenoid relay circuit
12	Short circuit in ABS solenoid relay circuit	• ABS solenoid relay circuit
13	Open circuit in ABS motor relay circuit	• ABS motor relay • ABS motor relay circuit
14	Short circuit in ABS motor relay circuit	• ABS motor relay circuit
21	Open or short circuit in 2-position solenoid circuit for right front wheel	• ABS actuator • SFRR or SFRH circuit
22	Open or short circuit in 2-position solenoid circuit for left front wheel	• ABS actuator • SFLR or SFLH circuit
23	Open or short circuit in 2-position solenoid circuit for right rear wheel	• ABS actuator • SRRR or SRRH circuit
24	Open or short circuit in 2-position solenoid circuit for left rear wheel	• ABS actuator • SRLR or SRLH circuit
31	Right front wheel speed sensor signal malfunction	• Right front, left front, right rear and left rear speed sensor • Each speed sensor circuit • Speed sensor rotor
32	Left front wheel speed sensor signal malfunction	
33	Right rear wheel speed sensor signal malfunction	
34	Left rear wheel speed sensor signal malfunction	
33, 34	Rear speed sensor rotor faulty	• Rear axle hub • Right rear, left rear speed sensor • Rear speed sensor circuit
41	Power source voltage down	• Battery • IC regulator • Power source circuit
49	Open circuit in stop light switch circuit	• Stop light switch • Stop light switch circuit
51	Pump motor is locked	• ABS pump motor
Always ON	Malfunction in ECU	• ECU • Battery

TY402970033800X

Fig. 59 Diagnostic trouble codes. 1997–99 Camry w/Nippondenso ABS

Code	ABS Warning Light Blinking Pattern	Diagnosis
11	ON/OFF	Open circuit in ABS solenoid relay circuit
12	ON/OFF	Short circuit in ABS solenoid relay circuit
13	ON/OFF	Open circuit in ABS motor relay circuit
14	ON/OFF	Short circuit in ABS motor relay circuit
21	ON/OFF	Open or short circuit in solenoid circuit for right front wheel
22	ON/OFF	Open or short circuit in solenoid circuit for left front wheel
23	ON/OFF	Open or short circuit in solenoid circuit for right rear wheel
24	ON/OFF	Open or short circuit in solenoid circuit for left rear wheel
31	ON/OFF	Right front wheel speed sensor signal malfunction
32	ON/OFF	Left front wheel speed sensor signal malfunction
33	ON/OFF	Right rear wheel speed sensor signal malfunction
34	ON/OFF	Left rear wheel speed sensor signal malfunction
35	ON/OFF	Open circuit in left front or right rear speed sensor circuit
36	ON/OFF	Open circuit in right front or left rear speed sensor circuit
37	ON/OFF	Faulty rear speed sensor rotor
41	ON/OFF	Low battery positive voltage or abnormally high battery positive voltage
51	ON/OFF	Pump motor is locked Open in pump motor ground
Always ON	ON/OFF	Malfunction in ECU

TY402940005200X

Fig. 58 Diagnostic trouble codes. Corolla & 1996 Celica & Camry w/Nippondenso ABS

Fig. 61 Diagnostic trouble codes. 1997–99 Camry w/Bosch ABS

DTC No.	Detection Item	Trouble Area
11	ABS solenoid valve relay faulty	• ABS solenoid valve relay • Valve supply voltage • ECU
13	ABS pump motor faulty	• ABS motor relay • Pump motor voltage • Pump motor lead disconnected • ECU
21	Right front solenoid valves faulty	• ABS actuator (right front inlet or outlet solenoid valve) • ECU
22	Left front solenoid valves faulty	• ABS actuator (left front inlet or outlet solenoid valve) • ECU
23	Right rear solenoid valves faulty	• ABS actuator (right rear inlet or outlet solenoid valve) • ECU
24	Left rear solenoid valves faulty	• ABS actuator (left rear inlet or outlet solenoid valve) • ECU
31	Right front wheel speed sensor signal malfunction	
32	Left front wheel speed sensor signal malfunction	• Right front, left front, right rear and left rear speed sensor • Each speed sensor circuit • Sensor installation • ECU
33	Right rear wheel speed sensor signal malfunction	
34	Left rear wheel speed sensor signal malfunction	
35	Open circuit in right front wheel speed sensor circuit	• Right front, left front speed sensor • Each speed sensor circuit • ECU
36	Open circuit in left front wheel speed sensor circuit	
37	Speed sensor rotor is wrong number of teeth on one of the 4 wheels	• Speed sensor • Sensor rotor • ECU
38	Open circuit in right rear wheel speed sensor circuit	• Right rear, left rear speed sensor • Each speed sensor circuit • ECU
39	Open circuit in left rear wheel speed sensor circuit	
41	Low battery positive voltage	• Battery • IC regulator • Power source circuit • ECU
58	Open circuit in stop light switch circuit	• Stop light switch • Stop light switch circuit • ECU
62	Malfunction in ECU	• ECU

Fig. 60 Diagnostic trouble codes. 1996 Camry w/Bosch ABS

DTC No.	Detection Item	Trouble Area
11	Open or short circuit in ABS solenoid relay circuit	• Open or short in ABS solenoid relay circuit • ECU
13	Open or short circuit in ABS motor relay circuit	• Pump motor • Open in ABS motor relay circuit • ECU
21	Open or short circuit in 3-position solenoid circuit for right front wheel	• ABS actuator (solenoid valve) • Open or short in right front solenoid circuit • ECU
22	Open or short circuit in 3-position solenoid circuit for left front wheel	• ABS actuator (solenoid valve) • Open or short in left front solenoid circuit • ECU
23	Open or short circuit in 3-position solenoid circuit for rear wheels	• ABS actuator (solenoid valve) • Open or short in rear solenoid circuit • ECU
31	Right front wheel speed sensor signal malfunction	• Right front, left front, right rear and left rear speed sensor • Open in each speed sensor circuit • Sensor installation • Sensor rotor • ECU
32	Left front wheel speed sensor signal malfunction	
33	Right rear wheel speed sensor signal malfunction	
34	Left rear wheel speed sensor signal malfunction	
35	Open circuit in right front speed sensor circuit	• Right front, left front, right rear and left rear speed sensor • Open in each speed sensor circuit • ECU
36	Open circuit in left front speed sensor circuit	
37	Faulty one of 4 speed sensor rotors	• Sensor rotor • Speed sensor • Wire harness for sensor circuit • Tires • ECU
38	Open circuit in right rear speed sensor circuit	• Right front, left front, right rear and left rear speed sensor • Open in each speed sensor circuit • ECU
39	Open circuit in left rear speed sensor circuit	
41	Low battery positive voltage	• Battery • IC regulator • Open or short in power source circuit • ECU
51	Pump motor is locked Open in pump motor circuit in actuator	• ABS pump motor
62	Malfunction in ECU	• ECU

DTC No.	Detection Item	Trouble Area
11	Open circuit in ABS & TRAC solenoid relay circuit	• ABS & TRAC solenoid relay • ABS & TRAC solenoid relay circuit • ECU
12	Short circuit in ABS & TRAC solenoid relay circuit	
13	Open circuit in ABS & TRAC motor relay circuit	• ABS & TRAC motor relay • ABS & TRAC motor relay circuit • ECU
14	Short circuit in ABS & TRAC motor relay circuit	
21	Open or short circuit in right front solenoid circuit	• ABS & TRAC actuator • SFRR or SFRH circuit • ECU
22	Open or short circuit in left front solenoid circuit	• ABS & TRAC actuator • SFLR or SFLH circuit • ECU
23	Open or short circuit in right rear solenoid circuit	• ABS & TRAC actuator • SRRR or SRRH circuit • ECU
24	Open or short circuit in left rear solenoid circuit	• ABS & TRAC actuator • SRLR or SRLH circuit • ECU
25	Open or short circuit in SMC1 circuit	• ABS & TRAC actuator • SMC1 circuit • ECU
26	Open or short circuit in SMC2 circuit	• ABS & TRAC actuator • SMC2 circuit • ECU
27	Open or short circuit in SRC1 circuit	• ABS & TRAC actuator • SRC1 circuit • ECU
28	Open or short circuit in SRC2 circuit	• ABS & TRAC actuator • SRC2 circuit • ECU
31	Right front wheel speed sensor signal malfunction	
32	Left front wheel speed sensor signal malfunction	• Right front, left front, right rear and left rear speed sensor • Each speed sensor circuit • Speed sensor rotor • ECU
33	Right rear wheel speed sensor signal malfunction	
34	Left rear wheel speed sensor signal malfunction	
41	Low battery positive voltage or abnormally high battery positive voltage	• Battery • IC regulator • Power source circuit • ECU

TY40297003390010X

Fig. 62 Diagnostic trouble codes (Part 1 of 3). 1997–99 Camry w/Traction Control

49	Open circuit in stop light switch circuit	• Stop light switch • Stop light switch circuit • ECU
51	Pump motor is locked	• ABS pump motor • ECU
Always ON	Malfunction in ECU	• ECU

TY40297003390020X

Fig. 62 Diagnostic trouble codes (Part 2 of 3). 1997–99 Camry w/Traction Control

DTC No.	Detection Item	Trouble Area
11	Open circuit in ABS solenoid relay circuit	• ABS solenoid relay • Open or short in ABS solenoid relay circuit
12	Short in ABS solenoid relay circuit	• ABS solenoid relay • B+ short in ABS solenoid relay circuit
13	Open circuit in ABS motor relay circuit	• ABS motor relay • Open or short in ABS motor relay circuit
14	Short circuit in ABS motor relay circuit	• ABS motor relay • B+ short in ABS motor relay circuit
21	Open or short circuit in solenoid circuit for right front wheel	• ABS actuator • Open or short in SFRH or SFRR circuit
22	Open or short circuit in solenoid circuit for left front wheel	• ABS actuator • Open or short in SFLH or SFLR circuit
23	Open or short circuit in solenoid circuit for right rear wheel	• ABS actuator • Open or short in SRRH or SRRR circuit
24	Open or short circuit in solenoid circuit for left rear wheel	• ABS actuator • Open or short in SRLH or SRLR circuit
31	Right front wheel speed sensor signal malfunction	• Right front, left front right rear and left rear speed sensor
32	Left front wheel speed sensor sirnal malfunction	• Open or short in each speed sensor circuit
33	Right rear wheel speed sensor signal malfunction	• Sensor rotor
34	Left rear wheel speed sensor signal malfunction	
41	Low battery positive voltage	• Battery • IC regulator
51	Pump motor is locked Open in pump motor ground	• Open or short in power source circuit • ABS pump motor
Always ON	Malfunction in ECU Abnormally high battery positive voltage	• ECU • Battery

Fig. 63 Diagnostic trouble codes. 1997–99 Celica

DTC No.	Detection Item	Trouble Area
43	Malfunction in ABS control system	• ABS control system
44	Open or short circuit in NE signal circuit	• NEO circuit • ECM • ECU
53	Malfunction in ECM communication circuit	• TRC+ or TRC– circuit • EFI+ or EFI– circuit • ECM • ECU
61	Malfunction in engine control system	• Engine control system
Always ON	Malfunction in ECU	• ECU

Fig. 62 Diagnostic trouble codes (Part 3 of 3). 1997–99 Camry w/Traction Control

Fig. 65 Diagnostic trouble codes. 1997–99 RAV4

DTC No.	Detection Item	Trouble Area
11	Open circuit in ABS control (solenoid) relay circuit	• ABS control (solenoid) relay • Open or short in ABS control (solenoid) relay circuit
12	Short circuit in ABS control (solenoid) relay circuit	• ABS control (solenoid) relay • B+ short in ABS control (solenoid) relay circuit
*3 13	Open circuit in ABS control (motor) relay circuit	• ABS control (motor) relay • Open or short in ABS control (motor) relay circuit
14	Short circuit in ABS control (motor) relay circuit	• ABS control (motor) relay • B+ short in ABS control (motor) relay circuit
21	Open or short circuit in 2-position solenoid circuit for right front wheel	• ABS actuator • Open or short in SFRR or SFRH circuit
22	Open or short circuit in 2-position solenoid circuit for left front wheel	• ABS actuator • Open or short in SFLR or SFLH circuit
23	Open or short circuit in 2-position solenoid circuit for right rear wheel	• ABS actuator • Open or short in SRRR or SRRH circuit
24	Open or short circuit in 2-position solenoid circuit for left rear wheel	• ABS actuator • Open or short in SRLR or SRLH circuit
*3 31	Right front wheel speed sensor signal malfunction	• Right front, left front, right rear and left rear speed sensor • Open or short in each speed sensor circuit • Speed sensor • Sensor rotor
*3 32	Left front wheel speed sensor signal malfunction	
*3 33	Right rear wheel speed sensor signal malfunction	
*3 34	Left rear wheel speed sensor signal malfunction	
*1 37	Some tire is different size from the other tires	• Tire size
41	Low battery positive voltage.	• Battery • IC regulator • Open or short in power source circuit
*2 43	Malfunction in deceleration sensor (constant output)	• Deceleration sensor • Wire harness for deceleration sensor system
*2 44	Open or short in deceleration sensor circuit	• Deceleration sensor • Open or short in deceleration sensor circuit
*3 45	Malfunction in deceleration sensor	• Deceleration sensor • Wire harness for deceleration sensor system
*2 49	Open circuit in stop light switch circuit	• Open in stop light switch circuit
51	Pump motor is locked Open in pump motor ground	• ABS pump motor
Always ON	Malfunction in ECU Abnormal high battery positive voltage	• Battery • IC regulator • ECU

*1: 2WD models only
*2: 4WD models only
*3: 4WD 2 Door models only
*4: As the DTC cannot be erased by replacing parts alone, do either of the following operations.
1. Clear DTC
2. At the vehicle speed of 20 km/h (12 mph), drive the vehicle for 30 sec. or more.

TY402970028I000X

Fig. 64 Diagnostic trouble codes. 1996 RAV4

DTC No.	Detection Item	Trouble Area
11	Open circuit in ABS control (solenoid) relay circuit	• ABS control (solenoid) relay • Open or short in ABS control (solenoid) relay circuit
12	Short circuit in ABS control (solenoid) relay circuit	• ABS control (solenoid) relay • B+ short in ABS control (solenoid) relay circuit
13	Open circuit in ABS control (motor) relay circuit	• ABS control (motor) relay • Open or short in ABS control (motor) relay circuit
14	Short circuit in ABS control (motor) relay circuit	• ABS control (motor) relay • B+ short in ABS control (motor) relay circuit
21	Open or short circuit in 2-position solenoid circuit for right front wheel	• ABS actuator • Open or short in SFRR or SFRH circuit
22	Open or short circuit in 2-position solenoid circuit for left front wheel	• ABS actuator • Open or short in SFLR or SFLH circuit
23	Open or short circuit in 2-position solenoid circuit for right rear wheel	• ABS actuator • Open or short in SRRR or SRRH circuit
24	Open or short circuit in 2-position solenoid circuit for left rear wheel	• ABS actuator • Open or short in SRLR or SRLH circuit
31	Right front wheel speed sensor signal malfunction	• Right front, left front, right rear and left rear speed sensor • Open or short in each speed sensor circuit • Speed sensor
32	Left front wheel speed sensor signal malfunction	
33	Right rear wheel speed sensor signal malfunction	
34	Left rear wheel speed sensor signal malfunction	
35	Open circuit in left speed sensor circuit	• Open in speed sensor circuit
*1 37	Some tire is different size from the other tires	• Tire size
41	Low battery positive voltage. Abnormally high battery positive voltage (4WD)	• Battery • IC regulator • Open or short in power source circuit
*2 43	Malfunction in deceleration sensor (constant output)	• Deceleration sensor • Wire harness for deceleration sensor system
*2 44	Open or short in deceleration sensor circuit	• Deceleration sensor • Open or short in deceleration sensor circuit
*2 45	Malfunction in deceleration sensor	• Deceleration sensor • Wire harness for deceleration sensor system
51	Pump motor is locked Open in pump motor ground	• ABS pump motor
Always ON	Malfunction in ECU Abnormal high battery positive voltage (2WD)	• ECU

*1: 2WD models
*2: 4WD models

TY402960019800X

ANTI-LOCK BRAKES

Fig. 67 Diagnostic trouble codes (Part 1 of 2). Tundra

DTC No.	Detection Item	Trouble Area
C0278/11	Open circuit in ABS solenoid relay circuit	• ABS solenoid relay • ABS solenoid relay circuit
C0279/12	B+ short circuit in ABS solenoid relay circuit	• ABS solenoid relay circuit
C0273/13*1	Open circuit in ABS motor relay circuit	• ABS motor relay • ABS motor relay circuit
C0274/14	B+ short circuit in ABS motor relay circuit	• ABS motor relay • ABS motor relay circuit
C0226/21	Open or short circuit in ABS actuator solenoid circuit (SFR circuit)	• ABS actuator • SFRR or SFRH circuit
C0236/22	Open or short circuit in ABS actuator solenoid circuit (SFL circuit)	• ABS actuator • SFLR or SFLH circuit
C0246/23	Open or short circuit in ABS actuator solenoid circuit (SRR circuit)	• ABS actuator • SRR or SRH circuit
C0200/31*1	Right front wheel speed sensor signal malfunction	
C0205/32*1	Left front wheel speed sensor signal malfunction	• Right front, left front, right rear and left rear speed sensor • Each speed sensor circuit • Sensor rotor
C0210/33*1	Right rear wheel speed sensor signal malfunction	
C0215/34*1	Left rear wheel speed sensor signal malfunction	
C1237/37	Some tire is different in size from the other tires Both rear speed sensor rotors are missing	• Tire size • Front sensor rotor • Front speed sensor • Front speed sensor circuit
C1241/41	Low battery positive voltage or abnormally high battery positive voltage	• Battery • Charging system • Power source circuit
C1243/43*2	Malfunction in deceleration sensor (constant output)	• Deceleration sensor • Wire harness for deceleration sensor system
C1244/44*2	Open or short circuit in deceleration sensor circuit	• Deceleration sensor • Deceleration sensor circuit
C1245/45*2	Malfunction in deceleration sensor	• Deceleration sensor • Wire harness for deceleration sensor system
C1249/49	Open circuit in stop light switch circuit	• Stop light switch • Stop light switch circuit

TY402900466010X

Fig. 66 Diagnostic trouble codes. Sienna

DTC No.	Detection Item	Trouble Area
11	Open circuit in ABS solenoid valve relay circuit	• ABS solenoid valve relay • Valve supply voltage
12	Short circuit in ABS solenoid valve relay circuit	• Valve supply voltage
13	Open circuit in ABS motor relay circuit	• ABS motor relay • Pump motor voltage
14	Short circuit in ABS motor relay circuit	• Pump motor voltage • Pump motor lead disconnected
21	Right front solenoid valve faulty	• Right front circuit • ABS actuator
22	Left front solenoid valves faulty	• Left front circuit • ABS actuator
23	Right rear solenoid valves faulty	• Right rear circuit • ABS actuator
24	Left rear solenoid valves faulty	• Left rear circuit • ABS actuator
*31	Right front wheel speed sensor signal malfunction	• Right front, left front speed sensor • Right rear, left rear axle hub • Each speed sensor circuit • Sensor installation • Sensor rotor
*32	Left front wheel speed sensor signal malfunction	
*33	Right rear wheel speed sensor signal malfunction	
*34	Left rear wheel speed sensor signal malfunction	
41	Low battery positive voltage or abnormally high battery positive voltage	• Battery • IC regulator • Power source circuit
49	Open circuit in stop light switch circuit	• Stop light switch • Stop light switch circuit
*51	Pump motor is locked	• ABS pump motor
Always ON	Malfunction in ECU IG power souce circuit	• Battery • ECU • IC regulator • Power souce circuit • ABS waring light circuit

TY402900558010X

*: As the DTC cannot be replacing parts alone, do either of the following operations.

(1) Clear DTC

(2) At the vehicle speed of 20 km/h (12 mph), drive the vehicle for 30 sec. or more.

Code No.	Light Pattern		Diagnosis
11		BE3931	Open circuit in solenoid relay circuit
12		BE3931	Short circuit in solenoid relay circuit
13		BE3931	Open circuit in pump motor relay circuit
14		BE3931	Short circuit in pump motor relay circuit
21		BE3932	Open or short circuit in 2 position solenoid of right front wheel
22		BE3932	Open or short circuit in 2 position solenoid of left front wheel
23		BE3932	Open or short circuit in 2 position solenoid of rear wheel
31		BE3933	Right front wheel speed sensor signal malfunction
32		BE3933	Left front wheel speed sensor signal malfunction
33		BE3933	Right rear wheel speed sensor signal malfunction
34		BE3933	Left rear wheel speed sensor signal malfunction
35		BE3933	Open circuit in left front or right rear wheel speed sensor
36		BE3933	Open circuit in right front or left rear wheel speed sensor
37		BE3933	• Neither front speed sensor rotor is missing • 2WD: Some tire is different size from the other tires
41		BE3934	Abnormally high or low battery voltage
*43		BE3934	Malfunction in deceleration sensor
*44		BE3934	Open or short circuit in deceleration sensor
51		BE3935	Actuator pump motor locked or open circuit in pump motor
Always on			Malfunction in ECU

* 4WD

TY402950015300 0X

Fig. 68 Diagnostic trouble codes. 1996 T100

C1251/51*1	Pump motor is locked Open circuit in pump motor circuit	• ABS pump motor
Always ON	Malfunction in ABS ECU	• Battery • Charging system • Power source circuit

*1: As long as the following operations are not performed, ABS warning light will not go OFF only by repairing the trouble area.
(1) Drive the vehicle at 20 km/h (12 mph) for 30 seconds or more and check that the ABS warning light goes off.
(2) Clear the DTC
*2: Only for 4WD.

TY402900466020X

Fig. 67 Diagnostic trouble codes (Part 2 of 2). Tundra

Fig. 70 Diagnostic trouble codes. 1997–98 T100

DTC NO.	Detection Item	Trouble Area
11	Open circuit in solenoid relay circuit	• Actuator inside wire harness • Solenoid relay • Wire harness and connector of solenoid relay circuit
12	Short circuit in solenoid relay circuit	• ECU
13	Open circuit in pump motor relay circuit	• Actuator inside wire harness • Pump motor relay • Wire harness and connector of pump motor relay circuit
14	Short circuit in pump motor relay circuit	• ECU
21	Open or short circuit in 2 position solenoid of right front wheel	• Actuator solenoid • Wire harness and connector of actuator solenoid circuit
22	Open or short circuit in 2 position solenoid of left front wheel	
23	Open or short circuit in 2 position solenoid of rear wheel	
31	Right front wheel speed sensor signal malfunction	• Speed sensor • Sensor rotor • Wire harness and connector of speed sensor
32	Left front wheel speed sensor signal malfunction	
33	Right rear wheel speed sensor signal malfunction	
34	Left rear wheel speed sensor signal malfunction	
35	Open circuit in left front or right rear wheel speed sensor	
36	Open circuit in right front or left rear wheel speed sensor	
37	• Faulty front speed sensor rotor • Tire (s) is different size from the other tires	• Front sensor rotor • Tire
41	Abnormally high or low battery voltage	• Battery • Voltage regulator • Wire harness and connector of power source circuit
*43	Malfunction in deceleration sensor	• Deceleration sensor • Deceleration sensor installation
*44	Open or short circuit in deceleration sensor	• Deceleration sensor • Wire harness and connector of deceleration sensor
49	Open or short circuit in stop circuit in stop light switch	• Stop light switch • Wire harness and connector of stop light circuit
51	Actuator pump motor locked or open circuit in pump motor	• Pump motor, relay and battery • Wire harness, connector and ground bolt or actuator pump motor circuit
Always ON	Malfunction in ECU IG power source circuit	• Battery • Voltage regulator • Wire harness and connector of power source circuit

*: 4 WD Models

TY402970030600X

Fig. 69 Diagnostic trouble codes. Tacoma

DTC No.	Detection Item	Trouble Area
11	Open circuit in ABS control (solenoid) relay circuit	• ABS control (solenoid) relay • Open or short in ABS control (solenoid) relay circuit • ECU
12	Short circuit in ABS control (solenoid) relay circuit	• ABS control (solenoid) relay • B+ short in ABS control (solenoid) relay circuit • ECU
13	Open circuit in ABS control (motor) relay circuit	• ABS control (motor) relay • Open or short in ABS control (motor) relay circuit • ECU
14	Short circuit in ABS control (motor) relay circuit	• ABS control (motor) relay • B+ short in ABS control (motor) relay circuit • ECU
21	Open or short circuit in 2-position solenoid circuit for right front wheel	• ABS actuator • Open or short in SFRR or SFRH circuit • ECU
22	Open or short circuit in 2-position solenoid circuit for left front wheel	• ABS actuator • Open or short in SFLR or SFLH circuit • ECU
23	Open or short circuit in 2-position solenoid for rear wheel	• ABS actuator • Open or short in SRR or SRH circuit • ECU
31	Right front wheel speed sensor signal malfunction	
32	Left front wheel speed sensor signal malfunction	• Right front, left front, right rear and left rear speed sensor
33	Right rear wheel speed sensor signal malfunction	• Open or short in each speed sensor circuit
34	Left rear wheel speed sensor signal malfunction	• ECU
*135	Open circuit in left front or right rear speed sensor circuit	• Open in left front or right rear speed sensor circuit • ECU
*136	Open circuit in right front or left rear speed sensor circuit	• Open in right front or left rear speed sensor circuit • ECU
37	Neither front speed sensor rotor missing	• Front axle hub • Right front, left front speed sensor • Wire harness for sensor system • ECU
37	Some tire is different size from the other tires	• Tire size • ECU
41	Low battery positive voltage or abnormally high battery positive voltage	• Battery • IC regulator • Open or short in power source circuit • ECU
*243	Malfunction in deceleration sensor	• Deceleration sensor • Wire harness for deceleration sensor system • ECU
*244	Open or short in deceleration sensor circuit	• Deceleration sensor • Open or short in deceleration sensor circuit • ECU
*248	Open or short circuit in rear differential lock circuit Rear differential is locking	• Rear differential lock
*249	Open or short circuit in stop light switch circuit	• Stop light switch • ECU
51	Pump motor is locked Open in pump motor ground	• ABS pump motor
Always ON	Malfunction in ECU	• ECU

*1: 2WD models *2: 4WD models *3: w/ Rear differential lock

TY402970031000X

CIRCUIT DESCRIPTION

This stop light switch senses whether the brake pedal is depressed or released, and sends the signal to the ECU.

WIRING DIAGRAM

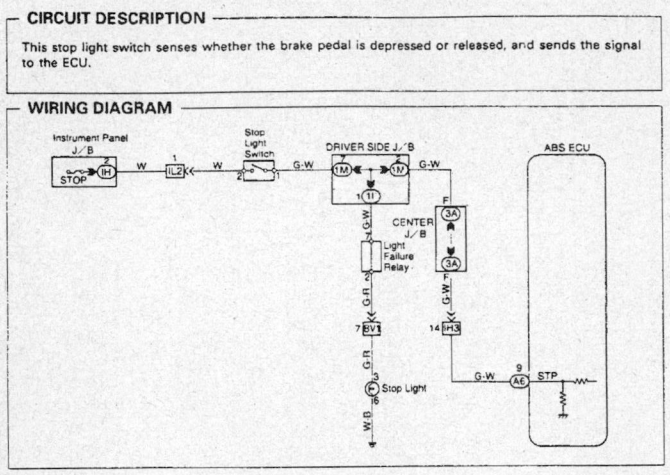

Fig. 71 Stop light switch circuit inspection (Part 1 of 2). 1996 Avalon

DTC No.	DTC Detecting Condition	Trouble Area
49	Battery voltage has never exceed more than 17.0 V and become less than 9.5 V within 2.16 sec. and the STP terminal voltage of ECU is under open circuit detecting limits continues for 3 sec. or more.	• Stop light switch • Stop light switch circuit • ECU

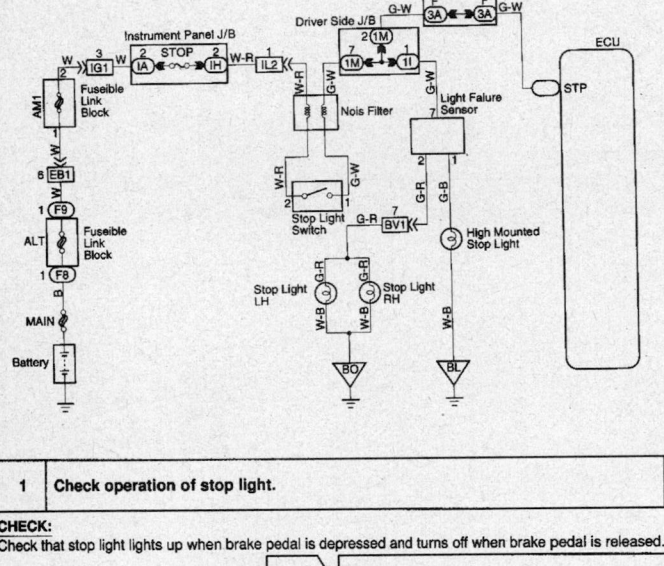

1 Check operation of stop light.

CHECK:
Check that stop light lights up when brake pedal is depressed and turns off when brake pedal is released.

NG ▷ Repair stop light circuit

OK

Fig. 72 Stop light switch circuit inspection (Part 1 of 2). 1997–99 Avalon

TY4029700237010X

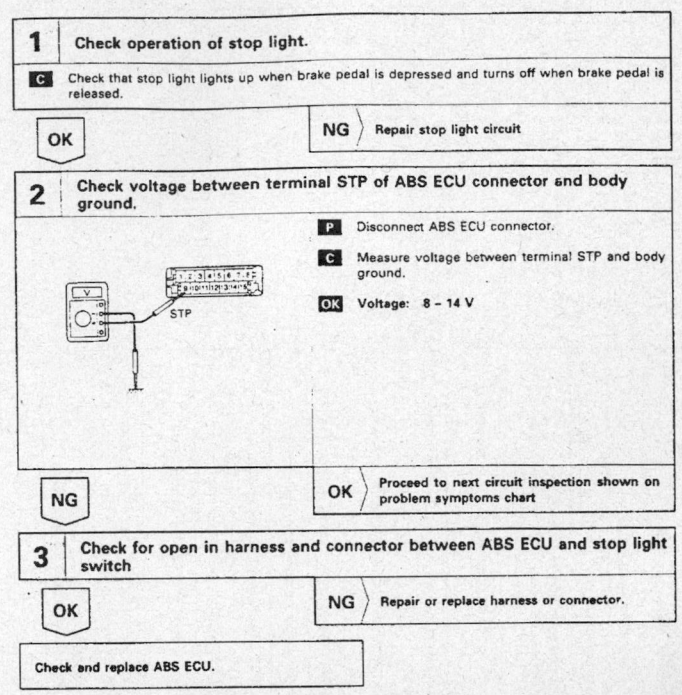

1 Check operation of stop light.

C Check that stop light lights up when brake pedal is depressed and turns off when brake pedal is released.

OK   NG ▷ Repair stop light circuit

2 Check voltage between terminal STP of ABS ECU connector and body ground.

P Disconnect ABS ECU connector.

C Measure voltage between terminal STP and body ground.

OK Voltage: 8 – 14 V

NG   OK ▷ Proceed to next circuit inspection shown on problem symptoms chart

3 Check for open in harness and connector between ABS ECU and stop light switch

OK   NG ▷ Repair or replace harness or connector.

Check and replace ABS ECU.

TY4029500160020X

Fig. 71 Stop light switch circuit inspection (Part 2 of 2). 1996 Avalon

2 Check voltage between terminal STP of ECU and body ground.

PREPARATION:
Remove ECU with connectors still connected.
CHECK:
Measure voltage between terminal STP of ECU and body ground when brake pedal is depressed.
OK:
Voltage: 8 – 14 V

OK ▷ Proceed to next circuit inspection under "Troubleshooting".

NG

3 Check for open in harness and connector between ECU and stop light Switch

NG ▷ Repair or replace harness or connector.

OK

Check and replace ECU.

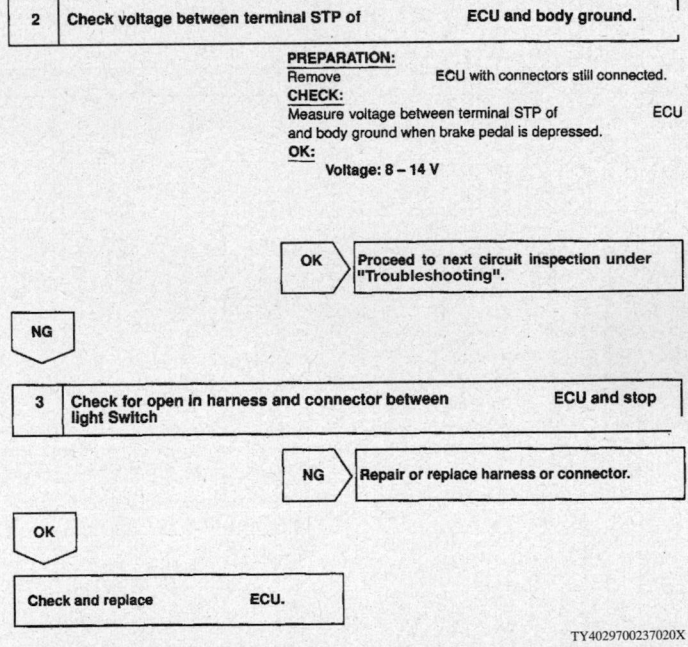

TY4029700237020X

Fig. 72 Stop light switch circuit inspection (Part 2 of 2). 1997–99 Avalon

This stop light switch senses whether the brake pedal is depressed or released, and sends the signal to the ECU.

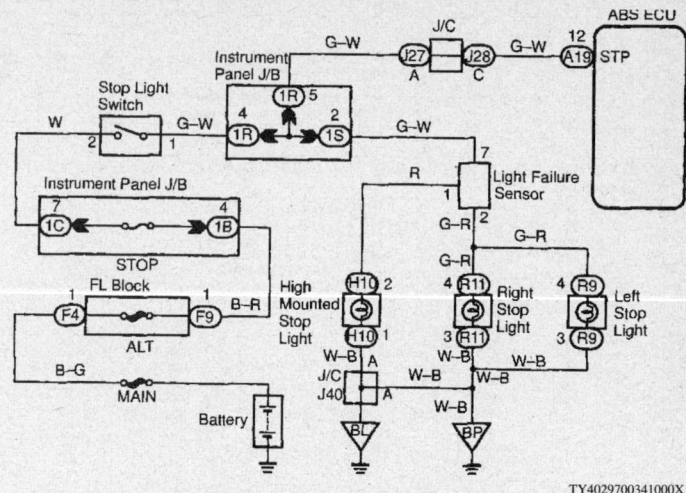

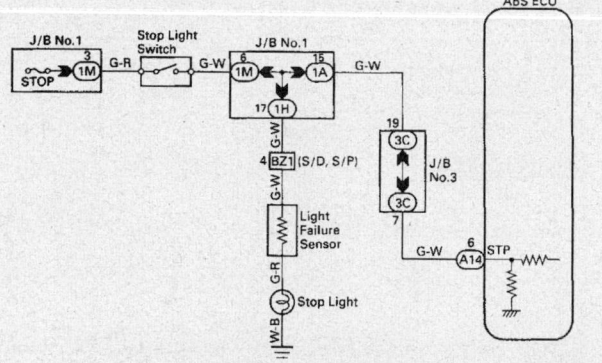

Fig. 73 Stop light circuit inspection (Part 1 of 2). 1996 Camry

Fig. 73 Stop light circuit inspection (Part 1 of 2). 1997–99 Camry

TY4029700341000X

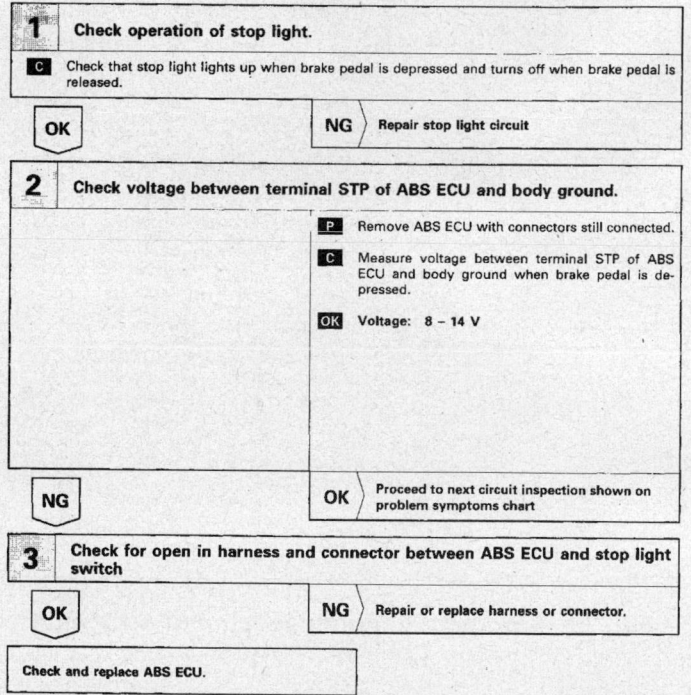

Fig. 73 Stop light circuit inspection (Part 2 of 2). Camry

TY4029500340020X

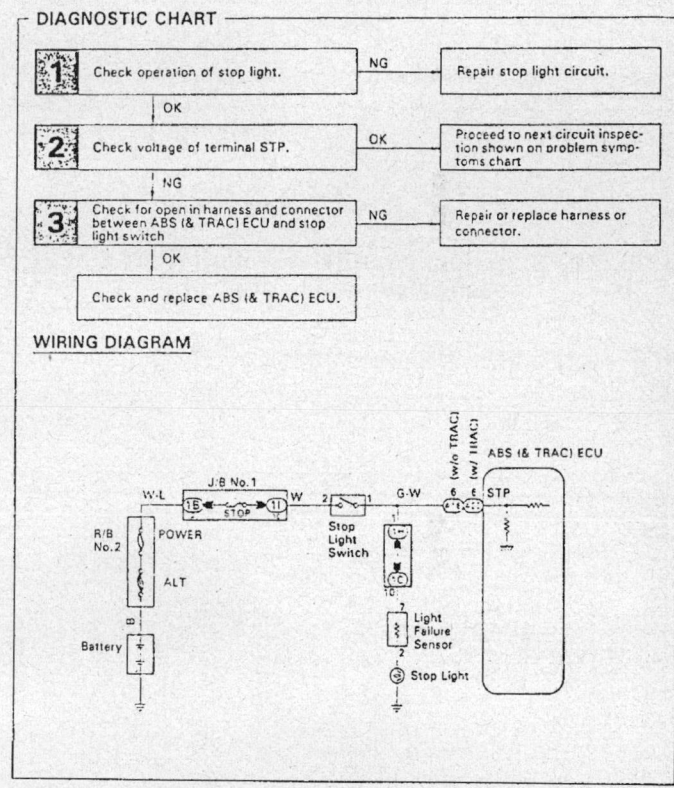

Fig. 74 Stop light circuit inspection (Part 1 of 2). Camry w/traction control

TY4029200057010X

1 Check operation of stop light.

C Check that stop light lights up when brake pedal is depressed and turns off when brake pedal is released.

OK		NG	Repair stop light circuit.

2 Check voltage between terminal STP of ABS (& TRAC) ECU and body ground.

w/o TRAC

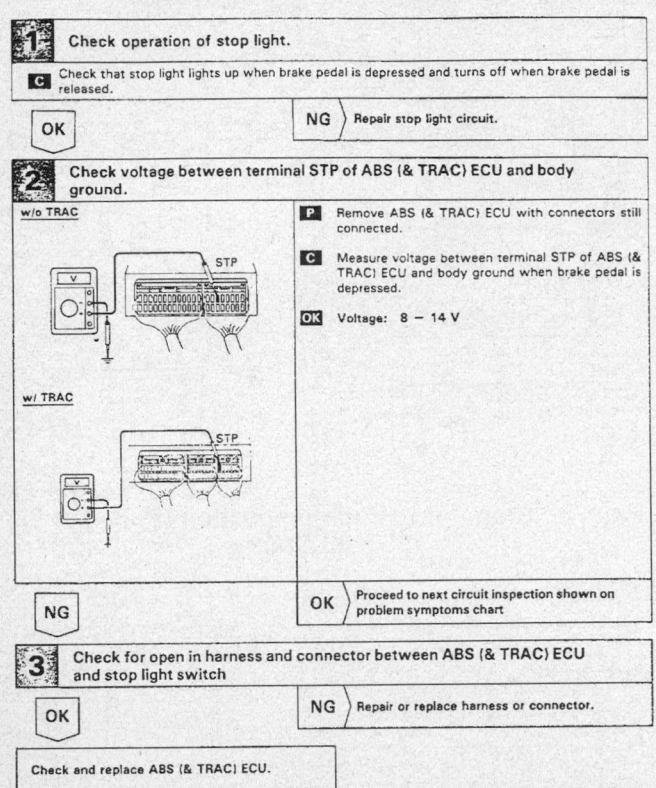

w/ TRAC

P Remove ABS (& TRAC) ECU with connectors still connected.

C Measure voltage between terminal STP of ABS (& TRAC) ECU and body ground when brake pedal is depressed.

OK Voltage: 8 – 14 V

NG		OK	Proceed to next circuit inspection shown on problem symptoms chart

3 Check for open in harness and connector between ABS (& TRAC) ECU and stop light switch

OK		NG	Repair or replace harness or connector.

Check and replace ABS (& TRAC) ECU.

TY4029200057020X

Fig. 74 Stop light circuit inspection (Part 2 of 2). Camry w/traction control

1 Check operation of stop light.

C Check that stop light lights up when brake pedal is depressed and turns off when brake pedal is released.

OK		NG	Repair stop light circuit

2 Check voltage between terminal STP of ABS ECU and body ground.

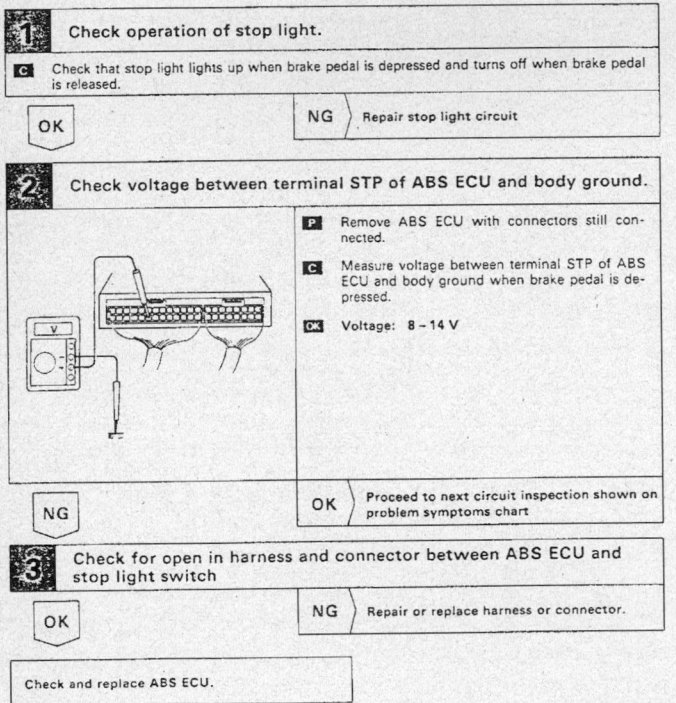

P Remove ABS ECU with connectors still connected.

C Measure voltage between terminal STP of ABS ECU and body ground when brake pedal is depressed.

OK Voltage: 8 – 14 V

NG		OK	Proceed to next circuit inspection shown on problem symptoms chart

3 Check for open in harness and connector between ABS ECU and stop light switch

OK		NG	Repair or replace harness or connector.

Check and replace ABS ECU.

TY4029400058020X

Fig. 75 Stop light circuit inspection (Part 2 of 2). 1996 Celica

---

CIRCUIT DESCRIPTION

This stop light switch senses whether the brake pedal is depressed or released, and sends the signal to the ECU.

DIAGNOSTIC CHART

1	Check operation or stop light.	NG	Repair stop light circuit
2	Check voltage of terminal STP.	OK	Proceed to next circuit inspection shown on problem symptoms chart
3	Check for open in harness and connector between ABS ECU and stop light switch	NG	Repair or replace harness or connector.

OK

Check and replace ABS ECU.

WIRING DIAGRAM

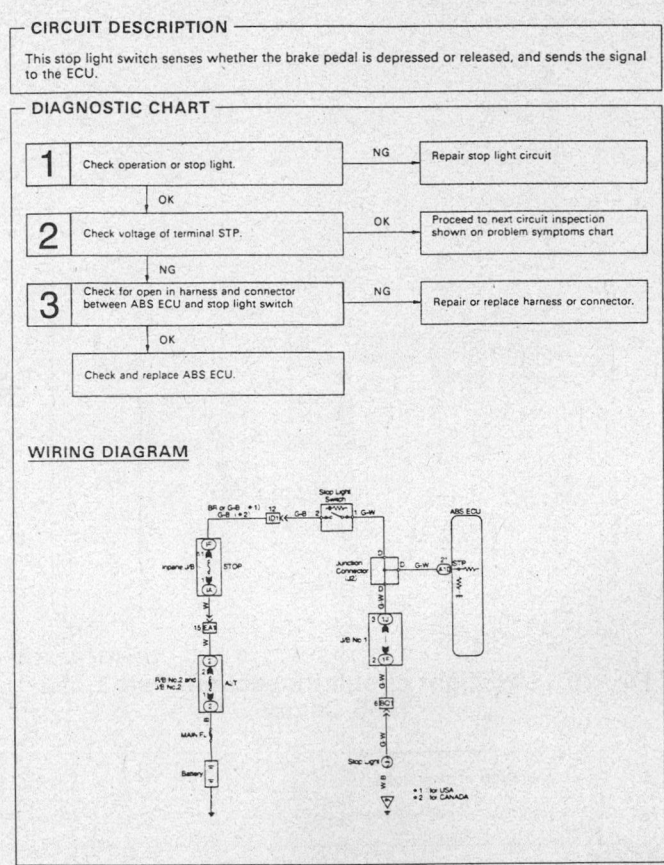

TY4029400058010X

Fig. 75 Stop light circuit inspection (Part 1 of 2). 1996 Celica

WIRING DIAGRAM

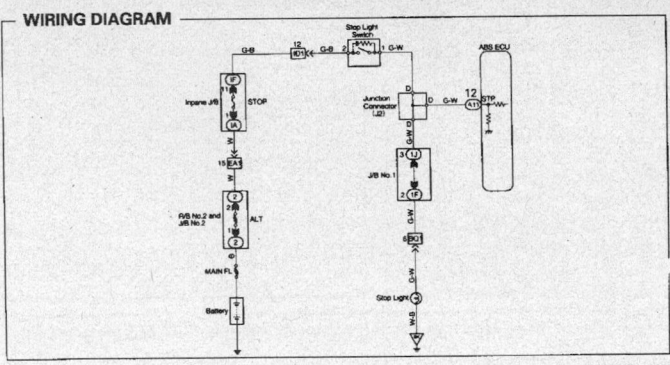

TY4029700389010X

Fig. 76 Stop light circuit inspection (Part 1 of 2). 1997–99 Celica

1   Check operation of stop light.

C   Check that stop light lights up when brake pedal is depressed and turns off when brake pedal is released.

OK   NG > Repair stop light circuit

2   Check voltage between terminal STP of ABS ECU and body ground.

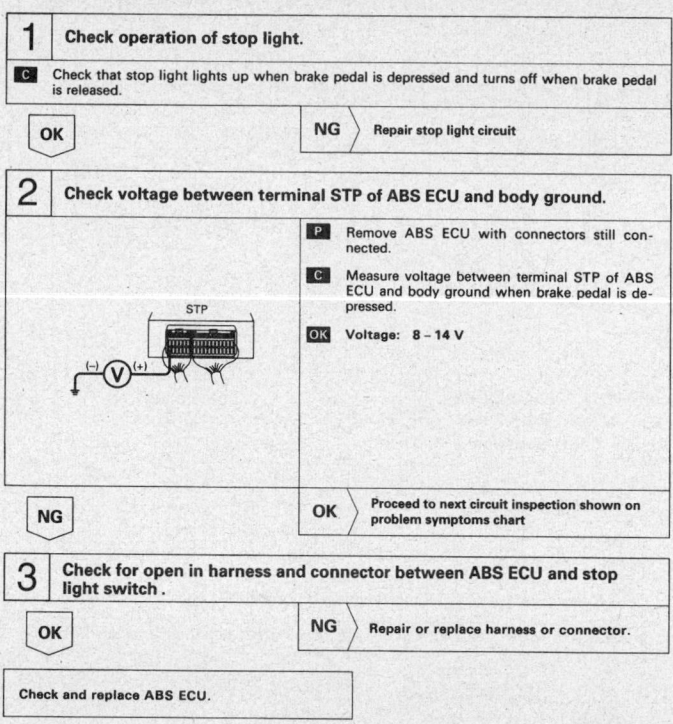

P   Remove ABS ECU with connectors still connected.

C   Measure voltage between terminal STP of ABS ECU and body ground when brake pedal is depressed.

OK   Voltage: 8 – 14 V

NG   OK > Proceed to next circuit inspection shown on problem symptoms chart

3   Check for open in harness and connector between ABS ECU and stop light switch .

OK   NG > Repair or replace harness or connector.

Check and replace ABS ECU.

TY4029700389020X

Fig. 76   Stop light circuit inspection (Part 2 of 2). 1997–99 Celica

INSPECTION PROCEDURE

1   Check operation of stop light.

C   Check that stop light lights up when brake pedal is depressed and turns off when brake pedal is released.

OK   NG > Repair stop light circuit

2   Check voltage between terminal STP of ABS ECU and body ground.

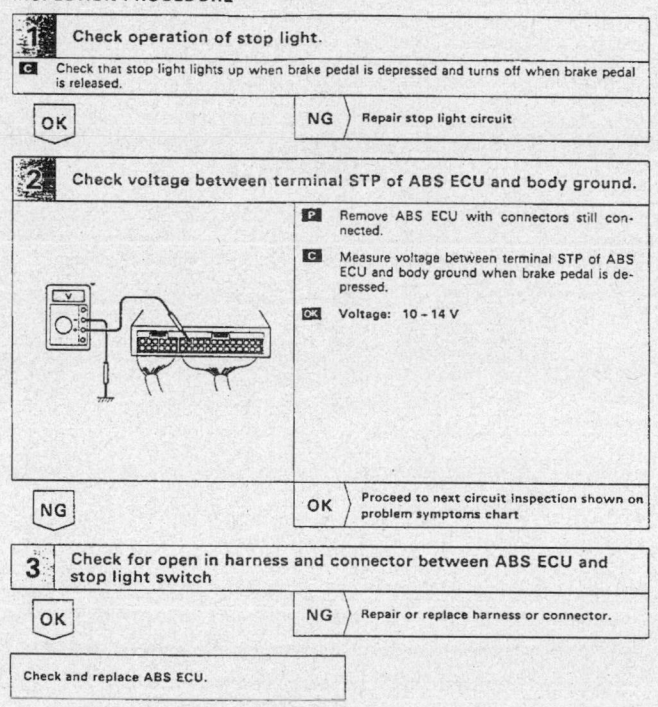

P   Remove ABS ECU with connectors still connected.

C   Measure voltage between terminal STP of ABS ECU and body ground when brake pedal is depressed.

OK   Voltage: 10 – 14 V

NG   OK > Proceed to next circuit inspection shown on problem symptoms chart

3   Check for open in harness and connector between ABS ECU and stop light switch

OK   NG > Repair or replace harness or connector.

Check and replace ABS ECU.

TY4029300055020X

Fig. 77   Stop light switch circuit inspection (Part 2 of 2). Corolla

— CIRCUIT DESCRIPTION —

This stop light switch senses whether the brake pedal is depressed or released, and send the signal to the ECU.

— DIAGNOSTIC CHART —

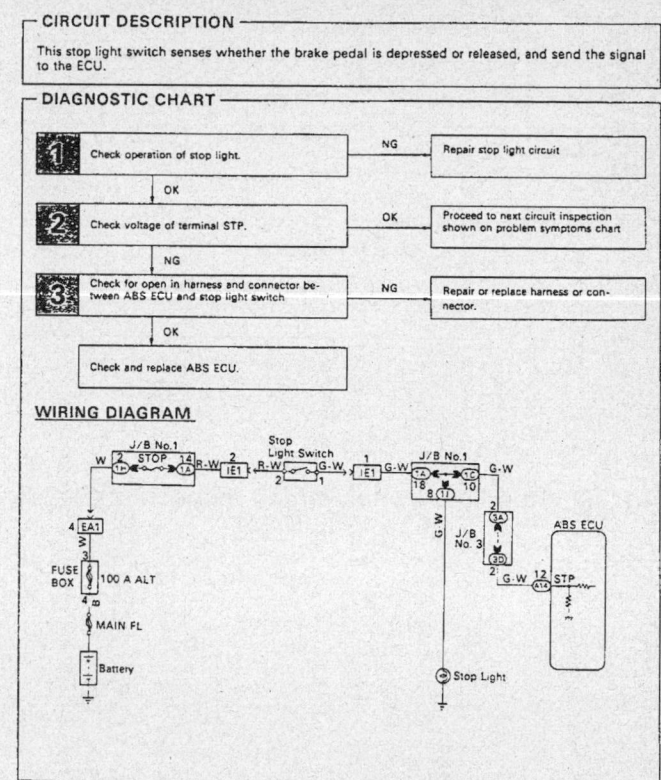

1   Check operation of stop light.   NG > Repair stop light circuit

OK

2   Check voltage of terminal STP.   OK > Proceed to next circuit inspection shown on problem symptoms chart

NG

3   Check for open in harness and connector between ABS ECU and stop light switch   NG > Repair or replace harness or connector.

OK

Check and replace ABS ECU.

WIRING DIAGRAM

TY4029300055010X

Fig. 77   Stop light switch circuit inspection (Part 1 of 2). Corolla

— CIRCUIT DESCRIPTION —

This stop light switch senses whether the brake pedal is depressed or released, and sends the signal to the ECU.

WIRING DIAGRAM

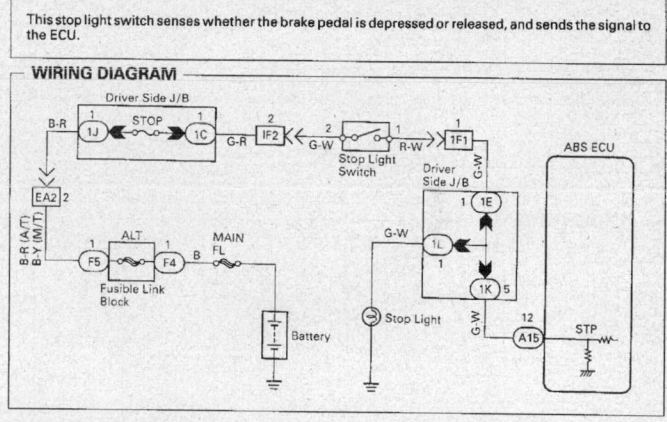

INSPECTION PROCEDURE

1   Check operation of stop light.

C   Check that stop light lights up when brake pedal is depressed and turns off when brake pedal is released.

OK   NG > Repair stop light circuit

2   Check voltage between terminal STP of ABS ECU and body ground.

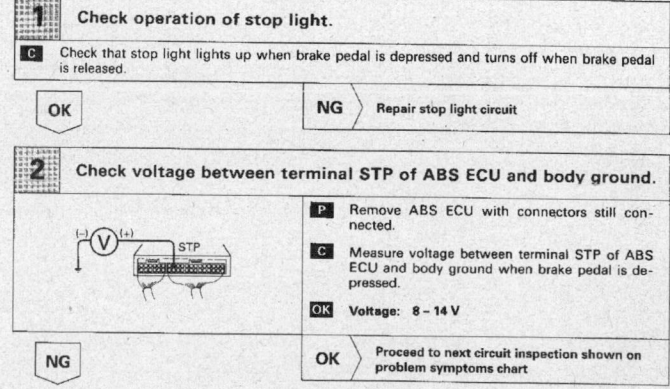

P   Remove ABS ECU with connectors still connected.

C   Measure voltage between terminal STP of ABS ECU and body ground when brake pedal is depressed.

OK   Voltage: 8 – 14 V

NG   OK > Proceed to next circuit inspection shown on problem symptoms chart

TY4029600272010X

Fig. 78   Stop light switch circuit inspection (Part 1 of 2). Paseo

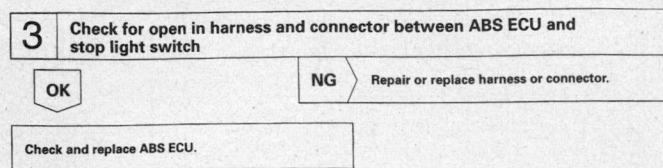

3 Check for open in harness and connector between ABS ECU and stop light switch

| OK | | NG | Repair or replace harness or connector. |

Check and replace ABS ECU.

TY4029600272020X

Fig. 78 Stop light switch circuit inspection (Part 2 of 2). Paseo

3 Check for open in harness and connector between ABS ECU stop light switch.

| OK | | NG | Repair or replace harness or connector. |

Check and replace ECU.

TY4029600201020X

Fig. 79 Stop light switch circuit inspection (Part 2 of 2). 1996 RAV4

CIRCUIT DESCRIPTION

The stop light switch senses whether the brake pedal is depressed or released, and sends a signal to the ECU.

DTC No.	DTC Detecting Condition	Trouble Area
49	1.2 – 1.7 V of STP voltage is continued for 0.3 sec. or more	• Open in stop light circuit

WIRING DIAGRAM

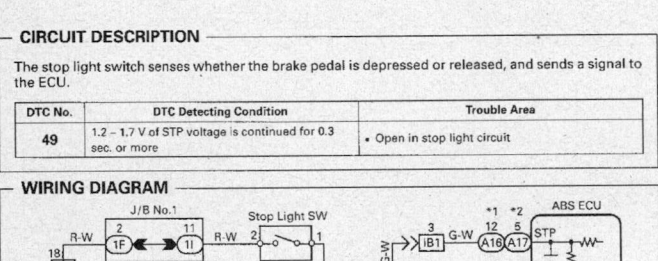

INSPECTION PROCEDURE

1 Check operation of stop light.

C Check that stop light lights up when brake pedal is depressed and turns off when brake pedal is released.

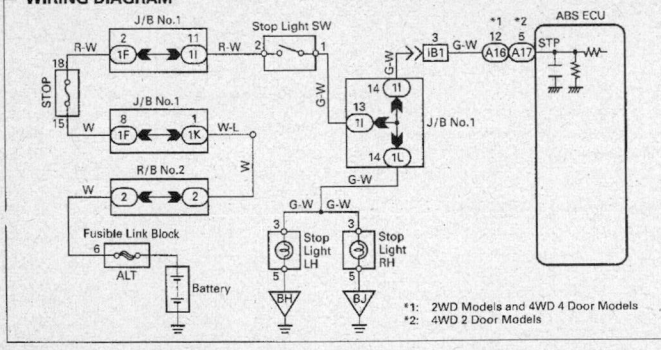

| OK | | NG | Repair stop light circuit |

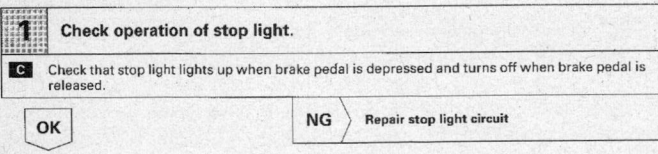

TY4029700282010X

Fig. 80 Stop light switch circuit inspection (Part 1 of 2). 1997–99 RAV4

WIRING DIAGRAM

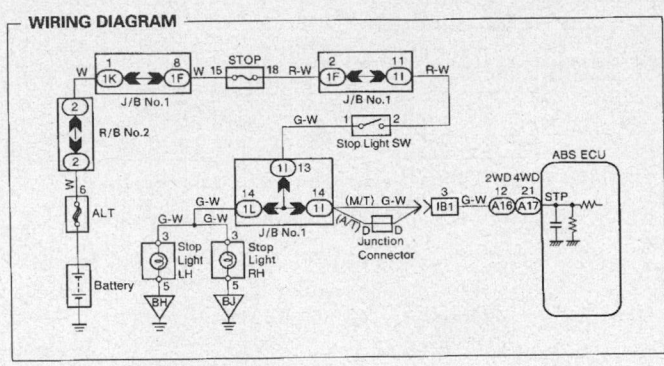

INSPECTION PROCEDURE

1 Check operation of stop light.

C Check that stop light lights up when brake pedal is depressed and turns off when brake pedal is released.

| OK | | NG | Repair stop light circuit. |

2 Check voltage between terminal STP of ABS ECU and body ground.

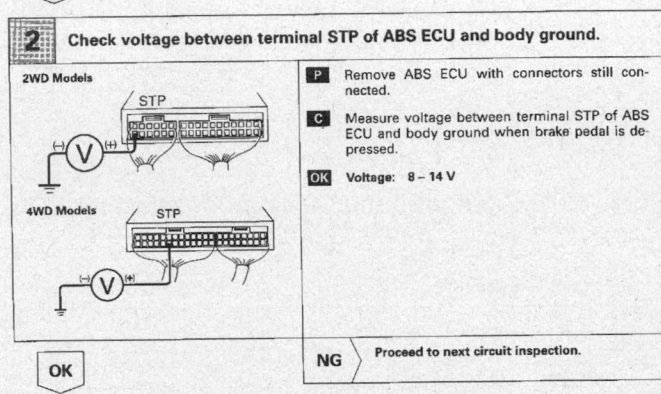

P Remove ABS ECU with connectors still connected.

C Measure voltage between terminal STP of ABS ECU and body ground when brake pedal is depressed.

OK Voltage: 8 – 14 V

| OK | | NG | Proceed to next circuit inspection. |

TY4029600201010X

Fig. 79 Stop light switch circuit inspection (Part 1 of 2). 1996 RAV4

2 Check voltage between terminal STP of ABS ECU and body ground.

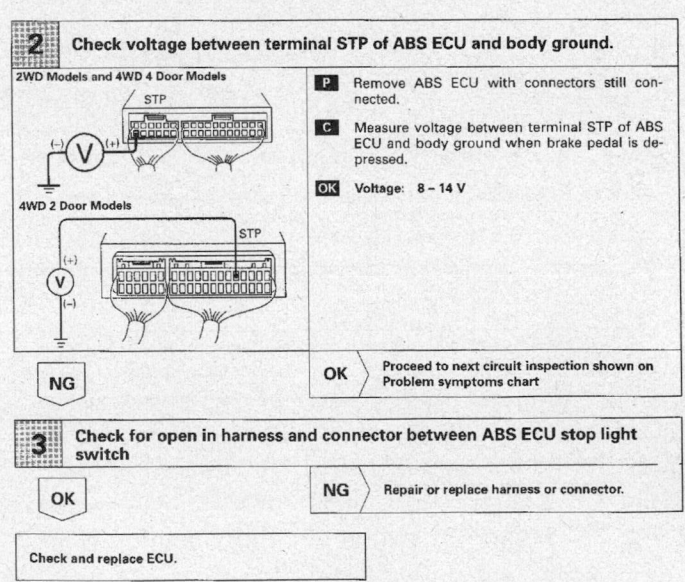

P Remove ABS ECU with connectors still connected.

C Measure voltage between terminal STP of ABS ECU and body ground when brake pedal is depressed.

OK Voltage: 8 – 14 V

| NG | | OK | Proceed to next circuit inspection shown on Problem symptoms chart |

3 Check for open in harness and connector between ABS ECU stop light switch

| OK | | NG | Repair or replace harness or connector. |

Check and replace ECU.

TY4029700282020X

Fig. 80 Stop light switch circuit inspection (Part 2 of 2). 1997–99 RAV4

CIRCUIT DESCRIPTION

The stop light switch senses whether the brake pedal is depressed or released, and sends a signal to the ECU.

WIRING DIAGRAM

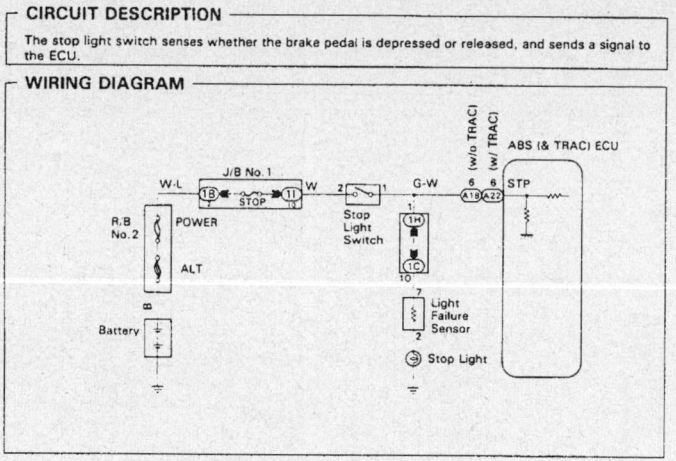

TY4029500154010X

Fig. 81 Stop light circuit inspection (Part 1 of 2). 1996 Supra

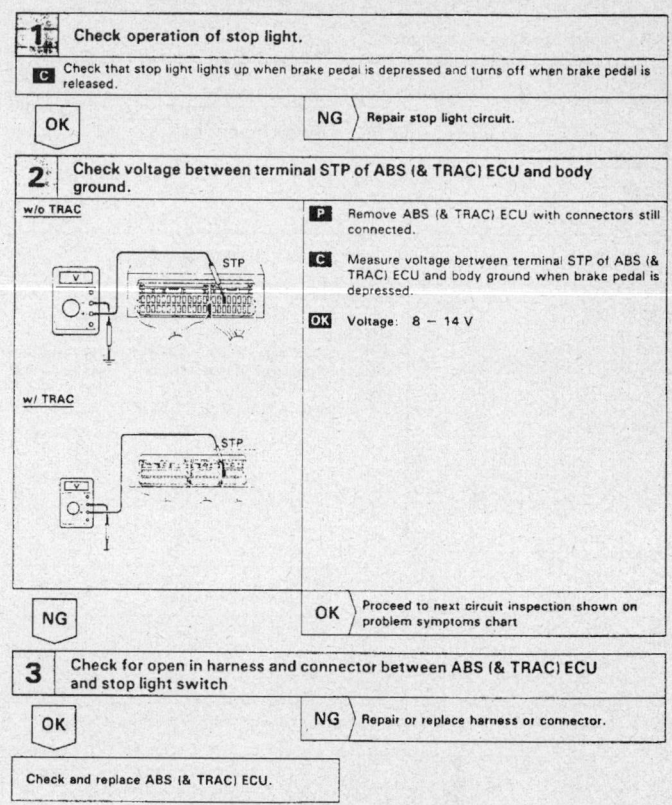

1 Check operation of stop light.

C Check that stop light lights up when brake pedal is depressed and turns off when brake pedal is released.

OK	NG	Repair stop light circuit.

2 Check voltage between terminal STP of ABS (& TRAC) ECU and body ground.

w/o TRAC

P Remove ABS (& TRAC) ECU with connectors still connected.

C Measure voltage between terminal STP of ABS (& TRAC) ECU and body ground when brake pedal is depressed.

OK Voltage: 8 – 14 V

w/ TRAC

NG	OK	Proceed to next circuit inspection shown on problem symptoms chart

3 Check for open in harness and connector between ABS (& TRAC) ECU and stop light switch

OK	NG	Repair or replace harness or connector.

Check and replace ABS (& TRAC) ECU.

TY4029500154020X

Fig. 81 Stop light circuit inspection (Part 2 of 2). 1996 Supra

CIRCUIT DESCRIPTION

The stop light switch senses whether the brake pedal is depressed or released, and sends a signal to the ECU.

DTC No.	DTC Detecting Condition	Trouble Area
49	1.2 – 1.7 V of STP voltage is continued for 0.3 sec. or more.	• Open in stop light circuit

WIRING DIAGRAM

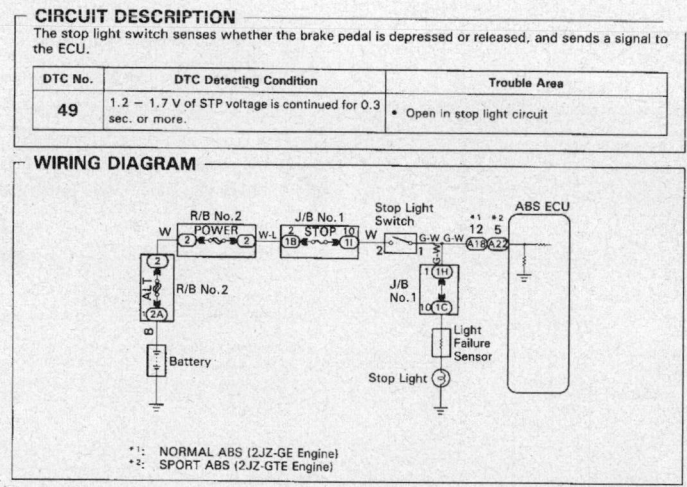

*1: NORMAL ABS (2JZ-GE Engine)
*2: SPORT ABS (2JZ-GTE Engine)

TY4029700406010X

Fig. 82 Stop light circuit inspection (Part 1 of 2). 1997–98 Supra

1   **Check operation of stop light.**

CHECK:
Check that stop light lights up when brake pedal is depressed and turns off when brake pedal is released.

> NG ▷ Replace stop light bulb.

OK ▽

2   **Check voltage between terminal STP of ABS ECU and body ground.**

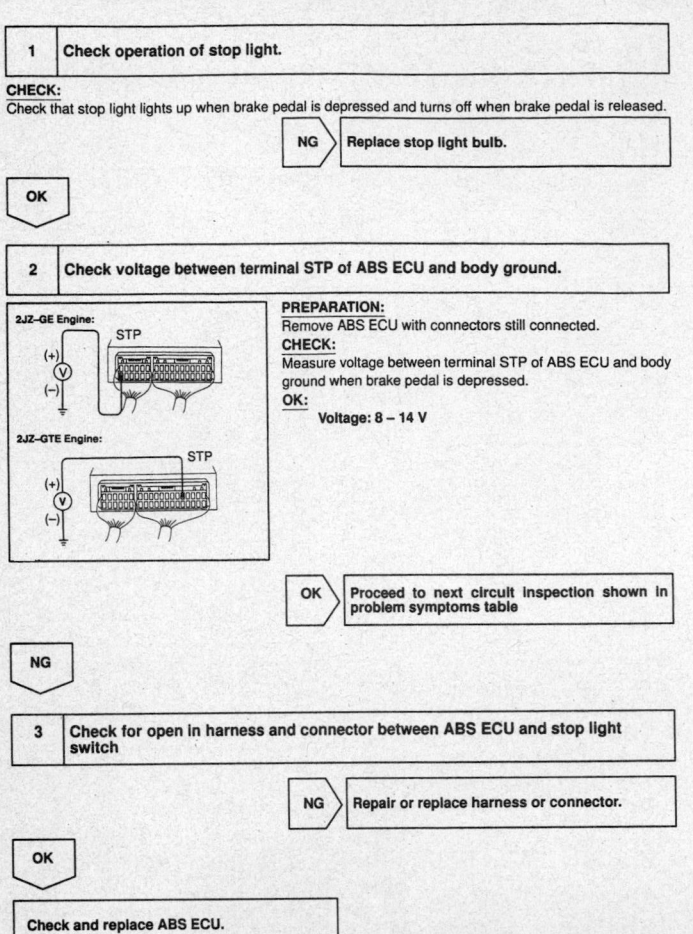

PREPARATION:
Remove ABS ECU with connectors still connected.
CHECK:
Measure voltage between terminal STP of ABS ECU and body ground when brake pedal is depressed.
OK:
    Voltage: 8 – 14 V

> OK ▷ Proceed to next circuit inspection shown in problem symptoms table

NG ▽

3   **Check for open in harness and connector between ABS ECU and stop light switch**

> NG ▷ Repair or replace harness or connector.

OK ▽

Check and replace ABS ECU.

TY4029700406020X

Fig. 82   Stop light circuit inspection (Part 2 of 2). 1997–98 Supra

This stop light switch senses whether the brake pedal is depressed or released, and sends the signal to the ECU.

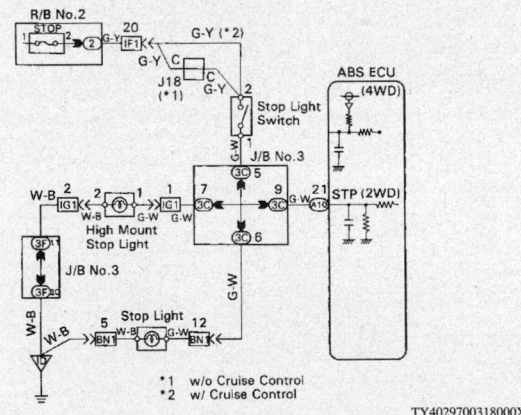

TY4029700318000X

Fig. 83   Stop light circuit inspection (Part 1 of 2). 1997–99 Tacoma

---

CIRCUIT DESCRIPTION

This stop light switch senses whether the brake pedal is depressed or released, and sends the signal to the ECU.

WIRING DIAGRAM

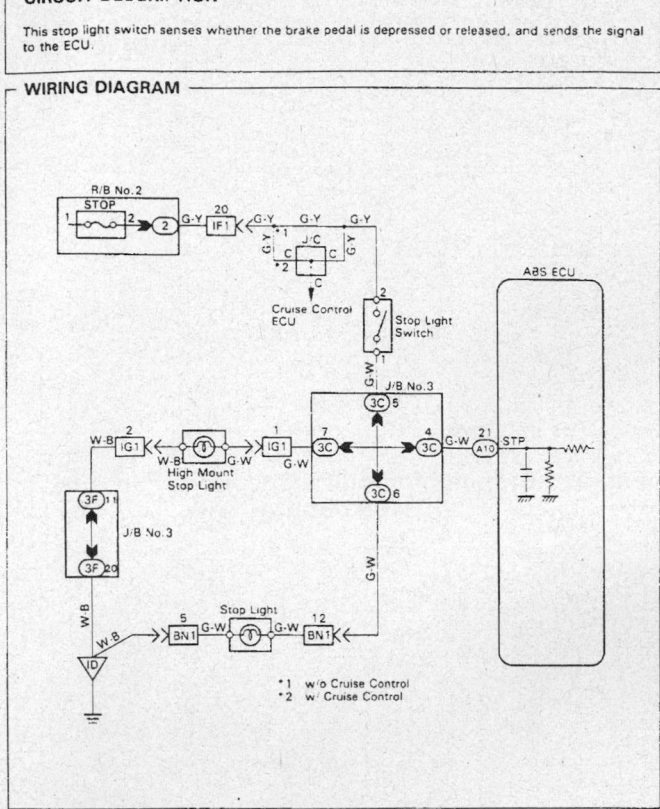

TY4029500174010X

Fig. 83   Stop light circuit inspection (Part 1 of 2). 1996 Tacoma

1   Check operation of stop light.

C Check that stop light lights up when brake pedal is depressed and turns off when brake pedal is released.

OK ▽

> NG ▷ Repair stop light circuit

2   Check voltage between terminal STP of ABS ECU and body ground.

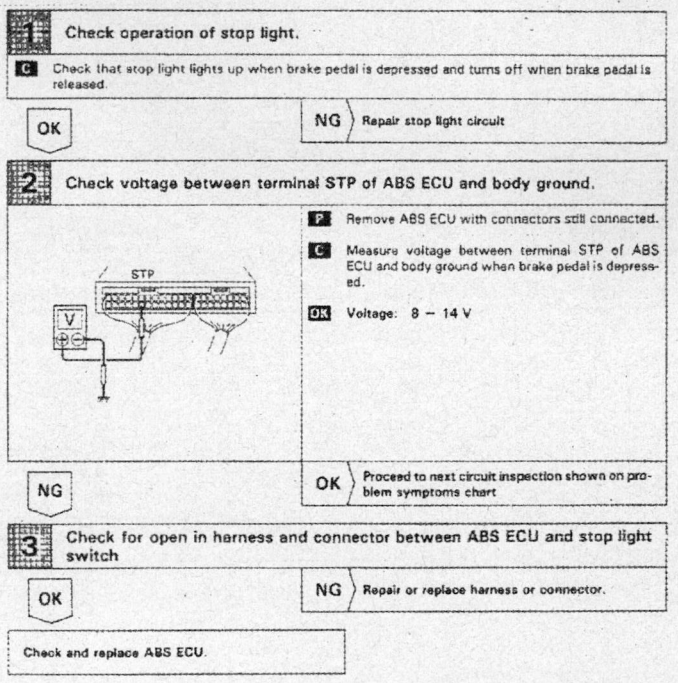

P Remove ABS ECU with connectors still connected.

C Measure voltage between terminal STP of ABS ECU and body ground when brake pedal is depressed.

OK Voltage: 8 – 14 V

NG ▽

> OK ▷ Proceed to next circuit inspection shown on problem symptoms chart

3   Check for open in harness and connector between ABS ECU and stop light switch

OK ▽

> NG ▷ Repair or replace harness or connector.

Check and replace ABS ECU.

TY4029500174020X

Fig. 83   Stop light circuit inspection (Part 2 of 2). Tacoma

CIRCUIT DESCRIPTION

This stop light switch senses whether the brake pedal is depressed or released, and sends the signal to the ECU.

WIRING DIAGRAM

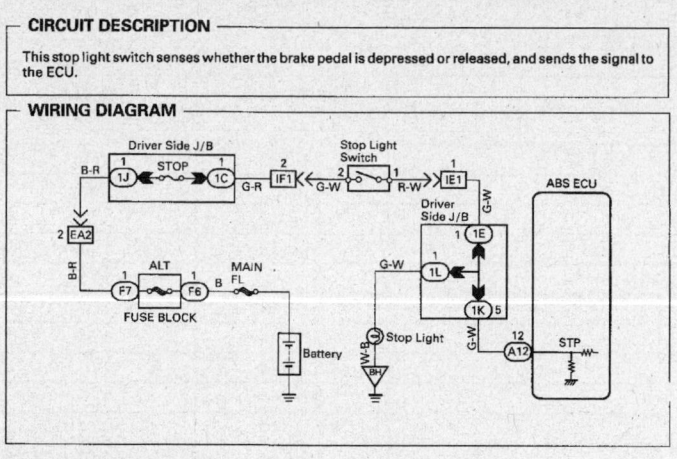

INSPECTION PROCEDURE

1 Check operation of stop light.

C Check that stop light lights up when brake pedal is depressed and turns off when brake pedal is released.

OK	NG	Repair stop light circuit

2 Check voltage between terminal STP of ABS ECU and body ground.

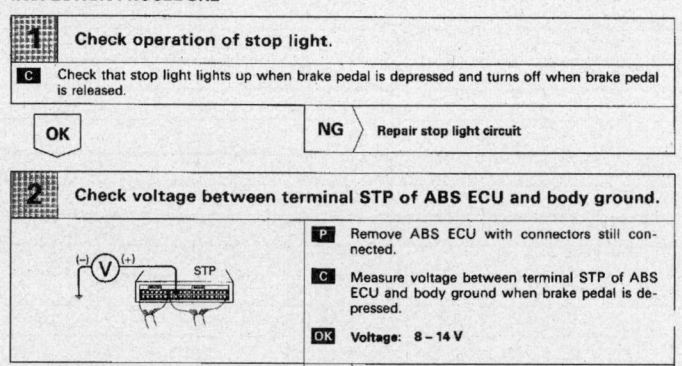

P Remove ABS ECU with connectors still connected.

C Measure voltage between terminal STP of ABS ECU and body ground when brake pedal is depressed.

OK Voltage: 8 – 14 V

NG	OK	Proceed to next circuit inspection shown on problem symptoms chart

TY4029500184010A

Fig. 84 Stop light circuit inspection (Part 1 of 2). Tercel

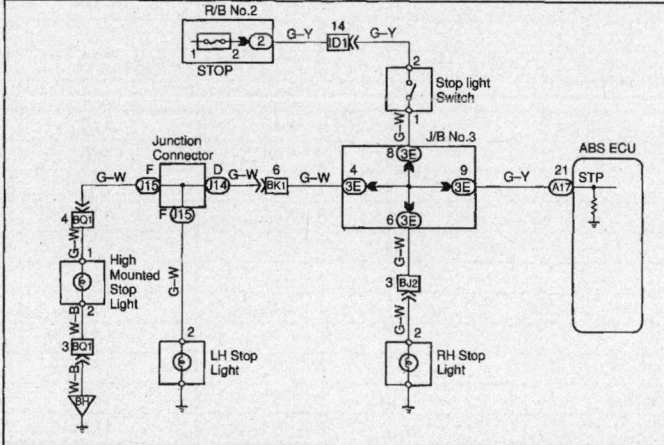

INSPECTION PROCEDURE

1 Check operation of stop light.

CHECK:
Check that stop light lights up when brake pedal is depressed and turns off when brake pedal is released.

NG	Repair stop light circuit.

OK

TY4029600225010X

Fig. 85 Stop light circuit inspection (Part 1 of 2). 4Runner

3 Check for open in harness and connector between ABS ECU and stop light switch

OK	NG	Repair or replace harness or connector.

Check and replace ABS ECU.

TY4029500184020A

Fig. 84 Stop light circuit inspection (Part 2 of 2). Tercel

2 Check voltage between terminal STP of ABS ECU and body ground.

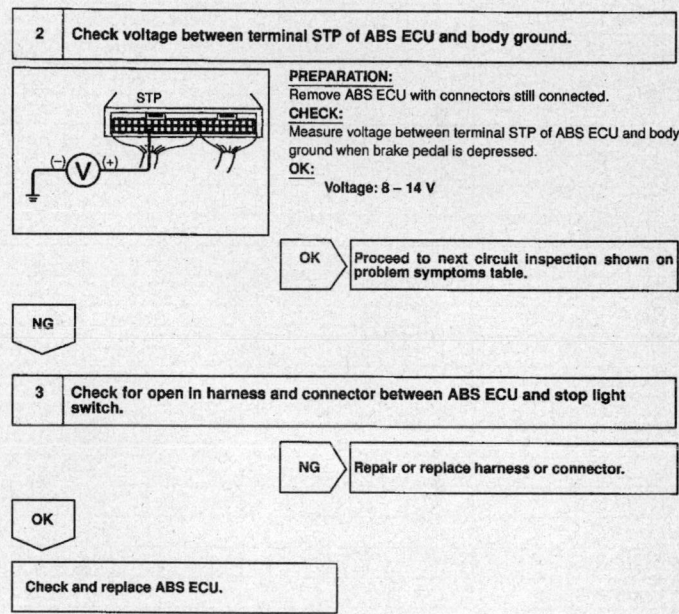

PREPARATION:
Remove ABS ECU with connectors still connected.
CHECK:
Measure voltage between terminal STP of ABS ECU and body ground when brake pedal is depressed.
OK:
Voltage: 8 – 14 V

OK	Proceed to next circuit inspection shown on problem symptoms table.

NG

3 Check for open in harness and connector between ABS ECU and stop light switch.

NG	Repair or replace harness or connector.

OK

Check and replace ABS ECU.

TY4029600225020X

Fig. 85 Stop light circuit inspection (Part 2 of 2). 4Runner

DIAGNOSTIC CHART INDEX

Code	Description	Page No.	Fig No.
1996 AVALON			
Code 11	ABS Solenoid & Motor Relay Circuit	51-539	166
Code 13	ABS Solenoid & Motor Relay Circuit	51-539	166
Code 21	ABS Actuator Solenoid Circuit	51-542	171
Code 22	ABS Actuator Solenoid Circuit	51-542	171
Code 23	ABS Actuator Solenoid Circuit	51-542	171
Code 31	Speed Sensor Circuit	51-544	174
Code 32	Speed Sensor Circuit	51-544	174
Code 33	Speed Sensor Circuit	51-544	174
Code 34	Speed Sensor Circuit	51-544	174
Code 35	Speed Sensor Circuit	51-544	174
Code 36	Speed Sensor Circuit	51-544	174
Code 38	Speed Sensor Circuit	51-544	174
Code 39	Speed Sensor Circuit	51-544	174
Code 41	+BS Power Source Circuit	51-546	177
Code 51	ABS Pump Motor Lock	51-550	182
1997–99 AVALON LESS TRACTION CONTROL			
Code 11	ABS Solenoid Valve Relay Circuit	51-539	167
Code 12	ABS Solenoid Valve Relay Circuit	51-540	168
Code 13	Pump Motor Circuit	51-541	169
Code 21	ABS Solenoid Valve Circuit	51-542	172
Code 22	ABS Solenoid Valve Circuit	51-542	172
Code 23	ABS Solenoid Valve Circuit	51-542	172
Code 24	ABS Solenoid Valve Circuit	51-542	172
Code 25	ABS Actuator Solenoid Circuit	51-543	173
Code 26	ABS Actuator Solenoid Circuit	51-543	173
Code 27	ABS Actuator Solenoid Circuit	51-543	173
Code 28	ABS Actuator Solenoid Circuit	51-543	173
Code 31	Speed Sensor Circuit	51-545	175
Code 32	Speed Sensor Circuit	51-545	175
Code 33	Speed Sensor Circuit	51-545	175
Code 34	Speed Sensor Circuit	51-545	175
Code 35	Speed Sensor Circuit	51-545	175
Code 36	Speed Sensor Circuit	51-545	175
Code 37	Speed Sensor Rotor Fault	51-546	176
Code 38	Speed Sensor Circuit	51-545	175
Code 39	Speed Sensor Circuit	51-545	175
Code 41	Power Source Circuit	51-547	178
Code 43	ABS Control System Fault	51-549	180
Code 44	NE Signal Circuit	51-549	181
Code 51	ABS Pump Motor Lock	51-550	183
Code 53	ECM Communication Circuit Fault	51-550	184
Code 61	ECM Communication Circuit Fault	51-551	185
Code 62	ECU Fault	51-551	186
1997–99 AVALON w/TRACTION CONTROL			
Code 11	ABS Solenoid Valve Relay Circuit	51-540	168
Code 12	ABS Solenoid Valve Relay Circuit	51-540	168
Code 13	ABS Motor Relay Circuit	51-541	170
Code 14	ABS Motor Relay Circuit	51-541	170
Code 21	ABS Actuator Solenoid Circuit	51-543	173
Code 22	ABS Actuator Solenoid Circuit	51-543	173
Code 23	ABS Actuator Solenoid Circuit	51-543	173
Code 24	ABS Actuator Solenoid Circuit	51-543	173
Code 25	ABS Actuator Solenoid Circuit	51-543	173
Code 26	ABS Actuator Solenoid Circuit	51-543	173
Code 27	ABS Actuator Solenoid Circuit	51-543	173
Code 28	ABS Actuator Solenoid Circuit	51-543	173

Continued

DIAGNOSTIC CHART INDEX—Continued

Code	Description	Page No.	Fig No.
1997–99 AVALON w/TRACTION CONTROL			
Code 31	Speed Sensor Circuit	51-545	175
Code 32	Speed Sensor Circuit	51-545	175
Code 33	Speed Sensor Circuit	51-545	175
Code 34	Speed Sensor Circuit	51-545	175
Code 35	Speed Sensor Circuit	51-545	175
Code 36	Speed Sensor Circuit	51-545	175
Code 37	Speed Sensor Rotor Fault	51-546	176
Code 38	Speed Sensor Circuit	51-545	175
Code 39	Speed Sensor Circuit	51-545	175
Code 41	Power Source Circuit	51-548	179
Code 43	ABS Control System Fault	51-549	180
Code 44	NE Signal Circuit	51-549	181
Code 51	ABS Pump Motor Lock	51-550	183
Code 53	ECM Communication Circuit Fault	51-550	184
Code 61	ECM Communication Circuit Fault	51-551	185
Code 62	ECU Fault	51-551	186
CAMRY SOLARA LESS TRACTION CONTROL			
—	ABS Warning Lamp Circuit	51-496	86
—	T_C Terminal Circuit	51-514	112
—	T_S Terminal Circuit	51-520	128
Code 11	ABS Solenoid Valve Relay Circuit	51-526	144
Code 13	Pump Motor Circuit	51-527	145
Code 21	ABS Solenoid Valve Circuit	51-527	146
Code 22	ABS Solenoid Valve Circuit	51-527	146
Code 23	ABS Solenoid Valve Circuit	51-527	146
Code 24	ABS Solenoid Valve Circuit	51-527	146
Code 31	Speed Sensor Circuit	51-528	147
Code 32	Speed Sensor Circuit	51-528	147
Code 33	Speed Sensor Circuit	51-528	147
Code 34	Speed Sensor Circuit	51-528	147
Code 35	Speed Sensor Circuit	51-528	147
Code 36	Speed Sensor Circuit	51-528	147
Code 37	Speed Sensor Rotor Faulty	51-529	148
Code 38	Speed Sensor Circuit	51-528	147
Code 39	Speed Sensor Circuit	51-528	147
Code 41	Power Source Circuit	51-529	149
Code 58	Stop Lamp Switch Circuit	51-530	150
Code 62	ABS ECU Fault	51-531	151
CAMRY SOLARA w/TRACTION CONTROL			
—	ABS Lamp Always On	51-538	163
—	ABS Warning Lamp Circuit	51-496	87
—	SLIP Indicator Lamp Circuit	51-539	165
—	TRAC OFF Indicator, TRAC Cut Switch Circuit	51-538	164
—	TC Terminal Circuit	51-514	113
—	TS Terminal Circuit	51-521	129
Code 11	ABS & TRAC Solenoid Relay Circuit	51-531	152
Code 12	ABS & TRAC Solenoid Relay Circuit	51-531	152
Code 13	ABS & TRAC Motor Relay Circuit	51-532	153
Code 14	ABS & TRAC Motor Relay Circuit	51-532	153
Code 21	ABS & TRAC Actuator Solenoid Circuit	51-533	154
Code 22	ABS & TRAC Actuator Solenoid Circuit	51-533	154
Code 23	ABS & TRAC Actuator Solenoid Circuit	51-533	154
Code 24	ABS & TRAC Actuator Solenoid Circuit	51-533	154
Code 25	ABS & TRAC Actuator Solenoid Circuit	51-533	154
Code 26	ABS & TRAC Actuator Solenoid Circuit	51-533	154
Code 27	ABS & TRAC Actuator Solenoid Circuit	51-533	154

Continued

DIAGNOSTIC CHART INDEX—Continued

Code	Description	Page No.	Fig No.
CAMRY SOLARA w/TRACTION CONTROL			
Code 28	ABS & TRAC Actuator Solenoid Circuit	51-533	154
Code 31	Speed Sensor Circuit	51-534	155
Code 32	Speed Sensor Circuit	51-534	155
Code 33	Speed Sensor Circuit	51-534	155
Code 34	Speed Sensor Circuit	51-534	155
Code 41	IG Power Source Circuit	51-535	156
Code 43	ABS Control System Fault	51-536	157
Code 44	NE Signal Circuit	51-536	158
Code 49	Stop Lamp Switch Circuit	51-536	159
Code 51	ABS Pump Motor Lock	51-537	160
Code 53	ECM Communication Fault	51-537	161
Code 61	Engine Control System Fault	51-537	162
1996 CAMRY w/BOSCH ABS			
Code 11	ABS Control Solenoid & Motor Relay Circuit	51-551	187
Code 13	ABS Control Solenoid & Motor Relay Circuit	51-551	187
Code 21	ABS Actuator Solenoid Circuit	51-559	195
Code 22	ABS Actuator Solenoid Circuit	51-559	195
Code 23	ABS Actuator Solenoid Circuit	51-559	195
Code 31	Speed Sensor Circuit	51-562	200
Code 32	Speed Sensor Circuit	51-562	200
Code 33	Speed Sensor Circuit	51-562	200
Code 34	Speed Sensor Circuit	51-562	200
Code 35	Speed Sensor Circuit	51-562	200
Code 36	Speed Sensor Circuit	51-562	200
Code 37	Rear Speed Sensor Rotor	51-568	205
Code 38	Speed Sensor Circuit	51-562	200
Code 39	Speed Sensor Circuit	51-562	200
Code 41	BS Power Source Circuit	51-568	207
Code 51	ABS Pump Motor Lock	51-572	212
1997–99 CAMRY w/BOSCH ABS			
Code 11	ABS Solenoid Valve Relay Circuit	51-552	188
Code 13	Pump Motor Circuit	51-556	191
Code 21	ABS Actuator Solenoid Circuit	51-560	196
Code 22	ABS Actuator Solenoid Circuit	51-560	196
Code 23	ABS Actuator Solenoid Circuit	51-560	196
Code 24	ABS Actuator Solenoid Circuit	51-560	196
Code 31	Speed Sensor Circuit	51-563	201
Code 32	Speed Sensor Circuit	51-563	201
Code 33	Speed Sensor Circuit	51-563	201
Code 34	Speed Sensor Circuit	51-563	201
Code 35	Speed Sensor Circuit	51-563	201
Code 36	Speed Sensor Circuit	51-563	201
Code 37	Speed Sensor Rotor	51-568	206
Code 38	Speed Sensor Circuit	51-563	201
Code 39	Speed Sensor Circuit	51-563	201
Code 41	BS Power Source Circuit	51-569	208
Code 43	ABS Control System Fault	51-571	210
Code 44	NE Signal Circuit Fault	51-572	211
Code 51	ABS Pump Motor Lock	51-572	212
Code 53	ECM Communication Circuit Fault	51-572	213
Code 61	ECM Communication Circuit Fault	51-573	214
Code 62	ABS ECU Fault	51-573	215
1996 CAMRY w/NIPPONDENSO ABS			
Code 11	ABS Control Solenoid Relay Circuit	51-552	189
Code 12	ABS Control Solenoid Relay Circuit	51-552	189
Code 13	ABS Control Motor Relay Circuit	51-556	192

Continued

DIAGNOSTIC CHART INDEX—Continued

Code	Description	Page No.	Fig No.
1996 CAMRY w/NIPPONDENSO ABS			
Code 14	ABS Control Motor Relay Circuit	51-556	192
Code 21	ABS Actuator Solenoid Circuit	51-560	197
Code 22	ABS Actuator Solenoid Circuit	51-560	197
Code 23	ABS Actuator Solenoid Circuit	51-560	197
Code 24	ABS Actuator Solenoid Circuit	51-560	197
Code 31	Speed Sensor Circuit	51-565	202
Code 32	Speed Sensor Circuit	51-565	202
Code 33	Speed Sensor Circuit	51-565	202
Code 34	Speed Sensor Circuit	51-565	202
Code 35	Speed Sensor Circuit	51-565	202
Code 36	Speed Sensor Circuit	51-565	202
Code 37	Rear Speed Sensor Rotor	51-568	205
Code 39	Speed Sensor Circuit	51-562	200
Code 41	IG Power Source Circuit	51-570	209
Code 51	ABS Pump Motor Lock	51-572	212
1997–99 CAMRY w/NIPPONDENSO ABS			
Code 11	ABS Control Solenoid Relay Circuit	51-554	190
Code 12	ABS Control Solenoid Relay Circuit	51-554	190
Code 13	ABS Control Motor Relay Circuit	51-557	193
Code 14	ABS Control Motor Relay Circuit	51-557	193
Code 21	ABS Actuator Solenoid Circuit	51-561	198
Code 22	ABS Actuator Solenoid Circuit	51-561	198
Code 23	ABS Actuator Solenoid Circuit	51-561	198
Code 24	ABS Actuator Solenoid Circuit	51-561	198
Code 31	Speed Sensor Circuit	51-566	203
Code 32	Speed Sensor Circuit	51-566	203
Code 33	Speed Sensor Circuit	51-566	203
Code 34	Speed Sensor Circuit	51-566	203
Code 34	Rear Speed Sensor Fault	51-568	204
Code 35	Rear Speed Sensor Fault	51-568	204
Code 37	Speed Sensor Rotor	51-568	206
Code 41	IG Power Source Circuit	51-570	209
Code 43	ABS Control System Fault	51-571	210
Code 44	NE Signal Circuit Fault	51-572	211
Code 51	ABS Pump Motor Lock	51-572	212
Code 53	ECM Communication Circuit Fault	51-572	213
Code 61	ECM Communication Circuit Fault	51-573	214
Code 62	ABS ECU Fault	51-573	215
1997–99 CAMRY w/TRACTION CONTROL			
Code 11	ABS Control Solenoid Relay Circuit (With Traction Control)	51-554	190
Code 12	ABS Control Solenoid Relay Circuit (With Traction Control)	51-554	190
Code 14	ABS Control Motor Relay Circuit (With Traction Control)	51-558	194
Code 21	ABS Actuator Solenoid Circuit (With Traction Control)	51-561	199
Code 22	ABS Actuator Solenoid Circuit (With Traction Control)	51-561	199
Code 23	ABS Actuator Solenoid Circuit (With Traction Control)	51-561	199
Code 24	ABS Actuator Solenoid Circuit (With Traction Control)	51-561	199
Code 25	ABS Actuator Solenoid Circuit (With Traction Control)	51-561	199
Code 26	ABS Actuator Solenoid Circuit (With Traction Control)	51-561	199
Code 27	ABS Actuator Solenoid Circuit (With Traction Control)	51-561	199
Code 28	ABS Actuator Solenoid Circuit (With Traction Control)	51-561	199
Code 31	Speed Sensor Circuit	51-566	203
Code 32	Speed Sensor Circuit	51-566	203
Code 33	Speed Sensor Circuit	51-566	203
Code 34	Speed Sensor Circuit	51-566	203
Code 37	Speed Sensor Rotor	51-568	206
Code 41	IG Power Source Circuit Traction Control	51-571	209

Continued

DIAGNOSTIC CHART INDEX—Continued

Code	Description	Page No.	Fig No.
1997–99 CAMRY w/TRACTION CONTROL			
Code 43	ABS Control System Fault	51-571	210
Code 44	NE Signal Circuit Fault	51-572	211
Code 51	ABS Pump Motor Lock	51-572	212
Code 53	ECM Communication Circuit Fault	51-572	213
Code 61	ECM Communication Circuit Fault	51-573	214
Code 62	ABS ECU Fault	51-573	215
1996 CELICA			
Code 11	ABS Solenoid Relay	51-573	216
Code 12	ABS Solenoid Relay	51-573	216
Code 13	ABS Motor Relay	51-575	217
Code 14	ABS Motor Relay	51-575	217
Code 21	ABS Actuator Solenoid	51-577	218
Code 22	ABS Actuator Solenoid	51-577	218
Code 23	ABS Actuator Solenoid	51-577	218
Code 24	ABS Actuator Solenoid	51-577	218
Code 31	Speed Sensor Circuit	51-578	219
Code 32	Speed Sensor Circuit	51-578	219
Code 33	Speed Sensor Circuit	51-578	219
Code 34	Speed Sensor Circuit	51-578	219
Code 35	Speed Sensor Circuit	51-578	219
Code 36	Speed Sensor Circuit	51-578	219
Code 41	IG Power Source Circuit	51-580	220
Code 51	ABS Pump Motor Lock	51-582	221
1997–99 CELICA			
Code 11	ABS Solenoid Relay	51-574	216
Code 12	ABS Solenoid Relay	51-574	216
Code 13	ABS Motor Relay	51-575	217
Code 14	ABS Motor Relay	51-575	217
Code 21	ABS Actuator Solenoid	51-577	218
Code 22	ABS Actuator Solenoid	51-577	218
Code 23	ABS Actuator Solenoid	51-577	218
Code 24	ABS Actuator Solenoid	51-577	218
Code 31	Speed Sensor Circuit	51-578	219
Code 32	Speed Sensor Circuit	51-578	219
Code 33	Speed Sensor Circuit	51-578	219
Code 34	Speed Sensor Circuit	51-578	219
Code 35	Speed Sensor Circuit	51-578	219
Code 36	Speed Sensor Circuit	51-578	219
Code 41	IG Power Source Circuit	51-580	220
Code 51	ABS Pump Motor Lock	51-582	222
COROLLA			
Code 11	ABS Control Solenoid Relay Circuit	51-582	223
Code 12	ABS Control Solenoid Relay Circuit	51-582	223
Code 13	ABS Control Motor Relay Circuit	51-583	224
Code 14	ABS Control Motor Relay Circuit	51-583	224
Code 21	ABS Actuator Solenoid Circuit	51-585	225
Code 22	ABS Actuator Solenoid Circuit	51-585	225
Code 23	ABS Actuator Solenoid Circuit	51-585	225
Code 24	ABS Actuator Solenoid Circuit	51-585	225
Code 31	Speed Sensor Circuit	51-585	226
Code 32	Speed Sensor Circuit	51-585	226
Code 33	Speed Sensor Circuit	51-585	226
Code 34	Speed Sensor Circuit	51-585	226
Code 35	Speed Sensor Circuit	51-585	226
Code 36	Speed Sensor Circuit	51-585	226
Code 37	Rear Speed Sensor Rotor	51-587	227

Continued

DIAGNOSTIC CHART INDEX—Continued

Code	Description	Page No.	Fig No.
COROLLA			
Code 41	IG Power Source	51-587	228
Code 51	ABS Pump Motor Lock	51-587	229
PASEO			
Code 11	ABS Control Solenoid Relay Circuit	51-588	230
Code 12	ABS Control Solenoid Relay Circuit	51-588	230
Code 13	ABS Control Motor Relay Circuit	51-588	231
Code 14	ABS Control Motor Relay Circuit	51-588	231
Code 21	ABS Actuator Solenoid Circuit	51-589	232
Code 22	ABS Actuator Solenoid Circuit	51-589	232
Code 23	ABS Actuator Solenoid Circuit	51-589	232
Code 24	ABS Actuator Solenoid Circuit	51-589	232
Code 31	Speed Sensor Circuit	51-590	233
Code 32	Speed Sensor Circuit	51-590	233
Code 33	Speed Sensor Circuit	51-590	233
Code 34	Speed Sensor Circuit	51-590	233
Code 41	IG Power Source Circuit	51-591	234
Code 51	ABS Pump Motor Lock	51-592	235
1996 RAV4			
Code 11	ABS Control Solenoid Relay Circuit	51-592	236
Code 12	ABS Control Solenoid Relay Circuit	51-592	236
Code 13	ABS Control Motor Relay Circuit	51-594	237
Code 14	ABS Control Motor Relay Circuit	51-594	237
Code 21	ABS Actuator Solenoid Circuit	51-596	239
Code 22	ABS Actuator Solenoid Circuit	51-596	239
Code 23	ABS Actuator Solenoid Circuit	51-596	239
Code 24	ABS Actuator Solenoid Circuit	51-596	239
Code 31	Speed Sensor Circuit	51-597	241
Code 32	Speed Sensor Circuit	51-597	241
Code 33	Speed Sensor Circuit	51-597	241
Code 34	Speed Sensor Circuit	51-597	241
Code 35	Speed Sensor Circuit	51-597	241
Code 37	Tires Of Different Size (2WD)	51-599	243
Code 41	IG Power Source Circuit	51-599	244
Code 43	Malfunction In Deceleration Sensor With 4WD	51-601	245
Code 45	Malfunction In Deceleration Sensor With 4WD	51-601	245
Code 44	Deceleration Sensor Circuit	51-601	246
Code 51	ABS Pump Motor Lock	51-602	248
1997–99 RAV4			
Code 11	ABS Control Solenoid Relay Circuit	51-592	236
Code 12	ABS Control Solenoid Relay Circuit	51-592	236
Code 13	ABS Control Motor Relay Circuit	51-594	238
Code 14	ABS Control Motor Relay Circuit	51-594	238
Code 21	ABS Actuator Solenoid Circuit	51-596	240
Code 22	ABS Actuator Solenoid Circuit	51-596	240
Code 23	ABS Actuator Solenoid Circuit	51-596	240
Code 24	ABS Actuator Solenoid Circuit	51-596	240
Code 31	Speed Sensor Circuit	51-598	242
Code 32	Speed Sensor Circuit	51-598	242
Code 33	Speed Sensor Circuit	51-598	242
Code 34	Speed Sensor Circuit	51-598	242
Code 37	Tires Of Different Size (2WD)	51-599	243
Code 41	IG Power Source Circuit	51-599	244
Code 43	Malfunction In Deceleration Sensor (With 4WD	51-601	245
Code 44	Deceleration Sensor Circuit	51-601	247
Code 45	Malfunction In Deceleration Sensor (With 4WD	51-601	245
Code 51	ABS Pump Motor Lock	51-602	248

Continued

DIAGNOSTIC CHART INDEX—Continued

Code	Description	Page No.	Fig No.
SIENNA			
—	ABS Lamp Always On	51-606	256
—	ABS Warning Light Circuit	51-496	88
—	TC Terminal Circuit	51-515	114
—	TS Terminal Circuit	51-521	130
Code 11	ABS Solenoid Relay Circuit	51-602	249
Code 12	ABS Solenoid Relay Circuit	51-602	249
Code 13	ABS Motor Relay Circuit	51-602	250
Code 14	ABS Motor Relay Circuit	51-602	250
Code 21	ABS Solenoid Valve Circuit	51-603	251
Code 22	ABS Solenoid Valve Circuit	51-603	251
Code 23	ABS Solenoid Valve Circuit	51-603	251
Code 24	ABS Solenoid Valve Circuit	51-603	251
Code 31	Speed Sensor Circuit	51-603	252
Code 32	Speed Sensor Circuit	51-603	252
Code 33	Speed Sensor Circuit	51-603	252
Code 34	Speed Sensor Circuit	51-603	252
Code 41	IG Power Source Circuit	51-604	253
Code 49	Stop Light Switch Circuit	51-605	254
Code 51	ABS Pump Motor Lock	51-606	255
1996 SUPRA LESS TRACTION CONTROL			
Code 11	ABS Solenoid Relay	51-607	257
Code 12	ABS Solenoid Relay	51-607	257
Code 13	ABS Motor Relay	51-611	260
Code 14	ABS Motor Relay	51-611	260
Code 21	ABS Actuator Solenoid	51-618	264
Code 22	ABS Actuator Solenoid	51-618	264
Code 23	ABS Actuator Solenoid	51-618	264
Code 24	ABS Actuator Solenoid	51-618	264
Code 31	Speed Sensor	51-623	272
Code 32	Speed Sensor	51-623	272
Code 33	Speed Sensor	51-623	272
Code 34	Speed Sensor	51-623	272
Code 35	Speed Sensor	51-623	272
Code 36	Speed Sensor	51-623	272
Code 41	IG Power Source Circuit	51-628	277
Code 44	Lateral Acceleration Sensor Circuit	51-632	283
Code 51	ABS Pump Motor Lock	51-635	288
1996 SUPRA WITH TRACTION CONTROL			
Code 15	TRAC Solenoid Relay	51-616	262
Code 16	TRAC Solenoid Relay	51-616	262
Code 17	TRAC Motor Relay	51-617	263
Code 18	TRAC Motor Relay	51-617	263
Code 24	Sub-Throttle Actuator Circuit	51-620	268
Code 25	TRAC Actuator Solenoid	51-622	271
Code 25	TRAC Sub-Throttle Valve	51-622	270
Code 26	TRAC Sub-Throttle Valve	51-622	270
Code 27	TRAC Actuator Solenoid	51-622	271
Code 31	Speed Sensor	51-624	273
Code 32	Speed Sensor	51-624	273
Code 33	Speed Sensor	51-624	273
Code 34	Speed Sensor	51-624	273
Code 41	IG Power Source Circuit	51-628	277
Code 43	ABS & TRAC ECU Fault	51-631	280
Code 44	NE Signal Circuit	51-633	284
Code 45	Main Throttle Position Sensor Circuit	51-634	286
Code 46	Main Throttle Position Sensor Circuit	51-634	286

Continued

DIAGNOSTIC CHART INDEX—Continued

Code	Description	Page No.	Fig No.
1996 SUPRA WITH TRACTION CONTROL			
Code 47	Sub-Throttle Position Sensor Circuit	51-635	287
Code 48	Sub-Throttle Position Sensor Circuit	51-635	287
Code 51	Engine Fault Detection Circuit	51-635	289
Code 53	ECM Communication Circuit	51-637	291
Code 55	Brake Fluid Level Warning Switch	51-637	292
Code 58	TRAC Pump Motor	51-637	293
Code 61	TRAC ECU Communication Circuit Fault	51-639	295
Code 61	ABS & TRAC ECU Communication Circuit Fault	51-638	294
Code 62	TRAC Vehicle Speed Malfunction	51-639	296
1997–98 SUPRA LESS TRACTION CONTROL			
Code 11	ABS Solenoid Relay	51-608	258
Code 12	ABS Solenoid Relay	51-608	258
Code 13	ABS Motor Relay	51-614	261
Code 14	ABS Motor Relay	51-614	261
Code 21	ABS Actuator Solenoid	51-618	265
Code 22	ABS Actuator Solenoid	51-618	265
Code 23	ABS Actuator Solenoid	51-618	265
Code 24	ABS Actuator Solenoid	51-618	265
Code 31	Speed Sensor	51-625	274
Code 32	Speed Sensor	51-625	274
Code 33	Speed Sensor	51-625	274
Code 34	Speed Sensor	51-625	274
Code 41	IG Power Source Circuit	51-628	277
Code 43	Deceleration Sensor Fault	51-632	281
Code 44	Deceleration Sensor Fault	51-633	285
Code 45	Deceleration Sensor Fault	51-632	281
Code 51	ABS Pump Motor Lock	51-635	288
1997–98 SUPRA WITH TRACTION CONTROL			
Code 11	Throttle Control Relay	51-610	259
Code 12	Throttle Control Relay (With Traction Control)	51-610	259
Code 21	Sub–Throttle Valve Motor	51-619	266
Code 22	Sub–Throttle Valve Motor	51-619	266
Code 23	Throttle Body Fault	51-620	267
Code 24	Sub–Throttle Position Sensor Leakage/Sub–Throttle Valve Stuck	51-621	269
Code 31	Throttle Position Sensor Circuit	51-626	275
Code 32	Sub-Throttle Position Sensor Circuit	51-627	276
Code 41	NE Signal Circuit	51-630	278
Code 42	Engine Control System Fault	51-631	279
Code 43	ECM Communication Circuit Fault	51-632	282
Code 44	Deceleration Sensor Fault	51-633	285
Code 51	Power Source Circuit	51-636	290
Code 61	Speed Sensor Circuit	51-639	297
Code 62	Speed Sensor Circuit	51-639	297
Code 63	Speed Sensor Circuit	51-639	297
Code 64	Speed Sensor Circuit	51-639	297
Code 71	Emergency Fuel Cut	51-640	298
Code 72	Emergency Fuel Cut	51-640	298
Code 81	ABS Control System Fault	51-641	299
4RUNNER			
Code 11	ABS Control Solenoid Relay Circuit	51-641	300
Code 12	ABS Control Solenoid Relay Circuit	51-641	300
Code 13	ABS Control Motor Relay Circuit	51-642	301
Code 14	ABS Control Motor Relay Circuit	51-642	301
Code 21	ABS Actuator Solenoid Circuit	51-643	302
Code 22	ABS Actuator Solenoid Circuit	51-643	302
Code 23	ABS Actuator Solenoid Circuit	51-643	302

Continued

DIAGNOSTIC CHART INDEX—Continued

Code	Description	Page No.	Fig No.
4RUNNER			
Code 31	Speed Sensor Circuit	51-644	303
Code 32	Speed Sensor Circuit	51-644	303
Code 33	Speed Sensor Circuit	51-644	303
Code 34	Speed Sensor Circuit	51-644	303
Code 37	Neither Front Speed Sensor Rotor Missing	51-645	304
Code 37	Tires Of Different Size	51-645	305
Code 41	IG Power Source Circuit	51-645	306
Code 43	Malfunction In Deceleration Sensor	51-646	307
Code 44	Deceleration Sensor Circuit	51-646	308
Code 48	Rear Differential Lock Circuit	51-647	309
Code 51	ABS Pump Motor Lock	51-647	310
1996 TACOMA			
Code 11	ABS Control Solenoid Relay Circuit	51-648	311
Code 12	ABS Control Solenoid Relay Circuit	51-648	311
Code 13	ABS Control Motor Relay Circuit	51-650	312
Code 14	ABS Control Motor Relay Circuit	51-650	312
Code 21	ABS Actuator Solenoid Circuit	51-652	313
Code 22	ABS Actuator Solenoid Circuit	51-652	313
Code 23	ABS Actuator Solenoid Circuit	51-652	313
Code 31	Speed Sensor Circuit	51-654	314
Code 32	Speed Sensor Circuit	51-654	314
Code 33	Speed Sensor Circuit	51-654	314
Code 34	Speed Sensor Circuit	51-654	314
Code 35	Speed Sensor Circuit	51-654	314
Code 36	Speed Sensor Circuit	51-654	314
Code 37	Neither Front Speed Sensor Rotor Missing	51-655	315
Code 37	Tires Of Different Size On 2WD Vehicles	51-656	316
Code 41	IG Power Source Circuit	51-656	317
Code 43	Fault In Deceleration Sensor	51-657	318
Code 44	Deceleration Sensor Circuit	51-657	319
Code 48	Rear Differential Lock Circuit	51-657	320
Code 51	ABS Pump Motor Lock	51-658	321
1997–99 TACOMA			
Code 11	ABS Control Solenoid Relay Circuit	51-648	311
Code 12	ABS Control Solenoid Relay Circuit	51-648	311
Code 13	ABS Control Motor Relay Circuit	51-651	312
Code 14	ABS Control Motor Relay Circuit	51-651	312
Code 21	ABS Actuator Solenoid Circuit	51-652	313
Code 22	ABS Actuator Solenoid Circuit	51-652	313
Code 23	ABS Actuator Solenoid Circuit	51-652	313
Code 31	Speed Sensor Circuit	51-654	314
Code 32	Speed Sensor Circuit	51-654	314
Code 33	Speed Sensor Circuit	51-654	314
Code 34	Speed Sensor Circuit	51-654	314
Code 35	Speed Sensor Circuit	51-654	314
Code 36	Speed Sensor Circuit	51-654	314
Code 37	Neither Front Speed Sensor Rotor Missing	51-655	315
Code 37	Tires Of Different Size On 2WD Vehicles	51-656	316
Code 41	IG Power Source Circuit	51-656	317
Code 43	Fault In Deceleration Sensor	51-657	318
Code 44	Deceleration Sensor Circuit	51-657	319
Code 48	Rear Differential Lock Circuit	51-657	320
Code 51	ABS Pump Motor Lock	51-658	322
TERCEL			
Code 11	ABS Control Solenoid Relay Circuit	51-659	323
Code 12	ABS Control Solenoid Relay Circuit	51-659	323

Continued

DIAGNOSTIC CHART INDEX—Continued

Code	Description	Page No.	Fig No.
TERCEL			
Code 13	ABS Control Motor Relay Circuit	51-660	324
Code 14	ABS Control Motor Relay Circuit	51-660	324
Code 21	ABS Actuator Solenoid Circuit	51-660	325
Code 22	ABS Actuator Solenoid Circuit	51-660	325
Code 23	ABS Actuator Solenoid Circuit	51-660	325
Code 24	ABS Actuator Solenoid Circuit	51-660	325
Code 31	Speed Sensor Circuit	51-661	326
Code 32	Speed Sensor Circuit	51-661	326
Code 33	Speed Sensor Circuit	51-661	326
Code 34	Speed Sensor Circuit	51-661	326
Code 35	Speed Sensor Circuit	51-661	326
Code 36	Speed Sensor Circuit	51-661	326
Code 41	IG Power Source Circuit	51-662	327
Code 51	ABS Pump Motor Lock	51-663	328
TUNDRA			
—	ABS Lamp Always On	51-668	339
—	ABS Warning Lamp Always On	51-497	89
—	T_C Terminal Circuit	51-515	115
—	T_S Terminal Circuit	51-521	131
Code C0200	Speed Sensor Circuit	51-664	329
Code C0205	Speed Sensor Circuit	51-664	329
Code C0210	Speed Sensor Circuit	51-664	329
Code C0215	Speed Sensor Circuit	51-664	329
Code C0226	ABS Solenoid Circuit	51-665	330
Code C0236	ABS Solenoid Circuit	51-665	330
Code C0246	ABS Solenoid Circuit	51-665	330
Code C0273	ABS Motor Relay Circuit	51-665	331
Code C0274	ABS Motor Relay Circuit	51-665	331
Code C0278	ABS Solenoid Relay Circuit	51-666	332
Code C0279	ABS Solenoid Relay Circuit	51-666	332
Code C1237	Both Front Speed Sensor Rotors Missing Or Tire Of Different Size	51-666	333
Code C1241	IG Power Source Circuit	51-666	334
Code C1243	Fault In Deceleration Sensor	51-667	335
Code C1244	Deceleration Sensor Circuit	51-667	336
Code C1245	Fault In Deceleration Sensor	51-667	335
Code C1249	Stop Lamp Switch Circuit	51-668	337
Code C1251	ABS Pump Motor Lock	51-668	338
Code 11	ABS Solenoid Relay Circuit	51-666	332
Code 12	ABS Solenoid Relay Circuit	51-666	332
Code 13	ABS Motor Relay Circuit	51-665	331
Code 14	ABS Motor Relay Circuit	51-665	331
Code 21	ABS Solenoid Circuit	51-665	330
Code 22	ABS Solenoid Circuit	51-665	330
Code 23	ABS Solenoid Circuit	51-665	330
Code 31	Speed Sensor Circuit	51-664	329
Code 32	Speed Sensor Circuit	51-664	329
Code 33	Speed Sensor Circuit	51-664	329
Code 34	Speed Sensor Circuit	51-664	329
Code 37	Both Front Speed Sensor Rotors Missing Or Tire Of Different Size	51-666	333
Code 41	IG Power Source Circuit	51-666	334
Code 43	Fault In Deceleration Sensor	51-667	335
Code 44	Deceleration Sensor Circuit	51-667	336
Code 45	Fault In Deceleration Sensor	51-667	335
Code 49	Stop Lamp Switch Circuit	51-668	337
Code 51	ABS Pump Motor Lock	51-668	338

CIRCUIT DESCRIPTION

If the ECU detects any trouble, it lights the ABS warning light while at the same time prohibiting ABS control. At this time, the ECU records a DTC in memory.

Connect terminals Tc and E_1 of the DLC1 or DLC2 to make the ABS warning light blink and output the DTC.

INSPECTION PROCEDURE

Troubleshoot in accordance with the chart below for each trouble symptom.

ABS warning light does not light up	Go to step 1
ABS warning light remains on	Go to step 2

1	Check ABS warning light.

Diagnose combination meter.

NG > Repair bulb or combination meter assembly.

OK

Check for open circuit in harness and connector between GAUGE fuse, DLC2 and ABS ECU.

TY4029900567010X

Fig. 86 ABS Warning Lamp Circuit (Part 1 of 2). Camry Solara less traction control

CIRCUIT DESCRIPTION

If the ECU detects a trouble, it lights the ABS warning light while at the same time prohibiting ABS control. At this time, the ECU records a DTC in memory.

Connect terminals Tc and E_1 of the DLC1 or DLC2 to make the ABS warning light blink and output the DTC.

INSPECTION PROCEDURE

Troubleshoot in accordance with the chart below for each trouble symptom.

ABS warning light does not light up	Go to step 1
ABS warning light remains on	Go to step 3

1	Check ABS warning light.

Diagnose combination meter.

NG > Repair bulb or combination meter assembly.

OK

TY4029900582010X

Fig. 87 ABS Warning Lamp Circuit (Part 1 of 3). Camry Solara w/traction control

3	Is DTC output?

Check DTC.

YES > Repair circuit indicated by the code output.

NO

4	Does ABS warning light go off?

NO > Check for short circuit in harness and connector between ABS warning light, DLC1 and ABS & TRAC ECU.

YES

5	Check ABS & TRAC solenoid relay (See step 2).

NG > Replace ABS & TRAC solenoid relay.

OK

Check for short circuit in harness and connector between DLC1 and ABS & TRAC solenoid relay.

TY4029900582030X

Fig. 87 ABS Warning Lamp Circuit (Part 3 of 3). Camry Solara w/traction control

2	Is DTC output

Check DTC.

YES > Repair circuit indicated by the code output.

NO

Check for short in harness and connector between ABS warning light, DLC1, DLC2, and ECU.

TY4029900567020X

Fig. 86 ABS Warning Lamp Circuit (Part 2 of 2). Camry Solara less traction control

2	Check ABS & TRAC solenoid relay.

PREPARATION:
Remove ABS & TRAC solenoid relay from Engine Room R/B No. 3.
CHECK:
Check continuity between each terminal of ABS & TRAC solenoid relay.
OK:

Terminals 4 and 6	Continuity (Reference value 80 Ω)
Terminals 2 and 3	Continuity
Terminals 1 and 3	Open

CHECK:
(a) Apply battery positive voltage between terminals 4 and 6.
(b) Check continuity between each terminal of ABS & TRAC solenoid relay.
OK:

Terminals 2 and 3	Open
Terminals 1 and 3	Continuity

CHECK:
Connect the ⊕ test lead to terminal 5 and the ⊖ lead to terminal 3. Check continuity between the terminals.
OK:
   Continuity
If there is no continuity, connect the ⊖ test lead to terminal 5 and the ⊕ lead to terminal 3. Recheck continuity between terminals.

NG > Replace ABS & TRAC solenoid relay.

 OK

Check for open circuit in harness and connector between DLC1, ABS & TRAC solenoid relay and body ground.

TY4029900582020X

Fig. 87 ABS Warning Lamp Circuit (Part 2 of 3). Camry Solara w/traction control

CIRCUIT DESCRIPTION

If the ECU detects trouble, it lights the ABS warning light while at the same time prohibiting ABS control. At this time, the ECU records a DTC in memory.

Connect terminals Tc and E_1 of the DLC1 make the ABS warning light blink and output the DTC.

TY4029900462010X

Fig. 88 ABS Warning Light Circuit (Part 1 of 2). Sienna

INSPECTION PROCEDURE
Troubleshoot in accordance with the table below for each trouble symptom.

ABS warning light does not light up	Go to step 1
ABS warning light remains on	Go to step 2

1	Check ABS warning light.

See combination meter troubleshooting

NG ▷ Repair bulb or combination meter assembly

OK

Check for open circuit in harness and connector between GAUGE fuse and ABS warning light.

2	Is DTC output?

Check DTC

YES ▷ Repair circuit indicated by the code output.

NO

Check for short circuit in harness and connector between ABS warning light, DLC1 and ABS ECU

TY4029900462020X

Fig. 88   ABS Warning Light Circuit (Part 2 of 2). Sienna

1	Check operation of the ABS warning light.

PREPARATION:
(a)   Connect the TOYOTA hand–held tester to the DLC3.
(b)   Turn the ignition switch ON and push the TOYOTA hand–held tester main switch ON.
(c)   Select the ACTIVE TEST mode on the TOYOTA hand–held tester.
CHECK:
Check that "ON" and "OFF" of the ABS warning light can be shown on the combination meter by the TOYOTA hand–held tester.

OK ▷ Check and replace ABS ECU.

NG

2	Check ABS warning light.

See combination meter troubleshooting

NG ▷ Repair bulb or combination meter assembly

OK

Check for open in harness and connector between GAUGE fuse and ABS ECU

3	Is DTC output?

Check DTC

YES ▷ Repair circuit indicated by the code output.

NO

TY4029900480020X

Fig. 89   ABS Warning Lamp Always On (Part 2 of 3). Tundra

CIRCUIT DESCRIPTION
If the ECU detects trouble, it lights the ABS warning light while at the same time prohibiting ABS control. At this time, the ECU records a DTC in memory.
After removing the short pin of the DLC1, connect terminals Tc and E_1 of the DLC1 to make the ABS warning light blink and output the DTC.

INSPECTION PROCEDURE
HINT:
Troubleshooting in accordance with the chart below for each trouble symptom.

ABS warning light does not light up	*1
ABS warning light remains on	*2

*1: Start the inspection from step 1 in case of using the TOYOTA hand–held tester and start from step 2 in case of not TOYOTA using hand–held tester.
*2: After inspection with step 3, start the inspection from step 4 in case of using the TOYOTA hand–held tester and start from step 5 in case of not using TOYOTA hand–held tester.

TY4029900480010X

Fig. 89   ABS Warning Lamp Always On (Part 1 of 3). Tundra

4	Check for short circuit in harness and connector between GAUGE fuse and ABS ECU

NG ▷ Repair or replace harness or connector.

OK

Check and repair ABS ECU.

TY4029900480030X

Fig. 89   ABS Warning Lamp Always On (Part 3 of 3). Tundra

CIRCUIT DESCRIPTION

If the ECU detects trouble, it lights the ABS warning light while at the same time prohibiting ABS control. At this time, the ECU records a diagnostic trouble code in memory.
Connect terminals Tc and E1 of the DLC1 or DLC2 to make the ABS warning light to blink and output the diagnostic trouble code.

WIRING DIAGRAM

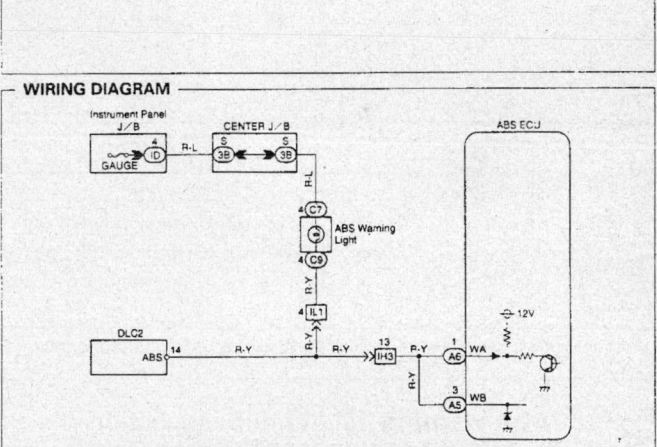

TY4029500161010X

Fig. 90   ABS warning light circuit inspection (Part 1 of 2). 1996 Avalon

Troubleshoot in accordance with the chart below for each trouble symptom.

ABS warning light does not light up	Go to step 1
ABS warning light remains on	Go to step 2

1 | Check ABS warning light.

See Combination Meter Troubleshooting

OK   NG ⟩ Replace bulb or combination meter assembly.

Check for open in harness and connector between GAUGE fuse and ECU

2 | Is diagnostic trouble code output?

Check diagnostic trouble code

NO   YES ⟩ Repair circuit indicated by the code output.

Check for short in harness and connector between warning light and ECU terminal WB, DLC 2 and ECU terminal WA

TY4029500161020X

Fig. 90 ABS warning light circuit inspection (Part 2 of 2). 1996 Avalon

2 | Is DTC output?

Check DTC

YES ⟩ Repair circuit indicated by the code output.

NO

Check for short in harness and connector between ABS warning light, DLC1, DLC2, and ECU

TY4029700240020X

Fig. 91 ABS warning light circuit inspection (Part 2 of 2). 1997–99 Avalon less Traction Control

If the ECU detects trouble, it lights the ABS warning light while at the same time prohibiting ABS control. At this time, the ECU records a DTC in memory.
Connect terminals Tc and E₁ of the DLC1 or DLC2 make the ABS warning light blink and output the DTC.

WIRING DIAGRAM

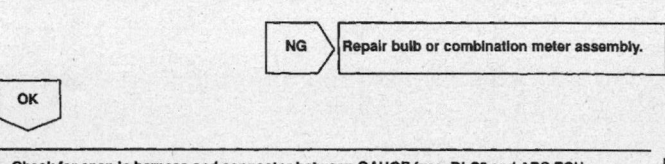

Troubleshooting in accordance with the chart below for each trouble symptom.

ABS warning light does not light up	Go to step 1
ABS warning light remains on	Go to step 2

1 | Check ABS warning light.

NG ⟩ Repair bulb or combination meter assembly.

OK

Check for open in harness and connector between GAUGE fuse, DLC2 and ABS ECU

TY4029700240010X

Fig. 91 ABS warning light circuit inspection (Part 1 of 2). 1997–99 Avalon less Traction Control

If the ECU detects trouble, it lights the ABS warning light while at the same time prohibiting ABS control. At this time, the ECU records a DTC in memory.
Connect terminals Tc and E₁ of the DLC1 or DLC2 make the ABS warning light blink and output the DTC.

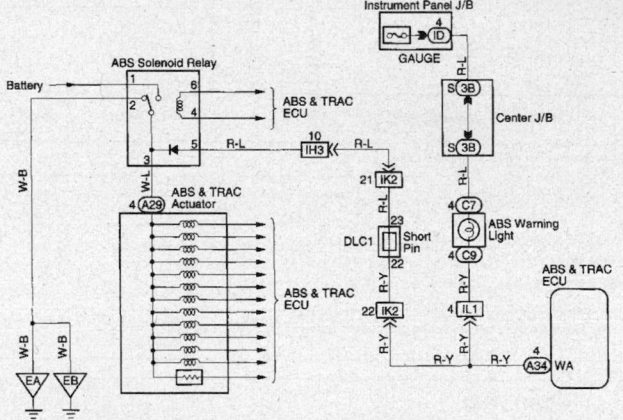

Troubleshooting in accordance with the chart below for each trouble symptom.

ABS warning light does not light up	Go to step 1
ABS warning light remains on	Go to step 3

1 | Check ABS warning light.

NG ⟩ Repair bulb or combination meter assembly.

OK

TY4029700241010X

Fig. 92 ABS warning light circuit inspection (Part 1 of 3). 1997–99 Avalon w/Traction Control

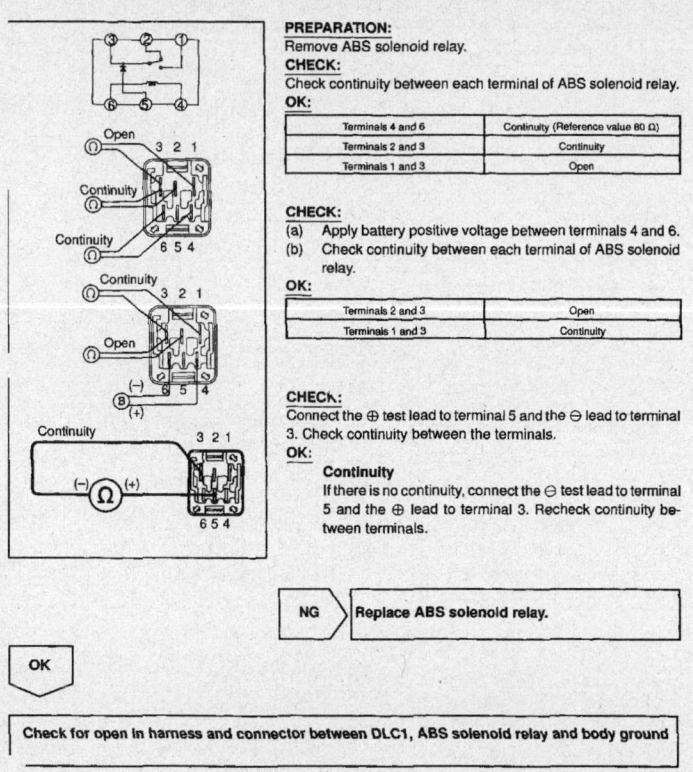

PREPARATION:
Remove ABS solenoid relay.
CHECK:
Check continuity between each terminal of ABS solenoid relay.
OK:

Terminals 4 and 6	Continuity (Reference value 80 Ω)
Terminals 2 and 3	Continuity
Terminals 1 and 3	Open

CHECK:
(a) Apply battery positive voltage between terminals 4 and 6.
(b) Check continuity between each terminal of ABS solenoid relay.
OK:

Terminals 2 and 3	Open
Terminals 1 and 3	Continuity

CHECK:
Connect the ⊕ test lead to terminal 5 and the ⊖ lead to terminal 3. Check continuity between the terminals.
OK:

Continuity
If there is no continuity, connect the ⊖ test lead to terminal 5 and the ⊕ lead to terminal 3. Recheck continuity between terminals.

NG ➤ Replace ABS solenoid relay.

OK

Check for open in harness and connector between DLC1, ABS solenoid relay and body ground

TY4029700241020X

Fig. 92 ABS warning light circuit inspection (Part 2 of 3). 1997–99 Avalon w/Traction Control

If the ECU detects trouble, it lights the ABS warning light while at the same time prohibiting ABS control. At this time, the ECU records a diagnostic trouble code in memory.
Connect terminals Tc and E1 of the DLC1 or DLC2 to make the ABS warning light blink and output the diagnostic trouble code.

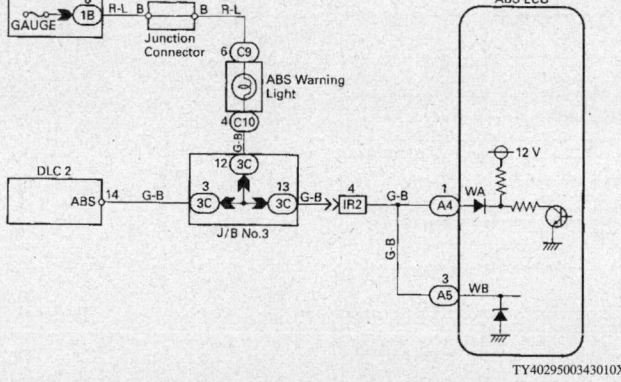

TY4029500343010X

Fig. 93 ABS warning light circuit inspection (Part 1 of 2). 1996 Camry w/Bosch ABS

3	Is DTC output?

Check DTC

YES ➤ Repair circuit indicated by the code output.

NO

4	Does ABS warning light go off?

NO ➤ Check for short in harness and connector between ABS warning light, DLC1 and ABS & TRAC ECU

YES

5	Check ABS solenoid relay (See step 2).

NG ➤ Replace ABS solenoid relay.

OK

Check for short in harness and connector between DLC1 and ABS solenoid relay

TY4029700241030X

Fig. 92 ABS warning light circuit inspection (Part 3 of 3). 1997–99 Avalon w/Traction Control

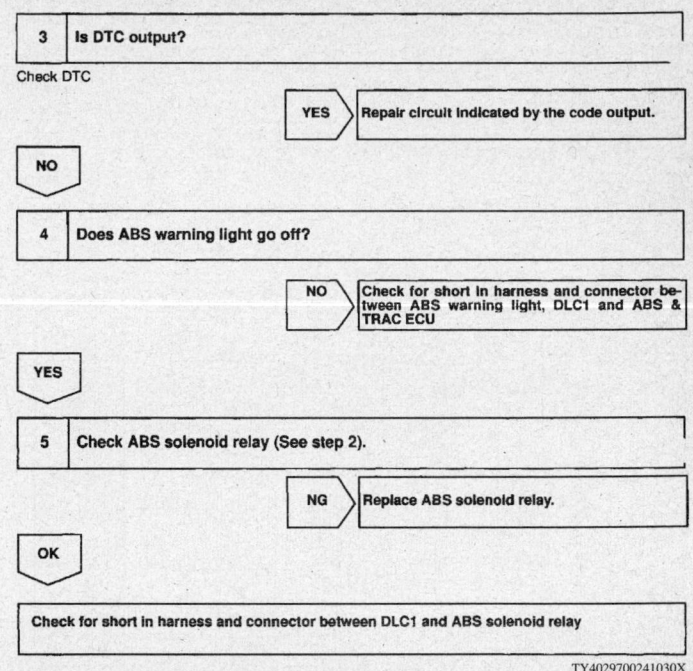

TY4029700344000X

Fig. 93 ABS warning light circuit inspection (Part 1 of 2). 1997–99 Camry w/Bosch ABS

ABS warning light does not light up	Go to step 1
ABS warning light remains on	Go to step 2

1	Check ABS warning light.

OK **NG** ➤ Replace bulb or combination meter assembly.

Check for open in harness and connector between GAUGE fuse and ECU

2	Is diagnostic trouble code output?

NO **YES** ➤ Repair circuit indicated by the code output.

Check for short in harness and connector between warning light and DLC1, and DLC2 and ECU terminal WA

TY4029500343020X

Fig. 93 ABS warning light circuit inspection (Part 2 of 2). Camry w/Bosch ABS

TOYOTA UNIT REPAIR

If the ECU detects trouble, it lights the ABS warning light while at the same time prohibiting ABS control. At this time, the ECU records a diagnostic trouble code in memory.
After removing the short pin of the DLC1, connect terminals Tc and E1 of the DLC1 or DLC2 to make the ABS warning light blink and output the diagnostic trouble code.

Troubleshoot in accordance with the chart below for each trouble symptom.

| ABS warning light does not light up | Go to step 1 |
| ABS warning light remains on | Go to step 3 |

1 | Check ABS warning light.

OK

NG — Replace bulb or combination meter assembly.

2 | Check ABS control relay.

P Disconnect the connectors from control relay.
C Check continuity between each terminal of ABS control relay.

OK

Terminals A7 1 and A6 3	Continuity (Reference value 80 Ω)
Terminals A7 5 and A7 6	Continuity
Terminals A7 2 and A7 5	Open

C 1. Apply battery voltage between terminals A7 1 and A6 3.
2. Check continuity between each terminal of ABS control relay.

OK

| Terminals A7 5 and A7 6 | Open |
| Terminals A7 2 and A7 5 | Continuity |

C Connect the ⊕ test lead to terminal 4 of A7 and the ⊖ lead to terminal 5 of A7. Check continuity between the terminals.

OK Continuity
If there is no continuity, connect the ⊖ test lead to terminal 4 of A7 and the ⊕ lead to terminal 5 of A7. Recheck continuity between terminals.

OK

NG — Replace ABS control relay.

Check for open in harness and connector between DLC1 and ABS control relay and body ground

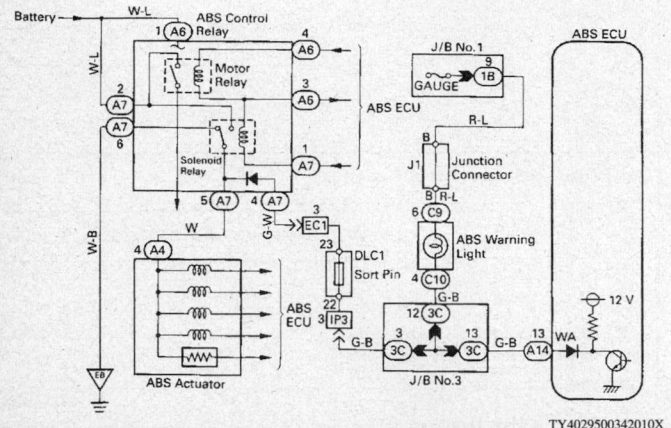

Fig. 94   ABS warning light circuit inspection (Part 1 of 3). 1996 Camry w/Nippondenso ABS

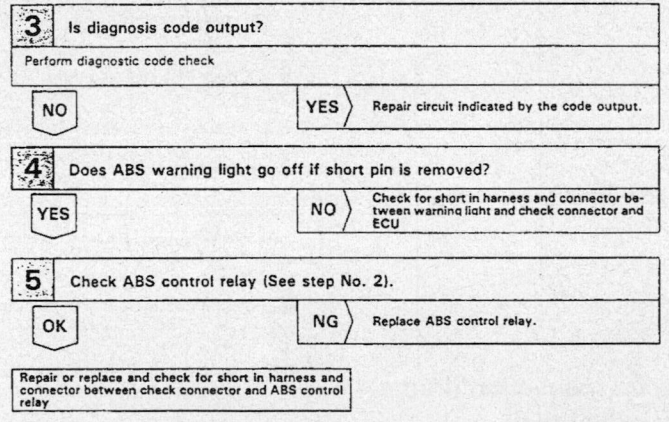

Fig. 94   ABS warning light circuit inspection (Part 2 of 3). 1996 Camry w/Nippondenso ABS

3 | Is diagnosis code output?
Perform diagnostic code check

NO

YES — Repair circuit indicated by the code output.

4 | Does ABS warning light go off if short pin is removed?

YES

NO — Check for short in harness and connector between warning light and check connector and ECU

5 | Check ABS control relay (See step No. 2).

OK

NG — Replace ABS control relay.

Repair or replace and check for short in harness and connector between check connector and ABS control relay

Fig. 94   ABS warning light circuit inspection (Part 3 of 3). 1996 Camry w/Nippondenso ABS

If the ECU detects trouble, it lights the ABS warning light while at the same time prohibiting ABS control. At this time, the ECU records a DTC in memory.
After removing the short pin of the DLC1, connect terminals Tc and E_1 of the DLC1 or DLC2 make the ABS warning light blink and output the DTC.

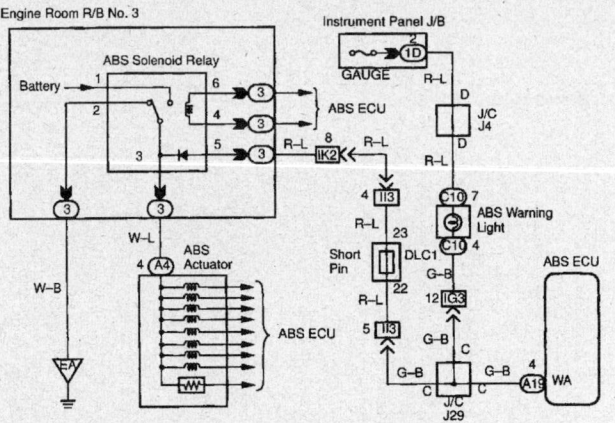

Troubleshooting in accordance with the chart below for each trouble symptom.

ABS warning light does not light up	Go to step 1
ABS warning light remains on	Go to step 3

1	Check ABS warning light.

NG ▷ Repair bulb or combination meter assembly.

OK

TY4029700345010X

Fig. 95   ABS warning light circuit inspection (Part 1 of 3). 1997–99 Camry w/traction control & Nippondenso ABS

2	Check ABS solenoid relay.

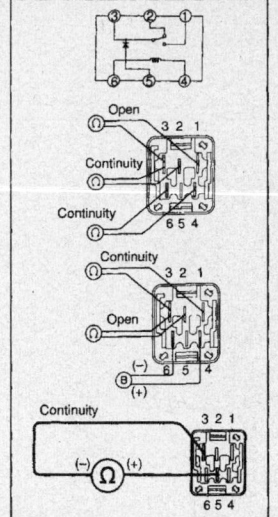

PREPARATION:
Remove ABS solenoid relay from Engine Room R/B No. 3.
CHECK:
Check continuity between each terminal of ABS solenoid relay.
OK:

Terminals 4 and 6	Continuity (Reference value 80 Ω)
Terminals 2 and 3	Continuity
Terminals 1 and 3	Open

CHECK:
(a) Apply battery positive voltage between terminals 4 and 6.
(b) Check continuity between each terminal of ABS solenoid relay.
OK:

Terminals 2 and 3	Open
Terminals 1 and 3	Continuity

CHECK:
Connect the ⊕ test lead to terminal 5 and the ⊖ lead to terminal 3. Check continuity between the terminals.
OK:

Continuity
If there is no continuity, connect the ⊖ test lead to terminal 5 and the ⊕ lead to terminal 3. Recheck continuity between terminals.

NG ▷ Replace ABS solenoid relay.

OK

Check for open in harness and connector between DLC1, ABS solenoid relay and body ground

TY4029700345020X

Fig. 95   ABS warning light circuit inspection (Part 2 of 3). 1997–99 Camry w/traction control & Nippondenso ABS

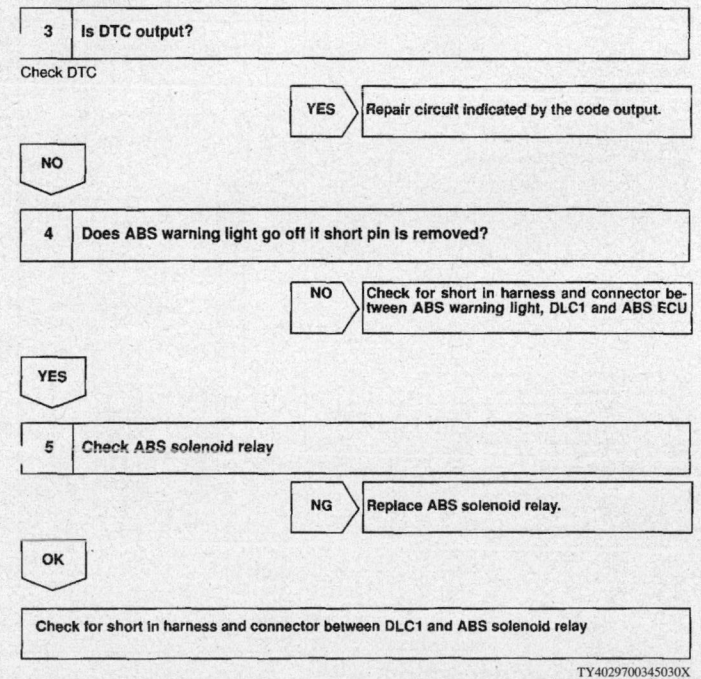

3	Is DTC output?

Check DTC

YES ▷ Repair circuit indicated by the code output.

NO

4	Does ABS warning light go off if short pin is removed?

NO ▷ Check for short in harness and connector between ABS warning light, DLC1 and ABS ECU

YES

5	Check ABS solenoid relay

NG ▷ Replace ABS solenoid relay.

OK

Check for short in harness and connector between DLC1 and ABS solenoid relay

TY4029700345030X

Fig. 95   ABS warning light circuit inspection (Part 3 of 3). 1997–99 Camry w/traction control & Nippondenso ABS

CIRCUIT DESCRIPTION

If the ECU detects trouble, it lights the ABS warning light while at the same time prohibiting ABS control. At this time, the ECU records a diagnostic trouble code in memory.
After removing the short pin of the DLC1 connect terminals Tc and E1 of DLC1 to make the ABS warning light blink and output the diagnostic trouble code.

DIAGNOSTIC CHART

Perform troubleshooting in accordance with the chart below for each trouble symptom.

| ABS warning light does not light up | Go to step |
| ABS warning light remains on | Go to step |

WIRING DIAGRAM

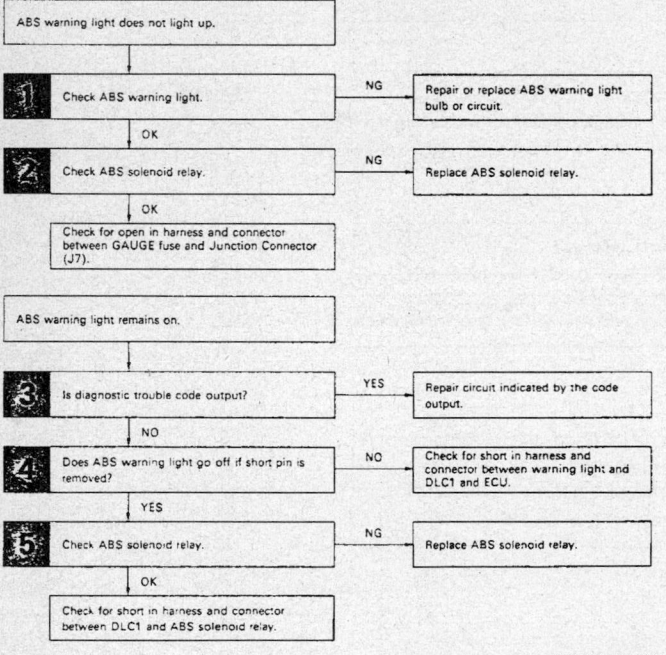

Fig. 96   ABS warning light switch circuit inspection (Part 1 of 4). 1996 Celica

ABS warning light does not light up.

| 1 | Check ABS warning light. | NG | Repair or replace ABS warning light bulb or circuit. |

OK

| 2 | Check ABS solenoid relay. | NG | Replace ABS solenoid relay. |

OK

Check for open in harness and connector between GAUGE fuse and Junction Connector (J7).

ABS warning light remains on.

| 3 | Is diagnostic trouble code output? | YES | Repair circuit indicated by the code output. |

NO

| 4 | Does ABS warning light go off if short pin is removed? | NO | Check for short in harness and connector between warning light and DLC1 and ECU. |

YES

| 5 | Check ABS solenoid relay. | NG | Replace ABS solenoid relay. |

OK

Check for short in harness and connector between DLC1 and ABS solenoid relay.

TY4029400062020X

Fig. 96   ABS warning light switch circuit inspection (Part 2 of 4). Celica

CIRCUIT DESCRIPTION

If the ECU detects trouble, it lights the ABS warning light while at the same time prohibiting ABS control. At this time, the ECU records DTC in memory.
After removing the short pin of the DLC1 connect terminals Tc and E1 of DLC1 to make the ABS warning light blink and output the DTC.

WIRING DIAGRAM

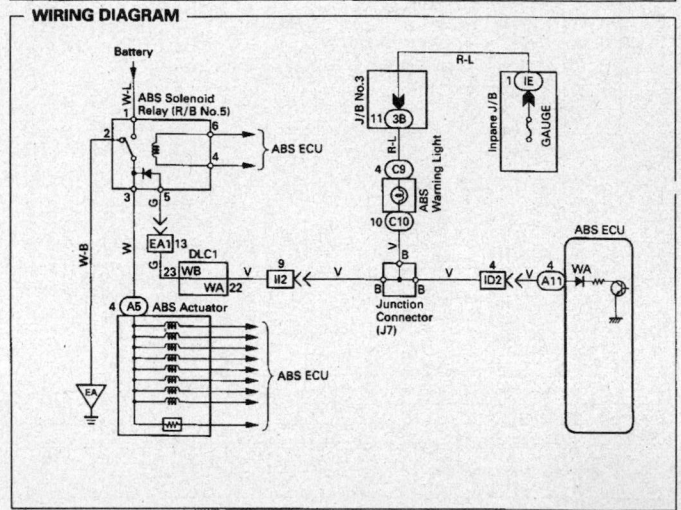

TY4029700390000X

Fig. 96   ABS warning light switch circuit inspection (Part 1 of 4). 1997–99 Celica

1	Check ABS warning light.		
	See Combination Meter Troubleshooting on		
	OK	NG	Replace bulb or combination meter assembly.

| 2 | Check ABS solenoid relay. | | |

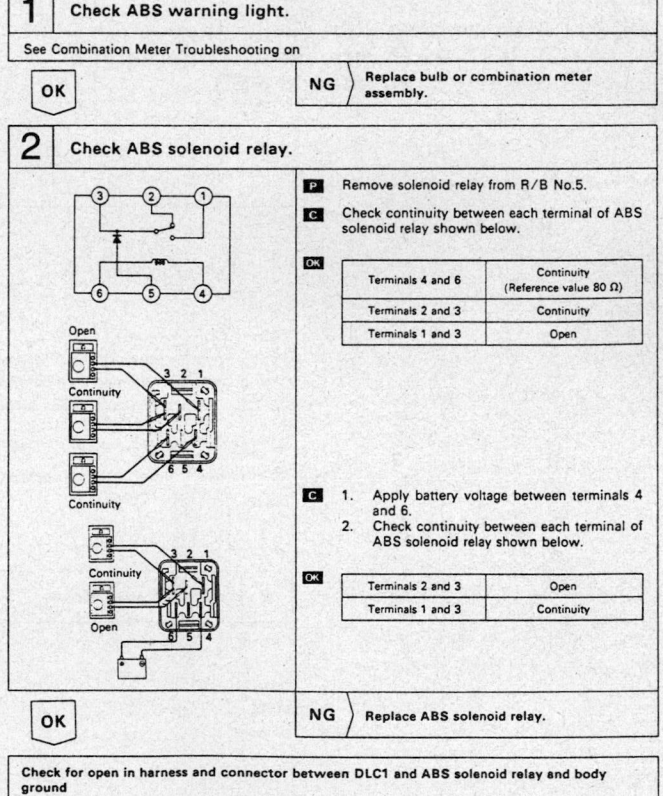

P Remove solenoid relay from R/B No.5.

C Check continuity between each terminal of ABS solenoid relay shown below.

OK		
Terminals 4 and 6	Continuity (Reference value 80 Ω)
Terminals 2 and 3	Continuity
Terminals 1 and 3	Open

C 1. Apply battery voltage between terminals 4 and 6.
2. Check continuity between each terminal of ABS solenoid relay shown below.

OK		
Terminals 2 and 3	Open
Terminals 1 and 3	Continuity

| OK | | NG | Replace ABS solenoid relay. |

Check for open in harness and connector between DLC1 and ABS solenoid relay and body ground

TY4029400062030X

Fig. 96   ABS warning light switch circuit inspection (Part 3 of 4). Celica

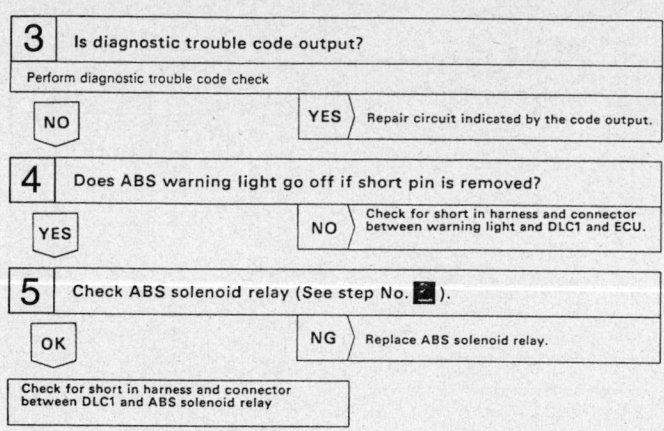

3	Is diagnostic trouble code output?	

Perform diagnostic trouble code check

| NO | | YES | Repair circuit indicated by the code output. |

4	Does ABS warning light go off if short pin is removed?	

| YES | | NO | Check for short in harness and connector between warning light and DLC1 and ECU. |

5	Check ABS solenoid relay (See step No. 2).	

| OK | | NG | Replace ABS solenoid relay. |

Check for short in harness and connector between DLC1 and ABS solenoid relay

TY4029400062040X

Fig. 96   ABS warning light switch circuit inspection (Part 4 of 4). Celica

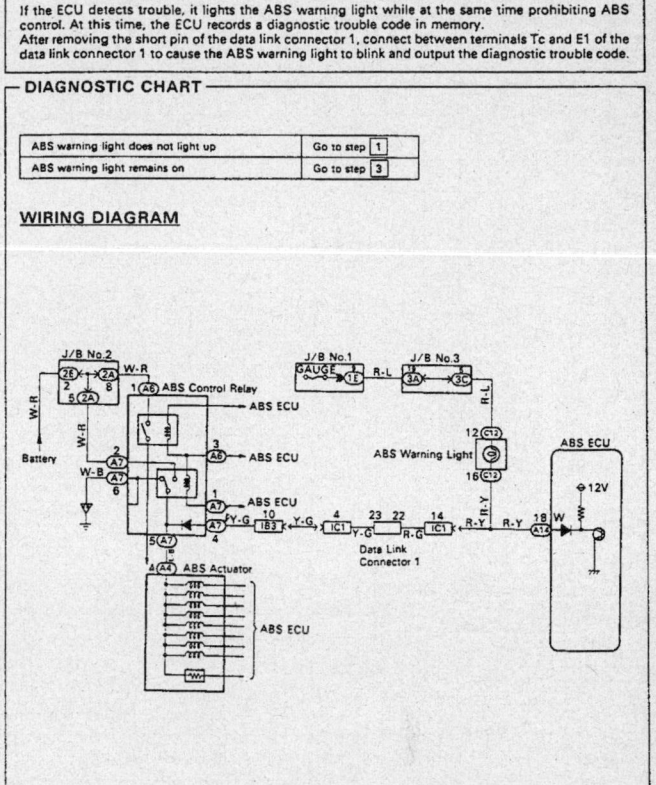

─ CIRCUIT DESCRIPTION ─

If the ECU detects trouble, it lights the ABS warning light while at the same time prohibiting ABS control. At this time, the ECU records a diagnostic trouble code in memory.
After removing the short pin of the data link connector 1, connect between terminals Tc and E1 of the data link connector 1 to cause the ABS warning light to blink and output the diagnostic trouble code.

─ DIAGNOSTIC CHART ─

ABS warning light does not light up	Go to step 1
ABS warning light remains on	Go to step 3

WIRING DIAGRAM

TY4029300060010X

Fig. 97   ABS warning light switch circuit inspection (Part 1 of 4). Corolla

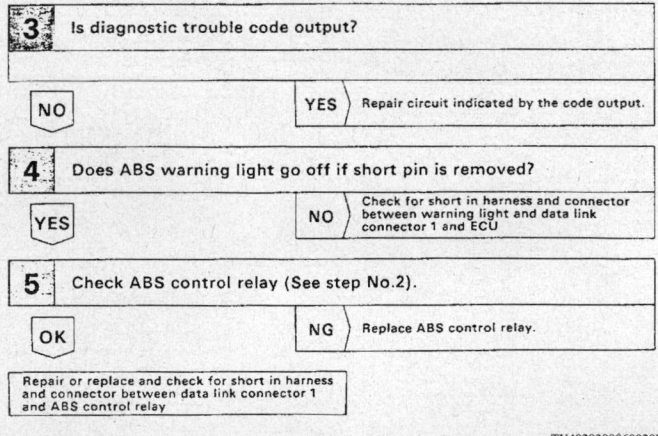

3	Is diagnostic trouble code output?	

| NO | | YES | Repair circuit indicated by the code output. |

4	Does ABS warning light go off if short pin is removed?	

| YES | | NO | Check for short in harness and connector between warning light and data link connector 1 and ECU. |

5	Check ABS control relay (See step No.2).	

| OK | | NG | Replace ABS control relay. |

Repair or replace and check for short in harness and connector between data link connector 1 and ABS control relay

TY4029300060020X

Fig. 97   ABS warning light switch circuit inspection (Part 2 of 4). Corolla

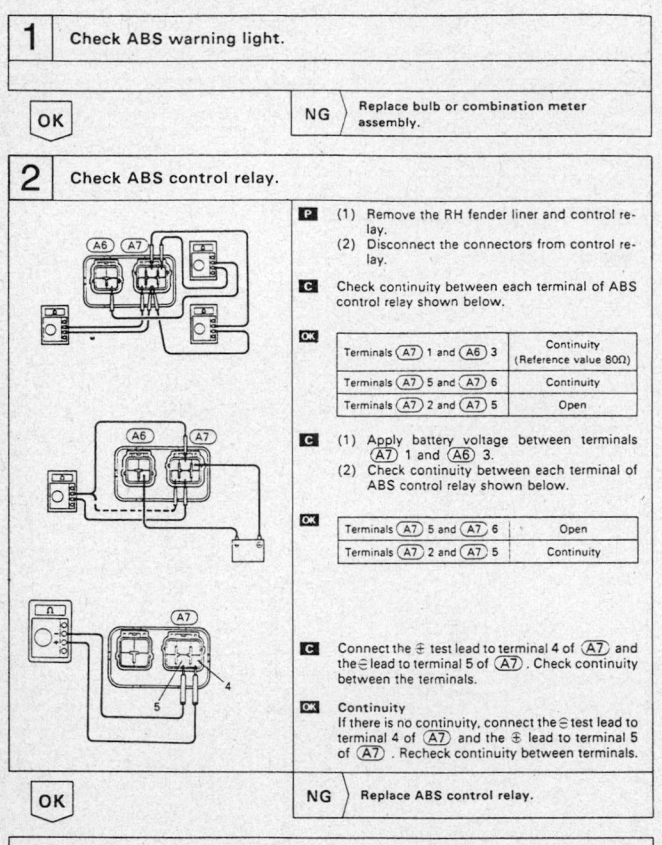

Fig. 97 ABS warning light switch circuit inspection
(Part 3 of 4). Corolla

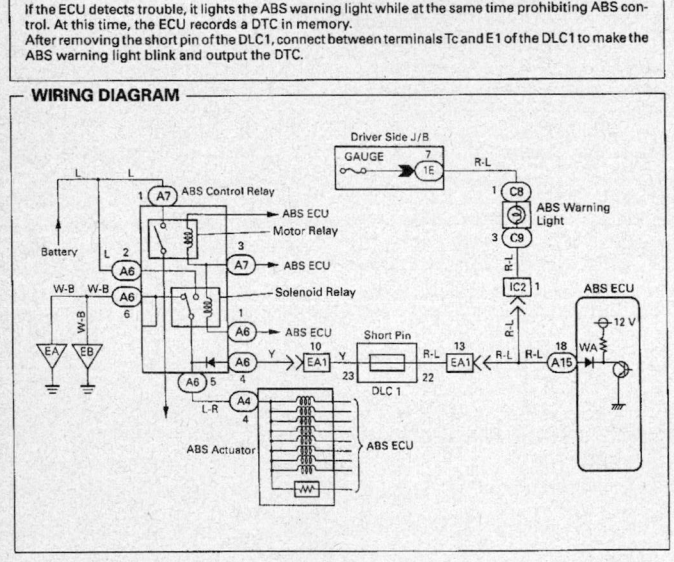

CIRCUIT DESCRIPTION

If the ECU detects trouble, it lights the ABS warning light while at the same time prohibiting ABS control. At this time, the ECU records a DTC in memory.
After removing the short pin of the DLC1, connect between terminals Tc and E1 of the DLC1 to make the ABS warning light blink and output the DTC.

WIRING DIAGRAM

Fig. 98 ABS warning light switch circuit inspection
(Part 1 of 3). Paseo

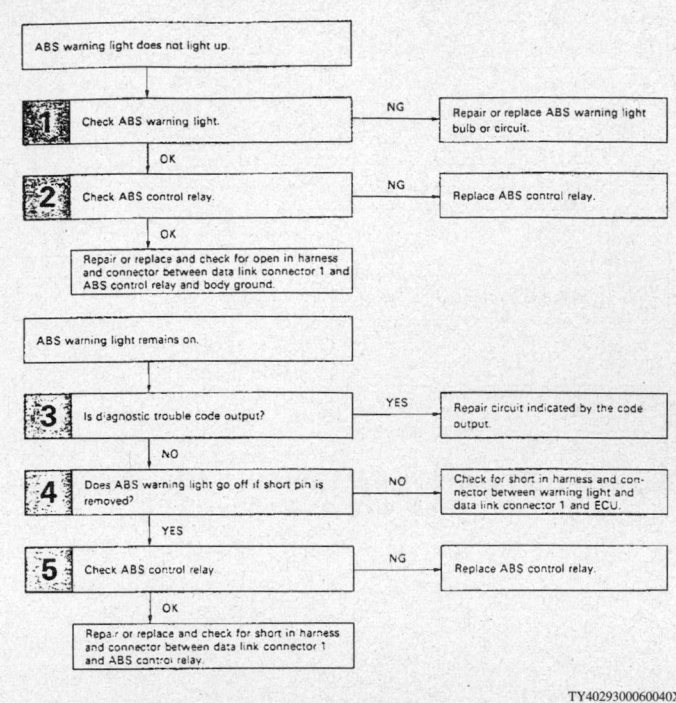

Fig. 97 ABS warning light switch circuit inspection
(Part 4 of 4). Corolla

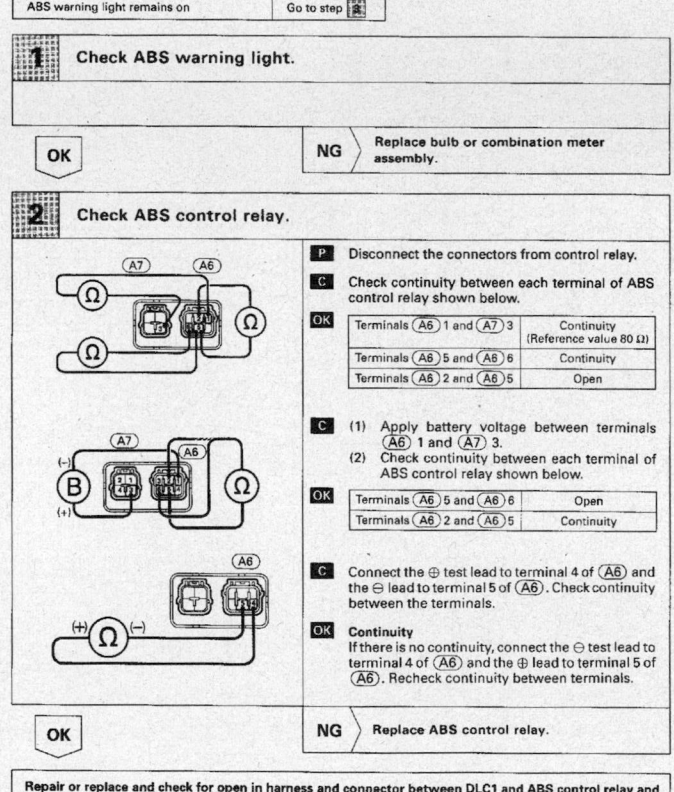

Fig. 98 ABS warning light switch circuit inspection
(Part 2 of 3). Paseo

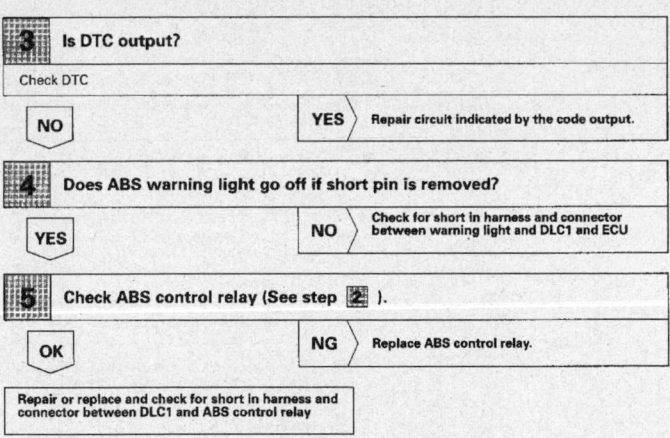

3 Is DTC output?

Check DTC

| NO | | YES | Repair circuit indicated by the code output. |

4 Does ABS warning light go off if short pin is removed?

| YES | | NO | Check for short in harness and connector between warning light and DLC1 and ECU |

5 Check ABS control relay (See step **2**).

| OK | | NG | Replace ABS control relay. |

Repair or replace and check for short in harness and connector between DLC1 and ABS control relay

TY4029600273030X

Fig. 98 ABS warning light switch circuit inspection (Part 3 of 3). Paseo

| ABS warning light does not light up | Go to step |
| ABS warning light remains on | Go to step |

1 Check ABS warning light.

Combination Meter Troubleshooting.

| OK | | NG | Replace bulb or combination meter assembly. |

2 Check ABS control relay.

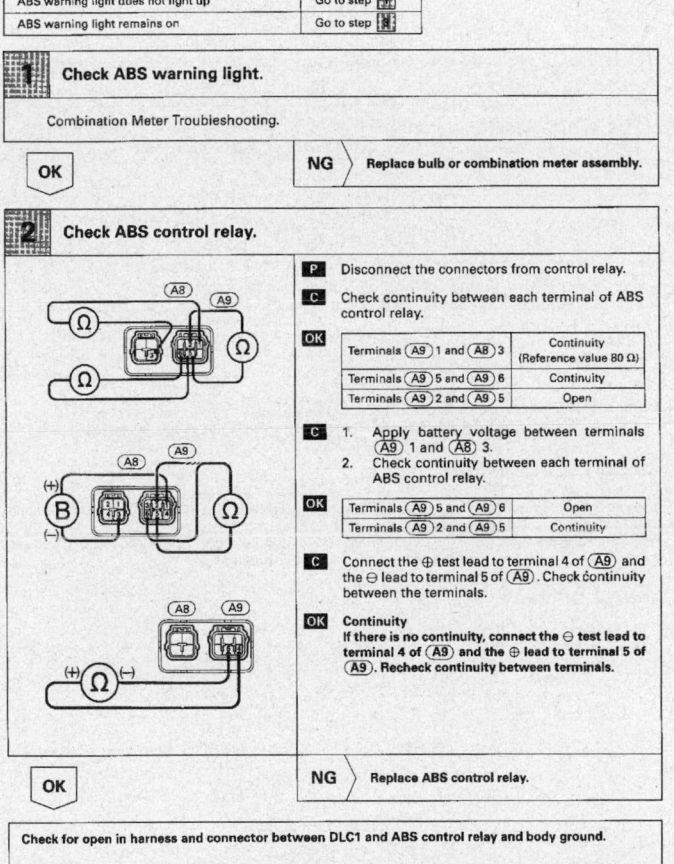

P Disconnect the connectors from control relay.

C Check continuity between each terminal of ABS control relay.

OK
Terminals (A9) 1 and (A8) 3	Continuity (Reference value 80 Ω)
Terminals (A9) 5 and (A9) 6	Continuity
Terminals (A9) 2 and (A9) 5	Open

C 1. Apply battery voltage between terminals (A9) 1 and (A8) 3.
2. Check continuity between each terminal of ABS control relay.

OK
| Terminals (A9) 5 and (A9) 6 | Open |
| Terminals (A9) 2 and (A9) 5 | Continuity |

C Connect the ⊕ test lead to terminal 4 of (A9) and the ⊖ lead to terminal 5 of (A9). Check continuity between the terminals.

OK Continuity
If there is no continuity, connect the ⊖ test lead to terminal 4 of (A9) and the ⊕ lead to terminal 5 of (A9). Recheck continuity between terminals.

| OK | | NG | Replace ABS control relay. |

Check for open in harness and connector between DLC1 and ABS control relay and body ground.

TY4029600202020X

Fig. 99 ABS warning light switch circuit inspection (Part 2 of 3). 1996 RAV4

CIRCUIT DESCRIPTION

If the ECU detects trouble, it lights the ABS warning light while at the same time prohibiting ABS control. At this time, the ECU records a DTC in memory.
After removing the short pin of the DLC1, connect terminals Tc and E1 of the DLC1 to make the ABS warning light blink and output the DTC.

WIRING DIAGRAM

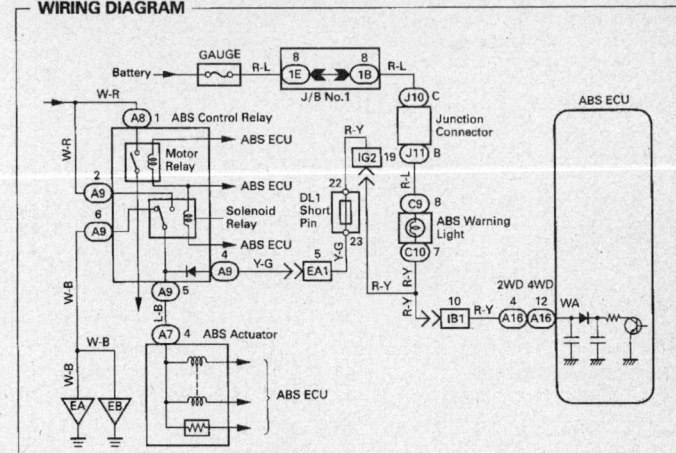

TY4029600202010X

Fig. 99 ABS warning light switch circuit inspection (Part 1 of 3). 1996 RAV4

3 Is DTC output?

Check DTC.

| NO | | YES | Repair circuit indicated by the code output. |

4 Does ABS warning light go off if short pin is removed?

| YES | | NO | Check for short in harness and connector between warning light and DLC1 and ECU. |

5 Check ABS control relay.

| OK | | NG | Replace ABS control relay. |

Check for short in harness and connector between DLC1 and ABS control relay.

TY4029600202030X

Fig. 99 ABS warning light switch circuit inspection (Part 3 of 3). 1996 RAV4

CIRCUIT DESCRIPTION

If the ECU detects trouble, it lights the ABS warning light while at the same time prohibiting ABS control. At this time, the ECU records a DTC in memory.
After removing the short pin of the DLC1, connect terminals Tc and E1 of the DLC1 to make the ABS warning light blink and output the DTC.

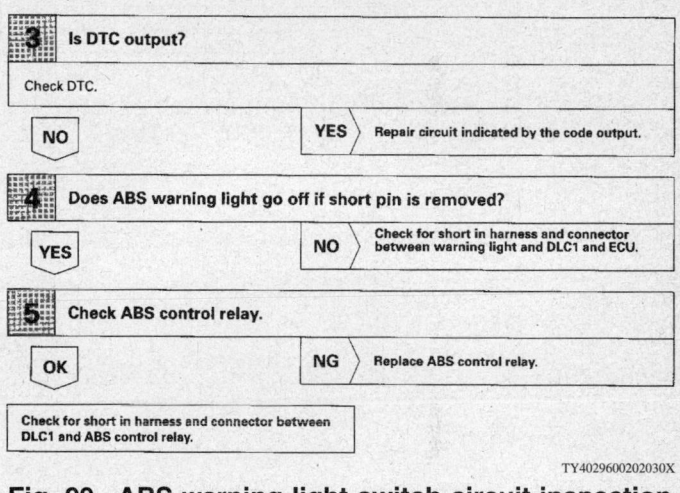

TY4029700283010X

Fig. 100 ABS warning light switch circuit inspection (Part 1 of 4). 1997–99 RAV4

WIRING DIAGRAM

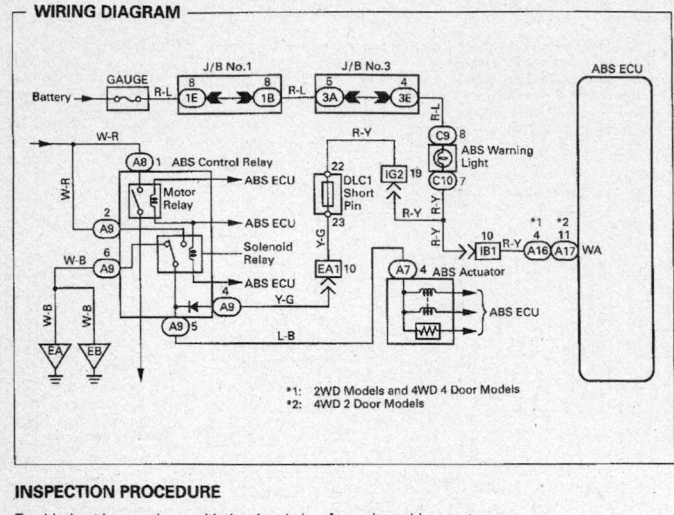

INSPECTION PROCEDURE

Troubleshoot in accordance with the chart below for each trouble symptom.

| ABS warning light does not light up | Go to step **1** |
| ABS warning light remains on | Go to step **3** |

1   **Check ABS warning light.**

See Combination Meter Troubleshooting

| OK | | NG | Replace bulb or combination meter assembly. |

TY4029700283020X

Fig. 100   ABS warning light switch circuit inspection (Part 2 of 4). 1997–99 RAV4

5   **Check ABS control relay**

| OK | | NG | Replace ABS control relay. |

Check for short in harness and connector between DLC1 and ABS control relay

TY4029700283040X

Fig. 100   ABS warning light switch circuit inspection (Part 4 of 4). 1997–99 RAV4

---

2   **Check ABS control relay.**

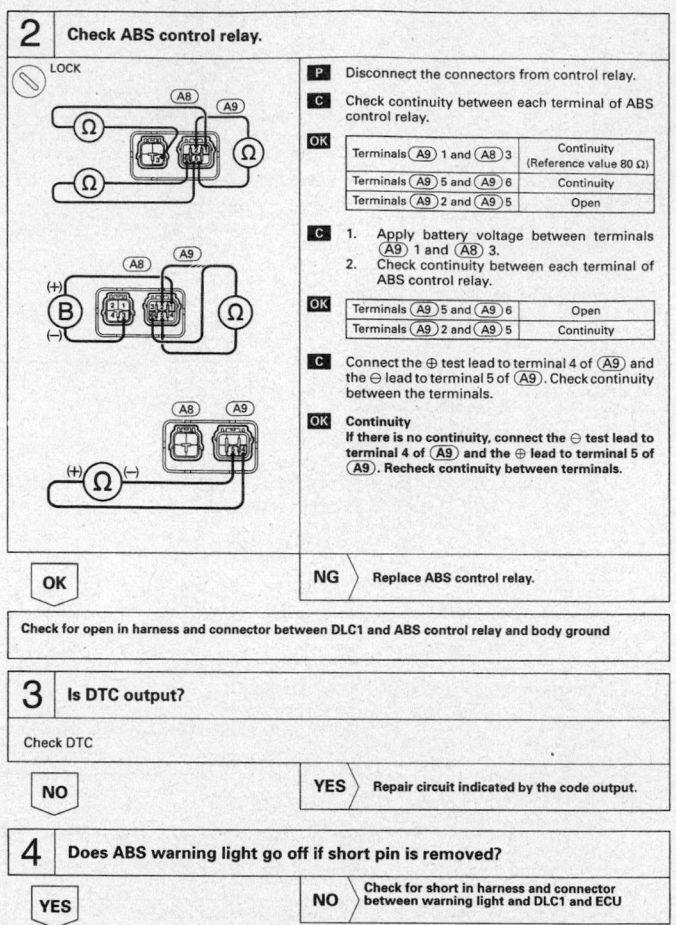

P   Disconnect the connectors from control relay.

C   Check continuity between each terminal of ABS control relay.

OK

Terminals (A9) 1 and (A8) 3	Continuity (Reference value 80 Ω)
Terminals (A9) 5 and (A9) 6	Continuity
Terminals (A9) 2 and (A9) 5	Open

C
1. Apply battery voltage between terminals (A9) 1 and (A8) 3.
2. Check continuity between each terminal of ABS control relay.

OK

| Terminals (A9) 5 and (A9) 6 | Open |
| Terminals (A9) 2 and (A9) 5 | Continuity |

C   Connect the ⊕ test lead to terminal 4 of (A9) and the ⊖ lead to terminal 5 of (A9). Check continuity between the terminals.

OK   **Continuity**
If there is no continuity, connect the ⊖ test lead to terminal 4 of (A9) and the ⊕ lead to terminal 5 of (A9). Recheck continuity between terminals.

| OK | | NG | Replace ABS control relay. |

Check for open in harness and connector between DLC1 and ABS control relay and body ground

3   **Is DTC output?**

Check DTC

| NO | | YES | Repair circuit indicated by the code output. |

4   **Does ABS warning light go off if short pin is removed?**

| YES | | NO | Check for short in harness and connector between warning light and DLC1 and ECU |

TY4029700283030X

Fig. 100   ABS warning light switch circuit inspection (Part 3 of 4). 1997–99 RAV4

CIRCUIT DESCRIPTION

If the ECU detects trouble, it lights the ABS warning light while at the same time prohibiting ABS control. At this time, the ECU records a diagnostic trouble code in memory.
After removing the short pin of the DLC1, connect terminals Tc and E1 of the DLC1 or DLC2 to make the ABS warning light to blink and output the diagnostic trouble code.

WIRING DIAGRAM

w/o TRAC

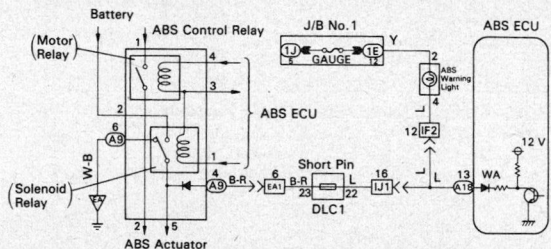

w/ TRAC

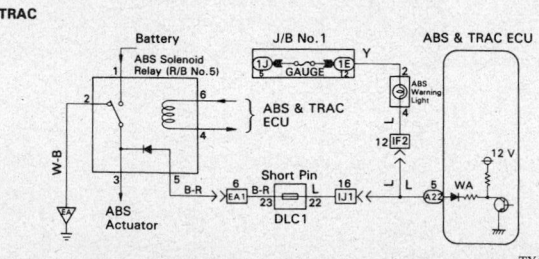

TY4029300061010X

Fig. 101   ABS warning light switch circuit inspection (Part 1 of 4). 1996 Supra

CIRCUIT DESCRIPTION

If the ECU detects trouble, it lights the ABS warning light while at the same time prohibiting ABS control.
At this time, the ECU records a DTC in memory.
After removing the short pin of the DLC1, connect terminals Tc and E1 of the DLC1 or DLC2 to make the ABS warning light to blink and output the DTC.

WIRING DIAGRAM

2JZ-GE Engine (NORMAL ABS):

2JZ-GTE Engine (SPORT ABS):

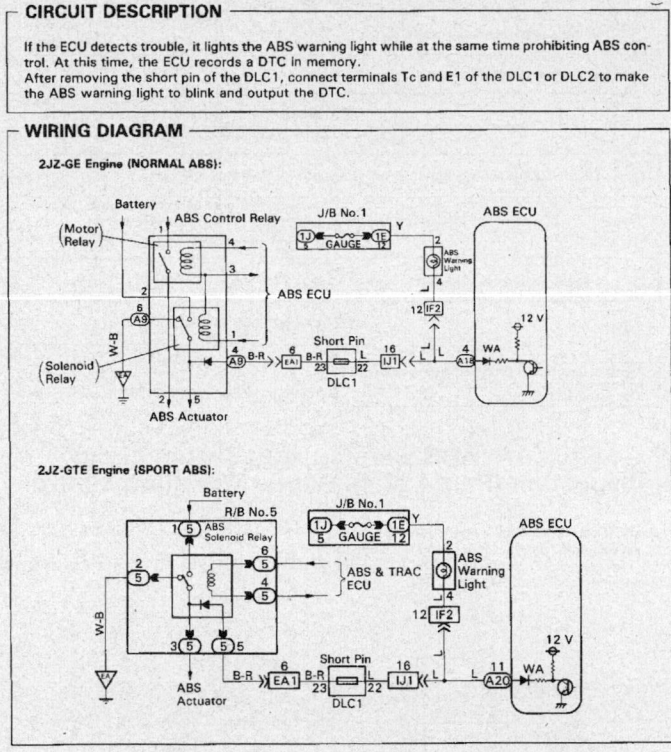

TY4029700407000X

Fig. 101 ABS warning light switch circuit inspection (Part 1 of 4). 1997–98 Supra

INSPECTION PROCEDURE (w/o TRAC)

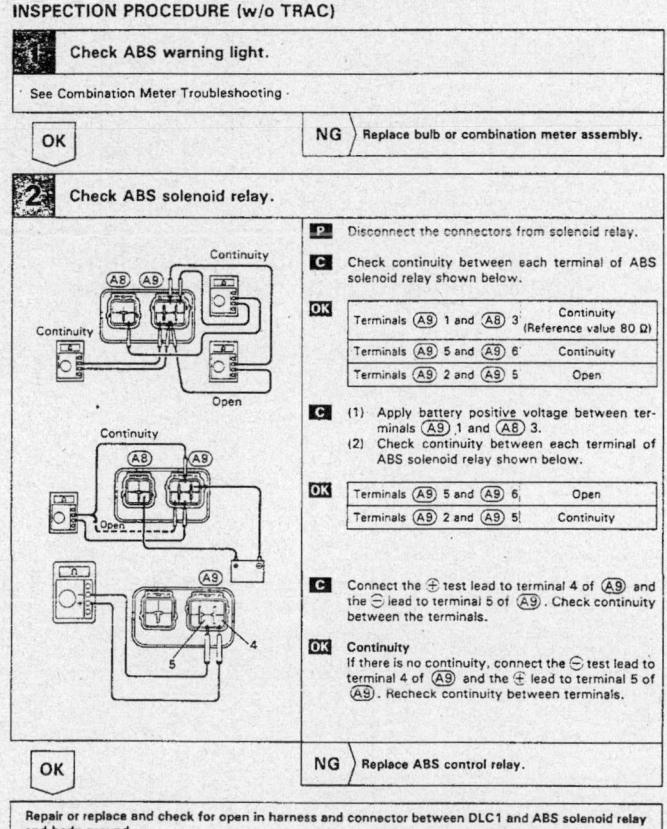

TY4029300061030X

Fig. 101 ABS warning light switch circuit inspection (Part 3 of 4). Supra less traction control

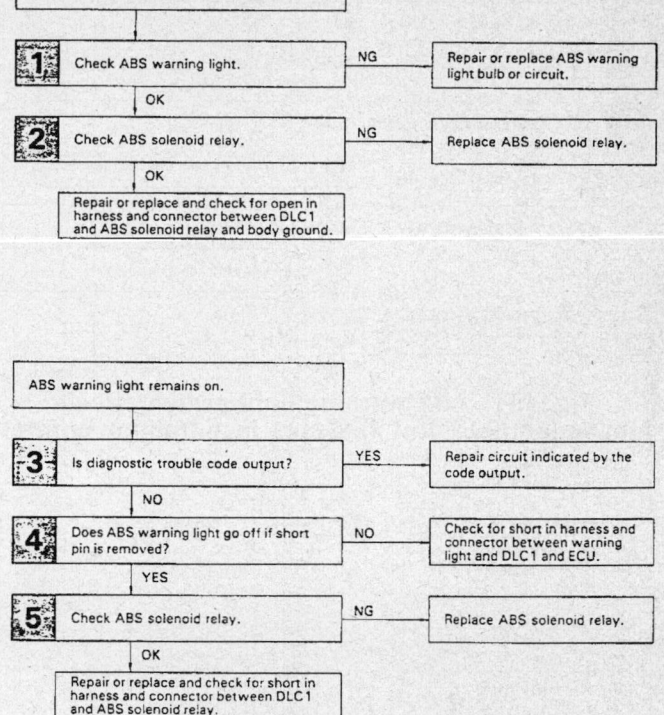

TY4029300061020X

Fig. 101 ABS warning light switch circuit inspection (Part 2 of 4). Supra

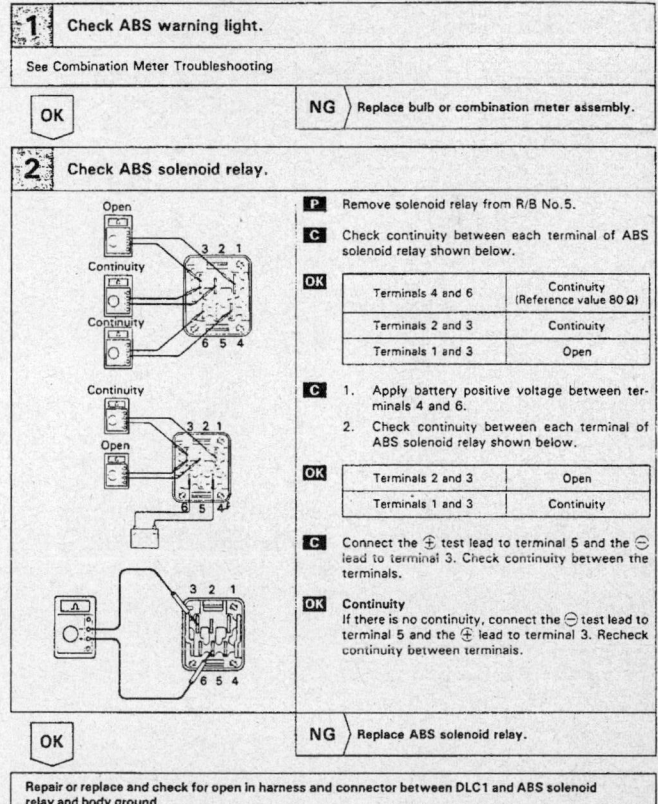

TY4029300061050X

Fig. 101 ABS warning light switch circuit inspection (Part 3 of 4). Supra w/traction control

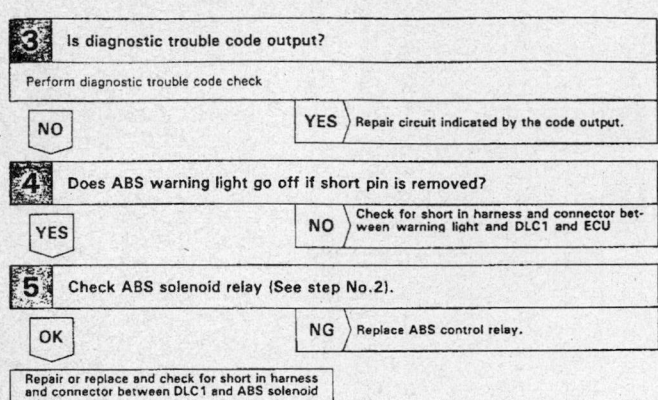

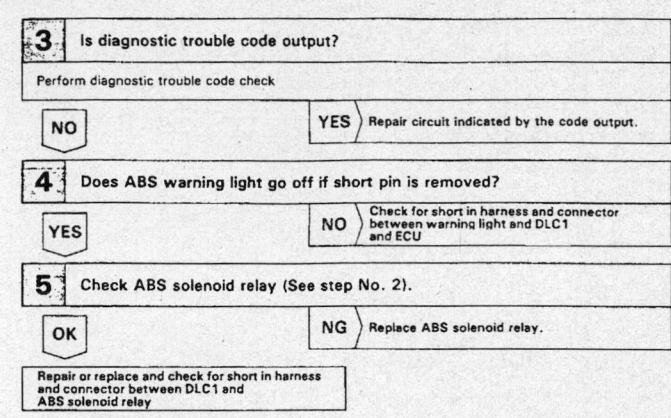

3	Is diagnostic trouble code output?
Perform diagnostic trouble code check	
NO	YES > Repair circuit indicated by the code output.

4	Does ABS warning light go off if short pin is removed?
YES	NO > Check for short in harness and connector between warning light and DLC1 and ECU

5	Check ABS solenoid relay (See step No.2).
OK	NG > Replace ABS control relay.

Repair or replace and check for short in harness and connector between DLC1 and ABS solenoid relay

TY4029300061040X

Fig. 101   ABS warning light switch circuit inspection (Part 4 of 4). Supra less traction control

CIRCUIT DESCRIPTION

If the ECU detects trouble, it lights the ABS warning light while at the same time prohibiting ABS control. At this time, the ECU records a DTC in memory.
After removing the short pin of the DLC1, connect terminals Tc and E1 of the DLC1 to make the ABS warning light blink and output the DTC.

WIRING DIAGRAM

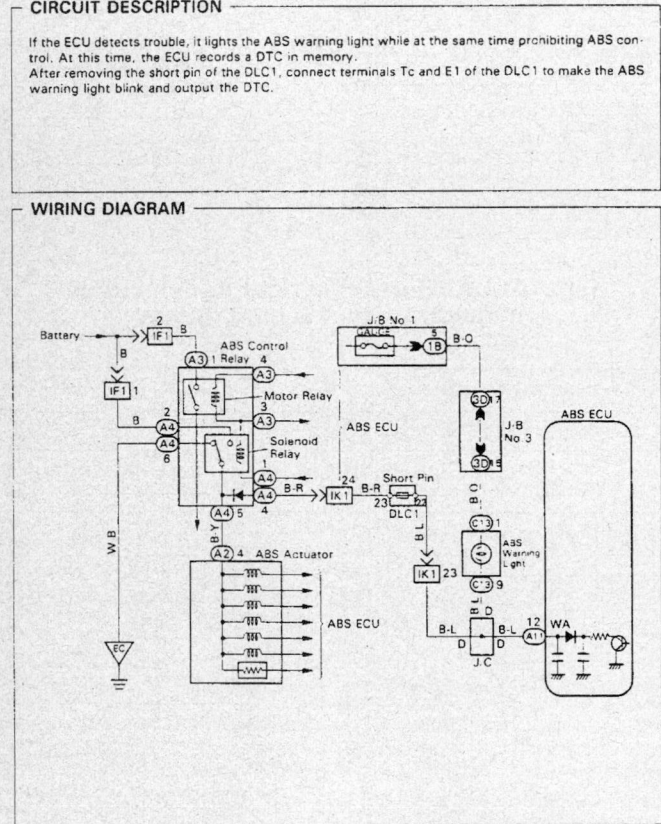

TY4029500175010X

Fig. 102   ABS warning light switch circuit inspection (Part 1 of 3). 1996 Tacoma

3	Is diagnostic trouble code output?
Perform diagnostic trouble code check	
NO	YES > Repair circuit indicated by the code output.

4	Does ABS warning light go off if short pin is removed?
YES	NO > Check for short in harness and connector between warning light and DLC1 and ECU

5	Check ABS solenoid relay (See step No. 2).
OK	NG > Replace ABS solenoid relay.

Repair or replace and check for short in harness and connector between DLC1 and ABS solenoid relay

TY4029300061060X

Fig. 101   ABS warning light switch circuit inspection (Part 4 of 4). Supra w/traction control

If the ECU detects trouble, it lights the ABS warning light while at the same time prohibiting ABS control. At this time, the ECU records a DTC in memory.
After removing the short pin of the DLC1, connect terminals Tc and E1 of the DLC1 to make the ABS warning light blink and output the DTC.

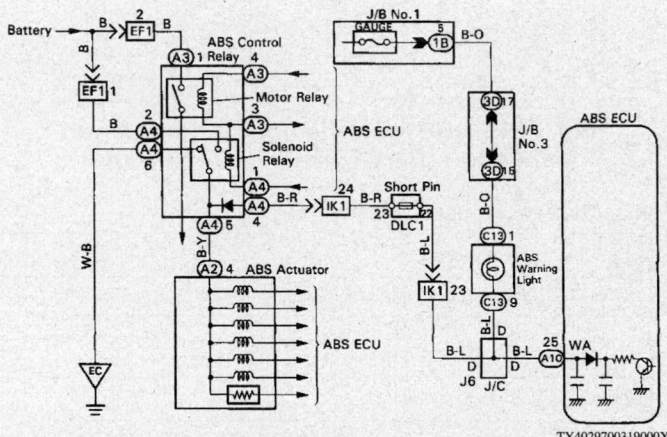

TY4029700319000X

Fig. 102   ABS warning light switch circuit inspection (Part 1 of 3). 1997–99 Tacoma

Troubleshoot in accordance with the chart below for each trouble symptom.

| ABS warning light does not light up | Go to step 🔳 |
| ABS warning light remains on | Go to step 🔳 |

1 **Check ABS warning light.**

See Combination Meter Troubleshooting

| **OK** ⬇ | **NG** ▷ Replace bulb or combination meter assembly. |

2 **Check ABS control relay.**

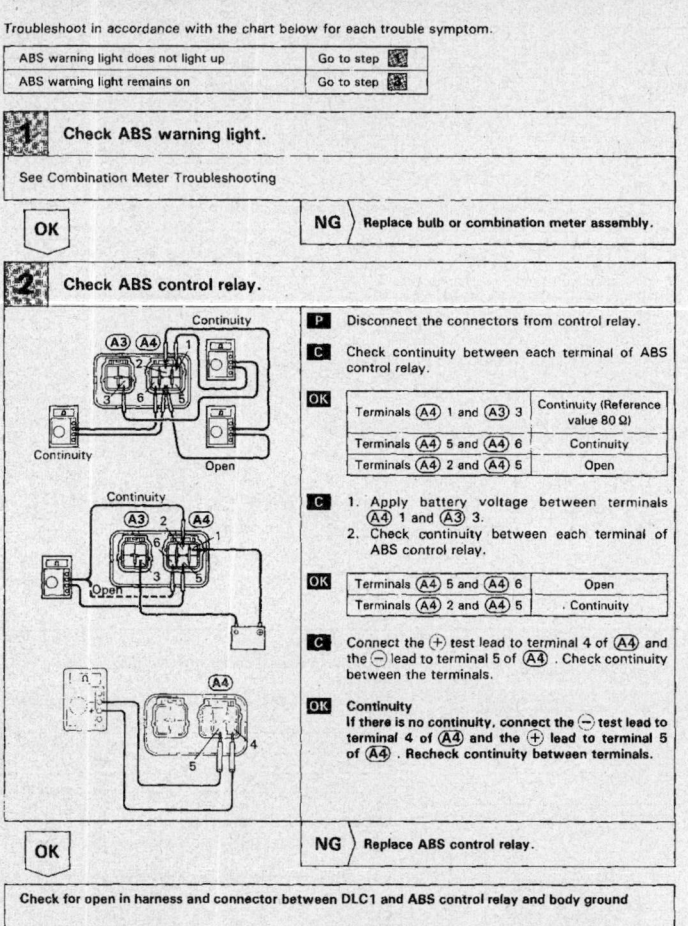

| **P** | Disconnect the connectors from control relay. |
| **C** | Check continuity between each terminal of ABS control relay. |

OK		
Terminals (A4) 1 and (A3) 3	Continuity (Reference value 80 Ω)	
Terminals (A4) 5 and (A4) 6	Continuity	
Terminals (A4) 2 and (A4) 5	Open	

| **C** | 1. Apply battery voltage between terminals (A4) 1 and (A3) 3.
 2. Check continuity between each terminal of ABS control relay. |

OK	
Terminals (A4) 5 and (A4) 6	Open
Terminals (A4) 2 and (A4) 5	Continuity

| **C** | Connect the ⊕ test lead to terminal 4 of (A4) and the ⊖ lead to terminal 5 of (A4). Check continuity between the terminals. |

| **OK** | Continuity
 If there is no continuity, connect the ⊖ test lead to terminal 4 of (A4) and the ⊕ lead to terminal 5 of (A4). Recheck continuity between terminals. |

| **OK** ⬇ | **NG** ▷ Replace ABS control relay. |

Check for open in harness and connector between DLC1 and ABS control relay and body ground

TY4029500175020X

Fig. 102   ABS warning light switch circuit inspection (Part 2 of 3). Tacoma

---

3 **Is DTC output?**

Check DTC

| **NO** | **YES** ▷ Repair circuit indicated by the code output. |

4 **Does ABS warning light go off if short pin is removed?**

| **YES** | **NO** ▷ Check for short in harness and connector between warning light and DLC1 and ECU |

5 **Check ABS control relay (See step No.2).**

| **OK** | **NG** ▷ Replace ABS control relay. |

Check for short in harness and connector between DLC1 and ABS control relay

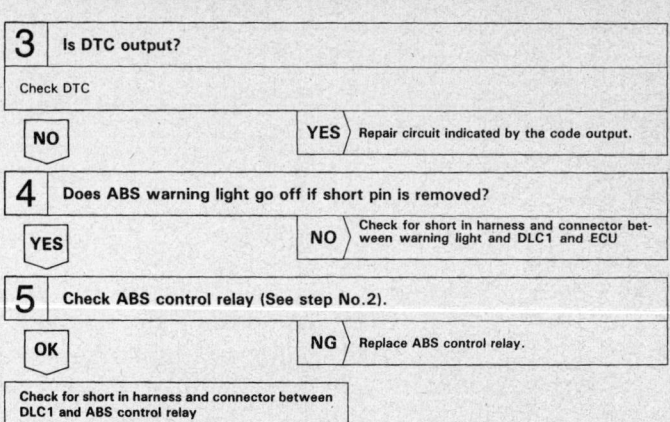

TY4029500175030X

Fig. 102   ABS warning light switch circuit inspection (Part 3 of 3). Tacoma

---

CIRCUIT DESCRIPTION

If the ECU detects trouble, it lights the ABS warning light while at the same time prohibiting ABS control. At this time, the ECU records a diagnostic trouble code in memory.

After removing the short pin of the data link connector 1, connect between terminals Tc and E1 of the data link connector 1 to make the ABS warning light blink and output the diagnostic trouble code.

WIRING DIAGRAM

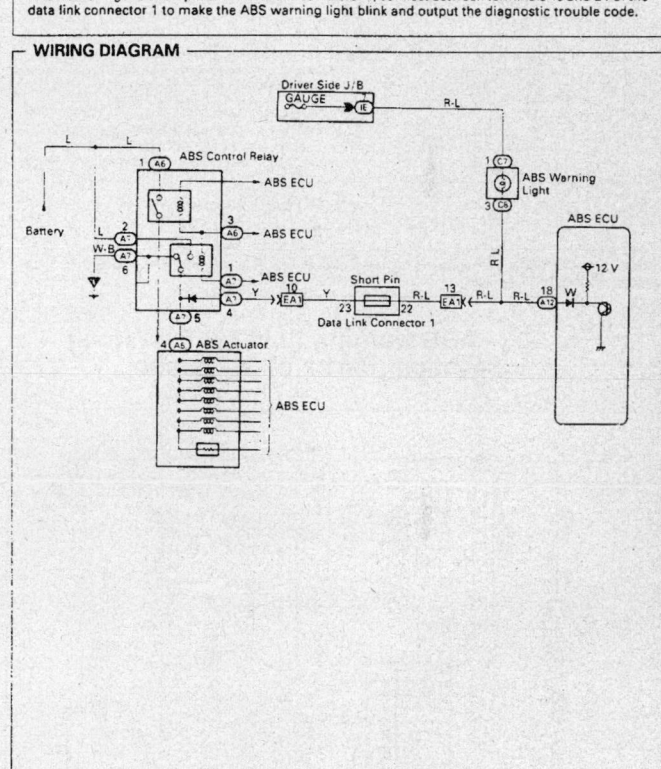

TY4029500185010X

Fig. 103   ABS warning light switch circuit inspection (Part 1 of 3). Tercel

Troubleshoot in accordance with the chart below for each trouble symptom.

| ABS warning light does not light up | Go to step 1 |
| ABS warning light remains on | Go to step 3 |

1 Check ABS warning light.

See Combination Meter

| OK | NG | Replace bulb or combination meter assembly. |

2 Check ABS control relay.

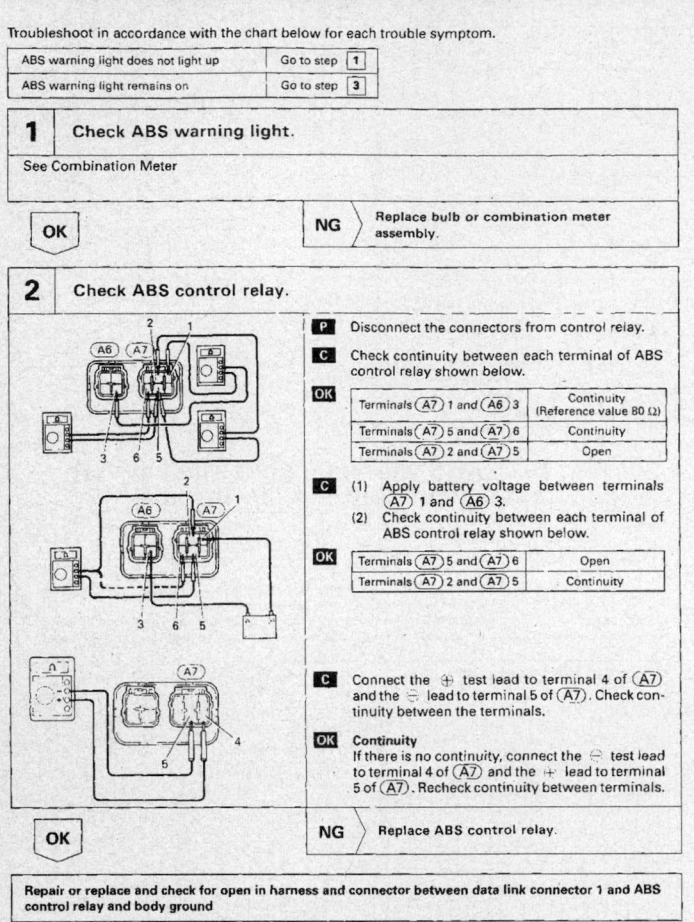

| P | Disconnect the connectors from control relay. |
| C | Check continuity between each terminal of ABS control relay shown below. |

OK		
Terminals (A7) 1 and (A6) 3	Continuity (Reference value 80 Ω)
Terminals (A7) 5 and (A7) 6	Continuity
Terminals (A7) 2 and (A7) 5	Open

| C | (1) Apply battery voltage between terminals (A7) 1 and (A6) 3. |
| | (2) Check continuity between each terminal of ABS control relay shown below. |

OK		
Terminals (A7) 5 and (A7) 6	Open
Terminals (A7) 2 and (A7) 5	Continuity

C	Connect the ⊕ test lead to terminal 4 of (A7) and the ⊖ lead to terminal 5 of (A7). Check continuity between the terminals.
OK	Continuity
	If there is no continuity, connect the ⊖ test lead to terminal 4 of (A7) and the ⊕ lead to terminal 5 of (A7). Recheck continuity between terminals.

| OK | NG | Replace ABS control relay. |

Repair or replace and check for open in harness and connector between data link connector 1 and ABS control relay and body ground

TY4029500185020X

Fig. 103 ABS warning light switch circuit inspection (Part 2 of 3). Tercel

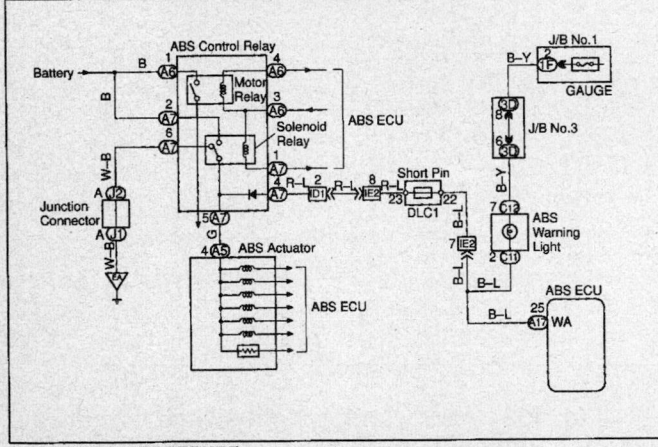

INSPECTION PROCEDURE

Troubleshooting in accordance with the chart below for each trouble symptom.

| ABS warning light does not light up | Go to step 1 |
| ABS warning light remains on | Go to step 3 |

1 Check ABS warning light.

See Combination Meter Troubleshooting.

| NG | Repair bulb or combination meter assembly. |

| OK |

TY4029600226010X

Fig. 104 ABS warning light circuit (Part 1 of 3). 4Runner

---

3 Is DTC output?

Check DTC

| NO | YES | Repair circuit indicated by the code output. |

4 Does ABS warning light go off if short pin is removed?

| YES | NO | Check for short in harness and connector between warning light and DLC1 and ECU |

5 Check ABS control relay (See step 2).

| OK | NG | Replace ABS control relay. |

Repair or replace and check for short in harness and connector between DLC1 and ABS control relay

TY4029500185030X

Fig. 103 ABS warning light switch circuit inspection (Part 3 of 3). Tercel

2 Check ABS control relay.

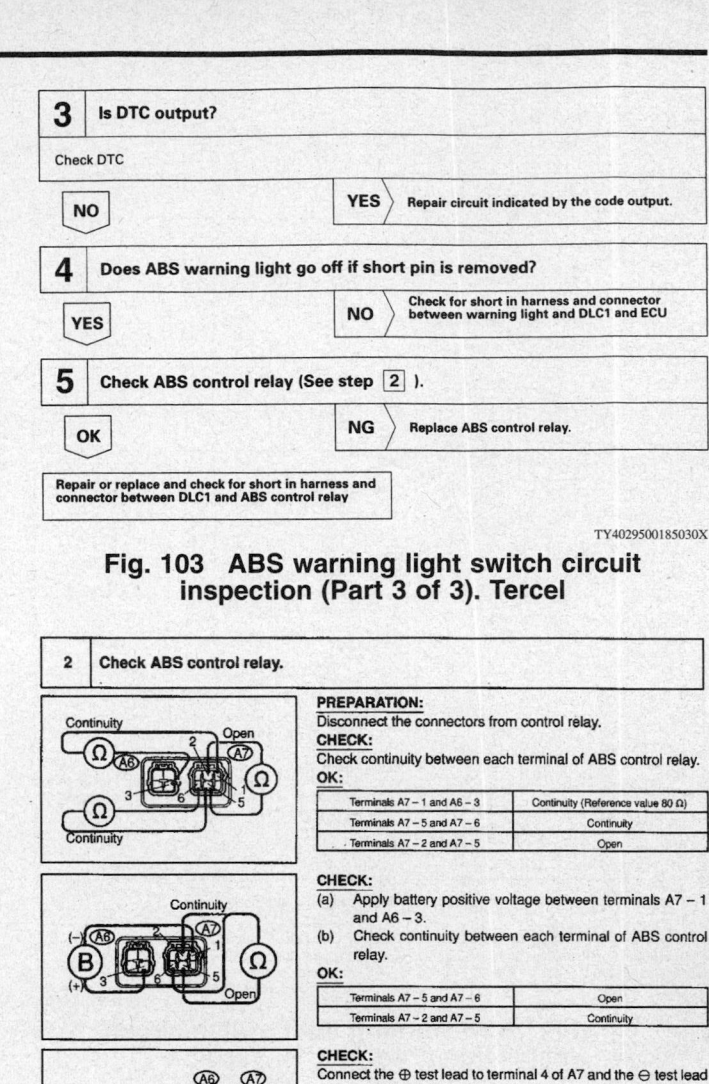

PREPARATION:
Disconnect the connectors from control relay.
CHECK:
Check continuity between each terminal of ABS control relay.
OK:

Terminals A7 – 1 and A6 – 3	Continuity (Reference value 80 Ω)
Terminals A7 – 5 and A7 – 6	Continuity
Terminals A7 – 2 and A7 – 5	Open

CHECK:
(a) Apply battery positive voltage between terminals A7 – 1 and A6 – 3.
(b) Check continuity between each terminal of ABS control relay.
OK:

| Terminals A7 – 5 and A7 – 6 | Open |
| Terminals A7 – 2 and A7 – 5 | Continuity |

CHECK:
Connect the ⊕ test lead to terminal 4 of A7 and the ⊖ test lead to terminal 5 of A7. Check continuity between the terminals.
OK:
Continuity
If there is no continuity, connect the ⊖ test lead to terminal 4 of A7 and the ⊕ lead to terminal 5 of A7. Recheck continuity between terminals.

| NG | Replace ABS control relay. |

| OK |

Check for open in harness and connector between DLC1 and ABS control relay and body ground.

TY4029600226020X

Fig. 104 ABS warning light circuit (Part 2 of 3). 4Runner

3	Is DTC output?

Check DTC.

YES ▶ Repair circuit indicated by the code output.

NO

4	Does ABS warning light go off if short pin is removed?

NO ▶ Check for short in harness and connector between warning light and DLC1 and ECU.

YES

5	Check ABS control relay (See step 2).

NG ▶ Replace ABS control relay.

OK

Check for short in harness and connector between DLC1 and ABS control relay.

TY4029600226030X

Fig. 104   ABS warning light circuit (Part 3 of 3). 4Runner

2	Check TRAC cut switch.

PREPARATION:
(a)   Remove TRAC cut switch.
(b)   Disconnect TRAC cut switch connector.
CHECK:
Measure resistance between terminals 1 and 4 of TRAC cut switch when TRAC cut switch is on and off.
OK:

TRAC cut switch	Resistance
Pushed in	Continuity
Released	1 MΩ or higher

NG ▶ Replace TRAC cut switch.

OK

3	Check for open and short in harness and connector between terminal CSW of ABS & TRAC ECU and TRAC cut switch and body ground

NG ▶ Repair or replace combination meter.

OK

4	Check TRAC OFF indicator light.

NG ▶ Repair or replace combination meter.

OK

TY4029700244020X

Fig. 105   Traction control lamp inspection (Part 2 of 3). 1997–99 Avalon

This is the TRAC control main switch. When the TRAC cut switch is pushed on, TRAC control goes off and the TRAC OFF indicator lights up. This indicator blinks for warnings when the trouble occurs and for displaying DTC.

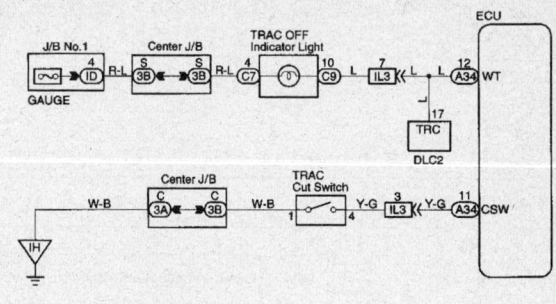

1	Check DTC.

Check DTC

YES ▶ Repair circuit indicated by the code output.

NO

TY4029700244010X

Fig. 105   Traction control lamp inspection (Part 1 of 3). 1997–99 Avalon

5	Check for open and short in harness and connector between terminal WT of ABS & TRAC ECU and TRAC OFF indicator light

NG ▶ Repair or replace harness connector.

OK

Check and replace   ECU.

TY4029700244030X

Fig. 105   Traction control lamp inspection (Part 3 of 3). 1997–99 Avalon

The SLIP indicator blinks during TRAC operation.

WIRING DIAGRAM

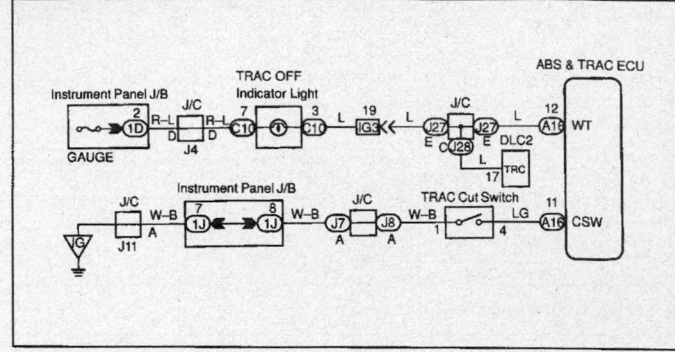

1 | Check SLIP indicator light.

NG ▷ Repair or replace combination meter.

OK

2 | Check for short in harness and connector between ABS & TRAC ECU and SLIP indicator light

NG ▷ Repair or replace harness or connector.

OK

Check and replace ABS & TRAC ECU.

TY4029700245000X

Fig. 106   Slip indicator lamp inspection. 1997–99 Avalon

2 | Check TRAC cut switch.

PREPARATION:
(a)   Remove TRAC cut switch.
(b)   Disconnect TRAC cut switch connector.
CHECK:
Measure resistance between terminals 1 and 4 of TRAC cut switch when TRAC cut switch is on and off.
OK:

TRAC cut switch	Resistance
Pushed in	Continuity
Released	1 MΩ or higher

NG ▷ Replace TRAC cut switch.

OK

3 | Check for open and short in harness and connector between terminal CSW of ABS & TRAC ECU and TRAC cut switch and body ground

NG ▷ Repair or replace combination meter.

OK

4 | Check TRAC OFF indicator light.

NG ▷ Repair or replace combination meter.

OK

TY4029700382020X

Fig. 107   Traction control lamp inspection (Part 2 of 3). 1997–99 Camry

CIRCUIT DESCRIPTION

This is the TRAC control main switch. When the TRAC cut switch is pushed on, TRAC control goes off and the TRAC OFF indicator lights up. This indicator blinks for warnings when the trouble occurs and for displaying DTC.

WIRING DIAGRAM

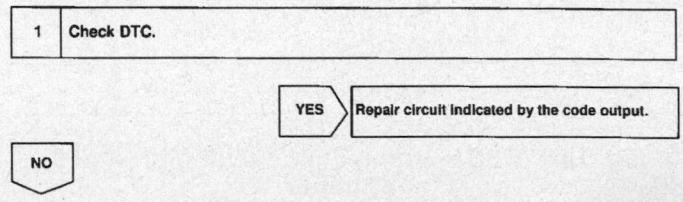

INSPECTION PROCEDURE

1 | Check DTC.

YES ▷ Repair circuit indicated by the code output.

NO

TY4029700382010X

Fig. 107   Traction control lamp inspection (Part 1 of 3). 1997–99 Camry

5 | Check for open and short in harness and connector between terminal WT of ABS & TRAC ECU and TRAC OFF indicator light

NG ▷ Repair or replace harness connector.

OK

Check and replace ABS & TRAC ECU.

TY4029700382030X

Fig. 107   Traction control lamp inspection (Part 3 of 3). 1997–99 Camry

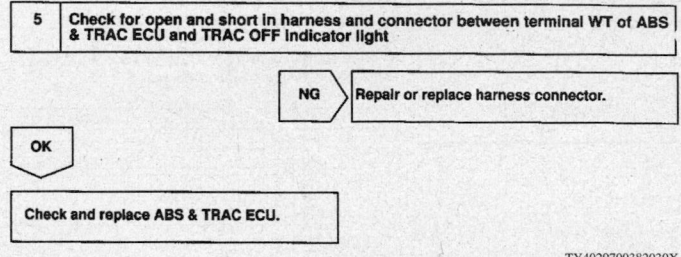

SLIP Indicator Light Circuit

CIRCUIT DESCRIPTION

The SLIP indicator blinks during TRAC operation.

WIRING DIAGRAM

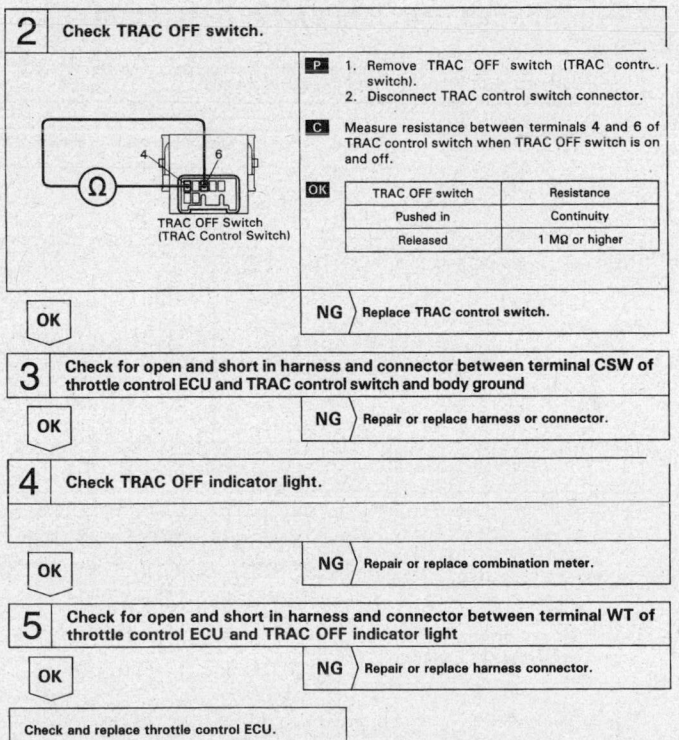

INSPECTION PROCEDURE

1. Check SLIP indicator light.

NG ▷ Repair or replace combination meter.

OK

2. Check for short in harness and connector between ABS & TRAC ECU and SLIP indicator light

NG ▷ Repair or replace harness or connector.

OK

Check and replace ABS & TRAC ECU.

TY4029700383000X

Fig. 108 Slip indicator lamp inspection. 1997–99 Camry

---

2. Check TRAC OFF switch.

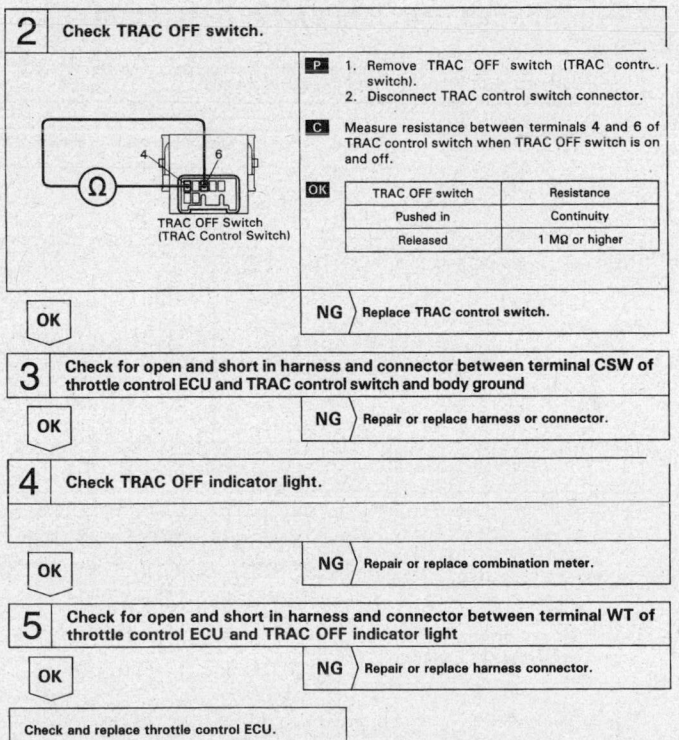

P 1. Remove TRAC OFF switch (TRAC control switch).
2. Disconnect TRAC control switch connector.

C Measure resistance between terminals 4 and 6 of TRAC control switch when TRAC OFF switch is on and off.

OK

TRAC OFF switch	Resistance
Pushed in	Continuity
Released	1 MΩ or higher

OK

NG ▷ Replace TRAC control switch.

3. Check for open and short in harness and connector between terminal CSW of throttle control ECU and TRAC control switch and body ground

OK

NG ▷ Repair or replace harness or connector.

4. Check TRAC OFF indicator light.

OK

NG ▷ Repair or replace combination meter.

5. Check for open and short in harness and connector between terminal WT of throttle control ECU and TRAC OFF indicator light

OK

NG ▷ Repair or replace harness connector.

Check and replace throttle control ECU.

TY4029700431020X

Fig. 109 TRAC off indicator lamp/TRAC off switch circuit (Part 2 of 2). 1997–98 Supra

---

CIRCUIT DESCRIPTION

This is the TRAC control main switch. When the TRAC OFF switch is pushed on, TRAC control goes off and the TRAC OFF indicator lights up. This indicator blinks for warnings when the trouble occurs and for displaying DTC.

WIRING DIAGRAM

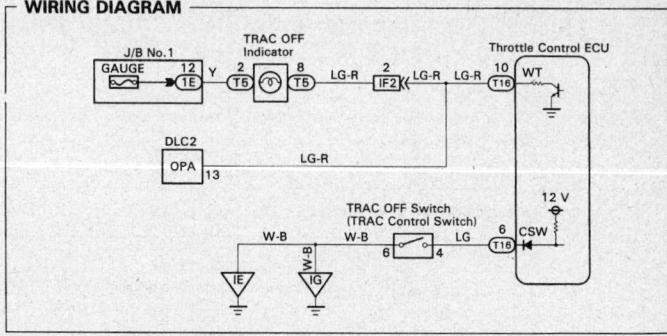

INSPECTION PROCEDURE

1. Check DTC.

NO ◁ ▷ YES ▷ Repair circuit indicated by the code output.

TY4029700431010X

Fig. 109 TRAC off indicator lamp/TRAC off switch circuit (Part 1 of 2). 1997–98 Supra

CIRCUIT DESCRIPTION

The SLIP indicator blinks during TRAC operation.

TY4029700432010X

Fig. 110 Slip indicator lamp (Part 1 of 2). 1997–98 Supra

WIRING DIAGRAM

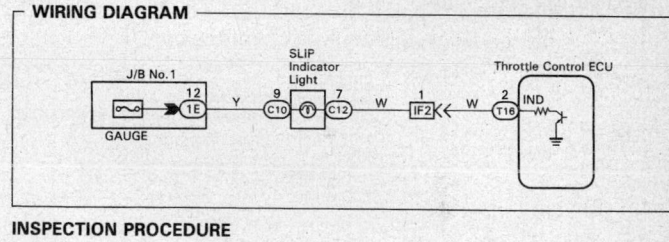

INSPECTION PROCEDURE

1. Check SLIP indicator light.

OK

NG ▷ Repair or replace combination meter.

2. Check for short in harness and connector between throttle control ECU and SLIP indicator light

OK

NG ▷ Repair or replace harness or connector.

Check and replace throttle control ECU.

TY4029700432020X

Fig. 110 Slip indicator lamp (Part 2 of 2). 1997–98 Supra

CIRCUIT DESCRIPTION

When you push the SNOW mode switch, TRAC control becomes SNOW mode operation and the SNOW indicator light on, and when you push the TRAC OFF switch, TRAC control will be released to normal mode operation and the SNOW indicator light goes off.

TY4029700433010X

Fig. 111 SNOW indicator lamp/SNOW mode switch circuit (Part 1 of 2). 1997–98 Supra

CIRCUIT DESCRIPTION

Connecting between terminals Tc and E_1 of the DLC1 or the DLC2 causes the ECU to display the DTC by flashing the ABS warning light.

INSPECTION PROCEDURE

1	Check voltage between terminals Tc and E_1 of DLC2 or DLC1.

CHECK:
(a) Turn the ignition switch ON.
(b) Measure voltage between terminals Tc and E_1 of DLC2 or DLC1.

OK:
Voltage: 10 – 14 V

OK	If ABS warning light does not blink even after Tc and E_1 are connected, the ECU may be defective.

NG

TY4029900568010X

Fig. 112 T_C Terminal Circuit (Part 1 of 2). Camry Solara less traction control

CIRCUIT DESCRIPTION

Connecting between terminals Tc and E_1 of the DLC1 or the DLC2 causes the ECU to display the DTC by blinking the ABS warning light and TRAC OFF indicator light.

INSPECTION PROCEDURE

1	Check voltage between terminals Tc and E_1 of DLC2 or DLC1.

CHECK:
(a) Turn the ignition switch ON.
(b) Measure voltage between terminals Tc and E_1 of DLC2 or DLC1.

OK:
Voltage: 10 – 14 V

OK	If ABS warning light does not blink even after Tc and E_1 are connected, the ECU may be defective.

NG

TY4029900585010X

Fig. 113 T_C Terminal Circuit (Part 1 of 2). Camry Solara w/traction control

WIRING DIAGRAM

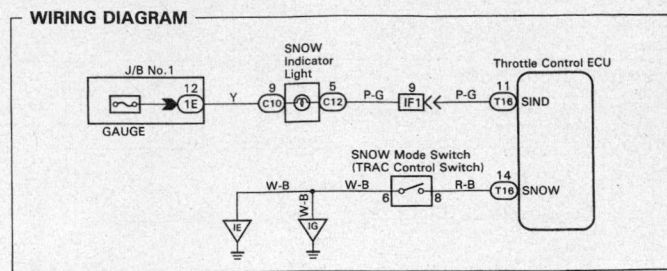

INSPECTION PROCEDURE

1	Check SNOW mode switch.

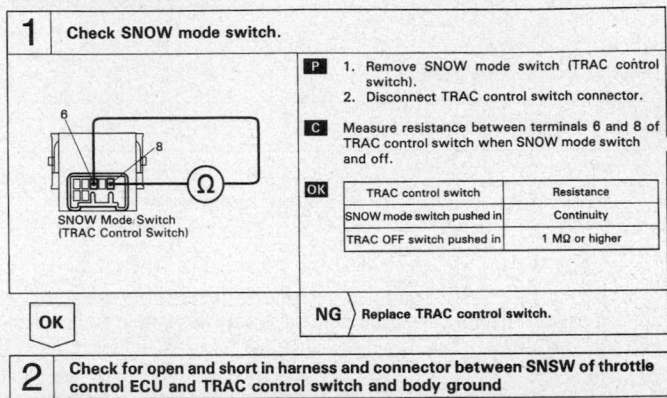

P	1. Remove SNOW mode switch (TRAC control switch).
	2. Disconnect TRAC control switch connector.

C	Measure resistance between terminals 6 and 8 of TRAC control switch when SNOW mode switch and off.

OK	TRAC control switch	Resistance
	SNOW mode switch pushed in	Continuity
	TRAC OFF switch pushed in	1 MΩ or higher

OK	NG	Replace TRAC control switch.

2	Check for open and short in harness and connector between SNSW of throttle control ECU and TRAC control switch and body ground

OK	NG	Repair or replace harness or connector.

3	Check SNOW indicator light.

OK	NG	Repair or replace combination meter.

TY4029700433020X

Fig. 111 SNOW indicator lamp/SNOW mode switch circuit (Part 2 of 2). 1997–98 Supra

2	Check for open and short circuit in harness and connector between ABS ECU and DLC2 or DLC1, DLC2 or DLC1 and body ground.

NG	Repair or replace harness or connector.

OK

Check and replace ABS ECU.

TY4029900568020X

Fig. 112 T_C Terminal Circuit (Part 2 of 2). Camry Solara less traction control

2	Check for open and short circuit in harness and connector between ABS & TRAC ECU and DLC2 or DLC1, DLC2 or DLC1 and body ground.

NG	Repair or replace harness or connector.

OK

Check and replace ABS & TRAC ECU.

TY4029900585020X

Fig. 113 T_C Terminal Circuit (Part 2 of 2). Camry Solara w/traction control

CIRCUIT DESCRIPTION

Connecting between terminals Tc and E_1 of the DLC1 causes the ECU to display the DTC by flashing the ABS warning light.

INSPECTION PROCEDURE

1	Check voltage between terminals Tc and E_1 of DLC1.

CHECK:
(a) Turn the ignition switch ON.
(b) Measure voltage between terminals Tc and E_1 of DLC1.
OK:
Voltage: 10 – 14 V

> OK > If ABS warning light does not blink even after Tc and E_1 are connected, the ECU may be defective.

NG

TY4029900463010X

Fig. 114 T_C Terminal Circuit (Part 1 of 2). Sienna

CIRCUIT DESCRIPTION

Connecting terminals Tc and E_1 of the DLC1 causes the ECU to display the DTC by flashing the ABS warning light.

INSPECTION PROCEDURE

1	Check voltage between terminals Tc and E_1 of DLC1.

CHECK:
(a) Turn the ignition switch ON.
(b) Measure voltage between terminals Tc and E_1 of DLC1.
OK:
Voltage: 10 – 14 V

> OK > If ABS warning light does not blink even after Tc and E_1 are connected, the ECU may be defective.

NG

TY4029900481010X

Fig. 115 T_C Terminal Circuit (Part 1 of 2). Tundra

2	Check for open and short circuit in harness and connector between ABS ECU and DLC1, DLC1 and body ground

NG > Repair or replace harness or connector.

OK

Check and replace ABS actuator assembly.

TY4029900463020X

Fig. 114 T_C Terminal Circuit (Part 2 of 2). Sienna

2	Check for open and short circuit in harness and connector between ABS actuator and DLC1, DLC1 and body ground

NG > Repair or replace harness or connector.

OK

Check and replace ABS ECU.

TY4029900481020X

Fig. 115 T_C Terminal Circuit (Part 2 of 2). Tundra

CIRCUIT DESCRIPTION

Connecting terminals Tc and E1 of the DLC1 or the DLC2 causes the ECU to display the diagnostic trouble code by flasing the ABS warning light.

WIRING DIAGRAM

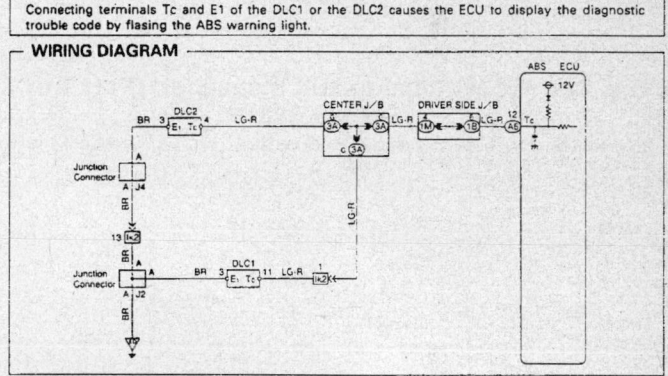

INSPECTION PROCEDURE

1	Check voltage between terminals Tc and E1 of DLC2 or DLC1.

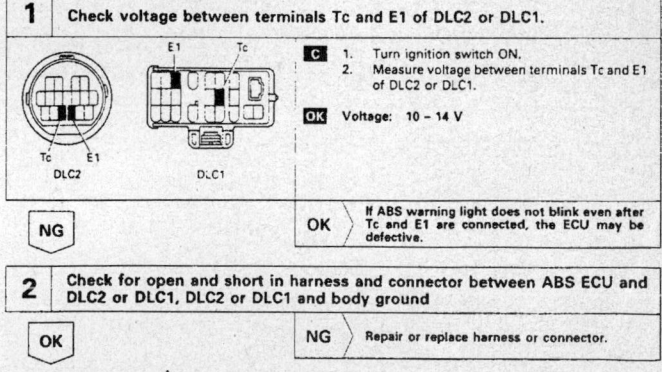

C
1. Turn ignition switch ON.
2. Measure voltage between terminals Tc and E1 of DLC2 or DLC1.

OK Voltage: 10 – 14 V

NG

OK > If ABS warning light does not blink even after Tc and E1 are connected, the ECU may be defective.

2	Check for open and short in harness and connector between ABS ECU and DLC2 or DLC1, DLC2 or DLC1 and body ground

OK

NG > Repair or replace harness or connector.

Check and replace ABS ECU.

TY4029500162000X

Fig. 116 Tc terminal circuit inspection. 1996 Avalon

Connecting between terminals Tc and E₁ of the DLC1 or the DLC2 causes the ECU to display the DTC by flashing the ABS warning light.

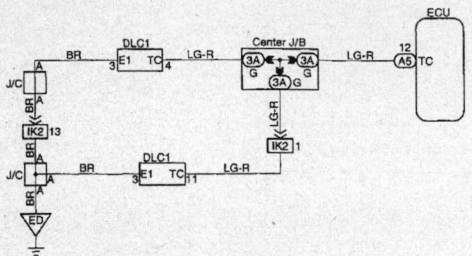

2 | Check for open and short in harness and connector between ABS ECU and DLC2 or DLC1, DLC2 or DLC1 and body ground

NG ▷ Repair or replace harness or connector.

OK

Check and replace ABS ECU.

TY4029700242020X

Fig. 117 Tc terminal circuit inspection (Part 2 of 2). 1997–99 Avalon

---

1 | Check voltage between terminals Tc and E₁ of DLC2 or DLC1.

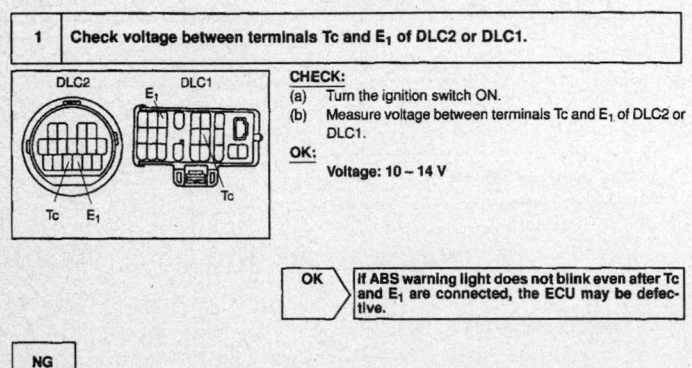

CHECK:
(a) Turn the ignition switch ON.
(b) Measure voltage between terminals Tc and E₁ of DLC2 or DLC1.

OK:
Voltage: 10 – 14 V

OK ▷ If ABS warning light does not blink even after Tc and E₁ are connected, the ECU may be defective.

NG

TY4029700242010X

Fig. 117 Tc terminal circuit inspection (Part 1 of 2). 1997–99 Avalon

Connecting terminals Tc and E1 of the DLC1 or the DLC2 causes the ECU to dispaly the diagnostic trouble code by flashing the ABS warning light.

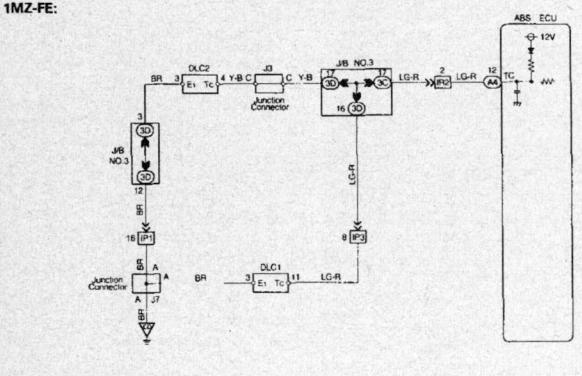

Fig. 118 Tc terminal circuit inspection (Part 1 of 2). 1996 Camry

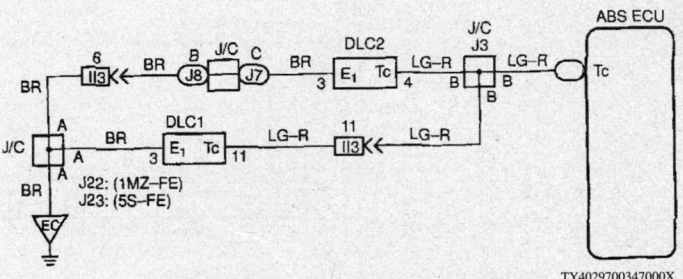

Fig. 118 Tc terminal circuit inspection (Part 1 of 2). 1997–99 Camry

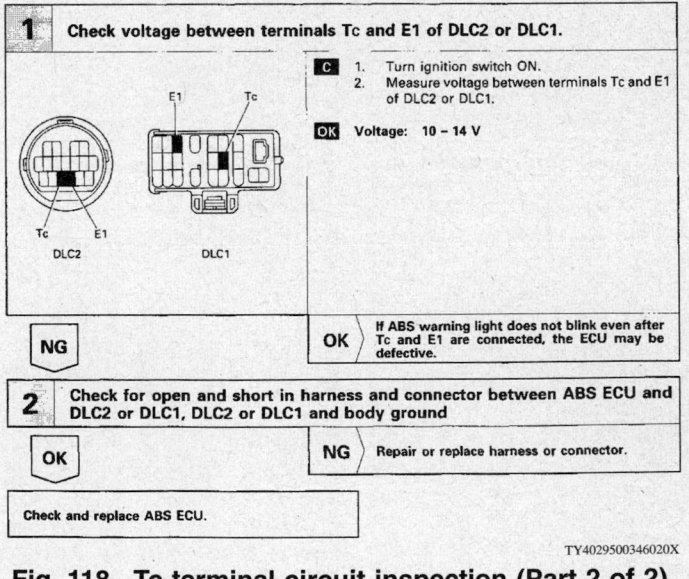

Fig. 118 Tc terminal circuit inspection (Part 2 of 2). Camry

TY4029500346020X

ANTI-LOCK BRAKES

CIRCUIT DESCRIPTION

Connecting terminals Tc and E1 of the DLC1 causes the ECU to display the diagnostic trouble code by flashing the ABS warning light.

DIAGNOSTIC CHART

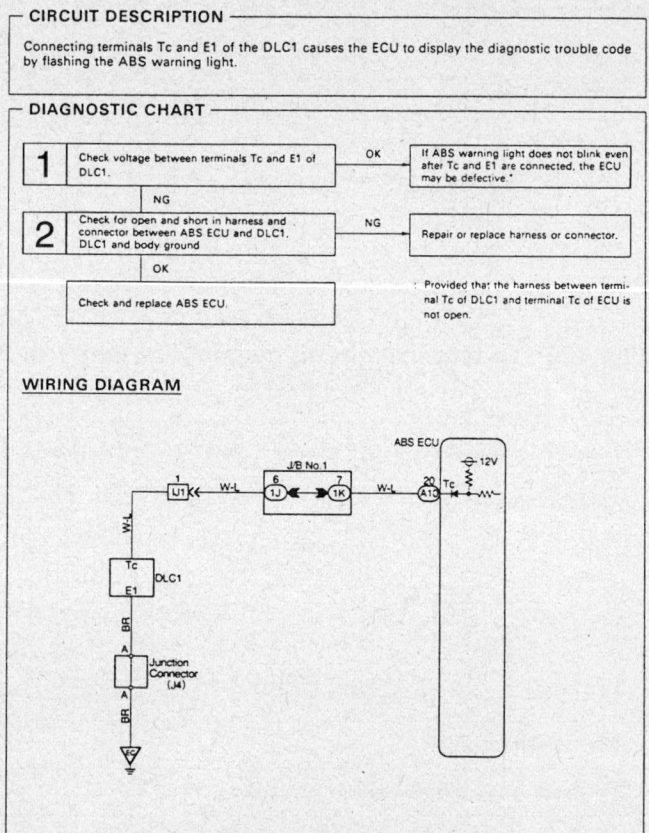

1	Check voltage between terminals Tc and E1 of DLC1.	OK →	If ABS warning light does not blink even after Tc and E1 are connected, the ECU may be defective.*
NG ↓			
2	Check for open and short in harness and connector between ABS ECU and DLC1, DLC1 and body ground.	NG →	Repair or replace harness or connector.
OK ↓			
Check and replace ABS ECU.			* Provided that the harness between terminal Tc of DLC1 and terminal Tc of ECU is not open.

WIRING DIAGRAM

Fig. 119   Tc terminal circuit inspection (Part 1 of 2). 1996 Celica

TY4029400066010X

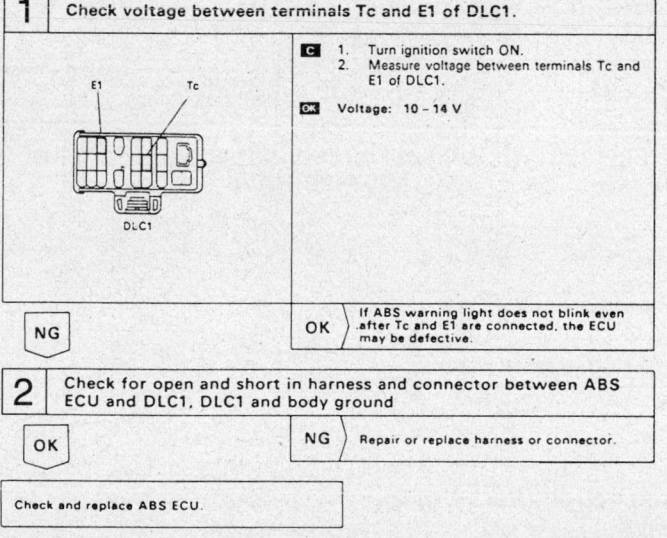

1	Check voltage between terminals Tc and E1 of DLC1.
	C 1. Turn ignition switch ON.
	2. Measure voltage between terminals Tc and E1 of DLC1.
	OK Voltage: 10 – 14 V
NG	OK → If ABS warning light does not blink even after Tc and E1 are connected, the ECU may be defective.
2	Check for open and short in harness and connector between ABS ECU and DLC1, DLC1 and body ground
OK	NG → Repair or replace harness or connector.
Check and replace ABS ECU.	

Fig. 119   Tc terminal circuit inspection (Part 2 of 2). Celica

TY4029400066020X

CIRCUIT DESCRIPTION

Connecting terminals Tc and E1 of the DLC1 causes the ECU to display the DTC by flashing the ABS warning light.

WIRING DIAGRAM

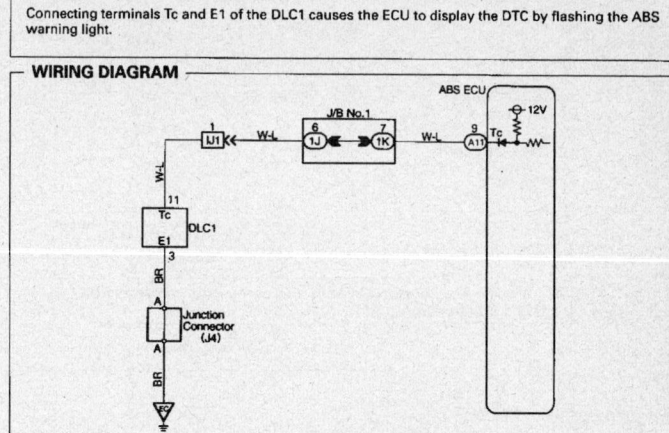

TY4029700391000X

Fig. 119   Tc terminal circuit inspection (Part 1 of 2). 1997–99 Celica

Connecting between terminals Tc and E1 of the DLC1 causes the ECU to display the diagnostic trouble code by flashing the ABS Warning light.

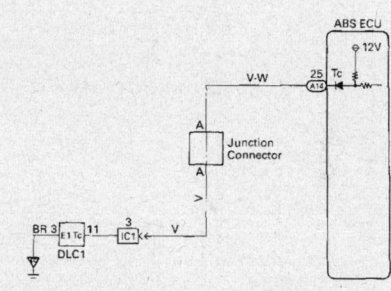

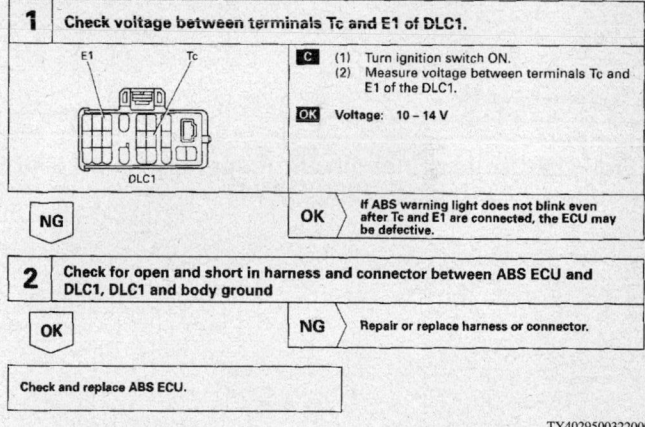

1	Check voltage between terminals Tc and E1 of DLC1.
	C (1) Turn ignition switch ON.
	(2) Measure voltage between terminals Tc and E1 of the DLC1.
	OK Voltage: 10 – 14 V
NG	OK → If ABS warning light does not blink even after Tc and E1 are connected, the ECU may be defective.
2	Check for open and short in harness and connector between ABS ECU and DLC1, DLC1 and body ground
OK	NG → Repair or replace harness or connector.
Check and replace ABS ECU.	

TY4029500322000X

Fig. 120   Tc terminal circuit inspection. Corolla

CIRCUIT DESCRIPTION

Connecting between terminals Tc and E1 of the DLC1 causes the ECU to display the DTC by flashing the ABS warning light.

WIRING DIAGRAM

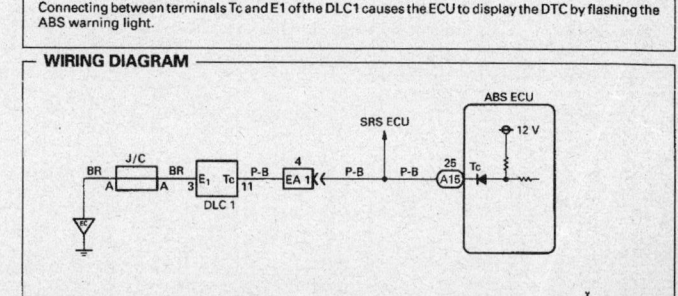

TY4029600274010X

Fig. 121   Tc terminal circuit inspection (Part 1 of 2). Paseo

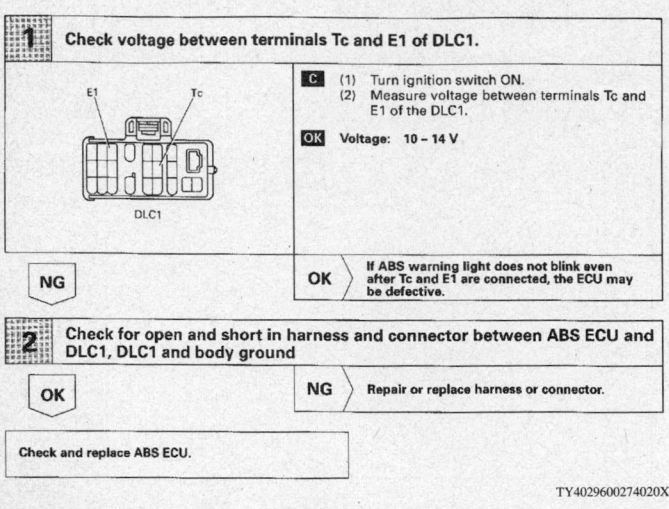

Fig. 121 Tc terminal circuit inspection (Part 2 of 2). Paseo

TY4029600274020X

INSPECTION PROCEDURE

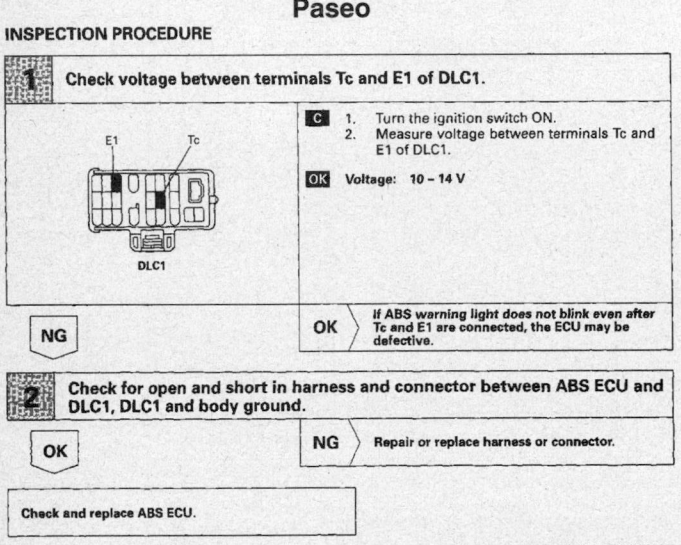

Fig. 122 Tc terminal circuit inspection (Part 2 of 2). 1996 RAV4

TY4029600203020X

CIRCUIT DESCRIPTION

Connecting terminals Tc and E1 of the DLC1 causes the ECU to display the DTC by flasing the ABS warning light.

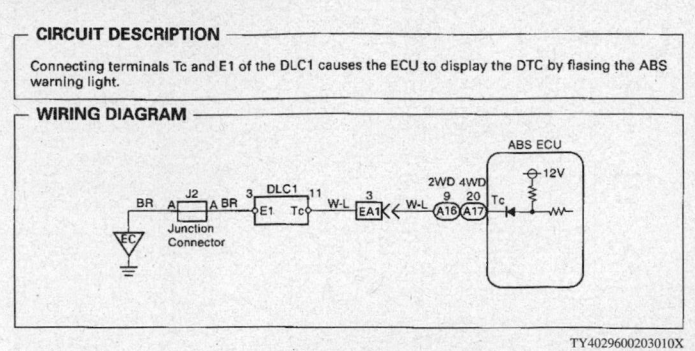

TY4029600203010X

Fig. 122 Tc terminal circuit inspection (Part 1 of 2). 1996 RAV4

CIRCUIT DESCRIPTION

Connecting terminals Tc and E1 of the DLC1 causes the ECU to display the DTC by flasing the ABS warning light.

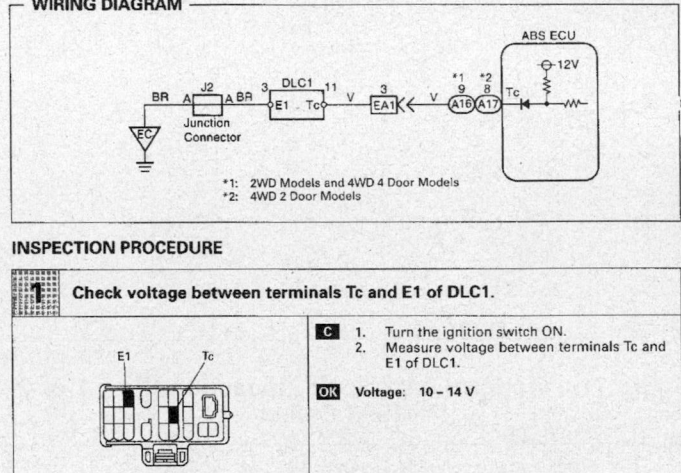

INSPECTION PROCEDURE

Fig. 123 Tc terminal circuit inspection (Part 1 of 2). 1997–99 RAV4

TY4029700284010X

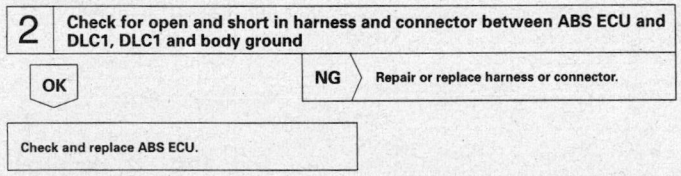

TY4029700284020X

Fig. 123 Tc terminal circuit inspection (Part 2 of 2). 1997–99 RAV4

CIRCUIT DESCRIPTION

Connecting terminals Tc and E1 of the DLC1 or the DLC2 causes the ECU to display the diagnostic trouble code by flashing the ABS warning light.

DIAGNOSTIC CHART

HINT: First confirm that the ABS warning light is operating normally.

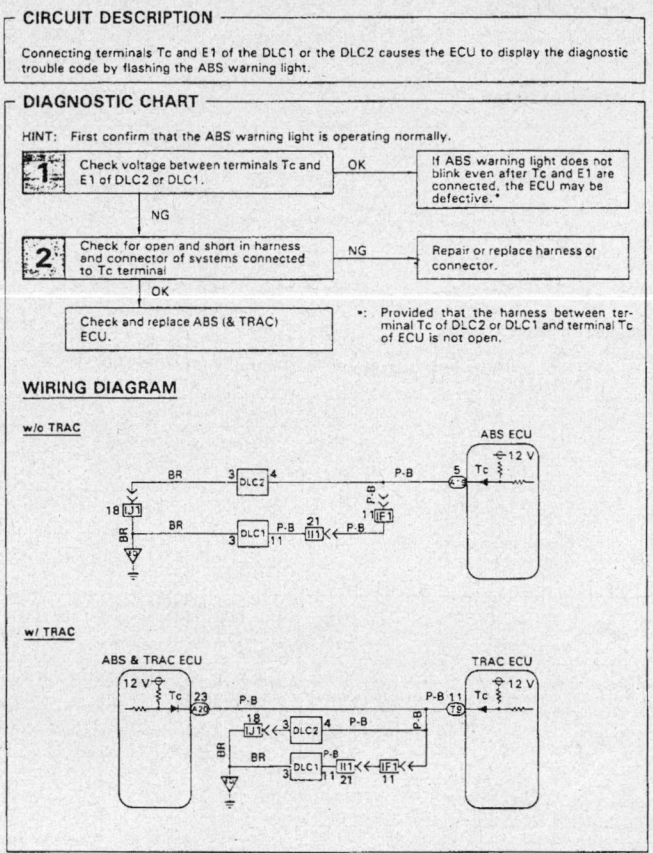

1 Check voltage between terminals Tc and E1 of DLC2 or DLC1. → OK → If ABS warning light does not blink even after Tc and E1 are connected, the ECU may be defective. *

↓ NG

2 Check for open and short in harness and connector of systems connected to Tc terminal → NG → Repair or replace harness or connector.

↓ OK

Check and replace ABS (& TRAC) ECU.

*: Provided that the harness between terminal Tc of DLC2 or DLC1 and terminal Tc of ECU is not open.

WIRING DIAGRAM

Fig. 124 Tc terminal circuit inspection (Part 1 of 2). 1996 Supra

CIRCUIT DESCRIPTION

By connecting terminals Tc and E1 of DLC1 or DLC2, the ECU displays the DTC by blinking the TRAC OFF indicator light.

WIRING DIAGRAM

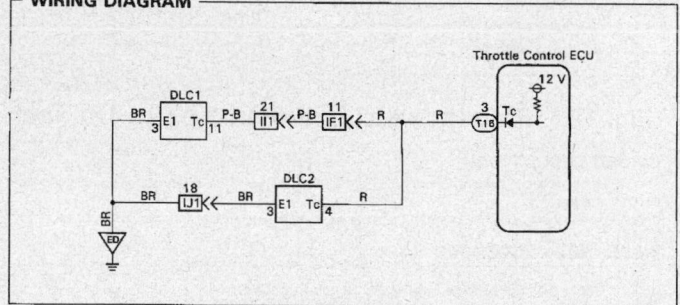

Fig. 124 Tc terminal circuit inspection (Part 1 of 2). 1997–98 Supra w/Traction Control

CIRCUIT DESCRIPTION

Connecting terminals Tc and E1 of the DLC1 or the DLC2 causes the ECU to display the DTC by flashing the ABS warning light.

WIRING DIAGRAM

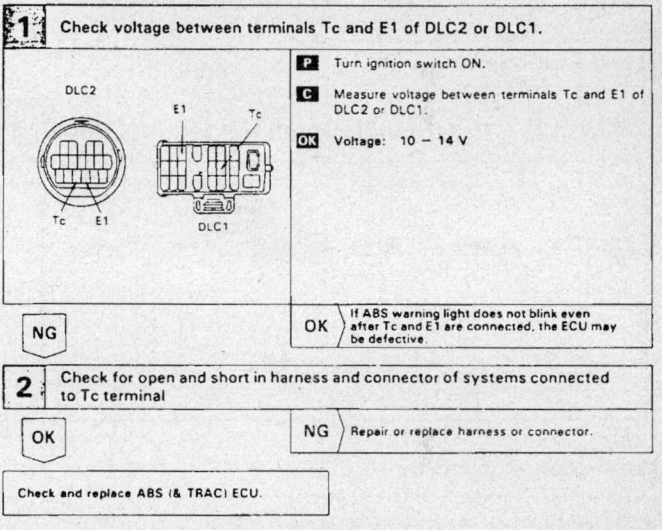

*1: NORMAL ABS (2JZ-GE Engine)
*2: SPORT ABS (2JZ-GTE Engine)

TY4029700408000X

Fig. 124 Tc terminal circuit inspection (Part 1 of 2). 1997–98 Supra less Traction Control

1 Check voltage between terminals Tc and E1 of DLC2 or DLC1.

P Turn ignition switch ON.

C Measure voltage between terminals Tc and E1 of DLC2 or DLC1.

OK Voltage: 10 – 14 V

NG

OK → If ABS warning light does not blink even after Tc and E1 are connected, the ECU may be defective.

2 Check for open and short in harness and connector of systems connected to Tc terminal

OK

NG → Repair or replace harness or connector.

Check and replace ABS (& TRAC) ECU.

TY4029300065020X

Fig. 124 Tc terminal circuit inspection (Part 2 of 2). Supra

CIRCUIT DESCRIPTION

Connecting terminals Tc and E1 of the DLC1 causes the ECU to display the DTC by flasing the ABS warning light.

WIRING DIAGRAM

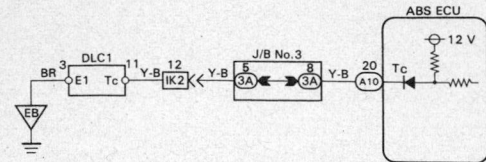

1 Check voltage between terminals Tc and E1 of DLC1.

C
1. Turn the ignition switch ON.
2. Measure voltage between terminals Tc and E1 of DLC1.

OK Voltage: 10 – 14 V

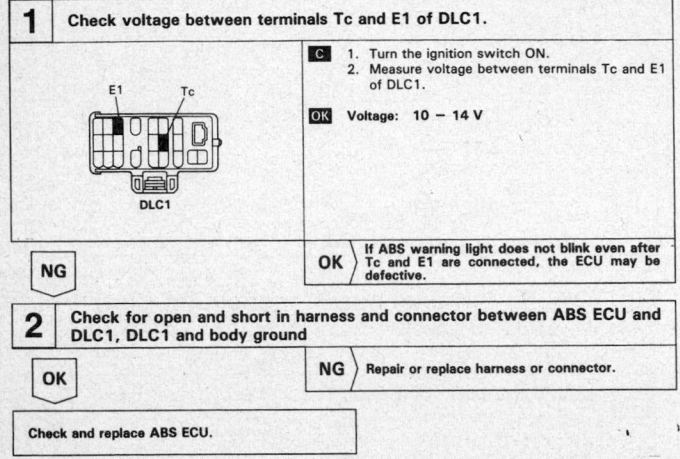

NG

OK If ABS warning light does not blink even after Tc and E1 are connected, the ECU may be defective.

2 Check for open and short in harness and connector between ABS ECU and DLC1, DLC1 and body ground

OK

NG Repair or replace harness or connector.

Check and replace ABS ECU.

TY4029500176000X

Fig. 125   Tc terminal circuit inspection. Tacoma

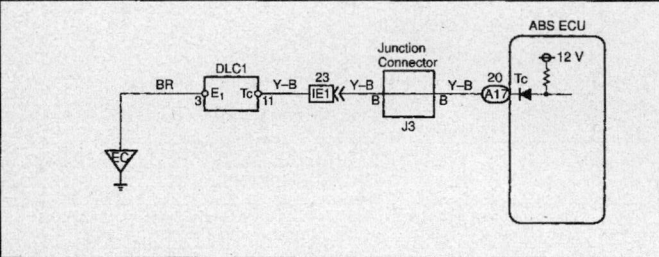

INSPECTION PROCEDURE

1 Check voltage between terminals Tc and E₁ of DLC1.

CHECK:
(a) Turn the ignition switch ON.
(b) Measure voltage between terminals Tc and E₁ of DLC1.
OK:
   Voltage: 10 – 14 V

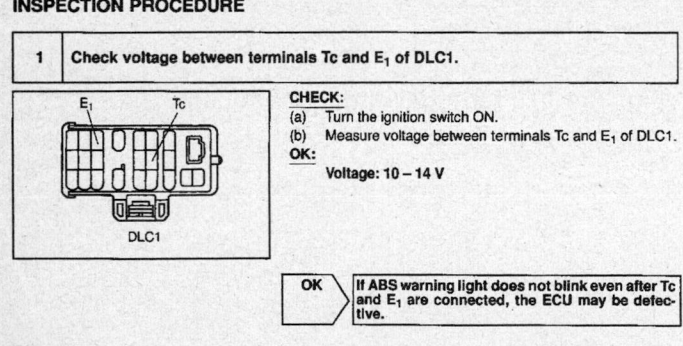

OK If ABS warning light does not blink even after Tc and E₁ are connected, the ECU may be defective.

NG

TY4029600227010X

Fig. 127   Tc terminal circuit (Part 1 of 2). 4Runner

CIRCUIT DESCRIPTION

Connecting between terminals Tc and E1 of the data link connector 1 causes the ECU to display the diagnostic trouble code by flashing the ABS warning light.

WIRING DIAGRAM

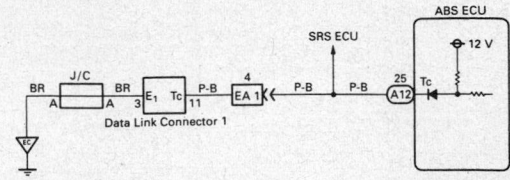

INSPECTION PROCEDURE

1 Check voltage between terminals Tc and E1 of Data Link Connector 1.

C
(1) Turn ignition switch ON.
(2) Measure voltage between terminals Tc and E1 of the data link connector 1.

OK Voltage: 10 – 14 V

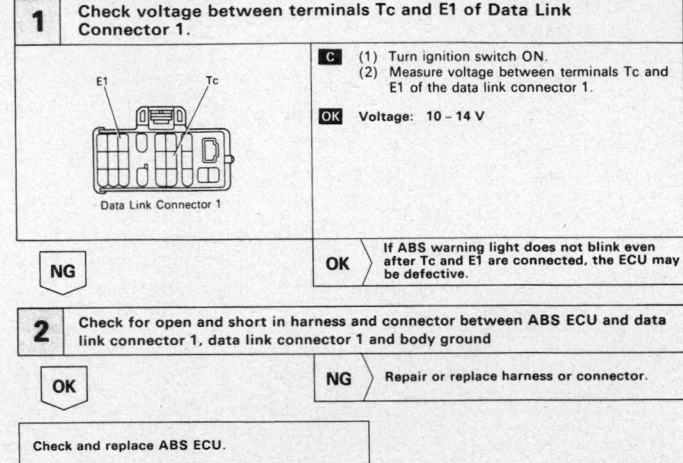

NG

OK If ABS warning light does not blink even after Tc and E1 are connected, the ECU may be defective.

2 Check for open and short in harness and connector between ABS ECU and data link connector 1, data link connector 1 and body ground

OK

NG Repair or replace harness or connector.

Check and replace ABS ECU.

TY4029500186000X

Fig. 126   Tc terminal circuit inspection. Tercel

2 Check for open and short in harness and connector between ABS ECU and DLC1, DLC1 and body ground.

NG Repair or replace harness or connector.

OK

Check and replace ABS ECU.

TY4029600227020X

Fig. 127   Tc terminal circuit (Part 2 of 2). 4Runner

CIRCUIT DESCRIPTION

The sensor check circuit detects abnormalities in the speed sensor signal which cannot be detected with the DTC check.
Connecting terminals Ts and E1 of the DLC1 in the engine compartment starts the check.

INSPECTION PROCEDURE

1 Check voltage between terminals Ts and E₁ of DLC1.

CHECK:
(a) Turn the ignition switch ON.
(b) Measure voltage between terminals Ts and E₁ of DLC1.
OK:
   Voltage: 10 – 14 V

OK If ABS warning light does not blink even after Ts and E₁ are connected, the ECU may be defective.

NG

TY4029900569010X

Fig. 128   T_s Terminal Circuit (Part 1 of 2). Camry Solara less traction control

| 2 | Check for open and short circuit in harness and connector between ABS ECU and DLC1, DLC1 and body ground. |

```
          NG >  Repair or replace harness or connector.
OK

Check and replace ABS ECU.
```

TY4029900569020X

Fig. 128 T_S Terminal Circuit (Part 2 of 2). Camry Solara less traction control

| 2 | Check for open and short circuit in harness and connector between ABS & TRAC ECU and DLC1, DLC1 and body ground . |

```
          NG >  Repair or replace harness or connector.

OK

Check and replace ABS & TRAC ECU.
```

TY4029900586020X

Fig. 129 T_S Terminal Circuit (Part 2 of 2). Camry Solara w/traction control

CIRCUIT DESCRIPTION

The sensor check circuit detects abnormalities which cannot be detected with the DTC check in the speed sensor signal.
Connecting terminals Ts and E_1 of the DLC1 in the engine compartment starts the check.

INSPECTION PROCEDURE

| 1 | Check voltage between terminals Ts and E_1 of DLC1. |

CHECK:
(a) Turn the ignition switch ON.
(b) Measure voltage between terminals Ts and E_1 of DLC1.
OK:
    Voltage: 10 – 14 V

```
          OK >  If ABS warning light does not blink even after Ts
                and E1 are connected, the ECU may be defec-
                tive.
NG
```

TY4029900464010X

Fig. 130 T_S Terminal Circuit (Part 1 of 2). Sienna

CIRCUIT DESCRIPTION

The sensor check circuit detects abnormalities in the speed sensor signal which cannot be detected with the DTC check.
Connecting terminals Ts and E_1 of the DLC1 in the engine compartment starts the check.

INSPECTION PROCEDURE

| 1 | Check voltage between terminals Ts and E_1 of DLC1. |

CHECK:
(a) Turn the ignition switch ON.
(b) Measure voltage between terminals Ts and E_1 of DLC1.
OK:
    Voltage: 10 – 14 V

```
          OK >  If ABS warning light does not blink even after Ts
                and E1 are connected, the ECU may be defec-
                tive.
NG
```

TY4029900482010X

Fig. 131 T_S Terminal Circuit (Part 1 of 2). Tundra

CIRCUIT DESCRIPTION

The sensor check circuit detects abnormalities in the speed sensor signal which cannot be detected with the DTC check.
Connecting terminals Ts and E_1 of the DLC1 in the engine compartment starts the check.

INSPECTION PROCEDURE

| 1 | Check voltage between terminals Ts and E_1 of DLC1. |

CHECK:
(a) Turn the ignition switch ON.
(b) Measure voltage between terminals Ts and E_1 of DLC1.
OK:
    Voltage: 10 – 14 V

```
          OK >  If ABS warning light does not blink even after Ts
                and E1 are connected, the ECU may be defec-
                tive.
NG
```

TY4029900586010X

Fig. 129 T_S Terminal Circuit (Part 1 of 2). Camry Solara w/traction control

| 2 | Check for open and short circuit in harness and connector between ABS ECU and DLC1, DLC1 and body ground |

```
          NG >  Repair or replace harness or connector.

OK

Check and replace ABS actuator assembly.
```

TY4029900464020X

Fig. 130 T_S Terminal Circuit (Part 2 of 2). Sienna

| 2 | Check for open and short circuit in harness and connector between ABS actuator and DLC1, DLC1 and body ground |

```
          NG >  Repair or replace harness or connector.

OK

Check and replace ABS ECU.
```

TY4029900482020X

Fig. 131 T_S Terminal Circuit (Part 2 of 2). Tundra

CIRCUIT DESCRIPTION

The sensor check circuit detects abnormalities in the speed sensor signal which cannot be detected with the diagnostic trouble code check.
Connecting terminals Ts and E1 of the DLC1 in the engine compartment starts the check.

WIRING DIAGRAM

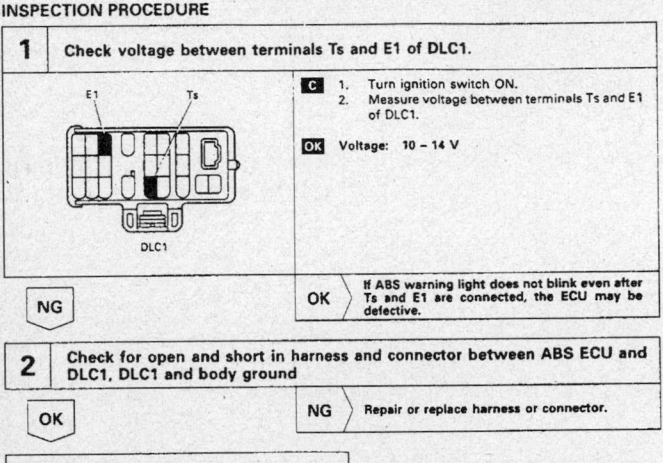

INSPECTION PROCEDURE

| 1 | Check voltage between terminals Ts and E1 of DLC1. |

C	1. Turn ignition switch ON.
	2. Measure voltage between terminals Ts and E1 of DLC1.
OK	Voltage: 10 – 14 V

NG

| OK | If ABS warning light does not blink even after Ts and E1 are connected, the ECU may be defective. |

| 2 | Check for open and short in harness and connector between ABS ECU and DLC1, DLC1 and body ground |

OK

| NG | Repair or replace harness or connector. |

Check and replace ABS ECU.

TY4029500163000X

Fig. 132 Ts terminal circuit inspection. 1996 Avalon

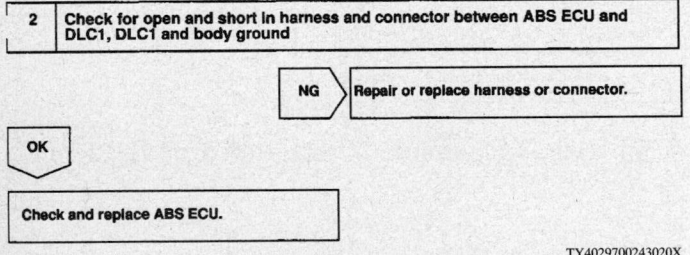

| 2 | Check for open and short in harness and connector between ABS ECU and DLC1, DLC1 and body ground |

| NG | Repair or replace harness or connector. |

OK

Check and replace ABS ECU.

TY4029700243020X

Fig. 133 Ts terminal circuit inspection (Part 2 of 2). 1997–99 Avalon

The sensor check circuit detects abnormalities in the speed sensor signal which cannot be detected with the DTC check.
Connecting terminals Ts and E1 of the DLC1 in the engine compartment starts the check.

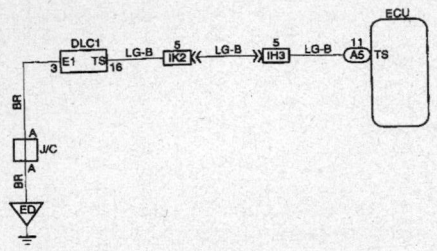

| 1 | Check voltage between terminals Ts and E1 of DLC1. |

CHECK:
(a) Turn the ignition switch ON.
(b) Measure voltage between terminals Ts and E1 of DLC1.
OK:
Voltage: 10 – 14 V

| OK | If ABS warning light does not blink even after Ts and E1 are connected, the ECU may be defective. |

NG

TY4029700243010X

Fig. 133 Ts terminal circuit inspection (Part 1 of 2). 1997–99 Avalon

The sensor check circuit detects abnormalities in the speed sensor signal which cannot be detected with the diagnostic trouble code check.
Connecting terminals Ts and E1 of the DLC1 in the engine compartment starts the check.

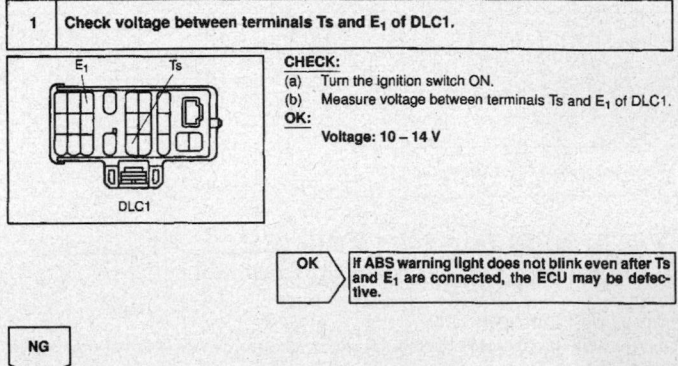

TY4029500348000X

Fig. 134 Ts terminal circuit inspection (Part 1 of 2). 1996 Camry

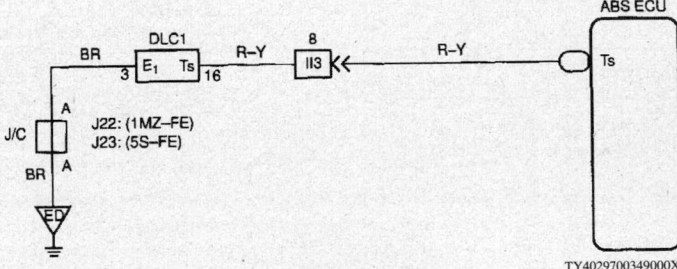

TY4029700349000X

Fig. 134 Ts terminal circuit inspection (Part 1 of 2). 1997–99 Camry

INSPECTION PROCEDURE

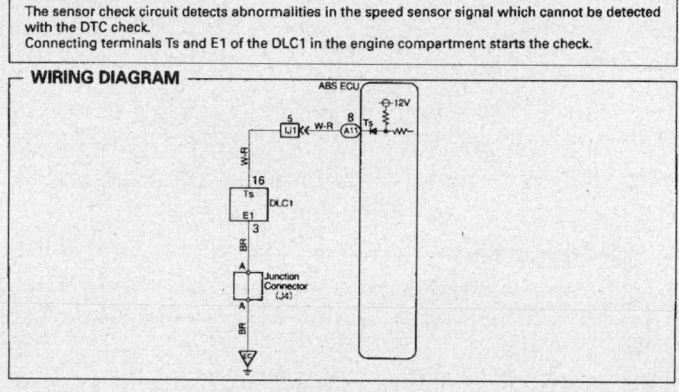

Ts	Check voltage between terminal Ts and E1 of check connector.		
	C	(1) Turn ignition switch ON. (2) Measure voltage between terminal Ts and E1 of check connector.	
	OK	Voltage: 10 – 14 V	
NG	**OK**	If ABS warning light does not blink even after Ts and E1 are connected, the ECU may be defective.	

2	Check for open and short in harness and connector between ABS ECU and check connector, check connector and body ground	
OK	**NG**	Repair or replace harness or connector.

Check and replace ABS ECU.

TY4029200067020X

Fig. 134 Ts terminal circuit inspection (Part 2 of 2). Camry

CIRCUIT DESCRIPTION

The sensor check circuit detects abnormalities in the speed sensor signal which cannot be detected with the DTC check.
Connecting terminals Ts and E1 of the DLC1 in the engine compartment starts the check.

WIRING DIAGRAM

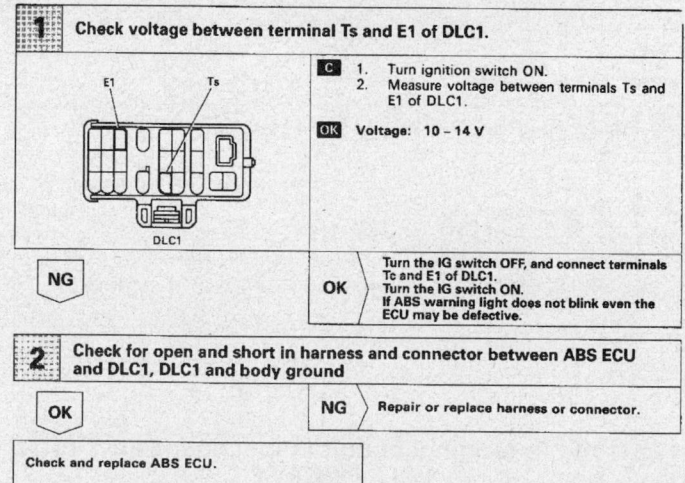

TY4029700392010X

Fig. 135 Ts terminal circuit inspection (Part 1 of 2). 1997–99 Celica

1	Check voltage between terminal Ts and E1 of DLC1.		
	C	1. Turn ignition switch ON. 2. Measure voltage between terminals Ts and E1 of DLC1.	
	OK	Voltage: 10 – 14 V	
NG	**OK**	Turn the IG switch OFF, and connect terminals Ts and E1 of DLC1. Turn the IG switch ON. If ABS warning light does not blink even the ECU may be defective.	

2	Check for open and short in harness and connector between ABS ECU and DLC1, DLC1 and body ground	
OK	**NG**	Repair or replace harness or connector.

Check and replace ABS ECU.

TY4029700392020X

Fig. 135 Ts terminal circuit inspection (Part 2 of 2). Celica

CIRCUIT DESCRIPTION

The sensor check circuit detects abnormalities in the speed sensor signal which cannot be detected with the diagnostic trouble code check.
Connecting terminals Ts and E1 of the DLC1 in the engine compartment starts the check.

DIAGNOSTIC CHART

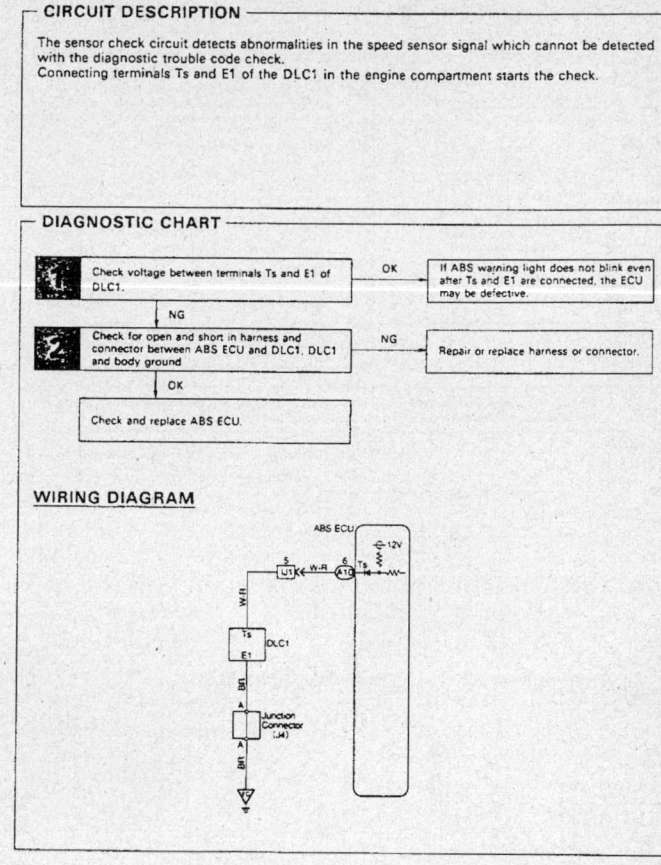

1	Check voltage between terminals Ts and E1 of DLC1.	OK	If ABS warning light does not blink even after Ts and E1 are connected, the ECU may be defective.
		NG	
2	Check for open and short in harness and connector between ABS ECU and DLC1, DLC1 and body ground	NG	Repair or replace harness or connector.
		OK	
Check and replace ABS ECU.			

WIRING DIAGRAM

TY4029400070010X

Fig. 135 Ts terminal circuit inspection (Part 1 of 2). 1996 Celica

CIRCUIT DESCRIPTION

The sensor check circuit detects abnormalities in the speed sensor signal which cannot be detected with the DTC check.
Connecting terminals Ts and E1 of the DLC1 in the engine compartment starts the check.

WIRING DIAGRAM

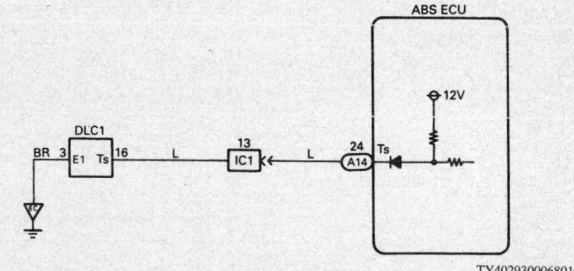

TY4029300068010X

Fig. 136 Ts terminal circuit inspection (Part 1 of 2). Corolla

INSPECTION PROCEDURE

1 Check voltage between terminals Ts and E1 of data link connector 1.

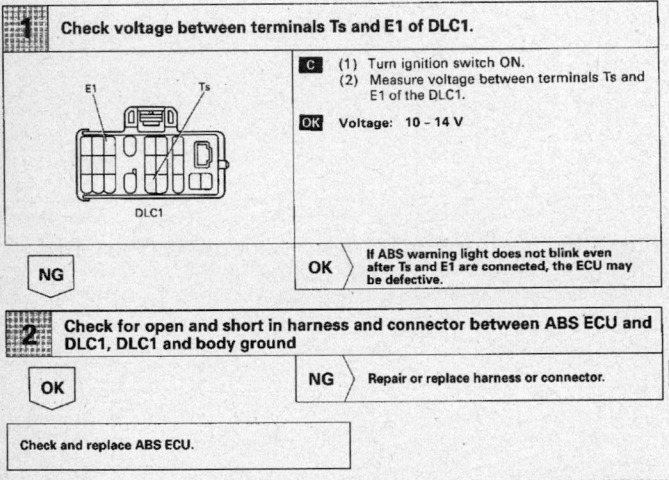

C
(1) Turn ignition switch ON.
(2) Measure voltage between terminals Ts and E1 of the data link connector 1.

OK Voltage: 10 – 14 V

Data Link Connector 1

NG ▽

OK ▷ If ABS warning light does not blink even after Ts and E1 are connected, the ECU may be defective.

2 Check for open and short in harness and connector between ABS ECU and data link connector 1, data link connector 1 and body ground

OK ▽

NG ▷ Repair or replace harness or connector.

Check and replace ABS ECU.

TY4029300068020X

Fig. 136 Ts terminal circuit inspection (Part 2 of 2). Corolla

1 Check voltage between terminals Ts and E1 of DLC1.

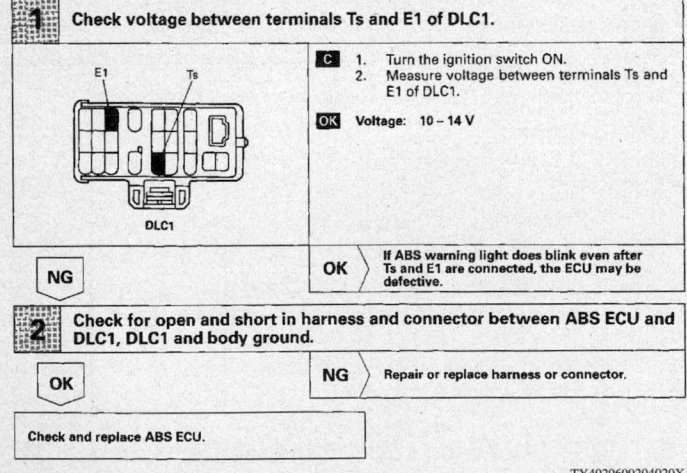

C
(1) Turn ignition switch ON.
(2) Measure voltage between terminals Ts and E1 of the DLC1.

OK Voltage: 10 – 14 V

DLC1

NG ▽

OK ▷ If ABS warning light does not blink even after Ts and E1 are connected, the ECU may be defective.

2 Check for open and short in harness and connector between ABS ECU and DLC1, DLC1 and body ground

OK ▽

NG ▷ Repair or replace harness or connector.

Check and replace ABS ECU.

TY4029600275020X

Fig. 137 Ts terminal circuit inspection (Part 2 of 2). Paseo

INSPECTION PROCEDURE

1 Check voltage between terminals Ts and E1 of DLC1.

C
1. Turn the ignition switch ON.
2. Measure voltage between terminals Ts and E1 of DLC1.

OK Voltage: 10 – 14 V

DLC1

NG ▽

OK ▷ If ABS warning light does blink even after Ts and E1 are connected, the ECU may be defective.

2 Check for open and short in harness and connector between ABS ECU and DLC1, DLC1 and body ground.

OK ▽

NG ▷ Repair or replace harness or connector.

Check and replace ABS ECU.

TY4029600204020X

Fig. 138 Ts terminal circuit inspection (Part 2 of 2). 1996 RAV4

CIRCUIT DESCRIPTION

The sensor check circuit detects abnormalities in the speed sensor signal which cannot be detected with the DTC check.
Connecting terminals Ts and E1 of the DLC1 in the engine compartment starts the check.

WIRING DIAGRAM

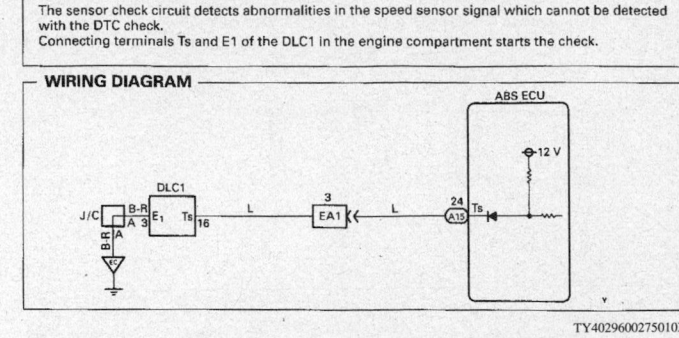

TY4029600275010X

Fig. 137 Ts terminal circuit inspection (Part 1 of 2). Paseo

CIRCUIT DESCRIPTION

The sensor check circuit detects abnormalities in the speed sensor signal which cannot be detected with the DTC check.
Connecting terminals Ts and E1 of the DLC1 in the engine compartment starts the check.

WIRING DIAGRAM

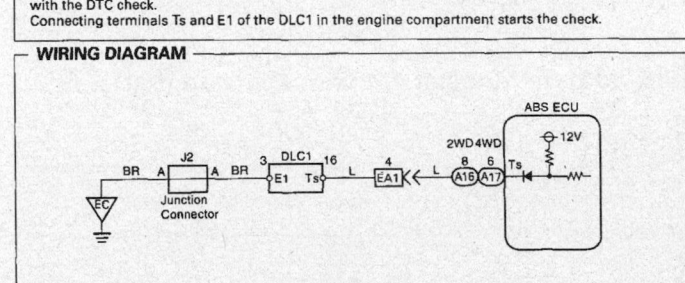

TY4029600204010X

Fig. 138 Ts terminal circuit inspection (Part 1 of 2). 1996 RAV4

CIRCUIT DESCRIPTION

The sensor check circuit detects abnormalities in the speed sensor signal which cannot be detected with the DTC check.
Connecting terminals Ts and E1 of the DLC1 in the engine compartment starts the check.

WIRING DIAGRAM

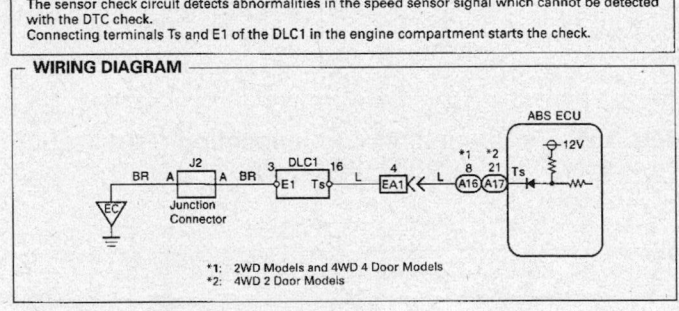

*1: 2WD Models and 4WD 4 Door Models
*2: 4WD 2 Door Models

INSPECTION PROCEDURE

1 Check voltage between terminals Ts and E1 of DLC1.

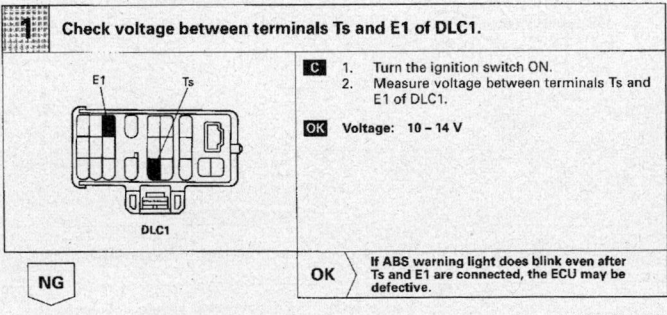

C
1. Turn the ignition switch ON.
2. Measure voltage between terminals Ts and E1 of DLC1.

OK Voltage: 10 – 14 V

DLC1

NG ▽

OK ▷ If ABS warning light does blink even after Ts and E1 are connected, the ECU may be defective.

TY4029700285010X

Fig. 139 Ts terminal circuit inspection (Part 1 of 2). 1997–99 RAV4

ANTI-LOCK BRAKES

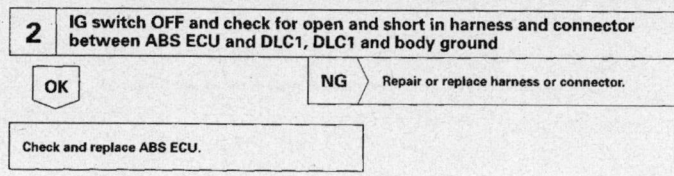

| 2 | IG switch OFF and check for open and short in harness and connector between ABS ECU and DLC1, DLC1 and body ground |

| OK | | NG | Repair or replace harness or connector. |

Check and replace ABS ECU.

TY4029700285020X

Fig. 139   Ts terminal circuit inspection (Part 2 of 2). 1997–99 RAV4

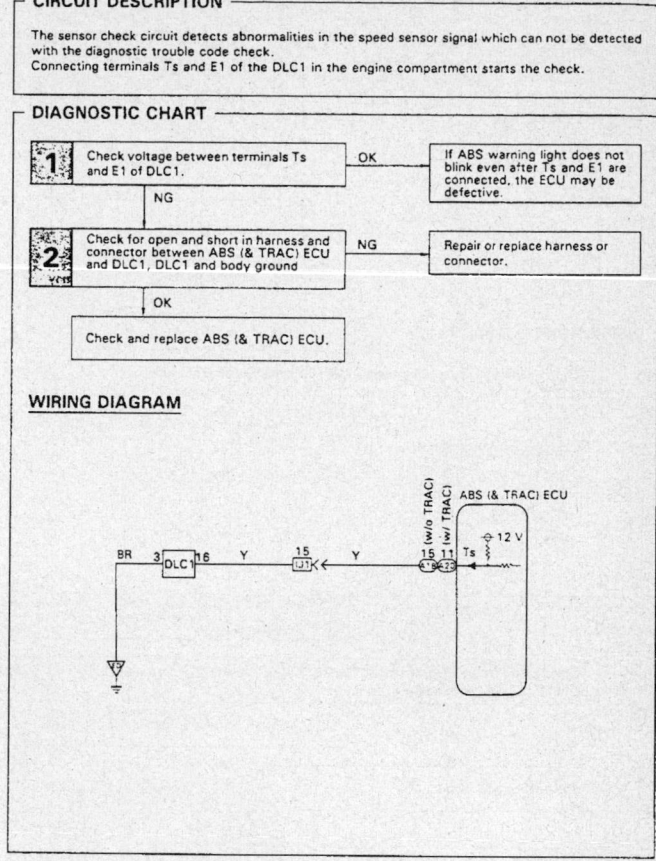

CIRCUIT DESCRIPTION

The sensor check circuit detects abnormalities in the speed sensor signal which can not be detected with the diagnostic trouble code check.
Connecting terminals Ts and E1 of the DLC1 in the engine compartment starts the check.

DIAGNOSTIC CHART

| 1 | Check voltage between terminals Ts and E1 of DLC1. | OK | If ABS warning light does not blink even after Ts and E1 are connected, the ECU may be defective. |

NG

| 2 | Check for open and short in harness and connector between ABS (& TRAC) ECU and DLC1, DLC1 and body ground | NG | Repair or replace harness or connector. |

OK

Check and replace ABS (& TRAC) ECU.

WIRING DIAGRAM

TY4029300069010X

Fig. 140   Ts terminal circuit inspection (Part 1 of 2). 1996 Supra

CIRCUIT DESCRIPTION

The sensor check circuit detects abnormalities in the speed sensor signal which cannot be detected with the DTC check.
Connecting terminals Ts and E1 of the DLC1 in the engine compartment starts the check.

WIRING DIAGRAM

*1:   NORMAL ABS (2JZ-GE Engine)
*2:   SPORT ABS (2JZ-GTE Engine)

TY4029700409000X

Fig. 140   Ts terminal circuit inspection (Part 1 of 2). 1997–99 Supra

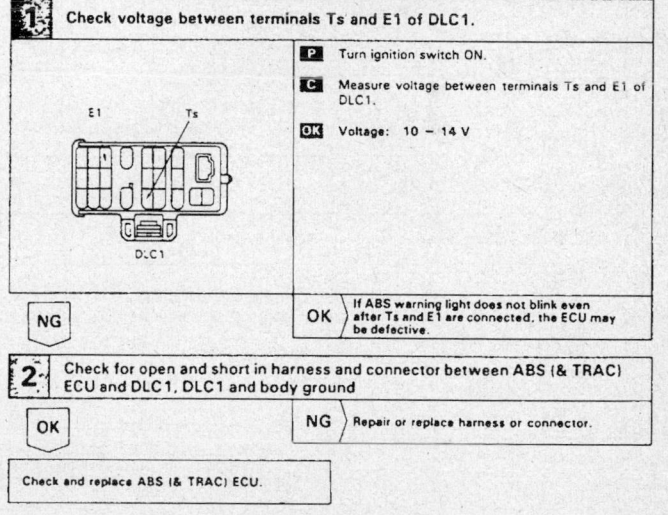

| 1 | Check voltage between terminals Ts and E1 of DLC1. |

P	Turn ignition switch ON.
C	Measure voltage between terminals Ts and E1 of DLC1.
OK	Voltage: 10 – 14 V

| NG | | OK | If ABS warning light does not blink even after Ts and E1 are connected, the ECU may be defective. |

| 2 | Check for open and short in harness and connector between ABS (& TRAC) ECU and DLC1, DLC1 and body ground |

| OK | | NG | Repair or replace harness or connector. |

Check and replace ABS (& TRAC) ECU.

TY4029300069020X

Fig. 140   Ts terminal circuit inspection (Part 2 of 2). Supra

CIRCUIT DESCRIPTION

The sensor check circuit detects abnormalities in the speed sensor signal which cannot be detected with the DTC check.
Connecting terminals Ts and E1 of the DLC1 in the engine compartment starts the check.

WIRING DIAGRAM

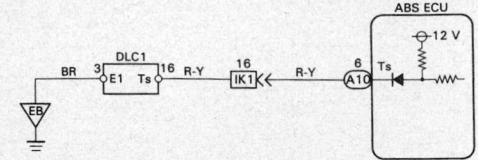

INSPECTION PROCEDURE

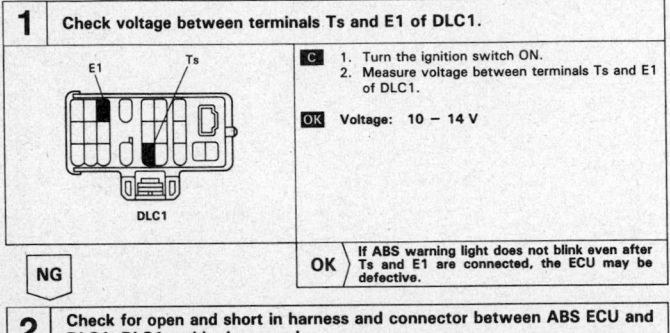

1 Check voltage between terminals Ts and E1 of DLC1.

C
1. Turn the ignition switch ON.
2. Measure voltage between terminals Ts and E1 of DLC1.

OK Voltage: 10 – 14 V

NG

OK If ABS warning light does not blink even after Ts and E1 are connected, the ECU may be defective.

2 Check for open and short in harness and connector between ABS ECU and DLC1, DLC1 and body ground

OK

NG Repair or replace harness or connector.

Check and replace ABS ECU.

TY4029500177000X

Fig. 141 Ts terminal circuit inspection. Tacoma

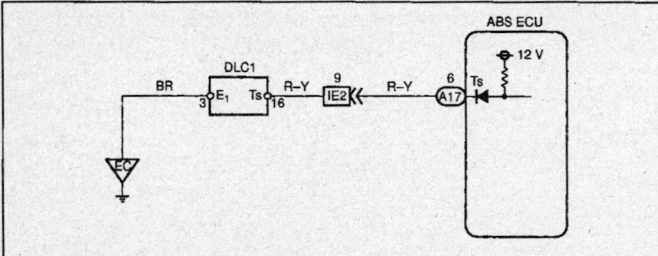

INSPECTION PROCEDURE

1 Check voltage between terminals Ts and E₁ of DLC1.

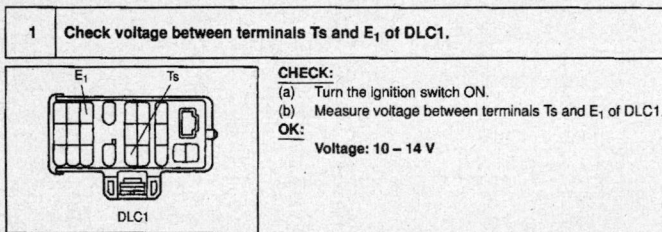

CHECK:
(a) Turn the ignition switch ON.
(b) Measure voltage between terminals Ts and E₁ of DLC1.
OK:
Voltage: 10 – 14 V

OK If ABS warning light does not blink even after Ts and E₁ are connected, the ECU may be defective.

NG

TY4029600228010X

Fig. 143 Ts terminal circuit (Part 1 of 2). 4Runner

CIRCUIT DESCRIPTION

The sensor check circuit detects abnormalities in the speed sensor signal which cannot be detected with the DTC check.
Connecting terminals Ts and E1 of the DLC1 in the engine compartment starts the check.

WIRING DIAGRAM

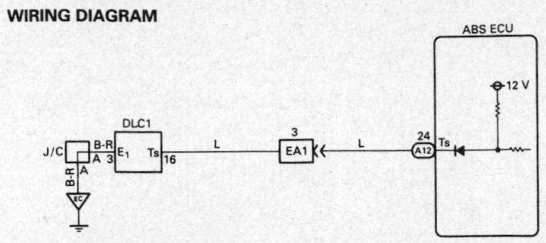

INSPECTION PROCEDURE

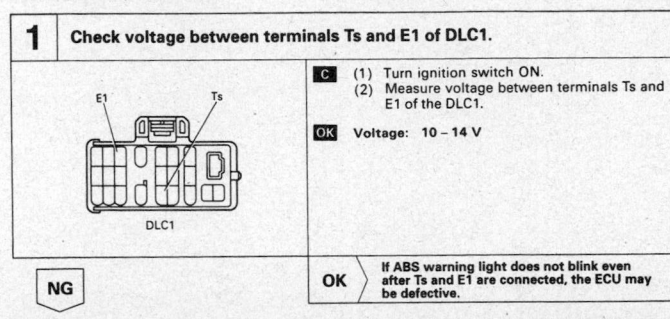

1 Check voltage between terminals Ts and E1 of DLC1.

C
(1) Turn ignition switch ON.
(2) Measure voltage between terminals Ts and E1 of the DLC1.

OK Voltage: 10 – 14 V

NG

OK If ABS warning light does not blink even after Ts and E1 are connected, the ECU may be defective.

2 Check for open and short in harness and connector between ABS ECU and DLC1, DLC1 and body ground

OK

NG Repair or replace harness or connector.

Check and replace ABS ECU.

TY4029500187000X

Fig. 142 Ts terminal circuit inspection. 1996 Tercel

2 Check for open and short in harness and connector between ABS ECU and DLC1, DLC1 and body ground.

NG Repair or replace harness or connector.

OK

Check and replace ABS ECU.

TY4029600228020X

Fig. 143 Ts terminal circuit (Part 2 of 2). 4Runner

CIRCUIT DESCRIPTION

This relay supplies power to each ABS solenoid. After the ignition switch is turned ON, if the initial check is OK, the relay goes on.

DTC No.	DTC Detecting Condition	Trouble Area
11	Detection of any conditions from 1. through 3.: 1. 3 or more solenoid valves are shown faulty in response and simultaneously valve supply voltage is detected faulty. 2. Solenoid valve relay will not be switched OFF. 3. Valve relay is frozen in spite of its high valve relay supply voltage.	• ABS solenoid valve relay • Valve supply voltage • ECU

Fail safe function:
If trouble occurs in the ABS solenoid valve relay circuit, the ECU cuts off current to the ABS solenoid valve relay and prohibits ABS control.

TY4029900559010X

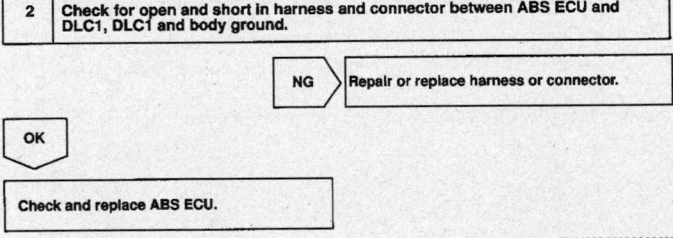

Fig. 144 Code 11: ABS Solenoid Valve Relay Circuit (Part 1 of 2). Camry Solara less traction control

INSPECTION PROCEDURE

1 Check voltage between terminals A5 – 17, 18 and A5 – 16, 19 of ABS actuator connector.

PREPARATION:
Disconnect the ABS actuator connector.
CHECK:
Measure the voltage between terminals A5 – 17, 18 and A5 – 16, 19 of ABS actuator harness side connector.
OK:
Voltage: 10 – 14 V

NG > Check and replace fuses.
Check and repair harness or connector.

OK

If the same code is still output after the DTC is deleted, check the contact condition of each connection. If the connections are normal, the ECU may be defective.

TY4029900559020X

Fig. 144 Code 11: ABS Solenoid Valve Relay Circuit (Part 2 of 2). Camry Solara less traction control

INSPECTION PROCEDURE

1 Check voltage between terminals A5 – 17, 18 and A5 – 16, 19 of ABS actuator connector.

PREPARATION:
Disconnect the ABS actuator connector.
CHECK:
Measure the voltage between terminals A5 – 17, 18 and A5 – 16, 19 of ABS actuator harness side connector.
OK:
Voltage: 10 – 14 V

NG > Check and replace fuses.
Check and repair harness or connector.

OK

If the same code is still output after the DTC is deleted, check the contact condition of each connection. If the connections are normal, the ECU may be defective.

TY4029900560020X

Fig. 145 Code 13: Pump Motor Circuit (Part 2 of 2). Camry Solara less traction control

CIRCUIT DESCRIPTION

The ABS motor relay supplies power to the ABS pump motor. While the ABS is activated, the ECU switches the ABS motor relay ON and operates the ABS pump motor.

DTC No.	DTC Detecting Condition	Trouble Area
13	Detection of any conditions from 1. through 3.: 1. After actuation of the motor relay, pump motor voltage will not be supplied within 0.4 sec. 2. Pump motor voltage is at a high level, motor relay will not actuate for 2.5 sec. or more. 3. Pump motor voltage keeps low level for longer than 0.4 sec. and the pump repeats activating for 7 sec. 3 times maximally since the last activation, the pump motor has been gone dead because of short circuit.	• ABS motor relay • Pump motor voltage • Pump motor lead disconnected • ECU

Fail safe function:
If trouble occurs in the ABS motor relay circuit, the ECU cuts off current to the ABS solenoid relay and prohibits ABS control.

TY4029900560010X

Fig. 145 Code 13: Pump Motor Circuit (Part 1 of 2). Camry Solara less traction control

CIRCUIT DESCRIPTION

This solenoid goes on when signals are received from the ECU and controls the pressure acting on the wheel cylinders thus controlling the braking force.

DTC No.	DTC Detecting Condition	Trouble Area
21, 22, 23, 24	Solenoid valve signal does not match to the check result.	• Each solenoid valve

Fail safe function:
If trouble occurs in the actuator solenoid valve circuit, the ECU cuts off current to the ABS solenoid valve relay and prohibits ABS control.

TY4029900561010X

Fig. 146 Codes 21, 22, 23 & 24: ABS Solenoid Valve Circuit (Part 1 of 2). Camry Solara less traction control

INSPECTION PROCEDURE

1	Check the DTC once more.

PREPARATION:
(a) Clear the DTC .
(b) Turn the ignition switch OFF.
CHECK:
Turn the ignition switch ON, and check if the same DTC is stored in the memory.

NO > No problem.

YES

Replace ABS ECU.

TY4029900561020X

Fig. 146   Codes 21, 22, 23 & 24: ABS Solenoid Valve Circuit (Part 2 of 2). Camry Solara less traction control

INSPECTION PROCEDURE

1	Check speed sensor.

Front:
PREPARATION:
(a)   Remove the front fender liner.
(b)   Disconnect the speed sensor connector.
CHECK:
Measure resistance between terminals 1 and 2 of speed sensor connector.
OK:
Resistance: (1.6 ± 0.2 kΩ at 20°C)
CHECK:
Measure resistance between terminals 1 and 2 of speed sensor connector and body ground.
OK:
Resistance: 1 MΩ or higher

Rear:
PREPARATION:
(a)   Remove the seat cushion and side seat back.
(b)   Disconnect the speed sensor connector.
CHECK:
Measure resistance between terminals 1 and 2 of speed sensor connector.
OK:
Resistance: (1.6 ± 0.1 kΩ at 20°C)
CHECK:
Measure resistance between terminals 1 and 2 of speed sensor connector and body ground.
OK:
Resistance: 1 MΩ or higher

NG > Replace speed sensor.

NOTICE:
Check the speed sensor signal last .

OK

TY4029900562020X

Fig. 147   Codes 31, 32, 33, 34, 35, 36, 38 & 39: Speed Sensor Circuit (Part 2 of 4). Camry Solara less traction control

CIRCUIT DESCRIPTION

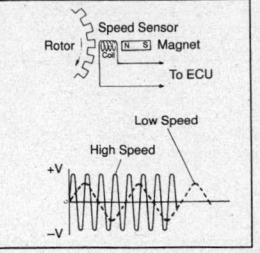

The speed sensor detects wheel speed and sends the appropriate signals to the ECU. These signals are used to control of the ABS system. The front and rear rotors each have 48 serrations.
When the rotors rotate, the magnetic field emitted by the permanent magnet in the speed sensor generates an AC voltage. Since the frequency of this AC voltage changes in direct proportion to the speed of the rotor, the frequency is used by the ECU to detect the speed of each wheel.

DTC No.	DTC Detecting Condition	Trouble Area
31, 32, 33, 34	Detection of any of conditions from 1. through 3.: 1. Vehicle speed is more than 40 km/h (25 mph), pulses are not input for 0.01 sec. 2. After the initial start or restart and when the vehicle speed has reached 12 km/h (7 mph), the wheel with 0 km/h (0 mph) of wheel speed is detected. 3. After the initial start or restart and when the vehicle speed has reached 70 km/h (44 mph), front wheel with 0 km/h (0 mph) of wheel speed is detected.	• Right front, left front, right rear, left rear speed sensor • Each speed sensor circuit • Sensor installation • ECU
35, 36, 38, 39	Detecting abnormality in the resistance value of each speed sensor.	• Right front, left front, right rear, left rear speed sensor • Each speed sensor circuit • ECU

HINT:
• DTC No. 31 and 35 are for the right front speed sensor.
• DTC No. 32 and 36 are for the left front speed sensor.
• DTC No. 33 and 38 are for the right rear speed sensor.
• DTC No. 34 and 39 are for the left rear speed sensor.
Fail safe function:
If trouble occurs in the speed sensor circuit, the ECU cuts off current to the ABS solenoid valve relay and prohibits ABS control.

TY4029900562010X

Fig. 147   Codes 31, 32, 33, 34, 35, 36, 38 & 39: Speed Sensor Circuit (Part 1 of 4). Camry Solara less traction control

2	Check for open and short in harness and connector between each speed sensor and ECU.

NG > Repair or replace harness or connector.

OK

3	Check speed sensor installation.

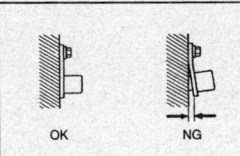

CHECK:
Check the speed sensor installation.
OK:
The installation bolt is tightened properly and there is no clearance between the sensor and steering knuckle or rear axle carrier.

NG > Replace speed sensor.

NOTICE:
Check the speed sensor signal last .

OK

4	Check sensor rotor and sensor tip.

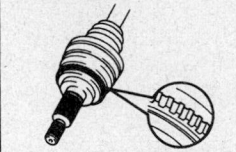

Front:
PREPARATION:
Remove the front drive shaft .
CHECK:
Check the sensor rotor serrations.
OK:
No scratches or missing teeth or foreign objects.
PREPARATION:
Remove the front speed sensor .
CHECK:
Check the sensor tip.
OK:
No scratches or foreign objects on the sensor tip.

TY4029900562030X

Fig. 147   Codes 31, 32, 33, 34, 35, 36, 38 & 39: Speed Sensor Circuit (Part 3 of 4). Camry Solara less traction control

Rear:
PREPARATION:
Remove the axle hub.
CHECK:
Check the sensor rotor serrations.
OK:

   No scratches or missing teeth or foreign objects.
PREPARATION:
Remove the rear speed sensor.
CHECK:
Check the sensor tip.
OK:

   No scratches or foreign objects on the sensor tip.

| NG | Replace sensor rotor or speed sensor. |

NOTICE:
Check the speed sensor signal last .

| OK |

| Check and replace ABS ECU. |

TY4029900562040X

Fig. 147   Codes 31, 32, 33, 34, 35, 36, 38 & 39: Speed Sensor Circuit (Part 4 of 4). Camry Solara less traction control

CIRCUIT DESCRIPTION

DTC No.	DTC Detecting Condition	Trouble Area
37	Detection of any of conditions from 1. through 3.: 1. Occurrence of differential to some degree in the wheel speed between the front and rear wheels of either left or right side of the vehicle and the front left and right wheels. (Detection of differential in mini tire size, spinning wheel and decelerating wheel.) 2. Continuous ABS control for 60 sec. or more. 3. Interference on 1 or more wheels for 20 sec. with the brake pedal depressed, or for 5 sec. when the brake pedal is not depressed.	• Speed sensor • Sensor rotor • ECU

INSPECTION PROCEDURE

| 1 | Check sensor rotor . |

| NG | Replace sensor rotor. |

| OK |

| 2 | Check speed sensor . |

| NG | Replace speed sensor. |

| OK |

| 3 | Check for open or short in harness and connector between speed sensor and ECU . |

| NG | Repair or replace harness and connector. |

| OK |

| Check and replace ABS ECU. |

TY4029900563000X

Fig. 148   Code 37: Speed Sensor Rotor Faulty. Camry Solara less traction control

CIRCUIT DESCRIPTION

This is the power source for the ECU, hence the actuator.

DTC No.	DTC Detecting Condition	Trouble Area
41	Vehicle speed at about 6 km/h (4 mph), low battery voltage is less than 9.4 V at the time of non–operation of ABS control or less than 8.8 V at the time of operation of ABS control, and high battery voltage is more than 17.4 V.	• Battery • Charging system • Power source circuit • ECU

Fail safe function:
If trouble occurs in the power source circuit, the ECU cuts off current to the ABS solenoid valve relay and prohibits ABS control.

TY4029900564010X

Fig. 149   Code 41: Power Source Circuit (Part 1 of 3). Camry Solara less traction control

INSPECTION PROCEDURE

| 1 | Check ECU–IG fuse. |

PREPARATION:
Remove ECU–IG fuse from Instrument Panel J/B.
CHECK:
Check continuity of ECU–IG fuse.
OK:

   Continuity

| NG | Check for short circuit in all the harness and components connected to ECU–IG fuse |

| OK |

| 2 | Check battery positive voltage. |

OK:

   Voltage: 10 – 14 V

| NG | Check and repair the charging system. |

| OK |

TY4029900564020X

Fig. 149   Code 41: Power Source Circuit (Part 2 of 3). Camry Solara less traction control

3	Check voltage between terminals IG1 and GND of ABS actuator connector.

PREPARATION:
Disconnect ABS actuator connector.
CHECK:
(a) Turn the ignition switch ON.
(b) Measure voltage between terminals IG1 and GND of ABS actuator harness side connector.
OK:
  Voltage: 10 – 14 V

OK > Check and replace ABS ECU.

NG

4	Check continuity between terminals GND of ABS actuator connector and body ground.

CHECK:
Measure resistance between terminal GND of ABS actuator harness side connector and body ground.
OK:
  Resistance: 1 Ω or less

NG > Repair or replace harness or connector.

OK

Check for open circuit in harness and connector between terminals IG1 of ABS & TRAC ECU and ECU–IG fuse.

TY4029900564030X

Fig. 149   Code 41: Power Source Circuit (Part 3 of 3). Camry Solara less traction control

---

CIRCUIT DESCRIPTION

DTC No.	DTC Detecting Condition	Trouble Area
58	Stop light switch circuit is open, and stop light switch voltage is in the level between 65 % or more and less than 93 % of the battery voltage.	• Stop light switch • Stop light switch circuit • ECU

TY4029900565010X

Fig. 150   Code 58: Stop Lamp Switch Circuit (Part 1 of 2). Camry less traction control

INSPECTION PROCEDURE

1	Check operation of stop light.

CHECK:
Check that stop light lights up when brake pedal is depressed and turns off when brake pedal is released.

NG > Repair stop light circuit.

OK

2	Check voltage between terminal STP of ABS actuator and body ground.

PREPARATION:
Disconnect ABS actuator connector.
CHECK:
Measure voltage between terminal STP of ABS actuator harness side connector and body ground when brake pedal is depressed.
OK:
  Voltage: 8 – 14 V

OK > Check and replace ABS ECU.

NG

3	Check for open circuit in harness and connector between ABS ECU and stop light switch.

NG > Repair or replace harness or connector.

OK

Proceed to next circuit inspection shown on problem symptoms table.

TY4029900565020X

Fig. 150   Code 58: Stop Lamp Switch Circuit (Part 2 of 2). Camry less traction control

ANTI-LOCK BRAKES

CIRCUIT DESCRIPTION

DTC No.	DTC Detecting Condition	Trouble Area
62	ABS ECU continuously detects the proper operation of ABS.	• Battery • ECU

Fail safe function:
If trouble occurs in the power source circuit, the ECU cuts off current to the ABS solenoid valve relay and prohibits ABS control.

INSPECTION PROCEDURE

1	Is DTC output?

Check DTC.

YES ▷ Repair circuit indicated by the code output.

NO

2	Is normal code displayed?

YES ▷ Check for short circuit in harness and connector between DLC1 or DLC2 and ABS ECU.

NO

3	Does ABS warning light go off?

YES ▷ Check open and short circuit of the harness and connector in the Tc circuit between ECU and DLC2 or DLC1.

NO

TY4029900566010X

Fig. 151   Code 62: ABS ECU Fault (Part 1 of 2). Camry Solara less traction control

4	Check voltage between terminals IG1 and GND of ABS actuator connector.

PREPARATION:
Disconnect ABS actuator connector.
CHECK:
(a) Turn the ignition switch ON.
(b) Measure voltage between terminals IG1 and GND of ABS actuator harness side connector.
OK:
Voltage: 10 – 14 V

NG ▷ Check for open or short circuit in harness and connector between ECU–IG fuse and ABS actuator.

OK

5	Check connection of ABS actuator connector.

NG ▷ Repair or replace harness or connector.

OK

6	Check the ABS warning light goes off.

NG ▷ Check and replace ABS ECU.

OK

Repair or replace harness or connector.

TY4029900566020X

Fig. 151   Code 62: ABS ECU Fault (Part 2 of 2). Camry Solara less traction control

CIRCUIT DESCRIPTION

This relay supplies power to each ABS & TRAC solenoid. After the ignition switch is turned ON, if the initial check is OK, the relay goes on.

DTC No.	DTC Detecting Condition	Trouble Area
11	Condition 1. to 3. are detected: 1. Malfunction of solenoid relay monitor. 2. Battery voltage will not exceed more than 17.0 V within 2.16 sec. 3. Battery voltage will not become less than 9.5 V within 2.16 sec., or after the solenoid relay is ON and AST voltage of ECU terminal does not become 8.0 V or more.	• ABS & TRAC solenoid relay • ABS & TRAC solenoid relay circuit • ECU
12	Solenoid relay is OFF in the midst of premain routine, and AST voltage of ECU terminal is 8.0 V or more, which continues for 2.04 sec. or more.	

Fail safe function:
If any trouble occurs in the ABS & TRAC solenoid relay circuit, the ECU cuts off current to the ABS & TRAC solenoid relay and prohibits ABS control and TRAC control.

TY4029900570010X

Fig. 152   Codes 11 & 12: ABS & TRAC Solenoid Relay Circuit (Part 1 of 3). Camry Solara w/traction control

ANTI-LOCK BRAKES

INSPECTION PROCEDURE

1 Check voltage between terminals 1 and 2 of Engine Room R/B No. 3 (for ABS & TRAC solenoid relay).

PREPARATION:
Remove ABS & TRAC solenoid relay from Engine Room R/B No. 3.
CHECK:
Measure the voltage between terminals 1 and 2 of Engine Room R/B No. 3 (for ABS & TRAC solenoid relay).
OK:
Voltage: 10 – 14 V

NG ▷ Check and repair harness or connector.

OK

2 Check continuity between terminal 3 of ABS & TRAC solenoid relay and terminal AST of ABS & TRAC ECU.

CHECK:
Check continuity between terminal 3 of Engine Room R/B No. 3 (for ABS & TRAC solenoid relay) and terminal AST of ABS & TRAC ECU.
OK:
Continuity
HINT:
There is a resistance of 4 – 6 Ω between terminals A7 – 4 and A7 – 5 of ABS actuator.

NG ▷ Repair or replace harness or ABS & TRAC actuator.

OK

TY4029900570020X

Fig. 152   Codes 11 & 12: ABS & TRAC Solenoid Relay Circuit (Part 2 of 3). Camry Solara w/traction control

3 Check ABS & TRAC solenoid relay.

CHECK:
Check continuity between each terminal of ABS & TRAC solenoid relay.
OK:

Terminals 4 and 6	Continuity (Reference value 80 Ω)
Terminals 2 and 3	Continuity
Terminals 1 and 3	Open

CHECK:
(a) Apply battery positive voltage between terminals 4 and 6.
(b) Check continuity between each terminal of ABS & TRAC solenoid relay.
OK:

Terminals 2 and 3	Open
Terminals 1 and 3	Continuity

NG ▷ Replace ABS & TRAC solenoid relay.

OK

4 Check for open and short circuit in harness and connector between ABS & TRAC solenoid relay and ABS & TRAC ECU.

NG ▷ Repair or replace harness or connector.

OK

If the same code is still output after the DTC is deleted, check the contact condition of each connection. If the connections are normal, the ECU may be defective.

TY4029900570030X

Fig. 152   Codes 11 & 12: ABS & TRAC Solenoid Relay Circuit (Part 3 of 3). Camry Solara w/traction control

CIRCUIT DESCRIPTION

The ABS & TRAC motor relay supplies power to the ABS & TRAC pump motor. While the ABS is activated, the ECU switches the ABS & TRAC motor relay ON and operates the ABS & TRAC pump motor.

DTC No.	DTC Detecting Condition	Trouble Area
13	Conditions 1. to 3. are detected: 1. Malfunction of motor relay monitor. 2. Battery voltage will not exceed more than 17.0 V within 2.16 sec. 3. Battery voltage will not become less than 9.5 V within 2.16 sec., or after the motor relay is ON and motor relay monitor does not ON.	• ABS & TRAC motor relay • ABS & TRAC motor relay circuit • ECU
14	Motor relay is OFF, and motor relay monitor is ON , which continues for 20.16 sec. or more.	

Fail safe function:
If any trouble occurs in the ABS & TRAC motor relay circuit, the ECU cuts off current to the ABS & TRAC solenoid relay and prohibits ABS control and TRAC control.

TY4029900571010X

Fig. 153   Codes 13 & 14: ABS & TRAC Motor Relay Circuit (Part 1 of 3). Camry Solara w/traction control

INSPECTION PROCEDURE

| 1 | Check voltage between terminal 1 of Engine Room R/B No. 3 (for ABS & TRAC motor relay) and body ground. |

PREPARATION:
Remove ABS & TRAC motor relay from Engine Room R/B No. 3.
CHECK:
Measure voltage between terminal 1 of Engine Room R/B No. 3 (for ABS & TRAC motor relay) and body ground.
OK:
Voltage: 10 – 14 V

| NG > | Check and repair harness or connector. |

OK

| 2 | Check continuity between terminal 2 of ABS & TRAC motor relay and terminal MT of ABS & TRAC ECU. |

CHECK:
Check continuity between terminal 2 of Engine Room R/B No. 3 (for ABS & TRAC motor relay) and terminal MT of ABS & TRAC ECU.
OK:
Continuity
HINT:
There is a resistance of 4 – 6 Ω between terminals A7 – 2 and A7 – 3 of ABS & TRAC actuator.

| NG > | Repair or replace harness or ABS & TRAC actuator. |

OK

TY4029900571020X

Fig. 153 Codes 13 & 14: ABS & TRAC Motor Relay Circuit (Part 2 of 3). Camry Solara w/traction control

| 3 | Check ABS & TRAC motor relay. |

CHECK:
Check continuity between each terminal of ABS & TRAC motor relay.
OK:

Terminals 3 and 4	Continuity (Reference value 62 Ω)
Terminals 1 and 2	Open

CHECK:
(a) Apply battery positive voltage between terminals 3 and 4.
(b) Check continuity between terminals of ABS & TRAC motor relay.
OK:

Terminals 1 and 2	Continuity

| NG > | Replace ABS & TRAC motor relay. |

OK

| 4 | Check for open and short circuit in harness and connector between ABS & TRAC motor relay and ABS & TRAC ECU. |

| NG > | Repair or replace harness or connector. |

OK

If the same code is still output after the DTC is deleted, check the contact condition of each connection. If the connections are normal, the ECU may be defective.

TY4029900571030X

Fig. 153 Codes 13 & 14: ABS & TRAC Motor Relay Circuit (Part 3 of 3). Camry Solara w/traction control

CIRCUIT DESCRIPTION

This solenoid goes on when signals are received from the ECU and controls the pressure acting on the wheel cylinders thus controlling the braking force.

DTC No.	DTC Detecting Condition	Trouble Area
21		• ABS actuator • SFRR or SFRH circuit • ECU
22		• ABS actuator • SFLR or SFLH circuit • ECU
23	Conditions 1. and 2. or 3. continue for 0.48 sec. or more: 1. Recovery prohibit run pulse is not output, solenoid relay is ON, AST voltage of ECU terminal is 8.0 V or more, and solenoid output has no change between the last time and this time. 2. Solenoid output is ON, pressure holding solenoid monitor voltage is more than 1.0 V or pressure reduction solenoid monitor voltage is more than 1.5 V. 3. Solenoid output is OFF, solenoid monitor voltage is more than –1.0 V AST voltage of ECU.	• ABS actuator • SRRH or SRRH circuit • ECU
24		• ABS actuator • SRLR or SRLH circuit • ECU
25		• ABS actuator • SMC1 circuit • ECU
26		• ABS actuator • SMC2 circuit • ECU
27		• ABS actuator • SRC1 circuit • ECU
28		• ABS actuator • SRC2 circuit • ECU

Fail safe function:
If any trouble occurs in the actuator solenoid circuit, the ECU cuts off current to the ABS & TRAC solenoid relay and prohibits ABS control and TRAC control.

TY4029900572010X

Fig. 154 Codes 21, 22, 23, 24, 25, 26, 27 & 28: ABS & TRAC Actuator Solenoid Circuit (Part 1 of 3). Camry Solara w/traction control

INSPECTION PROCEDURE

| 1 | Check ABS & TRAC actuator solenoid. |

PREPARATION:
Disconnect the 2 connectors from ABS & TRAC actuator.
CHECK:
Check continuity between terminals A7 – 4 and A6 – 1, 2, 3, 4, 5, 6, 7, 8, 9, 10, 11, 12 of ABS & TRAC actuator connector.
OK:
Continuity
HINT:
Resistance of each solenoid coil is 1.2 Ω.

| NG > | Replace ABS & TRAC actuator. |

OK

TY4029900572020X

Fig. 154 Codes 21, 22, 23, 24, 25, 26, 27 & 28: ABS & TRAC Actuator Solenoid Circuit (Part 2 of 3). Camry Solara w/traction control

2	Check for open and short circuit in harness and connector between ABS & TRAC ECU and actuator.

NG ⟩ Repair or replace harness or connector.

OK

If the same code is still output after the DTC is deleted, check the contact condition of each connection. If the connections are normal, the ECU may be defective.

TY4029900572030X

Fig. 154 Codes 21, 22, 23, 24, 25, 26, 27 & 28: ABS & TRAC Actuator Solenoid Circuit (Part 3 of 3). Camry Solara w/traction control

CIRCUIT DESCRIPTION

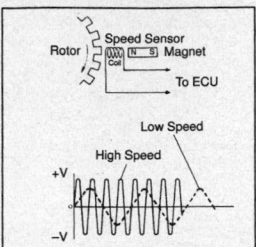

The speed sensor detects wheel speed and sends the appropriate signals to the ECU. These signals are used to control of the ABS and TRAC system. The front and rear rotors each have 48 serrations.
When the rotors rotate, the magnetic field emitted by the permanent magnet in the speed sensor generates an AC voltage. Since the frequency of this AC voltage changes in direct proportion to the speed of the rotor, the frequency is used by the ECU to detect the speed of each wheel.

DTC No.	DTC Detecting Condition	Trouble Area
31, 32, 33, 34	Detection of any of conditions from 1. through 3.: 1. ABS is in non–operation, wheel speed is 10 km/h or more, one eighth of maximum wheel speed is greater than the minimum wheel speed, one eighth of maximum wheel speed is smaller than the rear maximum wheel speed or momentary interruption of both the rear wheels are shown in the 15 sec. or more continuously. 2. ABS is in non–operation, momentary interruption of speed sensor occurs 7 times or more in the mean time of switching the ignition switch ON and OFF or vehicle speed is 20 km/h (12 mph) or more and the condition of noise interference or non–noise interference occurs 75 times or more within 5 sec.. 3. Vehicle is at a stop, malfunction signal of vehicle speed sensor hardware open circuit is ON for 1.02 sec. continuously since starting the checking of a certain vehicle.	• Right front, left front, right rear, left rear speed sensor • Each speed sensor circuit • Speed sensor rotor • ECU

HINT:
- DTC No. 31 is for the right front speed sensor.
- DTC No. 32 is for the left front speed sensor.
- DTC No. 33 is for the right rear speed sensor.
- DTC No. 34 is for the left rear speed sensor.

Fail safe function:
If any trouble occurs in the speed sensor circuit, the ECU cuts off current to the ABS & TRAC solenoid relay and prohibits ABS control and TRAC control.

TY4029900573010X

Fig. 155 Codes 31, 32, 33 & 34: Speed Sensor Circuit (Part 1 of 4). Camry Solara w/traction control

INSPECTION PROCEDURE

1	Check speed sensor.

Front:
PREPARATION:
(a) Remove the front fender liner.
(b) Disconnect the speed sensor connector.
CHECK:
Measure resistance between terminals 1 and 2 of speed sensor connector.
OK:
Resistance: (1.6 ± 0.2 kΩ at 20°C)
CHECK:
Measure resistance between terminals 1 and 2 of speed sensor connector and body ground.
OK:
Resistance: 1 MΩ or higher

Rear:
PREPARATION:
(a) Remove the seat cushion and side seat back.
(b) Disconnect the speed sensor connector.
CHECK:
Measure resistance between terminals 1 and 2 of speed sensor connector.
OK:
Resistance: (1.6 ± 0.1 kΩ at 20°C)
CHECK:
Measure resistance between terminals 1 and 2 of speed sensor connector and body ground.
OK:
Resistance: 1 MΩ or higher

NG ⟩ Replace speed sensor.

NOTICE:
Check the speed sensor signal last.

OK

TY4029900573020X

Fig. 155 Codes 31, 32, 33 & 34: Speed Sensor Circuit (Part 2 of 4). Camry Solara w/traction control

2 | Check for open and short circuit in harness and connector between each speed sensor and ECU.

NG ▷ Repair or replace harness or connector.

OK

3 | Check sensor installation.

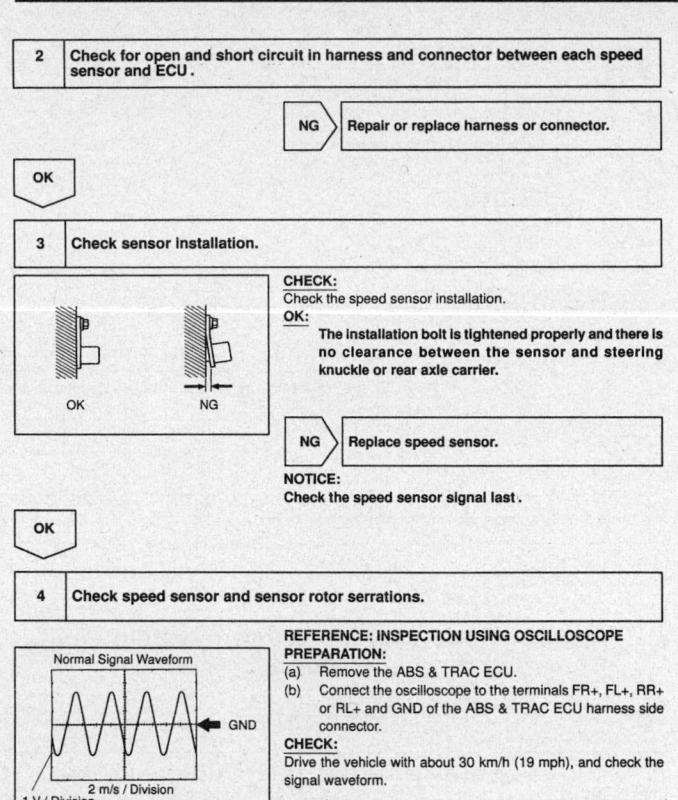

CHECK:
Check the speed sensor installation.
OK:
The installation bolt is tightened properly and there is no clearance between the sensor and steering knuckle or rear axle carrier.

NG ▷ Replace speed sensor.

NOTICE:
Check the speed sensor signal last.

OK

4 | Check speed sensor and sensor rotor serrations.

REFERENCE: INSPECTION USING OSCILLOSCOPE
PREPARATION:
(a) Remove the ABS & TRAC ECU.
(b) Connect the oscilloscope to the terminals FR+, FL+, RR+ or RL+ and GND of the ABS & TRAC ECU harness side connector.
CHECK:
Drive the vehicle with about 30 km/h (19 mph), and check the signal waveform.

OK ▷ Check and replace ABS & TRAC ECU.

NG

TY4029900573030X

Fig. 155   Codes 31, 32, 33 & 34: Speed Sensor Circuit (Part 3 of 4). Camry Solara w/traction control

CIRCUIT DESCRIPTION

This is the power source for the ECU, hence the actuators.

DTC No.	DTC Detecting Condition	Trouble Area
41	Detection of any conditions from 1. through 3.: 1. Vehicle speed is 3 km/h (1.9 mph) or more and battery voltage is less than 9.5 V continues for 10 sec. or more. 2. Battery voltage has never exceeded more than 17.0 V and has become less than 9.5 V within 2.16 sec., under malfunction of solenoid relay monitor after the solenoid relay is ON, at ECU AST terminal voltage of ECU has become 8.0 V or more or under malfunction of motor relay monitor and after the motor relay is ON, motor relay monitor has become ON. 3. Battery voltage is more than 17.0 V, which continues for 1.2 sec. or more or battery voltage has become more than 17.0 V within 2.16 sec. and solenoid or motor relay monitor is under malfunction condition.	• Battery • Charging system • Power source circuit • ECU

Fail safe function:
If any trouble occurs in the power source circuit, the ECU cuts off current to the ABS & TRAC solenoid relay and prohibits ABS control and TRAC control.

TY4029900574010X

Fig. 156   Code 41: IG Power Source Circuit (Part 1 of 3). Camry Solara w/traction control

5 | Check sensor rotor and sensor tip.

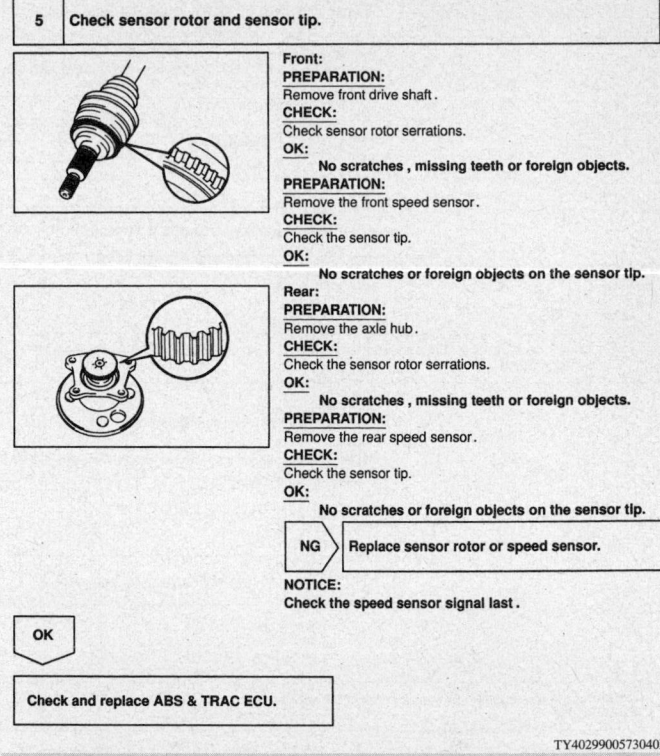

Front:
PREPARATION:
Remove front drive shaft.
CHECK:
Check sensor rotor serrations.
OK:
No scratches , missing teeth or foreign objects.
PREPARATION:
Remove the front speed sensor.
CHECK:
Check the sensor tip.
OK:
No scratches or foreign objects on the sensor tip.
Rear:
PREPARATION:
Remove the axle hub.
CHECK:
Check the sensor rotor serrations.
OK:
No scratches , missing teeth or foreign objects.
PREPARATION:
Remove the rear speed sensor.
CHECK:
Check the sensor tip.
OK:
No scratches or foreign objects on the sensor tip.

NG ▷ Replace sensor rotor or speed sensor.

NOTICE:
Check the speed sensor signal last.

OK

Check and replace ABS & TRAC ECU.

TY4029900573040X

Fig. 155   Codes 31, 32, 33 & 34: Speed Sensor Circuit (Part 4 of 4). Camry Solara w/traction control

INSPECTION PROCEDURE

1 | Check ECU–IG fuse.

PREPARATION:
Remove ECU–IG fuse from Instrument Panel J/B.
CHECK:
Check continuity of ECU–IG fuse.
OK:
Continuity

NG ▷ Check for short circuit in all the harness and components connected to ECU–IG fuse.

OK

2 | Check battery positive voltage.

OK:
Voltage: 10 – 14 V

NG ▷ Check and repair the charging system.

OK

TY4029900574020X

Fig. 156   Code 41: IG Power Source Circuit (Part 2 of 3). Camry Solara w/traction control

3	Check voltage between terminals IG1 and GND of ABS & TRAC ECU connector.

PREPARATION:
Remove ABS & TRAC ECU with connectors still connected.
CHECK:
(a) Turn the ignition switch ON.
(b) Measure voltage between terminals IG1 and GND of ABS & TRAC ECU connector.
OK:

Voltage: 10 – 14 V

OK ⟩ Check and replace ABS & TRAC ECU.

NG

4	Check continuity between terminals GND of ABS & TRAC ECU connector and body ground.

PREPARATION:
Disconnect the connector from the ABS & TRAC ECU.
CHECK:
Measure resistance between terminal GND of ABS & TRAC ECU connector and body ground.
OK:

Resistance: 1 Ω or less

NG ⟩ Repair or replace harness or connector.

OK

Check for open circuit in harness and connector between terminals IG1 of ABS & TRAC ECU and ECU–IG fuse.

TY4029900574030X

Fig. 156   Code 41: IG Power Source Circuit (Part 3 of 3). Camry Solara w/traction control

CIRCUIT DESCRIPTION

The ABS & TRAC ECU receives engine speed signals (NE signals) from the ECM.

DTC No.	DTC Detecting Condition	Trouble Area
44	Condition 1. or 2. is detected: 1. TRAC is in operation and engine speed is 0 rpm continues for 2.4 sec. or more. 2. TRAC is in non-operation, sift lever is not in P or N position, both the front right and left wheels' speed is 30 km/h (19 mph) or more, engine speed is 0 rpm and does not have communication malfunction, and malfunction information of engine system is OFF.	• NEO circuit • ECM • ECU

INSPECTION PROCEDURE

1	Check for open and short circuit in harness and connector between terminal NEO of ABS & TRAC ECU and terminal NEO of ECM.

NG ⟩ Repair or replace harness or connector.

OK

TY4029900576010X

Fig. 158   Code 44: NE Signal Circuit (Part 1 of 2). Camry Solara w/traction control

CIRCUIT DESCRIPTION

DTC No.	DTC Detecting Condition	Trouble Area
43	Detection of any conditions from 1. through 8.: 1. During TRAC is in non-operation and DTC of ABS is output, but TRAC is not during initial lamp checking, terminal WA of ECU is ON and engine speed is 500 rpm or more , which continues for 1 sec. or more. 2. Solenoid relay circuit is open or short. 3. Motor relay circuit is open or short. 4. ABS solenoid circuit is open or short. 5. TRAC solenoid circuit is open or short. 6. Speed sensor is under malfunction condition. 7. IG power source is down or raised. 8. Pump motor is locked.	• ABS control system

INSPECTION PROCEDURE

1	Check the DTC for the ABS.

*1 ⟩ Repair ABS control system according to the code output.

*2

Check for ECU connected to malfunction indicator lamp.

*1: Output NG code
*2: Malfunction indicator lamp remains ON.

TY4029900575000X

Fig. 157   Code 43: ABS Control System Fault. Camry Solara w/traction control

2	Check voltage between terminal NEO of ABS & TRAC ECU and body ground.

PREPARATION:
(a) Remove ABS & TRAC ECU with connectors still connected.
(b) Turn the ignition switch ON.
CHECK:
Measure voltage between terminal NEO of ABS & TRAC ECU and body ground for the engine conditions below.
OK:

Engine condition	Voltage
OFF (IG ON)	3 – 6 V or below 1 V
ON (Idling)	2 – 3 V (Pulse)

(Reference)

3 – 6 V

Below 1 V

3 ms. 3 ms.

NG ⟩ Check and replace ABS & TRAC ECU or ECM.

OK

If the same code is still output after the DTC is deleted, check the contact condition of each connection.

TY4029900576020X

Fig. 158   Code 44: NE Signal Circuit (Part 2 of 2). Camry Solara w/traction control

CIRCUIT DESCRIPTION

DTC No.	DTC Detecting Condition	Trouble Area
49	Battery voltage has never exceeded more than 17.0 V and become less than 9.5 V within 2.16 sec. and the STP terminal voltage of ECU is under open circuit detecting limits continues for 3 sec. or more.	• Stop light switch • Stop light switch circuit • ECU

TY4029900577010X

Fig. 159   Code 49: Stop Lamp Switch Circuit (Part 1 of 2). Camry Solara w/traction control

ANTI-LOCK BRAKES

INSPECTION PROCEDURE

1	Check operation of stop light.

CHECK:
Check that stop light lights up when brake pedal is depressed and turns off when brake pedal is released.

NG ▷ Repair stop light circuit.

OK ▽

2	Check voltage between terminal STP of ABS & TRAC ECU and body ground.

PREPARATION:
Remove ABS & TRAC ECU with connectors still connected.
CHECK:
Measure voltage between terminal STP of ABS & TRAC ECU and body ground when brake pedal is depressed.
OK:
Voltage: 8 – 14 V

OK ▷ Check and replace ABS & TRAC ECU.

NG ▽

3	Check for open circuit in harness and connector between ABS & TRAC ECU and stop light switch.

NG ▷ Repair or replace harness or connector.

OK ▽

Proceed to next circuit inspection shown on problem symptoms table.

TY4029900577020X

Fig. 159   Code 49: Stop Lamp Switch Circuit (Part 2 of 2). Camry Solara w/traction control

1	Check operation of ABS & TRAC pump motor.

PREPARATION:
Disconnect the ABS & TRAC actuator connector.
CHECK:
Connect positive ⊕ lead to terminal A7 – 2 and negative ⊖ lead to terminal A7 – 1 of the ABS & TRAC actuator connector, check that the pump motor is operates.
OK:
The running sound of the pump motor should be heard.

OK ▷ Check for open circuit in harness and connector between ABS & TRAC motor relay, ABS & TRAC actuator and ECU.

NG ▽

Replace ABS & TRAC actuator.

TY4029900578020X

Fig. 160   Code 51: ABS Pump Motor Lock (Part 2 of 2). Camry Solara w/traction control

CIRCUIT DESCRIPTION

DTC No.	DTC Detecting Condition	Trouble Area
51	In the midst of initial check, after the current flows to the motor for 3 sec. and motor relay is turned OFF, then within 0.66 sec., the condition that the motor relay monitor is OFF continues for 0.24 sec. or more.	• ABS pump motor

Fail safe function:
If any trouble occurs in the ABS & TRAC pump motor, the ECU cuts off current to the ABS & TRAC solenoid relay and prohibits ABS control and TRAC control.

TY4029900578010X

Fig. 160   Code 51: ABS Pump Motor Lock (Part 1 of 2). Camry Solara w/traction control

CIRCUIT DESCRIPTION

This circuit is used to send TRAC control information from the ABS & TRAC ECU to the ECM (TRC+, TRC–), and engine control information from the ECM to the ABS & TRAC ECU (EFI+, EFI–).

DTC No.	DTC Detecting Condition	Trouble Area
53	ECM communication data malfunction is detected.	• TRC+ or TRC– circuit • EFI+ or EFI– circuit • ECM • ECU

INSPECTION PROCEDURE

1	Check for open and short circuit in harness and connector between terminals EFI+, EFI–, TRC+, TRC– of ABS & TRAC ECU and ECM (See page IN–31).

NG ▷ Repair or replace harness or connector.

OK ▽

Check and replace ECM or ABS & TRAC ECU.

TY4029900579000X

Fig. 161   Code 53: ECM Communication Fault. Camry Solara w/traction control

CIRCUIT DESCRIPTION

If any trouble occurs in the engine control system, the ECU prohibits TRAC control.

DTC No.	DTC Detection Condition	Trouble Area
61	Conditions 1. and 2. are detected: 1. ECM communication is normal, malfunction information of engine system is ON, and engine speed is 500 rpm or more, which continues for 0.48 sec. or more, and TRAC operation start condition is concluded. 2. ECM communication is normal, malfunction information of engine system is ON, engine speed is 500 rpm and more which continues for 1 sec. or more, and the engine system memorizes DTC.	• Engine control system

INSPECTION PROCEDURE

1	Check the DTC for the engine.

*1 ▷ Repair engine control system according to the code output.

*2 ▽

Check for ECU connected to malfunction indicator light.

*1: Output NG code
*2: Malfunction indicator light remains ON.

TY4029900580000X

Fig. 162   Code 61: Engine Control System Fault. Camry Solara w/traction control

CIRCUIT DESCRIPTION

DTC No.	DTC Detecting Condition	Trouble Area
Always ON	ABS & TRAC ECU internal malfunction is detected.	• ECU

Fail safe function:
If any trouble occurs in the power source circuit, the ECU cuts off current to the ABS & TRAC solenoid relay and prohibits ABS control and TRAC control.

INSPECTION PROCEDURE

1	Is DTC output?

Check DTC.

YES	Repair circuit indicated by the code output.

NO

2	Is normal code displayed?

YES	Check ABS & TRAC solenoid relay. Check for short circuit in harness and connector between solenoid relay and DLC1.

NO

3	Does ABS warning light go off?

YES	Check for open or short circuit in harness and connector between ECU–IG fuse and ABS & TRAC ECU.

NO

TY4029900581010X

**Fig. 163   ABS Lamp Always On (Part 1 of 2).
Camry Solara w/traction control**

CIRCUIT DESCRIPTION

This is the TRAC control main switch. When the TRAC cut switch is pushed on, TRAC control goes off and the TRAC OFF indicator lights up. This indicator blinks for warnings when the trouble occurs and for displaying DTC.

INSPECTION PROCEDURE

1	Check the DTC.

Check DTC.

YES	Repair circuit indicated by the code output.

NO

TY4029900583010X

**Fig. 164   TRAC OFF Indicator, TRAC Cut Switch
Circuit (Part 1 of 3). Camry Solara w/traction
control**

4	Check battery positive voltage.

CHECK:
Check the battery positive voltage.
OK:
10 – 14 V

NG	Check and repair the charging system.

OK

5	Check ABS warning light.

PREPARATION:
(a) Turn the ignition switch OFF.
(b) Disconnect the connector from the ABS & TRAC ECU.
(c) Turn the ignition switch ON.
CHECK:
Check the ABS warning light goes off.

OK	Check and replace ABS & TRAC ECU.

NG

Check for short circuit in harness and connector between ABS warning light, DLC1, DLC2, and ABS & TRAC ECU

TY4029900581020X

**Fig. 163   ABS Lamp Always On (Part 2 of 2).
Camry Solara w/traction control**

2	Check TRAC cut switch.

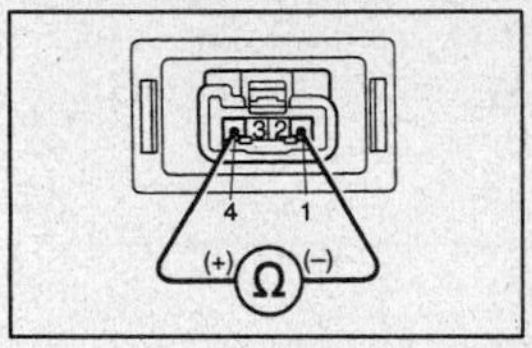

PREPARATION:
Remove TRAC cut switch, then disconnect TRAC cut switch connector
CHECK:
Measure resistance between terminals 1 and 4 of TRAC cut switch when TRAC cut switch is on and off.
OK:

TRAC cut switch	Resistance
Pushed in	Continuity
Released	1 MΩ or higher

NG	Replace TRAC cut switch.

OK

3	Check for open and short circuit in harness and connector between terminal CSW of ABS & TRAC ECU and TRAC cut switch and body ground.

NG	Repair or replace harness or connector.

OK

4	Check TRAC OFF indicator light.

Diagnose combination meter.

NG	Repair or replace combination meter.

OK

TY4029900583020X

**Fig. 164   TRAC OFF Indicator, TRAC Cut Switch
Circuit (Part 2 of 3). Camry Solara w/traction
control**

5	Check for open and short circuit in harness and connector between terminal WT of ABS & TRAC ECU and TRAC OFF indicator light .

NG ▷ Repair or replace harness connector.

OK

Check and replace ABS & TRAC ECU.

TY4029900583030X

Fig. 164 TRAC OFF Indicator, TRAC Cut Switch Circuit (Part 3 of 3). Camry Solara w/traction control

CIRCUIT DESCRIPTION

The solenoid relay supplies power to each ABS solenoid . After the ignition switch is turned ON, if the initial check is OK, the relay goes on. The motor relay supplies power to the ABS pump motor. While the ABS is activated, the ECU switches the motor relay ON and operates the ABS pump motor.

DTC No.	Diagnostic Trouble Code Detecting Condition	Trouble area
11	(1) 5V is applied to the solenoid voltage monitor terminal (AST) for 30 sec. with the IG switch ON and the warning light on. (2) 5V is applied to the solenoid voltage monitor terminal (AST) for 0.02 sec. or more, after the warning light goes off.	• Open or short in ABS solenoid relay circuit • ECU
13	(1) The motor voltage monitor terminal (MT) is ON for 5 sec. or more, with the motor relay operation signal OFF. (2) The motor voltage monitor terminal (MT) is OFF for 0.04 sec. with the motor relay operation signal ON.	• Pump motor • Open in ABS motor relay circuit • ECU

Fail safe function: If trouble occurs in the control (solenoid) relay circuit, the ECU cuts off current to the ABS solenoid relay and prohibits ABS control.

WIRING DIAGRAM

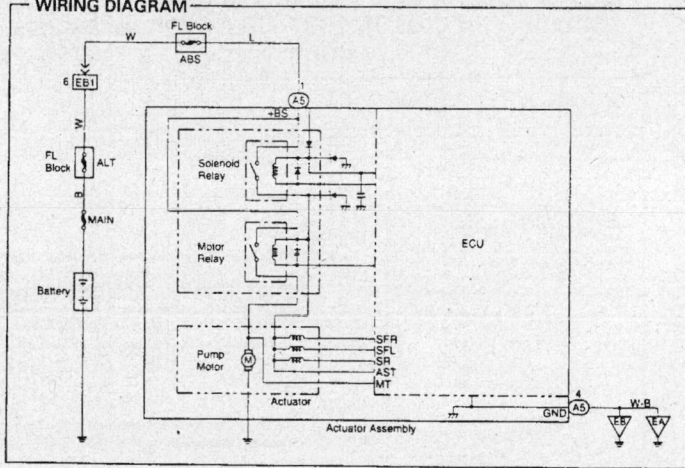

Fig. 166 Codes 11 & 13: ABS Solenoid & Motor Relay Circuit (Part 1 of 2). 1996 Avalon

TY4029500155010X

CIRCUIT DESCRIPTION
The SLIP indicator blinks during TRAC operation.

INSPECTION PROCEDURE

1	Check SLIP indicator light.

Diagnose combination meter .

NG ▷ Repair or replace combination meter.

OK

2	Check for short circuit in harness and connector between ABS & TRAC ECU and SLIP indicator light .

NG ▷ Repair or replace harness or connector.

OK

Check and replace ABS & TRAC ECU.

TY4029900584000X

Fig. 165 SLIP Indicator Lamp Circuit. Camry Solara w/traction control

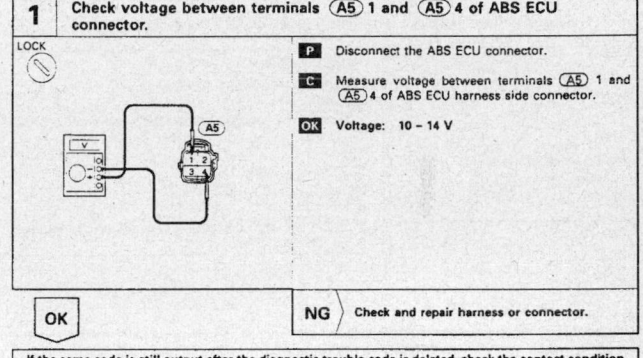

1	Check voltage between terminals (A5) 1 and (A5) 4 of ABS ECU connector.

P Disconnect the ABS ECU connector.

C Measure voltage between terminals (A5) 1 and (A5) 4 of ABS ECU harness side connector.

OK Voltage: 10 − 14 V

OK

NG ▷ Check and repair harness or connector.

If the same code is still output after the diagnostic trouble code is deleted, check the contact condition of each connection.
If the connections are normal, the ECU may be defective.

TY4029500155020X

Fig. 166 Codes 11 & 13: ABS Solenoid & Motor Relay Circuit (Part 2 of 2). 1996 Avalon

This relay supplies power to each ABS solenoid. After the ignition switch is turned ON, if the initial check is OK, the relay goes on.

DTC No.	DTC Detecting Condition	Trouble Area
11	Detection of any conditions from (1) through (3): (1) 3 or more solenoid valves are show faulty in response and simultaneously valve supply voltage is detected faulty. (2) Solenoid valve relay will not be switched OFF. (3) Valve relay is frozen in spite of its high valve supply voltage.	• ABS solenoid valve relay • Valve supply voltage • ECU

Fail safe function: If trouble in the ABS solenoid valve relay circuit, the ECU cuts off current to the ABS solenoid valve relay and prohibits ABS control.

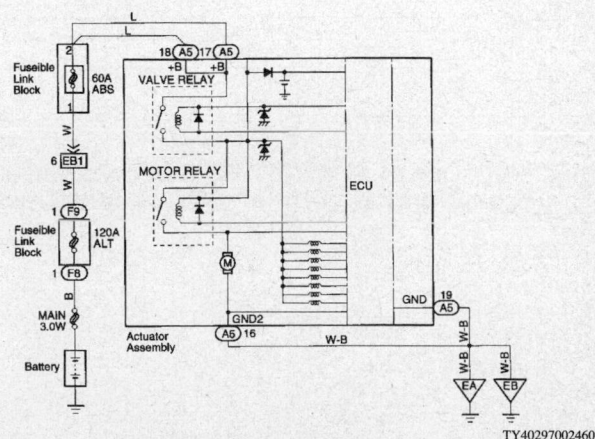

Fig. 167 Code 11: ABS Solenoid Valve Relay Circuit (Part 1 of 2). 1997–99 Avalon less Traction Control

1	Check voltage between terminals A5 – 17, 18 and A5 – 16, 19 of ABS actuator connector.

LOCK

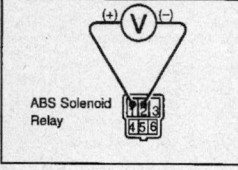

PREPARATION:
Disconnect the ABS actuator connector.
CHECK:
Measure the voltage between terminals A5 – 17, 18 and A5 – 16, 19 of ABS actuator harness side connector.
OK:
Voltage: 10 – 14 V

NG	Check and replace fuses. Check and repair harness or connector.

OK

If the same code is still output after the DTC is deleted, check the contact condition of each connection.
If the connector are normal, the ECU may be defective.

TY4029700246020X

Fig. 167 Code 11: ABS Solenoid Valve Relay Circuit (Part 2 of 2). 1997–99 Avalon less Traction Control

1	Check voltage between terminals 1 and 2 of ABS solenoid relay.

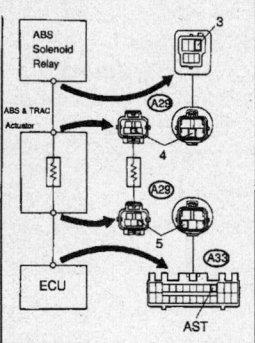

ABS Solenoid Relay

PREPARATION:
Remove ABS solenoid relay.
CHECK:
Measure the voltage between terminals 1 and 2 of ABS solenoid relay.
OK:
Voltage: 10 – 14 V

NG	Check and repair harness or connector.

OK

2	Check continuity between terminal 3 of ABS solenoid relay and terminal AST of ABS & TRAC ECU.

ABS Solenoid Relay

ABS & TRAC Actuator

ECU

AST

CHECK:
Check continuity between terminal 3 of ABS solenoid relay and terminal AST of ABS & TRAC ECU.
OK:
Continuity
HINT: There is a resistance of 4 ~ 6 Ω between terminals A29 – 4 and A29 – 5 of ABS & TRAC actuator.

NG	Repair or replace harness or ABS & TRAC actuator.

OK

TY4029700254020X

Fig. 168 Codes 11 & 12: ABS Solenoid Valve Relay Circuit (Part 2 of 3). 1997–99 Avalon w/Traction Control

This relay supplies power to each ABS & TRAC solenoid. After the ignition switch is turned ON, if the initial check is OK, the relay goes on.

DTC No.	DTC Detecting Condition	Trouble Area
11	Condition (1) to (3) are detected: (1) Malfunction of solenoid relay monitor. (2) Battery voltage will not exceed more than 17.0 V within 2.16 sec. (3) Battery voltage will not become less than 9.5 V within 2.16 sec., or after the solenoid relay is ON and AST voltage of ECU terminal does not become 8.0 V or more.	• ABS solenoid relay • ABS solenoid relay circuit • ECU
12	Solenoid relay is OFF in the midst of premain routine, and AST voltage of ECU terminal is 8.0 V or more continues for 2.04 sec. or more.	

Fail safe function: If trouble in the ABS solenoid relay circuit, the ECU cuts off current to the ABS solenoid relay and prohibits ABS control and TRAC control.

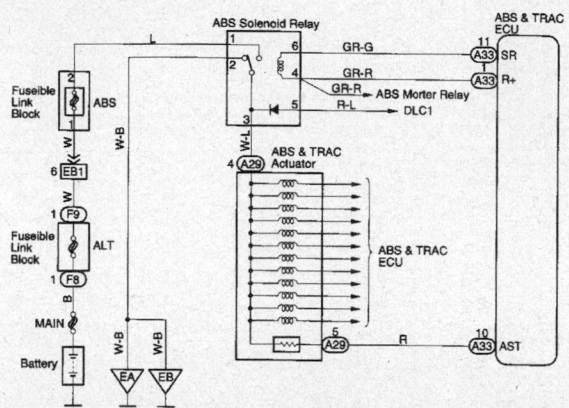

TY4029700254010X

Fig. 168 Codes 11 & 12: ABS Solenoid Valve Relay Circuit (Part 1 of 3). 1997–99 Avalon w/Traction Control

3	Check ABS solenoid relay.

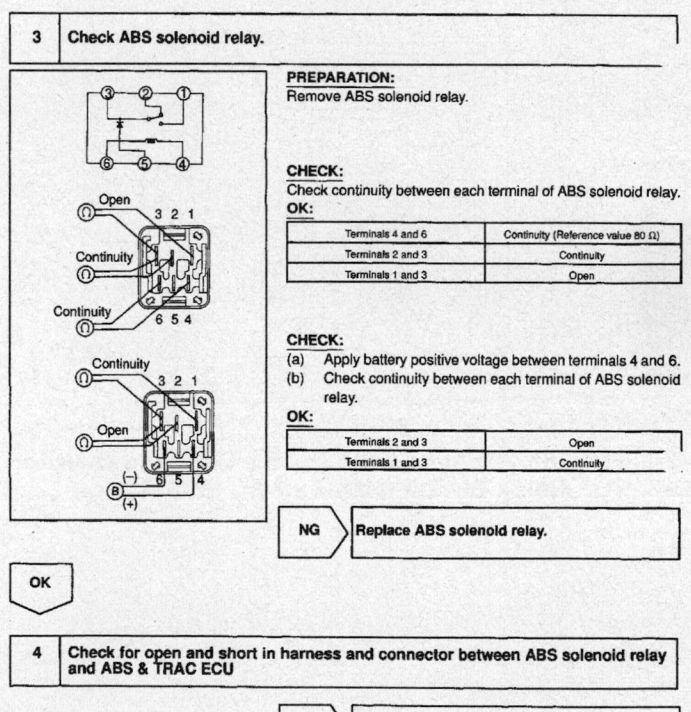

PREPARATION:
Remove ABS solenoid relay.

CHECK:
Check continuity between each terminal of ABS solenoid relay.
OK:

Terminals 4 and 6	Continuity (Reference value 80 Ω)
Terminals 2 and 3	Continuity
Terminals 1 and 3	Open

CHECK:
(a) Apply battery positive voltage between terminals 4 and 6.
(b) Check continuity between each terminal of ABS solenoid relay.
OK:

Terminals 2 and 3	Open
Terminals 1 and 3	Continuity

NG	Replace ABS solenoid relay.

OK

4	Check for open and short in harness and connector between ABS solenoid relay and ABS & TRAC ECU

NG	Repair or replace harness or connector.

OK

If the same code is still output after the DTC is deleted, check the contact condition of each connection.
If the connector are normal, the ECU may be defective.

TY4029700254030X

Fig. 168 Codes 11 & 12: ABS Solenoid Valve Relay Circuit (Part 3 of 3). 1997–99 Avalon w/Traction Control

The ABS motor relay supplies power to the ABS pump motor. While the ABS is activated, the ECU switches the ABS motor relay ON and operates the ABS pump motor.

DTC No.	DTC Detecting Condition	Trouble Area
13	Detection of any conditions from (1) through (3): (1) After actuation the motor relay, pump motor voltage will not supplied within 0.4 sec. (2) Pump motor voltage is in a high level, motor relay will not actuate for 2.5 sec. or more. (3) Pump motor voltage keeps low level for longer than 0.4 sec. and the pump repeats activating for 7 sec. 3times maximally. After the last activation, the pump motor has been gone dead because of short circuit.	• ABS motor relay • Pump motor voltage • Pump motor lead disconnected • ECU

Fail safe function: If trouble occurs in the ABS motor relay circuit, the ECU cuts off current to the ABS solenoid relay and prohibits ABS control.

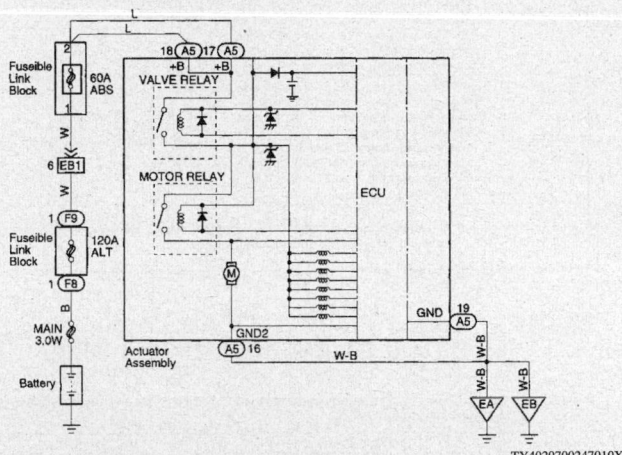

Fig. 169   Code 13: Pump Motor Circuit (Part 1 of 2). 1997–99 Avalon less Traction Control

The ABS motor relay supplies power to the ABS & TRAC pump motor. While the ABS is activated, the ECU switches the ABS motor relay ON and operates the ABS & TRAC pump motor.

DTC No.	DTC Detecting Condition	Trouble Area
13	Conditions (1) to (3) are detected: (1) Malfunction of motor relay monitor. (2) Battery voltage will not exceed more than 17.0 V within 2.16 sec. (3) Battery voltage will become less than 9.5 V within 2.16 sec., or after the motor relay is ON and motor relay monitor does not ON.	• ABS motor relay • ABS motor relay circuit • ECU
14	Motor relay is OFF, and motor relay monitor is ON continues for 20.16 sec. or more.	

Fail safe function: If trouble occurs in the ABS motor relay circuit, the ECU cuts off current to the ABS solenoid relay and prohibits ABS control and TRAC control.

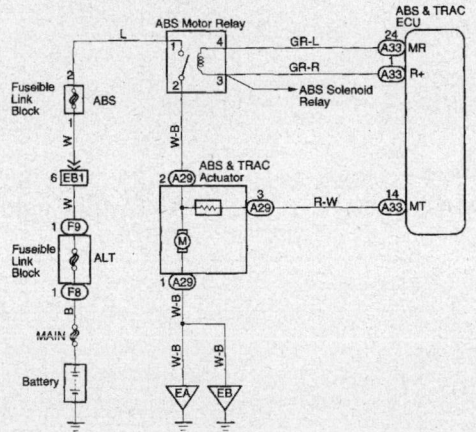

Fig. 170   Codes 13 & 14: ABS Motor Relay Circuit (Part 1 of 3). 1997–99 Avalon w/Traction Control

1	Check voltage between terminals A5 – 17, 18 and A5 – 16, 19 of ABS actuator connector.

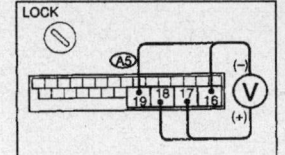

PREPARATION:
Disconnect the ABS actuator connector.
CHECK:
Measure the voltage between terminals A5 – 17, 18 and A5 – 16, 19 of ABS actuator harness side connector.
OK:
Voltage: 10 – 14 V

NG >	Check and replace fuses. Check and repair harness or connector.

OK

If the same code is still output after the DTC is deleted, check the contact condition of each connection.
If the connector are normal, the ECU may be defective.

TY4029700247020X

Fig. 169   Code 13: Pump Motor Circuit (Part 2 of 2). 1997–99 Avalon less Traction Control

1	Check voltage between terminal 1 of ABS motor relay and body ground.

PREPARATION:
Remove ABS motor relay.
CHECK:
Measure voltage between terminal 1 of ABS motor relay and body ground.
OK:
Voltage: 10 – 14 V

NG >	Check and repair harness or connector.

OK

2	Check continuity between terminal 2 of ABS motor relay and terminal MT of ABS & TRAC ECU.

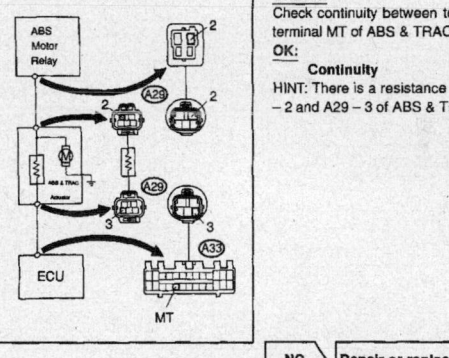

CHECK:
Check continuity between terminal 2 of ABS motor relay and terminal MT of ABS & TRAC ECU.
OK:
Continuity
HINT: There is a resistance of 4 – 6 Ω between terminals A29 – 2 and A29 – 3 of ABS & TRAC actuator.

NG >	Repair or replace harness or ABS & TRAC actuator.

OK

TY4029700255020X

Fig. 170   Codes 13 & 14: ABS Motor Relay Circuit (Part 2 of 3). 1997–99 Avalon w/Traction Control

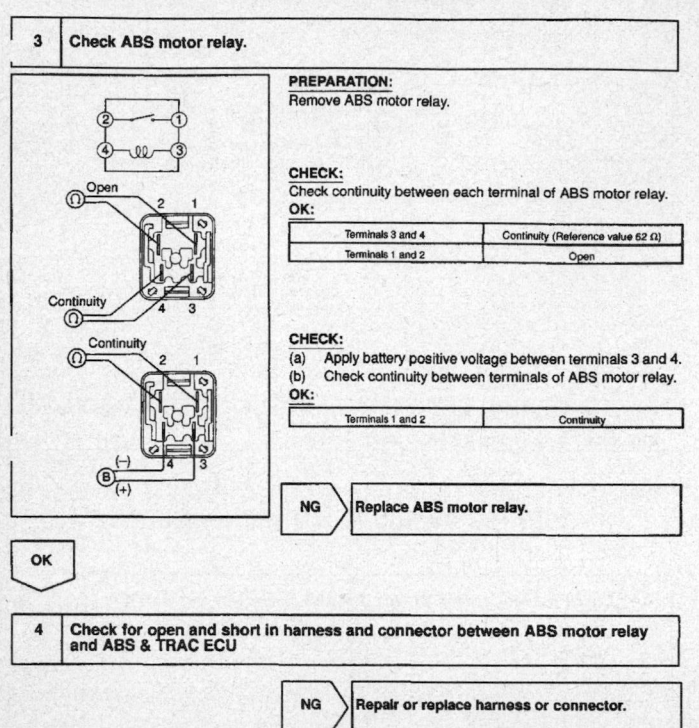

3	Check ABS motor relay.

PREPARATION:
Remove ABS motor relay.

CHECK:
Check continuity between each terminal of ABS motor relay.
OK:

Terminals 3 and 4	Continuity (Reference value 62 Ω)
Terminals 1 and 2	Open

CHECK:
(a) Apply battery positive voltage between terminals 3 and 4.
(b) Check continuity between terminals of ABS motor relay.
OK:

Terminals 1 and 2	Continuity

NG ▷	Replace ABS motor relay.

OK

4	Check for open and short in harness and connector between ABS motor relay and ABS & TRAC ECU

NG ▷	Repair or replace harness or connector.

OK

If the same code is still output after the DTC is deleted, check the contact condition of each connection.
If the connections are normal, the ECU may be defective.

TY4029700255030X

Fig. 170   Codes 13 & 14: ABS Motor Relay Circuit (Part 3 of 3). 1997–99 Avalon w/Traction Control

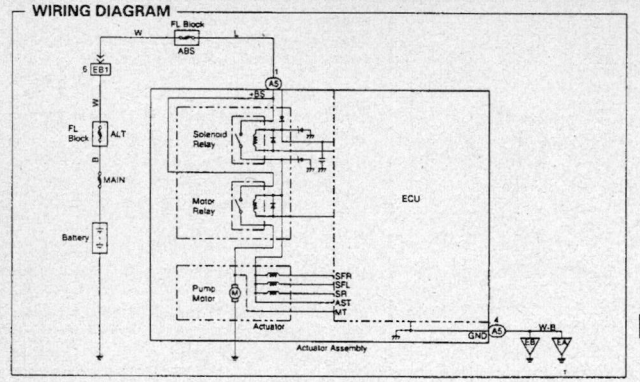

WIRING DIAGRAM

INSPECTION PROCEDURE

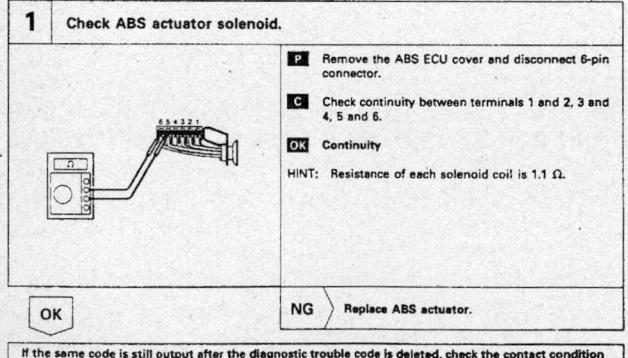

1	Check ABS actuator solenoid.

P Remove the ABS ECU cover and disconnect 6-pin connector.

C Check continuity between terminals 1 and 2, 3 and 4, 5 and 6.

OK Continuity

HINT: Resistance of each solenoid coil is 1.1 Ω.

NG ▷	Replace ABS actuator.

OK

If the same code is still output after the diagnostic trouble code is deleted, check the contact condition of each connection.
If the connections are normal, the ECU may be defective.

TY4029500156020X

Fig. 171   Codes 21, 22 & 23: ABS Actuator Solenoid Circuit (Part 2 of 2). 1996 Avalon

---

CIRCUIT DESCRIPTION

This solenoid goes on when signals are received from the ECU and controls the pressure acting on the wheel cylinders, thus controlling the braking force.

DTC No.	Diagnostic Trouble Code Detecting Condition	Trouble area
21	(1) 0V is applied to terminal SFR for 0.035 sec. while battery voltage is applied to the solenoid voltage monitor terminal (AST) and the ECM power transistor is OFF. (2) Battery voltage is applied to terminal SFR for 0.035 sec. while battery voltage is applied to the solenoid voltage monitor terminal (AST) and the ECM power transistor is ON.	• ABS actuator (soldnoid valve) • Open or short in right front solenoid circuit • ECU
22	(1) 0V is applied to terminal SFL for 0.035 sec. while battery voltage is applied to the solenoid voltage monitor terminal (AST) and the ECM power transistor is OFF. (2) Battery voltage is applied to terminal SFL for 0.035 sec. while battery voltage is applied to the solenoid voltage monitor terminal (AST) and the ECM power transistor is ON.	• ABS actuator (soldnoid valve) • Open or short in left front solenoid circuit • ECU
23	(1) 0V is applied to terminal SRA for 0.035 sec. while battery voltage is applied to the solenoid voltage monitor terminal (AST) and the ECM power transistor is OFF. (2) Battery voltage is applied to terminal SRA for 0.035 sec. while battery voltage is applied to the solenoid voltage monitor terminal (AST) and the ECM power transistor is ON.	• ABS actuator (solenoid valve) • Open or short in rear solenoid circuit • ECU

Fail safe function: If trouble occurs in the actuator solenoid circuit, the ECU cuts off current to the solenoid relay and prohibits ABS control.

TY4029500156010X

Fig. 171   Codes 21, 22 & 23: ABS Actuator Solenoid Circuit (Part 1 of 2). 1996 Avalon

This solenoid goes on when signals are received from the ECU and controls the pressure acting on the wheel cylinders thus controlling the braking force.

DTC No.	DTC Detecting Condition	Trouble Area
21, 22, 23, 24	Solenoid valve signal does not match for the check result.	• Each solenoid valve

Fail safe function: If trouble occurs in the actuator solenoid valve circuit, the ECU cuts off current to the ABS solenoid valve relay and prohibits ABS control.

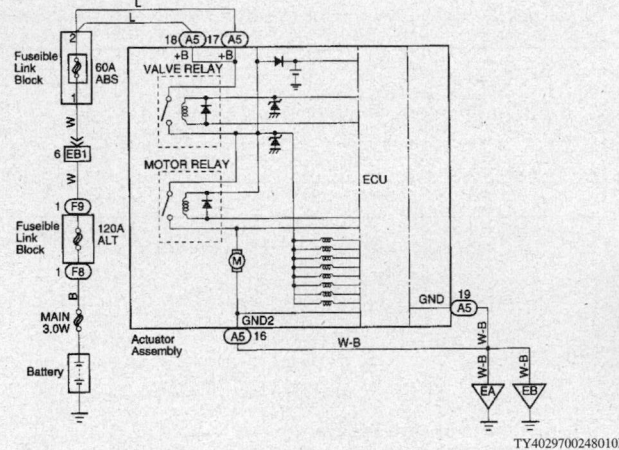

TY4029700248010X

Fig. 172   Codes 21, 22, 23 & 24: ABS Solenoid Valve Circuit (Part 1 of 2). 1997–99 Avalon less Traction Control

1	Check the DTC once more.

PREPARATION:
(a) Clear the DTC
(b) Turn the ignition switch OFF.
CHECK:
Turn the ignition switch ON, and check if the same DTC is stored in the memory.

NO ▷	No problem.

YES

Replace ABS ECU.

TY4029700248020X

Fig. 172   Codes 21, 22, 23 & 24: ABS Solenoid Valve Circuit (Part 2 of 2). 1997–99 Avalon less Traction Control

This solenoid goes on when signals are received from the ECU and controls the pressure acting on the wheel cylinders thus controlling the braking force.

DTC No.	DTC Detecting Condition	Trouble Area
21		• ABS actuator • SFRR or SFRH circuit • ECU
22		• ABS actuator • SFLR or SFLH circuit • ECU
23	Conditions (1) and (2) or (3) continued for 0.48 sec. or more:	• ABS actuator • SRRR or SRRH circuit • ECU
24	(1) Recovery prohibit run pulse is not output, solenoid relay is ON, AST voltage of ECU terminal is 8.0 V or more, and solenoid output has no change between the last time and this time.	• ABS actuator • SRLR or SRLH circuit • ECU
25	(2) Solenoid output is ON, pressure holding solenoid monitor voltage is more than 1.0 V or pressure reduction solenoid monitor voltage is more than 1.5 V.	• ABS actuator • SMC1 circuit • ECU
26	(3) Solenoid output is OFF, solenoid monitor voltage is more than −1.0 V AST voltage of ECU.	• ABS actuator • SMC2 circuit • ECU
27		• ABS actuator • SRC1 circuit • ECU
28		• ABS actuator • SRC2 circuit • ECU

Fail safe function: If trouble occurs in the actuator solenoid circuit, the ECU cuts off current to the ABS & TRAC solenoid relay and prohibits ABS control and TRAC control.

TY4029700256010X

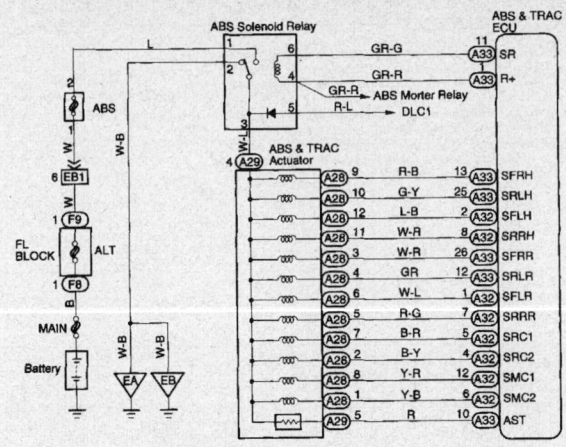

Fig. 173 Codes 21, 22, 23, 24, 25, 26, 27 & 28: ABS Actuator Solenoid Circuit (Part 1 of 3). 1997–99 Avalon w/Traction Control

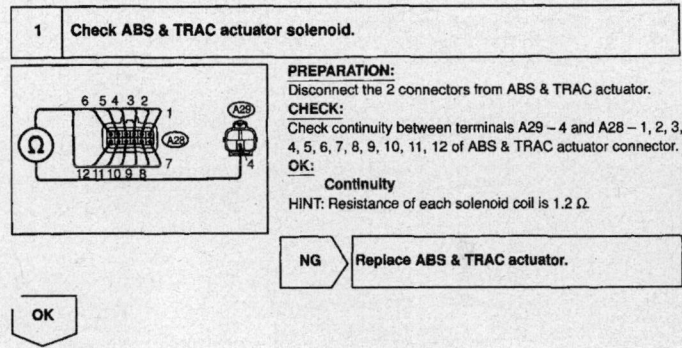

1 | Check ABS & TRAC actuator solenoid.

PREPARATION:
Disconnect the 2 connectors from ABS & TRAC actuator.
CHECK:
Check continuity between terminals A29 – 4 and A28 – 1, 2, 3, 4, 5, 6, 7, 8, 9, 10, 11, 12 of ABS & TRAC actuator connector.
OK:
  Continuity
HINT: Resistance of each solenoid coil is 1.2 Ω.

NG ▷ Replace ABS & TRAC actuator.

OK

TY4029700256020X

Fig. 173 Codes 21, 22, 23, 24, 25, 26, 27 & 28: ABS Actuator Solenoid Circuit (Part 2 of 3). 1997–99 Avalon w/Traction Control

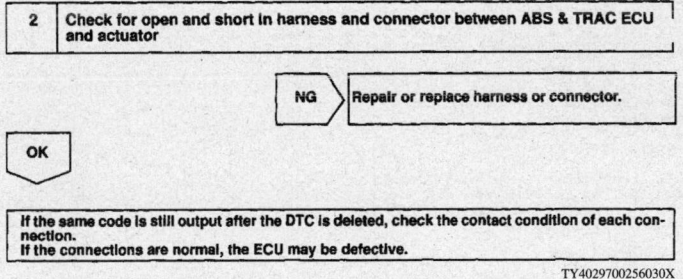

2 | Check for open and short in harness and connector between ABS & TRAC ECU and actuator

NG ▷ Repair or replace harness or connector.

OK

If the same code is still output after the DTC is deleted, check the contact condition of each connection.
If the connections are normal, the ECU may be defective.

TY4029700256030X

Fig. 173 Codes 21, 22, 23, 24, 25, 26, 27 & 28: ABS Actuator Solenoid Circuit (Part 3 of 3). 1997–99 Avalon w/Traction Control

CIRCUIT DESCRIPTION

The speed sensor detects the wheel speed and sends the appropriate signals to the ECU. These signals are used to control the ABS system. The front and rear rotors each have 48 serrations.

When the rotors rotate, the magnetic field emitted by the permanent magnet in the speed sensor generates an AC voltage. Since the frequency of this AC voltage changes in direct proportion to the speed of the rotor, the frequency is used by the ECU to detect the speed of each wheel.

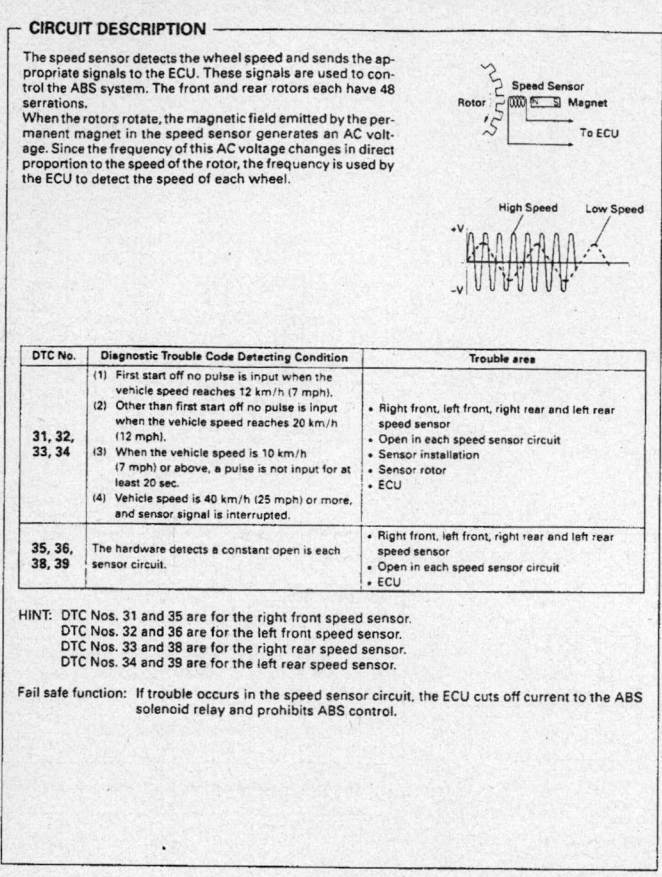

DTC No.	Diagnostic Trouble Code Detecting Condition	Trouble area
31, 32, 33, 34	(1) First start off no pulse is input when the vehicle speed reaches 12 km/h (7 mph). (2) Other than first start off no pulse is input when the vehicle speed reaches 20 km/h (12 mph). (3) When the vehicle speed is 10 km/h (7 mph) or above, a pulse is not input for at least 20 sec. (4) Vehicle speed is 40 km/h (25 mph) or more, and sensor signal is interrupted.	• Right front, left front, right rear and left rear speed sensor • Open in each speed sensor circuit • Sensor installation • Sensor rotor • ECU
35, 36, 38, 39	The hardware detects a constant open is each sensor circuit.	• Right front, left front, right rear and left rear speed sensor • Open in each speed sensor circuit • ECU

HINT: DTC Nos. 31 and 35 are for the right front speed sensor.
DTC Nos. 32 and 36 are for the left front speed sensor.
DTC Nos. 33 and 38 are for the right rear speed sensor.
DTC Nos. 34 and 39 are for the left rear speed sensor.

Fail safe function: If trouble occurs in the speed sensor circuit, the ECU cuts off current to the ABS solenoid relay and prohibits ABS control.

TY4029500157010X

Fig. 174 Codes 31, 32, 33, 34, 35, 36, 38 & 39: Speed Sensor Circuit (Part 1 of 4). 1996 Avalon

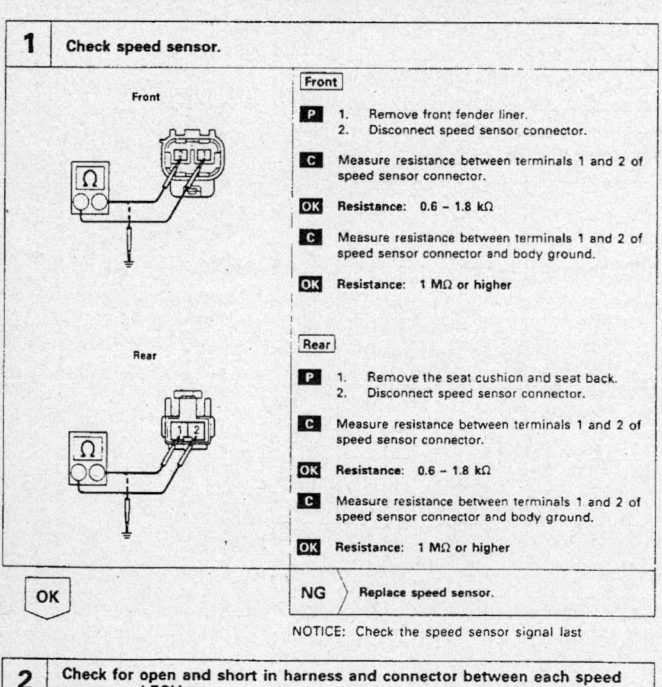

1	Check speed sensor.

Front

P 1. Remove front fender liner.
2. Disconnect speed sensor connector.

C Measure resistance between terminals 1 and 2 of speed sensor connector.

OK Resistance: 0.6 – 1.8 kΩ

C Measure resistance between terminals 1 and 2 of speed sensor connector and body ground.

OK Resistance: 1 MΩ or higher

Rear

P 1. Remove the seat cushion and seat back.
2. Disconnect speed sensor connector.

C Measure resistance between terminals 1 and 2 of speed sensor connector.

OK Resistance: 0.6 – 1.8 kΩ

C Measure resistance between terminals 1 and 2 of speed sensor connector and body ground.

OK Resistance: 1 MΩ or higher

OK		NG	Replace speed sensor.

NOTICE: Check the speed sensor signal last.

2	Check for open and short in harness and connector between each speed sensor and ECU

OK		NG	Repair or replace harness or connector.

TY4029500157030X

Fig. 174 Codes 31, 32, 33, 34, 35, 36, 38 & 39: Speed Sensor Circuit (Part 3 of 4). 1996 Avalon

WIRING DIAGRAM

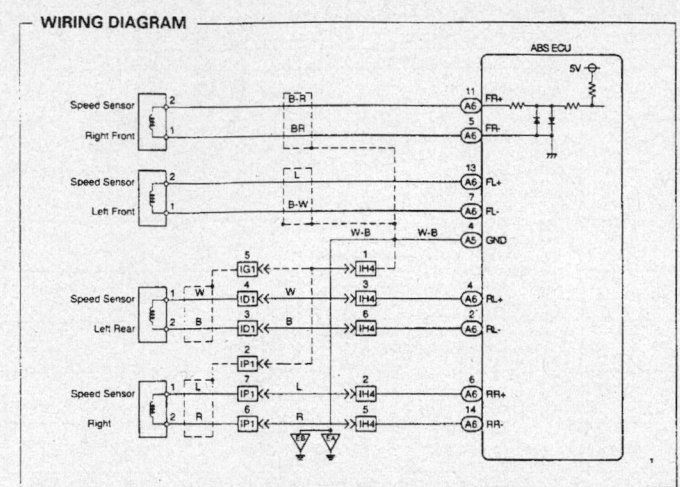

TY4029500157020X

Fig. 174 Codes 31, 32, 33, 34, 35, 36, 38 & 39: Speed Sensor Circuit (Part 2 of 4). 1996 Avalon

3	Check sensor rotor and sensor installation.

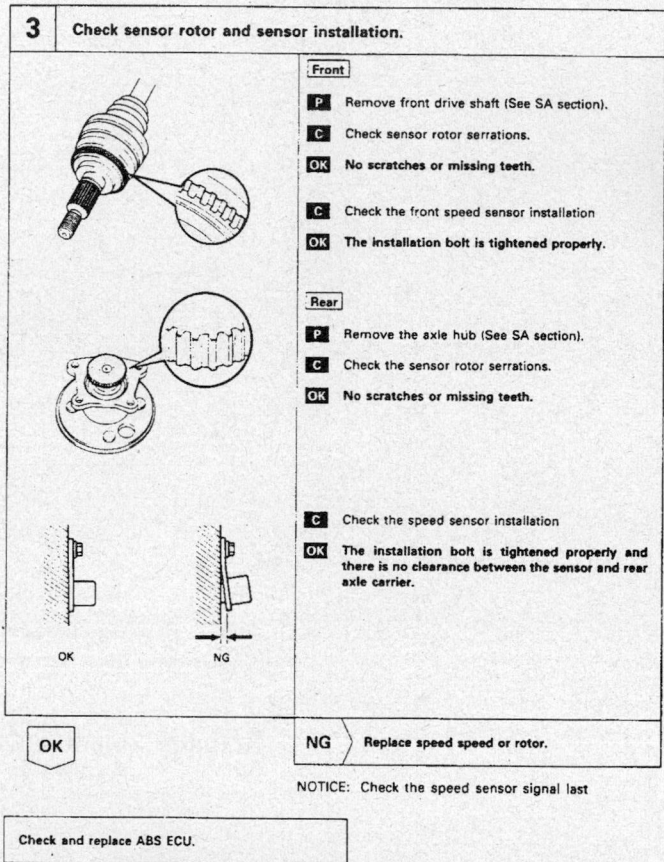

Front

P Remove front drive shaft (See SA section).

C Check sensor rotor serrations.

OK No scratches or missing teeth.

C Check the front speed sensor installation

OK The installation bolt is tightened properly.

Rear

P Remove the axle hub (See SA section).

C Check the sensor rotor serrations.

OK No scratches or missing teeth.

C Check the speed sensor installation

OK The installation bolt is tightened properly and there is no clearance between the sensor and rear axle carrier.

OK		NG	Replace speed speed or rotor.

NOTICE: Check the speed sensor signal last

Check and replace ABS ECU.

TY4029500157040X

Fig. 174 Codes 31, 32, 33, 34, 35, 36, 38 & 39: Speed Sensor Circuit (Part 4 of 4). 1996 Avalon

ANTI-LOCK BRAKES

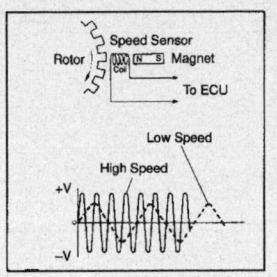

The speed sensor detects wheel speed and sends the appropriate signals to the ECU. These signals are used to control of the ABS system. The front and rear rotors each have 48 serrations.

When the rotors rotate, the magnetic field emitted by the permanent magnet in the speed sensor generates an AC voltage. Since the frequency of this AC voltage changes in direct proportion to the speed of the rotor, the frequency is used by the ECU to detect the speed of each wheel.

DTC No.	DTC Detecting Condition	Trouble Area
31, 32, 33, 34	Detection of any of conditions from (1) through (3): (1) Vehicle speed is more than 40 km/h (25 mph), pluses are not input for 0.1 sec. (2) After the initial start or restart and when the vehicle speed has reached 12 km/h (7 mph), the wheel with 0 km/h (0 mph) of wheel speed was detected. (3) After the initial start or restart and when the vehicle speed has reached 70 km/h (44 mph), front wheel with 0 km/h (0 mph) of wheel speed was detected.	• Right front, left front, right rear, left rear speed sensor • Each speed sensor circuit • Sensor installation • ECU
35, 36, 38, 39	Detecting abnormality in the resistance value of each speed sensor.	• Right front, left front, right rear, left rear speed sensor • Each speed sensor circuit • ECU

HINT:
DTC Nos. 31 and 35 are for the right front speed sensor.
DTC Nos. 32 and 36 are for the left front speed sensor.
DTC Nos. 33 and 38 are for the right rear speed sensor.
DTC Nos. 34 and 39 are for the left rear speed sensor.
Fail safe function: If trouble occurs in the speed sensor circuit, the ECU cuts off current to the ABS solenoid valve relay and prohibits ABS control.

TY4029700249010X

Fig. 175 Codes 31, 32, 33, 34, 35, 36, 38 & 39: Speed Sensor Circuit (Part 1 of 5). 1997–99 Avalon

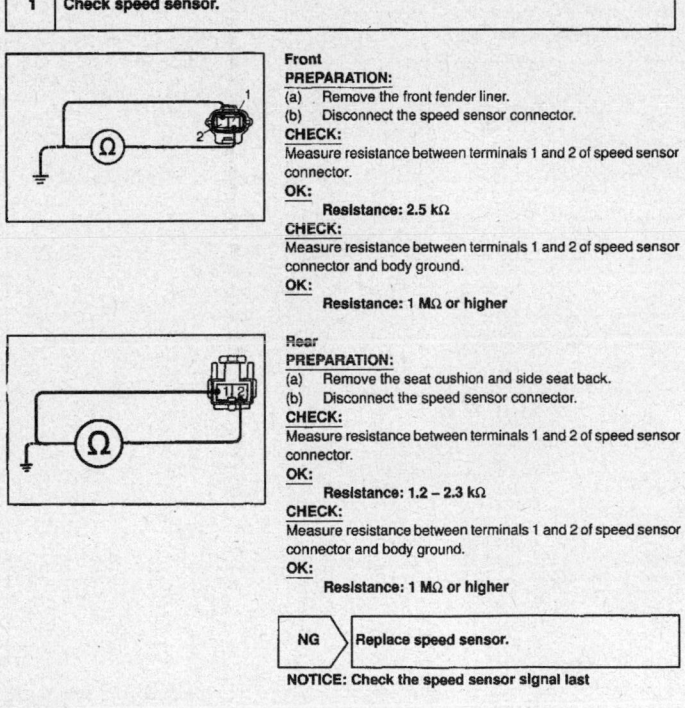

1 Check speed sensor.

Front
PREPARATION:
(a) Remove the front fender liner.
(b) Disconnect the speed sensor connector.
CHECK:
Measure resistance between terminals 1 and 2 of speed sensor connector.
OK:
Resistance: 2.5 kΩ
CHECK:
Measure resistance between terminals 1 and 2 of speed sensor connector and body ground.
OK:
Resistance: 1 MΩ or higher

Rear
PREPARATION:
(a) Remove the seat cushion and side seat back.
(b) Disconnect the speed sensor connector.
CHECK:
Measure resistance between terminals 1 and 2 of speed sensor connector.
OK:
Resistance: 1.2 – 2.3 kΩ
CHECK:
Measure resistance between terminals 1 and 2 of speed sensor connector and body ground.
OK:
Resistance: 1 MΩ or higher

NG ▷ Replace speed sensor.

NOTICE: Check the speed sensor signal last

OK

TY4029700249030X

Fig. 175 Codes 31, 32, 33, 34, 35, 36, 38 & 39: Speed Sensor Circuit (Part 3 of 5). 1997–99 Avalon

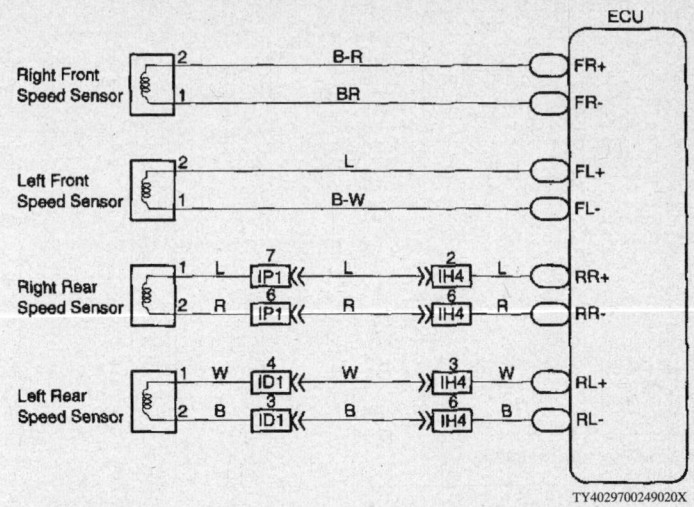

TY4029700249020X

Fig. 175 Codes 31, 32, 33, 34, 35, 36, 38 & 39: Speed Sensor Circuit (Part 2 of 5). 1997–99 Avalon

2 Check for open and short in harness and connector between each speed sensor and ECU

NG ▷ Repair or replace harness or connector.

OK

3 Check speed sensor installation.

CHECK:
Check the speed sensor installation.
OK:
The installation bolt is tightened properly and there is no clearance between the sensor and rear axle carrier.

OK   NG

NG ▷ Replace speed sensor.

NOTICE: Check the speed sensor signal last

OK

4 Check sensor rotor and sensor tip.

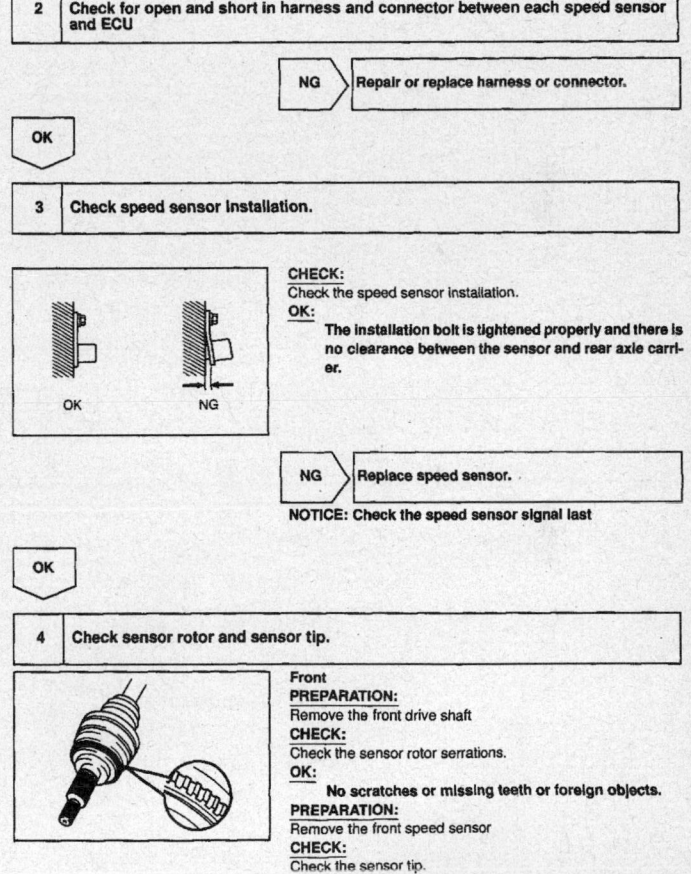

Front
PREPARATION:
Remove the front drive shaft
CHECK:
Check the sensor rotor serrations.
OK:
No scratches or missing teeth or foreign objects.
PREPARATION:
Remove the front speed sensor
CHECK:
Check the sensor tip.
OK:
No scratches or foreign objects on the sensor tip.

TY4029700249040X

Fig. 175 Codes 31, 32, 33, 34, 35, 36, 38 & 39: Speed Sensor Circuit (Part 4 of 5). 1997–99 Avalon

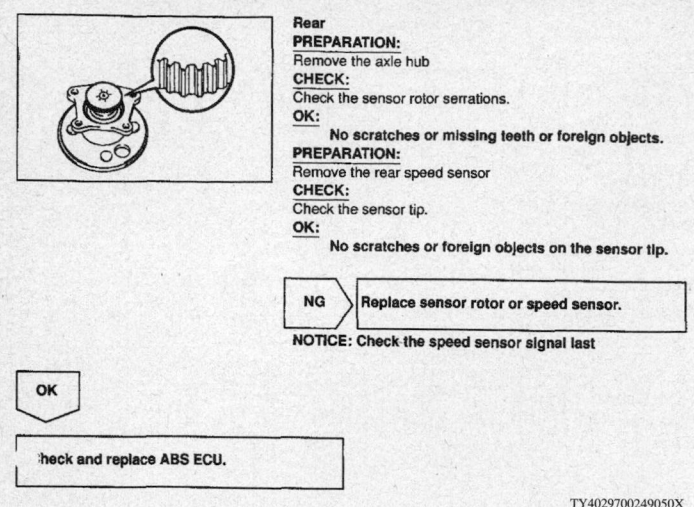

Rear
PREPARATION:
Remove the axle hub
CHECK:
Check the sensor rotor serrations.
OK:
    No scratches or missing teeth or foreign objects.
PREPARATION:
Remove the rear speed sensor
CHECK:
Check the sensor tip.
OK:
    No scratches or foreign objects on the sensor tip.

| NG | > | Replace sensor rotor or speed sensor. |

NOTICE: Check the speed sensor signal last

OK

Check and replace ABS ECU.

TY4029700249050X

Fig. 175   Codes 31, 32, 33, 34, 35, 36, 38 & 39: Speed Sensor Circuit (Part 5 of 5). 1997–99 Avalon

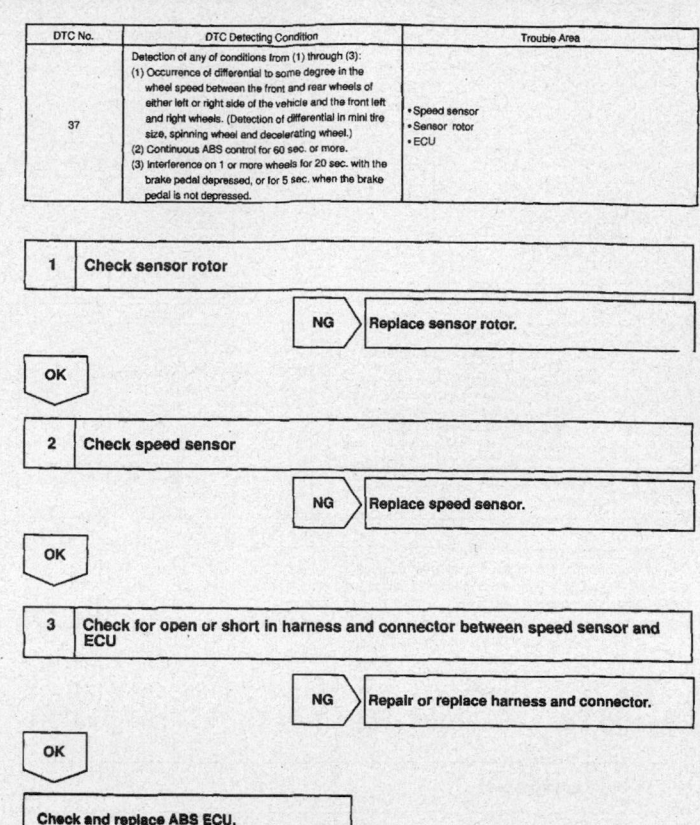

DTC No.	DTC Detecting Condition	Trouble Area
37	Detection of any of conditions from (1) through (3): (1) Occurrence of differential to some degree in the wheel speed between the front and rear wheels of either left or right side of the vehicle and the front left and right wheels. (Detection of differential in mini tire size, spinning wheel and decelerating wheel.) (2) Continuous ABS control for 60 sec. or more. (3) Interference on 1 or more wheels for 20 sec. with the brake pedal depressed, or for 5 sec. when the brake pedal is not depressed.	• Speed sensor • Sensor rotor • ECU

| 1 | Check sensor rotor |

| NG | > | Replace sensor rotor. |

OK

| 2 | Check speed sensor |

| NG | > | Replace speed sensor. |

OK

| 3 | Check for open or short in harness and connector between speed sensor and ECU |

| NG | > | Repair or replace harness and connector. |

OK

Check and replace ABS ECU.

TY4029700250000X

Fig. 176   Code 37: Speed Sensor Rotor Fault. 1997–99 Avalon

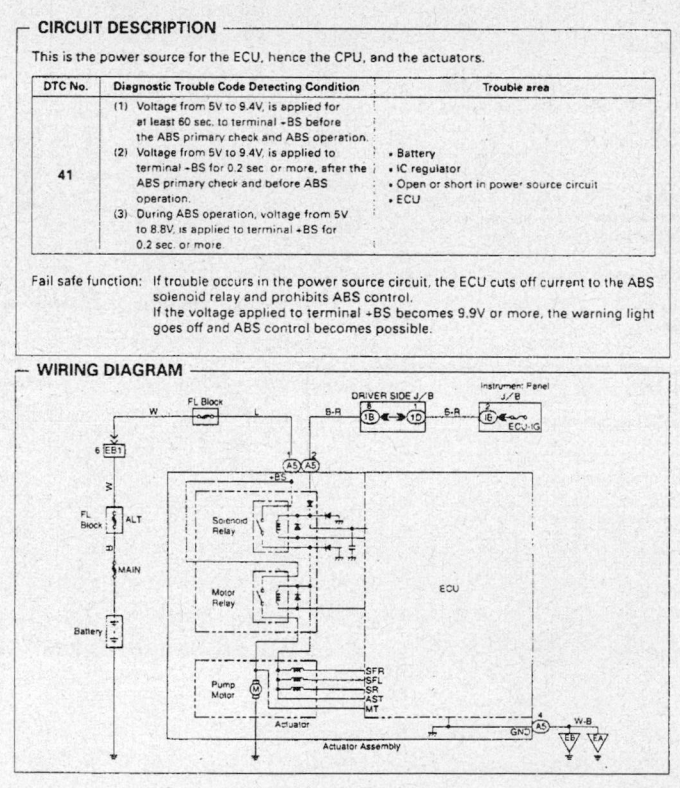

CIRCUIT DESCRIPTION

This is the power source for the ECU, hence the CPU, and the actuators.

DTC No.	Diagnostic Trouble Code Detecting Condition	Trouble area
41	(1) Voltage from 5V to 9.4V, is applied for at least 60 sec. to terminal +BS before the ABS primary check and ABS operation. (2) Voltage from 5V to 9.4V, is applied to terminal +BS for 0.2 sec. or more, after the ABS primary check and before ABS operation. (3) During ABS operation, voltage from 5V to 8.8V, is applied to terminal +BS for 0.2 sec. or more.	• Battery • IC regulator • Open or short in power source circuit • ECU

Fail safe function: If trouble occurs in the power source circuit, the ECU cuts off current to the ABS solenoid relay and prohibits ABS control.
If the voltage applied to terminal +BS becomes 9.9V or more, the warning light goes off and ABS control becomes possible.

WIRING DIAGRAM

TY4029500158010X

Fig. 177   Code 41: +BS Power Source Circuit (Part 1 of 3). 1996 Avalon

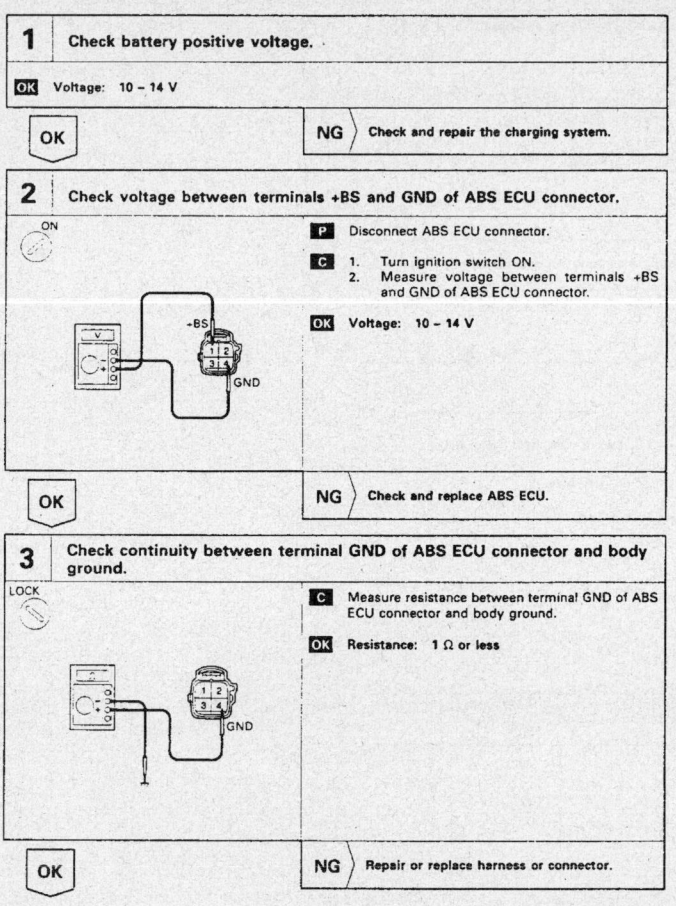

1	Check battery positive voltage.
OK Voltage: 10 – 14 V	

OK

NG ⟩ Check and repair the charging system.

2	Check voltage between terminals +BS and GND of ABS ECU connector.

P Disconnect ABS ECU connector.

C
1. Turn ignition switch ON.
2. Measure voltage between terminals +BS and GND of ABS ECU connector.

OK Voltage: 10 – 14 V

OK

NG ⟩ Check and replace ABS ECU.

3	Check continuity between terminal GND of ABS ECU connector and body ground.

C Measure resistance between terminal GND of ABS ECU connector and body ground.

OK Resistance: 1 Ω or less

OK

NG ⟩ Repair or replace harness or connector.

TY4029500158020X

Fig. 177 Code 41: +BS Power Source Circuit (Part 2 of 3). 1996 Avalon

This is the power source for the ECU, hence the actuators.

DTC No.	DTC Detecting Condition	Trouble Area
41	Vehicle speed at about 6 km/h (4 mph), low battery voltage is less than 9.4 V at the time of non-operation of ABS control or less than 8.8 V at the time of operation of ABS control, and high battery voltage is more than 17.4 V.	• Battery • IC regulator • Power source circuit • ECU

Fail safe function: If trouble occurs in the power source circuit, the ECU cuts off current to the ABS solenoid valve relay and prohibits ABS control.

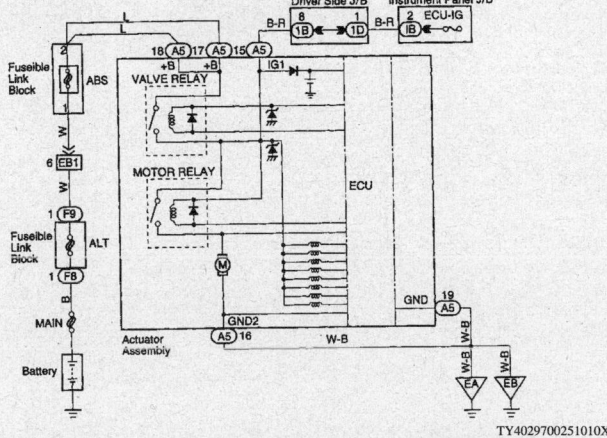

TY4029700251010X

Fig. 178 Code 41: Power Source Circuit (Part 1 of 3). 1997–99 Avalon less Traction Control

4	Check ECU-IG fuse.

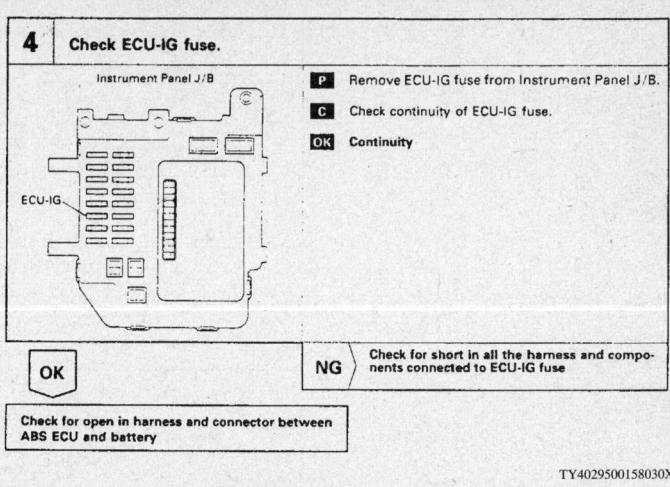

P Remove ECU-IG fuse from Instrument Panel J/B.

C Check continuity of ECU-IG fuse.

OK Continuity

OK

NG ⟩ Check for short in all the harness and components connected to ECU-IG fuse

Check for open in harness and connector between ABS ECU and battery

TY4029500158030X

Fig. 177 Code 41: +BS Power Source Circuit (Part 3 of 3). 1996 Avalon

1	Check battery positive voltage.

OK
Voltage: 10 – 14 V

NG ⟩ Check and replace fuses.
Check and repair the charging system.

OK

2	Check voltage between terminals IG1 and GND of ABS actuator connector.

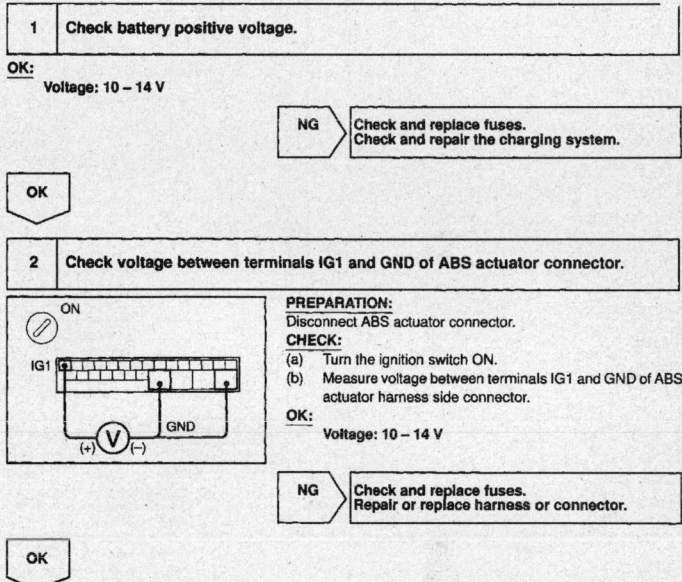

PREPARATION:
Disconnect ABS actuator connector.
CHECK:
(a) Turn the ignition switch ON.
(b) Measure voltage between terminals IG1 and GND of ABS actuator harness side connector.
OK:
Voltage: 10 – 14 V

NG ⟩ Check and replace fuses.
Repair or replace harness or connector.

OK

TY4029700251020X

Fig. 178 Code 41: Power Source Circuit (Part 2 of 3). 1997–99 Avalon less Traction Control

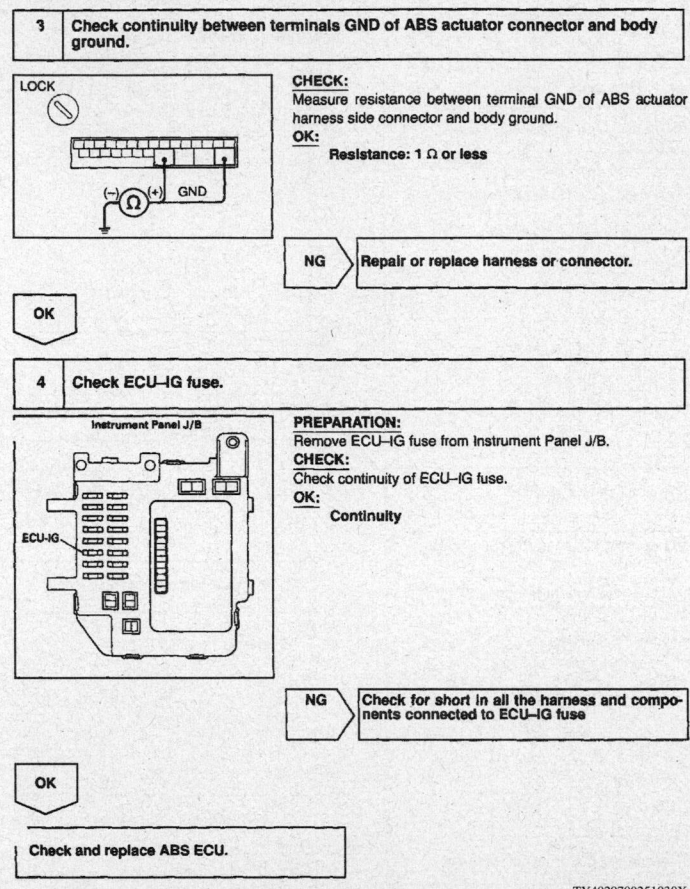

3 | Check continuity between terminals GND of ABS actuator connector and body ground.

LOCK

CHECK:
Measure resistance between terminal GND of ABS actuator harness side connector and body ground.
OK:
    Resistance: 1 Ω or less

NG ▷ Repair or replace harness or connector.

OK

4 | Check ECU–IG fuse.

Instrument Panel J/B

ECU–IG

PREPARATION:
Remove ECU–IG fuse from Instrument Panel J/B.
CHECK:
Check continuity of ECU–IG fuse.
OK:
    Continuity

NG ▷ Check for short in all the harness and components connected to ECU–IG fuse

OK

Check and replace ABS ECU.

TY4029700251030X

Fig. 178 Code 41: Power Source Circuit (Part 3 of 3). 1997–99 Avalon less Traction Control

This is the power source for the ECU, hence the actuators.

DTC No.	DTC Detecting Condition	Trouble Area
41	Detection of any conditions from (1) through (3): (1) Vehicle speed is 3 km/h (1.9 mph) or more and battery voltage is less than 9.5 V continues for 10 sec. or more. (2) Battery voltage has never exceeded more than 17.0 V and has become less than 9.5 V within 2.16 sec., under malfunction of solenoid relay monitor after the solenoid relay is ON, at ECU AST terminal voltage of ECU has become 8.0 V or more or under malfunction of motor relay monitor and after the motor relay is ON, motor relay monitor has become ON. (3) Battery voltage is more than 17.0 V continues for 1.2 sec. or more or battery voltage has become more than 17.0 V within 2.16 sec. and solenoid or motor relay monitor is under malfunction condition.	• Battery • IC regulator • Power source circuit • ECU

Fail safe function: If trouble occurs in the power source circuit, the ECU cuts off current to the ABS & TRAC solenoid relay and prohibits ABS control and TRAC control.

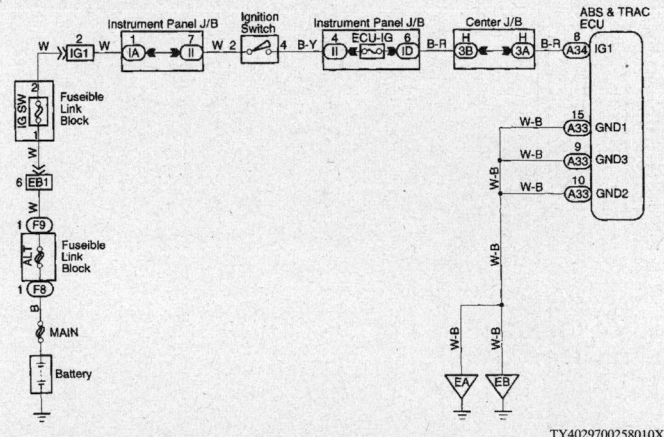

TY4029700258010X

Fig. 179 Code 41: Power Source Circuit (Part 1 of 3). 1997–99 Avalon w/Traction Control

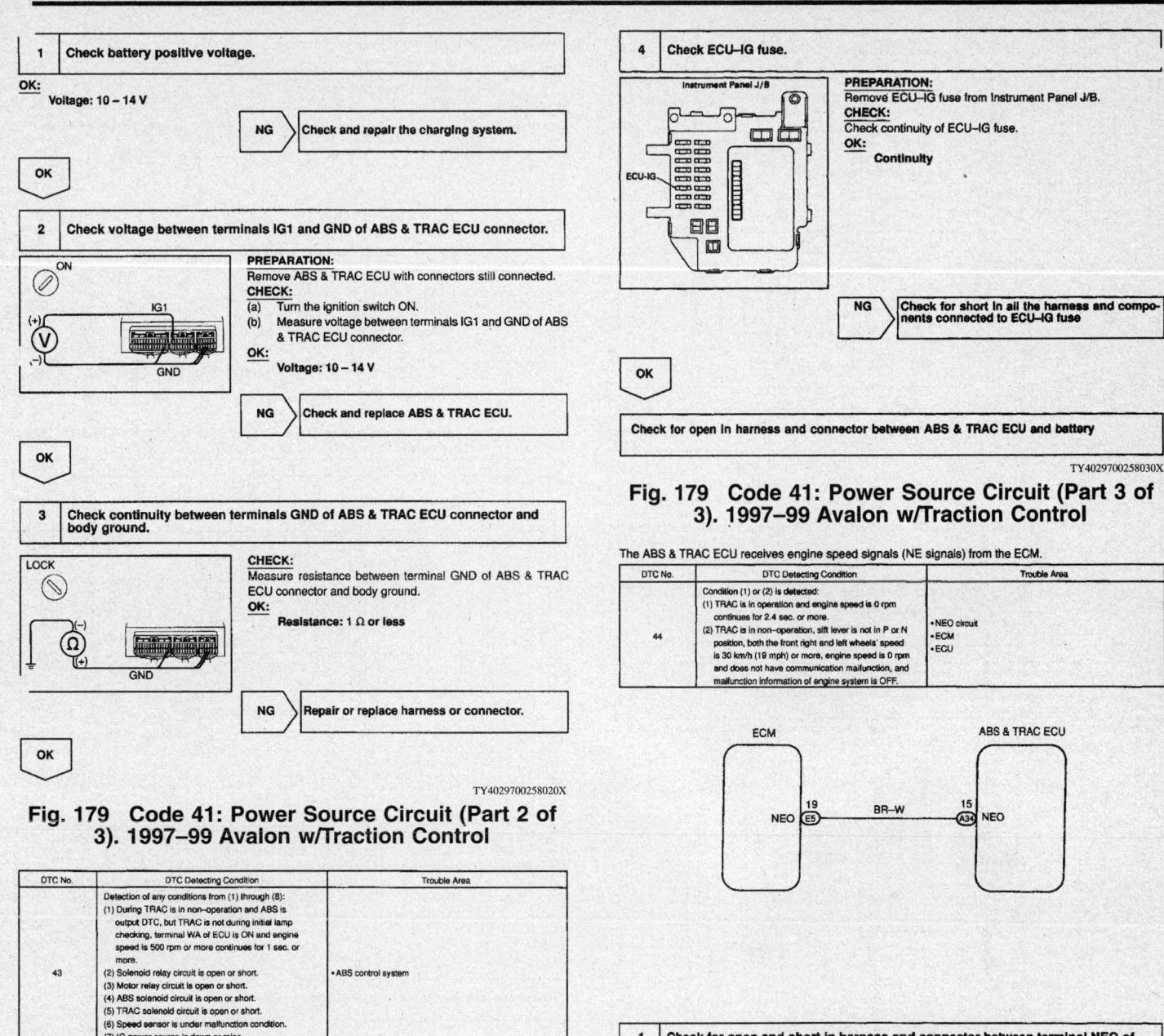

1 Check battery positive voltage.

OK:
   Voltage: 10 – 14 V

NG → Check and repair the charging system.

OK ↓

2 Check voltage between terminals IG1 and GND of ABS & TRAC ECU connector.

PREPARATION:
Remove ABS & TRAC ECU with connectors still connected.
CHECK:
(a) Turn the ignition switch ON.
(b) Measure voltage between terminals IG1 and GND of ABS & TRAC ECU connector.
OK:
   Voltage: 10 – 14 V

NG → Check and replace ABS & TRAC ECU.

OK ↓

3 Check continuity between terminals GND of ABS & TRAC ECU connector and body ground.

CHECK:
Measure resistance between terminal GND of ABS & TRAC ECU connector and body ground.
OK:
   Resistance: 1 Ω or less

NG → Repair or replace harness or connector.

OK ↓

TY4029700258020X

Fig. 179   Code 41: Power Source Circuit (Part 2 of 3). 1997–99 Avalon w/Traction Control

DTC No.	DTC Detecting Condition	Trouble Area
43	Detection of any conditions from (1) through (8): (1) During TRAC is in non–operation and ABS is output DTC, but TRAC is not during initial lamp checking, terminal WA of ECU is ON and engine speed is 500 rpm or more continues for 1 sec. or more. (2) Solenoid relay circuit is open or short. (3) Motor relay circuit is open or short. (4) ABS solenoid circuit is open or short. (5) TRAC solenoid circuit is open or short. (6) Speed sensor is under malfunction condition. (7) IG power source is down or raise. (8) Pump motor is lock.	• ABS control system

1 Check the DTC for the ABS

*1 → Repair ABS control system according to the code output.

*2 ↓

Check for ECU connected to malfunction indicator lamp.

*1: Output NG code
*2: Malfunction indicator lamp remains ON.

TY4029700260000X

Fig. 180   Code 43: ABS Control System Fault. Avalon

4 Check ECU–IG fuse.

Instrument Panel J/B

ECU–IG

PREPARATION:
Remove ECU–IG fuse from Instrument Panel J/B.
CHECK:
Check continuity of ECU–IG fuse.
OK:
   Continuity

NG → Check for short in all the harness and components connected to ECU–IG fuse

OK ↓

Check for open in harness and connector between ABS & TRAC ECU and battery

TY4029700258030X

Fig. 179   Code 41: Power Source Circuit (Part 3 of 3). 1997–99 Avalon w/Traction Control

The ABS & TRAC ECU receives engine speed signals (NE signals) from the ECM.

DTC No.	DTC Detecting Condition	Trouble Area
44	Condition (1) or (2) is detected: (1) TRAC is in operation and engine speed is 0 rpm continues for 2.4 sec. or more. (2) TRAC is in non–operation, shift lever is not in P or N position, both the front right and left wheels' speed is 30 km/h (19 mph) or more, engine speed is 0 rpm and does not have communication malfunction, and malfunction information of engine system is OFF.	• NEO circuit • ECM • ECU

ECM   ABS & TRAC ECU

NEO 19 (E5) ──BR–W── 15 (A34) NEO

1 Check for open and short in harness and connector between terminal NEO of ABS & TRAC ECU and terminal NEO of ECM

NG → Repair or replace harness or connector.

OK ↓

TY4029700261010X

Fig. 181   Code 44: NE Signal Circuit (Part 1 of 2). Avalon

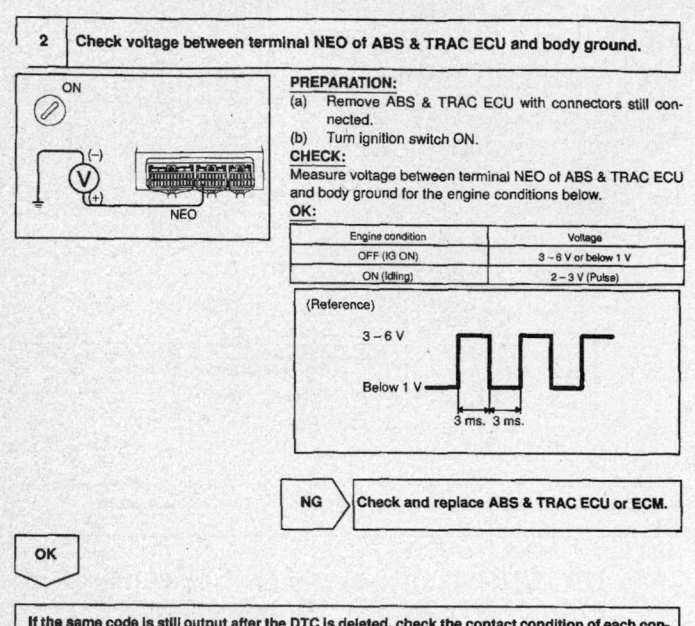

2   Check voltage between terminal NEO of ABS & TRAC ECU and body ground.

PREPARATION:
(a) Remove ABS & TRAC ECU with connectors still connected.
(b) Turn ignition switch ON.

CHECK:
Measure voltage between terminal NEO of ABS & TRAC ECU and body ground for the engine conditions below.

OK:

Engine condition	Voltage
OFF (IG ON)	3 ~ 6 V or below 1 V
ON (Idling)	2 ~ 3 V (Pulse)

(Reference)
3 ~ 6 V
Below 1 V
3 ms. 3 ms.

NG ▷ Check and replace ABS & TRAC ECU or ECM.

OK

If the same code is still output after the DTC is deleted, check the contact condition of each connection.

TY4029700261020X

Fig. 181 Code 44: NE Signal Circuit (Part 2 of 2). Avalon

DTC No.	DTC Detecting Condition	Trouble Area
51	In the midst of initial check, after the current flows to the motor for 3 sec. and motor relay is turned OFF , then within 0.66 sec., the condition that the motor relay monitor is OFF continues for 0.24 sec. or more.	• ABS pump motor

Fail safe function: If trouble occurs in the ABS & TRAC pump motor, the ECU cuts off current to the ABS & TRAC solenoid relay and prohibits ABS control and TRAC control.

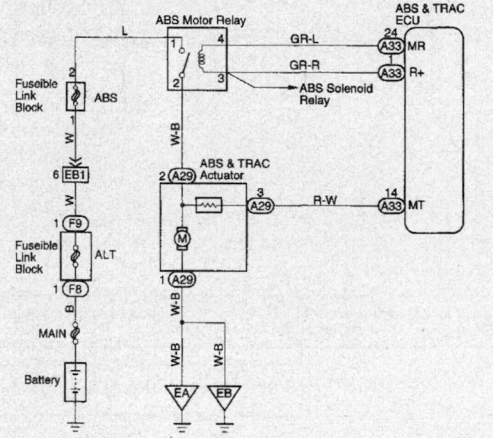

TY4029700259000X

Fig. 183 Code 51: ABS Pump Motor Lock. 1997–99 Avalon

CIRCUIT DESCRIPTION

DTC No.	Diagnostic Trouble Code Detecting Condition	Trouble area
51	Pump motor is not operating normally during initial check.	• ABS pump motor

Fail safe function: If trouble occurs in the ABS pump motor, the ECU cuts off current to the solenoid relay and prohibits ABS control.

INSPECTION PROCEDURE

Check that the pump motor ground wire is installed correctly.
If it is OK, replace the ABS actuator assembly.

TY4029500159000X

Fig. 182 Code 51: ABS Pump Motor Lock. 1996 Avalon

This circuit is used to send TRAC control information from the ABS & TRAC ECU to the ECM (TRC+, TRC–), and engine control information from the ECM to the ABS & TRAC ECU (EFI+, EFI–).

DTC No.	DTC Detecting Condition	Trouble Area
53	ECM communication data malfunction is detected.	• TRC+ or TRC– circuit • EFI+ or EFI– circuit • ECM • ECU

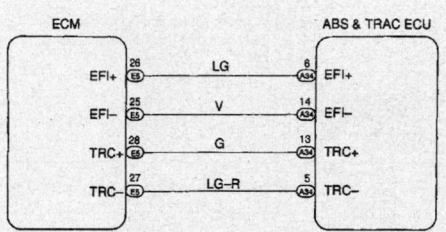

1   Check for open and short in harness and connector between terminals EFI+, EFI–, TRC+, TRC– of ABS & TRAC ECU and ECM

NG ▷ Repair or replace harness or connector.

OK

Check and replace ECM or ABS & TRAC ECU.

TY4029700262000X

Fig. 184 Code 53: ECM Communication Circuit Fault. Avalon

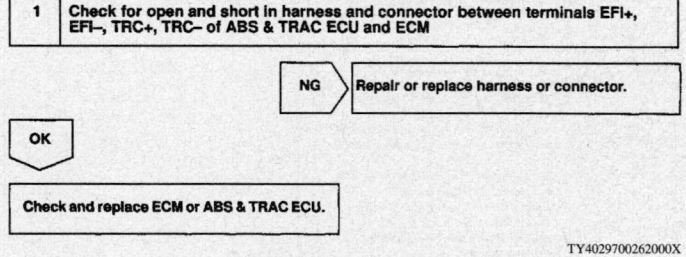

If trouble occurs in the engine control system, the ECU prohibits TRAC control.

DTC No.	DTC Detection Condition	Trouble Area
61	Conditions (1) and (2) is detected: (1) ECM communication is normal, malfunction information of engine system ON, and engine speed is 500 rpm or more continues for 0.48 sec. or more, and TRAC operation start condition is concluded. (2) ECM communication is normal, malfunction information of engine system is ON, engine speed is 500 rpm and more continues for 1 sec. or more, and the engine system memorizes DTC.	• Engine control system

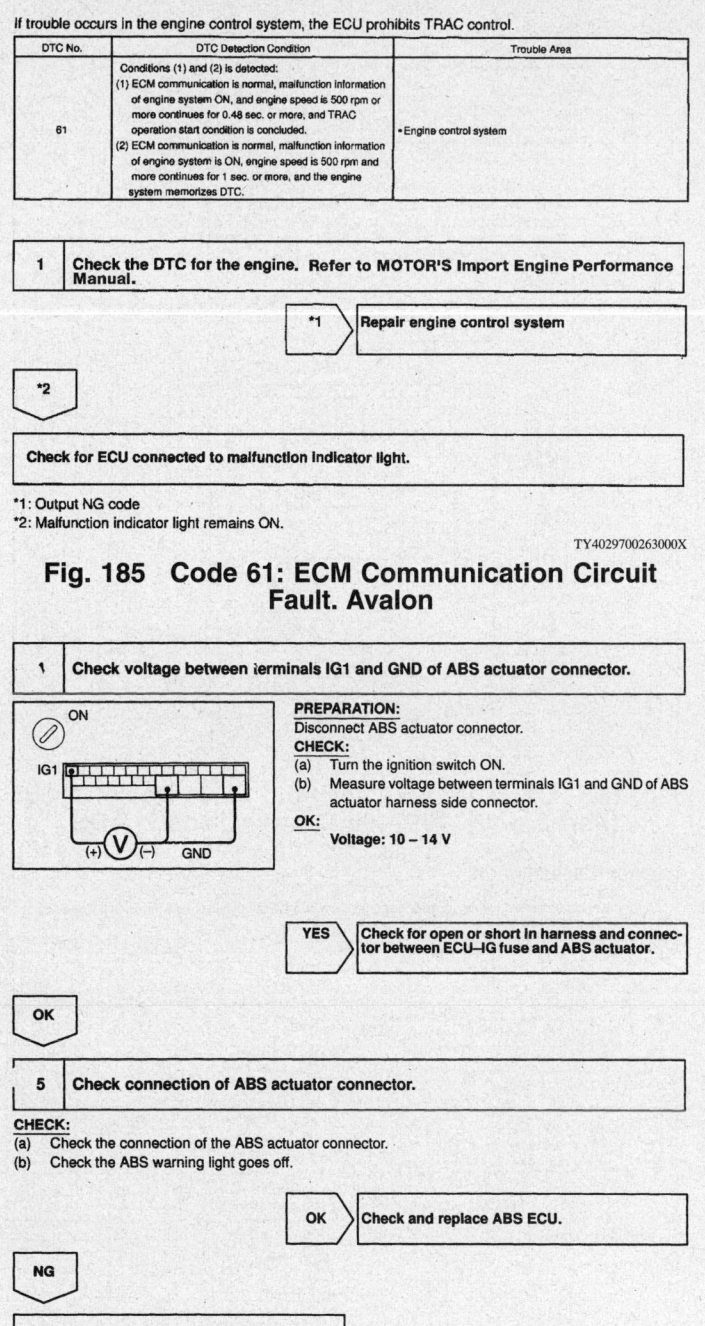

1 Check the DTC for the engine. Refer to MOTOR'S Import Engine Performance Manual.

*1 Repair engine control system

*2

Check for ECU connected to malfunction indicator light.

*1: Output NG code
*2: Malfunction indicator light remains ON.

TY4029700263000X

Fig. 185 Code 61: ECM Communication Circuit Fault. Avalon

1 Check voltage between terminals IG1 and GND of ABS actuator connector.

PREPARATION:
Disconnect ABS actuator connector.
CHECK:
(a) Turn the ignition switch ON.
(b) Measure voltage between terminals IG1 and GND of ABS actuator harness side connector.
OK:
Voltage: 10 – 14 V

YES Check for open or short in harness and connector between ECU–IG fuse and ABS actuator.

OK

5 Check connection of ABS actuator connector.

CHECK:
(a) Check the connection of the ABS actuator connector.
(b) Check the ABS warning light goes off.

OK Check and replace ABS ECU.

NG

Repair or replace harness or connector.

TY4029700253020X

Fig. 186 Code 62: ECU Fault (Part 2 of 2). Avalon

DTC No.	DTC Detecting Condition	Trouble Area
62	ABS ECU continuously detected the proper operation of ABS.	• Battery • ECU

Fail safe function: If trouble occurs in the power source circuit, the ECU cuts off current to the ABS solenoid valve relay and prohibits ABS control.

INSPECTION PROCEDURE

1 Is DTC output?

Check DTC

YES Repair circuit indicated by the code output.

NO

2 Is normal code displayed?

YES Check for short in harness and connector between DLC1 or DLC2 and ABS ECU

NO

3 Is ABS warning light go off?

YES Check open and short of the harness and connector in the Tc circuit between ECU and DLC2 or DLC1.

NO

TY4029700253010X

Fig. 186 Code 62: ECU Fault (Part 1 of 2). Avalon

CIRCUIT DESCRIPTION

The solenoid relay supplies power to each ABS solenoid. After the ignition switch is turned ON, if the initial check is OK, the relay goes on. The motor relay supplies power to the ABS pump motor. While the ABS is activated, the ECU switches the motor relay ON and operates the ABS pump motor.

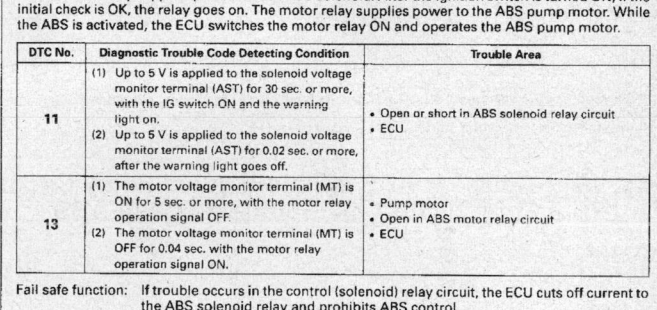

DTC No.	Diagnostic Trouble Code Detecting Condition	Trouble Area
11	(1) Up to 5 V is applied to the solenoid voltage monitor terminal (AST) for 30 sec. or more, with the IG switch ON and the warning light on. (2) Up to 5 V is applied to the solenoid voltage monitor terminal (AST) for 0.02 sec. or more, after the warning light goes off.	• Open or short in ABS solenoid relay circuit • ECU
13	(1) The motor voltage monitor terminal (MT) is ON for 5 sec. or more, with the motor relay operation signal OFF. (2) The motor voltage monitor terminal (MT) is OFF for 0.04 sec. with the motor relay operation signal ON.	• Pump motor • Open in ABS motor relay circuit • ECU

Fail safe function: If trouble occurs in the control (solenoid) relay circuit, the ECU cuts off current to the ABS solenoid relay and prohibits ABS control.

WIRING DIAGRAM

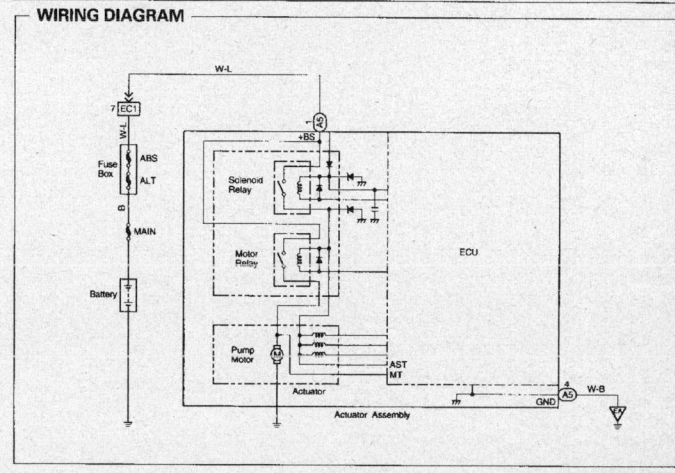

TY4029500357010X

Fig. 187 Codes 11 & 13: ABS Control Solenoid & Motor Relay Circuit (Part 1 of 2). 1996 Camry w/Bosch ABS

1 Check voltage between terminals Ⓐ5 1 and Ⓐ5 4 of ABS ECU connector.

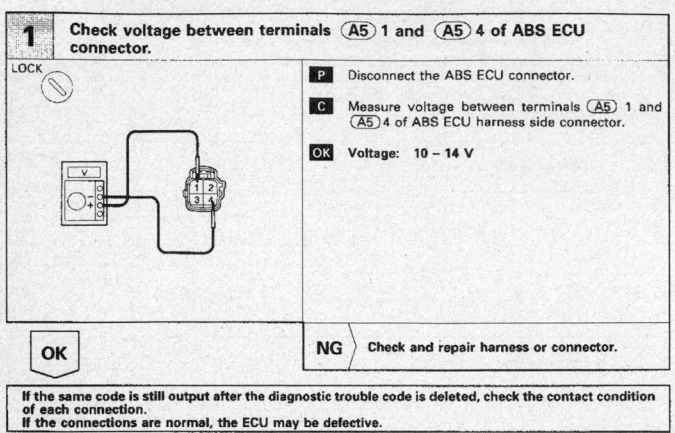

P Disconnect the ABS ECU connector.

C Measure voltage between terminals Ⓐ5 1 and Ⓐ5 4 of ABS ECU harness side connector.

OK Voltage: 10 – 14 V

OK ⟶ **NG** ⟩ Check and repair harness or connector.

If the same code is still output after the diagnostic trouble code is deleted, check the contact condition of each connection.
If the connections are normal, the ECU may be defective.

TY4029500357020X

Fig. 187   Codes 11 & 13: ABS Control Solenoid & Motor Relay Circuit (Part 2 of 2). 1996 Camry w/Bosch ABS

1 Check voltage between terminals A6 – 17, 18 and A6 – 16, 19 of ABS actuator connector.

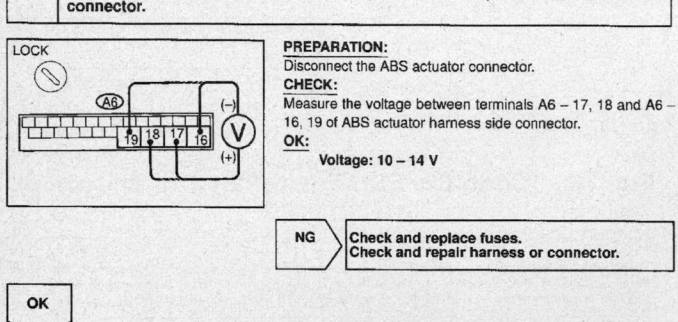

PREPARATION:
Disconnect the ABS actuator connector.

CHECK:
Measure the voltage between terminals A6 – 17, 18 and A6 – 16, 19 of ABS actuator harness side connector.

OK: Voltage: 10 – 14 V

NG ⟩ Check and replace fuses.
Check and repair harness or connector.

OK

If the same code is still output after the DTC is deleted, check the contact condition of each connection.
If the connector are normal, the ECU may be defective.

TY4029700367020X

Fig. 188   Code 11: ABS solenoid Valve Relay Circuit (Part 2 of 2). 1997–99 Camry w/Bosch ABS

CIRCUIT DESCRIPTION

This relay supplies power to each ABS solenoid. After the ignition switch is turned ON, if the initial check is OK, the relay goes on.

DTC No.	DTC Detecting Condition	Trouble Area
11	Detection of any conditions from (1) through (3): (1) 3 or more solenoid valves are show faulty in response and simultaneously valve supply voltage is detected faulty. (2) Solenoid valve relay will not be switched OFF. (3) Valve relay is frozen in spite of its high valve supply voltage.	• ABS solenoid valve relay • Valve supply voltage • ECU

Fail safe function: If trouble in the ABS solenoid valve relay circuit, the ECU cuts off current to the ABS solenoid valve relay and prohibits ABS control.

WIRING DIAGRAM

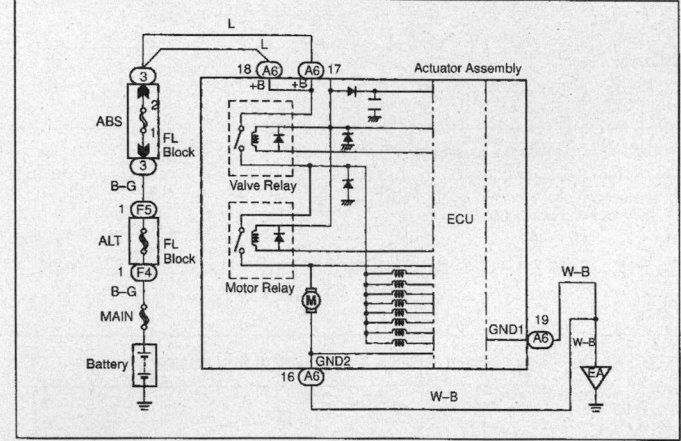

TY4029700367010X

Fig. 188   Code 11: ABS solenoid Valve Relay Circuit (Part 1 of 2). 1997–99 Camry w/Bosch ABS

CIRCUIT DESCRIPTION

This relay supplies power to each ABS solenoid. After the ignition switch is turned ON, if the initial check is OK, the relay goes on.

DTC No.	Diagnostic Trouble Code Detecting Condition	Trouble Area
11	Conditions (1) and (2) continue for 0.2 sec. or more: (1) ABS control (solenoid) relay terminal (SR) voltage: Battery positive voltage (2) ABS control (solenoid) relay monitor terminal (AST) voltage: 0 V	• ABS control (solenoid) relay • Open or short in ABS control (solenoid) relay circuit • ECU
12	Conditions (1) and (2) continue for 0.2sec. or more: (1) ABS control (solenoid) relay terminal (SR) voltage: 0 V (2) ABS control (solenoid) relay monitor terminal (AST) voltage: Battery positive voltage	• ABS control (solenoid) relay • B+ short in ABS control (solenoid) relay circuit • ECU

Fail safe function: If trouble occurs in the control (solenoid) relay circuit, the ECU cuts off current to the ABS control (solenoid) relay and prohibits ABS control.

WIRING DIAGRAM

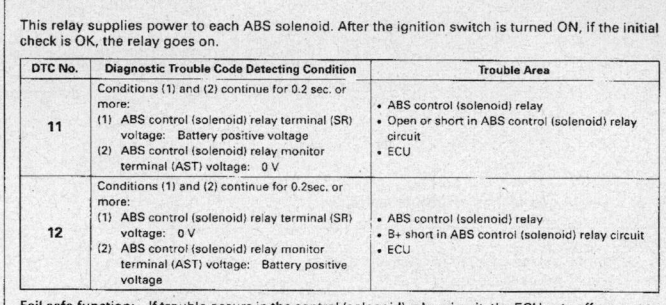
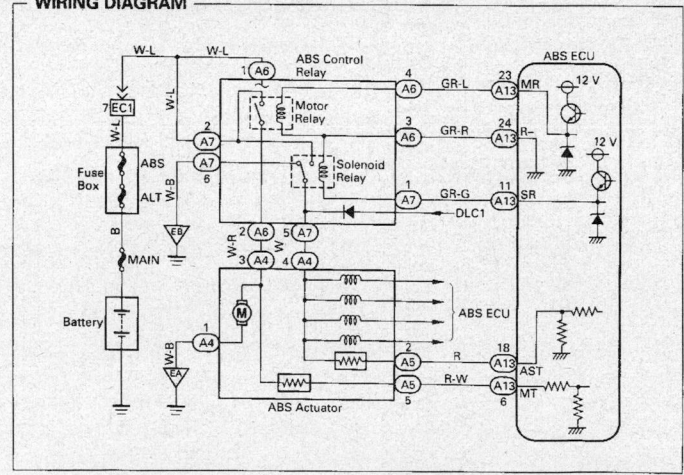

TY4029500350010X

Fig. 189   Codes 11 & 12: ABS Control Solenoid Relay Circuit (Part 1 of 3). 1996 Camry w/Nippondenso ABS

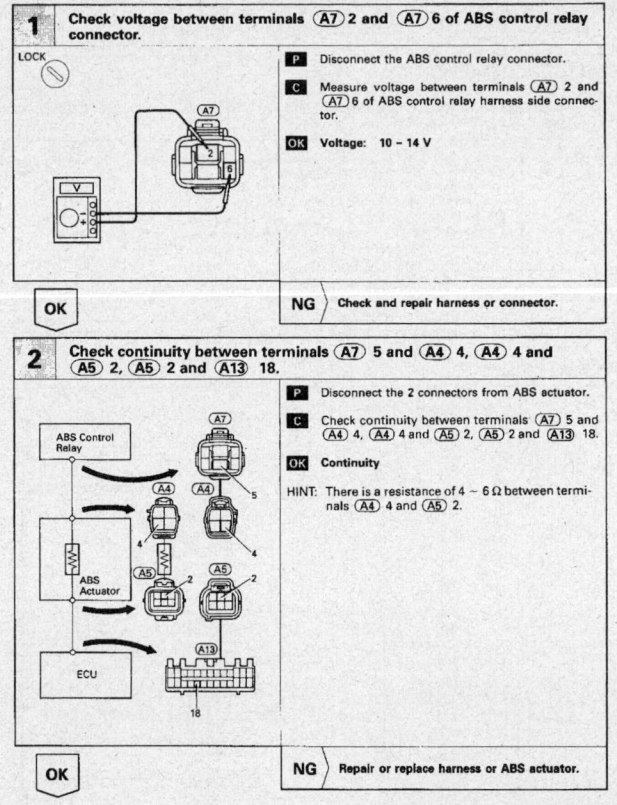

Fig. 189 Codes 11 & 12: ABS Control Solenoid Relay Circuit (Part 2 of 3). 1996 Camry w/Nippondenso ABS

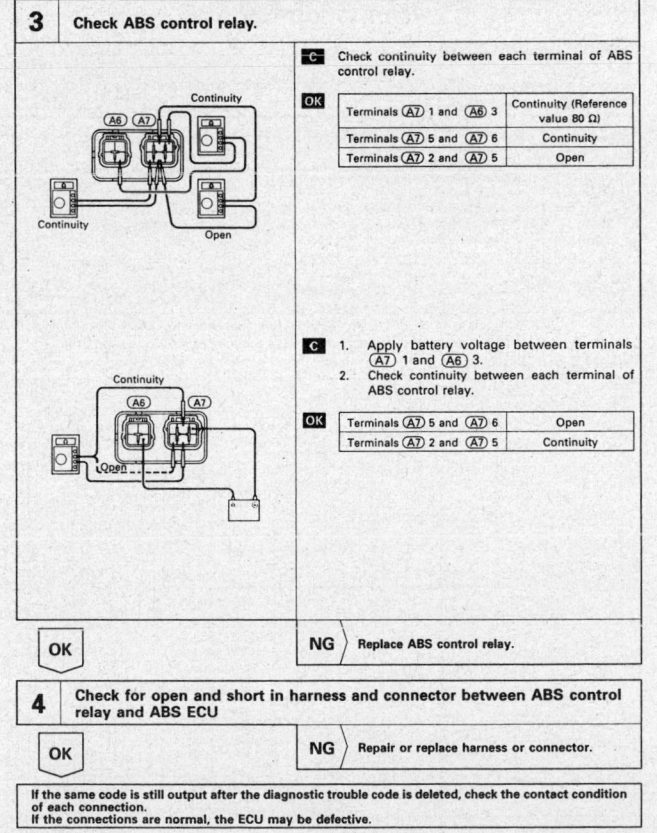

TY402920071040X

Fig. 189 Codes 11 & 12: ABS Control Solenoid Relay Circuit (Part 3 of 3). 1996 Camry w/Nippondenso ABS

DTC	11, 12	ABS Solenoid Relay Circuit

CIRCUIT DESCRIPTION

This relay supplies power to each ABS solenoid. After the ignition switch is turned ON, if the initial check is OK, the relay goes on.

DTC No.	DTC Detecting Condition	Trouble Area
11	Condition (1) or (2) continue for 0.2 sec. or more: (1) ABS ECU terminal IG1 voltage is 9.5 V to 18.0 V, and when solenoid relay is ON, ABS ECU terminal AST voltage is less than 4 V. (2) With solenoid relay is ON driving, ABS ECU terminal IG1 voltage becomes 9.5 V or less, and ABS ECU terminal AST voltage is less than 4 V.	• ABS solenoid relay • ABS solenoid relay circuit
12	Immediately after turning ignition switch ON, and when solenoid relay is OFF, ABS ECU terminal AST voltage is 4 V or more continues for 0.2 sec. or more.	

Fail safe function: If trouble in the ABS solenoid relay circuit, the ECU cuts off current to the ABS solenoid relay and prohibits ABS control.

WIRING DIAGRAM

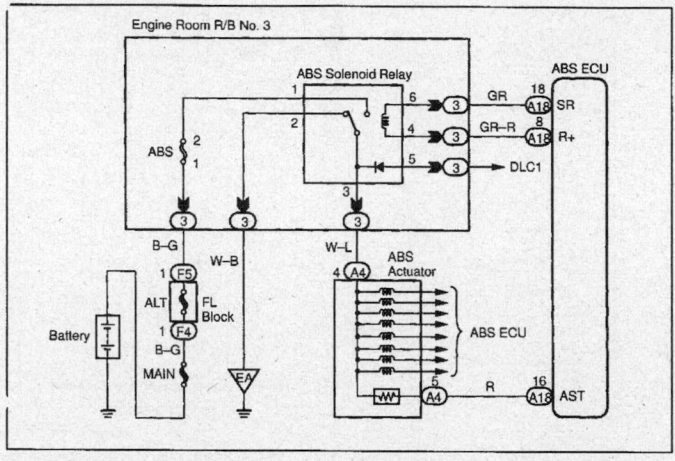

Fig. 190   Codes 11 & 12: ABS Control Solenoid Relay Circuit (Part 1 of 3). 1997–99 Camry w/Nippondenso ABS

CIRCUIT DESCRIPTION

This relay supplies power to each ABS & TRAC solenoid. After the ignition switch is turned ON, if the initial check is OK, the relay goes on.

DTC No.	DTC Detecting Condition	Trouble Area
11	Condition (1) to (3) are detected: (1) Malfunction of solenoid relay monitor. (2) Battery voltage will not exceed more than 17.0 V within 2.16 sec. (3) Battery voltage will not become less than 9.5 V within 2.16 sec., or after the solenoid relay is ON and AST voltage of ECU terminal does not become 8.0 V or more.	• ABS & TRAC solenoid relay • ABS & TRAC solenoid relay circuit • ECU
12	Solenoid relay is OFF in the midst of premain routine, and AST voltage of ECU terminal is 8.0 V or more continues for 2.04 sec. or more.	

Fail safe function: If trouble in the ABS & TRAC solenoid relay circuit, the ECU cuts off current to the ABS & TRAC solenoid relay and prohibits ABS control and TRAC control.

WIRING DIAGRAM

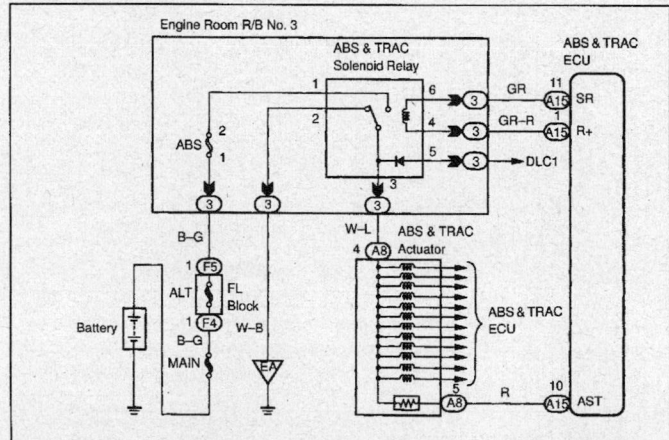

Fig. 190   Codes 11 & 12: ABS Control Solenoid Relay Circuit (Part 1 of 3). 1997–99 Camry w/Traction Control

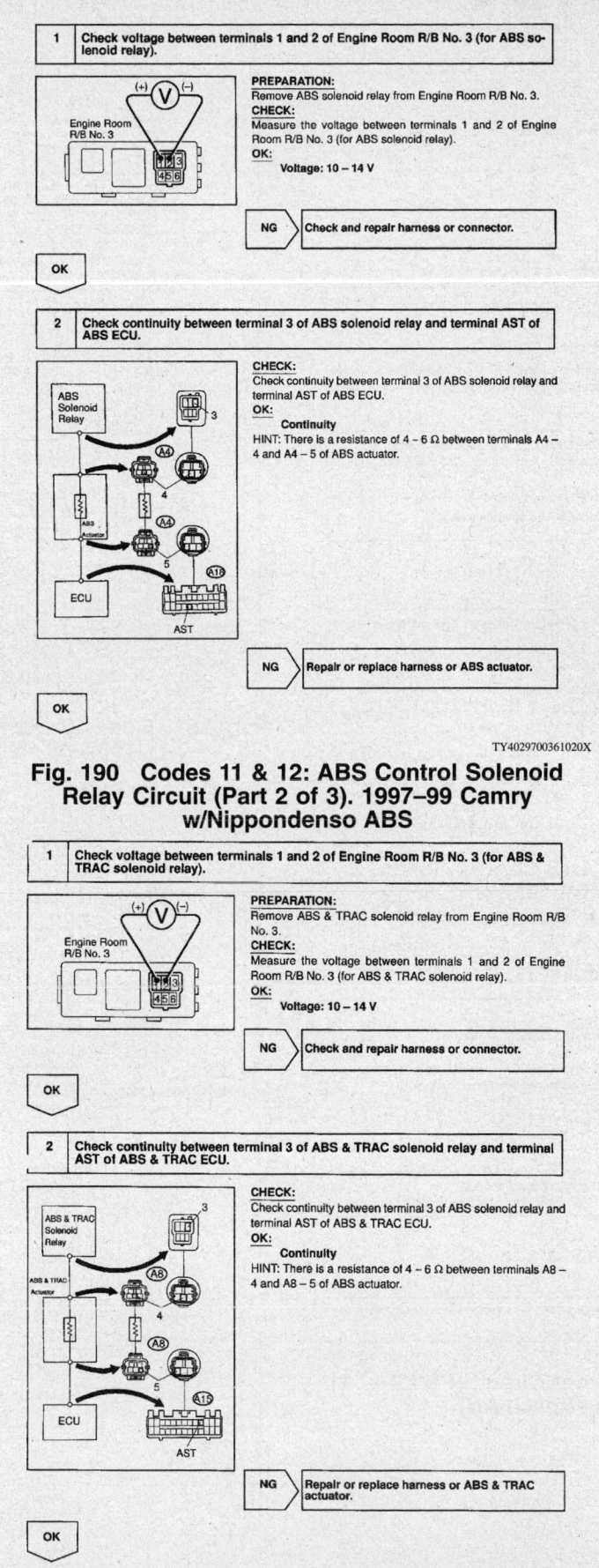

Fig. 190 Codes 11 & 12: ABS Control Solenoid Relay Circuit (Part 2 of 3). 1997–99 Camry w/Nippondenso ABS

Fig. 190 Codes 11 & 12: ABS Control Solenoid Relay Circuit (Part 2 of 3). 1997–99 Camry w/Traction Control

3	Check ABS solenoid relay.

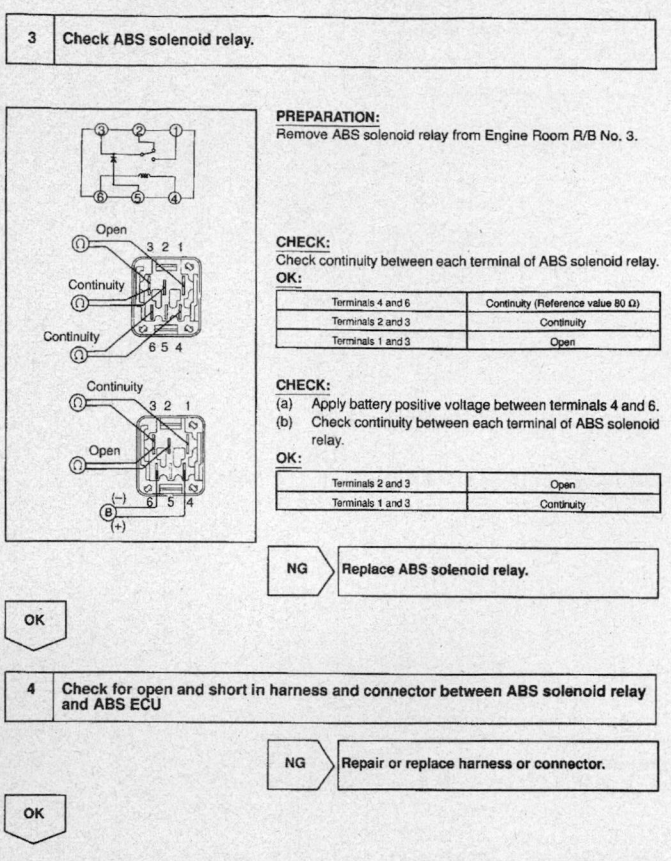

PREPARATION:
Remove ABS solenoid relay from Engine Room R/B No. 3.

CHECK:
Check continuity between each terminal of ABS solenoid relay.
OK:

Terminals 4 and 6	Continuity (Reference value 80 Ω)
Terminals 2 and 3	Continuity
Terminals 1 and 3	Open

CHECK:
(a) Apply battery positive voltage between terminals 4 and 6.
(b) Check continuity between each terminal of ABS solenoid relay.
OK:

Terminals 2 and 3	Open
Terminals 1 and 3	Continuity

> **NG** ⟩ Replace ABS solenoid relay.

OK

4	Check for open and short in harness and connector between ABS solenoid relay and ABS ECU

> **NG** ⟩ Repair or replace harness or connector.

OK

If the same code is still output after the DTC is deleted, check the contact condition of each connection.
If the connector are normal, the ECU may be defective.

TY4029700361030X

Fig. 190 Codes 11 & 12: ABS Control Solenoid Relay Circuit (Part 3 of 3). 1997–99 Camry w/Nippondenso ABS & Traction Control

1	Check voltage between terminals A6 – 17, 18 and A6 – 16, 19 of ABS actuator connector.

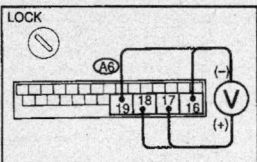

PREPARATION:
Disconnect the ABS actuator connector.
CHECK:
Measure the voltage between terminals A6 – 17, 18 and A6 – 16, 19 of ABS actuator harness side connector.
OK:
    Voltage: 10 – 14 V

> **NG** ⟩ Check and replace fuses.
> Check and repair harness or connector.

OK

If the same code is still output after the DTC is deleted, check the contact condition of each connection.
If the connector are normal, the ECU may be defective.

TY4029700368020X

Fig. 191 Code 13: Pump Motor Circuit (Part 2 of 2). 1997–99 Camry w/Bosch ABS

CIRCUIT DESCRIPTION

The ABS motor relay supplies power to the ABS pump motor. While the ABS is activated, the ECU switches the ABS motor relay ON and operates the ABS pump motor.

DTC No.	DTC Detecting Condition	Trouble Area
13	Detection of any conditions from (1) through (3): (1) After actuation the motor relay, pump motor voltage will not be supplied within 0.4 sec. (2) Pump motor voltage is in a high level, motor relay will not actuate for 2.5 sec. or more. (3) Pump motor voltage keeps low level for longer than 0.4 sec. and the pump repeats activating for 7 sec. 3 times maximally. After the last activation, the pump motor has been gone dead because of short circuit.	• ABS motor relay • Pump motor voltage • Pump motor lead disconnected • ECU

Fail safe function: If trouble occurs in the ABS motor relay circuit, the ECU cuts off current to the ABS solenoid relay and prohibits ABS control.

WIRING DIAGRAM

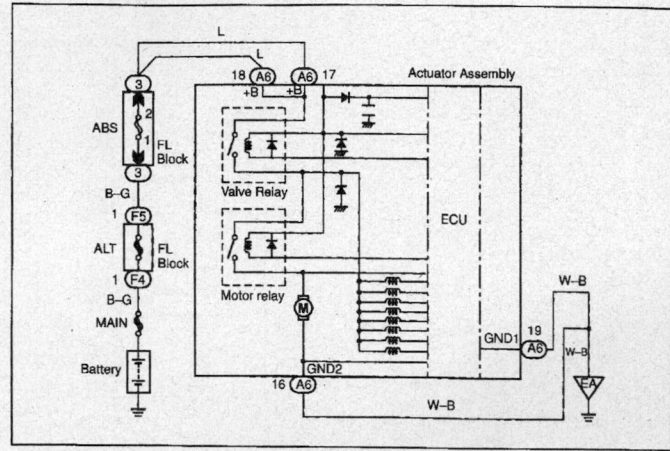

TY4029700368010X

Fig. 191 Code 13: Pump Motor Circuit (Part 1 of 2). 1997–99 Camry w/Bosch ABS

CIRCUIT DESCRIPTION

The ABS control (motor) relay supplies power to the ABS pump motor. While the ABS is activated, the ECU switches the control (motor) relay ON and operates the ABS pump motor.

DTC No.	DTC Detecting Condition	Trouble Area
13	Conditions (1) and (2) continued for 0.2 sec. or more. (1) ABS control (motor) relay terminal (MR) voltage: Battery positive voltage (2) ABS control (motor) relay monitor terminal (MT) voltage: 0 V	• ABS control (motor) relay • Open or short in ABS control (motor) relay circuit • ECU
14	Conditions (1) and (2) continued for 4 sec. or more. (1) ABS control (motor) relay terminal (MR) voltage: 0 V (2) ABS control (motor) relay monitor terminal (MT) voltage: Battery positive voltage	• ABS control (motor) relay • B+ short in ABS control (motor) relay circuit • ECU

Fail safe function: If trouble occurs in the ABS control (motor) relay circuit, the ECU cuts off current to the ABS control (solenoid) relay and prohibits ABS control.

WIRING DIAGRAM

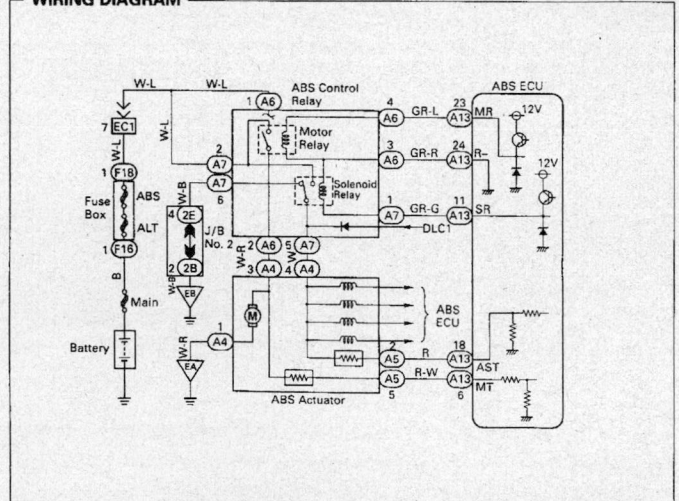

TY4029600351010X

Fig. 192 Codes 13 & 14: ABS Control Motor Relay Circuit (Part 1 of 3). 1996 Camry w/Nippondenso ABS

1 Check voltage between terminal (A7) 2 of ABS control relay and body ground.

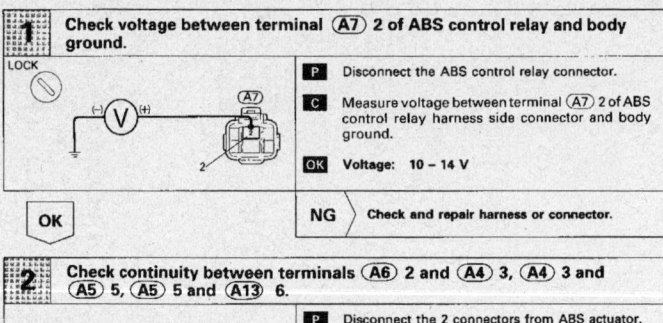

P	Disconnect the ABS control relay connector.
C	Measure voltage between terminal (A7) 2 of ABS control relay harness side connector and body ground.
OK	**Voltage: 10 – 14 V**

OK ↓ | **NG** ⟩ Check and repair harness or connector.

2 Check continuity between terminals (A6) 2 and (A4) 3, (A4) 3 and (A5) 5, (A5) 5 and (A13) 6.

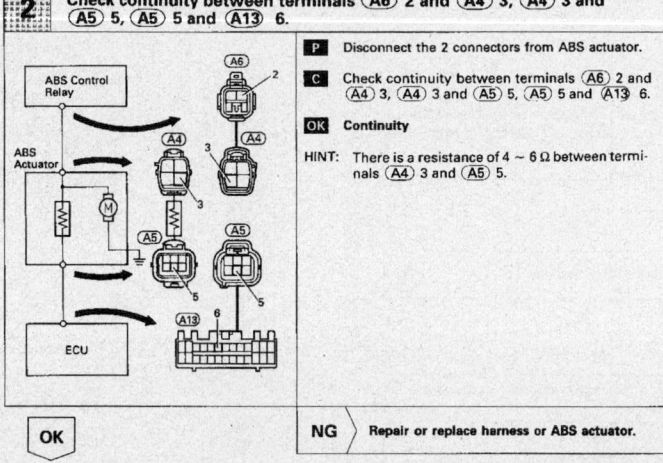

P	Disconnect the 2 connectors from ABS actuator.
C	Check continuity between terminals (A6) 2 and (A4) 3, (A4) 3 and (A5) 5, (A5) 5 and (A13) 6.
OK	**Continuity**

HINT: There is a resistance of 4 ~ 6 Ω between terminals (A4) 3 and (A5) 5.

OK ↓ | **NG** ⟩ Repair or replace harness or ABS actuator.

TY4029600351020X

Fig. 192 Codes 13 & 14: ABS Control Motor Relay Circuit (Part 2 of 3). 1996 Camry w/Nippondenso ABS

CIRCUIT DESCRIPTION

The ABS motor relay supplies power to the ABS pump motor. While the ABS is activated, the ECU switches the ABS motor relay ON and operates the ABS pump motor.

DTC No.	DTC Detecting Condition	Trouble Area
13	Condition (1) or (2) continued for 0.2 sec. or more: (1) ABS ECU terminal IG1 voltage is 9.5 V to 18.0 V, and when motor relay is ON in the midst of initial check or in operation of ABS control, ABS ECU terminal MT voltage is less than 4 V. (2) Motor relay is ON driving in the midst of initial check or in operation of ABS control, ABS ECU terminal IG1 voltage becomes 9.5 V or less and ABS ECU terminal MT voltage is less than 4 V.	• ABS motor relay • ABS motor relay circuit
14	When motor relay is OFF, ABS ECU terminal MT voltage is 4 V or more continues for 0.2 sec. or more.	

Fail safe function: If trouble occurs in the ABS motor relay circuit, the ECU cuts off current to the ABS solenoid relay and prohibits ABS control.

WIRING DIAGRAM

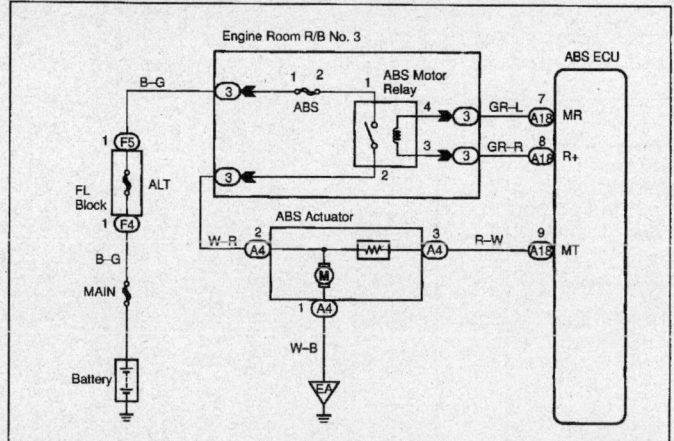

TY4029700362010X

Fig. 193 Codes 13 & 14: ABS Control Motor Relay Circuit (Part 1 of 3). 1997–99 Camry w/Nippondenso ABS

3 Check ABS control relay.

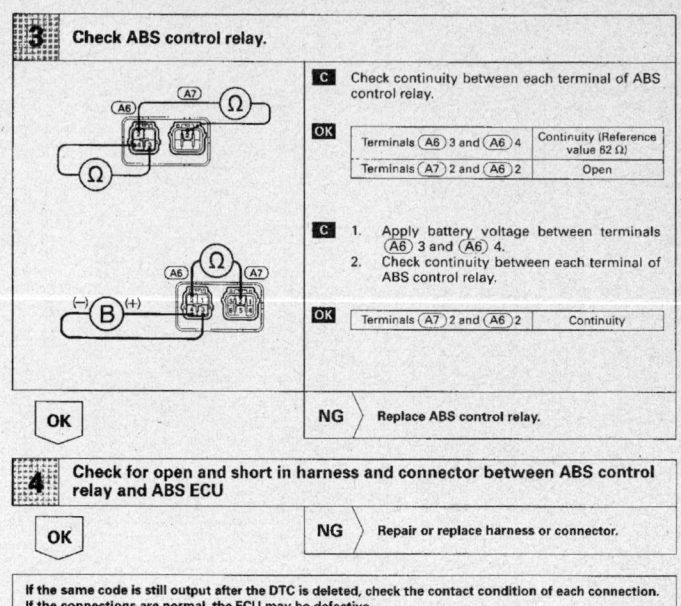

C	Check continuity between each terminal of ABS control relay.
OK	Terminals (A6) 3 and (A6) 4 — Continuity (Reference value 62 Ω) Terminals (A7) 2 and (A6) 2 — Open

C	1. Apply battery voltage between terminals (A6) 3 and (A6) 4. 2. Check continuity between each terminal of ABS control relay.
OK	Terminals (A7) 2 and (A6) 2 — Continuity

OK ↓ | **NG** ⟩ Replace ABS control relay.

4 Check for open and short in harness and connector between ABS control relay and ABS ECU

OK ↓ | **NG** ⟩ Repair or replace harness or connector.

If the same code is still output after the DTC is deleted, check the contact condition of each connection. If the connections are normal, the ECU may be defective.

TY4029600351030X

Fig. 192 Codes 13 & 14: ABS Control Motor Relay Circuit (Part 3 of 3). 1996 Camry w/Nippondenso ABS

1 Check voltage between terminal 1 of Engine Room R/B No. 3 (for ABS motor relay) and body ground.

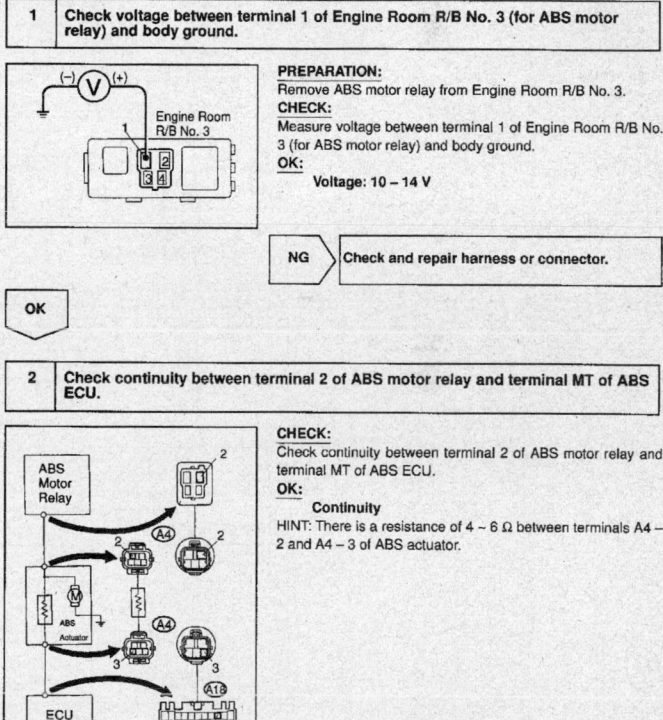

PREPARATION:
Remove ABS motor relay from Engine Room R/B No. 3.
CHECK:
Measure voltage between terminal 1 of Engine Room R/B No. 3 (for ABS motor relay) and body ground.
OK:
Voltage: 10 – 14 V

NG ⟩ Check and repair harness or connector.

OK ↓

2 Check continuity between terminal 2 of ABS motor relay and terminal MT of ABS ECU.

CHECK:
Check continuity between terminal 2 of ABS motor relay and terminal MT of ABS ECU.
OK:
Continuity
HINT: There is a resistance of 4 ~ 6 Ω between terminals A4 – 2 and A4 – 3 of ABS actuator.

NG ⟩ Repair or replace harness or ABS actuator.

OK ↓

TY4029700362020X

Fig. 193 Codes 13 & 14: ABS Control Motor Relay Circuit (Part 2 of 3). 1997–99 Camry w/Nippondenso ABS

3	Check ABS motor relay.

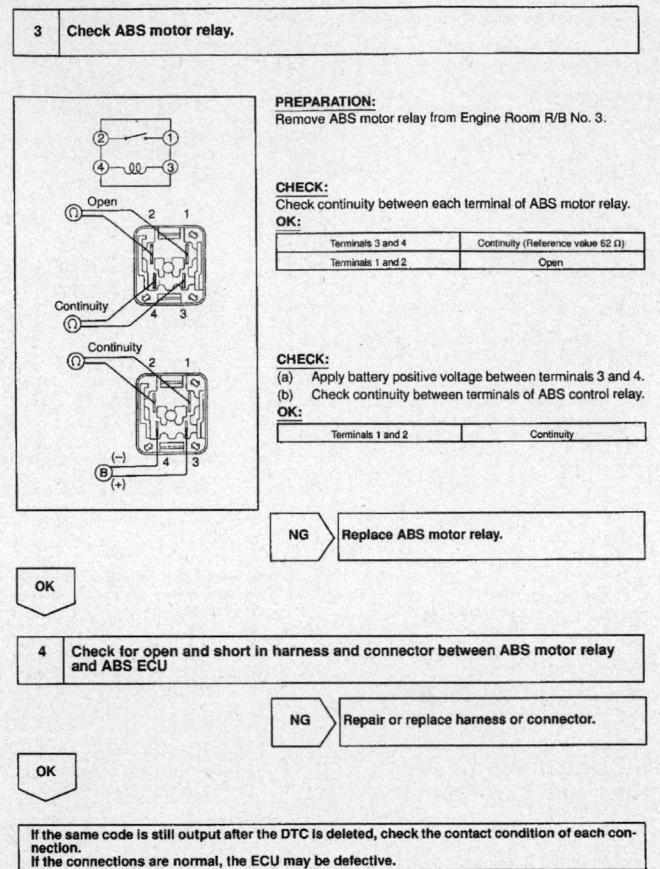

PREPARATION:
Remove ABS motor relay from Engine Room R/B No. 3.

CHECK:
Check continuity between each terminal of ABS motor relay.
OK:

Terminals 3 and 4	Continuity (Reference value 52 Ω)
Terminals 1 and 2	Open

CHECK:
(a) Apply battery positive voltage between terminals 3 and 4.
(b) Check continuity between terminals of ABS control relay.
OK:

Terminals 1 and 2	Continuity

NG >	Replace ABS motor relay.

OK

4	Check for open and short in harness and connector between ABS motor relay and ABS ECU

NG >	Repair or replace harness or connector.

OK

> If the same code is still output after the DTC is deleted, check the contact condition of each connection.
> If the connections are normal, the ECU may be defective.

TY4029700362030X

Fig. 193 Codes 13 & 14: ABS Control Motor Relay Circuit (Part 3 of 3). 1997–99 Camry w/Nippondenso ABS

CIRCUIT DESCRIPTION

The ABS & TRAC motor relay supplies power to the ABS & TRAC pump motor. While the ABS is activated, the ECU switches the ABS & TRAC motor relay ON and operates the ABS & TRAC pump motor.

DTC No.	DTC Detecting Condition	Trouble Area
13	Conditions (1) to (3) are detected: (1) Malfunction of motor relay monitor. (2) Battery voltage will not exceed more than 17.0 V within 2.16 sec. (3) Battery voltage will not become less than 9.5 V within 2.16 sec., or after the motor relay is ON and motor relay monitor does not ON.	• ABS & TRAC motor relay • ABS & TRAC motor relay circuit • ECU
14	Motor relay is OFF, and motor relay monitor is ON continues for 20.16 sec. or more.	

Fail safe function: If trouble occurs in the ABS & TRAC motor relay circuit, the ECU cuts off current to the ABS & TRAC solenoid relay and prohibits ABS control and TRAC control.

WIRING DIAGRAM

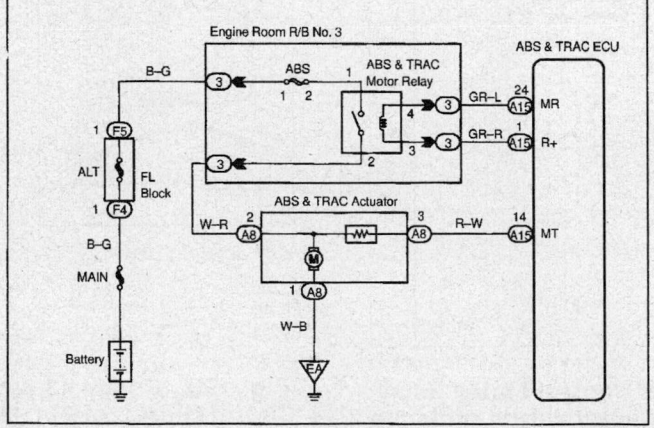

TY4029700375010X

Fig. 194 Codes 13 & 14: ABS Control Motor Relay Circuit (Part 1 of 3). 1997–99 Camry w/Traction Control

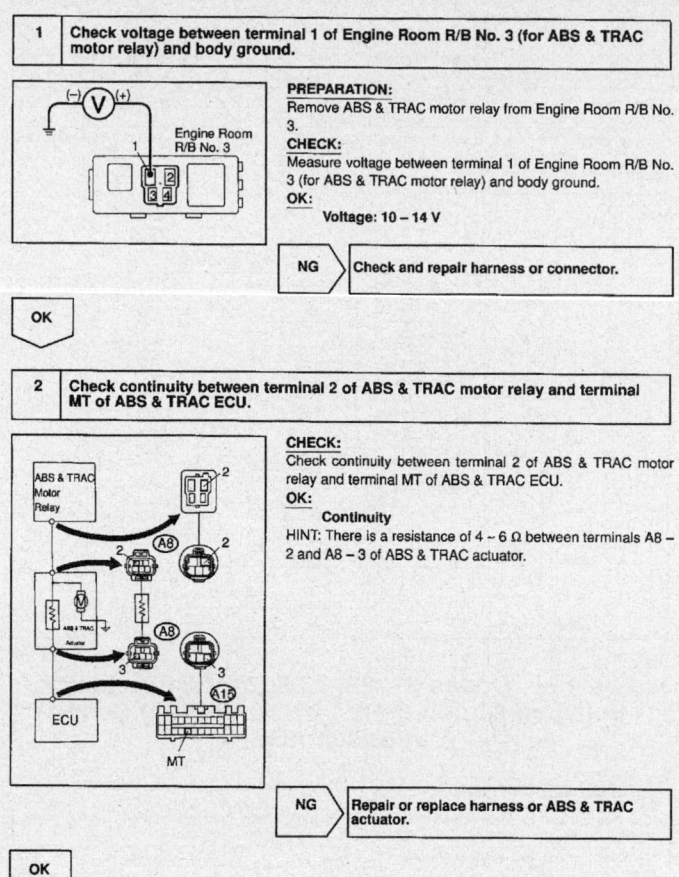

1 | Check voltage between terminal 1 of Engine Room R/B No. 3 (for ABS & TRAC motor relay) and body ground.

PREPARATION:
Remove ABS & TRAC motor relay from Engine Room R/B No. 3.

CHECK:
Measure voltage between terminal 1 of Engine Room R/B No. 3 (for ABS & TRAC motor relay) and body ground.

OK:

Voltage: 10 – 14 V

NG ▷ Check and repair harness or connector.

OK

2 | Check continuity between terminal 2 of ABS & TRAC motor relay and terminal MT of ABS & TRAC ECU.

CHECK:
Check continuity between terminal 2 of ABS & TRAC motor relay and terminal MT of ABS & TRAC ECU.

OK:

Continuity

HINT: There is a resistance of 4 ~ 6 Ω between terminals A8 – 2 and A8 – 3 of ABS & TRAC actuator.

NG ▷ Repair or replace harness or ABS & TRAC actuator.

OK

TY4029700375020X

Fig. 194 Codes 13 & 14: ABS Control Motor Relay Circuit (Part 2 of 3). 1997–99 Camry w/Traction Control

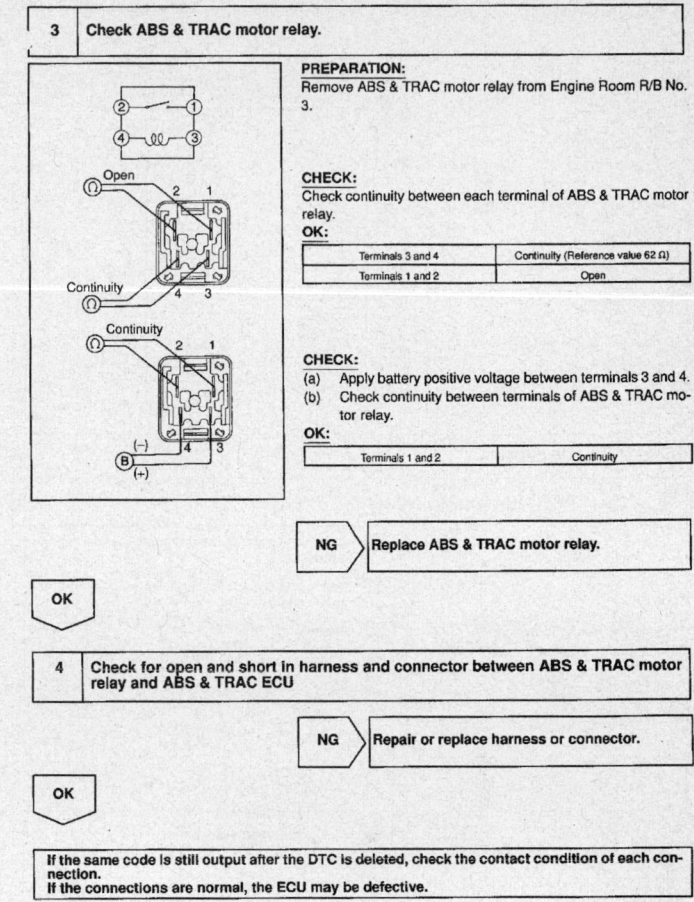

3 | Check ABS & TRAC motor relay.

PREPARATION:
Remove ABS & TRAC motor relay from Engine Room R/B No. 3.

CHECK:
Check continuity between each terminal of ABS & TRAC motor relay.

OK:

Terminals 3 and 4	Continuity (Reference value 62 Ω)
Terminals 1 and 2	Open

CHECK:
(a) Apply battery positive voltage between terminals 3 and 4.
(b) Check continuity between terminals of ABS & TRAC motor relay.

OK:

Terminals 1 and 2	Continuity

NG ▷ Replace ABS & TRAC motor relay.

OK

4 | Check for open and short in harness and connector between ABS & TRAC motor relay and ABS & TRAC ECU

NG ▷ Repair or replace harness or connector.

OK

If the same code is still output after the DTC is deleted, check the contact condition of each connection.
If the connections are normal, the ECU may be defective.

TY4029700375030X

Fig. 194 Codes 13 & 14: ABS Control Motor Relay Circuit (Part 3 of 3). 1997–99 Camry w/Traction Control

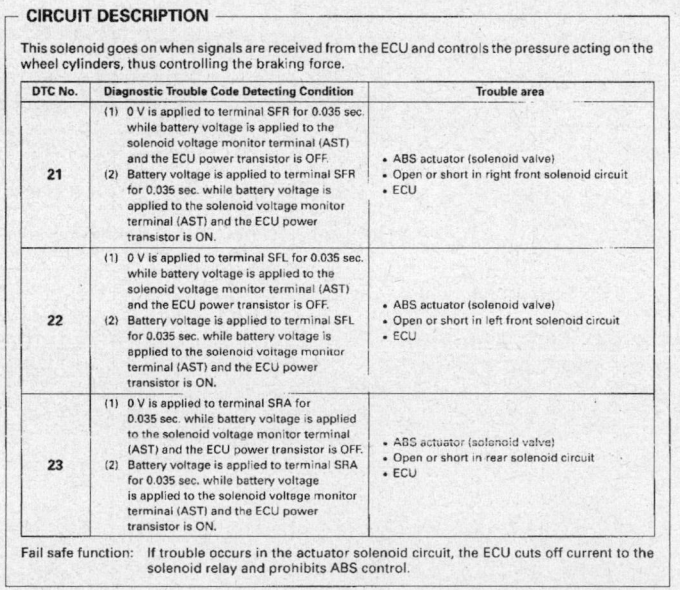

CIRCUIT DESCRIPTION

This solenoid goes on when signals are received from the ECU and controls the pressure acting on the wheel cylinders, thus controlling the braking force.

DTC No.	Diagnostic Trouble Code Detecting Condition	Trouble area
21	(1) 0 V is applied to terminal SFR for 0.035 sec. while battery voltage is applied to the solenoid voltage monitor terminal (AST) and the ECU power transistor is OFF. (2) Battery voltage is applied to terminal SFR for 0.035 sec. while battery voltage is applied to the solenoid voltage monitor terminal (AST) and the ECU power transistor is ON.	• ABS actuator (solenoid valve) • Open or short in right front solenoid circuit • ECU
22	(1) 0 V is applied to terminal SFL for 0.035 sec. while battery voltage is applied to the solenoid voltage monitor terminal (AST) and the ECU power transistor is OFF. (2) Battery voltage is applied to terminal SFL for 0.035 sec. while battery voltage is applied to the solenoid voltage monitor terminal (AST) and the ECU power transistor is ON.	• ABS actuator (solenoid valve) • Open or short in left front solenoid circuit • ECU
23	(1) 0 V is applied to terminal SRA for 0.035 sec. while battery voltage is applied to the solenoid voltage monitor terminal (AST) and the ECU power transistor is OFF. (2) Battery voltage is applied to terminal SRA for 0.035 sec. while battery voltage is applied to the solenoid voltage monitor terminal (AST) and the ECU power transistor is ON.	• ABS actuator (solenoid valve) • Open or short in rear solenoid circuit • ECU

Fail safe function: If trouble occurs in the actuator solenoid circuit, the ECU cuts off current to the solenoid relay and prohibits ABS control.

TY4029500358010X

Fig. 195 Codes 21, 22 & 23: ABS Actuator Solenoid Circuit (Part 1 of 2). 1996 Camry w/Bosch ABS

WIRING DIAGRAM

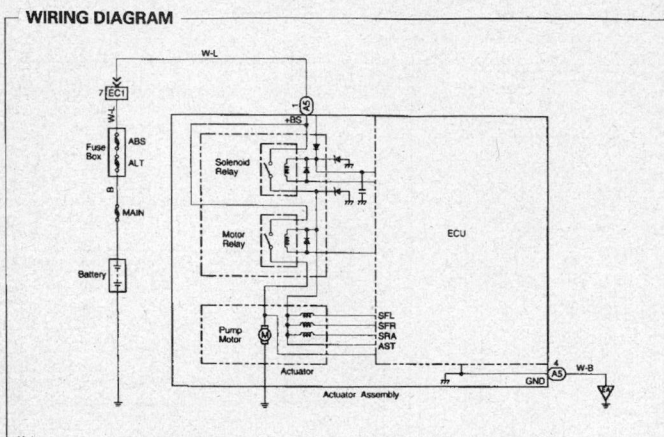

INSPECTION PROCEDURE

1 Check ABS actuator solenoid.

P Remove the ABS ECU cover and disconnect 6-pin connector.

C Check continuity between terminals 1 and 2, 3 and 4, and 5 and 6.

OK Continuity

HINT: Resistance of each solenoid coil is 1.1 Ω.

OK →

NG → Replace ABS actuator.

If the same code is still output after the diagnostic trouble code is deleted, check the contact condition of each connection.
If the connections are normal, the ECU may be defective.

TY4029500358020X

Fig. 195 Codes 21, 22 & 23: ABS Actuator Solenoid Circuit (Part 2 of 2). 1996 Camry w/Bosch ABS

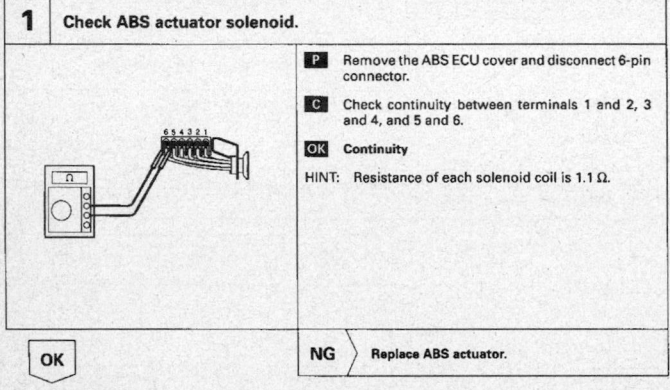

1 Check the DTC once more.

PREPARATION:
(a) Clear the DTC
(b) Turn the ignition switch OFF.
CHECK:
Turn the ignition switch ON, and check if the same DTC is stored in the memory.

NO → No problem.

YES

Replace ABS ECU.

TY4029700369020X

Fig. 196 Codes 21, 22, 23 & 24: ABS Actuator Solenoid Circuit (Part 2 of 2). 1997–99 Camry w/Bosch ABS

CIRCUIT DESCRIPTION

This solenoid goes on when signals are received from the ECU and controls the pressure acting on the wheel cylinders thus controlling the braking force.

DTC No.	DTC Detecting Condition	Trouble Area
21, 22, 23, 24	Solenoid valve signal does not match for the check result.	• Each solenoid valve

Fail safe function: If trouble occurs in the actuator solenoid valve circuit, the ECU cuts off current to the ABS solenoid valve relay and prohibits ABS control.

WIRING DIAGRAM

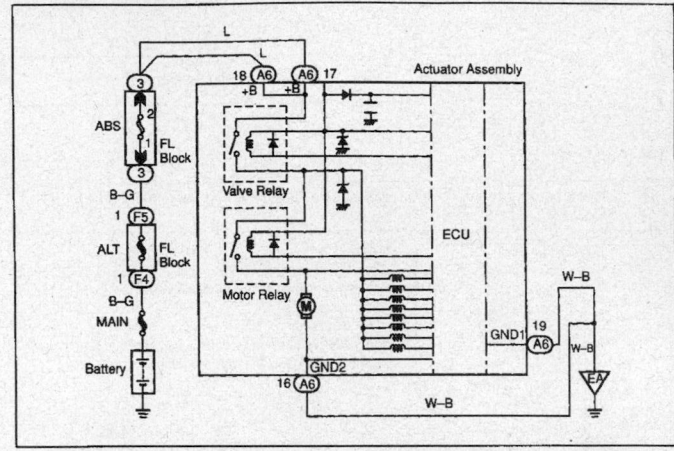

TY4029700369010X

Fig. 196 Codes 21, 22, 23 & 24: ABS Actuator Solenoid Circuit (Part 1 of 2). 1997–99 Camry w/Bosch ABS

CIRCUIT DESCRIPTION

This solenoid goes on when signals are received from the ECU and controls the pressure acting on the wheel cylinders, thus controlling the braking force.

DTC No.	Diagnostic Trouble Code Detecting Condition	Trouble area
21	Conditions (1) through (3) continue for 0.05 sec. or more: (1) ABS control (solenoid) relay terminal (SR) voltage: Battery positive voltage (2) Voltage of ABS ECU terminal AST: Battery positive voltage (3) When power transistor of ECU is ON, voltage of terminal SFR is 0 V or battery positive voltage.	• ABS actuator • Open or short in SFR circuit • ECU
22	Conditions (1) through (3) continue for 0.05 sec. or more: (1) ABS control (solenoid) relay terminal (SR) voltage: Battery positive voltage (2) Voltage of ABS ECU terminal AST: Battery positive voltage (3) When power transistor of ECU is ON, voltage of terminal SFL is 0 V or battery positive voltage.	• ABS actuator • Open or short in SFL circuit • ECU
23	Conditions (1) through (3) continue for 0.05 sec. or more: (1) ABS control (solenoid) relay terminal (SR) voltage: Battery positive voltage (2) Voltage of ABS ECU terminal AST: Battery positive voltage (3) When power transistor of ECU is ON, voltage of terminal SRR is 0 V or battery positive voltage.	• ABS actuator • Open or short in SRR circuit • ECU
24	Conditions (1) through (3) continue for 0.05 sec. or more: (1) ABS control (solenoid) relay terminal (SR) voltage: Battery positive voltage (2) Voltage of ABS ECU terminal AST: Battery positive voltage (3) When power transistor of ECU is ON, voltage of terminal SRL is 0 V or battery positive voltage.	• ABS actuator • Open or short in SRL circuit • ECU

Fail safe function: If trouble occurs in the actuator solenoid circuit, the ECU cuts off current to the control (solenoid) relay and prohibits ABS control.

TY4029500352010X

Fig. 197 Codes 21, 22, 23 & 24: ABS Actuator Solenoid Circuit (Part 1 of 2). 1996 Camry w/Nippondenso ABS

WIRING DIAGRAM

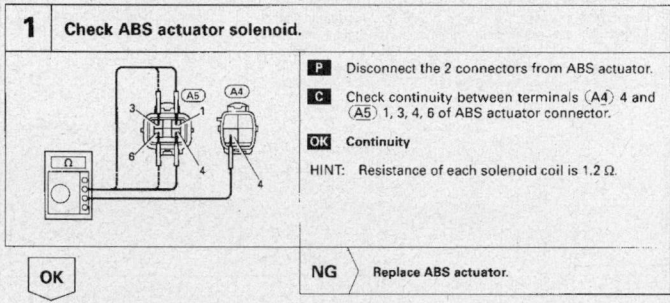

INSPECTION PROCEDURE

1 Check ABS actuator solenoid.

P	Disconnect the 2 connectors from ABS actuator.
C	Check continuity between terminals (A4) 4 and (A5) 1, 3, 4, 6 of ABS actuator connector.
OK	Continuity

HINT: Resistance of each solenoid coil is 1.2 Ω.

OK

NG > Replace ABS actuator.

2 Check for open and short in harness and connector between ABS ECU and actuator

OK

NG > Repair or replace harness or connector.

If the same code is still output after the diagnostic trouble code is deleted, check the contact condition of each connection.
If the connections are normal, the ECU may be defective.

TY4029500352020X

Fig. 197 Codes 21, 22, 23 & 24: ABS Actuator Solenoid Circuit (Part 2 of 2). 1996 Camry w/Nippondenso ABS

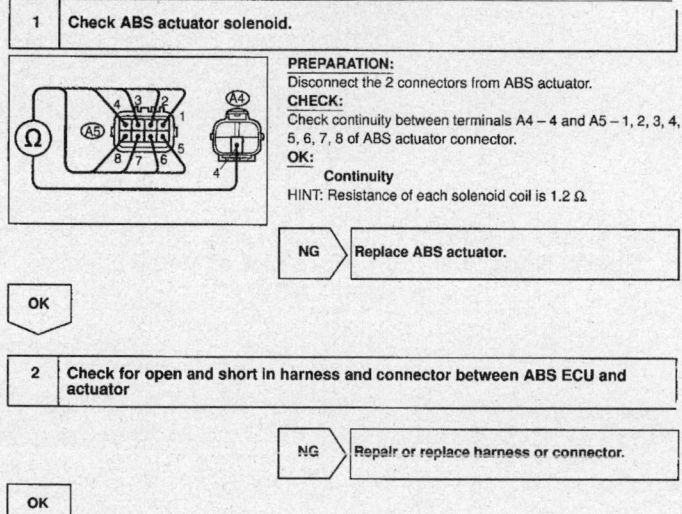

1 Check ABS actuator solenoid.

PREPARATION:
Disconnect the 2 connectors from ABS actuator.
CHECK:
Check continuity between terminals A4 – 4 and A5 – 1, 2, 3, 4, 5, 6, 7, 8 of ABS actuator connector.
OK:
Continuity
HINT: Resistance of each solenoid coil is 1.2 Ω.

NG > Replace ABS actuator.

OK

2 Check for open and short in harness and connector between ABS ECU and actuator

NG > Repair or replace harness or connector.

OK

If the same code is still output after the DTC is deleted, check the contact condition of each connection.
If the connections are normal, the ECU may be defective.

TY4029700363020X

Fig. 198 Codes 21, 22, 23 & 24: ABS Actuator Solenoid Circuit (Part 2 of 2). 1997–99 Camry w/Nippondenso ABS

CIRCUIT DESCRIPTION

This solenoid goes on when signals are received from the ECU and controls the pressure acting on the wheel cylinders thus controlling the braking force.

DTC No.	DTC Detecting Condition	Trouble Area
21	Actuator solenoid SFRR or SFRH is open or short circuit continues for 0.05 sec. or more.	• ABS actuator • SFRR or SFRH circuit
22	Actuator solenoid SFLR or SFLH is open or short circuit continues for 0.05 sec. or more.	• ABS actuator • SFLR or SFLH circuit
23	Actuator solenoid SRRR or SRRH is open or short circuit continues for 0.05 sec. or more.	• ABS actuator • SRRR or SRRH circuit
24	Actuator solenoid SRLR or SRLH is open or short circuit continues for 0.05 sec. or more.	• ABS actuator • SRLR or SRLH circuit

Fail safe function: If trouble occurs in the actuator solenoid circuit, the ECU cuts off current to the ABS solenoid relay and prohibits ABS control.

WIRING DIAGRAM

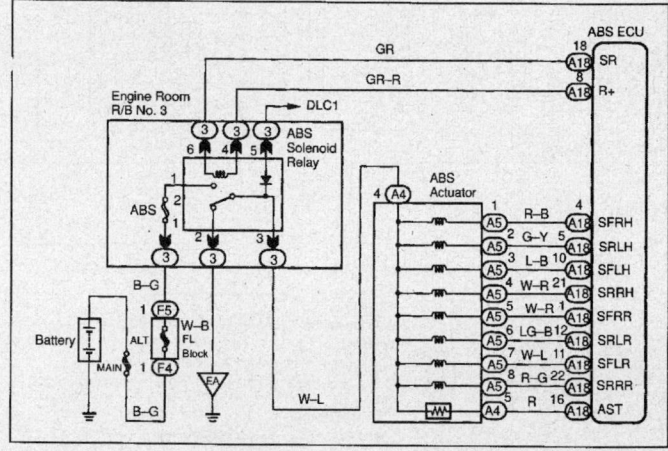

TY4029700363010X

Fig. 198 Codes 21, 22, 23 & 24: ABS Actuator Solenoid Circuit (Part 1 of 2). 1997–99 Camry w/Nippondenso ABS

CIRCUIT DESCRIPTION

This solenoid goes on when signals are received from the ECU and controls the pressure acting on the wheel cylinders thus controlling the braking force.

DTC No.	DTC Detecting Condition	Trouble Area
21		• ABS actuator • SFRR or SFRH circuit • ECU
22		• ABS actuator • SFLR or SFLH circuit • ECU
23	Conditions (1) and (2) or (3) continued for 0.48 sec. or more:	• ABS actuator • SRRR or SRRH circuit • ECU
24	(1) Recovery prohibit run pulse is not output, solenoid relay is ON, AST voltage of ECU terminal is 8.0 V or more, and solenoid output has no change between the last time and this time.	• ABS actuator • SRLR or SRLH circuit • ECU
25	(2) Solenoid output is ON, pressure holding solenoid monitor voltage is more than 1.0 V or pressure reduction solenoid monitor voltage is more than 1.5 V.	• ABS actuator • SMC1 circuit • ECU
26	(3) Solenoid output is OFF, solenoid monitor voltage is more than –1.0 V AST voltage of ECU.	• ABS actuator • SMC2 circuit • ECU
27		• ABS actuator • SRC1 circuit • ECU
28		• ABS actuator • SRC2 circuit • ECU

Fail safe function: If trouble occurs in the actuator solenoid circuit, the ECU cuts off current to the ABS & TRAC solenoid relay and prohibits ABS control and TRAC control.

TY4029700376010X

Fig. 199 Codes 21, 22, 23, 24, 25, 26, 27 & 28: ABS Actuator Solenoid Circuit (Part 1 of 3). 1997–99 Camry w/Traction Control

WIRING DIAGRAM

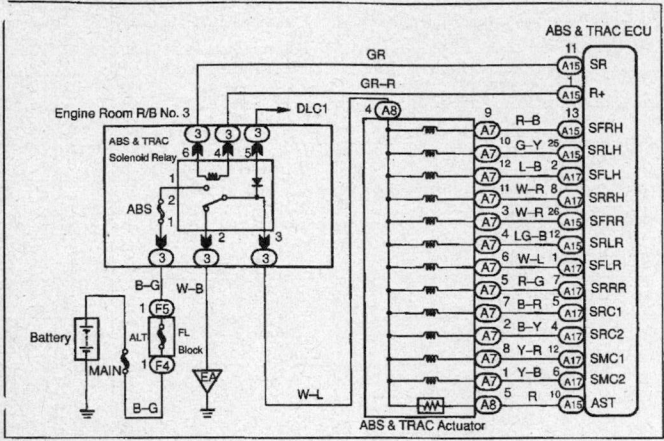

INSPECTION PROCEDURE

1	Check ABS & TRAC actuator solenoid.

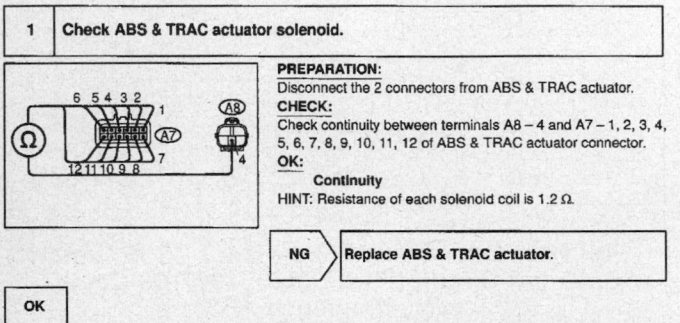

PREPARATION:
Disconnect the 2 connectors from ABS & TRAC actuator.
CHECK:
Check continuity between terminals A8 – 4 and A7 – 1, 2, 3, 4, 5, 6, 7, 8, 9, 10, 11, 12 of ABS & TRAC actuator connector.
OK:
  Continuity
HINT: Resistance of each solenoid coil is 1.2 Ω.

NG >	Replace ABS & TRAC actuator.

OK

TY4029700376020X

Fig. 199 Codes 21, 22, 23, 24, 25, 26, 27 & 28: ABS Actuator Solenoid Circuit (Part 2 of 3). 1997–99 Camry w/Traction Control

2	Check for open and short in harness and connector between ABS & TRAC ECU and actuator

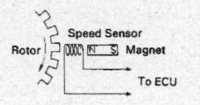

NG >	Repair or replace harness or connector.

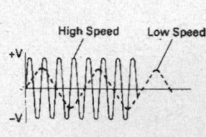

OK

• If the same code is still output after the DTC is deleted, check the contact condition of each connection.
• If the connections are normal, the ECU may be defective.

TY4029700376030X

Fig. 199 Codes 21, 22, 23, 24, 25, 26, 27 & 28: ABS Actuator Solenoid Circuit (Part 3 of 3). 1997–99 Camry w/Traction Control

CIRCUIT DESCRIPTION

The speed sensor detects the wheel speed and sends the appropriate signals to the ECU. These signals are used to control the ABS system. The front and rear rotors each have 48 serrations. When the rotors rotate, the magnetic field emitted by the permanent magnet in the speed sensor generates an AC voltage. Since the frequency of this AC voltage changes in direct proportion to the speed of the rotor, the frequency is used by the ECU to detect the speed of each wheel.

DTC No.	Diagnostic Trouble Code Detecting Condition	Trouble area
31, 32, 33, 34	(1) First start-off No pulse is input when the vehicle speed reaches 12 km/h (7 mph). (2) Other than first start-off No pulse is input when the vehicle speed reaches 20 km/h (12 mph). (3) When the vehicle speed is 10 km/h (7 mph) or above, a pulse is not input for at least 20 sec. (4) Vehicle speed is 40 km/h (25 mph) or more, and sensor signal is interrupted.	• Right front, left front, right rear and left rear speed sensor • Open in each speed sensor circuit • Sensor installation • Sensor rotor • ECU
35, 36, 38, 39	The hardware detects a constant open in each sensor circuit.	• Right front, left front, right rear and left rear speed sensor • Open in each speed sensor circuit • ECU

HINT: DCT Nos. 31 and 35 are for the right front speed sensor.
DTC Nos. 32 and 36 are for the left front speed sensor.
DTC Nos. 33 and 38 are for the right rear speed sensor.
DTC Nos. 34 and 39 are for the left rear speed sensor.

Fail safe function: If trouble occurs in the speed sensor circuit, the ECU cuts off current to the ABS solenoid relay and prohibits ABS control.

TY4029500359010X

Fig. 200 Codes 31, 32, 33, 34, 35, 36, 38 & 39: Speed Sensor Circuit (Part 1 of 4). 1996 Camry w/Bosch ABS

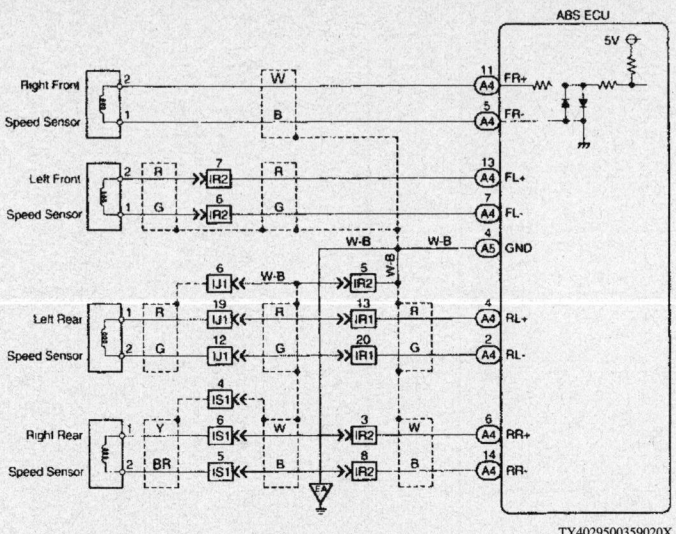

Fig. 200   Codes 31, 32, 33, 34, 35, 36, 38 & 39: Speed Sensor Circuit (Part 2 of 4). 1996 Camry w/Bosch ABS

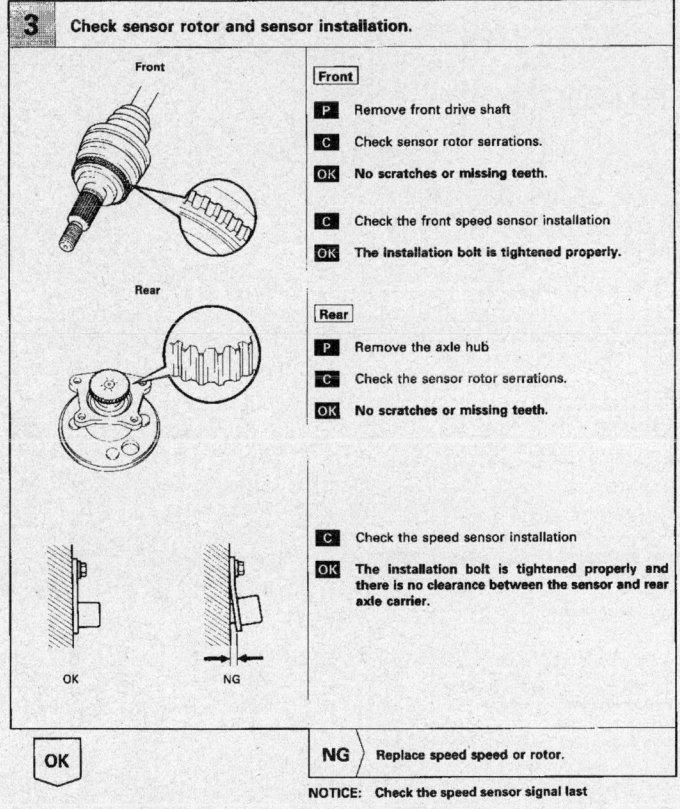

3   Check sensor rotor and sensor installation.

Front

P Remove front drive shaft

C Check sensor rotor serrations.

OK No scratches or missing teeth.

C Check the front speed sensor installation

OK The installation bolt is tightened properly.

Rear

P Remove the axle hub

C Check the sensor rotor serrations.

OK No scratches or missing teeth.

C Check the speed sensor installation

OK The installation bolt is tightened properly and there is no clearance between the sensor and rear axle carrier.

OK   NG

OK   **NG** Replace speed speed or rotor.

NOTICE: Check the speed sensor signal last.

Check and replace ABS ECU.

TY4029500359040X

Fig. 200   Codes 31, 32, 33, 34, 35, 36, 38 & 39: Speed Sensor Circuit (Part 4 of 4). 1996 Camry w/Bosch ABS

---

1   Check speed sensor.

Front

Front

P 1. Remove front fender liner.
2. Disconnect speed sensor connector.

C Measure resistance between terminals 1 and 2 of speed sensor connector.

OK Resistance: 0.6 - 1.8 kΩ

C Measure resistance between terminals 1 and 2 of speed sensor connector and body ground.

OK Resistance: 1 MΩ or higher

Rear

Rear

P 1. Remove the seat cushion (and side seat back).
2. Disconnect speed sensor connector.

C Measure resistance between terminals 1 and 2 of speed sensor connector.

OK Resistance: 0.6 - 1.8 kΩ

C Measure resistance between terminals 1 and 2 of speed sensor connector and body ground.

OK Resistance: 1 MΩ or higher

OK   **NG** Replace speed sensor.

2   Check for open and short in harness and connector between each speed sensor and ECU

OK   **NG** Repair or replace harness or connector.

TY4029500359030X

Fig. 200   Codes 31, 32, 33, 34, 35, 36, 38 & 39: Speed Sensor Circuit (Part 3 of 4). 1996 Camry w/Bosch ABS

CIRCUIT DESCRIPTION

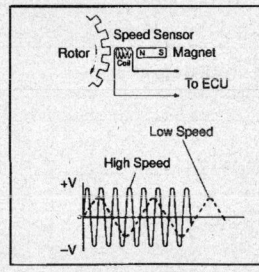

The speed sensor detects wheel speed and sends the appropriate signals to the ECU. These signals are used to control of the ABS system. The front and rear rotors each have 48 serrations.

When the rotors rotate, the magnetic field emitted by the permanent magnet in the speed sensor generates an AC voltage. Since the frequency of this AC voltage changes in direct proportion to the speed of the rotor, the frequency is used by the ECU to detect the speed of each wheel.

DTC No.	DTC Detecting Condition	Trouble Area
31, 32, 33, 34	Detection of any of conditions from (1) through (3): (1) Vehicle speed is more than 40 km/h (25 mph), pluses are not input for 0.1 sec. (2) After the initial start or restart and when the vehicle speed has reached 12 km/h (7 mph), the wheel with 0 km/h (0 mph) of wheel speed was detected. (3) After the initial start or restart and when the vehicle speed has reached 70 km/h (44 mph), front wheel with 0 km/h (0 mph) of wheel speed was detected.	• Right front, left front, right rear, left rear speed sensor • Each speed sensor circuit • Sensor installation • ECU
35, 36, 38, 39	Detecting abnormality in the resistance value of each speed sensor.	• Right front, left front, right rear, left rear speed sensor • Each speed sensor circuit • ECU

HINT:
DTC Nos. 31 and 35 are for the right front speed sensor.
DTC Nos. 32 and 36 are for the left front speed sensor.
DTC Nos. 33 and 38 are for the right rear speed sensor.
DTC Nos. 34 and 39 are for the left rear speed sensor.
Fail safe function: If trouble occurs in the speed sensor circuit, the ECU cuts off current to the ABS solenoid valve relay and prohibits ABS control.

TY4029700370010X

Fig. 201   Codes 31, 32, 33, 34, 35, 36, 38 & 39: Speed Sensor Circuit (Part 1 of 5). 1997–99 Camry w/Bosch ABS

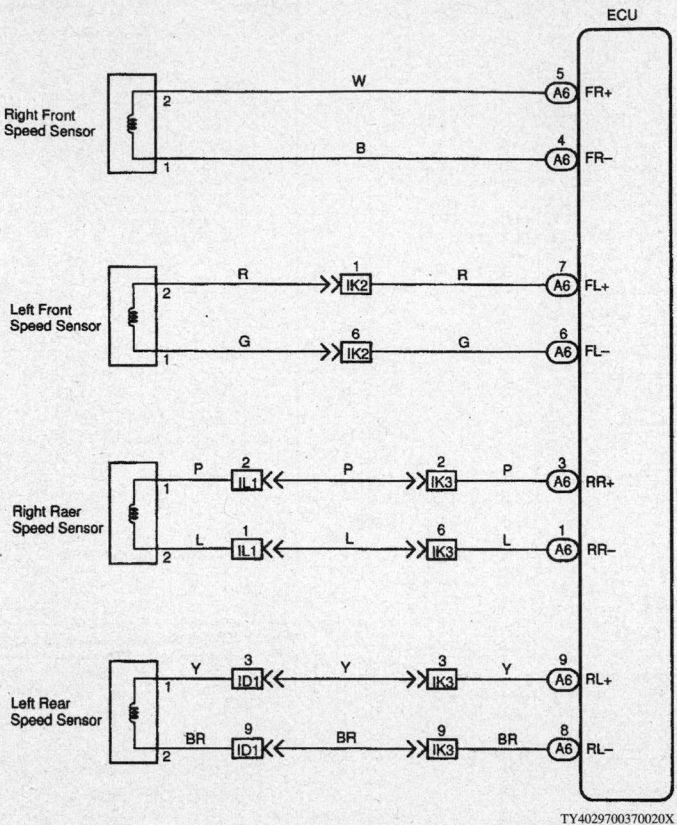

Fig. 201   Codes 31, 32, 33, 34, 35, 36, 38 & 39: Speed Sensor Circuit (Part 2 of 5). 1997–99 Camry w/Bosch ABS

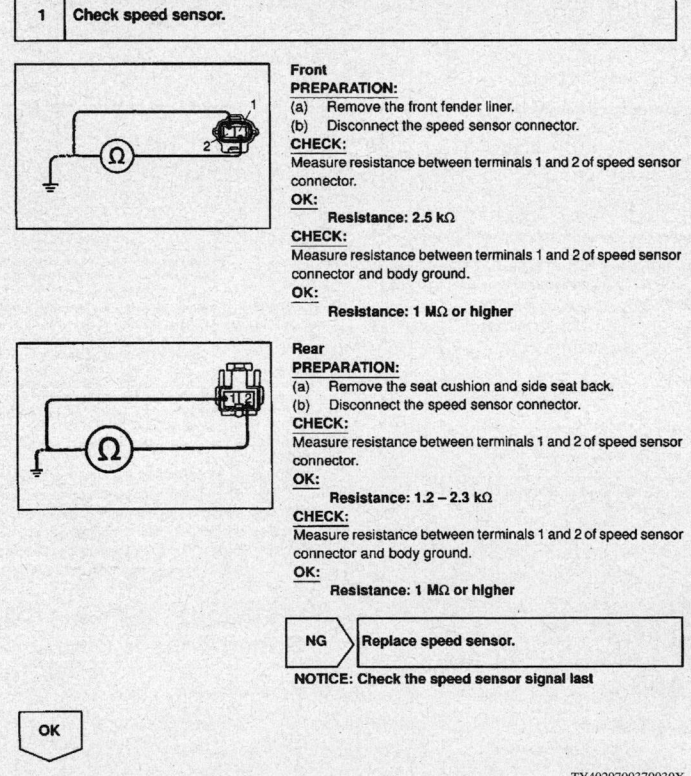

1	Check speed sensor.

Front

PREPARATION:
(a)   Remove the front fender liner.
(b)   Disconnect the speed sensor connector.

CHECK:
Measure resistance between terminals 1 and 2 of speed sensor connector.

OK:
Resistance: 2.5 kΩ

CHECK:
Measure resistance between terminals 1 and 2 of speed sensor connector and body ground.

OK:
Resistance: 1 MΩ or higher

Rear

PREPARATION:
(a)   Remove the seat cushion and side seat back.
(b)   Disconnect the speed sensor connector.

CHECK:
Measure resistance between terminals 1 and 2 of speed sensor connector.

OK:
Resistance: 1.2 – 2.3 kΩ

CHECK:
Measure resistance between terminals 1 and 2 of speed sensor connector and body ground.

OK:
Resistance: 1 MΩ or higher

NG	Replace speed sensor.

NOTICE: Check the speed sensor signal last

OK

Fig. 201   Codes 31, 32, 33, 34, 35, 36, 38 & 39: Speed Sensor Circuit (Part 3 of 5). 1997–99 Camry w/Bosch ABS

2	Check for open and short in harness and connector between each speed sensor and ECU

NG	Repair or replace harness or connector.

OK

3	Check speed sensor installation.

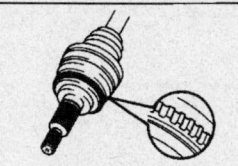

CHECK:
Check the speed sensor installation.
OK:
The installation bolt is tightened properly and there is no clearance between the sensor and rear axle carrier.

NG	Replace speed sensor.

NOTICE: Check the speed sensor signal last

OK

4	Check sensor rotor and sensor tip.

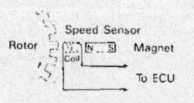
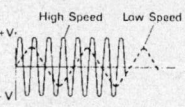

Front
PREPARATION:
Remove the front drive shaft
CHECK:
Check the sensor rotor serrations.
OK:
No scratches or missing teeth or foreign objects.
PREPARATION:
Remove the front speed sensor
CHECK:
Check the sensor tip.
OK:
No scratches or foreign objects on the sensor tip.

TY4029700370040X

Fig. 201 Codes 31, 32, 33, 34, 35, 36, 38 & 39: Speed Sensor Circuit (Part 4 of 5). 1997–99 Camry w/Bosch ABS

─CIRCUIT DESCRIPTION─

The speed sensor detects the wheel speed and sends the appropriate signals to the ECU. These signals are used for control of both the ABS and system. The front rotor and rear rotor have 48 serrations. When the rotors rotate, the magnetic field emitted by the permanent magnet in the speed sensor generates an AC voltage. Since the frequency of this AC voltage changes in proportion to the speed of the rotors (wheels), the frequency is used by the ECU to detect the speed of each wheel.

Code No.	Diagnostic Code Detecting Condition	Trouble area
31,32. 33,34	Detection of any of conditions (1) through (3): (1) At vehicle speed of 10 km/h (6 mph) or more, pulses are not input for 5 sec. (2) Momentary interruption of the vehicle speed signal occurs at least 7 times in the time between switching the ignition switch ON and switching it OFF. (3) Abnormal fluctuation of speed sensor signals with the vehicle speed 20 km/h (12 mph) or more.	• Right front, left front, right rear and left rear speed sensor. • Open or short in each speed sensor circuit. • ECU.
35	Vehicle speed sensor signal is not input for about 1 sec. while the left front and right rear vehicle speed sensor signals are being checked IG switch is turned ON.	• Open in left front, right rear speed sensor circuit. • ECU.
36	Vehicle speed sensor signal is not input for about 1 sec. while the right front and left rear vehicle speed sensor signals are being checked with the IG switch ON.	• Open in right front, left rear speed sensor circuit. • ECU.

HINT: Diag. code 31 is for the right front wheel speed sensor.
Diag. code 32 is for the left front wheel speed sensor.
Diag. code 33 is for the right rear wheel speed sensor.
Diag. code 34 is for the left rear wheel speed sensor.

Fail safe function: If trouble occurs in the speed sensor circuit, the ECU cuts off current to the ABS control (solenoid) relay and prohibits ABS control.

TY4029200074010X

Fig. 202 Codes 31, 32, 33, 34, 35 & 36: Speed Sensor Circuit (Part 1 of 4). 1996 Camry w/Nippondenso ABS

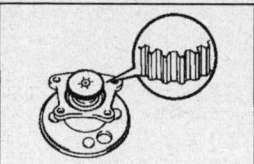

Rear
PREPARATION:
Remove the axle hub
CHECK:
Check the sensor rotor serrations.
OK:
No scratches or missing teeth or foreign objects.
PREPARATION:
Remove the rear speed sensor
CHECK:
Check the sensor tip.
OK:
No scratches or foreign objects on the sensor tip.

NG	Replace sensor rotor or speed sensor.

NOTICE: Check the speed sensor signal last

OK

Check and replace ABS ECU.

TY4029700370050X

Fig. 201 Codes 31, 32, 33, 34, 35, 36, 38 & 39: Speed Sensor Circuit (Part 5 of 5). 1997–99 Camry w/Bosch ABS

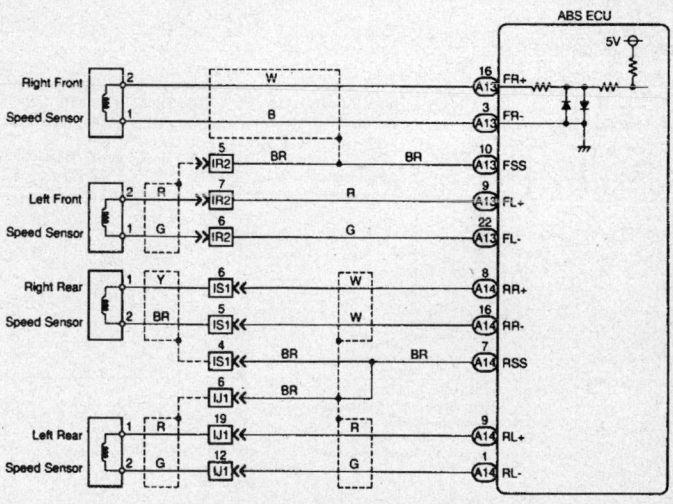

TY4029500353010X

Fig. 202 Codes 31, 32, 33, 34, 35 & 36: Speed Sensor Circuit (Part 2 of 4). 1996 Camry w/Nippondenso ABS

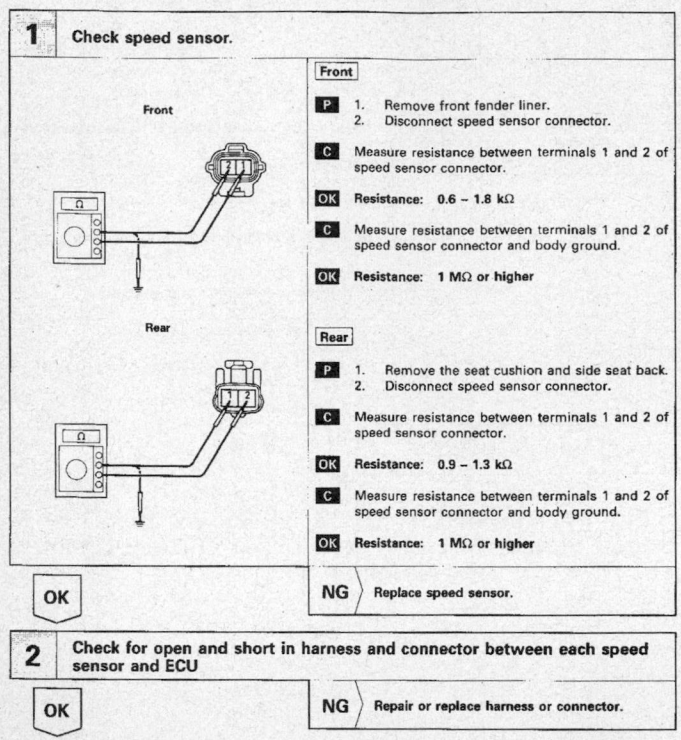

1 Check speed sensor.

Front

P	1. Remove front fender liner. 2. Disconnect speed sensor connector.
C	Measure resistance between terminals 1 and 2 of speed sensor connector.
OK	Resistance: 0.6 – 1.8 kΩ
C	Measure resistance between terminals 1 and 2 of speed sensor connector and body ground.
OK	Resistance: 1 MΩ or higher

Rear

P	1. Remove the seat cushion and side seat back. 2. Disconnect speed sensor connector.
C	Measure resistance between terminals 1 and 2 of speed sensor connector.
OK	Resistance: 0.9 – 1.3 kΩ
C	Measure resistance between terminals 1 and 2 of speed sensor connector and body ground.
OK	Resistance: 1 MΩ or higher

OK ↓

NG ▷ Replace speed sensor.

2 Check for open and short in harness and connector between each speed sensor and ECU

OK ↓   **NG** ▷ Repair or replace harness or connector.

TY4029500353020X

Fig. 202   Codes 31, 32, 33, 34, 35 & 36: Speed Sensor Circuit (Part 3 of 4). 1996 Camry w/Nippondenso ABS

3 Check sensor rotor and sensor installation.

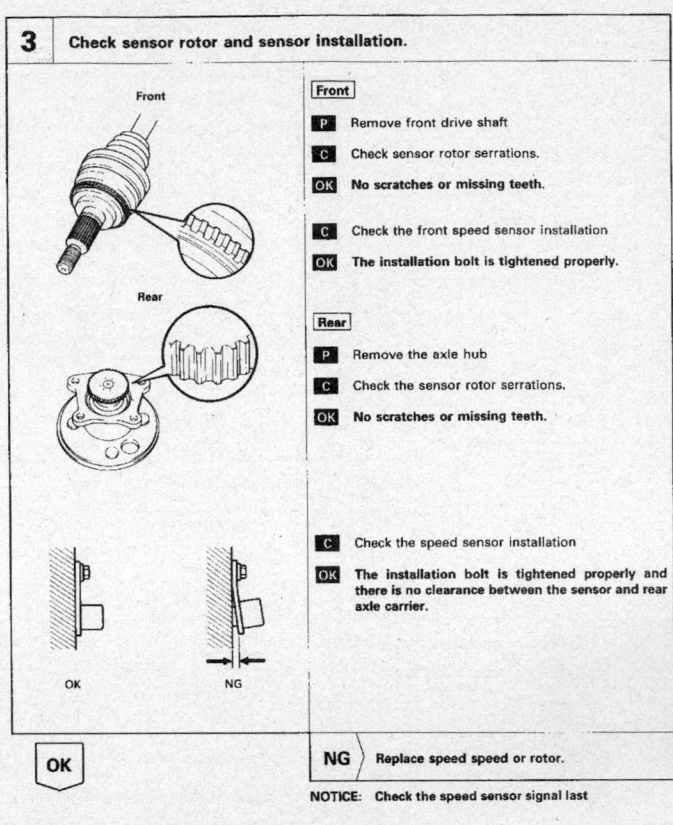

Front

P	Remove front drive shaft
C	Check sensor rotor serrations.
OK	No scratches or missing teeth.
C	Check the front speed sensor installation
OK	The installation bolt is tightened properly.

Rear

P	Remove the axle hub
C	Check the sensor rotor serrations.
OK	No scratches or missing teeth.
C	Check the speed sensor installation
OK	The installation bolt is tightened properly and there is no clearance between the sensor and rear axle carrier.

OK ↓   **NG** ▷ Replace speed speed or rotor.

NOTICE: Check the speed sensor signal last

Check and replace ABS ECU.

TY4029500353030X

Fig. 202   Codes 31, 32, 33, 34, 35 & 36: Speed Sensor Circuit (Part 4 of 4). 1996 Camry w/Nippondenso ABS

CIRCUIT DESCRIPTION

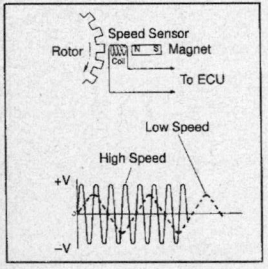

The speed sensor detects wheel speed and sends the appropriate signals to the ECU. These signals are used to control of the ABS system. The front and rear rotors each have 48 serrations.

When the rotors rotate, the magnetic field emitted by the permanent magnet in the speed sensor generates an AC voltage. Since the frequency of this AC voltage changes in direct proportion to the speed of the rotor, the frequency is used by the ECU to detect the speed of each wheel.

DTC No.	DTC Detecting Condition	Trouble Area
31, 32, 33, 34	Detection of any of conditions from (1) through (4): (1) Vehicle speed is at 10 km/h (6 mph) or more and the speed sensor signal circuit is open or short circuit continues for 15 sec. or more. (2) Momentary interruption of the speed sensor signal occurs 7 times or more. (3) Vehicle speed is at 20 km/h (12mph) or more and interference on the speed sensor signal continues for 5 sec. or more. (4) Open circuit condition of the speed sensor signal circuit continues for 0.5 sec. or more.	• Right front, left front, right rear, left rear speed sensor • Each speed sensor circuit • Speed sensor rotor

HINT:
DTC No. 31 is for the right front speed sensor.
DTC No. 32 is for the left front speed sensor.
DTC No. 33 is for the right rear speed sensor.
DTC No. 34 is for the left rear speed sensor.
Fail safe function: If trouble occurs in the speed sensor circuit, the ECU cuts off current to the ABS solenoid relay and prohibits ABS control.

TY4029700364010X

Fig. 203   Codes 31, 32, 33 & 34: Speed Sensor Circuit (Part 1 of 5). 1997–99 Camry w/Nippondenso ABS & Traction Control

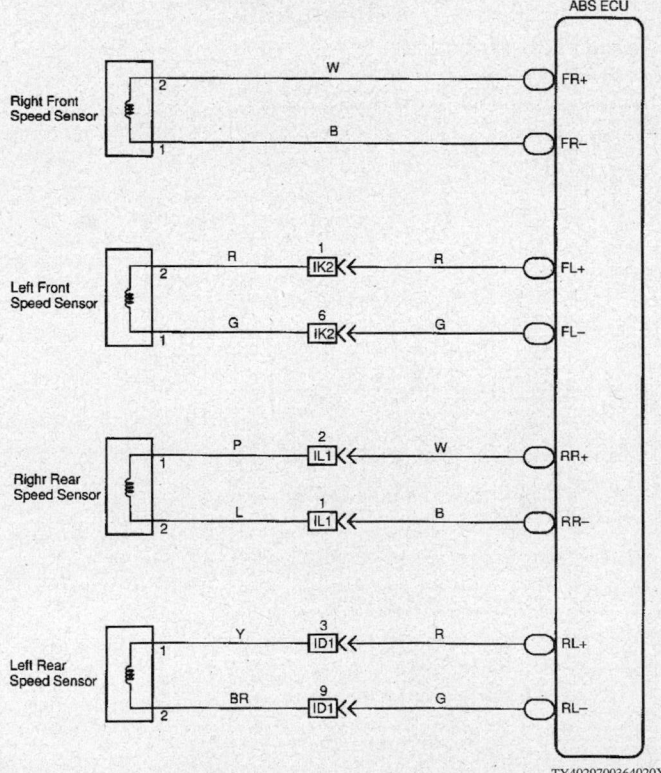

Fig. 203   Codes 31, 32, 33 & 34: Speed Sensor Circuit (Part 2 of 5). 1997–99 Camry w/Nippondenso ABS & Traction Control

ANTI-LOCK BRAKES

1	Check speed sensor.

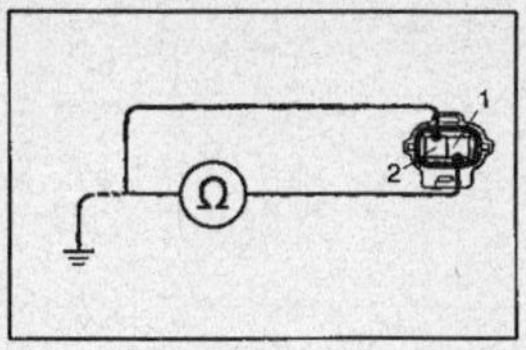

Front
PREPARATION:
(a)   Remove the front fender liner.
(b)   Disconnect the speed sensor connector.
CHECK:
Measure resistance between terminals 1 and 2 of speed sensor connector.
OK:
  Resistance: 2.5 kΩ
CHECK:
Measure resistance between terminals 1 and 2 of speed sensor connector and body ground.
OK:
  Resistance: 1 MΩ or higher

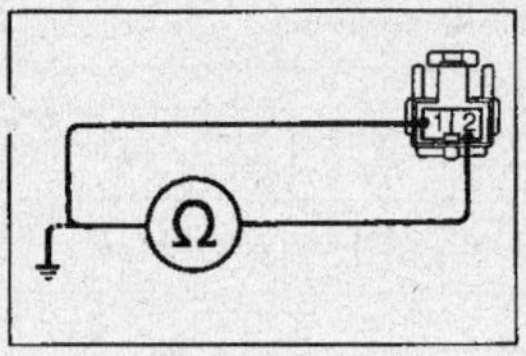

Rear
PREPARATION:
(a)   Remove the seat cushion and side seat back.
(b)   Disconnect the speed sensor connector.
CHECK:
Measure resistance between terminals 1 and 2 of speed sensor connector.
OK:
  Resistance: 1.2 – 2.3 kΩ
CHECK:
Measure resistance between terminals 1 and 2 of speed sensor connector and body ground.
OK:
  Resistance: 1 MΩ or higher

NG	Replace speed sensor.

NOTICE: Check the speed sensor signal last

OK

TY4029700364030X

Fig. 203   Codes 31, 32, 33 & 34: Speed Sensor Circuit (Part 3 of 5). 1997–99 Camry w/Nippondenso ABS & Traction Control

2	Check for open and short in harness and connector between each speed sensor and ECU

NG	Repair or replace harness or connector.

OK

3	Check speed sensor installation.

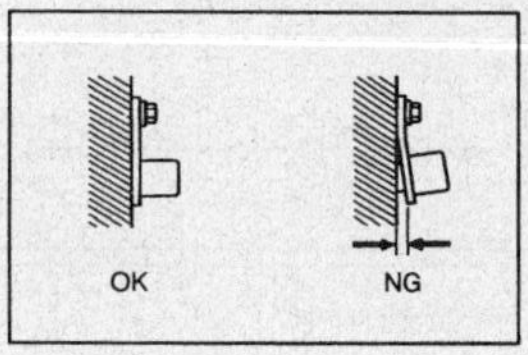

CHECK:
Check the speed sensor installation.
OK:
  The installation bolt is tightened properly and there is no clearance between the sensor and rear axle carrier.

OK   NG

NG	Replace speed sensor.

NOTICE: Check the speed sensor signal last

OK

4	Check sensor rotor and sensor tip.

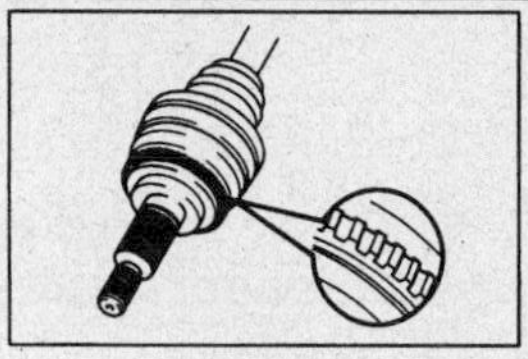

Front
PREPARATION:
Remove the front drive shaft
CHECK:
Check the sensor rotor serrations.
OK:
  No scratches or missing teeth or foreign objects.
PREPARATION:
Remove the front speed sensor
CHECK:
Check the sensor tip.
OK:
  No scratches or foreign objects on the sensor tip.

TY4029700364040X

Fig. 203   Codes 31, 32, 33 & 34: Speed Sensor Circuit (Part 4 of 5). 1997–99 Camry w/Nippondenso ABS & Traction Control

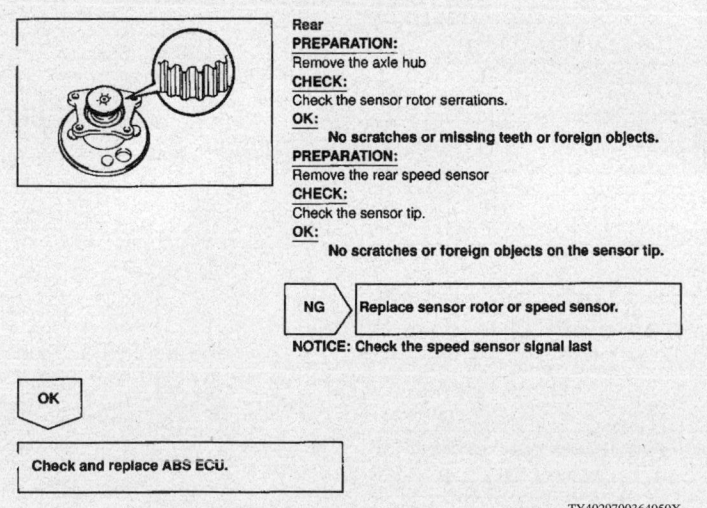

Rear
PREPARATION:
Remove the axle hub
CHECK:
Check the sensor rotor serrations.
OK:
  No scratches or missing teeth or foreign objects.
PREPARATION:
Remove the rear speed sensor
CHECK:
Check the sensor tip.
OK:
  No scratches or foreign objects on the sensor tip.

NG	Replace sensor rotor or speed sensor.

NOTICE: Check the speed sensor signal last

OK

Check and replace ABS ECU.

TY4029700364050X

Fig. 203   Codes 31, 32, 33 & 34: Speed Sensor Circuit (Part 5 of 5). 1997–99 Camry w/Nippondenso ABS & Traction Control

CIRCUIT DESCRIPTION

DTC No.	DTC Detecting Condition	Trouble Area
34, 35	The condition that the both rear side wheels' speed is lower than front wheels' speed at 20 km/h (12 mph) or more for 20 sec. or more when the IG switch turns ON and OFF is repeated in a sequence more than 8 times.	• Rear axle hub • Right rear, left rear speed sensor • Rear speed sensor circuit

INSPECTION PROCEDURE

1 Check rear axle hub

NG → Replace rear axle hub.

OK

2 Check rear speed sensor

NG → Replace rear speed sensor.

OK

3 Check for open or short in harness and connector between rear speed sensor and ECU

NG → Repair or replace harness and connector.

OK

Check and replace ABS ECU.

TY4029700365000X

Fig. 204   Codes 34 & 35: Rear Speed Sensor Fault. 1997–99 Camry w/Nippondenso ABS

CIRCUIT DESCRIPTION

DTC No.	DTC Detecting Condition	Trouble Area
37	Detection of any of conditions from (1) through (3): (1) Occurrence of differential to some degree in the wheel speed between the front and rear wheels of either left or right side of the vehicle and the front left and right wheels. (Detection of differential in mini tire size, spinning wheel and decelerating wheel.) (2) Continuous ABS control for 60 sec. or more. (3) Interference on 1 or more wheels for 20 sec. with the brake pedal depressed, or for 5 sec. when the brake pedal is not depressed.	• Speed sensor • Sensor rotor • ECU

INSPECTION PROCEDURE

1 Check sensor rotor

NG → Replace sensor rotor.

OK

2 Check speed sensor

NG → Replace speed sensor.

OK

3 Check for open or short in harness and connector between speed sensor and ECU

NG → Repair or replace harness and connector.

OK

Check and replace ABS ECU.

TY4029700371000X

Fig. 206   Code 37: Speed Sensor Rotor. 1997–99 Camry

CIRCUIT DESCRIPTION

DTC No.	DTC Detecting Condition	Trouble Area
37	With the rear wheels stationary and front wheels rotating at 20+ km/h (12+ mph) for 10+ secs, turn ignition switch ON then OFF 8 times in succession.	• Rear axle hub • Right rear, left rear speed sensor • Wire harness for rear sensor system • ECU

INSPECTION PROCEDURE

1 Check rear axle hub.

OK   NG → Replace rear axle hub.

2 Check rear speed sensor.

OK   NG → Replace rear speed sensor.

3 Check for open or short in harness and connector between rear speed sensor and ECU.

OK   NG → Repair or replace harness and connector.

Check and replace ABS ECU.

TY4029200075010X

Fig. 205   Code 37: Rear Speed Sensor Rotor. 1996 Camry

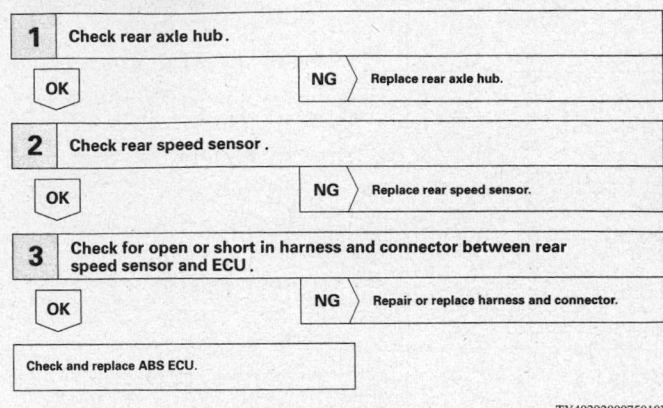

CIRCUIT DESCRIPTION

This is the power source for the ECU, hence the CPU, and the actuators.

DTC No.	Diagnostic Trouble Code Detecting Condition	Trouble area
41	(1) Voltage of 5 V or more, or less than 9.4 V, is applied for at least 60 sec. to terminal +BS before the ABS primary check and ABS operation. (2) Voltage of 5 V or more, or less than 9.4 V, is applied to terminal +BS for 0.2 sec. or more, after the ABS primary check and before ABS operation. (3) During ABS operation, voltage of 5 V or more, or less than 8.8 V, is applied to terminal +BS for 0.2 sec. or more.	• Battery • IC regulator • Open or short in power source circuit • ECU

Fail safe function: If trouble occurs in the power source circuit, the ECU cuts off current to the ABS solenoid relay and prohibits ABS control.
If the voltage applied to terminal +BS becomes 9.9 V or more, the warning light goes off and ABS control becomes possible.

WIRING DIAGRAM

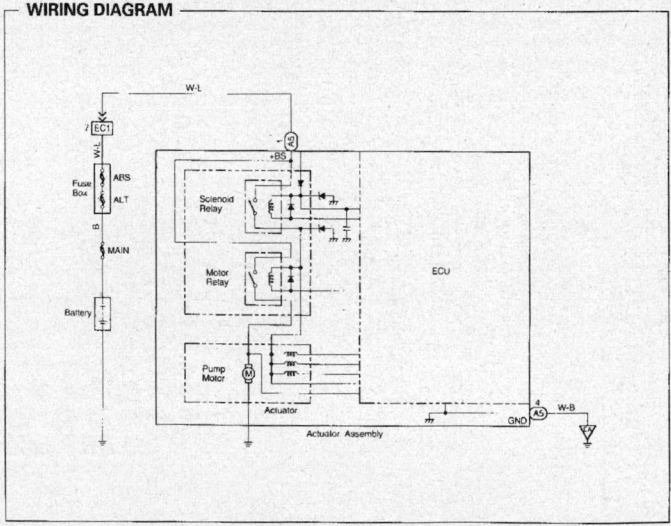

TY4029500360010X

Fig. 207   Code 41: BS Power Source Circuit (Part 1 of 3). 1996 Camry w/Bosch ABS

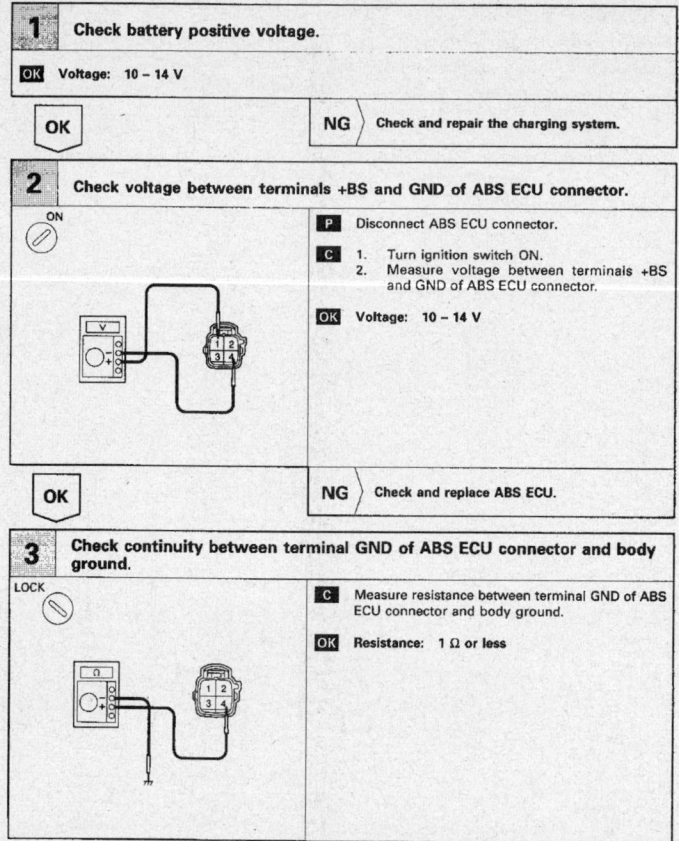

1 | Check battery positive voltage.

OK Voltage: 10 – 14 V

| OK | | NG | Check and repair the charging system. |

2 | Check voltage between terminals +BS and GND of ABS ECU connector.

ON

P Disconnect ABS ECU connector.

C 1. Turn ignition switch ON.
2. Measure voltage between terminals +BS and GND of ABS ECU connector.

OK Voltage: 10 – 14 V

| OK | | NG | Check and replace ABS ECU. |

3 | Check continuity between terminal GND of ABS ECU connector and body ground.

LOCK

C Measure resistance between terminal GND of ABS ECU connector and body ground.

OK Resistance: 1 Ω or less

| OK | | NG | Repair or replace harness or connector. |

TY4029500360020X

Fig. 207 Code 41: BS Power Source Circuit (Part 2 of 3). 1996 Camry w/Bosch ABS

CIRCUIT DESCRIPTION

This is the power source for the ECU, hence the actuators.

DTC No.	DTC Detecting Condition	Trouble Area
41	Vehicle speed at about 6 km/h (4 mph), low battery voltage is less than 9.4 V at the time of non-operation of ABS control or less than 8.8 V at the time of operation of ABS control, and high battery voltage is more than 17.4 V.	• Battery • IC regulator • Power source circuit • ECU

Fail safe function: If trouble occurs in the power source circuit, the ECU cuts off current to the ABS solenoid valve relay and prohibits ABS control.

WIRING DIAGRAM

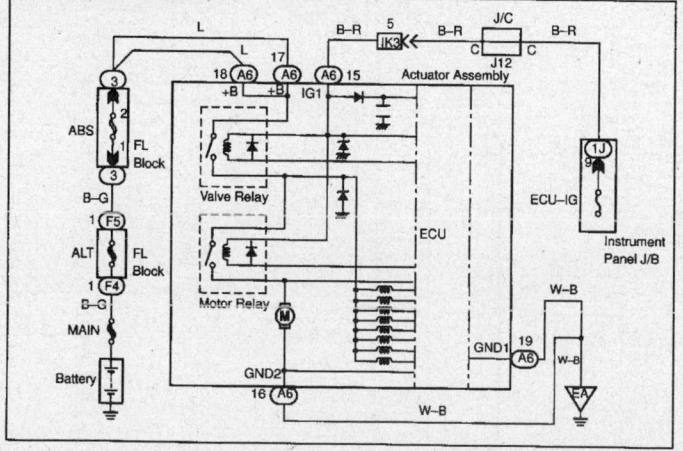

TY4029700372010X

Fig. 208 Code 41: BS Power Source Circuit (Part 1 of 3). 1997–99 Camry w/Bosch ABS

4 | Check ECU-IG fuse.

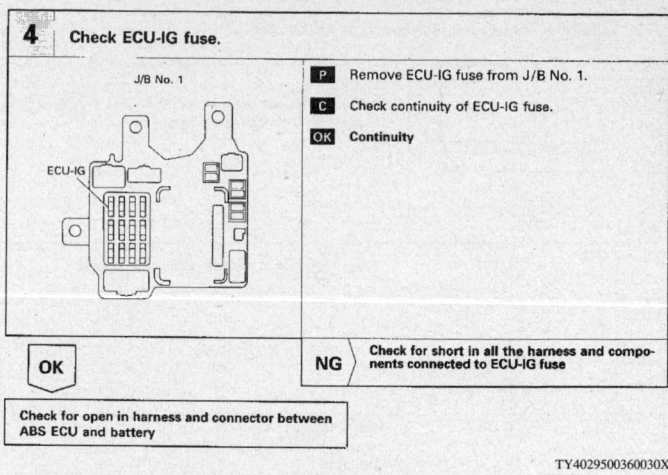

J/B No. 1

ECU-IG

P Remove ECU-IG fuse from J/B No. 1.

C Check continuity of ECU-IG fuse.

OK Continuity

| OK | | NG | Check for short in all the harness and components connected to ECU-IG fuse |

Check for open in harness and connector between ABS ECU and battery

TY4029500360030X

Fig. 207 Code 41: BS Power Source Circuit (Part 3 of 3). 1996 Camry w/Bosch ABS

1 | Check battery positive voltage.

OK:
Voltage: 10 – 14 V

| | NG | Check and replace fuses.
Check and repair the charging system. |

OK

2 | Check voltage between terminals IG1 and GND of ABS actuator connector.

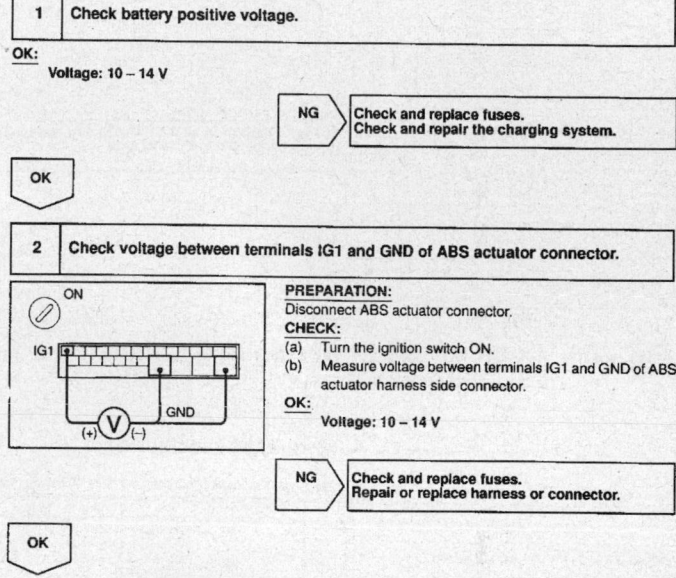

ON

IG1

GND

(+) V (−)

PREPARATION:
Disconnect ABS actuator connector.
CHECK:
(a) Turn the ignition switch ON.
(b) Measure voltage between terminals IG1 and GND of ABS actuator harness side connector.
OK:
Voltage: 10 – 14 V

| | NG | Check and replace fuses.
Repair or replace harness or connector. |

OK

TY4029700372020X

Fig. 208 Code 41: BS Power Source Circuit (Part 2 of 3). 1997–99 Camry w/Bosch ABS

3 Check continuity between terminals GND of ABS actuator connector and body ground.

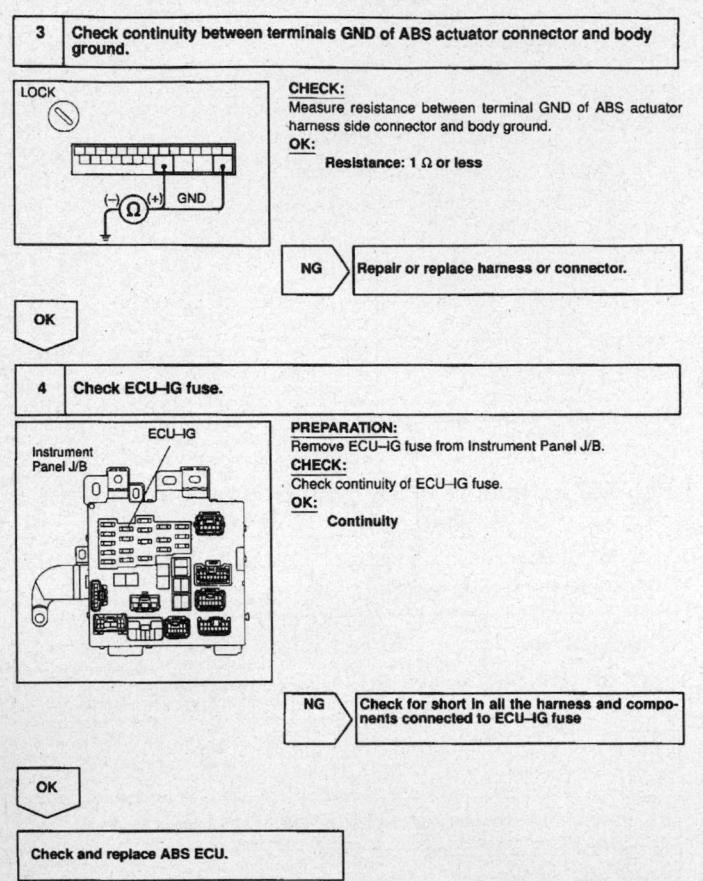

LOCK

CHECK:
Measure resistance between terminal GND of ABS actuator harness side connector and body ground.
OK:
 Resistance: 1 Ω or less

NG ▷ Repair or replace harness or connector.

OK

4 Check ECU–IG fuse.

Instrument Panel J/B

ECU–IG

PREPARATION:
Remove ECU–IG fuse from Instrument Panel J/B.
CHECK:
Check continuity of ECU–IG fuse.
OK:
 Continuity

NG ▷ Check for short in all the harness and components connected to ECU–IG fuse

OK

Check and replace ABS ECU.

TY4029700372030X

Fig. 208   Code 41: BS Power Source Circuit (Part 3 of 3). 1997–99 Camry w/Bosch ABS

CIRCUIT DESCRIPTION

This is the power source for the ECU, hence the CPU, and the actuators.

DTC No.	Diagnostic Trouble Code Detecting Condition	Trouble area
41	Vehicle speed is 3 km/h (1.9 mph) or more and voltage of ECU terminal IG1 remains at more than 17 V or below 9.5 V for more than 10 sec.	• Battery • IC regulator • Open or short in power source circuit • ECU

Fail safe function: If trouble occurs in power source circuit, the ECU cuts off current to the ABS control (solenoid) relay and prohibits ABS control.

WIRING DIAGRAM

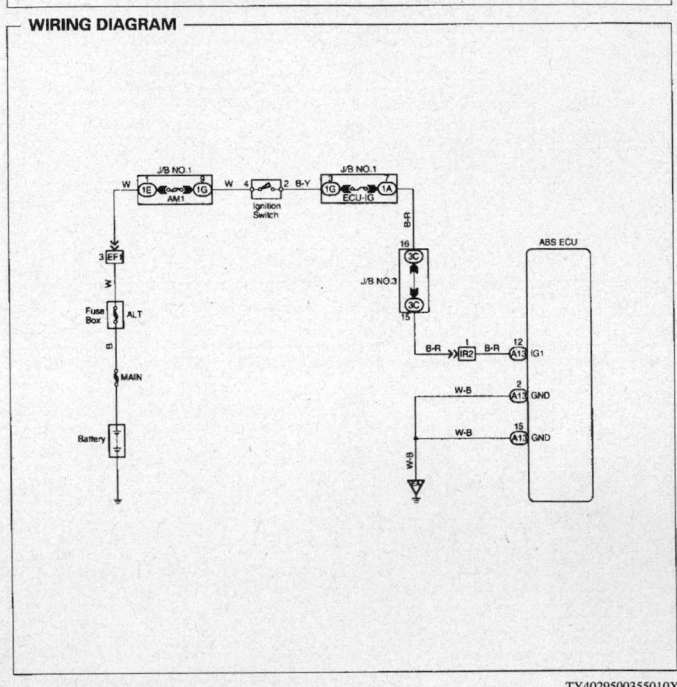

TY4029500355010X

Fig. 209   Code 41: IG Power Source Circuit (Part 1 of 3). 1996 Camry w/Nippondenso ABS

CIRCUIT DESCRIPTION

This is the power source for the ECU, hence the actuators.

DTC No.	DTC Detecting Condition	Trouble Area
41	Condition (1) or (2) is detected: (1) Vehicle speed is at 3 km/h (1.9 mph) or more and ECU terminal IG1 voltage is 9.5 V or less continues for 10 sec. or more. (2) While ABS solenoid or motor relay is ON, ABS ECU terminal IG1 voltage becomes 9.5 V or less and when ABS ECU terminal AST or MT voltage is less than 4 V continues for 0.2 sec. or more.	• Battery • IC regulator • Power source circuit

Fail safe function: If trouble occurs in the power source circuit, the ECU cuts off current to the ABS solenoid relay and prohibits ABS control.

WIRING DIAGRAM

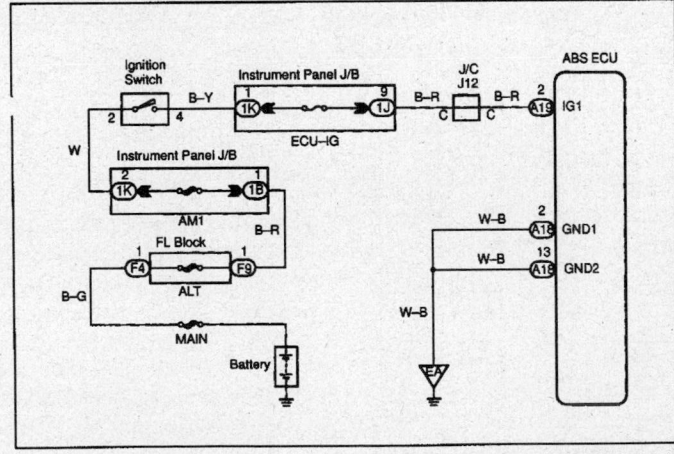

TY4029700366000X

Fig. 209   Code 41: IG Power Source Circuit (Part 1 of 3). 1997–99 Camry w/Nippondenso ABS

CIRCUIT DESCRIPTION

This is the power source for the ECU, hence the actuators.

DTC No.	DTC Detecting Condition	Trouble Area
41	Detection of any conditions from (1) through (3): (1) Vehicle speed is 3 km/h (1.9 mph) or more and battery voltage is less than 9.5 V continues for 10 sec. or more. (2) Battery voltage has never exceeded more than 17.0 V and has become less than 9.5 V within 2.16 sec., under malfunction of solenoid relay monitor after the solenoid relay is ON, at ECU AST terminal voltage of ECU has become 8.0 V or more or under malfunction of motor relay monitor and after the motor relay is ON, motor relay monitor has become ON. (3) Battery voltage is more than 17.0 V continues for 1.2 sec. or more or battery voltage has become more than 17.0 V within 2.16 sec. and solenoid or motor relay monitor is under malfunction condition.	• Battery • IC regulator • Power source circuit • ECU

Fail safe function: If trouble occurs in the power source circuit, the ECU cuts off current to the ABS & TRAC solenoid relay and prohibits ABS control and TRAC control.

WIRING DIAGRAM

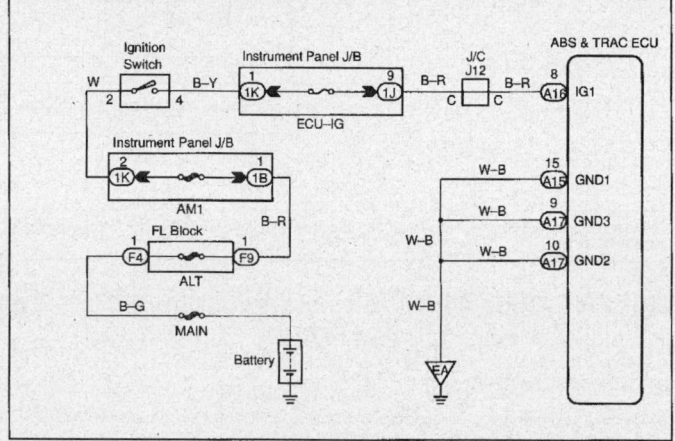

Fig. 209   Code 41: IG Power Source Circuit (Part 1 of 3). 1997–99 Camry w/Traction Control

TY4029700377000X

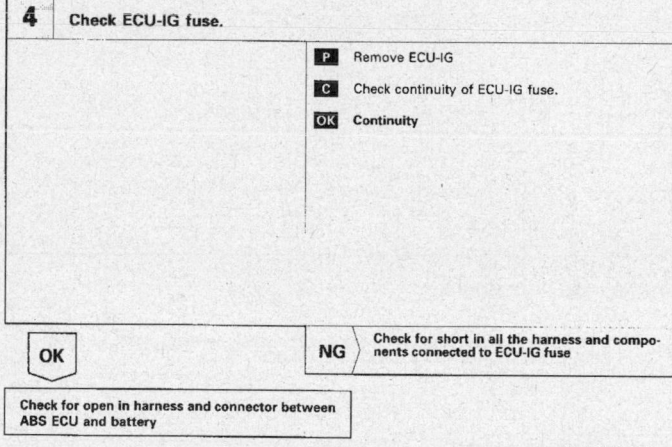

Fig. 209   Code 41: IG Power Source Circuit (Part 3 of 3). Camry w/Nippondenso ABS & Traction Control

TY4029500355030X

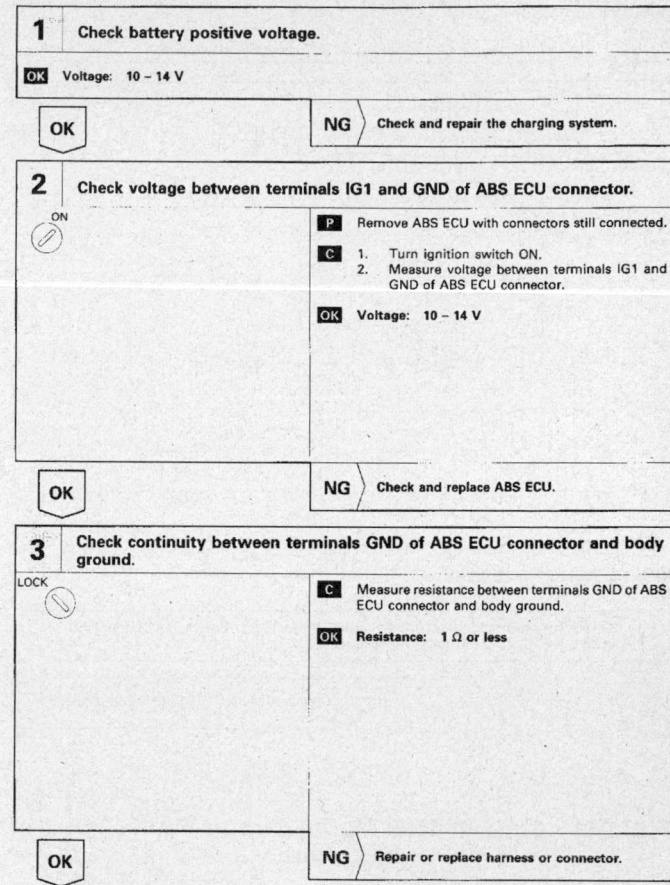

Fig. 209   Code 41: IG Power Source Circuit (Part 2 of 3). Camry w/Nippondenso ABS & Traction Control

TY4029500355020X

CIRCUIT DESCRIPTION

DTC No.	DTC Detecting Condition	Trouble Area
43	Detection of any conditions from (1) through (8): (1) During TRAC is in non-operation and ABS is output DTC, but TRAC is not during initial lamp checking, terminal WA of ECU is ON and engine speed is 500 rpm or more continues for 1 sec. or more. (2) Solenoid relay circuit is open or short. (3) Motor relay circuit is open or short. (4) ABS solenoid circuit is open or short. (5) TRAC solenoid circuit is open or short. (6) Speed sensor is under malfunction condition. (7) IG power source is down or raise. (8) Pump motor is lock.	• ABS control system

INSPECTION PROCEDURE

1	Check the DTC for the ABS

*1 Repair ABS control system according to the code output.

*2 Check for ECU connected to malfunction indicator lamp.

*1: Output NG code
*2: Malfunction indicator lamp remains ON.

TY4029700378000X

Fig. 210   Code 43: ABS Control System Fault. Camry

CIRCUIT DESCRIPTION

The ABS & TRAC ECU receives engine speed signals (NE signals) from the ECM.

DTC No.	DTC Detecting Condition	Trouble Area
44	Condition (1) or (2) is detected: (1) TRAC is in operation and engine speed is 0 rpm continues for 2.4 sec. or more. (2) TRAC is in non-operation, shift lever is not in P or N position, both the front right and left wheels' speed is 30 km/h (19 mph) or more, engine speed is 0 rpm and does not have communication malfunction, and malfunction information of engine system is OFF.	• NEO circuit • ECM • ECU

WIRING DIAGRAM

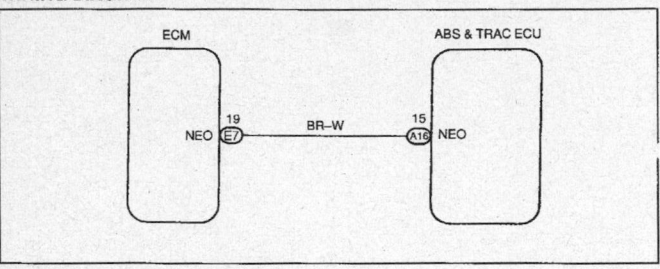

INSPECTION PROCEDURE

1	Check for open and short in harness and connector between terminal NEO of ABS & TRAC ECU and terminal NEO of ECM

NG → Repair or replace harness or connector.

OK

TY4029700379010X

Fig. 211   Code 44: NE Signal Circuit Fault (Part 1 of 2). Camry

CIRCUIT DESCRIPTION

DTC No.	Diagnostic Trouble Code Detecting Condition	Trouble area
51	Pump motor is not operating normally during initial check.	• ABS pump motor
Fail safe function:	If trouble occurs in the ABS pump motor, the ECU cuts off current to the control (solenoid) relay and prohibits ABS control.	

TY4029500356000X

Fig. 212   Code 51: ABS Pump Motor Lock. Camry

2	Check voltage between terminal NEO of ABS & TRAC ECU and body ground.

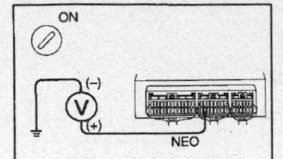

PREPARATION:
(a)   Remove ABS & TRAC ECU with connectors still connected.
(b)   Turn ignition switch ON.
CHECK:
Measure voltage between terminal NEO of ABS & TRAC ECU and body ground for the engine conditions below.
OK:

Engine condition	Voltage
OFF (IG ON)	3 – 6 V or below 1 V
ON (idling)	2 – 3 V (Pulse)

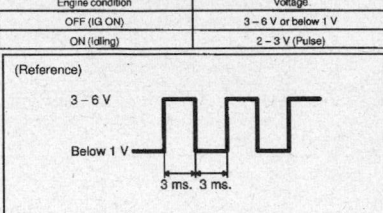

NG → Check and replace ABS & TRAC ECU or ECM.

OK

If the same code is still output after the DTC is deleted, check the contact condition of each connection.

TY4029700379020X

Fig. 211   Code 44: NE Signal Circuit Fault (Part 2 of 2). Camry

CIRCUIT DESCRIPTION

This circuit is used to send TRAC control information from the ABS & TRAC ECU to the ECM (TRC+, TRC–), and engine control information from the ECM to the ABS & TRAC ECU (EFI+, EFI–):

DTC No.	DTC Detecting Condition	Trouble Area
53	ECM communication data malfunction is detected.	• TRC+ or TRC– circuit • EFI+ or EFI– circuit • ECM • ECU

WIRING DIAGRAM

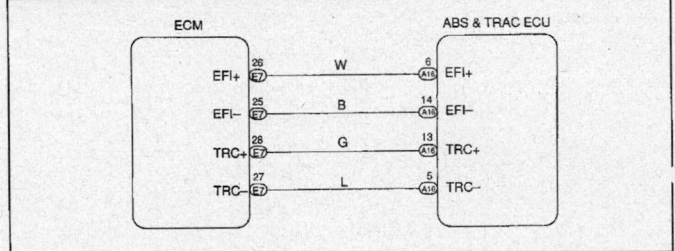

INSPECTION PROCEDURE

1	Check for open and short in harness and connector between terminals EFI+, EFI–, TRC+, TRC– of ABS & TRAC ECU and ECM

NG → Repair or replace harness or connector.

OK

Check and replace ECM or ABS & TRAC ECU.

TY4029700380000X

Fig. 213   Code 53: ECM Communication Circuit Fault. Camry

CIRCUIT DESCRIPTION

If trouble occurs in the engine control system, the ECU prohibits TRAC control.

DTC No.	DTC Detection Condition	Trouble Area
61	Conditions (1) and (2) is detected: (1) ECM communication is normal, malfunction information of engine system ON, and engine speed is 500 rpm or more continues for 0.48 sec. or more, and TRAC operation start condition is concluded. (2) ECM communication is normal, malfunction information of engine system is ON, engine speed is 500 rpm and more continues for 1 sec. or more, and the engine system memorizes DTC.	• Engine control system

INSPECTION PROCEDURE

```
1   Check the DTC for the engine
```

```
*1   Repair engine control system according to the
     code output.
```

```
*2
```

```
Check for ECU connected to malfunction indicator light.
```

*1: Output NG code
*2: Malfunction indicator light remains ON.

TY4029700381000X

Fig. 214   Code 61: ECM Communication Circuit Fault. Camry

```
4   Check voltage between terminals IG1 and GND of ABS actuator connector.
```

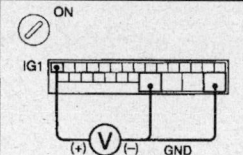

PREPARATION:
Disconnect ABS actuator connector.
CHECK:
(a) Turn the ignition switch ON.
(b) Measure voltage between terminals IG1 and GND of ABS actuator harness side connector.
OK:
Voltage: 10 – 14 V

```
YES   Check for open or short in harness and connec-
      tor between ECU–IG fuse and ABS actuator
```

```
OK
```

```
5   Check connection of ABS actuator connector.
```

CHECK:
(a) Check the connection of the ABS actuator connector.
(b) Check the ABS warning light goes off.

```
OK   Check and replace ABS ECU.
```

```
NG
```

```
Repair or replace harness or connector.
```

TY4029700373020X

Fig. 215   Code 62: ABS ECU Fault (Part 2 of 2). Camry

CIRCUIT DESCRIPTION

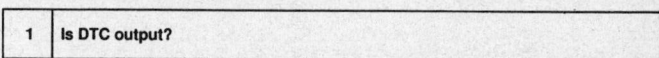

DTC No.	DTC Detecting Condition	Trouble Area
62	ABS ECU continuously detected the proper operation of ABS.	• Battery • ECU

Fail safe function: If trouble occurs in the power source circuit, the ECU cuts off current to the ABS solenoid valve relay and prohibits ABS control.

INSPECTION PROCEDURE

```
1   Is DTC output?
```

```
YES   Repair circuit indicated by the code output.
```

```
NO
```

```
2   Is normal code displayed?
```

```
YES   Check for short in harness and connector be-
      tween DLC1 or DLC2 and ABS ECU
```

```
NO
```

```
3   Is ABS warning light go off?
```

```
YES   Check open and short of the harness and con-
      nector in the Tc circuit between ECU and DLC2
      or DLC1.
```

```
NO
```

TY4029700373010X

Fig. 215   Code 62: ABS ECU Fault (Part 1 of 2). Camry

CIRCUIT DESCRIPTION

This relay supplies power to each ABS solenoid. After the ignition switch is turned ON, if the initial check is OK, the relay goes on.

DTC No.	Diagnostic Trouble Code Detecting Condition	Trouble area
11	Conditions (1) and (2) continue for 0.2 sec. or more: (1) ABS solenoid relay terminal (SR) voltage: Battery positive voltage (2) Solenoid relay monitor terminal (AST) voltage: 0 V	• ABS solenoid relay • Open or short in ABS solenoid relay circuit • ECU
12	Conditions (1) and (2) continue for 0.2 sec. or more: (1) ABS solenoid relay terminal (SR) voltage: 0 V (2) Solenoid relay monitor terminal (AST) voltage: Battery positive voltage	• ABS solenoid relay • B+ short in ABS solenoid relay circuit • ECU

Fail safe function: If trouble occurs in the solenoid relay circuit, the ECU cuts off current to the solenoid relay and prohibits ABS control.

DIAGNOSTIC CHART

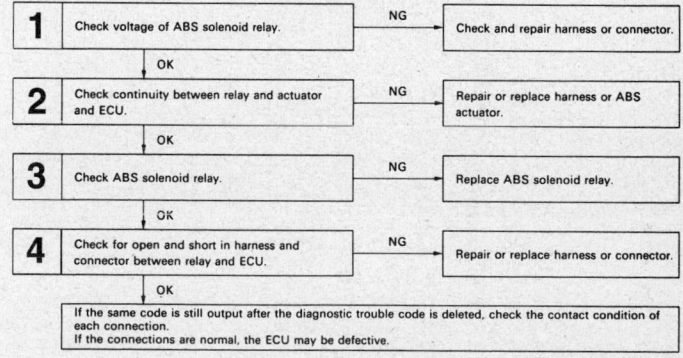

TY4029400097010X

Fig. 216   Codes 11 & 12: ABS Solenoid Relay (Part 1 of 4). 1996 Celica

CIRCUIT DESCRIPTION

This relay supplies power to each ABS solenoid. After the ignition switch is turned ON, if the initial check is OK, the relay goes on.

DTC No.	DTC Detecting Condition	Trouble Area
11	Conditions (1) and (2) continue for 0.2 sec. or more: (1) ABS solenoid relay terminal (SR) voltage: Below 1.5 V (2) Solenoid relay monitor terminal (AST) voltage: 0 V	• ABS solenoid relay • Open or short in ABS solenoid relay circuit
12	Conditions (1) and (2) continue for 0.2 sec. or more: (1) ABS solenoid relay terminal (SR) voltage: Battery positive voltage (2) Solenoid relay monitor terminal (AST) voltage: Battery positive voltage	• ABS solenoid relay • B+ short in ABS solenoid relay circuit

Fail safe function: If trouble occurs in the ABS solenoid relay circuit, the ECU cuts off current to the ABS solenoid relay and prohibits ABS control.

TY4029700393010X

Fig. 216 Codes 11 & 12: ABS Solenoid Relay (Part 1 of 4). 1997–99 Celica

WIRING DIAGRAM

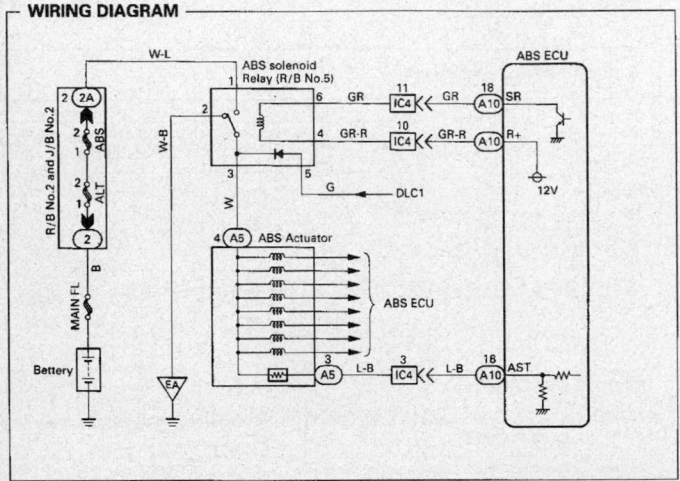

TY4029700393020X

Fig. 216 Codes 11 & 12: ABS Solenoid Relay (Part 2 of 4). 1997–99 Celica

WIRING DIAGRAM

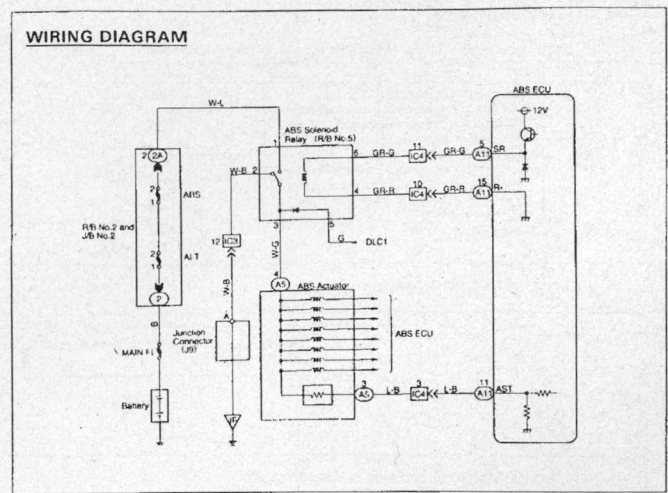

TY4029400097020X

Fig. 216 Codes 11 & 12: ABS Solenoid Relay (Part 2 of 4). 1996 Celica

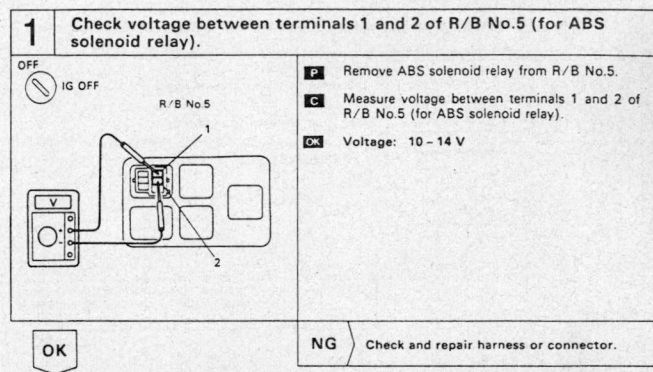

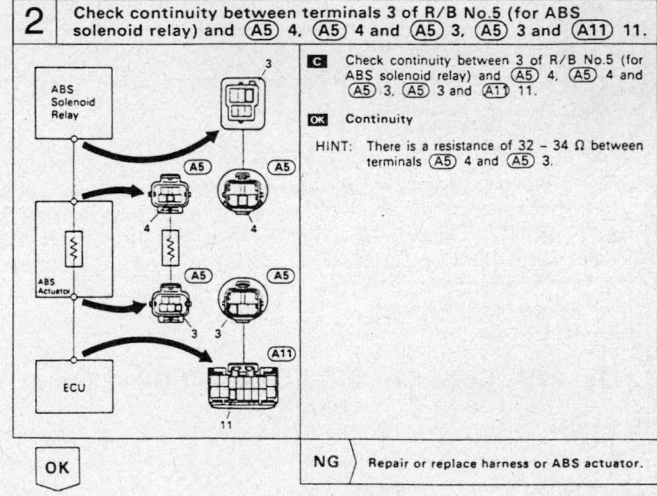

TY4029400097030X

Fig. 216 Codes 11 & 12: ABS Solenoid Relay (Part 3 of 4). 1996 Celica

ANTI-LOCK BRAKES

1 Check voltage between terminals 1 and 2 of R/B No.5 (for ABS solenoid relay).

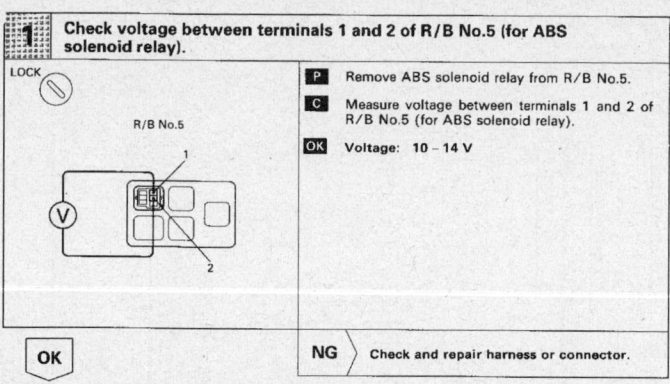

P Remove ABS solenoid relay from R/B No.5.

C Measure voltage between terminals 1 and 2 of R/B No.5 (for ABS solenoid relay).

OK Voltage: 10 – 14 V

OK ↓

NG ⟩ Check and repair harness or connector.

2 Check continuity between terminals 3 of R/B No.5 (for ABS solenoid relay) and (A5) 4, (A5) 4 and (A5) 3, (A5) 3 and (A10) 16.

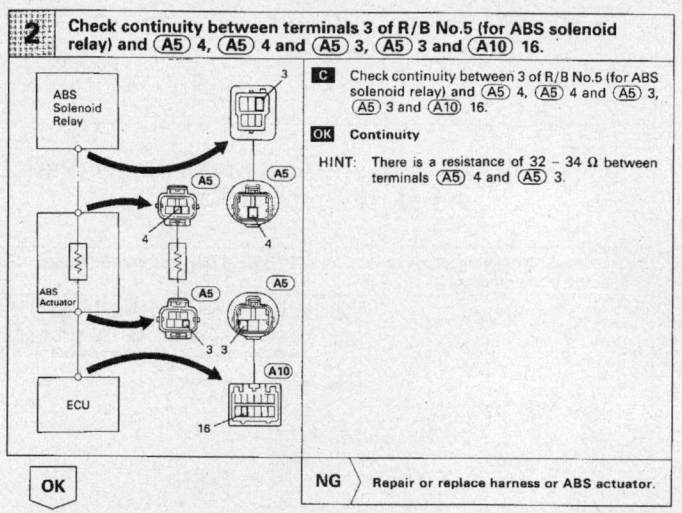

C Check continuity between 3 of R/B No.5 (for ABS solenoid relay) and (A5) 4, (A5) 4 and (A5) 3, (A5) 3 and (A10) 16.

OK Continuity

HINT: There is a resistance of 32 – 34 Ω between terminals (A5) 4 and (A5) 3.

OK ↓

NG ⟩ Repair or replace harness or ABS actuator.

TY4029700393030X

Fig. 216 Codes 11 & 12: ABS Solenoid Relay (Part 3 of 4). 1997–99 Celica

The ABS motor relay supplies power to the ABS pump motor. While the ABS activated, the ECU switches the motor relay ON and operates the ABS pump motor.

DTC No.	Diagnostic Trouble Code Detecting Condition	Trouble area
13	Conditions (1) and (2) continued for 0.2 sec. or more: (1) ABS motor relay terminal (MR) voltage: Battery positive voltage (2) Motor relay monitor terminal (MT) voltage: 0 V	• ABS motor relay • Open or short in ABS motor relay circuit • ECU
14	Conditions (1) and (2) continued for 4 sec. or more: (1) ABS motor relay terminal (MR) voltage: 0 V (2) Motor relay monitor terminal (MT) voltage: Battery positive voltage	• ABS motor relay • B+ short in ABS motor relay circuit. • ECU

Fail safe function: If trouble occurs in the motor relay circuit, the ECU cuts off the current to the solenoid relay and prohibits ABS control.

— DIAGNOSTIC CHART —

1 Check voltage of ABS motor relay. — NG → Check and repair harness or connector.

OK ↓

2 Check continuity between relay and pump motor and ECU. — NG → Repair or replace harness or ABS actuator.

OK ↓

3 Check ABS motor relay. — NG → Replace ABS motor relay.

OK ↓

4 Check for open and short in harness and connector between relay and ECU. — NG → Repair or replace harness or connector.

OK ↓

If the same code is still output after the diagnostic trouble code is deleted, check the contact condition of each connection.
If the connections are normal, the ECU may be defective.

TY4029400098010X

Fig. 217 Codes 13 & 14: ABS Motor Relay (Part 1 of 4). 1996 Celica

---

P Remove solenoid relay from R/B No.5.

C Check continuity between each terminal of ABS solenoid relay.

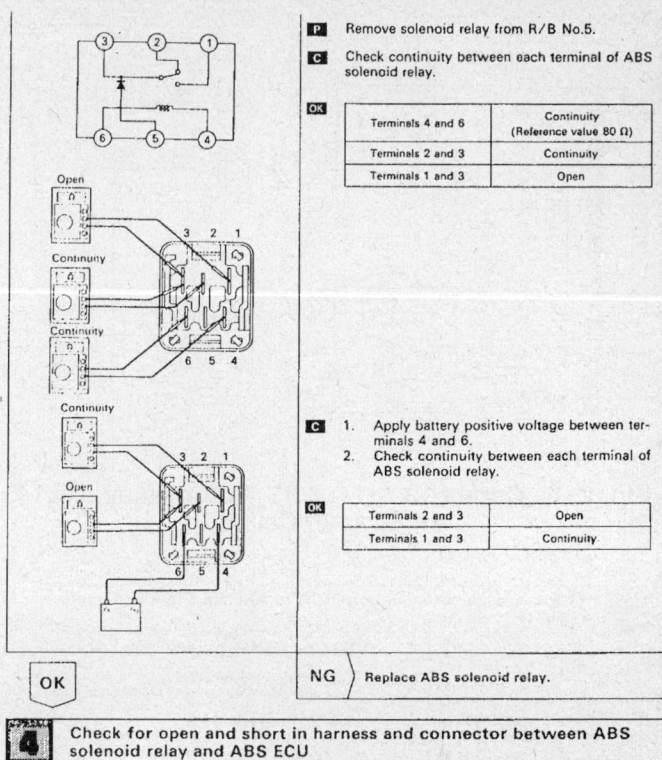

OK

Terminals 4 and 6	Continuity (Reference value 80 Ω)
Terminals 2 and 3	Continuity
Terminals 1 and 3	Open

C 1. Apply battery positive voltage between terminals 4 and 6.
2. Check continuity between each terminal of ABS solenoid relay.

OK

Terminals 2 and 3	Open
Terminals 1 and 3	Continuity

OK ↓

NG ⟩ Replace ABS solenoid relay.

4 Check for open and short in harness and connector between ABS solenoid relay and ABS ECU

OK ↓

NG ⟩ Repair or replace harness or connector.

If the same code is still output after the diagnostic trouble code is deleted, check the contact condition of each connection.
If the connections are normal, the ECU may be defective.

TY4029400097040X

Fig. 216 Codes 11 & 12: ABS Solenoid Relay (Part 4 of 4). Celica

— CIRCUIT DESCRIPTION —

The ABS motor relay supplies power to the ABS pump motor. While the ABS activated, the ECU switches the motor relay ON and operates the ABS pump motor.

DTC No.	DTC Detecting Condition	Trouble Area
13	Conditions (1) and (2) continued for 0.2 sec. or more: (1) ABS motor relay terminal (MR) voltage: Below 1.0 V (2) Motor relay monitor terminal (MT) voltage: 0 V	• ABS solenoid relay • Open or short in ABS solenoid relay circuit
14	Conditions (1) and (2) continued for 4 sec. or more: (1) ABS motor relay terminal (MR) voltage: Battery positive voltage (2) Motor relay monitor terminal (MT) voltage: Battery positive voltage	• ABS solenoid relay • B+ short in ABS solenoid relay circuit

Fail safe function: If trouble occurs in the ABS motor relay circuit, the ECU cuts off current to the ABS solenoid relay and prohibits ABS control.

TY4029700394010X

Fig. 217 Codes 13 & 14: ABS Motor Relay (Part 1 of 4). 1997–99 Celica

TOYOTA UNIT REPAIR

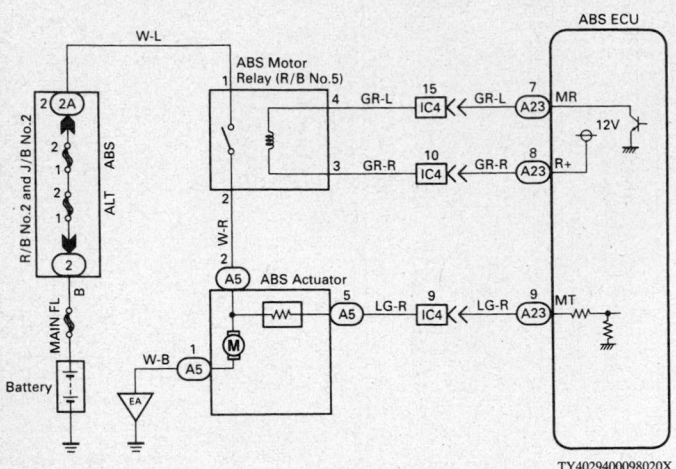

Fig. 217 Codes 13 & 14: ABS Motor Relay (Part 2 of 4). 1996 Celica

WIRING DIAGRAM

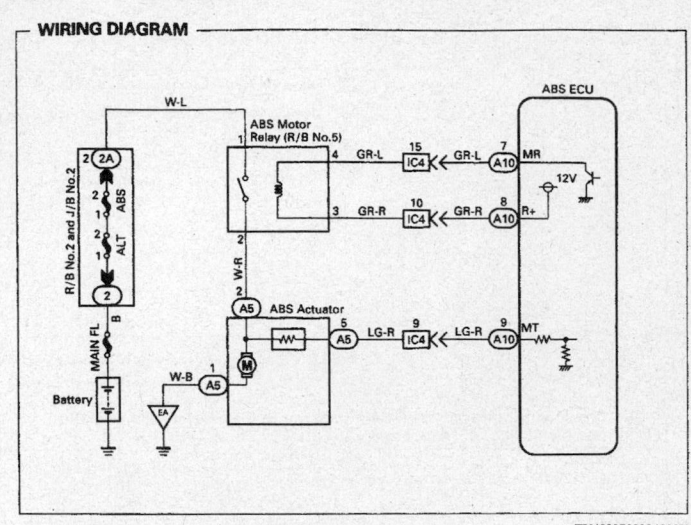

Fig. 217 Codes 13 & 14: ABS Motor Relay (Part 2 of 4). 1997–99 Celica

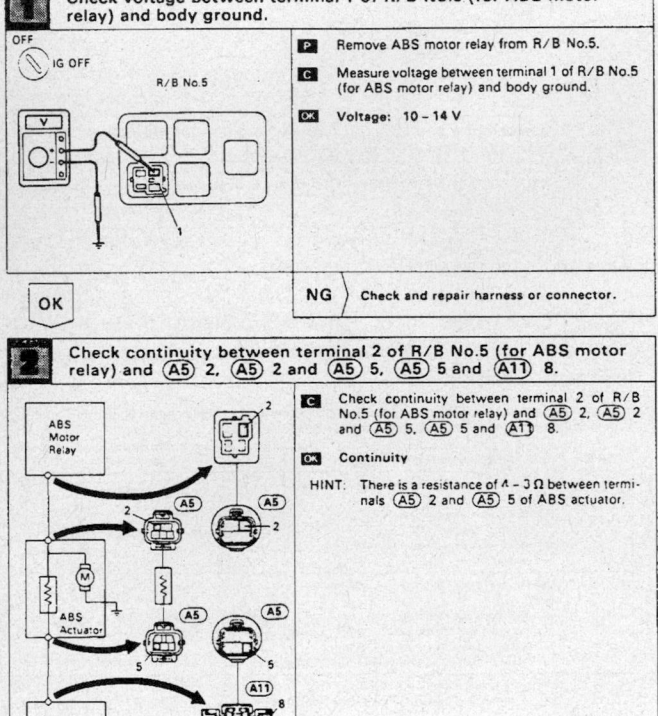

Fig. 217 Codes 13 & 14: ABS Motor Relay (Part 3 of 4). 1996 Celica

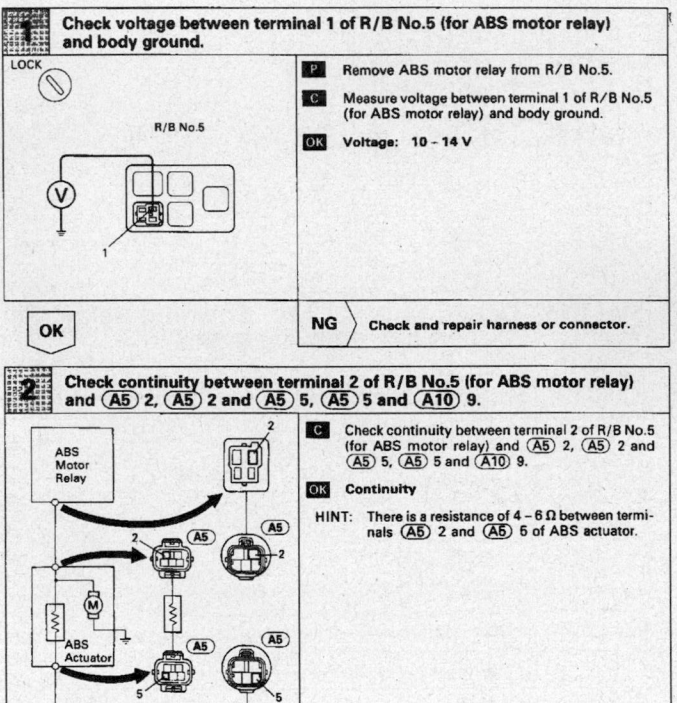

Fig. 217 Codes 13 & 14: ABS Motor Relay (Part 3 of 4). 1997–99 Celica

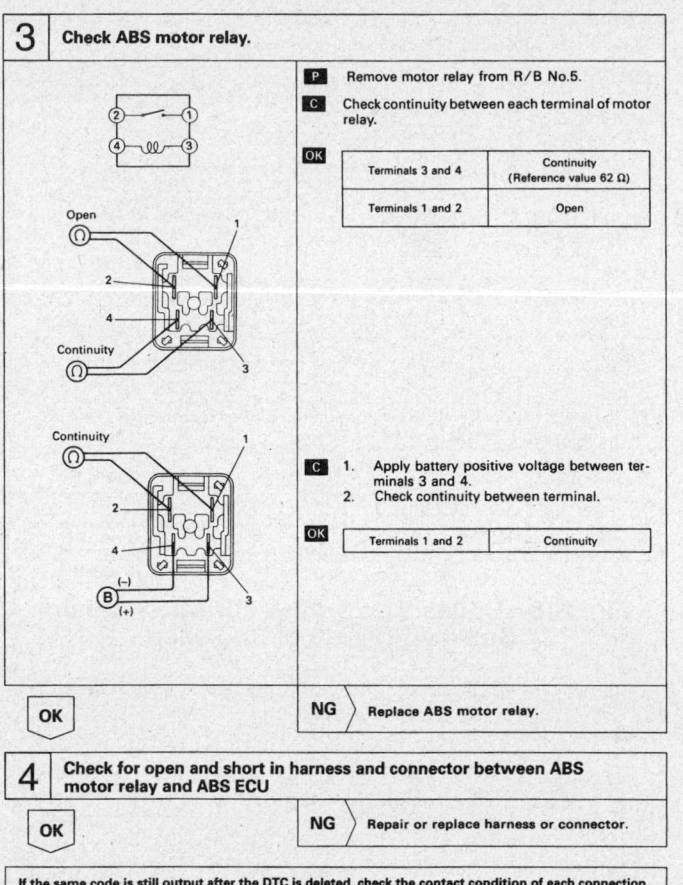

3 | Check ABS motor relay.

P Remove motor relay from R/B No.5.

C Check continuity between each terminal of motor relay.

OK

Terminals 3 and 4	Continuity (Reference value 62 Ω)
Terminals 1 and 2	Open

Open

Continuity

Continuity

C
1. Apply battery positive voltage between terminals 3 and 4.
2. Check continuity between terminal.

OK

Terminals 1 and 2	Continuity

OK

NG ▷ Replace ABS motor relay.

4 | Check for open and short in harness and connector between ABS motor relay and ABS ECU

OK

NG ▷ Repair or replace harness or connector.

If the same code is still output after the DTC is deleted, check the contact condition of each connection. If the connections are normal, the ECU may be defective.

TY4029700394040X

Fig. 217 Codes 13 & 14: ABS Motor Relay (Part 4 of 4). Celica

CIRCUIT DESCRIPTION

This solenoid goes on when signals are received from the ECU and controls the fluid pressure acting on the brake cylinders, thus controlling the braking force.

DTC No.	DTC Detecting Condition	Trouble Area
21	Conditions (1) through (3) continue for 0.05 sec. or more: (1) ABS solenoid relay terminal (SR) voltage: Below 1.5 V (2) Voltage of ABS ECU terminal AST: Battery positive voltage (3) When power transistor of ECU is ON, voltage of terminal SFRH or SFRR is 0 V or battery positive voltage.	• ABS solenoid relay • Open or short in SFRH or SFRR circuit
22	Conditions (1) through (3) continue for 0.05 sec. or more: (1) ABS solenoid relay terminal (SR) voltage: Below 1.5 V (2) Voltage of ABS ECU terminal AST: Battery positive voltage (3) When power transistor of ECU is ON, voltage of terminal SFLH or SFLR is 0 V or battery positive voltage.	• ABS solenoid relay • Open or short in SFLH or SFLR circuit
23	Conditions (1) through (3) continue for 0.05 sec. or more: (1) ABS solenoid relay terminal (SR) voltage: Below 1.5 V (2) Voltage of ABS ECU terminal AST: Battery positive voltage (3) When power transistor of ECU is ON, voltage of terminal SRRH or SRRR is 0 V or battery positive voltage.	• ABS solenoid relay • Open or short in SRRH or SRRR circuit
24	Conditions (1) through (3) continue for 0.05 sec. or more: (1) ABS solenoid relay terminal (SR) voltage: Below 1.5 V (2) Voltage of ABS ECU terminal AST: Battery positive voltage (3) When power transistor of ECU is ON, voltage of terminal SRLH or SRLR is 0 V or battery positive voltage.	• ABS solenoid relay • Open or short in SRLH or SRLR circuit

Fail safe function: If trouble occurs in the actuator solenoid circuit, the ECU cuts off current to the ABS solenoid relay and prohibits ABS control.

TY4029700395010X

Fig. 218 Codes 21, 22, 23 & 24: ABS Actuator Solenoid (Part 1 of 3). 1997–99 Celica

CIRCUIT DESCRIPTION

This solenoid goes on when signals are received from the ECU and controls the fluid pressure acting on the brake cylinders, thus controlling the braking force.

DTC No.	Diagnostic Trouble Code Detecting Condition	Trouble area
21	Conditions (1) through (3) continue for 0.05 sec. or more: (1) ABS solenoid relay terminal (SR) voltage: Battery positive voltage (2) Voltage of ABS ECU terminal AST: Battery positive voltage (3) When power transistor of ECU is ON, voltage of terminal SFRH or SFRR is 0 V or battery positive voltage.	• ABS actuator. • Open or short in SFRH or SFRR circuit. • ECU.
22	Conditions (1) through (3) continue for 0.05 sec. or more: (1) ABS solenoid relay terminal (SR) voltage: Battery positive voltage (2) Voltage of ABS ECU terminal AST: Battery positive voltage (3) When power transistor of ECU is ON, voltage of terminal SFLH or SFLR is 0 V or battery positive voltage.	• ABS actuator. • Open or short in SFLH or SFLR circuit. • ECU.
23	Conditions (1) through (3) continue for 0.05 sec. or more: (1) ABS solenoid relay terminal (SR) voltage: Battery positive voltage (2) Voltage of ABS ECU terminal AST: Battery positive voltage (3) When power transistor of ECU is ON, voltage of terminal SRRH or SRRR is 0 V or battery positive voltage.	• ABS actuator. • Open or short in SRRH or SRRR circuit. • ECU.
24	Conditions (1) through (3) continue for 0.05 sec. or more: (1) S solenoid relay terminal (SH) voltage: Battery positive voltage (2) Voltage of ABS ECU terminal AST: Battery positive voltage (3) When power transistor of ECU is ON, voltage of terminal SRLH or SRLR is 0 V or battery positive voltage.	• ABS actuator. • Open or short in SRLH or SRLR circuit. • ECU.

Fail safe function: If trouble occurs in the actuator solenoid circuit, the ECU cuts off current to the solenoid relay and prohibits ABS control.

TY4029400099020X

Fig. 218 Codes 21, 22, 23 & 24: ABS Actuator Solenoid (Part 1 of 3). 1996 Celica

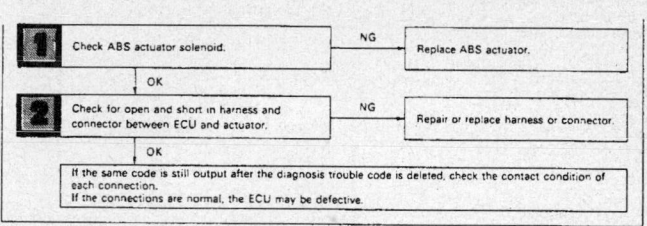

1 Check ABS actuator solenoid.
NG Replace ABS actuator.

OK

2 Check for open and short in harness and connector between ECU and actuator.
NG Repair or replace harness or connector.

OK

If the same code is still output after the diagnosis trouble code is deleted, check the contact condition of each connection.
If the connections are normal, the ECU may be defective.

WIRING DIAGRAM

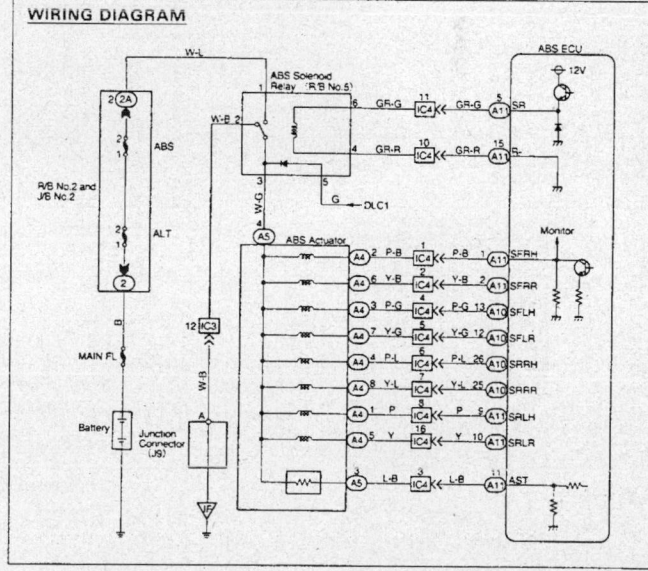

TY4029400099010X

Fig. 218 Codes 21, 22, 23 & 24: ABS Actuator Solenoid (Part 2 of 3). 1996 Celica

WIRING DIAGRAM

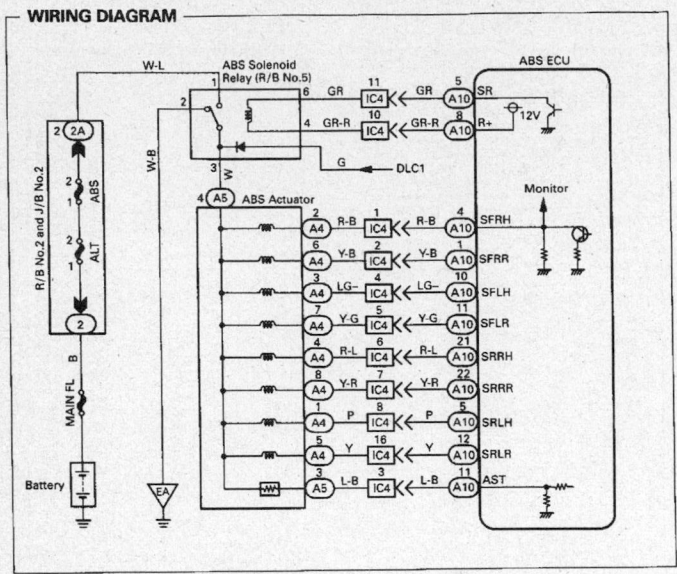

Fig. 218 Codes 21, 22, 23 & 24: ABS Actuator Solenoid (Part 2 of 3). 1997–99 Celica

TY4029700395020X

1 | **Check ABS actuator solenoid.**

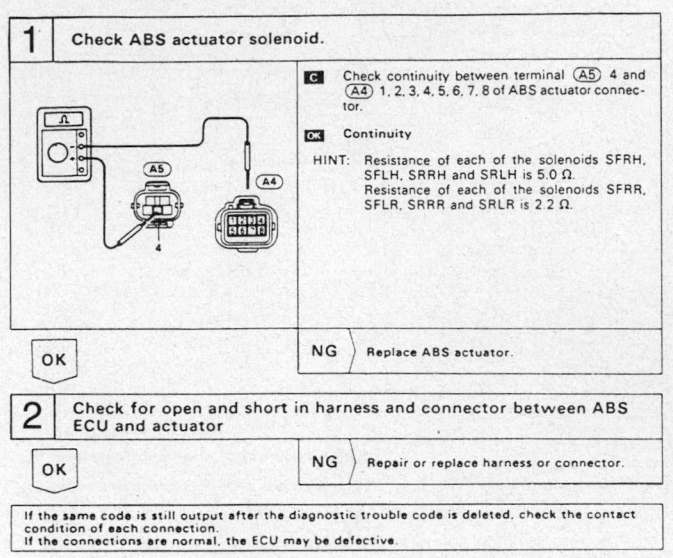

C: Check continuity between terminal Ⓐ5 4 and Ⓐ4 1, 2, 3, 4, 5, 6, 7, 8 of ABS actuator connector.

OK: Continuity

HINT: Resistance of each of the solenoids SFRH, SFLH, SRRH and SRLH is 5.0 Ω. Resistance of each of the solenoids SFRR, SFLR, SRRR and SRLR is 2.2 Ω.

| OK | | NG | Replace ABS actuator. |

2 | **Check for open and short in harness and connector between ABS ECU and actuator**

| OK | | NG | Repair or replace harness or connector. |

If the same code is still output after the diagnostic trouble code is deleted, check the contact condition of each connection.
If the connections are normal, the ECU may be defective.

TY4029400099030X

Fig. 218 Codes 21, 22, 23 & 24: ABS Actuator Solenoid (Part 3 of 3). Celica

CIRCUIT DESCRIPTION

The speed sensor detects the wheel speed and sends the appropriate signals to the ECU. These signals are used to control the ABS system. The front and rear rotors each have 48 serrations. When the rotors rotate, the magnetic field emitted by the permanent magnet in the speed sensor generates an AC voltage. Since the frequency of this AC voltage changes in direct proportion to the speed of the rotor, the frequency is used by the ECU to detect the speed of each wheel.

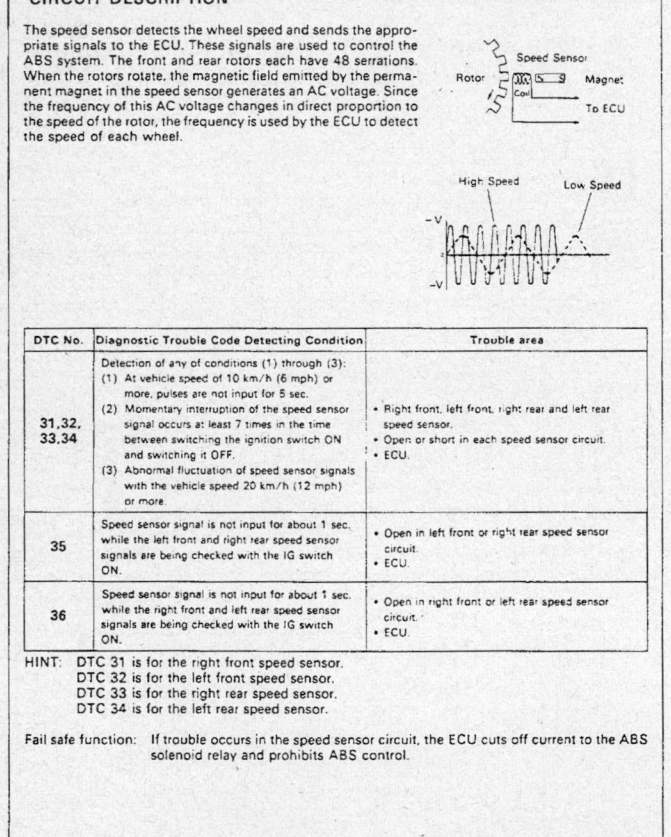

DTC No.	Diagnostic Trouble Code Detecting Condition	Trouble area
31, 32, 33, 34	Detection of any of conditions (1) through (3): (1) At vehicle speed of 10 km/h (6 mph) or more, pulses are not input for 5 sec. (2) Momentary interruption of the speed sensor signal occurs at least 7 times in the time between switching the ignition switch ON and switching it OFF. (3) Abnormal fluctuation of speed sensor signals at the vehicle speed 20 km/h (12 mph) or more.	• Right front, left front, right rear and left rear speed sensor. • Open or short in each speed sensor circuit. • ECU.
35	Speed sensor signal is not input for about 1 sec. while the left front and right rear speed sensor signals are being checked with the IG switch ON.	• Open in left front or right rear speed sensor circuit. • ECU.
36	Speed sensor signal is not input for about 1 sec. while the right front and left rear speed sensor signals are being checked with the IG switch ON.	• Open in right front or left rear speed sensor circuit. • ECU.

HINT: DTC 31 is for the right front speed sensor.
DTC 32 is for the left front speed sensor.
DTC 33 is for the right rear speed sensor.
DTC 34 is for the left rear speed sensor.

Fail safe function: If trouble occurs in the speed sensor circuit, the ECU cuts off current to the ABS solenoid relay and prohibits ABS control.

TY4029400100010X

Fig. 219 Codes 31, 32, 33, 34, 35 & 36: Speed Sensor Circuit (Part 1 of 4). Celica

DIAGNOSTIC CHART

1 | Check speed sensor. | NG → | Replace speed sensor. |

↓ OK

2 | Check for open and short in harness and connector between each speed sensor and ECU. | NG → | Repair or replace harness or connector. |

↓ OK

3 | Check sensor rotor and sensor installation. | NG → | Replace speed sensor or rotor. |

↓ OK

| Check and replace ABS ECU. |

HINT: Check the speed sensor signal last

WIRING DIAGRAM

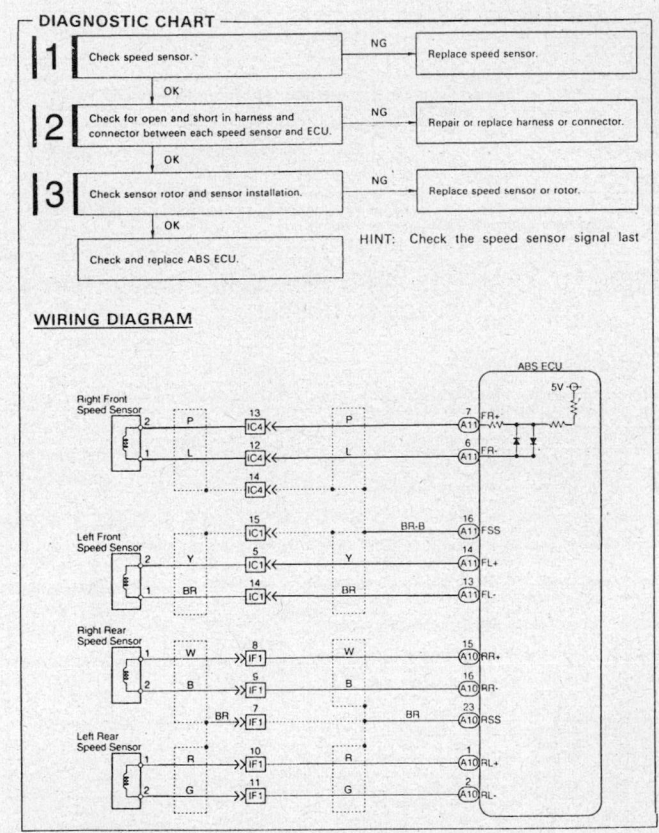

TY4029400100020X

Fig. 219 Codes 31, 32, 33, 34, 35 & 36: Speed Sensor Circuit (Part 2 of 4). 1996 Celica

WIRING DIAGRAM

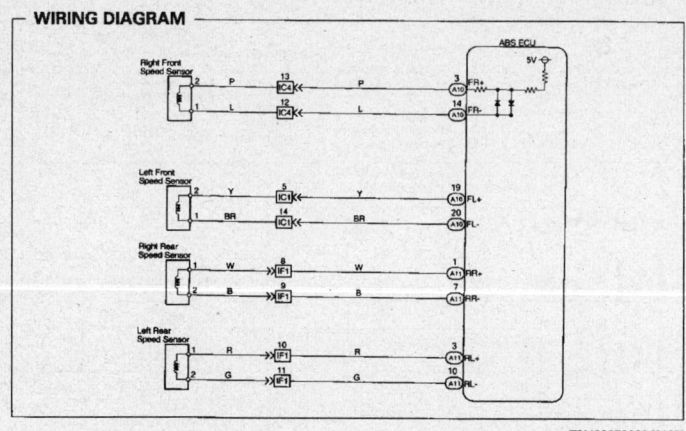

TY4029700396010X

Fig. 219   Codes 31, 32, 33, 34, 35 & 36: Speed Sensor Circuit (Part 2 of 4). 1997–99 Celica

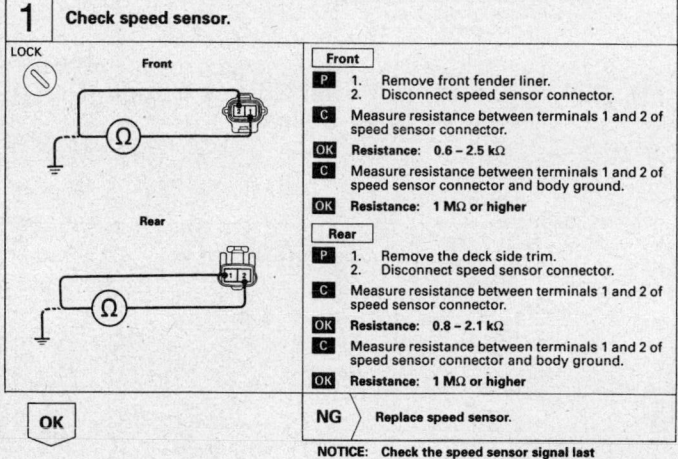

1	Check speed sensor.		
LOCK			

Front

P
1. Remove front fender liner.
2. Disconnect speed sensor connector.

C Measure resistance between terminals 1 and 2 of speed sensor connector.

OK Resistance: 0.6 – 2.5 kΩ

C Measure resistance between terminals 1 and 2 of speed sensor connector and body ground.

OK Resistance: 1 MΩ or higher

Rear

P
1. Remove the deck side trim.
2. Disconnect speed sensor connector.

C Measure resistance between terminals 1 and 2 of speed sensor connector.

OK Resistance: 0.8 – 2.1 kΩ

C Measure resistance between terminals 1 and 2 of speed sensor connector and body ground.

OK Resistance: 1 MΩ or higher

OK   NG ▷ Replace speed sensor.

NOTICE: Check the speed sensor signal last.

TY4029700396020X

Fig. 219   Codes 31, 32, 33, 34, 35 & 36: Speed Sensor Circuit (Part 3 of 4). 1997–99 Celica

INSPECTION PROCEDURE

1	Check speed sensor.

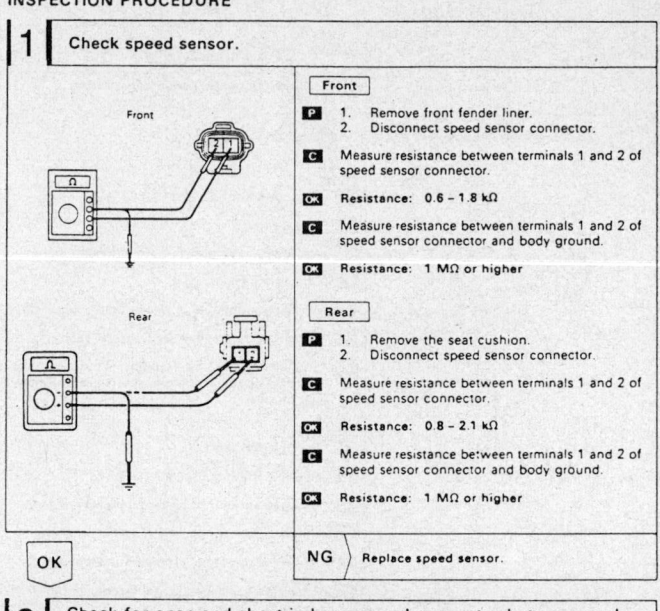

Front

P
1. Remove front fender liner.
2. Disconnect speed sensor connector.

C Measure resistance between terminals 1 and 2 of speed sensor connector.

OK Resistance: 0.6 – 1.8 kΩ

C Measure resistance between terminals 1 and 2 of speed sensor connector and body ground.

OK Resistance: 1 MΩ or higher

Rear

P
1. Remove the seat cushion.
2. Disconnect speed sensor connector.

C Measure resistance between terminals 1 and 2 of speed sensor connector.

OK Resistance: 0.8 – 2.1 kΩ

C Measure resistance between terminals 1 and 2 of speed sensor connector and body ground.

OK Resistance: 1 MΩ or higher

OK   NG ▷ Replace speed sensor.

2	Check for open and short in harness and connector between each speed sensor and ECU

OK   NG ▷ Repair or replace harness or connector.

TY4029400100030X

Fig. 219   Codes 31, 32, 33, 34, 35 & 36: Speed Sensor Circuit (Part 3 of 4). 1996 Celica

3	Check sensor rotor and sensor installation.

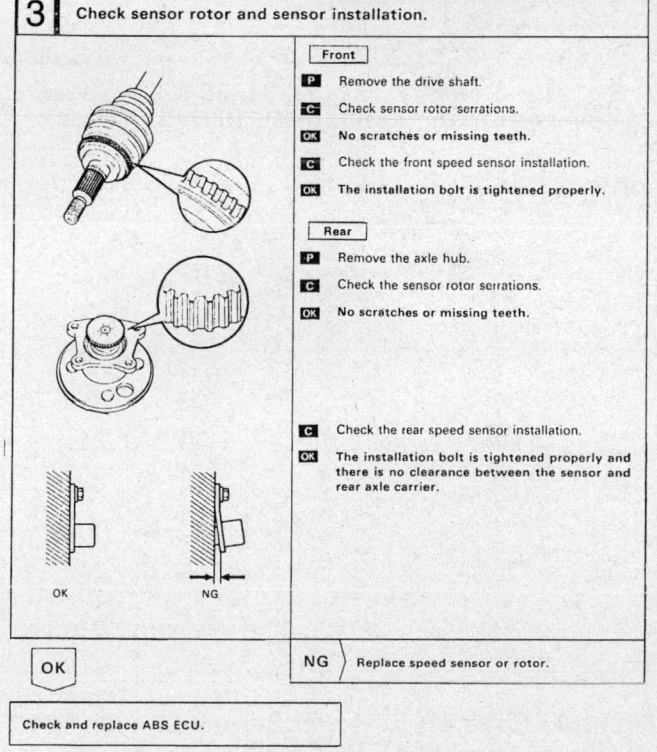

Front

P Remove the drive shaft.

C Check sensor rotor serrations.

OK No scratches or missing teeth.

C Check the front speed sensor installation.

OK The installation bolt is tightened properly.

Rear

P Remove the axle hub.

C Check the sensor rotor serrations.

OK No scratches or missing teeth.

C Check the rear speed sensor installation.

OK The installation bolt is tightened properly and there is no clearance between the sensor and rear axle carrier.

OK   NG ▷ Replace speed sensor or rotor.

Check and replace ABS ECU.

TY4029400100040X

Fig. 219   Codes 31, 32, 33, 34, 35 & 36: Speed Sensor Circuit (Part 4 of 4). 1996 Celica

2 Check for open and short in harness and connector between each speed sensor and ECU

OK		NG	Repair or replace harness or connector.

NOTICE: Check the speed sensor signal lsast

3 Check sensor rotor and sensor installation.

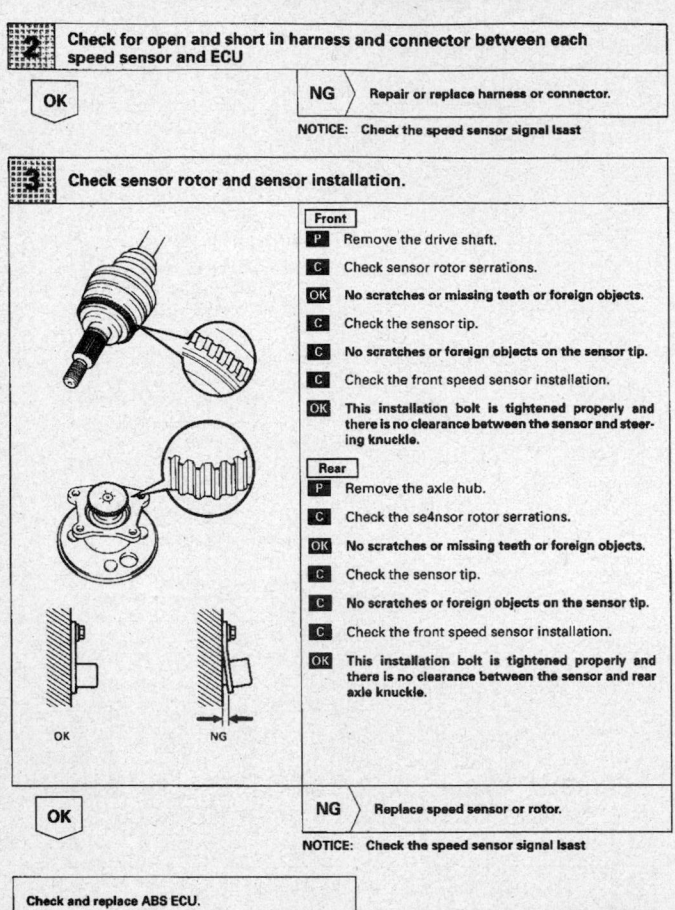

Front

P Remove the drive shaft.

C Check sensor rotor serrations.

OK No scratches or missing teeth or foreign objects.

C Check the sensor tip.

C No scratches or foreign objects on the sensor tip.

C Check the front speed sensor installation.

OK This installation bolt is tightened properly and there is no clearance between the sensor and steering knuckle.

Rear

P Remove the axle hub.

C Check the se4nsor rotor serrations.

OK No scratches or missing teeth or foreign objects.

C Check the sensor tip.

C No scratches or foreign objects on the sensor tip.

C Check the front speed sensor installation.

OK This installation bolt is tightened properly and there is no clearance between the sensor and rear axle knuckle.

OK		NG	Replace speed sensor or rotor.

NOTICE: Check the speed sensor signal lsast

Check and replace ABS ECU.

TY4029700396030X

Fig. 219 Codes 31, 32, 33, 34, 35 & 36: Speed Sensor Circuit (Part 4 of 4). 1997–99 Celica

WIRING DIAGRAM

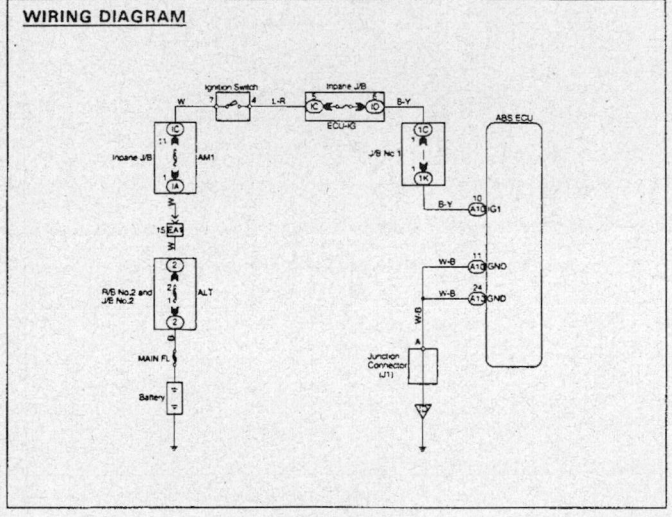

TY4029400101020X

Fig. 220 Code 41: IG Power Source Circuit (Part 2 of 4). 1996 Celica

---

CIRCUIT DESCRIPTION

This is the power source for the ECU, hence the CPU, and the actuators.

DTC No.	Diagnostic Trouble Code Detecting Condition	Trouble area
41	Vehicle speed is 3 km/h (1.9 mph) or more and voltage of ECU terminal IG1 remains at more than 17 V or below 9.5 V for more than 10 sec.	• Battery. • IC regulator. • Open or short in power source circuit. • ECU.

Fail safe function: If trouble occurs in the power source circuit, the ECU cuts off current to the ABS solenoid relay and prohibits ABS control.

DIAGNOSTIC CHART

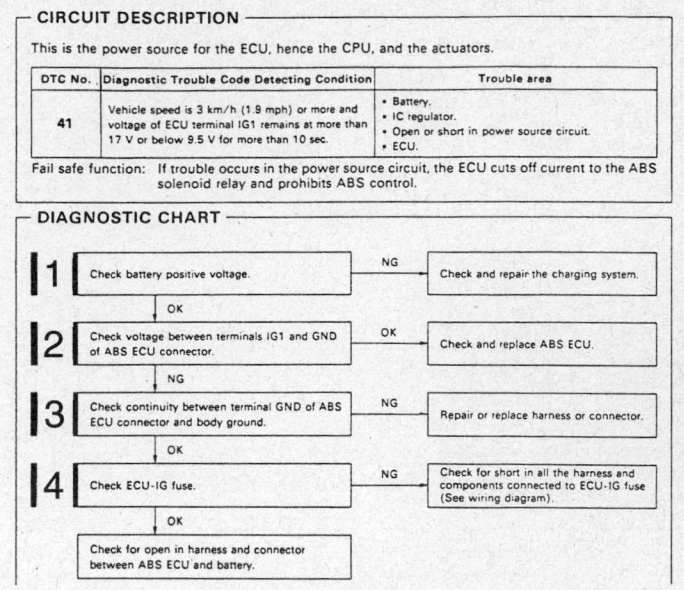

TY4029400101010X

Fig. 220 Code 41: IG Power Source Circuit (Part 1 of 4). Celica

WIRING DIAGRAM

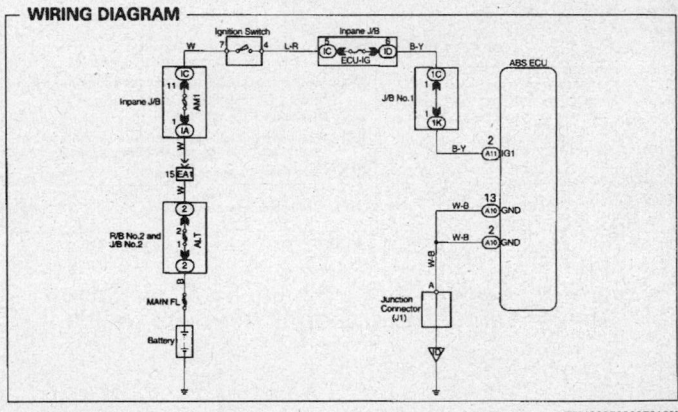

TY4029700397010X

Fig. 220 Code 41: IG Power Source Circuit (Part 2 of 4). 1997–99 Celica

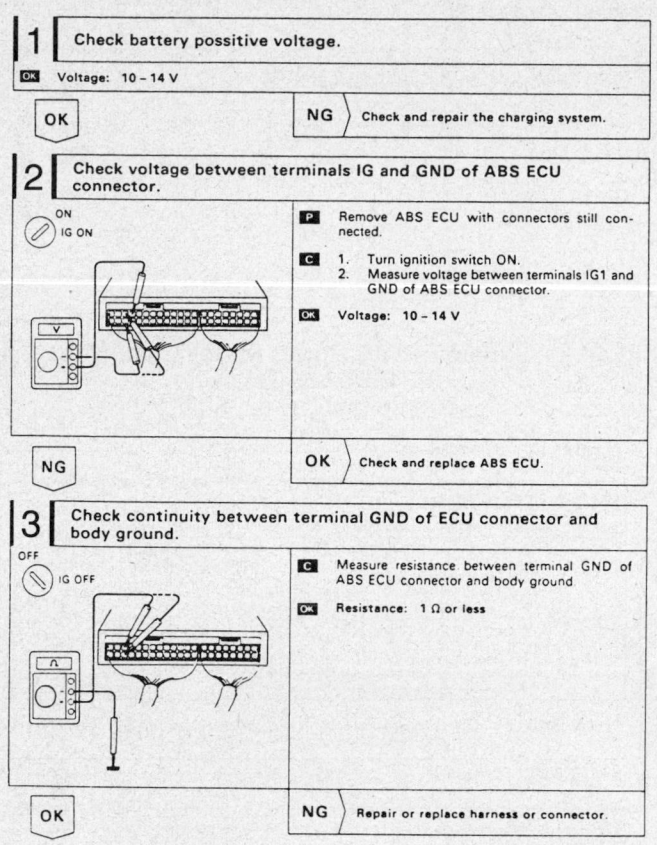

Fig. 220 Code 41: IG Power Source Circuit (Part 3 of 4). 1996 Celica

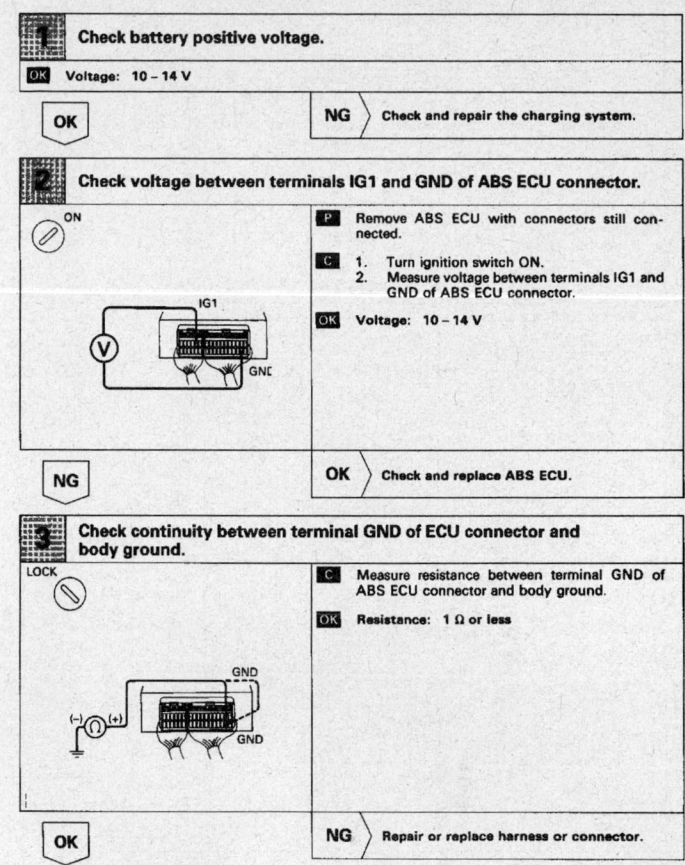

Fig. 220 Code 41: IG Power Source Circuit (Part 3 of 4). 1997–99 Celica

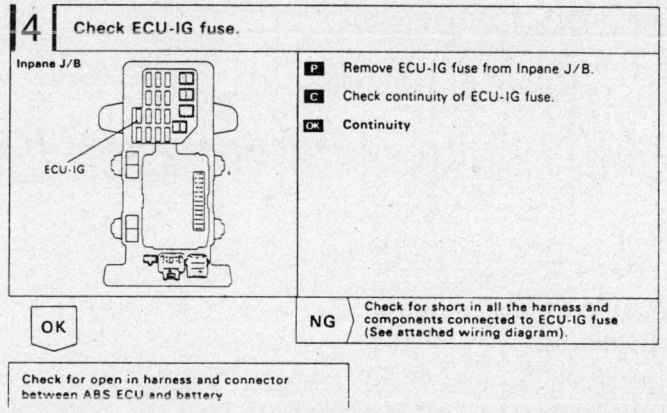

Fig. 220 Code 41: IG Power Source Circuit (Part 4 of 4). Celica

CIRCUIT DESCRIPTION

DTC No.	Diagnostic Trouble Code Detecting Condition	Trouble area
51	Pump motor is not operating normally during initial check.	• ABS pump motor.

Fail safe function: If trouble occurs in the ABS pump motor, the ECU cuts off the current to the solenoid relay and prohibits ABS control.

DIAGNOSTIC CHART

See inspection of ABS pump motor.

WIRING DIAGRAM

(Reference)

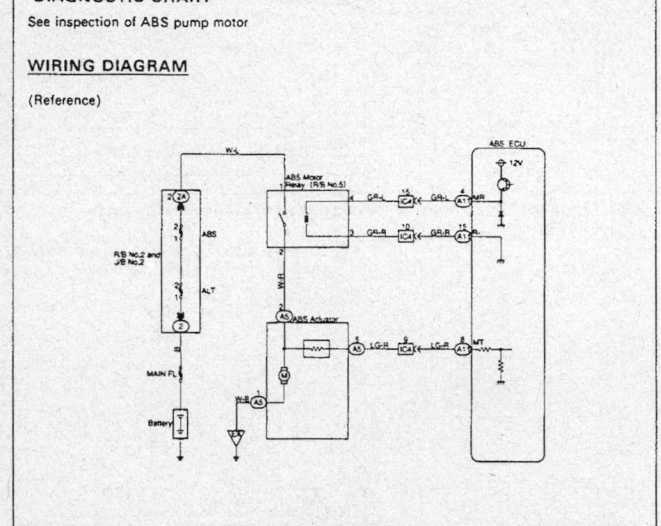

TY4029400102000X

Fig. 221 Code 51: ABS Pump Motor Lock. 1996 Celica

WIRING DIAGRAM

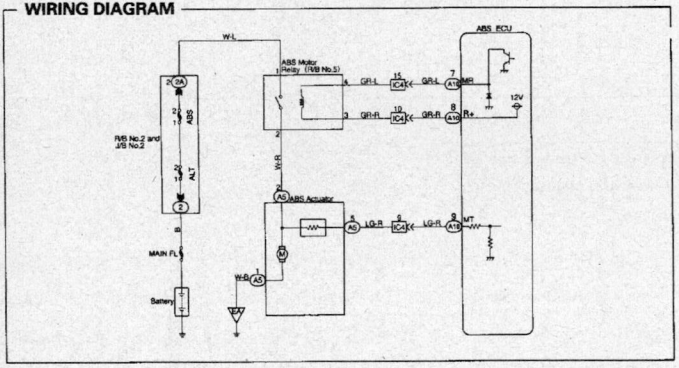

TY4029700398020X

Fig. 222 Code 51: ABS Pump Motor Lock (Part 2 of 2). 1997–99 Celica

---

CIRCUIT DESCRIPTION

DTC No.	DTC Detecting Condition	Trouble Area
51	Pump motor is not operating normally during initial check.	• ABS pump motor

Fail safe function: If trouble occurs in the ABS pump motor, the ECU cuts off current to the ABS solenoid relay and prohibits ABS control.

TY4029700398010X

Fig. 222 Code 51: ABS Pump Motor Lock (Part 1 of 2). 1997–99 Celica

CIRCUIT DESCRIPTION

This relay supplies power to each ABS solenoid. After the ignition switch is turned on, if the initial check is OK, the relay goes on.

DTC No.	Diagnostic Trouble Code Detecting Condition	Trouble Area
11	Conditions (1) and (2) continue for 0.2 sec. or more: (1) ABS control (solenoid) relay: ON (2) ABS control (solenoid) relay monitor terminal (AST) voltage: 0 V	• ABS control (solenoid) relay. • Open or short in ABS control (solenoid) relay circuit. • ECU.
12	Conditions (1) and (2) continue for 0.2 sec. or more: (1) ABS control (solenoid) relay: OFF (2) ABS control (solenoid) relay monitor terminal (AST) voltage: Battery voltage	• ABS control (solenoid) relay. • B+ short in ABS control (solenoid) relay circuit. • ECU.

Fail safe function: If trouble occurs in the control (solenoid) relay circuit, the ECU cuts off current to the ABS control (solenoid) relay and prohibits ABS control.

DIAGNOSTIC CHART

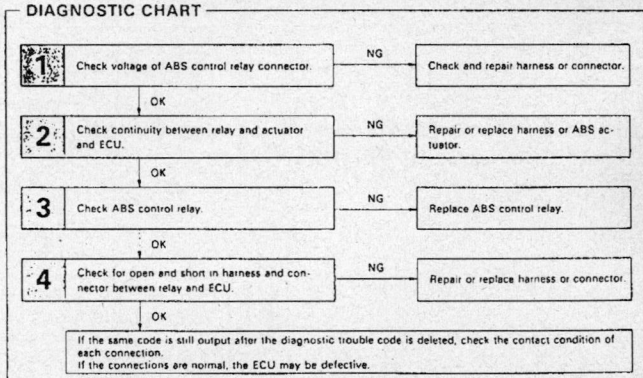

```
1  Check voltage of ABS control relay connector.   NG →  Check and repair harness or connector.
      │ OK
2  Check continuity between relay and actuator      NG →  Repair or replace harness or ABS ac-
   and ECU.                                               tuator.
      │ OK
3  Check ABS control relay.                         NG →  Replace ABS control relay.
      │ OK
4  Check for open and short in harness and con-     NG →  Repair or replace harness or connector.
   nector between relay and ECU.
      │ OK
```

If the same code is still output after the diagnostic trouble code is deleted, check the contact condition of each connection.
If the connections are normal, the ECU may be defective.

TY4029300077010X

Fig. 223 Codes 11 & 12: ABS Control Solenoid Relay Circuit (Part 1 of 4). Corolla

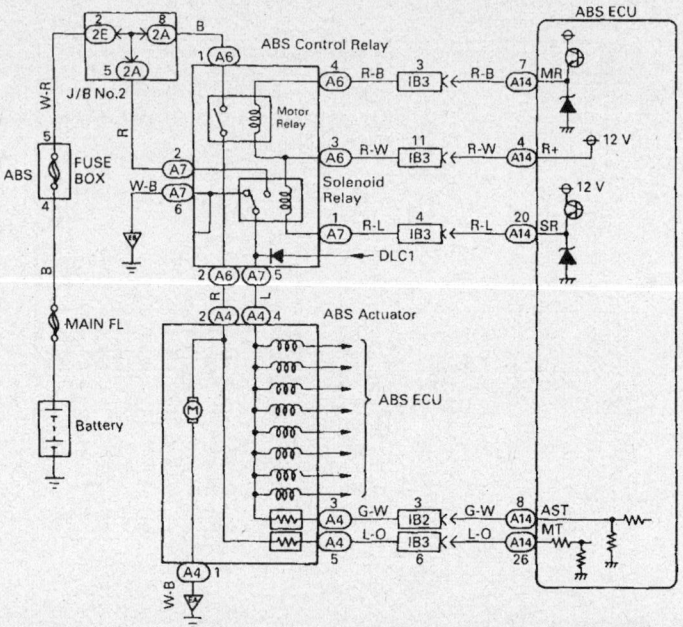

Fig. 223   Codes 11 & 12: ABS Control Solenoid Relay Circuit (Part 2 of 4). Corolla

TY4029700323000X

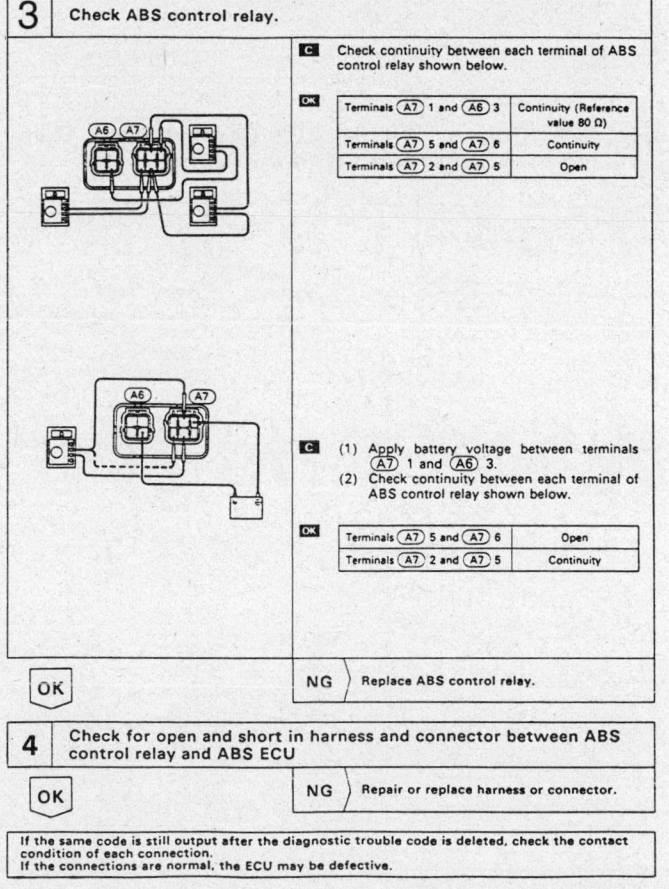

Fig. 223   Codes 11 & 12: ABS Control Solenoid Relay Circuit (Part 4 of 4). Corolla

TY4029300077040X

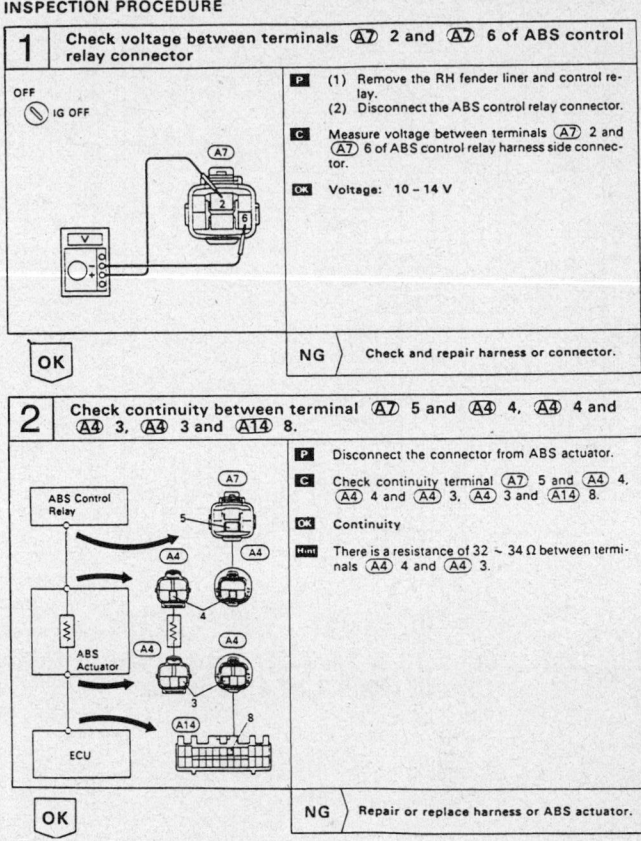

Fig. 223   Codes 11 & 12: ABS Control Solenoid Relay Circuit (Part 3 of 4). Corolla

TY4029300077030X

CIRCUIT DESCRIPTION

The ABS control (motor) relay supplies power to the ABS pump motor. If the accumulator pressure drops, the ECU switches the control (motor) relay ON and operates the ABS pump motor.

DTC No.	Diagnostic Trouble Code Detecting Condition	Trouble Area
13	Conditions (1) and (2) continue for 0.2 sec. or more: (1) ABS control (motor) relay: ON (2) ABS control (motor) relay monitor terminal (MT) voltage: 0 V	• ABS control (motor) relay. • Open or short in ABS control (motor) relay circuit. • ECU.
14	Conditions (1) and (2) continue for 4 sec. or more: (1) ABS control (motor) relay: OFF (2) ABS control (motor) relay monitor terminal (MT) voltage: Battery voltage	• ABS control (motor) relay. • B+ short in ABS control (motor) relay circuit. • ECU.

Fail safe function: If trouble occurs in the control (motor) relay circuit, the ECU cuts off the current to the ABS control (solenoid) relay and prohibits ABS control.

DIAGNOSTIC CHART

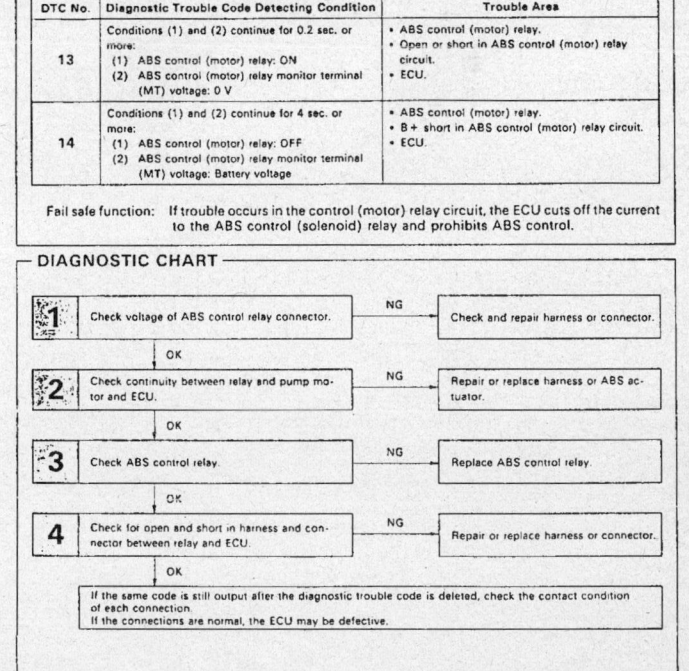

TY4029300078010X

Fig. 224   Codes 13 & 14: ABS Control Motor Relay Circuit (Part 1 of 4). Corolla

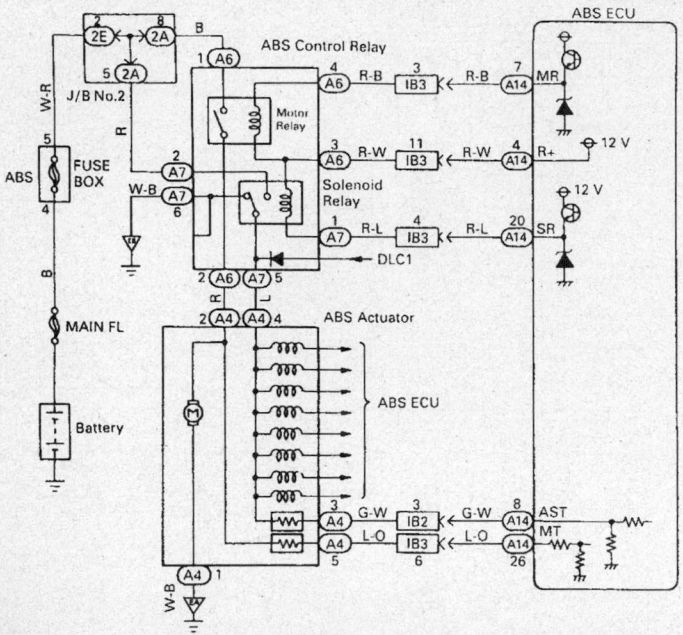

Fig. 224 Codes 13 & 14: ABS Control Motor Relay Circuit (Part 2 of 4). Corolla

TY4029700324000X

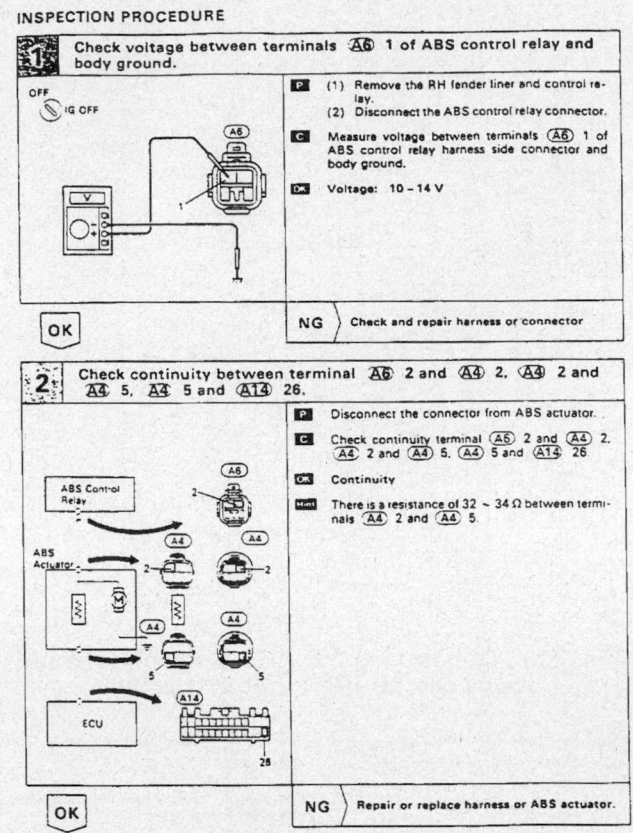

Fig. 224 Codes 13 & 14: ABS Control Motor Relay Circuit (Part 3 of 4). Corolla

TY4029300078030X

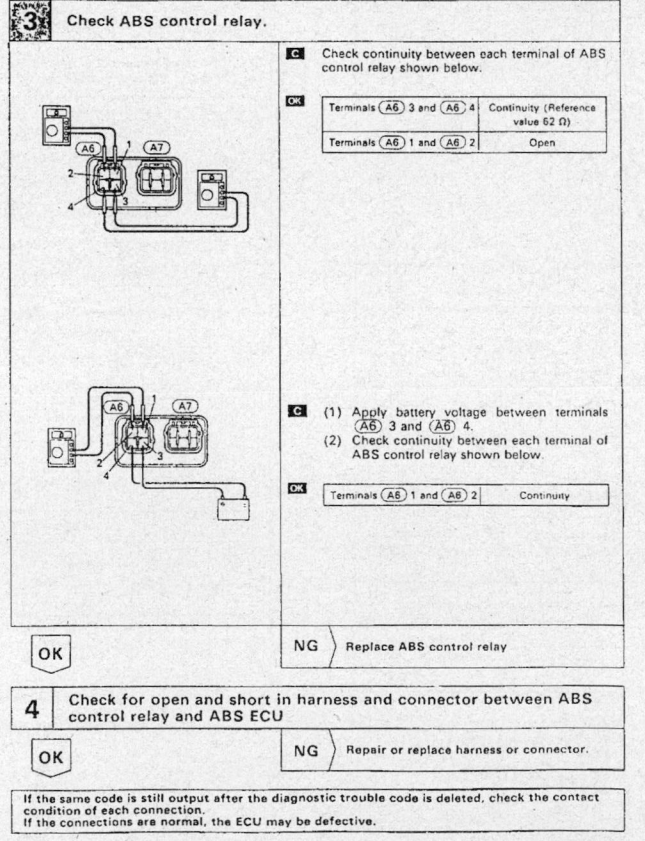

TY4029300078040X

Fig. 224 Codes 13 & 14: ABS Control Motor Relay Circuit (Part 4 of 4). Corolla

CIRCUIT DESCRIPTION

This solenoid goes on when signals are received from the ECU and controls the fluid pressure acting on the brake cylinders, thus controlling the braking force.

DTC No.	Diagnostic Trouble Code Detecting Condition	Trouble area
21	Conditions (1) through (3) continue for 0.05 sec. or more: (1) ABS solenoid relay (SR) terminal voltage: Battery positive voltage (2) Voltage of ABS ECU terminal AST: Battery positive voltage (3) When power transistor of ECU is ON, voltage of terminal SFR is 0 V or battery positive voltage.	• ABS actuator • Open or short in SFR circuit. • ECU
22	Conditions (1) through (3) continue for 0.05 sec. or more: (1) ABS solenoid relay (SR) terminal voltage: Battery positive voltage (2) Voltage of ABS ECU terminal AST: Battery positive voltage (3) When power transistor of ECU is ON, voltage of terminal SFL is 0 V or battery positive voltage.	• ABS actuator • Open or short in SFL circuit. • ECU
23	Conditions (1) through (3) continue for 0.05 sec. or more: (1) ABS solenoid relay (SR) terminal voltage: Battery positive voltage (2) Voltage of ABS ECU terminal AST: Battery positive voltage (3) When power transistor of ECU is ON, voltage of terminal SRR is 0 V or battery positive voltage.	• ABS actuator • Open or short in SRR circuit. • ECU
24	Conditions (1) through (3) continue for 0.05 sec. or more: (1) ABS solenoid relay (SR) terminal voltage: Battery positive voltage (2) Voltage of ABS ECU terminal AST: Battery positive voltage (3) When power transistor of ECU is ON, voltage of terminal SRL is 0 V or battery positive voltage.	• ABS actuator • Open or short in SRL circuit. • ECU

Fail safe function: If trouble occurs in the actuator solenoid circuit, the ECU cuts off current to the solenoid relay and prohibits ABS control.

DIAGNOSTIC CHART

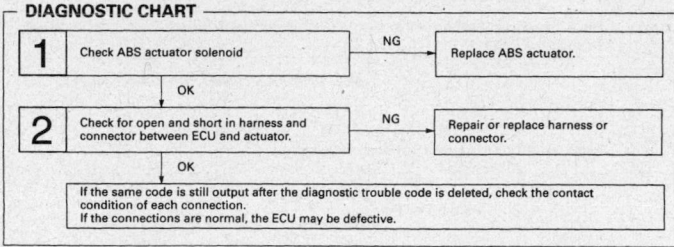

1. Check ABS actuator solenoid → NG → Replace ABS actuator.

OK

2. Check for open and short in harness and connector between ECU and actuator. → NG → Repair or replace harness or connector.

OK

If the same code is still output after the diagnostic trouble code is deleted, check the contact condition of each connection.
If the connections are normal, the ECU may be defective.

TY4029300079010X

Fig. 225 Codes 21, 22, 23 & 24: ABS Actuator Solenoid Circuit (Part 1 of 3). Corolla

INSPECTION PROCEDURE

1. **Check ABS actuator solenoid.**

P	(1) Remove the washer tank. (2) Disconnect the two connectors from ABS actuator.
C	Check continuity between terminal (A4) 4 and (A5) 1, 2, 3, 4, 5, 6, 7, 8 of ABS actuator connector.
OK	Continuity
Hint	Resistance of each of the solenoids SFRH, SFLH, SRRH and SRLH is 5.0 Ω. Resistance of each of the solenoids SFRR, SFLR, SRRR and SRLR is 2.2 Ω.

OK | NG > Replace ABS actuator.

2. **Check for open and short in harness and connector between ABS ECU and actuator**

OK | NG > Repair or replace harness or connector.

If the same code is still output after the diagnostic trouble code is deleted, check the contact condition of each connection.
If the connections are normal, the ECU may be defective.

TY4029300079030X

Fig. 225 Codes 21, 22, 23 & 24: ABS Actuator Solenoid Circuit (Part 3 of 3). Corolla

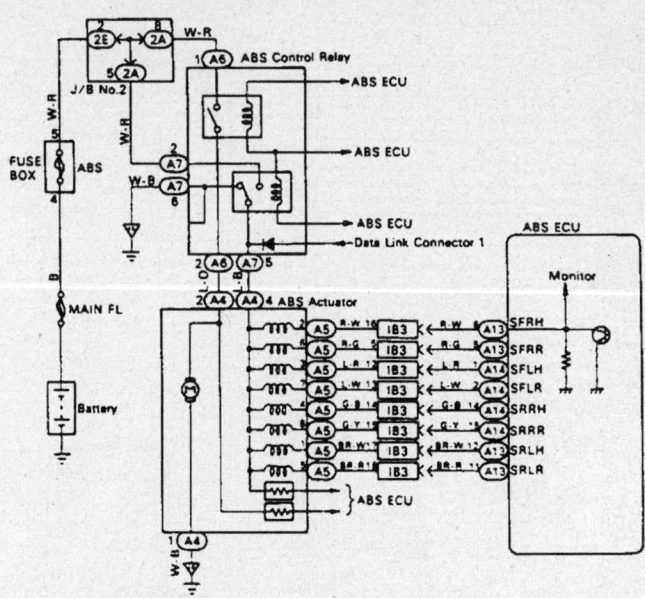

TY4029300079020X

Fig. 225 Codes 21, 22, 23 & 24: ABS Actuator Solenoid Circuit (Part 2 of 3). Corolla

CIRCUIT DESCRIPTION

The speed sensor detects the wheel speed and sends the appropriate signals to the ECU. These signals are used for control of the ABS system. The front rotor and rear rotor have 48 serrations. When the rotors rotate, the magnetic field emitted by the permanent magnet in the speed sensor generates an AC voltage. Since the frequency of this AC voltage changes in proportion to the speed of the rotors (wheels), the frequency is used by the ECU to detect the speed of each wheel.

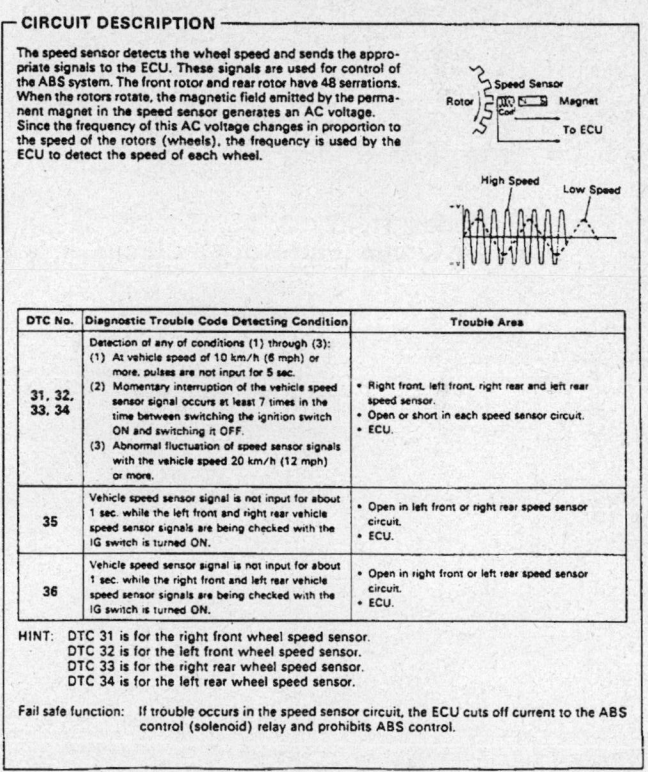

DTC No.	Diagnostic Trouble Code Detecting Condition	Trouble Area
31, 32, 33, 34	Detection of any of conditions (1) through (3): (1) At vehicle speed of 10 km/h (6 mph) or more, pulses are not input for 5 sec. (2) Momentary interruption of the vehicle speed sensor signal occurs at least 7 times in the time between switching the ignition switch ON and switching it OFF. (3) Abnormal fluctuation of speed sensor signals with the vehicle speed 20 km/h (12 mph) or more.	• Right front, left front, right rear and left rear speed sensor. • Open or short in each speed sensor circuit. • ECU.
35	Vehicle speed sensor signal is not input for about 1 sec. while the left front and right rear vehicle speed signals are being checked with the IG switch is turned ON.	• Open in left front or right rear speed sensor circuit. • ECU.
36	Vehicle speed sensor signal is not input for about 1 sec. while the right front and left rear vehicle speed signals are being checked with the IG switch is turned ON.	• Open in right front or left rear speed sensor circuit. • ECU.

HINT: DTC 31 is for the right front wheel speed sensor.
DTC 32 is for the left front wheel speed sensor.
DTC 33 is for the right rear wheel speed sensor.
DTC 34 is for the left rear wheel speed sensor.

Fail safe function: If trouble occurs in the speed sensor circuit, the ECU cuts off current to the ABS control (solenoid) relay and prohibits ABS control.

TY4029300080010X

Fig. 226 Codes 31, 32, 33, 34, 35 & 36: Speed Sensor Circuit (Part 1 of 4). Corolla

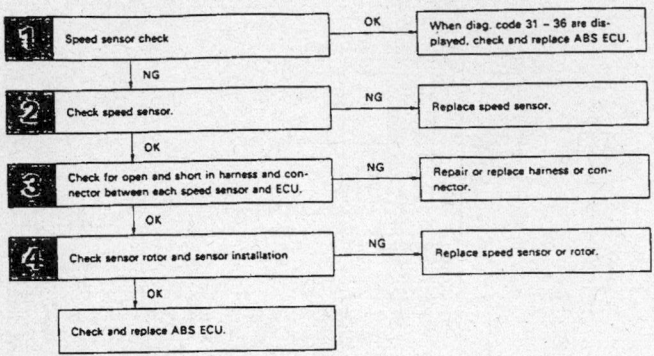

WIRING DIAGRAM

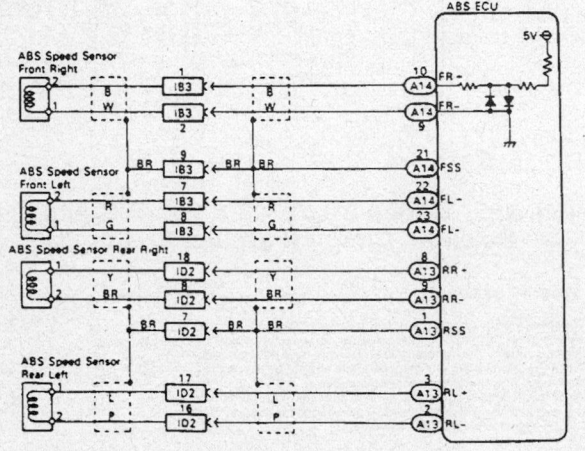

TY4029300080020X

Fig. 226   Codes 31, 32, 33, 34, 35 & 36: Speed Sensor Circuit (Part 2 of 4). Corolla

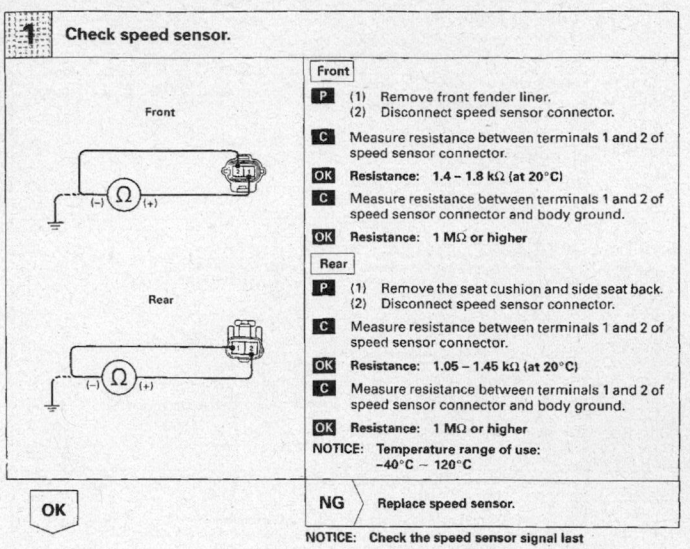

TY4029700325010X

Fig. 226   Codes 31, 32, 33, 34, 35 & 36: Speed Sensor Circuit (Part 3 of 4). Corolla

2	Check for open and short in harness and connector between each speed sensor and ECU
OK	NG > Repair or replace harness or connector.

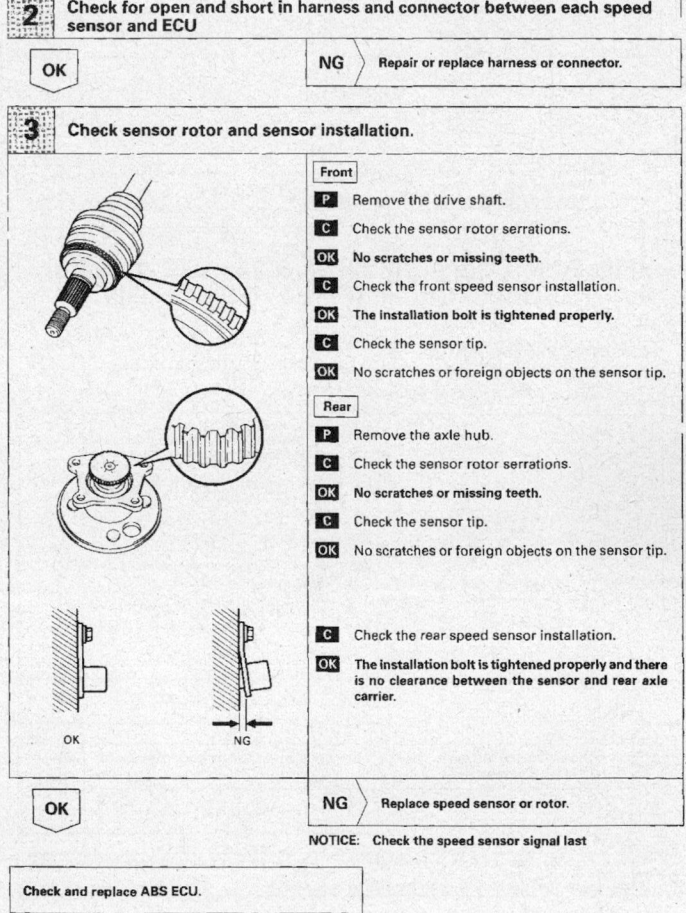

TY4029700325020X

Fig. 226   Codes 31, 32, 33, 34, 35 & 36: Speed Sensor Circuit (Part 4 of 4). Corolla

DTC No.	DTC Detecting Condition	Trouble Area
37	With the rear wheels stationary and front wheels rotating at 20+ km/h (12 mph) for 10 + secs, turn ignition switch ON then OFF 8 times in succession.	• Rear axle hub • Right rear, left rear speed sensor • Wire harness for rear sensor system • ECU

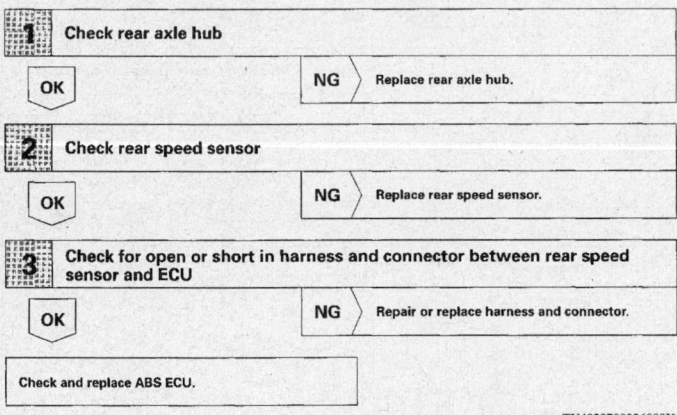

1	Check rear axle hub

OK		NG	Replace rear axle hub.

2	Check rear speed sensor

OK		NG	Replace rear speed sensor.

3	Check for open or short in harness and connector between rear speed sensor and ECU

OK		NG	Repair or replace harness and connector.

Check and replace ABS ECU.

TY4029700326000X

Fig. 227   Code 37: Rear Speed Sensor Rotor. Corolla

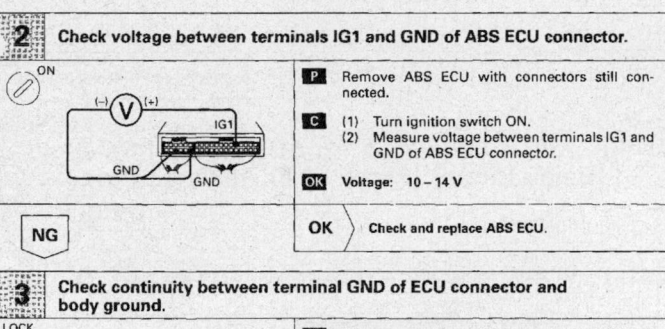

2	Check voltage between terminals IG1 and GND of ABS ECU connector.

P	Remove ABS ECU with connectors still connected.
C	(1) Turn ignition switch ON. (2) Measure voltage between terminals IG1 and GND of ABS ECU connector.
OK	Voltage: 10 – 14 V

NG		OK	Check and replace ABS ECU.

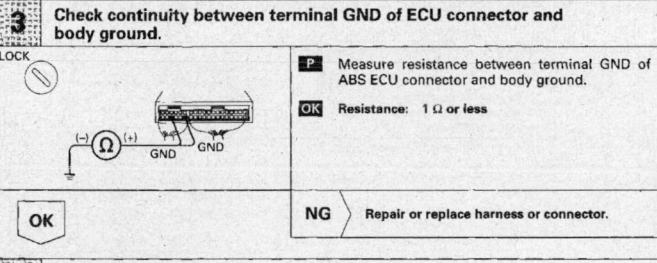

3	Check continuity between terminal GND of ECU connector and body ground.

P	Measure resistance between terminal GND of ABS ECU connector and body ground.
OK	Resistance: 1 Ω or less

OK		NG	Repair or replace harness or connector.

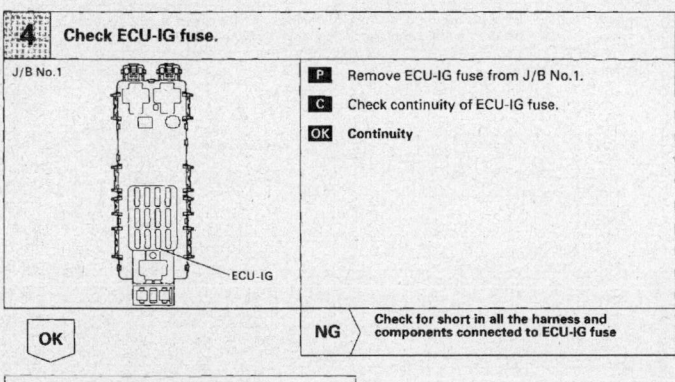

4	Check ECU-IG fuse.

P	Remove ECU-IG fuse from J/B No.1.
C	Check continuity of ECU-IG fuse.
OK	Continuity

OK		NG	Check for short in all the harness and components connected to ECU-IG fuse

Check for open in harness and connector between ABS ECU and battery

TY4029700327020X

Fig. 228   Code 41: IG Power Source (Part 2 of 2). Corolla

This is the power source for the ECU, hence the CPU and the actuators.

DTC No.	DTC Detecting Condition	Trouble Area
41	Vehicle speed is 3 km/h (1.9 mph) or more and voltage of ECU terminal IG1 remains at more than 17 V or below 9.5 V for more than 10 sec.	• Battery • IC regulator • Open or short in power source circuit • ECU

Fail safe function: If trouble occurs in the power source circuit, the ECU cuts off current to the ABS control (solenoid) relay and prohibits ABS control.

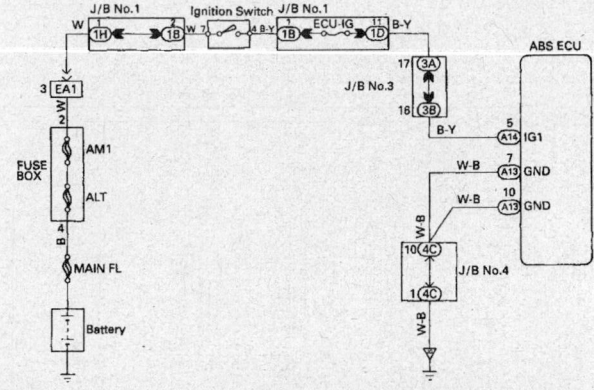

1	Check battery positive voltage

OK	Voltage: 10 – 14 V

OK		NG	Check and repair the charging system.

TY4029700327010X

Fig. 228   Code 41: IG Power Source (Part 1 of 2). Corolla

DTC No.	DTC Detecting Condition	Trouble Area
51	Pump motor is not operating normally during initial check	• ABS pump motor

Fail safe function: If trouble occurs in the ABS pump motor, the ECU cuts off the current to the ABS control (solenoid) relay and prohibits ABS control.

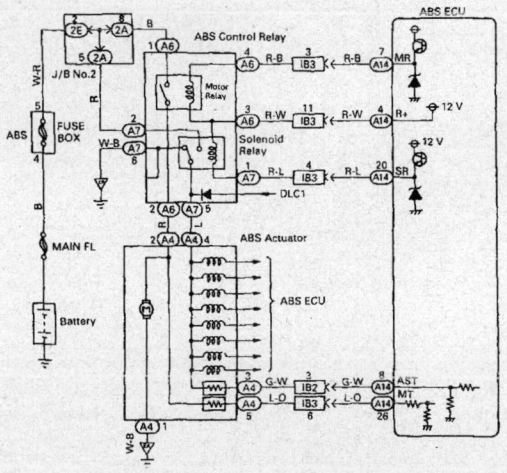

TY4029700329000X

Fig. 229   Code 51: ABS Pump Motor Lock. Corolla

CIRCUIT DESCRIPTION

This relay supplies power to each ABS solenoid. After the ignition switch is turned ON, if the initial check is OK, the relay goes on.

DTC No.	DTC Detecting Condition	Trouble Area
11	Conditions (1) and (2) continue for 0.2 sec. or more: (1) ABS control (solenoid) relay terminal (SR) voltage: Battery positive voltage (2) ABS control (solenoid) relay monitor terminal (AST) voltage: 0 V	• ABS control (solenoid) relay • Open or short in ABS control (solenoid) relay circuit • ECU
12	Conditions (1) and (2) continue for 0.2 sec. or more: (1) ABS control (solenoid) relay terminal (SR) voltage: 0 V (2) ABS control (solenoid) relay monitor terminal (AST) voltage: Battery positive voltage	• ABS control (solenoid) relay • B+ short in ABS control (solenoid) relay circuit • ECU

Fail safe function: If trouble occurs in the ABS control (solenoid) relay circuit, the ECU cuts off current to the ABS control (solenoid) relay and prohibits ABS control.

WIRING DIAGRAM

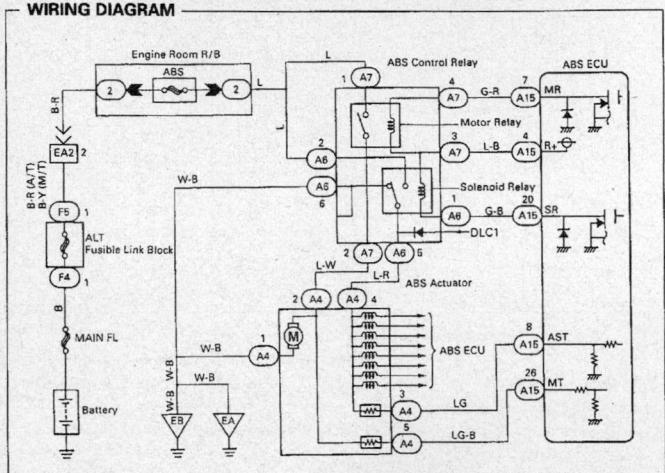

Fig. 230 Codes 11 & 12: ABS Control Solenoid Relay Circuit (Part 1 of 3). 1996–97 Paseo

TY4029600266010X

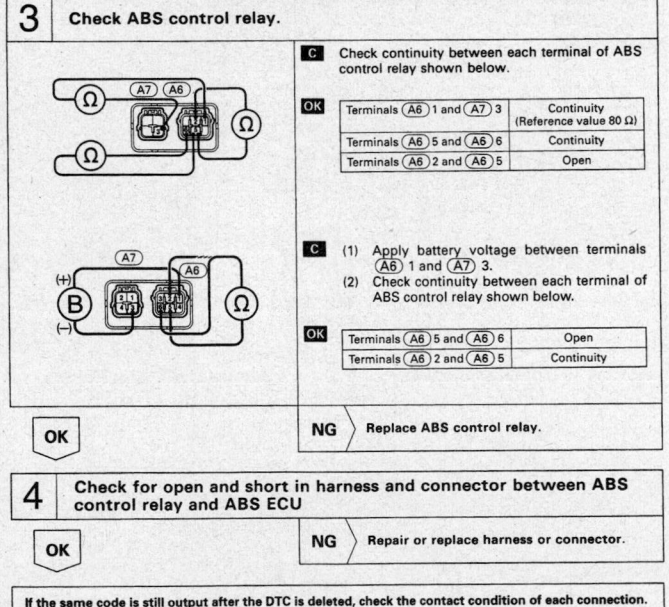

3 Check ABS control relay.

C Check continuity between each terminal of ABS control relay shown below.

OK

Terminals (A6) 1 and (A7) 3	Continuity (Reference value 80 Ω)
Terminals (A6) 5 and (A6) 6	Continuity
Terminals (A6) 2 and (A6) 5	Open

C (1) Apply battery voltage between terminals (A6) 1 and (A7) 3.
(2) Check continuity between each terminal of ABS control relay shown below.

OK

Terminals (A6) 5 and (A6) 6	Open
Terminals (A6) 2 and (A6) 5	Continuity

OK   **NG ▷ Replace ABS control relay.**

4 Check for open and short in harness and connector between ABS control relay and ABS ECU

OK   **NG ▷ Repair or replace harness or connector.**

If the same code is still output after the DTC is deleted, check the contact condition of each connection. If the connections are normal, the ECU may be defective.

TY4029600266030X

Fig. 230 Codes 11 & 12: ABS Control Solenoid Relay Circuit (Part 3 of 3). 1996–97 Paseo

1 Check voltage between terminals (A6) 2 and (A6) 6 of ABS control relay connector.

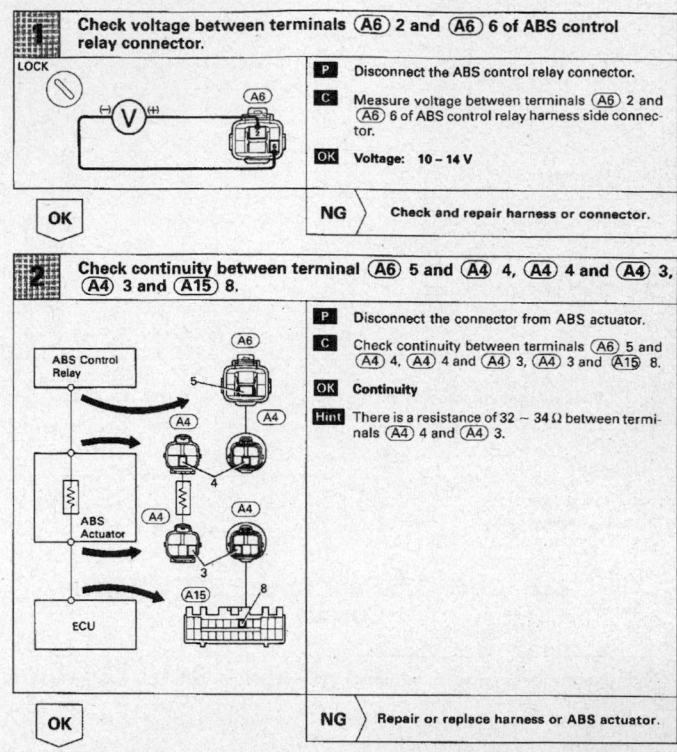

P Disconnect the ABS control relay connector.

C Measure voltage between terminals (A6) 2 and (A6) 6 of ABS control relay harness side connector.

OK Voltage: 10 – 14 V

OK   **NG ▷ Check and repair harness or connector.**

2 Check continuity between terminal (A6) 5 and (A4) 4, (A4) 4 and (A4) 3, (A4) 3 and (A15) 8.

P Disconnect the connector from ABS actuator.

C Check continuity between terminals (A6) 5 and (A4) 4, (A4) 4 and (A4) 3, (A4) 3 and (A15) 8.

OK Continuity

Hint There is a resistance of 32 – 34 Ω between terminals (A4) 4 and (A4) 3.

OK   **NG ▷ Repair or replace harness or ABS actuator.**

TY4029600266020X

Fig. 230 Codes 11 & 12: ABS Control Solenoid Relay Circuit (Part 2 of 3). 1996–97 Paseo

CIRCUIT DESCRIPTION

The ABS control (motor) relay supplies power to the ABS pump motor. While the ABS is activated, the ECU switches the ABS control (motor) relay on and operates the ABS pump motor.

DTC No.	DTC Detecting Condition	Trouble Area
13	Conditions (1) and (2) continue for 0.2 sec. or more: (1) ABS control (motor) relay terminal (MR) voltage: Battery positive voltage (2) ABS control (motor) relay monitor terminal (MT) voltage: 0 V	• ABS control (motor) relay • Open or short in ABS control (motor) relay circuit • ECU
14	Conditions (1) and (2) continued for 4 sec. or more: (1) ABS control (motor) relay terminal (MR) voltage: 0 V (2) ABS control (motor) relay monitor terminal (MT) voltage: Battery positive voltage	• ABS control (motor) relay • B+ short in ABS control (motor) relay circuit • ECU

Fail safe function: If trouble occurs in the ABS control (motor) relay circuit, the ECU cuts off the current to the ABS control (solenoid) relay and prohibits ABS control.

WIRING DIAGRAM

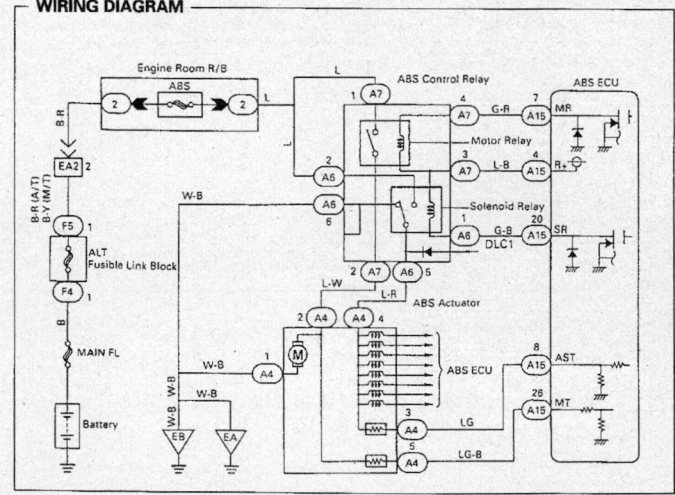

TY4029600267010X

Fig. 231 Codes 13 & 14: ABS Control Motor Relay Circuit (Part 1 of 3). 1996–97 Paseo

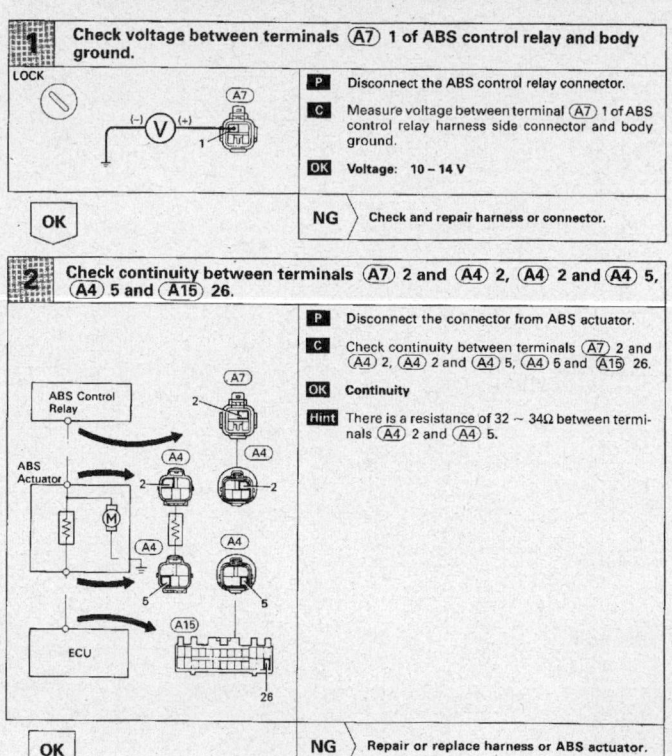

1 Check voltage between terminals (A7) 1 of ABS control relay and body ground.

P	Disconnect the ABS control relay connector.
C	Measure voltage between terminal (A7) 1 of ABS control relay harness side connector and body ground.
OK	Voltage: 10 – 14 V

OK →

NG > Check and repair harness or connector.

2 Check continuity between terminals (A7) 2 and (A4) 2, (A4) 2 and (A4) 5, (A4) 5 and (A15) 26.

P	Disconnect the connector from ABS actuator.
C	Check continuity between terminals (A7) 2 and (A4) 2, (A4) 2 and (A4) 5, (A4) 5 and (A15) 26.
OK	Continuity
Hint	There is a resistance of 32 ~ 34Ω between terminals (A4) 2 and (A4) 5.

OK →

NG > Repair or replace harness or ABS actuator.

TY4029600267020X

Fig. 231 Codes 13 & 14: ABS Control Motor Relay Circuit (Part 2 of 3). 1996–97 Paseo

CIRCUIT DESCRIPTION

This solenoid goes on when signals are received from the ECU and controls the pressure acting on the brake cylinders, thus controlling the braking force.

DTC No.	DTC Detecting Condition	Trouble Area
21	Conditions (1) through (3) continue for 0.05 sec. or more: (1) ABS control (solenoid) relay terminal (SR) voltage: Battery positive voltage (2) Voltage or ABS ECU terminal AST: Battery positive voltage (3) When power transistor of ECU is ON, voltage of terminal SFR is 0 V or battery positive voltage.	• ABS actuator • Open or short in SFR circuit • ECU
22	Conditions (1) through (3) continue for 0.05 sec. or more: (1) ABS control (solenoid) relay terminal (SR) voltage: Battery positive voltage (2) Voltage of ABS ECU terminal AST: Battery positive voltage (3) When power transistor of ECU is ON, voltage of terminal SFL is 0 V or battery positive voltage.	• ABS actuator • Open or short in SFL circuit • ECU
23	Conditions (1) through (3) continue for 0.05 sec. or more: (1) ABS control (solenoid) relay terminal (SR) voltage: Battery positive voltage (2) Voltage of ABS ECU terminal AST: Battery positive voltage (3) When power transistor of ECU is ON, voltage of terminal SRR is 0 V or battery positive voltage.	• ABS actuator • Open or short in SRR circuit • ECU
24	Conditions (1) through (3) continue for 0.05 sec. or more: (1) ABS control (solenoid) relay terminal (SR) voltage: Battery positive voltage (2) Voltage of ABS ECU terminal AST: Battery positive voltage (3) When power transistor of ECU is ON, voltage of terminal SRL is 0 V or battery positive voltage.	• ABS actuator • Open or short in SRL circuit • ECU

Fail safe function: If trouble occurs in the actuator solenoid circuit, the ECU cuts off current to the ABS control (solenoid) relay and prohibits ABS control.

TY4029600268010X

Fig. 232 Codes 21, 22, 23, & 24: ABS Actuator Solenoid Circuit (Part 1 of 2). 1996–97 Paseo

---

3 Check ABS control relay.

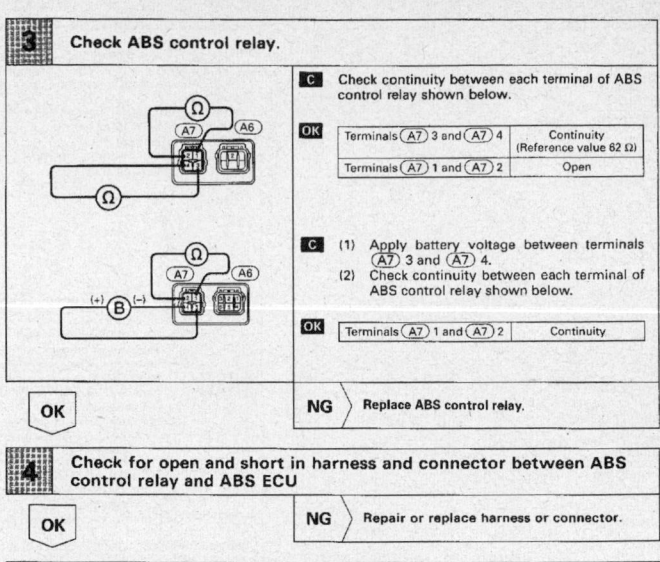

C	Check continuity between each terminal of ABS control relay shown below.

OK	Terminals (A7) 3 and (A7) 4	Continuity (Reference value 62 Ω)
	Terminals (A7) 1 and (A7) 2	Open

C	(1) Apply battery voltage between terminals (A7) 3 and (A7) 4. (2) Check continuity between each terminal of ABS control relay shown below.

OK	Terminals (A7) 1 and (A7) 2	Continuity

OK →

NG > Replace ABS control relay.

4 Check for open and short in harness and connector between ABS control relay and ABS ECU

OK →

NG > Repair or replace harness or connector.

If the same code is still output after the DTC is deleted, check the contact condition of each connection. If the connections are normal, the ECU may be defective.

TY4029600267030X

Fig. 231 Codes 13 & 14: ABS Control Motor Relay Circuit (Part 3 of 3). 1996–97 Paseo

WIRING DIAGRAM

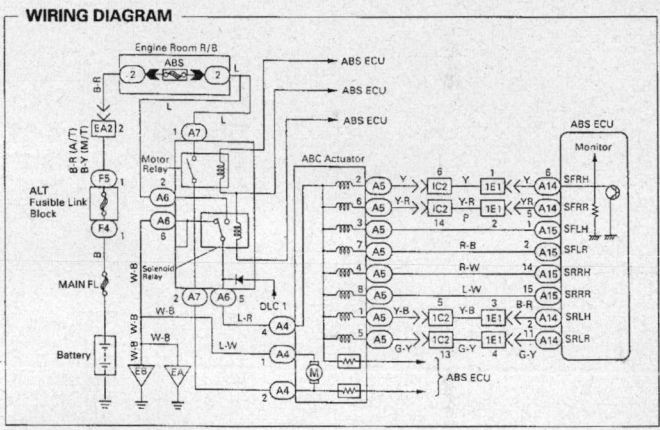

INSPECTION PROCEDURE

1 Check ABS actuator solenoid.

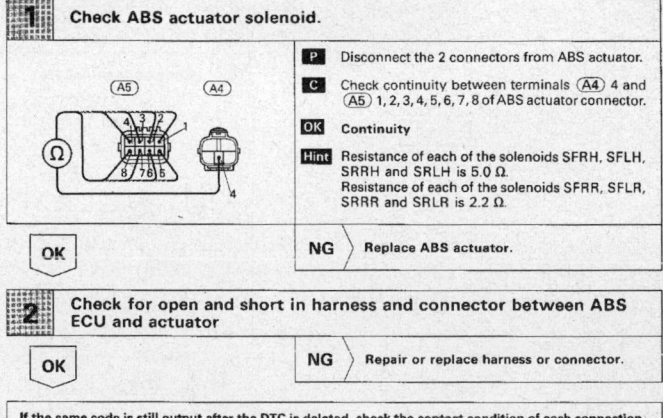

P	Disconnect the 2 connectors from ABS actuator.
C	Check continuity between terminals (A4) 4 and (A5) 1, 2, 3, 4, 5, 6, 7, 8 of ABS actuator connector.
OK	Continuity
Hint	Resistance of each of the solenoids SFRH, SFLH, SRRH and SRLH is 5.0 Ω. Resistance of each of the solenoids SFRR, SFLR, SRRR and SRLR is 2.2 Ω.

OK →

NG > Replace ABS actuator.

2 Check for open and short in harness and connector between ABS ECU and actuator

OK →

NG > Repair or replace harness or connector.

If the same code is still output after the DTC is deleted, check the contact condition of each connection. If the connections are normal, the ECU may be defective.

TY4029600268020X

Fig. 232 Codes 21, 22, 23, & 24: ABS Actuator Solenoid Circuit (Part 2 of 2). 1996–97 Paseo

CIRCUIT DESCRIPTION

The speed sensor detects the wheel speed and sends the appropriate signals to the ECU. These signals are used to control the ABS system. The front and rear rotors each have 48 serrations.

When the rotors rotate, the magnetic field emitted by the permanent magnet in the speed sensor generates an AC voltage.

Since the frequency of this AC voltage changes in direct proportion to the speed of the rotors, the frequency is used by the ECU to detect the speed of each wheel.

DTC No.	DTC Detecting Condition	Trouble Area
31, 32, 33, 34	Detection of any of conditions (1) through (3): (1) At vehicle speed of 10 km/h (6 mph) or more, pulses are not input for 5 sec. (2) Momentary interruption of the speed sensor signal occurs at least 7 times in the time between switching the ignition switch ON and switching it OFF. (3) Abnormal fluctuation of speed sensor signals with the vehicle speed 20 km/h (12 mph) or more.	• Right front, left front, right rear and left rear speed sensor • Open or short in each speed sensor circuit • ECU

HINT: DTC 31 is for the right front speed sensor.
DTC 32 is for the left front speed sensor.
DTC 33 is for the right rear speed sensor.
DTC 34 is for the left rear speed sensor.

Fail safe function: If trouble occurs in the speed sensor circuit, the ECU cuts off current to the ABS control (solenoid) relay and prohibits ABS control.

TY4029600269010X

Fig. 233   Codes 31, 32, 33, & 34: Speed Sensor Circuit (Part 1 of 3). 1996–97 Paseo

WIRING DIAGRAM

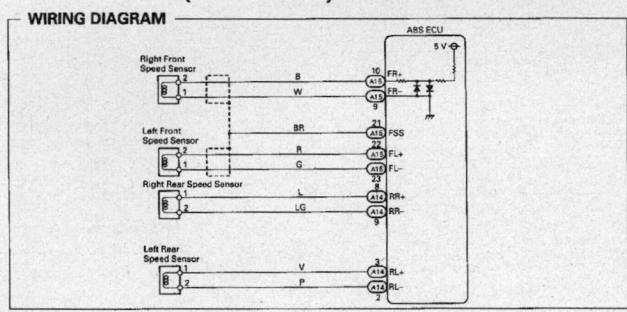

INSPECTION PROCEDURE

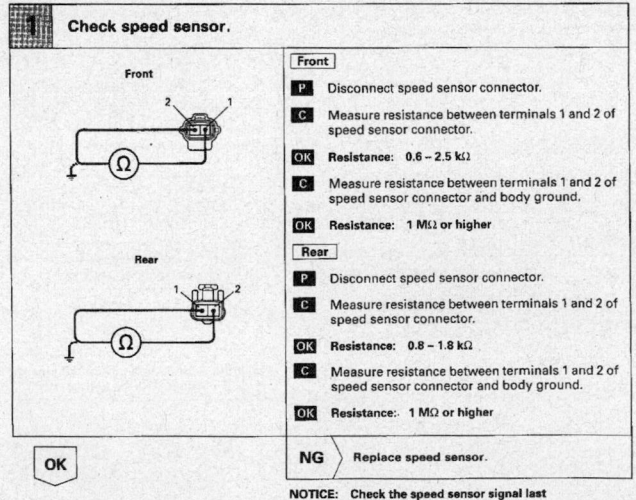

1 **Check speed sensor.**

Front

Front
- **P** Disconnect speed sensor connector.
- **C** Measure resistance between terminals 1 and 2 of speed sensor connector.
- **OK** Resistance: 0.6 – 2.5 kΩ
- **C** Measure resistance between terminals 1 and 2 of speed sensor connector and body ground.
- **OK** Resistance: 1 MΩ or higher

Rear

Rear
- **P** Disconnect speed sensor connector.
- **C** Measure resistance between terminals 1 and 2 of speed sensor connector.
- **OK** Resistance: 0.8 – 1.8 kΩ
- **C** Measure resistance between terminals 1 and 2 of speed sensor connector and body ground.
- **OK** Resistance: 1 MΩ or higher

OK

NG ▶ Replace speed sensor.

NOTICE: Check the speed sensor signal last.

TY4029600269020X

Fig. 233   Codes 31, 32, 33, & 34: Speed Sensor Circuit (Part 2 of 3). 1996–97 Paseo

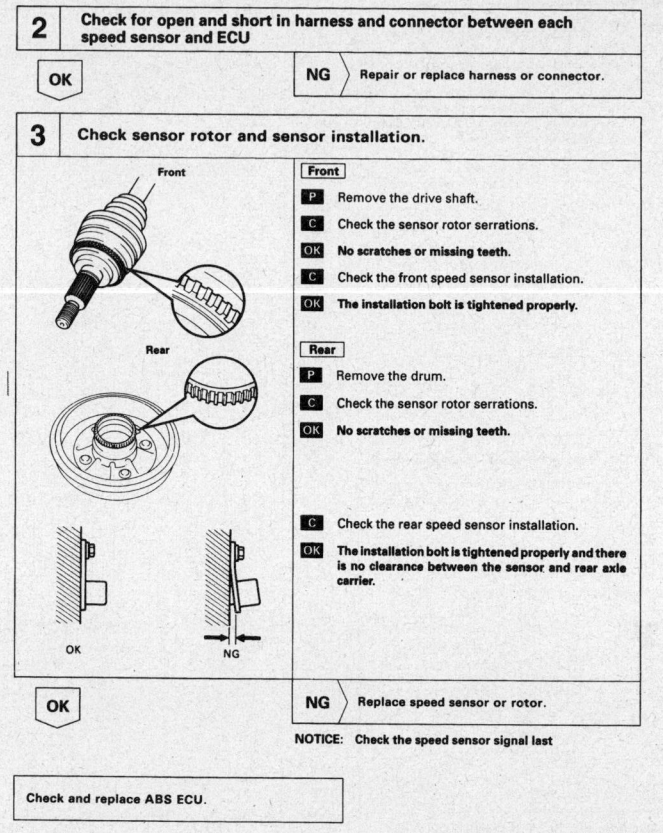

2	Check for open and short in harness and connector between each speed sensor and ECU		
	OK	NG	Repair or replace harness or connector.

3 Check sensor rotor and sensor installation.

Front
- **P** Remove the drive shaft.
- **C** Check the sensor rotor serrations.
- **OK** No scratches or missing teeth.
- **C** Check the front speed sensor installation.
- **OK** The installation bolt is tightened properly.

Rear
- **P** Remove the drum.
- **C** Check the sensor rotor serrations.
- **OK** No scratches or missing teeth.

- **C** Check the rear speed sensor installation.
- **OK** The installation bolt is tightened properly and there is no clearance between the sensor and rear axle carrier.

OK	NG	Replace speed sensor or rotor.

NOTICE: Check the speed sensor signal last

Check and replace ABS ECU.

TY4029600269030X

Fig. 233   Codes 31, 32, 33, & 34: Speed Sensor Circuit (Part 3 of 3). 1996–97 Paseo

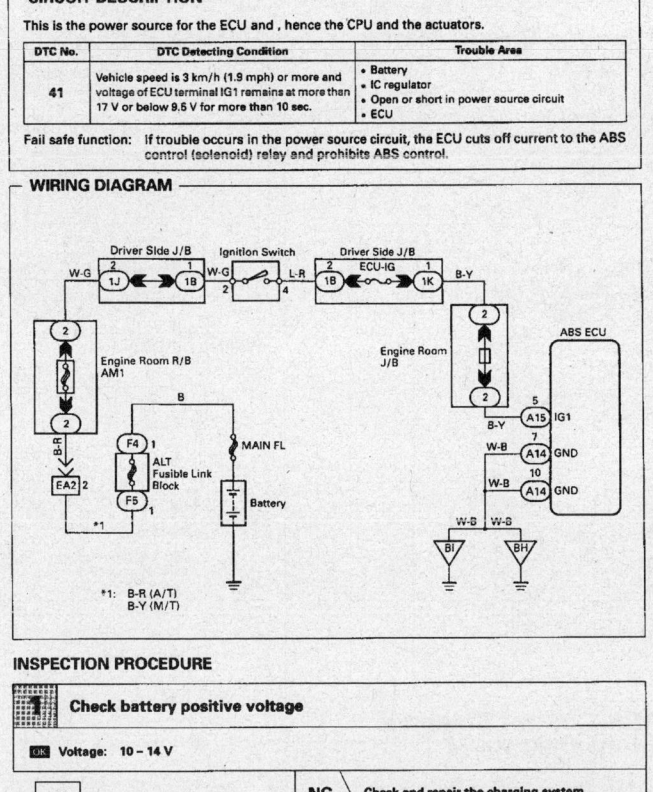

CIRCUIT DESCRIPTION

This is the power source for the ECU and , hence the CPU and the actuators.

DTC No.	DTC Detecting Condition	Trouble Area
41	Vehicle speed is 3 km/h (1.9 mph) or more and voltage of ECU terminal IG1 remains at more than 17 V or below 9.5 V for more than 10 sec.	• Battery • IC regulator • Open or short in power source circuit • ECU

Fail safe function: If trouble occurs in the power source circuit, the ECU cuts off current to the ABS control (solenoid) relay and prohibits ABS control.

WIRING DIAGRAM

INSPECTION PROCEDURE

1	Check battery positive voltage		
	OK Voltage: 10 – 14 V		
	OK	NG	Check and repair the charging system.

TY4029600270010X

Fig. 234   Code 41: IG Power Source Circuit (Part 1 of 2). 1996–97 Paseo

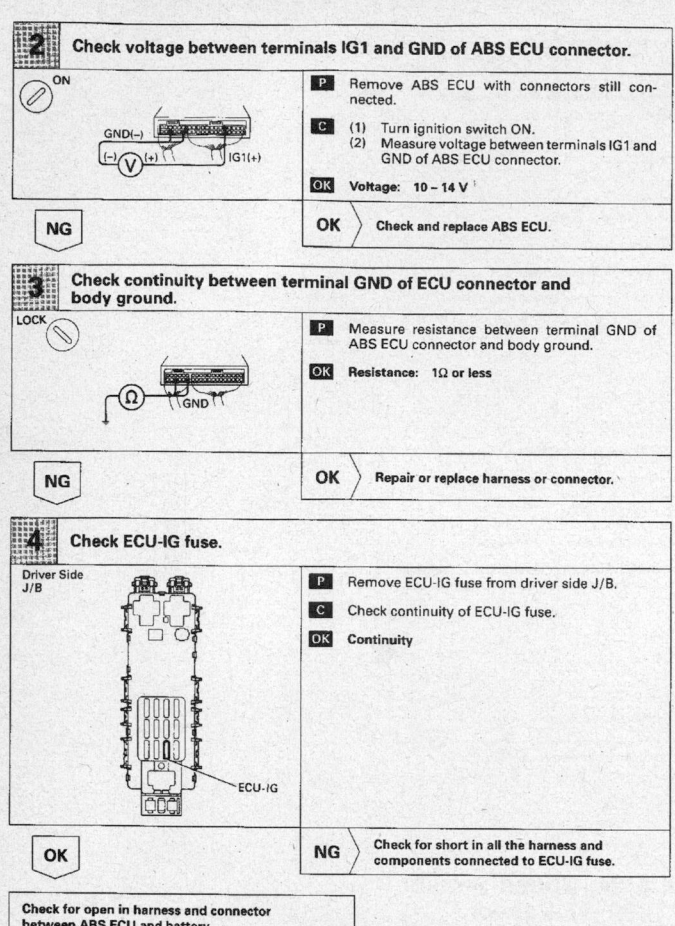

2 Check voltage between terminals IG1 and GND of ABS ECU connector.

P	Remove ABS ECU with connectors still connected.
C	(1) Turn ignition switch ON. (2) Measure voltage between terminals IG1 and GND of ABS ECU connector.
OK	**Voltage: 10 – 14 V**

NG → OK > Check and replace ABS ECU.

3 Check continuity between terminal GND of ECU connector and body ground.

P	Measure resistance between terminal GND of ABS ECU connector and body ground.
OK	**Resistance: 1Ω or less**

NG → OK > Repair or replace harness or connector.

4 Check ECU-IG fuse.

Driver Side J/B

P	Remove ECU-IG fuse from driver side J/B.
C	Check continuity of ECU-IG fuse.
OK	**Continuity**

OK → NG > Check for short in all the harness and components connected to ECU-IG fuse.

Check for open in harness and connector between ABS ECU and battery

TY4029600270020X

Fig. 234 Code 41: IG Power Source Circuit (Part 2 of 2). 1996–97 Paseo

WIRING DIAGRAM

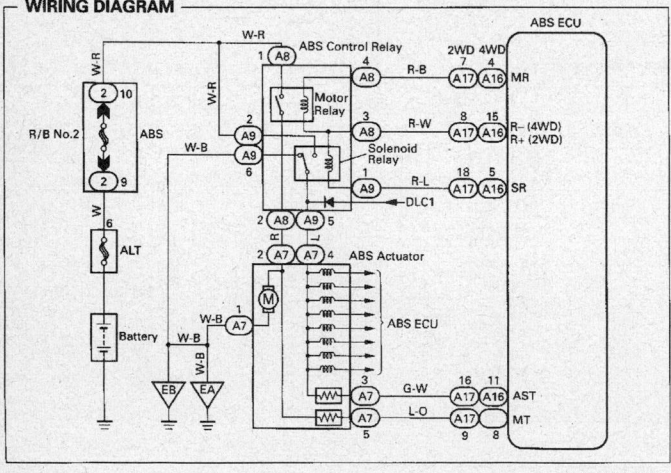

TY4029600205010X

Fig. 236 Codes 11 & 12: ABS Control Solenoid Relay Circuit (Part 1 of 3). 1996 RAV4

CIRCUIT DESCRIPTION

DTC No.	DTC Detecting Condition	Trouble Area
51	Pump motor is not operating normally during initial check.	• ABS pump motor

Fail safe function: If trouble occurs in the ABS pump motor, the ECU cuts off the current to the ABS control (solenoid) relay and prohibits ABS control.

WIRING DIAGRAM

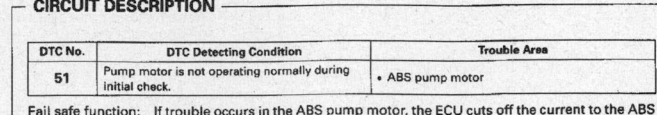
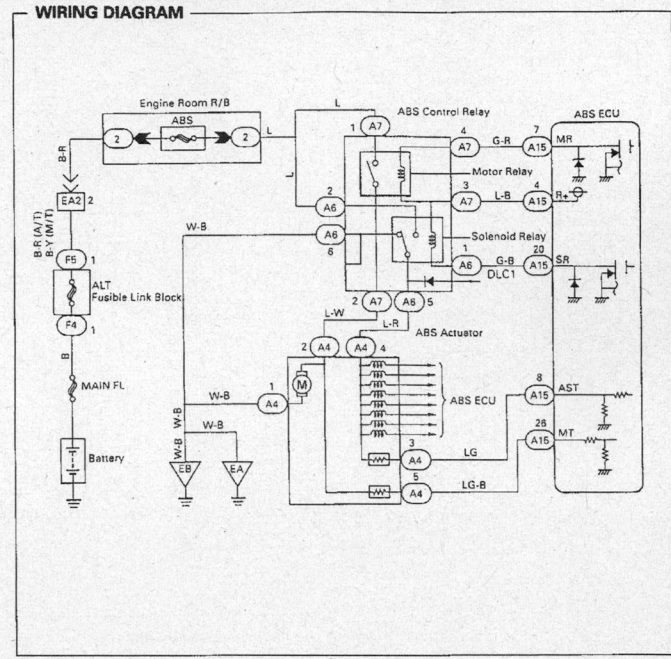

TY4029600271010X

Fig. 235 Code 51: ABS Pump Motor Lock. 1996–97 Paseo

CIRCUIT DESCRIPTION

This relay supplies power to each ABS solenoid. After the ignition switch is turned ON, if the initial check is OK, the relay goes on.

DTC No.	DTC Detecting Condition	Trouble Area
11	Conditions (1) and (2) continue for 0.2 sec. or more: (1) ABS control (solenoid) relay terminal (SR) voltage: Below 1.5 V (2) ABS control (solenoid) relay monitor terminal (AST) voltage: 0 V	• ABS control (solenoid) relay • Open or short in ABS control (solenoid) relay circuit • ECU
12	Conditions (1) and (2) continue for 0.2 sec. or more: (1) ABS control (solenoid) relay terminal (SR) voltage: 10 – 14 V (2) ABS control (solenoid) relay monitor terminal (AST) voltage: 10 – 14 V	• ABS control (solenoid) relay • B+ short in ABS control (solenoid) relay circuit • ECU

Fail safe function: If trouble occurs in the ABS control (solenoid) relay circuit, the ECU cuts off current to the ABS control (solenoid) relay and prohibits ABS control.

WIRING DIAGRAM

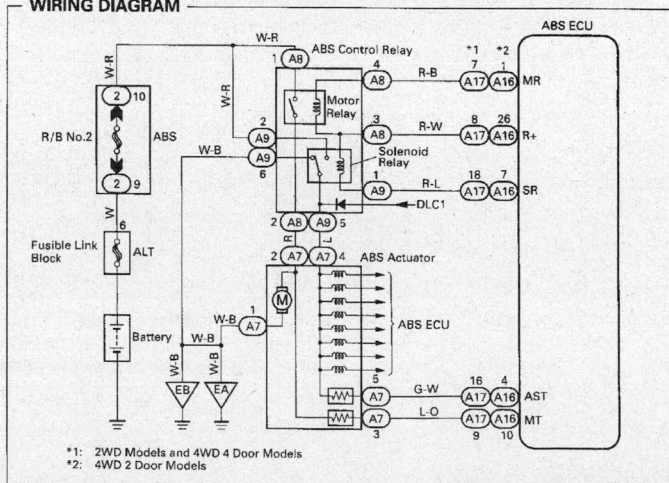

*1: 2WD Models and 4WD 4 Door Models
*2: 4WD 2 Door Models

TY4029700286010X

Fig. 236 Codes 11 & 12: ABS Control Solenoid Relay Circuit (Part 1 of 3). 1997–99 RAV4

INSPECTION PROCEDURE

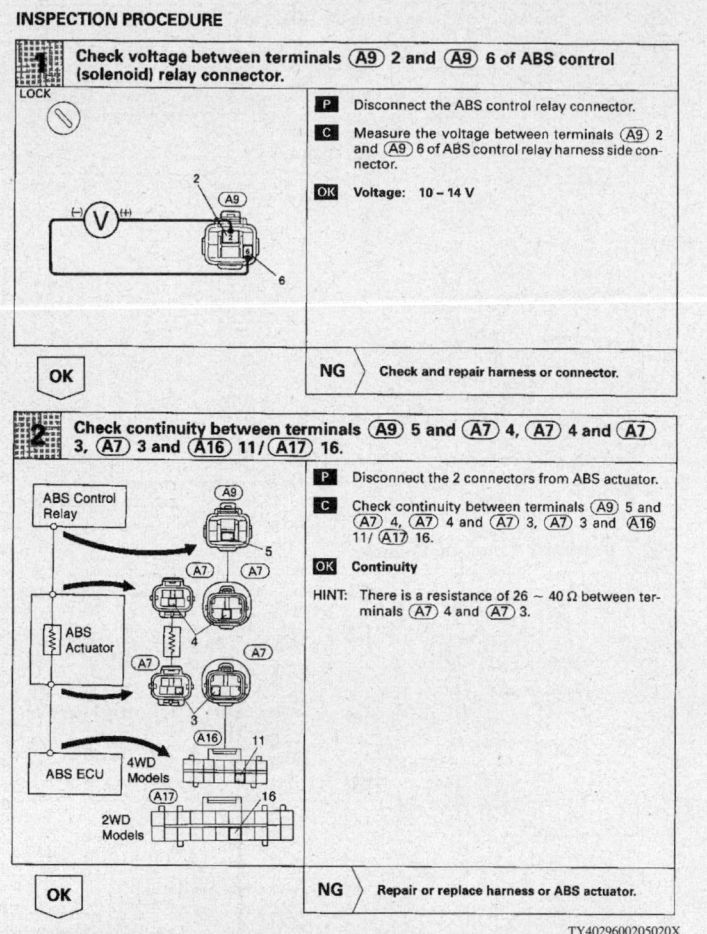

1 | Check voltage between terminals (A9) 2 and (A9) 6 of ABS control (solenoid) relay connector.

LOCK

P Disconnect the ABS control relay connector.

C Measure the voltage between terminals (A9) 2 and (A9) 6 of ABS control relay harness side connector.

OK Voltage: 10 – 14 V

OK | **NG** Check and repair harness or connector.

2 | Check continuity between terminals (A9) 5 and (A7) 4, (A7) 4 and (A7) 3, (A7) 3 and (A16) 11/ (A17) 16.

ABS Control Relay
ABS Actuator
ABS ECU
4WD Models
2WD Models

P Disconnect the 2 connectors from ABS actuator.

C Check continuity between terminals (A9) 5 and (A7) 4, (A7) 4 and (A7) 3, (A7) 3 and (A16) 11/ (A17) 16.

OK Continuity

HINT: There is a resistance of 26 ~ 40 Ω between terminals (A7) 4 and (A7) 3.

OK | **NG** Repair or replace harness or ABS actuator.

TY4029600205020X

Fig. 236 Codes 11 & 12: ABS Control Solenoid Relay Circuit (Part 2 of 3). 1996 RAV4

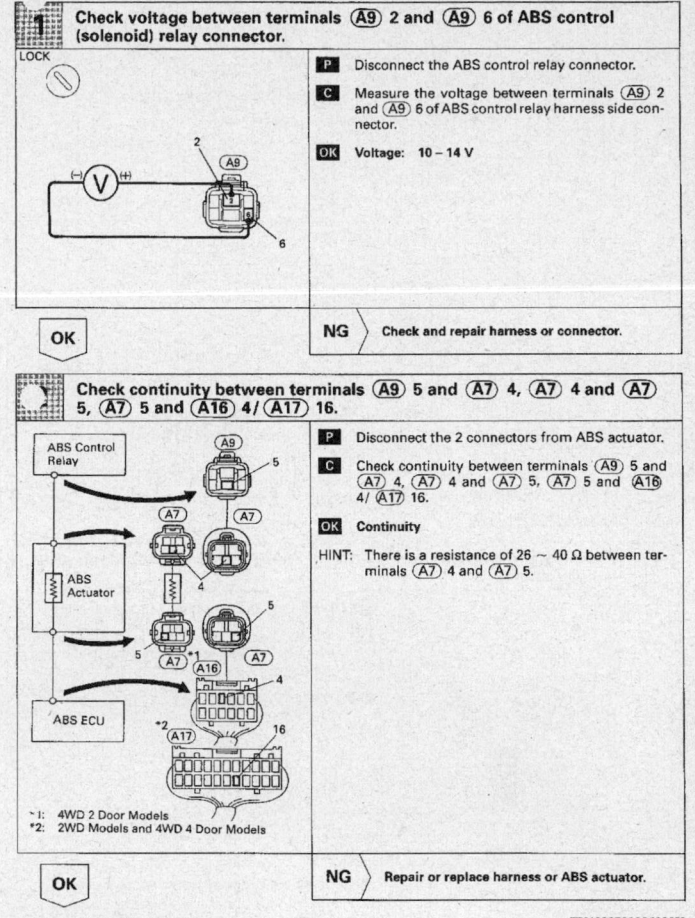

1 | Check voltage between terminals (A9) 2 and (A9) 6 of ABS control (solenoid) relay connector.

LOCK

P Disconnect the ABS control relay connector.

C Measure the voltage between terminals (A9) 2 and (A9) 6 of ABS control relay harness side connector.

OK Voltage: 10 – 14 V

OK | **NG** Check and repair harness or connector.

2 | Check continuity between terminals (A9) 5 and (A7) 4, (A7) 4 and (A7) 5, (A7) 5 and (A16) 4/ (A17) 16.

ABS Control Relay
ABS Actuator
ABS ECU

*1: 4WD 2 Door Models
*2: 2WD Models and 4WD 4 Door Models

P Disconnect the 2 connectors from ABS actuator.

C Check continuity between terminals (A9) 5 and (A7) 4, (A7) 4 and (A7) 5, (A7) 5 and (A16) 4/ (A17) 16.

OK Continuity

HINT: There is a resistance of 26 ~ 40 Ω between terminals (A7) 4 and (A7) 5.

OK | **NG** Repair or replace harness or ABS actuator.

TY4029700286020X

Fig. 236 Codes 11 & 12: ABS Control Solenoid Relay Circuit (Part 2 of 3). 1997–99 RAV4

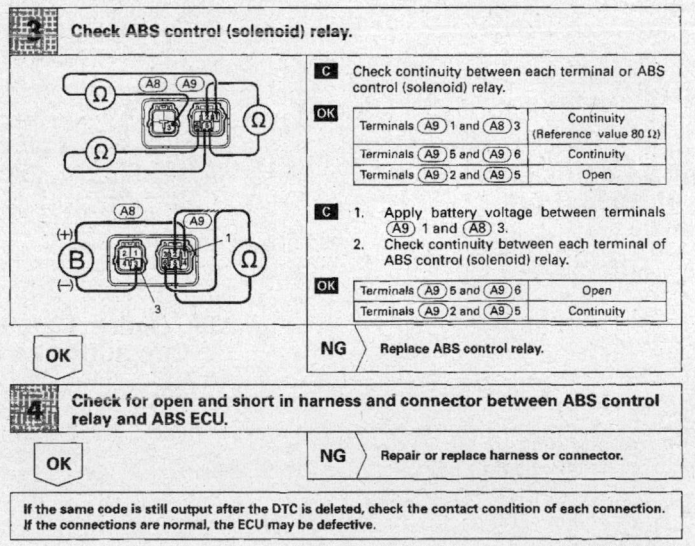

3 | Check ABS control (solenoid) relay.

C Check continuity between each terminal or ABS control (solenoid) relay.

OK

	Continuity
Terminals (A9) 1 and (A8) 3	Continuity (Reference value 80 Ω)
Terminals (A9) 5 and (A9) 6	Continuity
Terminals (A9) 2 and (A9) 5	Open

C 1. Apply battery voltage between terminals (A9) 1 and (A8) 3.
2. Check continuity between each terminal of ABS control (solenoid) relay.

OK

Terminals (A9) 5 and (A9) 6	Open
Terminals (A9) 2 and (A9) 5	Continuity

OK | **NG** Replace ABS control relay.

4 | Check for open and short in harness and connector between ABS control relay and ABS ECU.

OK | **NG** Repair or replace harness or connector.

If the same code is still output after the DTC is deleted, check the contact condition of each connection. If the connections are normal, the ECU may be defective.

TY4029600205030X

Fig. 236 Codes 11 & 12: ABS Control Solenoid Relay Circuit (Part 3 of 3). RAV4

WIRING DIAGRAM

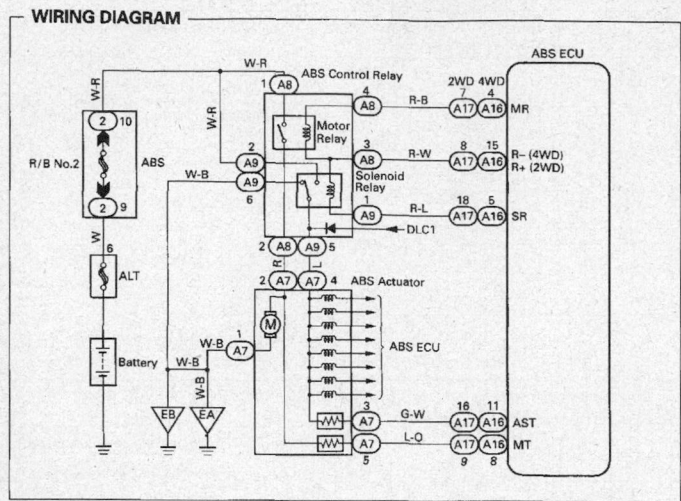

INSPECTION PROCEDURE

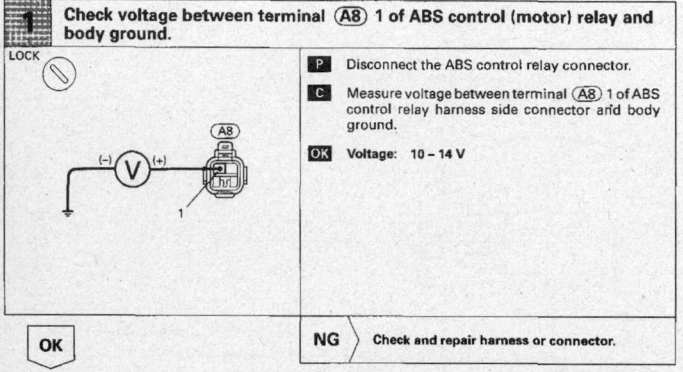

1 Check voltage between terminal (A8) 1 of ABS control (motor) relay and body ground.

- **P** Disconnect the ABS control relay connector.
- **C** Measure voltage between terminal (A8) 1 of ABS control relay harness side connector and body ground.
- **OK** Voltage: 10 – 14 V

OK | **NG** Check and repair harness or connector.

TY4029600206010X

Fig. 237 Codes 13 & 14: ABS Control Motor Relay Circuit (Part 1 of 3). 1996 RAV4

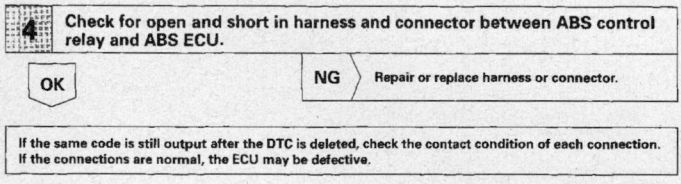

4 Check for open and short in harness and connector between ABS control relay and ABS ECU.

OK | **NG** Repair or replace harness or connector.

If the same code is still output after the DTC is deleted, check the contact condition of each connection. If the connections are normal, the ECU may be defective.

TY4029600206030X

Fig. 237 Codes 13 & 14: ABS Control Motor Relay Circuit (Part 3 of 3). 1996 RAV4

---

2 Check continuity between terminals (A8) 2 and (A7) 2, (A7) 2 and (A7) 5, (A7) 5 and (A16) 8/(A17) 9.

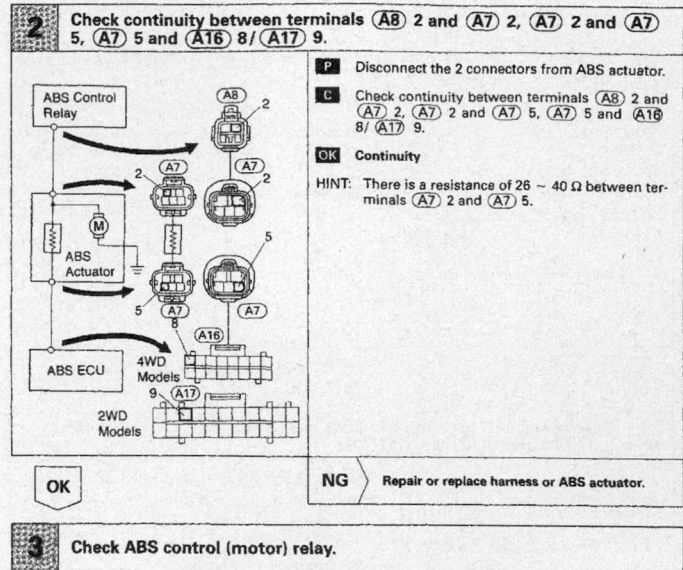

- **P** Disconnect the 2 connectors from ABS actuator.
- **C** Check continuity between terminals (A8) 2 and (A7) 2, (A7) 2 and (A7) 5, (A7) 5 and (A16) 8/ (A17) 9.
- **OK** Continuity

  HINT: There is a resistance of 26 ~ 40 Ω between terminals (A7) 2 and (A7) 5.

OK | **NG** Repair or replace harness or ABS actuator.

3 Check ABS control (motor) relay.

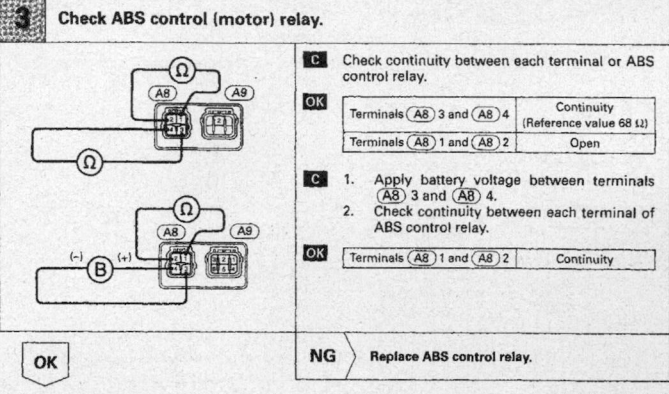

- **C** Check continuity between each terminal or ABS control relay.

OK		
Terminals (A8) 3 and (A8) 4	Continuity (Reference value 68 Ω)
Terminals (A8) 1 and (A8) 2	Open

- **C** 1. Apply battery voltage between terminals (A8) 3 and (A8) 4.
  2. Check continuity between each terminal of ABS control relay.

OK	
Terminals (A8) 1 and (A8) 2	Continuity

OK | **NG** Replace ABS control relay.

TY4029600206020X

Fig. 237 Codes 13 & 14: ABS Control Motor Relay Circuit (Part 2 of 3). 1996 RAV4

CIRCUIT DESCRIPTION

The ABS control (motor) relay supplies power to the ABS pump motor. While the ABS is activated, the ECU switches the control (motor) relay ON and operates the ABS pump motor.

DTC No.	DTC Detecting Condition	Trouble Area
13	Conditions (1) and (2) continued for 0.2 sec. or more: (1) ABS control (motor) relay terminal (MR) voltage: Below 1.5 V (2) ABS control (motor) relay monitor terminal (MT) voltage: 0 V	• ABS control (motor) relay • Open or short in ABS control (motor) relay circuit • ECU
14	Conditions (1) and (2) continued for 4 sec. or more: (1) ABS control (motor) relay terminal (MR) voltage: 10 – 14 V (2) ABS control (motor) relay monitor terminal (MT) voltage: Battery positive voltage	• ABS control (motor) relay • B+ short in ABS control (motor) relay circuit • ECU

Fail safe function: If trouble occurs in the ABS control (motor) relay circuit, the ECU cuts off current to the ABS control (solenoid) relay and prohibits ABS control.

TY4029700287010X

Fig. 238 Codes 13 & 14: ABS Control Motor Relay Circuit (Part 1 of 4). 1997–99 RAV4

WIRING DIAGRAM

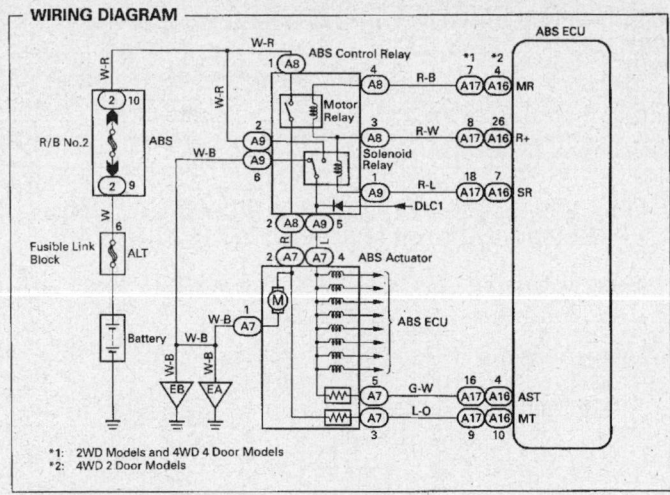

*1: 2WD Models and 4WD 4 Door Models
*2: 4WD 2 Door Models

INSPECTION PROCEDURE

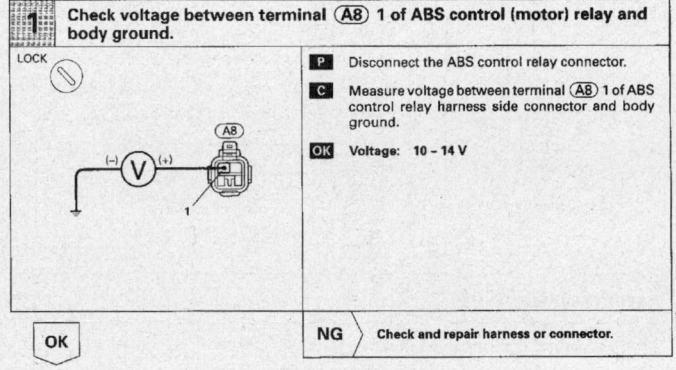

1 Check voltage between terminal (A8) 1 of ABS control (motor) relay and body ground.

P Disconnect the ABS control relay connector.

C Measure voltage between terminal (A8) 1 of ABS control relay harness side connector and body ground.

OK Voltage: 10 – 14 V

OK ⬇

NG ⟩ Check and repair harness or connector.

TY4029700287020X

Fig. 238   Codes 13 & 14: ABS Control Motor Relay Circuit (Part 2 of 4). 1997–99 RAV4

---

2 Check continuity between terminals (A8) 2 and (A7) 2, (A7) 2 and (A7) 5, (A7) 5 and (A16) 10/ (A17) 9.

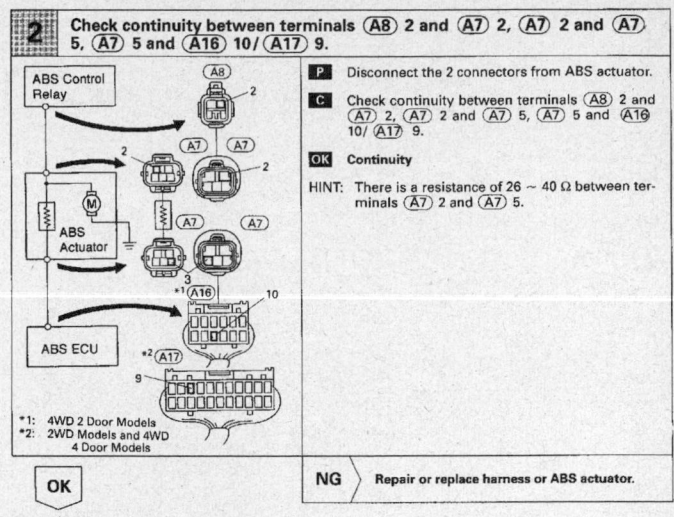

P Disconnect the 2 connectors from ABS actuator.

C Check continuity between terminals (A8) 2 and (A7) 2, (A7) 2 and (A7) 5, (A7) 5 and (A16) 10/ (A17) 9.

OK Continuity

HINT: There is a resistance of 26 ~ 40 Ω between terminals (A7) 2 and (A7) 5.

*1: 4WD 2 Door Models
*2: 2WD Models and 4WD 4 Door Models

OK ⬇

NG ⟩ Repair or replace harness or ABS actuator.

---

3 Check ABS control (motor) relay.

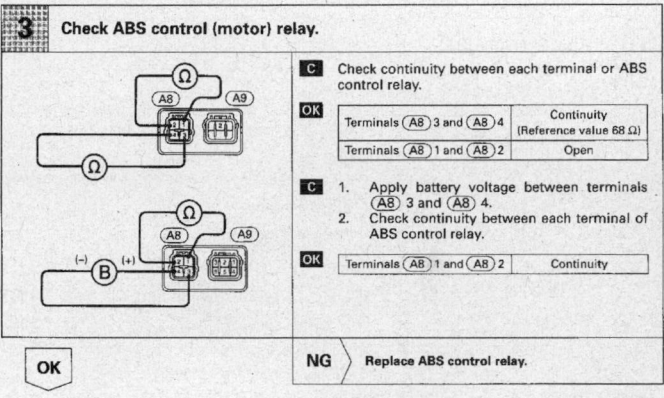

C Check continuity between each terminal or ABS control relay.

	Continuity (Reference value 68 Ω)
Terminals (A8) 3 and (A8) 4	Continuity (Reference value 68 Ω)
Terminals (A8) 1 and (A8) 2	Open

C 1. Apply battery voltage between terminals (A8) 3 and (A8) 4.
2. Check continuity between each terminal of ABS control relay.

Terminals (A8) 1 and (A8) 2	Continuity

OK ⬇

NG ⟩ Replace ABS control relay.

TY4029700287030X

Fig. 238   Codes 13 & 14: ABS Control Motor Relay Circuit (Part 3 of 4). 1997–99 RAV4

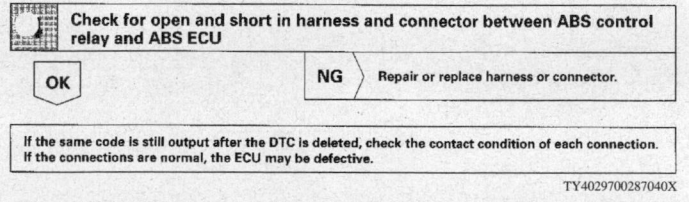

Check for open and short in harness and connector between ABS control relay and ABS ECU

OK ⬇

NG ⟩ Repair or replace harness or connector.

If the same code is still output after the DTC is deleted, check the contact condition of each connection. If the connections are normal, the ECU may be defective.

TY4029700287040X

Fig. 238   Codes 13 & 14: ABS Control Motor Relay Circuit (Part 4 of 4). 1997–99 RAV4

WIRING DIAGRAM

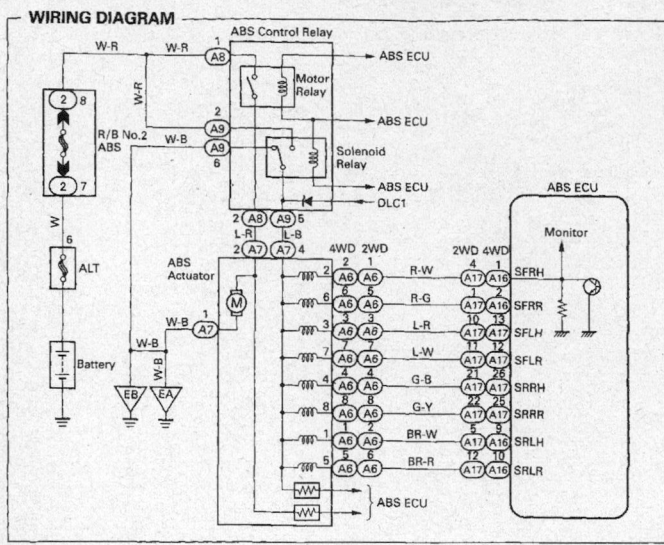

INSPECTION PROCEDURE

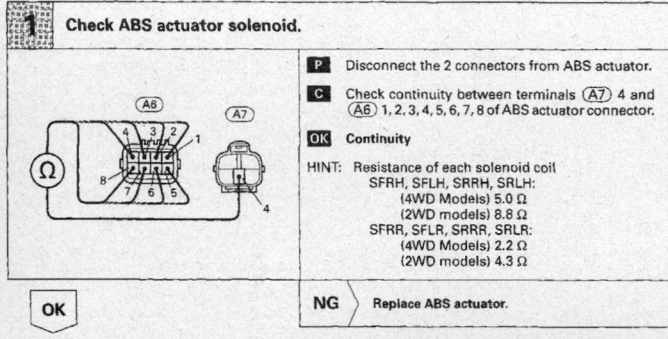

Fig. 239 Codes 21, 22, 23 & 24: ABS Actuator Solenoid Circuit (Part 1 of 2). 1996 RAV4

TY4029600207010X

CIRCUIT DESCRIPTION

This solenoid goes on when signals are received from the ECU and controls the pressure acting on the wheel cylinders, thus controlling the braking force.

DTC No.	DTC Detecting Condition	Trouble Area
21	Conditions (1) through (3) continue for 0.05 sec. or more: (1) ABS control (solenoid) relay terminal (SR) voltage: Below 1.5 V (2) Voltage of ABS ECU terminal AST: Battery positive voltage (3) When power transistor of ECU is ON, voltage of terminal SFRR or SFRH is 0 V or battery positive voltage.	• ABS actuator • Open or short in SFRR or SFRH circuit • ECU
22	Conditions (1) through (3) continue for 0.05 sec. or more: (1) ABS control (solenoid) relay terminal (SR) voltage: Below 1.5 V (2) Voltage of ABS ECU terminal AST: Battery positive voltage (3) When power transistor of ECU is ON, voltage of terminal SFLR or SFLH is 0 V or battery positive voltage	• ABS actuator • Open or short in SFLR or SFLH circuit • ECU
23	Conditions (1) through (3) continue for 0.05 sec. or more: (1) ABS control (solenoid) relay terminal (SR) voltage: Below 1.5 V (2) Voltage of ABS ECU terminal AST: Battery positive voltage (3) When power transistor of ECU is ON, voltage of terminal SRRR or SRRH is 0 V or battery positive voltage	• ABS actuator • Open or short in SRRR or SRRH circuit • ECU
24	Conditions (1) through (3) continue for 0.05 sec. or more: (1) ABS control (solenoid) relay terminal (SR) voltage: Below 1.5 V (2) Voltage of ABS ECU terminal AST: Battery positive voltage (3) When power transistor of ECU is ON, voltage of terminal SRLR or SRLH is 0 V or battery positive voltage.	• ABS actuator • Open or short in SRLR or SRLH circuit • ECU

Fail safe function: If trouble occurs in the actuator solenoid circuit, the ECU cuts off current to the ABS control (solenoid) relay and prohibits ABS control.

TY4029700288010X

Fig. 240 Codes 21, 22, 23 & 24: ABS Actuator Solenoid Circuit (Part 1 of 3). 1997–99 RAV4

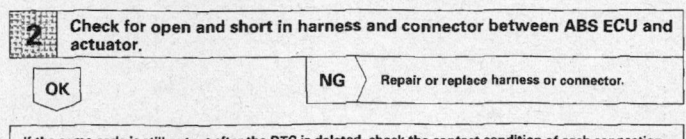

2 Check for open and short in harness and connector between ABS ECU and actuator.

OK → | NG > Repair or replace harness or connector.

If the same code is still output after the DTC is deleted, check the contact condition of each connection. If the connections are normal, the ECU may be defective.

TY4029600207020X

Fig. 239 Codes 21, 22, 23 & 24: ABS Actuator Solenoid Circuit (Part 2 of 2). 1996 RAV4

WIRING DIAGRAM

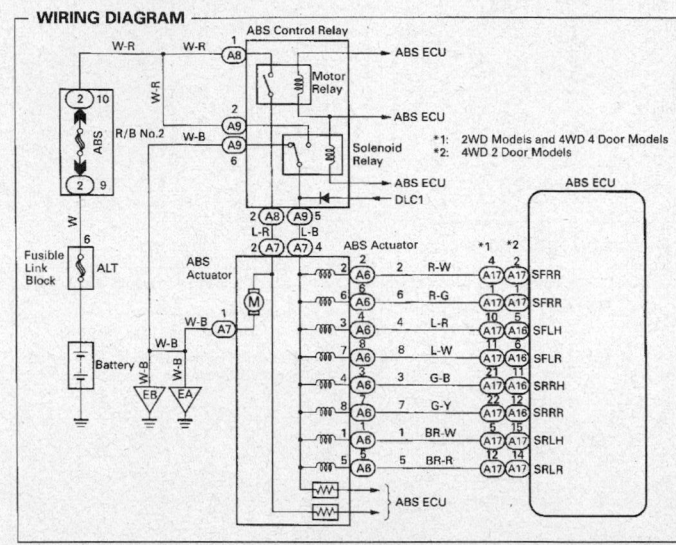

*1: 2WD Models and 4WD 4 Door Models
*2: 4WD 2 Door Models

INSPECTION PROCEDURE

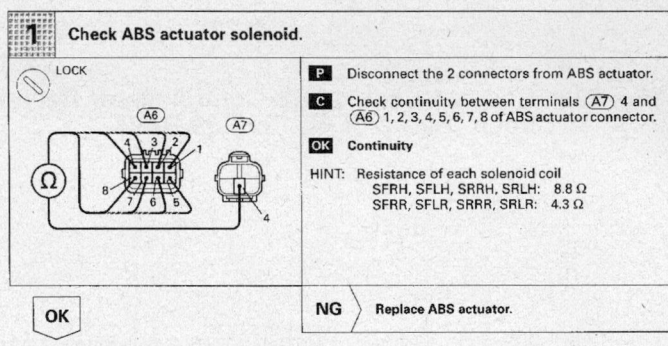

Fig. 240 Codes 21, 22, 23 & 24: ABS Actuator Solenoid Circuit (Part 2 of 3). 1997–99 RAV4

TY4029700288020X

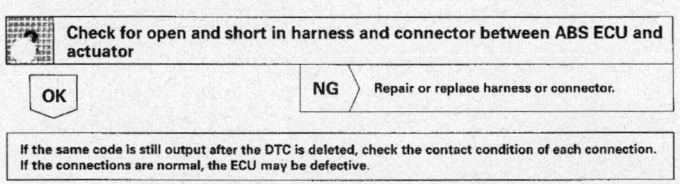

Check for open and short in harness and connector between ABS ECU and actuator

OK → | NG > Repair or replace harness or connector.

If the same code is still output after the DTC is deleted, check the contact condition of each connection. If the connections are normal, the ECU may be defective.

TY4029700288030X

Fig. 240 Codes 21, 22, 23 & 24: ABS Actuator Solenoid Circuit (Part 3 of 3). 1997–99 RAV4

ANTI-LOCK BRAKES

WIRING DIAGRAM

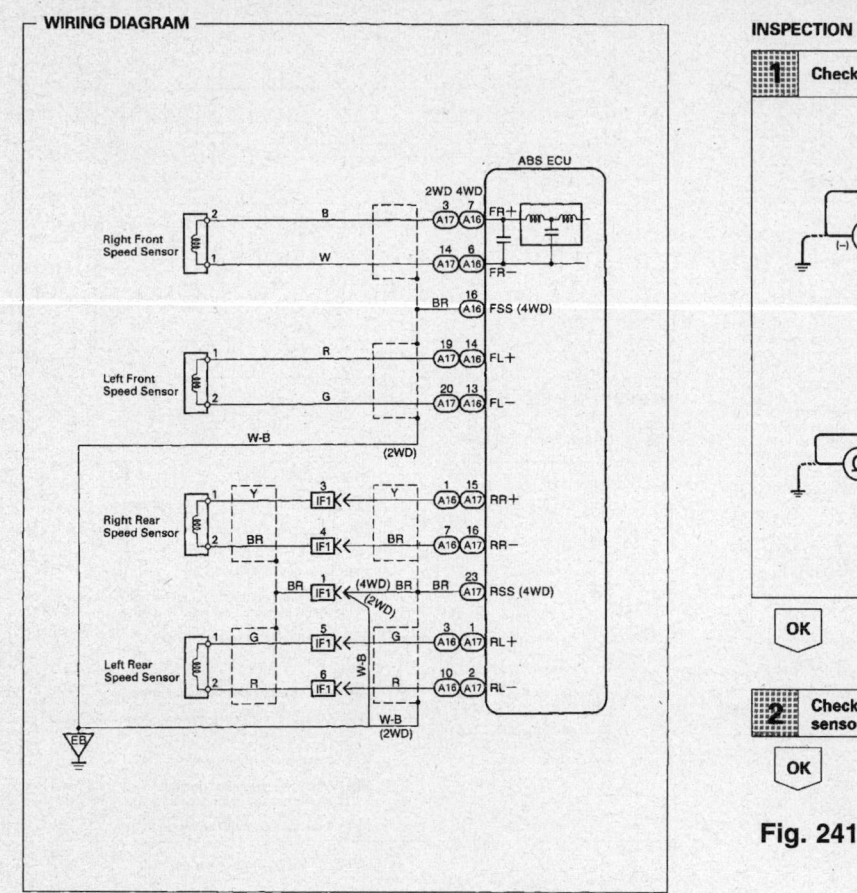

INSPECTION PROCEDURE

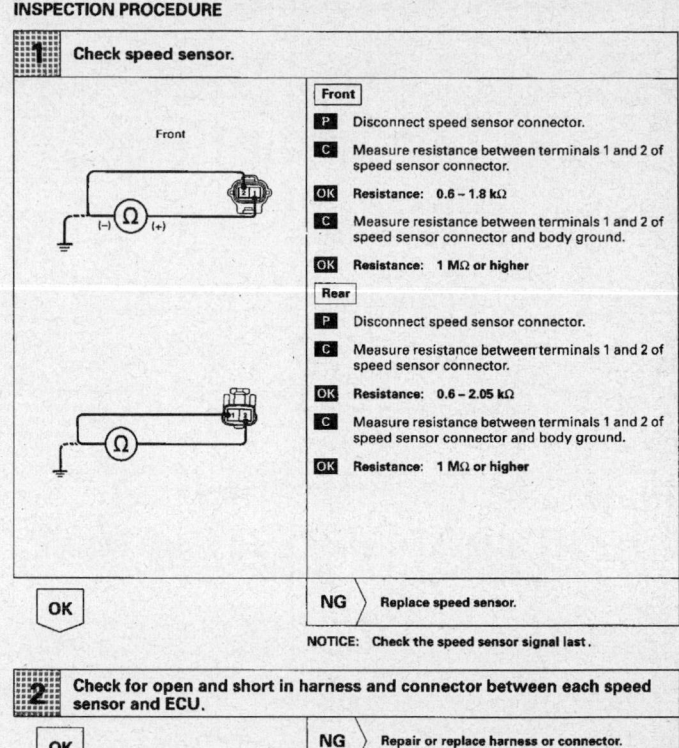

Fig. 241   Codes 31, 32, 33, 34 & 35: Speed Sensor Circuit (Part 2 of 3). 1996 RAV4

Fig. 241   Codes 31, 32, 33, 34 & 35: Speed Sensor Circuit (Part 1 of 3). 1996 RAV4

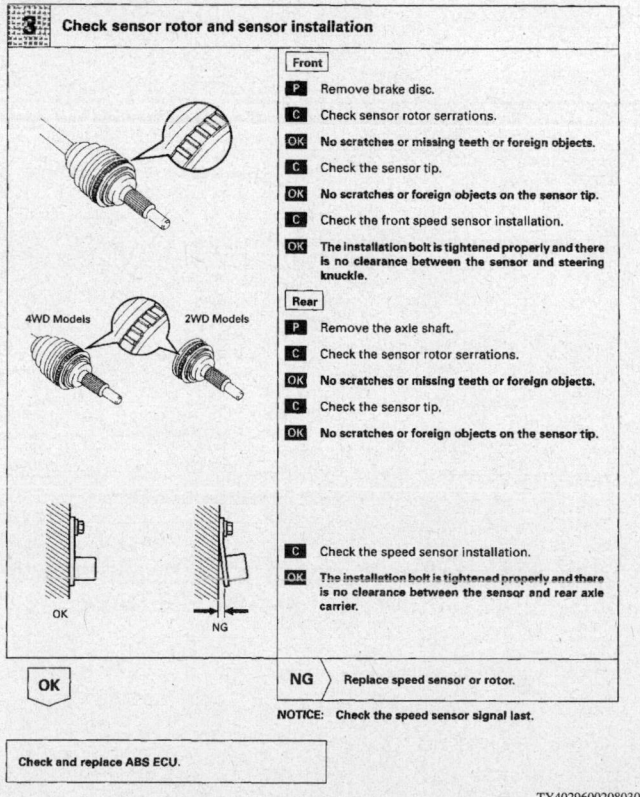

Fig. 241   Codes 31, 32, 33, 34 & 35: Speed Sensor Circuit (Part 3 of 3). 1996 RAV4

CIRCUIT DESCRIPTION

The speed sensor detects the wheel speed and sends the appropriate signals to the ECU. These signals are used to control the ABS system. The front and rear rotors each have 48 serrations.

When the rotors rotate, the magnetic field emitted by the permanent magnet in the speed sensor generates an AC voltage. Since the frequency of this AC voltage changes in direct proportion to the speed of the rotor, the frequency is used by the ECU to detect the speed of each wheel.

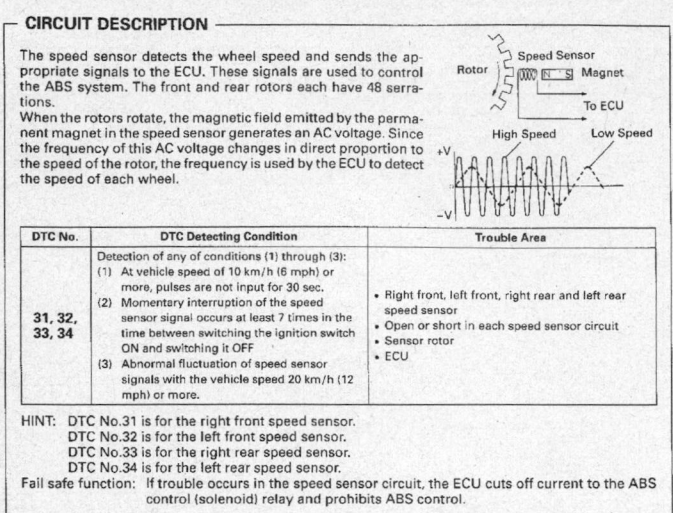

DTC No.	DTC Detecting Condition	Trouble Area
31, 32, 33, 34	Detection of any of conditions (1) through (3): (1) At vehicle speed of 10 km/h (6 mph) or more, pulses are not input for 30 sec. (2) Momentary interruption of the speed sensor signal occurs at least 7 times in the time between switching the ignition switch ON and switching it OFF (3) Abnormal fluctuation of speed sensor signals with the vehicle speed 20 km/h (12 mph) or more.	• Right front, left front, right rear and left rear speed sensor • Open or short in each speed sensor circuit • Sensor rotor • ECU

HINT: DTC No.31 is for the right front speed sensor.
DTC No.32 is for the left front speed sensor.
DTC No.33 is for the right rear speed sensor.
DTC No.34 is for the left rear speed sensor.

Fail safe function: If trouble occurs in the speed sensor circuit, the ECU cuts off current to the ABS control (solenoid) relay and prohibits ABS control.

TY4029700289010X

Fig. 242   Codes 31, 32, 33 & 34: Speed Sensor Circuit (Part 1 of 4). 1997–99 RAV4

WIRING DIAGRAM

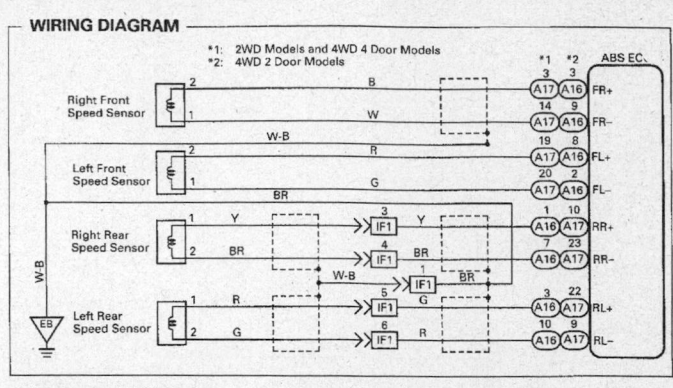

INSPECTION PROCEDURE

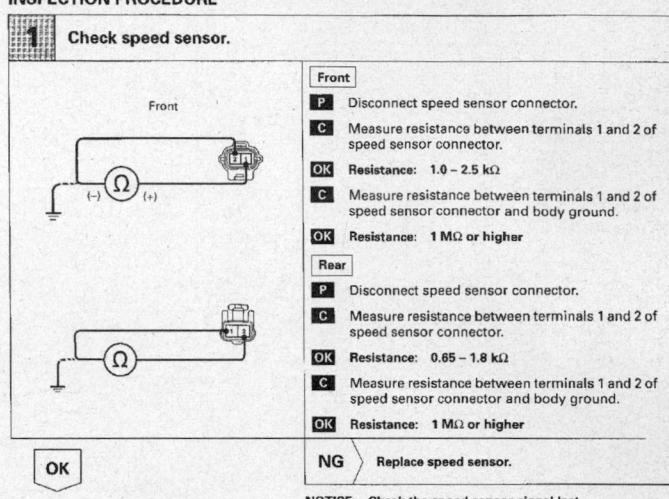

1   Check speed sensor.

Front

P Disconnect speed sensor connector.

C Measure resistance between terminals 1 and 2 of speed sensor connector.

OK Resistance: 1.0 – 2.5 kΩ

C Measure resistance between terminals 1 and 2 of speed sensor connector and body ground.

OK Resistance: 1 MΩ or higher

Rear

P Disconnect speed sensor connector.

C Measure resistance between terminals 1 and 2 of speed sensor connector.

OK Resistance: 0.65 – 1.8 kΩ

C Measure resistance between terminals 1 and 2 of speed sensor connector and body ground.

OK Resistance: 1 MΩ or higher

OK ▽

NG ▷ Replace speed sensor.

NOTICE: Check the speed sensor signal last.

TY4029700289020X

Fig. 242   Codes 31, 32, 33 & 34: Speed Sensor Circuit (Part 2 of 4). 1997–99 RAV4

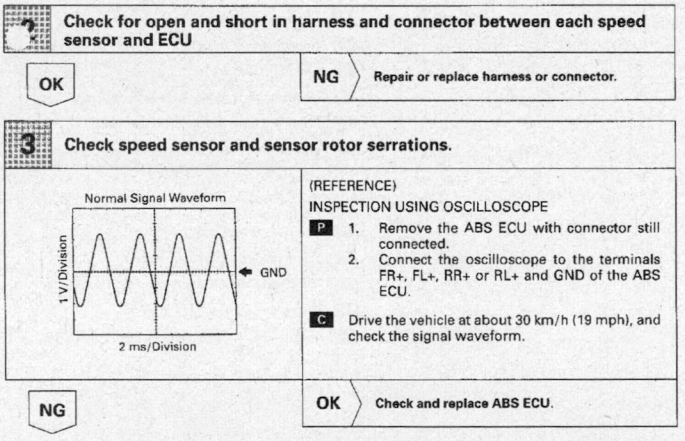

2   Check for open and short in harness and connector between each speed sensor and ECU

OK ▽

NG ▷ Repair or replace harness or connector.

3   Check speed sensor and sensor rotor serrations.

Normal Signal Waveform

1 V/Division

← GND

2 ms/Division

(REFERENCE)
INSPECTION USING OSCILLOSCOPE

P 1. Remove the ABS ECU with connector still connected.
2. Connect the oscilloscope to the terminals FR+, FL+, RR+ or RL+ and GND of the ABS ECU.

C Drive the vehicle at about 30 km/h (19 mph), and check the signal waveform.

NG ▽

OK ▷ Check and replace ABS ECU.

TY4029700289030X

Fig. 242   Codes 31, 32, 33 & 34: Speed Sensor Circuit (Part 3 of 4). 1997–99 RAV4

4 Check sensor rotor and sensor installation

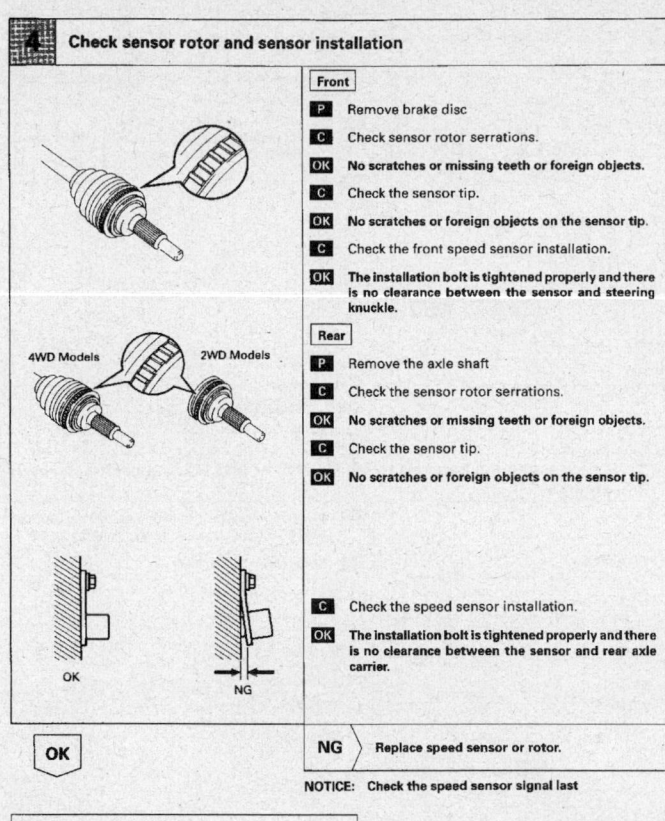

Front

P	Remove brake disc
C	Check sensor rotor serrations.
OK	No scratches or missing teeth or foreign objects.
C	Check the sensor tip.
OK	No scratches or foreign objects on the sensor tip.
C	Check the front speed sensor installation.
OK	The installation bolt is tightened properly and there is no clearance between the sensor and steering knuckle.

Rear

P	Remove the axle shaft.
C	Check the sensor rotor serrations.
OK	No scratches or missing teeth or foreign objects.
C	Check the sensor tip.
OK	No scratches or foreign objects on the sensor tip.
C	Check the speed sensor installation.
OK	The installation bolt is tightened properly and there is no clearance between the sensor and rear axle carrier.

4WD Models   2WD Models

OK   NG

OK ⟩ **NG** ⟩ Replace speed sensor or rotor.

NOTICE: Check the speed sensor signal last.

Check and replace ABS ECU.

TY4029700289040X

Fig. 242   Codes 31, 32, 33 & 34: Speed Sensor Circuit (Part 4 of 4). 1997–99 RAV4

CIRCUIT DESCRIPTION

This is the power source for the ECU, hence the CPU, and the actuators.

DTC No.	DTC Detecting Condition	Trouble Area
41	Vehicle speed is 3 km/h (1.9 mph) or more and voltage of ECU terminal IG1 remains at below 9.5 V for more than 10 sec.	• Battery • IC regulator • Open or short in power source circuit • ECU

Fail safe function: If trouble occurs in the power source circuit, the ECU cuts off current to the ABS control (solenoid)relay and prohibits ABS control.

TY4029700290010X

Fig. 244   Code 41: IG Power Source Circuit (Part 1 of 4). RAV4

INSPECTION PROCEDURE

1 Check tire size.

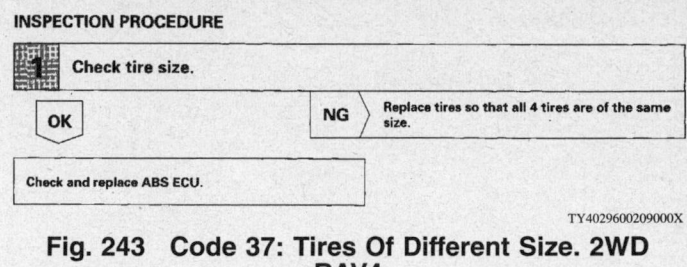

OK ⟩ **NG** ⟩ Replace tires so that all 4 tires are of the same size.

Check and replace ABS ECU.

TY4029600209000X

Fig. 243   Code 37: Tires Of Different Size. 2WD RAV4

WIRING DIAGRAM

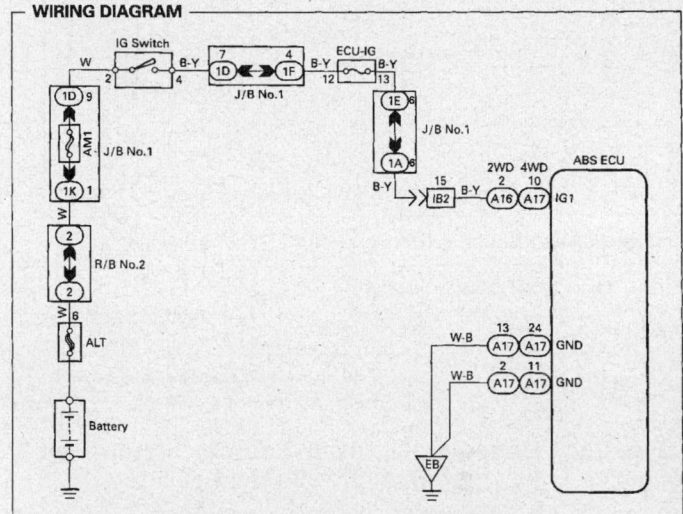

INSPECTION PROCEDURE

1 Check battery positive voltage.

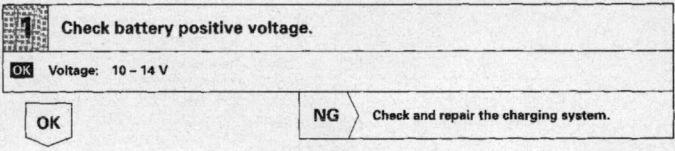

OK Voltage: 10 – 14 V

OK ⟩ **NG** ⟩ Check and repair the charging system.

TY4029600210010X

Fig. 244   Code 41: IG Power Source Circuit (Part 2 of 4). 1996 RAV4

WIRING DIAGRAM

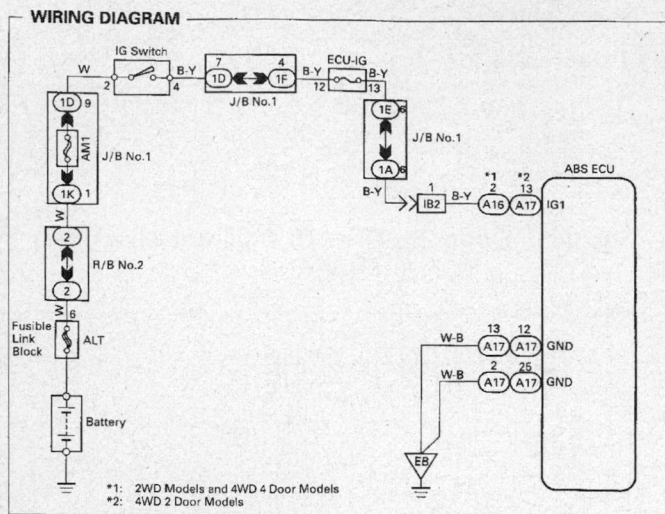

*1: 2WD Models and 4WD 4 Door Models
*2: 4WD 2 Door Models

INSPECTION PROCEDURE

1 | **Check battery positive voltage.**

OK Voltage: 10 – 14 V

OK

NG Check and repair the charging system.

TY4029700290020X

Fig. 244   Code 41: IG Power Source Circuit (Part 2 of 4). 1997–99 RAV4

---

2 | **Check voltage between terminals IG1 and GND of ABS ECU connector.**

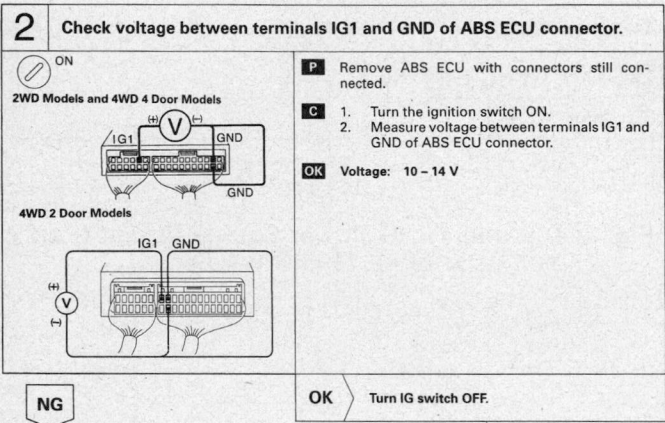

P Remove ABS ECU with connectors still connected.

C 1. Turn the ignition switch ON.
2. Measure voltage between terminals IG1 and GND of ABS ECU connector.

OK Voltage: 10 – 14 V

NG

OK Turn IG switch OFF.

---

3 | **Check continuity between terminals GND of ABS ECU connector and body ground.**

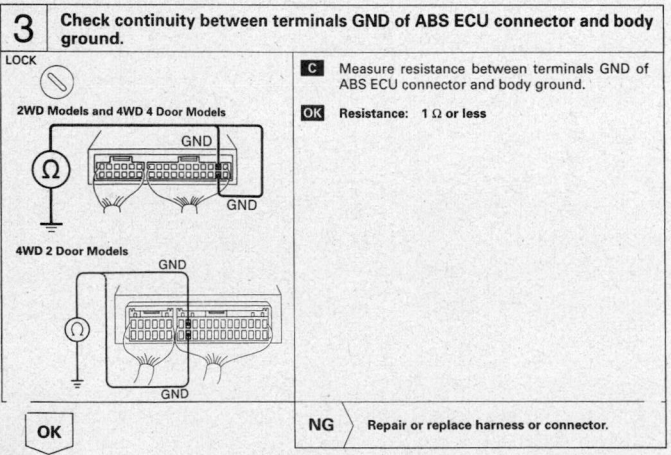

C Measure resistance between terminals GND of ABS ECU connector and body ground.

OK Resistance: 1 Ω or less

OK

NG Repair or replace harness or connector.

TY4029700290030X

Fig. 244   Code 41: IG Power Source Circuit (Part 3 of 4). 1997–99 RAV4

---

2 | **Check voltage between terminals IG1 and GND of ABS ECU connector.**

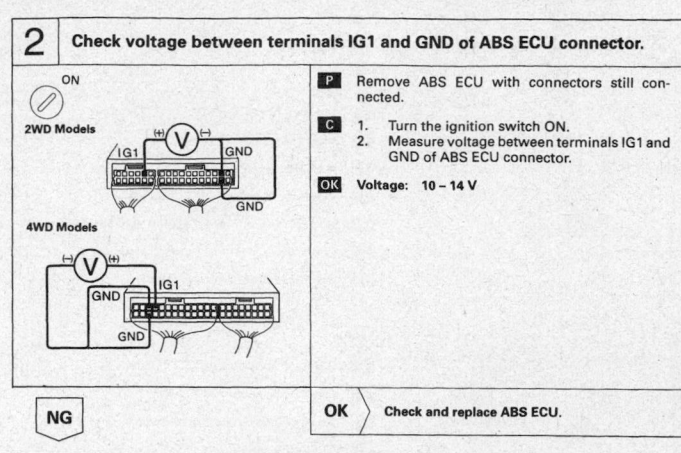

P Remove ABS ECU with connectors still connected.

C 1. Turn the ignition switch ON.
2. Measure voltage between terminals IG1 and GND of ABS ECU connector.

OK Voltage: 10 – 14 V

NG

OK Check and replace ABS ECU.

---

3 | **Check continuity between terminals GND of ABS ECU connector and body ground.**

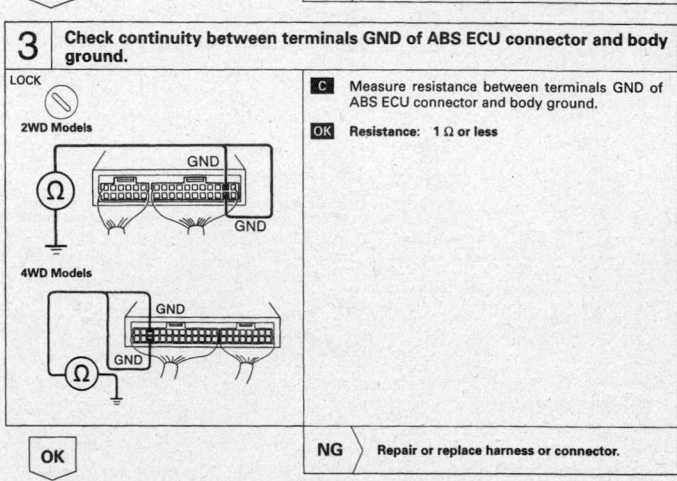

C Measure resistance between terminals GND of ABS ECU connector and body ground.

OK Resistance: 1 Ω or less

OK

NG Repair or replace harness or connector.

TY4029600210020X

Fig. 244   Code 41: IG Power Source Circuit (Part 3 of 4). 1996 RAV4

---

4 | **Check ECU-IG fuse.**

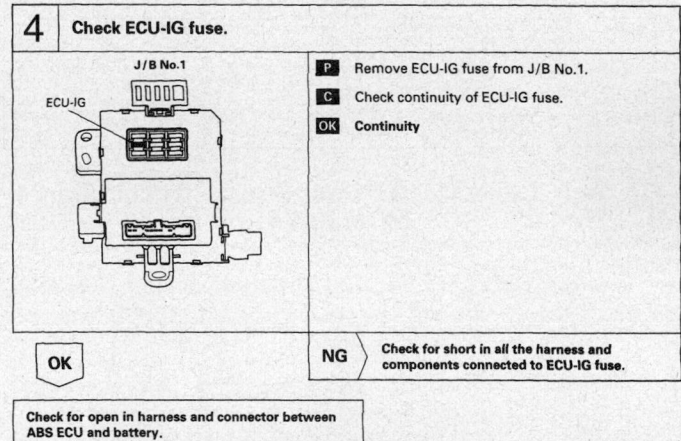

P Remove ECU-IG fuse from J/B No.1.

C Check continuity of ECU-IG fuse.

OK Continuity

OK

NG Check for short in all the harness and components connected to ECU-IG fuse.

Check for open in harness and connector between ABS ECU and battery.

TY4029600210030X

Fig. 244   Code 41: IG Power Source Circuit (Part 4 of 4). RAV4

INSPECTION PROCEDURE

1 Check deceleration sensor.

| OK | | NG | > | Replace deceleration sensor. |

2 Check for open or short in harness and connector between sensor and ECU.

| OK | | NG | > | Repair or replace harness and connector. |

Check and replace ABS ECU.

TY4029600211000X

Fig. 245 Codes 43 & 45: Malfunction In Deceleration Sensor. 4WD RAV4

INSPECTION PROCEDURE

1 Check for open and short in harness and connector between sensor and ECU.

| OK | | NG | > | Repair or replace harness or connector. |

2 Check voltage between terminals GL1, GL2, VGS of ECU and body ground.

P
1. Remove ABS ECU with connectors still connected.
2. Disconnect sensor connector.
3. Turn the ignition switch ON.

C Measure voltage between terminals GL1, GL2, VGS of ECU and body ground.

OK Voltage:
GL1, GL2:   0.5 – 4.5 V
VGS: 4.5 – 5.5 V

| OK | | NG | > | Check and replace ABS ECU. |

Check and replace deceleration sensor.

TY4029600212020X

Fig. 246 Code 44: Deceleration Sensor Circuit (Part 2 of 2). 1996 RAV4

WIRING DIAGRAM

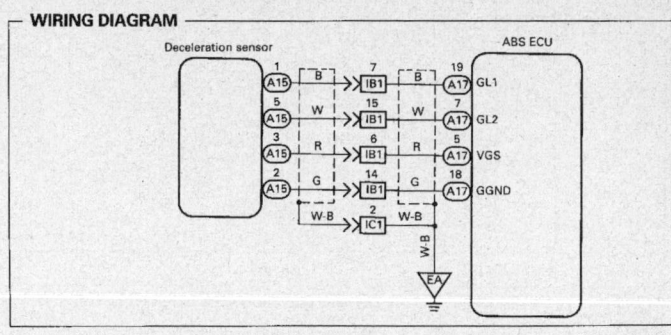

TY4029600212010X

Fig. 246 Code 44: Deceleration Sensor Circuit (Part 1 of 2). 1996 RAV4

CIRCUIT DESCRIPTION

This sensor detects deceleration on the vehicle. The sensor signal is used in ABS control. If the sensor functions abnormally, the ABS warning light comes on but the ABS still operates.

DTC No.	DTC Detecting Condition	Trouble Area
44	4 Door Models: Either of the following (1) or (2) is detected: (1) An open or short is detected in circuit GS1 or GS2 for 1 sec. (2) After the ignition is turned ON, the test signal is outptu by GST. During this time, a trouble signal is detected for 0.5 sec. 2 Door Models: Either of the following (1), (2) or (3) is detected: (1) IG switch ON and output voltage of GL1 or GL2 remains 0.5 V or less or 4.5 V or more for more than 1.2 sec. (2) At vehicle speed of 0 km/h, outputs of GL1 and of GL2 remains abnormally different for 60 sec. or more (3) IG switch ON and VGS $\leq$ 4.4 V, VGS $\geq$ 5.5 V continues for 1.2 sec. or more.	• Deceleration sensor • Open or short in deceleration sensor circuit • ECU

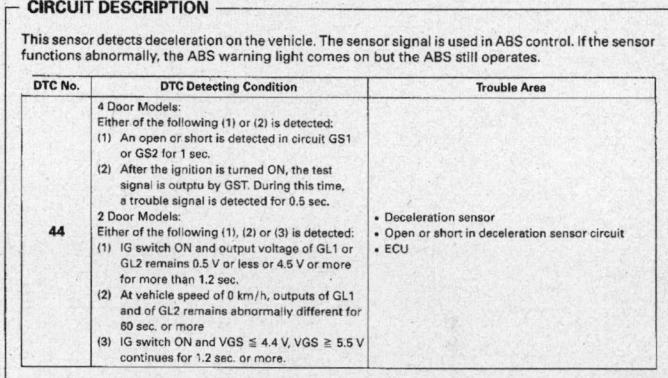

TY4029700291010X

Fig. 247 Code 44: Deceleration Sensor Circuit (Part 1 of 2). 1997–99 RAV4

WIRING DIAGRAM

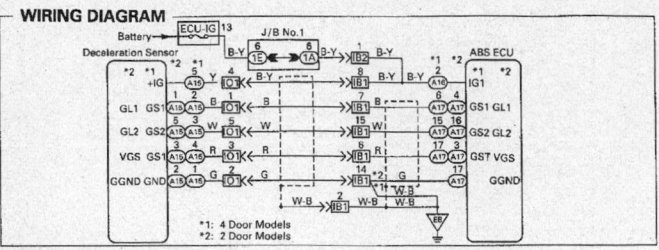

INSPECTION PROCEDURE

| 1 | Check for open and short in harness and connector between sensor and ECU |

OK →

NG → Repair or replace harness or connector.

| 2 | Check voltage between terminals GL1, GL2, VGS or GS1, GS2, GST of ECU and body ground. |

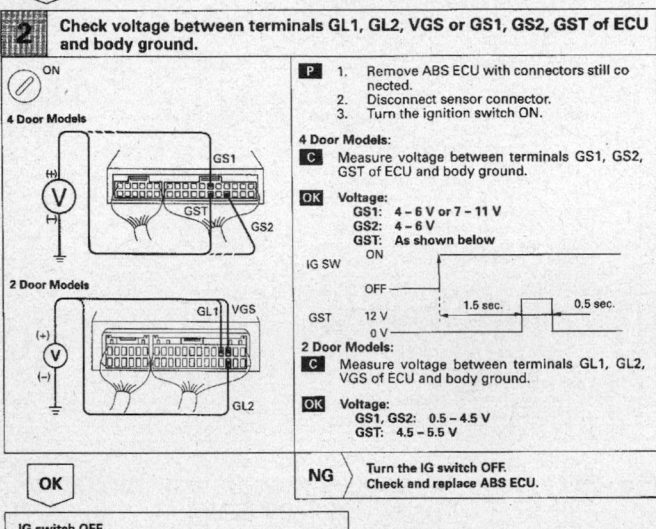

P
1. Remove ABS ECU with connectors still connected.
2. Disconnect sensor connector.
3. Turn the ignition switch ON.

4 Door Models:
C Measure voltage between terminals GS1, GS2, GST of ECU and body ground.

OK Voltage:
GS1: 4 – 6 V or 7 – 11 V
GS2: 4 – 6 V
GST: As shown below

IG SW ON / OFF
GST 12 V / 0 V   1.5 sec. 0.5 sec.

2 Door Models:
C Measure voltage between terminals GL1, GL2, VGS of ECU and body ground.

OK Voltage:
GS1, GS2: 0.5 – 4.5 V
GST: 4.5 – 5.5 V

OK →

NG → Turn the IG switch OFF.
Check and replace ABS ECU.

IG switch OFF.
Check and replace deceleration sensor.

TY4029700291020X

Fig. 247   Code 44: Deceleration Sensor Circuit (Part 2 of 2). 1997–99 RAV4

CIRCUIT DESCRIPTION

This relay supplies power to each ABS solenoid. After the ignition switch is turned ON, if the initial check is OK, the relay goes on.

DTC No.	DTC Detecting Condition	Trouble Area
11	With IG1 terminal voltage at 9.5V –18.5V, when solenoid relay is turned ON, relay contact is OFF[*1] for 0.2 sec. or longer.	• ABS solenoid valve relay • Valve supply voltage
12	Immediately after IG1 is turned ON, when solenoid relay is turned OFF, relay contact is ON[*2] for 0.2 sec. or longer.	

[*1] Relay contact OFF condition:
When all solenoid supplied voltage are below 2.5 V.
[*2] Relay contact ON condition:
Any of voltage supplied by solenoid is 6 V or more.
Fail safe function:
If any trouble occurs in the ABS solenoid valve relay circuit, the ECU cuts off current to the ABS solenoid valve relay and prohibits ABS control.

TY4029900454010X

Fig. 249   Codes 11 & 12: ABS Solenoid Relay Circuit (Part 1 of 2). Sienna

CIRCUIT DESCRIPTION

DTC No.	DTC Detecting Condition	Trouble area
51	Pump motor is not operating normally during initial check.	• ABS pump motor

Fail safe function: If trouble occurs in the ABS pump motor, the ECU cuts off current to the control (solenoid) relay and prohibits ABS control.

TY4029600213000X

Fig. 248   Code 51: ABS Pump Motor Lock. RAV4

INSPECTION PROCEDURE

| 1 | Check voltage between terminals 9 and 8, 15 and 8 of ABS ECU. |

PREPARATION:
Disconnect the ABS ECU connector.
CHECK:
Measure the voltage between terminals 9 and 8, 15 and 8 of ABS ECU harness side connector.
OK:
Voltage: 10 – 14 V

NG → Check and replace fuses.
Check and repair harness or connector.

OK →

If the same code is still output after the DTC is deleted, check the contact condition of each connection. If the connection is normal, the ECU may be defective.

TY4029900454020X

Fig. 249   Codes 11 & 12: ABS Solenoid Relay Circuit (Part 2 of 2). Sienna

CIRCUIT DESCRIPTION

The ABS motor relay supplies power to the ABS pump motor. While the ABS is activated, the ECU switches the ABS motor relay ON and operates the ABS pump motor.

DTC No.	DTC Detecting Condition	Trouble Area
13	Detection of any conditions in 1. and 2.: 1. When pump motor relay is ON, relay contact is OFF[*1] for 0.2 sec. or longer. 2. When pump motor relay is turned ON, relay contact is OFF for 0.5 sec. or longer.	• ABS motor relay • Pump motor voltage • Pump motor lead disconnected
14	Detection of any conditions in 1. and 2.: 1. When pump motor relay is OFF, relay contact is ON[*2] for 0.2 sec. or longer. 2. When pump motor relay is turned OFF, relay contact is ON for 2 sec. or longer.	

[*1] Relay contact OFF condition: BM terminal voltage is below 1.5 V.
[*2] Relay contact ON condition: BM terminal voltage is 4.0 V or above.
Fail safe function:
If any trouble occurs in the ABS motor relay circuit, the ECU cuts off current to the ABS solenoid valve relay and prohibits ABS control.

TY4029900455010X

Fig. 250   Codes 13 & 14: ABS Motor Relay Circuit (Part 1 of 2). Sienna

INSPECTION PROCEDURE

1	Check voltage between terminals 9 and 8, 24 and 23 of ABS ECU connector.

PREPARATION:
Disconnect the ABS ECU connector.
CHECK:
Measure the voltage between terminals 9 and 8, 24 and 23 of ABS ECU harness side connector.
OK:

> Voltage: 10 – 14 V

 NG ▷ | Check and replace fuses.
Check and repair harness or connector. |

 OK ▽

If the same code is still output after the DTC is deleted, check the contact condition of each connection. If the connection is normal, the ECU may be defective.

TY4029900455020X

Fig. 250 Codes 13 & 14: ABS Motor Relay Circuit (Part 2 of 2). Sienna

INSPECTION PROCEDURE

1	Check the DTC once more.

PREPARATION:
(a) Clear the DTC
(b) Turn the ignition switch OFF.
CHECK:
Turn the ignition switch ON, and check that the same DTC is stored in the memory.

NO ▷ | No problem. |

YES ▽

| Replace ABS actuator assembly. |

TY4029900456020X

Fig. 251 Codes 21, 22, 23 & 24: ABS Solenoid Valve Circuit (Part 2 of 2). Sienna

CIRCUIT DESCRIPTION

This solenoid goes on when signals are received from the ECU and controls the pressure acting on the wheel cylinders thus controlling the braking force.

DTC No.	DTC Detecting Condition	Trouble Area
21, 22, 23, 24	With IG1 terminal voltage at 9.5V – 18.5V, solenoid circuit is open or short for 0.05 sec. or longer.	• Each solenoid valves circuit • ABS actuator

HINT:
DTC No. 21 is for right front solenoid valve.
DTC No. 22 is for left front solenoid valve.
DTC No. 23 is for right rear solenoid valve.
DTC No. 24 is for left rear solenoid valve.
Fail safe function:
If any trouble occurs in the actuator solenoid valve circuit, the ECU cuts off current to the ABS solenoid valve relay and prohibits ABS control.

TY4029900456010X

Fig. 251 Codes 21, 22, 23 & 24: ABS Solenoid Valve Circuit (Part 1 of 2). Sienna

CIRCUIT DESCRIPTION

The speed sensor detects wheel speed and sends the appropriate signals to the ECU. These signals are used to control of the ABS system. The front and rear rotors each have 48 serrations.
When the rotors rotate, the magnetic field emitted by the permanent magnet in the speed sensor generates an AC voltage. Since the frequency of this AC voltage changes in direct proportion to the speed of the rotor, the frequency is used by the ECU to detect the speed of each wheel.

DTC No.	DTC Detecting Condition	Trouble Area
31, 32, 33, 34	Detection of any of conditions from 1. through 4.: 1. With vehicle speed at 10 km/h or more, sensor signal circuit of faulty wheel is open or short for 15 sec. or longer. 2. Momentary interruption of sensor signal of faulty wheel has occurred 7 times or more. 3. With vehicle speed at 20 km/h or more, sensor signal of faulty wheel generated noise for 5 sec. or longer. 4. Sensor signal circuit is open for 0.3 sec. or longer.	• Right front, left front, right rear, left rear speed sensor • Each speed sensor circuit • Sensor installation • Sensor rotor

HINT:
DTC No. 31 is for the right front speed sensor.
DTC No. 32 is for the left front speed sensor.
DTC No. 33 is for the right rear speed sensor.
DTC No. 34 is for the left rear speed sensor.
Fail safe function:
If any trouble occurs in the speed sensor circuit, the ECU cuts off current to the ABS solenoid valve relay and prohibits ABS control.

TY4029900457010X

Fig. 252 Codes 31, 32, 33 & 34: Speed Sensor Circuit (Part 1 of 4). Sienna

INSPECTION PROCEDURE

| 1 | Check speed sensor. |

Front:
PREPARATION:
(a) Remove the front fender liner.
(b) Disconnect the speed sensor connector.
CHECK:
Measure resistance between terminals 1 and 2 of speed sensor connector.
OK:
    Resistance: 1.4 – 1.8 kΩ
CHECK:
Measure resistance between each of terminals 1 and 2 of speed sensor connector and body ground.
OK:
    Resistance: 1 MΩ or higher

Rear:
PREPARATION:
(a) Remove the seat cushion and side seatback.
(b) Remove lower center garnish, rear door scuff plate and room partition trim.
(c) Disconnect the speed sensor connector.
CHECK:
Measure resistance between terminals 1 and 2 of speed sensor connector.
OK:
    Resistance: 0.9 – 1.3 kΩ
CHECK:
Measure resistance between each of terminals 1 and 2 of speed sensor connector and body ground.
OK:
    Resistance: 1 MΩ or higher

| NG > | Replace front speed sensor or rear axle hub. |

NOTICE:
Check the speed sensor signal last

| OK |

TY4029900457020X

Fig. 252   Codes 31, 32, 33 & 34: Speed Sensor Circuit (Part 2 of 4). Sienna

| 5 | Check front sensor rotor and sensor tip. |

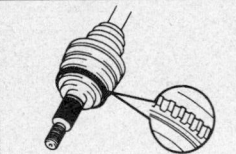

PREPARATION:
Remove the front drive shaft
CHECK:
Check the sensor rotor serrations.
OK:
    No scratches, missing teeth or foreign objects.
PREPARATION:
Remove the front speed sensor
CHECK:
Check the sensor tip.
OK:
    No scratches or foreign objects on the sensor tip.

| NG > | Replace sensor rotor or speed sensor. |

NOTICE:
Check the speed sensor signal last

| OK |

| Check and replace ABS actuator assembly. |

TY4029900457040X

Fig. 252   Codes 31, 32, 33 & 34: Speed Sensor Circuit (Part 4 of 4). Sienna

| 2 | Check for open and short circuit in harness and connector between each speed sensor and ECU |

| NG > | Repair or replace harness or connector. |

| OK |

| 3 | Check speed sensor and sensor rotor serrations. |

(REFERENCE) INSPECTION USING OSCILLOSCOPE
PREPARATION:
Connect the oscilloscope to the terminals FR+, FL+, RR+, or RL+ and GND of the ABS actuator assembly.
CHECK:
Drive the vehicle at 20 km/h (12 mph), and check the signal waveform.

| OK > | Replace front speed sensor or rear axle hub. |

| NG |

| 4 | Check front speed sensor installation. |

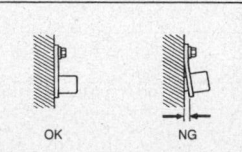

CHECK:
Check the speed sensor installation.
OK:
    The installation bolt is tightened properly and there is no clearance between the sensor and knucle.

| NG > | Replace speed sensor. |

NOTICE:
Check the speed sensor signal last

| OK |

TY4029900457030X

Fig. 252   Codes 31, 32, 33 & 34: Speed Sensor Circuit (Part 3 of 4). Sienna

CIRCUIT DESCRIPTION

This is the power source for the ECU, hence for the CPU, and actuator.

DTC No.	DTC Detecting Condition	Trouble Area
41	Detection of any of conditions from 1. through 3. 1. With vehicle speed at 3 km/h or more, IG1 or +BS terminal voltage is 9.5V or below for 10 sec. or longer. 2. With IG1 terminal voltage at 9.5V or below, solenoid relay open, pump motor relay open, solenoid fault detecting condition are established. 3. +BS terminal voltage is 19 V or above for 1 sec. or longer	• Battery • Charging system • Power source circuit

Fail safe function:
If any trouble occurs in the power source circuit, the ECU cuts off current to the ABS solenoid valve relay and prohibits ABS control.

TY4029900458010X

Fig. 253   Code 41: IG Power Source Circuit (Part 1 of 3). Sienna

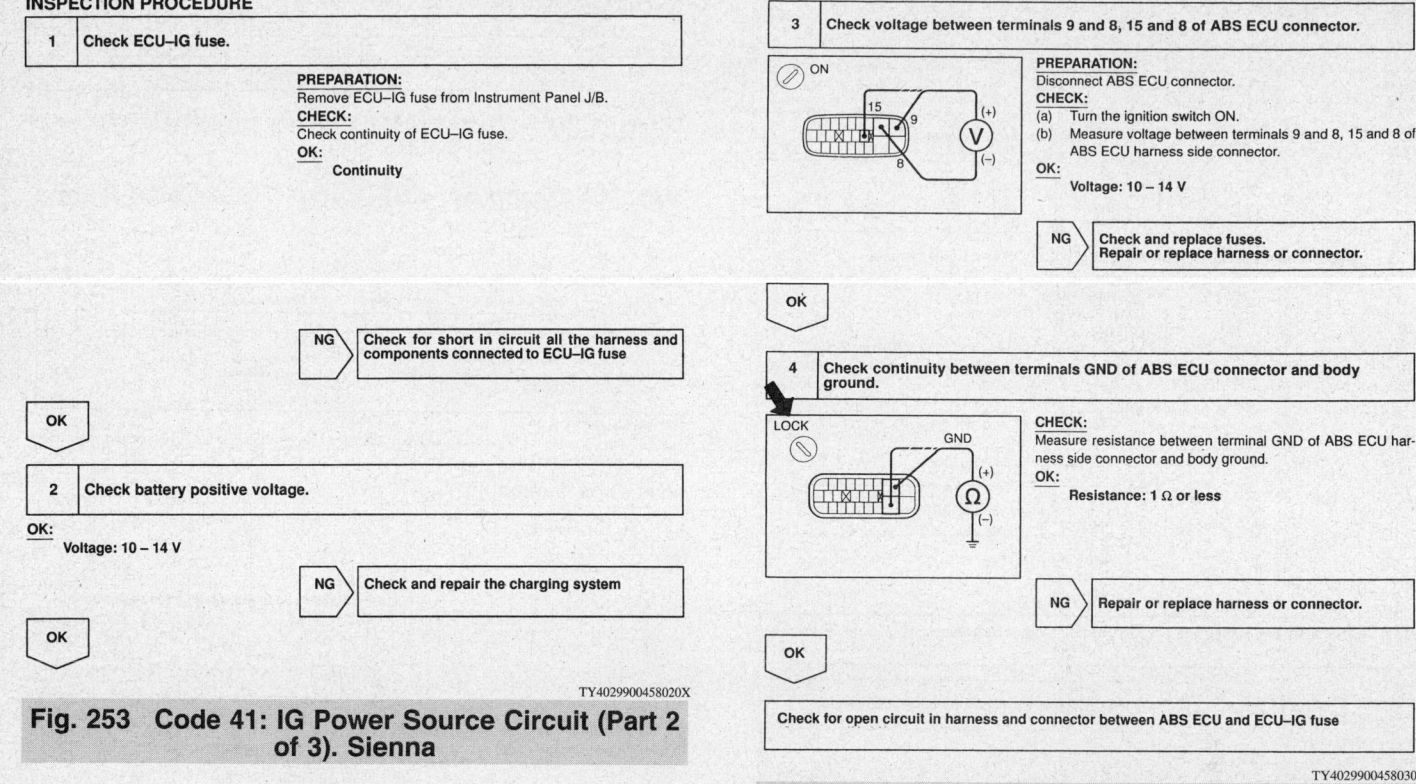

INSPECTION PROCEDURE

1	Check ECU–IG fuse.

PREPARATION:
Remove ECU–IG fuse from Instrument Panel J/B.
CHECK:
Check continuity of ECU–IG fuse.
OK:
    Continuity

| NG | Check for short in circuit all the harness and components connected to ECU–IG fuse |

OK

| 2 | Check battery positive voltage. |

OK:
    Voltage: 10 – 14 V

| NG | Check and repair the charging system |

OK

TY4029900458020X

Fig. 253   Code 41: IG Power Source Circuit (Part 2 of 3). Sienna

| 3 | Check voltage between terminals 9 and 8, 15 and 8 of ABS ECU connector. |

PREPARATION:
Disconnect ABS ECU connector.
CHECK:
(a) Turn the ignition switch ON.
(b) Measure voltage between terminals 9 and 8, 15 and 8 of ABS ECU harness side connector.
OK:
    Voltage: 10 – 14 V

| NG | Check and replace fuses. Repair or replace harness or connector. |

OK

| 4 | Check continuity between terminals GND of ABS ECU connector and body ground. |

CHECK:
Measure resistance between terminal GND of ABS ECU harness side connector and body ground.
OK:
    Resistance: 1 Ω or less

| NG | Repair or replace harness or connector. |

OK

| Check for open circuit in harness and connector between ABS ECU and ECU–IG fuse |

TY4029900458030X

Fig. 253   Code 41: IG Power Source Circuit (Part 3 of 3). Sienna

CIRCUIT DESCRIPTION

DTC No.	DTC Detecting Condition	Trouble Area
49	With IG1 terminal voltage at 9.5V–18.5V, and when ABS is in non–operation stop light switch circuit is open for 0.3 sec. or longer.	• Stop light switch circuit

TY4029900459010X

Fig. 254   Code 49: Stop Light Switch Circuit (Part 1 of 2). Sienna

TOYOTA UNIT REPAIR

INSPECTION PROCEDURE

| 1 | Check operation of stop light. |

CHECK:
Check that stop light lights up when brake pedal is depressed and turns off when brake pedal is released.

→ NG → Repair stop light circuit

↓ OK

| 2 | Check voltage between terminal STP of ABS ECU and body ground. |

PREPARATION:
Disconnect ABS ECU connector.
CHECK:
Measure the voltage between terminal STP of ABS ECU harness side connector and body ground when brake pedal is depressed.
OK:
Voltage: 8 – 14 V

→ OK → Check and replace ABS actuator assembly.

↓ NG

| 3 | Check for open circuit in harness and connector between ABS ECU and stop light switch |

→ NG → Repair or replace harness or connector.

↓ OK

Proceed to next circuit inspection shown on problem symptoms table

TY4029900459020X

Fig. 254 Code 49: Stop Light Switch Circuit (Part 2 of 2). Sienna

CIRCUIT DESCRIPTION

DTC No.	DTC Detecting Condition	Trouble Area
51	ABS actuator pump moter is not operating normally during initial check.	• ABS pump motor

Fail safe function:
If any trouble occurs in the ABS pump motor, the ECU cuts off current to the ABS solenoid valve relay and prohibits ABS control.

TY4029900460000X

Fig. 255 Code 51: ABS Pump Motor Lock. Sienna

CIRCUIT DESCRIPTION

This is the power source for the ECU, hence for the CPU and the actuator.

DTC No.	DTC Detecting Condition	Trouble Area
Always ON	Detection of any conditions in 1. and 2.: 1. ABS ECU internal malfunction is detected. 2. IG1 terminal voltage is 7 V or below.	• Battery • Charging system • Power source circuit • ECU • ABS warning light circuit

Fail safe function:
If any trouble occurs in the power source circuit, the ECU cuts off current to the ABS solenoid valve relay and prohibits ABS control.

INSPECTION PROCEDURE

| 1 | Is DTC output? |

Check DTC

→ YES → Repair circuit indicated by the code output.

↓ NO

| 2 | Check voltage between terminals IG1 and GND of ABS ECU connector. |

PREPARATION:
Disconnect ABS ECU connector.
CHECK:
(a) Turn the ignition switch ON.
(b) Measure voltage between terminals IG1 and GND of ABS ECU harness side connector.
OK:
Voltage: 10 – 14 V

→ NG → Check for open and short circuit in harness and connector between ECU–IG fuse and ABS actuator

↓ OK

TY4029900461010X

Fig. 256 ABS Lamp Always ON: ABS ECU Malfunction IG Power Source Circuit (Part 1 of 2). Sienna

3	Check combination meter.

PREPARATION:
Disconnect ABS ECU connector.
CHECK:
(a) Using service wire, connect terminal WA and GND1 of ABS ECU connector.
(b) Turn the ignition switch ON.
OK:

ABS warning light goes off

NG ▷ Repair or replace combination meter assembly.

OK

4	Check ABS warning light.

PREPARATION:
(a) Turn the ignition switch OFF.
(b) Disconnect the connector from the ABS ECU.
(c) Turn the ignition switch ON.
CHECK:
Check the ABS warning light goes off.

OK ▷ Check and replace ABS actuator assembly.

NG

Check for short circuit in harness and connector between ABS warning light, DLC1 and ABS ECU.

TY4029900461020X

Fig. 256   ABS Lamp Always ON: ABS ECU Malfunction IG Power Source Circuit (Part 2 of 2). Sienna

WIRING DIAGRAM

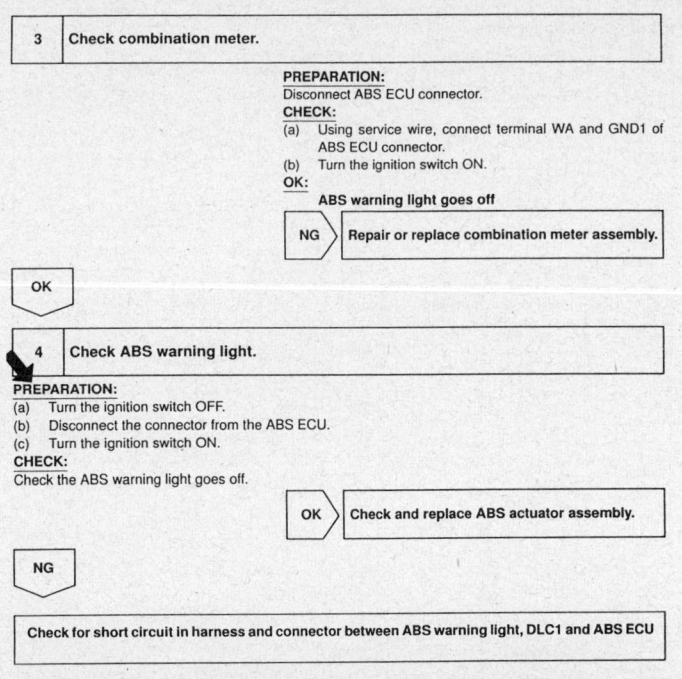

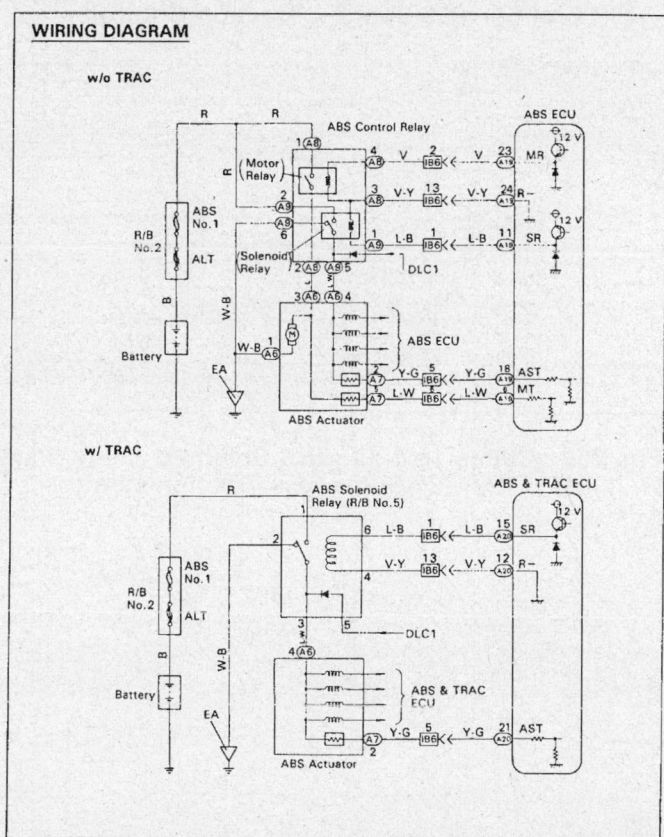

Fig. 257   Codes 11 & 12: ABS Solenoid Relay (Part 2 of 6). 1996 Supra

CIRCUIT DESCRIPTION

This relay supplies power to each ABS solenoid. After the ignition switch is turned on, if the initial check is OK, the relay goes on.

DTC No.	Diagnostic Trouble Code Detecting Condition	Trouble area
11	Conditions (1) and (2) continue for 0.2 sec. or more: (1) ABS solenoid relay (SR) terminal voltage: Battery positive voltage (2) Solenoid relay monitor terminal (AST) voltage: 0 V	• ABS solenoid relay • Open or short in ABS solenoid relay circuit • ECU
12	Conditions (1) and (2) continue for 0.2 sec. or more: (1) ABS solenoid relay (SR) terminal voltage: 0 V (2) Solenoid relay monitor terminal (AST) voltage: Battery positive voltage	• ABS solenoid relay • B+ short in ABS solenoid relay circuit • ECU

Fail safe function: If trouble occurs in the solenoid relay circuit, the ECU cuts off current to the solenoid relay and prohibits ABS control.

DIAGNOSTIC CHART

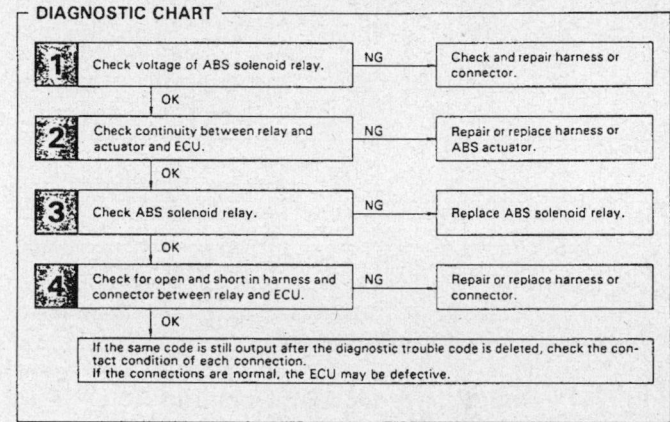

TY4029300083010X

Fig. 257   Codes 11 & 12: ABS Solenoid Relay (Part 1 of 6). 1996 Supra

INSPECTION PROCEDURE (w/o TRAC)

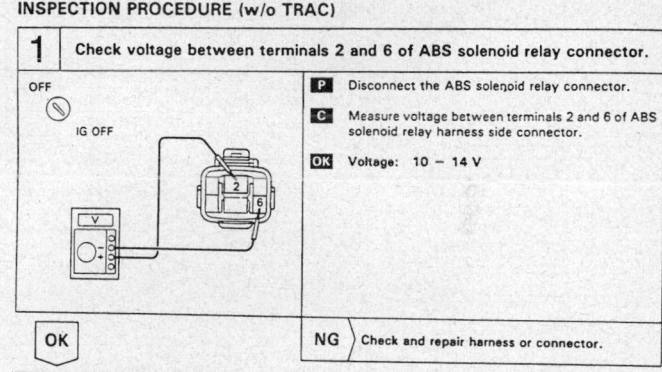

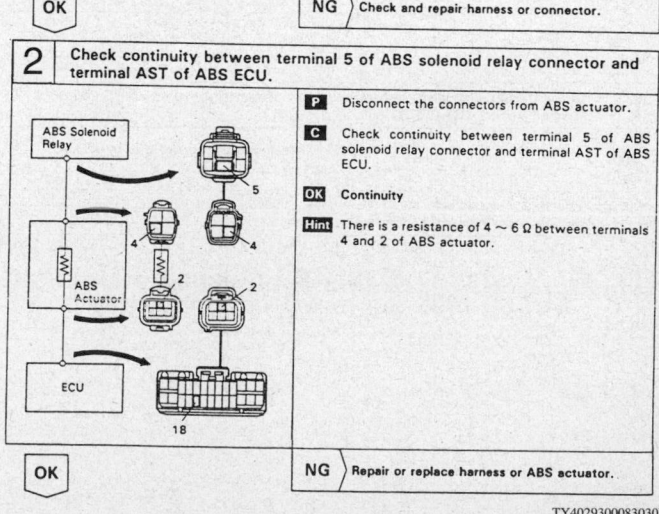

TY4029300083030X

Fig. 257   Codes 11 & 12: ABS Solenoid Relay (Part 3 of 6). 1996 Supra Less Traction Control

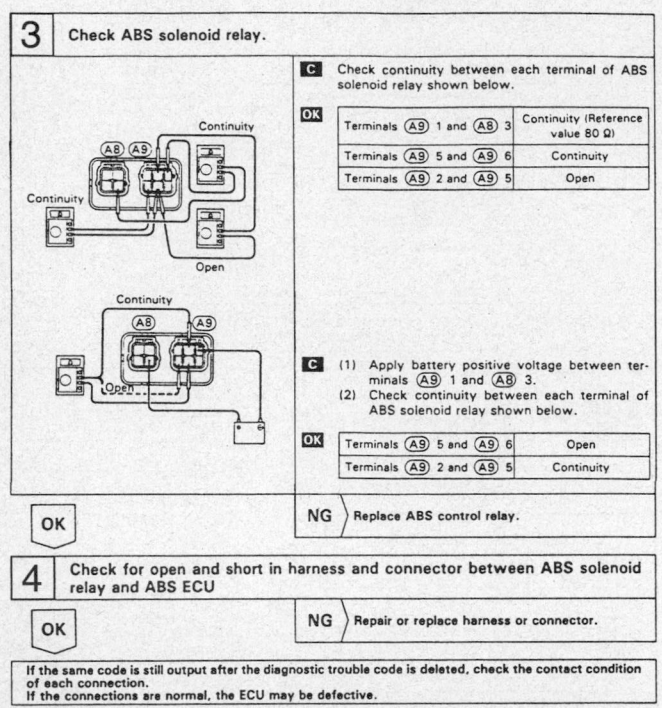

3 Check ABS solenoid relay.

C Check continuity between each terminal of ABS solenoid relay shown below.

OK

Terminals (A9) 1 and (A8) 3	Continuity (Reference value 80 Ω)
Terminals (A9) 5 and (A9) 6	Continuity
Terminals (A9) 2 and (A9) 5	Open

C
(1) Apply battery positive voltage between terminals (A9) 1 and (A8) 3.
(2) Check continuity between each terminal of ABS solenoid relay shown below.

OK

| Terminals (A9) 5 and (A9) 6 | Open |
| Terminals (A9) 2 and (A9) 5 | Continuity |

OK **NG** ▷ Replace ABS control relay.

4 Check for open and short in harness and connector between ABS solenoid relay and ABS ECU

OK **NG** ▷ Repair or replace harness or connector.

If the same code is still output after the diagnostic trouble code is deleted, check the contact condition of each connection.
If the connections are normal, the ECU may be defective.

TY4029300083040X

Fig. 257   Codes 11 & 12: ABS Solenoid Relay (Part 4 of 6). 1996 Supra Less Traction Control

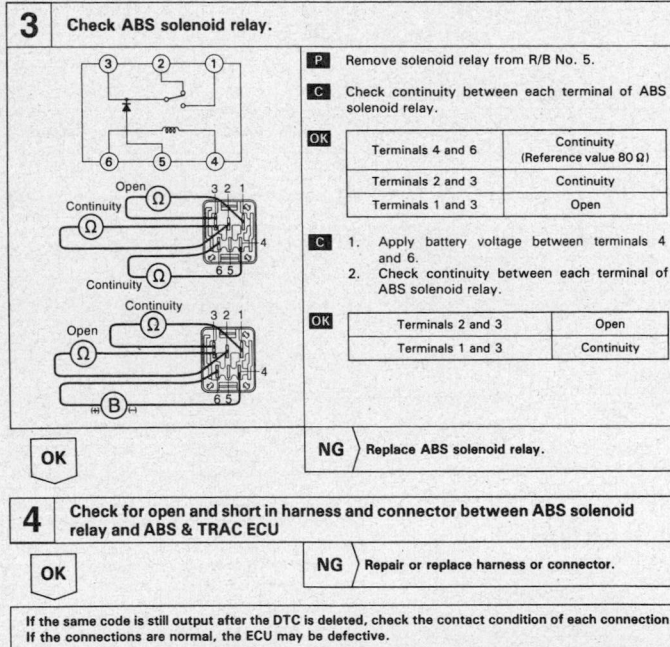

3 Check ABS solenoid relay.

P Remove solenoid relay from R/B No. 5.

C Check continuity between each terminal of ABS solenoid relay.

OK

Terminals 4 and 6	Continuity (Reference value 80 Ω)
Terminals 2 and 3	Continuity
Terminals 1 and 3	Open

C
1. Apply battery voltage between terminals 4 and 6.
2. Check continuity between each terminal of ABS solenoid relay.

OK

| Terminals 2 and 3 | Open |
| Terminals 1 and 3 | Continuity |

OK **NG** ▷ Replace ABS solenoid relay.

4 Check for open and short in harness and connector between ABS solenoid relay and ABS & TRAC ECU

OK **NG** ▷ Repair or replace harness or connector.

If the same code is still output after the DTC is deleted, check the contact condition of each connection.
If the connections are normal, the ECU may be defective.

TY4029300083060X

Fig. 257   Codes 11 & 12: ABS Solenoid Relay (Part 6 of 6). 1996 Supra w/Traction Control

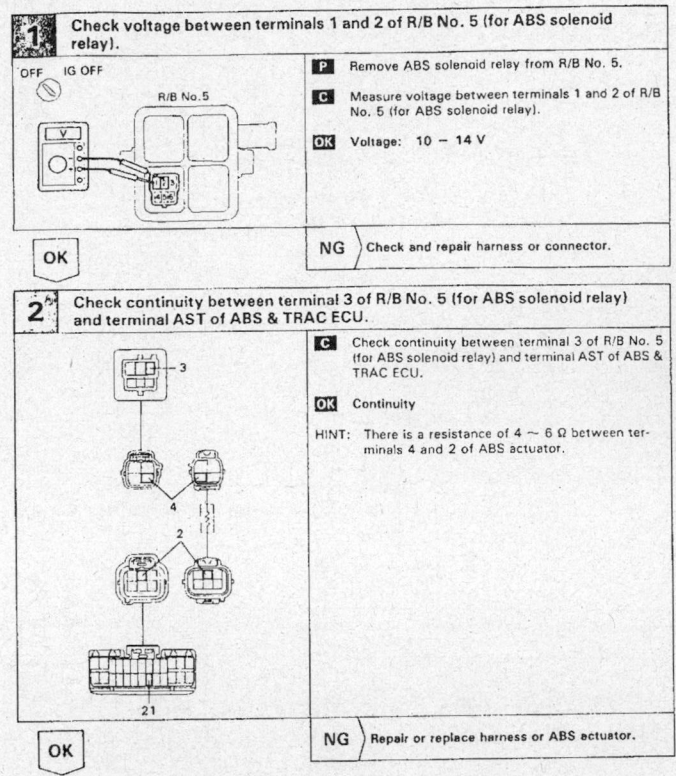

1 Check voltage between terminals 1 and 2 of R/B No. 5 (for ABS solenoid relay).

OFF   IG OFF   R/B No. 5

P Remove ABS solenoid relay from R/B No. 5.

C Measure voltage between terminals 1 and 2 of R/B No. 5 (for ABS solenoid relay).

OK Voltage: 10 ~ 14 V

OK **NG** ▷ Check and repair harness or connector.

2 Check continuity between terminal 3 of R/B No. 5 (for ABS solenoid relay) and terminal AST of ABS & TRAC ECU.

C Check continuity between terminal 3 of R/B No. 5 (for ABS solenoid relay) and terminal AST of ABS & TRAC ECU.

OK Continuity

HINT: There is a resistance of 4 ~ 6 Ω between terminals 4 and 2 of ABS actuator.

OK **NG** ▷ Repair or replace harness or ABS actuator.

TY4029300083050X

Fig. 257   Codes 11 & 12: ABS Solenoid Relay (Part 5 of 6). 1996 Supra w/Traction Control

---

CIRCUIT DESCRIPTION

This relay supplies power to each ABS solenoid. After the ignition switch is turned ON, if the initial check is OK, the relay goes on.

DTC No.	DTC Detecting Condition	Trouble Area
11	Conditions (1) and (2) continue for 0.2 sec. or more: (1) ABS solenoid relay terminal (SR) voltage: Below 1.5 V (2) Solenoid relay monitor terminal (AST) voltage: 0 V	• ABS solenoid relay • Open or short in ABS solenoid relay circuit
12	Conditions (1) and (2) continue for 0.2 sec. or more: (1) ABS solenoid relay terminal (SR) voltage: Battery positive voltage (2) Solenoid relay monitor terminal (AST) voltage: Battery positive voltage	• ABS solenoid relay • B+ short in ABS solenoid relay circuit

Fail safe function: If trouble occurs in the ABS solenoid relay circuit, the ECU cuts off current to the ABS solenoid relay and prohibits ABS control.

TY4029700410010X

Fig. 258   Codes 11 & 12: ABS Solenoid Relay (Part 1 of 7). 1997–98 Supra less Traction Control

WIRING DIAGRAM

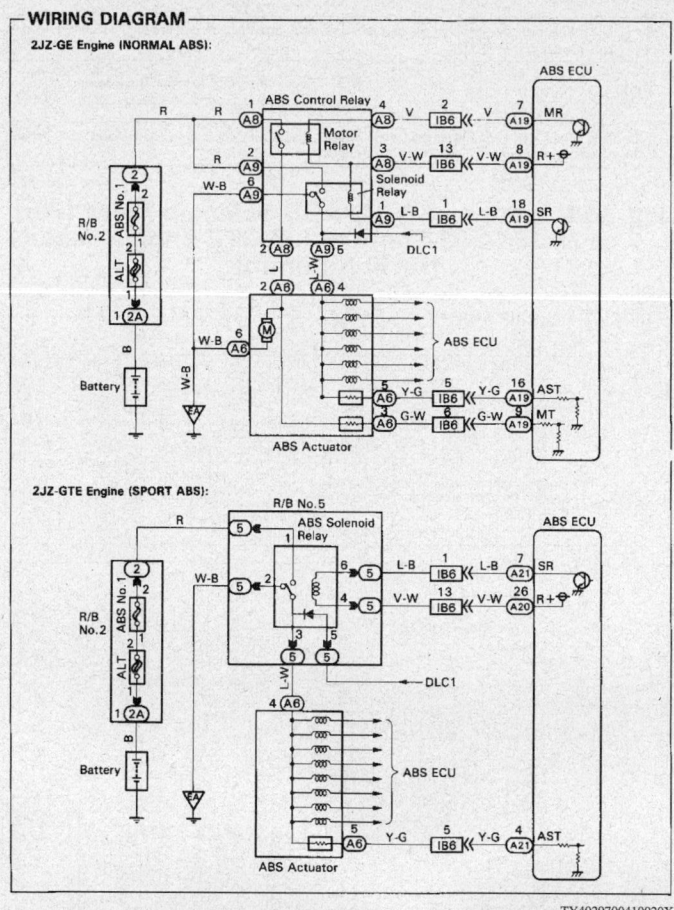

2JZ-GE Engine (NORMAL ABS):

2JZ-GTE Engine (SPORT ABS):

TY4029700410020X

Fig. 258   Codes 11 & 12: ABS Solenoid Relay (Part 2 of 7). 1997–98 Supra Less Traction Control

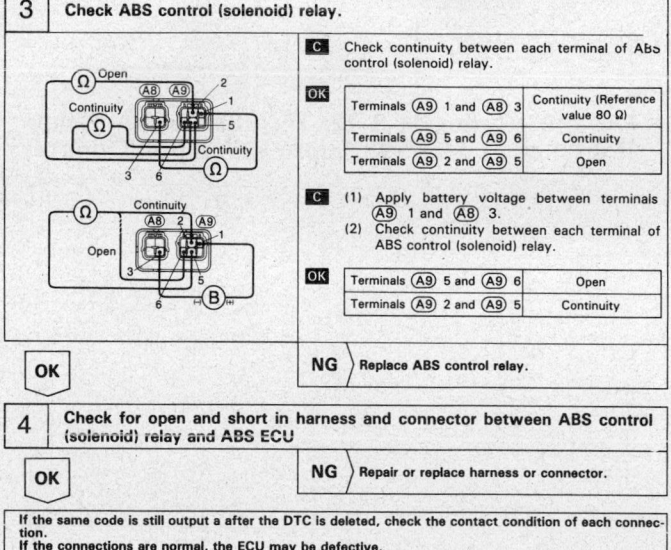

3	Check ABS control (solenoid) relay.

C Check continuity between each terminal of ABS control (solenoid) relay.

OK

Terminals (A9) 1 and (A8) 3	Continuity (Reference value 80 Ω)
Terminals (A9) 5 and (A9) 6	Continuity
Terminals (A9) 2 and (A9) 5	Open

C (1) Apply battery voltage between terminals (A9) 1 and (A8) 3.
(2) Check continuity between each terminal of ABS control (solenoid) relay.

OK

Terminals (A9) 5 and (A9) 6	Open
Terminals (A9) 2 and (A9) 5	Continuity

OK   **NG** Replace ABS control relay.

4	Check for open and short in harness and connector between ABS control (solenoid) relay and ABS ECU

OK   **NG** Repair or replace harness or connector.

If the same code is still output after the DTC is deleted, check the contact condition of each connection.
If the connections are normal, the ECU may be defective.

TY4029700410040X

Fig. 258   Codes 11 & 12: ABS Solenoid Relay (Part 4 of 7). 1997–98 Supra w/2JZ-GE Engine Less Traction Control

1	Check voltage between terminals (A9) 2 and (A9) 6 of ABS control (solenoid) relay connector.

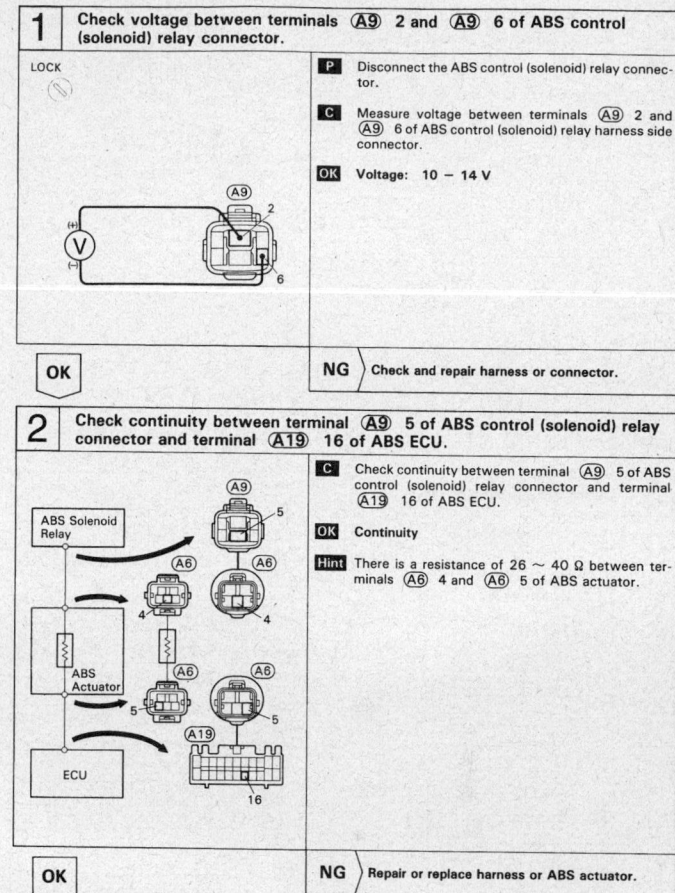

P Disconnect the ABS control (solenoid) relay connector.

C Measure voltage between terminals (A9) 2 and (A9) 6 of ABS control (solenoid) relay harness side connector.

OK Voltage: 10 – 14 V

OK   **NG** Check and repair harness or connector.

2	Check continuity between terminal (A9) 5 of ABS control (solenoid) relay connector and terminal (A19) 16 of ABS ECU.

C Check continuity between terminal (A9) 5 of ABS control (solenoid) relay connector and terminal (A19) 16 of ABS ECU.

OK Continuity

Hint There is a resistance of 26 ~ 40 Ω between terminals (A6) 4 and (A6) 5 of ABS actuator.

OK   **NG** Repair or replace harness or ABS actuator.

TY4029700410030X

Fig. 258   Codes 11 & 12: ABS Solenoid Relay (Part 3 of 7). 1997–98 Supra w/2JZ-GE Engine Less Traction Control

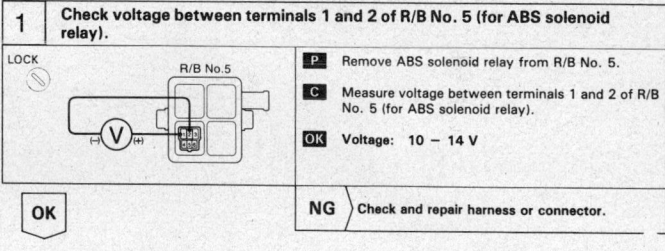

1	Check voltage between terminals 1 and 2 of R/B No. 5 (for ABS solenoid relay).

P Remove ABS solenoid relay from R/B No. 5.

C Measure voltage between terminals 1 and 2 of R/B No. 5 (for ABS solenoid relay).

OK Voltage: 10 – 14 V

OK   **NG** Check and repair harness or connector.

TY4029700410050X

Fig. 258   Codes 11 & 12: ABS Solenoid Relay (Part 5 of 7). 1997–98 Supra w/2JZ-GTE Engine Less Traction Control

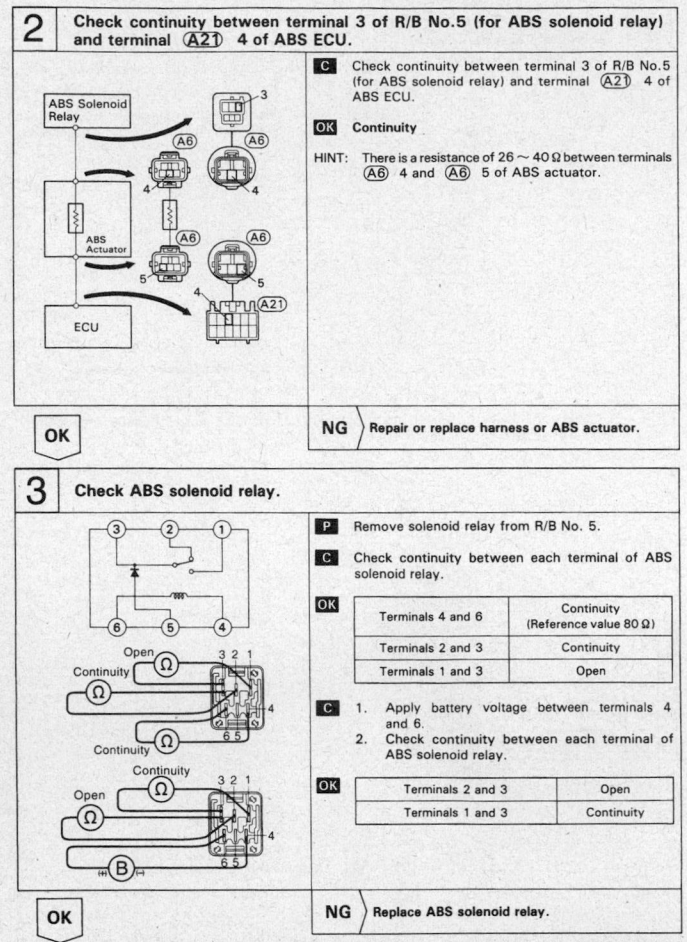

2 Check continuity between terminal 3 of R/B No.5 (for ABS solenoid relay) and terminal (A21) 4 of ABS ECU.

C Check continuity between terminal 3 of R/B No.5 (for ABS solenoid relay) and terminal (A21) 4 of ABS ECU.

OK Continuity

HINT: There is a resistance of 26 ~ 40 Ω between terminals (A6) 4 and (A6) 5 of ABS actuator.

OK

NG > Repair or replace harness or ABS actuator.

3 Check ABS solenoid relay.

P Remove solenoid relay from R/B No. 5.

C Check continuity between each terminal of ABS solenoid relay.

OK

Terminals 4 and 6	Continuity (Reference value 80 Ω)
Terminals 2 and 3	Continuity
Terminals 1 and 3	Open

C 1. Apply battery voltage between terminals 4 and 6.
2. Check continuity between each terminal of ABS solenoid relay.

OK

Terminals 2 and 3	Open
Terminals 1 and 3	Continuity

OK

NG > Replace ABS solenoid relay.

TY4029700410060X

Fig. 258   Codes 11 & 12: ABS Solenoid Relay (Part 6 of 7). 1997–98 Supra w/2JZ-GTE Engine Less Traction Control

4 Check for open and short in harness and connector between ABS solenoid relay and ABS ECU

OK

NG > Repair or replace harness or connector.

If the same code is still output after the DTC is deleted, check the contact condition of each connection. If the connections are normal, the ECU may be defective.

TY4029700410070X

Fig. 258   Codes 11 & 12: ABS Solenoid Relay (Part 7 of 7). 1997–98 Supra w/2JZ-GTE Engine Less Traction Control

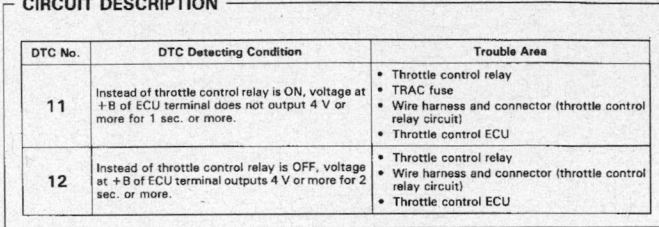

CIRCUIT DESCRIPTION

DTC No.	DTC Detecting Condition	Trouble Area
11	Instead of throttle control relay is ON, voltage at +B of ECU terminal does not output 4 V or more for 1 sec. or more.	• Throttle control relay • TRAC fuse • Wire harness and connector (throttle control relay circuit) • Throttle control ECU
12	Instead of throttle control relay is OFF, voltage at +B of ECU terminal outputs 4 V or more for 2 sec. or more.	• Throttle control relay • Wire harness and connector (throttle control relay circuit) • Throttle control ECU

WIRING DIAGRAM

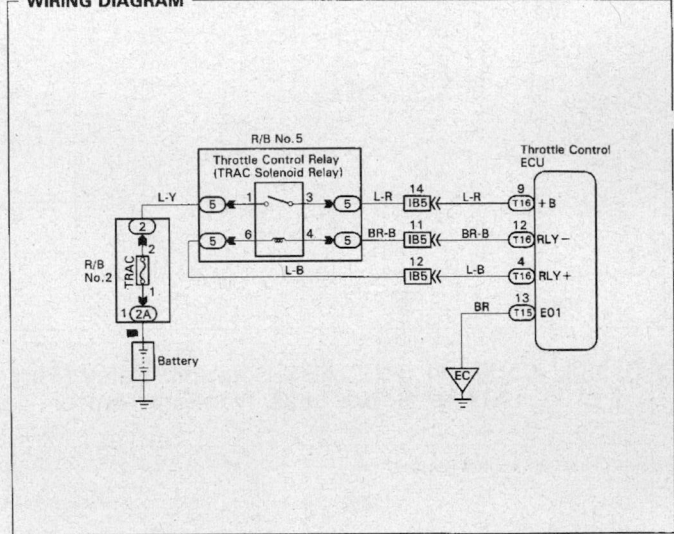

TY4029700412010X

Fig. 259   Codes 11 & 12: Throttle Control Relay (Part 1 of 3). 1997–98 Supra w/Traction Control

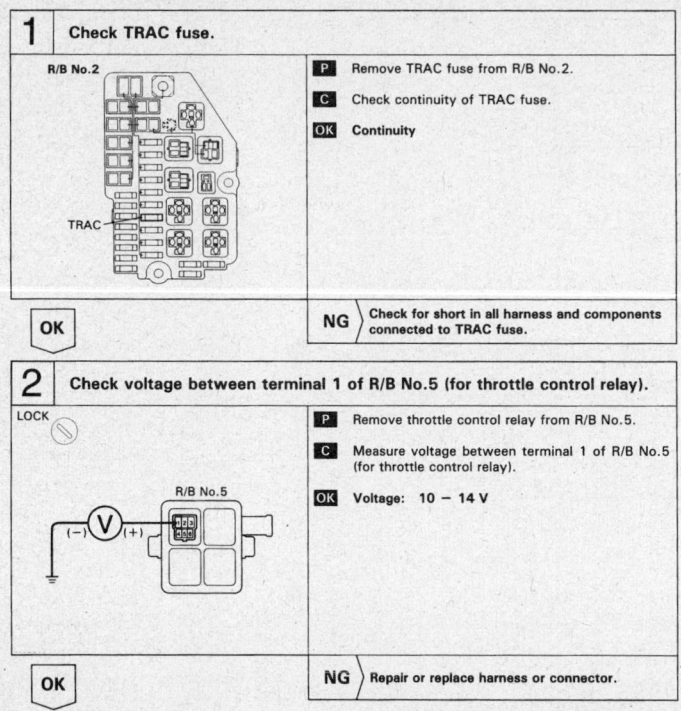

1 Check TRAC fuse.

R/B No.2

TRAC

P	Remove TRAC fuse from R/B No.2.
C	Check continuity of TRAC fuse.
OK	Continuity

OK

NG ▷ Check for short in all harness and components connected to TRAC fuse.

2 Check voltage between terminal 1 of R/B No.5 (for throttle control relay).

LOCK

R/B No.5

(−) V (+)

P	Remove throttle control relay from R/B No.5.
C	Measure voltage between terminal 1 of R/B No.5 (for throttle control relay).
OK	Voltage: 10 − 14 V

OK

NG ▷ Repair or replace harness or connector.

TY4029700412020X

Fig. 259 Codes 11 & 12: Throttle Control Relay (Part 2 of 3). 1997–98 Supra w/Traction Control

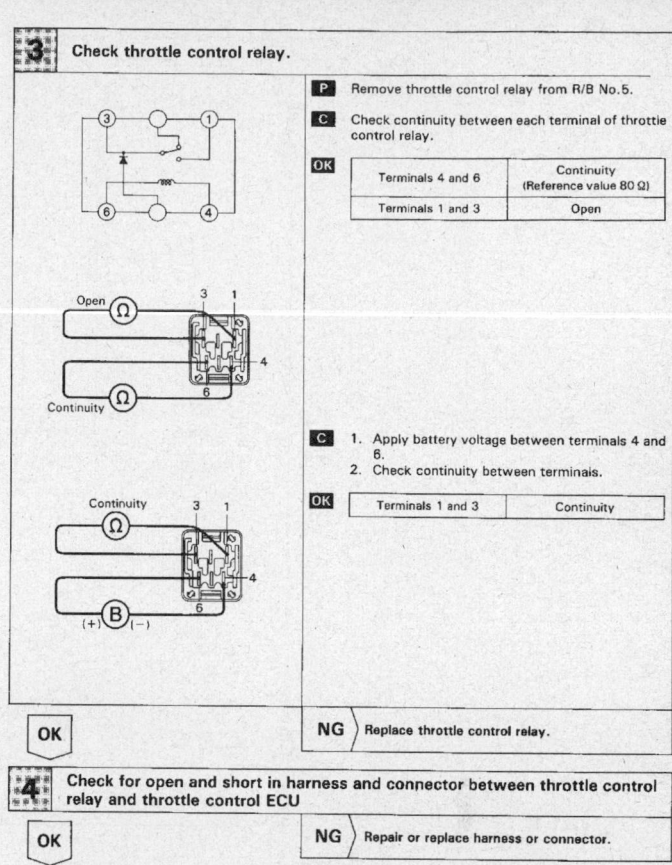

3 Check throttle control relay.

| P | Remove throttle control relay from R/B No.5. |
| C | Check continuity between each terminal of throttle control relay. |

| OK | Terminals 4 and 6 | Continuity (Reference value 80 Ω) |
| | Terminals 1 and 3 | Open |

Open Ω
Continuity Ω

| C | 1. Apply battery voltage between terminals 4 and 6. |
| | 2. Check continuity between terminals. |

| OK | Terminals 1 and 3 | Continuity |

Continuity Ω
B (+) (−)

OK

NG ▷ Replace throttle control relay.

4 Check for open and short in harness and connector between throttle control relay and throttle control ECU.

OK

NG ▷ Repair or replace harness or connector.

If the same code is still output after the DTC is deleted, check the contact condition of each connection. If the connections are normal, the ECU may be defective.

TY4029700412030X

Fig. 259 Codes 11 & 12: Throttle Control Relay (Part 3 of 3). 1997–98 Supra w/Traction Control

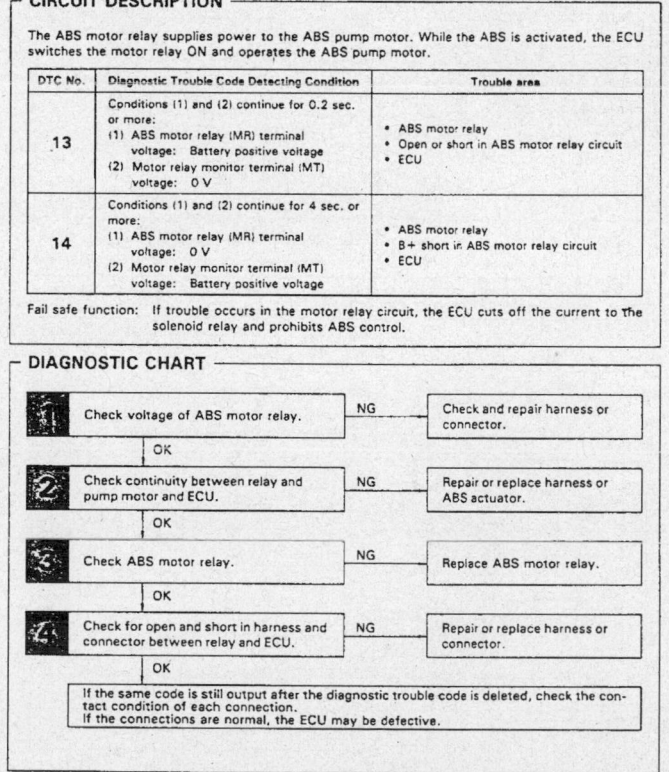

─ CIRCUIT DESCRIPTION ─

The ABS motor relay supplies power to the ABS pump motor. While the ABS is activated, the ECU switches the motor relay ON and operates the ABS pump motor.

DTC No.	Diagnostic Trouble Code Detecting Condition	Trouble area
13	Conditions (1) and (2) continue for 0.2 sec. or more: (1) ABS motor relay (MR) terminal voltage: Battery positive voltage (2) Motor relay monitor terminal (MT) voltage: 0 V	• ABS motor relay • Open or short in ABS motor relay circuit • ECU
14	Conditions (1) and (2) continue for 4 sec. or more: (1) ABS motor relay (MR) terminal voltage: 0 V (2) Motor relay monitor terminal (MT) voltage: Battery positive voltage	• ABS motor relay • B+ short in ABS motor relay circuit • ECU

Fail safe function: If trouble occurs in the motor relay circuit, the ECU cuts off the current to the solenoid relay and prohibits ABS control.

─ DIAGNOSTIC CHART ─

| 1 | Check voltage of ABS motor relay. | NG | Check and repair harness or connector. |
| OK |
| 2 | Check continuity between relay and pump motor and ECU. | NG | Repair or replace harness or ABS actuator. |
| OK |
| 3 | Check ABS motor relay. | NG | Replace ABS motor relay. |
| OK |
| 4 | Check for open and short in harness and connector between relay and ECU. | NG | Repair or replace harness or connector. |
| OK |

If the same code is still output after the diagnostic trouble code is deleted, check the contact condition of each connection.
If the connections are normal, the ECU may be defective.

TY4029300084010X

Fig. 260 Codes 13 & 14: ABS Motor Relay (Part 1 of 4). 1996 Supra

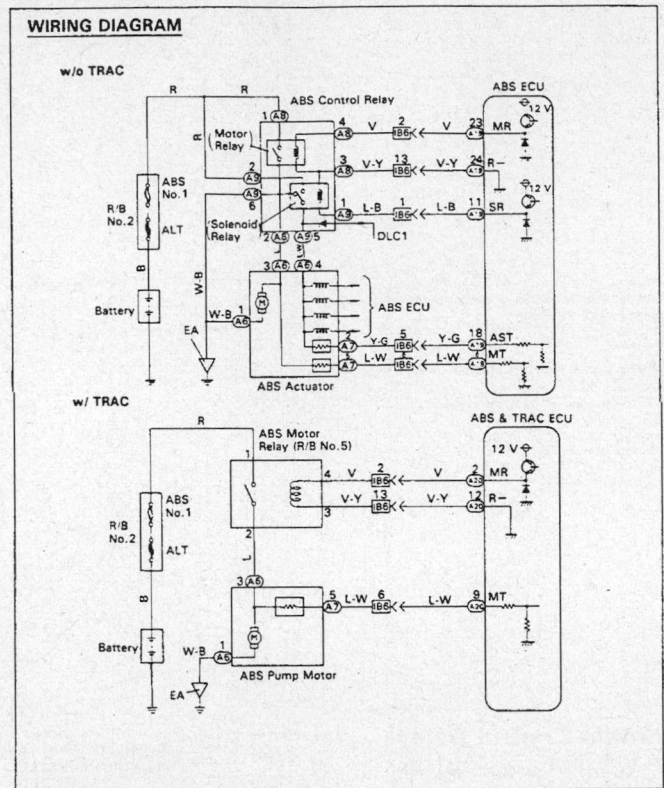

Fig. 260 Codes 13 & 14: ABS Motor Relay (Part 2 of 4). 1996 Supra

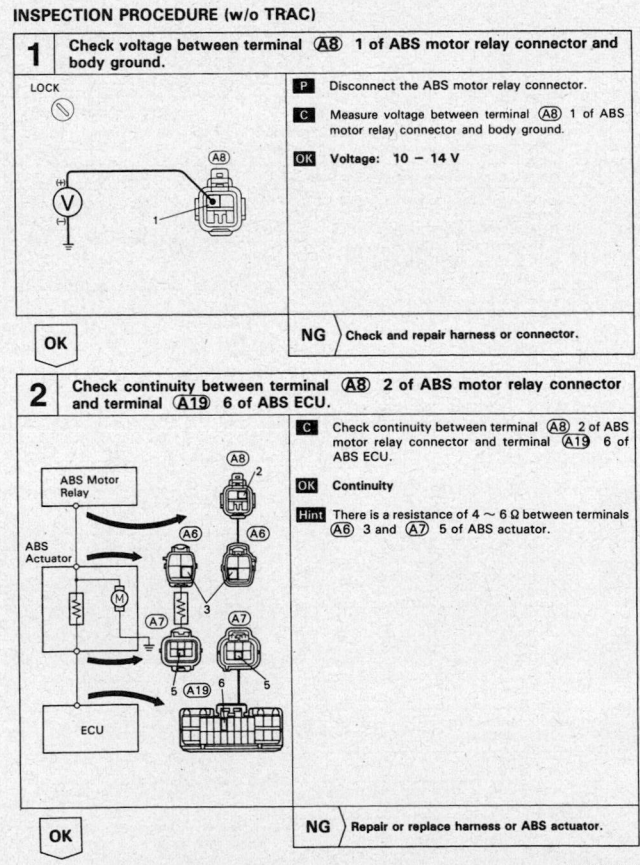

TY4029300084030X

Fig. 260 Codes 13 & 14: ABS Motor Relay (Part 3 of 4). 1996 Supra Less Traction Control

INSPECTION PROCEDURE (w/ TRAC)

1 Check voltage between terminal 1 of R/B No. 5 (for ABS motor relay) and body ground.

OFF IG OFF

R/B No.5

P Remove ABS motor relay from R/B No. 5.

C Measure voltage between terminal 1 of R/B No. 5 (for ABS motor relay) and body ground.

OK Voltage: 10 – 14 V

OK | NG > Check and repair harness or connector.

2 Check continuity between terminal 2 of R/B No. 5 (for ABS motor relay) and terminal MT of ABS & TRAC ECU.

C Check continuity between terminal 2 of R/B No. 5 (for ABS motor relay) and terminal MT of ABS & TRAC ECU.

OK Continuity

HINT: There is a resistance of 4 ~ 6 Ω between terminals 3 and 5 of ABS actuator.

OK | NG > Repair or replace harness or ABS actuator.

TY4029300084050X

Fig. 260 Codes 13 & 14: ABS Motor Relay (Part 3 of 4). 1996 Supra w/Traction Control

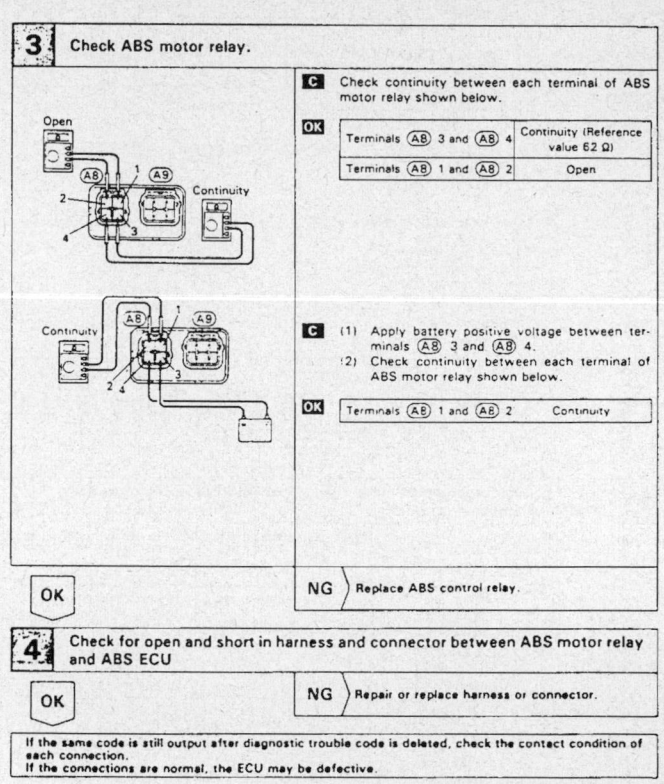

3 Check ABS motor relay.

Open

Continuity

Continuity

C Check continuity between each terminal of ABS motor relay shown below.

OK

| Terminals (AB) 3 and (AB) 4 | Continuity (Reference value 62 Ω) |
| Terminals (AB) 1 and (AB) 2 | Open |

C (1) Apply battery positive voltage between terminals (AB) 3 and (AB) 4.
(2) Check continuity between each terminal of ABS motor relay shown below.

OK | Terminals (AB) 1 and (AB) 2 | Continuity |

OK | NG > Replace ABS control relay.

4 Check for open and short in harness and connector between ABS motor relay and ABS ECU

OK | NG > Repair or replace harness or connector.

If the same code is still output after diagnostic trouble code is deleted, check the contact condition of each connection.
If the connections are normal, the ECU may be defective.

TY4029300084040X

Fig. 260 Codes 13 & 14: ABS Motor Relay (Part 4 of 4). 1996 Supra Less Traction Control

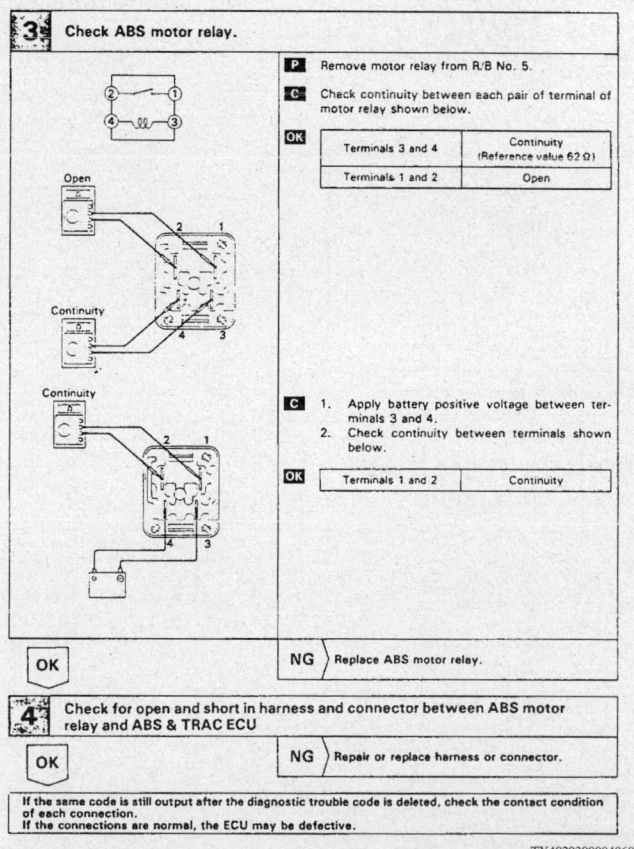

3 Check ABS motor relay.

P Remove motor relay from R/B No. 5.

C Check continuity between each pair of terminal of motor relay shown below.

OK

| Terminals 3 and 4 | Continuity (Reference value 62 Ω) |
| Terminals 1 and 2 | Open |

Open

Continuity

Continuity

C 1. Apply battery positive voltage between terminals 3 and 4.
2. Check continuity between terminals shown below.

OK | Terminals 1 and 2 | Continuity |

OK | NG > Replace ABS motor relay.

4 Check for open and short in harness and connector between ABS motor relay and ABS & TRAC ECU

OK | NG > Repair or replace harness or connector.

If the same code is still output after the diagnostic trouble code is deleted, check the contact condition of each connection.
If the connections are normal, the ECU may be defective.

TY4029300084060X

Fig. 260 Codes 13 & 14: ABS Motor Relay (Part 4 of 4). 1996 Supra w/Traction Control

CIRCUIT DESCRIPTION

The ABS motor relay supplies power to the ABS pump motor. While the ABS is activated, the ECU switches the motor relay ON and operates the ABS pump motor.

DTC No.	DTC Detecting Condition	Trouble Area
13	Conditions (1) and (2) continue for 0.2 sec. or more: (1) ABS motor relay terminal (MR) voltage: Below 1.5 V (2) Motor relay monitor terminal (MT) voltage: 0 V	• ABS motor relay • Open or short in ABS motor relay circuit
14	Conditions (1) and (2) continue for 4 sec. or more: (1) ABS motor relay terminal (MR) voltage: Battery positive voltage (2) Motor relay monitor terminal (MT) voltage: Battery positive voltage	• ABS motor relay • B+ short in ABS motor relay circuit

Fail safe function: If trouble occurs in the ABS motor relay circuit, the ECU cuts off the current to the ABS solenoid relay and prohibits ABS control.

TY4029700413010X

Fig. 261   Codes 13 & 14: ABS Motor Relay (Part 1 of 7). 1997–98 Supra

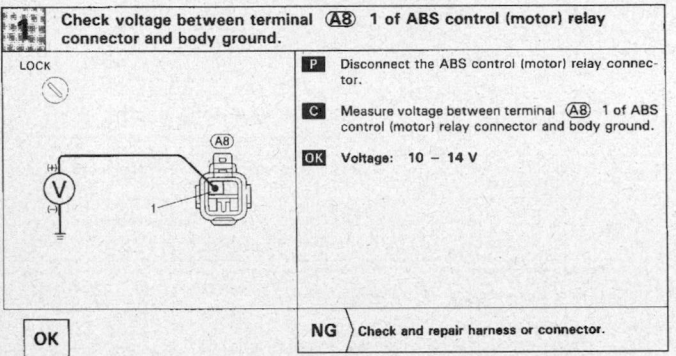

1 Check voltage between terminal (A8) 1 of ABS control (motor) relay connector and body ground.

P Disconnect the ABS control (motor) relay connector.

C Measure voltage between terminal (A8) 1 of ABS control (motor) relay connector and body ground.

OK Voltage: 10 – 14 V

OK ▷

NG ▷ Check and repair harness or connector.

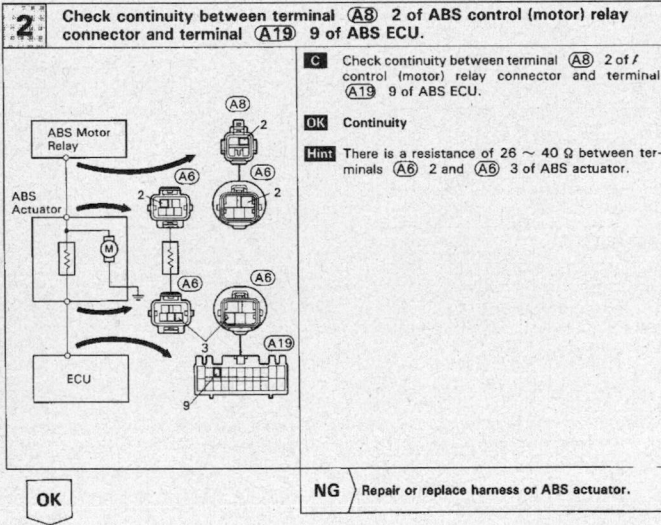

2 Check continuity between terminal (A8) 2 of ABS control (motor) relay connector and terminal (A19) 9 of ABS ECU.

C Check continuity between terminal (A8) 2 of ABS control (motor) relay connector and terminal (A19) 9 of ABS ECU.

OK Continuity

Hint There is a resistance of 26 ~ 40 Ω between terminals (A6) 2 and (A6) 3 of ABS actuator.

OK ▷

NG ▷ Repair or replace harness or ABS actuator.

TY4029700413030X

Fig. 261   Codes 13 & 14: ABS Motor Relay (Part 3 of 7). 1997–98 Supra w/2JZ-GE Engine

WIRING DIAGRAM

2JZ-GE Engine (NORMAL ABS):

2JZ-GTE Engine (SPORT ABS):

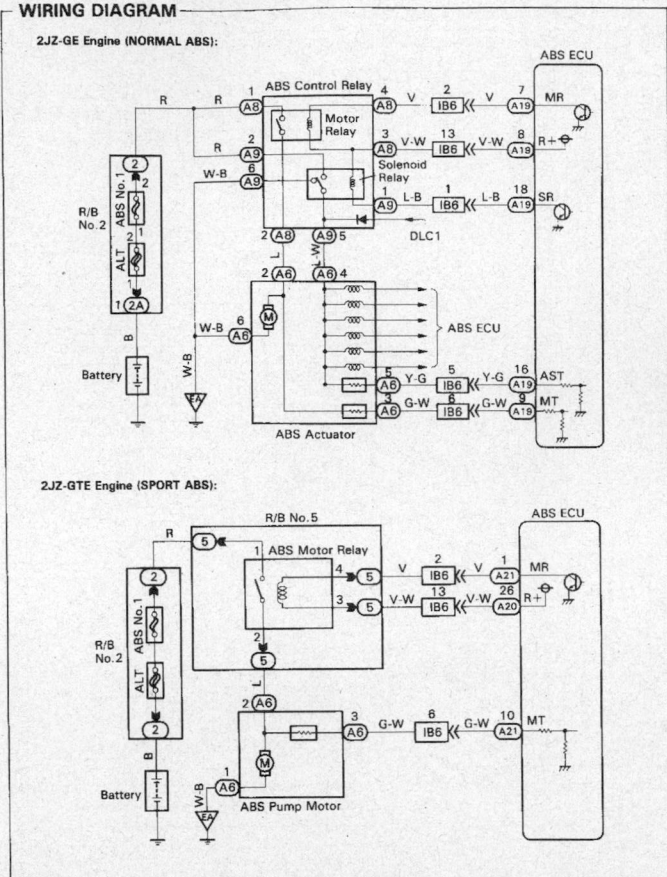

TY4029700413020X

Fig. 261   Codes 13 & 14: ABS Motor Relay (Part 2 of 7). 1997–98 Supra

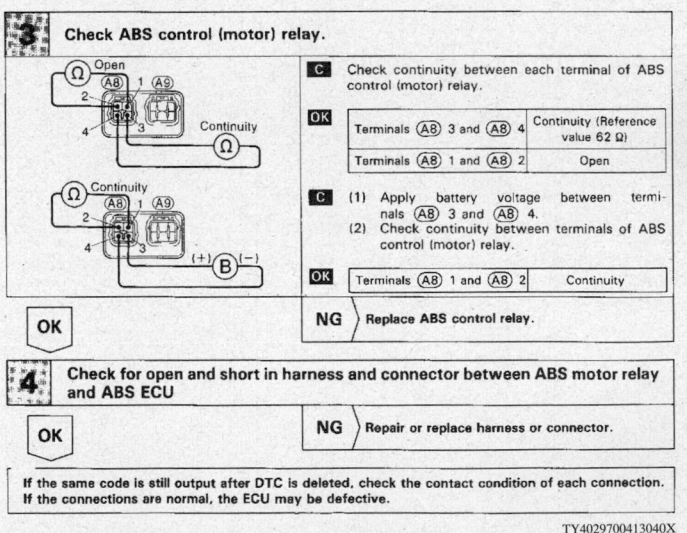

3 Check ABS control (motor) relay.

C Check continuity between each terminal of ABS control (motor) relay.

OK	Terminals (A8) 3 and (A8) 4	Continuity (Reference value 62 Ω)
	Terminals (A8) 1 and (A8) 2	Open

C (1) Apply battery voltage between terminals (A8) 3 and (A8) 4.
 (2) Check continuity between terminals of ABS control (motor) relay.

OK	Terminals (A8) 1 and (A8) 2	Continuity

OK ▷

NG ▷ Replace ABS control relay.

4 Check for open and short in harness and connector between ABS motor relay and ABS ECU

OK ▷

NG ▷ Repair or replace harness or connector.

If the same code is still output after DTC is deleted, check the contact condition of each connection. If the connections are normal, the ECU may be defective.

TY4029700413040X

Fig. 261   Codes 13 & 14: ABS Motor Relay (Part 4 of 7). 1997–98 Supra w/2JZ-GE Engine

1 Check voltage between terminal 1 of R/B No. 5 (for ABS motor relay) and body ground.

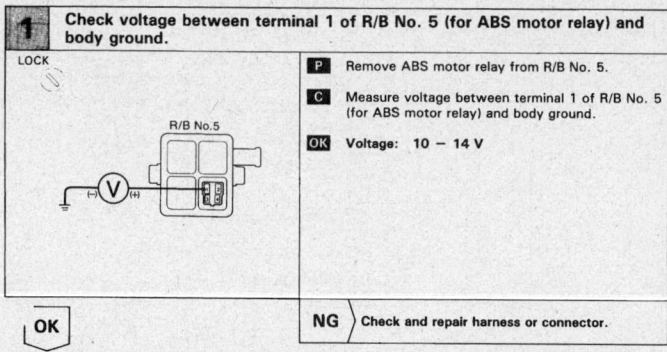

P Remove ABS motor relay from R/B No. 5.

C Measure voltage between terminal 1 of R/B No. 5 (for ABS motor relay) and body ground.

OK Voltage: 10 – 14 V

OK ↓

NG ▷ Check and repair harness or connector.

TY4029700413050X

Fig. 261   Codes 13 & 14: ABS Motor Relay (Part 5 of 7). 1997–98 Supra w/2JZ-GTE Engine

2 Check continuity between terminal 2 of R/B No.5 (for ABS motor relay) and terminal (A21) 10 of ABS ECU.

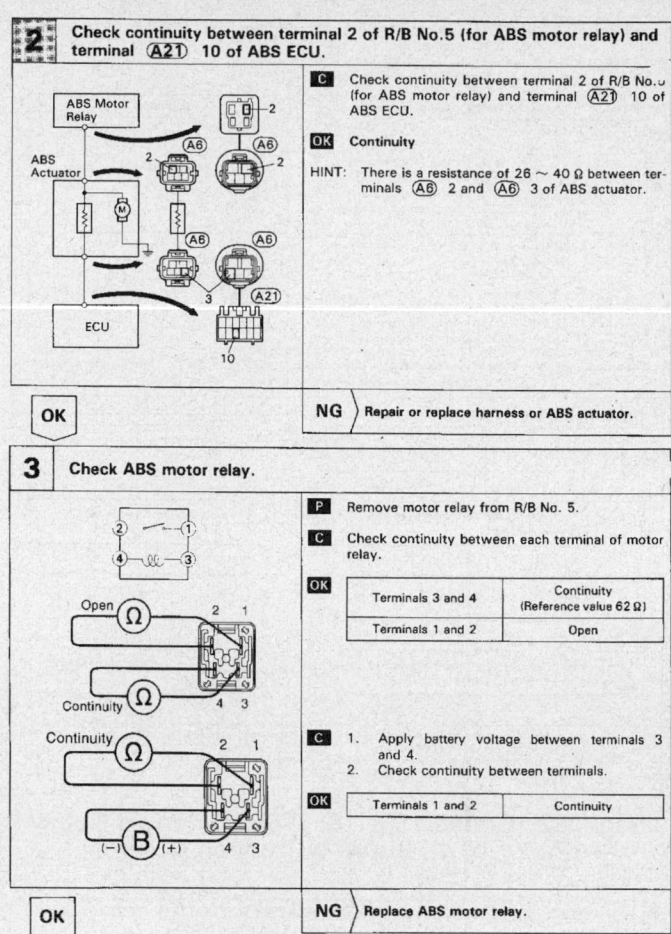

C Check continuity between terminal 2 of R/B No.5 (for ABS motor relay) and terminal (A21) 10 of ABS ECU.

OK Continuity

HINT: There is a resistance of 26 ~ 40 Ω between terminals (A6) 2 and (A6) 3 of ABS actuator.

OK ↓

NG ▷ Repair or replace harness or ABS actuator.

3 Check ABS motor relay.

P Remove motor relay from R/B No. 5.

C Check continuity between each terminal of motor relay.

OK

Terminals 3 and 4	Continuity (Reference value 62 Ω)
Terminals 1 and 2	Open

C 1. Apply battery voltage between terminals 3 and 4.
2. Check continuity between terminals.

OK

Terminals 1 and 2	Continuity

OK ↓

NG ▷ Replace ABS motor relay.

TY4029700413060X

Fig. 261   Codes 13 & 14: ABS Motor Relay (Part 6 of 7). 1997–98 Supra w/2JZ-GTE Engine

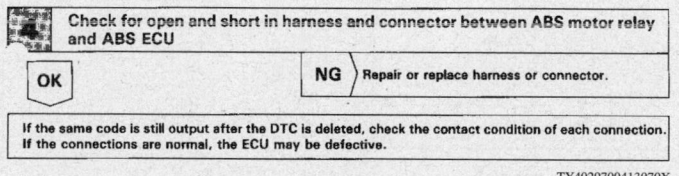

4 Check for open and short in harness and connector between ABS motor relay and ABS ECU

OK ↓

NG ▷ Repair or replace harness or connector.

If the same code is still output after the DTC is deleted, check the contact condition of each connection. If the connections are normal, the ECU may be defective.

TY4029700413070X

Fig. 261   Codes 13 & 14: ABS Motor Relay (Part 7 of 7). 1997–98 Supra w/2JZ-GTE Engine

CIRCUIT DESCRIPTION

This relay circuit supplies power to each traction actuator solenoid.
When the ignition switch is turned on, the relay goes on.

DTC No.	Diagnostic Trouble Code Detecting Condition	Trouble area
15	Conditions (1) through (3) continue for 0.2 sec. or more: (1) TRAC solenoid relay (TSR) terminal voltage: Battery positive voltage (2) All TRAC actuator solenoids: OFF (3) All TRAC actuator solenoid monitor voltages (in ECU): 0 V	• TRAC solenoid relay • Open or short in TRAC solenoid relay circuit • ECU
16	Conditions (1) through (3) continue for 0.2 sec. or more: (1) TRAC solenoid relay (TSR) terminal voltage: 0 V (2) All TRAC actuator solenoids: OFF (3) TRAC actuator solenoid monitor voltage (in ECU): Battery positive voltage	• TRAC solenoid relay • B+ short in TRAC solenoid relay circuit • ECU

Fail safe function: If trouble occurs in this relay circuit, the ECU cuts off current to the ABS and TRAC solenoid relays and prohibits ABS and TRAC control.

DIAGNOSTIC CHART

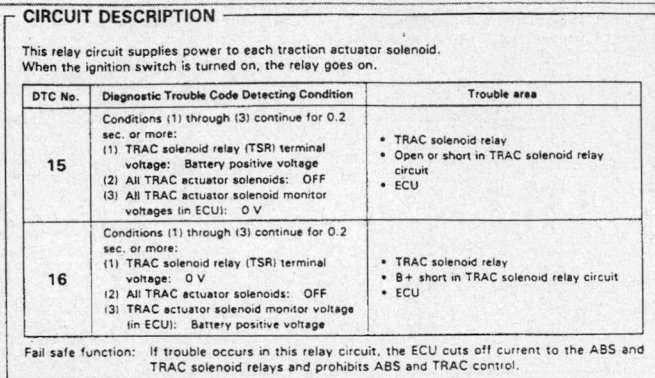

		NG	
1	Check voltage of TRAC solenoid relay.	→	Check and repair harness or connector.
2	Check continuity between relay and actuator and ECU.	→	Repair or replace harness or TRAC actuator.
3	Check TRAC solenoid relay.	→	Replace TRAC solenoid relay.
4	Check for open and short in harness and connector between relay and ECU.	→	Repair or replace harness or connector.

If the same code is still output after the diagnostic trouble code is deleted, check the contact condition of each connection.
If the connections are normal, the ECU may be defective.

TY4029300085010X

Fig. 262 Codes 15 & 16: TRAC Solenoid Relay (Part 1 of 4). Supra w/Traction Control

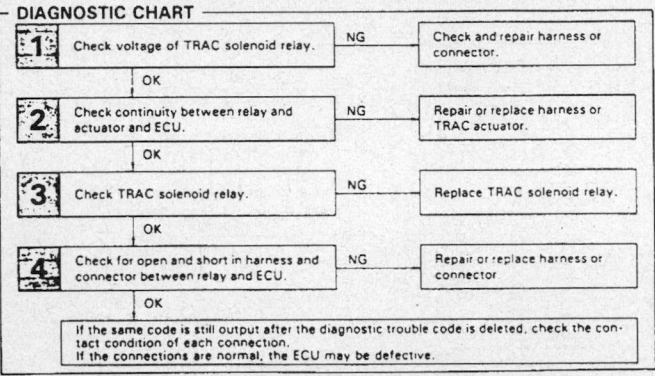

1 Check voltage between terminals 1 and 2 of R/B No. 5 (for TRAC solenoid relay).

P Remove TRAC solenoid relay from R/B No. 5.

C Measure voltage between terminals 1 and 2 of R/B No. 5 (for TRAC solenoid relay).

OK Voltage: 10 – 14 V

OFF IG OFF

OK | **NG** Repair or replace harness or connector.

2 Check continuity between terminal 3 of R/B No. 5 (for TRAC solenoid relay) and terminals SMC and SRC of ABS & TRAC ECU.

C Check continuity between terminal 3 of R/B No. 5 (for TRAC solenoid relay) and terminals SMC and SRC of ABS & TRAC ECU.

OK Continuity

HINT: Resistance of the TRAC actuator solenoid is 2 Ω.

OK | **NG** Repair or replace harness or TRAC actuator.

TY4029300085030X

Fig. 262 Codes 15 & 16: TRAC Solenoid Relay (Part 3 of 4). Supra w/Traction Control

WIRING DIAGRAM

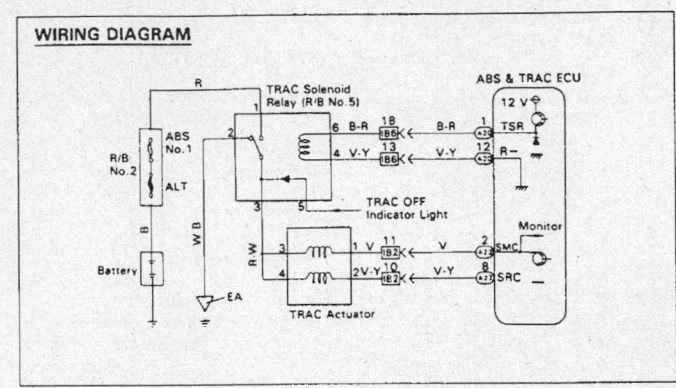

TY4029300085020X

Fig. 262 Codes 15 & 16: TRAC Solenoid Relay (Part 2 of 4). Supra w/Traction Control

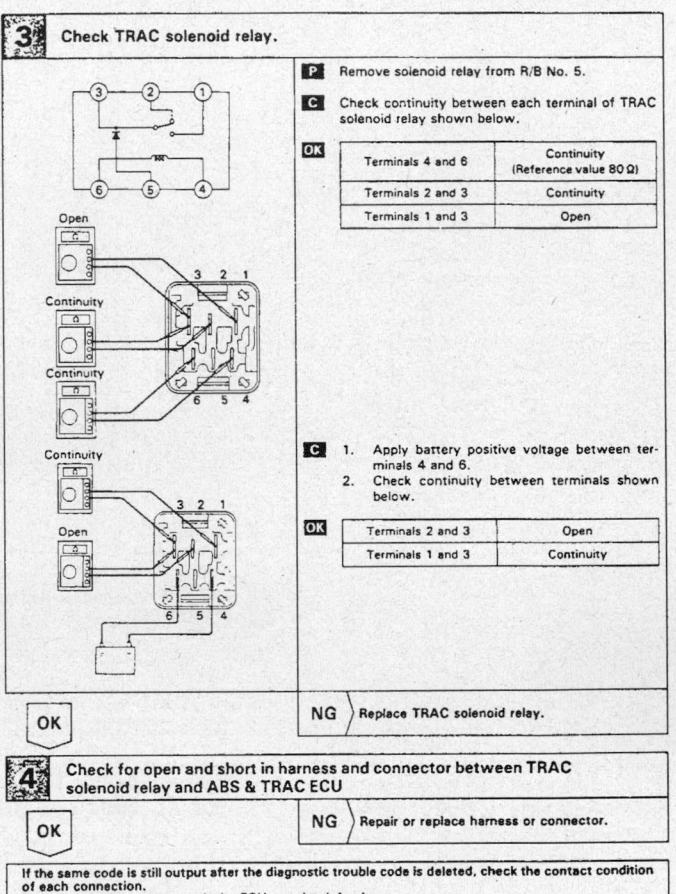

3 Check TRAC solenoid relay.

P Remove solenoid relay from R/B No. 5.

C Check continuity between each terminal of TRAC solenoid relay shown below.

OK

Terminals 4 and 6	Continuity (Reference value 80 Ω)
Terminals 2 and 3	Continuity
Terminals 1 and 3	Open

C
1. Apply battery positive voltage between terminals 4 and 6.
2. Check continuity between terminals shown below.

OK

Terminals 2 and 3	Open
Terminals 1 and 3	Continuity

OK | **NG** Replace TRAC solenoid relay.

4 Check for open and short in harness and connector between TRAC solenoid relay and ABS & TRAC ECU

OK | **NG** Repair or replace harness or connector.

If the same code is still output after the diagnostic trouble code is deleted, check the contact condition of each connection.
If the connections are normal, the ECU may be defective.

TY4029300085040X

Fig. 262 Codes 15 & 16: TRAC Solenoid Relay (Part 4 of 4). Supra w/Traction Control

CIRCUIT DESCRIPTION

This relay circuit supplies power to the TRAC pump motor. While the TRAC is activated, the ECU switches the motor relay ON and operates the TRAC pump motor.

DTC No.	Diagnostic Trouble Code Detecting Condition	Trouble area
17	Conditions (1) and (2) continue for 0.2 sec. or more. (1) TRAC motor relay terminal (TMR) voltage: Battery positive voltage (2) Voltage of ABS & TRAC ECU terminal MTT: 0 V	• TRAC motor relay • Open or short in TRAC motor relay circuit • ECU
18	Conditions (1) and (2) continue for 2 sec. or more. (1) TRAC motor relay terminal (TMR) voltage: 0 V (2) Voltage of ABS & TRAC ECU terminal MTT: Battery positive voltage	• TRAC motor relay • B+ short in TRAC motor relay circuit • ECU

Fail safe function: If trouble occurs in this relay circuit, the ECU cuts off current to the TRAC solenoid relay and prohibits TRAC control.

TY4029300086010X

Fig. 263   Codes 17 & 18: TRAC Motor Relay (Part 1 of 4). Supra w/Traction Control

INSPECTION PROCEDURE

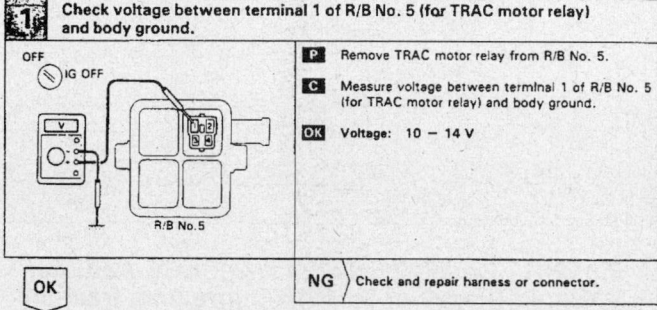

1 Check voltage between terminal 1 of R/B No. 5 (for TRAC motor relay) and body ground.

P Remove TRAC motor relay from R/B No. 5.

C Measure voltage between terminal 1 of R/B No. 5 (for TRAC motor relay) and body ground.

OK Voltage: 10 – 14 V

OK ↓

NG ▷ Check and repair harness or connector.

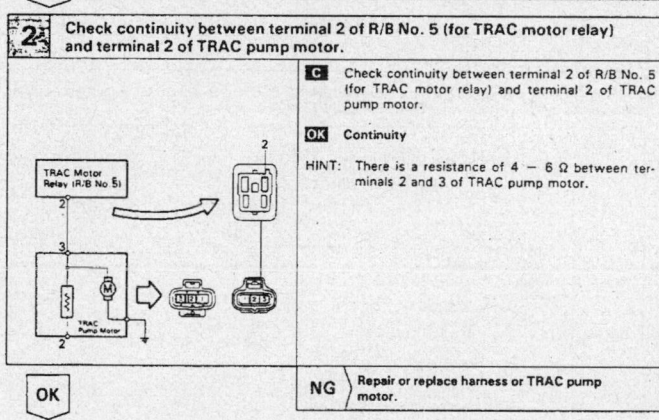

2 Check continuity between terminal 2 of R/B No. 5 (for TRAC motor relay) and terminal 2 of TRAC pump motor.

C Check continuity between terminal 2 of R/B No. 5 (for TRAC motor relay) and terminal 2 of TRAC pump motor.

OK Continuity

HINT: There is a resistance of 4 – 6 Ω between terminals 2 and 3 of TRAC pump motor.

OK ↓

NG ▷ Repair or replace harness or TRAC pump motor.

TY4029300086030X

Fig. 263   Codes 17 & 18: TRAC Motor Relay (Part 3 of 4). Supra w/Traction Control

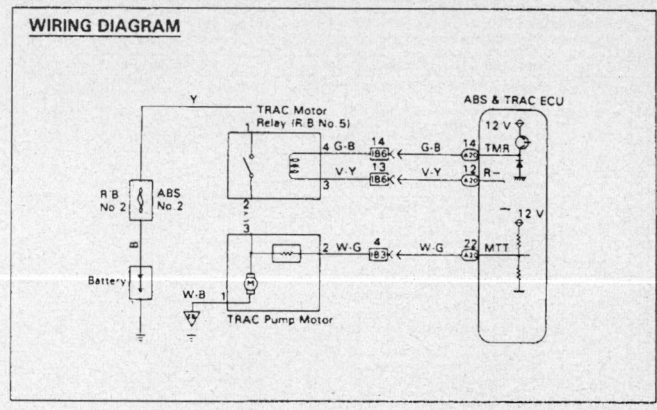

WIRING DIAGRAM

TY4029300086020X

Fig. 263   Codes 17 & 18: TRAC Motor Relay (Part 2 of 4). Supra w/Traction Control

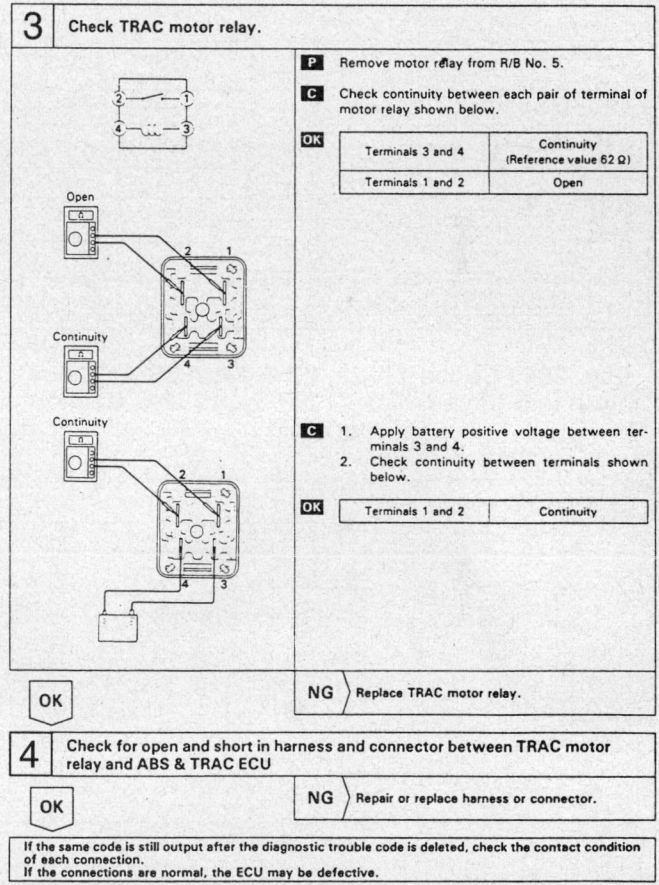

3 Check TRAC motor relay.

P Remove motor relay from R/B No. 5.

C Check continuity between each pair of terminal of motor relay shown below.

OK

Terminals 3 and 4	Continuity (Reference value 62 Ω)
Terminals 1 and 2	Open

C 1. Apply battery positive voltage between terminals 3 and 4.
 2. Check continuity between terminals shown below.

OK

Terminals 1 and 2	Continuity

OK ↓

NG ▷ Replace TRAC motor relay.

4 Check for open and short in harness and connector between TRAC motor relay and ABS & TRAC ECU

OK ↓

NG ▷ Repair or replace harness or connector.

If the same code is still output after the diagnostic trouble code is deleted, check the contact condition of each connection.
If the connections are normal, the ECU may be defective.

TY4029300086040X

Fig. 263   Codes 17 & 18: TRAC Motor Relay (Part 4 of 4). Supra w/Traction Control

CIRCUIT DESCRIPTION

This solenoid goes on when signals are received from the ECU and controls the fluid pressure acting on the brake cylinders, thus controlling the braking force.

DTC No.	Diagnostic Trouble Code Detecting Condition	Trouble area
21	Conditions (1) through (3) continue for 0.05 sec. or more: (1) ABS solenoid relay (SR) terminal voltage: Battery positive voltage (2) Voltage of ABS (& TRAC) ECU terminal AST: Battery positive voltage (3) When power transistor of ECU is ON, voltage of terminal SFR is 0 V or battery positive voltage.	• ABS actuator • Open or short in SFR circuit. • ECU
22	Conditions (1) through (3) continue for 0.05 sec. or more: (1) ABS solenoid relay (SR) terminal voltage: Battery positive voltage (2) Voltage of ABS (& TRAC) ECU terminal AST: Battery positive voltage (3) When power transistor of ECU is ON, voltage of terminal SFL is 0 V or battery positive voltage.	• ABS actuator • Open or short in SFL circuit. • ECU
23	Conditions (1) through (3) continue for 0.05 sec. or more: (1) ABS solenoid relay (SR) terminal voltage: Battery positive voltage (2) Voltage of ABS (& TRAC) ECU terminal AST: Battery positive voltage (3) When power transistor of ECU is ON, voltage of terminal SRR is 0 V or battery positive voltage.	• ABS actuator • Open or short in SRR circuit. • ECU
24	Conditions (1) through (3) continue for 0.05 sec. or more: (1) ABS solenoid relay (SR) terminal voltage: Battery positive voltage (2) Voltage of ABS (& TRAC) ECU terminal AST: Battery positive voltage (3) When power transistor of ECU is ON, voltage of terminal SRL is 0 V or battery positive voltage.	• ABS actuator • Open or short in SRL circuit. • ECU

Fail safe function: If trouble occurs in the actuator solenoid circuit, the ECU cuts off current to the solenoid relay and prohibits ABS control.

DIAGNOSTIC CHART

1️⃣ Check ABS actuator solenoid. — NG → Replace ABS actuator.

OK ↓

2️⃣ Check for open and short in harness and connector between ECU and actuator. — NG → Repair or replace harness or connector.

OK ↓

If the same code is still output after the diagnostic trouble code is deleted, check the contact condition of each connection.
If the connections are normal, the ECU may be defective.

TY4029300087010X

Fig. 264   Codes 21, 22, 23 & 24: ABS Actuator Solenoid (Part 1 of 3). 1996 Supra less traction control

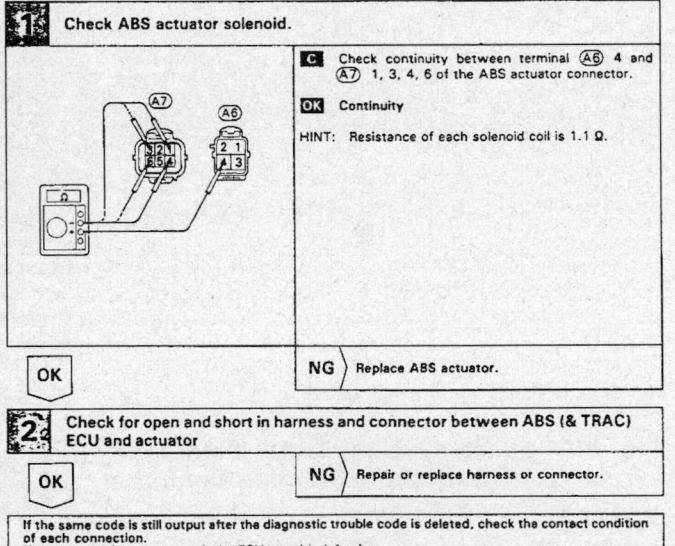

1️⃣ **Check ABS actuator solenoid.**

C Check continuity between terminal (A6) 4 and (A7) 1, 3, 4, 6 of the ABS actuator connector.

OK Continuity

HINT: Resistance of each solenoid coil is 1.1 Ω.

OK ↓

NG > Replace ABS actuator.

2️⃣ **Check for open and short in harness and connector between ABS (& TRAC) ECU and actuator**

OK ↓

NG > Repair or replace harness or connector.

If the same code is still output after the diagnostic trouble code is deleted, check the contact condition of each connection.
If the connections are normal, the ECU may be defective.

TY4029300087030X

Fig. 264   Codes 21, 22, 23 & 24: ABS Actuator Solenoid (Part 3 of 3). 1996 Supra less traction control

WIRING DIAGRAM

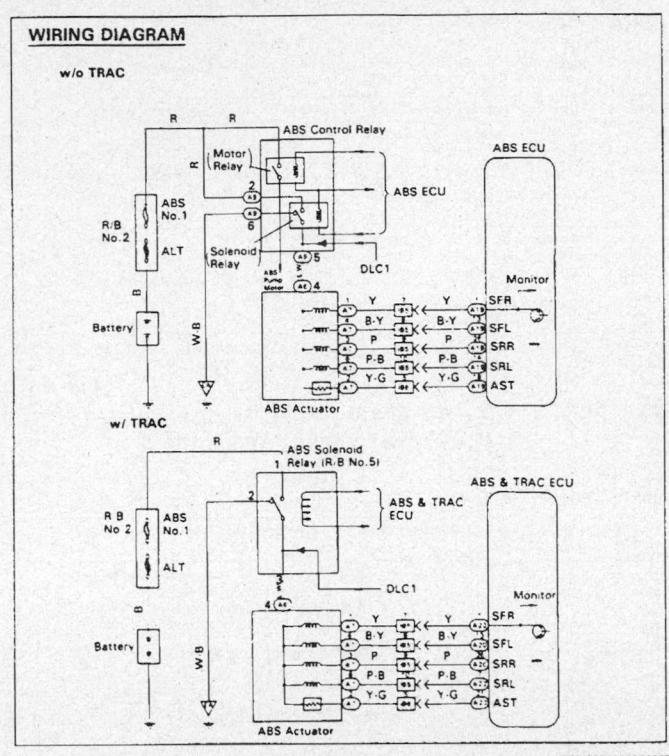

w/o TRAC

w/ TRAC

TY4029300087020X

Fig. 264   Codes 21, 22, 23 & 24: ABS Actuator Solenoid (Part 2 of 3). 1996 Supra less traction control

CIRCUIT DESCRIPTION

This solenoid goes on when signals are received from the ECU and controls the fluid pressure acting on the brake cylinders, thus controlling the braking force.

DTC No.	DTC Detecting Condition	Trouble Area
21	Conditions (1) through (3) continue for 0.05 sec. or more: (1) ABS solenoid relay terminal (SR) voltage: Below 1.5 V (2) Voltage of ABS ECU terminal AST: Battery positive voltage (3) When power transistor of ECU is ON, voltage of terminal SFR is 0 V or battery positive voltage.	• ABS actuator • Open or short in SFR circuit
22	Conditions (1) through (3) continue for 0.05 sec. or more: (1) ABS solenoid relay terminal (SR) voltage: Below 1.5 V (2) Voltage of ABS ECU terminal AST: Battery positive voltage (3) When power transistor of ECU is ON, voltage of terminal SFL is 0 V or battery positive voltage.	• ABS actuator • Open or short in SFL circuit
23	Conditions (1) through (3) continue for 0.05 sec. or more: (1) ABS solenoid relay terminal (SR) voltage: Below 1.5 V (2) Voltage of ABS ECU terminal AST: Battery positive voltage (3) When power transistor of ECU is ON, voltage of terminal SRH (SRRH) or SRR (SRRR) is 0 V or battery positive voltage.	• ABS actuator • Open or short in SRH (SRRH) or SRR (SRRR) circuit
24*	Conditions (1) through (3) continue for 0.05 sec. or more: (1) ABS solenoid relay terminal (SR) voltage: Below 1.5 V (2) Voltage of ABS ECU terminal AST: Battery positive voltage (3) When power transistor of ECU is ON, voltage of terminal SRLH or SRLR is 0 V or battery positive voltage.	• ABS actuator • Open or short in SRLH or SRLR circuit

Fail safe function: If trouble occurs in the ABS actuator solenoid circuit, the ECU cuts off current to the ABS solenoid relay and prohibits ABS control.

*: SPORT ABS (2JZ-GTE Engine) only

TY4029700414010X

Fig. 265   Codes 21, 22, 23 & 24: ABS Actuator Solenoid (Part 1 of 3). 1997–98 Supra less traction control

WIRING DIAGRAM

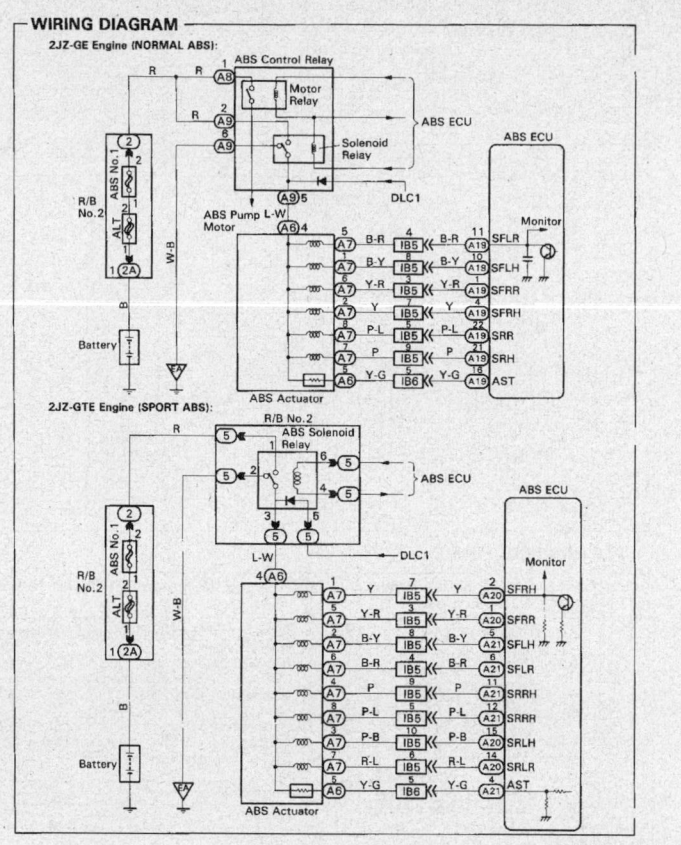

Fig. 265 Codes 21, 22, 23 & 24: ABS Actuator
Solenoid (Part 2 of 3). 1997–98 Supra less traction
control

TY4029700414020X

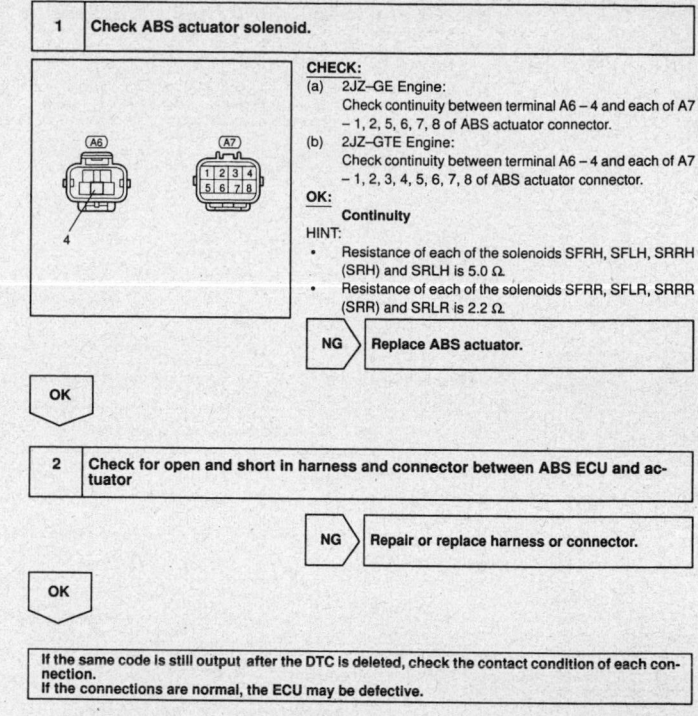

1	Check ABS actuator solenoid.

CHECK:
(a) 2JZ–GE Engine:
Check continuity between terminal A6 – 4 and each of A7 – 1, 2, 5, 6, 7, 8 of ABS actuator connector.
(b) 2JZ–GTE Engine:
Check continuity between terminal A6 – 4 and each of A7 – 1, 2, 3, 4, 5, 6, 7, 8 of ABS actuator connector.

OK:
Continuity

HINT:
• Resistance of each of the solenoids SFRH, SFLH, SRRH (SRH) and SRLH is 5.0 Ω.
• Resistance of each of the solenoids SFRR, SFLR, SRRR (SRR) and SRLR is 2.2 Ω.

NG	Replace ABS actuator.

OK

2	Check for open and short in harness and connector between ABS ECU and actuator

NG	Repair or replace harness or connector.

OK

If the same code is still output after the DTC is deleted, check the contact condition of each connection.
If the connections are normal, the ECU may be defective.

TY4029700414030X

Fig. 265 Codes 21, 22, 23 & 24: ABS Actuator
Solenoid (Part 3 of 3). 1997–98 Supra less traction
control

CIRCUIT DESCRIPTION

DTC No.	DTC Detecting Condition	Trouble Area
21	Sub-throttle valve motor circuit is open or short.	• Sub-throttle valve motor • Wire harness and connector (sub-throttle valve motor and E01 circuit) • Throttle control ECU
22	in case the sub-throttle valve open angie is tilted.	• Sub-throttle valve motor • Sub-throttle valve • Sub-throttle valve position sensor • Wire harness and connector (E1 circuit) • Throttle control ECU

WIRING DIAGRAM

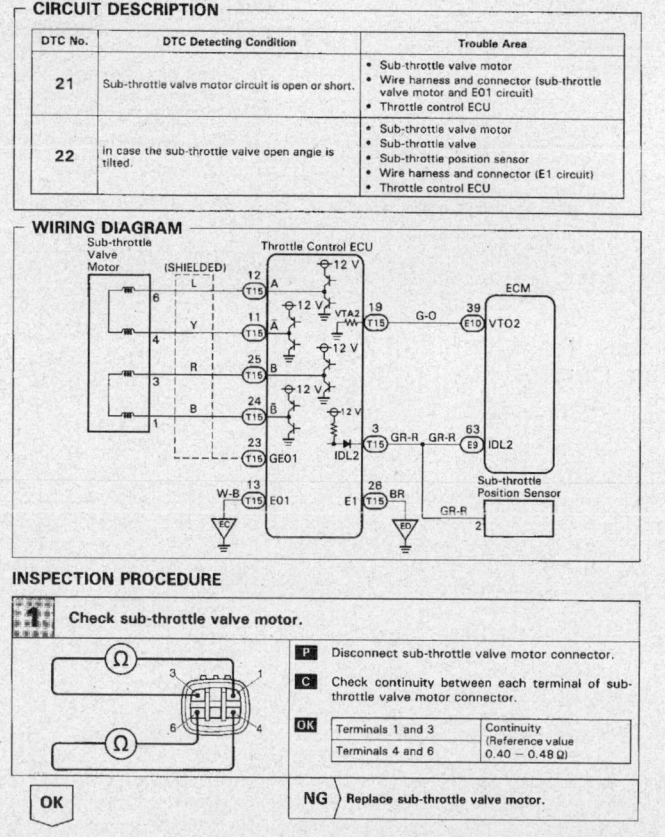

INSPECTION PROCEDURE

1	Check sub-throttle valve motor.

P Disconnect sub-throttle valve motor connector.

C Check continuity between each terminal of sub-throttle valve motor connector.

OK

	Continuity
Terminals 1 and 3	(Reference value)
Terminals 4 and 6	0.40 – 0.48 Ω

OK

NG	Replace sub-throttle valve motor.

TY4029700419010X

Fig. 266 Codes 21 & 22: Sub–Throttle Valve Motor
(Part 1 of 2). Supra w/Traction Control

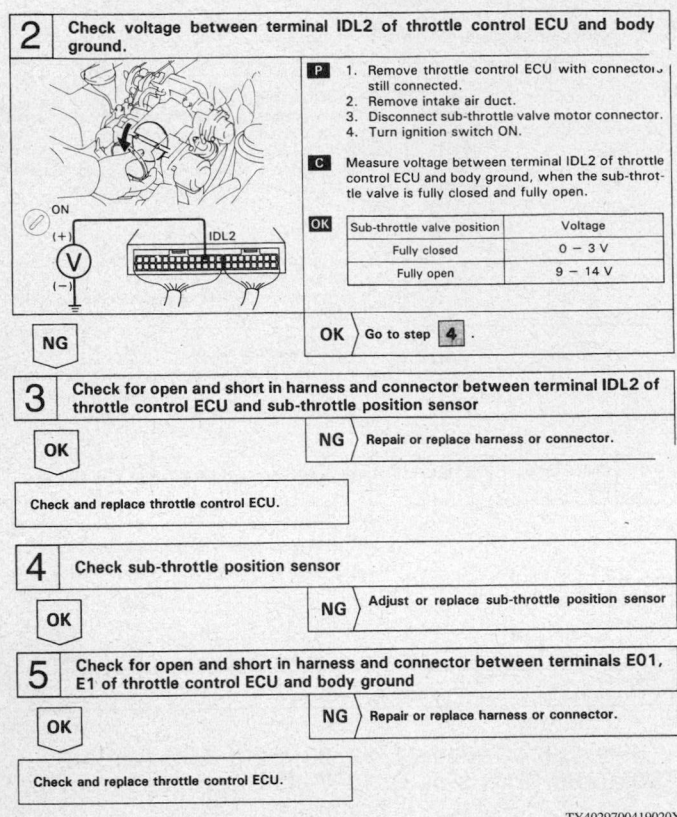

2	Check voltage between terminal IDL2 of throttle control ECU and body ground.

P	1. Remove throttle control ECU with connectors still connected. 2. Remove intake air duct. 3. Disconnect sub-throttle valve motor connector. 4. Turn ignition switch ON.
C	Measure voltage between terminal IDL2 of throttle control ECU and body ground, when the sub-throttle valve is fully closed and fully open.

OK	Sub-throttle valve position	Voltage
	Fully closed	0 – 3 V
	Fully open	9 – 14 V

NG

OK ▷ Go to step **4** .

3	Check for open and short in harness and connector between terminal IDL2 of throttle control ECU and sub-throttle position sensor

OK

NG ▷ Repair or replace harness or connector.

Check and replace throttle control ECU.

4	Check sub-throttle position sensor

OK

NG ▷ Adjust or replace sub-throttle position sensor.

5	Check for open and short in harness and connector between terminals E01, E1 of throttle control ECU and body ground

OK

NG ▷ Repair or replace harness or connector.

Check and replace throttle control ECU.

TY4029700419020X

Fig. 266 Codes 21 & 22: Sub–Throttle Valve Motor (Part 2 of 2). Supra w/Traction Control

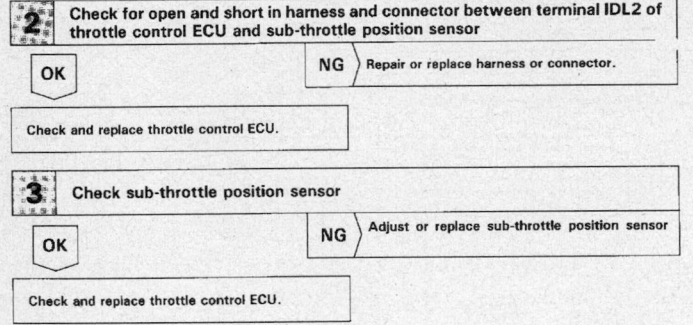

2	Check for open and short in harness and connector between terminal IDL2 of throttle control ECU and sub-throttle position sensor

OK

NG ▷ Repair or replace harness or connector.

Check and replace throttle control ECU.

3	Check sub-throttle position sensor

OK

NG ▷ Adjust or replace sub-throttle position sensor.

Check and replace throttle control ECU.

TY4029700420020X

Fig. 267 Code 23: Throttle Body Fault (Part 2 of 2). Supra w/Traction Control

CIRCUIT DESCRIPTION

DTC No.	DTC Detecting Condition	Trouble Area
23	In case the sub-throttle valve is fully open or full close angle becomes smaller.	• Sub-throttle valve • Sub-throttle position sensor • Throttle control ECU

WIRING DIAGRAM

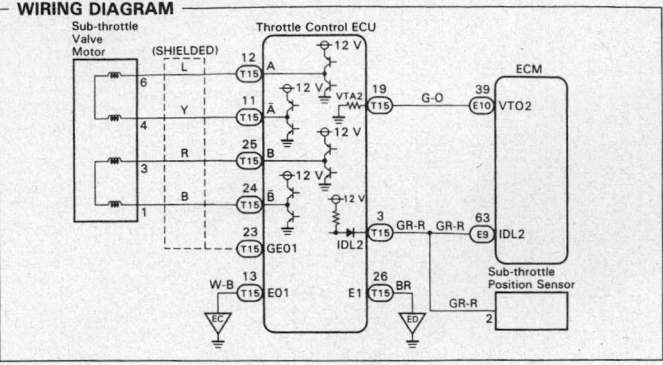

INSPECTION PROCEDURE

1	Check voltage between terminal IDL2 of throttle control ECU and body ground.

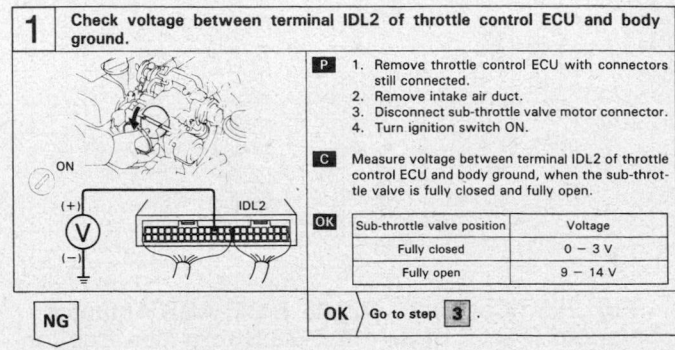

P	1. Remove throttle control ECU with connectors still connected. 2. Remove intake air duct. 3. Disconnect sub-throttle valve motor connector. 4. Turn ignition switch ON.
C	Measure voltage between terminal IDL2 of throttle control ECU and body ground, when the sub-throttle valve is fully closed and fully open.

OK	Sub-throttle valve position	Voltage
	Fully closed	0 – 3 V
	Fully open	9 – 14 V

NG

OK ▷ Go to step **3** .

TY4029700420010X

Fig. 267 Code 23: Throttle Body Fault (Part 1 of 2). Supra w/Traction Control

CIRCUIT DESCRIPTION

The sub-throttle actuator operates in accordance with signals from the ECU, controlling the opening and closing of the sub-throttle valve.

DTC No.	Diagnostic Trouble Code Detecting Condition	Trouble area
24	Open or short in sub-throttle actuator circuit.	• TRAC fuse • Open or short in BM circuit. • Sub-throttle actuator. • Open or short in sub-throttle actuator circuit. • ECU

WIRING DIAGRAM

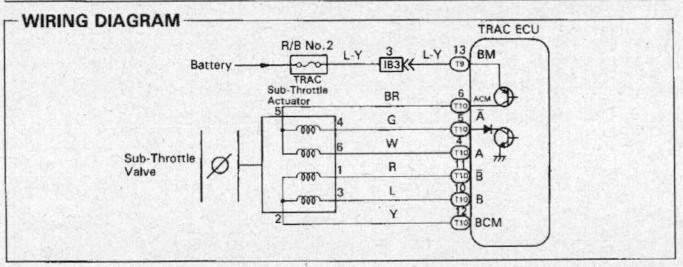

TY4029500439010X

Fig. 268 Code 24: Traction Sub Throttle Actuator Circuit (Part 1 of 3). 1996 Supra w/Traction Control

1 Check TRAC fuse.

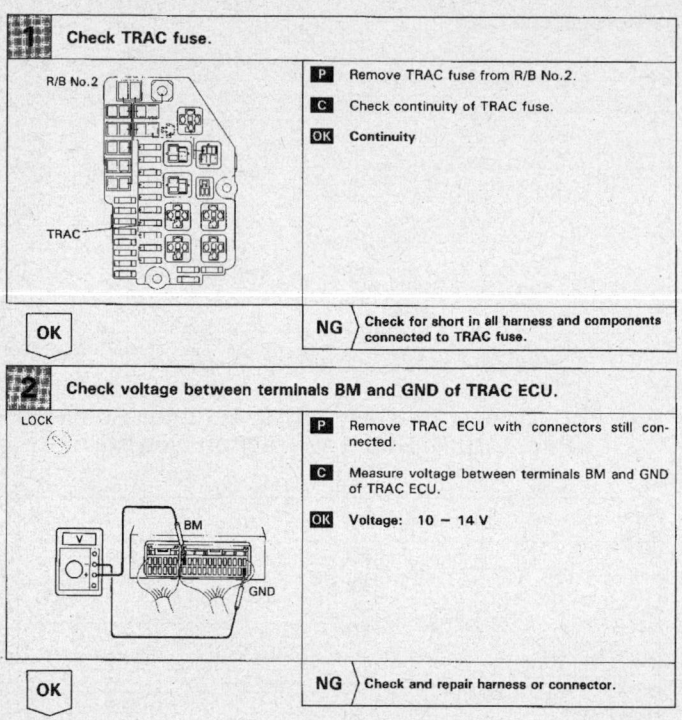

P	Remove TRAC fuse from R/B No.2.
C	Check continuity of TRAC fuse.
OK	Continuity

R/B No.2

TRAC

OK → **2**

NG → Check for short in all harness and components connected to TRAC fuse.

2 Check voltage between terminals BM and GND of TRAC ECU.

LOCK

P	Remove TRAC ECU with connectors still connected.
C	Measure voltage between terminals BM and GND of TRAC ECU.
OK	Voltage: 10 – 14 V

BM

GND

OK

NG → Check and repair harness or connector.

TY4029500439020X

Fig. 268 Code 24: Traction Sub Throttle Actuator Circuit (Part 2 of 3). 1996 Supra w/Traction Control

CIRCUIT DESCRIPTION

DTC No.	DTC Detecting Condition	Trouble Area
24	Instead of sub-throttle valve motor is driven fully open, voltage at VTA2 of ECU terminal does not output 3.2 V to 4.9 V or more.	• Sub-throttle valve • Sub-throttle position sensor • Wire harness and connector (E1 circuit) • Throttle control ECU

WIRING DIAGRAM

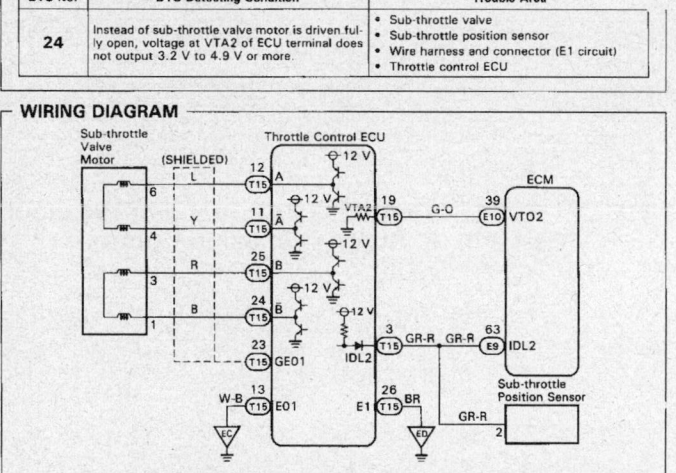

TY4029700421010X

Fig. 269 Code 24: Sub–Throttle Position Sensor Leakage/Sub–Throttle Valve Stuck (Part 1 of 2). 1997–98 Supra w/Traction Control

3 Check sub-throttle actuator.

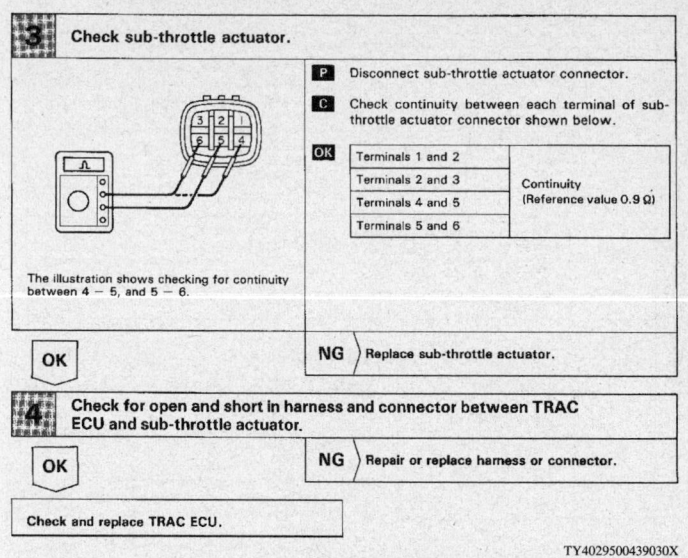

P	Disconnect sub-throttle actuator connector.
C	Check continuity between each terminal of sub-throttle actuator connector shown below.

OK		
Terminals 1 and 2		
Terminals 2 and 3	Continuity
Terminals 4 and 5	(Reference value 0.9 Ω)
Terminals 5 and 6	

The illustration shows checking for continuity between 4 – 5, and 5 – 6.

OK

NG → Replace sub-throttle actuator.

4 Check for open and short in harness and connector between TRAC ECU and sub-throttle actuator.

OK

NG → Repair or replace harness or connector.

Check and replace TRAC ECU.

TY4029500439030X

Fig. 268 Code 24: Traction Sub Throttle Actuator Circuit (Part 3 of 3). 1996 Supra w/Traction Control

1 Check voltage between terminal VTA2 of throttle control ECU and body ground.

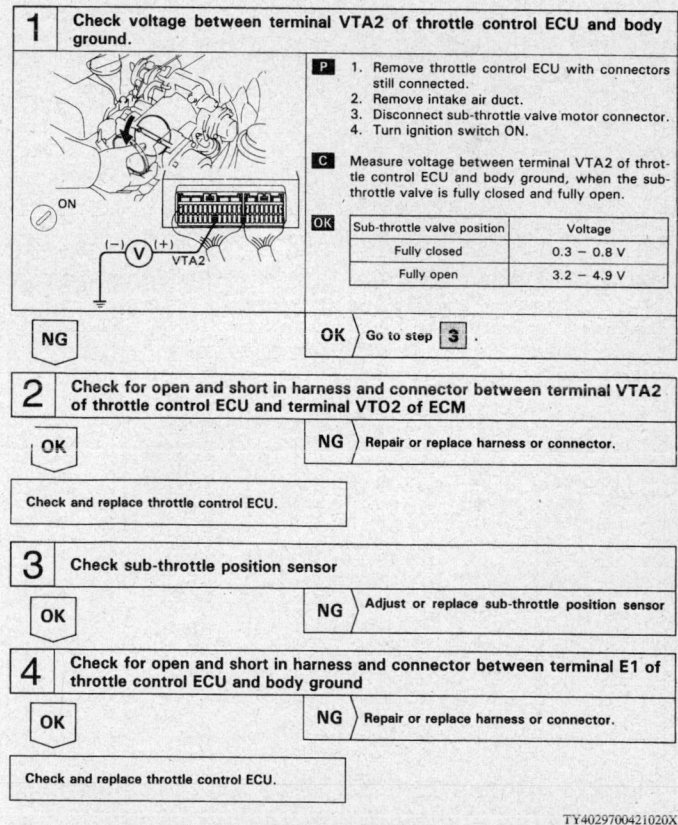

P	1. Remove throttle control ECU with connectors still connected. 2. Remove intake air duct. 3. Disconnect sub-throttle valve motor connector. 4. Turn ignition switch ON.
C	Measure voltage between terminal VTA2 of throttle control ECU and body ground, when the sub-throttle valve is fully closed and fully open.

OK	Sub-throttle valve position	Voltage
	Fully closed	0.3 – 0.8 V
	Fully open	3.2 – 4.9 V

NG

OK → Go to step **3**.

2 Check for open and short in harness and connector between terminal VTA2 of throttle control ECU and terminal VTO2 of ECM

OK

NG → Repair or replace harness or connector.

Check and replace throttle control ECU.

3 Check sub-throttle position sensor

OK

NG → Adjust or replace sub-throttle position sensor

4 Check for open and short in harness and connector between terminal E1 of throttle control ECU and body ground

OK

NG → Repair or replace harness or connector.

Check and replace throttle control ECU.

TY4029700421020X

Fig. 269 Code 24: Sub–Throttle Position Sensor Leakage/Sub–Throttle Valve Stuck (Part 2 of 2). Supra w/Traction Control

DTC No.	Diagnostic Trouble Code Detecting Condition	Trouble area
25	The difference between the sub-throttle sensor signal voltage and the voltage required by the step count is 1 V or more.	• Sub-throttle actuator. • Throttle body (sub-throttle valve is stuck or operation is faulty). • Sub-throttle position sensor. • Open or short in sub-throttle position sensor circuit. • ECM • TRAC ECU
26	Even when sub-throttle valve is driven to the fully open position, input voltage at terminal VTA2 of ECM does not come within range of the specifications 3 — 4.5 V.	• Sub-throttle actuator. • Throttle body (sub-throttle valve is stuck or operation is faulty). • Sub-throttle position sensor. • Open or short in sub-throttle position sensor circuit. • ECM • TRAC ECU

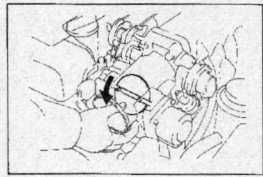

P Remove air duct.

C Open and close the sub-throttle valve manually and check the condition during operation.

OK The valve should operate smoothly without catching.

HINT: If sub-throttle actuator, sub-throttle valve, sub-throttle position sensor and harness are free from any defect, ECM may be defective.
If ECM is free from any defect, TRAC ECU may be defective.

TY4029500440000X

Fig. 270 Codes 25 & 26: Sub Throttle Valve. Supra w/Traction Control

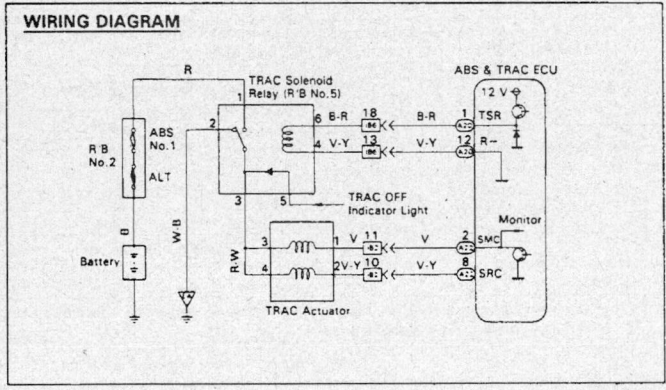

WIRING DIAGRAM

TY4029300088020X

Fig. 271 Codes 25 & 27: TRAC Actuator Solenoid (Part 2 of 3). Supra w/Traction Control

CIRCUIT DESCRIPTION

The TRAC actuator solenoid operates in accordance with signals from the ECU and raises the fluid pressure in and releases it from the brake cylinders.

DTC No.	Diagnostic Trouble Code Detecting Condition	Trouble area
25	Conditions (1) and (2) continue for 0.05 sec. or more: (1) TRAC solenoid relay terminal (TSR) voltage: Battery positive voltage (2) Voltage of ABS & TRAC ECU terminal SMC: 0 V	• TRAC actuator • Open or short in SMC circuit • ECU
27	Conditions (1) and (2) continue for 0.05 sec. or more: (1) TRAC solenoid relay terminal (TSR) voltage: Battery positive voltage (2) Voltage of ABS & TRAC ECU terminal SRC: 0V	• TRAC actuator • Open or short in SRC circuit • ECU

Fail safe function: If trouble occurs in this solenoid circuit, the ECU cuts off current to the ABS and TRAC solenoid relays and prohibits ABS and TRAC control.

TY4029300088010X

Fig. 271 Codes 25 & 27: TRAC Actuator Solenoid (Part 1 of 3). Supra w/Traction Control

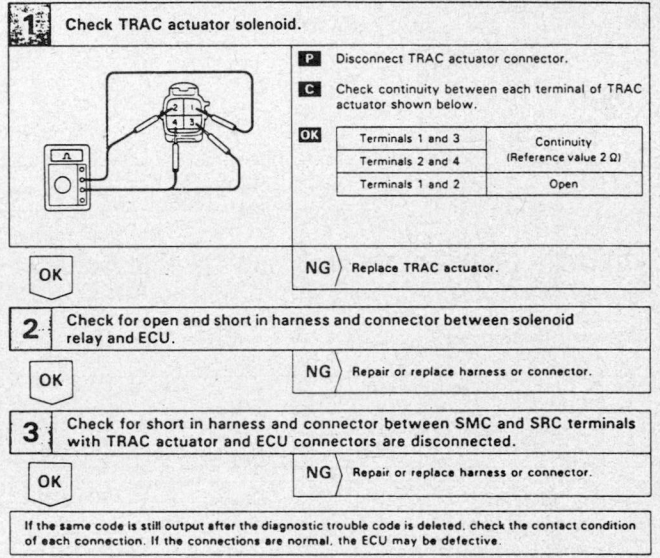

1 Check TRAC actuator solenoid.

P Disconnect TRAC actuator connector.

C Check continuity between each terminal of TRAC actuator shown below.

OK	Terminals 1 and 3	Continuity (Reference value 2 Ω)
	Terminals 2 and 4	
	Terminals 1 and 2	Open

OK ↓   **NG** ⟩ Replace TRAC actuator.

2 Check for open and short in harness and connector between solenoid relay and ECU.

OK ↓   **NG** ⟩ Repair or replace harness or connector.

3 Check for short in harness and connector between SMC and SRC terminals with TRAC actuator and ECU connectors are disconnected.

OK ↓   **NG** ⟩ Repair or replace harness or connector.

If the same code is still output after the diagnostic trouble code is deleted, check the contact condition of each connection. If the connections are normal, the ECU may be defective.

TY4029300088030X

Fig. 271 Codes 25 & 27: TRAC Actuator Solenoid (Part 3 of 3). Supra w/Traction Control

CIRCUIT DESCRIPTION

The speed sensor detects the wheel speed and sends the appropriate signals to the ECU. These signals are used to control both the ABS and TRAC control systems. The front and rear rotors each have 48 serrations. When the rotors rotate, the magnetic field emitted by the permanent magnet in the speed sensor generates an AC voltage. Since the frequency of this AC voltage changes in direct proportion to the speed of the rotor, the frequency is used by the ECU to detect the speed of each wheel.

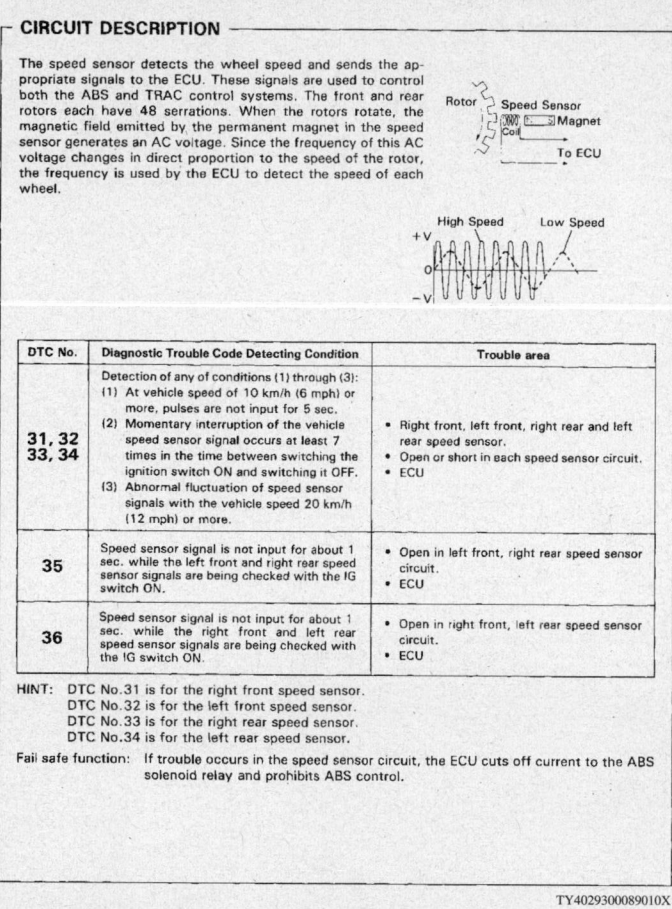

DTC No.	Diagnostic Trouble Code Detecting Condition	Trouble area
31, 32 33, 34	Detection of any of conditions (1) through (3): (1) At vehicle speed of 10 km/h (6 mph) or more, pulses are not input for 5 sec. (2) Momentary interruption of the vehicle speed sensor signal occurs at least 7 times in the time between switching the ignition switch ON and switching it OFF. (3) Abnormal fluctuation of speed sensor signals with the vehicle speed 20 km/h (12 mph) or more.	• Right front, left front, right rear and left rear speed sensor. • Open or short in each speed sensor circuit. • ECU
35	Speed sensor signal is not input for about 1 sec. while the left front and right rear speed sensor signals are being checked with the IG switch ON.	• Open in left front, right rear speed sensor circuit. • ECU
36	Speed sensor signal is not input for about 1 sec. while the right front and left rear speed sensor signals are being checked with the IG switch ON.	• Open in right front, left rear speed sensor circuit. • ECU

HINT: DTC No.31 is for the right front speed sensor.
DTC No.32 is for the left front speed sensor.
DTC No.33 is for the right rear speed sensor.
DTC No.34 is for the left rear speed sensor.

Fail safe function: If trouble occurs in the speed sensor circuit, the ECU cuts off current to the ABS solenoid relay and prohibits ABS control.

Fig. 272 Codes 31, 32, 33, 34, 35 & 36: Speed Sensor (Part 1 of 4). 1996 Supra less traction control

DIAGNOSTIC CHART

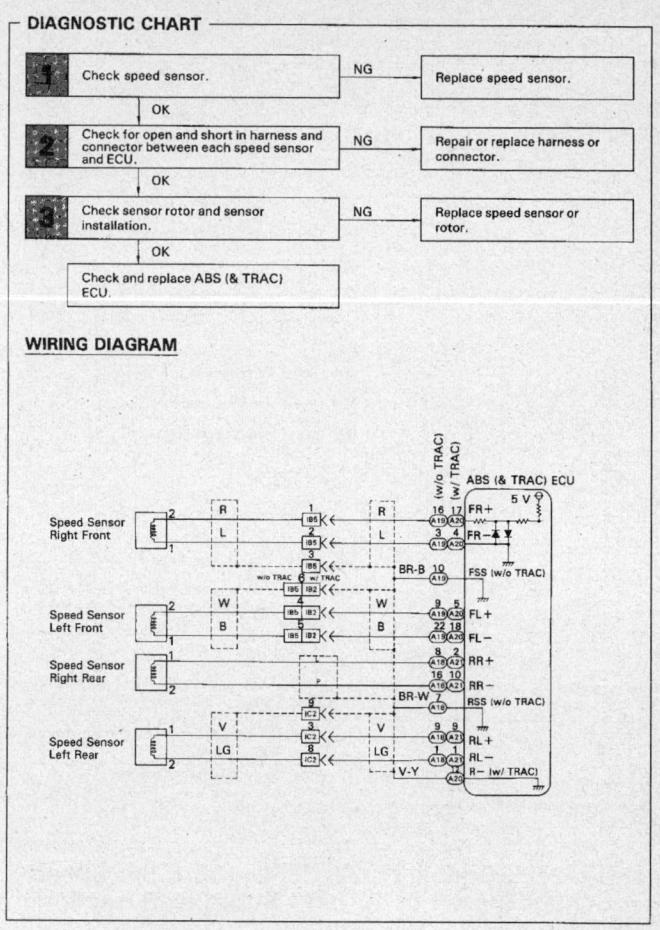

Fig. 272 Codes 31, 32, 33, 34, 35 & 36: Speed Sensor (Part 2 of 4). 1996 Supra less traction control

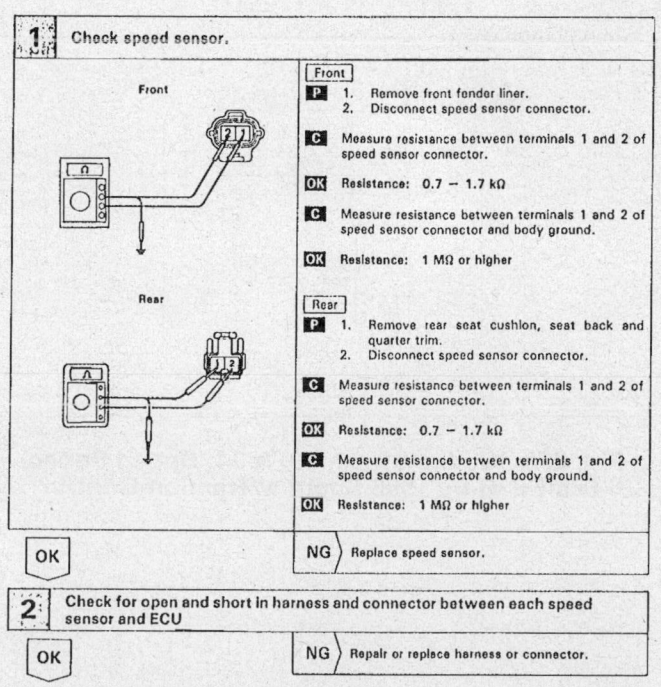

Fig. 272 Codes 31, 32, 33, 34, 35 & 36: Speed Sensor (Part 3 of 4). 1996 Supra less traction control

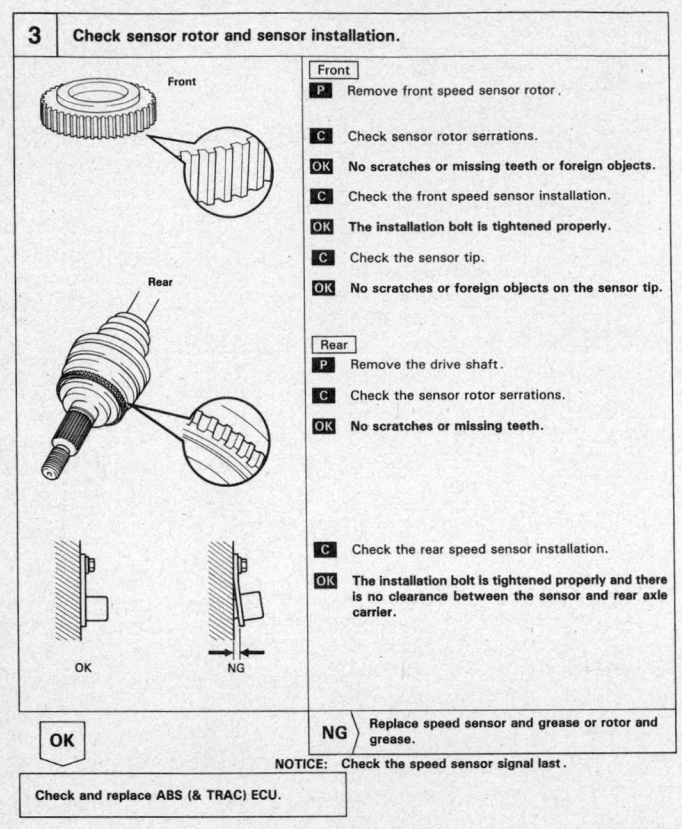

3 Check sensor rotor and sensor installation.

Front

Front

P Remove front speed sensor rotor .

C Check sensor rotor serrations.

OK No scratches or missing teeth or foreign objects.

C Check the front speed sensor installation.

OK The installation bolt is tightened properly.

C Check the sensor tip.

OK No scratches or foreign objects on the sensor tip.

Rear

Rear

P Remove the drive shaft .

C Check the sensor rotor serrations.

OK No scratches or missing teeth.

C Check the rear speed sensor installation.

OK The installation bolt is tightened properly and there is no clearance between the sensor and rear axle carrier.

OK | NG

OK | **NG** Replace speed sensor and grease or rotor and grease.

NOTICE: Check the speed sensor signal last .

Check and replace ABS (& TRAC) ECU.

TY4029300089040X

Fig. 272 Codes 31, 32, 33, 34, 35 & 36: Speed Sensor (Part 4 of 4). 1996 Supra less traction control

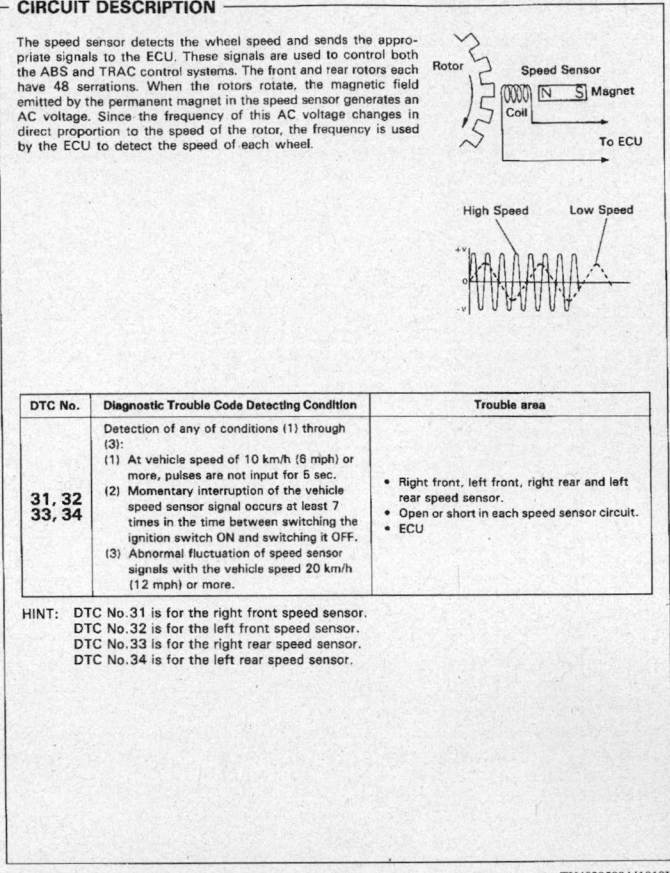

CIRCUIT DESCRIPTION

The speed sensor detects the wheel speed and sends the appropriate signals to the ECU. These signals are used to control both the ABS and TRAC control systems. The front and rear rotors each have 48 serrations. When the rotors rotate, the magnetic field emitted by the permanent magnet in the speed sensor generates an AC voltage. Since the frequency of this AC voltage changes in direct proportion to the speed of the rotor, the frequency is used by the ECU to detect the speed of each wheel.

DTC No.	Diagnostic Trouble Code Detecting Condition	Trouble area
31, 32 33, 34	Detection of any of conditions (1) through (3): (1) At vehicle speed of 10 km/h (6 mph) or more, pulses are not input for 5 sec. (2) Momentary interruption of the vehicle speed sensor signal occurs at least 7 times in the time between switching the ignition switch ON and switching it OFF. (3) Abnormal fluctuation of speed sensor signals with the vehicle speed 20 km/h (12 mph) or more.	• Right front, left front, right rear and left rear speed sensor. • Open or short in each speed sensor circuit. • ECU

HINT: DTC No.31 is for the right front speed sensor.
DTC No.32 is for the left front speed sensor.
DTC No.33 is for the right rear speed sensor.
DTC No.34 is for the left rear speed sensor.

TY4029500441010X

Fig. 273 Codes 31, 32, 33, & 34: Speed Sensor (Part 1 of 4). 1996 Supra w/Traction Control

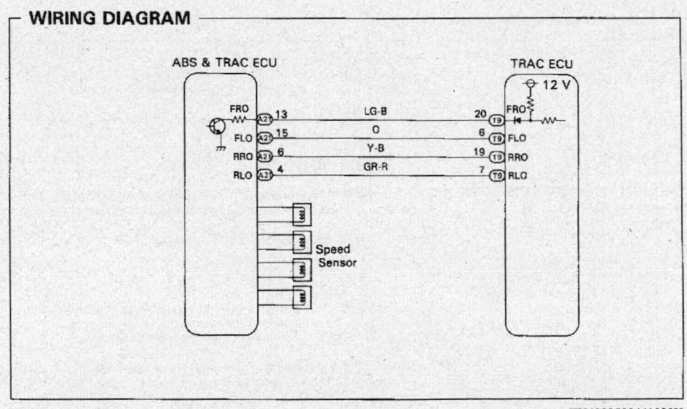

WIRING DIAGRAM

TY4029500441020X

Fig. 273 Codes 31, 32, 33, & 34: Speed Sensor (Part 2 of 4). 1996 Supra w/Traction Control

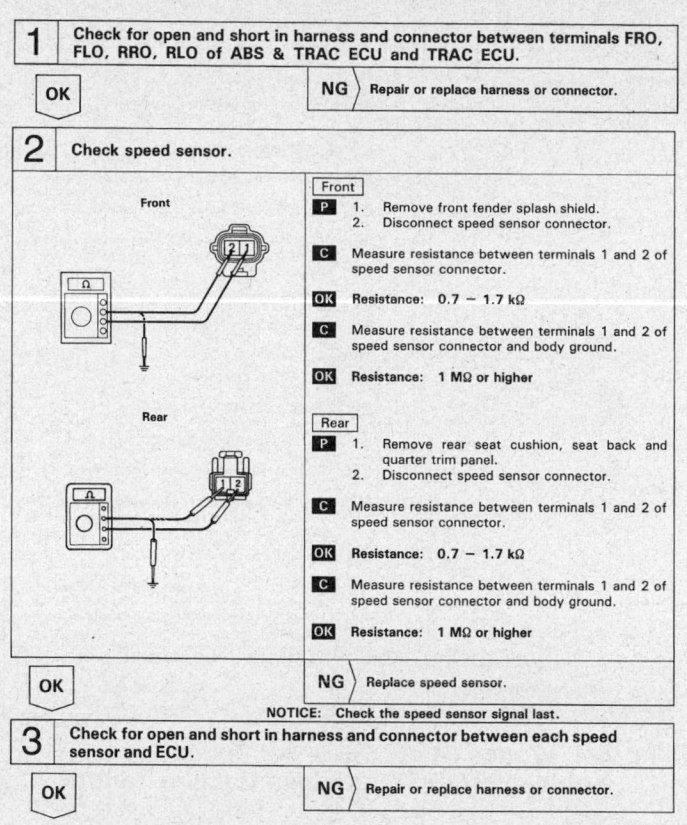

1 Check for open and short in harness and connector between terminals FRO, FLO, RRO, RLO of ABS & TRAC ECU and TRAC ECU.

OK ↓

NG ▷ Repair or replace harness or connector.

2 Check speed sensor.

Front

P
1. Remove front fender splash shield.
2. Disconnect speed sensor connector.

C Measure resistance between terminals 1 and 2 of speed sensor connector.

OK Resistance: 0.7 — 1.7 kΩ

C Measure resistance between terminals 1 and 2 of speed sensor connector and body ground.

OK Resistance: 1 MΩ or higher

Rear

P
1. Remove rear seat cushion, seat back and quarter trim panel.
2. Disconnect speed sensor connector.

C Measure resistance between terminals 1 and 2 of speed sensor connector.

OK Resistance: 0.7 — 1.7 kΩ

C Measure resistance between terminals 1 and 2 of speed sensor connector and body ground.

OK Resistance: 1 MΩ or higher

OK ↓

NG ▷ Replace speed sensor.

NOTICE: Check the speed sensor signal last.

3 Check for open and short in harness and connector between each speed sensor and ECU.

OK ↓

NG ▷ Repair or replace harness or connector.

TY4029500441030X

Fig. 273 Codes 31, 32, 33, & 34: Speed Sensor (Part 3 of 4). 1996 Supra w/Traction Control

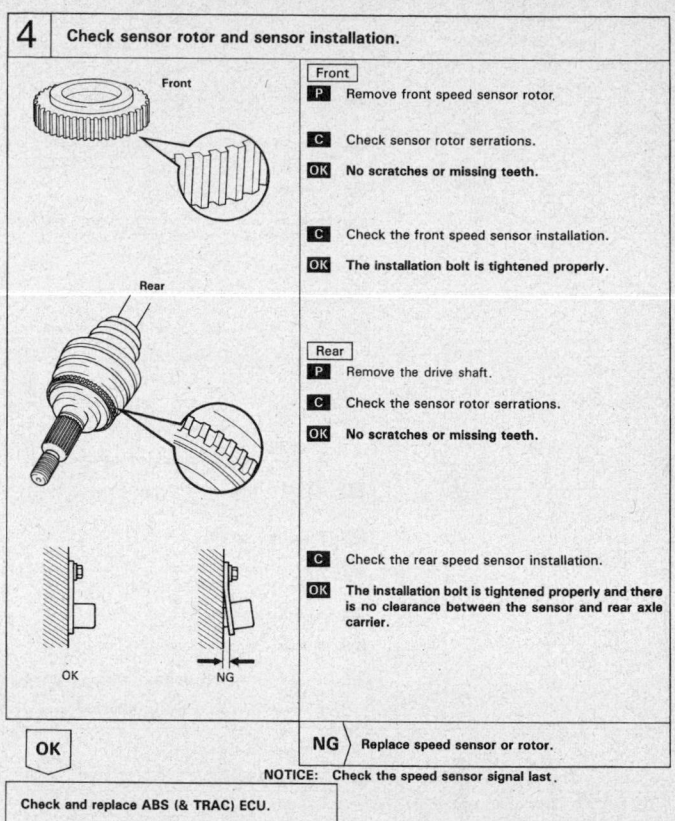

4 Check sensor rotor and sensor installation.

Front

P Remove front speed sensor rotor.

C Check sensor rotor serrations.

OK No scratches or missing teeth.

C Check the front speed sensor installation.

OK The installation bolt is tightened properly.

Rear

P Remove the drive shaft.

C Check the sensor rotor serrations.

OK No scratches or missing teeth.

C Check the rear speed sensor installation.

OK The installation bolt is tightened properly and there is no clearance between the sensor and rear axle carrier.

OK ↓

NG ▷ Replace speed sensor or rotor.

NOTICE: Check the speed sensor signal last.

Check and replace ABS (& TRAC) ECU.

TY4029500441040X

Fig. 273 Codes 31, 32, 33, & 34: Speed Sensor (Part 4 of 4). 1996 Supra w/Traction Control

CIRCUIT DESCRIPTION

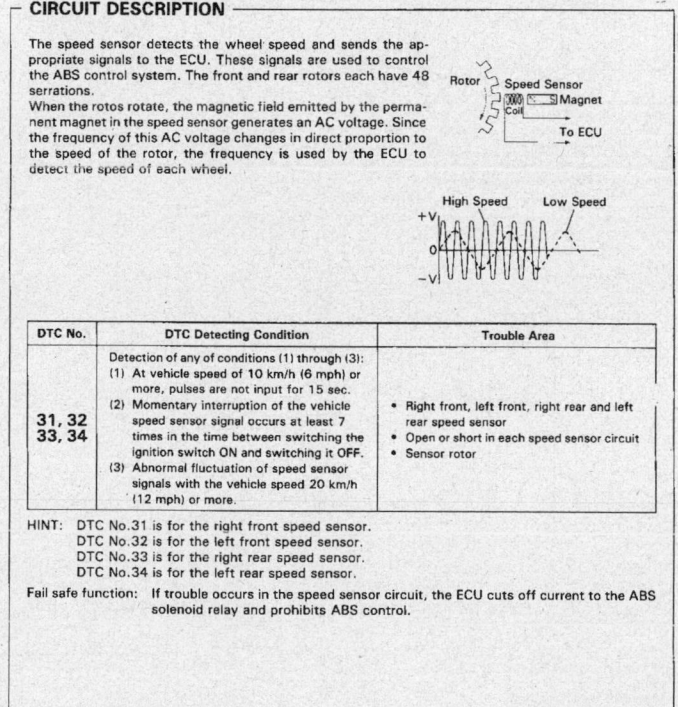

The speed sensor detects the wheel speed and sends the appropriate signals to the ECU. These signals are used to control the ABS control system. The front and rear rotors each have 48 serrations.

When the rotos rotate, the magnetic field emitted by the permanent magnet in the speed sensor generates an AC voltage. Since the frequency of this AC voltage changes in direct proportion to the speed of the rotor, the frequency is used by the ECU to detect the speed of each wheel.

DTC No.	DTC Detecting Condition	Trouble Area
31, 32 33, 34	Detection of any of conditions (1) through (3): (1) At vehicle speed of 10 km/h (6 mph) or more, pulses are not input for 15 sec. (2) Momentary interruption of the vehicle speed sensor signal occurs at least 7 times in the time between switching the ignition switch ON and switching it OFF. (3) Abnormal fluctuation of speed sensor signals with the vehicle speed 20 km/h (12 mph) or more.	• Right front, left front, right rear and left rear speed sensor • Open or short in each speed sensor circuit • Sensor rotor

HINT: DTC No.31 is for the right front speed sensor.
DTC No.32 is for the left front speed sensor.
DTC No.33 is for the right rear speed sensor.
DTC No.34 is for the left rear speed sensor.

Fail safe function: If trouble occurs in the speed sensor circuit, the ECU cuts off current to the ABS solenoid relay and prohibits ABS control.

TY4029700415010X

Fig. 274 Codes 31, 32, 33 & 34: Speed Sensor (Part 1 of 4). 1997–98 Supra less traction control

WIRING DIAGRAM

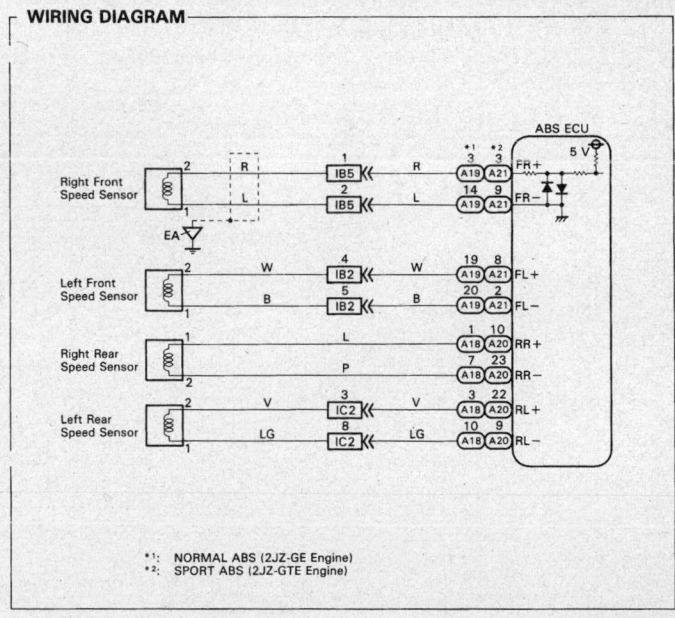

*1: NORMAL ABS (2JZ-GE Engine)
*2: SPORT ABS (2JZ-GTE Engine)

TY4029700415020X

Fig. 274 Codes 31, 32, 33 & 34: Speed Sensor (Part 2 of 4). 1997–98 Supra less traction control

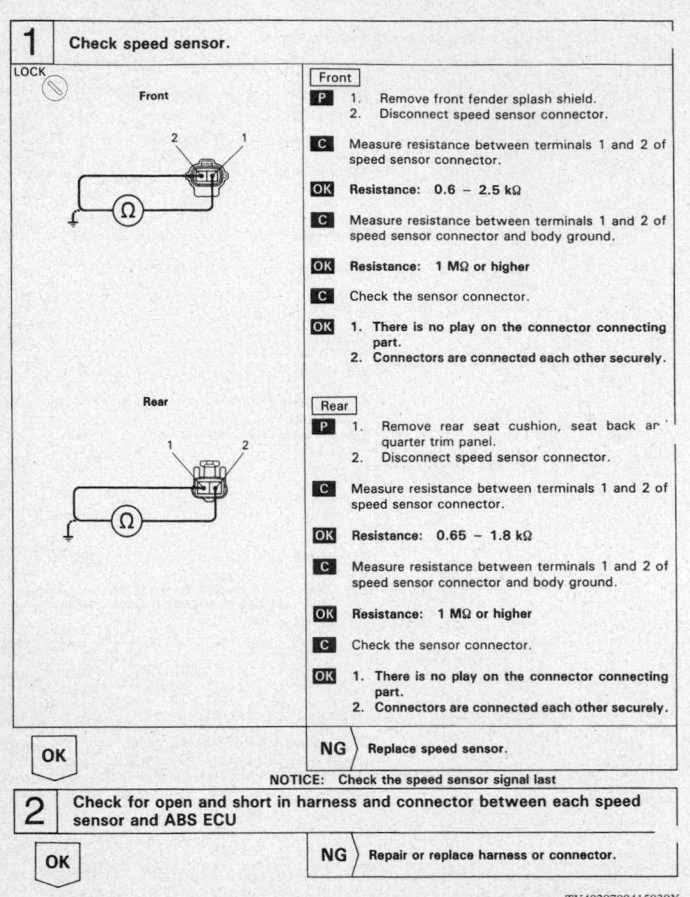

1 | Check speed sensor.

Front

P	1. Remove front fender splash shield. 2. Disconnect speed sensor connector.
C	Measure resistance between terminals 1 and 2 of speed sensor connector.
OK	Resistance: 0.6 – 2.5 kΩ
C	Measure resistance between terminals 1 and 2 of speed sensor connector and body ground.
OK	Resistance: 1 MΩ or higher
C	Check the sensor connector.
OK	1. There is no play on the connector connecting part. 2. Connectors are connected each other securely.

Rear

P	1. Remove rear seat cushion, seat back and quarter trim panel. 2. Disconnect speed sensor connector.
C	Measure resistance between terminals 1 and 2 of speed sensor connector.
OK	Resistance: 0.65 – 1.8 kΩ
C	Measure resistance between terminals 1 and 2 of speed sensor connector and body ground.
OK	Resistance: 1 MΩ or higher
C	Check the sensor connector.
OK	1. There is no play on the connector connecting part. 2. Connectors are connected each other securely.

OK → | NG | Replace speed sensor.

NOTICE: Check the speed sensor signal last.

2 | Check for open and short in harness and connector between each speed sensor and ABS ECU

OK → | NG | Repair or replace harness or connector.

TY4029700415030X

Fig. 274 Codes 31, 32, 33 & 34: Speed Sensor (Part 3 of 4). 1997–98 Supra less traction control

---

3 | Check sensor rotor and sensor installation.

Front

P	Remove front speed sensor rotor
C	Check sensor rotor serrations.
OK	No scratches, missing teeth or foreign objects.
C	Check the front speed sensor installation.
OK	The installation bolt is tightened properly and there is no clearance between sensor and steering knuckle.
C	Check the sensor tip.
OK	No scratches or foreign objects on the sensor tip.

Rear

P	Remove the drive shaft
C	Check the sensor rotor serrations.
OK	No scratches or missing teeth.
C	Check the rear speed sensor installation.
OK	The installation bolt is tightened properly and there is no clearance between the sensor and rear axle carrier.
C	Check the sensor tip.
OK	No scratches or foreign objects on the sensor tip.

OK → Check and replace ABS ECU.

NG → | Replace speed sensor and grease or rotor and grease.

NOTICE: Check the speed sensor signal last.

TY4029700415040X

Fig. 274 Codes 31, 32, 33 & 34: Speed Sensor (Part 4 of 4). 1997–98 Supra less traction control

---

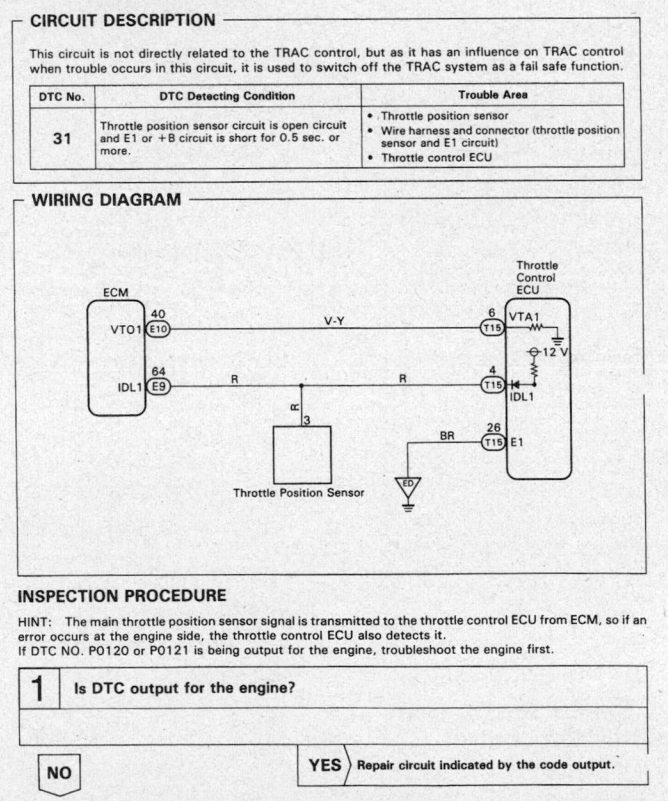

CIRCUIT DESCRIPTION

This circuit is not directly related to the TRAC control, but as it has an influence on TRAC control when trouble occurs in this circuit, it is used to switch off the TRAC system as a fail safe function.

DTC No.	DTC Detecting Condition	Trouble Area
31	Throttle position sensor circuit is open circuit and E1 or +B circuit is short for 0.5 sec. or more.	• Throttle position sensor • Wire harness and connector (throttle position sensor and E1 circuit) • Throttle control ECU

WIRING DIAGRAM

INSPECTION PROCEDURE

HINT: The main throttle position sensor signal is transmitted to the throttle control ECU from ECM, so if an error occurs at the engine side, the throttle control ECU also detects it.
If DTC NO. P0120 or P0121 is being output for the engine, troubleshoot the engine first.

1 | Is DTC output for the engine?

NO → | YES | Repair circuit indicated by the code output.

TY4029700422010X

Fig. 275 Code 31: Throttle Position Sensor Circuit (Part 1 of 3). Supra w/Traction Control

2 Check voltage between terminal IDL1 of throttle control ECU and body ground.

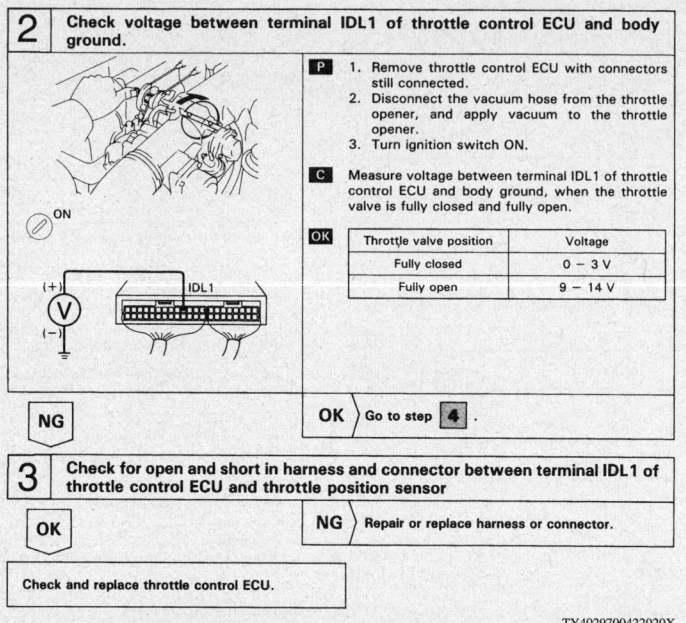

P
1. Remove throttle control ECU with connectors still connected.
2. Disconnect the vacuum hose from the throttle opener, and apply vacuum to the throttle opener.
3. Turn ignition switch ON.

C Measure voltage between terminal IDL1 of throttle control ECU and body ground, when the throttle valve is fully closed and fully open.

OK

Throttle valve position	Voltage
Fully closed	0 – 3 V
Fully open	9 – 14 V

NG

OK > Go to step **4**.

3 Check for open and short in harness and connector between terminal IDL1 of throttle control ECU and throttle position sensor

OK

NG > Repair or replace harness or connector.

Check and replace throttle control ECU.

TY4029700422020X

Fig. 275   Code 31: Throttle Position Sensor Circuit (Part 2 of 3). Supra w/Traction Control

---

4 Check voltage between terminal VTA1 of throttle control ECU and body ground.

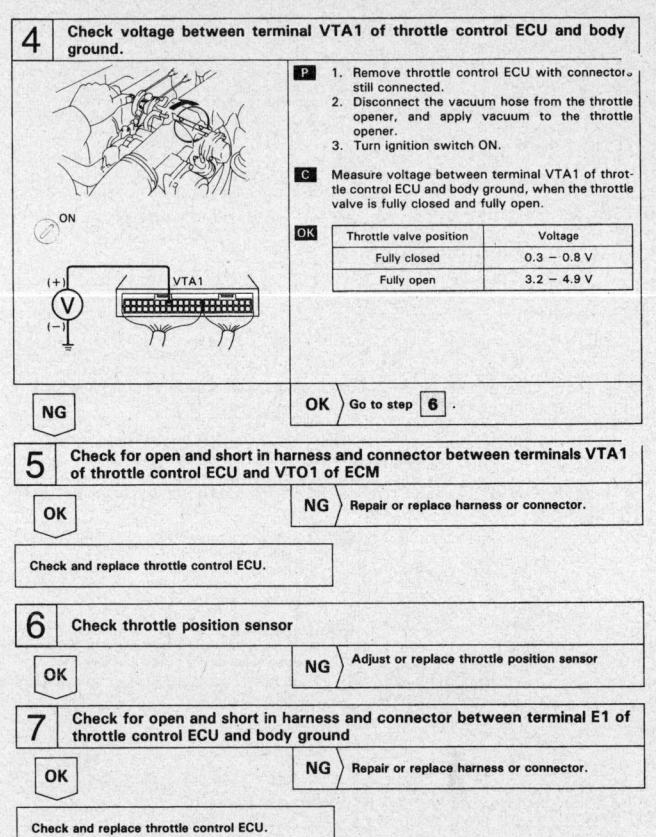

P
1. Remove throttle control ECU with connectors still connected.
2. Disconnect the vacuum hose from the throttle opener, and apply vacuum to the throttle opener.
3. Turn ignition switch ON.

C Measure voltage between terminal VTA1 of throttle control ECU and body ground, when the throttle valve is fully closed and fully open.

OK

Throttle valve position	Voltage
Fully closed	0.3 – 0.8 V
Fully open	3.2 – 4.9 V

NG

OK > Go to step **6**.

5 Check for open and short in harness and connector between terminals VTA1 of throttle control ECU and VTO1 of ECM

OK

NG > Repair or replace harness or connector.

Check and replace throttle control ECU.

6 Check throttle position sensor

OK

NG > Adjust or replace throttle position sensor

7 Check for open and short in harness and connector between terminal E1 of throttle control ECU and body ground

OK

NG > Repair or replace harness or connector.

Check and replace throttle control ECU.

TY4029700422030X

Fig. 275   Code 31: Throttle Position Sensor Circuit (Part 3 of 3). Supra w/Traction Control

---

CIRCUIT DESCRIPTION

This sensor detects the opening angle of the sub-throttle valve and sends the appropriate signals to the ECU. If a trouble signal is input, the ECU prohibits TRAC control.

DTC No.	DTC Detecting Condition	Trouble Area
32	Conditions (1) and (2) continue for 0.5 sec. or more: (1) Sub-throttle position sensor circuit is open and E1 or +B circuit is short. (2) Instead of sub-throttle valve motor is driven fully close, IDL2 of sub-throttle position sensor will not come ON.	• Sub-throttle position sensor • Sub-throttle valve motor • Sub-throttle valve • Wire harness and connector (sub-throttle position sensor and E1 circuit) • Throttle control ECU

WIRING DIAGRAM

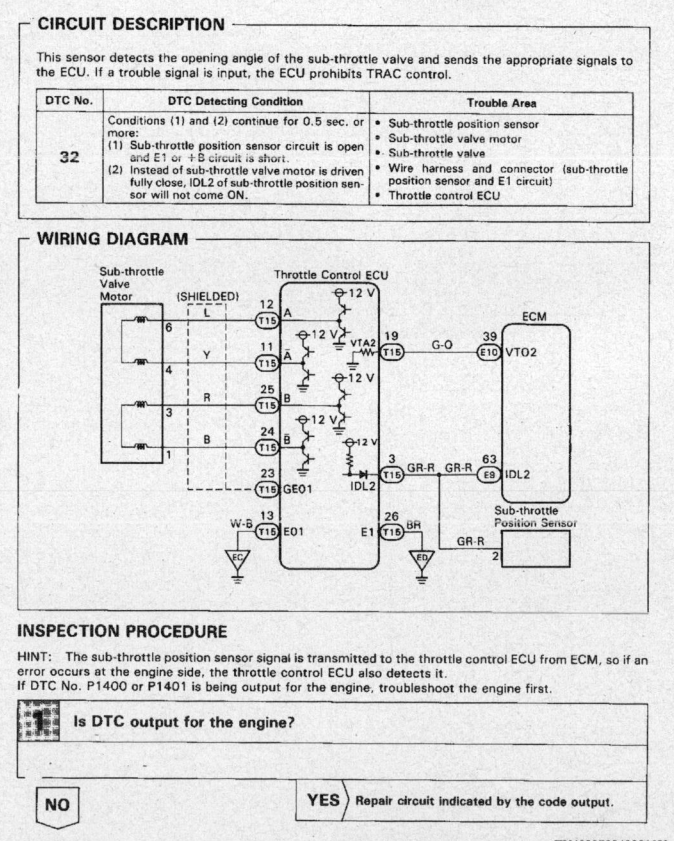

INSPECTION PROCEDURE

HINT: The sub-throttle position sensor signal is transmitted to the throttle control ECU from ECM, so if an error occurs at the engine side, the throttle control ECU also detects it.
If DTC No. P1400 or P1401 is being output for the engine, troubleshoot the engine first.

Is DTC output for the engine?

NO

YES > Repair circuit indicated by the code output.

TY4029700423010X

Fig. 276   Code 32: Sub-Throttle Position Sensor Circuit (Part 1 of 3). Supra w/Traction Control

2	Check voltage between terminal IDL2 of throttle control ECU and body ground.

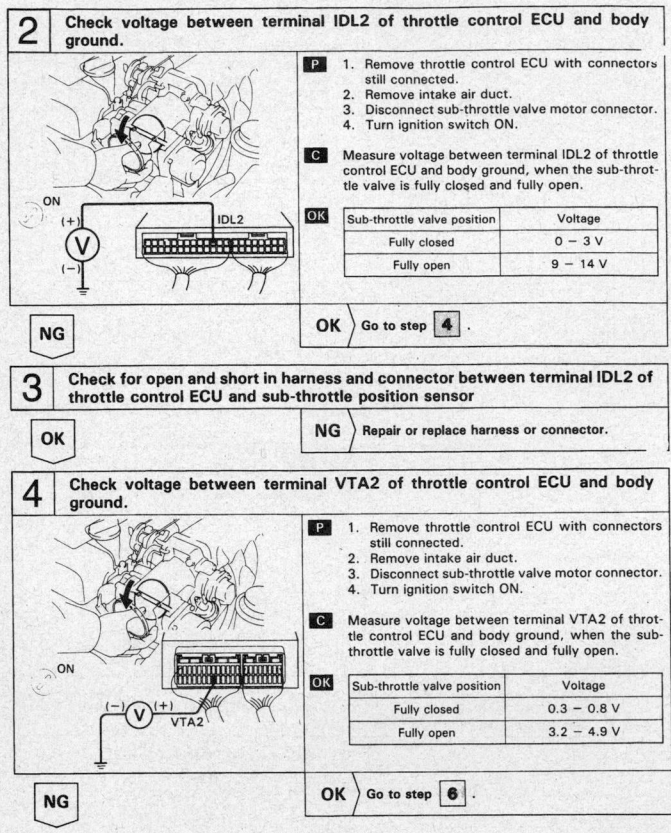

P
1. Remove throttle control ECU with connectors still connected.
2. Remove intake air duct.
3. Disconnect sub-throttle valve motor connector.
4. Turn ignition switch ON.

C Measure voltage between terminal IDL2 of throttle control ECU and body ground, when the sub-throttle valve is fully closed and fully open.

OK

Sub-throttle valve position	Voltage
Fully closed	0 – 3 V
Fully open	9 – 14 V

NG

OK Go to step **4**.

3	Check for open and short in harness and connector between terminal IDL2 of throttle control ECU and sub-throttle position sensor

OK

NG Repair or replace harness or connector.

4	Check voltage between terminal VTA2 of throttle control ECU and body ground.

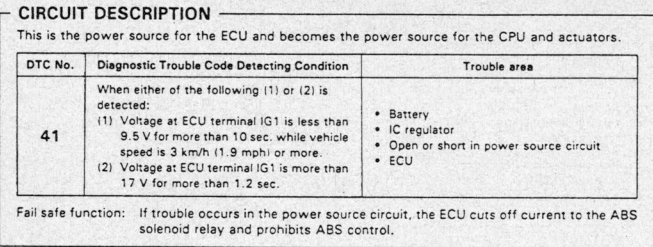

P
1. Remove throttle control ECU with connectors still connected.
2. Remove intake air duct.
3. Disconnect sub-throttle valve motor connector.
4. Turn ignition switch ON.

C Measure voltage between terminal VTA2 of throttle control ECU and body ground, when the sub-throttle valve is fully closed and fully open.

OK

Sub-throttle valve position	Voltage
Fully closed	0.3 – 0.8 V
Fully open	3.2 – 4.9 V

NG

OK Go to step **6**.

TY4029700423020X

Fig. 276   Code 32: Sub-Throttle Position Sensor Circuit (Part 2 of 3). Supra w/Traction Control

CIRCUIT DESCRIPTION

This is the power source for the ECU and becomes the power source for the CPU and actuators.

DTC No.	Diagnostic Trouble Code Detecting Condition	Trouble area
41	When either of the following (1) or (2) is detected: (1) Voltage at ECU terminal IG1 is less than 9.5 V for more than 10 sec. while vehicle speed is 3 km/h (1.9 mph) or more. (2) Voltage at ECU terminal IG1 is more than 17 V for more than 1.2 sec.	• Battery • IC regulator • Open or short in power source circuit • ECU

Fail safe function: If trouble occurs in the power source circuit, the ECU cuts off current to the ABS solenoid relay and prohibits ABS control.

DIAGNOSTIC CHART

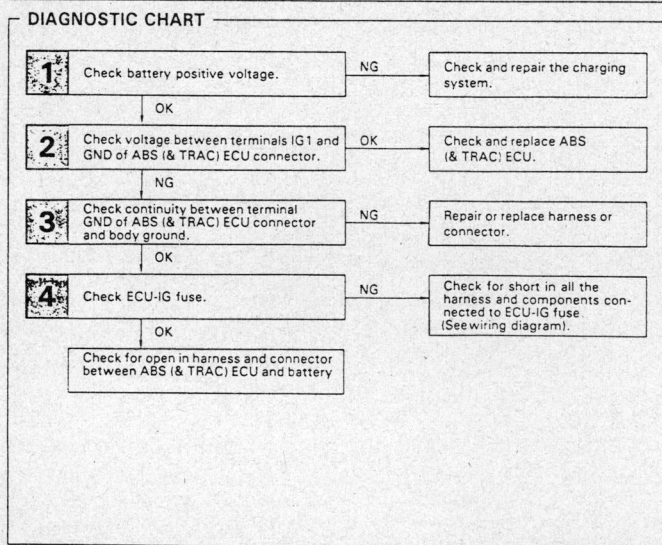

TY4029300090010X

Fig. 277   Code 41: IG Power Source Circuit (Part 1 of 4). Supra less Traction Control

5	Check for open and short in harness and connector between terminal VTA2 of throttle control ECU and terminal VTO2 of ECM

OK

NG Repair or replace harness or connector.

Check and replace throttle control ECU.

6	Check sub-throttle position sensor

OK

NG Adjust or replace sub-throttle position sensor

7	Check sub-throttle valve motor.

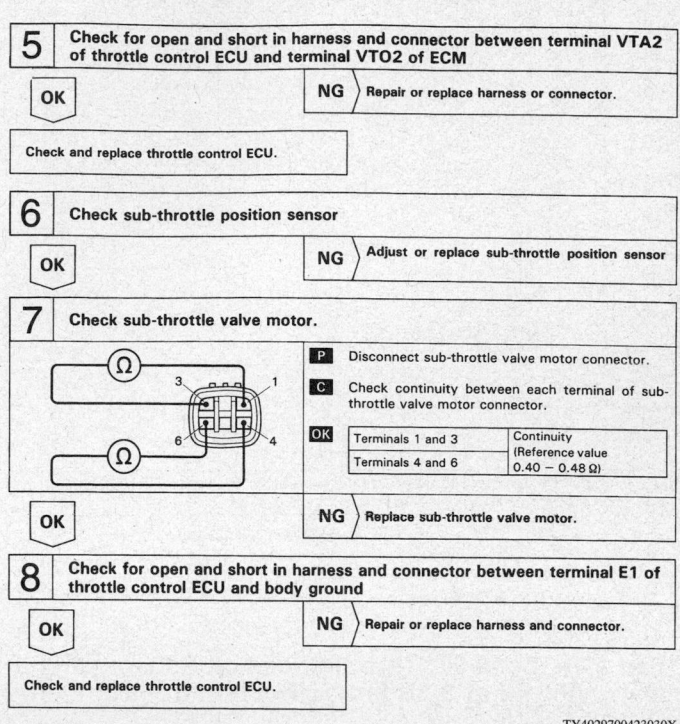

P Disconnect sub-throttle valve motor connector.

C Check continuity between each terminal of sub-throttle valve motor connector.

OK

Terminals 1 and 3	Continuity
Terminals 4 and 6	(Reference value 0.40 – 0.48 Ω)

OK

NG Replace sub-throttle valve motor.

8	Check for open and short in harness and connector between terminal E1 of throttle control ECU and body ground

OK

NG Repair or replace harness and connector.

Check and replace throttle control ECU.

TY4029700423030X

Fig. 276   Code 32: Sub-Throttle Position Sensor Circuit (Part 3 of 3). Supra w/Traction Control

1	Check battery positive voltage.

OK Voltage: 10 – 14 V

OK

NG Check and repair the charging system.

2	Check voltage between terminals IG1 and GND of TRAC ECU connector.

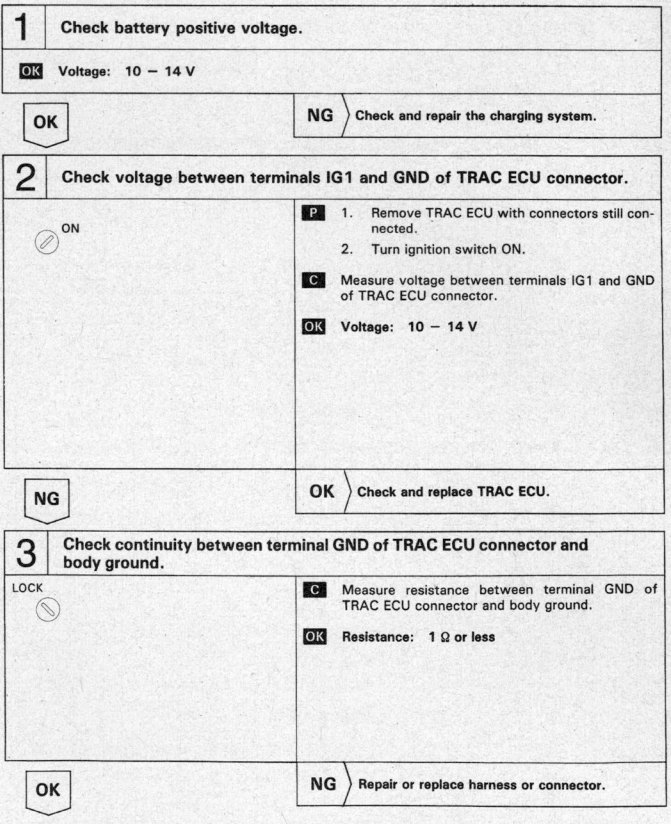

P
1. Remove TRAC ECU with connectors still connected.
2. Turn ignition switch ON.

C Measure voltage between terminals IG1 and GND of TRAC ECU connector.

OK Voltage: 10 – 14 V

NG

OK Check and replace TRAC ECU.

3	Check continuity between terminal GND of TRAC ECU connector and body ground.

C Measure resistance between terminal GND of TRAC ECU connector and body ground.

OK Resistance: 1 Ω or less

OK

NG Repair or replace harness or connector.

TY4029500442010X

Fig. 277   Code 41: IG Power Source Circuit (Part 2 of 4). 1996 Supra

WIRING DIAGRAM

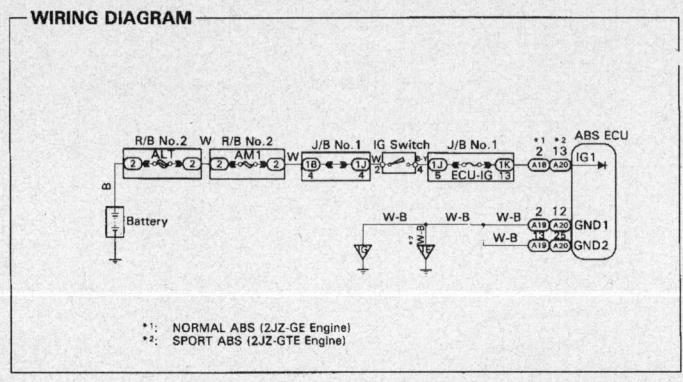

*1: NORMAL ABS (2JZ-GE Engine)
*2: SPORT ABS (2JZ-GTE Engine)

TY4029700416010X

Fig. 277 Code 41: IG Power Source Circuit (Part 2 of 4). 1997–98 Supra less Traction Control

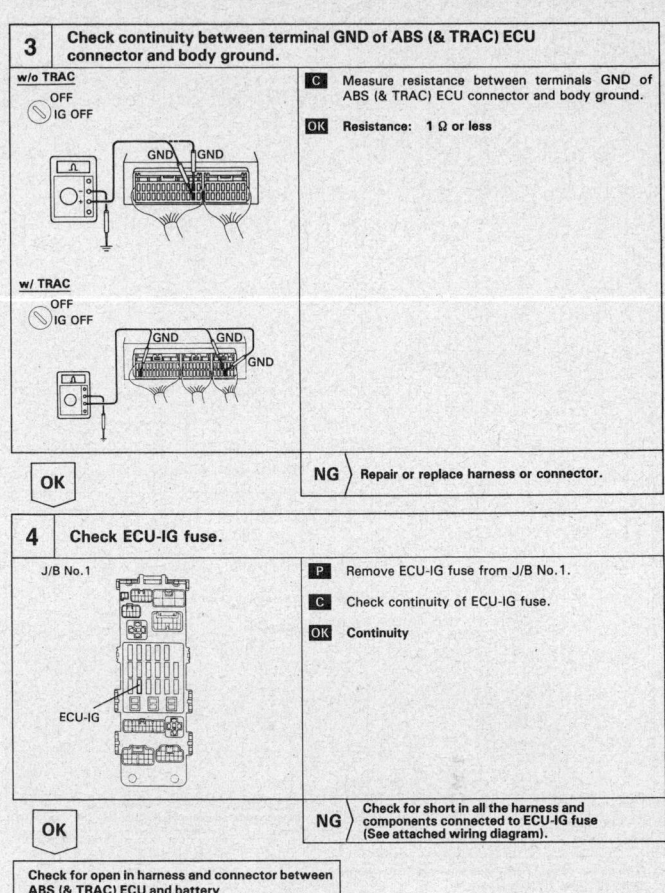

3	**Check continuity between terminal GND of ABS (& TRAC) ECU connector and body ground.**

w/o TRAC
OFF
IG OFF

w/ TRAC
OFF
IG OFF

C Measure resistance between terminals GND of ABS (& TRAC) ECU connector and body ground.

OK Resistance: 1 Ω or less

OK

NG ⟩ Repair or replace harness or connector.

4	**Check ECU-IG fuse.**

J/B No.1

ECU-IG

P Remove ECU-IG fuse from J/B No.1.

C Check continuity of ECU-IG fuse.

OK Continuity

OK

NG ⟩ Check for short in all the harness and components connected to ECU-IG fuse (See attached wiring diagram).

Check for open in harness and connector between ABS (& TRAC) ECU and battery

TY4029300442020X

Fig. 277 Code 41: IG Power Source Circuit (Part 3 of 4). 1996 Supra

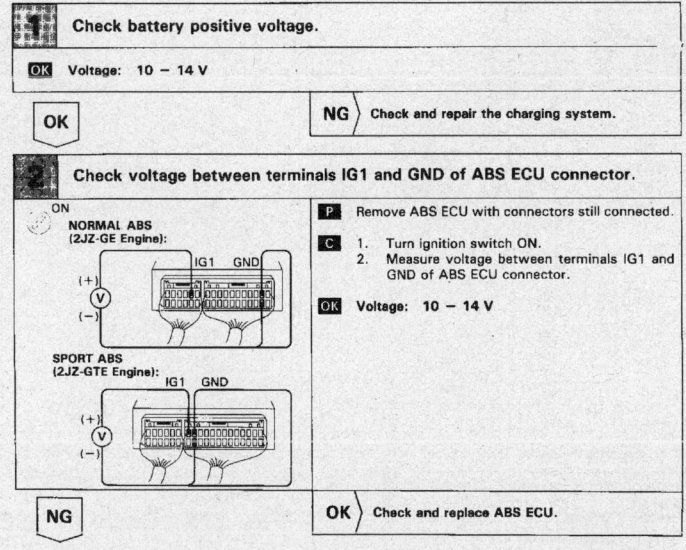

1	**Check battery positive voltage.**

OK Voltage: 10 – 14 V

OK

NG ⟩ Check and repair the charging system.

2	**Check voltage between terminals IG1 and GND of ABS ECU connector.**

ON

NORMAL ABS
(2JZ-GE Engine):
IG1 GND
(+)
(V)
(−)

SPORT ABS
(2JZ-GTE Engine):
IG1 GND
(+)
(V)
(−)

P Remove ABS ECU with connectors still connected.

C 1. Turn ignition switch ON.
2. Measure voltage between terminals IG1 and GND of ABS ECU connector.

OK Voltage: 10 – 14 V

NG

OK ⟩ Check and replace ABS ECU.

TY4029700416020X

Fig. 277 Code 41: IG Power Source Circuit (Part 3 of 4). 1997–98 Supra less Traction Control

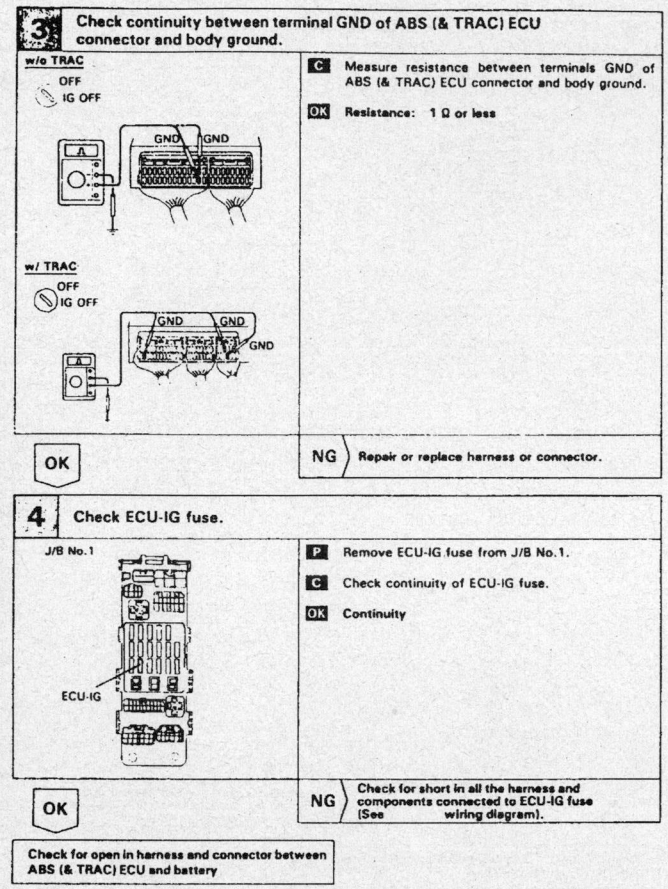

Fig. 277 Code 41: IG Power Source Circuit (Part 4 of 4). 1996 Supra less Traction Control

TY4029300090040X

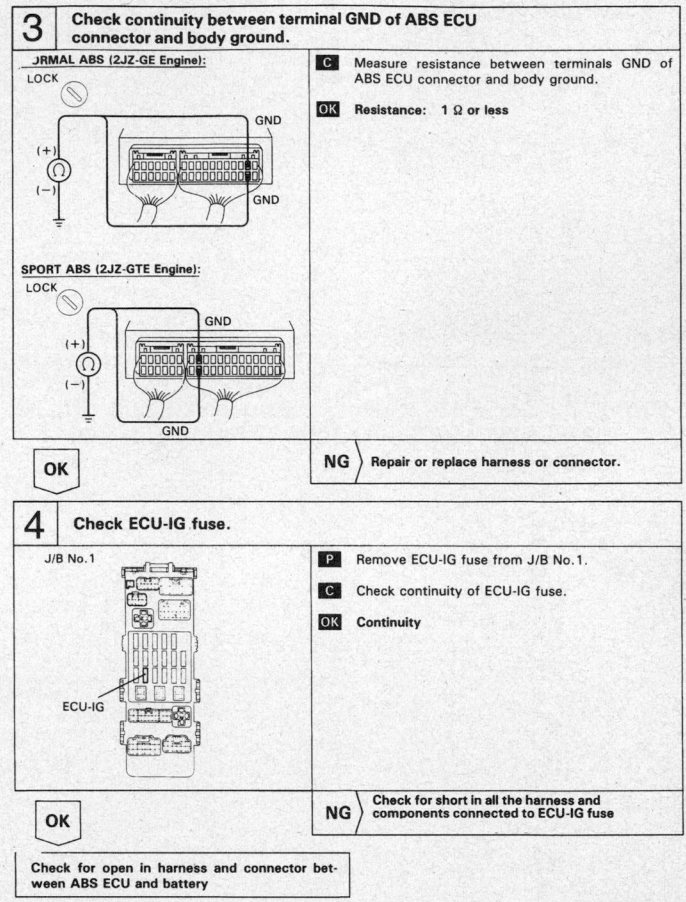

Fig. 277 Code 41: IG Power Source Circuit (Part 4 of 4). 1997–98 Supra less Traction Control

TY4029700416030X

CIRCUIT DESCRIPTION

The throttle control ECU receives engine speed signals (NE signals)from the ECM.

DTC No.	DTC Detecting Condition	Trouble Area
41	While engine is running, throttle control ECU detected 0 rpm signal for 0.8 sec. or more.	• Wire harness and connector (NE circuit) • ECM • Throttle control ECU

WIRING DIAGRAM

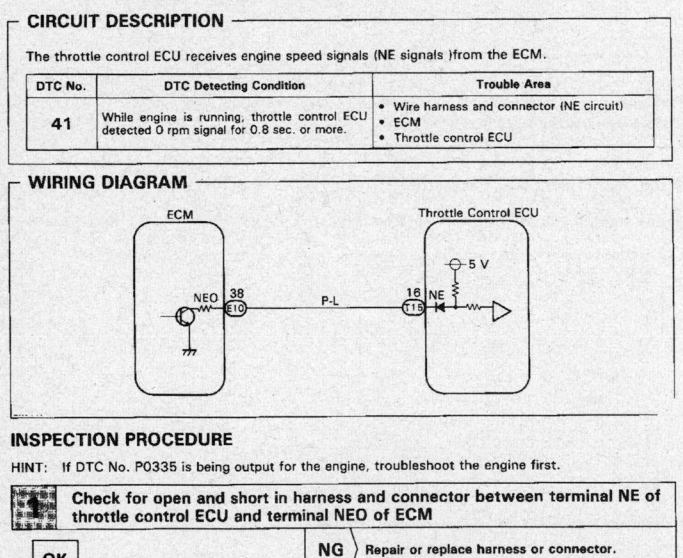

INSPECTION PROCEDURE

HINT: If DTC No. P0335 is being output for the engine, troubleshoot the engine first.

1	Check for open and short in harness and connector between terminal NE of throttle control ECU and terminal NEO of ECM.
OK	
NG	Repair or replace harness or connector.

TY4029700424010X

Fig. 278 Code 41: NE Signal Circuit (Part 1 of 2). Supra w/Traction Control

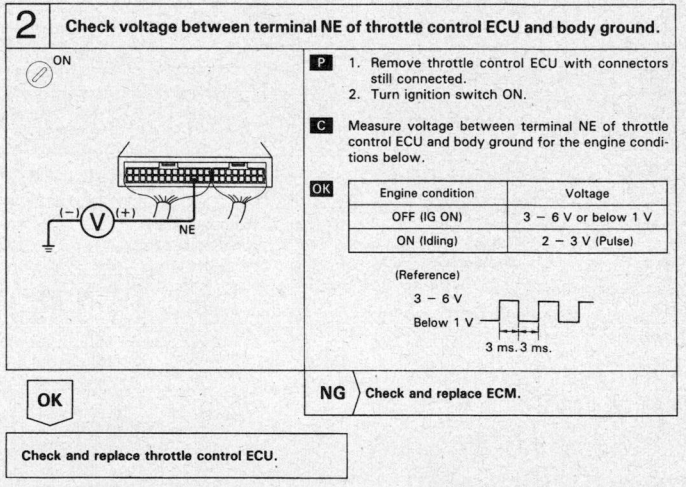

Check and replace throttle control ECU.

TY4029700424020X

Fig. 278 Code 41: NE Signal Circuit (Part 2 of 2). Supra w/Traction Control

CIRCUIT DESCRIPTION

If trouble in the engine control system causes the malfunction indicator light to light up, this information is transmitted from the ECM to the throttle control ECU. The throttle control ECU may prohibit TRAC control as a result.

DTC No.	DTC Detecting Condition	Trouble Area
42	ECM detected malfunction signal ON (output voltage at terminal EFIF is 4.5 V or more, or 5.5 V or less for 1 sec. or more).	• Wire harness and connector (EFIF circuit) • ECM • Throttle control ECU

TY4029700425010X

Fig. 279   Code 42: Engine Control System Fault (Part 1 of 2). Supra w/Traction Control

DTC	43	ABS & TRAC ECU Malfunction

CIRCUIT DESCRIPTION

DTC No.	Diagnostic Trouble Code Detecting Condition	Trouble area
43	ABS control system or TRAC (BRAKE) control system or communication circuit is abnormal.	• ABS & TRAC ECU • Open or short in BRFA circuit

WIRING DIAGRAM

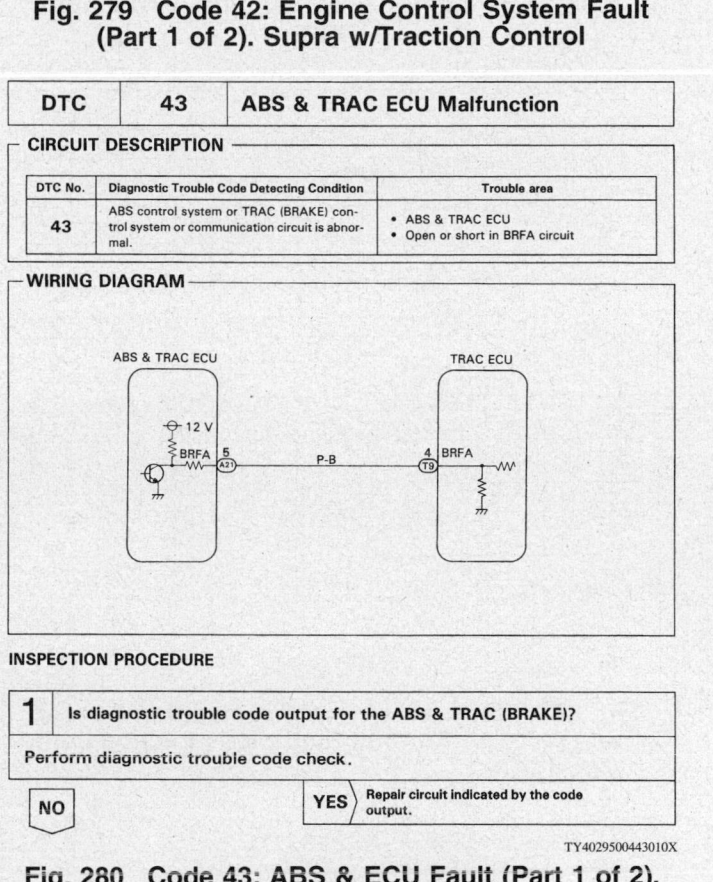

INSPECTION PROCEDURE

1	Is diagnostic trouble code output for the ABS & TRAC (BRAKE)?

Perform diagnostic trouble code check.

NO		YES	Repair circuit indicated by the code output.

TY4029500443010X

Fig. 280   Code 43: ABS & ECU Fault (Part 1 of 2). 1996 Supra w/Traction Control

WIRING DIAGRAM

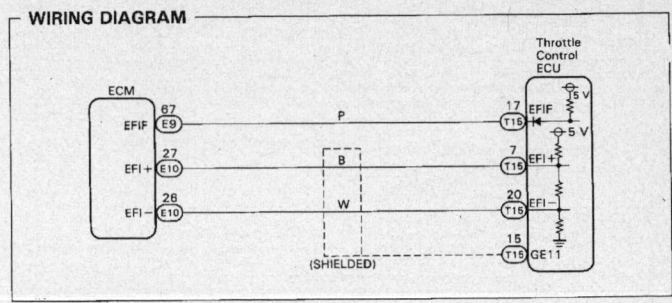

INSPECTION PROCEDURE

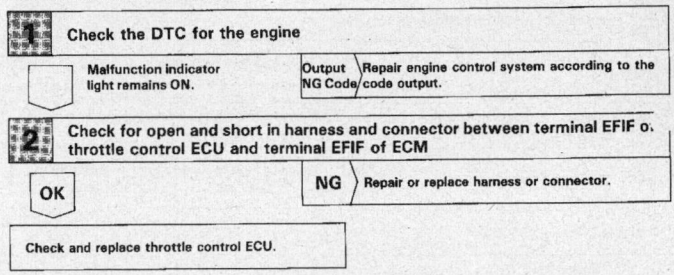

1	Check the DTC for the engine
Malfunction indicator light remains ON.	Output NG Code	Repair engine control system according to the code output.

2	Check for open and short in harness and connector between terminal EFIF of throttle control ECU and terminal EFIF of ECM
OK		NG	Repair or replace harness or connector.

Check and replace throttle control ECU.

TY4029700425020X

Fig. 279   Code 42: Engine Control System Fault (Part 2 of 2). Supra w/Traction Control

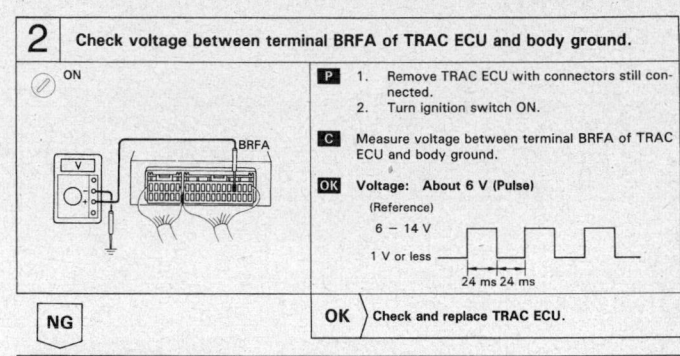

2	Check voltage between terminal BRFA of TRAC ECU and body ground.

P 1. Remove TRAC ECU with connectors still connected.
2. Turn ignition switch ON.

C Measure voltage between terminal BRFA of TRAC ECU and body ground.

OK Voltage: About 6 V (Pulse)

NG		OK	Check and replace TRAC ECU.

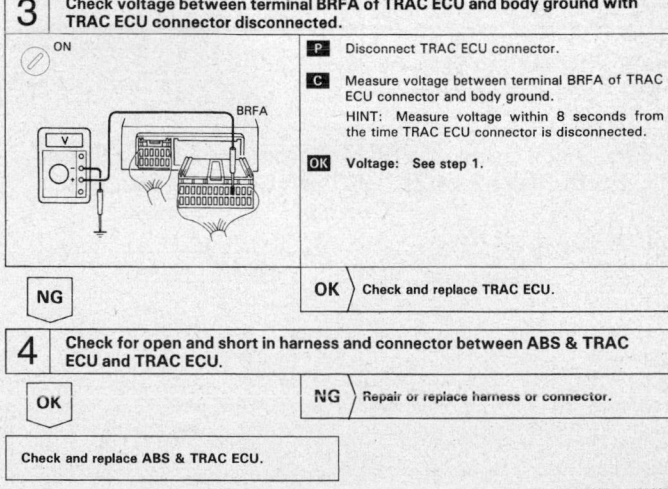

3	Check voltage between terminal BRFA of TRAC ECU and body ground with TRAC ECU connector disconnected.

P Disconnect TRAC ECU connector.

C Measure voltage between terminal BRFA of TRAC ECU connector and body ground.
HINT: Measure voltage within 8 seconds from the time TRAC ECU connector is disconnected.

OK Voltage: See step 1.

NG		OK	Check and replace TRAC ECU.

4	Check for open and short in harness and connector between ABS & TRAC ECU and TRAC ECU.
OK		NG	Repair or replace harness or connector.

Check and replace ABS & TRAC ECU.

TY4029500443020X

Fig. 280   Code 43: ABS & ECU Fault (Part 2 of 2). 1996 Supra w/Traction Control

CIRCUIT DESCRIPTION

DTC No.	DTC Detecting Condition	Trouble Area
43	Either of the following (1) or (2) is detected: (1) Input from the deceleration sensor does not change at one cycle (0 km/h → more than 30 km/h → 0 km/h) for 16 times continuously. (2) When the brake pedal is not depressed at vehicle speed of 5 km/h or more, forward and backward G (more than 0.4 G) is detected for 30 seconds or more.	• Deceleration sensor • Wire harness for deceleration sensor system
45	At vehicle speed of 30 km/h or more, the deceleration sensor output and vehicle acceleration from wheel speed remain abnormally different for 60 seconds or more.	• Deceleration sensor • Wire harness for deceleration sensor system

INSPECTION PROCEDURE

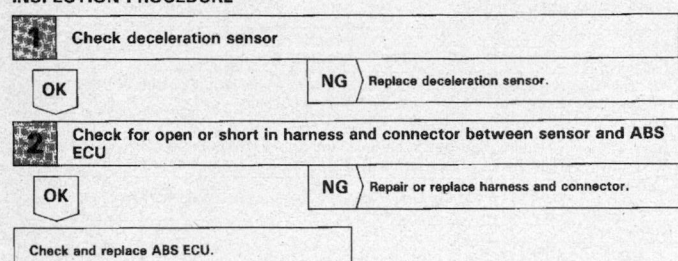

1 **Check deceleration sensor**

| OK | | NG | Replace deceleration sensor. |

2 **Check for open or short in harness and connector between sensor and ABS ECU**

| OK | | NG | Repair or replace harness and connector. |

Check and replace ABS ECU.

TY4029700417000X

Fig. 281 Code 43 & 45: Deceleration Sensor Fault. 1997–98 Supra less Traction Control

WIRING DIAGRAM

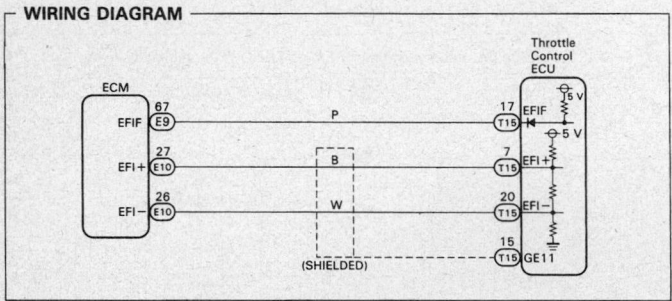

INSPECTION PROCEDURE

1 **Check for open and short in harness and connector between terminals EFI+ and EFI− of throttle control ECU and ECM**

| OK | | NG | Repair or replace harness or connector. |

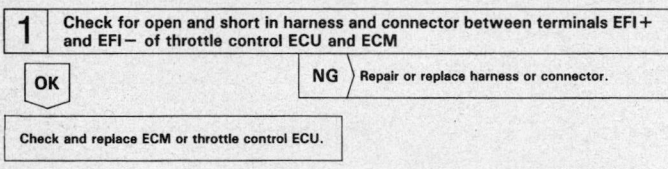

Check and replace ECM or throttle control ECU.

TY4029700426020X

Fig. 282 Code 43: ECM Communication Circuit Fault (Part 2 of 2). 1997–98 Supra w/Traction Control

CIRCUIT DESCRIPTION

DTC No.	DTC Detecting Condition	Trouble Area
43	ECM normal communication data is not received for 5 sec. or more.	• Wire harness and connector (EFI+ and EFI− circuit) • ECM • Throttle control ECU

TY4029700426010X

Fig. 282 Code 43: ECM Communication Circuit Fault (Part 1 of 2). 1997–98 Supra w/Traction Control

CIRCUIT DESCRIPTION

This sensor detects acceleration acting laterally on the vehicle. The sensor signal is used in ABS control. If the sensor functions abnormally, the ABS warning light comes on but the ABS still operates.

DTC No.	Diagnostic Trouble Code Detecting Condition	Trouble area
44	Either of the following (1) or (2) is detected: (1) An open or short is detected in circuit GS1 or GS2 for 1 sec. (2) After the ignition is turned ON, the test signal is output by GST. During this time, a trouble signal is detected for 0.5 sec.	• Lateral acceleration sensor • Open or short in lateral acceleration sensor circuit • ECU

DIAGNOSTIC CHART

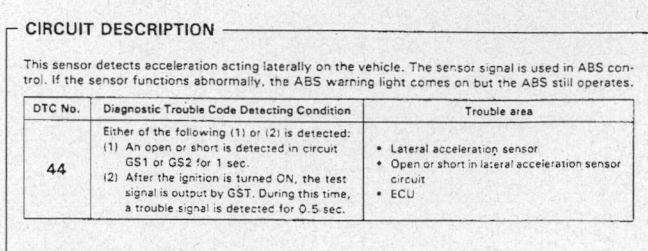

1 Check for open and short in harness and connector between sensor and ECU.

| | NG | Repair or replace harness or connector. |

OK

2 Check voltage between terminals GS1, GS2, GST of ECU and body ground.

| | NG | Check and replace ABS (& TRAC) ECU. |

OK

Check and replace lateral acceleration sensor.

TY4029300091010X

Fig. 283 Code 44: Lateral Acceleration Sensor Circuit (Part 1 of 3). 1996 Supra less traction control

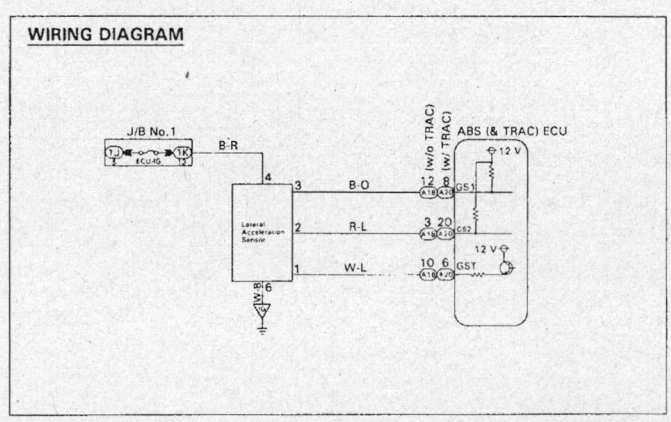

WIRING DIAGRAM

TY4029300091020X

Fig. 283 Code 44: Lateral Acceleration Sensor Circuit (Part 2 of 3). 1996 Supra less traction control

1 Check for open and short in harness and connector between sensor and ECU

OK

NG > Repair or replace harness or connector.

2 Check voltage between terminals GS1, GS2, GST of ECU and body ground.

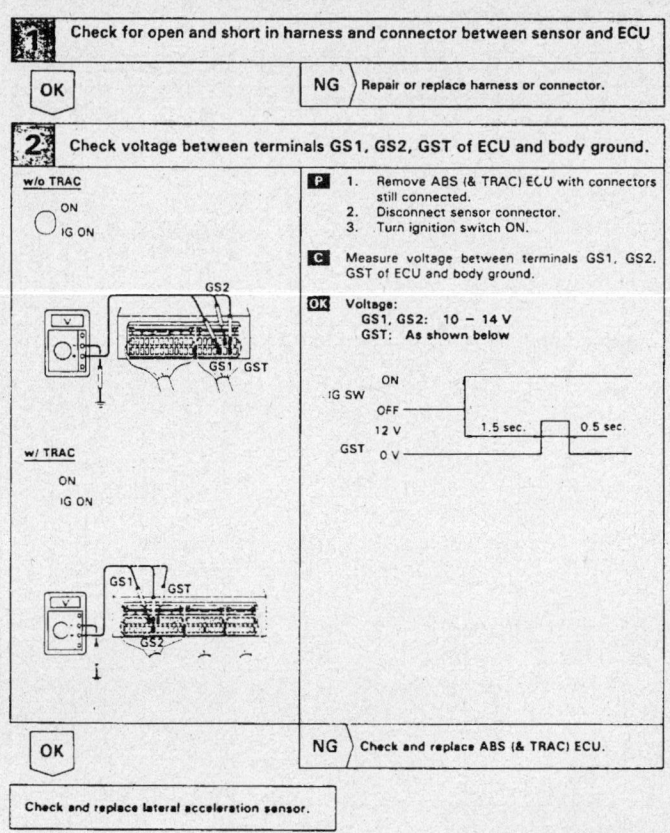

w/o TRAC
ON
○ IG ON

w/ TRAC
ON
IG ON

P 1. Remove ABS (& TRAC) ECU with connectors still connected.
2. Disconnect sensor connector.
3. Turn ignition switch ON.

C Measure voltage between terminals GS1, GS2, GST of ECU and body ground.

OK Voltage:
GS1, GS2: 10 – 14 V
GST: As shown below

OK

NG > Check and replace ABS (& TRAC) ECU.

Check and replace lateral acceleration sensor.

TY4029300091030X

Fig. 283 Code 44: Lateral Acceleration Sensor Circuit (Part 3 of 3). 1996 Supra less traction control

1 Check for open and short in harness and connector between terminal NEO of TRAC ECU and terminal NEO of ECM.

OK

NG > Repair or replace harness or connector.

2 Check voltage between terminal NEO of TRAC ECU and body ground.

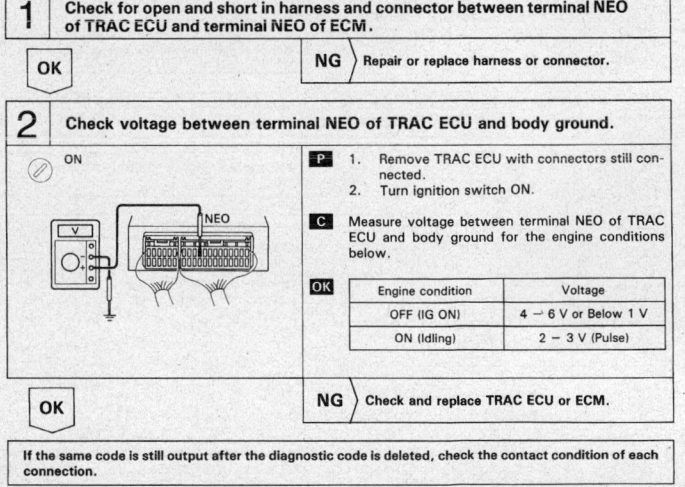

ON

P 1. Remove TRAC ECU with connectors still connected.
2. Turn ignition switch ON.

C Measure voltage between terminal NEO of TRAC ECU and body ground for the engine conditions below.

OK

Engine condition	Voltage
OFF (IG ON)	4 – 6 V or Below 1 V
ON (Idling)	2 – 3 V (Pulse)

OK

NG > Check and replace TRAC ECU or ECM.

If the same code is still output after the diagnostic code is deleted, check the contact condition of each connection.

TY4029500444020X

Fig. 284 Code 44: NE Signal Circuit Fault (Part 2 of 2). 1996 Supra w/Traction Control

CIRCUIT DESCRIPTION

The TRAC ECU receives engine speed signals (NE signals) from the ECM.

DTC No.	Diagnostic Trouble Code Detecting Condition	Trouble area
44	No signal is input to terminal NEO 0.24 sec. after traction control is initiated.	• Open or short in NEO circuit • ECM • TRAC ECU

WIRING DIAGRAM

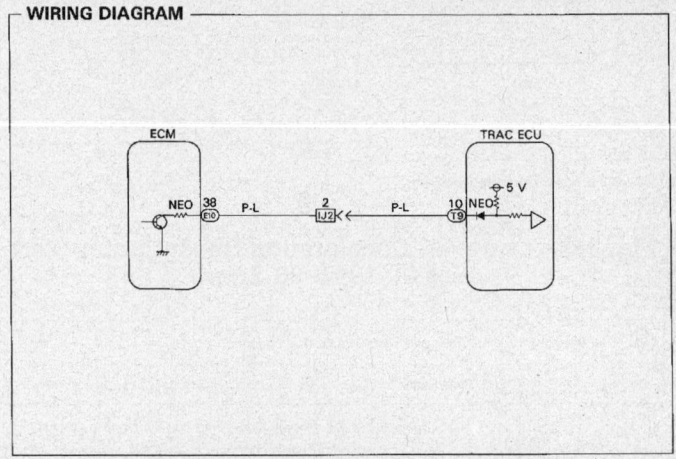

TY4029500444010X

Fig. 284 Code 44: NE Signal Circuit Fault (Part 1 of 2). 1996 Supra w/Traction Control

CIRCUIT DESCRIPTION

This sensor detects deceleration on the vehicle. The sensor signal is used in ABS control. If the sensor functions abnormally, the ABS warning light comes on but the ABS still operates.

DTC No.	DTC Detecting Condition	Trouble Area
44	Either of the following (1), (2) or (3) is detected: (1) IG switch ON and output voltage of GL1 or GL2 remains 0.5 V or less or 4.5 V or more for more than 1.2 sec. (2) At vehicle speed of 0 km/h, outputs of GL1 and GL2 remains abnormally different for 60 sec. or more (3) IG switch ON and VGS ≦ 4.4 V, VGS ≧ 5.5 V continues for 1.2 sec. or more.	• Deceleration sensor • Open or short in deceleration sensor circuit

WIRING DIAGRAM

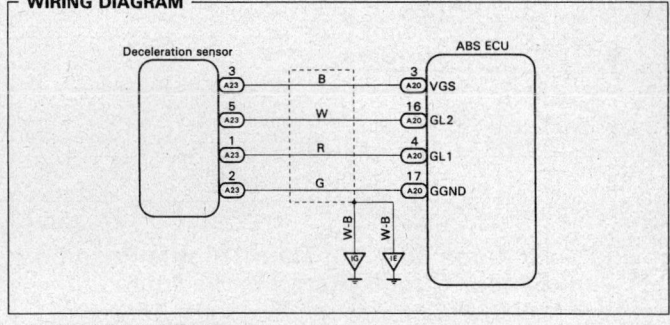

INSPECTION PROCEDURE

1 Check for open and short in harness and connector between sensor and ABS ECU

OK

NG > Repair or replace harness or connector.

TY4029700418010X

Fig. 285 Code 44: Deceleration Sensor Fault (Part 1 of 2). 1997–98 Supra

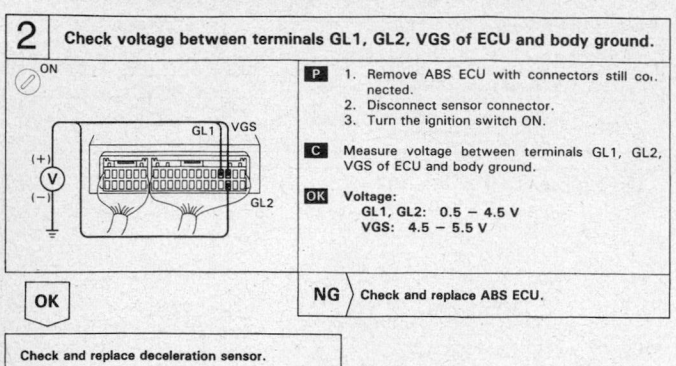

2 Check voltage between terminals GL1, GL2, VGS of ECU and body ground.

P
1. Remove ABS ECU with connectors still connected.
2. Disconnect sensor connector.
3. Turn the ignition switch ON.

C Measure voltage between terminals GL1, GL2, VGS of ECU and body ground.

OK Voltage:
GL1, GL2: 0.5 – 4.5 V
VGS: 4.5 – 5.5 V

OK | **NG** Check and replace ABS ECU.

Check and replace deceleration sensor.

TY4029700418020X

Fig. 285 Code 44: Deceleration Sensor Fault (Part 2 of 2). 1997–98 Supra

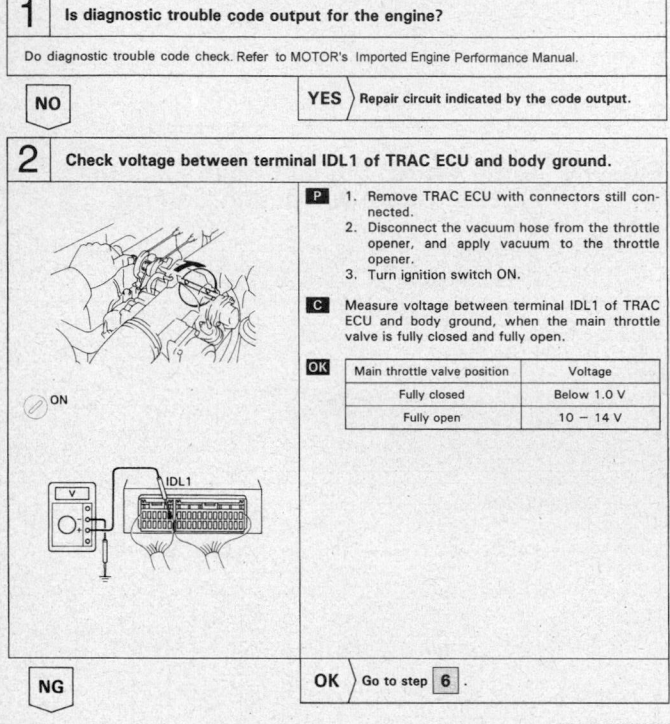

1 Is diagnostic trouble code output for the engine?

Do diagnostic trouble code check. Refer to MOTOR's Imported Engine Performance Manual.

NO | **YES** Repair circuit indicated by the code output.

2 Check voltage between terminal IDL1 of TRAC ECU and body ground.

P
1. Remove TRAC ECU with connectors still connected.
2. Disconnect the vacuum hose from the throttle opener, and apply vacuum to the throttle opener.
3. Turn ignition switch ON.

C Measure voltage between terminal IDL1 of TRAC ECU and body ground, when the main throttle valve is fully closed and fully open.

OK

Main throttle valve position	Voltage
Fully closed	Below 1.0 V
Fully open	10 – 14 V

NG | **OK** Go to step **6**.

TY4029500445020X

Fig. 286 Code 45 & 46: Main Throttle Position Sensor Circuit (Part 2 of 3). Supra

---

CIRCUIT DESCRIPTION

This circuit is not directly related to the TRAC control, but as it has an influence on TRAC control when trouble occurs in this circuit, it is used to switch off the TRAC system as a fail safe function.

DTC No.	Diagnostic Trouble Code Detecting Condition	Trouble area
45	Conditions (1) and (2) continue for 0.31 sec.: (1) CTP switch of main throttle position sensor is ON. (2) Input voltage of ECM terminal VTA1: 1.5 V or more.	• Main throttle position sensor • Short in IDL1 circuit • ECM • TRAC ECU
46	Either of the following (1) or (2) continues for 0.6 sec.: (1) Input voltage of ECM terminal VTA1: 4.9 V or more. (2) Input voltage of ECM terminal VTA1: 0.1 V or less.	• Main throttle position sensor • Open or short in VTA1 circuit • ECM

WIRING DIAGRAM

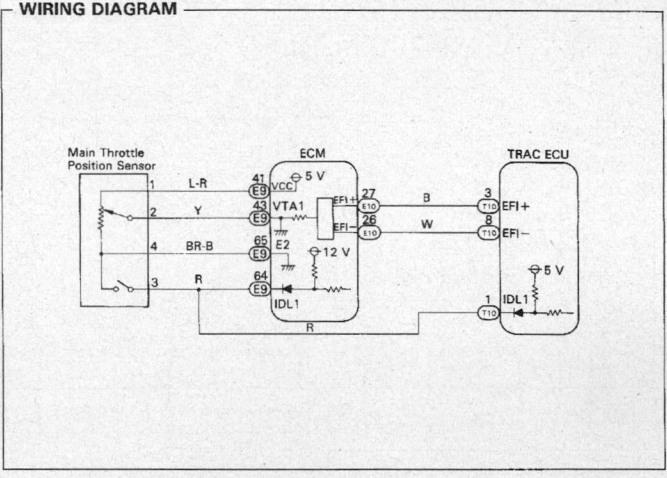

TY4029500445010X

Fig. 286 Code 45 & 46: Main Throttle Position Sensor Circuit (Part 1 of 3). Supra

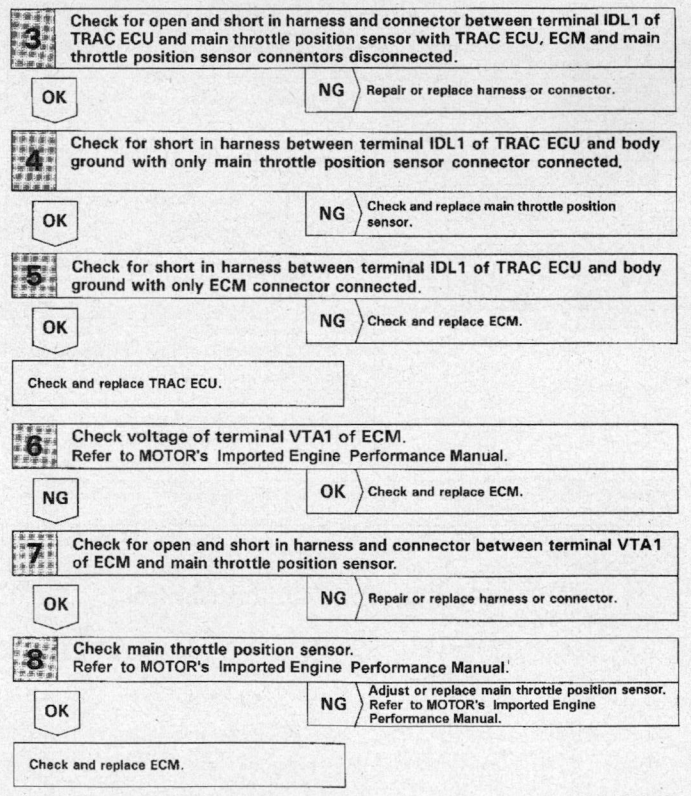

3 Check for open and short in harness and connector between terminal IDL1 of TRAC ECU and main throttle position sensor with TRAC ECU, ECM and main throttle position sensor connentors disconnected.

OK | **NG** Repair or replace harness or connector.

4 Check for short in harness between terminal IDL1 of TRAC ECU and body ground with only main throttle position sensor connector connected.

OK | **NG** Check and replace main throttle position sensor.

5 Check for short in harness between terminal IDL1 of TRAC ECU and body ground with only ECM connector connected.

OK | **NG** Check and replace ECM.

Check and replace TRAC ECU.

6 Check voltage of terminal VTA1 of ECM. Refer to MOTOR's Imported Engine Performance Manual.

NG | **OK** Check and replace ECM.

7 Check for open and short in harness and connector between terminal VTA1 of ECM and main throttle position sensor.

OK | **NG** Repair or replace harness or connector.

8 Check main throttle position sensor. Refer to MOTOR's Imported Engine Performance Manual.

OK | **NG** Adjust or replace main throttle position sensor. Refer to MOTOR's Imported Engine Performance Manual.

Check and replace ECM.

TY4029500445030X

Fig. 286 Code 45 & 46: Main Throttle Position Sensor Circuit (Part 3 of 3). Supra

CIRCUIT DESCRIPTION

This sensor detects the opening angle of the sub-throttle valve and sends the appropriate signals to the ECU. If a trouble signal is input, the ECU prohibits TRAC control.

DTC No.	Diagnostic Trouble Code Detecting Condition	Trouble area
47	When any of the following (1) through (3) is detected: (1) Deviation of 5 steps or more to the closed side of the idle step during sub-throttle initial check. (2) Voltage at terminal IDL2 does not become 0 V even after sub-throttle is driven to fully closed position during sub-throttle initial check. (3) Voltage at terminal VTA2 of ECM is 1.5 V or more for at least 0.31 sec. while CTP switch is ON.	• Sub-throttle position sensor • Open or short in IDL2 circuit • ECM • TRAC ECU
48	Either of the following (1) or (2) continues for more than 0.26 sec.: (1) Input voltage of ECM terminal VTA2: 4.9 V or more. (2) Input voltage of ECM terminal VTA2: 0.1 V or less.	• Sub-throttle position sensor • Open or short in VTA2 circuit • ECM

WIRING DIAGRAM

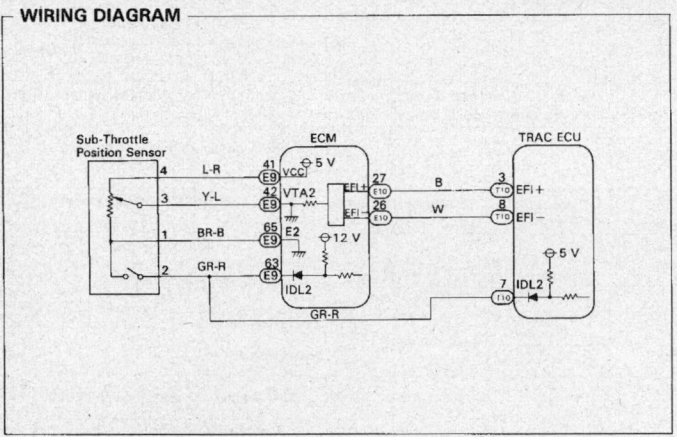

TY4029500446010X

Fig. 287 Code 47 & 48: Sub Throttle Position Sensor Circuit (Part 1 of 3). Supra

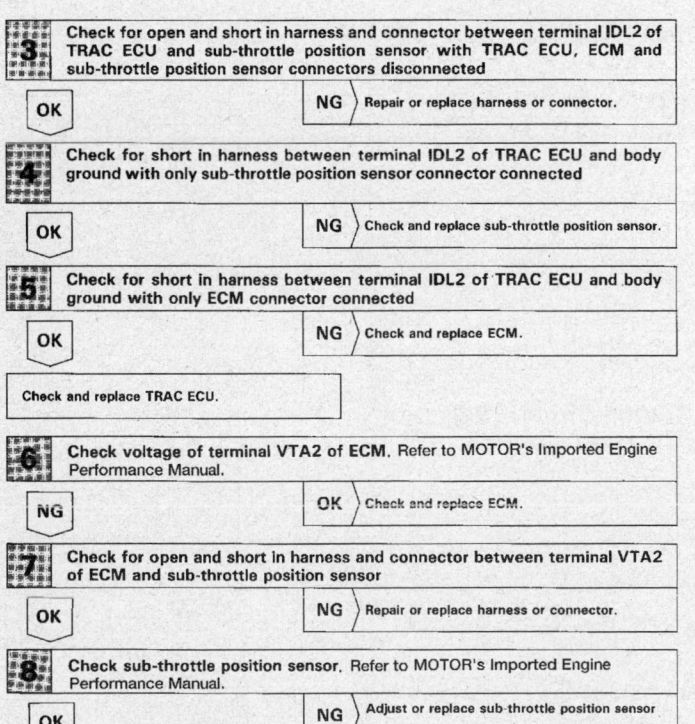

3 Check for open and short in harness and connector between terminal IDL2 of TRAC ECU and sub-throttle position sensor with TRAC ECU, ECM and sub-throttle position sensor connectors disconnected

OK │ NG ⟩ Repair or replace harness or connector.

4 Check for short in harness between terminal IDL2 of TRAC ECU and body ground with only sub-throttle position sensor connector connected

OK │ NG ⟩ Check and replace sub-throttle position sensor.

5 Check for short in harness between terminal IDL2 of TRAC ECU and body ground with only ECM connector connected

OK │ NG ⟩ Check and replace ECM.

Check and replace TRAC ECU.

6 Check voltage of terminal VTA2 of ECM. Refer to MOTOR's Imported Engine Performance Manual.

NG │ OK ⟩ Check and replace ECM.

7 Check for open and short in harness and connector between terminal VTA2 of ECM and sub-throttle position sensor

OK │ NG ⟩ Repair or replace harness or connector.

8 Check sub-throttle position sensor. Refer to MOTOR's Imported Engine Performance Manual.

OK │ NG ⟩ Adjust or replace sub-throttle position sensor.

Check and replace ECM.

TY4029500446030X

Fig. 310 Code 47 & 48: Sub Throttle Position Sensor Circuit (Part 3 of 3). Supra

ANTI-LOCK BRAKES

---

1 Is diagnostic trouble code output for the engine?

Do diagnostic trouble code check. Refer to MOTOR's Imported Engine Performance Manual.

NO │ YES ⟩ Repair circuit indicated by the code output.

2 Check voltage between terminal IDL2 of TRAC ECU and body ground.

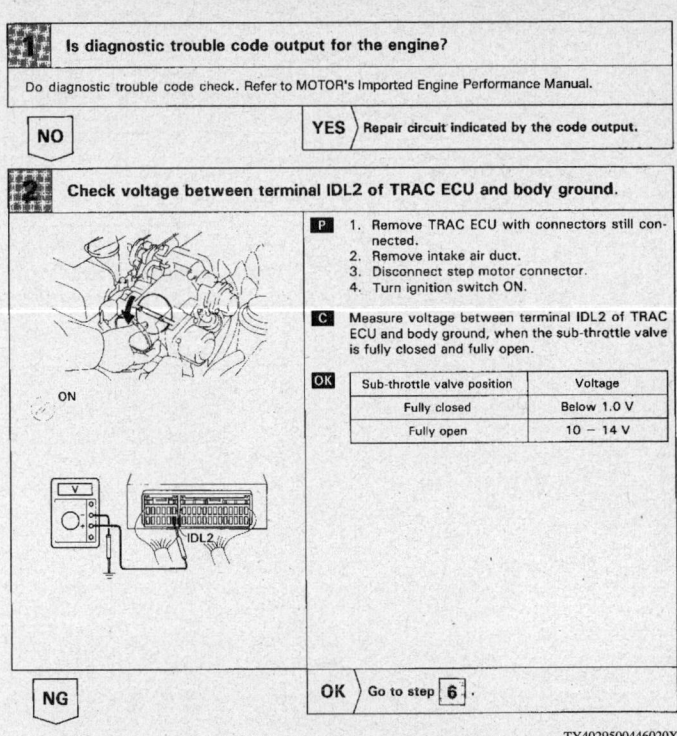

P 1. Remove TRAC ECU with connectors still connected.
2. Remove intake air duct.
3. Disconnect step motor connector.
4. Turn ignition switch ON.

C Measure voltage between terminal IDL2 of TRAC ECU and body ground, when the sub-throttle valve is fully closed and fully open.

OK

Sub-throttle valve position	Voltage
Fully closed	Below 1.0 V
Fully open	10 – 14 V

NG │ OK ⟩ Go to step **6**.

TY4029500446020X

Fig. 287 Code 47 & 48: Sub Throttle Position Sensor Circuit (Part 2 of 3). Supra

CIRCUIT DESCRIPTION

DTC No.	DTC Detecting Condition	Trouble Area
51	Pump motor is not operating normally during initial check.	• ABS pump motor

Fail safe function: If trouble occurs in the ABS pump motor, the ECU cuts off the current to the ABS solenoid relay and prohibits ABS control.

TY4029300092000X

Fig. 288 Code 51: ABS Pump Motor Lock. Supra less Traction Control

CIRCUIT DESCRIPTION

If trouble in the engine control system causes the malfunction indicator light to light up, this information is transmitted from the ECM to the TRAC ECU. The TRAC ECU may prohibit TRAC control as a result.

DTC No.	Diagnostic Trouble Code Detecting Condition	Trouble area
51	Conditions (1) and (2) continue for more than 1 sec.: (1) Engine speed: 500 rpm or more (2) Malfunction information is input from the ECM.	• Engine control system

INSPECTION PROCEDURE

1 Check the diagnostic trouble code for the engine. Refer to MOTOR's Imported Engine Performance Manual.

Malfunction indicator light remains ON. │ Output NG Code ⟩ Repair engine control system according to the code output.

Check for short in all the harness and ECU connected to malfunction indicator light.

TY4029500447000X

Fig. 289 Code 51: Engine Fault Detection Circuit. 1996 Supra w/Traction Control

CIRCUIT DESCRIPTION

DTC No.	DTC Detecting Condition	Trouble Area
51	In case power source voltage comes down, sub-throttle valve angle difference occurs.	• Wire harness and connector (+B and E01 circuit) • Throttle control ECU
52	Engine speed is 500 rpm or more and throttle relay is ON and ECU terminal +B voltage is less than 8 V for 10 sec. or more.	• Battery • IC regulator • Wire harness and connector (+B and E01 circuit) • Throttle control ECU

TY4029700427010X

Fig. 290   Code 51: Power Source Circuit (Part 1 of 3). 1997–98 Supra w/Traction Control

WIRING DIAGRAM

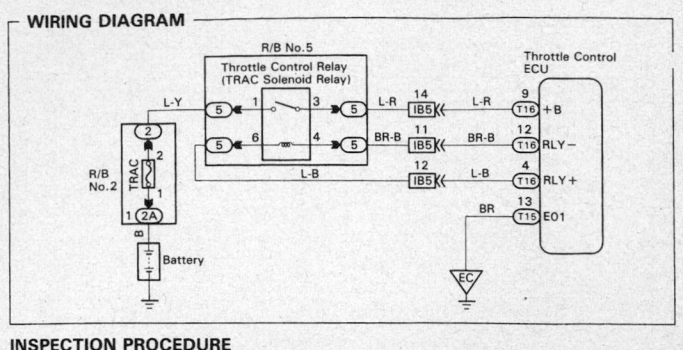

INSPECTION PROCEDURE

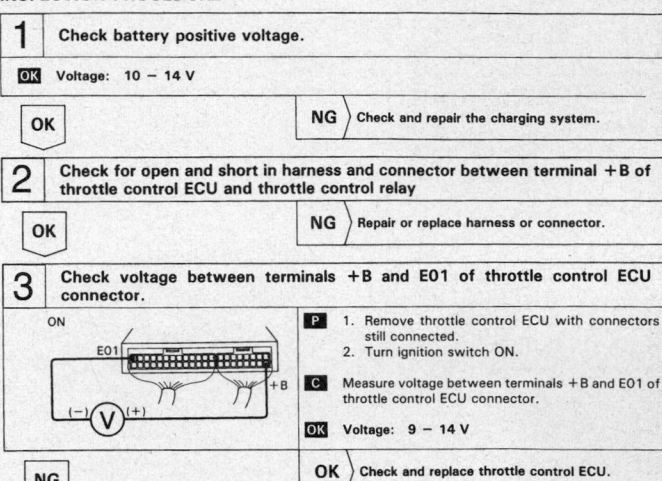

1   Check battery positive voltage.

OK   Voltage: 10 – 14 V

OK →

NG → Check and repair the charging system.

2   Check for open and short in harness and connector between terminal +B of throttle control ECU and throttle control relay

OK →

NG → Repair or replace harness or connector.

3   Check voltage between terminals +B and E01 of throttle control ECU connector.

P   1. Remove throttle control ECU with connectors still connected.
2. Turn ignition switch ON.

C   Measure voltage between terminals +B and E01 of throttle control ECU connector.

OK   Voltage: 9 – 14 V

NG →

OK → Check and replace throttle control ECU.

TY4029700427020X

Fig. 290   Code 51: Power Source Circuit (Part 2 of 3). 1997–98 Supra w/Traction Control

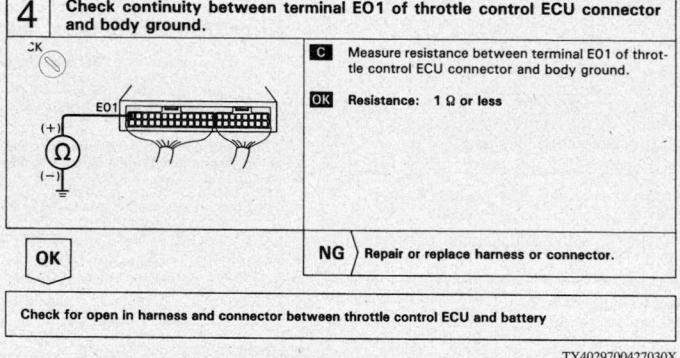

4   Check continuity between terminal E01 of throttle control ECU connector and body ground.

C   Measure resistance between terminal E01 of throttle control ECU connector and body ground.

OK   Resistance: 1 Ω or less

OK →

NG → Repair or replace harness or connector.

Check for open in harness and connector between throttle control ECU and battery

TY4029700427030X

Fig. 290   Code 51: Power Source Circuit (Part 3 of 3). 1997–98 Supra w/Traction Control

CIRCUIT DESCRIPTION

This circuit is used to send TRAC control information from the TRAC ECU to the ECM (TRC+, TRC−), and engine control information from the ECM to the TRAC ECU (EFI+, EFI−).

DTC No.	Diagnostic Trouble Code Detecting Condition	Trouble area
53	Either of the following (1) or (2) continues for 5 sec.: (1) A signal is received from the ECM indicating trouble in the TRC+ or TRC− circuit. (2) No EFI± data is received from the ECM when the engine speed is 500 RPM or more, or the vehicle speed is 60 km/h (37 mph) or more.	• Open or short in TRC+ or TRC− circuit • Open or short in EFI+ or EFI− circuit • ECM • TRAC ECU

WIRING DIAGRAM

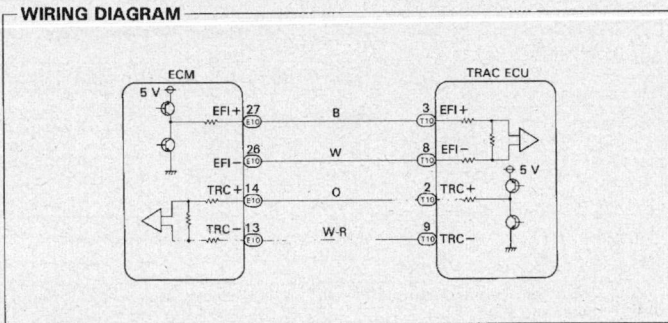

INSPECTION PROCEDURE

HINT: When the TRAC indicator light is ON, there is a problem in the EFI± circuit, and when the TRAC indicator light is OFF, there is a problem in the TRC± circuit.

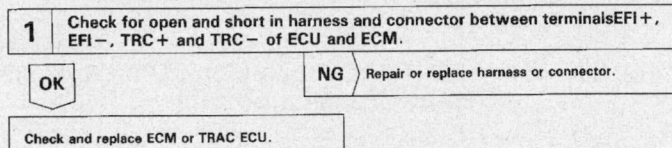

1 Check for open and short in harness and connector between terminals EFI+, EFI−, TRC+ and TRC− of ECU and ECM.

OK → NG ▷ Repair or replace harness or connector.

Check and replace ECM or TRAC ECU.

TY4029500448000X

Fig. 291 Code 53: ECM Communication Circuit Fault. Supra

INSPECTION PROCEDURE

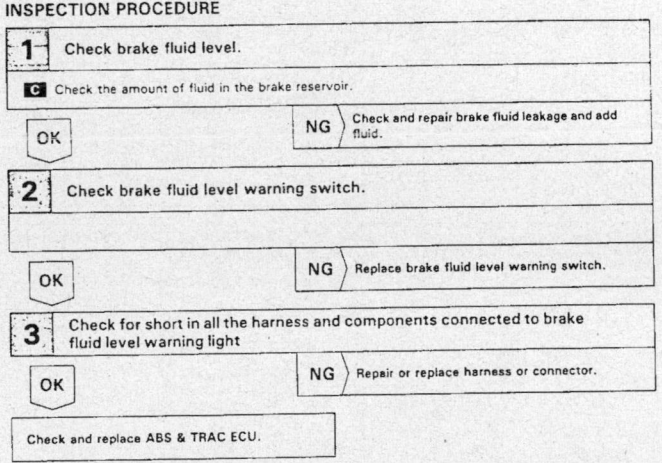

1 Check brake fluid level.

C Check the amount of fluid in the brake reservoir.

OK → NG ▷ Check and repair brake fluid leakage and add fluid.

2 Check brake fluid level warning switch.

OK → NG ▷ Replace brake fluid level warning switch.

3 Check for short in all the harness and components connected to brake fluid level warning light

OK → NG ▷ Repair or replace harness or connector.

Check and replace ABS & TRAC ECU.

TY4029300093020X

Fig. 292 Code 55: Brake Fluid Level Warning Switch (Part 2 of 2). Supra

CIRCUIT DESCRIPTION

The brake fluid level warning switch sends the appropriate signal to the ECU when the brake fluid level drops.

DTC No.	Diagnostic Trouble Code Detecting Condition	Trouble area
55	Voltage at ECU terminal LBL is 0 V continuously for 10 sec. or more.	• Brake fluid level • Brake fluid level warning switch • Short in brake fluid level warning switch circuit • ECU

Fail safe function: If trouble occurs in this circuit, the ECU cuts off current to the TRAC solenoid relay and prohibits TRAC control.

DIAGNOSTIC CHART

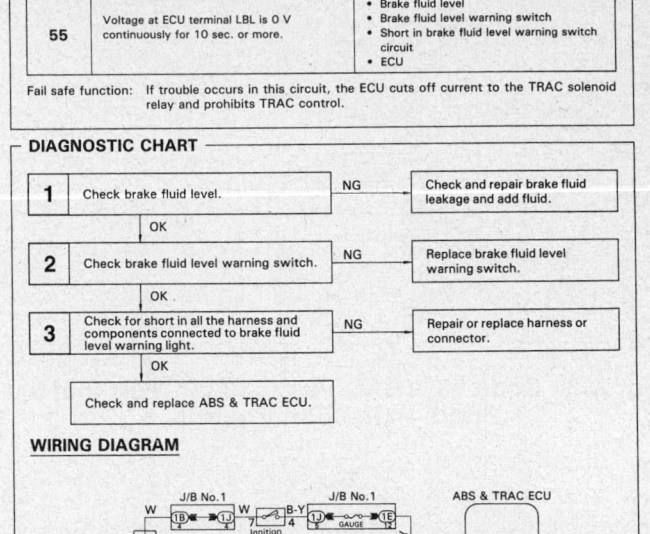

1 Check brake fluid level. — NG → Check and repair brake fluid leakage and add fluid.

OK

2 Check brake fluid level warning switch. — NG → Replace brake fluid level warning switch.

OK

3 Check for short in all the harness and components connected to brake fluid level warning light. — NG → Repair or replace harness or connector.

OK

Check and replace ABS & TRAC ECU.

WIRING DIAGRAM

TY4029300093010X

Fig. 292 Code 55: Brake Fluid Level Warning Switch (Part 1 of 2). Supra

CIRCUIT DESCRIPTION

This motor is used to apply hydraulic pressure for the rear wheel brakes during TRAC control.

DTC No.	Diagnostic Trouble Code Detecting Condition	Trouble area
58	Conditions (1) through (3) continue for 2 sec. or more. (1) TRAC motor relay: Normal (2) TRAC motor: OFF (3) Voltage of ABS & TRAC ECU terminal MTT: 4 − 8 V	• TRAC pump motor • Open in TRAC pump motor circuit • ECU

Fail safe function: If trouble occurs in this circuit, the ECU cuts off current to the TRAC solenoid relay and prohibits TRAC control.

DIAGNOSTIC CHART

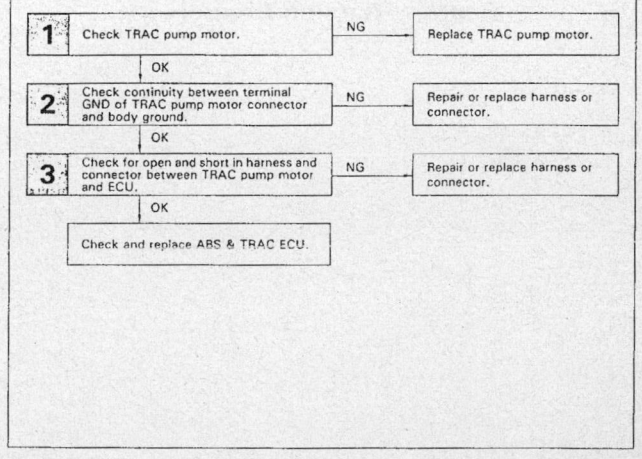

1 Check TRAC pump motor. — NG → Replace TRAC pump motor.

OK

2 Check continuity between terminal GND of TRAC pump motor connector and body ground. — NG → Repair or replace harness or connector.

OK

3 Check for open and short in harness and connector between TRAC pump motor and ECU. — NG → Repair or replace harness or connector.

OK

Check and replace ABS & TRAC ECU.

TY4029300094020X

Fig. 293 Code 58: TRAC Pump Motor (Part 1 of 3). Supra w/Traction Control

WIRING DIAGRAM

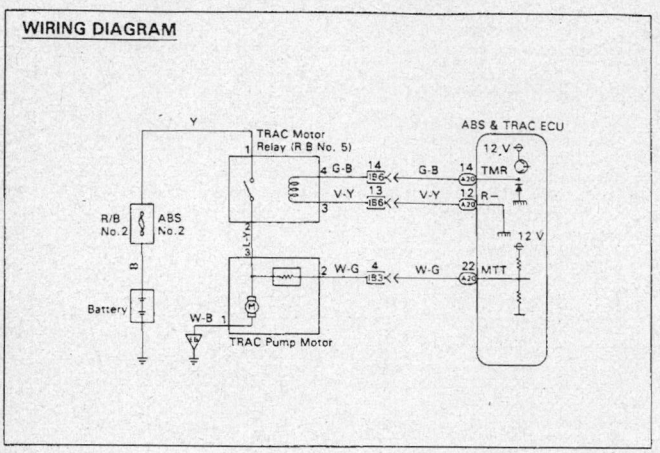

Fig. 293 Code 58: TRAC Pump Motor (Part 2 of 3).
Supra w/Traction Control

CIRCUIT DESCRIPTION

DTC No.	Diagnostic Trouble Code Detecting Condition	Trouble area
61	Malfunction in ABS & TRAC ECU communication circuit.	• Open or short in ABSO, BRC, BRP circuit • ABS & TRAC ECU • TRAC ECU

WIRING DIAGRAM

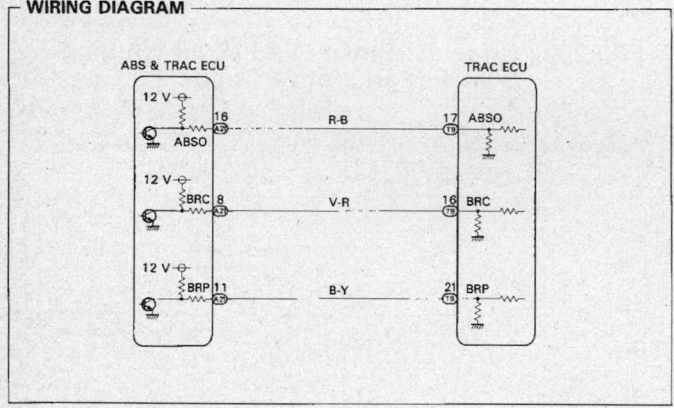

Fig. 294 Code 61: ABS & TRAC ECU
Communication Circuit Fault (Part 1 of 2). 1996
Supra w/Traction Control

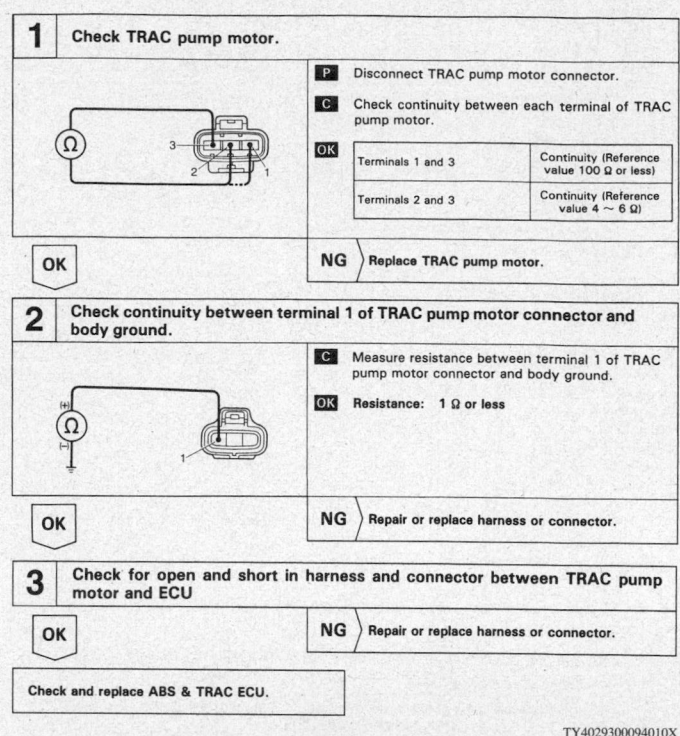

1 Check TRAC pump motor.

- **P** Disconnect TRAC pump motor connector.
- **C** Check continuity between each terminal of TRAC pump motor.
- **OK**

Terminals 1 and 3	Continuity (Reference value 100 Ω or less)
Terminals 2 and 3	Continuity (Reference value 4 ~ 6 Ω)

OK → **NG**) Replace TRAC pump motor.

2 Check continuity between terminal 1 of TRAC pump motor connector and body ground.

- **C** Measure resistance between terminal 1 of TRAC pump motor connector and body ground.
- **OK** Resistance: 1 Ω or less

OK → **NG**) Repair or replace harness or connector.

3 Check for open and short in harness and connector between TRAC pump motor and ECU.

OK → **NG**) Repair or replace harness or connector.

Check and replace ABS & TRAC ECU.

Fig. 293 Code 58: TRAC Pump Motor (Part 3 of 3).
Supra w/Traction Control

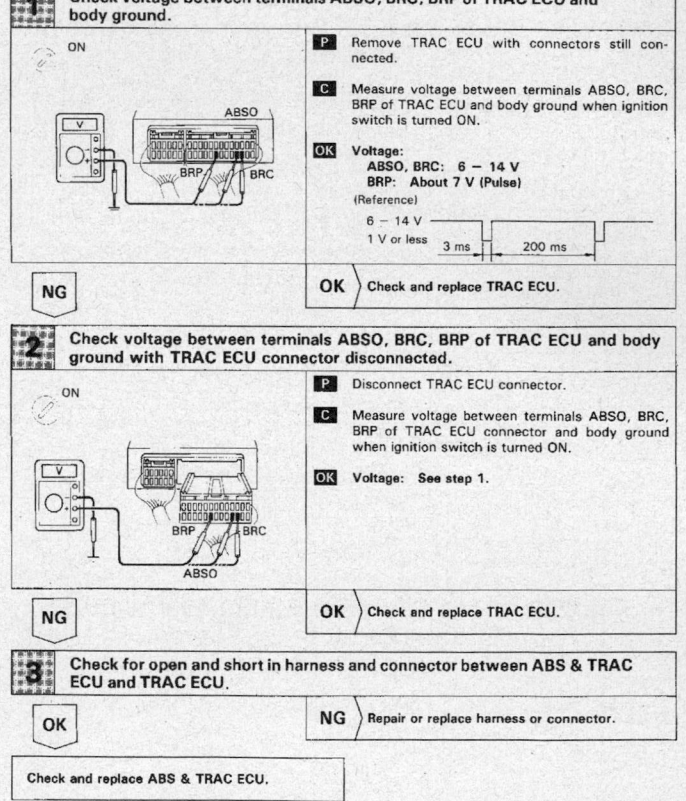

1 Check voltage between terminals ABSO, BRC, BRP of TRAC ECU and body ground.

- **P** Remove TRAC ECU with connectors still connected.
- **C** Measure voltage between terminals ABSO, BRC, BRP of TRAC ECU and body ground when ignition switch is turned ON.
- **OK** Voltage:
  ABSO, BRC: 6 – 14 V
  BRP: About 7 V (Pulse)
  (Reference)

NG → **OK**) Check and replace TRAC ECU.

2 Check voltage between terminals ABSO, BRC, BRP of TRAC ECU and body ground with TRAC ECU connector disconnected.

- **P** Disconnect TRAC ECU connector.
- **C** Measure voltage between terminals ABSO, BRC, BRP of TRAC ECU connector and body ground when ignition switch is turned ON.
- **OK** Voltage: See step 1.

NG → **OK**) Check and replace TRAC ECU.

3 Check for open and short in harness and connector between ABS & TRAC ECU and TRAC ECU.

OK → **NG**) Repair or replace harness or connector.

Check and replace ABS & TRAC ECU.

Fig. 294 Code 61: ABS & TRAC ECU
Communication Circuit Fault (Part 2 of 2). 1996
Supra w/Traction Control

ANTI-LOCK BRAKES

CIRCUIT DESCRIPTION

DTC No.	Diagnostic Trouble Code Detecting Condition	Trouble area
61	Either of the following (1) or (2) continues for more than 8 sec.: (1) Vehicle speed signal of 4 wheels is less than 1 km/h (1 mph) when TRCO signal is input. (2) Voltage of ABS & TRAC ECU terminal THFA is 0 V when TRCO signal is not input.	• Open or short in THFA, TRCO circuit • ABS & TRAC ECU • TRAC ECU

DIAGNOSTIC CHART

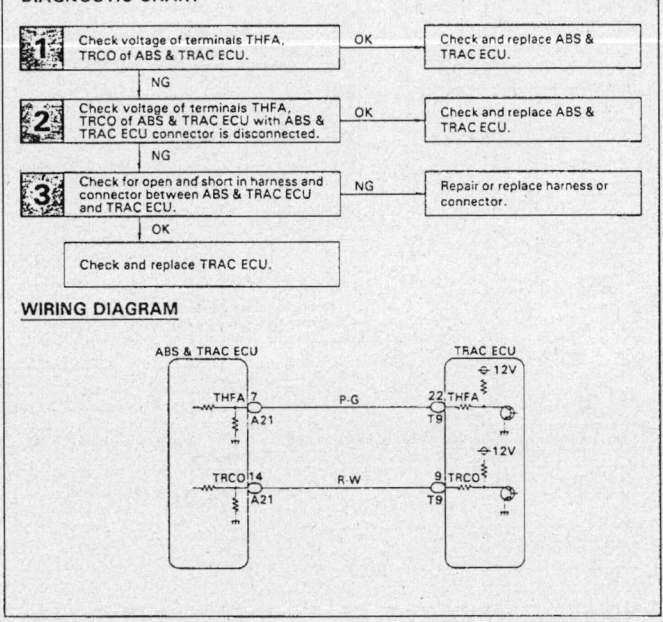

1 Check voltage of terminals THFA, TRCO of ABS & TRAC ECU. — OK → Check and replace ABS & TRAC ECU.

NG

2 Check voltage of terminals THFA, TRCO of ABS & TRAC ECU with ABS & TRAC ECU connector is disconnected. — OK → Check and replace ABS & TRAC ECU.

NG

3 Check for open and short in harness and connector between ABS & TRAC ECU and TRAC ECU. — NG → Repair or replace harness or connector.

OK

Check and replace TRAC ECU.

WIRING DIAGRAM

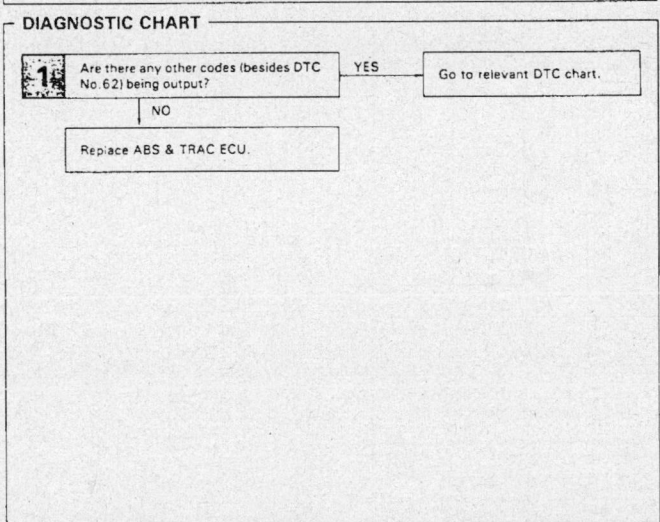

ABS & TRAC ECU   TRAC ECU

Fig. 295 Code 61: TRAC ECU Communication Circuit Fault (Part 1 of 2). 1996 Supra w/Traction Control

TY4029300095010X

CIRCUIT DESCRIPTION

DTC No.	Diagnostic Trouble Code Detecting Condition	Trouble area
62	At vehicle speed of 10 km/h (6 mph) or more, pulses are not input for 5 sec.	• ECU

HINT: When DTC Nos.31 – 36 are recorded in memory, DTC No.62 is not recorded.

DIAGNOSTIC CHART

1 Are there any other codes (besides DTC No.62) being output? — YES → Go to relevant DTC chart.

NO

Replace ABS & TRAC ECU.

TY4029300096000X

Fig. 296 Code 62: TRAC Vehicle Speed Malfunction. 1996 Supra w/Traction Control

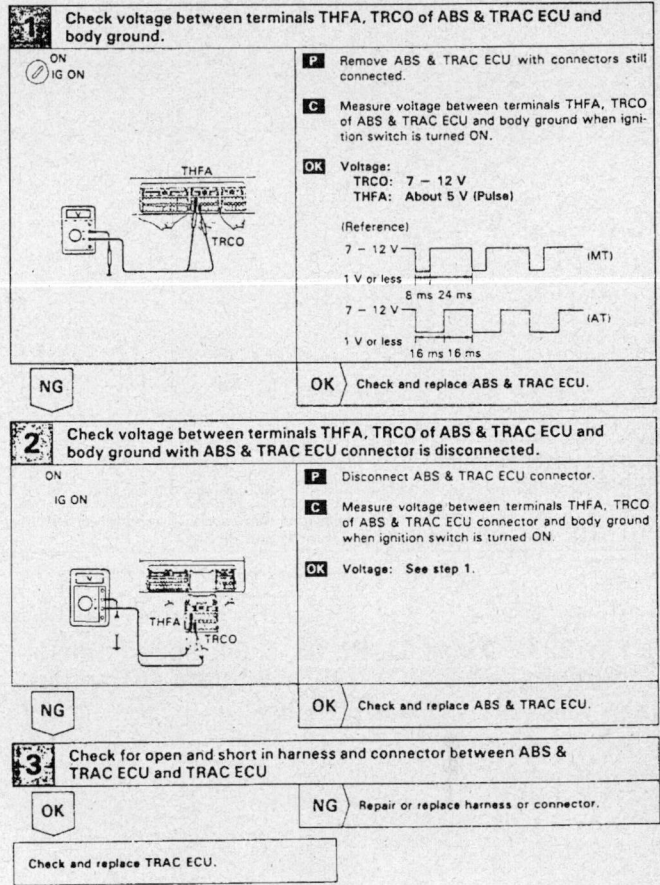

1 Check voltage between terminals THFA, TRCO of ABS & TRAC ECU and body ground.

ON / IG ON

P Remove ABS & TRAC ECU with connectors still connected.

C Measure voltage between terminals THFA, TRCO of ABS & TRAC ECU and body ground when ignition switch is turned ON.

OK Voltage:
TRCO: 7 – 12 V
THFA: About 5 V (Pulse)

(Reference)

7 – 12 V
1 V or less   8 ms 24 ms   (MT)

7 – 12 V
1 V or less   16 ms 16 ms   (AT)

NG   OK Check and replace ABS & TRAC ECU.

2 Check voltage between terminals THFA, TRCO of ABS & TRAC ECU and body ground with ABS & TRAC ECU connector is disconnected.

ON   IG ON

P Disconnect ABS & TRAC ECU connector.

C Measure voltage between terminals THFA, TRCO of ABS & TRAC ECU connector and body ground when ignition switch is turned ON.

OK Voltage: See step 1.

NG   OK Check and replace ABS & TRAC ECU.

3 Check for open and short in harness and connector between ABS & TRAC ECU and TRAC ECU

OK   NG Repair or replace harness or connector.

Check and replace TRAC ECU.

TY4029300095020X

Fig. 295 Code 61: TRAC ECU Communication Circuit Fault (Part 2 of 2). 1996 Supra w/Traction Control

CIRCUIT DESCRIPTION

The speed sensor detects the wheel speed and sends the appropriate signals to the ECU. These signals are used to control both the ABS and TRAC control systems. The front and rear rotors each have 48 serrations.

When the rotors rotate, the magnetic field emitted by the permanent magnet in the speed sensor generates an AC voltage. Since the frequency of this AC voltage changes in direct proportion to the speed of the rotor, the frequency is used by the ECU to detect the speed of each wheel.

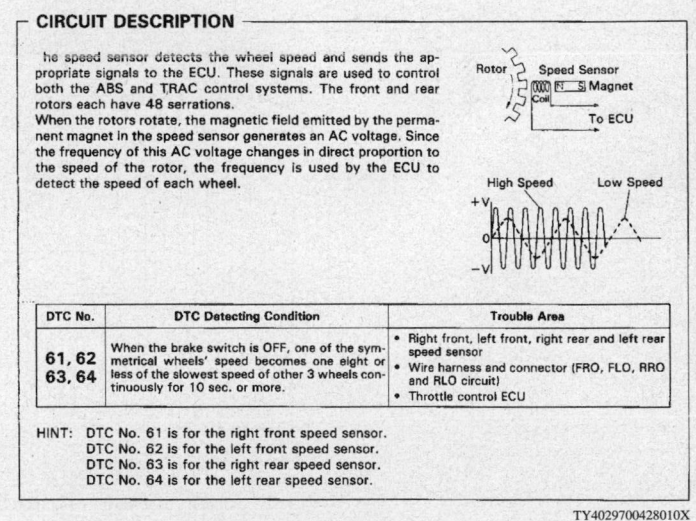

DTC No.	DTC Detecting Condition	Trouble Area
61, 62 63, 64	When the brake switch is OFF, one of the symmetrical wheels' speed becomes one eight or less of the slowest speed of other 3 wheels continuously for 10 sec. or more.	• Right front, left front, right rear and left rear speed sensor • Wire harness and connector (FRO, FLO, RRO and RLO circuit) • Throttle control ECU

HINT: DTC No. 61 is for the right front speed sensor.
DTC No. 62 is for the left front speed sensor.
DTC No. 63 is for the right rear speed sensor.
DTC No. 64 is for the left rear speed sensor.

TY4029700428010X

Fig. 297 Codes 61, 62, 63, & 64: Speed Sensor Circuit (Part 1 of 3). 1997–98 Supra w/Traction Control

WIRING DIAGRAM

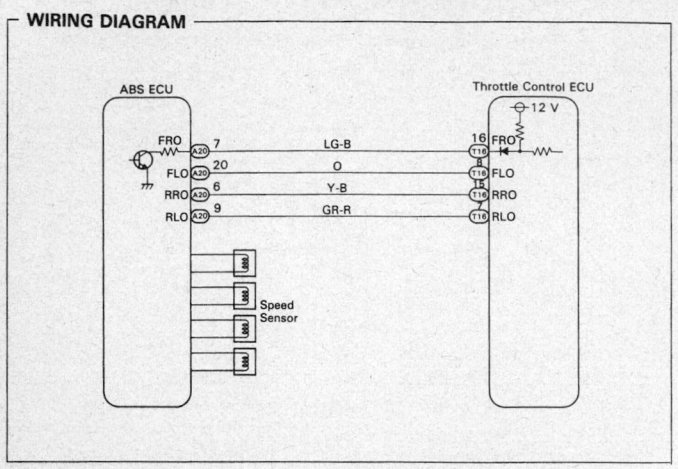

INSPECTION PROCEDURE

HINT: If the DTC is output from the ABS warning light, troubleshoot the ABS first.

1 | Check for open and short in harness and connector between terminals FRO, FLO, RRO, RLO of ABS ECU and throttle control ECU

| OK | | NG | Repair or replace harness or connector. |

TY4029700428020X

Fig. 297 Codes 61, 62, 63, & 64: Speed Sensor Circuit (Part 2 of 3). 1997–98 Supra w/Traction Control

---

2 | Check speed sensor.

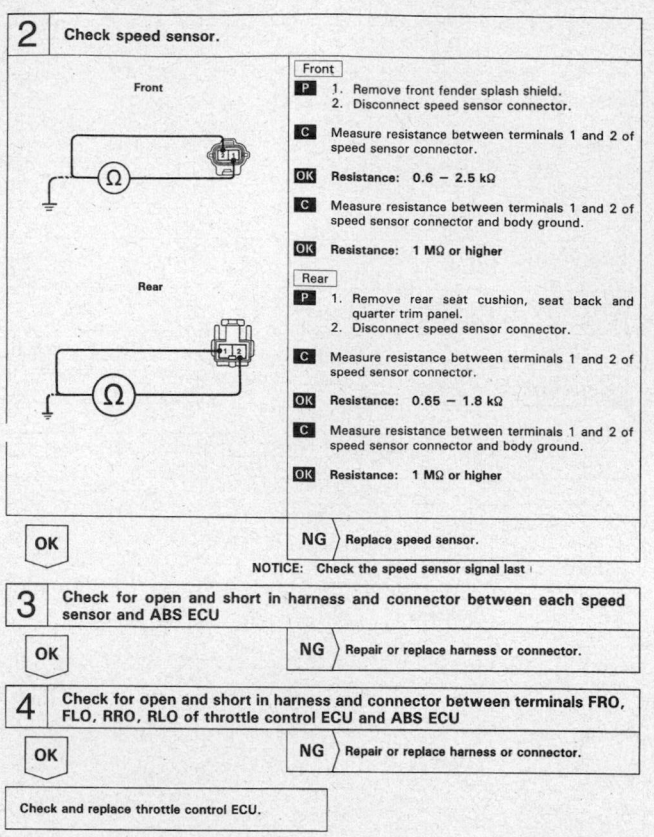

| OK | | NG | Replace speed sensor. |

NOTICE: Check the speed sensor signal last

3 | Check for open and short in harness and connector between each speed sensor and ABS ECU

| OK | | NG | Repair or replace harness or connector. |

4 | Check for open and short in harness and connector between terminals FRO, FLO, RRO, RLO of throttle control ECU and ABS ECU

| OK | | NG | Repair or replace harness or connector. |

Check and replace throttle control ECU.

TY4029700428030X

Fig. 297 Codes 61, 62, 63, & 64: Speed Sensor Circuit (Part 3 of 3). 1997–98 Supra w/Traction Control

---

CIRCUIT DESCRIPTION

DTC No.	DTC Detecting Condition	Trouble Area
71	Vehicle stability control required signal is received 2 times continuously from ECM and throttle control ECU is detected the motor system malfunction. The 2nd vehicle stability required signal is received more or less than 0.5 sec.	• Sub-throttle valve motor • Sub-throttle valve • Throttle control ECU
72	Vehicle stability control required signal is received 2 times continuously from ECM.	

WIRING DIAGRAM

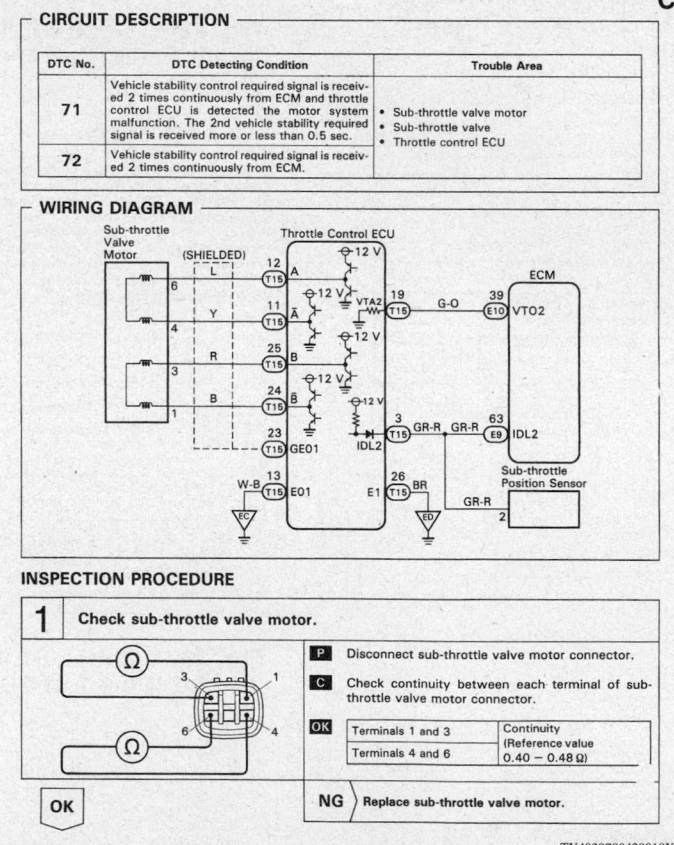

INSPECTION PROCEDURE

1 | Check sub-throttle valve motor.

| P | Disconnect sub-throttle valve motor connector. |
| C | Check continuity between each terminal of sub-throttle valve motor connector. |

| OK | Terminals 1 and 3 | Continuity (Reference value) |
| | Terminals 4 and 6 | 0.40 – 0.48 Ω |

| OK | | NG | Replace sub-throttle valve motor. |

TY4029700429010X

Fig. 298 Codes 71 & 72: Emergency Fuel Cut (Part 1 of 2). Supra w/Traction Control

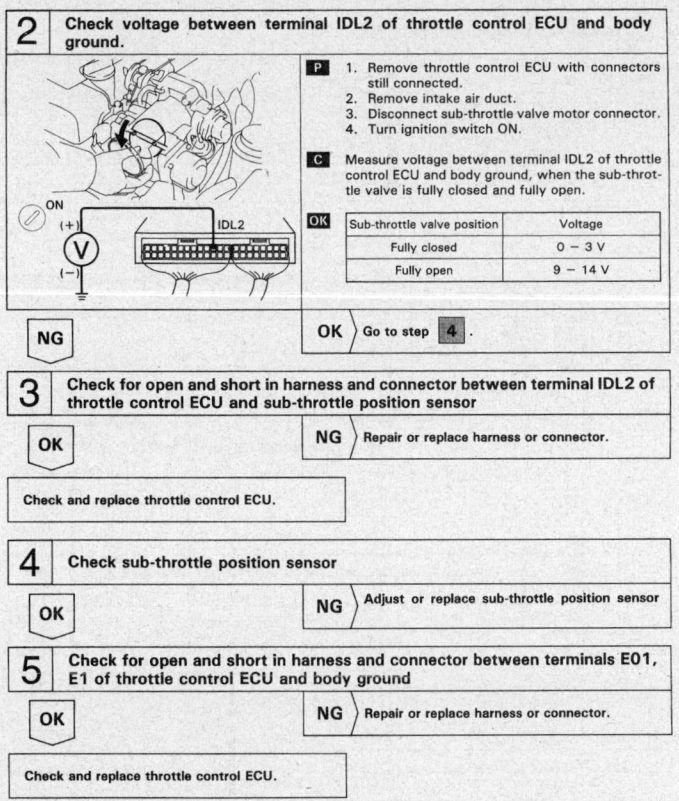

| 2 | Check voltage between terminal IDL2 of throttle control ECU and body ground. |

P
1. Remove throttle control ECU with connectors still connected.
2. Remove intake air duct.
3. Disconnect sub-throttle valve motor connector.
4. Turn ignition switch ON.

C Measure voltage between terminal IDL2 of throttle control ECU and body ground, when the sub-throttle valve is fully closed and fully open.

OK

Sub-throttle valve position	Voltage
Fully closed	0 – 3 V
Fully open	9 – 14 V

| NG | | OK ⟩ Go to step **4** . |

| 3 | Check for open and short in harness and connector between terminal IDL2 of throttle control ECU and sub-throttle position sensor |

| OK | | NG ⟩ Repair or replace harness or connector. |

Check and replace throttle control ECU.

| 4 | Check sub-throttle position sensor |

| OK | | NG ⟩ Adjust or replace sub-throttle position sensor |

| 5 | Check for open and short in harness and connector between terminals E01, E1 of throttle control ECU and body ground |

| OK | | NG ⟩ Repair or replace harness or connector. |

Check and replace throttle control ECU.

TY4029700429020X

Fig. 298 Codes 71 & 72: Emergency Fuel Cut (Part 2 of 2). Supra w/Traction Control

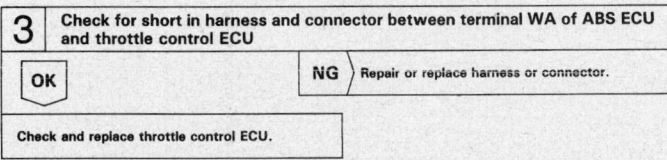

| 3 | Check for short in harness and connector between terminal WA of ABS ECU and throttle control ECU |

| OK | | NG ⟩ Repair or replace harness or connector. |

Check and replace throttle control ECU.

TY4029700430020X

Fig. 299 Code 81: ABS Control System Fault (Part 2 of 2). Supra w/Traction Control

CIRCUIT DESCRIPTION

DTC No.	DTC Detecting Condition	Trouble Area
81	Engine speed is 500 rpm or more and ABS warning light is ON for 12 sec. or more.	• Wire harness and connector (WA circuit) • ABS ECU • Throttle control ECU

WIRING DIAGRAM

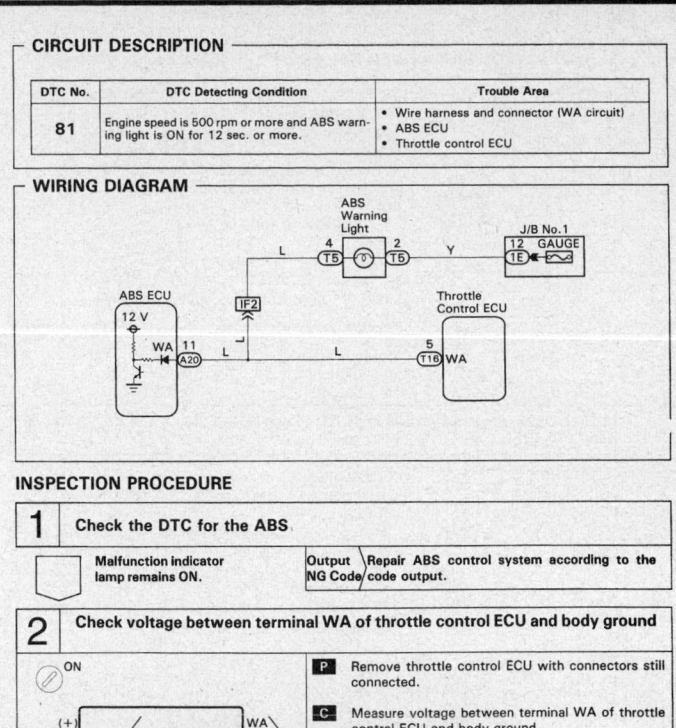

INSPECTION PROCEDURE

| 1 | Check the DTC for the ABS. |

Malfunction indicator lamp remains ON.   Output / NG Code ⟩ Repair ABS control system according to the code output.

| 2 | Check voltage between terminal WA of throttle control ECU and body ground |

P Remove throttle control ECU with connectors still connected.

C Measure voltage between terminal WA of throttle control ECU and body ground.

OK Voltage: 9 – 14 V

| OK | | NG ⟩ Check and replace ABS ECU. |

TY4029700430010X

Fig. 299 Code 81: ABS Control System Fault (Part 1 of 2). Supra w/Traction Control

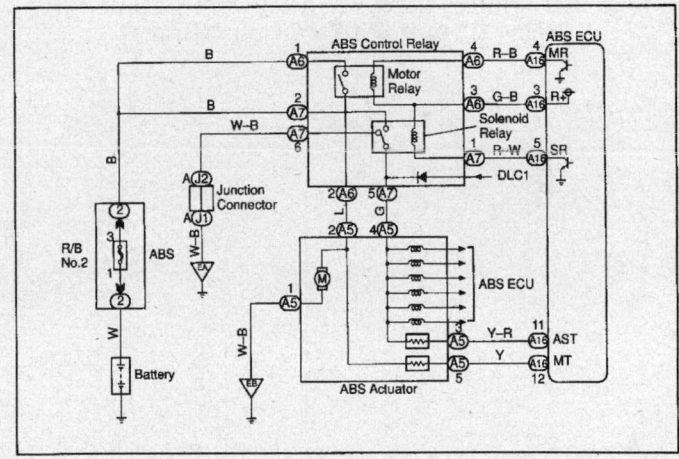

TY4029600214010X

Fig. 300 Codes 11 & 12: ABS Control Solenoid Relay Circuit (Part 1 of 3). 4Runner

1   Check voltage between terminals A7 – 2 and A7 – 6 of ABS control (solenoid) relay connector.

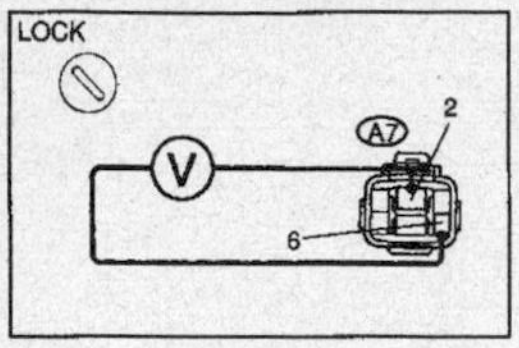

LOCK

PREPARATION:
Disconnect the ABS control relay connector.
CHECK:
Measure the voltage between terminals A7 – 2 and A7 – 6 of ABS control relay harness side connector.
OK:
    Voltage: 10 – 14 V

NG ▷ Check and repair harness or connector.

OK

2   Check continuity between terminals A7 – 5 and A5 – 4, A5 – 4 and A5 – 3, A5 – 3 and A16 – 11.

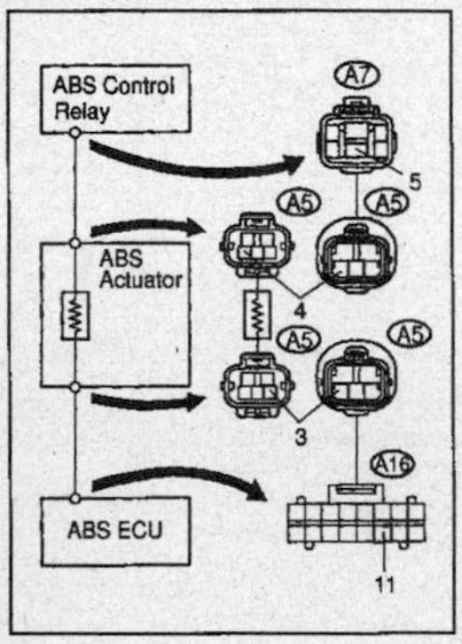

ABS Control Relay
ABS Actuator
ABS ECU

PREPARATION:
Disconnect the 2 connectors from ABS actuator.
CHECK:
Check continuity between terminals A7 – 5 and A5 – 4, A5 – 4 and A5 – 3, A5 – 2 and A16 – 11.
OK:
    Continuity
HINT: There is a resistance of 26 ~ 40 Ω between terminals A5 – 4 and A5 – 3.

NG ▷ Repair or replace harness or ABS actuator.

OK

TY4029600214020X

Fig. 300   Codes 11 & 12: ABS Control Solenoid Relay Circuit (Part 2 of 3). 4Runner

---

3   Check ABS control (solenoid) relay.

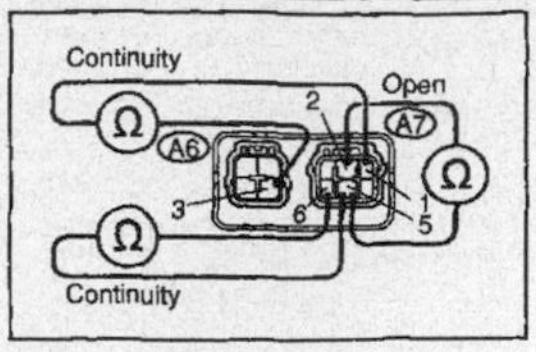

Continuity
Open
Continuity

CHECK:
Check continuity between each terminal of ABS control (solenoid) relay.
OK:

Terminals A7 – 1 and A6 – 3	Continuity (Reference value 80 Ω)
Terminals A7 – 5 and A7 – 6	Continuity
Terminals A7 – 2 and A7 – 5	Open

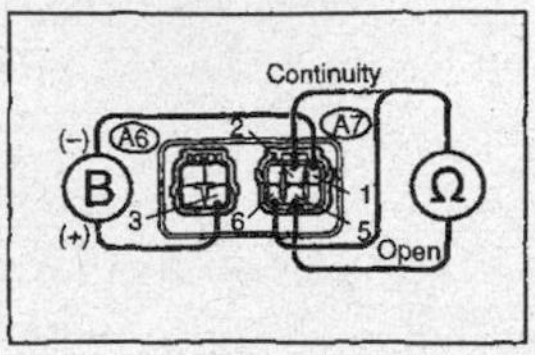

Continuity
Open

CHECK:
(a)   Apply battery positive voltage between terminals A7 – 1 and A6 – 3.
(b)   Check continuity between each terminal of ABS control (solenoid) relay.
OK:

Terminals A7 – 5 and A7 – 6	Open
Terminals A7 – 2 and A7 – 5	Continuity

NG ▷ Replace ABS control relay.

OK

4   Check for open and short in harness and connector between ABS control (solenoid) relay and ABS ECU.

NG ▷ Repair or replace harness or connector.

OK

If the same code is still output after the DTC is deleted, check the contact condition of each connection. If the connector are normal, the ECU may be defective.

TY4029600214030X

Fig. 300   Codes 11 & 12: ABS Control Solenoid Relay Circuit (Part 3 of 3). 4Runner

---

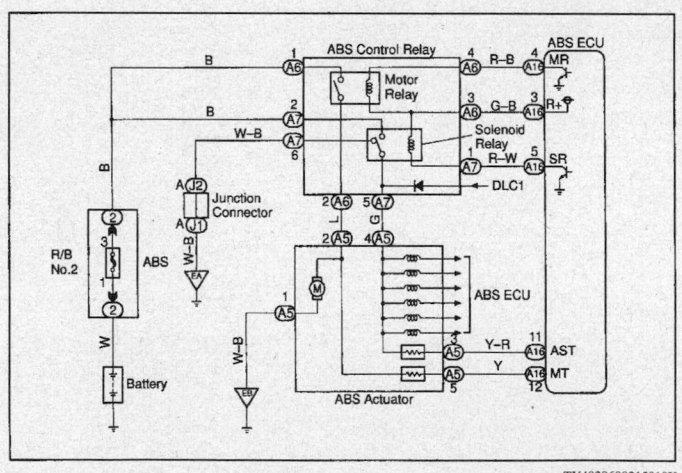

TY4029600215010X

Fig. 301   Codes 13 & 14: ABS Control Motor Relay Circuit (Part 1 of 3). 4Runner

1 | Check voltage between terminal A6 – 1 of ABS control (motor) relay and body ground.

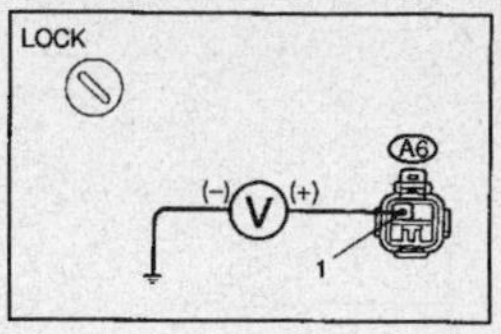

LOCK

PREPARATION:
Disconnect the ABS control relay connector.
CHECK:
Measure voltage between terminal A6 – 1 of ABS control relay harness side connector and body ground.
OK:
   Voltage: 10 – 14 V

NG ▷ Check and repair harness or connector.

OK

2 | Check continuity between terminals A6 – 2 and A5 – 2, A5 – 2 and A5 – 5, A5 – 5 and A16 – 12.

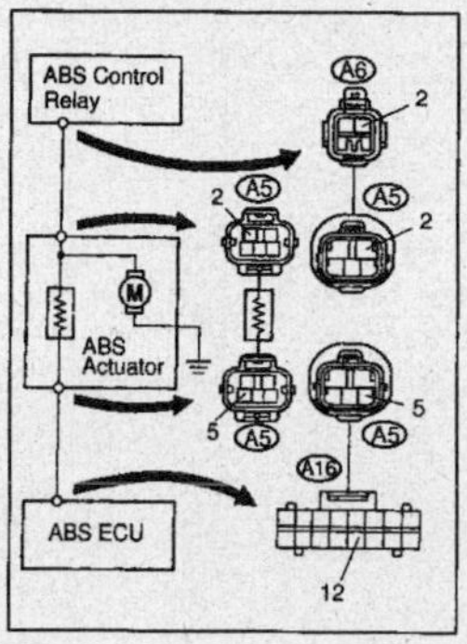

ABS Control Relay

ABS Actuator

ABS ECU

PREPARATION:
Disconnect the 2 connectors from ABS actuator.
CHECK:
Check continuity between terminals A6 – 2 and A5 – 2, A5 – 2 and A5 – 5, A5 – 5 and A16 – 12.
OK:
   Continuity
HINT: There is a resistance of 26 ~ 40 Ω between terminals A5 – 2 and A5 – 5.

NG ▷ Repair or replace harness or ABS actuator.

OK

TY4029600215020X

Fig. 301   Codes 13 & 14: ABS Control Motor Relay Circuit (Part 2 of 3). 4Runner

3 | Check ABS control (motor) relay.

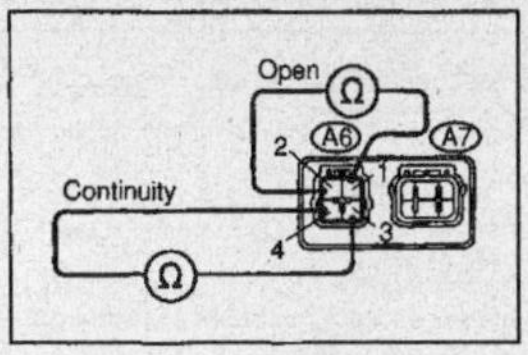

Open
Continuity

CHECK:
Check continuity between each terminal of ABS control (motor) relay.
OK:

Terminals A6 – 3 and A6 – 4	Continuity (Reference value 62 Ω)
Terminals A6 – 1 and A6 – 2	Open

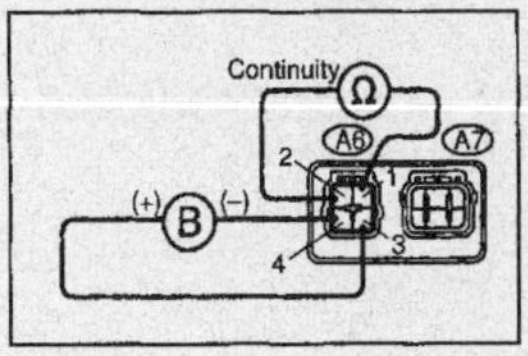

Continuity

CHECK:
(a)   Apply battery positive voltage between terminals A6 – 3 and A6 – 4.
(b)   Check continuity between each terminal of ABS control relay.
OK:

Terminals A6 – 1 and A6 – 2	Continuity

NG ▷ Replace ABS control relay.

OK

4 | Check for open and short in harness and connector between ABS control relay and ABS ECU.

NG ▷ Repair or replace harness or connector.

OK

If the same code is still output after the DTC is deleted, check the contact condition of each connection. If the connections are normal, the ECU may be defective.

TY4029600215030X

Fig. 301   Codes 13 & 14: ABS Control Motor Relay Circuit (Part 3 of 3). 4Runner

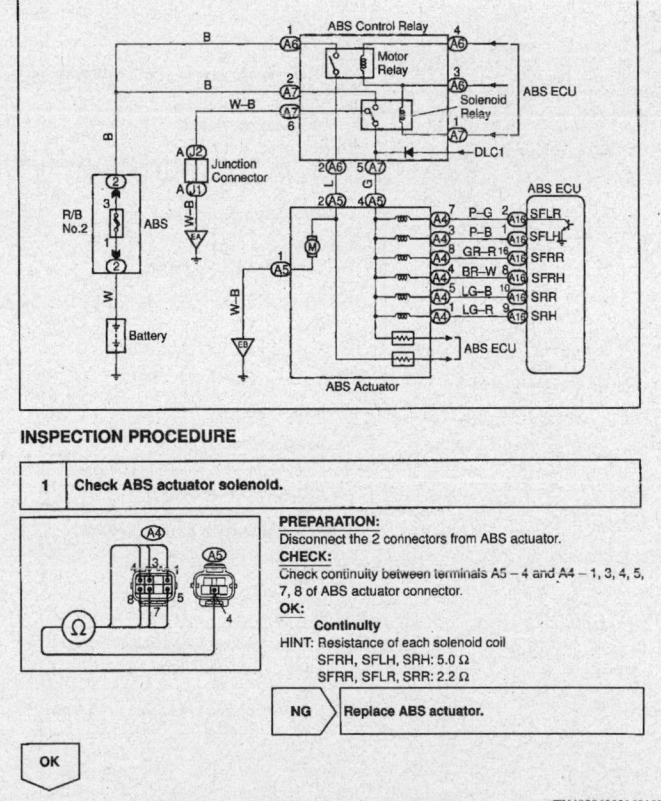

INSPECTION PROCEDURE

1 | Check ABS actuator solenoid.

PREPARATION:
Disconnect the 2 connectors from ABS actuator.
CHECK:
Check continuity between terminals A5 – 4 and A4 – 1, 3, 4, 5, 7, 8 of ABS actuator connector.
OK:
   Continuity
HINT: Resistance of each solenoid coil
   SFRH, SFLH, SRH: 5.0 Ω
   SFRR, SFLR, SRR: 2.2 Ω

NG ▷ Replace ABS actuator.

OK

TY4029600216010X

Fig. 302   Codes 21, 22 & 23: ABS Actuator Solenoid Circuit (Part 1 of 2). 4Runner

| 2 | Check for open and short in harness and connector between ABS ECU and actuator. |

NG > Repair or replace harness or connector.

OK

If the same code is still output after the DTC is deleted, check the contact condition of each connection. If the connector are normal, the ECU may be defective.

TY4029600216020X

Fig. 302   Codes 21, 22 & 23: ABS Actuator Solenoid Circuit (Part 2 of 2). 4Runner

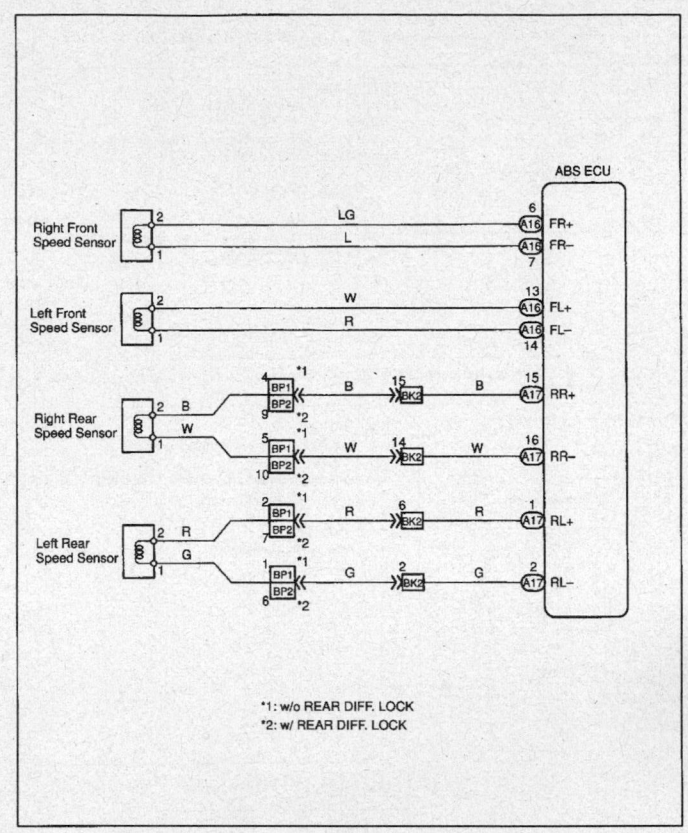

*1: w/o REAR DIFF. LOCK
*2: w/ REAR DIFF. LOCK

TY4029600217010X

Fig. 303   Codes 31, 32, 33 & 34: Speed Sensor Circuit (Part 1 of 3). 4Runner

| 1 | Check speed sensor. |

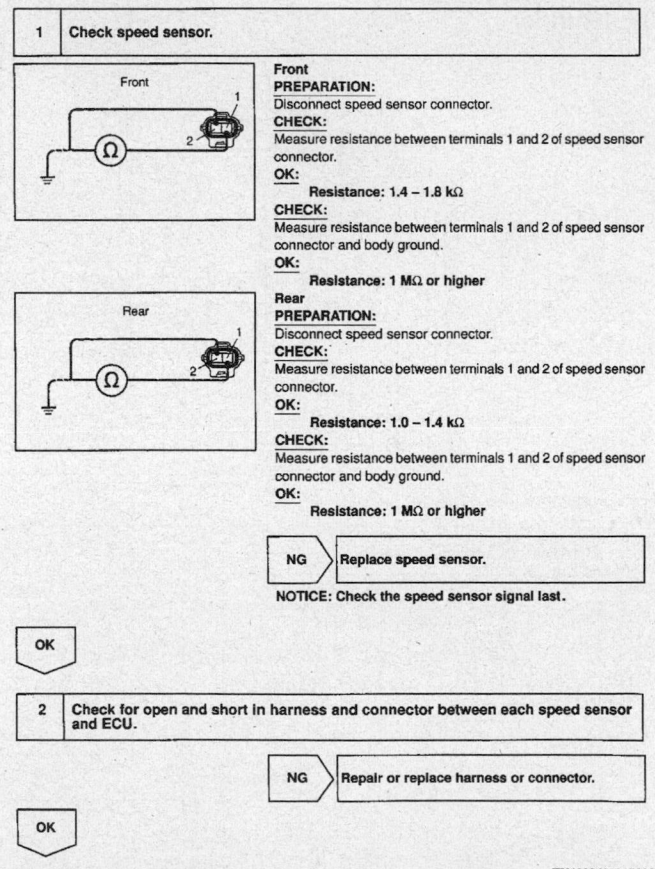

Front
PREPARATION:
Disconnect speed sensor connector.
CHECK:
Measure resistance between terminals 1 and 2 of speed sensor connector.
OK:
  Resistance: 1.4 – 1.8 kΩ
CHECK:
Measure resistance between terminals 1 and 2 of speed sensor connector and body ground.
OK:
  Resistance: 1 MΩ or higher
Rear
PREPARATION:
Disconnect speed sensor connector.
CHECK:
Measure resistance between terminals 1 and 2 of speed sensor connector.
OK:
  Resistance: 1.0 – 1.4 kΩ
CHECK:
Measure resistance between terminals 1 and 2 of speed sensor connector and body ground.
OK:
  Resistance: 1 MΩ or higher

NG > Replace speed sensor.

NOTICE: Check the speed sensor signal last.

OK

| 2 | Check for open and short in harness and connector between each speed sensor and ECU. |

NG > Repair or replace harness or connector.

OK

TY4029600217020X

Fig. 303   Codes 31, 32, 33 & 34: Speed Sensor Circuit (Part 2 of 3). 4Runner

ANTI-LOCK BRAKES

3 | Check sensor rotor and sensor installation.

Front
PREPARATION:
Remove brake disc.
CHECK:
Check sensor rotor serrations.
OK:
No scratches or missing teeth.
CHECK:
Check the sensor tip.
OK:
No scratches or foreign objects on the sensor tip.

Rear
PREPARATION:
Remove the axle shaft.
CHECK:
Check the sensor rotor serrations.
OK:
No scratches or missing teeth.
CHECK:
Check the sensor tip.
OK:
No scratches or foreign objects on the sensor tip.

CHECK:
Check the speed sensor installation.
OK:
The installation bolt is tightened properly and there is no clearance between the sensor and steering knuckle or rear axle carrier.

OK   NG

NG > Replace speed sensor or rotor.

NOTICE: Check the speed sensor signal last.

OK

Check and replace ABS ECU.

TY4029600217030X

Fig. 303   Codes 31, 32, 33 & 34: Speed Sensor Circuit (Part 3 of 3). 4Runner

1 | Check tire size.

NG > Replace tires so that all 4 tires are of the same size.

OK

Check and replace ABS ECU.

TY4029600219000X

Fig. 305   Code 37: Tires Of Different Size. 4Runner

1 | Check front axle hub.

NG > Replace front axle hub.

OK

2 | Check front speed sensor.

NG > Replace front speed sensor.

OK

3 | Check for open or short in harness and connector between speed sensor and ECU.

NG > Repair or replace harness and connector.

OK

Check and replace ABS ECU.

TY4029600218000X

Fig. 304   Code 37: Neither Front Speed Sensor Rotor Missing. 4Runner

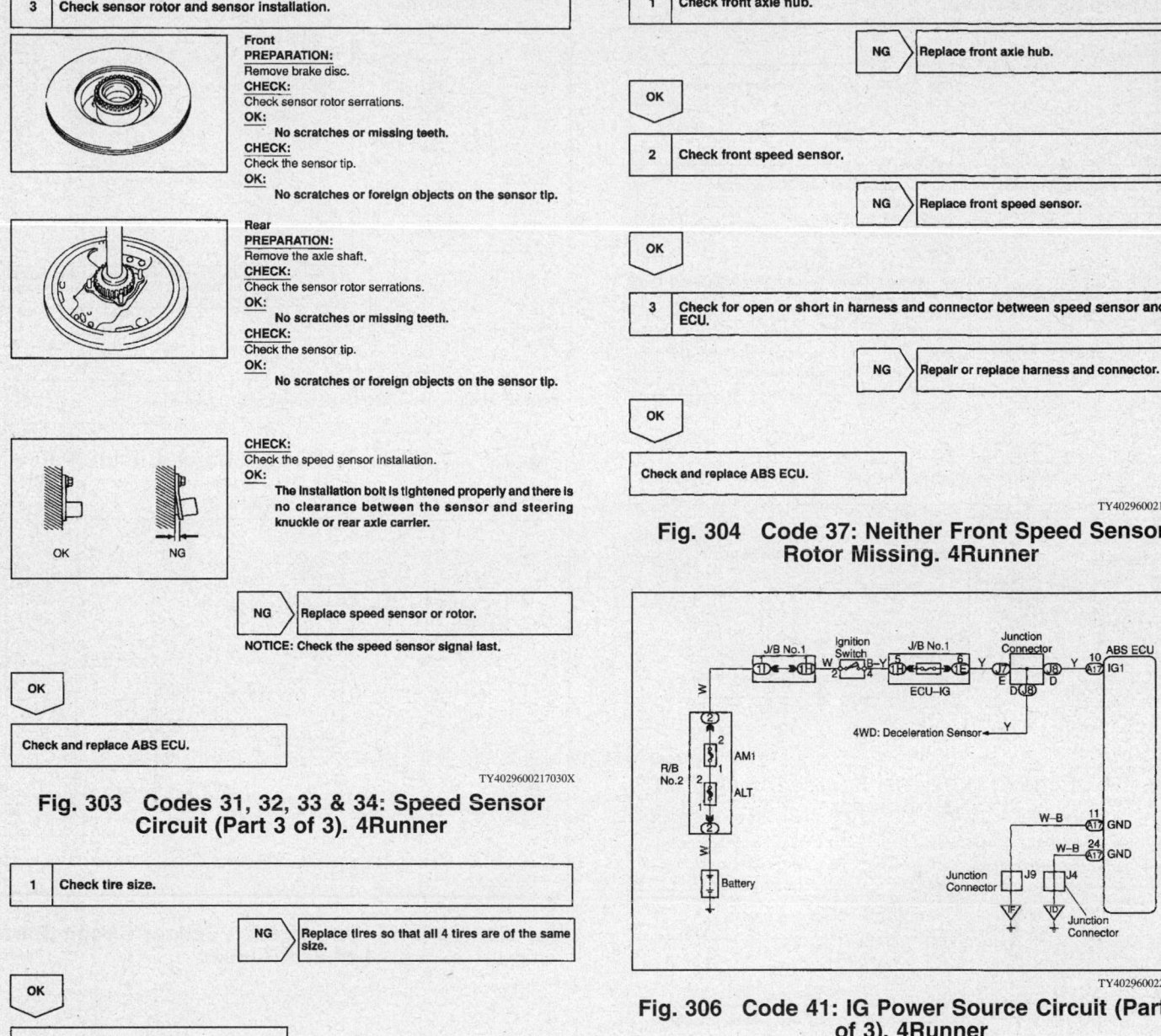

TY4029600220010X

Fig. 306   Code 41: IG Power Source Circuit (Part 1 of 3). 4Runner

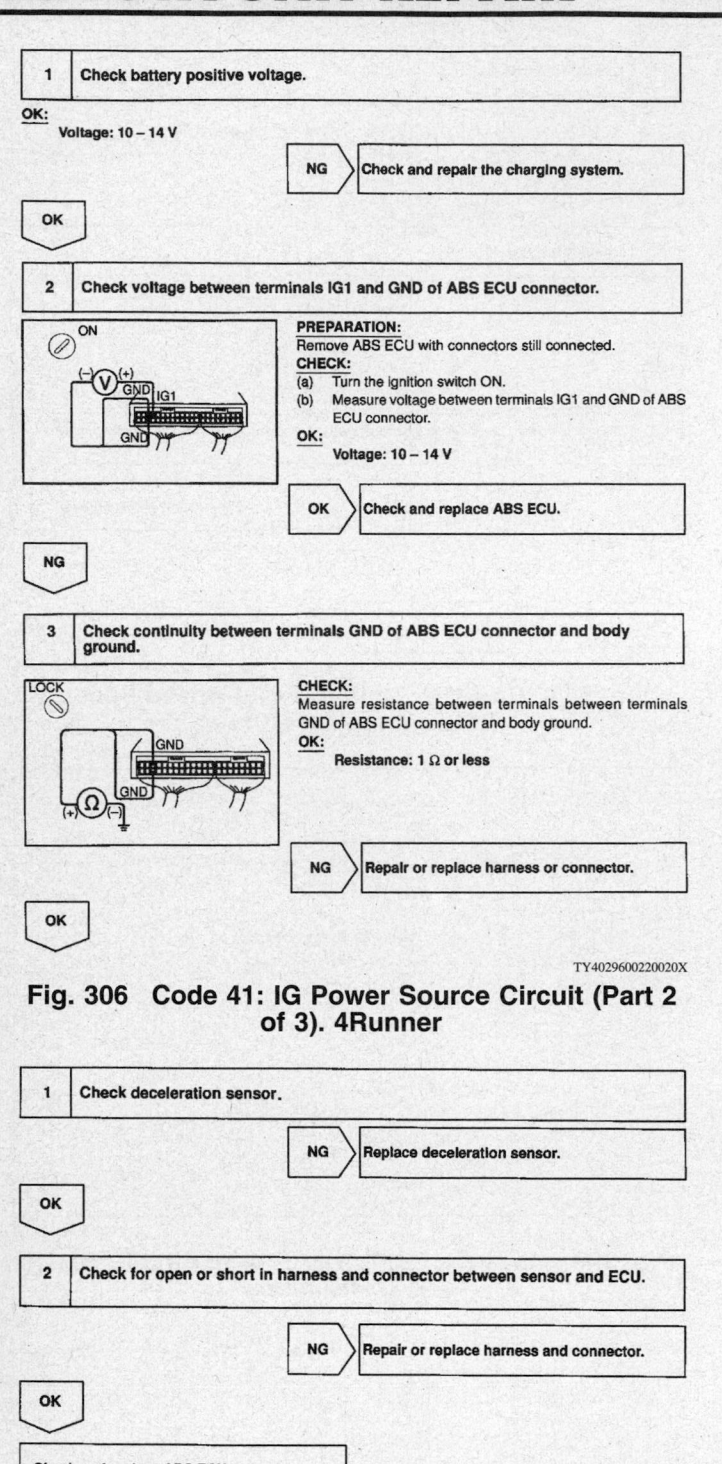

1 Check battery positive voltage.

OK:
Voltage: 10 – 14 V

NG ⟩ Check and repair the charging system.

OK

2 Check voltage between terminals IG1 and GND of ABS ECU connector.

PREPARATION:
Remove ABS ECU with connectors still connected.
CHECK:
(a) Turn the ignition switch ON.
(b) Measure voltage between terminals IG1 and GND of ABS ECU connector.
OK:
Voltage: 10 – 14 V

OK ⟩ Check and replace ABS ECU.

NG

3 Check continuity between terminals GND of ABS ECU connector and body ground.

CHECK:
Measure resistance between terminals between terminals GND of ABS ECU connector and body ground.
OK:
Resistance: 1 Ω or less

NG ⟩ Repair or replace harness or connector.

OK

TY4029600220020X

Fig. 306 Code 41: IG Power Source Circuit (Part 2 of 3). 4Runner

1 Check deceleration sensor.

NG ⟩ Replace deceleration sensor.

OK

2 Check for open or short in harness and connector between sensor and ECU.

NG ⟩ Repair or replace harness and connector.

OK

Check and replace ABS ECU.

TY4029600221000X

Fig. 307 Code 43: Malfunction In Deceleration Sensor. 4Runner

4 Check ECU–IG fuse.

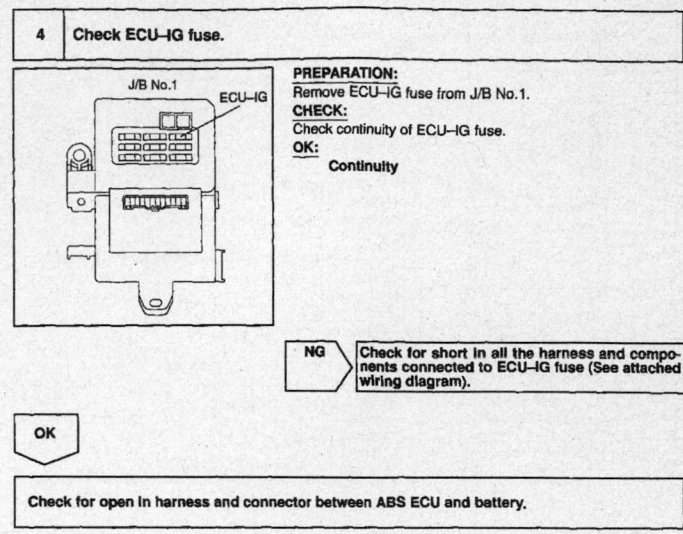

PREPARATION:
Remove ECU–IG fuse from J/B No.1.
CHECK:
Check continuity of ECU–IG fuse.
OK:
Continuity

NG ⟩ Check for short in all the harness and components connected to ECU–IG fuse (See attached wiring diagram).

OK

Check for open in harness and connector between ABS ECU and battery.

TY4029600220030X

Fig. 306 Code 41: IG Power Source Circuit (Part 3 of 3). 4Runner

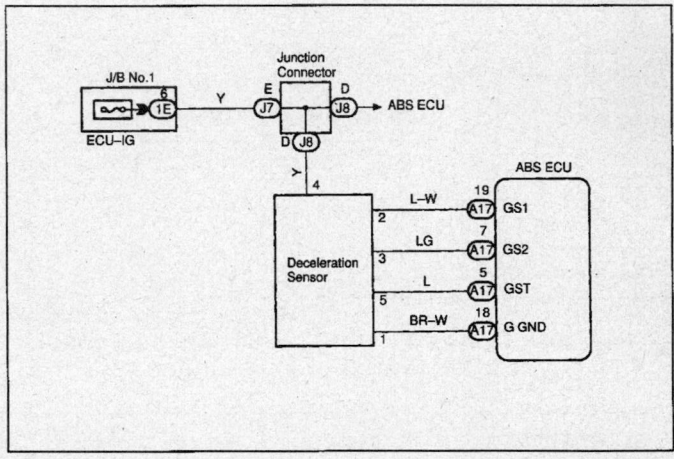

TY4029600222010X

Fig. 308 Code 44: Deceleration Sensor Circuit (Part 1 of 2). 4Runner

| 1 | Check for open and short in harness and connector between Deceleration sensor and ECU. |

NG ▷ Repair or replace harness or connector.

OK

| 2 | Check voltage between terminals GS1, GS2, GST of ABS ECU and body ground. |

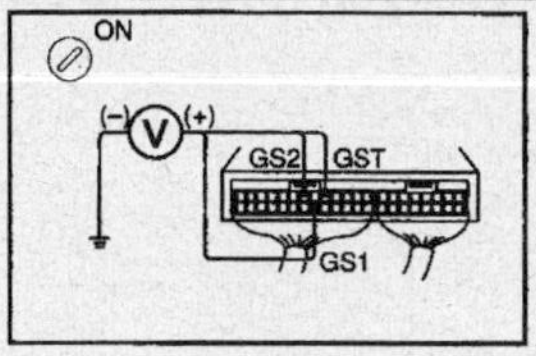

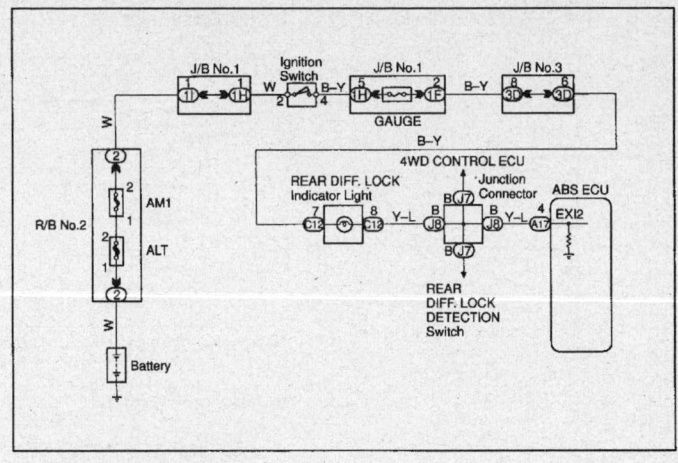

PREPARATION:
(a) Remove ABS ECU with connectors still connected.
(b) Disconnect deceleration sensor connector.
(c) Turn the ignition switch ON.

CHECK:
Measure voltage between terminals GS1, GS2, GST of ECU and Body ground.

OK:
Voltage:
GS1, GS2: 10 – 14 V
GST: As shown below

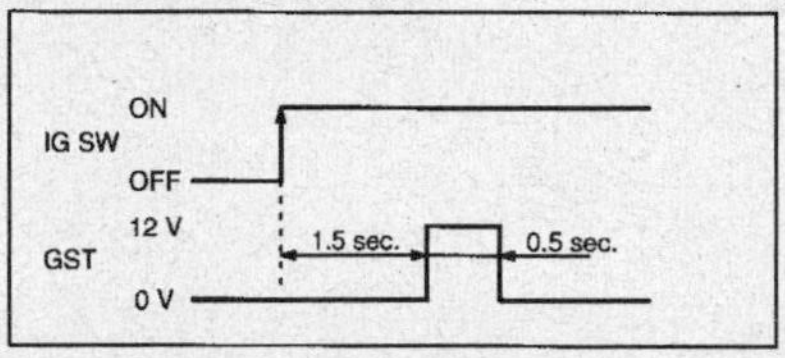

NG ▷ Check and replace ABS ECU.

OK

Check and replace deceleration sensor.

TY4029600222020X

Fig. 308 Code 44: Deceleration Sensor Circuit (Part 2 of 2). 4Runner

| 2 | Is DTC output? |

Check DTC.

NO ▷ Normal.

YES

| 3 | Check that REAR DIFF. LOCK indicator light does not go off. |

NO ▷ Go to step 6.

YES

| 4 | Check that bulb for REAR DIFF. LOCK indicator light is not burnt out. |

YES ▷ Replace indicator light.

NO

| 5 | Check for open in harness and connector between battery and REAR DIFF. LOCK indicator light, REAR DIFF. LOCK indicator light and ABS ECU. |

NG ▷ Repair or replace harness or connector.

OK

TY4029600223020X

Fig. 309 Code 48: Rear Differential Lock Circuit (Part 2 of 3). 4Runner

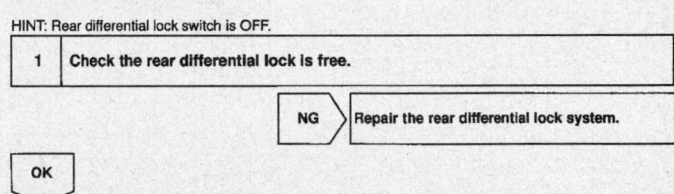

INSPECTION PROCEDURE

HINT: Rear differential lock switch is OFF.

| 1 | Check the rear differential lock is free. |

NG ▷ Repair the rear differential lock system.

OK

TY4029600223010X

Fig. 309 Code 48: Rear Differential Lock Circuit (Part 1 of 3). 4Runner

| 6 | Check for short in harness and connector between REAR DIFF. LOCK indicator light and ABS ECU. |

NG ▷ Repair or replace harness or connector.

OK

Check and replace ABS ECU.

TY4029600223030X

Fig. 309 Code 48: Rear Differential Lock Circuit (Part 3 of 3). 4Runner

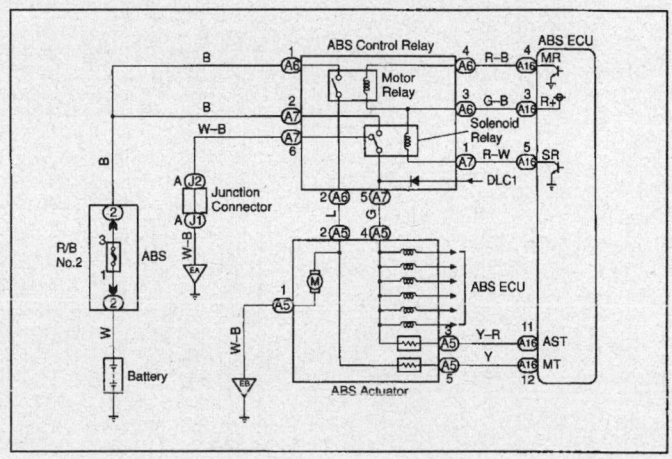

TY4029600224000X

Fig. 310 Code 51: ABS Pump Motor Lock. 4Runner

CIRCUIT DESCRIPTION

This relay supplies power to each ABS solenoid. After the ignition switch is turned ON, if the initial check is OK, the relay goes on.

DTC No.	DTC Detecting Condition	Trouble Area
11	Conditions (1) and (2) continue for 0.2 sec. or more: (1) ABS control (solenoid) relay terminal (SR) voltage: Battery positive voltage (2) ABS control (solenoid) relay monitor terminal (AST) voltage: 0 V	• ABS control (solenoid) relay • Open or short in ABS control (solenoid) relay circuit • ECU
12	Conditions (1) and (2) continue for 0.2 sec. or more: (1) ABS control (solenoid) relay terminal (SR) voltage: 0 V (2) ABS control (solenoid) relay monitor terminal (AST) voltage: Battery positive voltage	• ABS control (solenoid) relay • B+ short in ABS control (solenoid) relay circuit • ECU

Fail safe function: If trouble occurs in the ABS control (solenoid) relay circuit, the ECU cuts off current to the ABS control (solenoid) relay and prohibits ABS control.

WIRING DIAGRAM

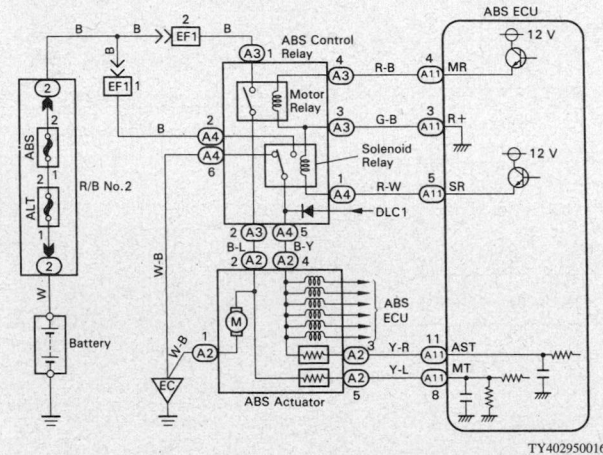

TY4029500164010X

Fig. 311   Codes 11 & 12: ABS Control Solenoid Relay Circuit (Part 1 of 3). 1996 Tacoma

This relay supplies power to each ABS solenoid. After the ignition switch is turned ON, if the initial check is OK, the relay goes on.

DTC No.	DTC Detecting Condition	Trouble Area
11	Conditions (1) and (2) continue for 0.2 sec. or more: (1) ABS control (solenoid) relay terminal (SR) voltage: Battery positive voltage (2) ABS control (solenoid) relay monitor terminal (AST) voltage: 0 V	• ABS control (solenoid) relay • Open or short in ABS control (solenoid) relay circuit • ECU
12	Conditions (1) and (2) continue for 0.2 sec. or more: (1) ABS control (solenoid) relay terminal (SR) voltage: 0 V (2) ABS control (solenoid) relay monitor terminal (AST) voltage: Battery positive voltage	• ABS control (solenoid) relay • B+ short in ABS control (solenoid) relay circuit • ECU

Fail safe function: If trouble occurs in the ABS control (solenoid) relay circuit, the ECU cuts off current to the ABS control (solenoid) relay and prohibits ABS control.

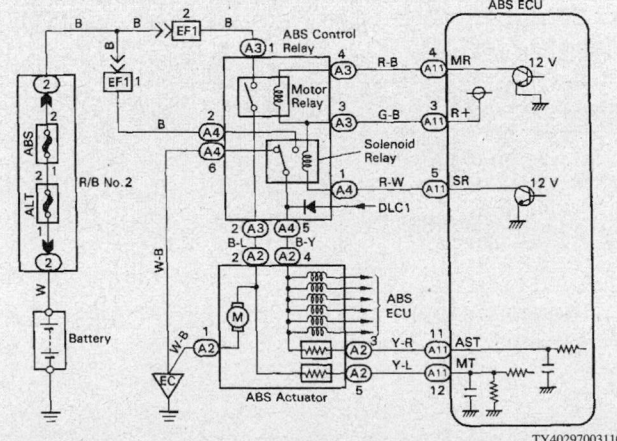

TY4029700311010X

Fig. 311   Codes 11 & 12: ABS Control Solenoid Relay Circuit (Part 1 of 3). 1997–99 Tacoma

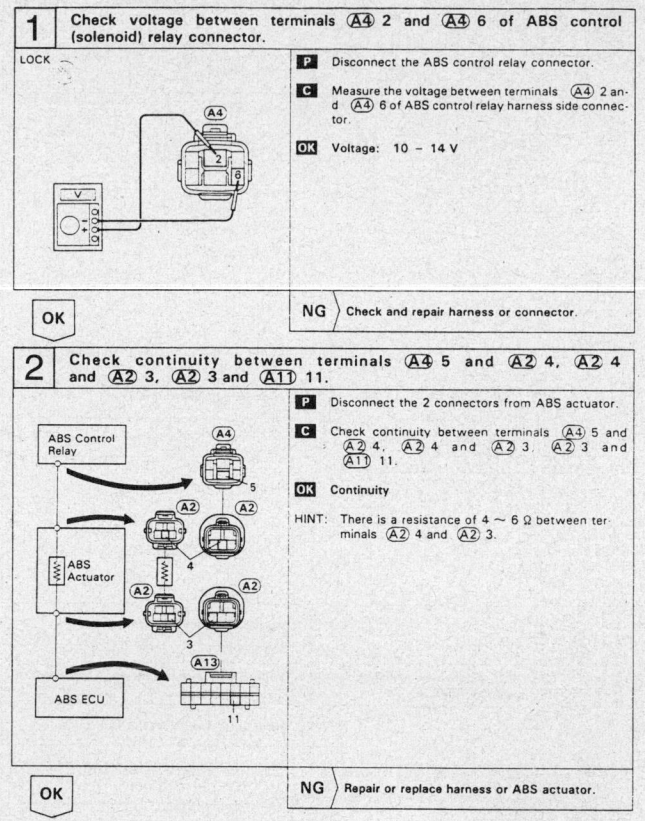

Fig. 311   Codes 11 & 12: ABS Control Solenoid Relay Circuit (Part 2 of 3). 1996 Tacoma

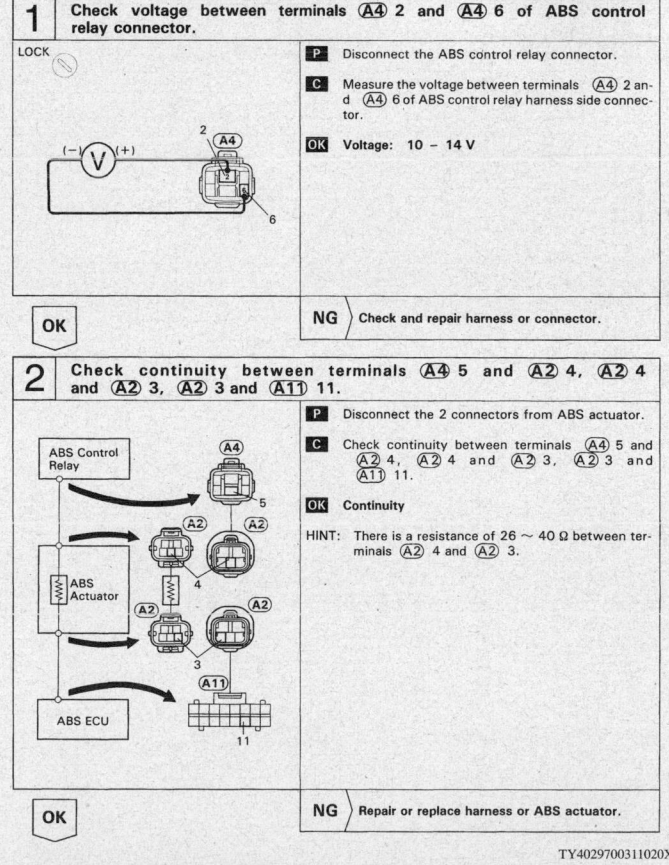

Fig. 311   Codes 11 & 12: ABS Control Solenoid Relay Circuit (Part 2 of 3). 1997–99 Tacoma

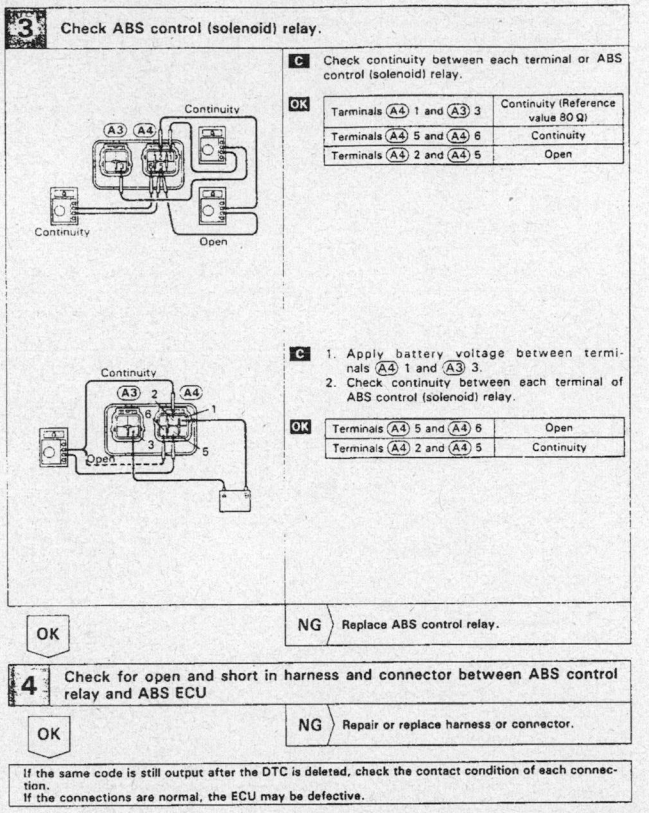

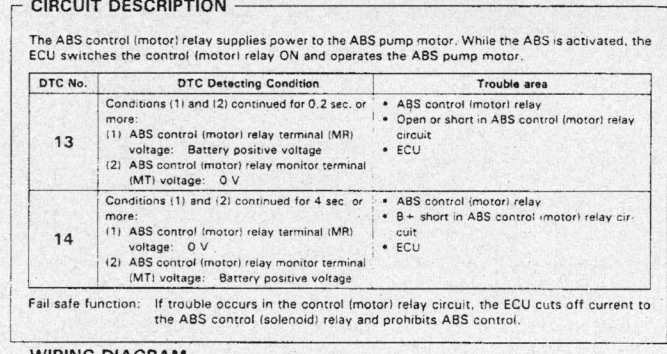

Fig. 311 Codes 11 & 12: ABS Control Solenoid Relay Circuit (Part 3 of 3). Tacoma

---CIRCUIT DESCRIPTION---

The ABS control (motor) relay supplies power to the ABS pump motor. While the ABS is activated, the ECU switches the control (motor) relay ON and operates the ABS pump motor.

DTC No.	DTC Detecting Condition	Trouble area
13	Conditions (1) and (2) continued for 0.2 sec. or more: (1) ABS control (motor) relay terminal (MR) voltage: Battery positive voltage (2) ABS control (motor) relay monitor terminal (MT) voltage: 0 V	• ABS control (motor) relay • Open or short in ABS control (motor) relay circuit • ECU
14	Conditions (1) and (2) continued for 4 sec. or more: (1) ABS control (motor) relay terminal (MR) voltage: 0 V (2) ABS control (motor) relay monitor terminal (MT) voltage: Battery positive voltage	• ABS control (motor) relay • B + short in ABS control (motor) relay circuit • ECU

Fail safe function: If trouble occurs in the control (motor) relay circuit, the ECU cuts off current to the ABS control (solenoid) relay and prohibits ABS control.

---WIRING DIAGRAM---

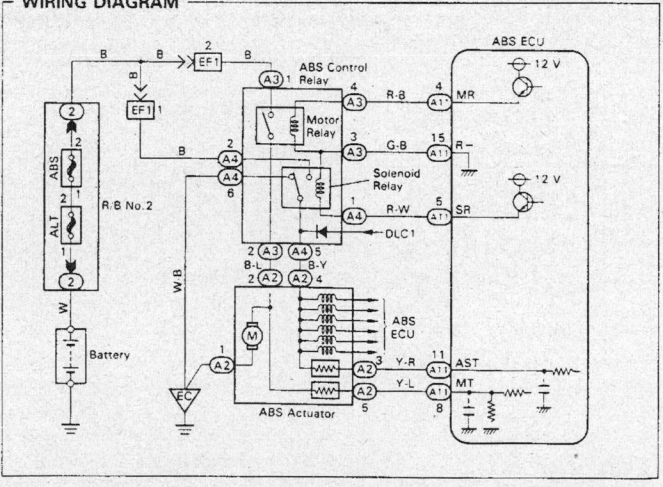

Fig. 312 Codes 13 & 14: ABS Control Motor Relay Circuit (Part 1 of 3). 1996 Tacoma

The ABS control (motor) relay supplies power to the ABS pump motor. While the ABS is activated, the ECU switches the control (motor) relay ON and operates the ABS pump motor.

DTC No.	DTC Detecting Condition	Trouble Area
13	Conditions (1) and (2) continued for 0.2 sec. or more: (1) ABS control (motor) relay terminal (MR) voltage: Battery positive voltage (2) ABS control (motor) relay monitor terminal (MT) voltage: 0 V	• ABS control (motor) relay • Open or short in ABS control (motor) relay circuit • ECU
14	Conditions (1) and (2) continued for 2.5 sec. or more: (1) ABS control (motor) relay terminal (MR) voltage: 0 V (2) ABS control (motor) relay monitor terminal (MT) voltage: Battery positive voltage	• ABS control (motor) relay • B+ short in ABS control (motor) relay circuit • ECU

Fail safe function: If trouble occurs in the ABS control (motor) relay circuit, the ECU cuts off current to the ABS control (solenoid) relay and prohibits ABS control.

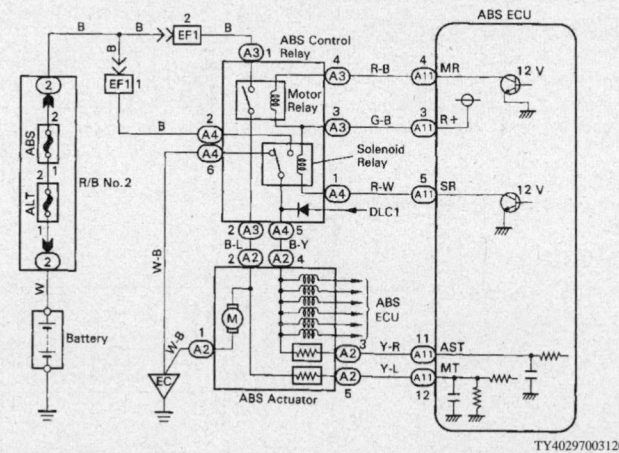

TY4029700312010X

Fig. 312   Codes 13 & 14: ABS Control Motor Relay Circuit (Part 1 of 3). 1997–99 Tacoma

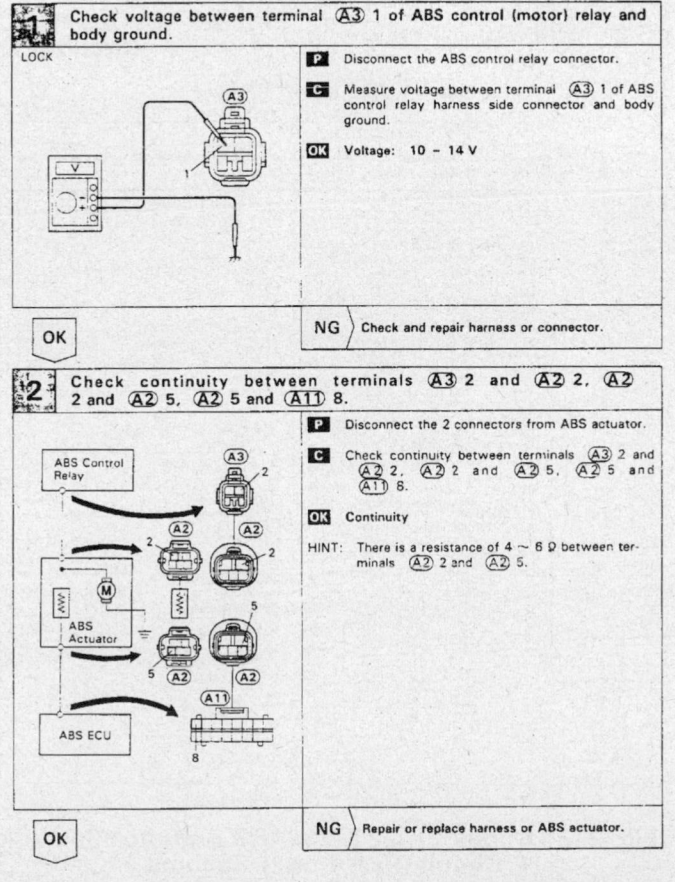

TY402950165020X

Fig. 312   Codes 13 & 14: ABS Control Motor Relay Circuit (Part 2 of 3). 1996 Tacoma

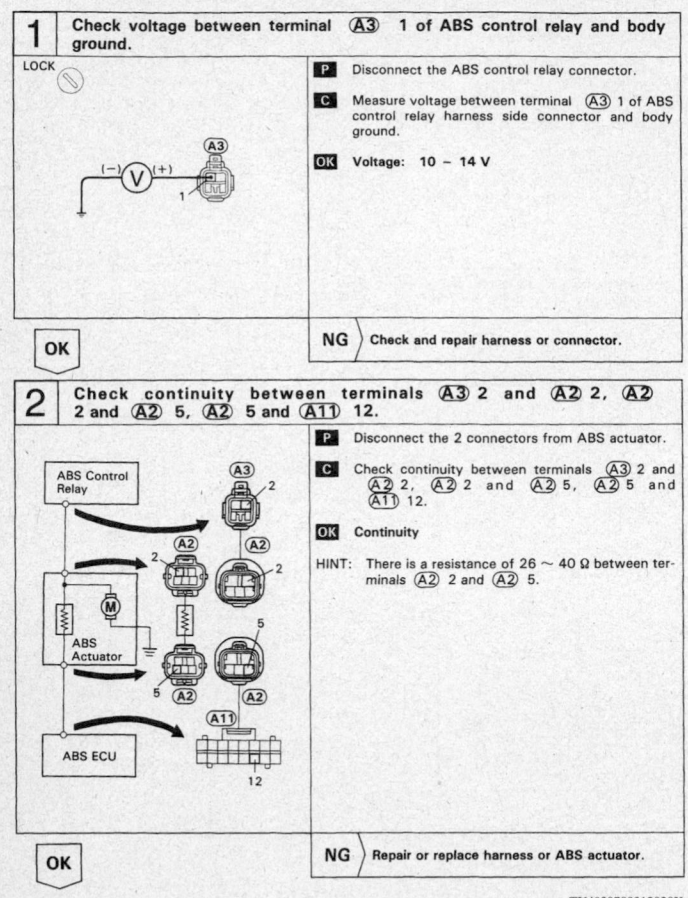

1 Check voltage between terminal Ⓐ3 1 of ABS control relay and body ground.

LOCK

P Disconnect the ABS control relay connector.

C Measure voltage between terminal Ⓐ3 1 of ABS control relay harness side connector and body ground.

OK Voltage: 10 – 14 V

OK ▽

NG ⟩ Check and repair harness or connector.

2 Check continuity between terminals Ⓐ3 2 and Ⓐ2 2, Ⓐ2 2 and Ⓐ2 5, Ⓐ2 5 and Ⓐ11 12.

ABS Control Relay

ABS Actuator

ABS ECU

P Disconnect the 2 connectors from ABS actuator.

C Check continuity between terminals Ⓐ3 2 and Ⓐ2 2, Ⓐ2 2 and Ⓐ2 5, Ⓐ2 5 and Ⓐ11 12.

OK Continuity

HINT: There is a resistance of 26 ~ 40 Ω between terminals Ⓐ2 2 and Ⓐ2 5.

OK ▽

NG ⟩ Repair or replace harness or ABS actuator.

TY4029700312020X

Fig. 312 Codes 13 & 14: ABS Control Motor Relay Circuit (Part 2 of 3). 1997–99 Tacoma

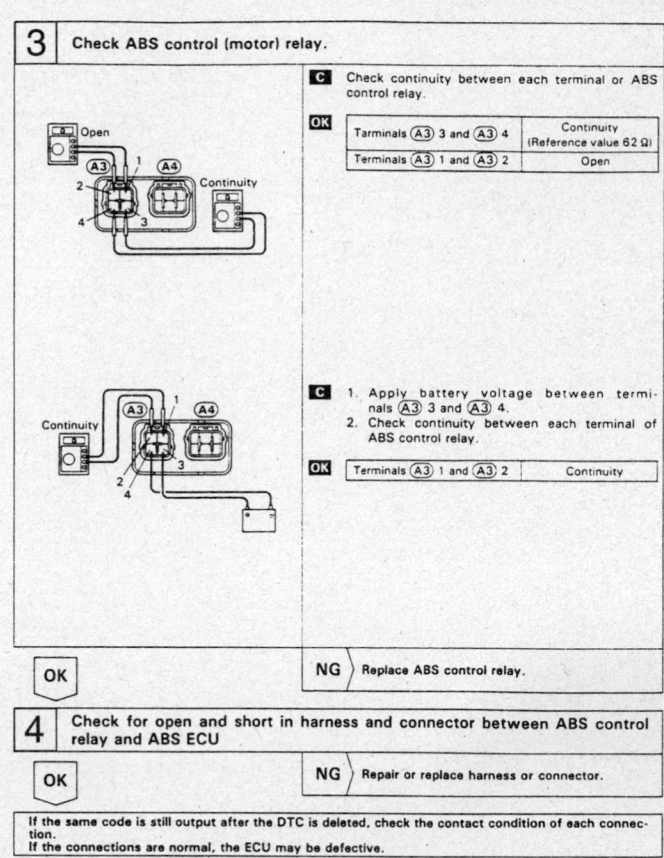

3 Check ABS control (motor) relay.

C Check continuity between each terminal or ABS control relay.

Open

Continuity

OK		
Terminals Ⓐ3 3 and Ⓐ3 4		Continuity (Reference value 62 Ω)
Terminals Ⓐ3 1 and Ⓐ3 2		Open

Continuity

C 1. Apply battery voltage between terminals Ⓐ3 3 and 4.
2. Check continuity between each terminal of ABS control relay.

OK		
Terminals Ⓐ3 1 and Ⓐ3 2		Continuity

OK ▽

NG ⟩ Replace ABS control relay.

4 Check for open and short in harness and connector between ABS control relay and ABS ECU

OK ▽

NG ⟩ Repair or replace harness or connector.

If the same code is still output after the DTC is deleted, check the contact condition of each connection.
If the connections are normal, the ECU may be defective.

TY4029500165030X

Fig. 312 Codes 13 & 14: ABS Control Motor Relay Circuit (Part 3 of 3). Tacoma

---

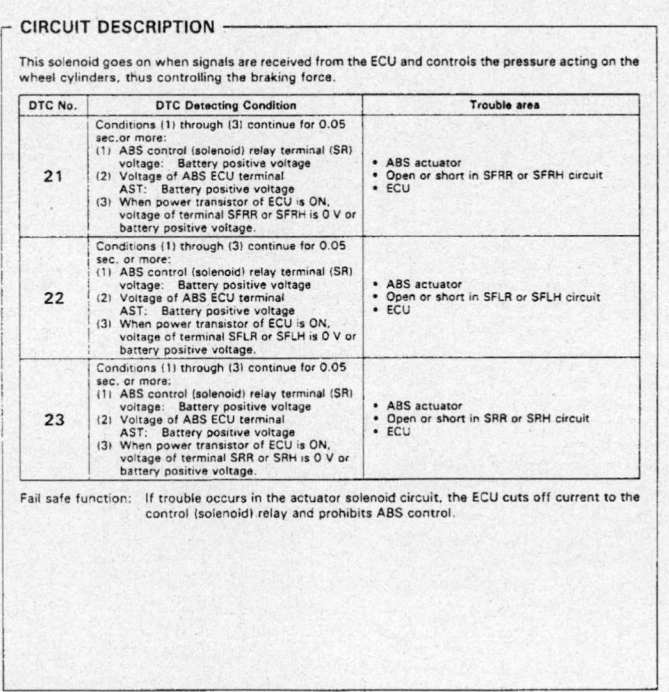

CIRCUIT DESCRIPTION

This solenoid goes on when signals are received from the ECU and controls the pressure acting on the wheel cylinders, thus controlling the braking force.

DTC No.	DTC Detecting Condition	Trouble area
21	Conditions (1) through (3) continue for 0.05 sec. or more: (1) ABS control (solenoid) relay terminal (SR) voltage: Battery positive voltage (2) Voltage of ABS ECU terminal AST: Battery positive voltage (3) When power transistor of ECU is ON, voltage of terminal SFRR or SFRH is 0 V or battery positive voltage.	• ABS actuator • Open or short in SFRR or SFRH circuit • ECU
22	Conditions (1) through (3) continue for 0.05 sec. or more: (1) ABS control (solenoid) relay terminal (SR) voltage: Battery positive voltage (2) Voltage of ABS ECU terminal AST: Battery positive voltage (3) When power transistor of ECU is ON, voltage of terminal SFLR or SFLH is 0 V or battery positive voltage.	• ABS actuator • Open or short in SFLR or SFLH circuit • ECU
23	Conditions (1) through (3) continue for 0.05 sec. or more: (1) ABS control (solenoid) relay terminal (SR) voltage: Battery positive voltage (2) Voltage of ABS ECU terminal AST: Battery positive voltage (3) When power transistor of ECU is ON, voltage of terminal SRR or SRH is 0 V or battery positive voltage.	• ABS actuator • Open or short in SRR or SRH circuit • ECU

Fail safe function: If trouble occurs in the actuator solenoid circuit, the ECU cuts off current to the control (solenoid) relay and prohibits ABS control.

TY4029500166010X

Fig. 313 Codes 21, 22 & 23: ABS Actuator Solenoid Circuit (Part 1 of 2). Tacoma

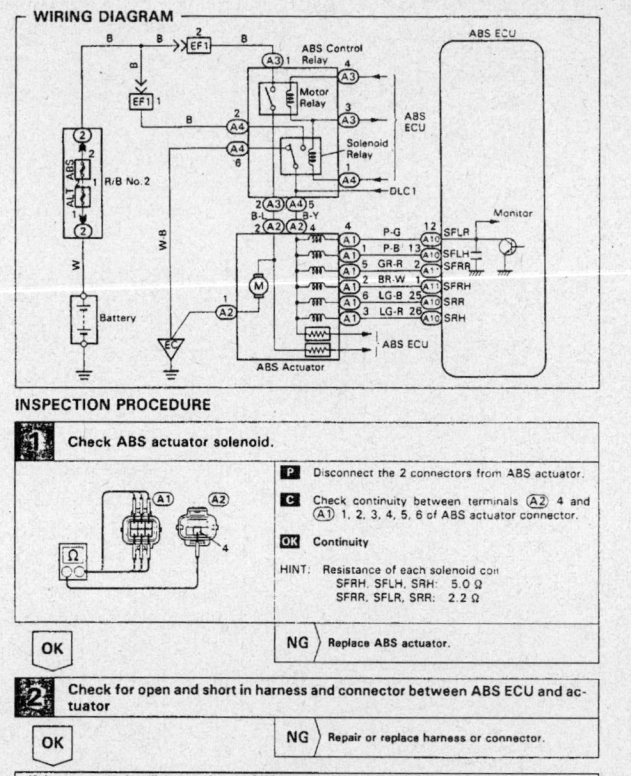

Fig. 313 Codes 21, 22 & 23: ABS Actuator Solenoid
Circuit (Part 2 of 2). 1996 Tacoma

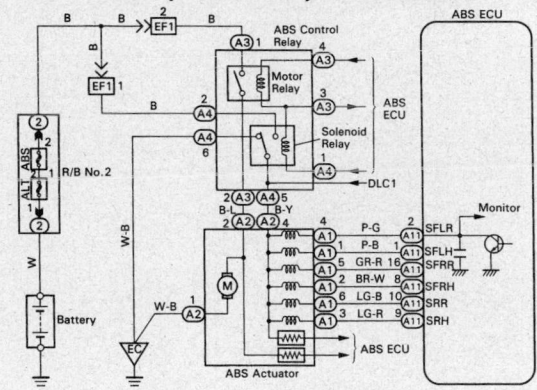

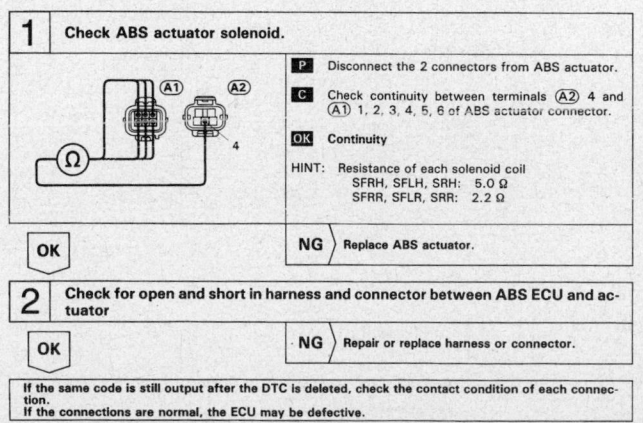

Fig. 313 Codes 21, 22 & 23: ABS Actuator Solenoid
Circuit (Part 2 of 2). 1997–99 Tacoma

CIRCUIT DESCRIPTION

The speed sensor detects the wheel speed and sends the appropriate signals to the ECU. These signals are used to control the ABS system. The front and rear rotors each have 48 serrations.

When the rotors rotate, the magnetic field emitted by the permanent magnet in the speed sensor generates an AC voltage. Since the frequency of this AC voltage changes in direct proportion to the speed of the rotor, the frequency is used by the ECU to detect the speed of each wheel.

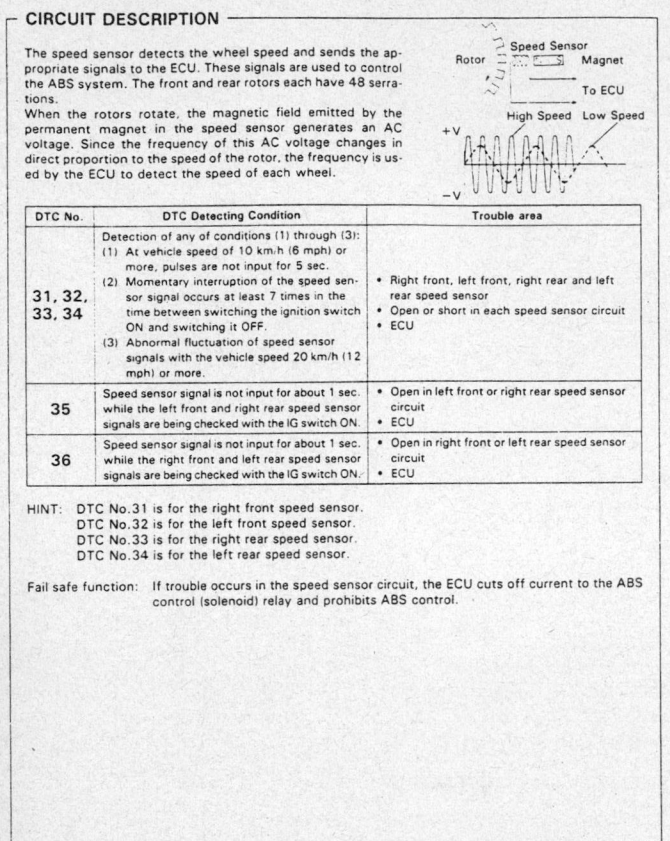

DTC No.	DTC Detecting Condition	Trouble area
31, 32, 33, 34	Detection of any of conditions (1) through (3): (1) At vehicle speed of 10 km/h (6 mph) or more, pulses are not input for 5 sec. (2) Momentary interruption of the speed sensor signal occurs at least 7 times in the time between switching the ignition switch ON and switching it OFF. (3) Abnormal fluctuation of speed sensor signals with the vehicle speed 20 km/h (12 mph) or more.	• Right front, left front, right rear and left rear speed sensor • Open or short in each speed sensor circuit • ECU
35	Speed sensor signal is not input for about 1 sec. while the left front and right rear speed sensor signals are being checked with the IG switch ON.	• Open in left front or right rear speed sensor circuit • ECU
36	Speed sensor signal is not input for about 1 sec. while the right front and left rear speed sensor signals are being checked with the IG switch ON.	• Open in right front or left rear speed sensor circuit • ECU

HINT: DTC No. 31 is for the right front speed sensor.
DTC No. 32 is for the left front speed sensor.
DTC No. 33 is for the right rear speed sensor.
DTC No. 34 is for the left rear speed sensor.

Fail safe function: If trouble occurs in the speed sensor circuit, the ECU cuts off current to the ABS control (solenoid) relay and prohibits ABS control.

TY4029500167010X

Fig. 314   Codes 31, 32, 33, 34, 35 & 36: Speed Sensor Circuit (Part 1 of 4). Tacoma

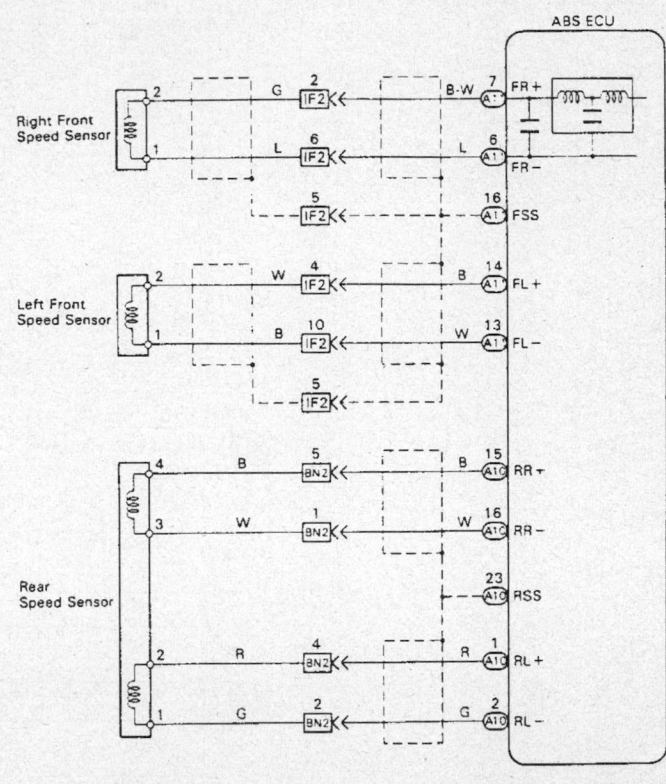

TY4029500167020X

Fig. 314   Codes 31, 32, 33, 34, 35 & 36: Speed Sensor Circuit (Part 2 of 4). 1996 Tacoma

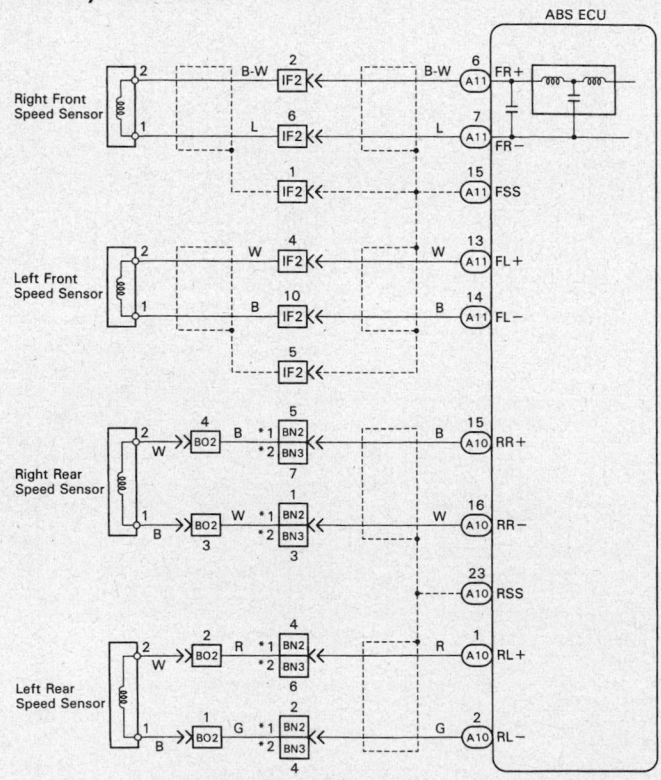

*1: w/o Rear Differential Lock
*2: w/ Rear Differential Lock

TY4029700314010X

Fig. 314   Codes 31, 32, 33, 34, 35 & 36: Speed Sensor Circuit (Part 2 of 4). 1997–99 Tacoma

INSPECTION PROCEDURE

1 Check speed sensor.

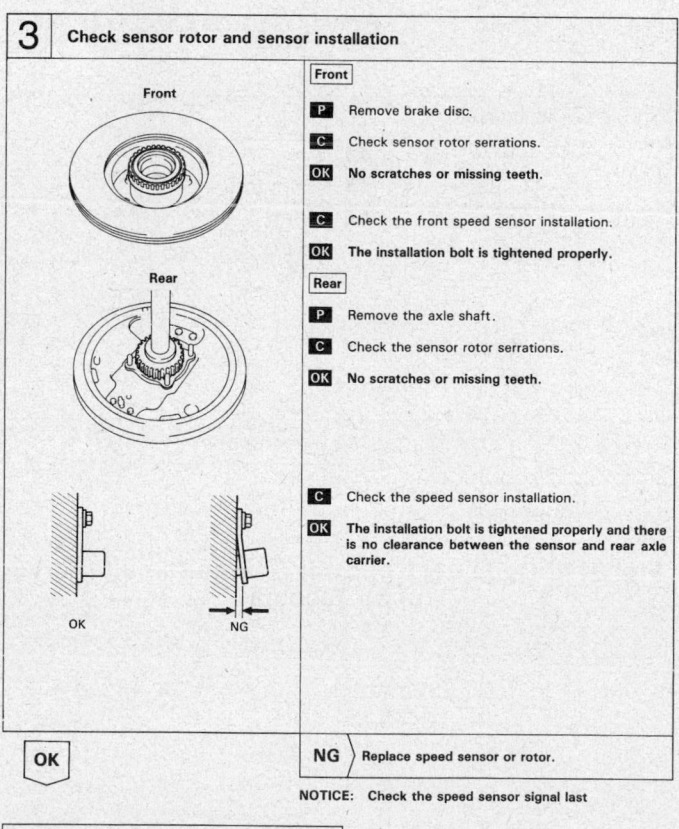

Front

P Disconnect speed sensor connector.

C Measure resistance between terminals 1 and 2 of speed sensor connector.

OK Resistance: 0.9 – 1.3 kΩ

C Measure resistance between terminals 1 and 2 of speed sensor connector and body ground.

OK Resistance: 1 MΩ or higher

Rear

P Disconnect speed sensor connector.

C Measure resistance between terminals 1 and 2, 3 and 4 of speed sensor connector.

OK Resistance: 0.9 – 1.3 kΩ

C Measure resistance between terminals 1 and 2, 3 and 4 of speed sensor connector and body ground.

OK Resistance: 1 MΩ or higher

OK → **NG** > Replace speed sensor.

NOTICE: Check the speed sensor signal last

2 Check for open and short in harness and connector between each speed sensor and ECU

OK → **NG** > Repair or replace harness or connector.

TY4029500167030X

Fig. 314 Codes 31, 32, 33, 34, 35 & 36: Speed Sensor Circuit (Part 3 of 4). 1996 Tacoma

3 Check sensor rotor and sensor installation

Front

P Remove brake disc.

C Check sensor rotor serrations.

OK No scratches or missing teeth.

C Check the front speed sensor installation.

OK The installation bolt is tightened properly.

Rear

P Remove the axle shaft.

C Check the sensor rotor serrations.

OK No scratches or missing teeth.

C Check the speed sensor installation.

OK The installation bolt is tightened properly and there is no clearance between the sensor and rear axle carrier.

OK → **NG** > Replace speed sensor or rotor.

NOTICE: Check the speed sensor signal last

Check and replace ABS ECU.

TY4029500167040X

Fig. 314 Codes 31, 32, 33, 34, 35 & 36: Speed Sensor Circuit (Part 4 of 4). Tacoma

---

1 Check speed sensor.

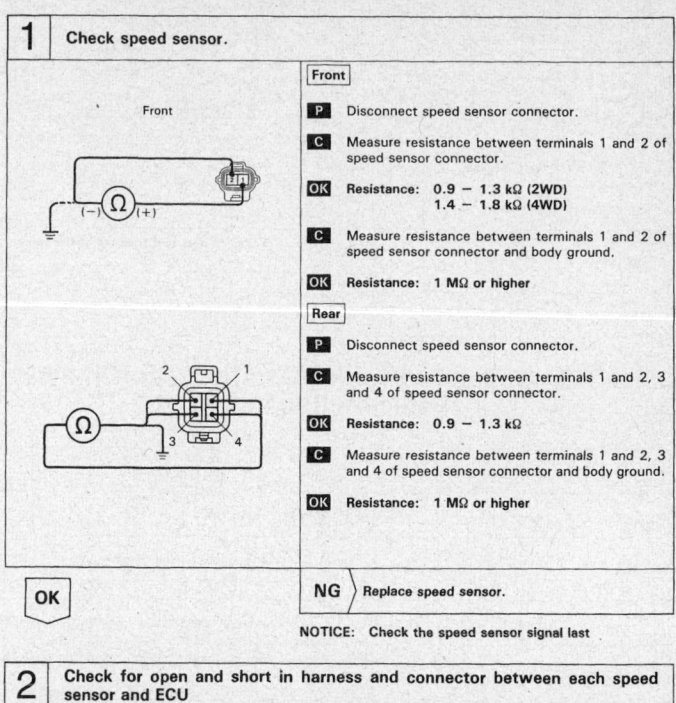

Front

P Disconnect speed sensor connector.

C Measure resistance between terminals 1 and 2 of speed sensor connector.

OK Resistance: 0.9 – 1.3 kΩ (2WD)
1.4 – 1.8 kΩ (4WD)

C Measure resistance between terminals 1 and 2 of speed sensor connector and body ground.

OK Resistance: 1 MΩ or higher

Rear

P Disconnect speed sensor connector.

C Measure resistance between terminals 1 and 2, 3 and 4 of speed sensor connector.

OK Resistance: 0.9 – 1.3 kΩ

C Measure resistance between terminals 1 and 2, 3 and 4 of speed sensor connector and body ground.

OK Resistance: 1 MΩ or higher

OK → **NG** > Replace speed sensor.

NOTICE: Check the speed sensor signal last

2 Check for open and short in harness and connector between each speed sensor and ECU

OK → **NG** > Repair or replace harness or connector.

TY4029700314020X

Fig. 314 Codes 31, 32, 33, 34, 35 & 36: Speed Sensor Circuit (Part 3 of 4). 1997–99 Tacoma

CIRCUIT DESCRIPTION

DTC No.	DTC Detecting Condition	Trouble area
37	With the rear wheels stationary and front wheels rotating at 20+ km/h (12+ mph) for 10+ secs, turn ignition switch ON then OFF 8 times, in succession.	• Front axle hub • Right front, left front speed sensor • Wire harness for sensor system • ECU

INSPECTION PROCEDURE

1 Check front axle hub

OK → **NG** > Replace front axle hub.

2 Check front speed sensor

OK → **NG** > Replace front speed sensor.

3 Check for open or short in harness and connector between speed sensor and ECU

OK → **NG** > Repair or replace harness and connector.

Check and replace ABS ECU.

TY4029500168000X

Fig. 315 Code 37: Neither Front Speed Sensor Rotor Missing. Tacoma

CIRCUIT DESCRIPTION

DTC No.	DTC Detecting Condition	Trouble area
37	Driving at more than 30 km/h (19 mph) for more than 60 seconds with 1 or 2 tires of different size.	• Tire size • ECU

INSPECTION PROCEDURE

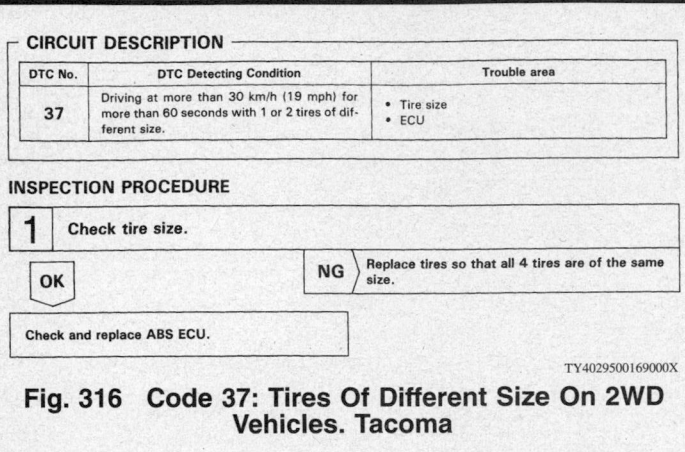

1 | Check tire size.

OK

NG > Replace tires so that all 4 tires are of the same size.

Check and replace ABS ECU.

TY4029500169000X

Fig. 316   Code 37: Tires Of Different Size On 2WD Vehicles. Tacoma

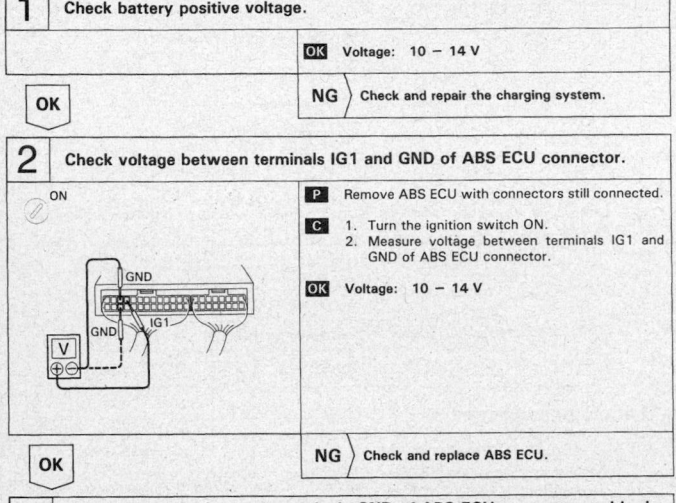

1 | Check battery positive voltage.

OK Voltage: 10 – 14 V

OK

NG > Check and repair the charging system.

2 | Check voltage between terminals IG1 and GND of ABS ECU connector.

ON

P Remove ABS ECU with connectors still connected.

C 1. Turn the ignition switch ON.
2. Measure voltage between terminals IG1 and GND of ABS ECU connector.

OK Voltage: 10 – 14 V

OK

NG > Check and replace ABS ECU.

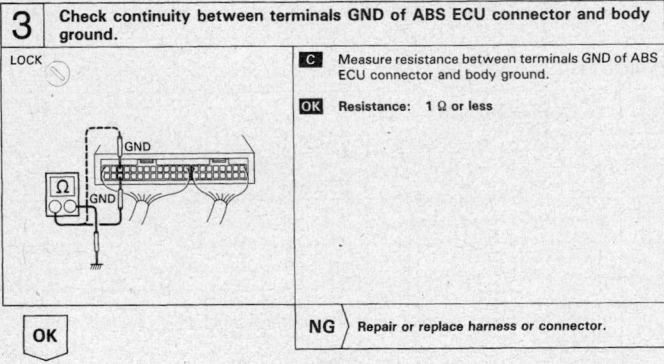

3 | Check continuity between terminals GND of ABS ECU connector and body ground.

LOCK

C Measure resistance between terminals GND of ABS ECU connector and body ground.

OK Resistance: 1 Ω or less

OK

NG > Repair or replace harness or connector.

TY4029500170020X

Fig. 317   Code 41: IG Power Source Circuit (Part 2 of 3). Tacoma

CIRCUIT DESCRIPTION

This is the power source for the ECU, hence the CPU, and the actuators.

DTC No.	DTC Detecting Condition	Trouble area
41	Vehicle speed is 3 km/h (1.9 mph) or more and voltage of ECU terminal IG1 remains at more than 17 V or below 9.5 V for more than 10 sec.	• Battery • IC regulator • Open or short in power source circuit • ECU

Fail safe function: If trouble occurs in the power source circuit, the ECU cuts off current to the ABS control (solenoid) relay and prohibits ABS control.

WIRING DIAGRAM

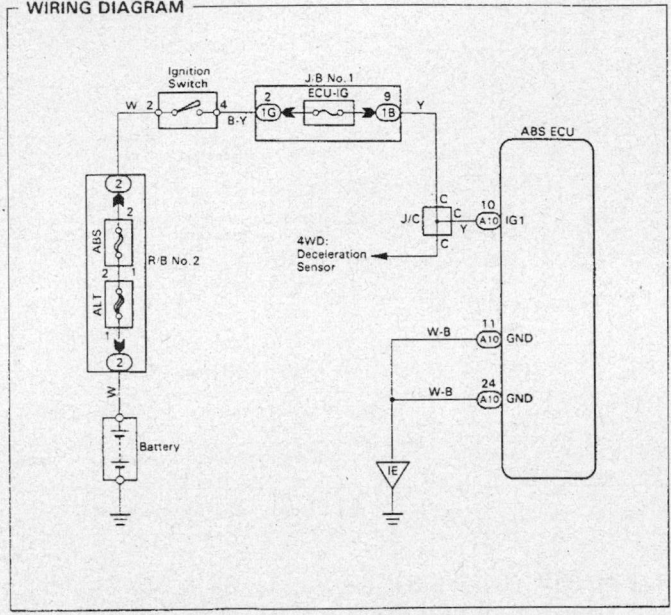

TY4029500170010X

Fig. 317   Code 41: IG Power Source Circuit (Part 1 of 3). Tacoma

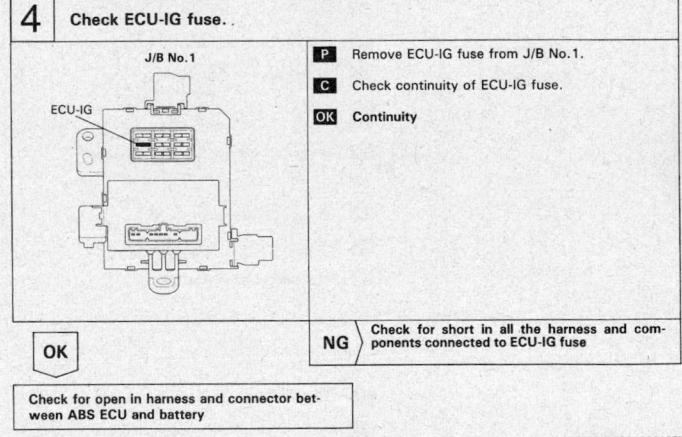

4 | Check ECU-IG fuse.

J/B No.1

ECU-IG

P Remove ECU-IG fuse from J/B No.1.

C Check continuity of ECU-IG fuse.

OK Continuity

OK

NG > Check for short in all the harness and components connected to ECU-IG fuse

Check for open in harness and connector between ABS ECU and battery

TY4029500170030X

Fig. 317   Code 41: IG Power Source Circuit (Part 3 of 3). Tacoma

DTC	43	Malfunction in Deceleration Sensor

CIRCUIT DESCRIPTION

DTC No.	DTC Detecting Condition	Trouble area
43	Either of the following (1) or (2) is detected: (1) After the battery terminal is connected, input from the deceleration sensor does not change at one cycle (0 km/h→ more than 30 km/h→ 0 km/h) for 16 times continuously. (2) When the brake pedal is not depressed at vehicle speed of 5 km/h or more, forward and backward G (more than 0.4G) is detected for 30 seconds or more.	• Deceleration sensor • Wire harness for deceleration sensor system • ECU

INSPECTION PROCEDURE

1 Check deceleration sensor

OK ↓   NG ▷ Replace deceleration sensor.

2 Check for open or short in harness and connector between sensor and ECU

OK ↓   NG ▷ Repair or replace harness and connector.

Check and replace ABS ECU.

TY4029500171000X

Fig. 318   Code 43: Fault In Deceleration Sensor. Tacoma

1 Check for open and short in harness and connector between sensor and ECU

OK ↓   NG ▷ Repair or replace harness or connector.

2 Check voltage between terminals GS1, GS2, GST of ECU and body ground.

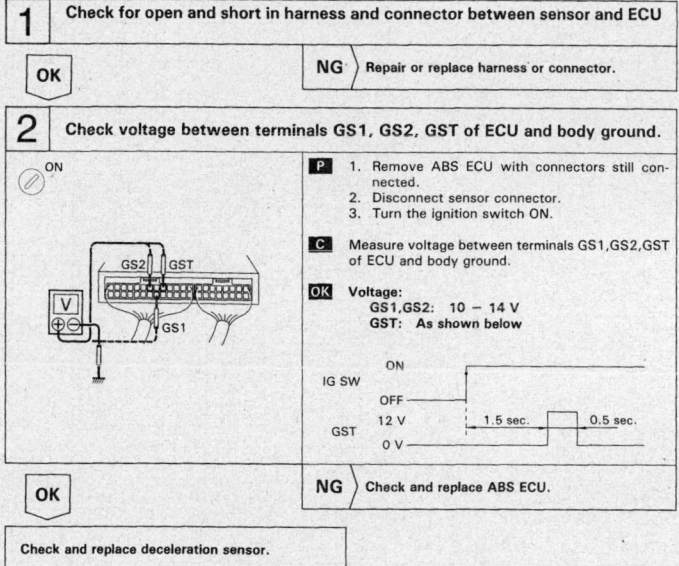

P
1. Remove ABS ECU with connectors still connected.
2. Disconnect sensor connector.
3. Turn the ignition switch ON.

C Measure voltage between terminals GS1,GS2,GST of ECU and body ground.

OK Voltage:
GS1,GS2: 10 – 14 V
GST: As shown below

OK ↓   NG ▷ Check and replace ABS ECU.

Check and replace deceleration sensor.

TY4029500172020X

Fig. 319   Code 44: Deceleration Sensor Circuit (Part 2 of 2). 1996 Tacoma

CIRCUIT DESCRIPTION

This sensor detects deceleration on the vehicle. The sensor signal is used in ABS control. If the sensor functions abnormally, the ABS warning light comes on but the ABS still operates.

DTC No.	DTC Detecting Condition	Trouble Area
44	Either of the following (1) or (2) is detected: (1) An open or short is detected in circuit GS1 or GS2 for 1 sec. (2) After the ignition is turned ON, the test signal is output by GST. During this time, a trouble signal is detected for 0.5 sec.	• Deceleration sensor • Open or short in deceleration sensor circuit • ECU

WIRING DIAGRAM

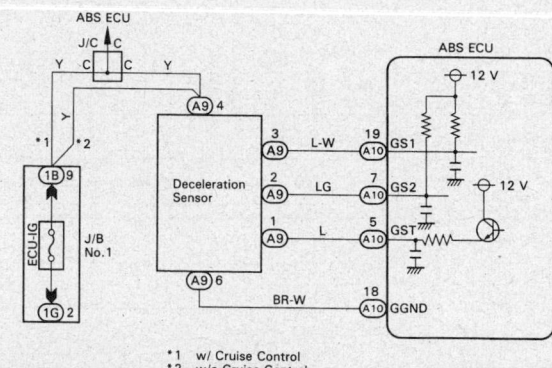

*1 w/ Cruise Control
*2 w/o Cruise Control

TY4029500172010X

Fig. 319   Code 44: Deceleration Sensor Circuit (Part 1 of 2). Tacoma

1 Check for open and short in harness and connector between sensor and ECU

OK ↓   NG ▷ Repair or replace harness or connector.

2 Check voltage between terminals GS1, GS2, GST of ECU and body ground.

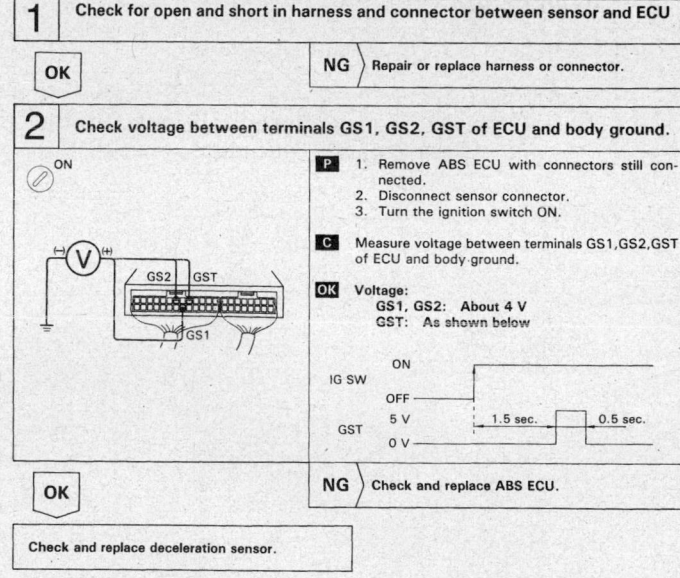

P
1. Remove ABS ECU with connectors still connected.
2. Disconnect sensor connector.
3. Turn the ignition switch ON.

C Measure voltage between terminals GS1,GS2,GST of ECU and body ground.

OK Voltage:
GS1, GS2: About 4 V
GST: As shown below

OK ↓   NG ▷ Check and replace ABS ECU.

Check and replace deceleration sensor.

TY4029700315000X

Fig. 319   Code 44: Deceleration Sensor Circuit (Part 2 of 2). 1997–99 Tacoma

DTC No.	DTC Detecting Condition	Trouble Area
48	Open or short circuit in rear differential lock circuit. Rear differential is locking.	• Rear differential lock • ECU

TY4029700316010X

Fig. 320   Code 48: Rear Differential Lock Circuit (Part 1 of 3). Tacoma

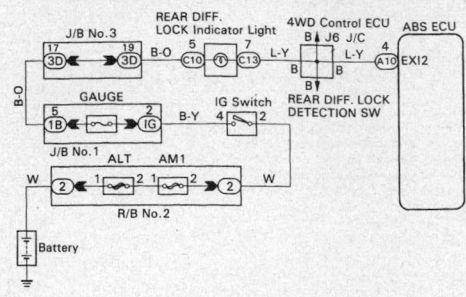

Fig. 320 Code 48: Rear Differential Lock Circuit (Part 3 of 3). Tacoma

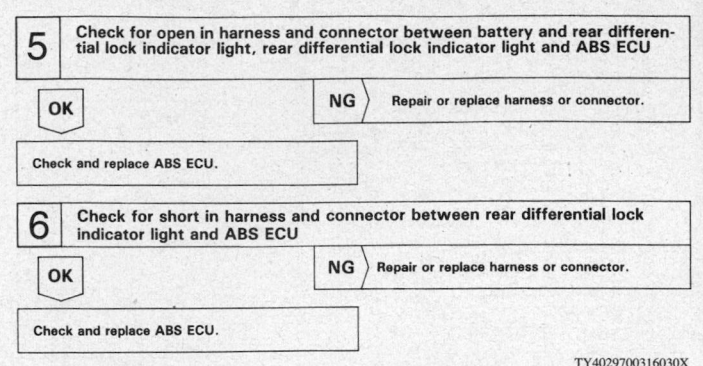

5 Check for open in harness and connector between battery and rear differential lock indicator light, rear differential lock indicator light and ABS ECU

| OK | | NG | Repair or replace harness or connector. |

Check and replace ABS ECU.

6 Check for short in harness and connector between rear differential lock indicator light and ABS ECU

| OK | | NG | Repair or replace harness or connector. |

Check and replace ABS ECU.

TY4029700316030X

Fig. 320 Code 48: Rear Differential Lock Circuit (Part 3 of 3). Tacoma

HINT: Rear differential lock switch is OFF.

1 Check the rear differential lock is free

| OK | | NG | Repair the rear differential lock system. |

2 Is DTC output?

Check DTC

| YES | | NO | Normal. |

3 Check that rear differential lock indicator light does not go off.

| YES | | NO | Go to step 6 . |

4 Check that bulb for rear differential lock indicator light is not burnt out.

| NO | | YES | Replace indicator light. |

TY4029700316020X

Fig. 320 Code 48: Rear Differential Lock Circuit (Part 2 of 3). Tacoma

CIRCUIT DESCRIPTION

DTC No.	DTC Detecting Condition	Trouble area
51	Pump motor is not operating normally during initial check.	• ABS pump motor

Fail safe function: If trouble occurs in the ABS pump motor, the ECU cuts off current to the control (solenoid) relay and prohibits ABS control.

WIRING DIAGRAM

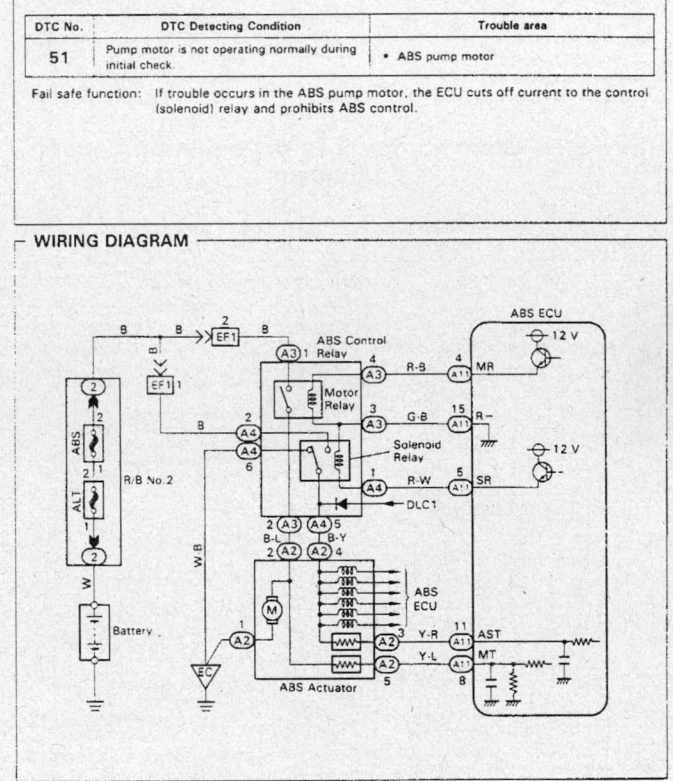

TY4029500173000X

Fig. 321 Code 51: ABS Pump Motor Lock. 1996 Tacoma

DTC No.	DTC Detecting Condition	Trouble Area
51	Pump motor is not operating normally during initial check.	• ABS pump motor

Fail safe function: If trouble occurs in the ABS pump motor, the ECU cuts off current to the ABS control (solenoid) relay and prohibits ABS control.

TY4029700317010X

Fig. 322 Code 51: ABS Pump Motor Lock (Part 1 of 2). 1997–99 Tacoma

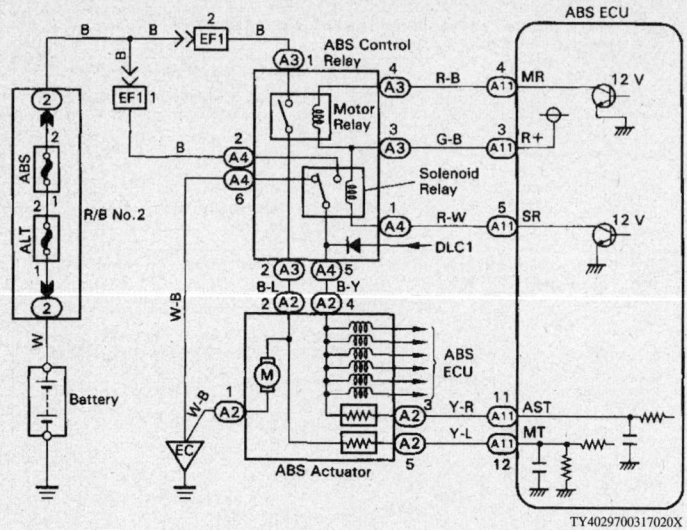

Fig. 322   Code 51: ABS Pump Motor Lock (Part 2 of 2). 1997–99 Tacoma

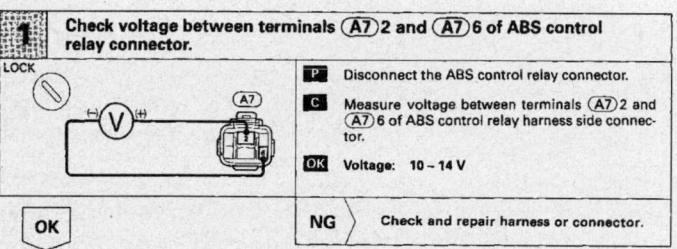

1	Check voltage between terminals (A7)2 and (A7)6 of ABS control relay connector.

P Disconnect the ABS control relay connector.

C Measure voltage between terminals (A7)2 and (A7)6 of ABS control relay harness side connector.

OK Voltage: **10 – 14 V**

OK ↓

NG ⟩ Check and repair harness or connector.

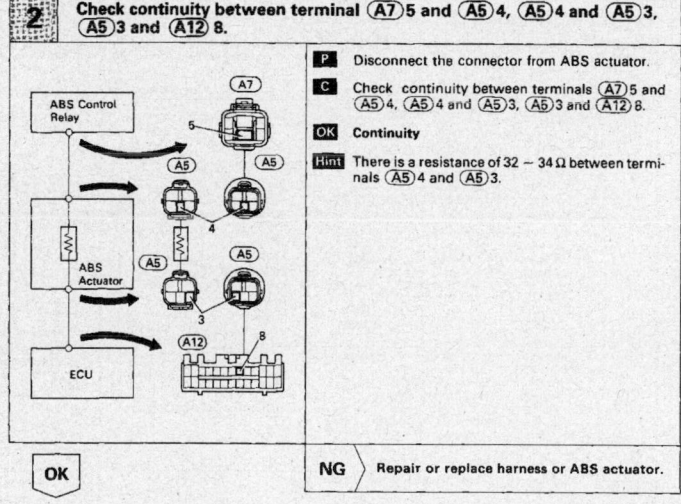

2	Check continuity between terminal (A7)5 and (A5)4, (A5)4 and (A5)3, (A5)3 and (A12)8.

P Disconnect the connector from ABS actuator.

C Check continuity between terminals (A7)5 and (A5)4, (A5)4 and (A5)3, (A5)3 and (A12)8.

OK Continuity

Hint There is a resistance of 32 ~ 34 Ω between terminals (A5)4 and (A5)3.

OK ↓

NG ⟩ Repair or replace harness or ABS actuator.

TY4029500178020X

Fig. 323   Codes 11 & 12: ABS Control Solenoid Relay Circuit (Part 2 of 3). Tercel

---

CIRCUIT DESCRIPTION

This relay supplies power to each ABS solenoid. After the ignition switch is turned ON, if the initial check is OK, the relay goes on.

DTC No.	DTC Detecting Condition	Trouble Area
11	Conditions (1) and (2) continue for 0.2 sec. or more: (1) ABS control (solenoid) relay terminal (SR) voltage: Battery positive voltage (2) ABS control (solenoid) relay monitor terminal (AST) voltage: 0 V	• ABS control (solenoid) relay • Open or short in ABS control (solenoid) relay circuit • ECU
12	Conditions (1) and (2) continue for 0.2sec. or more: (1) ABS control (solenoid) relay terminal (SR) voltage: 0 V (2) ABS control (solenoid) relay monitor terminal (AST) voltage: Battery positive voltage	• ABS control (solenoid) relay • B+ short in ABS control (solenoid) relay circuit • ECU

Fail safe function: If trouble occurs in the ABS control (solenoid) relay circuit, the ECU cuts off current to the ABS control (solenoid) relay and prohibits ABS control.

WIRING DIAGRAM

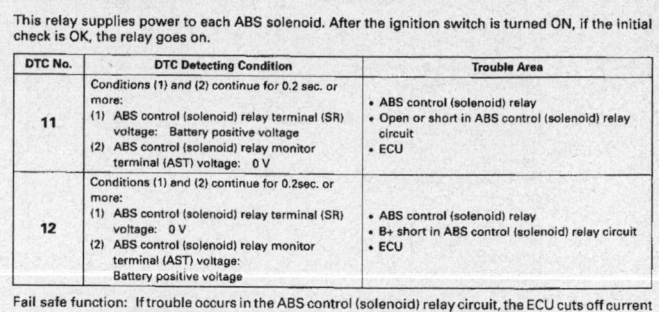

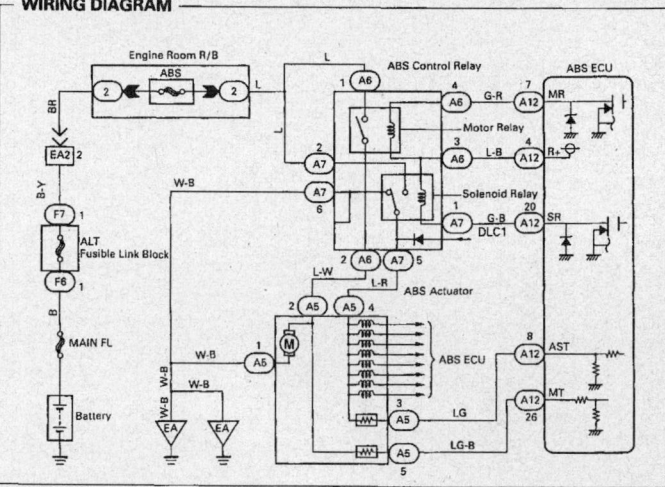

TY4029500178010X

Fig. 323   Codes 11 & 12: ABS Control Solenoid Relay Circuit (Part 1 of 3). Tercel

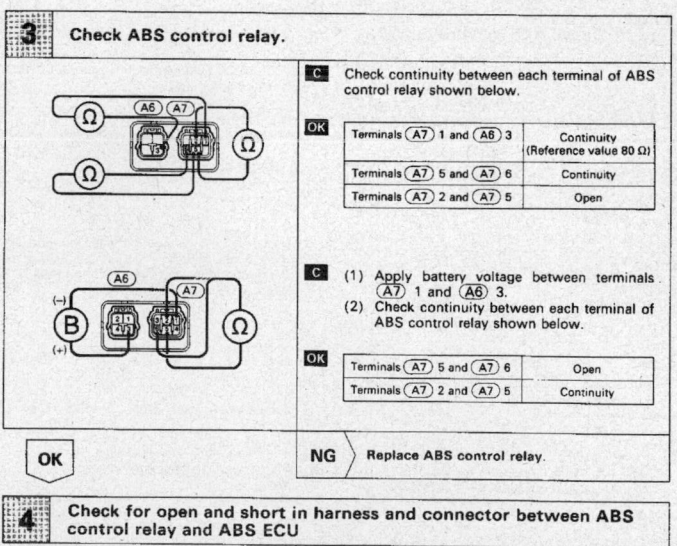

3	Check ABS control relay.

C Check continuity between each terminal of ABS control relay shown below.

OK

Terminals (A7)1 and (A6)3	Continuity (Reference value 80 Ω)
Terminals (A7)5 and (A7)6	Continuity
Terminals (A7)2 and (A7)5	Open

C
(1) Apply battery voltage between terminals (A7)1 and (A6)3.
(2) Check continuity between each terminal of ABS control relay shown below.

OK

Terminals (A7)5 and (A7)6	Open
Terminals (A7)2 and (A7)5	Continuity

OK ↓

NG ⟩ Replace ABS control relay.

4	Check for open and short in harness and connector between ABS control relay and ABS ECU

OK

NG ⟩ Repair or replace harness or connector.

If the same code is still output after the DTC is deleted, check the contact condition of each connection.
If the connections are normal, the ECU may be defective.

TY4029500178030X

Fig. 323   Codes 11 & 12: ABS Control Solenoid Relay Circuit (Part 3 of 3). Tercel

---

CIRCUIT DESCRIPTION

The ABS control (motor) relay supplies power to the ABS pump motor. While the ABS is activated, the ECU switches the ABS control (motor) relay on and operates the ABS pump motor.

DTC No.	DTC Detecting Condition	Trouble Area
13	Conditions (1) and (2) continue for 0.2 sec. or more: (1) ABS control (motor) relay terminal (MR) voltage: Battery positive voltage (2) ABS control (motor) relay monitor terminal (MT) voltage: 0 V	• ABS control (motor) relay • Open or short in ABS control (motor) relay circuit • ECU
14	Conditions (1) and (2) continued for 4 sec. or more: (1) ABS control (motor) relay terminal (MR) voltage: 0 V (2) ABS control (motor) relay monitor terminal (MT) voltage: Battery positive voltage	• ABS control (motor) relay • B+ short in ABS control (motor) relay circuit • ECU

Fail safe function: If trouble occurs in the ABS control (motor) relay circuit, the ECU cuts off the current to the ABS control (solenoid) relay and prohibits ABS control.

WIRING DIAGRAM

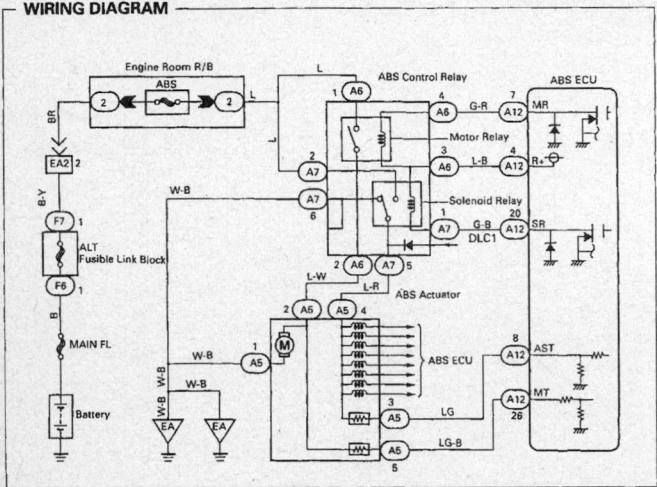

Fig. 324 Codes 13 & 14: ABS Control Motor Relay Circuit (Part 1 of 3). Tercel

TY4029500179010X

---

3 | **Check ABS control relay.**

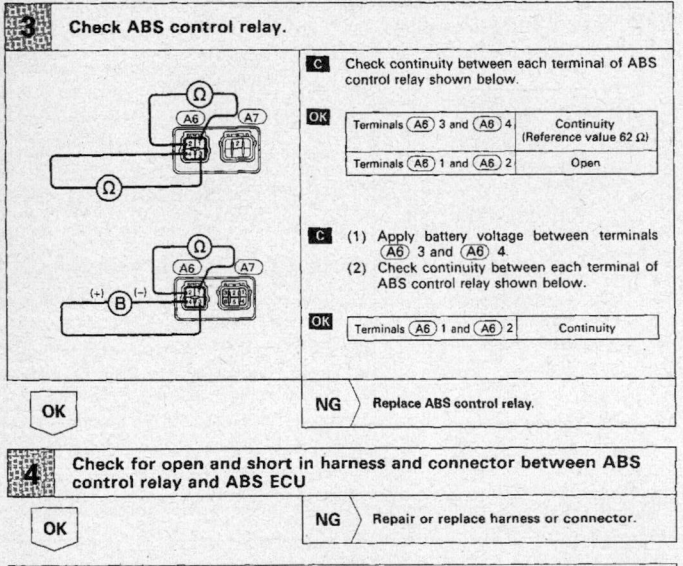

C Check continuity between each terminal of ABS control relay shown below.

OK	Terminals (A6) 3 and (A6) 4	Continuity (Reference value 62 Ω)
	Terminals (A6) 1 and (A6) 2	Open

C (1) Apply battery voltage between terminals (A6) 3 and (A6) 4.
(2) Check continuity between each terminal of ABS control relay shown below.

OK	Terminals (A6) 1 and (A6) 2	Continuity

OK → | NG → Replace ABS control relay.

4 | **Check for open and short in harness and connector between ABS control relay and ABS ECU.**

OK → | NG → Repair or replace harness or connector.

If the same code is still output after the DTC is deleted, check the contact condition of each connection. If the connections are normal, the ECU may be defective.

TY4029500179030X

Fig. 324 Codes 13 & 14: ABS Control Motor Relay Circuit (Part 3 of 3). Tercel

---

1 | **Check voltage between terminals (A6) 1 of ABS control relay and body ground.**

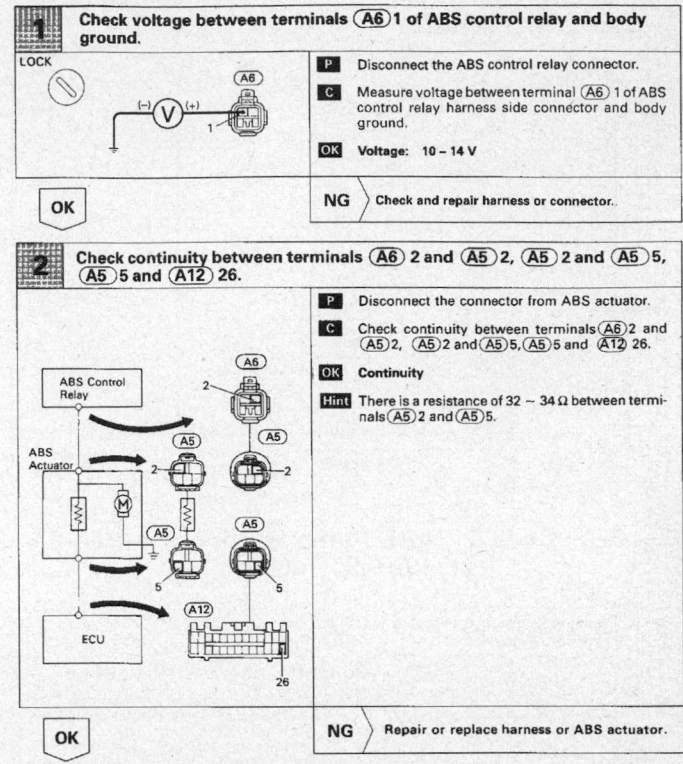

P Disconnect the ABS control relay connector.

C Measure voltage between terminal (A6) 1 of ABS control relay harness side connector and body ground.

OK Voltage: 10 – 14 V

OK → | NG → Check and repair harness or connector.

2 | **Check continuity between terminals (A6) 2 and (A5) 2, (A5) 2 and (A5) 5, (A5) 5 and (A12) 26.**

P Disconnect the connector from ABS actuator.

C Check continuity between terminals (A6) 2 and (A5) 2, (A5) 2 and (A5) 5, (A5) 5 and (A12) 26.

OK Continuity

Hint There is a resistance of 32 – 34 Ω between terminals (A5) 2 and (A5) 5.

OK → | NG → Repair or replace harness or ABS actuator.

TY4029500179020X

Fig. 324 Codes 13 & 14: ABS Control Motor Relay Circuit (Part 2 of 3). Tercel

CIRCUIT DESCRIPTION

This solenoid goes on when signals are received from the ECU and controls the pressure acting on the brake cylinders, thus controlling the braking force.

DTC No.	DTC Detecting Condition	Trouble Area
21	Conditions (1) through (3) continue for 0.05 sec. or more: (1) ABS control (solenoid) relay terminal (SR) voltage: Battery positive voltage (2) Voltage or ABS ECU terminal AST: Battery positive voltage (3) When power transistor of ECU is ON, voltage of terminal SFR is 0 V or battery positive voltage.	• ABS actuator • Open or short in SFR circuit • ECU
22	Conditions (1) through (3) continue for 0.05 sec. or more: (1) ABS control (solenoid) relay terminal (SR) voltage: Battery positive voltage (2) Voltage of ABS ECU terminal AST: Battery positive voltage (3) When power transistor of ECU is ON, voltage of terminal SFL is 0 V or battery positive voltage.	• ABS actuator • Open or short in SFL circuit • ECU
23	Conditions (1) through (3) continue for 0.05 sec. or more: (1) ABS control (solenoid) relay terminal (SR) voltage: Battery positive voltage (2) Voltage of ABS ECU terminal AST: Battery positive voltage (3) When power transistor of ECU is ON, voltage of terminal SRR is 0 V or battery positive voltage.	• ABS actuator • Open or short in SRR circuit • ECU
24	Conditions (1) through (3) continue for 0.05 sec. or more: (1) ABS control (solenoid) relay terminal (SR) voltage: Battery positive voltage (2) Voltage of ABS ECU terminal AST: Battery positive voltage (3) When power transistor of ECU is ON, voltage of terminal SRL is 0 V or battery positive voltage.	• ABS actuator • Open or short in SRL circuit • ECU

Fail safe function: If trouble occurs in the actuator solenoid circuit, the ECU cuts off current to the ABS control (solenoid) relay and prohibits ABS control.

TY4029500180010X

Fig. 325 Codes 21, 22, 23 & 24: ABS Actuator Solenoid Circuit (Part 1 of 3). Tercel

WIRING DIAGRAM

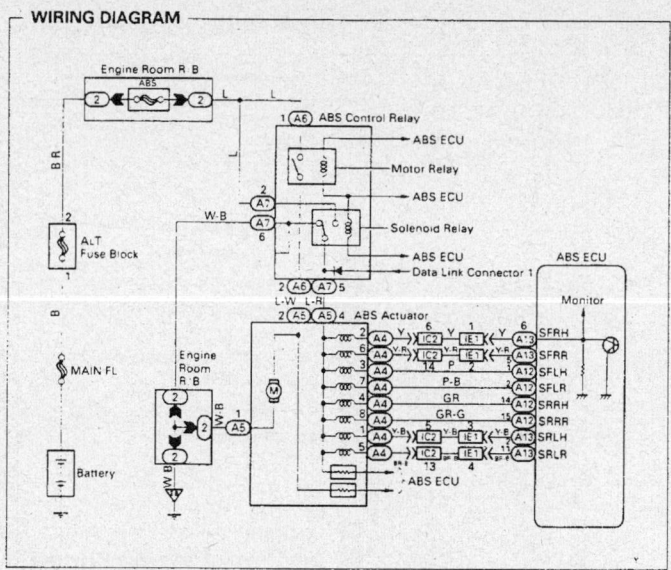

Fig. 325   Codes 21, 22, 23 & 24: ABS Actuator Solenoid Circuit (Part 2 of 3). Tercel

TY4029500180020X

CIRCUIT DESCRIPTION

The speed sensor detects the wheel speed and sends the appropriate signals to the ECU. These signals are used to control the ABS system. The front and rear rotors each have 48 serrations. When the rotors rotate, the magnetic field emitted by the permanent magnet in the speed sensor generates an AC voltage.
Since the frequency of this AC voltage changes in direct proportion to the speed of the rotors, the frequency is used by the ECU to detect the speed of each wheel.

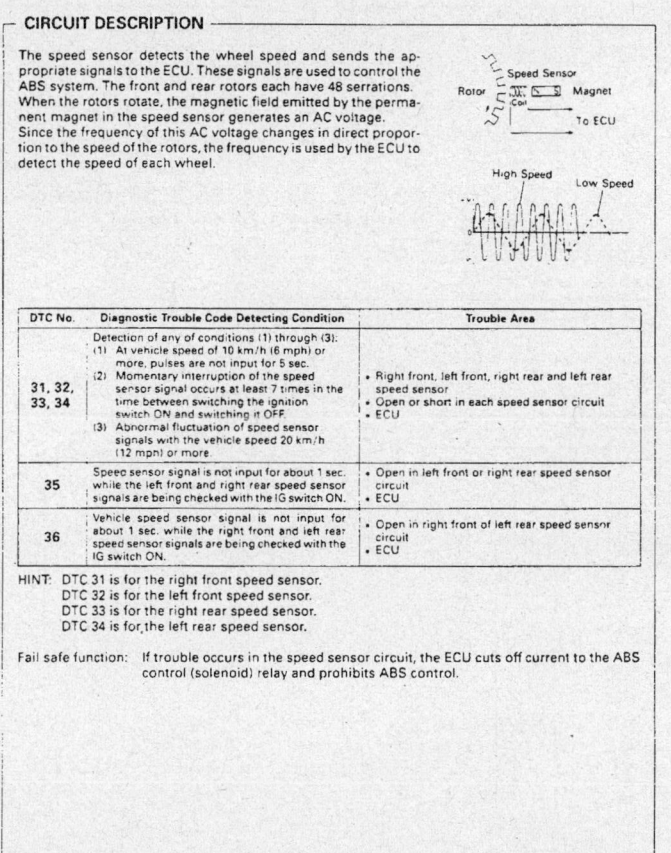

DTC No.	Diagnostic Trouble Code Detecting Condition	Trouble Area
31, 32, 33, 34	Detection of any of conditions (1) through (3): (1) At vehicle speed of 10 km/h (6 mph) or more, pulses are not input for 5 sec. (2) Momentary interruption of the speed sensor signal occurs at least 7 times in the time between switching the ignition switch ON and switching it OFF. (3) Abnormal fluctuation of speed sensor signals with the vehicle speed 20 km/h (12 mph) or more.	• Right front, left front, right rear and left rear speed sensor • Open or short in each speed sensor circuit • ECU
35	Speed sensor signal is not input for about 1 sec. while the left front and right rear speed sensor signals are being checked with the IG switch ON.	• Open in left front or right rear speed sensor circuit • ECU
36	Vehicle speed sensor signal is not input for about 1 sec. while the right front and left rear speed sensor signals are being checked with the IG switch ON.	• Open in right front of left rear speed sensor circuit • ECU

HINT: DTC 31 is for the right front speed sensor.
    DTC 32 is for the left front speed sensor.
    DTC 33 is for the right rear speed sensor.
    DTC 34 is for the left rear speed sensor.

Fail safe function: If trouble occurs in the speed sensor circuit, the ECU cuts off current to the ABS control (solenoid) relay and prohibits ABS control.

TY4029500181010X

Fig. 326   Codes 31, 32, 33, 34, 35 & 36: Speed Sensor Circuit (Part 1 of 4). Tercel

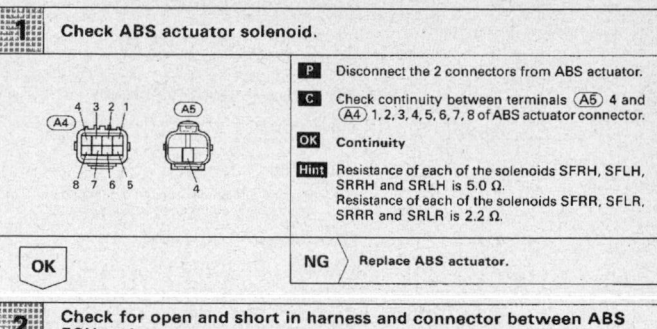

1	Check ABS actuator solenoid.	
P	Disconnect the 2 connectors from ABS actuator.	
C	Check continuity between terminals Ⓐ5 4 and Ⓐ4 1, 2, 3, 4, 5, 6, 7, 8 of ABS actuator connector.	
OK	Continuity	
Hint	Resistance of each of the solenoids SFRH, SFLH, SRRH and SRLH is 5.0 Ω. Resistance of each of the solenoids SFRR, SFLR, SRRR and SRLR is 2.2 Ω.	
OK		**NG** → Replace ABS actuator.

2	Check for open and short in harness and connector between ABS ECU and actuator.	
OK		**NG** → Repair or replace harness or connector.

If the same code is still output after the DTC is deleted, check the contact condition of each connection. If the connections are normal, the ECU may be defective.

TY4029500180030X

Fig. 325   Codes 21, 22, 23 & 24: ABS Actuator Solenoid Circuit (Part 3 of 3). Tercel

CIRCUIT DESCRIPTION

The speed sensor detects the wheel speed and sends the appropriate signals to the ECU. These signals are used to control the ABS system. The front and rear rotors each have 48 serrations.
When the rotors rotate, the magnetic field emitted by the permanent magnet in the speed sensor generates an AC voltage.
Since the frequency of this AC voltage changes in direct proportion to the speed of the rotors, the frequency is used by the ECU to detect the speed of each wheel.

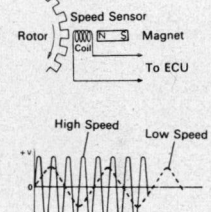

DTC No.	DTC Detecting Condition	Trouble Area
31, 32, 33, 34	Detection of any of conditions (1) through (3): (1) At vehicle speed of 10 km/h (6 mph) or more, pulses are not input for 5 sec. (2) Momentary interruption of the speed sensor signal occurs at least 7 times in the time between switching the ignition switch ON and switching it OFF. (3) Abnormal fluctuation of speed sensor signals with the vehicle speed 20 km/h (12 mph) or more.	• Right front, left front, right rear and left rear speed sensor • Open or short in each speed sensor circuit • ECU

HINT: DTC 31 is for the right front speed sensor.
    DTC 32 is for the left front speed sensor.
    DTC 33 is for the right rear speed sensor.
    DTC 34 is for the left rear speed sensor.

Fail safe function: If trouble occurs in the speed sensor circuit, the ECU cuts off current to the ABS control (solenoid) relay and prohibits ABS control.

TY4029500181020X

Fig. 326   Codes 31, 32, 33, 34, 35 & 36: Speed Sensor Circuit (Part 2 of 4). Tercel

1 Check speed sensor.

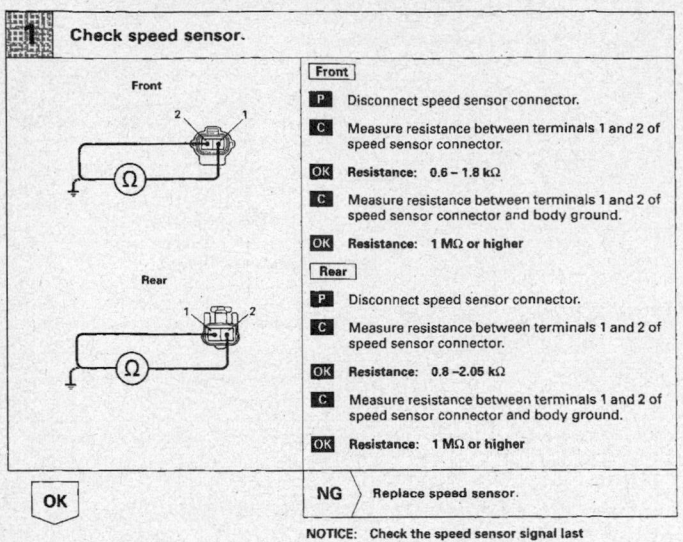

Front

P Disconnect speed sensor connector.

C Measure resistance between terminals 1 and 2 of speed sensor connector.

OK Resistance: 0.6 – 1.8 kΩ

C Measure resistance between terminals 1 and 2 of speed sensor connector and body ground.

OK Resistance: 1 MΩ or higher

Rear

P Disconnect speed sensor connector.

C Measure resistance between terminals 1 and 2 of speed sensor connector.

OK Resistance: 0.8 –2.05 kΩ

C Measure resistance between terminals 1 and 2 of speed sensor connector and body ground.

OK Resistance: 1 MΩ or higher

OK ▽

NG > Replace speed sensor.

NOTICE: Check the speed sensor signal last.

TY4029500181030X

Fig. 326   Codes 31, 32, 33, 34, 35 & 36: Speed Sensor Circuit (Part 3 of 4). Tercel

2 Check for open and short in harness and connector between each speed sensor and ECU.

OK ▽   **NG** > Repair or replace harness or connector.

3 Check sensor rotor and sensor installation.

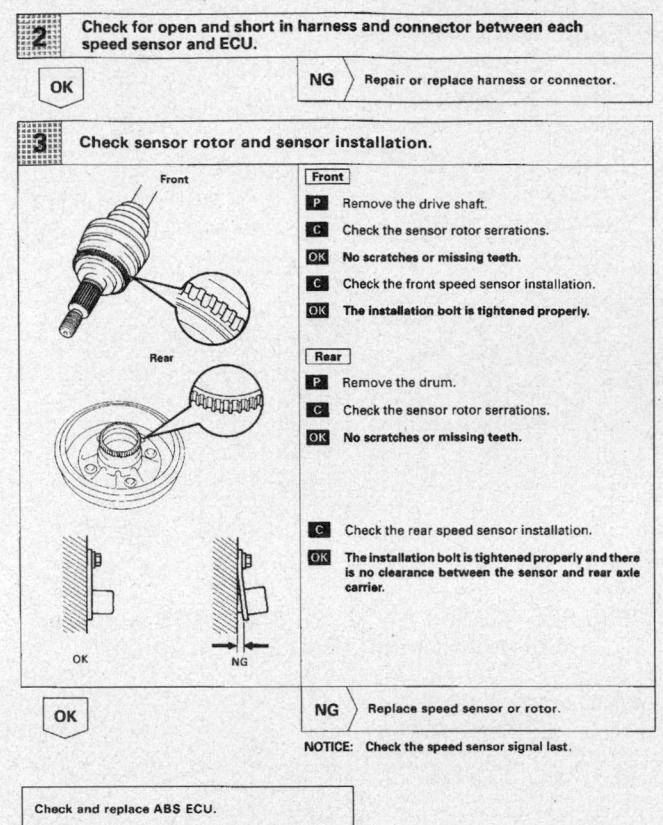

Front

P Remove the drive shaft.

C Check the sensor rotor serrations.

OK No scratches or missing teeth.

C Check the front speed sensor installation.

OK The installation bolt is tightened properly.

Rear

P Remove the drum.

C Check the sensor rotor serrations.

OK No scratches or missing teeth.

C Check the rear speed sensor installation.

OK The installation bolt is tightened properly and there is no clearance between the sensor and rear axle carrier.

OK   NG

OK ▽   **NG** > Replace speed sensor or rotor.

NOTICE: Check the speed sensor signal last.

Check and replace ABS ECU.

TY4029500181040X

Fig. 326   Codes 31, 32, 33, 34, 35 & 36: Speed Sensor Circuit (Part 4 of 4). Tercel

CIRCUIT DESCRIPTION

This is the power source for the ECU and , hence the CPU and the actuators.

DTC No.	Diagnostic Trouble Code Detecting Condition	Trouble Area
41	Vehicle speed is 3 km/h (1.9 mph) or more and voltage of ECU terminal IG1 remains at more than 17 V or below 9.5 V for more than 10 sec.	• Battery • IC regulator • Open or short in power source circuit • ECU

Fail safe function: If trouble occurs in the power source circuit, the ECU cuts off current to the ABS control (solenoid) relay and prohibits ABS control.

WIRING DIAGRAM

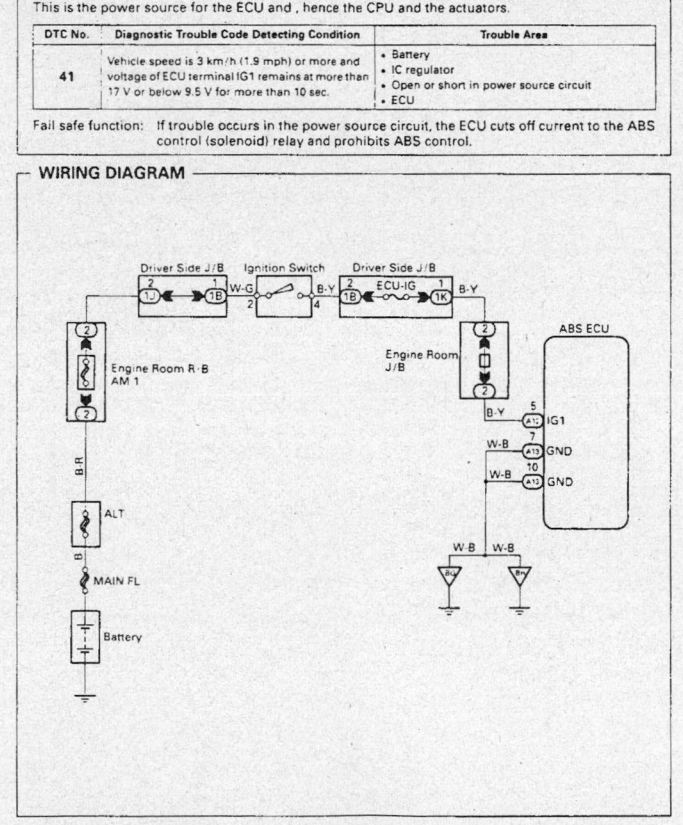

TY4029500182010X

Fig. 327   Code 41: IG Power Source Circuit (Part 1 of 3). Tercel

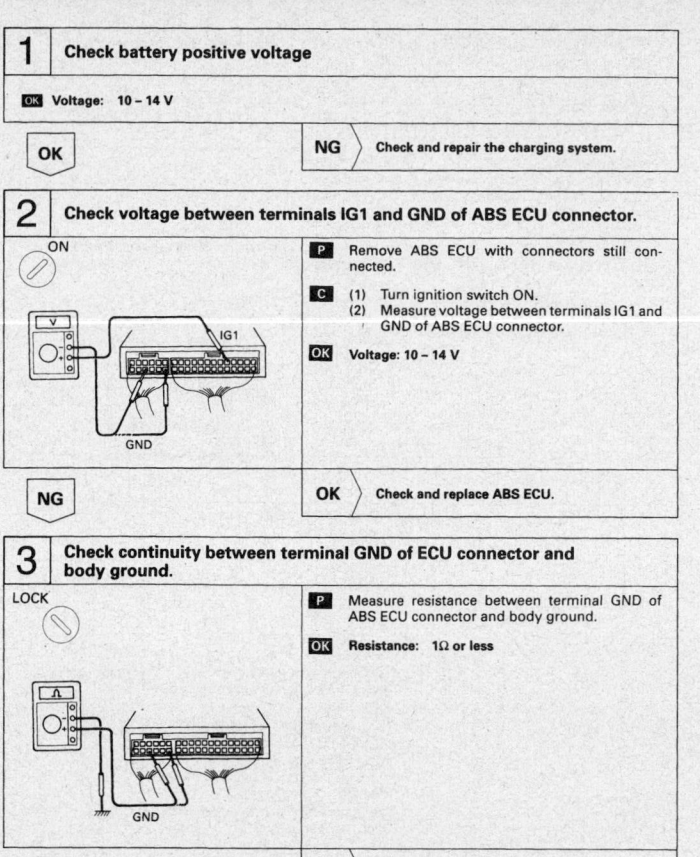

1   **Check battery positive voltage**

OK   Voltage: 10 – 14 V

OK | **NG** ⟩ Check and repair the charging system.

2   **Check voltage between terminals IG1 and GND of ABS ECU connector.**

ON

P   Remove ABS ECU with connectors still connected.

C   (1)   Turn ignition switch ON.
      (2)   Measure voltage between terminals IG1 and GND of ABS ECU connector.

OK   Voltage: 10 – 14 V

IG1

GND

NG | **OK** ⟩ Check and replace ABS ECU.

3   **Check continuity between terminal GND of ECU connector and body ground.**

LOCK

P   Measure resistance between terminal GND of ABS ECU connector and body ground.

OK   Resistance: 1Ω or less

GND

NG | **OK** ⟩ Repair or replace harness or connector.

TY4029500182020X

Fig. 327   Code 41: IG Power Source Circuit (Part 2 of 3). Tercel

4   **Check ECU-IG fuse.**

Driver Side
J/B

P   Remove ECU-IG fuse from driver side J/B.

C   Check continuity of ECU-IG fuse.

OK   Continuity

ECU-IG

OK | **NG** ⟩ Check for short in all the harness and components connected to ECU-IG fuse

Check for open in harness and connector between ABS ECU and battery

TY4029500182030X

Fig. 327   Code 41: IG Power Source Circuit (Part 3 of 3). Tercel

CIRCUIT DESCRIPTION

DTC No.	Diagnostic Trouble Code Detecting Condition	Trouble Area
51	Pump motor is not operating normally during initial check.	• ABS pump motor

Fail safe function: If trouble occurs in the ABS pump motor, the ECU cuts off the current to the ABS control (solenoid) relay and prohibits ABS control.

WIRING DIAGRAM

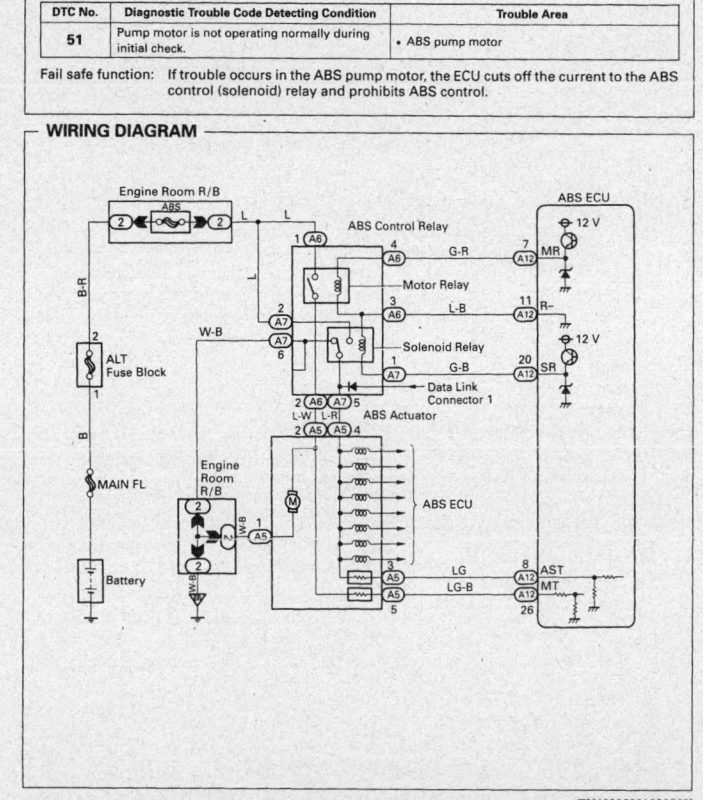

TY4029500183000X

Fig. 328   Code 51: ABS Pump Motor Lock. Tercel

CIRCUIT DESCRIPTION

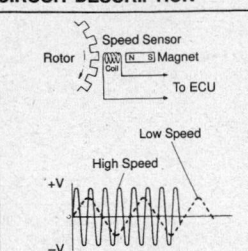

The speed sensor detects wheel speed and sends the appropriate signals to the ECU. These signals are used for control of the ABS control system. The front and rear rotors each have 48 serrations.

When the rotors rotate, the magnetic field emitted by the permanent magnet in the speed sensor generates an AC voltage. Since the frequency of this AC voltage changes in direct proportion to the speed of the rotor, the frequency is used by the ECU to detect the speed of each wheel.

DTC No.	DTC Detecting Condition	Trouble Area
C0200/31 C0205/32 C0210/33 C0215/34	Detection of any of conditions 1. through 4.: 1. At vehicle speed of 10 km/h (6 mph) or more, pulses are not input for 15 sec. 2. Momentary interruption of the speed sensor signal occurs at least 7 times in the time with the vehicle driving at 15 km/h (9 mph) or more. 3. Abnormal signal occurred in the pulse signal from the speed sensor 75 times or more in 5 sec. continuously with the vehicle driving at 20 km/h (12 mph) or more. 4. The condition that the speed sensor signal circuit is open circuit continues for 0.6 sec. or more.	• Right front, left front, right rear and left rear speed sensor • Each speed sensor circuit • Sensor rotor

HINT:
DTC No. C0200/31 is for the right front speed sensor.
DTC No. C0205/32 is for the left front speed sensor.
DTC No. C0210/33 is for the right rear speed sensor.
DTC No. C0215/34 is for the left rear speed sensor.
Fail safe function:
If any trouble occurs in the speed sensor circuit, the ECU cuts off current to the ABS solenoid relay and prohibits ABS control and brake system becomes normal.

TY4029900469010X

Fig. 329 Codes C0200/31, C0205/32, C0210/33 & C0215/34: Speed Sensor Circuit (Part 1 of 5). Tundra

INSPECTION PROCEDURE

HINT:
Start the inspection from step 1 in case of using the TOYOTA hand–held tester and start from step 2 case of not using TOYOTA hand–held tester.

1   Check output value of speed sensor.

PREPARATION:
(a)   Connect the TOYOTA hand–held tester to the DLC3.
(b)   Turn the ignition switch ON and push the TOYOTA hand–held tester main switch ON.
(c)   Select the DATALIST mode on the TOYOTA hand–held tester.
CHECK:
Check that there is no difference between the speed value output from the speed sensor displayed by the TOYOTA hand–held tester and the speed value displayed by the speedometer when driving the vehicle.
OK:
   There is almost no difference from the displayed speed value.
HINT:
There is tolerance in the speedometer indication.

OK > Check and replace ABS ECU.

NG

2   Check speed sensor.

FRONT SPEED SENSOR
PREPARATION:
Disconnect the speed sensor connector.
CHECK:
Measure resistance between terminals 1 and 2 of the speed sensor connector.
OK:
   Resistance: 1.4 – 1.8 kΩ
CHECK:
Measure resistance between each of terminals 1 and 2 of speed sensor connector and body ground.
OK:
   Resistance: 1 MΩ or higher
REAR SPEED SENSOR
PREPARATION:
Disconnect the speed sensor connector.
CHECK:
Measure resistance between terminals 1 – 2 and 3 – 4 of the speed sensor connector.
OK:
   Resistance: 1.07 – 1.11 kΩ

TY4029900469020X

Fig. 329 Codes C0200/31, C0205/32, C0210/33 & C0215/34: Speed Sensor Circuit (Part 2 of 5). Tundra

CHECK:
Measure resistance between terminals 1, 2, 3 and 4 of the speed sensor connector and body ground.
OK:
   Resistance: 1 MΩ or higher

NG > Replace speed sensor.

NOTICE:
Check the speed sensor signal last

OK

3   Check for open and short circuit in harness and connector between each speed sensor and ABS ECU

NG > Repair or replace harness or connector.

OK

4   Check speed sensor and sensor rotor serrations.

Normal Signal Waveform

2 m/s / Division
1 V / Division

(REFERENCE) INSPECTION USING OSCILLOSCOPE
PREPARATION:
Connect the oscilloscope to the terminals FR+, FL+, RR+ or RL+ and GND of the ABS ECU.
CHECK:
Drive the vehicle at about 20 km/h (12 mph), and check the signal waveform.
HINT:
Check if foreign objects stick on the sensor tip when noise occurs.

OK > Check and replace ABS ECU.

NG

TY4029900469030X

Fig. 329 Codes C0200/31, C0205/32, C0210/33 & C0215/34: Speed Sensor Circuit (Part 3 of 5). Tundra

5	Check sensor installation.

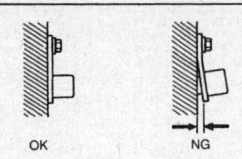

OK NG

CHECK:
Check the speed sensor installation.
OK:
  The installation bolt is tightened properly and there is no clearance between the sensor and front steering knuckle or rear axle carrier.

NG > Replace speed sensor.

NOTICE:
Check the speed sensor signal last

OK

6	Check sensor rotor and sensor tip.

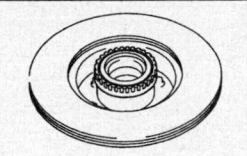

FRONT:
PREPARATION:
Remove the disc
CHECK:
Check the sensor rotor serrations.
OK:
  No scratches, missing teeth or foreign objects.
PREPARATION:
Remove the front speed sensor
CHECK:
Check the sensor tip.
OK:
  No scratches or foreign objects on the sensor tip.

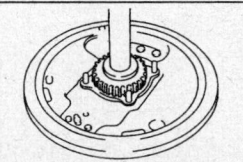

REAR:
PREPARATION:
Remove the axle shaft
CHECK:
Check the sensor rotor serrations.
OK:
  No scratches, missing teeth or foreign objects.
PREPARATION:
Remove the rear speed sensor

TY4029900469040X

Fig. 329   Codes C0200/31, C0205/32, C0210/33 & C0215/34: Speed Sensor Circuit (Part 4 of 5). Tundra

CIRCUIT DESCRIPTION

This solenoid goes on when signals are received from the ECU and controls the pressure acting on the wheel cylinders thus controlling the braking force.

DTC No.	DTC Detecting Condition	Trouble Area
C0226/21	The condition of open or short circuit in SFRH or SFRR circuit continues for 0.012 sec. or more when the solenoid relay is ON.	• ABS actuator • SFRH or SFRR circuit
C0236/22	The condition of open or short circuit in SFLH or SFLR circuit continues for 0.012 sec. or more when the solenoid relay is ON.	• ABS actuator • SFLH or SFLR circuit
C0246/23	The condition of open or short circuit in SRRH or SRRR circuit continues for 0.012 sec. or more when the solenoid relay is ON.	• ABS actuator • SRRH or SRRR circuit

Fail safe function:
If any trouble occurs in the actuator solenoid circuit, the ECU cuts off current to the ABS solenoid relay and prohibits ABS control and the brake system becomes normal.

TY4029900470010X

Fig. 330   Codes C0226/21, C0236/22 & C0246/23: ABS Solenoid Circuit (Part 1 of 2). Tundra

CIRCUIT DESCRIPTION

The ABS motor relay supplies power to the ABS pump motor. While the ABS is activated, the ECU switches the motor relay ON and operates the ABS pump motor.

DTC No.	DTC Detecting Condition	Trouble Area
C0273/13	The condition of open circuit in motor relay circuit continues for 0.2 sec. or more when the motor relay is ON.	• ABS motor relay • ABS motor relay circuit
C0274/14	The condition of short circuit in motor relay circuit continues for 2.5 sec. or more when the motor relay is OFF except during the ABS operation or the initial check.	

Fail safe function:
If any trouble occurs in the ABS motor relay circuit, the ECU cuts off current to the ABS solenoid relay and prohibits ABS control and teh brake system becomes normal.

TY4029900471010X

Fig. 331   Codes C0273/13 & C0274/14: ABS Motor Relay Circuit (Part 1 of 2). Tundra

---

CHECK:
Check the sensor tip.
OK:
  No scratches or foreign objects on the sensor tip.

NG > Replace speed sensor or rotor.

NOTICE:
Check the speed sensor signal last

OK

Check and replace ABS ECU.

TY4029900469050X

Fig. 329   Codes C0200/31, C0205/32, C0210/33 & C0215/34: Speed Sensor Circuit (Part 5 of 5). Tundra

INSPECTION PROCEDURE

1	Check DTC once more.

PREPARATION:
(a)   Clear the DTC
(b)   Turn the ignition switch OFF.
CHECK:
Turn the ignition switch ON, and check that the same DTC is stored in the memory.

NO > No problem.

YES

Replace ABS ECU.

TY4029900470020X

Fig. 330   Codes C0226/21, C0236/22 & C0246/23: ABS Solenoid Circuit (Part 2 of 2). Tundra

INSPECTION PROCEDURE

1	Check voltage between terminals +BM and GND of ABS ECU connector.

PREPARATION:
Disconnect the ABS ECU connector.
CHECK:
Measure the voltage between terminals +BM and GND of ABS ECU harness side connector.
OK:
  Voltage: 10 – 14 V

NG > Check and replace ABS1 fuses.
     Check and repair harness or connector.

OK

If the same code is still output after the DTC is deleted, check the contact condition of each connection. If the connections are normal, the ECU may be defective.

TY4029900471020X

Fig. 331   Codes C0273/13 & C0274/14: ABS Motor Relay Circuit (Part 2 of 2). Tundra

---

ANTI-LOCK BRAKES

CIRCUIT DESCRIPTION

This relay supplies power to each ABS solenoid. After the ignition switch is turned ON, if the initial check is OK, the relay goes on.

DTC No.	DTC Detecting Condition	Trouble Area
C0278/11	The condition of open circuit in solenoid relay circuit continues for 0.2 sec. or more when the solenoid relay is ON 2 sec. after turning ON the ignition switch.	• ABS solenoid relay • ABS solenoid relay circuit
C0279/12	The condition of short circuit in solenoid relay circuit continues for 0.2 sec. or more when the solenoid relay is OFF soon after turning the ignition switch ON.	

Fail safe function:

If any trouble occurs in the ABS solenoid relay circuit, the ECU cuts off current to the ABS solenoid relay and prohibits ABS control and the brake system becomes normal.

TY4029900472010X

Fig. 332 Codes C0278/11 & C0279/12: ABS Solenoid Relay Circuit (Part 1 of 2). Tundra

CIRCUIT DESCRIPTION

DTC No.	DTC Detecting Condition	Trouble Area
C1237/37	Detection of any of conditions 1. and 2. 1. Driving at more than 30 km/h (19 mph) for more than 60 seconds with 1 or 2 tires of different size. 2. The condition that the front wheels speed is not input in spite that the rear wheel speed is 20 km/h (12 mph) or more [wheels speed discrepancy between the front and rear wheel speed is 20 km/h (12 mph or more)] continues for 10 seconds, and this occurs more than 8 times in secession when the vehicle is driven after the ignition switch has been turned from OFF to ON.	• Tire size • Front speed sensor rotor • Front speed sensor • Front speed sensor circuit

INSPECTION PROCEDURE

1	Check tire size.

NG ▷ Replace tires so that all 4 tires are the same in size.

OK

2	Check front sensor rotor

NG ▷ Replace speed sensor rotor.

OK

3	Check front speed sensor

NG ▷ Replace speed sensor.

OK

TY4029900473010X

Fig. 333 Code C1237/37: Both Front Speed Sensor Rotors Missing Or Tire Of Different Size (Part 1 of 2). Tundra

CIRCUIT DESCRIPTION

DTC No.	DTC Detecting Condition	Trouble Area
C1241/41	Detection of any of conditions 1. and 2.: 1. The condition that the ECU terminal IG voltage is 9 to 10 V or less continues for 10 sec. or more with the vehicle driving at 3 km/h (1.9 mph) or more. 2. The condition the ECU terminal IG voltage rises up to 16 to 17 V continues for 0.6 sec. or more while the ignition switch is ON.	• Battery • Charging system • Power source circuit

Fail safe function:

If any trouble occurs in the power source circuit, the ECU cuts off current to the ABS solenoid relay and prohibits ABS control and the brake system becomes normal.

TY4029900474010X

Fig. 334 Code C1241/41: IG Power Source Circuit (Part 1 of 3). Tundra

INSPECTION PROCEDURE

1	Check voltage between terminals +BS and GND of ABS ECU connector.

PREPARATION:
Disconnect the ABS ECU connector.
CHECK:
Measure the voltage between terminals +BS and GND of ABS ECU harness side connector.
OK:
        Voltage: 10 – 14 V

NG ▷ Check and replace ABS2 fuses.
Check and repair harness or connector.

OK

If the same code is still output after the DTC is deleted, check the contact condition of each connection. If the connections are normal, the ECU may be defective.

TY4029900472020X

Fig. 332 Codes C0278/11 & C0279/12: ABS Solenoid Relay Circuit (Part 2 of 2). Tundra

4	Check for open and short circuit in harness and connector between rear speed sensor and ABS ECU

NG ▷ Repair or replace harness and connector.

OK

Check and replace ABS ECU.

TY4029900473020X

Fig. 333 Code C1237/37: Both Front Speed Sensor Rotors Missing Or Tire Of Different Size (Part 2 of 2). Tundra

INSPECTION PROCEDURE

1	Check ECU–IG fuse.

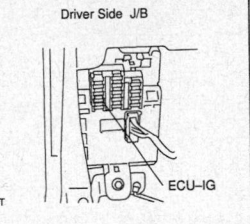

Driver Side J/B

ECU–IG

PREPARATION:
Remove ECU–IG fuse from the driver side J/B.
CHECK:
Check continuity of ECU–IG fuse.
OK:
        Continuity

NG ▷ Check for short circuit in all the harness and components connected to ECU–IG fuse

OK

2	Check battery position voltage.

OK:
        Voltage: 10 – 14 V

NG ▷ Check and repair the charging system.

OK

TY4029900474020X

Fig. 334 Code C1241/41: IG Power Source Circuit (Part 2 of 3). Tundra

3	Check voltage of the ECU IG power source.

IN CASE OF USING TOYOTA HAND–HELD TESTER:
PREPARATION:
(a) Connect the TOYOTA hand–held tester to the DLC3.
(b) Turn the ignition switch ON and push the TOYOTA hand–held tester main switch ON.
(c) Select the DATALIST mode on the TOYOTA hand–held tester.
CHECK:
Check the voltage condition output from the ECU displayed on the TOYOTA hand–held tester.
OK:
"Normal" is displayed.
IN CASE OF NOT USING TOYOTA HAND–HELD TESTER:

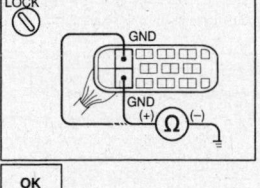

PREPARATION:
Disconnect the ABS ECU connector.
CHECK:
(a) Turn the ignition switch ON.
(b) Measure voltage between terminals IG and GND of ABS ECU harness side connector.
OK:
Voltage: 10 – 14 V

NG	Go to step 4.

OK

4	Check continuity between terminal GND of ABS ECU connector and body ground.

CHECK:
Measure resistance between terminal GND of ABS ECU harness side connector and body ground.
OK:
Resistance: 1 Ω or less

NG	Repair or replace harness or connector.

OK

Check for open circuit in harness and connector between ABS ECU and battery

TY4029900474030X

Fig. 334   Code C1241/41: IG Power Source Circuit (Part 3 of 3). Tundra

3	Check for open and short circuit in harness and connector between deceleration sensor and ABS ECU

NG	Repair or replace harness or connector.

OK

Check and replace ABS ECU.

TY4029900475020X

Fig. 335   Codes C1243/43 & C1245/45: Fault In Deceleration Sensor (Part 2 of 2). Tundra

CIRCUIT DESCRIPTION

DTC No.	DTC Detecting Condition	Trouble Area
C1243/43	While vehicle speed becomes 0 km/h (0 mph) from 30 km/h (18 mph), and the condition that GL1 signals of ECU terminals do not change 40 mV or less continues in a sequence 16 times.	• Deceleration sensor • Wire harness for deceleration sensor system
C1245/45	At the vehicle speed of 30 km/h (18 mph) or more, and the condition that the difference between acceleration and deceleration values of computation from deceleration sensor and vehicle speed becomes more than 0.35 G continues for 60 sec. or more.	

Fail safe function:
If any trouble occurs in the deceleration sensor circuit, the ECU cuts off current to the ABS solenoid relay and prohibits ABS control and the brake system becomes normal.

INSPECTION PROCEDURE

HINT:
Start the inspection from step 1 in case of using the TOYOTA hand–held tester and start from step 2 in case of not using the TOYOTA hand–held tester.

1	Check output value of the deceleration sensor.

PREPARATION:
(a) Connect the TOYOTA hand–held tester of the DLC3.
(b) Turn the ignition switch ON and push the TOYOTA hand–held tester main switch ON.
(c) Select the DATALIST mode on the TOYOTA hand–held tester.
CHECK:
Check that the deceleration value of deceleration sensor displayed by the TOYOTA hand–held tester changing when tilting the vehicle.
OK:

2	Check deceleration sensor

NG	Replace deceleration sensor.

OK

TY4029900475010X

Fig. 335   Codes C1243/43 & C1245/45: Fault In Deceleration Sensor (Part 1 of 2). Tundra

CIRCUIT DESCRIPTION

This sensor detects deceleration on the vehicle. The sensor signal is used in ABS control. If the sensor functions abnormally, the ABS warning light comes on.

DTC No.	DTC Detecting Condition	Trouble Area
C1244/44	Either of the following 1. 2. or 3. is detected: 1. The condition that ECU terminals GL1 values are –1.5 G or less or 1.5 G or more continues for 1.2 sec. or more. 2. The condition that the deceleration sensor terminal VGS voltage is 4.4 V or less or 5.6 V or more continues for 1.2 sec. or more. 3. Deceleration sensor signal momentary open occurs for 7 times or more.	• Deceleration sensor • Deceleration sensor circuit

Fail safe function:
If any trouble occurs in the deceleration sensor circuit, the ECU cuts off current to the ABS solenoid relay and prohibits ABS control and the brake system becomes normal.

TY4029900476010X

Fig. 336   Code C1244/44: Deceleration Sensor Circuit (Part 1 of 2). Tundra

INSPECTION PROCEDURE

1	Check for open and short circuit in harness and connector between deceleration sensor and ABS ECU

NG	Repair or replace harness or connector.

OK

2	Check deceleration sensor

NG	Replace deceleration sensor.

OK

Check and replace ABS ECU.

TY4029900476020X

Fig. 336   Code C1244/44: Deceleration Sensor Circuit (Part 2 of 2). Tundra

CIRCUIT DESCRIPTION

DTC No.	DTC Detecting Condition	Trouble Area
C1249/49	The condition that the ECU terminal STP voltage is 1.5 to 4 V continues for 0.3 sec. or more when the ignition switch is ON and stop light switch is ON.	• Stop light switch • Stop light switch circuit

TY4029900477010X

Fig. 337 Code C1249/49: Stop Lamp Switch Circuit (Part 1 of 2). Tundra

CIRCUIT DESCRIPTION

DTC No.	DTC Detecting Condition	Trouble Area
C1251/51	Pump motor does not operate during the initial check.	• ABS pump motor

Fail safe function:
If any trouble occurs in the ABS pump motor, the ECU cuts off current to the ABS solenoid relay and prohibits ABS control and brake system becomes normal.

TY4029900478010X

Fig. 338 Code C1251/51: ABS Pump Motor Lock (Part 1 of 2). Tundra

INSPECTION PROCEDURE

1 | Check operation of pump motor.

PREPARATION:
Disconnect the ABS ECU connector.
CHECK:
Connect positive ⊕ lead to M+ terminal and negative ⊖ lead to M– terminal of the ABS ECU side connector, check that the pump motor operates.
OK:
   The running sound of the pump motor should be heard.

OK ▷ Check for open circuit in harness and connector between ABS actuator and ABS ECU

NG

Replace ABS actuator.

TY4029900478020X

Fig. 338 Code C1251/51: ABS Pump Motor Lock (Part 2 of 2). Tundra

INSPECTION PROCEDURE

1 | Check operation of the stop light switch.

CHECK:
Check that the stop light lights up when brake pedal is depressed and turns OFF when the brake pedal is released.

NG ▷ Repair stop light circuit

OK

2 | Check voltage between terminal STP of ABS ECU and body ground.

PREPARATION:
Disconnect ABS ECU connector.
CHECK:
Measure voltage between terminal STP of ABS ECU harness side connector and body ground when the brake pedal is depressed.
OK:
   Voltage: 8 – 14 V

OK ▷ Check and replace ABS ECU.

NG

3 | Check for open circuit in harness and connector between ABS ECU and stop light switch

NG ▷ Repair or replace harness or connector.

OK

Proceed to next circuit inspection shown on problem symptoms table

TY4029900477020X

Fig. 337 Code C1249/49: Stop Lamp Switch Circuit (Part 2 of 2). Tundra

CIRCUIT DESCRIPTION

DTC No.	DTC Detecting Condition	Trouble Area
Always ON	Detection of any of conditions 1. and 2.: 1. There is a malfunction in the ECU internal circuit. 2. ECU power source voltage is 16 to 18 V or more.	• Battery • Charging system • Power source circuit • ABS ECU

HINT:
There is a case that TOYOTA hand–held tester cannot be used when ECU is abnormal.
Fail safe function:
If any trouble occurs in the ECU, the ECU cuts off current to the ABS solenoid relay and prohibits ABS control and the brake system becomes normal.

TY4029900479010X

Fig. 339 ABS Lamp Always On (Part 1 of 3). Tundra

INSPECTION PROCEDURE

| 1 | Check that the ABS ECU connectors are securely connected to the ABS ECU. |

NO > Connect the connector to the ABS ECU.

YES

| 2 | Is DTC output? |

Check DTC

YES > Repair circuit indicated by the output code.

NO

| 3 | Check voltage between terminals IG and GND of ABS ECU connector. |

PREPARATION:
Disconnect the ABS ECU connector.
CHECK:
(a) Turn the ignition switch ON.
(b) Measure voltage between terminals IG and GND of ABS ECU harness side connector.
OK:
Voltage: 10 – 14 V

NG > Check for open and short circuit in harness and connector between ECU–IG fuse and ABS ECU

OK

TY4029900479020X

Fig. 339   ABS Lamp Always On (Part 2 of 3). Tundra

| 4 | Check combination meter. |

PREPARATION:
Disconnect the ABS ECU connector.
CHECK:
(a) Using service wire, connect terminals WA and GND of ABS ECU harness side connector.
(b) Turn the ignition switch ON.
OK:
ABS warning light goes on.

NG > Repair or replace combination meter assembly

OK

| 5 | Check ABS warning light. |

PREPARATION:
(a) Turn the ignition switch OFF.
(b) Disconnect the service wire from the ABS ECU.
(c) Turn the ignition switch ON.
CHECK:
Check the ABS warning light goes off.

OK > Check and replace ABS ECU.

NG

| Check for short circuit in harness and connector between ABS warning light, DLC1 and ABS ECU |

TY4029900479030X

Fig. 339   ABS Lamp Always On (Part 3 of 3). Tundra

Code No.	Diagnosis	Trouble Area
71	Low output voltage of right front speed sensor	• Right front speed sensor • Sensor installation • Sensor rotor
72	Low output voltage of left front speed sensor	• Left front speed sensor • Sensor installation • Sensor rotor
73	Low output voltage of right rear speed sensor	• Right rear speed sensor • Sensor installation • Sensor rotor
74	Low output voltage of left rear speed sensor	• Left rear speed sensor • Sensor installation • Sensor rotor
75	Abnormal change in output voltage of right front speed sensor	• Right front speed sensor rotor
76	Abnormal change in output voltage of left front speed sensor	• Left front speed sensor rotor
77	Abnormal change in output voltage of right rear speed sensor	• Right rear speed sensor rotor
78	Abnormal change in output voltage of left rear speed sensor	• Left rear speed sensor rotor
*79	Deceleration sensor is faulty	• Deceleration sensor • Sensor installation

*: 4WD models only

TY402970029200X

Fig. 341   Speed sensor diagnostic trouble codes. RAV4 & Supra

Code No.	Diagnosis	Trouble Area
71	Low output voltage of right front speed sensor	• Right front speed sensor • Sensor installation • Right front speed sensor rotor
72	Low output voltage of left front speed sensor	• Left front speed sensor • Sensor installation • Left front speed sensor rotor
73	Low output voltage of right rear speed sensor	• Right rear speed sensor • Sensor installation • Right rear speed sensor rotor
74	Low output voltage of left rear speed sensor	• Left rear speed sensor • Sensor installation • Left rear speed sensor rotor
75	Abnormal change in output voltage of right front speed sensor	• Right front speed sensor rotor
76	Abnormal change in output voltage of left front speed sensor	• Left front speed sensor rotor
77	Abnormal change in output voltage of right rear speed sensor	• Right rear speed sensor rotor
78	Abnormal change in output voltage of left rear speed sensor	• Left rear speed sensor rotor

TY402970025200X

Fig. 340   Speed sensor diagnostic trouble codes. Except RAV4 & Supra

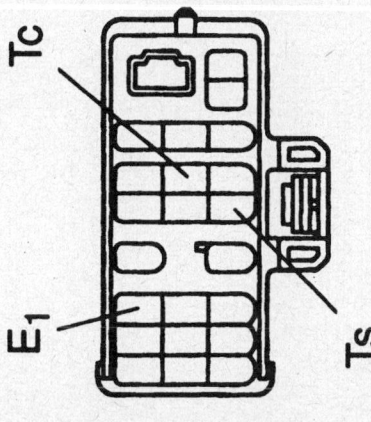

Fig. 343 DLC 1 terminal locations. Tundra

TY40290060200X

Code No.	Light Pattern	Diagnosis	Malfunctioning Part
	ON / OFF	All speed sensors and sensor rotors are normal	
71		Low voltage of front right speed sensor signal	• Front right speed sensor • Sensor installation
72		Low voltage of front left speed sensor signal	• Front left speed sensor • Sensor installation
73		Low voltage of rear right speed sensor signal	• Rear right speed sensor • Sensor installation
74		Low voltage of rear left speed sensor signal	• Rear left speed sensor • Sensor installation
75		Abnormal change of front right speed sensor signal	• Front right sensor rotor
76		Abnormal change of front left speed sensor signal	• Front left sensor rotor
77		Abnormal change of rear right speed sensor signal	• Rear right sensor rotor
78		Abnormal change of rear left speed sensor signal	• Rear left sensor rotor
79		Deceleration sensor is faulty	• Deceleration sensor • Sensor installation

TY40293001060000X

Fig. 342 Speed sensor diagnostic trouble codes. Land Cruiser, Previa, Tacoma, T100 & 4Runner

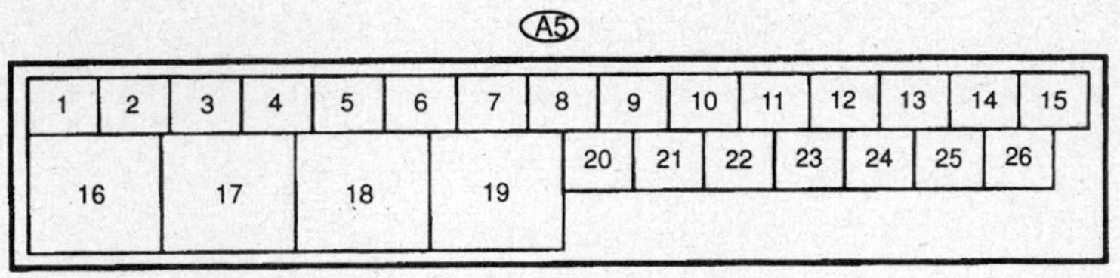

Symbols (Terminals No.)	Wiring Color	Condition	STD Voltage (V)
+B (A5 – 17, 18) – GND (A5 – 16, 19)	L ↔ W–B	Always	10 – 14
IG1 (A5 – 15) – GND (A5 – 16, 19)	B–R ↔ W–B	IG switch ON	10 – 14
WA (A5 – 21) – GND (A5 – 16, 19)	R–L ↔ W–B	IG switch ON, ABS warning light ON	Below 2.6
		IG switch ON, ABS warning light OFF	10 – 14
STP (A5 – 14) – GND (A5 – 16, 19)	G–W ↔ W–B	Stop light switch OFF	Below 1.5
		Stop light switch ON	5 – 14
Tc (A5 – 12) – GND (A5 – 16, 19)	LG–R ↔ W–B	IG switch ON	5.7 – 8.1
Ts (A5 – 11) – GND (A5 – 16, 19)	R–Y ↔ W–B	IG switch ON	5.7 – 8.1
FR+ (A5 – 5) – FR– (A5 – 4)	W ↔ B	IG switch ON, slowly turn right front wheel	AC generation
FL+ (A5 – 7) – FL– (A5 – 6)	R ↔ G	IG switch ON, slowly turn left front wheel	AC generation
RR+ (A5 – 2) – RR– (A5 – 1)	P ↔ L	IG switch ON, slowly turn right rear wheel	AC generation
RL+ (A5 – 9) – RL– (A5 – 8)	Y ↔ BR	IG switch ON, slowly turn left rear wheel	AC generation

TY40299060300X

Fig. 345 Anti-lock brake system circuit test. Camry Solara less traction control

DTC No.	Detection Item	Trouble Area
C1271/71	Low output voltage of right front speed sensor	• Right front speed sensor • Sensor installation
C1272/72	Low output voltage of left front speed sensor	• Left front speed sensor • Sensor installation
C1273/73	Low output voltage of right rear speed sensor	• Right rear speed sensor • Sensor installation
C1274/74	Low output voltage of left rear speed sensor	• Left rear speed sensor • Sensor installation
C1275/75	Abnormal change in output voltage of right front speed sensor	• Right front speed sensor rotor
C1276/76	Abnormal change in output voltage of left front speed sensor	• Left front speed sensor rotor
C1277/77	Abnormal change in output voltage of right rear speed sensor	• Right rear speed sensor rotor
C1278/78	Abnormal change in output voltage of left rear speed sensor	• Left rear speed sensor rotor
C1279/79*	Deceleration sensor is faulty	• Deceleration sensor • Sensor installation

*: Only for 4WD.

TY40299004650000X

Fig. 344 Speed sensor diagnostic trouble code identification. Tundra

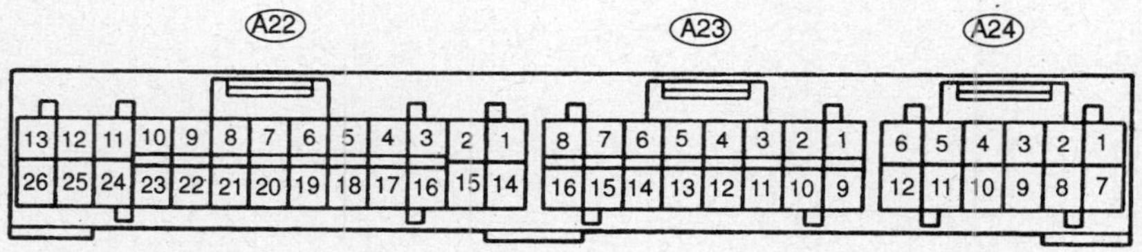

Fig. 346 Anti-lock brake system circuit test (Part 1 of 2). Camry Solara w/traction control

Symbols (Terminals No.)	Wiring Color	Condition	STD Voltage (V)
IG1 (A23 – 8) – GND (A22 – 15, A24 – 9, 10)	B-R ↔ W-B	IG switch ON	10 – 14
R+ (A22 – 1) – SR (A22 – 11)	GR-R ↔ GR	IG switch ON, ABS warning light OFF	9 – 14
R+ (A22 – 1) – MR (A22 – 24)	GR-R ↔ GR-L	IG switch ON	Below 1.0
SFRR (A22 – 26) – GND (A22 – 15, A24 – 9, 10)	G-B ↔ W-B	IG switch ON, ABS warning light OFF	10 – 14
SFRH (A22 – 13) – GND (A22 – 15, A24 – 9, 10)	R-B ↔ W-B	IG switch ON, ABS warning light OFF	10 – 14
SFLR (A24 – 1) – GND (A22 – 15, A24 – 9, 10)	W-L ↔ W-B	IG switch ON, ABS warning light OFF	10 – 14
SFLH (A24 – 2) – GND (A22 – 15, A24 – 9, 10)	L-B ↔ W-B	IG switch ON, ABS warning light OFF	10 – 14
SRRR (A24 – 7) – GND (A22 – 15, A24 – 9, 10)	R-G ↔ W-B	IG switch ON, ABS warning light OFF	10 – 14
SRRH (A24 – 8) – GND (A22 – 15, A24 – 9, 10)	W-R ↔ W-B	IG switch ON, ABS warning light OFF	10 – 14
SRLR (A22 – 12) – GND (A22 – 15, A24 – 9, 10)	LG-B ↔ W-B	IG switch ON, ABS warning light OFF	10 – 14
SRLH (A22 – 25) – GND (A22 – 15, A24 – 9, 10)	G-Y ↔ W-B	IG switch ON, ABS warning light OFF	10 – 14
AST (A22 – 10) – GND (A22 – 15, A24 – 9, 10)	R ↔ W-B	IG switch ON, ABS warning light OFF	10 – 14
WA (A23 – 4) – GND (A22 – 15, A24 – 9, 10)	R-L ↔ W-B	IG switch ON, ABS warning light ON	Below 2.0
		IG switch ON, ABS warning light OFF	10 – 14
STP (A23 – 16) – GND (A22 – 15, A24 – 9, 10)	G-W ↔ W-B	Stop light switch OFF	Below 1.5
		Stop light switch ON	8 – 14
D/G (A22 – 22) – GND (A22 – 15, A24 – 9, 10)	R-L ↔ W-B	IG switch ON, ABS warning light ON	10 – 14
Tc (A22 – 9) – GND (A22 – 15, A24 – 9, 10)	P-B ↔ W-B	IG switch ON	8 – 14
Ts (A22 – 23) – GND (A22 – 15, A24 – 9, 10)	R-Y ↔ W-B	IG switch ON	8 – 14
FR+ (A22 – 17) – FR– (A22 – 18)	W ↔ B	IG switch ON, slowly turn right front wheel	AC generation
FL+ (A22 – 5) – FL– (A22 – 4)	R ↔ G	IG switch ON, slowly turn left front wheel	AC generation
RR+ (A23 – 9) – RR– (A23 – 10)	W ↔ B	IG switch ON, slowly turn right rear wheel	AC generation
RL+ (A23 – 2) – RL– (A23 – 1)	R ↔ G	IG switch ON, slowly turn left rear wheel	AC generation

Fig. 346 Anti-lock brake system circuit test (Part 2 of 2). Camry Solara w/traction control

Symbols (Terminals No.)	Wiring Color	Condition	STD Voltage (V)
MT (A22 – 14) – GND (A22 – 15, A24 – 9, 10)	R-W ↔ W-B	IG switch ON	Below 1.5
SRC1 (A24 – 5) – GND (A22 – 9, 10)	B-R ↔ W-B	IG switch ON, TRAC OFF indicator light OFF	10 – 14
SRC2 (A24 – 4) – GND (A22 – 9, 10)	B-Y ↔ W-B	IG switch ON, TRAC OFF indicator light OFF	10 – 14
SMC1 (A24 – 12) – GND (A22 – 15, A24 – 9, 10)	Y-R ↔ W-B	IG switch ON, TRAC OFF indicator light OFF	10 – 14
SMC2 (A24 – 6) – GND (A22 – 15, A24 – 9, 10)	Y-B ↔ W-B	IG switch ON, TRAC OFF indicator light OFF	10 – 14
NEO (A23 – 15) – GND (A22 – 9, 10)	BR-W ↔ W-B	Idling	Pulse generation
EFI+ (A23 – 6) – GND (A22 – 9, 10)	W ↔ W-B	IG switch ON	Pulse generation
EFI– (A23 – 14) – GND (A22 – 9, 10)	B ↔ W-B	IG switch ON	Pulse generation
TRC+ (A23 – 13) – GND (A22 – 15, A24 – 9, 10)	LG ↔ W-B	TRAC control active	Pulse generation
TRC– (A23 – 5) – GND (A22 – 15, A24 – 9, 10)	L ↔ W-B	TRAC control active	Pulse generation
IND (A23 – 3) – GND (A22 – 9, 10)	LG ↔ W-B	IG switch ON, SLIP indicator light ON	Below 2.0
		IG switch ON, SLIP indicator light OFF	10 – 14
WT (A23 – 12) – GND (A22 – 9, 10)	L ↔ W-B	IG switch ON, TRAC OFF indicator light ON	Below 2.0
		IG switch ON, TRAC OFF indicator light OFF	10 – 14
CSW (A23 – 11) – GND (A22 – 9, 10)	LG ↔ W-B	IG switch ON, TRAC cut switch pushed in	Below 2.0
		IG switch ON, TRAC cut switch released	8 – 14

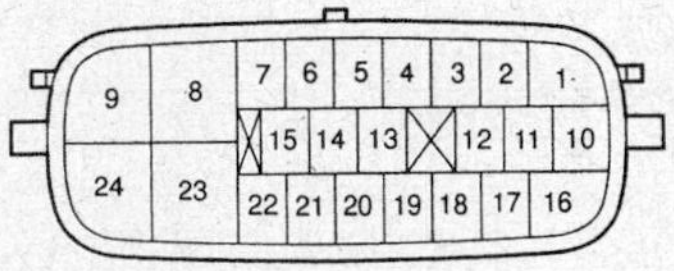

Fig. 347 Anti-lock brake system circuit test. Sienna

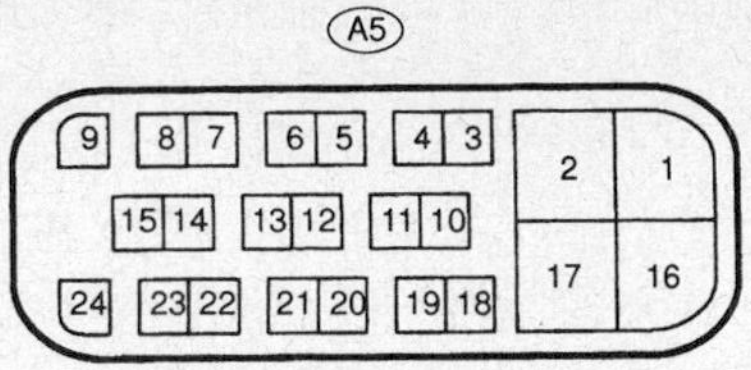

Symbols (Terminals No.)	Wiring Color	Condition	STD Voltage (V)
+BS (9) – GND (8, 23)	W–G ↔ W–B	Always	10 – 14
+BM (24) – GND (8, 23)	W–R ↔ W–B	Always	10 – 14
IG1 (15) – GND (8, 23)	B–R ↔ W–B	IG switch ON	10 – 14
WA (13) – GND (8, 23)	GR ↔ W–B	IG switch ON, ABS warning light ON	3 – 5
STP (5) – GND (8, 23)	G–W ↔ W–B	Stop light switch OFF	Below 1.0
		Stop light switch ON	10 – 14
FR + (22) – FR – (21)	BR ↔ Y	IG switch ON, Slowly turn right front wheel	AC generation
FL + (20) – FL – (19)	L ↔ P	IG switch ON, Slowly turn left front wheel	AC generation
RR + (18) – RR – (17)	W ↔ B	IG switch ON, Slowly turn right rear wheel	AC generation
RL + (16) – RL – (10)	R ↔ G	IG switch ON, Slowly turn left rear wheel	AC generation

TY402900452000X

Fig. 348 Anti-lock brake system circuit test. Tundra

Symbols (Terminals No.)	Wiring Color	Condition	STD Voltage (V)
+BS (A5 – 1) – GND (A5 – 2, 17)	B–R ↔ W–B	Always	10 – 14
GL1* (A5 – 3) – GGND (A5 – 11)	R ↔ B	IS switch ON, vehicle is placed on the horizontal surface	2.0 – 3.0
VGS* (A5 – 4) – GGND (A5 – 11)	W ↔ B	IG switch ON	4.5 – 5.5
RR+ (A5 – 6) – RR– (A5 – 5)	Y ↔ B	IG switch ON, slowly turn right rear wheel	AC generation
STP (A5 – 7) – GND (A5 – 2, 17)	G–W ↔ W–B	Stop light switch OFF	Below 1.5
		Stop light switch ON	8 – 14
RL+ (A5 – 8) – RL– (A5 – 9)	R ↔ W	IG switch ON, slowly turn left rear wheel	AC generation
Ts (A5 – 10) – GND (A5 – 2, 17)	R–L ↔ W–B	IG switch ON	10 – 14
EXI3 (A5 – 12) – GND (A5 – 2, 17)	L–R ↔ W–B	IG switch ON, transfer in L position	Below 1.5
		IG switch ON, transfer in any position except L position	8 – 14
IG (A5 – 13) – GND (A5 – 2, 17)	Y ↔ W–B	IG switch ON	10 – 14
D/G (A5 – 14) – GND (A5 – 2, 17)	W ↔ W–B	IG switch ON	10 – 14
WA (A5 – 15) – GND (A5 – 2, 17)	B–L ↔ W–B	IG switch ON, ABS warning light ON	Below 2.0
		IG switch ON, ABS warning light OFF	10 – 14
+BM (A5 – 16) – GND (A5 – 2, 17)	B ↔ W–B	Always	10 – 14
Tc (A5 – 19) – GND (A5 – 20)	W–G ↔ W–B	IG switch ON	10 – 14
FR+ (A5 – 21) – FR– (A5 – 20)	LG ↔ L	IG switch ON, slowly turn right front wheel	AC generation
EXI (A5 – 22) – GND (A5 – 2, 17)	GR ↔ W–B	IG switch ON, transfer in L4 or H4 position	Below 2.0
		IG switch ON, transfer in H2 position	10 – 14
FL+ (A5 – 23) – FL– (A5 –24)	P ↔ V	IG switch ON, slowly turn left front wheel	AC generation

*: Only for 4WD.

TY402900467000X

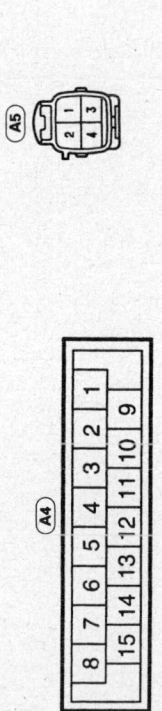

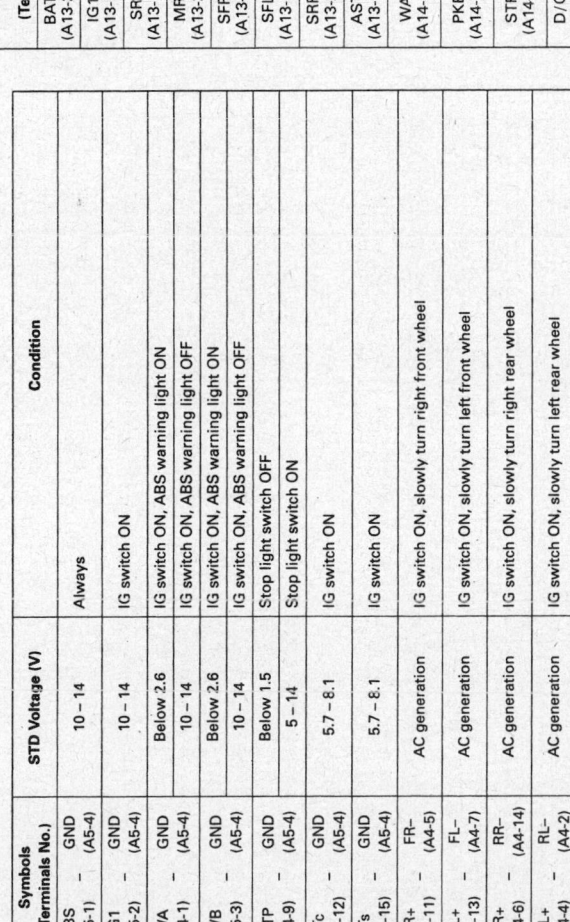

Symbols (Terminals No.)		STD Voltage (V)	Condition
+BS (A5-1)	GND (A5-4)	10 – 14	Always
IG1 (A5-2)	GND (A5-4)	10 – 14	IG switch ON
WA (A4-1)	GND (A5-4)	Below 2.6	IG switch ON, ABS warning light ON
WA (A4-1)	GND (A5-4)	10 – 14	IG switch ON, ABS warning light OFF
WB (A5-3)	GND (A5-4)	Below 2.6	IG switch ON, ABS warning light ON
WB (A5-3)	GND (A5-4)	10 – 14	IG switch ON, ABS warning light OFF
STP (A4-9)	GND (A5-4)	Below 1.5	Stop light switch OFF
STP (A4-9)	GND (A5-4)	5 – 14	Stop light switch ON
Tc (A4-12)	GND (A5-4)	5.7 – 8.1	IG switch ON
Ts (A4-15)	GND (A5-4)	5.7 – 8.1	IG switch ON
FR+ (A4-11)	FR- (A4-5)	AC generation	IG switch ON, slowly turn right front wheel
FL+ (A4-13)	FL- (A4-7)	AC generation	IG switch ON, slowly turn left front wheel
RR+ (A4-6)	RR- (A4-14)	AC generation	IG switch ON, slowly turn right rear wheel
RL+ (A4-4)	RL- (A4-2)	AC generation	IG switch ON, slowly turn left rear wheel

TY402940013802 0A

Fig. 349 Bosch anti-lock brake system circuit test. 1996 Avalon & Camry

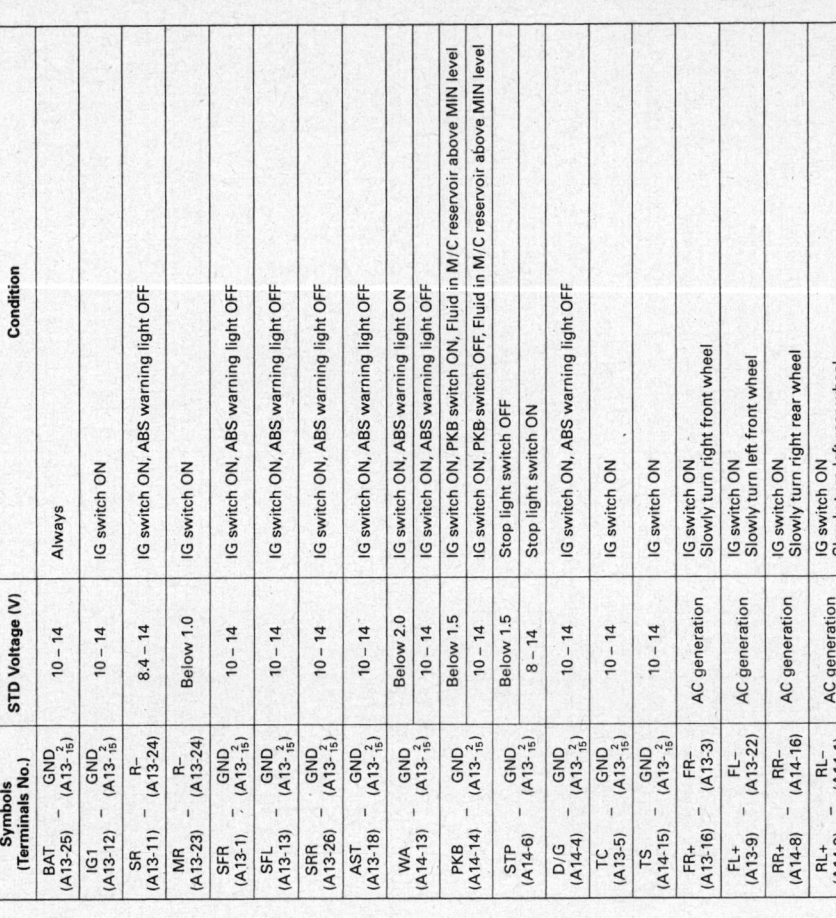

Symbols (Terminals No.)		STD Voltage (V)	Condition
BAT (A13-25)	GND (A13-$\frac{2}{15}$)	10 – 14	Always
IG1 (A13-12)	GND (A13-$\frac{2}{15}$)	10 – 14	IG switch ON
SR (A13-11)	R- (A13-24)	8.4 – 14	IG switch ON, ABS warning light OFF
MR (A13-23)	R- (A13-24)	Below 1.0	IG switch ON
SFR (A13-1)	GND (A13-$\frac{2}{15}$)	10 – 14	IG switch ON, ABS warning light OFF
SFL (A13-13)	GND (A13-$\frac{2}{15}$)	10 – 14	IG switch ON, ABS warning light OFF
SRR (A13-26)	GND (A13-$\frac{2}{15}$)	10 – 14	IG switch ON, ABS warning light OFF
AST (A13-18)	GND (A13-$\frac{2}{15}$)	10 – 14	IG switch ON, ABS warning light ON
WA (A14-13)	GND (A13-$\frac{2}{15}$)	Below 2.0	IG switch ON, ABS warning light ON
WA (A14-13)	GND (A13-$\frac{2}{15}$)	10 – 14	IG switch ON, ABS warning light OFF
PKB (A14-14)	GND (A13-$\frac{2}{15}$)	Below 1.5	IG switch ON, PKB switch ON, Fluid in M/C reservoir above MIN level
PKB (A14-14)	GND (A13-$\frac{2}{15}$)	10 – 14	IG switch ON, PKB switch OFF, Fluid in M/C reservoir above MIN level
STP (A14-6)	GND (A13-$\frac{2}{15}$)	Below 1.5	Stop light switch OFF
STP (A14-6)	GND (A13-$\frac{2}{15}$)	8 – 14	Stop light switch ON
D/G (A14-4)	GND (A13-$\frac{2}{15}$)	10 – 14	IG switch ON, ABS warning light OFF
TC (A13-5)	GND (A13-$\frac{2}{15}$)	10 – 14	IG switch ON
TS (A14-15)	GND (A13-$\frac{2}{15}$)	10 – 14	IG switch ON
FR+ (A13-16)	FR- (A13-3)	AC generation	IG switch ON, Slowly turn right front wheel
FL+ (A13-9)	FL- (A13-22)	AC generation	IG switch ON, Slowly turn left front wheel
RR+ (A14-8)	RR- (A14-16)	AC generation	IG switch ON, Slowly turn right rear wheel
RL+ (A14-9)	RL- (A14-1)	AC generation	IG switch ON, Slowly turn left rear wheel

TY402940013803 0A

Fig. 350 Nippondenso anti-lock brake system circuit test. 1996 Avalon & Camry

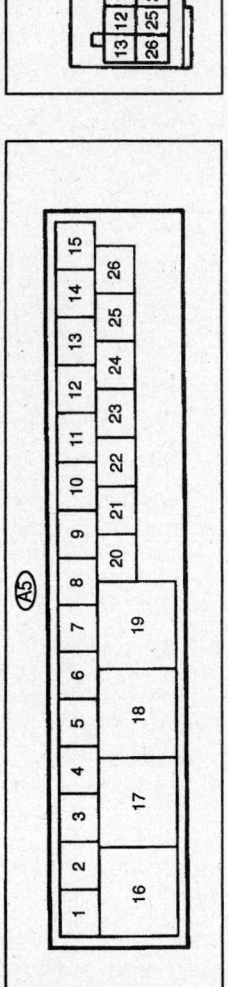

Fig. 352 table (A33, A34, A35 connectors)

Symbols (Terminals No.)	STD Voltage (V)	Condition
IG1 (A34 — 8) — GND (A33 — 15, A35 — 9, 10)	10 — 14	IG switch ON
R+ (A33 — 1) — SR (A33 — 11)	9 — 14	IG switch ON, ABS warning light OFF
R+ (A33 — 1) — MR (A33 — 24)	Below 1.0	IG switch ON
SFRR (A33 — 26) — GND (A33 — 15, A35 — 9, 10)	10 — 14	IG switch ON, ABS warning light OFF
SFRH (A33 — 13) — GND (A33 — 15, A35 — 9, 10)	10 — 14	IG switch ON, ABS warning light OFF
SFLR (A35 — 1) — GND (A33 — 15, A35 — 9, 10)	10 — 14	IG switch ON, ABS warning light OFF
SFLH (A35 — 2) — GND (A33 — 15, A35 — 9, 10)	10 — 14	IG switch ON, ABS warning light OFF
SRRR (A35 — 7) — GND (A33 — 15, A35 — 9, 10)	10 — 14	IG switch ON, ABS warning light OFF
SRRH (A35 — 8) — GND (A33 — 15, A35 — 9, 10)	10 — 14	IG switch ON, ABS warning light OFF
SRLR (A33 — 12) — GND (A33 — 15, A35 — 9, 10)	10 — 14	IG switch ON, ABS warning light OFF
SRLH (A33 — 25) — GND (A33 — 15, A35 — 9, 10)	10 — 14	IG switch ON, ABS warning light OFF
AST (A33 — 10) — GND (A33 — 15, A35 — 9, 10)	Below 2.0	IG switch ON
WA (A34 — 4) — GND (A33 — 15, A35 — 9, 10)	10 — 14	IG switch ON, ABS warning light OFF
STP (A34 — 18) — GND (A33 — 15, A35 — 9, 10)	Below 1.5	Stop light switch OFF
	8 — 14	Stop light switch ON
D/G (A33 — 22) — GND (A33 — 15, A35 — 9, 10)	10 — 14	IG switch ON, ABS warning light ON
Tc (A33 — 9) — GND (A33 — 15, A35 — 9, 10)	8 — 14	IG switch ON
Ts (A33 — 23) — GND (A33 — 15, A35 — 9, 10)	8 — 14	IG switch ON
FR+ (A33 — 17) — FR- (A33 — 18)	AC generation	Slowly turn right front wheel
FL+ (A33 — 5) — FL- (A33 — 4)	AC generation	Slowly turn left front wheel
RR+ (A34 — 9) — RR- (A34 — 10)	AC generation	Slowly turn right rear wheel
RL+ (A34 — 2) — RL- (A34 — 1)	AC generation	Slowly turn left rear wheel
MT (A33 — 14) — GND (A33 — 15, A35 — 9, 10)	Below 1.5	IG switch ON
SRC1 (A35 — 5) — GND (A33 — 15, A35 — 9, 10)	10 — 14	IG switch ON, TRAC OFF indicator light OFF
SRC2 (A35 — 6) — GND (A33 — 15, A35 — 9, 10)	10 — 14	IG switch ON, TRAC OFF indicator light OFF
SMC1 (A35 — 12) — GND (A33 — 15, A35 — 9, 10)	10 — 14	IG switch ON, TRAC OFF indicator light OFF
SMC2 (A35 — 6) — GND (A33 — 15, A35 — 9, 10)	10 — 14	IG switch ON, TRAC OFF indicator light OFF
NEO (A34 — 15) — GND (A33 — 15, A35 — 9, 10)	Pulse generation	Idling
EFI+ (A34 — 6) — GND (A33 — 15, A35 — 9, 10)	Pulse generation	IG switch ON
EFI- (A34 — 14) — GND (A33 — 15, A35 — 9, 10)	Pulse generation	IG switch ON

TY402970025701OX

Fig. 352 Anti-lock brake system circuit test (Part 1 of 2). 1997-99 Avalon w/traction control

Fig. 351 table (A5 connector)

Symbols (Terminals No.)	STD Voltage (V)	Condition
+B (A5 — 17, 18) — GND (A5 — 16, 19)	10 — 14	Always
IG1 (A5 — 15) — GND (A5 — 16, 19)	10 — 14	IG switch ON
WA (A5 — 21) — GND (A5 — 16, 26)	Below 2.6	IG switch ON, ABS warning light ON
	10 — 14	IG switch ON, ABS warning light OFF
STP (A5 — 2) — GND (A5 — 16, 19)	Below 1.5	Stop light switch OFF
	5 — 14	Stop light switch ON
Tc (A5 — 12) — GND (A5 — 16, 19)	5.7 — 8.1	IG switch ON
Ts (A5 — 11) — GND (A5 — 16, 19)	5.7 — 8.1	IG switch ON
FR+ (A5 — 5) — FR- (A5 — 4)	AC generation	Slowly turn right front wheel
FL+ (A5 — 7) — FL- (A5 — 6)	AC generation	Slowly turn left front wheel
RR+ (A5 — 3) — RR- (A5 — 1)	AC generation	Slowly turn right rear wheel
RL+ (A5 — 9) — RL- (A5 — 8)	AC generation	Slowly turn left rear wheel

TY402970026400OX

Fig. 351 Anti-lock brake system circuit test. 1997-99 Avalon less traction control

TRC+ (A34 – 13) – GND (A33 – 15, A35 – 9, 10)	Pulse generation	TRAC control active
TRC– (A34 – 5) – GND (A33 – 15, A35 – 9, 10)	Pulse generation	TRAC control active
IND (A34 – 3) – GND (A33 – 15, A35 – 9, 10)	Below 2.0	IG switch ON, SLIP indicator light ON
	10 – 14	IG switch ON, SLIP indicator light OFF
WT (A34 – 12) – GND (A33 – 15, A35 – 9, 10)	Below 2.0	IG switch ON, TRAC OFF indicator light ON
	10 – 14	IG switch ON, TRAC OFF indicator light OFF
CSW (A34 – 11) – GND (A33 – 15, A35 – 9, 10)	Below 2.0	IG switch ON, TRAC cut switch pushed in
	8 – 14	IG switch ON, TRAC cut switch released

TY4029700257020X

Fig. 352 Anti-lock brake system circuit test (Part 2 of 2). 1997–99 Avalon w/traction control

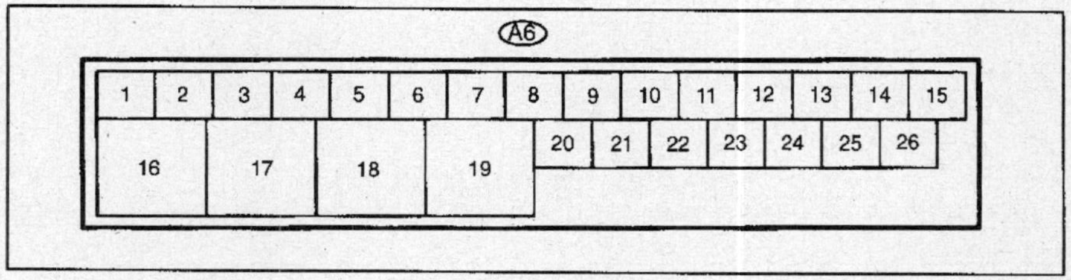

Symbols (Terminals No.)	STD Voltage (V)	Condition
+B (A6 – 17, 18) – GND (A6 – 16, 19)	10 – 14	Always
IG1(A6 – 15) – GND (A6 – 16, 19)	10 – 14	IG switch ON
WA (A6 – 21) – GND (A6 – 16, 26)	Below 2.6	IG switch ON, ABS warning light ON
	10 – 14	IG switch ON, ABS warning light OFF
STP (A6 – 2) – GND (A6 – 16, 19)	Below 1.5	Stop light switch OFF
	5 – 14	Stop light switch ON
Tc (A6 – 12) – GND (A6 – 16, 19)	5.7 – 8.1	IG switch ON
Ts (A6 – 11) – GND (A6 – 16, 19)	5.7 – 8.1	IG switch ON
FR+ (A6 – 5) – FR– (A6 – 4)	AC generation	IG switch ON Slowly turn right front wheel
FL+ (A6 – 7) – FL– (A6 – 6)	AC generation	IG switch ON Slowly turn left front wheel
RR+ (A6 – 3) – RR– (A6 – 1)	AC generation	IG switch ON Slowly turn right rear wheel
RL+ (A6 – 9) – RL– (A6 – 8)	AC generation	IG switch ON Slowly turn left rear wheel

TY4029700384000X

Fig. 353 Anti-lock brake system circuit test. 1997–99 Camry w/Bosch ABS

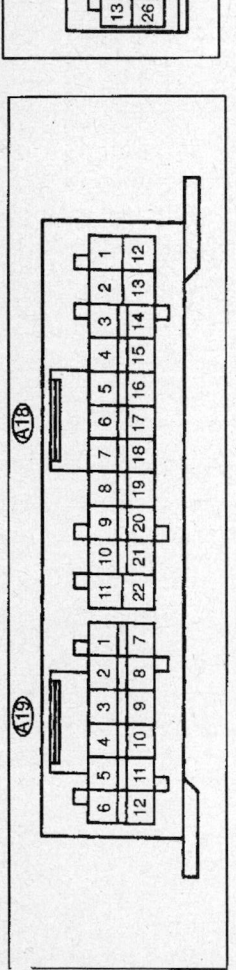

Fig. 355 Anti-lock brake system circuit test (Part 1 of 2). 1997–99 Camry w/Traction Control

Symbols (Terminals No.)	STD Voltage (V)	Condition
IG1 (A16 – 8) – GND (A15 – 15, A17 – 9, 10)	10 – 14	IG switch ON
R+ (A15 – 1) – SR (A15 – 11)	9 – 14	IG switch ON, ABS warning light OFF
R+ (A15 – 1) – MR (A15 – 24)	Below 1.0	IG switch ON
SFRR (A15 – 26) – GND (A15 – 15, A17 – 9, 10)	10 – 14	IG switch ON, ABS warning light OFF
SFRH (A15 – 13) – GND (A15 – 15, A17 – 9, 10)	10 – 14	IG switch ON, ABS warning light OFF
SFLR (A17 – 1) – GND (A15 – 15, A17 – 9, 10)	10 – 14	IG switch ON, ABS warning light OFF
SFLH (A17 – 2) – GND (A15 – 15, A17 – 9, 10)	10 – 14	IG switch ON, ABS warning light OFF
SRRR (A17 – 7) – GND (A15 – 15, A17 – 9, 10)	10 – 14	IG switch ON, ABS warning light OFF
SRRH (A17 – 8) – GND (A15 – 15, A17 – 9, 10)	10 – 14	IG switch ON, ABS warning light OFF
SRLR (A15 – 12) – GND (A15 – 15, A17 – 9, 10)	10 – 14	IG switch ON, ABS warning light OFF
SRLH (A15 – 25) – GND (A15 – 15, A17 – 9, 10)	10 – 14	IG switch ON, ABS warning light OFF
AST (A15 – 10) – GND (A15 – 15, A17 – 9, 10)	10 – 14	IG switch ON, ABS warning light ON
WA (A16 – 4) – GND (A15 – 15, A17 – 9, 10)	Below 2.0	IG switch ON, ABS warning light ON
STP (A16 – 16) – GND (A15 – 15, A17 – 9, 10)	Below 1.5	Stop light switch OFF
	8 – 14	Stop light switch ON
D/G (A15 – 22) – GND (A15 – 15, A17 – 9, 10)	10 – 14	IG switch ON, ABS warning light ON
Tc (A15 – 9) – GND (A15 – 15, A17 – 9, 10)	8 – 14	IG switch ON
Ts (A15 – 23) – GND (A15 – 15, A17 – 9, 10)	8 – 14	IG switch ON
FR+ (A15 – 17) – FR– (A15 – 18)	AC generation	Slowly turn right front wheel
FL+ (A15 – 5) – FL– (A15 – 4)	AC generation	Slowly turn left front wheel
RR+ (A16 – 9) – RR– (A16 – 10)	AC generation	Slowly turn right rear wheel
RL+ (A16 – 2) – RL– (A16 – 1)	AC generation	Slowly turn left rear wheel
MT (A15 – 14) – GND (A15 – 15, A17 – 9, 10)	Below 1.5	IG switch ON
SRC1 (A17 – 5) – GND (A15 – 15, A17 – 9, 10)	10 – 14	IG switch ON, TRAC OFF indicator light OFF
SMC1 (A17 – 12) – GND (A15 – 15, A17 – 9, 10)	10 – 14	IG switch ON, TRAC OFF indicator light OFF
SMC2 (A17 – 6) – GND (A15 – 15, A17 – 9, 10)	10 – 14	IG switch ON, TRAC OFF indicator light OFF
NEO (A16 – 15) – GND (A15 – 15, A17 – 9, 10)	Pulse generation	Idling
EFI+ (A16 – 6) – GND (A15 – 15, A17 – 9, 10)	Pulse generation	IG switch ON
EFI– (A16 – 14) – GND (A15 – 15, A17 – 9, 10)	Pulse generation	IG switch ON

Fig. 354 Anti-lock brake system circuit test. 1997–99 Camry w/Nippondenso ABS

Symbols (Terminals No.)	STD Voltage (V)	Condition
IG1 (A19 – 2) – GND (A18 – 2, 13)	10 – 14	IG switch ON
R+ (A18 – 8) – SR (A18 – 18)	9 – 14	IG switch ON, ABS warning light OFF
R+ (A18 – 8) – MR (A18 – 7)	Below 1.0	IG switch ON
SFRR (A18 – 1) – GND (A18 – 2, 13)	10 – 14	IG switch ON, ABS warning light OFF
SFRH (A18 – 4) – GND (A18 – 2, 13)	10 – 14	IG switch ON, ABS warning light OFF
SFLR (A18 – 11) – GND (A18 – 2, 13)	10 – 14	IG switch ON, ABS warning light OFF
SFLH (A18 – 10) – GND (A18 – 2, 13)	10 – 14	IG switch ON, ABS warning light OFF
SRRR (A18 – 22) – GND (A18 – 2, 13)	10 – 14	IG switch ON, ABS warning light OFF
SRRH (A18 – 21) – GND (A18 – 2, 13)	10 – 14	IG switch ON, ABS warning light OFF
SRLR (A18 – 12) – GND (A18 – 2, 13)	10 – 14	IG switch ON, ABS warning light OFF
SRLH (A18 – 5) – GND (A18 – 2, 13)	10 – 14	IG switch ON, ABS warning light OFF
AST (A18 – 16) – GND (A18 – 2, 13)	10 – 14	IG switch ON, ABS warning light ON
WA (A19 – 4) – GND (A18 – 2, 13)	Below 2.0	IG switch ON, ABS warning light ON
STP (A19 – 12) – GND (A18 – 2, 13)	Below 1.5	Stop light switch OFF
	8 – 14	Stop light switch ON
D/G (A19 – 11) – GND (A18 – 2, 13)	10 – 14	IG switch ON, ABS warning light ON
Tc (A19 – 9) – GND (A18 – 2, 13)	8 – 14	IG switch ON
Ts (A19 – 8) – GND (A18 – 2, 13)	8 – 14	IG switch ON
FR+ (A18 – 3) – FR– (A18 – 14)	AC generation	Slowly turn right front wheel
FL+ (A18 – 19) – FL– (A18 – 20)	AC generation	Slowly turn left front wheel
RR+ (A19 – 1) – RR– (A19 – 7)	AC generation	Slowly turn right rear wheel
RL+ (A19 – 3) – RL– (A19 – 10)	AC generation	Slowly turn left rear wheel
MT (A18 – 9) – GND (A18 – 2, 13)	Below 1.5	IG switch ON

ANTI-LOCK BRAKES

TY402940013902OA

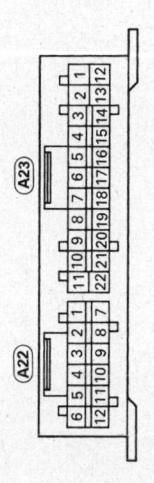

Symbols (Terminals No.)	STD Voltage (V)	Condition
SFRR (A23-1) – GND (A23-2)	10 – 14	IG switch ON, ABS warning light OFF
FR+ (A23-3) – FR– (A23-14)	AC generation	IG switch ON, Slowly turn right front wheel
SFRH (A23-4) – GND (A23-2)	10 – 14	IG switch ON, ABS warning light OFF
SRLH (A23-5) – GND (A23-2)	10 – 14	IG switch ON, ABS warning light OFF
MR (A23-7) – R+ (A23-8)	Below 1.0	IG switch ON
SFLH (A23-10) – GND (A23-2)	10 – 14	IG switch ON, ABS warning light OFF
SFLR (A23-11) – GND (A23-2)	10 – 14	IG switch ON, ABS warning light OFF
SRLR (A23-12) – GND (A23-2)	10 – 14	IG switch ON, ABS warning light OFF
AST (A23-16) – GND (A23-2)	10 – 14	IG switch ON, ABS warning light OFF
SR (A23-18) – R+ (A23-8)	9 – 14	IG switch ON
FL+ (A23-19) – FL– (A23-20)	AC generation	IG switch ON, Slowly turn left front wheel
SRRH (A23-21) – GND (A23-2)	10 – 14	IG switch ON, ABS warning light OFF
SRRR (A23-22) – GND (A23-2)	10 – 14	IG switch ON, ABS warning light OFF
RR+ (A22-1) – RR– (A27-7)	AC generation	IG switch ON, Slowly turn right rear wheel
IG1 (A22-2) – GND (A23-2)	10 – 14	IG switch ON
RL+ (A22-3) – RL– (A22-10)	AC generation	IG switch ON, Slowly turn left rear wheel
WA (A22-4) – GND (A23-2)	Below 2.0	IG switch ON, ABS warning light ON
	10 – 14	IG switch ON, ABS warning light OFF
Ts (A22-8) – GND (A23-2)	10 – 14	IG switch ON
Tc (A22-9) – GND (A23-2)	10 – 14	IG switch ON
STP (A22-12) – GND (A23-2)	Below 1.5	Stop light switch OFF
	8 – 14	Stop light switch ON

Fig. 356 Anti-lock brake system circuit test. 1996 Celica

TRC+ (A16–13) – GND (A15–15, A17–9, 10)	Pulse generation	TRAC control active
TRC– (A16–5) – GND (A15–15, A17–9, 10)	Pulse generation	TRAC control active
IND (A16–3) – GND (A15–15, A17–9, 10)	Below 2.0	IG switch ON, SLIP indicator light ON
	10 – 14	IG switch ON, SLIP indicator light OFF
WT (A16–12) – GND (A15–15, A17–9, 10)	Below 2.0	IG switch ON, TRAC OFF indicator light ON
	10 – 14	IG switch ON, TRAC OFF indicator light OFF
CSW (A16–11) – GND (A15–15, A17–9, 10)	Below 2.0	IG switch ON, TRAC out switch pushed in
	8 – 14	IG switch ON, TRAC out switch released

TY402970038602OX

Fig. 355 Anti-lock brake system circuit test (Part 2 of 2). 1997–99 Camry w/Traction Control

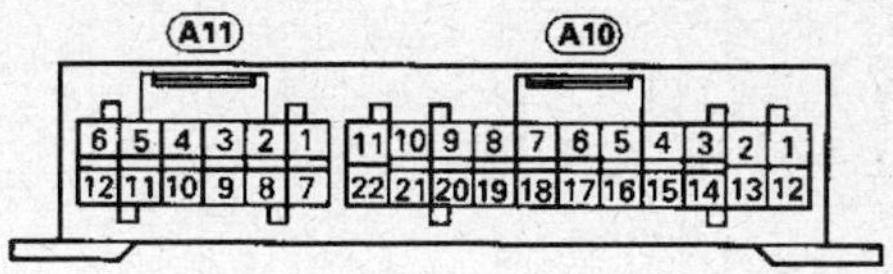

Connector face views (Corolla):

(A14)

```
     1                               14
   3   2                         16   15
   5   4                     19   18   17
   7   6                 21   20
   9   8             22
  11  10         24  23
  13  12     26  25
```

(A13)

```
   6   5   4   3   2   1
  12  11  10   9   8   7
```

Fig. 358 Anti-lock brake system circuit test. Corolla

Symbols (Terminals No.)	STD Voltage (V)	Condition
BAT (A14-17) – GND (A13-10)	10 – 14	Always
IG1 (A14-5) – GND (A13-10)	10 – 14	IG switch ON
SR (A14-20) – R+ (A14-11)	10 – 14	IG switch ON
MR (A14-7) – R+ (A14-11)	9 – 14	IG switch ON
SFRR (A13-5) – GND (A13-10)	Below 1.0	IG switch ON
SFRH (A13-6) – GND (A13-10)	10 – 14	IG switch ON, ABS warning light OFF
SFLR (A14-2) – GND (A13-7)	10 – 14	IG switch ON, ABS warning light OFF
SFLH (A14-1) – GND (A13-10)	10 – 14	IG switch ON, ABS warning light OFF
SRRR (A14-15) – GND (A13-7)	10 – 14	IG switch ON, ABS warning light OFF
SRRH (A14-14) – GND (A13-10)	10 – 14	IG switch ON, ABS warning light OFF
SRLR (A13-11) – GND (A13-7)	10 – 14	IG switch ON, ABS warning light OFF
SRLH (A13-12) – GND (A13-10)	10 – 14	IG switch ON, ABS warning light OFF
AST (A14-8) – GND (A13-7)	10 – 14	IG switch ON, ABS warning light OFF
WA (A14-18) – GND (A13-10)	Below 1.0	IG switch ON, ABS warning light ON
PKB (A14-3) – GND (A13-7)	Below 1.5	IG switch ON, PKB switch ON
PKB (A14-3) – GND (A13-10)	10 – 14	IG switch ON, PKB switch OFF
STP (A14-12) – GND (A13-10)	Below 1.0	Stop light switch OFF
STP (A14-12) – GND (A13-10)	8 – 14	Stop light switch ON
Tc (A14-25) – GND (A13-10)	10 – 14	IG switch ON
Ts (A14-24) – GND (A13-7)	10 – 14	IG switch ON
FR+ (A14-10) – FR- (A14-9)	AC generation	IG Switch ON, Slowly turn right front wheel
FL+ (A14-22) – FL- (A14-23)	AC generation	IG Switch ON, Slowly turn left front wheel
RR+ (A13-8) – RR- (A13-9)	AC generation	IG Switch ON, Slowly turn right rear wheel
RL+ (A13-3) – RL- (A13-2)	AC generation	IG Switch ON, Slowly turn left rear wheel

TY402970031000X

Connector face views (Celica):

(A10)

```
    1   2   3   4   5   6
    7   8   9  10
 11 10   9   8   ...
22 21 20 19 18 17 16 15 14 13
```

(A11)

```
   1   2   3   4   5   6
   7   8   9  10  11  12
```

Fig. 357 Anti-lock brake system circuit test. 1997–99 Celica

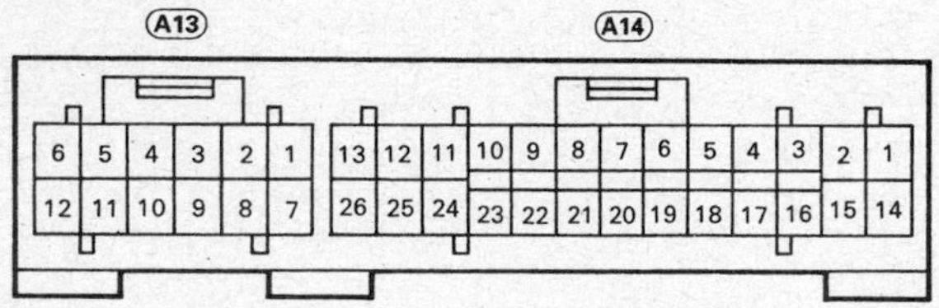

Symbols (Terminals No.)	STD Voltage (V)	Condition
SFRR (A10-1) – GND (A10-2)	10 – 14	IG switch ON, ABS warning light OFF
FR+ (A10-3) – FR- (A10-14)	AC generation	IG switch ON, Slowly turn right front wheel
SFRH (A10-4) – GND (A10-2)	10 – 14	IG switch ON, ABS warning light OFF
SRLH (A10-5) – GND (A10-2)	10 – 14	IG switch ON, ABS warning light OFF
MR (A10-7) – R+ (A10-8)	10 – 14	IG switch ON
SFLH (A10-10) – GND (A10-2)	10 – 14	IG switch ON, ABS warning light OFF
SFLR (A10-11) – GND (A10-2)	10 – 14	IG switch ON, ABS warning light OFF
SRLR (A10-12) – GND (A10-2)	10 – 14	IG switch ON, ABS warning light OFF
AST (A10-16) – GND (A10-2)	10 – 14	IG switch ON
SR (A10-18) – R+ (A10-8)	Below 1.5	IG switch ON
FL+ (A10-19) – FL- (A10-20)	AC generation	IG switch ON, Slowly turn left front wheel
SRRH (A10-21) – GND (A10-2)	10 – 14	IG switch ON, ABS warning light OFF
SRRR (A10-22) – GND (A10-2)	10 – 14	IG switch ON, ABS warning light OFF
RR+ (A11-7) – RR- (A11-7)	AC generation	IG switch ON, Slowly turn right rear wheel
IG1 (A11-1) – GND (A10-2)	10 – 14	IG switch ON
RL+ (A11-3) – RL- (A11-10)	AC generation	IG switch ON, Slowly turn left rear wheel
WA (A11-4) – GND (A10-2)	Below 2.0	IG switch ON, ABS warning light ON
Ts (A11-8) – GND (A10-2)	10 – 14	IG switch ON, ABS warning light OFF
Tc (A11-9) – GND (A10-2)	10 – 14	IG switch ON
STP (A11-12) – GND (A10-2)	Below 1.5	Stop light switch OFF
STP (A11-12) – GND (A10-2)	8 – 14	Stop light switch ON

TY402970039900X

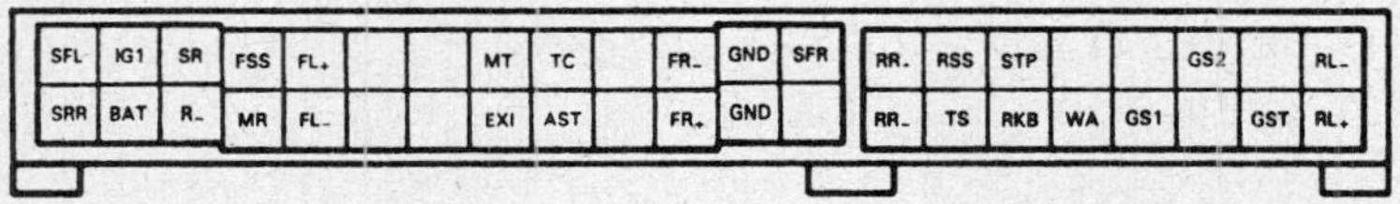

Tester Connection	Check Item	Condition	Specified Value	Trouble Part
SFL	Voltage	IG switch on and "ABS" warning light goes on	About 0 V	
		IG switch on and "ABS" warning light goes off	10~14 V	Actuator
AST	Voltage	IG switch on and "ABS" warning light goes on	About 0 V	
		IG switch on and "ABS" warning light goes off	Battery voltage	
EXI	Voltage	IG switch on and center differential lock indicator light goes off	10~14 V	GAUGE Fuse
FL–	Continuity	IG switch off	Continuity	ABS ECU
R–	Continuity	IG switch off	Continuity	
BAT	Voltage	IG switch off	10~14 V	DOME Fuse
SRR	Voltage	IG switch on and "ABS" warning light goes on	About 0 V	
		IG switch on and "ABS" warning light goes off	10~14 V	Actuator

TY402930012502OX

Fig. 359 Anti-lock brake system circuit test (Computer connector connected, Part 2 of 2). Land Cruiser

Tester Connection	Check Item	Condition	Specified Value	Trouble Part
RL–	Continuity	IG switch OFF	Continuity	ABS ECU
GS2	Voltage	IG switch ON	4 – 6 V	Deceleration Sensor
STP	Voltage	IG switch OFF and brake pedal depressed	10~14 V	Stop light switch / Stop light
		IG switch OFF and brake pedal returned	Below 1.5 V	Stop light
RSS	Continuity	IG switch OFF	Continuity	ABS ECU
GS1	Voltage	IG switch ON	4~6 V or 7~12 V	Deceleration Sensor
WA	Voltage	IG switch ON and "ABS" warning light goes on	About 0 V	ABS ECU
		IG switch ON and "ABS" warning light goes off	10~14 V	"ABS" warning light
PKB	Voltage	IG switch ON and PKB lever pulled	Below 1.5 V	Parking brake switch / Level warning switch
		IG switch ON and PKB lever returned	10~14 V	
TS	Voltage	IG switch ON and DLC1 T_s – E_1 connected	About 0 V	ABS ECU
RR–	Continuity	IG switch OFF	Continuity	
SFR	Voltage	IG switch ON and "ABS" warning light goes on	About 0 V	
		IG switch ON and "ABS" warning light goes off	10~14 V	Actuator
GND	Continuity	IG switch OFF	Continuity	Wiring harness
FR–	Continuity	IG switch OFF	Continuity	
TC	Voltage	IG switch ON and DLC1 T_c – E_1 not connected	10~14 V	
		IG switch ON and DLC1 T_c – E_1 connected	About 0 V	
FSS	Continuity	IG switch OFF	Continuity	ABS ECU
SR	Voltage	IG switch ON and "ABS" warning light goes on	About 0 V	
		IG switch ON and "ABS" warning light goes off	10~14 V	
IG1	Voltage	IG switch ON	10~14 V	ECU-IG fuse

TY402930012501OX

Fig. 359 Anti-lock brake system circuit test (Computer connector connected, Part 1 of 2). Land Cruiser

Connector pin layout:

SFL	IG1	SR	FSS	FL–	MT	TC	FR–	GND	SFR	RR–	RSS	STP		GS2		RL–
SRR	BAT	R–	MR	EXI	AST	FR–	GND	RKB	WA	TS	RR–			GS1	GST	RL+

TY4029700277000X

Fig. 361 — Anti-lock brake system circuit test. Paseo

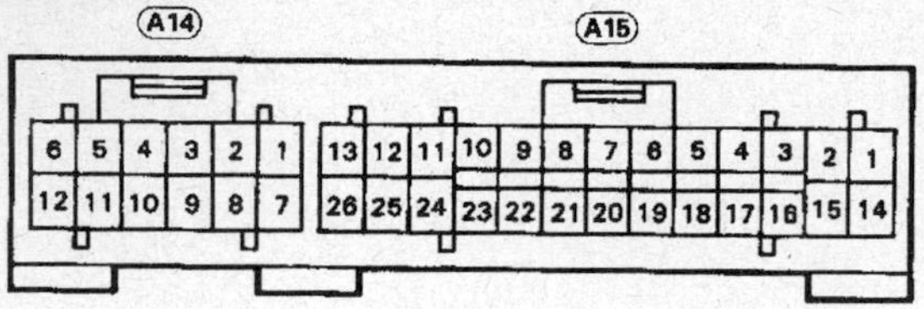

Symbols (Terminals No.)	STD Voltage (V)	Condition
IG1 (A15-5) – GND (A14-7)	10 – 14	IG switch ON
SR (A15-20) – R+ (A15-4)	9 – 14	IG switch ON
MR (A15-7) – R+ (A15-4)	Below 1.0	IG switch ON
SFRR (A14-5) – GND (A14-7)	10 – 14	IG switch ON, ABS warning light OFF
SFRH (A14-6) – GND (A14-7)	10 – 14	IG switch ON, ABS warning light OFF
SFLR (A15-2) – GND (A14-7)	10 – 14	IG switch ON, ABS warning light OFF
SFLH (A15-1) – GND (A14-7)	10 – 14	IG switch ON, ABS warning light OFF
SRRR (A15-15) – GND (A14-7)	10 – 14	IG switch ON, ABS warning light OFF
SRRH (A15-14) – GND (A14-7)	10 – 14	IG switch ON, ABS warning light OFF
SRLR (A14-11) – GND (A14-7)	10 – 14	IG switch ON, ABS warning light OFF
SRLH (A13-12) – GND (A14-7)	10 – 14	IG switch ON, ABS warning light OFF
AST (A15-8) – GND (A14-7)	10 – 14	IG switch ON, ABS warning light ON
WA (A15-18) – GND (A14-7)	Below 2.0	IG switch ON, ABS warning light ON
STP (A15-12) – GND (A14-7)	Below 1.5	Stop light switch OFF
	8 – 14	Stop light switch ON
Tc (A15-25) – GND (A14-7)	10 – 14	IG switch ON
Ts (A15-24) – GND (A14-7)	10 – 14	IG switch ON
FR+ (A15-10) – FR- (A15-9)	AC generation	IG switch ON, Slowly turn right front wheel
FL+ (A15-22) – FL- (A15-23)	AC generation	IG switch ON, Slowly turn left front wheel
RR+ (A14-8) – RR- (A14-9)	AC generation	IG switch ON, Slowly turn right rear wheel
RL+ (A14-3) – RL- (A14-2)	AC generation	IG switch ON, Slowly turn left rear wheel

TY4029300135000X

Fig. 360 — Anti-lock brake system circuit test (Computer connector disconnected). Land Cruiser

Tester Connection	Check Item	Specified Value	Trouble Part
RR+ ↔ RR-	Resistance	0.5 ~ 1.6 kΩ	RH rear speed sensor
RL+ ↔ RL-	Resistance	0.5 ~ 1.6 kΩ	LH rear speed sensor
SFR ↔ AST-	Resistance	About 6 Ω	Actuator
MT+ ↔ Body ground	Continuity	Continuity	Actuator
FL+ ↔ FL-	Resistance	0.97 ~ 1.77 kΩ	LH front speed sensor
SR ↔ R-	Resistance	60 ~ 100 Ω	Control relay

Taster Connection	Check Item	Specified Value	Trouble Part
SFL+ ↔ AST	Resistance	About 6 Ω	Actuator
FR+ ↔ FR-	Resistance	0.97 ~ 1.77 kΩ	RH front speed sensor
AST ↔ Body ground	Resistance	About 5 Ω	Actuator
MR ↔ R-	Resistance	55.8 ~ 68.2 kΩ	Control relay
SRR ↔ AST	Resistance	About 6 Ω	Actuator

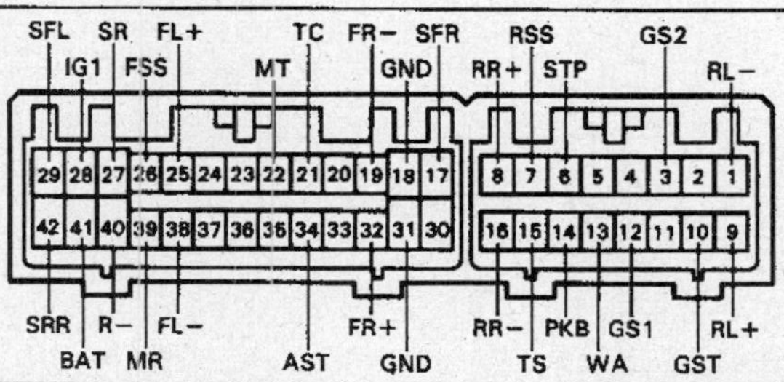

Tester Connection	Check Item	Condition	Specified Value	Trouble Part
GND	Continuity	IG switch OFF	Continuity	Wiring harness
AST	Voltage	IG switch ON and "ABS" warning light goes OFF	10 ~ 14 V	ABS ECU
		IG switch ON and "ABS" warning light goes ON	About 0 V	
FL–	Continuity	IG switch OFF	Continuity	
R–	Continuity	IG switch OFF	Continuity	
BAT	Voltage	IG switch ON	10 ~ 14 V	ECU-B Fuse
SRR	Voltage	IG switch ON and "ABS" warning light goes OFF	10 ~ 14 V	Actuator

TY4029600232020X

Fig. 362 Anti-lock brake system circuit test (Part 2 of 2). 1996 Previa

Connector pinout:
```
SFL  SR  FL+   TC  FR–  SFR  RSS  GS2  RL–
IG1  FSS   MT  GND  RR+  STP  GS1  RL+
     SRR  R–  FL–  BAT  MR  FR+  AST  GND  TS  WA  GST
RR–  PKB
```

Pin numbers: 29 28 27 26 25 24 23 22 21 20 19 18 17 16 15 14 13 12 11 10 9
42 41 40 39 38 37 36 35 34 33 32 31 30

Tester Connection	Check Item	Condition	Specified Value	Trouble Part
RL–	Continuity	IG switch OFF	Continuity	ABS ECU
GS2	Voltage	IG switch ON	4 ~ 6 V	Deceleration sensor
STP	Voltage	IG switch OFF and brake pedal depressed	8 ~ 14 V	Stop light switch
STP	Voltage	IG switch OFF and brake pedal returned	Below 1.5 V	Stop light
RSS	Continuity	IG switch OFF	Continuity	ABS ECU
SFR	Voltage	IG switch ON and "ABS" warning light goes OFF	10 ~ 14 V	Actuetor
GND	Continuity	IG switch OFF	Continuity	Wiring harness
FR–	Continuity	IG switch OFF	Continuity	
TC	Voltage	IG switch ON and data link connector 1 Tc – E_1 not connected	10 ~ 14 V	
TC	Voltage	IG switch ON and data link connector 1 Tc – E_1 connected	About 0 V	ABS ECU
FSS	Continuity	IG switch OFF	Continuity	
SR	Voltage	IG switch ON and "ABS" warning light goes OFF	About 0 V	
SR	Voltage	IG switch ON and "ABS" warning light goes ON	9 ~ 14 V	
IG1	Voltage	IG switch ON	10 ~ 14 V	ECU-IG Fuse
SFL	Voltage	IG switch ON and "ABS" warning light goes OFF	10 ~ 14 V	Actuator
GS1	Voltage	IG switch ON	4 ~ 6 V or 7 ~ 11 V	Deceleration sensor
WA	Voltage	IG switch ON and "ABS" warning light goes ON	Below 2.0 V	ABS ECU
WA	Voltage	IG switch ON and "ABS" warning light goes OFF	10 ~ 14 V	"ABS" warning light
PKB	Voltage	IG switch ON and PKB lever pulled	Below 1.5 V	Parking brake switch
PKB	Voltage	IG switch ON and PKB lever returned	10 ~ 14 V	Level warning switch
TS	Voltage	IG switch ON and data link connector 1 Ts – E_1 not connected	10 ~ 14 V	
TS	Voltage	IG switch ON and data link connector 1 Ts – E_1 connected	Below 1.0 V	ABS ECU
RR–	Continuity	IG switch OFF	Continuity	

TY4029600232010X

Fig. 362 Anti-lock brake system circuit test (Part 1 of 2). 1996 Previa

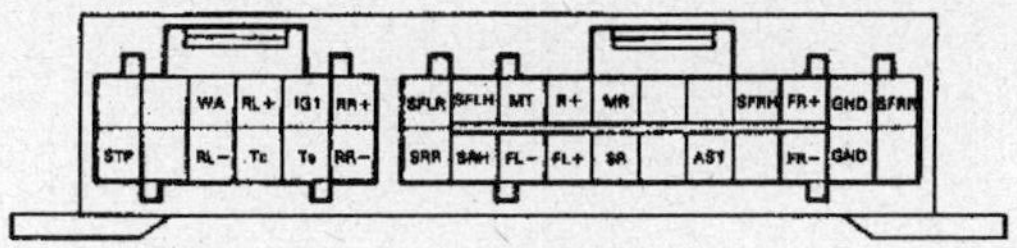

Fig. 364 Anti-lock brake system circuit test (Computer connector disconnected). 1997 Previa

Taster Connection	Check Item	Specified Value	Trouble Part	Taster Connection	Check Item	Specified Value	Trouble Part
SFLH↔Body Ground	Resistance	About 8.8 Ω	Actuator	SRH↔Body Ground	Resistance	About 8.8 Ω	Actuator
SFLR↔Body Ground	Resistance	About 4.3 Ω	Actuator	SRR↔Body Ground	Resistance	About 4.3 Ω	Actuator
MR↔R+	Resistance	56 – 68 Ω	Control relay	FL+↔FL+	Resistance	0.6 – 2.5 kΩ	LH front speed sensor
FR+↔FR-	Resistance	0.6 – 2.5 kΩ	RH front speed sensor	MT↔Body Ground	Continuity	Continuity	Actuator
R+↔SR	Resistance	72 – 88 Ω	Control relay	RR+↔RR-	Resistance	0.80 – 2.05kΩ	RH rear speed sensor
RL+↔RL-	Resistance	0.80 – 2.05kΩ	LH rear speed sensor	AST↔Body Ground	Resistance	About 5.0 Ω	Actuator
SFRR↔Body Ground	Resistance	About 4.3 Ω	Actuator				
SFRH↔Body Ground	Resistance	About 8.8 Ω	Actuator				

TY402970029900X

Fig. 363 Anti-lock brake system circuit test (Computer connector connected). 1997 Previa

Taster Connection	Check Item	Condition	Specified Value	Trouble Part
SFRR	Voltage	IG switch ON and "ABS" warning light goes OFF	10 – 14 V	Actuator Solenoid relay wiring harness
SFRH				
R+	Voltage	IG switch ON	10 – 14 V	ABS ECU
SFLR	Voltage	IG switch ON and "ABS" warning light goes OFF	10 – 14 V	Actuator Solenoid relay wiring harness
SFLH	Voltage	IG switch ON	10 – 14 V	
IG1	Voltage	IG switch ON	10 – 14 V	ECU–IG fuse
WA	Voltage	IG switch ON and "ABS" warning light goes ON	Below 1.5 V	ABS ECU "ABS" warning light wiring harness
	Voltage	IG switch ON and "ABS" warning light goes OFF	10 – 14 V	
FR-	Continuity	IG switch OFF	Continuity	ABS ECU wiring harness
AST	Voltage	IG switch ON and "ABS" warning light goes OFF	10 – 14 V	ABS ECU Solenoid relay wiring harness
SR	Voltage	IG switch ON and "ABS" warning light goes ON	About 0 V	
	Voltage	IG switch ON and "ABS" warning light goes OFF	9 – 14 V	
FL-	Continuity	IG switch OFF	Continuity	ABS ECU wiring harness
SRH	Voltage	IG switch ON and "ABS" warning light goes OFF	10 – 14 V	Actuator Solenoid relay wiring harness
SRR	Continuity	IG switch OFF	Continuity	
RR-	Voltage	IG switch ON and DLC1 Ts-E₁ not connected	10 – 14 V	
Ts	Voltage	IG switch ON and DLC1 Ts-E₁ connected	Below 1.0 V	ABS ECU wiring harness
Tc	Voltage	IG switch ON and DLC1 Tc-E₁ not connected	10 – 14 V	
	Voltage	IG switch ON and DLC1 Tc-E₁ connected	About 0 V	
RR-	Continuity	IG switch OFF	Continuity	
STP	Voltage	IG switch OFF and brake pedal depressed	8 – 14 V	Stop light switch Stop light wiring
	Voltage	IG switch OFF and brake pedal returned	Below 1.5 V	
GND	Continuity	IG switch OFF	Continuity	Wiring harness

If the circuit is not as specified, check and repair or replace the trouble part shown in the table above.

TY402970029800X

ANTI-LOCK BRAKES

Symbols (Terminals No.)			STD Voltage (V)	Condition
IG1 (A16-2)	–	GND (A17-2/13)	10 – 14	IG switch ON
SR (A17-18)	–	R+ (A17-8)	Below 1.5	IG switch ON, ABS warning light OFF
MR (A17-7)	–	R+ (A17-8)	10 – 14	IG switch ON
SFRH (A17-4)	–	GND (A17-2/13)	10 – 14	IG switch ON, ABS warning light OFF
SFRR (A17-1)	–	GND (A17-2/13)	10 – 14	IG switch ON, ABS warning light OFF
SFLH (A17-10)	–	GND (A17-2/13)	10 – 14	IG switch ON, ABS warning light OFF
SFLR (A17-11)	–	GND (A17-2/13)	10 – 14	IG switch ON, ABS warning light OFF
SRRR (A17-22)	–	GND (A17-2/13)	10 – 14	IG switch ON, ABS warning light OFF
SRRH (A17-21)	–	GND (A17-2/13)	10 – 14	IG switch ON, ABS warning light OFF
SRLR (A17-12)	–	GND (A17-2/13)	10 – 14	IG switch ON, ABS warning light OFF
SRLH (A17-5)	–	GND (A17-2/13)	10 – 14	IG switch ON, ABS warning light OFF
AST (A17-16)	–	GND (A17-2/13)	10 – 14	IG switch ON, ABS warning light OFF
WA (A16-4)	–	GND (A17-2/13)	Below 2.0	IG switch ON, ABS, warning light ON
			10 – 14	IG switch ON, ABS warning light OFF
STP (A16-12)	–	GND (A17-2/13)	Below 1.5	Stop light switch OFF
			8 – 14	Stop light switch ON
Tc (A16-9)	–	GND (A17-2/13)	10 – 14	IG switch ON
Ts (A16-8)	–	GND (A17-2/13)	10 – 14	IG switch ON
FR+ (A17-3)	–	FR– (A17-14)	AC generation	IG switch ON Slowly turn right front wheel
FL+ (A17-19)	–	FL– (A17-20)	AC generation	IG switch ON Slowly turn left front wheel
RR+ (A16-1)	–	RR– (A16-7)	AC generation	IG switch ON Slowly turn right rear wheel
RL+ (A16-3)	–	RL– (A16-10)	AC generation	IG switch ON Slowly turn left rear wheel

TY4029600230000X

Fig. 365 Anti-lock brake system circuit test. 1996 2WD RAV4

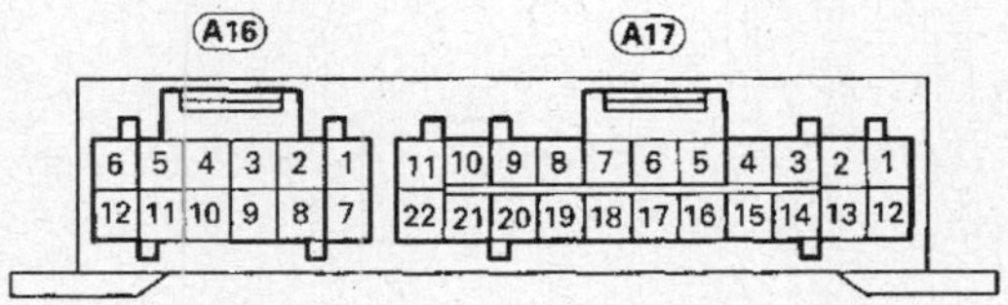

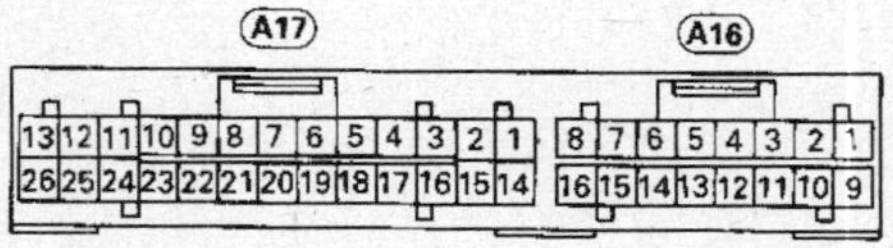

Symbols (Terminals No.)			STD Voltage (V)	Condition
BAT (A17-22)	–	GND (A17-11/24)	10 – 14	Always
IG1 (A17-10)	–	GND (A17-11/24)	10 – 14	IG switch ON
SR (A16-5)	–	R– (A16-15)	10 – 14	IG switch ON, ABS warning light OFF
MR (A16-4)	–	R– (A16-15)	Below 1.0	IG switch ON
SFRH (A16-1)	–	GND (A17-11/24)	10 – 14	IG switch ON, ABS warning light OFF
SFRR (A16-2)	–	GND (A17-11/24)	10 – 14	IG switch ON, ABS warning light OFF
SFLH (A17-13)	–	GND (A17-11/24)	10 – 14	IG switch ON, ABS warning light OFF
SFLR (A17-12)	–	GND (A17-11/24)	10 – 14	IG switch ON, ABS warning light OFF
SRRH (A17-26)	–	GND (A17-11/24)	10 – 14	IG switch ON, ABS warning light OFF
SRRR (A17-25)	–	GND (A17-11/24)	10 – 14	IG switch ON, ABS warning light OFF
SRLH (A16-9)	–	GND (A17-11/24)	10 – 14	IG switch ON, ABS warning light OFF
SRLR (A16-10)	–	GND (A17-11/24)	10 – 14	IG switch ON, ABS warning light OFF
AST (A16-11)	–	GND (A17-11/24)	10 – 14	IG switch ON, ABS warning light OFF
WA (A16-12)	–	GND (A17-11/24)	Below 2.0	IG switch ON, ABS warning light ON
			10 – 14	IG switch ON, ABS warning light OFF
PKB (A17-9)	–	GND (A17-11/24)	Below 1.5	IG switch ON, PKB switch ON
			10 – 14	IG switch ON, PKB switch OFF
STP (A17-21)	–	GND (A17-11/24)	Below 1.5	Stop light switch OFF
			8 – 14	Stop light switch ON
Tc (A17-20)	–	GND (A17-11/24)	10 – 14	IG switch ON
Ts (A17-6)	–	GND (A17-11/24)	10 – 14	IG switch ON
FR+ (A16-7)	–	FR– (A16-6)	AC generation	IG switch ON Slowly turn right front wheel
FL+ (A16-14)	–	FL– (A16-13)	AC generation	IG switch ON Slowly turn left front wheel
RR+ (A17-15)	–	RR– (A17-16)	AC generation	IG switch ON Slowly turn right rear wheel
RL+ (A17-1)	–	RL– (A17-2)	AC generation	IG switch ON Slowly turn left rear wheel
GL1 (A17-19)	–	GND (A17-11/24)	0.5 – 4.5 V	IG switch ON
GL2 (A17-7)	–	GND (A17-11/24)	0.5 – 4.5 V	IG switch ON
VGS (A17-5)	–	GND (A17-11/24)	4.5 – 5.5 V	IG switch ON

TY4029600231000X

Fig. 366 Anti-lock brake system circuit test. 1996 4WD RAV4

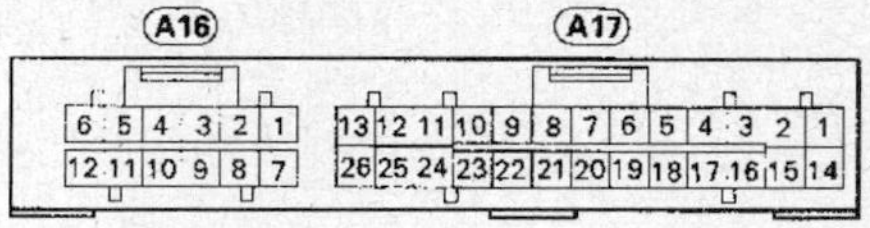

Fig. 368 — A16 / A17 connector

TY40297002940000X

Symbols (Terminals No.)		STD Voltage (V)	Condition
IG1 (A16-2)	GND (A17-13)	10 – 14	IG switch ON
SR (A17-18)	R+ (A17-8)	Below 1.5	IG switch ON, ABS warning light OFF
MR (A17-7)	R+ (A17-8)	Below 1.5	IG switch ON
R+ (A17-8)	GND (A17-13)	10 – 14	IG switch ON
SFRH (A17-4)	GND (A17-2, 13)	10 – 14	IG switch ON, ABS warning light OFF
SFRR (A17-1)	GND (A17-13)	10 – 14	IG switch ON, ABS warning light OFF
SFLH (A17-10)	GND (A17-2, 13)	10 – 14	IG switch ON, ABS warning light OFF
SFLR (A17-11)	GND (A17-2, 13)	10 – 14	IG switch ON, ABS warning light OFF
SRRR (A17-22)	GND (A17-13)	10 – 14	IG switch ON, ABS warning light OFF
SRLR (A17-12)	GND (A17-2, 13)	10 – 14	IG switch ON, ABS warning light OFF
SRLH (A17-5)	GND (A17-13)	10 – 14	IG switch ON, ABS warning light OFF
AST (A17-16)	GND (A17-2, 13)	10 – 14	IG switch ON, ABS warning light ON
WA (A16-4)	GND (A17-13)	Below 2.0	IG switch ON, ABS, warning light OFF
MT (A17-9)	GND (A17-2, 13)	10 – 14	IG switch ON, ABS warning light OFF
STP (A16-12)	GND (A17-13)	Below 1.5	Stop light switch OFF
		8 – 14	Stop light switch ON
Tc (A16-9)	GND (A17-2, 13)	10 – 14	IG switch ON
Ts (A16-8)	GND (A17-2, 13)	10 – 14	IG switch ON
FR- (A17-3)	FR- (A17-14)	AC generation	IG switch ON — Slowly turn right front wheel
FL+ (A17-19)	FL+ (A17-20)	AC generation	IG switch ON — Slowly turn left front wheel
RR+ (A16-1)	RR- (A16-7)	AC generation	IG switch ON — Slowly turn right rear wheel
RL+ (A16-3)	RL- (A16-10)	AC generation	IG switch ON — Slowly turn left rear wheel
*GS1 (A17-6)	GND (A17-13)	4 – 6 or 7 – 11	IG switch ON (Vehicle at horizontaly)
*GS2 (A17-15)	GND (A17-2, 13)	4 – 6	IG switch ON (Vehicle at horizontaly)

*: 4WD 4 Door Models only

Fig. 368 Anti-lock brake system circuit test. 1997–99 2WD & 4WD RAV4 w/4Door

Fig. 367 — A16 / A17 connector

TY40297002930000X

Symbols (Terminals No.)		STD Voltage (V)	Condition
IG1 (A17-13)	GND (A17-12, 25)	10 – 14	IG switch ON
SR (A16-7)	R- (A16-26)	10 – 14	IG switch ON, ABS warning light OFF
MR (A16-1)	R- (A16-26)	Below 1.0	IG switch ON
R+ (A17-26)	GND (A17-12, 25)	10 – 14	IG switch ON
SFRH (A17-2)	GND (A17-12, 25)	10 – 14	IG switch ON, ABS warning light OFF
SFRR (A17-1)	GND (A17-12, 25)	10 – 14	IG switch ON, ABS warning light OFF
SFLH (A16-5)	GND (A17-12, 25)	10 – 14	IG switch ON, ABS warning light OFF
SFLR (A16-6)	GND (A17-12, 25)	10 – 14	IG switch ON, ABS warning light OFF
SRRH (A16-11)	GND (A17-12, 25)	10 – 14	IG switch ON, ABS warning light OFF
SRRR (A16-12)	GND (A17-12, 25)	10 – 14	IG switch ON, ABS warning light OFF
SRLH (A17-15)	GND (A17-12, 25)	10 – 14	IG switch ON, ABS warning light OFF
SRLR (A17-14)	GND (A17-12, 25)	10 – 14	IG switch ON, ABS warning light OFF
AST (A16-4)	GND (A17-12, 25)	10 – 14	IG switch ON, ABS warning light ON
WA (A16-11)	GND (A17-12, 25)	Below 2.0	IG switch ON, ABS warning light OFF
MT (A16-10)	GND (A17-12, 25)	10 – 14	IG switch ON
STP (A17-5)	GND (A17-12, 25)	Below 1.5	Stop light switch OFF
		8 – 14	Stop light switch ON
Tc (A17-8)	GND (A17-12, 25)	10 – 14	IG switch ON
Ts (A17-21)	GND (A17-12, 25)	10 – 14	IG switch ON
FR+ (A16-9)	FR- (A16-9)	AC generation	IG switch ON — Slowly turn right front wheel
FL+ (A16-8)	FL- (A16-2)	AC generation	IG switch ON — Slowly turn left front wheel
RR+ (A17-10)	RR- (A17-23)	AC generation	IG switch ON — Slowly turn right rear wheel
RL+ (A17-22)	RL- (A17-9)	AC generation	IG switch ON — Slowly turn left rear wheel
GL1 (A17-4)	G GND (A17-17)	0.5 – 4.5 V	IG switch ON (Vehicle at horizontaly)
GL2 (A17-16)	G GND (A17-17)	0.5 – 4.5 V	IG switch ON (Vehicle at horizontaly)
VGS (A17-3)	G GND (A17-17)	4.5 – 5.5 V	IG switch ON

Fig. 367 Anti-lock brake system circuit test. 1997–99 4WD RAV4 w/2Door

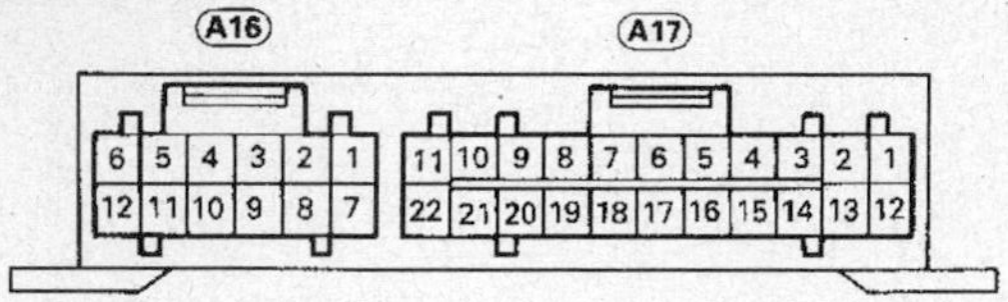

Anti-lock brake system circuit test (Part 2 of 2). 1996 Supra less traction control

TY4029400140020X

Symbols (Terminals No.)		STD Voltage (V)	Condition
BAT (A19-25)	GND (A19-15)	10 – 14	Always
IG1 (A19-12)	GND (A19-2)	10 – 14	IG switch ON
SR (A19-11)	R– (A19-24)	9 – 14	IG switch ON, ABS warning light OFF
MR (A19-23)	R– (A19-24)	Below 1.0	IG switch ON
SFR (A19-1)	GND (A19-2)	10 – 14	IG switch ON, ABS warning light OFF
SFL (A19-13)	GND (A19-2)	10 – 14	IG switch ON, ABS warning light OFF
SRR (A19-26)	GND (A19-15)	10 – 14	IG switch ON, ABS warning light OFF
SRL (A19-14)	GND (A19-15)	10 – 14	IG switch ON, ABS warning light OFF
AST (A19-18)	GND (A19-15)	10 – 14	IG switch ON, ABS warning light OFF
WA (A18-13)	GND (A19-15)	Below 2.0	IG switch ON, ABS warning light ON
PKB (A18-14)	GND (A19-15)	10 – 14	IG switch ON, PKB switch ON
		Below 1.5	IG switch ON, PKB switch OFF
STP (A18-6)	GND (A19-2)	8 – 14	Stop light switch ON
		Below 1.5	Stop light switch OFF
D/G (A18-4)	GND (A19-2)	8 – 14	IG switch ON, ABS warning light OFF
Tc (A19-5)	GND (A19-2)	10 – 14	IG switch ON
Ts (A18-15)	GND (A19-15)	8 – 14	IG switch ON
FR+ (A19-16)	FR– (A19-3)	8 – 14	IG switch ON
FL+ (A19-9)	FL– (A19-22)	AC generation	Slowly turn right front wheel
RR+ (A18-8)	RR– (A18-16)	AC generation	Slowly turn left front wheel
RL+ (A18-9)	RL– (A18-1)	AC generation	Slowly turn right rear wheel
GS1 (A18-12)	GND (A19-15)	AC generation	Slowly turn left rear wheel
GS2 (A18-3)	GND (A19-2)	4 – 6 or 7 – 11	IG switch ON, vehicle parked on a level surface
		4 – 6	IG switch ON, vehicle parked on a level surface

Fig. 369 Anti-lock brake system circuit test (Part 2 of 2). 1996 Supra less traction control

TY4029400140010X

Terminal No.	Symbol	Connection	Terminal No.	Symbol	Connection
A19- 1	SFR	Right front solenoid	A18- 1	RL–	Left rear speed sensor
2	GND1	Ground	2	GS2	Lateral acceleration sensor
3	FR–	Right front speed sensor	3	D/G	DLC2
4	--	--	4	--	--
5	Tc	DLC1, DLC2	5	STP	Stop light switch
6	MT	ABS motor relay monitor	6	RSS	Sealed wiring harness
7	--	--	7	RR+	Right rear speed sensor
8	--	--	8	RL+	Left rear speed sensor
9	FL+	Left front speed sensor	9	GST	Lateral acceleration sensor
10	FSS	Sealed wiring harness	10	GS1	Lateral acceleration sensor
11	SR	ABS solenoid relay	11	WA	ABS warning light
12	IG1	Ignition switch	12	PKB	Parking brake switch
13	SFL	Left front solenoid	13	Ts	DLC1
14	SRL	Left rear solenoid	14	RR–	Right rear speed sensor
15	GND2	Ground	15		
16	FR+	Right front speed sensor	16		
17	--	--			
18	AST	ABS solenoid relay monitor			
19	--	--			
20	--	--			
21	--	--			
22	FL–	Left front speed sensor			
23	MR	ABS motor relay			
24	R–	Relay ground			
25	BAT	Battery			
26	SRR	Right rear solenoid			

Fig. 369 Anti-lock brake system circuit test (Part 1 of 2). 1996 Supra less traction control

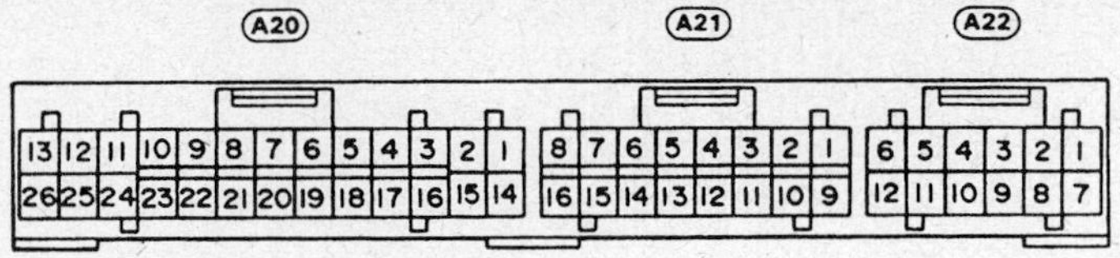

Symbols (Terminal No.)	STD Voltage (V)	Conditions
Tc (A20-23) — GND (A20-25)	8 – 14	IG switch ON
Ts (A20-11) — GND (A20-25)	8 – 14	IG switch ON
FR+ (A20-17) — FR– (A20-4)	AC generation	IG switch ON Slowly turn right front wheel.
FL+ (A20-5) — FL– (A20-18)	AC generation	IG switch ON Slowly turn left front wheel.
RR+ (A21-2) — RR– (A21-10)	AC generation	IG switch ON Slowly turn right rear wheel.
RL+ (A21-9) — RL– (A21-1)	AC generation	IG switch ON Slowly turn left rear wheel.
FRO (A21-13) — GND (A22-4)	Pulse generation	IG switch ON Slowly turn right front wheel.
FLO (A21-15) — GND (A22-4)	Pulse generation	IG switch ON Slowly turn left front wheel.
RRO (A21-6) — GND (A22-4)	Pulse generation	IG switch ON Slowly turn right rear wheel.
RLO (A21-4) — GND (A22-4)	Pulse generation	IG switch ON Slowly turn left rear wheel.
GS 1 (A20-8) — GND (A20-25)	4 – 6 or 7 – 11	IG switch ON, vehicle parked on a level surface
GS 2 (A20-20) — GND (A20-25)	4 – 6	IG switch ON, vehicle parked on a level surface
EXO (A21-12) — GND (A22-4)	10 – 14	IG switch ON

Fig. 370 Anti-lock brake system circuit test (Part 2 of 2). 1996 Supra w/traction control

Symbols (Terminals No.)	STD Voltage (V)	Condition
BAT (A20-7) — GND (A20-25)	10 – 14	Always
IG 1 (A20-24) — GND (A20-25)	10 – 14	IG switch ON
SR (A20-15) — R– (A20-12)	8.3 – 14	IG switch ON, ABS warning light OFF
MR (A20-2) — R– (A20-12)	Below 1.0	IG switch ON
TSR (A20-1) — R– (A20-12)	8.3 – 14	IG switch ON, TRAC and TRAC OFF indicator light OFF
TMR (A20-14) — R– (A20-12)	Below 1.0	IG switch ON
SFR (A22-1) — GND (A22-9)	10 – 14	IG switch ON, ABS warning light OFF
SFL (A22-13) — GND (A20-25)	10 – 14	IG switch ON, ABS warning light OFF
SRR (A20-26) — GND (A20-25)	10 – 14	IG switch ON, ABS warning light OFF
SRL (A22-7) — GND (A22-9)	10 – 14	IG switch ON, ABS warning light OFF
AST (A20-21) — GND (A20-25)	10 – 14	IG switch ON, ABS warning light OFF
SMC (A22-2) — GND (A22-9)	10 – 14	IG switch ON, TRAC and TRAC OFF indicator light OFF
SRC (A22-8) — GND (A22-9)	10 – 14	IG switch ON, TRAC and TRAC OFF indicator light OFF
WA (A22-5) — GND (A22-4)	Below 2.0	IG switch ON, ABS warning light ON
	10 – 14	IG switch ON, ABS warning light OFF
PKB (A22-12) — GND (A22-4)	Below 1.5	IG switch ON, PKB switch ON Fluid in M/C reservoir above MIN level.
	8 – 14	IG switch ON, PKB switch OFF Fluid in M/C reservoir above MIN level.
LBL (A20-10) — GND (A20-25)	8 – 14	IG switch ON Fluid in M/C reservoir above MIN level.
STP (A22-6) — GND (A22-4)	Below 1.5	Stop light switch OFF
	8 – 14	Stop light switch ON
D/G (A22-10) — GND (A22-9)	10 – 14	IG switch ON, ABS warning light OFF

Fig. 370 Anti-lock brake system circuit test (Part 1 of 2). 1996 Supra w/traction control

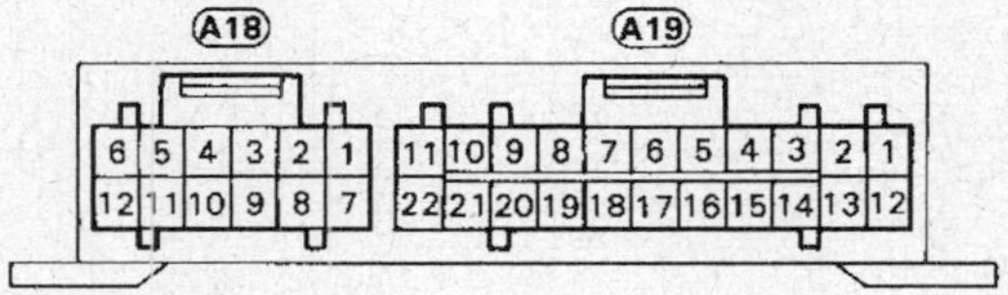

TY402970043600010X

Fig. 372 Anti-lock brake system circuit test (Part 1 of 2). 1997–98 Supra w/2JZ-GTE engine

Symbols (Terminals No.)	GND	STD Voltage (V)	Condition
IG1 (A20-13)	GND (A20-25)	10 – 14	IG switch ON
SR (A21-7)	R+ (A20-26)	10 – 14	IG switch ON, ABS warning light OFF
MR (A21-1)	R+ (A20-26)	Below 1.0	IG switch ON
SFRH (A20-2)	GND (A20-25)	10 – 14	IG switch ON, ABS warning lihgt OFF
SFRR (A20-1)	GND (A20-25)	10 – 14	IG switch ON, ABS warning light OFF
SFLH (A21-5)	GND (A20-25)	10 – 14	IG switch ON, ABS warning light OFF
SFLR (A21-6)	GND (A20-25)	10 – 14	IG switch ON, ABS warning light OFF
SRRH (A21-11)	GND (A20-25)	10 – 14	IG switch ON, ABS warning light OFF
SRRR (A21-12)	GND (A20-25)	10 – 14	IG switch ON, ABS warning light OFF
SRLH (A20-15)	GND (A20-25)	10 – 14	IG switch ON, ABS warning light OFF
SRLR (A20-14)	GND (A20-25)	10 – 14	IG switch ON, ABS warning light OFF
AST (A21-4)	GND (A20-25)	10 – 14	IG switch ON, ABS warning light OFF
WA (A20-11)	GND (A20-12)	Below 2.0	IG switch ON, ABS warning light ON
(A20-11)	GND (A20-25)	10 – 14	IG switch ON, ABS warning light OFF
STP (A20-5)	GND (A20-25)	Below 1.5	Stop light switch OFF
		8 – 14	Stop light switch ON
D/G (A20-24)	GND (A20-25)	10 – 14	IG switch ON, ABS warning light OFF
MT (A21-10)	GND (A20-25)	Below 1.5	IG switch ON
Tc (A20-8)	GND (A20-25)	10 – 14	IG switch ON
Ts (A20-21)	GND (A20-25)	10 – 14	IG switch ON
FR+ (A21-3)	FR- (A21-9)	AC generation	IG switch ON Slowly turn right front wheel
FL+ (A21-8)	FL- (A21-2)	AC generation	IG switch ON Slowly turn left front wheel
RR+ (A20-10)	RR- (A20-23)	AC generation	IG switch ON Slowly turn right rear wheel
RL+ (A20-22)	RL- (A20-9)	AC generation	IG switch ON Slowly turn left rear wheel

TY402970043500010X

Fig. 371 Anti-lock brake system circuit test. 1997–98 Supra w/2JZ-GE engine

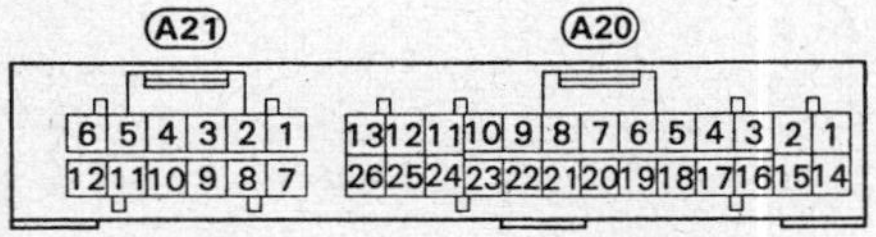

Symbols (Terminals No.)	GND	STD Voltage (V)	Condition
IG1 (A18-2)	GND (A19-13)	10 – 14	IG switch ON
SR (A19-18)	R+ (A19-8)	Below 1.5	IG switch ON, ABS warning light OFF
MR (A19-7)	R+ (A19-8)	10 – 14	IG switch ON
SFRH (A19-4)	GND (A19-13)	10 – 14	IG switch ON, ABS warning light OFF
SFRR (A19-1)	GND (A19-13)	10 – 14	IG switch ON, ABS warning light OFF
SFLH (A19-10)	GND (A19-13)	10 – 14	IG switch ON, ABS warning light OFF
SFLR (A19-11)	GND (A19-13)	10 – 14	IG switch ON, ABS warning light OFF
SRR (A19-22)	GND (A19-13)	10 – 14	IG switch ON, ABS warning light OFF
SRH (A19-21)	GND (A19-13)	10 – 14	IG switch ON, ABS warning light OFF
AST (A19-16)	GND (A19-13)	10 – 14	IG switch ON, ABS warning light OFF
WA (A18-4)	GND (A19-13)	Below 2.0	IG switch ON, ABS warning lihgt ON
	GND (A19-13)	10 – 14	IG switch ON, ABS warning light OFF
STP (A18-12)	GND (A19-13)	Below 1.5	Stop light switch OFF
	GND (A19-13)	8 – 14	Stop light switch ON
D/G (A18-11)	GND (A19-13)	10 – 14	IG switch ON, ABS warning light OFF
MT (A19-9)	GND (A19-13)	Below 1.5	IG switch ON
Tc (A18-9)	GND (A19-13)	10 – 14	IG switch ON
Ts (A18-8)	GND (A19-13)	10 – 14	IG switch ON
FR+ (A19-3)	FR- (A19-14)	AC generation	IG switch ON Slowly turn right front wheel
FL+ (A19-19)	FL- (A19-20)	AC generation	IG switch ON Slowly turn left front wheel
RR+ (A18-11)	RR- (A18-7)	AC generation	IG switch ON Slowly turn right rear wheel
RL+ (A18-3)	RL- (A18-10)	AC generation	IG switch ON Slowly turn left rear wheel

Symbols (Terminals No.)		STD Voltage (V)	Condition
BATT (T16-1)	– E1 (T15-26)	9 – 14	Always
+B (T16-9)	– E1 (T15-26)	9 – 14	IG switch ON, Engine stops
EFIB (T15-1)	– E1 (T15-26)	9 – 14	IG switch ON, Engine stops
IDL1 (T15-4)	– E1 (T15-26)	0 – 3	IG switch ON, Throttle valve fully closed
		9 – 14	IG switch ON, Throttle valve fully open
VTA1 (T15-6)	– E1 (T15-26)	0.3 – 0.8	IG switch ON, Throttle valve fully closed
		3.2 – 4.9	IG switch ON, Throttle valve fully open
IDL2 (T15-3)	– E1 (T15-26)	0 – 3	Engine running, Sub-throttle valve fully closed
		9 – 14	Engine running, Sub-throttle valve fully open
VTA2 (T15-19)	– E1 (T15-26)	0.3 – 0.8	Engine running, Sub-throttle valve fully closed
		3.2 – 4.9	Engine running, Sub-throttle valve fully open
FRO (T16-16)	– E1 (T15-26)	Pulse generation	Vehicle driving at about 30 km/h (19 mph)
FLO (T16-8)	– E1 (T15-26)	Pulse generation	Vehicle driving at about 30 km/h (19 mph)
RRO (T16-15)	– E1 (T15-26)	Pulse generation	Vehicle driving at about 30 km/h (19 mph)
RLO (T16-7)	– E1 (T15-26)	Pulse generation	Vehicle driving at about 30 km/h (19 mph)
WT (T16-10)	– E1 (T15-26)	0 – 3	IG switch ON, TRAC OFF indicator light ON
		9 – 14	IG switch ON, TRAC OFF indicator light OFF
IND (T16-2)	– E1 (T15-26)	0 – 3	IG switch ON, SLIP indicator light ON
		9 – 14	IG switch ON, SLIP indicator light OFF
CSW (T16-6)	– E1 (T15-26)	0 – 3	IG switch ON, TRAC OFF switch holded on pushing
		9 – 14	IG switch ON, TRAC OFF switch released
RLY+ (T16-4)	– RLY– (T16-12)	9 – 14	IG switch ON
SIND (T16-11)	– E1 (T15-26)	0 – 3	IG switch ON, SNOW indicator light ON
		9 – 14	IG switch ON, SNOW indicator light OFF
SNOW (T16-14)	– E1 (T15-26)	0 – 3	IG switch ON, SNOW mode switch holded on pushing
		9 – 14	IG switch ON, SNOW mode switch released
A (T15-12)	– EO1 (T15-13)	Pulse generation	Engine running, Throttle valve fully closed
Ā (T15-11)	– EO1 (T15-13)	Pulse generation	Engine running, Throttle valve fully closed
B (T15-25)	– EO1 (T15-13)	Pulse generation	Engine running, Throttle valve fully closed
B̄ (T15-24)	– EO1 (T15-13)	Pulse generation	Engine running, Throttle valve fully closed

Fig. 373 Anti-lock brake system circuit test (Part 1 of 2). 1997–98 Supra w/traction control

Symbols (Terminals No.)		STD Voltage (V)	Condition
FRO (A20-7)	– GND (A20-2, 25)	Pulse generation	Vehicle driving at about 30 km/h (19 mph)
FLO (A20-20)	– GND (A20-2, 25)	Pulse generation	Vehicle driving at about 30 km/h (19 mph)
RRO (A20-6)	– GND (A20-2, 25)	Pulse generation	Vehicle driving at about 30 km/h (19 mph)
RLO (A20-19)	– GND (A20-2, 25)	Pulse generation	Vehicle driving at about 30 km/h (19 mph)
GL1 (A20-4)	– GND (A20-2, 25)	0.5 – 4.5 V	IG switch ON
GL2 (A20-16)	– GND (A20-2, 25)	0.5 – 4.5 V	IG switch ON
VGS (A20-3)	– GND (A20-2, 25)	4.5 – 5.5 V	IG switch ON

Fig. 372 Anti-lock brake system circuit test (Part 2 of 2). 1997–98 Supra w/2JZ-GTE engine

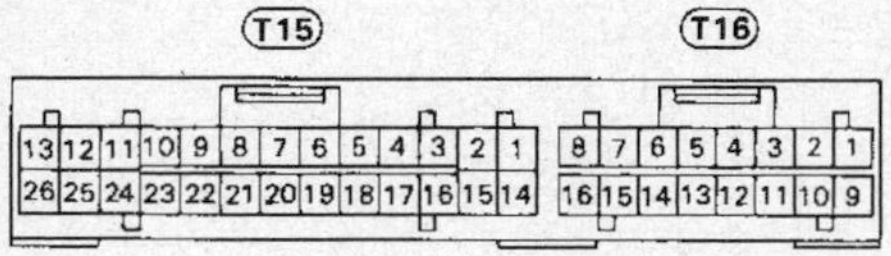

(A11)

(A10)

Fig. 374 Anti-lock brake system circuit test. 1996 Tacoma

TY40296003200000X

Symbols (Terminals No.)	STD Voltage (V)	Condition
BAT (A10-22) – GND (A10-24)	10 – 14	Always
IG1 (A10-10) – GND (A10-24)	10 – 14	IG switch ON
SR (A11-5) – R- (A11-15)	9 – 14	IG switch ON, ABS warning light OFF
MR (A11-4) – R- (A11-15)	Below 1.0	IG switch ON
SFRH (A11-1) – GND (A10-24)	10 – 14	IG switch ON, ABS warning light OFF
SFRR (A11-2) – GND (A10-24)	10 – 14	IG switch ON, ABS warning light OFF
SFLH (A10-13) – GND (A10-24)	10 – 14	IG switch ON, ABS warning light OFF
SFLR (A10-12) – GND (A10-24)	10 – 14	IG switch ON, ABS warning light OFF
SRR (A10-25) – GND (A10-24)	10 – 14	IG switch ON, ABS warning light OFF
SRH (A10-26) – GND (A10-24)	10 – 14	IG switch ON, ABS warning light OFF
AST (A11-11) – GND (A10-24)	10 – 14	IG switch ON, ABS warning light ON
WA (A11-12) – GND (A10-24)	Below 2.0	IG switch ON, ABS warning light ON
PKB (A10-9) – GND (A10-24)	Below 1.5	IG switch ON, PKB switch ON
	10 – 14	IG switch ON, PKB switch OFF
STP (A10-21) – GND (A10-24)	Below 1.5	Stop light switch OFF
	8 – 14	Stop light switch ON
Tc (A10-20) – GND (A10-24)	10 – 14	IG switch ON
Ts (A10-6) – GND (A10-24)	10 – 14	IG switch ON
FR+ (A11-7) – FR- (A11-6)	10 – 14	IG switch ON
	AC generation	Slowly turn right front wheel
FL+ (A11-14) – FL- (A11-13)	10 – 14	IG switch ON
	AC generation	Slowly turn left front wheel
RR+ (A10-15) – RR- (A10-16)	10 – 14	IG switch ON
	AC generation	Slowly turn right rear wheel
RL+ (A10-1) – RL- (A10-2)	10 – 14	IG switch ON
	AC generation	Slowly turn left rear wheel
GS1 (A10-19) – GND (A10-24)	4 – 6 or 7 – 11	IG switch ON
GS2 (A10-7) – GND (A10-24)	4 – 6	IG switch ON

Fig. 373 Anti-lock brake system circuit test (Part 2 of 2). 1997–98 Supra w/traction control

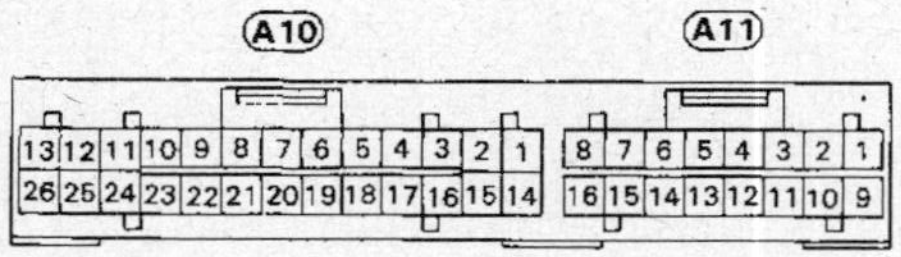

TY402970043702X

Symbols (Terminals No.)	STD Voltage (V)	Condition
NE (T15-16) – E1 (T15-26)	Pulse generation	Idling
FAIL (T15-9) – E1 (T15-26)	Pulse generation	IG switch ON (normal condition)
	9 – 14	IG switch ON (abnormal condition)
EFIF (T15-17) – E1 (T15-26)	0 – 2	IG switch ON, ECM normal condition
	4.5 – 5.5	IG switch ON, ECM abnormal condition
EFI+ (T15-7) – E1 (T15-26)	Pulse generation	IG switch ON
EFI- (T15-20) – E1 (T15-26)	Pulse generation	IG switch ON
ETC+ (T15-8) – E1 (T15-26)	Pulse generation	IG switch ON
ETC- (T15-21) – E1 (T15-26)	4.5 – 5.5	IG switch ON, Engine stops
TC (T16-3) – E1 (T15-26)	9 – 14	IG switch ON, ABS ECU normal condition
WA (T16-5) – E1 (T15-26)	0 – 3	IG switch ON, ABS ECU abnormal condition

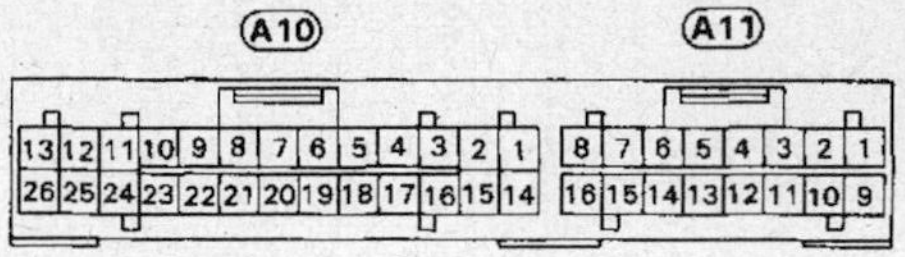

Anti-lock brake system circuit test. Tercel

Symbols (Terminals No.)		STD Voltage (V)	Condition
IG1 (A12-5)	GND (A13-7)	10 – 14	IG switch ON
SR (A12-20)	R+ (A12-4)	9 – 14	IG switch ON
MR (A12-7)	R+ (A12-4)	Below 1.0	IG switch ON
SFRR (A13-5)	GND (A13-7)	10 – 14	IG switch ON, ABS warning light OFF
SFRH (A13-6)	GND (A13-7)	10 – 14	IG switch ON, ABS warning light OFF
SFLR (A12-2)	GND (A13-7)	10 – 14	IG switch ON, ABS warning light OFF
SFLH (A12-1)	GND (A13-7)	10 – 14	IG switch ON, ABS warning light OFF
SRRR (A12-15)	GND (A13-7)	10 – 14	IG switch ON, ABS warning light OFF
SRRH (A12-14)	GND (A13-7)	10 – 14	IG switch ON, ABS warning light OFF
SRLR (A13-11)	GND (A13-7)	10 – 14	IG switch ON, ABS warning light OFF
SRLH (A13-12)	GND (A13-7)	10 – 14	IG switch ON, ABS warning light OFF
AST (A12-8)	GND (A13-7)	10 – 14	IG switch ON, ABS warning light ON
WA (A12-18)	GND (A13-7)	Below 2.0	IG switch ON, ABS warning light ON
		10 – 14	IG switch ON, ABS warning light OFF
STP (A12-12)	GND (A13-7)	Below 1.5	Stop light switch OFF
		8 – 14	Stop light switch ON
Tc (A12-25)	GND (A13-7)	10 – 14	IG switch ON
Ts (A12-24)	GND (A13-7)	10 – 14	IG switch ON
FR+ (A12-10)	FR− (A12-9)	AC generation	IG switch ON / Slowly turn right front wheel
FL+ (A12-22)	FL− (A12-23)	AC generation	IG switch ON / Slowly turn left front wheel
RR+ (A13-8)	RR− (A13-9)	AC generation	IG switch ON / Slowly turn right rear wheel
RL+ (A13-3)	RL− (A13-2)	AC generation	IG switch ON / Slowly turn left rear wheel

TY4029700278000X

Fig. 376   Anti-lock brake system circuit test. Tercel

Anti-lock brake system circuit test. 1997–99 Tacoma

Symbols (Terminals No.)		STD Voltage (V)	Condition
BAT (A10-22)	GND (A10-21)	10 – 14	Always
IG1 (A10-10)	GND (A10-21)	10 – 14	IG switch ON
SR (A11-5)	R+ (A11-3)	9 – 14	IG switch ON, ABS warning light OFF
MR (A11-4)	R+ (A11-3)	Below 1.0	IG switch ON
SFRH (A11-8)	GND (A10-21)	10 – 14	IG switch ON, ABS warning light OFF
SFRR (A11-16)	GND (A10-21)	10 – 14	IG switch ON, ABS warning light OFF
SFLH (A11-1)	GND (A10-21)	10 – 14	IG switch ON, ABS warning light OFF
SFLR (A11-2)	GND (A10-21)	10 – 14	IG switch ON, ABS warning light OFF
SRR (A11-10)	GND (A10-21)	10 – 14	IG switch ON, ABS warning light OFF
SRH (A11-9)	GND (A10-21)	10 – 14	IG switch ON, ABS warning light OFF
AST (A11-11)	GND (A10-21)	10 – 14	IG switch ON, ABS warning light ON
WA (A10-25)	GND (A10-21)	Below 2.0	IG switch ON, ABS warning light ON
		10 – 14	IG switch ON, ABS warning light OFF
EXI3	GND (A10-21)	Below 1.5	IG switch ON, transfer is in L4 position
		10 – 14	IG switch ON, transfer is in a position other than L4
STP (A10-9)	GND (A10-21)	Below 1.5	Stop light switch OFF
		8 – 14	Stop light switch ON
Tc (A10-21)	GND (A10-20)	10 – 14	IG switch ON
Ts (A10-20)	GND (A10-21)	10 – 14	IG switch ON
FR+ (A10-6)	FR− (A11-7)	AC generation	IG switch ON / Slowly turn right front wheel
FL+ (A11-13)	FL− (A11-14)	AC generation	IG switch ON / Slowly turn left front wheel
RR+ (A10-15)	RR− (A10-16)	AC generation	IG switch ON / Slowly turn right rear wheel
RL+ (A10-2)	RL− (A10-1)	AC generation	IG switch ON / Slowly turn left rear wheel
GS1 (A10-19)	GND (A10-21)	About 2 or About 4	IG switch ON
GS2 (A10-7)	GND (A10-21)	About 2	IG switch ON

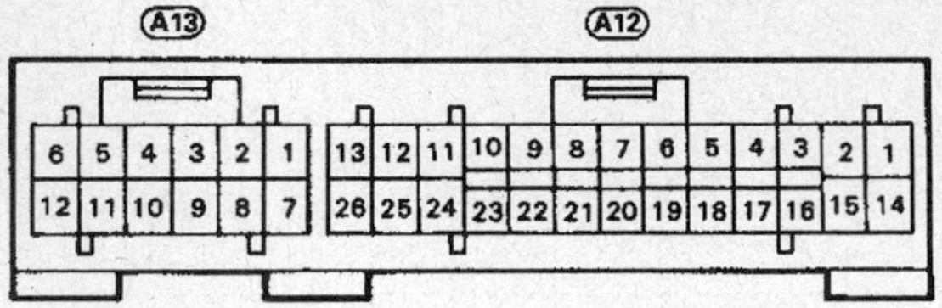

TY4029700321000X

Fig. 375   Anti-lock brake system circuit test. 1997–99 Tacoma

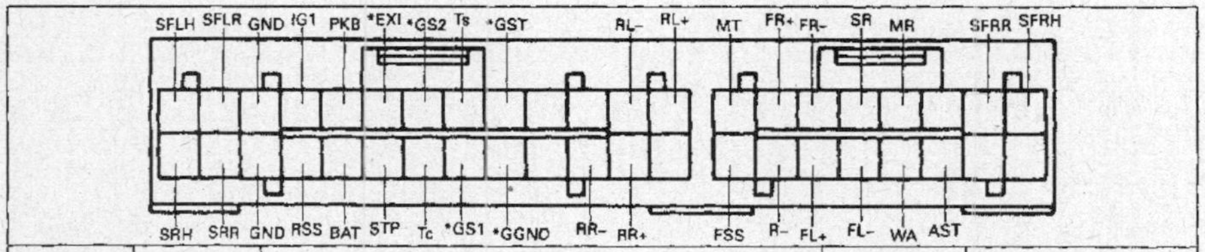

Part 2 of 2

Tester Connection	Check Item	Condition	Specified Value	Trouble Part
STP	Voltage	IG switch OFF and brake pedal depressed	8 ~ 14 V	Stop light switch, Stop light wiring harness
		IG switch OFF and brake pedal returned	Below 1.5 V	
BAT	Voltage	Always	10 ~ 14 V	ECU +B Fuse
RSS	Continuity	IG switch OFF	Continuity	ABS ECU, wiring harness
GND	Continuity	IG switch OFF	Continuity	Wiring harness
SRH / SRR	Voltage	IG switch ON and "ABS" warning light goes OFF	10 ~ 14 V	Actuator, Solenoid relay wiring harness

TY4029700302020X

Fig. 377 Anti-lock brake system circuit test (Computer connector connected, Part 2 of 2). 1996 T100

Connector pins: SFLH SFLR GND IG1 PKB *EXI *GS2 Ts *GST   —   SRH SRR GND RSS BAT STP Tc *GS1 *GGND   —   SFRR SFRH SR MR FR- FR+ RL- RL+ MT FSS R- FL+ FL- WA AST

Part 1 of 2

Tester Connection	Check Item	Condition	Specified Value	Trouble Part
SFRH / SFRR	Voltage	IG switch ON and "ABS" warning light goes OFF	10 ~ 14 V	Actuator, Solenoid relay wiring harness
SR	Voltage	IG switch ON and "ABS" warning light goes ON	About 0 V	ABS ECU, Solenoid relay wiring harness
		IG switch ON and "ABS" warning light goes OFF	9 ~ 14 V	
FR-	Continuity	IG switch OFF	Continuity	ABS ECU wiring harness
WA	Voltage	IG switch ON and "ABS" warning light goes ON	Below 1.5 V	ABS ECU "ABS" warning light wiring harness
		IG switch ON and "ABS" warning light goes OFF	10 ~ 14 V	
FL-, R-, FSS, RL-	Continuity	IG switch OFF	Continuity	ABS ECU wiring harness
Ts	Voltage	IG switch ON and check connector Ts – E₁ not connected	10 ~ 14 V	
		IG switch ON and check connector Ts – E₁ connected	Below 1.0 V	
PKB	Voltage	IG switch ON and PKB lever pulled	Below 1.5 V	Parking brake switch brake warning light wiring harness
		IG switch ON and PKB lever returned	10 ~ 14 V	
IG1	Voltage	IG switch ON	10 ~ 14 V	ECU-IG Fuse
GND	Continuity	IG switch OFF	Continuity	Wiring harness
SFLR / SFLH	Voltage	IG switch ON and "ABS" warning light goes OFF	10 ~ 14 V	Actuator, Solenoid relay wiring harness
RR-	Continuity	IG switch OFF	Continuity	ABS ECU wiring harness
Tc	Voltage	IG switch ON and check connector Tc – E₁ not connected	10 ~ 14 V	ABS ECU wiring harness
		IG switch ON and check connector Tc – E₁ connected	About 0 V	
AST	Voltage	IG switch ON and "ABS" warning light goes OFF	10 ~ 14 V	
*GS1	Voltage	IG switch ON	About 0 V	Deceleration Sensor
*GS2	Voltage	IG switch ON	4 ~ 8 V / 7 ~ 12 V	Deceleration Sensor
*EXI	Voltage	IG switch ON and 4WD indicator light goes OFF	10 ~ 14 V	GAUGE Fuse

* 4WD Vehicle

TY4029700302010X

Fig. 377 Anti-lock brake system circuit test (Computer connector connected, Part 1 of 2). 1996 T100

Tester Connection	Check Item	Condition	Specified Value	Trouble Part
SFRH / SFRR	Voltage	IG switch ON and "ABS" warning light goes OFF	10 – 14 V	Actuator Solenoid relay wiring harness
SR	Voltage	IG switch ON and "ABS" warning light goes ON	About 0 V	ABS ECU Solenoid relay wiring harness
		IG switch ON and "ABS" warning light goes OFF	9 – 14 V	ABS ECU Solenoid relay wiring harness
FR –	Continuity	IG switch OFF	Continuity	ABS ECU wiring harness
WA	Voltage	IG switch ON and "ABS" warning light goes ON	Below 1.5 V	ABS ECU "ABS" warning light wiring harness
		IG switch ON and "ABS" warning light goes OFF	10 – 14 V	ABS ECU "ABS" warning light wiring harness
FL –	Continuity	IG switch OFF	Continuity	ABS ECU wiring harness
FSS	Continuity	IG switch OFF	Continuity	ABS ECU wiring harness
RL –	Continuity	IG switch OFF	Continuity	ABS ECU wiring harness
Ts	Voltage	IG switch ON and DLC1 Ts-E1 not connected	10 – 14 V	
		IG switch ON and DLC1 Ts-E1 connected	Below 1.0 V	
IG1	Voltage	IG switch ON	10 – 14 V	ECU – IG fuse
GND	Continuity	IG switch OFF	Continuity	Wiring harness
SFLR / SFLH	Voltage	IG switch ON and "ABS" warning light goes OFF	10 – 14 V	Actuator Solenoid relay wiring harness
RR–	Continuity	IG switch OFF	Continuity	
Tc	Voltage	IG switch ON and DLC1 Tc-E1 not connected	10 – 14 V	ABS ECU wiring harness
		IG switch ON and DLC1 Tc-E1 connected	About 0 V	
AST	Voltage	IG switch ON and "ABS" warning light goes OFF	10 – 14 V	ABS ECU wiring harness
		IG switch ON and "ABS" warning light goes ON	About 0 V	
*GS1	Voltage	IG switch ON	About 2 or 4V	Deceleration sensor
*GS2	Voltage	IG switch ON	About 2 V	Deceleration sensor
*EX1	Voltage	IG switch ON and 4WD indicator light goes OFF	10 – 14 V	GAUGE fuse
		IG switch ON and 4WD indicator light goes ON	Below 2.0V	
*EX13	Voltage	IG switch ON and 4WD indicator light goes OFF	10 – 14 V	Deceleration sensor

*4WD Vehicle

Fig. 379 Anti-lock brake system circuit test (Computer connector connected, Part 1 of 2). 1997–98 T100

Tester Connection	Check Item	Specified Value	Trouble Part	Tester Connection	Check Item	Specified Value	Trouble Part
SFLH ↔ Body Ground	Resistance	About 5.0 Ω	Actuator	SRH ↔ Body Ground	Resistance	About 5.0 Ω	Actuator
SFLR ↔ Body Ground	Resistance	About 2.2 Ω	Actuator	SRR ↔ Body Ground	Resistance	About 2.2 Ω	Actuator
MR ↔ R–	Resistance	56 – 68 Ω	Control relay	FL+ ↔ FL–	Resistance	0.92 – 1.22 kΩ	Front LH speed sensor
FL+ ↔ FR–	Resistance	0.92 – 1.22 kΩ	Front RH speed sensor	MT ↔ Body Ground	Continuity	Continuity	Actuator
R– ↔ SR	Resistance	72 – 88 Ω	Control relay	RR+ ↔ RR–	Resistance	0.89 – 1.29 kΩ	Rear RH speed sensor
RL+ ↔ RL–	Resistance	0.89 – 1.29 kΩ	Rear LH speed sensor	AST ↔ Body Ground	Resistance	About 5.0 Ω	Actuator
SFRR ↔ Body Ground	Resistance	About 2.2 Ω	Actuator				
SFPH ↔ Body Ground	Resistance	About 5.0 Ω	Actuator				

Fig. 378 Anti-lock brake system circuit test (Computer connector disconnected). 1996 T100

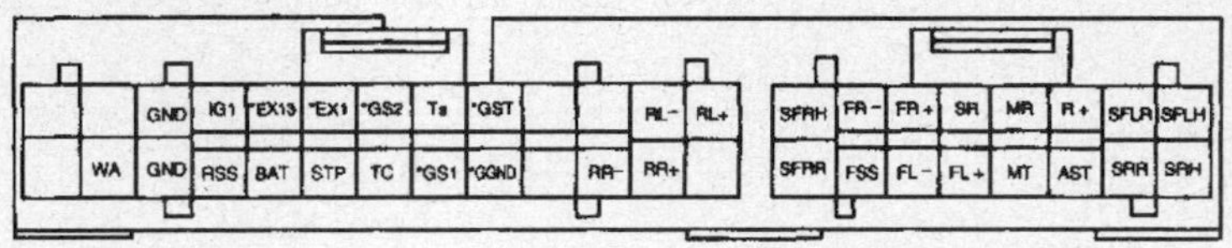

Tester Connection	Check Item	Condition	Specified Value	Trouble Part
STP	Voltage	IG switch OFF and brake pedal depressed	8 – 14V	Stop light switch
		IG switch OFF and brake pedal returned	Below 1.5V	Stop light wiring harness
BAT	Voltage	Always	10 – 14V	ECU – B fuse
RSS	Continuity	IG switch OFF	Continuity	ABS ECU, wiring harness
GND	Continuity	IG switch OFF	Continuity	Wiring harness
SRH	Voltage	IG switch ON and "ABS" warning light goes OFF	10 – 14V	Actuator
SRR				Solenoid relay wiring harness
R+	Voltage	IG switch ON ABS warning light goes ON	10 – 14V	ABS ECU
		IG switch ON ABS warning light goes OFF	Below 1.5V	ABS ECU
MT	Voltage	IG switch OFF	Below 1.5V	ABS ECU wiring harness

TY4029710030400X

Fig. 379 Anti-lock brake system circuit test (Computer connector connected, Part 2 of 2). 1997–98 T100

Tester Connection	Check Item	Specified Value	Trouble part	Tester Connection	Check Item	Specified Value	Trouble part
SFLH ↔ Body Ground	Resistance	About 5.0 Ω	Actuator	SRH ↔ Body Ground	Resistance	About 5.0 Ω	Actuator
SFLR ↔ Body Ground	Resistance	About 2.2 Ω	Actuator	SRR ↔ Body Ground	Resistance	About 2.2 Ω	Actuator
MR ↔ R–	Resistance	56 – 68 Ω	Control relay	FL+ ↔ FL–	Resistance	0.92 – 1.22 kΩ	Front LH speed sensor
FR+ ↔ FR–	Resistance	0.92 – 1.22 kΩ	Front RH speed sensor	MT ↔ Body Ground	Continuity	Continuity	Actuator
R– ↔ SR	Resistance	72 – 88 Ω	Control relay	RR+ ↔ RR–	Resistance	0.89 – 1.29 kΩ	Rear RH speed sensor
RL+ ↔ RL–	Resistance	0.89 – 1.29 kΩ	Rear LH speed sensor	AST ↔ Body Ground	Resistance	About 5.0 Ω	Actuator
SFRR ↔ Body Ground	Resistance	About 2.2 Ω	Actuator				
SFRH ↔ Body Ground	Resistance	About 5.0 Ω	Actuator				

TY4029300305000X

Fig. 380 Anti-lock brake system circuit test (Computer connector disconnected). 1997–98 T100

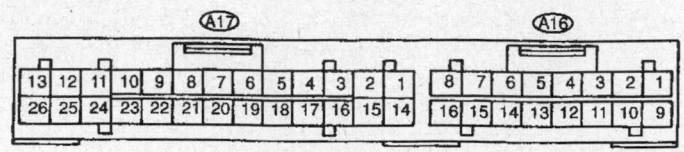

Symbols (Terminals No.)	STD Voltage (V)	Condition
BAT (A17 – 22) – GND (A17 – 11, 24)	10 – 14	Always
IG1 (A17 – 10) – GND (A17 – 11, 24)	10 – 14	IG switch ON
SR (A16 – 5) – R+ (A16 – 3)	9 – 14	IG switch ON, ABS warning light OFF
MR (A16 – 4) – R+ (A16 – 3)	Below 1.0	IG switch ON
SFRH (A16 – 8) – GND (A17 – 11, 24)	10 – 14	IG switch ON, ABS warning light OFF
SFRR (A16 – 16) – GND (A17 –11, 24)	10 – 14	IG switch ON, ABS warning light OFF
SFLH (A16 – 1) – GND (A17 – 11, 24)	10 – 14	IG switch ON, ABS warning light OFF
SFLR (A17 – 2) – GND (A17 – 11, 24)	10 – 14	IG switch ON, ABS warning light OFF
SRR (A17 – 10) – GND (A17 – 11, 24)	10 – 14	IG switch QN, ABS warning light OFF
SRH (A17 – 9) – GND (A17 – 11, 24)	10 – 14	IG switch ON, ABS warning light OFF
AST (A16 – 11) – GND (A17 – 11, 24)	10 – 14	IG switch ON, ABS warning light OFF
WA (A17 – 25) – GND (A17 – 11, 24)	Below 2.0	IG switch ON, ABS warning light ON
	10 – 14	IG switch ON, ABS warning light OFF
STP (A17 – 21) – GND (A17 – 11, 24)	Below 1.5	Stop light switch OFF
	8 – 14	Stop light switch ON
Tc (A17 – 20) – GND (A17 – 11, 24)	10 – 14	IG switch ON
Ts (A17 – 6) – GND (A17 – 11, 24)	10 – 14	IG switch ON
FR+ (A16 – 6) – FR– (A16 – 7)	AC generation	IG switch ON Slowly turn right front wheel
FL+ (A16 – 13) – FL– (A16 – 14)	AC generation	IG switch on Slowly turn left front wheel
RR+ (A17 – 15) – RR– (A17 – 16)	AC generation	IG switch ON Slowly turn right rear wheel
RL+ (A17 – 1) – RL– (A17 – 2)	AC generation	IG switch ON Slowly turn left rear wheel
GS1 (A17 – 19) – GND (A17 – 11, 24)	4 – 6 or 7 – 11	IG switch ON
GS2 (A17 – 7) – GND (A17 – 11, 24)	4 – 6	IG switch ON
EXI (A17 – 8) – GND (A17 – 11, 24)	Below 2.0	IG switch ON, center differential is locked
	10 – 14	IG switch ON, center differential is free
EXI2 (A17 – 4) – GND (A17 – 11, 24)	Below 2.0	IG switch ON, rear differential is locked (4WD)
	12 – 14	IG switch ON, rear differential is free (4WD)
	Below 2.0	Always (2WD)
EXI3 (A17 – 9) – GND (A17 – 11, 24)	Below 2.0	IG switch ON, transfer is in L4 position
	10 – 14	IG switch ON, transfer is in a position other than L4

TY4029600229000X

Fig. 381 Anti-lock brake system circuit test. 4Runner

Automatic Transmissions/ Transaxles

TABLE OF CONTENTS

Application Chart

Models	Transmission
1996	
Avalon	A541E
Camry	A140E, A541E
Celica	A140E, A246E
Corolla	A131L, A245E
Land Cruiser	A343F
Paseo	A244E
Tacoma	A43D, A340E, A340F
Previa	A340E, A340F
RAV4	A241E, A540H
Supra	A340E
Tercel	A132L, A242L
T100	A340E, A340F
4Runner	A340E, A340F
1997	
Avalon	A541E
Camry	A140E, A541E
Celica	A140E, A246E
Corolla	A131L, A245E
Land Cruiser	A343F
Paseo	A244E
Tacoma	A43D, A340E, A340F
Previa	A340E, A340F
RAV4	A241E, A540H
Supra	A340E
Tercel	A132L, A242L
T100	A340E, A340F
4Runner	A340E, A340F
1998	
Avalon	A541E
Camry	A140E & A541E

Continued

Models	Transmission
1998	
Celica	A140E
Corolla	A131L & A245E
ES300	A541E & U140E
GS300 & GS400	A650E
Land Cruiser	A343F
LS400	A650E
LX470	A343F
Paseo	A244E
RAV4	A247E & A540H
SC300 & SC400	A340E & A650E
Sienna	A540E
Supra	A340E
Tacoma	A43D, A340E & A340F
Tercel	A132L & A242L
T100	A340E & A340F
4Runner	A340E & A340F
1999	
Avalon	A541E
Camry	A140E & A541E
Celica	A140E
Corolla	A131L & A245E
ES300	A541E & U140E
GS300 & GS400	A650E
Land Cruiser	A343F
LS400	A650E
LX470	A343F
Tacoma	A43D, A340E & A340F
RAV4	A247E & A540H
RX300	U140E/F
SC300 & SC400	A340E & A650E
Sienna	A540E
Solara	A140E & A541E
Tercel	A132L & A242L
4Runner	A340E & A340F

A43D Automatic Transmission

NOTE: On Air Bag Equipped Models, Refer To "Air Bag System Precautions" Located In The Front Of This Manual For System Disarming & Arming Procedures.

INDEX

PRECAUTIONS

AIR BAG SYSTEMS

Refer to "Air Bag System Precautions" in the front of this manual for system disarming and arming procedures.

BATTERY GROUND CABLE

Prior to service disconnect battery ground cable and isolate as required.

AUDIO CODED ANTI-THEFT SYSTEM

Some models are equipped with an audio coded anti-theft system that will disable the radio when the battery cable is disconnected. The system can be identified by the "ANTI-THEFT SYSTEM" on the cassette lid. Obtain 3 digit code for input. Reset system after service as follows:

1. Obtain 3 digit audio theft code.
2. Depress 1 (PROG) while depressing righthand side of TUNE SEEK button, - - will appear in tape operation display.
3. To enter the first digit, depress 1 (PROG) button repeatedly until the number of times depressed equals the first digit (depress the 1 button six times if the first digit if five, first press equals 0).
4. To enter second digit, depress 2 (APS) button repeatedly until the number of times depressed equals the second digit.
5. To enter third digit, depress 3 (RPT) button repeatedly until the number of times depressed equals the third digit.
6. If - - - is displayed after inputting digits, repeat procedure.
7. When code appears in display, depress and hold SCAN button until SEC appears.
8. When SEC disappears audio system is operative.
9. If Err is displayed, repeat procedure. **Attempting to input code more than 9 times may permanently disable audio system.**

Problem	Possible cause	Remedy
Fluid discolored or smells burnt	Fluid contaminated Torque converter clutch faulty Transmission faulty	Replace fluid Replace torque converter clutch Disassemble and inspect transmission
Vehicle does not move in any forward position or reverse	Manual linkage out of adjustment Valve body or primary regulator faulty Parking lock pawl faulty Torque converter clutch faulty Converter drive plate broken Oil pump intake screen blocked Transmission faulty	Adjust linkage Inspect valve body Inspect parking lock pawl Replace torque converter clutch Replace drive plate Clean screen Disassemble and inspect transmission
Shift lever position incorrect	Manual linkage out of adjustment Manual valve and lever faulty Transmission faulty	Adjust linkage Inspect valve body Disassemble and inspect transmission
Harsh engagement into any drive position	Throttle cable out of adjustment Valve body or primary regulator faulty Accumulator pistons faulty Transmission faulty	Adjust throttle cable Inspect valve body Inspect accumulator pistons Disassemble and inspect transmission
Delayed 1-2, 2-3 or 3-O/D up-shift, or down-shift from O/D-3 or 3-2 then shifts back to O/D or 3	Throttle cable out of adjustment Valve body faulty Governor body faulty	Adjust throttle cable Inspect valve body Inspect governor body
Slips on 1-2, 2-3 or 3-O/D up-shift, or slips or shudders on acceleration	Manual linkage out of adjustment Throttle cable out of adjustment Valve body faulty Transmission faulty	Adjust linkage Adjust throttle cable Inspect valve body Disassemble and inspect transmission

TY5029501058010X

Fig. 1 Troubleshooting chart (Part 1 of 2). 1996–97

TROUBLESHOOTING

1996–97

Refer to **Fig. 1** for mechanical troubleshooting.

1998–99

Refer to **Fig. 2** for troubleshooting chart.

MAINTENANCE

FLUID CHECK

1. Operate vehicle, allow transmission fluid to reach normal operating temperature, 158–176°F.
2. Position vehicle on level surface, then apply parking brake.
3. With engine idling, depress brake pedal, then move shift lever through all positions from P to L, then return to P position.
4. Remove transmission dipstick and clean, then return dipstick, remove and check fluid level in HOT range.

FLUID CHANGE

1. Drain transmission fluid, then reinstall drain plug.
2. With ignition switch in Off position, add transmission fluid through filler tube.

Problem	Possible cause	Remedy
Drag, binding or tie-up on 1-2, 2-3 or 3-O/D up-shift	Manual linkage out of adjustment Valve body faulty Transmission faulty	Adjust linkage Inspect valve body Disassemble and inspect transmission
Harsh down-shift	Throttle cable out of adjustment Throttle cable and cam faulty Accumulator pistons faulty Valve body faulty Transmission faulty	Adjust throttle cable Inspect throttle cable and cam Inspect accumulator pistons Inspect valve body Disassemble and inspect transmission
No down-shift when coasting	Valve body faulty Governor body faulty	Inspect valve body Inspect governor body
Down-shift occurs too quickly or too late while coasting	Throttle cable faulty Valve body faulty Governor body faulty Transmission faulty	Inspect throttle cable Inspect valve body Inspect governor body Disassemble and inspect transmission
No O/D-3, 3-2 or 2-1 kick-down	Throttle cable out of adjustment Governor body faulty Valve body faulty	Adjust throttle cable Inspect governor body Inspect valve body
No engine braking in 2 or L position	Valve body faulty Transmission faulty	Inspect valve body Disassemble and inspect transmission
Vehicle does not hold in P	Manual linkage out of adjustment Parking lock pawl cam and spring faulty	Adjust linkage Inspect cam and spring

TY5029501058020X

Fig. 1   Troubleshooting chart (Part 2 of 2). 1996–97

Do not overfill.
3. Drain and refill capacity is 2.5 quarts. **Do not overfill.**
4. Start engine, then move shift lever through all positions.
5. With engine idling, check fluid level, add fluid to COOL level.
6. Operate vehicle, allow transmission fluid to reach normal operating temperature, 158–176°F, then recheck.

ADJUSTMENTS
MANUAL SHIFT LINKAGE
1. Remove cross shaft rod attaching nut.
2. Push cross shaft rod fully downward.
3. Return rod three notches to N position.
4. Set shift lever to N position.
5. While lightly holding shift lever toward R position, adjust cross shaft rod nut.
6. Tighten cross shaft rod nut.
7. Start engine, check transmission operation in all selector positions.

THROTTLE CABLE
1. Remove air cleaner, fully depress accelerator pedal and inspect throttle plate.
2. If throttle plate does not open fully with accelerator pedal depressed, adjust accelerator linkage.
3. With accelerator pedal held fully depressed, loosen adjusting nuts on throttle cable, **Fig. 3.**
4. Adjust cable to obtain 0–.04 inch (0–1 mm) clearance between cable housing and cable stop or painted mark, **Fig. 3.** **Service replacement cables do not have a cable stop and a mark must be painted on the inner cable for adjustment reference. If cable installed in vehicle does not have the stop or reference mark, refer to "Throttle Cable, Replace."**
5. Tighten adjuster nuts and release accelerator pedal.

6. Fully depress accelerator pedal and recheck adjustment, then install air cleaner.

NEUTRAL START SWITCH
1. Ensure engine can be started on in N or P range.
2. Loosen neutral switch attaching bolt, then set shift lever in N position.
3. Align groove and neutral basic line, **Fig. 4.**
4. Hold position, then tighten to specification.

PARK LOCK CABLE
1. Move shift lever to P position.
2. Turn ignition switch to lock position.
3. Loosen lower nuts, then ensure slide pin strikes rubber cushion.
4. Tighten attaching nuts to specification.

IN-VEHICLE REPAIRS
VALVE BODY, REPLACE
Removal
1. Raise and support vehicle, clean exterior of transmission and drain fluid.
2. Remove bolt from filler tube support, if equipped.
3. Remove oil pan retaining bolts, pan and gasket and filler tube. **Ensure filler tube seal is not damaged during removal.**
4. Remove oil feed tubes, if equipped, by prying at both ends with suitable levers.
5. Remove oil strainer retaining bolts, then the strainer and gasket.
6. Support valve body and remove 17 retaining bolts, noting position of each bolt for assembly reference, then lower valve body.
7. Disconnect throttle cable from cam, **Fig. 5,** and remove valve body.

Installation
1. Push throttle cable fitting into cam, position valve body with manual valve aligned with manual lever and loosely install several retaining bolts to hold valve body. **Valve body retaining bolts are of different lengths and must be properly positioned to avoid transmission damage. Proper position is shown in Fig. 6. Bolt lengths are given in millimeters.**
2. Remove accumulator piston retaining plate, install remaining valve body bolts and tighten all bolts hand tight.
3. Evenly tighten valve body bolts to specification.
4. Ensure oil strainer is clean, install strainer using a new gasket and tighten retaining bolts to specification.
5. Press oil feed tubes into position by hand, if equipped.
6. Install oil pan using a new gasket, evenly **torque** pan bolts to 48 inch lbs. and install filler tube retaining bolts, if equipped.
7. Install drain plug and tighten to specification.
8. Refill transmission to specified level and check transmission operation.

THROTTLE CABLE, REPLACE
Removal
1. Disconnect cable from throttle linkage, then remove PNP switch.
2. Remove bolt, then separate cable from transmission housing.
3. Remove valve body as outlined under "Valve Body, Replace."
4. Press cable out of transmission housing using a 10 mm socket.

Installation
1. Bend cable so there is a radius of 7.87 inches, as shown, **Fig. 7.**
2. Pull the inner cable lightly until a slight resistance is felt and hold.
3. Stake the stopper .031–.059 inch from end of outer cable as shown, **Fig. 7.**
4. Coat new O-ring with ATF and install onto cable.
5. Install cable into transmission case.
6. Install valve body as outlined under "Valve body Replace."
7. Connect throttle cable to transmission housing, then install PNP switch.
8. Connect throttle cable to engine.
9. Ensure transmission is filled to specified level.
10. Adjust throttle cable as outlined under "Adjustments," then road test vehicle.

GOVERNOR OR ROTOR SENSOR, REPLACE
1. Raise and support vehicle and remove driveshaft.
2. Disconnect speedometer cable and remove cable drive gear assembly.
3. Remove bolts securing rear mount to bracket, then raise transmission using a suitable jack.
4. Remove rear mount from extension housing.
5. Remove extension housing retaining

Fig. 2 Troubleshooting chart. 1998–99

Symptom	Suspect Area
Does not move in any forward position	1. Front clutch (C₁)
Does not move in reverse position	1. Rear clutch (C₂) 2. No.3 brake (B₃)
Does not move in any forward position or reverse position	1. Torque converter clutch 2. Oil pump 3. O/D direct clutch (C₀) 4. O/D one–way clutch (F₀) 5. Front planetary gear 6. Rear planetary gear
No–up shift (1st → 2nd)	1. No.2 brake (B₂) 2. No.1 one–way clutch (F₁)
No–up shift (2nd → 3rd)	1. Rear clutch (C₂)
No–up shift (3rd → O/D)	1. O/D brake (B₀)
Harsh engagement (N → R)	1. Rear clutch (C₂) 2. No.3 brake (B₃)
Harsh engagement (N → D)	1. Front clutch (C₁)
Harsh engagement (N → L)	1. No.3 brake (B₃)
Harsh engagement (1st → 2nd "D" position)	1. No.2 brake (B₂)
Harsh engagement (1st → 2nd "2" position)	1. No.1 brake (B₁) 2. No.2 brake (B₂)
Harsh engagement (2nd → 3rd)	1. Rear clutch (C₂)
Harsh engagement (3rd → O/D)	1. O/D brake (B₀)
Harsh engagement (O/D → 3rd)	1. O/D direct clutch (C₀)
Harsh engagement (3rd → 2nd)	1. No.2 brake (B₂)
Slip (Forward & Reverse)	1. O/D direct clutch (C₀) 2. Torque converter clutch 3. Oil pump 4. O/D one–way clutch (F₀)
Slip ("R" position)	1. O/D direct clutch (C₀) 2. Rear clutch (C₂) 3. No.3 brake (B₃) 4. O/D one–way clutch (F₀)
Slip (1st)	1. O/D direct clutch (C₀) 2. Front clutch (C₁) 3. O/D one–way clutch (F₀) 4. No.2 one–way clutch (F₂)
Slip (2nd)	1. O/D direct clutch (C₀) 2. Front clutch (C₁) 3. No.2 brake (B₂) 4. O/D one–way clutch (F₀) 5. No.1 one–way clutch (F₁)
Slip (3rd)	1. O/D direct clutch (C₀) 2. Front clutch (C₁) 3. Rear clutch (C₂) 4. No.2 brake (B₂) 5. O/D one–way clutch (F₀)
Slip (O/D)	1. Front clutch (C₁) 2. Rear clutch (C₂) 3. O/D brake (B₀)
No engine brake (1st "L" position)	1. No.3 brake (B₃)
No engine brake (2nd "2" position)	1. No.1 brake (B₁)
Poor acceleration	1. Torque converter clutch

TY5029901308000X

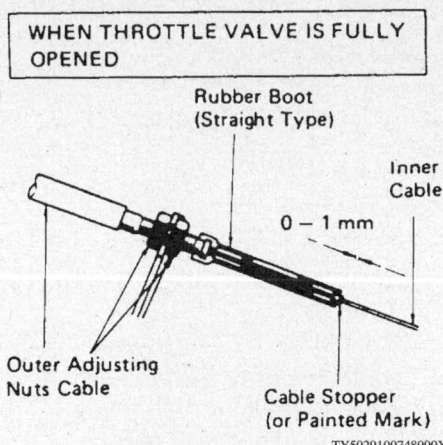

WHEN THROTTLE VALVE IS FULLY OPENED

Rubber Boot (Straight Type)

Inner Cable

0 – 1 mm

Outer Adjusting Nuts Cable

Cable Stopper (or Painted Mark)

TY5029100748000X

Fig. 3 Throttle cable adjustment

14. Remove engine wire from cabin.
15. Remove driveshaft, then disconnect speedometer cable.
16. Remove front exhaust pipe, then place jack under transmission.
17. Remove rear engine mounting bracket.
18. **On models equipped with A/C,** remove bolt and disconnect A/C compressor wire.
19. **On all models,** install engine hanger tool No. 12282–62030, or equivalent, then attach engine hoist chain to both hangers.
20. Remove four bolts and nuts securing front engine mounting insulators to frame.
21. Lift engine and transmission slowly out of vehicle. Ensure engine is clear of all wiring and hoses.
22. Place engine and transmission assembly onto suitable stand.
23. Remove stiffener plates and rear end plate.
24. Rotate crankshaft to gain access to and remove torque converter to flexplate bolts.
25. Remove starter, then separate engine from transmission.
26. Reverse procedure to install, noting the following:
    a. Measure installed distance of torque converter to front of transmission housing. Distance should be 1.25 inches or more.
    b. After installation, adjust shift lever position and throttle cable as outlined under "Adjustments."
    c. Fill transmission with specified fluid type and amount.

bolts, housing and gasket, noting position of bolts for assembly reference.
6. Remove and replace governor from output shaft as outlined for passenger cars.
7. Reverse procedure to complete installation.

TRANSMISSION
REPLACE

The engine and transmission are removed as an assembly. Refer to **Fig. 8** when replacing transmission.
1. Remove engine under cover, then drain coolant and engine oil into suitable containers.
2. Drain transmission fluid into suitable container, then remove hood.
3. Remove radiator assembly, then disconnect heater hoses.
4. Remove fan with fluid coupling and fan pulleys.
5. Remove air cleaner assembly, then disconnect accelerator, throttle and cruise control cables.
6. Disconnect EVAP, brake booster, fuel inlet and fuel return hoses.
7. Disconnect starter wire and connector, then remove wires from alternator.
8. Remove glove compartment door and lower trim panel, then disconnect four connectors from ECM.
9. Remove two bolts and the ECM.
10. Disconnect VSV connector for EVAP.
11. Disconnect vapor pressure sensor connector and clamp.
12. Disconnect VSV connector for vapor pressure sensor.
13. Disconnect igniter connector and ground strap, then remove bolt and two nuts.

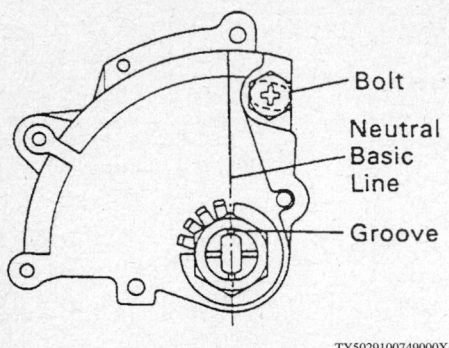

Fig. 4 Neutral safety switch adjustment

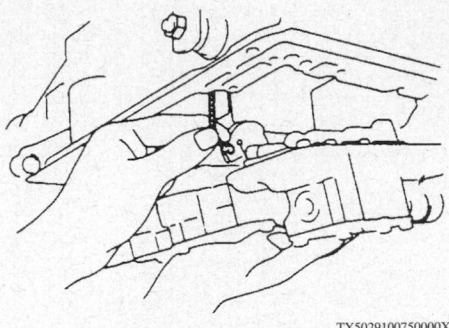

Fig. 5 Throttle cable connection

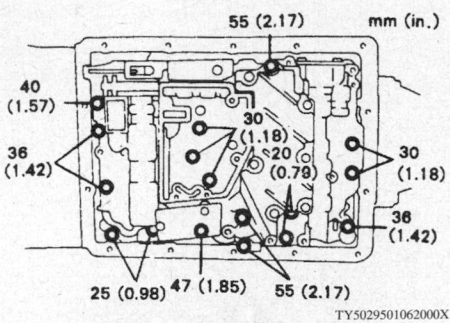

Fig. 6 Valve body bolt identification

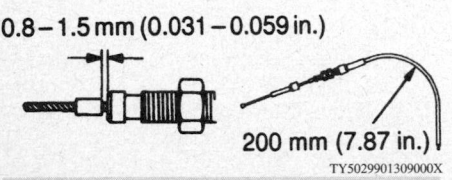

Fig. 7 Throttle cable positioning

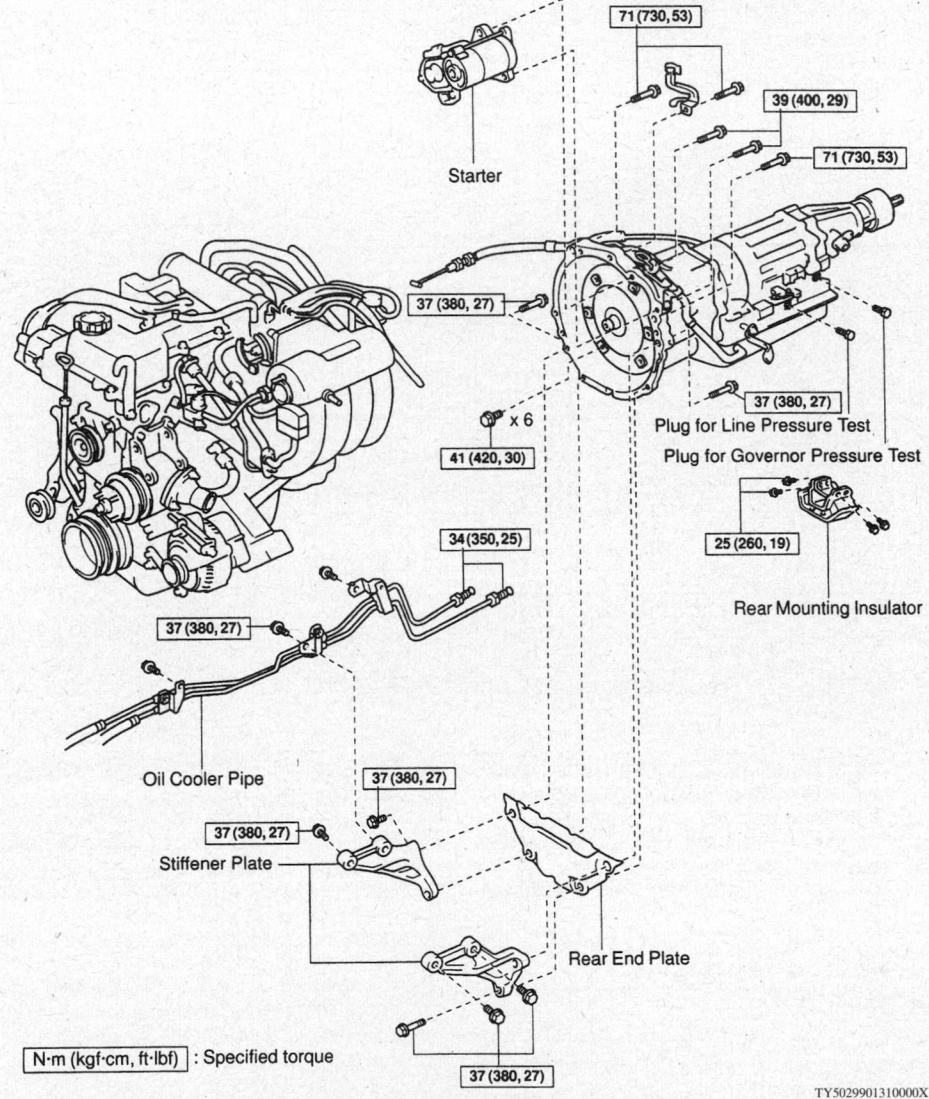

Fig. 8 Transmission replacement

TIGHTENING SPECIFICATIONS

Year	Component	Torque. Ft. Lbs.
1996-99	Auxiliary Crossmember (A43D)	70
	Center Support To Transmission	19
	Driveplate (A43D)	54
	Exhaust Pipe To Manifold	46
	Extension Housing	25
	Governor Lock Bolt	35①
	Neutral Start Switch	48①
	Oil Cooler Lines	25
	Oil Drain Plug	15
	Oil Pan Bolts	39①
	Oil Strainer	48①
	Rear Mount Bracket To Support Member	43
	Torque Converter	30
	Valve Body Bolts	84①

① — Inch lbs.

A241E Automatic Transaxle

NOTE: On Air Bag Equipped Models, Refer To "Air Bag System Precautions" Located In The Front Of This Manual For System Disarming & Arming Procedures.

NOTE: Prior To Performing Any Service Operations Listed In This Section, Consult The "Technical Service Bulletins" Section For Related Information.

INDEX

PRECAUTIONS

AIR BAG SYSTEMS

Refer to "Air Bag System Precautions" in the front of this manual for system disarming and arming procedures.

BATTERY GROUND CABLE

Prior to service disconnect battery ground cable and isolate as required.

AUDIO CODED ANTI-THEFT SYSTEM

Some models are equipped with an audio coded anti-theft system that will disable the radio when the battery cable is disconnected. The system can be identified by the "ANTI-THEFT SYSTEM" on the cassette lid. Obtain 3 digit code for input. Reset system after service as follows:

1. Obtain 3 digit audio theft code.
2. Depress 1 (PROG) while depressing righthand side of TUNE SEEK button, - - - will appear in tape operation display.
3. To enter the first digit, depress 1 (PROG) button repeatedly until the number of times depressed equals the first digit (depress the 1 button six times if the first digit if five, first press equals 0).
4. To enter second digit, depress 2 (APS) button repeatedly until the number of times depressed equals the second digit.
5. To enter third digit, depress 3 (RPT) button repeatedly until the number of times depressed equals the third digit.
6. If - - - is displayed after inputting digits, repeat procedure.
7. When code appears in display, depress and hold SCAN button until SEC appears.
8. When SEC disappears audio system is operative.
9. If Err is displayed, repeat procedure. **Attempting to input code more than 9 times may permanently disable audio system.**

TROUBLESHOOTING

FLUID DISCOLORED OR BURNED

1. Contaminated fluid.
2. Faulty torque converter.
3. Faulty transaxle.

VEHICLE DOES NOT MOVE IN ANY DRIVE GEAR

1. Incorrectly adjusted transaxle control cable.
2. Faulty valve body or primary regulator.
3. Faulty transaxle.

VEHICLE DOES NOT MOVE IN ANY RANGE

1. Faulty park lock pawl.
2. Faulty valve body or Primary regulator.
3. Faulty torque converter.
4. Broken converter driveplate.
5. Blocked oil pump intake strainer.
6. Faulty transaxle.

INCORRECT SHIFT LEVER POSITION

1. Incorrectly adjusted transaxle control cable.
2. Faulty manual valve and lever.
3. Faulty transaxle.

HARSH ENGAGEMENT INTO ANY DRIVE RANGE

1. Incorrectly adjusted throttle cable.
2. Incorrectly adjusted transaxle control cable.
3. Faulty valve body or primary regulator.
4. Faulty accumulator pistons.
5. Faulty transaxle.

DELAYED UPSHIFTS & DOWNSHIFTS

1. Incorrectly adjusted throttle cable.
2. Faulty governors.
3. Faulty valve body.
4. Faulty solenoid valve.

SLIPS ON UPSHIFTS OR SHUDDERS ON TAKEOFFS

1. Incorrectly adjusted transaxle control cable.
2. Incorrectly adjusted throttle cable.
3. Faulty valve body.
4. Faulty transaxle.
5. Faulty solenoid valve.

- If diagnostic code Nos 42, 61, 62 or 63 occur, the overdrive indicator light will begin to blink immediately to warn the driver However, an impact or shock may cause the blinking to stop; but, the code will still be retained in the ECT computer memory until canceled out
- There is no warning for diagnostic code No. 64
- In the event of a simultaneous malfunction of both No 1 and No 2 speed sensors, no diagnostic code will appear and the fail-safe system will not function. However, when driving in the D range, the transmission will not up-shift from first gear, regardless of the vehicle speed.

Trouble No. 1   Blinking overdrive indicator light (while driving)

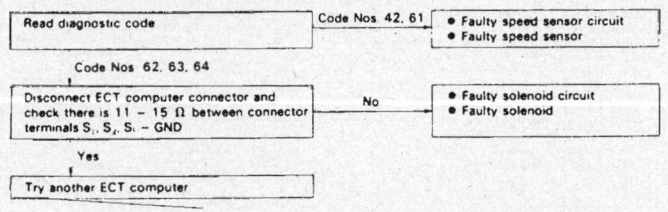

TY5028900090000X

Fig. 1   Blinking overdrive indicator lamp troubleshooting diagram

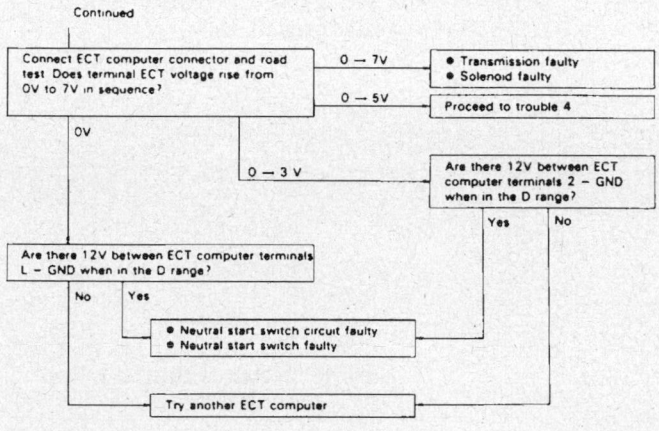

TY5028900091020X

Fig. 2   No shifting troubleshooting diagram (Part 2 of 2)

DRAG OR BINDING ON UPSHIFTS

1. Incorrectly adjusted transaxle control cable.
2. Faulty valve body.
3. Faulty transaxle.

HARSH DOWNSHIFT

1. Incorrectly adjusted throttle cable.
2. Faulty accumulator pistons.
3. Faulty valve body.
4. Faulty transaxle.

NO DOWNSHIFT WHEN COASTING

1. Faulty governor.
2. Faulty valve body.
3. Faulty solenoid valve.
4. Faulty electronic controls.

INCORRECT DOWNSHIFT

1. Incorrectly adjusted throttle cable.
2. Faulty governor.
3. Faulty valve body.
4. Faulty transaxle.
5. Faulty solenoid valve.
6. Faulty electronic control.

NO LOCK-UP IN 2, 3 OR O/D

1. Faulty valve body.

2. Faulty transaxle.
3. Faulty solenoid valve.
4. Faulty electronic control.
5. Faulty torque converter.

NO KICKDOWN

1. Incorrectly adjusted throttle cable.
2. Faulty governor.
3. Faulty valve body.
4. Faulty solenoid valve.
5. Faulty electronic control.

NO ENGINE BRAKING IN 2

1. Faulty valve body.
2. Faulty transaxle.
3. Faulty solenoid valve.
4. Faulty electronic control.

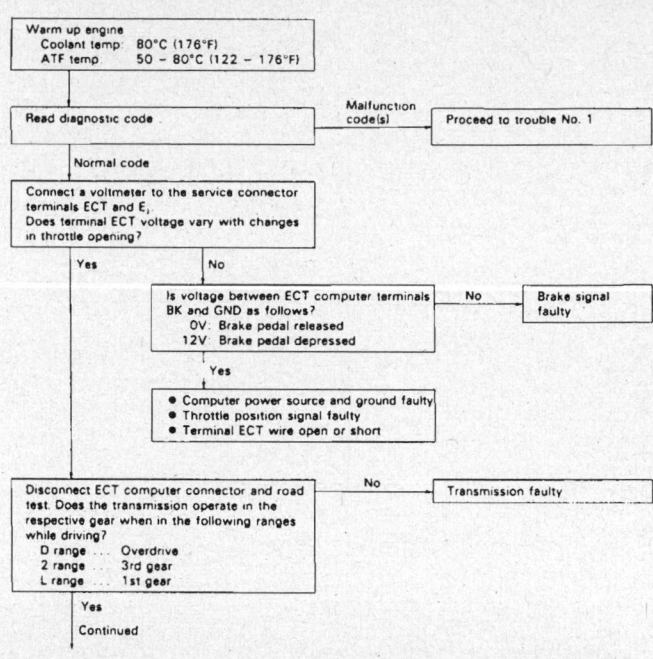

TY5028900091010X

Fig. 2   No shifting troubleshooting diagram (Part 1 of 2)

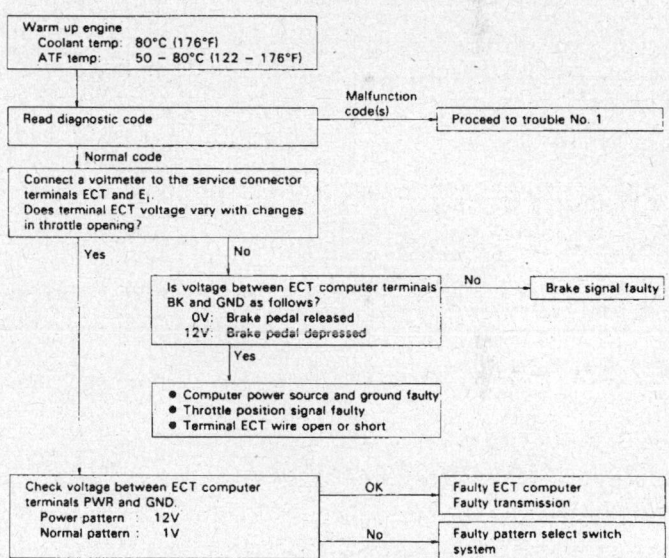

TY5028900092000X

Fig. 3   Incorrect shift point troubleshooting diagram

NO HOLD IN P

1. Incorrectly adjusted transaxle control cable.
2. Faulty parking lock pawl and rod.

NO CENTER DIFFERENTIAL CONTROL

1. Faulty electronic controls.
2. Faulty valve body.
3. Faulty transfer.
4. Faulty C/D clutch.

ELECTRIC CONTROL

For troubleshooting of electric control system, refer to **Figs. 1 through 5.**

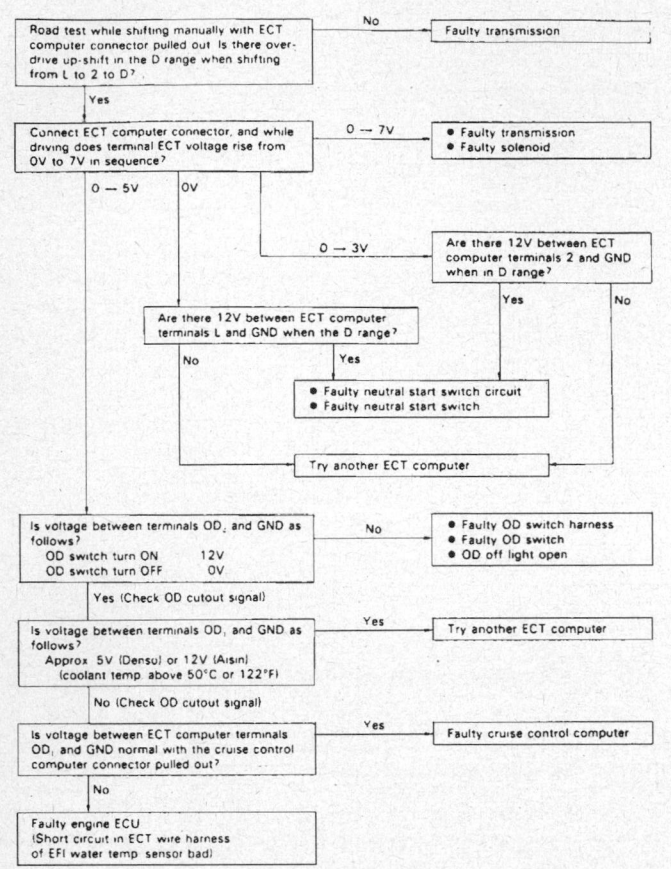

Fig. 4   No upshift to O/D troubleshooting diagram

Fig. 5   No lock-up after warm-up troubleshooting diagram.

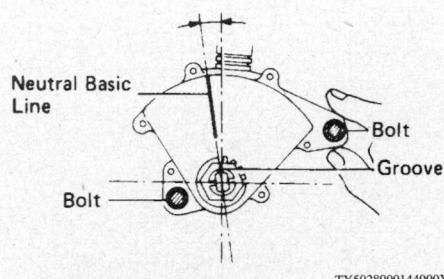

Fig. 8   Neutral start switch adjustment

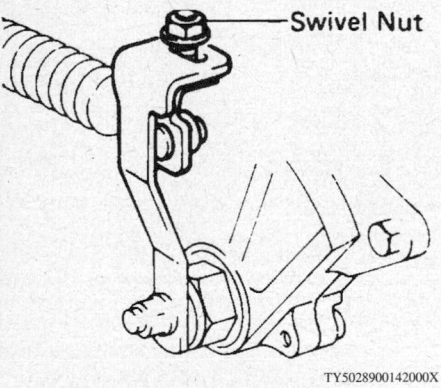

Fig. 6   Manual shift linkage adjustment

MAINTENANCE

FLUID CHECK

1. Start engine, allow transaxle fluid to reach 158–176°F.
2. Position vehicle on level surface, then set parking brake.
3. With engine idling, brake pedal depressed, move shift lever through all positions.
4. Remove transaxle dipstick, wipe clean, then replace.
5. Remove dipstick again, check fluid at HOT level.

Fig. 7   Throttle cable adjustment

FLUID CHANGE

1. Drain transaxle fluid.
2. Install drain plug and new gasket.
3. Add fluid through filler tube. **Do not overfill.**
4. Start engine, ensure smooth shift operation in all positions.
5. With engine at idle, check fluid COOL level, fill as required.
6. Allow vehicle to reach normal operating temperatures, then recheck level.

ADJUSTMENTS

MANUAL SHIFT LINKAGE

1. Loosen swivel nut on lever, then push manual lever fully toward right side of vehicle, **Fig. 6.**
2. Return lever two notches to Neutral position, then place selector lever in Neutral position.
3. Manually hold lever tightly toward R range, then tighten swivel nut to specification.

THROTTLE CABLE

1. Hold accelerator pedal in fully depressed position, then loosen cable adjusting nuts, **Fig. 7.**
2. Adjust cable to obtain .040 inch between end of boot and stopper on cable, then tighten adjusting nut.
3. Fully depress accelerator pedal and recheck adjustment, then road test vehicle.

NEUTRAL SAFETY SWITCH

1. Loosen neutral safety switch attaching bolts.
2. Place selector lever in Neutral position.
3. Disconnect electrical connector.
4. Align groove in with neutral basic line, **Fig. 8.**
5. Tighten switch retaining bolts to specification.
6. Reconnect electrical connector to

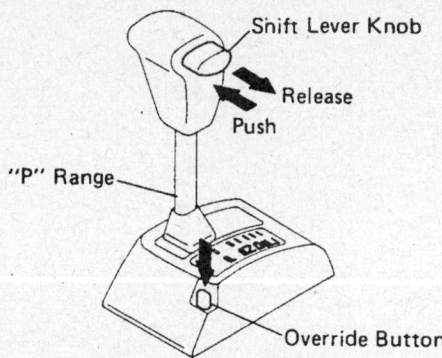

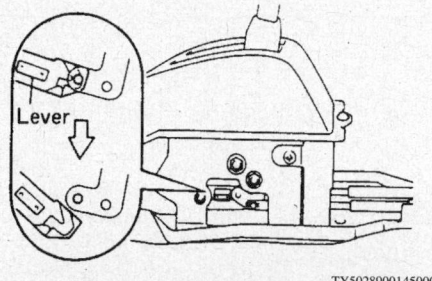

Fig. 9 Adjust park lock cable

switch, then ensure engine starts with selector lever in "N" and " P" only.

PARK LOCK CABLE

1. Remove slide key, then lightly pull park lock cable, to remove looseness.
2. Do not strongly pull on cable.
3. Install lock cable slide key.
4. Push set cable lever inward, **Fig. 9,** set cable lever should go down.
5. Move shift lever to P range.
6. While pushing shift lock override button, push shift lever knob, then release it. Ensure set cable lever is released.

IN-VEHICLE REPAIRS

VALVE BODY, REPLACE

REMOVAL

1. Clean area around pan, then drain transmission fluid, then remove engine undercover.
2. Remove oil pan and gasket, then the oil strainer.
3. Remove apply tube bracket attaching bolts, then the apply tube.
4. Remove oil tubes using a suitable screwdriver, then the manual detent spring.
5. Disconnect solenoid connector.
6. Remove valve body attaching bolts, then disconnect throttle cable.
7. Disconnect manual valve connecting rod.
8. Remove valve body, then the governor apply gasket.

INSTALLATION

1. Install governor apply gasket, then connect manual valve connecting rod.
2. Hold valve body in place, then manually retain cam in downward position and slip cable end into slot.

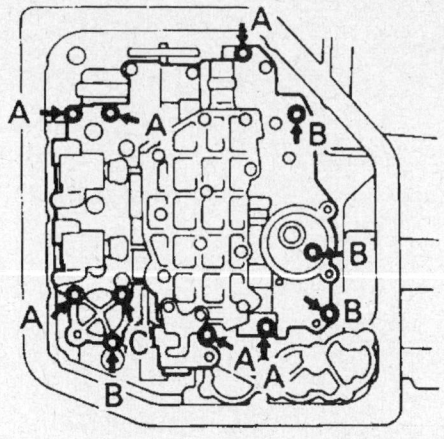

Fig. 10 Valve body bolt identification

3. Position valve body in installation position, then insert and finger tighten attaching bolts. Tighten bolts to specification. Attaching bolt lengths (mm) are indicated in, **Fig. 10.**
4. Connect solenoid connector.
5. Insert and finger tighten attaching bolts, then tighten to specification.
6. Install detent spring, then insert and finger tighten attaching bolt. Tighten attaching bolt to specification.
7. Ensure manual lever is in contact with center of roller at tip of detent spring, then install oil tubes.
8. Install and tighten tube clamp attaching bolt to specification.
9. Install oil strainer.
10. Insert magnet into pan, then install oil pan with new gasket.
11. Insert oil pan attaching bolts, then tighten to specification.
12. Install drain plug with new gasket, then tighten to specification.
13. Install engine undercover.
14. Fill transaxle to specifications, then ensure proper fluid level.

THROTTLE CABLE, REPLACE

Removal

1. Disconnect throttle cable from engine.
2. Drain transaxle fluid.
3. Remove engine undercover.
4. Remove neutral start switch.
5. Remove oil pan and gasket.
6. Disconnect throttle cable from cam.
7. Remove throttle cable attaching plate, then remove.

Installation

1. Install throttle cable, then plate.
2. Connect throttle cable to cam.
3. Install oil pan and drain plug.
4. Install and adjust neutral start switch.
5. Install engine undercover.
6. Position cable stop for reference as follows:
   a. Bend cable to a radius of approximately 7.87 inches as shown, **Fig. 11. Cable stop is not staked in place on replacement cable.**
   b. Lightly pull inner cable from housing until a slight resistance is felt,

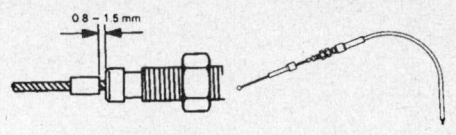

Fig. 11 Positioning throttle cable for stopper installation

   then hold in position.
   c. Stake stopper onto inner cable so that .031–.059 inch clearance exists between stop and cable housing.
   d. Connect and adjust throttle cable as described previously.
7. Ensure correct transaxle fluid level, then road test vehicle.

GOVERNOR VALVE, REPLACE

REMOVAL

1. Disconnect speedometer cable.
2. Remove governor cover, then the O-ring.
3. Remove governor body with thrust washer, then the gasket.

INSTALLATION

1. Install new gasket on governor body adapter, then install governor body adapter.
2. Install governor body with thrust washer.
3. Install governor cover with O-ring, then connect speedometer cable.
4. Ensure transaxle fluid level is to specifications, then road test vehicle.

DIFFERENTIAL CASE, REPLACE

REMOVAL

1. Remove neutral start switch, then the speedometer driven gear.
2. Remove governor body, then the oil pan.
3. Remove valve body, then the 11 transaxle rear cover attaching bolts. Tap cover from case using a suitable mallet.
4. Remove intermediate shaft, then the parking lock pawl bracket and rod.
5. Remove parking lock pawl, then the manual shaft and lever.
6. Remove manual shaft and lever, then the governor pressure adapter.
7. Remove carrier cover.

INSTALLATION

1. Install governor pressure adapter, then the manual shaft and lever.
2. Install parking lock pawl.
3. Install parking lock rod, then the bracket.
4. Install intermediate shaft.
5. Install transaxle rear cover with new gasket, then insert retaining bolts and tighten to specification.
6. Install valve body, then the governor body.
7. Install oil pan.
8. Install speedometer driven gear, then

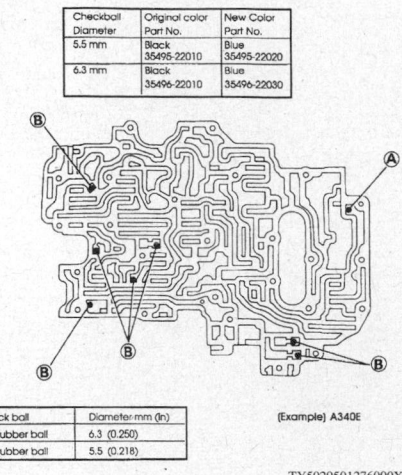

Checkball Diameter	Original color Part No.	New Color Part No.
5.5 mm	Black 35495-22010	Blue 35495-22020
6.3 mm	Black 35496-22010	Blue 35496-22030

Check ball	Diameter-mm (In)
Ⓐ Rubber ball	6.3 (0.250)
Ⓑ Rubber ball	5.5 (0.218)

(Example) A340E

TY5029501276000X

Fig. 13 Checkball diameters & locations

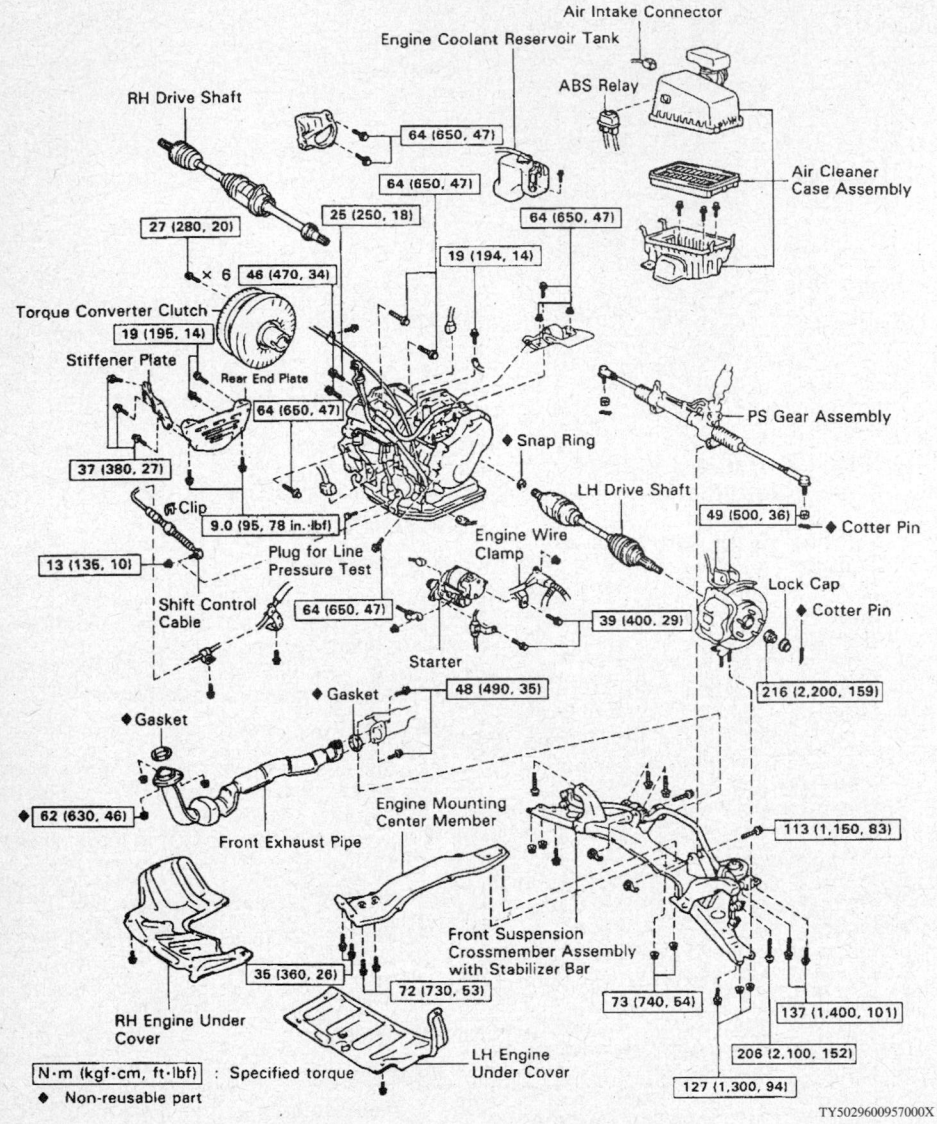

N·m (kgf·cm, ft·lbf) : Specified torque

◆ Non-reusable part

TY5029600957000X

Fig. 12 Transaxle replacement

the neutral start switch.

SECOND BRAKE SERVO ASSEMBLY, REPLACE

REMOVAL

1. Raise and support vehicle, then remove shift cable bracket at transaxle.
2. Remove snap ring.
3. Remove cover.
4. Remove piston, then the outer spring.

INSTALLATION

1. Insert piston, less outer spring, then install snap ring.
2. Install tool No. J-35679, or equivalent, then observe groove on plunger of tool.
3. Press button on tool, to allow tool to push brake apply rod into case. If groove is visible, piston stroke is correct (.059–.118 inch). If stroke is greater than specified, replace piston rod with 2.870 or 2.811 inch rod as needed.
4. Remove snap ring, then install piston and outer spring.
5. Install tool No. J-35549, or equivalent, to compress spring, then insert snap ring.
6. Install cover, then the shift cable bracket.
7. Lower vehicle.

TRANSAXLE

REPLACE

1. Remove as shown in, **Fig. 12.**
2. Reverse procedure to install.

TECHNICAL SERVICE BULLETINS

Harsh Shifts Due To Check Ball Failure

MODELS EQUIPPED w/ RUBBER CHECKBALLS

Harsh shift complaints are often cause by worn valve body checkballs. A more durable checkball available from the manufacture, original checkballs were black in color. The new designed checkballs are blue in color, **Fig. 13**

TIGHTENING SPECIFICATIONS

Year	Component	Torque/ Ft. Lbs.
1996–97	Apply Tube Bracket	84①
	Control Cable Bolt	108①
	Cooler Lines	20
	Exhaust Pipe Nut	46
	Kickdown Pressure Solenoid	56①
	Kickdown Pressure Switch	56①
	LH Engine Mount Bracket	32
	Neutral Safety Switch	58①
	Neutral Start Switch Bolt	48①
	Neutral Start Switch Nut	61①
	Oil Drain Plug	13
	Oil Pan Bolts	43①
	Oil Strainer	84①
	Oil Tube	84①
	Rear Engine Mount Bracket To Body	54
	Rear Engine Mount Bracket To Engine	43
	Rear Transaxle Cover	18
	Solenoid Wire Assembly Clamp	84①
	Speed Sensor	48①
	Speed Sensor Cover Bracket	108①
	Starter	29
	Test Plug	65①
	Torque Converter To Driveplate	18
	Transaxle Bolts (10 mm)	25
	Transaxle Bolts (12 mm)	47
	Transaxle Housing To Case	22
	Transaxle Rear Cover To Rear Case	18
	Valve Body Bolt	84①
	Valve Body Detent Spring	84①
	Valve Body To Case	84①

① — Inch lbs.

A131L & A132L Automatic Transaxles

NOTE: On Air Bag Equipped Models, Refer To "Air Bag System Precautions" Located In The Front Of This Manual For System Disarming & Arming Procedures.

INDEX

PRECAUTIONS

AIR BAG SYSTEMS

Refer to "Air Bag System Precautions" in the front of this manual for system disarming and arming procedures.

BATTERY GROUND CABLE

Prior to service disconnect battery ground cable and isolate as required.

AUDIO CODED ANTI-THEFT SYSTEM

Some models are equipped with an audio coded anti-theft system that will disable the radio when the battery cable is disconnected. The system can be identified by the "ANTI-THEFT SYSTEM" on the cassette lid. Obtain 3 digit code for input. Reset system after service as follows:
1. Obtain 3 digit audio theft code.
2. Depress 1 (PROG) while depressing righthand side of TUNE SEEK button, - - - will appear in tape operation display.
3. To enter the first digit, depress 1 (PROG) button repeatedly until the number of times depressed equals the first digit (depress the 1 button six times if the first digit if five, first press equals 0).
4. To enter second digit, depress 2 (APS) button repeatedly until the number of times depressed equals the second digit.
5. To enter third digit, depress 3 (RPT) button repeatedly until the number of times depressed equals the third digit.
6. If - - - is displayed after inputting digits, repeat procedure.
7. When code appears in display, de-press and hold SCAN button until SEC appears.
8. When SEC disappears audio system is operative.
9. If Err is displayed, repeat procedure. **Attempting to input code more than 9 times may permanently disable audio system.**

TROUBLESHOOTING

FLUID DISCOLORED OR BURNED

1. Contaminated fluid.
2. Faulty torque converter.
3. Faulty transaxle.

VEHICLE DOES NOT MOVE IN ANY DRIVE GEAR

1. Incorrectly adjusted transaxle control cable.
2. Faulty valve body or primary regulator.
3. Faulty transaxle.

VEHICLE DOES NOT MOVE IN ANY RANGE

1. Faulty park lock pawl.
2. Faulty valve body or Primary regulator.
3. Faulty torque converter.
4. Broken converter driveplate.
5. Blocked oil pump intake strainer.
6. Faulty transaxle.

INCORRECT SHIFT LEVER POSITION

1. Improperly adjusted transaxle control cable.
2. Faulty manual valve and lever.
3. Faulty transaxle.

HARSH ENGAGEMENT INTO ANY DRIVE RANGE

1. Incorrectly adjusted throttle cable.
2. Improperly adjusted transaxle control cable.
3. Faulty valve body or primary regulator.
4. Faulty accumulator pistons.
5. Faulty transaxle.

DELAYED UPSHIFTS & DOWNSHIFTS

1. Improperly adjusted throttle cable.
2. Faulty governors.
3. Faulty valve body.
4. Faulty solenoid valve.

SLIPS ON UPSHIFTS OR SHUDDERS ON TAKEOFF

1. Improperly adjusted transaxle control cable.
2. Improperly adjusted throttle cable.
3. Faulty valve body.
4. Faulty transaxle.
5. Faulty solenoid valve.

DRAG OR BINDING ON UPSHIFT

1. Improperly adjusted transaxle control cable.
2. Faulty valve body.
3. Faulty transaxle.

HARSH DOWNSHIFT

1. Improperly adjusted throttle cable.
2. Faulty accumulator pistons.
3. Faulty valve body.
4. Faulty transaxle.

Fig. 1 Manual shift linkage adjustment

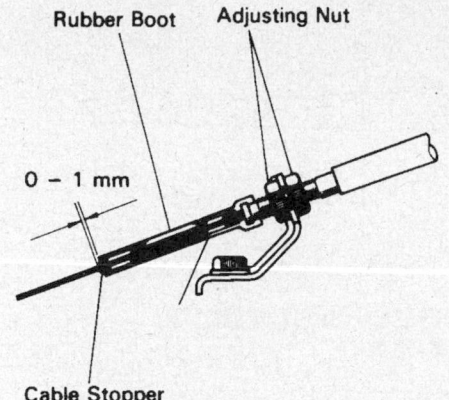

Fig. 2 Throttle cable adjustment

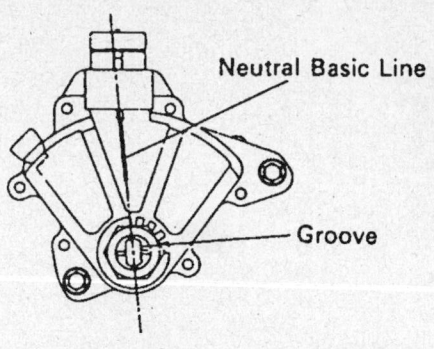

Fig. 3 Park/Neutral Position switch adjustment

NO DOWNSHIFT WHEN COASTING

1. Faulty governor.
2. Faulty valve body.
3. Faulty solenoid valve.
4. Faulty electronic controls.

INCORRECT DOWNSHIFT

1. Improperly adjusted throttle cable.
2. Faulty governor.
3. Faulty valve body.
4. Faulty transaxle.
5. Faulty solenoid valve.
6. Faulty electronic control.

NO LOCK-UP IN 2, 3 OR O/D

1. Faulty valve body.
2. Faulty transaxle.
3. Faulty solenoid valve.
4. Faulty electronic control.
5. Faulty torque converter.

NO KICKDOWN

1. Improperly adjusted throttle cable.
2. Faulty governor.
3. Faulty valve body.
4. Faulty solenoid valve.
5. Faulty electronic control.

NO ENGINE BRAKING IN 2

1. Faulty valve body.
2. Faulty transaxle.
3. Faulty solenoid valve.
4. Faulty electronic control.

NO HOLD IN P

1. Improperly adjusted transaxle Control Cable.
2. Faulty parking lock pawl and rod.

NO CENTER DIFFERENTIAL CONTROL

1. Faulty electronic controls.
2. Faulty valve body.
3. Faulty transfer.
4. Faulty C/D clutch.

MAINTENANCE

FLUID CHECK

1. Allow vehicle to reach operating temperature, 158–176°F.

2. Position vehicle on level surface, then apply parking brake.
3. With engine idling, move shift selector through all positions.
4. Remove transmission dipstick, wipe clean, then replace.
5. Remove dipstick again, check HOT fluid level.

FLUID CHANGE

1. Remove drain plug and drain fluid.
2. Install drain plug and new gasket.
3. Add fluid through filler tube. **Do not overfill.**
4. Refer to "Lubricant Data & Maintenance Charts," for capacity and fluid type.
5. Start engine, ensure smooth shift operation in all positions.
6. With engine at idle, check fluid COOL level, fill as required.
7. Allow vehicle to reach normal operating temperatures, then recheck level.

ADJUSTMENTS

MANUAL SHIFT LINKAGE

1. Loosen swivel nut on lever, then push manual lever fully toward right side of vehicle, **Fig. 1.**
2. Return lever two notches to Neutral position, then place selector lever in Neutral position.
3. Manually hold lever tightly toward R range, then tighten swivel nut to specifications.

THROTTLE CABLE

1. Hold accelerator pedal in fully depressed position, then loosen cable adjusting nuts, **Fig. 2.**
2. Adjust cable to obtain 0–.04 inch between end of boot and stopper on cable, then tighten adjusting nut to specifications.
3. Fully depress accelerator pedal and recheck adjustment, then road test vehicle.

PARK/NEUTRAL POSITION SWITCH

1. Loosen neutral safety switch attaching bolts.

2. Place selector lever in Neutral position.
3. Disconnect electrical connector.
4. Align groove in with neutral basic line, **Fig. 3.**
5. Reconnect electrical connector to switch, then ensure engine starts with selector lever in "N" and " P" only.

PARK LOCK CABLE

1. Remove slide key, then lightly pull park lock cable, to remove looseness.
2. Do not strongly pull on cable.
3. Install lock cable slide key.
4. Push set cable lever inward, **Fig. 9,** set cable lever should go down.
5. Move shift lever to P range.
6. While pushing shift lock override button, push shift lever knob, then release it. Ensure set cable lever is released.

IN-VEHICLE REPAIRS

VALVE BODY, REPLACE

Removal

1. Clean area around pan, remove engine undercover, then drain transmission fluid.
2. Remove oil pan and gasket, then the oil strainer.
3. Remove apply tube bracket attaching bolts, then the apply tube.
4. Remove oil tubes using a suitable screwdriver, then the manual detent spring.
5. Remove manual valve, then the manual valve body.
6. Remove valve body attaching bolts, then disconnect throttle cable.
7. Remove valve body, then the governor apply gasket.
8. Remove governor oil strainer.

Installation

1. Install governor oil strainer.
2. Install governor apply gasket.
3. Hold valve body in place, then manually retain cam in downward position and slip cable end into slot.
4. Position valve body in installation position, then insert and finger tighten attaching bolts. Attaching bolt lengths (mm) are indicated in, **Fig. 4.**
5. Align manual valve with pin on manual valve lever, then install manual valve body.

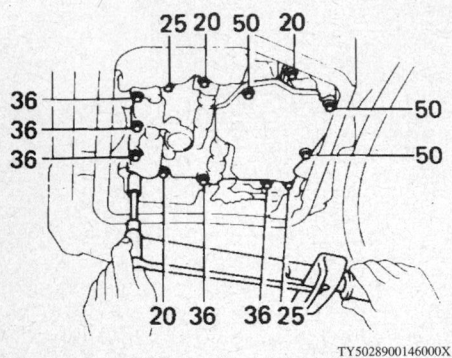

Fig. 4 Valve body bolt specifications (mm)

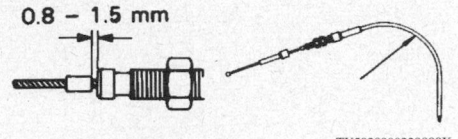

Fig. 5 Throttle cable positioning for installation

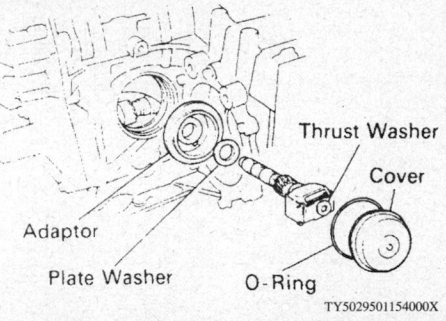

Fig. 6 Governor valve removal

6. Insert and finger tighten attaching bolts, then tighten as specified.
7. Install detent spring, then insert and finger tighten attaching bolt. Tighten as specified.
8. Ensure manual lever is in contact with center of roller at tip of detent spring, then install oil tubes.
9. Install apply tube bracket.
10. Install oil strainer.
11. Insert magnet into pan, then install oil pan with new gasket.
12. Insert oil pan attaching bolts.
13. Install drain plug with new gasket.
14. Install engine undercover.
15. Fill transaxle to specifications, then ensure proper fluid level.

THROTTLE CABLE, REPLACE

Removal

1. Disconnect throttle cable from throttle linkage.
2. Disconnect transaxle control cable from manual shift lever, then remove lever.
3. Remove neutral safety switch, then the valve body as previously described.
4. Remove cable retaining bolt, then the retaining plate.
5. Pull cable from transaxle case.

Installation

1. Insert cable into transaxle case, then install retaining plate and bolt.
2. Install valve body as previously described, then position cable stop for adjustment reference as follows:
   a. Bend cable to a radius of approximately 7.87 inches as shown, Fig. 5. Cable stop is not staked in place on replacement cable.
   b. Lightly pull inner cable from housing until a slight resistance is felt, then hold in position.
   c. Stake stopper onto inner cable so that .031–.059 inch clearance exists between stop and cable housing.
   d. Connect and adjust throttle cable as previously described.
3. Install neutral safety switch, then the manual shift lever. Adjust switch as previously described.
4. Connect transaxle control cable.

5. Ensure transaxle fluid level is to specifications, then road test vehicle.

GOVERNOR VALVE, REPLACE

Removal

1. Remove transaxle dust cover, then the righthand driveshaft and governor bracket.
2. Remove governor cover, then the O-ring, Fig. 6.
3. Remove governor body with thrust washer.
4. Remove washer, then the governor body adapter.

Installation

1. Install governor body adapter.
2. Install washer on governor body.
3. Install governor cover with O-ring.
4. Install righthand driveshaft, then the transaxle dust cover.
5. Ensure transaxle fluid level is to specifications, then road test vehicle.

DIFFERENTIAL CASE, REPLACE

Removal

1. Remove neutral start switch, then the speedometer driven gear.
2. Remove governor body, then the oil pan.
3. Remove valve body, then the 11 transaxle rear cover attaching bolts. Tap cover from case using a suitable mallet.
4. Remove intermediate shaft, then the parking lock pawl bracket and rod.
5. Remove parking lock pawl, then the manual shaft and lever.
6. Remove manual shaft and lever, then the governor pressure adapter.
7. Remove carrier cover.

Installation

1. Install governor pressure adapter, then the manual shaft and lever.
2. Install parking lock pawl.
3. Install parking lock rod, then the bracket.
4. Install intermediate shaft.
5. Install transaxle rear cover with new gasket, then insert retaining bolts and tighten to specification.
6. Install valve body, then the governor body.
7. Install oil pan.
8. Install speedometer driven gear, then the neutral start switch.

TRANSAXLE

REPLACE
COROLLA

1. Remove level gauge, throttle cable, engine upper side mounting bolts and ground cable, Fig. 7.
2. Disconnect harness wire and throttle cable clamps.
3. Remove speed sensor connectors, then raise vehicle.
4. Remove engine undercover, then disconnect driveshaft and suspend by cord.
5. Jack up transaxle.
6. Remove exhaust pipe, then install engine support fixture.
7. Remove suspension cover.
8. Remove starter, then disconnect neutral start switch.
9. Remove nut from control shaft lever, disconnect clip and remove shift control cable.
10. Remove two oil cooler tubes and filler tube.
11. Remove converter cover, turn crankshaft to gain access to remove six bolts, then remove seven bolts and transaxle.
12. Reverse procedure to install.

TERCEL

Refer to Fig. 8 when removing transaxle.
1. Remove battery, air cleaner assembly and throttle cable.
2. Remove upper side mounting bolts and starter motor.
3. Remove ground cables and bracket.
4. Install engine support fixture, then raise and support vehicle.
5. Remove engine under cover.
6. Remove right and left drive shafts.
7. Disconnect speedometer cable and control cable.
8. Disconnect park/neutral position switch connector.
9. Disconnect oil cooler hose from pipe.
10. Remove front exhaust pipe.
11. Remove torque converter mounting bolts.
12. Support transaxle with suitable jack, then disconnect left engine mounting bracket.
13. Remove rear engine mount.
14. Remove transaxle mounting bolts.
15. Remove transaxle from vehicle.
16. Reverse procedure to install.

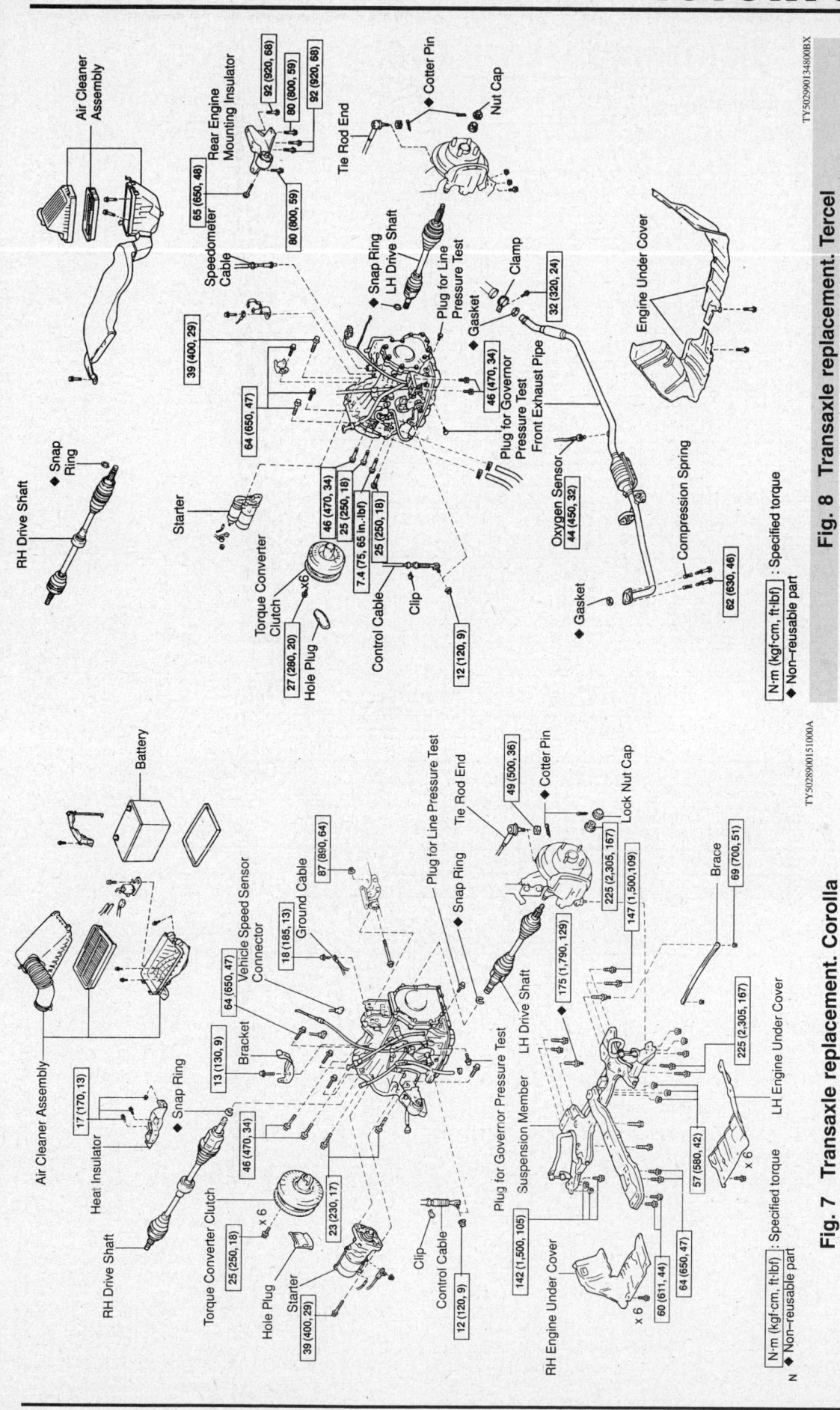

Fig. 8 Transaxle replacement. Tercel

TY50299013480OBX

Fig. 7 Transaxle replacement. Corolla

TY50289X00151000A

N·m (kgf·cm, ft·lbf) : Specified torque
◆ Non-reusable part

TIGHTENING SPECIFICATIONS

Component	Torque/Ft. Lbs.
A131L TRANSAXLE	
Accumulator Cover	84①
Cooler Pipe Union	22
Drain Plug	15
Lower Valve Body Cover	58①
Neutral Start Switch	61①
Oil Pan Bolts	49①
Oil Pump To Case	16
Oil Pump To Stator Shaft	84①
Oil Strainer	84①
Parking Lock Pawl Bracket	65①
Second Coast Brake Band Guide	48①
Solenoid Valve	58①
Transaxle Housing Bolts	22
Transaxle Rear Cover	18
Valve Body Bolts	84①
Valve Body Halves	58①
A132L TRANSAXLE	
Accumulator Cover	84①
Cooler Pipe Union	20
Drain Plug	15
Lower Valve Body Cover	58①
Neutral Start Switch	61①
Oil Pan Bolts	43①
Oil Pump To Case	18
Oil Pump To Stator Shaft	84①
Oil Strainer	84①
Parking Lock Pawl Bracket	65①
Second Coast Brake Band Guide	48①
Solenoid Valve	58①
Transaxle Housing Bolts	22
Transaxle Rear Cover	18
Valve Body Bolts	84①
Valve Body Halves	48①

① — Inch lbs.

A140E Automatic Transaxle

NOTE: On Air Bag Equipped Models, Refer To "Air Bag System Precautions" Located In The Front Of This Manual For System Disarming & Arming Procedures.

INDEX

PRECAUTIONS

AIR BAG SYSTEMS

Refer to "Air Bag System Precautions" in the front of this manual for system disarming and arming procedures.

BATTERY GROUND CABLE

Prior to service disconnect battery ground cable and isolate as required.

AUDIO CODED ANTI-THEFT SYSTEM

Some models are equipped with an audio coded anti-theft system that will disable the radio when the battery cable is disconnected. The system can be identified by the "ANTI-THEFT SYSTEM" on the cassette lid. Obtain 3 digit code for input. Reset system after service as follows:

1. Obtain 3 digit audio theft code.
2. Depress 1 (PROG) while depressing righthand side of TUNE SEEK button, - - - will appear in tape operation display.
3. To enter the first digit, depress 1 (PROG) button repeatedly until the number of times depressed equals the first digit (depress the 1 button six times if the first digit if five, first press equals 0).
4. To enter second digit, depress 2 (APS) button repeatedly until the number of times depressed equals the second digit.
5. To enter third digit, depress 3 (RPT) button repeatedly until the number of times depressed equals the third digit.
6. If - - - is displayed after inputting digits, repeat procedure.
7. When code appears in display, depress and hold SCAN button until SEC appears.
8. When SEC disappears audio system is operative.
9. If Err is displayed, repeat procedure. **Attempting to input code more than 9 times may permanently disable audio system.**

TROUBLESHOOTING

FLUID DISCOLORED OR SMELLS BURNED

1. Contaminated automatic transaxle fluid (ATF).
2. Faulty torque converter clutch.

VEHICLE DOES NOT MOVE IN ANY RANGE

1. Improperly adjusted control cable.
2. Faulty parking lock pawl control.
3. Faulty valve body or primary regulator.
4. Faulty torque converter clutch.
5. Broken converter driveplate.
6. Blocked oil pump intake screen.

INCORRECT SHIFT LEVER POSITION

1. Improperly adjusted control cable.
2. Faulty manual valve and lever.

HARSH ENGAGEMENT INTO ANY DRIVE RANGE

1. Improperly adjusted throttle cable.
2. Faulty valve body or primary regulator.
3. Faulty accumulator pistons.

NO DOWNSHIFT WHEN COASTING

1. Faulty valve body.
2. Faulty solenoid valve.
3. Malfunctioning electrical controls.

DOWNSHIFT OCCURS TOO QUICKLY OR TOO LATE WHILE COASTING

1. Faulty throttle cable.
2. Faulty valve body.
3. Faulty solenoid valve.
4. Malfunctioning electrical controls.

NO KICKDOWN

1. Faulty solenoid valve.
2. Malfunctioning electrical controls.
3. Faulty valve body.

NO ENGINE BRAKING IN 2 OR L RANGE

1. Faulty solenoid valve.
2. Malfunctioning electrical controls.
3. Faulty valve body.

VEHICLE DOES NOT HOLD IN P RANGE

1. Improperly adjusted control cable.
2. Faulty parking lock pawl cam and spring.

DELAYED UPSHIFTS OR DOWNSHIFTS

1. Malfunctioning electrical controls.
2. Faulty valve body.
3. Faulty solenoid valve.

SLIPS ON UPSHIFTS OR SLIPS/SHUDDERS ON ACCELERATION

1. Improperly adjusted control cable.
2. Improperly adjusted throttle cable.

3. Faulty valve body.
4. Faulty solenoid valve.

DRAG, BINDING OR TIE-UP ON UPSHIFTS

1. Improperly adjusted control cable.
2. Faulty valve body.

NO LOCK-UP IN 2, 3 OR OVERDRIVE (OD)

1. Malfunctioning electrical controls.
2. Faulty valve body.
3. Faulty solenoid valve.

HARSH DOWNSHIFTS

1. Improperly adjusted throttle cable.
2. Faulty throttle cable and cam.
3. Faulty accumulator pistons.
4. Faulty valve body.

ELECTRONIC CONTROL MODULE (ECM)

For troubleshooting of the electronic control system, refer to **Figs. 1 through 7.**

MAINTENANCE

FLUID CHECK

1. Operate vehicle, allow automatic transaxle fluid (ATF) temperature to reach 158–176°F.
2. Position vehicle on level surface, apply parking brake.
3. With engine at idle, move shift lever through all positions.
4. Remove transaxle dipstick, wipe clean, then replace.
5. Remove dipstick again, then check if ATF level is in HOT range.

FLUID CHANGE

1. Drain automatic transaxle fluid (ATF), then install drain plug and new gasket.
2. With engine Off, add ATF through dipstick tube. **Do not overfill.**
3. Start engine, then move shift selector through all positions, ensuring smooth operation.
4. Allow to idle, then check at COOL level.
5. Allow to reach normal operating temperature, then recheck.

ADJUSTMENTS

THROTTLE CABLE

1. Remove air intake hose, then fully depress accelerator pedal ensuring throttle valve is fully open. If not, adjust accelerator linkage.
2. Fully depress accelerator pedal and adjust cable to obtain 0–.04 inch clearance between end of housing and inner cable stop, **Fig. 8.**
3. Tighten adjusting nuts to secure adjustment, then release accelerator pedal.
4. Fully depress accelerator pedal and recheck adjustment.
5. Install air hose and road test vehicle.

SHIFT CONTROL CABLE

1. Loosen swivel nut on selector lever at transaxle.
2. Push manual lever all the way to right side of vehicle, then return lever two notches to neutral position.
3. Position selector lever to N.
4. Hold lever slightly toward R range side and tighten swivel nut to specifications.

PARK/NEUTRAL POSITION (NEUTRAL START) SWITCH

1. Loosen park/neutral position (neutral start) switch attaching bolts.
2. Position transaxle selector lever to N.
3. Align groove in neutral basic line, **Fig. 9.**
4. Maintain groove in position, then tighten attaching bolts to specification.
5. Adjust idle speed to specifications.

IN-VEHICLE REPAIRS

VEHICLE SPEED SENSOR, REPLACE

1. Disconnect speed sensor connector, then the bolt and bracket.
2. Remove speed sensor and O-ring.
3. Reverse procedure to install, **Torque** bracket retaining bolt to 12 ft. lbs.

THROTTLE CABLE, REPLACE

1. Disconnect throttle cable housing from bracket.
2. Disconnect throttle cable from throttle linkage.
3. Remove park/neutral position (neutral start) switch as follows:
   a. Disconnect clip, then the control cable from manual shift lever.
   b. Remove manual shift lever, then the park/neutral position (neutral start) switch.
4. Remove valve body.
5. Remove bolt and retaining plate, then pull throttle cable out of transaxle.
6. Install new cable in transaxle case, being sure to push cable all the way in, then install retaining plate and bolt.
7. Install valve body.
8. Install new stopper on inner cable of new throttle cable as follows:
   a. Bend cable approximately 7.87 inches in radius.
   b. Pull inner cable lightly until a slight resistance is felt and hold cable in position.
   c. Stake stopper on cable .031–.059 inch from end of outer cable, **Fig. 10.**
9. Connect throttle cable to throttle linkage.
10. Connect throttle cable housing to bracket and adjust throttle cable.
11. Install park/neutral position (neutral start) switch as follows:
    a. Install park/neutral position (neutral start) switch.
    b. Install manual shift lever.

c. Adjust park/neutral position (neutral start) switch.
d. Connect transaxle control cable, then adjust.
12. Test drive vehicle.

VALVE BODY, REPLACE

Removal

1. Raise and support vehicle.
2. Clean outside of transaxle and drain ATF.
3. Remove oil pan and gasket, then discard gasket.
4. Remove oil strainer.
5. Remove two bolts and apply tube bracket.
6. Disconnect solenoid electrical connectors.
7. Remove oil tubes.
8. Remove manual detent spring.
9. Remove manual valve body.
10. Remove valve body attaching bolts, disconnect throttle cable from cam and remove valve body.
11. Remove governor valve gasket.

Installation

1. Install governor valve gasket.
2. Hold cam down and slip throttle cable end into slot, then install valve body. **Be careful not to trap kickdown switch wire.**
3. Install valve body with attaching bolts, tighten to specification, **Fig. 11.**
4. Connect solenoid electrical connectors.
5. Install manual valve and body as follows:
   a. Align manual valve with pin on manual shift lever.
   b. Install manual valve body with attaching bolts, tighten to specification, **Fig. 12.**
6. Install detent spring, then tighten attaching bolts to specification.
7. Ensure manual valve lever is in contact with center of roller at tip of detent spring.
8. Using a suitable plastic hammer, tap oil tubes in proper locations. **Be careful not to bend or damage oil tubes.**
9. Install apply tube bracket, then the oil strainer.
10. Install magnets in pan, ensuring magnets do not interfere with oil tubes.
11. Install oil pan with gasket, **torquing** bolts to 43 inch lbs.
12. Install drain plug with gasket, **torquing** plug to 36 ft. lbs.
13. Add ATF, until fluid is of specified level.

DIFFERENTIAL OIL SEAL, REPLACE

1. Remove both driveshafts.
2. Using oil seal puller, tool No. 09308-00010, or equivalent, remove both side gear shaft oil seals.
3. Using oil seal replacer, tool No. 09351-32150, or equivalent, install left side oil seal to a depth of .09–.13 inch.
4. Using oil seal replacer, install right side oil seal to a depth of 0–.02 inch.
5. Install both driveshafts.

NOTE
- If diagnostic code Nos 42, 61, 62 or 63 occur, the overdrive indicator light will begin to blink immediately to warn the driver However, an impact or shock may cause the blinking to stop, however, the code will still be retained in the ECT computer memory until canceled out.
- There is no warning for diagnostic code No. 64
- In the event of a simultaneous malfunction of both No. 1 and No. 2 speed sensors, no diagnostic code will appear and the fail-safe system will not function. However, when driving in the "D" range, the transmission will not up-shift from first gear, regardless of the vehicle speed.

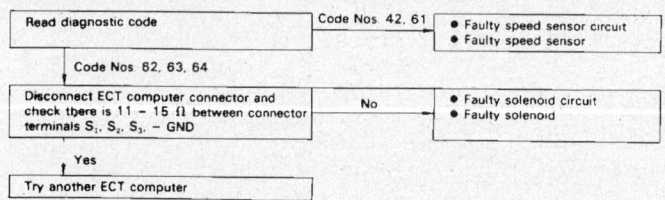

TY5028900256000X

Fig. 1 Troubleshooting, blinking overdrive indicator lamp troubleshooting chart. Celica

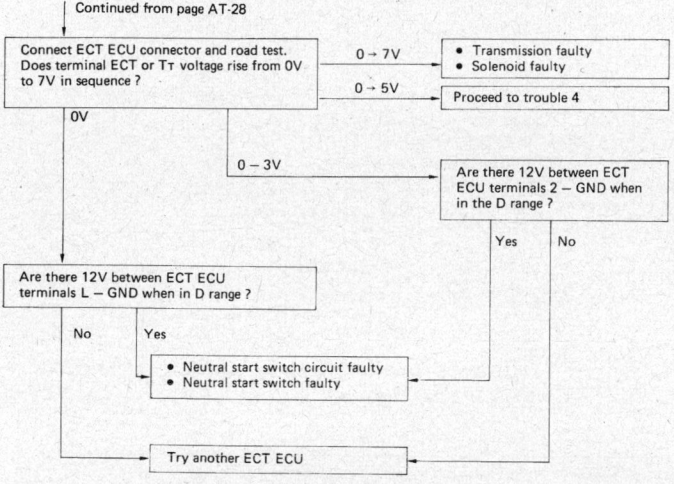

TY5028900257020X

Fig. 2 Troubleshooting, no shifting (Part 2 of 2). Celica

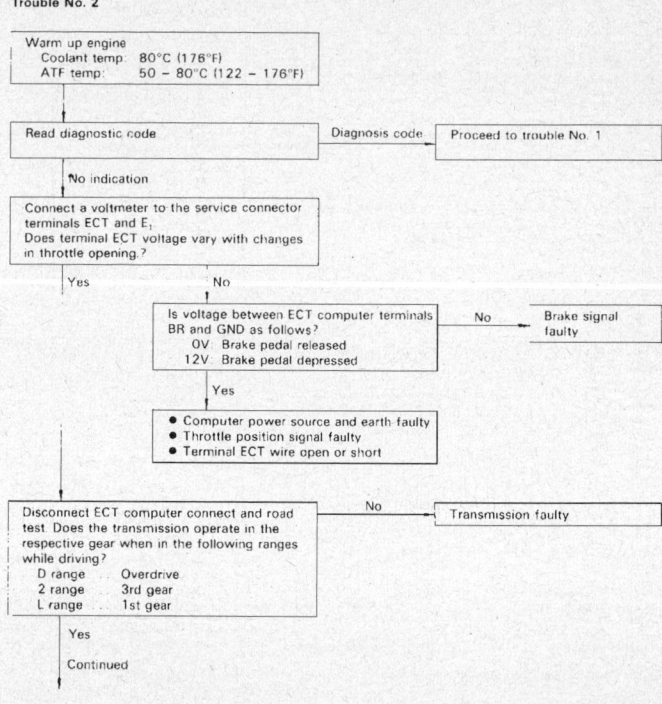

TY5028900257010X

Fig. 2 Troubleshooting, no shifting (Part 1 of 2). Celica

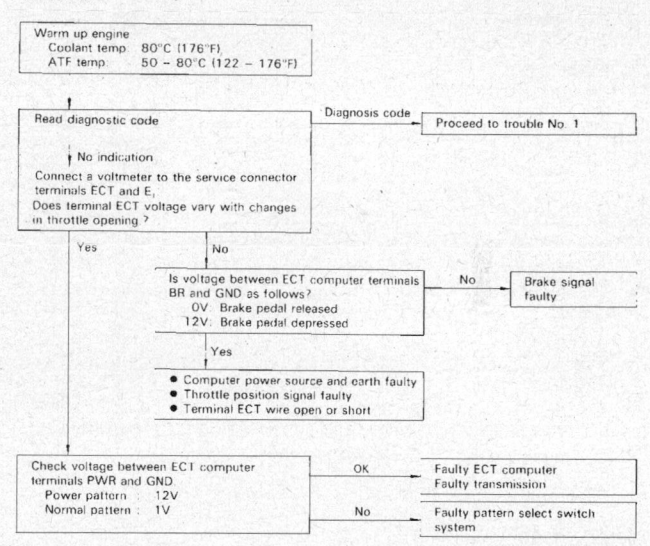

TY5028900258000X

Fig. 3 Troubleshooting, incorrect shift point. Celica

Trouble No. 3   Shift point too high or too low

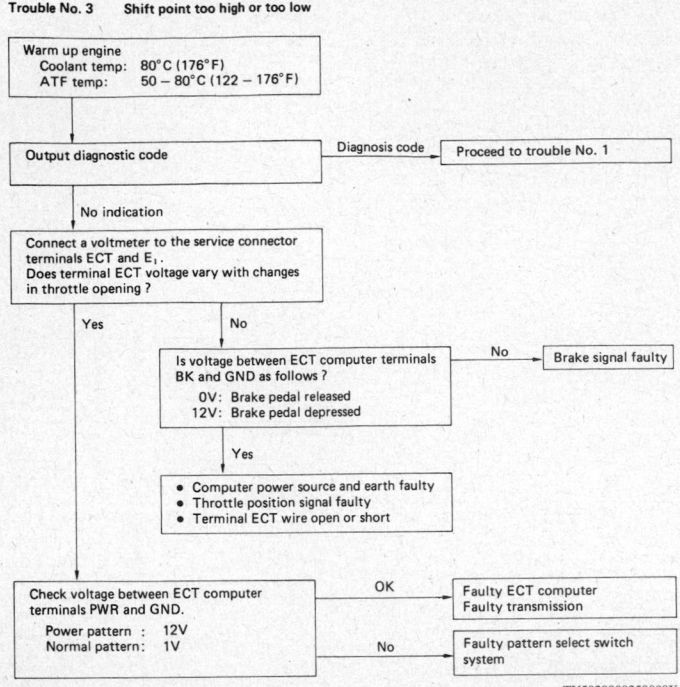

Fig. 4   Troubleshooting, incorrect shift point. Celica

TY5028900259000X

Trouble No. 5

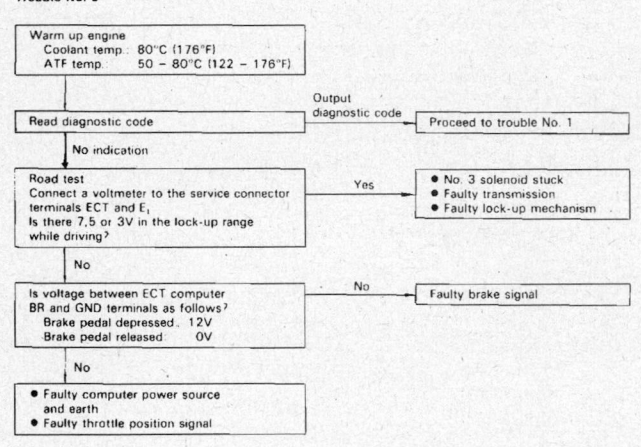

TY5028900261000X

Fig. 6   Troubleshooting, no lock-up after warm-up. Celica

Trouble No. 4

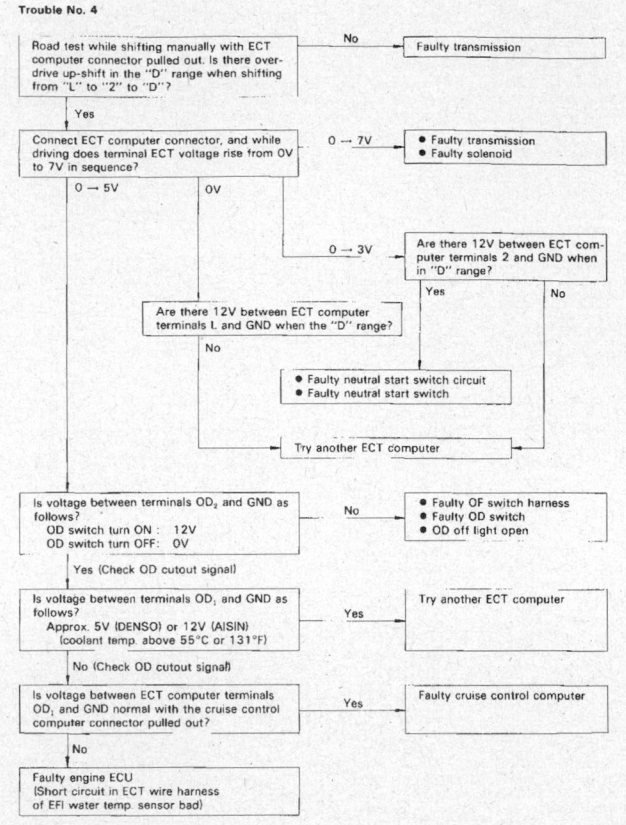

TY5028900260000X

Fig. 5   Troubleshooting, no upshift to O/D after warm-up. Celica

Trouble No.1   No shifting

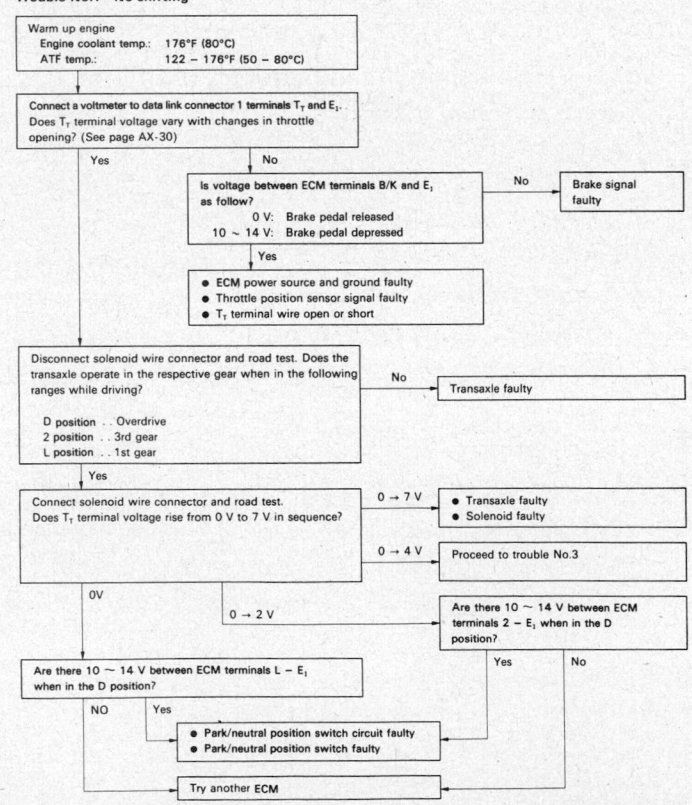

TY5029200263010X

Fig. 7   Troubleshooting, no shifting (Part 1 of 4). Camry

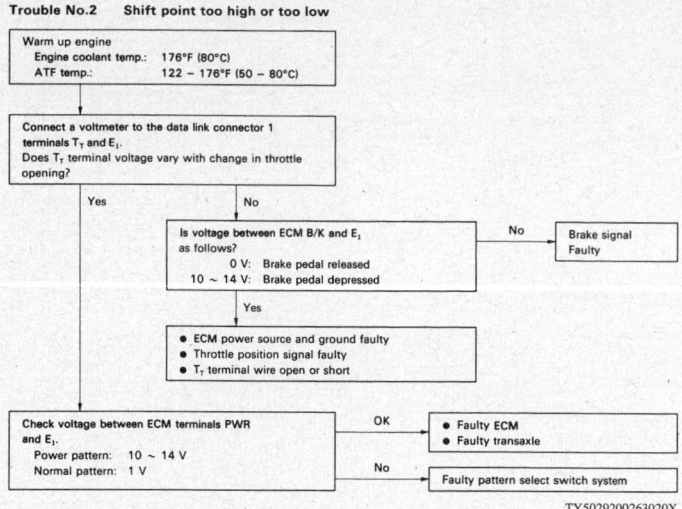

Fig. 7 Troubleshooting, shift point too high or too low (Part 2 of 4). Camry

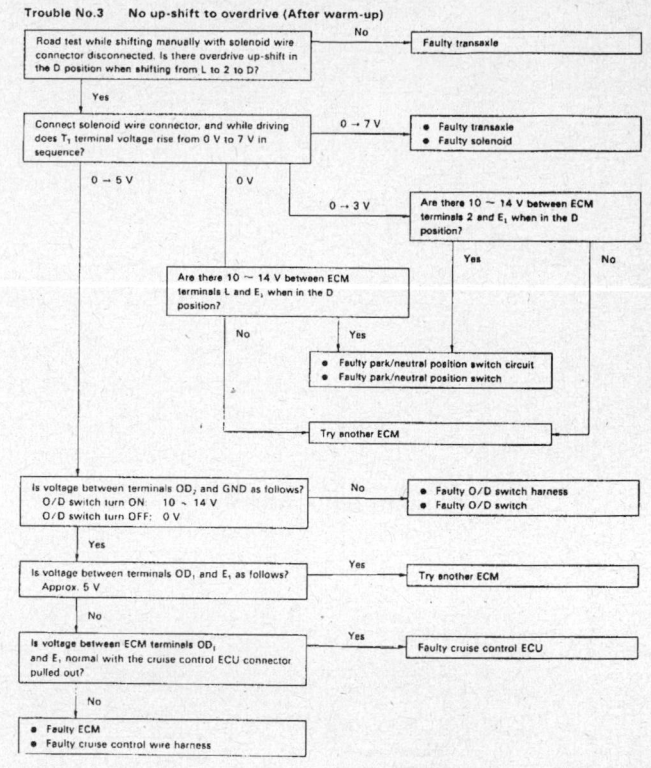

Fig. 7 Troubleshooting, no upshift to overdrive (Part 3 of 4). Camry

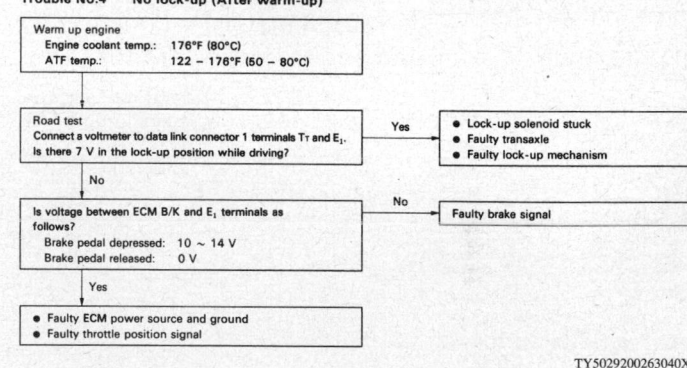

Fig. 7 Troubleshooting, no lock-up (Part 4 of 4). Camry

6. Check level of ATF.

MANUAL VALVE LEVER & SHAFT

1. Remove valve body, parking lock pawl bracket, parking lock rod and retaining spring.
2. Remove manual valve shaft, then using a screwdriver, remove oil seal. Drive in a new oil seal.
3. Assemble new collar to manual valve lever, then install manual valve shaft to transmission case through manual valve lever.
4. Drive in roll pin with slot at a right angle to shaft, then match collar hole to lever caulking hollow and caulk collar to lever.
5. Install retaining spring, then ensure lever moves smoothly.
6. Install parking lock rod, parking lock pawl bracket and valve body.

TRANSAXLE OIL SEAL, REPLACE

Lefthand Side

1. Remove dust cover and fender apron seal.
2. Drain out approximately one quart of ATF.
3. Remove righthand driveshaft.
4. Remove speed sensor.
5. Using oil seal puller, tool No. 09308-00010, or equivalent, drive out side gear shaft.
6. Remove side bearing retainer.
7. Press oil seal out of retainer, then using oil seal replacer, tool No. 09351-32150, or equivalent, press in seal to depth of .106 inch.
8. Coat lip of oil seal with suitable grease.
9. Clean bolt and case threads of side bearing retainer attaching bolts, coat threads of bolts with a suitable sealer, then **torque** bolts to 14 ft. lbs.
10. Using bearing replacer, tool No. 09351-32150, or equivalent, drive in side gear shaft until it contacts pinion shaft.
11. Install speed sensor.
12. Install righthand driveshaft.

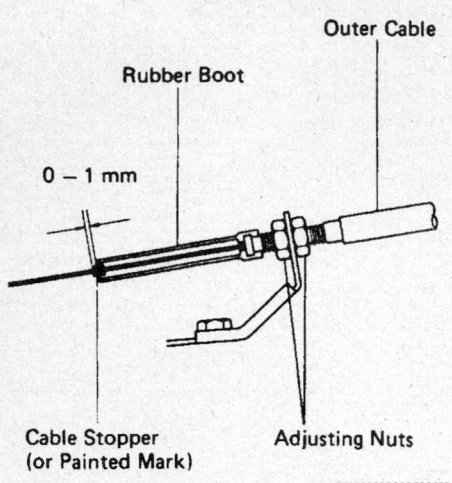

Fig. 8   Throttle cable adjustment

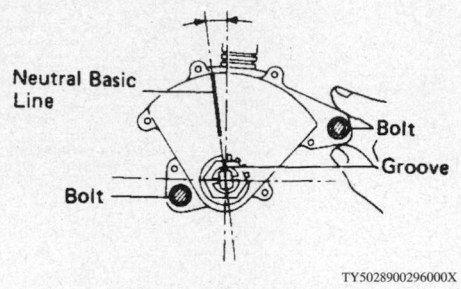

Fig. 9   Neutral safety switch adjustment

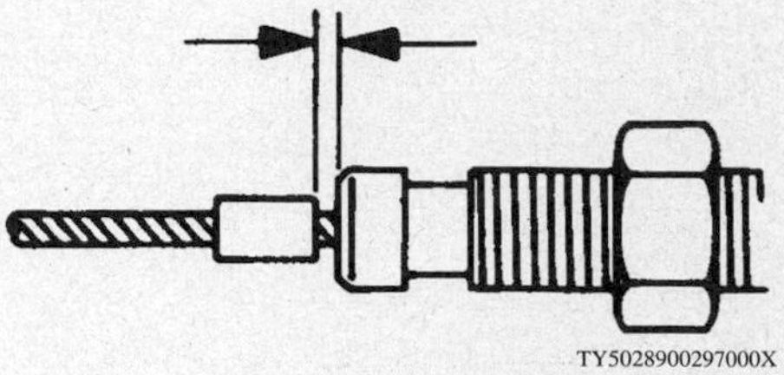

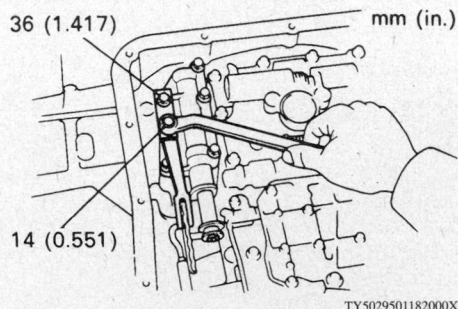

Fig. 10   Throttle cable installation

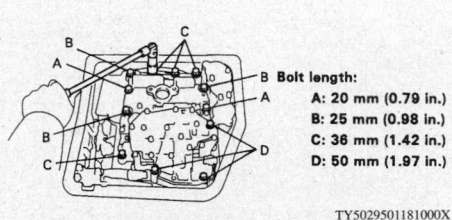

Fig. 11   Valve body bolt length identification

Fig. 12   Manual valve body bolt length identification

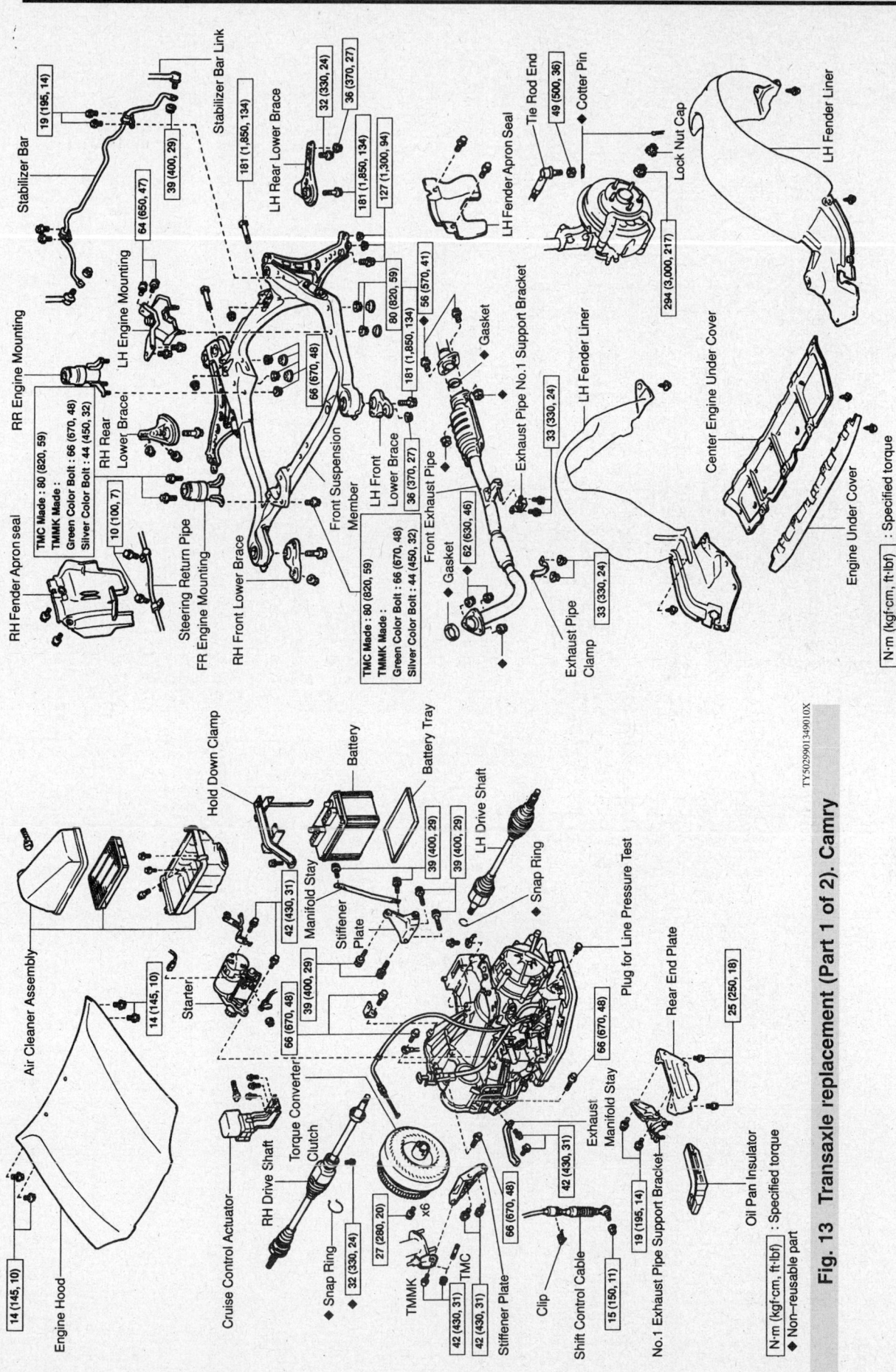

TY5029901349020X

Fig. 13 Transaxle replacement (Part 2 of 2). Camry

Stabilizer Bar

Stabilizer Bar Link

19 (195, 14)

32 (330, 24)

36 (370, 27)

Tie Rod End

49 (500, 36)

Cotter Pin

Lock Nut Cap

LH Fender Liner

181 (1,850, 134)

LH Rear Lower Brace

181 (1,850, 134)

127 (1,300, 94)

LH Fender Apron Seal

294 (3,000, 217)

64 (650, 47)

39 (400, 29)

80 (820, 59)

56 (570, 41)

Gasket

LH Engine Mounting

RR Engine Mounting

66 (670, 48)

181 (1,850, 134)

Exhaust Pipe No.1 Support Bracket

LH Fender Liner

Center Engine Under Cover

TMC Made : 80 (820, 59)
TMMK Made :
Green Color Bolt : 66 (670, 48)
Silver Color Bolt : 44 (450, 32)

RH Rear Lower Brace

33 (330, 24)

LH Front Lower Brace

36 (370, 27)

10 (100, 7)

Front Suspension Member

Front Exhaust Pipe

62 (630, 46)

Engine Under Cover

RH Fender Apron seal

Steering Return Pipe

FR Engine Mounting

RH Front Lower Brace

TMC Made : 80 (820, 59)
TMMK Made :
Green Color Bolt : 66 (670, 48)
Silver Color Bolt : 44 (450, 32)

Gasket

Gasket

Exhaust Pipe Clamp

33 (330, 24)

N·m (kgf·cm, ft·lbf) : Specified torque

◆ Non-reusable part

TY5029901349010X

Fig. 13 Transaxle replacement (Part 1 of 2). Camry

Hold Down Clamp

Battery

Battery Tray

LH Drive Shaft

Snap Ring

Plug for Line Pressure Test

39 (400, 29)

39 (400, 29)

42 (430, 31)

Manifold Stay

Stiffener Plate

14 (145, 10)

14 (145, 10)

Starter

39 (400, 29)

66 (670, 48)

Air Cleaner Assembly

Cruise Control Actuator

RH Drive Shaft

Torque Converter Clutch

Snap Ring

27 (280, 20)

x6

32 (330, 24)

TMMK

TMC

42 (430, 31)

42 (430, 31)

Stiffener Plate

66 (670, 48)

Clip

15 (150, 11)

Shift Control Cable

No.1 Exhaust Pipe Support Bracket

42 (430, 31)

19 (195, 14)

Exhaust Manifold Stay

66 (670, 48)

Rear End Plate

25 (250, 18)

Oil Pan Insulator

Engine Hood

14 (145, 10)

N·m (kgf·cm, ft·lbf) : Specified torque

◆ Non-reusable part

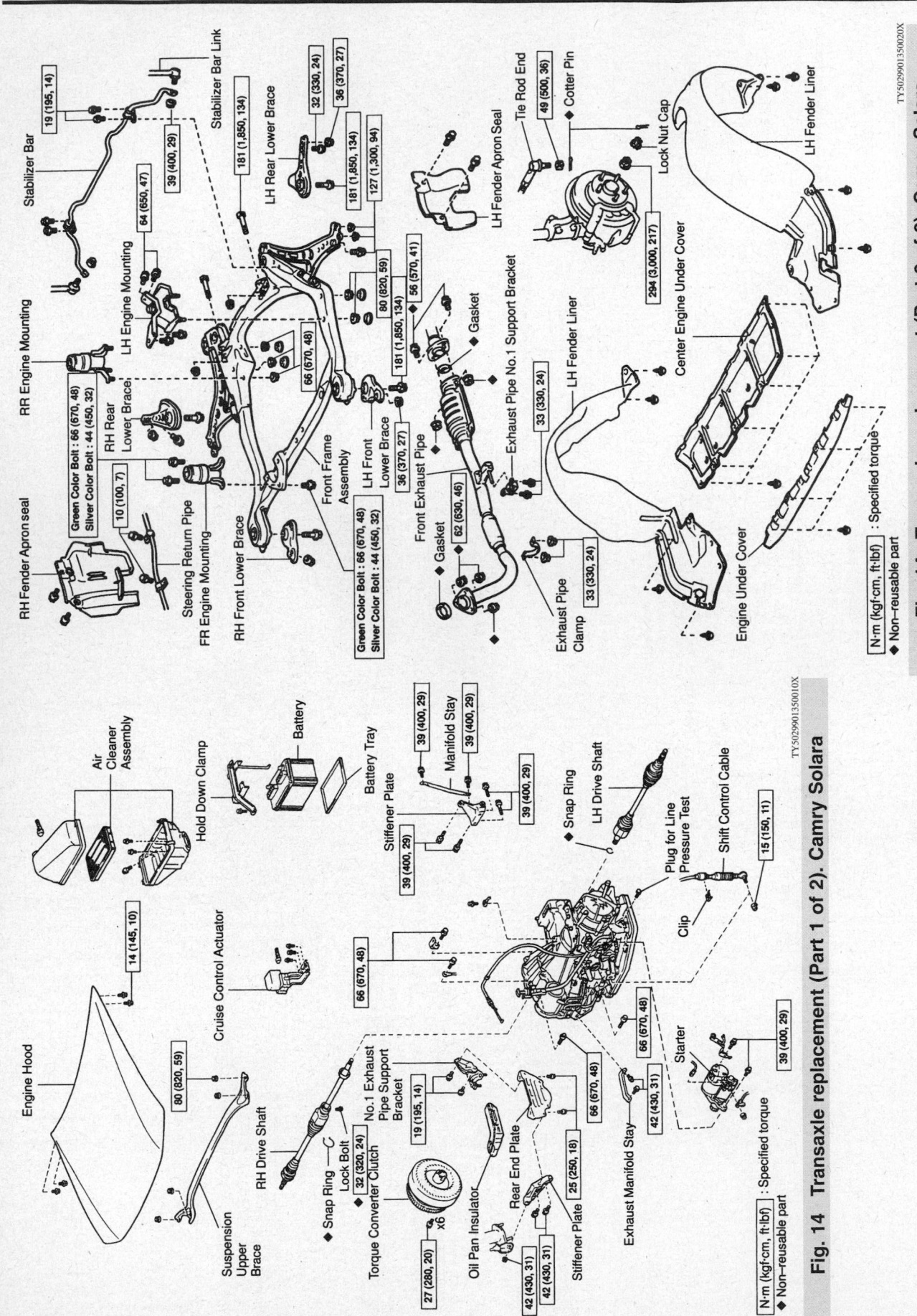

Fig. 14 Transaxle replacement (Part 2 of 2). Camry Solara

Fig. 14 Transaxle replacement (Part 1 of 2). Camry Solara

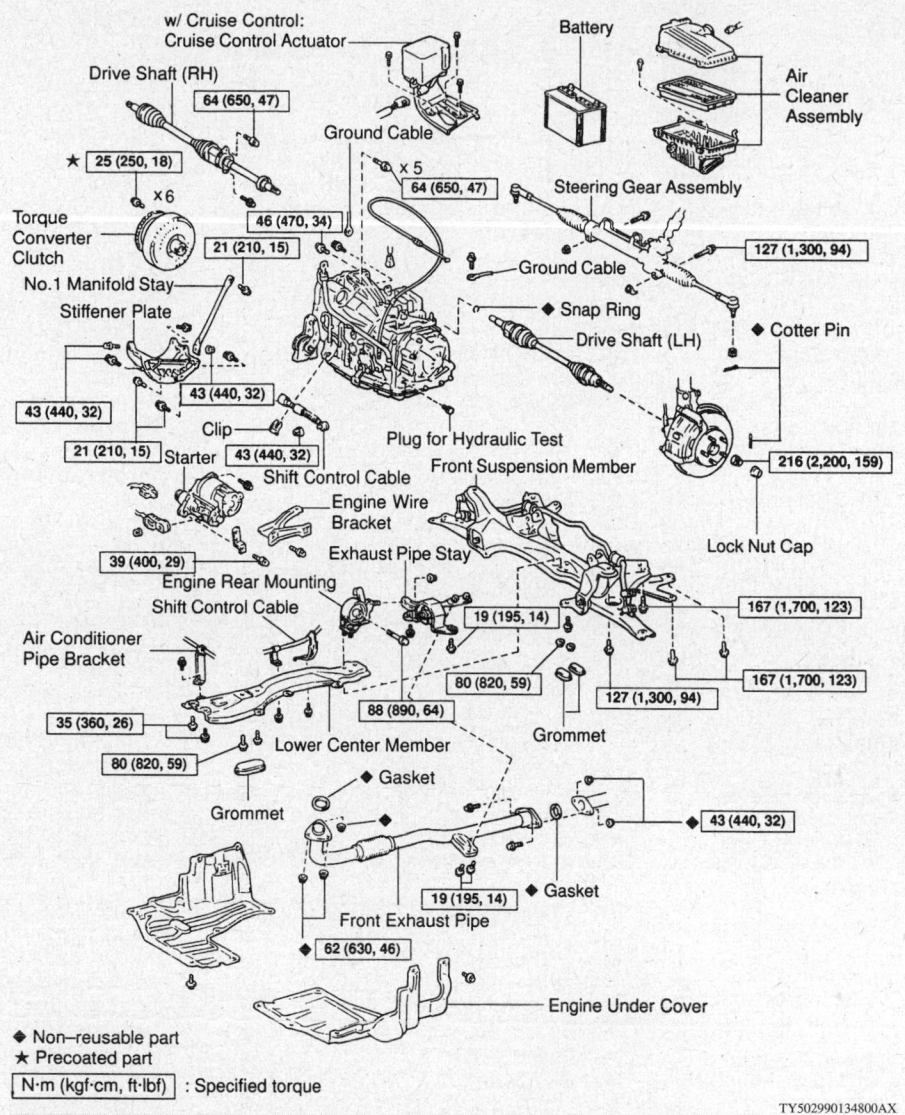

Fig. 15 Transaxle replacement. Celica

Labels in figure:

w/ Cruise Control:
Cruise Control Actuator

Drive Shaft (RH)

64 (650, 47)

★ 25 (250, 18)

Battery

Air Cleaner Assembly

Ground Cable

×5
64 (650, 47)

Steering Gear Assembly

Torque Converter Clutch

×6

46 (470, 34)

21 (210, 15)

127 (1,300, 94)

No.1 Manifold Stay

Stiffener Plate

Ground Cable

◆ Snap Ring

Drive Shaft (LH)

◆ Cotter Pin

43 (440, 32)

43 (440, 32)

43 (440, 32)

Clip

21 (210, 15)

Starter

Plug for Hydraulic Test

Shift Control Cable

Front Suspension Member

216 (2,200, 159)

Lock Nut Cap

Engine Wire Bracket

Exhaust Pipe Stay

39 (400, 29)

Engine Rear Mounting
Shift Control Cable

19 (195, 14)

167 (1,700, 123)

Air Conditioner Pipe Bracket

80 (820, 59)

127 (1,300, 94)

167 (1,700, 123)

35 (360, 26)

88 (890, 64)

Grommet

Lower Center Member

80 (820, 59)

◆ Gasket

43 (440, 32)

Grommet

19 (195, 14)

◆ Gasket

Front Exhaust Pipe

62 (630, 46)

Engine Under Cover

◆ Non–reusable part
★ Precoated part
N·m (kgf·cm, ft·lbf) : Specified torque

TY502990134800AX

13. Fill transaxle with approximately one quart of ATF.

Righthand Side

1. Remove fender apron seal.
2. Drain approximately one quart of ATF.
3. Remove driveshaft and intermediate shaft as follows:
   a. Remove cotter pin, dust cover and bearing locknut.
   b. Loosen nuts attaching driveshaft to intermediate shaft flange.
   c. Remove brake caliper from steering knuckle and secure out of way.
   d. Remove disc rotor.
   e. Using universal puller, tool No. 09950-20017, or equivalent, pull axle hub from driveshaft.
   f. Remove bearing bracket bolts and bracket from cylinder block.
   g. Remove intermediate shaft from universal joint.
4. Using universal puller, drive out universal joint.
5. Using oil seal puller, drive oil seal from case.
6. Using oil seal replacer, drive oil seal into case until surface of seal is flush with surface of case.
7. Coat lip of seal with suitable grease.
8. Drive in universal joint until joint contacts pinion shaft.
9. Install intermediate shaft and driveshaft as follows:
   a. Install intermediate shaft to universal joint.
   b. Install bearing bracket onto cylinder block, tighten bolts to specification.
   c. Install outboard joint side of driveshaft to axle hub.
   d. Finger-tighten nuts connecting driveshaft to intermediate shaft flange.
   e. Install disc rotor.
   f. Install brake caliper to steering knuckle, **torque** bolts to 70 ft. lbs.
   g. Installing bearing locknut, dust cover and cotter pin, **torque** nut to 137 ft. lbs.
   h. **Torque** six driveshaft to intermediate shaft flange attaching nuts to 25 ft. lbs.
   i. Fill transaxle with approximately one quart of ATF.
10. Install fender apron seal.

TRANSAXLE

REPLACE

CAMRY & CAMRY SOLARA

Refer to **Figs. 13 and 14** when replacing transaxle.

1. Remove battery and air cleaner assembly, then disconnect throttle cable.
2. **On models equipped with speed control,** remove speed control actuator and bracket.
3. **On all models,** Disconnect oil cooler hoses.
4. Disconnect park/neutral position and vehicle speed sensor connectors.
5. Disconnect shift solenoid valve connectors.
6. Remove two front side engine mounting bolts.
7. Disconnect two ground cables, then remove starter motor.
8. Remove exhaust manifold stay.
9. Remove engine to transaxle bolt located next to exhaust manifold stay.
10. Remove hood, then raise and support vehicle.
11. Remove front wheel and tire assemblies.
12. Remove engine undercovers.
13. Disconnect shift control cable.
14. Remove differential drain plug and drain differential fluid into suitable container.
15. Remove fender apron shields and driveshafts.
16. Remove front exhaust pipe.
17. Remove front side engine mounting insulator bolt.
18. Remove three rear side engine mounting nuts.
19. Remove two left side transaxle mounting nuts.
20. Remove steering gear housing. Secure housing to rear engine mounting bracket using suitable cord.
21. Attach suitable engine sling device to engine hangers.
22. Remove steering return pipe mounting brackets.
23. Remove screws, then turn over front side of left and right fender liners.
24. Remove screws, then turn over rear side of left and right fender liners.
25. Remove front frame assembly.
26. Support transaxle with suitable jack.

27. Remove front side stiffener plate and rear end plate.
28. Remove flexplate to torque converter mounting bolts.
29. Remove rear side stiffener plate.
30. Separate transaxle from engine, then lower transaxle assembly from vehicle.
31. Reverse procedure to install. Using suitable calipers and a straightedge, measure distance from installed surface to front surface of transaxle housing, distance should be .512 inch.

CELICA

Refer to **Fig. 15** when replacing the transaxle.

1. Remove battery and disconnect throttle cable.
2. **On models equipped with speed control,** remove speed control actuator.
3. **On all models,** remove air cleaner assembly.
4. Remove two ground cable mounting bolts.
5. Remove four left upper side engine mount bolts.
6. Remove starter motor, then disconnect vehicle speed sensor connector.
7. Disconnect park/neutral position switch connector and two solenoid connectors.
8. Remove three transaxle bolts, then disconnect oil cooler hoses.
9. Install engine support fixture, then raise and support vehicle.
10. Remove engine under covers, then drain transaxle fluid into suitable container.
11. Remove both driveshafts, then support transaxle using suitable jack.
12. Disconnect shift control cable, then remove rear engine mount bolt.
13. Remove front exhaust pipe and rear suspension member.
14. Remove stiffener plate.
15. Remove flexplate to torque converter mounting bolts.
16. Remove three lower transaxle mounting bolts, then lower transaxle from vehicle.
17. Reverse procedure to install. Using suitable calipers and a straightedge, measure distance from installed surface to front surface of transaxle housing, distance should be .512 inch.

TIGHTENING SPECIFICATIONS

Year	Component	Torque/Ft. Lbs.
1996–99	Accumulator Cover	84①
	Apply Tube Bracket	84①
	Driveplate	61
	Driveshaft To Intermediate Flange	25
	Front Engine Mount	59
	Front Exhaust Pipe	46
	Front Transaxle Assembly (12 mm Bolt)	24
	Front Transaxle Assembly (19 mm Bolt)	134
	Front Transaxle Assembly (Nut)	27
	Neutral Start Switch Bolt	48①
	Neutral Start Switch Nut	61①
	Oil Cooler Lines	25
	Oil Drain Plug	15
	Oil Pan	43①
	Oil Pump Body	84①
	Oil Pump	16
	Oil Strainer	84①
	Overdrive Case To Transaxle Case	18
	Rear Engine Mount	48
	Rear Exhaust Pipe	76
	Speed Sensor Bracket	108①
	Stabilizer Bar Bushing Bracket	14
	Solenoid valve	58①
	Starter	29
	Steering Gear Housing To Frame	134
	Stiffener Plate	27
	Test Plug	65①
	Throttle Cable	11
	Torque Converter	20
	Transaxle Case To Engine (10 mm)	34
	Transaxle Case To Engine (12 mm)	47
	Transaxle Mount	38
	Transaxle Rear Cover To Case	27
	Upper Valve Body To Lower	48①
	Valve Body	84①
	Valve Detent Spring	84①

① — Inch lbs.

A242L Automatic Transaxle

NOTE: On Air Bag Equipped Models, Refer To "Air Bag System Precautions" Located In The Front Of This Manual For System Disarming & Arming Procedures.

INDEX

PRECAUTIONS

AIR BAG SYSTEMS

Refer to "Air Bag System Precautions" in the front of this manual for system disarming and arming procedures.

BATTERY GROUND CABLE

Prior to service disconnect battery ground cable and isolate as required.

AUDIO CODED ANTI-THEFT SYSTEM

Some models are equipped with an audio coded anti-theft system that will disable the radio when the battery cable is disconnected. The system can be identified by the "ANTI-THEFT SYSTEM" on the cassette lid. Obtain 3 digit code for input. Reset system after service as follows:
1. Obtain 3 digit audio theft code.
2. Depress 1 (PROG) while depressing righthand side of TUNE SEEK button, - - - will appear in tape operation display.
3. To enter the first digit, depress 1 (PROG) button repeatedly until the number of times depressed equals the first digit (depress the 1 button six times if the first digit if five, first press equals 0).
4. To enter second digit, depress 2 (APS) button repeatedly until the number of times depressed equals the second digit.
5. To enter third digit, depress 3 (RPT) button repeatedly until the number of times depressed equals the third digit.
6. If - - - is displayed after inputting digits, repeat procedure.
7. When code appears in display, depress and hold SCAN button until SEC appears.
8. When SEC disappears audio system is operative.
9. If Err is displayed, repeat procedure. **Attempting to input code more than 9 times may permanently disable audio system.**

TROUBLESHOOTING

Refer to **Fig. 1** for troubleshooting infor-

mation. The numbers in the chart indicate the priority of the likely cause of the problem.

MAINTENANCE

FLUID CHECK

1. Run engine until transaxle fluid reaches normal operating temperature (158–176°F).
2. Park vehicle on level surface with parking brake set.
3. With engine idling, shift selector into each gear position and return to P position.
4. Remove transaxle dipstick and wipe clean, then push dipstick fully into fluid filler tube.
5. Remove dipstick and check if fluid level is in HOT range. If level is at low side of HOT range, add fluid.

FLUID CHANGE

1. Remove transaxle drain plug and drain fluid into suitable container.
2. Install drain plug securely.
3. Add new ATF fluid through filler pipe.
4. Start engine and move shift selector through all positions.
5. Check fluid level with engine idling. Add fluid level up to COOL level on dipstick, then check fluid level at normal operating temperature.

ADJUSTMENTS

THROTTLE CABLE

1. Fully depress accelerator pedal and ensure throttle valve opens fully.
2. Fully depress accelerator.
3. Loosen adjustment nuts.
4. Adjust outer cable so that distance between end of boot and stopper on cable is 0–.04 inch (0–1 mm), **Fig. 2.**
5. Tighten adjusting nuts to specifications.

SHIFT CONTROL CABLE

1. Remove engine under cover.
2. Loosen nut on manual shift lever, **Fig. 3.**

3. Push manual lever fully toward right side of vehicle.
4. Return lever two notches to neutral position.
5. Set shift lever in N position.
6. While holding lever lightly toward R position side, tighten swivel nut.

PARK/NEUTRAL POSITION SWITCH

1. Loosen park/neutral position switch bolts and set shift selector to N position.
2. Align groove and neutral basic line, **Fig. 4.**
3. Hold in position and tighten to specification.

IN-VEHICLE REPAIRS

VALVE BODY, REPLACE

1. Remove transaxle drain plug and drain transaxle fluid into suitable container.
2. Remove transaxle oil pan and gasket.
3. Remove three oil strainer attaching bolts and oil strainer, **Fig. 5.**
4. Remove two apply pipe bracket retaining bolts and bracket, **Fig. 5.**
5. Remove four oil pipes by prying up pipe ends with large screwdriver.
6. Remove manual detent spring.
7. Disconnect solenoid electrical connector.
8. Disconnect throttle cable and manual valve connecting rod from valve body.
9. Remove 12 valve body bolts and valve body. Refer to **Fig. 6** for valve body bolt lengths. (A) bolts are .79 inch, (B) bolts are 1.18 inches and (C) bolts are 2.17 inches.
10. Remove second brake apply gasket.
11. Reverse procedure to install, tighten all nuts and bolts to specification.

THROTTLE CABLE, REPLACE

1. Disconnect throttle cable from engine throttle linkage.
2. Remove park/neutral position switch as follows:
    a. Disconnect transaxle control cable from transaxle control shaft lever.

b. Using suitable screwdriver, pry off nut stopper.
c. Remove nut and nut stopper.
d. Remove park/neutral position switch, **Fig. 7**.
3. Remove valve body as described under "Valve Body, Replace."
4. Remove throttle cable retaining bolt and plate.
5. Pull throttle cable out from transaxle case.
6. Reverse procedure to install. **Since new throttle cables do not have a cable stopper staked, perform the following when installing a new throttle cable:**
   a. Bend cable so there is a radius of about 7.87 inches (200 mm), **Fig. 8**.
   b. Pull inner cable lightly until slight resistance is felt, then hold it in position.
   c. Stake stopper .031–.059 inch (.8–1.5 mm) from end of outer cable.

GOVERNOR VALVE, REPLACE

1. Disconnect speedometer cable.
2. Remove governor cover with O-ring.
3. Remove governor body with thrust washer, **Fig. 9**.
4. Remove governor body adapter.
5. Remove gasket.
6. Reverse procedure to install.

TRANSAXLE
REPLACE

1. Remove battery.
2. Remove air cleaner assembly, **Fig. 10**.
3. Remove throttle cable.
4. Remove ground cables and bracket.
5. Remove upper side mounting bolts and upper side starter bolt.
6. Install engine support fixture.
7. Raise and support vehicle.
8. Remove under cover.
9. Disconnect righthand and righthand driveshafts.
10. Disconnect speedometer cable.
11. Disconnect control cable from lever, **Fig. 11**.
12. Disconnect park/neutral position switch electrical connector, **Fig. 11**.
13. Disconnect O/D solenoid connector, **Fig. 11**.
14. Disconnect oil cooler hose from pipe.
15. Disconnect starter cable and connector.
16. Remove starter.
17. Remove front exhaust pipe as follows:
    a. Disconnect oxygen sensor.
    b. Remove bolts and springs from exhaust manifold and front exhaust pipe.
    c. Remove front exhaust pipe clamp and gaskets.
18. Remove torque converter cover.
19. Turn crankshaft to gain access to each torque converter clutch (TCC) mounting bolt.
20. Hold crankshaft pulley nut with wrench and remove six TCC mounting bolts.
21. Raise and support transaxle with suitable jack.
22. Disconnect righthand engine mounting bracket.
23. Remove rear mounting insulator through bolt, **Fig. 12**.
24. Remove five bolts and rear mounting insulator.
25. Remove transaxle mounting bolts, **Fig. 13**.
26. Reverse procedure to install, tighten bolts and nuts to specifications.

Trouble		Torque converter clutch	Parking lock pawl	Manual valve	1-2 shift valve	2-3 shift valve	Forward clutch (C1)	Direct clutch (C2)	No. 2 one-way clutch (F2)	Front planetary gear	Rear Planetary gear	1st and reverse brake (B3)	U/D one-way clutch (F3)	U/D clutch (C3)	U/D planetary gear	2nd brake (B2)	2nd coast brake (B1)	U/D brake (B0)	No. 1 one-way clutch (F1)	3-4 shift valve	Accumulator control valve	C1 accumulator	Low coast modulator valve	B2 accumulator	2nd coast modulator valve	Throttle modulator valve
Does not move in any forward position							1	5	2			3				4	4									
Does not move in reverse position					3	4		5	2	2	7			6				1								
Does not move in any forward position or reverse position		7	1	2						5	5	3	3	6					4							
No-up shift	1st → 2nd				2											3			4							
	2nd → 3rd					2		3																		
	3rd → O/D																2	3								
No-down shift	O/D → 3rd																2									
	3rd → 2nd					2																				
	2nd → 1st				2									3												
Shift point too high or too low																										
Up-shifts 3rd → O/D with O/D main switch "OFF"																										
Up-shifts 3rd → O/D when E/G is cold																										
Harsh engagement	"N" → "R"						1		2												3					
	"N" → "D"					1																2				
	"N" → "L"																						1			
	1st → 2nd ("D" position)								2															1		
	1st → 2nd ("2" position)																								1	
	1st → 2nd → 3rd																						1			2

TY5029500838010X

Fig. 1   Troubleshooting chart (Part 1 of 3)

Parts Name \ Trouble		Accumulator control valve	2nd coast brake (B1)	C2 accumulator	U/D clutch (C3)	U/D brake (B4)	U/D planetary gear	B4 accumulator	C3 accumulator	2nd coast modulator valve	B2 accumulator	1st and reverse brake	Lock-up relay valve	Torque converter clutch	U/D one-way clutch (F3)	Oil strainer	Pressure relief valve	Direct clutch (C2)	Forward clutch (C1)	No.2 one-way clutch (F2)	2nd brake (B2)	No.1 one-way clutch (F1)	Low coast modulator valve
Harsh engagement	1st → 2nd → 3rd → O/D	1																					
	2nd → 3rd		1	2																			
	3rd → O/D				1	2	3	4															
	O/D → 3rd							1	2														
	3rd → 2nd								1	2	3	4	5										
No lock-up													2	3									
No lock-up OFF													2	3									
Slip or shudder	Forward & Reverse (After warm-up)				3									1	2								
	Forward & Reverse (Directry after E/G start)													1		3	2						
	"R" position			2							3							1					
	1st																		1	2			
	2nd			1																	2	3	
	2nd → 3rd (Up-shift)																	1					
	3rd																	1					
	O/D					1																	
No engine braking	1st → 3rd				1																		
	1st											2											1
	2nd		1							2													

TY5029500838020X

Fig. 1 Troubleshooting chart (Part 2 of 3)

Parts Name \ Trouble		2nd coast brake (B1)	U/D clutch (C3)	U/D brake (B4)	U/D planetary gear	1st and reverse brake (B3)	Torque converter clutch	Direct clutch (C2)	Forward clutch (C1)	2nd brake (B2)	1-2 shift valve	2-3 shift valve	3-4 shift valve
Large shock during lock-up							2						
E/G stalls when starting off and stopping							2						
Poor acceleration	All-positions						1						
	O/D		1		2								
	Other than O/D			1	2								
	Other than 2nd	1								2			
	1st and 2nd								1				
	1st and "R"					1							
	"R"							1					

TY5029500838030X

Fig. 1 Troubleshooting chart (Part 3 of 3)

A242L AUTOMATIC TRANSAXLE

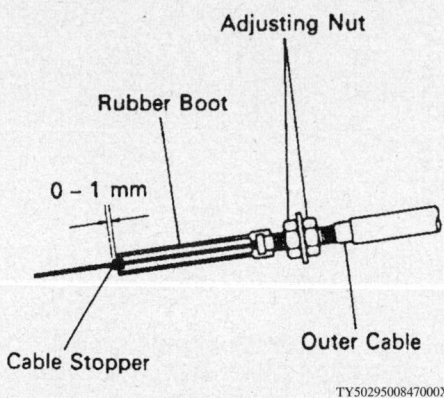

Adjusting Nut

Rubber Boot

0 – 1 mm

Cable Stopper

Outer Cable

TY5029500847000X

Fig. 2   Throttle cable adjustment

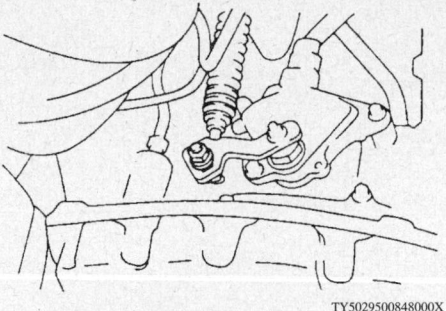

TY5029500848000X

Fig. 3   Shift control cable adjustment

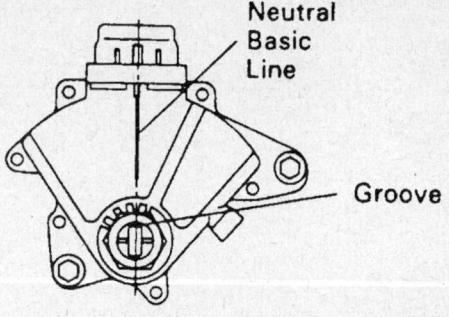

Neutral Basic Line

Groove

TY5029500849000X

Fig. 4   Park/neutral position switch adjustment

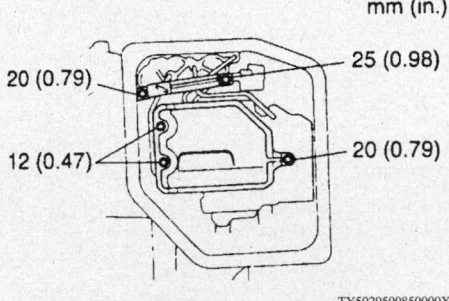

mm (in.)

20 (0.79)   25 (0.98)

12 (0.47)   20 (0.79)

TY5029500850000X

Fig. 5   Oil strainer & apply pipe bracket bolt removal

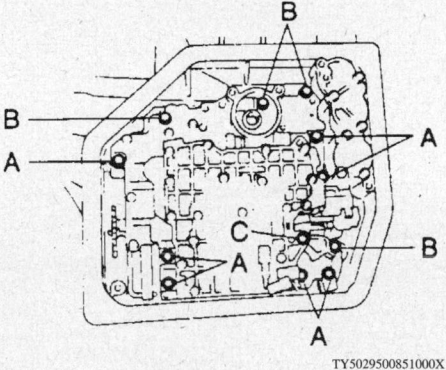

B

B

A

A

C

A

B

A

TY5029500851000X

Fig. 6   Valve body bolt removal

TY5029500852000X

Fig. 7   Park/neutral position switch removal

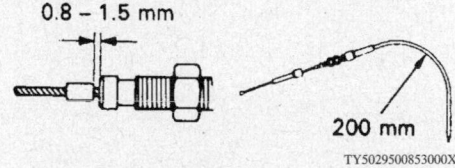

0.8 – 1.5 mm

200 mm

TY5029500853000X

Fig. 8   Throttle cable installation

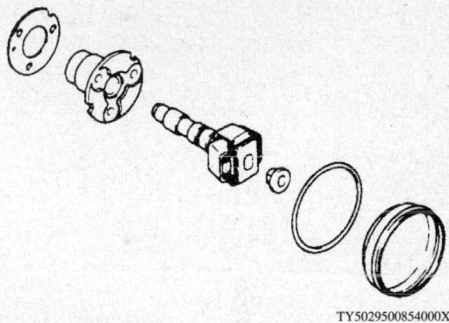

TY5029500854000X

Fig. 9   Governor valve replacement

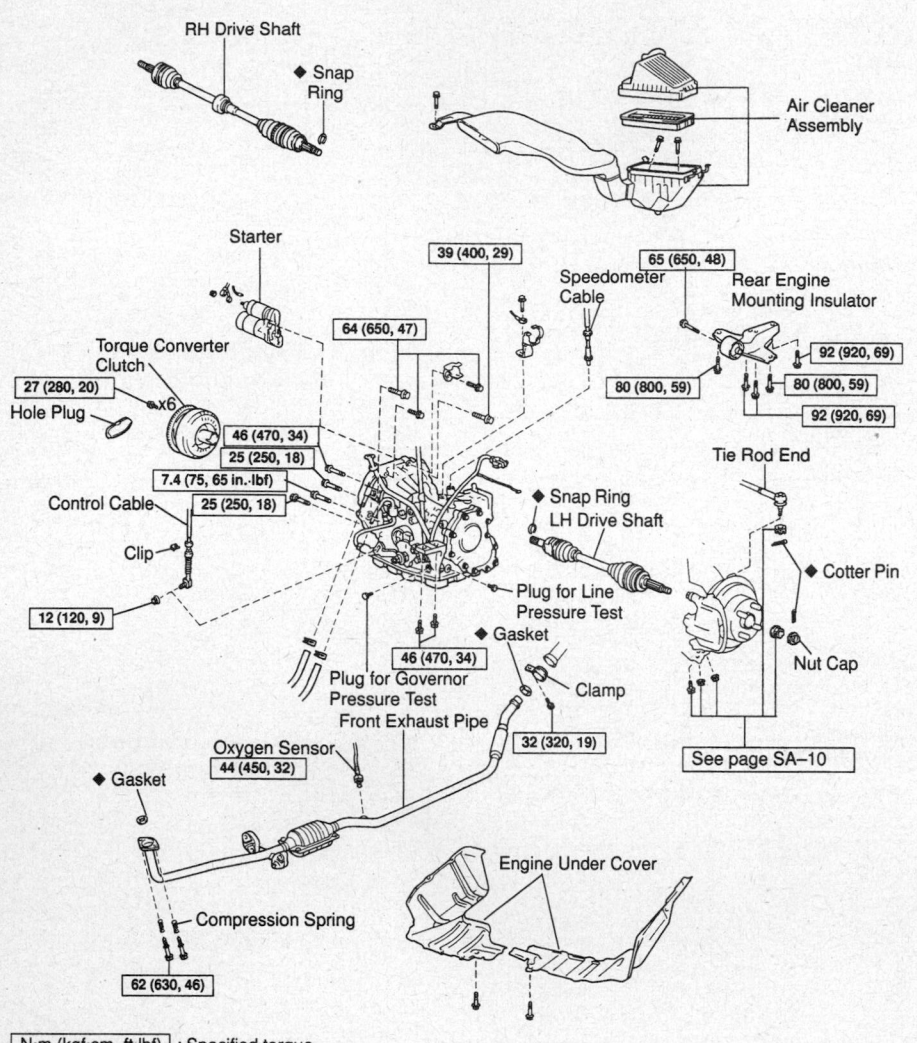

RH Drive Shaft

◆ Snap Ring

Air Cleaner Assembly

Starter

39 (400, 29)

64 (650, 47)

Speedometer Cable

65 (650, 48)

Rear Engine Mounting Insulator

92 (920, 69)

80 (800, 59)

80 (800, 59)

92 (920, 69)

Torque Converter Clutch

27 (280, 20)

Hole Plug

x6

46 (470, 34)

25 (250, 18)

7.4 (75, 65 in.·lbf)

25 (250, 18)

Control Cable

Clip

12 (120, 9)

◆ Snap Ring
LH Drive Shaft

Plug for Line Pressure Test

Tie Rod End

◆ Cotter Pin

Nut Cap

46 (470, 34)

◆ Gasket

Clamp

Plug for Governor Pressure Test
Front Exhaust Pipe

32 (320, 19)

See page SA–10

Oxygen Sensor

44 (450, 32)

◆ Gasket

Compression Spring

62 (630, 46)

Engine Under Cover

N·m (kgf·cm, ft·lbf) : Specified torque
◆ Non–reusable part

Fig. 10 Transaxle removal

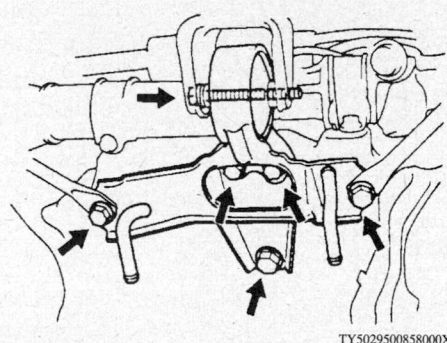

Fig. 11 Control cable, park/neutral position switch & O/D solenoid

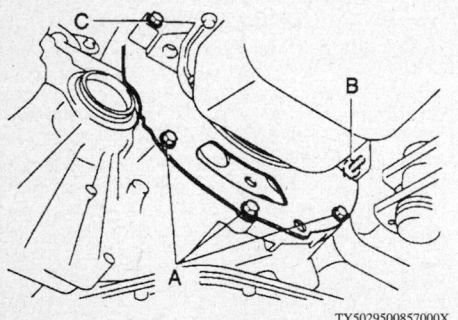

Fig. 12 Rear engine mount removal

Fig. 13 Transaxle mounting bolt removal

TIGHTENING SPECIFICATIONS

Year	Component	Torque/ Ft. Lbs.
1996–99	Engine Mounting Bracket Bolts	35
	Manual Detent Spring	7
	Neutral Safety Switch	48①
	Oil Pan Bolts	43①
	Oil Strainer bolts	7
	Oxygen Sensor	32
	Rear Mounting Insulator Through Bolt	47
	Rear Mounting Insulator Bolts	58
	TCC Mounting Bolts	20
	Upper Side Mounting Bolts	47
	Upper Side Starter Bolt	34
	Valve Body Bolts	7

① — Inch lbs.

A244E Automatic Transaxle

NOTE: On Air Bag Equipped Models, Refer To "Air Bag System Precautions" Located In The Front Of This Manual For System Disarming & Arming Procedures.

INDEX

PRECAUTIONS

AIR BAG SYSTEMS

Refer to "Air Bag System Precautions" in the front of this manual for system disarming and arming procedures.

BATTERY GROUND CABLE

Prior to service disconnect battery ground cable and isolate as required.

AUDIO CODED ANTI-THEFT SYSTEM

Some models are equipped with an audio coded anti-theft system that will disable the radio when the battery cable is disconnected. The system can be identified by the "ANTI-THEFT SYSTEM" on the cassette lid. Obtain 3 digit code for input. Reset system after service as follows:

1. Obtain 3 digit audio theft code.
2. Depress 1 (PROG) while depressing righthand side of TUNE SEEK button, - - - will appear in tape operation display.
3. To enter the first digit, depress 1 (PROG) button repeatedly until the number of times depressed equals the first digit (depress the 1 button six times if the first digit if five, first press equals 0).
4. To enter second digit, depress 2 (APS) button repeatedly until the number of times depressed equals the second digit.
5. To enter third digit, depress 3 (RPT) button repeatedly until the number of times depressed equals the third digit.
6. If - - - is displayed after inputting digits, repeat procedure.
7. When code appears in display, depress and hold SCAN button until SEC appears.
8. When SEC disappears audio system is operative.
9. If Err is displayed, repeat procedure. **Attempting to input code more than 9 times may permanently disable audio system.**

TROUBLESHOOTING

FLUID DISCOLORED OR SMELLS BURNED

1. Fluid contaminated.

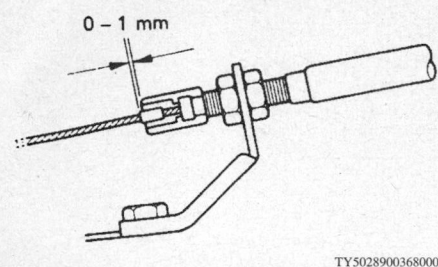

Fig. 1 Throttle cable adjustment

2. Torque converter clutch faulty.

VEHICLE DOES NOT MOVE IN ANY FORWARD RANGE OR REVERSE

1. Shift cable out of adjustment.
2. Valve body or primary regulator faulty.
3. Parking lock pawl faulty.
4. Torque converter clutch faulty.
5. Converter driveplate broken.
6. Oil strainer intake screen blocked.

SHIFT LEVER POSITION INCORRECT

1. Shift cable out of adjustment.
2. Manual valve and lever faulty.

HARSH ENGAGEMENT INTO ANY DRIVE RANGE

1. Throttle cable out of adjustment.
2. Valve body or primary regulator faulty.
3. Accumulator pistons faulty.

DELAYED UPSHIFTS & DOWNSHIFTS

1. Electronic control, valve body or solenoid valve faulty
2. Throttle cable out of adjustment.

SLIPS ON UPSHIFTS OR SLIPS/SHUDDERS ON ACCELERATION

1. Shift cable or throttle cable out of adjustment.
2. Valve body or solenoid valve faulty.

DRAG, BINDING OR TIE-UP ON UPSHIFTS

1. Shift cable out of adjustment.
2. Valve body faulty.

NO LOCK-UP IN 2, 3 OR OVERDRIVE (OD)

Electronic control, valve body or solenoid valve faulty.

HARSH DOWNSHIFT

1. Throttle cable out of adjustment.
2. Throttle cable and cam faulty.
3. Accumulator pistons or valve body faulty.

NO DOWNSHIFT WHEN COASTING

1. Valve body or solenoid valve faulty.
2. Electronic control faulty.

DOWNSHIFT OCCURS TOO QUICKLY OR TOO LATE WHILE COASTING

1. Throttle cable or valve body faulty.
2. Electronic control or solenoid valve faulty.

NO KICKDOWN

1. Electronic control, valve body or solenoid valve faulty.
2. Throttle cable out of adjustment.

NO ENGINE BRAKING IN 2 OR L RANGE

Electronic control, valve body or solenoid valve faulty.

VEHICLE DOES NOT HOLD IN P RANGE

1. Shift cable out of adjustment.
2. Parking lock pawl and spring faulty.

MAINTENANCE

FLUID CHECK

1. Operate vehicle until engine and transaxle are at normal operating temperature, 158–176°F.
2. Park vehicle on level surface, then set parking brake.
3. With engine idling and brake pedal depressed, shift gear lever through all positions smoothly, then return to P range.
4. Remove transaxle dipstick and wipe clean.
5. Push dipstick back fully into tube, then remove it and check that fluid level is in HOT range. If level is low, add fluid until fluid is of specified level. **Do not overfill.**
6. Check fluid condition. If fluid is black or smells burnt, replace.

FLUID CHANGE

1. Remove drain plug and gasket, then drain fluid.
2. Install gasket and drain plug.
3. Add fluid through filler tube.
4. Start engine, then shift gear selector through all positions. Return to P range.
5. With engine idling, check fluid level. Add fluid to COOL level on dipstick.
6. Check fluid level at normal fluid temperature, 158–176°F. Add, if necessary. **Do not overfill.**

ADJUSTMENTS

THROTTLE CABLE

1. Ensure throttle valve is fully closed and inner cable is not slack.
2. Loosen adjustment nuts.
3. Adjust outer cable so distance between end of boot and stopper measures 0–.04 inch, **Fig. 1.**
4. Tighten nuts, then recheck adjustments.

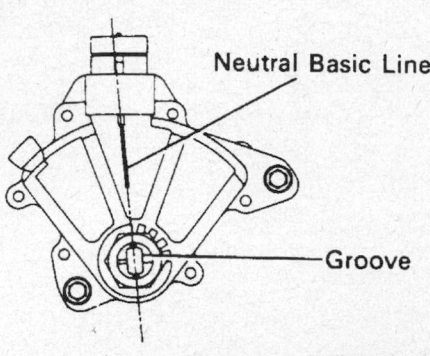

Fig. 2 Park/neutral position switch

SHIFT CONTROL CABLE

1. Loosen nut on lever, then push manual lever fully toward right side of vehicle.
2. Return lever to neutral (N) position, then set lever in N range.
3. Position lever lightly toward reverse (R) range side and tighten nut to specifications.

PARK/NEUTRAL POSITION SWITCH

If engine will start with shift selector in any range other than N or P range, adjustment is required.

1. Loosen neutral start switch bolts, then set shift selector to N range.
2. Align groove and neutral basic line, **Fig. 2.**
3. Hold in position and tighten bolts to specifications.
4. Inspect idle speed in N range. speed should be 800 RPM.

IN-VEHICLE REPAIRS

VALVE BODY, REPLACE

Removal

1. To help prevent contamination, clean exterior of transaxle.
2. Remove drain plug and gasket and drain fluid into suitable container.
3. Some fluid will remain in oil pan. Remove all pan bolts, then carefully remove oil pan assembly, **Fig. 3.** discard gasket.
4. Remove magnets to collect any steel chips. Examine chips to determine type of wear in transmission.
   a. Steel (magnetic) chips indicate bearing, gear and plate wear.
   b. Brass (non-magnetic) chips indicate bushing wear.
5. Remove bolts retaining oil strainer. **some oil will come out with strainer.** remove gasket.
6. Remove bolts, then oil tube bracket. Remove bolt, then oil tube clamp.
7. With large screwdriver, pry up both tube ends, then remove tubes.
8. Disconnect solenoid connectors, then remove wire clamp that holds solenoid wire assembly, **Fig. 4.**
9. Remove manual detent spring.
10. Remove bolts, then disconnect throttle

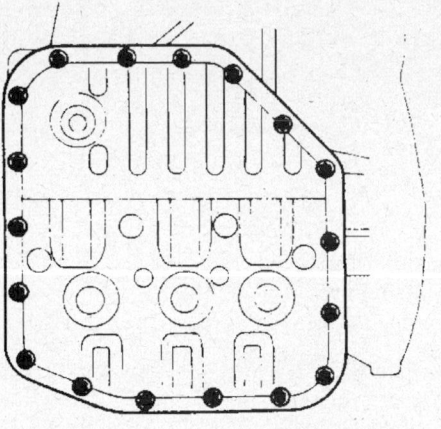

Fig. 3   Oil pan bolts

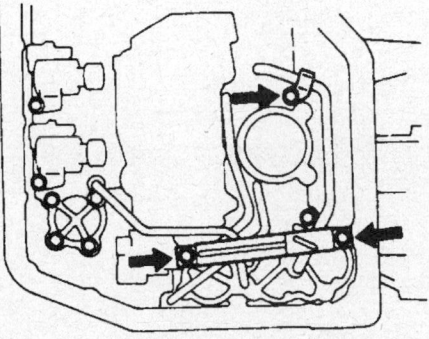

Fig. 6   Oil tube bracket & clamp bolt location

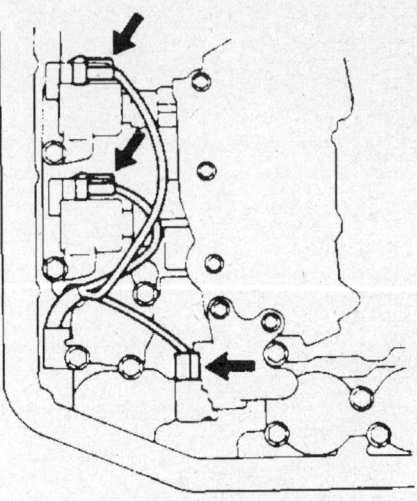

Fig. 4   Solenoid connector locations

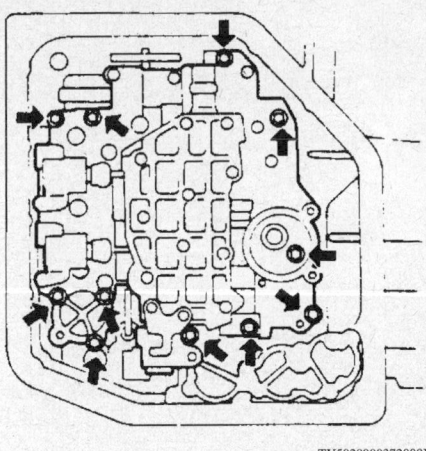

Fig. 5   Valve body bolts

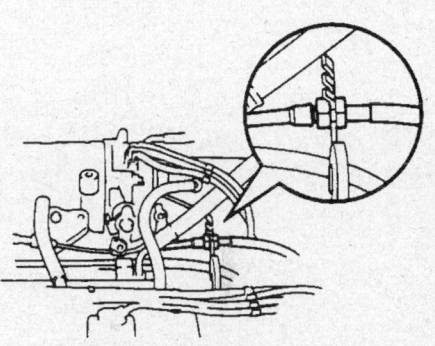

Fig. 7   Throttle cable disconnection

cable, **Fig. 5.** disconnect manual valve connecting rod and remove valve body.

Installation

1. Connect manual valve connecting rod.
2. Position cam down, then slip cable end into slot. position valve body into place being careful not to entangle solenoid wire.
3. Install and finger tighten all bolts, then tighten to specifications.
4. Install manual detent spring, then tighten to specification. Ensure lever is in contact with center of roller at tip of detent spring.
5. Install wire clamp to solenoid wire assembly.
6. Connect solenoid connectors, then install oil tubes. tap tubes with plastic hammer into position, being careful not to bend or damage tubes.
7. Install oil tube bracket and clamp, tighten to specification, **Fig. 6.**
8. Install gasket to oil strainer, then the oil strainer. Tighten bolts.
9. Install magnets in oil pan ensuring magnets do not interfere with oil tubes.
10. Install gasket to oil pan, then the oil pan. Tighten to specification.
11. Install gasket to drain plug, then the oil pan. Tighten to specification.
12. Fill transaxle with two liters of ATF. **Do not overfill.** check fluid level.

THROTTLE CABLE, REPLACE
Removal

1. Disconnect throttle cable from engine, then the cable from throttle linkage, **Fig. 7.**
2. Disconnect transmission control cable from transmission control shaft lever, then remove nut, washer and manual shift lever.
3. Remove nut, lock washer and packing. Remove bolts, then the park/neutral position switch (neutral start switch).
4. Remove bolt and plate, then the throttle cable retaining plate.
5. Remove throttle cable from valve body, then from transaxle case.

Installation

1. Install cable into transaxle case and check for full seating. **Do not roll case over cable to avoid breaking the cable fitting.** install throttle cable to valve body.
2. Bend and pull inner cable lightly until light resistance is felt, then hold it. Stake stopper from end of outer cable. if throttle cable is new, stake stopper or paint mark on inner cable.
3. Install throttle cable retaining plate and bolt, then park/neutral position switch (neutral start switch) to manual valve shaft.
4. Install packing, nut stopper and nut. Tighten to specification.
5. Align groove and neutral base line, **Fig. 2.**
6. Install bolts and tighten to specifications.
7. Stake nut with nut stopper, then install manual shift lever and washer. Tighten nut to specification.
8. Install and adjust throttle cable, then test drive vehicle.

DIFFERENTIAL OIL SEAL, REPLACE
Removal

1. Remove drain plug and transaxle fluid.

Remove engine undercover, then the righthand and righthand driveshafts.
2. Using oil seal puller, tool No. 09308-00010, or equivalent, drive out righthand and righthand oil seals.

Installation

1. Using side bearing race replacer and handle, tool Nos. 09351-32111 and 09351-32130, or equivalents, from transmission tool set, No. 09350-32014, or equivalent, drive in new righthand and righthand oil seals, then coat oil seal lips with MP grease.
2. Install righthand and righthand driveshafts, then the engine cover. fill transmission with ATF, then check fluid level. **Do not overfill.**

SPEEDOMETER DRIVEN GEAR, REPLACE

1. Using spring tension tool No. 09921-00010, or equivalent, remove oil seal.
2. Using valve guide bushing remover and replacer, tool No. 09201-60011, or equivalent, install oil seal.

TRANSAXLE
REPLACE

Refer to **Fig. 8** when replacing transaxle components.
1. Remove battery and air cleaner assembly.
2. Remove throttle cable from engine.

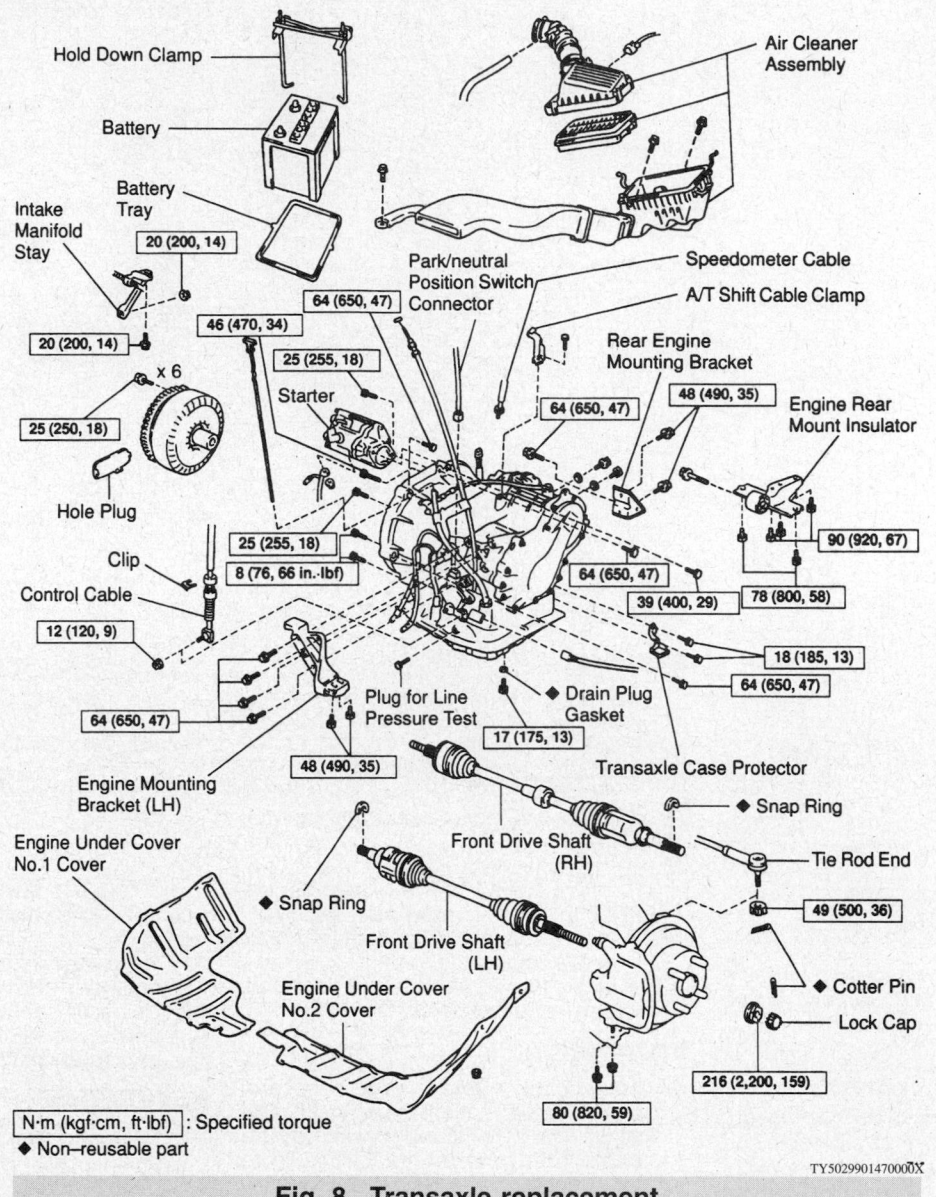

Fig. 8 Transaxle replacement

3. Remove ground cables, wire harness and throttle cable clamp bracket from transaxle.
4. Remove transaxle and starter upper side mounting bolts.
5. Install engine support fixture, then raise and support vehicle.
6. Remove front wheel and tire assemblies, then left and right engine undercovers.
7. Remove driveshafts, then disconnect solenoid connector.
8. Disconnect control cable from control shaft lever.
9. Disconnect all electrical connectors from transaxle.
10. Disconnect oil cooler pipes.
11. Remove starter and speedometer cable.
12. Secure stabilizer bar.
13. Remove torque converter mounting bolts.
14. Support transaxle using suitable jack.
15. Remove bolts from left side and rear engine mounting brackets.
16. Remove rear engine mount insulator.
17. Remove transaxle to engine mounting bolts, then lower transaxle from vehicle.
18. Reverse procedure to install.

TIGHTENING SPECIFICATIONS

Year	Component	Torque, Ft. Lbs.
1996–99	Driveshaft Locknut	152
	Engine Mount	32
	Lower Arm Bolts	59
	Manual Detent Spring	84①
	Oil Pan Bolts	43①
	Oil Pan Drain Plug	13
	Oil Tube Bracket Clamp	84①
	Starter Bolts	29
	Steering Knuckle Nut	36
	Torque Converter Mounting Bolts	13
	Transaxle Mounting Bolts	47
	Valve Body Mounting Bolts	84①

① — Inch lbs.

A245E, A246E & A247E Automatic Transaxles

NOTE: On Air Bag Equipped Models, Refer To "Air Bag System Precautions" Located In The Front Of This Manual For System Disarming & Arming Procedures.

INDEX

PRECAUTIONS

AIR BAG SYSTEMS

Refer to "Air Bag System Precautions" in the front of this manual for system disarming and arming procedures.

BATTERY GROUND CABLE

Prior to service disconnect battery ground cable and isolate as required.

AUDIO CODED ANTI-THEFT SYSTEM

Some models are equipped with an audio coded anti-theft system that will disable the radio when the battery cable is disconnected. The system can be identified by the "ANTI-THEFT SYSTEM" on the cassette lid. Obtain 3 digit code for input. Reset system after service as follows:
1. Obtain 3 digit audio theft code.
2. Depress 1 (PROG) while depressing righthand side of TUNE SEEK button, - - - will appear in tape operation display.
3. To enter the first digit, depress 1 (PROG) button repeatedly until the number of times depressed equals the first digit (depress the 1 button six times if the first digit if five, first press equals 0).
4. To enter second digit, depress 2 (APS) button repeatedly until the number of times depressed equals the second digit.
5. To enter third digit, depress 3 (RPT) button repeatedly until the number of times depressed equals the third digit.
6. If - - - is displayed after inputting digits, repeat procedure.
7. When code appears in display, depress and hold SCAN button until SEC appears.
8. When SEC disappears audio system is operative.
9. If Err is displayed, repeat procedure. **Attempting to input code more than**

9 times may permanently disable audio system.

TROUBLESHOOTING

DOES NOT MOVE IN ANY FORWARD RANGE

1. Faulty forward clutch

DOES NOT MOVE IN REVERSE

1. Faulty first and reverse brake.
2. Faulty U/D brake.
3. Faulty direct clutch.

DOES NOT MOVE IN ANY POSITION

1. Faulty manual valve.
2. Faulty throttle valve.
3. Faulty primary regulator valve.
4. Faulty torque converter clutch.
5. Faulty oil pump.
6. Faulty U/D one way clutch.
7. Faulty front or rear planetary gear.

NO 1-2 OR 2-3 UPSHIFT

1. Faulty vehicle speed sensor circuit.
2. Faulty No. 1, No. 2 solenoid circuit.
3. Fault in throttle position sensor circuit.
4. faulty park/neutral position switch.
5. Faulty ECM.
6. Faulty 1–2 or 2–3 shift valve.
7. Faulty second brake.
8. Faulty direct clutch.

NO 3-O/D UPSHIFT

1. Faulty vehicle speed sensor circuit.
2. Faulty No. 1, No. 2 solenoid circuit.
3. Fault in throttle position sensor circuit.
4. Faulty park/neutral position switch.
5. O/D cancel signal circuit.
6. Engine coolant temperature sensor circuit.
7. Faulty ECM.
8. Faulty 3rd-overdrive shift valve.
9. Faulty No. 1 or No. 2 solenoid.

NO O/D-3 OR 3-2 DOWNSHIFT

1. Fault in vehicle speed sensor circuit.
2. Faulty No. 1, No. 2 solenoid circuit.
3. Fault in throttle position sensor circuit.
4. Faulty ECM.
5. Faulty shift valve.
6. Faulty No. 1 or No. 2 solenoid.

NO 2-1 DOWNSHIFT

1. Fault in vehicle speed sensor circuit.
2. Faulty No. 1, No. 2 solenoid circuit.
3. Fault in throttle position sensor circuit.
4. Faulty ECM.
5. Fault in engine coolant temperature sensor circuit.
6. Faulty shift valve.
7. Faulty No. 1 solenoid.
8. Faulty No. 2 one way clutch.

SHIFT POINT TOO HIGH/ LOW

1. Fault in vehicle speed sensor circuit.
2. Fault in throttle position sensor circuit.

3. Faulty ECM.

NO LOCK-UP

1. Fault in vehicle speed sensor circuit.
2. Fault in SL solenoid circuit.
3. Fault in throttle position sensor circuit.
4. Faulty park/neutral position switch.
5. Fault in stop lamp switch circuit.
6. Faulty ECM.
7. Faulty lock-up relay valve.
8. Faulty torque converter clutch.

NO LOCK-UP OFF

1. Fault in vehicle speed sensor circuit.
2. Fault in SL solenoid circuit.
3. Fault in throttle position sensor circuit.
4. Fault in stop lamp switch circuit.
5. Faulty ECM.

UPSHIFTS TO 2ND OR 3RD WHILE IN "L" POSITION

1. Faulty park/neutral position switch.
2. Faulty ECM.

UPSHIFTS FROM 3RD TO O/D WHILE O/D SWITCH IS OFF

1. O/D main switch and O/D off indicator light circuit.
2. Faulty ECM.
3. Faulty No. 1 solenoid.

UPSHIFTS FROM 3RD TO O/D WHILE O/D SWITCH IS OFF

1. O/D main switch and O/D off indicator light circuit.
2. Faulty ECM.
3. Faulty No. 1 solenoid.

UPSHIFTS FROM 3RD TO O/D WHILE ENGINE IS COLD

1. Faulty park/neutral position switch.
2. Faulty engine coolant temperature sensor.
3. Faulty ECM.

HARSH ENGAGEMENT, "N" TO " D"

1. Faulty SL solenoid circuit.
2. Fault in throttle position sensor circuit.
3. Faulty park/neutral position switch.
4. Faulty ECM.
5. Faulty accumulator.
6. Faulty forward clutch.

HARSH ENGAGEMENT, "N" TO " R"

1. Faulty accumulator.
2. Faulty first and reverse brake.
3. Faulty direct clutch.

HARSH ENGAGEMENT IN ANY DRIVING POSITION

1. Fault in vehicle speed sensor circuit.
2. Fault in SL solenoid circuit.
3. Fault in throttle position sensor circuit.
4. Faulty ECM.
5. Faulty primary regulator valve.

6. Faulty coast modulator valve.
7. Faulty accumulator.

SLIPS IN FORWARD OR REVERSE

1. Primary regulator valve.
2. Faulty torque converter clutch.
3. Faulty oil pump.

SLIPS IN OVERDRIVE

1. Faulty forward clutch.
2. Faulty direct clutch.
3. Faulty U/D clutch.

NO KICKDOWN

1. Faulty vehicle speed sensor.
2. Faulty No. 1 and No. 2 solenoid circuit.
3. Faulty throttle position sensor circuit.
4. Faulty ECM.
5. Faulty shift valve.

POOR ACCELERATION

1. Faulty vehicle speed sensor.
2. Faulty No. 1 and No. 2 solenoid circuit.
3. Faulty throttle position sensor circuit.
4. Faulty ECM.
5. Faulty SL solenoid circuit.
6. Faulty primary regulator valve.
7. Faulty torque converter clutch.
8. Faulty forward clutch.

ENGINE STALLS WHEN STARTING OFF OR STOPPING

1. Fault in SL solenoid circuit.
2. Fault in stop light switch circuit.
3. Faulty ECM.

MAINTENANCE

FLUID CHECK

1. Start engine, allow transaxle fluid to reach 158–176°F.
2. Position vehicle on level surface, then set parking brake.
3. With engine idling, brake pedal depressed, move shift lever through all positions.
4. Remove transaxle dipstick, wipe clean, then replace.
5. Remove dipstick again, check fluid at hot level.
6. Add fluid until fluid is of specified level.

FLUID CHANGE

1. Drain transaxle fluid.
2. Install drain plug and new gasket.
3. Add fluid through filler tube. **Do not overfill.**
4. Start engine, ensure smooth shift operation in all positions.
5. With engine at idle, check fluid cool level, fill as required.
6. Allow vehicle to reach normal operating temperatures, then recheck level.

ADJUSTMENTS

THROTTLE CABLE

1. Check that throttle valve is fully closed.
2. Check that inner cable is not slack.

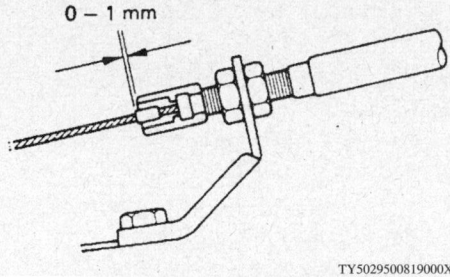

Fig. 1   Throttle Cable Adjustment

3. Measure distance between outer cable end and stopper on cable. Resistance should be 0–.04 inch (0–1 mm).
4. If distance is not within specifications, adjust cable by adjusting nuts, **Fig. 1**.

SHIFT LEVER POSITION

1. Loosen nut on control shaft lever, **Fig. 2**.
2. Push control shaft lever fully downward.
3. Return control shaft lever 2 notches to N position.
4. While holding shift lever lightly, toward R position side, tighten shift lever nut to specifications.
5. Start engine and ensure vehicle moves forward when shifting lever from N to D position and reverses when shifting to R position.

PARK/NEUTRAL POSITION SWITCH

1. Ensure engine can only be started in P or N positions. If engine can start on other positions, perform adjustment procedure.
2. Loosen park/neutral position switch bolt and set shift lever to N position.
3. Align groove and neutral basic line as shown in **Fig. 3**.
4. Hold in position and tighten to specification.

IN-VEHICLE REPAIRS

VALVE BODY, REPLACE

1. Drain transaxle fluid.
2. Remove transaxle oil pan and gasket.
3. Remove two magnets from oil pan.
4. Remove oil strainer.
5. Disconnect solenoid connectors.
6. Remove manual detent spring.
7. Remove valve body wire retainer and valve body.
8. **On A247E transaxles,** remove check ball body and 2nd brake apply gasket.
9. **On all transaxles,** disconnect throttle cable from cam. While disconnecting manual valve connecting rod from manual valve lever, remove valve body.
10. Reverse procedure to install, noting the following:
    a. **Torque** 18 oil pan attaching bolts to 48 inch lbs.
    b. **Torque** oil strainer bolts to 7 ft. lbs.
    c. **Torque** valve body bolts to 7 ft. lbs.

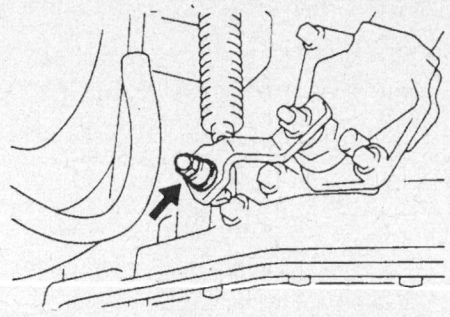

Fig. 2   Shift lever position adjustment

PARK/NEUTRAL POSITION SWITCH

1. Remove No. 2 engine under cover.
2. Disconnect park/neutral position switch connector.
3. Remove park/neutral position switch.
4. Reverse procedure to install. Ensure groove and neutral basic line are aligned.

DIFFERENTIAL OIL SEAL, REPLACE

1. Drain transaxle fluid.
2. Remove engine under cover.
3. Remove righthand and righthand driveshafts.
4. Pull out righthand and righthand oil seals using tool No. 09308–00010, or equivalent.
5. Using tool No. 09350–32014, or equivalent, install righthand side oil seal. Oil seal drive in depth should be .122–.020 inch.
6. Coat lip of oil seal with MP grease.
7. Install righthand side oil seal using tool No. 09350–32014, or equivalent.
8. Install righthand and righthand driveshafts.
9. Fill and check fluid level.
10. Install engine under cover.

TRANSAXLE

REPLACE

A245E TRANSAXLE

Refer to **Fig. 4** when replacing transaxle.
1. Remove air cleaner assembly, then disconnect throttle cable.
2. Remove battery and ground cable.
3. Remove wire harness clamp bracket.
4. Remove two upper transaxle mounting bolts from transaxle side.
5. Remove upper starter mounting bolt.
6. Disconnect vehicle speed sensor connector, then remove engine undercovers.
7. Remove drain plug and drain transaxle fluid into suitable container.
8. Remove both driveshafts.
9. Disconnect solenoid and park/neutral position switch connectors.
10. Remove shift control cable.
11. Remove suspension member and starter motor.

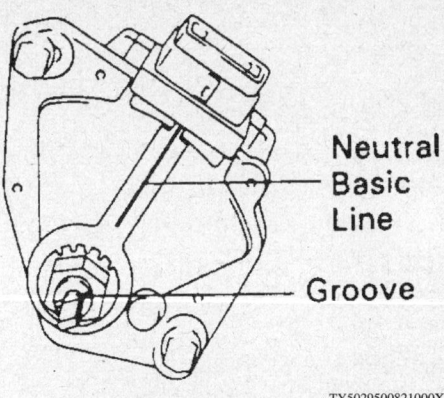

Fig. 3   Park/neutral position switch adjustment

12. Install engine support fixture, then remove left upper engine mounting bolt.
13. Remove oil cooler hoses and heat insulator.
14. Raise transaxle using suitable jack.
15. Remove torque converter mounting bolts.
16. Remove remaining transaxle to engine bolts, then carefully lower transaxle from vehicle.
17. Reverse procedure to install.

A246E TRANSAXLE

1. Remove transaxle fluid level gauge dipstick, **Fig. 5**.
2. Disconnect throttle cable.
3. Disconnect air cleaner electrical connector, then remove air cleaner assembly.
4. Remove battery.
5. Remove engine left mounting upper side bolt.
6. Remove throttle cable mounting bolt.
7. Remove ground cable bolt.
8. Remove wire harness clamp mounting bolt.
9. Remove starter upper side mounting bolt and two transaxle mounting bolts, **Fig. 6**.
10. Loosen clip and disconnect breather hose from filler pipe.
11. Remove filler pipe attaching bolt and filler pipe.
12. Disconnect two oil cooler hoses.
13. Install engine support fixture.
14. Support steering gear housing securely from engine support fixture, **Fig. 7**.
15. Raise and support vehicle.
16. Remove engine under covers.
17. Drain automatic transaxle fluid.
18. Remove left and right driveshafts.
19. Raise transaxle with suitable jack.
20. Remove engine rear mounting bolt.
21. Remove front exhaust pipe.
22. Remove suspension members as follows:
    a. Remove two shift cable mounting bolts.
    b. Disconnect air conditioner pipe.
    c. Remove two grommet cover bolts and cover.
    d. Remove two grommets and bolts.
    e. Remove suspension member mounting bolts.
    f. Remove eight bolts and front lover subframe.

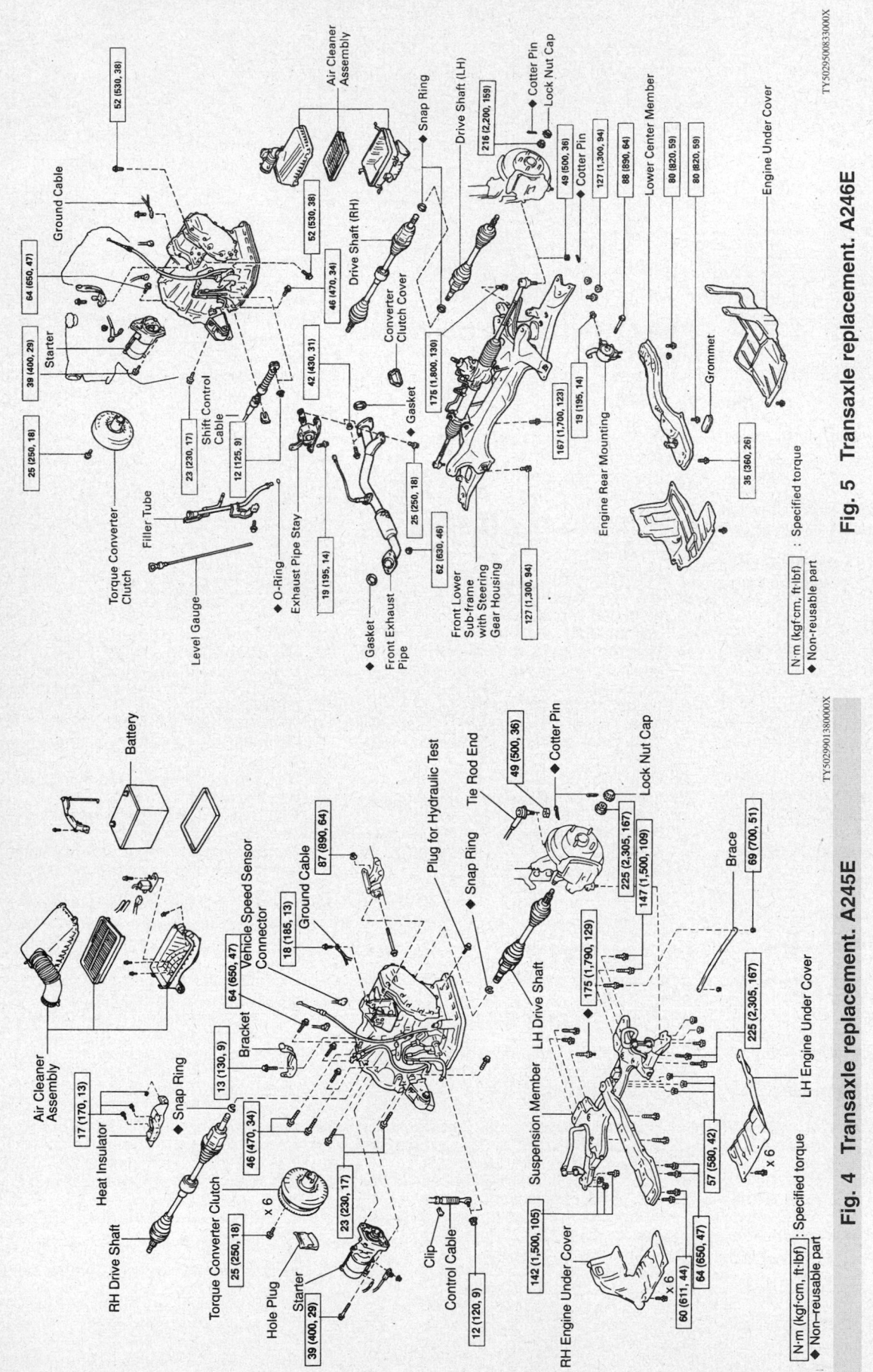

TY5029500833000X

Fig. 5 Transaxle replacement. A246E

52 (530, 38)

Air Cleaner Assembly

Snap Ring ◆

Drive Shaft (LH)

Cotter Pin

Lock Nut Cap

Engine Under Cover

Ground Cable

52 (530, 38)

Drive Shaft (RH)

216 (2,200, 159)

49 (500, 36)

Cotter Pin

127 (1,300, 94)

88 (890, 64)

Lower Center Member

80 (820, 59)

80 (820, 59)

64 (650, 47)

46 (470, 34)

Converter Clutch Cover

39 (400, 29)

Starter

42 (430, 31)

176 (1,800, 130)

167 (1,700, 123)

19 (195, 14)

Engine Rear Mounting

Grommet

25 (250, 18)

Shift Control Cable

23 (230, 17)

12 (125, 9)

Gasket ◆

35 (360, 26)

◆ : Non-reusable part

Torque Converter Clutch

Filler Tube

◆ O-Ring

Exhaust Pipe Stay

19 (195, 14)

62 (630, 46)

25 (250, 18)

Front Lower Sub-frame with Steering Gear Housing

127 (1,300, 94)

N·m (kgf·cm, ft·lbf) : Specified torque

Level Gauge

◆ Gasket

Front Exhaust Pipe

TY5029901380000X

Fig. 4 Transaxle replacement. A245E

Battery

Plug for Hydraulic Test

Tie Rod End

Snap Ring ◆

Cotter Pin

49 (500, 36)

Lock Nut Cap

87 (890, 64)

225 (2,305, 167)

Ground Cable

147 (1,500, 109)

Brace

69 (700, 51)

18 (185, 13)

Vehicle Speed Sensor Connector

64 (650, 47)

175 (1,790, 129)

LH Drive Shaft

225 (2,305, 167)

Bracket

13 (130, 9)

LH Engine Under Cover

Air Cleaner Assembly

Heat Insulator

17 (170, 13)

Snap Ring ◆

46 (470, 34)

Suspension Member

57 (580, 42)

× 6

RH Drive Shaft

Torque Converter Clutch

25 (250, 18)

× 6

23 (230, 17)

142 (1,500, 105)

RH Engine Under Cover

64 (650, 47)

× 6

60 (611, 44)

Hole Plug

Starter

39 (400, 29)

Clip

Control Cable

12 (120, 9)

N·m (kgf·cm, ft·lbf) : Specified torque

◆ : Non-reusable part

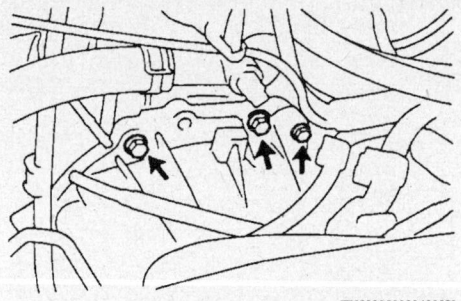

Fig. 6   Starter & transaxle side mounting bolt removal. A246E

Fig. 7   Engine support fixture installation. A246E

Fig. 8   Transaxle mounting bolt removal. A246E

23. Remove starter.
24. Disconnect vehicle speed sensor connector.
25. Disconnect shift control cable by removing nut from control shaft lever.
26. Disconnect solenoid connector and park/neutral position switch connector.
27. Remove torque converter clutch cover.
28. Turn crankshaft to gain access to transaxle mounting bolts.
29. Remove two engine left mounting lower side bolts.
30. Remove five transaxle mounting bolts and transaxle, **Fig. 8**.
31. Reverse procedure to install, tighten all bolts and nuts to specifications, **Fig. 9**.

A247E TRANSAXLE

Refer to **Fig. 10** when replacing transaxle.
1. Disconnect throttle cable, then remove coolant reservoir and air cleaner assembly.
2. Remove ground cable.

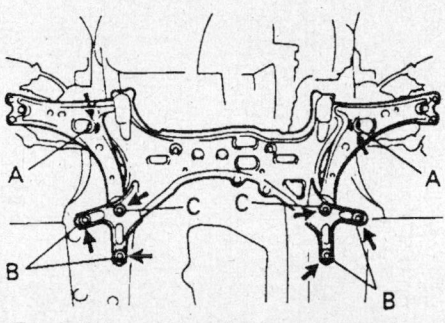

Fig. 9   Lower subframe bolt installation. A246E

3. Remove set nut of engine wire harness clamp.
4. Remove starter motor.
5. Remove three upper transaxle side mounting bolts.
6. Install engine support fixture.
7. Remove left engine mount nut and bolt.
8. Remove engine undercovers, then drain transaxle fluid into suitable container.
9. Remove driveshafts and front exhaust pipe.
10. Disconnect shift control cable.
11. Disconnect shift solenoid valve, park/neutral position switch and vehicle speed sensor connectors.
12. Disconnect oil cooler hoses.
13. Remove two power steering gear mounting bolts and nuts, then support housing securely.
14. Remove front suspension crossmember assembly with stabilizer bar.
15. Remove stiffener plate and rear end plate.
16. Remove torque converter mounting bolts.
17. Support transaxle using suitable jack.
18. Remove remaining transaxle mounting bolts, then carefully lower transaxle assembly.
19. Reverse procedure to install.

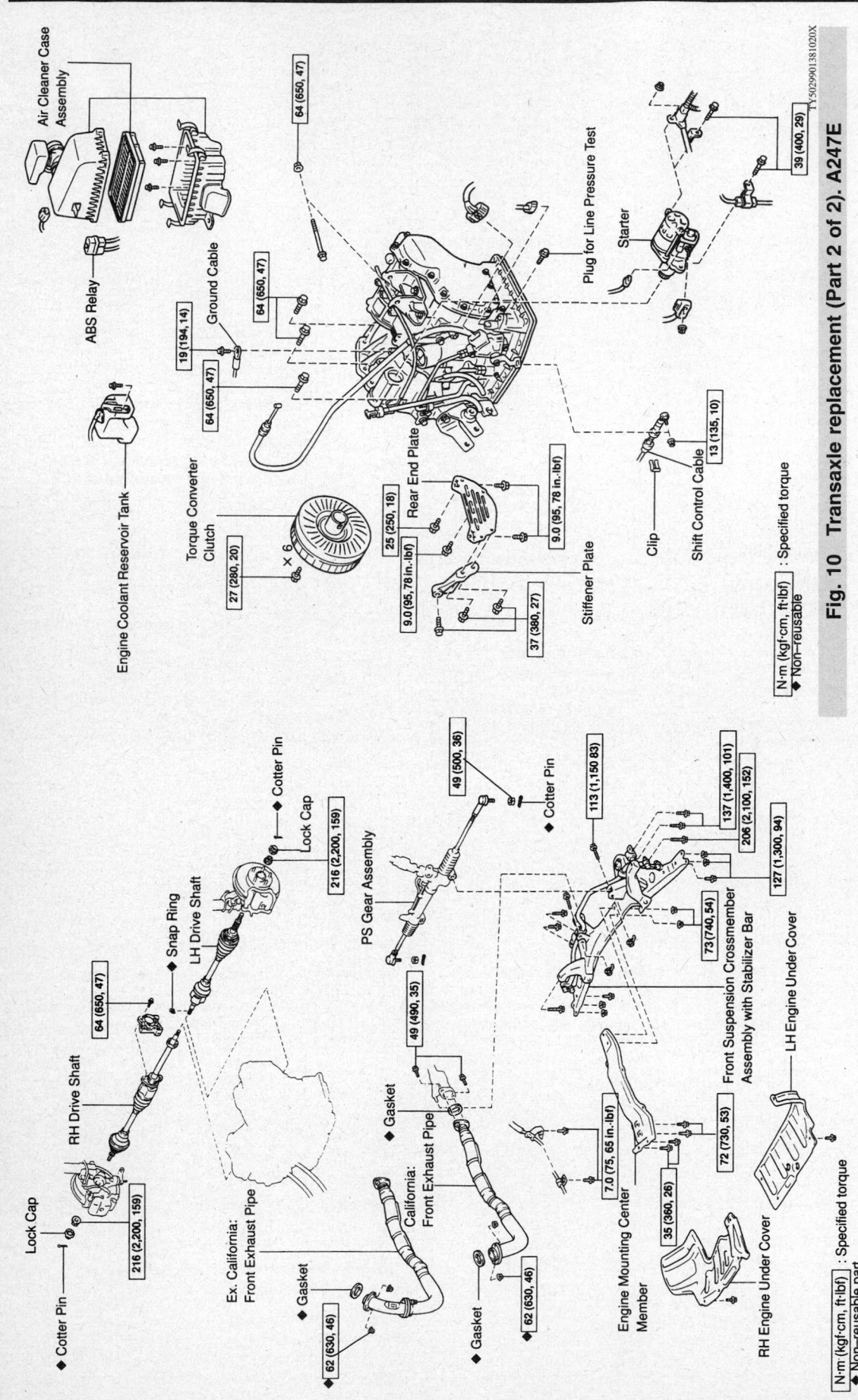

TY5029901381020X

Fig. 10 Transaxle replacement (Part 2 of 2). A247E

Air Cleaner Case Assembly

ABS Relay

Engine Coolant Reservoir Tank

64 (650, 47)

39 (400, 29)

Plug for Line Pressure Test

Starter

19 (194, 14)

Ground Cable

64 (650, 47)

64 (650, 47)

13 (135, 10)

Clip

Shift Control Cable

Torque Converter Clutch

27 (280, 20)

× 6

25 (250, 18)

Rear End Plate

9.0 (95, 78 in.·lbf)

9.0 (95, 78 in.·lbf)

37 (380, 27)

Stiffener Plate

N·m (kgf·cm, ft·lbf) : Specified torque

◆ Non-reusable

TY5029901381010X

Fig. 10 Transaxle replacement (Part 1 of 2). A247E

Cotter Pin

Lock Cap

216 (2,200, 159)

Snap Ring

LH Drive Shaft

64 (650, 47)

RH Drive Shaft

Lock Cap

Cotter Pin

216 (2,200, 159)

Ex. California: Front Exhaust Pipe

◆ Gasket

California: Front Exhaust Pipe

◆ Gasket

62 (630, 46)

◆ Gasket

◆ Gasket

62 (630, 46)

62 (630, 46)

49 (500, 36)

Cotter Pin

PS Gear Assembly

49 (490, 35)

113 (1,150 83)

137 (1,400, 101)

206 (2,100, 152)

127 (1,300, 94)

73 (740, 54)

Front Suspension Crossmember Assembly with Stabilizer Bar

LH Engine Under Cover

7.0 (75, 65 in.·lbf)

Engine Mounting Center Member

35 (360, 26)

72 (730, 53)

RH Engine Under Cover

N·m (kgf·cm, ft·lbf) : Specified torque

◆ Non-reusable part

TIGHTENING SPECIFICATIONS

Year	Component	Torque, Ft. Lbs.
1996–99	Engine Mount	47
	Lock Plate	108①
	Lower Subframe A Bolts	94
	Lower Subframe B Bolts	130
	Lower Subframe C Bolts	127
	Oil Pan Bolts	48①
	Oil Pan Drain Plug	13
	Oil Strainer Bolts	84①
	Starter Bolts	29
	Torque Converter Mounting Bolts	19
	Valve Body Mounting Bolts	84①

① — Inch lbs.

TOYOTA UNIT REPAIR

A340E, A340F & A343F Automatic Transmissions

NOTE: On Air Bag Equipped Models, Refer To "Air Bag System Precautions" Located In The Front Of This Manual For System Disarming & Arming Procedures.

INDEX

PRECAUTIONS

AIR BAG SYSTEMS

Refer to "Air Bag System Precautions" in the front of this manual for system disarming and arming procedures.

BATTERY GROUND CABLE

Prior to service disconnect battery ground cable and isolate as required.

AUDIO CODED ANTI-THEFT SYSTEM

Some models are equipped with an audio coded anti-theft system that will disable the radio when the battery cable is disconnected. The system can be identified by the "ANTI-THEFT SYSTEM" on the cassette lid. Obtain 3 digit code for input. Reset system after service as follows:
1. Obtain 3 digit audio theft code.
2. Depress 1 (PROG) while depressing righthand side of TUNE SEEK button, - - - will appear in tape operation display.
3. To enter the first digit, depress 1 (PROG) button repeatedly until the number of times depressed equals the first digit (depress the 1 button six times if the first digit if five, first press equals 0).
4. To enter second digit, depress 2 (APS) button repeatedly until the number of times depressed equals the second digit.
5. To enter third digit, depress 3 (RPT) button repeatedly until the number of times depressed equals the third digit.

6. If - - - is displayed after inputting digits, repeat procedure.
7. When code appears in display, depress and hold SCAN button until SEC appears.
8. When SEC disappears audio system is operative.
9. If Err is displayed, repeat procedure. **Attempting to input code more than 9 times may permanently disable audio system.**

TROUBLESHOOTING

FLUID DISCOLORED OR SMELLS BURNED

1. Contaminated fluid.
2. Faulty torque converter.
3. Faulty transmission.

VEHICLE DOES NOT MOVE IN ANY DRIVE GEAR

1. Improperly adjusted transmission control cable.
2. Faulty valve body or primary regulator.
3. Faulty parking lock pawl.
4. Faulty torque converter.
5. Broken converter driveplate.
6. Blocked oil pump intake screen.
7. Faulty transmission.

INCORRECT SHIFT LEVER POSITION

1. Improperly adjusted transmission control cable.
2. Faulty manual valve and lever.

3. Faulty transmission.

HARSH ENGAGEMENT INTO ANY DRIVE RANGE

1. Improperly adjusted transmission control cable.
2. Faulty valve body or primary regulator.
3. Faulty accumulator pistons.
4. Faulty transmission.

DELAYED UPSHIFTS & DOWNSHIFTS

1. Faulty electronic control.
2. Faulty valve body.
3. Faulty solenoid valve.

SLIPS ON UPSHIFTS OR SHUDDERS ON TAKEOFF

1. Improperly adjusted transmission control cable.
2. Improperly adjusted throttle cable.
3. Faulty valve body.
4. Faulty solenoid valve.
5. Faulty transmission.

DRAG OR BINDING ON UPSHIFTS

1. Improperly adjusted transmission control cable.
2. Faulty valve body.
3. Faulty transmission.

NO LOCK UP IN 2ND, 3RD OR O/D

1. Faulty electronic control
2. Faulty valve body.
3. Faulty solenoid valve.

4. Faulty transmission.

HARSH DOWNSHIFT

1. Improperly adjusted throttle cable.
2. Faulty throttle cable and cam.
3. Faulty accumulator pistons.
4. Faulty valve body.
5. Faulty transmission.

NO DOWNSHIFT WHEN COASTING

1. Faulty valve body.
2. Faulty solenoid valve.
3. Faulty electronic control.

INCORRECT DOWNSHIFT

1. Improperly adjusted throttle cable.
2. Faulty valve body.
3. Faulty transmission.
4. Faulty solenoid valve.
5. Faulty electronic control.

NO KICKDOWN

1. Faulty solenoid valve.
2. Faulty electronic control.
3. Faulty valve body.

NO ENGINE BRAKING IN 2 OR L

1. Faulty solenoid valve.
2. Faulty electronic control.
3. Faulty valve body.
4. Faulty transmission.

NO HOLD IN P

1. Improperly adjusted transmission control cable.
2. Faulty parking lock pawl cam and spring.

VEHICLE DOES NOT MOVE IN ANY RANGE

1. Improperly adjusted transfer linkage.
2. Faulty electronic control.
3. Faulty transfer valve body.
4. Faulty torque converter.
5. Faulty transmission.
6. Faulty transfer.

MAINTENANCE

FLUID CHECK

1. Operate vehicle, allow transaxle fluid temperature to reach 158–176°F.
2. Position vehicle on level surface, apply parking brake.
3. Allow engine to idle, depress brake pedal, then move shift lever through all positions.
4. Remove transaxle dipstick, wipe clean, then replace.
5. Remove again, then check fluid level in hot range.

FLUID CHANGE

1. Drain transaxle fluid, then reinstall drain plugs.
2. With engine off, add fluid through filler tube. **Do not overfill.**
3. Start engine, move shift lever through all positions, ensuring smooth operation.

4. Allow engine to idle, then check fluid level, add up to cool level.
5. Once fluid temperature reaches 158–176°F, recheck fluid level.

ADJUSTMENTS

SHIFT LINKAGE

1. Loosen shift linkage nut.
2. Push manual lever fully forward, then return lever two notches to Neutral position.
3. While holding selector slightly toward Reverse range, tighten shift linkage nut to specifications.

NEUTRAL SAFETY SWITCH

1. Check that vehicle can only be started in either " P" or "N" ranges.
2. If vehicle starts in any other position, adjust switch as follows:
   a. Loosen neutral start switch bolt and set shift lever to " N" range.
   b. Align groove and neutral basic line as shown in **Fig. 1.**
   c. Hold in position and tighten to specification.

THROTTLE CABLE

1. Ensure throttle valve is fully closed and that inner cable is not slack.
2. Adjust cable housing until distance between end of boot and stopper on cable is 0–.04 inch.
3. Tighten adjusting nuts to specifications, then recheck adjustment.

TRANSFER LINKAGE

1. Place transfer lever in "H2" position.
2. Disconnect No. 1 transfer linkage from cross shaft.
3. Position transfer indicator switch in "H2"position.
4. Connect No. 1 transfer linkage from cross shaft.

TRANSFER POSITION SWITCH

1. Loosen transfer position switch bolt, then place switch in " L4" position.
2. Disconnect electrical connector, then connect a suitable ohmmeter between terminals, **Fig. 2.**
3. Adjust switch until there is no continuity between terminals.
4. Connect electrical connector, then tighten to specification.
5. Ensure proper idle RPM.

IN-VEHICLE REPAIRS

VALVE BODY, REPLACE

Removal

1. Clean exterior of transmission.
2. Raise and support vehicle, then drain transmission fluid.
3. Remove oil pan attaching bolts, then remove oil pan by inserting oil pan seal cutter tool No. 09032-00100, or equivalent, between oil pan and transmission case and cut seal.
4. Being careful not to damage oil pan

flange, remove oil pan by lifting transmission case.
5. Remove attaching bolts, then oil strainer and two gaskets.
6. Note position of oil tubes to facilitate installation, then remove oil tubes.
7. Disconnect solenoid electrical connectors.
8. Remove attaching bolts, then disconnect throttle cable from cam and remove valve body.

Installation

1. Align groove of manual valve to pin of manual lever.
2. Connect throttle cable to cam, then ensure springs are correctly installed into accumulator pistons.
3. Install valve body, then tighten to specification.
4. Before installing solenoid wiring into case, coat a new O-ring with ATF and install it into grommet.
5. Insert solenoid wiring into case, then install stopper plate.
6. Connect remaining connectors to No. 1, No. 2 and lock-up solenoids.
7. Using a plastic hammer, install oil tubes into position.
8. Install two new gaskets and oil strainer, tighten to specification.
9. Install four magnets in indentations of oil pan.
10. Apply seal packing part No. 08826-00090, three bond 1281, or equivalent, to oil pan.
11. Install oil pan, tighten to specification.
12. Install drain plug, then tighten to specification.
13. Add transmission fluid to specifications, then road test vehicle.

TRANSFER VALVE BODY, REPLACE

Removal

1. Clean exterior of transfer case.
2. Raise and support vehicle, then drain transfer case fluid.
3. Support transmission, using suitable jack stands, then remove attaching bolts and disconnect rear support member from body.
4. Remove four attaching bolts, then rear support member.
5. Remove four attaching bolts, then the member bracket from transfer case.
6. Remove transfer case oil pan attaching bolts, then the oil pan.
7. Disconnect No. 4 solenoid electrical connector, then the solenoid attaching bolt and solenoid.
8. Remove six valve body attaching bolts, then the valve body.

Installation

1. Align manual valve lever with manual valve, then install attaching bolts as shown, **Fig. 3,** then tighten to specification. Attaching bolt lengths (mm) are indicated in **Fig. 3.**
2. Install No. 4 solenoid, then insert attaching bolt and tighten to specification.
3. Connect solenoid electrical connector.

4. Clean contacting surfaces of oil pan and case, then apply a suitable sealant to surfaces. Install oil pan within 10 minutes of application of sealant, then insert attaching bolts and tighten to specification.
5. Install drain plug, then tighten to specification.
6. Assemble member bracket to case.
7. Install engine rear support member, then insert attaching bolts and tighten to specification.
8. Install rear support member onto body, then insert attaching bolts and tighten to specification.
9. Fill transfer case to specifications, then ensure proper fluid level.
10. Remove transmission jack, then lower vehicle.
11. Road test vehicle.

THROTTLE CABLE, REPLACE

1. Disconnect cable housing from bracket on cylinder head cover, then the cable from throttle linkage.
2. Remove valve body as previously described.
3. Remove throttle cable mounting bolt from transmission case, then pull out cable.
4. Reverse procedure to install. Tighten throttle cable mount bolt to specification and adjust cable as outlined under "Adjustments."

PARKING LOCK PAWL, REPLACE

1. Remove valve body as outlined under "Valve Body, Replace."
2. Remove parking lock pawl bracket.
3. Remove pivot pin spring, then the pivot and pin.
4. Reverse procedure to install. Tighten bolts to specification.

EXTENSION HOUSING, REPLACE

1. Raise and support vehicle.
2. Position a pan to catch any fluid that may drip.
3. Remove propeller shaft together with center bearing.
4. Disconnect speedometer cable, then remove speedometer driven gear and speed sensor.
5. Remove output flange if equipped.
6. Jack up transmission slightly to remove weight from rear support member.
7. Remove No. 2 vehicle speed sensor.
8. Remove ground cable, then remove rear support member.
9. Remove extension housing and gasket.
10. Reverse procedure to install, tighten all nuts and bolts to specifications.

SENSOR ROTOR, REPLACE

1. Remove extension housing as outlined under "Extension Housing, Replace."
2. Using snap ring pliers, remove snap ring, then speedometer gear and lock ball.

3. Remove sensor rotor from output shaft.
4. Reverse procedure to install, ensuring that sensor rotor key is installed in groove.

REAR OIL SEAL, REPLACE

1. Raise vehicle, then position pan to catch any fluid that may drip.
2. Remove propeller shaft together with center bearing.
3. Remove oil seal with seal remover tool No. 09308-10010 or suitable equivalent.
4. Reverse procedure to install, using installation tool No. 09325-20010 or suitable equivalent, to install new seal.

TRANSMISSION

REPLACE
LAND CRUISER

Refer to **Fig. 4** when replacing transmission.
1. Remove battery and air cleaner cap.
2. Remove drive belt, fan and fluid coupling assembly.
3. Remove fan shroud and radiator reservoir.
4. Remove upper mounting bolt for filler tube.
5. Remove transfer shift lever boot.
6. Remove engine under covers.
7. Remove both front exhaust pipes.
8. Remove front and rear drive shafts.
9. Remove oil fill pipe and transmission shift control rod.
10. Disconnect transfer shift lever.
11. Disconnect all electrical connectors from transmission.
12. Remove torque converter access cover.
13. Remove torque converter mounting bolts.
14. Remove oil cooler pipe union nuts.
15. Support transmission using suitable jack, then remove crossmember.
16. Lower rear of transmission and remove engine to transmission mounting bolts.
17. Remove transmission from vehicle.
18. Reverse procedure to install.

SUPRA

Non-Turbocharged Engine

Refer to **Fig. 5** when replacing transmission.
1. Remove air cleaner assembly and engine under cover.
2. Remove exhaust pipe.
3. Remove exhaust manifold with catalytic converter.
4. Remove driveshaft and filler pipe.
5. Remove transmission control rod.
6. Disconnect oil cooler pipes from transmission.
7. Remove access hole plug and torque converter mounting bolts.
8. Using suitable jack, lift transmission and remove rear crossmember.
9. Remove starter motor, then disconnect all electrical connectors from transmission.

10. Remove transmission to engine mounting bolts, then remove transmission from vehicle.
11. Reverse procedure to install.

Turbocharged Engine

Refer to **Fig. 6** when replacing transmission.
1. Remove fluid filler pipe.
2. Remove engine under cover, exhaust pipe and driveshaft.
3. Disconnect shift control rod from shift lever.
4. Disconnect all electrical connectors from transmission.
5. Disconnect cable and connectors from starter motor.
6. Disconnect oil cooler union nuts, then remove front, center and rear oil cooler line brackets.
7. Remove intercooler pipe.
8. Remove access cover, then remove torque converter mounting bolts.
9. Set transmission using suitable jack, then support engine using suitable jack stands.
10. Remove rear transmission support and starter motor.
11. Disconnect wire harness from each clamp.
12. Remove transmission to engine mounting bolts, then lower transmission from vehicle.
13. Reverse procedure to install.

TACOMA

2WD Models

The engine and transmission are removed as an assembly. Refer to **Fig. 7** when replacing the transmission.
1. Remove engine under cover, then drain coolant and engine oil into suitable containers.
2. Drain transmission fluid into suitable container, then remove hood.
3. Remove radiator assembly, then disconnect heater hoses.
4. Remove fan with fluid coupling and fan pulleys.
5. Remove air cleaner assembly, then disconnect accelerator, throttle and cruise control cables.
6. Disconnect EVAP, brake booster, fuel inlet and fuel return hoses.
7. Disconnect starter wire and connector, then remove wires from alternator.
8. Remove glove compartment door and lower trim panel, then disconnect four connectors from ECM.
9. Remove two bolts and the ECM.
10. Disconnect VSV connector for EVAP.
11. Disconnect vapor pressure sensor connector and clamp.
12. Disconnect VSV connector for vapor pressure sensor.
13. Disconnect igniter connector and ground strap, then remove bolt and two nuts.
14. Remove engine wire from cabin.
15. Remove driveshaft, then disconnect speedometer cable.
16. Remove front exhaust pipe, then place jack under transmission.
17. Remove rear engine mounting bracket.

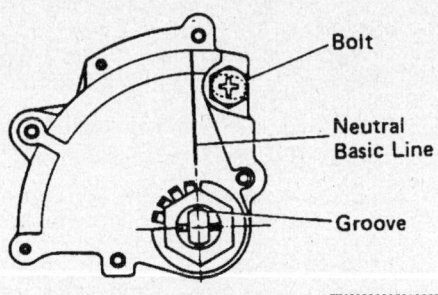

Fig. 1 Neutral safety switch adjustment

TY5028900521000X

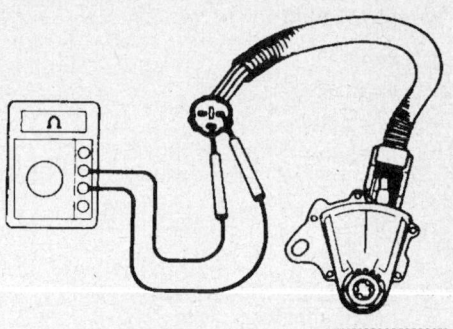

Fig. 2 Transfer indicator switch adjustment

TY5028900523000X

18. **On models equipped with A/C,** remove bolt and disconnect A/C compressor wire.
19. **On all models,** install engine hanger tool No. 12282–62030 or equivalent, then attach engine hoist chain to both hangers.
20. Remove four bolts and nuts securing front engine mounting insulators to frame.
21. Lift engine and transmission slowly out of vehicle. Ensure engine is clear of all wiring and hoses.
22. Place engine and transmission assembly onto suitable stand.
23. Remove filler pipe, then disconnect oil cooler pipes.
24. Disconnect any electrical connectors from transmission, then separate wire harness from transmission.
25. Remove flexplate inspection cover, then remove torque converter mounting bolts.
26. Remove starter motor, then separate transmission from engine.
    a. Measure installed distance of torque converter to front of transmission housing. Distance should be .7067 inch or more.
    b. After installation, adjust shift lever position and throttle cable as outlined under "Adjustments."
    c. Fill transmission with specified fluid type and amount.

4WD Models

Refer to **Figs. 8 and 9** when replacing the transmission.
1. Remove ATF level gauge and engine under cover.
2. Disconnect throttle cable, then remove No. 1 fan shroud.
3. Remove transmission shift lever assembly and transfer shift lever.
4. Remove ATF filler pipe.
5. Remove front and rear driveshafts.
6. Remove exhaust pipe.
7. Disconnect all electrical connectors from transmission and transfer unit.
8. Disconnect oil cooler pipes.
9. Remove starter motor.

10. Remove stabilizer bar bracket bolts.
11. Remove flexplate inspection cover and torque converter mounting bolts.
12. Lift up front differential using suitable support stand, then remove front differential rear mounting cushion.
13. Support rear of transmission using suitable support stand.
14. Remove crossmember, then support transmission using suitable transmission jack.
15. Separate wiring harness from transmission, then remove transmission to engine mounting bolts.
16. Lower transmission from vehicle.
17. Reverse procedure to install.

T100
A340E Transaxle

The engine and transmission are removed as an assembly. Refer to **Figs. 10 and 11** when replacing transmission.
1. Remove ATF level gauge.
2. Remove engine under cover, then disconnect throttle cable.
3. Remove No. 1 throttle cable clamp, then raise and support vehicle.
4. Remove ATF filler pipe and driveshaft.
5. Remove front exhaust pipe.
6. Disconnect speedometer cable, No. 2 speed sensor connector and solenoid connector.
7. Remove cross shaft and oil cooler pipes.
8. Disconnect ATF sensor and park/neutral position switch connectors.
9. Disconnect starter wires, then remove front stabilizer bar.
10. Remove rear end plate, then disconnect rear mounting insulator.
11. Remove torque converter mounting bolts, then lower vehicle.
12. Support transmission using suitable floor jack.
13. Drain oil, coolant and transmission fluid into suitable containers.
14. Remove hood, air cleaner assembly and MAF meter.
15. Remove radiator assembly.
16. Remove fan with fluid couplings and fan pulleys.
17. Remove A/C compressor bracket, if equipped.
18. Disconnect accelerator, throttle and cruise control cables, as equipped.
19. Disconnect heater hoses.
20. Disconnect EVAP and brake booster hoses.
21. Disconnect fuel inlet and return hoses.
22. Disconnect alternator wires.
23. Remove right front door scuff plate and cowl side trim panel.
24. Disconnect ECM connectors.
25. Disconnect two connectors from cowl wire harness.

26. Disconnect igniter connector and ground strap.
27. Disconnect six engine wire clamps.
28. Remove engine wiring harness from cabin area.
29. Install engine hanger, **Fig. 12.**
30. Attach engine hoist chain to hangers, then remove bolts and nuts securing engine mount insulators to frame.
31. Remove engine and transmission assembly from vehicle.
32. Remove transmission attaching bolts and separate engine from transmission.
33. Reverse procedure to install.

A340F Transaxle

Refer to **Fig. 13** when replacing transmission.
1. Remove engine under cover and disconnect throttle cable.
2. Remove transfer shift lever from inside vehicle.
3. Remove No. 1 throttle cable clamp, then lift and support vehicle.
4. Remove oil filler pipe and driveshafts.
5. Remove front exhaust pipe.
6. Disconnect speedometer cable.
7. Disconnect all electrical connectors from transmission, then separate wiring harness from transmission and transfer unit.
8. Remove cross shaft, then disconnect starter motor connectors.
9. Remove oil cooler pipes and starter motor.
10. Remove stiffener and rear end plates.
11. Remove front stabilizer bar.
12. Support transmission using suitable transmission jack.
13. Disconnect rear mounting insulator, then remove rear support member.
14. Remove torque converter mounting bolts.
15. Remove engine to transmission mounting bolts, then lower transmission from vehicle.
16. Reverse procedure to install.

4RUNNER

A340E

Refer to **Figs. 14 and 15** when replacing the transmission.
1. Disconnect throttle cable.
2. Remove ATF level gauge and oil filler pipe.
3. Remove engine under covers and driveshaft.
4. Remove front exhaust pipe.
5. Disconnect transmission control rod from shift lever.
6. Disconnect all electrical connectors from transmission.
7. Disconnect oil cooler pipes.
8. Remove flexplate inspection cover and torque converter mounting bolts.
9. Using suitable transmission jack, slightly lift transmission.
10. Remove No. 3 crossmember and rear engine mount.
11. Remove starter motor.
12. Remove engine to transmission mounting bolts, then lower transmission from vehicle.
13. Reverse procedure to install.

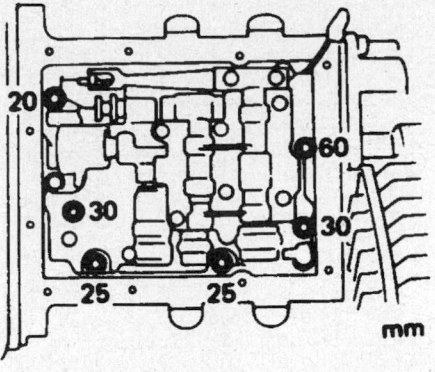

TY5028900524000X

Fig. 3 Transfer valve body bolt installation

A340F

Refer to **Figs. 16 through 18** when replacing transmission.
1. Disconnect throttle cable.
2. Remove ATF level gauge and oil filler pipe.

3. Remove transmission shift lever assembly and transfer shift lever.
4. Remove engine under covers and driveshafts.
5. Remove front exhaust pipe.
6. Disconnect all electrical connectors from transmission.
7. Disconnect oil cooler pipes.
8. Remove flexplate inspection cover and torque converter mounting bolts.
9. Using suitable jackstand, support rear of transmission.
10. Remove No. 3 crossmember and rear engine mount.
11. **On models equipped with VF3AM transfer unit,** remove No. 4 crossmember.
12. **On all models,** support transmission using suitable transmission jack.
13. Remove starter motor.
14. Remove engine to transmission mounting bolts, then lower transmission from vehicle.
15. Reverse procedure to install.

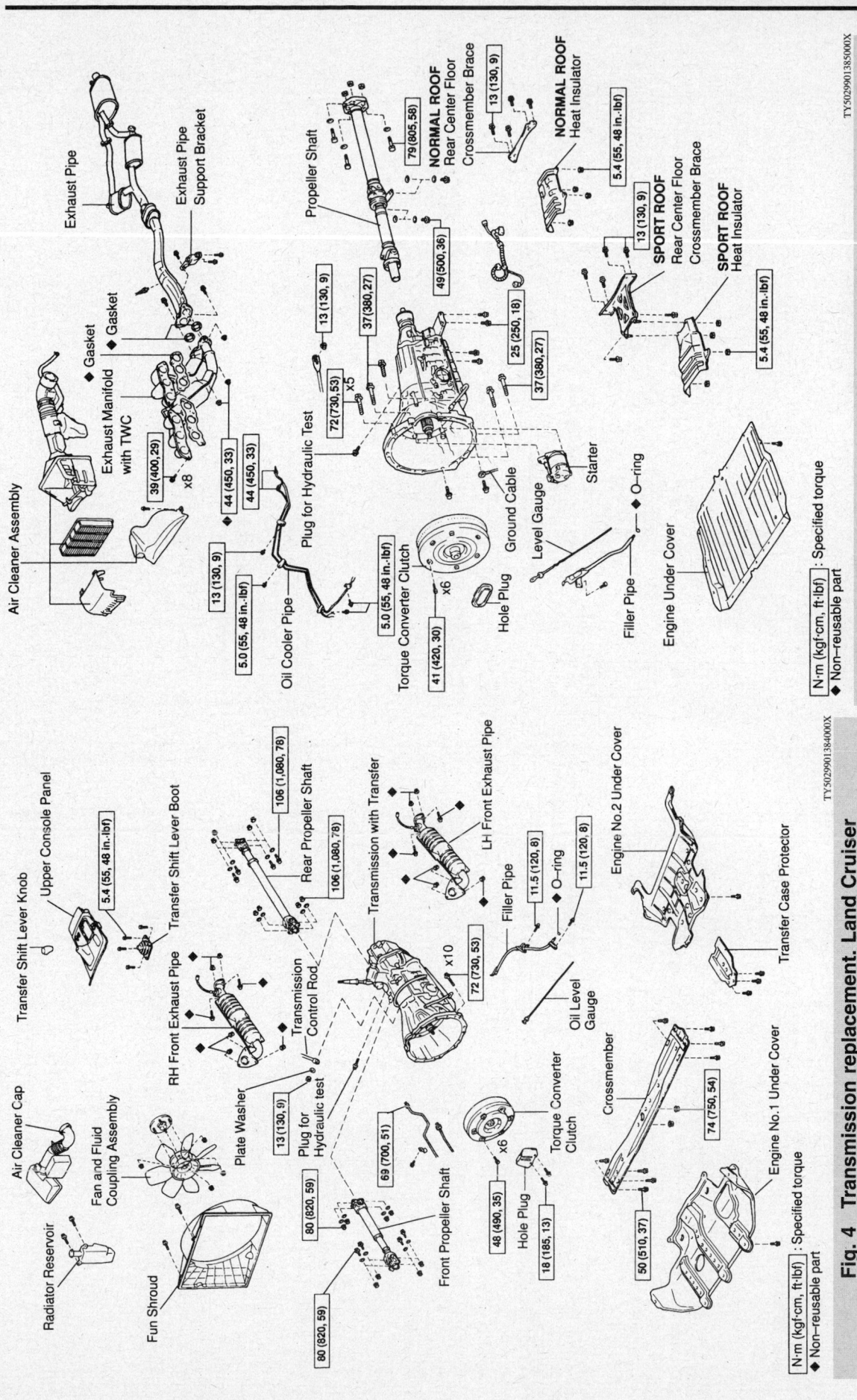

Fig. 5 Transmission replacement. Supra w/non-turbocharged engine

Fig. 4 Transmission replacement. Land Cruiser

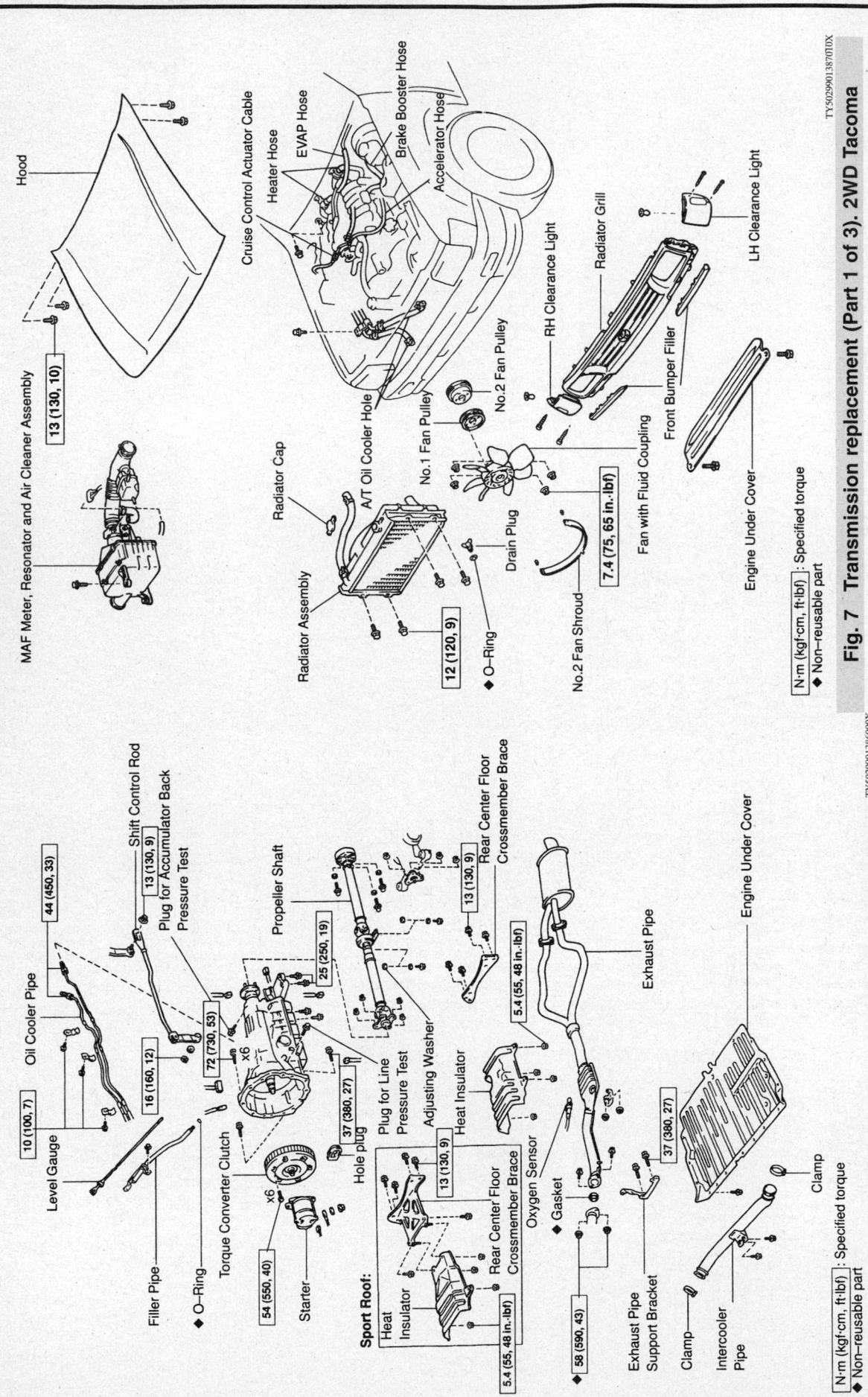

Fig. 7 Transmission replacement (Part 1 of 3). 2WD Tacoma

TY50299013870I0X

Hood

13 (130, 10)

MAF Meter, Resonator and Air Cleaner Assembly

Cruise Control Actuator Cable

Heater Hose

EVAP Hose

Brake Booster Hose

Accelerator Hose

Radiator Grill

RH Clearance Light

LH Clearance Light

No.2 Fan Pulley

No.1 Fan Pulley

A/T Oil Cooler Hole

Radiator Cap

Front Bumper Filler

Fan with Fluid Coupling

7.4 (75, 65 in.·lbf)

Engine Under Cover

Drain Plug

No.2 Fan Shroud

Radiator Assembly

12 (120, 9)

◆ O–Ring

N·m (kgf·cm, ft·lbf) : Specified torque
◆ Non-reusable part

Fig. 6 Transmission replacement. Supra w/turbocharged engine

TY50299013860I0X

Shift Control Rod

13 (130, 9)

Plug for Accumulator Back Pressure Test

Propeller Shaft

Rear Center Floor Crossmember Brace

13 (130, 9)

Exhaust Pipe

Engine Under Cover

44 (450, 33)

Oil Cooler Pipe

25 (250, 19)

16 (160, 12)

72 (730, 53) x6

37 (380, 27)

Plug for Line Pressure Test

Adjusting Washer

Heat Insulator

5.4 (55, 48 in.·lbf)

37 (380, 27)

Clamp

10 (100, 7)

Level Gauge

Filler Pipe

◆ O–Ring

54 (550, 40)

Torque Converter Clutch

x6

Starter

Hole plug

13 (130, 9)

Oxygen Sensor

◆ Gasket

58 (590, 43)

Exhaust Pipe Support Bracket

Clamp

Intercooler Pipe

Sport Roof:

Heat Insulator

Rear Center Floor Crossmember Brace

5.4 (55, 48 in.·lbf)

N·m (kgf·cm, ft·lbf) : Specified torque
◆ Non-reusable part

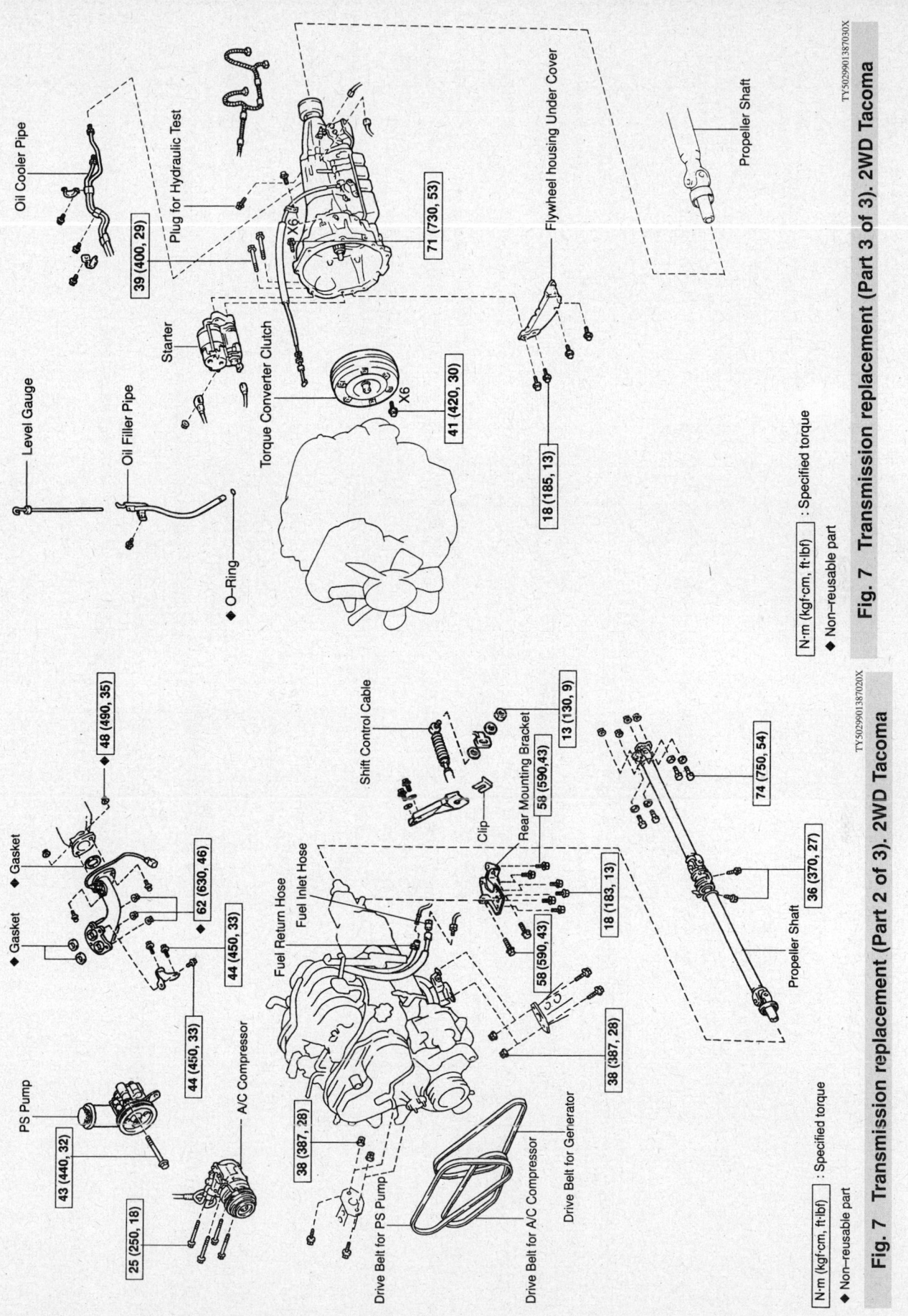

TY502990138703030X

Oil Cooler Pipe

Plug for Hydraulic Test

39 (400, 29)

71 (730, 53)

Flywheel housing Under Cover

Propeller Shaft

Starter

Torque Converter Clutch

X6

X6

41 (420, 30)

18 (185, 13)

Level Gauge

Oil Filler Pipe

◆ O-Ring

N·m (kgf·cm, ft·lbf) : Specified torque

◆ Non-reusable part

Fig. 7 Transmission replacement (Part 3 of 3). 2WD Tacoma

TY502990138702020X

48 (490, 35)

Gasket

62 (630, 46)

Gasket

44 (450, 33)

44 (450, 33)

PS Pump

43 (440, 32)

25 (250, 18)

A/C Compressor

Shift Control Cable

Clip

Rear Mounting Bracket

13 (130, 9)

58 (590, 43)

74 (750, 54)

Fuel Return Hose

Fuel Inlet Hose

18 (183, 13)

58 (590, 43)

36 (370, 27)

Propeller Shaft

38 (387, 28)

38 (387, 28)

Drive Belt for PS Pump

Drive Belt for A/C Compressor

Drive Belt for Generator

N·m (kgf·cm, ft·lbf) : Specified torque

◆ Non-reusable part

Fig. 7 Transmission replacement (Part 2 of 3). 2WD Tacoma

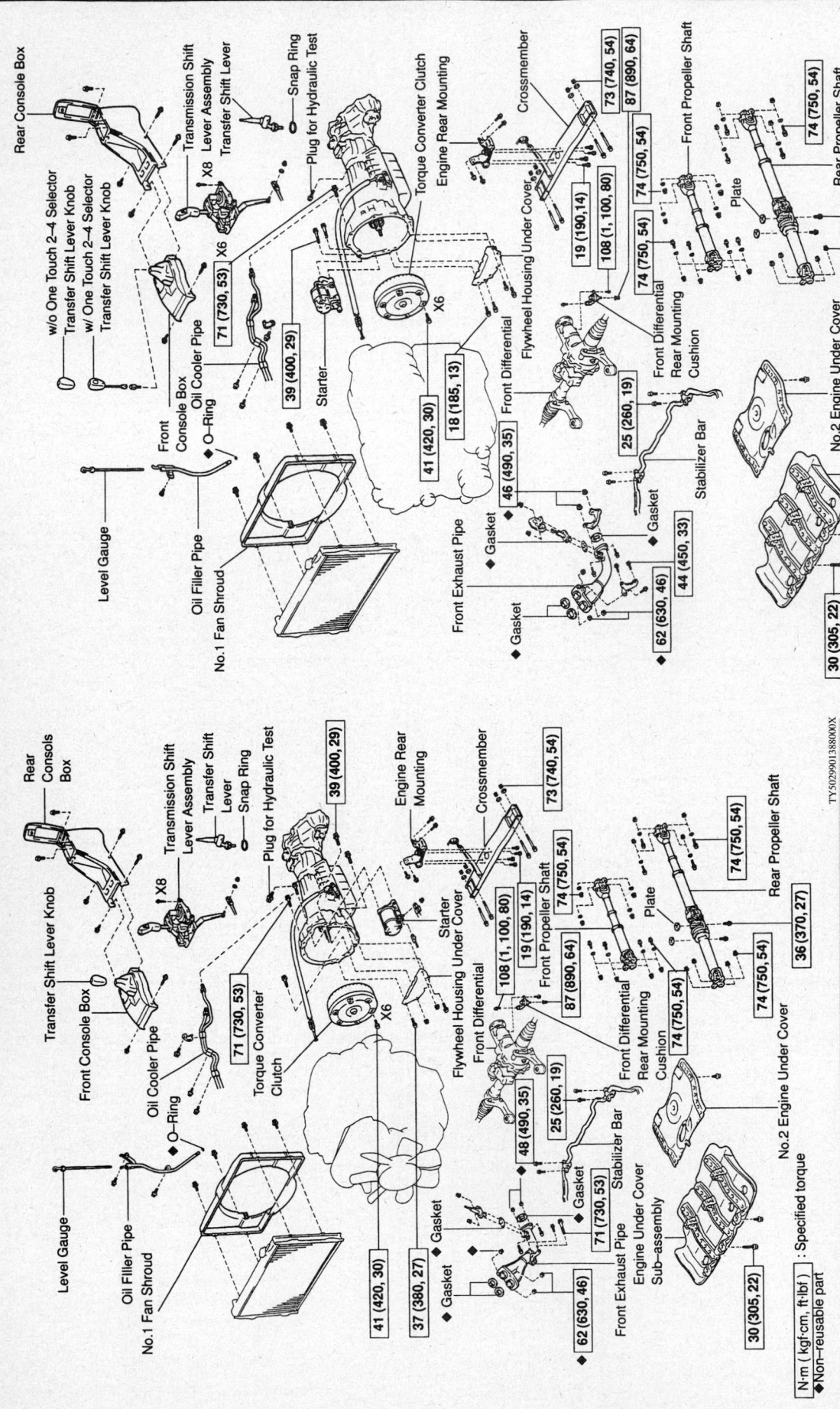

Fig. 9 Transmission replacement. 4WD Tacoma w/5VZ-FE engine

Fig. 8 Transmission replacement. 4WD Tacoma w/3RZ-FE engine

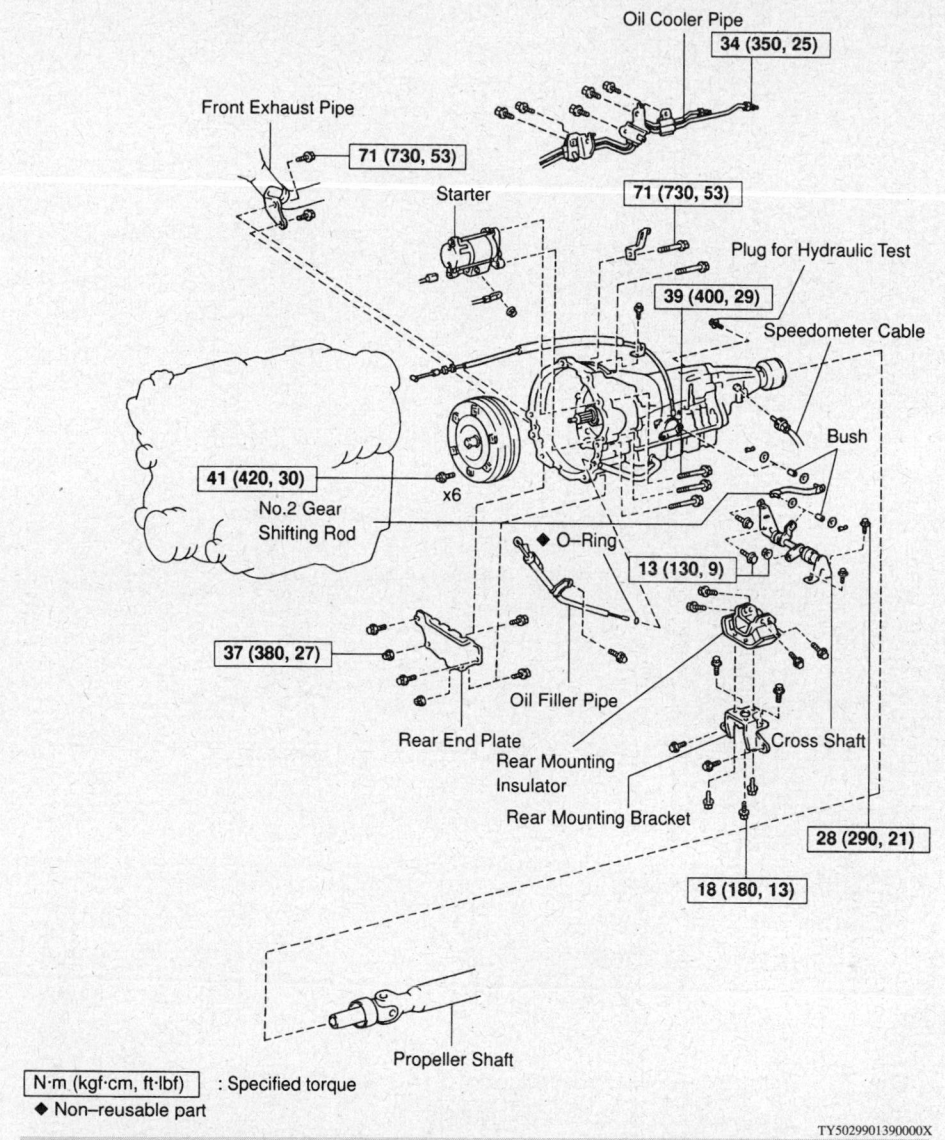

Oil Cooler Pipe
34 (350, 25)

Front Exhaust Pipe
71 (730, 53)

Starter

71 (730, 53)

Plug for Hydraulic Test

39 (400, 29)

Speedometer Cable

Bush

41 (420, 30)   x6

No.2 Gear
Shifting Rod

◆ O–Ring

13 (130, 9)

37 (380, 27)

Oil Filler Pipe

Rear End Plate

Rear Mounting
Insulator

Rear Mounting Bracket

Cross Shaft

28 (290, 21)

18 (180, 13)

Propeller Shaft

N·m (kgf·cm, ft·lbf) : Specified torque
◆ Non–reusable part

TY5029901390000X

Fig. 10   Transmission replacement. T100 w/3RZ-FE engine & A340E transaxle

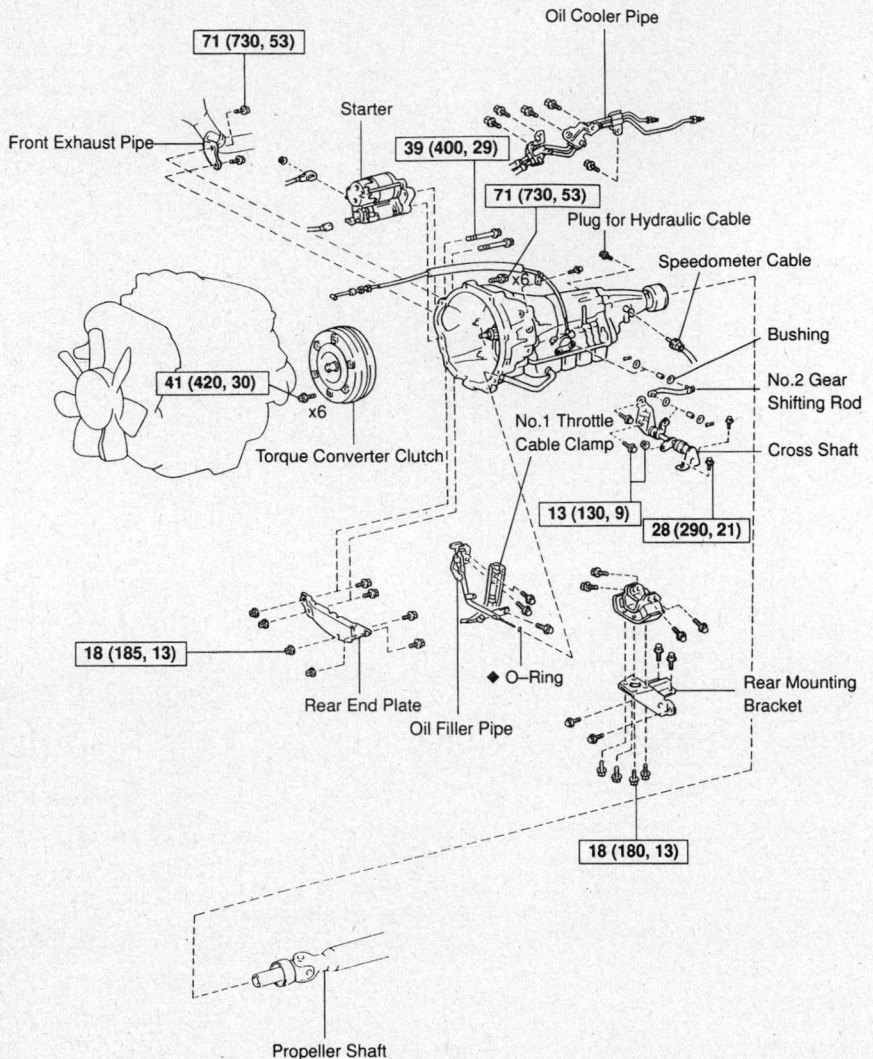

71 (730, 53)
Front Exhaust Pipe
Starter
Oil Cooler Pipe
39 (400, 29)
71 (730, 53)
Plug for Hydraulic Cable
Speedometer Cable
Bushing
No.2 Gear Shifting Rod
41 (420, 30)
x6
Torque Converter Clutch
No.1 Throttle Cable Clamp
Cross Shaft
13 (130, 9)
28 (290, 21)
18 (185, 13)
Rear End Plate
◆ O–Ring
Oil Filler Pipe
Rear Mounting Bracket
18 (180, 13)
Propeller Shaft

◆ Non–reusable part

TY5029901391000X

Fig. 11   Transmission replacement. T100 w/5VZ-FE engine & A340E transaxle

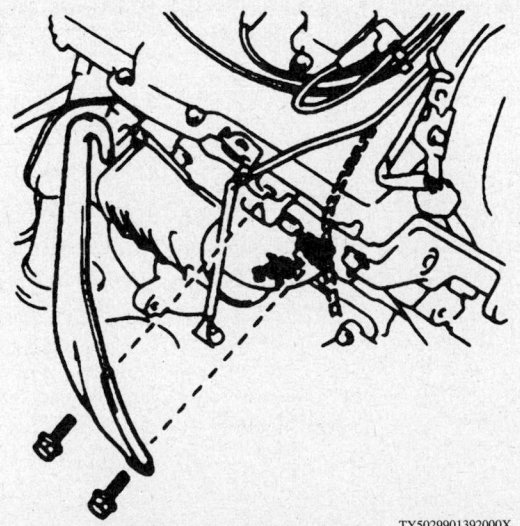

TY5029901392000X

Fig. 12   Engine hanger installation. T100 w/A340E Transaxle

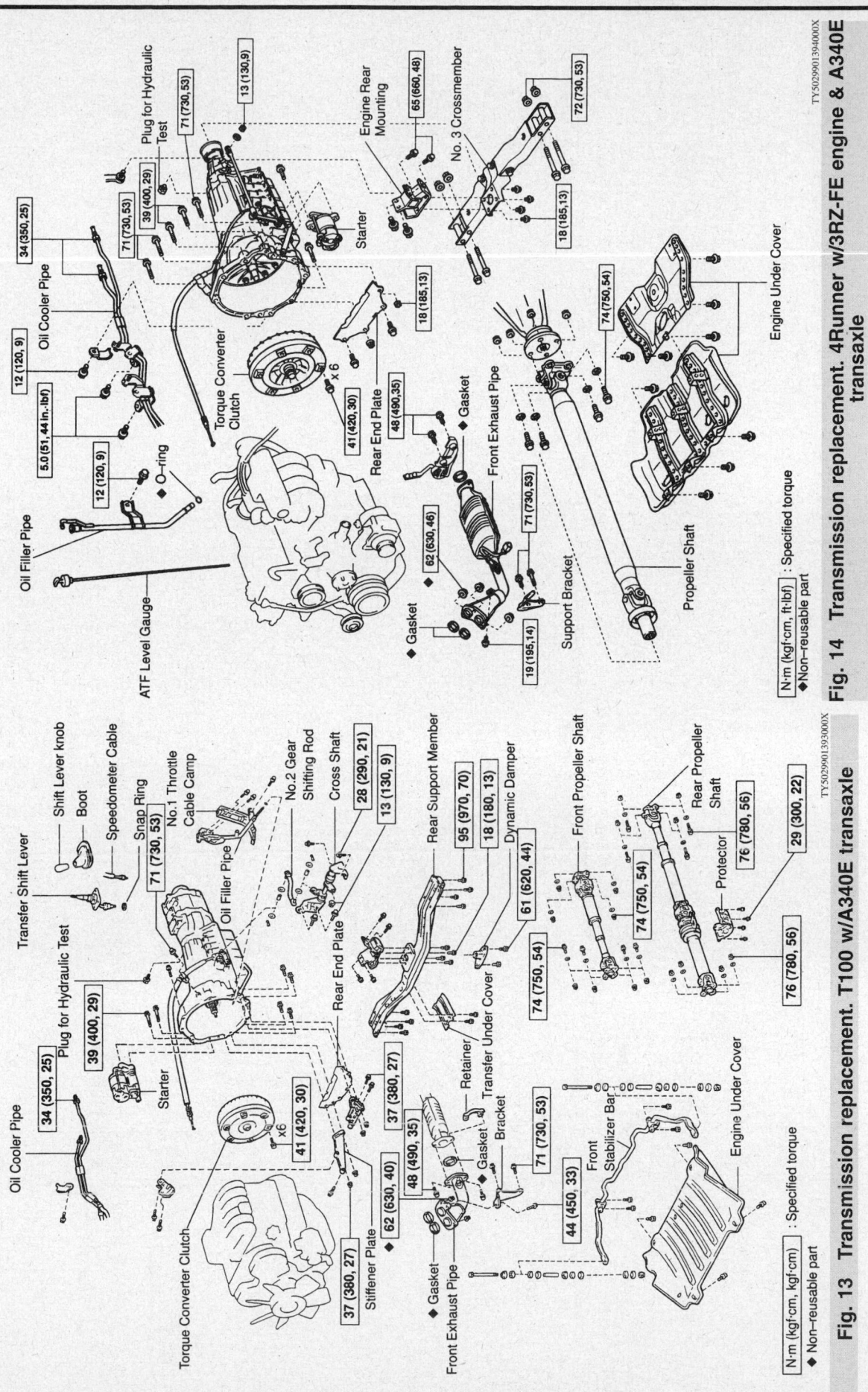

Fig. 14 Transmission replacement. 4Runner w/3RZ-FE engine & A340E transaxle

N·m (kgf·cm, ft·lbf) : Specified torque
◆ Non-reusable part

Fig. 13 Transmission replacement. T100 w/A340E transaxle

N·m (kgf·cm, kgf·cm) : Specified torque
◆ Non-reusable part

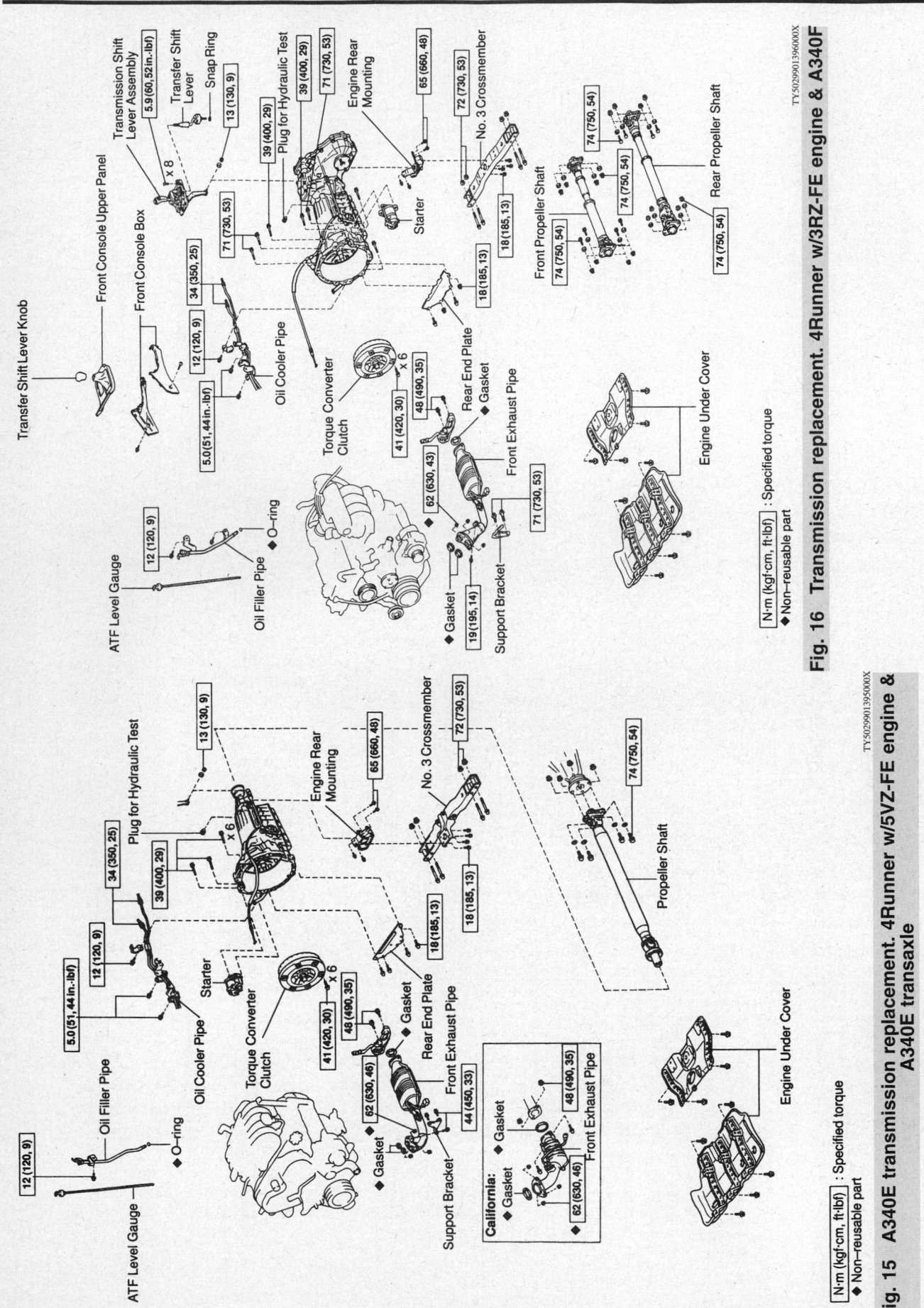

Fig. 16 Transmission replacement. 4Runner w/3RZ-FE engine & A340F

Fig. 15 A340E transmission replacement. 4Runner w/5VZ-FE engine & A340E transaxle

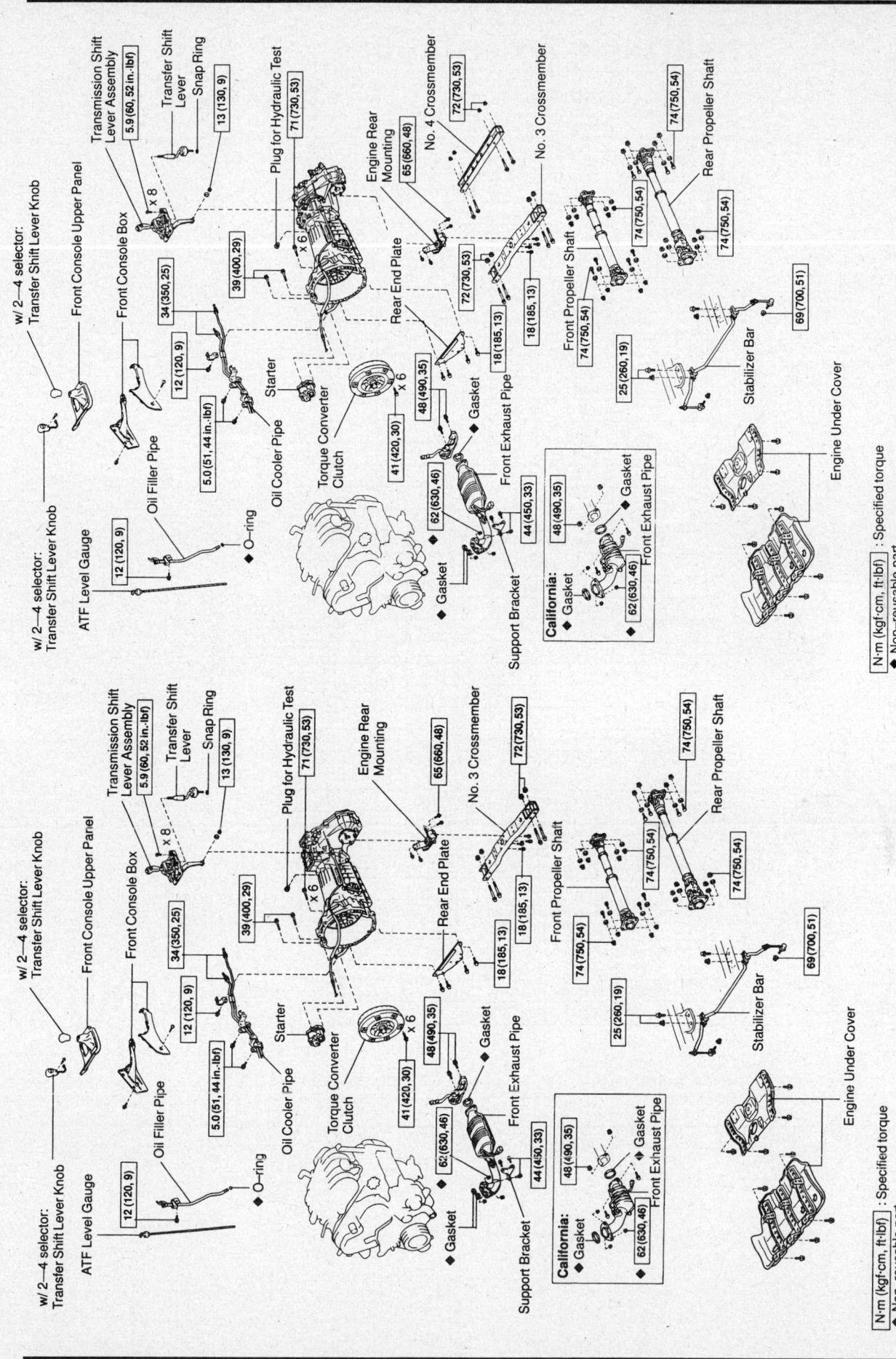

Fig. 18 Transmission replacement . 4Runner w/5VZ-FE engine, A340F & VF3AM transfer unit

N·m (kgf·cm, ft·lbf) : Specified torque
◆ Non-reusable part

TY502990139700BX

Fig. 17 Transmission replacement. 4Runner w/5VZ-FE engine, A340F & VF2A transfer unit

N·m (kgf·cm, ft·lbf) : Specified torque
◆ Non-reusable part

TY502990139700AX

TIGHTENING SPECIFICATIONS

Year	Component	Torque/ Ft. Lbs.
1996-99	Center Support Bolt	18
	Chain Case	25
	Control Shaft Lever	12
	Detent Spring To Valve Body	84①
	Driveplate To Crankshaft	②
	Extension Housing To Chain Rear Case	25
	Extension Housing To Transmission Case	27
	Fluid Temperature Sensor	11
	Front & Rear Companion Flanges	90
	Front Support To Transfer Case	25
	Neutral Start Switch (Bolt)	108①
	Neutral Start Switch (Nut)	61①
	No. 4 Solenoid To Valve Body	84①
	O/D Support To Transmission Case	19
	Oil Cooler Pipe Union Nut	25
	Oil Cooler Union	22
	Oil Drain Plug	15
	Oil Pan To Transfer Case	65①
	Oil Pan To Transmission	65①
	Oil Pump Body To Oil Pump Cover	84①
	Oil Strainer Case	84①
	Oil Strainer To Chain Rear Case	61①
	Parking Lock Pawl Bracket	65①
	Solenoid To Valve Body	84①
	Speed Sensor	12
	Speedometer Driven Gear Lock Plate	12
	Throttle Cable Bolt	84①
	Torque Converter To Driveplate	30
	Transfer Case To Transmission Case	25
	Transfer Chain Oil Receiver To Chain Front Case	84①
	Transfer Oil Cooler Tube Union Nut	25
	Transfer Oil Pump To Chain Rear Case	12
	Transfer Position Switch (Bolt)	108①
	Transfer Position Switch (Nut)	35①
	Transfer Pressure Switch To Valve Body	61①
	Transmission Housing To Transmission Case (10 mm Bolt)	25
	Transmission Housing To Transmission Case (12 mm Bolt)	42
	Upper Valve Body To Lower Valve Body	56①
	Valve Body Bolts	84①

① — Inch lbs.

② — Tacoma & 4Runner, 61 ft. lbs.; T100, 30 ft. lbs.; Supra, 54 ft. lbs.

A541E Automatic Transaxle

NOTE: On Air Bag Equipped Models, Refer To "Air Bag System Precautions" Located In The Front Of This Manual For System Disarming & Arming Procedures.

INDEX

PRECAUTIONS

AIR BAG SYSTEMS

Refer to "Air Bag System Precautions" in the front of this manual for system disarming and arming procedures.

BATTERY GROUND CABLE

Prior to service disconnect battery ground cable and isolate as required.

AUDIO CODED ANTI-THEFT SYSTEM

Some models are equipped with an audio coded anti-theft system that will disable the radio when the battery cable is disconnected. The system can be identified by the "ANTI-THEFT SYSTEM" on the cassette lid. Obtain 3 digit code for input. Reset system after service as follows:

1. Obtain 3 digit audio theft code.
2. Depress 1 (PROG) while depressing righthand side of TUNE SEEK button, - - - will appear in tape operation display.
3. To enter the first digit, depress 1 (PROG) button repeatedly until the number of times depressed equals the first digit (depress the 1 button six times if the first digit if five, first press equals 0).
4. To enter second digit, depress 2 (APS) button repeatedly until the number of times depressed equals the second digit.
5. To enter third digit, depress 3 (RPT) button repeatedly until the number of times depressed equals the third digit.
6. If - - - is displayed after inputting digits, repeat procedure.
7. When code appears in display, depress and hold SCAN button until SEC appears.

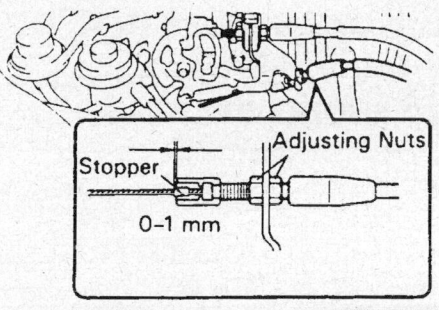

Fig. 1   Throttle cable adjustment

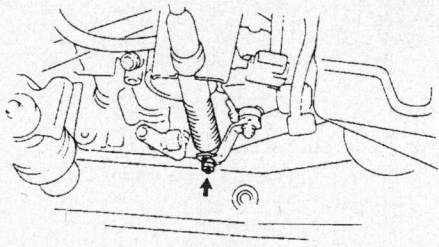

TY5029500879000X

Fig. 2   Shift lever position adjustment

8. When SEC disappears audio system is operative.
9. If Err is displayed, repeat procedure. **Attempting to input code more than 9 may permanently disable audio system.**

TROUBLESHOOTING

VEHICLE DOES NOT MOVE IN R POSITION

1. Faulty 1–2 shift valve.

2. Faulty 2–3 shift valve.
3. Faulty O/D direct clutch.
4. Faulty direct clutch.
5. Faulty 2nd coast brake.
6. Faulty 1st and reverse brake.
7. Faulty front or rear planetary gear.

VEHICLE DOES NOT MOVE IN ANY FORWARD POSITION

1. Faulty forward clutch.
2. Faulty direct clutch.
3. Faulty 2nd coast brake.
4. Faulty 2nd brake.
5. Faulty 1st and reverse brake.
6. Faulty No. 2 one-way clutch.

VEHICLE DOES NOT MOVE IN ANY POSITION

1. Faulty manual valve.
2. Faulty primary regulator valve.
3. Faulty lock-up relay valve.
4. Faulty parking lock pawl.
5. Faulty O/D direct clutch.
6. Faulty O/D brake.
7. Faulty O/D one-way clutch.
8. Faulty O/D planetary gear.
9. Faulty front or rear planetary gear.

NO LOCK-UP

1. Faulty torque converter clutch.
2. Faulty solenoid regulator valve.
3. Faulty lock-up relay valve.

NO KICK-DOWN

1. Faulty shift valve.

LARGE SHOCK DURING LOCK-UP

1. Faulty torque converter clutch.

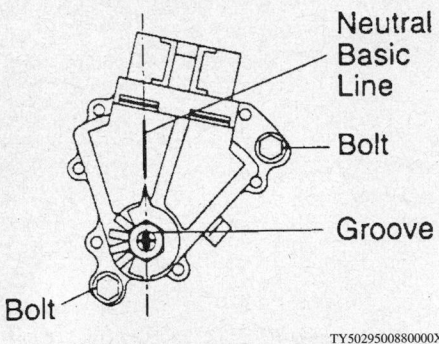

Fig. 3 Park/neutral position switch adjustment

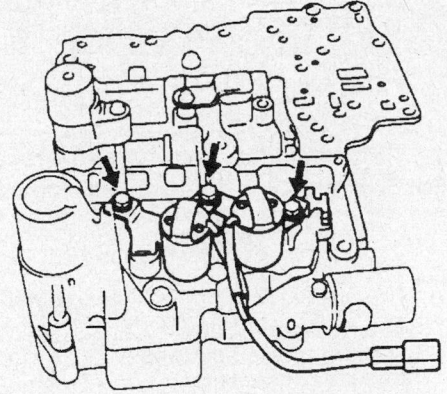

Fig. 4 Shift solenoid valve Nos. 1 & 2 removal

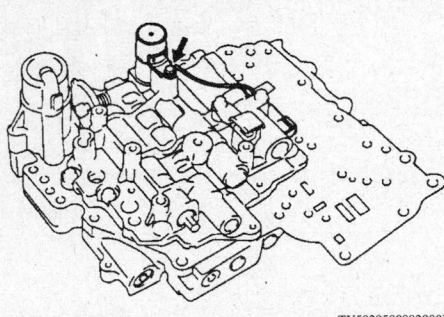

Fig. 5 Shift solenoid valve SL removal

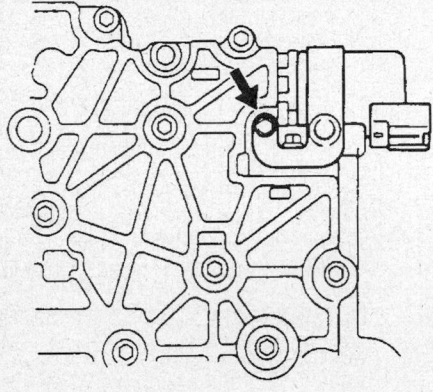

Fig. 6 Shift solenoid valve SLN removal

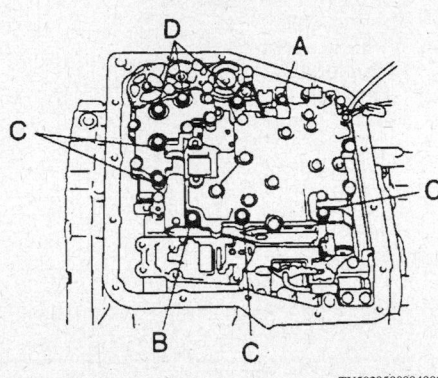

Fig. 7 Valve body bolts

NO ENGINE BRAKING

1. Faulty 2nd coast modulator valve.
2. Faulty low coast modulator valve.

NO UPSHIFT

1. Faulty shift valve.
2. Faulty direct clutch.
3. Faulty O/D brake.
4. Faulty 2nd brake.
5. Faulty No. 1 one-way clutch.

NO DOWNSHIFT

1. Faulty shift valve.
2. Faulty 2nd coast brake (2nd-1st gear).

SLIP OR SHUDDER IN FORWARD OR REVERSE (ENGINE WARM)

1. Faulty torque converter clutch.
2. Faulty O/D direct clutch.
3. Faulty No. 1 one-way clutch.

SLIP OR SHUDDER IN FORWARD OR REVERSE (ENGINE COLD)

1. Faulty torque converter clutch.
2. Faulty primary regulator valve.
3. Faulty throttle valve.
4. Faulty downshift plug.
5. Faulty pressure relief valve.

SLIP OR SHUDDER IN REVERSE

1. Faulty O/D direct clutch.

2. Faulty direct clutch.
3. Faulty O/D one-way clutch.

SLIP OR SHUDDER IN 1ST, 2ND OR 3RD

1. Faulty forward clutch.
2. Faulty direct clutch.
3. Faulty second brake.
4. Faulty No. 1 one-way clutch.
5. Faulty No. 2 one-way clutch.

SLIP OR SHUDDER IN O/D

1. Faulty O/D brake.

NO ENGINE BRAKING

1. Faulty O/D direct clutch.
2. Faulty 2nd coast brake.
3. Faulty 1st and reverse brake.

HARSH ENGAGEMENT (N-R, N-D, N-L & 1ST-2ND)

1. Faulty accumulator.
2. Faulty forward clutch.
3. Faulty direct clutch.
4. Faulty 1st and reverse brake

HARSH ENGAGEMENT (1ST-2ND-3RD-O/D)

1. Faulty primary regulator valve.
2. Faulty throttle valve.
3. Faulty downshift plug.
4. Faulty O/D direct clutch.
5. Faulty 2nd coast brake.

POOR ACCELERATION

1. Faulty torque converter clutch.
2. Faulty O/D direct clutch.
3. Faulty forward clutch.
4. Faulty O/D brake.
5. Faulty 2nd coast brake.
6. Faulty 2nd brake.
7. Faulty O/D planetary gear.

ENGINE STALLS WHEN STARTING OFF OR STOPPING

1. Faulty torque converter clutch.

MAINTENANCE

FLUID CHECK

1. Operate vehicle, allow transaxle fluid temperature to reach 158–176 °F.
2. Position vehicle on level surface, apply parking brake.
3. Allow engine to idle, depress brake pedal, then move shift lever through all positions.
4. Remove transaxle dipstick, wipe clean, then replace.
5. Remove again, then check fluid level in HOT range.

FLUID CHANGE

1. Drain transaxle fluid, then install drain plug and new gasket.
2. Add fluid through filler tube. **Do not overfill.**
3. Start engine, move shift lever through all positions, ensuring smooth operation.
4. Allow engine to idle, then check fluid level, add up to COOL level.
5. Once fluid temperature reaches 158–176°F, recheck fluid level.

ADJUSTMENTS

THROTTLE CABLE

1. Ensure throttle cable is not slack with accelerator pedal released.
2. Measure distance between outer cable end and stopper on cable, **Fig. 1.** Distance should be 0–.04 inch (0–1 mm).
3. If distance measured is not within specifications, rotate adjusting nuts to adjust cable.

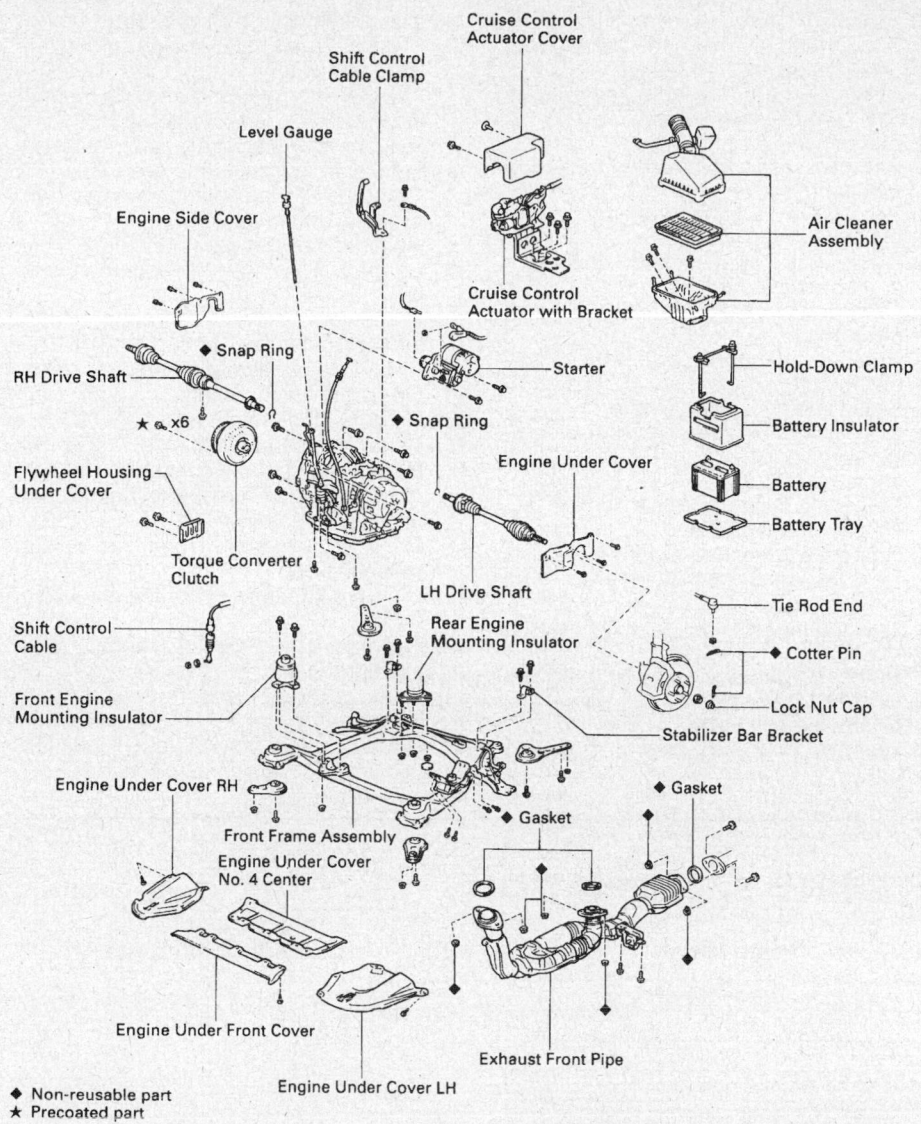

Fig. 8 Transaxle removal

◆ Non-reusable part
★ Precoated part

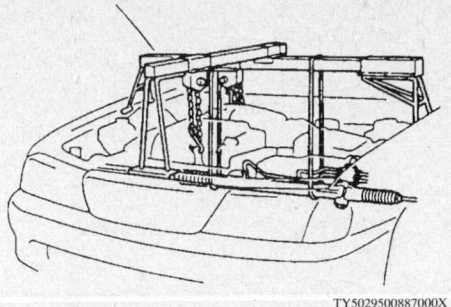

TY5029500887000X

Fig. 9 Support fixture installation

5. Pry off lock plate and remove park/neutral position switch retaining nut.
6. Remove park/neutral position switch.
7. Reverse procedure to install. Adjust park/neutral position switch as described under "Adjustments."

VALVE BODY, REPLACE

1. Remove transaxle drain plug and drain transaxle fluid into suitable container.
2. Remove transaxle oil pan and gasket.
3. Remove oil pan magnets and use them to collect any steel chips, present as a result of bearing, gear and plate wear.
4. Remove oil strainer and pipe bracket.
5. Pry up both ends of oil pipes with screwdriver and remove five pipes.
6. Disconnect solenoid connectors.
7. Remove shift solenoid valves No. 1 and No. 2 with retainer, **Fig. 4.**
8. Remove shift solenoid valve SL, **Fig. 5.**
9. Remove retaining bolt and shift solenoid valve SLN, **Fig. 6.**
10. Remove transfer lubrication apply pipe.
11. Remove five bolts and manual valve body.
12. Remove B_3 apply pipe.
13. Remove nine valve body retaining bolts, **Fig. 7.** Bolt lengths are as follows:
    a. Bolt A is 1.181 inches.
    b. Bolt B is 1.693 inches.
    c. Bolt C is 1.890 inches.
    d. Bolt D is 2.047 inches.
14. Disconnect throttle cable from cam and remove valve body.
15. Remove second brake apply gasket.
16. Reverse procedure to install.

THROTTLE CABLE, REPLACE

Removal

1. Disconnect throttle cable from engine throttle linkage.
2. Remove park/neutral position switch.
3. Remove valve body, refer to "Valve Body, Replace."
4. Remove throttle cable retaining plate.
5. Pull cable out from transaxle case.

Installation

1. Install throttle cable into transaxle case.
2. Install throttle cable retaining plate and bolt.
3. Install valve body.

SHIFT LEVER POSITION

1. Loosen swivel nut on manual shift lever, **Fig. 2.**
2. Push manual lever fully toward left side of vehicle.
3. Return lever two notches to N position.
4. Set shift lever to N position.
5. While holding shift lever lightly toward R position side, tighten swivel nut to specifications.
6. Start engine and ensure vehicle moves forward when shifting lever from N to D position and reverses when shifting to R position.

PARK/NEUTRAL POSITION SWITCH

1. Loosen park/neutral position switch bolt and set shift lever to N position.
2. Align groove and neutral basic line, **Fig. 3.**
3. Hold in position and tighten to specification.

IN-VEHICLE REPAIRS

VEHICLE SPEED SENSOR, REPLACE

1. Remove air cleaner assembly.
2. Disconnect vehicle speed sensor connector.
3. Remove vehicle speed sensor retaining bolt, then the sensor.
4. Remove driven gear from speed sensor.
5. Install vehicle speed sensor with new O-ring coated with transaxle fluid and tighten to specification.

PARK/NEUTRAL POSITION SWITCH, REPLACE

1. Remove air cleaner assembly.
2. Disconnect park/neutral position switch connector.
3. Disconnect park/neutral position switch control cable.
4. Remove nut and transaxle control shaft lever.

4. If throttle cable is new, stake stopper or paint mark on inner cable as follows:
   a. Bend cable so there is radius of about 7.87 inches.
   b. Pull inner cable lightly until light resistance is felt, then hold it in position.
   c. Stake stopper .031–.059 inch from end of outer cable.
5. Connect throttle cable to engine.
6. Adjust throttle cable as described under "Adjustments."
7. Install park/neutral position switch and test drive vehicle.

TRANSAXLE
REPLACE

1. Remove battery.
2. Remove air cleaner assembly, **Fig. 8.**
3. Remove throttle cable from engine.
4. Remove cruise control actuator cover.
5. Disconnect cruise control actuator connector.
6. Remove cruise control actuator with bracket.
7. Disconnect transaxle ground wire.
8. Disconnect vehicle speed sensor connector.
9. Disconnect direct clutch speed sensor connector.
10. Disconnect park/neutral position switch connector.
11. Disconnect shift control cable from park/neutral position switch.
12. Disconnect ground cable and remove shift control cable clamp.
13. Disconnect oil cooler hose.
14. Remove two front side transaxle mounting bolts.
15. Remove two front side engine mounting bolts.
16. Disconnect starter electrical connector and remove starter.
17. Remove exhaust manifold bracket mounting bolt.
18. Remove four upper transaxle to engine bolts.
19. Install engine support fixture.
20. Support steering gear housing securely from engine support fixture as shown in **Fig. 9.**
21. Raise and support vehicle.
22. Remove front wheels.
23. Remove front exhaust pipe.
24. Remove differential fluid drain plug and gasket.
25. Drain differential fluid into suitable container.
26. Remove righthand and righthand engine side cover No. 2.
27. Remove driveshafts.
28. Remove front side engine mounting nut.
29. Disconnect shift control cable.
30. Remove rear side engine mounting bolts and nuts.
31. Remove four left side transaxle mounting bolts.
32. Disconnect stabilizer bar bushing bracket from front frame assembly.
33. Remove steering gear housing mounting bolts and nuts.
34. Remove steering gear housing.
35. Support front frame assembly with jack.
36. Remove two set screws from right and left fender liners.
37. Remove power steering fluid reservoir pipe mounting brackets.
38. Remove front frame assembly.
39. Support transaxle with jack.
40. Remove torque converter clutch mounting bolts. Turn crankshaft to gain access to each bolt.
41. Remove exhaust manifold plate mounting nut.
42. Remove transaxle to engine mounting bolts.
43. Separate transaxle and engine and lower transaxle.
44. Remove torque converter clutch from transaxle.
45. Reverse procedure to install, tighten all nuts and bolts to specifications.

TIGHTENING SPECIFICATIONS

Year	Component	Torque, Ft. Lbs.
1996–99	Drain Plug	43①
	Front Engine Mount Nut	59
	Front Frame Bolts	24
	Front Frame Nut	27
	Left Transaxle Mounting Bolts	134
	Neutral Safety Switch	48
	Shift Control Cable Nut	11
	Shift Solenoid Retaining Bolts	58①
	TCC Mounting Bolts	20
	Throttle Cable	11
	Transaxle To Engine 17mm Bolts	47
	Transaxle To Engine 12mm Bolts	34
	Valve Body Bolts	96①
	Vehicle Speed Sensor	12

① — Inch lbs.

A540H Automatic Transaxle

NOTE: On Air Bag Equipped Models, Refer To "Air Bag System Precautions" Located In The Front Of This Manual For System Disarming & Arming Procedures.

INDEX

PRECAUTIONS

AIR BAG SYSTEMS

Refer to "Air Bag System Precautions" in the front of this manual for system disarming and arming procedures.

BATTERY GROUND CABLE

Prior to service disconnect battery ground cable and isolate as required.

AUDIO CODED ANTI-THEFT SYSTEM

Some models are equipped with an audio coded anti-theft system that will disable the radio when the battery cable is disconnected. The system can be identified by the "ANTI-THEFT SYSTEM" on the cassette lid. Obtain 3 digit code for input. Reset system after service as follows:

1. Obtain 3 digit audio theft code.
2. Depress 1 (PROG) while depressing righthand side of TUNE SEEK button, - - will appear in tape operation display.
3. To enter the first digit, depress 1 (PROG) button repeatedly until the number of times depressed equals the first digit (depress the 1 button six times if the first digit if five, first press equals 0).
4. To enter second digit, depress 2 (APS) button repeatedly until the number of times depressed equals the second digit.
5. To enter third digit, depress 3 (RPT) button repeatedly until the number of times depressed equals the third digit.
6. If - - - is displayed after inputting digits, repeat procedure.
7. When code appears in display, depress and hold SCAN button until SEC appears.
8. When SEC disappears audio system is operative.
9. If Err is displayed, repeat procedure. **Attempting to input code more than 9 may permanently disable audio system.**

Suspect Area / Symptom	Oil strainer	Parking lock pawl	Manual valve	1-2 shift valve	2-3 shift valve	3-4 shift valve	C₁ accumulator	B₃ accumulator	2nd lock valve
Vehicle does not move in R position				1	2				
Vehicle does not move in any forward position or reverse position			1						
No lock-up									
No lock-up OFF									
No kick-down				2	3	4			
No engine braking — 1st (L position)									
No engine braking — 2nd (2 position)									2
No up-shift — 1st → 2nd				1					
No up-shift — 2nd → 3rd					1				
No up-shift — 3rd → O/D						1			
No down-shift — O/D → 3rd						1			
No down-shift — 3rd → 2nd					1				
No down-shift — 2nd → 1st				1					
Harsh engagement — N → R									
Harsh engagement — N → D							1		
Harsh engagement — N → L									
Harsh engagement — 1st → 2nd (D position)								1	
Harsh engagement — 1st → 2nd (2 position)									
Harsh engagement — 1st → 2nd → 3rd									
Harsh engagement — 1st → 2nd → 3rd → O/D									
Harsh engagement — 2nd → 3rd									
Harsh engagement — 3rd → O/D									
Harsh engagement — O/D → 3rd									
Harsh engagement — 3rd → 2nd									1
Sliper shudder in forward and reverse (Directly after E/G start)	2								
Front or rear wheel is slipping									
Shift point too high or too low									

TY5029601233010X

Fig. 1 Transaxle on vehicle troubleshooting (Part 1 of 2)

TROUBLESHOOTING

Refer to **Figs. 1 and 2** for A540H general troubleshooting.

MAINTENANCE

FLUID CHECK

1. Operate vehicle, allow transaxle fluid temperature to reach 158–176 °F.
2. Position vehicle on level surface, apply parking brake.
3. Allow engine to idle, depress brake pedal, then move shift lever through all positions.
4. Remove transaxle dipstick, wipe clean, then replace.
5. Remove again, then check fluid level in HOT range.

FLUID CHANGE

1. Drain transaxle fluid, then install drain plug and new gasket.
2. Add fluid through filler tube. **Do not overfill.**

Fig. 1 — Transaxle on vehicle troubleshooting (Part 2 of 2)

C₂ accumulator	B₀ accumulator	C₀ accumulator	No. 1 and No. 2 accumulator control valve	Low coast modulator valve	2nd coast modulator valve	Throttle modulator valve	Lock-up relay valve	Pressure relief valve	Throttle valve	Down shift plug	Secondary regulator valve	Primary regulator valve	Shift restrict reverse ball	Solenoid modulator valve	Differential control valve	Throttle cable	Low coast modulator valve	OFF-vehicle repair matrix chart
									3									4
											3	2						4
										1								2
										1								2
													5			1		
					1												2	3
						1												3
																		2
																		2
																		2
																		2
					1													2
																		2
					1													2
				1														2
		2			1													2
		1																2
1																		
	1																	2
2	1																	
3	2		4															5
																1		3
													1	2	3			4
										1								

TY5029601233020X

Fig. 2 — Transaxle off vehicle troubleshooting (Part 1 of 2)

Symptom (Suspect Area)		Torque converter clutch	Parking lock pawl	O/D direct clutch (C₀)	Forward clutch (C₁)	Direct clutch (C₂)	O/D brake (B₀)	Oil pump
Vehicle does not move in any forward position					1	6		
Vehicle does not move in reverse position				5		4		
Vehicle does not move in any forward position and reverse position				4			5	2
No lock-up		1						
No lock-up OFF		1						
Large shock during lock-up		1						
E/G stalls when starting off and stopping		1						
No up-shift	1st → 2nd							
	2nd → 3rd					1		
	3rd → O/D						1	
No down shift 2nd → 1st								
Harsh engagement	N → R				1			
	N → D			1				
	1st → 2nd (D position)							
	2nd → 3rd							
	3rd → O/D			1			2	
Slip on shudder	Forward and reverse (After warm-up)	1	4				2	
	Forward and reverse (Directly after E/G start)							
	R range			2		1		
	1st					1		
	2nd							
	2nd → 3rd (Up-shift)					1		
	3rd					1		
	O/D						1	
No engine braking	1st ~ 3rd			1				
	1st (L position)							
	2nd (2 position)							
Poor acceleration	All positions	1						2
	O/D			1				
	Other than O/D						1	
	Other than 2nd						1	
	1st and 2nd							
	1st and R position							
	R position							
Front or rear wheel is slipping								

TY5029601234010X

---

3. Start engine, move shift lever through all positions, ensuring smooth operation.
4. Allow engine to idle, then check fluid level, add up to COOL level.
5. Once fluid temperature reaches 158–176°F, recheck fluid level.

ADJUSTMENTS

THROTTLE CABLE

1. Ensure throttle valve is fully closed and that inner cable is not slack.
2. Loosen adjustment nuts.
3. Adjust outer cable so that distance between end of boot and stopper on cable is at .04 inch.

SHIFT LEVER POSITION

1. Loosen swivel nut on manual shift lever.
2. Push manual lever fully toward left side of vehicle.
3. Return lever two notches to N position.
4. Set shift lever to N position.
5. While holding shift lever lightly toward R position side, tighten swivel nut.
6. Start engine and ensure vehicle moves forward when shifting lever from N to D position and reverses when shifting to R position.

PARK/NEUTRAL POSITION SWITCH

1. Loosen park/neutral position switch bolt and set shift lever to N position.

2. Align groove and neutral basic line.
3. Hold in position and tighten to specification.

IN-VEHICLE REPAIRS

VEHICLE SPEED SENSOR, REPLACE

1. Remove air cleaner assembly.
2. Disconnect front speed sensor connector.
3. Remove bolt, then the front speed sensor.
4. Remove clip and speedometer driven gear from speed sensor.
5. Remove O-ring from front speed sensor.
6. Reverse procedure to install.

PARK/NEUTRAL POSITION SWITCH, REPLACE

1. Remove air cleaner assembly.
2. Disconnect park/neutral position switch connector.
3. Disconnect park/neutral position switch control cable.
4. Remove nut and transaxle control shaft lever.
5. Pry off lock plate and remove park/neutral position switch retaining nut.
6. Remove park/neutral position switch.
7. Reverse procedure to install. Adjust park/neutral position switch as described under "Adjustments."

VALVE BODY

1. Remove transaxle drain plug and drain transaxle fluid into suitable container.
2. Remove transaxle oil pan and gasket.
3. Remove oil pan magnets and use them to collect any steel chips, present as a result of bearing, gear and plate wear.
4. Remove oil strainer and pipe bracket.
5. Pry up both ends of oil pipes with screwdriver and remove five pipes.
6. Remove five bolts and manual valve body.
7. Disconnect solenoid connectors.
8. Remove B₃ apply pipe.
9. Remove shift solenoid valves No. 1 and No. 2 with retainer, **Fig. 3.**
10. Remove shift solenoid valve SL, **Fig. 4.**
11. Remove shift solenoid valve ST from check valve sleeve, then the key, two check valves and check ball, **Fig. 5.**
12. Remove the ten valve body bolts, **Fig. 6**, disconnect throttle cable from cam, then the valve body.
13. Reverse procedure to install.

THROTTLE CABLE, REPLACE

Removal

1. Disconnect throttle cable from engine throttle linkage.
2. Remove park/neutral position switch.
3. Remove valve body, refer to "Valve Body, Replace."
4. Remove throttle cable retaining plate.
5. Pull cable out from transaxle case.

2nd coast brake (B₁)	2nd brake (B₂)	1st and reverse brake (B₃)	O/D one-way clutch (F₀)	No.1 one-way clutch (F₁)	No.2 one-way clutch (F₂)	O/D planetary gear	Front planetary gear	Rear planetary gear	Center differential clutch
4	5	3			2				
1		6					2	3	
		3				8	6	7	
	1			2					
1									
		2							
		1							
1									
						3			
				3					
			3						
					2				
	1			2					
		1							
1									
							2		
							2		
1	2								
		1							
									1

TY5029601234020X

Fig. 2 Transaxle off vehicle troubleshooting (Part 2 of 2)

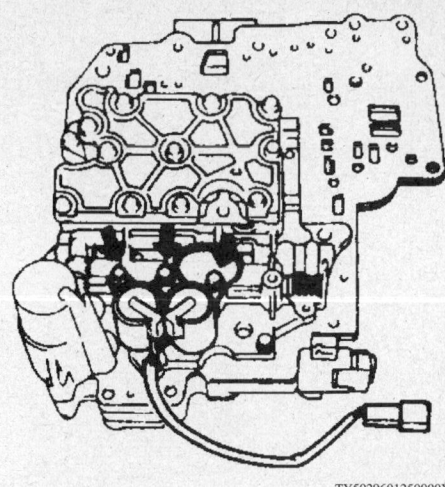

TY5029601250000X

Fig. 3 Solenoid valve removal

Installation

1. Install throttle cable into transaxle case.
2. Install throttle cable retaining plate and bolt.
3. Install valve body.
4. If throttle cable is new, stake stopper or paint mark on inner cable as follows:
   a. Bend cable so there is radius of about 7.87 inches.
   b. Pull inner cable lightly until light resistance is felt, then hold it in position.
   c. Stake stopper .031–.059 inch from end of outer cable.
5. Connect throttle cable to engine.
6. Adjust throttle cable as described under "Adjustments."
7. Install park/neutral position switch and test drive vehicle.

TRANSAXLE
REPLACE

Refer to **Fig. 7,** for transaxle replacement.

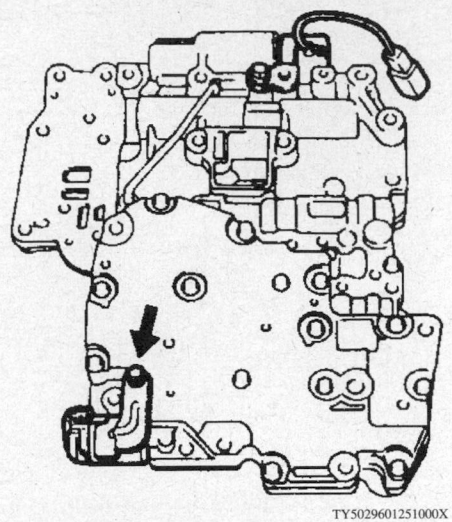

Fig. 4   Solenoid valve SL removal

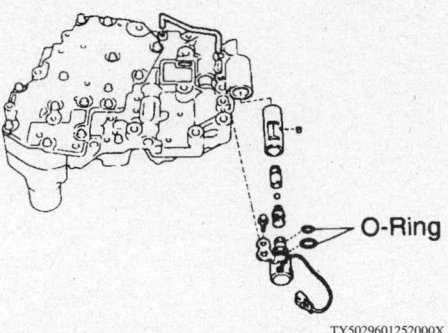

Fig. 5   Shift solenoid valve ST removal

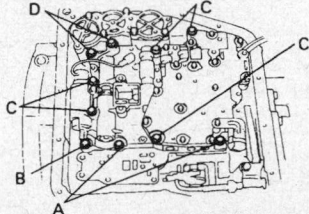

Bolt length:
    Bolt A: 22 mm (0.87 in.)
    Bolt B: 32 mm (1.26 in.)
    Bolt C: 43 mm (1.69 in.)
    Bolt D: 55 mm (2.17 in.)
Torque: 11 N·m (110 kgf·cm, 8 ft·lbf)

Fig. 6   Valve body removal

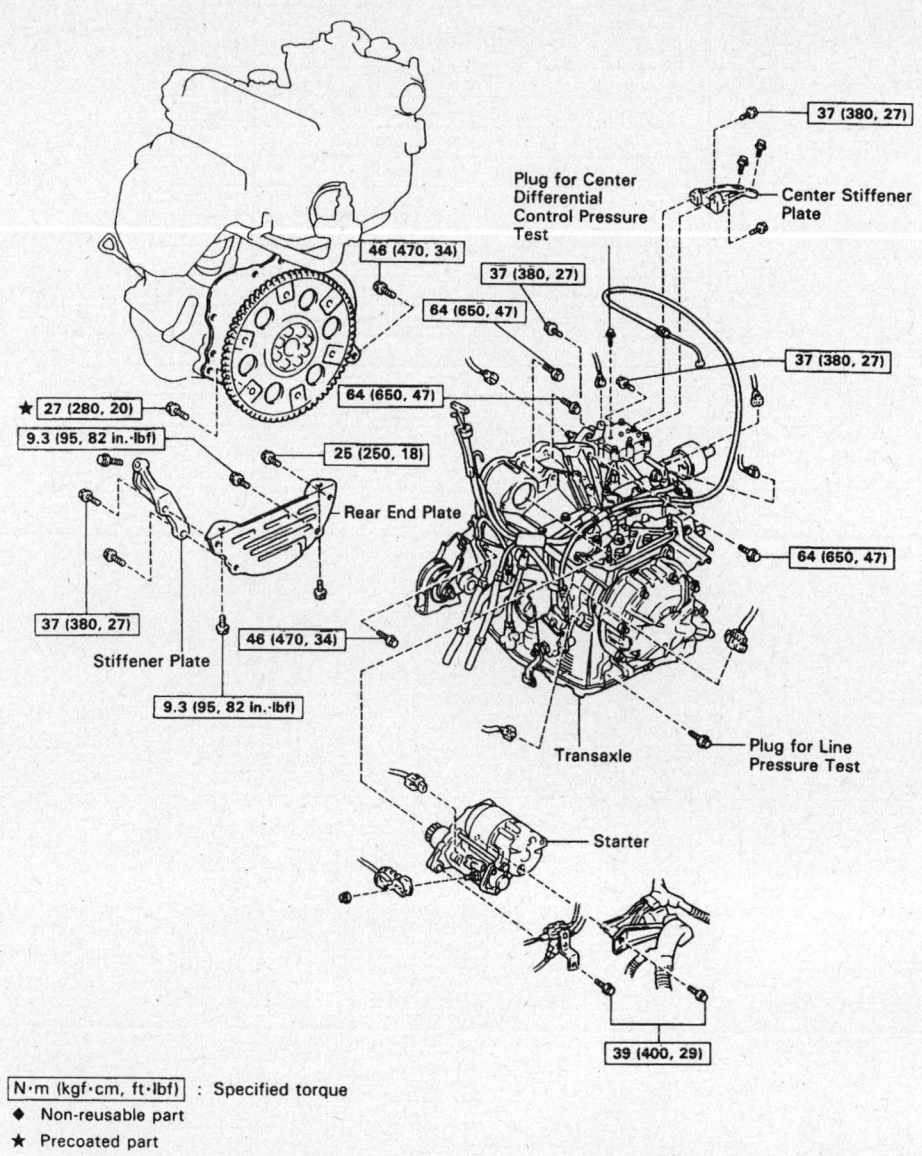

37 (380, 27)

Plug for Center
Differential
Control Pressure
Test

Center Stiffener
Plate

46 (470, 34)

37 (380, 27)

64 (650, 47)

37 (380, 27)

64 (650, 47)

★ **27 (280, 20)**

9.3 (95, 82 in.·lbf)

25 (250, 18)

64 (650, 47)

Rear End Plate

37 (380, 27)

Stiffener Plate

46 (470, 34)

9.3 (95, 82 in.·lbf)

Transaxle

Plug for Line
Pressure Test

Starter

39 (400, 29)

N·m (kgf·cm, ft·lbf) : Specified torque
◆ Non-reusable part
★ Precoated part

TY5029601254000X

Fig. 7 Transaxle replacement

TIGHTENING SPECIFICATIONS

Year	Component	Torque, Ft. Lbs.
1996–99	Center Stiffener Plate	27
	Engine To Transaxle 14mm Bolt	47
	Engine To Transaxle 12mm Bolt	34
	Manual Valve Body Bolts	96①
	Neutral Safety Switch	48①
	Oil Pan Bolts	43①
	Oil Strainer To Valve Body	96①
	Pipe Bracket To Valve Body	84①
	Rear End Plate To Torque Converter Housing	29
	Speed Sensor	48①
	Starter Bolts	29
	Stiffener Plate To Engine	27
	Torque Converter Clutch To Drive Plate	20
	Valve Body Bolts	96①

① — Inch lbs.

Front Wheel Drive Axles

NOTE: On Air Bag Equipped Models, Refer To "Air Bag System Precautions" Located In The Front Of This Manual For System Disarming & Arming Procedures.

INDEX

PRECAUTIONS

AIR BAG SYSTEMS

Refer to "Air Bag System Precautions" in the front of this manual for system disarming and arming procedures.

AUDIO CODED ANTI-THEFT SYSTEM

Some models are equipped with an audio coded anti-theft system that will disable the radio when the battery cable is disconnected. The system can be identified by the "ANTI-THEFT SYSTEM" on the cassette lid. Obtain 3 digit code for input. Reset system after service as follows:
1. Obtain 3 digit audio theft code.
2. Depress 1 (PROG) while depressing righthand side of TUNE SEEK button, - - - will appear in tape operation display.
3. To enter the first digit, depress 1 (PROG) button repeatedly until the number of times depressed equals the first digit (depress the 1 button six times if the first digit if five, first press equals 0).
4. To enter second digit, depress 2 (APS) button repeatedly until the number of times depressed equals the second digit.
5. To enter third digit, depress 3 (RPT) button repeatedly until the number of times depressed equals the third digit.
6. If - - - is displayed after inputting digits, repeat procedure.
7. When code appears in display, depress and hold SCAN button until SEC appears.
8. When SEC disappears audio system is operative.
9. If Err is displayed, repeat procedure. **Attempting to input code more than 9 times may permanently disable audio system.**

BATTERY GROUND CABLE

Prior to service, disconnect battery ground cable and isolate as required.

DESCRIPTION

AVALON, CAMRY & CELICA

These models use an intermediate (center) shaft to allow the use of equal length driveshafts. This shaft is supported at one end in the transaxle and the other end by a bearing and bearing carrier secured to the engine **Figs. 1 through 3.**

Two types of inner joint are used on these model. A tripod type and a constant velocity type.

COROLLA, PASEO & TERCEL

These models use unequal length driveshaft that connect directly to the output of the transaxle **Figs. 4 and 5.**

LAND CRUISER

This model uses a solid type front axle which incorporates axle shafts, joints and differential within a solid housing **Fig. 6.**

4WD T100, AWD PREVIA & 4RUNNER

These models use equal length driveshafts connected to a center differential unit. This unit incorporates a side gear shaft and extension housing to compensate for differential offset, **Figs. 7 and 8.**

RAV4

These models use equal length driveshafts connected to a center differential unit, **Figs. 9 and 10.** The front driveshaft of the 2WD manual transaxle model uses the double offset type constant velocity joints (CVJs) on the differential side and Rzeppa type CVJs on the wheel side. The front driveshaft of the 4WD and 2WD automatic transaxle models use the tripod type CVJs on the differential side and Rzeppa type CVJs on the wheel side.

DRIVESHAFT

REPLACE

AVALON, CAMRY & CELICA

1. Raise and support vehicle, then remove front wheels as necessary and front fender apron seal.
2. Remove cotter pin, locknut cap and locknut from axle spline **Figs. 1 through 3.**
3. Drain transmission fluid, then using a suitable puller, disconnect tie rod end from steering knuckle.
4. Disconnect stabilizer bar link from lower control arm.
5. Disconnect ball joint from steering knuckle.
6. **On models with constant velocity type inner joints,** using paint or chalk, place match marks on driveshaft inner joint and side gear shaft or center driveshaft, then proceed as follows:
   a. Have an assistant apply brakes to prevent axle from turning.
   b. Use a suitable drive socket to loosen, **but do not remove,** six hexagon bolts connecting inner joint to side gear shaft or center drive shaft.
7. **On all models,** remove outer joint from hub by using a plastic hammer to gently tap drive shaft spline to separate joint from axle hub.
8. Push front axle hub toward outside of vehicle to remove shaft from hub. **Use a suitable hanger or jack stand to support shaft, do not allow shaft to hang from inner joint.**
9. To separate LH driveshaft from transmission, gently pry shaft out of transaxle with suitable tool, then remove snap ring from splined end of side gear shaft.
10. To separate RH driveshaft from transmission proceed as follows:
    a. **On Celica models,** remove two bolts and retainer holding center bearing into support.
    b. **Except Celica models,** remove

---

center drive shaft support bearing lock bolt and snap ring.

c. Using a suitable pry bar and/or soft face hammer pry and/or tap center drive shaft with support bearing from transaxle and support bearing housing

d. Using suitable pliers, remove snap ring from splined end of center driveshaft.

11. Reverse procedure to install, noting the following:

a. Always use new snap ring on splined end of shaft inserted into transaxle.

b. Ensure positive engagement of snap ring into transaxle.

c. Tighten fasteners to specifications.

d. Fill transaxle to correct level using a suitable fluid.

COROLLA, PASEO & TERCEL

1. Raise and support vehicle, then remove wheels and engine undercover.
2. Drain transmission fluid, then remove cotter pin and lock cap. While applying brakes, remove axle spline nut **Figs. 4 through 5.**
3. Disconnect tie rod end from steering knuckle, then lower ball joint from lower control arm.
4. Remove brake disc if necessary, then using suitable puller, remove driveshaft outer joint from axle hub.
5. To remove driveshafts from transaxle, gently tap with hammer and brass drift to release shaft, or use a suitable pry bar to lever shaft from transaxle, then remove snap ring from transaxle end of shaft.
6. Reverse procedure to install, noting the following:

a. Always use new snap ring on splined end of shaft inserted into transaxle.

b. Ensure positive engagement of snap ring into transaxle.

c. Tighten fasteners to specifications.

d. Fill transaxle to correct level using a suitable fluid.

LAND CRUISER

REPLACEMENT

1. Raise and support vehicle, then remove tire and wheel assembly.
2. Remove axle hub.
3. Remove dust seal and gasket, then the dust cover, **Fig. 6.**
4. Remove knuckle spindle and gasket, then position flattened part of outer axle shaft upward and remove axle shaft.
5. Remove oil seal retainer, then disconnect drag link from knuckle arm.
6. Disconnect tie rod from knuckle arm, then remove knuckle arm and shim using a suitable brass brand hammer to tap cone washers loose.
7. Remove bearing cap and shim using pusher tool No. 09606-60020, or equivalent. Identify upper and lower bearings and shims for reference during assembly. **If original axle shaft is being reused, original shims may be used. If new axle shaft is to be in-**

stalled, new shims must be used. Refer to "Adjustments" to determine shim thickness.

ADJUSTMENT

Whenever axle housing or steering knuckle is replaced, the steering knuckle alignment and knuckle bearing preload should be adjusted using a suitable alignment and preload measurement tool set.

Axle Shaft Alignment

1. Assemble a suitable axle alignment tool using tool manufactures instructions to knuckle and axle housing.
2. Thickness of steering knuckle lower bearing shim will be distance between two scribe marks less .12 inch (3 mm).
3. Thickness of steering knuckle upper bearing shim will be difference between shim selected in step 4 and shim selected in step 6 under " Bearing Preload." Adjusting shims are available in .004 inch (.1 mm), .008 inch (.2 mm), .02 inch (.5 mm) and .04 inch (1 mm) thicknesses.

Bearing Preload

1. Using puller tool No. 09308-00010, or equivalent, remove oil seal.
2. Lubricate bearing with suitable grease, then install bearing and a suitable preload measurement tool into axle housing.
3. Install a suitable spring scale and measure bearing preload.
4. Bearing preload should be 5.6–9.9 lbs. Tighten nut at top of suitable preload measurement tool until specified bearing preload is obtained.
5. Measure distance A as shown in **Fig. 11,** then measure distance B as shown in **Fig. 12.**
6. Subtract measurement A from measurement B to obtain total adjusting shim thickness required to maintain correct bearing preload.

4WD T100 & AWD PREVIA

Removal

1. Raise and support vehicle, then remove tire and wheel assembly.
2. Depress brake pedal, then loosen six front driveshaft attaching nuts, **Fig. 7.**
3. Remove manual locking hub as follows:

a. Place control handle to "Free" position.

b. Remove cover attaching bolts, then the cover.

c. Remove axle bolt with washer, then the hub body attaching nuts and washers.

d. Remove cone washer by tapping on heads of bolts using a hammer and suitable drift.

e. Remove manual locking hub body.

4. Remove automatic locking hub as follows:

a. Remove hub cover.

b. Remove axle bolt, then the washer.

c. Remove hub body attaching nuts.

d. Remove cone washer by tapping

on heads of bolts, using a hammer and suitable drift.

e. Remove automatic locking hub body.

5. **On models less locking hubs,** remove hub as follows:

a. Remove grease cap from hub flange.

b. Remove hub bolt and washer, then hub flange attaching nuts.

c. Tap hub flange attaching studs with brass drift and hammer to remove cone washers.

d. Install two bolts into hub flange opposite from each other, then tighten evenly to remove hub flange.

6. **On all models,** remove driveshaft snap ring, then the spacer.
7. Pull front shaft from side gear shaft, then pull from steering knuckle.

Installation

1. Apply molybdenum disulphide lithium base grease to outboard joint shaft, then insert it into steering knuckle and side gear shaft. Install 6 retaining nuts, **Fig. 7.**
2. Install spacer and snap ring to outboard joint shaft.
3. Install free wheeling hub as follows:

a. Place new gasket on front axle hub.

b. Install hub body with six cone washers and nuts, then **torque** attaching nuts to 23 ft. lbs.

c. Install hub bolt with washer, then **torque** to 13 ft. lbs.

d. Apply a suitable grease to inner hub splines, then place control handle in "Free" position.

e. Install new gasket on cover, then install cover on body with follower pawl tabs aligned with non-toothed portions of body.

f. Install cover attaching bolts and **torque** to 7 ft. lbs.

4. Install automatic locking hub as follows:

a. Position new gasket on axle hub, then apply suitable multipurpose grease to automatic locking hub splines.

b. Align spring ends of brake assembly in hub with hub flange alignment pins.

c. Ensure locking hub outer cam stopper is securely in inner cam groove, then position inner cam protrusion so it is centered between outer cam protrusions and aligned with hub alignment pin holes.

d. Install locking hub to axle hub ensuring inner cam protrusion is set between ends of hub brake spring.

e. Install 6 cone washers and nuts and **torque** nuts to 23 ft. lbs. **If hub does not fit perfectly on axle hub, remove and reinstall.**

f. Install axle bolt with washer, then **torque** to 13 ft. lbs.

g. Install cover, then insert attaching bolts and **torque** to 7 ft. lbs.

5. **On models less locking hubs,** install hubs as follows:

a. Position new gasket on axle hub, then install hub flange on axle.

b. Install cone washers and attaching

nuts. **Torque** attaching nuts to 23 ft. lbs.

c. Install washer and bolt in driveshaft. **Torque** to 13 ft. lbs.

d. Install grease cap on hub flange.

6. **On all models,** while an assistant depresses brake pedal, **Torque** side gear shaft to driveshaft attaching nuts to 61 ft. lbs.

TACOMA & 4RUNNER

1. Raise and support vehicle, then remove front wheel.
2. Drain differential oil.
3. Using a screwdriver, remove grease cap, **Fig. 8.**
4. Remove driveshaft locknut cotter pin, lock cap and locknut.
5. Disconnect driveshaft using brass bar and hammer. If driveshaft is difficult to remove, tap screwdriver between differential tube/carrier and driveshaft.
6. Remove lower suspension arm cotter pin and nut.
7. Using tool No. 09628-62011, or equivalent, disconnect lower suspension arm.
8. Push steering knuckle outward and remove driveshaft.
9. Remove snap ring from inboard shaft.
10. Reverse procedure to install.

RAV4

1. Raise and support vehicle, then remove front wheel.
2. Remove engine under cover.
3. Drain gear oil.
4. **On models with ABS,** remove ABS speed sensor.
5. **On all models,** remove cotter pin, lock cap and driveshaft locknut.
6. Disconnect tie rod end from steering knuckle.
7. Disconnect stabilizer bar link from lower suspension arm.
8. Disconnect lower ball joint from lower suspension arm.
9. Disconnect driveshaft from axle hub.
10. **On 2WD models with manual transaxle,** remove RH driveshaft as follows:
    a. Using a screwdriver and hammer, remove snap ring from center bearing bracket.
    b. Remove bolt from center bearing bracket.
    c. Remove driveshaft with center driveshaft.
    d. Remove center bearing bracket.
11. **On 2WD models with automatic transaxle,** remove RH driveshaft as follows:
    a. Remove two center bearing bracket bolts and pull out driveshaft together with center bearing case and center driveshaft.
    b. Remove three bolts and the center bearing bracket.
12. **On 2WD models,** remove LH side driveshaft using brass bar and hammer, then pry off snap ring with a screwdriver.
13. **On 4WD models,** remove RH side driveshaft using brass bar and hammer, then pry off snap ring and O-ring with a screwdriver.

14. **On 4WD models,** remove LH side driveshaft as follows:
    a. Remove air cleaner.
    b. Remove transmission case protector.
    c. Using hub nut wrench, remove driveshaft.
    d. Using screwdriver, remove snap ring.
15. **On all models,** reverse procedure to install, noting the following.
    a. After installation, ensure there is .08–.12 inch of play in axial direction.
    b. **Torque** driveshaft locknut to 159 ft. lbs.
    c. **Torque** ABS speed sensor bolt to 69 inch lbs.

DRIVESHAFT SERVICE

AVALON, CAMRY & CELICA

DISASSEMBLE

1. Check driveshaft for excessive wear and/or damage.
2. For righthand driveshaft, proceed as follows:
   a. **On driveshafts with constant velocity type joints,** remove bolts and disconnect center driveshaft, then remove boot clamps and pull back boot **Figs. 1 through 3.**
   b. **On driveshafts with constant velocity type joints,** pry off inboard joint cover, using suitable tools.
   c. **On driveshafts with tripod type joints,** remove boot clamps, pull back boot then, disconnect center driveshaft.
3. For lefthand driveshaft, proceed as follows:
   a. **On driveshafts with constant velocity type joints,** remove boot clamps and pull back boot.
   b. **On driveshafts with constant velocity type joints,** pry off inboard joint cover, using suitable tools.
   c. **On driveshafts with tripod type joints,** remove boot clamps, then pull back boot and remove outer housing.
4. **On all driveshafts,** place matchmarks on the shaft and inboard joint inner race.
5. Using suitable pliers, remove snap ring retaining inboard joint.
6. Using suitable press tools and press, remove inboard joint from driveshaft. **Mark position of chamfers on joints for later assembly.**
7. Remove any remaining inboard joint clips or washers.
8. Remove both boots by sliding off inboard end of shaft.
9. Outboard joints are serviced with shaft. **Do not remove outboard joints from shaft.**

ASSEMBLE

1. Install outboard joint boot and new boot clamps.
2. Using a suitable grease, pack boot and joint then assemble boot to outboard joint. **Do not tighten clamps at this time.**

3. Install new boot clamps and inboard joint boot.
4. **On driveshafts with constant velocity type joints,** assemble a new inboard joint cover to inboard joint. Align bolt holes of cover with those of the inboard joint, then insert attaching bolts. Using a suitable hammer, tap rim of the inboard joint cover into place.
5. Temporarily install the attaching nuts, bolts and washers to keep the inboard joint together during installation of joint to shaft. Tighten bolts hand tight.
6. **On all driveshafts,** install any required snap rings and washers, then assemble the inboard joint to shaft as follows:
   a. Align marks made during disassembly, then using a brass bar and hammer, tap inboard joint into the driveshaft. Ensure brass bar is contacting the inner race and not the bearing cage.
   b. Install inboard joint retaining snap ring, then using a suitable grease pack inboard joint and boot.
7. **On driveshafts with tripod type joints,** install outer housing to joint, then install boot. **Do not tighten clamps at this time.**
8. **On driveshafts with constant velocity type joints,** install boot to inboard joint cover. **Do not tighten clamps at this time.**
9. **On all driveshafts,** ensure the boots are properly located when installing. **On righthand driveshafts with constant velocity type joints,** install center driveshaft. Ensure the boot is not stretched or contracted when the driveshaft is at standard length, **Figs. 13 through 15.**
10. Bend back boot band and lock it.
11. Check driveshaft for smooth operation. Ensure there is no play in the inboard joint and outboard joint. Ensure the inboard joint slides smoothly in the thrust direction.

COROLLA, PASEO & TERCEL

DISASSEMBLE

Before disassembling driveshaft, ensure there is no play in the inboard or outboard joints and that the inboard joint slides smoothly in the thrust direction.

1. Remove boot clamps, **Figs. 4 and 5.**
2. Place matchmarks on inboard joint. **Do not use a sharp tool to place matchmarks on inboard joint.**
3. Remove inboard joint from driveshaft.
4. Using snap ring pliers, remove snap ring.
5. Using a suitable punch and hammer, place matchmarks on driveshaft and tripod joint.
6. Using suitable press tools, press tripod joint from driveshaft.
7. Remove boots for inboard and outboard joints from shaft.
8. **Do not disassemble outboard joint, it is serviced as an assembly with the shaft.**

ASSEMBLE

Before installing boot, wrap vinyl tape around driveshaft splines.

1. Install outboard joint boot and new boot clamp onto shaft.
2. **On right side driveshaft,** install damper assembly.
3. **On all shafts,** install inboard joint boot and new boot clamp onto shaft. **The boot and clamp for the inboard joint are larger than those of the outboard joint.**
4. Assemble tripod joint as follows:
   a. Face the beveled side of tripod axial spline toward the outboard joint.
   b. Align matchmarks placed during disassembly.
   c. Using a suitable brass bar and hammer, tap tripod joint onto driveshaft.
5. Install a new snap ring onto driveshaft.
6. Pack inboard and outboard joints and boots with a suitable grease, then install boot and clamps onto outboard joint. **Do not tighten clamps at this time.**
7. Install inboard joint onto driveshaft, then install boot and clamps onto inboard joint.
8. Ensure boots are not stretched or damaged in any way and that driveshaft is at assembled length, **Fig. 13 through 15.**
9. Install both boot clamps onto boots. Ensure boot is on the driveshaft groove. Bend clamp band and lock.

LAND CRUISER

1. Place axle shaft in vise, then separate outer shaft from axle shaft using drift , **Fig. 6.**
2. Remove six ball bearings by rotating inner cage until bearings can be removed.
3. Remove cage and inner race from outer shaft. Remove inner race from cage.
4. Inspect all parts for damage or wear, then assemble inner race into cage as shown in **Fig. 16.**
5. Assemble cage and inner race onto outer shaft by positioning two large openings of cage against protruded parts of outer shaft.
6. Assemble inner race and cage, then install ball bearings. Lubricate outer shaft cavity with suitable grease.
7. Install new snap ring onto inner shaft then assemble inner and outer shafts.

RAV4

2WD w/MANUAL TRANSAXLE

Disassemble

1. Using a screwdriver, remove two inboard joint boot clamps, **Fig. 9.**
2. Using a side cutter, cut small outboard joint boot clamp and remove.
3. Using pliers, draw hooks together and remove large outboard joint boot clamp.
4. Place matchmarks on inboard joint tulip or center driveshaft and driveshaft.

5. Using a screwdriver, remove snap ring.
6. Remove inboard joint tulip from driveshaft.
7. Place matchmarks on driveshaft inner race and outer cage.
8. Remove six balls and cage.
9. Using a snap ring expander, remove snap ring.
10. Using brass bar and hammer, remove inner race.
11. Slide out inboard and outboard joint boots.
12. Using a press, remove dust cover from RH side center driveshaft.
13. Using tool No. 09950-00020, or equivalent, remove dust cover from LH side inboard joint tulip.
14. Using tool No. 09950-00020, or equivalent, remove dust cover from center driveshaft.
15. Using a snap ring expander, remove snap ring.
16. Using suitable press, remove bearing.
17. Mount outboard joint shaft in soft jaw vise and remove No. 2 dust deflector.

Assemble

1. Using tool Nos. 09309-36010 and 09316-20011, or equivalents, install new No. 2 dust deflector.
2. Using suitable press, install snap ring and bearing.
3. Using suitable press, install new dust cover.
4. Place new boot clamp on small ends of new outboard joint boot and install boot to driveshaft.
5. Temporarily install new inboard joint boot to driveshaft.
6. Install cage with new snap ring to driveshaft.
7. Align matchmarks and install inner race to driveshaft using hammer and brass bar.
8. Install boot to outboard joint.
9. Pack boot and inboard joint tulip with grease.
10. Align matchmarks and install cage to inner race.
11. Install six balls.
12. Align matchmarks and install inboard joint tulip or center driveshaft to driveshaft.
13. Install new snap ring.
14. Temporarily install boot to the inboard joint tulip.
15. Ensure both boots are on shaft groove and place new boot clamps on inboard joint boot. Ensure boots are not stretched when driveshaft is at standard length, **Fig. 15.**
16. Secure clamps by drawing closing hooks together.
17. Place tool No. 09521-24010, or equivalent, onto clamp and tighten tool so that clamp is pinched.
18. Using tool No. 09240-00020, or equivalent, adjust clearance of clamp to .075 inch or less.

2WD w/AUTOMATIC TRANSAXLE & 4WD MODELS

Disassemble

1. Using a screwdriver, remove inboard

and outboard joint boot clamps, **Fig. 10.**
2. Place matchmarks on tripod, inboard joint tulip or center driveshaft and driveshaft.
3. Remove inboard joint tulip from driveshaft.
4. Using a snap ring expander, remove snap ring.
5. Place matchmarks on driveshaft and tripod, then use brass bar and hammer to remove tripod from driveshaft.
6. Remove snap ring and slide out two inboard and outboard joint boots.
7. Using suitable press, remove dust cover from center driveshaft.
8. **On 4WD models and 2WD LH side driveshaft,** remove dust cover from inboard joint tulip using tool No. 09950-00020, or equivalent.
9. **On 2WD model RH side driveshaft,** disassemble center driveshaft as follows:
   a. Using a screwdriver, remove snap ring.
   b. Using suitable press, remove bearing case.
   c. Using pin punch and hammer, remove straight pin from bearing case.
   d. Using tool No. 09950-00020, or equivalent, and a suitable press, remove dust cover.
   e. Using snap ring expander, remove snap ring.
   f. Using suitable press, remove bearing.
10. **On all models,** mount outboard shaft in soft jaw vise.
11. Using screwdriver and hammer, remove No. 2 dust deflector.

Assemble

1. Using suitable press, install new No. 2 dust deflector.
2. Using pin punch and hammer, install straight pin into bearing case.
3. Using tool Nos. 09950-60010 and 09950-70010, or equivalents, install new bearing into bearing case.
4. Using a screwdriver, install new snap ring.
5. Using tool No. 09710-30021, or equivalent, install bearing with bearing case assembly to center driveshaft.
6. Using tool No. 09506-35010, or equivalent, an extension bar and press, install new dust cover.
7. Temporarily install new outboard joint boot to driveshaft.
8. Temporarily install new inboard joint boot to driveshaft.
9. Place beveled side of tripod axial spline toward outboard joint.
10. Align matchmarks and tap in tripod to driveshaft using brass bar and hammer.
11. Install new snap ring using snap ring expander.
12. Pack outboard joint and boot with grease and install boot to outboard joint.
13. Pack boot and inboard joint tulip with grease.
14. Align matchmarks and install inboard

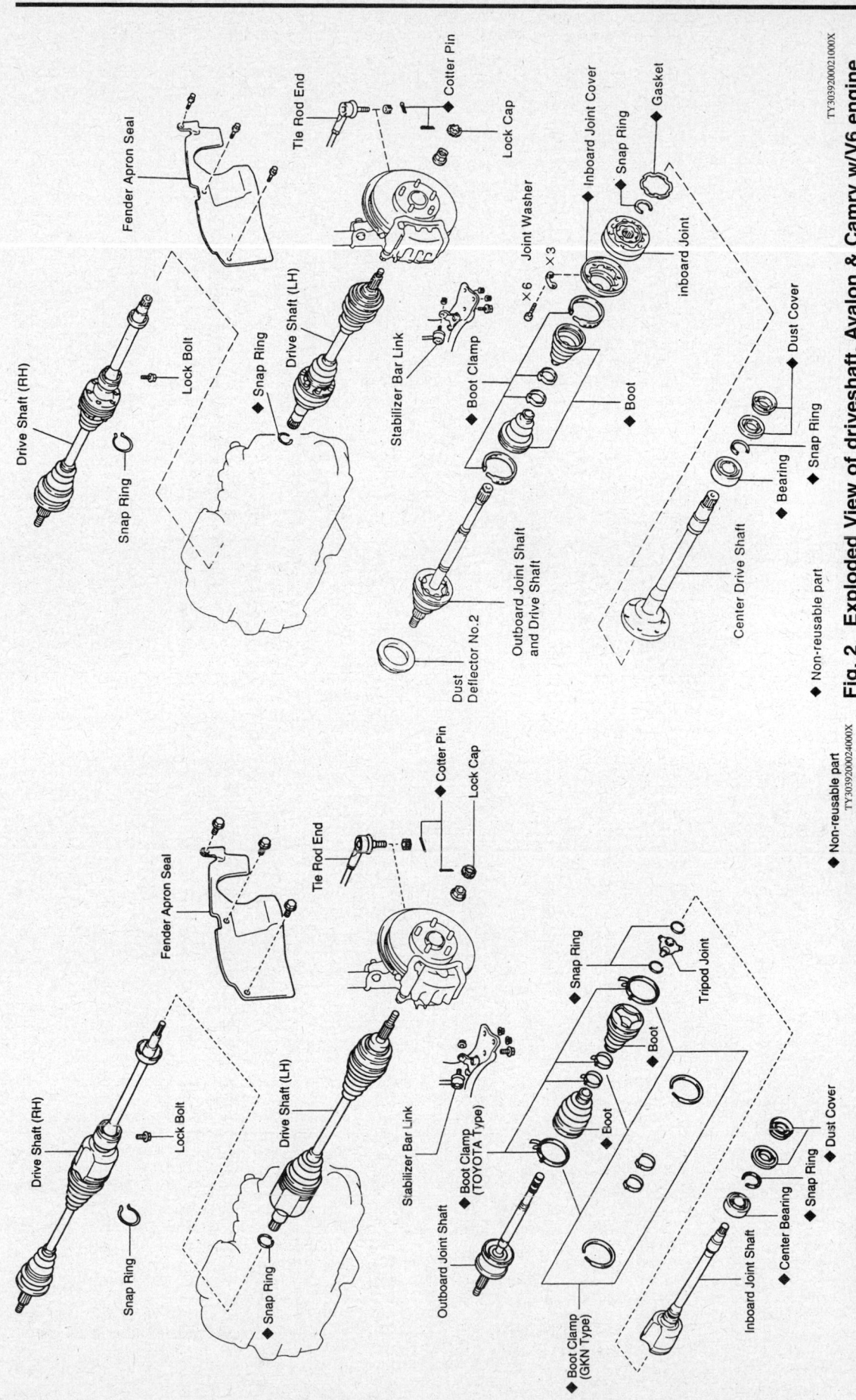

TY3039200021000X

Fender Apron Seal

Cotter Pin

Tie Rod End

Lock Cap

Inboard Joint Cover

Snap Ring

Gasket

Drive Shaft (RH)

Lock Bolt

Snap Ring

Drive Shaft (LH)

Joint Washer
×6
×6
×3

inboard Joint

Dust Cover

Snap Ring

Bearing

Snap Ring

Stabilizer Bar Link

Boot Clamp

Boot

Center Drive Shaft

Outboard Joint Shaft and Drive Shaft

Dust Deflector No. 2

Snap Ring

◆ Non-reusable part

Fig. 2   Exploded View of driveshaft. Avalon & Camry w/V6 engine

---

Fender Apron Seal

Cotter Pin

Tie Rod End

Lock Cap

Snap Ring

Tripod Joint

Drive Shaft (RH)

Lock Bolt

Snap Ring

Drive Shaft (LH)

Snap Ring

Boot

Stabilizer Bar Link

Boot Clamp (TOYOTA Type)

Boot

Dust Cover

Outboard Joint Shaft

Center Bearing

Snap Ring

Boot Clamp (GKN Type)

Inboard Joint Shaft

TY3039200024000X

◆ Non-reusable part

Fig. 1   Exploded View of driveshaft. Camry w/4 cylinder engine

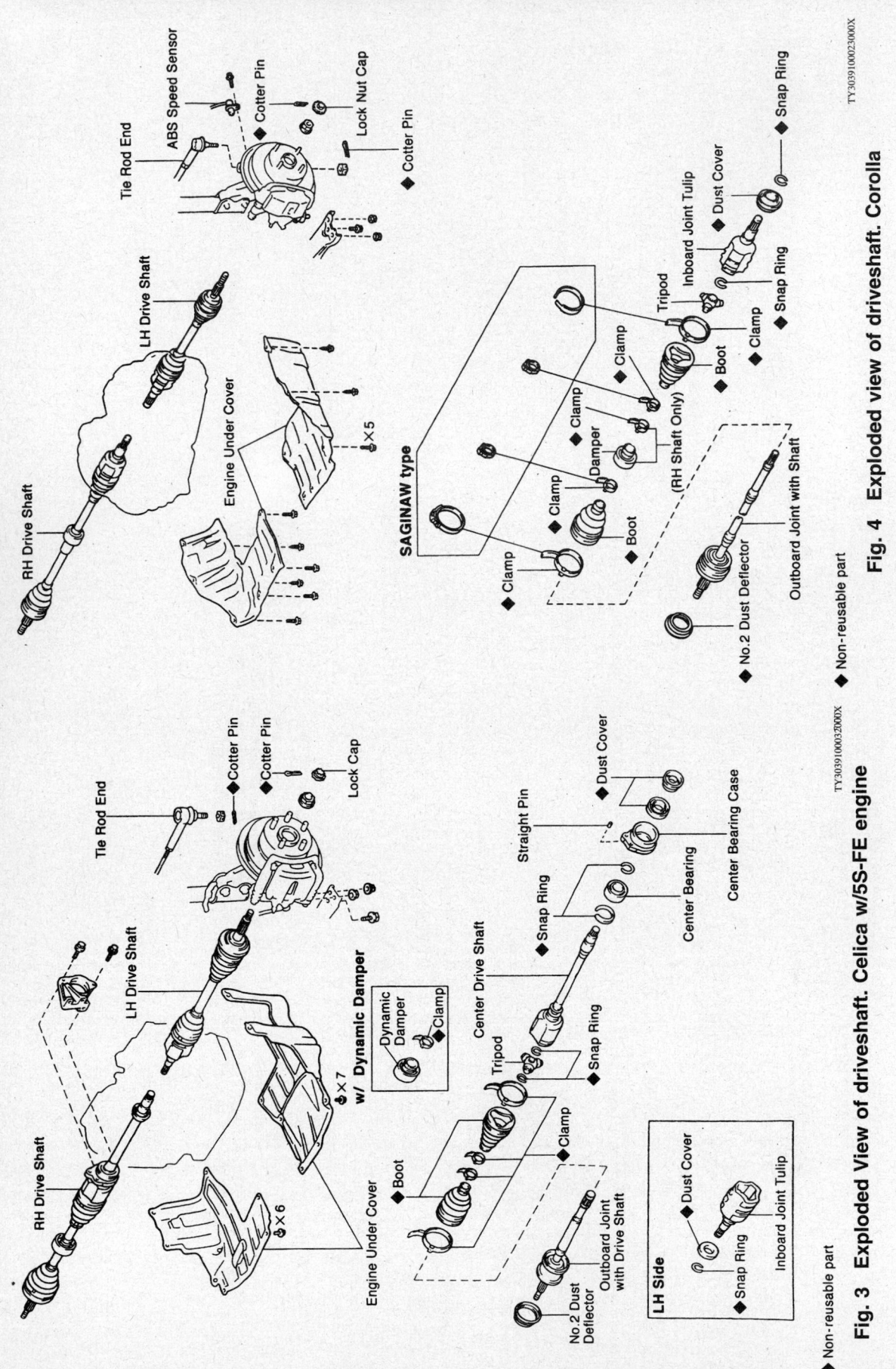

TY303910002300X

Fig. 4   Exploded view of driveshaft. Corolla

SAGINAW type

Tie Rod End

ABS Speed Sensor

Cotter Pin

Cotter Pin

Lock Nut Cap

LH Drive Shaft

RH Drive Shaft

Engine Under Cover

☆×5

Clamp

Clamp

Clamp

Clamp

Clamp

Damper

Boot

Boot

Boot

Tripod

Inboard Joint Tulip

Dust Cover

Snap Ring

Snap Ring

Snap Ring

(RH Shaft Only)

Outboard Joint with Shaft

No.2 Dust Deflector

◆ Non-reusable part

TY30391000320 00X

Fig. 3   Exploded View of driveshaft. Celica w/5S-FE engine

Tie Rod End

Cotter Pin

Cotter Pin

Lock Cap

LH Drive Shaft

RH Drive Shaft

Engine Under Cover

☆×7

☆×6

w/ Dynamic Damper

Dynamic Damper

Clamp

Center Drive Shaft

Tripod

Boot

Clamp

Snap Ring

Snap Ring

Straight Pin

Dust Cover

Center Bearing

Center Bearing Case

No.2 Dust Deflector

Outboard Joint with Drive Shaft

LH Side

Dust Cover

Snap Ring

Inboard Joint Tulip

◆ Non-reusable part

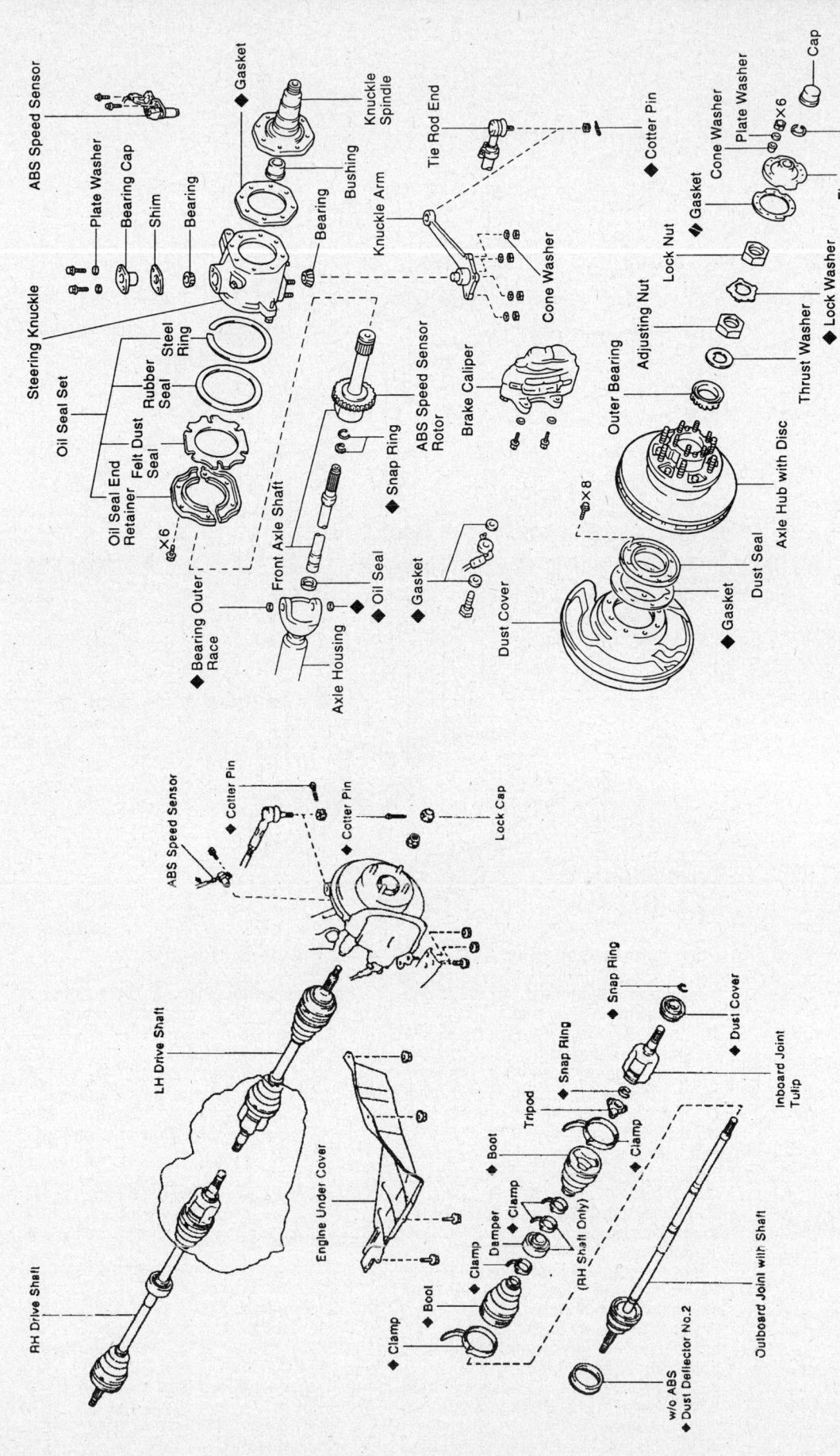

TY303910002900X

◆ Non-reusable part

Fig. 6   Front axle shaft & steering knuckle. Land Cruiser

TY303910002700A

◆ Non-reusable part

Fig. 5   Exploded view of driveshaft. Paseo & Tercel

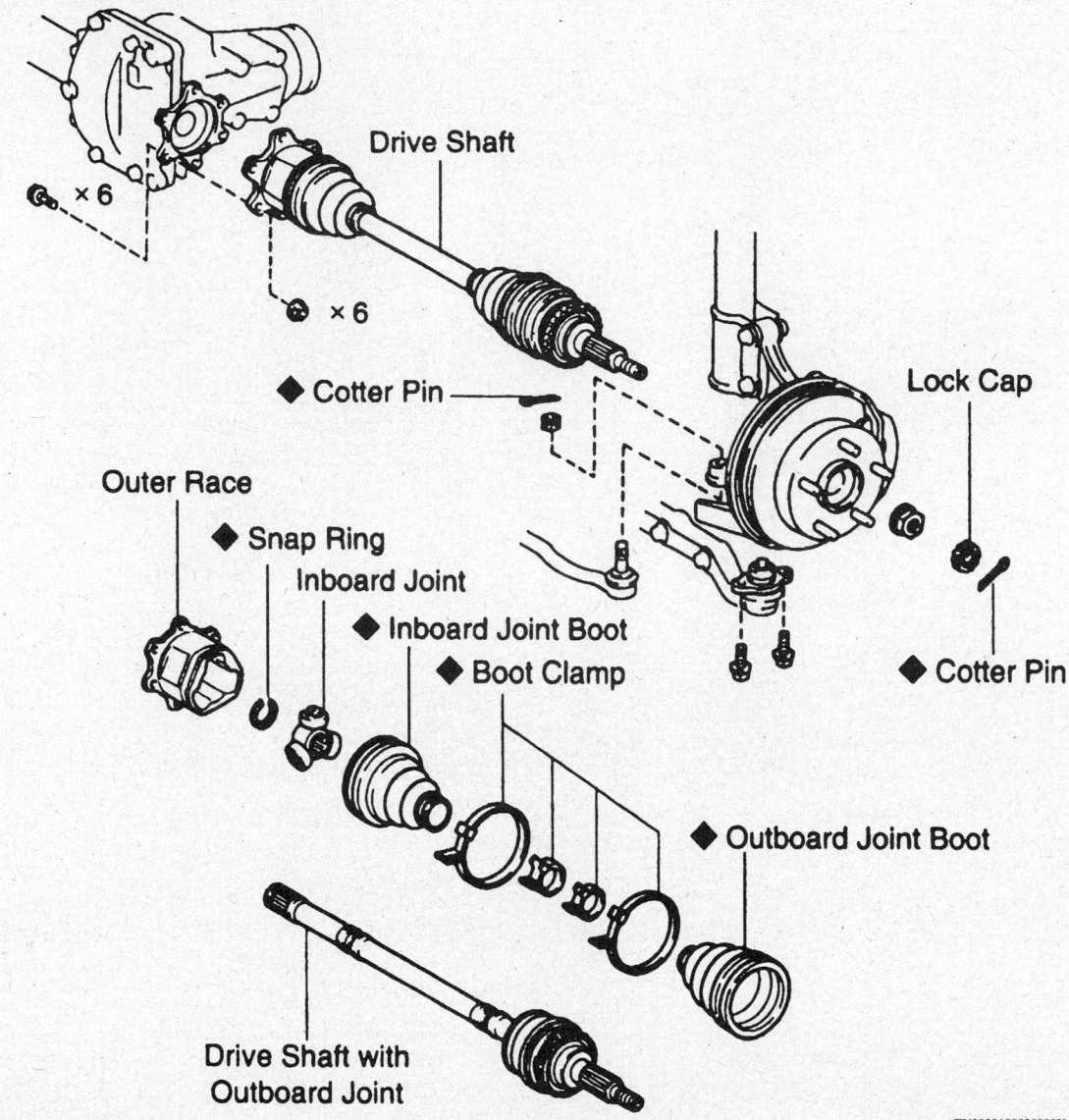

Drive Shaft

Lock Cap

◆ **Cotter Pin**

Outer Race

◆ **Snap Ring**

Inboard Joint

◆ **Inboard Joint Boot**

◆ **Boot Clamp**

◆ **Cotter Pin**

◆ **Outboard Joint Boot**

Drive Shaft with Outboard Joint

× 6

× 6

TY3039100030000X

◆ **Non-reusable part**

Fig. 7 Exploded view of front driveshaft assembly. 4WD T100, AWD Previa & 4Runner

joint tulip or center driveshaft to drive shaft.
15. Temporarily install boot to inboard joint tulip.
16. Ensure both boots are on shaft groove and are not stretched or compressed when driveshaft is at standard length, **Fig. 15.**
17. Install four new boot clamps and bend clamp bands with a screwdriver to lock.

4WD T100 & AWD PREVIA

1. Place axle shaft in a suitable vise, then make sure there is no play in inboard and outboard joints.
2. Ensure inboard boot slides smoothly in thrust direction and that there in no radial play in U-joints.
3. Check boots for damage, then remove inboard joint clamps **Fig. 7.**
4. Place matchmarks on inboard joint tulip and tripod, then separate inboard joint tulip from driveshaft.
5. Remove snap ring from tripod joint,

then place matchmarks on shaft and tripod, using paint or chalk.
6. Remove tripod joint from shaft, using a hammer and brass drift.
7. Remove inboard joint boot, then the outboard joint boot clamps and boot. **Do not attempt to disassemble outboard joint.**
8. Remove dust deflector.
9. Temporarily install new dust deflector, then wrap vinyl tape around spline of shaft and install boot with new clamps to outboard joint.
10. Temporarily install boot with new clamps to inboard joint and driveshaft.
11. Place beveled side of tripod axial spline toward outboard joint, then align matchmarks previously marked. Tap tripod joint into driveshaft using a suitable drift, then install snap ring.
12. Apply .39–.41 lbs. of grease included with boot kit into boot, then assemble boot to outboard joint.
13. Apply .60–.62 lbs. of grease included in boot kit to inboard tulip and boot,

then assemble inboard joint to inboard joint tulip. Align matchmarks, then insert inboard tulip to driveshaft. Install boot to inboard tulip.
14. Install both boot clamps, then bend bands rearward and close clamps.
15. Measure assembled length of axle without boots stretched or contracted, **Figs. 13 through 15.**

TACOMA & 4RUNNER

Disassemble

1. Using a screwdriver, remove inboard joint boot clamps, **Fig. 8.**
2. Slide inboard joint boot toward outboard joint.
3. Place matchmarks on inboard joint and driveshaft.
4. Remove inboard joint tulip from driveshaft.
5. Using snap ring expander, remove tripod snap ring.
6. Place matchmarks on shaft and tripod.

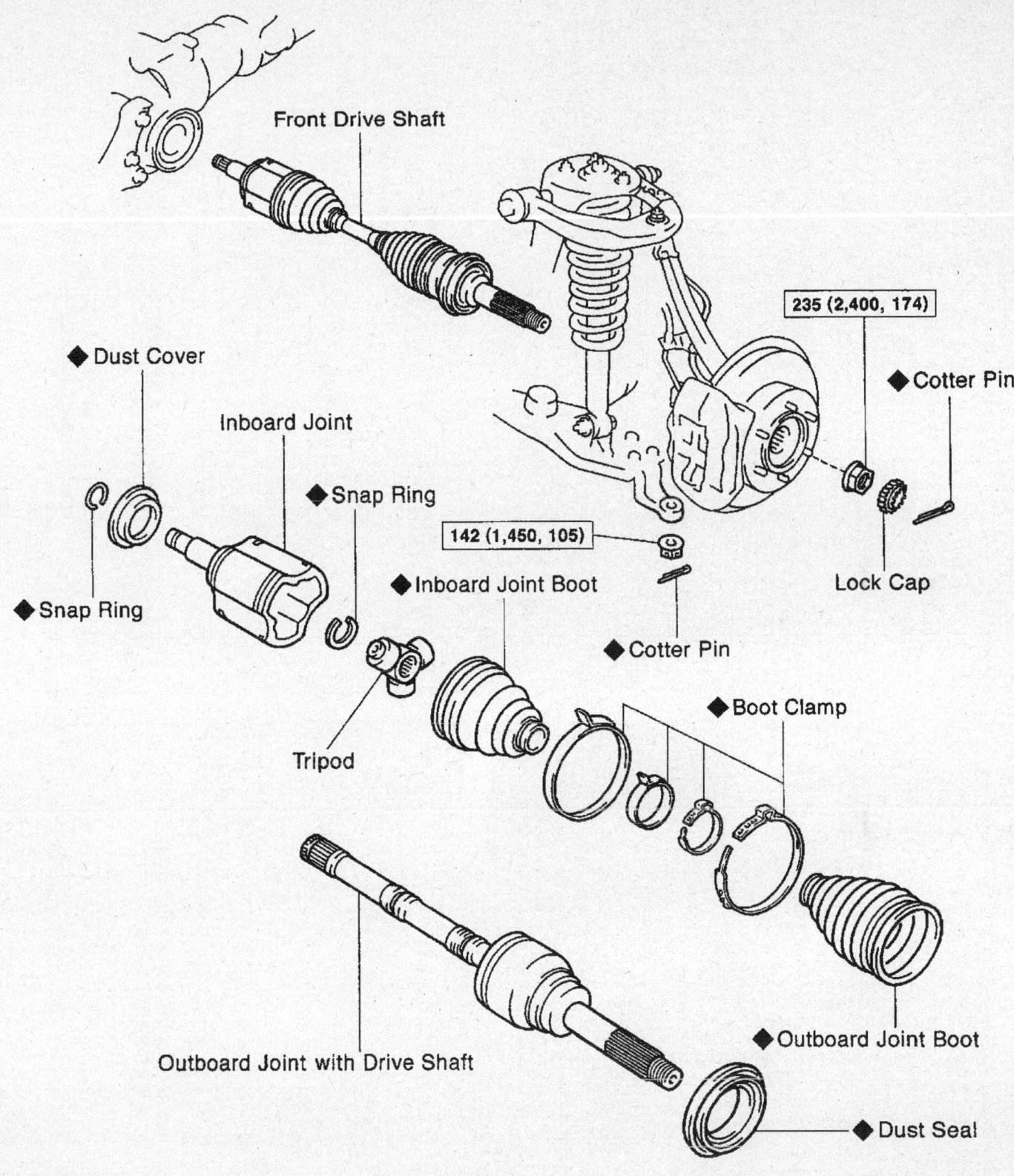

Front Drive Shaft

235 (2,400, 174)

◆ Dust Cover

◆ Cotter Pin

Inboard Joint

◆ Snap Ring

◆ Snap Ring

142 (1,450, 105)

Lock Cap

◆ Inboard Joint Boot

◆ Cotter Pin

Tripod

◆ Boot Clamp

Outboard Joint with Drive Shaft

◆ Outboard Joint Boot

◆ Dust Seal

N·m (kgf·cm, ft·lbf) : Specified torque

◆ Non-reusable part

TY3039600106000X

Fig. 8 Exploded view of front driveshaft assembly. Tacoma & 4Runner

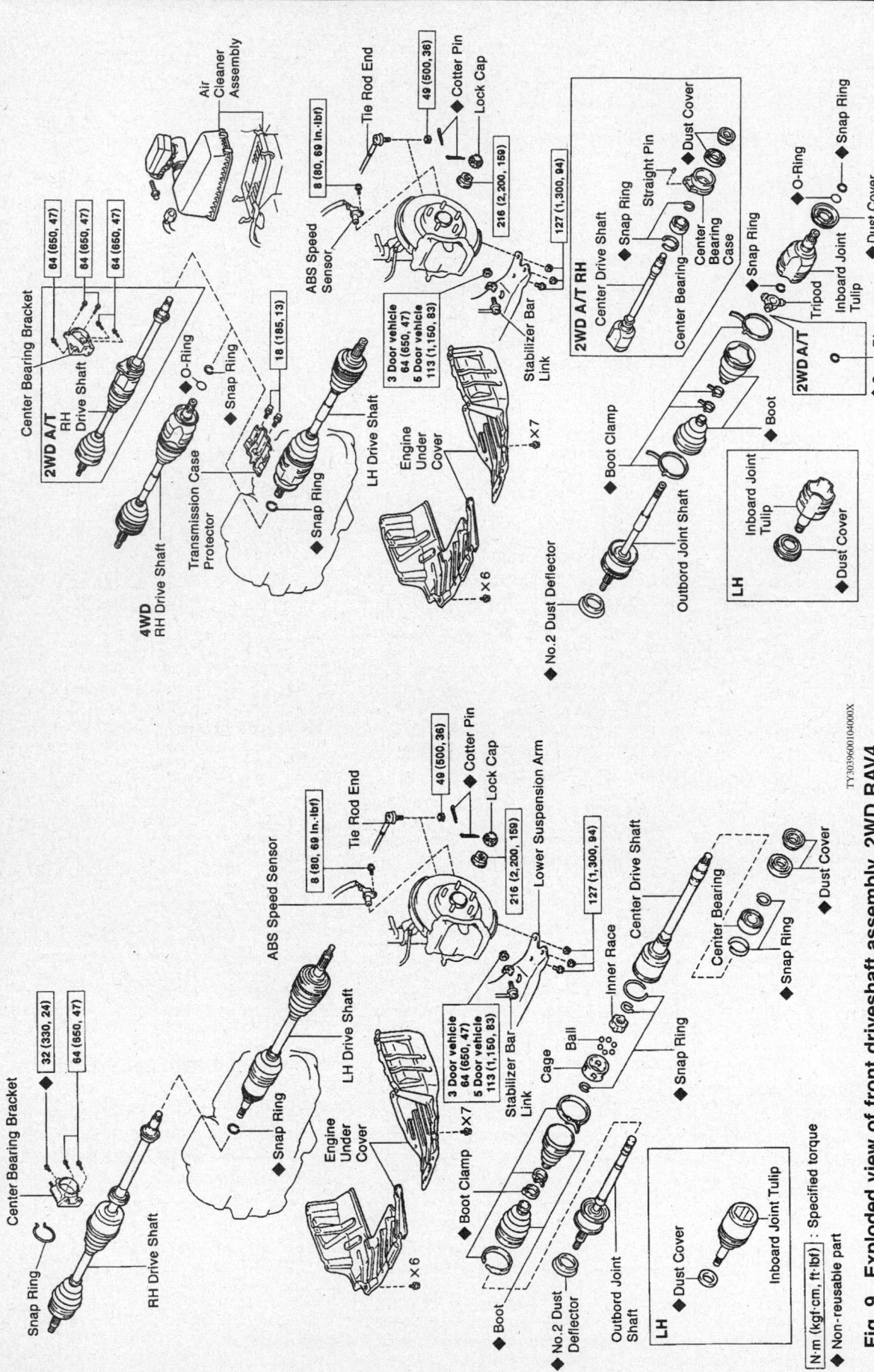

Fig. 10 Exploded view of front driveshaft assembly. 2WD RAV4 w/automatic transaxle & 4WD models

Fig. 9 Exploded view of front driveshaft assembly. 2WD RAV4 w/manual transaxle

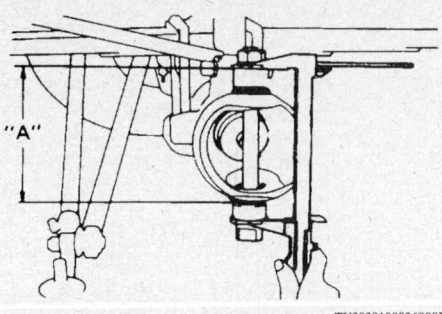

TY3039100036000X

Fig. 11 Axle housing dimension A inspection. Land Cruiser

7. Using brass bar and hammer, remove tripod.
8. Remove inboard joint boot from driveshaft.
9. Using a side cutter, cut two outboard boot clamps.
10. Remove outboard joint boot from driveshaft.
11. Using a screwdriver, remove dust seal from driveshaft.

Assemble

1. Using a screwdriver and hammer, install new dust cover and dust seal.
2. Place two new clamps to outboard joint boot and install to driveshaft.
3. Place beveled side of tripod axial spline toward outboard joint.
4. Align matchmarks and install tripod onto driveshaft using brass bar and hammer.
5. Install new snap ring.
6. Pack outboard joint and boot with grease and assemble boot to outboard joint.
7. Pack inboard joint and boot with grease, align matchmarks and install inboard joint tulip to driveshaft.
8. Temporarily install boot to inboard joint tulip.

9. Ensure both boots are in shaft groove and not stretched or contracted with driveshaft at standard length, **Fig. 15.**
10. Install new inboard joint boot clamps and bend the bands with a screwdriver to lock.
11. Install outboard joint boot clamps and pinch clamps to tighten. Use tool No. 09521-24010, or equivalent, to adjust clamp clearance to .031 inch or less.

INTERMEDIATE SHAFT SERVICE

CAMRY w/4 CYLINDER ENGINE & COROLLA

The following procedure applies only to the right side driveshaft on Camry models.

1. Using suitable tools, press out dust covers.
2. Remove snap ring.
3. Using press tool 09950-00020, or equivalent, remove bearing.
4. Remove the snap ring.
5. Install snap ring over shaft, then, using press tool 09527-20011, or equivalent, press on a new bearing.
6. Install new snap ring.
7. Using suitable press, press in a new dust cover on driveshaft side to a clearance of .04–.08 inch, ensuring that there is clearance between dust cover and bearing.
8. Using suitable press, press in a new dust cover on transaxle side to a distance of 3.39–3.43 inches from end of shaft.

AVALON & CAMRY w/V6 ENGINE

Disassemble

1. Using a suitable press, remove dust cover from transaxle side.

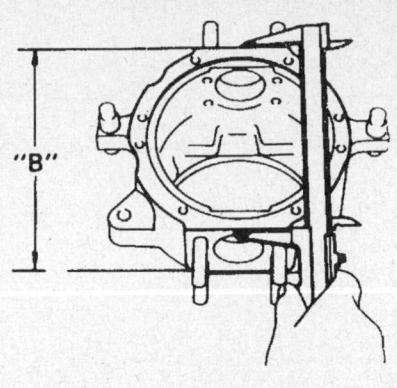

TY3039100037000X

Fig. 12 Steering knuckle dimension B inspection. Land Cruiser

2. Using press tool 09950-00020, or equivalent, and a suitable press, remove driveshaft side dust cover.
3. Remove snap ring.
4. Using a suitable press, remove bearing.

Assemble

1. Install snap ring to the center driveshaft.
2. Using a suitable press and a extension bar, press in the bearing.
3. Install a new snap ring.
4. Install dust covers, as follows:
   a. Using a suitable press, install driveshaft side dust cover. Clearance between the dust cover and the bearing should be .04–.08 inch.
   b. Using a suitable press, install transaxle side dust cover. Clearance between dust cover and transaxle end should be 3.94–3.98 inches.

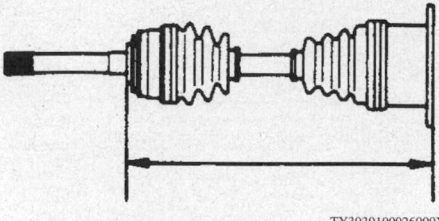

Fig. 13 Front axle shaft assembled length measurement. Models with constant velocity type inner joints

4A-FE Engine

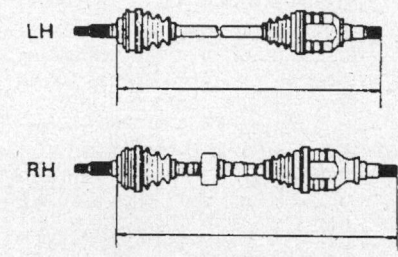

5S-FE Engine

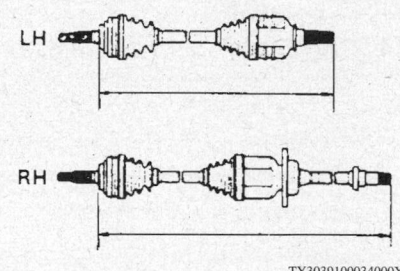

Fig. 14 Front axle shaft standard length measurement. Celica, other models w/tripod joints similar

Year	Model/Type	Damper Position, Inch⑬	Driveshaft Length, Inch⑬	
			Righthand	Lefthand
AVALON				
1996	—	—	17.81	17.81
1997–99	—	—	34.70	23.07
CAMRY				
1996	①③	—	17.81	17.81
	①②	—	17.95	17.95
	④②	—	34.10	23.94
	④③	—	34.68	23.98
1997–99	⑨	—	34.31	23.68
	⑩	—	34.71	23.07
CELICA				
1996	⑦⑨	7.87	33.76	22.53
	⑦⑩	7.87	33.94	22.71
	⑧	15.45	34.54	22.02
1997–99	⑨	—	33.76	22.53
	⑩	—	33.93	22.71
COROLLA				
1996	②	14.14	33.17	20.80
	⑫	14.14	33.75	21.26
1997–99	②	16.99	33.69	21.31
	⑫	16.58	33.75	21.26
PASEO				
1996–97	—	16.36	30.88	21.81
PREVIA				
1996–97	⑥	—	19.35	19.35
RAV4				
1996–99	⑤⑩	—	33.25	21.59
	⑤⑨	—	33.19	21.36
	⑭	—	20.13	20.00
TACOMA				
1996–99	—	—	17.17	17.17
TERCEL				
1996–98	—	14.34	30.90	21.42
T100				
1996–98	—	—	19.14	19.14
4RUNNER				
1996–99	—	—	20.90	20.90

① — Models w/V6 engines.
② — Toyota type boot & clamp.
③ — GKN type boot & clamp.
④ — Models w/4 cylinder engines.
⑤ — 2WD. ⑥ — AWD.
⑦ — 5S-FE engine.
⑧ — 7A-FE engine.
⑨ — Manual transaxle.
⑩ — Automatic transaxle.
⑪ — 4A-FE engine.
⑫ — Saginaw type boot & clamp.
⑬ — ± .20 inches,
⑭ — 4WD

Fig. 15 Front driveshaft length specification chart

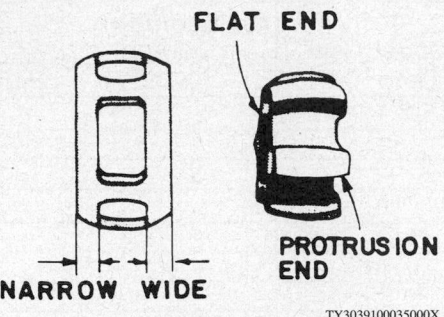

FLAT END

NARROW WIDE

PROTRUSION END

TY3039100035000X

Fig. 16 Inner race into cage installation. Land Cruiser

TIGHTENING SPECIFICATIONS

Year	Component	Torque/ Ft. Lbs.
AVALON		
1996–99	Axle Hub Nut	217
	Lower Ball Joint To Steering Knuckle	90
	Steering Knuckle To Shock Absorber	156
	Suspension Support To Body	59
	Suspension Support To Piston Rod	36
	Tie Rod To Lock Nut	54
	Tie Rod To Steering Knuckle	36
CAMRY		
1996–99	Axle Hub Nut	217
	Brake Caliper To Steering Knuckle	79
	Shock Absorber To Steering Knuckle	156
	Stabilizer Bar Link Nut	47
	Steering Knuckle To Lower Arm	90
	Tie Rod To Steering Knuckle	36
CELICA		
1996–99	Axle Hub Nut	159
	Lower Arm To Steering Knuckle	76
	Stabilizer Bar To Lower Suspension Arm	33
	Steering Knuckle To Brake Caliper	76
	Tie Rod End To Steering Knuckle	36
	Tie Rod End Lock Nut	54
COROLLA		
1996–99	Axle Hub Nut	159
	Brake Caliper To Steering Knuckle	65
	Lower Ball Joint To Steering Knuckle	87
	Shock Absorber To Steering Knuckle	203
	Stabilizer Bar Link Nut	33
	Tie Rod To Steering Knuckle	36
	Tie Rod End Lock Nut	41
LAND CRUISER		
1996–99	Disc Brake Caliper To Axle Hub	90
	Flange To Axle Hub	26
	Front Axle Hub Bearing Locknut	47
	Shock Absorber To Axle Housing	51
	Shock Absorber To Body	51
	Steering Knuckle To Bearing Cap	71
	Steering Knuckle To Knuckle Arm	71
	Steering Knuckle To Knuckle Spindle	34
	Tie Rod End To Steering Knuckle	67

Continued

TIGHTENING
SPECIFICATIONS—Continued

Year	Component	Torque/ Ft. Lbs.
PASEO		
1996-97	Brake Caliper To Steering Knuckle	65
	Driveshaft Lock Nut	159
	Shock Absorber To Steering Knuckle	①
	Stabilizer Bar To Lower Suspension Arm	13
	Tie Rod Locknut	35
PREVIA		
1996-97	Drive Shaft Lock Nut	152
	Drive Shaft To Differential Side Gear Shaft	51
	Steering Knuckle To Lower Ball Joint	94
	Steering Knuckle To Tie Rod End	36
	Steering Knuckle To Shock Absorber Set Bolt	232
4RUNNER		
1996-99	Driveshaft Locknut	174
	Lower Suspension Arm	105
RAV4		
1996-99	ABS Speed Sensor Bolt	72②
	Driveshaft Locknut	159
	Lower Ball Joint To Lower Suspension Arm	94
	Lower Ball Joint To Steering Knuckle Bolts	94
	Tie Rod End Locknut	41
TACOMA		
1996-99	Hub Nut	83
	Rack End Lock Nut	40
	Stabilizer Bar To Link	22
	Steering Knuckle To Brake Caliper	90
	Steering Knuckle To Lower Ball Joint	59
	Strut Bar To Frame	221
TERCEL		
1996-98	Brake Caliper To Steering Knuckle	65
	Driveshaft Locknut	159
	Piston Rod To Suspension Support	34
	Shock Absorber To Steering Knuckle	①
	Tie Rod Locknut	36
T100		
1996-98	Brake Caliper To Steering Knuckle	80
	Hub Nut	76
	Steering Knuckle To Upper Ball Joint	105
	Tie Rod End Locknut	41

① — 1996 models, 180 ft. lbs.; 1997–99 models, 113 ft. lbs.

② — Inch lbs.

All-Wheel Drive Systems

NOTE: On Air Bag Equipped Models, Refer To "Air Bag System Precautions" Located In The Front Of This Manual For System Disarming & Arming Procedures.

INDEX

PRECAUTIONS

AIR BAG SYSTEMS

Refer to "Air Bag System Precautions" in the front of this manual for system disarming and arming procedures.

AUDIO CODED ANTI-THEFT SYSTEM

Some models are equipped with an audio coded anti-theft system that will disable the radio when the battery cable is disconnected. The system can be identified by the "ANTI-THEFT SYSTEM" on the cassette lid. Obtain 3 digit code for input. Reset system after service as follows:

1. Obtain 3 digit audio theft code.
2. Depress 1 (PROG) while depressing righthand side of TUNE SEEK button, - - - will appear in tape operation display.
3. To enter the first digit, depress 1 (PROG) button repeatedly until the number of times depressed equals the first digit (depress the 1 button six times if the first digit if five, first press equals 0).
4. To enter second digit, depress 2 (APS) button repeatedly until the number of times depressed equals the second digit.
5. To enter third digit, depress 3 (RPT) button repeatedly until the number of times depressed equals the third digit.
6. If - - - is displayed after inputting digits, repeat procedure.
7. When code appears in display, depress and hold SCAN button until SEC appears.
8. When SEC disappears audio system is operative.
9. If Err is displayed, repeat procedure. **Attempting to input code more than 9 times may permanently disable audio system.**

BATTERY GROUND CABLE

Prior to service, disconnect battery ground cable and isolate as required.

DESCRIPTION

PREVIA

These automatic transmissions are four-speed, electronically controlled transmissions developed for use with high performance engines.

The A46DF & A340F automatic transmissions are equipped with a full time four wheel drive transfer cases.

These transmissions are mainly composed of a torque converter, the overdrive planetary gear, a 3-speed planetary gear unit, a hydraulic control system and electronic control system.

A lock-up mechanism is built into the torque converter clutch.

DRIVESHAFT SERVICE

FRONT

Refer to "Front Wheel Drive Axles" for front driveshaft repair procedures.

REAR

PREVIA

Refer to "Rear Axle & Suspension" section for rear axle service procedures.

DIFFERENTIAL SERVICE

PREVIA

Disassemble

1. Place differential carrier into a suitable working fixture.
2. Remove differential carrier cover, **Fig. 1.**
3. Measure side gear backlash while holding on pinion gear toward case. Backlash should be .0020–.0079 inch.
4. If backlash is not within specifications, install correct thrust washer, **Fig 2.**
5. Remove side gear shaft, differential tube and side gear shaft oil seals.
6. Using a dial indicator, measure ring gear runout. Maximum runout should be .0028 inch.
7. If runout is greater than maximum, replace ring gear and drive pinion as a set.
8. Check ring gear backlash as follows:
   a. Fix dial indicator on tooth surface at 90° angle.
   b. Holding drive pinion flange, measure ring gear backlash. Backlash should be .0051–.0071 inch.
   c. If backlash is not within specifications, adjust ring gear backlash. Measure from three of more places on circumference of ring gear.
   d. Inspect tooth contact between ring gear and drive pinion.
9. Using remover tool No. 09557-22022, or equivalent, remove companion flange.
10. Using oil seal puller tool No. 09308-00010, or equivalent, remove oil seal and oil slinger.
11. Using bearing remover tool No. 09556-22010, or equivalent, remove rear bearing and bearing spacer.
12. Remove differential case assembly as follows:
    a. Place alignment marks on bearing cap and differential carrier.
    b. Remove four bolts and two bearing caps.
    c. Using differential remover tool No. 09504-22011, or equivalent, remove drive pinion side plate washer.
    d. Measure plate washer and note thickness.
    e. Remove differential case and bearing outer race from carrier.
    f. Tag bearing outer race for identification.
13. Remove drive pinion from differential carrier.
14. Using bearing remover tool No. 09950-00020, or equivalent, remove bearing from drive pinion.
15. If drive pinion or ring gear are damaged, replace as a set.
16. Using a brass bar and hammer, drive out outer races from differential carrier.
17. Place marks on ring gear and differential case, then using a screwdriver unstake lock plate.
18. Remove eight bolts and four lock plates, then using plastic hammer tap on ring gear to separate it from differential case.
19. Check differential case runout as follows:
    a. Place bearing outer races on respective bearings. Ensure the left and right outer races are not interchanged.
    b. Install differential case in differential carrier.

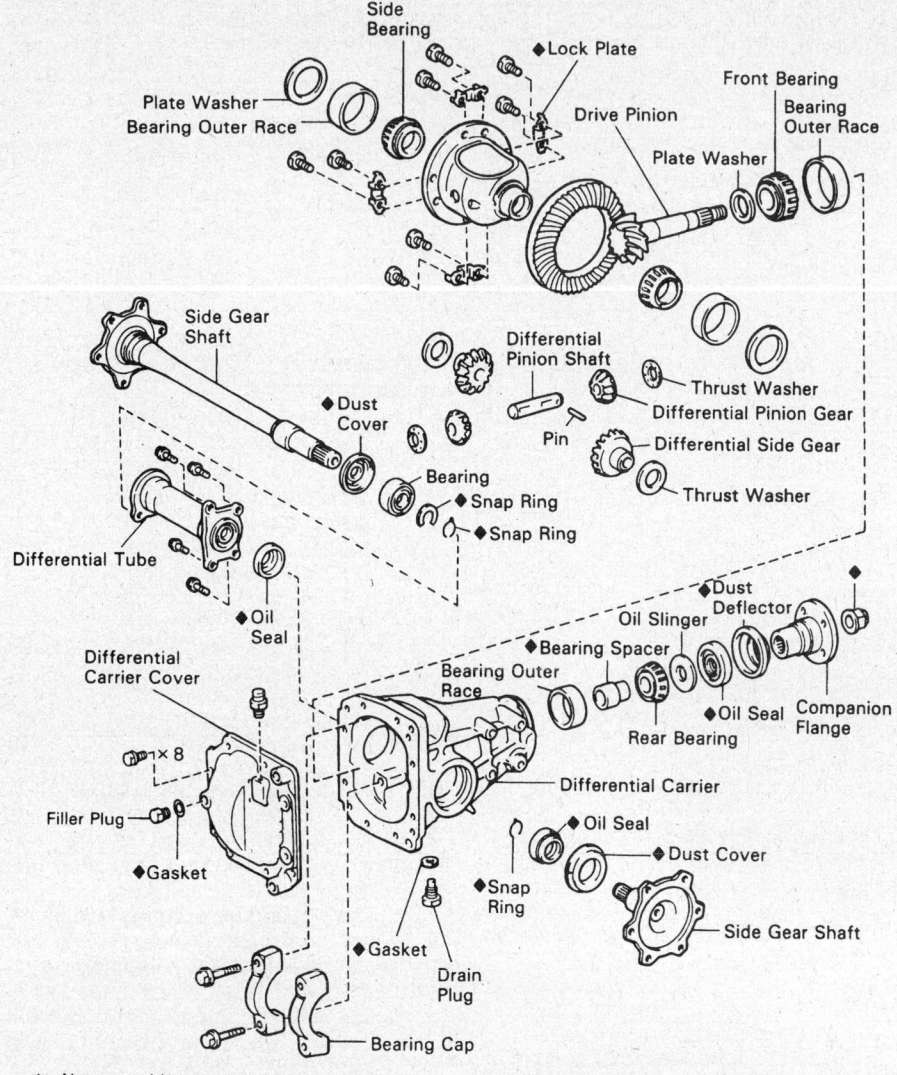

Thrust washer thickness
0.95 mm (0.037 in.)
1.00 mm (0.039 in.)
1.05 mm (0.041 in.)
1.10 mm (0.043 in.)
1.15 mm (0.045 in.)
1.20 mm (0.047 in.)

TY3039100054000X

Fig. 2 Side gear thrust washers. Previa

◆ Non-reusable part

TY3039100053000X

Fig. 1 Exploded view of AWD differential. Previa

c. When there no play left in side bearings, install plate washers.
d. Align marks on bearing cap and differential carrier.
e. Install and uniformly tighten four bearing caps in several passes.
f. Using dial indicator, measure differential case runout. Runout should be .016 inch.
g. Remove differential case.
20. Using puller tool No. 09950-20017, or equivalent, remove side bearing from differential case.
21. Using pin punch and hammer, drive out straight pin.
22. Remove pinion shaft, pinion gear, pinion gear thrust washers, side gears and side gear thrust washers from differential case.

Assemble

1. Adjust differential side gear shaft backlash as follows:
   a. Install proper thrust washers on side gears.
   b. Refer to **Fig. 2,** select thrust washers which will ensure backlash is within specification.
   c. Install side gears, pinion gears, pinion gear thrust washers and pinion shaft in differential case.
   d. Align holes of differential case and pinion shaft.
   e. Push side gear shafts carefully into differential case by hand and install.
   f. Measure side gear backlash while holding on pinion gear toward differential case. Backlash should be .0020–.0079 inch.
   g. If backlash is not within specifications, install side gear thrust washers with differential thickness.
   h. Remove side gear shafts.
2. Using a hammer and punch, install straight pin through case and hole of pinion shaft.
3. Stake differential case.
4. Install side bearings into differential case.
5. Heat ring gear in boiling water. After moisture on ring gear has completely evaporated, install ring gear to differential case.
6. Align marks on ring gear and differential case, then temporarily install five new lock plates and ten bolts so that bolt holes in ring gear and differential case are not misaligned. **Ring gear set bolts should not be tightened until ring gear has cooled sufficiently. Torque** ring gear set bolt to 71 ft. lbs.
7. Stake lock plates. Stake one claw flush with the flat surface of the nut. For claw contacting the protruding portion of the nut, stake only half on the tightening side.
8. Using a dial indicator, check ring gear runout. Ring gear runout should be .0028 inch.
9. Install drive pinion front bearing.
10. Temporarily adjust drive pinion preload as follows:
    a. Install drive pinion, rear bearing and oil slinger.
    b. Assemble spacer and oil seal after adjusting gear contact pattern.

Thickness	mm(in.)
2.21 – 2.23 (0.0870 – 0.0878)	2.72 – 2.74 (0.1071 – 0.1079)
2.24 – 2.26 (0.0881 – 0.0890)	2.75 – 2.77 (0.1083 – 0.1091)
2.27 – 2.29 (0.0894 – 0.0902)	2.78 – 2.80 (0.1095 – 0.1102)
2.30 – 2.32 (0.0906 – 0.0913)	2.81 – 2.83 (0.1106 – 0.1114)
2.33 – 2.35 (0.0917 – 0.0925)	2.84 – 2.86 (0.1118 – 0.1126)
2.36 – 2.38 (0.0929 – 0.0937)	2.87 – 2.89 (0.1130 – 0.1138)
2.39 – 2.41 (0.0941 – 0.0949)	2.90 – 2.92 (0.1142 – 0.1150)
2.42 – 2.44 (0.0953 – 0.0961)	2.93 – 2.95 (0.1154 – 0.1161)
2.45 – 2.47 (0.0965 – 0.0972)	2.96 – 2.98 (0.1165 – 0.1173)
2.48 – 2.50 (0.0976 – 0.0984)	2.99 – 3.01 (0.1177 – 0.1185)
2.51 – 2.53 (0.0988 – 0.0996)	3.02 – 3.04 (0.1189 – 0.1197)
2.54 – 2.56 (0.1000 – 0.1008)	3.05 – 3.07 (0.1201 – 0.1209)
2.57 – 2.59 (0.1012 – 0.1020)	3.08 – 3.10 (0.1213 – 0.1220)
2.60 – 2.62 (0.1024 – 0.1031)	3.11 – 3.13 (0.1224 – 0.1232)
2.63 – 2.65 (0.1035 – 0.1043)	3.14 – 3.16 (0.1236 – 0.1244)
2.66 – 2.68 (0.1047 – 0.1055)	3.17 – 3.19 (0.1248 – 0.1256)
2.69 – 2.71 (0.1059 – 0.1067)	3.20 – 3.22 (0.1260 – 0.1268)

TY3039100055000X

Fig. 3   Side bearing thrust washers. Previa

Thickness	mm(in.)
2.27 (0.0894)	2.51 (0.0988)
2.30 (0.0906)	2.54 (0.1000)
2.33 (0.0917)	2.57 (0.1012)
2.36 (0.0929)	2.60 (0.1024)
2.39 (0.0941)	2.63 (0.1035)
2.42 (0.0953)	2.66 (0.1047)
2.45 (0.0965)	2.69 (0.1059)
2.48 (0.0976)	

TY3039100056000X

Fig. 4   Tooth contact between ring gear & drive pinion. Previa

Thickness	mm(in.)
2.27 (0.0894)	2.51 (0.0988)
2.30 (0.0906)	2.54 (0.1000)
2.33 (0.0917)	2.57 (0.1012)
2.36 (0.0929)	2.60 (0.1024)
2.39 (0.0941)	2.63 (0.1035)
2.42 (0.0953)	2.66 (0.1047)
2.45 (0.0965)	2.69 (0.1059)
2.48 (0.0976)	

TY3039100057000X

Fig. 5   Tooth thrust washers. Previa

c. Using companion flange replacer tool No. 09557-22022, or equivalent, install companion flange.

d. Adjust drive pinion preload by tightening plate washer and companion flange nut.

e. Using companion flange replacer tool No. 09557-22022, or equivalent, hold flange to tighten nut. **As there is no spacer, tighten nut little at a time, ensuring not to overtighten.**

f. Using a torque meter, measure preload. Preload should be 8.7–13.9 inch lbs., for new bearing or 4.3–6.9 lbs., for used bearing.

11. Install differential case in differential carrier. Place bearing outer on their respective bearings. Ensure the left and right outer races are not interchanged.

12. Install differential case in the differential carrier.

13. Check ring gear backlash, backlash should be .0051–.0071 inch, If not, adjust backlash by either increasing or decreasing the number of washers on both sides by an equal amount. There should be no clearance between plate, washer and case, **Fig. 3.**

14. Adjust side bearing preload as follows:
  a. Remove drive pinion side plate washer, then measure thickness.
  b. Using backlash as a reference, install a new washer of .0024–.0035 inch thicker than washer removed.
  c. Select a washer which can be pressed in 2/3 of the way in by hand.
  d. Using suitable tool, tap in plate washer.
  e. Recheck ring gear backlash. Backlash should be .0051–.0071 inch. Backlash will change approximately .0008 inch with a .0012 inch alteration of the side washer. If backlash is incorrect, adjust by either increasing or decreasing the number of washers on both sides by equal amounts.
  f. Install bearing caps. Align marks on cap and carrier. **Torque** attaching bolts to 58 ft. lbs.

15. Measure total preload. Total preload at the (start plus drive pinion preload) should be 2.6–4.3 inch lbs.

16. Inspect tooth contact between ring gear and drive pinion as follows:
  a. Coat 3 or 4 teeth at three different positions on ring gear with red lead.
  b. Hold companion flange firmly, then rotate ring gear in both directions, **Fig. 4.**
  c. Inspect tooth pattern.
  d. If teeth are not contacting properly, use proper washers for correction, **Fig. 5.**

17. Install bearing spacer, oil seal and companion flange.

18. Check drive pinion preload as follows:
  a. Using a torque meter, measure drive pinion preload using backlash of drive pinion and ring gear. Preload (at the start) should be 8.7–13.9 inch lbs., for new bearing or 4.3–6.9 lbs., for used bearing.
  b. If preload is greater than specified, replace bearing spacer.
  c. If preload is less than specified, retighten nut to 9 ft. lbs. at a time until specified preload is reached.
  d. If maximum torque exceeds 174 ft. lbs. while tightening nut, replace bearing spacer and repeat procedure.
  e. Do not back off the pinion nut to reduce preload.

19. Check ring gear backlash. Backlash should be .0051–.0071 inch.

20. Recheck tooth contact between ring gear and drive pinion. Refer to step 16.

21. Using dial indicator, measure vertical and lateral runout of companion flange. Maximum runout should be .0039 inch. Maximum lateral runout should be .0039 inch.

22. If runout is greater than maximum, inspect bearings.

23. Stake drive pinion nut.

24. Install side gear shaft oil seals.

25. Install differential tube. **Torque** attaching bolt to 65 ft. lbs.

26. Install side gear shafts.

27. Install differential carrier cover. **Torque** attaching bolts to 34 ft. lbs.

Drive Axles

NOTE: On Air Bag Equipped Models, Refer To "Air Bag System Precautions" Located In The Front Of This Manual For System Disarming & Arming Procedures.

INDEX

PRECAUTIONS

AIR BAG SYSTEMS

Refer to "Air Bag System Precautions" in the front of this manual for system disarming and arming procedures.

AUDIO CODED ANTI-THEFT SYSTEM

Some models are equipped with an audio coded anti-theft system that will disable the radio when the battery cable is disconnected. The system can be identified by the "ANTI-THEFT SYSTEM" on the cassette lid. Obtain 3 digit code for input. Reset system after service as follows:

1. Obtain 3 digit audio theft code.
2. Depress 1 (PROG) while depressing righthand side of TUNE SEEK button, - - will appear in tape operation display.
3. To enter the first digit, depress 1 (PROG) button repeatedly until the number of times depressed equals the first digit (depress the 1 button six times if the first digit if five, first press equals 0).
4. To enter second digit, depress 2 (APS) button repeatedly until the number of times depressed equals the second digit.
5. To enter third digit, depress 3 (RPT) button repeatedly until the number of times depressed equals the third digit.
6. If - - - is displayed after inputting digits, repeat procedure.
7. When code appears in display, depress and hold SCAN button until SEC appears.
8. When SEC disappears audio system is operative.
9. If Err is displayed, repeat procedure. **Attempting to input code more than 9 times may permanently disable audio system.**

BATTERY GROUND CABLE

Prior to service, disconnect battery ground cable and isolate as required.

IDENTIFICATION

Refer to **Fig. 1** for drive axle identification.

REMOVABLE TYPE CARRIER DIFFERENTIAL

RAV4

Disassemble

1. Using a hammer and chisel, unstake staked part of companion flange nut, **Fig. 2.**
2. Using tool No. 09330-00021, or equivalent, to hold flange, remove companion flange nut.
3. Using tool Nos. 09950-30010 and 09954-03010, or equivalents, remove companion flange.
4. Using tool No. 09308-10010, or equivalent, remove oil seal and oil slinger from housing.
5. Using tool No. 09556-22010, or equivalent, remove front bearing from drive pinion.
6. Remove bearing spacer.
7. **On models with torque sensing limited slip differential,** proceed as follows:
   a. Using tool No. 09520-24010, or equivalent, remove two side gear shafts from differential.
   b. Using a screwdriver, remove two snap rings from side gear shafts.
8. **On models with 2 pinion differential,** proceed as follows:
   a. Use needle nose pliers to remove two snap rings from side gear shafts.
   b. Remove side gear shafts.
9. **On all models,** use tool No. 09308-00010, or equivalent, to remove oil seals from housing.
10. Place matchmarks on bearing and differential carrier, then remove bearing caps.
11. Using tool No. 09504-22010, or equivalent, remove two plate washers.
12. Remove differential case and two bearing outer races from carrier.

13. Remove drive pinion from differential carrier.
14. Using tool No. 09950-00020, or equivalent, and a suitable press, remove bearing from drive pinion.
15. Remove plate washer.
16. Remove front and rear bearing outer races using brass bar and hammer.
17. Place matchmarks on ring gear and differential case.
18. Using a screwdriver, unstake four ring gear lock plates.
19. Remove 8 ring gear set bolts and four lock plates.
20. Using a plastic hammer, tap on ring gear to separate it from differential case.
21. Remove side bearings from differential case using tool No. 09950-00020, or equivalent.
22. **On models with 2 pinion differential,** proceed as follows:
    a. Using pin punch and hammer, remove differential case straight pin.
    b. Remove pinion shaft, two pinion gears, two pinion gear thrust washers, two side gears and side gear thrust washers.

Assemble

1. **On models with 2 pinion differential,** proceed as follows:
   a. Install two proper thrust washers on two side gears. Select shim from selection chart, **Fig. 3,** to ensure side gear backlash is .0020–.0079 inch.
   b. Install two side gears, two pinion gears, two pinion gear thrust washers and pinion shaft into differential case.
   c. Measure side gear backlash while holding one pinion gear toward differential case. If backlash is not .0020–.0079 inch, install two side gear thrust washers of different thicknesses.
   d. Install straight pin and stake outside of differential case pin hole.
2. **On all models,** clean contact surfaces of differential case and ring gear.
3. Heat ring gear in boiling water.
4. Carefully remove ring gear from boiling

water and install to differential case.

5. Align matchmarks on ring gear and differential case.
6. Temporarily install 4 lock plates and 8 bolts.
7. After ring gear has cooled, **torque** 8 lock plate bolts to 71 ft. lbs.
8. Using a chisel and hammer, stake outside of differential case pin hole.
9. Using tool No. 09710-22021, or equivalent, and a press, install two side bearings into differential case.
10. Install differential case on carrier and install 2 plate washers where no play exists in bearing.
11. Install bearing caps.
12. Using dial indicator, measure runout of ring gear. Maximum runout should be .0028 inch.
13. Remove two bearing caps, two plate washers and differential carrier.
14. Install front and rear bearing outer races.
15. Install reused washer on drive pinion.
16. Using tool No. 09506-30012, or equivalent, and a press, install rear bearing onto drive pinion.
17. Install drive pinion and front bearing.
18. Using tool Nos. 09950-30010 and 09954-03010, or equivalents, install companion flange.
19. Adjust drive pinion preload by tightening companion flange nut.
20. Using tool No. 09330-00021, or equivalent, to hold flange, **torque** nut to 80 ft. lbs.
21. Using a torque wrench to measure preload, ensure preload is within specifications.
22. Place two bearing outer races in their respective bearings, then install differential case in carrier.
23. Adjust ring gear backlash as follows:
    a. Install plate washer on ring gear back side.
    b. Snug down washer and bearing by tapping on ring gear with plastic hammer.
    c. Using dial indicator, hold side bearing boss on teeth surface of ring gear and measure ring gear backlash. Backlash should be .0051 inch.
    d. Select ring gear back side plate washer to ensure backlash is correct.
    e. Select a ring gear teeth side washer with thickness that eliminates any clearance between outer race and case.
    f. Remove plate washer and differential case.
    g. Install plate washer into ring gear back side.
    h. Place outer plate washer onto differential case together with outer race.
    i. Install differential case with outer race onto carrier.
    j. Using a plastic hammer, snug down washer and bearing by tapping ring gear.
24. Remove companion flange and front bearing.
25. Install new bearing spacer and front bearing.

26. Install oil slinger and new front oil seal. Apply grease to oil seal lip.
27. Install companion flange, then check drive pinion preload. If preload is greater than specification, replace bearing spacer. If preload is less than specification, **retorque** nut 9 ft. lbs. at a time until proper preload is reached.
28. **Do not back off pinion nut to reduce preload.**
29. Stake drive pinion nut, then install side gear shaft oil seals.
30. Install side gear shafts with new snap rings.
31. **On models with 2 pinion differential,** install two side gear shafts to differential case with new snap rings.
32. **On all models,** install differential carrier cover. **Torque** to 34 ft. lbs.

LAND CRUISER, PREVIA, TACOMA, T100 & 4RUNNER

Disassemble

1. Place carrier assembly on a suitable workbench, **Fig. 4.**
2. Loosen staked portion of companion flange locknut, then retain flange using tool No. 09330-00021, or equivalent, and remove nut.
3. Remove companion flange using tool No. 09557-22022, or equivalent.
4. Remove oil seal, using tool No. 09557-22022, or equivalent, then the oil slinger.
5. Remove front bearing front drive pinion, using tool No. 09556-30010, or equivalent, then the bearing spacer.
6. Mark relative position between bearing cap and differential carrier, then remove 2 adjusting locknuts, bearing caps, adjusting nuts, bearing outer races and differential case from carrier. **Tag components as to original location to facilitate installation.**
7. Remove drive pinion from differential carrier.
8. If necessary to replace drive pinion rear bearing, proceed as follows:
    a. Remove rear bearing from drive pinion, using tool No. 09950-00020, or equivalent.
    b. Install washer on drive pinion with chamfer end facing pinion gear.
    c. Press washer and new rear bearing onto drive pinion, using tool No. 09506-30011, or equivalent.
9. If necessary to replace drive pinion front and rear bearing outer race, proceed as follows:
    a. Drive out outer bearing race using a hammer and suitable drift.
    b. Press in new outer race using suitable tool.
10. Remove side bearing from differential case using tool No. 09950-20016, or equivalent.
11. Remove ring gear attaching bolts and lock plates, then mark relative position between ring gear and differential case. Separate ring gear from case by tapping on ring gear, using a suitable mallet.
12. Drive out straight pin, then remove pin-

ion shaft, two pinion gears, side gears and thrust washers from differential case.

Assemble

1. Select suitable thrust washers from chart, **Figs. 5 and 6,** that will bring backlash to .0020–.0079 inch, then install thrust washers into differential case.
2. Drive in straight pin, using a hammer and suitable drift, through case and hole in pinion shaft, then stake pin to differential case.
3. Install side bearings using tool No. 09608-30012, or equivalent.
4. Clean mating surfaces of differential case, then heat ring gear in a suitable oil bath to approximately 212°F.
5. Install ring gear into differential case, aligning mating marks on gear and case.
6. Apply a suitable lubricant to ring gear, then install lock plates and attaching bolts. **Torque** bolts uniformly to 71 ft. lbs.
7. Stake lock plates using a hammer and suitable drift.
8. Check ring gear runout. Maximum runout should be .0028 inch on Previa models, or .0039 inch on 4WD 4Runner models.
9. Temporarily adjust drive pinion preload as follows:
    a. Install drive pinion and front bearing.
    b. Install companion flange using tool No. 09557-22022, or equivalent.
    c. Retain companion flange using tool No. 09330-0021, or equivalent, then adjust drive pinion preload to 5.2–8.7 inch lbs. on Previa, 7.8–11.3 inch lbs. on 4WD and 4Runner models.
10. Place bearing outer races on their respective bearings, then insert case into carrier.
11. Install adjusting nuts on their respective carrier, ensuring backlash exists between ring gear and drive pinion.
12. Align mating marks on bearing caps and carrier, then rotate cap bolts 2–3 turns and manually depress cap.
13. Tighten cap bolts until adjusting nut on ring gear side until backlash is approximately .008 inch.
14. Tighten adjusting nut from drive pinion side as shown, **Fig. 7,** then check for backlash. If tightening nut causes backlash, loosen nut until backlash is eliminated.
15. Install a suitable dial indicator on top of adjusting nut, then adjust side bearing for zero preload, or until indicator begins to move. **Tighten nut 1 ½ notches from zero preload position.**
16. Adjust ring gear backlash to .0051–.0071 inch, by rotating both left and right adjusting nuts equal amounts, then **torque** bearing cap bolts to 58 ft. lbs.
17. Measure total preload. Preload should be 3.5–5.2 inch lbs., with a preload of .0051–.0071 inch.
18. Inspect gear tooth contact as shown,

Fig. 8. If contacting pattern is not correct, select a suitable shim from chart, **Fig. 6,** that will ensure proper contact.

19. Install new bearing spacer and front bearing.
20. Install oil slinger, then drive in new oil seal to a depth of .059 inch on Previa or .039 inch on 4WD 4Runner models.
21. Install companion flange, using tool No. 09557-22022, or equivalent, then apply a suitable lubricant to new nut. Retain companion flange, using tool No. 09330-00021, or equivalent, then install nut and **torque** to 80–173 ft. lbs. on Previa, 145–253 ft. lbs. on 1 ton and 4WD 4Runner models.
22. Check drive pinion preload. Drive pinion preload should be 7.8–11.3 inch lbs.
23. If preload is greater than specified, replace bearing spacer. If preload is less than specified **torque** nut 9 ft. lbs. at a time until specified preload is obtained. **If maximum torque is exceeded during tightening procedure, replace bearing spacer and repeat preload adjustment.**
24. Check companion flange deviation. Deviation in any direction should not exceed .0039 inch.
25. Stake drive pinion nut.
26. Install bearing cap nut lock, then **torque** attaching bolt to 9 ft. lbs.

INTEGRAL TYPE CARRIER DIFFERENTIAL w/INDEPENDENT REAR SUSPENSION

EXCEPT LIMITED SLIP

SUPRA

Disassemble

1. Drain lubricant, then remove differential carrier cover attaching bolts and the cover, **Fig. 9.**
2. Using suitable dial indicator, measure ring gear runout. If runout exceeds .0028 inch, replace ring gear.
3. With dial indicator positioned 90° to ring gear teeth surface, hold drive pinion flange while measuring ring gear backlash. Backlash should be .0051–.0071 inch. If backlash is not within specifications, it must be adjusted.
4. Using suitable inch lbs. torque wrench mounted on pinion nut, **Fig. 10,** measure and record starting preload of the ring and pinion backlash. Preload should be 4.3–6.9 inch lbs.
5. With wrench positioned as above, measure and record the total starting preload of ring and pinion assembly. Total preload should be 3.5–5.2 inch lbs. plus drive pinion preload measured in step 4, above.
6. Using suitable hammer and chisel, unstake pinion nut.
7. While holding companion flange from turning with tool 09330-00021, remove pinion nut.
8. Remove companion flange with suitable puller.

9. Remove pinion oil seal and oil slinger from differential carrier.
10. Remove pinion rear bearing using suitable puller, then the spacer.
11. Remove side gear shaft from differential with puller tool No. 09520-24010, or equivalent.
12. Remove side gear shaft oil seal with puller tool No. 09308-00010, or equivalent.
13. Place reference marks between bearing caps and differential carrier, then remove bearing cap bolts and caps.
14. Remove two side bearing preload adjusting shims.
15. Lift differential case with bearing outer races from differential carrier.
16. Tag outer races to show which side they were removed from.
17. Remove drive pinion from differential carrier.
18. If necessary to replace drive pinion rear bearing, remove rear bearing from drive pinion, using press and tool No. 09950-00020, or equivalent. **If drive pinion or ring gear are damaged, they must be replaced as a set.**
19. If necessary to replace drive pinion front and rear bearing outer race, drive out outer bearing race using a hammer and suitable drift.
20. If necessary to replace differential side bearings, remove with puller tool No. 09950-20017, or equivalent.
21. If ring gear replacement is necessary, proceed as follows:
    a. Make reference marks between ring gear and differential case.
    b. Bend back attaching bolt lock plates, then remove ring gear attaching bolts and lock plates.
    c. Tap on ring gear with plastic mallet to separate it from differential case.

Differential Case Service

1. Make reference marks between left and right side differential case halves.
2. Remove 8 case halves attaching bolts, then separate halves by tapping with plastic hammer.
3. Remove two side gears, two side gear thrust washers, spider, four pinion gears and four pinion thrust washers.
4. Install side gear thrust washer on side gear, then install in right side of case.
5. Install four pinion gears and thrust washers to spider, then install spider in right side of case.
6. While holding side gear, measure side gear backlash. Backlash should be .002–.0079 inch. **Measure backlash at right side case and at left side case.**
7. If backlash is not within specifications, install a different thickness thrust washer. **Washers of same thickness must be used on both right and left sides.**
8. Install side gears and thrust washers to right side case.
9. Install pinion gears and spider to right side case.
10. Install side gear and thrust washer to left side case.
11. Lubricate differential case parts with gear oil.

12. Align right and left side case reference marks and position together.
13. Install 8 attaching bolts and **torque** to 35 ft. lbs.

Assemble

1. Place ring gear in oil bath heated to 212°F, then clean differential case to ring gear contact surface with suitable solvent. **Do not heat ring gear to more than 230°F.**
2. Align ring gear and differential case alignment marks, then install ring gear on case.
3. Install ring gear attaching bolts and lock plates, then **torque** ring gear attaching bolts to 71 ft. lbs. Bend over lock plates.
4. Press on side bearings using press and tool Nos. 09316-60010 and 09608-30012, or equivalents.
5. Install differential case into carrier and tighten adjusting nut until all play is removed, then check ring gear runout. Maximum runout is .004 inch. Remove differential.
6. Press in pinion front and rear bearing outer races using tool No. 09608-35014, or equivalent.
7. Install washer on drive pinion with chamfer end facing pinion gear.
8. Install new rear bearing onto drive pinion, using press and tool No. 09506-30012, or equivalent.
9. Temporarily adjust drive pinion preload as follows:
    a. Install drive pinion and front bearing.
    b. Install companion flange using tool No. 09557-22022, or equivalent.
    c. Retain companion flange using tool No. 09330-00021, or equivalent, then adjust drive pinion preload to 8.7–13.9 inch lbs. for new bearings or 4.3–6.9 inch lbs. for used bearings.
10. Place bearing outer races on their respective bearings, then insert differential case into carrier.
11. Install shim on ring gear side of case side bearing, then ensure ring gear has backlash.
12. Tap on ring gear, using a suitable mallet to snug down washer and bearing, then retain side bearing boss on tooth surface and measure backlash. Backlash should be .0039 inch.
13. Select proper ring gear side of case side bearing shim, using backlash as reference.
14. Select ring gear side of case side bearing shim with a thickness that will eliminate clearance between outer race and carrier.
15. Remove shims and differential case, then install shim into lower part of carrier.
16. Place second shim onto differential case with outer races, then insert differential case, shim and outer races into carrier.
17. Snug down shim and bearing, by tapping on ring gear, using a suitable mallet.
18. Measure ring gear backlash, using a suitable dial indicator. Backlash should

Model	Size①	Ratio
Land Cruiser	9.5	4.100
Previa	7.5	3.72
RAV4	⑧	2.928
1996 Tacoma	8.0	⑤
1997–99 Tacoma	⑭	⑭
1996 T100	8.0	③
1997–98 T100	8.0	⑮
1996 Supra	8.0	④
1997–98 Supra	⑱	⑱
1996 4Runner 2WD	8.0	⑥
1996 4Runner 4WD	8.0	⑦
1997–99 4Runner 2WD	8.0	⑯
1997–99 4Runner 4WD	8.0	⑰

① — Inches.
② — A340F transmission, 4.556; A340H transmission, 4.100; G58 transmission, 4.100; R150F transmission, 4.100; R150F transmission and 10.5R15 tire with 7JJ wheel, 4.556; W56 transmission, 4.100.
③ — 3RZ-FE engine w/manual transmission, 3.615; 3RZ-FE engine w/auto transmission, 3.916; 5VZ-FE engine w/manual transmission 2WD, 3.769; 5VZ-FE engine w/manual transmission 4WD, 3.909; 5VZ-FE engine w/manual transmission 4WD & 31 inch tires, 4.100.
④ — 2JZ-GE engine, W58 & A340E transmissions, 4.272; 2JZ-GTE engine, V160 manual transmission, 3.133; A340E automatic transmission, 3.769.
⑤ — 2RZ-FE engine w/manual transmission, 3.416; 3RZ-FE engine w/manual transmission, 3.583; 2RZ-FE engine w/auto transmission, 3.583; 3RZ-FE engine w/auto transmission, 3.410; 5VZ-FE engine w/manual transmission 2WD, 3.153; 5VZ-FE engine w/manual transmission 4WD, 3.909; 5VZ-FE engine w/manual transmission 4WD & 31 inch tires, 4.100.
⑥ — 3RZ-FE engine w/manual transmission & 5VZ-FE engine w/automatic transmission, 3.727; 3RZ-FE engine w/automatic transmission, 3.909.
⑦ — 3RZ-FE engine w/A340F & W59 transmissions, 4.100 (4.556 w/P265/70R16 Tire); 5VZ-FE engine w/R150 & A340F transmissions, 3.909 (4.100 w/P265/70R16 Tire).
⑧ — LH side, 21.787 inches; RH side, 23.598 inches.
⑨ — 3S-GTE engine.
⑩ — 5S-FE engine.
⑪ — LH side & RH side halfshafts.
⑫ — LH side, 21.272 inches; RH side, 32.732 inches.
⑬ — S54 manual transaxle, 4.176; A241 automatic transaxle, 3.034.
⑭ — 2RZ-FE manual transaxle, 7.5 ring gear & 3.41 ratio; 2RZ-FE w/automatic transmission, 7.5 ring gear & 3.58 ratio; 3RZ-FE & 5RZ-FE engine w/10.5R tire and 7JJ wheel, 8.0 ring gear & 4.10 ratio; 3RZ-FE & 5RZ-FE engine less 10.5R tire and 7JJ wheel, 7.5 ring gear & 3.58 ratio; 5VZ-FE engine w/R150 manual transmission or A340E automatic transmission, 8.0 ring gear & 3.15 ratio;
⑮ — 3RZ-FE engine w/manual transmission, 3.61; 3RZ-FE engine w/automatic transmission, 4.08; 5VZ-FE engine w/R150 transmission and P235R tire, 3.91; 5VZ-FE engine w/R150 transmission less P235R tire, 3.91; 5VZ-FE engine w/R150F transmission and 265R tire, 4.10; 5VZ-FE engine w/R150F transmission less 265R tire, 3.90; 5VZ-FE engine w/A340E transmission, 3.91; 5VZ-FE engine w/A340F transmission and 265R tire, 4.30; 5VZ-FE engine w/A340F transmission less 265R tire, 4.10
⑯ — Manual transmission, less P265 70R15, 3.72; w/P265 70R15, 4.10; 3RZ-FE engine w/automatic transmission, less P265 70R15, 3.90; w/P265 70R15, 4.30; 5VZ-FE engine w/automatic transmission, 4.10.
⑰ — 3RZ-FE engine, less P265 70R15, 4.10; w/P265 70R15, 4.56; 5VZ-FE engine w/manual transmission less P265 70R15 3.90; w/P265 70R15, 4.10; 5VZ-FE engine w/automatic transmission, 4.10 STD. 4.30 optional.
⑱ — 2JZ-GE engine, 8.0 ring gear, 4.08 ratio; 2JZ-GTE engine w/manual transmission, 8.74 ring gear, 3.13 ratio; 2JZ-GTE engine w/automatic transmission, 8.0 ring gear, 3.76 ratio.

Fig. 1 Identification chart

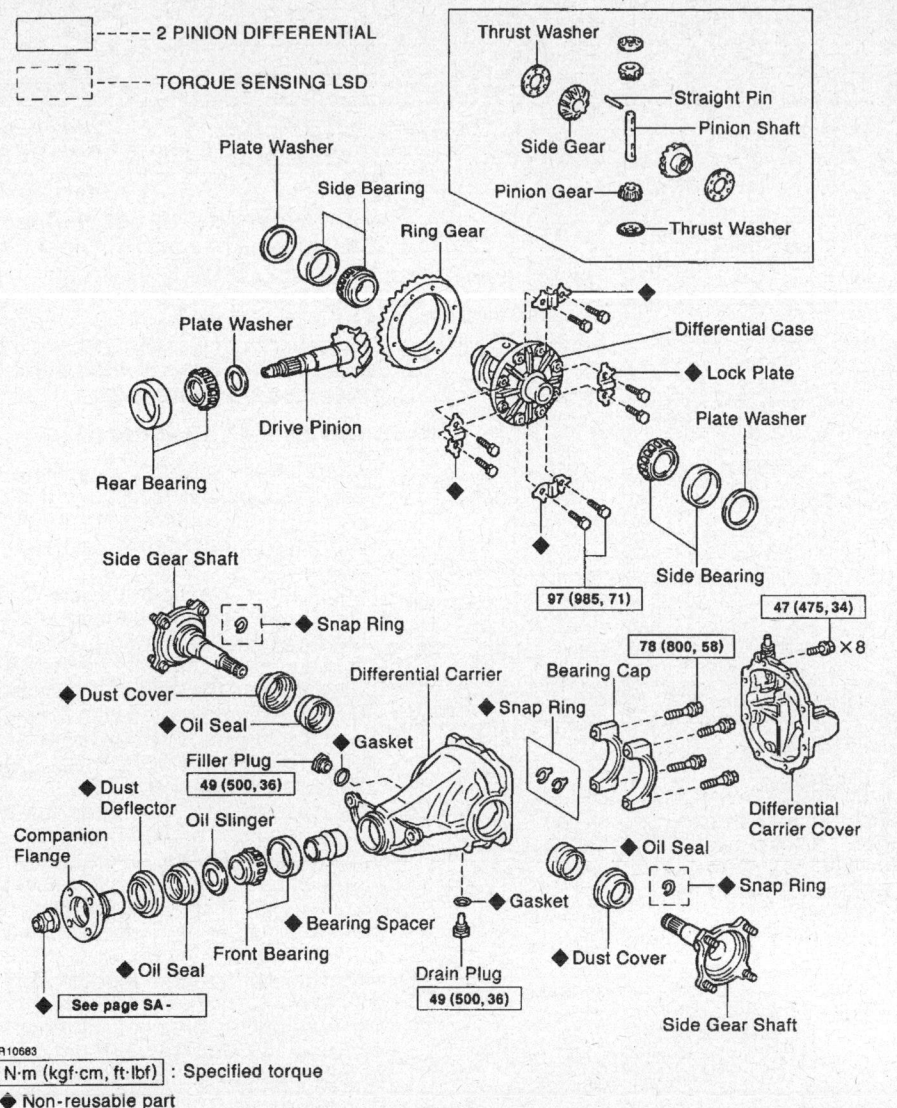

- ☐ ----- 2 PINION DIFFERENTIAL
- ⌐⌐ ----- TORQUE SENSING LSD

Thrust Washer
Straight Pin
Side Gear
Pinion Shaft
Pinion Gear
Thrust Washer

Plate Washer
Side Bearing
Ring Gear

Plate Washer
Differential Case
Lock Plate
Plate Washer
Drive Pinion
Rear Bearing

97 (985, 71)
Side Bearing

Side Gear Shaft
47 (475, 34)
Snap Ring ◆
78 (800, 58)
×8
Dust Cover ◆
Differential Carrier
Bearing Cap
Oil Seal ◆
Snap Ring
Gasket
Filler Plug
49 (500, 36)
Differential Carrier Cover
Dust Deflector ◆
Oil Slinger
Oil Seal
Companion Flange
Snap Ring ◆
Oil Seal ◆
Bearing Spacer ◆
Gasket
Dust Cover ◆
Front Bearing
Drain Plug
Oil Seal ◆
49 (500, 36)
Side Gear Shaft
◆ See page SA-

R10683

N·m (kgf·cm, ft·lbf) : Specified torque
◆ Non-reusable part

TY3039600108000X

Fig. 2 Exploded view of differential carrier. RAV4

Thickness	mm (in.)	Thickness	mm (in.)
0.93–0.97	(0.0366–0.0382)	1.08–1.12	(0.0425–0.0441)
0.98–1.02	(0.0386–0.0402)	1.13–1.17	(0.0445–0.0461)
1.03–1.07	(0.0406–0.0421)	1.18–1.22	(0.0465–0.0480)

TY3039600107000X

Fig. 3 Shim selection chart adjustment. RAV4

firmly and rotate ring gear in either direction.

24. Inspect gear tooth contact as shown, **Fig. 8.** If contacting pattern is not correct, select a suitable shim from chart, **Fig. 12,** that will ensure proper contact.
25. Remove companion flange and front bearing.
26. Install new bearing spacer and front bearing.
27. Install oil slinger, then drive in new oil seal to a depth of .059 inch.
28. Install companion flange, using tool No. 09557-22022, or equivalent, then apply a suitable lubricant to new nut. Retain companion flange, using tool No. 09330-00021, or equivalent, then install nut and **torque** to 134 ft. lbs.
29. Check preload of backlash between ring and pinion (measure pinion preload). Preload should be 8.7–13.9 inch lbs. on new bearings or 4.3–6.9 inch lbs. on used bearings.
30. If preload is greater than specified, replace bearing spacer. If preload is less that specified, **torque** nut 9 ft. lbs. at a time until specified preload is obtained. If a maximum **torque** of 250 ft. lbs. is exceeded during tightening procedure, replace bearing spacer and repeat preload adjustment.
31. Check companion flange runout. Runout in any direction should not exceed .004 inch. If runout exceeds specifications, inspect pinion bearing.
32. Stake drive pinion nut.
33. Apply a suitable lubricant to new side gear shaft oil seal, then drive in new oil seal using tool Nos. 09608-10010 and 09608-35014, or equivalents, until flush with carrier end surface.
34. Install new snap ring on side gear shaft, then using tool No. 09520-24010, or equivalent, drive in side gear shaft until it contacts pinion shaft.
35. Check side gear shaft runout. If runout exceeds .008 inch in either direction, replace side gear shaft.
36. Install differential carrier cover. **Torque** attaching bolts to 34 ft. lbs.

LIMITED SLIP DIFFERENTIAL

For replacement of differential carrier and adjustment of pinion depth, backlash

be .0051–.0071 inch. If backlash is not as specified, adjust number of shims on both sides an equal amount.

19. Adjust side bearing preload as follows:
    a. Remove ring gear side of case side bearing shim, then measure and record thickness.
    b. Install a new shim approximately .0024–.0035 inch thicker.
20. Measure ring gear backlash, using a suitable dial indicator. Backlash should be .0051–.0071 inch. If backlash is not as specified, adjust number of shims on both sides an equal amount. Refer to **Fig. 11,** for shim sizes available.
21. Align reference marks on cap and carrier, then install side bearing caps and **torque** evenly to 58 ft. lbs.
22. Measure total preload with inch lbs. wrench on pinion nut. Preload should be 3.5–5.2 inch lbs. in addition to drive pinion preload.
23. Paint 3 or 4 ring gear teeth at 3 different positions on ring gear with red lead paint, then hold companion flange

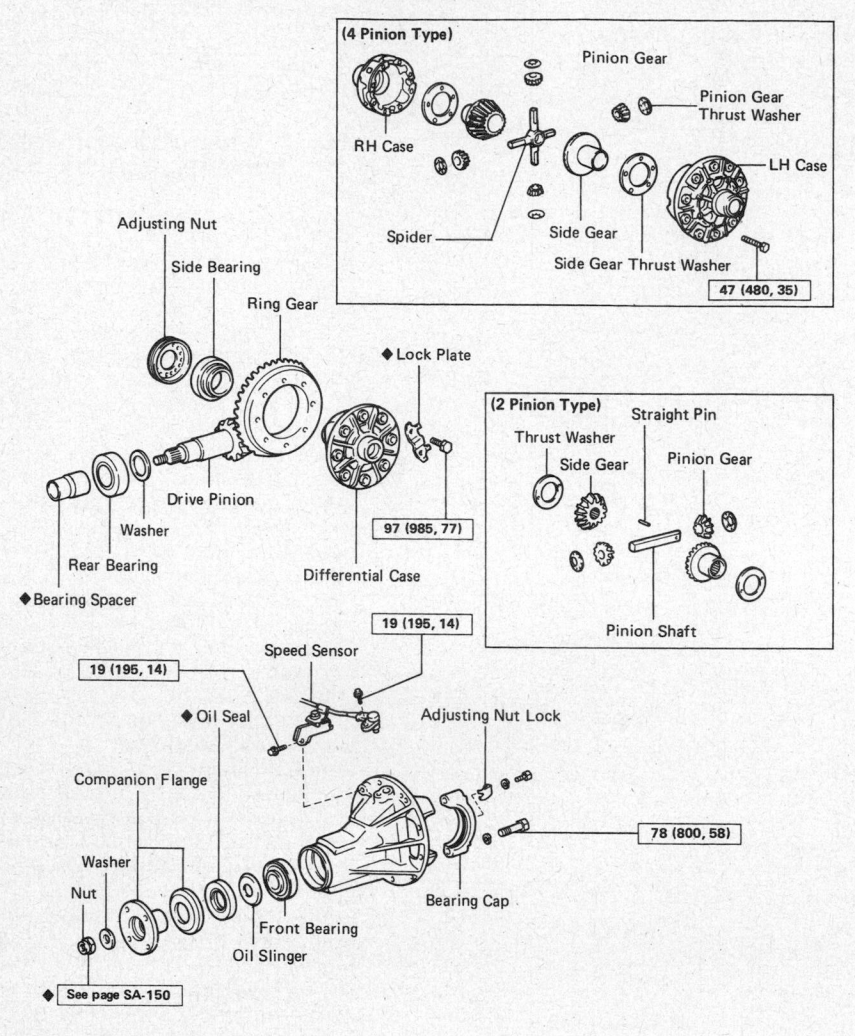

Thickness	mm (in)
1/2 ton and 3/4 ton (except*)	C&C and 4WD (incl.*)
1.0 (0.039)	1.6 (0.063)
1.1 (0.043)	1.7 (0.067)
1.2 (0.047)	1.8 (0.071)
1.3 (0.051)	
*: Short wheel base, 22R Engine vehicle.	

TY3039100073000X

Fig. 5 Side gear thrust washer identification. Land Cruiser, Tacoma, T100 & 4Runner

gear, righthand retainer, side gear, 5 side gear thrust washers and 4 clutch plates. **Keep disassembled parts in order they were removed.**

Inspection & Adjustment

1. Inspect parts for signs of damage or wear. Replace as necessary. **If side gear requires replacement, replace the thrust washer that contacts it also.**
2. Inspect thrust washers for damage or wear. Ensure contact surface is even with no bare metal showing.
3. Using a suitable micrometer, measure thrust washer thickness. If less than .0685 (1.74 mm), replace thrust washers. If thrust washers require replacement, replace clutch plate that contacts thrust washer.
4. Check clutch plates for wear or damage and replace as necessary. **These differentials may be assembled with either of two type clutch plates, Fig. 13.** If clutch plates require replacement, they must be replaced with the same type that was removed.
5. Measure spring free length. Spring should be 1.232 inch (31.3 mm).
6. Measure and record right side case dimension "A," **Fig. 14,** then determine required side bearing shim thickness as follows:
   a. Assemble thrust washers and clutch plates on side gear. **Do not assemble side gear shims at this time.**
   b. Using tool No. 09726-35010, or equivalent, apply approximately 22 lbs. of pressure to thrust washer and clutch pack while measuring dimension "B," **Fig. 15.**
   c. To determine side bearing shim thickness "C," use the following formula: "C"= "A" – "B" –.6358 inch (16.15 mm).
   d. Refer to **Figs. 16 and 17** to select proper shims.
   e. Install selected shim(s) between

N·m (kgf·cm, ft·lbf) : Specified torque
◆ Non-reusable part

TY3039100072000X

Fig. 4 Exploded view of differential assembly. Land Cruiser, Previa, Tacoma, T100 & 4Runner

and preload, refer to procedure for models "Except Limited Slip Differential."

SUPRA

Disassemble

1. Make reference marks on left and right side differential case halves, then place righthand case in suitable vise.
2. Loosen case halves attaching bolts a little at a time, then remove attaching bolts and separate lefthand case from righthand case, **Fig. 13.**
3. From lefthand side case, remove side gear, 5 side gear thrust washers and 4 clutch plates. **Keep disassembled parts in order.**
4. From righthand case, remove lefthand retainer, spring, spider with pinion

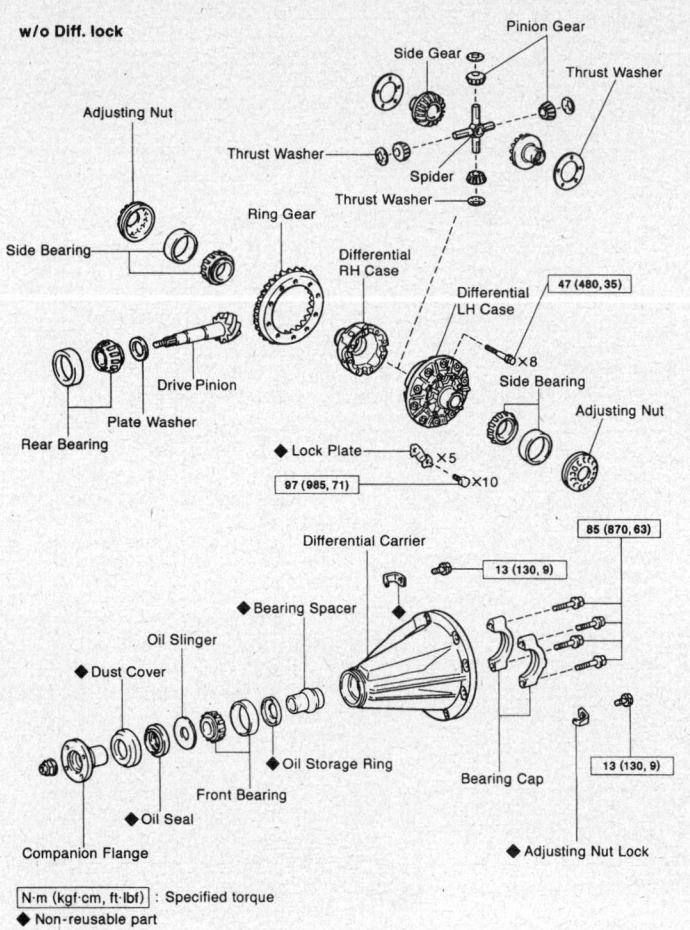

w/o Diff. lock

N·m (kgf·cm, ft·lbf) : Specified torque
◆ Non-reusable part

TY3039100074000X

Fig. 6 Drive pinion shim identification. Land Cruiser, Previa, Tacoma, T100 & 4Runner

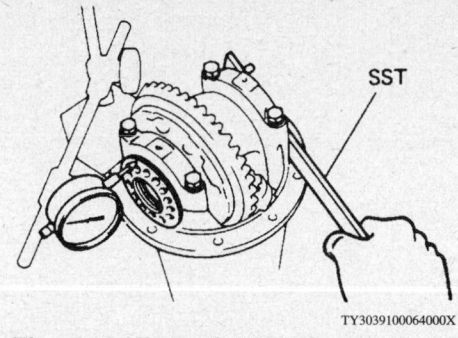

TY3039100064000X

Fig. 7 Differential bearing preload adjustment

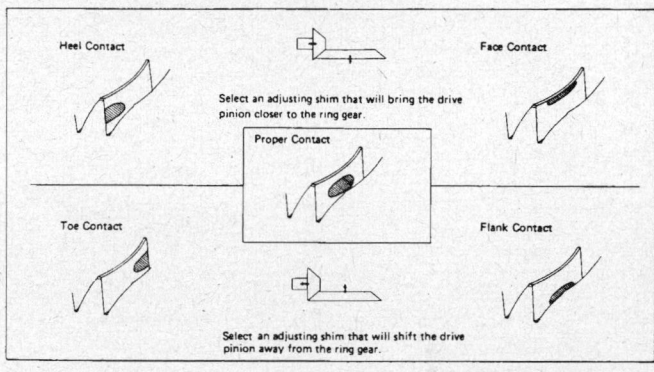

TY3039100066000X

Fig. 8 Ring gear & pinion tooth contact inspection

outer thrust washer and case.

7. Determine side bearing shim thickness for left side case by following procedures in step 6, above.

Assemble

1. Lubricate all components with limited slip differential lubricant.
2. Into righthand case, install adjusting shim, thrust washers and clutch plates. **Install thrust washer without oil groove on outer side so it makes contact with the side of the case with no oil groove.**
3. Into lefthand case, install adjusting shim, thrust washers and clutch plates. **Install thrust washer without oil groove on outer side so it makes contact with the side of the case with no oil groove.**
4. Install pinion gears and washers to spider, then align righthand retainer holes with spider lockpins and install retainer.
5. Install spider, pinion, washers and righthand retainer assembly to righthand case.
6. Secure side gear, then measure backlash while pushing on spider retainer. Backlash should be .002–.0079 inch (.05–.20 mm). If not within specifications, select suitable adjusting shim.
7. Measure backlash in left side case as outlined in step 6.
8. Install spring and lefthand retainer in spider.
9. Align reference marks, then install lefthand case on righthand case.
10. Lightly oil attaching bolts, then install bolts and tighten evenly and gradually. When snug, **torque** to 35 ft. lbs.

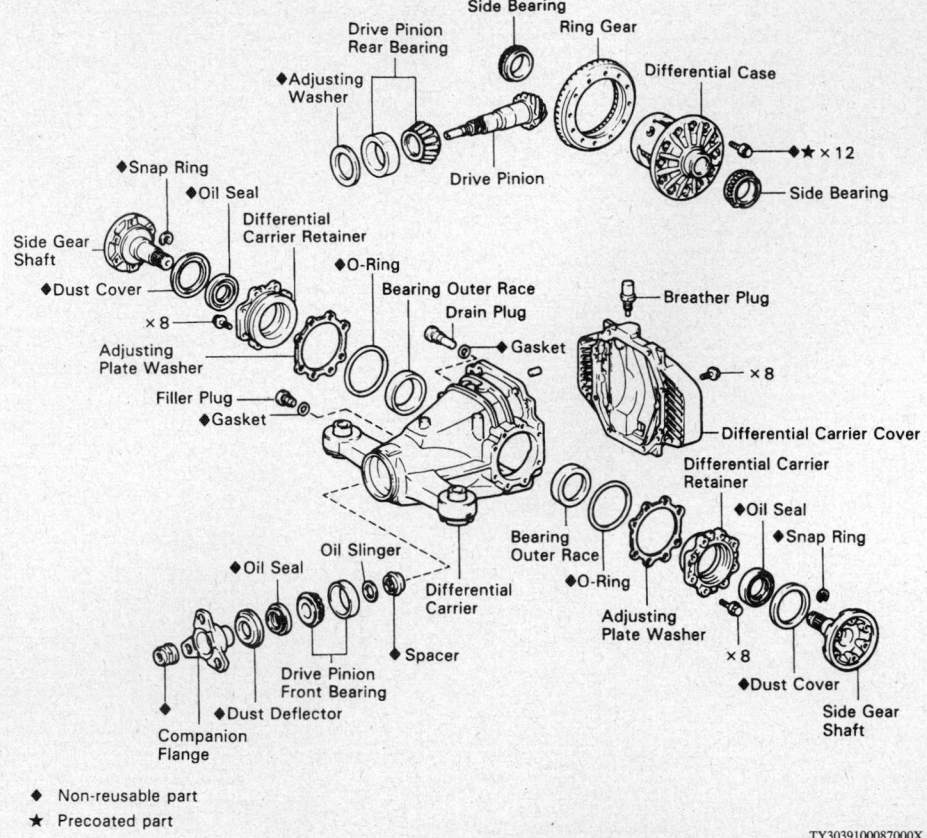

◆ Non-reusable part
★ Precoated part

TY3039100087000X

Fig. 9   Exploded view of differential assembly. Supra

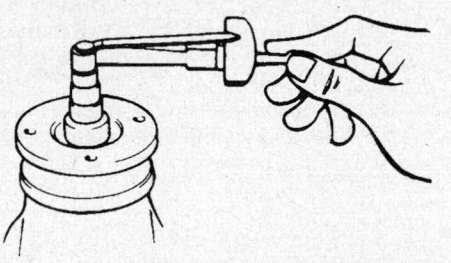

TY3039100063000X

**Fig. 10   Preload (rotating torque)
                 measurement**

Washer thickness

Thickness		mm (in.)
2.57 – 2.59 (0.1012 – 0.1020)	2.90 – 2.92 (0.1142 – 0.1150)	3.23 – 3.25 (0.1272 – 0.1280)
2.60 – 2.62 (0.1024 – 0.1031)	2.93 – 2.95 (0.1154 – 0.1161)	3.26 – 3.28 (0.1283 – 0.1291)
2.63 – 2.65 (0.1035 – 0.1043)	2.96 – 2.98 (0.1165 – 0.1173)	3.29 – 3.31 (0.1295 – 0.1303)
2.66 – 2.68 (0.1047 – 0.1055)	2.99 – 3.01 (0.1177 – 0.1185)	3.32 – 3.34 (0.1307 – 0.1315)
2.69 – 2.71 (0.1059 – 0.1067)	3.02 – 3.04 (0.1189 – 0.1197)	3.35 – 3.37 (0.1319 – 0.1327)
2.72 – 2.74 (0.1071 – 0.1079)	3.05 – 3.07 (0.1201 – 0.1209)	3.38 – 3.40 (0.1331 – 0.1339)
2.75 – 2.77 (0.1083 – 0.1091)	3.08 – 3.10 (0.1213 – 0.1220)	3.41 – 3.43 (0.1343 – 0.1350)
2.78 – 2.80 (0.1094 – 0.1102)	3.11 – 3.13 (0.1224 – 0.1232)	3.44 – 3.46 (0.1354 – 0.1362)
2.81 – 2.83 (0.1106 – 0.1114)	3.14 – 3.16 (0.1236 – 0.1244)	3.47 – 3.49 (0.1366 – 0.1374)
2.84 – 2.86 (0.1118 – 0.1126)	3.17 – 3.19 (0.1248 – 0.1256)	
2.87 – 2.89 (0.1130 – 0.1138)	3.20 – 3.22 (0.1260 – 0.1268)	

TY3039100088000X

Fig. 11   Side gear bearing shim identification chart. Supra

Washer thickness

Thickness		mm (in.)	
1.70	(0.0669)	2.03	(0.0799)
1.73	(0.0681)	2.06	(0.0811)
1.76	(0.0693)	2.09	(0.0823)
1.79	(0.0705)	2.12	(0.0835)
1.82	(0.0717)	2.15	(0.0846)
1.85	(0.0728)	2.18	(0.0858)
1.88	(0.0740)	2.21	(0.0870)
1.91	(0.0752)	2.24	(0.0882)
1.94	(0.0764)	2.27	(0.0894)
1.97	(0.0776)	2.30	(0.0906)
2.00	(0.0787)	2.33	(0.0317)

TY3039100089000X

Fig. 12   Drive pinion shim identification chart. Supra

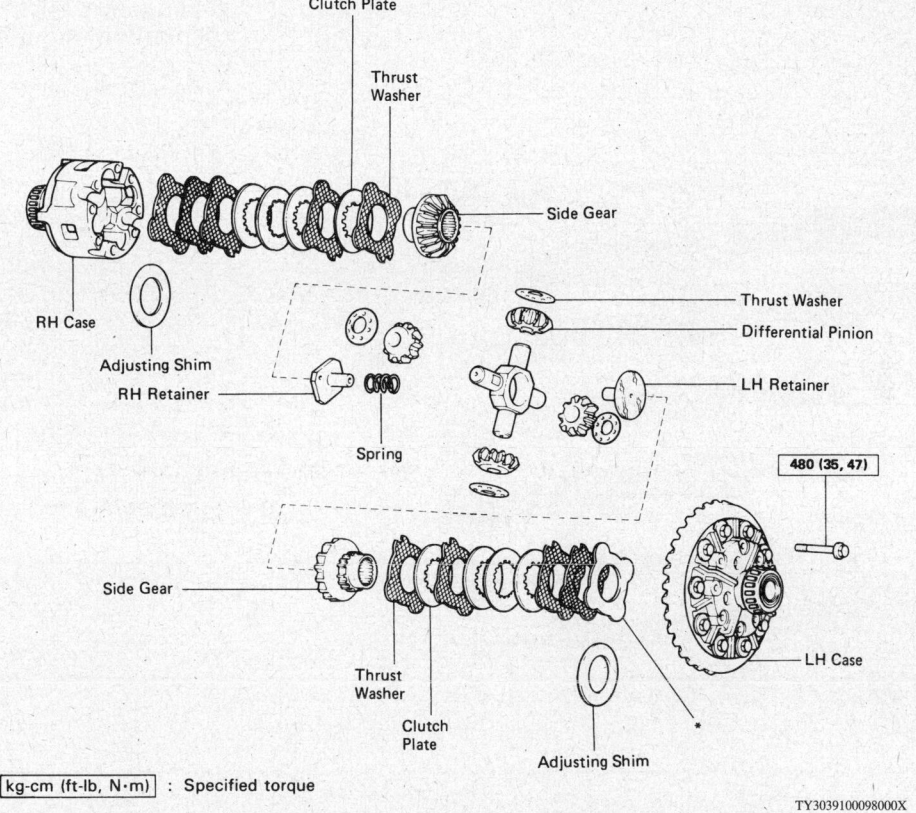

kg-cm (ft-lb, N·m) : Specified torque

TY3039100098000X

Fig. 13   Exploded view of limited slip differential. Supra

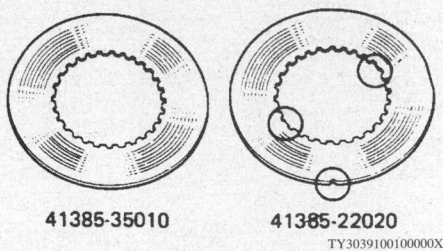

41385-35010   41385-22020

TY3039100100000X

Fig. 14   Righthand case dimension "A" measurement. Supra w/limited slip differential

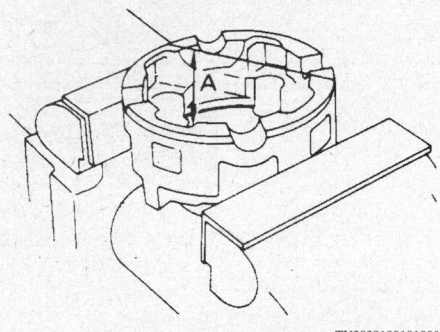

TY3039100101000X

Fig. 15   Dimension "B" to determine side gear bearing shim pack measurement. Supra w/ limited slip differential

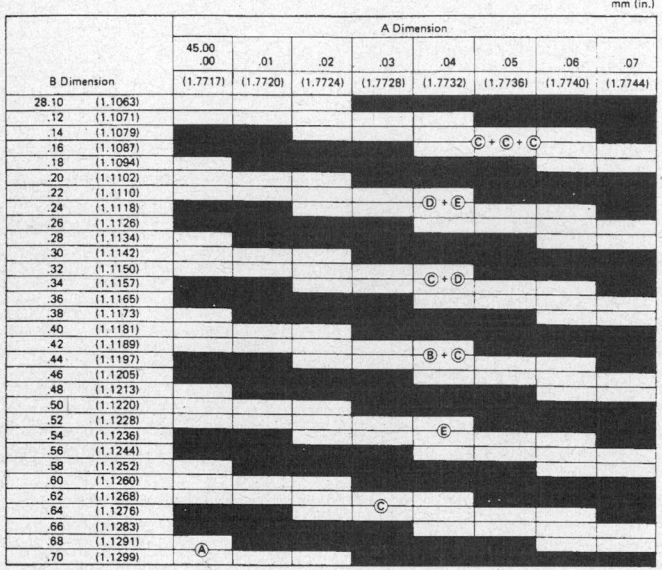

mm (in.)

B Dimension	A Dimension							
	45.00 .00 (1.7717)	.01 (1.7720)	.02 (1.7724)	.03 (1.7728)	.04 (1.7732)	.05 (1.7736)	.06 (1.7740)	.07 (1.7744)
28.10 (1.1063)								
.12 (1.1071)								
.14 (1.1079)								
.16 (1.1087)					Ⓒ + Ⓒ + Ⓒ			
.18 (1.1094)								
.20 (1.1102)								
.22 (1.1110)								
.24 (1.1118)				Ⓓ + Ⓔ				
.26 (1.1126)								
.28 (1.1134)								
.30 (1.1142)								
.32 (1.1150)								
.34 (1.1157)			Ⓒ + Ⓓ					
.36 (1.1165)								
.38 (1.1173)								
.40 (1.1181)								
.42 (1.1189)								
.44 (1.1197)		Ⓑ + Ⓒ						
.46 (1.1205)								
.48 (1.1213)								
.50 (1.1220)								
.52 (1.1228)		Ⓔ						
.54 (1.1236)								
.56 (1.1244)								
.58 (1.1252)								
.60 (1.1260)								
.62 (1.1268)		Ⓒ						
.64 (1.1276)								
.66 (1.1283)								
.68 (1.1291)								
.70 (1.1299)	Ⓐ							

TY3039100102000X

Fig. 16   Shim selection chart. Supra w/limited slip differential

Mark	Thickness	Mark	Thickness
A	0.15 (0.0059)	D	0.30 (0.0118)
B	0.20 (0.0079)	E	0.35 (0.0138)
C	0.25 (0.0098)		

TY3039100103000X

Fig. 17   Adjusting shim sizes. Supra w/limited slip differential

DRIVE AXLE SPECIFICATIONS

Year	Model	Ring Gear & Pinion		Pinion Bearing Preload			Differential Bearing Preload		
		Backlash Method	Adjustment, Inch	Method	New Bearing In. Lbs.	Used Bearing In. Lbs.	Method	New Bearing In. Lbs.	Used Bearing In. Lbs.
1996–99	Land Cruiser	Shims	.006–.008	Spacer & Shims	11.3–17.4	6.1–8.7	Shims	3.5–5.2①	3.5–5.2①
	Previa⑤⑥	Threaded Adjust	.005–.007	Spacer & Shims	10.4–16.5	5.2–8.7	Threaded adj.	3.5–5.2①	3.5–5.2①
	T100	Shim	.002–.008	Spacer & Shims	8.7–13.9	4.3–6.9	Shim	3.5–5.2①	3.5–5.2①
1996	Supra	Shim	.002–.007	Spacer & Shims	17.3–21.7⑨	8.9–10.6⑩	Shim	3.5–5.2①⑩	3.5–5.2①⑩
1997–98	Supra	Shim	.003–.005	Spacer & Shims	17.3–21.7	8.9–10.6	Shim	3.5–5.2①	3.5–5.2①
1996	Tacoma	Shim	.002–.008	Spacer & Shims	12.2–18.3	5.2–8.7	Shim	3.5–5.2①	3.5–5.2①
1997-99	Tacoma	Shim	.002–.008	Spacer & Shims	10.0–15.2	5.7–8.3	Shim	3.5–5.2①	3.5–5.2①
1996–99	RAV4	Shim	.005–.007	Spacer & Shim	8.7–13.9	4.3–6.9	Shim	2.6–4.3①	2.6–4.3①
1996	4Runner	Threaded Adjust	.002–.008	Spacer & Shims	8.7–13.9	4.3–6.9	Shims	3.5–5.2①	3.5–5.2①
1997-99	4Runner	Threaded Adjust	.005–.007	Spacer & Shims	8.7–13.9	4.3–6.9	Shims	3.5–5.2①	3.5–5.2①
1997	Previa	Threaded Adjust	.005–.007	Spacer & Shims	12.2–18.3	5.2–8.7	Threaded Adj.	3.5–5.2①	3.5–5.2①

① — Total preload, add this to drive pinion preload.
② — 2 pinion type, 7.8–11.3 inch lbs.; 4 pinion type, 4.3–6.9 inch lbs.
③ — 2 pinion type, 16.5–22.6 inch lbs.; 4 pinion type, 8.7–13.9 inch lbs.

④ — 8 inch ring gear.
⑤ — Rear axle.
⑥ — 7.5 inch ring gear.
⑦ — Front axle.
⑧ — 22R-E engine, 7.8–11.3 inch lbs.; 3VZ-E engine, 4.3–9.6 inch lbs.

⑨ — Except 2JZ-GTE engine, 10.8–16.0 inch lbs.
⑩ — Except 2JZ-GTE engine, 4.3–6.9 inch lbs.
⑪ — 22R-E engine, 16.5–22.6 inch lbs.; 3VZ-E engine, 8.7–13.9 inch lbs.

Engine Rebuilding Specifications

INDEX

CYLINDER HEAD, VALVE GUIDE & VALVE SEATS

All measurements given are in inches unless otherwise specified.

Year	Engine Liters (ID Code)	Cylinder Head Warpage Limit	Valve Guides			Seat Angle, Degree	Valve Seats	
			Standard Inside Diameter	Stem To Guide Clearance			Seat Width	
				Intake	Exhaust		Intake	Exhaust
1996	1.5L (5E-FE)	.020	.2366–.2374	.0010–.0024	.0012–.0026	45	.039–.055	.039–.055
	1.6L (4A-FE)	③	.2366–.2374	.0010–.0024	.0012–.0026	45	.047–.063	.047–.063
	1.8L (7A-FE)	③	.2366–.2374	.0010–.0024	.0012–.0026	45	.039–.055	.039–.055
	2.0L (3S-FE)	②	.2366–.2374	.0010–.0024	.0012–.0026	45	.039–.055	.039–.055
	2.2L (5S-FE)	②	.2366–.2374	.0010–.0024	.0012–.0026	45	.039–.055	.039–.055
	2.4L (2RZ-FE)	②	.2366–.2374	.0010–.0024	.0012–.0026	45	.039–.055	.039–.055
	2.4L (2TZ-FZE)	④	.2366–.2374	.0010–.0024	.0012–.0026	45	.039–.055	.039–.055
	2.7L (3RZ-FE)	②	.2366–.2374	.0010–.0024	.0012–.0026	45	.039–.055	.039–.055
	3.0L (1MZ-FE)	.0039	.2169–.2177	.0010–.0024	.0012–.0026	45	.039–.055	.039–.055
	3.0L (2JZ-GE)	.0039	.2366–.2374	.0010–.0024	.0012–.0026	45	.039–.055	.047–.063
	3.0L (2JZ-GTE)	.0039	.2366–.2374	.0010–.0024	.0012–.0026	45	.039–.055	.047–.063
	3.4L (5VZ-FE)	.0039	.2348–.2356	.0010–.0024	.0012–.0026	45	.039–.055	.039–.055
	4.5L (1FZ-FE)	①	.2760–.2768	.0010–.0024	.0012–.0026	45	.047–.063	.039–.055
1997	1.5L (5E-FE)	.020	.2366–.2374	.0010–.0024	.0012–.0026	45	.039–.055	.039–.055
	1.6L (4A-FE)	③	.2366–.2374	.0010–.0024	.0012–.0026	45	.039–.055	.039–.055
	1.8L (7A-FE)	③	.2366–.2374	.0010–.0024	.0012–.0026	45	.039–.055	.039–.055
	2.0L (3S-FE)	②	.2366–.2374	.0010–.0024	.0012–.0026	45	.039–.055	.039–.055
	2.2L (5S-FE)	②	.2366–.2374	.0010–.0024	.0012–.0026	45	.039–.055	.039–.055
	2.4L (2RZ-FE)	③	.2366–.2374	.0010–.0024	.0012–.0026	45	.039–.055	.039–.055
	2.4L (2TZ-FZE)	④	.2366–.2374	.0010–.0024	.0012–.0026	45	.039–.055	.039–.055
	2.7L (3RZ-FE)	③	.2366–.2374	.0010–.0024	.0012–.0026	45	.039–.055	.039–.055
	3.0L (1MZ-FE)	.0039	.2169–.2177	.0010–.0024	.0012–.0026	45	.039–.055	.039–.055
	3.0L (2JZ-GE)	.0039	.2366–.2374	.0010–.0024	.0012–.0026	45	.039–.055	.047–.063
	3.0L (2JZ-GTE)	.0039	.2366–.2374	.0010–.0024	.0012–.0026	45	.039–.055	.047–.063
	3.4L (5VZ-FE)	.0039	.2366–.2374	.0010–.0024	.0012–.0026	45	.039–.055	.039–.055
	4.5L (1FZ-FE)	①	.2760–.2768	.0010–.0024	.0012–.0026	45	.047–.063	.039–.055
1998	1.5L (5E-FE)	.0020	.2366 - .2374	.0010 - .0024	.0012 - .0026	45	.039 - .055	.039 - .055
	1.8L (1ZZ-FE)	.0020	.2169 - .2177	.0010 - .0024	.0012 - .0026	45	.039 - .055	.039 - .055
	2.0L (3S-FE)	②	.2366 - .2374	.0010 - .0024	.0012 - .0026	45	.039 - .055	.039 - .055
	2.2L (5S-FE)	②	.2366 - .2374	.0010 - .0024	.0012 - .0026	45	.039 - .055	.039 - .055
	2.4L (2RZ-FE)	③	.2366 - .2374	.0010 - .0024	.0012 - .0026	45	.039 - .055	.039 - .055
	2.7L (3RZ-FE)	③	.2366 - .2374	.0010 - .0024	.0012 - .0026	45	.039 - .055	.039 - .055
	3.0L (1MZ-FE)	.039	.2169 - .2177	.0010 - .0024	.0012 - .0026	45	.039 - .055	.039 - .055
	3.0L (2JZ-GE)	.0039	.2366 - .2374	.0010 - .0024	.0012 - .0026	45	.039 - .055	.047 - .063
	3.0L (2JZ-GTE)	.0039	.2366 - .2374	.0010 - .0024	.0012 - .0026	45	.039 - .055	.047 - .063
	3.4L (5VZ-FE)	.039	.2366 - .2374	.0010 - .0024	.0012 - .0026	45	.039 - .055	.039 - .055
	4.7L (2UZ-FE)	.039	.2169 - .2374	.0010 - .0024	.0012 - .0026	45	.039 - .055	.039 - .055

Continued

CYLINDER HEAD, VALVE GUIDE & VALVE SEATS—Continued

All measurements given are in inches unless otherwise specified.

Year	Engine Liters (ID Code)	Cylinder Head Warpage Limit	Valve Guides			Valve Seats		
			Standard Inside Diameter	Stem To Guide Clearance		Seat Angle, Degree	Seat Width	
				Intake	Exhaust		Intake	Exhaust
1999	1.8L (1ZZ-FE)	.0020	.2169 - .2177	.0010 - .0024	.0012 - .0026	45	.039 - .055	.039 - .055
	2.0L (3S-FE)	②	.2366 - .2374	.0010 - .0024	.0012 - .0026	45	.039 - .055	.039 - .055
	2.2L (5S-FE)	②	.2366 - .2374	.0010 - .0024	.0012 - .0026	45	.039 - .055	.039 - .055
	2.4L (2RZ-FE)	③	.2366 - .2374	.0010 - .0024	.0012 - .0026	45	.039 - .055	.039 - .055
	2.7L (3RZ-FE)	③	.2366 - .2374	.0010 - .0024	.0012 - .0026	45	.039 - .055	.039 - .055
	3.0L (1MZ-FE)	.039	.2169 - .2177	.0010 - .0024	.0012 - .0026	45	.039 - .055	.039 - .055
	3.4L (5VZ-FE)	.039	.2366 - .2374	.0010 - .0024	.0012 - .0026	45	.039 - .055	.039 - .055
	4.7L (2UZ-FE)	.039	.2169 - .2374	.0010 - .0024	.0012 - .0026	45	.039 - .055	.039 - .055
2000	3.4L (5VZ-FE)	.039	.2169 - .2374	.0010 - .0024	.0012 - .0026	45	.039 - .055	.039 - .055
	4.7L (2UZ-FE)	.039	.2169 - .2374	.0010 - .0024	.0012 - .0026	45	.039 - .055	.039 - .055

① — Cylinder block side, .0059 inch, manifold side .0039 inch.

② — Cylinder block side, .0020 inch, manifold side .0031 inch.

③ — Cylinder block side, .0020 inch, manifold side .0039 inch.

④ — Cylinder block side, .0059 inch, manifold side .0079 inch.

VALVE SPRINGS

All measurements given are in inches, unless otherwise specified.

Year	Engine Liter (ID Code)	Valve Springs			
		Free Length	Installed Height	Pressure @ Installed Height	Out Of Square Limit
1996	1.5L (5E-FE)	1.5669	1.252	33.3–36.8	.079
	1.6L (4A-FE)②	1.774	1.366	34.8	.079
	1.6L (4A-FE)③	1.5185	1.248	37.3	.079
	1.8L (7A-FE)	1.5185	1.248	37.3	.079
	2.0L (3S-FE)	1.6520–1.6531	1.366	36.8–42.5	.079
	2.2L (5S-FE)	1.5669	1.252	33.3–36.8	.0079
	2.4L (2RZ-FE)	—	1.406	39.7	.079
	2.4L (2TZ-FZE)	1.6425	1.406	38.7	.079
	2.7L (3RZ-FE)	—	1.406	39.7	.079
	3.0L (1MZ-FE)	①	1.7913	33.8	.079
	3.0L (2JZ-GE)	①	1.358	34.5	.079
	3.0L (2JZ-GTE)	①	1.358	34.5	.079
	3.4L (5VZ-FE)	1.7630	1.311	41.9–46.3	.079
	4.5L (1FZ-FE)	1.7299–1.7740	1.437	48.1–53.4	.079
1997	1.5L (5E-FE)	2.109	1.252	33.3–36.8	.079
	1.6L (4A-FE)	1.669	1.248	35.5–39.0	.079
	1.8L (7A-FE)	1.5185	1.248	37.3	.079
	2.0L (3S-FE)	1.6520–1.6531	1.366	36.8–42.5	.079
	2.2L (5S-FE)	1.612–1.685	1.366	36.8–42.5	.0079
	2.4L (2RZ-FE)	—	1.406	39.7–45.9	.079
	2.4L (2TZ-FZE)	1.6425	1.406	38.7	.079
	2.7L (3RZ-FE)	—	1.406	39.7–45.9	.079
	3.0L (1MZ-FE)	1.791	1.331	41.9–46.3	.079
	3.0L (2JZ-GE)	1.641	1.358	42–46	.079
	3.0L (2JZ-GTE)	1.641	1.358	42–46	.079
	3.4L (5VZ-FE)	1.7630	1.311	41.9–46.3	.079
	4.5L (1FZ-FE)	1.7299–1.7740	1.437	48.1–53.4	.079
1998	1.5L (5E-FE)	2.109	1.252	33.3 - 36.8	.079
	1.8L (1ZZ-FE)	1.807	1.323	31.3 - 34.8	.063
	2.0L (3S-FE)	1.6520 - 1.6531	1.366	36.8 - 42.5	.079
	2.2L (5S-FE)	1.612 - 1.685	1.366	36.8 - 42.5	.079
	2.4L (2RZ-FE)	—	1.406	39.7 - 45.9	.079
	2.7L (3RZ-FE)	—	1.406	39.7 - 45.9	.079
	3.0L (1MZ-FE)	1.791	1.331	41.9 - 46.3	.079
	3.0L (2JZ-GE)	④	1.358	41.9 - 46.3	.079
	3.0 (2JZ-GTE)	1.641	1.358	42 - 46	.079
	3.4L (5VZ-FE)	1.7630	1.311	41.9 - 46.3	.079
	4.7L (2UZ-FE)	2.130	1.378	45.9 - 50.7	.079
1999	1.8L (1ZZ-FE)	1.807	1.323	31.3 - 34.8	.063
	2.0L (3S-FE)	1.6520 - 1.6531	1.366	36.8 - 42.5	.079
	2.2L (5S-FE)	1.612 - 1.685	1.366	36.8 - 42.5	.079
	2.4L (2RZ-FE)	—	1.406	39.7 - 45.9	.079
	2.7L (3RZ-FE)	—	1.406	39.7 - 45.9	.079
	3.0L (1MZ-FE)	1.791	1.331	41.9 - 46.3	.079
	3.4L (5VZ-FE)	1.7630	1.311	41.9 - 46.3	.079
	4.7L (2UZ-FE)	2.130	1.378	45.9 - 50.7	.079
2000	3.4L (5VZ-FE)	1.7630	1.311	41.9 - 46.3	.079
	4.7L (2UZ-FE)	2.130	1.378	45.9 - 50.7	.079

① — Blue paint, 1.6433 inches; yellow paint, 1.6417 inches.

② — Celica.

③ — Corolla.

④ — Pink paint, 1.7209 inches; yellow paint, 1.7362 inches.

VALVES

All measurements given are in inches, unless otherwise specified.

Year	Engine Liter (ID Code)	Stem Diameter		Face Angle, De-gree	Margin		Clearance	
		Intake	Exhaust		Intake	Exhaust	Intake	Exhaust
1996	1.5L (5E-FE)	.2350–.2356	.2348–.2354	44.5	.031–.047	.031–.047	.006–.010	.012–.016
	1.6L (4A-FE) ③	.2350–.2356	.2348–.2354	44.5	.031–.047	.031–.047	.006–.010	.008–.012
	1.6L (4A-FE) ①	.2350–.2356	.2348–.2354	44.5	.031–.047	.031–.047	.006–.010	.008–.012
	1.8L (7A-FE)	.2350–.2356	.2348–.2354	44.5	.031–.047	.031–.047	.006–.010	.008–.012
	2.0L (3S-FE)	.2350–.2356	.2348–.2354	44.5	.031–.047	.031–.047	.007–.011	.011–.015
	2.2L (5S-FE)	.2350–.2356	.2348–.2354	44.5	.031–.047	.031–.047	.007–.011	.011–.015
	2.4L (2RZ-FE)	.2350–.2356	.2348–.2354	44.5	.039	.039	.006–.010	.010–.014
	2.4L (2TZ-FZE)	.2350–.2356	.2348–.2354	44.5	.020 ②	.020 ②	.006–.010	.010–.014
	2.7L (3RZ-FE)	.2350–.2356	.2348–.2354	44.5	.039	.039	.006–.010	.010–.014
	3.0L (1MZ-FE)	.2154–.2159	.2152–.2157	44.5	.039	.039	.006–.010	.010–.014
	3.0L (2JZ-GE)	.2350–.2356	.2348–.2354	44.5	.031–.047	.031–.047	.006–.010	.010–.014
	3.0L (2JZ-GTE)	.2350–.2356	.2348–.2354	44.5	.031–.047	.031–.047	.006–.010	.010–.014
	3.4L (5VZ-FE)	.2350–.2356	.2348–.2354	44.5	.020–.039	.020–.039	.001–003	.001–.004
	4.5L (1FZ-FE)	.2744–.2750	.2742–.2748	44.5	.047	.047	.006–.010	.010–.014
1997	1.5L (5E-FE)	.2350–.2356	.2348–.2354	44.5	.031–.047	.031–.047	.006–.010	.012–.016
	1.6L (4A-FE) ①	.2350–.2356	.2348–.2354	44.5	.031–.047	.031–.047	.006–.010	.010–.014
	1.8L (7A-FE)	.2350–.2356	.2348–.2354	44.5	.031–.047	.031–.047	.006–.010	.010–.014
	2.0L (3S-FE)	.2350–.2356	.2348–.2354	44.5	.031–.047	.031–.047	.007–.011	.011–.015
	2.2L (5S-FE)	.2350–.2356	.2348–.2354	44.5	.031–.047	.031–.047	.007–.011	.011–.015
	2.4L (2RZ-FE)	.2350–.2356	.2348–.2354	44.5	.039	.039	.006–.010	.010–.014
	2.4L (2TZ-FZE)	.2350–.2356	.2348–.2354	44.5	.039	.039	.006–.010	.010–.014
	2.7L (3RZ-FE)	.2350–.2356	.2348–.2354	44.5	.039	.039	.006–.010	.010–.014
	3.0L (1MZ-FE)	.2154–.2159	.2152–.2157	44.5	.039	.039	.006–.010	.010–.014
	3.0L (2JZ-GE)	.2350–.2356	.2348–.2354	44.5	.031–.047	.031–.047	.006–.010	.010–.014
	3.0L (2JZ-GTE)	.2350–.2356	.2348–.2354	44.5	.031–.047	.031–.047	.006–.010	.010–.014
	3.4L (5VZ-FE)	.2350–.2356	.2348–.2354	44.5	.020–.039	.020–.039	.006–.009	.011–.014
	4.5L (1FZ-FE)	.2744–.2750	.2742–.2748	44.5	.047	.047	.006–.010	.010–.014
1998	1.5L (5E-FE)	.2350–.2356	.2348–.2354	44.5	.031-.047	.037-.047	.006-.010	.012-.016
	1.8L (1ZZ-FE)	.2154–.2159	.2152–.2157	44.5	.039	.039	.006-.010	.010-.014
	2.0L (3S-FE)	.2350–.2356	.2348–.2354	44.5	.031-.047	.031-.047	.007-.011	.011-.015
	2.2L (5S-FE)	.2350–.2356	.2348–.2354	44.5	.031-.047	.031-.047	.007-.011	.011-.015
	2.4L (2RZ-FE)	.2350–.2356	.2348–.2354	44.5	.039	.039	.006-.010	.010-.014
	2.7L (3RZ-FE)	.2350–.2356	.2348–.2354	44.5	.039	.039	.006-.010	.010-.014
	3.0L (1MZ-FE)	.2154–.2159	.2152–.2157	44.5	.039	.039	.006-.010	.010-.014
	3.0L (2JZ-GE)	.2350–.2356	.2348–.2354	44.5	.031-.047	.031-.047	.006-.010	.010-.014
	3.0L (2JZ-GTE)	.2350–.2356	.2348–.2354	44.5	.031-.047	.031-.047	.006-.010	.010-.014
	3.4L (5VZ-FE)	.2350–.2356	.2348–.2354	44.5	.039	.039	.006-.009	.011-.014
	4.7L (2UZ-FE)	.2154–.2159	.2152–.2157	44.5	.049	.055	.006-.010	.010-.014
1999	1.8L (1ZZ-FE)	.2154–.2159	.2152-2157	44.5	.039	.039	.006-.010	.010-.014
	2.0L (3S-FE)	.2350–.2356	.2348–.2354	44.5	.031-.047	.031-.047	.007-.011	.011-.015
	2.2L (5S-FE)	.2350–.2356	.2348–.2354	44.5	.031-.047	.031-.047	.007-.011	.011-.015
	2.4L (2RZ-FE)	.2350–.2356	.2348–.2354	44.5	.039	.039	.006-.010	.010-.014
	2.7L (3RZ-FE)	.2350–.2356	.2348–.2354	44.5	.039	.039	.006-.010	.010-.014
	3.0L (1MZ-FE)	.2154–.2159	.2152-2157	44.5	.039	.039	.006-.010	.010-.014
	3.4L (5VZ-FE)	.2350–.2356	.2348–.2354	44.5	.039	.039	.006-.009	.011-.014
	4.7L (2UZ-FE)	.2154-.2159	.2152-.2157	44.5	.049	.055	.006-.010	.010-.014
2000	3.4L (5VZ-FE)	.2350–.2356	.2348–.2354	44.5	.039	.039	.006-.009	.011-.014
	4.7L (2UZ-FE)	.2154-.2159	.2152-.2157	44.5	.039	.039	.006-.010	.010-.014

① — Corolla.   ② — Limit.   ③ — Celica.

CAMSHAFT

All measurements given are in inches, unless otherwise specified.

Year	Engine Liters (ID Code)	Journal Dia.	Max. Journal Runout	Bearing Clearance	Camshaft Endplay	Lifter Dia.	Lifter To Bore Clearance
1996	1.5L (5E-FE)	①	.0016	.0014–.0028	.0018–.0039	1.1014–1.1018	.0006–.0018
	1.6L (4A-FE)⑤	①	.0016	.0014–.0028	②	1.1014–1.1018	.0008–.0020
	1.6L (4A-FE)④	.9822–.9829	.0016	.0014–.0028	②	1.2191–1.2195	.0009–.0023
	1.8L (7A-FE)	.9822–.9829	.0016	.0014–.0028	②	1.2191–1.2195	.0009–.0023
	2.0L (3S-FE)	1.0614–1.0620	.0016	.0010–.0024	.0008–.0079	1.2191–1.2195	.0009–.0020
	2.2L (5S-FE)	1.0614–1.0620	.0016	.0010–.0024	③	1.1014–1.1018	.0006–.0018
	2.4L (2RZ-FE)	1.0614–1.0620	.0024	.0010–.0024	.0016–.0037	1.1576–1.2195	.0009–.0022
	2.4L (2TZ-FZE)	1.0614–1.0620	.0024	.0010–.0024	.0016–.0037	1.2191–1.2195	.0009–.0020
	2.7L (3RZ-FE)	1.0614–1.0620	.0024	.0010–.0024	.0016–.0037	1.1576–1.2195	.0009–.0022
	3.0L (1MZ-FE)	1.0610–1.0616	.0024	.0014–.0028	.0016–.0035	1.2191–2.195	.0009–.0020
	3.0L (2JZ-GE)	1.1397–1.1404	.0031	.0014–.0028	.0031–.0075	1.2191–1.2195	.0009–.0020
	3.0L (2JZ-GTE)	1.1397–1.1404	.0031	.0014–.0028	.0031–.0075	1.2191–1.2195	.0009–.0020
	3.4L (5VZ-FE)	1.0610–1.0616	.0024	.0014–.0028	.0008–.0079	1.2191–1.2195	.0009–.0020
	4.5L (1FZ-FE)	1.0614–1.0620	.0024	.0010–.0024	.0012–.0031	1.3372–1.3376	.0009–.0022
1997	1.5L (5E-FE)	①	.0016	.0014–.0028	.0018–.0039	1.1014–1.1018	.0006–.0018
	1.6L (4A-FE)④	①	.0016	.0014–.0028	②	1.2191–1.2195	.0009–.0023
	1.8L (7A-FE)	①	.0016	.0014–.0028	②	1.2191–1.2195	.0009–.0023
	2.0L (3S-FE)	1.0614–1.0620	.0016	.0010–.0024	③	1.2191–1.2195	.0009–.0020
	2.2L (5S-FE)	1.0614–1.0620	.0016	.0010–.0024	③	1.2191–1.2195	.0009–.00020
	2.4L (2RZ-FE)	1.0614–1.0620	.0024	.0010–.0024	.0016–.0037	1.1578–1.2195	.0009–.0020
	2.4L (2TZ-FZE)	1.0614–1.0620	.0024	.0010–.0024	.0016–.0037	1.2191–1.2195	.0009–.0020
	2.7L (3RZ-FE)	1.0614–1.0620	.0024	.0010–.0024	.0016-.0037	1.1578–1.2195	.0009–.0022
	3.0L (1MZ-FE)	1.0610–1.0616	.0024	⑥	.0016–.0035	1.2191–1.2195	.0009–.0020
	3.0L (2JZ-GE)	1.1397–1.1404	.0031	.0014–.0028	.0031–.0075	1.2191–1.2195	.0009–.0020
	3.0L (2JZ-GTE)	1.1397–1.1404	.0031	.0014–.0028	.0031–.0075	1.2191–1.2195	.0009–.0020
	3.4L (5VZ-FE)	1.0610–1.0616	.0024	.0014–.0028	.0013–0031	1.2191–1.2195	.0009–.0020
	4.5L (1FZ-FE)	1.0614–1.0620	.0024	.0010–.0024	.0012–.0031	1.3372–1.3376	.0009–.0022
1998	1.5L (5E-FE)	①	.0016.	.0014-.0028	.0018-.0039	1.1014-1.1018	.0006-.0018
	1.8L (1ZZ-FE)	⑦	.0012	.0006-.0020	.0016-.0037	1.2191-1.2195	.0009-.0023
	2.0L (3S-FE)	1.0614-1.0620	.0016	.0010-.0024	③	1.2191-1.2195	.0009-.0020
	2.2L (5S-FE)	1.0614-1.0620	.0016	.0010-.0024	③	1.2191-1.2195	.0009-.0020
	2.4L (2RZ-FE)	1.0614-1.0620	.0024	.0010-.0024	.0016-.0037	1.1578-1.2195	.0009-.0020
	2.7L (3RZ-FE)	1.0614-1.0620	.0024	.0010-.0024	.0016-.0037	1.1578-1.2195	.0009-.0020
	3.0L (1MZ-FE)	1.0610-1.0616	.0024	.0014-.0028	.0016-.0035	1.2191-1.2195	1.2191-1.2195
	3.0L (2JZ-GE)	1.1397-1.1404	.0031	.0014-.0028	.0031-.0075	1.2191-1.2195	.0009-.0020
	3.0L (2JZ-GTE)	1.1397-1.1404	.0031	.0014-.0028	.0031-.0075	1.2191-1.2195	.0009-.0020
	3.4L (5VZ-FE)	1.0610-1.0616	.0024	.0014-.0028	.0013-.0031	1.2191-1.2195	.0009-.0020
	4.7L (2UZ-FE)	1.0612-1.0618	.0031	.0012-.0026	.0016-.0035	1.2191-1.2195	.0009-.0020

Continued

ENGINE REBUILDING SPECIFICATIONS

CAMSHAFT—Continued

All measurements given are in inches, unless otherwise specified.

Year	Engine Liters (ID Code)	Journal Dia.	Max. Journal Runout	Bearing Clearance	Camshaft Endplay	Lifter Dia.	Lifter To Bore Clearance
1999	1.8L (1ZZ-FE)	⑦	.0012	.0006-.0020	.0016-.0037	1.2191-1.2195	.0009-.0023
	2.0L (3S-FE)	1.0614-1.0620	.0016	.0010-.0024	③	1.2191-1.2195	.0009-.0020
	2.2L (5S-FE)	1.0614-1.0620	.0016	.0010-.0024	③	1.2191-1.2195	.0009-.0020
	2.4L (2RZ-FE)	1.0614-1.0620	.0024	.0010-.0024	.0016-.0037	1.1578-1.2195	.0009-.0020
	2.7L (3RZ-FE)	1.0614-1.0620	.0024	.0010-.0024	.0016-.0037	1.1578-1.2195	.0009-.0020
	3.0L (1MZ-FE)	1.0610-1.0616	.0024	.0014-.0028	.0016-.0035	1.2191-1.2195	1.2191-1.2195
	3.4L (5VZ-FE)	1.0610-1.0616	.0024	.0014-.0028	.0013-.0031	1.2191-1.2195	.0009-.0020
	4.7L (2UZ-FE)	1.0612-1.0618	.0031	.0012-.0026	⑧	1.2191-1.2195	.0009-.0020
2000	3.4L (5VZ-FE)	1.0610-1.0616	.0024	.0014-.0028	.0013-.0031	1.2191-1.2195	.0009-.0020
	4.7L (2UZ-FE)	1.0612-1.0618	.0031	.0012-.0026	⑨	1.2191-1.2195	.0009-.0020

① — No. 1 Exhaust, .9822–.9829 inch; all others, .9035–.9041 inch.

② — Intake, .0012–.0033 inch; exhaust, .0014–.0035 inch.

③ — Intake, .0018–.0039 inch; exhaust, .0012–.0033 inch.

④ — Corolla.

⑤ — Celica.

⑥ — Intake, .0014–.0028; exhaust, .0010–.0024 inch.

⑦ — No. 1 Exhaust, 1.3563–1.3569 inch; all others, .9035–.9041 inch.

⑧ — Intake, .0016–.0035 inch; exhaust, .0016–.0033 inch.

⑨ — Intake, .0016–.0033 inch; exhaust, .0011–.0030 inch.

CRANKSHAFT, BEARINGS & RODS
All measurements given are in inches, unless otherwise specified.

Year	Engine Liters (ID Code)	Crankshaft Std. Journal Dia. ①		Bearing Clearance			Connecting Rod Side Clearance
		Main Bearing	Crank Pin	Main Bearing	Connecting Rod Bearing	Thrust Bearing	
1996	1.5L (5E-FE)	③	1.6923–1.6929	.0006–.0014	.0006–.0019	.0008–.0087	.0059–.0138
	1.6L (4A-FE)	1.8891–1.8898	1.5742–1.5748	.0006–.0013	.0008–.0020	.0008–.0087	.0059–.0098
	1.8L (7A-FE)	1.8891–1.8898	1.8891–1.8898	.0006–.0013	.0008–.0020	.0008–.0087	.0059–.0098
	2.0L (3S-FE)	2.1653–2.1655	2.0466–2.0472	.0006–.0013	.0009–.0022	.0008–.0087	.0063–.0123
	2.2L (5S-FE)	2.1653–2.1655	2.0466–2.0472	②	.0009–.0022	.0008–.0087	.0063–.0123
	2.4L (2RZ-FE)	2.3617–2.3622	2.0861–2.0866	④	.0012–.0022	.0008–.0087	.0063–.0123
	2.4L (2TZ-FZE)	2.3617–2.3622	2.0861–2.0866	.0009–.0019	.0012–.0023	.0008–.0087	.0063–.0123
	2.7L (3RZ-FE)	2.3617–2.3622	2.0861–2.0866	④	.0012–.0022	.0008–.0087	.0063–.0123
	3.0L (1MZ-FE)	2.4011–2.4016	2.0864–2.0866	.0010–.0018	.0015–.0025	.0016–.0095	.0059–.0118
	3.0L (2JZ-GE)	2.4403–2.4409	2.0465–2.0472	.0010–.0016	.0014–.0021	.0008–.0087	.0098–.0158
	3.0L (2JZ-GTE)	2.4403–2.4409	2.0465–2.0472	.0010–.0016	.0014–.0021	.0008–.0087	.0098–.0158
	3.4L (5VZ-FE)	2.5191–2.5197	2.1648–2.1654	.0008–.0025	.0009–.0027	.0008–.0087	.0059–.0130
	4.5L (1FZ-FE)	2.7158–2.7165	2.2434–2.2441	.0017–.0024	.0013–.0020	.0008–.0087	.0063–.0103
1997	1.5L (5E-FE)	1.9679–1.9685	1.6923–1.6929	.0006–.0014	.0006–.0019	.0008–.0078	.0059–.0138
	1.6L (4A-FE)	1.8891–1.8898	1.5742–1.5748	.0006–.0013	.0008–.0020	.0008–.0087	.0059–.0098
	1.8L (7A-FE)	1.8891–1.8898	1.8893–1.8898	.0006–.0013	.0008–.0017	.0006–.0087	.0059–.0098
	2.0L (3S-FE)	2.1653–2.1655	2.0466–2.0472	②	.0009–.0022	.0008–.0087	.0063–.0123
	2.2L (5S-FE)	2.1653–2.1655	2.0466–2.0472	②	.0009–.0022	.0008–.0087	.0063–.0123
	2.4L (2RZ-FE)	⑧	2.0861–2.0866	⑦	.0012–.0022	.0008–.0087	.0063–.0123
	2.4L (2TZ-FZE)	⑧	2.0861–2.0866	⑦	.0012–.0022	.0008–.0087	.0063–.0123
	2.7L (3RZ-FE)	⑧	2.0861–2.0866	⑦	.0012–.0022	.0008–.0087	.0063–.0123
	3.0L (1MZ-FE)	2.4011–2.4016	2.0863–2.0866	⑥	.0015–.0025	.0016–.0095	.0059–.0118
	3.0L (2JZ-GE)	2.4403–2.4409	2.0465–2.0472	.0010–.0016	.0009–.0016	.0008–.0087	.0098–.0158
	3.0L (2JZ-GTE)	2.4403–2.4409	2.0465–2.0472	.0010–.0016	.0009–.0016	.0008–.0087	.0098–.0158
	3.4L (5VZ-FE)	2.5191–2.5197	2.1648–2.1654	⑤	.0009–.0021	.0008–.0087	.0059–.0130
	4.5L (1FZ-FE)	2.7158–2.7165	2.2434–2.2441	.0014–.0021	.0013–.0020	.0008–.0087	.0063–.0103
1998	1.5L (5E-FE)	1.9679–1.9685	1.6923–1.6929	.0006–.0014	.0006–.0019	.0008–.0078	.0059–.0138
	1.8L (1ZZ-FE)	1.8893–1.8893	1.7320–1.7323	.0006–.0013	.0011–.0024	.0016–.0094	.0063–.0135
	2.0L (3S-FE)	2.1653–2.1655	2.0466–2.0472	②	.0009–.0022	.0008–.0087	.0063–.0123
	2.2L (5S-FE)	2.1653–2.1655	2.0466–2.0472	②	.0009–.0022	.0008–.0087	.0063–.0123
	2.4L (2RZ-FE)	⑧	2.0861–2.0866	⑦	.0012–.0022	.0008–.0087	.0063–.0123
	2.7L (3RZ-FE)	⑧	2.0861–2.0866	⑦	.0012–.0022	.0008–.0087	.0063–.0123
	3.0L (1MZ-FE)	2.4011–2.4016	2.0863–2.0866	⑥	.0015–.0025	.0016–.0095	.0059–.0118
	3.0L (2JZ-GE)	2.4403–2.4409	2.0465–2.0472	.0010–.0016	.0009–.0016	.0008–.0087	.0098–.0158
	3.0L (2JZ-GTE)	2.4403–2.4409	2.0465–2.0472	.0010–.0016	.0009–.0016	.0008–.0087	.0098–.0158
	3.4L (5VZ-FE)	2.5191–2.5197	2.1648–2.1654	⑤	.0009–.0021	.0008–.0087	.0059–.0130
	4.7L (2UZ-FE)	2.6373–2.6378	2.0465–2.0472	.0016–.0023	.0011–.0021	.0008–.0087	.0063–.0138
1999	1.8L (1ZZ-FE)	1.8893–1.8893	1.7320–1.7323	.0006–.0013	.0011–.0024	.0016–.0094	.0063–.0135
	2.0L (3S-FE)	2.1653–2.1655	2.0466–2.0472	②	.0009–.0022	.0008–.0087	.0063–.0123
	2.2L (5S-FE)	2.1653–2.1655	2.0466–2.0472	②	.0009–.0022	.0008–.0087	.0063–.0123
	2.4L (2RZ-FE)	⑧	2.0861–2.0866	⑦	.0012–.0022	.0008–.0087	.0063–.0123
	2.7L (3RZ-FE)	⑧	2.0861–2.0866	⑦	.0012–.0022	.0008–.0087	.0063–.0123
	3.0L (1MZ-FE)	2.4011–2.4016	2.0863–2.0866	⑥	.0015–.0025	.0016–.0095	.0059–.0118
	3.4L (5VZ-FE)	2.5191–2.5197	2.1648–2.1654	⑤	.0009–.0021	.0008–.0087	.0059–.0130
	4.7L (2UZ-FE)	2.6373–2.6378	2.0465–2.0472	.0016–.0023	.0011–.0021	.0008–.0087	.0063–.0138

Continued

ENGINE REBUILDING SPECIFICATIONS

CRANKSHAFT, BEARINGS & RODS—Continued

All measurements given are in inches, unless otherwise specified.

Year	Engine Liters (ID Code)	Crankshaft Std. Journal Dia. ①		Bearing Clearance			Connecting Rod Side Clearance
		Main Bearing	Crank Pin	Main Bearing	Connecting Rod Bearing	Thrust Bearing	
2000	3.4L (5VZ-FE)	2.5191-2.5197	2.1648-2.1654	⑤	.0009-.0021	.0008-.0087	.0059-.0130
	4.7L (2UZ-FE)	2.6373-2.6378	2.0465-2.0472	.0016-.0023	.0011-.0021	.0008-.0087	.0063-.0138

① — Max. taper and out of round, .0008 inch.

② — No. 3, .0010–.0017 inch; all others, .0006–.0013 inch.

③ — Mark 0, 1.9683-1.69685 inches; Mark 1, 1.9681-1.9683 inches; Mark 2, 1.9679–1.9681 inches.

④ — No. 0, 1.9683–1.9685 inches; No. 1, 1.9681–1.9683 inches; No. 2, 1.9679-1.9681 inches.

⑤ — No. 1, .0008–.0015 inch; all others .0009–.0017 inch.

⑥ — No. 1 and 4, .0006–.0014 inch; No. 2 and 3, .0011–.0019 inch.

⑦ — No. 3 .0012–.0022 inch; all others .0009–.0019 inch.

⑧ — No. 3, 2.2615–2.3620 inches; all others 2.3617–2.3622 inches.

PISTONS, PINS & RINGS

All measurements given are in inches, unless otherwise specified.

Year	Engine Liters (ID Code)	Piston Dia. Std.	Piston Clearance	Piston Pin Dia.	Piston Ring End Gap			Piston Ring Side Clearance	
					Top	Second	Oil	Top	Second
1996	1.5L (5E-FE)	④	.0035–.0043	—	.0102–.0189	.0118–.0224	.0059–.0197	.0016–.0031	.0012–.0028
	1.6L (4A-FE)⑧	⑤	.0024–.0031	—	.0098–.0177	.0059–.0157	.0039–.0276	.0016–.0032	.0012–.0028
	1.6L (4A-FE)⑨	②	.0033–.0041	—	.0098–.0177	.0138–.0197	.0059–.0177	.0018–.0033	.0012–.0028
	1.8L (7A-FE)	②	.0033–.0041	—	.0098–.0177	.0138–.0197	.0059–.0177	.0018–.0033	.0012–.0028
	2.0L (3S-FE)	①	.0047–.0063	.8660–.8665	.0106–.0197	.0106–.0201	.0079–.0217	.0012–.0028	.0012–.0028
	2.2L (5S-FE)	3.4193–3.4205	.0055–.0063	.8660–.8665	.0106–.0197	.0138–.0234	.0079–.0217	.0016–.0031	.0012–.0028
	2.4L (2RZ-FE)	3.7371–3.7375	.0022–.0031	.9449–.9452	.0118–.0157	.0157–.0194	.0157–.0194	.0008–.0028	.0012–.0028
	2.4L (2TZ-FZE)	3.7382–3.7386	.0012–.0020	.9449–.9452	.0118–.0169	.0177–.0236	.0051–.0150	.0008–.0028	.0012–.0028
	2.7L (3RZ-FE)	3.7375–3.7379	.0019–.0028	.9449–.9452	.0118–.0157	.0157–.0194	.0157–.0194	.0008–.0028	.0012–.0028
	3.0L (1MZ-FE)	3.4412–3.4416	.0033–.0042	—	.0098–.0138	.0138–.0177	.0059–.0157	.0008–.0028	.0008–.0024
	3.0L (2JZ-GE)	3.3833–2.3837	.0022–.0031	—	.0118–.0185	.0138–.0205	.0051–.0177	.0004–.0028	.0012–.0028
	3.0L (2JZ-GTE)	3.3833–3.3837	.0022–.0031	—	.0118–.0157	.0138–.0178	.0051–.0150	.0016–.0031	.0012–.0028
	3.4L (5VZ-FE)	3.6754–3.6758	.0053–.0060	.8660–.8665	.0118–.0197	.0157–.0236	.0059–.0217	.0016–.0031	.0012–.0028
	4.5L (1FZ-FE)	⑥	.0016–.0024	1.0236–1.0241	.0118–.0205	.0177–.0264	.0059–.0205	.0016–.0031	.0012–.0028

PISTONS, PINS & RINGS—Continued

All measurements given are in inches, unless otherwise specified.

Year	Engine Liters (ID Code)	Piston Dia. Std.	Piston Clear-ance	Piston Pin Dia.	Piston Ring End Gap			Piston Ring Side Clearance	
					Top	Second	Oil	Top	Second
1997	1.5L (5E-FE)	④	.0035–.0043	—	.0102–.0189	.0142–.0224	.0059–.0197	.0016–.0031	.0012–.0028
	1.6L (4A-FE)	②	.0033–.0041	—	.0098–.0138	.0138–.0197	.0039–.0157	.0018–.0033	.0012–.0028
	1.8L (7A-FE)	②	.0033–.0041	—	.0098–.0138	.0138–.0197	.0059–.0157	.0018–.0033	.0012–.0028
	2.0L (3S-FE)	①	.0047–.0055	.8660–.8665	.0106–.0197	.0106–.0201	.0079–.0217	.0012–.0028	.0012–.0028
	2.2L (5S-FE)	⑩	.0055–.0063	.8660–.8665	.0106–.0197	.0138–.0236	.0079–.0217	.0016–.0031	.0012–.0028
	2.4L (2RZ-FE)	3.7371–3.7375	.0022–.0031	.9449–.9452	.0118–.0157	.0157–.0197	.0157–.0197	.0008–.0028	.0012–.0028
	2.4L (2TZ-FZE)	3.7376–3.7380	.0017–.0026	.9449–.9452	.0118–.0169	.0177–.0236	.0051–.0150	.0008–.0028	.0012–.0028
	2.7L (3RZ-FE)	3.7375–3.7379	.0019–.0028	.9449–.9452	.0118–.0157	.0157–.0194	.0157–.0194	.0008–.0028	.0012–.0028
	3.0L (1MZ-FE)	⑪	③	.8660–.8664	.0098–.0138	.0138–.0177	.0059–.0157	.0008–.0028	.0008–.0024
	3.0L (2JZ-GE)	3.3833–3.3837	.0022–.0031	.8660–.8664	.0118–.0185	.0138–.0205	.0051–.0177	.0004–.0028	.0012–.0028
	3.0L (2JZ-GTE)	3.3826–3.3830	.0029–.0038	.8660–.8664	.0118–.0157	.0138–.0178	.0051–.0150	.0016–.0031	.0012–.0028
	3.4L (5VZ-FE)	⑦	.0053–.0060	.8660–.8665	.0118–.0197	.0157–.0236	.0059–.0217	.0016–.0031	.0012–.0028
	4.5L (1FZ-FE)	⑥	.0016–.0024	1.0236–1.0241	.0118–.0205	.0177–.0264	.0059–.0205	.0016–.0031	.0012–.0028
1998	1.5L (5E-FE)	④	.0035-.0043		.0102-.0189	.0142-.0224	.0059-.0197	.0016-.0031	.0012-.0028
	1.8L (1ZZ-FE)	3.1073 - 3.1077	.0033-.0042	—	.0098-.0138	.0138-.0177	.0059-.0157	.0012-.0028	.0012-.0028
	2.0L (3S-FE)	⑫	.0056-.0064	.8660-.8665	.0106-.0185	.0177-.0256	.0039.0177	.0012-.0028	.0012-.0028
	2.2L (5S-FE)	⑬	.0068-.0076	.8660-.8665	.0106-.0192	.0177-.0263	.0039-.0185	.0012-.0028	.0012-.0028
	2.4L (2RZ-FE)	3.7371-3.7375	.0022-.0031	.9449-.9452	.0118-.0157	.0157-.0197	.0157-.0197	.0008-.0028	.0012-.0028
	2.7L (3RZ-FE)	3.7572-3.7576	.0019-.0028	.9449-.9452	.0118-.0157	.0157-.0197	.0157-.0197	.0008-.0028	.0012-.0028
	3.0L (1MZ-FE)	⑪	③	.8660-.8667	.0098-.0138	.0138-.0177	.0059-.0157	.0008-.0028	.0008-.0024
	3.0L (2JZ-GE)	3.3833-3.3837	.0022-.0031	.8660-.8664	.0118-.0185	.0138-.0205	.0051-.0177	.0004-.0028	.0012-.0028
	3.0L (2JZ-GTE)	3.3826-3.3830	.0029-.0038	.8660-.8664	.0118-.0157	.0138-.0178	.0051-.0150	.0016-.0031	.0012-.0028
	3.4L (5VZ-FE)	⑦	.0053-.0060	.8660-.8665	.0118-.0197	.0157-.0236	.0059-.0217	.0016-.0031	.0012-.0028
	4.7L 2UZ-FE)	⑭	.0035-.0044	.8660-.8664	.0118-.0197	.0157-.0256	.0051-.0189	.0012-.0031	.0012-.0028

Continued

ENGINE REBUILDING SPECIFICATIONS

PISTONS, PINS & RINGS—Continued
All measurements given are in inches, unless otherwise specified.

Year	Engine Liters (ID Code)	Piston Dia. Std.	Piston Clearance	Piston Pin Dia.	Piston Ring End Gap			Piston Ring Side Clearance	
					Top	Second	Oil	Top	Second
1999	1.8L (1ZZ-FE)	3.1073 - 3.1077	.0033-.0042	—	.0098-.0138	.0138-.0177	.0059-.0157	.0012-.0028	.0012-.0028
	2.0L (3S-FE)	⑫	.0056-.0064	.8660-.8665	.0106-.0185	.0177-.0256	.0039.0177	.0012-.0028	.0012-.0028
	2.2L (5S-FE)	⑬	.0068-.0076	.8660-.8665	.0106-.0192	.0177-.0263	.0039-.0185	.0012-.0028	.0012-.0028
	2.4L (2RZ-FE)	3.7371-3.7375	.0022-.0031	.9449-.9452	.0118-.0157	.0157-.0197	.0157-.0197	.0008-.0028	.0012-.0028
	2.7L (3RZ-FE)	3.7572-3.7576	.0019-.0028	.9449-.9452	.0118-.0157	.0157-.0197	.0157-.0197	.0008-.0028	.0012-.0028
	3.0L (1MZ-FE)	⑪	③	.8660-.8667	.0098-.0138	.0138-.0177	.0059-.0157	.0008-.0028	.0008-.0024
	3.4L (5VZ-FE)	⑦	.0053-.0060	.8660-.8665	.0118-.0197	.0157-.0236	.0059-.0217	.0016-.0031	.0012-.0028
	4.7L 2UZ-FE)	⑭	.0035-.0044	.8660-.8664	.0118-.0197	.0157-.0256	.0051-.0189	.0012-.0031	.0012-.0028
2000	3.4L (5VZ-FE)	⑦	.0053-.0060	.8660-.8665	.0118-.0197	.0157-.0236	.0059-.0217	.0016-.0031	.0012-.0028
	4.7L 2UZ-FE)	⑭	.0035-.0044	.8660-.8664	.0118-.0197	.0157-.0256	.0051-.0189	.0012-.0031	.0012-.0028

① — Standard No. 1, 3.3807–3.3811 inches; No. 2, 3.3811–3.3815 inches; No. 3, 3.3815-3.3819 inches.

② — Mark 1, 3.1852–3.1856 inches; Mark 2, 3.1856–3.1860 inches; Mark 3, 3.1860–3.1864 inches.

③ — Aisin piston, .0033–.0042 inch; Mahle piston, .0013–.0023 inch.

④ — Mark 1, 2.9094-2.9098 inches; Mark 2, 2.9098-2.9102 inches; Mark 3, 2.9102-2.9106 inches.

⑤ — Mark 1, 3.1862–3.1866 inches; Mark 2, 3.1866–3.1870 inches; Mark 3, 3.1870–3.1874 inches.

⑥ — Mark 1, 3.9350–3.9354 inches; Mark 2, 3.9354–3.9358 inches; Mark 3, 3.9358–3.9362 inches.

⑦ — Mark 1, 3.6754–3.6758 inches; Mark 2, 3.6759–3.6762 inches; Mark 3, 3.6763–3.6766 inches.

⑧ — Celica.

⑨ — Corolla.

⑩ — Mark 1, 3.4193–3.4197 inches; Mark 2, 3.4197–3.4201 inches; Mark 3, 3.4201–3.4205 inches.

⑪ — Aisin piston, 3.4412–3.4416 inches; Mahle piston, 3.4430–3.4436 inches.

⑫ — Mark 1, 3.3798–3.3802 inches; Mark 2, 3.3798–3.3806 inches; Mark 3, 3.3866–3.3870 inches.

⑬ — Mark 1, 3.4179–3.4183 inches; Mark 2, 3.4183–3.4186 inches; Mark 3, 3.4201–3.4205 inches.

⑭ — Mark 1, 3.6969–3.6973 inches; Mark 2, 3.6973–3.6976 inches; Mark 3, 3.6976–3.6980 inches.

CYLINDER BLOCK
All measurements given are in inches unless otherwise specified.

Year	Engine Liters (ID Code)	Cylinder Bore Dia. (Std.)			Cylinder Bore Dia. (Max.)
		Mark 1	Mark 2	Mark 3	
1996	1.5L (5E-FE)		2.9134–2.9138		2.8831
	1.6L (4A-FE)	3.1890–3.1894	3.1894–3.1898	3.1898–3.1902	3.1982
	1.8L (7A-FE)	3.1890–3.1894	3.1894–3.1898	3.1898–3.1902	3.1982
	2.0L (3S-FE)	3.3858–3.3862	3.3862–3.3866	3.3866–3.3870	3.3949
	2.2L (5S-FE)	3.4252–3.4256	3.4256–3.4260	3.4260–3.4264	3.4342
	2.4L (2RZ-FE)		3.7398–3.7403		3.7425
	2.4L (2TZ-FZE)		3.3798–3.27402		3.7425
	2.7L (3RZ-FE)		3.7398–3.7403		3.7425
	3.0L (1MZ-FE)		3.4449–3.4453		3.4457
	3.0L (2JZ-GE)		3.3858–3.3863		3.3866
	3.0L (2JZ-GTE)		3.3858–3.3863		3.3866
	3.4L (5VZ-FE)		3.6811–3.6819		3.6902
	4.5L (1FZ-FE)	3.9370–3.9374	3.9374–3.9378	3.9378–3.9382	3.9461

Continued

CYLINDER BLOCK—Continued
All measurements given are in inches unless otherwise specified.

Year	Engine Liters (ID Code)	Cylinder Bore Dia. (Std.)			Cylinder Bore Dia. (Max.)
		Mark 1	Mark 2	Mark 3	
1997	1.5L (5E-FE)	2.9134–2.9138	2.9138–2.9142	2.9142–2.9146	2.9244
	1.6L (4A-FE)	3.1890–3.1894	3.1894–3.1898	3.1898–3.1902	3.1982
	1.8L (7A-FE)	3.1890–3.1894	3.1894–3.1898	3.1898–3.1902	3.1982
	2.0L (3S-FE)	3.3858–3.3862	3.3862–3.3866	3.3866–3.3870	3.3949
	2.2L (5S-FE)	3.4252–3.4256	3.4256–3.4260	3.4260–3.4264	3.4342
	2.4L (2RZ-FE)		3.7398–3.7403		3.7425
	2.4L (2TZ-FZE)		3.7398–3.7403		3.7425
	2.7L (3RZ-FE)		3.7398–3.7403		3.7425
	3.0L (1MZ-FE)		3.4449–3.4453		3.4457
	3.0L (2JZ-GE)		3.3858–3.3863		3.3866
	3.0L (2JZ-GTE)		3.3858–3.3863		3.3866
	3.4L (5VZ-FE)	3.6811–3.6815	3.6815–3.6819	3.6819–3.6823	3.6902
	4.5L (1FZ-FE)	3.9370–3.9374	3.9374–3.9378	3.9378–3.9382	3.9461
1998	1.5L (5E-FE)	2.9134–2.9138	2.9138–2.9142	2.9142–2.9146	2.9244
	1.8L (1ZZ-FE)		3.1102–3.1107		3.1107
	2.0L (3S-FE)	3.3858–3.3862	3.3862–3.3866	3.3866–3.3870	3.3949
	2.2L (5S-FE)	3.4252–3.4256	3.4256–3.4260	3.4260–3.4264	3.4342
	2.4L (2RZ-FE)		3.7400–3.7403		3.7425
	2.7L 3RZ-FE)		3.7400–3.7403		3.7425
	3.0L (1MZ-FE)		3.4449–3.4453		3.4457
	3.0L (2JZ-GE)		3.3585–3.3863		3.3866
	3.0L (2JZ-GTE)		3.3858–3.3863		3.3866
	3.4L (5VZ-FE)	3.6811–3.6815	3.6815–3.6819	3.6819–3.6823	3.6902
	4.7L (2UZ-FE)	3.7009–3.7012	3.7012–3.7017	3.7017–3.7020	3.7099
1999	1.8L (1ZZ-FE)		3.1102–3.1107		3.1107
	2.0L (3S-FE)	3.3858–3.3862	3.3862–3.3866	3.3866–3.3870	3.3949
	2.2L (5S-FE)	3.4252–3.4256	3.4256–3.4260	3.4260–3.4264	3.4342
	2.4L (2RZ-FE)		3.7400–3.7403		3.7425
	2.7L 3RZ-FE)		3.7400–3.7403		3.7425
	3.0L (1MZ-FE)		3.4449–3.4453		3.4457
	3.4L (5VZ-FE)	3.6811–3.6815	3.6815–3.6819	3.6819–3.6823	3.6902
	4.7L (2UZ-FE)	3.7009–3.7012	3.7012–3.7017	3.7017–3.7020	3.7099
2000	3.4L (5VZ-FE)	3.6811–3.6815	3.6815–3.6819	3.6819–3.6823	3.6902
	4.7L (2UZ-FE)	3.7009–3.7012	3.7012–3.7017	3.7017–3.7020	3.7099

OIL PUMP
All measurements given are in inches, unless otherwise specified.

Year	Engine Liters (ID Code)	Gear Backlash	Gear To Body Clearance	Tip Clearance	Side Clearance
1996	1.5L (5E-FE)	—	.0039–.0083	.0024–.0059	.1146–.1169
	1.6L (4A-FE)	—	.0031–.0071	.0010–.0033	.0010–.0033
	1.8L (7A-FE)	—	.0031–.0071	.0010–.0033	.0010–.0033
	2.0L (3S-FE)	—	.0039–.0063	.0016–.0063	—
	2.2L (5S-FE)	—	.0039–.0063	.0016–.0063	—
	2.4L (2RZ-FE)	—	.0039–.0069	.0043–.0094	.0012–.0035
	2.4L (2TZ-FZE)	—	.0039–.0069	.0043–.0094	.0012–.0035
	2.7L (3RZ-FE)	—	.0039–.0069	.0043–.0094	.0012–.0035
	3.0L (1MZ-FE)	—	.0039–.0069	.0043–.0094	.0012–.0035
	3.0L (2JZ-GE)	—	.0039–.0069	.0122–.0193	.0012–.0035
	3.0L (2JZ-GTE)	—	.0039–.0069	.0022–.0128	.0007–.0026
	3.4L (5VZ-FE)	—	.0039–.0069	.0043–.0094	.0012–.0035
	4.5L (1FZ-FE)	—	.0039–.0067	.0012–.0063	.0012–.0035

Continued

ENGINE REBUILDING SPECIFICATIONS

OIL PUMP—Continued
All measurements given are in inches, unless otherwise specified.

Year	Engine Liters (ID Code)	Gear Backlash	Gear To Body Clearance	Tip Clearance	Side Clearance
1997	1.5L (5E-FE)	—	.0039–.0063	.0012–.0055	.1145–.1169
	1.6L (4A-FE)	—	.0031–.0071	.0010–.0033	.0010–.0033
	1.8L (7A-FE)	—	.0031–.0071	.0010–.0033	.0010–.0033
	2.0L (3S-FE)	—	.0039–.0063	.0016–.0063	—
	2.2L (5S-FE)	—	.0039–.0063	.0016–.0063	—
	2.4L (2RZ-FE)	—	.0039–.0069	.0043–.0094	.0012–.0035
	2.4L (2TZ-FZE)	—	.0039–.0069	.0043–.0094	.0012–.0035
	2.7L (3RZ-FE)	—	.0039–.0069	.0043–.0094	.0012–.0035
	3.0L (1MZ-FE)	—	.0039–.0069	.0043–.0094	.0012–.0035
	3.0L (2JZ-GE)	—	.0039–.0069	.0024–.0094	.0012–.0035
	3.0L (2JZ-GTE)	—	.0031–.0053	.0022–.0128	.0007–.0026
	3.4L (5VZ-FE)	—	.0039–.0069	.0043–.0094	.0012–.0035
	4.5L (1FZ-FE)	—	.0039–.0067	.0012–.0063	.0012–.0035
1998	1.5L (5E-FE)	—	.0039–.0063	.0012–.0055	.1145–.1169
	1.8L (1ZZ-FE)	—	.0031–.0071	.0024–.0071	.0010–.0030
	2.0L (3S-FE)	—	.0039–.0063	.0016–.0063	—
	2.2L (5S-FE)	—	.0039–.0063	.0016–.0063	—
	2.4L (2RZ-FE)	—	.0039–.0069	.0043–.0094	.0012–.0035
	2.7L (3RZ-FE)	—	.0039–.0069	.0043–.0094	.0012–.0035
	3.0L (1MZ-FE)	—	.0039–.0069	.0043–.0094	.0012–.0035
	3.0L (2JZ-GE)	—	.0036–.0069	.0024–.0094	.0012–.0035
	3.0L (2JZ-GTE)	—	.0031–.0035	.0022–.0128	.0007–.0026
	3.4L (5VZ-FE)	—	.0039–.0069	.0043–.0094	.0012–.0035
	4.7L (2UZ-FE)	—	.0039–.0069	.0043–.0094	.0012–.0035
1999	1.8L (1ZZ-FE)	—	.0031–.0071	.0024–.0071	.0010–.0030
	2.0L (3S-FE)	—	.0039–.0063	.0016–.0063	—
	2.2L (5S-FE)	—	.0039–.0063	.0016–.0063	—
	2.4L (2RZ-FE)	—	.0039–.0069	.0043–.0094	.0012–.0035
	2.7L (3RZ-FE)	—	.0039–.0069	.0043–.0094	.0012–.0035
	3.0L (1MZ-FE)	—	.0039–.0069	.0043–.0094	.0012–.0035
	3.4L (5VZ-FE)		.0039–.0069	.0043–.0094	.0012–.0035
	4.7L (2UZ-FE)	—	.0039–.0069	.0043–.0094	.0012–.0035
2000	3.4L (5VZ-FE)	—	.0039–.0069	.0043–.0094	.0012–.0035
	4.7L (2UZ-FE)	—	.0039–.0069	.0043–.0094	.0012–.0035

Manual Information Locator

All Wheel Drive Models

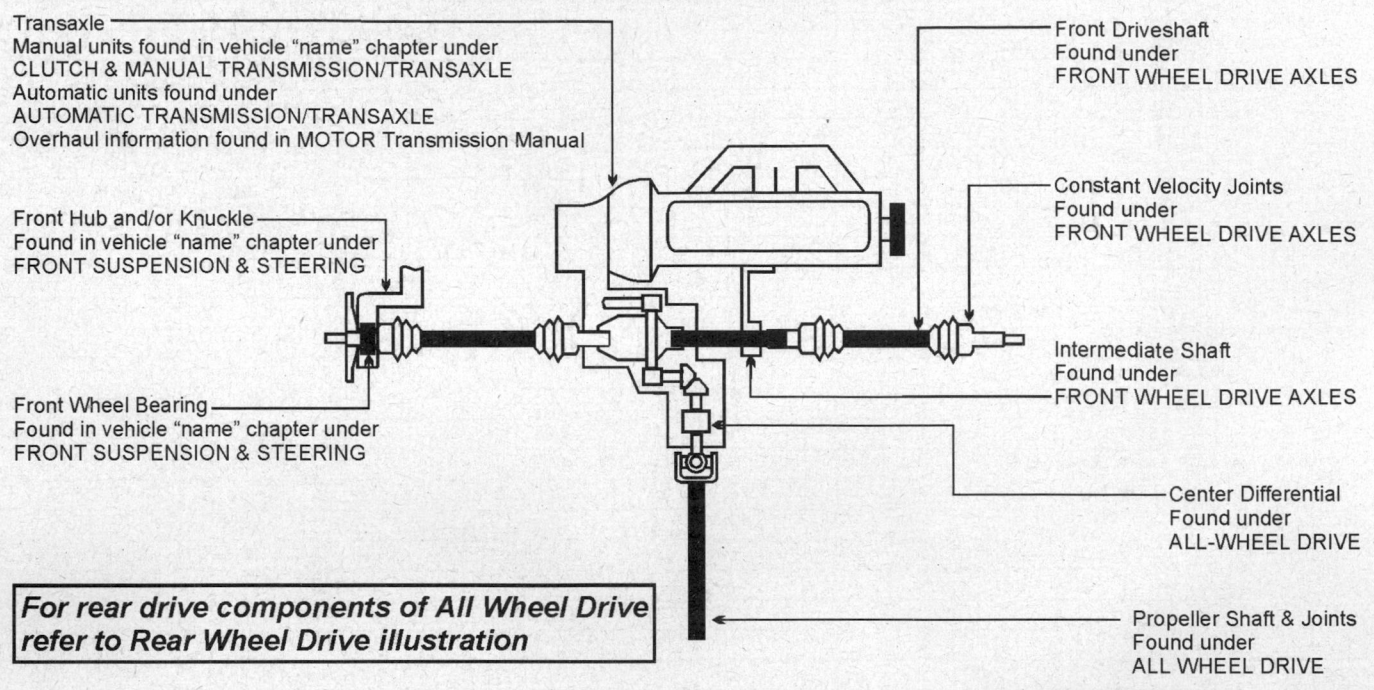

Transaxle
Manual units found in vehicle "name" chapter under
CLUTCH & MANUAL TRANSMISSION/TRANSAXLE
Automatic units found under
AUTOMATIC TRANSMISSION/TRANSAXLE
Overhaul information found in MOTOR Transmission Manual

Front Hub and/or Knuckle
Found in vehicle "name" chapter under
FRONT SUSPENSION & STEERING

Front Wheel Bearing
Found in vehicle "name" chapter under
FRONT SUSPENSION & STEERING

Front Driveshaft
Found under
FRONT WHEEL DRIVE AXLES

Constant Velocity Joints
Found under
FRONT WHEEL DRIVE AXLES

Intermediate Shaft
Found under
FRONT WHEEL DRIVE AXLES

Center Differential
Found under
ALL-WHEEL DRIVE

Propeller Shaft & Joints
Found under
ALL WHEEL DRIVE

For rear drive components of All Wheel Drive refer to Rear Wheel Drive illustration

Rear Wheel Drive Models

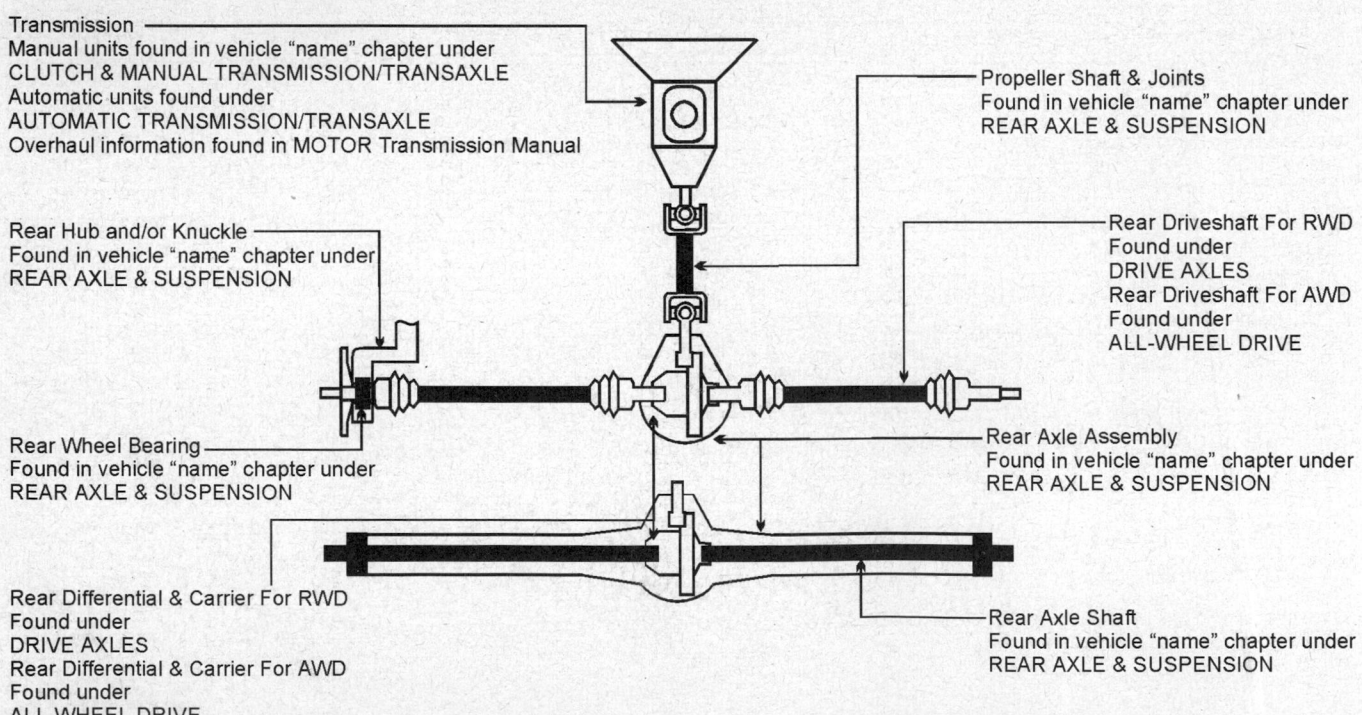

Transmission
Manual units found in vehicle "name" chapter under
CLUTCH & MANUAL TRANSMISSION/TRANSAXLE
Automatic units found under
AUTOMATIC TRANSMISSION/TRANSAXLE
Overhaul information found in MOTOR Transmission Manual

Rear Hub and/or Knuckle
Found in vehicle "name" chapter under
REAR AXLE & SUSPENSION

Rear Wheel Bearing
Found in vehicle "name" chapter under
REAR AXLE & SUSPENSION

Propeller Shaft & Joints
Found in vehicle "name" chapter under
REAR AXLE & SUSPENSION

Rear Driveshaft For RWD
Found under
DRIVE AXLES
Rear Driveshaft For AWD
Found under
ALL-WHEEL DRIVE

Rear Axle Assembly
Found in vehicle "name" chapter under
REAR AXLE & SUSPENSION

Rear Axle Shaft
Found in vehicle "name" chapter under
REAR AXLE & SUSPENSION

Rear Differential & Carrier For RWD
Found under
DRIVE AXLES
Rear Differential & Carrier For AWD
Found under
ALL-WHEEL DRIVE

Manual Information Locator - Continued

Front Wheel Drive Models

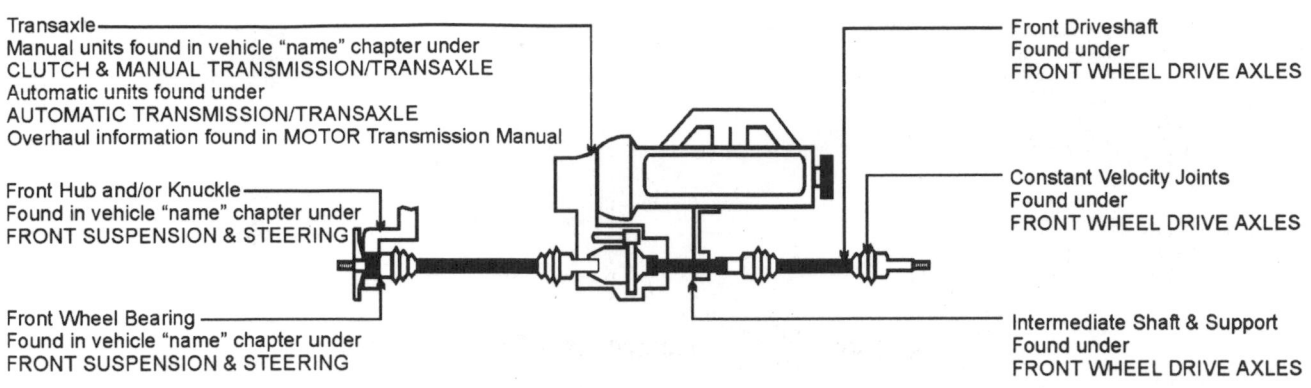

Transaxle—
Manual units found in vehicle "name" chapter under
CLUTCH & MANUAL TRANSMISSION/TRANSAXLE
Automatic units found under
AUTOMATIC TRANSMISSION/TRANSAXLE
Overhaul information found in MOTOR Transmission Manual

Front Hub and/or Knuckle—
Found in vehicle "name" chapter under
FRONT SUSPENSION & STEERING

Front Wheel Bearing —
Found in vehicle "name" chapter under
FRONT SUSPENSION & STEERING

Front Driveshaft
Found under
FRONT WHEEL DRIVE AXLES

Constant Velocity Joints
Found under
FRONT WHEEL DRIVE AXLES

Intermediate Shaft & Support
Found under
FRONT WHEEL DRIVE AXLES

Four Wheel Drive Models

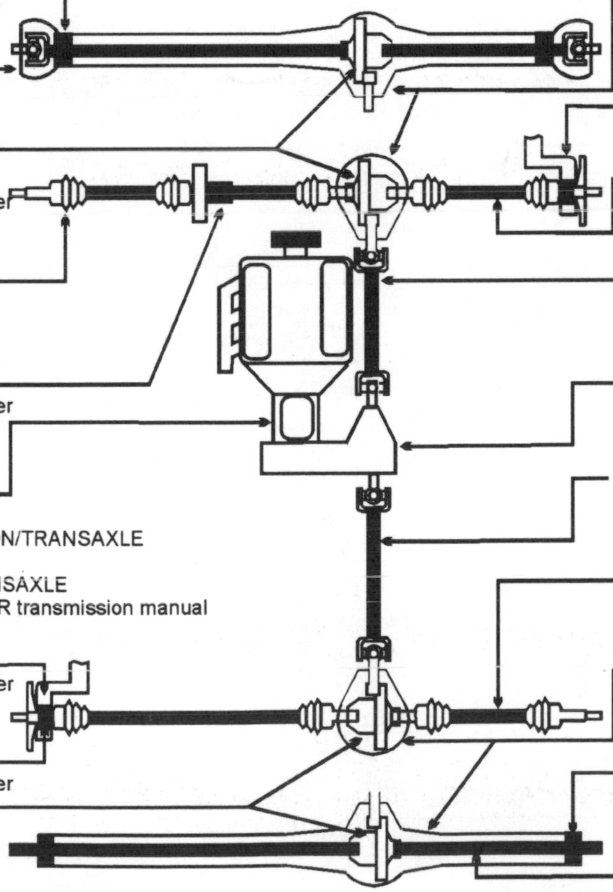

Front Wheel Bearing —
Found in vehicle "name" chapter
FRONT SUSPENSION & STEERING

Front Hub and/or Knuckle —
Found under
FRONT WHEEL DRIVE

Differential & Carrier —
Found in vehicle "name" chapter under
FRONT WHEEL DRIVE

Constant Velocity Joints —
Found under
FRONT WHEEL DRIVE AXLES

Intermediate Shaft —
Found in vehicle "name" chapter under
FRONT WHEEL DRIVE

Transmission Units —
Manual units found under
CLUTCH & MANUAL TRANSMISSION/TRANSAXLE
Automatic units found under
AUTOMATIC TRANSMISSION/TRANSAXLE
Overhaul information found in MOTOR transmission manual

Rear Hub and/or Knuckle —
Found in vehicle "name" chapter under
FRONT WHEEL DRIVE

Rear Wheel Bearing —
Found in vehicle "name" chapter under
FRONT WHEEL DRIVE

Differential and Carrier —
Found under
DRIVE AXLES

Front Axle Assembly
Found in vehicle "name chapter under
FRONT SUSPENSION & STEERING

Front Hub and/or Knuckle
Found under
FRONT WHEEL DRIVE

Front Driveshaft
Found in vehicle "name" chapter under
FRONT SUSPENSION & STEERING

Front Propeller Shaft
Found under
FRONT WHEEL DRIVE AXLE

Transfer Case
Found in vehicle "name" chapter under
TRANSFER CASE

Rear Propeller Shaft
Found in vehicle "name" chapter under
REAR AXLE & SUSPENSION

Rear Driveshaft
Found under
FRONT WHEEL DRIVE AXLES

Rear Axle Assembly
Found in vehicle "name" chapter under
REAR AXLE & SUSPENSION

Rear Wheel Bearing
Found in vehicle "name" chapter under
REAR AXLE & SUSPENSION

Rear Axle Shaft
Found in vehicle "name" chapter under
REAR AXLE & SUSPENSION

Operation/Subject/Topic	Imported Car Repair Manual, Asian	Imported Engine Performance & Driveability, Asian
Air Bags	X	—
Air Bag System Precautions	X	X
Air Conditioning	X	—
AIR Systems	—	X
All-Wheel Drive Systems	X	—
Alternator Specifications	X	—
Alternator Systems	X	—
Anti-Lock Brake Systems	X	—
Automatic Seat Belts	X	—
Automatic Transaxle In-Vehicle Service	X	—
Automatic Transmission In-Vehicle Service	X	—
Axle Shaft Service	X	—
Back-Up Light Switch, Replace	X	—
Balance Shaft Service	X	—
Ball Joint Service	X	—
Belt Tension Data	X	—
Blower Motor, Replace	X	—
Brake Booster Service	X	—
Brake Service	X	—
Camber Adjustment	X	—
Camshaft Service	X	—
Capacity Data	X	—
Caster Adjustment	X	—
Catalytic Converters	—	X
Clutch Service	X	—
Clutch Start Switch, Replace	X	—
Coil Pack, Replace	X	X
Coil Spring, Replace	X	—
Compression Pressure	X	X
Computer Relearn Procedures	X	X
Computer System Diagnostics	—	X
Computer System Identification	X	X
Computer Terminal Connector Identification	X	X
Computerized Engine Control Systems	—	X
Control Arm Service	X	—
Cooling System Bleed	X	—
Cooling System Data	X	—
Crankshaft Pulley, Replace	X	—
Crankshaft Rear Oil Seal Service	X	—
Cruise Control Systems	X	—
Cylinder Block Specifications	X	—
Cylinder Head Service	X	—
Cylinder Head Specifications	X	—
Cylinder Head, Replace	X	—
Cylinder Liner, Replace	X	—
Dash Panel Service	X	—
Differential Service	X	—
Dimmer Switch, Replace	X	—
Disc Brake Service	X	—
Distributor Service	—	X
Distributor, Replace	X	X
Distributorless Ignition Systems	—	X
Drive Axle Service	X	—
Drive Belt Tension Data	X	—

Operation/Subject/Topic	Imported Car Repair Manual, Asian	Imported Engine Performance & Driveability, Asian
Drum Brake Service	X	—
EGR System	—	X
Electric Engine Cooling Fans	X	—
Electric Fuel Pumps	X	X
Electrical Symbol Identification	X	X
Electronic Fuel Injection	—	X
Electronic Ignition	—	X
Electronic Instrumentation	—	X
Electronic Level Controls	X	—
Emission Control Application Charts	—	X
Emission Controls	—	X
Emission Vacuum Hose Routings	—	X
Engine Compartment Reference Diagrams	—	X
Engine Cooling Fans	X	—
Engine Control Module, Replace	—	X
Engine Control Unit, Replace	—	X
Engine Front Cover Service	X	—
Engine Mounts, Replace	X	—
Engine Oil Seal Service	X	—
Engine Rebuilding Specifications	X	—
Engine Repairs	X	—
Engine Sensor Location	—	X
Engine Sensor Replacement	—	X
Engine Sensor Specifications	—	X
Engine Specifications	X	—
Engine System Identification Charts	—	X
Engine Tightening Specifications	X	—
Engine, Replace	X	—
Evaporator Core, Replace	X	—
Exhaust Gas Recirculation (EGR) Systems	—	X
Exhaust Manifold, Replace	X	—
Fast Idle Speed Adjustment	—	X
Federal Air Quality Standards	—	X
Flasher Location	X	—
Front Drive Axle Service	X	—
Front Wheel Alignment	X	—
Fuel Control System Identification	—	X
Fuel Filter, Replace	X	—
Fuel Injection Systems	—	X
Fuel Injector Cleaning Procedures	—	X
Fuel Injector, Replace	—	X
Fuel Pump Pressure Specifications	X	X
Fuel Pump Pressure Test	—	X
Fuel Pump Relay Location	X	X
Fuel Pump Replacement	X	X
Fuse Panel Location	X	—
General Engine Specifications	X	—
Headlight Switch, Replace	X	—
Heated Air Cleaners	—	X
Heater Core, Replace	X	—
Hub & Bearing Assembly Service	X	—
Hydraulic Brake System Service	X	—
Hydraulic Valve Lifter Service	X	—
Idle Mixture Adjustments	—	X
Idle Speed Adjustments	—	X